2001

72ND EDITION

INTERNATIONAL MOTION PICTURE ALMANAC

Editorial Director
TRACY STEVENS

QUIGLEY PUBLISHING COMPANY, INC.
6639 LA JOLLA BLVD., LA JOLLA, CA 92037
9 RAILROAD WAY, LARCHMONT, NY 10538

(858) 459-1159

2001 72nd Edition
INTERNATIONAL MOTION PICTURE ALMANAC

ISSN: 0074-7084
ISBN: 0-900610-67-0

PRINTED IN THE UNITED STATES OF AMERICA

TABLE OF CONTENTS

THE YEAR

THE MOTION PICTURE YEAR IN REVIEW 5

STATISTICS 9

TOP GROSSING FILMS 14

AWARDS AND POLLS 15

ENTERTAINMENT INDUSTRY MERGERS AND ACQUISITIONS, 1999-2000 22

BIOGRAPHIES

WHO'S WHO: ENTERTAINMENT INDUSTRY BIOGRAPHIES 34

OBITUARIES 456

FEATURE FILMS

U.S. FEATURE FILM RELEASES — 1999-2000 459

FOREIGN FILM RELEASES — 1999-2000 485

FEATURE FILM RELEASES — 1990-1999 530

INTERNATIONAL FILM & TV FESTIVALS AND MARKETS 630

PRODUCERS AND DISTRIBUTORS

HISTORIES OF THE MOTION PICTURE STUDIOS 636

PRODUCERS AND DISTRIBUTORS 645

NON-THEATRICAL MOTION PICTURE COMPANIES 704

PRODUCTION SERVICES

ADVERTISING & PUBLICITY 706

ANIMATION 712

CASTING DIRECTORS 721

CONSULTANTS AND TECHNICAL ADVISORS 724

COSTUME AND PROP RENTALS 726

ENTERTAINMENT LAWYERS 730

FILM PRESERVATION, PROCESSING AND REPAIR 735

FILM STOCK 736

FINANCIAL SERVICES 737

MARKET RESEARCH AND ANALYSIS 741

SOUND STUDIOS AND SERVICES 742

SPECIAL EFFECTS 746

STOCK SHOTS 753

STUDIO AND EDITING EQUIPMENT RENTALS 755

SUBTITLES AND CAPTIONS 759

TALENT AGENCIES 760

Exhibition

Theatre Circuits .771
Circuit Theatres by State .819
Circuit Theatres by Market .831
Independent Theaters .848
Specialty Exhibitors .876
Specialty Exhibitor Services & Equipment .878
Theatre Equipment Services .879
Concession Suppliers .896
Screening Rooms 900
Preview and Policy Trailers .901
Buying and Booking Agencies .902
Film Distributors in Key Cities .904
Exhibitor Organizations .905

Professional Organizations and Government Offices

Motion Picture Organizations .908
Guilds & Unions .915
State and City Film Commissions .921
Federal Government Offices and Film and Media Services .929
The Press 931

The World Market

The Industry in Canada .936
The Industry in Great Britain & Ireland .972
Guide to European Multiplexes .1002
The World Market: Europe, Latin America, Asia and the Pacific .1007

Index

Website Guide .1042
Index 1045

Motion Picture Year in Review

BY WILLIAM J. QUIGLEY

What a difference a year makes. After years of sharp upward trends at the box-office, the year 2000 ends with results that are just comparable to those achieved in 1999. North American Box-office over $7.5 billion for the year 2000 sounds all well and good, especially considering that 1999 capped many years of increasing box-office. However, the expectation was that the incredible theatrical building boom of the last few years would increase the total box-office pie. The truth is that for the most part the new multiplexes just grabbed market share from older theatres and did not in fact appreciably increase the size of the market. Many of these, formerly profitable older theatres, are part of the excess capacity plaguing Exhibitors. While the baby boomers have provided a significant demographic bulge to film-going demographics, it is clear that the slight increase in attendance will not justify the enormous capital outlays for new mega-multiplexes or the cost of shuttering older theatres. There is a significant excess of screens that will have to be closed before this segment of the Industry returns to profitability.

Wall Street fueled the explosion of theatre building that continued in 2000 and that boom of stadium-seated movie palaces looked to change the landscape of the Industry. Ironically, it was the easy availability of capital that created much of the current crisis. Exhibitors that have deployed enormous sums to re-screen and reseat much of the world with mega-multiplexes now find themselves in substantial financial difficulties. With the exception of drive-ins, the total number of screens in the US is dropping for the first time in memory. More than 360 theatres with over 2,000 screens have gone dark this year, while only 130 theatres with 1,350 screens have opened. By November six major circuits including United Artists Theatre Circuit, General Cinema, Mann, Edwards and Carmike had gone into Chapter 11. There will be many more closings in the next year.

Prospects appear significantly better from the Production and Distribution point of view.

The proliferation of theatres Internationally and the expansion of the traditional ancillary markets continue to augur well for those in the business of making and marketing films. The year 2000 started to look like it would considerably exceed 1999's results. Through Memorial Day the domestic box-office was consistently 8% to 9% ahead of 1999. However, disappointing Summer and early Fall pictures left the performance to that date as far as 15% behind last year's results. A number of strong late Fall and Holiday releases brought the results even to 1999 by year-end. The most improved Studio by far was Dreamworks, which in its sixth year delivered on the promise it had been showing with a full "Major Studio" release slate and spectacular box-office.

Of somewhat greater concern was the Federal Trade Commission report that was highly critical of the Studios practices of marketing inappropriate product to children. Ours is an Industry where the specter of censorship has reared its ugly head periodically throughout its history. Hollywood drew the ire of politicians and initially Industry leaders were not very responsive to the outcry. The politicos pointed the finger at Hollywood specifically for marketing violence to children. The attendant Senate hearings gave journalists plenty to write about, especially in an Election Year ,and many politicians were quick to espouse theories about the role of the motion picture in the moral decay of America's youth. All of the Majors quickly signed off on the MPAA initiatives, which were essentially a restatement of policies already in place. NATO was quick to call for renewed care in enforcing the ratings system at the theatres and making sure that appropriate trailers were playing for the audiences at all times. The heat died down after the tumult from the Presidential election ended.

THE STUDIOS

Disney had another extraordinary year at the box-office as has been the case in many of the years in the 1990s. "Toy Story 2," which opened in 1999, continued to do great grosses into 2000 and ended up with $245 million in North America alone. Two other animated films in the first half of the year, "Fantasia 2000" and "Dinosaur" also were strong performers. Disney led the Summer's results for the fifth straight year with "Shanghai Noon," "Gone in Sixty Seconds," "The Kid" and "Coyote Ugly." Denzel Washington starred in the Fall smash, "Remember the Titans," and Glenn Close reprised her role as Cruella De Vil in "201 Dalmatians." Bruce Willis starred in M. Night Shyamalan's "Unbreakable," which did not do anywhere near the business of "Sixth Sense." The two holiday features were the animated, "The Emperor's New Groove" and the Coen Brothers' "O Brother, Where Art Thou?" which was a co-production with Universal. Disney's two big films for 2001 are "Pearl Harbor" at Memorial Day and the animated Summer release, "Atlantis, The Lost Empire."

Disney took the lead in another arena, the digital or electronic distribution of "films" to theatres. Under the direction of Phil Barlow, the ex-head of Buena Vista Distribution, Disney assembled and tested delivering films to more than 30 theatres around the world in an electronic format. Utilizing Texas Instrument Cinema Chips, a Qu-Vis player and delivery via DVDs, Disney demonstrated that films could be distributed and screened electronically in theatres with quality that is close if not comparable to 35 millimeter. There are many technical and financial hurdles to overcome, but this event marks the advent of electronic distribution in theatres.

Warner Bros. had "The Whole Nine Yards," "Romeo Must Die," which did well, and John Travolta in the forgettable "Battlefield Earth" at the beginning of the year. Summer started out like a tidal wave with "The Perfect Storm" which did over $180 million in the US alone. Both "Pokemon" and "My Dog Skip" did fine with family audiences and Clint Eastwood helped turn "Space Cowboys" into a huge hit. The re-issue of "The Exorcist" with new footage also performed well. "Pay It Forward" did not do as well as expected in October. The holiday pictures were "Red Planet" with Val Kilmer, Taylor Hackford's "Proof of Life" and "Miss Congeniality" with Sandra Bullock. "Harry Potter and the Sorcerer's Stone" directed by Chris Columbus will be their much anticipated November 2001 release.

Dreamworks has finally come into its own and delivered films that were critical and commercial successes in sufficient quantity to thrill theatre owners around the world. "Gladiator" with Russell Crowe was a huge hit that did $440 million worldwide after opening in May. The teen-oriented "Road Trip" did excellent business in June and the animated "Chicken Run" earned $170 million worldwide. "What Lies Beneath" was also a smash Summer hit for the studio. Cameron Crowe's "Almost Famous" was terrific in the Fall and Robert Redford's "The Legend of Bagger Vance" with Will Smith, Charlize Theron and Matt Damon garnered critical plaudits and commercial success. Their sole holiday offering was "An Everlasting Piece" which was directed by Barry Levinson and a co-production with Columbia. In the first quarter of 2001 they will release "The Mexican" starring Julia Roberts and Brad Pitt.

Universal built on 1999's success with a huge hit in the early part of the year, "Erin Brokovitch" starring Julia Roberts. "U-571" and "The Flintstones in Viva Rock Vegas," did well in Spring. Summer brought the $122 million grossing "Nutty Professor II: The Klumps," with Eddie Murphy and the surprise hit about rival cheerleading squads, "Bring It On." The co-production with Dreamworks, "Meet the Parents" with Robert De Niro and Ben Stiller was big and "Billy Elliot" from

Working Title did well on a much smaller release. Imagine Entertainment produced the Holiday smash starring Jim Carrey in "Dr. Seuss' How the Grinch Stole Christmas." "The Family Man" with Nicholas Cage was released in December. For 2001, one of Universal's Summer releases will be "Jurassic Park III," directed by Joe Johnson.

Paramount did substantial business in the first six months of the year with "Wonder Boys," "Snow Day" and "Rules of Engagement." Tom Cruise provided a smash hit in "Mission Impossible 2" which did $215 million in the US and has a worldwide total of $524 million. "The Original Kings of Comedy" opened in August to great reviews and good business. John Travolta in "Lucky Numbers" did not have it but "Rugrats In Paris - The Movie," which was produced by Nickelodeon, played at Thanksgiving to its family followers. The Holidays brought Mel Gibson in the Nancy Meyers directed "What Women Want," which also starred Helen Hunt and Jean-Jacques Annaud's "Enemy at the Gates." In April of 2001 Paramount will release the third in a series, "Crocodile Dundee in Los Angeles" and the much-anticipated film based on a videogame "Tomb Raider" will star Angelina Jolie as Lara Croft.

Twentieth Century Fox's only film that did business in the first half of the year was the Leonardo DiCaprio film, "The Beach" which grossed $40 million in the US but did an excellent $140 million worldwide. The Summer product started out strong with Martin Lawrence in "Big Momma's House," which did $170 million worldwide and the Farrelly Brothers' "Me, Myself and Irene," which starred Jim Carrey and Renee Zellweger. "X-Men" was Fox's big hit which attained $277 million around the world. It was also notable that Fox teamed up with Cisco Systems and did a demonstration where they delivered the animated film, "Titan A.E." over the Internet to Atlanta and used a digital projector to put the motion picture on the screen. Joel Schumacher's "Tigerland" was released on a limited basis in early Fall and "Bedazzled" from director Harold Ramis did well. "Men of Honor" starring Robert De Niro and Cuba Gooding Jr. opened in November and the Holiday picture featured Tom Hanks in "Cast Away" which is interesting to consider in light of the television phenomenon, "Survivor" from CBS which played out to small-screen audiences this Summer. Audiences can expect "Moulin Rouge," with Nicole Kidman, Eddie Murphy in "Doctor Doolittle 2" and Tim Burton's take on "Planet of the Apes" in 2001.

Columbia was in a bit of a slump for the first ten months of the year, although Mel Gibson in "The Patriot" and the creepy "Hollow Man" did respectably. All that changed with the November opening of "Charlies' Angels" with Drew Barrymore, Cameron Diaz, Lucy Liu and Bill Murray which did over $40 million the opening week in North America. Arnold Schwarzenegger did not deliver as expected in "The 6th Day." The two Holiday offerings were the extraordinary "Vertical Limit" and the Gus Van Sant directed film, "Finding Forrester," featuring Sean Connery. Former Disney topper Joe Roth's Revolution Films will deliver three films for Columbia in 2001.

Miramax and Dimension continue to deliver a mix of critically well-received specialized product and mass-market youth-oriented films. The Dimension label produced their highest grossing "Scary Movie" which did $218 million and Scream 3 produced $147 million worldwide. Jackie Chan's "Legend of the Drunken Master," which was made in 1994 did well in its US release in October and Wes Craven's "Dracula 2000" was Dimension's Christmas offering. Miramax released "Down to You" and "Boys and Girls" which did over $20 million each in the US. "Bounce" with Ben Affleck and Gwyneth Paltrow opened in November and "The Yards" opened on a limited release. Christmas brought Matt Damon in Billy Bob Thornton's "All The Pretty Horses" and three of Miramax's intended Oscar-contenders: "Chocolat" directed by Lasse Hallstrom; "Malena" by the director of "Cinema Paradiso," Giusseppe Tornatore; and Roland Joffe's "Vatel" which stars Uma Thurman and Gerard Depardieu.

New Line continues to be a consistent supplier of commercial product. In the first six months of the year there were three films that delivered more than $50 million at the box-office: "Next Friday," "Frequency" and "Final Destination." "The Cell" came in at over $60 million in the US from a late August start. "Little Vampire" only opened to $5.5 million on over 2000 screens, but Adam Sandler's "Little Nicky" brightened a lot of November screens. December brought the film based on the fantasy role-playing game, "Dungeons and Dragons" and Kevin Costner headlined "Thirteen Days." The most anticipated release of 2001 is the first installment of "The Lord of the Rings," which is based on the beloved trilogy written by J.R.R. Tolkein.

MGM spent most of the year 2000 on the sidelines. "Return to Me" with David Duchovy and Minnie Driver and "Autumn in New York" with Richard Gere and Winona Ryder both did over $30 million in the US. "Supernova" only managed $14 million. Hopefully the management and ownership difficulties of the studio are a thing of the past and the 2001 release schedule, which includes the Ridley Scott directed "Hannibal" with Anthony Hopkins, will make the Lion roar again.

STUDIO RELATED INDEPENDENTS

Sony Classics continued their incredibly long and consistent string of critical and commercial success this year with pictures such as "Crouching Tiger, Hidden Dragon," "East West," "Bossa Nova" and films like "The Tao of Steve" and "Color of Paradise."

This distributor has often been criticized for not taking more production or distribution release risk, but they have repeatedly demonstrated that they know how to wring the maximum amount of profit from every film they release.

Fine Line also had a fine year with films like "Saving Grace" which won the audience award at Sundance and has done $12 million in the US alone. The singer Bjork turned in a powerful role in the Palme d'Or winning "Dancer in the Dark." The Holidays brought Julian Schnabel's "Before Night Falls" and David Mamet's "State and Main."

Paramount Classics also had a strong year. "Virgin Suicides" and "Sunshine" did $4 and $5 million respectively. "Girl on the Bridge" and "Passion of Mind" also did well.

Fox Searchlight did not repeat the success of last year's "Boys Don't Cry" and the man who had been in charge of production, Lindsay Law, left to produce "The Full Monty" on Broadway. Searchlight did release "Woman on Top" and is looking forward to their 2001 release slate.

THE INDEPENDENTS

USA Films won two Academy Awards in their first year of operation last year for "Topsy- Turvy" and did fine in their second year of operation. "Pitch Black" produced $39 million and "Nurse Betty" did $24 million. Director Steven Soderbergh's "Traffic" with Michael Douglas and Catherine Zeta-Jones was the Christmas release. Next year will bring the Michael Douglas produced "One Night at McCools" and "Possession" starring Gwyneth Paltrow.

Destination had a year that was continually subject to the rumor mills about their impending collapse. They did release "Mysteries of Egypt" to $40 million of business in the US. "Drowning Mona" was an interesting, quirky film that did $15 million and "Thomas and the Magic Railroad" produced $16 million box-office.

There is no way that Artisan could replicate the unbelievable success of "The Blair Witch Project" and "Blair Witch 2: Book of Shadows" did not. However, the company continued to release an interesting and eclectic group of films including Roman Polanski's "The Ninth Gate" which did $15 million and Robert Altman's "Dr T and the Women" which starred Richard Gere and delivered a similar number. "Blair Witch 3" will come in 2001.

Lions Gate released the controversial "American Psycho" to $15 million and had some success with "The Big Kahuna," "But I'm A Cheerleader" and the wrestling expose, "Beyond the Mat."

Shooting Gallery had great limited release success with "Croupier" which did over $6.5 million, but the most interesting thing was the distribution pattern and marketing alliances created by the company. Shooting Gallery got corporate sponsors to pay most of the marketing and distribution costs for a festival of films that played initially for two week runs each in Loews Cineplex theatres in about fifteen cities around the US. After the two-week runs Shooting Gallery was free to move the prints to other theatres.

The producers got their films played, Loews Cineplex had 24 weeks of quality product in fifteen theatres, the sponsors got exposure, the audiences and critics got to see films that might not have been released theatrically, and Shooting Gallery got the rest of the Industry's admiration or envy.

Trimark did almost $5 million worth of business with "Held Up" and Zeitgeist did well with "Aimee & Jaguar." Kino had two interesting films with "Time Regained" and "Kadosh." Other specialized distributors such as Castle Hill, Cowboy Booking, First Run, the new company Lot 47 and New Yorker continue to bring controversial, engaging and challenging fare to the screens. Phaedra, Rialto, Strand and Windstar all cater to niche audiences that help bring an extraordinary richness and diversity of product to the theatres.

EXHIBITORS

This sector of the Industry is in the midst of a period of uncertainty and the litany of woes is loud and substantial. Six major circuits were in Chapter 11 by November and many people are speculating that Regal will be the next to go if the investment house owners, Kohlberg, Kravis and Roberts and Hicks, Muse, Tate & Furst cannot restructure the debt. Industry pundits state that the number of screens in the US needs to be reduced by twenty to twenty-five percent from current levels before Exhibition is healthy and profitable again. The quality of the film-going experience in the new theatres has raised the bar so high that the older theatres just cannot compete. The cost to build a theatre has gone from $100,000 per screen to as high as $1 million per screen. Exhibitors are locked into losing, long-term leases on those smaller multiplexes that have been made obsolete by the huge category killer mega-multiplexes. Chapter 11 is an increasingly compelling strategy to shed wasting assets. Journalists delight in pointing fingers at theatre owners for overbuilding and over-leveraging their companies. Increased competition forces theatre operators to run the same film on many screens, shortening the length of the run and subsequently driving up film rental. Capital and cash flow have dried up. There is increasing competition from home entertainment, particularly the Internet. Many households have huge TV sets and sophisticated home entertainment centers that deliver filmed content via cable, satellite, DVD, VHS or free TV with superb sound. There is increasing competition for all leisure time dollars. Is the sky falling? Is this the end of Exhibition, as we know it? No way.

The demise of motion picture theatres has been predicted since the invention of television, probably even before that. Pay-per-view, cable, videotape, satellite and DVD all in turn, and now, "streaming media" were all supposed to be the death knell for theatres. But showmen always adapt. Periodically, there are currents of change that sweep through Exhibition and the entire Industry. Change creates uncertainty, but it also creates opportunity. Mega-multiplexes with stadium seating, superb sound, perfect sight lines and all the other wonderful amenities present in the new theatres are all there for a simple reason: audiences love them. The quality of the environment, the attention to customer service and playing the best films are all part of the way that Exhibitors brand their theatres, build their audiences and turn their theatres into true entertainment destinations. The new theatres show films the way that Filmmakers intend them to be seen. Entrepreneurs, major circuits and niche players alike will experiment with different programming and different approaches to the business of running theatres and the customer's theatrical experience. It has been clear for some time that the number of theatre locations would decline, while the number of screens per location would increase. What is happening in Exhibition is uncomfortable and creates anxiety, but it is part of the natural evolution of the Industry.

Many theatre circuits and individual operators are looking at ways to weather the recent financial storms. The first step is usually by trying to improve the quality of the theatre and the quality of the presentation of the film. The second is usually in the food and beverage department. Concessions have been the major, sometimes only, source of profit for theatres for many years and the plethora of food and drinks offered in theatres today are astounding. Also, there have been efforts to focus on niche programming and marketing it to children, seniors, ethnic or affinity groups, particularly in non-peak times. In spite of some significant customer resistance, revenue-generating screen advertising on slide and moving stock is ubiquitous throughout the Exhibition community. In fact, some theatres are using virtually every square inch of their lobbies as marketing, promotional, advertising or rental spaces. Smart marketers are making forays into database marketing and using web sites and email to promote films and their theatres. Many companies are looking into alternative uses for the theatres during non-peak times. There are obvious business reasons for this in that these very expensive physical plants are operated 365 days each year for up to twelve hours daily, yet are only really used on Friday and Saturday night. The utilization of most theatres in the US is considerably below 15%. Most theatres are now distributing their show times electronically to both paid and unpaid media. There have also been significant strides in electronic ticketing in the lobby, at remote kiosks and over the Internet by groups of theatre owners and third parties.

Probably the best proof of the long-term viability of motion picture theatres is the fact that investors from within and outside the Industry are starting to nose around some of the distressed circuits in the hope of picking up a bargain. Those circuits that did not take on inordinate debt are in a position to scoop up attractive theatres or circuits. Whoever figures out alternative uses for the space vacated by the closing theatres will be wealthy. Someone will. It has been stated that one of the alternatives for Regal Cinemas rather than Chapter 11 is to have it acquire other circuits and get even bigger. Outside value investors like billionaire Philip Anschutz, who has invested in United Artists Theatre Circuit, may well view his investment as the start of a move to roll up and consolidate this segment. The next twelve months will prove to be challenging for Exhibition and the landscape may change considerably, but large audiences will still go to see their films in theatres that are continually getting better.

NEW CENTURY, NEW HORIZONS

Significant change seems to come to the Motion Picture Industry very slowly. After all, stadium-style seating has been around for thousands of years. Twenty-four frames per second has been the film speed rate for a long time and stereo sound, Cinemascope and 3-D were all invented a half century ago. The way films are made, distributed and displayed has changed very little and very slowly in 100 years. However, this seems to be one of the times when there will be fairly significant change, quickly.

Financial, technical and artistic concerns are driving this change. Filmmaking is an expensive and laborious process and the costs are increasing each year. The physical distribution and traditional marketing costs of films also are huge. Separate from the current problem of an over-supply of screens, Exhibitors' theatres are empty much more than they are full. Producers and Distributors need to reduce costs and Exhibitors need to drive traffic and increase revenue.

Technology has created new markets for filmed entertainment delivered to the home, which in turn creates demand for more production. The good news for Exhibitors is that they tend to be the first beneficiary of increased production. Studios, Distributors and other rights holders have proven adroit at exploiting their films as new distribution channels develop. This helps insure the continued profitability of Filmmakers and Distributors. What remains to be done is to figure out how to use new technologies such as the Internet to cost-effectively market the films to audiences and help deliver them to the theatres. One of the exciting things about digital filmmaking and distribution is that it has the potential to substantially reduce the cost to produce and distribute films. If theatres can use digital projectors for other revenue producing purposes in non-peak times, or dramatically expand the product they offer, then this part of the Industry could get healthy in a hurry.

No matter what the next year will bring, 2001 promises to an exciting, interesting and challenging time to be in the Industry.

Motion Picture Statistics

EXHIBITION

GROSSES AND ADMISSIONS

Domestic theatrical grosses were reported at $6,949 million in 1998, up 9.2% vs. 1997 and a 38.4% increase vs. 1990. Total U.S. theatre admissions in 1998 were 1,480.7 million, a 6.7% increase vs. 1997 and a 24.6% increase vs. 1990.

	Gross ($ millions)	Admissions (millions)	Per week (millions)
1999	7,448.0	1,465.2	28.2
1998	6,949.0	1480.7	28.5
1997	6,365.9	1,387.7	26.7
1996	5,911.5	1,338.6	25.7
1995	5,493.5	1,262.6	24.3
1994	5,396.2	1,291.7	24.8
1993	5,154.2	1,244.0	23.9
1992	4,871.0	1,173.2	22.6
1991	4,803.2	1,140.6	21.9
1990	5,021.8	1,188.6	22.9
1989	5,033.4	1,262.8	24.3
1988	4,458.4	1,084.8	20.9
1987	4,252.9	1,088.5	20.9
1986	3,778.0	1,017.2	19.6
1985	3,749.4	1,056.1	20.3
1984	4,030.6	1,199.1	23.1
1983	3,766.0	1,196.9	23.0
1982	3,452.7	1,175.4	22.6
1981	2,965.6	1,067.0	20.5
1980	2,748.5	1,021.5	19.6
1979	2,821.3	1,120.9	21.6
1978	2,643.4	1,128.2	21.7
1977	2,372.3	1,063.2	20.4
1976	2,036.4	957.1	18.4
1975	2,114.8	1,032.8	19.9
1974	1,908.5	1,010.7	19.4
1973	1,523.5	864.6	16.6
1972	1,583.1	934.1	18.0
1971	1,349.5	820.3	15.8
1970	1,429.2	920.6	17.7
1969	1,294.0	911.9	17.5
1968	1,282.0	978.6	18.8
1967	1,110.0	926.5	17.8
1966	1,067.1	975.4	18.8
1965	1,041.8	1,031.5	19.8
1964	947.6	1,024.4	19.7
1963	925.0	1,093.4	21.0
1962	874.9	1,080.1	20.8
1961	945.5	1,224.7	23.6
1960	984.4	1,304.5	25.1
1959	1,006.0	1,488.2	28.6
1958	1,010.0	1,553.8	29.9
1957	1,078.0	1,727.6	33.2
1956	1,125.0	1,893.9	36.4
1955	1,204.0	2,072.3	39.9
1954	1,251.0	2,270.4	43.7
1953	1,339.0	2,630.6	50.6
1952	1,325.0	2,777.7	53.4
1951	1,332.0	2,840.1	54.6
1950	1,379.0	3,017.5	58.0
1949	1,448.0	3,168.5	60.9
1948	1,506.0	3,422.7	65.8
1947	1,594.0	3,664.4	70.5
1946	1,692.0	4,067.3	78.2

Source: MPAA

ADMISSIONS PER CAPITA

	Admissions Per Capita	Yearly Change (%)	1999 Versus (%)
1999	5.4	-1.9	-
1998	5.5	5.8	-1.9
1997	5.2	2.7	3.7
1996	5.0	5.1	7.4
1995	4.8	-3.2	11.2
1994	5.0	2.8	7.4
1993	4.8	4.9	11.2
1992	4.6	1.7	14.9
1991	4.5	-5.1	16.7

ADMISSION PRICES

Average admission prices increased in 1999 to $5.08, an increase of 8.3% vs. 1998. Since 1980, admission prices have risen by 89% (from $2.69, dollars not adjusted).

	Average Admission Price ($)	Annual change (%)	1999 Versus (%)
1999	5.080	8.3	-
1998	4.690	1.6	8.3
1997	4.587	3.9	10.8
1996	4.416	1.5	15.0
1995	4.351	4.1	16.8
1994	4.178	0.8	21.6
1993	4.143	-0.2	22.6
1992	4.152	-1.4	22.4
1991	4.211	-0.3	20.6
1990	4.225	6.0	20.2
1989	3.986	-0.6	27.5
1988	4.110	5.2	23.6
1987	3.907	5.2	30.0
1986	3.714	4.6	36.8
1985	3.550	5.6	43.1
1984	3.361	6.8	51.1
1983	3.146	7.1	61.5
1982	2.937	5.7	72.9
1981	2.779	3.3	82.7
1980	2.690	--	88.8

ADMISSION DEMOGRAPHICS

The following admission demographics are compiled from the Motion Picture Association of America. These definitions apply with respect to frequency data: "Frequent" means "at least once per month," "Occasional" means "once in two to six months," "Infrequent" means "less than once in six months."

ATTENDANCE BY AGE GROUP

Age	% Resident Civilian Population as of 1/99	% of Total Annual Admissions 1999	1998	1997
12-15	7	11	10	9
16-20	9	20	18	17
21-24	6	10	6	9
25-29	8	12	10	12
30-39	19	18	17	19
40-49	18	14	16	15
50-59	13	7	11	9
60 +	20	8	9	9

FREQUENCY OF ATTENDANCE BY AGE GROUP, 1999

Age	Frequent %	Occasional %	Infrequent %	Never %
12-17	49	40	5	7
18 and over	28	29	13	30

FREQUENCY OF ATTENDANCE BY GENDER AND AGE, 1999

Gender and Age	Frequent %	Occasional %	Infrequent %	Never %
Males 12 and older	32	27	12	28
Females 12 and older	28	33	13	26
Males 18 and older	30	26	12	31
Females 18 and older	25	32	14	29

FREQUENCY OF ATTENDANCE BY MARITAL STATUS, 1999

Marital Status	Frequent %	Occasional %	Infrequent %	Never %
Married	21	36	11	32
Single	34	32	7	28

FREQUENCY OF ATTENDANCE BY FAMILY COMPOSITION, 1999

Family Type	Frequent %	Occasional %	Infrequent %	Never %
Adults with children under 18	30	35	14	20
Adults without children	26	25	12	36
Adults with teens, 12-17	32	31	12	25

FREQUENCY OF ATTENDANCE BY EDUCATIONAL BACKGROUND, 1999

Education	Frequent %	Occasional %	Infrequent %	Never %
Did not complete high school	19	23	11	46
Completed high school	20	25	15	39
At least some college	33	31	12	23

U.S. THEATRE AND SCREEN STATISTICS

Year	Total Screens	1999 Versus (%)	Indoor Screens	1999 Versus (%)	Drive-In Screens	1999 Versus (%)
1999	37,185	--	36,448	--	737	--
1998	34,186	8.8	33,440	9.0	746	-1.2
1997	31,640	17.5	30,825	18.2	815	-9.6
1996	29.690	25.2	28,864	26.3	826	-10.8
1995	27,805	33.7	26,958	35.2	847	-13.0
1994	26,586	39.9	25,701	41.8	885	-16.7
1993	25,737	44.5	24,887	46.5	850	-13.3
1990	23,689	57.0	22,774	60.0	915	-19.5
1985	21,147	75.8	18,327	98.9	2,820	-73.5
1980	17,590	111.4	14,029	159.8	3,561	-79.1

THE TOP 10 U.S. THEATRE CIRCUITS, 1999

Circuit	U.S. Theatres	U.S. Screens	% of All U.S. Screens	% of Top 10
Regal Cinemas	431	4464	12.0	24.0
Carmike	360	2424	6.5	13.0
Loews Cineplex	241	1956	5.3	10.5
United Artists	226	1685	4.5	9.0
AMC	188	2611	7.0	14.0
Cinemark	188	2180	5.9	11.7
National Amusements	109	1121	3.0	6.0
Hoyts	105	889	2.4	4.8
General Cinema	93	784	2.1	4.2
Kerasotes	90	521	1.4	2.8

PRODUCTION

NUMBER OF FILMS RATES & RELEASED, INCLUDING REISSUES

	Films Rated	Films Released
1999	677	461
1998	661	509
1997	679	510
1996	713	471
1995	697	411
1990	N/A	410

HIGH GROSSING FEATURES (FILM RENTALS)

	Films Grossing > 10 million	Films Grossing > 20 million
1999	71	42
1998	69	37
1997	66	39
1996	69	31
1995	75	36
1994	57	33
1993	64	28
1992	57	36
1991	68	30
1990	59	30
1985	42	13
1980	36	17

AVERAGE COSTS OF NEW FEATURES: PRODUCTION, ADVERTISING AND PRINTS*

	Production costs ($ millions)	Advertising ($ millions)	Print ($ millions)	Total ($ millions)
1999	51.50	21.4	3.1	76.0
1998	52.70	22.1	3.2	78.0
1997	53.42	19.2	3.0	75.7
1996	39.84	17.2	2.6	59.6
1995	36.37	15.4	2.3	54.0
1994	34.29	13.9	2.2	50.4
1993	29.91	12.1	1.9	44.0
1992	28.86	11.5	1.9	42.3
1991	26.14	10.4	1.6	38.2
1990	26.78	10.2	1.7	38.8
1985	16.80	5.2	1.2	23.3
1980	9.4	3.5	.8	13.7

*All figures in this table are for MPAA member companies

INDUSTRY FILM RATING SYSTEM (CARA RATINGS)

In the first three columns of the following table, "#" is the number of films released in the given year that received the corresponding rating, and "%" is the percentage of the total number of films released in the given year that received the corresponding rating. In the fourth (rightmost) column, "#" and "%" represent cumulative figures for the range 1968-1998.

	1999		1998		1997		1968-1998	
	#	%	#	%		#	%	
G	36	.5	40	.6	23	3.4	1,141	.8
PG	64	.9	70	11	97	14.4	3,746	.25
PG-13	107	.16	115	.17	117	.17.4	1,408	.9
R	468	.70	432	.65	432	.64.2	8173	.55
NC-17/X	0	.0	4	.6	4	0.6	418	.3
Totals	675	100.0	661	100.0	673	100.0	14,886	100.0

EMPLOYMENT

	Total (millions)	Production & Services (millions)	Exhibition (millions)	Video Tape Rental (millions)	Other (millions)
1999	600.1	265.5	144.2	170.5	19.9
1998	564.8	240.2	133.5	171.9	19.2
1997	548.1	233.4	131.8	162.9	20.0
1996	524.7	222.5	123.9	155.1	23.2
1995	487.6	200.7	118.7	146.1	22.1
1994	441.2	169.9	113.4	138.8	19.4
1993	412.0	152.7	110.6	132.4	16.3
1992	400.9	148.8	110.2	127.1	14.8
1991	410.9	153.1	112.0	131.2	14.6
1990	407.7	147.8	112.1	133.7	14.1

TOP TEN MEDIA GROUPS

All figures below reflect 1999-2000 annual revenue in billions and include all subsidiaries.

AOL Time Warner	34.2
Walt Disney	23.4
Vivendi Universal	22.6
Viacom	20.3
Sony	16.9
News Corp.	14.3
AT&T Broadband	8.6
Comcast	6.2
Tribune	6.0
Cox Enterprises	6.0

Sources: MPAA, Quigley Publishing Co.

TOP GROSSING FILMS 1990-2000

The ten top grossing films per year from 1990-2000, as selected by Quigley Publishing. Some films may have been held over from the previous year. The 2000 films are for the year as of October 15, 2000.

2000

Mission Impossible 2 (Par) 1
Gladiator (DrmWks) 2
The Perfect Storm (WB) 3
X-Men (Fox) 4
Scary Movie (Mir) 5
What Lies Beneath (DrmWks) 6
Dinosaur (BV) 7
Nutty Professor II: The Klumps (Uni) 8
Big Momma's House (20th/New Regency) 9
The Patriot (Sony) 10

1999

Star Wars: Episode 1 (20th Fox) 1
The Matrix (WB) 2
The Mummy (Univ) 3
Notting Hill (Univ) 4
The Sixth Sense (BV) 5
Austin Powers: The Spy Who Shagged Me (New Line) 6
Tarzan (BV) 7
Runaway Bride (Par) 8
Wild Wild West (WB) 9
Big Daddy (Sony) 10

1998

Saving Private Ryan (DrmWks) 1
Armageddon (BV) 2
There's Something About Mary (Fox) 3
A Bug's Life (BV) 4
The Waterboy (BV) 5
Doctor Dolittle (Fox) 6
Rush Hour (New Line) 7
Deep Impact (Par) 8
Good Will Hunting (Mir) 9
Patch Adams (Uni) 10

1997

Men In Black (Sony) 1
The Lost World (Uni) 2
Liar Liar (Uni) 3
Jerry Maguire (Sony) 4
Star Wars (reissue) 5
Ransom (BV) 6
101 Dalmations (BV) 7
Air Force One (Sony) 8
My Best Friend's Wedding (Sony) 9
Face/Off (Par) 10

1996

Independence Day (Fox) 1
Twister (WB) 2
Mission: Impossible (Par) 3
The Rock (BV) 4
Eraser (WB) 5
The Hunchback of Notre Dame (BV) 6
The Birdcage (MGM) 7
The Nutty Professor (Par) 8
Phenomenon (BV) 9
A Time to Kill (WB) 10

1995

Batman Forever (Warner) 1
Apollo 13 (Uni) 2
Toy Story (BV) 3
Pocahontas (BV) 4
Ace Ventura: When Nature Calls (Warner) 5
Casper (Uni) 6
Die Hard With A Vengeance (Fox) 7
Goldeneye (UA) 8
Crimson Tide (BV) 9
Waterworld (Uni) 10

1994

The Lion King (BV) 1
Forrest Gump (Par) 2
True Lies (Fox) 3
The Santa Clause (BV) 4
The Flintstones (Univ) 5
Dumb and Dumber (New Line) 6
The Mask (New Line) 7
Speed (Univ) 8
Clear and Present Danger (Par) 9
The Client (WB) 10

1993

Jurassic Park (Univ) 1
Mrs. Doubtfire (Fox) 2
The Fugitive (WB) 3
The Firm (Par) 4
Sleepless In Seattle (TriStar) 5
Indecent Proposal (Par) 6
Maverick (WB) 7
The Pelican Brief (WB) 8
In the Line of Fire (Col) 9
Schindler's List (Univ) 10

1992

Aladdin (BV) 1
Batman Returns (WB) 2
Lethal Weapon 3 (WB) 3
A Few Good Men (Col) 4
Sister Act (BV) 5
The Bodyguard (WB) 6
Wayne's World (Par) 7
A League of Their Own (Col) 8
Basic Instinct (TriStar) 9
Bram Stoker's Dracula (Col) 10

1991

Terminator 2 (TriStar) 1
Home Alone 2: Lost In New York (Fox) 2
Robin Hood: Prince of Thieves (Warner) 3
Beauty and the Beast (BV) 4
Hook (TriStar) 5
City Slickers (Col) 6
The Silence of the Lambs (Orion) 7
The Addams Family (Par) 8
Sleeping With the Enemy (Fox) 9
The Naked Gun 2 1/2: The Smell of Fear (Par) 10

1990

Home Alone (Fox) 1
Ghost (Par) 2
Pretty Woman (BV) 3
Dances With Wolves (Orion) 4
Teenage Mutant Ninja Turtles (New Line) 5
Die Hard 2 (Fox) 6
Total Recall (TriStar) 7
Dick Tracy (BV) 8
The Hunt for Red October (Par) 9
Back to the Future, Part III (Univ) 10

QP Top Ten Money-Makers Poll

QP Top Ten Poll of Money-Making Stars

In the 67th annual poll of circuit exhibitors and independent theater owners in the United States conducted by Quigley Publishing, these stars were voted the top ten money-makers of 1999:

Julia Roberts	1
Tom Hanks	2
Adam Sandler	3
Bruce Willis	4
Mike Myers	5
Tom Cruise	6
Will Smith	7
Mel Gibson	8
Meg Ryan	9
Sandra Bullock	10

The runners up: (11) Ashley Judd; (12) Gwyneth Paltrow; (13) Robin Williams; (14) Matt Damon; (15) Pierce Brosnan; (16) Jim Carrey; (17) Harrison Ford; (18) Liam Neeson; (19) Anthony Hopkins; (20) Keanu Reeves.

QP Stars of Tomorrow

Major and independent exhibitors were asked to name those stars they thought would be top money-makers within the next 5-10 years. The overwhelming choices were:

Christian Bale	1
Chloe Sevigny	2

QP Money-Making Stars of 1933-1998

1998: (1) Tom Hanks; (2) Jim Carrey; (3) Leonardo DiCaprio; (4) Robin Williams; (5) Meg Ryan; (6) Mel Gibson; (7) Adam Sandler; (8) Eddie Murphy; (9) Cameron Diaz; (10) Julia Roberts.

1997: (1) Harrison Ford; (2) Julia Roberts; (3) Leonardo DiCaprio; (4) Will Smith; (5) Tom Cruise; (6) Jack Nicholson; (7) Jim Carrey; (8) John Travolta; (9) Robin Williams; (10) Tommy Lee Jones.

1996: (1) Tom Cruise & Mel Gibson; (3) John Travolta; (4) Arnold Schwarzenegger; (5) Sandra Bullock; (6) Robin Williamsl (7) Sean Connery; (8) Harrison Ford; (9) Kevin Costner; (10) Michelle Pfeiffer.

1995: (1) Tom Hanks; (2) Jim Carrey; (3) Brad Pitt; (4) Harrison Ford; (5) Robin Williams; (6) Sandra Bullock; (7) Mel Gibson; (8) Demi Moore; (9) John Travolta; (10) Kevin Costner & Michael Douglas.

1994: (1) Tom Hanks; (2) Jim Carrey (3) Arnold Schwarzenegger; (4) Tom Cruise; (5) Harrison Ford; (6) Tim Allen; (7) Mel Gibson; (8) Jodie Foster; (9) Michael Douglas; (10) Tommy Lee Jones.

1993: (1) Clint Eastwood; (2) Tom Cruise; (3) Robin Williams; (4) Kevin Costner; (5) Harrison Ford; (6) Julia Roberts; (7) Tom Hanks; (8) Mel Gibson; (9) Whoopi Goldberg; (10) Sylvester Stallone.

1992: (1) Tom Cruise; (2) Mel Gibson; (3) Kevin Costner; (4) Jack Nicholson; (5) Macaulay Culkin; (6) Whoopi Goldberg; (7) Michael Douglas; (8) Clint Eastwood; (9) Steven Seagal; (10) Robin Williams.

1991: (1) Kevin Costner; (2) Arnold Schwarzenegger; (3) Robin Williams; (4) Julia Roberts; (5) Macaulay Culkin; (6) Jodie Foster; (7) Billy Crystal; (8) Dustin Hoffman; (9) Robert De Niro; (10) Mel Gibson.

1990: (1) Arnold Schwarzenegger; (2) Julia Roberts; (3) Bruce Willis; (4) Tom Cruise; (5) Mel Gibson; (6) Kevin Costner; (7) Patrick Swayze; (8) Sean Connery; (9) Harrison Ford; (10) Richard Gere.

1989: (1) Jack Nicholson; (2) Tom Cruise; (3) Robin Williams; (4) Michael Douglas; (5) Tom Hanks; (6) Michael J. Fox; (7) Eddie Murphy; (8) Mel Gibson; (9) Sean Connery; (10) Kathleen Turner.

1988: (1) Tom Cruise; (2) Eddie Murphy; (3) Tom Hanks; (4) Arnold Schwarzenegger; (5) Paul Hogan; (6) Danny De Vito; (7) Bette Midler; (8) Robin Williams; (9) Tom Selleck; (10) Dustin Hoffman.

1987: (1) Eddie Murphy; (2) Michael Douglas; (3) Michael J. Fox; (4) Arnold Schwarzenegger; (5) Paul Hogan; (6) Tom Cruise; (7) Glenn Close; (8) Sylvester Stallone; (9) Cher; (10) Mel Gibson.

1986: (1) Tom Cruise; (2) Eddie Murphy; (3) Paul Hogan; (4) Rodney Dangerfield; (5) Bette Midler; (6) Sylvester Stallone; (7) Clint Eastwood; (8) Whoopi Goldberg; (9) Kathleen Turner; (10) Paul Newman.

1985: (1) Sylvester Stallone; (2) Eddie Murphy; (3) Clint Eastwood; (4) Michael J. Fox; (5) Chevy Chase; (6) Arnold Schwarzenegger; (7) Chuck Norris; (8) Harrison Ford; (9) Michael Douglas; (10) Meryl Streep.

1984: (1) Clint Eastwood; (2) Bill Murray; (3) Harrison Ford; (4)Eddie Murphy; (5) Sally Field; (6) Burt Reynolds; (7) Robert Redford; (8) Prince; (9) Dan Aykroyd; (10) Meryl Streep.

1983: (1) Clint Eastwood; (2) Eddie Murphy; (3) Sylvester Stallone; (4) Burt Reynolds; (5) John Travolta; (6) Dustin Hoffman; (7)Harrison Ford; (8) Richard Gere; (9) Chevy Chase; (10) Tom Cruise.

1982: (1) Burt Reynolds; (2) Clint Eastwood; (3) Sylvester Stallone; (4) Dudley Moore; (5) Richard Pryor; (6) Dolly Parton; (7) Jane Fonda; (8) Richard Gere; (9) Paul Newman; (10) Harrison Ford.

1981: (1) Burt Reynolds; (2) Clint Eastwood; (3) Dudley Moore; (4)Dolly Parton; (5) Jane Fonda; (6) Harrison Ford; (7) Alan Alda; (8) Bo Derek; (9) Goldie Hawn; (10) Bill Murray.

1980: (1) Burt Reynolds; (2) Robert Redford; (3) Clint Eastwood; (4) Jane Fonda; (5) Dustin Hoffman; (6) John Travolta; (7) Sally Field; (8) Sissy Spacek; (9) Barbra Streisand; (10) Steve Martin.

1979: (1) Burt Reynolds; (2) Clint Eastwood; (3) Jane Fonda; (4) Woody Allen; (5) Barbra Streisand; (6) Sylvester Stallone; (7) John Travolta; (8) Jill Clayburgh; (9) Roger Moore; (10) Mel Brooks.

1978: (1) Burt Reynolds; (2) John Travolta; (3) Richard Dreyfuss; (4) Warren Beatty; (5) Clint Eastwood; (6) Woody Allen; (7) Diane Keaton; (8) Jane Fonda; (9) Peter Sellers; (10) Barbra Streisand.

1977: (1) Sylvester Stallone; (2) Barbra Streisand; (3) Clint Eastwood; (4) Burt Reynolds; (5) Robert Redford; (6) Woody Allen; (7) Mel Brooks; (8) Al Pacino; (9) Diane Keaton; (10) Robert De Niro.

1976: (1) Robert Redford; (2) Jack Nicholson; (3) Dustin Hoffman; (4) Clint Eastwood; (5) Mel Brooks; (6) Burt Reynolds; (7) Al Pacino; (8) Tatum O'Neal; (9) Woody Allen; (10) Charles Bronson.

1975: (1) Robert Redford; (2) Barbra Streisand; (3) Al Pacino; (4)Charles Bronson; (5) Paul Newman; (6) Clint Eastwood; (7) Burt Reynolds; (8) Woody Allen; (9) Steve McQueen; (10) Gene Hackman.

1974: (1) Robert Redford; (2) Clint Eastwood; (3) Paul Newman; (4) Barbra Streisand; (5) Steve McQueen; (6) Burt Reynolds; (7) Charles Bronson; (8) Jack Nicholson; (9) Al Pacino; (10) John Wayne.

1973: (1) Clint Eastwood; (2) Ryan O'Neal; (3) Steve McQueen; (4) Burt Reynolds; (5) Robert Redford; (6) Barbra Streisand; (7) Paul Newman; (8) Charles Bronson; (9) John Wayne; (10) Marlon Brando.

1972: (1) Clint Eastwood; (2) George C. Scott; (3) Gene Hackman; (4) John Wayne; (5) Barbra Streisand; (6) Marlon Brando; (7) Paul Newman; (8) Steve McQueen; (9) Dustin Hoffman; (10) Goldie Hawn.

1971: (1) John Wayne; (2) Clint Eastwood; (3) Paul Newman; (4) Steve McQueen; (5) George C. Scott; (6) Dustin Hoffman; (7) Walter Matthau; (8) Ali MacGraw; (9) Sean Connery; (10) Lee Marvin.

1970: (1) Paul Newman; (2) Clint Eastwood; (3) Steve McQueen; (4) John Wayne; (5) Elliott Gould; (6) Dustin Hoffman; (7) Lee Marvin; (8) Jack Lemmon; (9) Barbra Streisand; (10) Walter Matthau.

1969: (1) Paul Newman; (2) John Wayne; (3) Steve McQueen; (4) Dustin Hoffman; (5) Clint Eastwood; (6) Sidney Poitier; (7) Lee Marvin; (8) Jack Lemmon; (9) Katharine Hepburn; (10) Barbra Streisand.

1968: (1) Sidney Poitier; (2) Paul Newman; (3) Julie Andrews; (4) John Wayne; (5) Clint Eastwood; (6) Dean Martin; (7) Steve McQueen; (8) Jack Lemmon; (9) Lee Marvin; (10) Elizabeth Taylor.

1967: (1) Julie Andrews; (2) Lee Marvin; (3) Paul Newman; (4) Dean Martin; (5) Sean Connery; (6) Elizabeth Taylor; (7) Sidney Poitier; (8) John Wayne; (9) Richard Burton; (10) Steve McQueen.

1966: (1) Julie Andrews; (2) Sean Connery; (3) Elizabeth Taylor; (4) Jack Lemmon; (5) Richard Burton; (6) Cary Grant; (7) John Wayne; (8) Doris Day; (9) Paul Newman; (10) Elvis Presley.

1965: (1) Sean Connery; (2) John Wayne; (3) Doris Day; (4) Julie Andrews; (5) Jack Lemmon; (6) Elvis Presley; (7) Cary Grant; (8) James Stewart; (9) Elizabeth Taylor; (10) Richard Burton.

1964: (1) Doris Day; (2) Jack Lemmon; (3) Rock Hudson; (4) John Wayne; (5) Cary Grant; (6) Elvis Presley; (7) Shirley MacLaine; (8) Ann-Margret; (9) Paul Newman; (10) Jerry Lewis.

1963: (1) Doris Day; (2) John Wayne; (3) Rock Hudson; (4) Jack Lemmon; (5) Cary Grant; (6) Elizabeth Taylor; (7) Elvis Presley; (8) Sandra Dee; (9) Paul Newman; (10) Jerry Lewis.

1962: (1) Doris Day; (2) Rock Hudson; (3) Cary Grant; (4) John Wayne; (5) Elvis Presley; (6) Elizabeth Taylor; (7) Jerry Lewis; (8)Frank Sinatra; (9) Sandra Dee; (10) Burt Lancaster.

1961: (1) Elizabeth Taylor; (2) Rock Hudson; (3) Doris Day; (4) John Wayne; (5) Cary Grant; (6) Sandra Dee; (7) Jerry Lewis; (8)William Holden; (9) Tony Curtis; (10) Elvis Presley.

1960: (1) Doris Day; (2) Rock Hudson; (3) Cary Grant; (4) Elizabeth Taylor; (5) Debbie Reynolds; (6) Tony Curtis; (7) Sandra Dee; (8) Frank Sinatra; (9) Jack Lemmon; (10) John Wayne.

1959: (1) Rock Hudson; (2) Cary Grant; (3) James Stewart; (4) Doris Day; (5) Debbie Reynolds; (6) Glenn Ford; (7) Frank Sinatra; (8) John Wayne; (9) Jerry Lewis; (10) Susan Hayward.

1958: (1) Glenn Ford; (2) Elizabeth Taylor; (3) Jerry Lewis; (4) Marlon Brando; (5) Rock Hudson; (6) William Holden; (7) Brigitte Bardot; (8) Yul Brynner; (9) James Stewart; (10) Frank Sinatra.

1957: (1) Rock Hudson; (2) John Wayne; (3) Pat Boone; (4) Elvis Presley; (5) Frank Sinatra; (6) Gary Cooper; (7) William Holden; (8) James Stewart; (9) Jerry Lewis; (10) Yul Brynner.

1956: (1) William Holden; (2) John Wayne; (3) James Stewart; (4) Burt Lancaster; (5) Glenn Ford; (6) Dean Martin & Jerry Lewis; (7) Gary Cooper; (8) Marilyn Monroe; (9) Kim Novak; (10) Frank Sinatra.

1955: (1) James Stewart; (2) Grace Kelly; (3) John Wayne; (4) William Holden; (5) Gary Cooper; (6) Marlon Brando; (7) Dean Martin & Jerry Lewis; (8) Humphrey Bogart; (9) June Allyson; (10) Clark Gable.

1954: (1) John Wayne; (2) Martin & Lewis; (3) Gary Cooper; (4) James Stewart; (5) Marilyn Monroe; (6) Alan Ladd; (7) William Holden; (8) Bing Crosby; (9) Jane Wyman; (10) Marlon Brando.

1953: (1) Gary Cooper; (2) Martin & Lewis; (3) John Wayne; (4) Alan Ladd; (5) Bing Crosby; (6) Marilyn Monroe; (7) James Stewart; (8) Bob Hope; (9) Susan Hayward; (10) Randolph Scott.

1952: (1) Martin & Lewis; (2) Gary Cooper; (3) John Wayne ; (4) Bing Crosby; (5) Bob Hope; (6) James Stewart; (7) Doris Day; (8) Gregory Peck; (9) Susan Hayward; (10) Randolph Scott.

1951: (1) John Wayne; (2) Martin & Lewis; (3) Betty Grable; (4) Abbott & Costello; (5) Bing Crosby; (6) Bob Hope; (7) Randolph Scott; (8) Gary Cooper; (9) Doris Day; (10) Spencer Tracy.

1950: (1) John Wayne; (2) Bob Hope; (3) Bing Crosby; (4) Betty Grable; (5) James Stewart; (6) Abbott & Costello; (7) Clifton Webb; (8) Esther Williams; (9) Spencer Tracy; (10) Randolph Scott.

1949: (1) Bob Hope; (2) Bing Crosby; (3) Abbott & Costello; (4) John Wayne; (5) Gary Cooper; (6) Cary Grant; (7) Betty Grable; (8) Esther Williams; (9) Humphrey Bogart; (10) Clark Gable.

1948: (1) Bing Crosby; (2) Betty Grable; (3) Abbott & Costello; (4) Gary Cooper; (5) Bob Hope; (6) Humphrey Bogart; (7) Clark Gable; (8) Cary Grant; (9) Spencer Tracy; (10) Ingrid Bergman.

1947: (1) Bing Crosby; (2) Betty Grable; (3) Ingrid Bergman; (4) Gary Cooper; (5) Humphrey Bogart; (6) Bob Hope; (7) Clark Gable; (8) Gregory Peck; (9) Claudette Colbert; (10) Alan Ladd.

1946: (1) Bing Crosby; (2) Ingrid Bergman; (3) Van Johnson; (4) Gary Cooper; (5) Bob Hope; (6) Humphrey Bogart; (7) Greer Garson; (8) Margaret O'Brien; (9) Betty Grable; (10) Roy Rogers.

1945: (1) Bing Crosby; (2) Van Johnson; (3) Greer Garson; (4) Betty Grable; (5) Spencer Tracy; (6) Humphrey Bogart, Gary Cooper; (7) Bob Hope; (8) Judy Garland; (9) Margaret O'Brien; (10) Roy Rogers.

1944: (1) Bing Crosby; (2) Gary Cooper; (3) Bob Hope; (4) Betty Grable; (5) Spencer Tracy; (6) Greer Garson; (7) Humphrey Bogart; (8) Abbott & Costello; (9) Cary Grant; (10) Bette Davis.

1943: (1) Betty Grable; (2) Bob Hope; (3) Abbott & Costello; (4) Bing Crosby; (5) Gary Cooper; (6) Greer Garson; (7) Humphrey Bogart; (8) James Cagney; (9) Mickey Rooney; (10) Clark Gable.

1942: (1) Abbott & Costello; (2) Clark Gable; (3) Gary Cooper; (4) Mickey Rooney; (5) Bob Hope; (6) James Cagney; (7) Gene Autry; (8) Betty Grable; (9) Greer Garson; (10) Spencer Tracy.

1941: (1) Mickey Rooney; (2) Clark Gable; (3) Abbott & Costello; (4) Bob Hope; (5) Spencer Tracy; (6) Gene Autry; (7) Gary Cooper; (8) Bette Davis; (9) James Cagney; (10) Judy Garland.

1940: (1) Mickey Rooney; (2) Spencer Tracy; (3) Clark Gable; (4) Gene Autry; (5) Tyrone Power; (6) James Cagney; (7) Bing Crosby; (8) Wallace Beery; (9) Bette Davis; (10) Judy Garland.

1939: (1) Mickey Rooney; (2) Tyrone Power; (3) Spencer Tracy; (4) Clark Gable; (5) Shirley Temple; (6) Bette Davis; (7) Alice Faye; (8) Errol Flynn; (9) James Cagney; (10) Sonja Henie.

1938: (1) Shirley Temple; (2) Clark Gable; (3) Sonja Henie; (4) Mickey Rooney; (5) Spencer Tracy; (6) Robert Taylor; (7) Myrna Loy; (8) Jane Withers; (9) Alice Faye; (10) Tyrone Power.

1937: (1) Shirley Temple; (2) Clark Gable; (3) Robert Taylor; (4) Bing Crosby; (5) William Powell; (6) Jane Withers; (7) Fred Astaire and Ginger Rogers; (8) Sonja Henie; (9) Gary Cooper; (10)Myrna Loy.

1936: (1) Shirley Temple; (2) Clark Gable; (3) Fred Astaire and Ginger Rogers; (4) Robert Taylor; (5) Joe E. Brown; (6) Dick Powell; (7) Joan Crawford; (8) Claudette Colbert; (9) Jeanette MacDonald; (10) Gary Cooper.

1935: (1) Shirley Temple; (2) Will Rogers; (3) Clark Gable; (4) Fred Astaire and Ginger Rogers; (5) Joan Crawford; (6) Claudette Colbert; (7) Dick Powell; (8) Wallace Beery; (9) Joe E. Brown; (10) James Cagney.

1934: (1) Will Rogers; (2) Clark Gable; (3) Janet Gaynor; (4) Wallace Beery; (5) Mae West; (6) Joan Crawford; (7) Bing Crosby; (8) Shirley Temple; (9) Marie Dressler; (10) Norma Shearer.

1933: (1) Marie Dressler; (2) Will Rogers; (3) Janet Gaynor; (4)Eddie Cantor; (5) Wallace Beery; (6) Jean Harlow; (7) Clark Gable; (8) Mae West; (9) Norma Shearer; (10) Joan Crawford.

1932: (1) Marie Dressler; (2) Janet Gaynor; (3) Joan Crawford; (4) Charles Farrell; (5) Greta Garbo; (6) Norma Shearer; (7) Wallace Beery; (8) Clark Gable; (9) Will Rogers; (10) Joe E. Brown.

NATIONAL & INTERNATIONAL AWARDS

ACADEMY AWARD WINNERS 1999

The 72nd annual Academy Awards were presented on March 26, 2000 by the Academy of Motion Picture Arts and Sciences.

PICTURE
American Beauty, A Jinks/Cohen Co. production; Bruce Cohen and Dan Jinks, producers. DreamWorks.

ACTOR
Kevin Spacey, American Beauty, DreamWorks.

ACTRESS
Hilary Swank, Boys Don't Cry, Fox Searchlight.

SUPPORTING ACTOR
Michael Caine, The Cider House Rules, Miramax.

SUPPORTING ACTRESS
Angelina Jolie, Girl Interrupted, Sony.

DIRECTOR
Sam Mendes, American Beauty, DreamWorks.

FOREIGN LANGUAGE FILM
All About My Mother, An El Desea SA/Renn/France 2 Cine production, Spain.

ORIGINAL SCREENPLAY
Alan Ball, American Beauty.

ADAPTED SCREENPLAY
John Irving, The Cider House Rules.

CINEMATOGRAPHER
Conrad Hall, American Beauty.

ART DIRECTION
Rich Heinrichs (art direction), **Peter Young** (set decoration), Sleepy Hollow.

COSTUME DESIGN
Lindy Heming, Topsy-Turvy.

FILM EDITING
Zach Staenberg, The Matrix.

ORIGINAL SCORE
John Corigliano, The Red Violin.

ORIGINAL SONG
Phil Collins, "You'll Be in My Heart" from Tarzan.

SHORT SUBJECT—ANIMATED
The Old Man and the Sea, A Productions Pascal Blais/ Imagica Corp./Dentsu Tech./NHK Enterprise 21/ Panorama Studio of Yaroslvl production; Alexandre Petrov, producer.

SHORT SUBJECT—LIVE ACTION
My Mother Dreams the Satan's Disciples in New York, A Kickstart production; Barbara Schock and Tamara Tiehel, producers.

SOUND
John Reitz, Gregg Rudloff, David Campbell and David Lee, The Matrix.

SOUND EFFECTS EDITING
Dane A. Davis, The Matrix

MAKE-UP
Christine Blundell and Trefor Proud, Topsy-Turvy.

VISUAL EFFECTS
John Gaeta, Janek Sirrs, Steve Courtley and Jon Thum, The Matrix.

DOCUMENTARY—FEATURE
One Day in September, An Arthur Cohn Production; Arthur Cohn and Kevin Macdonald.

DOCUMENTARY—SHORT SUBJECT
King Gimp, A Whiteford-Hadary/University of Maryland/ Tapestry International Production; Susan Hannah Hadary and William A. Whiteford.

THE IRVING G. THALBERG AWARD
Warren Beatty.

THE GORDON E. SAWYER AWARD
Dr. Roderick T. Ryan.

THE JOHN A. BONNER MEDAL OF COMMENDATION
Edmund M. DiGiulio and Takuo Miyagishima.

ACADEMY AWARD WINNERS 1995-1998

Productions, players, directors and craftspersons named for superior merit by the Academy of Motion Picture Arts and Sciences, from 1995-1998. For a complete list of winners from the inception of the awards, please see Vols. 1995 and earlier.

1998

PICTURE
Shakespeare In Love, A Miramax Films, Universal Pictures, Bedford Falls Co. production, David Parfitt, Donna Gigliotti, Harvey Weinstein, Edward Zwick and Marc Norman, producers.

ACTOR
Roberto Benigni, Life Is Beautiful, Miramax.

ACTRESS
Gwyneth Paltrow, Shakespeare In Love, Miramax.

SUPPORTING ACTOR
James Coburn, Affliction, Lions Gate.

SUPPORTING ACTRESS
Judi Dench, Shakespeare In Love, Miramax.

DIRECTOR
Steven Spielberg, Saving Private Ryan, DreamWorks.

FOREIGN LANGUAGE FILM
Life Is Beautiful, A Melampo Cinematografica production, Italy.

ORIGINAL SCREENPLAY
Shakespeare In Love, Marc Norman and Tom Stoppard.

ADAPTED SCREENPLAY
Gods and Monsters,written for the screen by Bill Condon.

CINEMATOGRAPHER
Saving Private Ryan, Janusz Kaminski.

ART DIRECTION
Martin Childs (art direction), **Jill Qiertier** (set decoration), Shakespeare In Love.

COSTUME DESIGN
Sandy Powell, Shakespeare In Love.

FILM EDITING
Michael Kahn, Saving Private Ryan.

ORIGINAL DRAMATIC SCORE
Nicola Piovani, Life Is Beautiful.

ORIGINAL MUSICAL OR COMEDY SCORE
Stephen Warbeck, Shakespeare In love.

ORIGINAL SONG
"When You Believe," from The Prince of Egypt; music and lyrics by Stephen Schwartz.

SHORT SUBJECT—ANIMATED
Bunny, A Blue Sky Studios, Inc. production; Chris Wedge, producer.

SHORT SUBJECT—LIVE ACTION
Election Night, An M&M production; Kim Magnusson and Anders Thomas Jensen, producers.

SOUND
Gary Rydstrom, Gary Summers, Andy Nelson and Ronald Judkins, Saving Private Ryan.

SOUND EFFECTS EDITING
Gary Rydstrom and Richard Hymns, Saving Private Ryan.

MAKE-UP
Jenny Shircore, Elizabeth.

VISUAL EFFECTS
Joel Hynk, Nicholas Brooks, Stuart Robertson and Kevin Mack, What Dreams May Come.

DOCUMENTARY—FEATURE
The Last Days, A Survivors of the Shoah Visual History Foundation production, James Moll and Ken Lipper.

DOCUMENTARY—SHORT SUBJECT
The Personals: Improvisations on Romance in the Golden Years, A Keiko Ibi Film, Keiko Ibi.

THE IRVING G. THALBERG AWARD
Norman Jewison.

HONORARY AWARD
Elia Kazan.

1997

PICTURE
Titanic, A 20th Century Fox and Paramount production, Jon Landau and James Cameron, producers.

ACTOR
Jack Nicholson, As Good As It Gets, a TriStar production.

ACTRESS
Helen Hunt, As Good As It Gets, a TriStar production.

SUPPORTING ACTOR
Robin Williams, Good Will Hunting, a Miramax production.

SUPPORTING ACTRESS
Kim Basinger, L.A. Confidential, Warner Bros.

DIRECTOR
James Cameron, Titanic.

FOREIGN LANGUAGE FILM
Character, A First Floor Features Production (The Netherlands).

ORIGINAL SCREENPLAY
Ben Affleck and Matt Damon, Good Will Hunting.

ADAPTED SCREENPLAY
Brian Helgeland and Curtis Hanson, L.A. Confidential, Warner Bros.

CINEMATOGRAPHER
Russell Carpenter, Titanic.

ART DIRECTION
Peter Lamont (art direction), **Michael Ford** (set decoration), Titanic.

COSTUME DESIGN
Deborah L. Scott, Titanic.

FILM EDITING
Conrad Buff, James Cameron and Richard A. Harris, Titanic.

ORIGINAL DRAMATIC SCORE
James Horner, Titanic.

ORIGINAL MUSICAL OR COMEDY SCORE
Anne Dudley, The Full Monty, a Fox Searchlight production.

ORIGINAL SONG
"My Heart Will Go On," from Titanic; Music by James Horner, lyric by Will Jennings.

SHORT SUBJECT—ANIMATED
Geri's Game, A Pixar Animation Studios production, produced by Jan Pinkava.

SHORT SUBJECT—LIVE ACTION
Visas and Virtue, A Cedar Grove production, produced by Chris Tashima and Chris Donahue

SOUND
Gary Rydstrom, Tom Johnson, Gary Sumers and Mark Ulano, Titanic.

SOUND EFFECTS EDITING
Tom Bellfort and Christopher Boyes, Titanic.

MAKE-UP
Rick Baker and David LeRoy Anderson, Men In Black, Columbia Pictures.

VISUAL EFFECTS
Robert Legato, Mark Lasoff, Thomas L. Fisher and Michael Kanfer, Titanic.

DOCUMENTARY—FEATURE
The Long Way Home, A Moriah Films production at the Simon Wiesenthal Center, produced by Rabbi Marvin Hier and Richard Trank.

DOCUMENTARY—SHORT SUBJECT
A Story of Healing, A Dewey-Obenchain Films production, produced by Donna Dewey and Carol Pasternak.

HONORARY AWARD
Stanley Donen, in appreciation of a body of work marked by grace, elegance, wit and visual innovation.

JOHN A. BONNER MEDAL OF COMMENDATION
Pete Clark, for outstanding service and dedication in upholding the high standards of the Academy.

ACADEMY AWARD OF MERIT
Gunnar P. Michelson, for the engineering and development of an improved, electronic, high-speed, precision light valve for use in motion picture printing machines.

1996

PICTURE
The English Patient, A Tiger Moth production, Saul Zaentz, producer.

ACTOR
Geoffrey Rush, Shine, Momentum Films, Fine Line Features.

ACTRESS
Frances McDormand, Fargo, a Working Title production.

SUPPORTING ACTOR
Cuba Gooding, Jr., Jerry Maguire, a TriStar Pictures production, Sony Pictures Entertainment.

SUPPORTING ACTRESS
Juliette Binoche, The English Patient.

DIRECTOR
Anthony Minghella, The English Patient.

FOREIGN LANGUAGE FILM
Kolya, Biograf Jan Sverak/Portobello Pictures/Ceska Televize/Pandora Cinema production Miramax (Czech Republic).

ORIGINAL SCREENPLAY
Ethan Coen & Joel Coen, Fargo.

ADAPTED SCREENPLAY
Billy Bob Thornton, Slingblade, A Shooting Gallery production, Miramax.

CINEMATOGRAPHER
John Seale, The English Patient.

ART DIRECTION
Stuart Craig (art direction), **Stephanie McMillan** (set decoration), The English Patient.

COSTUME DESIGN
Ann Roth, The English Patient.

FILM EDITING
Walter Murch, The English Patient.

ORIGINAL DRAMATIC SCORE
Gabriel Yared, The English Patient.

ORIGINAL MUSICAL OR COMEDY SCORE
Rachel Portman, Emma, a Matchmaker Films production in association with Haft Entertainment, Miramax.

ORIGINAL SONG
"You Must Love Me," from Evita; Music by Andrew Lloyd Webber, lyric by Tim Rice.

SHORT SUBJECT—ANIMATED
Quest, A Thomas Stellmach Animation production; Stellmach, Tyron Montgomery, producers.

SHORT SUBJECT—LIVE ACTION
Dear Diary, A Dreamworks production; David Frankel, Barry Jossen, producers.

SOUND
Walter Murch, Mark Berger, David Parker, Chris Newman, The English Patient.

SOUND EFFECTS EDITING
Bruce Stambler, The Ghost and the Darkness, a Douglas/Reuther production, Paramount.

MAKE-UP
Rick Baker, David Leroy Anderson, The Nutty Professor, an Imagine Entertainment production, Universal.

VISUAL EFFECTS
Voker Engel, Douglas Smith, Clay Pinney, Joseph Viskocil, Independence Day, a Centropolis Entertainment production, 20th Century Fox.

DOCUMENTARY—FEATURE
When We Were Kings, UFA Non-Fiction/USA, Gramercy, DASFilms Ltd; Leon Gast, David Sonenberg, producers.

DOCUMENTARY—SHORT SUBJECT
Breathing Lessons: The Life and Work of Mark O'Brien, an Inscrutable Films/Pacific News Service production; Jessica Yu, producer.

IRVING G. THALBERG MEMORIAL AWARD
Saul Zaentz

CAREER ACHIEVEMENT AWARD
Michael Kidd

SCIENTIFIC AND TECHNICAL
Imax Corp., for its large format movies.

1995

PICTURE
Braveheart, An Icon Productions/Ladd Company production.

ACTOR
Nicolas Cage, Leaving Las Vegas.

ACTRESS
Susan Sarandon, Dead Man Walking.

SUPPORTING ACTOR
Kevin Spacey, The Usual Suspects.

SUPPORTING ACTRESS
Mira Sorvino, Mighty Aphrodite.

DIRECTOR
Mel Gibson, Braveheart.

FOREIGN LANGUAGE FILM
Antonia's Line, A Bergen Theatre-Film-Television Prod., (Dutch).

ORIGINAL SCREENPLAY
Christopher McQuarrie, The Usual Suspects.
ADAPTED SCREENPLAY
Emma Thompson, Sense and Sensibility.
CINEMATOGRAPHER
John Toll, Braveheart.
ART DIRECTION
Eugenio Zanetti, Restoration.
COSTUME DESIGN
James Acheson, Restoration.
FILM EDITING
Mike Hill, Dan Hanley, Apollo 13.
ORIGINAL SCORE
Luis Bacalov, Il Postino (The Postman).
ORIGINAL SONG
"Colors of the Wind," from Pocahontas; Music by Alan Menken, lyric by Steven Schwartz.
SHORT SUBJECT—ANIMATED
A Close Shave, An Aardman Animations production; Nick Park.
SHORT SUBJECT—LIVE ACTION
Lierberman In Love, A Chanticleer Films production; Christine Lahti and Jana Sue Memel.
SOUND
Rick Dior, Steve Pederswon, Scott Millan and David MacMillan, Apollo 13.
SOUND EFFECTS EDITING
Lon Bender, Per Hallberg, Braveheart.
MAKE-UP
Peter Frampton, Paul Pattison, Lois Burwell, Braveheart.
VISUAL EFFECTS
Scott E. Anderson, Charles Gibson, Neal Scanlan, John Cox, Babe.
DOCUMENTARY—FEATURE
Anne Frank Remembered, A Jon Blair Film Company Limited Production; Jon Blair, producer.
DOCUMENTARY—SHORT SUBJECT
One Survivor Remembers, An HBO and The United States Holocaust Memorial Museum production; Kathy Antolis, producer.
HONORARY ACADEMY AWARDS
Kirk Douglas, for 50 years as a creative and moral force in the motion picture community.
Chuck Jones, for the creation of classic cartoons and cartoon characters whose animated lives have brought joy to our real ones for more than half a century.
John Lasseter, for the development and inspired application of techniques that have made possible the first feature-length computer animated film.
SPECIAL AWARDS
Gordon E. Sawyer Award (Academy Statuette); **Donald C. Rogers**.

American Film Institute Lifetime Achievement Award

2000 RECIPIENT
Harrison Ford
PAST RECIPIENTS

Dustin Hoffman 1999
Robert Wise 1998
Martin Scorcese 1997
Clint Eastwood 1996
Steven Spielberg 1995
Jack Nicholson 1994
Elizabeth Taylor 1993
Sidney Poitier 1992
Kirk Douglas 1991
Sir David Lean 1990
Gregory Peck 1989
Jack Lemmon 1988
Barbara Stanwyck 1987
Billy Wilder 1986
Gene Kelly 1985
Lillian Gish 1984
John Huston 1983
Frank Capra 1982
Fred Astaire 1981
James Stewart 1980
Alfred Hitchcock 1979
Henry Fonda 1978
Bette Davis 1977
William Wyler 1976
Orson Welles 1975
James Cagney 1974
John Ford 1973

American Society of Cinematographers Awards

BEST CINEMATOGRAPHY
Conrad Hall, American Beauty.
LIFETIME ACHIEVEMENT AWARD
William A. Fraker

British Academy of Film & Television Arts (BAFTA) Awards

BEST FILM
American Beauty.
THE DAVID LEAN AWARD FOR BEST ACHIEVEMENT IN DIRECTION
Pedro Almodovar, All About My Mother.
BEST ORIGINAL SCREENPLAY
Being John Malkovich, Charlie Kaufman.
BEST ADAPTED SCREENPLAY
Neil Jordan, The End of the Affair.
BEST ACTRESS
Annette Bening, American Beauty.
BEST ACTOR
Kevin Spacey, American Beauty.
BEST SUPPORTING ACTRESS
Maggie Smith, Tea With Mussolini.
BEST SUPPORTING ACTOR
Jude Law, The Talented Mr. Ripley.
BEST FILM NOT IN THE ENGLISH LANGUAGE
All About My Mother.
BEST CINEMATOGRAPHY
Conrad Hall, American Beauty.
BEST PRODUCTION DESIGN
Rick Heinrichs, Sleepy Hollow.
BEST COSTUME DESIGN
Colleen Atwood, Sleepy Hollow.
BEST EDITING
Tariq Anwar and Christopher Greenbury, American Beauty.
BEST SOUND
David Lee, John Reitz, Gregg Rudloff, David Campbell and Dane A. Davis, The Matrix.
ACHIEVEMENT IN SPECIAL VISUAL EFFECTS
John Gaeta, Stee Courtley, Janek Sirrs and Jon Thum, The Matrix.
BEST MAKE-UP/HAIR
Christine Blundell, Topsy-Turvy.
BEST SHORT FILM
Who's My Favourite Girl, Joern Utliken, Kara Johnston and Adrian McDowall.
BEST SHORT ANIMATION
The Man With Beautiful Eyes, Jonathan Bairstow and Jonathan Hodgson.
THE FELLOWSHIP
Michael Caine, Stanley Kubrick.
THE ANTHONY ASQUITH AWARD FOR ACHIEVEMENT IN FILM MUSIC
Thomas Newman, American Beauty.
THE ALEXANDER KORDA AWARD FOR THE OUTSTANDING BRITISH FILM OF THE YEAR
East is East, Leslee Udwin and Damien O'Donnell.
THE MICHAEL BALCON AWARD FOR OUTSTANDING BRITISH CONTRIBUTION TO CINEMA
Joyce Herlihy.
THE CARL FOREMAN AWARD FOR THE MOST PROMISING NEWCOMER IN BRITISH FILM
Lynne Ramsay.
THE ORANGE AUDIENCE AWARD
Notting Hill.

Cannes Film Festival Awards

PALME D'OR
Dancer in the Dark, Lars Von Trier.
GRAND PRIZE
Guizi Lai Le, Wen Jiang.
JURY PRIZE
Takhte Siah, Samira Makhmalbaf.
Sanger Fran Andra Vaningen, Roy Andersson.
CAMERA D'OR
Djomeh, Hassan Yektapanah.
Zamani Baraye Masti Asbha, Bahman Ghobadi.
BEST ACTOR
Tony Leung, In The Mood For Love.
BEST ACTRESS
Bjork, Dancer in the Dark.
BEST DIRECTOR
Edward Yang, Yi Yi.
BEST SCREENPLAY
Neil LaBute, Nurse Betty.
SHORT FILM PALME D'OR
Anino, Raymond Red.

Directors Guild of America Award

FILM DIRECTOR'S AWARD
Sam Mendes, American Beauty.
DOCUMENTARY AWARD
Nanette Burstein and Brett Morgan, On The Ropes.
LIFETIME ACHIEVEMENT AWARD
Steven Spielberg.

Golden Globe Awards

BEST PICTURE—DRAMA
American Beauty.
BEST ACTOR—DRAMA
Denzel Washington, The Hurricane.
BEST ACTRESS—DRAMA
Hilary Swank, Boys Don't Cry.
BEST PICTURE—COMEDY OR MUSICAL
Toy Story 2.
BEST ACTOR—COMEDY OR MUSICAL
Jim Carrey, Man on the Moon.
BEST ACTRESS—COMEDY OR MUSICAL
Janet McTeer, Tumbleweeds.
BEST SUPPORTING ACTOR
Tom Cruise, Magnolia.
BEST SUPPORTING ACTRESS
Angelina Jolie, Girl Interrupted.
BEST DIRECTOR
Sam Mendes, American Beauty.
BEST SCREENPLAY
Alan Ball, American Beauty.
BEST ORIGINAL SCORE
Ennio Morricone, The Legend of 1900.
BEST ORIGINAL SONG
Phil Collins, "You'll Be In My Heart," Tarzan.
BEST FOREIGN FILM
All About My Mother.

Independent Spirit Awards

Awarded by the Independent Feature Project West in recognition of the contributions of independent filmmakers.

BEST FEATURE
Election.
BEST FIRST FEATURE (OVER $500,000)
Being John Malkovich.
BEST FIRST FEATURE (UNDER $500,000)
The Blair Witch Project.
BEST DIRECTOR
Alexander Payne, Election.
BEST ACTOR
Richard Farnsworth, The Straight Story.
BEST ACTRESS
Hilary Swank, Boys Don't Cry.
BEST SUPPORTING ACTOR
Steve Zahn, Happy Texas.
BEST SUPPORTING ACTRESS
Chloe Sevigny, Boys Don't Cry.
BEST SCREENPLAY
Alexander Payne and Jim Taylor, Election.
BEST FIRST SCREENPLAY
Charlie Kaufman, Being John Malkovich.
BEST CINEMATOGRAPHY
Lisa Rinzler, Three Seasons.
BEST FOREIGN FILM
Run Lola Run, Germany.
BEST DEBUT PERFORMANCE
Kimberly J. Brown, Tumbleweeds.

Los Angeles Film Critics Awards

BEST PICTURE
The Insider.
BEST ACTOR
Russell Crowe, The Insider.
BEST ACTRESS
Hilary Swank, Boys Don't Cry.
BEST SUPPORTING ACTOR
Christopher Plummer, The Insider.
BEST SUPPORTING ACTRESS
Chloe Sevigny, Boys Don't Cry.
BEST DIRECTOR
Sam Mendes, American Beauty.
BEST SCREENPLAY
Charlie Kaufman, Being John Malkovich.
BEST CINEMATOGRAPHY
Dante Spinotti, The Insider.
BEST MUSICAL SCORE
Trey Parker and **Marc Shaiman**, South Park: Bigger, Longer and Uncut.
BEST FOREIGN FILM
All About My Mother.
BEST ANIMATION
Iron Giant.
BEST DOCUMENTARY
The Buena Vista Social Club.

National Board of Review

BEST PICTURE
American Beauty.
BEST DIRECTOR
Anthony Mighella, The Talented Mr. Ripley.
BEST ACTOR
Russell Crowe, The Insider.
BEST ACTRESS
Janet McTeer, Tumbleweeds.
BEST SUPPORTING ACTOR
Philip Seymour Hoffman, Magnolia, The Talented Mr. Ripley.
SUPPORTING ACTRESS
Julianne Moore, An Ideal Husband, Cookie's Fortune, A Map of the World, Magnolia.
BEST DOCUMENTARY
The Buena Vista Social Club.
FIVE BEST FOREIGN FILMS
All About My Mother, East-West, Run Lola Run, Cabaret Balkan, The Emperor and the Assassin.
CAREER ACHIEVEMENT AWARD
Clint Eastwood.
SPECIAL ACHIEVEMENT IN FILMMAKING
Tim Robbins, Cradle Will Rock.

National Society of Film Critics Awards

BEST PICTURE
Topsy-Turvy and **Being John Malkovich (tie).**
BEST DIRECTOR
Mike Leigh, Topsy-Turvy.
BEST ACTOR
Russell Crowe, The Insider.
BEST ACTRESS
Reese Witherspoon, Election.
BEST SUPPORTING ACTOR
Christopher Plummer, The Insider.
BEST SUPPORTING ACTRESS
Chloe Sevigny, Boys Don't Cry.
BEST SCREENPLAY
Charlie Kaufman, Being John Malkovich.
BEST FOREIGN FILM
An Autumn Tale.

New York Film Critics Circle

BEST PICTURE
Topsy-Turvy.
BEST DIRECTOR
Mike Leigh, Topsy-Turvy.
BEST ACTOR
Richard Farnsworth, The Straight Story.
BEST ACTRESS
Hilary Swank, Boys Don't Cry.
BEST SUPPORTING ACTOR
John Malkovich, Being John Malkovich.
BEST SUPPORTING ACTRESS
Catherine Keener, Being John Malkovich.
BEST SCREENPLAY
Alexander Payne and Jim Taylor, Election.
BEST FOREIGN FILM
All About My Mother.
BEST CINEMATOGRAPHY
Freddie Francis, The Straight Story.
BEST FIRST FEATURE FILM
Spike Jonze, Being John Malkovich.
BEST ANIMATED FEATURE
South Park: Bigger, Longer and Uncut.
BEST NON-FICTION FEATURE
The Buena Vista Social Club.

Screen Actors Guild Awards

BEST ACTOR
Kevin Spacey, American Beauty.
BEST ACTRESS
Annette Bening, American Beauty.
BEST SUPPORTING ACTOR
Michael Caine, The Cider House Rules.
BEST SUPPORTING ACTRESS
Angelina Jolie, Girl Interrupted.
BEST ENSEMBLE CAST
American Beauty.

Industry Mergers & Acquisitions

(October 1, 1999—September 30, 2000)

The following list shows active merger & acquisition information through September, 2000. Pending transactions do not have effective dates. Included here are motion picture, video and television (including cable, satellite and wireless) companies as well as corporations from other industries with interests in entertainment or ancillary media.

Date Announced	Date Effective	Acquisition Target	Target Country	Acquired by	Acquiror Country	Status
			October 1999			
10/01/1999	04/07/2000	Haarlem Cable	Netherlands	United Pan-Europe Comm NV	Netherlands	Completed
10/01/1999	10/01/1999	Triangle MultiMedia Ltd	United States	Acciaierie Valbruna SRL	Italy	Completed
10/02/1999	10/06/1999	Fox Sports Australia	Australia	Publishing & Broadcasting Ltd	Australia	Completed
10/04/1999	02/28/2000	RCN Corp.	United States	Vulcan Ventures, Inc.	United States	Completed
10/04/1999	07/12/2000	TV Guide (Tele-Communications)	United States	Gemstar International Group	United States	Completed
10/04/1999	10/04/1999	Trixter Films GmbH	Germany	Das Werk Digitale Bildbearbeit	Germany	Completed
10/05/1999		Elnet	Greece	Despec Hellas	Greece	Pending
10/05/1999	10/05/1999	Plus Licens AB	Sweden	EM.TV & Merchandising AG	Germany	Completed
10/05/1999	10/05/1999	Sonics Associates Inc.	Canada	Imax Corp.	Canada	Completed
10/06/1999	10/06/1999	Thai Film Industries Ltd	Thailand	Bangkok Bank Public Co. Ltd	Thailand	Completed
10/07/1999	10/07/1999	Central European Media Entrp	Bermuda	Investor	Russia	Completed
10/08/1999	10/08/1999	Brand Union Ltd	United Kingdom	WPP Group PLC	United Kingdom	Completed
10/08/1999		ProSieben Media AG	Germany	KirchMedia KGAA (Kirch-Gruppe)	Germany	Pending
10/09/1999	10/09/1999	Mocom AG	Switzerland	Ruag Suisse AG	Switzerland	Completed
10/11/1999	10/11/1999	DK 4 (Tele Danmark)	Denmark	Euro909.com	Denmark	Completed
10/11/1999		VMH VideoMovieHouse.com	Canada	First American Scientific Corp.	United States	Pending
10/11/1999		WKBT-TV	United States	Television Wisconsin Inc.	United States	Pending
10/11/1999		Win's Movie Production Ltd	Hong Kong	China Prospect Group	Hong Kong	Pending
10/12/1999	10/12/1999	Chesapeake Microwave	United States	Andrew Corp.	United States	Completed
10/13/1999	10/13/1999	Facts & Fiction GmbH	Germany	Wunderman Cato Johnson GmbH	Germany	Completed
10/13/1999	10/13/1999	Harmon Cable Investments Inc.	United States	Cable One Inc. (Washington Post	United States	Completed
10/13/1999	10/13/1999	Harmon Cable Investments Inc.	United States	American MediaGroup, LLC	United States	Completed
10/13/1999	10/13/1999	Mesilla Valley Cable Co.	United States	TCI Cablevision of New Mexico	United States	Completed
10/13/1999		Sky Entertainment	Japan	J Sports	Japan	Pending
10/13/1999	10/13/1999	White Sands Cable	United States	TCI Cablevision of New Mexico	United States	Completed
10/14/1999	02/16/2000	Star Cable Associates	United States	Classic Communications Inc.	United States	Completed
10/15/1999	10/15/1999	Blue Zone Productions Ltd	Canada	Blue Zone Entertainment Inc.	Canada	Completed
10/15/1999	04/03/2000	Canadian Satellite Commun Inc.	Canada	Shaw Communications Inc.	Canada	Completed
10/15/1999		Sat 1 Schweiz AG	Switzerland	Ringier AG	Switzerland	Pending
10/15/1999	10/15/1999	Story Board	Spain	Indice Multimedia	Spain	Completed
10/15/1999	04/03/2000	WIC Western Int'l Comm-TV Stn	Canada	CanWest Global Communications	Canada	Completed
10/15/1999	04/03/2000	WIC Western Int'l-Specialty	Canada	CORUS Entertainment Inc.	Canada	Completed
10/18/1999	10/18/1999	Ogden Corp.	United States	Investor Group	United States	Completed
10/18/1999	10/26/1999	Virgin Group-Cinema Business	United Kingdom	UGC SA	France	Completed
10/19/1999	10/19/1999	Jugendfilm-Verleih GmbH	Germany	Kinowelt Medien AG	Germany	Completed
10/19/1999	10/19/1999	Pegasus Broadcasting Inc.	United States	LIN Television Corp.	United States	Completed
10/20/1999		Ascent Entertainment Group Inc.	United States	Liberty Media Group (AT&T Corp.)	United States	Withdrawn
10/20/1999	10/20/1999	Challenger Ppty-Complexes (4)	New Zealand	St Lukes Group	New Zealand	Completed
10/21/1999	10/21/1999	Barcika-TV Kft	Hungary	Investor Group	Hungary	Completed
10/21/1999	10/25/2000	Rogers Communications Inc.	Canada	Rogers Communications Inc.	Canada	Completed
10/21/1999	10/21/1999	Supercanal SA (Supercanal SA)	Spain	Union Electrica Fenosa SA	Spain	Completed
10/21/1999		TV 8 Brabant BV	Netherlands	Omroep Brabant	Netherlands	Pending
10/21/1999	10/21/1999	Television Eighteen India	India	Undisclosed Acquiror	Unknown	Completed
10/21/1999	10/21/1999	TT&T	Thailand	Seeking Buyer	Unknown	Completed
10/22/1999		Pullman Cinemas Ltd	United Kingdom	Seeking Buyer	Unknown	S Buyer
10/22/1999		Time Telecom	Malaysia	Seeking Buyer	Unknown	S Buyer
10/22/1999	10/22/1999	Videotron Bay Area (Sprint)	United States	Sprint Corp.	United States	Completed
10/25/1999	10/25/1999	Chinese Channel (TVB Int'll)	China	TVB	Hong Kong	Completed
10/25/1999		LNR Trexcom Inc. (Trex Comm)	United States	L-3 Communications Holdings	United States	Pending
10/25/1999	05/30/2000	NTL Inc.	United States	France Telecom SA (France)	France	Completed
10/26/1999	01/03/2000	Corporate Technologies	United States	Vicom Inc.	United States	Completed
10/26/1999		Knight Ridder Inc.	United States	Knight Ridder Inc.	United States	Intended
10/26/1999	10/29/1999	Stanford Telecom Mnfr Unit	United States	DII Group	United States	Completed
10/26/1999	12/09/1999	KirchMedia KGaA (Kirch-Gruppe)	Germany	Capital Research & Mangement	United States	Completed
10/26/1999	10/26/1999	Triptych Media Inc.	Canada	Salter Street Films Ltd	Canada	Completed
10/27/1999		Ofuna Studio, Kamakura, Japan	Japan	Kamakura Women's College	Japan	Pending
10/27/1999	11/19/1999	Portman Entertainment Group	United Kingdom	South Beach Concepts PLC	United Kingdom	Completed
10/27/1999	12/31/1999	Zugloi Kommunikacios Rt	Hungary	KFKI Szamitastechnikai Rt	Hungary	Completed
10/28/1999	10/28/1999	Larsen	United States	Radiall SA	France	Completed
10/28/1999	10/28/1999	Stamptronic SA	France	Adcon Telemetry AG	Austria	Completed
10/29/1999		Sonera-Mobicentrex Svc Sys Co.	Finland	Trio Information Systems AB	Sweden	Pending
10/31/1999	10/31/1999	Cologne Sitcom Prod GmbH & Co.	Germany	Pearson Television (Pearson)	United Kingdom	Completed
			November 1999			
11/01/1999	04/10/2000	Four Media Co.	United States	Liberty Media Group (AT&T Corp.)	United States	Completed
11/01/1999	11/01/1999	Keremeos Cable Ltd Cable Sys	Canada	Regional Cablesystems Inc.	Canada	Completed
11/01/1999	10/24/2000	Pontiac Cable Co.	Canada	Regional Cablesystems Inc.	Canada	Completed
11/01/1999		Shawville Cable Co.	Canada	Regional Cablesystems Inc.	Canada	Pending
11/01/1999	11/01/1999	Wood Lake Cable-Cbl Sys (2), BC	Canada	Regional Cablesystems Inc.	Canada	Completed
11/02/1999	11/02/1999	Antennentechnik R Busler GmbH	Germany	PrimaCom AG	Germany	Completed
11/02/1999		Golden Channels & Co.	Israel	Investor Group	Israel	Pending
11/02/1999	11/02/1999	Kabelcom Halberstadt	Germany	PrimaCom AG	Germany	Completed
11/03/1999		Harte-Hanks Inc.	United States	Harte-Hanks Inc.	United States	Intended
11/03/1999		KCBD-TV, Lubbock, Texas	United States	Cosmos Broadcasting Corp.	United States	Pending
11/03/1999	11/03/1999	Nova Televisia	Bulgaria	Antena TV	Greece	Completed
11/03/1999	11/03/1999	Serviradio SL	Spain	Taylor Nelson Sofres PLC	United Kingdom	Completed
11/03/1999	02/07/2000	Seven Network Ltd	Australia	Granada Group PLC	United Kingdom	Completed
11/03/1999	11/03/1999	Viva Fernsehen GmbH & Co. KG	Germany	Edel Music AG	Germany	Completed

Date Announced	Date Effective	Acquisition Target	Target Country	Acquired by	Acquiror Country	Status
11/04/1999	11/04/1999	ESPN Brasil (Tevecap SA)	Brazil	ESPN Inc.	United States	Completed
11/04/1999		Matthews Studio Equm Grp Prd	United States	Rio Grande Media Technology	United States	Pending
11/05/1999	11/05/1999	Behavior Interactive Inc.	Canada	3470172 Canada Inc.	Canada	Completed
11/05/1999		Cable Communications Ashiya	Japan	Kobe Cable Television Co.	Japan	Pending
11/05/1999	11/05/1999	Ogden Corp.	United States	Fir Tree Partners, LP	United States	Completed
11/05/1999	11/05/1999	Thomson-CSF (France)	France	Alcatel SA	France	Completed
11/06/1999	02/17/2000	ONPA International PLC	Thailand	Broadcasting Network Thailand	Thailand	Completed
11/08/1999		Jp Digital Broadcasting-Satell	Japan	NTT Satellite Communications	Japan	Pending
11/09/1999	02/02/2000	Qwest Broadcasting, LLC	United States	Tribune Co.	United States	Completed
11/09/1999	11/09/1999	Stan Lee Media	United States	Macromedia Inc.	United States	Completed
11/11/1999		April Films Entertainment	Australia	Macquarie Film and Television	Australia	Pending
11/11/1999		Matsushita Comm Ind-Brdcstg	Japan	Matsushita Electric Industrial	Japan	Pending
11/11/1999	12/08/1999	V-Bits Inc.	United States	Cisco Systems Inc.	United States	Completed
11/11/1999	03/01/2000	Nexus Telecommunications	Israel	Investor Group	Israel	Completed
11/12/1999	11/30/1999	Atlantic Telecom Group PLC	United Kingdom	Marconi PLC	United Kingdom	Completed
11/12/1999	11/12/1999	Cencom Cable Income-Cert Asts	United States	Galaxy Systems Management Inc.	United States	Completed
11/12/1999	11/12/1999	Triax Midwest-Cable TV Systems	United States	Mediacom, LLC	United States	Completed
11/13/1999	11/13/1999	Replay Networks Inc.	United States	Matsushita Kotobuki	Japan	Completed
11/15/1999	11/30/1999	Bob & Partners	Hong Kong	Star East Holdings Ltd	Hong Kong	Completed
11/15/1999	11/15/1999	Animasia International	Singapore	Pentafour Software & Exports	India	Completed
11/15/1999		HBO Brasil	Brazil	Seeking Buyer	Unknown	S Buyer
11/15/1999	11/15/1999	Metrocine	Switzerland	Europlex Cinemas	Netherlands	Completed
11/15/1999		Shin Corp. PLC	Thailand	United Communication Industry	Thailand	Rumor
11/15/1999		Star East Holdings Ltd	Hong Kong	Ananda Wing On Travel Holdings	Hong Kong	Pending
11/15/1999	11/15/1999	Wireless Communications A/S	Norway	Logisoft ASA	Norway	Completed
11/16/1999	12/03/1999	AimTV Inc.	United States	Netzero Inc.	United States	Completed
11/16/1999		Alenia Spazio SpA	Italy	Astrium	United Kingdom	Pending
11/16/1999		Comcast Corp. Cable Systems	United States	Time Warner Cable Corp.	United States	Pending
11/16/1999	06/26/2000	KRON-TV, San Francisco, CA	United States	Young Broadcasting Inc.	United States	Completed
11/16/1999	01/18/2000	Lenfest Communications Inc.	United States	Comcast Corp.	United States	Completed
11/16/1999		Nostalgia Network Inc.	United States	Crown Communications Corp.	United States	Pending
11/16/1999		WIngs-TV, Buffalo, New York	United States	Granite Broadcasting Corp.	United States	Pending
11/17/1999		Chambers Communication Cable	United States	AT&T Broadband & Internet Svcs	United States	Pending
11/18/1999	11/18/1999	Denver News Channel, LLC	United States	KWGN Inc. (Tribune Co.)	United States	Completed
11/18/1999	03/31/2000	WOWT-TV, KS; KAKE-TV, NE	United States	Benedek Broadcasting Corp.	United States	Completed
11/18/1999	01/22/2000	ZDTV (Ziff-Davis/Softbank)	United States	Vulcan Ventures Inc.	United States	Completed
11/19/1999	12/02/1999	Atlas Communication Engines	United States	Polycom Inc.	United States	Completed
11/19/1999	10/06/2000	Sinclair Brdcstg Grp Radio (6)	United States	Emmis Communications Corp.	United States	Completed
11/19/1999		TCL International Holdings Ltd	Hong Kong	Luks Industrial Co. Ltd	Hong Kong	Pending
11/22/1999	11/22/1999	American Comm Network Corp.	United States	Black Box Corp.	United States	Completed
11/22/1999	12/15/1999	Carrington Productions Ltd.	United Kingdom	SKD Media PLC	United Kingdom	Completed
11/22/1999	11/22/1999	Gemini Filmproduktion GmbH	Germany	Team Communication Group Inc.	United States	Completed
11/22/1999		Korea Telecom Powertel	South Korea	Motorola Inc.	United States	Pending
11/22/1999	01/17/2000	Lolafilms	Spain	Telefonica Multimedia	Spain	Completed
11/22/1999	11/22/1999	Tele Tell AG	Switzerland	Neue Luzerner Zeitung	Switzerland	Completed
11/22/1999		Tiberius Broadcasting Inc.	United States	Tribune Co.	United States	Pending
11/23/1999		Videotron Telecom	Canada	Carlyle Group LP	United States	Pending
11/23/1999	11/23/1999	Central European Media Entrp	Bermuda	Investor	Russia	Completed
11/24/1999	11/24/1999	Cable Plus Operating Co.-Assets	United States	Time Warner Cable Corp.	United States	Completed
11/24/1999	11/24/1999	Audiofina	Luxembourg	Groupe Bruxelles Lambert SA	Belgium	Completed
11/24/1999		Tebecai Netwerken, Telecom BV	Netherlands	United Pan-Europe Comm NV	Netherlands	Pending
11/24/1999	11/24/1999	Ukrainian Indep TV Corp.	Ukraine	Dilovyy Svit	Ukraine	Completed
11/25/1999	11/25/1999	Albacete Sistemas de Cable	Spain	Caja de Castilla-La Mancha	Spain	Completed
11/25/1999	11/25/1999	Matra Nortel-Termina Prods	France	Doro Telefoni AB	Sweden	Completed
11/25/1999	01/31/2000	AJ Gale Ltd	Canada	Regional Cablesystems Inc.	Canada	Completed
11/25/1999	04/12/2000	Titus Communications Corp.	Japan	Microsoft Corp.	United States	Completed
11/26/1999	03/01/2000	Canal 4 Multivision	Costa Rica	Undisclosed Acquiror	Unknown	Completed
11/26/1999		Carlton Communications PLC	United Kingdom	United News & Media PLC	United Kingdom	Withdrawn
11/26/1999		GMA Network Inc.	Philippines	First Pacific Co. Ltd	Hong Kong	Pending
11/26/1999		Korea Wireless CATV	South Korea	CJ 39 Shopping	South Korea	Pending
11/26/1999		PK Cable Systems Oy	Finland	PK Cable Systems Oy	Finland	Intended
11/29/1999	11/29/1999	Linkon Corp.	United States	PacketPort Inc.	United States	Completed
11/29/1999		Audiofina	Luxembourg	Groupe Bruxelles Lambert SA	Belgium	Pending
11/29/1999		Mike Mansfield Television Ltd	United Kingdom	Coastplan Ltd	United Kingdom	Pending
11/30/1999	11/30/1999	APT Satellite Co. Ltd	Hong Kong	China Telecommunications	China	Completed
11/30/1999	07/05/2000	Atlantida Comunicaciones, ACE	Argentina	Telefonica Media	Spain	Completed
11/30/1999		Audio Follow	France	Netia (EVS Broadcasting)	France	Pending
11/30/1999		Cable Vision Nishinomiya	Japan	Channel Wave Amagasaki	Japan	Pending
11/30/1999		Cable Vision I Inc.	Japan	Channel Wave Amagasaki	Japan	Pending
11/30/1999		CanWest Global Communications	Canada	CanWest Global Communications	Canada	Intended
11/30/1999	11/30/1999	Pacific Place Cable	Canada	Novus Telecom Group Inc.	Canada	Completed

December 1999

12/01/1999		City Kabel	Hungary	Seeking Buyer	Unknown	S Buyer
12/01/1999	12/01/1999	GPA Cable of Virginia	United States	GS Communications Inc.	United States	Completed
12/01/1999		Regional Cablesystems Inc.	Canada	Regional Cablesystems Inc.	Canada	Intended
12/01/1999	12/01/1999	Simoco Europe Ltd Ireland Op	Ireland	NTL Inc.	United States	Completed
12/01/1999		AT&T Broadband-Cert Cable Sys	United States	Charter Communications Inc.	United States	Pending
12/01/1999	12/01/1999	Trison Ltd	United Kingdom	Saville Audio Visual Ltd	United Kingdom	Completed
12/02/1999	12/27/1999	Magna Pacific Pty Ltd	Australia	Becker Entertainment	China	Completed
12/03/1999	12/15/1999	Minotaur International Ltd	United Kingdom	Flextech PLC	United Kingdom	Completed
12/03/1999		Video Image	United States	MCSi	United States	Intended
12/04/1999	12/04/1999	Bosch Tlom GmbH-Beam Wveguide	Germany	ESC Elktrnk Svc GmbH (Kthn Wke)	Germany	Completed
12/06/1999	03/03/2000	KMCI-TV, Lawrence, Kansas	United States	EW Scripps (Edward Scripps Tr)	United States	Completed
12/06/1999	05/04/2000	KirchPay TV GmbH (Kirch Gruppe)	Germany	British Sky Broadcasting Group	United Kingdom	Completed
12/07/1999	12/07/1999	Bucklebridge Ltd	United Kingdom	CTL Manufacturing	United Kingdom	Completed
12/07/1999		Cablevision-Sytems, Cleveland	United States	Adelphia Communications Corp.	United States	Pending
12/07/1999	03/27/2000	Spartan Communications Inc.	United States	Media General Inc.	United States	Completed
12/08/1999	12/08/1999	Amstrad Distribution GmbH	Germany	Metabox AG	Germany	Completed
12/08/1999	12/08/1999	Central Film Vertriebs GmbH	Germany	Senator Film AG	Germany	Completed
12/08/1999		M Fernsehen fuer Muenchen GmbH	Germany	Stadtfernsehen Programm	Germany	Pending
12/08/1999		Media General Inc.	United States	Media General Inc.	United States	Intended
12/08/1999		Media-Most Private Joint Stock	Russia	Gazprom	Russia	Pending
12/09/1999		Ingenious Design Inc.	United States	USA Networks Inc.	United States	Pending
12/09/1999	12/09/1999	Jack Nicklaus Productions	United States	Gaylord Entertainment Co.	United States	Completed
12/09/1999	12/09/1999	Northwest Teleproductions Inc.	United States	Sharon Harrison	United States	Completed
12/10/1999		Golden Village Pictures Film	Singapore	Warner Bros Int'l Theatrical	Singapore	Pending
12/10/1999		VTV	Slovak Repub.	Polska Telewizja Satelitarna	Poland	Pending

Date Announced	Date Effective	Acquisition Target	Target Country	Acquired by	Acquiror Country	Status
12/13/1999	03/28/2000	Cablecom Holding AG	Switzerland	NTL Inc.	United States	Completed
12/13/1999	12/13/1999	Money Channel PLC	United Kingdom	Primark Corp.	United States	Completed
12/13/1999	03/31/2000	WWLP-FM, Springfield, MA	United States	WGRC-FM, Lewisburgh, PA	United States	Completed
12/14/1999	01/29/2000	CTV Inc.	Canada	CORUS Entertainment Inc.	Canada	Completed
12/14/1999	12/14/1999	Imaginon Inc. Imon.Com TV	United States	Rockwindow Television Network	United States	Completed
12/14/1999	05/31/2000	MPI Productions Inc.	United States	eCONTENT Inc.	United States	Completed
12/15/1999		Columbia Communications Corp.	United States	GE American Communications	United States	Withdrawn
12/15/1999	12/15/1999	Pacific Title/Mirage Inc.	United States	Finacopro NV	Netherlands	Completed
12/15/1999	12/15/1999	Unique Broadband Systems Inc.	Canada	Tina Livchits Spousal Trust	Barbados	Completed
12/16/1999	12/16/1999	De Otr & De Vries Prdtins GmbH	Germany	Jack Morton (Interpublic Group)	United States	Completed
12/16/1999	12/16/1999	Famous Players Coliseum	Canada	Riocan Real Estate Invest Trust	Canada	Completed
12/16/1999		Skyview Media Group	United States	EchoStar Communications Corp.	United States	Withdrawn
12/17/1999		Matav Cable Systems Media Ltd	Israel	Tevel Israel Int Comms Ltd	Israel	Pending
12/17/1999		Salter Street Films Ltd	Canada	Salter Street Films Ltd	Canada	Intended
12/20/1999	12/20/1999	Ascent Entertainment Group Inc.	United States	Investor Group	United States	Completed
12/20/1999	12/20/1999	Cable Plus Operating Co.-Assets	United States	MediaOne Group Inc.	United States	Completed
12/20/1999	12/20/1999	Iceberg Media.Com Inc.	Canada	Newcap Inc. (Newfoundland Cap)	Canada	Completed
12/20/1999	12/20/1999	Stereo Vision Entertainment	United States	Kestrel Equity Corp.	United States	Completed
12/20/1999	12/20/1999	Sunrise Television Inc.	United States	BusinessNet Holdings Corp.	United States	Completed
12/21/1999	12/21/1999	Adatel TV E Communicacoes SA	Brazil	TV Jacaranda Ltd (Canbras)	Brazil	Completed
12/21/1999	12/21/1999	Cable Plus Operating Co. LP	United States	Dallas Wireless Broadband LP	United States	Completed
12/21/1999	12/20/1999	Hispano Television Ventures	United States	American Independent Network	United States	Completed
12/21/1999	01/20/2000	Telesta AB	Sweden	Aspiro Information AB	Sweden	Completed
12/22/1999	03/28/2000	Intercomm France Holding SA	France	United Pan-Europe Comm NV	Netherlands	Completed
12/22/1999	03/02/2000	Jones Intercable Inc.	United States	Comcast Corp.	United States	Completed
12/22/1999	12/22/1999	Marine Electro Process AB	Norway	Saab Marine Electronics (Saab)	Sweden	Completed
12/22/1999		N24 (Pro Sieben Media AG)	Germany	Frankfurter Allgemeine	Germany	Withdrawn
12/22/1999	04/07/2000	Neighbourhood Cable Ltd	Australia	National Investments Ltd	Australia	Completed
12/22/1999	12/22/1999	Oy Ruutunelonen AB	Finland	Sanoma WSOY Oyj	Finland	Completed
12/22/1999	01/03/2000	PrimaCom AG	Germany	United Pan Europe Comm NV	Netherlands	Completed
12/23/1999	12/23/1999	Cablevision of Riverside	United States	Adelphia Communications Corp.	United States	Completed
12/23/1999	02/06/2000	Comcast MHCP Holdings LLC	United States	Comcast Corp.	United States	Completed
12/23/1999	01/13/2000	Mann Theatres (WestStar Cinema)	United States	WF Cinema Holdings LP	United States	Completed
12/23/1999	01/17/2000	Video Arts Ltd Selmore Films	United Kingdom	Investor Group	United Kingdom	Completed
12/23/1999	12/23/1999	Vox Film Und Fernseh	Germany	CLT-UFA (Cie Luxembourgeoise)	Luxembourg	Completed
12/24/1999	12/24/1999	Canadian Satellite Comm Inc.	Canada	Shaw Communications Inc.	Canada	Completed
12/24/1999	12/29/1999	Latvijas Neatkariga Televizija	Latvia	Polska Telewizja Satelitarna	Poland	Completed
12/27/1999	12/27/1999	Advanced Frequency Products	United States	Signal Technology Corp.	United States	Completed
12/27/1999	12/27/1999	Hantro Products Oy	Finland	Menire Oyj	Finland	Completed
12/27/1999	06/14/2000	Harman International Inds Inc.	United States	Circuit Research Laboratories	United States	Completed
12/27/1999		VDI Multimedia	United States	Bain Capital	United States	Withdrawn
12/28/1999	12/28/1999	Wavespan Corp.	United States	Proxim Inc.	United States	Completed
12/29/1999	12/29/1999	Hot Entertainment Group	United States	Jack White Productions AG	Germany	Completed
12/30/1999	12/30/1999	DirecTV Inc. Direct	United States	US Satellite Broadcasting Inc.	United States	Completed
12/30/1999	12/30/1999	Kabel Elektro Kft	Hungary	Fibernet Communications RT	Hungary	Completed
12/30/1999		Team TV	Italy	Stream (Telecom Italia SpA)	Italy	Intended
12/31/1999	12/31/1999	ACC Entertainment GmbH & Co.	Germany	Legend Entertainments Inc.	United States	Completed
12/31/1999	12/31/1999	Lion's Gate Entertainment Corp.	Canada	Fidelity Management & Research	United States	Completed

January 2000

Date Announced	Date Effective	Acquisition Target	Target Country	Acquired by	Acquiror Country	Status
01/03/2000		Cablevision SA de Argentina	Argentina	Investor Group	Argentina	Pending
01/03/2000	01/03/2000	Capetronic Int'l (Thailand) PCL	Thailand	Krittika International	Hong Kong	Completed
01/03/2000	04/14/2000	Dattelkabel	Czech Republic	United Pan Europe Comm NV	Netherlands	Completed
01/04/2000	01/04/2000	GMTV Ltd	United Kingdom	Scottish Media Group PLC	United Kingdom	Completed
01/04/2000	01/04/2000	GMTV Ltd	United Kingdom	Granada Group PLC	United Kingdom	Completed
01/04/2000	01/04/2000	GMTV Ltd	United Kingdom	Carlton Communications PLC	United Kingdom	Completed
01/04/2000		Galaxy Satellite Broadcasting	Hong Kong	Astro Broadcast Corp. (BVI) Ltd	Br. Virgin I.	Pending
01/05/2000	01/05/2000	CET 21	Czech Republic	Edikon	Czech Republic	Completed
01/05/2000	01/05/2000	CET 21	Czech Republic	MEF Media	Czech Republic	Completed
01/05/2000	01/05/2000	Faziscom R. Cable TV Network	Hungary	Fibernet Communications RT	Hungary	Completed
01/05/2000	01/05/2000	Korors Kabel Kft	Hungary	Delkabel Kft	Hungary	Completed
01/05/2000		Lion's Gate Entertainment Corp.	Canada	Investor Group	United States	Pending
01/06/2000	01/06/2000	Doty Moore	United States	SpectraSite Holdings Inc.	United States	Completed
01/06/2000		Grupo Televisa SA de CV	Mexico	Seeking Buyer	Unknown	S Buyer
01/06/2000	01/06/2000	StreamQuest	United States	Sonicbox Inc.	United States	Completed
01/06/2000		TT&T	Thailand	TelecomAsia Corp. Ltd	Thailand	Pending
01/07/2000	02/02/2000	Ericsson AB Private Radio Ops	United States	Com. Net Critical Communication	United States	Completed
01/07/2000	01/07/2000	Mediascape Communications	Germany	Emprise Management Consulting	Germany	Completed
01/07/2000	01/07/2000	Patagonik Film Group	Argentina	Telefonica Media	Spain	Completed
01/10/2000		GEA	Argentina	Telefonica Media	Spain	Pending
01/10/2000	01/24/2000	17th Street Productions Inc.	United States	Alloy Online Inc.	United States	Completed
01/10/2000		Time Warner	United States	America Online Inc.	United States	Pending
01/11/2000	05/05/2000	Golden Sky Holdings	United States	Pegasus Communications Corp.	United States	Completed
01/11/2000		Shaw Communications Inc.	Canada	Shaw Communications Inc.	Canada	Intended
01/11/2000	01/11/2000	Synergy International	United States	Pinnacle Systems Inc.	United States	Completed
01/11/2000	01/11/2000	Undisclosed Television	United States	Hispanic Television Network	United States	Completed
01/12/2000	02/17/2000	CarsTV.com Inc.	United States	Fidelity Holdings (JetLease)	United States	Completed
01/12/2000	03/28/2000	Eneco C&T	Netherlands	United Pan Europe Comm NV	Netherlands	Completed
01/12/2000	03/14/2000	Ginger Media Group	United Kingdom	Scottish Media Group PLC	United Kingdom	Completed
01/12/2000	01/12/2000	Northwire and Cable Telecom	Philippines	SkyCable TV Baguio	Philippines	Completed
01/13/2000	01/13/2000	AMC Entertainment Inc.	United States	Syufy Century Corp.	United States	Completed
01/13/2000	01/13/2000	Bioskop Film GmbH & Co.	Germany	Kinowelt Medien AG	Germany	Completed
01/13/2000	01/13/2000	Canal Satellite (Canal Plus SA)	France	Lagardere Group	France	Completed
01/13/2000	10/06/2000	Hughes Electronics Satellite	United States	Boeing Co.	United States	Completed
01/13/2000	03/27/2000	Multithematiques	France	Lagardere Group	France	Completed
01/13/2000	01/13/2000	Studio Munich Animation GmbH	Germany	Kinowelt Medien AG	Germany	Completed
01/13/2000	07/10/2000	Telefonica del Peru SA	Peru	Telefonica SA	Spain	Completed
01/14/2000		Golden Harvest Asia Cinema Op	Hong Kong	Village Roadshow Corp. Ltd	Australia	Pending
01/14/2000		Hahn Film AG	Germany	Constantin Film Holding GmbH	Germany	Intended
01/14/2000	04/14/2000	Orius Corp.	United States	Willis Stein & Partners	United States	Completed
01/14/2000	01/17/2000	Tblga Film Und Produktion GmbH	Germany	EM.TV & Merchandising AG	Germany	Completed
01/17/2000	01/17/2000	All America Cables & Radio Inc.	Dominican Rep.	Centennial Cellular Corp.	United States	Completed
01/17/2000		Broadcast.Com Japan KK	Japan	Yahoo Japan (Yahoo!,Softbank)	Japan	Pending
01/17/2000		Cameo Interactive Ltd	Japan	Visual Communication	Japan	Pending
01/17/2000	01/17/2000	Newmarket Capital Group	United States	Helkon Media Group AG	Germany	Completed
01/18/2000		Film Consortium Ltd	United Kingdom	WhiteCliff Film and Television	United Kingdom	Pending
01/18/2000	01/18/2000	NVS	United States	Launch Media Inc.	United States	Completed
01/18/2000		Research In Motion Ltd	Canada	Nortel Networks Corp.	Canada	Pending

Date Announced	Date Effective	Acquisition Target	Target Country	Acquired by	Acquiror Country	Status
01/18/2000	04/25/2000	Scientific Atlanta, Satellite	United States	ViaSat Inc.	United States	Completed
01/18/2000	04/03/2000	Telefon AB Ericsson Energy Sys	Sweden	Emerson Electric Co.	United States	Completed
01/18/2000	01/24/2000	Via Digital (Telefonica Media)	Spain	Investor Group	Netherlands	Completed
01/19/2000		Broadcast Worldwide Pte Ltd	India	News Corp. Ltd	Australia	Pending
01/19/2000		MTV Asia Ventures (India) Pte	Mauritius	MTV Asia (MTV Networks Inc.)	Singapore	Pending
01/19/2000	01/19/2000	Red Ant Media AG	Germany	BMP Mobility AG	Germany	Completed
01/20/2000	01/20/2000	Cinergon	Greece	Epiphania Intertyp. SA	Greece	Completed
01/20/2000	01/20/2000	Railway Film Centre Ltd	Canada	Investor Group	Canada	Completed
01/20/2000	03/15/2000	StarComm Products Inc.	United States	GDI Global Data	Canada	Completed
01/21/2000	01/21/2000	MTV Russia	Russia	MTV Networks Inc. (Viacom Int'l.)	United States	Completed
01/21/2000		RAISAT (RAI)	Italy	RCS Editori SpA	Italy	Pending
01/21/2000	02/15/2000	Singapore Cablevision Pte. Ltd	Singapore	Singapore Press Holdings Ltd	Singapore	Completed
01/21/2000		Singapore Cablevision Pte. Ltd,	Singapore	ST Telecomm. (SG Telecomm.)	Singapore	Pending
01/21/2000	01/21/2000	Virgin Multiplex Cinema, Dundee	United Kingdom	Undisclosed Acquiror	Unknown	Completed
01/24/2000		EMI Group PLC Music Business	United Kingdom	Time Warner Inc. Music Business	United States	Withdrawn
01/24/2000	02/25/2000	PairGain Technologies Inc.	United States	GlobeSpan Inc.	United States	Completed
01/24/2000	01/24/2000	Replay TV	United States	Omnicom Group Inc.	United States	Completed
01/26/2000	01/26/2000	Innovative Technologies, LLC	United States	MUSIC Semiconductors	United States	Completed
01/27/2000		Gaumont Television	France	Tele Images	France	Pending
01/28/2000		Britt Allcroft Co.. PLC	United Kingdom	HIT Entertainment PLC	United Kingdom	Dis Rumor
01/28/2000	05/05/2000	Canal Plus Belgique SA	Belgium	Canal Plus SA	France	Completed
01/28/2000		Chris Craft Industries Inc.	United States	CBS Corp..	United States	Dis Rumor
01/28/2000	01/28/2000	SAC	Argentina	Cinemark USA Inc..	United States	Completed
01/28/2000	04/05/2000	North Coast Productions Inc.	United States	Storm High Performance Snd Co.	United States	Completed
01/28/2000		SBC Communications Inc.	United States	SBC Communications Inc.	United States	Pendind
01/28/2000		Toyo Communication Equipment	Japan	Seeking Buyer	Unknown	S Buyer
01/28/2000		Warner Mycal	Japan	Tokuma Shoten Co.. Ltd	Japan	Pending
01/31/2000		Avatar Holdings Inc.	United States	Avatar Holdings Inc.	United States	Intended
01/31/2000	01/31/2000	Enstar Incom, Growth Program	United States	Charter Communications Inc.	United States	Completed
01/31/2000	01/31/2000	FOOTAGE.net	United States	eMotion Inc.	United States	Completed
01/31/2000	02/07/2000	Hamburg 1 GmbH	Germany	Kirch Gruppe	Germany	Completed

Feburary 2000

Date Announced	Date Effective	Acquisition Target	Target Country	Acquired by	Acquiror Country	Status
02/01/2000	02/01/2000	AmPro Corp..	United States	Video Display Corp..	United States	Completed
02/01/2000	02/01/2000	Observer RTV Medienauswert	Germany	Argus Media (Sifo, Media Inter)	Germany	Completed
02/01/2000	02/01/2000	Pathe Sport (Pathe SA)	France	Pathe SA	France	Completed
02/02/2000	02/02/2000	CBB	Spain	Euskaltel	Spain	Completed
02/02/2000	02/02/2000	Class Financial Network	Italy	Mediaset SpA	Italy	Completed
02/02/2000		iTV Public Co.. Ltd	Thailand	Investor	Thailand	Pending
02/02/2000	02/02/2000	Networx Media Logistics GmbH	Germany	EM.TV & Merchandising AG	Germany	Completed
02/02/2000	02/02/2000	Ste du Casino d'Antibes	France	Moliflor SA	France	Completed
02/04/2000	02/04/2000	Cogeco Cable Inc.	Canada	Shaw Communications Inc.	Canada	Completed
02/04/2000		Gyor Cable TV	Hungary	Nemet Cable Asset Management	Hungary	Pending
02/04/2000	02/04/2000	Leading Edge Entertainment Inc.	United States	Dynamic Imaging Systems	United States	Completed
02/04/2000		MediaServe (Mitsui, Toshiba)	Japan	Wink Communications Inc.	United States	Pending
02/04/2000	04/04/2000	UPN (BHC Comm., Viacom Inc.)	United States	Viacom Inc. (Nat'l. Amusements)	United States	Completed
02/07/2000	02/07/2000	Hamburg 1 GmbH	Germany	Kirch Gruppe	Germany	Completed
02/07/2000		Hammer Films Ltd	United Kingdom	Investor Group	United Kingdom	Pending
02/07/2000	02/07/2000	K&A Communications Inc.	United States	Black Box Corp..	United States	Completed
02/07/2000	04/27/2000	Ortel Corp..	United States	Lucent Technologies Inc.	United States	Completed
02/07/2000	02/07/2000	Seven Network-Int'l. Prod. Svcs.	Australia	Granda Media Artist Services	Australia	Completed
02/07/2000		Groupe Videotron Ltd	Canada	Rogers Communications Inc.	Canada	Withdrawn
02/08/2000	04/25/2000	Advanced Broadcast Systems Inc.	United States	EMCEE Broadcast Prod. Partners	United States	Completed
02/08/2000	02/08/2000	Lunaris Film Und Fernsehprod	Germany	Odeon Film AG	Germany	Completed
02/09/2000	03/09/2000	Harris Corp.. TV Antenna	United States	Dielectric Communications	United States	Completed
02/09/2000		iTract, LLC	United States	Margo Caribe Inc.	United States	Pending
02/09/2000	02/09/2000	Production Design Group	United States	Interpublic Group of Cos Inc.	United States	Completed
02/09/2000		Segilink Co.. Ltd	South Korea	Starmax Co.. Ltd	South Korea	Pending
02/10/2000	07/13/2000	Ellipse Programme (StudioCanal)	France	Expand SA	France	Completed
02/10/2000		Expand SA	France	StudioCanal (Canal Plus)	France	Intended
02/10/2000	02/10/2000	ITI TV Holdings	Poland	McCann Erickson (Interpublic)	United States	Completed
02/10/2000	02/10/2000	SHS Multimedia	Italy	Hopa SpA	Italy	Completed
02/11/2000	02/11/2000	Vivendi SA	France	Morgan Stanley Dean Witter	United States	Completed
02/11/2000	02/11/2000	Telaxis Comm. Co.. Millitech Div	United States	Millitech, LLC	United States	Completed
02/14/2000	02/14/2000	Incoms Blagoevgrad Plant	Bulgaria	Communication Equipment	Bulgaria	Completed
02/14/2000	03/01/2000	S Media Vision AG	Switzerland	Viva Fernsehen GmbH & Co.. KG	Germany	Completed
02/14/2000	10/01/2000	Yagi Antenna Co..	Japan	Kokusai Electric Co.. Ltd	Japan	Completed
02/15/2000		Behaviour New Media Inc.	Canada	Tube Images	Canada	Pending
02/15/2000		Boyana Film (Bulgaria)	Bulgaria	Seeking Buyer	Unknown	S Buyer
02/15/2000	02/15/2000	Canal Satellite Digital SL	Spain	Warner Brothers International	United States	Completed
02/15/2000	02/15/2000	Channel 5 Television Group Ltd	United Kingdom	Pearson Television (Pearson)	United Kingdom	Completed
02/15/2000	02/15/2000	Channel 5 Television Group Ltd	United Kingdom	United News & Media PLC	United Kingdom	Completed
02/15/2000	02/15/2000	Channel 5 Television Group Ltd	United Kingdom	CLT-UFA Holding SA	Luxembourg	Completed
02/15/2000	02/15/2000	Cinemania SL	Spain	Warner Brothers International	United States	Completed
02/15/2000		Citizens Utilities Co.. Arizona	United States	Cap Rock Electric Corp.. Inc.	United States	Pending
02/15/2000	02/15/2000	E-News (Nihon Sogo Television)	Japan	Investor	Japan	Completed
02/15/2000		Ericsson Sulmona Facilities	Italy	Finmek SpA	Italy	Pending
02/15/2000		Pacific Data Images	United States	DreamWorks SKG	United States	Pending
02/15/2000		Reach Satellite Network	United States	Salem Communications Corp..	United States	Pending
02/15/2000		Sofia Film (Bulgaria)	Bulgaria	Globus Roihmann Group	Israel	Pending
02/15/2000		Sunset Productions	United States	Soundworks International Inc.	United States	Pending
02/16/2000		Broadcasting Network Thailand	Thailand	QUILVEST Fund of Canada	Canada	Pending
02/16/2000	05/25/2000	Viacom Inc. (Nat'l. Amusements)	United States	Viacom Inc. (Nat'l. Amusements)	United States	Completed
02/16/2000	02/16/2000	X-Vrleh AG Distrbution Actvties	Germany	Senator Film AG	Germany	Completed
02/16/2000		Golden Harvest Entertainment	Hong Kong	Media Corporation of Singapore	Singapore	Pending
02/17/2000	02/17/2000	Telefriuli	Italy	Investor Group	Italy	Completed
02/17/2000	02/17/2000	Tobis Filmkunst GmbH Verleih	Germany	Le Studio Canal (Canal Plus SA)	France	Completed
02/18/2000	02/18/2000	Galaxy Ent. Inc. (Onex Corp..)	Canada	Investor Group	Canada	Completed
02/18/2000	02/18/2000	Orbita Max	Spain	SCR Barcelona Empren	Spain	Completed
02/18/2000		Shanghai Guangdian Information	China	Shanghai Vacuum and Electron	China	Pending
02/19/2000		Television Sonido Telson SA	Spain	Radiotronica SA (Banesto)	Spain	Pending
02/21/2000		Fujian EastNet	China	Leading Spirit High-Tech Hldgs	Hong Kong	Pending
02/21/2000	03/22/2000	Jim Henson Productions Inc.	United States	EM.TV & Merchandising AG	Germany	Completed
02/21/2000	02/21/2000	Rank Group PLC Odeon Cinemas	United Kingdom	Cinven	United Kingdom	Completed
02/22/2000	06/08/2000	Ascent Entertainment Group Inc.	United States	Liberty Media Group (AT&T Corp..)	United States	Completed
02/22/2000	06/08/2000	Faroudja Inc.	United States	Sage Inc.	United States	Completed
02/22/2000	02/22/2000	MPT New Media GmbH	Germany	Plenum AG Technologie	Germany	Completed
02/22/2000	02/22/2000	OptaPhone Systems Inc.	United States	Zhone Technologies Inc.	United States	Completed

Date Announced	Date Effective	Acquisition Target	Target Country	Acquired by	Acquiror Country	Status
02/22/2000	02/22/2000	Pinewood Studios (Rank Group)	United Kingdom	Investors	United Kingdom	Completed
02/22/2000	04/17/2000	SDL Communications Inc.	United States	SBS Technologies Inc.	United States	Completed
02/22/2000		Television Gijon	Spain	Grupo Alonso	Spain	Pending
02/22/2000	05/19/2000	VSI Network Inc.	United States	PentaStar Communications Inc.	United States	Completed
02/23/2000	02/23/2000	Eagle Pictures SpA	Italy	B & S Electra	Italy	Completed
02/23/2000	02/23/2000	Energee Entertainment Pty. Ltd	Australia	RTV Family Entertainment AG	Germany	Completed
02/23/2000		Gannett Co.. Inc.	United States	Gannett Co.. Inc.	United States	Intended
02/23/2000	03/31/2000	Saturn Communications	New Zealand	Telstra New Zealand Ltd	New Zealand	Completed
02/23/2000	05/16/2000	Stento ASA	Norway	SAIT Radio Holland S	Belgium	Completed
02/23/2000		TV3 (CME)	Hungary	RTL Klub	Hungary	Pending
02/24/2000		Makedonia TV	Greece	Antenna TV SA	Greece	Intended
02/25/2000	02/25/2000	BMS Inc.	United States	Interspot Inc.	United States	Completed
02/25/2000		Vox Film Und Fernseh	Germany	RTL Multimedia GmbH	Germany	Pending
02/26/2000	06/02/2000	CTV Inc.	Canada	BCE Inc.	Canada	Completed
02/28/2000		Elecplay.com Productions Inc.	Canada	Hip Interactive Corp..	Canada	Pending
02/28/2000		Japan Digital Broadcasting	Japan	Investor Group	United States	Pending
02/28/2000		Kangjegyu Film Ltd	South Korea	Korea Technology Banking Corp..	South Korea	Pending
02/28/2000		Zeppelin	Spain	Endemol Entertainment NV	Netherlands	Pending
02/29/2000	03/09/2000	Aran	Italy	Endemol Entertainment NV	Netherlands	Completed
02/29/2000		DirecTV Japan	Japan	Hughes Electronics Corp..	United States	Pending
02/29/2000	02/29/2000	Eizo-Grmn Lgstc Repair Bus	Germany	Teleplan International NV	Netherlands	Completed
02/29/2000	02/29/2000	Francis Industries Inc.	United States	Barjan Products, LLC	United States	Completed
02/29/2000	02/29/2000	Golf Channel	United States	Comcast Corp..	United States	Completed
02/29/2000	03/15/2000	STV Communications Inc.	United States	Sonic Foundry Inc.	United States	Completed

March 2000

03/01/2000	03/01/2000	Cablevision VI Inc.	United States	Rock Port Cablevision Inc.	United States	Completed
03/01/2000	03/01/2000	Communikabel NV	Netherlands	Multikabel NV	Netherlands	Completed
03/01/2000		KXTX-TV Channel 39, TX	United States	Pappas Telecasting Cos	United States	Pending
03/01/2000		Lee Entrp. Broadcasting Segment	United States	Seeking Buyer	Unknown	S Buyer
03/01/2000		Satellite Microcable Corp..	United States	Telecom Wireless Corp..	United States	Pending
03/01/2000	06/02/2000	Strategic Technologies Inc.	United States	FSN Cable Ltd	United States	Completed
03/01/2000	03/01/2000	Swizz Music Television	Switzerland	Viva Fernsehen GmbH & Co.. KG	Germany	Completed
03/01/2000	08/07/2000	TVN	Poland	SBS Broadcasting SA	Luxembourg	Completed
03/01/2000		Telia AB-Cable Television	Sweden	Seeking Buyer	Unknown	Withdrawn
03/02/2000		DirectTV Japan	Japan	SkyPerfectTV	Japan	Pending
03/02/2000	03/02/2000	Helen Duval Visuals BV	Netherlands	Beate Uhse AG	Germany	Completed
03/02/2000		Meaga SA	Greece	Antenna TV SA	Greece	Pending
03/02/2000	03/02/2000	Modern Film Effects Inc.	United States	Cinema Investment Group Inc.	United States	Completed
03/03/2000	03/03/2000	Cable Plus Operating Co.. LP-Cer	United States	AT&T Broadband & Internet Svcs.	United States	Completed
03/03/2000	05/30/2000	iTV Public Co.. Ltd	Thailand	Siam Commercial Bank PLC	Thailand	Completed
03/03/2000	03/03/2000	Pay Per View Japan Inc.	Japan	Japan Digital Broadcasting	Japan	Completed
03/03/2000	08/31/2000	Reigncom Ltd	Hong Kong	AV Concept Holdings Ltd	Hong Kong	Completed
03/03/2000	03/03/2000	SVC Television Ltd	United Kingdom	Four Media Co..	United States	Completed
03/06/2000	08/24/2000	Clear Channel Communications	United States	Infinity Broadcasting Corp..	United States	Completed
03/06/2000	08/30/2000	Clear Channel Communications	United States	Cox Radio Inc.	United States	Completed
03/06/2000		Complete Rider.com	United States	Sierra-Rockies Corp..	United States	Pending
03/06/2000	03/06/2000	Consolidated Film Industries	United States	Technicolor Inc.	United States	Completed
03/06/2000	09/11/2000	Destron Fearing Corp.	United States	Applied Digital Solutions Inc.	United States	Completed
03/07/2000	03/07/2000	Big Sky Community TV Inc.	United States	Mallard Cablevision LLC	United States	Completed
03/07/2000	09/08/2000	Cablevision Systems Cable Sys	United States	Charter Communications Inc.	United States	Completed
03/07/2000	03/28/2000	Eitele Ostfold	Norway	United Pan Europe Comm NV	Netherlands	Completed
03/07/2000	03/09/2000	Himachal Futuristic Comm.	India	Consolidated Press Hldgs Ltd	Australia	Completed
03/07/2000	03/07/2000	Pen Interconnect Inc. Incirt	United States	Comtel Corp.	United States	Completed
03/07/2000		TT&T	Thailand	Investor Group	Thailand	Pending
03/08/2000	03/08/2000	Digital Media Online	United States	Primedia Inc.	United States	Completed
03/08/2000	03/08/2000	Queensgate Instruments Ltd	United Kingdom	SDL Inc.	United States	Completed
03/08/2000		Railway Film Centre Ltd	Canada	Sextant Entertainment Group Inc.	Canada	Pending
03/08/2000		SSM Freesports Ltd	United Kingdom	Sportsworld Media Group PLC	United Kingdom	Pending
03/08/2000		Undisclosed Satellite	Hong Kong	Oriental Union Holdings Ltd	Hong Kong	Pending
03/09/2000		SBS Broadcasting SA	Luxembourg	United Pan Europe Comm NV	Netherlands	Withdrawn
03/12/2000	04/12/2000	Icons Production House Pty Ltd	Australia	POS Media Online Ltd	Australia	Completed
03/13/2000	05/11/2000	Electrohome Broadcasting Inc.	Canada	BCE Inc.	Canada	Completed
03/13/2000	05/17/2000	Holland Media Group	Netherlands	CLT-UFA (Cie Luxembourgeoise)	Luxembourg	Completed
03/13/2000		Natural Health Channel Ltd	United Kingdom	West 175 Media Group Inc.	United Kingdom	Pending
03/13/2000	04/04/2000	Quickband Networks	United States	On2com Inc.	United States	Completed
03/13/2000	03/13/2000	Telewizja Familijna	Poland	KGHM Polska Miedz SA (Poland)	Poland	Completed
03/13/2000	06/12/2000	Times Mirror Co.	United States	Tribune Co.	United States	Completed
03/14/2000	03/14/2000	Kwangju Cable TV	South Korea	Hanaro Telecom	South Korea	Completed
03/14/2000	03/14/2000	Measat Broadcast Network Sys.	Malaysia	Microsoft Corp.	United States	Completed
03/14/2000	06/02/2000	Xros Inc.	United States	Nortel Networks Corp.	Canada	Completed
03/15/2000		Border Television PLC	United Kingdom	Scottish Radio Holdings PLC	United Kingdom	Withdrawn
03/15/2000		CNBC India	India	Sony Entertainment Television	United States	Pending
03/15/2000	03/15/2000	Filmhaus GmbH	Germany	Jack White Productions AG	Germany	Completed
03/15/2000		HiTV	China	DVB Holdings Ltd	Hong Kong	Pending
03/15/2000	04/11/2000	Media Merchants Television Co.	United Kingdom	Britt Allcroft Co.. PLC	United Kingdom	Completed
03/15/2000		Pulse Engineering	United States	Titan Corp.	United States	Pending
03/15/2000		Telewizja Familijna	Poland	Investor Group	Poland	Pending
03/16/2000	03/16/2000	Kelly Broadcasting Systems Inc.	United States	EchoStar Communications Corp.	United States	Completed
03/16/2000	05/22/2000	Shaw Brothers-Film Library	Hong Kong	East Asia Filmed Entertainment	Hong Kong	Completed
03/16/2000		Strateurop International BV	Netherlands	Investor Group	Luxembourg	Pending
03/17/2000	08/02/2000	Endemol Entertainment NV	Netherlands	Telefonica SA	Spain	Completed
03/17/2000	03/17/2000	MFP Munich Film Partners GmbH	Germany	KG Allgemeine Leasing GmbH und	Germany	Completed
03/17/2000	03/30/2000	Magnavision Corp.-Private Cable	United States	Lamont Television Systems Inc.	United States	Completed
03/17/2000	03/17/2000	PPC Film Management GmbH	Germany	LHI Leasing Und Beteiligungsq	Germany	Completed
03/17/2000	03/17/2000	Primedia Ltd	South Africa	Mineworkers Investment Co.	South Africa	Completed
03/17/2000	03/17/2000	Seven Network Ltd	Australia	Granada Group PLC	United Kingdom	Completed
03/20/2000	03/20/2000	Dishnet DSL	India	CenturyTel Inc.	United States	Completed
03/20/2000		Induslnd Media & Comm Ltd	India	Richman Investrade	India	Pending
03/20/2000		Raiway	Italy	Seeking Buyer	Unknown	S Buyer
03/20/2000	03/20/2000	Sogecable	Spain	Investor Group	Spain	Completed
03/21/2000	03/21/2000	AAPT Sat-Tel Pty Ltd	Australia	New Skies Satellites NV	Netherlands	Completed
03/21/2000	03/21/2000	Telecor SA	Argentina	Group Clarin	Argentina	Completed
03/21/2000	03/21/2000	Top Dog Video Productions Inc.	United States	NewAgeCities.com Inc.	United States	Completed
03/21/2000		Golden Harvest Entertainment	Hong Kong	Lai Sun Hotels International	Hong Kong	Withdrawn
03/22/2000	03/22/2000	Alma Media Oy	Finland	Bonnier Group	Sweden	Completed
03/22/2000	03/22/2000	CIC Video GmbH	Germany	Viacom Inc. (Natl Amusements)	United States	Completed
03/22/2000	03/22/2000	Carant Antenn AB	Sweden	Smarteq	Sweden	Completed

Date Announced	Date Effective	Acquisition Target	Target Country	Acquired by	Acquiror Country	Status
03/23/2000		Cable One Inc. Cable System	United States	Insight Midwest	United States	Pending
03/23/2000		Cable One Inc. Midwestern Cable	United States	AT&T Broadband & Internet Svcs	United States	Pending
03/23/2000	03/24/2000	Canadian Satellite Commun Inc.	Canada	Shaw Communications Inc.	Canada	Completed
03/23/2000	03/24/2000	Cogeco Group Inc.	Canada	Rogers Communications Inc.	Canada	Completed
03/23/2000		Momentum Productions Inc.	United States	Buffalo Capital VIII Ltd	United States	Pending
03/23/2000		Rogers Comm. Inc. Cable Ops, BC	Canada	Shaw Commun Inc.-Cable Ops,ON	Canada	Pending
03/23/2000		TV 1000	Sweden	MTG	Sweden	Pending
03/24/2000	03/24/2000	TQS Inc.	Canada	Quebecor Communications Inc.	Canada	Completed
03/24/2000	03/24/2000	Telset	Estonia	Tele2	Estonia	Completed
03/25/2000		Antenna Hungaria	Hungary	UPC Hungary	Hungary	Pending
03/25/2000	0/24/2000	Groupe Videotron Ltee	Canada	Investor Group	Canada	Completed
03/27/2000		Nippon Eiga Eisei Hoso	Japan	Toho	Japan	Pending
03/27/2000	03/27/2000	Westpark Studios Gesellschaft	Germany	Das Werk Digitale Bildbearbeit	Germany	Completed
03/28/2000		iTV Public Co.., Ltd	Thailand	Merrill Lynch & Co. Inc.	United States	Pending
03/29/2000		Advent Communications Ltd	United Kingdom	Vislink PLC	Ireland	Pending
03/29/2000	03/29/2000	Cable Plus (United Pan-Europe)	Czech Republic	United Pan-Europe Comm NV	Netherlands	Completed
03/29/2000		ConnectBlue AB	Sweden	Investor	Sweden	Pending
03/29/2000		ConnectBlue AB	Sweden	Midway Holding AB	Sweden	Pending
03/29/2000		ConnectBlue AB	Sweden	Malmohus Invest	Sweden	Pending
03/29/2000	03/29/2000	Entertainment Concepts LLC	United States	Kinowelt Medien AG	Germany	Completed
03/29/2000	03/29/2000	MCP-Records Produktions Und	Austria	Kinowelt Medien AG	Germany	Completed
03/29/2000	03/29/2000	UPC Hungary	Hungary	United Pan Europe Comm NV	Netherlands	Completed
03/30/2000		CellularVision of New York LP	United States	SpeedUs.com Inc.	United States	Pending
03/30/2000		Coast To Coast Film Classics	United Kingdom	PrimeEnt PLC	United Kingdom	Pending
03/30/2000	05/26/2000	Motion Int'l. Inc.	Canada	TVA International (TVA Group)	Canada	Completed
03/30/2000	03/30/2000	Palomar	Italy	Endemol Entertainment NV	Netherlands	Completed
03/30/2000		CJ 39 Shopping	South Korea	Cheil Jedang Corp.	South Korea	Pending
03/30/2000		Television Azteca SA de CV	Mexico	Telefonica Media	Spain	Pending
03/31/2000	04/03/2000	Destiny Cable Inc.	Philippines	Solid Group	Philippines	Completed
03/31/2000	03/31/2000	Falcon/Capital Cable Partners	United States	Charter Communications Inc.	United States	Completed
03/31/2000	03/31/2000	KDD Submarine Cable Systems	Japan	Investor Group	Japan	Completed
03/31/2000	06/06/2000	PRIMEDIA Inc.	United States	CMGI Inc.	United States	Completed
03/31/2000	04/20/2000	PRIMEDIA Inc.	United States	Liberty Media Group (AT&T Corp.)	United States	Completed
03/31/2000	03/31/2000	Tennessee Cable Inc.	United States	Comcast Cable Communications	United States	Completed

April 2000

Date Announced	Date Effective	Acquisition Target	Target Country	Acquired by	Acquiror Country	Status
04/01/2000	09/13/2000	Columbia Communications Corp.	United States	GE American Communications	United States	Completed
04/01/2000		e-Cell Tech. Inc.	United States	Hing Kong Holdings Ltd	Hong Kong	Pending
04/03/2000	04/04/2000	EWT Nachrichtentechnik GmbH	Germany	UPC Germany GmbH	Germany	Completed
04/03/2000	06/23/2000	Lusomundo SGPS SA	Portugal	PT Multimedia Servicos de	Portugal	Completed
04/03/2000	04/03/2000	Pacifica Entertainment	United States	Intermedia Films	United States	Completed
04/03/2000	04/03/2000	Radix Wireless Inc.	United States	Bell Atlantic Corp.	United States	Completed
04/03/2000	04/03/2000	Themusicchannel BV	Netherlands	LCI Technology Group NV	Netherlands	Completed
04/04/2000	03/31/2000	Canadian Satellite Commun Inc.	Canada	Shaw Communications Inc.	Canada	Completed
04/04/2000		Dongnam Cable Vision Ltd	South Korea	Seeking Buyer	Unknown	S Buyer
04/04/2000	05/18/2000	GVN Technologies Inc.	United States	Advanced Fibre Communications	United States	Completed
04/04/2000	04/04/2000	Itron Inc.-Automated Meter Syst	United States	Datacom Information Systems	United States	Completed
04/04/2000	04/04/2000	max.mobil.Telekommunikation	Austria	DeTeMobil	Germany	Completed
04/04/2000	04/04/2000	Networks North Inc.	Canada	Chell.com	Canada	Completed
04/05/2000	04/05/2000	Apoio Tecnico Brazil	Brazil	Richardson Electronics Ltd	United States	Completed
04/05/2000		Darling Land Ltd	Hong Kong	Amazing Growth Profits Ltd	Hong Kong	Pending
04/05/2000	04/05/2000	Gaumont SA-Cinema Complex	Belgium	UGC SA	France	Completed
04/05/2000		MV Video Publishing Group Ltd	Canada	GLS Global Assets Ltd	Canada	Pending
04/05/2000		Receivable Agents Ltd	Hong Kong	Amazing Growth Profits Ltd	Hong Kong	Pending
04/05/2000	10/31/2000	Rodin	Canada	Cheni Resources Inc.	Canada	Completed
04/05/2000		State Broadcasting Centre	Estonia	Seeking Buyer	Unknown	S Buyer
04/05/2000	04/26/2000	TM3 Fernseh GmbH & Co. KG	Germany	News Corp. Ltd	Australia	Completed
04/05/2000		Tomei International (BVI) Ltd	Hong Kong	Tomei Technologies Ltd	Hong Kong	Pending
04/06/2000	04/06/2000	Ascom Holding AG-Solothurn	Switzerland	Flextronics International Ltd	Singapore	Completed
04/06/2000	04/06/2000	Cable & Wireless-Videoconf Act	France	Genesys SA	France	Completed
04/06/2000	04/06/2000	ScriptShark.com	United States	iFilm Corp.	United States	Completed
04/06/2000	04/06/2000	Signal Tech. Inc.	United States	ParkerVision Inc.	United States	Completed
04/06/2000		Tele Lyon Metropole	France	Le Progres (Delaroche SA)	France	Pending
04/06/2000	04/06/2000	Unicabo	Brazil	Globo Cabo SA (Globo Cabo Hldg)	Brazil	Completed
04/07/2000	04/07/2000	AB Transistor (GN Store Nord)	Sweden	GN Store Nord A/S	Denmark	Completed
04/07/2000	04/07/2000	DES	United States	Pinnacle Systems Inc.	United States	Completed
04/07/2000	04/07/2000	Ikusasa Communications	South Africa	Millennium Property Holdings	South Africa	Completed
04/07/2000	04/07/2000	Jaguar Communications PLC	United Kingdom	Cable & Wireless Communications	United Kingdom	Completed
04/07/2000		Midi Television	South Africa	Rembrandt Group Ltd	South Africa	Pending
04/07/2000		Pacific Cyber	Hong Kong	Multi-Asia International	Hong Kong	Withdrawn
04/07/2000	07/26/2000	Pearson Television (Pearson)	United Kingdom	CLT-UFA (Cie Luxembourgeoise)	Luxembourg	Completed
04/07/2000	04/07/2000	Report On Business Television	Canada	WIC Television Ltd	Canada	Completed
04/07/2000	04/07/2000	World Access Inc.-Wireless	United States	Nera AS	Norway	Completed
04/08/2000		Telefonica de Espana-Mobile	Spain	Shareholders	Spain	Pending
04/10/2000	04/10/2000	DBC Sports	United States	SportsLine.Com Inc.	United States	Completed
04/10/2000	04/10/2000	Daybreak Corp.	Japan	SCN	Japan	Completed
04/10/2000	04/10/2000	Garden State Communications	United States	Council Tree Communications	United States	Completed
04/10/2000	04/10/2000	Grupo Argos	Mexico	Telefonos de Mexico SA de CV	Mexico	Completed
04/10/2000	04/10/2000	Microtronic A/S	Denmark	Investor Group	Sweden	Completed
04/10/2000	04/10/2000	NVS Pty Ltd	Australia	Cambrian Resources Ltd	Australia	Completed
04/10/2000	04/10/2000	Second Line Search	United States	FootageNow	United States	Completed
04/11/2000	04/11/2000	Astral Commun Inc.-AstralTech	Canada	Technicolor Inc.	United States	Completed
04/11/2000		beeb.com	United Kingdom	Seeking Buyer	Unknown	S Buyer
04/11/2000	04/11/2000	DS2	Spain	Endesa SA	Spain	Completed
04/11/2000		Izhtel	Russia	Siemens AG	Germany	Pending
04/11/2000		Kamatel	Russia	Siemens AG	Germany	Pending
04/11/2000		Radioshack Corp.	United States	Radioshack Corp.	United States	Intended
04/11/2000	04/11/2000	Rapid Comms Partners-Cable Sys	United States	Mediacom Communications Corp.	United States	Completed
04/11/2000	04/11/2000	Golden Harvest Entertainment	Hong Kong	Investor Group	Taiwan	Completed
04/12/2000	04/12/2000	Cogeco Group Inc.	Canada	Rogers Communications Inc.	Canada	Completed
04/12/2000	04/12/2000	New Legend Media AG	Germany	Investor Group	Germany	Completed
04/12/2000	07/12/2000	PRASARA Technologies Inc.	United States	PowerTV Inc.	United States	Completed
04/12/2000	05/30/2000	Philsar Semiconductor Inc.	Canada	Conexant Systems Inc.	United States	Completed
04/12/2000	04/12/2000	Play Inc.	United States	Lynx Technology Group LLC	United States	Completed
04/13/2000	04/13/2000	AlfaNett AS	Norway	Telenor Avidi AS	Norway	Completed
04/13/2000	04/13/2000	Asianet Communication	India	Zee Telefilms Ltd	India	Completed
04/13/2000		Border Television PLC	United Kingdom	Capital Radio PLC	United Kingdom	Unconditional
04/14/2000	04/14/2000	CJ Entertainment Co. Ltd	South Korea	Cheil Jedang Corp.	South Korea	Completed

Date Announced	Date Effective	Acquisition Target	Target Country	Acquired by	Acquiror Country	Status
04/14/2000	04/14/2000	Prima TV	Romania	SBS Broadcasting SA	Luxembourg	Completed
04/14/2000	09/01/2000	Titus Communications Corp.	Japan	Jupiter Telecommunications	Japan	Completed
04/15/2000	04/15/2000	TeleTicino SA	Switzerland	Azienda Electtrica Ticinese	Switzerland	Completed
04/17/2000		Border TV-Television Assets	United Kingdom	Granada Group PLC	United Kingdom	Pending
04/17/2000	07/06/2000	Gadline Ltd	Israel	COM21 Inc.	United States	Completed
04/17/2000	04/17/2000	Reelfinder.com (Reelscreen)	United Kingdom	Future Network PLC	United Kingdom	Completed
04/17/2000	04/17/2000	Reelscreen.com Ltd (Reelscreen)	United Kingdom	Future Network PLC	United Kingdom	Completed
04/18/2000		Across Wireless AB	Sweden	Sonera Corp.	Finland	Pending
04/18/2000	04/18/2000	B&L Cable Communications Inc.	United States	Mallard Cablevision LLC	United States	Completed
04/18/2000	04/18/2000	Blackstone Cable	United States	Mallard Cablevision LLC	United States	Completed
04/18/2000		Cablevision Sys-Cable Sys, MA	United States	AT&T Corp.	United States	Pending
04/18/2000		CinemaxX AG	Germany	Senator Film AG	Germany	Pending
04/18/2000		Ericsson-NA Cordless System	United States	Ascom Holding AG (Hasler Works)	Switzerland	Pending
04/18/2000	04/18/2000	Filmtel SA	Spain	Filmax	Spain	Completed
04/18/2000		Golden Harvest (Marks) Ltd	Hong Kong	Golden Harvest Entertainment	Hong Kong	Pending
04/18/2000		Golden Harvest Film	Hong Kong	Golden Harvest Entertainment	Hong Kong	Pending
04/18/2000	04/18/2000	SIC TV	Portugal	Impresa Sociedade Gestora de	Portugal	Completed
04/18/2000		Space Yacht	Japan	Nichii Gakkan Co.	Japan	Pending
04/18/2000		Telema	France	TF-1	France	Pending
04/18/2000	04/18/2000	Trebitsch Produktion Holding	Germany	Kinowelt Medien AG	Germany	Completed
04/18/2000	07/06/2000	Wireless Link Corp.	United States	Communication Systems Intl	Canada	Completed
04/19/2000	04/19/2000	Alltech Cable TV Inc.	United States	Mallard Cablevision LLC	United States	Completed
04/19/2000	04/19/2000	Channel V Music Networks Ltd	Hong Kong	Satellite Television Asia	Hong Kong	Completed
04/19/2000	04/19/2000	High Mountain Communications	United States	Mallard Cablevision LLC	United States	Completed
04/19/2000	04/19/2000	Hurst Cable Inc.	United States	Mallard Cablevision LLC	United States	Completed
04/19/2000	04/19/2000	KFBT-TV, Las Vegas, NV	United States	Sinclair Broadcast Group Inc.	United States	Completed
04/19/2000		Nokia M T-Multimedia Dvlp Gp	Sweden	SCI Systems Inc.	United States	Pending
04/19/2000	04/19/2000	Sociedade Independente de	Portugal	Impresa Sociedade Gestora de	Portugal	Completed
04/19/2000		Trimark Holdings Inc.	United States	Trimark Holdings Inc.	United States	Intended
04/19/2000		Video Ezy International	Malaysia	Internet Group	New Zealand	Pending
04/20/2000		Coach's Edge	United States	Sportsvision	United States	Pending
04/20/2000		Dongfang Lianhe Audio	China	Continental Mariner Investment	Hong Kong	Pending
04/20/2000	04/20/2000	Televerda	United States	Council Tree Communications	United States	Completed
04/21/2000	04/21/2000	Applied Graphics-Photo Busn	United States	Photobition Group PLC	United Kingdom	Completed
04/21/2000		Cablodistribution G Inc.	Canada	Cogeco Cable Inc.	Canada	Pending
04/21/2000		Karrie International	Hong Kong	Host Smart Ltd	Hong Kong	Pending
04/21/2000		Lindsay CATV Systems Ltd	Canada	Cogeco Cable Inc.	Canada	Pending
04/21/2000	07/05/2000	TRT Lucent Technologies	United States	Harris Corp.	United States	Completed
04/21/2000		Telecable Provincial Inc.	Canada	Cogeco Cable Inc.	Canada	Pending
04/24/2000		Fuji Television Network	Japan	Sony Corp.	Japan	Withdrawn
04/24/2000	04/24/2000	Zee Telefilms Ltd	India	Goldman Sachs Invest MV Ltd	Mauritius	Completed
04/25/2000	04/25/2000	BHG Hiradastechniki Rt (APV Rt)	Hungary	Eminvest Tanacsado Kft	Hungary	Completed
04/25/2000		ECI Telecom Ltd	Israel	ECI Telecom Ltd	Israel	Intended
04/25/2000		Point Classics (UK) Ltd	United Kingdom	Seeking Buyer	Unknown	S Buyer
04/25/2000		Point Entertainment Ltd	United Kingdom	Seeking Buyer	Unknown	S Buyer
04/25/2000	04/25/2000	Trinity Communication Inc.	Taiwan	Compal Electronics Inc.	Taiwan	Completed
04/25/2000	04/25/2000	USN Wireless Inc.	United States	Alexandra Telephone Acquisition	United States	Completed
04/26/2000	04/26/2000	Antenna Man	Australia	Comet Satellite & Cable Ltd	Australia	Completed
04/26/2000		Hot Vision	Sweden	Ledstiernan Investment AB	Sweden	Pending
04/26/2000		IndusInd Media & Comm Ltd	India	Grant Investrade Ltd	India	Pending
04/26/2000	04/26/2000	MidAmer Cable Sys LP-Midwest	United States	Mediacom Communications Corp.	United States	Completed
04/26/2000		Yaroslavsky Radio Plant	Russia	Investors	Unknown	Withdrawn
04/27/2000		Artsworld	United Kingdom	British Sky Broadcasting Group	United Kingdom	Pending
04/27/2000		Artsworld	United Kingdom	Guardian Media Group PLC	United Kingdom	Pending
04/27/2000		Asianet Communication	India	Zee Telefilms Ltd	India	Pending
04/27/2000	04/27/2000	In-Motion AG	Germany	Gold-Zack AG	Germany	Completed
04/27/2000	06/28/2000	IndusInd Media & Comm Ltd	India	Intel Pacific Inc. (Intel Corp.)	Hong Kong	Completed
04/27/2000	04/27/2000	WTN Specialty TV Network	Canada	Moffat Communications Ltd	Canada	Completed
04/27/2000	07/31/2000	Sony Trans Com Inc.	United States	Rockwell Collins	United States	Completed
04/28/2000		FFP-Film and Television Assets	Germany	TEAM FFP	Germany	Pending
04/28/2000	04/28/2000	Konjic Radio-TV (Bosnia)	Bosnia	Investors	Unknown	Completed
04/28/2000		PC Card International AB	Sweden	TPC Security AB	Sweden	Pending
04/28/2000		Reliance Distributors	Canada	Shaw Communications Inc.	Canada	Pending
04/28/2000	04/28/2000	West Media Events (West 175)	United Kingdom	West 175 Media Group Inc.	United Kingdom	Completed

May 2000

05/01/2000		First Ent Hldg Corp.-Radio Stn	United States	American Comm. Entrp Inc.	United States	Pending
05/01/2000	05/01/2000	Marcali Cable TV	Hungary	MATAVkabelTV Kft	Hungary	Completed
05/01/2000		Nippon Eiga Eisei Hoso	Japan	Kadokawa Shoten Publishing	Japan	Pending
05/01/2000		Surya Citra Televisi PT	Indonesia	Bhakti Investama PT	Indonesia	Withdrawn
05/02/2000	05/02/2000	Florida RF Labs Inc.	United States	Smiths Industries PLC	United Kingdom	Completed
05/02/2000		Indra Sistemas SA	Spain	Seeking Buyer	Unknown	S Buyer
05/02/2000	05/24/2000	Television Azteca SA de CV	Mexico	NBC	United States	Completed
05/03/2000	05/24/2000	Alation Systems Inc.	United States	Cypress Semiconductor Corp.	United States	Completed
05/03/2000	05/03/2000	DIVA Systems Corp.	United States	OpenTV Corp.	United States	Completed
05/04/2000	08/02/2000	DDST	Spain	ACESA	Spain	Completed
05/04/2000		Holdiko Perkasa PT-Indosair	Indonesia	Seeking Buyer	Unknown	S Buyer
05/04/2000	05/04/2000	SMA Real Time Inc.	United States	PSA Inc.	United States	Completed
05/04/2000	05/04/2000	Sit Telecommunication	Italy	B&S Ventures	Italy	Completed
05/04/2000	05/11/2000	Vox Film Und Fernseh	Germany	CLT-UFA (Cie Luxembourgeoise)	Luxembourg	Completed
05/05/2000	05/05/2000	Asia Television	Hong Kong	Investor	Hong Kong	Completed
05/05/2000	05/05/2000	Empire Communications	United States	Empire Communications Corp.	United States	Completed
05/05/2000		Home Team Sports	United States	Comcast Corp.	United States	Pending
05/06/2000		En Efecto SA	Spain	Das Werk Digitale Bildbearbeit	Germany	Pending
05/08/2000	05/08/2000	Gahrens & Battermann GmbH	Germany	Cinemedia Film AG	Germany	Completed
05/08/2000		KJEO-TV, Fresno, CA	United States	Ackerley Group Inc.	United States	Pending
05/08/2000	10/10/2000	Lee Enterprises-TV Station (15)	United States	Emmis Communications Corp.	United States	Completed
05/08/2000	05/08/2000	PEN	India	Transatlantic Corp.	Spain	Completed
05/08/2000	05/08/2000	Theile Hoyts Kinepolis Gruppe	Germany	Kinowelt Medien AG	Germany	Completed
05/09/2000		Arcade Movie Company	Netherlands	Investor Group	Netherlands	Pending
05/09/2000		Ceotronics AG	Germany	Ceotronics AG	Germany	Intended
05/09/2000		Gahrens & Battermann GmbH	Germany	Cinemedia Film AG	Germany	Intended
05/09/2000	05/09/2000	525 Studios Inc. (Virgin Media)	United States	Four Media Co.	United States	Completed
05/09/2000	05/09/2000	Rushes Post-Production	United Kingdom	Four Media Co.	United States	Completed
05/09/2000		Telemozi (Hungary)	Hungary	Seeking Buyer	Unknown	S Buyer
05/09/2000	05/09/2000	Virgin Television de Mexico	Mexico	Four Media Co.	United States	Completed
05/09/2000	05/09/2000	West One Television (Virgin)	United Kingdom	Four Media Co.	United States	Completed
05/10/2000	08/08/2000	AXIS	Australia	AdultShop.com Ltd	Australia	Completed
05/10/2000	05/10/2000	Bichsel & Burger	Switzerland	Endemol Entertainment NV	Netherlands	Completed
05/10/2000		Overseas Filmgroup Inc.	United States	Rosemary Street Production LLC	United States	Pending

Date Announced	Date Effective	Acquisition Target	Target Country	Acquired by	Acquiror Country	Status
05/10/2000		S-Midi Com (Dong Won)	South Korea	Undisclosed Acquiror	Unknown	Pending
05/11/2000	05/11/2000	Documit Inc.	United States	Incunet.com Inc.	United States	Completed
05/11/2000	05/11/2000	TVS Systems Inc.	United States	Quanta Services Inc.	United States	Completed
05/12/2000		Cable Satisfaction Intl Inc.	Canada	Undisclosed Acquiror	Unknown	Withdrawn
05/12/2000	05/12/2000	Colibria AS	Norway	Aspiro Ventures (Aspiro)	Sweden	Completed
05/12/2000	05/31/2000	iTV Public Co. Ltd	Thailand	Shin Corp. PLC	Thailand	Completed
05/15/2000	05/15/2000	Active-Film.com	Germany	G&J Multimedia Ventures GmbH	Germany	Completed
05/15/2000	05/15/2000	Black Canyon Productions	United States	SFX Entertainment Inc.	United States	Completed
05/15/2000		Technicolor Inc.	United States	Seeking Buyer	Unknown	S Buyer
05/15/2000	05/15/2000	Warren Miller Entertainment	United States	Times Mirror Magazines	United States	Completed
05/16/2000		AVT Electronics Ltd	Hong Kong	CIL Holdings	Hong Kong	Pending
05/16/2000		Allied Electronics Corp. Ltd	South Africa	Investor Group	South Africa	Pending
05/16/2000	05/16/2000	Avalon Pictures Inc.	United States	SecureWorks	United States	Completed
05/16/2000	05/16/2000	Boston University-TV (4)	United States	Paxson Communications Corp.	United States	Completed
05/16/2000	05/16/2000	Medical Info & Broadcasting	United Kingdom	British Sky Broadcasting Group	United Kingdom	Completed
05/16/2000	05/16/2000	Primedia Ltd	South Africa	Active Value Advisors Ltd	United Kingdom	Completed
05/17/2000	09/18/2000	Pegasus Communications Corp.	Puerto Rico	Centennial Communications Corp.	United States	Completed
05/17/2000	05/31/2000	US Wireless Corp.	United States	American Tower Corp.	United States	Completed
05/17/2000	05/17/2000	Unified Film Organization	United States	Advanced Medien AG	Germany	Completed
05/18/2000		Dalton Group-Charlotte Radio	United States	Clear Channel Communications	United States	Pending
05/18/2000		Filmgroup Plc	United Kingdom	Intertainment AG	Germany	Intended
05/18/2000		Metropolis (Cristalerias de CE)	Chile	Cordillera Communications	Chile	Pending
05/18/2000	05/18/2000	Salter New Media	Canada	Salter Street Films Ltd	Canada	Completed
05/18/2000	05/18/2000	SAF SA	France	CS Communications & Systemes	France	Completed
05/18/2000	08/23/2000	Theater Radio Network	United States	Distributedmedia.com Inc.	United States	Completed
05/19/2000	05/19/2000	DIVA Systems Corp.	United States	NTL Inc.	United States	Completed
05/19/2000	05/19/2000	Eurosport International (TF1)	France	Investor Group	France	Completed
05/19/2000	05/19/2000	Eurosport France	France	Investor Group	France	Completed
05/19/2000	05/19/2000	Foxcom Ltd	Israel	CDB Web Tech Investments SA	Italy	Completed
05/19/2000	05/19/2000	MLR	France	Thomson-CSF (France)	France	Completed
05/19/2000		Magic TV	France	Seeking Buyer	Unknown	S Buyer
05/19/2000		Sky Argentina SA	Argentina	Sky Argentina DTH Holding LLC	Argentina	Pending
05/19/2000	05/19/2000	Trio, Newsworld International	United States	USA Networks Inc.	United States	Completed
05/19/2000		Golden Harvest Entertainment	Hong Kong	Undisclosed Acquiror	Unknown	Pending
05/20/2000	05/20/2000	Karol Film Produktions GmbH	Germany	Dieter Schwartz	Germany	Completed
05/20/2000	05/20/2000	Katira Media Productions GmbH	Germany	Gothaer Versicherungsbank VVaG	Germany	Completed
05/22/2000		Destiny Inc.	Philippines	Seeking Buyer	Unknown	S Buyer
05/22/2000	05/22/2000	Screenvision Cinema Network	United States	Carlton Communications PLC	United Kingdom	Completed
05/22/2000	05/22/2000	Golden Harvest Entertainment	Hong Kong	Prudential Asset Management	Hong Kong	Completed
05/23/2000		Antena 3 Television	Spain	Bertelsmann AG	Germany	Pending
05/23/2000		Ericsson-Shelter Operations	Sweden	Applied Power Inc.	United States	Pending
05/23/2000	05/23/2000	Kabel plus Vychodne Slovensko	Slovak Repub.	UPC Slovakia	Slovak Repub.	Completed
05/23/2000		Siam UATC Co. Ltd	Thailand	BEC World PLC	Thailand	Pending
05/24/2000	05/24/2000	Baker Cable TV Co.	United States	Mallard Cablevision LLC	United States	Completed
05/24/2000	05/24/2000	CanalWeb	France	Investor Group	France	Completed
05/24/2000	05/24/2000	PlentyWood Cable TV	United States	Mallard Cablevision LLC	United States	Completed
05/24/2000	05/24/2000	Solo Tango	Argentina	Gaylord Cable Networks	United States	Completed
05/24/2000	05/24/2000	TV Argentina	Argentina	Gaylord Cable Networks	United States	Completed
05/25/2000		Adventure Photo & Film	United States	ImageState Ltd (Convergence)	United Kingdom	Pending
05/25/2000	05/25/2000	Canal Digital Norge AS	Norway	Telenor AS (Norway)	Norway	Completed
05/25/2000	08/28/2000	International Image	United States	Sonic Foundry Inc.	United States	Completed
05/25/2000		Promark Entertainment Group	United States	PrimeEnt PLC	United Kingdom	Withdrawn
05/25/2000	05/25/2000	Sypro System Professionals Oy	Finland	TietoEnator Oyj	Finland	Completed
05/26/2000		Viacom Inc. (Natl Amusements)	United States	Viacom Inc. (Natl Amusements)	United States	Intended
05/27/2000	05/27/2000	Canal Plus Belgique SA	Belgium	Canal Plus SA	France	Completed
05/27/2000	05/27/2000	New Economy Media	Germany	Investor Group	Austria	Completed
05/29/2000	05/29/2000	Hubert Productions	France	Endemol Developpement	France	Completed
05/29/2000	05/29/2000	Koeln Comedy Festival GmbH	Germany	Brainpool TV AG	Germany	Completed
05/29/2000	09/14/2000	Mark IV Industries Inc.	United States	Investor Group	United Kingdom	Completed
05/29/2000		New Economy Media	Germany	Investor Group	Austria	Intended
05/29/2000		Surf TV Pty Ltd	Australia	Min-Tech 8 Ltd	Australia	Pending
05/30/2000	05/30/2000	Astral	Romania	AIG Funds	United States	Completed
05/30/2000		Delkabel Kft	Hungary	MATAVkabelTV Kft	Hungary	Pending
05/30/2000	05/30/2000	Elmeg GmbH	Germany	BinTec Communications AG	Germany	Completed
05/30/2000	05/30/2000	Hollywood Entertainment	United States	Cyber Group Network Corp.	United States	Completed
05/30/2000	05/30/2000	Rapid Comm Partners-Certain	United States	Cox Classic Cable Inc.	United States	Completed
05/30/2000		Rights Picture (ONPA Intl)	Thailand	ONPA International PLC	Thailand	Pending
05/31/2000	05/31/2000	APT Satellite Co. Ltd	Hong Kong	SingaSat (Singapore Telecomm)	Singapore	Completed
05/31/2000	05/31/2000	Black Pencil AG	Switzerland	Phenomedia AG	Germany	Completed
05/31/2000	05/31/2000	Chunan Cable TV Co. Ltd	South Korea	Taekwang Industrial Co. Ltd	South Korea	Completed
05/31/2000	05/31/2000	Korea Cable TV Chungbu Bdcstg	South Korea	Taekwang Industrial Co. Ltd	South Korea	Completed

June 2000

Date Announced	Date Effective	Acquisition Target	Target Country	Acquired by	Acquiror Country	Status
06/01/2000	08/10/2000	iTV Public Co. Ltd	Thailand	Shin Corp. PLC	Thailand	Completed
06/01/2000	06/01/2000	Two Way TV Ltd	United Kingdom	NTL Inc.	United States	Completed
06/02/2000	06/02/2000	FFP Media GmbH	Germany	Traumwerk (Das Werk AG)	Germany	Completed
06/02/2000	09/05/2000	Midwestern Broadcasting Co.	United States	Cox Radio Inc.	United States	Completed
06/05/2000		KLDT, Channel 55, Lake Dallas,TX	United States	Hispanic Television Network	United States	Pending
06/06/2000	06/06/2000	Arles Animation	France	BKN International AG	Germany	Completed
06/06/2000	06/06/2000	DP Media-TV Stations (6)	United States	Paxson Communications Corp.	United States	Completed
06/06/2000		Sun TV	India	Seeking Buyer	Unknown	S Buyer
06/06/2000		Telediscount Company Inc.	United States	Elite Technologies Inc.	United States	Pending
06/06/2000	10/13/2000	Trimark Holdings Inc.	United States	Lion's Gate Entertainment Corp.	Canada	Completed
06/07/2000	06/07/2000	ABC Sports Inc.-Mobile Prod	United States	National Mobile TV	United States	Completed
06/07/2000	06/07/2000	America TV SA	Argentina	Avila Enterprises SA	Argentina	Completed
06/07/2000	06/07/2000	North Lowndes Cable Co.	United States	Mallard Cablevision LLC	United States	Completed
06/08/2000	06/08/2000	Woestijnvis NV	Belgium	Vlaamse Uitgeversmaatschappij	Belgium	Completed
06/12/2000	06/12/2000	General Cinema Mexico	Mexico	Grupo Cinemex	Mexico	Completed
06/12/2000		Maxon Electronics Co. Ltd	South Korea	Sewon Telecom	South Korea	Pending
06/12/2000		Motorola-Campinas	Brazil	CommScope Inc.	United States	Pending
06/12/2000		News TV India Pte Ltd	India	Buzzer Investments Ltd	Mauritius	Pending
06/12/2000	06/12/2000	Soincom (Grupo Balsemao)	Portugal	Impresa Sociedade Gestora de	Portugal	Completed
06/13/2000		Cable Comm. Nagaragawa	Japan	Himawari Network	Japan	Pending
06/13/2000	06/13/2000	Channel TV (Channel TV Grp Ltd)	United Kingdom	Investor Group	United Kingdom	Completed
06/13/2000	06/13/2000	Star TV AG (Reflection Film AG)	Switzerland	Edipresse SA	Switzerland	Completed
06/13/2000	06/20/2000	VidiPax Inc.	United States	Loudeye Technologies Inc.	United States	Completed
06/13/2000	06/13/2000	Watch! Entertainment AG	Germany	Cinemedia Film AG	Germany	Completed
06/14/2000		GS Communications Inc.	United States	Adelphia Communications Corp.	United States	Pending
06/14/2000		Interruption Television Inc.	United States	Time Financial Services Inc.	United States	Pending
06/14/2000	06/14/2000	TalkBack Productions Ltd	United Kingdom	Pearson Television (Pearson)	United Kingdom	Completed
06/14/2000	09/22/2000	TiVo Inc.	United States	America Online Inc.	United States	Completed

Date Announced	Date Effective	Acquisition Target	Target Country	Acquired by	Acquiror Country	Status
06/15/2000	06/15/2000	iTV Public Co. Ltd	Thailand	Nation Multimedia Group PLC	Thailand	Completed
06/16/2000	06/19/2000	Ronin Entertainment AG	Switzerland	Brainpool TV AG	Germany	Completed
06/16/2000	06/16/2000	Talent Television Ltd	United Kingdom	Write Good Co. Ltd	United Kingdom	Completed
06/17/2000	06/17/2000	South Kentucky Services Corp.	United States	Mediacom Southeast LLC	United States	Completed
06/19/2000	09/15/2000	Dynamic Media Inc.	United States	Dynamic Media Inc.	United States	Completed
06/19/2000	06/19/2000	Grupo Televicentro SA de CV	Mexico	Investor Group	Mexico	Completed
06/20/2000		Canal Plus SA	France	Vivendi SA	France	Pending
06/20/2000		Civic Communications	United States	Liberty Corp.	United States	Pending
06/20/2000	06/23/2000	Mafilm Rt (Mafilm Befektetesi)	Hungary	Investor Group	Hungary	Completed
06/20/2000		Seagram Co. Ltd	Canada	Vivendi SA	France	Pending
06/20/2000		Shanghai Shang Kai Telecom	China	Shenzhen Motion Telecom Svc	China	Pending
06/21/2000		WAOM TV-67, Lexington, Kentucky	United States	Paxson Communications Corp.	United States	Pending
06/21/2000	06/21/2000	Black & White TV Mobiles Ltd	United Kingdom	Avesco PLC	United Kingdom	Completed
06/21/2000		First Entertainment Hldg Corp.	United States	Choice Sports Network Inc.	United States	Pending
06/21/2000	06/21/2000	MDF.1 Lokales Fernsehen GmbH	Germany	PrimaCom AG	Germany	Completed
06/21/2000		TIL-TEK Antennas Inc.	Canada	Wi-LAN Inc.	Canada	Pending
06/22/2000		DirecTV-Rural Affiliates (12)	United States	Pegasus Communications Corp.	United States	Pending
06/22/2000		Shibuya Tsutaya	Japan	Culture Convenience Club	Japan	Pending
06/22/2000		UMG Telecom, Napanee Deseronto	Canada	Cogeco Cable Inc.	Canada	Pending
06/23/2000		Novosibirsk Tele Network Co.	Russia	Electrosvyaz of Novosibirsk	Russia	Pending
06/23/2000	06/23/2000	AT&T BIS-Cable Systems (4)	United States	Adelphia Comm Corp.-Cable (3)	United States	Completed
06/23/2000	06/23/2000	TelePartners LLC	United States	Cable One Inc. (Washington Post)	United States	Completed
06/23/2000		Tomen Corp.-Cable Television	Japan	Pacific Century CyberWorks Ltd	Hong Kong	Pending
06/26/2000	06/26/2000	Magmasters Sound Studios	United Kingdom	4MC Ltd (Four Media)	United Kingdom	Completed
06/26/2000	06/26/2000	Wireless Entertainment Oy	Finland	Conventum Oy	Finland	Completed
06/27/2000	07/06/2000	Antenna Hungaria	Hungary	Investors	Unknown	Completed
06/27/2000	06/27/2000	Ford Microelectronics Inc.	United States	Intel Corp.	United States	Completed
06/27/2000	07/26/2000	Microwave Radio Corp.	United States	Vislink PLC	Ireland	Completed
06/27/2000	10/02/2000	ProSieben Media AG	Germany	KirchMedia KGaA (Kirch-Gruppe)	Germany	Completed
06/27/2000	08/22/2000	SAT-1Kirch Gruppe	Germany	ProSieben Media AG	Germany	Completed
06/27/2000		Young Broadcasting Inc.	United States	Young Broadcasting Inc.	United States	Intended
06/28/2000	06/28/2000	B TV Television GmbH & Co. KG	Germany	Kinowelt Medien AG	Germany	Completed
06/28/2000		Liberty Media-Broadband Assets	United Kingdom	UnitedGlobalCom Inc.	United States	Pending
06/28/2000	06/28/2000	Pro-Active Projects Ltd	United Kingdom	Sportsworld Media Group PLC	United Kingdom	Completed
06/28/2000	07/26/2000	Triumph Communications Inc.	United States	Liberty Livewire Corp.	United States	Completed
06/29/2000	06/29/2000	ARF Test	France	Integrated Test Engineering NV	Belgium	Completed
06/29/2000	06/29/2000	Frontier Design Inc. GSM Comm.	United States	Parthus Technologies PLC	Ireland	Completed
06/29/2000	06/29/2000	Telesicel, Telelavaux, Urbanet	Switzerland	Cablecom AG	Switzerland	Completed
06/29/2000		3C Ltd-Certain Assets	Hong Kong	interWAVE Communications	Bermuda	Pending
06/30/2000	06/30/2000	HSQ Technology	United States	RailWorks Corp.	United States	Completed
06/30/2000		Quarterwave Corp.	United States	PSA Inc.	United States	Pending
06/30/2000	06/30/2000	Saco Defense Corp.	United States	General Dynamics Corp.	United States	Completed
06/30/2000	09/20/2000	Tokyo Cable Television	Japan	Sony Corp.	Japan	Completed
06/30/2000	06/30/2000	Werber Kommunikation	Germany	Kommunikations Design Studio	Germany	Completed

July 2000

07/01/2000		Happyfish	United Kingdom	Frontline Group Ltd	United Kingdom	Pending
07/03/2000		B4U South	India	GV Films Ltd	India	Pending
07/03/2000		Full Immersion Television Ltd	United Kingdom	Adaptive Venture Managers PLC	United Kingdom	Pending
07/03/2000		Okaya Electric Industries Co.	Japan	Okaya Electric Industries Co.	Japan	Intended
07/04/2000	07/04/2000	Delaney Holdings-Cable & Satel	Australia	Comet Satellite & Cable Ltd	Australia	Completed
07/04/2000		Jeil Broadcasting System Inc.	South Korea	Cheil Jedang Corp.	South Korea	Pending
07/04/2000	07/04/2000	Peak Broadcast Systems AS	Norway	Real Time Synthesized Ent	Israel	Completed
07/04/2000		Sofia Film (Bulgaria)	Bulgaria	Seeking Buyer	Unknown	S Buyer
07/04/2000		Yangcheon Net Co. Ltd	South Korea	Cheil Jedang Corp.	South Korea	Pending
07/05/2000		Belvidere Broadcasting	United States	NextMedia Group Inc.	United States	Pending
07/05/2000	07/05/2000	Exalink Ltd	Israel	Comverse Technology Inc.	United States	Completed
07/05/2000		Jordan Radio & Television Corp.	Jordan	Seeking Buyer	Unknown	S Buyer
07/06/2000	07/06/2000	Cabel Tec GmbH-Stassfurt Cable	Germany	PrimaCom AG	Germany	Completed
07/06/2000	07/06/2000	Davies Industrial Commun Ltd	United Kingdom	Marconi PLC	United Kingdom	Completed
07/06/2000	07/06/2000	Spirit Lake Cable TV-Cable TV	United States	Mediacom Communications Corp.	United States	Completed
07/06/2000		Suncorp Technologies Ltd	Hong Kong	Inventel Systemes	France	Pending
07/06/2000	07/06/2000	Szeged Cable Television Rt	Hungary	Magyar Tavkozlesi (MagyarCom)	Hungary	Completed
07/07/2000	07/07/2000	Dynatex GmbH	Germany	Gamesite GmbH	Germany	Completed
07/07/2000	07/07/2000	Fuji Television Network	Japan	Investor Group	Japan	Completed
07/07/2000		WJAC-TV, Johnstown, PA, WTOV-TV	United States	Cox Broadcasting Corp.	United States	Pending
07/08/2000		Scandinature AB	Sweden	Telia Infomedia International	Sweden	Pending
07/10/2000	07/10/2000	Jydsk Central Antenne A/S	Denmark	Telia Stofa A/S (Telia AB)	Denmark	Completed
07/10/2000		StarGuide Digital Networks Inc.	United States	Digital Generation Systems	United States	Pending
07/10/2000		TCL-Telital Mobile Commun	Hong Kong	TCL Holdings (BVI) Ltd	China	Pending
07/10/2000	07/10/2000	Venner TV Ltd	United Kingdom	Television Corporation PLC	United Kingdom	Completed
07/10/2000	07/10/2000	Video Cable Mex SA de CV	Mexico	Mandeville Partners	United States	Completed
07/11/2000	07/11/2000	Cable y Comunicacion de Merida	Mexico	Mandeville Mexico SA de CV	Mexico	Completed
107/11/2000	07/11/2000	Marlboro Cablevision Const	United States	Quanta Services Inc.	United States	Completed
07/11/2000	07/11/2000	Societe du Spectacles	France	Endemol Entertainment NV	Netherlands	Completed
07/11/2000	07/11/2000	Videoreport SA	Spain	Television y Sonido Telson SA	Spain	Completed
07/12/2000		CAA Satelite TV Ltd	Hong Kong	G-Prop (Holdings) Ltd	Hong Kong	Pending
07/12/2000		Midwest Sports Channel (Viacom)	United States	Comcast Corp.	United States	Pending
07/12/2000	08/23/2000	USA Digital Radio Inc.	United States	Lucent Digital Radio Inc.	United States	Completed
07/13/2000		Great North Communications Ltd	Canada	Alliance Atlantis Comm Inc.	Canada	Pending
07/13/2000		LogiMetrics Inc.	United States	L-3 Communications Holdings	United States	Pending
07/13/2000	07/13/2000	Quantel (Carlton Commun)	United Kingdom	Investor Group	United Kingdom	Completed
07/13/2000	07/13/2000	Sony Entertainment Television	India	Capital Japan (Capital Intl)	Japan	Completed
07/14/2000	07/14/2000	Allied Artists Entertainment	United States	Merit Diversified Intl Inc.	United States	Completed
07/14/2000		Canadian Satellite Commun Inc.	Canada	Shaw Communications Inc.	Canada	Part Comp
07/14/2000		Lockheed Martin-Aerospace	United States	BAE SYSTEMS North America	United States	Pending
07/15/2000		WCA-TV, Ashlund, Minnesota	United States	EIS Broadcasting Corp.	United States	Pending
07/17/2000	07/17/2000	American Multi-Television Ntwk	United States	Silki La Silk	Saudi Arabia	Completed
07/17/2000	07/17/2000	Europool GmbH	Germany	Advanced Medien AG	Germany	Completed
07/17/2000		Open	United Kingdom	British Sky Broadcasting Group	United Kingdom	Pending
07/19/2000	07/19/2000	e18 (Television Eighteen India)	India	ICICI Venture Funds Mgmt Co.	India	Completed
07/19/2000		Spool Media Pty Ltd	Australia	Central Kalgoorlie Gold Mines	Australia	Pending
07/19/2000		Zeppotron.com Ltd	United Kingdom	GMG Endemol Entertainment PLC	United Kingdom	Pending
07/20/2000		Hyundai Electronics Industries	South Korea	Credit Agricole Lazard Finl	United Kingdom	Pending
07/20/2000	07/20/2000	ICTV (Ukraine)	Ukraine	Vulychne Telebachennia	Ukraine	Completed
07/20/2000		Indosiar Visual Mandiri PT	Indonesia	Seeking Buyer	Unknown	S Buyer
07/20/2000		Needs Media	India	Glenair Engineering India	India	Pending
07/20/2000	09/06/2000	Nickel Palace Inc.	United States	North Coast Productions Inc.	United States	Completed
07/20/2000	08/28/2000	Precision Cable Manufacturing	United States	Insilco Holding Co.	United States	Completed
07/20/2000		Valencia Entertainment Intl	United States	SBI Communications Inc.	United States	Withdrawn
07/21/2000		Media Asia Group Ltd	Hong Kong	eSun Holdings Ltd	Hong Kong	Pending

Date Announced	Date Effective	Acquisition Target	Target Country	Acquired by	Acquiror Country	Status
07/21/2000	08/28/2000	Televisao Independente {TVI}	Portugal	Kimberley Trading	Portugal	Completed
07/23/2000		Alice	Italy	Merloni Elettrodomestici	Italy	Pending
07/24/2000	07/24/2000	Channel V Music Networks Ltd	Hong Kong	Satellite Television Asia	Hong Kong	Completed
07/25/2000		Cogeco Group Inc.	Canada	Cogeco Group Inc.	Canada	Intended
07/25/2000	07/25/2000	Javad Positioning Systems	United States	Topcon Corp.	Japan	Completed
07/25/2000		Pinnacle Systems Inc.	United States	Pinnacle Systems Inc.	United States	Intended
07/25/2000	07/25/2000	Zugloi Kommunikacios Rt	Hungary	UPC Magyarorszag Kft	Hungary	Completed
07/26/2000	07/26/2000	Cable Plus Operating-CA Cable	United States	Adelphia Communications Corp.	United States	Completed
07/26/2000		Canal Satelite Digital	Spain	Walt Disney Co.	United States	Pending
07/26/2000	07/26/2000	Crown Media Holdings Inc.	United States	EM.TV & Merchandising AG	Germany	Completed
07/26/2000		Doordarshan (India)	India	Seeking Buyer	Unknown	S Buyer
07/26/2000		Lusomundo SGPS SA	Portugal	Investor Group	Portugal	Pending
07/26/2000	07/31/2000	RespondTV Inc.	United States	Liberty Digital (Liberty Media)	United States	Completed
07/26/2000		Theater Television Co. Ltd	Japan	Creamont Capital Holding	Japan	Pending
07/26/2000		Video Services Corp.	United States	Liberty Livewire Corp.	United States	Pending
07/27/2000	07/27/2000	Autocue Holdings Ltd (Cue Corp.)	United Kingdom	Investor Group	United Kingdom	Completed
07/27/2000	07/27/2000	Digitale Telekabel AG	Germany	Telecolumbus GmbH	Germany	Completed
07/27/2000	07/27/2000	Endemol International Dstrbtn	Netherlands	CanWest Global Communications	Canada	Completed
07/27/2000	07/11/2000	MGB Entertainment Inc.	United State	Hispanic Television Network	United States	Completed
07/27/2000	07/27/2000	MuchMusic USA	United States	Rainbow Media Holdings Inc.	United States	Completed
07/27/2000	07/27/2000	Octal TV (Novabase)	Portugal	PT Multimedia Servicos de	Portugal	Completed
07/27/2000	07/27/2000	Octal TV (Novabase)	Portugal	PTM.com (PT Multimedia)	Portugal	Completed
07/27/2000		Parfitel (Metalgiste Sociedade)	Portugal	Privatel	Portugal	Pending
07/27/2000	07/11/2000	Televideo Inc.	United States	Hispanic Television Network	United States	Completed
07/27/2000	07/28/2000	Tomen Mediacom (Tomen)	Japan	Pacific Century CyberWorks Ltd	Hong Kong	Completed
07/28/2000		AH Belo Corp.	United States	AH Belo Corp.	United States	Intended
07/28/2000		Family Channel Canada	Canada	Astral Communications Inc.	Canada	Pending
07/28/2000	07/28/2000	Himachal Futuristic Commun	India	Janus Capital Corp.	United States	Completed
07/28/2000	07/28/2000	Igel Media AG	Germany	Beuttenmueller Wertpapier	Germany	Completed
07/28/2000	07/28/2000	Myriad Pictures	United States	In-Motion AG	Germany	Completed
07/28/2000		Nokia Oy AB	Finland	Nokia Oy AB	Finland	Intended
07/28/2000		United News-Broadcast,Prod,Int	United Kingdom	Granada Media Group	United Kingdom	Pending
07/31/2000	07/31/2000	Sereli Hufaco Industries	France	Barco NV	Belgium	Completed
07/31/2000	10/06/2000	Village Roadshow Corp. Ltd	Australia	Granada Media Group	United Kingdom	Completed

August 2000

Date Announced	Date Effective	Acquisition Target	Target Country	Acquired by	Acquiror Country	Status
08/01/2000	08/01/2000	Helkon Media Group AG	Germany	Investor Group	Germany	Completed
08/01/2000		WMP	Germany	TV Media	Germany	Pending
08/02/2000		Cinar Corp.	Canada	Seeking Buyer	Unknown	S Buyer
08/02/2000		First Entertainment Network	Philippines	ATN Holdings Inc.	Philippines	Pending
08/02/2000		Moffat Communications Ltd	Canada	Moffat Communications Ltd	Canada	Intended
08/02/2000		PMP Communications Ltd	Australia	UBS Warburg	Switzerland	Rumor
08/02/2000		Rankine Group of Cos-Key Asset	Canada	Axia NetMedia Corp.	Canada	Pending
08/02/2000		Television Azteca SA de CV	Mexico	Comunicaciones Avanzadas SA de	Mexico	Pending
08/03/2000	08/03/2000	Golden Village	Hong Kong	Golden Harvest Entertainment	Hong Kong	Completed
08/03/2000		Vijay TV	India	Satellite Television Asia	Hong Kong	Pending
08/04/2000	08/04/2000	Film Finders	United States	iFilm Corp.	United States	Completed
08/04/2000	08/04/2000	Hippo-TV Prod GmbH	Germany	Digital Advertising AG	Germany	Completed
08/04/2000		Undisclosed Cable Franchise	United States	Mediacom Communications Corp.	United States	Pending
08/07/2000	08/07/2000	Career Channel Ltd	Australia	Broadcast 2020 (Australian)	Australia	Completed
08/07/2000		TVN	Poland	SBS Broadcasting SA	Luxembourg	Intended
08/07/2000		WPEK-FM, Greenvile, SC	United States	Radio One Inc.	United States	Pending
08/08/2000		Comcast Corp.	United States	Comcast Corp.	United States	Intended
08/08/2000	08/08/2000	Japan Business Television Inc.	Japan	Toyota Motor Corp.	Japan	Completed
08/08/2000	08/08/2000	Multimex	Bulgaria	Antena TV	Greece	Completed
08/08/2000	08/08/2000	Nova Televisia (Antena TV)	Bulgaria	Antena TV	Greece	Completed
08/08/2000		Telemontecarlo	Italy	Seat Pagine Gialle SPA	Italy	Intended
08/08/2000		Telemontecarlo	Italy	Telecom Italia (Ing C Olivetti)	Italy	Pending
08/09/2000	08/09/2000	Broadcast Worldwide Pte ltd	India	Unit Trust of India (India)	India	Completed
08/09/2000	08/09/2000	GMG Endemol Entertainment PLC	United Kingdom	Endemol Entertainment NV	Netherlands	Completed
08/09/2000	08/09/2000	Hopstener Kabel TV GmbH	Germany	PrimaCom AG	Germany	Completed
08/10/2000		Magellan Filmed Entertainment	United States	Storm High Performance Snd Co.	United States	Pending
08/10/2000		N-TV Nachrichtenfernsehen GmbH	Germany	Investor	Germany	Rumor
08/10/2000	08/10/2000	SBSi	South Korea	Aria Investment Partners LP	Hong Kong	Completed
08/10/2000		Super RTL (Walt Disney, CLT UFA)	Germany	Seeking Buyer	Unknown	Rumor
08/11/2000	08/11/2000	Eesti Soltumatu Television TV1	Estonia	Polska Telewizja Satelitarna	Poland	Completed
08/11/2000	09/18/2000	Multikable NV (Primacom AG)	Netherlands	PrimaCom AG	Germany	Completed
08/11/2000	08/11/2000	Rapid Comms Partner-Certain	United States	ICE Cable Holdings LLC	United States	Completed
08/11/2000	08/11/2000	Soho Group Ltd	United Kingdom	Four Media Co.	United States	Completed
08/11/2000	08/11/2000	THE (John Menzies PLC)	United Kingdom	Investor Group	United Kingdom	Completed
08/14/2000		BHC Communications Inc.	United States	News Corp. Ltd	Australia	Pending
08/14/2000		Chris-Craft Industries Inc.	United States	News Corp. Ltd	Australia	Pending
08/14/2000		Shepperton Studios	United Kingdom	Pinewood Studios Ltd	United Kingdom	Pending
08/14/2000		Surya Citra Televisi PT	Indonesia	Artha Graha Investama Sentral	Indonesia	Pending
08/14/2000		United Television Inc.	United States	News Corp. Ltd	Australia	Pending
08/16/2000		Television del Valle de Mexico	Mexico	Television Azteca SA de CV	Mexico	Pending
08/17/2000	08/17/2000	DST Video Promotion AG	Switzerland	Feratel Media Technologies AG	Austria	Completed
08/17/2000	08/17/2000	Media Classics Group Inc.	United States	ePersonnelManagement.com	United States	Completed
08/17/2000	08/17/2000	Nevada Media Partners	United States	Media Classics Group Inc.	United States	Completed
08/17/2000	08/17/2000	Shaw Communications Inc.	Canada	Berkshire Hathaway Inc.	United States	Completed
08/18/2000		Cable-Axion Digitel	Canada	Videotron Communications Ltd	Canada	Pending
08/18/2000		Game Show Network (Sony Pic.)	United States	Liberty Digital (Liberty Media)	United States	Pending
08/18/2000		Grant Television Inc.	United States	Sinclair Broadcast Group Inc.	United States	Pending
08/18/2000		RTL Group	Luxembourg	Recoletos Cia Editorial SA	Spain	Pending
08/21/2000		Barrandov Film Studios	Czech Republic	Kodiak Group	Canada	Pending
08/21/2000		ECI Telecom Ltd-Hi-TV Tech	Israel	Optibase Ltd	Israel	Pending
08/21/2000	10/01/2000	Higashiosaka Cable Television	Japan	Suita Cable Television Co. Ltd	Japan	Completed
08/21/2000	10/01/2000	Ikeda Multi Media Co Ltd	Japan	Suita Cable Television Co. Ltd	Japan	Completed
08/21/2000		Image Entertainment Inc.	United States	Image Entertainment Inc.	United States	Intended
08/21/2000	08/21/2000	Leitch Tech-Server & News	Canada	Bell ExpressVu	Canada	Completed
08/21/2000		LT-Global Provisioning Center	France	Viasystems (PCB Investments)	United States	Pending
08/21/2000	10/01/2000	Moriguchi Kadoma CATV	Japan	Suita Cable Television Co. Ltd	Japan	Completed
08/21/2000	10/01/2000	Takatsuki Cable Network	Japan	Suita Cable Television Co. Ltd	Japan	Completed
08/21/2000	10/01/2000	Toyonaka Community CATV	Japan	Suita Cable Television Co. Ltd	Japan	Completed
08/22/2000	08/22/2000	AccelerateTV	United States	RespondTV Inc.	United States	Completed
08/22/2000		Valencia Entertainment Intl	United States	SBI Communications Inc.	United States	Pending
08/23/2000		Blackwatch Communications Inc.	Canada	Wotan Capital Inc.	Canada	Pending
08/23/2000		KMnTV	United States	Feratel Media Technologies AG	Austria	Pending
08/23/2000		Red Sky Entertainment Ltd	Canada	International Keystone	Canada	Pending
08/24/2000		Cablevue (Quinte) Ltd	Canada	Cogeco Cable Inc.	Canada	Pending
08/25/2000		Antenna Hungaria	Hungary	Seeking Buyer	Unknown	S Buyer

Date Announced	Date Effective	Acquisition Target	Target Country	Acquired by	Acquiror Country	Status
08/25/2000		International Broadcasting	Philippines	Seeking Buyer	Unknown	S Buyer
08/26/2000		Full Moon Universe Inc.	United States	Cimarron-Grandview Group Inc.	United States	Pending
08/29/2000	08/29/2000	Alfa TV	Hungary	ViaSat AB (Modern Times Group)	Sweden	Completed
08/29/2000	08/29/2000	Channel 2	Chile	Torneos y Competencias SA	Argentina	Completed
08/30/2000		CTV Sportsnet	Canada	Rogers Communications Inc.	Canada	Pending
08/30/2000		Regional Cable TV (Western)	Canada	Regional Cablesystems Inc.	Canada	Pending
08/31/2000		Myanmar-State Enterprises (11)	Burma	Seeking Buyer	Unknown	S Buyer

September 2000

09/01/2000		Barco Communication Systems	Belgium	Shareholders	Belgium	Pending
09/01/2000	09/01/2000	Better Life TV Corp.	Japan	Rakuten Inc.	Japan	Completed
09/01/2000		Multipark	Spain	Telecinco	Spain	Pending
09/01/2000		Ring SV	Bulgaria	Antenna TV SA	Greece	Pending
09/01/2000	09/01/2000	Via Digital	Spain	RTL Group	Luxembourg	Completed
09/04/2000	09/04/2000	IE Intertainment	Malaysia	AD Venture Co.	Malaysia	Completed
09/04/2000		Telenor Bus Sol-Data&Voice Ops	Norway	EDB Intech (EDB AS)	Norway	Pending
09/04/2000	09/04/2000	Telemagination Ltd	United Kingdom	TV-Loonland AG	Germany	Completed
09/04/2000	09/04/2000	Video Ezy (Malaysia) Sdn Bhd	Malaysia	Video Ezy Australasia Pty Ltd	Australia	Completed
09/05/2000	09/05/2000	Antena 3 Television	Spain	RTL Group	Luxembourg	Completed
09/05/2000		Lavender Industries Inc.	United States	Cable Link Inc. (A Novo SA)	United States	Pending
09/05/2000		Mentorn Group Ltd (Sagitas AG)	United Kingdom	Television Corporation PLC	United Kingdom	Intended
09/05/2000	09/15/2000	ProTeleVision Technologies A/S	Denmark	Unique Broadband Systems Inc.	Canada	Completed
09/05/2000		Rainmaker Entertainment Group	Canada	Rainmaker Entertainment Group	Canada	Intended
09/05/2000		Valsystems	Canada	Cable Link Inc. (A Novo SA)	United States	Pending
09/07/2000	09/07/2000	Shin Corp. PLC	Thailand	Investors	Thailand	Completed
09/07/2000		WMUR-TV, Manchester, NH	United States	Hearst-Argyle Television Inc.	United States	Pending
09/08/2000	09/08/2000	Iceberg Media.Com Inc.	Canada	Newcap Inc. (Newfoundland Cap)	Canada	Completed
09/08/2000	09/08/2000	Latgales Teevi Zijas	Latvia	Latvijas Neatkariga Televizija	Latvia	Completed
09/08/2000	09/08/2000	Naive	France	Part'Com (Caisse des Depots)	France	Completed
09/08/2000	09/08/2000	KirchPayTV GmbH (Kirch Gruppe)	Germany	Kingdom Holdings 8 BV	Netherlands	Completed
09/08/2000	09/08/2000	KirchPayTV GmbH (Kirch Gruppe)	Germany	Capital Research & Mangement	United States	Completed
09/11/2000	09/11/2000	Journal de Chez Vous	France	Investor Group	France	Completed
09/11/2000	09/11/2000	TV3 (Ireland) Television	Ireland	Granada Media PLC	United Kingdom	Completed
09/12/2000		Esztergom Town Council Cable	Hungary	MATAVkabelTV Kft	Hungary	Pending
09/12/2000	09/12/2000	Five Star Productions	United States	Flat Spin Media LLC	United States	Completed
09/12/2000		Sat-Elit 2000 Kft	Hungary	MATAVkabelTV Kft	Hungary	Pending
09/12/2000	09/12/2000	KirchMedia KGaA (Kirch-Gruppe)	Germany	Mediaset SpA	Italy	Completed
09/12/2000	09/12/2000	Turbo Productions	Costa Rica	Flat Spin Media LLC	United States	Completed
09/12/2000		Wirepress Kft	Hungary	MATAVkabelTV Kft	Hungary	Pending
09/13/2000	09/13/2000	Antena 3 Television	Spain	RTL Group	Luxembourg	Completed
09/13/2000	09/13/2000	Antena 3 Television	Spain	Banco Santander Central Hispan	Spain	Completed
09/13/2000	09/13/2000	Mobilask Kft	Hungary	3 TS Venture Partners	Hungary	Completed
09/13/2000		Sportscope Television Network	Canada	Investor Group	United States	Pending
09/13/2000		Swisscom-Bdcstg Act	Switzerland	Seeking Buyer	Unknown	S Buyer
09/14/2000		Cablevision SA de Argentina	Argentina	UnitedGlobalCom Inc.	United States	Pending
09/14/2000	09/14/2000	Conan Properties Inc.	United States	Stan Lee Media	United States	Completed
09/14/2000	09/14/2000	Entertainment Channel Network	Germany	Phenomedia AG	Germany	Completed
09/14/2000		ERG Ltd-Telecom Mnfg Busns	Australia	SCI Systems Inc.	United States	Pending
09/14/2000	09/14/2000	Promofilm SA	Argentina	Grupo Arbol Producciones SA	Spain	Completed
09/14/2000		Regal Cinema, Larne	United Kingdom	Seeking Buyer	Unknown	S Buyer
09/14/2000		Sky Global Networks Inc.	United States	Shareholders	United States	Pending
09/15/2000		Inmarsat	United Kingdom	Telenor AS (Norway)	Norway	Pending
09/15/2000		Nelvana Ltd	Canada	Seeking Buyer	Unknown	S Buyer
09/15/2000	09/15/2000	Off The Fence	Netherlands	RTV Family Entertainment AG	Germany	Completed
09/15/2000		Thomson Multimedia (Thomson)	France	Investors	Unknown	Pending
09/15/2000	09/15/2000	Webshow TV	South Korea	Freechal	South Korea	Completed
09/17/2000		SKY Perfect Communications Inc.	Japan	Seeking Buyer	Unknown	S Buyer
09/18/2000		Cable Atlantic Inc.	Canada	Rogers Communications Inc.	Canada	Pending
09/18/2000		Nelvana Ltd	Canada	CORUS Entertainment Inc.	Canada	Pending
09/18/2000		VDI Multimedia	United States	VDI Multimedia	United States	Intended
09/19/2000		Classlane Ltd	United Kingdom	ePromo.com	United States	Pending
09/19/2000	09/19/2000	Gregoire Furrer Productions SA	Switzerland	Brainpool TV AG	Germany	Completed
09/19/2000	09/19/2000	M News SARL	France	Maximal Productions SA	France	Completed
09/20/2000		Ninox Films Ltd	New Zealand	West 175 Media Group Inc.	United Kingdom	Pending
09/20/2000		WSAH-TV, Bridgeport, CT	United States	Azteca America Stations Group	United States	Pending
09/21/2000	09/21/2000	Alcatel-Poznan Manufacturing	Poland	Kimball International Inc.	United States	Completed
09/21/2000	09/21/2000	Erim Intl-Holovision	United States	X-Rite	United States	Completed
09/21/2000	09/21/2000	KirchPayTV GmbH (Kirch Gruppe)	Germany	Lehman Bro Merchant Bk Prts II	United States	Completed
09/22/2000		M6-Certain Assets	France	TF1-Certain Assets	France	Pending
09/22/2000		Scanbox Medien (Scanbox)	Germany	VCL Film & Medien AG	Germany	Pending
09/22/2000		Transmast Oy (IVO Transmission)	Finland	IVO Transmission Engineering	Finland	Pending
09/25/2000		Delux Video Services Ltd	United Kingdom	Seeking Buyer	Unknown	S Buyer
09/25/2000	09/25/2000	Olive Jar Studios	United States	Red Sky Interactive Inc.	United States	Completed
09/25/2000	09/25/2000	Research Systems Inc.	United States	Eastman Kodak Co. Inc.	United States	Completed
09/25/2000	09/25/2000	Salsa Distribution SARL	France	TV-Loonland AG	Germany	Completed
09/26/2000	09/26/2000	ComingSoon TV	Japan	Investor Group	Japan	Completed
09/26/2000	10/12/2000	Nickel Palace Inc.	United States	Magellan Filmed Entertainment	United States	Completed
09/27/2000	09/27/2000	AmpliComm Inc.	United States	Aeroflex Inc.	United States	Completed
09/27/2000		Fox Nederland BV (News Corp.)	Netherlands	SBS Broadcasting SA	Luxembourg	Pending
09/27/2000		Imax Corp.	Canada	Seeking Buyer	Unknown	Withdrawn
09/27/2000	09/27/2000	Monogram Pictures Inc.	United States	ePersonnelManagement.com	United States	Completed
09/27/2000		Sky Global Networks Inc.	United States	Liberty Media Group (AT&T Corp.)	United States	Pending
09/27/2000		TQS Inc.	Canada	Seeking Buyer	Unknown	S Buyer
09/27/2000		Village Roadshow Exhibition	Germany	Kinowelt Medien AG	Germany	Pending
09/28/2000		Allgon AB	Sweden	Remec Inc.	United States	Pending
09/28/2000		Beijing Total Solution System	China	Hartcourt Cos Inc.	United States	Pending
09/28/2000	09/28/2000	Canbras Communications Corp.	Canada	Bell Canada International Inc.	Canada	Completed
09/28/2000	09/28/2000	Multimedia Development Corp.	United States	Efficient Networks Inc.	United States	Completed
09/28/2000	09/28/2000	Starman (Telia AB)	Estonia	Emerging Europe Capital	Unknown	Completed
09/28/2000		Videotron Telecom	Canada	Seeking Buyer	Unknown	S Buyer
09/29/2000	09/29/2000	Fiat SpA	Italy	Nuova Holding San Paolo IMI	Italy	Completed
09/29/2000		ID MEDIA AG	Germany	Deutsche Telekom AG	Germany	Pending
09/29/2000		MTV Draama (MTV OY)	Finland	Jarowskij Draama Suomi Oy	Finland	Pending
09/29/2000		Singapore Cablevision Pte Ltd	Singapore	Starhub Pte Ltd	Singapore	Pending
09/29/2000		Sony Wonder (Sony Corp.)	United States	TV-Loonland AG	Germany	Pending
09/30/2000	09/30/2000	Ren TV (LUKoil)	Russia	Unified Energy System	Russia	Completed

Biographies

A . . . 34
B . . . 52
C . . . 92
D . . . 123
E . . . 146
F . . . 151
G . . . 167
H . . . 191
I . . . 218
J . . . 221
K . . . 230
L . . . 247
M . . . 271
N . . . 305
O . . . 313
P . . . 318
Q . . . 339
R . . . 340
S . . . 363
T . . . 407
U . . . 420
V . . . 422
W . . . 428
Y . . . 451
Z . . . 454

WHO'S WHO

IN THE ENTERTAINMENT WORLD

A

AARON, PAUL
Director, Producer, Writer.
THEATRE: *B'way*: Salvation, Paris Is Out, '70 Girls '70, Love Me Love My Children, That's Entertainment, The Burnt Flowerbed.
PICTURES: A Different Story, A Force of One, The Octagon (co-s.p.), Imperial Navy, Deadly Force, Maxie, Home Front, Bill & Ted's Bogus Journey (co-prod.), In Too Deep (prod., s.p.).
TELEVISION: *Movies*: The Miracle Worker, Thin Ice, Maid in America, When She Says No, Casebusters (exec. prod.), Save the Dog!, In Love and War, Laurel Avenue (creator, co-writer, exec. prod.),Untamed Love (prod.), Under One Roof (co-creator, co-writer, exec. prod.), Grand Avenue (creator, exec. prod.).

AARON, ROY H.
Executive, Entertainment Industry Consultant. b. Los Angeles, CA, April 8, 1929. e. UC Berkeley, BA; USC, LLB. Attorney in L.A. law firm of Pacht, Ross, Warne, Bernhard & Sears (1957-78). Joined Plitt Companies in 1978 as sr. v.p. & gen. counsel. In 1980 was named pres. & CEO of Plitt Theatres, Inc. and related Plitt companies. 1985-93, pres. & CEO of Showscan Corp. 1993, business consultant, pres. of Plitt Entertainment Group Inc. & chmn. of Pacific Leisure Entertainment Group, L.L.C. Chmn. & CEO Intra-Asia Ent. Corp., 1997-.

ABARBANEL, SAM X.
Producer, Writer, Publicist. b. Jersey City, NJ, March 27, 1914. e. Cornell U., U. of Illinois, B.S. 1935. Newspaperman in Chicago before joining NY exploitation dept. of Republic, then to studio as asst. publicity director. WWII in Europe with 103rd Div. After war became independent publicist and producer. Formed own co. in Spain, 1966. A founder of the Publicists Guild in Hollywood.
PICTURES: *Producer/Co-Prod./Exec. Prod./Assoc. Prod.*: Argyle Secrets, Prehistoric Women (also co-s.p.), Golden Mistress, Gunfighters of Casa Grande, The Sound of Horror (s.p.) Son of Gunfighter, Narco Men, The Last Day of War (also s.p.), Summertime Killer (s.p).

ABEND, SHELDON
Executive. b. New York, NY, June 13, 1929. Maritime Labor-Rel. Negotiator, 1954-56; chmn., Maritime Union, 1954-56. Head, exec. dir. Authors' Research Co. (est. 1957) representing estates of deceased authors. Ind't literary negotiator: CC films, A.A.P., RKO General Inc., David O. Selznick, 7 Arts, Warner Bros., 1959-65. Pres. American Play Co. Inc. & Century Play Co. Inc., 1961-present. Est. Million Dollar Movie Play Library, 1962. Pres. Amer. Literary Consultants, est. 1965. Exec. v.p. Chantec Enterprises Inc. 1969-72. Mktg. literary cons. for Damon Runyon Estate. Copyright analyst and literary rights negotiator, United Artists Corp. Founder and chmn., Guild for Author's Heirs, 1970-72. Literary negotiator and prod. cons. for Robert Fryer, 1972. Founder, Copyright Royalty Co. for Authors' Heirs, 1974. Copyright consultant, Films, Inc. 1975; literary agent for Bway. play, Chicago, 1975. Owner of 53 classic RKO motion pictures for the non-theatrical markets, distributed by Films, Inc. Revived publishing of Damon Runyon stories in quality paperback. Published Cornell Woolrich mystery stories-all prod. by Alfred Hitchcock for TV & motion pictures, 1976. Assoc. prod. of film, Why Would I Lie?, 1978. Originator of Million Dollar Movie Book Theatre and Million Dollar Movie Sound Track Co., 1980. Assoc. prod. of B'way revival, Shanghai Gesture, 1981. Publ. 5 Cornell Woolrich books owned by S. Abend, 1982-83. Co-authored, The Guardians, 1985 and Romance of the Forties by Damon Runyon, 1986. Founder and pres. American Concerts, Inc. and American Theatre Collections, Inc., 1985. Published Into the Night by Cornell Woolrich. Packaged m.p. Bloodhounds of Broadway, 1988; co-author s.p. Ultimate Deman; stage adapt. of Bloodhounds of Broadway, Madam La Gimp, 1990. Exec. prod. adaptation of Cornell Woolrich stories for TV and movies. Won landmark copyright case before U.S. Supreme Court protecting Woolrich estate, also affecting other deceased authors, songwriters and their copywright renewals of their work, 1990. Acquired Damon Runyon copywrights, 1992. Guys & Dolls handbook published by Viking, 1993.

ABRAHAM, F. MURRAY
Actor. r.n. Fahrid Murray Abraham. b. Pittsburgh, PA, Oct. 24, 1939. e. U. of Texas, 1959-61; trained for stage at Herbert Berghof Studios with Uta Hagen. First NY acting job was as Macy's Santa Claus. Stage debut in Los Angeles in The Wonderful Ice Cream Suit, 1965. New York debut in The Fantasticks, 1966. Full professor of theatre at CUNY Brooklyn College. Honorary Doctorate, Ryder College.
THEATER: Antigone (NYSF, 1982), Uncle Vanya (Obie, LaMamma, etc.), The Golem (NYSF), Madwoman of Chaillot, Othello, Cyrano, A Life in the Theatre, Sexual Perversity in Chicago, Duck Variations, The David Show, Adaptation/Next, Don't Drink the Water, And Miss Reardon Drinks a Little, Where Has Tommy Flowers Gone?, A Christmas Carol, The Seagull, Landscape of the Body, 6 Rms Riv Vu, Survival of St. Joan, Scuba Duba, Teibele & Her Demon, The Ritz, Legend, Bad Habits, Frankie & Johnnie in the Claire De Lune, Twelfth Night, Macbeth, A Midsummer's Night Dream, Waiting for Godot, King Lear, Angels in America: Millenium Aproaches/Perestroika, Little Murders, A Month in the Country; also 5 Children's musicals, Theatreworks.
PICTURES: They Might Be Giants (debut, 1971), Serpico, The Prisoner of 2nd Avenue, The Sunshine Boys, All the President's Men, The Ritz, Madman, The Big Fix, Scarface, Amadeus (Academy Award, 1984), The Name of the Rose, Slipstream, The Favorite, Russicum (The Third Solution), An Innocent Man, Beyond the Stars, Eye of the Widow, The Bonfire of the Vanities, Cadence, Mobsters, National Lampoon's Loaded Weapon 1, By the Sword, Last Action Hero, Sweet Killing, The Final Card, Surviving the Game, Nostradamus, The Case, Jamila, Quiet Flows the Dawn, Money, Dillinger and Capone, Mighty Aphrodite., Baby Face Nelson, Looking for Richard, Children of the Revolution, Eruption, Mimic, Star Trek: Insurrection, All New Adventures of Laurel and Hardy: For Love or Mummy, Muppets from Space, Excellent Cadavers, Finding Forrester, The Knights of the Quest.
TELEVISION: *Movies*: Sex and the Married Woman, A Season of Giants, Journey to the Center of the Earth, Color of Justice, Falcone, Esther. *Mini-Series*: The Betrothed, Marco Polo, Dream West., Dead Man's Walk, Noah's Ark, Esther, The Darkling. *Series*: Love of Life, How to Survive a Marriage. *Guest*: Kojak, All in the Family. *Specials*: Largo Desolato.

ABRAHAMS, JIM
Producer, Writer, Director. b. Shorewood, WI, May 10, 1944. e. U. of Wisconsin. Former private investigator. 1971, with friends David and Jerry Zucker, opened the Kentucky Fried Theatre in Madison, WI, a multimedia show specializing in live improvisational skits mixed with videotaped and film routines and sketches, with the threesome writing and appearing in most. Opened new theatre in Los Angeles in 1972 and developed large following. Co-wrote, co-dir., and co-exec. prod. TV series Police Squad!
PICTURES: *With Zuckers*: The Kentucky Fried Movie (co-s.p.), Airplaine! (co-dir., co-exec. prod., co-s.p.), Top Secret! (co-dir., co-s.p.,co-exec. prod.), Ruthless People (co-dir.). *Also*: Big Business (dir.), The Naked Gun (exec. prod., co-s.p.), Cry-Baby (co-exec. prod.), Welcome Home Roxy Carmichael (dir.), The Naked Gun 2-1/2 (co-exec. prod.), Hot Shots! (dir., co-s.p.), Hot Shots Part Deux!. (dir., co-s.p.), Naked Gun 33 1/3: The Final Insult (co-exec. prod.), Jane Austen's Mafia (dir.).
TELEVISION: *Movies:* First do No Harm (dir.).

ABRAHAMS, MORT
Producer. b. New York, NY. Dir. programming, prod., NTA, 1958-60. Exec. prod. Cooga Mooga Prod. Inc., 1960-61. Prod.: Target, The Corruptors 1961, Route 66, 1962-63; writer TV shows, 1963-64. Prod., Kraft Suspense Theatre, 1965; prod., Man from U.N.C.L.E., 1965-66; exec. v.p., APJAC Prod., 1966; v.p. in chg. of prod., Rastar Prods., 1969; exec. prod. American Film Theatre & v.p. Ely Landau Organization, in charge of West Coast prod., 1971-74. Member of Faculty and prod.-in-residence, Center for Advanced Film and TV Studies of A.F.I. Vice-pres. Alph Productions, 1993-present.
PICTURES: *Assoc. Prod.*: Doctor Dolittle, Planet of the Apes, The Chairman, Goodbye Mr. Chips, Beneath the Planet of the Apes (also s.p.). *Exec. Prod.*: Luther, Homecoming, The Man in the Glass Booth, The Greek Tycoon, Hopscotch, The Chosen (exec. in chg. prod.), Beatlemania (exec. in chg. prod.), The Deadly Game, Arch of Triumph, The Holcroft Covenant, Seven Hours to Judgment (prod.).

ACKERMAN, ANDY
Director, Producer, Editor.
TELEVISION: *Series Dir.*: Cheers (also co-prod., editor, Emmy Award, 1988, 1991), Wings, Seinfeld (also prod., Directors' Guild Award, 1997-98), Frasier, Almost Perfect, Suddenly Susan, Public Morals, Jenny, LateLine (also prod.), Becker (also prod.), It's Like, You Know...., The Trouble with Normal.

ACKERMAN, BETTYE
Actress. r.n. Bettye Louise Ackermann. b. Cottageville, SC, Feb. 28, 1928. e. Columbia U., 1948-52. Taught dancing, 1950-54.
THEATER: No Count Boy, 1954; Tartuffe, Sophocles' Antigone and Oedipus at Colonus, The Merchant of Venice.
PICTURES: Face of Fire, Rascal, Ted & Venus, Pre-Hysteria II.
TELEVISION: *Movies*: Companions in Nightmare, A Day for Thanks on Walton's Mountain, Confessions of a Married Man, Trouble in High Timber Country. *Series*: Ben Casey. *Guest*: Alcoa Premiere, Alfred Hitchcock Presents, Perry Mason, Breaking Point, Hope-Chrysler Theatre, Bonanza, FBI Story, Mannix, Ironside, Medical Center, Columbo, Sixth Sense, Heat of Anger, Return to Peyton Place, The Rookies, Barnaby Jones, Police Story, Gunsmoke, Harry O, Streets of San Francisco, S.W.A.T., Petrocelli, Wonder Woman, Police Woman, Chips, 240-Robert, The Waltons, Dynasty, Falcon Crest, Me and Mom, Trapper John M.D., St. Elsewhere.

ACKLAND, JOSS
Actor. b. North Kensington, London, England, Feb. 29, 1928. e. Central Sch. of Speech Training & Dramatic Art. Spent time in Central Africa as a tea planter. Over 400 TV appearances. Autobiography, I Must Be in There Somewhere.
THEATER: The Old Vic (3 yrs.), Mermaid Theatre (artistic dir., 3 yrs.); Hotel in Amsterdam, Jorrocks Come as You Are, The Collaborators, A Streetcar Named Desire, The Madras House, Captain Brassbound's Conversion, Never the Sinner, Henry IV Parts I & II, Peter Pan (dramatic & musical versions), A Little Night Music, Evita, The Visit, etc.
PICTURES: Seven Days to Noon, Crescendo, Trecolonne in Cronaca, The House That Dripped Blood, The Happiness Cage, Villain, England Made Me, The Black Windmill, S.P.Y.S, The Little Prince, Royal Flash, Operation Daybreak, Who Is Killing the Great Chefs of Europe, Saint Jack, The Apple, Rough Cut, Lady Jane, A Zed and Two Noughts, The Sicilian, White Mischief, To Kill a Priest, It Couldn't Happen Here, Lethal Weapon 2, The Hunt for Red October, Object of Beauty, Bill and Ted's Bogus Journey, The Palermo Connection, The Mighty Ducks, Nowhere to Run, Mother's Boys, The Princess and the Goblin (voice), Miracle on 34th Street, Giorgino, Mad Dogs and Englishmen, A Kid in the Court of King Arthur, Occhio Pinocchio, Daisies in December, To the Ends of Time, Mighty Ducks 3, Surviving Picasso, Deadly Voyage, Firelight, Milk, Passion of Mind, Mumbo Jumbo.
TELEVISION: *Movies/Specials*: Queenie, Shadowlands, The Man Who Lived at the Ritz, A Quiet Conspiracy, Jekyll and Hyde, First and Last, A Murder of Quality, A Woman Named Jackie, Ashenden, Voices in the Garden, Queenie, The Bible, Citizen X, Heat of the Sun, The Son of Sandokan.

ADAM, KEN
Art Director, Prod. Designer. b. Berlin, Germany, Feb. 5, 1921. e. St. Pauls Sch., London; London U., student of architecture. 6 years war service as RAF pilot. In 1947 entered motion picture industry as draughtsman for movie, This Was a Woman.
PICTURES: *Art Dir.*: The Devil's Pass, Soho Incident, Around the World in 80 Days. *Prod. Designer*: Spin a Dark Web, Night of the Demon, Gideon's Day, The Angry Hills, Beyond This Place, The Rough and the Smooth, In the Nick, Let's Get Married, Trials of Oscar Wilde, Dr. No, Sodom and Gomorrah, In the Cool of the Day, Dr. Strangelove, Goldfinger, Woman of Straw, Thunderball, The Ipcress File, Funeral in Berlin, You Only Live Twice, Chitty Chitty Bang Bang, Goodbye Mr. Chips, The Owl and the Pussycat, Diamonds Are Forever, Sleuth, The Last of Sheila, Barry Lyndon (Acad. Award, 1975), Madam Kitty, The Seven Percent Solution, The Spy Who Loved Me, Moonraker, Pennies From Heaven (visual consult., assoc. prod.), King David, Agnes of God, Crimes of the Heart, The Deceivers, Dead-Bang, The Freshman, The Doctor, Company Business, Undercover Blues, Addams Family Values, The Madness of King George (Acad. Award, 1994), Boys on the Side, Bogus, In & Out, The Out of Towners, The White Hotel.

ADAMS, BROOKE
Actress. b. New York, NY, Feb. 8, 1949. e. H.S. of Performing Arts; Inst. of American Ballet. Studied with Lee Strasberg. Made professional debut at six in Finian's Rainbow. Worked steadily in summer stock and TV until age 18. After hiatus resumed acting career.
THEATER: Petrified Forest, Split, Key Exchange, Linda Her, Over Mother's Dead Body, Old Neighborhood, Heidi Chronicles, Lost in Yonkers. *Director*: Two Faced. Helps run small summer theater upstate NY.
PICTURES: Shock Waves (Death Corps), Car Wash, Days of Heaven, Invasion of the Body Snatchers, Cuba, The Great Train Robbery, A Man a Woman and a Bank, Tell Me a Riddle, Utilities, The Dead Zone, Almost You, Key Exchange, The Stuff, Man on Fire, The Unborn, Gas Food Lodging, Sleepless, The Fire This Time, The Baby Sitter's Club.
TELEVISION: *Movies*: F. Scott Fitzgerald and the Last of the Belles, The Daughters of Joshua Cabe Return, James Dean, Who is the Black Dahlia?, Murder on Flight 502, Lace, Haunted, Special People, Lace II, The Lion of Africa, Bridesmaids, Sometimes They Come Back, The Last Hit, Gun, Song of the Succubus. *Specials*: Paul Reiser: Out on a Whim. *Series*: O.K. Crackerby. *Pilot*: A Girl's Life, Nero Wolfe, The Lords of Flatbush. *Guest*: Kojack, Family, Police Woman, Moonlighting, Tony Randall Show, Bob Newhart Show, thirtysomething, Frasier.

ADAMS, CATLIN
Actress, Director. r.n. Barab. b. Los Angeles, CA, Oct. 11, 1950. Began career as actress then studied directing at American Film Institute. Made directorial debut with, Wanted: The Perfect Guy. Also directed Little Shiny Shoes (short, written and prod. with Melanie Mayron), Stolen: One Husband (TV), Toothless (TV).
THEATER: Safe House, Scandalous Memories, Dream of a Blacklisted Actor, The Candy Store, Ruby Ruby Sam Sam, Bermuda Avenue Triangle (dir.).
PICTURES: *Actress*: The Jerk, The Jazz Singer. *Director*: Sticky Fingers (also co-s.p., co-prod.).
TELEVISION: *Movies*: Panic in Echo Park, Freaky Friday. *Series*: Square Pegs. *Guest*: thirtysomething. *Specials*: How to Survive the 70's and Maybe Even Bump into a Little Happiness, She Loves Me She Loves Me Not.

ADAMS, DON
Actor. r.n. Donald James Yarmy. b. New York, NY, April 13, 1926. Won Arthur Godfrey talent contest. Was nightclub impressionist before starting in TV.
PICTURES: The Nude Bomb, Jimmy the Kid, Back to the Beach, Inspector Gadget (voice).
TELEVISION: *Movies*: The Love Boat, Get Smart Again! *Series*: Perry Como's Kraft Music Hall, The Bill Dana Show, Tennessee Tuxedo (voice), Get Smart (3 Emmy Awards, 2 Clio Awards), The Partners, Don Adams' Screen Test, Three Times Daley, Inspector Gadget (voice), Check It Out!, Get Smart (1995), Gadget Boy and Heather (voice), Gadget Boy's Adventures In History (voice), Pepper Ann (voice). *Guest:* The Andy Williams Show, Wait til Your Father Gets Home, The New Scooby-Doo Movies, Empty Nest.

ADAMS, EDIE
Actress, Singer. r.n. Elizabeth Edith Enke. b. Kingston, PA, April 16, 1931. e. Juilliard Sch. of Music, Columbia Sch. of Drama.
THEATER: *NY*: Wonderful Town, Lil Abner (Tony Award), Mame.
PICTURES: The Apartment, Lover Come Back, Call Me Bwana, It's a Mad Mad Mad Mad World, Under the Yum Yum Tree, Love With the Proper Stranger, The Best Man, Made in Paris, The Oscar, The Honey Pot, Up in Smoke, The Happy Hooker Goes Hollywood, Boxoffice, Adventures Beyond Belief.
TELEVISION: *Movies*: Evil Roy Slade, Return of Joe Forrester, Superdome, Fast Friends, Make Me an Offer, A Cry for Love, Ernie Kovacs' Between the Laughter. *Series*: Ernie in Kovacsland, The Ernie Kovacs Show (1952-54, 1955-56), The Chevy Show, Take a Good Look (panelist), Here's Edie, The Edie Adams Show. *Guest*: Miss U.S. Television, Three to Get Ready, Kovacs on the Corner, Kovacs Unlimited, Jack Paar, Ed Sullivan Show, Perry Como Show, Pat Boone Show, G.E. Theatre, Colgate Comedy House, Dinah Shore Show, Palace, Bob Hope Show, Bosom Buddies, Designing Women. *Specials*: Cinderella, Tales of the City.

ADAMS, JOEY LAUREN
Actress. b. Little Rock, AR, Jan. 6, 1971.
PICTURES: Dazed and Confused (debut, 1993), Coneheads, The Program, Sleep with Me, S.F.W., The Pros & Cons of Breathing, Mallrats, Drawing Flies, Bio-Dome, Michael, Chasing Amy (Chicago Crits. Award, Most Promising New Actress, 1997), A Cool Dry Place, Bruno, Big Daddy, Reaching Normal, Bruno, Beautiful, In the Shadows, Harvard Man.
TELEVISION: *Series*: Top of the Heap, Vinnie & Bobby, Second Noah. *Guest:* Married...with Children, Double Rush, Hercules.

ADAMS, JULIE
Actress. r.n. Betty May Adams. b. Waterloo, IA, Oct. 17, 1928. e. jr. coll., Little Rock, AK. Coll. dramatics.
PICTURES: Red Hot and Blue (debut, 1949), The Dalton Gang, Crooked River, Hostile Country, West of the Brazos, Colorado Ranger, Fast on the Draw, Marshal of Heldorado. *As Julie Adams*: Hollywood Story, Finders Keepers, Bend of the River, Bright Victory, Treasure of Lost Canyon, Horizons West, Lawless Breed, Mississippi Gambler, Man From the Alamo, The Stand of Apache River, Wings of the Hawk, The Creature From the Black Lagoon, Francis Joins the WACS, The Looters, One Desire, The Private War of Major Benson, Six Bridges to Cross, Away All Boats, Four Girls in Town, Slim Carter, Slaughter on 10th Avenue, Tarawa Beachhead, Gunfight at Dodge City, Raymie, Underwater City, Tickle Me, Valley of Mystery, The Last Movie, McQ, Psychic Killer, The Wild McCullochs, Killer Inside Me, Goodbye Franklin High, The Fifth Floor, Black Roses, Backtrack.
TELEVISION: *Movies:* The Trackers, Go Ask Alice, Code Red, Backtrack, The Conviction of Kitty Dodds. *Series:* Yancy Derringer, General Hospital, The Jimmy Stewart Show, Code Red, Capitol. *Guest:* Vega$, Cagney & Lacey, Beverly Hills, 90210, Murder She Wrote, Melrose Place, Diagnosis Murder, Sliders, Family Law.

ADAMS, MASON
Actor. b. New York, NY, Feb. 26, 1919. e. U. Wisconsin. B.A., 1940; M.A., 1941. Trained for stage at Neighborhood Playhouse. Began on radio in 1946, spending nearly two decades in starring role of Pepper Young's Family. Made B'way. debut in, Get Away Old Man, 1943.
THEATER: Career Angel, Public Relations, Violet, Shadow of My Enemy, Inquest, The Sign in Sidney Brustein's Window, Tall Story, The Trial of the Catonsville Nine, Foxfire, Checking Out, Danger Memory, The Day Room, The Rose Quartet.
PICTURES: God Told Me To, Raggedy Ann and Andy (voice), Northstar, The Final Conflict, F/X, Toy Soldiers, Son-in-Law, Houseguest, Not of This Earth, Touch, Hudson River Blues, The Lesser Evil.
TELEVISION: *Movies/Specials:* The Deadliest Season, And Baby Makes Six, The Shining Season, Flamingo Road, The Revenge of the Stepford Wives, The Kid with the Broken Halo, Adam, Passions, Solomon Northrup's Odyssey, The Night They Saved Christmas, Who is Julia?, Under Siege, Rage of Angels: The Story Continues, Perry Mason, Jonathan: The Boy Nobody Wanted, Buying a Landslide, Assault at West Point, From the Earth to the Moon. *Series*: Lou Grant, Morningstar/Eveningstar, Knight and Daye, Murder One.

ADAMS, MAUD
Actress. r.n. Maud Wikstrum. b. Lulea, Sweden, Feb. 12, 1945. Formerly a model. Acting debut as model in, The Boys in the Band.
PICTURES: The Boys in the Band, The Christian Licorice Store, U-Turn, Mahoney's Estate, The Man With the Golden Gun, Rollerball, Killer Force, The Merciless Man, Tattoo, Octopussy, Target Eagle, Jane and the Lost City, The Women's Club, A Man of Passion, The Favorite, Soda Cracker, Deadly Intent, Angel III, The Kill Reflex, Forbidden Sun, Favorite, Ringer.
TELEVISION: *Documenttary:* The James Bond Story. *Movies*: Big Bob Johnson and His Fantastic Speed Circus, The Hostage Tower, Playing for Time, Nairobi Affair, The Case of the Wicked Wives. *Series*: Hawaii Five-O, , Chicago Story, Emerald Point, N.A.S., Walker, Texas Ranger, Radioskugga, Vita logner.

ADAMS, TONY
Producer. b. Dublin, Ireland, Feb. 15, 1953. Began career as asst. to dir. John Boorman and was associated with Burt Reynolds prior to joining Blake Edwards as a prod., 1971. Then president, The Blake Edwards Entertainment; Pres. & CEO, The Blake Edwards Company, 1988.
PICTURES: *Assoc. Prod.*: Return of the Pink Panther, The Pink Panther Strikes Again. *Exec. Prod.*: Revenge of the Pink Panther. Prod.: ``10", S.O.B., Victor/Victoria, Trail of the Pink Panther, Curse of the Pink Panther, The Man Who Loved Women, Micki & Maude, That's Life, A Fine Mess, Blind Date, Sunset, Skin Deep, Switch, Son of the Pink Panther.
TELEVISION: Julie Andrews (series and specials), Justin Case, Peter Gunn, Julie.

ADEFARASIN, REMI
Cinematographer.
PICTURES: Truly Madly Deeply, The Hummingbird Tree, Captives, Hollow Reed, The English Patient (second unit), Sliding Doors, Elizabeth (Acad. Award nom.), Onegin, The House of Mirth, Unconditional Love.
TELEVISION: *Movies/Specials:* Grown-Ups, Home Sweet Home, four Days in July, Amy, Shoot for the Sun, Sweet as You Are, Christabel, The Land of Dreams, Children Crossing, The Lost Language of Cranes, Sleepers, Memento Mori, Great Moments in Aviation, Wide-Eyed and Lesless, Midnight Movie, Into the Fire, The Buccaneers, Human Bomb, Emma, Arabian Nights, Band of Brothers.

ADELMAN, GARY
Executive. b. Los Angeles, CA, March 16, 1944. e. California State U., Long Beach State Coll. Asst. dir. on feature, The Masterpiece, 1969; assoc. prod. on The Candy Snatchers. Produced first feature film, The Severed Arm, 1974. Assisted Winston Hock in development of 3-D process, 1975. Pres. & COO of Monarch Prods, 1976-93. Post-prod. consultant for Jerry Gross Organization. Founder and partial owner of New Image Releasing Inc., a prod. & dist. co., 1983. Had post of secty./treas. then named v.p., chg. prod., All-American Group, 1987. Assoc. prod. on Nobody's Perfect, 1990.

ADELMAN, JOSEPH A.
Executive. b. Winnipeg, Manitoba, Canada, Dec. 27, 1933. e. NYU, B.A., 1954; Harvard Law Sch., J.D., graduated cum laude, 1957. Attorney, United Artists Corp., New York, 1958; named west coast counsel, Hollywood, 1964; named exec. asst. to the v.p. in charge of prod. 1968; named v.p., west coast business and legal affairs, 1972. Appointed exec. v.p., Association of Motion Pictures and Television Producers, 1977. Appointed v.p. in chg. of business affairs, Paramount Pictures Corp., 1979. Co-founder Kidpix, Inc.,1984. Founder and CEO of Kidpix Theaters Corp. 1985. Appointed sr. v.p. for business/legal affairs, Color Systems Technology, Inc. 1986. Named pres. of CST Entertainment, 1987. Appointed mng. dir., Broadway Video Entertainment, 1990. CEO, Intl. Entertainment Enterprises 1991. Admitted to NY, California and U.S. Supreme Court bars.
Member: Phi Beta Kappa, American Bar Association, Los Angeles Copyright Society, Academy of Motion Picture Arts and Sciences, National Assn. of Television Programming Executives. On bd. of dirs., AMPTP, 1969-1979; bd. of trustees, Theatre Authority, 1970-79. Recipient of Alumni Achievement Award, NYU, 1982

ADELSON, GARY
Producer. b. 1954. e. UCLA, B.A. Son of Merv Adelson. Joined Lorimar Prods. 1970 as prod. asst. on TV movie Helter Skelter. In 1989, formed Adelson/Baumgarten Prods. with Craig Baumgarten.
PICTURES: The Last Starfighter, The Boy Who Could Fly, In The Mood, Tap, Hard to Kill (also s.p.), Hook, Universal Soldier, Nowhere to Run, Blank Check, It Could Happen to You, Jade, Rolling Thunder, The Shooter.
TELEVISION: Helter Skelter (asst. prod.), Sybil (assoc. prod.), Eight Is Enough (prod.), The Blue Knight (prod.). *Exec. prod.*: Too Good To Be True, Our Family Business, Cass Malloy, John Steinbeck's The Winter of Our Discontent, Lace, Detective in the House, Lace II, Critical Choices, The Hunchback, Love in Another Town, Everything to Gain. *Series*: Spies.

ADELSON, MERV
Producer. b. Los Angeles, CA, Oct. 23, 1929. e. UCLA. Pres., Markettown Builders Emporium, Las Vegas, 1953-63. Managing partner Paradise Dev., 1958-. Pres. Realty Holdings, 1962-. Bd. chmn., Lorimar Inc., 1969-86. Bd. dirs. chmn. & CEO, Lorimar Telepictures, 1986-.
PICTURES: Twilight's Last Gleaming, The Choirboys, Who Is Killing the Great Chefs of Europe?, Avalanche Express, The Big Red One.
TELEVISION: *Movies/Mini-Dir.*: Sybil, A Man Called Intrepid, The Blue Knight, Helter-Skelter. *Series*: The Waltons, Eight Is Enough, Dallas, Kaz, The Waverly Wonders, Knots Landing.

ADJANI, ISABELLE
Actress, Producer. b. Gennevilliers, France, June 27, 1955.
PICTURES: Le Petit Bougnat, Faustine and the Beautiful Summer, The Slap, The Story of Adele H. (Acad. Award nom.), The Tenant, Barocco, Violette and Francois, The Driver, Nosferatu—The Vampire, The Bronte Sisters, Clara et les Chics Types, Possession, Quartet, Next Year If All Goes Well, One Deadly Summer, Antonieta, Deadly Circuit, Subway, Ishtar, Camille Claudel (also co-prod.; Acad. Award nom.), Toxic Affair, Queen Margot, Diabolique, Paparazzi.

ADLER, ALLEN
Writer, Producer. b. New York, NY, 1946. e. Princeton U., B.A.; Harvard Business Sch., M.B.A. Started with Standard & Poor's Inter-Capital then joined Alan Hirschfield at American Diversified Enterprises. Moved to Columbia Pictures as corporate officer, 1973; named sr. v.p., Columbia, 1979. Teamed with Daniel Melnick in IndieProd Co., 1981. *Writer:* Forbidden Planet, Behemoth,the Sea Monster, Parasite, The Concrete Jungle, Metalstorm:The Destruction of Jared-Syn, The Alchemist. Exec. prod., Making Love.

ADLON, PERCY
Director, Writer, Producer. b. Munich, Germany, June 1, 1935. e. Munich Univ. m. Eleonore Adlon, with whom he has worked on several film projects. Created more than forty tv documentaries.
PICTURES: Celeste, The Last Five Days (dir. only), The Swing, Sugarbaby, Bagdad Cafe, Rosalie Goes Shopping, Salmonberries, Younger and Younger, Hotel Adlon, Eat Your Heart Out (prod. only), Forever Flirt.
TELEVISION: The Guardian and His Poet (Adolf Grimme Award).

AFFLECK, BEN
Actor, Writer, Director. b. Berkeley, CA, Aug. 15, 1972. Began acting at age 8.
PICTURES: School Ties (debut, 1992), Buffy the Vampire Slayer, Dazed and Confused, Mallrats, I Killed My Lesbian Wife Hung Her on a Meat Hook, and Now I Have a Three-Picture Deal at Disney (dir. only), Glory Daze, Office Killer, Chasing Amy, Going All the Way, Good Will Hunting (also s.p., Acad. Award, Golden Globe Award, Best Screenplay, 1997), Phantoms, Armageddon, Reindeer Games, Shakespeare in Love, Forces of Nature, Dogma, Daddy and Them, 200 Cigarettes, The Boiler Room, Bounce, The Third Wheel, Daddy and Them, Pearl Harbor.
TELEVISION: *Movies*: Hands of a Stranger, Daddy. *Specials:* A People's History of the United States (prod. only). *Series*: Voyage of the Mimi, Against the Grain, Lifestories: Families in Crisis. *Guest:* Almost Home.

AGAR, JOHN
Actor. b. Chicago, IL, Jan. 31, 1921. In service WWII.
PICTURES: Fort Apache (debut, 1948), Adventure in Baltimore, I Married a Communist, Sands of Iwo Jima, She Wore a Yellow Ribbon, Breakthrough, Woman on Pier 13, Magic Carpet, Along the Great Divide, Woman of the North Country, Man of Conflict, Bait, Rocket Man, Shield for Murder, Golden Mistress, Revenge of the Creature, Hold Back Tomorrow, Tarantula, Star in the Dust, The Lonesome Trail, The Mole People, Flesh and the Spur, Daughter of Dr. Jekyll, Cavalry Command, The Brain from Planet Arous, Attack of the Puppet People, Ride a Violent Mile,

Joe Butterfly, Jet Attack, Frontier Gun, Invisible Invaders, Raymie, Hand of Death, Lisette, Journey to the 7th Planet, Of Love and Desire, The Young and the Brave, Law of the Lawless, Stage to Thunder Rock, Young Fury, Waco, Johnny Reno, Curse of the Swamp Creature, Zontar: The Thing from Venus, Women of the Prehistoric Planet, St. Valentine's Day Massacre, Big Jake, Chisum, King Kong, Perfect Bride, Miracle Mile, Nightbreed, Fear, Invasion of Privacy, Body Bags, Pandora Directive (CD-ROM).

AGOGLIA, JOHN J.
Executive. Worked for 14 years for CBS Entertainment in New York, becoming v.p. business affairs. Joined NBC in 1979 as v.p., program and talent negotiations; named sr. v.p. business affairs NBC, 1980; exec. v.p. NBC Prods., 1984; exec. v.p., business affairs NBC-TV Network, 1986; in charge of foreign marketing relating to NBC Productions products, 1987; pres. of NBC Enterprises, 1990; pres. of NBC Prods., 1993.

AGUTTER, JENNY
Actress. b. Taunton, Devonshire, England, Dec. 20, 1952. e. Elmhurst Ballet Sch. Received Variety Club of Great Britain Most Promising Artiste Award, 1971.
THEATER: School for Scandal, Rooted, Arms and the Man, The Ride Across Lake Constance, The Tempest, Spring Awakening, Hedda, Betrayal. Member, Royal Shakespeare Co.-King Lear, Arden of Taversham, The Body. Breaking the Silence, Shrew (Los Angeles), Love's Labour's Lost, Mothers and Daughters.
PICTURES: East of Sudan (debut, 1964), Ballerina (tv in U.S.), Gates of Paradise, Star!, I Start Counting, Walkabout, The Railway Children, Logan's Run, The Eagle Has Landed, Equus (BAFTA Award, 1977), Dominique, China 9 Liberty 37, The Riddle of the Sands, Sweet William, The Survivor, Amy, An American Werewolf in London, Secret Places, Dark Tower, King of the Wind, Dark Man, Child's Play 2, Freddie as F.R.O. 7 (voice), Blue Juice.
TELEVISION: *Movies*: The Great Mr. Dickens, The Wild Duck, The Cherry Orchard, The Snow Goose (Emmy Award, 1972), As Many as Are Here Present, A War of Children, The Man in the Iron Mask, A House in Regent Place, There's Love and Dove, Kiss Me and Die, A Legacy, The Waiting Room, Six Million Dollar Man, School Play, The Mayflower, Voyage of the Pilgrims, Beulah Land, Love's Labour's Lost, This Office Life, Magnum, The Two Ronnies, Silas Marner, The Twilight Zone, Murder She Wrote, No a Penny More Not a Penny Less, Dear John, The Equalizer, The Outsiders, Breaking the Code, Boon, Love Hurts, Heartbeat, The Buccaneers, September, Bramwell: Our Brave Boys, Bramwell: Loose Women. *Mini-series*: A Respectable Trade, The Railway Children.

AIELLO, DANNY
Actor. b. New York, NY, June 20, 1936.
THEATER: Lampost Reunion (Theatre World Award), Wheelbarrow Closers, Gemini (Obie Award), Knockout, The Floating Light Bulb, Hurlyburly (LA Drama Critics Award), The House of Blue Leaves.
PICTURES: Bang the Drum Slowly (debut, 1973), The Godfather Part II, The Front, Fingers, Blood Brothers, Defiance, Hide in Plain Sight, Fort Apache the Bronx, Chu Chu and the Philly Flash, Deathmask, Once Upon a Time in America, Old Enough, The Purple Rose of Cairo, Key Exchange, The Protector, The Stuff, Radio Days, The Pick-Up Artist, Man on Fire, Moonstruck, The January Man, Crack in the Mirror, Do the Right Thing (LA, Chicago & Boston Film Critics Awards; Acad. Award nom.), Russicum (The Third Solution), Harlem Nights, Jacob's Ladder, Once Around, Hudson Hawk, The Closer, 29th Street, Ruby, Mistress, The Cemetery Club, The Pickle, Me and the Kid, The Professional, Ready to Wear (Pret-a-Porter), City Hall, Power of Attorney, He Ain't Heavy, Two Much, 2 Days in the Valley, Mojave Moon, A Brooklyn State of Mind, Bring Me The Head of Mavis Davis, Wilbur Falls, Prince of Central Park, Mambo Cafe, 18 Shades of Dust, Off Key, Dinner Rush.
TELEVISION: *Movies*: The Last Tenant, Lovey: A Circle of Children Part 2, A Question of Honor, Blood Feud, Lady Blue, Daddy, Alone in the Neon Jungle, The Preppie Murder. *Mini Series:* The Last Don, The Last Don II *Series*: Lady Blue, Dellaventura (also prod). *Specials*: Family of Strangers (Emmy Award), Lieberman in Love.

AIMEE, ANOUK
Actress. r.n. Francoise Soyra Dreyfus. b. Paris, France, April 27, 1932. Studied dancing at Marseilles Opera, acting at Bauer-Therond dramatic school, Paris. Started in films as teenager billed as Anouk.
PICTURES: La Maison Sous la Mer (debut, 1946), La Fleur de l'age, Les Amants De Verone, The Golden Salamander, Noche de Tormenta, Le Rideau Cramoisi, The Man Who Watched the Trains Go By (Paris Express), Contraband Spain, Forever My Heart, Les Mauvaises Rencontres, Ich Suche Dich, Nina, Stresemann, Pot Bouille, Montparnasse 19, Tous Peuvent Me Tuer, Le Tete Contre Les Murs, The Journey, Les Dragueurs, La Dolce Vita, Le Farceur, Lola, L'Imprevu, Quai Notre-Dame, Il Giudizio Universale, Sodom and Gomorrah, Les Grand Chemins, 8 1/2, Il Terrorista, Il Successo, Liola, Le Voci Bianche, La Fuga, La Stagione del Nostro Amore, A Man and a Woman (Acad. Award nom.), Lo Sacandalo, Il Morbidonne, Un Soir Un Train, The Model Shop, Justine, The Appointment, Si C'Etait d Refaire, Mon Premier Amour, Salto nel Vuoto (Leap Into the Void), Tragedy of a Ridiculous Man, What Makes David Run?, Le General de l'Armee Morte, Success is the Best Revenge, Viva la Vie, A Man and A Woman: 20 Years Later, Arrivederci e Grazie, La Table Tournante, The House of the Lord, Dr. Bethune, Rabbit Face, Ready to Wear (Pret-a-Porter), A Hundred and One NIghts, Ruptures, Marmottes, Men, Women: A Users Manual, LA Without a Map, Riches, Belles, etc, One 4 All, 1999 Madeline, 2000 Eve, .
TELEVISION: Voices in the Garden, Solomon, Victorie,ou la douleur de femmes.

ALBECK, ANDY
Executive. b. U.S.S.R., Sept. 25, 1921. Industry career began in 1939 with Columbia Pictures Intl. Corp. Central Motion Picture Exchange, 1947. Eagle Lion Classics, Inc., 1949. Joined UA in intl. dept., functioning in the area of operations, 1951. After filling a number of key posts, named asst. treas., 1970; v.p. of UA and its subsidiary, UA Broadcasting, Inc., 1972; pres. of UA Broadcasting, 1973; sr. v.p. operations, 1976; UA Corp. pres. & chief exec. officer in 1978. Retired, 1981.

ALBERGHETTI, ANNA MARIA
Singer, Actress. b. Pesaro, Italy, May 15, 1936. d. Daniele Alberghetti, cellist. Concert debut in 1948 in Pesaro, then toured Italy, Scandinavia, Spain; Am. debut Carnegie Hall, 1950, sang with NY Philharmonic Society, Phila. Symphony, on television. Made B'way debut in Carnival, 1962 (Tony Award).
PICTURES: The Medium (debut, 1951), Here Comes the Groom, The Stars Are Singing, The Last Command, Duel at Apache Wells, Ten Thousand Bedrooms, Cinderfella, The Whole She-Bang, Friends and Family.
TELEVISION: *Guest*: Toast of the Town, Cavalcade of Stars, Arthur Murray Show, Bob Hope, Eddie Fisher, Red Skelton, Dinah Shore, Desilu Playhouse, G.E. Theatre, Chevy Show, Dupont Show, Voice of Firestone, Colgate Hour, Climax, Loretta Young, Ford Jubilee, Perry Como.

ALBERT, EDDIE
Actor. r.n. Eddie Albert Heimberger. b. Rock Island, IL, April 22, 1908. e. U. of Minnesota. Son is actor Edward Albert. Performer on Radio NBC.
THEATER: *B'way*: Brother Rat, Say Darling, The Music Man, Room Service, The Boys from Syracuse, Seven Year Itch, Our Town, No Hard Feelings, Reuben Reuben, Miss Liberty, You Can't Take It With You.
PICTURES: Brother Rat (debut, 1938), On Your Toes, Four Wives, Brother Rat and a Baby, Angel from Texas, My Love Came Back, Dispatch from Reuter's, Four Mothers, The Wagons Roll at Night, Out of the Fog, Thieves Fall Out, The Great Mr. Nobody, Treat 'em Rough, Eagle Squadron, Ladies' Day, Lady Bodyguard, Bombadier, Strange Voyage, Rendezvous With Annie, Perfect Marriage, Smash-Up, Time Out of Mind, Hit Parade of 1947, Dude Goes West, You Gotta Stay Happy, Fuller Brush Girl, You're in the Navy Now, Meet Me After the Show, Carrie, Actors and Sin, Roman Holiday (Acad. Award nom.), Girl Rush, I'll Cry Tomorrow, Oklahoma!, Attack, Teahouse of the August Moon, The Sun Also Rises, The Joker is Wild, Orders to Kill, Gun Runners, The Roots of Heaven, Beloved Infidel, The Young Doctors, Two Little Bears, Madison Avenue, Who's Got the Action?, The Longest Day, Captain Newman M.D., Miracle of the White Stallions, The Party's Over, Seven Women, The Heartbreak Kid (Acad. Award nom.), McQ, The Take, The Longest Yard, Escape to Witch Mountain, The Devil's Rain, Hustle, Whiffs, Birch Interval, Moving Violations, Yesterday, The Concorde — Airport 79, Foolin' Around, How to Beat the High Cost of Living, Take This Job and Shove It, Yes Giorgio, Dreamscape, The Act, Stitches, Head Office, The Big Picture, Brenda Starr, Headless!
TELEVISION: *Movies/Specials*: The Yeagers, Benjamin Franklin, The Borrowers, Killer Bees, Nutcracker, Anything Goes, Crash, The Word, Evening in Byzantium, Pirates Key, Living in Paradise, Oklahoma Dolls, The Plan, Peter and Paul, Goliath Awaits, Concord, Beyond Witch Mountain, Rooster, Demon Murder Case, Coalfire, In Like Flynn, Dress Gray, Mercy or Murder?, War and Remembrance, Return to Green Acres, The Girl from Mars, The Barefoot Executive, The Rodgers & Hart Story:Thou Swell, Thou Witty. *Series*: Leave It To Larry, Nothing But the Best, Saturday Night Revue, Green Acres, Switch!, Falcon Crest, General Hospital. *Guest*: The Fall Guy, Love Boat, Highway to Heaven, Falcon Crest, Murder She Wrote, thirtysomething, Ray Bradbury Theatre, Twilight Zone, Time Trax, Golden Palace, Dr. Quinn–Medicine Woman.

ALBERT, EDWARD
Actor. b. Los Angeles, CA, Feb. 20, 1951. e. UCLA. Son of actor Eddie Albert and late actress Margo. Was prod. asst. on Patton in Spain. Has appeared with father on radio and TV shows. Is photographer and has exhibited work in L.A.
THEATER: Room Service, Our Town, The Glass Menagerie, Hamlet.

PICTURES: The Fool Killer (debut, 1965), Wild Country, Butterflies Are Free, Forty Carats, Midway, The Domino Principle, The Purple Taxi, The Greek Tycoon, When Time Ran Out, The Squeeze, Galaxy of Terror, Butterfly, The House Where Evil Dwells, A Time to Die, Ellie, Getting Even, Distortions, Terminal Entry, The Rescue, Mind Games, Sight Unseen, Fist Fighter, Shootfighter:Fight to the Death, Broken Trust, Red Sun Rising, The Ice Runner, Demon Keeper, Guarding Tess, Sexual Malice, Sorceress, The Royal Affair, Space Marines, The Secret Agent Club, Kid Cop, The Man in the Iron Mask, Unbowed, Stagehost, Finding Home.
TELEVISION: *Movies*: Killer Bees, Death Cruise, The Millionaire, Silent Victory: The Kitty O'Neil Story, Blood Feud, The Girl from Mars, Body Language, Star Witness. *Mini-Series*: Black Beauty, The Last Convertible, Invasion America. *Series*: The Yellow Rose, Falcon Crest, Beauty and the Beast, The Fantastic Four (voice), Port Charles. *Host:* Viva, Different Point of View, On Call*Specials:* Daddy Can't Read, Orson Welles' Great Mysteries (BBC). *Guest*: Beauty and the Beast, Houston Knights, Murder She Wrote, Police Story, Hitchhiker, The Love Boat, The Rookies, Profiler, Dr. Quinn, Medicine Woman, Nash Bridges, Martial Law, Chicken Soup for the Soul, Sabrina,the Teenage Witch, The Sentinel.

ALBRIGHT, LOLA
Actress. b. Akron, OH, July 20, 1925. e. Studied piano 12 years. Switchboard operator and stenographer NBC; stenographer with WHAM and bit player; photographers' model. Made screen debut in The Pirate, 1947.
PICTURES: The Pirate (debut, 1947), Easter Parade, Julia Misbehaves, The Girl From Jones Beach, Tulsa, Champion, Bodyhold, Beauty on Parade, The Good Humor Man, When You're Smiling, Sierra Passage, The Killer That Stalked New York, Arctic Flight, The Silver Whip, The Treasure of Ruby Hills, The Magnificent Matador, The Tender Trap, The Monolith Monsters, Pawnee, Oregon Passage, Seven Guns to Mesa, A Cold Wind in August, Kid Galahad, Joy House (The Love Cage), Lord Love a Duck, The Way West, Where Were You When the Lights Went Out?, The Impossible Years, The Money Jungle.
TELEVISION: *Movies*: Helicopter Spies, How I Spent My Summer Vacation, Delta County USA, Terraces. *Series*: Peter Gunn, Peyton Place. *Guest*: Switch, The Eddie Capra Mysteries, Quincy, Airwolf.

ALCAINE, JOSE LUIS
Cinematographer. b. Tangier, Algeria, Dec. 26, 1938. e. Spanish Cinema Sch., Madrid. After graduation joined Madrid's Studio Moros doing commercials.
PICTURES: El Puente, El Sur, Taseo, Rustlers' Rhapsody, Bluebeard Bluebeard, Women on the Verge of a Nervous Breakdown, The Mad Monkey, Tie Me Up Tie Me Down, Ay Carmela, Lovers, Ham Ham, Sevillanas, The Age of Beauty, The Bird of Happiness, Golden Balls, Intruder, The Tit & the Moon, La Pasion.Turca, Libertarias, Tramway to Malvarrosa, In Praise of Older Women, Two Much, La Pistola de Mi Hermano, My West, Blast from the Past, Antonio: Rapaz de Lisboa, Se quien eres, That Girl from Rio.

ALDA, ALAN
Actor, Writer, Director r.n. Alphonso D'Abruzzo b. New York, NY, Jan. 28, 1936. e. Fordham U., 1956. Son of actor Robert Alda. Studied at Cleveland Playhouse on Ford Foundation Grant; performed with Second City, then on TV in That Was The Week That Was. For work as director, writer and actor on M*A*S*H won 5 Emmys, 2 Writers Guild Awards, 3 Directors Guild Awards, 6 Golden Globes, 7 People's Choice Awards, Humanitas Award (for Writing).
THEATER: *B'way*: Only in America, The Owl and The Pussycat, Purlie Victorious, Fair Game For Lovers (Theatre World Award), The Apple Tree (Tony nom.), Jake's Women (Tony Award nom.). *London:* Our Town.
PICTURES: Gone Are The Days (debut, 1963), Paper Lion, The Extraordinary Seaman, Jenny, The Moonshine War, The Mephisto Waltz, To Kill a Clown, Same Time Next Year, California Suite, The Seduction of Joe Tynan (also s.p.), The Four Seasons (also dir., s.p.), Sweet Liberty (also dir., s.p.), A New Life (also dir., s.p.), Crimes and Misdemeanors (D.W. Griffith Award, NY Film Critics Award), Betsy's Wedding (also dir., s.p.), Whispers in the Dark, Manhattan Murder Mystery, Canadian Bacon, Flirting With Disaster, Everyone Says I Love You, Murder at 1600, Mad City, The Object of My Affection, Keepers of the Frame, What Women Want.
TELEVISION: *Movies*: The Glass House, Playmates, Isn't It Shocking?, Kill Me If You Can (Emmy nom.), And the Band Played On, Jake's Women, White Mile. *Series*: That Was the Week That Was, M*A*S*H (11 years), Scientific American Frontiers (PBS, host), We'll Get By, The Four Seasons (creator), E.R., Club Land. *Specials*: Free to Be You and Me, 6 Rms Riv Vu (also dir.), Life's Big Questions (host). *Guest*: Phil Silvers Show, The Nurses, Route 66, Trials of O'Brien, Coronet Blue, Carol Burnet Show. *Pilots*: Where's Everett, Higher and Higher.

ALDREDGE, THEONI V.
Costume Designer. b. Salonika, Greece, Aug. 22, 1932. m. actor Tom Aldredge. e. American School, Athens; Goodman Theatre School, Chicago, 1949-52.
THEATER: *B'way.*: Sweet Bird of Youth, That Championship Season, Sticks and Bones, Two Gentlemen of Verona, A Chorus Line, Annie (Tony Award), Ballroom, Much Ado About Nothing, Barnum (Tony Award), Dream Girls, Woman of the Year, Onward Victoria, La Cage aux Folles (Tony Award), 42nd Street, Merlin, Private Lives, The Corn is Green, The Rink, Blithe Spirit, Chess, Gypsy, Oh Kay!, The Secret Garden, High Rollers.
PICTURES: You're A Big Boy Now, No Way to Treat a Lady, Uptight, Last Summer, I Never Sang for My Father, Promise at Dawn, The Great Gatsby (Acad. Award, 1974), Network, Semi-Tough, The Cheap Detective, The Fury, Eyes of Laura Mars (Sci Fi. Acad. Honor), The Champ, The Rose, Can't Stop the Music, Circle of Two, Loving Couples, A Change of Seasons, Middle Age Crazy, Rich and Famous, Annie, Monsignor, Ghostbusters, Moonstruck, We're No Angels, Stanley & Iris, Other People's Money, Milk Money, The First Wives Club, Mrs. Winterbourne, Addams Family Values, The Mirror Has Two Faces, The Rage: Carrie 2.

ALEANDRO, NORMA
Actress. b. Buenos Aires, Argentina, May 2, 1936. Sister is actress Maria Vaner. As child, performed with parents in theater troupe. In Argentina performed in every theatrical genre and epoch and also directed. Has written & published short stories (1986), poems and the screenplay for Argentinian film, Los Herederos. Was in exile in Uruguay (18 months) and Spain 1976-82 because of the military junta in Argentina. Before exile had made 12 films; after return in 1982 starred in theatre and 7 films.
THEATER: *U.S.*: About Love and Other Stories (one-woman show, toured South America, then at La Mama and later off-B'way at Public Theater 1986); The Senorita of Tacna (written for her by Mario Vargas-Llosa, 1987).
PICTURES: The Official Story (Cannes Film Fest. Award, 1986), Gaby: A True Story (Acad. Award nom.), Cousins, Vital Signs, The Tombs, Facundo: The Tiger's Shadow, The Lighthouse, Foolish Heart, El Faro de Sur.
TELEVISION: *Movies*: Autumn Sun, Dark Holiday, One Man's War, Operacion Rescate, Una Noche con Sabrina Love.

ALEXANDER, JANE
Actress. r.n. Jane Quigley. b. Boston, MA, Oct. 28, 1939. e. Sarah Lawrence Coll., U. of Edinburgh. m. director Edwin Sherin. Mother of actor Jace Alexander. Stage career includes appearances on B'way; at Arena Stage, Washington D.C.; Kennedy Center, D.C.; Music Center, L.A.; and Shakespeare Festival at Stamford, Conn. Appointed chair of the National Endowment for the Arts, 1993.
THEATER: *NY:* The Great White Hope (Tony & Theatre World Awards, 1969), 6 Rms Riv Vu, Find Your Way Home, Hamlet, The Heiress, First Monday in October, Goodbye Fidel, Losing Time, Monday After the Miracle, Old Times, Night of the Iguana, Approaching Zanzibar, Shadowlands, The Visit, The Sisters Rosensweig.
PICTURES: The Great White Hope (debut, 1970), A Gunfight, The New Centurions, All the President's Men, The Betsy, Kramer vs. Kramer, Brubaker, Night Crossing, Testament, City Heat, Square Dance, Sweet Country, Glory, Women Don't Want To, Buck and the Magic Bracelet, The Cider House Rules.
TELEVISION: *Movies*: Welcome Home Johnny Bristol, Miracle on 34th St., This is the West That Was, Death Be Not Proud, Eleanor and Franklin, Eleanor and Franklin: The White House Years, A Circle of Children, Lovey: A Circle of Children Part II, A Question of Love, Playing for Time (Emmy Award), In the Custody of Strangers, When She Says No, Calamity Jane, Malice in Wonderland, Blood & Orchids, In Love and War, Open Admissions, A Friendship in Vienna, Daughter of the Streets, Stay the Night. *Guest:* Law and Order, Law and Order:Special Victims Unit. *Specials*: Mountain View, A Marriage: Georgia O'Keeffe and Alfred Stieglitz. *Pilot*: New Year.

ALEXANDER, JASON
Actor. r.n. Jay Scott Greenspan. b. Newark, NJ, Sept. 23, 1959. e. Boston Univ. Received an honorary doctorate from Boston University.
THEATER: *NY:* Merrily We Roll Along, Forbidden Broadway, The Rink, Personals, Stop the World, Light Up the Sky, Broadway Bound, Jerome Robbins' Broadway (Tony, Drama Desk & Outer Critics' Circle Awards, 1989), Accomplice. *Regional*: Give 'em Hell Harry.
PICTURES: The Burning (debut, 1981), Brighton Beach Memoirs, The Mosquito Coast, Pretty Woman, White Palace, Jacob's Ladder, I Don't Buy Kisses Anymore, The Return of Jafar (voice), Down on the Waterfront, Coneheads, The Paper, North, Blankman, For Better or Worse (also dir.), The Last Supper, Dunston Checks In, The Hunchback of Notre Dame (voice), Love! Valour! Compassion!, Denial, Love and Action in Chicago, The Adventures of Rocky and Bullwinkle, Just Looking (dir. only) On Edge, The Hunchback of Notre Dame II.
TELEVISION: *Movies*: Senior Trip, Rockabye, Favorite Son, Bye Bye Birdie, Cinderella. *Series*: E/R, Everything's Relative, Seinfeld, Duckman (voice), Aladdin (voice). *Guest*: Dinosaurs, Newhart, Dream On, The Larry Sanders Show, Remember WENN, Dilbert (voice). *Special*: Sexual Healing.

ALEXANDER, RALPH
Executive. Began career with Universal Pictures in sales, 1949. Had various sls. jobs with 20th Century Fox and Lorimar. Appointed v.p., theatrical foreign sls., Filmway Pictures, 1981-82. Appoined v.p., sls, for Latin America & Southeast Asia, Embassy Pictures Intl., 1982-84. Named exec. v.p., multi-media foreign sls. for Robert Meyers Intl., 1984. Joined Dino De Laurentiis Corp. as intl. sls. dir. in chg. all foreign sls. theatrical and ancillary rights except tv., 1985. Promoted to v.p., intl. sls., DEG, 1986. Appointed pres. mktg. and sales, Kings Road Intl., 1989. Joined Scotti Bros. Pictures as pres. intl. sales and mktg., 1989.

ALIN, MORRIS
Editor, Writer, Publicist, Lyricist. e. City Coll. of New York. Entered motion picture industry as auditor of Hunchback of Notre Dame roadshow oper., 1924. Appointed asst. sls. prom. mgr. Universal, 1926-27; slsmn., Universal, 1927. Named assoc. editor The Distributor, MGM publication, 1927; editor, 1928-33; writer, publicist, MGM Studio, 1933-34; writer, publicist, Hollywood, New York, 1935-38. Rejoined Universal, Progress (Univ. publication) editor, 1938; senior publicist and Progress editor, Universal, 1961-67. Twice winner of International Competition on Industrial Journalism. Editor Enterprise Press, 1968. Member: exec., Enterprise Press, 1973; American Guild of Authors and Composers; American Society of Composers, Authors and Publishers; National Academy of Popular Music; Motion Picture Pioneers.

ALLEN, COREY
Director, Actor. r.n. Alan Cohen. b. Cleveland, OH, June 29, 1934. e. UCLA, 1951-54; UCLA law sch. 1954-55. Actor turned dir. starred in Oscar-winning UCLA student film, appeared in 20 plays at Players Ring, Players Gallery and other L.A. theaters. TV: Perry Mason, Alfred Hitchcock Presents. With partner John Herman Shaner, prod. Freeway Circuit Theatre. Led Actors Workshop with actor Guy Stockwell for 10 years.
PICTURES: *Actor*: Rebel Without a Cause, Key Witness, Sweet Bird of Youth, Private Property, Party Girl, The Chapman Report. *Director*: The Erotic Adventures of Pinocchio, Thunder and Lightning, Avalanche.
TELEVISION: *Movies*: See the Man Run, Cry Rape!, Yesterday's Child, Stone (pilot), Man in the Santa Claus Suit, The Return of Frank Cannon, Code Name: Foxfire (pilot), Brass, Destination America, Beverly Hills Cowgirl Blues, The Last Fling, Ann Jillian Story, Moment of Truth:Stalking Back. *Series Dir.*: This is the Life, Mannix, High Chaparral, Dr. Kildare, Streets of San Francisco (DGA nom.), Ironside, Barnaby Jones, Police Woman, Rockford Files, Quincy, Dallas, Lou Grant, McClain's Law, Family Novak, T.J. Hooker, Paper Chase: The Second Year, Hill Street Blues (Emmy), Road Home, Deep Space Nine. *Pilots:* Man Undercover, Capitol, Simon and Simon, Whiz Kids, Murder She Wrote, Code Name: Foxfire, Star Trek: The Next Generation, The Search.

ALLEN, DAYTON
Performer. b. New York, NY, Sept. 24, 1919. e. Mt. Vernon H.S. Motion picture road shows, 1936-40. Disc jockey, WINS, N.Y., 1940-41. Writer, vaudeville comedy bits, 1941-45, then radio comic, puppeteer and voices. In television since 1948, film commercials and shows. Acted in the film The Cotton Club.
TELEVISION: (voices): Terrytoons, Deputy Dwag, Heckle & Jeckle, Lancelot Link: Secret Chimp, Lariat Sam, Oaky Doky, Bonny Maid Varieties, Howdy Doody, Jack Barry's Winky Dink, The Steve Allen Show. 130 Dayton Allen 5 min. shows (synd.).

ALLEN, DEBBIE
Actress, Choreographer, Director. b. Houston, TX, Jan. 16, 1950. e. Howard U. Sister is actress Phylicia Rashad.
THEATER: Ti-Jean and His Brothers (debut, 1972), Purlie, Raisin, Ain't Misbehavin', West Side Story (revival), Sweet Charity (revival, Tony Award, 1986), Carrie (choreographer).
PICTURES: The Fish That Saved Pittsburgh (1979), Fame, Ragtime, Jo Jo Dancer Your Life is Calling, Blank Check, Out of Sync, Everything's Jake.
TELEVISION: *Movies*: The Greatest Thing That Almost Happened, Ebony—Ivory and Jade, Women of San Quentin, Celebrity, Polly (dir.), Polly-Comin' Home (dir.), Stompin' at the Savoy, Cool Women (dir.). *Series*: The Jim Stafford Show, 3 Girls 3, Fame (series; 3 Emmys as choreographer, 1 nom. as actress), Family Ties (dir.), A Different World (also dir.,prod.), In the House, Between Brothers (dir.), Linc's, C. Bear and Jamal (voice). *Mini-Series*: Roots-The Next Generation. *Specials*: Ben Vereen-His Roots, Loretta Lynn in Big Apple Country, Texaco Star Theater—Opening Night, The Kids from Fame, John Schneider's Christmas Holiday, A Tribute to Martin Luther King Jr.—A Celebration of Life, Motown Returns to the Apollo, The Debbie Allen Special (also dir., chor.), Sinbad Live (Afros and Bell Bottoms), Academy Awards (choreographer: 1991-96,99), Michael Jordan: An American Hero.

ALLEN, DEDE
Film Editor. r.n. Dorothea Carothers Allen b. Cleveland, OH, 1924. Started as messenger at Columbia Pictures, moved to editing dept., then to commercials and features. Theatrical Production v.p. then pres. at Warner Brothers, 1992-1997. A.C.E. Honorary Lifetime Achievement Award, 1994.
PICTURES: Odds Against Tomorrow (1959), The Hustler, America America, Bonnie and Clyde, Rachel Rachel, Alice's Restaurant, Little Big Man, Slaughterhouse 5, Serpico, Night Moves, Dog Day Afternoon (Acad. award nom.), The Missouri Breaks, Slap Shot, The Wiz, Reds (also exec. prod. Acad. award nom.), Harry and Son, Mike's Murder, The Breakfast Club, Off Beat, The Milagro Beanfield War (co-ed.), Let It Ride (co-ed.), Henry and June, The Addams Family, Wonder Boys.

ALLEN, IOAN
Executive. b. Stafford, England, Oct. 25, 1938. e. Rossall School and Dartmouth Naval College, England. Artist mgmt. and record prod., 1964-1969. Responsible for origination and devt. of Dolby Stereo film program. Fellow of Society of Motion Picture & Television Engineers, Audio Engineering Society and the British Kinematographic Sound & Television Society. Past Pres., Intl. Theatre Equipment Assn. U.S. correspondent on the Intl. Standards Org. cinematographic subcommittee. Adjunct prof., USC School of Cinema-Television. Vice pres., Dolby Laboratories. Recipient: Acad. Scientific & Technical Awards, 1979 & 1987. Acad. award for work in Dolby Laboratories film program, 1989; Samuel L. Warner Award for contribution to motion picture sound, 1985.

ALLEN, JAY PRESSON
Writer, Producer. r.n. Jacqueline Presson. b. Fort Worth, TX, March 3, 1922. m. prod. Lewis M. Allen.
THEATER: *Writer*:The First Wife, The Prime of Miss Jean Brodie, Forty Carats, Tru (also dir.), The Big Love (also dir.).
PICTURES: *Writer:* Marnie, The Prime of Miss Jean Brodie, Cabaret, Travels with My Aunt, Funny Lady, Just Tell Me What You Want (also prod.), It's My Turn (exec. prod. only), Prince of the City (also exec. prod.), Deathtrap (also exec. prod.), The Celluloid Closet (act. only).
TELEVISION: *Series*: Family (creator), Hot House (also exec. prod.).

ALLEN, JOAN
Actress. b. Rochelle, IL, Aug. 20, 1956. Founding member of Steppenwolf Theatre Co., in Chicago where she performed in over 20 shows.
THEATER: *Chicago*: A Lesson from Aloes, Three Sisters, The Miss Firecracker Contest, Cloud 9, Balm in Gilead, Fifth of July, Reckless, Earthly Possessions. *Off B'way*: The Marriage of Bette and Boo, And a Nightingale Sang (Clarence Derwent, Drama Desk, Outer Critics' Circle and Theatre World Awards). *B'way.*: Burn This (debut, 1987; Tony Award), The Heidi Chronicles.
PICTURES: Compromising Positions (debut, 1985), Manhunter, Peggy Sue Got Married, Tucker: The Man and His Dream, In Country, Ethan Frome, Searching for Bobby Fischer, Josh and S.A.M., Mad Love, Nixon, The Crucible, The Ice Storm, Face Off, Pleasantville, All the Rage, When the Sky Falls, The Contender.
TELEVISION: *Movie*: Say Goodnight, Gracie, The Room Upstairs, All My Sons, Without Warning: The James Brady Story. *Mini-Series*: Evergreen, New York:A Documentary Film, The Mists of Avalon.

ALLEN, KAREN
Actress. b. Carrollton, IL, Oct. 5, 1951. e. George Washington U., U. of Maryland. Auditioned for theatrical company in Washington, DC and won a role in Saint, touring with it for 7 months. Spent several years with Washington Theatre Laboratory Co. Moved to NY, acted in student films at NYU and studied acting at Theatre Institute with Lee Strasberg.
THEATER: *NY*: Monday After the Miracle (B'way debut, 1982; Theatre World Award), Extremities, The Miracle Worker, The Country Girl. *Williamstown (MA) Theatre*: Tennessee Williams--A Celebration, The Glass Menagerie.
PICTURES: National Lampoon's Animal House (debut, 1978), Manhattan, The Wanderers, Cruising, A Small Circle of Friends, Raiders of the Lost Ark, Shoot the Moon, Split Image, Until September, Starman, Terminus, The Glass Menagerie, Backfire, Scrooged, Animal Behavior, Secret Places of the Heart, Sweet Talker, Exile, Malcolm X, The Sandlot, Ghost in the Machine, 'Til There Was You, Wind River, Falling Sky, The Basket, The Perfect Storm, In the Bedroom.
TELEVISION: *Movies*: Lovey: A Circle of Children Part II, Secret Weapon, Challenger, Rapture, Voyage, Hostile Advances: The Kerry Ellison Story, All the Winters That Have Been. *Mini-Series*: East of Eden, Shaka Zulu: The Citadel. *Guest*: Alfred Hitchcock Presents (1986), Law & Order.

ALLEN, LEWIS M.
Producer. b. Berryville, VA, June 27, 1922. e. Univ. of VA. m. writer-producer Jay Presson Allen.
PICTURES: *Prod./Exec. prod./Co-prod.*:The Connection, The Balcony, Lord of the Flies, Fahrenheit 451, The Queen, Fortune and Men's Eyes, Never Cry Wolf, 1918, Valentine's Day, Swimming to Cambodia, O.C. & Stiggs, End of the Line, Miss Firecracker.

ALLEN, NANCY
Actress. b. New York, NY, June 24, 1950. e. H.S. Performing Arts, N.Y.
PICTURES: The Last Detail (debut, 1973), Carrie, I Wanna Hold Your Hand, 1941, Home Movies, Dressed to Kill, Blow Out, Strange Invaders, The Buddy System, The Philadelphia Experiment, The Last Victim, Not for Publication, Terror in the Aisles, Sweet Revenge, Robocop, Poltergeist III, Limit Up, Robocop 2, Robocop 3, The Patriots, Dusting Cliff Seven, Against the Law, Secret of the Andes, The Pass, Out of Sight, Children of the Corn 666: Isaac's Return, Kiss Toledo Goodbye, Quality Time.
TELEVISION: *Movies*: The Gladiator, Memories of Murder, Acting on Impulse, The Man Who Wouldn't Die. *Guest:* The Outer Limits, The Commish, Touched by an Angel.

ALLEN, REX
Actor. b. Wilcox, AZ, Dec. 31, 1922. e. Wilcox H.S., 1939. Vaudeville & radio actor, WLS, Chicago, 5 yrs. Was rodeo star appearing in shows through U.S.
PICTURES: Arizona Cowboy, Hills of Oklahoma, Under Mexicali Stars, Thunder in God's Country, Rodeo King & the Senorita, I Dream of Jeannie, Last Musketeer, South Pacific Trail, Old Overland Trail, Down Laredo Way, Phantom Stallion, For the Love of Mike, Tomboy and the Champ. Narrator: The Legend of Lobo, The Incredible Journey, Charlotte's Web, Vanishing Wilderness, The Secret of Navajo Cave.
TELEVISION: *Series*: Frontier Doctor, Five Star Jubilee. *Guest:* Perry Como Special. *Voice only*: commercials, Wonderful World of Color.
(d. Dec. 17, 1999)

ALLEN, STEVE
Performer. b. New York, NY, Dec 26, 1921. e. Arizona St. Univ. m. actress Jayne Meadows. U.S. Army 1942. Radio shows, Los Angeles. TV, N.Y., 1950. On NY stage in The Mikado. Composer or lyricist of numerous songs including This Could Be the Start of Something Big, Pretend You Don't See Her, South Rampart St. Parade, Picnic, Houseboat, On the Beach, Sleeping Beauty, Bell Book and Candle, Gravy Waltz, Impossible; score for B'way musical Sophie; score for TV musicals: The Bachelor, and Alice in Wonderland.
AUTHOR: Fourteen For Tonight, Steve Allen's Bop Fables, The Funny Men, Wry On the Rocks, The Girls on the Tenth Floor, The Question Man, Mark It and Strike It, Not All of Your Laughter, Not All of Your Tears, Bigger Than a Breadbox, A Flash of Swallows, The Wake, Princess Snip-Snip and the Puppykittens, Curses, Schmock-Schmock!, Meeting of Minds, Ripoff, Meeting of Minds-Second Series, Rip-off, Explaining China, The Funny People, Talk Show Murders, Beloved Son: Story of the Jesus Cults, More Funny People, How To Make a Speech and How To Be Funny, Murder on the Glitter Box, The Passionate Non-smoker's Bill of Rights, Dumbth and 81 Ways to Make Americans Smarter, Murder in Manhattan, Steve Allen on the Bible, Religion and Morality, The Public Hating, Murder in Vegas, Hi-Ho Steverino!: My Adventures in the Wonderful Wacky World of TV, The Murder Game, More Steve Allen on the Bible, Religion & Morality Book II, Make 'em Laugh, Reflections, Murder on the Atlantic, The Man Who Turned Back the Clock and Other Short Stories, Die Laughing.
PICTURES: Down Memory Lane (debut, 1949), I'll Get By, The Benny Goodman Story, The Big Circus, College Confidential, Don't Worry We'll Think of a Title, Warning Shot, Where Were You When the Lights Went Out?, The Comic, The Sunshine Boys, Heart Beat, Amazon Women on the Moon, Great Balls of Fire!, The Player, Casino, Let Me In,I Hear Laughter.
TELEVISION: *Movies*: Now You See It Now You Don't, Stone, The Gossip Columnist, Lenny Bruce: Swear to Tell the Truth. *Mini-Series*: Rich Man Poor Man. *Series*: The Steve Allen Show (1950-52), Songs for Sale, Talent Patrol, What's My Line, Steve Allen Show, Tonight, Steve Allen Show (1956-61), (1962-64), (1964-67), I've Got a Secret, Steve Allen Comedy Hour (1967), Steve Allen Show (1967-69), I've Got a Secret (1972-73) Steve Allen's Laugh Back, Meeting of Minds, Steve Allen Comedy Hour (1980-81), Life's Most Embarrassing Moments. *Specials:* James Dean: A Portrait, Steve Allen's 75th Birthday Celebration
(d. Oct. 30, 2000)

ALLEN, TIM
Actor. r.n. Timothy Allen Dick. b. Denver, CO, June 13, 1953. e. W. Michigan Univ., Univ. of Detroit, studied acting. Worked as creative dir. for adv. agency before becoming stand up comedian. Made stand up tv debut on Showtime Comedy Club All-Stars, 1988. Author: Don't Stand Close to a Naked Man (1994).
PICTURES: Comedy's Dirtiest Dozen, The Santa Clause, Toy Story (voice), Meet Wally Sparks, Jungle2Jungle, For Richer or Poorer, Toy Story 2 (voice), Galaxy Quest, The Cat in the Hat, Cletis Tout, Big Trouble, Buzz Lightyear of Star Command:The Adventure Begins.
TELEVISION: *Series*: Home Improvement. *Specials*: Tim Allen: Men Are Pigs (also writer), Tim Allen Rewrites America (also exec. prod., writer), AFI's 100 Years,100 Laughs:America's Funniest Movies.

ALLEN, WILLIAM
Executive. e. USC Cinema/TV Sch., Pepperdine Univ. 1979. Exec. trainee in CBS Entertainment division, eventually serving as assoc. program exec. in the Comedy Series Programming Dept.; mngr./dir. of the CBS Comedy Program Development. Dept. Joined MTM as sr. v.p., Comedy Programming, 1986-87; sr. v.p. creative affairs, 1987-88; exec. v.p. MTM Television, 1989-1991; pres., MTM Television, 1992.

ALLEN, WOODY
Actor, Director, Writer. r.n. Allan Stewart Konigsberg. b. New York, NY, Dec. 1, 1935. e. NYU, 1953; City Coll. NY, 1953. Began writing comedy at age 17, contributing to various magazines (Playboy, New Yorker) and top TV comedy shows incl. Sid Caesar (1957), Art Carney (1958-59), Herb Shriner (1953). Appeared in nightclubs starting in 1961 as stand-up comic; later performed as a jazz musician at Michael's Pub, NY. Special Award, Berlin Film Fest., 1975.
AUTHOR: Getting Even, Without Feathers, Side Effects.
THEATER: *Author*: Play It Again Sam (also actor), Don't Drink The Water, The Floating Lightbulb, Central Park West (from Death Defying Acts).
PICTURES: *Actor-Screenplay:* What's New Pussycat?, What's Up Tiger Lily? (also dubbed and compiled footage; assoc. prod.), Casino Royale (actor only). Play It Again Sam. *Director/Screenplay/Actor:* Take the Money and Run, Bananas, Everything You Always Wanted to Know About Sex* But Were Afraid to Ask, Sleeper, Love and Death, The Front (actor only), Annie Hall (Acad. Awards for Best Director and Original Screenplay, 1977), Interiors (dir., s.p. only), Manhattan, Stardust Memories, A Midsummer Night's Sex Comedy, Zelig, Broadway Danny Rose, The Purple Rose of Cairo (dir., s.p. only), Hannah and Her Sisters (Acad. Award for Best Original Screenplay, 1986), Radio Days (dir., s.p., narrator only), September (dir., s.p. only), King Lear (actor only), Another Woman (dir., s.p. only), New York Stories (Oedipus Wrecks segment), Crimes and Misdemeanors, Alice (dir., s.p. only), Scenes From a Mall (actor only), Shadows and Fog, Husbands and Wives, Manhattan Murder Mystery, Bullets Over Broadway (dir., s.p. only), Mighty Aphrodite, Everyone Says I Love You (dir. & actor), Deconstructing Harry, The Imposters (actor only), Antz (voice), Wild Man Blues, Company Man (actor only), Picking Up the Pieces (actor only), Celebrity, Count Mercury Goes to the Suburbs (writer only), Light Keeps Me Company (actor only), Sweet and Lowdown, Small Time Crooks .
TELEVISION: *Movies*: Don't Drink the Water (also dir., writer), The Sunshine Boys. *Specials:* The Best on Record, Gene Kelly in New York New York, The Woody Allen Special (also writer, co-dir.), Woody Allen Looks at 1967 (Kraft Music Hall; also writer), Plimpton: Did You Hear the One About ...? ,Cannes...lee 400 Coups, AFI'S 100 Years...100 Movies. *Guest*: That Was the Week That Was, Hullabaloo, Andy Williams, Hippodrome, Just Shoot Me.

ALLEY, KIRSTIE
Actress. b. Wichita, KS, Jan. 12, 1955. e. KS State U., U. of Kansas. On L.A. stage in Cat on a Hot Tin Roof.
PICTURES: Star Trek II: The Wrath of Khan (debut, 1982), Blind Date, Champions, Runaway, Summer School, Shoot to Kill, Loverboy, Look Who's Talking, Madhouse, Sibling Rivalry, Look Who's Talking Too, Look Who's Talking Now, Village of the Damned, It Takes Two, Nevada (also co-prod.), Deconstructing Harry, For Richer or Poorer, The Mao Game, Drop Dead Gorgeous.
TELEVISION: *Movies*: Sins of the Past, A Bunny's Tale, Stark: Mirror Image, Prince of Bel Air, Infidelity, David's Mother (Emmy Award, 1994), Radiant City, Peter and the Wolf, Toothless. *Mini-Series*: North and South, North and South Book II, The Last Don, The Last Don II. *Series*: Masquerade, The Hitchhiker, Cheers (Emmy Award, 1991), Veronica's Closet, Blonde. *Guest*: The Love Boat.

ALLYSON, JUNE
Actress. r.n. Ella Geisman. b. Westchester, NY, Oct. 7, 1917. Started as chorus girl. Voted one of ten top money-making stars in Motion Picture Herald-Fame poll, 1955.
THEATER: *B'way*: Sing Out the News, Panama Hattie, Best Foot Forward, 40 Carats. *Tour*: No No Nanette.
PICTURES: Best Foot Foward (debut, 1943), Girl Crazy, Thousands Cheer, Meet the People, Two Girls and a Sailor, Music For Millions, Her Highness and the Bellboy, The Sailor Takes a Wife, Two Sisters From Boston, Till the Clouds Roll By, Secret Heart, High Barbaree, Good News, The Bride Goes Wild, The Three Musketeers, Words and Music, Little Women, The Stratton Story, Meet the People, Reformer and the Redhead, Right Cross, Too Young to Kiss, Girl in White, Battle Circus, Remains to be Seen, Executive Suite, Glenn Miller Story, Woman's World, Strategic Air Command, The Shrike, McConnell Story, Opposite Sex, You Can't Run Away From It, Interlude, My Man Godfrey, Stranger in My Arms, They Only Kill Their Masters, Blackout, That's Entertainment III.
TELEVISION: *Movies*: See the Man Run, Letters from Three Lovers, Curse of the Black Widow, Vega$, Three on a Date, The Kid With the Broken Halo. *Series*: DuPont Show With June Allyson. *Guest*: Murder She Wrote, Misfits of Science. *Special*: 20th Century Follies.

ALMODOVAR, PEDRO
Director, Writer. b. La Mancha, Spain, Sept. 25, 1951. r.n.Pedro Almodovar Cabellero. Grew up in Calzada de Calatrava. At 17 moved to Madrid where worked 10 years for telephone co. while writing comic strips and articles for underground newspapers and working as actor with independent theater co., Los Goliardos. Upon the end of Francoist repression in 1975, made Super-8 experimental films starring friends. Wrote fiction, sang with rock band and created character of porn star, Patty Diphusa, whose fictionalized confessions he published in the magazine La Luna.
PICTURES: Pepi Lucy Bom and Other Girls on the Heap (debut, 1980), Labyrinth of Passion (also prod.), Dark Habits, What Have I Done to Deserve This?, Matador, Law of Desire, Women on the Verge of a Nervous Breakdown (also prod.), Tie Me Up! Tie Me Down!, Madonna:Truth or Dare (actor only), High Heels, Kika, The Flower of My Secret, Live Flesh, All About My Mother, The Paperboy.

ALONSO, MARIA CONCHITA
Actress, Singer. b. Cienfuegos, Cuba, June 29, 1957. Family moved to Venezuela when she was five. 1971, named Miss Teenager of the World. 1975, Miss Venezuela. 6th runner up, Miss World. Appeared in four feature films and 10 soap operas before coming to U.S. Recorded several albums as singer: 5 gold albums, 1 platinum, 3 Grammy noms.
THEATER: Aurora. *B'way*: Kiss of the Spider Woman.
PICTURES: Fear City, Moscow on the Hudson, Touch and Go, A Fine Mess, Extreme Prejudice, The Running Man, Colors, Vampire's Kiss, Predator 2, McBain, The House of the Spirits, Roosters, Caught, For Which He Stands, Caught, El Crito en el Cieto, Catherine's Grove, Acts of Betrayal, Knockout, Expose, Blackheart, Chain of Command, The Code Conspiracy, Blind Heat, Babylon Revisited.
TELEVISION: *Movies*: Teamster Boss: The Jackie Presser Story, MacShayne: The Final Roll of the Dice, Texas, The Gun, Sudden Terror, Fx, My Husband's Secret Life, Best Actress, High Noon. *Specials*: Viva Miami!, The Night of the Super Sounds (host) An American Cousin (RAI mini-series),. *Guest*: One of the Boys, Chicago Hope, The Outer Limits, Touched by an Angel.

ALONZO, JOHN A
Cinematographer, Director. b. Dallas, TX, 1934.
PICTURES: Bloody Mama, Vanishing Point, Harold and Maude, Get to Know Your Rabbit, Lady Sings the Blues, Sounder, Pete-n-Tillie, Hit, The Naked Ape, Conrack, Chinatown, Farewell My Lovely, The Fortune, I Will ... I Will ... For Now, Once Is Not Enough, The Bad News Bears, Black Sunday, Beyond Reason, Close Encounters of the Third Kind (addtl. photog.), Which Way Is Up?, Casey's Shadow, FM (dir. only), The Cheap Detective, Norma Rae, Tom Horn, Back Roads, Zorro the Gay Blade, Blue Thunder, Cross Creek, Scarface, Out of Control, Terror in the Aisles, Runaway, Jo Jo Dancer Your Life Is Calling, Nothing in Common, 50 Years of Action, Real Men, Overboard, Physical Evidence, Steel Magnolias, Internal Affairs, The Guardian, Navy Seals, Housesitter, Cool World, The Meteor Man, Clifford, Star Trek: Generations, The Grass Harp, Letters from a Killer, The Dancing Cow, Deuces Wild.
TELEVISION: Champions: A Love Story , Belle Star, Blinded By the Light, The Kid From Nowhere, Roots: The Gift, Knights of the City, World War II, When Lions Roared Lansky, Portrait of a Stripper.*Specials:* High Def.

ALTERMAN, JOSEPH GEORGE
Executive. b. New Haven, CT., Dec. 17, 1919. e. Wesleyan U., B.A., 1942; Inst. for Organization Management, Yale U., 1957-59. Exec. assist., SoundScriber Corp., 1945-48. District mgr., Industrial Luncheon Service, 1948-55. Asst. secretary and admin. secretary, Theatre Owners of America, 1955; exec. dir. and vice pres., Natl. Assn. of Theatre Owners, 1966. Exec. v.p. COMPO., 1970. Retired 1988 from NATO. Consultant m.p. industry, conventions and meetings. Chmn., bd. govs., Institute for Learning in Retirement, Albertus Magnus College.

ALTMAN, ROBERT
Director, Writer, Producer. b. Kansas City, MO, Feb. 20, 1925. e. U. of Missouri. Early film writer credits: Bodyguard (co-story), Corn's-a-Poppin (co-s.p.). Made industrial films and documentaries for the Calvin Company in Kansas City, before dir. first indept. feature in 1957. Received D.W. Griffith Lifetime Achievement Award from Directors Guild of America, 1994.
THEATER: NY: Two By South, Come Back to the Five and Dime Jimmy Dean Jimmy Dean. Operas: The Rake's Progress, McTeague.
PICTURES: *Director*: The Delinquents (also s.p., prod.), The James Dean Story (also co-prod., edit.), Countdown, That Cold Day in the Park, M*A*S*H (Cannes Film Fest. Golden Palm Award, 1970; Acad. Award nom.), Brewster McCloud, McCabe & Mrs. Miller (also co-s.p.), Images (also s.p.), The Long Goodbye, Thieves Like Us (also co-s.p.), California Split (also co-prod.), Nashville (also prod.; NY Film Critics, Natl. Society of Film Critics & Natl. Board of Review Awards for Best Director & Picture, 1975; Acad. Award noms. for dir. & picture), Buffalo Bill and the Indians: Or Sitting Bull's History Lesson (also co-s.p., prod.), Three Women (also s.p., prod.), A Wedding (also co-s.p., prod., co-story), Quintet (also co-s.p., prod., co-story), A Perfect Couple (also co-s.p., prod.), Health (also co-s.p., prod.), Popeye, Come Back to the Five and Dime Jimmy Dean Jimmy Dean, Streamers (also co-prod.), Secret Honor (also prod.), Fool for Love, Beyond Therapy (also co-s.p.), O.C. and Stiggs (also co-prod.), Aria (dir. Les Boreades sequence; also s.p.), Vincent & Theo, The Player (BAFTA & Cannes Film Fest. Awards for Best Director, 1991; Acad. Award nom.), Short Cuts (also co-s.p.; Acad. Award nom. for dir.), Ready to Wear/Pret-a-Porter (also co-s.p., prod.), Jazz '34, Kansas City (also s.p., prod.), Cookie's Fortune (also s.p., prod.), Dr. T and the Women, Another City,Not My Own. *Producer:* The Late Show, Welcome to L.A., Remember My Name, Rich Kids (exec.), Mrs. Parker and the Vicious Circle, Trixie, Dr. T and the Women, Roads and Bridges (exec.).
TELEVISION: *Series*: *Director/Writer &/or Producer*: The Roaring Twenties, The Millionaire, Alfred Hitchcock Presents, Whirlybirds, Maverick, U.S. Marshall, The Lawman, Peter Gunn, Troubleshooters, Bonanza, Route 66, Bus Stop, Combat!, Kraft Mystery Theatre, The Gallant Men (pilot), The Long Hot Summer (pilot), Tanner '88 (also co-exec. prod.; Emmy Award for dir. episode The Boiler Room, 1989), Gun (also exec. prod.). *Specials*: Two by South (also prod.), Nightmare in Chicago (also prod.), The Laundromat, The Dumb Waiter (also prod.), The Room, The Real McTeague, Precious Blood, The Caine Mutiny Court-Martial (also co-prod.).

ALVARADO, TRINI
Actress. b. New York, NY, Jan. 10, 1967. e. Fordham U. m. actor Robert McNeill. Began performing at age 7 as flamenco dancer with her parents' troupe. Prof. acting debut at 9 in stage musical Becca.
THEATER: Runaways, Yours Anne, Maggie Magalita, I Love You—I Love You Not, Reds, The Magic Show, Godspell.
PICTURES: Rich Kids (debut, 1989), Times Square, Mrs. Soffel, Sweet Lorraine, Satisfaction, The Chair, Stella, American Blue Note, The Babe, American Friends, Little Women, The Perez Family, The Frighteners, Paulie.
TELEVISION: *Movies*: Dreams Don't Die, Prisoner Without a Name, Nitti, The Last Dance. *Guest*: Kay O'Brien, Kate and Allie, Spenser: For Hire. *Specials*: Private Contentment, Unicorn Tales, A Movie Star's Daughter, Stagestruck, Sensibility and Sense, The Christmas Tree.

ALVIN, JOHN
Actor. r.n. John Alvin Hoffstadt. b. Chicago, IL, Oct. 24, 1917. e. Pasadena Playhouse, CA. Attended Morgan Park Military Acad. On radio Chicago & Detroit; on N.Y. stage Leaning on Letty, Life of the Party. Screen debut 1944 in Destination Tokyo. Under contract four years to Warner Bros., featured in 25 films.
PICTURES: Destination Tokyo, Objective Burma, San Antonio, The Beast With Five Fingers, Night and Day, Cheyenne, Missing Women, Two Guys From Texas, Bold Frontiersman, Train to Alcatraz, Shanghai Chest, Carrie, April In Paris, Roughly Speaking, The Very Thought of You, Shadow of a Woman, Three Strangers, Romance on the High Seas, Torpedo Alley, Irma La Douce, Marnie, Inside Daisy Clover, The Legend of Lylah Clare, They Shoot Horses Don't They?, They Call Me Mr. Tibbs, Somewhere in Time, Beethoven's 2nd, Milk Money.
TELEVISION: Meet Millie, Burns and Allen, Death Valley Days, Asphalt Jungle, Climax, Dragnet, Jack Benny Show, My Three Sons, The Texan, Adventures in Paradise, Rawhide, Rifleman, Omnibus, Wells Fargo, Alfred Hitchcock, Mannix, I Spy, Legend of Lizzie Borden, All in the Family, McDuff, Lineup, My Favorite Husband, Family Affair, Get Smart, The Incredible Hulk, The Lucy Show, Ironside, Nightstalker, M*A*S*H, Lou Grant Show, Hart to Hart, Yellow Rose, Dennis the Menace (2 Hour Pilot), Murder She Wrote, Monster Squad, House of Evil, Aftermash, General Hospital, Starsky & Hutch, Policewoman, Amazing Stories, Capitol, Passions, The Quest, Visions/KCET, Rachel Sweet Rachel, Swallows Came Back, Return to Green Acres, Moving Target, From Out of the Night, The Walkers, The Bold and the Beautiful.

AMATEAU, ROD
Director. b. New York, NY, Dec. 20, 1923. U.S. Army, 1941. 20th Century-Fox, 2nd unit dir.
PICTURES: The Statue, Where Does It Hurt?, The Wilby Conspiracy, Drive-In, Lovelines, Garbage Pail Kids (also s.p., prod.), Sunset (story only).
TELEVISION: *Movies*: Uncommon Valor, High School U.S.A., Swimsuit (prod.). *Series*: Schlitz Playhouse of Stars, Four Star Playhouse, General Electric Theatre, Private Secretary, Dennis Day Show, Lassie, Ray Milland Show, Bob Cummings Show, Burns & Allen Show (also prod.), Dobie Gillis.

AMENABAR, ALEJANDRO
Director, Writer. b. 1972.
PICTURES: Himenoptero, Luna, Thesis, Open Your Eyes, The Others.

AMES, LOUIS B.
Executive. b. St. Louis, MO, Aug. 9, 1918. e. Washington U., St. Louis. m. Jetti Ames. Began as music consultant and staff dir. of musical programs for NBC; appt. music dir., WPIX, 1948; program mgr., WPIX, 1951. Assoc. prod., Today, NBC TV, 1954. Feature editor Home, 1957. Adm.-prod. NBC Opera, 1958. Dir. cultural prog. N.Y. World's Fair, 1960-63; dir. RCA Pavillion, N.Y. World's Fair, 1963-65; dir., Nighttime, TV, 1966; dir. of programming N.W. Ayer & Sons, Inc., 1969. Mgr. Station Services, Television Information Office. NY, 1973.

AMIEL, JON
Director, Producer. b. London, England, May 20, 1948. e. Cambridge. Was in charge of the Oxford & Cambridge Shakespeare Co., then literary mgr. for Hamptead Theatre Club where he started directing. Became story edit. for BBC, then director.
PICTURES: Silent Twins, Queen of Hearts, Tune in Tomorrow, Sommersby, Copycat, The Man Who Knew Too Little, Entrapment, Simply Irresistible (prod. only).
TELEVISION: A Sudden Wrench, Gates of Gold, Busted. *Mini-Series:* The Singing Detective. *Series:* Tandoori Nights.

AMIN, MARK
Producer, Executive. b. Rafsanjan, Iran, 1950. e. M.B.A., marketing, John Anderson School of Business (UCLA), 1975. Began career in business ventures, 1975-81; co-founder, 20/20 Video, 1981-87; founder, Vidmark (now Trimark), 1984. Currently chairman & CEO, Trimark Holdings, Inc. (parent company of Trimark Pictures).
PICTURES: Exec. producer, Eve's Bayou, Kama Sutra: A Tale of Love, Sprung, Diplomatic Siege, The Eternal.

AMIS, SUZY
Actress. b. Oklahoma City, OK, Jan. 5, 1962. e. Heritage Hall, Oklahoma City. At 16 was introduced on the Merv Griffin Show by Eileen Ford whose modeling agency she worked for, as "The Face of the Eighties." After modeling and living in Europe, made film debut in Fandango (1985). Off-B'way debut: Fresh Horses (Theatre World Award).
PICTURES: Fandango, The Big Town, Plain Clothes, Rocket Gibraltar, Twister, Where the Heart Is, Rich in Love, Watch It, The Ballad of Little Jo, Two Small Bodies, Blown Away, The Usual Suspects, Nadja, One Good Turn, Titanic, The Ex, Cadillac Ranch, Firestorm, Judgement Day.
TELEVISION: *Movies*: The Beneficiary, Dead by Midnight, Last Stand at Saber River.

AMOS, JOHN
Actor. b. Newark, NJ, Dec. 27, 1941. e. East Orange H.S., Colorado State U, Long Beach City Col. Inducted as honorary Master Chief Petty Officer in U.S. Navy 1993. Worked as professional football player, social worker (heading the Vera Institute of Justice in NY), and advertising copywriter before writing television comedy material (for the Leslie Uggams Show) and performing as stand-up comedian in Greenwich Village. Has also dir. theatre with Bahamian Rep. Co. Artistic dir., John Harms Theatre, Englewood, NJ.
THEATER: *L.A.*: Norman Is That You?, Master Harold...And the Boys, Split Second, The Emperor Jones. *B'way*: Tough to Get Help. NYSF: Twelfth Night. *Off-B'way*: The Past is the Past. Regional: Fences, Halley's Comet (also writer). *Foreign:* Life and Death of a Buffalo Sodier.
PICTURES: Vanishing Point (debut, 1971), Sweet Sweetback's Baadasssss Song, The World's Greatest Athlete, Let's Do It Again, Touched By Love, The Beastmaster, Dance of the Dwarfs, American Flyers, Coming to America, Lock Up, Die Hard 2, Ricochet, Two Evil Eyes (The Black Cat), Mac, Night Trap (Mardi Gras for the Devil), Hologramman, For Better or Worse, A Woman Like That, The Player's Club, All Over Again.
TELEVISION: *Movies*: The President's Plane is Missing, Future Cop, Cops and Robin, Willa, Alcatraz-The Whole Shocking Story, Bonanza-the Next Generation, The Rockford Files: Murder and Misdemeanors. *Mini-Series*: Roots. *Series*: Mary Tyler Moore, The Funny Side, Maude, Good Times, Hunter, South by Southwest, 704 Hauser, The District. *Pilots:* Clippers, 704 Hauser Street. *Special*: Without a Pass. *Guest:* Bill Cosby Show, Love American Style, Sanford and Son, The Love Boat, Cosby Show, The Fresh Prince of Bel Air, Martin, King of the Hill.

ANDERS, ALLISON
Director, Writer. b. Ashland, KY, Nov. 16, 1954. e. UCLA; Los Angeles.
PICTURES: Border Radio (debut, 1987), Gas Food Lodging, Mi vida loca, Four Rooms (The Missing Ingredient segment), Grace of My Heart, Lover Girl (exec. prod. only), Sugar Town, Things Behind the Sun. *Television:* Sex and the City.

ANDERSON, DAVID LEROY
Special Effects.
PICTURES: Shocker, Cadence, Beyond the Law, Alien 3, Loaded Weapon 1, The Chase, The Nutty Professor, Men in Black (Acad. Award, Best Makeup, 1997), Jane Austen's Mafia.

ANDERSON, GERRY
Hon. F.B.K.S., Producer, Director, Writer. b. London, England, April 14, 1929. Entered industry in 1946. Chmn./man. dir. Gerry Anderson Productions, Ltd. Over 320 pictures produced for TV worldwide. Co-founded Anderson Burr Pictures, 1981. Prod. Terrahawks in association with London Weekend Television, 1982; second series, Terrahawks, 1984. Space Police pilot for series in assoc. with TVS, 1985-6. Dick Spanner stop motion series for Channel Four, 1987. Entered commercials as a dir.: numerous commercials incl. Royal Bank of Scotland, Children's World, Domestos, Shout, Scotch Tape, etc. Anglo Russian Cartoon Series Astro Force and lecture tour An Evening with Garry Anderson, 1992
PICTURES: Thunderbirds Are Go, Thunderbird 6, Journey to the Far Side of the Sun.
TELEVISION: *Series*: The Adventures of Twizzle, Torchy the Battery Boy, Four Feather Falls, Supercar, Fireball XL5, Stingray, Thunderbirds, Captain Scarlet, Joe 90, The Secret Service, The Protectors, UFO, Space 1999, Terrahawks, Dick Spanner, Space Precinct, Lavender Castle.

ANDERSON, GILLIAN
Actress. b. Chicago, IL, Aug. 9, 1968. e. Cornell University, NY; DePaul University, Chicago.
PICTURES: The Turning, Playing by Heart, The Mighty, Chicago Cab, The X-Files: Fight the Future, The House of Mirth.
TELEVISION: Series: The X-Files, Future Fantastic. *Guest:* Class of '96, The Simpsons (voice), Frasier (voice), Harsh Realm (voice).

ANDERSON, HARRY
Actor. b. Newport, RI, Oct. 14, 1952. m. actress-magician Leslie Pollack. Performed magic show prior to plays at Oregon Shakespeare Festival. Also opening act for Kenny Rogers, Debbie Reynolds and Roger Miller in Las Vegas. Owner of magic shop in Ashland OR. Received Stage Magician of Year Award, National Acad. of Magician Arts and Sciences.
PICTURE: The Escape Artist.
TELEVISION: *Movies*: Spies, Lies and Naked Thighs; The Absent-Minded Professor, Stephen King's It, Harvey. *Series*: Night Court (Emmy nom.), Our Time, Dave's World, The Science of Magic. *Guest*: Cheers, The Tonight Show, David Letterman, Saturday Night Live, Wil Shriner. *Specials*: The Best of the Big Laff Off, Comic Relief, Harry Anderson's Sideshow (also exec. prod., writer), Comic Relief II, The Best of Gleason, Magic with the Stars, Nell Carter: Never Too Old to Dream, Hello Sucker.

ANDERSON, J. WAYNE
Executive. b. Clifton Forge, VA, Feb. 19, 1947. e. USA Signal School (1965-67); USN Service Schools (1967). USMC, 1965-69; opened and operated 1st military 35mm m.p. theatre, DaNang, Vietnam, 1967-69. R/C Theatres, dist. mgr., 1971-75; v.p., 1976-83; pres./COO, 1983-present. Bd. of dirs., Maryland Permanent Bank & Trust co., 1988-present; chmn., 1992-present. Member of NATO, bd. of dirs., 1987-present; technical advancement committee, 1981-present; chmn., 1991-present. Inter-Society for the Enhancement of Theatrical Presenation, 1986-present. Huntsman bd. of dirs., 1979-83; pres., 1982-83. Member: NRA, 1970-life; Will Rogers Inst., 1988-present; Presidential Task Force, 1990-life.

ANDERSON, KEVIN
Actor. b. Gurnee, Illinois, Jan. 13, 1960. e. Goodman School. Member of Chicago's Steppenwolf Theatre where he starred in Orphans. Moved with the play to New York (1985) and later starred in the London production, as well as the film version.
THEATER: *NY*: Orphans (Theatre World Award), Moonchildren, Brilliant Tracers, Orpheus Descending. *London*: Sunset Boulevard.
PICTURES: Risky Business (debut, 1983), Pink Nights, A Walk on the Moon, Orphans, Miles From Home, In Country, Sleeping With the Enemy, Liebestraum, Hoffa, The Night We Never Met, Rising Sun, A Thousand Acres, Eye of God, Firelight, A Thousand Acres, Gregory's Two Girls, Shearer's Breakfast, Doe Boy.
TELEVISION: *Movies*: Orpheus Descending, The Wrong Man, The Hunt for the Unicorn Killer. *Series*: Nothing Sacred. *Special:* Hale the Hero.

ANDERSON, LONI
Actress. b. St. Paul, MN, Aug. 5. 1946. e. U. of Minnesota. Taught school before acting.
PICTURES: Stroker Ace, The Lonely Guy (cameo), All Dogs Go to Heaven (voice), Munchie, A Night at the Roxbury, 3 Ninjas: High Noon at Mega Mountain.
TELEVISION: *Movies:* The Magnificent Magnet of Mesa, Three on a Date, The Jayne Mansfield Story, Sizzle, Country Gold, My Mother's Secret Life, A Letter to Three Wives, Stranded, Necessity, A Whisper Kills, Too Good to Be True, Sorry Wrong Number, Coins in the Fountain, White Hot: The Mysterious Murder of Thelma Todd, The Price She Paid, Gambler V: Playing for Keeps, Deadly Family Secrets. *Series*: WKRP in Cincinnati, Partners in Crime, Easy Street, Nurses. *Specials:* Christmas in Opryland, Shaun Cassidy Special, Bob Hope specials, Intimate Portrait:Loni Anderson. *Guest:* Bob Newhart Show, The Love Boat, The Incredible Hulk, Sabrina, The Teenage Witch, Clueless, Melrose Place.

ANDERSON, MELISSA SUE
Actress. b. Berkeley, CA, Sept. 26, 1962. Took up acting at suggestion of a dancing teacher. Did series of commercials; guest role in episode of Brady Bunch; episode of Shaft. Gained fame as Mary Ingalls on Little House on the Prairie series (Emmy nom.).
PICTURES: Happy Birthday to Me, Chattanooga Choo Choo, Dead Men Don't Die.
TELEVISION: *Movies*: Little House on the Prairie (pilot), The Loneliest Runner, James at 15 (pilot), Survival of Dana, Which Mother is Mine? (Emmy Award, 1980), Midnight Offerings, Advice to the Lovelorn, An Innocent Love, First Affair, Dark Mansions, Forbidden Nights, Earthquake in New York. *Specials:* Intimate Portrait:Melissa Gilbert. *Series*: Little House on the Prairie.

ANDERSON, MICHAEL
Director. b. London, England, Jan. 30, 1920. e. France, Germany. Ent. motion picture industry as actor, 1936. Son is actor Michael Anderson Jr.
PICTURES: Private Angelo (debut, 1949; co-dir. with Peter Ustinov), Waterfront, Hell Is Sold Out, Night Was Our Friend, Will Any Gentleman?, The Dam Busters, 1984, Around the World in 80 Days, Yangtse Incident (Battle Hell), Chase a Crooked Shadow, Shake Hands With the Devil (also prod.), The Wreck of the Mary Deare, All the Fine Young Cannibals, The Naked Edge, Flight From Ashiya, Wild and Wonderful, Operation Crossbow, The Quiller Memorandum, The Shoes of the Fisherman, Pope Joan, Doc Savage: The Man of Bronze, Conduct Unbecoming, Logan's Run, Orca, Dominique (Avenging Spirit), Murder By Phone, Second Time Lucky, Separate Vacations, Jeweller's Shop, Millenium, Summer of the Monkeys.
TELEVISION: *Movies*: Regina Vs. Nelles, The Sea Wolf, Harry Oakes, Rugged Gold, Captain's Courageous, 20,000 Leagues Under the Sea. *Mini-Series*: The Martian Chronicles, Sword of Gideon, Young Catherine.

ANDERSON, MICHAEL, JR.
Actor. b. London, England, Aug. 6, 1943. Father is director Michael Anderson. Ent. films as child actor, 1954.
PICTURES: The Moonraker, Tiger Bay, The Sundowners, In Search of the Castaways, Play It Cool, Reach For Glory, Greatest Story Ever Told, Dear Heart, Major Dundee, The Glory Guys, The Sons of Katie Elder, The Last Movie, Logan's Run, Sunset Grill, Terminal Rush, Rent-a-Kid, Mulholland Drive.
TELEVISION: *Movies*: The House That Would Not Die, In Search of America, The Family Rico, The Daughters of Joshua Cabe, Coffee Tea or Me? Shootout in a One-Dog Town, Kiss Me Kill Me, The Million Dollar Face, Making of a Male Model, Love Leads the Way, Undue Influence, Elvis Meets Nixon. *Mini-Series*: Washington Behind Closed Doors, The Martian Chronicles. *Series*: The Monroes.

ANDERSON, PAUL THOMAS
Director, Writer, Producer. b. Studio City, CA, Jan. 1, 1970. LA Film Crits. Award, New Generation, 1997. BSFC Award for Best New Filmmaker for Boogie Nights in 1997. Garnered Best Screenplay Academy Award Nominations for Boogie Nights and Magnolia. Won the Golden Berlin Bear award for Magnolia as best picture at Berlin International Film Festival.
PICTURES: The Dirk Diggler Story (short), Cigarettes and Coffee (short), Sydney (aka Hard Eight), Boogie Nights, Flagpole Special (short), Magnolia.

ANDERSON, RICHARD
Actor. b. Long Branch, NJ, Aug. 8, 1926. e. University H.S., W. Los Angeles. Served in U.S. Army, WWII. Began acting career in summer theatre in Santa Barbara and Laguna Playhouse where spotted by MGM executives who signed him to six year contract. Appeared in 26 films for MGM before leaving studio. Spokesperson for Kiplinger Washington Letter since 1985.
PICTURES: 12 O'Clock High, The People Against O'Hara, Scaramouche, The Story of Three Loves, Escape from Fort Bravo, Forbidden Planet, The Search for Bridey Murphy, Paths of Glory, The Long Hot Summer, Curse of the Faceless Man, Compulsion, A Gathering of Eagles, Johnny Cool, Seven Days in May, Seconds, The Ride to Hangman's Tree, Tora! Tora! Tora!, Macho Callahan, Doctors' Wives, Play It As It Lays, The Honkers, The Player, The Glass Shield, An American in Saigon, Gettysburg.
TELEVISION: *Movies*: Along Came a Spider, Kane & Abel, The Return of the Six Million Dollar Man and the Bionic Woman, Pearl, Perry Mason Returns, Hoover vs. the Kennedys, Emminent Domain, Danger High, Stranger on My Land, The Bionic Showdown: The Six Million Dollar Man & The Bionic Woman (also co-prod.), Return of the Six Million Dollar Man and the Bionic Woman III, Kung Fu Revisted, Bionic Breakdown: The Six Million Dollar Man & The Bionic Woman (exec. prod.), Bionic Ever After? (also co-exec. prod.), In the Lake of The Woods. *Series*: Mama Rosa, Bus Stop, The Lieutenant, Perry Mason, Dan August, The Six Million Dollar Man, The Bionic Woman (Emmy nom.), Dynasty, Cover-Up. *Guest*: Ironside, The Big Valley, Mannix, My Friend Tony, The Mod Squad, Land of the Giants, The FBI, Gunsmoke.

ANDERSON, RICHARD DEAN
Actor. b. Minneapolis, MN, Jan. 23, 1950. Planned to become professional hockey player. Became a street mime and jester. Performed with his own rock band, Ricky Dean and Dante.
PICTURES: Young Doctors in Love, Ordinary Heroes, Odd Jobs, Firehouse, Fallout (voice).
TELEVISION: *Movies*: In the Eyes of a Stranger, Through the Eyes of a Killer, MacGyver: Lost Treasure of Atlantis (also co-exec. prod.), MacGyver: Trail to Doomsday, Beyond Betrayal, Past the Bleachers, Firehouse. *Mini-series*: Pandora's Clock. *Series*: General Hospital (1976-81), Seven Brides for Seven Brothers, Emerald Point N.A.S., MacGyver, Legend, Stargate SG-1(also exec. prod.).

ANDERSON, SYLVIA
Producer, Writer (Pinewood Studios). b. London, England. e. London U. Entered m.p. ind. 1960. First pub. novel, Love and Hisses. UK rep for Home Box Office of America.
PICTURES: Thunderbird Six (prod.), Thunderbirds Are Go, Journey to the Far Side of the Sun .
TELEVISION: *Creator &/or Prod.*: Space 1999, UFO, Thunderbirds, Journey Throught the Black Sun, Destination Moonbase Alpha, Alien Attack.

ANDERSON, WES
Director, Writer.
PICTURES: Bottle Rocket, Rushmore (also exec. prod.).

ANDERSSON, BIBI
Actress. b. Stockholm, Sweden, Nov. 11, 1935. e. Royal Dramatic Theatre School (Kungliga Dramatiska Teatern).
PICTURES: Dum-Bom (debut, 1953), Sir Arne's Treasure, Smiles of a Summer Night, The Seventh Seal, Wild Strawberries, The Magician, Brink of Life, The Face, The Devil's Eye, Square of Violence, Pleasure Garden, The Swedish Mistress, Not to Mention These Women, My Sister My Love, Persona, Duel at Diablo, A Question of Rape, Black Palm Trees, The Girls, Story of a Woman, The Passion of Anna, The Kremlin Letter, The Touch, Scenes From a Marriage, It Is Raining on Santiago, Blondy (Vortex), The Hounds of Spring, I Never Promised You a Rose Garden, An Enemy of the People, Quintet, The Concorde: Airport '79, Prosperous Times, The Marmalade Revolution, Black Crows, Exposed, The Hill on the Other Side of the Moon, Babette's Feast, Manika, Fordringsagare, A Passing Season, The Butterfly's Dream, Little Big Sister.
TELEVISION: Rabies, Wallenberg—A Hero's Story, Tul Julia.

ANDRESS, URSULA
Actress. b. Bern, Switzerland, Mar. 19, 1936. To Rome as teen where she landed roles in Italian Films.
PICTURES: Sins of Casanova (debut, 1954), An American in Rome, The Tempest Has Gone, La Catena dell'Odio, Anyone Can Play, Dr. No, Four For Texas, Fun in Acapulco, Nightmare in the Sun, She, The Tenth Victim, What's New Pussycat?, Up to His Ears, Once Before I Die, The Blue Max, Casino Royale, The Southern Star, Perfect Friday, Red Sun, Africa Express, Scaramouche, The Sensuous Nurse, Slave of the Cannibal God, Tigers in Lipstick, The Fifth Musketeer, Primitive Desires, Four Tigers in Lipstick, Clash of the Titans, Reporters, Mexico in Flames, Liberte/Egalite/Choucroute, Class Reunion, Cremaster 5.
TELEVISION: *Movies*: Man Against the Mob: The Chinatown Murders, Cave of the Golden Rose III, Cave of the Golden Rose IV. *Mini-Series*: Peter the Great. *Series:* Falcon Crest.

ANDREWS, ANTHONY
Actor, Producer. b. London, England, Dec. 1, 1948. e. Royal Masonic Sch., Herts. Regional stage debut, 1967.
PICTURES: Take Me High/Hot Property (debut, 1973), Operation Daybreak, Under the Volcano, The Holcroft Covenant, The Second Victory, The Lighthorsemen, Hanna's War, Lost in Siberia, The Law Lord, Haunted (also co-prod.).
TELEVISION: A Beast With Two Backs, Upstairs Downstairs, A War of Children, Romeo and Juliet, QB VII, Ivanhoe, The Scarlet Pimpernel, Danger UXB, Brideshead Revisited, Sparkling Cyanide, A.D., Bluegrass, Suspicion, The Woman He Loved, Columbo Goes to the Guillotine, Danielle Steel's Jewels, Strange Case of Dr. Jekyll and Mr. Hyde, Hands of a Murderer, Heartstones, Mothertime.

ANDREWS, JULIE
Actress, Singer. r.n. Julia Wells. b. Walton-on-Thames, England. Oct. 1, 1935. m. dir./writer Blake Edwards. Debut, England Starlight Roof Revue London Hippodrome, 1948. Author of Mandy, Last of the Really Great Whangdoodles, 1973.
THEATER: *NY:* The Boy Friend, My Fair Lady, Camelot, Putting It Together, Victor/Victoria.
PICTURES: Mary Poppins (debut, 1964; Acad. Award), The Americanization of Emily, The Sound of Music (Acad. Award nom.), Hawaii, Torn Curtain, Thoroughly Modern Millie, Star!, Darling Lili, The Tamarind Seed, ``10," S.O.B, Victor/Victoria (Acad. Award nom.), The Man Who Loved Women, That's Life, Duet For One, A Fine Romance.

TELEVISION: *Movies*: Our Sons. *Series:* The Julie Andrews Hour (1972-73), Julie. *Specials*: High Tor, Julie and Carol at Carnegie Hall, The Julie Andrews Show, An Evening with Julie Andrews and Harry Belafonte, The World of Walt Disney, Julie and Carol at Lincoln Center, Julie on Sesame Street, Julie Andrews' Christmas Special, Julie and Dick in Covent Garden, Julie Andrews and Jackie Gleason Together, Julie Andrews: My Favorite Things, Julie Andrews:The Sound of Christmas, Julie and Carol: Together Again.

ANDREWS, NAVEEN
Actor. b. Enland, 1971. e. Guildhall School of Music and Drama.
PICTURES: London Kills Me, Wild West, True Love and Chaos, Kama Sutra: A Tale of Love, The English Patient, Mighty Joe Young.
TELEVISION: Double Vision, The Buddha of Suburbia, The Peacock Spring.

ANGELOPOULOS, THEO
Director, Writer, Producer, Actor. b. Athens, Greece, April 17, 1935.
PICTURES: Reconstruction, Days of 36, The Travelling Players, The Hunters, Alexander the Great, Voyage to Kythera (Cannes Film Fest. Award, Best Screenplay, 1984), The Beekeeper, Landscape in the Mist, The Suspended Step of the Stork, The Gaze of Odysseus (Cannes Film Fest. Award, Jury Prize, 1995), Lumiere and Company, Eternity and a Day (Cannes Film Fest. Award, Palm D'Or, 1998).

ANGERS, AVRIL
Actress, Comedienne, Singer. b. Liverpool, England, April 18, 1922. Stage debut at age of 14; screen debut in 1947 in Lucky Mascot (The Brass Monkey).
THEATER: The Mating Game, Cockie, Murder at the Vicarage, Little Me, Norman, Is That You?, Blithe Spirit, Oklahoma!, Gigi, The Killing of Sister George, Cards on the Table, When We Are Married, Cinderella, Easy Virtue, Post Mortem, Crazy for You.
PICTURES: Miss Pilgrim's Progress, Don't Blame the Stork, Women Without Men, Green Man, Devils of Darkness, Be My Guest, Three Bites of the Apple, The Family Way, Two a Penny, The Best House in London, Staircase, There's a Girl in My Soup, Forbush and the Penguins, Gollocks, Confessions of a Driving Instructor, Dangerous Davies.
TELEVISION: How Do You View, Friends and Neighbors, Dear Dotty, Holiday Town, Charlie Fainsbarn Show, Arthur Askey Show, All Aboard, The Gold Hunter, Bob Monkhouse Show, Before The Fringe, Hudd, Coronation Street, Dick Emery Show, Dad's Army, Bright Boffins, The More We Are Together, The Millionairess, Liver Birds, Looks Familiar, No Appointment Necessary, The Songwriters, All Creatures Great and Small, Coronation Concert, Minder, Smuggler, Just Liz, Give Us a Clue, Are You Being Served, Trelawney of the Wells, Cat's Eye, C.A.B., Rude Health, Victoria Wood Playhouse, Common As Muck.

ANHALT, EDWARD
Writer. b. New York, NY, March 28, 1914. e. Columbia U.
PICTURES: Crime Doctor's Diary, Gentleman From Nowhere, Avalanche, Strange Voyage, Bulldog Drummond Strikes Back, Panic in the Streets (Acad. Award for Best Original Story, 1950), Red Mountain, The Member of the Wedding (also prod.), The Sniper (Acad. award nom.), My Six Convicts, Eight Iron Men, Not as a Stranger, The Pride and the Passion, The Young Lions, In Love and War, The Restless Years, The Sins of Rachel Cade, The Young Savages, Girls Girls Girls, A Girl Named Tamiko, Wives and Lovers, Becket (Acad. Award for Best Adapted Screenplay, 1964), The Satan Bug, Boeing-Boeing, Hour of the Gun, In Enemy Country, The Boston Strangler, The Madwoman of Chaillot, Jeremiah Johnson, The Man in the Glass Booth, Luther, Escape to Athena, Green Ice, The Holcroft Covenant.
TELEVISION: A Time for Killing, Madame X, Peter the Great, QB VII, Contract on Cherry Street, Day That Christ Died, The Neon Empire, The Take, Alexander the Great, The Life and Times of Santa Claus, The Apostles.

ANISTON, JENNIFER
Actress. b. Sherman Oaks, CA, Feb. 11, 1969. e. NY High School of the Performing Arts. Daughter of actor John Aniston. m. Brad Pitt. Started training as a drama student in high school. In 1987, after graduation, appeared in For Dear Life and Dancing on Checker's Grave (off B'way.).
PICTURES: Leprechaun, Dream for an Insomniac, Waiting for Woody, She's the One, 'Til There Was You, Picture Perfect, The Object of My Affection, Office Space.
TELEVISION: *Movies*: How I Spent My Summer, Camp Cucamonga. *Series*: Molloy (debut, 1989), Ferris Bueller, The Edge, Muddling Through, Friends. *Guest*: Quantum Leap, Herman's Head, The Larry Sanders Show, Burke's Law, Partners, Ellen, Hercules (voice), South Park (voice).

ANN-MARGRET
Actress, Singer, Dancer. r.n. Ann-Margret Olsson. b. Valsjobyn, Sweden, April 28, 1941. e. New Trier H.S., Winnetka, IL; Northwestern U. m. Roger Smith, actor, dir., prod. Radio shows, toured with band; worked with George Burns in Las Vegas. TV debut, Jack Benny Show, 1961.
PICTURES: Pocketful of Miracles (debut, 1961), State Fair, Bye Bye Birdie, Viva Las Vegas, Kitten With a Whip, The Pleasure Seekers, Bus Riley's Back in Town, Once A Thief, The Cincinnati Kid, Made in Paris, Stagecoach, The Swinger, Murderer's Row, The Prophet, The Tiger and the Pussycat, Rebus, Criminal Affair, RPM, C. C. & Company, Carnal Knowledge (Acad. Award nom.), The Outside Man, The Train Robbers, Tommy (Acad. Award nom.), The Last Remake of Beau Geste, The Twist, Joseph Andrews, The Cheap Detective, Magic, The Villain, Middle Age Crazy, I Ought To Be in Pictures, Lookin' to Get Out, The Return of the Soldier, Twice in a Lifetime, 52 Pick-up, A Tiger's Tail, A New Life, Newsies, Grumpy Old Men, Grumpier Old Men, The Limey, The Last Producer, Any Given Sunday.
TELEVISION: *Movies*: Who Will Love My Children?, A Streetcar Named Desire, The Two Mrs. Grenvilles, Our Sons, Nobody's Children, Following Her Heart, Blue Rodeo, Life of the Party: The Pamela Harriman Story, Happy Face, Any Given Sunday. *Mini-Series*: Queen, Scarlett, Seduced By Madness: The Diane Borchardt Story. *Series*: Four Corners. *Specials*: The Ann-Margret Show, From Hollywood With Love, Dames at Sea, When You're Smiling, Ann-Margret Smith, Ann-Margret Olsson, Memories of Elvis, Rhinestone Cowgirl, Hollywood Movie Girls.

ANNAUD, JEAN-JACQUES
Writer, Director. b. Draveil, France, Oct. 1, 1943. Began career as film dir. in French army, making educational pictures. Also directed 500 commercials. Received 1989 cinema prize from French Acad. for career's work. Directed IMAX film Wings of Courage.
PICTURES: Black and White in Color (winner of Best Foreign Language Film Oscar, 1978), Coup de Tete (Hothead), Quest for Fire (Cesar Award for best dir., 1982), The Name of the Rose, The Bear (Cesar Award for best dir., 1989), The Lover, Wings of Courage, Seven Years In Tibet, Too Shy to Try (writer only), Hoofbeats (writer, prod. only).

ANSARA, MICHAEL
Actor. b. Lowell, MA, April 15, 1922. e. Pasadena Playhouse. Served in U.S. Army; then summer stock, little theatre, road shows.
PICTURES: Soldiers Three, Only the Valiant, The Robe, Julius Caesar, Sign of the Pagan, Bengal Brigade, New Orleans Uncensored, Diane, Lone Ranger, Sol Madrid, Daring Game, Dear Dead Delilah, The Bears and I, Mohammad Messenger of God, The Manitou, Gas, Access Code, Knights of the City, Assasination, Lethal (KGB: The Secret War), Border Shootout.
TELEVISION: *Movies*: How I Spent My Summer Vacation, Powderkeg, A Call to Danger, Ordeal, Shootout in a One-Dog Town, Barbary Coast, The Fantastic World of D.C. Collins. *Series*: Broken Arrow, Law of the Plainsman, Buck Rogers in the 25th Century, Batman: The Animated Series (voice), The New Batman/Superman Adventures (voice). *Mini-Series*: Centennial. *Guest*: The Westerner, Lost in Space, Simon and Simon, Gavilan, George Burns Comedy Week, Hunter, Hardcastle and McCormick.

ANSPACH, SUSAN
Actress. b. New York, NY, Nov. 23, 1945. e. Catholic U., Washington, DC. After school returned to NY and in 3 years had performed in 11 B'way and off-B'way prods. Moved to Los Angeles and entered films.
PICTURES: The Landlord (debut, 1970), Five Easy Pieces, Play It Again Sam, Blume in Love, The Big Fix, Running, The Devil and Max Devlin, Gas, Montenegro, Misunderstood, Blue Monkey, Into the Fire, Blood Red, Back to Back.
TELEVISION: *Movies*: I Want to Keep My Baby, The Secret Life of John Chapman, Rosetti & Ryan, Mad Bull, The Last Giraffe, Portrait of an Escort, The First Time, Deadly Encounter, Cagney & Lacey: The Return. *Series*: The Yellow Rose, The Slap Maxwell Story. *Mini-Series*: Space.

ANSPAUGH, DAVID
Director, Producer. b. Decatur, IN, Sept. 24, 1946. e. Indiana U., 1965-70; U. of Southern CA, 1974-76. School teacher, Aspen, CO, 1970-74.
PICTURES: *Director*: Hoosiers (debut, 1986), Fresh Horses, Rudy, Moonlight and Valentino, Swing Vote.
TELEVISION: *Movies*: Deadly Care, In the Company of Darkness. *Series*: Hill St. Blues (assoc. prod. 1980-81; prod.-dir. 1981-82; prod.-dir. 1983-84, dir. 1985. DGA Award: 1983, 2 Emmy Awards for producing: 1982, 1983), St. Elsewhere (dir.), Miami Vice (dir.).

ANTHONY, LYSETTE
Actress. r.n. Lysette Chodzko. b. London, England, 1963. Stage work incl. Bristol Old Vic, 1988-90.
PICTURES: Krull, The Emperor's New Clothes, Without a Clue, 29 Days in February, Switch, Husbands and Wives, The Pleasure Principle, Face the Music, Look Who's Talking Now, The Hard Truth, The Advocate, Dr. Jekyll and Ms. Hyde, Dead Cold, Dracula: Dead and Loving It, Robinson Crusoe, Man of Her Dreams, Russell Mulcahy's Talos the Mummy, Dead Man's Gun.
TELEVISION: *Movies/Specials:* Ivanhoe, Oliver Twist, Dombey and Son, Jemima Shore, Night Train to Murder, The Bretts, Princess Daisy, The Lady and the Highwayman, Jack the Ripper, A Ghost in Monte Carlo, Target of Suspicion, Sweet Danger, Trilogy of Terror II. *Series:* Crossroads, Lovejoy (BBC), Three Up Two Down (BBC), Campion, Dark Shadows, Dead Man's Gun. *Guest:* Tales from the Crypt, Night Man, Highlander: The Raven.

ANTHONY, TONY
Actor, Producer, Writer. b. Clarksburg, WV, Oct. 16, 1939. e. Carnegie Mellon.
PICTURES: Force of Impulse, Pity Me Not, The Wounds of Hunger, A Stranger in Town, The Stranger Returns, A Stranger in Japan, Come Together, Blindman, Pete Pearl and the Pole, Let's Talk About Men, Get Mean, The Treasure of the Four Crowns, Comin' at Ya, For Better or For Worse.
TELEVISION: Dollar for the Dead (prod. only).

ANTON, SUSAN
Actress. b. Oak Glen, CA, Oct. 12, 1950. Concert & night club singer. Country album & single Killin' Time went top 10 on Country charts, received Gold Record in Japan. Made B'way debut in Hurlyburly, 1985. Also in The Will Rogers Follies. Off-B'way in X-mas a Go-Go. 1992, hon. chmn. of Amer. Cancer Soc., Calif. Special Olympics, & hon. capt. U.S. Woman's Olympic Volleyball Team..
PICTURES: Goldengirl, Spring Fever, Cannonball Run II, Options (cameo), Making Mr. Right, Lena's Holiday.
TELEVISION: *Movies*: The Great American Beauty Contest, Baywatch: River of No Return. *Series*: Stop Susan Williams (Cliff Hangers), Presenting Susan Anton, Baywatch. *Guest:* Quantum Leap, Blossom, Murder She Wrote, Night Court, The Famous Teddy Z, Circus of the Stars, The Ben Stiller Show, The Larry Sanders Show.

ANTONIO, LOU
Actor, Writer, Producer, Director. b. Oklahoma City, OK. e. U. of OK. Two Emmy Nominations for TV Movies.
THEATER: *Actor:* The Buffalo Skinner (Theatre World Award), The Girls of Summer, The Good Soup, The Garden of Sweets, Andorra, The Lady of the Camellias, The Ballad of the Sad Cafe, Ready When You Are, C.B. *Director*: Private Lives (w Taylor/Burton).
PICTURES: *Actor*: The Strange One, Splendor in the Grass, America America, Hawaii, Cool Hand Luke, The Phynx. *Also*: Mission Batangas (s.p.), Micki and Maude (exec. prod.).
TELEVISION: *Movies*: Lanigan's Rabbi, Someone I Touched, Something for Joey, The Girl in the Empty Grave, The Critical List, Silent Victory-The Kitty O'Neil Story, A Real American Hero, The Contender, We're Fighting Back, Something So Right, A Good Sport, Threesome, Rearview Mirror, Face to Face, The Outside Woman (also prod.), Dark Holiday (also exec. prod.), Between Friends, Mayflower Madam, One Terrific Guy, Pals, 13 at Dinner, This Gun for Hire, Lies Before Kisses, The Last Prostitute, The Rape of Dr. Willis, A Taste for Killing, Nightmare in the Daylight. *Series*: Snoop Sisters, Dog and Cat, Making It, Piece of Blue Sky, The Power and the Glory, Danny Thomas Hour, Partners in Crime, Sole Survivor, Where the Ladies Go, Star Trek. *Director: Mini-Series:* Rich Man, Poor Man (co-dir.), Breaking Up Is Hard to Do, The Star Maker. *Series:* Diagnosis Murder, Party of Five, American Gothic, Dark Skies, Vengeance Unlimited, Picket Fences , Chicago Hope.

ANTONIONI, MICHELANGELO
Director, Writer. b. Ferrara, Italy, Sept. 29, 1912. e. Centro Spiremintale di Cinematografia; degree in economics. Film critic on local newspaper; film critic with Corriere Padano, 1936-40; script writer for Un Pilota Ritorna, I due Foscari and asst. dir. for Les Visiteurs du Soir, 1942; with Italia Libera and on edit. staff of Cinema, 1944-45. First films as dir. were short documentaries including: Gente del Po (1943-47), N.U., L'Amorosa Menzogna, Superstizione, Sette canne un vestito, followed by latter works La Villa dei Mostri, La Funivia del Faloria, Kumbha Mela, Roma, Noto—Mandorli—Vulcano—Stromboli—Carnevale. Recipient of: Palme d'Or, 1987; Prix Lumiere, 1990; h.c. degree, Univ. of Berkeley, 1993; honorary Academy Award, 1995; Legion d'Honneur, Paris 1996 and many others. Prof. at Cornell Univ., NY.
PICTURES: *Director/Writer*: Story of a Love Affair (feature debut as dir., 1950), The Vanquished, Lady Without Camelias, Love in the City (segment: When Love Fails), The Girl Friends, The Outcry, I Am a Camera, L'Avventura, The Night, Eclipse, Red Desert, I Tre Volti/Three Faces of a Woman (dir. only; segment: Prefazione), Blow-Up (Acad. Award nom. for dir.), Zabriskie Point, Chung Kuo (documentary), The Passenger, The Oberwald Mystery, Identification of a Woman, The Crew, Beyond the Clouds (co-dir., co-s.p., with Wim Wenders), Just to Be Together, Destinazione Verna.

ANTONOWSKY, MARVIN
Executive. b. New York, NY, Jan. 31, 1929. e. City Coll. of New York, B.A., M.B.A. Joined Kenyon and Eckhart in 1957 for which was media research dir. then mktg. v.p. With Norman, Craig, & Kummel as v.p., mktg. svcs. Became v.p. in charge of media research and spot buying at J. Walter Thompson, 1965. Joined ABC-TV as v.p. in charge of research, 1969. Left to become v.p. in charge of programming at NBC-TV. Became sr. v.p., Universal-TV, 1976. Joined Columbia Pictures as pres., mktg. & research, 1979. Rejoined MCA/Universal Pictures as pres, mktg., 1983. Formed Marvin Antonowsky & Assoc., mktg. consultancy firm, 1989. Rejoined Columbia Pictures in 1990 as exec. v.p. and asst. to chmn. Joined Price Entertainment as exec. v.p., 1993.

ANWAR, GABRIELLE
Actress. b. Laleham, England, Feb. 4,1970.
PICTURES: Manifesto (debut, 1989), If Looks Could Kill, Wild Hearts Can't Be Broken, Scent of a Woman, For Love or Money, The Three Musketeers, Body Snatchers, Things to Do in Denver When You're Dead, Innocent Lies, The Grave, Kimberly, The Guilty, The Manor.
TELEVISION: *Movies*: Prince Caspian and the Voyage of the Dawn Treader, First Born, In Pursuit of Honor, The Ripper, White Chapel, Nevada (also co-prod.), Sub Down. *Specials*: The Storyteller, Summer's Lease, Fallen Angels.

APATOW, JUDD
Producer, Writer. b. 1968
PICTURES: Crossing the Bridge (Assoc. prod. only), Heavyweights (exec., also actor), Happy Gilmore (s.p. only), Celtic Pride (exec.), The Cable Guy, The Wedding Singer (s.p. only), The Whistlebower.
TELEVISION: *Series*: The Larry Sanders Show (dir. only), Freaks and Geeks (exec.). *Guest*: The Ben Stiller Show (actor only).

APFEL, EDWIN R.
Writer, Executive. b. New York, NY, Jan. 2, 1934. e. Franklin and Marshall Coll., B.A., 1955. Mktg. exec.: Metro-Goldwyn-Mayer, Verve Records, Embassy Pictures. Freelance copywriter. Writer of, Edward R. Murrow: This Reporter, Amer. Masters (PBS), 1990. Council member, WGA East, 1992.

APPLEGATE, CHRISTINA
Actress. b. Hollywood, CA, Nov. 25, 1972.
PICTURES: Jaws of Satan (debut, 1980), Streets, Don't Tell Mom the Babysitter's Dead, Across the Moon, Wild Bill, Mars Attacks!, Nowhere, The Big Hit, Jane Austen's Mafia, The Giving Tree, Out in Fifty, The Visitors..
TELEVISION: *Movies*: Grace Kelly, Dance 'til Dawn. *Series*: Washingtoon, Heart of the City, Married... With Children, Jesse. *Guest*: Quincy M.E., Silver Spoons, Family Ties, Charles in Charge, The New Leave It to Beaver, Amazing Stories, 21 Jump Street, Top of the Heap, Prince Charming.

APTED, MICHAEL
Director, Producer. b. Aylesbury, England, Feb. 10, 1941. e. Cambridge. Broke into show business at Granada TV in England in early 1960's as trainee, researcher and finally director. By 1965, was prod.-dir. for local programs and current affairs then staff drama dir. for TV series, plays and serials. In late 1960's, left Granada to freelance.
PICTURES: Triple Echo, Stardust, The Squeeze, Agatha, Coal Miner's Daughter, Continental Divide, Gorky Park, Firstborn, Bring on the Night, 28 Up, Critical Condition, Gorillas in the Mist, Class Action, 35 Up, Thunderheart, Incident at Oglala, Bram Stoker's Dracula (exec. prod. only), Blink, Nell, Moving the Mountain, Extreme Measures, Inspirations, 42 Up, Fortune's Fools, The World is Not Enough, Enigma.
TELEVISION: *Director:* Seven Up, Big Breadwinner Hogg (series), Seven Plus Seven, The Lovers (series), Another Sunday and Sweet F.A., Follyfoot, Joy The Style of the Countess, The Reporters, The Collection, Stronger Than the Sun, Buggins' Ermine, Jackpoint, Kisses at 50, High Kampf, Poor Girl, Wednesday Love, Ptang Yang Kipperbang, The Long Way Home, My Life and Times (series), Crossroads, New York News (pilot), Always Outnumbered, Nathan Dixon. *Exec. Prod*: Criminal Justice, Age 7 in America, Intruders, Strapped, Nathan Dixon.

ARAKI, GREGG
Director, Editor, Producer, Writer. b. Los Angeles, CA. 1959.
PICTURES: Three Bewildered People in The Night, The Living End, Totally F***ed Up, The Doom Generation, Nowhere, Splendor.
TELEVISION: This Is How The World Ends.

ARAU, ALFONSO
Director, Actor. b. Mexico City, Mexico, 1933. e. Univ. of Mexico. Studied drama there and with Saki Sano in Mexico; UCLA film school; studied pantomime in Paris.
PICTURES: *Actor*: The Wild Bunch, El Topo, Scandalous John, Run Cougar Run, Tivoli, Posse, Used Cars, Romancing the Stone, Three Amigos, Walker, Camino Largo a Tijuana, Committed. *Director*: The Barefoot Eagle (also actor), Clazonian Inspector, Mojado Power (also prod.), Chido One, Like Water for Chocolate (also prod., Mexico's Ariel Award), A Walk in the Clouds, Picking up the Pieces (also actor, prod.).
TELEVISION: *Movies*: Stones for Ibarra, Dynamite and Gold. *Series*: El Show de Arau.

ARCAND, DENYS
Director. b. Deschambault, Quebec, Canada, June 25, 1941. e. U. of Montreal, 1963. While still history student, co-prod. Seul ou avec D'Autres (1962). Joined National Film Board of Canada, where he began making documentary shorts (Champlain, Les Montrealistes and La Route de l'ouest) forming a trilogy dealing with colonial Quebec. In 1970 socio-political doc. about Quebec textile workers, On Est au Coton, generated controversy resulting in the NFB banning film until 1976.

PICTURES: On Est au Coton (doc.), Un Maudite Galette (1st fiction feature, 1971). *Dir. &/or Writer*: Seoul ou Avec D'autres, Entre la Mer et L'eau Douce, Quebec: Duplessis et Apres... (doc.), Dirty Money, Rejeanne Padovani, Gina, Comfort and Indifference, Le Crime d'Ovide Plouffe, The Decline of the American Empire, Night Zoo (actor only), Jesus of Montreal (Cannes Film Fest. jury prize, 1989), Leolo (actor only), Montreal Sextet (also actor), Love and Human Remains, Poverty and Other Delights, 15 Moments.
TELEVISION: *Series:* Duplessis (s.p.), Empire Inc. (dir.), Murder in the Family (mini).

ARCHER, ANNE
Actress. b. Los Angeles, CA, Aug. 25, 1947. Daughter of actress Marjorie Lord and actor John Archer. m. Terry Jastrow, TV network sports producer-director and pres. Jack Nicklaus Prods.
THEATER: A Coupla White Chicks Sitting Around Talking (off-B'way, 1981), Les Liaisons Dangereuses (Williamstown Fest., 1988).
PICTURES: The Honkers (debut, 1972), Cancel My Reservation, The All-American Boy, Trackdown, Lifeguard, Paradise Alley, Good Guys Wear Black, Hero at Large, Raise the Titanic, Green Ice, Waltz Across Texas (also co-story), The Naked Face, Too Scared to Scream, The Check Is in the Mail, Fatal Attraction (Acad. Award nom.), Love at Large, Narrow Margin, Eminent Domain, Patriot Games, Body of Evidence, Family Prayers, Short Cuts, Clear and Present Danger, There Goes My Baby (narrator), Mojave Moon, Nico the Unicorn, Whispers (voice), Dark Summer, Rules of Engagement, The Art of War.
TELEVISION: *Movies*: The Blue Knight, The Mark of Zorro, The Log of the Black Pearl, A Matter of Wife...and Death, The Dark Side of Innocence, Harold Robbins' The Pirate, The Sky's No Limit, A Different Affair, A Leap of Faith, The Last of His Tribe, Nails, Jane's House, Because Mommy Works (also co-prod.), The Man in the Attic. *Series*: Bob and Carol and Ted and Alice, The Family Tree, Falcon Crest. *Mini-Series*: Seventh Avenue. *Special*: Leslie's Folly.

ARCHERD, ARMY
Columnist, TV commentator. r.n. Armand Archerd. b. New York, NY, Jan. 13, 1922. e. UCLA, grad. '41, U.S. Naval Academy Post Graduate Sch., 1943. m. actress Selma Archerd. Started as usher at Criterion Theatre, N.Y., while in high school. After grad. UCLA, worked at Paramount studios before entering Navy. Joined AP Hollywood bureau 1945, Herald-Express, Daily Variety as columnist, 1953. M.C. Hollywood premieres, Emmys and Academy Awards. Pres., found., Hollywood Press Club. Awards from Masquers, L.A. Press Club, Hollywood Foreign Press Club, and Newsman of the Year award from Publicists Guild, 1970; Movie Game. Co-host on TV series, People's Choice. Received Hollywood Women's Press Club Man of the Year Award, 1987.

ARDANT, FANNY
Actress. b. Monte Carlo, March 22, 1949. Majored in political science in college. Served a 5-year apprenticeship in the French theater acting in Polyeucte, Esther, The Mayor of Santiago, Electra and Tete d'Or. TV debut in Les Dames de la Cote.
PICTURES: Les Chiens (debut, 1979), Les uns et les Autres, The Woman Next Door, The Ins and Outs, Life Is a Novel, Confidentially Yours, Benevenuta, Desire, Swann in Love, Love Unto Death, Les Enrages, L'Ete Prochain, Family Business, Affabulazione, Melo, The Family, La Paltoquet, Three Sisters, Australia, Pleure pas My Love, Adventure of Catherine C., Afraid of the Dark, Rien Que des Mensonges, La Femme du Deserteur, Amok, Colonel Chabert, Beyond the Clouds, Ridicule, Elizabeth, La Cena.

ARGENTO, DARIO
Director, Writer. b. Rome, Italy, 1940. Son of prod. Salvatore Argento.
PICTURES: *Writer/Co-s.p.*: Today It's Me...Tomorrow It's You, Cemetery Without Crosses, Once Upon a Time in the West, Commandos, Zero Probability, The Five Man Army, One Night at Dinner, Sexual Revoultion, Legion of the Damned, Seasons of Love .*Also Dir./Prod./Co-Prod.*: Bird With the Crystal Plumage, Cat O'Nine Tails (also story), Four Flies on Grey Velvet, The Five Days of Milan, Deep Red, Suspiria (also music), Dawn of the Dead (prod., also music), Inferno (also story), Tenebrae Unsane (also story), Creepers, Demons, Demons 2: The Nightmare is Back, Opera (Terror at the Opera), The Church (also story), Two Evil Eyes (episode: The Black Cat), Devil's Daughter, Innocent Blood (actor only), Trauma, Stendhal's Syndrome, The Wax Mask, Phantom of the Opera, ICan't Sleep.
TELEVISION: *Series:* Door Into Darkness (It.).

ARKIN, ADAM
Actor. b. Brooklyn, NY, Aug. 19, 1956. Father is actor Alan Arkin. Made acting debut in short film prod. by father, People Soup.
THEATER: I Hate Hamlet (Theatre World Award), Four Dogs and a Bone.
PICTURES: Made for Each Other, Baby Blue Marine, Improper Channels (s.p.), Under the Rainbow, Chu Chu and the Philly Flash, Full Moon High, The Doctor, With Friends Like These, Halloween: H20, With Friends Like These, Lake Placid, East of A, Hanging Up, Mission, Dropping Out.
TELEVISION: *Movies*: It Couldn't Happen to a Nicer Guy, All Together Now, In the Line of Duty: Hunt for Justice, Not in This Town, Thirst, A Slight Case of Murder.. *Specials*: Mark Twain's America: Tom Edison, The Fourth Wise Man, Baseball (voice). *Series*: Busting Loose, Teachers Only, Tough Cookies, A Year in the Life, Northern Exposure, Chicago Hope. *Mini-Series:* Pearl, Lewis & Clark: The Journey of the Corps of Discovery (voice), Not for Ourselves Alone: The Story of Elizabeth Cady Stanton & Susan B. Anthony. *Guest:* St. Elsewhere, China Beach, Law & Order, Picket Fences.

ARKIN, ALAN
Actor, Director, b. New York, NY, March 26, 1934. e. Los Angeles City Col., Los Angeles State Col., Bennington (VT) Col. m. Barbara Dana, actress-author. Father of actor Adam Arkin. Was member of folk singing group The Tarriers, then one of the original members of Chicago's Second City improvisational group. Directed short films T.G.I.F., People Soup (Acad. Award nom.). Author: Tony's Hard Work Day, The Lemming Condition, Halfway Through the Door, The Clearing, Some Fine Grandpa.
THEATER: *B'way*: Enter Laughing (Tony & Theatre World Awards, 1963), Luv. *Off-B'way:* Second City, Man Out Loud, From the Second City. *Director*: Eh?, Little Murders, White House Murder Case (Obie Award), Joan of Lorraine, Rubbers and Yanks Three, The Sunshine Boys, The Sorrows of Stephen, Room Service.
PICTURES: Calypso Heat Wave (debut, 1957), The Russians Are Coming The Russians Are Coming (Golden Globe Award, Acad. Award nom.), Woman Times Seven, Wait Until Dark, Inspector Clouseau, The Heart Is a Lonely Hunter (NY Film Critics Award, Acad. Award nom.), Popi, The Monitors, Catch-22, Little Murders (also dir.), Deadhead Miles, Last of the Red Hot Lovers, Freebie and the Bean, Rafferty and the Gold Dust Twins, Hearts of the West (NY Film Critics Award), The 7 Per Cent Solution, Fire Sale (also dir.), The In-Laws (also exec. prod.), The Magician of Lublin, Simon, Improper Channels, Chu Chu and the Philly Flash, Full Moon High, The Last Unicorn (voice), The Return of Captain Invincible, Joshua Then and Now, Bad Medicine, Big Trouble, Coupe de Ville, Edward Scissorhands, Havana, The Rocketeer, Glengarry Glen Ross, Indian Summer, So I Married an Axe Murderer, North, The Jerky Boys, Steal Big Steal Little, Mother Night, Grosse Point Blank, Gattaca, The Slums of Beverly Hills, Jakob the Liar, Arigo (also dir. & s.p.).
TELEVISION: *Movies*: The Defection of Simas Kurdirka, The Other Side of Hell, A Deadly Business, Escape from Sobibor, Cooperstown, Taking the Heat, Doomsday Gun. *Specials*: The Love Song of Barney Kempinski, The Fourth Wise Man, A Matter of Principle, Fay (pilot; dir.), Twigs (dir.), The Emperor's New Clothes (Faerie Tale Theatre), The Visit (Trying Times; dir.), The Boss (Trying Times; dir.), Necessary Parties (also co-s.p., co-prod.). *Series*: Harry, Chicago Hope. *Guest*: East Side/West Side, St. Elsewhere.

ARKOFF, SAMUEL Z.
Producer, Executive. b. Fort Dodge, IA, June 12, 1918. e. U. of Colorado, U. of Iowa, Loyola U. Law Sch. Chmn. & pres. of the Samuel Z. Arkoff Company (formed 1980) and Arkoff Int'l Pictures (formed 1981). Served in USAF as cryptographer WWII. Exec. prod. of The Hank McCune Show, 1948-51. Co-founder American Releasing, 1954, and American International Pictures, 1955. Pres. and chmn. of bd. AIP until 1979. Named with partner James H. Nicholson, Producers of the Year by Allied States Assoc. of MP Theatre Owners, 1963. Named Master Showmen of the Decade by the Theatre Owners of America, 1964. Along with Nicholson, named Pioneers of the Year by the Foundation of the MP Pioneers, Inc., 1971. Since appointment in 1973, has served as intl. v.p. of Variety Clubs Intl. V.p., Permanent Charities Committee. Member of the bd. of Trustees of Loyola Marymount U., L.A., 1979. Hollywood Walk of Fame Star, 1993. Author of Flying Through Hollywood By the Seat of My Pants, with Richard Trubo.
PICTURES: *Exec. Prod./Producer:* Reform School Girl, Motorcycle Gang, Machine Gun Kelly, The Bonnie Parker Story, The Fall of the House of Usher, The Pit and the Pendulum, Tales of Terror, Master of The World, Premature Burial, Panic in the Year Zero, The Raven, Beach Party, Haunted Palace, Comedy of Terrors, Bikini Beach, Masque of the Red Death, Muscle Beach Party, Pajama Party Tomb of Ligeia, Wild Angels, Devil's Angels, The Trip, Three in the Attic, Wild in the Streets, The Oblong Box, Scream and Scream Again, Murders in the Rue Morgue, Cry of the Banshee, Bloody Mama, Wuthering Heights, The Abominable Dr. Phibes, Frogs, Blacula, Dillinger, Heavy Traffic, Hennessy, Cooley High, Food of the Gods, Futureworld, The Great Scout and Cathouse Thursday, The Land That Time Forgot, The People That Time Forgot, At the Earth's Core, Island of Dr. Moreau, Our Winning Season, The Amityville Horror, C.H.O.M.P.S., Dressed to Kill, How to Beat the High Cost of Living, The Final Terror, Up the Creek, I Was a Teenage Werewolf, I Was a Teenage Frankenstein, Amazing Colossal Man, Force 10 From Navarone, California Dreaming, Coffy, Foxy Brown, War of the Colossal Beast, Beast With a Million Eyes, Dementia 13, Mad Max, X the Man With X-ray Eyes, How to Make a Monster.

ARKUSH, ALLAN
Director. b. Jersey City, NJ, April 30, 1948. e. Franklin & Marshall, NYU. Film Sch. With New World Pictures as film, music and trailer editor, 1974-79. Co-dir. Hollywood Boulevard and Death Sport and was 2nd unit dir. of Grand Theft Auto before directing on own. Dir. rock videos with Bette Midler and Mick Jagger, Elvis Costello, Christine McVie.
PICTURES: Hollywood Boulevard (co-dir., co-edit.), Deathsport (co-dir.), Rock 'n' Roll High School (also story), Heartbeeps, Get Crazy, Caddyshack II, Shake Rattle and Rock.
TELEVISION: *Movies*: XXX & OOOs (co-exec. prod.), Young at Heart, Desert Breeze (co-exec. prod.), Elvis Meets Nixon. *Mini-Series:* The Temptations. *Series*: Fame, St. Elsewhere, L.A. Law, Moonlighting (Emmy nom.), Shannon's Deal (spv. prod.), Tattinger's, The Twilight Zone, Mann & Machine, I'll Fly Away, Middle Ages, Johnny Bago, Central Park West (co-exec. prod.), Ally McBeal, The Visitor, Timecop, Players, Total Security, The Practice, Dawson's Creek. *Pilots*: The Bronx Zoo, Capital News (prod.), Parenthood (co-exec. prod.), Bodies of Evidence, Moon Over Miami (exec. prod.).

ARLEDGE, ROONE
Executive. b. Forest Hills, NY, July 8, 1931. e. Columbia U. Entered industry with Dumont Network in 1952. Joined U.S. Army, 1953, serving at Aberdeen Proving Ground in Maryland, prod. and dir. radio programs. Joined NBC, held various production positions, 1954. Went to ABC TV, 1960; named v.p. in charge of ABC Sports, 1964; created ABC's Wide World of Sports, 1961; named pres. of ABC News, 1968; pres. of ABC News and Sports, 1977. Holds four George Foster Peabody Awards for sports reporting; 19 Emmy awards.

ARMSTRONG, BESS
Actress. b. Baltimore, MD, Dec. 11, 1953. e. Brown U. m. producer John Fiedler.
PICTURES: The House of God (debut, 1979), The Four Seasons, Jekyll and Hyde—Together Again, High Road to China, Jaws 3-D, Nothing in Common, Second Sight, Mother Mother, The Skateboard Kid, The Perfect Daughter, That Darn Cat, Pecker.
TELEVISION: *Movies*: Getting Married, How to Pick Up Girls, Walking Through the Fire, 11th Victim, This Girl for Hire, Lace, Take Me Home Again, She Stood Alone: The Tailhook Scandal, Stolen Innocence, She Cried No, Christmas Every Day, Forever Love. *Special*: Barefoot in the Park. *Series*: On Our Own, All is Forgiven, Married People, My So-Called Life.

ARMSTRONG, GILLIAN
Director. b. Melbourne, Australia, Dec. 18, 1950. e. Swinburne Coll. Among 1st class in dirs. course at National Aust. Film & TV School, Sydney. Worked as art dir. on a number of films. Dir. numerous shorts (One Hundred a Day, The Singer and the Dancer) and documentaries (A Busy Kind of Bloke, Bingo Bridesmaids and Braces) before turning to features.
PICTURES: My Brilliant Career (Australian Film Inst. Award), Starstruck, Mrs. Soffel, Hard to Handle, High Tide, Fires Within, The Last Days of Chez Nous, Little Women, Not Fourteen Again (also prod., s.p.), Oscar & Lucinda.

ARMSTRONG, GORDON
Executive, b. East Orange, NJ, Nov. 26, 1937. e. Arizona State U., graduate studies at NYU. Joined 20th Century-Fox as nat. pub. dir., 1970. Was appointed dir. of adv.-pub.-promo. for Dino De Laurentiis Corp., 1975; became vice pres., worldwide marketing for the company, 1978. Named v.p., adv.-pub.-prom., Universal Pictures, 1970; exec. v.p., mktg. MCA Recreation, 1984; pres. mktg., Morgan Creek Prods., 1991. Pres., Entertainment Marketing Group, 1993. V.p., sales and mktg., ATTICA Cybernetics ,1995; v.p., sales and mktg., Doubleclick Network, 1996.

ARNALL, ELLIS GIBBS
Lawyer, executive. b. Newnan, GA, March 20, 1907. e. Mercer U., U. of the South, A.B. 1928, D.C.L. 1947; U. of Georgia LL.B. 1931; Atlanta Law Sch., LL.D. 1941; Piedmont Coll., LL.D 1943; Bryant Coll., LL.D. 1948. Georgia state rep. from Coweta County, 1936-38; asst. Attorney-General (GA), 1938-42; Attorney-General (GA), 1942-43; Governor of GA, 1943-47. Pres. Dixie Life Insurance Co; pres., Columbus Natl Life Insurance Co; sr. member, law firm Arnall Golden & Gregory; pres. Georgia State Jr. Chamber of Commerce ,1939. Author: The Shore Dimly Seen (1946), What The People Want (1948). Member, U.S. Natl. Com. on UNESCO; member, U.S. delegation to 4th annual conference UNESCO, Paris, 1949. SIMPP pres., 1948 & 1952; pres. Indept. Film Prod. Export Corp., 1953. Bd. of dir., exec. com., U.S. Nat'l Comm. for UNESCO, 1964-65; AMPAS.

ARNAZ, JR., DESI
Actor, Singer. b. Los Angeles, CA, Jan. 19, 1953. e. Beverly Hills H.S. Son of Lucille Ball and Desi Arnaz. Sister is actress Lucie Arnaz. Gained fame as rock singer and musician with the Dino, Desi and Billy group. Video: A Day at the Zoo. Regional theatre includes Sunday in New York, Grease, Promises Promises, Alone Together, I Love My Wife, Is There Life After High School?, Love Letters, The Boys Next Door.
PICTURES: Red Sky at Morning (debut, 1971), Marco, Billy Two Hats, Joyride, A Wedding, Fake-Out, House of the Long Shadows, The Mambo Kings.
TELEVISION: *Movies*: Mr. & Mrs. Bo Jo Jones, Voyage of the Yes, She Lives, Having Babies, Flight to Holocaust, Black Market Baby, To Kill a Cop, The Courage and the Passion, How to Pick Up Girls, Crisis in Mid-Air, Gridlock, Advice to the Lovelorn, The Night the Bridge Fell Down. *Series*: Here's Lucy, Automan. *Guest*: The Love Boat, Fantasy Island, Paul Reiser: Out on a Whim, Matlock.

ARNAZ, LUCIE
Actress. b. Los Angeles, CA, July 17, 1951. Daughter of Lucille Ball and Desi Arnaz. m. actor Laurence Luckinbill. Brother is actor Desi Arnaz Jr. B'way: They're Playing Our Song (Theatre World Award), Lost in Yonkers. National touring companies: Whose Life is It Anyway?, Educating Rita, My One and Only, Social Security. Nightclubs: Lucie Arnaz-Latin Roots, Irving Berlin in Concert-In Sicily.
PICTURES: Billy Jack Goes to Washington, The Jazz Singer, Second Thoughts.
TELEVISION: *Movies*: Who is the Black Dahlia, The Mating Season, The Washington Mistress, Who Gets the Friends?, Abduction of Innocence. *Series*: Here's Lucy, The Lucy Arnaz Show, Sons and Daughters. *Pilot*: One More Try. *Specials*: Lucy & Desi: A Home Movie (host, co-exec. prod., co-dir.), The Wizard of Oz in Concert: Dreams Come True.

ARNESS, JAMES
Actor. r.n. James Aurness. b. Minneapolis, MN, May 26, 1923. e. Beloit Coll. Brother of actor Peter Graves. Served in U.S. Army; worked in advertising, real estate. Started in films in late 1940's appearing under his real name.
PICTURES: The Farmer's Daughter (debut 1947), Roses Are Red, The Man From Texas, Battleground, Sierra, Two Lost Worlds, Wyoming Mail, Wagon Master, Double Crossbones, Stars in My Crown (1st billing as James Arness), Cavalry Scout, Belle le Grand, Iron Man, The People Against O'Hara, The Girl in White, The Thing, Carbine Williams, Hellgate, Big Jim McLain, Horizons West, Lone Hand, Ride the Man Down, Island in the Sky, Veils of Bagdad, Hondo, Her Twelve Men, Them!, Many Rivers to Cross, Flame of the Islands, The Sea Chase, The First Travelling Saleslady, Gun the Man Down, Alias Jesse James (cameo).
TELEVISION: *Movies*: The Macahans, The Alamo: 13 Days to Glory, Gunsmoke: Return to Dodge, Red River, Gunsmoke: The Last Apache, Gunsmoke: To the Last Man, Gunsmoke: The Long Ride (also exec. prod.), Gunsmoke: One Man's Justice (also exec. prod.). *Series*: Gunsmoke (20 years), How the West Was Won, McClain's Law. *Mini-Series*: How the West Was Won.

ARNOLD, EDDY
Singer. b. Henderson, TN, May 15, 1918. Radio performer, Nashville, TN. Recording star since 1946; records include That's How Much I Love You, Anytime, Bouquet of Roses (on the Country Music charts longer than any record in the history of country music), Make the World Go Away. Holds the record for most Country Records on the charts. Elected to Country Music Hall of Fame, 1966; Entertainer of the Year, 1967; Pioneer Award from Acad. of Country Music, 1984; President's Award from Songwriter's Guild, 1987.
TELEVISION: *Series*: Eddy Arnold Show (1952-3), Eddy Arnold Time, Eddy Arnold Show (1956), The Kraft Music Hall (1967-71). Hosted Music from the Land, Tonight Show, more than 20 specials.

ARNOLD, TOM
Actor. b. Ottumwa, IA, June 3, 1959.
PICTURES: Freddy's Dead: The Final Nightmare, Hero, Undercover Blues, True Lies, Nine Months, Big Bully, Carpool, The Stupids, Hacks, Touch, McHale's Navy (also co-prod.), Buster and Chauncey's Silent Night (voice), Golf Punks, The Day October Died, Blue Ride Fall, Bar Hopping, Ablaze, Exit Wounds, Just Sue Me, Lloyd, I Know What You Screamed.
TELEVISION: *Movies*: Backfield in Motion, Body Bags, The Woman Who Loved Elvis, Jackie's Back! *Series*: The Roseanne Barr Show, Roseanne (also prod.), The Jackie Thomas Show (also creator, exec. prod.), Tom, The Tom Show (also creator, exec. prod.). *Guest*: The Ben Stiller Show, Saturday Night Live, The Larry Sanders Show, High Society, The Naked Truth, L.A. Doctors.

ARNOW, TED J.
Executive. b. Brooklyn, NY. e. St. Johns U., Washington and Lee U. Served as dir. of recreation for 262nd General Hospital in Panama. Veteran of over 50 yrs. in amusement industry. Was v.p. for adv., pub., & promo. for Loew's Theatres. Member: Motion Picture Pioneers, Variety Clubs, Will Rogers Hospital. Former pres. of AMPA (Assoc. M.P. Advertisers). Retired.

ARONOFSKY, DARREN
Director, Writer. b. Brooklyn, New York, Feb. 12, 1969.
PICTURES: Protozoa (dir. only), Pi, Requiem for a Dream, Batman: Year One.

ARQUETTE, DAVID
Actor. b. Sept. 8, 1971. m. actress Courtney Cox. Brother of actresses Patricia and Rosanna Arquette and actors Richmond and Alexis Arquette.
PICTURES: Where the Day Takes You, Buffy the Vampire Slayer, The Webbers, The Killing Box, Airheads, Fall Time, Wild Bill, Skin and Bone, Beautiful Girls, Johns, Scream, Life During Wartime, Dream with the Fishes (also co-prod.), Scream 2, Ravenous, Never Been Kissed, Muppets From Space, Scream 3, Ready to Rumble, The Shrink is In, The Mile High Club, 3000 Miles in Graceland, See Spot Run, The Grey Zone.
TELEVISION: *Movies:* Cruel Doubt, Roadracers. *Mini-Series:* Dead Man's Walk. *Series:* The Outsiders, Parenthood, Double Rush, Pelswick. *Guest:* Blossom, Beverly Hills, 90210, Friends.

ARQUETTE, PATRICIA
Actress. b. Chicago, IL, April 8, 1968. Sister of actress Rosanna Arquette and actors Richmond, Alexis and David Arquette. Prof. debut in children's version of Story Theatre. Studied acting with Milton Katselis.
PICTURES: A Nightmare on Elm Street 3: Dream Warriors (debut, 1987), Pretty Smart, Time Out, Far North, Prayer of the Rollerboys, The Indian Runner, Ethan Frome, Trouble Bound, Inside Monkey Zetterland, True Romance, Holy Matrimony, Ed Wood, Beyond Rangoon, Infinity, Flirting With Disaster, The Secret Agent, Nightwatch, Lost Highway, The Hi-Lo Country, Goodbye Lover, Stigmata, Bringing Out the Dead, Little Nicky, In the Boom Boom Room, Human Nature.
TELEVISION: *Movies*: Daddy, Dillinger, Wildflower, Betrayed by Love. *Special*: The Girl With the Crazy Brother. *Guest*: The Edge (Indian Poker), thirtysomething, Tales From the Crypt.

ARQUETTE, ROSANNA
Actress. b. New York, NY, Aug. 10, 1959. Granddaughter of humorist Cliff Arquette (Charlie Weaver). Daughter of actor-producer Lewis Arquette. Sister of actress Patricia Arquette and actors Richmond, Alexis and David Arquette. Prof. debut in children's version of Story Theatre. Studied acting in San Francisco. Role in LA play led to bit parts on tv then regular role as Shirley Jones' teenage daughter on series Shirley (1979).
PICTURES: More American Graffiti (debut, 1979), Gorp, S.O.B., Baby It's You, Off the Wall, The Aviator, Desperately Seeking Susan, Silverado, After Hours, 8 Million Ways To Die, Nobody's Fool, Amazon Women on the Moon, The Big Blue, New York Stories (Life Lessons), Flight of the Intruder, Wendy Cracked a Walnut, The Linguini Incident, Fathers and Sons, Nowhere to Run, Pulp Fiction, Search and Destroy, Gone Fishin, Crash, Do Me a Favor, Liar, I'm Losing You, Hell's Kitchen, Buffalo '66, Sugar Town, Palmer's Pick Up, The Whole Nine Yards, Pigeon Holed, Interview With A Dead Man, Too Much Flesh, Things Behind the Sun, Good Advice, Diary of a Sex Addict, Big Bad Love .
TELEVISION: *Movies*: Having Babies II, The Dark Secret of Harvest Home, Zuma Beach, The Ordeal of Patty Hearst, A Long Way Home, The Wall, The Executioner's Song, Johnny Belinda, One Cooks the Other Doesn't, The Parade, Survival Guide, Promised a Miracle, Sweet Revenge, Separation, Son of the Morning Star, Black Rainbow, In the Deep Woods, The Wrong Man, Nowhere to Hide, I Know What You Did, Switched at Birth, Poison. *Mini-Series:* The '60's. *Series*: Shirley, Gun. *Guest:* Eight is Enough, Homicide: Life on the Street. *Specials*: Mom and Dad Can't Hear Me, A Family Tree (Trying Times).

ARTHUR, BEATRICE
Actress. r.n. Bernice Frankel. b. New York, NY, May 13, 1926. Franklin Inst. of Sciences & Art. Studied with Erwin Piscator at New School for Social Research; first stage role as Lysistrata; professional stage debut in Dog Beneath the Skin, 1947.
THEATER: Gas, Yerma, No Exit, Six Characters in Search of an Author, The Taming of the Shrew, (1948) The Owl and the Pussycat, The Threepenny Opera (1953 revival), The ShoeString Revue, What's the Rush?, Nature's Way, Ulysses in Nighttown, Gay Divorcee, Fiddler on the Roof, Mame (Tony Award, 1966), The Floating Light Bulb, Night of the 100 Stars.
PICTURES: That Kind of Woman, Lovers and Other Strangers, Mame, History of the World Part I.
TELEVISION: Once Upon a Time (debut, 1951), Numerous guest appearances. *Series*: Caesar's Hour, Maude (Emmy Award, 1977), Amanda's, Golden Girls (Emmy Award, 1988). *Specials*: All Star Gala at Ford's Theater (host), Jay Leno's Family Comedy Hour. *Movie*: My First Love.

ARTHUR, KAREN
Director. b. Omaha, NB, Aug. 24, 1941. Ballet dancer, choreographer and musical comedy singer, dancer and actress, 1950-68; actress, film, tv and theatre, 1968-75; film, tv director, 1970-95.
PICTURES: *Actress*: A Guide for the Married Man, Winning. *Director*: Legacy (1975, Int'l Film Critics & Josef Von Sternberg Awards, 1975), The Mafu Cage, Lady Beware, Labor of Love.
TELEVISION: *Movies*: Charleston, Victims for Victims: The Theresa Saldana Story (Christopher Award), A Bunny's Tale, The Rape of Richard Beck, Evil in Clear River (Christopher Award), Cracked Up, Bridge to Silence, Fall from Grace, Bump in the Night, Shadow of a Doubt, The Secret, The Disappearance of Christina, Against Their Will: Women in Prison, Journey of the Heart, The Staircase. *Mini-Series*: Love and Betrayal: The Mia Farrow Story, Crossings, Return to Eden, The Jacksons: An American Dream, Dead by Sunset, A Will of Their Own, True Women. *Series*: Rich Man Poor Man Book II, Emerald Point, Boone, Two Marriages, Hart to Hart, Remington Steele, Cagney & Lacey (Emmy Award, 1985). *Pilots*: Tin Man, Blue Bayou.

ARTZ, BOB
Theatre executive. b. Spokane, WA, Aug 21, 1946. e., B.T.A. Pasadena Playhouse College of Theatre Arts. Began in 1968 as doorman, became asst. mgr. to mgr. with National General Theatre Corporation. Joined Plitt Theatres in 1978 as dist. mgr. and ad/pub. dir., West Coast. Joined General Cinema Theatres in 1986 as reg. mktg. dir., Western region. Became dir., film mktg. in 1993. National dir., Entertainment Mktg. & Operations in 1996. Dir. client svc's., Global Cinema Network, 1998. Member: Variety Club, Film Information Council, Pasadena PlayHouse Alumni & Assoc (life mem.).

ASH, RENE
Producer. b. Brussels, Belgium, March 14, 1939. e. U. of Omaha. Employed with I.A.T.S.E. 1968-1979, prior to which was assoc. editor, Greater Amusements. Eastern v.p. of Pub. Guild, 1973-1981; editor-in-chief, Backstage, 1979-80; pres., Cinereal Pictures, 1984-85; co-pres., Eagle Films Corp., 1985-94; pres. Rea Film Prods. Author of various articles published in foreign film magazines and The Film Editor in Motion Pictures & Television. Member of the Pub. Guild since 1968.

ASHER, JANE
Actress. b. London, England, April 5, 1946.
PICTURES: Mandy (Crash of Silence; debut, 1952), Third Party Risk, Dance Little Lady, Adventure in the Hopfields, The Quatermass Experiment (The Creeping Unknown), Charley Moon, Greengage Summer (Loss of Innocence), The Girl in the Headlines (The Model Murder Case), The Masque of the Red Death, Alfie, The Winter's Tale, Deep End, The Buttercup Chain, Henry VIII and His Six Wives (from the BBC series the Six Wives of Henry VIII), Runners, Success Is the Best Revenge, Dream Child, Paris By Night, Closing Numbers.
TELEVISION: *Movies/Specials*: Brideshead Revisited, Voyage 'Round My Father, East Lynne, The Mistress, Wish Me Luck, Tonight at 8:30, The Volunteer. *Mini-series*: The Choir, *Series:* Good Living.

ASHLEY, ELIZABETH
Actress. b. Ocala, FL, Aug. 30, 1939. e. Studied ballet LA State U., 1957-58; grad. Neighborhood Playhouse, 1961. Author: Postcards From the Road.
THEATER: Take Her She's Mine (1962 Tony & Theatre World Awards), The Highest Tree, Barefoot in the Park, Ring 'Round the Bathtub, The Skin of Our Teeth, Legend, Cat on a Hot Tin Roof (B'way revival), Caesar and Cleopatra, Agnes of God, The Milk Train Doesn't Stop Here Anymore, When She Danced.
PICTURES: The Carpetbaggers (debut, 1964), Ship of Fools, The Third Day, The Marriage of a Young Stockbroker, Paperback Hero, Golden Needles, Rancho DeLuxe, 92 in the Shade, The Great Scout and Cathouse Thursday, Coma, Windows, Paternity, Split Image, Dragnet, Vampire's Kiss, Dangerous Curves, Lost Memories, Sleeping Together, Happiness, Just the Ticket.
TELEVISION: *Movies*: Harpy, The Face of Fear, When Michael Calls, Second Chance, The Heist, Your Money or Your Wife, The Magician, One of My Wives is Missing, The War Between the Tates, A Fire in the Sky, Svengali, He's Fired She's Hired, Stagecoach, Warm Hearts Cold Feet, The Two Mrs. Grenvilles, Blue Bayou, Reason for Living: The Jill Ireland Story, Love and Curses... and All That Jazz, In the Best Interest of the Children. *Mini-Series:* The Buccaneers, *Series*: Evening Shade. *Pilot*: Tom and Joann. *Guest*: Mission Impossible, Miami Vice, Hunter, Murder She Wrote, B.L. Stryker, Caroline in the City.

ASHTON, JOHN
Actor. b. Springfield, MA, Feb. 22, 1948. e. USC, BA in theatre.
THEATER: The Last Meeting of the Knights of the White Magnolia (L.A. Drama Critics Circle Award), True West (Drama-Logue Award), A Flea in Her Ear (L.A. Drama Critics Circle Award).
PICTURES: Oh God!, Breaking Away, Borderline, Honky Tonk Freeway, The Adventures of Buckaroo Banzai Across the 8th Dimension, Beverly Hills Cop, The Last Resort, King Kong Lives, Some Kind of Wonderful, Beverly Hills Cop II, She's Having a Baby, Midnight Run, I Want to Go Home, Curly Sue, Little Big League, Trapped in Paradise, The Shooter, Fast Money, Meet the Deedles, Instinct.

TELEVISION: *Movies*: Elvis and the Beauty Queen, A Death in California, The Deliberate Stranger, I Know My First Name is Steven, Dirty Work, Stephen King's The Tommyknockers. *Mini-Series*: The Rhinemann Exchange. Love Lies and Murder, Asteroid. *Series*: Dallas, Breaking Away, Hardball, The Day Lincoln Was Shot. *Guest*: M*A*S*H*, Police Squad!, The Twilight Zone, JAG, King of the Hill (voice), Fantasy Island.

ASNER, EDWARD

Actor. r.n. Isaac Edward Asner. b. Kansas City, MO, Nov. 15, 1929. e. U. of Chicago, where affiliated with campus acting group. Served two years with U.S. Army in France. Returned to Chicago to join Playwright's Theatre Club. Moved to NY and joined NY Shakespeare Festival, 1960 and American Shakespeare Festival, 1961. In 1961, moved to Hollywood to become active in films and tv. National pres. Screen Actors Guild, 1981-85. Prod. tv & feature projects through his company, Quince. Winner of numerous humanitarian awards.
THEATER: *B'way*: Face of a Hero, Born Yesterday (debut, 1989). *Off-B'way*: Ivanov, Threepenny Opera, Legend of Lovers, The Tempest, Venice Preserved.
PICTURES: Kid Gallahad (debut, 1962), The Slender Thread, The Satan Bug, The Venetian Affair, El Dorado, Gunn, Change of Habit, Halls of Anger, They Call Me Mister Tibbs, The Todd Killings, Skin Game, The Wrestler, Gus, Teach Our Children, Americas in Transition, Fort Apache-The Bronx, O'Hara's Wife, Daniel, Pinocchio and the Emperor of the Night (voice), Moon Over Parador, JFK, Happily Ever After (voice), Cat's Don't Dance (voice), Earth and the American Dream, Down on the Waterfront, Prep, 187: Documented, The Long Way Home, Hard Rain, Perfect Game, Mars and Beyond, The Confidence Game, Bring Him Home.
TELEVISION: *Movies*: Fanfare for a Death Scene, The Doomsday Flight, Daughter of the Mind, The House on Greenapple Road, The Old Man Who Cried Wolf, The Last Child, They Call It Murder, Haunts of the Very Rich, The Police Story, The Girl Most Likely To..., The Imposter, Death Scream, Hey I'm Alive, Life and Assassination of the Kingfish, The Gathering, The Family Man, The Marva Collins Story, A Small Killing, A Case of Libel, Anatomy of an Illness, Vital Signs, Kate's Secret, The Christmas Star, Cracked Up, A Friendship in Vienna, Not a Penny More Not a Penny Less, Good Cops Bad Cops, Switched at Birth, Silent Motive, Yes Virginia There Is a Santa Claus, Cruel Doubt, Gypsy, Heads, Dog's Best Friend, Higher Education, The Story of Santa Claus, Payback (also prod.). *Mini-Series*: Rich Man Poor Man (Emmy Award, 1976), Roots (Emmy Award, 1977), Tender Is the Night, More Tales of the City. *Series*: Slattery's People, The Mary Tyler Moore Show (3 Emmy Awards: 1971, 1972, 1975), Lou Grant (2 Emmy Awards: 1978, 1980), Off the Rack, The Bronx Zoo, The Trials of Rosie O'Neill, Fish Police (voice), Hearts Afire, Gargoyles, Thunder Alley, Spider-Man, Freakazoid, Bruno the Kid (voice), Batman: Gotham Knights, Ask Harriet, The Closer. *Guest*: Gunsmoke, Hawaii Five-O, Roseanne, Mad About You, The Practice, The X-Files, Common Ground, Becoming Dick.

ASPEL, SIR MICHAEL

Radio/TV Presenter. b. London, England, Jan. 12, 1933. Entered industry in 1954 as actor/presenter for BBC Radio, and announcer/newsreader for BBC TV. Presentations incl: Miss World, Crackerjack, Give Us A Clue, Ask Aspel, Family Favourites, Child's Play, ITV Telethon 1988, 1990 & 1992, Aspel and Company, This Is Your Life, BAFTA Awards, Strange ... But True?, Caught on Camera, Light Camera Action, ITN's V.E. Day Programme 1995, Blockbusters. Received OBE in 1993.

ASSANTE, ARMAND

Actor. b. New York, NY, Oct. 4, 1949. e. American Acad. of Dramatic Arts. Appeared with regional theatre groups incl. Arena Stage, DC; Long Wharf, New Haven; Actor's Theatre of Louisville.
THEATER: *B'way*: Boccaccio, Comedians, Romeo and Juliet, Kingdoms. *Off-B'way*: Why I Went Crazy, Rubbers, The Beauty Part, Lake of the Woods, Yankees 3 Detroit 0.
PICTURES: Paradise Alley, Prophecy, Little Darlings, Private Benjamin, Love and Money, I the Jury, Unfaithfully Yours, Belizaire the Cajun, The Penitent, Animal Behavior, Q & A, Eternity, The Marrying Man, The Mambo Kings, 1492: Conquest of Paradise, Hoffa, Fatal Instinct, Trial by Jury, Judge Dredd, Striptease, Looking for an Echo, Hunt for the Devil, The Road to El Dorado, One Eyed King, After the Storm.
TELEVISION: *Movies*: Human Feelings, Lady of the House, The Pirate, Sophia Loren-Her Own Story, Rage of Angels, Why Me?, A Deadly Business, Stranger in My Bed, Hands of a Stranger, Jack the Ripper, Passion and Paradise, Fever, Blind Justice, Kidnapped, Gotti (Emmy Award, 1997), C.S.S. Hunley, On The Beach. *Mini-Series*: Napoleon and Josephine: A Love Story, Evergreen, The Odyssey. *Series*: How to Survive a Marriage, The Doctors (1975).

ASSEYEV, TAMARA

Producer. e. Marymont College; UCLA, MA, theatre arts. Began career as asst. to Roger Corman, working on 8 films with him. In 1967 started to produce films independently. Then co-produced films with Alex Rose, starting with Drive-In. In 1966 at 24, became youngest member of Producers Guild of Amer. Member: Costume Council, LA City Museum; founding member, LA Museum of Contemporary Art.
PICTURES: The Wild Racers, Paddy, The Arousers, The History of Atlantic Records. *Co-prod. with Ms. Rose*: Drive-In, I Wanna Hold Your Hand, Big Wednesday, Norma Rae.
TELEVISION: *Movies: Exec. prod.*: Penalty Phase, After the Promise, A Shadow on the Sun (also actress), The Secret Life of Kathy McCormick, The Hijacking of the Achille Lauro, Murder By Moonlight.

ASTIN, JOHN

Actor. b. Baltimore, MD, March 30, 1930. e. Washington and Jefferson Coll., Washington Drama Sch., Johns Hopkins U., grad. BA, U. of Minnesota Graduate School. Father of actors Sean and Mackenzie Astin. Theatre debut on Off-B'way stage, Threepenny Opera. B'way debut, Major Barbara. Dir., co-prod., A Sleep of Prisoners, Phoenix Theatre. Did voices in cartoons, commercials, 1955-59. Prod. & dir. short subject Prelude.
THEATER: The Cave Dwellers, Ulysses in Nighttown, Tall Story, Lend Me a Tenor, H.M.S. Pinafore.
PICTURES: The Pusher (debut, 1958), West Side Story, That Touch of Mink, Move Over Darling, The Wheeler Dealers, The Spirit is Willing, Candy, Viva Max!, Bunny O'Hare, Get to Know Your Rabbit, Every Little Crook and Nanny, The Brothers O'Toole, Freaky Friday, National Lampoon's European Vacation, Body Slam, Teen Wolf Too, Return of the Killer Tomatoes, Night Life, Gremlins 2, Killer Tomatoes Eat France, Stepmonster, The Silence of the Hams, Frighteners, Harrison Bergeron.
TELEVISION: *Movies*: Two on a Bench, Evil Roy Slade, Skyway to Death, Only with Married Men, The Dream Makers, Operation Petticoat (also dir.), Rossetti and Ryan: Men Who Love Women (dir. only), Huck and the King of Hearts. *Series*: I'm Dickens... He's Fenster, The Addams Family, The Pruitts of Southampton, Operation Petticoat, Mary, The Addams Family (voice for animated series), The Adventures of Brisco County Jr., Recess (voice). *Guest*: Batman, The Flying Nun, Bonanza, Odd Couple, Night Gallery, Partridge Family, Police Woman, Love Boat, Night Court. *Specials*: Harry Anderson's Sideshow, Halloween With the Addams Family. *Pilots*: Phillip and Barbara, Ethel Is an Elephant.

ASTIN, MACKENZIE

Actor. b. Los Angeles, CA, May 12, 1973. Parents are actors John Astin and Patty Duke. Brother is actor Sean Astin.
PICTURES: The Garbage Pail Kids Movie, Widow's Kiss, Iron Will, Wyatt Earp, In Love and War, Dream for an Insomniac, The Evening Star, The Last Days of Disco, Stranger Than Fiction.
TELEVISION: The Facts of Life Down Under, Lois Gibbs and the Love Canal, I Dream of Jeannie: 15 Years Later, A Child Lost Forever, The Long Island Incident, Selma, Lord Slema. *Series:* The Facts of Life.

ASTIN, SEAN

Actor. b. Santa Monica, Feb. 25, 1971. Parents are actors John Astin and Patty Duke. Brother is actor Mackenzie Astin. First acting job at 7 opposite mother in Afterschool Special, Please Don't Hit Me Mom. Dir. short films On My Honor, Kangaroo Court (Acad. Award nom.). On LA stage in Lone Star.
PICTURES: The Goonies (debut, 1985), White Water Summer, Like Father Like Son, Staying Together, The War of the Roses, Memphis Belle, The Willies, Toy Soldiers, Encino Man, Where the Day Takes You, Rudy, Safe Passage, The Low Life, Courage Under Fire, The Long Way Home (voice), Deterrence, Bulworth, The Sky is Falling, The Last Producer, Kimberly.
TELEVISION: *Movies*: The Rules of Marriage, The Brat Patrol, Harrison Bergeron. *Pilot*: Just Our Luck.

ATHERTON, WILLIAM

Actor. r.n. William Knight. b. New Haven, CT, June 30, 1947. While in high school became youngest member of Long Wharf Theatre Co. Given scholarship to Pasadena Playhouse; then switched to Carnegie Tech Sch. of Drama in 1965. In college years toured with USO prods in Europe and in stock and industrial shows. Came to NY where first prof. job was in nat'l co. of Little Murders.
THEATER: The House of Blue Leaves, The Basic Training of Pavlo Hummel, The Sign in Sidney Brustein's Window, Suggs (Theatre World Award, Outer Circle Critics Award, Drama Desk Award), Rich and Famous, Passing Game, Happy New Year, The American Clock, Three Acts of Recognition, The Caine Mutiny Court-Martial, Child's Play, Loco Motives.
PICTURES: The New Centurions (debut, 1972), Class of '44, The Sugarland Express, The Day of the Locust, The Hindenburg, Looking for Mr. Goodbar, Ghostbusters, Real Genius, No Mercy, Frank and Jesse, Die Hard, Die Hard 2, Grim Prairie Tales, Oscar, The Pelican Brief, Bio-Dome, Hoods, Executive Power, Mad City, Michael Kael in Katango, Butterfly Legend.
TELEVISION: *Movies*: Tomorrow's Child, Malibu, Intrigue, Buried Alive, Diagnosis of Murder, Chrome Soldiers, Robin Cook's Virus, Broken Trust. *Mini-Series*: Centennial. *Guest*: The Equalizer, Twilight Zone, Murder She Wrote, Tales From the Crypt, *Special*: The House of Mirth.

ATKINS, CHRISTOPHER

Actor. b. Rye, NY, Feb. 21, 1961. e. Dennison U., Ohio. Early modeling jobs before being hired for theatrical film debut in The Blue Lagoon (1980).

PICTURES: The Blue Lagoon, The Pirate Movie, A Night in Heaven, Beaks, Mortuary Academy, Listen to Me, Shakma, King's Ransom, Outrage, Dracula Rising, Die Watching, Exchange Lifeguards, A Bullet Down Under, Trigger Fast, Project Shadowchaser III, It's My Party, Mutual Needs, Breaking the Silence, Beings (writer only), Deadly Delusions, The Day October Died.
TELEVISION: *Movies*: Child Bride of Short Creek, Secret Weapons, Fatal Charm, Guns of Honor, The Black Rose, Miami Killer, The Floating Outfit, Deadman's Island, Angel Flight Down. *Series*: Dallas. *Guest*: The Black Stallion, Silk Stalkings.

ATKINSON, ROWAN
Actor, Writer. b. England, Jan. 6, 1955. e. Newcastle U., Oxford.
THEATER: Rowan Atkinson in Revue (also writer), Not in Front of an Audience, The Nerd, Rowan Atkinson at the Atkinson (also writer; NY), Mime Gala, The Sneeze.
PICTURES: The Secret Policeman's Ball (also co-s.p.), Fundamental Frolics, The Secret Policeman's Other Ball, Dead on Time, Never Say Never Again, The Appointments of Dennis Jennings, The Tall Guy, The Witches, Hot Shots Part Deux, Four Weddings and a Funeral, The Lion King (voice), Bean (also prod.), Black Adder Back and Forth, Maybe Baby, Rat Race, .
TELEVISION: *Series*: Not the Nine O'Clock News (also writer; BAFTA Award for acting), Blackadder, Blackadder II, Blackadder the Third, Mr Bean, Blackadder Goes Forth, The Thin Blue Line. *Specials*: Canned Laughter, Just for Laughs II, Live from London, Blackadder's Christmas Carol, Blackadder: The Cavalier Years, The Driven Man, Mr. Bean Rides Again, A Royal Birthday Celebration, Doctor Who and the Curse of Fatal Death.

ATTENBOROUGH, BARON RICHARD (SAMUEL)
Actor, Producer, Director. 1993, Life Peer of Richmond Upon Thames; Kt 1976; CBE 1967. b. Cambridge, England, Aug. 29, 1923. e. Wyggeston Grammar Sch., Leicester; Leverhulme Scholarship to Royal Acad. of Dramatic Art, 1941 (Bancroft Medal). m. Sheila Beryl Grant Sim, 1945. Stage debut in Ah Wilderness (Palmers Green, 1941). West End debut in Awake and Sing (1942), then The Little Foxes, Brighton Rock. Joined RAF, 1943; seconded to RAF Film Unit, and appeared in training film Journey Together, 1945; demobilized, 1946. Returned to stage, 1949, in The Way Back (Home of the Brave), To Dorothy a Son, Sweet Madness, The Mousetrap (original cast: 1952-54), Double Image, The Rape of the Belt. Formed Beaver Films with Bryan Forbes, 1959; formed Allied Film Makers, 1960.
PICTURES: *Actor*: In Which We Serve (debut, 1942), Schweik's New Adventures, The Hundred Pound Window, Journey Together, A Matter of Life and Death (Stairway to Heaven), School for Secrets (Secret Flight), The Man Within (The Smugglers), Dancing With Crime, Brighton Rock (Young Scarface), London Belongs to Me (Dulcimer Street), The Guinea Pig, The Lost People, Boys in Brown, Morning Departure (Operation Disaster), Hell Is Sold Out, The Magic Box, Gift Horse (Glory at Sea), Father's Doing Fine, Eight O'Clock Walk, The Ship That Died of Shame, Private's Progress, The Baby and the Battleship, Brothers in Law, The Scamp, Dunkirk, The Man Upstairs, Sea of Sand (Desert Patrol), Danger Within (Breakout), I'm All Right Jack, Jet Storm, SOS Pacific, The Angry Silence (also co-prod.), The League of Gentlemen, Only Two Can Play, All Night Long, The Dock Brief (Trial & Error), The Great Escape, Seance on a Wet Afternoon (also prod.; San Sebastian Film Fest. & Brit. Acad. Awards for Best Actor), The Third Secret, Guns at Batasi (Brit. Acad. Award), The Flight of the Phoenix, The Sand Pebbles (Golden Globe Award), Dr. Dolittle (Golden Globe Award), The Bliss of Mrs Blossom, Only When I Larf, The Magic Christian, David Copperfield (TV in U.S.), The Last Grenade, A Severed Head, Loot, 10 Rillington Place, Ten Little Indians (And Then There Were None), Rosebud, Brannigan, Conduct Unbecoming, The Chess Players, The Human Factor, Jurassic Park, Miracle on 34th Street, Hamlet, The Lost World: Jurassic Park, Elizabeth I, E=MC^2, Light Keeps Me Company. *Producer*: Whistle Down the Wind, The L-Shaped Room. *Director*: Oh! What a Lovely War (also prod.; 16 Intl. Awards incl. Golden Globe and BAFTA UN Award), Young Winston (Golden Globe), A Bridge Too Far (Evening News Best Drama Award, 1977), Magic, Gandhi (also prod.; 8 Oscars, 5 BAFTA Awards, 5 Golden Globes, DGA Award, 1982), A Chorus Line, Cry Freedom (also prod.; Berlinale Kamera, 1987; BFI Award for Tech. Achievement), Chaplin (also prod.), Shadowlands (also prod.; BAFTA Award for Best British Film of 1993), In Love and War (also prod.), Grey Owl (also prod.).

ATTENBOROUGH, SIR DAVID
Broadcaster. b. London, England, May 8, 1926. Brother of Baron Richard Attenborough. e. Wyggeston Sch., Leicester; Clare Coll., Cambridge. Early career, editor in educational publishing house. Ent. BBC-TC, 1952. Prod. Zoo Quest series, Travellers Tales, Adventure and other prog., travel, Eastward with Attenborough, The Tribal Eye, Life on Earth, The Living Planet, The First Eden, The Trials of Life. Controller BBC-2, 1965-68; Dir. of Prog. BBC-TV, 1969-72. Received Desmond Davis Award, 1970 and a Fellowship, 1979. Narrator of A Zed and Two Noughts, Survival Island (also writer), Cities of the Wild (also writer), The Life of Birds.

AUBERJONOIS, RENE
Actor. b. New York, NY, June 1, 1940. e. attended Carnegie Mellon U.
THEATER: Dark of the Moon, Beyond the Fringe, Tartuffe, King Lear, Fire, Julius Caesar, Charley's Aunt, Coco (Tony Award, 1970), Tricks, The Ruling Class, Twelfth Night, The Good Doctor (Tony nom.), Break a Leg, The New York Idea, Every Good Boy Deserves Favor, Richard III, The Misanthrope, Flea in Her Ear, Big River (Tony nom.), Metamorphosis, City of Angels (Tony nom.).
PICTURES: Lilith (debut, 1964), Petulia, M*A*S*H*, Brewster McCloud, McCabe and Mrs. Miller, Pete 'n Tillie, Images, Hindenberg, The Big Bus, King Kong, Eyes of Laura Mars, Where the Buffalo Roam, The Last Unicorn (voice), 3:15, Walker, Police Academy 5: Assignment Miami Beach, My Best Friend is a Vampire, The Little Mermaid (voice), The Feud, Star Trek VI: The Undiscovered Country (unbilled), The Player, Little Nemo (voice), The Ballad of Little Jo, Burning Down the House, Los Locos, Snide and Prejudice, Gepetto.
TELEVISION: *Movies*: The Birdmen, Shirts/Skins, Panache, Dark Secret of Harvest Home, Wild Wild West Revisted, More Wild Wild West, Smoky Mountain Christmas, The Christmas Star, Gore Vidal's Billy the Kid, Longarm, A Connecticut Yankee in King Arthur's Court, Absolute Strangers, Ned Blessing: The True Story of My Life, Wild Card. *Mini-Series:* The Rhineman Exchange. *Series*: Benson (Emmy nom.), Star Trek: Deep Space Nine. *Episode Director*: Marble Head Manor, Star Trek: Deep Space Nine. *Specials*: Faerie Tale Theatre (The Frog Prince, Sleeping Beauty), King Lear, Legend of Sleepy Hollow (Emmy nom.), Fort Necessity, Incident at Vichy, The Booth, The Cask of Amontillado, Ashenden (BBC), The Lost Language of Cranes (BBC).

AUDRAN, STEPHANE
Actress. r.n. Collette Suzanne Dacheville. b. Versailles, France, Nov. 8, 1938. Former wife of French star Jean-Louis Trintignant and director Claude Chabrol.
PICTURES: Les Cousins (debut under direction of Chabrol, 1959), Les Bonnes Femmes, Bluebeard, The Third Lover, Six in Paris, The Champagne Murders, Les Biches, La Femme Infidele, The Beast Must Die, The Lady in the Car, Le Boucher, Without Apparent Motive, Dead Pigeon on Beethoven Street, La Rupture, Just Before Nightfall, The Discreet Charm of the Bourgeoisie, Blood Wedding, The Devil's Advocate, Le Cri de Couer, Vincent Francois Paul and the Others, The Black Bird (U.S. film debut), Ten Little Indians, The Silver Bears, Eagle's Wing, The Big Red One, Coup de Torchon, La Cage aux Folles III: The Wedding, Cop au Vin, Babette's Feast, Seasons of Pleasure, Faceless, Body-To-Body, Sons, Manika: The Girl Who Lived Twice, Quiet Days in Clichy, Mass in C Minor, Betty, Poulet au Vinaigre, Au Petit Marguery, Arlette, Maximum Risk, Arlette, Madeline, Belle Maman.
TELEVISION: *Movies:* Mistral's Daughter, The Blood of Others, The Sun Also Rises, Poor Little Rich Girl: The Barbara Hutton Story, Champagne Charlie, Petit, Un Printemps de Chien. *Series:* TECX

AUERBACH, NORBERT T.
Executive. b. Vienna, Austria, 1923. e. UCLA, business administration. Served with U.S. Army Intelligence in Europe during WWII. Entered motion picture industry after grad., 1946. First asst. dir. at Service Studios in CA. Moved to N.Y. to join domestic sales dept. of Film Classics. Joined Columbia Pictures in foreign dept. In 1950 assigned to Paris office, where remained for over decade, except for 18 mos. in Portugal as mgr. Returned to Paris in 1953 and filled number of exec. sls. positions for Columbia, ultimately rising to continental mgr. Left Columbia to produce films in France, 1961. Resumed career in dist. as continental mgr. at Paris office of United Artists. Returned to prod. to make The Thief of Paris, 1966. Joined Seven Arts Prods. heading theatrical and TV sls. operations in Paris, 1967. When Seven Arts acquired Warner Bros., he became continental sls. mgr. for Warners in Paris. Set up European prod. and dist. org. for CBS Cinema Center Films, operating from London, 1968. Moved to L.A. as v.p., foreign mgr. for CCF, 1972. Returned to London to be consultant in prod. and dist., 1973. Rejoined UA as sls. mgr. for Europe and the Middle East, 1977; named sr. v.p. & foreign mgr., 1978; named pres. & COO, Jan. 1981; pres. & CEO, Feb. 1981. Co-pres., United Int'l Pictures, London, until 1982. Acting pres. and chief exec. officer of Almi Distribution Corp., 1982. Formed packaging and financing Co., Eliktra, Inc., 1983. Now Almi consultant, exec. v.p. American Screen Co.

AUGUST, BILLE
Director. b. Brede, Denmark, Nov. 9, 1948. e. trained in advertising photography, Danish Film School, grad. 1971, cinematography. As cinematographer shot: Christiania, Homeward in the Night, Man kan inte valdtas (Men Can't Be Raped), Karleken, The Grass is Singing. Became dir. 1978 with short Kim G. and dramas for Danish TV.
PICTURES: Honning Maane (also sp.), Zappa (also s.p.), Buster's World, Twist and Shout (also s.p.), Pelle the Conquerer (also s.p.), The Best Intentions (Cannes Film Festival Palm d'Or Award, 1992), The House of the Spirits (also s.p.), Jerusalem (also s.p.), Smilla's Sense of Snow, Les Miserables
TELEVISION: *Movies:* Maj. *Mini-Series:* Den Goda viljan.

AUMONT, JEAN-PIERRE
Actor. b. Paris, France, Jan. 5, 1911. e. Conservatoire of Drama. Roles French stage and films. In 1943 enlisted in Free French Army. Film debut, Jean de la Lune, 1932.
THEATER: *U.S.*: Tovarich, Incident at Vichy, Hostile Witness, Carnival, Camino Real, Murderous Angels, Gigi, A Talent for Murder.
PICTURES: Hotel du Nord, Assignment in Brittany, The Cross of Lorraine, Heartbeat, Song of Scheherazade, Siren of Atlantis, Affairs of a Rogue, Wicked City, Lili, Life Begins Tomorrow, Gay Adventure, Charge of the Lancers, Hilda Crane, The Seventh Sin, John Paul Jones, The Enemy General, The Devil at 4 O'Clock, Carnival of Crime, Five Miles to Midnight, Cauldron of Blood, Castle Keep, Day for Night, Turn the Other Cheek, The Happy Hooker, Mahogany, Catherine & Co., Entire Days Among the Trees, Cat and Mouse, Blackout, Two Solitudes, Something Short of Paradise, Nana, Sweet Country, The Free Frenchman, Senso, A Star for Two, Becoming Colette, Giorgino, Jefferson in Paris.
TELEVISION: *Mini-Series:* Sins, Windmills of the Gods, A Tale of Two Cities, The Count of Monte Cristo, *Series:* The Young Indiana Jones Chronicles.

AURELIUS, GEORGE M.
Executive. b. Grasston, MN, Sept. 16, 1911. e. U. of Minnesota. Entered motion picture industry in 1927 as usher Finkelstein & Ruben, St. Paul; asst. mgr. 1929-30. To Warner Theatres, New York, 1931; mgr. Moss' B'way. Minnesota Amusement Co., 1932-41. City mgr. Publix-Rickards-Nace; Paramount-Nace Theatres, Tucson, Ariz. 1941-46. V.p. ABC Theatres. of Arizona, Inc., 1949-67; pres. ABC North Central Theatres, Inc., 1967-72; v.p., ABC Intermountain Theatres, Inc., & v.p. ABC Theatres of California, Inc. 1972-1974. Mgmt. Consulting and ShoWest Convention & Trade Show since 1975, named exec. dir., 1979. Retired 1985.

AUSTIN, RAY
Baron Devere-Austin of Delvin, Lord of Bradwell. Producer, Director, Writer. b. London, England, Dec. 5, 1932. Has written, produced and directed many TV series, specials and movies. Lecturer, film & tv techniques, etc., 1978-93. Lecturer U. of VA.
PICTURES: Virgin Witches, House of the Living Dead, Fun & Games (One Woman And A 1,000 Men).
TELEVISION: *Series: Dir.:* Avengers, The Champions, Department S, Randall & Hopkirk, Ugliest Girl in Town, Journey into the Unknown, Magnum P.I., Simon and Simon, House Calls, Kings Crossing, Fall Guy, Lime Street (pilot), Spencer for Hire, Heaven Help Us, JAG. It's the Only Way to Go, Fun and Games, Space 1999, New Avengers, Hawaii Five-O, Sword of Justice, Webb, Barnaby Jones, Hardy Boys, Wonder Woman, Salvage, B.J. and the Bear, Hart to Hart, The Yeagers, Man Called Sloane, From Here to Eternity, Bad Cats, Westworld, Tales of the Gold Monkey (2-hr. pilot), The Return of the Man from U.N.C.L.E. *Dir./Writer*: Randall & Hopkirk, Black Beauty, Zany Adventures of Robin Hood, The Master, Hart to Hart, V, Air Wolf, Lime Street (pilot and episodes), Spenser for Hire (several episodes), Magnum P.I. (season premiere 2-hr. episode); Return of the Six Million Dollar Man (pilot); Our House (episodes), Dirty Dozen, Alfred Hitchcock Presents, A Fine Romance, Zorro, Boys of Twilight, Crossroads, Highlander, High Tide, CI5: The New Professionals *Prod./Dir.*: The Perfumed Garden. *Prod./Writer*: Department S

AUTANT-LARA, CLAUDE
Director. b. Luzerches, France, Aug. 5, 1901. Began career as scenic designer for French films in early 1920s, then asst. dir. to Rene Clair. First solo venture experimental film, 1923; in Hollywood, dir., Parlor, Bedroom and Bath, Incomplete Athlete, 1930-32.
PICTURES: Nana (actor only), Construire un feu, Pur sang, .Le Fils du royal, Buster se marie, Un Chien serieux, Le Plombier amoureux, La Peur des coups, Monsieur le duc, Invite monsieur a diner, Le Gendarme est sans pitie, L'Athlete incomplet, Ciboulette (also writer), My Partner Mr. Davis, Fric-Frac, Le Mariage de chiffon, Lettres d'amour, Love Story, Sylvia and the Ghost, Devil in the Flesh, Oh Amelia!, The Red Inn (also writer), The Seven Deadly Sins (also writer), Le Bon Dieu sans confession, The Red and the Black (also writer), The Game of Love (also writer), Marguerite de la nuit (also writer), Four Bags Full, Love Is My Profession, Le Joueur, The Green Mare, Le Bois des amants, Les Regates de San Francisco, Vive Henri IV... vive l'amour, Thou Shalt Not Kill, The Story of Monte Crisco, Enough Rope, Black Humor, Le Magot de Josefa (also writer), A Woman in White, Une Femme en blanc se revolte, The Oldest Profession, Flash 29 (actor only), Le Franciscain de Bourges, Les Patates (also writer), Le Rouge et le blanc.

AUTEUIL, DANIEL
Actor. b. Algeria, Jan. 24, 1950. Parents were lyric opera singers in roving troupe. Lived in Avignon. Performed in Amer. prod. in Paris of Godspell. Then did musical comedy for 2 years. Provided voice of baby for French print of U.S. film Look Who's Talking.
PICTURES: L'Aggression/Sombres Vacanes, Attention Les Yeaux, La Nuit de Saint-Germain des Pres, Monsieuer Papa, L'Amour Viole (Rape of Love), Les Heroes n'ont pas Froid aux Oreilles, A Nous Deux, Bete Mais Discipline, Les Sous-Doues, La Banquiere, Clara et les Chic Types, Men Prefer Fat Girls, Pour 100 Briques t'as Plus Rien Maintentant, Que les Gros Salaires Levent le Doigt!!!, L'Indic, P'tit Con, The Beast, L'Arbalete, Palace, L'Amour en Douce, Jean de Florette, Manon of the Spring, Romuald and Juliette (Mama There's a Man in Your Bed), A Few Days With Me, My Life is Hell, L'Elegant Criminel, Un Coeur en Hiver (A Heart in Winter), Ma Saison Preferee (My Favorite Season), Queen Margot, The Separation, Un Femme Francais, According to Pereira, The Eighth Day (Best actor, Cannes 1996), Thieves, Death in Therapy, Lucie Aubrac, On Guard, The Wrong Blonde, An Interesting State, The Lost Son.

AVALON, FRANKIE
Singer, Actor. r.n. Francis Thomas Avalone. b. Philadelphia, PA, Sept 18, 1940. e. South Philadelphia H.S. Trumpet prodigy age 9 yrs. Recording contract, Chancellor Records, Inc., 1957; Gold Record: Venus 1959; Gold Album: Swingin' on a Rainbow, 1959.
PICTURES: Jamboree (debut, 1957), Guns of the Timberland, The Alamo, Alakazam the Great (voice), Voyage to the Bottom of the Sea, Sail a Crooked Ship, Panic in the Year Zero, Beach Party, The Castilian, Drums of Africa, Operation Bikini, Bikini Beach, Pajama Party, Muscle Beach Party, How to Stuff a Wild Bikini, Beach Blanket Bingo, Ski Party, I'll Take Sweden, Sgt. Deadhead, Dr. Goldfoot and the Bikini Machine, Fireball 500, The Million Eyes of Su-Muru, Skidoo, Horror House, The Take, Grease, Blood Song, Back to the Beach (also co-exec. prod.), Troop Beverly Hills, The Stoned Age, Casino
TELEVISION: *Movies:* A Dream Is A Wish Your Heart Makes: The Annette Funicello Story. *Series*: Easy Does It... Starring Frankie Avalon. *Guest*: Ed Sullivan, Perry Como, Pat Boone, Arthur Murray, Dick Clark Shows, Milton Berle, Golden Circle Spectacular, Dinah Shore Show, Steve Allen Show, The Patty Duke Show, Hullabaloo, Happy Days, Full House.

AVEDON, DOE
Actress, b. Old Westbury, NY, 1928. Bookkeeper, then actress.
THEATER: Young and the Fair, My Name Is Aquilon.
PICTURES: The High and the Mighty, Deep in My Heart, The Boss.
TELEVISION: *Series*: Big Town.

AVILDSEN, JOHN G.
Director, Cinematographer, Editor. b. Chicago, IL, Dec. 21, 1935. m. actress Tracy Brooks Swope. e. NYU. After service in Army made film with friend, Greenwich Village Story, then joined ad agency to write, direct, photograph & edit industrial films. Entered motion picture industry as ass't cameraman on Below the Hill, followed with prod. mgr. job on two Italian films made in U.S. Afterwards, made first theatrical short, Smiles. Asst. dir., Black Like Me; prod. mgr., Mickey One, Una Moglie Americana; 2nd unit dir., Hurry Sundown. Produced, photographed & edited a short, Light—Sound—Diffuse. Returned to industry to make industrial films for ad agencies before resuming theatrical career.
PICTURES: *Dir./photo./edit.*: Turn on to Love (debut), Out of It (assoc. prod., dir. of photog.), Sweet Dreams (aka Okay, Bill), Guess What We Learned in School Today?, Joe, Cry Uncle, The Stoolie, Save the Tiger, W. W. and the Dixie Dancekings, Foreplay, Rocky (Acad. Award, 1976), Slow Dancing in the Big City (also prod.), The Formula, Neighbors (also supv. edit.), Traveling Hopefully (documentary; Acad. Award nom.), A Night in Heaven, The Karate Kid, The Karate Kid: Part II, Happy New Year, For Keeps, Lean On Me (also exec. prod.), The Karate Kid Part III (also co-edit.), Rocky V (also co-edit.), The Power of One, Steal This Video Abbie Hoffman (documentary), 8 Seconds, Save The Everglades (documentary), A fine and Private Place, Coyote Moon.
TELEVISION: From No House to Options House (2 On the Town, Emmy Award).

AVNET, JON
Producer, Director. b. Brooklyn, NY, Nov. 17, 1949. e. U. of PA, Sarah Lawrence Coll. Began career as director of off-B'way prods. Produced and directed low-budget film, Confusion's Circle, which brought a directing fellowship at American Film Institute. Joined Weintraub/Heller Prods. as assoc. prod., where met Steve Tisch, with whom formed Tisch/Avnet Prods. Formed Avnet/Kerner Co., 1986.
PICTURES: Checkered Flag or Crash (assoc. prod.), Outlaw Blues (assoc. prod.). *Producer:* Coast to Coast, Risky Business, Deal of the Century (exec. prod.), Less Than Zero, Tango & Cash, Men Don't Leave, Funny About Love, Fried Green Tomatoes (also dir., co-s.p.), The Mighty Ducks, The Mighty Ducks II, The Mighty Ducks III, The Three Musketeers (co-exec. prod.), When a Man Loves a Woman, The War (also dir.), Miami Rhapsody (co-exec. prod.), Up Close and Personal (also dir.), Red Corner (also. dir.), George of the Jungle, Steal This Move (exec. prod.).

TELEVISION: *Producer*: No Other Love, Homeward Bound, Prime Suspect, Something So Right, Silence of the Heart, Calendar Girl Murders, Call to Glory (pilot and series), The Burning Bed, In Love and War (also exec. prod.), Between Two Women (also dir., co-s.p.), My Last Love. *Exec. Prod.*: Side By Side, My First Love, Breaking Point, O Do You Know the Muffin Man?, Heatwave, Backfield in Motion, The Nightman, The Switch, For Their Own Good, Naomi and Wynona: Love Can Build a Bridge, Poodle Springs, Mama Flora's Family, Parting the Waters (mini-series).

AXEL, GABRIEL
Director. b. Denmark, 1918. e. France, then studied acting at Danish National Conservatory. Returned to France where joined the Paris theater co. of Louis Jouvet as stagehand. Worked as actor in Copenhagen Boulevard theater where made directing debut. Went on to dir. Danish TV, mostly classic plays.
PICTURES: Golden Mountains (debut, 1957), Crazy Paradise, The Red Mantle, Danish Blue, Babette's Feast (also s.p.; Acad. Award for Best Foreign-Language Feature, 1988), Christian (also s.p.), Prince of Jutland (Royal Deceit; also s.p.), Lumiere & Company. *Actor*: The Reluctant Sadist, Love Me Darling, and numerous other Danish films. *Writer*: Crazy Paradise, The Red Mantle, Det Kaere legetoj, Babette's Feast.

AXELMAN, ARTHUR
Executive. b. Philadelphia, PA, Dec. 10, 1944. e. Florida Atlantic U., B.A., 1969. Entered NY offices of William Morris Agency, June 1972; transferred to Bev. Hills offices, 1976, as literary agent. Founded company's original TV Movie dept., 1977; appointed v.p. in 1980; sr. v.p. in 1991. Among clients represented while overseeing network sales, negotiation, packaging, development, etc. of some 100 TV movies have been EMI TV, Bob Banner, Edward S. Feldman, Lee Grant, Thom Mount, Edward Anhalt, Zev Braun, Marvin Worth, Gilbert Cates, Jerry London, Jeremy Kagan, Dick Berg, Patty Duke, Finnegan-Pinchuk Prods.

AXELROD, GEORGE
Writer, Producer, Director. b. New York, NY, June 9, 1922. Stage mgr., actor, summer stock, 1940-41; radio writer, 1941-52.
AUTHOR: *Novels*: Beggar's Choice, Blackmailer; co-writer, night-club musical: All About Love, 1951. *Memoirs*: Where Am I Now When I Need Me?
THEATER: *B'way*: The Seven Year Itch, Will Success Spoil Rock Hunter?, Visit to a Small Planet, Once More with Feeling, Goodbye Charlie (also dir.).
PICTURES: *Writer*: Phffft, The Seven Year Itch, Bus Stop, Breakfast at Tiffany's, The Manchurian Candidate (also co-prod.), Paris When It Sizzles (also co-prod.), How to Murder Your Wife, Lord Love a Duck (also dir., prod.), The Secret Life of an American Wife (also dir., prod.), The Lady Vanishes, The Holocroft Covenant, The Fourth Protocol.

AXELROD, JONATHAN
Writer, Producer. b. New York, NY, July 9, 1952. Stepson of writer George Axelrod. Started as on-set "gofer" before writing screenplays. V.p. primetime drama dev., ABC Entertainment,1978-80; v.p. exec. dir. in charge dev. ABC Ent., 1980-82. Exec. v.p., Columbia Pictures TV, 1983-85. Pres. New World Pictures, 1985-87. Co-owner, Camden Artists, 1987-. Exec. v.p. Ventura Entertainment Group, 1989. Pres. & CEO Producers Entertainment Group, 1990-93. Exec. Prod. of Hollywood Detective series. Formed Axelrod Woddoes Productions, 1994.
TELEVISION: *Exec. Prod.*: Dave's World, Can't Hurry Love, A Day With, Manhattan Match, Late Bloomer, Brother's Keeper, The Price She Paid. *Writer:* Every Little Crook and Nanny.

AYKROYD, DAN
Actor, Writer. b. Ottawa, Canada, July 1, 1952. m. actress Donna Dixon. Member of Toronto Co. of Second City Theater. Worked as mgr. of Club 505, after-hours Toronto nightclub 1970-73. Performed and recorded (Briefcase Full of Blues, Made in America) with John Belushi as the Blues Brothers. Co-owner, Hard Rock Cafe.
PICTURES: Love at First Sight (debut, 1977; also co-s.p.), Mr. Mike's Mondo Video, 1941, The Blues Brothers (also co-s.p.), Neighbors, It Came From Hollywood, Doctor Detroit, Trading Places, Twilight Zone—The Movie, Indiana Jones and the Temple of Doom (cameo), Ghostbusters (also co-s.p.), Nothing Lasts Forever, Into the Night, Spies Like Us (also co-s.p.), One More Saturday Night (exec. prod. only), Dragnet (also co-s.p.), The Couch Trip, The Great Outdoors, Caddyshack II, My Stepmother Is an Alien, Ghostbusters II (also co-s.p.), Driving Miss Daisy (Acad. Award nom.), Loose Cannons, Nothing But Trouble (also dir., s.p.), Masters of Menace, My Girl, This Is My Life, Sneakers, Chaplin, Coneheads (also co-s.p.), My Girl 2, North, Exit to Eden, Tommy Boy, Casper (cameo), Canadian Bacon (cameo), Getting Away With Murder, Sgt. Bilko, Celtic Pride, Feeling Minnesota, My Fellow Americans, Grosse Pointe Blank, Susan's Plan, Antz (voice), Blues Brothers 2000 (also prod., s.p.), The House of Mirth, Stardom, Loser, On the Nose, Hitting the Wall, Unconditional Love, Pearl Harbor.
TELEVISION: Series: Coming Up Rosie (Canada), Saturday Night Live 1975-79 (writer and performer; Emmy Award for writing: 1977). Steve Martin's Best Show Ever (performer, writer), Soul Man (also sup. prod.). *Guest*: Tales From the Crypt, Home Improvement.

AZARIA, HANK
Actor. b. Forest Hills, NY, April 25, 1964. e. Tufts Univ.
PICTURES: Pretty Woman, Cool Blue, Quiz Show, Now and Then, Heat, The Birdcage, Grosse Pointe Blank, Anastasia (voice), Mystery Alaska, Homegrown, Celebrity, Godzilla, Great Expectations, The Cradle Will Rock, Mystery Men.
TELEVISION: *Movies:* Tuesday's With Morrie (Emmy Award), Bartok the Magnificent. *Series:* The Simpsons (voice, Emmy Award), Herman's Head, If Not for You, Mad About You, Stressed Eric (voice). *Guest:* Fresh Prince of Bel-Air, Growing Pains, Friends.

AZNAVOUR, CHARLES
Singer, Songwriter, Actor. r.n. Shahnour Varenagh Aznavourian. b. Paris, France, May 22, 1924. Studied dance and drama as a child and was performing at the age of 10. Encouraged by Edith Piaf, became one of France's leading performers by the mid-1950s and an international concert star by the 1970s. Has also composed music for film.
PICTURES: Adieu Cherie (1947), C'est arrive a 36 Chandelles, Les Dragueurs, Shoot the Piano Player, Le testament d'Orphee, Le Passage du Rhin, Un taxi pour Tobrouk, Horace 62, Tempo di Roma, Les Quatres Verites, Le Rat'd Amerique, Pourquoi Paris?, Paris in August, Candy, The Games, The Adventurers, The Blockhouse, Ten Little Indians, The Twist, Sky Riders, Ciao Les Mecs, The Tin Drum, The Magic Mountain, Hatter's Ghosts, What Makes David Run?, Edith and Marcel, Long Live Life!, Mangeclous, Friend to Friend, Il Maestro, Double Game, The Country Years, L'Alibienor.
TELEVISION: Sans Ceremonie. *Series:* Baldi.
Mondo Beyondo, The Paul Daniels Magic Show (BBC), The Last Mile. *Guest*: Tonight Show, Cosby Show, Northern Exposure.

B

BABENCO, HECTOR
Director. b. Buenos Aires, Argentina, Feb. 7, 1946. Early years spent in Mar del Plata. Left home at 17 and traveled throughout Europe for 8 years working as a writer, house-painter, salesman, and, in Rome, as an extra at Cinecitta. Moved to Sao Paulo, Brazil where he made several short documentaries, before turning to features in 1975.
PICTURES: Rei Da Noite (King of the Night; debut, 1975), Lucio Flavio—Passageiro da Agonia, Pixote (also co-s.p.), Kiss of the Spider Woman, Ironweed, Besame Mucho (prod. only), At Play in the Fields of the Lord (also co-s.p.), Foolish Heart (also prod. and s.p.).

BACALL, LAUREN
Actress. r.n. Betty Joan Perske. b. New York, NY, Sept. 16, 1924. e. American Acad. Dram. Arts. Was m. Jason Robards, late Humphrey Bogart. *Autobiographies*: By Myself (1979), Now (1994).
THEATER: *B'way*: Cactus Flower, Goodbye Charlie, Applause (Tony Award), Woman of the Year (Tony Award). *Foreign*: Sweet Bird of Youth. *Tour*: Wonderful Town.
PICTURES: To Have and Have Not (debut, 1944), Two Guys From Milwaukee (cameo), Confidential Agent, The Big Sleep, Dark Passage, Key Largo, Young Man With a Horn, Bright Leaf, How to Marry a Millionaire, Woman's World, Cobweb, Blood Alley, Written on the Wind, Designing Woman, Gift of Love, Flame Over India, Shock Treatment, Sex and the Single Girl, Harper, Murder on the Orient Express, The Shootist, Health, The Fan, Appointment With Death, Mr. North, Innocent Victim, Misery, A Star for Two, All I Want for Christmas, Le Jour et La Nuit, Ready to Wear (Pret-a-Porter), The Mirror Has Two Faces (Golden Globe Award, 1996; Screen Actors Guild Award), My Fellow Americans, Day and Night, Diamonds, The Venice Project, Presence of Mind.
TELEVISION: *Movies*: Perfect Gentlemen, Dinner at Eight, A Little Piece of Sunshine (BBC), The Portrait, From the Mixed Up Files of Mrs. Basil E. Frankweiler, Too Rich: The Secret Life of Doris Duke. *Specials*: The Girls in Their Summer Dresses, Blithe Spirit, The Petrified Forest, Applause, Bacall on Bogart, A Foreign Field (BBC).

BACH, CATHERINE
Actress. r.n. Catherine Bachman. b. Warren, Ohio, March 1, 1954.
PICTURES: The Midnight Man, Thunderbolt and Lightfoot, Hustle, Cannonball Run II, Tunnels (Criminal Act), Music City Blues, Driving Force, Street Justice.
TELEVISION: *Series*: The Dukes of Hazzard (1979-85), The Dukes (cartoon, voice), African Skies. Guest on many specials. *Movies*: Matt Helm, Strange New World, Murder in Peyton Place, White Water Rebels, Masters of Menace, Rage & Honor, The Nutt House, The Dukes of Hazard Reunion.

BACHARACH, BURT
Composer, Conductor, Arranger. b. Kansas City, MO, May 12, 1928. e. McGraw U., Mannes Sch. of Music, Music Acad. of the West. Studied with composers Darius Milhaud, Henry Cowell, and Bohuslav Martinu. Has conducted for Marlene Dietrich, Vic Damone. As a performer albums include: Burt Bacharach; Futures, Man! His Songs. Book: The Bacharach-David Song Book (1978).
THEATER: Promises Promises (Tony Award, 1969).
PICTURES: Lizzie, The Sad Sack, The Blob, Country Music Holiday, Love in a Goldfish Bowl, Wives and Lovers, Who's Been Sleeping in My Bed?, Send Me No Flowers, A House Is Not a Home, What's New Pussycat?, Alfie, Made in Paris, After the Fox, Promise Her Anything, Casino Royale, The April Fools, Butch Cassidy and the Sundance Kid (*2* Acad. Awards: Best Original Score & Best Song: Raindrops Keep Fallin' on My Head; 1969), Something Big, Lost Horizon, Together?, Arthur (Acad. Award for Best Song: Arthur's Theme; 1981), Night Shift, Best Defense, Tough Guys, Baby Boom, Arthur 2 on the Rocks, Love Hurts, Grace of My Heart, Austin Powers—International Man of Mystery (actor only), Austin Powers: The Spy Who Shagged Me (actor only).
TELEVISION: *Special*: Singer Presents Burt Bacharach (Emmy Award for Best Variety Special, 1971) *Series:* Any Day Now.

BACK, LEON B.
Exhibitor. b. Philadelphia, PA, Oct. 23, 1912. e. Johns Hopkins U., B.E., 1932; U. of Baltimore, LL.B., 1933. Entered motion picture industry as mgr. for Rome Theatres, Inc., Baltimore, Md., 1934; booker, ass't buyer, 1936; ass't to gen. mgr. 1939; U.S. Navy 1944-46; v.p., gen. mgr., Rome Theatres, 1946. Allied MPTO of Md. 1952-55; nat'l dir. Allied States, 1952-55; nat'l secy. 1954. Pres. NATO of Maryland 1969-80. Pres. USO Council, Greater Baltimore 1969-75. Chmn., bd. of trustees, Employees Benefit Trust for Health & Welfare Council of Central Maryland, 1970-79.

BACON, KEVIN
Actor. b. Philadelphia, PA, July 8, 1958. m. actress Kyra Sedgwick. Studied at Manning St. Actor's Theatre. Apprentice at Circle-in-the-Square in N.Y. B'way debut in Slab Boys with Sean Penn. Narrated short film A Little Vicious.
THEATER: *B'way*: Slab Boys. *Off-B'way*: Getting Out (debut), Album, Forty Deuce (Obie Award), Poor Little Lambs, Flux, Men Without Dates, The Author's Voice, Loot, Road, Spike Heels.
PICTURES: National Lampoon's Animal House (debut, 1978), Starting Over, Hero at Large, Friday the 13th, Only When I Laugh, Forty Deuce, Diner, Footloose, Enormous Changes at the Last Minute, Quicksilver, White Water Summer (Rites of Summer), End of the Line, Planes Trains and Automobiles, She's Having a Baby, Criminal Law, The Big Picture, Tremors, Flatliners, Queens Logic, He Said/She Said, Pyrates, JFK, A Few Good Men, The Air Up There, The River Wild, Murder in the First, Apollo 13, Balto (voice), Sleepers, Picture Perfect, Telling Lies in America, Elizabeth Jane, Digging to China, Wild Things (also exec. prod.), My Dog Skip, Stir of Echoes, The Hollow Man, Novocaine, We Married Margo.
TELEVISION: *Movies*: The Gift, The Demon Murder Case, The Tender Age (The Little Sister), Lemon Sky, Losing Chase (dir. only). *Specials*: Mr. Roberts. *Series*: Search for Tomorrow, The Guiding Light. Guest: Mad About You, Frasier (voice).

BADALAMENTI, ANGELO
Composer, orchestrator. b. New York, NY, March 22, 1937.
PICTURES: Gordon's War, law and Disorder, Blue Velvet, Weeds, A Nightmare on Elm Street 3: Dream Warriors, Tough Guys Don't Dance, Wait Until Spring Bandini, Parents, National Lampoon's Christmas Vacation, Cousins, The Comfort of Strangers, Wild at Heart, Twin Peaks: Fire Walk with Me, Naked in New York, The City of Lost Children, The Blood Oranges, Lost Highway, Story of a Bad Boy, Arlington Road.
TELEVISION: *Movies/Specials:* Industrial Symphony No. 1: The Dream of the Broken Hearted, The Last Don. *Series:* Twin Peaks, On the Air, Hotel Room, Inside the Actors Studio (main theme), Cracker, Profiler (main title theme), Mulholland Drive.

BADER, DIEDRICH
Actor. b. Alexandria, VA, Dec. 24, 1968.
PICTURES: The Beverly Hillbillies, Teresa's Tattoo, Office Space.
TELEVISION: *Movies:* The Preppie Murder, The Assassination. *Series:* Danger Theatre, The Drew Carey Show, Disney's Hercules. *Guest:* 21 Jump Street, Star Trek: The Next Generation, The Fresh Prince of Bel-Air, Cheers, Quantum Leap, Frasier, Gargoyles (voice), Murphy Brown.

BADHAM, JOHN
Director. b. Luton, England, Aug. 25, 1939. Raised in Alabama. e. Yale U., B.A.; Yale Drama School, M.F.A. Sister is actress Mary Badham. Landed first job at Universal Studio mailroom; later was Universal tour guide, a casting dir. and assoc. prod. to William Sackheim. Twice nominated for Emmy Awards for TV movies. Recipient of George Pal Award.
PICTURES: The Bingo Long Traveling All-Stars and Motor Kings (debut 1976), Saturday Night Fever, Dracula (Best Horror Film award, Science Fiction/Fantasy Academy), Whose Life Is It Anyway? (San Rafael Grand Prize), Blue Thunder, War Games (Best Directing award, Science Fiction/Fantasy Academy), American Flyers, Short Circuit, Stakeout (also exec. prod.), Disorganized Crime (exec. prod. only), Bird on a Wire, The Hard Way, Point of No Return, Another Stakeout (also exec. prod.), Drop Zone (also exec. prod.), Nick of Time (also prod.), Incognito, Floating Away.
TELEVISION: *Movies*: Night Gallery (assoc. prod. only), Neon Ceiling (assoc. prod. only), The Impatient Heart, Isn't It Shocking?, The Law, The Gun, Reflections of Murder, The Godchild, The Keegans, Relentless: Mind of a Killer (co-exec. prod. only), Rebound: The Legend of Earl "The Goat" Manigault (exec. prod. only), The Jack Bull. *Series episodes*: The Senator (also assoc. prod.), Kung Fu, Night Gallery, Streets of San Francisco, The Doctors, Owen Marshall - Counsellor at Law, Sunshine, Nichols, Sarge, The Sixth Sense, Cannon.

BAILEY, JOHN
Cinematographer. b. Moberly, MO, Aug. 10, 1942. m. film editor Carol Littleton. e. U. of Santa Clara, Loyola U., U.S.C., U. of Vienna. Lecturer, American Film Institute, 1982, 1984, 1994.
PICTURES: Premonition, End of August, Legacy, The Mafu Cage (visual consult.), Boulevard Nights, Winter Kills (add. photog.), American Gigolo, Ordinary People, Honky Tonk Freeway, Continental Divide, Cat People, That Championship Season, Without a Trace, The Big Chill, Racing With the Moon, The Pope of Greenwich Village, Mishima, Silverado, Crossroads, Brighton Beach Memoirs, Light of Day, Swimming to Cambodia, Tough Guys Don't Dance (visual consult.), Vibes, The Accidental Tourist, My Blue Heaven, The Search for Signs of Intelligent Life in the Universe (also dir.), A Brief History of Time, Groundhog Day, In the Line of Fire, China Moon (dir. only), Nobody's Fool, Mariette in Ecstasy (dir. only), Extreme Measures, As Good As It Gets, Living Out Loud, Forever Mine, The Out-of-Towners.
TELEVISION: Battered, City in Fear, Always Outnumbered.

BAIO, SCOTT
Actor. b. New York, NY, Sept. 22, 1961. Started career at 9 doing commercials and voice-overs.
PICTURES: Bugsy Malone, Skatetown USA, Foxes, Zapped!, I Love New York, Detonator, Bar Hopping, Face to Face, Very Mean Men.
TELEVISION: *Movies*: The Boy Who Drank Too Much, Senior Trip, Alice in Wonderland, Perry Mason: The Case of the Fatal Fashion, Mixed Blessings. *Specials*: Luke Was There, Muggsy, Stoned, How to Be a Man, Gemini, The Truth About Alex. *Series*: Blansky's Beauties, Happy Days, Who's Watching the Kids?, We're Movin' (host), Joanie Loves Chachi, Charles in Charge (also dir.), Luke Was There, Baby Talk, Diagnosis Murder, Before They Were Stars (host). *Guest*: Hotel, The Fall Guy, Full House, Can't Hurry Love. *Director*: Lassie, Out of This World, First Time Out, Wayans Brothers, Jamie Foxx Show, Nick Freno: Licensed Teacher, Harry and the Hendersons, Kirk.

BAKER, BLANCHE
Actress. r.n. Blanche Garfein. b. New York, NY, Dec. 20, 1956. Daughter of actress Carroll Baker and dir. Jack Garfein. e. Wellesley, Coll., studied acting with Uta Hagen. Acting debut, White Marriage, Yale Repertory Co. (1978), Regional Theater. B'way debut in Lolita (1981).
PICTURES: The Seduction of Joe Tynan (debut, 1979), French Postcards, Sixteen Candles, Raw Deal, Cold Feet, Nobody's Child, Shakedown, The Handmaid's Tale, Livin' Large, Bum Rap, Dead Funny.
TELEVISION: *Movies*: Mary and Joseph, The Day the Bubble Burst, The Awakening of Candra, Nobody's Child. *Mini-Series*: Holocaust (Emmy Award, 1978). *Specials*: Romeo & Juliet. *Guest:* The Equalizer, Spenser: For Hire, Law & Order.

BAKER, CARROLL
Actress. b. Johnstown, PA, May 28, 1931. e. schools there and St. Petersburg (FL) Junior Coll. Career started as dancer in nightclubs. Actors' Studio N.Y. Made stage debut in Escapade, then acted in All Summer Long. *Autobiography*: Baby Doll.
PICTURES: Easy to Love (debut, 1953), Giant, Baby Doll, The Big Country, But Not for Me, The Miracle, Bridge to the Sun, Something Wild, How the West Was Won, The Carpetbaggers, Station Six Sahara, Cheyenne Autumn, The Greatest Story Ever Told, Sylvia, Mister Moses, Harlow, Jack of Diamonds, The Sweet Body of Deborah, Paranoia, A Quiet Place to Kill, Captain Apache, The Harem, Honeymoon, My Father's Wife, Bloodbath (The Sky Is Falling), Andy Warhol's Bad, The World is Full of Married Men, Watcher in the Woods, Star 80, The Secret Diary of Sigmund Freud, Native Son, Ironweed, Red Monarch, Kindergarten Cop, Blonde Fist, Cybereden, Undercurrent, Skeletons, Just Your Luck, The Game, Nowhere to Go.
TELEVISION: *Movies*: Hitler's SS: Portrait in Evil, On Fire, Judgement Day: The John List Story, Men Don't Tell, A Kiss to Die For, North Shore Fish, Heart Full of Rain, Big Guns Talk: The Story of the Western. *Specials*: Rain, On Fire, Sharing Time, Coward's: What Mad Pursuit. *Guest*: Tales from the Crypt, L.A. Law, Chicago Hope.

BAKER, DIANE
Actress. b. Hollywood, CA, Feb. 25, 1938. e. USC.
PICTURES: The Diary of Anne Frank (debut, 1959), The Best of Everything, Journey to the Center of the Earth, Tess of the Storm Country, The Wizard of Baghdad, Hemingway's Adventures of a Young Man, 300 Spartans, Nine Hours to Rama, Stolen Hours, The Prize, Straight Jacket, Marnie, Mirage, Sands of Beersheba, The Horse in the Grey Flannel Suit, Krakatoa — East of Java, Baker's Hawk, The Pilot, The Silence of the Lambs, The Closer, The Joy Luck Club, Twenty Bucks, Imaginary Crimes, The Net, The Cable Guy, Murder at 1600.
TELEVISION: *Movies*: Dangerous Days of Kiowa Jones, Trial Run, The D.A.: Murder One, The Old Man Who Cried Wolf, Do You Take This Stranger?, Sarge: The Badge or the Cross, Congratulations It's a Boy!, A Little Game, Killer By Night, Police Story (pilot), A Tree Grows in Brooklyn, The Dream Makers, The Last Survivors, Fugitive Family, The Haunted, Perry Mason: The Case of the Heartbroken Bride, About Sarah. *Mini-Series*: The Blue and the Gray, A Woman of Substance (also prod.). *Series*: Here We Go Again. *Guest:* Murder, She Wrote, Chicago Hope, Mission: Impossible, Bonanza, The Fugitive, Wagon Train.

BAKER, DYLAN
Actor. b. Syracuse, NY. e. Southern Methodist Univ. (BFA), Yale Sch. of Drama (MFA).
THEATER: *B'way:* Eastern Standard (Theatre World Award), La Bete (Tony nom.). *Off-B'way:* Not About Heroes (Obie Award).
PICTURES: Ishtar (debut, 1987), Planes Trains and Automobiles, The Wizard of Loneliness, The Long Walk Home, Delirious, Passed Away, Love Potion No. 9, The Last of the Mohicans, Life With Mikey, Radioland Murders, Disclosure, The Stars Fell on Henrietta, True Blue, Happiness, Celebrity, Oxygen, Simply Irresistible, Random Hearts.
TELEVISION: *Movies:* A Case of Deadly Force, The Murder of Mary Phagan, Judgment, Love Honor and Obey: The Last Mafia Marriage, Forbidden Territory: Stanley's Search for Livingstone. *Mini-Series:* Return to Lonesome Dove, From the Earth to the Moon. *Series:* Murder One, Feds. *Guest:* Spenser: For Hire, Miami Vice, Law & Order, The Cosby Mysteries, Northern Exposure.

BAKER, GEORGE
Actor. b. Varna, Bulgaria, April 1, 1931. e. Lancing College, Sussex. Stage debut Deal Repertory Theatre, 1946. AUTHOR: The Fatal Spring, Imaginary Friends, Going for Broke, The Marches of Wales, The Hopkins, Just a Hunch, Sister, Dear Sister, From Doom With Death, Mouse in the Corner, The Strawberry Tree, Talking About Mira Beau, Dead on Time, The Last Silence.
PICTURES: The Intruder (debut, 1953), The Dam Busters, The Ship That Died of Shame, Woman for Joe, The Extra Day, The Feminine Touch, A Hill in Korea, No Time for Tears, These Dangerous Years, The Moonraker, Tread Softly Stranger, Lancelot and Guinevere, Curse of the Fly, Mister Ten Per Cent, Goodbye Mr. Chips, Justine, The Executioners, On Her Majesty's Secret Service, A Warm December, The Fire Fighters, The Spy Who Loved Me, Thirty-Nine Steps, A Nightingale Sang in Berkeley Square, Hopscotch, North Sea Hijack, For Queen and Country.
TELEVISION: Fan Show, Ron Raudell's programme 1956, Guinea Pig, Death of a Salesman, The Last Troubadour, The Square Ring, Nick of the River, Mary Stuart, Probation Officers, Far Away Music, It Happened Like This, Boule de Suif, Maigret, Zero One, Rupert Henzau, Miss Memory, Any Other Business, The Navigators, Common Ground, Alice, The Queen and Jackson, The Big Man Coughed and Died, Up and Down, Call My Bluff, The Baron, St. Patrick, Love Life, Seven Deadly Virtues, The Prisoner, The Sex Games, Z Cars, Paul Temple, Candida, Fenn Street, Man Outside, The Persuaders, Main Chance, Ministry of Fear, Bowler, Voyage in the Dark, Dial M for Murder, Zodiac, The Survivors, I, Claudius, Print Out, Goodbye, Darling, Chinese Detective, Triangle, Minder, Hart to Hart, Goodbye Mr. Chips, Woman of Substance, The Bird Fancier, Robin of Sherwood, Time after Time, If Tomorrow Comes, Coast to Coast, Dead Head, The Canterville Ghost, Room at the Bottom, Ruth Rendell Mysteries (From Doon With Death; adap.), Journey's End, No Job for a Lady, The Means of Evil, Kissing the Gunner's Daughter, Little Lord Fauntleroy (mini-series), Simisola, Road Rage (also s.p.).

BAKER, JOE DON
Actor. b. Groesbeck, TX, Feb. 12, 1936. e. North Texas State Coll., B.B.A., 1958. Began career on N.Y. stage, in Marathon 33 and Blues for Mr. Charlie. L.A. stage in The Caine Mutiny Court Martial.
PICTURES: Cool Hand Luke (debut, 1967), Guns of the Magnificent Seven, Adam at Six A.M., Wild Rovers, Welcome Home Soldier Boys, Junior Bonner, Walking Tall, Charley Varrick, The Outfit, Golden Needles, Mitchell, Framed, Checkered Flag or Crash, Speedtrap, The Pack, Wacko, Joysticks, The Natural, Fletch, Getting Even, The Living Daylights, The Killing Time, Leonard Part 6, Criminal Law, The Children, Cape Fear, The Distinguished Gentleman, Reality Bites, Panther, The Underneath, Congo, The Grass Harp, Goldeneye, Mars Attacks!, Tomorrow Never Dies.
TELEVISION: *Movies*: Mongo's Back in Town, That Certain Summer, To Kill a Cop, Power, The Abduction of Kari Swenson, Edge of Darkness (BBC mini-series), Defrosting the Fridge (BBC), Citizen Cohn, Complex of Fear, Ruby Ridge: An American Tragedy, To Dance with Olivia, George Wallace, Poddle Springs, Too Rich: The Secret Life of Doris Duke. *Series*: Eischeid. *Guest*: In the Heat of the Night, Gunsmoke, Mission: Impossible, The Streets of San Francisco.

BAKER, KATHY
Actress. B. Midland, TX, June 8, 1950. Raised in Albuquerque, NM. e. UC/Berkeley. Stage debut in San Francisco premiere of Fool for Love, won Obie and Theatre World Awards for New York debut in same. Also appeared in Desire Under the Elms, Aunt Dan and Lemon.
PICTURES: The Right Stuff (debut, 1983), Street Smart (Natl. Society of Film Critics Award), Permanent Record, A Killing Affair, Clean and Sober, Jacknife, Dad, Mr. Frost, Edward Scissorhands, Article 99, Jennifer Eight, Mad Dog and Glory, To Gillian on Her 37th Birthday, Inventing the Abbotts, The Cider House Rules.
TELEVISION: *Movies*: Nobody's Child, The Image, One Special Victory, Lush Life, Not In This Town, Weapons of Mass Destruction, Oklahoma City: A Survivor's Story. *Series*: Picket Fences (2 Emmy Awards: 1993, 1995). *Guest*: Amazing Stories, Gun, Ally McBeal, The Practice.

BAKER, RICK
Makeup Artist, Performer. b. Binghamton, NY, Dec. 8, 1950. Started as assist. to makeup artist Dick Smith before creating his own designs in 1972. Frequent film appearances in makeup, usually as gorillas. Worked on Michael Jackson's video Thriller.
PICTURES: *Actor*: The Thing With Two Heads, King Kong, The Kentucky Fried Movie, The Incredible Shrinking Woman, Into the Night. *Makeup Design*: Shlock, Zebra Force, It's Alive, The Incredible Melting Man, Star Wars (2nd unit, also actor), It Lives Again, The Howling (consultant), Funhouse, An American Werewolf in London (Acad. Award, 1981), Videodrome, Greystoke: The Legend of Tarzan Lord of the Apes (also costume design; Acad. Award nom.), Ratboy, Harry and the Hendersons (Acad. Award, 1987), Coming to America (Acad. Award nom.), Gorillas in the Mist (also assoc. prod.), Missing Link, Wolf, Ed Wood (Acad, Award, 1994), Batman and Robin, Mighty Joe Young, Batman Forever (also designed monster bat), Escape From L.A. The Nutty Professor (Acad. Award, 1996), Men in Black (Acad. Award, Best Makeup, 1997), A Thousand Acres, The Devil's Advocate, Critical Care, Psycho, Mighty Joe Young, Life. *Other*: Tanya's Island (beast design), Starman (transformation scenes), Cocoon (consultant), My Science Project (Tyrannosaurus Rex sequences consultant), Max My Love (chimpanzee consultant), Gremlins 2: The New Batch (co-prod., f/x supervisor), Baby's Day Out (baby f/x), Just Cause (special bodies), Little Panda (panda suits).
TELEVISION: *Movies*: The Autobiography of Miss Jane Pittman (Emmy Award), An American Christmas Carol, Something Is Out There. *Makeup Design*: *Series*: Werewolf, Beauty and the Beast, Harry and the Hendersons.

BAKER, ROY
Producer, Director. b. London, England. e. Lycaee Corneille, Rouen; City of London School. Ass't dir. with Gainsborough 1934-40; served in Army 1940-46.
PICTURES: Operation Disaster, Don't Bother to Knock, Inferno, One That Got Away, A Night to Remember, The Singer Not the Song (also prod.), Flame in the Streets (also prod.), Quartermass and the Pit, The Anniversary, Vampire Lovers, Dr. Jekyll and Mr. Hyde, Asylum (Paris Grand Prize), Seven Golden Vampires, The Monster Club.
TELEVISION: The Human Jungle, The Saint, Gideon's Way, The Baron, The Avengers, The Champions, Department S., The Persuaders, Danger UXB, The Flame Trees of Thika (mini-series), Q.E.D., Sherlock Holmes and the Masks of Death, Fairly Secret Army, Minder: An Officer and a Car Salesman.

BAKER, DR. WILLIAM F.
Executive. b. 1944. e. Case Western Reserve U., B.A., M.A., Ph.D. Began broadcasting career in Cleveland while still a student. Joined Scripps-Howard Broadcasting, 1971. Joined Group W as v.p. and general mgr., WJZ-TV, 1978; served as pres. and CEO, Group W Productions; pres. of Group W. Television, 1979; chmn., Group W Satellite Communications, 1981. Carried Explorers Club flag to top of world, becoming one of few in history to visit both North and South Poles, 1983. Appointed pres. and CEO, WNET/Thirteen, NY PBS station, 1987. Pres., NY Chapter, Natl. Acad. Television Arts & Sciences. Recipient of 4 Emmy Awards, 2 Columbia Dupont Journalism Awards. Author of, Down the Tube, 1998.

BAKER, WILLIAM M.
Executive. b. Newark, NJ, Dec. 26, 1939. e. University of Virginia 1961. Joined FBI in 1965. From 1987 to 1989, took a haitus from the FBI to serve as dir. of Public Affairs for the CIA. Retired from position as asst. dir., Criminal Investigative Division of FBI in 1991. Currently pres. and COO Motion Picture Assoc. and exec. v.p., Motion Picture Assoc. of America.

BAKSHI, RALPH
Animator, Writer, Director. b. Haifa, Israel, Oct. 29, 1938. Began career at Terrytoons at age 18 as cell painter and animator, then creative dir. 1965, headed Paramount Cartoons, 1967. Pres., Bakshi Prods. Inc., 1973-.
PICTURES: *Dir./S.P./Writer*: Fritz the Cat, Heavy Traffic, Coonskin. *Also Prod/Co-prod.*: Wizards, The Lord of the Rings, American Pop, Hey Good Lookin', Fire and Ice, Cool World.
TELEVISION: Mighty Mouse: The New Adventures (dir., prod.) This Ain't Bebop (Amer. Playhouse, dir., s.p.), The Cool and the Crazy (dir., writer), Spider-Man (also prod.), Spicy City (also exec. prod.).

BAKULA, SCOTT
Actor. b. St. Louis, MO, Oct. 9, 1955. e. Kansas Univ.
THEATER: *NY*: Marilyn: An American Fable, Three Guys Naked from the Waist Down, Romance/Romance (Tony nom.). *LA*: Nite Club Confidential.
PICTURES: Sibling Rivalry, Necessary Roughness, Color of Night, A Passion to Kill, My Family/Mi Familia, Lord of Illusions, Cats Don't Dance (voice), Major League: Back to the Minors, Luminarias, American Beauty, The Trial of Old Drum, Above Suspicion.
TELEVISION: *Movies*: The Last Fling, An Eye for an Eye, In the Shadow of a Killer, Mercy Mission: The Rescue of Flight 771, Nowhere to Hide, The Invaders, The Bachelor's Baby (also exec. prod.), Mean Streak, Netforce, In the Name of the People, Papa's Angels. *Series*: Gung Ho, Eisenhower & Lutz, Quantum Leap (Emmy noms., Golden Globe Award, also dir.), Murphy Brown, Mr. & Mrs. Smith, It's A Girl Thing. *Guest:* Matlock, Designing Women, My Sister Sam, .

BALABAN, BOB
Actor, Director. b. Chicago, IL, Aug. 16, 1945. Began studying with Second City troupe while still in high school. Attended Colgate U. and NYU while appearing on Broadway in Plaza Suite.
THEATER: You're a Good Man Charlie Brown, The Inspector General, Who Wants to Be the Lone Ranger?, The Basic Training of Pavlo Hummel, The Children, The White House Murder Case, Some of My Best Friends, The Three Sisters, The Boys Next Door, Speed-the-Plow, Some Americans Abroad.
PICTURES: *Actor*: Midnight Cowboy (debut, 1969), Me Natalie, The Strawberry Statement, Catch-22, Making It, Bank Shot, Report to the Commissioner, Close Encounters of the Third Kind, Girlfriends, Altered States, Prince of the City, Absence of Malice, Whose Life Is It Anyway?, 2010, In Our Hands (doc.), End of the Line, Dead-Bang, Alice, Little Man Tate, Bob Roberts, For Love or Money, Greedy, Pie in the Sky, Deconstructing Harry, Waiting For Guffman, Conversation with the Beast, The Definite Maybe (also prod.), Clockwatchers, Natural Selection, The Cradle Will Rock, Jakob the Liar. *Director*: Parents, My Boyfriend's Back, The Last Good Time (also prod, co-s.p.).
TELEVISION: *Movies*: Marriage: Year One, The Face of Fear, Unnatural Pursuits, The Late Shift, Giving Up the Ghost, Swing Vote. *Series*: Miami Vice, Seinfeld. *Director*: Tales From the Darkside, Amazing Stories, Penn & Teller's Invisible Thread, Eerie Indiana, Subway Stories: Tales from the Underground, Legend.

BALDWIN, ADAM
Actor. b. Chicago, IL, Feb. 27, 1962. While in high school in Winnetka, was chosen by dir. Tony Bill for role in My Bodyguard. Made stage debut in Album, Chicago.
PICTURES: My Bodyguard (debut, 1980), Ordinary People, D.C. Cab, Reckless, Hadley's Rebellion, Bad Guys, 3:15, Full Metal Jacket, The Chocolate War, Cohen and Tate, Next of Kin, Predator 2, Guilty By Suspicion, Radio Flyer, Where the Day Takes You, Deadbolt, Bitter Harvest, Eight Hundred Leagues Down the Amazon, Wyatt Earp, How to Make an American Quilt, Independence Day, Lover's Knot, Starquest II, The Patriot, The Right Temptaions, Pursiot of Happiness, Jackpot.
TELEVISION: *Movies*: Off Sides, Poison Ivy, Welcome Home Bobby, Murder in High Places, Cruel Doubt, Cold Sweat, Sawbones, Smoke Jumpers, The Cape, Indiscreet, From the Earth to the Moon, Gargantua. *Special*: The Last Shot. *Series:* The Cape. *Guest:* The Outer Limits, The Visitor, VR5.

BALDWIN, ALEC
Actor. r.n. Alexander Rae Baldwin III. b. Massapequa, NY, April 3, 1958. e. George Washington U., NYU. m. actress Kim Basinger. Brother of actors Stephen, William and Daniel Baldwin. Trained at Lee Strasberg Theatre Inst. and with Mira Rostova, Elaine Aiken. Started career in daytime TV on serial The Doctors. Member, The Creative Coalition.
THEATER: A Midsummer Night's Dream, The Wager, Summertree, A Life in the Theatre (Hartman), Study in Scarlet (Williamstown). *NY*: Loot (B'way debut; Theatre World Award, 1986), Serious Money, Prelude to a Kiss, A Streetcar Named Desire.
PICTURES: Forever Lulu (debut, 1987), She's Having a Baby, Beetlejuice, Married to the Mob, Working Girl, Talk Radio, Great Balls of Fire!, The Hunt for Red October, Miami Blues, Alice, The Marrying Man, Prelude to a Kiss, Glengarry Glen Ross, Malice, The Getaway, The Shadow, Heaven's Prisoners (also exec. prod.), The Juror, Looking For Richard, Ghosts of Mississippi, The Edge, Mercury Rising, Thick as Thieves, Notting Hill, The Confession (also prod.), Outside Providence, Thomas and the Magic Railroad, State and Main, The Acting Class, Pearl Harbor, Like Cats & Dogs, Final Fantasy (voice).
TELEVISION: *Movies*: Sweet Revenge, Love on the Run, Dress Gray, The Alamo: 13 Days to Glory, Nuremberg. *Series*: The Doctors (1980-2), Cutter to Houston, Knots Landing. *Guest*: Hotel, Saturday Night Live, The Simpsons.

BALDWIN, DANIEL
Actor. b. Long Island, NY, Oct. 5, 1960. e. Nassau Comm. Col., Ball St. Univ. Brother of actors Alec, William and Stephen Baldwin.
PICTURES: Born on the Fourth of July, Harley Davidson and the Marlboro Man, Knight Moves, Car 54 Where Are You?, Bodily Harm, Yesterday's Target, Trees Lounge, Lone Justice, Mullholland Drive, The Invader, The Treat, Phoenix, The Pandora Project, On the Border, Love Kills, John Carpenter's Vampires, Water Damage, Net Worth, In Pursuit, Fall, Silver Man.
TELEVISION: *Movies:* Too Good to Be True, L.A. Takedown, The Heroes of Desert Storm, Ned Blessing: The True Story of My Life, Attack of the 50 Foot Woman, Family of Cops, Twisted Desire, Killing Moon. *Series:* Sydney, Homicide: Life on the Street. *Specials:* Curse of the Corn People. *Guest:* Family Ties, Charles in Charge, The Larry Sanders Show, Dead Man's Gun.

BALDWIN, STEPHEN
Actor. b. Long Island, NY, 1966. Brother of actors Alec, William and Daniel Baldwin. Stage debut in Off-B'way prod., Out of America.
PICTURES: The Beast, Born on the Fourth of July, Last Exit to Brooklyn, Crossing the Bridge, Bitter Harvest, Posse, New Eden, 8 Seconds, Threesome, A Simple Twist of Fate, Mrs. Parker and the Vicious Circle, Fall Time, The Usual Suspects, Under the Hula Moon, Bio-Dome, Fled, Sub Down, Scar City, One Tough Cop, Half Baked, The Sex Monster, The Flintstones in Viva Rock Vegas, Friends & Lovers, The Sex Monster, Mercy, Cutaway, Exchange, Table One, Wild Awake. TELEVISION: *Movies*: Jury Duty: The Comedy, Dead Weekend, Absence of the Good. *Specials*: The Lawrenceville Stories, In a New Light: Sex Unplugged (co-host). *Series*: The Young Riders. *Guest*: Family Ties, Kate and Allie, China Beach.

BALDWIN, WILLIAM
Actor. b. Massapequa, NY, Feb. 21, 1963. e. SUNY/Binghamton. Degree in political science; worked in Washington on staff of rep. Thomas J. Downey. Brother of actors Alec, Stephen and Daniel Baldwin. With Ford Model agency, appearing in tv ads while studying acting. Member, The Creative Coalition.
PICTURES: Born on the Fourth of July (debut, 1989), Internal Affairs, Flatliners, Backdraft, Three of Hearts, Sliver, A Pyromaniac's Love Story, Fair Game, Curdled, Virus, Primary Suspect, Relative Values, One Eyed King, Double Bang.
TELEVISION: *Movie*: The Preppie Murder.

BALE, CHRISTIAN
Actor. b. Pembrokeshire, Wales, Jan. 30, 1974. Acting debut at age 9 in U.S. Pac-Man commercial. London stage debut following year in The Nerd.
PICTURES: Empire of the Sun, Land of Faraway, Henry V, Newsies, Swing Kids, Prince of Jutland, Little Women, Pocahontas (voice), The Secret Agent, The Portrait of a Lady, Metroland, Velvet Goldmine, All the Little Animals, A Midsummer Night's Dream, American Psycho, Shaft, Reign of Fire, Librium, Captain Corelli's Mandolin.
TELEVISION: *Specials/Movies*: Heart of the Country (BBC), Anastasia: The Mystery of Anna, Treasure Island (released theatrically in U.K.), A Murder of Quality.

BALK, FAIRUZA
Actress. b. Point Reyes, CA, May 21, 1974.
PICTURES: Return to Oz, Discovery, The Outside Chance of Maximilian Glick, Valmont, Gas Food Lodging, Tollbooth, Imaginary Crimes, Things to Do in Denver When You're Dead, The Craft, The Island of Dr. Moreau, The Maker, American Perfekt, What Is It? (voice), American History X, The Waterboy, There's No Fish Food In Heaven, Red Letters, Great Sex, Deuces Wild.
TELEVISION: *Movies/Specials:* Best Christmas Pageant Ever, Deceptions, The Worst Witch, Poor Little Rich Girl: The Barbara Hutton Story, Deadly Intentions...Again?, Shame, The Danger of Love, Shadow of a Doubt, The Witching Hour.

BALL, ALAN
Writer, Producer. b. Atlanta,GA, 1957.e. Florida State University School of Theatre.
PICTURES: American Beauty (s.p.).
TELEVISION: *Series:* Grace Under Fire (writer), Cybill (exec. prod.), Oh Grow Up (prod. only), Six Feet Under (dir. & prod.)

BALLARD, CARROLL
Director. b. Los Angeles, Oct. 14, 1937. e. UCLA. Prod. of 1967 film Harvest. Camera operator on Star Wars.
PICTURES: The Black Stallion (debut, 1979), Never Cry Wolf, Nutcracker: The Motion Picture, Wind, Fly Away Home.

BALLARD, KAYE
Actress. r.n. Catherine Gloria Balotta. b. Cleveland, OH, Nov. 20, 1926. Began career as impressionist-singer-actress, toured vaudeville. 17 recordings incl.: The Fanny Brice Story, Peanuts, Oklahoma (w/ Nelson Eddy), Unsung Sondheim, Then & Again. Appeared in short film Walking to Waldheim.
THEATER: Three to Make Ready, Carnival, Molly, The Pirates of Penzance, Hey Ma It's Me, Working 42nd Street at Last, Chicago, Touch & Go (London), Nymph Errant (concert version), Hello Dolly, She Stoops to Conquer, Funny Girl, High Spirits, Crazy Words Crazy Times: The Cole Porter-Irving Berlin Revue, Beloved Enemies.
PICTURES: The Girl Most Likely, A House is Not a Home, Which Way to the Front?, The Ritz, Freaky Friday, Falling in Love Again, Pandemonium, Tiger Warsaw, Modern Love, Eternity, Ava's Magical Adventure, Anna Petrovic: You Rock!, Fortune Hunters, Baby Geniuses .
TELEVISION: *Movies*: The Dream Merchants, Alice in Wonderland, Due South. *Series*: Henry Morgan's Great Talent Hunt, The Perry Como Show, The Mothers-in-Law, The Doris Day Show, The Steve Allen Comedy Hour, What a Dummy. *Pilot*: Makin' Out. Guest appearances incl. over 100 spots on The Tonight Show.

BALLHAUS, MICHAEL
Cinematographer. b. Berlin, Germany, Aug. 5, 1935.
PICTURES: Deine Zartlichkeiten, Two of Us, Whity, Beware of a Holy Whore, Tschetan, The Indian Boy, The Bitter Tears of Petra von Kant, Fox and His Friends, Mother Kusters Goes to Heaven, Summer Guests, Satan's Brew, I Only Want You To Love Me, Adolf and Marlene, Chinese Roulette, Bolweiser (The Stationmaster's Wife), Willie and the Chinese Cat, Women in New York, Despair, The Marriage of Maria Braun, Germany in Autumn, German Spring, The Uprising, Big and Little, Malou, Looping, Baby It's You, Friends and Husbands, Dear Mr. Wonderful, Magic Mountain, Edith's Diary, Aus der Familie der Panzereschen, The Autograph, Heartbreakers, Old Enough, Reckless, After Hours, Under the Cherry Moon, The Color of Money, The Glass Menagerie, Broadcast News, The House on Carroll Street,The Last Temptation of Christ, Working Girl, Dirty Rotten Scoundrels, The Fabulous Baker Boys, GoodFellas, Postcards from the Edge, Guilty by Suspicion, What About Bob?, The Mambo Kings, Bram Stoker's Dracula, The Age of Innocence, Quiz Show, Outbreak, Sleepers, Air Force One, Primary Colors, Wild, Wild West, The Thirteenth Floor (exec. prod. only), What Planet Are You From?, The Legend of Bagger Vance, Gone Underground, The Gangs of New York.

BANCROFT, ANNE
Actress. r.n. Anna Maria Italiano. b. New York, NY, Sept. 17, 1931. m. dir.-comedian Mel Brooks. e. American Acad. of Dramatic Arts. Acting debut on TV, Studio One as Anne Marno in Torrents of Spring.
THEATER: Two For the Seesaw (Tony Award, Theatre World Award: 1958), The Miracle Worker (Tony Award, 1960), Mother Courage, The Devils, A Cry of Players, Golda, Duet For One, Mystery of the Rose Bouquet, The Little Foxes.
PICTURES: Don't Bother to Knock (debut, 1952), Tonight We Sing, Treasure of the Golden Condor, The Kid from Left Field, Gorilla at Large, Demetrius and the Gladiators, The Raid, New York Confidential, Life in the Balance, The Naked Street, The Last Frontier, Walk the Proud Land, Nightfall, The Restless Breed, The Girl in Black Stockings, The Miracle Worker (Acad. Award for Best Actress, 1962), The Pumpkin Eater, The Slender Thread, Seven Women, The Graduate, Young Winston, The Prisoner of Second Avenue, The Hindenburg, Lipstick, Silent Movie, The Turning Point, Fatso (also dir., s.p.), The Elephant Man, To Be or Not to Be, Garbo Talks, Agnes of God, 'night Mother, 84 Charing Cross Road, Torch Song Trilogy, Bert Rigby You're a Fool, Honeymoon in Vegas, Love Potion No. 9, Point of No Return, Malice, Mr. Jones, How to Make an American Quilt, Home for the Holidays, Dracula–Dead & Loving It, The Sunchaser, Great Expectations, Critical Care, G.I. Jane, Antz (voice), Mark Twain's America in 3D (voice), Keeping the Faith, Up in the Villa, Breakers.
TELEVISION: *Movies*: Broadway Bound, Oldest Living Confederate Widow Tells All, Homecoming, Deep in My Heart. *Mini-Series*: Jesus of Nazareth, Marco Polo. *Specials*: I'm Getting Married, Annie and the Hoods, Annie: The Women in the Life of a Man (also dir.; Emmy Award for Best Variety Special, 1970), Mrs. Cage, The Mother, A Salute to Dustin Hoffman. *Guest:* The Simpsons.

BAND, ALBERT
Producer, Director. b. Paris, France, May 7, 1924. e. Lyceum Louis le Grand, won French-English Lit. Prize 1938. Entered m.p. industry as cutter Pathe Lab.; prod. ass't to John Huston at MGM. First screen credit adaptation Red Badge of Courage novel; first direction, The Young Guns. Formed Maxim Prods., Inc., Sept. 1956. Recently formed Albert Band Intl. Prods., Inc.
PICTURES: The Young Guns, I Bury the Living, Face of Fire, The Avenger, Grand Canyon Massacre, The Tramplers, The Hellbenders (prod. only), A Minute to Pray a Second to Die, Little Cigars, Mansion of the Doomed, Dracula's Dog, She Came to the Valley, Metalstorm: The Destruction of Jared-Syn, Swordkill, Buy and Cell (exec. prod. only), Troll, Terrorvision, Ghoulies II, Robot Jox, Trancers III; Honey, I Blew Up the Kid; Pet Shop, Oblivion, Oblivion 2: Backlash, Zarkorr! The Invader, Prehysteria, Prehysteria 2.

BAND, CHARLES
Producer, Director. b. Los Angeles, CA, Dec. 27, 1951. e. Overseas Sch. of Rome. Son of Albert Band. Formed Media Home Ent., 1978; formed Empire Ent., 1983; formed Full Moon Ent., 1988; formed Moonbeam Productions, 1993.
PICTURES: *Prod.*: Mansion of the Doomed, Cinderella, End of the World, Laserblast, Fairytales, Swordkill, Dungeonmaster, Puppet Master 4, Eliminators. *Dir./Prod.*: Crash, Parasite, Metalstorm, Trancers, Pulsepounders, Meridian, Crash & Burn, Trancers II, Dr. Mordrid, Dollman vs. Demonic Toys, Hideous, The Creeps. *Exec. Prod.*: Tourist Trap, Day Time Ended, Ghoulies, Re-Animator, Zone Troopers, Troll, Terrorvision, Crawlspace, Dolls, From Beyond, The Caller, Spellcaster, Cellar Dweller, Ghoulies II, Enemy Territory, Deadly Weapon, Robot Jox, Prison, Buy & Cell, Ghost Town, Catacombs, Arena, Puppet Master, Shadowzone, Puppet Master II, The Pit and the Pendulum, Subspecies, Puppet Master III, Arcade, Dollman, Netherworld, Bad Channels, Trancers III, Shrunken Heads, Oblivion, Seed People, Bad Channels, Robot Wars, Subspecies II, Mandroid, Invisible, Prehysteria, Remote, Dragonworld, Beanstalk, Pet Shop, Prehysteria II, Curse IV: The Ultimate Sacrifice, Bloodstone: Subspecies III, Puppet Master 5, Lurking Fear, Trancers 5, Castle Freak, Oblivion 2: Backlash, Magic in the Mirror, Kraa! The Sea Monster, Curse of the Puppet Master, Subspecies 4: Bloodstorm.

BANDERAS, ANTONIO
Actor. r.n. Jose Antonio Dominguez Banderas. b. Malaga, Spain, Aug. 10, 1960. e. School of Dramatic Art, Malaga. Moved to Madrid in 1981 where he made his stage debut in Los Tarantos. Other theatre incl.: The City and the Dogs, Daughter of the Air, The Tragedy of Edward II of England.
PICTURES: Labyrinth of Passion (debut, 1982), Pesantas Positzas, Y Del Seguro... Libranos Senor!, Pestanas Positzas, El Senor Galindez, El Caso Almeria, Los Zancos, Casa Cerrado, La Corte de Faraon, Requiem por un Campesino Espanol, 27 Horas, Puzzle, Matador, Asi Como Habian Sido, Law of Desire, The Pleasure of Killing, Baton Rouge, Bajarse Al Moro, Women on the Verge of a Nervous Breakdown, Si Te Dicen Que Cai, Tie Me Up! Tie Me Down!, Contra el Viento, La Blanca Paloma, Truth or Dare, The Mambo Kings, Philadelphia, Dispara, Of Love and Shadows, The House of the Spirits, Interview With the Vampire, Miami Rhapsody, Desperado, Four Rooms, Never Talk to Strangers, Two Much, Assassins, Evita, The Mask of Zorro, White River Kid (also prod.), The Thirteenth Warrior, Play it to the Bone, Original Sin, The Body, Spy Kids, Frida Kahlo. *Director:* Crazy in Alabama.
TELEVISION: La llave de Hierro, Fragmentos de Interior, La Mujer de Tu Vida.

BANDY, MARY LEA
Director, Dept. of Film, Museum of Modern Art. b. Evanston, IL, June 16, 1943. e. Stanford U., B.A., 1965. Asst. editor, Harry Abrams and Museum of Modern Art dir., 1980-93; chief Curator 1993-. Dept. of Film, Museum of Modern Art Editor of MOMA film publications incl.: Rediscovering French Film (1983). Member: Advisory Bd., AFI's National Center for Preservation of Film and Video; Film Advisory Comm., American Federation of Arts; Advisory Comm. on Film, Japan Society; Advisory Comm., NY State Motion Picture and Television. Co-pres., National Alliance of Media Arts Center, 1986-88. Bd. mem.: Intl. Film Seminars; MacDowell Colony; Natl. Film Preservation Bd.; Library of Congress; Advisory Board, Film Foundation; Bd. of Directors., Third World Newsreel.

BANERJEE, VICTOR
Actor. b. Calcutta, India, Oct. 15, 1946. Was instrumental in forming the first Screen Extras Union in India, presently founding secretary. Won int'l recognition for A Passage to India. On stage in: Pirates of Penzance, An August Requiem (dir.), Desert Song, Godspell.
PICTURES: The Chess Players (debut), Hullabaloo, Madhurban, Tanaya, Pratidan, Prarthana, Dui Prithri, Kalyug, Arohan, Jaipur Junction (German), A Passage to India, Foreign Body, The Home and the World, Hard to Be a God, Bitter Moon, Mahaprithivi.
TELEVISION: *Movie*: Dadah Is Death.

BANNEN, IAN
Actor. b. Airdrie, Scotland, June 29, 1928. Early career Shakespeare Memorial Theatre (now RSC), Stratford-on-Avon.
THEATER: A View From the Bridge, The Iceman Cometh, Long Days Journey Into Night, Sergeant Musgrave's Dance. Royal Shakespeare Thea. Co. 1961-62. Toys in the Attic, Hamlet, As You Like It (with Vanessa Redgrave), Romeo and Juliet, Othello, The Blood Knot, Devil's Disciple, The Iceman Cometh, Hedda Gabler, Translations (Drama Critics Award, 1981); Riverside Mermaid Theatres, 1983; Moon for the Misbegotten (London, Boston, Broadway), All My Sons.

PICTURES: Private's Progress (debut, 1956), The Third Key (The Long Arm), Battle Hell, Miracle in Soho, The Birthday Present, Behind the Mask, A Tale of Two Cities, She Didn't Say No, The French Mistress, Carlton-Browne of the F.O. (Man in Cocked Hat), On Friday at 11, A French Mistress, The Risk (Suspect), Macbeth, Station Six Sahara, Psyche 59, Mister Moses, Rotten to the Core, The Hill, The Flight of the Phoenix (Acad. Award nom.), Penelope, Sailor From Gibraltar, Lock Up Your Daughters!, Too Late the Hero, The Deserter, Fright, Doomwatch, The Offence (BAFTA nom.), The Macintosh Man, The Driver's Seat, The Voyage, Bite the Bullet, From Beyond the Grave, Sweeney!, Inglorious Bastards, Ring of Darkness, The Watcher in the Woods, Eye of the Needle, Night Crossing, Gandhi, The Prodigal, Gorky Park, Defense of the Realm, Lamb, Hope and Glory (BAFTA nom.), The Courier, The Match, Ghost Dad, Crossing the Line, George's Island, The Gamble, Damage, A Pin for the Butterfly, Braveheart, Dead Sea Reels, Something to Believe In, Waking Ned Devine, To Walk with Lions, Best.
TELEVISION: Johnny Belinda, Jane Eyre, Jesus of Nazareth, Tinker Tailor Soldier Spy, Dr. Jekyll and Mr. Hyde, Fifteen Streets, Murder in Eden, Ashenden, Uncle Vanya, The Sound and the Silence, The Treaty, Doctor Finlay, The Politician's Wife, Original Sin.

BANNER, BOB
Producer, Director. b. Ennis, TX, Aug. 15, 1921. e. Southern Methodist U., B.A., 1939-43; Northwestern U., M.A., 1946-48. U.S. Naval Reserve 1943-46. Faculty, Northwestern U., 1948-50. Staff dir., NBC-TV in Chicago, 1949-50. Pres., Bob Banner Assocs. Visiting Prof.: Southern Methodist U.
TELEVISION: *Movies*: Mongo's Back in Town, The Last Survivors, Journey From Darkness, My Sweet Charlie, Bud and Lou, Yes Virginia There is a Santa Claus, Crash Landing, With Murder in Mind, The Sea Wolf, Angel Flight Down. *Specials*: Garroway at Large (dir.), Fred Waring Show (prod., dir.), Omnibus (dir.), Nothing But the Best (prod. dir.), Dave Garroway Show (prod. dir), Dinah Shore Show, Garry Moore Show (exec. prod.), Candid Camera TV Show (exec. prod.), Carnegie Hall Salutes Jack Benny (exec. prod.), Julie & Carol at Carnegie Hall, Carol & Co., Jimmy Dean Show, Calamity Jane, Once Upon a Mattress, The Entertainers, Kraft Summer Music Hall, Carol & Co., Ice Follies, Carol Burnett Show, Peggy Fleming at Madison Square Garden, John Davidson at Notre Dame, Here's Peggy Fleming, Peggy Fleming at Sun Valley, The American West of John Ford, Love! Love! Love!—Hallmark Hall of Fame, To Europe with Love, Peggy Fleming Visits the Soviet Union, Perry Como's Lake Tahoe Holiday, Perry Como's Christmas In Mexico, Perry Como's Hawaiian Holiday, Perry Como's Spring In New Orleans, Don Ho Show, Perry Como Las Vegas Style, Perry Como's Christmas in Austria, All-Star Anything Goes, Peggy Fleming and Holiday on Ice at Madison Square Garden, Julie Andrews, One Step Into Spring, Leapin' Lizards, It's Liberace, Perry Como's Easter By The Sea, Ford Motor Company's 75th Anniversary; Gift of Music, specials starring Bob Hope, Julie Andrews, Andy Williams, Los Angeles Music Center 25th Anniversay, Amazing Music Series, Happy Birthday George Gershwin. *Series*: Almost Anything Goes, Solid Gold, Star Search, It's Showtime at the Apollo, Uptown Comedy Club.

BAR, JACQUES JEAN LOUIS
Executive, Producer, Exhibitor. b. Chateauroux, France, Sept. 12, 1921. e. Lycees Lakanal and Saint Louis, France. Formed Citae-Films S.A., 1947; CIPRA in assoc. with MGM, 1961; S.C.B., Bourges, 8 cinemas; S.C.M., Le Mans, 9 cinemas. Hollywood films incl.: Bridge to the Sun, Once A Thief, Guns for San Sebastian. Prod. 57 films in France, Spain, Italy, Switzerland, Japan and Brazil 1948-89.
PICTURES: Where the Hot Wind Blows, Bridge to the Sun, Rififi in Tokyo, A Very Private Affair, Swordsmen of Siena, Monkey in Winter, The Turfist, Any Number Can Win, The Day and the Hour, Joy House, Guns for San Sebastian, Last Known Address, The Homecoming, Dancing Machine, The Candidate, Once a Thief, My Father the Hero.

BARANSKI, CHRISTINE
Actress. b. Buffalo, NY, May 2, 1952. e. Juilliard Sch. of Music & Dramatic Arts.
THEATER: *NY*: Private Lives, One Crack Out, Says I Says He, Shadow of a Gunman, Hide and Seek (B'way debhut, 1980), Company, Coming Attractions, Operation Midnight Climax, A Midsummer Night's Dream (Obie Award, 1982), Sally and Marsha, The Real Thing (Tony Award, 1984), Hurlyburly, It's Only a Play, The House of Blue Leaves, Rumors (Tony Award, 1989), Elliot Loves, Nick and Nora, Lips Together Teeth Apart, The Loman Family Picnic.
PICTURES: Soup for One (debut, 1982), Lovesick, Crackers, 9-1/2 Weeks, Legal Eagles, The Pick-Up Artist, Reversal of Fortune, The Night We Never Met, Life With Mikey, Addams Family Values, New Jersey Drive, The Ref, Jeffrey, The Birdcage, The Odd Couple II, Bulworth, Cruel Intentions, Bowfinger.
TELEVISION: *Movie*: Playing for Time, To Dance With the White Dog. *Special*: The Addams Chronicles. *Series*: Cybill (Emmy Award, 1995), Welcome to New York. Guest: Law & Order, Frasier, 3rd Rock from the Sun.

BARBEAU, ADRIENNE
Actress. b. Sacramento, CA, June 11, 1947. e. Foothill Col.
THEATER: *B'way*: Fiddler on the Roof, Grease (Tony nom., Theatre World Award). *L.A.*: Women Behind Bars, Strange Snow, Pump Boys & Dinettes, Drop Dead. Canadian Premiere: Lost in Yonkers. Regional: Love Letters, Best Little Whorehouse in Texas.
PICTURES: The Fog, Cannonball Run, Escape From New York, Swamp Thing, Creepshow, The Next One, Back to School, Open House, Two Evil Eyes, Cannibal Women & the Avocado Jungle of Death, Father Hood, Bimbo Movie Bash.
TELEVISION: *Movies*: The Great Houdinis, Having Babies, Red Alert, Return to Fantasy Island, Crash, Someone's Watching Me!, The Darker Side of Terror, The Top of the Hill, Valentine Magic on Love Island, Tourist, Charlie and the Great Balloon Chase, Seduced, Bridge Across Time, Blood River, Double Crossed, The Burden of Proof, The Parsley Garden, Jailbreakers, Bram Stoker's Burial of the Rats, A Champion's Fight, Scooby Doo on Zombie Island (voice). *Series*: Maude, Batman (voice). *Guest*: Quincy, 8 Is Enough, Tony Orlando and Dawn, The David Frost Special, Bobby Vinton Show, FBI, Head of the Class, Love Boat, Hotel, Twlight Zone, Murder She Wrote, Dream On, Daddy Dearest, The Carlin Show, Babylon 5, The Drew Carey Show, Love Boat: The Next Wave, Star Trek: Deep Space Nine.

BARBER, FRANCES
Actress. b. Wolverhampton, England, May 13, 1957. e. Bangor U.; grad. studies in theatre, Cardiff U. Stage experience with fringe theaters including improvisational troupe Hull Truck Theatre Company, Glasgow Citizens and Tricycle Theatre (Killburn) before joining Royal Shakespeare Co. (Camille, Hamlet).
PICTURES: The Missionary (debut, 1982), A Zed and Two Noughts, White City, Castaway, Prick Up Your Ears, Sammy and Rosie Get Laid, We Think the World of You, The Grasscutter, Separate Bedrooms, Young Soul Rebels, Secret Friends; Soft Top, Hard Shoulder; Germaine and Benjamin, Giorgino, Tea, Photographing Fairies, Still Crazy.
TELEVISION: Clem, Jackie's Story, Home Sweet Home, Flame to the Phoenix, Reilly, Ace of Spies, Those Glory Glory Days; Hard Feelings, Behaving Badly, The Nightmare Years, The Leaving of Liverpool, Three Steps to Heaven, A Royal Scandal, The Ice House. *Mini-Series:* Rhodes, Real Women, Plastic Man.

BARBER, GARY
Executive Producer. COO, Morgan Creek Prod.; pres. Morgan Creek Int'l.
PICTURES: Midnight Crossing, Communion, Young Guns II, Pacific Heights, Robin Hood: Prince of Thieves, Freejack, White Sands, The Crush, True Romance, Imaginary Crimes, Ace Ventura: Pet Detective, Chasers, Silent Fall, Trial by Jury, Ace Ventura: When Nature Calls, Two if by Sea, Big Bully, Diabolique, Bad Moon, Wild America, Incognito, Major League: Back to the Minors, Wrongfully Accused, A Course in Miracles.

BARBERA, JOSEPH R.
Executive. b. New York, NY, Mar. 24, 1911. e. NYU, American Institute of Banking. After schooling joined Irving Trust Co. in N.Y.; started submitting cartoon drawings to leading magazines selling one to Collier's. Joined Van Buren Assocs. as sketch artist, later going to work in animation dept. of MGM Studios. At MGM met William Hanna, who became his lifelong business associate. Made first animated short together in 1937, starting the famous Tom & Jerry series which they produced for 20 years. Left MGM in 1957 to form Hanna-Barbera Productions to make cartoons for TV. Hanna-Barbera became a subsidiary of Taft Ent. Co. in 1968 with both men operating the studio under long-term agreements with Taft. Taft and the studio were sold to Great American Broadcasting, 1988. Hanna-Barbera Prods. acquired by Turner Bdcstg. System, 1991; Barbera is co-founder, chmn. Team received Governor's Award from the Acad. of Television Arts & Sciences, 1988.
PICTURES: Hey There It's Yogi Bear, A Man Called Flintstone, Charlotte's Web, C.H.O.M.P.S., Heidi's Song, Jetsons: The Movie, The Flintstones (exec. prod. of live action film; also cameo appearance).
TELEVISION: *Specials/Movies*: The Gathering (Emmy Award), I Yabba Dabba Do!, Hollyrock-a-Bye Baby. *Series*: The Huckleberry Hound Show (Emmy Award), Quick Draw McGraw, Yogi Bear, The Flintstones, The Jetsons, Top Cat, Jonny Quest, Scooby-Doo, The Smurfs.

BARBOUR, ALAN G.
Writer, Editor, Publisher. b. Oakland, CA, July 25, 1933. e. Rutgers U. m. Catherine Jean Callovini, actress, Teacher, AADA, American Mime Theatre. U.S. Army, worked as computer programmer. Formed Screen Facts Press in 1963, Screen Facts Magazine. Compiled, edited: The Serials of Republic, The Serials of Columbia, Great Serial Ads, The B Western, Serial Showcase, Hit the Saddle, The Wonderful World of B-Films, Days of Thrills and Adventure, Serial Quarterly, Serial Pictorial, Karloff—A Pictorial History, Errol Flynn—A Pictorial Biography, A Pictorial History of the Serial, A Thousand and One Delights, Cliffhanger, The Old-Time Radio Quiz Book. Direct Mktg. Div., RCA Records. Mgr., A & R, RCA, BMG Video Club.

BARBOUR, MALCOLM
Executive. b. London, England, May 3, 1934. e. Radley Coll., Oxford, England, A.B., Columbia Coll. At National Broadcasting Co., was press info. asst., 1958-59; asst. magazine ed., 1959-62; assoc. mag. ed., 1962-64; sr. mag. ed., 1964-65; mgr. of magazine pub., 1965-67. Pub. mgr., Buena Vista, 1967-68; relations, Buena Vista, 1969. Eastern story ed., Walt Disney Prod., 1968-69; dir. of adv. & pub. Partner, Producers Creative Services, 1976-79. Pres., The International Picture Show, 1980-81 (Tim Conway comedies The Billion Dollar Hobo and They Went That-A-Way & That-A-Way; Slayer. Distributor: Soldier of Orange, The Magic of Lassie, The Visitor, etc.). Pres., Barbour/Langley Productions, 1982-present. Prod., Geraldo Rivera specials: American Vice, Innocence Lost, Sons of Scarface, Murder: Live from Death Row, Satan Worship. Prod., Jack Anderson specials. Writer, prod., Cocaine Blues. Co-screenplay, P.O.W. The Escape. *Exec. producer*: Cops, Code 3, Inside the KGB, Cop Files, Deadly Sins (also writer).

BARCLAY, PARIS
Director, Actor.
PICTURES: America's Dream, Don't Be a Menace to South Central While Drinking Your Juice in the Hood.
TELEVISION: *Movies*: The Cherokee Kid (also actor). *Series*: NYPD Blue (Emmy Award, 1998), Diagnosis: Murder, ER, Sliders, Clueless, Brooklyn South.

BARDEN, EARL
Executive. b. 1941. e. Whitworth Coll. Hist./Educ., 1963. Began career as doorman at Yakima Theatre, Yakima, WA. Became gen'l mgr. of Yakima Theatres, Inc., 1968. VP, 1979. Pres. Yakima Audio Svcs. Co., 1974.

BARDOT, BRIGITTE
Actress. b. Paris, France, Sept. 28, 1934. e. Paris Conservatory. Studied ballet, before becoming model. Studied acting with Rene Simon. On stage in L'Invitation au Chateau. Awarded French Legion of Honor, 1985. Active in the movement to preserve endangered animals. Created the Brigitte Bardot Foundation for animal protection, April 1986.
PICTURES: Le Trou Normand (debut, 1952), Nanina la Fille san Voiles, Les Dents Longues, Act of Love, Le Portrait de Son Pere, Royal Affairs in Versailles, Tradita, Le Fils de Caroline Cherie, Helen of Troy, Futures Vedettes, Les Grandes Maneuvres, Doctor at Sea, La Lumiere d'En Face, Cette Sacre Gamine, Mi Figlio Nerone, En Effeuillant la Marguerite, The Bride is Much Too Beautiful, And God Created Woman, Une Parisienne, The Night Heaven Fell, En Cas de Malheur, Le Femme et le Pantin, Babette Goes to War, Come Dance With Me, La Verite, La Bride sur le Cou, Les Amours Celebres, A Very Private Affair, Love on a Pillow, Contempt, A Ravishing Idiot, Dear Brigitte, Viva Maria, Masculine-Feminine, Two Weeks in September, Spirits of the Dead, Shalako, Les Femmes, L'Ours et la Poupee, Les Novices, Boulevard du Rhum, Les Petroleuses, Ms. Don Juan, L'Historie Tres Bonne et Tres Joyeuse de Colinot Troussechemise.

BARE, RICHARD L.
Producer, Director. b. Turlock, CA. Started as dir. for Warners. SDG Best Dir. TV award, 1959. Author of The Film Director (Macmillan, 1971). Pres., United National Film Corp.
PICTURES: *Director*: Smart Girls Don't Talk, Flaxy Martin, This Side of the Law, House Across The Street, This Rebel Breed, Girl on the Run, Return of Frontiersman. *Dir./Prod./Writer*: Wicked Wicked, Story of Chang & Eng, City of Shame, Sudden Target, Purple Moon.
TELEVISION: 77 Sunset Strip, Maverick, So This is Hollywood, The Islanders, Dangerous Robin, This Rebel Breed, Twilight Zone, Bus Stop, Adventures in Paradise, The Virginian, Kraft Theatre, Run For Your Life, Green Acres, Farraday and Son, Westwind.

BAREN, HARVEY M.
Executive. b. New York, NY, Nov. 25, 1931. e. State U. of New York. Served in U.S. Army, 1952-54. United Artists Corp., 1954-59 (contract dept., print dept., booker—NY branch). Asst. to general sls. mgr., Magna Pictures Corp., 1959-61. Road show mgr., nat'l. sls. coordinator, 20th Century-Fox, 1961-71. Asst. general sls. manager, Allied Artists Pictures, 1971-79. V.p., gen. sls. mgr., Nat'l. Screen Service, 1978-79. V.p., gen. sls. mgr., Cannon Pictures, 1979-80. Pres. of Summit Feature Distributors, 1980. Exec. v.p., dir., MGM/UA Classics, 1983. Joined New Century/Vista as v.p., sls. admin, 1986. Pres., Sea Movies Inc., 1991.

BARENHOLTZ, BEN
Executive. b. Kovel, Poland, Oct. 5, 1935. Asst. theatre mngr., RKO Bushwick, Brooklyn, 1959-60. Mngr., Village Theatre, NY, 1966-68. Owner, operator, Elgin Cinema, 1968-75; originated Midnight Movie concept with El Topo. Pres., owner., Libra Film Corp., 1972-84. V.p. & partner, Circle Releasing (which launched and distributed The Family Game, Therese, Blood Simple and prod. Raising Arizona) 1984-1992. Pres., Barenholtz Prods. Inc.
PICTURES: *Exec. Prod.*: Miller's Crossing, Barton Fink, Cheat, White Man's Burden, Georgia.

BARISH, KEITH
Producer. b. Los Angeles, CA. Background in finance. Founded Keith Barish Prods., 1979. In partnership with Taft Broadcasting Co., Entertainment Div., 1984-88. Founder and chmn. of Planet Hollywood. Appeared in film Last Action Hero.
PICTURES: Sophie's Choice, Light of Day, Ironweed. *Exec. prod.*: Endless Love, Kiss Me Goodbye, Misunderstood, Nine 1/2 Weeks, Big Trouble in Little China, The Running Man, The Monster Squad, The Serpent and the Rainbow, Her Alibi, Firebirds, The Fugitive, U.S. Marshals.
TELEVISION: *Movie*: A Streetcar Named Desire (exec. prod.).

BARKER, BOB
TV host. b. Darrington, WA, Dec. 12. e. Springfield Central H.S., Drury Coll. News writer, announcer, disc jockey KTTS until 1949. News editor, staff announcer, Station WWPG. Pres. Bob Barker Prod., Inc. Started as M.C. for both Miss USA Pageant and Miss Universe Pageant, 1966. First time as M.C. of both Rose Bowl Parade and Pillsbury Bakeoff. Series, 1970.
PICTURES: Happy Gilmore.
TELEVISION: *Emcee or host*: The End of the Rainbow, Truth or Consequences (daytime: 1956-65; nighttime synd: 1966-74), Lucky Pair (prod.), That's My Line (1980-1), The Price Is Right (exec. prod. & m.c.; 1972-; received several Emmy Awards as host). *Narrator*: 500 Festival Parade, Indianapolis 1969-81.

BARKER, CLIVE
Writer, Producer, Director. b. Liverpool, England, Oct. 5, 1952. e. Liverpool Univ. Moved to London at twenty-one, forming theatre company. Began writing short stories which were subsequently published as Books of Blood (Vols. 1-3 & Vols. 4-6). Author of: *Novels*: Damnation Game, Weaveworld, The Great and Secret Show, Imajica, The Thief of Always, Everville, Sacrament. *Books*: Clive Barker: Illustrator, The Art of Clive Barker, Incarnations. *Plays*: History of the Devil, Colossus, Frankenstein In Love. Painter with exhibitions in NY, California.
PICTURES: Rawhead Rex (from his story), Transmutations (from his story), Hellraiser (dir., s.p.; from his novella The Hellbound Heart), Hellbound: Hellraiser II (co-exec. prod.; from his story), Nightbreed (dir., s.p.; from his novel Cabal), Sleepwalkers (actor), Hellraiser III: Hell on Earth (exec. prod.; from his story), Candyman (exec. prod.; from his story The Forbidden), Candyman: Farewell to the Flesh (exec. prod.; from his story), Lord of Illusions (dir., s.p., co-prod.; from his story The Last Illusion), Hellraiser: Bloodline, The Thief of Always (from his novel), Gods and Monsters (exec. prod.), Candyman: Day of the Dead.
TELEVISION: Quicksilver Highway (story).

BARKER, MICHAEL W.
Executive. b. Nuremberg, Germany, Jan. 9, 1954. e. U. of Texas at Austin, B.S. in International Communications, 1976. Joined Films Inc. 1979-80; then United Artists 1980-83, first as non-theatrical sls. mngr., then as nat'l. sls. mngr. of UA Classics. Co-founder and v.p., sls. & mktg. for Orion Classics, a div. of Orion, 1983-1992. Co-founder and co-pres., Sony Pictures Classics, 1992-present. Member bd. of dirs. of BAFTA NY, and Independent Features Project.

BARKETT, STEVE
Actor, Director, Producer, Film Editor, Writer. b. Oklahoma City, OK, Jan. 1, 1950. Exhibited and scored over 52 feature length classic silent films 1966-1968 as dir. of two film series at the Oklahoma Art Center and Science and Arts Foundation, prior to coming to LA in 1970. Toured in stage prod. 1971-72: Pajama Tops, Winnie the Pooh. Exec. in several non-theatrical releasing cos., incl. Independent Film Associates and Thunderbird Films. Active in film preservation and restoration work on early silent and sound films, 1968-1974. Founded The Hollywood Book and Poster Company, 1978; est. The Nautilus Film Co., 1978. Founded and operated Capt. Nemo's Video, 1985-87; co-wrote and performed 42 episodes of Capt. Nemo's Video Review for radio.
PICTURES: *Actor*: The Egyptians are Coming, Corpse Grinders, Dillinger, Night Caller, Cruise Missile, Beverly Hills Vampire, Wizard of the Demon Sword, Bikini Drive-In, Cyber Zone, Hard Bounty, Masseuse, Star Hunter, Rapid Assault. *Prod./Dir./S.P./Edit.*: Collecting, Empire of the Dark, Angels of Death. *Also Actor*: The Movie People, Cassavetes, The Aftermath, Angels of Death, Empire of the Dark. *Actor/FX*: Dark Universe, Dinosaur Island, Attack of the 60's Centerfold, Invisible Mom. *FX Only*: Warlords, Sorceress. *Editor only*: Hurricane Express.

BARKIN, ELLEN
Actress. b. Bronx, NY, Apr. 16, 1954. e. Hunter Coll.; Actors Studio.
THEATER: Irish Coffee (debut, Ensemble Studio Theatre), Shout Across the River, Killings Across the Last, Tobacco Road, Extremities, Eden Court.
PICTURES: Diner (debut, 1982), Tender Mercies, Daniel, Eddie and the Cruisers, Harry and Son, The Adventures of Buckaroo Banzai Across the Eighth Dimension, Enormous Changes at the Last Minute, Terminal Choice, Desert Bloom, Down by Law, The Big Easy, Siesta, Made in Heaven, Sea of Love, Johnny Handsome, Switch, Man Trouble, Mac, This Boy's Life, Into the West, Bad Company, Wild Bill, Mad Dog Time, Fear and Loathing in Las Vegas, Popcorn, Drop Dead Gorgeous, The White River Kid, Crime and Punishment in Suburbia, Mercy, In the Boom Boom Room, Animal Husbandry.

TELEVISION: *Movies*: Kent State, We're Fighting Back, Parole, Terrible Joe Moran, Act of Vengeance, Clinton and Nadine, Before Women Had Wings (Emmy Award, 1998). *Series*: Search for Tomorrow. *Special*: Faerie Tale Theatre (The Princess Who Never Laughed), Before Women Had Wings.

BARNHOLTZ, BARRY
Executive. b. St. Louis, MO, Oct. 12, 1945. e. California State U., Northridge; USC; UCLA; WLAU, studied law. Concert promotions in So. Calif. 1963-71. With Medallion TV as v.p. in chg. sls. Barnholtz Organization, representing ind't. prod. cos. for feature films for cable. Founder, sr. v.p. of Vidmark Inc., and Trimark Films.

BARONE, TRACY
Producer. b. Nov. 1, 1962. m. actor Paul Michael Glaser.
PICTURES: Writer's Block (writer). *Exec prod.*: Money Train, My Fellow Americans, Rosewood.

BARR, ANTHONY
Producer, Director, Actor. r.n. Morris Yaffe. b. St. Louis, MO, March 14, 1921. e. Washington U., B.S. 1942. Actor, asst. stage mgr., 1944-46; stage mgr., Katherine Dunham Dancers, 1946-47. Teacher, actor, dir. in chg. Film Actors' Workshop, Professional Theatre Workshop, Hollywood. V.p. current prime time series, ABC-TV. V.p., current dramatic program production, CBS-TV; v.p., CBS Entertainment Prods. Author of Acting for the Camera, 1982.
THEATER: Jacobowsky and the Colonel, Winters' Tale, Embezzled Heaven.
PICTURES: *Actor*: People Against O'Hara, Border Incident, The Hollywood Story, The Mozart Story, Murder in the First. *Co-prod.*: Dime with a Halo.
TELEVISION: *Director*: Art Linkletter's Houseparty, About Faces. *Assoc. dir.*: Climax, Shower of Stars. *Producer.*: Climax, Summer Studio One. *Assoc. prod.*: Climax, Playhouse 90, Pursuit, G.E. Theatre, The Law and Mr. Jones, Four-Star.

BARR, JULIA
Actress. b. Ft. Wayne, IN, Feb. 8, 1949.
PICTURES: I, the Jury.
TELEVISION: *Series*: All My Children (Emmy Awards, 1990, 1998), Ryan's Hope.

BARRAULT, MARIE-CHRISTINE
Actress. b. Paris, France, March 21, 1944. m. dir. Roger Vadim.
PICTURES: My Night at Maud's, Le Distrait, Lancelot of the Lake, The Aspern Papers, Les Intrus, La Famille Grossfeld, Chloe in the Afternoon, John Glueckstadt, Cousin Cousine (Acad. Award nom.), By the Tennis Courts, Perceval, The Medusa Touch, Tout est a nous, Femme Entre Chien et Loup, Ma Cherie, Stardust Memories, Table for Five, Josephs Tochter, A Love in Germany, Les Mots Pour le Dire, Swann in Love, Grand Piano, Prisonnieres, Un Etae de orages, Savage State, Necessary Love, Next Time the Fire, Bonsoir, C'est la tangente que je prefere, Obsession.
TELEVISION: *Movies*: Mon pere avait raison, Les Braconniers de Belledombre.

BARRETT, RONA
News Correspondent b. New York, NY, Oct. 8, 1936. e. NYU (communications major). Created the column, Rona Barrett's Young Hollywood, which led to featured column in 1960 in Motion Picture Magazine and a nationally syndicated column distributed to 125 newspapers by the North American Newspaper Alliance. Turned to TV; initial appearances on ABC Owned Stations in 5 cities, providing two-minute reports for local newscasts. Resulted in Dateline Hollywood a network morning prog., co-hosted by Joanna Barnes. 1969, created first daily syndicated TV news segment for Metromedia. 1975, became arts and entertainment editor for ABC's Good Morning America. 1980, joined NBC News. Publ. and exec. editor, newsletter, The Rona Barrett Report. 1985, pres., Rona Barrett Enterprises, Inc., sr. corresp., Entertainment Tonight; Mutual Radio Network. 1988, creator of original novels for television, for NBC prods. Appeared in films Sextette, An Almost Perfect Affair.

BARRIE, BARBARA
Actress. b. Chicago, IL, May 23, 1931. e. U. of TX, B.F.A., 1953. Trained for stage at Herbert Berghof Studio. NY stage debut, The Wooden Dish, 1955. Author of, Lone Star (1990), Adam Zigzag (1994), Second Act (1997).
THEATER: The Crucible, The Beaux Stratagem, The Taming of the Shrew, Conversations in the Dark, All's Well That Ends Well, Happily Never After, Horseman Pass By, Company, The Selling of the President, The Prisoner of Second Avenue, The Killdeer, California Suite, Big and Little, Isn't It Romantic, Torch Song Trilogy, Fugue, After-play.
PICTURES: Giant (debut, 1956), The Caretakers, One Potato Two Potato (best actress, Cannes Film Fest, 1964), The Bell Jar, Breaking Away (Acad. Award nom.), Private Benjamin, Real Men, End of the Line, The Passage, Hercules (voice), Spent, Judy Berlin.

TELEVISION: *Movies*: Tell Me My Name, Summer of My German Soldier, To Race the Wind, The Children Nobody Wanted, Not Just Another Affair, Two of a Kind, The Execution, Vital Signs, Winnie, My First Love, Guess Who's Coming for Christmas?, The Odd Couple: Together Again, My Breast, A Chance of Snow. *Specials*: To Be Young Gifted and Black, Barefoot in the Park, What's Alan Watching?, Lovejoy: The Lost Colony, My Summer As a Girl. *Mini-Series*: 79 Park Avenue, Backstairs at the White House, Roots: The Next Generation, Scarlett. *Series*: Love of Life, Diana, Barney Miller, Breaking Away, Tucker's Witch, Reggie, Double Trouble, Love of Life, Big City Story, Suddenly Susan. *Guest*: Ben Casey, The Fugitive, Dr. Kildare, Alfred Hitchcock Presents, The Defenders, Mary Tyler Moore Show, Lou Grant, Trapper John, M.D., Babes, Kojak, Island Son, thirtysomething, Law & Order, The Commish.

BARRON, ARTHUR RAY
Executive. b. Mt. Lake, MN, July 12, 1934, e. San Diego State U. 1956-60, B.S. Accounting. Certified public acc't, Calif., 1960. Coopers & Lybrand, 1960-63; Desilu Productions, Inc., 1963-67. V.p. finance and admin., Paramount TV, 1967-70; v.p. finance, Paramount Pictures Corp., 1970; sr. v.p. finance and admin., 1971; exec. v.p., finance & admin., 1974; exec. v.p. 1980. Exec. v.p., Gulf & Western Industries, entertainment & communications group, 1983; promoted to pres., 1984-88. Chmn, Time Warner Enterprises, 1990.

BARRY, GENE
Actor. r.n. Eugene Klass. b. New York, NY. e. New Utrecht H.S., Brooklyn.
BROADWAY: Rosalinda, Catherine Was Great, Happy As Larry, Bless You All, The Would-Be Gentleman, La Cage aux Folles (Tony nom.).
PICTURES: Atomic City (debut, 1952), The Girls of Pleasure Island, The War of the Worlds, Those Redheads From Seattle, Alaska Seas, Red Garters, Naked Alibi, Soldier of Fortune, The Purple Mask, The Houston Story, Back From Eternity, China Gate, The 27th Day, Forty Guns, Thunder Road, Hong Kong Confidential, Maroc 7, Subterfuge, The Second Coming of Suzanne, Guyana: Cult of the Damned.
TELEVISION: *Movies*: Prescription Murder, Istanbul Express, Do You Take This Stranger?, The Devil and Miss Sarah, Ransom for Alice!, A Cry for Love, The Girl the Gold Watch and Dynamite, Adventures of Nellie Bly, Turn Back the Clock. *Mini-Series*: Aspen. *Series*: Our Miss Brooks, Bat Masterson, Burke's Law (1963-66), The Name of the Game, Burke's Law (1994-95).

BARRY, JOHN
Composer, Arranger, Conductor. r.n. John Barry Prendergast. b. York, England, Nov. 3, 1933. Started as rock 'n' roll trumpeter. Artist and prod., CBS Records.
PICTURES: Beat Girl, Never Let Go, The L-Shaped Room, The Amorous Mr. Prawn, From Russia With Love, Seance on a Wet Afternoon, Zulu, Goldfinger, The Ipcress File, The Knack, King Rat, Mister Moses, Thunderball, The Chase, Born Free (2 Acad. Awards: Best Music Scoring and Best Song: title song, 1966), The Wrong Box, The Quiller Memorandum, The Whisperers, Deadfall, You Only Live Twice, Petulia, The Lion in Winter (Acad. Award, 1968), Midnight Cowboy, The Appointment, On Her Majesty's Secret Service, Monte Walsh, The Last Valley, They Might Be Giants, Murphy's War, Walkabout, Diamonds Are Forever, Mary Queen of Scots, Alice's Adventures in Wonderland, The Public Eye, A Doll's House, The Tamarind Seed, The Dove, The Man With the Golden Gun, The Day of the Locust, Robin and Marian, King Kong, The Deep, The Betsy, Hanover Street, Moonraker, The Black Hole, Starcrash, Game of Death, Raise the Titanic, Somewhere in Time, Inside Moves, Touched By Love, Body Heat, The Legend of the Lone Ranger, Frances, Hammett, High Road to China, Octopussy, The Golden Seal, Mike's Murder, Until September, The Cotton Club, A View to a Kill, Jagged Edge, Out of Africa (Acad. Award, 1985), Howard the Duck, Peggy Sue Got Married, The Living Daylights, Hearts of Fire, Masquerade, A Killing Affair, Dances With Wolves (Acad. Award, 1990), Chaplin, Indecent Proposal, Deception, My Life, The Specialist, Cry the Beloved Country, Across the Sea of Time, The Scarlett Letter, Swept from the Sea, Playing by Heart, Mercury Rising.
TELEVISION: Elizabeth Taylor in London, Sophia Loren in Rome.

BARRYMORE, DREW
Actress. b. Los Angeles, CA, Feb. 22, 1975. Father is actor John Barrymore, Jr. (John Drew Barrymore). At 11 months appeared in first commercial. Author of Little Girl Lost (1990).
PICTURES: Altered States (debut, 1980), E.T.: The Extra Terrestrial, Firestarter, Irreconcilable Differences, Cat's Eye, See You in the Morning, Far From Home, No Place to Hide, Waxwork II, Poison Ivy, Motorama, Doppelganger, Wayne's World 2, Bad Girls, Inside the Goldmine, Boys on the Side, Mad Love, Batman Forever, Everyone Says I Love You, Scream, Home Fries, The Wedding Singer, Ever After: A Cinderella Story, Never Been Kissed (also prod.), Titan A.E. (voice), Charlie's Angels: The Movie (also prod.), Barbarella, Donnie Darko, Riding in Cars With Boys, So Love Returns.

TELEVISION: *Movies*: Bogie, Suddenly Love, Babes in Toyland, Conspiracy of Love, The Sketch Artist, Guncrazy (also released theatrically), The Amy Fisher Story. *Specials*: Disneyland's 30th Anniversary, Night of 100 Stars II, Con Sawyer and Hucklemary Finn, 15 & Getting Straight. *Series*: 2000 Malibu Road.

BARRYMORE, JOHN DREW
Actor. r.n. John Blythe Barrymore Jr. b. Beverly Hills, CA, June 4, 1932. e. St. John's Military Acad., various public and private schools. Son of actors John Barrymore and Delores Costello. Daughter is actress Drew Barrymore. Started acting at age 18 under the name John Barrymore Jr.
PICTURES: Sundowners (debut, 1950), High Lonesome, Quebec, The Big Night, Thunderbirds, While the City Sleeps, Shadow on the Window, Never Love a Stranger, High School Confidential, Night of the Quarter Moon, The Cossacks, The Night They Killed Rasputin, The Pharaoh's Woman, The Trojan Horse, The Centurion, Invasion 1700, War of the Zombies.

BART, PETER
Executive. b. Martha's Vineyard, MA, July 24, 1932. e. Swarthmore Coll. and The London School of Economics. Eight years as corrp. for New York Times and wrote for such magazines as Harper's, The Atlantic, Saturday Review, etc. Joined Paramount Pictures in 1965. Named exec. ass't. to Robert Evans, exec. in charge of world-wide prod. Appointed v.p. prod. Resigned 1973 to develop and produce own films for Paramount. Appointed pres. Lorimar Films, 1978. Resigned, 1979, to be indept. prod. 1983, joined MGM as sr. v.p., prod., m.p. div. Resigned, 1985, to be indep. prod. Editor, Variety. Author of novels: Thy Kingdom Come (1983), Destinies (1979), Fade Out.
PICTURES: *Producer*: Islands in the Stream, Fun with Dick and Jane, Revenge of the Nerds (exec. prod.), Youngblood, Revenge of the Nerds II.

BARTEK, STEVE
Composer, orchestrator. Co-founded musical group Oingo Boingo with composer Danny Elfman. With group performed in film Back to School.
PICTURES: *Composer*: Guilty as Charged, Cabin Boy, Coldblooded, Romy and Michele's High School Reunion, Meet the Deedles (also act.). *Orchestrator*: Forbidden Zone, Beetlejuice, Batman, Nightbreed, Darkman, Edward Scissorhands, Batman Returns, Tim Burton's The Nightmare Before Christmas, The Frighteners, Extreme Measures, Psycho. *Also songs*: Sommersby, Dolores Claiborne, Black Beauty , To Die For, Dead Presidents.
TELEVISION: *Series:* Dilbert (music producer/arranger)

BARTEL, PAUL
Director, Writer, Actor. b. New York, NY, Aug. 6, 1938. e. UCLA, B.A. At 13 spent summer working at UPA Cartoons. Later at UCLA won acting and playwriting awards and prod. animated and doc. films. Awarded Fulbright schl. to study film dir. at Centro Sperimentale di Cinematograpfia in Rome where dir. short Progetti (presented Venice Fest., 1962). Then at Army Pictorial Center, L.I. City. Asst. dir. military training films. After discharge from army worked for Hearst Metrotone News as writer-dir. monthly news doc. series, Horizontes for U.S. Information Agency. The Naughty Nurse. Appeared in 1984 short film Frankenweenie.
PICTURES: *Director:* Lust in the Dust, The Longshot, Shelf Life. *Actor:* Hi Mom!, Private Parts (also dir. debut), Big Bad Mama (2nd unit. dir. only), Death Race 2000, Cannonball (also dir., co-s.p.), Eat My Dust!, Hollywood Boulevard, Grand Theft Auto, Mr. Billion, Piranha, Rock 'n' Roll High School, Heart Like a Wheel, Eating Raoul (also dir., s.p.), Trick or Treats, White Dog, Get Crazy, Not for Publication (also dir., s.p.), Into the Night, Sesame Street Presents Follow That Bird, Chopping Mall, Killer Party, Munchies, Amazon Women on the Moon, Mortuary Academy, Out of the Dark (also exec. prod.), Scenes From the Class Struggle in Beverly Hills (also dir., s.p.), Pucker Up and Bark Like a Dog, Far Out Man, Gremlins 2: The New Batch, The Pope Must Die, Liquid Dreams, Desire and Hell at Sunset Motel, Posse, Grief, The Jerky Boys, The Usual Suspects, Red Ribbon Blues, Basquiat, Escape from L.A., Dreamers, Billy's Hollywood Screen Kiss.
TELEVISION: *Director*: Amazing Stories (The Secret Cinema, Gershwin's Truck; also writer, actor), The Hustler of Muscle Beach, Clueless (2 episodes). *Actor*: Alfred Hitchcock Presents, Fame, L.A. Law, Acting on Impulse (movie), A Bucket of Blood (movie), Inheritance, Armistead Maupin's More Tales of the City (mini-series).

BARTKOWIAK, ANDRZEJ
Cinematographer. b. Lodz, Poland, 1950. Attended Polish Film School. Moved to US in 1972, gaining experience in TV commercials and low-budget features. Protege of Sidney Lumet, for whom did several pictures.
PICTURES: Deadly Hero, Prince of the City, Deathtrap, The Verdict, Daniel, Terms of Endearment, Garbo Talks, Prizzi's Honor, The Morning After, Power, Nuts, Twins, Q&A, Hard Promises, A Stranger Among Us, Falling Down, Guilty As Sin, Speed, A Good Man in Africa, Losing Isaiah, Species, Jade, The Mirror Has Two Faces, Dante's Peak, The Devil's Advocate, U.S. Marshals, Lethal Weapon 4, Romeo Must Die, Gossip.

BARTY, BILLY
Actor. b. Millsboro, PA, Oct. 25, 1924. e. LA City Col., LA State U. Began performing at age 3 appearing as Mickey Rooney's little brother in the Mickey McGuire shorts. Founded Little People of America, 1957; Billy Barty Foundation, 1975.
PICTURES: Golddigers of 1933, Footlight Parade, Roman Scandals, Gift of Gab, A Midsummer Night's Dream, Nothing Sacred, The Clown, The Undead, Billy Rose's Jumbo, Roustabout, Harum Scarum, Pufnstuf, The Day of the Locust, The Amazing Dobermans, W.C. Fields and Me, Foul Play, Firepower, Hardly Working, Under the Rainbow, Night Patrol, Legend, Tough Guys, Body Slam, Rumplestiltskin, Willow, Lobster Man From Mars, UHF, The Rescuers Down Under (voice), Life Stinks, The Naked Truth, Radioland Murders, Burn Hollywood Burn, I/O Error.
TELEVISION: *Movies*: Punch and Jody, Twin Detectives. *Series*: Ford Festival, The Spike Jones Show, Circus Boy, Club Oasis, Ace Crawford—Private Eye, Vendetta, Secrets of a Mafia Bride.

BARUCH, RALPH M.
Executive. b. Frankfurt, Germany, Aug. 5, 1923. e. The Sorbonne. m. Jean Ursell de Mountford. Administrative aide, SESAC, Inc. 1944-48. Account exec., DuMont Television Network, 1950-54. Account exec., CBS Films, 1954; account supr., 1957; dir. int'l sales, 1959; CBS Group President 1961-70. Pres. and CEO Viacom International, 1971-1983; chmn. 1983-87. Currently a consultant to Viacom International. Trustee of Lenox Hill Hospital. Chmn. Emeritus of the Nat'l Academy of Cable Programming and recipient of the Academy's first Governor's Award. Past-pres., the International Radio & Television Society and was honored by an IRTS gold medal award. Founder and fellow of the International Council of the Nat'l Academy of Television Arts & Sciences. Recipient of an Emmy Award. Former dir., Exec. Committee of the Nat'l Cable Television Assoc. Co-founder of C-Span. Recipient of the Vanguard Award, three NCTA President's Awards and NCTA Chmn. of the Year Award. Chmn. of the USIA's Television Communications Board of Advisors under Pres. Reagan. Elected to the Broadcasting/Cable Hall of Fame in 1992. Appointed to New York City Cultural Affairs Advisory Comm. Member of New York Yacht Club.

BARWOOD, HAL
Writer, Producer, Director. e. U. of Southern California Sch. of Cinema. Has written scripts in collaboration with Matthew Robbins. Barwood branched out into producing with Corvette Summer, 1978 and directing with Warning Sign, 1985.
PICTURES: *Screenplays* (all with Robbins): The Sugarland Express, The Bingo Long Traveling All-Stars and Motor Kings, MacArthur, Corvette Summer (also prod.), Dragonslayer (also prod.), Warning Sign (also dir.).

BARYSHNIKOV, MIKHAIL
Dancer, Actor. b. Riga, Latvia, Jan. 27, 1948. Joined Kirov Ballet, Leningrad, 1969-74; defected to U.S. With American Ballet Theatre 1974-78; New York City Ballet Company 1978-79; named dir. of the American Ballet Theatre. B'way stage debut, Metamorphosis (1989).
PICTURES: The Turning Point (debut, 1977; Acad. Award nom.), That's Dancing!, White Nights (also co-choreog.), Dancers (also choreog.), Company Business, The Cabinet of Dr. Ramirez.
TELEVISION: Baryshnikov at the White House (Emmy Award, 1979), Bob Hope on the Road to China, Baryshnikov on Broadway (Emmy Award, 1980), AFI Salute to Fred Astaire, Baryshnikov in Hollywood, AFI Salute to Gene Kelly, David Gordon's Made in USA, All Star Gala at Ford's Theater, Dance in America: Baryshnikov Dances Balanchine (Emmy Award, 1989).

BASCH, BUDDY
Print Media Syndicater, Publicist, Producer. b. South Orange, NJ, June 28, 1922. e. Columbia U. Began career as youngest radio editor in U.S. at 15. Has since written for nat'l mags, syndicates, wire services, and newspapers. Edit. & pub. Top Hit Club News for 7 yrs. Joined Donahue and Coe 1940 on m.p. accounts, U.S. Army in Europe 1942-45. 1945-67, own publicity and promotion office, working on m.p. company accounts and stars such as Burl Ives, Dinah Shore, Tony Martin, Danny Kaye, Peter Lorre, Tony Bennett, Gloria De Haven, McGuire Sisters, Rhonda Fleming, Sammy Davis, Jr., Anna Maria Alberghetti, Polly Bergen, Meyer Davis, The Beatles, Glenn Miller and Tommy Dorsey Orchestras. Produced many shows for radio, TV and stage in New York, Newark, Chicago, Hartford. Asst. to publisher, The Brooklyn Eagle 1962. 1966, formed Buddy Basch Feature Syndicate, covering assignments on show business, travel, health, medicine, food, human interest and general subjects for such pulications as N.Y. Daily News, A.P., Grit Magazine, Travel/Holiday, Frontier Magazine, Kaleidoscope, True, United Features, Gannett Westchester-Rockland Newspapers, Bergen (NJ) Record, Argosy, N.A.N.A., Womens' News Service, Today Magazine, Christian Science Monitor, New York Post, Inflight Magazine, Deseret News, California Canadian and Diversion. Provided Associated Press with worldwide exclusives on a number of national and intl. events. Member: Friars Club since 1959; Admission Comm. and House Comm. Organized & appointed permanent chmn. of VIP Reception and Security for Friars luncheons and dinners since 1970. Served as chmn. of Elections (6 times). Contributing ed. Friars Epistle.

BASINGER, KIM
Actress. b. Athens, GA, Dec. 8, 1953. e. Neighborhood Playhouse. m. actor Alec Baldwin. Began career as Ford model in New York.
PICTURES: Hard Country (debut, 1981), Mother Lode, Never Say Never Again, The Man Who Loved Women, The Natural, Fool for Love, 9-1/2 Weeks, No Mercy, Blind Date, Nadine, My Stepmother is an Alien, Batman, The Marrying Man, Final Analysis, Cool World, The Real McCoy, Wayne's World 2, Pret-a-Porter, The Getaway, L.A. Confidential (Acad. Award, Golden Globe Award, Best Supporting Actress), I Dreamed of Africa, Bless the Child.
TELEVISION: *Movies*: Dog and Cat (pilot), The Ghost of Flight 401, Katie: Portrait of a Centerfold, Killjoy. *Series*: From Here to Eternity, Dog and Cat, *Guest*: Charlie's Angels, The Simpsons, McMillian and Wife.

BASS, RONALD
Writer. b. Los Angeles, CA. e. Yale, Harvard Law School. Entered industry as entertainment lawyer, while writing novels: The Perfect Thief, Lime's Crisis, The Emerald Illusion.
PICTURES: Code Name: Emerald, Black Widow, Gardens of Stone, Rain Man (Academy Award, 1988), Sleeping With the Enemy, The Joy Luck Club (prod.), When a Man Loves a Woman (also exec. prod), Dangerous Minds, Waiting to Exhale (exec. prod.), How Stella Got Her Groove Back (also exec. prod.), My Best Friend's Wedding (prod.), What Dreams May Come (also exec. prod.), Stepmom (also exec. prod.), Snow Falling on Cedars (also prod.), New Kid on the Block, Good Nigh Moon, Entrapment (story, also exec. prod.), Passion of Mind (also prod.), Memoirs of a Geisha .
TELEVISION: *Movies:* Border Line, Invisible Child, Swing Vote. *Series*: Dangerous Minds, Moloney.

BASSETT, ANGELA
Actress. b. New York, NY, Aug. 16, 1958. Moved to St. Petersburg, FL, at 5 yrs. old. e. Yale.
THEATER: *B'way*: Ma Rainey's Black Bottom, Joe Turner's Come and Gone. *Off-B'way*: Colored People's Time, Antigone, Black Girl, Henry IV Part 1. *Regional*: Beef No Chicken.
PICTURES: F/X (debut, 1986), Kindergarten Cop, Boyz N the Hood, City of Hope, Critters 4, Innocent Blood, Malcolm X, Passion Fish, What's Love Got to Do With It (Acad. Award nom.; Golden Globe Award), Strange Days, Waiting to Exhale, A Vampire in Brooklyn, Panther, Contact, Wings Against the Wind, How Stella Got Her Groove Back, Supernova, Boesman and Lena, The Score.
TELEVISION: *Movies/Specials*: Line of Fire: The Morris Dees Story, The Jacksons: An American Dream, Africans in America: America's Journey Through Slavery. *Guest*: Cosby Show, 227, thirty-something, Tour of Duty, Equal Justice, The Flash, Nightmare Cafe.

BATEMAN, JASON
Actor. b. Rye, NY, Jan. 14, 1969. Brother of actress Justine Bateman. Son of prod.-theatrical mgr. Kent Bateman. Started career in commercials until cast in Little House on the Prairie at 12 (1981).
PICTURES: Teen Wolf Too, Necessary Roughness, Breaking the Rules, Love Stinks.
TELEVISION: *Movies*: The Fantastic World of D.C. Collins, The Thanksgiving Promise, Can You Feel Me Dancing, The Bates Motel, Moving Target, A Taste for Killing, Confessions: Two Faces of Evil, This Can't Be Love, Hart to Hart: Secrets of the Hart. *Specials:* Just a Little More Love, Candid Camera: Eat! Eat! Eat! *Mini-Series:* Robert Kennedy and His Times. *Series*: Little House on the Prairie, Silver Spoons, It's Your Move, Valerie (Valerie's Family, The Hogan Family), Simon, Chicago Sons, George & Leo.

BATEMAN, JUSTINE
Actress, b. Rye, NY, Feb. 19, 1966. Brother is actor Jason Bateman.
THEATER: Lulu, Self-Storage, The Crucible, Love Letters, Carnal Knowledge, Speed-the-Plow.
PICTURES: Satisfaction, The Closer, Primary Motive, Deadbolt, The Night We Never Met, God's Lonely Man, Kiss & Tell, Bucket of Blood.
TELEVISION: *Movies:* Right to Kill?, Family Ties Vacation, Can You Feel Me Dancing?, The Fatal Image, In the Eyes of a Stranger, The Hunter, Terror in the Night, Another Woman. *Specials:* First the Egg, Whatta Year... 1986, Fame Fortune and Romance, Candid Camera: Eat! Eat! Eat!, Merry Christmas Baby, A Century of Women, *Series*: Family Ties, Men Behaving Badly. *Guest*: Tales from the Dark Side, One to Grow On, It's Your Move, Glitter, Lois & Clark.

BATES, ALAN
Actor. b. Allestree, Derbyshire, England, Feb. 17, 1934. e. Herbert Strutt Grammar Sch.; after natl. service with the RAF studied at RADA with Albert Finney, Peter O'Toole and Tom Courtenay. Professional stage debut 1955 with the Midland Theatre Co. in You and Your Wife.
THEATER: *London*: The Mulberry Tree, Look Back in Anger (also NY, Moscow), Long Day's Journey Into Night, Poor Richard, Richard III, In Celebration, Hamlet, Butley (also NY; Tony Award, 1973), The Taming of the Shrew, Life Class, Otherwise Engaged, The Seagull, Stage Struck, A Patriot for Me, One for the Road, Victoria Station, Dance of Death, Yonadab, Melon, Much Ado About Nothing, Ivanov, Stages, The Showman, Simply Disconnected, Fortune's Fool, Life Support.
PICTURES: The Entertainer (debut, 1960), Whistle Down the Wind, A Kind of Loving, The Caretaker, The Running Man, Nothing But the Best, Zorba the Greek, Georgy Girl, King of Hearts, Far From the Madding Crowd, The Fixer (Acad. Award nom.), Women in Love, Three Sisters, The Go-Between, A Day in the Death of Joe Egg, Impossible Object, Butley, In Celebration, Royal Flash, An Unmarried Woman, The Shout, The Rose, Nijinsky, Quartet, The Return of the Soldier, Britannia Hospital, The Wicked Lady, Duet for One, A Prayer for the Dying, We Think the World of You, Mr. Frost, Hamlet, Force Majeure, Dr. M, Shuttlecock, Secret Friends, Silent Tongue, Losing Track, The Grotesque, Varya.
TELEVISION: The Thug, A Memory of Two Mondays, The Jukebox, The Square Ring, The Wind and the Rain, Look Back in Anger, Three on a Gasring, Duel for Love, A Hero for Our Time, Plaintiff & Defendant, Two Sundays, The Collection, The Mayor of Casterbridge, The Trespasser, Very Like a Whale, Voyage Round My Father, An Englishman Abroad, Separate Tables, Dr. Fischer of Geneva, One for the Road, Pack of Lies, 102 Boulevard Haussmann, Unnatural Pursuits, Hard Times, Oliver's Travels, Hard Times, Nicholas' Gift.

BATES, KATHY
Actress. b. Memphis, TN, June 28, 1948. e. S. Methodist U. Regional theatre incl. D.C. and Actor's Theatre in Louisville.
THEATER: Vanities (Off-B'way debut, 1976), Semmelweiss, Crimes of the Heart, The Art of Dining, Goodbye Fidel (B'way debut, 1980), Chocolate Cake and Final Placement, Fifth of July, Come Back to the 5 & Dime Jimmy Dean Jimmy Dean, 'night Mother (Tony nom., Outer Critics Circle Award), Two Masters: The Rain of Terror, Curse of the Starving Class, Frankie and Johnny in the Clair de Lune (Obie, L.A. Drama Critics Award), The Road to Mecca.
PICTURES: Taking Off (debut, 1971), Straight Time, Come Back to the Five & Dime Jimmy Dean Jimmy Dean, Two of a Kind, Summer Heat, My Best Friend is a Vampire, Arthur 2: On the Rocks, Signs of Life, High Stakes, Men Don't Leave, Dick Tracy, White Palace, Misery (Acad. Award, Golden Globe & Chicago Film Critics Awards, Best Actress 1990), At Play in the Fields of the Lord, Fried Green Tomatoes, Shadows and Fog, The Road to Mecca, Prelude to a Kiss, Used People, A Home of Our Own, North, Dolores Claiborne, Angus, Diabolique, The War at Home, Titanic, Swept from the Sea, Primary Colors (Acad. Award nom.), The Waterboy, Bruno, Unconditiona Love, Rat Race, Dragonfly, American Outlaws.
TELEVISION: *Movies*: Johnny Bull, No Place Like Home, Roe vs. Wade, Hostages, Curse of the Starving Class. *Mini-Series*: Murder Ordained, The Stand, The Night Shift (Golden Globe Award, 1997).*Special*: Talking With (also dir.). *Guest*: The Love Boat, St. Elsewhere, Cagney and Lacey, L.A. Law, China Beach.

BATTY, PETER
Producer, Director, Writer. b. Sunderland, England, June 18, 1931. e. Bede Grammar Sch. and Queen's Coll., Oxford. Feature-writer both sides Atlantic 1954-58. Joined BBC TV 1958 dir. short films. Edited Tonight programme 1963-4. Exec. prod. ATV 1964-68. Awarded Grand Prix for doc. at 1965 Venice and Leipzig festivals. Official entries 1970 and 1971 San Francisco and Melbourne festivals. Nominated Int'l. Emmy, 1986. Own company since 1968 prod. TV specials, series, commercials.
TELEVISION: The Quiet Revolution, The Big Freeze, The Katanga Affair, Sons of the Navvy Man, The Fall and Rise of the House of Krupp, The Road to Suez, The Suez Affair, Battle for the Desert, Vietnam Fly-In, The Plutocrats, The Aristocrats, Battle for Cassino, Battle for the Bulge, Birth of the Bomb, Search for the Super, Operation Barbarossa, Farouk: Last of the Pharaohs, Superspy, Spy Extraordinary, Sunderland's Pride and Passion, A Rothschild and His Red Gold, The World of Television, The Story of Wine, The Rise and Rise of Laura Ashley, The Gospel According to Saint Michael, Battle for Warsaw, Battle for Dien Bien Phu, Nuclear Nightmares. A Turn Up in A Million, Il Poverello, Swindle!, The Algerian War, Fonteyn and Nureyev: The Perfect Partnership, The Divided Union, A Time for Remembrance, Swastika Over British Soil. Contributed 6 episodes to Emmy-winning World at War series.

BAUER, STEVEN
Actor. r.n. Rocky Echaveria. b. Havana, Cuba, Dec. 2, 1956. Moved with family to Miami at age 3. e. Miami Dade Jr. Coll. where studied acting. Breakthrough came with selection for role in Que Pasa U.S.A.? for Public TV. Signed by Columbia TV and moved to California.
PICTURES: Scarface, Thief of Hearts, Running Scared, The Beast, Wildfire, Gleaming the Cube, Bloody Murder!, Raising Cain, Woman of Desire, Improper Conduct, Stranger by Night, The Wild Side, Codename: Silencer, Primal Fear, Navajo Blues, Plato's Run, Kickboxing Academy, The Blackout, Star Portal, Rave, Naked Lies, Forever Lulu, Traffic, Glory Glory.

TELEVISION: *Movies*: Doctors' Private Lives, She's in the Army Now, Nichols and Dymes, An Innocent Love, Sword of Gideon, Sweet Poison, False Arrest, Drive Like Lightning, Sisters and Other Strangers, The Versace Murder. *Mini-Series*: Drug Wars: The Camarena Story. *Series*: Wiseguy. *Guest*: The Rockford Files, From Here to Eternity, One Day at a Time, Hill Street Blues.

BAUM, MARTIN
Executive. b. New York, NY, March 2, 1924. 1968-1971, Pres. of Theatrical Motion Pictures for ABC Pictures. Previously partner Baum & Newborn Theatrical Agency. Head of West Coast office General Artists Corp. Head of m.p. dept., Ashley Famous Agency. Pres., Martin Baum Agency. Sr. exec. v.p. Creative Management Assoc. Pres., Optimus Productions, Inc. Partner with Michael Ovitz, Ron Meyer, Rowland Perkins, Bill Haber in Creative Artists Agency, Inc.
PICTURES: Bring Me the Head of Alfredo Garcia, The Wilby Conspiracy, The Killer Elite, They Shoot Horses Don't They?, Lovers and Other Strangers, Straw Dogs, Kotch, Cabaret.

BAUMGARTEN, CRAIG
Executive. b. Aug. 27, 1949. Partner in independent prod. co., New America Cinema. Joined Paramount Pictures as prod. exec.; named v.p., prod. In 1980 went to Keith Barish Prods., of which was pres. three years. In 1983 appt. exec. v.p. & exec. asst. to the pres. & CEO, Columbia Pictures; resigned 1985. Joined Lorimar Motion Pictures as pres. Joined 20th Century Fox m.p. div. as exec. v.p. of prod., 1987; resigned. Formed Adelson/Baumgarten Prods. with Gary Adelson, 1989. Co-Prod.: Hard to Kill, Hook, Universal Soldier, Nowhere to Run, Blank Check, It Could Happen to You, Jade, The Shooter, Esmeralda, Michael Hayes. Formed Baumgarten/Prophet Entertainment Inc., 1994.

BAXTER, BILLY
Executive. b. New York, NY, Feb. 8, 1926. e. Holy Cross, 1948. Mgr., Ambassador Brokerage Group, Albany, 1957-58. Bill Doll & Co., 1959-63. Organ., prod., radio show, Earl Wilson Celebrity Column, 1962; prod. B'way show, Mandingo, with Franchot Tone, 1962. Dir. of promotion, spec. events, Rumrill Ad Agency, 1963-64; dir. of promotion, exploitation, Landau Co., 1964-65; dir. of adv. and pub., Rizzoli Co., 1965-86. Consultant on special events to the Philip Morris Corp. and American Express.
PICTURES: *Co-prod.*: Love and Anarchy, Daughters-Daughters, Outrageous, One Man, Dawn of the Dead. *Prod.*: Diary of the Cannes Film Festival with Rex Reed, 1980. *Prod./dir.*: documentaries: Artists of the Old West, Remington & Russell, Buffalo Bill Cody (1988).

BAXTER, KEITH
Actor. b. Monmouthshire, Wales, April 29, 1933. e. Wales, entered Royal Acad. of Dramatic Art in 1951. 1952-55 in national service; returned to RADA. Did years of repertory work in Dublin, Croydon, Chichester, London's West End, and New York. Biggest stage hit in Sleuth, both London and NY. Later in Corpse (London, NY).
PICTURES: The Barretts of Wimpole Street, Peeping Tom, Chimes at Midnight, With Love in Mind, Ash Wednesday, Berlin Blues.
TELEVISION: For Tea on Sunday, Hold My Hand Soldier, Saint Joan, *Mini-Series:* Merlin.

BAXTER, MEREDITH
Actress. b. Los Angeles, CA, June 21, 1947. e. Interlochen Arts Academy. On stage in Guys and Dolls, Butterflies Are Free, Vanities, Country Wife, Talley's Folly, Love Letters, Diaries of Adam & Eve.
PICTURES: Ben, Stand Up and Be Counted, Bittersweet Love, All the President's Men, Jezebel's Kiss.
TELEVISION: *Movies*: Cat Creature, The Stranger Who Looks Like Me, Target Risk, The Imposter, The Night That Panicked America, Little Women, The Family Man, Beulah Land, Two Lives of Carol Letner, Take Your Best Shot, The Rape of Richard Beck, Kate's Secret, The Long Journey Home (also co-exec. prod.), Winnie: My Life in the Institution, She Knows Too Much, The Kissing Place, Burning Bridges, Bump in the Night, A Mother's Justice, A Woman Scorned: The Betty Broderick Story, Her Final Fury: Betty Broderick—The Last Chapter, Darkness Before Dawn (also co-exec. prod.), For the Love of Aaron, One More Mountain, My Breast (also co-exec. prod.), Betrayed: A Story of Three Women (also co-exec. prod.).Dog's Best Friend (voice), Inheritance, Miracle in the Woods, Let Me Call You Sweetheart, Holy Joe, Down Will Come Baby. *Specials:* The Diaries of Adam and Eve, Vanities, Other Mothers (Afterschool Special). *Series*: The Interns, Bridget Loves Bernie, Family, Family Ties, The Faculty.

BAXTER, STANLEY
Actor. b. Glasgow, Scotland, May, 1926. e. Hillhead H.S., Glasgow. Principal comedian in Howard & Wyndham pantomimes. Summer revues. Televised regularly on BBC-TV, and also frequent broadcaster. M.P. debut in Geordie, 1955.
THEATER: The Amorous Prawn, On the Brighter Side, Chase Me Comrade (Australia), Cinderella, What the Butler Saw, Phil The Fluter, Mother Goose Pantomime seasons 1970-74. Jack & The Beanstalk, Cinderella, Mother Goose, Aladdin, Cinderella.
PICTURES: Geordie (debut, 1955), Very Important Person, Crooks Anonymous, The Fast Lady, Father Came Too, Joey Boy, Arabian Knight (voice).
TELEVISION: Baxter on (series) 1964; The Confidence Course, The World of Stanley Baxter, Stanley Baxter Show, Time for Baxter, The Stanley Baxter Big Picture Show, The Stanley Baxter Moving Picture Show, Part III, Stanley Baxter's Christmas Box, Bing Crosby's Merrie Olde Christmas, Stanley Baxter's Greatest Hits, Baxter on Television, Stanley Baxter Series, The Stanley Baxter Hour, Children's Royal, Stanley Baxter's Christmas Hamper, Stanley Baxter's Picture Annual 1986; Mr. Majeika (series, 1988-89), Fitby, Stanley Baxter Is Back, Stanley Baxter in Reel Terms.

BAY, MICHAEL
Director. b. 1964. e. Wesleyan U.; Pasadena's Art Center College of Design. Worked on advertisements and created music videos for Tina Turner, Meatloaf, Lionel Richie, Wilson Phillips. Recipient of the Gold Lion for The Best Beer campaign for Miller Lite; Silver Lion & Grand Prix Clio for Commercial of the Year, for the Got Milk/AaronBurr commercial; Commercial Dir. of the Year, Directors Guild of America, 1995.
PICTURES: Vengeance (actor only), Bad Boys, The Rock, Armageddon (also prod.), Pearl Harbor, Coyote Ugly (actor).

BEACHAM, STEPHANIE
Actress. b. Casablanca, Morocco, Feb. 28, 1947. e. RADA. On London stage in The Basement, On Approval, London Cuckolds, etc.
PICTURES: The Games, Tam Lin, The Nightcomers, Dracula A.D., And Now the Screaming Stars, House of Whipcord, Schizo, The Confessional, Horror Planet (Inseminoid), The Wolves of Willoughby Chase, Troop Beverly Hills, Wedding Bell Blues.
TELEVISION: *Movies/Specials*: Napoleon & Josephine: A Love Story, Lucky/Chances, Secrets, To Be the Best, Foreign Affairs, Marked Personal, Jane Eyre, A Sentimental Education, A Change of Place.*Series*: Tenko (PBS), The Colbys, Dynasty, Sister Kate, SeaQuest DSV, Beverly Hills 90210, Riders.

BEALS, JENNIFER
Actress. b. Chicago, IL, Dec. 19, 1963. Started as fashion model before making film debut in small role in My Bodyguard, 1980.
PICTURES: My Bodyguard, Flashdance, The Bride, Split Decisions, Vampire's Kiss, Layover, Rider in the Dark, The Lizard's Tale, Sons, Jackal's Run, A Reasonable Doubt, Dr. M, Blood and Concrete, In the Soup, Day of Atonement, Caro Diario, Mrs. Parker and the Vicious Circle, Arabian Knight (voice), Devil in a Blue Dress, Four Rooms, The Search for One-Eye Jimmy, Wishful Thinking, The Prophecy II, Body and Soul, The Last Days of Disco.
TELEVISION: *Movies*: Terror Strikes the Class Reunion, Indecency, Night Owl, The Twilight of the Golds, The Spree. *Specials*: The Picture of Dorian Grey, Cinderella (Faerie Tale Theatre). *Series*: 2000 Malibu Road, Nothing Sacred.

BEAN, ORSON
Actor. r.n. Dallas Burrows. b. Burlington, VT, July 22, 1928. Performed in nightclubs as comic and on Broadway (Never Too Late, Will Success Spoil Rock Hunter?, Subways Are for Sleeping, Roar of the Grease Paint, the Smell of the Crowd, Ilya Darling.) Author of Me and the Orgone. Founder, administrator, dir. 15th St. School, NY.
PICTURES: How to Be Very Very Popular (debut, 1955), Anatomy of a Murder, Lola, Forty Deuce, Innerspace, Instant Karma, Final Judgement, One of Those Nights, Being John Malkovich.
TELEVISION: *Movies/Specials*: Arsenic and Old Lace, Chance of a Lifetime, Just My Imagination. *Series*: The Blue Angel (host), I've Got a Secret (panelist), Keep Talking, To Tell the Truth (panelist), Mary Hartman Mary Hartman, One Life to Live, Dr. Quinn: Medicine Woman.

BEAN, SEAN
Actor. b. Sheffield, Yorkshire, England, Apr. 17, 1958.
THEATER: Romeo and Juliet, Fair Maid of the West, Midsummer Night's Dream, Who Knew Mackenzie and Gone, Deathwatch, Last Days of Mankind.
PICTURES: Winter Flight, Caravaggio, Stormy Monday, War Requeim, The Field, Patriot Games. Shopping, Black Beauty, Goldeneye, When Saturday Comes, Leo Tolstoy's Anna Karenina, Ronin, Bravo Two Zero, Airborne.
TELEVISION: Troubles, Small Zones, 15 Street, My Kingdom for a Horse, Winter Flight, Samson & Delilah, The True Bride, Prince, Tell Me That You Love Me, Clarissa, Scarlett, Jacob, The "Sharpe" teleplays.

BEART, EMMANUELLE
Actress. b. Gassin, France, Aug. 14, 1965. Moved to Montreal at age 15. Returned to France and enrolled in drama school.
THEATER: La Repetition ou l'Amour Puni, La Double Inconstance.

PICTURES: Premiers Desirs, L'Enfant Trouve, L'Amour en Douce, Manon of the Spring, Date With an Angel, A Gauche en Sortant de L'Ascenseur, Les Enfants du Desordre, Capitaine Fracasse, La Belle Noiseuse, J'Embrasse Pas, Un Coeur en Hiver, Ruptures, Divertimento, L'Enfer, Une Femme Francaise, Nelly & Mr. Arnaud, Mission: Impossible, Voleur de Vie, Le Temps Retrouve, Don Juan.
TELEVISION: Zacharius, Raison Perdue.

BEATTY, NED
Actor. b. Lexington, KY, July 6, 1937. Worked at Barter Theatre in Virginia appearing in over 70 plays, 1957-66; with Arena Stage, Washington D.C. 1963-71. Made Bway debut in The Great White Hope.
PICTURES: Deliverance (debut, 1972), The Life and Times of Judge Roy Bean, The Thief Who Came to Dinner, The Last American Hero, White Lightning, Nashville, W.W. and the Dixie Dance Kings, All the President's Men, The Big Bus, Network, Mikey and Nicky, Silver Streak, Exorcist II: The Heretic, Gray Lady Down, The Great Georgia Bank Hoax, Superman, Alambrista!, Promises in the Dark, 1941, Wise Blood, American Success Company, Hopscotch, The Incredible Shrinking Woman, Superman II, The Toy, Touched, Stroker Ace, Back to School, The Big Easy, The Fourth Protocol, The Trouble With Spies, Switching Channels, Rolling Vengeance, The Unholy, Midnight Crossing, After the Rain, Purple People Eater, Physical Evidence, Time Trackers, Big Bad John, Chattahoochee, A Cry in the Wild, Repossessed, Blind Vision, Going Under, Hear My Song, Prelude to a Kiss, Ed and His Dead Mother, Rudy, Black Water, Radioland Murders, Just Cause, The Curse of Inferno, He Got Game, Life, Cookie's Fortune.
TELEVISION: *Movies*: Footsteps, Marcus-Nelson Murders, Dying Room Only, The Execution of Private Slovik, Attack on Terror: The FBI vs. the Ku Klux Klan, The Deadly Tower, Tail Gunner Joe, Lucan, A Question of Love, Friendly Fire, Guyana Tragedy: The Story of Jim Jones, All God's Children, The Violation of Sarah McDavid, Splendor in the Grass, Pray TV, A Woman Called Golda, Kentucky Woman, Hostage Flight, Go Toward the Light, Spy, Last Train Home, Back to Hannibal, The Tragedy of Flight 103: The Inside Story, Trial: The Price of Passion, T Bone N Weasel, Gulliver's Travels. *Mini-Series:* Celebrity, The Last Days of Pompeii, Robert Kennedy and His Times, Streets of Laredo. *Special*: Our Town. *Series*: Szysznyk, The Boys, Homicide: Life on the Street, The Great War (voice). *Guest*: Murder She Wrote, M*A*S*H, Rockford Files, Alfred Hitchcock, B.L. Stryker, Roseanne.

BEATTY, WARREN
Actor., Producer, Director, Writer. r.n. Henry Warren Beaty. b. Richmond, VA, March 30, 1937. e. Northwestern U. Sister is actress Shirley MacLaine. m. actress Annette Bening. Studied with Stella Adler. Small roles on television; on stage in Compulsion (winter stock, North Jersey Playhouse); B'way debut: A Loss of Roses (Theatre World Award).
PICTURES: Splendor in the Grass (debut, 1961), The Roman Spring of Mrs. Stone, All Fall Down, Lilith, Mickey One, Promise Her Anything, Kaleidoscope, Bonnie and Clyde (also prod.), The Only Game in Town, McCabe and Mrs. Miller, $ (Dollars), The Parallax View, Shampoo (also prod., co-s.p.), The Fortune, Heaven Can Wait (also prod., co-dir., co-s.p.), Reds (also prod., dir., co-s.p.; Acad. Award for Best dir., 1981), Ishtar (also prod.), Dick Tracy (also prod., dir.), Bugsy (also co-prod.), Madonna: Truth or Dare, Love Affair (also prod, co-s.p.), Bulworth (also prod., dir., s.p.; Acad. Award nom.), Forever Hollywood, Town and Country
TELEVISION: *Specials*: AFI's Salute to Dustin Hoffman. *Series*: The Many Loves of Dobie Gillis (1959-60). *Guest*: Kraft Television Theatre, Studio One, Suspicion, Alcoa Presents, One Step Beyond, Wagon Train.

BECK, ALEXANDER J.
Executive. b. Ung. Brod, Czechoslovakia, Nov. 5, 1926. e. Charles U., Prague; NYU. Owns 500 features and westerns for foreign distribution and library of 1400 shorts, importer and exporter. Pres., chmn. of bd. Alexander Beck Films, 1955. Formed Albex Films and A.B. Enterprises, 1959; formed & pres., Beckman Film Corp., 1960; formed Alexander Beck Productions, 1964. In 1969 formed Screencom Int'l Corp., 1986, formed Beck Int'l Corp., 1987; formed Challenger Pictures Corp., 1988.

BECK, JACKSON
Actor, announcer, narrator. b. New York, NY. TV and radio commercials, children's records, comm. industrial films; Narrator.

BECK, MICHAEL
Actor. r.n. Michael Beck Tucker. b. Memphis, TN, Feb. 4, 1949. e. Millsaps Coll. on football scholarship (quarterback). Became active in college theatre. In 1971 attended Central Sch. of Speech and Drama, London; studied 3 years, following which toured England with repertory companies for 2 years. Returned to U.S.; cast as lead in independent film, Madman (shot in Israel in 1977).
PICTURES: Madman, The Warriors, Xanadu, Megaforce, War Lords of the 21st Century, The Golden Seal, Triumphs of a Man Called Horse, Final Judgment, Forest Warrior.
TELEVISION: *Movies*: Mayflower: the Pilgrim's Adventure, Alcatraz: The Whole Shocking Story, Fly Away Home, The Last Ninja, Rearview Mirror, Chiller, Blackout, Only One Survived, The Reckoning, Houston: Legend of Texas, Deadly Game, Deadly Aim, Stranger at My Door, Fade to Black. *Series*: Houston Knights. *Mini-Series*: Holocaust, Celebrity.

BECKER, HAROLD
Director. b. New York, NY. Dir. documentaries, Eugene Atget Interview with Bruce Gordon, Blind Gary Davis, Signet, Ivanhoe Donaldson.
PICTURES: The Ragman's Daughter (debut, 1972), The Onion Field, The Black Marble, Taps, Vision Quest, The Boost, Sea of Love, Malice (also co-prod.), City Hall (also co-prod.), Mercury Rising, Solo.

BEDELIA, BONNIE
Actress. r.n. Bonnie Bedelia Culkin. b. New York, NY, March 25, 1946. e. Hunter Coll.
THEATER: Enter Laughing, The Playroom, My Sweet Charlie (Theatre World Award).
PICTURES: The Gypsy Moths (debut, 1969), They Shoot Horses Don't They?, Lovers and Other Strangers, The Strange Vengeance of Rosalie, The Big Fix, Heart Like a Wheel, Death of an Angel, Violets Are Blue, The Boy Who Could Fly, The Stranger, Die Hard, The Prince of Pennsylvania, Fat Man and Little Boy, Die Hard 2, Presumed Innocent, Needful Things, Speechless, Judicial Consent, Homecoming, Bad Manners, Gloria.
TELEVISION: *Movies*: Then Came Bronson, Sandcastles, A Time for Love, Hawkins on Murder (Death and the Maiden), Message to My Daughter, Heatwave!, A Question of Love, Walking Through the Fire, Salem's Lot, Tourist, Fighting Back, Million Dollar Infield, Memorial Day, Alex: The Life of a Child, The Lady from Yesterday, Somebody Has to Shoot the Picture, Switched at Birth, A Mother's Right: The Elizabeth Morgan Story, The Fire Next Time, Judicial Consent, Legacy of Sin: The William Coit Story, Shadow of a Doubt, Her Costly Affair, A Season in Purgatory, Any Mother's Son, To Live Again, Locked in Silence. *Special:* The Gift. *Series*: Love of Life (1961-67), The New Land, Partners. Guest: Fallen Angels, Bonanza, The Outer Limits.

BEGLEY, ED, JR.
Actor. b. Los Angeles, CA, Sept. 16, 1949. Son of late actor Ed Begley. Debut in a guest appearance on My Three Sons at 17. On NY stage in The Cryptogram.
PICTURES: The Computer Wore Tennis Shoes (debut, 1970), Now You See Him Now You Don't, Showdown, Superdad, Cockfighter, Stay Hungry, Citizens Band, Blue Collar, The One and Only, Goin' South, Hardcore, Battlestar Gallactica, The In-Laws, The Concorde: Airport '79, Private Lessons, Cat People, Eating Raoul, Get Crazy, This Is Spinal Tap, Streets of Fire, Protocol, Transylvania 6-5000, Amazon Women on the Moon, The Accidental Tourist, Scenes From the Class Struggle in Beverly Hills, She-Devil, Meet the Applegates, Dark Horse, Greedy, Even Cowgirls Get the Blues, Renaissance Man, The Pagemaster, Batman Forever, The Lay of the Land, Joey, I'm Losing You, Addams Family Reunion.
TELEVISION: *Movies*: Family Flight, Amateur Night at the Dixie Bar and Grill, Elvis, Hot Rod, A Shining Season, Rascals and Robbers - The Secret Adventures of Tom Sawyer and Huck Finn, Tales of the Apple Dumpling Gang, Voyagers, Not Just Another Affair, Still the Beaver, An Uncommon Love, Insight/The Clearing House, Roman Holiday, Spies Lies & Naked Thighs, Not a Penny More Not a Penny Less, In the Best Inerest of the Child, The Big One: The Great Los Angeles Earthquake, Chance of a Lifetime, The Story Lady, In the Line of Duty: Siege at Marion, Exclusive, Running Mates. Cooperstown, World War II: When Lions Roared, Columbo: Undercover, Incident at Deception Ridge, The Shaggy Dog, Murder She Purred: A mrs. Murphy Mystery. *Specials*: Mastergate, Partners. *Series*: Roll Out, St. Elsewhere (1982-88), Parenthood, Winnetka Road. *Guest*: Room 222, Love American Style, Happy Days, Columbo, M*A*S*H, Barnaby Jones, Doris Day Show, Mary Hartman Mary Hartman, Faerie Tale Theatre, Meego, Ellen, The Simpsons, The Drew Carey Show, The Larry Sanders Show.

BEINEIX, JEAN-JACQUES
Director, Writer. b. Paris France, October, 8, 1946.
PICTURES: Diva, The Moon in the Gutter, Betty Blue (also prod.), Roselyne et les lions, IP 5: The Island of Pachyderms (also prod.), Otaku (dir. & prod. only), Mortel transfert.

BELAFONTE, HARRY
Actor, Singer, Producer. b. New York, NY, March 1, 1927. Trained for stage at the Actors Studio, New Sch. for Social Research and American Negro Theatre. Professional debut, Royal Roost nightclub, N.Y., Village Vanguard, 1950. Broadway debut: John Murray Anderson's Almanac, 1953. Recording, concert artist. Emmy Award for Tonight With Harry Belafonte, 1961.
THEATER: Juno and the Paycock, John Murray Anderson's Almanac. (Tony Award, 1953), Three for Tonight, A Night With Belafonte, To Be Young Gifted and Black (prod.), Asinamali (co-prod.).

PICTURES: Bright Road (debut, 1953), Carmen Jones, Island in the Sun, Odds Against Tomorrow, The World the Flesh and the Devil, The Angel Levine, Buck and the Preacher, Uptown Saturday Night (also prod.), Beat Street (prod. only), The Player, Ready to Wear (Pret-a-Porter), White Man's Burden, Kansas City (NY Society of Film Critics Award, 1997), Jazz '34, Swing Vote.
TELEVISION: *Movies*: Grambling's White Tiger, Parting the Waters (exec. prod. only). Many variety specials. *Series*: Sugar Hill Times.

BELAFONTE, SHARI
Actress. b. New York, NY, Sept. 22, 1954. e. Carnegie-Mellon U., BFA, 1976. Daughter of actor-singer Harry Belafonte. Worked as publicist's asst. at Hanna Barbera Prods. before becoming successful model (appearing on more than 200 magazine covers and in numerous TV commercials).
PICTURES: If You Could See What I Hear, Time Walker, Murder One Murder Two, The Player, Fire—Ice & Dynamite, Mars, Loving Evangeline.
TELEVISION: *Movies*: The Night the City Screamed, The Midnight Hour, Kate's Secret, Perry Mason: The Case of the All-Star Assassin, French Silk, Heidi Chronicles, Babylon 5, Babylon 5: Thirdspace. *Host*: Big Hex of Little Lulu, AM Los Angeles, Living the Dream: a Tribute to Dr. Martin Luther King Jr., Lifestyles with Robin Leach and Shari Belafonte, First Edition, The Caribbean with Shari Belafonte. *Series*: Hotel. *Pilot*: Velvet, Beyond Reality. *Guest*: Hart to Hart, Code Red, Trapper John M.D., Different Strokes, The Love Boat, Matt Houston.

BELFER, HAL B.
Executive Producer, Director, Choreographer. b. Los Angeles, CA, Feb. 16. e. USC; U. of CA (writing). Head of choreography depts. at both 20th Century-Fox and Universal Studios. Dir. of entertainment, in Las Vegas, Riviera and Flamingo Hotels. Prod., musical shows for Mexico City, Aruba, Puerto Rico, Montreal, Las Vegas. Dir., TV commercials and industrials. H.R. Pufnstuf TV series. Prod., dir., choreographer, Premore, Inc. Develop TV specials and sitcom, tape and film. Exec. prod.: Once Upon a Tour and Dora's World, Rose on Broadway, Secret Sleuth, Inn by the Side of the Road, Imagine That! Special staging Tony The Pony Series and prod., segment of What a Way to Run a Railroad; TV specials. Talent dev't. programs, Universal Studios, 20th Century-Fox. Personal mgr. and show packager. 1982, exec. prod.: Enchanted Inn (TV Special), Cameo Music Hall I; stage mgr.: Promises, Promises, A Chorus Line (Sahara Hotel, Las Vegas). Created: Hal Belfer Associates Talent and Production Consultant; Convention Destination & Services Consultant.

BEL GEDDES, BARBARA
Actress. r.n. Barbara Geddes Lewis. b. New York, NY, Oct 31, 1922. Father was Norman Bel Geddes, scenic designer. B'way debut in Out of the Frying Pan. Toured USO camps in Junior Miss, 1941; voted Star of Tomorrow, 1949. Author-illustrator children's books: I Like to Be Me (1963), So Do I (1972). Also designer of greeting cards for George Caspari Co.
THEATER: Out of the Frying Pan, Deep Are the Roots, Burning Bright, The Moon Is Blue, Living Room, Cat on a Hot Tin Roof, The Sleeping Prince, Silent Night Holy Night, Mary Mary, Everything in the Garden, Finishing Touches.
PICTURES: The Long Night (debut, 1947), I Remember Mama (Acad Award nom.), Blood on the Moon, Caught, Panic in the Streets, Fourteen Hours, Vertigo, The Five Pennies, Five Branded Women, By Love Possessed, Summertree, The Todd Killings.
TELEVISION: Live TV in 1950s: Robert Montgomery Presents (The Philadelphia Story), Schlitz Playhouse of the Stars; several Alfred Hitchcock Presents episodes (incl. Lamb to the Slaughter), Our Town. *Series*: Dallas (Emmy Award, 1980).

BELL, TOM
Actor. b. Liverpool, England, 1932. Early career in repertory and on West End stage. First TV appearance in Promenade.
PICTURES: The Concrete Jungle (The Criminal; debut, 1960), Echo of Barbara, Payroll, The Kitchen, H.M.S. Defiant (Damn the Defiant!), A Prize of Arms, The L-Shaped Room, Ballad in Blue (Blues for Lovers), He Who Rides a Tiger, Sands of Beersheba, In Enemy Country, The Long Day's Dying, Lock Up Your Daughters, All the Right Noises, The Violent Enemy, Quest for Love, Straight on Till Morning, Royal Flash, The Sailor's Return, Stronger Than the Sun, The Innocent, Wish You Were Here, Resurrected, The Magic Toy Shop, The Krays, Let Him Have It, Angels, Seconds Out, Feast of July, Swept for the Sea, Preaching to the Perverted, The Boxer, Swing.
TELEVISION: No Trams to Lime Street, Love on the Dole, A Night Out, The Seekers, Long Distance Blue, Summer Lightning, Hard Travelling, White Knight, The Virginian, The Rainbow, Prime Suspect 3, Dalziel and Pascoe: Recalled to Life. *Mini-Series:* The Cinder Path, No Bananas, The Great Kandinsky.

BELLAMY, EARL
Producer, Director. b. Minneapolis, MN, March 11, 1917. e. Los Angeles City Coll. President, The Bellamy Productions Co.
PICTURES: Seminole Uprising (debut, 1955), Blackjack Ketchum: Desperado, Toughest Gun in Tombstone, Stagecoach to Dancers' Rock (also prod.), Fluffy, Gunpoint, Munster Go Home!, Incident at Phantom Hill, Three Guns for Texas, Sidecar Racers, Seven Alone, Part 2: Walking Tall, Against a Crooked Sky, Sidewinder 1, Speedtrap, Magnum Thrust.
TELEVISION: Bachelor Father, Wells Fargo, Lone Ranger, Alcoa Premiere, Arrest and Trial, The Virginian, The Crusaders, Schlitz Playhouse, Rawhide, The Donna Reed Show, Andy Griffith Show, Wagon Train, Laramie, Laredo, I Spy, Mod Squad, Medical Center.

BELLFORT, JOSEPH
Executive. b. New York, NY, Sept. 20, 1912. e. NYU, Brooklyn Law Sch. Joined RKO Service Corp., 1930; trans. to RKO Radio Pictures, legal dept., 1942; joined RKO Fgn. dept., 1944; handled Far Eastern division, 1946; then asst. to European gen. mgr.; gen. European mgr., 1949-1958. Gen. sales mgr. Nat'l Screen Service, 1959. Home office supv., Europe & Near East, 20th Century-Fox, 1963; home office intl. mgr., 20th Century-Fox, 1966; asst. v.p. & foreign mgr. 20th Cent.-Fox, 1967; v.p. 20th Century-Fox, Intl. Corp. & Inter-America, Inc. 1968; named sr. v.p., 1975. Resigned from Fox, 1977, to become v.p., Motion Picture Export Assn. of America in New York. Retired 1983.

BELLFORT, TOM
Sound.
PICTURES: Rumble Fish, The Cotton Club, The Journey of Natty Gann, Seize the Day, Tucker: The Man and His Dream, The Godfather: Part III, Bingo!, The Last Supper, One Fine Day, Titanic (Acad. Award, Best Sound Editing, 1997), Star Wars: Episode I-The Phantom Menace.

BELLOCCHIO, MARCO
Director, Writer. b. Piacenza, Italy, Nov. 9, 1939. e. Academy of Cinematografia, Rome (studying acting, then film directing); Slade School of Fine Arts, London 1959-63.
PICTURES: Fist in His Pocket (debut, 1965), China Is Near, Amore e Rabbia (segment: Discutiamo Discutiamo), Nel Nome del Padre, Slap the Monster on the Front Page (also co-s.p.), Madmen to Be Released, Triumphal March, Il Gabbiano, The Film Machine, Leap Into the Void, The Eyes and the Mouth, Henry IV, Devil in the Flesh, The Sabba's Vision, The Conviction, The Butterfly's Dream, Broken Dreams, The Prince of Homburg, The Nanny.

BELMONDO, JEAN-PAUL
Actor. b. Neuilly-sur-Seine, France, April 9, 1933. e. private drama school of Raymond Girard, and the Conservatoire d'Art Dramatique. Formed a theater group with Annie Girardot and Guy Bedos.
THEATER: (Jean Marais' production) Caesar and Cleopatra, Treasure Party, Oscar, Kean, Cyrano de Bergerac, Tailleur pour Dames, La Puce a L'Oreille.
PICTURES: A Pied a Cheval et En Voiture (By Foot Horse and Car), Look Pretty and Shut Up, Drole de Dimanche, Les Tricheurs, Les Copains du Dimanche, Charlotte et Son Jules, A Double Tour, Breathless, Classe Tous Risques, Moderato Cantabile, La Francaise et l'Amour, Les Distractions, Mademoiselle Ange, La Novice, Two Women, La Viaccia, Une Femme Est une Femme, Leon Morin Pretre, Les Amours Celebres, Un Singe en Hiver, Le Doulos, L'Aine des Ferchaux, La Mer A Boire, Banana Peel, That Man From Rio, Cent Mille Dollars au Soleil, Echappement Libre, La Chasse a l'Homme, Dieu a Choisi Paris, Weekend a Zuydcocte, Par Un Beau Matin d'Ete, Up to His Ears, Is Paris Burning?, Casino Royale, The Thief of Paris, Pierrot le Fou, The Brain, Love Is a Funny Thing, Mississippi Mermaid, Borsalino, A Man I Like, The Burglars, Tender Scoundrel, Inheritor, Stavisky, Fear Over the City, L'Animal, The Professional, Ace of Aces, The Vultures, Happy Easter, Hold Up, Le Solitaire, Itinerary of a Spoiled Child (also prod., Cesar Award), L'Inconnu dans la Maison, Les Miserables, Les Cent et une Nuits, Desire, Une chance sur deux, Peut-etre, Les Acteurs, Amazone.

BELSON, JERRY
Producer, Director, Writer. With Garry Marshall, writer of The Dick Van Dyke Show, prod. of The Odd Couple. Co-authoring the Broadway play The Roast (1980).
PICTURES: How Sweet It Is (prod., s.p.), The Grasshopper (s.p., prod.), Smile (s.p.), Fun With Dick and Jane (s.p.), Smokey and the Bandit II (s.p.), Student Bodies (exec. prod.), The End (s.p.), Jekyll and Hyde Together Again (dir.), Surrender (dir., s.p.), For Keeps (prod.), Always (co-s.p.).
TELEVISION: *Special*: Billy Crystal: Midnight Train to Moscow (co-writer; Emmy Award). *Series*: The Dick Van Dyke Show, The Odd Couple, The Tracey Ullmann Show (co-creator, co-exec. prod.; Emmy Awards), Tracey Takes On..., The Norm Show (consulting prod.).

BELUSHI, JAMES
Actor. b. Chicago, IL, June 15, 1954. e. DuPage Coll., Southern Illinois U. Brother was late actor John Belushi. Began at Chicago's Second City Theatre.
THEATER: Sexual Perversity in Chicago, The Pirates of Penzance, True West, Conversations With My Father, Baal.

PICTURES: Thief (debut, 1981), Trading Places, The Man with One Red Shoe, Salvador, About Last Night, Jumpin' Jack Flash, Little Shop of Horrors, Number One With a Bullet (co-s.p. only), The Principal, Real Men, Red Heat, Who's Harry Crumb?, K-9, Homer and Eddie, Wedding Band, Taking Care of Business, Mr. Destiny, The Palermo Connection, Only the Lonely, Masters of Menace (cameo), Curly Sue, Once Upon a Crime, Diary of a Hitman (cameo), Traces of Red, Last Action Hero (cameo), The Pebble and the Penguin (voice), Destiny Turns on the Radio, Separate Lives, Canadian Bacon, Race the Sun, Jingle All the Way, Gold in the Streets, Retroactive, Bad Baby (voice), Living in Peril, Gang Related, Wag the Dog, Justice,The Florentine, Angel's Dance, Made Men, Return to Me.
TELEVISION: *Movies:* Royce, Parallel Lives, Sahara, K-9 II, Who Killed Atlanta's Children? *Mini-Series*: Wild Palms. *Specials*: The Joseph Jefferson Awards, The Best Legs in the 8th Grade, Cinemax's Comedy Experiment's Birthday Boy (also prod., writer). *Series*: Who's Watching the Kids?, Working Stiffs, Saturday Night Live, Mighty Ducks, Superman, It's Good to Be King, Total Security, Hercules.

BELZER, RICHARD
Actor, Comedian. b. Bridgeport, CT, Aug. 4, 1944.
PICTURES: The Groove Tube (debut, 1974), Fame, Author Author, Night Shift, Scarface, America, Flicks, The Wrong Guys, Freeway, Fletch Lives, The Big Picture, The Bonfire of the Vanities, Off and Running, Mad Dog and Glory, Girl 6, A Very Brady Sequel, Get on the Bus, Species II, The Bar Channel, Man on the Moon, Jump.
TELEVISION: *Movies:* Not of This Earth, Prince for a Day, Homicide: The Movie. *Specials*: On Location: Richard Belzer in Concert (also writer), Belzer on Broadway (also writer, exec. prod.). *Series*: The Late Show (host), Homicide: Life on the Street, Law & Order: Special Victims Unit. *Guest*: The X-Files, Law & Order.

BENBEN, BRIAN
Actor. b. Winchester, VA, June 18. Raised in Marlboro, NY. m. actress Madeleine Stowe. In regional and alternative theatre before making B'way debut in Slab Boys.
PICTURES: Clean and Sober (debut, 1988), Dangerous Obsession (Mortal Sins), I Come in Peace, Radioland Murders.
TELEVISION: *Movies/Specials*: Conspiracy: The Trial of the Chicago 8, Comfort, Texas. *Series*: The Gangster Chronicles, Kay O'Brien, Dream On (Cable ACE Award, 1992), The Brian Benben Show (also co-exec. prod.).

BENDICK, ROBERT
Indep. documentary prod., dir. b. New York, NY, Feb. 8, 1917. e. NYU, White School Photography. U.S. Air Force, W.W.II. Documentary and still cameraman before joining CBS Television as cameraman and dir., 1940; rejoined CBS Television as dir. special events, 1946; promoted dir. news & special events; acting program dir. 1947; resigned 1951. Collaborated with Jeanne Bendick on: Making the Movies, Electronics for Young People, Television Works Like This, Filming Works Like This, 1971. Prod. Peabody Award-winning U.N. show The U.N. in Action. V.p., Cinerama Prod. Co-prod., This Is Cinerama; co-dir., Cinerama Holiday; prod., Dave Garroway Show Today and Wide Wide World, 1955-56. NBC prod. dir. C.V. Whitney Pict., 1956; Merian C. Cooper Ent., 1957; prod. NBC, 1958. Prod.: Garroway Today Show, Bob Hope 25 Yrs. of Life Show, 1961; Bell Telephone Threshold Science Series, Groucho Marx, Merrily We Roll Along, US Steel Opening New York World's Fair, 1964; First Look Series 1965 (Ohio St. Award); also dir. American Sportsman, ABC; prod., pilot, Great American Dream Machine (NET) (Emmy Award, 1971 and 1972); co-exec. prod., Dick Cavett—Feeling Good, 1975. Pres. Bendick Assoc. Inc.; prod. of education audio-visual systems. Bd. of Govs., NY Academy of TV Arts and Sciences. 1976, co-author with Jeanne Bendick, TV Reporting. Consultant, Warner Qube Cable Co. Prod., dir., Fight for Food (PBS), 1978. Program consultant to Times-Mirror Cable Co., L.A. Prod. segment ABC 20/20. Member awards committee, National TV Acad. Arts & Science. Co-author with Jeanne Bendick of Eureka It's Television (1993). Inducted into Natl. TV Academy Arts & Science, NY chapter, Silver Circle, 1994. Co-author with Jeanne Bendick of Markets—From Barter to Bar Codes, 1998.

BENDER, LAWRENCE
Producer.
PICTURES: Intruder (also story), Reservoir Dogs, Fresh, Killing Zoe (exec. prod.), Pulp Fiction, Four Rooms, White Man's Burden, From Dusk Till Dawn (exec. prod.), Good Will Hunting, Jackie Brown, A Price Above Rubies, From Dusk Till Dawn: The Hangman's Daughter (exec. prod), Anna and the King, From Dusk Till Dawn 2: Texas Blood Money (exec. prod.), Knockaround Guys, The Mexican.

BENEDICT, DIRK
Actor. r.n. Dirk Niewoehner. b. Helena, MT, March 1, 1945. e. Whitman Coll., Walla Walla, WA. Enrolled in John Fernald Academy of Dramatic Arts, Rochester, MI, after which had season with Seattle Repertory Theatre; also in summer stock at Ann Arbor, MI. Made B'way debut in Abelard and Heloise, 1970. Author: Confessions of a Kamikaze Cowboy, And Then We Went Fishing. Film debut, Georgia, Georgia, 1972.
PICTURES: Ssssss, W, Battlestar Galactica, Scavenger Hunt, Ruckus, Underground Aces, Body Slam, Blue Tornado, Shadow Force, Cahoots, Tales From the Crypt Presents Demon Knight, Alaska, The Feminine Touch.
TELEVISION: *Movies*: Journey from Darkness, The Georgia Peaches, Scruples, Trenchcoat in Paradise, Abduction of Innocence. *Series*: Chopper One, Battlestar Galactica, The A Team, Steel Stomach (host). *Guest*: Love Boat, Murder She Wrote, Hawaii Five-O.

BENEDICT, PAUL
Actor, Director. b. Silver City, NM, Sept. 17, 1938. Acted with the Theatre Company of Boston, Arena Stage, D.C.; Trinity Rep., Providence; Playhouse in the Park, Cincinnati; Center Stage, Baltimore; A.R.T., Cambridge.
THEATER: *NY*: Little Murders, The White House Murder Case, Bad Habits, It's Only a Play, Richard III, The Play's the Thing. *LA*: The Unvarnished Truth, It's Only a Play. *Director*: Frankie & Johnnie in the Clair de Lune, Bad Habits, The Kathy and Mo Show, Beyond Therapy, Geniuses, Any Given Day.
PICTURES: The Virgin President, They Might Be Giants (debut, 1971), The Gang that Couldn't Shoot Straight, Cold Turkey, Taking Off, Up the Sandbox, Deadhead Miles, Jeremiah Johnson, The Front Page, Mandingo, The Goodbye Girl, Billy in the Lowlands, The Man With Two Brains, This Is Spinal Tap, Arthur 2 on the Rocks, Cocktail, The Chair, The Freshman, Sibling Rivalry, The Addams Family, Waiting for Guffman.
TELEVISION: *Movies*: Hustling, Baby Cakes, Attack of the 50 Ft. Woman. *Mini-Series*: The Blue and the Gray. *Series*: Sesame Street (1969-74), The Jeffersons, Mama Malone. *Guest*: Kojak, Maude, All in the Family, Harry-O, Seinfeld.

BENIGNI, ROBERTO
Actor, Writer, Director, Producer. b. Misericordia, Arezzo, Italy, Oct. 27, 1952. Won Best Actor and Best Foreign Film Oscar for Life is Beautiful.
PICTURES: Berlinguer ti voglio bene (also s.p.), Giorni cantati, Chiedo asilo (also s.p.), Clair de femme, La Luna, In the Pope's Eye, Il Minestrone, Tu mi turbi (also s.p., dir.), F.F.S.S. cioe che mi hai portato a fare sopra Posillipo se non mi vuoi piu bene, Nothing Left to Do But Cry (also s.p., dir.), Coffee and Cigarettes, Down by Law, The Little Devil (also s.p., dir.), The Voice of the Moon, Johnny Toothpick (also s.p., dir.), Night on Earth, Son of the Pink Panther, The Monster (also s.p., dir., prod.), Life Is Beautiful (also s.p., dir.; Acad. Award for Best Actor, nom. for dir., s.p.), Asterix and Obelix vs. Caesar, Pinocchio.

BENING, ANNETTE
Actress. b. Topeka, KS, May 29, 1958. Raised in San Diego. e. San Francisco St. Univ. m. actor Warren Beatty. Acted with San Francisco's American Conservatory Theatre. Voted Star of the Year, 2000 at ShoWest.
THEATER: Coastal Disturbances (Tony Award nom., Theatre World & Clarence Derwent Awards), Spoils of War.
PICTURES: The Great Outdoors (debut, 1988), Valmont, Postcards from the Edge, The Grifters (Natl. Society of Film Critics Award, Acad. Award nom., 1990), Guilty by Suspicion, Regarding Henry, Bugsy, Love Affair, The American President, Richard III, Mars Attacks.!, The Seige, In Dreams, American Beauty (SAG, BAFTA awards), Forever Hollywood, What Planet Are You From?.
TELEVISION: *Movies*: Manhunt for Claude Dallas, Hostage. *Guest*: Miami Vice, Wiseguy. *Pilot*: It Had to Be You.

BENJAMIN, RICHARD
Actor, Director. b. New York, NY, May 22, 1939. e. Northwestern U. m. actress Paula Prentiss.
THEATER: (Central Park productions) The Taming of the Shrew, As You Like It; toured in Tchin Tchin, A Thousand Clowns, Barefoot in the Park, The Odd Couple. Star Spangled Girl (B'way debut; Theatre World Award, 1966). *Also*: The Little Black Book, The Norman Conquests, Barefoot in the Park (dir. only; London prod).
PICTURES: *Actor*: Goodbye Columbus, Catch-22, Diary of a Mad Housewife, The Marriage of a Young Stockbroker, The Steagle, Portnoy's Complaint, The Last of Sheila, Westworld, The Sunshine Boys (Golden Globe Award), House Calls, Love at First Bite, Scavenger Hunt, The Last Married Couple in America, Witches' Brew, How to Beat the High Cost of Living, First Family, Saturday the 14th, Deconstructing Harry. *Director*: My Favorite Year, Racing with the Moon, City Heat, The Money Pit, Little Nikita, My Stepmother Is an Alien, Downtown, Mermaids, Made in America, Milk Money, Mrs. Winterbourne, The Shrink is In.
TELEVISION: *Movies*: No Room to Run (Australia), Packin' It In, The Pentagon Wars (also dir.) *Special*: Arthur Miller's Fame. *Series*: He and She (with Paula Prentiss, 1967), Quark.

BENNETT, ALAN
Author, Actor. b. Leeds, England, May 9, 1934. e. Oxford U. With Jonathan Miller, Dudley Moore and Peter Cook co-authored and starred in satirical revue Beyond the Fringe in London (1961) and on B'way (special Tony Award, 1963).
THEATER: Forty Years On (actor, author), Getting On, Habeas Corpus (also actor), The Old Country, Enjoy, Kafka's Dick, Single Spies (also dir.), The Madness of George III.

PICTURES: *Actor*: Pleasure at Her Majesty's, The Secret Policeman's Other Ball, Long Shot, Dream Child (voice), Little Dorrit, The Wind in the Willows (voice), In Love And War, The Land Girls. *Writer:* A Private Function, Prick Up Your Ears, The Madness of King George (also actor).
TELEVISION: Famous Gossips, On the Margin (also actor), An Evening With, A Day Out, Sunset Across the Bay, A Little Outing, A Visit from Miss Prothero, Me—I'm Afraid of Virginia Wood, Doris and Doreen, The Old Crowd, Afternoon Off, All Day on the Sands, The Insurance Man, Talking Heads (6 TV monologues), One Fine Day, Our Winnie, A Woman of No Importance, Rolling Home, Marks, An Englishman Abroad, Intensive Care (also actor), 102 Boulevard Haussmann, Poetry in Motion. *Mini-Series*: A Dance to the Music of Time (actor), Talking Heads 2.

BENNETT, BRUCE
Actor. r.n. Herman Brix. b. Tacoma, WA, May 19, 1909. e. U. of W.
PICTURES: My Son Is Guilty, Lone Wolf Keeps a Date, Atlantic Convoy, Sabotage, Underground Agent, The More the Merrier, Sahara, Mildred Pierce, The Man I Love, A Stolen Life, Nora Prentiss, Cheyenne, Dark Passage, Treasure of the Sierra Madre, Smart Girls Don't Talk, Task Force, The Second Face, The Great Missouri Raid, Angels in the Outfield, Sudden Fear, Dream Wife, Dragonfly Squadron, Robber's Roost, Big Tipoff, Hidden Guns, Bottom of the Bottle, Strategic Air Command, Danger Signal, Silver River, Younger Brothers, Without Honor, Mystery Street, The Last Outpost, Three Violent People, The Outsider, Deadhead Miles, The Clones.

BENNETT, HARVE
Producer. r.n. Harve Fischman. b. Chicago, IL, Aug. 17, 1930. e. UCLA. Quiz Kids radio show, 5 yrs.; newspaper columnist, drama critic; freelance writer; Assoc. prod., CBS-TV; freelance TV writer; prod. of special events. CBS-TV; dir., Television film commercials; program exec., ABC, vice pres., programs west coast, ABC-TV. Pres., Bennett-Katleman. Productions at Columbia Studios.
PICTURES: Star Trek II: The Wrath of Khan (exec. prod., co-story), Star Trek IV: The Voyage Home (also co-s.p.), Star Trek V: The Final Frontier (also co-story).
TELEVISION: *Movies*: A Woman Named Golda (exec. prod.; Emmy Award), The Jesse Owens Story (exec. prod.), Crash Landing: The Rescue of Flight 232 (writer). *Mini-Series*: Rich Man Poor Man. *Series*: Mod Squad (prod., writer), The Young Rebels (creator-writer), Six Million Dollar Man (exec. prod.), Bionic Woman (exec. prod.). American Girls (exec. prod.). From Here to Eternity, Salvage 1, Time Trax (exec. prod.), Invasion America (also developer).

BENNETT, HYWEL
Actor, Director. b. Garnant, South Wales, Apr. 8, 1944. Early career National Youth Theatre where he played many leading Shakespearean roles followed by extensive work in British theatre. 1971-81: directed numerous stage productions.
PICTURES: The Family Way (debut, 1967), Drop Dead My Love, Twisted Nerve, The Virgin Soldiers, The Buttercup Chain, Loot, Percy, Endless Night, Alice in Wonderland, Murder Elite, War Zone, Deadline, Deadly Advice, Married 2 Malcolm.
TELEVISION: Where The Buffalo Roam, Malice Aforethought, Artemis 81, Myself A Mandarin, Frankie and Johnnie, Check Point Chiswick, Twilight Zone, The Idiot, The Traveller, Death of a Teddy Bear, Three's One, Pennies From Heaven, The Critic, The Consultant, Absent Friends, The Secret Agent, A Mind to Kill, Virtual Murder, The Other Side of Paradise, NeverWhere, Karaoke, Hospital! *Series:* Tinker Tailor Soldier Spy, Shelley.

BENNIS, JEFFREY D.
Executive. e. Penn. State U and U. Conn., MBA. Started with Clairol, Inc., Hair and Skin Care Divs. as marketing dir. VP Marketing/Programming of Rifkin & Assocs., 1991-94. Elected to bds. of Nat'l Cable TV Assoc. and C-SPAN in 1995. Pres. and COO, Rifkin & Assocs., 1994-.

BENSON, HUGH
Producer. Exec. Prod., Screen Gems; exec. prod., MGM Television. On staff Col.-TV, pilots and long form.
PICTURES: Nightmare Honeymoon, Logan's Run (assoc. prod.), Billy Jack Goes to Washington.
TELEVISION: Contract On Cherry St., Child Stealers, Goldie and the Boxer, A Fire in the Sky, Shadow Riders, Confessions of a Lady Cop, The Dream Merchants, Goldie and the Boxer Go to Hollywood, Goliath Awaits, The Blue and the Gray, Hart to Hart, Master of Ballantrae, Anna Karenina, The Other Lover, I Dream of Jeannie 15 Yrs. Later, Miracle of the Heart: A Boy's Town Story, Crazy Like a Fox, In the Heat of the Night (pilot and series), Daughter of the Streets, Back to Hannibal: Tom and Huck Return, Danielle Steele's Fine Things, Danielle Steele's Changes, Shadow of a Stranger, Diana: Her True Story, Danielle Steele's Message From 'Nam, A Season of Hope, Liz: The Elizabeth Taylor Story.

BENSON, ROBBY
Actor, Writer, Director. r.n. Robert Segal. b. Dallas, TX, Jan. 21, 1956. m. actress Karla DeVito. Father is Jerry Segal, novelist and screenwriter, mother is Ann Benson, veteran of Dallas stage and nat'l summer stock and nat'l spokesperson for Merrill Lynch. Appeared in commercials and summer stock at age 5. B'way debut at age 12 in Zelda. Made dir. debut with White Hot (a.k.a. Crack in the Mirror), 1989. Composed music for Diana Ross, Karla DeVito and soundtrack of film The Breakfast Club.
THEATER: *NY*: Zelda, The Rothschilds, Dude, The Pirates of Penzance. *Regional*: Oliver!, Evita, The King and I, King of Hearts, Do Black Patent Leather Shoes Really Reflect Up?
PICTURES: Jory (debut, 1973), Jeremy, Lucky Lady, Ode to Billy Joe, One on One (also co-s.p. with father), The End, Ice Castles, Walk Proud (also co-s.p. & co-composer with father), Die Laughing (also prod., co-s.p., co-composer), Tribute, National Lampoon Goes to the Movies, The Chosen, Running Brave, Harry and Son, City Limits, Rent-a-Cop, White Hot (also dir.), Modern Love (also dir., s.p., composed songs), Beauty and the Beast (voice), Betrayal of the Dove (s.p. only), At Home with the Webbers, Deadly Exposure, Belle's Magical World (voice), Beauty and the Beast: The Enchanted Christmas (voice).
TELEVISION: *Movies*: Death Be Not Proud, The Death of Richie, Remember When, Virginia Hill Story, All the Kind Strangers, Two of a Kind, California Girls, Invasion of Privacy, Homewrecker, Precious Victims. *Specials:* Our Town, The Last of Mrs. Lincoln. *Series*: Search for Tomorrow, Tough Cookies. Guest: One Day at a Time, Alfred Hitchcock Presents, Sabrina the Teenage Witch.. *Writer:* Animsed. *Episode dir.*: True Confessions, Thunder Alley, Evening Shade, Good Advice, Muddling Through, Monty, Dream On, Friends, Family Album, Ellen, House Rules, Jesse, Brother's Keeper, Reunited. *Pilot dir.*: Bringing Up Jack, George Wendt Show, Game Nigh, Commonlaw, Family Beat, Style & Substance, Sabrina the Teenage Witch (also episodes), The Naked Truth.

BENTON, ROBERT
Writer, Director. b. Waxahachie, TX, 1932. e. U. of Texas, B.A. Was art dir. and later consulting ed. at Esquire Magazine where he met David Newman, a writer-editor, and formed writing partnership. Together wrote a monthly column for Mademoiselle (10 years). Made dir. debut with Bad Company, 1972.
THEATER: It's a Bird... It's a Plane... It's Superman (libretto), Oh! Calcutta (one sketch).
PICTURES: *Co-writer* (with Newman): Bonnie and Clyde, There Was a Crooked Man, What's Up, Doc?, Superman (with Mario Puzo and Tom Mankiewicz). *Dir./Writer*: Bad Company, The Late Show, Kramer vs. Kramer (Acad. Awards for Best Dir. and Adapted Screenplay, 1979), Still of the Night, Places in the Heart (Acad. Award for Best Original Screenplay, 1984), Nadine, The House on Carroll Street (co-exec. prod. only), Billy Bathgate (dir. only), Nobody's Fool, Twilight, Double Jeopardy.

BERENGER, TOM
Actor. r.n. Thomas Michael Moore. b. Chicago, IL, May 31, 1950. e. U. of Missouri (drama). Studied acting at H.B. Studios. Acted in regional theatres and off-off-Broadway. Plays include Death Story, The Country Girl, National Anthems, The Rose Tattoo, Electra, Streetcar Named Desire, End as a Man (Circle Rep.).
PICTURES: The Sentinel (debut, 1977), Looking for Mr. Goodbar, In Praise of Older Women, Butch and Sundance: The Early Days, The Dogs of War, Beyond the Door, The Big Chill, Eddie and the Cruisers, Fear City, Rustler's Rhapsody, Platoon (Acad. Award nom.), Someone to Watch Over Me, Shoot to Kill, Betrayed, Last Rites, Major League, Born on the Fourth of July, Love at Large, The Field, Shattered, At Play in the Fields of the Lord, Sniper, Sliver, Gettysburg, Major League 2, Chasers, Last of the Dogmen, The Substitute, An Occasional Hell (also exec. prod.), Shadow of a Doubt, The Gingerbread Man, Takedown, One Man's Hero (also prod.), Diplomatic Siege, A Murder of Crows.
TELEVISION: *Movies*: Johnny We Hardly Knew Ye, The Avenging Angel, Body Language, Rough Riders (also prod.), In the Company of Spies. *Mini-Series:* Flesh and Blood, If Tomorrow Comes. *Special*: Dear America: Letters Home From Vietnam (reader). *Series*: One Life to Live (1975-76).

BERENSON, MARISA
Actress. b. New York, NY, Feb. 15, 1947. Granddaughter of haute couture fashion designer Schiaparelli. Great niece of art critic and historian Bernard Berenson. Former model.
PICTURES: Death in Venice (debut, 1971), Cabaret, Barry Lyndon, Casanova & Co., Killer Fish, S.O.B., The Secret Diary of Sigmund Freud, La Tete Dans Le Sac, L'Arbalete, Desire, Quel Treno da Vienna, Il Giardino Dei Cigliegi, Winds of the South, White Hunter Black Heart, Night of the Cyclone, The Cherry Orchard, Flagrant Desire, Tonka; Rich, belles, etc.
TELEVISION: *Movies*: Tourist, Playing for Time, Notorious. *Mini-Series*: Sins, Hemingway, Lo Scialo, Blue Blood, Have a Nice Night, L'Enfant Des Loups, Oceano, Hollywood Detective, Bel Ami, *Guest:* Murder She Wrote.

BERESFORD, BRUCE
Director, Writer. b. Sydney, Australia, Aug. 16, 1940. e. U. of Sydney, B.A. 1962. Worked as teacher in London, 1961. Film editor, East Nigerian Film Unit, 1966; sect. and head of prod., British Film Inst. Production Board, 1966-71.

PICTURES: The Adventures of Barry McKenzie (also co-s.p.), Barry McKenzie Holds His Own (also prod., co-s.p.), Don's Party, The Getting of Wisdom, Money Movers, Breaker Morant (also s.p.), The Club, Puberty Blues, Tender Mercies, King David, The Fringe Dwellers (also s.p.), Crimes of the Heart, Aria (sequence), Her Alibi, Driving Miss Daisy, Mister Johnson (also co-s.p.), Black Robe, Rich in Love, A Good Man in Africa, Silent Fall, The Last Dance, Paradise Road (also s.p.), Double Jeopardy.
TELEVISION: *Movie*: Curse of the Starving Class (writer, exec. prod.)

BERG, DICK
Writer, Producer. b. New York, NY. e. Lehigh U. 1942; Harvard Business Sch. 1943. Prior to 1960 writer for TV shows Playhouse 90 Studio One, Robert Montgomery Presents, Kraft Television Playhouse. Prod., writer for Universal Studios, 1961-69; exec. prod., The Chrysler Theatre, Alcoa Premiere, Checkmate. Created and wrote Staccato (series). Prod., writer of over 50 TV movies via his Stonehenge Prods, 1971-85. TV films won 15 Emmies, 23 nominations. Twice elected pres. National Acad. of Television Arts and Sciences.
PICTURES: *Prod.*: Counterpoint, House of Cards, Banning Shoot (also s.p.), Fresh Horses.
TELEVISION: *Prod. and/or writer: Movies:* Rape and Marriage: The Rideout Case, An Invasion of Privacy, Thief, Footsteps, Firehouse, American Geisha, Class of '63, Louis Armstrong, Chicago Style, Everybody's Baby: The Rescue of Jessica McClure (exec. prod.), White Mile, Bloodlines: Murder in the Family (exec. prod.), For the Love of My Child: The Anissa Ayala Story (exec. prod.), Sin & Redemption (exec. prod.), Pronto. *Mini-Series*: A Rumor of War, The Martian Chronicles, The Word, Space, Wallenberg: A Hero's Story.

BERG, JEFF
Executive. b. Los Angeles, CA, May 26, 1947. e. U of California, Berkeley, B.A., 1969. V.P., head lit. div., Creative Mgt. Associates, Los Angeles, 1969-75; v.p., m.p. dept., International Creative Associates, 1975-80; pres., 1980-. Dir., Joseph Intl. Industries. Named chmn. ICM.

BERG, PETER
Actor. b. New York, NY, 1964. e. Malcalester Col., St. Paul, MN.
PICTURES: Miracle Mile, Heart of Dixie, Race for Glory, Shocker, Genuine Risk, Crooked Hearts, Late for Dinner, A Midnight Clear, Aspen Extreme, Fire in the Sky, Girl 6, The Great White Hype, Cop Land, Dill Scallion, Very Bad Things (writer, dir. only).
TELEVISION: *Movies*: Rise and Walk: The Dennis Byrd Story, The Last Seduction (also released theatrically). *Series*: Chicago Hope.

BERGEN, CANDICE
Actress. b. Beverly Hills, CA, May 9, 1946. e. U. of PA. m. late dir. Louis Malle. Father was late ventriloquist Edgar Bergen. Modeled during college; freelance photo-journalist. Autobiography: Knock Wood (1984). B'way debut in Hurlyburly.
PICTURES: The Group (debut, 1966), The Sand Pebbles, The Day the Fish Came Out, Live for Life, The Magus, The Adventurers, Getting Straight, Soldier Blue, Carnal Knowledge, The Hunting Party, T. R. Baskin, 11 Harrowhouse, The Wind and the Lion, Bite the Bullet, The Domino Principle, A Night Full of Rain, Oliver's Story, Starting Over (Acad. Award nom.), Rich and Famous, Gandhi, Stick, Belly Talkers.
TELEVISION: *Movies*: Arthur the King, Murder: By Reason of Insanity, Mayflower Madam, Mary & Tim (also co-exec. prod.). *Mini-Series*: Hollywood Wives. *Specials*: Woody Allen Special, Moving Day, A Century of Women (voice), AFI's 100 Years...100 Movies. *Series*: Murphy Brown (5 Emmy Awards: 1989, 1990, 1992, 1994, 1995).

BERGEN, POLLY
Singer, Actress. r.n. Nellie Burgin b. Bluegrass, TN, July 14, 1930. e. Compton Jr. Coll., CA. Prof. debut radio at 14; in light opera, summer stock; sang with orchestra and appeared in night clubs; Columbia recording star. Bd. chmn. Polly Bergen Co.; chmn. Culinary Co., Inc.; co-chmn. Natl. Business Council for Equal Rights Amendment. Humanitarian Award: Asthmatic Research Inst. & Hosp., 1971; Outstanding Mother's Award, 1984.
THEATRE:*B'way.*:John Murray Anderson's Almanac, Champagne Complex, First Impressions, Top Man, Plaza Suit, Love Letters.
PICTURES: At War With the Army (debut, 1950), That's My Boy, Warpath, The Stooge, Half a Hero, Cry of the Hunted, Arena, Fast Company, Escape from Fort Bravo, Belle Sommers, Cape Fear, The Caretakers, Move Over Darling, Kisses for My President, A Guide for the Married Man, Making Mr. Right, Mother Mother, Cry-Baby, Dr. Jekyll and Ms. Hyde, Once Upon a Time... When We Were Colored.
TELEVISION: *Movies*: Death Cruise, Murder on Flight 502, Telethon, How to Pick Up Girls, The Million Dollar Face, Born Beautiful, Velvet, Addicted to His Love, She Was Marked For Murder, The Haunting of Sarah Hardy, My Brother's Wife, Lightning Field, Lady Against the Odds, Perry Mason: The Case of the Skin-Deep Scandal, Leave of Absence (also story, co-exec. prod.), Hand In the Glove, Blink Of an Eye, The Surrogate, For Hope. *Mini-Series*: 79 Park Avenue, The Winds of War, War and Remembrance. *Special*: The Helen Morgan Story (Emmy Award, 1958). *Series*: Pepsi-Cola Playhouse (host 1954-55), To Tell the Truth (panelist), The Polly Bergen Show, Baby Talk. *Guest*: G.E. Theatre, Schlitz Playhouse, Playhouse 90, Studio One, Perry Como, Ed Sullivan Show, Bob Hope Show, Bell Telephone, Wonderful World of Entertainment, Dinah Shore Show, Dean Martin Show, Andy Williams Show, Red Skelton Show, Mike Douglas Show.

BERGER, HELMUT
Actor. r.n. Helmut Steinberger. b. Salzburg, Austria, May 29, 1943. e. Feldkirk College and U. of Perugia. First film, small role in Luchino Visconti's The Witches (Le Streghe) in 1966.
PICTURES: The Young Tigers, The Damned, Do You Know What Stalin Did To Women?, The Garden of the Finzi-Continis, Dorian Gray, A Butterfly with Bloody Wings, The Greedy Ones, The Strange Love Affair, Ludwig, Ash Wednesday, Conversation Piece, The Romantic Englishwoman, Orders to Kill, Madam Kitty, Merry-Go-Round, Code Name: Emerald, The Glass Heaven, Faceless, The Betrothed, The Godfather Part III, Once Arizona, Ludwig 1881, Exit II - Transfigured Night, Still Waters, Die 120 Tage von Bottrop, Unter den Palmen, Die Haupter Meiner.

BERGER, RICHARD L.
Executive. b. Tarrytown, NY, Oct. 25, 1939. e. Cornell U., UCLA 1963, B.S. In 1964 joined acct. dept., 20th Century-Fox; promoted to exec. position in Fox-TV; was dir. of programming, then v.p. of programs.; asst. v.p. prod. 20th-Fox. Left in 1975 to join CBS-TV as v.p. dramatic development. Returned to 20th-Fox in 1977 as v.p., domestic prod., 20th Century-Fox Pictures. Joined Disney as pres. Walt Disney Pictures; resigned 1984. Named sr. v.p., United Artists Corp., promoted to pres. MGM/UA Film Group, 1988.

BERGER, SENTA
Actress. b. Vienna, Austria, May 13, 1941. Studied ballet, then acting at Vienna's Reinhardt Seminar. Debuted in German films as teen.
PICTURES: Die Lindenwirtin vom Donanstrand (debut, 1957), The Journey, Katia, The Good Soldier Schweik, The Secret Ways, Sherlock Holmes and the Deadly Necklace, The Testament of Dr. Mabuse, The Victors, Major Dundee, The Glory Guys, Cast a Giant Shadow, Bang! Bang! You're Dead, The Poppy Is Also a Flower, The Quiller Memorandum, To Commit a Murder, The Treasure of San Gennaro, The Ambushers, Diabolically Yours, If It's Tuesday This Must Be Belgium, De Sade, When Women Had Tails, Percy, The Scarlet Letter, Merry-Go-Round, White Mafia, The Swiss Conspiracy, Cross of Iron, Nest of Nipers, The Two Lives of Mattia Pascal, The Flying Devils, Swiss Cheese, Am I Beautiful?.

BERGERAC, JACQUES
Actor. b. Biarritz, France, May 26, 1927. Career includes Five Minutes With Jacques Bergerac on radio; in the theatre, on tour in Once More with Feeling; on most major network TV shows.
PICTURES: Twist of Fate, The Time is Now, Strange Intruder, Come Away With Me, Les Girls, Gigi, Man and His Past, Thunder in the Sun, Hypnotic Eye, A Sunday in Summer, Fear No More, Achilles, A Global Affair, Taffy and the Jungle Hunter, The Emergency Operation: Lady Chaplin, The Last Party, One Plus One.

BERGIN, PATRICK
Actor. b. Ireland, 1954.
PICTURES: Those Glory Glory Days, Taffin, The Courier, Mountains of the Moon, Sleeping With the Enemy,.Love Crimes, Highway to Hell, Patriot Games, Map of the Human Heart, Double Cross, Soft Deceit, Lawnmower Man 2: Beyond Cyberspace, Whitechapel, The Proposition, The Island on Bird Street, The Lost World, One Man's Hero, Merlin: The Return, Eye of the Beholder.
TELEVISION: *Movies:* Act of Betrayal, Robin Hood, They, Frankenstein, Triple Cross; Stolen Women, Captured Hearts;. Robert Ludlum's The Apocalypse Watch, The Ripper, Durango. *Specials:* Morphine and Dolly Mixtures (BBC), The Real Carlotte. *Guest:* Twilight Zone: Lost Classics.

BERGMAN, ALAN
Songwriter. b. Brooklyn, NY. e. U. of North Carolina, UCLA. m. Marilyn Bergman with whom he collaborates.
THEATER: Ballroom, Something More, The Lady and the Clarinet.
PICTURES: *Lyrics*: Harlow, Harper, In the Heat of the Night, Fitzwilly, The Thomas Crown Affair (Acad. Award for Best Song: The Windmills of Your Mind, 1968), John and Mary, The Happy Ending, Gaily Gaily, The Magic Garden of Stanley Sweetheart, Move, Pieces of Dreams, Wuthering Heights, Doctor's Wives, Sometimes a Great Notion, Pete 'n' Tillie, The Life and Times of Judge Roy Bean, Breezy, 40 Carats,

The Way We Were (Acad. Award for title song, 1973), Summer Wishes Winter Dreams, Harry and Walter Go to New York, Ode to Billy Joe, A Star Is Born, Same Time Next Year, The Promise, And Justice for All, A Change of Seasons, Back Roads, Author Author, Yes Giorgio, Best Friends, Tootsie, Never Say Never Again, Yentl (Academy Award for song score, 1983), The Man Who Loved Women, Micki and Maude, The January Man, Major League, Shirley Valentine, Welcome Home, Switch, For the Boys, Sabrina, Bogus.
TELEVISION: Queen of the Stardust Ballroom (Emmy Award), Hollow Image, Sybil (Emmy Award). *Themes*: Bracken's World, Maude, The Sandy Duncan Show, Good Times, Alice, The Dumplings, Nancy Walker Show, The Powers That Be, Brooklyn Bridge, etc.

BERGMAN, ANDREW
Writer, Director, Producer. b. Queens, NY, Feb. 20, 1945. e. Harpur Coll., magna cum laude; U. of Wisconsin, Ph.D, history, 1970. Worked as publicist at United Artists. Author: We're in the Money, a study of Depression-era films, and the mysteries: The Big Kiss-Off of 1944, Hollywood and Levine, Sleepless Nights. Also wrote Broadway comedy, Social Security.
PICTURES: *Writer:* Blazing Saddles, The In Laws, So Fine (also dir.) Oh God You Devil, Fletch, The Freshman (also dir.), Soapdish, Honeymoon in Vegas (also dir.), The Scout, Striptease (also dir.), Isn't She Great? *Director*: It Could Happen to You. *Exec. Prod.:* Chances Are, Undercover Blues, Little Big League.

BERGMAN, INGMAR
Writer, Director. b. Uppsala, Sweden, July 14, 1918. e. Stockholm U. Directed university play prods.; wrote & dir. Death of Punch, 1940; first theatrical success, dir., Macbeth, 1940; writer-dir., Svensk Film-industri, 1942-present; first s.p, Frenzy, 1943; first directorial assignment, Crisis, 1945; chief prod., Civic Malmo, 1956-60. Directed Swedish prod. Hamlet for stage at Brooklyn Acad. of Music, 1988.
PICTURES: *Writer:* Torment, Woman Without a Face, Eva, The Last Couple Out, Pleasure Garden, Best Intentions, Sunday's Children, Faithless. *Dir./Writer:* Crisis It Rains on Our Love, A Ship to India, Night is My Future (dir. only), Port of Call, The Devil's Wanton, Three Strange Loves, To Joy, This Can't Happen Here (dir. only), Summer Interlude, Secrets of Women, Summer With Monika, The Naked Night, A Lesson in Love, Dreams, Smiles of a Summer Night, The Seventh Seal, Wild Strawberries, Brink of Life, The Magician, The Virgin Spring (dir. only), The Devil's Eye, Through a Glass Darkly, Winter Light, The Silence, All These Women, Persona, Stimulantia (episode), Hour of the Wolf, Shame, The Ritual, The Passion of Anna, The Touch, Cries and Whispers, Scenes from a Marriage, The Magic Flute, Face to Face, The Serpent's Egg, Autumn Sonata, From the Life of the Marionettes, Fanny and Alexander, After the Rehearsal.
TELEVISION: The Lie, The Last Gasp, Private Confessions (writer only), In the Presence of a Clown.

BERGMAN, MARILYN
Songwriter. b. Brooklyn, NY. e. NYU. m. Alan Bergman with whom she collaborates. Became pres. of ASCAP, 1994.
THEATER: Ballroom, Something More, The Lady and the Clarinet.
PICTURES: *Lyrics*: Harlow, Harper, In the Heat of the Night, Fitzwilly, The Thomas Crown Affair (Acad. Award for Best Song: The Windmills of Your Mind, 1968), John and Mary, The Happy Ending, Gaily Gaily, The Magic Garden of Stanley Sweetheart, Move, Pieces of Dreams, Wuthering Heights, Doctor's Wives, Sometimes a Great Notion, Pete 'n' Tillie, The Life and Times of Judge Roy Bean, Breezy, 40 Carats, The Way We Were (Acad. Award for title song, 1973), Summer Wishes Winter Dreams, Harry and Walter Go to New York, Ode to Billy Joe, A Star Is Born, Same Time Next Year, The Promise, And Justice for All, A Change of Seasons, Back Roads, Author Author, Yes Giorgio, Best Friends, Tootsie, Never Say Never Again, Yentl (Academy Award for song score, 1983), The Man Who Loved Women, Micki and Maude, The January Man, Major League, Shirley Valentine, Welcome Home, Switch, For the Boys.
TELEVISION: Queen of the Stardust Ballroom (Emmy Award), Hollow Image, Sybil (Emmy Award). *Themes:* Bracken's World, Maude, The Sandy Duncan Show, Good Times, Alice, The Dumplings, Nancy Walker Show, The Powers That Be, Brooklyn Bridge.

BERKOFF, STEVEN
Actor, Director, Writer. b. London, England, Aug. 3, 1937. e. studied drama in London and Paris. Founder of London Theatre Group. Author of plays; East, West, Greek Decadence, Sink the Belgrano, Kvetch (London, NY). Staged, adapted and toured with: Kafka's In the Penal Colony, The Trial and Metamorphosis; Agamemnon, The Fall of the House of Usher. Starred in Hamlet and Macbeth. NY theater: Dir.: Kvetch (also writer, actor), Coriolanus, Metamorphosis (starring Baryshnikov). Also dir. Roman Polanski in Metamorphosis in Paris.
PICTURES: *Actor*: Nicholas and Alexandra, A Clockwork Orange, Barry Lyndon, The Passenger, Outland, McVicar, Octopussy, Beverly Hills Cop, Rambo: First Blood II, Revolution, Underworld, Absolute Beginners, Under the Cherry Moon, The Krays, Decadence (also dir., s.p.), Fair Game, Flynn, Doppelganger (voice), Love in Paris, Rancid Aluminium.

TELEVISION: Beloved Family, Knife Edge, War and Remembrance, A Season of Giants, Intruders.

BERLE, MILTON
Actor. r.n. Milton Berlinger. b. New York, NY, July 12, 1908. e. Professional Children's Sch., N.Y. Early appearances as child actor incl. film Tillie's Punctured Romance. In vaudeville; on N.Y. stage (Ziegfeld Follies 1936, Life Begins at 8:40, etc.): nightclubs; concurrently on radio & screen. Author: Out of My Trunk (1945), Earthquake (1959), Milton Berle: An Autobiography (1974).
PICTURES: New Faces of 1937, Radio City Revels, Tall Dark and Handsome, Sun Valley Serenade, Rise and Shine, A Gentleman at Heart, Whispering Ghosts, Over My Dead Body, Margin for Error, Always Leave Them Laughing, Let's Make Love, The Bellboy, It's a Mad Mad Mad Mad World, The Loved One, The Oscar, Don't Worry We'll Think of a Title, The Happening, Who's Minding the Mint?, Where Angels Go... Trouble Follows, For Singles Only, Can Hieronymus Merkin Ever Forget Mercy Humppe and Find True Happiness?, Lepke, Won Ton Ton the Dog Who Saved Hollywood, The Muppet Movie, Cracking Up, Broadway Danny Rose, Driving Me Crazy, Storybook, Legend of Forrest Tucker.
TELEVISION: *Movies*: Seven in Darkness, Evil Roy Slade, Legend of Valentino, Side By Side. *Series*: Texaco Star Theatre, Kraft Music Hall TV Show, Jackpot Bowling, Milton Berle Show. *Guest*: Doyle Against the House, Dick Powell Show, Chrysler TV special, Lucy Show, F Troop, Batman, Love Boat, many others.

BERLINGER, WARREN
Actor. b. Brooklyn, NY, Aug. 31, 1937. e. Columbia U.
THEATER: Annie Get Your Gun, The Happy Time, Bernardine, Take A Giant Step, Anniversary Waltz, Roomful of Roses, Blue Denim (Theatre World Award), Come Blow Your Horn, How To Succeed in Business Without Really Trying, (London) Who's Happy Now?, California Suite (1977-78 tour), Lead Me a Tenor-Toup.
PICTURES: Teenage Rebel, Three Brave Men, Blue Denim, Because They're Young, Platinum High School, The Wackiest Ship in the Army, All Hands on Deck, Billie, Spinout, Thunder Alley, Lepke, The Four Deuces, I Will I Will... for Now, Harry and Walter Go to New York, The Shaggy D.A., The Magician of Lublin, The Cannonball Run, The World According to Garp, Going Bananas, Outlaw Force, Ten Little Indians, Hero, Crime and Punishment, Feminine Touch, That Thing You Do!, Dear God.
TELEVISION: *Movies*: The Girl Most Likely To..., The Red Badge of Courage, Ellery Queen, Wanted: The Sundance Woman, Sex and the Single Parent, The Other Woman, Trial By Jury, Death Hits the Jackspot. *Series*: Secret Storm (serial), The Joey Bishop Show, The Funny Side, A Touch of Grace, Operation Petticoat, Small & Frye, Shades of L.A. *Guest*: Alcoa, Goodyear, Armstrong, Matinee Theatre, The London Palladium, Kilroy, Bracken's World, Columbo, Friends.

BERMAN, BRUCE
Executive. b. New York, NY, April 25, 1952. e. California Inst. of the Arts Film School; UCLA, magna cum laude, history degree 1975; Georgetown Law School and California Bar, 1978. Entered motion picture industry while in law school, as assistant to Jack Valenti, MPAA. Assistant to Peter Guber, Casablanca Filmworks, 1979. Assistant to Sean Daniel & Joel Silver, Universal Pictures, 1979; v.p. prod., Universal, 1982. V.p. prod., Warner Bros., 1984; sr. v.p., prod.,1988; pres., Theatrical Prod.,1989; pres., Worldwide Prod., 1991-96. Founded Plan B Ent., an independent motion picture prod. co., funded by Warner Bros., Inc., 1996.

BERMAN, JOEL P.
Executive. b. Forest Hills, NY, Dec. 3, 1951. e. Ohio University, BS communications, 1973. Acct. exec., Petry Television, NY, 1976-79. Dir. ad. sales, Westwood One, NY, 1979-80. East. div. mgr., Paramount Pictures Domestic Television, NY, 1981-84, VP, East. reg. mgr., 1985-87. Sr. VP/sales mgr., GTG Marketing, NY, 1987-89. Back to Paramount Pics. Domestic TV, VP, off-network and features, 1989-90, Sr. VP/nat'l sales mgr., 1990-92, Exec. VP/sales and mktng., LA, 1992-94, pres. of distribution, 1994-97, co-pres., 1997-present.

BERMAN, RICK
Producer. r.n. Richard Keith Berman. b. Dec. 25, 1944. e. Univ. of Wisconsin-Madison, BA in speech, 1963-67.
PICTURES: Star Trek: Generations (also story), Star Trek: First Contact (also story), Star Trek: The Experience, Star Trek: Insurrection (also story), Star Trek: 3D (also story).
TELEVISION: *Series*: Star Trek: The Next Generation, Star Trek: Deep Space Nine, Star Trek: Voyager.

BERMAN, STEVEN H.
Executive. b. Middletown, OH, March 22, 1952. e. Ohio U., B.F.A. in playwriting, 1974; USC, Annenberg Sch. of Communication studied management, 1977. Special research projects Paramount and ABC TV, 1977. Account exec., Gardner Advertising, 1978. Devt. exec., CBS Television, 1979-82; dir. of comedy devt., CBS Television, 1982-84; five years at CBS in series devt., comedy and drama. Vice pres., dramatic devt., Columbia Pictures TV, 1984-85; sr. v.p., Creative Affairs, Columbia Pictures TV, 1985-87; exec. v.p., Columbia TV, div. of Columbia Entertainment TV, 1987-90; ind. prod., Columbia Pictures TV, 1990-present.

BERNARD, MARVIN A.
Executive. b. New York, NY, Oct. 1, 1934. e. NYU. Lab technician to v.p. in charge of sales, Rapid Film Technique, Inc., 1949-63; developed technological advances in film rejuvenation and preservation, responsible for public underwriting; real estate sales & investments in Bahamas, then with Tishman Realty (commercial leasing div.), 1964-69; est. B-I-G Capital Properties; v.p. and operating head of International Filmtreat 1970-1973; authored Film Damaged Control Chart, a critical analysis of film care and repair, 1971; founded Filmlife Inc. with latest chemical/mechanical and technical advancement in field of film rejuvenation and preservation. Bd. chmn. and chief executive officer of Filmlife Inc., m. p. film rejuvenation, storage and distribution company, 1973-75. Elected president in addition to remaining bd. chairman, Feb. 1975. Consultant to National Archives of U.S. on m.p. preservation, 1979. Dev. m.p. rejuvenation and preservation for 8mm and S8mm, 1981. Introduced this technology to private home movie use before and after transfer to videotape, 1986. Active mem. of awards comm. for tech. achievements, National Acad. TV Arts & Sciences, 1987. Recognition as leading authority and m.p. conservator from Intl. Communications Industries Assn. (ICIA), 1988. Filmlife became 1st national film to video transfer lab in U.S., 1989. Elected to Princeton Film Preservation Group. Established Film/Video Hospital, repairing broken tapes & videocassettes, 1990.

BERNARD, TOM
Executive. e. University of Maryland at College Park, BA in Radio/Film/TV. Held positions in theatrical sales at New Line Cinema. 1980, established specialized distribution company, United Artists Classics. 1983, co-founded Orion Classics. 1992, founding partner and co-president, Sony Pictures Classics. Member of the A.M.P.A.S., Sundance Institute Advisory Board. Chairman of the Board of Advisors for the Independent Feature Project/West.

BERNHARD, HARVEY
Producer. b. Seattle, WA, March 5, 1924. e. Stanford U. In real estate in Seattle, 1947-50; started live lounge entertainment at the Last Frontier Hotel, Las Vegas, 1950. Partner with Sandy Howard, 1958-60; v.p. in chg. prod., David L. Wolper Prods., dividing time between TV and feature films, 1961-68; with MPC, v.p., chg. prod., 1968-70. Now pres. of Harvey Bernhard Ent., Inc.
PICTURES: The Mack (1973), The Omen, Damien: Omen II, Omen III: The Final Conflict, The Beast Within, Ladyhawke (exec. prod.), The Goonies, The Lost Boys.
TELEVISION: *Movies:* Omen IV: The Awakening.

BERNHARD, SANDRA
Actress, Comedian, Singer. b. Flint, MI, June 6, 1955. Moved to Scottsdale, AZ at 10. Began career in Los Angeles 1974 as stand-up comedian while supporting herself as manicurist in Beverly Hills. Has written articles for Vanity Fair, Interview, Spin, recorded and written lyrics for debut album I'm Your Woman (1985) and starred in one-woman off-B'way show Without You I'm Nothing (1988). Published collection of essays, short stories and memoirs, Confessions of a Pretty Lady (1988). Frequent guest on Late Night with David Letterman and Robin Byrd Show.
PICTURES: Cheech and Chong's Nice Dreams (debut, 1981), The King of Comedy, Sesame Street Presents: Follow That Bird, The Whoopee Boys, Track 29, Heavy Petting, Without You I'm Nothing, Hudson Hawk, Inside Monkey Zetterland, Dallas Doll, Madonna: Truth or Dare, Unzipped, The Reggae Movie, Plump Fiction, Lover Girl, The Apocalypse, An Alan Smithee Film: Burn Hollywood Burn, Somewhere in the City, I Woke Up Early the Day I Died, Wrongfully Accused, Expose, Dinner Rush.
TELEVISION: *Movies*: Freaky Friday, The Late Shift, Hercules Zero to Hero, Sandra Bernhard: I'm Still Here Damn It! *Series*: The Richard Pryor Show, Roseanne, Hercules.

BERNSEN, CORBIN
Actor. b. North Hollywood, CA, Sept. 7, 1954. e. UCLA, B.A. theater arts; M.F.A playwriting. m. actress Amanda Pays. Son of actress Jeanne Cooper. Teaching asst. at UCLA while working on playwriting degree. 1981 studied acting in NY while supporting self as carpenter and model (Winston cigarettes). Built own theater in loft. Formed theatre co. Theatre of the Night.
PICTURES: Three the Hard Way (debut, 1974), Eat My Dust!, King Kong, S.O.B., Hello Again, Bert Rigby You're a Fool, Major League, Disorganized Crime, Shattered, Frozen Assets, The Killing Box, Savage Land, Major League 2, Trigger Fast, A Brilliant Disguise, The New Age, Radioland Murders, Tales From the Hood, The Great White Hype, The Dentist, Menno's Mind, Circuit Breaker, An American Affair, Recipe for Revenge, The Misadventures of Margaret, Drop Dead, Beings, Major League: Back to the Minors, Young Hearts Unlimited.
TELEVISION: *Movies*: Breaking Point, Line of Fire: The Morris Dees Story, Dead on the Money, Grass Roots, Love Can Be Murder, Beyond Suspicion, I Know My Son is Alive, Where Are My Children?, Voice From Within, Dangerous Intentions, In the Heat of the Night: By Duty Bound, Bloodhounds, The Cape, Tidalwave: No Escape, Loyal Opposition: Terror in the White House, Nightworld: Riddler's Moon, Recipe for Revenge. *Series*: Ryan's Hope, L.A. Law, A Whole New Ballgame, The Cape. *Guest*: Anything But Love, Roc, The Larry Sanders Show, Love and War, The Nanny, Night Watch, Seinfeld, Dear John.

BERNSEN, HARRY
Producer, Executive. b. Chicago, IL, June 14, 1935. Served in US Marine Corp., 1953-55. Had own agency, Continental Management, 1956-70. Became prod., 1970.
THEATER: *Producer*: Beyond the Rainbow, The Boys in Autumn.
PICTURES: *Producer/Assoc. prod.*: Fool's Parade, Something Big, Three the Hard Way, Take a Hard Ride, Fatal Inheritance.
TELEVISION: *Movies*: *Exec. prod.*: The Awakening Land, ABC After School Specials.

BERNSTEIN, ARMYAN
Director, Writer, Producer.
PICTURES: Thank God It's Friday (s.p.), One From the Heart (co-s.p.), Windy City (dir., s.p.), Cross My Heart (dir., co-s.p.), Satisfaction (co-exec. prod.), The Commitments (co-exec. prod.), A Midnight Clear (co-exec. prod.), The Baby-sitters Club (co-exec. prod.), Airforce One, A Thousand Acres, Playing God (exec. prod.), Disturbing Behaviour (prod.), For Love of the Game, Lazarus & Hurrican (s.p.), End of Days (prod.), Thirteen Days (prod.).

BERNSTEIN, BOB
Executive. Began public relations career 1952 at DuMont TV Network, followed by 2 yrs. as press agent for Liberace. With Billboard Magazine as review editor 3 yrs. Joined Westinghouse Bdg. Co. as p.r. dir., 1959. In 1963 named p.r. dir. for Triangle Publications, serving in various capacities to 1971. Joined Viacom Intl. as dir. of information services. In 1975 formed own co., March Five Inc., p.r. and promotion firm.

BERNSTEIN, ELMER
Composer, Conductor. b. New York, NY, April 4, 1922. e. Scholarship, Juilliard; Walden Sch., NYU., U.S. Army Air Force radio unit. After war 3 yrs. recitals, musical shows, United Nations radio dept. Pres., Young Musicians Found. 1st v.p. Academy of Motion Picture Arts & Sciences; co-chmn. music branch. Music dir. Valley Symphony. Recording artist, United Artists. More than 90 major films. Pres. of Composers & Lyricists Guild of America.
THEATER: How Now Dow Jones?
PICTURES: Never Wave at a WAC, Sudden Fear, Robot Monster, Cat Women of the Moon, It's a Dog's Life, Man With the Golden Arm, Storm Fear, The View From Pompey's Head, The Ten Commandments, Fear Strikes Out, Desire Under the Elms, Drango, The Naked Eye, Sweet Smell of Success, The Tin Star, Anna Lucasta, The Buccaneer, God's Little Acre, Kings Go Forth, Some Came Running, The Miracle, The Story on Page One, From the Terrace, The Magnificent Seven, The Rat Race, By Love Possessed, The Commancheros, Summer and Smoke, The Young Doctors, Birdman of Alcatraz, Walk on the Wild Side, A Girl Named Tamiko, To Kill a Mockingbird, The Great Escape, The Caretakers, Hud, Kings of the Sun, Rampage, Love With the Proper Stranger, The Carpetbaggers, Four Days in November, The World of Henry Orient, The Hallelujah Trail, The Reward, Seven Women, Cast a Giant Shadow, Hawaii, Thoroughly Modern Millie (Acad. Award, 1967), I Love You Alice B. Toklas, The Scalphunters, True Grit, The Gypsy Moths, Midas Run, Where's Jack?, Cannon for Cordoba, The Liberation of L.B. Jones, A Walk in the Spring Rain, Doctor's Wives, See No Evil, Big Jake, The Magnificent Seven Ride, Cahill U.S. Marshall, McQ., Gold, The Trial of Billy Jack, Report to the Commissioner, From Noon Till Three, The Incredible Sarah, The Shootist, Slap Shot, National Lampoon's Animal House, Bloodbrothers, Meatballs, The Great Santini, Saturn 3, The Blues Brothers, Airplane!, Zulu Dawn, Going Ape, Stripes, An American Werewolf in London, Honky Tonk Freeway, The Chosen, Five Days One Summer, Airplane II: The Sequel, Spacehunter, Trading Places, Class, Bolero, Ghostbusters, The Black Cauldron, Spies Like Us, Legal Eagles, Three Amigos, Amazing Grace and Chuck, Leonard Part 6, Da, Funny Farm, The Good Mother, Slipstream, My Left Foot, The Grifters, The Field, Oscar, A Rage in Harlem, Rambling Rose, Cape Fear (adapt.), The Babe, The Cemetery Club, Mad Dog and Glory, Lost in Yonkers, The Age of Innocence, The Good Son, I Love Trouble, Roommates, Canadian Bacon, Devil in a Blue Dress, Buddy, Hoodlums, The Rainmaker, Twilight, The Deep End of the Ocean, Wild Wild West.
TELEVISION: *Movies*: Gulag, Guyana Tragedy, Today's FBI, Rough Riders. *Specials*: Hollywood: The Golden Years, The Race for Space: Parts I & II, D-Day, The Making of the President—1960 (Emmy Award), Hollywood and the Stars, Voyage of the Brigantine Yankee, Crucifiction of Jesus, NBC Best Sellers Theme (1976). *Mini-series:* A Personal Journey with Martin Scorcese Through American Movies. *Series*: Julia, Owen Marshall, Ellery Queen, Serpico, The Chisholms.

BERNSTEIN, FRED
Executive. Was sr. v.p. of business affairs and pres. of worldwide prod. for Columbia Pictures in 1980's before serving as sr. v.p. of MCA Inc.'s Motion Picture Group, 1987-94. Named pres. of Coumbia TriStar Motion Pictures, 1994.

BERNSTEIN, JACK B.
Executive. b. New York, NY, May 6, 1937. e. City U. of New York, B.A., sociology. U.S. Army-Europe, 1956-58; research bacteriologist, 1959-61. Entered industry in 1962 with S.I.B. Prods., Paramount, as v.p. gen. mgr.; 1964-66, v.p. gen. mgr. C.P.I. Prods.; 1966-73, prod. mgr. asst. dir., free lance. 1973-1982, assoc. prod. exec. prod. at several studios. 1983-86, v.p. worldwide prod., Walt Disney Pictures; 1987, sr. v.p., worldwide prod., United Artists Pictures; 1988-90, sr. v.p. worldwide prod., MGM Pictures. Member: DGA, Friars, Academy of MP Arts & Sciences, Academy of TV Arts & Sciences, AFI.
PICTURES: *Asst. dir.* Hearts of the West. *Prod. mngr.*: Silver Streak. *Assoc. prod.*: The Other Side of Midnight, The Fury, Butch and Sundance: The Early Days, Six Pack, Unfaithfully Yours. *Exec. prod.*: North Dallas Forty, Monsignor, The Beast Within. *Co-prod.*: The Mambo Kings, Under Siege.

BERNSTEIN, JAY
Producer, Personal manager. b. Oklahoma City, OK. e. Pomona Coll. 1963-76, pres. of Jay Bernstein Public Relations, representing over 600 clients. Formed Jay Bernstein Enterprises, acting as personal manager for Farrah Fawcett, Suzanne Somers, Kristy McNichol, Susan Hayward, Donald Sutherland, Bruce Boxleitner, Robert Conrad, Susan Saint James, Robert Blake, William Shatner, Linda Evans, Cicely Tyson, etc. Past pres., Bernstein Thompson Entertainment Complex, entertainment and personal mgt. firm.
PICTURES: *Exec. prod.:* Sunburn, Nothing Personal.
TELEVISION: *Exec. prod. Movies*: The Return of Mike Hammer, Mickey Spillane's Margin for Murder, Wild—Wild—West Revisited, More Wild—Wild West, Murder Me Murder You, More Than Murder, The Return of Mike Hammer, Murder Takes All, The Diamond Trap, Final Notice, Double Jeopardy, Come Die with Me: A Mickey Spillane's Mike Hammer Mystery. *Series*: Bring 'Em Back Alive, Mike Hammer, Houston Knights.

BERNSTEIN, WALTER
Writer, Director. b. New York, NY. Aug. 20, 1919. e. Dartmouth. Wrote for NY Magazine; in W.W.II was roving correspondent for Yank Magazine. Returned to NY after war. Wrote TV scripts; published Keep Your Head Down (collection of articles).
PICTURES: *Writer.* Kiss the Blood Off My Hands (co-s.p.), That Kind of Woman, Heller in Pink Tights, A Breath of Scandal (co-s.p.), Paris Blues, The Magnificent Seven (uncredited), Fail Safe, The Money Trap, The Train, The Molly Maguires, The Front, Semi-Tough, The Betsy (co-s.p.), An Almost Perfect Affair, Yanks, Little Miss Marker (dir. debut), The House on Carroll Street.
TELEVISION: Women & Men 2: In Love There Are No Rules (also dir.), Doomsday Gun, The Affair (story), Miss Evers' Boys, Durango.

BERNSTEIN, WILLIAM
Executive. b. New York, NY, Aug. 30, 1933. e. New York U., B.A. 1954; Yale U., L.L.B. 1959. Joined United Artists as an attorney in 1959; v.p., business affairs, 1967-72; promoted to sr. v.p., 1972. Executive v.p., Orion Pictures, 1978-91. Pres. and CEO Orion Pictures, 1991-92. Exec. v.p., Paramount Pictures 1992-present. Member, A.B.A., A.M.P.A.S.

BERRI, CLAUDE
Director, Actor, Producer. r.n. Claude Langmann. b. Paris, France, July 1, 1934. Started as actor, playing roles in French films and on stage in the 1950s. Began dir. career with short film Jeanine, followed by Le Poulet (The Chicken; also prod.; Acad. Award for best live action short subject, 1965). 1963, created Renn Productions. 1973, became partner in AMLF distribution co.
PICTURES: *Director.* The Two of Us (feature debut, 1967), Marry Me Marry Me (also s.p., actor), Le Pistonne (The Man with Connections), Le Cinema de Papa (also prod.), Le Sex Shop (also s.p.), Male of the Century (also s.p., actor), The First Time (also s.p.), Tess (prod.), Inspecteur la Bavure (prod.), Je Vous Aime (prod., s.p.), In a Wild Moment, Je Vous Aime, Le Maitre d' Ecole (also prod., s.p.), A Quarter to Two Before Jesus Christ (prod.), L'Africain (prod.), Banzai (prod.), L'Homme Blesse (prod.), Tchao Pantin (also prod., s.p.), Jean la Florette, Manon of the Spring, The Bear (exec. prod.), Valmont (exec. prod.), Uranus (also s.p., prod.), Germinal (also prod., co-s.p.), Queen Margot (prod.), La Separation (prod.), French Twist (exec. prod.), Les Trois Freres (prod., actor), Arlette (prod.), The Ogre (prod.), Didier (Prod.), Le Pari (exec. prod.), Lucie Aubrac (s.p.), Asterix and Obelix vs. Ceasar (prod.).

BERRIDGE, ELIZABETH
Actress. b. New Rochelle, NY, May 2, 1962. Studied acting at Lee Strasberg Inst., Warren Robertson Theatre Workshop.
THEATER: *NY*: The Vampires, The Incredibly Famous Willy Rivers, Outside Waco, Ground Zero Club, Cruise Control, Sorrows and Sons, Crackwalker, Coyote Ugly, Briar Patch. *Regional*: Tuesday's Child, Hedda Gabler, Lulu, Venus and Thumbtacks.
PICTURES: Natural Enemies, The Funhouse, Amadeus, Smooth Talk, Five Corners, When the Party's Over.
TELEVISION: *Movies:* Silence of the Heart, Home Fires Burning, Montana. *Series:* One of the Boys, The Powers That Be, The John Larroquette Show.

BERRY, HALLE
Actress. b. Cleveland, OH, Aug. 14, 1968. Named Miss Teen Ohio, Miss Teen All-American, runner up to Miss U.S.A.
PICTURES: Jungle Fever, Strictly Business, The Last Boy Scout, Boomerang, Father Hood, The Program, The Flintstones, Losing Isaiah, Race the Sun, Girl 6, Executive Decision, Rich Man's Wife, B.A.P.S., Bulworth, Why Do Fools Fall in Love, X-Men, Swordfish.
TELEVISION: *Movie*: Solomon and Sheba, Dorothy Dandridge. *Mini-Series*: Queen, The Wedding. *Series*: Living Dolls, Knot's Landing. *Guest:* A Different World, Frasier (voice).

BERRY, JOHN
Director. b. New York, NY, 1917. Directed films in Hollywood mid and late '40s; went abroad during McCarthy era in U.S. where worked in French film industry. Later went to London to do stage work, acting as well as directing. Returned to U.S. to do stage work; returned to Hollywood to do TV.
PICTURES: Cross My Heart, From This Day Forward, Miss Susie Slagle's, Casbah, Tension, He Ran All the Way, CCa Va Barder, The Great Lover, Je Suis un Sentimental, Tamango, On Que Mambo, Claudine, Maya, The Bad News Bears Go to Japan, Thieves, Il y a maldonne, 'Round Midnight (actor only), A Man in Love (actor only), La Voyage a Paimpol (also prod.), A Captive in the Land (also prod., s.p.), Hantises (actor), Boesman and Lena (also s.p.).
TELEVISION: One Drink at a Time, Farewell Party, Mr. Broadway, Sister Sister (also prod.), Angel on My Shoulder, Honeyboy, Legitimate Defense. *Series:* Tales

BERRY, KEN
Actor. b. Moline, IL, Nov. 3, 1933.
PICTURES: Two for the Seesaw, Hello Down There, Herbie Rides Again, The Cat from Outer Space.
TELEVISION: *Movies*: Wake Me When the War Is Over, The Reluctant Heroes, Every Man Needs One, Letters from Three Lovers, Love Boat II, The Legend of Forrest Tucker. *Series*: The Ann Sothern Show, Bob Newhart Show (1962), F Troop, Mayberry RFD, Ken Berry Wow Show, Mama's Family. *Guest*: Dick Van Dyke Show, Hazel, Lucy Show, Carol Burnett, Sonny & Cher.

BERSTEIN, WILLIAM
Executive. e. Yale Law School and New York U. Joined United Artists Corp. as a member of its legal dept. in 1959, then moved to senior v.p. of business affairs and became a member of its board of directors. Exec. v.p. and member of the board of directors, Orion Pictures Corp., 1978-91; named president and CEO of Orion in 1991. Currently exec. v.p., Paramount Pictures (since 1992), where he oversees business affairs, legal, finance, and gov't. operations and studio administration depts.

BERTINELLI, VALERIE
Actress. b. Wilmington, DE, April 23, 1960. m. musician Eddie Van Halen. Dramatic training at Tami Lynn Academy of Artists in California. Made early TV appearances in the series, Apple's Way, in commercials, and in public service announcements. Started own prod. company to acquire properties for self.
PICTURE: Number One with a Bullet.
TELEVISION: *Movies*: Young Love First Love, The Promise of Love, The Princess and the Cabbie, I Was a Mail Order Bride, The Seduction of Gina, Shattered Vows, Silent Witness, Rockabye, Pancho Barnes, In a Child's Name, What She Doesn't Know, Murder of Innocence, The Haunting of Helen Walker, Two Mothers for Zachary, A Case for Life. *Mini-Series*: I'll Take Manhattan, Night Sins. *Specials*: The Secret of Charles Dickens, The Magic of David Copperfield. *Series*: One Day at a Time, Sydney, Cafe Americain,.

BERTOLUCCI, BERNARDO
Director, Writer, b. Parma, Italy, May 16, 1940. e. Rome U. Son of Attilio Bertolucci, poet and film critic. At age 20 worked as asst. dir. to Pier Paolo Pasolini on latter's first film, Accatone. Made debut film, The Grim Reaper, from script by Pasolini, 1962; published poetry book, In Cerca del Mistero, 1962. Directed and wrote 3-part TV documentary, La vie del Petrolio for Ital. Oil co. in Iran, 1965-66. Collaborated on s.p. for Ballata de un Milliardo, Sergio Leone's Once Upon a Time in the West, L'inchiesta. Prod.: Sconcerto Rock, Lo Con Te Non Ci Sto Piu, Lost and Found.
PICTURES: The Grim Reaper, Before the Revolution, Love and Rage (episode: Agony), Partner, The Spider's Strategem, The Conformist, Last Tango in Paris, 1900, Luna, Tragedy of a Ridiculous Man, The Last Emperor (Acad. Awards for Best Dir. & Screenplay, 1987), The Sheltering Sky, Little Buddha, Stealing Beauty, L'Assedio, Paradiso e Inferno, Heaven and Hell.

BESSON, LUC
Director, Writer, Producer. b. Paris, France, March 18, 1959. Formed Les Films de Loups, which later changed name to Les Films de Dauphins.
PICTURES: Le Dernier Combat, Le Grand Carnaval (2nd unit dir.), Subway, Kamikaze (prod., s.p.), Taxi Boy (tech. advis.), The Big Blue (also lyrics, camera op.), La Femme Nikita (also song), The Professional, The Fifth Element (dir.), Taxi (s.p., prod.), Joan of Arc (dir.), Nil by Mouth (prod., BAFTA Award, Outstanding Brit. Film, 1997), The Dancer (prod & writer), Taxi 2 (writer).

BEST, BARBARA
Publicist. b. San Diego, CA, Dec. 2, 1921. e. U. of Southern California, AB, 1943. Pub., 20th Century-Fox, 1943-49; reporter, San Diego Journal, 1950 Stanley Kramer Co. 1950-53; own agency, Barbara Best & Associates, 1953-66; exec. v.p. Jay Bernstein Public rel., 1966; Freeman and Best, 1967-74; Barbara Best Inc. publ. rel. 1975-85; Barbara Best Personal Management, 1997. Retired, 1998.

BEST, JAMES
Actor. r.n. Jules Guy. b. Corydon, IN, July 26, 1926. Magazine model; on stage in European roadshow cast of My Sister Eileen. Served as M.P. with USAAF, WWII.
PICTURES: One Way Street (debut, 1950), Commanche Territory, Winchester 73, Peggy, Kansas Raiders, Air Cadet, Cimarron Kid, Target Unknown, Apache Drums, Ma & Pa Kettle at the Fair, Steel Town, Francis Goes to West Point, Battle at Apache Pass, Flat Top, About Face, The Beast from 20000 Fathoms, Seminole, The President's Lady, City of Bad Men, Column South, Riders to the Stars, The Raid, The Caine Mutiny, Return from the Sea, They Rode West, Seven Angry Men, The Eternal Sea, A Man Called Peter, Forbidden Planet, Calling Homicide, When Gangland Strikes, Come Next Spring, Gaby, The Rack, Man on the Prowl, Hot Summer Night, Last of the Badmen, Verboten!, The Naked and the Dead, The Left Handed Gun, Cole Younger—Gunfighter, The Killer Shrews, Ride Lonesome, Cast a Long Shadow, The Mountain Road, Shock Corridor, Black Gold, The Quick Gun, Black Spurs, Shenandoah, Three on a Couch, First to Fight, Firecreek, The Brain Machine, Sounder, Ode to Billy Joe, Gator (also assoc. prod.), Nickelodeon, Rolling Thunder, The End (also assoc. prod.), Hooper, Death Mask.
TELEVISION: *Movies*: Run Simon Run, Savages, The Runaway Barge, The Savage Bees, The Dukes of Hazzard: Reunion!. *Mini-Series*: Centennial. *Series*: Dukes of Hazzard, Dukes of Hazzard 2000. *Guest*: Alfred Hitchcock Presents, Twilight Zone, The Andy Griffith Show, Hawkins, Enos, In the Heat of the Night.

BETHUNE, ZINA
Actress, Dancer, Singer. b. New York, NY, Feb. 17, 1950. New York City Ballet (Balanchine), Zina Bethune & Company Dance Theatre, Bethune Theatredanse. Special performance at the White House and Kennedy Center.
THEATER: *B'way*: Most Happy Fella, Grand Hotel. National tours: Sweet Charity, Carnival, Oklahoma!, Damn Yankees, Member of the Wedding, The Owl and The Pussycat, Nutcracker.
PICTURES: Sunrise At Campobello, Who's That Knocking at My Door, The Boost.
TELEVISION: *Movies*: Party of Five, Nutcracker: Money Madness Murder (also choreographer). *Specials*: The Gymnast (An ABC Afterschool Special), Heart Dancing, From the Heart. *Series*: The Nurses, The Guiding Light, Love of Life. *Guest*: Lancer, Cains Hundred, Naked City, Route 66, Little Women, Santa Barbara, Judy Garland Show, Jackie Gleason Show, Gunsmoke, Dr. Kildare, Emergency, Planet of The Apes, Police Story, Chips, Hardy Boys, Dirty Dancing.

BETTGER, LYLE
Actor b. Philadelphia, PA, Feb. 13, 1915. e. Haverford School, Philadelphia, American Acad. of Dramatic Art, N.Y. m. Mary Rolfe, actress. Started in summer stock; in road cos. of Brother Rat, Man Who Came to Dinner.
THEATER: John Loves Mary, Love Life, Eve of St. Mark, The Male Animal, Sailor Beware, The Moon is Down.
PICTURES: No Man of Her Own, Union Station, First Legion, Greatest Show on Earth, The Denver & Rio Grande, Vanquished, Forbidden, The Great Sioux Uprising, All I Desire, Drums Across the River, Destry, Carnival Story, Sea Chase, Showdown at Abilene, Gunfight at OK Corral, Town Tamer, Johnny Reno, Nevada Smith, Return of The Gunfighter, Impasse, The Hawaiians, The Seven Minutes.
TELEVISION: Court of Last Resort, Grand Jury, Hawaii 5-0, Police Story, Bonanza, Combat, Gunsmoke.

BEVILLE, HUGH M., JR.
Executive; b. April 18, 1908. e. Syracuse U., NYU (MBA). To NBC 1930 statistician, chief statistician; research mgr., dir., research. U.S. Army 1942-46. Dir. of research and planning for NBC then v.p., planning and research, 1956; v.p., planning, 1964; consultant, 1968. Professor Business Admin., Southampton Coll., 1968. Exec. dir., Broadcast Rating Council, 1971-82. Author, cons., contributing ed., TV/Radio Age, 1982-85. Author of Audience Ratings; Radio, Television, Cable, 1985, Elected member, Research Hall of Fame, 1986.

BEY, TURHAN
Actor. b. Vienna, Austria, March 30, 1922. Came to U.S. in 1930's studying acting at Ben Bard's School of Dramatic Arts, Pasadena Playhouse.
PICTURES: Footsteps in the Dark (debut, 1941), Burma Convoy, Raiders of the Desert, Shadows on the Stairs, The Gay Falcon, Junior G-Men of the Air (serial), The Falcon Takes Over, A Yank on the Burma Road, Bombay Clipper, Drums of the Congo, Destination Unknown, Arabian Nights, The Unseen Enemy, The Mummy's Tomb, Danger in the Pacific, Adventures of Smilin' Jack (serial), White Savage, The Mad Ghoul, Background to Danger, Follow the Boys, The Climax, Dragon Seed, Bowery to Broadway, Ali Baba and the 40 Thieves, Frisco Sal, Sudan, Night in Paradise, Out of the Blue, The Amazing Mr. X, Adventures of Casanova, Parole Inc., Song of India, Prisoners of the Casbah, Stolen Identity (prod. only), Healer, Possessed by the Night, The Skateboard Kid II, Virtual Combat.
TELEVISION: *Guest*: Seaquest, Murder She Wrote, Babylon 5

BEYMER, RICHARD
Actor. r.n. George Richard Beymer, Jr., b. Avoca, IA, Feb. 21, 1939. e. N. Hollywood H.S., Actors Studio. Performer, KTLA, Sandy Dreams, Fantastic Studios, Inc., 1949, Playhouse 90.
PICTURES: Indiscretion of an American Wife (debut, 1953), So Big, Johnny Tremain, The Diary of Anne Frank, High Time, West Side Story, Bachelor Flat, Five Finger Exercise, Hemingway's Adventures of a Young Man, The Longest Day, The Stripper, Grass (Scream Free!), Cross Country, Silent Night Deadly Night 3: Better Watch Out, My Girl 2, The Little Death, Foxfire.
TELEVISION: *Movies*: Generation, With a Vengeance, A Face to Die For, Elvis Meets Nixon. *Series*: Paper Dolls, Twin Peaks. *Guest*: The Virginian, Walt Disney (Boston Tea Party), Dr. Kildare, Man from U.N.C.L.E., Moonlighting, Murder She Wrote, The Bronx Zoo.

BIALIK, MAYIM
Actress. b. San Diego, CA, Dec. 12, 1976.
PICTURES: Pumpkinhead (debut, 1988), Beaches.
TELEVISION: *Movies:* Blossom in Paris, Don't Drink the Water. *Specials:* Earth Day Special, Sea World Mother Earth Celebration (host), Surviving a Break-Up, The Kingdom Chums: Original Top Ten (voice), I Hate the Way I Look, For Our Children: The Concert (host), Recess (voice). *Series:* Blossom. *Pilot:* Molly. *Guest:* Webster, The Facts of Life, MacGyver, Empty Nest, The John Larroquette Show.

BICK, JERRY
Producer. b. New York, NY, April 26, 1923. e. Columbia U., Sorbonne. Taught English at U. of Georgia, before entering film industry in pub. dept. of MGM, N.Y. Opened own literary agency in Hollywood after stint with MCA. Began career as producer in London; debut film, Michael Kohlhaas, 1969. 1986-89, exec. v.p. worldwide prod., Heritage Entertainment.
PICTURES: The Long Goodbye, Thieves Like Us, Russian Roulette, The Big Sleep, Against All Odds (exec. prod.), Swing Shift.

BIEHN, MICHAEL
Actor. b. Anniston, AL, July 31, 1956. Raised in Lincoln, NB, and Lake Havisu, AZ. At 18 years moved to Los Angeles and studied acting with Vincent Chase. First professional job in 1977 in TV pilot for Logan's Run.
PICTURES: Grease (debut, 1978), Coach, Hog Wild, The Fan, The Lords of Discipline, The Terminator, Aliens, The Seventh Sign, Rampage, In a Shallow Grave, The Abyss, Navy Seals, Time Bomb, K2, DeadFall, Tombstone, Deep Red, Jade, The Rock, Mojave Moon, The Ride, American Dragon, Dead Men Can't Dance, Susan's Plan, Wonderland, Silver Wolf, Cherry Falls.
TELEVISION:. *Movies*: Zuma Beach, A Fire in the Sky, China Rose, Deadly Intentions, A Taste for Killing, Strapped, Conundrum, Asteroid. *Series*: The Runaways, The Magnificent Seven. *Guest*: Logan's Run, Hill Street Blues, Police Story, Family *Pilots*: James at 15, The Paradise Connection.

BIGELOW, KATHRYN
Director, Writer. b. San Carlos, CA, 1951. e. SF Art Inst., Columbia. Studied to be painter before turning to film with short Set-Up, 1978. Was script supervisor on Union City; appeared in film Born in Flames.
PICTURES: The Loveless (feature debut as co-dir. with Monty Montgomery, 1981; also co-s.p.), Near Dark (also co-s.p.), Blue Steel (also co-s.p.), Point Break, Strange Days, Undertow (s.p.).
TELEVISION: *Mini-Series:* Wild Palms (co-dir.). Series: Homicide: Life on the Streets (3 episodes).

BIGGS, JASON
Actor. b. Pompton Plains, NJ, May 12, 1978.
PICTURES: Camp Stories, American Pie, Boys and Girls, Loser, Prozac Nation, Saving SIlverman, American Pie II.
TELEVISION: *Series:* Drexel's Class, As The World Turns, Total Security.

BIKEL, THEODORE
Actor. b. Vienna, Austria, May 2, 1924. Moved to Palestine (Israel) as teen where he made stage debut in Tevye the Milkman. Studied acting at Royal Academy of Dramatic Arts in London. London stage debut in 1948. Autobiography: Theo (1995).
THEATER: Tonight in Samarkland, The Lark, The Rope Dancers, The Sound of Music, Cafe Crown, Fiddler on the Roof.
PICTURES: The African Queen, Melba, Desperate Moment, The Divided Heart, The Little Kidnappers, The Vintage, The Pride and the Passion, The Enemy Below, Fraulein, The Defiant Ones (Acad. Award nom.), I Want to Live, The Angry Hills, The Blue Angel, A Dog of Flanders, My Fair Lady, Sands of the Kalahari,

he Russians Are Coming the Russians Are Coming, Sweet November, My Side of the Mountain, Darker Than Amber, 200 Motels, The Little Ark, Prince Jack, Dark Tower, See You in the Morning, Shattered, Crisis in the Kremlin, My Family Treasure, Benefit of the Doubt, Shadow Conspiracy, Trickle.
TELEVISION: *Movies:* The Eternal Light, Look Up and Live, Who Has Seen the Wind?, The Diary of Anne Frank, Killer by Night, Murder on Flight 502, Victory at Entebbe, Christine Cromwell: Things That Go Bump in the Night, The Final Days, Babylon 5: In the Beginning. *Mini-series:* Testimony of Two Men, Loose Change.

BILBY, KENNETH W.
Executive. b. Salt Lake City, UT, Oct. 7, 1918. e. Columbia U; U. of Arizona, B.A. With N.Y. Herald-Tribune, 1947-50. Author of New Star in the Near East, 1950. Pub. rel. rep. to RCA Victor, Camden, NJ, 1950-54. Exec. v.p. National Broadcasting Co., N.Y., 1954-60. V.p. public affairs, RCA, 1960-62; exec. v.p., 1962-75; exec. v.p. corporate affairs, 1976-present.

BILL, TONY
Director, Producer, Actor. b. San Diego, CA, Aug. 23, 1940. e. Notre Dame U. Founded Bill/Phillips Prods. with Julia and Michael Phillips, 1971-73; Tony Bill Prods. 1973-92; Barnstorm Films, 1993-. Acad. of M.P. Arts & Sciences, bd. of govs., bd of trustees, chmn. prods. branch.
PICTURES: *Director*: My Bodyguard (debut, 1980), Six Weeks, Five Corners (also co-prod.), Crazy People, Untamed Heart (also co-prod.), A Home of Our Own. *Prod.*: Hearts of the West (exec. prod.), Harry and Walter Go to New York, Boulevard Nights (exec. prod.), Going in Style, Little Dragons (also actor). *Co-producer*: Deadhead Miles, Steelyard Blues, The Sting (Acad. Award for Best Picture, 1973), Taxi Driver. *Actor*: Come Blow Your Horn (debut, 1963), Soldier in the Rain, Marriage on the Rocks, None But the Brave, You're a Big Boy Now, Ice Station Zebra, Never a Dull Moment, Castle Keep, Flap, Shampoo, Heartbeat, Pee-wee's Big Adventure, Less Than Zero, Barb Wire.
TELEVISION: *Director*: Dirty Dancing (pilot), Love Thy Neighbor, Next Door, One Christmas, Oliver Twist, A Chance of Snow. *Actor*: *Movies*: Haunts of the Very Rich, Having Babies II, The Initiation of Sarah, With This Ring, Are You in the House Alone?, Portrait of an Escort, Freedom, Washington Mistress, Running Out, The Killing Mind, Naked City: Justice with a Bullet, The Fixer (also prod.). *Mini-Series*: Washington Behind Closed Doors. *Series*: What Really Happened to the Class of '65? *Guest*: Alfred Hitchcock Presents (Night Caller, 1985). *Special*: Lee Oswald - Assassin (BBC).

BILLS, ELMER E.
Executive. b. Salisbury, MO, July 12, 1936. e. University of Missouri, B.S. Partner B & B Theatres, Inc.

BILSON, BRUCE
Director. b. Brooklyn, NY, May 19, 1928. e. UCLA, BA, Theater Arts, 1950. m. actress Renne Jarrett. Father was prod. George Bilson, son is prod.-dir. Danny Bilson, daughter is prod. Julie Ahlberg. Asst. film ed. 1951-55; USAF photo unit 1952-53; asst. dir. 1955-65. Dir. since 1965 of more than 390 TV shows.
PICTURES: The North Avenue Irregulars, Chattanooga Choo Choo.
TELEVISION: *Movies/pilots:* The Odd Couple, The Dallas Cowboys Cheerleaders, BJ and the Bear, The Misadventures of Sheriff Lobo, Half Nelson, Finder of Lost Loves, The Girl Who Came Gift Wrapped, The Ghosts of Buxley Hall, The New Gidget, Barefoot in the Park, The Bad News Bears, Harper Valley PTA, Deadly Games. *Series*: The Sentinel, Touched by an Angel, Viper, The Flash, Dinosaurs, Barney Miller, Get Smart (Emmy Award, 1968), Andy Griffith Show (asst. dir.), Route 66 (asst. dir.), The Baileys of Balboa (also assoc. prod.), Hogan's Heroes, House Calls, Alice, Private Benjamin, Life With Lucy, Spenser: For Hire, Hotel, Dallas, Hawaii Five-O, Dynasty, The Fall Guy, Nightingales, The Love Boat: The Next Wave.

BINDER, STEVE
Producer, Director, Writer. b. Los Angeles, CA, Dec. 12. e. Univ. of Southern California. 1960-61, announcer in Austria and Germany with AFN, Europe. Prof. of Cinema, Univ. Southern CA. Mem.: DGA, Producers Guild of America, Writers Guild of America, NARAS, ATAS.
PICTURES: *Director*: The T.A.M.I. Show, Give 'Em Hell Harry!, Melissa, Father Guido Sarducci Goes to College.
TELEVISION: *Prod./Dir.*: Soupy Sales Show, Jazz Scene U.S.A., Hullaballoo, The Danny Kaye Show, Hallelujah Leslie!, TJ's, Petula, America, A Funny Thing Happened on the Way to the White House, Comedy of the 60's, Don Kirshner's Rock Concert, Olivia Newton-John, Norman Corwin Theater, Mac Davis Series, The Big Show, Primetime Emmy's, Motown Revue, Peggy Fleming Special, Dorothy Hammil Special, Shields & Yarnell Series (also writer) The Magic Castle Special, Star Wars Holiday Special, Father Guido Sarducci at UCSB, A Tribute to Sam Kinison, Smhatar, Jane Fonda In Search of the Missing Smhatar, Steve Allen Show (1963-65, 1973), Elvis Presley Comeback Special, Barry Manilow Special (also exec. prod., writer, Emmy Award, 1977), Diana Ross '81, Ringling Bros & Barnum Bailey Circus (also writer), Pee-wee's Playhouse (exec. prod., writer), Barry Manilow Big Fun on Swing Street, Pee-wee's Playhouse Christmas Special, A Tribute to Sam Kinison, Diana Ross at Wembley, Diana Ross Sings Jazzy Blues, Diana Ross—World Tour, Diana Ross in Central Park (Cable Ace Award, also writer), Diana Ross (also writer), The International Special Olmpics, 65th Anniversary of the Grand Ole Opry, The First Annual ESPY Awards, Liza Minneli, Lucy in London, Fiesta Texas, Eddie Rabbit Special, One Night With You, Disney's First Lady of Magic (exec. prod.). *Exec. Prod./Writer.*: Soul Train Music Awards, Zoobilee Zoo, Disney's Greatest Hits on Ice, Disney's Alladin on Ice, Disney's Beauty and the Beast on Ice, Innocent Love (MOW), The Chevy Chase Show, SK8 TV, On the Television Series, Tales From the Whoop, The Beach Boys Summer Series, Television's Greatest Performances.

BINOCHE, JULIETTE
Actress. b. Paris, France, March 9, 1964. e. Natl Schl. of Dramatic Art, Paris. Began acting career while in school, performing on stage. In 1984, after some small roles in films and TV prods., appeared in Jean-Luc Godard's, Je Vous Salue Marie. In 1985, gained recognition at the Cannes Film Festival for her role in Andre Techine's Rendez-Vous.
PICTURES: Liberty Bell, Le Meilleur de la Vie, Adieu Blaireau, La Vie de la Familie, Je Vous Salue Marie, Les Nanas, Rendez-Vous, Mauvais Sang, Mon Beau-Frere a Tue Ma Soeur, The Unbearable Lightness of Being, Un Tour de Manege, Les Amants du Pont-Neuf, Mara, Wuthering Heights, Damage, Red, White, Blue, Le Hussard Sur le Toit, The English Patient (Acad. Award, 1996; BAFTA), A Couch in New York, Alice et Martin, Les Enfants du Siecle, La Veuve de Saint-Pierre, Code Unknown: Incomplete Tales of Several Journeys, Chocolat.

BIONDI, JR. FRANK J.
Executive. b. Jan. 9, 1945. e. Princeton U.; Harvard U., MBA (1968). Various investment banking positions, 1968-74. Asst. treas. Children's TV Workshop 1974-78. V.p. programming HBO 1978-82; pres. HBO 1983, then chmn. & chief exec. off. Joined Coca-Cola Co. as exec. v.p., entertainment business arm, 1984. Resigned 1987 to join Viacom International as pres. and CEO. Pres., MCA, 1996. Resigned, 1998.

BIRCH, THORA
Actress. b. Los Angeles, CA, March 11, 1982. Began acting at age 4. First appeared in commericals.
PICTURES: Paradise, All I Want for Christmas, Patriot Games, Hocus Pocus, Monkey Trouble, Clear and Present Danger, Now and Then, Alaska, American Beauty, Anywhere But Here, The Smokers, Dungeons & Dragons, Ghost World, The Hole.
TELEVISION: *Movie:* Night Ride Home. *Series*: Parenthood, Day by Day. *Guest*: Amen, Doogie Howser M.D.

BIRKIN, JANE
Actress. b. London, England, Dec. 14, 1946. Daughter is actress Charlotte Gainsbourg. Sister of dir.-writer Andrew Birkin. Was subject of Agnes Vardas` 1988 documentary Jane B. par Agnes V.
PICTURES: Blow-Up, Kaleidoscope, Wonderwall, Les Chemins de Katmandou, La Piscine, Cannabis, Romance of a Horse Thief, Trop jolies pour etre honnetes, Dark Places, Projection Privee, La Moutarde me monte au nex, Le Mouton Enrage, 7 Morts sur Ordonnance, Catherine et Cie, La Course a l'echalote, Je T'Aime Moi Non Plus, Seriex comme let plaisir, Le Diable au Coeur, L'Animal, Death on the Nile, Au bout du bout du banc, Melancolie Baby, La Miel, La Fille Prodigue, Evil Under the Sun, L'Ami de Vincent, Circulez u'a rien a voir, Love on the Ground, le Garde du Corps, The Pirate, Beethoven's Nephew, Dust, Leave All Fair, la Femme de ma vie, Comedie!, Kung Fu Master (also story), Soigne ta droite, Daddy Nostalgia, Between the Devil and the Deep Blue Sea (voice), A Soldier's Daughter Never Cries, The Last September..

BIRNBAUM, ROGER
Producer, Executive. b. Teaneck, NJ. e. Univ. of Denver. Was v.p. of both A&M Records and Arista records before becoming m.p. prod.. Headed Guber/Peters Company, then named pres. of worldwide prod., United Artists; pres. of worldwide prod. and exec. v.p. of 20th Century Fox. Left Fox in 1993 to become co-founder of Caravan Pictures.
PICTURES: *Prod./Exec. Prod.*: The Sure Thing, Young Sherlock Homes, Who's That Girl, The Three Musketeers, Angie, Angels in the Outfield, A Low Down Dirty Shame, Houseguest, Tall Tale, While You Were Sleeping, Dead Presidents, Powder, Celtic Pride, The Beautician and the Beast, G.I. Jane, Gone Fishin', Grosse Pointe Blank, Washington Square, Metro, Rocket Man, A Small Miracle, Holy Man, Six Days Seven Nights, Simon Birch, Rush Hour, Stretch Armstrong (exec. prod.), A Course in Miracles, Inspector Gadget, Shanghai Noon, The Hitchhiker's Guide to the Galaxy.
TELEVISION: Flash (exec. prod.).

BIRNEY, DAVID
Actor. b. Washington, DC, April 23, 1940. e. Dartmouth Coll., B.A., UCLA, M.A. Phd. Southern Utah St. (hon.). Following grad. sch. and the Army spent 2 yrs. in regional theatre, Amer. Shakespeare Festival, Lincoln Center Repertory Theatre, Great Lakes Theatre Festival, Mark Taper Forum, Shakespeare Theatre Washington DC, Hartford Stage Co., Barter Theatre, to N.Y. where appeared in Lincoln Center prod. of Summertree (Theatre World Award). Appeared for two yrs. on TV daytime series, Love Is a Many Splendored Thing, doing other stage roles in same period. Theatre panelist, Natl. Endowment for the Arts; bd. mem., Hopkins Center, Dartmouth College; bd. of Foundation for Biomedical Research.
THEATER: Comedy of Errors (NY debut; NY Shakespeare Fest). *NY & Regional*: Amadeus, Benefactors, Anthony & Cleopatra, Man and Superman, Macbeth, Hamlet, Richard II, III, Romeo & Juliet, Much Ado About Nothing, King John, Titus Andronicus, Major Barbara, Biko Inquest, Playboy of the Western World, The Miser, Antigone, My Fair Lady, Camelot, Love Letters, Present Laughter, Twelfth Night, Talley's Folley, Rumors, Social Security, Enemy of the People, Mark Twain's The Diaries of Adam & Eve.
PICTURES: Caravan to Vaccares, Trial by Combat, Oh God Book II, Prettykill, Nightfall.
TELEVISION: *Movies*: Murder or Mercy, Bronk, Serpico: The Deadly Game, Someone's Watching Me!, High Midnight, Only With Married Men, OHMS, Mom The Wolfman & Me, The Five of Me, The Long Journey Home (also co-exec. prod.), Love and Betrayal, Always Remember I Love You, Touch and Die, Keeping Secrets, The Champions. *Mini-Series*: Night of the Fox, Seal Morning, Adam's Chronicles, Testimony of Two Men, Master of the Game, Valley of the Dolls, The Bible. *Specials*: Missing: Have You Seen This Person? Drop Everything and Read, 15 and Getting Straight, Mark Twain's The Diaries of Adam and Eve (co-prod.), St. Joan. *Series*: Bridget Loves Bernie, Serpico, St. Elsewhere, Glitter, Live Shot, Beyond 2000 (host), Raising Kids (host), Great American TV Poll (host). Guest appearances in series & anthology shows.

BISHOP, LARRY
Actor.
MOVIES: Wild in the Street, The Savage Seven, The Devil's Eight, Angel Unchained, Chrome and Hot Leather, Shanks, How Come Nobody's on Our Side?, The Big Fix, Hey Good Lookin' (voice), The Sting II, Mad Dog Time (also dir., prod., writer), Underworld (also writer).

BISSET, JACQUELINE
Actress. r.n. Winnifred Jacqueline Fraser-Bisset, b. Weybridge, England, September 13, 1944. e. French Lycaee, London. After photographic modeling made film debut in The Knack, 1965.
PICTURES: The Knack... and How to Get It (debut, 1965), Cul de Sac, Two For The Road, Casino Royale, The Cape Town Affair, The Sweet Ride, The Detective, Bullitt, The First Time, Secret World, Airport, The Grasshopper, The Mephisto Waltz, Believe in Me, Stand Up and Be Counted, The Life & Times of Judge Roy Bean, The Thief Who Came to Dinner, Day for Night, Le Manifique, Murder on the Orient Express, End of the Game, The Spiral Staircase, St. Ives, Sunday Woman, The Deep, The Greek Tycoon, Secrets, Who Is Killing the Great Chefs of Europe?, Together?, When Time Ran Out, Rich and Famous, Inchon, Class, Under the Volcano, High Season, Scenes From the Class Struggle in Beverly Hills, La Maison de Jade, Wild Orchid, The Maid, A Judgment in Stone, Dangerous Beauty,.
TELEVISION: *Movies*: Forbidden, Anna Karenina, Choices, Leave of Absence, End of Summer, September, Witch Hunt, Britannic. *Mini-Series:* Napoleon and Josephine: A Love Story, Joan of Arc, Jesus.

BJORK
Actress, Composer. b. Reykjavik, Iceland, November 21, 1965. Winner of best actress award for Dancer in the Dark at Cannes. Solo recording artist. Former member of pop band The Sugarcubes.
PICTURES: Juniper Tree (act. only), The Young Americans (comp. only) Pret A Porter (act. only), Anton (comp. only), Dancer in the Dark.

BLACK, ALEXANDER F.
Publicist. b. New Rochelle, NY, Dec. 27, 1918. e. Brown U., BA, 1940. Joined Universal 1941. U.S. Navy 1942-45, Lt. Sr. Grade. Rejoined Universal 1946 serving in various capacities in Foreign Department, becoming dir. of foreign publicity for Universal International Films, Inc. in 1967. Named exec. in chg. intl. promotion for MCA-TV, 1974.

BLACK, KAREN
Actress. b. Park Ridge, IL, July 1, 1942. r.n. Karen Ziegler. e. Northwestern U. Left school for NY to join the Hecscher House, appearing in several Shakespearean plays. In 1965 starred in Playroom, which ran only 1 month but won her NY Drama Critic nom. as best actress.
THEATER: Happily Never After, Keep It in the Family, Come Back to the Five and Dime Jimmy Dean Jimmy Dean.
PICTURES: You're a Big Boy Now (debut, 1966), Hard Contact, Easy Rider, Five Easy Pieces (Acad. Award nom.), Drive He Said, A Gunfight, Born To Win, Cisco Pike, Portnoy's Complaint, The Pyx, Little Laura and Big John, Rhinoceros, The Outfit, The Great Gatsby, Airport 1975, Law and Disorder, Day of the Locust, Nashville, Family Plot, Crime and Passion, Burnt Offerings, Capricorn One, Killer Fish, In Praise of Older Women, The Squeeze, The Last Word, Chanel Solitaire, Come Back to the Five and Dime Jimmy Dean Jimmy Dean, Killing Heat, Can She Bake a Cherry Pie?, Martin's Day, Bad Manners, Cut and Run, Invaders from Mars, Flight of the Spruce Goose, It's Alive III, Hostage, Eternal Evil, The Invisible Kid, Out of the Dark, Homer and Eddie, Night Angel, Miss Right, Dixie Lanes, Sister City, Zapped Again, Twisted Justice, Over Exposure, The Children, Mirror Mirror, Haunting Fear, Quiet Fire, Children of the Night, Hotel Oklahoma, Killer's Edge, Club Fed, Evil Spirits, Moon Over Miami, The Legend of the Rollerblade 7, Hitz, FInal Judgment, Caged Fear, Bound & Gagged: A Love Story, The Player, Rubin & Ed, The Trust, The Double O Kid, Sister Island, Plan 10 From Outer Space, The Wacky Adventures of Dr. Boris & Mrs. Duluth, Odyssey, Every Minute Is Goodbye, A Thousand Stars, Children of the Corn III: The Fever, Crimetime, Children of the Corn IV: The Gathering, Stir, Invisible Dad, Dogtown, Conceiving Ada, Men (also s.p.), I Woke Up Early the Day I Died, Felons, Fallen Arches, Bury the Evidence, Spoken in Silence, Mascara.
TELEVISION: *Movies:* Trilogy of Terror, The Strange Possession of Mrs. Oliver, Mr. Horn, Power, Where the Ladies Go, Because He's My Friend, Full Circle Again (Canadian TV), My Neighbor's Daugher. *Guest:* In the Heat of the Night, Moon Over Miami, Murder She Wrote.

BLACK, NOEL
Director. b. Chicago, IL, June 30, 1937. e. UCLA, B.A., 1959; M.A. 1964. Made short film Skaterdater and won numerous awards including the Cannes' Grand Prix for Best Short Film.
PICTURES: Pretty Poison (debut, 1968), Cover Me Babe, Jennifer on My Mind, Mirrors, A Man a Woman and a Bank, Private School, Mischief (s.p., exec. prod.).
TELEVISION: *Movies:* Mulligan's Stew, The Other Victim, Prime Suspect, Happy Endings, Quarterback Princess, Promises to Keep, A Time to Triumph, My Two Loves, Conspiracy of Love, The Town Bully, Trilogy: The American Boy; The World Beyond; I'm a Fool, The Golden Honeymoon, The Electric Grandmother, The Doctors Wilde, Meet the Munceys, Eyes of the Panther, The Hollow Boy, Swan's Crossing, The Baby Sitter's Club, Dolphin Cove. *Mini-series:* Deadly Intentions.

BLACK, STANLEY
Composer, Conductor, Musical director. OBE. b. London, Eng. Resident conductor, BBC, 1944-52. Musical director 105 feature films and Pathe Newsreel music: Music dir. Associated British Film Studios 1958-64. Guest conductor, Royal Philharmonic Orchestra and London Symphony. Orchestra; many overseas conducting engagements including (1977) Boston Pops and Winnipeg Symphony. Associated conductor Osaka Philharmonic Orchestra. Exclusive recording contract with Decca Record Co. since 1944.
PICTURES: Crossplot, The Long the Short and The Tall, Rattle of a Simple Man, The Young Ones, Hell Is a City, Top Secret, Valentino.

BLACKMAN, HONOR
Actress. b. London, England, Aug. 22, 1926. Stage debut. The Gleam 1946.
PICTURES: Fame Is the Spur (debut, 1947), Quartet, Daughter of Darkness, A Boy A Girl and a Bike, Diamond City, Conspirator, So Long at the Fair, Set a Murderer, Green Grow the Rushes, Come Die My Love, Rainbow Jacket, Outsiders, Delavine Affair, Three Musketeers, Breakaway, Homecoming, Suspended Alibi, Dangerous Drugs, A Night to Remember, The Square Peg, A Matter of Who, Present Laughter, The Recount, Serena, Jason & the Golden Fleece, Goldfinger, The Secret of My Success, Moment to Moment, Life at the Top, A Twist of Sand, Shalako, Struggle for Rome, Twinky, The Last Grenade, The Virgin and the Gypsy, Fright, Something Big, Out Damned Spot, Summer, Cat and the Canary, Russell Mulcahy's Talos the Mummy, To Walk with Lions.
TELEVISION: African Patrol, The Witness, Four Just Men, Top Secret, Ghost Squad, Invisible Man, Voice of the Heart, The Upper Hand, The Secret Garden (voice). *Series:* The Avengers, Probation Officer, The Saint.

BLADES, RUBEN
Actor, Composer, Singer, Writer. b. Panama City, Panama, July 16, 1948. e. U. of Panama (law and political science, 1974), Harvard U., L.L.M., 1985. Has recorded more than 14 albums, winning 3 Grammy Awards (1986, 1988, 1997). With his band Seis del Solar has toured U.S., Central America and Europe. President of Panama's Papa Egoro political party.
PICTURES: *Actor:* The Last Fight (debut, 1982), Crossover Dreams (also co-s.p.), Critical Condition, The Milagro Beanfield War, Fatal Beauty, Homeboy, Disorganized Crime, The Lemon Sisters, Mo' Better Blues, The Two Jakes, Predator 2, Homeboy, The Super, Life With Mikey, A Million to Juan, Color of Night. Music: Beat Street, Oliver & Company, Caminos Verdes (Venezuela), Q&A (also composer), Scorpion Spring, The Devil's Own, The Chinese Box, The Cradle Will Rock, All the Pretty Horses.

TELEVISION: *Movies:* Dead Man Out (ACE Award), One Man's War, The Josephine Baker Story (Emmy nom.), Crazy from the Heart (Emmy nom.), The Heart of the Deal, Miracle on I-880. *Guest:* Sesame Street, The X-Files.

BLAIN, GERARD
Actor, Director. b. Paris, France, Oct. 23, 1930. Began his professional career in 1943 as an extra in Marcel Carne's The Children of Paradise. Appeared on stage in Marcel Pagnol's Topaze (1944). Military service in a parachute regiment. In 1955 Julien Duvivier gave him his first major role in Voici le Temps des Assassins (Murder a la Carte). By 1969 had appeared in more than 30 stage and film roles before becoming a dir. and co-author.
PICTURES: *Actor:* Voice le temps des assassins, Les Mistons, Giovani mariti, Charlotte et son Jules, Le Beau Serge, Les Cousins, Match contre la mort, Il Gobbo, I Delfini, L'Oro di Roma, Hatari!, Les Vierges, La Smania addosso, La Bonne soupe, Un Amore, Joe Caligula, Negresco -- Eine toedliche Affaere, Un homme de trop, Le Pelican (also dir.), Der Amerikanische Freund, Un dimance de flic, Pas de vieux os, Poussiere d'ange, Der Schnee der Anden, L'Enfant de l'hiver, Jour apres jour, Faut-il aimer Mathilde?, Chasse gardee, Jusqu'au Bout de la Nuit (also dir.), Le Radeau de la Meduse. *Director:* Les Amis (also s.p.), Un enfant dans la foule, Un second souffle, Le Rebelle, Pierre et Djemila (also s.p.).

BLAIR, JANET
Actress. r.n. Martha Janet Lafferty. b. Altoona, PA, April 23, 1921. With Hal Kemp's Orchestra; toured in South Pacific, 1950-52.
PICTURES: Three Girls About Town (debut, 1941), Blondie Goes to College, Two Yanks in Trinidad, Broadway, My Sister Eileen, Something to Shout About, Once Upon a Time, Tonight and Every Night, Tars and Spars, Gdallant Journey, The Fabulous Dorseys, I Love Trouble, The Black Arrow, Fuller Brush Man, Public Pigeon No. 1, Boys Night Out, Burn Witch Burn, The One and Only Genuine Original Family Band, Won Ton Ton the Dog Who Saved Hollywood.
TELEVISION: *Special:* Arabian Nights, Tom Sawyer. *Series:* Leave it to the Girls (panelist), Caesar's Hour, The Chevy Show, The Smith Family. *Guest:* Bell Telephone Hour, Ed Sullivan, Murder She Wrote.

BLAIR, LINDA
Actress. b. St. Louis, MO, Jan. 22, 1959. Model and actress on TV commercials before going into films.
PICTURES: The Sporting Club (debut, 1971), The Exorcist, Airport '75, Exorcist II: The Heretic, Roller Boogie, Wild Horse Hank, Hell Night, Ruckus, Chained Heat, Savage Streets, Savage Island, Red Heat, Night Patrol, Night Force, Silent Assassins, Grotesque (also prod.), Witchery, The Chilling, Bad Blood, Moving Target, Up Your Alley, Repossessed, Aunt Millie's Will, Zapped Again, Dead Sleep, Double Blast, Temptress, Prey of the Jaguar, Scream.
TELEVISION: *Movies:* Born Innocent, Sarah T.: Portrait of a Teenage Alcoholic, Sweet Hostage, Victory at Entebbe, Stranger in Our House, Calendar Girl Cop Killer? The Bambi Bembenek Story, Perry Mason: The Case of the Heartbroken Bride. *Guest:* Fantasy Island, Murder She Wrote.

BLAIR, STEWART
Executive. b. Scotland. e. Univ. of Glasgow. Was v.p. of Chase Manhattan Bank N.A. in NY, before joining Tele-Communications Inc. in 1981. Served as vice-chmn. & CEO of United Artists Entertainment Company. 1992, appointed chmn. and CEO of United Artists Theatre Circuit Inc.; removed, 1996. Bd. member of Foundation of Motion Picture Pioneers, exec. v.p. of Will Rogers Memorial Fund.

BLAKE, JEFF
Executive. e. B.A., economics, Northwestern U. and J.D., Whittier College of Law. Began career as sales broker and mgr., Paramount Pictures, 1974-78; asst. gen. sales mgr., Buena Vista Distribution (Walt Disney Co.) 1980. mgr., Western Div., Paramount, 1981; v.p., theatrical distribution, Paramount, 1984-1987; exec. v.p. & gen. sales mgr., Columbia Pictures (Sony Pictures Entertainment-SPE); 1987-92; president, domestic distribution, SPE, 1992-94; president, Sony Pictures Releasing, 1994-99. Currently president, Worldwide Sales & Distribution, Columbia Pictures, overseeing all theatrical sales and distribution activities worldwide for Sony Pictures Releasing and Columbia TriStar Film Distributors Intl. Member, Calif. Bar Assn. and Academy of Motion Picture Arts & Sciences, v.p., Motion Picture Pioneer Found.

BLAKE, ROBERT
Actor. r.n. Michael Gubitosi. b. Nutley, NJ, Sept. 18, 1933. Started as a child actor in Our Gang comedies as Mickey Gubitosi, also appeared as Little Beaver in Red Ryder series. Later was Hollywood stunt man in Rumble on the Docks and The Tijuana Story. First adult acting job was at the Gallery Theater in Hatful of Rain.
PICTURES: I Love You Again (debut, 1940, as Bobby Blake), Andy Hardy's Double Life, China Girl, Mokey, Salute to the Marines, Slightly Dangerous, The Big Noise, Lost Angel, Red Ryder series (as Little Beaver), Meet the People, Dakota, The Horn Blows at Midnight, Pillow to Post, The Woman in the Window, A Guy Could Change, Home on the Range, Humoresque, In Old Sacramento, Out California Way, The Last Round-Up, Treasure of the Sierra Madre, The Black Rose, Blackout (also co-prod.), Apache War Smoke, Treasure of the Golden Condor, Veils of Bagdad, The Rack, Screaming Eagles, Three Violent People, Beast of Budapest, Revolt in the Big House, Pork Chop Hill, The Purple Gang, Town Without Pity, PT 109, The Greatest Story Ever Told, The Connection, This Property Is Condemned, In Cold Blood, Tell Them Willie Boy is Here, Ripped-Off, Corky, Electra Glide in Blue, Busting, Coast to Coast, Second-Hand Hearts, Money Train, Lost Highway.
TELEVISION: *Movies:* The Big Black Pill (also creator & exec. prod.), The Monkey Mission (also creator & exec. prod.), Of Mice and Men (also exec. prod.), Blood Feud, Murder 1--Dancer 3 (also exec. prod.), Heart of a Champion: The Ray Mancini Story, Judgment Day: The John List Story. *Series:* The Richard Boone Show, Barretta (Emmy Award, 1975), Hell Town (also exec. prod.). *Guest:* One Step Beyond, Have Gun Will Travel, Bat Masterson.

BLAKELY, SUSAN
Actress. b. Frankfurt, Germany, Sept. 7, 1948, where father was stationed in Army. Studied at U. of Texas. m. prod., media consultant Steve Jaffe. Became top magazine and TV commercial model in N.Y.
PICTURES: Savages (debut, 1972), The Way We Were, The Lords of Flatbush, The Towering Inferno, Report to the Commissioner, Shampoo, Capone, Dreamer, The Concorde—Airport '79, Over the Top, Dream a Little Dream, My Mom's a Werewolf, Russian Holiday, Seven Sundays.
TELEVISION: *Movies:* Secrets, Make Me an Offer, A Cry For Love, The Bunker, The Oklahoma City Dolls, Will There Really Be A Morning?, The Ted Kennedy Jr. Story, Blood & Orchids, April Morning, Fatal Confession: A Father Dowling Mystery, Broken Angel, Hiroshima Maiden, Ladykillers, Sight Unseen, The Incident, End Run, Dead Reckoning, Murder Times Seven, And the Sea Will Tell, Sight Unseen, Blackmail, Wildflower, Against Her Will: An Incident in Baltimore, Intruders, No Child of Mine, Honor Thy Father and Mother: The True Story of the Menendez Murders, Color Me Perfect, Co-ed Call Girl, Race Against Fear. *Special:* Torn Between Two Fathers. *Mini-Series:* Rich Man Poor Man. *Series:* Falcon Crest, The George Carlin Show. *Guest:* Step by Step, Murder She Wrote, Father Dowling Mysteries, Diagnosis Murder. *Pilot:* Dad's a Dog.

BLAKLEY, RONEE
Actress. Singer. b. Stanley, ID, 1946. Wrote and performed songs for 1972 film Welcome Home Soldier Boys.
PICTURES: Nashville (debut, 1975; Acad. Award nom.), The Private Files of J. Edgar Hoover, The Driver, Renaldo and Clara, Good Luck Miss Wyckoff (Secret Yearnings/The Sin), The Baltimore Bullet, A Nightmare on Elm Street, Return to Salem's Lot, Student Confidential, Someone to Love, Murder by Numbers.

BLANC, MICHEL
Actor. b. France, June 16, 1952.
PICTURES: Que la Fete Commence, The Tenant, Les Bronzes, The Adolescent, Les Bronzes font du Ski, Le Cheval d'Orgueil, Walk in the Shadow, Les Fugitives, Evening Dress, Menage, I Hate Actors!, Story of Women, Monsieur Hire, Chambre a Part, Strike It Rich, Uranus, Merci la Vie, Prospero's Books, The Favor the Watch and the Very Big Fish, Ready to Wear (Pret-a-Porter), Grosse Fatigue (also dir., s.p.), The Monster, The Grand Dukes.

BLANCHETT, CATE
Actress. b. Melbourne, Australia, May 14, 1969. e. National Institute of Dramatic Art, Australia.
THEATER: Top Girls, Kafka Dances, Oleanna, Hamlet, Sweet Phoebe, The Tempest, The Blind Giant is Dancing.
PICTURES: Police Rescue, Parklands, Paradise Road, Thank God He Met Lizzie, Oscar and Lucinda, Pushing Tin, Elizabeth (Acad. Award nom.), Dreamtime Alice (also prod.), The Talented Mr. Ripley, An Ideal Husband.
TELEVISION: *Movie:* Heartland, Bordertown. *Guest*: G.P., Police Rescue.

BLANCO, RICHARD M.
Executive. b. Brooklyn, NY. e. electrical engineering, Wentworth Institute. J.C., 1925-27; bus. admin., U. of CA, 1939-40; U.S. Govt. Coll., 1942. Superv. Technicolor Corp., 1931-56; organ. and operator Consumer Products, Kodachrome film process., Technicolor, 1956-62; dir. of MP Govt. and theatre sales, NY & DC, 1963-65; gen. mgr. of Technicolor Florida photo optns. at Kennedy Space Center.; prod. doc. & educ. films for NASA, 1965; v.p. of tv div., Technicolor Corp. of America; 1967 elected corporate v.p. Technicolor, Inc.; 1971 pres., Technicolor Graphic Services, Inc.; 1974, elected chmn. of bd. of Technicolor Graphic Services; 1977, elected to bd. of dirs. of Technicolor Inc.

BLANK, MIKE
Executive. e. U. Michigan, 1933. Began career as poster clerk for Pathe, 1927. Head of const., maint., concessions, Central States Theatres, 1933. US Navy, 1942, in charge of visual ed. for 7th Naval Dist. in Miami. Pres., CEO, chmn., Central States 1950. B. V. Sturdivant Award, NATO/ShoWest, 1990.

BLANK, MYRON
Circuit executive. b. Des Moines, IA, Aug. 30, 1911. e. U. of Michigan. Son of A. H. Blank, circuit operator. On leaving coll. joined father in operating Tri-States and Central States circuits. On leave 1943-46 in U.S. Navy, officer in charge visual educ. Now pres. Central States Theatre Corp.; pres. TOA, 1955; chmn. bd. TOA Inc. 1956-57; exec. chmn. of NATO. Pres. of Greater Des Moines Comm. Built Anne Blank Child Guidance Center-Raymond Blank Hospital for Children. Endowed chair for gifted and talented children at Univ. of Iowa; permanent scholarship at Wertzman Inst., Israel. Sturdevant Award from NATO, Humanitarian Award from Variety Club in 1980. Partial scholarship for 80 students annually for 3-week seminar at Univ. of Iowa.

BLATT, DANIEL
Producer. e. Philips Andover Acad., Duke U., Northwestern U Sch. of Law.Indt. prod. since 1976; prior posts: resident counsel, ABC Pictures; exec. v.p. Palomar Pictures.
PICTURES: I Never Promised You a Rose Garden, Winter Kills, The American Success Company, The Howling, Independence Day, Cujo, Restless, The Boost.
TELEVISION: *Movies:* Circle of Children, Zuma Beach, The Children Nobody Wanted, Sadat, V: The Final Battle, Badge of the Assassin, Raid on Entebbe, Sacred Vows, A Winner Never Quits, Sworn to Silence, Common Ground, Beyond Betrayal (exec. prod.), Kissinger and Nixon (exec. prod.), It Was Him or Us (exec. prod.), Sins of Silence (exec. prod.), Childhood Sweethearts? (exec. prod.). *Series:* V, Against the Law.

BLATTY, WILLIAM PETER
Writer, Director, Producer. b. New York, NY, Jan. 7, 1928. e. George Washington U., Seattle U. Worked as editor for U.S. Information Bureau, publicity dir. for USC and Loyola U. before becoming novelist and screenwriter. Novels include: John Goldfarb Please Come Home (filmed), Twinkle Twinkle Killer Kane, The Exorcist, Legion (filmed as Exorcist III).
PICTURES: The Man From the Diner's Club, A Shot in the Dark, Promise Her Anything, What Did You Do in the War Daddy?, Gunn, The Great Bank Robbery, Darling Lili, The Exorcist (also prod.; Academy Award for Best Adapted Screenplay, 1973), The Ninth Configuration (also dir., prod.), The Exorcist III (also dir.), Dimiter (dir.), Exorcist IV: The Beginning.

BLAU, MARTIN
Executive. b. New York, NY, June 6, 1924. e. Ohio U., 1948. Employed on newspapers in OH, TX, WV. Pub. dept., Columbia Pictures, 1951; asst. pub. mgr. 1959; pub. mgr., Columbia Int'l, 1961; admin. asst. to v.p. of adv. & pub. Columbia Pictures, 1966. Dir. adv. and publicity, Columbia Pictures Int'l, 1970; v.p., 1971; sr. v.p., 1985. Retired, 1988.

BLAY, ANDRE
Executive. In 1979, sold Magnetic Video to 20th Century Fox, named pres., CEO, 20th Century Fox Home Video; 1981, formed The Blay Corporation; 1982, joined with Norman Lear and Jerry Perenchio, founders of Embassy Communications, as chairman and CEO of Embassy Home Entertainment; 1986, when Embassy sold to Nelson Group, left to form Palisades Entertainment Group with Elliott Kastner.
PICTURES: *Exec. Prod.:* Prince of Darkness, They Live, Jack's Back, Homeboy, Braindamage, The Blob, A Chorus of Disapproval, Village of the Damned (prod.).

BLECKNER, JEFF
Director, Producer. b. Brooklyn, NY, Aug. 12, 1943. e. Amherst College, BA., 1965; Yale Sch. of Drama, MFA 1968. Taught drama at Yale, also participated in the theater co. 1965-68. 1968-75 theater dir. NY Shakespeare Fest. Public Theatre (2 Drama Desk Awards, Tony nom. for Sticks and Bones); Basic Training of Pavlo Hummel (Obie Award, 1971), The Unseen Hand (Obie Award). Began TV career directing The Guiding Light, 1975.
TELEVISION: Hill Street Blues (Emmy Award, DGA Award, 1983), Concealed Enemies (Emmy Award, 1984), Daddy, I'm Their Momma Now (Emmy nom.), Do You Remember Love (Christopher, Humanitas, Peabody Awards, Emmy nom.), Fresno, Terrorist on Trial, Brotherly Love, My Father My Son, Favorite Son, Mancuso F.B.I. (exec. prod.), Lifestories (exec. prod.), Last Wish, In Sickness and In Health, The Round Table (pilot), 7th Avenue (pilot), Serving In Silence (Emmy nom.), A Father For Charlie, Any Day Now, Rear Window. *Mini-series:* In The Best of Families, Beast, The Advocate's Devil, Blackout Effect.

BLEES, ROBERT
Writer, Producer. b. Lathrop, MO, June 9, 1925. e. Dartmouth, Phi Beta Kappa. Writer/photographer, Time and Life Magazines. Fiction: Cosmopolitan, etc. Exec. boards of WGA, Producers Guild. Executive consultant, QM Prods.; BBC (England). Trustee, Motion Picture & TV Fund. Expert witness, copyright and literary litigation, U.S. Federal Court, California Superior Court.
PICTURES: Magnificent Obsession, Autumn Leaves, The Glass Web.
TELEVISION: *Producer:* Combat!, Bonanza, Bus Stop, Kraft Theater. *Writer:* Alfred Hitchcock, Cannon, Barnaby Jones, Harry O, Columbo. *Co-creator:* The New Gidget.

BLEIER, EDWARD
Executive. b. New York, NY, October 16, 1929. e. Syracuse U., 1951, C.U.N.Y., grad. courses. Reporter/sportscaster: Syracuse and NY newspapers/stations: 1947-50. Prog. service mgr., DuMont Television Network, 1951; v.p., radio-television-film, Tex McCrary, Inc. 1958. American Broadcasting Company, 1952\-57; 1959-68 v.p. in chg. pub. relations (marketing, advertising, publicity), & planning, broadcast div.; v.p. in chg. of daytime sales & programming; v.p./gen. sales mgr., ABC-TV Network. U.S. Army Psy. War School; Ex-chmn., TV Committee, NASL; Trustee, NATAS; founder-dir. & vice-chmn., International TV Council (NATAS); past-pres., IRTS; trustee, Keystone Center for Scientific & Environmental Policy, Council on Foreign Relations; ATAS; AMPAS; guest lecturer at universities. Chmn., Steering comm., Aspen B'dcaster's Conference. 1969-present: Warner Bros. Inc.: Pres, pay-TV, cable & network features.

BLETHYN, BRENDA
Actress. b. Ramsgate, Kent, England, Feb. 20, 1946.
PICTURES: The Witches, A River Runs Through It, Secrets & Lies (Acad. Award. nom.; Golden Globe Award, 1997; L.A. Film Critics Award; BAFTA Award), Remember Me?, Girls Night, Music From Another Room, RKO 281, In the Winter Dark, Little Voice (Acad. Award nom.), Keeping Time, Saving Grace, On the Nose, Delaney's Flutter, Daddy and Them, Untitled Nicole Holofcener, The Sleeping Dictionary.
TELEVISION: *Movies:* Grown-Ups, King Lear, Henry VI (Part One), The Bullion Boys. *Mini-series:* The Buddha of Suburbia. Series: Chance In a Million, The Labours of Erica, Outside Edge. *Guest:* Yes Minister, Alas Smith & Jones.

BLIER, BERTRAND
Director. b. Paris, France, 1939. Son of late actor Bernard Blier. Served as asst. dir. to Georges Lautner, John Berry, Christian-Jaque, Denys de la Paatelliere and Jean Delannoy for two years before dir. debut.
PICTURES: Hitler Connais Pas (debut, 1963), Breakdown, C'Est une Valse (s.p. only), Going Places, Femme Fatales (Calmos), Get Out Your Handkerchiefs (Academy Award for Best Foreign-Language Film, 1978), Buffet Froid, Beau-pere, My Best Friend's Girl, Notre Historie, Menage, Too Beautiful for You, Thank You Life, Patrick Deware (actor only), 1-2-3 Sun, Mon Homme.

BLOCK, BILL H.
Executive. Began career as a talent agent at ICM, then began his own agency, InterTalent, 1988, which later merged with ICM, where he served as head of West Coast operations, representing a spectrum of top-level talent in motion picture production and entertainment. Currently president, Artisan Entertainment.

BLOCK, WILLARD
Executive. b. New York, NY, March 18, 1930.; e. Columbia Coll., Columbia U. Law Sch., 1952. Counter-Intelligence Corps., U.S. Army, 1952-54, account exec., Plus Marketing, Inc. 1954-55; joined sales staff, NBC Television Network, 1955-57; sales staff, CBS Enterprises, Inc., 1957; intl. sales mgr, 1960; dir., intl. sales, 1965; v.p., 1967; v.p., Viacom Enterprises, 1971; pres., 1972; v.p. MCA-TV, 1973; v.p., gen. mgr., Taft, H-B International, Inc.; pres. Willard Block, Ltd.; 1979, named pres., Viacom Enterprises; 1982-89, pres. Viacom Worldwide Ltd.; 1989, retired. Currently consultant to Sumitomo Corp., TCI, Int'l. Telecommunications, Jupiter Telecommunications, Ltd. Past consultant & mem. bd. dirs, Starsight Telecast.

BLOODWORTH-THOMASON, LINDA
Producer, Writer. b. Poplar Bluff, MO, April 15, 1947. With husband Harry Thomason co-owner of Mozark Productions.
TELEVISION: *Series:* M*A*S*H (writer), Rhoda (writer), Filthy Rich (prod.), Lime Street (co-exec. prod., creator), Designing Women (co-exec. prod., creator, writer), Evening Shade (co-exec. prod., creator, writer), Women of the House. Pilots: Dribble (prod.), Over and Out (writer), London and Davis in New York (prod.).

BLOOM, CLAIRE
Actress. r.n. Patricia Claire Blume. b. London, England, Feb. 15, 1931.e. Guildhall School of Music & Drama, Central Sch. To U.S. in 1940 during London evacuation. Returned to England in 1943. Stage debut with Oxford Rep 1946 in It Depends What You Mean. Author: Limelight and After: The Education of an Actress (1982).
THEATER: The White Devil (London debut), The Lady's Not for Burning, Ring Round the Moon, A Streetcar Named Desire; at Stratford-on-Avon, Old Vic seasons, etc. B'way: Rashomon, A Doll's House, Hedda Gabler, Vivat Vivat Regina, Cherry Orchard, Long Day's Journey Into Night.

PICTURES: The Blind Goddess (debut, 1948), Limelight, Innocents in Paris, The Man Between, Richard III, Alexander the Great, The Brothers Karamazov, The Buccaneer, Look Back in Anger, The Royal Game, The Wonderful World of the Brothers Grimm, The Chapman Report, The Haunting, 80000 Suspects, High Infidelity, Il Maestro di Vigevano, The Outrage, The Spy Who Came in From the Cold, Charly, The Illustrated Man, Three Into Two Won't Go, A Severed Head, Red Sky at Morning, A Doll's House, Islands in the Stream, Clash of the Titans, Deja Vu, Sammy and Rosie Get Laid, Crimes and Misdemeanors, The Princess and the Goblin (voice), Mighty Aphrodite, Daylight, Wrestling With Alligators.
TELEVISION: *Specials/Movies (US/UK):* Cyrano de Bergerac, Caesar and Cleopatra, Misalliance, Anna Karenina, Wuthering Heights, Ivanov, Wessex Tales, An Imaginative Woman, A Legacy, In Praise of Love, The Orestaia, Henry VIII, Backstairs at the White House, Brideshead Revisited, Hamlet, Cymbeline, King John, Ann and Debbie, The Going Up of David Lev, Ellis Island, Separate Tables, Florence Nightingale, The Ghost Writer, Time and the Conways, Shadowlands, Liberty, Promises to Keep, The Belle of Amherst, Hold the Dream, Anastasia, Queenie, Intimate Contact, Beryl Markham: A Shadow on the Sun, Oedipus the King, The Lady and the Highwayman, The Camomile Lawn, The Mirror Crack'd From Side to Side, It's Nothing Personal, Barbara Taylor Bradford's Remember., Family Money, Imogen's Face.

BLOOM, VERNA
Actress. b. Lynn, MA, Aug. 7, 1938. e. Boston U. Studied drama at Uta Hagen-Herbert Berghof School. Performed with small theatre groups all over country; then started repertory theatre in Denver.
THEATER: B'way: Marat/Sade, Brighton Beach Memoirs. Off B'way.: Messiah, Bits and pieces, The Cherry Orchard.
PICTURES: Medium Cool (debut, 1969), The Hired Hand, High Plains Drifter, Badge 373, National Lampoon's Animal House, Honkytonk Man, After Hours, The Journey of Natty Gann, The Last Temptation of Christ.
TELEVISION: *Movies:* Where Have All the People Gone?, Sarah T.: Portrait of a Teenage Alcoholic, The Blue Knight, Contract on Cherry Street, Playing for Time, Rivkin–Bounty Hunter, Gibbsville, Dr. Quinn Medicine Woman.

BLOUNT, LISA
Actress. b. Fayetteville, AK, July 1, 1957. e. Univ. of AK. Auditioned for role as extra in film September 30, 1955 and was chosen as the female lead.
PICTURES: September 30, 1955, Dead and Buried, An Officer and a Gentleman, Cease Fire, What Waits Below, Radioactive Dreams, Prince of Darkness, Nightflyers, South of Reno, Out Cold, Great Balls of Fire, Blind Fury, Femme Fatale, Cut and Run, Stalked, Box of Moonlight.
TELEVISION: *Movies:* Murder Me Murder You, Stormin' Home, The Annihilator, Unholy Matrimony, In Sickness and in Health, An American Story, Murder Between Friends, Judicial Consent, Get to the Heart: The Barbara Mandrell Story. *Series:* Sons and Daughters, Profit. *Pilot:* Off Duty. *Guest:* Moonlighting, Magnum P.I., Starman, Murder She Wrote, Hitchhiker, Picket Fences.

BLUM, HARRY N.
Executive. b. Cleveland, OH, Oct. 3, 1932. e. U. of Michigan, B.B.A., LL.B. Toy & hobby industry exec., gen. mngr. Lionel division of General Mills, mngt. consultant, and venture capital mngr. before entering industry. Now heads The Blum Group, entertainment financing, packaging, production, licensing, and worldwide distrib. of motion pictures, documentaries, and television programming.
PICTURES: Executive Action (assoc. prod.), The Land That Time Forgot (assoc. prod.), At the Earth's Core (exec. prod.), Drive-In (assoc. prod.), Diamonds (exec. prod.), The Bluebird (prod.), Obsession (prod.), Skateboard (prod.), The Magician of Lublin (exec. prod.), Duran Duran—Arena (exec. prod.), Young Lady Chatterly II (exec. prod.), Eminent Domain (exec. prod.).

BLUM, MARK
Actor. b. Newark, NJ, May 14, 1950. Studied drama at U. of Minnesota and U. of Pennsylvania. Also studied acting with Andre Gregory, Aaron Frankel and Daniel Seltzer. Extensive Off-B'way work after debut in The Cherry Orchard (1976).
THEATER: *NY*: Green Julia, Say Goodnight Gracie, Table Settings, Key Exchange, Loving Reno, Messiah, It's Only a Play, Little Footsteps, Cave of Life, Gus & Al (Obie Award), Lost in Yonkers (Broadway). *Regional:* Brothers (New Brunswick, NJ), Close Ties (Long Wharf), The Cherry Orchard (Long Wharf), Iago in Othello (Dallas). *Mark Taper Forum:* American Clock, Wild Oats, Moby Dick Rehearsed and An American Comedy.
PICTURES: Lovesick, Desperately Seeking Susan, Just Between Friends, Crocodile Dundee, Blind Date, The Presidio, Worth Winning, Emma & Elvis, The Low Life, Miami Rhapsody, Denise Calls Up, Sudden Manhattan, Stag, You Can Thank Me Later, Getting to Know You.
TELEVISION: *Movies*: Condition: Critical, Indictment: The McMartin Trial. *Series*: Sweet Surrender, Capitol News. *Pilot*: Critical Condition. *Guest*: Miami Vice, St. Elsewhere, Roseanne.

BLUMOFE, ROBERT F.
Producer. b. New York, NY, Sept. 23, 1909. e. Columbia Coll., AB, Columbia U. Sch. of Law, JD. v.p., West Coast oper., U.A., 1953-66; indept. prod., pres. RFB Enterprises, Inc; American Film Institute, dir., AFI—West, 1977-81. Now indep. prod.

BLUNDELL, CHRISTINE
Make-Up.
PICTURES: Life is Sweet, Naked, I.D., Hackers, Secrets and Lies, Carla's Song, Career Girls, The Full Monty, Seven Years in Tibet, Martha, Meet Frank, Daniel and Laurence, Topsy-Turvey, The Man Who Killed Don Quixote.
TELEVISION: Lady Chatterly.

BLUTH, DON
Animator, Director, Producer, Writer. b. El Paso, TX, Sept. 13, 1938.e. Brigham Young U. Animator with Walt Disney Studios 1956 and 1971-79; animator with Filmation 1967; Co-founder and dir. with Gary Goldman and John Pomery, Don Bluth Productions, 1979-85; animator, Sullivan Studios, 1986. Joined Fox Animation as dir./prod., 1995.
PICTURES: *Animation director*: Robin Hood, The Rescuers, Pete's Dragon, Xanadu. *Director/Co-Producer*: The Secret of NIMH (also co-s.p.), An American Tail, The Land Before Time, All Dogs Go to Heaven (also co-story), Rock-a-Doodle, Hans Christian Andersen's Thumbelina (also s.p.), A Troll in Central Park, The Pebble and the Penguin, Anastasia, Titan A.E..
TELEVISION: Banjo the Woodpile Cat (prod., dir., story, music and lyrics).

BLYTH, ANN
Actress. b. Mt. Kisco, NY, Aug. 16, 1928. e. New Wayburn's Dramatic Sch. On radio in childhood; with San Carlos Opera Co. 3 years; Broadway debut in Watch on the Rhine.
PICTURES: Chip Off the Old Block (debut, 1944), The Merry Monahans, Babes on Swing Street, Bowery to Broadway, Mildred Pierce (Acad. Award nom.), Swell Guy, Brute Force, Killer McCoy, A Woman's Vengeance, Another Part of the Forest, Mr. Peabody and the Mermaid, Red Canyon, Once More My Darling, Free for All, Top o' the Morning, Our Very Own, The Great Caruso, Katie Did It, Thunder on the Hill, I'll Never Forget You, Golden Horde, One Minute to Zero, The World in His Arms, Sally and Saint Anne, All the Brothers Were Valiant, Rose Marie, The Student Prince, King's Thief, Kismet, Slander, The Buster Keaton Story, The Helen Morgan Story.
TELEVISION: *Guest*: Lux Video Theatre (A Place in the Sun).

BOCHCO, STEVEN
Producer, Writer. b. New York, NY, Dec. 16, 1943. m. actress Barbara Bosson. e. Carnegie Tech, MFA. Won MCA fellowship in college, joined U-TV as apprentice. Awards incl. Humanitas, NAACP Image, Writers Guild, George Foster Peabody, & Edgar Allen Poe Awards.
PICTURES: *Co-Writer:* The Counterfeit Killer, Silent Running.
TELEVISION: Name of the Game, Columbo, McMillan and Wife; Delvecchio (writer-prod.), Paris (exec. prod.), Richie Brockelman (co-creator), Turnabout (writer), Invisible Man (writer), Vampire (writer), Hill St. Blues (creator, prod., writer; Emmys 1981, 1982, 1983, 1984), Every Stray Dog and Kid (exec. prod.), Bay City Blues (exec. prod., writer, creator), L.A. Law (Emmy Awards: 1987, 1989), Hooperman, Cop Rock, NYPD Blue (Emmy Award, 1995), Byrds of Paradise, Murder One, Public Morals, Total Security (prod.), Brooklyn South (prod.), City of Angels.

BOCHNER, HART
Actor, Director. b. Toronto, Canada, Oct. 3, 1956. Son of actor Lloyd Bochner. e. U. of. San Diego. Wrote, prod., dir. short film The Buzz (1992) starring Jon Lovitz.
PICTURES: Islands in the Stream (debut, 1977), Breaking Away, Terror Train, Rich and Famous, The Wild Life, Supergirl, Making Mr. Right, Die Hard, Apartment Zero, Mr. Destiny, Mad at the Moon, Fellow Traveller, Batman: Mask of the Phantasm (voice), The Innocent, The Break Up, Anywhere But Here. *Dir.:* High School High, PCU.
TELEVISION: *Movies*: Having It All, Complex of Fear. *Mini-Series*: Haywire, East of Eden, The Sun Also Rises, War and Remembrance, And the Sea Will Tell, Children of the Dust. *Special*: Teach 109.

BOCHNER, LLOYD
Actor. b. Toronto, Canada, July 29, 1924. Father of actor Hart Bochner.
PICTURES: Drums of Africa, The Night Walker, Sylvia, Tony Rome, Point Blank, The Detective, The Horse in the Gray Flannel Suit, Tiger By the Tail, Ulzana's Raid, The Man in the Glass Booth, The Lonely Lady, Millenium, The Naked Gun 2 1/2, Morning Glory, It Seemed Like A G ood Idea At The Time, Hot Touch, The Crystal Cage, Berlin Lady, Landslide, Lolita's Affair, The Dozier Case, Fine Gold, Legend of the Mummy.

TELEVISION: *Series*: One Man's Family, Hong Kong, The Richard Boone Show, Dynasty, Batman: The Animated Series (voice). *Movies*: Scalplock, Stranger on the Run, Crowhaven Farm, They Call It Murder, Satan's School for Girls, Richie Brockelman: Missing 24 Hours, Terraces, Immigrants, A Fire in the Sky, The Best Place to Be, The Golden Gate Murders, Mary and Joseph: A Story of Faith, Mazes & Monsters, Blood Sport, Race For the Bomb, Double Agent, Eagle One, Our Man Flint, Morning Glory, Loyal Opposition: Terror in the White House. *Guest*: Fantasy Island, Masquerade, The A-Team, Hotel, Crazy Like a Fox, Greatest Heroes of the Bible, Murder She Wrote, Designing Women, Hart To Hart, Who's The Boss, Golden Girls, The Love Boat.

BODE, RALF
Cinematographer. b. Berlin, Germany. Attended Yale where was actor with drama school and acquired degree in directing. Received on-job training teaching combat photography and making films for Army at Ft. Monmouth. First professional job in films was gaffer on Harry, followed by long association with dir. John G. Avildsen, for whom served as gaffer and lighting designer on Guess What We Learned in School Today, Joe, and Cry Uncle. Later dir. of photography for Avildsen on Inaugural Ball and as East Coast dir. phot. for Rocky.
PICTURES: There is No. 13, Saturday Night Fever, Slow Dancing in the Big City, Rich Kids, Coal Miner's Daughter, Dressed to Kill, Raggedy Man, A Little Sex, Gorky Park, First Born, Bring on the Night, Violets Are Blue, Critical Condition, The Big Town, The Accused, Distant Thunder, Cousins, Uncle Buck, One Good Cop, Love Field, Made in America, George Balanchine's The Nutcracker, Bad Girls, Safe Passage, Don Juan DeMarco, A Simple Wish, The Big Green, Women Without Implants, Hacks, Unglued.
TELEVISION: PBS Theatre in America, lighting designer and dir. of photo. Also many TV commercials. *Movie*: Gypsy, A Streetcar Named Desire, Cinderella, The Hunt for the Unicorn Killer.

BOETTICHER, BUDD
Director, Writer. Producer. r.n. Oscar Boetticher, Jr. b. Chicago, IL, July 29, 1916. e. Culver Military Acad., Ohio State U. bullfighter Novillero; then technical dir., Blood and Sand, 1941; asst. dir., Hal Roach studios and Columbia 1941-44; became feature dir. at Columbia in 1944; dir. Eagle Lion, 1946; dir., Universal; independ. prod., 1954. Autobiography: When in Disgrace.
PICTURES: *As Oscar Boetticher*: Behind Locked Doors, Assigned to Danger, Black Midnight, Killer Shark, Wolf Hunters. *As Budd Boetticher*: The Bullfighter and the Lady (also co-story), The Sword of D'Artagnan, The Cimarron Kid, Bronco Busters, Red Ball Express, Horizons West, City Beneath the Sea, Seminole, The Man from the Alamo, Wings of the Hawk, East of Sumatra, The Magnificent Matador (also story), The Killer Is Loose, Seven Men From Now, Decision at Sundown, The Tall T, Buchanan Rides Alone, Ride Lonesome (also prod.), Westbound, The Rise and Fall of Legs Diamond, Comanche Station (also prod.), Arruza (also prod., co-s.p.), A Time For Dying (also s.p.), My Kingdom For a... (also s.p.).
TELEVISION: *Movies:* Big Guns Talk: The Story of the Western (actor only).

BOGART, PAUL
Director. b. New York, NY, Nov. 13, 1919. Puppeteer-actor with Berkeley Marionettes 1946-48; TV stage mgr., assoc. dir. NBC 1950-52. Won numerous Christopher Awards; recipient homage from French Festival Internationale Programmes Audiovisuelle, Cannes '91.
PICTURES: Marlowe (debut, 1969), Halls of Anger, Skin Game, Cancel My Reservation, Class of '44 (also prod.), Mr. Ricco, Oh God! You Devil, Torch Song Trilogy.
TELEVISION: *Series*: U.S. Steel Hour, Kraft Theatre, Armstrong Circle Theatre, Goodyear Playhouse, The Defenders (Emmy Award, 1965), All in the Family (Emmy Award, 1978), The Golden Girls (Emmy Award, 1986). *Specials*: Ages of Man, Mark Twain Tonight, The Final War of Ollie Winter, Dear Friends (Emmy Award, 1968). Secrets, Shadow Game (Emmy Award, 1970), The House Without a Christmas Tree, Look Homeward Angel, The Country Girl, Double Solitaire, The War Widow, The Thanksgiving Treasure; The Adams Chronicles, Natica Jackson. Movies: In Search of America, Tell Me Where It Hurts, Winner Take All, Nutcracker: Money, Madness and Murder, Broadway Bound, The Gift of Love, The Heidi Chronicles.

BOGDANOVICH, PETER
Director, Producer, Writer, Actor. b. Kingston, NY, July 30, 1939. e. Collegiate Sch., Stella Adler Theatre Sch., N.Y. 1954-58. Stage debut, Amer. Shakespeare Festival, Stratford, CT, followed by N.Y. Shakespeare Festival, 1958. Off-Bway: dir./prod.: The Big Knife, Camino Real, Ten Little Indians, Rocket to the Moon, Once in a Lifetime. Film critic and feature writer, Esquire, New York Times, Village Voice, Cahiers du Cinema, Los Angeles Times,New York Magazine, Vogue, Variety, etc. 1961–. Owner: The Holly Moon Company Inc. (L.A.), 1992-present. LA Film Crits. Career Achievement Award, 1997.
PICTURES: Voyage to the Planet of the Prehistoric Women (dir., s.p., narrator; billed as Derek Thomas), The Wild Angels (2nd unit dir., co-s.p., actor). *Director*: Targets (also prod., co-s.p., actor), The Last Picture Show (also co-s.p; N.Y. Film Critics' Award, best s.p., British Academy Award, best s.p. 1971), Directed by John Ford (also s.p., interviewer), What's Up Doc? (also prod., co-s.p.; Writer's Guild of America Award, best s.p., 1972), Paper Moon (also prod.; Silver Shell, Mar del Plata, Spain 1973), Daisy Miller (also prod.; Best Director, Brussels Festival, 1974), At Long Last Love (also prod., s.p.), Nickelodeon (also co-s.p.), Saint Jack (also co-s.p., actor; Pasinetti Award, Critics Prize, Venice Festival, 1979), Opening Night (actor only), They All Laughed (also co-s.p.), Mask, Illegally Yours (also prod.), Texasville (also co-prod., s.p.), Noises Off (also co-exec. prod.), The Thing Called Love. *Actor*: Jean Renior, The Battle Over Citizen Kane, Ben Johnson: Third Cowboy on the Right, Mr. Jealousy, Highball, 54, The Shore Store.
TELEVISION: *Movies*: To Sir with Love 2 (dir.), The Price of Heaven (dir.), Naked City: A Killer Christmas, A Saintly Switch. *Special*: The Great Professional: Howard Hawks (co-dir., writer, interviewer; BBC). *Series*: CBS This Morning (weekly commentary; 1987-89). *Mini-series*: Bella Mafia. *Guest*: Northern Exposure (actor), Moonlighting (actor), The Price of Heaven.
AUTHOR: The Cinema of Orson Welles (1961), The Cinema of Howard Hawks (1962), The Cinema of Alfred Hitchcock, (1963), John Ford (1968; enlarged 1978), Fritz Lang in America, (1969), Allan Dwan—The Last Pioneer (1971), Pieces of Time (1973, enlarged 1985), The Killing of the Unicorn: Dorothy Stratten: 1960-1980 (1984), This Is Orson Welles (1992). Also edit., intro. writer to annual Year and a Day Engagement Calendar (1991-).

BOGOSIAN, ERIC
Actor, Writer. b. Woburn, MA, Apr. 24, 1953. e. studied 2 years at U. of Chicago, then Oberlin, theater degree, 1976. In high school, acted in plays with Fred Zollo (now prod.) and Nick Paleologus (now MA congressman). Moved to NY and worked briefly as gofer at Chelsea Westside Theater. Then joined downtown performance space, the Kitchen, first acting in others pieces, then creating his own incl. character Ricky Paul, a stand-up comedian in punk clubs. Theater pieces include: The New World, Men Inside, Voices of America, FunHouse, Drinking in America (Drama Desk and Obie Awards), Talk Radio, Sex Drugs Rock & Roll, Pounding Nails in the Floor With My Forehead (Obie Award), SubUrbia (author only). Author of Notes From Underground.
PICTURES: Special Effects, Talk Radio (also s.p.; Silver Bear Award 1988 Berlin Film Fest.), Sex Drugs Rock & Roll (also s.p.), Naked in New York, Dolores Claiborne, Under Siege 2: Dark Territory, Arabian Knight (voice), Beavis and Butt-Head Do America (voice), Suburbia (s.p. only), Deconstructing Harry.
TELEVISION: *Movies:* The Caine Mutiny Court Martial, Last Flight Out, Witch Hunt, A Bright Shining Lie. *Special:* Drinking in America. *Guest:* Miami Vice, Twilight Zone, Law & Order, The Larry Sanders Show.

BOLAM, JAMES
Actor. b. Sunderland, England. Entered industry in 1960.
PICTURES: The Kitchen, A Kind of Loving, Loneliness of the Long Distance Runner, HMS Defiant, Murder Most Foul, In Celebration, Clockwork Mice, Stella Does Tricks, Island on Bird Street.
TELEVISION: Likely Lads, When The Boat Comes In, Only When I Laugh, The Beiderbecke Affair, Father Matthews Daughter, Room at the Bottom, Andy Capp, The Beiderbecke Tapes, The Beiderbecke Connection, Second Thoughts, Have Your Cake, The Missing Postman, The Stalker's Apprentice.

BOLOGNA, JOSEPH
Actor, Writer. b. Brooklyn, NY., Dec. 30, 1938. e. Brown U. m. actress-writer Renee Taylor. Service in Marine Corps and on discharge joined ad agency, becoming dir.-prod. of TV commercials. Collaborated with wife on short film, 2, shown at 1966 N.Y. Film Festival. Together they wrote Lovers and Other Strangers, B'way play, in which both also acted; wrote s.p. for film version. Both wrote and starred in Made for Each Other, and created and wrote TV series, Calucci's Dept.
PICTURES: Lovers and Other Strangers (co.-s.p. only), Made for Each Other (also co.-s.p.), Cops and Robbers, Mixed Company, The Big Bus , Chapter Two, My Favorite Year, Blame It on Rio , The Woman in Red, Transylvania 6-5000, It Had to Be You (also co-dir., co-s.p.), Coupe de Ville, Jersey Girl, Alligator II: The Mutation, Love Is All There Is (dir., s.p.), Heaven Before I Die, Big Daddy.
TELEVISION: *Movies:* Honor Thy Father, Woman of the Year (also co-writer), Torn Between Two Lovers, One Cooks The Other Doesn't, Copacabana, A Time To Triumph, Prime Target, Thanksgiving Day, Citizen Cohn, The Danger of Love: The Carolyn Warmus Story, Revenge of the Nerds IV: Nerds in Love, The Don's Analyst, The Batman/Superman Movie (voice). Special: Acts of Love and Other Comedies (Emmy Award, 1974). *Mini-Series:* Sins. *Series:* Calucci's Dept. (creator, co-writer only), Rags to Riches, Top of the Heap.

BONANNO, LOUIE
Actor. a.k.a. Louix Dor Dempriey. b. Somerville, MA, Dec. 17, 1961. e. Bentley Coll., Waltham, MA, BS-economics, finance; AS accountancy, 1983. In Who's Who Among Students in American Univ. & Colleges; Who's Who Among Rising Young Americans. Moved to NY, 1983 to study at Amer. Acad. of Dramatic Arts. Toured U.S. 1985-86 as Dangermouse for MTV/Nickelodeon. Stand-up comedian 1987-89. Stage debut in The Head, 1990.
PICTURES: Sex Appeal (debut, 1986), Wimps, Student Affairs, Cool as Ice, Auntie Lee's Meat Pies.
TELEVISION: *Series:* Eisenhower & Lutz, 227, Tour of Duty, TV 101, Santa Barbara, New York Story.

BONET, LISA
Actress. b. Los Angeles, CA, Nov. 16, 1967. First gained recognition on The Cosby Show as Denise Huxtable at the age of 15.
PICTURES: Angel Heart, Dead Connection, Bank Robber, New Eden, Serpent's Lair, Enemy of the State, High Fidelity.
TELEVISION: *Special*: Don't Touch. *Series:* The Cosby Show, A Different World. *Guest:* Tales From the Dark Side, St. Elsewhere.

BONET, NAI
Actress, Producer. Worked in entertainment field since age of 13, including opera, films, TV, stage, night clubs and records.
PICTURES: *Actress:* The Soul Hustlers, The Seventh Veil, Fairy Tales, The Soul of Nigger Charlie, The Spy with the Cold Nose, John Goldfarb Please Come Home, Nocturna (also s.p.), Hoodlums, (also s.p.).
TELEVISION: Johnny Carson Show, Merv Griffin Show, Joe Franklin Show, Beverly Hillbillies, Tom Snyder Show.

BONHAM CARTER, HELENA
Actress. b. London, England, May 26, 1966. Great granddaughter of Liberal Prime Minister Lord Asquith. e. Westminster. Appeared on BBC in A Pattern of Roses; seen by dir. Trevor Nunn who cast her in Lady Jane, 1986, theatrical film debut. On London stage in Trelawny of the Wells.
PICTURES: Lady Jane, A Room with a View, Maurice (cameo), Francesco, La Mascheral (The Mask), Getting It Right, Hamlet, Where Angles Fear to Tread, Howards End, Mary Shelley's Frankenstein, Mighty Aphrodite, Margaret's Museum, Twelfth Night, Shadow Play, The Wings of the Dove (LA Film Crits. Award, Best Actress, 1997), Keep the Aspidistra Flying, The Theory of Flight, The Revengers of Comedy, Fight Club, Women Talking Dirty, Carnivale, Novcaine, Planet of the Apes, Till Human Voices Wake Us.
TELEVISION: *Movies:* A Hazard of Hearts (U.S.), The Vision, Beatrix Potter, Fatal Deception: Mrs. Lee Harvey Oswald, Dancing Queen. *Mini-Series:* Merlin. *Series*: The Great War (voice). *Guest:* Miami Vice, Absolutely Fabulous.

BOOKMAN, ROBERT
Executive. b. Los Angeles, CA, Jan. 29, 1947. e. U. of California, Yale Law Sch. Motion picture literary agent, IFA 1972-74, ICM 1974-79. 1979-84, ABC Motion Pictures v.p., worldwide production; 1984-6, Columbia Pictures, exec. v.p., world-wide prod. 1986, Creative Artists Agency, as motion picture literary and directors' agent.

BOONE, PAT
Singer, Actor. r.n. Charles Eugene Boone. b. Jacksonville, FL, June 1, 1934. e. David Lipscomb Coll., North Texas State Coll., grad. magna cum laude, Columbia U. Winner of Ted Mack's Amateur Hour TV show; joined Arthur Godfrey TV show, 1955. Most promising new male star, Motion Picture Daily-Fame Poll 1957. One of top ten moneymaking stars, M.P. Herald-Fame Poll, 1957. Daughter is singer Debby Boone. Author: Twixt Twelve and Twenty, Between You & Me and the Gatepost, The Real Christmas, A New Song, others.
RECORDINGS: Ain't That a Shame, I Almost Lost My Mind, Friendly Persuasion, Love Letters in the Sand, April Love, Tutti Frutti, many others.
PICTURES: Bernardine (debut, 1957), April Love, Mardi Gras, Journey to the Center of the Earth, All Hands on Deck, State Fair, The Main Attraction, The Yellow Canary, The Horror of It All, Never Put It in Writing, Goodbye Charlie, The Greatest Story Ever Told, The Perils of Pauline, The Cross and the Switchblade, Roger and Me.
TELEVISION: *Movie:* The Pigeon. *Series:* Arthur Godfrey and His Friends, The Pat Boone-Chevy Showroom (1957-60), The Pat Boone Show (1966-8).

BOORMAN, JOHN
Director, Producer, Writer. b. London, England, Jan. 18, 1933. Wrote film criticism at age of 17 for British publications incl. Manchester Guardian; founder TV Mag. Day By Day; served in National Service in Army; Broadcaster and BBC radio film critic 1950-54; film editor Independent Television News; prod. documentaries for Southern Television; joined BBC, headed BBC Documentary Film Unit 1960-64, indep. doc. about D.W. Griffith; chmn. Natl. Film Studios of Ireland 1975-85; governor Brit. Film Inst. 1985-.
PICTURES: *Director:* Catch Us If You Can (debut, 1965), Point Blank, Hell in the Pacific, Leo the Last (also co-s.p., Cannes Film Fest. Award, Best Director 1970), Deliverance (also prod.; 2 Acad. Award noms.), Zardoz (also prod., s.p.), Exorcist II: The Heretic (also co-prod.), Excalibur (also exec. prod., co-s.p., Cannes Film Fest. Award, Best Art. Contribution, 1981), Danny Boy (exec. prod. only), The Emerald Forest (also prod.), Hope and Glory (also prod., s.p., actor; 3 Acad. Award noms., Nat'l Film Critics Awards for dir., s.p.; L.A. Film Critics Awards for picture, s.p., dir.; U.K. Critics Awards for picture), Where the Heart Is (also prod., co-s.p.), I Dreamt I Woke Up (also s.p., actor), Two Nudes Bathing (also s.p., prod.), Beyond Rangoon (also co-prod.), The General (also s.p., prod.).
TELEVISION: *Series:* Citizen '63 (dir.), The Newcomers (dir.).

BOOTH, MARGARET
Film editor. b. Los Angeles, CA, 1898. Awarded honorary Oscar, 1977.
PICTURES: Why Men Leave Home, Husbands and Lovers, Bridge of San Luis Rey, New Moon, Susan Lenox, Strange Interlude, Smilin' Through, Romeo and Juliet, Barretts of Wimpole Street, Mutiny on the Bounty, Camille, etc. Supervising editor on Owl and the Pussycat, The Way We Were, Funny Lady, Murder by Death, The Goodbye Girl, California Suite, The Cheap Detective (also assoc. prod.), Chapter Two (also assoc. prod.), The Toy (assoc. prod. only), Annie, The Slugger's Wife (exec. prod. only).

BOOTHE, POWERS
Actor. b. Snyder, TX, June 1, 1949. e. Southern Methodist U. On B'way in Lone Star.
PICTURES: The Goodbye Girl, Cruising, Southern Comfort, A Breed Apart, Red Dawn, The Emerald Forest, Extreme Prejudice, Stalingrad, Rapid Fire, Tombstone, Blue Sky, Sudden Death, Nixon, U-Turn.
TELEVISION: *Movies:* Skag, Plutonium Incident, Guyana Tragedy—The Story of Jim Jones (Emmy Award, 1980), A Cry for Love, Into the Homeland, Family of Spies, By Dawn's Early Light, Wild Card, Marked for Murder, Web of Deception, The Spree. *Mini-Series:* True Women, Joan of Arc. *Series:* Skag, Philip Marlowe.

BORGE, VICTOR
Comedian, Pianist. b. Copenhagen, Denmark, Jan. 3, 1909. Child prodigy at age 8. Awarded scholarship to study in Berlin and Vienna. Later became humorous concert artist. Wrote and starred in musical plays and films in Denmark. Fled Nazis in 1940, came to America. Appeared on Bing Crosby radio show, concert and nightclub tours, tv variety shows. One-man Broadway shows: Comedy in Music, 1953, 1965, 1977, 1989. Guest conductor with major symphonies around the world. Recent recording, The Two Sides of Victor Borge. Author: My Favorite Intermissions and My Favorite Comedies in Music. Awarded Medal of Honor by Statue of Liberty Centennial Comm. Knighted by 5 Scandinavian countries, honored by U.S. Congress and U.N. Created Thanks to Scandinavia Scholarship Fund, Dana College, Univ. of Conn., SUNY—Purchase Scholarships. Recent video: Onstage with Victor Borge.

BORGNINE, ERNEST
Actor. r.n. Ermes Effron Borgnino. b. Hamden, CT, Jan. 24, 1917. e. Randall Sch. of Dramatic Art, Hartford, CT. Joined Barter Theatre in Viginia. Served in U.S. Navy; then little theatre work, stock companies; on Broadway in Harvey, Mrs. McThing; many TV appearances. Honors: 33rd Degree of the Masonic Order, Order of the Grand Cross, from same. Named honorary Mayor of Universal City Studios.
PICTURES: China Corsair (debut, 1951), The Mob, Whistle at Eaton Falls, From Here to Eternity, The Stranger Wore a Gun, Demetrius & the Gladiators, Johnny Guitar, Bounty Hunter, Vera Cruz, Bad Day at Black Rock, Marty (Acad. Award for Best Actor, 1955), Run for Cover, Violent Saturday, Last Command, Square Jungle, Catered Affair, Jubal, Best Things in Life are Free, Three Brave Men, The Vikings, Badlanders, Torpedo Run, Rabbit Trap, Season of Passion, Man on a String, Pay or Die, Go Naked in the World, Barabbas, McHales's Navy, Flight of the Phoenix, The Oscar, Chuka, The Dirty Dozen, Ice Station Zebra, Legend of Lylah Clare, The Split, The Wild Bunch, The Adventurers, Suppose They Gave a War and Nobody Came?, A Bullet for Sandoval, Bunny O'Hare, Willard, Rain for a Dusty Summer, Hannie Caulder, The Revengers, Ripped Off, The Poseidon Adventure, Emperor of the North Pole, The Neptune Factor, Manhunt, Law and Disorder, Sunday in the Country, The Devil's Rain, Hustle, Shoot, Love By Appointment, The Greatest, Crossed Swords, Convoy, Strike Force, Diary of Madam X, The Black Hole, The Double McGuffin, The Ravagers, When Time Ran Out, High Risk, Super Fuzz, Escape from New York, Deadly Blessing, Young Warriors, Codename: Wild Geese, Skeleton Coast, Spike of Bensonhurst, The Opponent, Any Man's Death, Laser Mission, Turnaround, Captain Henkel, Real Men Don't Eat Gummy Bears, Moving Target, The Last Match, Mistress, All Dogs Go to Heaven 2 (voice) McHale's Navy, Gattaca, BASEketball, An All Dogs Christmas Carol, 12 Bucks, Small Soldiers (voice), Mel, The Last Great Ride, Abilene.

TELEVISION: *Movies*: Sam Hill: Who Killed the Mysterious Mr. Foster?, The Trackers, Twice in a Lifetime, Future Cop, Jesus of Nazareth, Fire!, The Ghost of Flight 401, Cops and Robin, All Quiet on the Western Front, Blood Feud, Carpool, Love Leads the Way, Last Days of Pompeii, The Dirty Dozen: The Next Mission, Alice in Wonderland, The Dirty Dozen: The Deadly Mission, Treasure Island (Ital. TV), The Dirty Dozen: The Fatal Mission, Jake Spanner-Private Eye, Appearances, The Burning Shore, Mountain of Diamonds (Ital TV). *Specials:* Billy the Kid, Legend in Granite: The Vince Lombardi Story, Big Guns Talk: The Story of the Western. *Series:* McHale's Navy, Air Wolf, The Single Guy, The Married Guy. *Guest:* Philco Playhouse, General Electric Theater, Wagon Train, Laramie, Zane Grey Theater, Alcoa Premiere, The Love Boat, Little House on the Prairie, Murder She Wrote, Home Improvement, The Simpsons (voice), Pinky and the Brain (voice).

BORIS, ROBERT
Writer, Director. b. NY, NY, Oct. 12, 1945. Screenwriter before also turning to direction with Oxford Blues, 1984.
PICTURES: Electra Glide in Blue, Some Kind of Hero, Doctor Detroit, Oxford Blues (also dir.), Steele Justice (dir.), Extreme Justice, Diplomatic Siege, Buy and Cell (dir.).
TELEVISION: Birds of Prey, Blood Feud, Deadly Encounter, Izzy and Moe, Frank and Jesse (also dir.), Marilyn and Me.

BORODINSKY, SAMUEL
Executive. b. Brooklyn, NY, Oct. 25, 1941. e. Industrial Sch. of Arts & Photography. Expert in film care and rejuvenation. Now exec. v.p., Filmtreat International Corp. Previously with Modern Film Corp. (technician) and Comprehensive Filmtreat, Inc. & International Filmtreat (service manager). 1998 Emmy Award for pionerring development of scratch removal systems.

BOSCO, PHILIP
Actor. b. Jersey City, NJ, Sept. 26, 1930. e. Catholic U., Washington, DC, BA. drama, 1957. Studied for stage with James Marr, Josephine Callan and Leo Brady. Consummate stage actor (in over 100 plays, 61 in NY) whose career spans the classics (with NY Shakespeare Fest. and American Shakespeare Fest, CT.), 20 plays with Arena Stage 1957-60, to modern classics as a resident actor with Lincoln Center Rep. Co. in the 1960s, winning Tony and Drama Desk Awards for the farce Lend Me a Tenor, 1988. Recipient: Clarence Derwent Award for General Excellence, Outer Critics Circle Award & Obie for Lifetime Achievement.
THEATER: Auntie Mame (B'way debut, City Center revival, 1958), Measure for Measure, The Rape of the Belt (Tony nom.), Donnybrook, Richard III, The Alchemist, The East Wind, The Ticket of Leave Man, Galileo, Saint Joan, Tiger at the Gates, Cyrano de Bergerac, Be Happy for Me, King Lear, The Miser, The Time of Your Life, Camino Real, Operation Sidewinder, Amphitryon, In the Matter of J. Robert Oppenheimer, The Good Woman of Setzuan, The Playboy of the Western World, An Enemy of the People, Antigone, Mary Stuart, The Crucible, Enemies, Mrs. Warren's Profession, Henry V, The Threepenny Opera, Streamers, Stages, The Biko Inquest, Whose Life Is It Anyway? A Month in the Country, Don Juan in Hell, Inadmissible Evidence, Ah! Wilderness, Man and Superman, Major Barbara, The Caine Mutiny Court Martial, Heartbreak House (Tony nom.), Come Back Little Sheba, Loves of Anatol, Be Happy for Me, Master Class, You Never Can Tell, A Man for All Seasons, Devil's Disciple, Lend Me a Tenor (Tony Award, 1989), The Miser, Breaking Legs, An Inspector Calls, The Heiress, Moon Over Buffalo.
PICTURES: Requiem for a Heavyweight, A Lovely Way to Die, Trading Places, The Pope of Greenwich Village, Walls of Glass, Heaven Help Us, Flanagan, The Money Pit, Children of a Lesser God, Suspect, Three Men and a Baby, Another Woman, Working Girl, The Luckiest Man in the World, Dream Team, Blue Steel, Quick Change, True Colors, FX2, Shadows and Fog, Straight Talk, Angie, Milk Money, Nobody's Fool, Safe Passage, It Takes Two, My Best Friend's Wedding, Critical Care, Frank Lloyd Wright (voice), Brooklyn Sonnet.
TELEVISION: *Movies:* Echoes in the Darkness, Second Effort, Internal Affairs, Murder in Black and White, The Return of Eliot Ness, Against the Wall, The Forget-Me-Not Murders, Attica: Line of Fire, Janek: A Silent Betrayal, Young at Heart, Carriers, Twelfth Night. *Mini-series:* LIBERTY!: The American Revolution. *Specials:* Prisoner of Zenda, An Enemy of the People, A Nice Place to Visit, Read Between the Lines (Emmy Award). *Series:* TriBeCa. *Guest:* Nurses, Trials of O'Brien, Law & Order, Spenser: For Hire, The Equalizer, Against the Law, Janek, Spin City.

BOSLEY, TOM
Actor. b. Chicago, IL, Oct. 1, 1927. e. DePaul U. Had roles on radio in Chicago and in stock productions before moving to New York. Appeared off-Broadway and on road before signed to play lead in Fiorello! for George Abbott on Broadway. First actor to win Tony, Drama Critics, ANTA and Newspaper Guild awards in one season for that role.
PICTURES: Love with the Proper Stranger, The World of Henry Orient, Divorce American Style, Yours Mine and Ours, The Secret War of Harry Frigg, To Find a Man, Mixed Company, Gus, O'Hara's Wife, Million Dollar Mystery, Wicked Stepmother.
TELEVISION: *Specials*: Alice in Wonderland (1953), Arsenic and Old Lace, The Drunkard, Profiles in Courage. *Guest*: Focus, Naked City, The Right Man, The Nurses, Route 66, The Perry Como Show, The Drew Carey Show. *Series*: That Was the Week That Was, The Debbie Reynolds Show, The Dean Martin Show, Sandy Duncan Show, Wait Til Your Father Gets Home (voice), Happy Days, That's Hollywood (narrator), Murder She Wrote, Father Dowling Mysteries. *Movies*: Marcus Welby M.D.: A Matter of Humanities (pilot), Night Gallery, A Step Out of Line, Vanished, Congratulations It's a Boy!, Mr. & Mrs. Bo Jo Jones, Streets of San Francisco (pilot), No Place to Run, Miracle on 34th Street, The Girl Who Came Gift Wrapped, Death Cruise, Who Is the Black Dahlia?, Last Survivors, The Night That Panicked America, Love Boat, Testimony of 2 Men, Black Market Baby, With This Ring, The Bastard, The Triangle Factory Fire Scandal, The Castaways on Gilligan's Island, The Rebels, Return of the Mod Squad, For the Love of It, Jesse Owens Story, Fatal Confession: A Father Dowling Mystery, The Love Boat: A Valentine Voyage.

BOSTWICK, BARRY
Actor. b. San Mateo, CA, Feb. 24, 1945. e. USIU Sch. of Performing Arts, San Diego, BFA in acting; NYU Grad. Sch. of the Arts. Made prof. stage debut while in coll. working with Walter Pidgeon in Take Her She's Mine. Joined APA Phoenix Rep. Co. making his B'way debut in Cock-A-Doodle Dandy.
THEATER: Salvation, House of Leather, Soon, The Screens, Colette, Grease (created role of Danny Zuko, 1972), They Knew What They Wanted, The Robber Bridegroom (Tony Award, 1977), She Loves Me, L'Historie du Soldat, Nick and Nora.
PICTURES: The Rocky Horror Picture Show, Movie Movie, Megaforce, Eight Hundred Leagues Down the Amazon, Weekend at Bernie's 2, Spy Hard, The Secret Agent Club,.
TELEVISION: *Series*: Foul Play, Dads, Spin City. *Movies*: The Chadwick Family, The Quinns, Murder By Natural Causes, Once Upon a Family, Moviola—The Silent Lovers, Red Flag: The Ultimate Game, Summer Girl, An Uncommon Love, Deceptions, Betrayed by Innocence, Body of Evidence, Addicted to His Love, Parent Trap III, Till We Meet Again, Challenger, Captive, Between Love and Hate, Praying Mantis, Danielle Steel's Once in a Lifetime, The Return of Hunter, The Secretary, Lexx: The Dark Zone, One Hot Summer, National Lampoon's Men in White. *Mini-Series*: Scruples, George Washington, I'll Take Manhattan, War and Remembrance. *Specials*: A Woman of Substance, You Can't Take It With You, Working.

BOSUSTOW, NICK
Producer. b. Los Angeles, CA, March 28, 1940. e. Menlo Coll., administration. MCA, intl. sales, 1963. Pres., Stephen Bosustow Productions, 1967. Pres., ASIFA-West. Pres., Bosustow Entertainment Inc., 1973. Founded Animation Consultants International, 1995.
PICTURES: Is It Always Right to Be Right?(Acad. award) The Legend of John Henry (Acad. award nom.).
TELEVISION: *Specials*: The Incredible Book Escape, Misunderstood Monsters, A Tale of Four Wishes, Wrong Way Kid (Emmy, 1984). *Series*: The Hayley Mills Story Book.

BOSWALL, JEFFERY
Producer, Director, Writer. b. Brighton, England, 1931. e. Taunton House School, Montpelier Coll., Brighton. Started career as an ornithologist for the Royal Society for the Protection of Birds. Joined BBC in 1958 as radio prod., moving to TV 1964 making films in diverse locations (Ethiopia and Antarctica). Contributed to 50 films as wildlife cameraman. Co-founder of British Library of Wildlife Sounds. 1987: returned to RSPB. Head of Film and Video Unit, 1987. 1992, sr. lecturer in Biological Film & Video, Derby Univ. Chairmanship BKSTS Intl Wildlife Filmmakers' Symposium.
AUTHOR: Birds for All Seasons. Ed. Look and Private Lives. Contrib.: Times, Countryman, the Field, Wildlife and Countryside, BBC Wildlife, Scientific Film, Journal of the Society of Film and TV Arts, Image Technology. Has written for scientific journals and writes annual update for Encyclopedia Britannica on ornithology.
TELEVISION: 18 films in the Private Lives series of which 4 (about the Kingfisher, Cuckoo, Starling and Jackass Penguin) won intl awards. Animal Olympians, Birds For All Seasons, Where the Parrots Speak Mandarin, Wildlife Safari to Ethiopia.

BOTTOMS, JOSEPH
Actor. b. Santa Barbara, CA, April 22, 1954. Brother of Sam and Timothy Bottoms. Did plays in jr. high school in Santa Barbara and then with community theatre.
PICTURES: The Dove (debut, 1974), Crime and Passion, The Black Hole, Cloud Dancer, King of the Mountain, Blind Date, Open House, Born to Race, Inner Sanctum.
TELEVISION: *Movies*: Trouble Comes to Town, Unwed Father, Stalk the Wild Child, The Intruder Within, Side By Side: The True Story of the Osmond Family, I Married Wyatt Earp, The Sins of Dorian Gray, Time Bomb, Braker, Island Sons, Cop Killer, Gunsmoke: To the Last Man, Treacherous Crossing, Liar's Edge. *Mini-Series:* Holocaust, Celebrity. *Special*: Winesburg Ohio. *Series:* The Net. *Guest*: Owen Marshall, Murder She Wrote.

BOTTOMS, SAM
Actor. b. Santa Barbara, CA, Oct. 17, 1955. Brother of Timothy, Joseph and Ben Bottoms. Co-prod. documentary Picture This. Appeared in documentary Hearts of Darkness.
PICTURES: The Last Picture Show (debut, 1971), Class of '44, Zandy's Bride, Up From the Depths, The Outlaw Josey Wales, Apocalypse Now, Bronco Billy, Hunter's Blood, Gardens of Stone, After School, Hearts of Darkness: A Filmmaker's Apocalypse, Picture This--The Times of Peter Bogdanovich in Archer City Texas, Ragin' Cajun, Dolly Dearest, In 'n Out, North of Chiang Mai, Prime Risk, The Trust, Sugar Hill, Sunny Side Up, Project Showchaser 3000, Angel Blue.
TELEVISION: *Series*: Santa Barbara. *Movies*: Savages, Cage Without a Key, Desperate Lives, Island Sons, The Witching of Ben Wagner, Zooman, My Neighbor's Daughter. *Mini-Series*: East of Eden, Return to Eden. *Guest*: Greatest Heroes of the Bible, Murder She Wrote, Marcus Welby M.D., Doc Elliot, Eddie Capra, Lucas Tanner, 21 Jump Street, X Files.

BOTTOMS, TIMOTHY
Actor. b. Santa Barbara, CA, Aug. 30, 1951. Brother of actors Joseph and Sam Bottoms. Early interest in acting; was member of S.B. Madrigal Society, touring Europe in 1967. Sang and danced in West Side Story local prod. With brother Sam co-prod. documentary Picture This about making of the Last Picture Show and Texasville.
PICTURES: Johnny Got His Gun (debut, 1971), The Last Picture Show, Love and Pain and the Whole Damn Thing, The Paper Chase, The White Dawn, The Crazy World of Julius Vrooder, Operation Daybreak, A Small Town in Texas, Rollercoaster, The Other Side of the Mountain: Part 2, Hurricane, The High Country, Tin Man, The Census Taker, Hambone and Hillie, In the Shadow of Kilimanjaro, The Sea Serpent, The Fantasist, Invaders from Mars, The Drifter, Mio in the Land of Faraway, Return to the River Kwai, A Case of Law, Texasville, Istanbul, I'll Met By Moonlight, Top Dog, Uncle Sam, Ringer, Fox Hunt, Mr. Atlas, Absolute Force, Mixed Blessings, The Man in the Iron Mask, The Prince and the Surfer, The Boy with the X-Ray Eyes.
TELEVISION: *Special*: Look Homeward Angel. *Mini-Series*: The Money Changers, East of Eden. Movies: The Story of David, The Gift of Love, A Shining Season, Escape, Perry Mason: The Case of the Notorious Nun. Island Sons, Ben Johnson: Third Cowboy on the Right. *Series*: Land of the Lost, The Great War (voice).

BOUCHEZ, ELODIE
Actress.
PICTURES: Stan the Flasher, The Stolen Diary, Tango, Good Old Daze, Les mots de l'amour, The Wild Reeds, Those Were the Days, Clubbed to Death, Mademoiselle Personne, Full Speed, The Proprietor, Fire in Paradise, La divine poursuite, Le ciel est a nous, The Dreamlife of Angels (Cannes Film Fest. Award, Best Actress, 1998), Louise, J'aimerais pas crever un dimanche, Zonzon, Les Kidnappeurs, Shooting Vegetarians, Lovers.

BOUQUET, CAROLE
Actress. b. Neuilly-sur-Seine, France, Aug. 18, 1957. e. Sorbonne, Paris, Paris Conservatoire. Also model for Chanel No. 5 perfume.
PICTURES: That Obscure Object of Desire (debut, 1977), Buffet Froid, Il Cappotto di Astrakan, For Your Eyes Only, Bingo Bongo, Mystere, Nemo, Le Bon Roi Dagobert, Rive Droite Rive Gauche, Special Police, Double Messieurs, Le Mal d'aimer, Jenatsch, Bunker Palace Hotel, New York Stories, Too Beautiful for You, Against Oblivion, Tango, Women in Skirts, Grosse Fatigue, A Business Affair, Lucie Aubrac, In All Innocence, Un Pont Entre Deux Rives.
TELEVISION: *Mini-series:* Le Rouge et le Noir.

BOUTSIKARIS, DENNIS
Actor. b. Newark, NJ, Dec. 21, 1952. e. Hampshire Col.
THEATER: *Off-B'way:* Another Language (debut, 1975), Funeral March for a One Man Band, All's Well That Ends Well, Nest of the Wood Grouse, Cheapside, Rum and Coke, The Boys Next Door, Sight Unseen. *B'way:* Filomena, Bent, Amadeus.
PICTURES: The Exterminator, Very Close Quarters, Batteries Not Included, Crocodile Dundee II, The Dream Team, Talent for the Game, The Boy Who Cried Bitch, Boys on the Side, Chasing the Dragon, Surviving Picasso, Blue Vision, In Dreams.
TELEVISION: *Series:* Nurse, Stat, The Jackie Thomas Show, Misery Loves Company. *Movies:* Rappaccini's Daughter, Internal Affairs, Thunderboat Row, The Keys, Love Lies and Murder, The Hit Man, Victim of Love: The Shannon Mohr Story, The Yarn Princess, Tonya & Nancy: The Inside Story, Beyond Betrayal, Love and Betrayal: The Mia Farrow Story, The Three Lives of Karen, Survival on the Mountain. *Mini Series*: The Last Don. *Guest*: Murphy Brown, Law & Order, The Burning Zone, ER.

BOWIE, DAVID
Singer, Actor. r.n. David Robert Jones. b. Brixton, South London, England, Jan. 8, 1947. m. model-actress Iman. Broadway debut: The Elephant Man (1980).
PICTURES: The Virgin Soldiers (debut, 1969), Ziggy Stardust and the Spiders from Mars (1973; U.S. release 1983), The Man Who Fell to Earth, Just a Gigolo, Radio On, Christiane F, Cat People (performed song), The Hunger, Yellowbeard, Merry Christmas Mr. Lawrence, Into the Night, Absolute Beginners (also songs), Labyrinth (also songs), When the Wind Blows (songs), The Last Temptation of Christ, Imagine—John Lennon, The Linguini Incident, Twin Peaks: Fire Walk With Me, Basquiat, Inspirations, Exhuming Mr Rice, My West.
TELEVISION: *Specials*: Christmas With Bing Crosby, The Midnight Special, Glass Spider Tour, Closure.

BOWSER, EILEEN
Curator, Film Archivist, Historian. b. Ohio, Jan. 18, 1928. e. Marietta Coll., B.A., 1950; U. of North Carolina, M.A., history of art, 1953. Joined Dept. of Film, Museum of Modern Art, 1954. Curator, Dept. of Film (1976-1993). Organized major exhib. of the films of D.W. Griffith, Carl-Theodor Dreyer, Art of the Twenties, recent acquisitions and touring shows. On exec. comm. of Federation Internationale des Archives du Film 1969-91, v.p. FIAF 1977-85; pres. FIAF Documentation Commission 1972-81. Film Archives Advisory Comm. since 1971. Assoc. of Univ. Seminars on Cinema and Interdisciplinary Interpretation. Publications: The Transformation of Cinema: 1907-15, Vol II, History of the American Film Series, The Movies, David Wark Griffith, Biograph Bulletins 1908-1912. A Handbook for Film Archives. Has written numerous articles on film history.

BOXLEITNER, BRUCE
Actor. b. Elgin, IL, May 12, 1950. m. actress Melissa Gilbert. After high school enrolled in Chicago's Goodman Theatre, staging productions and working with lighting and set design in addition to acting.
PICTURES: Six-Pack Annie, The Baltimore Bullet, Tron, The Crystal Eye, Breakaway, Diplomatic Immunity, Kuffs, The Babe.
TELEVISION: *Series*: How the West Was Won, Bring 'Em Back Alive, Scarecrow and Mrs. King, Babylon 5. *Movies*: The Chadwick Family, A Cry for Help, The Macahans, Kiss Me—Kill Me, Murder at the World Series, Happily Ever After, Wild Times, Kenny Rogers as The Gambler, Fly Away Home, Bare Essence, I Married Wyatt Earp, Kenny Rogers as The Gambler: The Adventure Continues, Passion Flower, Angel in Green, Kenny Rogers as the Gambler: The Legend Continues, Red River, The Town Bully, From the Dead of Night, The Road Raiders, Till We Meet Again, Murderous Vision, The Secret, Perfect Family, Double Jeopardy (also co-exec. prod.), House of Secrets, Gambler V: Playing for Keeps, Danielle Steel's Zoya, Babylon 5: In the Beginning, Babylon 5: Thirdspace, Babylon 5: A Call to Arms. *Mini-Series*: How the West Was Won, East of Eden, The Last Convertible. *Special*: Wyatt Earp: Return to Tombstone. *Guest:* Tales from the Crypt.

BOYER, PHIL
TV Executive. b. Portland, OR, Dec. 13, 1940. e. Sacramento State U. Began broadcasting career as 12-year-old in Portland, establishing nation's first youth radio facility—a 5-watt facility in the basement of his home. At 16 began working at KPDQ, Portland; two years later joined KPTV, Portland, as announcer. In 1960 joined KEZI-TV, Eugene, OR, heading prod. and prog. depts. In 1965 named staff prod.-dir. for KCRA, TV, Sacramento, CA, becoming prod. mgr. in 1967 and prog. mgr. in 1969. In 1972 joined KNBC-TV, Los Angeles, as prog. dir. In 1974 named v.p., programming, of ABC Owned TV Stations; 1977, v.p.-gen. mgr., WLS-TV, Chicago; 1979, v.p.-gen. mgr. of WABC-TV, NY, 1981; v.p., gen mgr., ABC-owned TV station div.; 1984, joined ABC Video Enterprises as v.p. intl. dev.; 1986-97 sr. v.p., intl and prog. dev., CC/ABC Video Ent.

BOYES, CHRISTOPHER
Sound.
PICTURES: Rush, Terminator 2: Judgment Day, Bingo!, Single White Female, Jurassic Park, Under Siege 2: Dark Territory, The Rock, Broken Arrow, Eraser, Titanic (Acad. Award, Best Sound Effects Editing, 1997), Volcano, The Lost World: Jurassic Park, Con Air, Big Daddy.

BOYETT, ROBERT LEE
Producer. e. Duke U., B.A.; Col. U., M.A., marketing. Began career in media and mkt. research at Grey Advertising, Inc. Was program development consultant for PBS. In 1973 joined ABC as dir. of prime time series TV, East Coast. In 1975 named ABC TV v.p. & asst. to v.p. programs for West Coast. In 1977 joined Paramount Pictures in newly created position of v.p., exec. asst. to pres. & chief operating officer. 1979, joined Miller-Milkis-Boyett Productions to produce for Paramount Television.
TELEVISION: *Exec. prod.*: Laverne and Shirley, Happy Days, Bosom Buddies, Mork and Mindy, Valerie, Perfect Strangers, Family Matters, Meego, Step By Step, Full House, Family Matters, Going Places, The Family Man, Getting By, On Our Own, Two-N-Two Together, Hogan Family, Two of a Kind.

BOYLE, BARBARA D.
Executive. b. New York, NY. e. U. of California, Berkeley, B.A., 1957; UCLA, J.D., 1960. Named to bar: California, 1961; New York, 1964; Supreme Court, 1964. Atty. in busn. affairs dept. & corp. asst. secty., American Intl. Pictures, Los Angeles, 1965-67; partner in entertainment law firm, Cohen & Boyle, L.A., 1967-74; exec. v.p. & gen. counsel, COO, New World Pictures, L.A., 1974-82. Sr. v.p. worldwide prod., Orion Pictures, L.A., 1982-86; exec. v.p., prod., RKO Pictures, L.A., 1986-87. President, Sovereign Pictures, L.A., 1988-92; Boyle-Taylor Prods., 1993-. Exec. prod: Eight Men Out, Battle Rocket. Prod.: Mrs. Munch, Phenomenon, Instinct. Co-chmn. 1979-80, Entertainment Law Symposium Advisory Committee, UCLA Law Sch. Member, AMPAS, Women in Film (pres., 1977-78, mem. of bd., chairperson 1981-84), Women Entertainment Lawyers Assn., California Bar Assn., N.Y. State Bar Assn., Beverly Hills Bar Assn., Hollywood Women's Political Committee, American Film Institute. Bd. mem.: Women Director's Workshop, Independent Feature Project/West (pres. 1994-), Los Angeles Women's Campaign Fund. Founding mem. UCLA Sch. of Law's Entertainment Advisory Council (& co-chairperson 1979 & 80).

BOYLE, LARA FLYNN
Actress. b. Davenport, IA, Mar. 24, 1970. e. Chicago Academy for the Visual and Performing Arts. First studied acting at the Piven Theatre. Professional debut at age 15 in tv mini-series Amerika.
PICTURES: Poltergeist III (debut, 1988), How I Got Into College, Dead Poets Society, May Wine, The Rookie, The Dark Backward, Mobsters, Wayne's World, Where the Day Takes You, The Temp, Eye of the Storm, Equinox, Red Rock West, Threesome, Baby's Day Out, The Road to Wellville, Farmer & Chase, Cafe Society, The Big Squeeze, Afterglow, Red Meat, Susan's Plan, Happiness, Speaking of Sex, Chain of Fools, Susan's Plan.
TELEVISION: *Series*: Twin Peaks, The Practice. *Mini-Series*: Amerika. *Movies*: Terror on Highway 91, Gang of Four, The Preppie Murder, The Hidden Room, Since You've Been Gone, Jacob.

BOYLE, PETER
Actor. b. Philadelphia, PA, Oct. 18, 1933. e. LaSalle Coll. Was monk in Christian Bros. order before leaving in early 60s to come to N.Y. Acted in off-Broadway shows and joined The Second City in Chicago. Also did TV commercials.
THEATER: *NY*: Shadow of Heroes, Paul Sills' Story Theatre, The Roast, True West, Snow Orchid.
PICTURES: The Virgin President (debut, 1968), The Monitors, Medium Cool, Joe, Diary of a Mad Housewife, T.R. Baskin, The Candidate, Steelyard Blues, Slither, The Friends of Eddie Coyle, Kid Blue, Ghost in the Noonday Sun, Crazy Joe, Young Frankenstein, Taxi Driver, Swashbuckler, F.I.S.T., The Brink's Job, Hardcore, Beyond the Poseidon Adventure, Where the Buffalo Roam, In God We Trust, Outland, Hammett, Yellowbeard, Johnny Dangerously, Turk 182, Surrender, Walker, The In Crowd, Red Heat, The Dream Team, Speed Zone, Funny, Men of Respect, Solar Crisis, Kickboxer 2, Honeymoon in Vegas, Nervous Ticks, Malcolm X, The Shadow, The Santa Clause, Bulletproof Heart, Born to Be Wild, While You Were Sleeping, That Darn Cat, Doctor Doolittle.
TELEVISION: *Series*: Comedy Tonight, Joe Bash, Everybody Loves Raymond. *Mini-Series*: From Here to Eternity. *Movies*: The Man Who Could Talk to Kids, Tail Gunner Joe, Echoes in the Darkness, Disaster at Silo 7, Guts and Glory: The Rise and Fall of Oliver North, Challenger, In the Line of Duty: Street War, Taking the Heat, Royce. *Specials*: 27 Wagons Full of Cotton, Conspiracy: The Trial of the Chicago Eight. *Guest*: Cagney & Lacey, Midnight Caller, X-Files (Emmy Award, 1996), NYPD Blue, The Single Guy. *Pilot*: Philly Heat.

BRABOURNE, LORD JOHN
Producer. b. London, England, Nov. 9, 1924.
PICTURES: Harry Black and the Tiger, Sink the Bismarck, H.M.S. Defiant (Damn the Defiant!), Othello, The Mikado, Up the Junction, Romeo and Juliet, Dance of Death, Peter Rabbit and Tales of Beatrix Potter, Murder on the Orient Express, Death on the Nile, Stories from a Flying Trunk, The Mirror Crack'd, Evil Under the Sun, A Passage to India, Little Dorrit.

BRACCO, LORRAINE
Actress. b. Brooklyn, NY, Oct. 2, 1955. m. actor Edward James Olmos. At 16 began modelling for Wilhelmina Agency appearing in Mademoiselle, Seventeen, Teen magazine. Moved to Paris where modelling career continued and led to TV commercials. After making her film debut in Duo sur Canape became a disc jockey on Radio Luxembourg, Paris. 1983 produced a TV special on fashion and music. In Lincoln Center workshop performance of David Rabe's Goose and Tom Tom, 1986.
PICTURES: Cormorra, The Pick-up Artist, Someone to Watch Over Me, Sing, The Dream Team, On a Moonlit Night, Good Fellas (Acad. Award nom.), Talent for the Game, Switch, Medicine Man, Radio Flyer, Traces of Red, Being Human, The Basketball Diaries, Hackers, The Liars, Ladies Room.
TELEVISION: *Movies*: Scam, Getting Gotti, Lifeline, The Taking of Pelham One-Two-Three. *Series:* The Sopranos.

BRACKEN, EDDIE
Actor. b. New York, NY, Feb. 7, 1920. e. Prof. Children's Sch. for Actors, N.Y. m. Connie Nickerson, actress. Vaudeville & night club singer: stage debut in Lottery, 1930.
THEATER: Lady Refuses, Iron Men, So Proudly We Hail, Brother Rat, What A Life, Too Many Girls, Seven Year Itch, Shinbone Alley, Teahouse of the August Moon, You Know I Can't Hear You When The Water's Running, The Odd Couple, Never Too Late, Sunshine Boys, Hotline to Heaven, Hello Dolly, Damn Yankees, Sugar Babies, Show Boat, The Wizard of Oz, It Runs in the Family, These Golden Years, No No Nanette.
PICTURES: Too Many Girls (debut, 1940), Life With Henry, Reaching for the Sun, Caught in the Draft, The Fleet's In, Sweater Girl, Star Spangled Rhythm, Happy Go Lucky, Young and Willing, The Miracle of Morgan's Creek, Hail the Conquering Hero, Rainbow Island, Bring on the Girls, Duffy's Tavern, Hold That Blonde, Out of This World, Ladies' Man, Fun on a Weekend, The Girl From Jones Beach, Summer Stock, Two Tickets to Broadway, About Face, We're Not Married, Slight Case of Larceny, Wild Wild World (narrator), Shinbone Alley (voice), National Lampoon's Vacation, Preston Sturges: The Rise and Fall of an American Dreamer, Oscar, Home Alone 2: Lost in New York, Rookie of the Year, Baby's Day Out, The Brave Little Toaster (voice).
TELEVISION: *Series*: I've Got a Secret (panelist), Make the Connection (panelist), Masquerade Party (host, 1957), Winnetka Road. *Guest*: Goodyear Playhouse, Studio One, Climax, Murder She Wrote, Blacke's Magic, Amazing Stories, Tales of the Dark Side, Golden Girls, Wise Guy, Empty Nest, Monsters. *Movies*: The American Clock, Assault at West Point.

BRADEN, WILLIAM
Executive, Producer. b. Alberta, Canada. e. U.S., Canada, and abroad. Began career as stuntman in Hollywood, and has worked in all aspects of industry Worked for Elliott Kastner as prod. exec. and with Jeffrey Bloom, of Feature Films, Inc., as prod. and v.p. in chg. of prod. Also with Dunatai Corp., as head of film and TV prod. With Completion Bond Co. one yr. as prod. exec., Australia then with Filmaker Completion as pres. 4 years. Now indep. prod.
PICTURES: Pyramid (assoc. prod., prod. supv.), Russian Roulette (prod. exec.), 92 in the Shade (prod. exec.), Breakheart Pass (prod. exec.), Dogpound Shuffle (asst. dir.), Dublin Murders (supvr. re-edit), He Wants Her Back (prod.), Goldengirl (prod. exec.), Running Scared (prod.), Death Valley (asst. dir.), The Seduction (prod. exec.), Slapstick of Another Kind (prod. exec.).
TELEVISION: Requiem for a Planet (series, prod./creator). *Specials*: Nothing Great is Easy (exec. prod.), King of the Channel (exec. prod.), I Believe (prod.), If My People... (prod.), America: Life in the Family (dir./prod.). Also various Movies of the Week for networks and many industrial and doc. films.

BRADFORD, JESSE
Actor. b. May 28, 1979. Made first appearance as infant in Q-tip commercial.
PICTURES: Falling in Love (debut, 1984), Prancer, Presmued Innocent, My Blue Heaven, The Boy Who Cried Bitch, King of the Hill, Far From Home: The Adventures of Yello Dog, Hackers, Romeo & Juliet, A Soldier's Daughter Never Cries, Speedway Junky.
TELEVISION: *Movie:* The Boys. *Special:* Classified Love. *Guest:* Tribeca.

BRADLEY, ED
Newscaster. b. Philadelphia, Pa., June 22, 1941. e. Cheyney State Coll, B.S. Worked way up through the ranks as local radio reporter in Philadelphia 1963-67 and NY 1967-71. Joined CBS News as stringer in Paris bureau, 1971; then Saigon bureau. Named CBS news correspondent, 1973. Became CBS News White House corr. and anchor of CBS Sunday Night News, 1976-81; principal corr. and anchor, CBS Reports, 1978-81; co-editor and reporter 60 Minutes since 1980. Recipient: Alfred I. duPont-Columbia University and Overseas Press Club Awards, George Foster Peabody and Ohio State Awards, George Polk Award.
TELEVISION: *Special reports*: What's Happened to Cambodia, The Boat People, The Boston Goes to China, Blacks in America—With All Deliberate Speed, Return of the CIA, Miami... The Trial That Sparked the Riot (Emmy Award), The Saudis, Too Little Too Late (Emmy Award), Murder—Teenage Style (Emmy Award, 1981), In the Belly of the Beast (Emmy Award, 1982), Lena (Emmy Award, 1982).

BRAEDEN, ERIC
Actor. r.n. Hans Gudegast. b. Kiel, Germany, Apr. 3, 1941. Awarded Federal Medal of Honor by pres. of Germany for promoting positive, realistic image of Germans in America.
PICTURES: Morituri, Dayton's Devils, 100 Rifles, Colossus: The Forbin Project, Escape from the Planet of the Apes, Lady Ice, The Adulteress, The Ultimate Thrill, Herbie Goes to Monte Carlo, The Ambulance, Titanic, Meet the Deedles.
TELEVISION: *Series*: The Rat Patrol, The Young and the Restless (People's Choice Award, Soap Opera Award, 2 Emmy noms., Emmy Award, 1998). *Movies*: Honeymoon With a Stranger, The Mask of Sheba, The Judge and Jake Wyler, Death Race, Death Scream, The New Original Wonder Woman (pilot), Code Name: Diamond Head, Happily Ever After, The Power Within, The Aliens Are Coming, The Case of the Wicked Wives. *Mini-series:* Jackie Collins' Lucky Chances.

BRAGA, SONIA
Actress. b. Maringa, Parana, Brazil, 1950. Began acting at 14 on live children's program on Brazilian TV, Gardin Encantado. Stage debut at 17 in Moliere's Jorge Dandin, then in Hair! Starred in many Brazilian soap operas including Gabriella, as well as a prod. of Sesame Street in Sao Paulo.
PICTURES: The Main Road, A Moreninha, Captain Bandeira Vs. Dr. Moura Brasil, Mestica, The Indomitable Slave, The Couple, Dona Flor and Her Two Husbands, Gabriella, I Love You, A Lady in the Bus, Kiss of the Spider Woman, The Milagro Beanfield War, Moon Over Parador, The Rookie, Roosters, Two Deaths, Tieta do Agreste (also co-prod.).
TELEVISION: *Movies*: The Man Who Broke 1000 Chains, The Last Prostitute, The Burning Season, Money Plays, Streets of Laredo, A Will of Their Own. *Series:* Four Corners. *Guest*: The Cosby Show, Tales From the Crypt.

BRANAGH, KENNETH
Actor, Director, Producer, Author. b. Belfast, Northern Ireland, Dec. 10, 1960. Moved to Reading, England at age 9. e. RADA. Went from drama school into West End hit Another Country, followed by Gamblers, The Madness, Francis. Royal Shakespeare Co.: Love Labors Lost, Hamlet, Henry V. Left Royal Shakespeare Company to form his own Renaissance Theater Co. with actor David Parfitt for which he wrote a play Public Enemy (also produced Off-B'way), wrote-directed Tell Me Honestly, directed Twelfth Night, produced-directed-starred in Romeo & Juliet, and played Hamlet, Benedick and Touchstone in a sold-out nationwide tour and London season. L.A.: King Lear, A Midsummer Night's Dream. Author: Beginning (1990). Received BAFTA's Michael Balcon Award for Outstanding Contribution to Cinema (1993). Made short film Swan Song (Acad. Award nom.).
PICTURES: High Season (debut, 1987), A Month in the Country, Henry V (also dir., adapt.; BAFTA & Natl. Board of Review Awards for Best Dir., 1989), Dead Again (also dir.), Peter's Friends (also dir., prod.), Swing Kids, Much Ado About Nothing (also dir., adapt.), Mary Shelley's Frankenstein (also dir., co-prod.), In the Bleak Mid-Winter (dir., s.p. only), Anne Frank Remembered (narrator), Othello, Looking for Richard, Hamlet (also dir, prod.), The Theory of Flight, Celebrity, The Gingerbread Man, The Proposition, The Dance of Shiva, Love's Labour's Lost (also, dir., s.p.),The Betty Schimmel Story (dir. only), Wild Wild West, Galapagos: The Enchanted Voyage (voice), Love's Labourls Lost, The Road to El Dorado (voice), How to KIll Your Neighbor's Dog, Alien Love Triangle, Rabbit Proof Fence. TELEVISION: The Boy in the Bush (series), The Billy Plays, Maybury, To the Lighthouse, Coming Through, Ghosts, The Lady's Not For Burning, Fortunes of War (mini-series) Thompson (series), Strange Interlude, Look Back in Anger, cold War (voice) Great Composers (narrator).

BRANDAUER, KLAUS MARIA
Actor, Director. r.n. Klaus Maria Steng. b. Bad Ausse, Steiermark, Austria, June 22, 1944. m. film and TV dir.-screen-writer Karin Mueller. e. Acad. of Music and Dramatic Arts, Stuttgart, W. Germany. Was established in the German and Austrian theater before film debut.
PICTURES: The Salzburg Connection (debut, 1972), Mephisto (Cannes Film Fest. Award, 1981). Never Say Never Again, Colonel Redl, Out of Africa, The Lightship, Streets of Gold, Burning Secret, Hanussen, Hitlerjunge Salomon, Das Spinnennetz (The Spider's Web) The French Revolution, The Russia House, White Fang, The Resurrected, Seven Minutes (also dir.), Becoming Colette, Felidae (voice), Marco and the Magician (also dir.), Die Wand (dir. only), Rembrandt.
TELEVISION: Quo Vadis?, Jeremiah, Dorothy Dandridge.

BRANDIS, BERNARDINE
Executive. e. B.A., (magna cum laude) UCLA, 1975. J.D., UCLA, 1978. Began career as private practice attorney. senior dist & mktg./prod. counsel, 20th Century Fox Film Corp.; dir., business affairs, Universal Pictures, 1983-85; v.p., business affairs, Walt Disney Pictures, 1985-89; senior v.p., business and legal affairs, Hollywood Pictures, 1989-present. Currently exec. v.p., The Walt Disney Motion Pictures Group, overseeing all aspects of business and legal affairs for the motion pictures division, studio administration, and theme park film productions.

BRANDIS, JONATHAN
Actor. b. Danbury, CT, April 13, 1976. Started as print model at age 4; followed by several tv commercials.
PICTURES: Fatal Attraction, Stepfather 2, Never Ending Story II: The Next Chapter, Ladybugs, Sidekicks, Ride with the Devil, Outside Providence.
TELEVISION: *Series*: SeaQuest DSV, Aladdin (voice). *Movies*: Poor Little Rich Girl, Stephen King's IT, SeaQuest DSV, Good King Wenceslas, Born Free: A New Adventure, Her Last Chance, Fall Into Darkness, Two Came Back. *Guest:* Murder, She Wrote, L.A. Law, The Wonder Years, Alien Nation, The Flash, Saved by the Bell: The College Years.

BRANDO, MARLON
Actor. b. Omaha, NB, April 3, 1924. Sister is actress Jocelyn Brando. e. Shattuck Military Acad., Faribault, MN. Studied acting at New School's Dramatic Workshop, NY, with Stella Adler; played stock in Sayville, Long Island. Broadway debut: I Remember Mama, followed by Truckline Cafe, Candida, A Flag Is Born, A Streetcar Named Desire. Voted one of top ten Money-Making Stars, M.P. Herald-Fame poll, 1954-55. Autobiography: Brando: Songs My Mother Taught Me (1994).
PICTURES: The Men (debut, 1950), A Streetcar Named Desire, Viva Zapata!, Julius Caesar, The Wild One, On the Waterfront (Academy Award, 1954), Desiree, Guys and Dolls, The Teahouse of the August Moon, Sayonara, The Young Lions, The Fugitive Kind, One-Eyed Jacks (also dir.), Mutiny on the Bounty, The Ugly American, Bedtime Story, The Saboteur—Code Name: Morituri, The Chase, The Appaloosa, A Countess From Hong Kong, Reflections in a Golden Eye, Candy, The Night of the Following Day, Burn!, The Nightcomers, The Godfather (Academy Award, 1972), Last Tango in Paris, The Missouri Breaks, Superman, Apocalypse Now, The Formula, A Dry White Season, The Freshman, Christopher Columbus: The Discovery, Don Juan DeMarco, Divine Rapture, The Island of Dr. Moreau, The Brave, Free Money, The Score.
TELEVISION: *Mini-Series*: Roots: The Next Generations (Emmy Award, 1979).

BRANDON, MICHAEL
Actor. r.n. Michael Feldman. b. Brooklyn, NY, April 20, 1945. e. AADA. Appeared on B'way in Does Tiger Wear a Necktie?
PICTURES: Lovers and Other Strangers, Jennifer on My Mind, Four Flies on Grey Velvet, Heavy Traffic (voice), FM, Promises in the Dark, A Change of Seasons, Rich and Famous, Deja Vu.
TELEVISION: *Series*: Emerald Point, Dempsey & Makepeace, Home Fires. *Movies*: The Impatient Heart, The Strangers in 7A, The Third Girl From the Left, Hitchhike!, The Red Badge of Courage, Queen of the Stardust Ballroom, Cage Without a Key, James Dean, Scott Free, Red Alert, The Comedy Company, A Vacation in Hell, A Perfect Match, Between Two Brothers, The Seduction of Gina, Deadly Messages, Rock 'n' Roll Mom, Dynasty: The Reunion, Not in My Family, Moment of Truth: Murder or Memory?, The Apocalypse Watch.

BRANDT, RICHARD PAUL
Executive. b. New York, NY, Dec. 6, 1927. e. Yale U., BS, Phi Beta Kappa. Chmn. Trans Lux Corp.; chmn., Brandt Theatres; dir., Presidential Realty Corp.; chmn. emeritus & trustee, American Film Institute; trustee, American Theatre Wing; vice-chmn. & trustee, College of Santa Fe; board member for Taos Talking Pictures Festival.

BRAUGHER, ANDRE
Actor. b. Chicago, IL, July 1, 1962.
PICTURES: Glory, Striking Distance, Primal Fear, Get on the Bus, Thick as Thieves, City of Angels, A Better Way to Die, Duets, All the Rage.
TELEVISION: *Movies*: Kojak: Fatal Flaw, Kojak: Ariana, Kojak: None So Blind, Murder in Mississippi, Somebody Has to Shoot the Picture, The Court-Martial of Jackie Robinson, Simple Justice, Class of '61, Without Warning: Terror in the Towers, The Tuskegee Airmen, Passing Glory, Love Songs (also dir.). *Series*: Kojak, Homicide: Life in the Street (Emmy Award, 1998), City of Angels. *Guest:* Law & Order.

BRAUNSTEIN, GEORGE GREGORY
Producer. b. New York, NY, May 23, 1947. e. Culver Military Acad., U. of California, B.A., biology, chemistry, 1970. U. W.L.A. Law School, J.D. 1987. Father is Jacques Braunstein (Screen Televideo Prods. At War with the Army, Young Lions.).
PICTURES: Train Ride to Hollywood, Fade to Black, Surf II, And God Created Woman, Out Cold, Don't Tell Her It's Me, Uncle Sam, Meltdown.

BRAVERMAN, CHARLES
Producer, Director. b. Los Angeles, CA, March 3, 1944. e. Los Angeles City Coll., U. of Southern California, B.A. m. Kendall Carly Browne, actress. Child actor, 1950-57. Two time Emmy winner.
PICTURES: Dillinger, Soylent Green, Same Time Next Year (all montages, titles), Can't Stop the Music (titles), Hit and Run (prod./dir.), The Hank Gather Story.
TELEVISION: An American Time Capsule, The Smothers Brothers Racing Team Special, How to Stay Alive, David Hartman... Birth and Babies, Breathe a Sigh of Relief, The Television Newsman, Getting Married, The Making of a Live TV Show, Televisionland, Nixon: Checkers to Watergate, Braverman's Condensed Cream of Beatles, Two Cops, Peanuts to the Presidency: The Jimmy Carter Campaign, The Making of Beatlemania, Willie Nelson Plays Lake Tahoe, Tony Bennett Sings, What's Up, America?, The Big Laff Off, Engelbert at the MGM Grand, Oscar's First 50 Years, Frankie Valli Show, The Sixties, Showtime Looks at 1981, Roadshow, Kenny Rodger's America, St. Elsewhere, DTV (Disney Channel), Crazy Like a Fox, Dreams, The Richard Lewis Special, Prince of Bel Air, Brotherhood of Justice, The Wizard; Heart of the City, Rags to Riches, The New Mike Hammer, Sledge Hammer!, Gabriel's Fire, Life Goes On, Beverly Hills 90210, FBI: Untold Stories, Final Shot: The Hank Gathers Story, Melrose Place, Northern Exposure (DGA nom.), Haunted Lives II.

BRECHER, IRVING
Writer. b. New York, NY, Jan. 17, 1914. e. Roosevelt H.S. in Yonkers. Yonkers Herald reporter; network programs writer for Milton Berle, Willie Howard, Al Jolson, etc., m.p. writer since 1937. On B'way in Sweet Charity, 1942.
PICTURES: At the Circus, Go West, Du Barry Was a Lady, Shadow of the Thin Man, Best Foot Forward, Meet Me in St. Louis, Summer Holiday, Yolanda and the Thief, Life of Riley (also dir.), Somebody Loves Me (also dir.), Cry for Happy, Sail a Crooked Ship (also dir.), Bye Bye Birdie.
TELEVISION: The People's Choice, The Life of Riley.

BREGMAN, MARTIN
Producer, Writer. b. New York, NY, May 18, 1931. m. actress Cornelia Sharpe. e. Indiana U., NYU. Began career as business and personal mgr. to Barbra Streisand, Faye Dunaway, Candice Bergen, Al Pacino. Chairman NY Advisory Council for Motion Pictures, Radio and TV (co-founder, 1974).
PICTURES: Serpico, Dog Day Afternoon, The Next Man, The Seduction of Joe Tynan, Simon, The Four Seasons, Eddie Macon's Run, Venom, Scarface, Sweet Liberty, Real Men, A New Life, Sea of Love, Nesting, Betsy's Wedding, Whispers in the Dark, The Real McCoy, Carlito's Way, The Shadow, Gold Diggers: The Secret of Bear Mountain, Matilda (exec. prod.), Nothing to Lose, The Bone Collector.
TELEVISION: S*H*E (movie), The Four Seasons (series).

BRENNAN, EILEEN
Actress. b. Los Angeles, CA, Sept. 3, 1935. e. Georgetown U., American Acad. of Dramatic Arts, N.Y. Daughter of silent film actress Jean Manahan. Big break came with lead in off-Broadway musical, Little Mary Sunshine (Obie & Theatre World Awards, 1960).
THEATER: The Miracle Worker (tour), Hello Dolly! (Broadway), and revivals of The King and I, Guys and Dolls, Camelot, Bells Are Ringing; also An Evening with Eileen Brennan, A Couple of White Chicks Sitting Around Talking.
PICTURES: Divorce American Style (debut, 1967), The Last Picture Show (BAFTA nom.), Scarecrow, The Sting, Daisy Miller, At Long Last Love, Hustle, Murder by Death, FM, The Cheap Detective, The Last of the Cowboys (The Great Smokey Roadblock), Private Benjamin (Acad. Award nom.), Pandemonium, The Funny Farm, Clue, Sticky Fingers, Rented Lips, The New Adventures of Pippi Longstocking, It Had to Be You, Stella, Texasville, White Palace, Joey Takes a Cab, I Don't Buy Kisses Anymore, Reckless, Pants on Fire, Nuncio's Second Cousin, Changing Bad Habits, Boy's Life 2, The Last Great Ride.
TELEVISION: *Series*: Rowan & Martin's Laugh-In, All My Children, 13 Queens Boulevard, A New Kind of Family, Private Benjamin (Emmy Award, 1981), Off the Rack, 7th Heaven. *Specials*: Working, In Search of Dr. Seuss. *Movies*: Playmates, My Father's House, The Night That Panicked America, The Death of Richie, When She Was Bad..., My Old Man, When the Circus Came to Town, Incident at Crestridge, Going to the Chapel, Deadly Intentions... Again?, Taking Back My Life: The Nancy Ziegenmeyer Story, Poisoned by Love: The Kern County Murders, Precious Victims, My Name Is Kate, Take Me Home Again, Freaky Friday, Trail of Tears, Toothless. *Mini-Series*: The Blue Knight, Black Beauty. *Guest:* Taxi, Magnum P.I., Newhart, All in the Family, Murder She Wrote, Blossom, Mad About You, Veronica's Closet, ER, McMillian and Wife.

BRENNEMAN, AMY
Actress. b. Glastonbury, Connecticut, June 22, 1964.
PICTURES: Bye Bye Love, Casper, Heat, Fear, Daylight, Nevada (also prod.), Lesser Prophets, Your Friends and Neighbors, The Suburbans, Things You Can Tell Just By Looking At Heart.
TELEVISION: *Series*: Middle Ages, NYPD Blue, ATF, Judging Amy. *Guest*: Frasier, Murder She Wrote.

BREST, MARTIN
Director. b. Bronx, NY, Aug. 8, 1951. e. NYU Sch. of Film. m. prod. Lisa Weinstein. Made award-winning short subject, Hot Dogs for Gauguin (featuring Danny DeVito). Accepted into fellowship program at American Film Institute, making first feature, Hot Tomorrows (dir., prod., s.p.), as AFI project. Appeared in Fast Times at Ridgemont High, Spies Like Us. Produced film Josh and S.A.M.
PICTURES: Going in Style (also s.p.), Beverly Hills Cop, Midnight Run (also prod.), Scent of a Woman (also prod.), Meet Joe Black (also prod.).

BRIALY, JEAN-CLAUDE
Actor. b. Aumale, Algeria, March 30, 1933. e. Strasbourg U. (philosophy) also attended drama classes at Strasbourg Conservatoire. Made several short films with Jacques Rivette and Jean-Luc Godard. Appeared in several French TV movies.
PICTURES: Paris Does Strange Things, Elevator to the Gallows, Les Cousins, Three Faces of Sin, A Woman Is a Woman, Seven Capitol Sins, The Devil and Ten Commandments, Two Are Guilty, Nutty Naughty Chateau, Carless Love, Male Hunt, Circle of Love, King of Hearts, The Oldest Profession, Shock Troops, The Bride Wore Black, Claire's Knee, A Murder is a Murder, The Phantom of Liberty, Catherine et Cie, The Accuser, L'Annee Sainte, Robert and Robert, Eglantine, Les Violets Clos, L'oiseau Rare, Un Amour De Pluie, Bobo Jacco, L'oeil Du Maitre, La Banquiere, La Nuit de Varennes, Cap Canaille, Le Demon Dan L'Isle, Edith and Marcel, Sarah, Stella, The Crime, Papy Fait de la Resistance, Pinot, Simple Flic, Comedie dété, My New Partner 2, No Fear-No Die, August, Pakt mit dem Tod, The Monster, Queen Margot, The Son of Gascogne, A French Woman, A Hundred and One Nights, Shadow Play, Beaumarchais the Scoundrel.
TELEVISION: Les Heritiers, La Grande Beke, Le Comte de Monte Cristo (mini-series).

BRICK, RICHARD A.
Producer. b. New York, NY, Sept. 20, 1945. e New York University, B.A.; Columbia University, M.F.A. 1988-89, Chair. Columbia Univ., Film Division School of the Arts. 1992-94, Comm. of New York City Mayor's Office of Film, Theatre, and Broadcasting. Presently, Prof., Columbia Univ.; on the Board of Dir. for the Independent Feature Project.
PICTURES: Ragtime (unit mgr.), Part of the Family (prod. mgr), Andrea Doria: The Final Chapter (assoc. prod.), The Trials of Alger Hiss (assoc. prod.), Pilgrim...Farewell (assoc. prod.), Little Gloria...Happy at Last (unit prod. mgr), Silkwood (unit. prod. mgr.), Places in the Heart (unit prod. mgr.), Arizona Dream (co-prod.), Deconstructing Harry (co-prod.), Celebrity (co-prod.), Sweet and Lowdown (co-prod.), Hangin' with the Homeboys, Caught.

BRICKMAN, MARSHALL
Writer, Director. b. Rio de Janeiro, Brazil, Aug. 25, 1941. e. U. of Wisconsin. Banjoist, singer, writer with folk groups The Tarriers and The Journeymen before starting to write for TV. Appeared in films Funny and That's Adequate.
PICTURES: *Co-writer* (with Woody Allen): Sleeper, Annie Hall (Acad. Award, 1977), Manhattan, Manhattan Murder Mystery. *Dir./Writer*: Simon (dir. debut, 1980), Lovesick, The Manhattan Project (also prod.). *Co-Writer*: For the Boys, Intersection.
TELEVISION: *Writer*: Candid Camera 1966, The Tonight Show 1966-70. *Specials*: Johnny Carson's Repertory Co. in an Evening of Comedy (1969), Woody Allen Special, Woody Allen Looks at 1967. *Prod.:* Dick Cavett Show (1970-72, Emmy Award).

BRICKMAN, PAUL
Writer, Director. b. Chicago, IL, April 23, 1949. e. Claremont Men's Coll. Worked as camera asst., then story analyst at Paramount, Columbia, and Universal.
PICTURES: Handle With Care (assoc. prod., s.p.), The Bad News Bears in Breaking Training (s.p.), Risky Business, Deal of the Century (s.p., co-exec. prod.), That's Adequate, Men Don't Leave (also co-s.p.), True Crime (writer), Uprising (writer).

BRIDGES, ALAN
Director. b. England, Sept. 28, 1927. Started dir. for the BBC before moving into feature films.
PICTURES: An Act of Murder (debut, 1965), Invasion, Shelley, The Hireling, Out of Season, Summer Rain, The Return of the Soldier, The Shooting Party, Displaced Persons, Apt Pupil, Secret Places of the Heart, Fire Princess.
TELEVISION: The Father, Dial M For Murder, The Intrigue, The Ballade of Peckham Rye, The Initiation, Alarm Call: Z Cars, The Fontenay Murders, The Brothers Karamazov, The Idiot, Days to Come, Les Miserables, Born Victim, The Wild Duck, The Lie, Brief Encounter, Forget Me Not Lane, Double Echo, Saturday—Sunday—Monday, Crown Matrimonial.

BRIDGES, BEAU
Actor. r.n. Lloyd Vernet Bridges III. b. Hollywood, CA, Dec. 9, 1941. e. UCLA; U. of Hawaii. Father was late actor Lloyd Bridges, brother is actor Jeff Bridges.
PICTURES: Force of Evil (debut, 1948), No Minor Vices, The Red Pony, Zamba, The Explosive Generation, Village of the Giants, The Incident, For Love of Ivy, Gaily Gaily, The Landlord, Adam's Woman, The Christian Licorice Store, Hammersmith Is Out, Child's Play, Your Three Minutes Are Up, Lovin' Molly, The Other Side of the Mountain, Dragonfly (One Summer Love), Swashbuckler, Two-Minute Warning, Greased Lightning, Norma Rae, The Fifth Musketeer, The Runner Stumbles, Silver Dream Racer, Honky Tonk Freeway, Night Crossing, Love Child, Heart Like a Wheel, The Hotel New Hampshire, The Killing Time, The Wild Pair (also dir.), Seven Hours to Judgement (also dir.), The Iron Triangle, Signs of Life, The Fabulous Baker Boys, The Wizard, Daddy's Dyin'...Who's Got the Will?, Married to It, Sidekicks, Jerry Maguire, Rocket Man, Meeting Daddy, The White River Kid, Sordid Lives.
TELEVISION: *Movies*: The Man Without a Country, The Stranger Who Looks Like Me, Medical Story, The Four Feathers, Shimmering Light, The President's Mistress, The Child Stealer, The Kid from Nowhere (also dir.), Dangerous Company, Witness for the Prosecution, The Red-Light Sting, Alice in Wonderland, Outrage!, Fighting Choice, The Thanksgiving Promise (also dir., co-prod.), Everybody's Baby: The Rescue of Jessica McClure, Just Another Secret, Women & Men: Stories of Seduction, Guess Who's Coming for Christmas?, Without Warning: The James Brady Story (Emmy Award, 1992), Wildflower, Elvis and the Colonel, The Man With 3 Wives, The Positively True Adventures of the Alleged Texas Cheerleader-Murdering Mom (Emmy Award, 1993), Secret Sins of the Fathers (also dir.), Kissinger and Nixon, Losing Chase, The Defenders: Choice of Evils,

The Defenders: Taking the First, Inherit the Wind, Common Ground, Songs in Ordinary Time. *Series*: Ensign O'Toole, United States, Harts of the West, Maximum Bob. *Mini-series*: The Second Civil War (Emmy Award, 1997), Voyage of the Unicorn. *Guest*: Sea Hunt, Ben Casey, Dr. Kildare, Mr. Novak, Combat, Eleventh Hour, Cimarron Strip, Amazing Stories, The Outer Limits, My Three Sons.

BRIDGES, JEFF
Actor. b. Los Angeles, CA, Dec. 4, 1949. Appeared as infant in 1950 film The Company She Keeps. Made acting debut at eight in the TV series Sea Hunt starring his father, Lloyd Bridges. Studied acting at Herbert Berghof Studio, NY. Mil. service in Coast Guard reserves. Brother is actor-dir. Beau Bridges. Composed and performed song for film John and Mary. Named Male Star of the Year (1990) by NATO.
PICTURES: Halls of Anger (debut, 1970), The Yin and Yang of Mr. Go, The Last Picture Show (Acad. Award nom.), Fat City, Bad Company, The Iceman Cometh, The Last American Hero, Lolly-Madonna XXX, Thunderbolt and Lightfoot (Acad. Award nom.), Hearts of the West, Rancho Deluxe, Stay Hungry, King Kong, Somebody Killed Her Husband, The American Success Company, Winter Kills, Heaven's Gate, Cutter's Way (Cutter and Bone), Tron, The Last Unicorn (voice only), Kiss Me Goodbye, Against All Odds, Starman (Acad. Award nom.), Jagged Edge, 8 Million Ways to Die, The Morning After, Nadine, Tucker: The Man and His Dream, See You in the Morning, Cold Feet, The Fabulous Baker Boys, Texasville, The Fisher King, The Vanishing, American Heart (also co-prod.), Fearless, Blown Away, Wild Bill, White Squall, The Mirror Has Two Faces, The Big Lebowski, Arlington Road, A Soldier's Daughter Never Cries, The Muse, Forever Hollywood, Simpatico, The Contender.
TELEVISION: *Movies*: Silent Night, Lonely Night; In Search of America, The Thanksgiving Promise (cameo), Raising the Mammoth (voice). *Special*: Faerie Tale Theatre (Rapunzel). *Guest*: Lloyd Bridges Show, The FBI, Most Deadly Game.

BRIGHT, KEVIN
Producer, Director.
TELEVISION: Dream On (prod. only), The Adventures of Brisco County Jr. (dir. only), Friends (exec. prod.), Veronica's Closet (exec. prod.), Jesse (exec. prod.).

BRIGHT, RICHARD
Actor. b. Brooklyn, NY, June 11, 1937. e. trained for stage with Frank Corsaro, John Lehne and Paul Mann.
THEATER: The Balcony (1959), The Beard, The Salvation of St. Joan, Gogol, The Basic Training of Pavlo Hummel, Richard III, Kid Twist, Short Eyes as well as regional theater.
PICTURES: Odds Against Tomorrow, Lion's Love, Panic in Needle Park, The Getaway, Pat Garrett and Billy the Kid, The Godfather, The Godfather II, Rancho Deluxe, Marathon Man, Citizens Band, Looking For Mr. Goodbar, On the Yard, Hair, The Idolmaker, Vigilante, Two of a Kind, Once Upon a Time in America, Crackers, Crimewave, Cut and Run, Brighton Beach Memoirs, 52-Pick-up, Time Out, Red Head, The Godfather III, Who's the Man, The Ref, Sweet Nothing, Ripper, Jaded, Beautiful Girls, Night Falls of Manhattan, OK Garage, Anima.
TELEVISION: *Series*: Lamp Unto My Feet, Armstrong Circle Theater, The Verdict Is Yours, Kraft Television Theatre, Studio One, Cagney and Lacey, Beacon Hill, Hill Street Blues, From These Roots. *Movies*: A Death of Innocence, The Connection, The Gun, Cops and Robin, Sizzle, There Must Be A Pony, Penalty Phase. *Mini-series*: From Here to Eternity, Skag, Calm of Sunset, Witness to the Mob.

BRIGHT, RICHARD S.
Executive. b. New Rochelle, NY, Feb. 28, 1936. e. Hotchkiss Sch., 1953-54; Wharton Sch. of Finance, U. of Pennsylvania, 1954-58. With U.S. Army Finance Corp., 1959-60. Was corporate exec. prior to founding Persky-Bright Organization in 1973, private investment group to finance films. Now bd. chmn, Persky-Bright Productions, Inc.
THEATER: A History of the American Film, Album (Off-B'way, co-prod.).
PICTURES: Last Detail, Golden Voyage of Sinbad, For Pete's Sake, California Split, The Man Who Would Be King, Funny Lady, The Front, and Equus. Financing/production services for: Hard Times, Taxi Driver, Missouri Breaks, Bound for Glory, Sinbad and the Eye of the Tiger, Hair, Body Heat, Still of the Night. Exec. prod.: Tribute.
TELEVISION: The President's Mistress (co-prod.).

BRILLSTEIN, BERNIE
Producer, Talent Manager. b. New York, NY. 1931. e. NYU, B.S. advertising. Manager whose clients have incl. Lorne Michaels, John Belushi, Jim Henson and the Muppets. Chairman and chief exec. officer, Lorimar Film Entertainment. Founder, chmn., pres., The Brillstein Company. Former co-partner of Brillstein-Grey Entertainment and Brillstein-Grey Communications.
PICTURES: *Exec. Prod.*: The Blues Brothers, Up the Academy, Continental Divide, Neighbors, Doctor Detroit, Ghostbusters, Spies Like Us, Summer Rental, Armed and Dangerous, Dragnet, Ghostbusters II, Hexed, The Celluloid Closet, Cat and Mouse, Happy Gilmore, The Cable Guy, Bulletproof, Dirty Work, The Replacement Killers.
TELEVISION: *Exec. prod.*: Burns and Schreiber Comedy Hour, Buckshot, Open All Night, Show Business, Sitcom, Buffalo Bill, Jump, The Faculty, The Real Ghostbusters (exec. consultant), It's Garry Shandling's Show, The Days and Nights of Molly Dodd, The "Slap" Maxwell Show, The Boys (pilot), The Wickedest Witch, Normal Life, The Larry Sanders Show, Newsradio, Def Comedy Jam—Prime Time, Hightower 411, The Naked Truth, The Steve Harvey Show, Mr. Show, Just Shoot Me.

BRIMLEY, WILFORD
Actor. b. Salt Lake City, UT, Sept. 27, 1934. Formerly a blacksmith, ranch hand and racehorse trainer; began in films as an extra and stuntman. Also acted as A. Wilford Brimley. Original member of L.A. Actors Theatre.
PICTURES: True Grit, Lawman, The China Syndrome, The Electric Horseman, Brubaker, Borderline, Absence of Malice, Death Valley, The Thing, Tender Mercies, Tough Enough, High Road to China, 10 to Midnight, Hotel New Hampshire, Harry and Son, The Stone Boy, The Natural, Country, Cocoon, Remo Williams: The Adventure Begins, American Justice, End of the Line, Cocoon: The Return, Eternity, The Firm, Hard Target, Last of the Dogmen, My Fellow Americans, In & Out, Summer of the Monkeys, All My Friends are Cowboys, The Progeny.
TELEVISION: *Movies*: The Oregon Trail, The Wild Wild West Revisited, Amber Waves, Roughnecks, Rodeo Girl, The Big Black Pill, Ewoks: The Battle for Endor, Murder in Space, Thompson's Last Run, Act of Vengeance, Gore Vidal's Billy the Kid, Blood River, Tom Clancy's Op Center. *Series*: Our House, Boys of Twilight. *Guest*: The Waltons, Seinfeld.

BRINKLEY, DAVID
TV news correspondent. b. Wilmington, NC, July 10, 1920. e. U. of North Carolina; Vanderbilt U. Started writing for hometown newspaper. Joined United Press before entering Army, WWII. After discharge in 1943, joined NBC News in Washington as White House corr. Co-chmn. for many years with late Chet Huntley on NBC Nightly News. Then began David Brinkley's Journal. Moved to ABC to host This Week with David Brinkley.

BRISKIN, MORT
Producer, Writer. b. Oak Park, IL, 1919. e. U. of Southern California; attended Harvard and Northwestern law schools, being admitted to the bar at 20. Practiced law before entering m.p. industry in management with such stars as Mickey Rooney. Turned to production and also wrote screenplays for 16 of his 29 films. Created nine TV series and was prod. or exec. prod. of some 1,350 TV segments of which he wrote more than 300.
PICTURES: The River, The Magic Face, No Time for Flowers, The Second Woman, Quicksand, The Big Wheel, The Jackie Robinson Story, Ben, Willard, Walking Tall, Framed.
TELEVISION: Sheriff of Cochise, U.S. Marshal, The Texan, Grand Jury, The Walter Winchell File, Official Detective, Whirlybirds.

BRITTANY, MORGAN
Actress. r.n. Suzanne Cupito. b. Hollywood, CA, Dec. 5, 1951.
PICTURES: Gypsy, The Birds, Marnie, Yours Mine and Ours, Gable and Lombard, Sundown: The Vampire in Retreat, The Prodigal, Last Action Hero, The Saint, Riders in the Storm, The Protector, Legend of the Spirit Dog.
TELEVISION: *Series*: Dallas, Glitter, Melrose Place. *Guest*: B. L. Stryker, L.A. Law, Buck Rogers in the 25th Century. *Movies*: Amazing Howard Hughes, Delta County U.S.A., The Initiation of Sarah, Samurai, Stunt Seven, Death on the Freeway, The Dream Merchants, Moviola: The Scarlett O'Hara War, The Wild Women of Chastity Gulch, LBJ: The Early Years, Perry Mason: The Case of the Scandalous Scoundrel, National Lampoon's Favorite Deadly Sins.

BROADBENT, JIM
Actor, Writer. b. England. Member of the National Theatre and the Royal Shakespeare Company. Wrote and starred in short film A Sense of History (Clermont-Ferrand Intl. Film Fest. Award).
THEATER: The Recruiting Officer, A Winter's Tale, The Government Inspector, A Flea in Her Ear, Goose Pimples.
PICTURES: The Shout (debut, 1978), The Passage, Breaking Glass, The Dogs of War, Time Bandits, Brazil, The Good Father, Superman IV: The Quest for Peace, Life Is Sweet, Enchanted April, The Crying Game, Widow's Peak, The Wedding Gift, Princess Caraboo, Bullets Over Broadway, Rough Magic, The Secret Agent, Richard III, The Borrowers, Little Voice, The Avengers.
TELEVISION: Not the Nine O'Clock News, Gone to Seed, Sense of History (also writer), Murder Most Horrid, Gone to the Dogs, Only Fools and Horses, The Victoria Wood Show, Silas Marner, Blackladder, Birth of a Nation, The Peter Principles.

BROADHEAD, PAUL E.
Executive. e. Univ. of MS. Founder of Paul Broadhead & Assocs. real estate development. 1984, sold his interests in that company. Became chmn. of bd. of Theatre Properties, Cinemark USA.

BROADNAX, DAVID
Actor, Producer, Writer. b. Columbus, GA, Dec. 16.
PICTURES: The Landlord, Come Back Charleston Blue, Sharpies (also prod., co-s.p.), Zombie Island Massacre (also prod., story).
TELEVISION: As the World Turns, Another World, Edge of Night, Love Is a Many Splendored Thing, Search for Tomorrow, Saturday Night Live.

BROCKMAN, MICHAEL
Executive. b. Brooklyn, NY, Nov. 19, 1938. e. Ithaca Coll. Became v.p., daytime programming, ABC Entertainment, 1974; later v.p., tape prod. operations and admin. Left to become v.p., daytime programs, NBC Entertainment, 1977-1980. Became v.p. programs, Lorimar Prods. 1980-82; v.p. daytime and children's prog. CBS Entertainment, 1982-89. 1986, title changed to v.p. daytime, children's and late night. Became pres. ABC daytime, children's & late night entertainment 1989-90. Joined Mark Goodson Prods. as v.p. 1991. Became sr. v.p. in 1993. Pres., M. Brockman Broadcast Inc., 1995.

BRODERICK, MATTHEW
Actor, Producer, Director. b. New York, NY, Mar. 21, 1962. Son of late actor James Broderick and writer-dir./artist Patricia Broderick. Acted in a workshop prod. of Horton Foote's Valentine's Day with his father (1979).
THEATER: *NY*: Torch Song Trilogy, Brighton Beach Memoirs (Tony & Theatre World Awards, 1983), Biloxi Blues, The Widow Claire, How to Succeed in Business Without Really Trying (Tony Award, 1995).
PICTURES: Max Dugan Returns (debut, 1983), WarGames, Ladyhawke, 1918, On Valentine's Day, Ferris Bueller's Day Off, Project X, Biioxi Blues, Torch Song Trilogy, Glory, Family Business, The Freshman, Out on a Limb, The Night We Never Met, The Lion King (voice), The Road to Wellville, Mrs. Parker and the Vicious Circle, Arabian Knight (voice), Infinity (also dir., co-prod.), The Cable Guy, Infinity (also dir.), Addicted to Love, Lion King II: Simba's Pride (voice), Godzilla, Election, Inspector Gadget, Walking to the Waterline, You Can Count On Me.
TELEVISION: *Specials*: Master Harold... and the Boys, Cinderella (Faerie Tale Theatre), The Year of the Generals (voice), A Simple Melody. *Movie:* A Life in the Theatre. *Guest*: Lou Grant, Frasier.

BRODNEY, OSCAR
Writer. b. Boston, MA, 1906. e. Boston U., LL.B., 1927; Harvard, LL.M., 1928. Atty., MA Bar, 1928-35.
PICTURES: She Wrote the Book, If You Knew Susie, Are You With It?, For the Love of Mary, Mexican Hayride, Arctic Manhunt, Yes Sir, That's My Baby, Double Crossbones, Gal Who Took the West, South Sea Sinner, Comanche Territory, Harvey, Frenchie, Francis Goes to the Races, Little Egypt, Francis Covers the Big Town, Willie and Joe Back at the Front, Scarlet Angel, Francis Goes to West Point, Walking My Baby Back Home, Sign of the Pagan, Black Shield of Falworth, Captain Lightfoot, The Spoilers, Purple Mask, Lady Godiva, Day of Fury, Star in the Dust, Tammy and the Bachelor, When Hell Broke Loose, Bobbikins (also prod.), Tammy Tell Me True, The Right Approach, All Hands on Deck, Tammy and the Doctor, The Brass Bottle, I'd Rather Be Rich.

BRODSKY, JACK
Producer. b. Brooklyn, NY, July 3, 1932. e. George Washington H.S. Writer for N.Y. Times. Joined 20th-Fox publicity in N.Y. in 1956. Left in 1961 to head national ad-pub for Filmways. Joined Rastar Productions to work on Funny Girl; later named v.p. in charge of prod. In 1976 named v.p. in chg. film prod. prom., Rogers & Cowan; 1978, Columbia Pictures v.p. of adv., pub., promo.; 1979, named exec. v.p. of Michael Douglas' Big Stick Productions; 1983; joined 20th-Fox as exec. v.p., worldwide adv., pub., exploit. Resigned 1985 to resume career as prod..
PICTURES: Harry & Walter Go to New York (actor only), Two Minute Warning (actor only), Little Murders, Everything You Always Wanted To Know About Sex But Were Afraid to Ask (exec. prod.), Summer Wishes Winter Dreams, The Jewel of the Nile, Dancers (co-exec. prod., actor), King Ralph, Scenes From a Mall (actor), Rookie of the Year (co-exec. prod.).
AUTHOR: The Cleopatra Papers, with Nat Weiss.

BROKAW, CARY
Executive, Producer. b. Los Angeles, CA, June 21, 1951. e. Univ. of CA/Berkeley, UCLA Grad. Sch. Worked at several positions at 20th Century Fox before serving as exec. v.p. for Cineplex Odeon Corp. 1983 became co-chmn., pres. of Island Alive; 1985, became co-chmn., pres. & CEO of Island Pictures. 1987, formed Avenue Pictures; 1991, became pres. & CEO for Avenue Entertainment Group.
PICTURES: *Executive Producer*: Trouble in Mind, Down by Law, Nobody's Fool, Slamdance, Pascali's Island, Signs of Life, Cold Feet, Drugstore Cowboy, After Dark My Sweet, The Object of Beauty, Sex Drugs Rock & Roll, The Player, American Heart, Stained Glass. *Producer*: Short Cuts, Restoration, Voices From a Locked Room, Finding Graceland, Stand by Your Man, Letters from a Wayward Son.
TELEVISION: *Movies*: In the Eyes of a Stranger, Amelia Earhart: The Final Flight, See Jane Run, Stranger in Town, Two Mothers for Zachary. Tell Me No Secrets, The Almost Perfect Bank Robbery, Path to Paradise, The Time Shifters *Series*: The Player.

BROKAW, NORMAN R.
Executive. b. New York, NY, April 21, 1927. Joined William Morris Agency as trainee in 1943; junior agent, 1948; sr. agent, company exec. in m.p. and TV, 1951; 1974, v.p., William Morris Agency, World Wide all areas. 1981, named exec. v.p. & mem. of bd., William Morris Agency, worldwide; 1986, named co-chmn. of bd., WMA, worldwide. 1989, named pres. & CEO, William Morris Inc. worldwide. 1991, named Chmn. of Board of CEO. Member Acad. of TV Arts & Sciences, AMPAS. Member bd. of dir. of Cedars-Sinai Medical Center, Los Angeles; pres., The Betty Ford Cancer Center. Clients include former President and Mrs. Gerald R. Ford, Bill Cosby, Gen. Alexander Haig, Priscilla Presley, Andy Griffith, Dr. C. Everett Koop, Marcia Clark, Christopher Darden.

BROKAW, TOM
TV Host, Anchorman. b. Yankton, S.D., Feb. 6, 1940, e. U. of South Dakota. Newscaster, weatherman, staff announcer KTIV, Sioux City, IA, 1960-62. Joined KMTV, NBC affiliate in Omaha, in 1962; 1965, joined WSB-TV, Atlanta. Worked in L.A. bureau of NBC News, anchored local news shows for KNBC, NBC station (1966-73). In 1973 named NBC News' White House correspondent; was anchor of NBC Saturday Night News. Named host of Today show in August, 1976. In 1982 co-anchor, NBC Nightly News. Co-anchor 1993 series NBC newsmagazine, Now With Tom Brokaw & Katie Couric. Special: Conversation with Mikhail S. Gorbachev.

BROLIN, JAMES
Actor, Producer, Director. b. Los Angeles, CA, July 18, 1940. r.n. James Bruderlin. e. UCLA. Son is actor Josh Brolin. Debut in Bus Stop (TV series); named most promising actor of 1970 by Fame and Photoplay magazines. Winner, Emmy and Golden Globe Awards. Also nominated for 3 additional Emmys and 2 Golden Globes.
PICTURES: Take Her She's Mine (debut, 1963), John Goldfarb Please Come Home, Goodbye Charlie, Dear Brigitte, Von Ryan's Express, Morituri, Fantastic Voyage, Way ... Way Out, The Cape Town Affair, Our Man Flint, The Boston Strangler, Skyjacked, Westworld, Gable and Lombard, The Car, Capricorn One, The Amityville Horror, Night of the Juggler, High Risk, Pee-wee's Big Adventure, Bad Jim, Super High Score, Ted & Venus, Gas Food Lodging, Cheatin' Hearts (also exec. prod.), Back Stab, Savate, Relative Fear, Parallel Lives, Indecent Bahavior, The Expert, Tracks of a Killer, Lewis and Clark and George, Blood Money, My Brother's War, Haunted Sea, Goodbye America.
TELEVISION: *Series*: Marcus Welby M.D. (Emmy Award, 1970), Hotel, Angel Falls, Extreme, Pensacola: Wings of Gold, Beyond Belief. *Movies*: Marcus Welby M.D., Short Walk to Daylight, Class of '63, Trapped, Steel Cowboys, The Ambush Murders, Mae West, White Water Rebels, Cowboy, Beverly Hills Cowgirl Blues, Hold the Dream, Intimate Encounters, Voice of the Heart, Finish Line, Nightmare on the 13th Floor, And the Sea Will Tell, Deep Dark Secrets, The Sands of Time, Visions of Murder, Gunsmoke: The Long Ride, The Calling, Parallel Lives, A Perry Mason Mystery: The Case of the Grimacing Governor, Terminal Virus, A Marriage of Convenience, To Love Honor and Betray. *Special*: City Boy (PBS), Body Human 2000: Love Sex & the Miracle of Birth. *Director:* Hotel (12 episodes), The Young Riders, Hijacked: Flight 285, Pensacola Wings of Gold (also exec. prod.), Beyond Belief, Fact or Fiction. *Guest:* Roseanne, Batman.

BROMHEAD, DAVID M.
Executive. b. Teaneck, NJ, Jan. 7, 1960. e. Leighton Park Sch., Reading, England, 1973-78. Overseas sls. exec., Rank Film Dist., 1980; joined New World Pictures, 1984, dir. intl. dist.; named dir., TV dist., 1986.

BRON, ELEANOR
Actress, Writer. b. Stanmore, Middlesex, England, March 14, 1938. Started career in Establishment Club, London, and on American tour. Leading lady on British TV show Not So Much a Programme—More a Way of Life. Author of Double Take, The Pillowbook of Eleanor Bron, Life and Other Punctures. Translator of Desdemona—If You Had Only Spoken, by Christine Bruckner.
THEATER: The Doctor's Dilemma, Howards End, The Prime of Miss Jean Brodie, Hedda Gabler, The Duchess of Malfi, The Madwoman of Chaillot, Uncle Vanya, A Delicate Balance, A Perfect Ganesh, Dona Rosita, The Cherry Orchard, A Month In the Country.
PICTURES: Help!, Alfie, Two for the Road, Bedazzled, The Turtle Diary, Thank You All Very Much, Women in Love, The Millstone, Little Dorrit, Black Beauty, A Little Princess, Saint-Ex, Deadly Advice.
TELEVISION: *Movies*: The Day Christ Died, The Attic: The Hiding of Anne Frank, Intrigue, Changing Step, The Blue Boy, Vanity Fair. *Series*: Where Was Spring? (also co-wrote), After That This. *Guest*: Rumpole of the Bailey, Yes Minister, Absolutely Fabulous.

BRONDFIELD, JEROME
Writer. b. Cleveland, OH, Dec. 9, 1913. e. Ohio State U., 1936. Reporter, ed. on Columbus Dispatch, Associated Press, story ed., script head, RKO Pathe, Oct., 1944; writer, dir. & supvr. of many doc. shorts incl. This Is America series; TV writer; short story writer; collab. s.p., Below the Sahara; s.p. Louisiana Territory; doc. film writer. Author: Woody Hayes, The 100-Yard War, Knute Rockne, The Man and the Legend. Sr. editor, Scholastic, Inc.

BRONFMAN, EDGAR, JR.
Executive. Joined Seagram 1982 as asst. to officeof the pres.; served as mng. dir. of Seagram Europe until he was appointed pres. of The House of Seagram, 1984-88; became pres. & COO in 1989. June 1994 named pres. & CEO of The Seagram Company Ltd. Upon acquisition of MCA Inc. was named acting chairman, 1995. Currently President & CEO of Seagram which has merged with Vivendi.

BRONSON, CHARLES
Actor. r.n. Charles Buchinsky. b. Ehrenfeld, PA, Nov. 3, 1921. Worked as a coal miner. Served in Air Force (1943-46) as tail gunner on B29s in Pacific. Studied acting at Pasadena Playhouse. Started in films billed under real name. Guest in numerous TV shows in addition to those below.
PICTURES: You're in the Navy Now (debut, 1951), The People Against O'Hara, The Mob, Red Skies of Montana, My Six Convicts, The Marrying Kind, Pat and Mike, Diplomatic Courier, Bloodhounds of Broadway, House of Wax, The Clown, Miss Sadie Thompson, Crime Wave, Tennessee Champ, Riding Shotgun, Apache, Drum Beat (Ist billing as Charles Bronson), Vera Cruz, Big House U.S.A., Target Zero, Jubal, Run of the Arrow, Machine Gun Kelly, Gang War, Showdown at Boot Hill, When Hell Broke Loose, Ten North Frederick, Never So Few, The Magnificent Seven, Master of the World, A Thunder of Drums, X-15, Kid Galahad, The Great Escape, Four for Texas, The Sandpiper, The Battle of the Bulge, This Property Is Condemned, The Dirty Dozen, Villa Rides, Guns for San Sebastian, Farewell Friend, Once Upon a Time in the West, Rider on the Rain, You Can't Win Em All, The Family, Cold Sweat, Twinky (Lola), Someone Behind the Door, Red Sun, Chato's Land, The Mechanic, The Valachi Papers, The Stone Killer, Chino, Mr. Majestyk, Death Wish, Breakout, Hard Times, Breakheart Pass, From Noon Till Three, St. Ives, The White Buffalo, Telefon, Love and Bullets, Caboblanco, Borderline, Death Hunt, Death Wish II, Ten to Midnight, The Evil That Men Do, Death Wish 3, Murphy's Law, Assassination, Death Wish 4: The Crackdown, Messenger of Death, Kinjite: Forbidden Subjects, The Indian Runner, Death Wish V: The Face of Death, Family of Cops II & III.
TELEVISION: *Series*: Man With a Camera, Empire, Travels of Jamie McPheeters. *Guest*: Philco Playhouse (Adventure in Java), Medic, A Bell for Adano, Gunsmoke, Have Gun Will Travel, Meet McGraw, The FBI, The Fugitive, The Virginian. *Movies*: Raid on Entebbe, Act of Vengeance, Yes Virginia There Is a Santa Claus, The Sea Wolf, Donato and Daughter, A Family of Cops.

BROOK, PETER
Director. b. London, England, March 21, 1925. e. Magdalen Coll., Oxford. To London 1943 to dir. his first play, Doctor Faustus; other stage incl. Man and Superman, Marat/Sade, A Midsummer Night's Dream, etc.
PICTURES: The Beggar's Opera (debut, 1953), Moderato Cantabile (also co-s.p.), Lord of the Flies (also s.p., edit), The Persecution and Assassination of Jean-Paul Marat as Performed by the Inmates of the Asylum of Charenton Under the Direction of the Marquis de Sade, Tell Me Lies (also prod.), King Lear (also s.p.), Meetings With Remarkable Men (also s.p.), The Tragedy of Carmen, Swann in Love (s.p. only), The Mahabharata.

BROOKS, ALBERT
Director, Writer, Actor. r.n. Albert Einstein. b. Los Angeles, CA, July 22, 1947. e. Carnegie Tech. Son of late comedian Harry Einstein (Parkyakarkus). Brother is performer Bob Einstein. Sports writer KMPC, L.A. 1962-63. Recordings: Comedy Minus One, A Star is Bought (Grammy nom.).
PICTURES: Taxi Driver, Real Life (also dir., co-s.p.), Private Benjamin, Modern Romance (also dir., co-s.p.), Twilight Zone—The Movie, Terms of Endearment (voice), Unfaithfully Yours, Lost in America (also dir., co-s.p.), Broadcast News (Acad. Award nom.), Defending Your Life (also dir., s.p.), I'll Do Anything, The Scout (also co-s.p.), Mother (also dir.; NY Society of Film Critics Award, Natl Society of Film Critics Award for best s.p., 1997), Doctor Dolittle (voice), Out of Sight, The Muse, My First Mister (actor).
TELEVISION: *Series*: Dean Martin Presents the Golddiggers, Saturday Night Live (prod., dir. short films 1975-76), Hot Wheels (voices), The Associates (wrote theme song). *Specials*: Milton Berle's Mad Mad Mad World of Comedy, General Electric's All-Star Anniversary. *Guest*: Love American Style, The Odd Couple, Ed Sullivan Show, Tonight Show, The Simpsons (voice).

BROOKS, JAMES L.
Director, Producer, Writer. b. North Bergen, NJ, May 9, 1940. e. NYU. Copyboy for CBS News, N.Y.; promoted to newswriter. 1965 moved to L.A. to work for David Wolper's documentary prod. co. In 1969 conceived idea for series, Room 222; formed partnership with fellow writer Allan Burns. Together they created Mary Tyler Moore Show in 1970. 1977, established prod. co. on Paramount lot with other writers, producing and creating the series, The Associates and Taxi. Formed Gracie Films. Directed play Brooklyn Laundry, in L.A.
PICTURES: Real Life (actor), Starting Over (s.p., co-prod.), Modern Romance (actor), Terms of Endearment (dir., prod., s.p.; Acad. Awards for Best Picture, Dir. and Screenplay, 1983), Broadcast News (dir., prod., s.p.), Big (co-prod.), Say Anything... (exec. prod.), The War of the Roses (co-prod.), I'll Do Anything (dir., prod., s.p.), Bottle Rocket, Jerry Maguire, As Good As It Gets (dir., s.p.), The Simpsons Movie (exec. prod.), Riding in Cars with Boys.
TELEVISION: *Movie*: Thursday's Game (writer, prod., 1971). *Series*: The Mary Tyler Moore Show (co-creator, writer, exec. prod.; 2 Emmy Awards for writing: 1971, 1977; 3 Emmy Awards as exec. prod.: 1975, 1976, 1977), Rhoda (writer, prod.), The New Lorenzo Music Show (writer), Lou Grant (co-exec. prod.). Series (co-creator, and/or exec. prod.): Taxi (3 Emmy Awards as exec. prod.: 1979, 1980, 1981), Cindy, The Associates, Cheers, Tracey Ullman Show (Emmy Award as exec. prod., 1989), The Simpsons (2 Emmy Awards as exec. prod.: 1990, 1991), Sibs, Phenom, The Critic.

BROOKS, JOSEPH
Producer, Director, Writer, Composer, Conductor. Well-known for composing music for TV commercials before turning to producing, directing, writing and scoring theatrical feature, You Light Up My Life, in 1977. Winner of 21 Clio Awards (advertising industry), Grammy, Golden Globe, People's Choice, Amer. Music Awards; created music for 100 commercials. Has also composed for theatrical films. Winner of Cannes Film Festival Advertising Award.
PICTURES: *Scores*: The Garden of the Finzi-Continis, Marjoe, Jeremy, The Lords of Flatbush. *Prod.-Dir.-Writer-Composer*: You Light Up My Life (Academy Award for Best Song: title song, 1977), If Ever I See You Again (also actor), Headin' for Broadway, Invitation to the Wedding, Eddie and the Cruisers.

BROOKS, MEL
Writer, Director, Actor. r.n. Melvin Kaminsky. b. Brooklyn, NY, June 28, 1926. . m. actress Anne Bancroft. e. VA Military Inst. 1944. U.S. Army combat engineer 1944-46. As child, did impressions and was amateur drummer and pianist. First appearance as actor in play Separate Rooms in Red Bank, NJ. Was also social dir. of Grossinger's Resort in the Catskills. Became writer for Sid Caesar on TV's Broadway Review and Your Show of Shows. Teamed with Carl Reiner for comedy record albums: The 2000 Year Old Man, The 2000 and 13 Year Old Man. Founded Brooksfilms Ltd., 1981. Won Academy Award for Best Short Subject (animated): The Critic (dir., s.p., narrator). Co-writer of Shinbone Alley.
THEATER: *Writer*: New Faces of 1952 (sketches), Shinbone Alley (book), All-American (book).
PICTURES: New Faces (co-s.p.), The Producers (dir., s.p.; Academy Award for Best Original Screenplay, 1968), The Twelve Chairs (dir., s.p., actor), Blazing Saddles (dir., co-s.p., actor), Young Frankenstein (dir., co-s.p.; Acad. Award nom. for s.p.), Silent Movie (dir., co-s.p., actor), Frances (exec.-prod), High Anxiety (dir., prod., co-s.p., actor), The Muppet Movie (actor), History of the World Part 1 (dir., prod., s.p., actor, lyrics), To Be or Not To Be (exec-prod., actor), Spaceballs (dir., prod., co-s.p., actor), , Look Who's Talking Too (voice), Life Stinks (dir., prod., co-s.p., actor), Robin Hood: Men in Tights (dir., prod., co-s.p., actor), The Silence of the Hams (actor), The Little Rascals (actor),, Dracula: Dead and Loving It (dir., prod., co-s.p., actor), The Prince of Egypt (voice), Svitati (actor, s.p.). *Exec. Prod.*: The Elephant Man, My Favorite Year, The Doctor and the Devils, The Fly, 84 Charing Cross Road, Solarbabies, The Vagrant, The Fly II.
TELEVISION: *Special*: The Sid Caesar-Imogene Coca-Carl Reiner-Howard Morris Special (co-writer; Emmy Award, 1967), I am Your Child. *Series*: Get Smart (co-creator, co-writer), When Things Were Rotten (co-creator, co- writer, prod.), The Nutt House (prod., co-writer). *Guest*: Mad About You (Emmy Award, 1997), The Simpsons (voice), Frasier.

BROSNAN, PIERCE
Actor. b. Navan, County Meath, Ireland, May 16, 1953. Left County Meath, Ireland for London at 11. Worked as commercial illustrator, then joined experimental theater workshop and studied at the Drama Center. On London stage (Wait Until Dark, The Red Devil Battery Sign, Filumenia, etc.)
PICTURES: The Mirror Crack'd (debut, 1980), The Long Good Friday, Nomads, The Fourth Protocol, Taffin, The Deceivers, Mister Johnson, The Lawnmower Man, Entangled, Mrs. Doubtfire, Love Affair, Goldeneye, Mars Attacks, The Mirror Has Two Faces, Dante's Peak, Tomorrow Never Dies, Quest for Camelot (voice), The Nephew (also prod.), Grey Owl, The Thomas Crown Affair (also prod.), The World is Not Enough, Dolphins, The Tailor of Panama, Blood and Champagne, Beyond the Ice.

TELEVISION: *Series*: Remington Steele, Frame-Up (NBC Friday Night Mystery). *Movies/Specials*: Murphy's Stroke, The Manions of America, Nancy Astor, Noble House, Around the World in 80 Days, The Heist, Murder 101, Victim of Love, Live Wire, Death Train (Detonator), The Broken Chain, Don't Talk to Strangers, Alistair MacLean's Night Watch.

BROUGH, WALTER
Producer, Writer. b. Phila. PA, Dec. 19, 1935. e. La Salle U. (B.A.), USC (M.A.). Began career with Stage Society Theatre, LA. Currently CEO, Orb Enterprises, Inc.
PICTURES: Gabriella, A New Life, No Place to Hide, Run Wild Run Free, The Desperadoes, Funeral for an Assassin (also prod.), On a Dead Man's Chest (also prod.), Jed and Sonny (also prod.).
TELEVISION: Doctor Kildare, The Fugitive, Branded, Name of the Game, Mannix, Mission Impossible, The Magician, Man From Atlantis, Police Story, Wildside, Heart of the City (also prod.), Thunder Guys (pilot), Spencer for Hire (also co-prod.), Law & Harry McGraw, New Mission Impossible (also co-prod.), Over My Dead Body, Hunter, Tequila & Bonetti, Sirens.

BROUGHTON, BRUCE
Composer. b. Los Angeles, CA , March 8, 1945. e. U. of Southern California, B.M., 1967. Music supvr., CBS-TV, 1967-77. Since then has been freelance composer for TV and films. Member of Academy of TV Arts & Sciences Society of Composers & Lyricists (past pres.), AMPAS (governor). Nominated 17 times for Emmy. Nominated for Grammy for Young Sherlock Holmes.
PICTURES: The Prodigal, The Ice Pirates, Silverado (Acad. Award nom.), Young Sherlock Holmes, Sweet Liberty, The Boy Who Could Fly, Square Dance, Harry and the Hendersons, Monster Squad, Big Shots, Cross My Heart, The Rescue, The Presidio, Last Rites, Moonwalker, Jacknife, Betsy's Wedding, Narrow Margin, The Rescuers Down Under, All I Want for Christmas, Honey I Blew Up the Kid, Stay Tuned, Homeward Bound: The Incredible Journey, So I Married an Axe Murderer, For Love or Money, Tombstone, Holy Matrimony, Baby's Day Out, Miracle on 34th Street, Infinity, Carried Away, House Arrest, Homeward Bound II: Lost in San Francisco, The Shadow Conspiracy, A Simple Wish, One Tough Cop, Krippendorf's Tribe, Lost in Space.
TELEVISION: *Series*: Hawaii Five-0, Gunsmoke, Quincy, How the West Was Won, Logan's Run, The Oregon Trail, Buck Rogers (Emmy Award), Dallas (Emmy Award), Dinosaurs (theme), Capitol Critters (theme), Tiny Toon Adventures (Emmy Award). *Movies*: The Paradise Connection, Desperate Voyage, The Return of Frank Cannon, Desperate Lives, Killjoy, One Shoe Makes It Murder, The Master of Ballantrae, MADD, The Candy Lightner Story, Cowboy, A Thanksgiving Promise, The Old Man and the Sea, O Pioneers! (Emmy Award), Night Ride Home. *Mini-Series*: The Blue and the Gray, The First Olympics—Athens: 1896 (Emmy Award), George Washington II, True Women.

BROUMAS, JOHN G.
Executive. b. Youngstown, OH, Oct. 12, 1917. e. Youngstown. Usher, Altoona Publix Theatres, 1933, usher to asst. mgr., Warner Thea. 1934-39; mgr. Grand 1939-40; mgr. Orpheum 1940-41. WWII active, Officer Chemical Corps, commanding officer 453rd Chem. Battalion (Reserve); Life member Reserve Officers Assoc.; Gen. mgr. Pitts & Roth Theatres 1946-54; pres., Broumas Theatres; v.p. NATO, 1969; bd. of dir. of NATO of VA, MD, D.C.; pres., Broumas Theatre Service 1954-82; bd. chmn., Showcase Theatres 1965-82; past pres. & bd. chmn. Maryland Theatre Owners; v.p. & bd. of dir., Virginia Theatre Owners; bd. of dir. NATO of D.C.; pres. B.C. Theatres; Past dir. and mem. Motion Picture Pioneers; Advisory Council: Will Rogers Memorial Hospital; Washington, D.C. Variety Club, Tent No. 11, bd. of gov. 1959, 1st asst. chief. barker, 1964 & 71, chief barker 1965-66, 1972, and 1978-79, and bd. chmn., 1980; lecturer, Georgetown Univ., 1972-; Life Patron, Variety Clubs Int'l, 1978 Life Liner, Variety Clubs Intl.; member: Screen Actors Guild. 1994.

BROWN, BLAIR
Actress. b. Washington, DC, 1948. e. National Theatre Sch. of Canada.
THEATER: *NY*: The Threepenny Opera (NY Shakespeare Fest), Comedy of Errors, The Secret Rapture, Arcadia. Acted with Old Globe, San Diego; Stratford, Ont. Shakespeare Fest.; Guthrie Theatre MN; Arena Stage, Wash.; Long Wharf, New Haven; Shaw Festival.
PICTURES: The Paper Chase, The Choirboys, One-Trick Pony, Altered States, Continental Divide, A Flash of Green, Stealing Home, Strapless, Passed Away, The Good Policeman, The Astronaut's Wife, Random Hearts.
TELEVISION: *Series*: The Days and Nights of Molly Dodd, Talk It Over, Feds. *Mini-series*: Captains and the Kings, James Michener's Space, Arthur Hailey's Wheels, Kennedy, A Season in Purgatory. *Movies*: The 3,000 Mile Chase, And I Alone Survived, The Child Stealer, The Bad Seed, Hands of a Stranger, Eleanor and Franklin: The White House Years, Extreme Close-Up, Those Secrets, Majority Rule, Rio Shannon (pilot), The Day My Parents Ran Away, Moment of Truth: To Walk Again, The Gift of Love, The Ultimate Lie, Convictions. *Specials*: School for Scandal, The Skin of Your Teeth, Lethal Innocence, Oregon Trail, The Quinns, Space.

BROWN, BRYAN
Actor. b. Sydney, Australia, June 23, 1947. m. actress Rachel Ward. Began acting professionally in Sydney. Worked in repertory theatres in England with the National Theatre of Great Britain. Returned to Australia to work in films while continuing stage work with Theatre Australia.
PICTURES: Love Letters From Teralba Road (debut, 1977), The Irishman, Weekend of Shadows, Newsfront, Third Person Plural, Money Movers, Palm Beach, Cathy's Child, The Odd Angry Shot, Breaker Morant, Blood Money, Stir, Winter of Our Dreams, Far East, Give My Regards to Broad Street, Parker (Bones), The Empty Beach, F/X, Tai-Pan, Rebel, The Good Wife, Cocktail, Gorillas in the Mist, Shall We Dance, FX2 (also co-exec. prod.), Sweet Talker (also co-wrote story), Prisoners of the Sun, Blame It on the Bellboy, The Chart of Jimmy Balcksmith, Age of Treason, Dead Heart, On the Border, Dear Claudia.
TELEVISION: *Mini-Series*: Against the Wind, A Town Like Alice, The Thorn Birds. *Movies*: The Shiralee (Aust.), Dead in the Water, Devlin, The Last Hit, Eureka Stockade, Full Body Massage, Twisted Tales, 20,000 Leagues Under the Sea, Dogboys, Journey to the Center of the Earth.

BROWN, CLANCY
Actor. b. Ohio. e. Northwestern Univ.
PICTURES: Bad Boys (debut, 1983), The Adventures of Buckaroo Banzai, The Bride, Highlander, Extreme Prejudice, Shoot to Kill, Season of Fear, Blue Steel, Waiting for the Light, Ambition, Past Midnight, Pet Sematary II, Thunder Alley, The Shawshank Redemption, Dead Man Walking, Donor Unknown, Female Perversions, Starship Troopers, Flubber, Vendetta.
TELEVISION: *Series*: Earth 2, ER, Voltron: The Third Dimension (voice), SpongBob SquarePants (voice). *Movies*: Johnny Ryan, Love Lies & Murder, Cast a Deadly Spell, Desperate Rescue: The Cathy Mahone Story, Bloodlines, Last Light, The Patron Saint of Liars, The Batman/Superman Movie (voice), In the Company of Spies.

BROWN, DAVID
Executive, Producer. b. New York, NY, July 28, 1916. m. writer-editor Helen Gurley Brown. e. Stanford U., A.B., 1936; Columbia U. Sch. of Journalism, M.S., 1937. Apprentice reporter, copy-editing, San Francisco News & Wall Street Journal, 1936; night ed. asst. drama critic, Fairchild Publications, N.Y., 1937-39; edit. dir. Milk Research Council, N.Y., 1939-40; assoc. ed., Street & Smith Publ., N.Y., 1940-43; assoc. ed., exec. ed., then ed.-in-chief, Liberty Mag., N.Y., 1943-49; edit. dir., nat'l education campaign, Amer. Medical Assn., 1949; assoc. ed., mng. ed., Cosmopolitan Mag., N.Y., 1949-52; contrib. stories & articles to many nat'l mags.; man. ed., story dept., 20th-Fox, L.A., Jan., 1952; story ed. & head of scenario dept., 1953-56; appt'd. member of exec. staff of Darryl F. Zanuck, 1956; mem. of exec. staff, 20th-Fox studios, and exec. studio story editor, 1956-60; Prod. 20th-Fox Studios, Sept. 1960-62; Editorial v.p. New American Library of World Literature, Inc., 1963-64; exec. story opers., 20th Century-Fox, 1964-67; vp. dir. of story operations, 1967; exec. v.p., creative optns. and mem. bd. of dir., 1969-71. Exec. v.p., mem. bd. of directors Warner Bros., 1971-72; partner and dir., The Zanuck/Brown Co., 1972-88. Pres., Manhattan Project Ltd., 1988-; mem., bd. of trustees, American Film Institute, 1972-80. Recipient with Richard D. Zanuck of the Mo. Pic. Acad. of Arts & Sciences' Irving G. Thalberg Memorial Award. Books: Brown's Guide to Growing Gray, Delacorte, Let Me Entertain You, Morrow, The Rest of Your Life is the Best of Your Life, Barricade.
PICTURES: Sssssss, The Sting (Academy Award for Best Picture, 1973), The Sugarland Express, The Black Windmill, Willie Dynamite, The Girl from Petrovka, The Eiger Sanction, Jaws, MacArthur, Jaws 2, The Island, Neighbors, The Verdict, Cocoon, Target, Cocoon: The Return, Driving Miss Daisy (exec. prod.), The Player, A Few Good Men, The Cemetery Club, Watch It, Canadian Bacon, The Saint, Kiss the Girls, The Saint, Deep Impact, Angela's Ashes, Along Came a Spider.

BROWN, GEORG STANFORD
Actor, Director. b. Havana, Cuba, June 24, 1943. Acted on stage with the New York Shakespeare Fest. in the 1960s. Gained fame as one of the rookie cops in the 1970s TV series, The Rookies, before turning to TV directing.
THEATER: All's Well That Ends Well, Measure for Measure, Macbeth, Murderous Angels, Hamlet, Detective Story.
PICTURES: The Comedians, Dayton's Devils, Bullitt, Colossus: The Forbin Project, The Man, Black Jack, Stir Crazy, House Party 2.
TELEVISION: *Series*: The Rookies, Linc's. *Movies*: The Young Lawyers, Ritual of Evil, The Rookies (pilot), Dawn: Portrait of a Teenage Runaway, The Night the City Screamed, The Kid With the Broken Halo, In Defense of Kids, The Jesse Owens Story, Murder Without Motive. *Dir. of movies*: Grambling's White Tiger, Kids Like These, Alone in the Neon Jungle, Stuck With Each Other (also exec. prod.), Father & Son: Dangerous Relations. *Dir. of episodes*: Charlie's Angels, Starsky and Hutch, Dynasty, Hill Street Blues, Great American Hero, Cagney & Lacey (Emmy Award, 1986), Miami Vice, Police Squad.

BROWN, HIMAN
Producer, Director, b. New York, NY, July 21, 1910. e. City Coll. of New York, St. Lawrence U. Radio & TV package prod. since 1927 include: Inner Sanctum, Thin Man, Bulldog Drummond, Dick Tracy, Terry and the Pirates, Joyce Jordan MD, Grand Central Station, CBS Radio Mystery Theatre, pres. Production Center, Inc.
PICTURES: The Thin Man, Nero Wolfe, Bulldog, Drummond, That Night, Violators, The Stars Salute, The Price of Silence, The Road Ahead.

BROWN, JIM
Actor. b. St. Simons Island, GA, Feb. 17, 1936. e. Manhasset H.S., Syracuse U. For nine years played football with Cleveland Browns; in 1964 won Hickock Belt as Professional Athlete of the year. Founder, Black Economic Union.
PICTURES: Rio Conchos (debut, 1964), The Dirty Dozen, Ice Station Zebra, The Split, Riot, Dark Of The Sun, 100 Rifles, Kenner, El Condor, The Phynx, ... tick ... tick ... tick ..., The Grasshopper, Slaughter, Black Gunn, I Escaped from Devil's Island, The Slams, Slaughter's Big Rip-Off, Three the Hard Way, Take a Hard Ride, Adios Amigo, Mean Johnny Barrows, Kid Vengeance, Fingers, One Down Two to Go (also exec. prod.), Richard Pryor: Here and Now (exec. prod. only), Pacific Inferno (also exec. prod.), Abducted, The Running Man, I'm Gonna Git You Sucka, L.A. Heat, Crack House, Twisted Justice, The Divine Enforcer, Original Gangstas, Mars Attacks!, He Got Game, Small Soldiers (voice), Any Given Sunday.
TELEVISION: *Movie*: Lady Blue.

BROWNE, ROSCOE LEE
Actor, Director, Writer. b. Woodbury, NJ, May 2, 1925. e. Lincoln U., PA; postgraduate studies in comparative literature and French at Middlebury Coll., VT, Columbia U., N.Y. Taught French and lit. at Lincoln U. until 1952. National sales rep. for Schenley Import Corp. 1946-56; United States' intl. track star and a member of ten A.A.U. teams. Twice American champion in the 1000-yard indoor competition, twice all-American and, in 1951 in Paris, ran the fastest 800 meters in the world for that year. Professional acting debut, 1956, in Julius Caesar at the NY Shakespeare Fest.; published poet and short story writer. Trustee: Millay Colony Arts, NY; Los Angeles Free Public Theatre.
THEATER: *NY*: The Ballad of the Sad Cafe, The Cool World, General Seeger, Tiger Tiger Burning Bright!, The Old Glory, A Hand Is on the Gate (dir., actor), My One and Only. Off-Broadway: The Connection, The Blacks, Aria da Capo, Benito Cereno (Obie Award), Joe Turner's Come and Gone (L.A., S.F., Pittsburgh), Two Trains Running.
PICTURES: The Connection (debut, 1961), Black Like Me, The Comedians, Uptight, Topaz, The Liberation of L. B. Jones, Cisco Pike, The Cowboys, The World's Greatest Athlete, Superfly T.N.T., The Ra Expeditions (narrator), Uptown Saturday Night, Logan's Run, Twilight's Last Gleaming, Nothing Personal, Legal Eagles, Jumpin' Jack Flash, Oliver & Company (voice), Moon 44, The Mambo Kings, Naked in New York, Brother Minister: The Assassination of Malcolm X (narrator), Babe (voice), The Pompatus of Love, Last Summer in the Hamptons, Dear God, Babe: Pig in the City (voice), Morgan's Ferry.
TELEVISION: *Series*: McCoy, Miss Winslow and Son, Soap, Falcon Crest. *Movies*: The Big Ripoff, Dr. Scorpion, Lady in a Corner, Columbo: Rest in Peace Mrs. Columbo, Meeting of Minds (Peabody Award), A Connecticut Yankee in King Arthur's Court (Peabody Award), Hard Time. *Guest*: All in the Family, Maude, Barney Miller, Soap, Head of the Class, The Cosby Show (Emmy Award, 1986), Falcon Crest, ER. *Mini-Series*: King, Space.

BROWNING, KIRK
Director. b. New York, NY, March 28, 1921. e. Brooks School, Andover, MA, Avon Old Farms, Avon, CT., and Cornell U. 1940. Reporter for News-Tribune in Waco, TX; with American Field Service, 1942-45; adv. copywriter for Franklin Spier, 1945-48; became floor mgr. NBC-TV 1949; app't asst. dir. NBC-TV Opera Theatre in 1951 directing NBC Opera Theatre, TV Recital Hall, and Toscanini Simulcasts.
TELEVISION: Trial of Mary Lincoln, Jascha Heifetz Special, Harry and Lena, NBC Opera Theatre, Producers Showcase, Evening with Toscanini, Bell Telephone, The Flood, Beauty and the Beast, Lizzie Borden, World of Carl Sandburg, La Gioconda (Emmy Award, 1980), Big Blonde, Working, Ian McKellan Acting Shakespeare, Fifth of July, Alice in Wonderland, You Can't Take it with You, The House of Blue Leaves, O Pioneers!, Live From the Met—Centennial.

BROWNLOW, KEVIN
Film Historian, Writer, Director, Film Editor. b. Crowborough, England, June 2, 1938. e. University College Sch. Asst. ed./editor, World Wide Pictures, London, 1955-61; film editor, Samaritan Films, 1961-65; film editor, Woodfall Films, 1965-68. Dir., Thames Television 1975-90. Dir., Photoplay Productions 1990-present.
PICTURES: It Happened Here (dir. with Andrew Mollo) 1964, Charge of the Light Brigade (editor), Winstanley (with Andrew Mollo), Napoleon (restoration of 1927 film, re-released 1980).
TELEVISION: Charm of Dynamite (dir., ed.), All with David Gill: Hollywood (dir., writer), Unknown Chaplin (dir., prod.; Emmy Award), Buster Keaton: A Hard Act to Follow (prod.; 2 Emmy Awards), Harold Lloyd—The Third Genius, D.W. Griffith: Father of Film, Cinema Europe–The Other Hollywood.
AUTHOR: How It Happened Here (1968), The Parade's Gone By... (1968), Adventures with D.W. Griffith (editor, 1973), The War the West and the Wilderness (1979), Hollywood: The Pioneers (1980), Napoleon: Abel Gance's Classic Film (1983), Behind the Mask of Innocence (1990), David Lean–A Biography (1996).

BRUBAKER, JAMES D.
Producer. b. Hollywood, CA, March 30, 1937. e. Eagle Rock H.S. Transportation coordinator for 15 years before becoming unit prod. mgr., 1978-84. Then assoc. prod., exec. prod. & prod. Prod. tv movie, Runnng Mates.
PICTURES: *Assoc. Prod.*: True Confessions (also prod. mgr.), Rocky III (also prod. mgr.), Rhinestone (also prod. mgr.). *Unit Prod. Mgr.*: New York New York, Comes a Horseman, Uncle Joe Shannon, Rocky II, Raging Bull, Staying Alive, K-9, Problem Child, Mr. Baseball. *Exec. Prod.*: The Right Stuff, Beer, Rocky IV, Cobra, Over the Top, Problem Child (also prod. mgr.), Brain Donors (also prod. mgr.), A Walk in the Clouds, Liar Liar, The Nutty Professor, Life, The Nutty Professor II.
TELEVISION: Gia

BRUCKHEIMER, BONNIE
Producer. b. Brooklyn, NY. Started in advertising and public relations eventually working for treasurer of Columbia Pictures. Later worked as asst. to Arthur Penn and Ross Hunter. Became partner with Bette Midler in All Girl Productions, 1985.
PICTURES: Big Business (assoc. prod.), Beaches, Stella, For the Boys, Hocus Pocus, Man of the House, That Old Feeling.
TELEVISION: *Movie*: Gypsy (exec. prod.).

BRUCKHEIMER, JERRY
Producer. b. Detroit, MI. e. U. of Arizona. Was art dir./prod. of TV commercials before becoming prod. of films. 1983, formed Don Simpson/Jerry Bruckheimer Prods. with the late Don Simpson and entered into deal with Paramount Pictures to produce; company moved over to Walt Disney in early 1990's. Formed Jerry Bruckheimer Films in 1997.
PICTURES: *Assoc. Prod.*: The Culpepper Cattle Company, Rafferty and the Gold Dust Twins. *Producer*: Farewell My Lovely, March or Die, Defiance, American Gigolo, Thief, Cat People (exec. prod.), Young Doctors in Love, Flashdance, Thief of Hearts, Beverly Hills Cop, Top Gun, Beverly Hills Cop II, Days of Thunder, The Ref, Bad Boys, Crimson Tide, Dangerous Minds, The Rock, Con Air, Enemy of the State, Armageddon, The Rock Star, Gone in 60 Seconds, Coyote Ugly, Bad Boys 2, National Treasure, Down And Under, Pearl Harbor.
TELEVISION: *Exec Prod*: Dangerous Minds (series), Soldier of Fortune Inc. (series), Max Q, Swing Vote.

BRYAN, DORA
Actress. r.n. Dora Broadbent. b. Southport, Lancashire, England, Feb. 7, 1924. e. Council Sch. Stage debut 1935.
PICTURES: Once Upon a Dream, (debut, 1947), The Fallen Idol, No Room at the Inn, Blue Lamp, Cure for Love, Now Barabas, The Ringer, Women of Twilight, The Quiet Woman, The Intruder, You Know What Sailors Are, Mad About Men, See How They Run, Cockleshell Heroes, Child in the House, Green Man, Carry on Sergeant, Operation Bullshine, Desert Mice, The Night We Got the Bird, A Taste of Honey, Two a Penny, Apartment Zero, Up to Front, Screamtime, Apartment Zero.
TELEVISION: Virtual Murder, Casualty, Presenting Frank Subbs, Heartbeat, Both Ends Meet, Mothers Ruin.

BUCHHOLZ, HORST
Actor. r.n. Henry Bookholt. b. Berlin, Germany, Dec. 4, 1933. e. high school. In radio and stage plays. Started in films dubbing foreign movies. Work with Berlin's Schiller Theatre result in film debut in French film.
PICTURES: Marianne (debut, 1955), Emil and the Detectives, Himmel Ohne Sterne (Sky Without Stars), Regine, Teenage Wolfpack, The King in Shadow, The Confessions of Felix Krull, The Legend of Robinson Crusoe, Mompti, Endstation Liebe, Nasser Asphalt, Resurrection, Das Totenschiff, Tiger Bay (English-language debut, 1959), The Magnificent Seven, Fanny, One Two Three, Nine Hours to Rama, The Empty Canvas, Andorra, Marco the Magnificent, That Man in Istanbul, Johnny Banco, Cervantes (The Young Rebel), L'Astragale, How When and With Whom, La Sauveur, La Columba non deve Volare, The Great Waltz, The Catamount Killing, Women in Hospital, The Amazing Captain Nemo, From Hell to Victory, Avalanche Express, Aphrodite, Sahara, Fear of Falling, Code Name: Emerald, And the Violins Stopped Playing, Escape From Paradise, Aces: Iron Eagle III, Far Away So Close, Ptak Ohnivak, Life is Beautiful, Mulan (voice).
TELEVISION: *Movies*: The Savage Bees, Raid on Entebbe, Return to Fantasy Island, Berlin Tunnel 21, Family Affairs, The Lion of Granada, Come Back to Kampen, Cave of the Golden Rose IV, Voyage of Terror. *Mini-Series*: The French Atlantic Affair, Clan der Anna Voss.

BUCKLEY, BETTY
Actress. b. Fort Worth, TX, July 3, 1947. e. Texas Christian U., BA. Studied acting with Stella Adler. NY Stage debut: 1776 (1969); London debut: Promises Promises. Appeared in interactive short film Race for Your Life.

THEATER: Johnny Pott, What's a Nice Country Like You Doing in a State Like This?, Pippin, I'm Getting My Act Together and Taking It on the Road, Cats (Tony Award, 1983), Juno's Swans, The Mystery of Edwin Drood, Song and Dance, Carrie, The Fourth Wall, The Perfectionist, Sunset Boulevard (London/B'way; Olivier Award nom.).
PICTURES: Carrie (debut, 1976), Tender Mercies, Wild Thing, Frantic, Another Woman, Rain Without Thunder, Wyatt Earp, Simply Irresistible.
TELEVISION: *Series*: Eight is Enough. *Movies*: The Ordeal of Bill Carney, Roses Are for the Rich, The Three Wishes of Billy Grier, Babycakes, Bonnie & Clyde: The True Story (Emmy nom.), Betrayal of Trust, Critical Choices. *Specials*: Bobby and Sarah, Salute to Lady Liberty, Taking a Stand (Afterschool Special; Emmy nom.), Stephen Sondheim Carnegie Hall Gala. *Mini-Series*: Evergreen. *Guest*: L.A. Law, Tribeca.

BUCKLEY, DONALD
Executive. b. New York, NY, June 28, 1955. e. C.W. Post Coll, NY, Sch. of Visual Arts. Ad. mgr., United Artists Theatres, 1975-78. Acct. exec., Grey Advertising, 1978-80. Joined Warner Bros. in 1980 as NY adv. mgr.; 1986; promoted to east. dir. of adv./promo. for WB; 1988, named eastern dir. of adv. and publicity; 1991, promoted to v.p., East Coast Adv. & Publicity; 1996, promoted to v.p., Adv. & Publicity, v.p., WB On-Line; 1997, promoted to senior v.p., Theatrical Marketing & New Media.

BUFF, CONRAD
Editor.
PICTURES: The Empires Strikes Back (effects ed.), Raiders of the Lost Ark (effects ed.), Poltergeist (effects ed.), E.T.: The Extra-Terrestrial (effects ed. superv.), Return of the Jedi (asst. ed.), Jagged Edge, Solarbabies, Spaceballs, Short Circuit 2, The Abyss, Side Out, Terminator 2: Judgment Day, Jennifer Eight, The Getaway, True Lies, Species, Titanic (Acad. Award, 1997), Dante's Peak, Switchback, Arlington Road, Mystery Men.

BUJOLD, GENEVIEVE
Actress. b. Montreal, Canada, July 1, 1942. e. Montreal Conservatory of Drama. Worked in a Montreal cinema as an usher; American TV debut: St. Joan.
THEATER: The Barber of Seville, A Midsummer Night's Dream, A House...A Day.
PICTURES: La Guerre est Finie, La Fleur de L'Age, Entre La Mer et L'eau Douce, King of Hearts, The Thief of Paris, Isabel, Anne of the Thousand Days, Act of the Heart, The Trojan Women, The Journey, Kamouraska, Earthquake, Swashbuckler, Obsession, Alex and the Gypsy, Another Man Another Chance, Coma, Murder by Decree, Final Assignment, The Last Flight of Noah's Ark, Monsignor, Tightrope, Choose Me, Trouble in Mind, The Moderns, Dead Ringers, False Identity, Secret Places of the Heart, A Paper Wedding, An Ambush of Ghosts, Mon Amie Max, Dead Innocent, The Adventures of Pinocchio, The House of Yes, You Can Thank Me Later, Last Night.
TELEVISION: *Specials*: Saint Joan, Antony and Cleopatra. *Movies*: Mistress of Paradise, Red Earth White Earth.

BULLOCK, SANDRA
Actress. b. Arlington, VA, 1964. e. East Carolina Univ., drama major. Raised in Germany; studied piano in Europe. First prof. acting job in NY in Off-B'way prod. No Time Flat.
PICTURES: Who Shot Patakango?, Love Potion No. 9, When the Party's Over, The Vanishing, The Thing Called Love, Demolition Man. Speed, Me and the Mob, While You Were Sleeping, The Net, Two If by Sea, A Time to Kill, In Love and War, Speed 2 Cruise Control, The Prince of Egypt (voice), Making Sandwiches (also dir., s.p.), Hope Floats, Practical Magic, Forces of Nature, 28 Days, Welcome to Hollywood, Gun Shy, Famous, Miss Congeniality, Exactly 3:30.
TELEVISION: *Series*: Working Girl. *Movies:* The Preppie Murder, Bionic Showdown: The Six Million Dollar Man and the Bionic Woman, Jackie Collins' Lucky/Chances.

BURGHOFF, GARY
Actor. b. Bristol, CT, May 24, 1943. Winner of Student Hallmark Award while in high school, 1961. Also wildlife artist, with work exhibited in many U.S. galleries.
THEATER: *NY*: You're a Good Man Charlie Brown, The Nerd. *Also*: Finian's Rainbow, Bells Are Ringing, Sound of Music, The Boy Friend, Romanoff and Juliet, Whose Life Is It Anyway?
PICTURES: M*A*S*H*, B.S. I Love You, Small Kill (also co-dir.), Behind the Waterfall.
TELEVISION: *Series*: The Don Knotts Show, M*A*S*H (Emmy Award, 1977). *Guest*: Good Guys, Name of the Game, Love American Style, Fernwood 2-Night, Sweepstakes, Love Boat, Fantasy Island. *Movies*: The Man in the Santa Claus Suit, Casino. *Special*: Twigs.

BURKE, ALFRED
Actor. b. London, England, February 28, 1918.
PICTURES: Touch and Go, The Man Upstairs, The Angry Silence, Moment of Danger, The Man Inside, No Time To Die, Children of the Damned, The Nanny, One Day in the Life of Ivan Denisovitch, Law and Disorder, Yangtse Incident, Interpol, Bitter Victory, The Nanny, Guns in the Heather, One Day in the Life of Ivan Denisovich.
TELEVISION: The Crucible, Mock Auction, Parole, No Gun, No Guilt, The Big Knife, Parnell, The Strong Are Lonely, Home of the Brave, The Birthday Party, The Watching Eye, Public Eye (series), The Brontes of Haworth, Enemy at the Door (series), The House on Garibaldi Street, The Borgias, The Glory Boys, Kim, Sophia and Constance (series).

BURKE, DELTA
Actress. b. Orlando, FL, July 30, 1956. e. LAMDA. m. actor Gerald McRaney. Competed in Miss America contest as Miss Florida, prior to studying acting in England.
TELEVISION: *Series*: The Chisholms, Filthy Rich, 1st & Ten, Designing Women, Delta (also co-exec. prod.), Women of the House (also exec. prod.), Any Day Now. *Movies*: Charleston, A Last Cry for Help, Mickey Spillane's Mike Hammer: Murder Me Murder You, A Bunny's Tale, Where the Hell's That Gold?!!? Love and Curses... And All That Jazz (also co-exec. prod.), Day-O, Simon & Simon: In Trouble Again, A Promise to Carolyn, Melanie Darron (also prod.).
PICTURES: Maternal Instincts (also exec. prod.).

BURNETT, CAROL
Actress, Singer, Producer, Director. b. San Antonio, TX, April 26, 1933. e. Hollywood H.S., UCLA. Daughter is actress Carrie Hamilton. Introduced comedy song "I Made a Fool of Myself Over John Foster Dulles," 1957; regular performer Garry Moore Show, 1959-62. Recipient outstanding commedienne award Am. Guild Variety Artists, 5 times; TV Guide award for outstanding female performer 1961, 62, 63; Peabody Award, 1963; 5 Golden Globe awards for outstanding comedienne of year; Woman of Year award Acad. TV Arts and Scis. Voted one of the world's 20 most admired women in 1977 Gallup Poll. First Annual National Television Critics Award for Outstanding Performance, 1977. Best Actress Award at San Sebastian Film Fest. for film A Wedding, 1978. Inducted Acad. of Television Arts and Sciences Hall of Fame, 1985. *Author:* Once Upon a Time (1986).
THEATER: *NY*: Once Upon a Mattress (debut, 1959; Theatre World Award), Fade Out-Fade In, Moon Over Buffalo. *Regional:* Calamity Jane, Plaza Suite, I Do I Do, Same Time Next Year.
PICTURES: Who's Been Sleeping in My Bed? (debut, 1963), Pete 'n' Tillie, The Front Page, A Wedding, H.E.A.L.T.H., The Four Seasons, Chu Chu and the Philly Flash, Annie, Noises Off, Get Bruce.
TELEVISION: *Movies*: The Grass Is Always Greener Over the Septic Tank, Friendly Fire, The Tenth Month, Life of the Party: The Story of Beatrice, Between Friends, Hostage, Seasons of the Heart, Grace, Happy Birthday Elizabeth. *Series*: Stanley, Pantomime Quiz, The Garry Moore Show (Emmy Award, 1962), The Entertainers, The Carol Burnett Show (1967-78; in syndication as Carol Burnett & Friends), Carol Burnett & Company, Carol & Company, The Carol Burnett Show (1991). *Mini-Series*: Fresno. *Specials*: Julie & Carol at Carnegie Hall, Carol and Company (Emmy Award for previous 2 specials, 1963), An Evening with Carol Burnett, Calamity Jane, Once Upon a Mattress, Carol + 2, Julie & Carol at Lincoln Center, 6 Rms Riv Vu, Twigs, Sills & Burnett at the Met, Dolly & Carol in Nashville, All-Star Party for Carol Burnett, Burnett Discovers Domingo, The Laundromat, Carol Carl Whoopi & Robin, Julie & Carol—Together Again, The Carol Burnett Show: A Reunion (also co-exec. prod.), Men Movies & Carol. *Guest*: Twilight Zone, The Jack Benny Program, Get Smart, The Lucy Show, Fame, Magnum P.I., Mad About You (Emmy Award, 1997).

BURNETT, CHARLES
Director, Writer, Cinematographer. b. Vicksburg, MI, 1944. e. LA Community Col., UCLA.
PICTURES: *Director*: Killer of Sheep (also prod., s.p., photog., edit.), My Brother's Wedding (also prod., s.p., photog.), To Sleep With Anger (also s.p.), The Glass Shield (also s.p.), When it Rains, Dr Endesha Ida Mae Holland. *Cinematographer:* Bless Their Little Hearts (also s.p.), Guest of Hotel Astoria.
TELEVISION: Nightjohn, The Wedding.

BURNS, EDWARD J.
Actor, Director, Producer. b. Valley Stream, NY, Jan. 28, 1968.
PICTURES: *Actor//dir./s.p.*: The Brothers McMullen, She's the One (also prod.), No Looking Back, Saving Private Ryan (actor only), Sidewalks of New York, Fifteen Minutes (actor).

BURNS, KEN
Producer, Director, Cinematographer, Writer. b. July 29, 1953. e. Hampshire Col. *Co-author:* Shakers: Hands to Work Hearts to God: The History and Visions of the United Society of Believers in Christ's Second Appearance from 1774 to Present, The Civil War: An Illustrated History, Baseball: An Illustrated History. Appeared in film Gettysburg.
TELEVISION: Prod. and dir. of the following documentaries: Brooklyn Bridge (also photog., edit.; Acad. Award nom.), The Shakers: Hands to Work Hearts to God (also co-writer), The Statue of Liberty (also photog.; Acad. Award nom.), Huey Long (also co-writer), Thomas Hart Benton (also photog.), The Congress, The Civil War (also photog., co-writer; numerous awards incl. Peabody and Emmy), Lindbergh (co-prod. only), Empire of the Air: The Men Who Made Radio (also photog., music dir.), Baseball (co- writer, prod., dir.), Lewis & Clark: The Journey of the Corps of Discovery (also photog.), Frank Lloyd Wright (also photog.), The West (exec. prod only), Thomas Jefferson (prod. only).

BURNS, RALPH
Musical Conductor, Composer. b. Newton, MA, June 29, 1922.
PICTURES: Lenny, Cabaret (Academy Award, 1972), Lucky Lady, New York New York, Movie Movie, All That Jazz (Academy Award, 1979), Urban Cowboy, Annie, My Favorite Year, Jinxed, Kiss Me Goodbye, Star 80, National Lampoon's Vacation, Perfect, Bert Rigby You're a Fool.
TELEVISION: *Specials*: Baryshnikov on Broadway, Liza and Goldie Special. *Movies*: Ernie Kovacs—Between the Laughter, After the Promise, Sweet Bird of Youth.

BURRILL, TIMOTHY
Producer, Executive. b. North Wales, June 8, 1931. e. Eton Coll., Sorbonne U., Paris. Grenadier Guards 2 yrs, then London Shipping Co. Ent. m.p. ind. as resident prod. mgr. Samaritan Films working on shorts, commercials, documentaries, 1954. Ass't. dir.: The Criminal, The Valiant Years (TV series), On The Fiddle, Reach for Glory, War Lover, Prod. mgr: The Cracksman, Night Must Fall, Lord Jim, Yellow Rolls Royce, The Heroes of Telemark, Resident prod. with World Film Services. 1970 prod. two films on pop music for Anglo-EMI. 1972 first prod. administrator National Film School in U.K. 1974 Post prod. administrator The Three Musketeers. Prod. TV Special The Canterville Ghost; assoc. prod, That Lucky Touch; UK Administrator, The Prince and the Pauper; North American Prod. controller, Superman; 1974-1983 council member of BAFTA; mng. dir., Allied Stars (Breaking Glass, Chariots of Fire); 1979-80 V. chmn. Film BAFTA; 1980-83 chmn. BAFTA; 1981-92, Gov. National Film School, executive BFTPA mem. Cinematograph Films Council. 1982-88 Gov Royal National Theatre; 1987-93, chmn., Film Asset Developments, Formed Burrill Prods, 1979-; chmn. First Film Foundation. Exec. member PACT, 1991. Vice-chmn. (film) PACT, 1993.
PICTURES: Privilege, Oedipus the King, A Severed Head, Three Sisters, Macbeth (assoc. prod.), Alpha Beta, Tess (co-prod.), Pirates of Penzance (co-prod.), Supergirl, The Fourth Protocol, To Kill a Priest (co-prod.), Return of the Musketeers (tv in U.S.), Valmont, The Rainbow Thief, The Lover, Bitter Moon, Sweet Killing.

BURROWS, JAMES
Director, Producer. b. Los Angeles, CA, Dec. 30, 1940. e. Oberlin, B.A.; Yale, M.F.A. Son of late Abe Burrows, composer, writer, dir. Directed off-B'way.
PICTURE: Partners.
TELEVISION: *Series: Dir.*: Mary Tyler Moore, Bob Newhart, Laverne and Shirley, Rhoda, Phyllis, Tony Randall Show, Betty White Show, Fay, Taxi (2 Emmy Awards: 1980, 1981), Lou Grant, Cheers (also prod.; 4 Emmy Awards as prod.: 1983, 1984, 1989, 1991; 2 Emmy Awards as dir.: 1983, 1991), Dear John, Night Court, All is Forgiven (also exec. prod.), The Fanelli Boys, Frasier (Emmy Award, 1994), Friends, NewsRadio, Men Behaving Badly, Chicago Sons, 3rd Rock from the Sun, Pearl, Fired Up (pilot), George & Leo, Dharma & Greg, Veronica's Closet, Union Square, Will & Grace (pilot) Conrad Bloom, Jesse, The Secret Lives of Men. *Movie*: More Than Friends.

BURROWS, ROBERTA
Executive. e. Brandeis U; Academia, Florence, Italy. Career includes freelance writing for natl. magazines: GQ, Italian Bazaar, US, Family Circle. Dir. of pub. for Howard Stein Enterprises and with Rogers & Cowan and Billings Associates. Joined Warner Bros. as sr. publicist 1979; named dir. east coast publicity, 1986. Resigned 1989 to dev. novelty products. Proj. co-ordinator at Orion Pictures in NY for The Silence of the Lambs, Little Man Tate, Married to It, Bill & Ted's Bogus Journey. Columnist, Max publication.

BURSTYN, ELLEN
Actress. r.n. Edna Rae Gilhooley. b. Detroit, MI, Dec. 7, 1932. Majored in art; was fashion model in Texas at 18. Moved to Montreal as dancer; then N.Y. to do TV commercials (under the name of Ellen McRae), appearing for a year on the Jackie Gleason show (1956-57). In 1957 turned to dramatics and won lead in B'way show, Fair Game. Then went to Hollywood to do TV and films. Returned to N.Y. to study acting with Lee Strasberg; worked in TV serial, The Doctors. Co-artistic dir. of Actor's Studio. 1982-88. Pres. Actors Equity Assn. 1982-85. On 2 panels of Natl. Endowment of the Arts and Theatre Advisory Council (NY).
THEATER: *NY*: Same Time Next Year (Tony Award, 1975), 84 Charing Cross Road, Shirley Valentine, Shimada. L.A.: Love Letters. Regional: The Trip to Bountiful.
PICTURES: *As Ellen McRae:* For Those Who Think Young (debut, 1964), Goodbye Charlie, Pit Stop. *As Ellen Burstyn:* Tropic of Cancer, Alex in Wonderland, The Last Picture Show, The King of Marvin Gardens, The Exorcist, Harry and Tonto, Alice Doesn't Live Here Anymore (Academy Award, 1974), Providence, A Dream of Passion, Same Time Next Year, Resurrection, Silence of the North, The Ambassador, In Our Hands (doc.), Twice in a Lifetime, Hanna's War, Dying Young, The Color of Evening, The Cemetery Club, When a Man Loves a Woman, Roommates, The Baby-sitters Club, How to Make an American Quilt, The Spitfire Grill, Liar, You Can Thank Me Later, Playing by Heart, The Yards.
TELEVISION: *Movies*: Thursday's Game, The People Vs. Jean Harris, Surviving, Act of Vengeance, Into Thin Air, Something in Common, Pack of Lies, When You Remember Me, Mrs. Lambert Remembers Love, Taking Back My Life: The Nancy Ziegenmeyer Story, Grand Isle, Shattered Trust: The Shari Karney Story, Getting Out, Getting Gotti, Trick of the Eye, My Brother's Keeper, Follow the River, A Deadly Vision, Flash, The Patron Saint of Liars, A Will of Their Own, Night Ride Home. *Special*: Dear America: Letters Home From Vietnam (reader). *Series*: The Doctors, The Ellen Burstyn Show. *Guest*: Cheyenne, Dr. Kildare, 77 Sunset Strip, Perry Mason, The Iron Horse.

BURTON, KATE
Actress. b. Geneva, Switzerland, Sept. 10, 1957. e. Brown Univ. (B.A.), Yale Drama Sch. Daughter of late Richard Burton. m. stage manager Michael Ritchie. Worked at Yale Repertory Theatre, Hartford, Stage Co., the Hartman, Huntington Theatre, Williamstown, Berkshire Theatre festivals, The O'Neil Playwright's Conference, Pray Street Theatre.
THEATER: Present Laughter (debut, 1982; Theatre World Award), Alice in Wonderland, Winners, The Accrington Pals, Doonesbury, The Playboy of the Western World, Wild Honey, Measure For Measure, Some Americans Abroad (Drama Desk nom.), Jake's Women, London Suite, Company.
PICTURES: Big Trouble in Little China (debut, 1986), Life With Mikey, August, First Wives Club, Looking for Richard, The Ice Storm.
TELEVISION: *Mini-Series*: Ellis Island, Evergreen. *Movies*: Alice in Wonderland, Uncle Tom's Cabin, Love Matters, Mistrial, Notes For My Daughter, Ellen Foster. *Series*: Home Fires, Monty.

BURTON, LEVAR
Actor. b. Landstuhl, W. Germany, Feb. 16, 1957. e. U. of Southern California. Signed to play role of Kunta Kinte in TV mini-series, Roots, while still in school. Has hosted Public TV children's shows, Rebop, and Reading Rainbow.
PICTURES: Looking for Mr. Goodbar, The Hunter, The Supernaturals, Star Trek: Generations, Star Trek: First Contact, Trekkies, Star Trek: Insurrection.
TELEVISION: *Mini-Series*: Roots. *Special*: Almos' a Man. *Movies*: Billy: Portrait of a Street Kid, Battered, One in a Million: The Ron Leflore Story, Dummy, Guyana Tragedy: The Story of Jim Jones, The Acorn People, Grambling's White Tiger, Emergency Room, The Jesse Owens Story, A Special Friendship, Roots: The Gift, Firestorm: 72 Hours in Oakland, Parallel Lives. *Series*: Star Trek: The Next Generation, Reading Rainbow (PBS; host, co-exec. prod.). Guest: Voyager.

BURTON, STEVE
Actor. b. Indianapolis, IN, June 28, 1970.
PICTURES: Red Sun Rising, CyberTracker CyberTracker 2.
TELEVISION: *Series*: Out of This World, Days of Our Lives, General Hospital (Emmy Award, 1998).

BURTON, TIM
Director, Producer. b. Burbank, CA, Aug. 25, 1958. Cartoonist since grade school in suburban Burbank. Won Disney fellowship to study animation at California Institute of the Arts. At 20 went to Burbank to work as apprentice animator on Disney lot, working on such features as The Fox and the Hound, The Black Cauldron. Made Vincent, 6-minute stop-motion animation short on his own which was released commercially in 1982 and won several film fest. awards. Also made Frankenweenie, 29 minute live-action film. Appeared in film Singles. Wrote and illustrated children's book based on The Nightmare Before Christmas.
PICTURES: *Director*: Pee-wee's Big Adventure, Beetlejuice, Batman, Edward Scissorhands (also co-story, prod.), Batman Returns (also co-prod.), The Nightmare Before Christmas (also story, prod. design, co-prod.), Ed Wood (also co-prod.), Mars Attacks! (also prod, s.p..), Sleepy Hollow, Planet of the Apes Co-Prod.:Cabin Boy, James and the Giant Peach, Batman Forever, The Corpse Bride.
TELEVISION: *Episode Director*: Aladdin (Faerie Tale Theatre), Alfred Hitchcock Presents, Amazing Stories (Family Dog). *Exec. Prod.:* Beetlejuice, Family Dog, Lost in Oz (also creator).

BURWELL, LOIS
Make-Up.
PICTURES: Gregory's Girl, The Draughtsman's Contract, Legend, No Surrender, Highlander, Mona Lisa, The Princess Bride, The Lonely Passion of Judith Hearne, Without A Clue, Dirty Rotten Scoundrels, Shirley Valentine, Air America, Hamlet, Blue Ice, The Muppet Christmas Carol, Widows' Peak, Braveheart, Mission: Impossible, The Fifth Element, The Rainmaker, Saving Private Ryan, Hilary and Jackie, The Green Mile, Magnolia, Almost Famous, Captaon Corelli's Mandolin.
TELEVISION: *Movies:* Jack the Ripper, Charles and Diana: Unhappily Ever After, Jekyll & Hyde. *Mini-Series:* Master of the Game.

BUSCEMI, STEVE
Actor. b. Brooklyn, NY, 1957. Started as standup comedian in New York City, also wrote and acted in numerous one-act plays in collaboration with Mark Boone Jr. Acted in many plays by John Jesurun and worked briefly with the Wooster Group; worked as fireman. Studied acting at Lee Strasberg Inst. in NY.

PICTURES: The Way It Is/Eurydice in the Avenue, No Picnic, Parting Glances, Sleepwalk, Heart, Kiss Daddy Good Night, Call Me, Force of Circumstance, Vibes, Heart of Midnight, Bloodhounds of Broadway, Borders, New York Stories (Life Lessons), Slaves of New York, Mystery Train, Tales from the Dark Side, Miller's Crossing, King of New York, Zandalee, Barton Fink, Billy Bathgate, Crisscross, In the Soup, Reservoir Dogs, Trusting Beatrice, Rising Sun, Twenty Bucks, Ed and His Dead Mother, The Hudsucker Proxy, Floundering, Airheads, Me and the Mob, Pulp Fiction, Billy Madison, Desperado, Somebody to Love, The Search for One-Eye Jimmy, Living in Oblivion, Things to Do in Denver When You're Dead, Pistolero, Fargo, Kansas City, Trees Lounge (also dir., s.p.), John Carpenter's Escape From L.A., Con Air, The Impostors, The Big Lebowski, The Wedding Singer, Armageddon, Louis & Frank, Big Daddy, 28 Days, Final Fantasy (voice), Ghost World, Monsters,Inc. (voice), The Grey Zone, Double Whammy, The Animal Factory (also dir.).
TELEVISION: *Mini-Series*: Lonesome Dove. *Movie*: The Last Outlaw. *Guest*: Miami Vice, The Equalizer, L.A. Law, Mad About You, Homicide: Life on the Streets, The Drew Carey Show.

BUSCH, H. DONALD
Exhibitor. b. Philadelphia, PA, Sept. 21, 1935. e. U. of Pennsylvania, physics, math, 1956; law school, 1959. Practiced law, anti-trust & entertainment, 1960-87. 1984, pres., Budco Theatres, Inc. 1975-87. Pres., Busch, Grafman & Von Dreusche, P.C. 1987. Pres. & CEO, AMC Philadelphia, Inc., 1986-96. NATO chmn.,1990-91; chmn. emeritus, 1992. Showeast, gen. chmn., 1990-91. Will Rogers Memorial Fund, dir. Pres. of NATO of Pennsylvania, 1988. Motion Picture Pioneers, Inc., dir., 1995

BUSEY, GARY
Actor, Musician. b. Goose Creek, TX, June 29, 1944. e. Coffeyville Jr. Coll. A.B., 1963; attended Kansas State Coll, Okla. State U. Played drums with the Rubber Band 1963-70. Also drummer with Leon Russell, Willie Nelson (as Teddy Jack Eddy).
PICTURES: Angels Hard as They Come (debut, 1971), Didn't You Hear?, Dirty Little Billy, The Magnificent Seven Ride, The Last American Hero, Lolly Madonna XXX, Hex, Thunderbolt and Lightfoot, The Gumball Rally, A Star Is Born, Straight Time, Big Wednesday, The Buddy Holly Story (Natl. Society of Film Critics Award; Acad. Award nom., 1978), Foolin' Around, Carny, Barbarosa, D.C. Cab, The Bear, Insignificance, Stephen King's Silver Bullet, Let's Get Harry, Eye of the Tiger, Lethal Weapon, Bulletproof, Act of Piracy, Predator 2, My Heroes Have Always Been Cowboys, Hider in the House, Point Break, The Player, Under Siege, South Beach, The Firm, Rookie of the Year. Surviving the Game, Chasers, Breaking Point, Drop Zone, Man With a Gun, Black Sheep, Carried Away, 18 Suspicious Minds, Rough Draft, The Rage, Plato's Run, Livers Ain't Cheap, Lost Highway, Lethal Tender, Steel Sharks, Deadly Current, Warriors, Fear and Loathing in Las Vegas, Detour, Soldier, Jacob Two Two Meets the Hooded Fang, Apocalypse III: Tribulation, G-Men from Hell, Glory Glory, Down and Dirty, A Crack in the Floor, Joe Dirt.
TELEVISION: *Series*: The Texas Wheelers, Bonanza. *Guest*: High Chaparral (debut, 1970), Gunsmoke, Saturday Night Live, The Hitchhiker (ACE Award). *Movies*: Bloodsport, The Execution of Private Slovik, The Law, Wild Texas Wind, Chrome Soldiers, Universal Soldier II: Brothers in Arms, Rough Riders, The Girl Next Door. *Mini-Series*: A Dangerous Life, The Neon Empire.

BUSFIELD, TIMOTHY
Actor. b. Lansing, MI, June 12, 1957. e. East Tennessee State U; Actor's Theatre of Louisville (as apprentice and resident). Founded Fantasy Theatre in Sacramento, 1986, a professional acting co., which performs in Northern CA schools, providing workshops on playwriting for children and sponsors annual Young Playwrights contest.
THEATER: Richard II, Young Playwrights Festival (Circle Rep.), A Tale Told, Getting Out (European tour), Green Mountain Guilds Children Theatre, Mass Appeal, The Tempest, A Few Good Men (B'way). Founded & co-prod. The "B" Theatre, 1992, prods. Mass Appeal, Hidden in This Picture.
PICTURES: Stripes, Revenge of the Nerds, Revenge of the Nerds II, Field of Dreams, Sneakers, The Skateboard Kid, Striking Distance, Little Big League, Quiz Show, First Kid, The Souler Opposite, Erasable You, Wanted, Time at the Top.
TELEVISION: *Series*: Reggie, Trapper John M.D., thirtysomething (Emmy Award, 1991; also dir. 3 episodes), Byrds of Paradise, Champs. *Guest*: Family Ties, Matlock, Paper Chase, Love American Style, After M.A.S.H, Hotel. *Movies*: Strays, Calendar Girl-Cop-Killer?: The Bambi Bembenek Story, Murder Between Friends, In the Shadow of Evil, In the Line of Duty: Kidnapped, When Secrets Kill, Buffalo Soldiers.

BUTTONS, RED
Actor. r.n. Aaron Chwatt. b. New York, NY, Feb. 5, 1919. Attended Evander Child H.S. in the Bronx. Singer at the age of 13; comic, Minsky's. Served in U.S. Army, during WWII; in Army stage prod. and film version of Winged Victory. Received Golden Globe Award noms. for Harlow and They Shoot Horses Don't They?; Best Comedian Award for The Red Buttons Show. Performed in most major Variety nightclubs shows.
PICTURES: Winged Victory (1944, debut), 13 Rue Madeleine, Footlight Varieties of 1951, Sayonara (Acad. Award for Best Supporting Actor, 1957; also Golden Globe Award), Imitation General, The Big Circus, One Two Three, The Longest Day, Gay Purr-ee (voice), Five Weeks in a Balloon, Hatari!, A Ticklish Affair, Your Cheatin' Heart, Harlow, Up From the Beach, Stagecoach, They Shoot Horses Don't They?, Who Killed Mary What's 'er Name?, The Poseidon Adventure, Gable and Lombard, Viva Knievel!, Pete's Dragon, Movie Movie, C.H.O.M.P.S., When Time Ran Out..., 18 Again!, The Ambu-lance, It Could Happen to You, Off Your Rocker.
TELEVISION: *Series*: The Red Buttons Show (1952-55), The Double Life of Henry Phyfe, Knots Landing, Rosanne, Bill Cosby, E.R.. *Movies*: Breakout, The New Original Wonder Woman, Louis Armstrong: Chicago Style, Telethon, Vega$, The Users, Power, The Dream Merchants, Leave 'Em Laughing, Reunion at Fairborough, Alice in Wonderland, Hansel & Gretel. Barefoot Boy With Cheek, Hold It, The Admiral Had a Wife, Winged Victory, Tender Trap, Play It Again Sam, The Teahouse of the August Moon, Red Buttons on Broadway, Finian's Rainbow.

BUZZI, RUTH
Actress. b. Westerly, RI, July 24, 1939. e. Pasadena Playhouse Col. of Theatre Arts. On Country Music charts with You Oughta Hear the Song. Has received 5 Emmy nominations; Golden Globe winner, AGVA Variety Artist of the Year, 1977, Rhode Island Hall of Fame, Presidential commendation for outstanding artist in the field of entertainment, 1980, NAACP Image Award.
THEATER: Sweet Charity (Broadway), 4 off-Broadway shows incl. A Man's A Man, Little Mary Sunshine, Cinderella, Wally's Cafe, 18 musical revues and Las Vegas club act.
PICTURES: Record City, Freaky Friday, The Apple Dumpling Gang Rides Again, The North Avenue Irregulars, The Villain, Surf Two, Skatetown USA, Chu Chu and the Philly Flash, The Being, The Bad Guys, Dixie Lanes, Up Your Alley, Diggin' Up Business, My Mom's a Werewolf, It's Your Life Michael Angelo, The Trouble Makers, Boys Will Be Boys.
TELEVISION: *Series*: Rowan & Martin's Laugh-In, The Steve Allen Comedy Hour, Donny & Marie, The Lost Saucer, Betsy Lee's Ghost Town Jamboree, Carol Burnett's The Entertainers, Days of Our Lives, Sesame Street; semi-regular on 12 other series including Flip, Tony Orlando & Dawn, That Girl, Glen Campbell's Goodtime Hour, Leslie Uggums Show, The Dean Martin Variety Hour. *Guest:* Medical Center, Adam 12, Trapper John M.D., Love Boat, They Came from Outer Space, Major Dad, Alice, Here's Lucy, Saved by the Bell. *Movie*: In Name Only. Many cartoon voice-over series and over 150 on-camera commercials.

BYGRAVES, MAX
Comedian, Actor. b. London, England, October 16, 1922. e. St. Joseph's R.C. School, Rotherhithe. After RAF service, touring revues and London stage. TV debut in 1953, with own show. Autobiography: I Wanna Tell You A Story, 1976. Novel: The Milkman's on His Way, 1977. Received O.B.E., New Year's Honours 1983.
PICTURES: Skimpy in the Navy (debut, 1949), Bless 'em All, Nitwits on Parade, Tom Brown's Schooldays, Charley Moon, A Cry from the Streets, Bobbikins, Spare the Rod, The Alf Garnett Saga.
TELEVISION: Roamin' Holiday (series).

BYRD, CARUTH C.
Production Executive. b. Dallas, TX, March 25, 1941. e. Trinity U, San Antonio. Multi-millionaire businessman, chmn. of Caruth C. Byrd Enterprises, Inc., who entered entertainment industry forming Communications Network Inc. in 1972. Was principal investor in film Santee (1972) and in 1973 formed Caruth C. Byrd Prods. to make theatrical features. 1983, chmn., Lone Star Pictures. 1987, formed Caruth C. Byrd Television. Formed Caruth C. Byrd Entertainment Inc. May, 1989. Concerts incl. Tom Jones, Natalie Cole, B.J. Thomas, Tammy Wynette, Seals & Croft, Eddie Rabbit, Helen Reddy, Jim Stafford, Tanya Tucker and many more.
PICTURES: Murph the Surf, The Monkeys of Bandapur (both exec. prod.), Santee, Sudden Death, Hollywood High II, Lone Star Country, Trick or Treats.
TELEVISION: Fishing Fever, Kids Are People Too, Tribute to Mom and Dad, Back to School, Texas 150: A Celebration Special.

BYRNE, DAVID
Actor, Singer, Director. b. Dumbarton, Scotland, May 14, 1952. Moved to Baltimore at 7. e. Rhode Island Sch. of Design studying photography, performance and video, and Maryland Inst. Coll. of Art 1971-72. Prod. and dir. music videos. Awarded MTV's Video Vanguard Award, 1985. Best known as the lead singer and chief songwriter of Talking Heads. Composed and performed original score for choreographer Twyla Tharp's The Catherine Wheel (B'way). Wrote music for Robert Wilson's The Knee Plays.
PICTURES: Stop Making Sense (conceived and stars in concert film), True Stories (dir., s.p., narrator), The Last Emperor (music, Academy Award, 1987), Married to the Mob (music), Heavy Petting, Between the Teeth (also co-dir.). Also contributed music to such films as Times Square, The Animals' Film, King of Comedy, America is Waiting, Revenge of the Nerds, Down and Out in Beverly Hills, Dead End Kids, Cross My Heart, Somebody Is Waiting.

TELEVISION: A Family Tree, Alive From Off-Center (also composed theme), Survival Guides; Rolling Stone Magazine's 20 Years of Rock and Roll.

BYRNE, GABRIEL
Actor. b. Dublin, Ireland, 1950. e. University Coll., Ireland. Worked as archaeologist, then taught Spanish at girls' school. Participated in amateur theater before acting with Ireland's Focus Theatre, an experimental rep. co. and joining Dublin's Abbey Theatre Co. Cast in long-running TV series the Riordans. Also worked with National Theater in London. Author: Pictures in My Head (1994).
PICTURES: On a Paving Stone Mounted, The Outsider, Excalibur, Hanna K, The Keep, Defence of the Realm, Gothic, Lionheart, Siesta, Hello Again, Julia and Julia, A Soldier's Tale, The Courier, Miller's Crossing, Shipwrecked, Dark Obsession, Cool World, Point of No Return, Into the West (also assoc. prod.), A Dangerous Woman, In the Name of the Father (co-prod. only), Prince of Jutland, A Simple Twist of Fate, Trial by Jury, Little Women, The Usual Suspects, Frankie Starlight, Dead Man, Last of the High Kings (also co-s.p.), Mad Dog Time, Somebody Is Waiting (also prod.), The End of Violence, Toby's Story, Polish Wedding, This Is the Sea, The Man in the Iron Mask, Quest for Camelot (voice), The Brylcreem Boys (also prod.), Stigmata, End of Days, Mad About Mambo (exec. prod.), Canone inverso - Making Love, When Brendan Met Trudy, Semana Santa.
TELEVISION: *Series*: The Riordan's, Branken, Madigan Men. *Movies/ Specials*: Wagner, The Search for Alexander the Great, Treatment, Joyce, Mussolini, Christopher Columbus, Lark in the Clear Air (also dir., writer), Buffalo Girls, Weapons of Mask Destruction.

BYRNES, EDD
Actor. r.n. Edward Breitenberger. b. New York, NY, July 30, 1933. e. Harren H.S. Prof. debut, Joe E. Brown's Circus Show. Author of Edd Byrnes: Kookie No More.
THEATER: Tea and Sympathy, Picnic, Golden Boy, Bus Stop, Ready When You Are C.B., Storm in Summer.
PICTURES: Reform School Girl, Darby's Rangers, Up Periscope, Marjorie Morningstar, Yellowstone Kelly, Girl on the Run, The Secret Invasion, Wicked Wicked, Grease, Stardust, Go Kill and Come Back, Payment in Blood, Troop Beverly Hills.
TELEVISION: *Series*: 77 Sunset Strip, Sweepstake$. Has appeared in over 300 TV shows incl.: Matinee Theatre, Crossroads, Jim Bowie, Wire Service, Navy Log, Oh Susanna!, Throb, Rags to Riches, Murder She Wrote. *Movies*: The Silent Gun, Mobile Two, Telethon, Vega$, Twirl.

BYRON, KATHLEEN
Actress. b. London, England, Jan. 11, 1922. e. London U., Old Vic. co. student, 1942. Screen debut in Young Mr. Pitt, 1943.
PICTURES: Silver Fleet, Black Narcissus, Matter of Life and Death, Small Back Room, Madness of the Heart, Reluctant Widow, Prelude to Fame, Scarlet Thread, Tom Brown's Schooldays, Four Days, Hell Is Sold Out, I'll Never Forget You, Gambler and the Lady, Young Bess, Night of the Silvery Moon, Profile, Secret Venture, Hand in Hand, Night of the Eagle, Hammerhead, Wolfshead, Private Road, Twins of Evil, Craze, Abdication, One of Our Dinosaurs Is Missing, The Elephant Man, From a Far Country, Emma, Remembering Sister Ruth (documentary), The Frighteners, Saving Private Ryan.
TELEVISION: The Lonely World of Harry Braintree, All My Own Work, Emergency Ward 10, Probation Officer, Design for Murder, Sergeant Cork, Oxbridge 2000, The Navigators, The Worker, Hereward the Wake, Breaking Point, Vendetta, Play To Win, Who Is Sylvia, Portrait of a Lady, Callan, You're Wrecking My Marriage, Take Three Girls, The Confession of Mariona Evans, Paul Temple, The Worker, The Moonstone, The Challengers, The Golden Bowl, The Edwardians, The New Life, Menace, The Rivals of Sherlock Holmes, The Brontes, On Call, Edward VII, Sutherland's Law, Crown Court, Anne of Avonlea, Heidi, Notorious Woman, General Hospital, North & South, Angelo, Within these Walls, Jubilee, Z Cars, Tales from the Supernatural, Secret Army, An Englishman's Castle, The Professionals, Forty Weeks, Emmerdale Farm, Blake Seven, The Minders, Together, Hedda Gabler, Nancy Astor, God Speed Co-operation, Take Three Women, Reilly, Memoirs of Sherlock Holmes, Moon And Son, The Bill, Casualty, Portrait of a Marriage, Gentlemen & Players.

BYRUM, JOHN
Writer, Director. b. Winnetka, IL, March 14, 1947. e. New York U. Film School. First job as gofer on industrial films and cutting dailies for underground filmmakers. Went to England where wrote 1st s.p., Comeback. From 1970-73, was in NY writing and re-writing scripts for low-budget films.
PICTURES: *Writer*: Mahogany, Inserts (also dir.) Harry and Walter Go to New York, Heart Beat (also dir), Sphinx, Scandalous, The Razor's Edge (also dir.), The Whoopee Boys (also dir.), The War at Home (also dir.), Duets (also prod.).
TELEVISION: *Movie*: Murder in High Places (dir., writer). *Series*: Alfred Hitchcock Presents (1985), Middle Ages (creator, writer, exec. prod.), South of Sunset (creator, writer, exec. prod.), Winnetka Road (creator, writer, exec. prod.).

C

CAAN, JAMES
Actor. b. Bronx, NY, March 26, 1940. e. Hofstra U. Studied with Sanford Meisner at the Neighborhood Playhouse. Appeared off-B'way in La Ronde, 1961. Also on B'way in Mandingo, Blood Sweat and Stanley Poole.
PICTURES: Irma La Douce (debut, 1963), Lady in a Cage, The Glory Guys, Red Line 7000, El Dorado, Games, Countdown, Journey to Shiloh, Submarine X-1, The Rain People, Rabbit Run, T.R. Baskin, The Godfather (Acad. Award nom.), Slither, Cinderella Liberty, The Gambler, Freebie and the Bean, The Godfather Part II, Funny Lady, Rollerball, The Killer Elite, Harry and Walter Go To New York, Silent Movie, A Bridge Too Far, Another Man Another Chance, Comes a Horseman, Chapter Two, Hide in Plain Sight (also dir.), Thief, Bolero, Kiss Me Goodbye, Gardens of Stone, Alien Nation, Dick Tracy, Misery, The Dark Backward, For the Boys, Honeymoon in Vegas, The Program, Flesh & Bone, A Boy Called Hate, Things to Do in Denver When You're Dead, Bottle Rocket, Eraser, Bulletproof, This is My Father, The Yards, Mickey Blue Eyes.
TELEVISION: Much series guest work (Naked City, Route 66, Wagon Train, Ben Casey, Alfred Hitchcock Presents, NewsRadio, etc.). *Movie*: Brian's Song (Emmy nom.), Poodle Springs.

CACOYANNIS, MICHAEL
Producer, Director, Writer. b. Limassoc, Cyprus, June 11, 1922. Studied law in London, admitted to bar at age 21. Became a producer of BBC's wartime Greek programs while attending dramatic school. After acting on the stage in England, left in 1952 for Greece, where he made his first film, Windfall in Athens, with his own script. While directing Greek classical plays, he continued making films.
PICTURES: *Director/Writer*: Windfall in Athens (Sunday Awakening; debut, 1954), Stella, Girl in Black, A Matter of Dignity (The Final Lie), Our Last Spring (Eroica), The Wastrel, Electra, Zorba the Greek, The Day the Fish Came Out, The Trojan Women, Attila '74, Iphigenia, Sweet Country, Up Down and Sideways, Varya.

CAESAR, SID
Actor. b. Yonkers, NY, Sept. 8, 1922. Studied saxophone at Juilliard School; then appeared in service revue Tars and Spars. Cast by prod. Max Liebman in B'way revue Make Mine Manhattan in 1948. Voted best comedian in M.P. Daily's TV poll, 1951, 1952. Best Comedy Team (with Imogene Coca) in 1953. Received Sylvania Award, 1958. Formed Shelbrick Corp. TV, 1959. Appeared in B'way musical Little Me (1962), Off-B'way & B'way revue Sid Caesar & Company (1989). Author: Where Have I Been? (autobiography, 1982).
PICTURES: Tars and Spars (debut, 1945), The Guilt of Janet Ames, It's a Mad Mad Mad Mad World, The Spirit Is Willing, The Busy Body, A Guide for the Married Man, Airport 1975, Silent Movie, Fire Sale, Grease, The Cheap Detective, The Fiendish Plot of Dr. Fu Manchu, History of the World Part 1, Grease 2, Over the Brooklyn Bridge, Cannonball Run II, Stoogemania, The Emperor's New Clothes, Vegas Vacation, The Wonderful Ice Cream Suit.
TELEVISION: *Series*: Admiral Broadway Revue, Your Show of Shows (Emmy Award for Best Actor, 1952), Caesar's Hour (Emmy Award for Best Comedian, 1956), Sid Caesar Invites You (1958), As Caesar Sees It, The Sid Caesar Show. *Movies*: Flight to Holocaust, Curse of the Black Widow, The Munsters' Revenge, Found Money, Love Is Never Silent, Alice in Wonderland, Freedom Fighter, Side By Side, The Great Mom Swap. *Guest*: U.S. Steel Hour, G.E. Theatre, The Ed Sullivan Show, Carol Burnett Show, Lucy Show, That's Life, Love American Style, When Things Were Rotten, The Love Boat, Amazing Stories, Mad About You. *Specials:* Tiptoe Through TV, Variety—World of Show Biz, Sid Caesar and Edie Adams Together, The Sid Caesar Imogene Coca Carl Reiner Howard Morris Special, Christmas Snow.

CAGE, NICOLAS
Actor. b. Long Beach, CA, Jan. 7, 1964. r.n. Nicholas Coppola. Nephew of dir. Francis Ford Coppola. Joined San Francisco's American Conservatory Theatre at age 15. While attending Beverly Hills High School won role on tv pilot Best of Times.
PICTURES: Fast Times at Ridgemont High (debut, 1982; billed as Nicholas Coppola), Valley Girl, Rumble Fish, Racing with the Moon, The Cotton Club, Birdy, The Boy in Blue, Peggy Sue Got Married, Raising Arizona, Moonstruck, Vampire's Kiss, Fire Birds, Wild at Heart, Tempo di Mecidere (Time to Kill), Zandalee, Honeymoon in Vegas, Amos & Andrew, DeadFall, Red Rock West, Guarding Tess, It Could Happen to You, Trapped in Paradise, Kiss of Death, Leaving Las Vegas (Academy Award, Chicago Film Critics Award, Nat'l Society of Film Critics Award; Golden Globe Award), The Rock, Con Air, Face/Off, Tom Slick: Monster Hunter, 8mm, City of Angels, Snake Eyes, Defective Detective, Bringing Out the Dead.

CAINE, MICHAEL
Actor. r.n. Maurice Micklewhite. b. London, England, March 14, 1933. Asst. stage mgr. Westminster Rep. (Sussex, UK 1953); Lowestoft Rep. 1953-55. London stage: The Room, The Dumbwaiter, Next Time I'll Sing For You (1963). Author: Michael Caine's Moving Picture Show or: Not Many People Know This Is the Movies, Acting on Film, What's It All About? (autobiography, 1993). Awarded C.B.E., 1992. Video: Michael Caine—Acting on Film.
PICTURES: A Hill in Korea (debut, 1956; aka Hell in Korea), How to Murder A Rich Uncle, The Key, Two-Headed Spy, Blind Spot, Breakout (Danger Within), Foxhole in Cairo, Bulldog Breed, The Day the Earth Caught Fire, Solo for Sparrow, Zulu, The Ipcress File, Alfie (Acad. Award nom.), The Wrong Box, Gambit, Funeral in Berlin, Hurry Sundown, Woman Times Seven, Billion Dollar Brain, Deadfall, The Magus, Play Dirty, The Italian Job, The Battle of Britain, Too Late the Hero, The Last Valley, Get Carter, Kidnapped, Zee and Company (X,Y & Zee), Pulp, Sleuth (Acad. Award nom.), The Black Windmill, The Destructors (The Marseille Contract), The Wilby Conspiracy, Peeper, The Romantic Englishwoman, The Man Who Would Be King, Harry and Walter Go to New York, The Eagle Has Landed, A Bridge Too Far, The Silver Bears, The Swarm, California Suite, Ashanti, Beyond the Poseidon Adventure, The Island, Dressed to Kill, The Hand, Victory, Deathtrap, Educating Rita (Acad. Award nom.), Beyond the Limit, Blame It on Rio, The Jigsaw Man, The Holcroft Covenant, Hannah and Her Sisters (Academy Award for Best Supporting Actor, 1986), Water, Sweet Liberty, Mona Lisa, Half Moon Street, Jaws—The Revenge, The Whistle Blower, The Fourth Protocol (also exec. prod.), Surrender, Without a Clue, Dirty Rotten Scoundrels, A Shock to the System, Mr. Destiny, Bullseye!, Noises Off, The Muppet Christmas Carol, On Deadly Ground, Bullet in Beijing, Blood & Wine, Shadow Run, Little Voice, Curtain Call, The Cider House Rules, Quills, Shiner, Get Carter, Miss Congeniality, The Quiet American, Last Orders.
TELEVISION: *Series*: Rickles (1975). In more than 100 British teleplays 1957-63 incl. The Compartment, The Playmates, Hobson's Choice, Funny Noises with Their Mouths, The Way with Reggie, Luck of the Draw, Hamlet, The Other Man. *Movies*: Jack the Ripper, Jekyll and Hyde, Blue Ice (also prod.), World War II: When Lions Roared, 20,000 League under the Sea, Mandela and De Klerk.

CALLAN, MICHAEL
Actor, Singer, Dancer. b. Philadelphia, PA, Nov. 22, 1935. Singer, dancer, Philadelphia nightclubs; to New York in musicals including The Boy Friend and West Side Story; dancer at Copacabana nightclub; in short-run plays, Las Vegas: That Certain Girl, Love Letters.
PICTURES: They Came to Cordura (debut, 1958) The Flying Fontaines, Because They're Young, Pepe, Mysterious Island, Gidget Goes Hawaiian, 13 West Street, Bon Voyage, The Interns, The Victors, The New Interns, Cat Ballou, You Must Be Joking!, The Magnificent Seven Ride!, Frasier the Sensuous Lion, Lepke, The Photographer, The Cat and The Canary, Record City, Double Exposure (also prod.), Chained Heat, Freeway, Leprechaun III, Hello Muddah—Hello Fadduh (prod. only).
TELEVISION: *Series*: Occasional Wife, Superboy. *Guest*: Murder She Wrote, Superboy, T.J Hooker, The Fall Guy. *Movies*: In Name Only, Donner Pass: The Road to Survival, Last of the Great Survivors. *Mini-Series*: Blind Ambition, Scruples.

CALLEY, JOHN
Producer, Executive. b. Jersey City, NJ, 1930. Exec., Ted Bates advertising and NBC; exec. v.p., Filmways, Inc., 1961-1968; president, vice chairman, exec. v.p., Warner Bros., Inc., 1968-81; indpt. producer, Postcards from the Edge, Remains of the Day, 1989-93; president & COO, United Artists (MGM); CEO, Sony Pictures Entertainment (SPE), 1996; chairman & CEO, SPE, 1999-present.

CALLOW, SIMON
Actor, Writer, Director. b. London, June 15, 1949. e. Queens, U. of Belfast, The Drama Centre. Originated role of Mozart in London premiere of Amadeus and Burgess/Chubb in Single Spies. Author: Being an Actor, Acting in Restoration Comedy, Charles Laughton: A Difficult Actor, Shooting the Actor, Orson Welles: The Road to Xanadu.
THEATER: *London*: Plumber's Progress, The Doctor's Dilemma, Soul of the White Ant, Blood Sports, The Resistible Rise of Arturo Ui, Amadeus, Restoration, The Beastly Beatitudes of Balthazar B, Titus Andronicus (Bristol Old Vic), Faust. Shakespeare's Sonnets. Director: Loving Reno, The Infernal Machine (also translator), Jacques and His Master (also trans.; *L.A.*), Single Spies, Shades, My Fair Lady (Natl. tour), Shirley Valentine (*London, NY*), Carmen Jones.
PICTURES: Amadeus, A Room With a View, The Good Father, Maurice, Manifesto, Postcards From the Edge, Mr. and Mrs. Bridge, The Ballad of the Sad Cafe (dir. only), Howards End, Four Weddings and a Funeral, Street Fighter, Jefferson in Paris, Ace Ventura: When Nature Calls, James and the Giant Peach, The Scarlet Tunic, Bedroom and Hallways, Shakespeare in Love, Notting Hill.
TELEVISION: Man of Destiny, La Ronde, All the World's a Stage, Wings of Song, The Dybbuk, Instant Enlightenment, Chance of a Lifetime (series), David Copperfield, Honour, Profit and Pleasure, Old Flames, Revolutionary Witness: Palloy, The Woman in White.

CALVET, CORINNE
Actress. r.n. Corinne Dibos. b. Paris, France, April 30, 1925. e. U. of Paris School of Fine Arts, Comedie Francaise. On French stage and radio; screen debut in French films, then to U.S. in 1949. Author: Has Corinne Been a Good Little Girl?, The Kirlian Aura.
PICTURES: La Part de L'Ombre (debut, 1946), Nous ne Sommes pas Maries, Petrus, La Chateau de la Derniere Chance, Rope of Sand (U.S. debut), When Willie Comes Marching Home, My Friend Irma Goes West, Quebec, On the Riviera, Peking Express, Sailor Beware, Thunder in the East, What Price Glory?, Powder River, Flight to Tangier, The Far Country, So This Is Paris, The Adventures of Casanova (Sins of Casanova), The Girls of San Frediano, Four Women in the NIhgt, Bonnes a Tuer (One Step to Eternity), Napoleon, Plunderers of Painted Flats, Bluebeard's Ten Honeymoons, Hemingway's Adventures of a Young Man, Apache Uprising, Pound, Too Hot to Handle, Dr. Heckle and Mr. Hype, The Sword and the Sorcerer, Side Roads.
TELEVISION: *Movies*: The Phantom of Hollywood, She's Dressed to Kill, The French Atlantic Affair. *Series:* General Hospital.

CAMERON, JAMES
Director, Writer. b. Kapuskasing, Ontario, Canada, Aug. 16, 1954. e. Fullerton Junior Col. (physics). 1990, formed Lightstorm Entertainment.
PICTURES: Piranha II—The Spawning (dir.), The Terminator (dir., s.p.), Rambo: First Blood Part II (co-s.p.), Aliens (dir., s.p.), The Abyss (dir., s.p.), Terminator 2: Judgment Day (dir., co-s.p., prod.), Point Break (exec. prod.), True Lies (dir., co-s.p., prod.), Strange Days (co-prod., co-s.p., story), Titanic (dir., prod., story, Acad. Award, Golden Globe Award, Best Pic., Best Dir., Best Film Edit., 1997), True Lies 2, Terminator 3.
TELEVISION: *Series:* Dark Angel.

CAMERON, JOANNA
Actress, Director. r.n. Patricia Cameron. b. Aspen, CO, Sept. 20, 1951. e. U. of California, Sorbonne, Pasadena Playhouse, 1968. Guinness Record: Most network programmed TV commercials. TV Director: Various commercials, CBS Preview Special, closed circuit program host U.S.N., all TV equipped ships–actress and dir. Documentaries: Razor Sharp (prod., dir.), El Camino Real (dir., prod.).
PICTURES: How To Commit Marriage (debut), P.S. I Love You, Pretty Maids All in a Row.
TELEVISION: *Movies*: The Great American Beauty Contest, Night Games, It Couldn't Happen to a Nicer Guy, High Risk, Swan Song. *Series*: Isis. *Guest*: The Survivors, Love American Style, Daniel Boone, Mission Impossible, The Partners, Search, Medical Center, Name of the Game, The Bold Ones, Marcus Welby, Petrocelli, Columbo, Switch, MacMillan, Spiderman. *Specials*: Bob Hope Special, Bob Hope 25th NBC Anniversary Special.

CAMERON, KIRK
Actor. b. Canoga Park, CA, Oct. 12, 1970. m. actress Chelsea Noble. Sister is actress Candace Cameron. Started doing TV commercials at age 9.
PICTURES: The Best of Times, Like Father, Like Son, Listen to Me, You Lucky Dog.
TELEVISION: *Series*: Two Marriages, Growning Pains, Kirk. *Movies*: Goliath Awaits, Starflight: The Plane That Couldn't Land, A Little Piece of Heaven, Star Struck, The Computer Wore Tennis Shoes, You Lucky Dog. *Specials*: The Woman Who Willed a Miracle, Andrea's Story. Ice Capades with Kirk Cameron.

CAMP, COLLEEN
Actress. b. San Francisco, CA, 1953. Spent 2 years as a bird trainer at Busch Gardens before being noticed by an agent and cast on TV. TV debut on The Dean Martin Show. Assoc. prod. on Martha Coolidge's film The City Girl. Sang several songs in They All Laughed and made Billboard charts with song One Day Since Yesterday.
PICTURES: Battle for the Planet of the Apes (debut, 1973), Swinging Cheerleaders, Death Game (The Seducers), Funny Lady, Smile, The Gumball Rally, Cats in a Cage, Game of Death, Apocalypse Now, Cloud Dancer, They All Laughed, The Seduction, Valley Girl, Smokey and the Bandit III, Rosebud Beach Hotel, The Joy of Sex, Police Academy II, Doin' Time, D.A.R.Y.L., Clue, Walk Like a Man, Illegally Yours, Track 29, Wicked Stepmother, My Blue Heaven, Wayne's World, The Vagrant, Un-Becoming Age, Sliver, Last Action Hero, Greedy, Naked in New York, Die Hard With a Vengeance, The Baby-sitter's Club, Three Wishes, Plump Fiction, House Arrest, The Ice Storm, Speed 2: Cruise Control, Jazz Night, Election.
TELEVISION: *Movies*: Amelia Earhart, Lady of the House, Sisterhood, Addicted to His Love, Backfield in Motion, For Their Own Good, The Right to Remain Silent. *Mini-Series*: Rich Man Poor Man Book II. *Series:* Dallas. *Guest*: George Burns Comedy Week, Happy Days, Dukes of Hazzard, WKRP in Cincinnati, Magnum PI, Murder She Wrote, Tales from the Crypt, Roseanne. *Special*: Going Home Again.

CAMP, JOE
Producer, Director, Writer. b. St. Louis, MO, Apr. 20, 1939. e. U. of Mississippi, B.B.A. Acct. exec. McCann-Erickson Advt., Houston 1961-62; owner Joe Camp Real Estate 1962-64; acct. exec. Norsworthy-Mercer, Dallas 1964-69; dir. TV commercials; founder and pres. Mulberry Square Prods, 1971-present. Author: Underdog.
PICTURES: *Dir./Prod./Writer*: Benji, Hawmps, For the Love of Benji, The Double McGuffin, Oh Heavenly Dog, Benji the Hunted.
TELEVISION: *Specials*: The Phenomenon of Benji (dir., writer, prod.), Benji's Very Own Christmas Story (dir., prod., writer), Benji at Work (prod., writer), Benji at Marineland (dir., writer), Benji Zax and the Alien Prince (dir.).

CAMPANELLA, TOM
Executive. b. Houston, TX, 1944. e. City U. of NY. Joined Paramount Pictures 1968 as asst. business mgr.; later worked for corporate div. and Motion Picture Group. Named exec. dir., nat'l adv. 1979, made v.p., nat'l adv. 1982, appt. sr. v.p., adv., for M.P. Group. of Paramount, 1984. Appointed exec. v.p., adv. & promo., 1990.

CAMPBELL, BRUCE
Actor, Producer. b. Birmingham, MI, June 22, 1958.
PICTURES: The Evil Dead (debut, 1983; also exec. prod.), Crimewave (also co-prod.), Evil Dead 2 (also co-prod.), Maniac Cop, Moontrap, Darkman, Maniac Cop 2, Sundown: The Vampire in Retreat, Mindwarp, Lunatics: A Love Story (also prod.), Waxwork II: Lost in Time, Army of Darkness (also co-prod.), The Hudsucker Proxy, The Demolitionist, Congo, Assault on Dome 4, Menno's Mind, John Carpenter's Escape From L.A., Running Time, McHale's Navy, The Ice Rink, From Dusk Till Dawn 2: Texas Blood Money.
TELEVISION: *Series:* The Adventures of Brisco County Jr., Timecop, Ellen. *Guest*: Xena, Hercules: The Legendary Journies, The X Files, American Gothic. *Movies*: Tornado!, Missing Links, The Love Bug, In the Line of Duty: Blaze of Glory, Goldrush: A Real Life Alaskan Adventure.

CAMPBELL, CHRISTIAN
Actor. b. Toronto, Canada, May 12, 1972. Sister is actress Neve Campbell,
PICTURES: Next Time, Trick, Cold Hearts.
TELEVISION: *Movies*: School's Out, City Boy, Born to Run, Picture Perfect, Seduced by Madness, I've Been Waiting for You. *Series*: Malibu Shores.

CAMPBELL, GLEN
Actor, Singer. b. Delight, AK, April 22, 1936. After forming local band became studio guitarist in Hollywood on records for such performers as Frank Sinatra and Elvis Presley. Won two Grammy awards for record By the Time I Get to Phoenix, 1967. Appeared frequently on Shindig on TV.
PICTURES: The Cool Ones, True Grit, Norwood, Any Which Way You Can, Rock a Doodle (voice).
TELEVISION: *Series*: The Smothers Brothers Comedy Hour, The Glen Campbell Goodtime Hour, The Glen Campbell Music Show; many specials. *Movie*: Strange Homecoming.

CAMPBELL, MICHAEL L.
Executive. b. Knoxville, TN, Jan. 22, 1954. Worked for White Stores, Inc. in a management position until 1982. Founded first theatre venture, Premiere Cinemas in 1982. Premiere grew to 150 screens and was sold to Cinemark in 1989. Founded Regal Cinemas in 1989. President and CEO Regal Cinemas, Inc which has more than 3,900 screens (1998). Named Coopers & Lybrand regional entreprenuer of the year, 1993. Dir. NATO and serves on NATO executive committee.

CAMPBELL, NEVE
Actress. b. Guelph, Ontario, Canada, Oct. 3, 1973.
PICTURES: Paint Cans, The Dark, Love Child, The Craft, Scream, Simba's Pride (voice), Scream 2, Hairshirt (also prod.), Wild Things, 54, Three to Tango, Scream 3, Investigating Sex, Panic, Drowning Mona.
TELEVISION: *Series*: Catwalk, Party of Five. *Movies*: Web of Deceit, Baree, I Know My Son is Alive, The Forget-Me-Not Murders, The Canterville Ghost. *Guest*: The Kids in the Hall, Are You Afraid of the Dark?

CAMPBELL, WILLIAM
Actor. b. Newark, NJ, Oct. 30, 1926. e. Feagin Sch. of Drama. Appeared in summer stock; B'way before film debut.
PICTURES: The Breaking Point (debut, 1950), Breakthrough, Inside the Walls of Folsom Prison, Operation Pacific, The People Against O'Hara, Holiday for Sinners, Battle Circus, Small Town Girl, Code Two, The Big Leaguer, Escape from Fort Bravo, The High and the Mighty, The Fast and the Furious, Man Without a Star, Cell 2455— Death Row, Battle Cry, Running Wild, Man in the Vault, Backlash, Love Me Tender, Walk the Proud Land, Eighteen and Anxious, The Naked and the Dead, Money Women and Guns, The Sheriff of Fractured Jaw, Natchez Train, Night of Evil, The Young Racers, The Secret Invasion, Dementia 13, Hush Hush Sweet Charlotte, Blood Bath, Track of the Vampire, Pretty Maids All in a Row, Black Gunn, Dirty Mary Crazy Larry.
TELEVISION: *Series*: Cannonball, Dynasty, Crime Story. *Pilot*: The Heat: When You Lie Down With Dogs. *Movie*: Return of the Six Million Dollar Man and the Bionic Woman.

CAMPION, JANE
Director, Writer. b. Wellington, New Zealand, April 30, 1954. e. Victoria Univ. of Wellington (BA, anthropology, 1975), Sydney Coll. of Arts (BA, painting, 1979). Attendend Australian Sch. of Film & TV in early 1980's, where she debuted as dir. & writer with short film Peel (1982; Palme d'Or at Cannes Film Fest., 1986). Other short films: A Girl's Own Story, Passionless Moments, After Hours, Two Friends, Mishaps of Seduction & Conquest.
PICTURES: *Director/Writer*: Sweetie (feature debut, 1989; Australian Film Awards for Best Director & Film; LA Film Critics New Generation Award, American Indept. Spirit Award), An Angel at My Table (Venice Film Fest. Silver Lion Award, Indept. Spirit Award), The Piano (Academy Award, WGA, LA Film Critics, NY Film Critics, & Natl. Society of Film Critics Awards for best screenplay; LA Film Critics & NY Film Critics Awards for best director; Cannes Film Fest. Award for best film), The Portrait of a Lady, Holy Smoke, In the Cut.
TELEVISION: *Series*: *Episode director*: Dancing Daze.

CANBY, VINCENT
Journalist, Critic. b. Chicago, IL, July 27, 1924. e. Dartmouth Coll. Navy officer during WWII. Worked on newspapers in Paris and Chicago. Joined Quigley Publications in 1951 in editorial posts on Motion Picture Herald. Reporter for Weekly Variety 1959-1965. Joined New York Times film news staff, 1965; named film critic, 1969. Author: Living Quarters (1975); End of the War (play, 1978); Unnatural Scenery (1979); After All (play, 1981); The Old Flag (1984).

CANNELL, STEPHEN J.
Writer, Producer. b. Los Angeles, CA, Feb. 5, 1942. e. U. of Oregon, B.A., 1964. After coll. worked at father's decorating firm for 4 years while writing scripts in evening. Sold 1st script for Adam 12, 1966. Asked to serve as head writer at Universal Studios. Chief exec. officer, Stephen J. Cannell Prods. TV prod. co. he formed 1979. Also formed The Cannell Studios, parent co. 1986. Natl. chmn., Orton Dyslexia Society. Received Mystery Writers award 1975; 4 Writers Guild Awards. Acted in films: Identity Crisis, Posse.
TELEVISION: The Rockford Files (creator, writer, prod.; Emmy Award), The Jordan Chance, The Duke, Stone, 10 Speed and Brownshoe, Nightside, Midnight Offerings, The Greatest American Hero, The Quest, Them, The Rockford Files: Crime and Punishment, The Rockford Files: Murder and Misdemeanors. *Prod.:* The A-Team, Hardcastle and McCormick, The Rousters, Riptide, Brothers-in-Law, *Creator/Prod.*: Baa Baa Black Sheep, Richie Brockelman, Hunter, Wise Guy, 21 Jump Street, J.J. Starbuck, Sonny Spoon, Sirens (co-exec. prod.), Unsub (exec. prod., writer, pilot), Booker (exec. prod.), Top of the Hill (exec. prod.), Scene of the Crime (exec.-prod., creator), The Commish, The Hat Squad, Traps, Greyhounds (exec. prod., writer), Hawkeye, Marker (exec. prod., creator), Renegade (exec. prod., creator), U.S. Customs Classified (exec. prod., host), Profit (exec.).

CANNON, DYAN
Actress. r.n. Samille Diane Friesen. b. Tacoma, WA, Jan. 4, 1937. e. U. of Washington. Studied with Sanford Meisner. Modelled before becoming actress. Directed, produced and wrote short film Number One (Acad. Award nom.).
THEATER: *B'way*: The Fun Couple, Ninety-Day Mistress. *Tour*: How to Succeed in Business Without Really Trying.
PICTURES: The Rise and Fall of Legs Diamond (debut, 1960), This Rebel Breed, Bob & Carol & Ted & Alice (Acad. Award nom.), Doctors' Wives, The Anderson Tapes, The Love Machine, The Burglars, Such Good Friends, Shamus, The Last of Sheila, Child Under a Leaf, Heaven Can Wait (Acad. Award nom.), Revenge of the Pink Panther, Honeysuckle Rose, Coast To Coast, Deathtrap, Author Author, Caddyshack II, The End of Innocence (also dir., prod., s.p.), The Pickle, Out to Sea, That Darn Cat, 8 Heads in a Duffel Bag, Kiss of a Stranger.
TELEVISION: *Mini-Series*: Master of the Game. *Movies*: The Virginia Hill Story, Lady of the House, Having It All, Arthur the King, Jenny's War, Rock 'n' Roll Mom, Jailbirds, Christmas in Connecticut, Based on an Untrue Story, A Perry Mason Mystery: The Case of the Jealous Jokester, Black Jaq, Diamond Girl. *Series:* Ally McBeal. *Guest*: Playhouse 90.

CANNON, WILLIAM
Writer, Producer, Director. b. Toledo, OH, Feb. 11, 1937. e. Columbia Coll., B.A., 1959; M.B.A., 1962. Wrote, prod., dir., Square Root of Zero, Locarno and San Francisco Film Festivals, 1963-65. Distrib., at Doran Enterprises, Ltd. Publisher of Highlife and Movie Digest, 1978 and The Good Guys, 1987. Co-inventor: Cardz (TM), 1988. Author: Authorship: The Dynamic Principles of Writing Creatively, 1993; The Veteran, (novel) 1974; The Trojan Head (play), 1997.
THEATER: *Off-B'Way*: Death of a Salesman, Pirates of Penzance, 1960.
PICTURES: *Writer*: Skidoo, Brewster McCloud, Hex.
TELEVISION: *Writer*: Knots Landing, Heaven on Earth.

CANOVA, DIANA
Actress. b. West Palm Beach, FL, June 1, 1952. r.n. Diana Rivero. Daughter of actress Judy Canova and musician Filberto Rivero. NY theater: They're Playing Our Song (1981). People's Choice award, favorite female performer, 1981. On B'way in, Company. In film, The First Nudie Musical.
TELEVISION: *Series*: Dinah and Her New Best Friends, Soap, I'm a Big Girl Now, Foot in the Door, Throb, Home Free. *Guest*: Ozzie's Girls (debut), Happy Days, Love Boat, Fantasy Island, Hotel, Chico and the Man, Barney Miller, Murder She Wrote. *Movies*: The Love Boat II, With This Ring, Death of Ocean View Park, Night Partners.

CANTON, ARTHUR H.
Motion Picture Producer. b. New York, NY. e. NYU, Columbia U. Capt. USAF. Pres., Canton-Weiner Films, indep. foreign films importers, 1947; Van Gogh (Academy Award for best 2-reel short subject, 1949); MGM Pictures, eastern div. publicity mgr., executive liaison, advertising-publicity, Independent Productions; public relations executive, v.p.; pres., Blowitz, Thomas & Canton Inc., 1964; pres., Arthur H. Canton Co. Inc.; prod. exec., Warner Bros., 1968-70; advertising-publicity v.p., Columbia Pictures, 1971; exec. v.p. of advertising and publicity, Billy Jack Productions, 1974-76. Co-founder of Blowitz & Canton Co. Inc., 1976, chmn of bd. Pres. of Arthur H. Canton Co. Member Academy of Motion Picture Arts and Sciences. Now exec. v.p. of Filmroos.

CANTON, MARK
Executive. b. New York, NY, June 19, 1949. e. UCLA, 1978. v.p., m.p. dev., MGM; 1979, exec. v.p., JP Organization; 1980, v.p. prod., Warner Bros.; named sr. v.p., 1983 and pres. worldwide theatrical prod. div., 1985; v.p. worldwide m.p. production, 1989; appointed chmn. of Columbia Pictures, 1991. Promoted to chmn. of Columbia TriStar Motion Pictures, 1994. Resigned, 1996.

CAPELIER, MARGOT
Casting Director
PICTURES: Behold a Pale Horse, :Lady L, The Night of the Generals, The Day of the Jackal, The Destructors, Julia, Moonraker, Le Coup du parapluie, Psy, What Makes David Run?, Five Days One Summer, Hanna K, The Outsider, He Died With His Eyes Open, The Original, Family Business, Vent de panique, Europa, Europa, The Double Life of Veronique, The Favour, the Watch, and the Very Big Fish, Olivier, Olivier, Blue, Red, Total Eclipse, Those Who Love Me Can Take the Train, Ronin.

CAPRA, JR., FRANK,
Executive. Son of famed director Frank Capra. Served in various creative capacities on TV series (Zane Grey Theatre, Gunsmoke, The Rifleman, etc.). Associate producer on theatrical films (Planet of the Apes, Play It Again Sam, Marooned, etc.). Joined Avco Embassy Pictures, 1981, as v.p., worldwide production. In July, 1981, became pres. of A-E. Resigned May, 1982 to become indep. producer. Now with Pinehurst Industry Studios, NC.
PICTURES: *Producer*: Tom Sawyer (assoc. prod.), Billy Jack Goes to Washington, Born Again, The Black Marble, An Eye for an Eye, Vice Squad, Firestarter, Marie, Waterproof. *Exec. prod.*: Death Before Dishonor.

CAPSHAW, KATE
Actress. r.n. Kathleen Sue Nail. b. Ft. Worth, TX, Nov. 3, 1953. e. U. of Missouri. m. director Steven Spielberg. Taught school before moving to New York to try acting.
PICTURES: A Little Sex (debut, 1982), Indiana Jones and the Temple of Doom, Best Defense, Dreamscape, Windy City, Power, SpaceCamp, Black Rain, Love at Large, My Heroes Have Always Been Cowboys, Love Affair, Just Cause, Duke of Groove (short), How to Make an American Quilt, The Locusts, Life During Wartime, The Love Letter (also prod.).
TELEVISION: *Series*: The Edge of Night, Black Tie Affair, It's A Girl Thing. *Movies*: Missing Children: A Mother's Story, The Quick and the Dead, Her Secret Life, Internal Affairs, Next Door.

CARA, IRENE
Singer, Actress. b. New York, NY, March 18, 1959. Off-B'way shows include The Me Nobody Knows, Lotta. On B'way in Maggie Flynn, Ain't Misbehavin', Via Galactica. Received Academy Award for co-writing theme song from Flashdance, 1983.
THEATER: *B'way.*: Maggie Flynn, The Me Nobody Knows, Via Galactica, Got to Go Disco. *Off-B'way.*: Ain't Misbehavin'. *Regional*: Lotta, The Wiz, Jesus Christ Superstar. *Foreign*: Mo' Magic.
PICTURES: Aaron Loves Angela, Sparkle, Fame, D.C. Cab, City Heat, Certain Fury, Killing 'em Softly, Paradiso, Busted Up, Maximum Security, Happily Ever After (voice), The Magic Voyage (voice).
TELEVISION: *Series*: Hearts are Wild, Love of Life, The Electric Company. *Mini-Series*: Roots—The Next Generation. *Movies*: Guyana Tragedy, Sisters, For Us the Living, Gabriel's Fire. *Special*: Tribute to Martin Luther King, Jr., Bob Hope Thanksgiving Special, Tribute to Ray Charles.

CARDIFF, JACK
Cinematographer, Director. b. Yarmouth, Eng., Sept. 18, 1914. Early career as child actor, before becoming cinematographer, then dir. in 1958.
PICTURES: *Cinematographer*: A Matter of Life and Death (Stairway to Heaven), Black Narcissus (Acad. Award, 1947), The Red Shoes, Scott of the Antarctic, Black Rose, Under Capricorn, Pandora and the Flying Dutchman, The African Queen, The Magic Box, The Master of Ballantrae, The Barefoot Contessa, The Brave One, War and Peace, Legend of the Lost, The Prince and the Showgirl, The Vikings, The Journey, Fanny, Scalawag, Crossed Swords (The Prince and the Pauper), Death on the Nile, Avalanche Express, The Fifth Musketeer, A Man a Woman and a Bank, The Awakening, The Dogs of War, Ghost Story, The Wicked Lady, Scandalous, Conan the Destroyer, Cat's Eye, Rambo: First Blood II, Blue Velvet, Tai-Pan, Million Dollar Mystery, Delius, Call from Space, The Magic Balloon, Vivaldi's Four Seasons, The Dance of Shiva. *Director*: Intent to Kill (debut, 1958), Beyond This Place, Scent of Mystery, Sons and Lovers, My Geisha, The Lion, The Long Ships, Young Cassidy (co-dir.), The Liquidator, Dark of the Sun, Girl on a Motorcycle, Penny Gold, The Mutations, Ride a Wild Pony.
TELEVISION: *Cinematographer*: The Far Pavillions, The Last Days of Pompeii.

CARDINALE, CLAUDIA
Actress. b. Tunis, Tunisia, April 15, 1939. Raised in Italy. Studied acting at Centro Sperimentale film school in Rome. Debuted 1956 in short French film Anneaux d'Or.
PICTURES: Goha (feature debut, 1957), Big Deal on Madonna Street, The Facts of Murder, Upstairs and Downstairs, The Battle of Austerlitz, Il Bell' Antonio, Rocco and His Brothers, Senilita, Girl With a Suitcase, The Love Makers, Cartouche, The Leopard, 8 1/2, Bebo's Girl, The Pink Panther, Circus World, Time of Indifference, The Magnificent Cuckold, Sandra, Blindfold, Lost Command, The Professionals, Don't Make Waves, Mafia, The Queens, Day of the Owl, The Hell With Heroes, Once Upon a Time in the West, A Fine Pair, The Butterfly Affair, The Red Tent, The Legend of Frenchy King, Conversation Piece, Escape to Athena, The Salamander, Careless, Immortal Bachelor, History, The French Revolution, Hiver '54, L'abbe Pierre, Mother, 588 Rue Paradis, Women Only Have One Thing on Their Minds..., A Summer in La Goulette, Sous les pieds des Femmes, Rich Belles Etc, My Best Friend.
TELEVISION: Princess Daisy, Jesus of Nazareth, 10-07: L'affaire Zeus, Nostromo, Deserto di Fuoco.

CAREY, DREW
Comedian, Actor. b. Cleveland, OH, May 23, 1958. First break was as contestant on TV show Star Search.
PICTURES: Coneheads, The Big Tease, Gepetto.
TELEVISION: *Specials*: Sex, Drugs, and Freedom of Choice. *Series*: The Good Life, The Drew Carey Show (also prod., creator), Whose Line Is It Anyway? (also exec. prod.). *Guest*: The Torkelsons, The George Carlin Show, Lois & Clark: The New Adventures of Superman, Home Improvement, Ellen, Sabrina the Teenage Witch, Dharma & Greg.

CAREY, HARRY JR.
Actor. b. Saugus, CA, May 16, 1921. e. Newhall, CA, public school, Black Fox Military Acad., Hollywood. m. Marilyn Fix. Son of Harry Carey. Appeared in Railroads on Parade at 1939-40 NY World's Fair. Summer stock, Skowhegan, ME., with father; page boy, NBC, New York; U.S. Navy 1942-45. Author of Company of Heroes - My Life as an Actor in the John Ford Stock Co.
PICTURES: Rolling Home (debut, 1946), Pursued, Red River, Three Godfathers, She Wore a Yellow Ribbon, Wagonmaster, Rio Grande, Copper Canyon, Warpath, Wild Blue Yonder, Monkey Business, San Antone, Island in the Sky, Gentlemen Prefer Blondes, Beneath the 12-Mile Reef, Silver Lode, The Outcast, Long Gray Line, Mister Roberts, House of Bamboo, The Great Locomotive Chase, The Searchers, The River's Edge, Rio Bravo, The Great Imposter, Two Rode Together, Alvarez Kelly, Bandolero, The Undefeated, Dirty Dingus Magee, Big Jake, Something Big, One More Train To Rob, Cahill: U.S. Marshal, Take a Hard Ride, Nickelodeon, The Long Riders, Endangered Species, Mask, Crossroads, The Whales of August, Cherry 2000, Illegally Yours, Breaking In, Bad Jim, Back to the Future Part III, The Exorcist III, Tombstone.
TELEVISION: *Movies*: Black Beauty, The Shadow Riders, Wild Times, Once Upon a Texas Train, Last Stand at Saber River. *Guest*: Gunsmoke, Rifleman, Laramie, Wagon Train, Have Gun Will Travel, John Ford's America, Legends of the American West. Disney *Series*: Spin & Marty. *Special*: Wyatt Earp: Return to Tombstone.

CARIOU, LEN
Actor. b. Winnipeg, Manitoba, Canada, Sept. 30, 1939. e. St. Paul's Col.
THEATER: *NY stage*: House of Atreus, Henry V, Applause (Theatre World Award), Night Watch, A Sorrow Beyond Dreams, Up from Paradise, A Little Night Music, Cold Storage, Sweeney Todd—The Demon Barber of Fleet Street (Tony Award), Master Class, Dance a Little Closer, Teddy & Alice, Measure for Measure, Mountain, The Speed of Darkness, Papa.

PICTURES: Drying Up the Streets, A Little Night Music, One Man, The Four Seasons, There Were Times Dear, Lady in White, Getting In, Never Talk to Strangers, Executive Decision.
TELEVISION: *Movies*: Who'll Save Our Children?, Madame X, The Four Seasons, Louisiana, Surviving, Killer in the Mirror, Miracle on Interstate 880, Class of '61, The Sea Wolf, Witness to the Execution, Love on the Run, The Man in the Attic, A Dream Is a Wish Your Heart Makes: The Annette Funicello Story, Derby, The Summer of Ben Tyler, In the Company of Spies. *Series*: Swift Justice. *Specials*: The Master Builder, Juno and the Paycock, Kurt Vonnegut's Monkey House (All the King's Men).

CARLIN, GEORGE
Actor, Comedian. b. New York, NY, May 12, 1937. Stand-up comedian and recording artist. Recipient of 1972 Grammy Award for Best Comedy Album: FM & AM; 1993 Grammy Award for Best Comedy Album: Jammin'. Has released 15 comedy albums between 1960-90. Has guested on many TV shows including Talent Scouts, On B'way Tonight, Merv Griffin Show, Saturday Night Live. *Author*: Sometimes a Little Brain Damage Can Help (1984), Braindroppings (1997).
PICTURES: With Six You Get Eggroll, Car Wash, Americathon (narrator), Outrageous Fortune, Bill & Ted's Excellent Adventure, Bill and Ted's Bogus Journey, The Prince of Tides, Dogma.
TELEVISION: *Series*: Kraft Summer Music Hall, That Girl, Away We Go, Tony Orlando and Dawn, Shining Time Station, The George Carlin Show. *Movies*: Justin Case, Working Trash, Streets of Laredo. *Specials*: George Carlin: Jammin' in New York, also appeared in 10 HBO comedy specials. *Guest:* Welcome Back Kotter, The Simpsons.

CARLINER, MARK
Producer.
PICTURES: Viva Max!, Heaven Help Us, Crossroads.
TELEVISION: *Movies*: A Death of Innocence, Revenge, Strangers in 7A, Nightmare, The Phoenix (pilot), Disaster at Silo 7 (also story), Stalin, George Wallace (Emmy Award, 1998). *Series*: The Phoenix. *Mini-series*: The Shining, Storm of the Century.

CARLINO, LEWIS JOHN
Writer, Director. b. New York, NY, Jan. 1, 1932. e. U. of Southern California. Early interest in theatre, specializing in writing 1-act plays. Winner of Obie award (off-B'way play). Won Rockefeller Grant for Theatre, the Int'l. Playwriting Competition from British Drama League, Huntington Hartford Fellowship.
THEATER: Cages, Telemachus Clay, The Exercise, Double Talk, Objective Case, Used Car for Sale, Junk Yard.
PICTURES: *Writer*: Seconds, The Brotherhood, The Fox (co-s.p.), A Reflection of Fear, The Mechanic (also prod.), Crazy Joe, The Sailor Who Fell From Grace With the Sea (also dir.), I Never Promised You a Rose Garden (co-s.p.), The Great Santini (also dir.), Resurrection, Class (dir. only), Haunted Summer.
TELEVISION: Honor Thy Father, In Search of America, Where Have All the People Gone?

CARLTON, RICHARD
Executive. b. New York, NY, Feb. 9, 1919. e. Columbia U., Pace Inst. Columbia Pictures 1935-41; U.S. Army 1941-45; National Screen Serv. 1945-51; Sterling Television 1951-54; U.M. & M. TV Corp. 1955; v.p. in charge of sales, Trans-Lux Television Corp., 1956; exec. v.p., Television Affiliates Corp., 1961; exec. v.p. Trans-Lux Television Corp.; v.p. Entertainment Div. Trans-Lux Corp., 1966. Pres., Schnur Appel, TV, Inc. 1970; Deputy Director, American Film Institute, 1973. Pres., Carlton Communications Corporation, 1982; exec. dir., International Council, National Academy of Television Arts and Sciences, 1983-93. Became writer/consultant, 1994.

CARLYLE, ROBERT
Actor. b. Glasgow, Scotland, April 14, 1961.
PICTURES: Silent Scream, Riff-Raff, Safe, Being Human, Priest, Go Now, Trainspotting, Carla's Song, Face, The Full Monty (BAFTA Award, Best Actor, 1997), Ravenous, Plunkett & MacCleane, The World is Not Enough, Angela's Ashes, The Beach, There's Only One Jimmy Grimble, To End All Wars, The 51st State.
TELEVISION: *Series*: Hamish Macbeth. *Mini-series*: Looking After Jo Jo.

CARMEN, JULIE
Actress. b. New York, NY, Apr. 4, 1954. Studied acting at Neighborhood Playhouse. On NY stage in The Creation of the Universe, Cold Storage, Zoot Suit. Also acted with INTAR and the New Conservatory Theater. Recipient of 1992 National Council of La Raza Pioneer Award.
PICTURES: Night of the Juggler, Gloria, Man on the Wall, Comeback, Blue City, The Penitent, The Milagro Beanfield War, Fright Night 2, Kiss Me a Killer, Paint It Black, Cold Heaven, In the Mouth of Madness, Africa, Everything's George.
TELEVISION: *Series:* Condo, Falcon Crest. *Mini-Series*: True Women. *Movies:* Can You Hear the Laughter?: The Story of Freddie Prinze, Three Hundred Miles for Stephanie, She's in the Army Now, Fire on the Mountain, Neon Empire, Manhunt: Search for the Night Stalker, Billy the Kid, Drug Wars: The Cocaine Cartel, Finding the Way Home, Curacao, The Omen, Gargantua. *Mini-Series:* True Women.

CARMICHAEL, IAN
Actor. b. Hull, England, June 18, 1920. e. Scarborough Coll., Bromsgrove Sch. Stage debut: R.U.R. 1939. B'way debut: Boeing-Boeing (1965). One of the top ten British money making stars Motion Picture Herald Fame Poll 1957, 1958.
PICTURES: Bond Street (debut, 1948), Trottie True (Gay Lady), Mr. Prohack, Time Gentlemen Please, Ghost Ship!, Miss Robin Hood, Meet Mr. Lucifer, Betrayed, The Colditz Story, Storm Over the Nile, Simon and Laura, Private's Progress, The Big Money, Brothers in Law, Lucky Jim, Happy Is the Bride, Left Right and Center, I'm All Right Jack, School for Scoundrels, Light Up the Sky, Double Bunk, The Amorous Prawn, Hide and Seek, Heavens Above, The Case of the 44's, Smashing Time, The Magnificent Seven Deadly Sins, From Beyond the Grave, The Lady Vanishes, Dark Obsession (Diamond Skulls).
TELEVISION: New Faces, Twice Upon a Time, Passing Show, Tell Her The Truth, Lady Luck, Give My Regards to Leicester Square, Jill Darling, Don't Look Now, Regency Room, Globe Revue, Off the Record, Here and Now, The Girl at the Next Table, Gilt and Gingerbread, The Importance of Being Earnest, Simon and Laura, 90 Years On, The World of Wooster (series), The Last of the Big Spenders, The Coward Revue, Odd Man In, Bachelor Father (series), Lord Peter Wimsey (series), Alma Mater, Comedy Tonight, Song by Song, Country Calendar, Down at the Hydro, Obituaries, Strathblair, The Great Kandinsky. *Guest*: Under The Hammer, Bramwell.

CARNEY, ART
Actor. r.n. William Matthew Carney. b. Mt. Vernon, NY, Nov. 4, 1918. Started as band singer with the Horace Heidt Orchestra. On many radio shows before and after war. Served in U.S. Army, 1944-45. Regular on Morey Amsterdam's radio show which eventually moved to television.
THEATER: The Rope Dancers. B'way: Take Her She's Mine, The Odd Couple, Lovers, The Prisoner of Second Avenue.
PICTURES: Pot o' Gold (debut, 1941), The Yellow Rolls Royce, A Guide for the Married Man, Harry and Tonto (Academy Award for Best Actor, 1974), W. W. and the Dixie Dancekings, Won Ton Ton the Dog Who Saved Hollywood, The Late Show, Scott Joplin, House Calls, Movie Movie, Ravagers, Sunburn, Going in Style, Defiance, Roadie, Steel, St. Helens, Take This Job and Shove It, Better Late Than Never, Firestarter, The Naked Face, The Muppets Take Manhattan, Night Friend, Last Action Hero.
TELEVISION: *Series*: The Morey Amsterdam Show, Cavalcade of Stars, Henry Morgan's Great Talent Hunt, The Jackie Gleason Show (1951-55; 2 Emmy Awards: 1953, 1954), The Honeymooners (Emmy Award, 1955), The Jackie Gleason Show (1956-57), The Jackie Gleason Show (1966-70; 2 Emmy Awards: 1967, 1968), Lanigan's Rabbi. Guest: Studio One, Kraft Theatre, Playhouse 90, Alfred Hitchcock Presents (Safety for the Witness), Sid Caesar Show, Twilight Zone (Night of the Meek), Bob Hope Chrysler Theater (Timothy Heist), Danny Kaye Show, Men From Shiloh, Batman, Carol Burnett Show, Jonathan, Winters Show, Faerie Tale Theatre (The Emperor's New Clothes). *Specials*: Peter and the Wolf, Harvey, Our Town, Charley's Aunt, Art Carney Meets the Sorcerer's Apprentice, Very Important People, Jane Powell Special: Young at Heart, Man in the Dog Suit, The Great Santa Claus Switch. Movies: The Snoop Sisters, Death Scream, Katherine, Letters From Frank, Terrible Joe Moran (Emmy Award, 1984), The Night They Saved Christmas, A Doctor's Story, Izzy and Moe, Blue Yonder, Where Pigeons Go to Die.

CARNEY, FRED
Producer, Director. b. Brooklyn, NY, June 10, 1914. e. Mt. Vernon H.S., 1932. Actor on B'way & summer stock; prod. mgr. for radio show, Truth or Consequences; asst. to prod.-dir of Kraft TV Theatre, 3 yrs.; dir., Kraft, Pond's Show; creator-prod., Medical Horizons; dir., Lux Video Theatre; prod. commercials at Cunningham & Walsh. Assoc. Prod. Everybody's Talking for ABC-TV. Ass't. exec. dir., Hollywood Chpt., Nat'l Acad. TV; Assoc. prod. 40th Acad. Award show, ABC-TV Arts & Sciences.

CARON, GLENN GORDON
Writer, Director, Producer. Started as tv writer for James L. Brooks, Steve Gordon. Prod. of tv series Breaking Away. Formed prod. co., Picturemaker Productions, 1985.
PICTURES: *Director*: Clean and Sober (debut, 1988), Wilder Napalm, Love Affair, Picture Perfect (also s.p.).
TELEVISION: *Series*: Moonlighting (creator, prod., writer). *Movies:* Long Time Gone.

CARON, LESLIE
Actress, Dancer. b. Paris, France, July 1, 1931. e. Convent of Assumption, Paris; Nat'l Conservatory of Dance, Paris 1947-50; joined Roland Petit's Ballet des Champs Elysees where she was spotted by Gene Kelly who chose her as his co-star in An American in Paris. Also with Ballet de Paris.
THEATER: Orvet, Ondine, Gigi (London), 13 Rue de l'Amour, The Rehearsal, Women's Games, On Your Toes, One For the Tango.

PICTURES: An American in Paris (debut, 1951), The Man With a Cloak, Glory Alley, The Story of Three Loves, Lili (Acad. Award nom.; BFA Award), The Glass Slipper, Daddy Long Legs, Gaby, Gigi, The Doctor's Dilemma, The Man Who Understood Women, The Subterraneans, Austerlitz, Fanny, Guns of Darkness, Three Fables of Love, The L-Shaped Room (Acad. Award nom.; BFA Award), Father Goose, A Very Special Favor, Promise Her Anything, Is Paris Burning?, Head of the Family, The Beginners, Madron, Chandler, Purple Night, Valentino, The Man Who Loved Women, Golden Girl, Contract, Imperative, The Unapproachable, Dangerous Moves, Warriors and Prisoners, Courage Mountain, Damage, Funny Bones, Let It Be Me, The Reef.
TELEVISION: *Mini-Series*: QB VIII, Master of the Game. *Guest*: Love Boat, Tales of the Unexpected, Carola, Falcon Crest. *Movie*: The Man Who Lived at the Ritz. *Special*: The Sealed Train. *Series*: The Great War.

CARPENTER, CARLETON
Actor. b. Bennington, VT, July 10, 1926 e. Bennington H.S., Northwestern U. (summer scholarship). Began career with magic act, clubs, camps, hospitals in New Eng.; then toured with carnival; first N.Y. stage appearance in Bright Boy. Appeared in nightclubs, radio; as magazine model. TV debut, Campus Hoopla show. Screen debut Lost Boundaries (also wrote song for film, I Wouldn't Mind). Member: SAG, AFTRA, AEA, ASCAP, Dramatists Guild, Mystery Writers of Amer. (ex.-treas., bd. mem.).
THEATER: *NY*: Career Angel, Three To Make Ready, The Magic Touch, The Big People, Out of Dust, John Murray Anderson's Almanac, Hotel Paradiso, Box of Watercolors, A Stage Affair, Greatest Fairy Story Ever Told, Something for the Boys, Boys in the Band, Dylan, Hello Dolly!, Light Up the Sky, Murder at Rutherford House, Rocky Road, Apollo of Bellac, Sweet Adaline, Geo. White's Scandals, Life on the L.I.E. Miss Stanwyck is Still in Hiding, Good Ole Fashioned Revue, What is Turning Gilda So Grey?, Crazy for You, Many Thousands Gone.
PICTURES: Lost Boundries (debut, 1949), Summer Stock, Father of the Bride, Three Little Words, Two Weeks With Love, The Whistle at Eaton Falls, Fearless Fagan, Sky Full of Moon, Vengeance Valley, Up Periscope, Take the High Ground, Some of My Best Friends Are..., The Prowler, Simon, Byline, Cauliflower Cupids, The Bar, Carnegie Hall.
TELEVISION: Over 6,000 shows (live & filmed) since 1945.

CARPENTER, CHARISMA
Actress. b. Las Vegas, NV, July 23, 1970. Was cheerleader for NFL's San Diego Chargers before turning to modeling, then acting.
TELEVISION: *Movies*: Josh Kirby...Time Warrior: The Human Pets, Josh Kirby...Time Warrior: Planet of the Dino-Knights, Josh Kirby...Time Warrior: Last Battle for the Universe. *Series*: Malibu Shores, Buffy the Vampire Slayer, Angel. *Guest*: Baywatch, Boy Meets World.

CARPENTER, JOHN
Director, Writer, Composer. b. Carthage, NY, Jan. 16, 1948. e. Western Kentucky U., U. of Southern California. At U.S.C. became involved in film short, Resurrection of Bronco Billy, which won Oscar as best live-action short of 1970. Also at U.S.C. began directing what ultimately became Dark Star, science fiction film that launched his career.
PICTURES: *Director*: Dark Star (also co-s.p., music), Assault on Precinct 13 (also s.p., music), Halloween (also s.p., music), The Fog (also co-s.p., music), Escape from New York (also co-s.p., music), The Thing, Christine (also music), Starman, Big Trouble in Little China (also music), Prince of Darkness (also music, and s.p. as Martin Quatermass), They Live (also music, and s.p. as Frank Armitage), Memoirs of an Invisible Man, In the Mouth of Madness (also co-music), Village of the Damned (also s.p., co-music), Escape From L.A, Meltdown (also s.p.), Eyes of Laura Mars (co-sp., co-story), Halloween II (co- s.p., co-prod., co-music), Halloween III: Season of the Witch (co-prod., co-music), The Philadelphia Experiment (co-exec. prod.), Black Moon Rising (co-s.p., story), The Silence of the Hams (actor), Vampires, (also s.p. and music), Ghosts of Mars.
TELEVISION: *Movies* (director): Elvis, Someone Is Watching Me (also writer), John Carpenter Presents Body Bags (also co-exec. prod., actor). *Movies* (writer): Zuma Beach, El Diablo, Blood River, Silent Predators.

CARPENTER, ROBERT L.
Executive. b. Memphis, TN, March 20, 1927. Joined Universal Pictures in 1949 as booker in Memphis exchange; promoted to salesman, 1952, then branch mgr., 1958; 1963 named Los Angeles branch mgr. 1971, moved to New York to become asst. to gen. sales mgr. Named gen. sales mgr. 1972, replacing Henry H. Martin when latter became pres. of Universal. Left in 1982 to become consultant and producer's rep. 1984, joined Cannon Releasing Corp. as east. div. mgr. Left in 1989 to become consultant and producers rep.

CARPENTER, RUSSELL
Cinematographer, Actor.
PICTURES: The Wizard of Speed and Time (also actor), Lady in White, Critters 2: The Main Course, Cameron's Closet, Solar Crisis, Lionheart, Death Warrant, The Perfect Weapon, The Lawnmower Man, Pet Sematary II, Hard Target, True Lies, The Indian in the Cupboard, Titanic (Acad. Award, Chicago Film Crits. Award, Best Cinematography, 1997), Ghosts, Money Talks, The Negotiator.
TELEVISION: *Movies*: Attack of the 50 Ft. Woman.

CARR, MARTIN
Producer, Director, Writer. b. New York, NY, Jan. 20, 1932. e. Williams Coll. Recepient of: 5 Emmys, 3 Peabody awards, 2 Du-Pont Col. Journalism awards, Robert F. Kennedy award, Sidney Hillman award, Writers Guild Award.
TELEVISION: PBS Smithsonian World (exec. prod.). For CBS prod., wrote and dir. CBS Reports: Hunger in America, The Search for Ulysses, Gauguin in Tahiti, Five Faces of Tokyo, Dublin Through Different Eyes. For NBC prod., wrote and dir. NBC White Paper: Migrant, NBC White Paper: This Child Is Rated X. Also directed drama, dance, music, opera specials and daytime serial for CBS-TV. ABC Close-Up. The Culture Thieves. PRS Global Paper: Waging Peace, ABC News 20/20; NBC, The Human Animal.

CARRADINE, DAVID
Actor. r.n. John Arthur Carradine. b. Hollywood, CA, Dec. 8, 1936. e. San Francisco State U. Son of late actor John Carradine. Brother of actors Keith and Robert Carradine. Began career in local repertory; first TV on Armstrong Circle Theatre and East Side, West Side; later TV includes Shane series and Kung Fu; N.Y. stage in The Deputy, Royal Hunt of The Sun (Theatre World Award).
PICTURES: Taggart, Bus Riley's Back in Town, The Violent Ones, Young Billy Young, The McMasters, Heaven with a Gun, The Bood Buys and the Bad Guys, Macho Callahan, Boxcar Bertha, Mean Streets, House of Dracula's Daughter, Death Race 2000, Cannonball, Bound for Glory, Thunder and Lightning, A Look at Liv, The Serpent's Egg, Dray Lady Down, Deathsport, Fast Charlie the Moonbeam Rider, Circle of Iron, Cloud Dancer, The Long Rides, Americana, Trick or Treats, Safari 3000, Q, Lone Wolf McQuade, The Warrior and the Sorceress, Rio Abajo, A Distant Scream, Armed Response, P.O.W. the Escape, The Misfit Brigade, Wizards of the Lost Kingdom II, Warlords, Open Fire, Fatal Secret, Crime Zone, Animal Protector, Thry This One for Size, Tropical Snow, Sundown: The Vampire in Retreat, Nowhere to Run, The Mad Bunch, Las Huellas del lince, Crime of Crimes, Thing Big, Sonny Boy, Night Children, Midnight Fear, Future Zone, Future Force, Evil Toons, Dune Warriors, Bird on a Wire, Karate Cop, Field of Fire, Capital Punishment, Waxwork II: Lost in Time, Night Rhythms, Martial Law, Double Trouble, Distant Justice, Animal Instincts, Roadside Prophets, Kill Zine, Dead Center, The Rage, Full Blast, Crossroads of Destiny, Light Speed, Drop-Dead, The New Swiss Family Robinson, Americana (also s.p., dir., ed.).
TELEVISION: *Movies*: Maybe I'll Come Home in the Spring, Kung Fu (1972 pilot), Mr. Horn, Johnny Belinda, Gaugin the Savage, High Noon Part II, Jealousy, The Bad Seed, Kung Fu: The Movie, Oceans of Fire, Six Against the Rock, The Cover Girl & the Cop, I Saw What You Did, The Cover Girl and the Cop, Deadly Surveillance, Brotherhood of the Gun, The Gambler Returns: Luck of the Draw, Kung Fu: The Legend Continues, The Eagle and the Horse, Lost Treasure of Dos Santos, Last Stand at Saber River. *Mini-series*: North & South Books I & II. *Series*: Shane, Kung Fu, Kung Fu: The Legend Continues. *Guest:* Darkroom, Amazing Stories, Charmed, Matlock.

CARRADINE, KEITH
Actor. b. San Mateo, CA, Aug. 8, 1949. e. Colorado State U. Daughter is actress Martha Plimpton. Son of late actor John Carradine, brother of David and Robert Carradine. First break in rock opera Hair.
THEATER: Wake Up It's Time to Go to Bed, Foxfire, The Will Rogers Follies.
PICTURES: A Gunfight (debut, 1971), McCabe and Mrs. Miller, Hex, Emperor of the North Pole, Thieves Like Us, Antoine et Sebastien, Run Joe Run, Idaho Transfer, Nashville (also composed songs; Acad. Award for best song: I'm Easy, 1975), You and Me, Lumiere, Welcome to L.A. (also composed songs), The Duellists, Pretty Baby, Sgt. Pepper's Lonely Heart Club Band (cameo), Old Boyfriends, An Almost Perfect Affair, The Long Riders, Southern Comfort, Choose Me, Maria's Lovers (also composed song), Trouble in Mind, The Inquiry (The Investigation), Backfire, The Moderns, Street of No Return, Cold Feet, Daddy's Dyin'...Who's Got the Will?, The Ballad of the Sad Cafe, Crisscross, The Bachelor, Andre, Mrs. Parker and the Vicious Circle, The Tie That Binds, Wild Bill, A Thousand Acres, Standoff, Out of the Cold, The Hunter's Moon.
TELEVISION: *Movies*: Man on a String, Kung Fu, The Godchild, A Rumor of War, Scorned and Swindled, A Winner Never Quits, Murder Ordained, Eye on the Sparrow, Blackout, Stones for Ibarra, My Father My Son, The Revenge of Al Capone, Judgment, Payoff, In the Best of Families: Marriage Pride & Madness, Is There Life Out There?, Trial by Fire, Hard Time: Hide and Seek, Night Ride Home. *Mini-Series*: Chiefs. *Series:* Outreach. *Guest*: Bonanza, Love American Style, Kung Fu.

CARRADINE, ROBERT
Actor. b. Hollywood, CA, March 24, 1954. Son of late actor John Carradine; brother of Keith and David Carradine.
PICTURES: The Cowboys (debut, 1972), Mean Streets, Aloha Bobby and Rose, Jackson County Jail, The Pom Pom Girls, Cannonball, Massacre at Central High, Joyride, Orca, Blackout, Coming Home, The Long Riders, The Big Red One, Heartaches, Tag: The Assassination Game, Wavelength, Revenge of the Nerds, Just the Way You Are, Number One With a Bullet, Revenge of the Nerds II: Nerds in Paradise, Buy and Cell, All's Fair, Rude Awakening, The Player, Bird of Prey, Escape From L.A., Scorpio One, Lycanthrope, Stray Bullet, Gunfighter, Palmer's Pick Up
TELEVISION: *Series*: The Cowboys. *Movies*: Footsteps, Rolling Man, Go Ask Alice, The Hatfields and the McCoys, The Survival of Dana, The Sun Also Rises, Monte Carlo, The Liberators, I Saw What You Did, The Incident, Clarence, Doublecrossed, Revenge of the Nerds III: The Next Generation, Body Bags, The Disappearance of Christina, Revenge of the Nerds IV: Nerds in Love (also co-prod.), A Part of the Family, The Tommyknockers, Young Hearts Unlimited. *Guest*: Alfred Hitchcock Presents (1985), The Hitchhiker, Twilight Zone (1986), ER, Kung Fu: The Legend Continues, The Fall Guy. *Specials*: Disney's Totally Minnie, As Is.

CARRERA, BARBARA
Actress. b. Nicaragua, Dec. 31, 1951. Fashion model before film career; had part in film Puzzle of a Downfall Child.
PICTURES: The Master Gunfighter, Embryo, The Island of Dr. Moreau, When Time Ran Out, Condorman, I the Jury, Lone Wolf McQuade, Never Say Never Again, Wild Geese II, The Underachievers, Love at Stake, Wicked Stepmother, Loverboy, Spanish Rose, Night of the Archer, Tryst, Oh No Not Her (Love Is All There Is), Moscow Connection, Ghost Ships of the Kalahari, Love Is All There Is, Illusion of Infinity.
TELEVISION: *Mini-Series*: Centennial, Masada, Emma: Queen of the South Seas. *Series*: Dallas. *Movies*: Sins of the Past, Murder in Paradise, Lakota Moon, The Rockford Files. *Guest*: Fortune Hunter

CARRERE, TIA
Actress. r.n. Althea Janairo. b. Honolulu, HI, 1967. Was prof. model before turning to acting. Received NATO/ShoWest award for Female Star of 1994.
PICTURES: Zombie Nightmare (debut, 1987), Aloha Summer, Fatal Mission, Instant Karma, Showdown in Little Tokyo, Harley Davidson and the Marlboro Man, Wayne's World, Rising Sun, Wayne's World 2, True Lies, Jury Duty, My Generation, The Immortals, Hollow Point, Bad With Numbers, High School High, Top of the World, Dumped, Kull the Conqueror, Scar City, 20 Dates (also exec. prod), Merlin: The Return, Meet Prince Charming, Shi.
TELEVISION: *Series:* General Hospital. *Mini-Series:* James Clavell's Noble House. *Movies:* The Road Raiders, Fine Gold, Natural Enemy, Dogboys. *Guest:* The A-Team, MacGyver, Tales From the Crypt.

CARREY, JIM
Actor. b. Newmarket, Ontario, Canada, Jan. 17, 1962. Began performing act at Toronto comedy clubs while teenager. Moved to LA at 19, performing at the Comedy Store.
PICTURES: Finders Keepers (debut, 1984), Once Bitten, Peggy Sue Got Married, The Dead Pool, Earth Girls Are Easy, Pink Cadillac, High Strung, Ace Ventura: Pet Detective (also co-s.p.), The Mask, Dumb and Dumber, Batman Forever, Ace Ventura: When Nature Calls, The Cable Guy, Liar Liar, The Truman Show, Simon Birch, Man on the Moon, How the Grinch Stole Christmas.
TELEVISION: *Series*: The Duck Factory, In Living Color. *Movies*: Mickey Spillane's Mike Hammer—Murder Takes All, Doin' Time on Maple Drive, In My Life. *Special*: Jim Carrey's Unnatural Act. *Canadian TV*: Introducing Janet, Copper Mountain: A Club Med Experience.

CARROLL, DIAHANN
Actress, Singer. r.n. Carol Diahann Johnson. b. Bronx, NY, July 17, 1935. r.n. Carol Diahann Johnson. m. singer Vic Damone. Started singing as teen, winning 1st place on tv's Chance of a Lifetime talent show resulting in engagement at Latin Quarter nightclub in New York. Autobiography: Diahann! (1986).
THEATER: *B'way*: House of Flowers, No Strings (Tony Award, 1962), Agnes of God.
PICTURES: Carmen Jones (debut, 1954), Porgy and Bess, Goodbye Again, Paris Blues, Hurry Sundown, The Split, Claudine (Acad. Award nom.), The Five Heartbeats, Eve's Bayou.
TELEVISION: *Series*: Julia, The Diahann Carroll Show, Dynasty, Sister Sister. *Movies*: Death Scream, I Know Why the Caged Bird Sings, From the Dead of Night, Murder in Black and White, A Perry Mason Mystery: The Case of the Lethal Lifestyle. The Sweetest Gift, Having Our Say: The Delany Sisters' First 100 Years, Jackie's Back! *Mini-Series*: Roots: The Next Generations; many specials; guest appearances incl. The Naked City, Andy Williams, Judy Garland, Dean Martin Shows, Ellen.

CARROLL, GORDON
Producer. b. Baltimore, MD, Feb. 2, 1928. e. Princeton U. Advtg. exec., Foote, Cone & Belding, 1954-58; Ent. industry, Seven Arts Prods., 1958-61; v.p., prod., Jalem Prods., 1966-1969; independent producer to present.
PICTURES: How to Murder Your Wife, Luv, Cool Hand Luke, The April Fools, Pat Garrett and Billy the Kid, Alien, Blue Thunder, The Best of Times, Aliens, Red Heat, Alien 3, Alien: Resurrection.

CARROLL, PAT
Actress. b. Shreveport, LA, May 5, 1927. e. Immaculate Heart Coll., L.A, Catholic U., Washington, DC. Joined U.S. Army in capacity of Civilian Actress Technician. Night club entertainer in N.Y., 1950.
THEATER: Catch a Star (debut, 1955), Gertrude Stein Gertrude Stein (Drama Desk, Outer Critics Circle, Grammy Awards), Dancing in the End Zone, The Show Off. Shakespeare Theatre at the Folger: Romeo and Juliet (Helen Hayes Award), The Merry Wives of Windsor (Helen Hayes Award), Mother Courage (Helen Hayes Award), H.M.S. Pinafore, Volpone.
PICTURES: With Six You Get Eggroll, The Brothers O'Toole, The Last Resort, The Little Mermaid (voice), Invader, A Goofy Movie.
TELEVISION: *Series*: Red Buttons Show, Saturday Night Revue, Caesar's Hour (Emmy Award, 1957), Masquerade Party (panelist), Keep Talking, You're in the Picture (panelist), Danny Thomas Show, Getting Together, Busting Loose, The Ted Knight Show, She's the Sheriff, The Little Mermaid (voice). *Specials*: Cinderella, Gertrude Stein. *Guest*: Carol Burnett, Danny Kaye, Red Skelton. *Movie*: Second Chance, Just My Imagination.

CARSEY, MARCY
Producer. b. Weymouth, MA, Nov. 21, 1944. e. Univ. NH. Was actress in tv commercials, tour guide at Rockefeller Center. Served as exec. story editor, Tomorrow Ent., 1971-74; sr. v.p. for prime time series, ABC-TV, 1978-71; founded Carsey Prods., 1981; owner, Carsey-Werner Co., 1982-.
TELEVISION: *Series* (exec. prod.): Oh Madeline, The Cosby Show, A Different World, Roseanne, Chicken Soup, Grand, Davis Rules, Frannie's Turn, You Bet Your Life (synd.), Grace Under Fire, Cybill, Cosby (1996-), Men Behaving Badly, Townies, Damon, That '70s Show (exec.). *Pilots:* Callahan, I Do I Don't. *Special:* Carol Carl Whoopi and Robin. *Movie:* Single Bars Single Women.

CARSON, JEANNIE
Actress. r.n. Jean Shufflebottom. b. Yorkshire, England, May 23, 1928. Became Amer. citizen, 1966. Founded Hyde Park Festival Theatre with husband William "Biff" McGuire, 1979. Has taught a musical drama class at U. of WA. Awards: TV Radio Mirror, 1st Recipient of the Variety Club Theatre Award in England.
THEATER: *U.K.*: Ace of Clubs, Love From Judy, Starlight Roof, Casino Reviews, Aladdin. *U.S.*: The Sound of Music, Blood Red Roses, Finian's Rainbow (revival). *Tours*: Camelot, 110 in the Shade, Cactus Flower. Also extensive work with the Seattle Repertory Theatre as actress, and dir. with Seattle Bathhouse Theatre.
PICTURES: A Date with a Dream (debut, 1948), Love in Pawn, As Long as They're Happy, An Alligator Named Daisy, Mad Little Island (Rockets Galore), Seven Keys.
TELEVISION: Best Foot Forward, Little Women, Berkeley Square, The Rivals, Frank Sinatra Show, Heidi, What Every Woman Knows, Jimmy Durante Show, Pat Boone Show, A Kiss for Cinderella. Series: Hey Jeannie, Jeannie Carson Show.

CARSON, JOHNNY
Host, Comedian. b. Corning, IA, Oct. 23, 1925. e. U. of Nebraska, B.A. 1949. U.S. Navy service during WWII; announcer with station KFAB, Lincoln, Neb.; WOW radio-TV, Omaha, 1948; announcer, KNXT-TV, Los Angeles, 1950; then hosted own program, Carson's Cellar (1951-53); latter resulted in job as writer for Red Skelton Show. 1958 guest hosting for Jack Paar on The Tonight Show led to his becoming regular host 4 years later. President, Carson Productions. Recipient: ATAS Governor's Award, 1980. Author: Happiness Is a Dry Martini (1965).
PICTURES: *Movies*: Looking for Love, Cancel My Reservation, The Newton Boys.
TELEVISION: *Series*: Earn Your Vacation (emcee; 1954), The Johnny Carson Show (daytime, 1955; later moved to nighttime, 1955-56), Who Do You Trust? (1957-62), The Tonight Show Starring Johnny Carson (1962-92). *Movies:* James Stewart: A Wonderful Life, The Poistively True Adventures of the Alleged Texas Cheerleader-Murdering Mom. *Guest*: Playhouse 90, U.S. Steel Hour, Get Smart, Here's Lucy, The Simpsons, Cheers. Pilot: Johnny Come Lately.

CARTER, CHRIS
Producer, Composer, Writer, Director. b. Bellflower, CA, Oct. 13, 1957.
PICTURES: The X Files: Fight the Future.
TELEVISION: *Producer/Composer/Writer/Director*: In the Shadow of the Sun, The B.R.A.T. Patrol, Rags to Riches (co-prod. only), Millenium (also creator), The X-Files (also creator), Harsh Realm.

CARTER, DIXIE
Actress. b. McLemoresville, TN, May 25, 1939. m. actor Hal Holbrook. e. U. of Tennessee, Knoxville, Rhodes Coll.; Memphis, Memphis State U. Off-B'way debut, A Winter's Tale with NY Shakespeare Fest (1963). London debut, Buried Inside Extra (1983). Lincoln Center musicals: The King & I, Carousel, The Merry Widow. Video: Dixie Carter's Unworkout.
THEATER: Pal Joey (1976 revival), Jesse and the Bandit Queen (Theatre World Award), Fathers and Sons, Taken in Marriage, A Coupla White Chicks Sitting Around Talking, Buried Inside Extra, Sextet, Pal Joey.
PICTURE: Going Berserk.
TELEVISION: *Series*: The Edge of Night, On Our Own, Out of the Blue, Filthy Rich, Diff'rent Strokes, Designing Women, Family Law. *Movies*: OHMS, The Killing of Randy Webster, Dazzle, Gambler V: Playing for Keeps, A Perry Mason Mystery: The Case of the Lethal Lifestyle, Gone in the Night.

CARTER, JACK
Actor, r.n. Jack Chakrin. b. New York, NY, June 24, 1923. e. New Utrecht H.S., Brooklyn Coll., Feagin Sch. of Dramatic Arts. Worked as comm. artist for adv. agencies. Debut B'way in Call Me Mister, 1947; starred in TV Jack Carter Show, NBC Sat. Nite Revue. Hosted first televised Tony Awards. Seen on most major variety, dram. programs, incl. Ed Sullivan Show. Emmy nom. 1962 for Dr. Kildare seg. Played most major nightclubs. On B'way in Top Banana, Mr. Wonderful, Dir. several Lucy Shows. TV incl. specials, HA Comedy Special, Top Banana, Girl Who Couldn't Lose.
PICTURES: The Horizontal Lieutenant, Viva Las Vegas, The Extraordinary Seaman, The Resurrection of Zachary Wheeler, Red Nights, Hustle, The Amazing Dobermans, Alligator, The Octagon, History of the World Part 1, Heartbeeps (voice), The Arena, Deadly Embrace, In the Heat of Passion, Social Suicide, The Opposite Sex, W.A.R., Natl. Lampoon's Last Resort.
TELEVISION: *Series*: American Minstrels of 1949, Cavalcade of Stars, The Jack Carter Show, Make Me Laugh. *Movies*: The Lonely Profession, The Family Rico, The Sex Symbol, The Great Houdinis, The Last Hurrah, Human Feelings, Rainbow, The Gossip Columnist, The Hustler of Muscle Beach, For the Love of It, Double Deception. *Guest:* Blossom, Empty Nest, Nurses, Murder She Wrote, Time Trax, Burke's Law, New Adventures of Superman, Sanford and Son.

CARTER, LYNDA
Actress. r.n. Lynda Jean Cordoba. b. Phoenix, AZ, July 24, 1951. e. Arcadia H.S. Wrote songs and sang professionally in Ariz. from age of 15; later toured 4 yrs. with rock 'n roll band. Won beauty contests in Ariz. and became Miss World-USA 1973. Dramatic training with Milton Katselas, Greta Seacat, and Sandra Seacat.
PICTURE: Lightning in a Bottle.
TELEVISION: *Series*: Wonder Woman, Hawkeye. *Specials*: The New Original Wonder Woman Specials; 5 variety specials, Hawkeye. *Movies*: The New Original Wonder Woman, A Matter of Wife... and Death, Baby Brokers, Last Song, Hotline, Rita Hayworth: The Love Goddess, Stillwatch (also exec. prod.), Mickey Spillane's Mike Hammer, Murder Takes All, Danielle Steel's Daddy, Posing: Inspired By 3 Real Stories, She Woke Up Pregnant, A Secret Between Friends, Family Blessings, A Prayer in the Dark.

CARTER, NELL
Actress. b. Birmingham, AL. Sept. 13, 1948.
THEATER: Hair, Dude, Don't Bother Me I Can't Cope, Jesus Christ Superstar, Ain't Misbehavin' (Tony & Theatre World Awards, 1978), Ain't Misbehaving (1988 revival), Hello Dolly! (L.A.).
PICTURES: Hair, Quartet, Back Roads, Modern Problems, Bebe's Kids (voice), The Grass Harp, The Crazysitter, The Proprietor, Fakin' Da Funk.
TELEVISION: *Series*: Lobo, Gimme a Break, You Take the Kids, Hangin' With Mr. Cooper. *Specials*: Baryshnikov on Broadway, The Big Show, An NBC Family Christmas, Ain't Misbehavin' (Emmy Award), Christmas in Washington, Nell Carter, Never Too Old To Dream, Morton's By the Bay (pilot). *Movies*: Cindy, Maid for Each Other, Final Shot: The Hank Gathers Story.

CARTLIDGE, WILLIAM
Director, Producer. b. England, June 16, 1942. e. Highgate Sch. Ent. m.p. ind. 1959. Early career in stills dept., Elstree Studio. Later worked as an asst. dir. on The Young Ones, Summer Holiday, The Punch & Judy Man, The Naked Edge. As 1st asst. dir. on such pictures as Born Free, Alfie, You Only Live Twice, The Adventurers, Young Winston, Friends. As assoc. prod., Paul and Michelle, Seven Nights in Japan, The Spy Who Loved Me, Moonraker, An Ideal Husband. *Prod.:* Educating Rita, Not Quite Paradise, Consuming Passions, Dealers, The Playboys. Producer of Haunted, Incognito, The Scarlet Tunic (exec.).

CARTWRIGHT, VERONICA
Actress. b. Bristol, Eng., April 20, 1949. m. writer-dir. Richard Compton. Sister is actress Angela Cartwright. Began career as child actress. On stage in, The Hands of Its Enemies (Mark Taper Forum, LA 1984), The Triplet Connection (off-B'way).
PICTURES: In Love and War (debut, 1958), The Children's Hour, The Birds, Spencer's Mountain, One Man's Way, Inserts, Goin' South, Invasion of the Body Snatchers, Alien, Nightmares, The Right Stuff, My Man Adam, Flight of the Navigator, Wisdom, The Witches of Eastwick, Valentino Returns, False Identity, Man Trouble, Candyman: Farewell to the Flesh, Money Talks, Sparkler, My Engagement Party, A Slipping Down Life, Trash.
TELEVISION: *Series*: Daniel Boone. *Guest*: Leave It to Beaver, Twilight Zone, The X-Files. *Mini-series*: Robert Kennedy and His Times. *Movies*: Guyana Tragedy—The Story of Jim Jones, The Big Black Pill, Prime Suspect, Intimate Encounters, Desperate for Love, A Son's Promise, Hitler's Daughter, Dead in the Water, It's Nothing Personal, My Brother's Keeper, The Lottery, The Rat Pack, The Last Man on Planet Earth. *Specials*: Who Has Seen the Wind?, Bernice Bobs Her Hair, Tell Me Not the Mournful Numbers (Emmy Award), Joe Dancer, Abby My Love, On Hope.

CARUSO, DAVID
Actor. b. Queens, NY, Jan. 7, 1956.
PICTURES: Without Warning (debut, 1980), An Officer and a Gentleman, First Blood, Thief of Hearts, Blue City, China Girl, Twins, King of New York, Hudson Hawk, Mad Dog and Glory, Kiss of Death, Jade, Cold Around the Heart, The Split.
TELEVISION: *Series*: N.Y.P.D. Blue, Michael Hayes (also prod.). *Movies*: Crazy Times, The First Olmypics—Athens 1896, Into the Homeland, Rainbow Drive, Mission of the Shark, Judgment Day: The John List Story, Gold Coast. *Guest*: Crime Story, Hill Street Blues.

CARVER, STEVE
Director. b. Brooklyn, NY, April 5, 1945. e. U. of Buffalo; Washington U., MFA. Directing, writing fellow, Film Inst. Center for Advanced Studies, 1970. (Writer, dir. films Patent and the Tell-Tale Heart). Teacher of filmmaking art and photo. Florissant Valley Col., MO 1966-68. News photographer, UPI. Instructor, film and photography, Metropolitan Ed. Council in the Arts; St. Louis Mayor's Council on the Arts, Give a Damn (dir., prod.); asst. dir. Johnny Got His Gun; writer, editor with New World Pictures. Member: Sierra Club, Natl. Rifle Assn.
PICTURES: Arena, Big Bad Mama, Capone, Drum, Fast Charlie, The Moonbeam Rider, Steel, An Eye for an Eye, Lone Wolf McQuade (also prod.), Oceans of Fire, Jocks (also co-s.p.), Bulletproof (also co-s.p.), River of Death, Crazy Joe, The Wolves.

CARVEY, DANA
Actor. b. Missoula, MT, Apr. 2, 1955. e. San Francisco State Coll. Won San Francisco Stand-Up Comedy Competition which led to work as stand-up comedian in local S.F., then L.A. comedy clubs. TV debut as Mickey Rooney's grandson on series, One of the Boys, 1982. Received American Comedy Award (1990, 1991) as TV's Funniest Supporting Male Performer.
PICTURES: Halloween II, Racing With the Moon, This is Spinal Tap, Tough Guys, Moving, Opportunity Knocks, Wayne's World, Wayne's World 2, Clean Slate, The Road to Wellville, Trapped in Paradise, The Shot.
TELEVISION: *Series*: One of the Boys, Blue Thunder, Saturday Night Live (Emmy Award, 1993), The Dana Carvey Show. *Specials*: Superman's 50th Anniversary (host), Salute to Improvisation, Wayne & Garth's Saturday Night Live Music a Go-Go. *Guest*: The Larry Sanders Show, Just Shoot Me, Lateline. *Pilots*: Alone at Last, Whacked Out.

CASEY, BERNIE
Actor. b. Wyco, WV, June 8, 1939. e. Bowling Green U. Played pro-football with San Francisco 49ers and L.A. Rams.
PICTURES: Guns of the Magnificent Seven (debut, 1969), Tick...Tick...Tick, Boxcar Bertha, Black Gunn, Hit Man, Cleopatra Jones, Maurie, Cornbread Earl and Me, The Man Who Fell to Earth, Dr. Black/Mr. Hyde, Brothers, Sharky's Machine, Never Say Never Again, Revenge of the Nerds, Spies Like Us, Steele Justice, Rent-a-Cop, I'm Gonna Git You Sucka, Backfire, Bill and Ted's Excellent Adventure, Another 48 HRS, Under Siege, The Cemetery Club, Street Knight, The Glass Shield, In the Mouth of Madness, Once Upon a Time...When We Were Colored, The Dinner (also prod., dir., s.p.).
TELEVISION: *Series*: Harris and Company, Bay City Blues. *Movies*: Brian's Song, Gargoyles, Panic on the 5:22, Mary Jane Harper Cried Last Night, It Happened at Lake Wood Manor, Ring of Passion, Love is Not Enough, Sophisticated Gents, Hear No Evil, The Fantastic World of D.C. Collins, The Simple Life of Noah Dearborn. Mini-*Series*: Roots—The Next Generations, The Martian Chronicles.

CASSAVETES, NICK
Actor, Director, Writer. b. New York, NY, May 21, 1959. Son of director/actor John Cassavetes and actress Gena Rowlands.
PICTURES: A Woman Under the Influence, Mask, The Wraith, Quiet Cool, Black Moon Rising, Assault of the Killer Bimbos, Blind Fury, Backstreet Dreams, Delta Force 3: The Killing Game, Twogether, Sins of the Night, Sins of Desire, Body of Influence, Class of 1999 II: The Substitute, Mrs. Parker and the Vicious Circle, Just Like Dad, Black Rose of Harlem, Face/Off, Life, The Astronaut's Wife. *Director:* Unhook the Stars (also s.p.), She's So Lovely.
TELEVISION: *Movies*: Reunion, Shooter.

CASSEL, ALVIN I.
Executive. b. New York , NY, July 26. e. U. of Michigan, B.A., 1938. Capt. in U.S. Army European Theatre, 1941-45. Surveyed Central Africa for MGM, 1946-50, then assumed duties as asst. mgr. for MGM South Africa. Continued with MGM in West Indies, 1950-51 and Philippines, 1951-57. In 1957 joined Universal as mgr./supvr. for Southeast Asia; back to MGM in 1963 as supvr. S.E. Asia; 1967, with CBS Films as Far East supvr. In 1972, established Cassel Films to secure theatrical films for foreign distributors, principally in Far East. 1979, consultant for Toho-Towa and the Toho Co. of Japan and other Far East distributors.

CASSEL, JEAN-PIERRE
Actor.r.n. Jean-Pierre Crochon. b. Paris, France, Oct. 27, 1932. Began as dancer, attracting attention of Gene Kelly at Left Bank nightspot, resulting in film debut. Also appeared in plays before becoming established as leading French screen star.
PICTURES: The Happy Road (debut, 1956), A Pied a Cheval et en Voiture, Le Desorde et la Nuit, Love Is My Profession, The Love Game, The Joker, Candide, The Five-Day Lover, Seven Capital Sins, La Gamberge, The Elusive Corporal, Arsene Lupin contre Arsene Lupin, Cyrano and D'Artagnan, The Beautiful Swindlers, The Male Companion, High Infidelity, La Ronde, Les Fetes Galantes, Those Magnificent Men in Their Flying Machines, Is Paris Burning?, Anyone Can Play, The Killing Game, The Bear and the Doll, Oh! What a Lovely War, The Army of the Shadows, The Break Up, The Boat on the Grass, Baxter!, Malpertuis, The Discreet Charm of the Bourgeoisie, The Three Musketeers, Le Mouton Enrage, Murder on the Orient Express, The Twist, That Lucky Touch, No Time for Breakfast, The Four Musketeers, Les Oeufs Brouilles, The Meetings of Anna, Who Is Killing the Great Chefs of Europe?, Alice, Chouans! Grandeson, From Hell to Victory, La Ville des Silence, The Green Jacket, Ehrengard, La Vie Continue, Portrait of a Nude Woman, The Trout, Vive la Sociale! Tranches de Vie, Mangeclous, The Return of the Musketeers, Mr. Frost, Vincent & Theo, Tha Maid, The Favor the Watch and the Very Big Fish, Lieutenant Lorena, Love and Tiny Toes, Between Heaven and Earth, Coup de Jeune, The Secret Coach of 13, Petain, Blue Helmet, Metisse, Cha Forte Com Limao, L'Enfer, Ready to Wear (Pret-a-Porter), La Ceremonie (A Judgment in Stone), The Ice Rink.
TELEVISION: La Lune d'Omaha, Liberty, A Matter of Convenience, Sentimental Journey, Tu Crois Pa si Bien Dire, Casanova, The Burning Shore, Warburg, Young Indiana Jones Chronicles, From Earth and Blood, Elissa Rhais, The Fatal Image, The Phantom of the Opera, Cave of the Golden Rose, Notorious, Tatort - Eine Todsichere Falle, Flairs Ennemis, Un Printemps de Chien. *Mini-series*: The Secret of the Sahara, La Misere des Riches, Disperatamente Giulia

CASSEL, SEYMOUR
Actor. b. Detroit, MI, Jan. 22, 1937. As a boy travelled with a troupe of burlesque performers including his mother. After high school appeared in summer stock in Michigan. Studied acting at American Theatre Wing and Actor's Studio. After joining a workshop taught by John Cassavetes, began a long creative association with the director-actor. On B'way in, The World of Suzy Wong, The Disenchanted.
PICTURES: Murder Inc., Shadows, Too Late Blues, Juke Box Racket, The Killers, The Sweet Ride, Coogan's Bluff, Faces (Acad. Award nom.), The Revolutionary, Minnie and Moskowitz, Black Oak Conspiracy, Death Game (The Seducers), The Killing of a Chinese Bookie, The Last Tycoon, Scott Joplin, Opening Night, Valentino, Convoy, California Dreaming, Ravagers, Sunburn, The Mountain Men, King of the Mountain, I'm Almost Not Crazy..., John Cassavetes–The Man and His Work (doc.), Love Streams, Eye of the Tiger, Survival Game, Tin Men, Johnny Be Good, Plain Clothes, Colors, Track 29, Wicked Stepmother, Dick Tracy, White Fang, Cold Dog Soup, Mobsters, Diary of a Hitman, Honeymoon in Vegas, In the Soup, Trouble Bound, Indecent Proposal, Boiling Point, Chain of Desire, Chasers, There Goes My Baby, When Pigs Fly, Hand Gun, It Could Happen to You, Tollbooth, Dark Side of Genius, Imaginary Crimes, Things I Never Told You, Dead Presidents, The Last Home Run, Dream for an Insomniac, Four Rooms, Cameleone, Things I Never Told You, Seed, Motel Blue, This World Then the Fireworks, Obsession, The Treat, Snapped, Rushmore, Me and Will, Kubanisch Rauchen, Dream for an Insomniac, Relax...It's Just Sex,.
TELEVISION: *Movies*: The Hanged Man, Angel on My Shoulder, Blood Feud, I Want to Live, Beverly Hills Madame, Sweet Bird of Youth, My Shadow, Dead in the Water, Face of a Stranger, The Last Don, Emma's Wish. *Pilot*: Rose City. *Special*: Partners. *Series*: Good Company.

CASSIDY, DAVID
Actor, Singer. b. New York, NY, April 12, 1950. Son of late actor Jack Cassidy; brother of Shaun and Patrick. Composed and performed theme song for The John Larroquette Show.
THEATER: *B'way*: The Fig Leaves Are Falling (debut, 1968), Joseph and the Amazing Technicolor Dreamcoat, Blood Brothers. Regional: Little Johnny Jones, Tribute. London: Time.
PICTURES: Instant Karma, The Spirit of '76.
TELEVISION: *Series*: The Partridge Family, David Cassidy-Man Undercover. *Movie*: The Night the City Screamed. *Guest*: The Mod Squad, Bonanza, Adam-12, Ironside, Marcus Welby M.D., Police Story (Emmy nom.), The Love Boat, Alfred Hitchcock Presents, The Flash, The Ben Stiller Show, The John Larroquette Show.

CASSIDY, JOANNA
Actress. r.n. Joanna Virginia Caskey. b. Camden, NJ, Aug. 2, 1944. e. Syracuse U.
PICTURES: Bullitt (debut, 1968), Fools, The Laughing Policeman, The Outfit, Bank Shot, The Stepford Wives, Stay Hungry, The Late Show, Stunts, The Glove, Our Winning Season, Night Games, Blade Runner, Under Fire, Club Paradise, The Fourth Protocol, Who Framed Roger Rabbit, 1969, The Package, Where the Heart Is, Don't Tell Mom the Babysitter's Dead, All-American Murder, May Wine, Vampire in Brooklyn, Chain Reaction, Loved, Executive Power, Dangerous Beauty.
TELEVISION: *Series*: Shields and Yarnell, The Roller Girls, 240-Robert, Family Tree, Buffalo Bill, Code Name: Foxfire, Hotel Malibu, Superman. *Movies*: She's Dressed to Kill, Reunion, Invitation to Hell, The Children of Times Square, Pleasures, A Father's Revenge, Nightmare at Bitter Creek, Wheels of Terror, Grass Roots, Taking Back My Life, Live! From Death Row, Perfect Family, Barbarians at the Gate, Stephen King's The Tommyknockers, The Rockford Files: I Still Love L.A, Sleep Baby Sleep, The Second Civil War, Circle of Deceit, To Serve and Protect. *Mini-Series*: Hollywood Wives. *Special*: Roger Rabbit and the Secrets of Toontown (host), Other Mothers (Afterschool Special), Tribe. *Pilot*: Second Stage. *Guest*: Taxi, Love Boat, Hart to Hart, Charlie's Angels, Lou Grant, Melrose Place.

CASSIDY, PATRICK
Actor. b. Los Angeles, CA, Jan. 4, 1961. Son of late actor Jack Cassidy and actress-singer Shirley Jones.
THEATER: *NY*: The Pirates of Penzance, Leader of the Pack, Assassins. Regional: Conrack.
PICTURES: Off the Wall, Just the Way You Are, Fever Pitch, Nickel Mountain, Love at Stake, Longtime Companion, I'll Do Anything, Lord Protector, Man of Her Dreams.
TELEVISION: *Series*: Bay City Blues, Dirty Dancing. *Movies*: Angel Dusted, Midnight Offerings, Choices of the Heart, Christmas Eve, Dress Gray, Something in Comon, Follow Your Heart, Three on a Match, How the West Was Fun. *Mini-Series*: Napoleon and Josephine: A Love Story. Pilot: The Six of Us.

CASTELLANETA, DAN
Actor. b. Chicago, IL, 1958.
PICTURES: Nothing in Common, The War of the Roses, K-9, Don't Tell Mom the Babysitter's Dead (voice), The Return of Jafar (voice), Super Mario Bros., The Client, Love Affair, Forget Paris, Space Jam, Plump Fiction, Rhapsody in Bloom, My Giant.
TELEVISION: *Movies*: Working Tra$h, Lady Against the Odds, The Online Adventures of Ozzie the Elf (voice). *Series*: The Tracey Ullman Show, The Simpsons (voice), Darkwing Duck (voice), Taz-Mania (voice), Sibs, Back to the Future (voice), Eek! the Cat, Aladdin (voice), The Tick (voice), Earthworm Jim, Hey Arnold (voice), Cow and Chicken (voice). *Guest*: ALF, Married...with Children, Rugrats (voice), Dream On, L.A. Law, Animaniacs (voice), The Critic (voice), Grace Under Fire, Cybil, Murphy Brown, Friends, NYPD Blue, The Drew Carey Show, Duckman (voice), Everybody Loves Raymond, Futurama (voice).

CASTLE, NICK
Writer, Director. b. Los Angeles, CA, Sept. 21, 1947. e. Santa Monica Coll., U. of Southern California film sch. Son of late film and TV choreographer Nick Castle Sr. Appeared as child in films Anything Goes, Artists and Models. Worked with John Carpenter and other USC students on Acad. Award-winning short, The Resurrection of Bronco Billy.
PICTURES: Skatedown USA (s.p.), Tag: The Assassination Game (Kiss Me Kill Me; dir., s.p.), Escape from New York (co-s.p.), The Last Starfighter (dir.), The Boy Who Could Fly (dir.), Tap (dir., s.p.), Hook (co-story), Dennis the Menace (dir.), Major Payne (dir.), Mr. Wrong (dir.). *Actor:* Halloween.

CATES, GILBERT
Director, Producer. r.n. Gilbert Katz. b. New York, NY, June 6, 1934. e. Syracuse U. Brother is dir.-prod. Joseph Cates. Began TV career as guide at NBC studios in N.Y., working way up to prod. and dir. of game shows (Camouflage, Haggis Baggis, Mother's Day, etc.). Created Hootenanny and packaged and directed many TV specials. Pres. Directors Guild of America 1983-87. Awarded DGA's Robert B. Aldrich award 1989. Dir. short film The Painting.
THEATER: *Director*: Tricks of the Trade, Voices, The Price (Long Wharf Theatre). *Producer*: Solitaire/Double Solitaire, The Chinese and Mr. Fish, I Never Sang for My Father, You Know I Can't Hear You When the Water's Running.
PICTURES: Rings Around the World (debut, 1966), I Never Sang for My Father (also prod.), Summer Wishes Winter Dreams, One Summer Love (Dragonfly; also prod.), The Promise, The Last Married Couple in America, Oh God!—Book II (also prod.), Backfire.

TELEVISION: *Specials*: *Prod. &/or Dir. unless otherwise noted*: International Showtime (1963-65 exec. prod.), Electric Showcase Specials, Academy Awards (prod. 1990-95, 1997-98; Emmy Award, 1991), After the Fall. Movies: To All My Friends on Shore, The Affair, Johnny, We Hardly Knew Ye, The Kid from Nowhere, Country Gold, Hobson's Choice, Burning Rage, Consenting Adult, Fatal Judgement, My First Love, Do You Know the Muffin Man, Call Me Anna, Absolute Strangers (exec. prod.), In My Daughter's Name (co-exec. prod.), Confessions: Two Faces of Evil, To Life: America Celebrates Israel's 50th.

CATES, PHOEBE
Actress. r.n. Phoebe Katz. b. New York, NY, July 16, 1962. e. Juilliard. Daughter of late prod-dir. Joseph Cates. m. actor Kevin Kline. Dance prodigy and fashion model before launching acting career. NY stage debut The Nest of the Wood Grouse (1984).
PICTURES: Paradise (debut, 1982), Fast Times at Ridgemont High, Private School, Gremlins, Date With an Angel, Bright Lights Big City, Shag, Heart of Dixie, I Love You to Death (unbilled), Gremlins 2: The New Batch, Drop Dead Fred, Bodies Rest and Motion, My Life's in Turnaround, Princess Caraboo.
TELEVISION: *Movies*: Baby Sister, Lace, Lace II. *Special*: Largo Desolato.

CATON-JONES, MICHAEL
Director. b. Broxburn, Scotland, 1958.
PICTURES: Scandal (debut, 1989), Memphis Belle, Doc Hollywood (also cameo), This Boy's Life, Rob Roy (also exec. prod.), The Jackal (also exec.)
TELEVISION: Series: Trinity.

CATTRALL, KIM
Actress. b. Liverpool, Eng., Aug. 21, 1956. e. American Acad. of Dramatic Arts, N.Y. Started stage career in Canada's Off-B'way in Vancouver and Toronto; later performed in L.A. in A View from the Bridge, Agnes of God, Three Sisters, etc. On B'way in Wild Honey. Chicago Goodman Theatre in the Misanthrope. Regional: Miss Julie (Princeton).
PICTURES: Rosebud (debut 1975), The Other Side of the Mountain Part II, Tribute, Ticket to Heaven, Porky's, Police Academy, Turk 182, City Limits, Hold-Up, Big Trouble in Little China, Mannequin, Masquerade, Midnight Crossing, Palais Royale, Honeymoon Academy, The Return of the Musketeers, Brown Bread Sandwiches, Bonfire of the Vanities, Star Trek VI: The Undiscovered Country, Split Second, Double Vision, Breaking Point, Unforgettable, Live Nude Girls, Where Truth Lies, Baby Geniuses, Modern Vampires.
TELEVISION: *Series*: Angel Falls, Sex and the City. *Movies*: Good Against Evil, The Bastard, The Night Rider, The Rebels, The Gossip Columnist, Sins of the Past, Miracle in the Wilderness, Running Delilah, Above Suspicion, The Heidi Chronicles, Two Golden Balls, Outer Limits, 36 Hours to Die. *Mini-Series*: Scruples, Wild Palms, Tom Clancy's Op Center, Invasion, Creature.

CAULFIELD, MAXWELL
Actor. b. Glasgow, Scotland, Nov. 23, 1959. m. actress Juliet Mills. First worked as a dancer at a London nightclub. After coming to NY in 1978, ran the concession stand at the Truck and Warehouse Theatre. Won a Theatre World Award for Class Enemy.
THEATER: Entertaining Mr. Sloane, Salonika, Journey's End, Sleuth, The Elephant Man, An Inspector Calls, Sweet Bird of Youth, The Woman In Black.
PICTURES: Grease 2, Electric Dreams, The Boys Next Door, The Supernaturals, Sundown: The Vampire in Retreat, Mind Games, Alien Intruder, Midnight Witness, Ipi/Tombi, In a Moment of Passion, Calendar Girl, Gettysburg, Inevitable Grace, Empire Records, Prey of the Jaguar, Oblivion 2: Backlash, The Real Blonde, The Man Who Knew Too Little.
TELEVISION: *Series*: Dynasty, The Colbys, All My Children, Spider Man (voice). *Movies*: The Parade, Till We Meet Again, Blue Bayou, Dynasty: The Reunion.

CAVANAUGH, ANDREW
Executive. Held positions with Norton Simon, Inc. and Equitable Life Insurance Co. before joining Paramount Pictures in 1984 as v.p., human resources. 1985, appt. sr. v.p., administration, mng. personnel depts. on both coasts. Also oversees corp. admin. function for Paramount.

CAVANI, LILIANA
Director. b. near Modena, in Emilia, Italy, Jan. 12, 1937. e. U. of Bologna, diploma in classic literature, 1960; Ph.D. in linguistics. In 1960 took courses at Centro Sperimentale di Cinematografia in Rome where made short films Incontro Notturno and L'Evento. 1961 winner of RAI sponsored contest and started working for the new second Italian TV channel, 1962-66 directing progs. of serious political and social nature incl. History of 3rd Reich, Women in the Resistance, Age of Stalin, Philippe Petain–Trial at Vichy (Golden Lion Venice Fest.), Jesus My Brother, Day of Peace, Francis of Assisi. Has also directed operas Wozzeck, Iphigenia in Tauris and Medea on stage; also dir. opera liriche: Cardillac, Jenufa, Traviata, Vestale, Cena Delle Beffe, Iphigenia in Tauride, Medea.
PICTURES: Galileo, I Cannibali, Francesco d'Assissi, L'Ospite, Milarepa, Night Porter, Beyond Good and Evil, The Skin, Oltre la Porta, The Berlin Affair, Francesco, Sans Pouvoir le Dire, Dissociated States.
TELEVISION: Movies: Where Are You? I'm Here (also s.p.).

CAVETT, DICK
Actor, Writer. b. Kearny, NE, Nov. 19, 1936. e. Yale U. Acted in TV dramas and Army training films. Was writer for Jack Paar and his successors on the Tonight Show. Also wrote comedy for Merv Griffin, Jerry Lewis, Johnny Carson. In 1967 began performing own comedy material in night clubs. On TV starred in specials Where It's At (ABC Stage 67) and What's In. Author of, Cavett (with Christopher Porter) 1974.
THEATER: *B'way*: Otherwise Engaged, Into the Woods.
PICTURES: Annie Hall, Power Play, Health, Simon, A Nightmare on Elm Street 3, Beetlejuice, Moon Over Parador, After School, Funny, Year of the Gun, Forrest Gump.
TELEVISION: *Series*: This Morning (ABC daytime talk show, 1968), The Dick Cavett Show (ABC primetime talk show, summer 1969), The Dick Cavett Show (ABC late night talk show, 1969-72: Emmy Award, 1972), ABC Late Night (talk show, 1973-74; Emmy Award, 1974), The Dick Cavett Show (CBS primetime variety; 1975), Dick Cavett Show (talk show: PBS, 1977-82; USA, 1985-86; CBS, 1986), The Edge of Night (1983), The Dick Cavett Show (CNBC talk show: 1989). *Guest:* The Simpsons, Cheers.

CAZENOVE, CHRISTOPHER
Actor. b. Winchester, Eng., Dec. 17, 1945. m. Angharad Rees. e. Eton, Oxford U., trained at Bristol Old Vic Theatre School.
THEATER: Hamlet (1969), The Lionel Touch, My Darling Daisy, The Winslow Boy, Joking Apart, In Praise of Rattigan, The Life and Poetry of T.S. Eliot, The Sound of Music, Goodbye Fidel (B'way debut, 1980).
PICTURES: There's a Girl in My Soup, Royal Flash, East of Elephant Rock, The Girl in Blue Velvet, Zulu Dawn, Eye of the Needle, From a Far Country, Heat and Dust, Until September, Mata Hari, The Fantastist, Hold My Hand I'm Dying, Three Men and a Little Lady, Aces: Iron Eagle III, The Proprietor.
TELEVISION: *Series*: The Regiment, The Duchess of Duke Street, Dynasty, A Fine Romance, Tales From the Crypt. *Specials/Movies:* The Rivals of Sherlock Holmes (1971), Affairs of the Heart, Jennie: Lady Randolph Churchill, The Darkwater Hall Mystery, Ladykillers—A Smile Is Sometimes Worth a Million, The Red Signal, Lou Grant, The Letter, Jenny's War, Lace 2, Kane and Abel, Windmills of the Gods, Shades of Love, Souvenir, The Lady and the Highwayman, Tears in the Rain, Ticket to Ride (A Fine Romance), To Be the Best, The Way to Dusty Death.

CELENTINO, LUCIANO
Producer, Director, Writer. b. Naples, Italy, 1940. e. Rome, Paris, London. Entered. ind. 1959. Wrote, prod., dir. many plays incl: Infamita di Questa Terra, Black Destiny, Honour, Stranger's Heart, Youth's Sin, Wanda Lontano Amore. Stage musicals such as Songs...Dots...And Fantasies, Night Club's Appointment, Filumena, Serenada, Mamma. Since 1964, film critic of Il Meridionale Italiano. From 1962, co-writer and first asst. director to Luigi Capuano and Vittorio De Sica. In 1972, formed own company, Anglo-Fortunato Films. Honorary President Accademia Di Arte Drammatica Eduardo de Filippo teaching film acting, writing, directing.
PICTURES: Blood Money, Bandito (dir. only), Toujours (dir., s.p.), Parole (dir.,s.p.), Jackpot (dir., s.p.),Panache (dir.only), Was There a Way Out? (dir. only), Hobo, Gallan (dir. only), The Pinch.

CELLAN-JONES, JAMES
Director. b. Swansea, Wales, July 13, 1931. e. St. John's Coll., Cambridge. Best known for his adaptations of classic novels for the BBC and PBS (shown on Masterpiece Theatre). Won Nymphe d'Or at Monaco Festival.
PICTURE: The Nelson Affair, Chou Chou, Une Vie de Debussy, Married 2 Malcolm.
TELEVISION: The Scarlet and the Black, The Forsythe Saga, Portrait of a Lady, The Way We Live Now, Solo, The Roads to Freedom, Eyeless In Gaza, The Golden Bowl, Jennie (DGA series award), Caesar and Cleopatra, The Adams Chronicles, The Day Christ Died, The Ambassadors, Unity Mitford, Oxbridge Blues (also prod.), Sleeps Six (also prod.), The Comedy of Errors, Fortunes of War, You Never Can Tell, Arms and the Man, A Little Piece of Sunshine, A Perfect Hero (also prod.), The Gravy Train Goes East, Maigret, Harnessing Peacocks, Brighton Belles, The Vacillations of Poppy Carew, La Musique de l'Amour, McLibel.

CHABROL, CLAUDE
Director. b. Paris, France, June 24, 1930. Worked as newsman for Fox, then writer for Cahiers du Cinema. A founding director of the French New Wave.
PICTURES: Le Beau Serge, The Cousins, A Double Tour, Les Bonnes Femmes, Les Godelureaux, The Third Lover, Seven Capital Sins, Ophelia, Landru, Le Tigre Aime la Chair Fraiche, Marie-Chantal Contre le Docteur Kah, Le Tigre Se Parfume a la Dunamite, Paris vu par... Chabrol, La Ligne de Demarcation, The Champagne Murders, The Route to Corinth, Les Biches,

Le Femme Infidele, This Man Must Die, Le Boucher, La Rapture, Ten Days' Wonder, Just Before Nightfall, Dr. Popaul, Les Noces Rouges, Nada, The Blood of Others, The Horse of Pride, Alouette je te plumera, Poulet au Vinaigre, Inspector Lavardin, Masques, Le Cri du Hibou, Story of Women, Clichy Days (Quiet Days in Clichy), The Lark (actor only), Doctor M (Club Extinction), Madame Bovary, Betty, Through the Eyes of Vichy, L'Enfer (Hell; also s.p.), A Judgment in Stone (also co-s.p.), Rien Ne Va Plus, The Color of Lies (also s.p.).

CHAKERES, MICHAEL H.
Executive. b. Ohio. e. Wittenberg U, 1935. Pres. and chmn. of bd. of Chakeres Theatres of Ohio and Kentucky. U.S. Army AF 1942-45. Bd. of Dir.: National NATO, NATO of Ohio, Will Rogers Hospital, Motion Picture Pioneers, Society National Bank, Wittenberg U., Springfield Foundation, Variety Club of Palm Beach, Tent No. 65. Member: Masonic Temple, Scottish Rite, I.O.O.F., AHEPA, Leadership 100, ARCHON-Order of St. Andrew, Rotary Club, City of Hope, University Club.

CHAKIRIS, GEORGE
Actor. b. Norwood, OH, Sept. 16, 1933. Entered m.p. industry as chorus dancer.
PICTURES: Song of Love (debut, 1947), The Great Caruso, The 5000 Fingers of Dr. T, Give a Girl a Break, Gentlemen Prefer Blondes, There's No Business Like Show Business, White Christmas, Brigadoon, The Girl Rush, Meet Me in Las Vegas, Under Fire (1st acting role), West Side Story (Academy Award for Best Supporting Actor, 1961), Two and Two Make Six, Diamond Head, Bebo's Girl, Kings of the Sun, Flight From Ashiya, 633 Squadron, McGuire Go Home! (The High Bright Sun), Is Paris Burning?, The Young Girls of Rochefort, The Big Cube, The Day the Hot Line Got Hot, Why Not Stay for Breakfast?, Jekyll and Hyde... Together Again, Pale Blood.
TELEVISION: *Series*: Dallas (1985-86). *Guest*: Fantasy Island, CHiPs, Matt Houston, Scarecrow and Mrs. King, Hell Town, Murder She Wrote. *Movie*: Return to Fantasy Island. *Specials*: You're the Top, Highways of Melody, Kismet, Notorious Woman (PBS).

CHAMBERLAIN, RICHARD
Actor. r.n. George Richard Chamberlain. b. Los Angeles, CA, March 31, 1935. Studied voice, LA Conservatory of Music 1958; acting with Jeff Corey. Founding mem. City of Angels, LA Theater Company. Became TV star in Dr. Kildare series, 1961-66. Founded prod. co. Cham Enterprises. Had hit record Three Stars Will Shine Tonight (them from Dr. Kildare) in 1962.
THEATER: Breakfast at Tiffany's, Night of the Iguana, Fathers & Sons, Blithe Spirit.
PICTURES: The Secret of the Purple Reef (debut, 1960), A Thunder of Drums, Twilight of Honor, Joy in the Morning, Petulia, The Madwoman of Chaillot, Julius Caesar, The Music Lovers, Lady Caroline Lamb, The Three Musketeers, The Towering Inferno, The Four Musketeers, The Slipper and the Rose, The Swarm, The Last Wave, Murder by Phone (Bells), King Solomon's Mines, Alan Quartermain and the Lost City of Gold, The Return of the Musketeers (tv in U.S.), Bird of Prey.
TELEVISION: *Specials*: Hamlet, Portrait of a Lady, The Woman I Love, The Lady's Not for Burning. *Movies*: F. Scott Fitzgerald and the Last of the Belles, The Count of Monte Cristo, The Man in the Iron Mask, Cook and Perry: The Race to the Pole, Wallenberg: A Hero's Story, Casanova, Aftermath: A Test of Love, The Night of the Hunter, Ordeal in the Arctic, The Thorn Birds: The Missing Year, All the Winters that Have Been. *Mini-Series*: Centennial, Shogun, The Thorn Birds, Dream West, The Bourne Identity, Too Rich: The Secret Life of Doris Duke. *Series*: Dr. Kildare, Island Son (also co-exec. prod.) *Host*: The Astronomers. *Guest*: Gunsmoke, Thriller, The Deputy, Alfred Hitchcock Presents, The Lost Daughter.

CHAMBERS, EVERETT
Producer, Writer, Director. b. Montrose, CA; Aug. 19, 1926. e. New School For Social Research, Dramatic Workshop, N.Y. Entered industry as actor; worked with Fred Coe as casting dir. and dir., NBC, 1952-57; Author: Producing TV Movies.
PICTURES: *Actor*: Too Late Blues. Writer: Tess of the Storm Country, Run Across the River, The Kiss (short; dir.: Acad. Award nom.), The Lollipop Cover (also prod., dir.; Acad. award, Chicago Film Fest.), Private Duty Nurses, A Girl to Kill For.
TELEVISION: *Series*: *Producer:* Johnny Staccato (also writer), Target the Corrupters, The Dick Powell Theatre, The Lloyd Bridges Show (also writer), Peyton Place, Columbo, Future Cop, Timeslip (exec. prod., writer), Lucan (also writer), Airwolf, Partners in Crime, Rin Tin Tin K-9 Cop (also creative consultant). *Movies*: Beverly Hills Madam, A Matter of Sex (exec. prod., 1985 Christopher & A.W.R.T. Awards), Will There Really Be a Morning?, Berlin Tunnel 21 (sprv. prod.), Night Slaves (also writer), Moon of the Wolf, Trouble Comes to Town, The Great American Beauty Contest, Can Ellen Be Saved? (also writer), Jigsaw John, Street Killing, Nero Wolfe, Twin Detectives (also writer), The Girl Most Likely to..., Sacrifice the Queen, Paris Conspiracy, Family Secret, Incident in a Small Town (spv. prod.). *Co-writer*: The Perfect Town for Murder, Last Chance (pilot).

CHAMPION, JOHN C.
Director, Producer, Writer. b. Denver, CO, Oct. 13, 1923. e. Stanford U., Wittenberg Coll. p. Lee R. Champion, Supreme Court judge. Entered m.p. in Fiesta; did some radio work; in stock at MGM briefly; co-pilot Western Air Lines, Inc., 1943; served in U.S. Army Air Force, air transport command pilot 1943-45; public relations officer AAF; writer & prod. for Allied Artists; v.p. prod. Commander Films Corp.: press. Champion Pictures, Inc.; prod., MGM, Warner, Paramount, Universal, Member: SAG, SWG, SIMPP, SPG; TV Academy, Prod. Writer, Mirisch-U.A.; prod. TV Laramie series; created McHales Navy; author, novel, The Hawks of Noon, 1965; National Cowboy Hall of Fame Award, 1976.
PICTURES: Panhandle, Stampede, Hellgate, Dragonfly Squadron, Shotgun, Zero Hour, The Texican, Attack on the Iron Coast, Submarine X-1, The Last Escape, Brother of the Wind, Mustang Country (dir-prod-writer).

CHAMPION, MARGE
Dancer, Actress, Choreographer. r.n. Marjorie Celeste Belcher. b. Los Angeles, CA, Sept. 2, 1921. e. Los Angeles public schools. Father was Ernest Belcher, ballet master. Was model for Snow White for Disney's animated feature. Debuted in films as Marjorie Bell. Made debut in 1947, with former husband Gower Champion as dancing team; team was signed by MGM; voted Star of Tomorrow, 1952. Received Lifetime Achievement award from the American Dance Foundation, 1997.
THEATER: Blossom Time, Student Prince (LA Civic Opera), Dark of the Moon. Beggar's Holiday (NY), 3 for Tonight (NY), nvitation to a March (tour). Director: Stepping Out, Lute Song (Berkshire Theatre Fest, 1989), She Loves Me, No No Nanette.
PICTURES: Honor of the West (debut, 1939), The Story of Vernon and Irene Castle, Sorority House, Mr. Music, Show Boat, Lovely to Look At, Everything I Have Is Yours, Give a Girl a Break, Three for the Show, Jupiter's Darling, The Swimmer, The Party, The Cockeyed Cowboys of Calico County. *Choreographer only:* The Day of the Locust, Whose Life Is It Anyway?.
TELEVISION: *Series*: Admiral Broadway Revue, Marge and Gower Champion Show. *Guest*: GE Theatre, Chevy Show, Bell Telephone Hour, Ed Sullivan, Shower of Stars, Fame. *Movie*: Queen of the Stardust Ballroom (choreographer; Emmy Award, 1975).

CHAN, JACKIE
Actor, Director, Writer. r.n. Chan Kwong-Sang. b. Hong Kong, Apr. 7, 1955. Trained in acrobatics, mime and martial arts at Peking Opera Sch. Was child actor in several films; later became stuntman before being launched as action star by prod.-dir. Lo Wei.
PICTURES: Little Tiger From Canton, New Fist of Fury, Shaolin Wooden Men, To Kill With Intrigue, Snake in the Eagle's Shadow, Snake & Crane Arts of Shaolin, Magnificent Bodyguards, Drunken Master (Drunk Monkey in the Tiger's Eyes), Spiritual Kung Fu, The Fearless Hyena, Dragon Fist, The Young Master (also dir., co-s.p.), Half a Loaf of Kung Fu, The Big Brawl, The Cannonball Run, Dragon Lord (also dir., co-s.p.), Winners and Sinners, The Fearless Hyena Part 2, Cannonball Run II, Project A (also co-dir., co-s.p.), Wheels on Meals, My Lucky Stars, The Protector, Twinkle Twinkle Lucky Stars, Heart of the Dragon (First Mission), Police Story (also dir., co-s.p.), Armour of God (also dir., co-s.p.), Project A Part 2 (also dir., co-s.p.), Dragons Forever, Police Story II (also dir., co-s.p.), Mr. Canton and Lady Rose (Miracle; also dir., co-s.p.), Armour of God II: Operation Condor (also dir., co-s.p.), Island of Fire, Twin Dragons, Police Story III: Super Cop (also dir., co-s.p.), City Hunter, Crime Story, Project S, Drunken Master II, Rumble in the Bronx, Thunderbolt, First Strike, Burn Hollywood Burn, Mr. Nice Guy, Rush Hour, Who Am I? (also dir., s.p.), Gorgeous (also exec. prod.), Shanghai Noon (also prod.)

CHANNING, CAROL
Actress. b. Seattle, WA, Jan. 31, 1921. e. Bennington Coll.
THEATER: B'way: Gentlemen Prefer Blondes, Lend an Ear (Theatre World Award), Hello Dolly! (Tony Award, 1964), Show Girl, Lorelei. Tour: Legends.
PICTURES: Paid in Full (debut, 1950), The First Traveling Saleslady, Thoroughly Modern Millie (Acad. Award nom.), Skidoo, Shinbone Alley (voice), Sgt. Pepper's Lonely Hearts Club Band (cameo), Happily Ever After (voice), Hans Christian Andersen's Thumbelina (voice), Edie & Pen, The Line King: Al Hirschfeld, Homo Heights.
TELEVISION: *Specials*: Svengali and the Blonde, Three Men on a Horse, Crescendo, The Carol Channing Special. *Guest*: Omnibus, George Burns Show, Lucy Show, Carol Burnett Show, The Love Boat, The Drew Carey Show.

CHANNING, STOCKARD
Actress. r.n. Susan Williams Antonia Stockard. b. New York, NY, Feb. 13, 1944. e. Radcliffe Coll., B.A., 1965. With Theater Co. of Boston, experimental drama company, 1967.
THEATER: Two Gentlemen of Verona, No Hard Feelings, Vanities (Mark Taper Forum, LA), They're Playing Our Song, The Lady and the Clarinet, Golden Age, The Rink, Joe Egg (Tony Award, 1985), Love Letters, Woman in Mind, House of Blue Leaves, Six Degrees of Separation, Four Baboons Adoring the Sun.

PICTURES: The Hospital (debut, 1971), Up the Sandbox, The Fortune, The Big Bus, Sweet Revenge, Grease, The Cheap Detective, The Fish That Saved Pittsburgh, Safari 3000, Without a Trace, Heartburn, The Men's Club, A Time of Destiny, Staying Together, Meet the Applegates, Married to It, Six Degrees of Separation (Acad. Award nom.), Bitter Moon, Smoke, To Wong Foo—Thanks for Everything—Julie Newmar, Up Close and Personal, Moll Flanders, Edie and Pen, The First Wives Club, Practical Magic, Baby Dance, Twilight, Lulu on the Bridge (voice), Practical Magic, Isn't She Great, The Venice Project, Where the Heart Is.
TELEVISION: *Series*: Stockard Channing in Just Friends, The Stockard Channing Show, Batman Beyond (voice), It's A Girl Thing. *Movies*: The Girl Most Likely To..., Lucan, Silent Victory: The Kitty O'Neil Story, Not My Kid, The Room Upstairs, Echoes in the Darkness, The Perfect Witness, David's Mother, An Unexpected Family, Lily Dale, The Prosecutors, An Unexpected Life, The Baby Dance. *Guest*: Medical Center, Trying Times (The Sad Professor), King of the Hill (voice). *Special*: Tidy Endings.

CHAPIN, DOUG
Producer. Began career as actor; then switched to film production, making debut with When a Stranger Calls, 1979.
PICTURES: Pandemonium, American Dreamer, What's Love Got to Do With It, Love! Valour! Compassion!, The Passion of Ayn Rand (co-exec.).
TELEVISION: *Movies*: All Lies End in Murder, Belle Starr, Missing Pieces, Second Sight, When A Stranger Calls Back, Jackie's Back (exec.). *Series*: Tim Conway's Funny America.

CHAPLIN, CHARLES S.
Executive. b. Toronto, Ont., Canada, June 24, 1911. Studied law. Entered m.p. ind. in 1930 as office boy with United Artists; then office mgr. booker, St. John, N.B., 1933; br. mgr. 1935; to Montreal in same capacity, 1941; 1945-62, Canadian gen. mgr.; v.p. Canadian sls. mgr., 7 Arts Prod., 1962; CEO, v.p., dir. TV sls., Europe-Africa, Middle East-Socialist countries, 1968-70; v.p., WB-7 Arts, 1970-72; exec. v.p. intl. film dist., NTA (Canada) Ltd., Toronto Intl. Film Studios, 1972-80; pres., Charles Chaplin Enterprises, specializing in theatrical and TV sls. and prod. Pres.: B'nai Brith, Toronto Bd. of Trade, various charitable org., many trade assns., past pres. Canadian M.P. Dist. Assn., Chmn. m.p. section Com. Chest, chmn. publ. rel. comm. & past-chmn., M.P. Industry Council; Natl. Board Council Christians & Jews, etc. Representing many indept. producers in Europe, Canada, Far East, South America, etc.

CHAPLIN, GERALDINE
Actress. b. Santa Monica, CA, July 3, 1944. e. Royal Ballet School, London. Father was actor-director Charles Chaplin. Starred in over 20 European productions, including seven with Spanish filmmaker, Carlos Saura. On NY stage in The Little Foxes.
PICTURES: Limelight (debut, 1952), Par un Beau Matin d'Ete, Doctor Zhivago, Andremo in Citta, A Countess from Hong Kong, Stranger in the House (Cop-Out), I Killed Rasputin, Peppermint Frappe, Stres es Tres Tres, Honeycomb, Garden of Delights, The Hawaiians, Sur un Arbre Perche, Z.P.G. (Zero Population Growth), Innocent Bystanders, La Casa sin Fronteras, Ana and the Wolves, The Three Musketeers, Le Marriage a la Mode, The Four Musketeers, Summer of Silence, Nashville, Elisa My Love, Noroit, Buffalo Bill and the Indians or Sitting Bull's History Lesson, Welcome to L.A., Cria, In Memorium, Une Page d'Amour, Roseland, Remember My Name, Los Ojos Vendados, The Masked Bride, L'Adoption, A Wedding, The Mirror Crack'd, Le Voyage en Douce, Bolero, Life Is a Bed of Roses, Love on the Ground, The Moderns, White Mischief, Mama Turns 100, The Return of the Musketeers (tv in U.S.), I Want to Go Home, The Children, Buster's Bedroom, Chaplin, The Age of Innocence, Words Upon the Window Pane, Home for the Holidays, Jane Eyre, Crimetime, The Eyes of Asia, Mother Theresa: In the Name of God's Poor, Cousin Bette, To Walk with Lions.
TELEVISION: *Specials*: The Corsican Brothers, My Cousin Rachel, The House of Mirth, A Foreign Field. *Mini-Series:* The World, The Odyssey. *Movie*: Duel of Hearts, Gulliver's Travels.

CHAPMAN, MICHAEL
Cinematographer, Director. b. New York, NY, Nov. 21, 1935. m. writer-dir. Amy Jones. Early career in N.Y. area working on documentaries before becoming camera operator for cinematographer Gordon Willis on The Godfather, Klute, End of the Road, The Landlord. Also camera operator on Jaws.
PICTURES: *Cinematographer*: The Last Detail, White Dawn, Taxi Driver, The Front, The Next Man, Fingers, The Last Waltz, Invasion of the Body Snatchers, Hardcore, The Wanderers, Raging Bull, Dead Men Don't Wear Plaid, Personal Best, The Man With Two Brains, Shoot to Kill, Scrooged, Ghostbusters II, Quick Change, Kindergarten Cop, Whispers in the Dark, Rising Sun, The Lost Boys, The Fugitive, Primal Fear, Space Jam, Six Days Seven Nights. *Director:* All the Right Moves, The Clan of the Cave Bear, The Viking Sagas (also s.p.).
TELEVISION: Death Be Not Proud, King, Gotham. *Dir.*: The Annihilator (pilot).

CHARBONNEAU, PATRICIA
Actress. b. Valley Stream, Long Island, NY, 1959. Stage appearances with Actors Theatre of Louisville, KY. Also in NY in My Sister in This House.
PICTURES: Desert Hearts, Manhunter, Stalking Danger, Call Me, Shakedown, Brain Dead, Captive, The Owl, K2, Portraits of a Killer, Kiss the Sky, She's All That.
TELEVISION: *Series:* Crime Story. *Pilots:* C.A.T. Squad, Dakota's Way. *Guest:* Spenser: For Hire, The Equalizer, Wiseguy, UNSUB, Matlock. *Movies:* Disaster at Silo 7, Desperado: Badlands Justice.

CHAREST, MICHELINE
Producer.
PICTURES: Bonjour Timothy, The Whole of the Moon, The Sleep Room.
TELEVISION: *Series*: The Wonderful Wizard of Oz, Arthur (Emmy Award, 1998), Lassie, The Country Mouse and the City Mouse Adventures, Emily of the New Moon. *Mini-series*: Million Dollar Babies.

CHARISSE, CYD
Dancer, Actress. r.n. Tula Ellice Finklea. b. Amarillo, TX, March 8, 1921. e. Hollywood Prof. Sch. m. Tony Martin, singer. Toured U.S. & Europe with Ballet Russe starting at age 13. Began in films as bit player using the name Lily Norwood. Signed contract with MGM in 1946. Named Star of Tomorrow 1948. B'way debut 1991 in Grand Hotel.
PICTURES: Something to Shout About (debut, 1943; billed as Lily Norwood), Mission to Moscow; Ziegfeld Follies (1st film billed as Cyd Charisse), The Harvey Girls, Three Wise Fools, Till the Clouds Roll By, Fiesta, Unfinished Dance, On an Island with You, Words and Music, Kissing Bandit, Tension, East Side West Side, Mark of the Renegade, Wild North, Singin' in the Rain, Sombrero, The Band Wagon, Brigadoon, Deep in My Heart, It's Always Fair Weather, Meet Me in Las Vegas, Silk Stockings, Twilight for the Gods, Party Girl, Five Golden Hours, Black Tights, Two Weeks in Another Town, The Silencers, Maroc 7, Won Ton Ton the Dog Who Saved Hollywood, Warlords of Atlantis, That's Entertainment III.
TELEVISION: *Movies*: Portrait of an Escort, Swimsuit, Cinderalla Summer.

CHARLES, MARIA
Actress. b. London, England, Sept. 22, 1929. Trained at RADA. London stage debut 1946 in Pick Up Girl.
THEATER: *London*: Women of Twilight, The Boy Friend, Divorce Me Darling!, Enter A Free Man, They Don't Grow on Trees, Winnie the Pooh, Jack the Ripper, The Matchmaker, Measure for Measure, Annie (1979-80), Fiddler on the Roof, Steaming, Peer Gynt, The Lower Depths, When We Are Married, Follies, Party Piece, School for Scandal, Driving Miss Daisy, Hay Fever, Blithe Spirit. *Dir.*: Owl and the Pussycat. *Dir./prod.*: The Boy Friend, 40, Starting Here Starting Now.
PICTURES: Folly To Be Wise, The Deadly Affair, Eye of the Devil, Great Expectations, The Return of the Pink Panther, Cuba, Victor/Victoria, Savage Hearts, The Fool.
TELEVISION: The Likes of 'Er, The Moon and the Yellow River, Down Our Street, Easter Passion, Nicholas Nickleby, The Voice of the Turtle, The Fourth Wall, The Good Old Days, Turn Out the Lights, Angel Pavement, The Ugliest Girl in Town, Other Peoples Houses, Rogues Gallery, The Prince and the Pauper, Crown Court, Bar Mitzvah Boy, Secret Army, Agony, Never the Twain, La Ronde, Shine of Harvey Moon, Sheppey, La Ronde, Brideshead Revisited, A Perfect Spy, Casualty, The Fallout Guy, Lovejoy, Anna, Agony Again, Oliver Twist, Crime and Punishment.

CHARTOFF, ROBERT
Producer. b. New York, NY., Aug. 26, 1933. e. Union College, A.B.; Columbia U., LL.B. Met Irwin Winkler through mutual client at William Morris Agency (N.M.) and established Chartoff-Winkler Prods. Currently pres., Chartoff Prods., Inc.
PICTURES: Double Trouble, Point Blank, The Split, They Shoot Horses Don't They?, The Strawberry Statement, Leo the Last, Believe in Me, The Gang That Couldn't Shoot Straight, The New Centurions, Up the Sandbox, The Mechanic, Thumb Tripping, Busting, The Gambler, S*P*Y*S, Breakout, Nickelodeon, Rocky, New York New York, Valentino, Comes a Horseman, Uncle Joe Shannon, Rocky II, Raging Bull, True Confessions, Rocky III, The Right Stuff, Rocky IV, Beer, Rocky V, Straight Talk.

CHASE, BRANDON
Producer, Director. President MPA Feature Films, Inc.; newscaster-news director NBC-TV 1952-57. Executive director Mardi Gras Productions, Inc. and member of Board of Directors. Now pres., Group I Films, Ltd., and V.I. Prods., Ltd.
PICTURES: The Dead One, The Sinner and the Slave Girl, Bourbon Street Shadows, Verdict Homicide, Face of Fire, Four for the Morgue, Mission To Hell, The Wanton, Harlow, Girl In Trouble, Threesome, Wild Cargo, Alice in Wonderland, The Models, The Four of Us, Against All Odds, The Giant Spider Invasion, House of 1000 Pleasures, The Rogue, Eyes of Dr. Chaney, Alligator, Crash!, Take All of Me, The Psychic, UFOs Are Real, The Actresses, The Sword and the Sorcerer, Alligator II.

TELEVISION: Wild Cargo (series prod.-dir.); This Strange and Wondrous World (prod.-dir.), Linda Evans: Secrets to Stay Young Forever.

CHASE, CHEVY
Actor. r.n. Cornelius Crane Chase. b. New York, NY, Oct. 8, 1943. e. Bard Coll.; B.A. Studied audio research at CCS Institute. Worked as writer for Mad Magazine 1969. Teamed with Kenny Shapiro and Lane Sarasohn while still in school to collaborate on material for underground TV, which ultimately became off-off-Broadway show and later movie called Groove Tube. Co-wrote and starred in Saturday Night Live on TV, winning 2 Emmys as continuing single performance by a supporting actor and as writer for show. Wrote Paul Simon Special (Emmy Award, 1977).
PICTURES: The Groove Tube (debut, 1974), Tunnelvision, Foul Play, Caddyshack, Oh Heavenly Dog, Seems Like Old Times, Under the Rainbow, Modern Problems, National Lampoon's Vacation, Deal of the Century, Fletch, National Lampoon's European Vacation, Sesame Street Presents Follow That Bird (cameo), Spies Like Us, Three Amigos!, The Couch Trip (cameo), Funny Farm, Caddyshack II, Fletch Lives, National Lampoon's Christmas Vacation, L.A. Story (cameo), Nothing But Trouble, Memoirs of an Invisible Man, Hero (unbilled), Last Action Hero (cameo), Cops and Robbersons, Man of the House, Vegas Vacation, Dirty Work, Snow Day.
TELEVISION: *Series*: Saturday Night Live, The Chevy Chase Show.

CHASE, STANLEY
Producer. b. Brooklyn, NY, May 3. e. NYU, B.A.; Columbia U, postgraduate. m. actress/artist Dorothy Rice. Began career as assoc. prod. of TV show Star Time; story dept., CBS-TV; then produced plays Off-B'way and on B'way, winner Tony and Obie awards for The Threepenny Opera. Joined ABC-TV as dir. in chg. programming; prod., Universal Pictures & TV; exec. consultant, Metromedia Producers Org.; prod. & exec. Alan Landsburg Productions. Formed Stanley Chase Productions, Inc. in 1975, which heads as pres.
THEATER: *B'way Producer*: The Potting Shed, The Cave Dwellers, A Moon for the Misbegotten, European Tour: Free and Easy. *Off-B'way*: The Threepenny Opera.
PICTURES: The Hell with Heroes, Colossus: The Forbin Project, Welcome to Blood City, High-Ballin', Fish Hawk, The Guardian, Mack the Knife.
TELEVISION: Inside Danny Baker (pilot), Al Capp special (prod., writer), Happily Ever After (pilot; prod., writer), Bob Hope Presents the Chrysler Theatre series, Jigsaw (pilot), Fear on Trial (Emmy nom.), Courage of Kavik: The Wolf Dog (exec. prod.), An American Christmas Carol, Grace Kelly.

CHASMAN, DAVID
Executive. b. New York, NY, Sept. 28, 1925. e. Sch. of Industrial Art, 1940-43; Academie De La Grande-Chaumiere, 1949-50. Monroe Greenthal Co., Inc. 1950-53; Grey Advertising Agency, Inc., 1953-60. Freelance consultant to industry 1950-60; worked on pictures for UA, 20th-Fox, Columbia, Samuel Goldwyn, City Film; Adv. mgr. United Artists, 1960; exec. dir. adv., United Artists, 1962; exec. production, United Artists, London, 1964; v.p. in prod. United Artists, 1969; v.p. of west coast operations, U.A. 1970; sr. v.p. in charge of prod., U.A. 1972; president, Convivium Productions Inc., 1974. Joined Columbia 1977, named exec. v.p. worldwide theatrical prod. 1979. Joined MGM 1980; named exec. v.p.-worldwide theatrical prod.
PICTURES: *Exec. prod.*: Brighton Beach Memoirs, The Secret of My Success.

CHAUDHRI, AMIN QAMAR
Director, Producer, Cinematographer, Editor. b. Punjab, India, April 18, 1942. e. Hampstead Polytechnic, London, City U. of New York. Pres., Filmart Enterprises Ltd. & Filmart Int'l Ltd., Pres./CEO, Continental Film Group Ltd. Pres./CEO, Continental Entertainment Group, Ltd., Heron Int'l Pictures, Ltd.
PICTURES: *Director*: Kashish, Khajuraho, Eternal, Urvasi, Konarak, The Land of Buddha. *Producer*: Night Visitors, Diary of a Hit Man, The Master Mechanic. *Producer/Director*: Once Again, An Unremarkable Life, Tiger Warsaw, The Last Day of School, Gunga Din, Golden Chute, Wings of Grey, Call It Sleep, The Bookie. *Cinematography*: Right On, Sweet Vengeance, The Hopefuls, The Wicked Die Slow, Who Says I Can't Ride a Rainbow, Black Rodeo, Medium Is the Message, Death of a Dunbar Girl, Kashish, The Last Day of School.
TELEVISION: Reflections of India (prod.-dir.), Wild Wild East (camera), Nehru (edit.), Medium is the Message (photog.), America... Amerika (prod., dir.).

CHAYKIN, MAURY
Actor. b. Brooklyn, NY, July 27, 1949. e. Univ. of Buffalo. Formed theatre co. Swamp Fox; later acted with Buffalo rep. co., Public Theatre in NY. Moved to Toronto in 1980.
PICTURES: The Kidnapping of the President, Death Hunt, Soup for One, Of Unknown Origin, Harry and Son, Highpoint, Mrs. Soffel, Turk 182!, Meatballs III, The Bedroom Window, Wild Thing, Stars and Bars, Caribe, Iron Eagle II, Twins, Millenium, Breaking In, Where the Heart Is, Mr. Destiny, Dances With Wolves, George's Island, My Cousin Vinny, Leaving Normal, The Adjuster, Hero, Sommersby, Money for Nothing, Josh and S.A.M., Beethoven's 2nd, Camilla, Whale Music (Genie Award), Unstrung Heroes, Devil in a Blue Dress, Cutthroat Island, Love and Death on Long Island, Pale Saints, Strip Search, The Sweet Hereafter, A Life Less Ordinary, Mouse Hunt, Jerry & Tom, Mystery Alaska, Shegalla, Jacob Two Two Meets the Hooded Fang, Entrapment.
TELEVISION: *Special:* Canada's Sweetheart: The Saga of Hal Banks (Nellie Award). *Series*: Emily of New Moon. *Movies*: If Looks Could Kill, Northern Lights, Joan of Arc.

CHELSOM, PETER
Director, Writer. b. Blackpool, England. Studied acting at London's Central School of Drama. Acted with Royal Shakespeare Co., Royal Natl. Theatre, Royal Court Theatre. Dir. at Central School of Drama, taught acting at Actors Ints. and at Cornell Univ. Wrote and directed short film Treacle for Channel 4/British Screen. Director of many commercials for television in London and U.S.
PICTURES: Hear My Song (dir., story, co-s.p.), Funny Bones (dir., co-prod., co-s.p.), The Mighty, Town and Country.

CHEN, JOAN
Actress. r.n. Chen Chung. b. Shanghai, China, 1961. Studied acting with actress Zhang Rei Fang at Shanghai Film Studio. Debuted as teenager in Chinese films. Moved to U.S. in 1981.
PICTURES: Little Flower, Awakening, Dim Sum: A Little Bit of Heart, Tai-Pain, The Last Emperor, The Blood of Heroes, Turtle Beach, When Sleeping Dogs Lie, Night Stalker, Heaven and Earth, Golden Gate, On Deadly Ground, Temptation of a Monk, Deadlock, The Hunted, Red Rose/White Rose, Judge Dredd, The Wild Side (also assoc. prod.), Precious Find, Purple Storm, What's Cookin. *Director/Writer:* Xiu Xiu: The Sent Down Girl (also exec. prod.), Autumn in New York.
TELEVISION: *Series*: Twin Peaks. *Movie*: Shadow of a Stranger. *Guest*: Miami Vice.

CHER
Singer, Actress. r.n. Cherilyn Sarkisian. b. El Centro, CA, May 20, 1946. Began singing as backup singer for Crystals and Ronettes then with former husband Sonny Bono in 1965; first hit record I Got You Babe, sold 3 million copies. Made two films and then debuted nightclub musical-comedy act in 1969. CBS comedy-variety series started as summer show in 1971; became regular series the following December. NY stage debut: Come Back to the Five and Dime Jimmy Dean Jimmy Dean (1982).
PICTURES: Wild on the Beach (debut, 1965), Good Times, Chastity, Come Back to the Five and Dime Jimmy Dean Jimmy Dean, Silkwood, Mask (Cannes award), The Witches of Eastwick, Suspect, Moonstruck (Academy Award), Mermaids, The Player, Ready to Wear (Pret- a-Porter), Faithful, Tea with Mussolini.
TELEVISION: *Series*: Sonny & Cher Comedy Hour (1971-74), Cher, The Sonny and Cher Show (1976-77). *Specials*: Cher, Cher... Special, Cher and Other Fantasies, Cher: A Celebration at Caesar's Palace, Cher at the Mirage. *Movie*: If These Walls Could Talk (also dir.). *Guest*: Shindig, Hullabaloo, Hollywood Palace, The Man from U.N.C.L.E., Laugh-In, Glen Campbell, Love American Style.

CHERMAK, CY
Producer, Writer. b. Bayonne, NJ, Sept. 20, 1929. e. Brooklyn Coll., Ithaca Coll.
TELEVISION: *Writer, prod., exec. prod.*: Ironside, The Virginian, The New Doctors, Amy Prentiss, Kolchak: The Night Stalker, Barbary Coast, CHiPS. *Movie*: Murder at the World Series (prod., s.p.).

CHERNIN, PETER
Executive. Began career as assoc. publicity director, St. Martin's Press; editor, Warner Books. v.p. of development & prod., David Gerber Co.; exec. v.p., programming & mktg., Showtime/The Movie Channel, Inc.; president & COO, Lorimar Film Entertainment. president, Fox Entertainment Group of Fox Broadcasting Co.; chairman & CEO, Fox Filmed Entertainment, 1992-96. Currently president & COO, News Corporation and Fox Entertainment Group, under which the top grossing movie of all time, Titanic, was developed and produced. Also currently chairman & CEO, Fox Group, the North American Operations of News Corp.; member of the board, News Corp. and Office of the Chairman.

CHERTOK, JACK
Producer. b. Atlanta, GA, July 13, 1906. Began career as script clerk, MGM; later asst. cameraman, asst. dir., head of music dept., short subjects prod. (including Crime Does Not Pay, Robert Benchley, Pete Smith series). Feature prod. MGM 1939-42 (The Penalty, Joe Smith, American, Kid Glove Killer, The Omaha Trail, Eyes in the Night, etc.). In 1942, apptd. Hollywood prod. chief, Co-Ord. Inter-Amer. Affairs, serving concurrently with regular studio work. Left MGM in 1942 and prod. for Warner Bros. to late 1944; Produced The Corn is Green and Northern Pursuit for Warner Bros. Pres. Jack Chertok TV, Inc.

TELEVISION: *Prod.*: My Favorite Martian, The Lone Ranger, Sky King, Cavalcade, Private Secretary, My Living Doll, Western Marshal, The Lawless Years.

CHETWYND, LIONEL
Executive, Writer, Director. b. London, England. m. actress Gloria Carlin. Emigrated to Canada, 1948. e. Sir George Williams U., Montreal, BA, economics; BCL-McGill U., Montreal. Graduate Work-Law, Trinity Coll. Oxford. Admitted to bar, Province of Quebec, 1968. C.B.C., TV-Public Affairs and Talks, 1961-1965. CTV network 1965-67. Controller commercial TV and film rights, Expo '67. Freelance writer and consultant 1961-68. Asst. mng. dir. Columbia Pictures (U.K.) Ltd. London 1968-72. Asst. mng. dir. Columbia-Warner UK, 1971. Story and book for musical Maybe That's Your Problem, 1971-1973. Then Bleeding Great Orchids (staged London, and Off-B'way). Also wrote The American 1776, official U.S. Bi-centennial film and We the People/200 Constitutional Foundation. Former mem. of NYU grad. film sch. faculty, lecturer on screenwriting at Frederick Douglass Ctr. Harlem. Mem of Canadian Bar Assc. Served on bd. of gov., Commission on Battered Children, and the Little League.
PICTURES: *Director and/or Writer*: The Apprenticeship of Duddy Kravitz (Acad. Award nom.), Morning Comes, Two Solitudes (also prod., Grand Award Salonika), Quintet, The Hanoi Hilton, Redline, The Hot Touch.
TELEVISION: *Producer and/or Writer*: Johnny We Hardly Knew Ye (George Washington Honor Medal, Freedom Fdn.), It Happened One Christmas, Goldenrod, A Whale for the Killing , Miracle on Ice (Christopher Award), Escape From Iran: The Canadian Caper, Sadat (NAACP Image Award), Children in the Crossfire, To Heal a Nation (also exec. prod.), Evil in Clear River (exec. prod. only, Christopher Award), So Proudly We Hail (also exec. prod.), The Godfather Wars, The Heroes of Desert Storm, Reverse Angle (also exec. prod.), Doom's Day Gun, The Bible... Moses, The Bible... Jacob, The Bible... Joseph (Emmy award), The Man Who Captured Eichmann, Kissinger & Nixon (also exec. prod.), Ruby Ridge, An American Tragedy, The Doom's Day Gun, Freefall, Goldenrod.

CHEUNG, MAGGIE
Actress. b. Hong Kong, Sept. 20, 1964. Extensive work in Hong Kong. Cinema.
PICTURES: Jackie Chan's Police Story, Happy Ghost 3, Kino Countdown (cameo), The Game They Call Sex, Police Story 2, Song of Exile, The Dragon from Russia, Heart Against Hearts (cameo), The Banquet, Days of Being Wild, The Actress, Dragon Inn, The Heroic Trio, Double Dragon, Police Story 3: Supercop, Family Happiness, Chasing Boys, Moon Warriors, Heroic Trio 2: Executioners, Seven Maidens, The Eagle Shooting Heroes, Green Snake, Ashes of Time, Comrades: Almost a Love Story, Irma Vep, Chinese Box, The Soong Sisters, Augustin: King of Kung-Fu, Memoirs of a Geisha.

CHINICH, MICHAEL
Producer. b. New York, NY. e. Boston U. Began career as casting agent in N.Y.; moved to L.A. to join MCA-Universal Pictures as executive in casting. Named head of feature film casting; then prod. v.p.
PICTURES: *Casting dir.*: Dog Day Afternoon, Coal Miner's Daughter, Animal House, Melvin and Howard, The Blues Brothers, Mask, Midnight Run, Twins, Ghostbusters II, Kindergarten Cop, Dave, Junior, The Late Shift, Father's Day, Six Days Seven Nights. *Exec. Prod.*: Pretty in Pink, Ferris Bueller's Day Off, Some Kind of Wonderful, Planes Trains and Automobiles (co-exec. prod.), Commandments (prod.).

CHOMSKY, MARVIN J.
Director, Producer. b. Bronx, NY, May 23, 1929. e. Syracuse U., B.S.; Stanford U., M.A. Started in theatre business at early age as art dir. with such TV credits as U.S. Steel Hour, Playhouse 90, Studio One, etc. Later worked with Herbert Brodkin who advanced him to assoc. prod. with such TV shows as The Doctors and The Nurses. Brought to Hollywood in 1965 as assoc. prod. for Talent Associates, producing series of TV pilots. Art dir.: The Bubble.
PICTURES: Evel Knievel, Murph the Surf, Mackintosh and T.J., Good Luck Miss Wycoff, Tank.
TELEVISION: *Series*: The Wild Wild West, Gunsmoke, Star Trek, Then Came Bronson. *Movies*: Assault on the Wayne, Mongo's Back in Town, Family Flight, Fireball Forward, Female Artillery, The Magician, The F.B.I. Story: The F.B.I. Vs. Alvin Karpas, Mrs. Sundance, Attack on Terror: The F.B.I. Vs. the Ku Klux Klan, Kate McShane, Brink's: The Great Robbery, Law and Order, A Matter of Wife and Death, Victory at Entebbe, Little Ladies of the Night, Roots (co-dir.), Danger in Paradise, Holocaust (Emmy Award, 1978), Hollow Image, King Crab, Attica (Emmy Award, 1980), Inside the Third Reich (Emmy Award, 1982), My Body My Child, The Nairobi Affair, I Was a Mail Order Bride, Robert Kennedy and His Times, Evita Peron (also prod.), Peter the Great (also prod.; Emmy Award as prod., 1986), The Deliberate Stranger (also prod.), Anastasia: The Mystery of Anna (also prod.), Billionaire Boys Club (also spv. prod.), Angel in Green, I'll Be Home for Christmas (also prod.), Brotherhood of the Rose (also prod.), Telling Secrets, Strauss Dynasty (also prod.), Hurricane Andrew (also prod.), Catherine the Great (also prod.).

CHONG, RAE DAWN
Actress. b. Edmonton Alta, Canada, Feb. 28, 1961. Father is director-comedian Tommy Chong. Debut at 12 in The Whiz Kid of Riverton (TV). B'way debut 1991 in Oh Kay!
PICTURES: Stony Island (debut, 1978), Quest for Fire, Beat Street, The Corsican Brothers, Choose Me, Fear City, City Limits, American Flyers, Commando, The Color Purple, Soul Man, The Squeeze, The Principal, Walking After Midnight, Tales From the Darkside, Far Out Man, The Borrower, Amazon, Chaindance, Time Runner, When the Party's Over, In Exile, Boulevard, Boca, Hideaway, The Break, Starlight, Mask of Death, Waiting for the Man, Goodbye America.
TELEVISION: *Movies*: The Top of the Hill, Badge of the Assassin, Curiosity Kills, Prison Stories: Women on the Inside, Father & Son: Dangerous Relations, Thing I Forgot to Remember, Valentine's Day. *Series*: Nitecap, Martian Law.

CHONG, TOMMY
Actor, Writer, Director. b. Edmonton, Alta., Canada, May 24, 1938. Daughter is actress Rae Dawn Chong. Was guitar player with various Canadian rhythm and blues combinations, before teaming with Richard (Cheech) Marin in improvisational group. Has made comedy recordings.
PICTURES: Up in Smoke, Cheech and Chong's Next Movie (also dir., co-s.p.), Cheech and Chong's Nice Dreams (also dir., co-s.p.), Things Are Tough All Over, It Came from Hollywood, Still Smokin', Yellowbeard, The Corsican Brothers (also dir., s.p.), After Hours, Tripwire (cameo), Far Out Man (also dir., s.p.), The Spirit of 76, FernGully (voice), National Lampoon's Senior Trip, McHale's Navy, Best Buds (also s.p., exec. prod.), Half Baked (actor only).
TELEVISION: Trial and Error (co-exec. prod.).

CHOOLUCK, LEON
Producer, Director. b. New York, NY, March 19, 1920. e. City Coll. of New York, 1938. Production, distribution, editing Consolidated Film Industries Ft. Lee 1936-40; staff sgt., Army Pictorial Service as news photographer 1941-45; prod. for Regal Films (Fox) Clover Prods. (Col.), Hugo Haas Prods. and Orbit Pro. (Col), 1957-58; dir. Highway Patrol, 1958. Prod. mgr., Captain Sinbad, prod. sprv. Encyclopedia Britannica Films, in Spain, 1964; prod. supv., U.S. Pictures, Battle of the Bulge; v.p. Fouad Said Cinemobile Systems, 1969-70; ABC Pictures 1970-71 (Grissom Gang, Kotch). 1983-present, consultant, intl. film services.
PICTURES: Hell on Devil's Island, Plunder Road, Murder by Contract, City of Fear (prod.), The Fearmakers, Day of the Outlaw, Bramble Bush, Rise and Fall of Legs Diamond (assoc. prod.), Studs Lonigan, Three Blondes in His Life (dir.), El Cid, Midas Run (assoc. prod.), Payday; Three the Hard Way, Take a Hard Ride, Apocalypse Now, Loving Couples, Square Dance, Wonders of China (Disney Circlevision Epcot).
TELEVISION: Prod. supv.: 1/4 hr. Fireside Theatre, Stoney Burke, The Outer Limits (assoc. prod.), I Spy (assoc. prod.), Lock Up (dir.). *Specials*: Strange Homecoming, James Mitchener's Dynasty, Judge Horton and the Scottsboro Boys, Pearl, A Rumor of War, Murder in Texas, Love Boat, Dynasty, Breakdown (Alfred Hitchcock), On Wings of Eagles.

CHOW, RAYMOND
O.B.E. Producer. b. Hong Kong, 1927. e. St. John's U., Shanghai. Worked for Hong Kong Standard; then joined the Hong Kong office of the U.S. Information Service. In 1959 joined Shaw Brothers as head of publicity, became head of production before leaving in 1970 to start Golden Harvest to produce Chinese-language films in Hong Kong. Kung-fu films featuring Bruce Lee put Harvest into int'l market. Started English-language films in 1977, beginning with The Amsterdam Kill and The Boys in Company C. Named Showman of the Year 1984 by NATO. Awarded O.B.E. in 1988.
PICTURES: Armour of God, The Big Boss (and subsequent Bruce Lee films), The Cannonball Run (and Part II), High Road to China, Lassiter, Miracles, Mr. Boo (a.k.a. The Private Eyes; and many subsequent Michael Hui films), Painted Faces, Police Story (and Part II), Project A (and Part II), Rouge, The Story of the Flying Fox, Love on the Rooftops, A Show of Force, China O'Brien (and Part II), Teenage Mutant Ninja Turtles (and Part II), Lord of East China Sea, The Reincarnation of Golden Lotus, Summer Snow, Rumble in the Bronx, Lost & Found, Viva Erotica, The Stunt Woman, Hold You Tight, The Soong Sisters, Kitchen, Portland Street Blues, Gorgeous.

CHRISTIANSEN, ROBERT W.
Producer. b. Porterville, CA. e. Bakersfield Coll. Spent 3 years in Marine Corps. Worked on Hollywood Reporter in circulation and advertising. Joined Cinema Center Films; P.A. on Monte Walsh and Hail Hero. Co-produced first feature in 1970, Adam at Six A.M., with Rick Rosenberg, with whom co-produced all credits listed.
PICTURES: Adam at Six A.M., Hide in Plain Sight.
TELEVISION: *Features*: Suddenly Single, The Glass House, Gargoyles, A Brand New Life, The Man Who Could Talk to Kids, The Autobiography of Miss Jane Pittman, I Love You...Goodbye, Queen of the Stardust Ballroom, Born Innocent, A Death in Canaan, Strangers, Robert Kennedy and His Times, Kids Don't Tell, As Summers Die, Gore Vidal's Lincoln, Red Earth, White Earth, The Heist, A House of Secrets and Lies, The Last Hit, Heart of Darkness, Tad, Kingfish: A Story of Huey P. Long, Redwood Curtain.

CHRISTIE, JULIE
Actress. b. Chukua, Assam, India, April 14, 1941. Father had tea plantation in India. e. in Britian, at 16 studied art in France, then attended Central Sch. of Music & Drama in London. 3 yrs. with Frinton-on-Sea Rep., before TV debut in A for Andromeda. Birmingham Rep.; Royal Shakespeare Co.; East European and American tour. NY stage: Uncle Vanya. London stage: Old Times.
PICTURES: Crooks Anonymous (debut, 1962), Fast Lady, Billy Liar, Young Cassidy, Darling (Academy Award & BFA Award, 1965), Dr. Zhivago, Farenheit 451, Far From the Madding Crowd, Petulia, In Search of Gregory, The Go-Between, McCabe and Mrs. Miller, Don't Look Now, Shampoo, Nashville (cameo), Demon Seed, Heaven Can Wait, Memoirs of a Survivor, The Return of the Soldier, Heat and Dust, Golddiggers, Power, Miss Mary, La Memoire tatouree (Secret Obsession), Fools of Fortune, Dragonheart, Hamlet, Afterglow (NY Film Crits. Circle Award, Best Actress, 1997; Academy Award nom.), Belphegor, Monster.
TELEVISION: Debut: A is for Andromeda (UK series, 1962), Sins of the Fathers (Italian TV), Separate Tables, Dadah Is Death (Amer. TV debut, 1988), The Railway Station Man.

CHRISTOPHER, DENNIS
Actor. r.n. Dennis Carelli. b. Philadelphia, PA, Dec. 2, 1955. e. Temple U. NY stage debut, Yentl the Yeshiva Boy (1974). Other NY theater: Dr. Needle and the Infectious Laughter Epidemic, The Little Foxes, Brothers, Exmass, A Pound on Demand, Advice from a Caterpillar. Regional theater incl. Balm in Gilead, American Buffalo. Appeared in 1991 short The Disco Years.
PICTURES: Blood and Lace, Didn't You Hear?, The Young Graduates, Fellini's Roma, Salome, 3 Women, September 30, 1955, A Wedding, California Dreaming, The Last Word, Breaking Away, Fade to Black, Chariots of Fire, Don't Cry It's Only Thunder, Alien Predator, Flight of the Spruce Goose, Jake Speed, Friends, A Sinful Life, Circuitry Man, Dead Women in Lingerie, Doppelganger, Circuitry Man II: Plughead Rewired, Skeletons, The Silencers, It's My Party.
TELEVISION: *Movies*: The Oregon Trail, Stephen King's IT, False Arrest, Willing to Kill: The Texas Cheerleader Story, Curacao, Deadly Invasion: The Killer Bee Nightmare. *Specials*: Bernice Bobs Her Hair, Jack and the Beanstalk (Faerie Tale Theatre), Cristabel. *Series:* Profiler. *Guest*: Trapper John M.D., Tales of the Unexpected, Stingray, Cagney & Lacey, Moonlighting, Hooperman, The Equalizer, Matlock, Murder She Wrote, Monsters, Civil Wars, Dark Justice, The Watcher, The Cosby Mysteries.

CHRISTOPHER, JORDAN
Actor, Musician. b. Youngstown, OH. Oct. 23, 1941. e. Kent State U. Led rock 'n' roll group, The Wild Ones. B'way debut, Black Comedy, 1967.
PICTURES: Return of the Seven, The Fat Spy, The Tree, Angel Angel Down We Go, Pigeons, Brainstorm, Star 80, That's Life!
TELEVISION: *Series*: Secrets of Midland Heights.

CHUNG, CONNIE
TV News Anchor. r.n. Constance Yu-Hwa Chung. m. anchor Maury Povich. b. Washington, D.C., Aug. 20, 1946. e. U. of Maryland, B.S. Entered field 1969 as copy person, writer then on-camera reporter for WTTG-TV, Washington; 1971, named Washington corr., CBS News; 1976, anchor KNXT, Los Angeles; 1983, anchor, NBC News at Sunrise; anchor, NBC Saturday Nightly News and news specials; 1989 moved to CBS as anchor, Sunday Night Evening News; anchor and reporter, Saturday Night with Connie Chung (later Face ot Face With Connie Chung), 1989-90. Received Emmy Award for Shot in Hollywood (1987), Interview With Marlon Brando (1989); 2 additional Emmy Awards: 1986, 1990. Became co-anchor, with Dan Rather, of CBS Evening News, 1993-95. Prime time series: Eye to Eye With Connie Chung, 1993. Many other awards incl. Peabody, 2 LA Emmy Awards, Golden Mike, Women in Business Award, etc.

CHURCH, THOMAS HADEN
Actor. b.El Paso, TX, March 31, 1960
PICTURES: Tombstone, Tales From the Crypt Presents: Demon Knight, George of the Jungle, One Night, Free Money, Scotch and Milk (prod.), The Specials.
TELEVISION: *Series*: Wings, Ned and Stacey. *Movies*: Fugitive Nights: Danger in the Desert. *Guest*: China Beach, Cheers, Booker, 21 Jump Street, Flying Blind, Partners. *Mini-series:* Mr. Murder.

CILENTO, DIANE
Actress. b. Queensland, Australia, April 2, 1934. e. Toowoomba. Went to New York and finished schooling and then American Acad. of Dramatic Art. First theatre job at 16; toured U.S. with Barter Co.; returned to London and joined Royal Acad. of Dramatic Art; several small parts and later repertory at Manchester's Library Theatre.
THEATER: *London stage*: Tiger at the Gates (also NY: Theatre World Award), The Third Secret, The Four Seasons, The Bonne Soup, Heartbreak House. NY: The Big Knife, Orpheus, Altona, Castle in Sweden, Naked, Marys, I've Seen You Cut Lemons.
PICTURES: Wings of Danger (Dead on Course; debut, 1952), Moulin Rouge, Meet Mr. Lucifer, All Halloween, The Angel Who Pawned Her Harp, The Passing Stranger, Passage Home, The Woman for Joe, The Admirable (Paradise Lagoon), The Truth About Women, Jet Storm, Stop Me Before I Kill! (The Full Treatment), I Thank a Fool, The Naked Edge, Tom Jones (Acad. Award nom.), Rattle of a Simple Man, The Third Secret, The Agony and the Ecstacy, Hombre, Negatives, Z.P.G. (Zero Population Growth), Hitler: The Last Ten Days, The Wicker Man, The Tiger Lily, The Boy Who Had Everything, Duet for Four.
TELEVISION: La Belle France (series), Court Martial, Blackmail, Dial M for Murder, Rogues Gallery, Rain, Lysistrata, The Kiss of Blood, For the Term of His Natural Life.

CIMINO, MICHAEL
Writer, Director. b. New York, NY, Nov. 16, 1943. e. Yale U. BFA, MFA. Was tv commecial director before becoming screen writer.
PICTURES: Silent Running (co-s.p.), Magnum Force (co-s.p.). Director: Thunderbolt and Lightfoot (also s.p.), The Deer Hunter (also co-wrote story, co-prod.; Academy Awards for Best Picture & Director, 1978.), Heaven's Gate (also s.p.), Year of the Dragon (also co-s.p.), The Sicilian (also co-prod.), Desperate Hours (also co-prod.), The Sunchasers (also co-s.p., co-prod.), The Dreaming Place.

CIPES, ARIANNE ULMER
Executive. b. New York, NY, July 25, 1937. e. Royal Acad. of Dramatic Art, London, U. of London. Daughter of film dir. Edgar G. Ulmer. Actress, then production and dubbing, Paris; CDC, Rome; Titra, New York; 1975-77, v.p., Best Intl Films (intl film distributor), Los Angeles; 1977 co-founder and sr. v.p./sales & services of Producers Sales Organization; 1981, named exec. v.p., American Film Marketing Assn.; 1982, founded AUC Films, consulting and intl. and domestic sales-prods. rep.; Pres. of the Edgar G. Ulmer Preservation Corp.-committed to the preservation and propagation of the work of independent, pioneering filmmakers.

CIPES, JAY H.
Executive. b. Mt. Vernon, NY, Dec. 14, 1928. e. Cornell U. 1960-66, indt producer-packager-distributor European features for U.S. TV sales; 1967, prod., 20th Century-Fox TV; 1970, prod., Four Star TV; 1971, mktg. exec. Technicolor, Inc.; 1973, v.p., mktg. Technicolor, Inc.; 1979 sr. v.p., dir. worldwide mktg, Technicolor, Inc. Professional Film Division. 1992, indt. consultant to prod. & post-prod. facilities.

CLAPP, GORDON
Actor. b. Canada, Sept. 24, 1948.
PICTURES: Running, Return of the Secaucus 7, Matewan, Eight Men Out, Termini Station, Gross Anatomy, April One, The Rage: Carrie 2.
TELEVISION: *Movies*: The Other Kingdom, Letting Go, The Right of the People, Hands of a Stranger, Small Sacrifices, Family of Spies, Blind Faith, The Secret Life of Archie's Wife, Fever, Mission of the Shark: The Saga of the U.S.S. Indianapolis, Bonds of Love, Kiss of a Killer, Family of Strangers, In the Line of Duty: Ambush in Waco, Her Hidden Truth, Abandoned and Deceived, The Morrison Murders, Badge of Betrayal. *Mini-series*: Evergreen. *Series*: Check It Out, NYPD Blue (Emmy Award, 1998).

CLARK, BILL
Producer.
TELEVISION: *Series*: NYPD Blue (Emmy Award, 1998), Brooklyn South.

CLARK, BOB
Director, Writer, Producer. r.n. Benjamin Clark. b. New Orleans, LA, Aug. 5, 1941.
PICTURES: *Director*: The She Man, The Emperor's New Clothes, Children Shouldn't Play with Dead Things (credited as Benjamin Clark), Deathdream (Dead of Night), Deranged (prod. only), Black Christmas (Silent Night Evil Night), Breaking Point, Murder by Decree, Tribute, Porky's (also s.p., prod.), Porky's II—The Next Day (also s.p., prod.), A Christmas Story (also s.p., prod.), Rhinestone, Turk 182, From the Hip (also co-s.p.), Loose Cannons (also co-s.p.), It Runs in the Family (also co-s.p.), Baby Geniuses.
TELEVISION: *Movies*: The American Clock, Stolen Memories, Secrets from the Rose Garden, Fudge-A-Mania, Derby, Ransom of the Red Chief. *Series episode*: Amazing Stories (Remote Control Man).

CLARK, CANDY
Actress. b. Norman, OK, June 20. Was successful model in N.Y. before landing role in Fat City, 1972. Off-B'way debut 1981: A Couple of White Chicks Sitting Around Talking; followed by It's Raining on Hope Street. Appeared in short Blind Curve.
PICTURES: Fat City (debut, 1972), American Graffiti (Acad. Award nom.), I Will I Will... For Now, The Man Who Fell To Earth, Citizens Band (Handle With Care), The Big Sleep, When You Comin' Back Red Ryder, More American Graffiti, National Lampoon Goes to the Movies, Q, Blue Thunder, Amityville 3-D, Hambone and Hillie, Cat's Eye, At Close Range, The Blob, Original Intent, Deuce Coupe, Cool as Ice, Buffy the Vampire Slayer, Radioland Murders, Cherry Falls.

TELEVISION: *Movies*: James Dean, Amateur Night at the Dixie Bar and Grill, Where the Ladies Go, Rodeo Girl, Johnny Belinda, Cocaine and Blue Eyes, The Price She Paid.

CLARK, DICK
Performer; Chairman, CEO, dick Clark Prods., Inc. b. Mt. Vernon, NY, Nov. 30, 1929. e. Syracuse U. graduated 1951, summer announcer WRUN, Utica 1949, staff announcer WOLF, Syracuse 1950. After grad. 1951, took regular job with WOLF. Rejoined WRUN, Utica, then joined WKTV, Utica. Announcer WFIL Philadelphia 1952. Formed Dick Clark productions 1956, TV and motion picture production with in-person concert division, cable TV programing dept. Host of two weekly synd. radio programs: U.S. Music Survey and Rock Roll & Remember. Founder and principal owner of Unistar Communications Group. Took company public in January, 1987 (NASDAQ: DCPI), serves as chmn. & CEO. Received Emmy Lifetime Achievement Award, 1994.
PICTURES: *Actor*: Because They're Young (debut, 1960), The Young Doctors, Killers Three. *Producer*: Psychout, The Savage Seven, Remo Williams: The Adventure Begins.
TELEVISION: *Host*: American Bandstand (also exec. prod.; Emmy Award as exec. prod., 1982-83), The Dick Clark Beechnut Show, Dick Clark's World of Talent, Record Years, Years of Rock. $25,000 Pyramid (3 Emmy Awards as host: 1979, 1985, 1986), $100,000 Pyramid, The Challengers. Producer: Where The Action Is, Swinging Country, Happening, Get It Together, Shebang, Record Years, Years of Rock. *Executive Producer*: American Music Awards, Academy of Country Music Awards, Dick Clark's New Year's Rockin' Eve, ACE Awards, Daytime Emmy Awards, Golden Globe Awards, Soap Opera Awards, Superstars and Their Moms, Caught in the Act (pilot). *Series*: TV's Bloopers & Practical Jokes, Puttin' on the Hits, Puttin' on the Kids, Dick Clark's Nitetime, Inside America, In Person From the Palace, Getting in Touch, Live! Dick Clark Presents!, VH-1's Best of American Bandstand, Strange Truth: Fact or Fiction, Primetime Country, No Relation, The Weird Al Show, Meet Hanson. *Movies*: Elvis, Man in the Santa Claus Suit, Murder in Texas, Reaching for the Stars, The Demon Murder Case, The Woman Who Willed a Miracle (Emmy Award, 1983), Birth of the Beatles, Copacabana, Promised a Miracle, The Town Bully, Liberace, Backtrack, Death Dreams, Elvis and the Colonel, Secret Sins of the Father, Deep Family Secrets. *Specials:* Live Aid—An All-Star Concert for African Relief, Farm Aid III, Super Bloopers & New Practical Jokes, American Bandstand's 33 1/3 Celebration, America Picks the No. 1 Songs, You Are the Jury, Thanks for Caring, Supermodel of the World, Freedom Festival '89, What About Me I'm Only Three, 1992 USA Music Challenge, The Good Doctor, TV Censored Bloopers '98, Motown 40: The Music Is Forever.
WRITER: Your Happiest Years, 1959; Rock, Roll & Remember, 1976; To Goof or Not to Goof, 1963; Dick Clark's Easygoing Guide to Good Grooming, 1986; The History of American Bandstand, 1986, Dick Clark's American Bandstand, 1997.

CLARK, DUNCAN C.
Executive. b. Sutton, Surrey, England. Entered industry in 1972. Appointed dir. of publicity and adv., CIC, Jan. 1979, taking up similar post in 1981 for United Artists. On formation of U.I.P. in 1982, appt. dir., pub. and adv., & deputy mng. dir., 1983. 1987 appt. v.p. adv. & pub., Columbia Pictures Intl (NY). In 1987, sr. v.p. intl marketing for Columbia (Burbank); appt. sr. v.p., Columbia Tri-Star Film Distribs., Inc., (NY). Relocated to corp. headquarters in Culver City, 1991. Appointed exec. v.p. Worldwide Marketing, 1994. In 1996, appointed presdient Columbia TriStar Film Distributors Intl.

CLARK, GREYDON
Producer, Director, Writer. b. Niles, MI, Feb. 7, 1943. e. Western Michigan U., B.A., theatre arts, 1963. Heads own company, World Amusement Corp., Sherman Oaks, CA.
PICTURES: *Director:* Danse Macabre, Satan's Sadists (actor only), Hell's Bloody Devils (actor only), The Blood Seekers (actor only), The Bad Bunch (also writer, actor), Black Shampoo (also writer), Satan's Cheerleaders, Hi-Riders (also writer), Angels' Revenge (also prod., writer), Without Warning (also prod.), The Return, Wacko (also prod.), Joysticks, Final Justice, Uninvited, Skinheads (also prod., writer), Out of Sight Out of Mind, The Forbidden Dance, Killer Instinct, Dark Future (also prod.), Stargames (also s.p.).
TELEVISION: *Series*: Star Games.

CLARK, HILARY J.
Executive. e. U. of Southern California, B.A., 1976. Began industry career 1978 as ad-pub admin. in co-op adv. dept., Buena Vista Dist. Co. Promoted to mgr. of natl. field pub & promo., 1980. Acted as unit publicist on numerous films (Explorers, Sylvester, Swing Shift, Twilight Zone, Crossroads, etc.) before returning to BV 1986 as natl. pub. dir. for Walt Disney Pictures. Became exec. dir. of Natl. Publicity for Disney and Touchstone Pictures, 1988; v.p. Intl. Publicity for Buena Vista Intl., 1990.

CLARK, MATT
Actor, Director. b. Washington, DC, Nov. 25, 1936.
THEATER: *NY*: A Portrait of the Artist as a Young Man, The Subject Was Roses, The Trial of the Catonsville Nine; Regional: One Flew Over the Cuckoo's Nest, Tonight We Improvise.
PICTURES: Black Like Me (debut, 1964), In the Heat of the Night, Will Penny, The Bridge at Remagen, Macho Callahan, Homer (co-s.p. only), Monte Walsh, The Beguiled, The Grissom Gang, The Cowboys, The Culpepper Cattle Company, The Great Northfield Minnesota Raid, Jeremiah Johnson, The Life and Times of Judge Roy Bean, Emperor of the North Pole, The Laughing Policeman, Pat Garrett and Billy the Kid, White Lightning, The Terminal Man, Hearts of the West, Outlaw Blues, Kid Vengeance, The Driver, Dreamer, Brubaker, An Eye for an Eye, Legend of the Lone Ranger, Ruckus, Some Kind of Hero, Honkytonk Man, Love Letters, The Adventures of Buckaroo Banzai, Country, Tuff Turf, Return to Oz, Let's Get Harry, Da (dir. only), The Horror Show, Back to the Future Part III, Cadence, Class Action, Frozen Assets, Fortunes of War, The Harvest, Candyman: Farewell to the Flesh, Mother, Hacks, Claudine's Return, Homegrown, Five Aces.
TELEVISION: *Series*: Dog and Cat, The Jeff Foxworthy Show. *Mini-Series*: The Winds of War, War and Remembrance, Trilogy of Special Terror II. *Movies*: The Execution of Private Slovik, The Great Ice Rip-Off, Melvin Purvis: G-Man, This is the West That Was, The Kansas City Massacre, Dog and Cat (pilot), Lacy and the Mississippi Queen, The Last Ride of the Dalton Gang, The Children Nobody Wanted, In the Custody of Strangers, Love Mary, Out of the Darkness, The Quick and the Dead, The Gambler III: The Legend Continues, Terror on Highway 91, Blind Witness, Deceptions, Dead Before Dawn, Barbarians at the Gate, A Season of Hope, Raven Hawk. *Specials*: Shadow of Fear, Andrea's Story. *Pilots*: The Big Easy, Highway Honeys, Traveling Man. Guest: Hardcastle and McCormick, Midnight Caller, Bodies of Evidence. *Director*: Midnight Caller, My Dissident Mom (Schoolbreak Special).

CLARK, PETULA
Actress, Singer. b. Ewell, Surrey, England, Nov. 15, 1932. On British stage in The Sound of Music, Candida, Someone Like You (also composer, co-writer). B'way debut in Blood Brothers (1993). Starred in own BBC TV series 1967-8. Winner of two Grammy Awards, 1964 (Best Rock and Roll Recording: Downtown), 1965 (Best Contemporary R & R Vocal Performance Female: I Know a Place).
PICTURES: Medal for the General (debut, 1944), Strawberry Roan, Murder in Reverse, I Know Where I'm Going, London Town (My Heart Goes Crazy), Vice Versa, Easy Money, Here Come the Huggets, Vote for Hugget, Don't Ever Leave Me, The Huggets Abroad, The Romantic Age (Naughty Arlette), Dance Hall, White Corridors, Madame Louise, The Card (The Promoter), Made In Heaven, The Gay Dog, The Runaway Bus, The Happiness of Three Women, Track the Man Down, That Woman Opposite (City After Midnight), Six-Five Special, A Couteaux Tires (Daggers Drawn), Questi Pazzi Pazzi Italiani, The Big T.N.T. Show, Finian's Rainbow, Goodbye Mr. Chips, Never Never Land.

CLARK, SUSAN
Actress. r.n. Nora Golding. b. Sarnid, Ontario, Canada, March 8, 1943. Trained at Royal Acad. of Dramatic Art, London and Stella Adler Academy.
PICTURES: Banning (debut, 1967), Coogan's Bluff, Madigan, Tell Them Willie Boy Is Here, Colossus: The Forbin Project, Skullduggery, Skin Game, Valdez Is Coming, Showdown, The Midnight Man, Airport 1975, Night Moves, The Apple Dumpling Gang, The North Avenue Irregulars, Murder by Decree, City on Fire, Promises in the Dark, Double Negative, Nobody's Perfekt, Porky's.
TELEVISION: *Series*: Webster, Emily of New Moon. *Movies*: Something for a Lonely Man, The Challengers, The Astronaut, Trapped, Babe (Emmy Award, 1976), McNaughton's Daughter, Amelia Earhart, Jimmy B. and Andre (also co-prod.), The Choice, Maid in America (also co-prod.), Snowbound: The Jim and Jennifer Stolpa Story, Tonya and Nancy: The Inside Story, Butterbox Babies. *Specials*: Hedda Gabler, Double Solitaire.

CLAYBURGH, JILL
Actress. b. New York, NY, April 30, 1944. m. playwright David Rabe. e. Sarah Lawrence Coll. 1966. Former member of Charles Playhouse, Boston.
THEATER: The Nest (*off-B'way*), The Rothschilds, Jumpers, Pippin, In the Boom Boom Room, Design For Living.
PICTURES: The Wedding Party (debut, 1969), The Telephone Book, Portnoy's Complaint, The Thief Who Came to Dinner, Terminal Man, Gable and Lombard, Silver Streak, Semi-Tough, An Unmarried Woman (Acad. Award nom.), Luna, Starting Over (Acad. Award nom.), It's My Turn, First Monday in October, I'm Dancing as Fast as I Can, Hannah K, Where Are The Children?, Shy People, Beyond the Ocean, Whispers in the Dark, Rich in Love, Day of Atonement, Naked in New York, Going All the Way, Fools Rush In.
TELEVISION: *Series*: Search For Tomorrow, Trinity, Everything's Relative. *Movies*: The Snoop Sisters, Miles To Go, Hustling, The Art of Crime, Griffin and Phoenix, Who Gets the Friends?, Fear Stalk, Unspeakable Acts, Reason for Living: The Jill Ireland Story, Trial: The Price of Passion, Firestorm: 72 Hours in Oakland, Honor Thy Father and Mother: The True Story of the Menedez Murders, For the Love of Nancy, The Face on the Milk Carton, Crowned & Dangerous, Sins of the Mind, Crowned and Dangerous. *Guest*: Medical Center, Rockford Files, Frasier (voice).

CLEESE, JOHN
Actor, Writer. b. Weston-Super-Mare, England, Oct. 27, 1939. e. Clifton Coll., Cambridge U. Began acting with Cambridge University Footlights revue. With classmate Graham Chapman wrote for British TV. Co-creator of Monty Python's Flying Circus. Co-author (with psychiatrist Robin Skynner): Families and How to Survive Them (1983), Life and How to Survive It (1995).
PICTURES: Interlude (debut, 1968), The Bliss of Mrs. Blossom, The Best House in London, The Rise and Rise of Michael Rimmer (also co-s.p.), The Magic Christian (also co-s.p.), The Statue, And Now for Something Completely Different (also co-s.p.), Monty Python and the Holy Grail (also co-s.p.), The Life of Brian (also co-s.p.), The Great Muppet Caper, Time Bandits, The Secret Policeman's Other Ball, Monty Python Live at the Hollywood Bowl (also co-s.p.), Monty Python's The Meaning of Life (also co-s.p.), Yellowbeard, Privates on Parade, Silverado, Clockwise, A Fish Called Wanda (also co-s.p., exec. prod., BAFTA Award, Writer's Guild of America nom., Oscar nom.), The Big Picture (cameo), Erik the Viking, An American Tail: Fievel Goes West (voice), Splitting Heirs, Mary Shelley's Frankenstein, The Swan Princess (voice), Rudyard Kipling's The Jungle Book, George of the Jungle, Fierce Creatures, Parting Shots, The Out-of-Towners, Isn't She Great, The World is Not Enough, Harry Potter.
TELEVISION: *Special*: Taming of the Shrew, Funny Women, Laughter in the House: The Story of British Sitcom. *Series*: The Frost Report, At Last the 1948 Show, Monty Python's Flying Circus, Fawlty Towers, Look at the State We're In! *Guest*: Cheers (Emmy Award, 1987), Third Rock from the Sun.

CLEMENS, BRIAN
Writer, Producer, Director. b. Croydon, England. Early career in advertising then wrote BBC TV play. Later TV filmed series as writer, script editor and features. Script editor Danger Man; Won Edgar Allen Poe Award for Best TV Thriller of 1962 (Scene of the Crime for U.S. Steel Hour). Various plays for Armchair Theatre; ATV Drama 70; Love Story. Winner two Edgar Allan Poe Awards, Cinema Fantastique Award for best s.p.
PICTURES: The Tell-Tale Heart, Station Six-Sahara, The Peking Medallion, And Soon The Darkness, The Major, When The Wind Blows, See No Evil, Dr. Jekyll and Sister Hyde, Golden Voyage of Sinbad, Watcher in the Woods, Stiff, Highlander 2, Justine (France), Bugs (UK).
TELEVISION: *Writer/Prod.*: The Avengers (2 Emmy noms.), The New Avengers, The Professionals, Escapade (U.S.), Perry Mason, Loose Cannon, Fther Dowling..

CLENNON, DAVID
Actor. b. Waukegan, IL. e. Univ. of Notre Dame, Yale Drama School.
THEATER: *Off-B'way.*: The Unseen Hand, Forensic and the Navigators, As You Like It, Little Eyolf, Welcome to Andromeda, Medal of Honor Rag, The Cherry Orchard. *Regional*: Saved, Blood Knot, Loot, Marat/Sade, Beyond Therapy, others.
PICTURES: The Paper Chase, Bound for Glory, The Greatest, Coming Home, Gray Lady Down, Go Tell the Spartans, On the Yard, Being There, Hide in Plain Sight, Missing, The Escape Artist, The Thing, Ladies and Gentlemen the Fabulous Stains, The Right Stuff, Hannah K., Star 80, Falling in Love, Sweet Dreams, Legal Eagles, He's My Girl, The Couch Trip, Betrayed, Downtown, Man Trouble, Light Sleeper, Matinee, Two Crimes (Dos Crimenes), Grace of My Heart.
TELEVISION: *Series*: Rafferty, Park Place, thirtysomething, Almost Perfect. *Movies*: The Migrants, Crime Club, Helter Skelter, Gideon's Trumpet, Marriage is Alive and Well, Reward, Special Bulletin, Best Kept Secrets, Blood and Orchids, Conspiracy: The Trial of the Chicago 8, Nurses on the Line: The Crash of Flight 7, Black Widow Murders, Original Sins, Tecumseh: The Last Warrior, From the Earth to the Moon, The Staircase. *Guest*: Alfred Hitchcock Presents, Murder She Wrote, Barney Miller, Dream On (Emmy Award, 1993), Just Shoot Me, NewsRadio. *Special*: The Seagull.

CLIFFORD, GRAEME
Director. b. England. Worked as film editor on such films as Don't Look Now, The Rocky Horror Picture Show, The Man Who Fell to Earth, F.I.S.T., The Postman Always Rings Twice, before turning to directing.
PICTURES: Frances, Burke & Wills, Gleaming the Cube, Deception, Caracara.
TELEVISION: The New Avengers, Barnaby Jones, Faerie Tale Theatre, The Turn of the Screw, Twin Peaks, Crossroads, Past Tense, A Loss of Innocence, The Last Don, The Last Don II.

CLOONEY, GEORGE
Actor. b. Augusta, KY, 1962. Father is tv newscaster-host Nick Clooney. Aunt is singer Rosemary Clooney. e. Northern KY Univ.
PICTURES: Return to Horror High, Return of the Killer Tomatoes, Red Surf, Unbecoming Age, The Harvest, One Fine Day, Full Tilt Boogie, From Dusk Till Dawn, Batman and Robin, The Peacemaker, The Thin Red Line, Out of Sight, South Park: Bigger Longer and Uncut (voice), Three Kings, The Perfect Storm, Ocean's Eleven, O Brother, Where Art Thou, .
TELEVISION: *Series:* The Facts of Life, Roseanne, Sunset Beat, Baby Talk, Sisters, Bodies of Evidence, ER. *Guest*: Hunter, Murder She Wrote, The Golden Girls, The Building, Friends, South Park (voice). *Movies:* Playmate Pajama Party, Fail Safe.

CLOONEY, ROSEMARY
Singer, Actress. b. Maysville, KY, May 23, 1928. Was singer with sister Betty on radio and with Tony Pastor's band. Won first place on Arthur Godfrey's Talent Scouts in early 1950's. Had first million selling record in 1951 with Come on-a My House. Son is actor Miguel Ferrer. *Autobiography:* This for Remembrance (1977).
PICTURES: The Stars Are Singing (debut, 1953), Here Come the Girls, Red Garters, White Christmas, Deep in My Heart, Radioland Murders.
TELEVISION: *Series:* Songs for Sale, The Johnny Johnston Show, The Rosemary Clooney Show (1956-57), The Lux Show Starring Rosemary Clooney (1957-58). *Movie:* Sister Margaret and the Saturday Night Ladies. *Guest:* Ed Sullivan, Steve Allen, Perry Como's Kraft Music Hall, Red Skelton, Dick Powell Show, Bing Crosby, Hardcastle and McCormick, ER. *Special*: Danny Kaye: A Legacy of Laughter.

CLOSE, GLENN
Actress. b. Greenwich, CT, Mar. 19, 1947. e. Coll. of William and Mary. Began performing with a repertory group Fingernails, then toured country with folk-singing group Up With People. Professional debut at Phoenix Theatre, New York. Also accomplished musical performer (lyric soprano).
THEATER: *NY*: Love for Love, Rules of the Game, Member of the Wedding, Rex, Uncommon Women and Others, The Crucifer of Blood, Wine Untouched, The Winter Dancers, Barnum, Singular Life of Albert Nobbs (Obie Award), The Real Thing (Tony Award, 1984), Childhood, Joan of Arc at the Stake, Benefactors, Death and the Maiden (Tony Award, 1992), Sunset Boulevard (Tony Award, 1995). Regional: King Lear, Uncle Vanya, The Rose Tattoo, A Streetcar Named Desire, Brooklyn Laundry, Sunset Boulevard.
PICTURES: The World According to Garp (debut, 1982), The Big Chill, The Natural, The Stone Boy, Greystoke: The Legend of Tarzan Lord of the Apes (dubbed voice), Jagged Edge, Maxie, Fatal Attraction, Light Years (voice), Dangerous Liaisons, Immediate Family, Reversal of Fortune, Hamlet, Meeting Venus, Hook (cameo), The Paper, The House of the Spirits, Anne Frank Remembered (voice), Mary Reilly, Mars Attacks!, 101 Dalmatians, Paradise Road, In the Gloaming, Airforce One, In & Out, Cookie's Fortune, Tarzan (voice), Cast and Crew, Things You Can Tell Just By Looking At Her, 102 Dalmatians, The Safety of Objects.
TELEVISION: *Movies*: Too Far To Go, The Orphan Train, Something About Amelia, Stones for Ibarra, Sarah: Plain and Tall, Skylark (also co-exec. prod.), Serving in Silence: The Margarethe Cammermeyer Story (Emmy Award, 1995; also co-exec. prod.), South Pacific, Baby *Specials*: The Elephant Man, Broken Hearts Broken Homes (host, co-exec. prod.). *Guest:* The Simpsons, Ellen.

COATES, ANNE V.
Film editor, Producer. b. Reigate, Surrey, Eng. e. Bartrum Gables Coll. m. late dir. Douglas Hickox. Worked as nurse at East Grinstead Plastic Surgery Hospital. Recipient of 1995 A.C.E. Career Achievement award.
PICTURES: Pickwick Papers, Grand National Night, Forbidden Cargo, To Paris With Love, The Truth About Women, The Horse's Mouth, Tunes of Glory, Don't Bother to Knock, Lawrence of Arabia (Academy Award, 1962; also ACE nom.), Becket (Acad. Award & ACE noms.), Young Cassidy, Those Magnificent Men in Their Flying Machines (co-ed.), Hotel Paridiso, Great Catherine, The Bofors Guns, The Adventurers, Friends, The Public Eye, The Nelson Affair, 11 Harrowhouse, Murder on the Orient Express (BAFTA nom.), Man Friday, Aces High, The Eagle Has Landed, The Medusa Touch (prod. & sprv. ed.), The Legacy, The Elephant Man (Acad. Award nom., BAFTA nom.), The Bushido Blade, Ragtime (co-ed.), The Pirates of Penzance, Greystoke: The Legend of Tarzan Lord of the Apes, Lady Jane, Raw Deal, Masters of the Universe, Farewell to the King (co-ed.), Listen to Me, I Love You to Death, What About Bob?, Chaplin, In the Line of Fire (Acad. Award nom., A.C.E. nom., BAFTA nom., G.B.F.E. award), Pontiac Moon, Congo, Striptease, Out to Sea, Out of Sight.

COBE, SANDY
Executive, Producer, Distributor. b. New York, NY, Nov. 30, 1928. e. Tulane U., B.A., fine arts. U.S. Army WWII & Korea, combat photographer; produced 11 features for Artmark Pictures, N.Y. General Studios, exec. v.p., distribution; First Cinema Releasing Corp., pres. Formed Sandy Cobe Productions, Inc., producer, packager, European features for U.S. theatrical & television. 1974 pres., Intercontinental Releasing Corporation, domestic and foreign distribution of theatrical features; 1989, named chmn. of bd. and CEO. Member, dir. of bd., American Film Marketing Assn., Dir. of bd., Scitech Corp. USA, 14 year mem., Academy of Television Arts and Sciences, 32nd degree Mason, Shriner, Variety Club Int'l. Special commendations from: Mayor of Los Angeles, California State Senate, City and County of L.A., California Assembly and Senate, and Governor of CA.
PICTURES: Terror on Tour (prod.), Access Code (exec. prod.), A.R.C.A.D.E. (prod.), Terminal Entry (exec. prod.), Open House (prod.).

COBE, SHARYON REIS
Executive, Producer. b. Honolulu, HI, e. U. of Hawaii, Loyola Marymount U. Dancer Fitzgerald, & Sample, N.Y. United Air Lines, N.Y.; v.p., story editor, Gotham Publishing N.Y.; v.p., distribution-foreign sales, World Wide Film Distributors, L.A.; pres. and chief operating officer, Intercontinental Releasing Corp., L.A. Member of Variety Clubs Intl., Industry Rltns. Com., Amer. Film Mktg. Assoc., Indpt. Feature Projects West. (tent 25), Women in Film.
PICTURES: Home Sweet Home (prod. mgr.), To All a Good Night (assoc. prod.), Access Code (co-prod.), Terminal Entry (prod.), Open House (exec. in chg. of prod.).

COBLENZ, WALTER
Producer.
PICTURES: The Candidate, All the President's Men, The Onion Field, The Legend of the Lone Ranger, Strange Invaders, Sister Sister, 18 Again!, For Keeps, The Babe, Money Talks.
TELEVISION: *Movie*: Jack Reed: Badge of Honor, House of Secrets, Not Our Son, A Dream for Christmas. *Series*: Apples Way. *Mini Series*: The Blue Knight.

COBURN, JAMES
Actor. b. Laurel, NB, Aug. 31, 1928. e. Los Angeles City Coll., where he studied drama. Also studied with Stella Adler in NY for 5 years. Served in U.S. Army. First acting role in coast production of Billy Budd. Later to New York, where he worked on TV commercials, then in live teleplays on Studio One, GE Theatre, Robert Montgomery Presents. Summer stock in Detroit before returning to Hollywood. Commercial: Remington Rand.
PICTURES: Ride Lonesome (debut, 1959), Face of a Fugitive, The Magnificent Seven, Hell Is for Heroes, The Great Escape, Charade, The Americanization of Emily, The Loved One, Major Dundee, A High Wind in Jamaica, Our Man Flint, What Did You Do in the War Daddy?, Dead Heat on a Merry-Go-Round, In Like Flint, Waterhole No. 3, The President's Analyst, Duffy, Candy, Hard Contract, Last of the Mobile Hot-Shots, The Carey Treatment, The Honkers, Duck You Sucker, Pat Garrett and Billy the Kid, The Last of Sheila, Harry in Your Pocket, A Reason to Live—A Reason to Die, The Internecine Project, Bite the Bullet, Hard Times, Sky Riders, The Last Hard Men, Midway, Cross of Iron, California Suite (cameo), The Muppet Movie, Goldengirl, Firepower, The Baltimore Bullet, Loving Couples, Mr. Patman, High Risk, Looker, Martin's Day, Death of a Soldier, Phoenix Fire, Walking After Midnight, Train to Heaven, Young Guns II, Hudson Hawk, The Player, Hugh Hefner: Once Upon a Time (narrator), Deadfall, Sister Act 2: Back in the Habit, Maverick, Skeletons, The Nutty Professor, Eraser, Keys to Tulsa, Affliction (Acad. Award for Support. Actor), Payback.
TELEVISION: *Series*: Klondike, Acapulco, Darkroom (host), Hollywood Stuntmakers (host), Fifth Corner. *Movies*: Draw!, Sins of the Fathers, Malibu, The Dain Curse, Valley of the Dolls, Crash Landing: The Rescue of Flight 232, The Hit List, Greyhounds, The Avenging Angel, Ray Alexander: A Menu for Murder, The Set Up, The Disappearance of Kevin Johnson, Ben Johnson: Third Cowboy on the Right, The Cherokee Kid, The Second Civil War, Mr. Murder, Atticus, Noah's Ark. *Specials*: Pinocchio (Faerie Tale Theater), Mastergate. *Pilot*: Silver Fox.

COCA, IMOGENE
Actress. b. Philadelphia, PA, Nov. 18, 1908. p. the late Joe Coca, orchestra leader, and Sadie Brady, vaudevillian. At 11, debut tap dancer in New York vaudeville; solo dancer B'way musicals; as comedienne, in New Faces of 1934; with former husband, Bob Burton, in Straw Hat Revue in 1939, and others through 1942. New York night clubs, Cafe Society and Le Ruban Bleu, Palmer House, Chicago; Park Plaza, St. Louis, and at Tamiment resort. Seen on early experimental TV telecasts in 1939.1949 to TV via B'way Revue, co-starring with Sid Caesar. Emmy Award, 1951. Returned to B'way in Musical On the Twentieth Century.
PICTURES: Under the Yum Yum Tree, Promises! Promises!, Rabbit Test, National Lampoon's Vacation, Nothing Lasts Forever, Buy and Cell.
TELEVISION: *Series*: Buzzy Wuzzy (host, 1948), Admiral Broadway Revue (1949), Your Show of Shows (1950-54). Imogene Coca Show (1954-55), Sid Caesar Invites You (1958), Grindl (1963-64), It's About Time (1966-67). Special: Ruggles of Red Gap. *Guest*: Fireside Theatre, Hollywood Palace, Love American Style, Moonlighting. *Movies*: Alice in Wonderland, Return of the Beverly Hillbillies, Papa Was a Preacher.

COCCHI, JOHN
Writer, Critic. b. Brooklyn, NY, June 19, 1939. e. Fort Hamilton H.S., 1957; Brooklyn College, A.A.S., 1961. U.S. Army, 1963-65. Puritan Film Labs, manager, 1967-69. Independent-International Pictures, biographer-researcher, 1969. Boxoffice Magazine, critic, reporter, columnist, 1970-79. Co-author: The American Movies Reference Book (Prentice-Hall). Contributor: Screen Facts, Film Fan Monthly, Films in Review. Actor in: The Diabolical Dr. Ongo, Thick as Thieves, Captain Celluloid vs. the Film Pirates. Worked on dubbing: Dirtymouth, 1970. Author of film books incl. The Westerns: a Movie Quiz Book, Second Feature, Best of the B Films. Now free lance writer, researcher, agent. Recent credits: contributor to books, 500 Best American Films, 500 Best British and Foreign-Language Films. Consultant to Killiam Shows, Prof. Richard Brown, Photofest, Star Magazine; research chief for AMC channel, 1984-present; Global Producers Group associate.

COCHRAN, BARBARA
Executive, Writer. b. Akron, OH, June 16 1945. e. Swarthmore, BA English Lit., 1967. Columbia U., MA journalism, 1968. Various positions and finally managing ed., Washington *Times*, 1968-79. VP news, NPR, 1979-83. Political ed., NBC, 1983-85. Exec. prod., NBC's *Meet the Press*, 1985-89. VP news/Wash. bureau chief, CBS news, 1989-95. Exec. prod. for political coverage, CBS, 1996. Pres., Radio-Television News Directors Assoc., 1997-.

COEN, ETHAN
Producer, Writer. b. St. Louis Park, MN, Sep. 21, 1957. e. Princeton U. Co-wrote s.p. with brother, Joel, XYZ Murders (renamed Crimewave).
PICTURES: *Producer/Co-Writer:* Blood Simple (also co-edited under pseudonym Roderick James), Raising Arizona, Miller's Crossing, Barton Fink, The Hudsucker Proxy, Fargo (original s.p. Acad. Award, 1996; Chicago Film Critics Award for s.p.; LA Film Critics Award for s.p.), The Naked Man, The Big Lebowski, O Brother, Where Art Thou?, The Barber Project..

COEN, GUIDO
Producer, Executive. In 1959 became production exec. Twickenham Studios, 1963 Appt. a dir. there, then producer and executive prod. series pictures for Fortress Films and Kenilworth Films.
PICTURES: One Jump Ahead, Golden Link, The Hornet's Nest, Behind the Headlines, Murder Reported, There's Always a Thursday, Date with Disaster, The End of the Line, The Man Without a Body, Woman Eater, Kill Her Gently, Naked Fury, Operation Cupid, Strictly Confidential, Dangerous Afternoon, Jungle Street, Strongroom, Penthouse, Baby Love, One Brief Summer, Burke and Hare, Au Pair Girls, Intimate Games.

COEN, JOEL
Director, Writer. b. St. Louis Park, MN, Nov. 29, 1954. e. Simon's Rock College, MA; studied film at NYU. m. actress Frances McDormand. Was asst. editor on Fear No Evil and Evil Dead. Co-wrote with brother, Ethan, s.p. for XYZ Murders (renamed Crime Wave.) Cameo role in film Spies Like Us, 1985.
PICTURES: *Director/Co-Writer*: Blood Simple (also co-editor, under pseudonym Roderick Jaynes), Raising Arizona, Miller's Crossing, Barton Fink (also co-editor, as Roderick Jaynes), The Hudsucker Proxy, Fargo (Best director, Cannes 1996; original s.p. Acad. Award, 1997; Chicago Film Critics Award for s.p., and dir.; LA Film Critics Award for s.p.; BAFTA for achievement in dir.), The Big Lebowski, O Brother, Where Art Thou?, The Barber Project.

COHEN, ARTHUR
Executive. President, Bloomingdale's, 1975-78. Founder & president, Lansdowne Advertising, a division of J. Walter Thompson, 1978-82, creating billings to $14 million in four years. President, Tele1st, a division of ABC Video Enterprises, 1982-85; partner with Robert Nederlander, 1985-86; exec. v.p., advertising, Revlon, 1986-89, during which time Revlon restored its consumer image to record highs. Currently president, Worldwide Mktg., Paramount Pictures Motion Picture Grp. (since 1989), where he is responsible for marketing, advertising, publicity, and promotion of all feature films.

COHEN, ELLIS A.
Producer, Writer. b. Baltimore, MD, Sept. 15, 1945. e. Baltimore Jr. Coll., A.A. 1967, Univ. of W. LA, mini-law sch., 1992. 1963, talent coord., Cerebral Palsy Telethon, WBAL-TV, Baltimore; 1964, p.r. asst. Campbell-Ewald Adv. Agency, L.A.; 1966, retail mgr.; 1968-69, talent booking; 1968, journalist & ed.; 1969-72, p.r. & adv. Camera Mart, NY; 1972-74, creator & ed.-in-chief, TV/NY Magazine; 1974-76 dir., worldwide pub./adv., William Morris Agency. 1973-74, prod., NY Emmy Awards Telecast; WOR-TV (prod.), chmn., exec. prod. of TV Academy Celebrity drop-in luncheon series; 1972, talent coordinator Bob Hope's Celebrity Flood Relief Telethon; 1976, exec. prod., Democratic Nat'l Conv. Gala. 1978, acc. exec., Solters & Roskin P.R., L.A.; 1978, dir. of TV Network Boxing Events, Don King Prod., NY; 1979, prod., Henry Jaffe Ent., Inc.; 1980, prod.-writer, CBS Entertainment & pres. Ellis A. Cohen Prods. Since 1983, pres., Hennessey Ent., Ltd. Author: Avenue of the Stars, (novel 1990), Dangerous Evidence (1995). Member: WGA, Producers Guild of America, World Affairs Council, Friars Club, Amer. Newspaper Guild, Intl. Press Corp., Israeli Press Corp., Acad. of TV Arts & Sciences, SAG. Comm. Public Interest for NYC; Natl. Writers Union, and many others.
TELEVISION: *Movies*: *Producer*: Aunt Mary (also story); First Steps, Love Mary, Dangerous Evidence (also story). *Specials*: NY Area Emmy Awards (1973-74).

COHEN, IRWIN R.
Exhibition Executive. b. Baltimore, MD, Sept. 4, 1924. e. U. of Baltimore, (LLB) 1948, admitted to Maryland and U.S. Bar same year. Active limited practice. R/C Theatres outgrowth of family business started in 1932. One of founders of Key Bank and Trust, chairman of board Loan Comm., director and member of exec. comm. Pres. NATO of Virginia 1976-78, chairman 1978-80. Director, member of exec. comm., treasurer, former chairman of finance comm. National NATO. Member of Motion Picture Pioneers, Will Rogers Hospital, and various other orgs.

COHEN, LARRY
Director, Producer, Writer. b. New York, NY, July 15, 1946. e. CCNY. Started as writer for TV series incl. Kraft Mystery Theatre, The Defenders, Arrest and Trial. Creator of series Branded, The Invaders, Cool Million, Blue Light, Cop Talk.
PICTURES: *Dir./prod./s.p.*: Daddy's Gone A-Hunting (co-s.p.), El Condor, Bone, Black Caesar, It's Alive, Demon, The Private Files of J. Edgar Hoover, It Lives Again, Success (story), Full Moon High, Q, I The Jury, Perfect Strangers, The Man Who Wasn't There (story), Special Effects, Scandalous (story), The Stuff (exec. prod.), Spies Like Us (actor), It's Alive III: Island of the Alive (exec. prod.), Return to Salem's Lot (exec. prod.), Best Seller, Deadly Illusion, Maniac Cop, Wicked Stepmother (exec. prod.), Maniac Cop II, The Ambulance, The Apparatus, Guilty As Sin, Original Gangstas, Invasion of Privacy (writer), The Ex, Misbegotten.
TELEVISION: *Movies*: *Writer*: Cool Million, Man on the Outside, Shootout in a One Dog Town (co-writer, story) Desperado: Avalanche at Devil's Ridge, As Good as Dead (also dir., prod.), 87th Precint–Ice. *Series*: *Writer*: NYPD Blue, 87th Precinct Heatwave.

COHEN, PAUL
Executive. b. New York, NY, Apr. 16, 1948. e. Hofstra U.; New School for Social Research; Jungian Inst. NY. Started in industry as exec. prod., distributor, screenwriter, producer for Masada Prods. Served as v.p. of Grand Slam Prods., exec. prod. for Moonbeam Assocs. Head of Analysis Films, 1976-84. Founded Aries Film Releasing, 1989, becoming pres. & CEO. Professor, Florida State Univ., 1995-97. Currently pres., Stratosphere Entertainment; oversaw Stratosphere's acquisition of The Thief, One Tough Cop, Bandits, Six Ways to Sunday, Divine Trash, The Last Big Thing, The Inheritors.
PICTURES: Caligula, My Brilliant Career, Maniac, Basket Case, The Chosen, Butterfly, The Innocent, Mephisto. The Icicle Thief, My Twentieth Century, Superstar: The Life and Times of Andy Warhol, Overseas, The Story of Boys and Girls, Thank You and Goodnight, Lovers, Bad Lieutenant.

COHEN, ROB
Producer, Director. b. Cornwall-on-the-Hudson, NY, March 12, 1949. e. Harvard U. BA. Formerly exec. v.p. in chg of m.p. and TV for Motown. Started as dir. of m.p. for TV at 20th Century-Fox. Joined Motown at age of 24 to produce films. Headed own production co. 1985, appt. pres., Keith Barish Prods.
PICTURES: Mahogany (prod.), The Bingo Long Traveling All-Stars (prod.), Scott Joplin (prod.), Almost Summer (prod.), Thank God It's Friday (prod.), The Wiz (prod.), A Small Circle of Friends (dir.), Scandalous (dir., co-s.p.), The Razor's Edge (prod.), The Legend of Billie Jean (prod.), Light of Day (co-prod.), The Witches of Eastwick (co-exec. prod.), The Monster Squad (co-exec. prod.), Ironweed (co-exec. prod.), The Running Man (co-exec. prod.), The Serpent and the Rainbow (exec. prod.), Disorganized Crime (exec. prod.), Bird on a Wire (prod.), The Hard Way (prod.), Dragon: The Bruce Lee Story (dir., co-s.p., actor), Dragonheart, Daylight, The Rat Pack.
TELEVISION: Miami Vice (dir.), Cuba and Claude (exec. prod.), Vanishing Son (exec. prod.).

COHEN, ROBERT B.
Executive. e. George Washington U., B.A., Southern Texas Sch. of Law. 1980-84. Atty. for Pillsbury Madison's Sutro and for Greenberg, Glusker, Fields, Clamans and Machtinger (L.A.). Was asst. gen. counsel for Columbia Pictures. Joined Paramount 1985 as sr. atty. for M.P. Group. to oversee legal functions for assigned feature films; 1988 named v.p. in charge of legal affairs, Motion Picture Group of Paramount; 1990, named sr. v.p. legal affairs, motion picture group, Paramount.

COHEN, SID
Executive. e. Univ. of RI Col. of Business. Served as western div. mngr. for WB tv distrib. in 1970's. 1979-84, v.p. feature planning & sls. develop. for domestic tv distrib. div. of Paramount Pictures Corp. There he created the first satellite- delivered feature-film package for free over-the-air tv on a regularly scheduled natl. basis. 1985-91, pres. of domestic tv distrib. at King World Prods. Sept. 1991, became pres. of MGM Domestic TV Distrib.

COLBY, RONALD
Producer, Director, Writer. b. New York, NY. e. Hofstra U., NYU. Began career as playwright at Cafe La Mama and Caffe Cino; performed in off-B'way shows; spent year as actor-writer in residence at Pittsburgh Playhouse. Served as dialogue coach and asst. to Francis Coppola; was v.p. of Zoetrope Studios. Directed several documentaries and short films.
PICTURES: Finian's Rainbow (act. only), The Rain People (prod.), Hammett (prod.), Some Kind of Wonderful (exec. prod.), She's Having a Baby (exec. prod.), Jailbait (co-prod).
TELEVISION: Margaret Bourke-White (co-prod.), Lush Life (co-prod.).

COLE, GARY
Actor. b. Park Ridge, IL, Sept. 20. e. Illinois State, theater major. Dropped out of coll. after 3 years and moved to Chicago where he tended bar, painted houses and worked with Steppenwolf Theatre group. In 1979 helped to form Remains Theatre, left in 1986 to become ensemble member of Steppenwolf.
PICTURES: Lucas, In the Line of Fire, The Brady Bunch Movie.
TELEVISION: *Series*: Midnight Caller, American Gothic. *Movies*: Heart of Steel, Fatal Vision, Vital Signs, Those She Left Behind, The Old Man and the Sea, Son of the Morning Star, The Switch, When Love Kills: The Seduction of John Hearn, A Time to Heal, Fall from Grace. *Mini-Series*: Echoes in the Darkness.

COLE, GEORGE
Actor. b. London, Eng., Apr. 22, 1925. e. secondary sch. Surrey. Stage debut in White Horse Inn, 1939; motion picture debut in Cottage to Let, 1941.
PICTURES: Henry V, Quartet, My Brother's Keeper, Laughter in Paradise, Scrooge, Lady Godiva Rides Again, Who Goes There (Passionate Sentry), Morning Departure (Operation Disaster), Top Secret (Mr. Potts Goes to Moscow), Happy Family, Will Any Gentleman, Apes of the Rock, The Intruder, Happy Ever After (Tonight's the Night), Our Girl Friday (Adventures of Sadie), Belles of St. Trinian's, Prize of Gold, Where There's a Will, Constant Husband, Quentin Durward, The Weapon, It's a Wonderful Life, Green Man, Bridal Path, Too Many Crooks, Blue Murder at St. Trinians, Don't Panic Chaps, Dr. Syn, One Way Pendulum, Legend of Young Dick Turpin, The Great St. Trinian's Train Robbery, Cleopatra, The Green Shoes, Vampire Lovers, Fright, The Bluebird, Mary Reilly.
TELEVISION: Life of Bliss, A Man of Our Times, Don't Forget To Write, The Good Life. *Series*: Minder, Root Into Europe, My Good Friend, An Independent Man, Dad.

COLEMAN, DABNEY
Actor. b. Austin, TX, Jan. 3, 1932. e. VA Military Inst. 1949-51; U. Texas 1951-57; Neighborhood Playhouse School Theater 1958-60.
PICTURES: The Slender Thread (debut, 1965), This Property Is Condemned, The Scalphunters, The Trouble With Girls, Downhill Racer, I Love My Wife, Cinderella Liberty, The Dove, The Towering Inferno, The Other Side of the Mountain, Bite the Bullet, The Black Streetfighter, Midway, Rolling Thunder, Viva Knievel, North Dallas Forty, Nothing Personal, How to Beat the High Cost of Living, Melvin and Howard, Nine to Five, On Golden Pond, Modern Problems, Young Doctors in Love, Tootsie, WarGames, The Muppets Take Manhattan, Cloak and Dagger, The Man with One Red Shoe, Dragnet, Hot to Trot, Where the Heart Is, Short Time, Meet the Applegates, There Goes the Neighborhood, Amos & Andrew, The Beverly Hillbillies, Clifford, You've Got Mail, Inspector Gadget.
TELEVISION: *Movies*: Brotherhood of the Bell, Savage, Dying Room Only, The President's Plane is Missing, Bad Ronald, Attack on Terror: The FBI Versus the Ku Klux Klan, Returning Home, Kiss Me Kill Me, Maneaters Are Loose!, More Than Friends, Apple Pie, When She Was Bad, Murrow, Guilty of Innocence, Sworn To Silence (Emmy Award, 1987), Baby M, Maybe Baby, Never Forget, Columbo and the Murder of a Rock Star, Judicial Consent, In the Line of Duty: Kidnapped, Devil's Food, Target Earth, My Date with the President's Daughter, Exiled, The Slap Maxwell Story. *Mini-Series*: Fresno, Idols of the Game (host). *Series*: That Girl, Bright Promise, Mary Hartman Mary Hartman, Apple Pie, Forever Fernwood, Buffalo Bill, Drexell's Class, Madman of the People, Recess (voice). *Special*: Plaza Suite, Texan.

COLEMAN, GARY
Actor. b. Zion, IL, Feb. 8, 1968. Gained fame as star of TV's Diff'rent Strokes.
PICTURES: The Fish That Saved Pittsburgh, On the Right Track, Jimmy the Kid, S.F.W., Party, Dirty Work.
TELEVISION: *Series*: Diff'rent Strokes. *Guest*: America 2-Night, Good Times, The Jeffersons, Lucy Moves to NBC, The Big Show, Martin, Married... With Children, Fresh Prince of Bel-Air, The Steve Allen Show. *Movies*: *Actor/Producer*: The Kid from Left Field, Scout's Honor, The Kid With the Broken Halo; The Kid with the 200 I.Q., The Fantastic World of D.C. Collins, Playing With Fire, Like Father Like Santa.

COLEMAN, NANCY
Actress. b. Everett, WA, Dec. 30, 1912. e. U. of Washington. In radio serials; on NY stage in Susan and God, Liberty Jones, Desperate Hours, 1955; American Theatre Guild Rep. Co. tour of Europe and So. America, 1961.
PICTURES: Dangerously They Live, Kings Row (debut, 1941), The Gay Sisters, Desperate Journey, Edge of Darkness, In Our Time, Devotion, Her Sister's Secret, Violence, Mourning Becomes Electra, That Man from Tangier, Slaves.
TELEVISION: Valiant Lady, Producers Showcase, Kraft Theatre, Philco Playhouse, Robert Montgomery Presents, Lux Theatre, Alcoa Hour, Theatre Guild Playhouse, Play of the Week, Silver Theatre, Adams Chronicles. *Series:* Ryan's Hope.

COLEMAN, THOMAS J.
Executive. b. Connecticut, Apr. 13, 1950. e. Boston U. Pres., Twalzo Music Corp., 1972-73; v.p., natl. sls. mgr., United Intl. Pictures, 1973-74; founded Atlantic Releasing Corp., 1974; Atlantic Television, Inc., 1981. All Atlantic corps. consolidated into Atlantic Entertainment Group, 1986. Co. has distributed over 100 films and produced 30 features and TV movies. Sold Atlantic, March, 1989. Formed Independent Entertainment Group, named chmn. Feb., 1992 formed Rocket Pictures.

PICTURES: *Producer or Exec. Prod.*: Valley Girl, Alphabet City, Roadhouse, Night of the Comet, Starchaser, Teen Wolf, Extremities, The Men's Club, Modern Girls, Nutcracker, Teen Wolf Too, Cop, Patty Hearst, 1969, Bad Golf Made Easier, Fluke, A New York Minute, Cannes Man, The Love Master.

COLER, JOEL H.
Executive. b. Bronx, NY, July 27, 1931. e. Syracuse U., B.A., journalism. Worked as adv. asst. NBC; acct. exec. Grey advertising. Joined 20th Century-Fox 1964 as adv. coordinator Fox Intl.; 1967, named intl. adv./pub. mgr. 1974, named v.p. dir., intl. adv./pub. Nov. 1990, named v.p. publicity/promotions Fox Intl. 1991, v.p. Worldwide Distrib. Services. 1984, memb. L.A. Olympic Org. Com. Left Fox in 1992 to form Joel Coler & Friends intl. mktg. consultants. Memb. L.A. Philarmonic Business & Professional Com.

COLIN, MARGARET
Actress. b. Brooklyn, NY, 1958. Raised on Long Island. Studied acting at Stella Adler Conservatory, Juilliard, Hofstra U. Left Hofstra to pursue acting career in Manhattan where she was cast in daytime TV series The Edge of Night. NY Theatre incl. work at Ensemble Studio, Geva Theatre and Manhattan Theatre Club (Aristocrats, Sight Unseen).
PICTURES: Pretty in Pink, Something Wild, Like Father Like Son, Three Men and a Baby, True Believer, Martians Go Home, The Butcher's Wife, Amos & Andrew, Terminal Velocity, Independence Day, The Devil's Own.
TELEVISION: *Movies*: Warm Hearts Cold Feet, The Return of Sherlock Holmes, The Traveling Man, Good Night Sweet Wife: A Murder in Boston, In the Shadow of Evil. *Series*: The Edge of Night, As the World Turns, Foley Square, Leg Work, Sibs. *Guest*: Chicago Hope.

COLLERAN, BILL
Producer, Director. b. Edgerton, WI, Nov. 6, 1922. Story department 20th Century-Fox 1945-46; Director Louis de Rochemont 1946-50; stage mgr. NBC 1951; assoc. dir. The Hit Parade 1952-53; dir. The Hit Parade, various TV specs. 1954-56; dir. Cinerama Windjammer film 1956; tv specs. with Bing Crosby, Frank Sinatra, Debbie Reynolds 1957-60; exec. Prod. Judy Garland Show, Dean Martin Show, 1965-66; dir. Richard Burton's Hamlet film; prod. Popendipity ABC-TV spec. and various other TV specs. and series 1967-77. 1978-83, prod., dir., writer for Hill-Eubanks Group and Little Joey, Inc.; 1984-86, dir. music video for Simba; developing film and TV projects for own production co. 1988, semi-retired.

COLLET, CHRISTOPHER
Actor. b. New York, NY, March 13, 1968. Started acting in commercials as teenager.
THEATER: *NY*: Off-B'way: Coming of Age in SoHo, An Imaginary Life, Unfinished Stories. B'way: Torch Song Trilogy, Spoils of War. Regional: The Lion in Winter, The Old Boy, Pterodactyls.
PICTURES: Sleepaway Camp (debut, 1983), Firstborn, The Manhattan Project, Prayer of the Rollerboys.
TELEVISION: *Movies*: Right to Kill?, Stephen King's The Langoliers. *Specials*: Pigeon Feathers, First Love and Other Sorrows, Welcome Home Jelly Bean. *Guest*: The Equalizer, The Cosby Show.

COLLETTE, TONI
Actress. b. Sydney, Australia, November 1, 1972. Was nominated for Best Supporting Actress Oscar for The Sixth Sense.
PICTURES: Spotswood, Muriel's Wedding, This Marching Girl Thing, Arabian Knight, Lilian's Story, Cosi, The Pallbearer, Emma, Clockwatchers, The James Gang, Dianna & Me, The Boys, Velvet Goldmine, 8 1/2 Women, The Sixth Sense, Shaft, Hotel Splendide.

COLLINS, GARY
Actor. b. Boston, MA, Apr. 30, 1938.
TELEVISION: *Series*: The Wackiest Ship in the Army, The Iron Horse, Sixth Sense, Born Free, Hour Magazine (host), Home. *Movies*: Quarantined, Getting Away from It All, Houston We've Got a Problem, The Night They Took Miss Beautiful, The Kid From Left Field, Jacqueline Susann's Valley of the Dolls, Danielle Steel's Secrets. *Mini-Series*: Roots.
PICTURES: The Pigeon That Took Rome, The Longest Day, Cleopatra, Stranded, Angel in My Pocket, Airport, Killer Fish, Hangar 18.

COLLINS, JOAN
Actress. b. London, Eng., May 23, 1933. e. Francis Holland Sch., London. Sister is writer Jackie Collins. Made stage debut in A Doll's House, Arts Theatre 1946. Author: Past Imperfect (autobiography, 1978), Katy, A Fight For Life, Joan Collins Beauty Book, Prime Time, Love & Desire & Hate, My Secrets, Too Damn Famous. On London, LA and NY stage in Private Lives. Video: Secrets of Fitness and Beauty (also exec. prod.)
PICTURES: I Believe in You (debut, 1951), Lady Godiva Rides Again, Judgment Deferred, Decameron Nights, Cosh Boy, The Square Ring, Turn the Key Softly, Our Girl Friday (Adventures of Sadie), The Good Die Young, Land of the Pharaohs, Virgin Queen, Girl in the Red Velvet Swing, Opposite Sex, Sea Wife, Island in the Sun, Wayward Bus, Stopover Tokyo, The Bravados, Rally Round the Flag Boys, Seven Thieves, Esther and the King, Road to Hong Kong, Warning Shot, Can Hieronymus Merkin Ever Forget Mercy Humppe and Find True Happiness?, If It's Tuesday This Must Be Belgium, Subterfuge, The Executioner, Up in the Cellar, Quest for Love, Inn of the Frightened People, Fear in the Night, Tales from the Crypt, Tales That Witness Madness, Dark Places, Alfie Darling, The Devil Within Her, The Bawdy Adventures of Tom Jones, Empire of the Ants, The Big Sleep, The Stud, Zero to Sixty, The Bitch, Game of Vultures, Sunburn, Homework, Nutcracker, Decadence, In the Bleak Mid-Winter, Decadence, In The Bleak Midwinter, Annie: A Royal Adventure, The Line King: Al Hirschfield.
TELEVISION: *Series*: Dynasty, Pacific Palisades. *Movies*: The Cartier Affair, The Making of a Male Model, Her Life as a Man, Paper Dolls, The Wild Women of Chastity Gulch, Drive Hard Drive Fast, Dynasty: The Reunion. *Specials*: Hansel and Gretel (Faerie Tale Theater), Mama's Back, Hidden Hollywood: Treasures from the 20th Century Fox Film Vaults (Host). *Mini-Series*: The Moneychangers, Sins, Monte Carlo (also exec. prod.).

COLLINS, PAULINE
Actress. b. Exmouth, Devon, Eng., Sept. 3, 1940. m. actor John Alderton (Thomas on Upstairs, Downstairs). e. Central School of Speech and Drama. Stage debut A Gazelle in Park Lane (Windsor, 1962). Best known to US audiences as Sarah in Upstairs, Downstairs.
THEATER: Passion Flower Hotel (London debut, 1965), The Erpingham Camp, The Happy Apple, The Importance of Being Earnest, The Night I Chased the Women with an Eel, Come as You Are, Judies, Engaged, Confusions, Romantic Comedy, Woman in Mind, Shirley Valentine (in London won Olivier Award as best actress, in NY won Tony, Drama Desk and Outer Critics Circle Awards.)
PICTURES: Secrets of a Windmill Girl, Shirley Valentine, City of Joy, My Mother's Courage.
TELEVISION: *Series*: Upstairs Downstairs, Thomas and Sarah, Forever Green, No—Honestly (all with husband), Tales of the Unexpected, Knockback, Tropical Moon Over Dorking.

COLLINS, STEPHEN
Actor. b. Des Moines, IA, Oct. 1, 1947. Appeared off-B'way in several Joseph Papp productions before B'way debut in Moonchildren, followed by No Sex We're British, The Ritz, Loves of Anatol, Censored Scenes from King Kong. Off-B'way: Twelfth Night, The Play's the Thing, Beyond Therapy, One of the Guys, The Old Boy, Putting It Together. Author of play Super Sunday (Williamstown Fest.), and novel Eye Contact (1994).
PICTURES: All the President's Men, Between the Lines, The Promise, Fedora, Star Trek: The Motion Picture, Loving Couples, Brewster's Millions, Jumpin' Jack Flash, Choke Canyon, The Big Picture, Stella, My New Gun, The First Wives Club, An Unexpected Life.
TELEVISION: *Series*: Tales of the Gold Monkey, Tattinger's (revamped as Nick & Hillary), Working it Out, Seventh Heaven. *Movies*: Brink's: The Great Robbery, The Henderson Monster, Dark Mirror, Threesome, Weekend War, A Woman Scorned: The Betty Broderick Story, Her Final Fury: Betty Broderick--The Last Chapter, The Disappearance of Nora, Barbara Taylor Bradford's Remember, A Family Divided, On Seventh Avenue, The Babysitter's Seduction, An Unexpected Family. *Mini-Series*: The Rhinemann Exchange, Hold the Dream, Inside the Third Reich, Chiefs, The Two Mrs. Grenvilles, A Woman Named Jackie, Scarlett.

COLT, MARSHALL
Actor, Writer. b. New Orleans, LA, Oct. 26. e. Tulane U., B.S. Physics; Pepperdine U., M.A. Clinical Psychology; Fielding Inst., PhD. candidate student, Clinical Psychology. Combat tour in Southeast Asia during Vietnam War. Captain, U.S. Naval Reserve. Stage productions: (Hotel Universe, Who's Afraid of Virginia Woolf?, Zoo Story, Killer's Head, etc.).
PICTURES: Bimbo (short), North Dallas Forty, Those Lips, Those Eyes, Jagged Edge, Flowers in the Attic, Illegally Yours, Deceptions.
TELEVISION: *Guest*: Family, Paper Chase, Streets of San Francisco, Barnaby Jones, Murder She Wrote. *Series*: McClain's Law, Lottery! *Movies*: Colorado C-1, Sharon: Portrait of a Mistress, Once an Eagle, To Heal a Nation, Mercy or Murder, Guilty of Innocence.

COLTRANE, ROBBIE
Actor. b. Glasgow, Scotland, 1950. Ent. ind. 1977.
THEATER: San Quentin theatre workshop, Oxford Theatre Group, Citizens Theatre, Traverse Theatre, Borderline Theatre, Hampstead Theatre, Bush Theatre; one man shows: Your Obedient Servant,Mistero Buffo.
PICTURES: Bad Business (dir.); Flash Gordon, Death Watch, Subway Riders, Britannia Hospital, Scrubbers, Ghost Dance, Krull, National Lampoon's European Vacation, Caravaggio, Defence of the Realm, Chinese Boxes, The Supergrass, Mona Lisa, Eat the Rich, Bert Rigby You're a Fool, Wonderland (The Fruit Machine), Let It Ride, Henry V, Slipstream, Nuns on the Run, Perfectly Normal, The Pope Must Die, Triple Bogey on a Par 5 Hole, Oh What a Night, The Adventures of Huck Finn, Goldeneye, Buddy, Montana, Frogs for Snakes, The World Is Not Enough, On the Nose, Delaney's Flutter, Harry Potter and the Sorcerer's Stone, From Hell..

TELEVISION: 1981 Take Two, Seven Deadly Sins, Keep It in the Family, Kick Up The Eighties, The Green Door, The Sheep Stealer, House With Green Shutters, The Lost Tribe, Alfresco, Laugh? I Nearly Paid My Licence Fee, Comic Strip Presents Five Go Mad in Dorset, Beat Generation, Susie, Gino, The Bullshitters, Miner's Strike, Tutti Frutti, Danny the Champion of the World (theatrical release in Europe), Jealousy (also dir., co-writer), Space Sluts From Planet Sex, French and Aunders, The Lenny Henry Show, Robbie Coltrane Special, Mistero Buffo (series), Alive & Kicking, The Secret Ingredients, The Bogie Man, Rednose of Courage, A Tour of the Western Isles, Coltrane in a Cadillac (also co-writer), Cracker (BAFTA & Cable ACE Awards).

COLUMBUS, CHRIS
Director, Writer: b. Spangler, PA, 1959. Grew up in Ohio. Started making short super 8 films in high school, studied screenwriting at New York U. Film Sch., graduated 1980. Sold first s.p., Jocks, while at college. Wrote for and developed TV cartoon series, Galaxy High School.
PICTURES: *Writer*: Reckless, Gremlins, The Goonies, Young Sherlock Holmes, Little Nemo: Adventures in Slumberland (co-s.p.). *Director*: Adventures in Babysitting (debut, 1987), Heartbreak Hotel (also s.p.), Home Alone, Only the Lonely (also s.p.), Home Alone 2: Lost in New York, Mrs. Doubtfire, Nine Months (also co-prod.), Jingle All the Way, (prod. only), Stepmom, Bicentennial Man, Harry Potter and the Sorcerer's Stone..
TELEVISION: Amazing Stories, Twilight Zone, Alfred Hitchcock Presents.

COMDEN, BETTY
Writer. b. Brooklyn, NY, May 3, 1917. e. Erasmus Hall, NYU sch. of ed., B.S. Nightclub performer and writer with The Revuers, 1939-44. NY City Mayor's Award Art and Culture, 1978. Named to Songwriters Hall of Fame, 1980. NYU Alumnae Assn.'s Woman of Achievement award, 1987. Kennedy Center Honors for Life Achievement, 1991.
THEATER: With Adolph Green: writer book, sketches & lyrics for B'way shows: On the Town (book, lyrics, actress, 1944), Billion Dollar Baby (bk., Lyrics), Bonanza Bound! (bk., lyrics), Two on the Aisle (sketches and lyrics), Wonderful Town (lyrics; Tony Award, 1953), Peter Pan (lyrics), Bells Are Ringing (bk., lyrics), Say Darling (lyrics), A Party With Comden and Green (bk., lyrics, star; 1959 and 1977); Do Re Mi (lyrics), Subways Are For Sleeping (bk., lyrics), Fade Out-Fade In (bk., lyrics), Leonard Bernstein's Theatre Songs, Hallelujah, Baby (lyrics; Tony Award, 1968), Applause (book; Tony Award, 1970), Lorelei (revision to book), By Bernstein (book and some lyrics), On the Twentieth Century (2 Tony Awards, book and lyrics, 1978); A Doll's Life (bk., lyrics), The Will Rogers Follies (Tony Award, 1991). Actress only: Isn't It Romantic.
PICTURES: *Writer with Adolph Green*: Good News, Take Me Out to the Ballgame (lyrics), On the Town, Barkleys of Broadway, Singin' in the Rain, The Band Wagon, It's Always Fair Weather (also lyrics), Auntie Mame, Bells Are Ringing (also lyrics), What a Way to Go, The Addams Family (lyrics). *Actress*: Greenwich Village, Garbo Talks, Slaves of New York.

COMO, PERRY
Singer. r.n. Pierino Como. b. Canonsburg, PA, May 18, 1912. e. Canonsburg local schools. Barber at 15; joined Carlone Band, then Ted Weems Orchestra, 1936-42; played many night clubs; records for RCA Victor. Voted Best Male vocalist M.P. Daily, TV poll, 1952-56; radio poll, 1954. Best TV performer M.P.D. Fame poll 1957. Recipient of Emmy Awards: Best Male Singer (1954, 1955), Best Emcee (1955), Best Male Personality (1956), Best Actor in a Musical or Variety Show (1956).
PICTURES: Something for the Boys (debut, 1944), Doll Face, If I'm Lucky, Words and Music.
TELEVISION: *Series*: The Chesterfield Supper Club, The Perry Como Show (1950-61), The Kraft Music Hall (1961-63); numerous annual holiday specials.

CONAWAY, JEFF
Actor. b. New York, NY, Oct. 5, 1950. Started in show business at the age of 10 when he appeared in B'way production, All the Way Home. Later toured in Critics Choice before turning to fashion modeling. Toured with musical group, 3 1/2, as lead singer and guitarist. Entered theatre arts program at NYU. Film debut at 19 in Jennifer on My Mind.
THEATER: Grease, The News.
PICTURES: Jennifer on My Mind (debut, 1971), The Eagle Has Landed, Pete's Dragon, I Never Promised You a Rose Garden, Grease, The Patriot, Elvira: Mistress of the Dark, Cover Girl, Tale of Two Sisters, The Banker, The Sleeping Car, A Time to Die, Total Exposure, Mirror Images, Sunset Strip, Bikini Summer II, Almost Pregnant, L.A. Goddess, In a Moment of Passion, Alien Intruder, 2002: The Rape of Eden, Jawbreaker, Man on the Moon.
TELEVISION: *Series*: Taxi, Wizards and Warriors, Berrenger's, The Bold and the Beautiful, Babylon 5, Crusade: The Babylon Project. *Guest*: From Sea to Shining Sea (1974), Joe Forrester, The Mary Tyler Moore Show, Happy Days, Movin' On, Barnaby Jones, Kojak, Mickey Spillane's Mike Hammer. *Movies*: Having Babies, Delta County, U.S.A., Breaking Up Is Hard to Do, For the Love of It, Nashville Grab, The Making of a Male Model, Bay Coven, The Dirty Dozen: The Fatal Mission, Ghost Writer, Eye of the Storm, Babylon 5: Thirdspace, Babylon 5: The River of Souls, Babylon 5: A Call to Arms.

CONDON, BILL
Director, Writer.
PICTURES: Dead Kids (s.p. only), Strange Invaders (s.p. only), Sister Sister, F/X 2 (s.p. only), Candyman: Farewell to the Flesh (dir. only), Gods and Monsters (Acad. Award for s.p. adapt.)
TELEVISION: *Movies:* Murder 101, White Lie, Dead in the Water, Deadly Relations, The Man Who Wouldn't Die (also co-exec. prod.)

CONDON, CHRIS J.
Producer, Director, Motion Equipment Designer. b. Chicago, IL, Dec. 7, 1922. e. Davidson Inst., U. of Southern California. U.S. Air Force 1943-46. Founded Century Precision Optics, 1948. Designed Athenar telephoto lenses, Century Super wide-angle lenses and Duplikins. Co-founded StereoVision International, Inc. 1969 specializing in films produced in new 3-D process. Member SMPTE. Lecturer and consultant on motion picture optics and 3-D motion picture technology.
PICTURES: The Wild Ride, The Surfer, Girls, Airline, The New Dimensions.

CONN, ROBERT A.
Executive. b. Philadelphia, PA, Jan. 16, 1926. e. Lehigh U. 1944; U. of Pennsylvania, 1948. 1st Lt. Days of Eden Army Security Agency, 1944-46, 1951-52; band & act. dept., MCA, 1952-53; dir. of adv. & prom. Official Films NY 1954; head of Official Films Philadelphia sales office serving PA, Baltimore, Washington, Cleveland and Detroit, 1956. Eastern Reg. Sls. Mgr. Flamingo Films, 1957; acct. exec. Dunnan and Jeffrey, Inc., 1961; v.p., Dunnan and Jeffrey, 1962; pres., adv. mgr., Suburban Knitwear Co., 1963; exec. v.p. Rogal Travel Service, 1964-68. 1968-78, pres. RAC Travel, Inc., Jenkintown, PA. and pres. Royal Palm Travel, Inc. Palm Beach, Florida, 1978; Rosenbluth Travel Service, 1979; v.p., natl. retail mktg., E.F. Hutton & Co. (N.Y.), 1983.

CONNELLY, JENNIFER
Actress. b. New York, NY, Dec. 12, 1970. e. Yale, Stamford U.
PICTURES: Once Upon a Time in America (debut, 1983), Creepers, Labyrinth, Seven Minutes in Heaven, Etoile, Some Girls, The Hot Spot, Career Opportunities, The Rocketeer, Of Love and Shadows, Higher Learning, Mulholland Falls, Far Harbor, Inventing the Abbotts, Dark City, Waking the Dead, Requiem for a Dream, Pollock.
TELEVISION: *Movie:* The Heart of Justice. *Series:* The Street.

CONNERY, SEAN
Actor. r.n. Thomas Sean Connery. b. Edinburgh, Scotland, Aug. 25, 1930. Worked as a lifeguard and a model before landing role in chorus of London prod. of South Pacific, 1953. Prod. dir., The Bowler and the Bonnet (film doc.), I've Seen You Cut Lemons (London stage). Director of Tantallon Films Ltd. (First production: Something Like the Truth). Recipient of Golden Globe Cecil B. Demille Award, 1996.
PICTURES: No Road Back (debut, 1957), Time Lock, Hell Drivers, Action of the Tiger, Another Time Another Place, Darby O'Gill and the Little People, Tarzan's Greatest Adventure, Frightened City, On the Fiddle, The Longest Day, Dr. No, From Russia With Love, Marnie, Woman of Straw, Goldfinger, The Hill, Thunderball, A Fine Madness, You Only Live Twice, Shalako, The Molly Maguires, The Red Tent, The Anderson Tapes, Diamonds Are Forever, The Offence, Zardoz, Murder on the Orient Express, The Terrorists, The Wind and the Lion, The Man Who Would Be King, Robin and Marian, The Next Man, A Bridge Too Far, The Great Train Robbery, Meteor, Cuba, Outland, Time Bandits, Wrong Is Right, Five Days One Summer, Sword of the Valiant, Never Say Never Again, Highlander, The Name of the Rose, The Untouchables (Academy Award, best supporting actor, 1987), The Presidio, Memories of Me (cameo), Indiana Jones and the Last Crusade, Family Business, The Hunt for Red October, The Russia House, Robin Hood: Prince of Thieves (cameo), Highlander 2: The Quickening, Medicine Man (also exec. prod.), Rising Sun (also exec. prod.), A Good Man in Africa, Just Cause (also exec. prod.), First Knight, Dragonheart (voice), The Rock (also exec. prod.), Playing by Heart, The Avengers, Entrapment (also prod.), Finding Forrester.
TELEVISION: Requiem for a Heavyweight, Anna Christie, Boy with the Meataxe, Women in Love, The Crucible, Riders to the Sea, Colombe, Adventure Story, Anna Karenina, Macbeth (Canadian TV).

CONNICK, HARRY, JR.
Musician, Actor. b. New Orleans, LA, Sept. 11, 1967. Began performing with Bourbon Street jazz combos at age 6. Studied classical piano. Albums: Harry Connick, 20, When Harry Met Sally..., Lofty's Roach Souffle, We Are in Love (Grammy Award, 1991), Blue Light Red Light, 25, Eleven, When My Heart Finds Christmas, She, Star Turtle. Acting debut in Memphis Belle (1990). B'way debut 1990 in An Evening with Harry Connick Jr.

PICTURES: When Harry Met Sally... (special musical performances and arrangements), Memphis Belle, The Godfather Part III (performed theme song), Little Man Tate, Sleepless in Seattle (performed song), Copycat, Independence Day, Excess Baggage, Hope Floats, The Iron Giant (voice), Wayward Son, My Dog Skip (voice), The Simian Line.
TELEVISION: *Specials*: Swingin' Out Live, The New York Big Band Concert, The Harry Connick Jr. Christmas Special, South Pacific. *Guest*: Cheers, Mad TV.

CONNORS, MIKE
Actor. r.n. Krekor Ohanian. b. Fresno, CA, Aug. 15, 1925. e. UCLA. Film debut in Sudden Fear (1952) as Touch Connors.
PICTURES: Sudden Fear (debut, 1952), Sky Commando, 49th Man, Island in the Sky, Day of Triumph, Five Guns West, The Twinkle in God's Eye, Oklahoma Woman, Swamp Woman, The Day the World Ended, The Ten Commandments, Flesh and Spur, Shake Rattle and Rock, Voodoo Woman, Live Fast Die Young, Suicide Battalion, Panic Button, Seed of Violence, Good Neighbor Sam, Where Love Has Gone, Harlow, Situation Hopeless–But Not Serious, Stagecoach, Kiss the Girls and Make Them Die, Avalanche Express, Nightkill, Too Scared to Scream, Fist Fighter, Friend to Friend.
TELEVISION: *Series*: Tightrope, Mannix (Golden Globe Award), Today's FBI, Crimes of the Century (host). *Movies*: High Midnight, Beg Borrow or Steal, The Killer Who Wouldn't Die, Revenge for a Rape, Long Journey Back, The Death of Ocean View Park, Casino, Hart to Hart Returns. *Mini-Series*: War and Remembrance.

CONRAD, ROBERT
Actor, Director. r.n. Conrad Robert Falk. b. Chicago, IL, March 1, 1935. e. public schools, Northwestern U. Prof. debut, nightclub singer. Formed Robert Conrad Productions, 1966 (later A Shane Productions, then Black Sheep Productions).
PICTURES: Thundering Jets (debut, 1958), Palm Springs Weekend, Young Dillinger, The Bandits (also dir.), Murph the Surf (Live a Little Steal a Lot), The Lady in Red, Wrong Is Right, Moving Violations, Uncommon Courage, Jingle All the Way, Wild Wild West.
TELEVISION: *Series*: Hawaiian Eye, Wild Wild West, The D.A., Assignment Vienna, Baa Baa Black Sheep, The Duke, A Man Called Sloane, High Mountain Rangers, Jesse Hawkes, Search and Rescue. *Guest*: Lawman, Maverick, 77 Sunset Strip. *Mini-Series*: Centennial. *Movies*: Weekend of Terror, The D.A.: Conspiracy to Kill, Five Desperate Women, Adventures of Nick Carter, The Last Day, Smash-Up on Interstate 5, Wild Wild West Revisited, Breaking Up Is Hard To Do, More Wild Wild West, Coach of the Year, Will: G. Gordon Liddy, Confessions of a Married Man, Hard Knox, Two Fathers' Justice, Assassin, Charley Hannah, The Fifth Missile, One Police Plaza, High Mountain Rangers (also dir., co-story), Glory Days (also dir.), Anything to Survive, Mario and the Mob, Sworn to Vengeance, Two Fathers: Justice for the Innocent, Search and Rescue.

CONSTANTINE, MICHAEL
Actor. b. Reading, PA, May 22, 1927.
PICTURES: The Hustler, Hawaii, Skidoo, Justine, If It's Tuesday This Must Be Belgium, Peeper, Voyage of the Damned, The North Avenue Irregulars, Pray for Death, In the Mood, Prancer, Dead Fall, My Life, The Juror, Stephen King's Thinner.
TELEVISION: *Series*: Hey Landlord, Room 222 (Emmy Award, 1970), Sirota's Court. *Mini-Series*: 79 Park Avenue, Roots: The Next Generations. *Movies*: Suddenly Single, Deadly Harvest, Say Goodbye Maggie Cole, The Bait, Death Cruise, The Night That Panicked America, Conspiracy of Terror, Wanted: The Sundance Woman, The Pirate, Crisis in Mid-Air, The Love Tapes, Evita Peron, My Palikari, Finder of Lost Loves, Leap of Faith, Because Mommy Works. Numerous guest appearances.

CONTE, JOHN
Actor, Singer. b. Palmer, MA, Sept. 15, 1915. e. Lincoln H.S., Los Angeles. Actor, Pasadena Playhouse; radio anncr., m.c.; Armed Forces, WWII. Pres. KMIR-TV, Channel 36, Desert Empire Television Corp., Palm Springs, NBC Affiliate.
THEATER: On B'way in Windy City, Allegro, Carousel, Arms and the Girl.
PICTURES: Thousands Cheer, Lost in a Harem, Trauma, Man With the Golden Arm, The Carpetbaggers.
TELEVISION: *Series*: Van Camp's Little Show (1950-52), Mantovani. *Specials*: Max Liebman Spectaculars and dramatic shows, host and star of NBC Matinee Theatre, TV Hour of Stars.

CONTI, BILL
Composer. b. Providence, RI, April 13, 1942. Studied piano at age 7, forming first band at age 15. e. Louisiana State U., Juilliard School of Music. Moved to Italy with jazz trio where scored first film, Candidate for a Killing. Was: music supvr. on Blume in Love for Paul Mazursky.
PICTURES: Harry and Tonto, Next Stop Greenwich Village, Rocky, Handle With Care, Slow Dancing in the Big City, An Unmarried Woman, F.I.S.T., The Big Fix, Paradise Alley, Uncle Joe Shannon, Rocky II, A Man a Woman and A Bank, Goldengirl, The Seduction of Joe Tynan, The Formula, Gloria, Private Benjamin, Carbon Copy, Victory, For Your Eyes Only, I The Jury, Rocky III, Neighbors, Split Image, Bad Boys, That Championship Season, Unfaithfully Yours, The Right Stuff (Academy Award, 1983), Mass Appeal, The Karate Kid, The Bear, Big Trouble, Gotcha, Beer, Nomads, F/X, The Karate Kid II, A Prayer for the Dying, Masters of the Universe, Baby Boom,
Broadcast News, For Keeps, A Night in the Life of Jimmy Reardon, Betrayed, Cohen and Tate, Big Blue, Lean On Me, The Karate Kid Part III, Lock Up, The Fourth War, Backstreet Dreams, Rocky V, Necessary Roughness, Year of the Gun, A Captive in the Land, The Adventures of Huck Finn, Bound By Honor, By the Sword, Rookie of the Year, Yellowstone, 8 Seconds, The Next Karate Kid, Bushwhacked, The Scout, Spy Hard, Wrongfully Accused, The Real Macaw, The Thomas Crown Affair.
TELEVISION: Kill Me If You Can, Stark, North and South, The Pirate, Smashup on Interstate 5, Papa & Me, Napoleon and Josephine, Murderers Among Us: The Simon Wiesenthal Story. *Series themes*: Cagney and Lacy, Dynasty, Falcon Crest, The Colbys, Kenya, Heartbeat, Lifestyles of the Rich and Famous, Emerald Point N.A.S., Dolphin Cove, The Elite, Instant Recall, Inside Edition.

CONTI, TOM
Actor. b. Paisley, Scotland, Nov. 22, 1941. Trained at Royal Scottish Academy of Music, Glasgow. Did repertory work in Scotland before London stage debut appearing with Paul Scofield in Savages, 1973.
THEATER: *London*: Devil's Disciple, Whose Life Is It Anyway?, They're Playing Our Song, Romantic Comedy, Two Into One, Italian Straw Hat, Jeffrey Bernard is Unwell, Present Laughter. *Director*: Before the Party, The Housekeeper. NY: Whose Life Is It Anyway? (Tony Award, 1979), Last Licks (dir.), Present Laughter (dir.), Chapter Two.
PICTURES: Galileo (debut, 1975), Eclipse, The Duellists, The Haunting of Julia (Full Circle), Merry Christmas Mr. Lawrence, Reuben Reuben (Acad. Award nom.), American Dreamer, Miracles, Saving Grace, Beyond Therapy, The Gospel According to Vic, That Summer of White Roses, Shirley Valentine, Someone Else's America, Subdown, Something to Believe in.
TELEVISION: Mother of Men (1959), The Glittering Prizes, Madame Bovery, Treats, The Norman Conquests, The Wall, Nazi Hunter, The Quick and the Dead, Roman Holiday, The Dumb Waiter, Faerie Tale Theater (The Princess and the Pea), Fatal Judgement, Blade on the Feather, Voices Within: The Lives of Truddi Chase, The Wright Verdicts (series).

CONVERSE, FRANK
Actor. b. St. Louis, MO, May 22, 1938. e. Carnegie-Mellon. Early training on stage in New York. Active in repertory theatres. Two seasons with Amer. Shakespeare Fest.
THEATER: The Seagull, Death of a Salesman, Night of the Iguana, A Man for All Seasons, The House of Blue Leaves, First One Asleep Whistle, Arturo Ui, The Philadelphia Story (1980 revival), Brothers, A Streetcar Named Desire (1988 revival), Design for Living, The Crucible, Hobson's Choice, The Ride Down Mount Morgan, etc.
PICTURES: Hurry Sundown, Hour of the Gun, The Rowdyman, The Pilot, The Bushido Blade, Spring Fever, Everybody Wins, Primary Motive.
TELEVISION: *Movies*: Dr. Cook's Garden, A Tattered Web, In Tandem, Killer on Board, Cruise Into Terror, Sgt. Matlovich Vs. the U.S. Air Force, Marilyn: The Untold Story, The Miracle of Kathy Miller, Anne of Green Gables—The Sequel, Alone in the Neon Jungle. *Guest*: Mod Squad, Medical Center, Wonderworks, Guests of the Nation. *Series*: Coronet Blue, N.Y.P.D., Movin' On, The Family Tree, Dolphin Cove, One Life to Live.

CONWAY, GARY
Actor. r.n. Gareth Carmody. b. Boston, MA, Feb. 4, 1936. e. UCLA. As college senior was chosen for title role in Teen-Age Frankenstein. After graduating served in military at Ford Ord, CA. In 1960 began contract with Warner Bros., appearing in films and TV. Has also appeared on stage. Has given several one-man shows as painter and is represented in public and private collections.
PICTURES: I Was a Teenage Frankenstein, Young Guns of Texas, Once Is Not Enough, The Farmer (also prod.), American Ninja (also s.p.), Over The Top, American Ninja III: Blood Hunt (s.p.).
TELEVISION: *Series*: Burke's Law, Land of the Giants. *Movie*: The Judge and Jake Wyler. *Guest*: 77 Sunset Strip, Columbo, Police Story, Love Boat.

CONWAY, KEVIN
Actor. b. New York, NY, May 29, 1942.
THEATER: *Actor*: One Flew Over the Cuckoo's Nest, When You Comin' Back Red Ryder? (Obie & Drama Desk Awards), Of Mice and Men, Moonchildren, Life Class, Saved, The Elephant Man, Other Places, King John (NYSF), Other People's Money (Outer Critics Circle Award; also L.A. prod.), The Man Who Fell in Love with His Wife, Ten Below, On the Waterfront. *Director*: Mecca, Short Eyes (revival), One Act Play Fest (Lincoln Center), The Milk Train Doesn't Stop Here Anymore (revival), The Elephant Man (tour), Other People's Money (Chicago, L.A. & S.F.).

PICTURES: Believe in Me, Portnoy's Complaint, Slaughterhouse Five, Shamus, F.I.S.T., Paradise Alley, The Fun House, Flashpoint, Homeboy, The Sun and the Moon (dir., prod.), Funny Farm, One Good Cop, Rambling Rose, Jennifer Eight, Gettysburg, The Quick and the Dead, Lawnmower Man II, Looking for Richard.
TELEVISION: *Series*: All My Children. *Movies*: Johnny We Hardly Knew Ye, The Deadliest Season, Rage of Angels, The Lathe of Heaven, Attack on Fear, Something About Amelia, Jesse, When Will I Be Loved?, Breaking the Silence, The Whipping Boy. *Specials*: The Scarlet Letter, The Elephant Man, Calm at Sunset. *Mini-Series*: Streets of Laredo.

CONWAY, TIM
Actor. b. Willoughby, OH, Dec. 15, 1933. e. Bowling Green State U. After 2 yrs. Army service joined KYW-TV in Cleveland as writer-director and occasional performer. Comedienne Rose Marie discovered him and arranged audition for the Steve Allen Show on which he became regular. In 1962 signed for McHale's Navy, series. Also has done night club appearances.
PICTURES: McHale's Navy (debut, 1964), McHale's Navy Joins the Air Force, The World's Greatest Athlete, The Apple Dumpling Gang, Gus, The Shaggy D.A., Billion Dollar Hobo, The Apple Dumpling Gang Rides Again, The Prize Fighter, The Private Eyes (also co-s.p.), Cannonball Run II, The Longshot, Dear God, Speed 2: Cruise Control, Air Bud: Golden Receiver.
TELEVISION: *Series*: The Steve Allen Show, McHale's Navy, Rango, The Tim Conway Show (1970), The Tim Conway Comedy Hour, The Carol Burnett Show (3 Emmy Awards as actor: 1973, 1977, 1978; Emmy Award as writer: 1976), The Tim Conway Show (1980-81), Ace Crawford: Private Eye, Tim Conway's Funny America. *Guest*: Hollywood Palace, and shows starring Garry Moore, Carol Burnett, Red Skelton, Danny Kaye, Dean Martin, Cher, Doris Day, Coach (Emmy Award, 1996), The Simpsons (voice), The Drew Carey Show. *Movie*: Roll Freddy Roll.

COOGAN, KEITH
Actor. b. Palm Springs, CA, Jan. 13, 1970. e. Santa Monica City Col. Grandson of late actor Jackie Coogan. Formerly acted as Keith Mitchell. Appeared in shorts All Summer in a Day and The Great O'Grady.
PICTURES: The Fox and the Hound (voice), Adventures in Babysitting, Hiding Out, Under the Boardwalk, Cousins, Cheetah, Book of Love, Toy Soldiers, Don't Tell Mom the Babysitter's Dead, Forever, In the Army Now, Life 101, The Power Within, A Reason to Believe, Downhill Willy, Ivory Tower.
TELEVISION: *Series*: The MacKenzies of Paradise Cove, The Waltons, Gun Shy. *Movies*: A Question of Love, Million Dollar Infield, Kid With the Broken Halo, Battered, Memorial Day, Spooner. *Specials*: Wrong Way Kid, The Treasure of Alpheus T. Winterborn, Rascal, Over the Limit, A Town's Revenge. *Guest*: Growing Pains, Silver Spoons, Fame, CHips, The Love Boat, Mork and Mindy, 21 Jump Street, 8 is Enough, Fantasy Island, Just the Ten of Us, Sibs, Tales From the Crypt, others. *Pilots*: Norma Rae, Apple Dumpling Gang, Wonderland Cove.

COOK, FIELDER
Director, Producer. b. Atlanta, GA. e. Washington & Lee U., B.A.; U. of Birmingham, Eng., post grad. Served with 7th Amphibious Force, WWII.
PICTURES: Patterns (debut, 1956), Home Is the Hero, A Big Hand for the Little Lady (also prod.), How to Save a Marriage and Ruin Your Life, Prudence and the Pill, Eagle in a Cage, From the Mixed Up Files of Mrs. Basil E. Frankweiler.
TELEVISION: *Movies*: Sam Hill: Who Killed the Mysterious Mr. Foster?, Goodbye Raggedy Ann (also exec. prod.), The Homecoming, Miracle on 34th Street, This is the West That Was, Miles to Go Before I Sleep, Judge Horton and the Scottsboro Boys, Beauty and the Beast, A Love Affair: The Eleanor and Lou Gehrig Story, Too Far to Go (also released theatrically), I Know Why the Caged Bird Sings, Gaugin the Savage, Family Reunion, Will There Really Be a Morning?, Why Me?, A Special Friendship. *Mini-Series*: Evergreen. *Specials*: The Hands of Carmac Joyce, Teacher Teacher, The Rivalry, Valley Forge, The Price (Emmy Award), Harvey, Brigadoon (also prod.; 2 Emmy Awards), Seize the Day, Third and Oak: The Pool Hall, A Member of the Wedding. *Pilots*: Ben Casey, The 11th Hour, The Waltons.

COOK, RACHAEL LEIGH
Actress. b. Minneapolis, MN, Oct. 4, 1979.
PICTURES: The Baby-Sitters Club, Tom and Huck, 26 Summer Street, Carpool, The House of Yes, The Eighteenth Angel, Strike, The Naked Man, Living Out Loud, The Hi-Line, The Bumblebee Flies Anyway, She's All That, Texas Rangers, Anti-Trust, Tangled, Josie and the Pussycats, Get Carter.
TELEVISION: Movies: The Defenders: Payback, Country Justice, True Women. Guest: The Outer Limits, Dawson's Creek, Batman Beyond (voice).

COOK, RICHARD
Executive. b. Bakersfield, CA, Aug. 20, 1950.e. USC. Began career as a ride operator at Disneyland, 1970. Disneyland sales rep. & manager of sales, 1971-76; manager, pay TV and non-theatrical releases, The Disney Channel, 1977-80; asst. domestic sales mgr., v.p. & general sales mgr., senior v.p., domestic dist., Buena Vista Pictures, 1980-87; president and head of dist. & mktg., Buena Vista Pictures Distribution, 1988-present; established Buena Vista as a pioneer in new methods of film delivery, helped prohibit paid screen advertising in theaters exhibiting products from any of the Disney Studios' banners; promoted restoration of the classic movie palace and award-winning landmark, the El Capitan, 1989-91; noted for spectacular showmanship in launching new films with live stage shows, parades and gala outdoor premieres; member, Academy of Motion Picture Arts & Sciences; member of the board of trustees, The Chandler School; recipient of the George Washington Medal of Freedom, Freedom Found. of Valley Forge. Currently chairman, The Walt Disney Motion Pictures Group and head of production for Walt Disney, Touchstone, and Hollywood Pictures. Oversees worldwide home video operations and is directly responsible for domestic theatrical mktg. & dist., intl., mktg. & dist. and feature film acquisitions.

COOKE, ALISTAIR
Journalist, Broadcaster. b. Manchester, Eng., Nov. 20, 1908. e. Jesus Coll., Cambridge U.; Yale U.; Harvard U. Film crit. of BBC 1934-37. London corr. NBC 1936-37. BBC commentator in U.S. since 1937. Weekly 15 min. talk on radio show, Letter From America, starting in 1946. Chief Amer. corr., Manchester Guardian, 1948-72; English narrator, The March of Time, 1938-39. Became U.S. citizen in 1941. Peabody award winner for International reporting, 1952, 1973-83. Hon. Knighthood, KBE, 1973.
AUTHOR: Douglas Fairbanks, Garbo & The Night Watchmen, A Generation on Trial, One Man's America, Christmas Eve, The Vintage Mencken, etc. America, 1973; Six Men, 1977; Talk About America, 1968; The Americans, 1979; Above London (with Robert Cameron), 1980; Masterpieces, 1981; The Patient Has the Floor, 1986, America Observed, 1988; Fun and Games with Alistair Cooke, 1995.
PICTURES: *Narrator*: Sorrowful Jones, The Three Faces of Eve, Hitler—The Last Ten Days
TELEVISION: *Series*: Omnibus (host; 1952-61), m.c. prod. U.N.'s International Zone (host, prod.; Emmy Award, 1958); Masterpiece Theatre (host, 1971-92). *Special doc.*: America: A Personal History of The United States (writer and narrator; 5 Emmy Awards, 1973; Franklin Medal, Royal Society of Arts, 1973).

COOLIDGE, MARTHA
Director, Writer, Producer. b. New Haven, CT, Aug. 17, 1946. e. Rhode Island Sch. of Design. NYU Inst. of Film and TV grad. sch. m. writer Michael Backes. Dir. short films while in school. Wrote and prod. daily children's tv show Magic Tom in Canada Worked on commercials and political doc. film crews. Prod., dir. and writer of docs. which have won festival awards, including Passing Quietly Through; David: Off and On (American Film Fest.), Old Fashioned Woman (CINE Golden Eagle Award, Blue Ribbon Award, American film festival), Bimbo (short), Magic Tom in Canada. First feature film Not a Pretty Picture (won Blue Ribbon Award, Amer. Film Fest.) Helped start assn. of Indep. Video and Filmmakers, Inc. As an AFI/Academy Intern worked with Robert Wise on his film Audrey Rose, 1976. Wrote orig. story that was filmed as the The Omega Connection. DGA, member of bd. of dirs.; WIF, member bd. of dirs. Acted in film Beverly Hills Cop III.
PICTURES: Not a Pretty Picture, The City Girl, Valley Girl, Joy of Sex, Real Genius, Plain Clothes, That's Adequate (interviewee), Rambling Rose (IFP Spirit Award, 1991), Lost in Yonkers, Angie, Three Wishes, Out to Sea.
TELEVISION: The Twilight Zone, Sledge Hammer (pilot), House and Home (pilot). *Movies*: Trenchcoat in Paradise, Bare Essentials, Crazy in Love.

COONEY, JOAN GANZ
Executive, Producer. b. Phoenix, AZ, Nov. 30, 1929. e. U. of Arizona. After working as a reporter in Phoenix, moved to NY in 1953 where she wrote soap-opera summaries at NBC. Then was publicist for U.S. Steel Hour. Became producer of live weekly political TV show Court of Reason (Emmy Award) and documentaries (Poverty, Anti-Poverty and the Poor) before founding Children's Television Workshop and Sesame Street in 1969. Currently chmn., exec. committe, CTW.

COOPER, BEN
Actor. b. Hartford, CT, Sept. 30, 1933. e. Columbia U. On stage in Life with Father (1942); over 3200 radio, TV appearances starting from 1945.
PICTURES: Side Street (debut, 1950), Thunderbirds, The Woman They Almost Lynched, A Perilous Journey, Sea of Lost Ships, Flight Nurse, The Outcast, Johnny Guitar, Jubilee Trail, Hell's Outpost, The Eternal Sea, The Last Command, Headline Hunters, Finghting Chance, The Rose Tattoo, Rebel in Town, A Strange Adventure, Duel at Apache Wells, Outlaw's Son, Chartroose Caboose, The Raiders, Gunfight at Comanche Creek, Arizona Raiders, Waco, The Fastest Gun Alive, Red Tomahawk, One More Train to Rob, Support Your Local Gunfighter, Lighting Jack.

COOPER, HAL
Director, Performer. b. New York, NY, Feb. 22, 1923. e. U. of Michigan. m. Marta Salcido; child actor in various radio prog. starting in 1932; featured Bob Emery's Rainbow House, Mutual, 1936-46; asst. dir. Dock St. Theatre, Charleston, SC, 1946-48.
TELEVISION: Your School Reporter, TV Baby Sitter, The Magic Cottage (writer, prod.). *Director*: Valiant Lady, Search for Tomorrow, Portia Faces Life, Kitty Foyle (also assoc. prod.), Indictment (also prod.), The Happy Time (also assoc. prod.), For Better or Worse (also prod.), The Clear Horizon, Surprise Package (also assoc. prod.), Dick Van Dyke Show, The Art Linkletter Show (also prod.), The Object Is, Death Valley Days, I Dream of Jeannie, That Girl, I Spy, Hazel, Gidget, Gilligan's Island, NYPD, Mayberry, Courtship of Eddie's Father, My World and Welcome to It, The Brady Bunch, The Odd Couple, Mary Tyler Moore, All in the Family. *Exec. prod./Director:* Maude, Phyl and Mikky, Love, Sidney, Gimme a Break, Empty Nest, Dear John, The Powers That Be.

COOPER, JACKIE
Actor, Director, Producer. b. Los Angeles, CA, Sept. 15, 1922. Began theatrical career at age of 3 as m.p. actor; was member of Our Gang comedies (first short was Boxing Gloves in 1929). First starring role in 1931 in Skippy. Worked at every major studio, always with star billing. At 20 enlisted in Navy. After three-yr. tour of duty went to N.Y. to work in live TV. Appeared in 3 plays on B'way stage and in Mr. Roberts on natl. tour and in London. Directed as well as acted in live and filmed TV. Served as v.p. in chg. of TV prod., for Screen Gems, 1964-69, when resigned to return to acting, directing, producing. 2 Emmy Awards for directing M*A*S*H and The White Shadow. Retired 1989.
PICTURES: Fox Movietone Follies (feature debut, 1929), Sunny Side Up, Skippy (Acad. Award nom.), Young Donovan's Kid, Sooky, The Champ, When a Feller Needs a Friend, Divorce in the Family, Broadway to Hollywood, The Bowery, Lone Cowboy, Treasure Island, Peck's Bad Boy, Dinky, O'Shaughnessy's Boy, Tough Guy, The Devil Is a Sissy, Boy of the Streets, White Banners, Gangster's Boy, That Certain Age, Newsboys' Home, Scouts to the Rescue (serial), Spirit of Culver, Streets of New York, What a Life, Two Bright Boys, The Big Guy, The Return of Frank James, Seventeen, Gallant Sons, Life With Henry, Ziegfeld Girl, Glamour Boy, Her First Beau, Syncopation, Men of Texas, The Navy Comes Through, Where Are Your Children?, Stork Bites Man, Kilroy Was Here, French Leave, Everything's Ducky, The Love Machine, Stand Up and Be Counted (dir. only), Chosen Survivors, Superman, Superman II, Superman III, Superman IV: The Quest for Peace, Surrender.
TELEVISION: *Series*: People's Choice (also directed 71 episodes), Hennesey (also dir. 91 epsiodes), Dean Martin Comedy World (host), Mobile One. *Movies*: Shadow on the Land, Maybe I'll Come Home in the Spring, The Astronaut, The Day the Earth Moved, The Invisible Man, Mobile Two, Operation Petticoat. *Director*: Having Babies III, Rainbow, White Mama, Rodeo Girl, Sex and the Single Parent, The Ladies, Deacon Street Deer, Perfect Gentlemen, Marathon, Leave 'Em Laughing, Rosie (also prod.), Glitter, The Night They Saved Christmas, Izzy and Moe.

COOPER, JEANNE
Actress. r.n. Wilma Jean Cooper. b. Taft, CA, Oct. 25. e. College of the Pacific, Pasadena Playhouse. Son is actor Corbin Bernsen. Recipient: 3 Soap Opera Update MVP Awards, Soap Opera Digest, Pasadena Playhouse Woman of the Year and Hollywood Entertainment Museum Award.
THEATER: The Miracle Worker, Plain and Fancy, Picnic, On the Town, The Big Knife, Tonight at 8:30, Dark Side of the Moon, Plaza Suite.
PICTURES: Man From the Alamo, The Redhead From Wyoming, The Houston Story, Red Nightmare, Plunder Road, 5 Steps to Danger, The Intruder, House of Women, 13 West Street, Let No Man Write My Epitaph, The Glory Guys, Tony Rome, The Boston Strangler, There Was a Crooked Man, Kansas City Bomber, All-American Boy, Frozen Assets.
TELEVISION: *Series:* Bracken's World, The Young and the Restless (1973-). *Movie*: Sweet Hostage, Beyond Suspicion. *Guest*: Perry Mason, The Twilight Zone, Wanted: Dead or Alive, Gunsmoke, The Big Valley, L.A. Law.

COOPER, SHELDON
Executive. e. Indiana U. Joined WGN Television, 1950 holding various positions in prod. including floor mgr., dir., prod.; 1961, named mgr. prod.; 1961 became exec. prod. for station; 1964, named asst. prog. mgr.; 1965, mgr. of dept.; 1966, v.p. prog. dev. with WGN Continental Productions Co.; elected to bd. of dir., Continental Broadcasting Co. and appointed station mgr., WGN TV, April 1974.; 1975, named v.p. and gen. mrg., WGN Continental Broadcasting.; 1977, dir., broadcasting; 1979, pres. and gen. mgr., WGN Television; 1982, chief exec. of newly formed Tribune Entertainment Co. and dir. of Tribune Co. Syndicate, Inc., 1982-present. One of founders of Operation Prime Time, consortium of independent stations. Awarded Emmys: 1960 as television's man of the year behind the cameras and 1964 for continuing excellence as writer, prod., executive, WGN TV. Chmn., Assoc. of Independent TV Stations, Inc. (INTV), 1980 and 1981; National v.p., Muscular Dystrophy Assoc.; 1980, on bd. National Assoc. of TV Prog. Executives (NATPE); first v.p., Chicago chap. Acad. of TV Arts and Sciences; v.p., trustee of national chap.

COOPERMAN, ALVIN
Producer. b. Brooklyn, NY. Prod., Untouchables, 1961-63; exec. dir., Shubert Theatre Ent. 1963; v.p., special programs, NBC, 1967-68; exec. v.p., Madison Square Garden Center, 1968-72; pres., Madison Square Garden Center, Inc.; founder , Madison Sq. Garden Prods. and Network; chmn. of the board, Athena Communications Corp.; pres., NY Television Academy, 1987-89.
TELEVISION: *Producer*: Romeo and Juliet (Emmy nom.), Pele's Last Game, The Fourth King, Amahl and the Night Visitors, Live from Studio 8H—A Tribute to Toscanini (Emmy Award), Live from Studio 8H—An Evening with Jerome Robbins and the New York City Ballet (Emmy Award), Live from Studio 8H—Caruso Remembered, Ain't Misbehavin' (Emmy nom., NAACP Image Award), Pope John Paul II, My Two Loves, Safe Passage, Family Album, U.S.A. (26 half hrs.), Witness to Survival (26 half hrs.), Mobs and Mobsters, Follow The River, Susan B. Anthony Slept Here (docu.).

COPELAND, STEWART
Composer. b. Alexandria, Egypt, July 16, 1952. Drummer and singer for The Police. Member of pop group, Animal Logic.
PICTURES: Rumble Fish, Out of Bounds, Wall Street, Talk Radio, Sge's Having a Baby, See No Evil Hear No Evil, Riff-Raff, Hidden Agenda, The First Power, Men at Work, Highlander II: The Quickening, Taking Care of Business, Wide Sargasso Sea, Bank Robber, Airborne, Raining Stones, Surviving the Game, Decadence, Fresh, Rapa Nui, Silent Fall, The Girl You Want, The Pallbearer, Boys, The Leopard Son, O Que E Isso Companheiro?, Little Boy Blue, Gridlock'd, Good Burger, Welcome to Woop-Woop, Very Bad Things, Pecker, She's All That, Made Men. *Actor:* Urgh! A Music War, South Park: Bigger Longer and Uncut.
TELEVISION: *Series*: The Equalizer, TV 101, Afterburn, Babylon 5. *Movies*: White Dwarf, Tyson The Taking of Pelham One Two Three, Futuresport, Legalese.

COPPOLA, FRANCIS FORD
Director, Writer, Producer. b. Detroit, MI, April 7, 1939. Raised in NYC. Son of late composer Carmine Coppola. Sister is actress Talia Shire. e. Hofstra U, B.A., 1958; UCLA, 1958-68, M.F.A., cinema. While at UCLA was hired as asst. to Roger Corman as dialogue dir., sound man and assoc. prod. 1969; est. American Zoetrope, (later Zoetrope Studios), a prod. center in San Francisco. Publisher, City (magazine, 1975-6). Appeared in documentary Hearts of Darkness: A Filmmaker's Apocalypse.
PICTURES: Tonight for Sure (dir., prod.), The Playgirls and the Bellboy (co-dir., co-s.p. of addtl. sequences for U.S. version), Premature Burial (asst. dir.), Tower of London (dialog. dir.), Battle Beyond the Sun (adapt.), The Young Races (sound, 2nd unit dir.), The Terror (assoc. prod., 2nd unit dir.), Dementia 13 (dir., s.p.), Is Paris Burning? (co-s.p.), This Property Is Condemned (co-s.p.), You're a Big Boy Now (dir., s.p.), The Wild Races (2nd unit dir.), Reflections in a Golden Eye (s.p.), Finian's Rainbow (dir.), The Rain People (dir., s.p.), Patton (co-s.p.; Academy Award, 1970), THX 1138 (exec. prod.), The Godfather (dir., co-s.p.; Academy Award for Best Screenplay, 1972), American Graffiti (exec. prod.), The Great Gatsby (s.p.), The Conversation (dir., co-prod., s.p.), The Godfather Part II (dir., co-s.p., prod.; Academy Awards for Best Picture, Director & Screenplay, 1974), Apocalypse Now (dir., prod., co-s.p., cameo), The Black Stallion (exec. prod.), Kagemusha (co-exec. prod.), One From the Heart (dir., co-s.p.), Hammett (exec. prod.), The Escape Artist (co-exec. prod.), The Black Stallion Returns (exec. prod.), The Outsiders (dir.), Rumble Fish (dir., exec. prod., co-s.p.), The Cotton Club, (dir., co-s.p.), Mishima (co-exec. prod.), Peggy Sue Got Married (dir.), Gardens of Stone (dir., co-prod.), Tough Guys Don't Dance (co-exec. prod.), Lionheart (exec. prod.), Tucker: The Man and His Dream (dir.), New York Stories (Life Without Zoe; dir., co-s.p.), The Godfather Part III (dir., co-s.p., prod.), Wind (co-exec. prod.), Bram Stoker's Dracula (dir., co-prod.), The Secret Garden (exec. prod.), Mary Shelley's Frankenstein (prod.), Don Juan DeMarco (exec. prod.), My Family/Mi Familia (exec. prod.), Haunted (co-exec. prod.), Jack, Buddy (exec. prod.), Lanai-Loa (prod.), The Rainmaker (dir., s.p.), The Third Miracle (exec. prod.), Grapefruit Miracle (prod.), Goosed (exec. prod.), The Florentine (prod.), Sleepy Hollow (exec. prod.), Grapefruit Moon (prod.), Monster (exec. prod.).
TELEVISION: *Movies*: The People (exec. prod.), White Dwarf (co-prod), Tecumseh: The Last Warrior (co-exec. prod.), Dark Angel (exec. prod.), The Odyssey (exec. prod.), Outrage (exec. prod.), Moby Dick (exec. prod.), The Third Miracle (exec. prod.). *Special*: Rip Van Winkle (Faerie Tale Theatre; dir.). *Series*: The Outsiders (exec. prod.), First Wave (exec. prod.).

CORBIN, BARRY
Actor. b. Dawson County, TX, Oct. 16, 1940. e. Texas Tech. Univ.
PICTURES: Urban Cowboy, Stir Crazy, Any Which Way You Can, Dead and Buried, The Night the Lights Went Out in Georgia, The Best Little Whorehouse in Texas, Six Pack, Honkytonk Man, The Ballad of Gregorio Cortez, WarGames, The Man Who Loved Women, Hard Traveling, What Comes Around, My Science Project, Nothing in Common, Under Cover, Off the Mark, Permanent Record, Critters 2: The Main Course, It Takes Two, Who is Harry Crumb?, Short Time, Ghost Dad, The Hot Spot, Career Opportunities, Solo, Kiss and Tell, Curdled.

TELEVISION: *Series*: Boone, Spies, Northern Exposure, The Big Easy. *Mini-Series*: The Thorn Birds, Lonesome Dove. *Movies*: Rage, This House Possessed, The Killing of Randy Webster, Murder in Texas, Bitter Harvest, A Few Days in Weasel Creek, Fantasies, Prime Suspect, Travis McGee, Flight #90: Disaster on the Potomac, The Jesse Owens Story, Fatal Vision, I Know My First Name is Steven, Last Flight Out, The Chase, Conagher, Siringo, The Keys, Robin Cook's Virus, Moon Shot, Deadly Family Secrets, My Son Is Easy, Columbo: A Trace of Murder, The Hired Heart. *Guest*: Mash, Call to Glory, Murder She Wrote, Hill Street Blues, Matlock, Murphy Brown, Ellen, The Drew Carey Show.

CORD, ALEX
Actor. r.n. Alexander Viespi. b. Floral Park, NY, May 3, 1933. Early career in rodeo; left to become actor. Studied at Shakespeare Academy (Stratford, Conn.) and Actor's Studio (N.Y.). Spent two yrs. in summer stock; in 1961 went on tour with Stratford Shakespeare Co. Author of novel Sandsong. Co-founder of Chuckers for Charity polo team which has raised more than $2 million for various charities. Champion rodeo team roper and cutting horse rider.
PICTURES: Synanon (debut, 1965), Stagecoach, A Minute to Pray A Second to Die, The Brotherhood, Stiletto, The Last Grenade, The Dead Are Alive, Chosen Survivors, Inn of the Damned, Sidewinder One, Grayeagle, Jungle Warriors, Street Asylum.
TELEVISION: *Series*: W.E.B., Cassie & Company, Airwolf. *Movies*: The Scorpio Letters, Hunter's Man; Genesis II, Fire !, Beggerman Thief, Goliath Awaits, The Dirty Dozen: The Fatal Mission.

CORDAY, BARBARA
Executive. b. New York, NY, Oct. 15, 1944. Began career as publicist in N.Y. and L.A. Turned to writing for TV; named v.p., ABC-TV, in chg. of comedy series development. 1982-84, headed own production co. in association with Columbia Pictures TV; June, 1984-87 pres., Columbia Pictures TV; 1988, appointed CBS Entertainment, exec. v.p. primetime programs. Member: Caucus of Writers, Producers & Directors; Hollywood Women's Coalition.
TELEVISION: *Writer*: American Dream (pilot), Cagney and Lacey (also co-creator).

COREY, JEFF
Actor. b. New York, NY, Aug. 10, 1914. e. Feagin Sch. of Dram. Art. On stage in Leslie Howard prod. of Hamlet, 1936; Life and Death of an American, In the Matter of J. Robert Oppenheimer, Hamlet-Mark Taper Forum, King Lear, Love Suicide at Schofield Barracks.
PICTURES: All That Money Can Buy, Syncopation, The Killers, Ramrod, Joan of Arc, Roughshod, Black Shadows, Bagdad, Outriders, The Devil and Daniel Webster, My Friend Flicka, Canyon City, Singing Guns, Seconds, In Cold Blood, Golden Bullet, Boston Strangler, True Grit, Butch Cassidy and The Sundance Kid, Beneath the Planet of the Apes, Getting Straight, Little Big Man, They Call Me Mister Tibbs, Clear and Present Danger, High Flying Lowe, Catlow, Something Evil, Premonition, Shine, Rooster, Oh God!, Butch and Sundance: The Early Days, Up River, Conan the Destroyer, Cognac, Messenger of Death, Bird on a Wire, The Judas Project, Deception, Beethoven's 2nd, Surviving the Game, Color of Night, Home of the Brave.
TELEVISION: *Guest*: The Untouchables, The Beachcomber,, Outer Limits, Channing, The Doctors and the Nurses, Perry Mason, Gomer Pyle, Wild Wild West, Run for Your Life, Bonanza, Iron Horse, Judd for Defense, Garrisons Gorillas, Gunsmoke, Hawaii Five O, Star Trek, The Psychiatrist, Night Gallery, Alias Smith and Jones, Sixth Sense, Hawkins, Owen Marshall, Police Story, Bob Newhart Show, Six Million Dollar Man, Doctors Hospital, Starsky and Hutch, Land of the Free, Kojak, McCloud, Captains Courageous, Bionic Woman, Barney Miller, One Day at a Time, The Pirate, Lou Grant, The Powers of Jonathan Starr, Cry for the Strangers, Today's FBI, Knots Landing, Archie Bunker's Place, Faerie Tale Theatre, Night Court, Helltown, Morning Star/Evening Star, New Love American Style, Starman, The A Team, Roseanne, Wolf, Jake and the Fatman, Rose and the Jackal, To My Daughter, Payoff, Sinatra, The Marshal, Home Court, Picket Fences, Murphy Brown, Nothing Sacred. *Movies*: A Deadly Silence, The Balcony, Yellow Canary, Lady in a Cage.

CORMAN, GENE
Producer. r.n. Eugene H. Corman. b. Detroit, MI, Sept. 24, 1927. e. Stanford U. Went to work for MCA as agent 1950-57; left to produce his first feature film, Hot Car Girl. Partner with brother Roger in Corman Company and New World Distributors. Vice pres. 20th Century Fox Television, 1983-87; exec. v.p. worldwide production, 21st Century Film Corp.
PICTURES: Attack of the Giant Leeches, Not of This Earth, Blood and Steel, Valley of the Redwoods, Secret of the Purple Reef, Beast from Haunted Cave, Cat Burglar, The Intruder, Tobruk, You Can't Win Em All, Cool Breeze, Hit Man, The Slams, Von Richthofen and Brown, I Escaped from Devil's Island, Secret Invasion, Vigilante Force, F.I.S.T. (exec. prod.), The Big Red One, If You Could See What I Hear, Paradise, A Man Called Sarge.
TELEVISION: What's In It For Harry, A Woman Called Golda (Emmy and Christopher Awards as prod.), Mary and Joseph, a Love Story, Blood Ties.

CORMAN, ROGER WILLIAM
Executive, Director, Producer, Writer, Distributor. b. Detroit, MI, April 5, 1921. e. Stanford U. 1947; Oxford U., England 1950. U.S. Navy 1944; 20th Century-Fox, production dept., 1948, story analyst 1948-49; Literary agent, 1951-52; story, s.p., assoc. prod., Highway Dragnet. Formed Roger Corman Prod. and Filmgroup. Prod. over 200 feature films and dir. over 60 of them. Formed production-releasing company, org., New World Pictures, Inc., 1970. Formed prod. co., Concorde, 1984; distribution co., New Horizons, 1985. On TV acted in film Body Bags. Recipient of LA Film Critics Award for Career Achievement, 1997.
PICTURES: *Director*: Five Guns West (dir. debut, 1955), Apache Woman, Swamp Women, The Day the World Ended, The Oklahoma Woman, The Gunslinger, It Conquered the World, Not of This Earth, Naked Paradise (Thunder Over Hawaii), Attack of the Crab Monsters, Rock All Night, Teenage Doll, Carnival Rock, Sorority Girl, Saga of the Viking Women and Their Voyage to the Waters of the Great Sea Serpent, The Undead, War of the Satellites, She Gods of Shark Reef, Machine Gun Kelly, Teenage Caveman, I Mobster, A Bucket of Blood, The Wasp Woman, Ski Troop Attack, House of Usher, The Little Shop of Horrors, The Last Woman on Earth, Creature From the Haunted Sea, Atlas, The Pit and the Pendulum, The Intruder, The Premature Burial, Tales of Terror, Tower of London, The Raven, The Terror, X—The Man With the X Ray Eyes, The Haunted Palace, The Young Racers, The Secret Invasion, The Masque of the Red Death, Tomb of Ligeia, The Wild Angels, The St. Valentine's Day Massacre, The Trip, Target: Harry (credited as Henry Neill), Bloody Mama, Gas-s-s-s, Von Richtofen and Brown, Frankenstein Unbound (also s.p.). *Producer:* Boxcar Bertha, Big Bad Mama, Death Race 2000, Eat My Dust, Capone, Jackson County Jail, Fighting Mad, Thunder & Lightning, Grand Theft Auto, I Never Promised You A Rose Garden, Deathsport, Avalanche, Battle Beyond the Stars, St. Jack, Love Letters, Smokey Bites the Dust, Galaxy of Terror, Slumber Party Massacre Part II, Death Stalker, Barbarian Queen, Munchies, Stripped To Kill, Big Bad Mama II, Daddy's Boys, Lords of the Deep (also actor), The Terror Within, Two to Tango, Time Trackers, Heroes Stand Alone, Bloodfist, Silk 2, Edgar Allan Poe's The Masque of Red Death, Haunted Symphony, Midnight Tease. *Exec. Prod.:* Black Scorpion, Black Scorpion 2, Not of This Earth, Not Like Us, Sweet Revenge (co-exec. prod.), The Drifter, Singles, Crime Zone, Watcher, The Lawless Land, Stripped to Kill 2, Hollywood Boulevard II, Rock and Roll High School Forever, Bloodfist II (prod.), One Night Stand, Haunted Sea, Future Fear, Falling fire, Eruption, Don't Sleep Alone, Detonator, Criminal Affairs, Club Vampire, Circuit Breaker, Born Bad, Alien Avengers II, Spacejacked, Stray Bullet, The Protector. *Actor:* The Godfather Part II, Cannonball, The Howling, The State of Things, Swing Shift, The Silence of the Lambs, Philadelphia., Apollo 13.
TELEVISION: *Movie Series:* Roger Corman Presents (exec. prod.). Movie: The Second Civil War.
AUTHOR: How I Made a Hundred Movies in Hollywood and Never Lost a Dime.

CORNELL, JOHN
Producer, Director, Writer. b. Kalgoorlie, Western Australia, 1941. m. actress Delvene Delancy. Grew up Bunbury. e. studied pharmacy for two years in Perth. Won internship at Western Australian Newspapers at 19, becoming columnist then London editor at 26. As Melbourne prod. of TV show, A Current Affair, discovered bridge rigger Paul Hogan. Put him on show, became his manager and formed JP Productions with him in 1972. Prod. and appeared on The Paul Hogan Show. Formed movie co. with Hogan, Rimfire Films.
PICTURES: Crocodile Dundee (prod., co-s.p.), Crocodile Dundee II (prod., dir., editor), Almost an Angel (dir., prod.).

CORNFELD, STUART
Producer. b. Los Angeles, CA. e. U. of California, Berkeley. Entered America Film Institute's Center for Advanced Film Studies as producing fellow, 1975. Joined Brooksfilm as asst. to Mel Brooks on High Anxiety. Assoc. prod., History of the World Part I.
PICTURES: Fatso, The Elephant Man, (exec. prod.), Fast Times at Richmont High (actor only), National Lampoon's European Vacation (co-prod.), Girls Just Want to Have Fun (exec. prod.), The Fly, Moving, The Fly II (exec. prod.), Hider in the House (co-prod.), Darkman (actor only), Kafka, Wilder Napalm, Mimic (co-exec. prod.).

CORRI, ADRIENNE
Actress. r.n. Adrienne Riccoboni. b. Glasgow, Scotland, Nov. 13, 1933. e. RADA at 13; parts in several stage plays including The Human Touch. Numerous TV appearances.
PICTURES: The Romantic Age (Naughty Arlette; debut, 1949), The River, Quo Vadis, The Little Kidnappers, The Sinners, Devil Girl From Mars, Meet Mr. Callaghan, Lease of Life, Make Me an Offer, Triple Blackmail, The Feminine Touch, Behind the Headlines, The Shield of Faith, Three Men in a Boat, Second Fiddle, The Surgeon's Knife, The Big Chance, Corridors of Blood, The Rough and the Smooth (Portrait of a Sinner), The Tell-Tale Heart, Sword of Freedom, The Hellfire, Dynamite Jack, Sword of Lancelot, A Study in Terror, Bunny Lake Is Missing, Doctor Zhivago, Woman Times Seven, The Viking Queen, Africa—Texas Style!, The File of the Golden Goose, Cry Wolf, Moon Zero Two, Vampire Circus, A Clockwork Orange, Madhouse, Rosebud, Revenge of the Pink Panther, The Human Factor.

CORT, BUD
Actor. r.n. Walter Edward Cox. b. New Rochelle, NY, March 29, 1950. e. NYU School of the Arts. Stage debut in Wise Child, B'way. L.A. theatre includes Forget-Me-Not Lane, August 11 1947, Endgame (Dramalogue Award), Demon Wine, The Seagull, He Who Gets Slapped. Founding member of L.A. Classical Theatre. Theatrical film debut as extra in Up the Down Staircase 1967. Television debut in The Doctors.
PICTURES: Sweet Charity, M*A*S*H, Gas-s-s-s, The Traveling Executioner, Brewster McCloud, Harold and Maude, Die Laughing, Why Shoot the Teacher?, She Dances Alone, Hysterical, Electric Dreams (voice), Love Letters, The Secret Diary of Sigmund Freud, Maria's Lovers, Invaders from Mars, Love at Stake, The Chocolate War, Out of the Dark, Brain Dead, Going Under, Ted and Venus (also dir., co-s.p.), Girl in the Cadillac, Heat, Theodore Rex, Sweet Jane, I Woke Up Early the Day I Died, Dogma, But I'm a Cheerleader.
TELEVISION: *Special*: Bernice Bobs Her Hair. *Guest*: Faerie Tale Theatre (The Nightingale), The Hitchhiker (Made for Each Other), The New Twilight Zone, Midnight Caller, Gun. *Movies*: Brave New World, The Bates Motel, And the Band Played On, Jitters.

CORT, ROBERT W.
Executive. e. U. of Pennsylvania (Phi Beta Kappa). Moved into feature prod. after having worked primarily in marketing/advertising. Joined Columbia Pictures as v.p., 1976; elevated to v.p., adv./pub./promo. Named exec. v.p. of mktg. for 20th-Fox, 1980. Moved into feature prod. as senior v.p., 1981. In 1983 named exec. v.p., prod., 20th-Fox Prods. 1985, joined Interscope Communications as pres.
PICTURES: *Prod.*: Critical Condition, Outrageous Fortune, Revenge of the Nerds II, Three Men and a Baby, The Seventh Sign, Cocktail, Bill & Ted's Excellent Adventure (exec. prod.), Renegades (exec. prod.), Blind Fury (exec. prod.), An Innocent Man, The First Power (exec. prod.), Bird on a Wire, Arachnophobia, Three Man and a Little Lady, Eve of Destruction, Class Action, Bill & Ted's Bogus Journey, Paradise, The Hand That Rocks the Cradle, The Cutting Edge, FernGully, The Gun in Betty Lou's Handbag, Out on a Limb, Jersey Girl, Holy Matrimony, Imaginary Crimes, Operation Dumbo Drop, The Tie That Binds, Mr. Holland's Opus, The Associate (exec. prod.), Snow White (exec.), The Odd Couple II.
TELEVISION: *Movies (co-exec. prod.):* A Mother's Courage (Emmy Award), A Part of the Family, Body Language.

CORTESE, VALENTINA
Actress. b. Milan, Italy, Jan. 1, 1924. Started career at 15 in Orizzonte Dipinto while studying at Rome Acad. of Dramatic Art. Following several appearances in European films brought to Hollywood by 20th Century-Fox, 1949; billed in U.S. films as Valentina Cortesa. Experience on dramatic stage in variety of roles inc. Shakespeare, O'Neill, Shaw.
PICTURES: Orrizonte Dipinto (debut, 1940), Primo Amore, A Yank in Rome, A Bullet for Strefano, Les Miserables, The Glass Mountain (English-language debut, 1950), Black Magic, Malaya, Thieves Highway, Shadow of the Eagle, The House on Telegraph Hill, Secret People, Lulu, Forbidden Women (Angels of Darkness), The Barefoot Contessa, Le Amiche, Magic Fire, Calabuch, Barabbas, The Evil Eye, The Visit, The Possessed, Juliet of the Spirits, Black Sun, The Legend of Lylah Clare, The Secret of Santa Vittoria, First Love, Give Her the Moon, The Assassination of Trotsky, Brother Sun Sister Moon, Day for Night (Acad. Award nom.), Tendre Dracula, Widow's Nest, When Time Ran Out, La Ferdinanda, Blue Tango, The Adventures of Baron Munchausen, The Betrothed, Young Toscanini, Buster's Bedroom, Sparrow.

CORWIN, BRUCE CONRAD
Exhibitor. b. Los Angeles, CA, June 11, 1940. e. Wesleyan U. Pres., Metropolitan Theatres Corp.; Past pres., Variety Children's Charities Tent 25; Board of Trustees U.C.S.B. Foundation; pres. emeritus, L.A. Children's Museum; chmn., Coro Natl. Board of Governors; Past President of the Foundation of Motion Picture Pioneers and Pioneer of the Year, 1977.

CORWIN, NORMAN
Writer, Producer, Director. b. Boston, MA, May 3, 1910. Sports ed. Greenfield, Mass. Daily Recorder, 1926-29; radio ed., news commentator, Springfield Republican & Daily News, 1929-36; prog. dir., CBS, 1938. Author of Thirteen by Corwin, More by Corwin, Untitled & Other Plays, The Plot to Overthrow Christmas, Dog in the Sky, Overkill and Megalove, Prayer for the 70's, Holes in a Stained Glass Window, Trivializing America; taught courses at UCLA, USC, San Diego State U. Faculty, U.S.C. Sch. of Journalism, 1980-.; sec., M.P. Academy Foundation, 1985. First v.p., Motion Picture Acad., 1989. Inducted into Radio Hall of Fame, Chicago Museum, 1993. Writer-host Academy Leaders (PBS). Chmn. Doc. Award Com., Motion Picture Acad. 1965-91; elected to bd. of gov., 1980; first v.p., 1988-89; chmn., writers' exec. comm., M.P. Academy; co-chmn. scholarship com., M.P. Academy; mem.: Film Advisory Bd.; bd. of trustees, Advisory Board, Filmex; bd. of dirs., WGA. Books incl. Directors Guild Oral History, Years of the Electric Ear, Norman Corwin's Letters.
THEATER: The Rivalry, The World of Carl Sandburg, The Hyphen, Overkill and Megalove, Cervantes. Together Tonight: Jefferson Hamilton and Burr.
PICTURES: Once Upon a Time, The Blue Veil, The Grand Design, Scandal in Scourie, Lust for Life (Acad. Award nom. best adapt. s.p.), The Story of Ruth.
TELEVISION: Inside the Movie Kingdom, The FDR series, The Plot to Overthrow Christmas, Norman Corwin Presents, The Court Martial of General Yamashita, Network at 50.

COSBY, BILL
Actor, Comedian. b. Philadelphia, PA, July 12, 1938. e. Temple U., U. of Mass., Ed.D. Served in United States Navy Medical Corps. Started as night club entertainer.
AUTHOR: The Wit and Wisdom of Fat Albert, Bill Cosby's Personal Guide to Power Tennis, Fatherhood, Time Flies.
COMEDY ALBUMS: Bill Cosby Is a Very Funny Fellow... Right! (Grammy Award, 1964), I Started Out As a Child (Grammy Award, 1965), Why Is There Air? (Grammy Award, 1966), Wonderfulness (Grammy Award, 1967), Revenge (Grammy Award, 1967), To Russell My Brother Whom I Slept With (Grammy Award, 1969), Bill Cosby Is Not Himself These Days, Rat Own Rat Own Rat Own, My Father Confused Me... What Must I Do? What Must I Do?, Disco Bill, Bill's Best Friend, Cosby and the Kids, It's True It's True, Bill Cosby - Himself, 200 MPH, Silverthroat, Hooray for the Salvation Army Band, 8:15 12:15, For Adults Only, Bill Cosby Talks to Kids About Drugs, Inside the Mind of Bill Cosby.
RADIO: The Bill Cosby Radio Program.
PICTURES: Hickey and Boggs (debut, 1972), Man and Boy, Uptown Saturday Night, Let's Do It Again, Mother Jugs and Speed, A Piece of the Action, California Suite, The Devil and Max Devlin, Bill Cosby Himself, Leonard Part VI (also co-prod., story), Ghost Dad, The Meteor Man, Jack, 4 Little Girls.
TELEVISION: *Series*: I Spy (3 Emmy Awards for Best Actor: 1966, 1967, 1968), The Bill Cosby Show (1969-71), The New Bill Cosby Show (1972-73), Fat Albert and the Cosby Kids, Cos, The New Fat Albert Show (Emmy Award, 1981), The Cosby Show (1984-92), A Different World (exec. prod. only), You Bet Your Life, Here and Now (exec. prod. only), The Cosby Mysteries, Cosby (also prod., 1996-), Kids Say the Darndest Things. *Specials*: The Bill Cosby Special, The Second Bill Cosby Special, Fat Albert Easter Special (voice), Cosby Salutes Alvin Ailey. *Movies:* To All My Friends on Shore (also exec. prod., story, music), Top Secret, I Spy Returns (also co-exec. prod.).

COSMATOS, GEORGE PAN
Director, Producer, Writer. b. Tuscany, Italy, Jan. 4, 1947. e. London U., London Film School. Asst. on such films as Exodus, Zorba the Greek.
PICTURES: *Director*: Restless (also co-prod., s.p.), Massacre in Rome (also co-s.p.), The Cassandra Crossing (also co-s.p.), Escape to Athena (also co-s.p.), Of Unknown Origin, Rambo: First Blood Part II, Cobra, Leviathan, Tombstone, Shadow Conspiracy.

COSTA-GAVRAS (CONSTANTIN)
Director, Writer. r.n. Konstaninos Gavras. b. Athens, Greece, Feb. 13, 1933. French citizen. e. Studied at the Sorbonne; Hautes Etudes Cinematographique, (IDHEC). Was leading ballet dancer in Greece before the age of 20. Worked as second, then first assistant to Marcel Ophuls, Rene Clair, Rene Clement and Jacques Demy. Pres. of the Cinematheque Francaise, 1982-87. Appeared as actor in film Madame Rosa.
PICTURES: *Director*: The Sleeping Car Murders (also s.p.; debut, 1965), Un Homme De Trop/Shock Troops (also s.p.), Z (also co-s.p.; 2 Acad. Award noms.), The Confession, State of Siege (also co- s.p.), Special Section (also co-s.p.), Clair de Femme (also s.p.), Missing (also co-s.p.; Acad. Award for Best Adapted s.p., 1982; Palm d'Or at Cannes Film Fest.), Hannah K. (also prod.), Spies Like Us (actor only), Family Business (also s.p.), Betrayed, Music Box (Golden Bear, Berlin Festival, 1989), The Little Apocalypse, Lumiere & Company, Mad City.

COSTNER, KEVIN
Actor. b. Lynwood, CA, Jan. 18, 1955. e. CA. State U, Fullerton majored in marketing. Acted with South Coast Actors' Co-op, community theater gp. while at coll. After grad. took marketing job which lasted 30 days. Early film work in low budget exploitation film, Sizzle Beach, 1974. Then one line as Luther Adler in Frances. Role in The Big Chill was edited from final print. 1989, set up own prod. co. Tig Prods. at Raleigh Studios.
PICTURES: Sizzle Beach U.S.A., Shadows Run Black, Night Shift, Chasing Dreams, Table for Five, Testament, Stacy's Knights, The Gunrunner, Fandango, Silverado, American Flyers, The Untouchables, No Way Out, Bull Durham, Field of Dreams, Revenge (also exec. prod.), Dances With Wolves (also dir., co-prod.; Academy Awards for Best Picture & Director, 1990), Robin Hood: Prince of Thieves, JFK, The Bodyguard (also co-prod.), A Perfect World, Wyatt Earp (also co-prod.), Rapa Nui (co-prod. only), The War, Waterworld (also co-prod.), Tin Cup, The Postman (also dir., co-prod), For Love of the Game, Message in a Bottle (also prod.), Play it to the Bone, Thirteen Days, 3000 Miles to Graceland, Dragonfly, Beyond Borders.
TELEVISION: *Special*: 500 Nations (co-exec. prod., host)

COURIC, KATIE
Newcaster. b. Arlington, VA, Jan. 7, 1957. e. Univ. of VA. Started as desk asst. at ABC News, then assignment editor for CNN, reporter for WTVJ, NBC affiliate in Miami. Moved to NBC's Washington D.C. station WRC. Became natl. correspondent for The Today Show, 1989, then co-host in 1991. Served as co-host of Macy's Thanksgiving Day Parade, 1991-present. Co-host of nighttime series Now With Tom Brokaw & Katie Couric.

COURTENAY, TOM
Actor. b. Hull, England, Feb. 25, 1937 e. University Coll., London, Royal Acad. of Dramatic Art, 1960-61; Old Vic.
THEATER: Billy Liar, Andorra, Hamlet, She Stoops to Conquer, Otherwise Engaged (N.Y. debut), The Dresser, Poison Pen, Uncle Vanya, Moscow Stations, etc.
PICTURES: The Loneliness of the Long Distance Runner (debut, 1962), Private Potter, Billy Liar, King and Country, Operation Crossbow, King Rat, Doctor Zhivago (Acad. Award nom.), The Night of the Generals, The Day the Fish Came Out, A Dandy in Aspic, Otley, One Day in the Life of Ivan Denisovich, Catch Me a Spy, The Dresser (Acad. Award nom.), Happy New Year, Leonard Part VI, Let Him Have It, The Last Butterfly.
TELEVISION: *Series*: The Lads, Ghosts, Private Potter. *Movies/Specials*: I Heard the Owl Call My Name, Jesus of Nazareth, Absent Friends, Chekhov in Yalta, Redemption, The Old Curiosity Shop.

COURTLAND, JEROME
Actor, Producer, Director. b. Knoxville, TN, Dec. 27, 1926. Began career in 40s as actor, then turned to directing and producing.
PICTURES: *Actor*: Kiss and Tell, Man from Colorado, Battleground, The Barefoot Mailman, The Bamboo Prison, Tonka, Black Spurs. *Director*: Run, Cougar, Run, Diamond on Wheels. *Producer*: Escape to Witch Mountain, Ride a Wild Pony, Return from Witch Mountain, Pete's Dragon.
TELEVISION: *Actor*: The Saga of Andy Burnett, Tonka. *Director*: Hog Wild (also co-prod.), Harness Fever. Knots Landing, Dynasty, Hotel, Love Boat, Fantasy Island.

COUTARD, RAOUL
Cinematographer. b. Paris, France, Sept. 16, 1924. Spent 4 years in Vietnam working for French Military Info. Service, later a civilian photographer for Time and Paris-Match. During WWII worked in photo labs. After war returned to France and formed prod. co. making documentaries. Joined Jean-Luc Godard as his cinematographer on Breathless (1960). His use of hand-held camera and natural light established him as a seminal cameraman of the French New Wave, working with Godard, Truffaut and later with Costa Gavras. Director: Hoa Binh (1971).
PICTURES: Breathless, Shoot the Piano Player, Lola, Jules and Jim, The Army Game, My Life to Live, Love at Twenty (segment), Les Carabiniers, Contempt, Alphaville, The Soft Skin, Male Companion, Pierrot le Fou, Made in USA, Weekend, Sailor From Gibraltar, The Bride Wore Black, Z, The Confession, Le Crabe Tambour, Passion, First Name: Carmen, Dangerous Moves, Salt on the Skin, La Garce, Max My Love, Burning Beds, Let Sleeping Cops Lie, Bethune: The Making of a Hero.

COWAN, WARREN J.
Publicist. b. New York, NY, Mar. 13. e. Townsend Harris H.S., UCLA, graduated 1941. Entered public relations, 1941, with Alan Gordon & Associates; three yrs. Air Force; joined Henry C. Rogers office in 1945; became partner, 1949, and changed name to Rogers & Cowan Public Relations; advisor, Rogers & Cowan, Inc., 1960; pres., Rogers & Cowan, Inc., 1964; named bd. chmn., 1983. Retired as Rogers & Cowan chmn. in 1992. 1994, started new P.R. company, Warren Cowan & Assocs. Served as natl. communications chmn. for United Way of America. On advisory bd. of the Natl. Assoc. of Film Commissioners; 2nd Decade Council of American Film Inst. On bd. L.A. County High School for the Arts, Scott Newman Center, Young Musicians Foundation.

COX, ALEX
Director, Writer. b. Liverpool, England, Dec. 15, 1954. Studied law at Oxford U. where he dir. and acted in plays for school drama society. Studied film prod. Bristol U. Received Fulbright Scholarship to study at UCLA film school, 1981.
PICTURES: Repo Man (also s.p.), Sid and Nancy (also co-s.p.), Straight to Hell (also co-s.p.), Walker (also co-editor), Highway Patrolman, Floundering (actor only), Dead Beat (actor only), The Queen of the Night (actor only), The Winner (also actor), Death and the Compass (also actor), Perdita Durango (actor only), Waldo's Hawaiian Holiday, Fear and Loathing in Las Vegas (s.p. only), Three Businessmen (also dir.).

COX, BRIAN
Actor. b. Dundee, Scotland, June 1, 1946. e. London Acad. of Music & Dramatic Art. Acted with Royal Lyceum Edinburgh and Birmingham Rep. Theatre; also season with Royal Shakespeare Company. Video: Acting and Tragedy. Author: The Lear Diaries, Salem in Moscow.
THEATER: The Master Builder, King Lear, Richard III, Fashion, Rat in the Skull (Olivier Award; also B'way), Titus Andronicus (Olivier Award), Penny for a Song, Misalliance, St. Nicholas, Skylight.
PICTURES: Nicholas and Alexandra, In Celebration, Manhunter, Shoot for the Sun, Hidden Agenda, Prince of Jutland, Iron Will, Rob Roy, Braveheart, Chain Reaction, The Boxer, The Long Kiss Goodnight, Kiss the Girls, Rushmore, Desperate Measures, The Minus Man, The Corruptor. *Director/Writer:* Scorpion Spring.
TELEVISION: Inspector Morse, Therese Raquin, Pope John Paul II, Florence Nightingale, Beryl Markham: A Shadow on the Sun, Murder by Moonlight, Six Characters in Search of an Author, Picasso, The Negotiator, The Big Battalions, Bach, Bothwell, Churchill's People, Master of Ballantrae, Lost Language of Cranes, The Changeling, Secret Weapon, Witness Against Hitler, Poddle Springs.

COX, COURTENEY
Actress. b. Birmingham, AL, June 15, 1964. m. actor David Arquette. Left AL to pursue modelling career in NY. Dir. Brian DePalma selected her to be the young woman who jumps out of audience and dances with Bruce Springsteen in his music video Dancing in the Dark. This break led to featured role in short-lived TV series Misfits of Science (1985-86).
PICTURES: Masters of the Universe, Down Twisted, Cocoon: The Return, Mr. Destiny, Blue Desert, Shaking the Tree, The Opposite Sex, Ace Ventura—Pet Detective, Scream, Commandments, Scream 2, The Runner, Scream 3, The Shrink is In, Alien Love Triangle, 3000 Miles to Graceland.
TELEVISION: *Series*: Misfits of Science, Family Ties, The Trouble With Larry, Friends. *Movies*: I'll Be Home for Christmas, Roxanne: The Prize Pulitzer, Till We Meet Again, Curiosity Kills, Battling for Baby, Topper, Sketch Artist II: Hands That See.

COX, RONNY
Actor. b. Cloudcroft, NM, July 23, 1938. e. Eastern New Mexico Univ.
PICTURES: The Happiness Cage (debut, 1972), Deliverance, Hugo the Hippo (voice), Bound for Glory, The Car, Gray Lady Down, Harper Valley P.T.A., The Onion Field, Taps, The Beast Within, Some Kind of Hero, Courage (Raw Courage), Beverly Hills Cop, Vision Quest, Hollywood Vice Squad, Steele Justice, Beverly Hills Cop II, Robocop, One Man Force, Loose Cannons, Martians Go Home!, Total Recall, Scissors, Captain America, Past Midnight, Murder at 1600, Frog and Wombat, Forces of Nature, Deep Blue Sea.
TELEVISION: *Series*: Apple's Way, Spencer, St. Elsewhere, Cop Rock, Sweet Justice. *Movies*: The Connection, A Case of Rape, Who Is the Black Dahlia?, Having Babies, Corey: For the People, The Girl Called Hatter Fox, Lovey: A Circle of Children Part II, Transplant, When Hell Was in Session, Fugitive Family, Courage of Kavik: The Wolf Dog, The Last Song, Alcatraz—The Whole Shocking Story, Fallen Angel, Two of a Kind, The Jesse Owens Story, The Abduction of Kari Swenson, Baby Girl Scott, In the Line of Duty: The FBI Murders, The Comeback, When We Were Young, With Murder in Mind, Perry Mason: The Case of the Heartbroken Bride, A Part of the Family. *Mini-Series*: Favorite Son, From the Earth to the Moon. *Specials*: Our Town, Chicago 7 Trial.

COYOTE, PETER
Actor. r.n. Peter Cohon. b. New York, NY, 1942. Studied with San Francisco Actors Workshop. Theatre includes The Minstrel Show (dir.), Olive Pits (also co-writer), The Red Snake, True West, The Abduction of Kari Swenson, Baby Girl Scott.
PICTURES: Die Laughing (debut, 1980), Tell Me a Riddle, Southern Comfort, The Pursuit of D.B. Cooper, E.T.: The Extra Terrestrial, Endangered Species, Timerider, Cross Creek, Slayground, Stranger's Kiss, Heartbreakers, The Legend of Billie Jean, Jagged Edge, Outrageous Fortune, A Man in Love, Stacking, Heart of Midnight, The Man Inside, Crooked Hearts, Exposure, Bitter Moon, Kika, That Eye The Sky, Moonlight and Valentino, Unforgettable, Sphere, Patch Adams, The Basket, Last Call, Random Hearts.
TELEVISION: *Movies*: Alcatraz: The Whole Shocking Story, The People vs. Jean Harris, Isabel's Choice, Best Kept Secrets, Scorned and Swindled, Time Flyer, Child's Cry, Sworn to Silence, Echoes in the Darkness, Unconquered, A Seduction in Travis County, Living a Lie, Keeper of the City, Breach of Conduct. Buffalo Girls. *Special*: Abraham Lincoln: A New Birth of Freedom (voice).

CRAIG, MICHAEL
Actor. r.n. Michael Gregson. b. Poona, India, Jan. 27, 1929. At 16 joined Merchant Navy. 1949, returned to England and made stage debut in repertory. Entered industry as extra in 1949.
PICTURES: Passport to Pimlico (debut, 1949), The Magic Box, The Cruel Sea, Malta Story, The Love Lottery, Passage Home, The Black Tent, Yield to the Night, Eye-Witness, House of Secrets, High Tide At Noon, Sea of Sand, Sapphire, Upstairs and Downstairs, The Angry Silence, Cone of Silence, Doctor In Love, Mysterious Island, Payroll, No My Darling Daughter, A Pair of Briefs, A Life for Ruth, The Iron Maiden, Captive City, Summer Flight, Stolen Flight, Of a Thousand Delights, Life at the Top, Modesty Blaise, Star!, Twinky, The Royal Hunt of the Sun, Brotherly Love (Country Dance), A Town Called Bastard, The Fourth Mrs. Anderson, Vault of Horror, Inn of the Damned, Ride a Wild Pony, The Irishman, Turkey Shoot, Stanley, Appointment With Death.

TELEVISION: *Movie:* Spoiled, Tartuffe. *Series:* G.P.. Guest: Doctor Who, The Professionals, Shoestring. *Mini-Series:* The Timeless Land.

CRAIN, JEANNE
Actress. b. Barstow, CA, May 25, 1925. Model; crowned Miss Long Beach of 1941: Camera Girl of 1942.
PICTURES: The Gang's All Here (debut, 1943), Home in Indiana, In the Meantime Darling, Winged Victory, State Fair, Leave Her to Heaven, Margie, Centennial Summer, You Were Meant for Me, Apartment for Peggy, Letter to Three Wives, The Fan, Pinky, Cheaper by the Dozen, I'll Get By (cameo), Take Care of My Little Girl, People Will Talk, Model and the Marriage Broker, Belles on Their Toes, O. Henry's Full House, City of Bad Men, Dangerous Crossing, Vicki, Duel in the Jungle, Man Without a Star, The Second Greatest Sex, Gentlemen Marry Brunettes, Fastest Gun Alive, Tattered Dress, The Joker is Wild, Guns of the Timberland, Queen of the Nile, Twenty Plus Two, Madison Avenue, Pontius Pilate, Hot Rods to Hell, The Night God Screamed, Skyjacked, .

CRAMER, DOUGLAS S.
Executive. e. Northwestern U., Sorbonne, U. of Cincinnati, B.A.; Columbia U.M.F.A. m. Joyce Haber, columnist. Taught at Carnegie Inst. of Tech., 1954-55; Production asst. Radio City Music Hall 1950-51; MGM Script Dept. 1952; Manag. Dir. Cincinnati Summer Playhouse 1953-54. TV supvr. Procter and Gamble 1956-59; Broadcast supvr. Ogilvy Benson and Mather adv. 1959-62; v.p. program dev. ABC-TV 1962-66; v.p. program dev. 20 Cent.-Fox TV 1966; exec. v.p. in chg. of prod., Paramount TV, 1968-71; exec. v.p. Aaron Spelling Prods. 1976-89; pres. Douglas S. Cramer Co, 1989-.
THEATER: Call of Duty, Love is a Smoke, Whose Baby Are You, Last Great Dish.
PICTURES: *Exec. prod.*: Sleeping Together.
TELEVISION: *Exec. prod.*: Bridget Loves Bernie, QB VII, Dawn: Portrait of a Teenage Runaway, Nightmare in Badham County, Sex Symbol, Danielle Steel's Fine Things, Kaleidoscope, Changes, Message from Nam, Daddy, Palamino, Once in a Lifetime, The Ring, Zoya: Trade Winds, Lake Success, Wonder Woman. *Co-exec. prod.*: Love Boat (1977-86), Vegas (1978-81), Dynasty, Matt Houston, Hotel, Colbys.

CRANE, DAVID
Producer. b. 1957.
TELEVISION: *Movies:* Ngaio Marsh's Alleyn Mysteries: Death at the Bar (s.p. editor). *Series:* Dream On (creator), Ngaio Marsh's Alleyn Mysteries (s.p. editor), Friends (co-exec., co-creator), Veronica's Closet (co-exec., co-creator), Jesse (co-exec.)

CRAVEN, GEMMA
Actress. b. Dublin, Ireland, June 1, 1950. e. Loretto Coll. Studied acting at Bush Davies School. London stage debut, Fiddler on the Roof (1970).
THEATER: *London*: Audrey, Trelawny, Dandy Dick, They're Playing Our Song, Song and Dance, Loot, A Chorus of Disapproval, Three Men on a Horse, Jacobowsky and the Colonel, The Magistrate, South Pacific, The London Vertigo, Private Lives, Present Laughter.
PICTURES: Kingdom of Gifts, Why Not Stay for Breakfast, The Slipper and the Rose, Wagner, Double X: The Name of the Game, Words Upon the Windowpane, Still Life.
TELEVISION: Pennies From Heaven, Must Wear Tights, She Loves Me, Song by Song by Noel Coward, Song by Song by Alan Jay Lerner, East Lynne, Robin of Sherwood, Treasure Hunt, Gemma Girls and Gershwin, Boon, The Bill, The Marshal.

CRAVEN, WES
Director, Writer. b. Cleveland, OH, Aug. 2, 1939. e. Wheaton Coll., B.A.; Johns Hopkins, M.A., philosophy. Worked as humanities prof. prior to film.
PICTURES: The Last House on the Left (also s.p., ed.), The Hills Have Eyes (also s.p., ed.), Deadly Blessing, Swamp Thing (also s.p.), A Nightmare on Elm Street (also s.p.), The Hills Have Eyes Part II (also s.p.), Deadly Friend, A Nightmare on Elm Street III: Dream Warriors (co-s.p., co-exec. prod. only), The Serpent and the Rainbow, Shocker (also exec. prod., s.p.), The People Under the Stairs (also s.p., co-exec. prod.), Wes Craven's New Nightmare (also actor, s.p.), Vampire in Brooklyn, The Fear (actor only), Scream, Wishmaster (prod. only), Scream 2, Music of the Heart, Scream 3, Carnival of Souls (exec. prod. only).
TELEVISION: *Series*: Twilight Zone (1985, 7 episodes: Word Play, A Little Peace and Quiet, Shatterday, Chameleon, Dealer's Choice, The Road Less Traveled, Pilgrim Soul). The People Next Door (exec. prod.). *Movies*: A Stranger in Our House, Invitation to Hell, Chiller, Casebusters, Night Visions (also exec. prod., co-writer), Laurel Canyon (exec. prod. only), Body Bags (actor only).

CRAWFORD, MICHAEL
O.B.E. Actor. r.n. Michael Dumbell-Smith. b. Salisbury, England, Jan.19, 1942. Early career as boy actor in children's films, as a boy soprano in Benjamin Britten's Let's Make an Opera and on radio. Later star of TV's Not So Much a Programme, More a Way of Life. Solo albums: Songs from the Stage and Screen, With Love, Performs Andrew Lloyd Weber, A Touch of Music in the Night. Appeared for MGM Grand in production EFX.
THEATER: Come Blow Your Horn, Traveling Light, The Anniversary, White Lies and Black Comedy (N.Y.), No Sex Please We're British, Billy, Same Time Next Year, Flowers for Algernon, Barnum, The Phantom of the Opera (London: Laurence Olivier Award; New York: Tony, Drama Desk, Drama League & Outer Circle Critics Awards, 1988; also L.A.), The Music of Andrew Lloyd Weber (U.S., Canada, U.K. & Australia).
PICTURES: Soap Box Derby (debut, 1957), Blow Your Own Trumpet, A French Mistress, Two Living One Dead, Two Left Feet, The War Lover, The Knack... and How to Get It, A Funny Thing Happened on the Way to the Forum, The Jokers, How I Won the War, Hello Dolly!, The Games, Hello-Goodbye, Alice's Adventures in Wonderland, Condorman, Once Upon a Forest (voice).
TELEVISION: Still Life, Destiny, Byron, Move After Checkmate, Three Barrelled Shotgun, Home Sweet Honeycomb, Some Mothers Do 'ave 'em, Chalk and Cheese, BBC Play for Today, Private View, Barnum.

CRENNA, RICHARD
Actor. b. Los Angeles, CA, Nov. 30, 1927. e. Belmont H.S., USC.
RADIO: Boy Scout Jamboree, A Date With Judy, The Hardy Family, The Great Gildersleeve, Burns & Allen, Our Miss Brooks.
PICTURES: Red Skies of Montana (debut, 1951), Pride of St. Louis, It Grows on Trees, Our Miss Brooks, Over-Exposed, John Goldfarb Please Come Home, Made in Paris, The Sand Pebbles, Wait Until Dark, Star!, Midas Run, Marooned, The Deserter, Doctors' Wives, Red Sky at Morning, Catlow, A Man Called Noon, Dirty Money (Un Flic), Jonathan Livingston Seagull (voice), Breakheart Pass, The Evil, Wild Horse Hank, Death Ship, Stone Cold Dead, Body Heat, First Blood, Table for Five, The Flamingo Kid, Rambo: First Blood Part II, Summer Rental, Rambo III, Leviathan, Hot Shots! Part Deux, A Pyromaniac's Love Story (unbilled), Jade, Sabrina, Wrongfully Accused.
TELEVISION: *Series*: Our Miss Brooks, The Real McCoys, Slattery's People, All's Fair, It Takes Two, Pros & Cons. *Movies*: Footsteps, Thief, Passions, A Case of Deadly Force, The Day the Bubble Burst, Centennial, The Rape of Richard Beck (Emmy Award, 1985), Doubletake, The Price of Passion, Police Story: The Freeway Killings, Plaza Suite, Kids Like These, On Wings of Eagles, Internal Affairs, Blood Brothers: The Case of the Hillside Stranglers, Murder in Black and White, Stuck with Each Other, Montana, Last Flight Out, Murder Times Seven, And the Sea Will Tell, Intruders, Terror on Track 9, A Place to Be Loved, The Forget-Me-Not Murders, Jonathan Stone: Threat of Innocence, Janek: A Silent Betrayal, In the Name of Love: A Texas Tragedy, Texas Graces, Race Against Time: The Search for Sarah, Heart Full of Rain, Cold Case, 20,000 Leagues Under the Sea, To Serve and Protect.

CRICHTON, CHARLES
Director. b. Wallasey, England, Aug. 6, 1910. e. Oundle & Oxford.
PICTURES: For Those in Peril (debut, 1944), Painted Boats (The Girl on the Canal), Dead of Night (Golfing segment), Hue and Cry, Against the Wind, Another Shore, Train of Events (Orchestra Conductor segment), Dance Hall, The Lavender Hill Mob, Hunted (The Stranger in Between), The Titfield Thunderbolt, The Love Lottery, The Divided Heart, Man in the Sky (Decision Against Time), Floods of Fear (also s.p.), The Battle of the Sexes, The Boy Who Stole a Million (also co-s.p.), The Third Secret, He Who Rides a Tiger, Tomorrow's Island (also s.p.), A Fish Called Wanda (also story; 2 Acad. Award noms.).
TELEVISION: The Wild Duck, Danger Man, The Avengers, Man in a Suitcase, The Strange Report, Shirley's World, Black Beauty, The Protectors, Space 1999, Return of the Saint, Dick Turpin 1 & 2 Series, Smuggler, Video Arts Shorts.

CRICHTON, MICHAEL
Writer, Director. r.n. John Michael Crichton. b. Chicago, IL, Oct. 23, 1942. e. Harvard U. Medical School (M.D.), 1969. Postdoctoral fellow, Salk Inst. for Biological Sciences, La Jolla, 1969-70. Visiting writer, MIT, 1988. Recipient Edgar Award, Mystery Writers Amer.: A Case of Need (1968), The Great Train Robbery (1980). Named medical writer of year, Assn. of Amer. Med. Writers: Five Patients (1970). Received Scientific and Technical Achievement Academy Award, 1995.
AUTHOR: *Novels*: (as John Lange): Odds On, Scratch One, Easy Go (The Last Tomb), The Venom Business, Zero Cool, Grave Descend, Drug of Choice, Binary. (as Jeffery Hudson): A Case of Need (filmed as The Carey Treatment). (as Michael Douglas, with brother Douglas Crichton): Dealing or the Berkeley-to-Boston Forty-Brick Lost-Bag Blues (filmed). (as Michael Crichton): The Andromeda Strain (filmed), The Terminal Man (filmed), The Great Train Robbery, Eaters of the Dead, Congo, Sphere, Jurassic Park, Rising Son, Disclosure, The Lost World, Airframe (filmed), The Lost World (filmed). *Non-Fiction* (as Michael Crichton): Five Patients, Jasper Johns, Electronic Life, Travels, Spare, The 13th Warrior.
PICTURES: Westworld (dir., s.p.), Coma (dir., s.p.), The Great Train Robbery (dir., s.p.), Looker (dir., s.p.), Runaway (dir., s.p.), Physical Evidence (dir.), Jurassic Park (co-s.p.), Rising Sun (co-s.p.), Disclosure (co-exec. prod.), Congo (co-s.p.), Twister (co-s.p., co-prod.), The Lost World: Jurassic Park (s.p.), Sphere (s.p., prod.), Airframe, The 13th Warrior (s.p., dir., prod.).

TELEVISION: *Movie*: Pursuit (dir.; based on Binary). *Series*: ER (creator, co-exec. prod.; Emmy Award, 1996). *Pilot*: ER (Writers Guild Award, 1996).

CRIST, JUDITH
Journalist, Critic. b. New York, NY, May 22, 1922. e. Hunter College, Columbia U. School of Journalism. Joined NY Herald Tribune, serving as reporter, arts editor, assoc. drama critic, film critic. Contributing editor Columbia Magazine. Continued as film critic for NY World Journal Tribune, NBC-TV Today Show, New York Magazine, NY Post, Saturday Review, TV Guide, WWOR-TV. Teaches at Col. Grad. School of Journalism.
AUTHOR: The Private Eye the Cowboy and the Very Naked Girl, Judith Crist's TV Guide to the Movies, Take 22: Moviemakers on Moviemaking.

CROMWELL, JAMES
Actor. b. Los Angeles, CA, Jan. 27, 1940. e. Carnegie Mellon Univ. Father was director John Cromwell, mother was actress Kate Johnson.
PICTURES: Murder by Death, The Cheap Detective, The Man With Two Brains, House of God, Tank, Revenge of the Nerds, Oh God You Devil, Explorers, A Fine Mess, Revenge of the Nerds II: Nerds in Paradise, The Rescue, Pink Cadillac, The Runnin' Kind, The Babe, Romeo Is Bleeding, Babe, Eraser, The People vs. Larry Flynt, Star Trek: First Contact, L.A. Confidential, The Education of Little Tree, Deep Impact, Babe: Pig in the City,.Species 2, Snow Falling on Cedars, The Green Mile, The General's Daughter.
TELEVISION: *Series:* All in the Family, Hot L Baltimore, The Nancy Walker Show, The Last Precinct, Easy Street, Mama's Boy. *Mini-Series:* Once an Eagle. *Movies:* The Girl in the Empty Grave, Deadly Game, A Christmas Without Snow, The Wall, Spraggue, The Shaggy Dog. *Guest:* M*A*S*H, Dallas, L.A. Law, Star Trek: The Next Generation, Hill Street Blues.

CRONENBERG, DAVID
Writer, Director. b. Toronto, Ont., May 15, 1943. e. U. of Toronto. In college produced two short movies on 16mm. 1971, to Europe on a Canadian Council grant where in 1975 he shot his first feature, They Came From Within (Shivers).
PICTURES: *Director*: Transfer (also prod, s.p. and edit.), From the Drain (also s.p. and edit.), Stereo, Crimes of the Future, Jim Ritche Sculptor, They Came From Within (Shivers; also s.p.), Rabid (also s.p.), Fast Company, The Brood (also s.p.), Scanners (also s.p.), Videodrome, The Dead Zone, The Fly (also co-s.p., cameo), Dead Ringers (also co-prod., co-s.p.), Naked Lunch (also s.p.), M. Butterfly, Crash, eXistenZ (also s.p. and prod.), Camera. *Actor*: Into the Night, Nightbreed, Trial by Jury, Blue, Henry & Verlin, Trial By Jury, To Die For, Blood and Donuts, The Stupids, Extreme Measures, The Grace of God, Last Night, Resurrection, The American Nightmare, Jason X.
TELEVISION: *Movie:* Moonshine Highway.

CRONKITE, WALTER
Correspondent. b. St. Joseph, MO, Nov. 4, 1916. e. U. of Texas. Reporter and editor Scripps-Howard News Service, TX; radio reporter; U.P. correspondent. WW II corres. British Isles, N. Africa. Foreign Correspondent, France, Belgium, Netherlands, Soviet Union. Joined CBS as Washington news correspondent, 1950; anchorman and mng. editor, CBS Evening News, 1962-81; special correspondent, CBS News, 1981-present. Many TV shows including You Are There, Twentieth Century, Eyewitness to History: CBS Reports: 21st Century, Walter Cronkite's Universe. Past nat'l pres. & mem. bd. Trustees, Acad. TV Arts & Sciences. Mng. editor of CBS Evening News 1963-81. Special correspondent, Children of Apartheid, Walter Cronkite at Large, Cronkite Remembers. Chairman, Cronkite Ward & Company, which has produced more than 25 award winning documentary hours for the Discovery Channel, PBS and others, 1993-98. Host/commentator of The Cronkite Reports, on the Discovery Channel which investigates current, global news issues. Other Cronkite Ward & Co. productions: Great Books series for the Learning Channel and Understanding: Science programs for the Discovery Channel. Supplied voice for 1995 B'way revival of How to Succeed in Business Without Really Trying. Autobiography, A Reporter's Life, 1996.

CRONYN, HUME
Actor, Writer, Director. b. London, Ont., Canada, July 18, 1911. Was married to late actress Jessica Tandy. e. Ridley Coll., McGill U., Amer. Acad. of Dramatic Art.
THEATER: *N.Y.*: *Actor*: High Tor, Escape This Night, Three Men on a Horse, Boy Meets Girl, Three Sisters, Mr. Big, The Survivors, Now I Lay Me Down to Sleep (dir.), Hilda Crane (dir.), The Fourposter (dir.), Madam Will You Walk, The Honeys, A Day by the Sea, The Man in the Dog Suit, The Egghead (dir.), Triple Play (dir. and toured with wife), Big Fish Little Fish (also in London), The Miser, The Three Sisters, Hamlet, The Physicists, Slow Dance on The Killing Ground (prod.), appeared at the White House, Hear America Speaking, Richard III, The Miser, A Delicate Balance (1966 and tour, 1967), Hadrian VII (tour), Caine Mutiny Court Martial, Promenade All, Krapp's Last Tape, Happy Days, Act Without Words, Many Faces Of Love (concert recital), Noel Coward in Two Keys (National tour), Merchant of Venice and A Midsummer Night's Dream (Stratford Festival Theatre). *Canada*: The Gin Game (with Miss Tandy; Long Wharf Thea., New Haven, B'way, 1977, co-prod. with Mike Nichols; also toured U.S., Toronto, London, U.S.S.R., 1978-79). *Also*: Foxfire (co-author, actor, at Stratford, Ont., 1980, Minneapolis, 1981 and N.Y., 1982-83); Traveler in the Dark (Amer. Repertory Theatre, Cambridge, MA), Foxfire (Ahmanson, LA 1985-86), The Petition (NY 1986).
PICTURES: Shadow of a Doubt (debut, 1943), Phantom of the Opera, The Cross of Lorraine, Lifeboat, The Seventh Cross (Acad. Award nom.), Main Street After Dark, The Sailor Takes a Wife, A Letter for Evie, The Green Years, The Postman Always Rings Twice, Ziegfeld Follies, The Secret Heart (narrator), The Beginning or the End, Brute Force, Rope (adapt. only), The Bride Goes Wild, Top o' the Morning, Under Capricorn (adapt. only), People Will Talk, Crowded Paradise, Sunrise at Campobello, Cleopatra, Hamlet, Gaily Gaily, The Arrangement, There Was a Crooked Man, Conrack, The Parallax View, Honky Tonk Freeway, Rollover, The World According to Garp, Impulse, Brewster's Millions, Cocoon, Batteries Not Included, Cocoon: The Return, The Pelican Brief, Camilla, Marvin's Room.
TELEVISION: *Series*: The Marriage. *Movies*: The Dollmaker (co-writer only), Foxfire (also co-writer), Day One, Age-old Friends, Christmas on Division Street, Broadway Bound (Emmy Award, 1992), To Dance With the White Dog (Emmy Award, 1994), Alone, Twelve Angry Men (Emmy nom., 1997),.Love on the Land.

CROSBY, CATHY LEE
Actress. b. Los Angeles, CA. e. Grad. of U. of Southern California. Studied with Lee Strasberg. Author of Let The Magic Begin.
THEATER: Downside Risk, Almost Perfect (Off-B'way debut), Jellyroll Shoes, They Shoot Horses, Don't They? (wrote, dir. starred in 1st theatrical adapt. Hollywood Amer. Legion), Zoot Suit—The Real Story (writer, dir., actress, adapt., Beverly Hills).
PICTURES: The Laughing Policeman (debut, 1973), Trackdown, The Dark, Coach, Training Camp (s.p.), San Sebastian (s.p.), Call Me By My Rightful Name, The Player.
TELEVISION: *Movies*: Wonder Woman, Keefer, Roughnecks, World War III, Intimate Strangers, One Child, North & South III: Heaven and Hell, Untamed Love (also co-exec. prod.), When the Cradle Falls, Treasure of Dos Santos. *Series*: That's Incredible. *Specials*: A Spectacular Evening in Egypt, Battle of the Network Stars, Circus of the Stars, Bob Hope Specials, Get High on Yourself, Bob Hope: USO Tour of Lebanon & the Mediterranean.

CROSBY, KATHRYN
Actress. r.n. Olive Kathryn Grandstaff. b. Houston, TX. e. U. of Texas, Queen of Angels Sch. of Nursing, Immaculate Heart Col. m. late actor-singer Bing Crosby. Author: Bing and Other Things, My Life With Bing.
THEATER: Mama's Baby Boy, The Enchanted, Sunday in New York, Sabrina Fair, The Guardsman, Guys and Dolls, Same Time Next Year, The Crucible, Cyrano de Bergerac, Tonight at 8:30, The Cocktail Hour, Oh Coward, I Do I Do, The Heiress, The Seagull, Hello Dolly, State Fair, The Music Man, Lion In Winter, and many others.
PICTURES: Forever Female, Rear Window, Living It Up, Sabrina, Arrowhead, Casanova's Big Night, Unchained, Cell 2455 Death Row, Tight Spot, Five Against the House, Reprisal, Guns of Fort Petticoat, The Phenix City Story, Wild Party, Mister Cory, Gunman's Walk, The Librarian, Anatomy of a Murder, The Brothers Rico, Operation Mad Ball, The Seventh Voyage of Sinbad, The Big Circus, The Wild Party.
TELEVISION: *Guest*: Bob Hope Chrysler Theatre, Bing Crosby Christmas Specials, Suspense Theatre, Ben Casey, The Kathryn Crosby Show (KPIX-TV, San Francisco). *Movie*: The Initiation of Sarah.

CROSBY, MARY
Actress. b. Los Angeles, CA, Sept. 14, 1959. e. U. TX; American Conservatory Theatre. Daughter of performers Kathryn Crosby and the late Bing Crosby. Formerly acted as Mary Frances Crosby. Appeared from an early age in several TV variety specials with her parents. On stage in: Rome & Juliet, A Gentleman of Verona (L.A.), As You Like It (L.A.), The Seagull (L.A.).
PICTURES: The Last Plane Out, The Ice Pirates, Tapeheads, Body Chemistry, Corporate Affairs, Eating, The Berlin Conspiracy, Desperate Motive (Distant Cousins).
TELEVISION: *Series*: Brothers and Sisters, Dallas. *Movies*: With This Ring, A Guide for the Married Woman, Midnight Lace, Golden Gate, Confessions of a Married Man, Final Jeopardy, Stagecoach, Johnann Strauss: The King Without a Crown. *Mini-Series*: Pearl, Hollywood Wives, North and South Book II. *Pilot*: Golden Gate, The Big Easy, Cover Up. *Specials*: Goldilocks, Bing Crosby's Christmas Show (1970-73, 1976-77), Battle of the Network Stars, The 21st Annual Academy of Country Music Awards, Crazy Dan, Tube Test Two, Best Sellers: Men Who Hate Women and the Wome Who Love Them. *Guest*: Knots Landing, The Love Boat, The Fall Guy, Hotel, In the Heat of the Night, Murder She Wrote, Beverly Hills 90210, and many others.

CROSS, BEN
Actor. r.n. Bernard Cross. b. London, England, Dec. 16, 1947. e. Royal Acad. of Dramatic Art. Worked as stagehand, prop-master, and master carpenter with Welsh Natl. Opera and as set builder, Wimbledon Theatre.

THEATER: The Importance of Being Earnest (Lancaster, debut, 1972), I Love My Wife, Privates on Parade, Chicago, Lydie Breeze (NY debut, 1982), Caine Mutiny Court Martial.
PICTURES: A Bridge Too Far (debut, 1977), Chariots of Fire, The Unholy, The Goldsmith's Shop, Paperhouse, The House of the Lord, Eye of the Widow, Haunted Symphony, The Ascent, First Knight, Turbulence.
TELEVISION: *Movies/Specials*: Melancholy Hussar of the German Legion (1973, BBC), The Flame Trees of Thika, The Citadel, The Far Pavilions, Coming Out of the Ice, The Assisi Underground, Arthur Hailey's Strong Medicine, Steal the Sky, Pursuit, Twist of Fate, Nightlife, She Stood Alone, Diamond Fleece, Live Wire, Deep Trouble, Cold Sweat. *Series*: Dark Shadows (1991).

CROUSE, LINDSAY
Actress. b. New York, NY, May 12, 1948. Daughter of playwright Russel Crouse. e. Radcliffe.
THEATER: *With Circle Repertory Co. N.Y.*: Hamlet, Twelfth Night, Richard II, Childe Byron, Reunion (Obie Award). *NY*: Serenading Louie, The Shawl, The Stick Wife, The Homecoming (B'way debut; Theatre World Award). *With L.A. Matrix Theatre Co.*: The Tavern, Habeus Corpus.
PICTURES: All the President's Men (debut, 1976), Slap Shot, Between the Lines, Prince of the City, The Verdict, Daniel, Iceman, Places in the Heart (Acad. award nom.), House of Games, Communion, Desperate Hours, Being Human, Bye Bye Love, The Indian in the Cupboard, The Arrival, The Juror, Prefontaine.
TELEVISION: *Movies*: Eleanor and Franklin, Chantilly Lace, Final Appeal, Out of Darkness, Parallel Lives, Traps. *Mini-Series*: The Kennedys of Massachusetts. *Specials*: Kennedy's Children, Lemon Sky, Between Mother and Daughter, If These Walls Could Talk. *Guest*: Colombo, Murder She Wrote, LA Law, Hill Street Blues, Civil Wars, Law and Order, E.R. *Series*: American Nuclear (pilot), NYPD Blue, Millenium.

CROWE, CAMERON
Writer, Director. b. Palm Springs, CA, July 13, 1957. e. Calif. St. Univ., San Diego. Began career as journalist and editor for Rolling Stone. Adapted his book Fast Times at Ridgemont High into Writers Guild Award-nominated screenplay for 1982 film.
PICTURES: American Hot Wax (actor). Fast Times at Ridgemont High (s.p. only), The Wild Life (s.p.,co-prod.), Say Anything..., Singles, Jerry Maguire (dir. & prod. only), Almost Famous.
TELEVISION: *Series*: Fast Times (creative consultant).

CROWE, KEN
Executive. b. Sewickley, PA, Sept. 3, 1939. e. San Diego U. CPA, public accounting, Coopers & Lybrand, 1968-77. Mann Theatres, treas./CFO, 1977-86; Paramount Mann Theatres, sr. v.p./CFO, 1986-88. Cinamerica Theatres, exec. v.p./CFO, 1988-present. Member of Motion Picture Pioneers, AICPA, FEI, Variety Club of So. Calif and Sertoma.

CROWE, RUSSELL
Actor. b. New Zealand, 1964. Raised in Australia. Worked as professional musician while appearing on Australian stage in Bad Boy Johnny and the Profits of Doom, Blood Brothers, Rocky Horror Show.
PICTURES: For the Moment, The Silver Brumby, Hammers Over the Anvil, Prisoners of the Sun, Love in Limbo, For the Moment, Proof (Australian Film Inst. Award), The Efficiency Expert, Romper Stomper (Australian Film Inst. Award), The Quick and the Dead, The Sum of Us, Virtuosity, Rough Magic, No Way Back, Breaking Up, L.A. Confidential, Heaven's Burning, Breaking Up, Mystery Alaska, The Insider, Gladiator, Proof of Life.

CROWN, DANIEL
Executive. Pres., Crown Theatres, S. Norwalk, CT., 1990-. Bd. or dirs., NY Yankees, 1985-. Other bds.: Lenox Hill Hosp., Mt. Sinai Children's Ctr. Fdn., Jerusalem Fdn., Jewish Nat'l. Fund, New York, NY. Member NATO, 1991-.

CRUEA, EDMOND D.
Executive. b. Jersey City, NJ, June 3. Joined Grand Natl. Pictures, LA, 1935; Monogram Pictures, 1938-41, LA & Seattle; U.S. Army Signal Corps., 1942-46; Monogram Pictures, Seattle, 1946; branch mgr. & district mgr. Allied Artists, 1950-65 (Seattle, Portland, San Francisco, LA); v.p. & gen. sls. mgr., Allied Artists, 1965-71; dir. distbn., Abkco Films div. of Abkco Industries Inc., 1971-73; pres. Royal Dist. Corp, 1974; joined Film Ventures Intl. 1976 as exec. v.p. succeeding to pres. & COO in 1976. Co-founded New Image Releasing Inc., 1982, as pres. & CEO. 1985, v.p. theatrical, Cinetel Films; V.P. Distrib. Jerry Gross Org.; 1987 theatrical distbn. cons., Sony Pictures (NY), Sony Video Softwear plus and Shining Armour Commun (London). Acquisitions & distbn. cons. to Columbia TriStar Home Video, Triumph Pictures and Healing Arts Documentary Prods.; 1995, chmn. and CEO Global International Films Inc.; 1996, pres. Capstone films; cons. to Intic Productions. Theatrical consult to Croatian Embassy, NY.

CRUISE, TOM
Actor. r.n. Thomas Cruise Mapother IV. b. Syracuse, NY, July 3, 1962. m. actress Nicole Kidman. Acted in high school plays; secured role in dinner theatre version of Godspell. Studied acting at Neighborhood Playhouse, before landing small part in Endless Love. Received American Cinema Award for Distinguished Achievement in Film, 1991.
PICTURES: Endless Love (debut, 1981), Taps, Losin' It, The Outsiders, Risky Business, All the Right Moves, Legend, Top Gun, The Color of Money, Cocktail, Rain Man, Born on the 4th of July (Golden Globe Award; Acad. Award nom., 1989), Days of Thunder (also co-wrote story), Far and Away, A Few Good Men, The Firm, Interview With the Vampire, Mission: Impossible, Jerry Macguire (Golden Globe Award, 1997), Eyes Wide Shut, Magnolia, Mission Impossible 2 (also prod.), Without Limits (prod. only) Vanilla Sky, Minority Report.
TELEVISION: *Director*: The Frightening Framis (episode of series Fallen Angels).

CRUZ, PENELOPE
Actress. b. Madrid, Spain, April 28, 1974.
PICTURES: The Greek Labyrinth, The Age of Beauty, Salami, Salami, The Rebel, For Love, Only For Love, Alegre ma non troppo, Life's a Bitch, Entre rojas, Brujas, La Celestina, Not Love, Just Frenzy, Love Can Seriously Damage Your Health, A Corner of Paradise, Live Flesh, Open Your Eyes, Don Juan, Twice Upon A Yesterday, Talk of Angels, The Girl of Your Dreams, The Hi-Lo Country, Nada en la nevera, All About My Mother, Volaverunt, Blow, All the Pretty Horses, Vanilla Sky, Captain Corelli's Mandolin.

CRYER, JON
Actor. b. New York, NY, Apr. 16, 1965. Son of actor David Cryer and songwriter-actress Gretchen Cryer. On B'way stage in Brighton Beach Memoirs.
PICTURES: No Small Affair (debut, 1984), Pretty in Pink, Morgan Stewart's Coming Home, O.C. and Stiggs, Superman IV: The Quest for Peace, Hiding Out, Dudes, Penn and Teller Get Killed, Hot Shots!, The Pompatus of Love, Plan B, Went to Coney Island on a Mission from God...Back By 5, Die Wholesale, Holy Man.
TELEVISION: *Series*: The Famous Teddy Z, Partners, It's Good to Be King, Getting Personal. *Special*: Kurt Vonnegut's Monkey House. *Movie*: Heads.

CRYSTAL, BILLY
Actor, Writer, Producer, Director. b. Long Island, NY, Mar. 14, 1947. e. Marshall U., Nassau Commun. Col., NYU (BFA in tv & film direction). Father, Jack, produced jazz concerts; family owned Commodore jazz record label. Worked with Alumni Theatre Group at Nassau Commun. College. Later teamed with two friends (billed as We the People, Comedy Jam, 3's Company) and toured coffee houses and colleges. Became stand-up comedian on own, appearing at Catch a Rising Star, The Comedy Story and on TV. Album: Mahvelous!. Book: Absolutely Mahvelous!
PICTURES: Rabbit Test (debut, 1978), Animalympics (voice), This Is Spinal Tap, Running Scared, The Princess Bride, Throw Mama From the Train, Memories of Me (also co-prod., co-s.p.), When Harry Met Sally..., City Slickers (also exec. prod.), Mr. Saturday Night (also dir., prod., co-s.p.), City Slickers II: The Legend of Curly's Gold (also prod., co-s.p.), Forget Paris (also dir., prod., co-s.p.), Hamlet, Father's Day, Deconstructing Harry, My Giant, Analyze This, Monsters, Inc. (voice).
TELEVISION: *Series*: Soap, The Billy Crystal Comedy Hour (also writer), Saturday Night Live (also writer), Sessions (creator, exec. prod. only). *Guest*: Saturday Night Live with Howard Cosell, Tonight Show, Dinah, Mike Douglas Show, That Was the Year That Was, All in the Family, Love Boat. Specials include: Battle of the Network Stars, Billy Crystal: A Comic's Line (also writer), A Comedy Salute to Baseball (also writer), On Location: Billy Crystal - Don't Get Me Started (also dir., writer), The Three Little Pigs (Faerie Tale Theatre), The Lost Minutes of Billy Crystal, Midnight Train to Moscow (also exec. prod., co-writer; Emmy Award 1990). *Movies*: SST—Death Flight, Human Feelings, Breaking Up Is Hard to Do, Enola Gay: The Men the Mission and the Atomic Bomb. *Host*: Grammy Awards (Emmy Awards for hosting, 1988, 1989), Academy Awards (Emmy Award for hosting, 1991, 1997; Emmy Award for co-writing, 1992).

CULBERG, PAUL S.
Executive. b. Chicago, IL, June 14, 1942. Began career in record industry, holding positions with Elektra Records & Wherehouse Record; 1977-80; v.p. sls. mktg., Cream Records.; 1980-82, dir. sls. Paramount Home Video; 1982, v.p. sls. mktg., Media Home Entertainment; 1984-89, pres., New World Video; 1989-present, COO, RCA Columbia/TriStar Home Video.

CULKIN, MACAULAY
Actor. b. New York, NY, Aug. 26, 1980. Acting debut at 4 yrs. old in Bach Babies at NY's Symphony Space. Appeared in several TV commercials. Studied ballet at George Ballanchine's School of American Ballet and danced in NY productions of H.M.S. Pinafore and The Nutcracker. Received Comedy Award and Youth in Film Award for role in Home Alone. Appeared in Michael Jackson video Black and White.

THEATER: *NY*: Afterschool Special, Mr. Softee, Buster B. and Olivia.
PICTURES: Rocket Gibraltar (debut, 1988), See You in the Morning, Uncle Buck, Jacob's Ladder, Home Alone, Only the Lonely, My Girl, Home Alone 2: Lost in New York, The Good Son, George Balanchine's The Nutcracker, Getting Even With Dad, The Pagemaster, Richie Rich.
TELEVISION: *Guest*: The Equalizer, Saturday Night Live, Bob Hope Christmas Special.

CULLUM, JOHN
Actor. b. Knoxville, TN, Mar. 2, 1930. e. Univ. of TN. Son is actor John David (J.D.) Cullum.
THEATER: *NY*: Camelot, On a Clear Day You Can See Forever (Theatre World Award, Tony nom.), Hamlet, Man of La Mancha, 1776, Shenandoah (Tony Award, Drama Desk & Outer Circle Critics Awards, 1975), The Trip Back Down, On the Twentieth Century (Tony Award, 1978), Deathtrap, Private Lives, Doubles, The Boys in Autumn, Aspects of Love, Showboat.
PICTURES: All the Way Home, 1776, The Prodigal, The Act, Marie, Sweet Country.
TELEVISION: *Series*: Buck James, Northern Exposure. *Guest*: Quantum Leap (also dir.). *Movies*: The Man Without a Country, The Day After, Shoot Down, With a Vengeance.

CULP, ROBERT
Actor, Writer, Director. b. Berkeley, CA, Aug. 16, 1930. e. Stockton, College of the Pacific, Washington U., San Francisco State. To N.Y. to study with Herbert Berghof (played Potzo in 1st U.S. prod. of Waiting for Godot. Starred in off-Bway prod. He Who Gets Slapped. Best Actor of the Year in an off-Bway Play; motion picture debut, 1962; P.T. 109. Television guest appearances in Rawhide, Wagon Train, Bob Hope Presents the Chrysler Theatre; wrote and acted in Rifleman, Cain's Hundred, The Dick Powell Show.
THEATER: *Bway.:* The Prescott Proposals, A Clearing in the Woods, Diary of a Scoundrel.
PICTURES: PT 109 (debut, 1963), Sunday in New York, Rhino!, Bob & Carol & Ted & Alice, The Grove, Hannie Caulder, Hickey & Boggs (also dir., uncredited co-s.p.), A Name for Evil, The Castaway Cowboy, Inside Out (Golden Heist), Sky Riders, Breaking Point, The Great Scout and Cathouse Thursday, Goldengirl, National Lampoon Goes to the Movies, Turk 182!, Big Bad Mama II, Silent Night Deadly Night 3: Better Watch Out, Pucker Up and Bark Like a Dog, Timebomb, The Pelican Brief, Panther.
TELEVISION: *Series*: Trackdown, I Spy (also wrote pilot and 6 shows; Emmy noms. as writer and actor), The Greatest American Hero (also wrote 2 shows). *Guest:* The Cosby Show. *Movies*: Sammy The Way Out Seal, The Raiders, The Hanged Man, See the Man Run, A Cold Night's Death, Outrage!, Houston We've Got a Problem, Strange Homecoming, A Cry for Help, Flood, Spectre, Last of the Good Guys, Women in White, Hot Rod, The Dream Merchants, The Night the City Screamed, Killjoy, Thou Shalt Not Kill, Her Life as a Man, The Calendar Girl Murders, Brothers-in-Law, The Blue Lightning, The Gladiator, The Key to Rebecca, Combat High, Voyage of Terror: The Achille Lauro Affair, Columbo Goes to College, I Spy Returns.

CUMMING, ALAN
Actor. b. Perthshire, Scotland, Jan. 27, 1965.
PICTURES: Prague, Second Best, Black Beauty (voice), Circle of Friends, GoldenEye, Burn Your Phone, Emma, Spice World, For My Baby, Romy and Michele's High School Reunion, Buddy, The Flintstones in Viva Rock Vegas, Eyes Wide Shut, Plunkett & MaCleane, Titus, Urbania, Company Man, Spy Kids, Josie and the Pussycats, The Anniversary Party..
TELEVISION: *Movies:* Bernard and the Genie, The Airzone Solution, Micky Love, That Sunday, Annie. *Guest:* Mr. Bean.

CUMMINS, PEGGY
Actress. b. Prestatyn, North Wales, Dec. 18, 1925. e. Alexandra Sch., Dublin, Gate Theatre, Dublin. Starred in Let's Pretend on London Stage 1938, followed by Junior Miss, Alice in Wonderland, Peter Pan.
PICTURES: Dr. O'Dowd (debut, 1939), Salute John Citizen, Old Mother Riley—Detective, Welcome Mr. Washington, English Without Tears (Her Man Gilbey), The Late George Apley, Moss Rose, Green Grass of Wyoming, Escape, That Dangerous Age (If This Be Sin), Gun Crazy, My Daughter Joy (Operation X), Who Goes There (Passionate Sentry), Street Corner (Both Sides of the Law), Meet Mr. Lucifer, Always a Bride, The Love Lottery, To Dorothy a Son (Cash on Delivery), The March Hare, Carry on Admiral, Night of the Demon, Hell Drivers, The Captain's Table, Your Money or Your Wife, Dentist in the Chair, In the Doghouse.
TELEVISION: The Human Jungle, Looks Familiar.

CUNNINGHAM, SEAN S.
Producer, Director. b. New York, NY, Dec. 31 1941. e. Franklin & Marshall, B.A.; Stanford U., M.F.A. Worked briefly as actor, moving into stage-managing. Became producer of Mineola Theatre (Long Island, NY) and took several productions to B'way. Formed Sean S. Cunningham Films, Ltd., 1971. Produced commercials, industrial film, documentaries, features.
PICTURES: Together (prod., dir.), Last House on the Left (prod.), The Case of the Full Moon Murders (prod.), Here Come the Tigers (prod., dir.), Kick (prod., dir.), Friday the 13th (prod., dir.), A Stranger Is Watching (prod., dir.), Spring Break (prod., dir.), The New Kids (prod., dir.), House (prod.), House II: The Second Story (prod.), Deepstar Six (prod., dir.), The Horror Show (House III; prod.), House IV (prod.), My Boyfriend's Back (prod.), Jason Goes to Hell: The Final Friday (prod.).

CURLEY, JOHN J
Executive. b. Dec. 31, 1938. e. Dickinson Coll., BA, 1960; Columbia U., MS, 1963. Reporter, editor Associated Press, 1961-66. With Gannett Co., Inc., 1969-; pres. mid-Atlantic newspaper group Gannett Co., Inc, 1980-82; sr. v.p., Gannett Co., Inc, 1983-84; pres., 1984-; COO, 1984-86; CEO, 1986-; chmn., and bd. dirs., 1989-.

CURRY, TIM
Actor. b. Cheshire, England, Apr. 19, 1946. e. Birmingham U. Albums: Read My Lips, Fearless, Simplicity.
THEATER: Hair, A Midsummer Night's Dream, The Rocky Horror Show, Travesties, Amadeus (Tony nom.), The Pirates of Penzance, Me and My Girl (U.S. tour), The Art of Success, My Favorite Year (Tony nom.).
PICTURES: The Rocky Horror Picture Show (debut, 1975), The Shout, Times Square, Annie, The Ploughman's Lunch, Blue Money, Clue, Legend, Pass the Ammo, The Hunt for Red October, Oscar, FernGully... The Last Rainforest (voice), Passed Away, Home Alone 2: Lost in New York, National Lampoon's Loaded Weapon 1, The Three Musketeers, The Shadow, Lovers' Knot, The Pebble and the Penguin (voice), Congo, The Muppet Treasure Island, Lover's Knot, McHale's Navy, The Rugrats Movie (voice), The Titanic Chronicles, Pirates of Plain, Four Dogs Playing Poker.
TELEVISION: *Movies*: Oliver Twist, Stephen King's IT, Jackie's Back. *Voice work—series*: Peter Pan and the Pirates (Emmy Award, 1991), Captain Planet and the Planeteers, Fish Police, Over the Top, The Net, The Wild Thornberrys, Voltron: The Third Dimension. *Specials*: The Life of Shakespeare, Three Men in a Boat, Rock Follies, City Sugar. *Guest*: Dinosaurs (voice), Earth 2, Duckman (voice).

CURTIN, JANE
Actress. b. Cambridge, MA, Sept. 6, 1947. e. Northeastern U. On stage in Proposition, Last of the Red Hot Lovers, Candida. Author, actress off-B'way musical revue Pretzel 1974-75.
PICTURES: Mr. Mike's Mondo Video, How to Beat the High Cost of Living, O.C. and Stiggs, Coneheads, Antz (voice).
TELEVISION: *Series*: Saturday Night Live (1974-79), Kate & Allie (Emmy Awards: 1984, 1985), Working It Out, 3rd Rock from the Sun, Recess (voice). *Movies*: What Really Happened to the Class of '65, Divorce Wars—A Love Story, Suspicion, Maybe Baby, Common Ground, Tad, Christmas in Washington. *Special*: Candida.

CURTIS, DAN
Producer, Director. b. Bridgeport, CT, Aug. 12, 1928. e. U. of Bridgeport, Syracuse U., B.A. Was sales exec. for NBC and MCA before forming own company, Dan Curtis Productions, which he now heads. Producer/owner of CBS Golf Classic (1963-73).
PICTURES: *Dir./Prod.*: House of Dark Shadows, Night of Dark Shadows, Burnt Offerings (also co-s.p.), Me and the Kid.
TELEVISION: *Series*: *Producer*: Dark Shadows (ABC daytime serial, 1966-71), Dark Shadows (prime time series, 1991). *Movies: Director*: The Night Stalker, Frankenstein, The Picture of Dorian Gray, The Last Ride of the Dalton Gang, The Long Days of Summer, Mrs. R's Daughter, Intruders (also co-exec. prod.). *Prod./Dir.*: The Night Strangler, The Norliss Tapes, Scream of the Wolf, Dracula, Melvin Purvis: G-Man, The Turn of the Screw, The Great Ice-Rip Off, Trilogy of Terror, Kansas City Massacre, Curse of the Black Widow, When Every Day Was the Fourth of July (also co-story), The Love Letter. *Mini-Series (prod./dir.)*: The Winds of War, War and Remembrance (also co-writer).

CURTIS, JAMIE LEE
Actress. b. Los Angeles, CA, Nov. 22, 1958. e. Choat Rosemary Hall, CT; Univ. of the Pacific. m. actor-director Christopher Guest. Daughter of Janet Leigh and Tony Curtis. While in school won contract with Universal Studios appearing in small parts in several tv shows.
PICTURES: Halloween (debut, 1978), The Fog, Prom Night, Terror Train, Halloween II, Roadgames, Trading Places, Love Letters, Grandview USA, Perfect, Amazing Grace and Chuck, A Man in Love, Dominick and Eugene, A Fish Called Wanda, Blue Steel, Queens Logic, My Girl, Forever Young, My Girl 2, Mother's Boys, True Lies, House Arrest, Fierce Creatures, Halloween H2O: Twenty Years Later, Homegrown, Virus, Drowning Mona, The Tailor of Panama, Daddy and Them, Halloween H2K: Evil Never Dies.
TELEVISION: *Special*: Tall Tales (Annie Oakley). *Series*: Operation Petticoat (1977-78), Anything But Love (also, dir., Golden Globe Award). *Movies*: Operation Petticoat (pilot), She's in the Army Now, Death of a Centerfold: The Dorothy Stratten Story, Money on the Side, As Summers Die, The Heidi Chronicles, Nicholas' Gift. *Pilot*: Callahan. *Guest*: Quincy, Nancy Drew Mysteries, The Love Boat, The Drew Carey Show, Buck Rogers in the 25th Century.

CURTIS, TONY
Actor. r.n. Bernard Schwartz. b. New York, NY, June 3, 1925. e. Seward Park H.S. Daughter is actress Jamie Lee Curtis. In U.S. Navy, amateur dramatics, N.Y., started Empire Players Theatre, Newark, NJ. With Dramatic Workshop, Cherry Lane Theatre, Junior Drama workshop of Walt Whitman School. First prod. work with Stanley Woolf Players. Made m.p. debut unbilled in Criss-Cross; signed with U-I. Star of Tomorrow, 1953. Author: Tony Curtis: The Autobiography (1993).
PICTURES: Criss Cross (debut, 1948), City Across the River, The Lady Gambles, Johnny Stool Pigeon, Francis, Sierra, I Was a Shoplifter, Winchester 73, Sierra, Kansas Raiders, Prince Who Was a Thief, Flesh and Fury, Son of Ali Baba, No Room for the Groom, Houdini, All American, Forbidden, Beachhead, Johnny Dark, Black Shield of Falworth, 6 Bridges to Cross, So This Is Paris, Purple Mask, Square Jungle, Rawhide Years, Trapeze, Mister Cory, Midnight Story, Sweet Smell of Success, The Vikings, Kings Go Forth, The Defiant Ones (Acad. Award nom.), The Perfect Furlough, Some Like It Hot, Operation Petticoat, Who Was That Lady?, The Rat Race, Spartacus, Pepe (cameo), The Great Impostor, The Outsider, Taras Bulba, 40 Pounds of Trouble, The List of Adrian Messenger, Captain Newman, M.D., Paris When it Sizzles, Wild and Wonderful, Sex and the Single Girl, Goodbye Charlie, The Great Race, Boeing-Boeing, Chamber of Horrors (cameo), Not With My Wife You Don't!, Arrivederci Baby!, Don't Make Waves, On My Way to the Crusades I Met a Girl Who—(The Chastity Belt), The Boston Strangler, Rosemary's Baby (voice), Those Daring Young Men in Their Jaunty Jalopies (Monte Carlo or Bust), Suppose They Gave a War and Nobody Came, You Can't Win 'Em All, Lepke, The Last Tycoon, Casanova & Co., The Manitou, The Bad News Bears Go to Japan, Sextette, Little Miss Marker, The Mirror Crack'd, Brainwaves, King of the City, Insignificance, Club Life, The Last of Philip Banter, Balboa, Midnight, Lobster Man From Mars, The High-Flying Mermaid, Prime Target, Center of the Web, Naked in New York, The Reptile Man, The Immortals, The Celluloid Closet, Hardball, Brittle Glory.
TELEVISION: *Series*: The Persuaders, McCoy, Vega$, Hollywood Babylon (host). *Movies*: The Third Girl from the Left, The Count of Monte Cristo, Vega$, The Users, Moviola: The Scarlett O'Hara War, Inmates: A Love Story, Harry's Back, The Million Dollar Face, Mafia Princess, Murder in Three Acts, Portrait of a Showgirl, Tarzan in Manhattan, Thanksgiving Day, Christmas in Connecticut, A Perry Mason Mystery: The Case of the Grimacing Governor, Elvis Meets Nixon.

CUSACK, JOAN
Actress. b. Evanston, IL, Oct. 11, 1962. Brother is actor John Cusack. e. U. of Wisconsin, Madison. Studied acting at Piven Theatre Workshop, Evanston, IL. While in coll. joined The Ark, local improvisational comedy group.
THEATER: Road, Brilliant Traces (Theatre World Award for both), Cymbeline, The Celestial Alphabet Event, 'Tis Pity She's a Whore, A Midsummer Night's Dream.
PICTURES: My Bodyguard (debut, 1980), Class, Sixteen Candles, Grandview U.S.A., The Allnighter, Broadcast News, Stars and Bars, Married to the Mob, Working Girl (Acad. Award nom.), Say Anything..., Men Don't Leave, My Blue Heaven, The Cabinet of Dr. Ramirez, Hero, Toys, Addams Family Values, Corrina Corrina, Nine Months, Mr. Wrong, Grosse Pointe Blank, A Smile Like Yours, In & Out (NY Film Crits. Circle Award, Best Supporting Actress, 1997), Runaway Bride, The Cradle Will Rock, Arlington Road, Toy Story 2 (voice), High Fidelity, Where the Heart Is.
TELEVISION: *Series*: Saturday Night Live (1985-86). *Special*: The Mother.

CUSACK, JOHN
Actor. b. Evanston, IL, June 28, 1966. Sister is actress Joan Cusack. Member of Piven Theatre Workshop in Evanston for 10 years beginning when he was 9 years old. Appeared on several tv commercials as teen. Formed Chicago theatrical company, New Criminals.
PICTURES: Class (debut, 1983), Sixteen Candles, Grandview U.S.A., The Sure Thing, The Journey of Natty Gann, Better Off Dead, Stand By Me, One Crazy Summer, Hot Pursuit, Eight Men Out, Tapeheads, Say Anything..., Fat Man and Little Boy, The Grifters, True Colors, Shadows and Fog, Roadside Prophets, The Player, Bob Roberts, Map of the Human Heart, Money for Nothing, Bullets Over Broadway, The Road to Wellville, Floundering, City Hall, Grosse Pointe Blank (also co-prod. & s.p.), Con Air, Midnight in the Garden of Good and Evil, Anastasia (voice), This Is My Father, The Thin Red Line, Pushing Tin, Chicago Cab, Arigo (also prod.), High Fidelity (also s.p.), Cradle Will Rock, Being John Malkovich, White Jazz, Life of the Party, Arigo, Serendipity.
TELEVISION: *Movies:* Eastwood on Eastwood. *Mini-Series*: Baseball (voice).

CZERNY, HENRY
Actor. b. Toronto, Canada, 1959. Began acting career performing in musicals at Humberside collegiate in Toronto.
PICTURES: I Love a Man in Uniform, Cold Sweat, Buried on Sunday, Anchor Zone, Clear and Present Danger, Notes From Underground, The Michelle Apartments, The Interview, When Night Is Falling, Mission Impossible, Promise the Moon, Kayla, The Ice Storm, Glory & Honor.
TELEVISION: *Movies*: Deadly Matrimony, A Town Torn Apart, Lifeline to Victory, The Boys of St. Vincent, Ultimate Betrayal, Choices of the Heart: The Margaret Sanger Story, For Hope. *Guest*: Street Legal, Counterstrike, Kung Fu: The Legend Continues.

D

D'ABO, OLIVIA
Actress. b. England. Parents, singer Michael d'Abo, actress Maggie London.
THEATER: *LA:* Scenes From an Execution, It's a Girl.
PICTURES: Conan the Destroyer, Bolero, Bullies, Into the Fire, Beyond the Stars, The Spirit of 76, Point of No Return, Wayne's World 2, Bank Robber, Greedy, Clean Slate, The Last Good Time, The Big Green, Kicking and Screaming, Live Nude Girls, Hacks, The Velocity of Gary, It had To Be You, Texas Funeral.
TELEVISION: *Series:* The Wonder Years, The Single Guy, Mortal Kombat: The Animated Series (voice). *Movies:* Not My Kid, Crash Course, Midnight's Child, Dad's Week Off. *Guest:* Party of Five.

DAFOE, WILLEM
Actor. r.n. William Dafoe. b. Appleton, WI, July 22, 1955. Worked with experimental group Theatre X on the road before coming to New York. Built sets and debuted with the Wooster Group at the Performing Garage playing (literally) a chicken heart in Elizabeth Le Compte's Nayatt School. Current member of the Wooster Group, performing with them frequently in U.S. and Europe. For them appeared in independent film The Communists Are Comfortable.
PICTURES: Heaven's Gate (debut, 1980), The Loveless, The Hunger, Streets of Fire, Roadhouse 66, To Live and Die in L.A., Platoon (Acad. Award nom.), Off Limits, The Last Temptation of Christ, Mississippi Burning, Triumph of the Spirit, Born on the Fourth of July, Cry-Baby, Wild at Heart, Flight of the Intruder, White Sands, Light Sleeper, Body of Evidence, Faraway So Close!, Clear and Present Danger, Tom and Viv, The Night and the Moment, Basquiat, The English Patient, Speed 2: Cruise Control, Affliction, Lulu on the Bridge, New Rose Hotel, eXistenZ, Bullfighter, Boondock Saints, American Psycho, The Animal Factory, Morality Play, Edges of the Lord.

DAHL, ARLENE
Actress, Writer, Designer. b. Minneapolis, MN, Aug. 11, 1928. e. MN Business Coll.; U. of Minnesota, summers 1941-44; Minneapolis. Coll. of Music. m. Marc A. Rosen. Mother of actor Lorenzo Lamas. At age 8, played heroine of children's adventure serials on radio. Internationally syndicated beauty columnist, Chgo. Tribune-N.Y. News Syndicate, 1951-71; Pres. Arlene Dahl Enterprises, 1951-75; Sleepwear Designer, A.N. Saab & Co., 1952-57; Natl. Beauty Advisor, Sears Roebuck & Co., 1970-75; v.p. Kenyon & Eckhart Advg. Agcy., pres., Women's World Div., Kenyon-Eckhart, 1967-72; Fashion Consultant, O.M.A. 1975-78, Int'l. Director of S.M.E.I., 1973-76, Designer, Vogue Patterns 1978-85. Pres., Dahlia Parfums Inc., 1975-80, pres., Dahlia Prods., 1978-81: pres. Dahlmark Prods. 1981-. Honrs. include: 8 Motion Picture Laurel Awards, 1948-63; Hds. of Fame Award, 1971, Woman of the Year, N.Y. Adv. Council, 1969. Mother of the Year, 1979; Coup de Chapeau, Deauville Film Fest 1983. Received star on Hollywood Walk of Fame. Lifetime Achievement Award Filmfest 1994.
THEATER: *B'way*: Mr. Strauss Goes to Boston (debut, 1946), Cyrano de Bergerac, Applause. *Major US tours include*: Questionable Ladies, The King and I, One Touch of Venus, I Married an Angel, Mame, Pal Joey, Bell Book and Candle, The Camel Bell, Life With Father, A Little Night Music, Lilliom, Marriage Go Round, Blithe Spirit, Forty Carats, Dear Liar, Murder Among Friends.
PICTURES: My Wild Irish Rose (debut, 1947), The Bride Goes Wild, A Southern Yankee, Ambush, Reign of Terror (The Black Book), Scene of the Crime, The Outriders, Three Little Words, Watch the Birdie, Inside Straight, No Questions Asked, Caribbean, Jamaica Run, Desert Legion, Here Come the Girls, Sangaree, The Diamond Queen, Wicked as They Come, Fortune is a Woman, Bengal Brigade, Woman's World, Slightly Scarlet, She Played With Fire, Journey to the Center of the Earth, Kisses for My President, Les Ponyettes, DuBle en Liasse, Le Chemin du Katmandu. The Landraiders, A Place to Hide, Night of the Warrior.
TELEVISION: Max Factor Playhouse, Lux Television Theater, Pepsi Cola Playhouse, Opening Night, Arlene Dahl's Beauty Spot, Hostess, Model of the Year Show, Arlene Dahl's Starscope, Arlene Dahl's Lovescopes, One Life to Live (1981-84), Night of One Hundred Stars, Happy Birthday Hollywood, Who Killed Max Thorn?, Love Boat, Love American Style, Fantasy Island, Burke's Law, Renegade.
WRITER: Always Ask a Man, 1965, Your Beautyscope, 1969, Secrets of Hair Care, 1971, Secrets of Skin Care, 1973, Your Beautyscope 1977-78, Beyond Beauty, 1980, Lovescopes, 1983.

DAHL, JOHN
Director, Writer. b. Montana, 1956. e. Univ. of MT, Montana St. In collaboration with David Warfield made 30 minute rock musical, Here Come the Pugs and indept. feature, The Death Mutants.
PICTURES: Private Investigations (co-s.p.), Kill Me Again (dir., co-s.p.), Red Rock West (dir., co-s.p.), The Last Seduction (dir.), Unforgettable (dir., co-s.p.), Striking Back: A Jewish Commando's War Against the Nazis (dir., prod.), Rounders (dir.), Meltdown (s.p.).

DALE, JIM
Actor. b. Rothwell, Northhamptonshire, England, Aug. 15, 1935. Debut as solo comedian at the Savoy, 1951. Joined National Theatre Co. in 1969 playing in Love's Labour's Lost, The Merchant of Venice, The National Health, The Card. Has written songs and music for films: Twinky, Shalako, Joseph Andrews, Georgy Girl (Acad. Award nom.). Many TV appearances. Director: Asprin and Elephants. In TV movie, The American Clock.
THEATER: *U.S.*: Mark Taper Forum: Comedians, Scapino. *N.Y.*: Theater: Taming of the Shrew, Scapino, Barnum (Tony and Drama Desk Awards, 1980), Joe Egg (Tony Award nom.), Me and My Girl, Privates on Parade, Travels With My Aunt. PICTURES: Six-Five Special (debut, 1958), Raising the Wind, Nurse on Wheels, The Iron Maiden, Carry on Cabby, Carry on Jack, Carry on Spying, Carry on Cleo, The Big Job, Carry on Cowboy, Carry on Screaming, Don't Lose Your Head, The Winter's Tale, The Plank, Follow That Camel, Carry on Doctor, Lock Up Your Daughters, Carry on Again Doctor, The National Health, Digby—The Biggest Dog in the World, Joseph Andrews, Pete's Dragon, Hot Lead Cold Feet, Unidentified Flying Oddball, Scandalous, Carry on Columbus.

DALEY, ROBERT
Producer. e. UCLA. Began career in pictures at Universal International and TV at Desilu.
PICTURES: Play Misty For Me, Dirty Harry (exec. prod.), Joe Kidd, High Plains Drifter, Breezy, Magnum Force, Thunderbolt and Lightfoot, The Eiger Sanction, The Outlaw Josey Wales, The Enforcer, The Gauntlet, Every Which Way But Loose, Escape from Alcatraz (exec. prod.), Any Which Way You Can (exec. prod.), Bronco Billy (exec. prod.), Stick (exec. prod.), Real Genius (exec. prod.).
TELEVISION: The Untouchables, Ben Casey, The FBI, 12 O'Clock High, The Invaders, etc.

DALSIMER, SUSAN
Executive. Editor for E.P. Dutton before joining Lorimar Prods., as v.p. of east coast development. Left to become consultant for original programming at Home Box Office. 1987, named v.p., creative affairs, east coast, for Warner Bros. 1994, v.p., publishing for Miramax Films.

DALTON, TIMOTHY
Actor. b. Colwyn Bay, No. Wales, March 21, 1946. Started acting at Natl. Youth Theatre, then studied at RADA. Prof. stage debut in Richard III and As You Like It at Birmingham Rep.
THEATER: Coriolanus, The Merchant of Venice, Richard III, The Doctor's Dilemna, St. Joan, Macbeth, Henry IV, Henry V, The Samaritan, Black Comedy, White Liars, Lunatic Lover and Poet, Love Letters (1991).
PICTURES: The Lion in Winter (debut, 1968), Cromwell, The Voyeur, Wuthering Heights, Mary Queen of Scots, Permission to Kill, Sextette, Agatha, Flash Gordon, El Hombre Que Supo Amar, Anthony and Cleopatra, Chanel Solitaire, The Doctor and the Devils, The Living Daylights, Brenda Starr, Hawks, Licence to Kill, The King's Whore, The Rocketeer, Naked in New York, Saltwater Moose, The Reef, The Informant, The Beautician and the Beast, Made Men.
TELEVISION: *Mini-Series*: Centennial, Mistral's Daughter, Sins, Scarlett, Framed, Cleopatra. *Movies*: The Master of Ballantrae, Lie Down With Lions, Field of Blood. *Specials*: The Three Princes, Five Finger Exercise, Candida, Daerie Tale Theater: The Emperor's New Clothes (narr.), Nature: In The Company of Wolves (docu.). *Series*: Sat'day While Sunday, Judge Dee, Hooked International, Charlie's Angels: Fallen Angel, Tales From the Crypt: Werewolf Concerto, Survival Factor Series (narr.).

DALTREY, ROGER
Singer, Actor. b. London, England, March 1, 1944. Lead vocalist with The Who.
PICTURES: Woodstock, Tommy, Lisztomania, The Legacy, The Kids Are Alright, McVicar (also prod.), Mack the Knife, The Teddy Bear Habit, Father Jim, If Looks Could Kill, Buddy's Song, Lightning Jack.
TELEVISION: *Movie*: Forgotten Prisoners: The Amnesty Files.

DALY, JIM
Executive Director. b. 1938. Managing director of Film and Television division which includes: Pinewood Studios, Rank Film Laboratories, Odeon Cinemas, Rank Film Distributors, Deluxe Hollywood, Deluxe Toronto, Rank Advertising Films, Rank Theatres, Rank Video Services, Rank Video Services America, Rank Video Services Europe, Film House Company, Rank Brimar, Rank Cintel, Strand Lighting, Rank Taylor Hobson. Appt. exec. dir., Rank Org., 1982.

DALY, JOHN
Executive. b. London, England, July 16, 1937. After working in journalism joined Royal Navy. On leaving Service after three years, trained as underwriter with an Assurance Company. In 1966 became David Hemmings manager and in 1967 formed the Hemdale Company with Hemmings (who later sold interest) Chmn. Hemdale Holdings Ltd.
PICTURES: Images, Sunburn (co-prod., co-s.p.), High Risk, Going Ape, Deadly Force, Carbon Copy, Yellowbeard, The Terminator, The Falcon and the Snowman, Salvador, River's Edge, At Close Range, Hoosiers, Platoon, Best Seller, Shag (exec. prod.), Vampire's Kiss (exec. prod.), Miracle Mile (prod.), Criminal Law (co-exec. prod.), War Party (prod.), The Boost, Out Cold (exec. prod.), Staying Together (exec. prod.).

DALY, ROBERT A.
Executive. b. New York, NY, Dec. 8, 1936. e. Brooklyn Coll., Hunter Coll. Joined CBS-TV in 1955; dir. of program acct.; dir. of research and cost planning; dir. of business affairs. Later named v.p., business affairs, NY; exec. v.p. of network on April, 1976. Named president, CBS Entertainment, Oct. 1977. In Oct. 1979 became responsible for CBS Theatrical Films as well as the TV operation. In 1981, appointed chmn. of bd. and co-CEO of Warner Bros.; 1982, named chmn. of bd. and CEO; 1994, named chmn. of bd. and co-CEO, sharing office with Terry Semel; 1995, also named chmn. and co-CEO of the Warner Bros. Music Group.

DALY, TIM
Actor. b. New York, NY, March 1, 1956. m. actress Amy Van Nostrand. Son of late actor James Daly, brother of actress Tyne Daly. e. Bennington Coll., B.A. Acted in summer stock while in college. Moved to NY where had own rock and roll band. Has performed in cabaret at Williamstown Theater Festival.
THEATER: Fables for Friends, Oliver Oliver, Mass Appeal, Bus Stop, Coastal Disturbances (Theatre World Award).
PICTURES: Diner, Just the Way You Are, Made in Heaven, Spellbinder, Love or Money, Year of the Comet, Caroline at Midnight, Dr. Jekyll and Ms. Hyde, Denise Calls Up, The Associate, The Object of My Affection, Seven Girlfriends.
TELEVISION: *Special*: The Rise and Rise of Daniel Rocket. *Mini-Series*: I'll Take Manhattan, Queen, From the Earth to the Moon, Storm of the Century. *Series*: Ryan's Four, Almost Grown, Wings, Superman (voice). *Movies*: I Married a Centerfold, Mirrors, Red Earth White Earth, In the Line of Duty: Ambush in Waco, Dangerous Heart, Execution of Justice. *Guest*: Midnight Caller, Hill Street Blues, Alfred Hitchcock Presents.

DALY, TYNE
Actress. r.n. Ellen Tyne Daly. b. Madison, WI, Feb. 21, 1946. Daughter of late actor James Daly and actress Hope Newell; brother is actor Timothy Daly.
THEATER: The Butter and Egg Man, That Summer That Fall, Skirmishes, The Black Angel, Rimers of Eldritch, Ashes, Three Sisters, Come Back Little Sheba (L.A., 1987), Gypsy (Tony Award, 1990), Queen of the Stardust Ballroom, The Seagull, On the Town, Call Me Madam (in concert).
PICTURES: John and Mary, Angel Unchained, Play It As It Lays, The Adulteress, The Enforcer, Telefon, Speedtrap, Zoot Suit, The Aviator, Movers & Shakers, The Lay of the Land, Vig, Autumn Heart.
TELEVISION: *Series*: Cagney & Lacey (4 Emmy Awards), Christy (Emmy Award, 1996), Judging Amy. *Movies*: In Search of America, A Howling in the Woods, Heat of Anger, The Man Who Could Talk to Kids, Larry, The Entertainer, Better Late Than Never, Intimate Strangers, The Women's Room, A Matter of Life or Death, Your Place or Mine, Kids Like These, Stuck With Each Other, The Last to Go, Face of a Stranger, Columbo: A Bird in the Hand, Scattered Dreams: The Kathryn Messenger Story, The Forget-Me-Not Murders, Columbo: Undercover, Cagney & Lacey: The Return, Cagney & Lacey: Together Again, Bye Bye Birdie. *Guest*: Medical Center, Columbo, Ray Bradbury Theatre, Wings.

DAMON, MARK
Executive, Actor. b. Chicago, IL, April 22, 1933. e. UCLA, B.A. literature, M.A. business administration. Actor: 1958 under contract to 20th Century Fox, 1960 winner Golden Globe Award-Newcomer of the Year; early career includes The Fall of The House of Usher, The Longest Day; 1961 moved to Italy, stayed 16 years appearing in leading roles in 50 films; 1974 head of foreign dept. for PAC, a leading film distributor in Italy; 1976 returned to the U.S. as exec. prod. of The Choirboys and in charge of its foreign distribution; 1979 founder and pres. of Producers Sales Organization, intl. distribution org. 1987 formed Vision Int'l.; 1993, formed MDP Worlwide, intl. prod. & distrib. co.
PICTURES: *Exec. prod. or prod.*: The Arena, The Choirboys, The Neverending Story, Das Boot, Nine 1/2 Weeks, Short Circuit, Flight of the Navigator, Lost Boys, High Spirits, Bat 21 (co-prod.), Diary of a Hit Man, Wild Orchid, Wild Orchid II: Two Shades of Blue, Stalingrad, The Jungle Book, The Jungle Book 2, The Blackout, The Winner, Orgazmo, Loved, Deceiver (also actor), Eye of the Beholder. *Actor*: Inside Detroit, Screaming Eagles, Between Heaven and Hell, Young and Dangerous, The Party Crashers, Life Begins at 17, House of Usher, This Rebel Breed, The Reluctant Saint, The Longest Day (uncredited), Beauty and the Beast, The Young Racers, Black Christmas, Pedro el Cruel,

Son of Cleopatra, Hundred Horsemen, Ringo and His Golden Pistol, Agente segreto 777 operzione Mistero, Dio—come ti amo, One for All, Train for Durango, Death Does Not Count the Dollars, Johnny Yuma, Morti non si contano I, Kill and Pray, School Girl Killer, Anzio, Long Live Robin Hood, The Norman Swordsman, La Spada Normanna, Posate le pistole reverendo, Leoni di Petersburgo, Monta in sella figlio di...!, The Devil's Wedding Night, Little Mother, Crypt of the Living Death, Byleth, There Is No 13, Lo matas tu o lo mato yo, Do I Kill You or Do You Kill Me?, Stuck on You.

DAMON, MATT
Actor, Writer. b. Cambridge, MA, Oct. 8, 1970. Chicago Film Crits. Award, Most Promising New Actor, 1997.
PICTURES: *Actor*: Mystic Pizza (debut, 1988), School Ties, Geronimo: An American Legend, Courage Under Fire, Glory Daze, Chasing Amy, The Rainmaker, Good Will Hunting (also s.p., Acad. Award, Golden Globe Award, Best Screenplay, 1997), Rounders, Saving Private Ryan, The Talented Mr. Ripley, Dogma, All the Pretty Horses, Titan A.E. (voice), The Legend of Bagger Vance, All the Pretty Horses, Ocean's Eleven, The Third Wheel, The Bourne Identity.
TELEVISION: *Movies*: Rising Son, The Good Old Boys.

DAMONE, VIC
Singer, Actor. r.n. Vito Farinola. b. Brooklyn, NY, June 12, 1928. m. actress-singer Diahann Carroll. e. Lafayette H.S., Brooklyn. Winner Arthur Godfrey talent show, 1947; then night clubs, radio, theatres. U.S. Army, 1951-53.
PICTURES: Rich Young and Pretty (debut, 1951), The Strip, Athena, Deep in My Heart, Hit the Deck, Kismet, Hell to Eternity.
TELEVISION: *Series*: The Vic Damone Show (1956-57), Lively Ones (1962-63), The Vic Damone Show (1967).

DAMSKI, MEL
Director. b. New York, NY, July 21, 1946. e. Colgate U., AFI. Worked as reporter, journalism professor. USC Cinema instructor.
PICTURES: Yellowbeard, Mischief, Happy Together.
TELEVISION: *Series*: M*A*S*H, Lou Grant, Dolphin Cove. *Movies*: Long Journey Back, The Child Stealer, Word of Honor, The Legend of Walks Far Woman, American Dream, For Ladies Only, Making the Grade, An Invasion of Privacy, Badge of the Assassin, A Winner Never Quits, Attack on Fear, Hero in the Family, Murder by the Book, Hope Division, The Three Kings, Everybody's Baby: The Rescue of Jessica McClure, Back to the Streets of San Francisco.

DANA, BILL
Actor, Writer. b. Quincy, MA, Oct. 5, 1924. In night clubs and on TV.
PICTURES: The Busy Body, The Barefoot Executive, The Nude Bomb (also s.p.).
TELEVISION: *Series*: The Steve Allen Show (performer, head writer, 1961), The Bill Dana Jose Jimenez Show (star, writer), Spike Jones Show (prod., writer, performer), Milton Berle Show (prod., writer, performer), No Soap Radio, Zorro and Son, All in the Family (writer). *Movies*: The Snoop Sisters, Rosetti & Ryan: Men Who Love Women, A Guide for the Married Woman, Murder in Texas. *Actor*: Facts of Life, Too Close for Comfort, Golden Girls, Hollywood Palace, St. Elsewhere.

DANCE, CHARLES
Actor. b. Worcestershire, England, Oct. 10, 1946. e. Plymouth Coll. Art., Leicester Coll. of Art (graphic design degree). After first working as a West End theatre stagehand, made acting debut in 1970 in a touring company of It's a Two-Foot-Six-Inches-above-the Ground World. Worked in provincial repertory theaters. Joined the Royal Shakespeare Company 1975-80: Hamlet, Richard III, As You Like It. Lead in Henry V (1975, N.Y.), Coriolanus (Paris, London, Stratford).
THEATER: Plenty, McGuffin, revival of Irma La Douce (West End), Turning Over (London's Bush Theatre).
PICTURES: The Spy Who Loved Me (debut, 1977), For Your Eyes Only, Plenty, The Golden Child, Good Morning Babylon, White Mischief, The Hidden City, Pascali's Island, Alien 3, The Valley of Stone, Last Action Hero, China Moon, Century, Kabloonak, Exquisite Tenderness, Shortcut to Paradise, Undertow, Michael Collins, Space Truckers, In the Presence of Mine Enemies.
TELEVISION: Very Like a Whale, The McGuffin, The Jewel in the Crown, Lightning Always Strikes Twice, Edward VII, The Fatal Spring, Little Eyolf, Frost in May, Nancy Astor, Saigon—The Last Day, Out On a Limb, BBC's The Secret Servant, Rainy Day Woman, Out of the Shadows, First Born, Goldeneye, Rebecca, Phantom of the Opera (mini-series), Darling of the Gods.

D'ANGELO, BEVERLY
Actress. b. Columbus, OH, Nov. 15, 1954. Studied visual arts and was exchange student in Italy before working as cartoonist for Hanna-Barbera Studios in Hollywood. Toured Canada's coffeehouse circuit as singer and appeared with rock band called Elephant. Joined Charlotte Town Festival Company. B'way debut in rock musical, Rockabye Hamlet. Off-B'way: Simpatico (Theatre World Award).
PICTURES: The Sentinel (debut 1977), Annie Hall, First Love, Every Which Way But Loose, Hair, Highpoint, Coal Miner's Daughter, Honky Tonk Freeway, Paternity, National Lampoon's Vacation, Finders Keepers, National Lampoon's European Vacation, Big Trouble, Maid to Order, In the Mood, Aria, Trading Hearts, High Spirits, National Lampoon's Christmas Vacation, Daddy's Dyin', Pacific Heights (unbilled), The Miracle, The Pope Must Die, Man Trouble, Lonely Hearts, Lightning Jack, Eye for an Eye, Edie and Pen, Pterodactyl Woman from Beverly Hills, Vegas Vacation, A Ratls Take, Nowhere, Love Always, With Friends Like These, Illuminata, American History X, Sugar Town, Jazz Night, High Fidelity.
TELEVISION: *Mini-Series*: Captains and the Kings. *Movies*: A Streetcar Named Desire, Doubletake, Slow Burn, Hands of a Stranger, Trial: The Price of Passion, A Child Lost Forever, The Switch, Judgment Day: The John List Story, Jonathan Stone: Threat of Innocence, Menendez: A Killing in Beverly Hills, Lansky. *Special*: Sleeping Beauty (Faerie Tale Theater). *Guest*: The Simpsons.

DANES, CLAIRE
Actress. b. New York, NY, April 12, 1979. e. Professional Performing Arts School, NY; Lee Strasberg Studio. Acting career began with off-off-B'way appearances in Happiness, Punk Ballet and Kids on Stage.
PICTURES: Dreams of Love (debut), Thirty (short), The Pesky Suitor (short), Little Women, How to Make an American Quilt, Home for the Holidays, I Love You I Love You Not, Romeo + Juliet, To Gillian on Her 37th Birthday, Polish Wedding, U-Turn, The Rainmaker, Polish Wedding, Les Miserables, The Mod Squad, Brokedown Palace.
TELEVISION: *Series*: My So Called Life. *Guest*: Law and Order. *Movies*: No Room for Opal, The Coming Out of Heidi Leiter.

DANGERFIELD, RODNEY
Actor, Comedian. r.n. Jacob Cohen. b. Babylon, NY, Nov. 22, 1921. Performer in nightclubs as Jack Roy 1941-51. Worked as businessman 1951-63, before becoming stand-up comedian. Founder Dangerfields' Nightclub, 1969.
PICTURES: The Projectionist, Caddyshack, Easy Money (also co-s.p.), Back to School, Moving, Rover Dangerfield (voice, exec. prod., s.p., co-story, co-wrote songs), Ladybugs, Natural Born Killers, Casper (cameo), Meet Wally Sparks (also co-s.p.), The Godson, Everything's George.
TELEVISION: *Movies:* Benny and Barney: Las Vegas Undercover. *Series:* The Dean Martin Show. *Guest:* The Simpsons.

DANIEL, SEAN
Executive. b. Aug. 15, 1951. e. California Inst. of Arts film school. BFA, 1973. Was journalist for Village Voice before starting m.p. career as documentary filmmaker and asst. dir. for New World Pictures. In 1976 joined Universal Pictures as prod. exec.; 1979, named v.p., then pres., production. Resigned March, 1989 to become pres., The Geffen Co., film div.; resigned from Geffen, Nov. 1989. 1990, with Jim Jacks started own prod. co. Alphaville, in partnership with Universal Pictures.
PICTURES: Pure Luck, American Me, CB4, Hard Target, Heart and Souls, Tombstone, Michael.

DANIELS, JEFF
Actor. b. Athens, Georgia. Feb. 19, 1955. e. Central Michigan U. Apprentice with Circle Repertory Theatre, New York. Established Purple Rose Theatre Co. in Chelsea, Michigan. Playwright: The Kingdom's Coming, The Vast Difference.
THEATER: Brontosaurus, Short-Changed Review, The Farm, Fifth of July, Johnny Got His Gun (Obie Award), Lemon Sky, The Three Sisters, The Golden Age, Redwood Curtain.
PICTURES: Ragtime (debut, 1981), Terms of Endearment, The Purple Rose of Cairo, Marie, Heartburn, Something Wild, Radio Days, The House on Carroll Street, Sweet Hearts Dance, Checking Out, Arachnophobia, Welcome Home Roxy Carmichael, Love Hurts, The Butcher's Wife, There Goes the Neighborhood, Rain Without Thunder, Gettysburg, Speed, Terminal Velocity, Dumb & Dumber, 2 Days in the Valley, Fly Away Home, 101 Dalmations, Trial and Error, Pleasantville, All the Rage, My Favorite Martian, The Crossing, Cheaters, Chasing Sleep, Escanabia in da Moonlight.
TELEVISION: *Movies*: A Rumor of War, Invasion of Privacy, The Caine Mutiny Court Martial, No Place Like Home, Disaster in Time, Teamster Boss: The Jackie Presser Story, Redwood Curtain, The Crossing. *Specials*: Fifth of July, The Visit (Trying Times). *Guest*: Breaking Away (pilot), Hawaii 5-0.

DANIELS, PAUL
TV performer, Magician. b. South Bank, England, April 6, 1938. Early career starring in British and overseas theatres. 1983, Magician Of The Year Award by Hollywood's Academy of Magical Arts. 1985, his BBC TV special awarded Golden Rose of Montreux trophy. Presenter of Every Second Counts and Paul Daniels Magic Show. Devised children's TV series, Wizbit and radio series Dealing With Daniels, Secret Magic and Game Show Wipeout.

DANIELS, WILLIAM
Actor. b. Brooklyn, NY, Mar 31, 1927. e. Northwestern U. m. actress Bonnie Bartlett. Traveled around NY as part of The Daniels Family song and dance troupe. Appeared with family on experimental TV in 1941. Stage debut in Life with Father. Brought to national attention in A Thousand Clowns in original B'way play and film version.
THEATER: The Zoo Story, On a Clear Day You Can See Forever, 1776, Dear Me, The Sky Is Falling, A Little Night Music.
PICTURES: Ladybug Ladybug, A Thousand Clowns, Two for the Road, The Graduate, The President's Analyst, Marlowe, 1776, The Parallax View, Black Sunday, Oh God!, The One and Only, Sunburn, The Blue Lagoon, All Night Long, Reds, Blind Date, Her Alibi, Magic Kid.
TELEVISION: *Series*: Captain Nice, The Nancy Walker Show, Freebie and the Bean, Knight Rider (voice), St. Elsewhere (Emmy Awards, 1985, 1986), Boy Meets World. *Guest*: East Side/West Side, For the People, Toma, The Rockford Files. *Movies*: Rooster, Rehearsal for a Murder, Murdock's Gang, A Case of Rape, Sarah T.—Portrait of a Teenage Alcoholic, One of Our Own, Francis Gary Powers, Killer on Board, The Bastard, Big Bob Johnson and His Fantastic Speed Circus, Sgt. Matlovich Vs. the U.S. Air Force, The Rebels, City in Fear, Damien: The Leper Priest, Million Dollar Face, Drop Out Father, The Little Match Girl, Knight Rider 2000 (voice), Back to the Streets of San Francisco. *Mini-series*: Blind Ambition, The Adams Chronicles, The Lottery.

DANNER, BLYTHE
Actress. b. Philadelphia, PA, Feb. 3, 1943. e. Bard Coll. m. writer-prod. Bruce Paltrow. Daughter is actress Gwyneth Paltrow. Appeared in repertory cos. in U.S. before Lincoln Center productions of Cyrano de Bergerac, Summertree, and The Miser (Theatre World Award for last).
THEATER: *NY*: Butterflies Are Free (Tony Award, 1971), Major Barbara, Twelfth Night, The Seagull, Ring Around The Moon, Betrayal, Blithe Spirit, A Streetcar Named Desire, Much Ado About Nothing, Sylvia. Williamstown: Picnic.
PICTURES: To Kill a Clown (debut, 1972), 1776, Lovin' Molly, Hearts of the West, Futureworld, The Great Santini, Man Woman and Child, Brighton Beach Memoirs, Another Woman, Mr. and Mrs. Bridge, Alice, The Prince of Tides, Husbands and Wives, To Wong Foo—Thanks for Everything—Julie Newmar, Homage, The Myth of Fingerprints, Mad City, The Farmhouse, The Proposition, No Looking Back, The X Files: Fight the Future, Invisible Circus, Forces of Nature, The Love Letter.
TELEVISION: *Movies*: Dr. Cook's Garden, F. Scott Fitzgerald and The Last of the Belles, Sidekicks, A Love Affair: The Eleanor and Lou Gehrig Story, Too Far to Go, Eccentricities of a Nightingale, Are You in the House Alone?, Inside the Third Reich, In Defense of Kids, Helen Keller: The Miracle Continues, Guilty Conscience, Money Power Murder, Judgment, Never Forget, Cruel Doubt, Getting Up and Going Home, Oldest Living Confederate Widow Tells All, Leave of Absence, A Call to Remember, Saint Maybe, Murder She Purred: A Mrs. Murphy Mystery (voice). *Series*: Adam's Rib, Tattingers (revamped as Nick & Hillary). *Specials*: To Confuse the Angel, George M, To Be Young Gifted and Black, The Scarecrow., Kiss Kiss Dahlings.

DANSON, TED
Actor, Producer. b. San Diego, CA, Dec. 29, 1947. e. Kent Sch., Stanford U., Carnegie-Mellon U, 1972. m. actress Mary Steenburgen. Studied at Actors Inst. New York stage debut, The Real Inspector Hound, 1972; mgr. and teacher, Actors Inst., L.A., 1978. Tv debut, The Doctors. Founded Amer. Oceans Campaign; bd. mem. Futures for Children.
PICTURES: The Onion Field (debut, 1979), Body Heat, Creepshow, Little Treasure, Just Between Friends, A Fine Mess, Three Men and a Baby, Cousins, Dad, Three Men and a Little Lady, Made in America, Getting Even With Dad, Pontiac Moon (also co-exec. prod.), Loch Ness, Mumford, Jerry and Tom, Homegrown, Saving Private ryan .
TELEVISION: An Affectionate Look at Fatherhood (special). *Series*: Somerset, Cheers (2 Emmy Awards: 1990, 1993), Ink (also co-exec. prod.), Becker. *Movies*: The Women's Room, Once Upon a Spy, Our Family Business, Cowboy, Something About Amelia, When the Bough Breaks (also prod.), We Are the Children, Mercy Mission: The Rescue of Flight 771, On Promised Land, Fight For Justice, The Canterville Ghost, Gulliver's Travels, Thanks of a Grateful Nation. *Guest*: Laverne & Shirley, Magnum P.I., Taxi, The Simpsons, Frasier.

DANTE, JOE
Director. b. Morristown, NJ, Nov. 28, 1946. Managing editor for Film Bulletin before going to Hollywood to work in advertising, creating campaigns for many films. Became protege of Roger Corman, co-directing Hollywood Boulevard. Edited film Grand Theft Auto; co-wrote story for Rock 'n' Roll High School.
PICTURES: *Director*: Piranha (also co-editor), The Howling (also co-editor), Twilight Zone-The Movie (dir. segment), Gremlins, Innerspace, Amazon Women on the Moon (co-dir.), The 'burbs, Gremlins II: The New Batch (also cameo), Matinee, Cat and Mouse, Small Soldiers. *Actor:* Cannonball, Slumber Party Massacre, Eating Raoul, Sleepwalkers, Beverly Hills Cop III, The Silence of the Hams.
TELEVISION: Amazing Stories, Eerie Indiana, The Warlord: Battle for the Galaxy. *Movie*: Runaway Daughters, The Second Civil War.

D'ANTONI, PHILIP
Producer. Director. b. New York, NY, Feb. 19, 1929. e. Fordham U., business administration. Joined CBS in mailroom, advanced into prod., sales development, prog. analysis, mkt. rsrch. Became indep. radio-TV repr. in 1954 for two years; then joined Mutual Broadcasting as sales manager; later, exec. v.p. Resigned in 1962 to form own prod. co. Made theatrical film debut with Bullitt as prod.; directing debut with The Seven Ups. Heads D'Antoni Prods.
PICTURES: *Producer*: Bullitt, The French Connection (Acad. Award for Best Picture, 1971). *Prod.-Dir.*: The Seven Ups.
TELEVISION: Movin' On (series) Elizabeth Taylor in London, Sophia Loren in Rome, Melina Mercouri in Greece, Jack Jones Special, This Proud Land. *Movies*: Mr. Inside/Mr. Outside, The Connection, Strike Force, In Tandem, Rubber Gun Squad, Cabo.

DANZ, FREDRIC A.
Executive. b. Seattle, WA, Feb. 28, 1918. Is chmn. of Sterling Recreation Organization Co., Seattle. Member, Foundation of M.P. Pioneers; v.p., Variety Club Intl.

DANZA, TONY
Actor, Producer. b. Brooklyn, NY, April 21, 1951. e. U. of Dubuque, IA on a wrestling scholarship. After grad. professional boxer before tested for role in TV pilot (Fast Lane Blues) which he won. Back to New York and fighting until called to coast to appear as Tony Banta in Taxi series. On L.A. & NY Stage: Wrong Turn at Lungfish.
PICTURES: Hollywood Knights, Going Ape, Cannonball Run II, She's Out of Control, Mob Justice, Angels in the Outfield, The Jerky Boys (co-exec. prod. only), Noah.
TELEVISION: *Series*: Taxi, Who's the Boss, Baby Talk (voice), The Mighty Jungle (voice), George (co-exec. prod. only), Hudson Street (also co-exec. prod.), The Tony Danza Show (also prod.), Family Law. *Movies*: Murder Can Hurt You!, Doing Life (also exec. prod.), Single Bars Single Women, Freedom Fighter (also co-exec. prod.), The Whereabouts of Jenny (also co-exec. prod.), Dead and Alive (also co-exec. prod.), Deadly Whispers, Garbage Picking Field Goal Kicking etc., 12 Angry Men, The Girl Gets Moe, A Brooklyn State of Mind.

DARABONT, FRANK
Writer, Director. b. January 28, 1959.
PICTURES: *Writer:* A Nightmare on Elm Street 3: Dream Warriors, The Blob, The Fly II, Frankenstein, The Shawshank Redemption, Eraser, The Fan, Saving Private Ryan, The Green Mile, Collateral Damage, Minority Report. *Director:* The Woman in the Room, The Shawshank Redemption, The Green Mile (also prod.).
TELEVISION: Two-Fisted Tales (s.p.), The Young Indiana Jones Chronicles (s.p.), Young Indiana Jones Travels with Father (s.p.), Buried Alive (dir.), Till Death Us Do Part (dir.), Black Cat Run (s.p. and dir.), The Adventures of Young Indiana Jones in the Secret Service (s.p.).

D'ARBANVILLE-QUINN, PATTI
Actress. b. New York, NY, 1951. Grew up in Greenwich Village. Landed first job as baby in Ivory Soap commercials. In early teens worked as disc jockey where discovered by Andy Warhol and cast in small role in film Flesh. Moved to Paris at 15 where she became successful model and was featured in book *Scavullo on Beauty*. Made film debut in Gerard Brach's 1969 film La Maison. Fluent in French, worked in French films until 1973 when moved to Los Angeles. Won Dramalogue Award for John Patrick Shanley's Italian-American Reconciliation (L.A., 1987).
PICTURES: La Maison, La Saigne, The Crazy American Girl, Rancho DeLuxe, Bilitis, Big Wednesday, The Main Event, Time After Time, The Fifth Floor, Hog Wild, Modern Problems, Contract: Kill, The Boys Next Door, Real Genius, Call Me, Fresh Horses, Wired, Frame-Up II: The Cover Up, The Fan, Father's Day, I Know What You Did Last Summer, Celebrity, Archibald the Rainbow Painter.
TELEVISION: *Movies*: Crossing the Mob, Blind Spot, Bad to the Bone. *Mini-Series*: Once an Eagle. *Series:* New York Undercover, Another World, South Beach, The Guiding Light. *Guest*: Crime Story, R.E.L.A.X., Tough Cookies, Charlie's Angels, Barnaby Jones, Miami Vice, Murder She Wrote, My So-Called Life.

DARBY, KIM
Actress. r.n. Deborah Zerby. b. Hollywood, CA, July 8, 1948. e. Swanson's Ranch Sch., Van Nuys H.S. Studied at the Desilu Workshop in Hollywood. Professional debut on the Mr. Novak TV series; screen debut as extra in Bye Bye Birdie.
PICTURES: Bus Riley's Back in Town, The Restless Ones, True Grit, Generation, Norwood, The Strawberry Statement, The Grissom Gang, The One and Only, Better Off Dead, Teen Wolf Too, Halloween: The Curse of Michael Myers, The Last Best Sunday.
TELEVISION: *Movies*: The Karate Killers, Ironside (pilot), The People, Streets of San Francisco (pilot), Don't Be Afraid of the Dark, Story of Pretty Boy Floyd, This Was the West That Was, Flatbed Annie & Sweetiepie: Lady Truckers, Enola Gay, Embassy. *Mini-Series*: Rich Man Poor Man, The Last Convertible. *Guest*: Eleventh Hour, Gunsmoke. *Special*: Flesh and Blood.

DARK, JOHN
Producer. Pres. of J.D.Y.T. Producciones S.L., Coin Film City.
PICTURES: Light Up the Sky, Wind of Change, Loss of Innocence (Greengage Summer), The 7th Dawn, Casino Royale, Half a Sixpence, Bachelor of Arts, There's a Girl in My Soup, From Beyond the Grave, Madhouse, Land That Time Forgot, At the Earth's Core, The People That Time Forgot, Warlords of Atlantis, Arabian Adventure, Slayground, Shirley Valentine, Stepping Out.

DARREN, JAMES
Actor. b. Philadelphia, PA, June 8, 1936. e. Thomas Jefferson h.s., South Philadelphia h.s. Studied acting with Stella Adler, NYC.
PICTURES: Rumble on the Docks (debut, 1956), The Brothers Rico, The Tijuana Story, Operation Mad Ball, Gunman's Walk, Gidget, The Gene Krupa Story, Because They're Young, All the Young Men, Let No Man Write My Epitaph, Guns of Navarone, Gidget Goes Hawaiian, Diamond Head, Gidget Goes to Rome, For Those Who Think Young, The Lively Set, Venus in Furs, The Boss' Son.
TELEVISION: *Series*: The Time Tunnel, T.J. Hooker. *Guest*: Police Story, Hawaii Five-0, Vega$, Baa Baa Blacksheep, One Day at a Time. *Movies*: City Beneath the Sea, Police Story, The Lives of Jenny Dolan, Turnover Smith, Scruples. *Episode Director*: T.J. Hooker, The A Team, Stingray, Werewolf, Hardball, Hunter, Tequila and Bonetti, Raven, Silk Stalkings, Walker: Texas Ranger, Renegade, Nowhere Man, Beverly Hills 90210, Savannah, Melrose Place.

DARRIEUX, DANIELLE
Actress. b. Bordeaux, France, May 1, 1917. e. Lycee LaTour, Conservatoire de Musique.
THEATER: Coco, The Ambassador (B'way).
PICTURES: Le Bal (debut, 1932), La Crise Est Finis, Mayerling, Tarass Boulba, Port Arthur, Un Mauvais Garcon, Club de Femmes, Abus de Confiance, Mademoiselle ma Mere, The Rage of Paris, Katia, Retour a l'Aube, Battlement de Coeur, Premier Rendezvous, Caprices, Adieu Cherie, Au Petit Bonbeur, Bethsabee, Ruy Blas, Jean de le Lune, Occupe-toi d'Amelie, La Ronde, Rich Young and Pretty, Five Fingers, Le Plaisir, La Verite sur Bebe Donge, Adorable Creatures, Le Bon Dieu sans Confession, The Earrings of Madame De, Le Rouge et le Noir, Bonnes a Tuer, Napoleon, Alexander the Great, A Friend of the Family, Loss of Innocence (Greengage Summer), Les Lions sont Laches, Les Bras de lat Nuit, Bluebeard (Landru), Patate, Le Coup de Grace, L'Or du Duc, Le Dimanche de la Vie, The Young Girls of Rochefort, La Maison de Campagne, Scene of the Crime, A Few Days With Me.

DARTNALL, GARY
Executive. b. Whitchurch, England, May 9, 1937. e. Kings Col., Taunton. Overseas div., Associate British Pathe. European rep., 1958-60; Middle & Far East rep., Lion Intl. Films; U.S. rep., 1962; pres. Lion Intl. 1963; U.S. rep., Alliance Intl. Films Distributors Ltd., and London Indept. Prods. Ltd.; pres. Alliance Intl. Films Corp. and Dartnall Films Ltd., 1966; mng. dir., Overseas div. Walter Reade Org., 1969; pres. EMI Film Distribs., 1971; vice chmn. EMI TV Programs Inc., 1976; pres. EMI Videograms Inc., 1979; pres. VHD Programs Inc. & VHD Disc Mfg. Co, 1980; chmn. Thorn EMI Cinemas; CEO, Thorn EMI Screen Entertainment Ltd. 1987; acquired Southbrook Intl. TV and formed Palladium Inc., chmn. & CEO. 1993 formed The Douris Corporation to acquire and distribute the 700 title Rohauer Collection of classic titles.

DASSIN, JULES
Director, Writer, Actor. b. Middletown, CT, Dec. 18, 1911. Was married to late actress Melina Mercouri. Actor on dramatic stage several years; radio writer. Joined MGM, 1940, as dir. short subjects; later dir. features.
PICTURES: *Director*: Nazi Agent, Affairs of Martha, Reunion in France, Young Ideas, The Canterville Ghost, A Letter for Evie, Two Smart People, Brute Force, The Naked City, Thieves' Highway, Night and the City, Rififi (also co-s.p., actor), He Who Must Die (also co-s.p.), Where the Hot Wind Blows (also co-s.p.), Never on Sunday (also actor, prod., s.p.), Phaedra (also prod., co-s.p., actor), Topkapi (also prod.), 10:30 p.m. Summer (also prod., co-s.p.), Survival (also co-prod.), Uptight (also prod., co-s.p.), Promise at Dawn (also actor, prod., s.p.), The Rehearsal, A Dream of Passion (also s.p., prod.), Circle of Two.
PLAYS: Ilya Darling, Medicine Show, Magdalena, Joy to the World, Isle of Children, Two's Company, Heartbreak House, Threepenny Opera, Sweet Bird of Youth, A Month in the Country, Who's Afraid of Virginia Woolf?, The Road to Mecca, Death of a Salesman.

DAVENPORT, NIGEL
Actor. b. Cambridge, England, May 23, 1928. e. Trinity Coll., Oxford. Began acting after stint in British military at 18 years. First 10 years of professional career in theatre. Majority of screen work in British films in 1960s and 70s.
PICTURES: Look Back in Anger (debut, 1959), Desert Mice, Peeping Tom, The Entertainer, Lunch Hour, In the Cool of the Day, Operation Snatch, Return to Sender, Ladies Who Do, The Third Secret, Sands of the Kalahari, A High Wind in Jamaica, Where the Spies Are, Life at the Top, A Man for All Seasons, Sebastian, The Strange Affair, Play Dirty, Sinful Davey, The Virgin Soldiers, The Royal Hunt of the Sun, The Mind of Mr. Soames, The Last Valley, No Blade of Grass, Villain, Mary Queen of Scots, L'Attentat, Living Free, Charley-One-Eye, Phase IV, La Regenta, Stand Up Virgin Soldiers, The Island of Dr. Moreau, Zulu Dawn, The Omega Connection, Nighthawks, Chariots of Fire, Greystoke: The Legend of Tarzan Lord of the Apes, Caravaggio, Without a Clue, The Circus Trap.
TELEVISION: A Christmas Carol, Dracula, The Picture of Dorian Gray, The Ordeal of Dr. Mudd, Masada, The Upper Crust.

DAVIAU, ALLEN
Cinematographer. b. New Orleans, LA, June 14, 1942. Started as still photographer and stage lighting designer. Received Gold Clio Award for Tackle (Levi's 501).
PICTURES: Harry Tracy, E.T.: The Extra-Terrestrial (Acad. Award nom.), Twilight Zone: The Movie (co-photog.), Indiana Jones and the Temple of Doom (Calif. unit), The Falcon and the Snowman, The Color Purple (Acad. Award nom.), Harry and the Hendersons, Empire of the Sun (Acad. Award nom.; BAFTA & ASC Awards), Avalon (Acad. Award nom.), Defending Your Life, Bugsy (Acad. Award nom.; ASC Award), Fearless, Congo.
TELEVISION: *Movies*: Streets of L.A., Rage, Legs. *Specials*: The Boy Who Drank Too Much. *Series*: Amazing Stories (pilot).

DAVID, KEITH
Actor. b. New York, NY, June 4, 1954. e. Juilliard.
THEATER: *NY*: The Pirates of Penzance, A Midsummer Night's Dream, Waiting for Godot, Miss Waters to You, La Boheme, Coriolanus, Titus Andronicus, A Map of the World, The Haggadah, Alec Wilder: Clues to a Life, Boesman & Lena, Jelly's Last Jam, Hedda Gabler, Seven Guitars.
PICTURES: The Thing, Platoon, Hot Pursuit, Braddock: Missing in Action III, Off Limits, Stars and Bars, Bird, They Live, Road House, Always, Men at Work, Marked for Death, Final Analysis, Article 99, Reality Bites, The Puppet Masters, The Quick and the Dead, Clockers, Dead Presidents, Johns, Dead Cold (prod.), Marked Man (prod.), Daddy's Girl (prod.), The Dentist (prod.), The Nurse (prod.), The Stranger In The House (prod.), Voodoo (exec. prod.), Serial Killer (prod./dir.), Flipping, Larger than Life, Eye for an Eye, Johns, Hercules (voice), Fallout (voice), Executive Target, Volcano, Armageddon, There's Something About Mary, Where the Heart Is.
TELEVISION: *Movies*: Ladykillers, Murder in Black and White, There Are No Children Here, Vanishing Point, Murder She Wrote: South by Southwest, Don King: Only in America, The Tiger Woods Story. *Series*: Spawn, Hercules (voice). *Mini-Series*: Roots: The Next Generations. *Special*: Hallelujah. *Guest*: The Equalizer, A Man Called Hawk, New York Undercover.

DAVID, PIERRE
Executive, Producer. b. Montreal, Canada, May 17, 1944. e. U. of Montreal. Joined radio station CJMS 1966 as pub. rel. & spec. events dir., 1969, while running Mutual Broadcasting Network of Canada's live entertainment div., created new film dist. co. Mutual Films. 1972 added prod. unit and as prod. or exec. prod., prod. and dist. 19 French language. Canadian films. With filmmaker Roger Corman est. Mutual Pictures of Canada, Ltd to dist. films in English Canada; 1978 teamed Mutual Films with Victor Solnicki and Claude Heroux to prod. English language films. Pioneered 3-picture concept for Canadian m.p. investors. Moved to L.A. 1983 where became pres., Film Packages Intl. where prod. exec. on Platoon. Then joined Larry Thompson Org. as partner involved in dev. and/or prod. of m.p., Jan., 1987, named chmn. of bd. and chief exec. officer, Image Org., Inc. intl. dist. co. formed by David and Rene Malo. Also pres. Lance Entertainment, prod. co. Sold Image Organization in 1997 and is currently Chairman of WIN Ventures, LLC. Also Chairman of AFMA's producers committee
PICTURES: *Prod.*: The Brood, Hog Wild, Scanners, Dirty Tricks, Gas, The Funny Farm, Visiting Hours, Videodrome, Going Berserk, Of Unknown Origin, Covergirl, Breaking All the Rules, For Those I Loved, Blind-Fear (co-prod.), The Perfect Bride, Hot Pursuit, The Perfect Weapon, Bounty Tracker, Distant Cousins, Deep Cover, Marital Outlaw, Stalked, Open Fire, The Force, The Secretary, Scanner Cop 2, The Wrong Woman, Scenes from the Goldmine, My Demon Lover, The Great Land of Small, Voodoo, Marked Man, Dead Cold, The Nurse, Man of Her Dreams, Daddy's Girl, The Dentist, Kid Cop, Stranger in the House, The Night Caller, Never Too Late, Little Men, Cupid, Wishmaster, Catured, The Dentist 2, The Landlady, Wanted, Rites of Passage, A Clean Kill, Someone is Watching, Dead Simple. *Exec. Prod.*: Quiet Cool, Scanners II: The New Order, Desire and Hell at Sunset Motel, Martial Law, Scanners III, Dolly Dearest, Mission of Justice, Deadbolt, Internal Affairs, Twin Sisters, Pin, The Neighbor, The Paperboy. *Prod.-Dir.*: Scanner Cop, Serial Killer.

DAVIDOVICH, LOLITA
Actress. b. Ontario, Canada, 1961. Also acted under the name Lolita David.
PICTURES: Class, Adventures in Babysitting, The Big Town, Blaze, The Object of Beauty, JFK, The Inner Circle, Raising Cain, Leap of Faith, Boiling Point, Younger and Younger, Cobb, For Better or Worse, Now and Then, Jungle 2 Jungle, Touch, Gods and Monsters, Mystery Alaska.

TELEVISION: *Movies*: Two Fathers' Justice, Prison Stories: Women on the Inside (Parole Board), Keep the Change, Indictment: The McMartin Trial, McMartin Trial, Dead Silence.

DAVIDSON, JOHN
Actor, Singer. b. Pittsburgh, PA, Dec. 13, 1941. e. Denison U. In numerous school stage prods. before coming to N.Y. in 1964 to co-star with Bert Lahr in B'way show, Foxy. Signed as regular on The Entertainers with Carol Burnett.
PICTURES: The Happiest Millionaire, The One and Only Genuine Original Family Band, The Concorde—Airport '79, The Squeeze, Edward Scissorhands.
TELEVISION: *Special*: The Fantasticks. *Guest*: The FBI, The Interns, Owen Marshall, The Tonight Show, (also frequent guest host). *Series*: The Entertainers, Kraft Summer Music Hall, The John Davidson Show (1969), The Girl With Something Extra, The John Davidson Show (1976), The John Davidson Talk Show (1980), That's Incredible, New Hollywood Squares, Time Machine (game show), Incredible Sunday, The $100,000 Pyramid. *Movies*: Coffee Tea or Me?, Shell Game, Roger & Harry: The Mitera Target, Dallas Cowboys Cheerleaders II.

DAVIDSON, MARTIN
Director, Writer. b. New York, NY, Nov. 7, 1939.
PICTURES: The Lords of Flatbush, Almost Summer, Hero at Large, Eddie and the Cruisers, Heart of Dixie (also exec. prod.), Hard Promises.
TELEVISION: *Series*: Our Family Honor, Call to Glory, Law and Order, My Life and Times, Picket Fences, Chicago Hope. *Movies*: Long Gone, A Murderous Affair: The Carolyn Warmus Story, Follow the River.

DAVIDTZ, EMBETH
Actress. b. Trenton, New Jersey, 1966.
PICTURES: Sweet Murder, Mutator, Schindler's List, Army of Darkness, Murder in the First, Feast of July, Matilda, Fallen, The Gingerbread Man, Bicentennial Man.
TELEVISION: A Private Life, 'Till Death Us Do Part, Deadly Matrimony, The Garden of Redemption.

DAVIES, JOHN HOWARD
Producer, Director. b. London, England, March 9, 1939. e. Haileybory, IS.C. and Grenoble Univ. Former child actor played leading roles in Oliver Twist, The Rocking Horse Winner, Tom Brown's Schooldays.
TELEVISION: *Prod./Dir.*: Monty Python's Flying Circus, Steptoe and Son, Fawlty Towers, The Good Life, The Goodies, The Other One, No Job for a Lady, Mr. Bean.

DAVIS, ANDREW
Director. b. Chicago, IL. e. Univ. of IL. Former journalist and photographer before landing job as asst. cameraman on 1969 film Medium Cool. Was dir. of photog. on several TV commercials and documentaries.
PICTURES: Lepke (dir. of photog.), Stony Island (dir., prod., co-s.p.), Over the Edge (dir. of photog.), Angel (dir. of photog.), Beat Street (co-s.p.). *Director*: The Final Terror, Code of Silence, Above the Law (also co-prod., co-story), The Package, Under Siege, The Fugitive, Steal Big Steal Little (also co-prod., co-s.p., co-story), Chain Reaction, A Perfect Murder.

DAVIS, CARL
Composer. b. New York, NY, Oct. 28, 1936. e. Queens Coll., Bard Coll. and New England Coll. of Music. Worked as pianist with Robert Shaw Chorale and wrote music for revue Diversions (1958) and Twists (London), Moved to England 1961 writing incidental music for Joan Littlewood's Theatre Workshop Co., Royal Shakespeare Co. and National Theatre. Other theater music includes Jonathan Miller's Tempest, Forty Years On, and the musical The Vackees. Best known for composing new scores for silent classics (Napoleon, The Crowd, Greed, Intolerance, etc.) for screenings at which he conducts and for Thames TV The Silents series. Concert work: Paul McCartney's Liverpool Oratorio.
PICTURES: The Bofors Gun, Up Pompeii, Rentadick, Man Friday, The Sailor's Return, Birth of the Beatles, The French Lieutenant's Woman, Praying Mantis, The Aerodrome, Champions, Weather in the Streets, George Stevens: A Filmmaker's Journey, King David, The Rainbow, Scandal, Girl in a Swing, Fragments of Isabella, Frankenstein Unbound, Diary of a Madman, Raft of the Medusa, The Voyage, Liberation, Widow's Peak, Anne Frank Remembered.
TELEVISION: That Was the Week That Was, Hollywood, the Pioneers, World at War, Mayor of Casterbridge, Lorna Doone, Unknown Chaplin, Buster Keaton—A Hard Act to Follow, Treasure Island, The Snow Goose, Our Mutual Friend, Naked Civil Servant, Silas Marner, The Accountant, Secret Life of Ian Fleming, Why Lockerbie?, Buried Mirro, A Christmas Carol, Royal Collection, Hotel du Lac, Black Velvet Gown, Lie Down With Lions, The Return of the Native. *Mini-series*: Pride & Prejudice, Oliver's Travels, Cinema Europe: The Other Hollywood, Real Women.

DAVIS, COLIN
Executive. Held executive positions in Canada in adv., bdcst., & p.r. with several companies, including Procter & Gamble, Young & Rubicam. Joined MCA TV Canada as v.p. & gen. mgr., 1977. Named dir. intl. sls., 1978. In 1986 appt. pres., MCA TV Int'l.

DAVIS, FRANK I.
Executive. b. Poolesville, MD, Feb. 18, 1919. e. U. of Maryland, A.B., 1941; Harvard Law School, LL.B., 1948. Law firm, Donovan, Leisure, Newton, Lombard and Irvine, 1948-50; v.p., gen. counsel, Vanguard Films, 1951; v.p., gen. counsel, Selznick Releasing Org., 1951-53; pres., The Selznick Company, 1953-55; v.p., Famous Artists Corp., 1956-62; v.p. George Stevens Productions Inc., 1962-65; exec. prod., The Greatest Story Ever Told; v.p. in charge of m.p. affairs, Seven Arts, 1966; exec. in chg. talent and exec. asst. to v.p. in chg. prod., MGM, 1967; dir. m.p. business affairs, MGM, 1970; v.p., business affairs, MGM, 1972; sr. v.p., motion picture business affairs, MGM/UA, 1983, exec. v.p., business affairs, MGM Pictures, 1986-88; sr. exec. v.p., business affairs, Pathe Entertainment Inc., 1989-90; sr. exec. v.p. of bus. affairs, MGM, 1990.

DAVIS, GEENA
Actress. r.n. Virginia Elizabeth Davis. b. Wareham, MA, Jan. 21, 1957. e. Boston U. Acted with Mount Washington Repertory Theatre Co., NH. Was NY model before winning role Tootsie, 1982.
PICTURES: Tootsie (debut, 1982), Fletch, Transylvania 6-5000, The Fly, Beetlejuice, The Accidental Tourist (Acad. Award, supporting actress, 1988), Earth Girls Are Easy, Quick Change, Thelma & Louise, A League of Their Own, Hero, Angie, Speechless (also prod.), Cutthroat Island, The Long Kiss Goodnight (also prod.), Stuart Little, Stuart Little 2.
TELEVISION: *Series*: Buffalo Bill (also wrote one episode), Sara, The Geena Davis Show. *Movie*: Secret Weapons. *Guest*: Family Ties, Riptide, Remington Steele, Trying Times.

DAVIS, JOHN
Executive, Producer. e. Bowdoin Col., Harvard Bus. Sch. Served as v.p. at 20th Century Fox before forming Davis Entertainment.
PICTURES: Predator, Three O'Clock High, License to Drive, Little Monsters, The Last of the Finest, Shattered, Storyville, The Firm, The Thing Called Love, Fortress, Gunmen, Grumpy Old Men, Richie Rich, The Hunted, Waterworld, The Grass Harp, Courage Under Fire, Daylight, Out to Sea.
TELEVISION: *Movies:* Tears and Laughter: The Joan and Melissa Rivers Story, The Last Outlaw, This Can't Be Love.

DAVIS, JUDY
Actress. b. Perth, Australia, 1955. m. actor Colin Friels. Left convent school as teenager to become a singer in a rock band. Studied at West Australia Inst. of Technology and National Inst. of Dramatic Art, Sydney. Worked with theatre companies in Adelaide and Sydney and at Royal Court Theatre, London. Los Angeles stage debut Hapgood.
PICTURES: High Rolling (debut, 1977), My Brilliant Career, Hoodwink, Heatwave, Winter of Our Dreams, The Final Option, A Passage to India (Acad. Award nom.), Kangaroo, High Tide, Georgia, Alice, Impromtu, Barton Fink, Naked Lunch, Where Angels Fear to Tread, Husbands and Wives (Acad. Award nom.), On My Own (Australian Film Inst. Award), The Ref, The New Age, Absolute Power, Deconstructing Harry, Blood and Wine, Celebrity, Absolute Power, A Cooler Climate, Gaudi Afternoon.
TELEVISION: Rocket to the Moon, A Woman Called Golda, One Against the Wind, Serving in Silence: The Margarethe Cammermeyer Story (Emmy Award, 1995), The Echo of Thunder, Dash and Lilly, Rosamunde Pilcher, Me & My Shadows.

DAVIS, LUTHER
Writer, Producer. b. New York, NY, Aug. 29, 1921. e. Yale, B.A.
THEATER: *Writer*: Kiss Them for Me, Kismet (Tony Award), Timbuktu! (also prod.), Grand Hotel (Tony nom.). Co-Prod.: Eden Court, Not About Heroes.
PICTURES: *Writer*: The Hucksters, B.F.'s Daughter, Black Hand, A Lion Is in the Streets, The Gift of Love, Holiday for Lovers, The Wonders of Aladdin, Lady in a Cage (also prod.), Across 110th Street.
TELEVISION: *Writer/Prod.*: Kraft Suspense Theatre and many pilots for series (Run for Your Life, The Silent Force, Eastside, Westside, etc.). *Specials*: Arsenic and Old Lace, The People Trap (prod.). *Movies*: Daughter of the Mind, The Old Man Who Cried Wolf.

DAVIS, MAC
Singer, Songwriter, Actor. b. Lubbock, TX, Jan 21, 1942. e. Emory U., Georgia State Coll. Employed as ditch digger, service station attendant, laborer, probation officer and record company salesman before gaining fame as entertainer-singer in 1969. Recording artist and composer of many popular songs. On B'way 1992 in The Will Rogers Follies.
PICTURES: North Dallas Forty, Cheaper to Keep Her, The Sting II.
TELEVISION: *Series*: The Mac Davis Show. *Movies*: Brothers-In-Law, What Price Victory?, Blackmail.

DAVIS, OSSIE
Actor, Writer, Director. b. Cogdell, GA, Dec. 18, 1917. e. Howard U., Washington, DC. m. actress Ruby Dee. Studied acting in N.Y. with Rose McLendon Players, leading to Broadway debut in 1946 in Jeb. For years thereafter was one of best-known black actors on Bway stage in: Anna Lucasta, Jamaica, The Green Pastures, Wisteria Tree, A Raisin in the Sun, I'm Not Rappaport. Wrote and starred in Purlie Victorious, repeating role for film version. Directed and appeared with Ms. Dee in her musical Take It From the Top. Co-hosted Ossie Davis and Ruby Dee Story Hour on radio (3 years). Published plays: Purlie Victorious, Langston, Escape to Freedom, Curtain Call, Mr. Aldredge, Sir.
PICTURES: *Actor*: No Way Out, Fourteen Hours, The Joe Louis Story, Gone Are the Days, The Cardinal, Shock Treatment, The Hill, Man Called Adam, The Scalphunters, Sam Whiskey, Slaves, Let's Do It Again, Hot Stuff, House of God, Harry and Son, Avenging Angel, School Daze, Do the Right Thing, Joe Versus the Volcano, Jungle Fever, Gladiator, Malcolm X (voice), Grumpy Old Men, The Client, I'm Not Rappaport, Get on the Bus. *Director:* Cotton Comes to Harlem (also co-s.p.), Black Girl, Gordon's War, Countdown at Kusini (also actor, prod.), Get on the Bus, Doctor Dolittle.
TELEVISION: *Writer*: East Side/West Side, The Eleventh Hour. *Guest:* Name of the Game, Night Gallery, Bonanza, etc. *Specials*: Martin Luther King: The Dream and the Drum, With Ossie and Ruby (also co-prod.), Today is Ours (writer, dir.). *Movies*: All God's Children, Don't Look Back, Roots: The Next Generations, King, Teacher Teacher, The Ernest Green Story, Ray Alexander: A Taste for Justice, Ray Alexander: A Menu for Murder, The Android Affair. *Series*: B.L. Stryker, Evening Shade, John Grisham's The Client. *Mini-Series*: Queen, Stephen King's The Stand, Miss Evers' Boys.

DAVIS, PETER
Author, Filmmaker. b. Santa Monica, CA, Jan. 2, 1937. e. Harvard Coll., 1955-57. Parents were screenwriter Frank Davis, and novelist-screenwriter Tess Slesinger. Writer-interviewer, Sextant Prods., FDR Series, 1964-65. Host: The Comers, PBS 1964-65. Author: Hometown (1982), Where Is Nicaragua? (1987), If You Came This Way (1995), articles for Esquire, NY Times Mag., The Nation, NY Woman, TV Guide.
PICTURES: Hearts and Minds (prod., dir.; Acad. Award, best documentary, 1975; Prix Sadoul, 1974), Jack (writer/prod.).
TELEVISION: *Writer-prod.*: Hunger in America (assoc. prod., WGA Award, 1968), The Heritage of Slavery, The Battle of East St. Louis, (Saturday Review Award, 1970; 2 Emmy nom.), The Selling of the Pentagon (WGA, Emmy, Peabody, George Polk, Ohio State, Sat. Review Awards, 1971), 60 Minutes (segment prod.), Middletown (series, prod., Dupont Citation, Emmy noms. 1983), The Best Hotel on Skidrow (ACE Award noms., 1992).

DAVIS, PRESTON A.
Executive. b. Norfolk, VA. Served in US Army. 1976, joined ABC as engineer in Washington DC, later becoming sprv. of Electronic News Gathering; 1979, became tech. mngr. of ENG; 1983, named tech. mngr. then manager of ENG for southeast region, Atlanta; 1986, promoted to gen. mngr. ENG Operations, New York; 1988, named v.p. TV Operations, Broadcast Operations & Engineering, East Coast; 1993, named pres. of Broadcast Operations and Engineering for ABC Television Network Group.

DAVIS, SAMMI
Actress. b. Kidderminster, Worcestershire, England, June 21, 1964. Convent-educated before taking drama course. Performed in stage prods. with local drama society in Midlands, then Birmingham Rep. and Big Brum Theatre Co. Plays include The Home Front, The Apple Club, Nine Days, Databased, Choosey Susie. London stage debut: A Collier's Friday.
PICTURES: Mona Lisa, Lionheart, Hope and Glory, A Prayer for the Dying, Consuming Passions, The Lair of the White Worm, The Rainbow, The Horseplayer, Shadow of China, Four Rooms, Death Do Us Part, Assignment Berlin.
TELEVISION: Auf Wiedersehn Pet, The Day After the Fair, Pack of Lies, Chernobyl: The Final Warning, The Perfect Bride, Indecency, Spring Awakening. *Series:* Homefront.

DAVIS, WARWICK
Actor. b. 1970
PICTURES: Star Wars: Episode VI-Return of the Jedi, Labyrinth, Willow, Leprechaun, Leprechaun 2, Leprechaun 3, Leprechaun 4: In Space, Prince Valiant, A Very Unlucky Leprechaun, The Bacchae, Star Wars: Episode I-The Phantom Menace.
TELEVISION: *Movies:* The Ewok Adventure, Ewoks: The Battle for Endor, Prince Caspian and the Voyage of the Dawn Treader, The Silver Chair, Gulliver's Travels. *Guest:* Seinfeld.

DAVISON, BRUCE
Actor. b. Philadelphia, PA, June 28, 1946. e. Pennsylvania State U., NYU. debut, Lincoln Center Repertory prod. of Tiger at the Gates, 1967.
THEATER: NY: King Lear (Lincoln Center), The Elephant Man, Richard III (NY Shakespeare Fest.), The Glass Menagerie, The Cocktail Hour. *Regional:* Streamers (LA Critics Award), The Caine Mutiny Court-Martial, The Normal Heart, To Kill a Mockingbird, A Life in the Theatre, The Front Page, Downside, Breaking the Silence.
PICTURES: Last Summer (debut, 1969), The Strawberry Statement, Willard, Been Down So Long It Looks Like Up To Me, The Jerusalem File, Ulzana's Raid, Mame, Mother Jugs and Speed, Grand Jury, Short Eyes, Brass Target, French Quarter, High Risk, A Texas Legend, Lies, Crimes of Passion, Spies Like Us, The Ladies Club, The Misfit Brigade, Longtime Companion (NY Film Critics, Natl. Society of Film Critics, & Golden Globe Awards, 1990; Acad. Award nom.), Steel and Lace, Short Cuts, An Ambush of Ghosts, Six Degrees of Separation, Far From Home: The Adventures of Yellow Dog, The Cure, The Baby-sitters Club, Homage, Grace of My Heart, The Crucible, Lovelife, Apt Pupil, Paulie, Vendetta, At First Sight, X-Men, The Other Side, Summer Catch, At Seventeen.
TELEVISION: *Movies*: Owen Marshall: Counsellor at Law (A Pattern of Morality), The Affair, The Last Survivors, Deadman's Curve, Summer of My German Soldier, Mind Over Murder, The Gathering, Tomorrow's Child, Ghost Dancing, Poor Little Rich Girl: The Barbara Hutton Story, Lady in a Corner, Stolen: One Husband, Live! From Death Row, Desperate Choices: To Save My Child, A Mother's Revenge, Someone Else's Child, Down Out and Dangerous, The Color of Justice, Hidden in Silence, Little Girl Fly Away, A Memory in My Heart. *Specials:* Taming of the Shrew, The Lathe of Heaven, The Wave. *Guest*: Medical Center, Marcus Welby, Love American Style, Police Story, Lou Grant, Murder She Wrote, Alfred Hitchcok Presents (1985), Amazing Stories. *Series*: Hunter, Harry and the Hendersons.

DAVISON, DALE
Executive. b. North Hollywood, CA, March 21, 1955. e. U.C.L.A., B.A., 1978. Entered the motion picture industry in 1973 working for Pacific Theatres. Employed with Great Western Theatres 1974-77 as manager, dir. of concessions, and asst. vice pres. Partner with Great Western Theatres, 1978-1984. Founder and CEO, CinemaCal Enterprises, Inc., 1985-present. NATO Board of Directors 1994-present. NATO of CA Executive Committee 1996-present. Chief Barker Variety Club of Northern CA 1997-present.

DAVISON, JON
Producer. b. Haddonfield, NJ, July 21, 1949. e. NYU Film School. 1972, joined New World Pictures as natl. dir. of publ./adv.; 1972, named in charge of prod.; 1980, became indep. prod.
PICTURES: Hollywood Boulevard, Grand Theft Auto, Piranha, Airplane!, White Dog, Twilight Zone—The Movie (episode), Top Secret! Robocop, Robocop 2, Trapped in Paradise, Starship Troopers.

DAWBER, PAM
Actress, Singer. b. Detroit, MI, Oct. 18, 1954. m. actor Mark Harmon. e. Farmington H.S., Oakland Community Coll. Worked as model and did commercials. First professional performance as singer in Sweet Adeleine at Goodspeed Opera House, East Haddam, CT.
THEATER: Regional: My Fair Lady, The Pirates of Penzance, The Music Man, She Loves Me, Love Letters.
PICTURES: A Wedding, Stay Tuned, I'll Remember April.
TELEVISION: *Series*: Mork and Mindy, My Sister Sam, 101 Dalmations: The Series (voice), Life...and Stuff. *Movies*: The Girl the Gold Watch and Everything, Remembrance of Love, Through Naked Eyes, Last of the Great Survivors, This Wife For Hire, Wild Horses, Quiet Victory: The Charlie Wedemeyer Story, Do You Know the Muffin Man, The Face of Fear, The Man With Three Wives, Web of Deception, Trail of Tears, A Child's Cry for Help, Don't Look Behind You. *Specials*: Kennedy Center Honors, Salute to Andy Gibb, Night of the 100 Stars, 3rd Annual TV Guide Special.

DAY, DORIS
Singer, Actress. r.n. Doris Kappelhoff. b. Cincinnati, OH, April 3, 1924. e. dancing, singing. Toured as dancer; radio and band singer; screen debut in Romance on the High Seas, 1948. Voted one of Top Ten Money-Making Stars in Motion Picture Herald-Fame poll, 1951-52. Best female vocalist. M. P. Daily radio poll, 1952.
PICTURES: Romance on the High Seas (debut, 1948), My Dream is Yours, It's a Great Feeling, Young Man With a Horn, Tea for Two, Storm Warning, West Point Story, Lullaby of Broadway, On Moonlight Bay, I'll See You in My Dreams, Starlift, The Winning Team, April in Paris, By the Light of the Silvery Moon, Calamity Jane, Lucky Me, Young at Heart, Love Me or Leave Me, The Man Who Knew Too Much, Julie, The Pajama Game, Teacher's Pet, Tunnel of Love, It Happened to Jane, Pillow Talk (Acad. Award nom.), Please Don't Eat the Daisies, Midnight Lace, Lover Come Back, That Touch of Mink, Bill Rose's Jumbo, The Thrill of It All, Move Over Darling, Send Me No Flowers, Do Not Disturb, Glass Bottom Boat, Caprice, The Ballad of Josie, Where Were You When the Lights Went Out?, With Six You Get Eggroll.
TELEVISION: *Series*: The Doris Day Show (1968-73), Doris Day's Best Friends (educational cable show; 1985-86).

DAY, LARAINE
Actress. r.n. Laraine Johnson. b. Roosevelt, UT, Oct. 13, 1920. e. Long Beach Polytechic H.S., Paramount Studio School. In school dramatics; with Players Guild, Long Beach, Calif.; toured in church prod. Conflict; Professionally on stage in Lost Horizon, The Women, Time of the Cuckoo, Angel Street.

PICTURES: Stella Dallas (debut, 1937 as Laraine Johnson), Scandal Sheet, Border G-Man, Young Dr. Kildare (and subsequent series), And One Was Beautiful, My Son My Son, Foreign Correspondent, The Trial of Mary Dugan, The Bad Man, Unholy Partners, Fingers at the Window, Journey for Margaret, Mr. Lucky, The Story of Dr. Wassell, Bride by Mistake, Those Endearing Young Charms, Keep Your Powder Dry, The Locket, Tycoon, My Dear Secretary, I Married a Communist (Woman on Pier 13), Without Honor, The High and the Mighty, Toy Tiger, Three for Jamie Dawn, The Third Voice, Painted Desert, Sergeant Madden, Arizona Legion, Tarzan Finds A Son, I Take This Woman, Kathleen, Yank On the Burma Road.
TELEVISION: Appearances include Climax, Playhouse 90, Alfred Hitchcock, Wagon Train, Let Freedom Ring, Name of the Game, FBI, Sixth Sense, Medical Center, Murder on Flight 504 (movie), Fantasy Island, Love Boat, Lou Grant, Airwolf, Hotel, Murder She Wrote.

DAY, ROBERT
Director. b. England, Sept. 11, 1922. Started as cinematographer before turning to direction.
PICTURES: *Director*: The Green Man (debut, 1956), Stranger's Meeting, Grip of the Strangler (The Haunted Strangler), First Man Into Space, Bobbikins, Two-Way Stretch, Tarzan the Magnificent (also co-s.p.), The Rebel (Call Me Genius), Corridors of Blood, Operation Snatch, Tarzan's Three Challenges (also co-s.p.), She, Tarzan and the Valley of Gold, Tarzan and the Great River, Tarzan and the Jungle Boy (prod. only), The Man with Bogart's Face.
TELEVISION: *Pilots include:* Banion, Kodiak, Dan August, Sunshine, Switch, Logan's Run, Kingston, Dallas, Matlock. Movies include: Ritual of Evil, The House of Greenapple Road, In Broad Daylight, Having Babies, The Grass Is Always Greener Over the Septic Tank, Peter and Paul, Running Out, Scruples, Cook and Peary—The Race to the Pole, Hollywood Wives, The Lady from Yesterday, Diary of a Perfect Murder, Celebration, Higher Ground, Walking Through the Fire.

DAY-LEWIS, DANIEL
Actor. b. London, England, April 29, 1957. Son of late C. Day-Lewis, poet laureate of Eng., and actress Jill Balcon. Grandson of late Sir Malcolm Balcon who prod. Hitchcock's Brit. films. e. Bristol Old Vic. Theatre School. First professional job at 12 as ruffian scratching cars with broken bottle in film, Sunday Bloody Sunday. Then acted with Bristol Old Vic and Royal Shakespeare Co.
THEATER: *London*: Dracula, Funny Peculiar, Troilus & Cressida, A Midsummer Night's Dream, Class Enemy, Edward II, Look Back in Anger, Another Country, Romeo and Juliet The Futurists Hamlet.
PICTURES: Gandhi, The Bounty, A Room With a View, My Beautiful Laundrette, The Unbearable Lightness of Being, Stars and Bars, Nanou, Ever Smile New Jersey, My Left Foot (Acad. Award, 1989; also BAFTA, NY Film Critics, L.A. Film Critics, Natl. Society of Film Critics Awards), The Last of the Mohicans, The Age of Innocence, In the Name of the Father, The Crucible, The Boxer, The Gans of New York.
TELEVISION: *BBC Movies/Specials*: Eddie Shoestring, Artemis 11, The Lost Traveller, The Sugar House, Beyond the Glass, Thenk You P.G. Woodhouse, Dangerous Corner, A Frost in May, How Many Miles to Babylon?, My Brother Jonathan, The Insurance Man, History of Hamlet (host).

DEAKINS, ROGER
Cinematographer. b. Devon, England, May 24, 1949. Accepted into National Film School in 1972. Working as professional filmmaker from 1975 directing and photographing documentary films including Around the World With Ridgeway, Zimbabwe, Eritrea—Behind the Lines, When the World Changed, Worlds Apart S.E. Nuba, Worlds Apart Rajgonds. Photographed first feature, Another Time Another Place in 1982.
PICTURES: 1984, The Innocent, Sid & Nancy, Shadey, Defense of the Realm, White Mischief, Personal Services, Stormy Monday, Pascali's Island, The Kitchen Toto, Mountains of the Moon, Air America, The Long Walk Home, Barton Fink, Homicide, Thunderheart, Passion Fish, The Secret Garden, The Hudsucker Proxy, The Shawshank Redemption (Acad. Award nom.; ASC Award), Rob Roy, Dead Man Walking, Fargo, Courage Under Fire, Kundun, Martial Law, The Big Lebowski, The Siege, Anywhere But Here, O Brother, Where Art Thou?, Thirteen Days.

DEAN, JIMMY
SONGS: *Composer*: Big Bad John, Little Black Book, I.O.U., To a Sleeping Beauty, PT-109, Dear Ivan.
PICTURES: Diamonds Are Forever, Big Bad John.
TELEVISION: *Series*: The Jimmy Dean Show (1957; 1963-66), Daniel Boone, J.J. Starbuck. *Specials*: Sunday Night at the Palladium (London), Celebrities Offstage. *Movies*: The Ballad of Andy Crocker, Rolling Man, The City.

DEAN, MORTON
Television Newsman. b. Fall River, MA, Aug. 22, 1935. e. Emerson Coll. News dir., N.Y. Herald Tribune Net, 1957; corr. WBZ, 1960, corr. WCBS-TV, 1964; anchor, WCBW-TV News, 1967; corr., CBS News, 1967; anchor, CBS Sunday Night News, 1975; anchor, Sunday edition CBS Evening News, 1976; co-anchor, Independent Network News, 1985.

DEARDEN, JAMES
Writer, Director, b. London, England, Sept. 14, 1949. Son of late British director Basil Dearden. e. New Coll., Oxford U. Entered film industry in 1967 as production runner. After editing commercials and documentaries, and working as asst. dir., wrote, prod. and dir. first short film, The Contraption (Silver Bear Award, 1978 Berlin Film Fest.). 1978, began dir. commercials and made short, Panic (Cert. of Merit, 1980 Chicago Film Fest.). 1979, made 45-min film Diversion, which became basis for Fatal Attraction (Gold Plaque, best short drama, 1980 Chicago Film Fest.).
PICTURES: Fatal Attraction (s.p.), Pascali's Island (dir., s.p.), A Kiss Before Dying (dir., s.p.), Rogue Trader (dir., s.p., prod.).
TELEVISION: The Cold Room (dir., writer, Special Jury Prize, dir., 1985 Fest. Intl. d'Avoriaz du Film Fantastique).

De BONT, JAN
Cinematographer, Director. b. Holland, Oct. 22, 1943.Trained at Amsterdam Film Acad. Recipient of Kodak Camera Award and Rembrandt Award.
PICTURES: *Cinematographer:* Turkish Delight, Keetje Tippel, Max Heuelaar, Soldier of Orange, Private Lessons (U.S. debut, 1981), Roar, I'm Dancing as Fast as I Can, Cujo, All the Right Moves, Bad Manners, The Fourth Man, Mischief, The Jewel of the Nile, Flesh + Blood, The Clan of the Cave Bear, Ruthless People, Who's That Girl, Leonard Part 6, Die Hard, Bert Rigby You're a Fool, Black Rain, The Hunt for Red October, Flatliners, Shining Through, Basic Instinct, Lethal Weapon 3. *Director:* Speed (debut, 1994), Twister, Speed 2: Cruise Control (also s.p., story), The Haunting (also prod.), Cosm (also s.p., prod.). *Producer*: S.L.C. Punk!, Zero Hour, Like a Hole in the Head.
TELEVISION (Photography): *Movie:* The Ray Mancini Story. *Episode:* Tales From the Crypt (Split Personality).

De BROCA, PHILIPPE
Director, Writer. b. Paris, France, March 15, 1933. e. Paris Technical School of Photography and Cinematography.
PICTURES: *Director/Writer*: Les Jeux de l'Amour (The Love Game), The Joker, The Five Day Lovers, Seven Capitol Sins (dir. segment only), Cartouche (also actor), Les Veinards (segment), That Man From Rio, Male Companion (Un Monsieur de Compagnie), Les Tribulations d'un Chinois en Chine (Up to His Ears), King of Hearts (also prod.), Devil by the Tail, Give Her the Moon, Chere Louise, Le Magnifique, Dear Inspector (also s.p.), The Skirt Chaser, Someone's Stolen the Thigh of Jupiter, The African, Louisiana (TV in U.S.), The Gypsy, Chouans! (dir., co-s.p.), Scheherazade.

De CAMP, ROSEMARY
Actress. b. Prescott AZ, Nov. 14, 1913.
PICTURES: Cheers for Miss Bishop (debut, 1941), Hold Back the Dawn, Jungle Book, Yankee Doodle Dandy, Eyes in the Night, THe Commandos Strike at Dawn, Smith of Minnesota, Without Men, This is the Army, The Merry Monahans, Bowery to Broadway, Blood on the Sun, Practically Yours, Rhapsody in Blue, Pride of the Marines, Danger Signal, Too Young to Know, From This Day Forward, Nora Prentiss, Night Unto Night, The Life of Riley, Look for the Silver Lining, Story of Seabiscuit, The Big Hangover, Night Into Morning, On Moonlight Bay, Scandal Sheet, Treasure of Lost Canyon, By the Light of the Silvery Moon, Main Street to Broadway, So This Is Love, Many Rivers to Cross, Strategic Air Command, 13 Ghosts, Saturday the 14th.
TELEVISION: *Series*: The Life of Reilly (with Jackie Gleason), The Bob Cummings Show, That Girl. *Guest*: Death Valley Days, Partridge Family, Love American Style, Police Story, Rockford Files, Days of Our Lives, Misadventures of Sheriff Lobo, Love Boat, B.J. & the Bear. *Mini-Series*: Blind Ambition. *Movie*: The Time Machine.

De CAPRIO, AL
Producer, Director. e. Brooklyn Tech., NYU. Started as radio engineer, cameraman, tech. dir., prod. & dir. CBS; dir. series episodes of Sgt. Bilko, Car 54 Where Are You?, Musical specials for ABC, CBS, NBC; v.p. exec. prod. dir., MPO Videotronics, Pres. World Wide Videotape; retired.

DECHERD, ROBERT WILLIAM
Newspaper & Broadcasting Executive. b. April 9, 1951. e. Harvard U., AB cum laude, 1973. Exec. v.p., Dallas Morning News, 1980-83. Exec. v.p. A.H. Belo Corp., 1981-84; pres., COO, 1985-86; chmn., CEO, 1987-94; chmn., pres., CEO & bd. dirs., 1994-. Pres.: Dallas Symphony Assn., 1979-80; Dallas Symphony Found., 1984-86; St. Mark's Sch., Tex., 1988-91. Chmn.: Dallas Parks Found., 1985-87; Dallas Soc. Profl. Journalists, 1978. Trustee:
Tomas Rivera Ctr., 1992-. Incorporator, pres.. Freedom of Info. Found. Tex., 1978. Mem.: Tex., Soc. of Archs (hon.); Newspaper assn. Am. (exec. bd., 1992-). Recipient of: Disting. Svc. award Dallas Jaycees, 1985; Am. Newspaper Exec. of Yr. award Adweek mag., 1985; citation of honor Am. Inst. Arch., 1988; Seymour Preston award Nat. Assn. Ind. Schs. Coun. Advancement and Support Edn., 1989; James Madison award Freedom of Info. Found. Tex., 1989; Henry Cohn Humanitarian award Anti-Defamation League, 1992.

De CARLO, YVONNE
Actress. b. Vancouver, B.C., Sept. 1, 1922. e. June Roper School of Dance, Britsh Columbia; Fanchon & Marco, Hollywood. Specialty dancing at Florentine Gardens, Earl Carroll's; motion picture debut in This Gun for Hire, 1942. One-woman club act and 7-person club act. Autobiography, Yvonne (1987).
PICTURES: This Gun for Hire (debut, 1942), Harvard Here I Come, Youth on Parade, Road to Morocco, Let's Face It, The Crystal Ball, Salute for Three, For Whom the Bell Tolls, True to Life, So Proudly We Hail, The Deerslayer, Practically Yours, Salome Where She Danced, Frontier Gal, Brute Force, Song of Scheherazade, Slave Girl, Black Bart, Casbah, River Lady, Criss Cross, Gal Who Took the West, Calamity Jane and Sam Bass, Buccaneer's Girl, The Desert Hawk, Tomahawk, Hotel Sahara, Silver City, Scarlet Angel, San Francisco Story, Hurricane Smith, Sombrero, Sea Devils, Fort Algiers, Captain's Paradise, Border River, Passion, Tonight's the Night, Shotgun, Magic Fire, Flame of the Islands, Ten Commandments, Raw Edge, Death of a Scoundrel, Band of Angels, Timbuktu, McLintock!, A Global Affair, Law of the Lawless, Munster Go Home, Hostile Guns, The Power, Arizona Bushwhackers, The Seven Minutes, Play Dead, It Seemed Like a Good Idea at the Time, Won Ton Ton the Dog Who Saved Hollywood, Blazing Stewardesses, Satan's Cheerleaders, Nocturna, Silent Scream, Guyana Cult of the Damned, The Man With Bogart's Face, Liar's Moon, American Gothic, Cellar Dweller, Mirror Mirror, Oscar, The Naked Truth.
TELEVISION: *Series*: The Munsters. *Movies*: The Girl on the Late Late Show, The Mark of Zorro, The Munsters' Revenge, A Masterpiece of Murder. *Guest*: Bonanza, Man From U.N.C.L.E., Murder She Wrote, Hollywood Sign (special), Johnny Carson, Merv Griffin, Steve Allen, David Frost, Perry Como, Tales from the Crypt, Dream On.

De CORDOVA, FREDERICK
Director. b. New York, NY, Oct. 27, 1910. e. Northwestern U., B.S. 1931. Gen. stage dir. Shubert enterprises, N.Y., 1938-41; same for Alfred Bloomingdale Prods., N.Y., and prod. Louisville (Ky.) Amphitheatre 1942-43. Dir., program planning, Screen Gems, 1964. Author: Johnny Came Lately, 1988.
PICTURES: *Dialogue Director*: San Antonio, Janie, Between Two Worlds. *Director*: Too Young to Know (debut, 1945), Her Kind of Man, That Way with Women, Love and Learn, Always Together, Wallflower, For the Love of Mary, The Countess of Monte Cristo, Illegal Entry, The Gal Who Took the West, Buccaneer's Girl, Peggy, The Desert Hawk, Bedtime for Bonzo, Katie Did It, Little Egypt, Finders Keepers, Here Come the Nelsons, Yankee Buccaneer, Bonzo Goes to College, Column South, I'll Take Sweden, Frankie and Johnny.
TELEVISION: *Series* (prod., dir.): The Burns and Allen Show, December Bride, Mr. Adams and Eve, George Gobel Show, The Jack Benny Program, The Smothers Bros. Show, My Three Sons (dir.), Tonight Show (prod.; 6 Emmy Awards).

DeCUIR, JR., JOHN F.
Art Director, Production Designer. b. Burbank, CA, Aug. 4, 1941. e. U. of Southern California, bachelor of architecture, 1965. Son of John F. De Cuir, Sr. 1966-68, U.S. Coast Guard (holds commission with rank of Lt. Commander, USCGR). 1968-72, project designer, Walt Disney World, Walt Disney Prods. 1972-74, dir. of design, Six Flags Corp. 1974-9, project designer, EPCOT, Walt Disney Prods. 1980-86, pres., John F. De Cuir, Jr. Design Consultants, Inc.; 1987-pres., Cinematix Inc.
PICTURES: *Illustrator*: Cleopatra, The Honey Pot. Design Concepts: The Agony and the Ecstasy. *Art Director*: Raise the Titanic, Ghosbusters. *Special Effects Consultant*: Dead Men Don't Wear Plaid, Monsignor. *Producer*: Jazz Club, The Baltimore Clipper, The Building Puzzle. Prod. *Designer*: Fright Night, Top Gun, Apt Pupil, Elvira Mistress of the Dark, Turner & Hooch, True Identity, Sleepwalkers, Sister Act 2: Back in the Habit.
TELEVISION: *Art Director*: Frank Sinatra Special—Old Blue Eyes Is Back, Annual Academy Awards Presentation 1971, Double Agent. *Production Design*: Double Switch, Earth * Star Voyager.

DEE, RUBY
Actress. b. Cleveland, OH, Oct. 27, 1924. r.n. Ruby Ann Wallace. e. Hunter Coll. m. actor-dir.-writer Ossie Davis. Worked as apprentice at Amer. Negro Theatre, 1941-44, studied at Actor's Workshop. Stage appearances include Jeb, Anna Lucasta, The World of Sholom Aleichem, A Raisin in the Sun, Purlie Victorious, Wedding Band, Boseman and Lena, Hamlet, Checkmates.
PICTURES: No Way Out, The Jackie Robinson Story, The Tall Target, Go Man Go!, Edge of the City, St. Louis Blues, Take a Giant Step, Virgin Island, A Raisin in the Sun, Gone Are the Days, The Balcony, The Incident, Up Tight, Buck and the Preacher, Black Girl, Countdown at Kusini, Cat People, Do the Right Thing, Love at Large, Jungle Fever, Cop and a Half, Just Cause, A Simple Wish.
TELEVISION: *Movies*: Deadlock, The Sheriff, It's Good to Be Alive, I Know Why the Caged Bird Sings, All God's Children, The Atlanta Child Murders, Go Tell it on the Mountain, Windmills of the Gods, The Court-Martial of Jackie Robinson, Decoration Day (Emmy Award, 1991), The Ernest Green Story. *Specials*: Actor's Choice, Seven Times Monday, Go Down Moses, Twin-Bit Gardens, Wedding Band, To Be Young Gifted and Black, Long Day's Journey into Night, Edgar Allan Poe: Terror of the Soul (narrator). *Mini-Series*: Roots: The Next Generation, Gore Vidal's Lincoln, The Stand. *Series*: Peyton Place, With Ossie and Ruby, Middle Ages.

DEE, SANDRA
Actress. r.n. Alexandra Zuck. b. Bayonne, NJ, April 23, 1942. Modeled, Harry Conover and Huntington Hartford Agencies, N.Y., 1954-56; signed long term exclusive contract, U-I, 1957.
PICTURES: Until They Sail (debut, 1957), The Reluctant Debutante, The Restless Years, Stranger in My Arms, Imitation of Life, Gidget, The Wild and the Innocent, A Summer Place, The Snow Queen (voice), Portrait in Black, Romanoff and Juliet, Come September, Tammy Tell Me True, If a Man Answers, Tammy and the Doctor, Take Her She's Mine, I'd Rather Be Rich, That Funny Feeling, A Man Could Get Killed, Doctor You've Got to Be Kidding!, Rosie, The Dunwich Horror.
TELEVISION: *Movies*: The Daughters of Joshua Cabe, Houston We've Got a Problem, The Manhunter, Fantasy Island (pilot). *Guest*: Steve Allen Show, Night Gallery, Love American Style, Police Woman.

DEELEY, MICHAEL
Producer. b. London, England, August 6, 1932. Ent. m.p. ind. 1951 and TV, 1967, as alt. dir. Harlech Television Ltd. Film editor, 1951-58. MCA-TV 1958-61, later with Woodfall as prod. and assoc. prod. Assoc. prod. The Knack, The White Bus, Ride of the Valkyrie. Great Western Investments Ltd.; 1972; Great Western Festivals Ltd.; 1973, mng. dir. British Lion Films Ltd. 1975, purchased BLF, Ltd. Appt. Jnt. man. dir. EMI Films Ltd., 1977; pres., EMI Films, 1978, Member Film Industry Interim Action Committee, 1977-82; Deputy Chairman, British Screen Advisory Council, 1985. Appt. Chief Executive Officer, Consolidated Television Production & Distribution Inc., 1984.
PICTURES: *Prod.*: One Way Pendulum, Robbery, The Italian Job, Long Days Dying (exec. prod.), Where's Jack, Sleep Is Lovely, Murphy's War, The Great Western Express, Conduct Unbecoming, The Man Who Fell to Earth, Convoy, The Deer Hunter (Acad. Award for Best Picture, 1978), Blade Runner.
TELEVISION: *Movie:* A Gathering of Old Men (exec. prod.).

DE FINA, BARBARA
Producer. Started as prod. asst. before working at various jobs for such filmmakers as Woody Allen and Sidney Lumet. Became assoc. prod. of development for King/Hitzig Prods., working on Happy Birthday Gemini, Cattle Annie and Little Britches. Was unit mgr./assoc. prod. on Prince of the City. First worked with Martin Scorsese on The King of Comedy as unit mgr. Produced music video Bad.
PICTURES: *Producer*: The Color of Money, The Last Temptation of Christ, New York Stories (segment: Life Lessons), GoodFellas (exec. prod.), The Grifters (exec. prod.), Cape Fear, Mad Dog and Glory, The Age of Innocence, Casino, Kicked in the Head, Kundun, The Hi-Lo Country, Bringing Out the Dead, Dino.

DEGENERES, ELLEN
Actress. b. New Orleans, LA, Jan 26, 1958.
PICTURES: Wisecracks, Coneheads, Mr. Wrong, Doctor Dolittle (voice), Edtv, Goodbye Lover, The Love Letter.
TELEVISION: *Series*: Open House, Laurie Hill, Ellen (also prod.). *Special:* If These Walls Could Talk 2. *Guest*: Roseanne.

De HAVILLAND, OLIVIA
Actress b. Tokyo, Japan, July 1, 1916. e. California schools and Notre Dame Convent, Belmont. Acting debut, Max Reinhardt's stage prod., A Midsummer Night's Dream; going to Warner Bros. for film debut in m.p. version, 1935. Recipient: The Snake Pit (NY Film Critics & Look Awards), The Heiress (NY Film Critics, Women's Natl. Press Club & Look Awards). Autobiography: Every Frenchman Has One (1962).
THEATER: A Midsummer Night's Dream (Hollywood Bowl). B'way: Romeo and Juliet (1951), A Gift of Time. U.S. Tour: Candida (1951-52).
PICTURES: A Midsummer Night's Dream (debut, 1935), Alibi Ike, The Irish in Us, Captain Blood, Anthony Adverse, The Charge of the Light Brigade, Call It a Day, It's Love I'm After, The Great Garrick, Gold is Where You Find It, The Adventures of Robin Hood, Four's a Crowd, Hard to Get, Wings of the Navy, Dodge City, The Private Lives of Elizabeth and Essex, Gone With the Wind, Raffles, My Love Came Back, Santa Fe Trail, Strawberry Blonde, Hold Back the Dawn, They Died With Their Boots On, The Male Animal, In This Our Life, Princess O'Rourke, Thank Your Lucky Stars, Government Girl, The Well Groomed Bride, To Each His Own (Acad. Award, 1946), Devotion, Dark Mirror, The Snake Pit, The Heiress (Acad. Award, 1949), My Cousin Rachel, That Lady, Not as a Stranger, Ambassador's Daughter, Proud Rebel, Libel, Light in the Piazza, Lady in a Cage, Hush ... Hush Sweet Charlotte, The Adventurers, Pope Joan, Airport '77, The Swarm, The Fifth Musketeer.
TELEVISION: *Special*: Noon Wine (Stage 67). *Movies & Mini-series*: The Screaming Woman, Roots: The Next Generations, Murder is Easy, Charles & Diana: A Royal Romance, North & South Book II, Anastasia, The Woman He Loved.

DELANY, DANA
Actress. b. New York, NY, March 13, 1956. e. Phillips Acad., Wesleyan U.
THEATER: *B'way:* Translations, A Life. *Off-B'way*: Blood Moon.
PICTURES: Almost You, Where the River Runs Black, Masquerade, Moon Over Parador, Patty Hearst, Housesitter, Light Sleeper, Batman: Mask of the Phantasm (voice), Tombstone, Exit to Eden, Live Nude Girls, Fly Away Home, Wide Awake, Looking for Lulu, The Curve, The Outfitters.

TELEVISION: *Series*: Love of Life, As the World Turns, Sweet Surrender, China Beach (2 Emmy Awards: 1989, 1992). *Guest*: Moonlighting, Magnum P.I. *Movies*: A Promise to Keep, Donato and Daughter, The Enemy Within, Choices of the Heart: The Margaret Sanger Story, For Hope, The Patron St. of Liars, Resurrection. *Mini-Series*: Wild Palms, True Women. *Specials*: Texan, Fallen Angels (Good Housekeeping), The Rescuers.

De LAURENTIIS, DINO
Producer, Executive. b. Torre Annunziata, Italy, Aug. 8, 1919. Took part in Rome Experimental Film Center; dir., prod. chmn. of the bd. and CEO, De Laurentiis Entertainment Group Inc.; founded in 1984 the DEG Film Studios in Wilmington, NC. Resigned 1988. Started Dino De Laurentiis Communications, 1990.
PICTURES: L'amore Canta, Il Bandito, La Figlia del Capitano, Riso Amaro, La Lupa, Anna, Ulysses, Mambo, La Strada, Gold of Naples, War and Peace, Nights of Cabiria, The Tempest, Great War, Five Branded Women, Everybody Go Home, Under Ten Flags, The Best of Enemies, The Unfaithfuls, Barabbas, The Bible, Operation Paradise, The Witches, The Stranger, Diabolik, Anzio, Barbarella, Waterloo, The Valachi Papers, The Stone Killer, Serpico, Death Wish, Mandingo, Three Days of the Condor, Drum, Face to Face, Buffalo Bill and the Indians, King Kong, The Shootist, Orca, White Buffalo, The Serpent's Egg, King of the Gypsies, The Brink's Job, Hurricane, Flash Gordon, Halloween II, Ragtime, Conan the Barbarian, Fighting Back, Amityville II: The Possession, Halloween III: Season of the Witch, The Dead Zone, Amityville 3-D, Firestarter, The Bounty, Conan the Destroyer, Stephen King's Cat's Eye, Red Sonja, Year of the Dragon, Marie, Stephen King's Silver Bullet, Raw Deal, Maximum Overdrive, Tai-Pan, Blue Velvet, The Bedroom Window, Crimes of the Heart, King Kong Lives, Million Dollar Mystery, Weeds, Desperate Hours, Kuffs, Once Upon a Crime, Body of Evidence, Army of Darkness, Unforgettable, Assassins.

De LAURENTIIS, RAFFAELLA
Producer. Daughter of Dino De Laurentiis. Began career as prod. asst. on father's film Hurricane. Independent prod..
PICTURES: Beyond the Reef, Conan the Barbarian, Conan the Destroyer, Dune, Tai-Pan, Prancer, Dragon: The Bruce Lee Story, Trading Mom, Dragonheart, Backdraft (exec. prod.), Timebomb, Daylight (exec. prod.), Kull the Conqueror, Black Dog.
TELEVISION: *Series*: Vanishing Son.

De La VARRE, ANDRE, JR.
Producer, Director. b. Vienna, Austria, Oct. 26, 1934. Prod. Grand Tour travelogues; prod. of promotion films for KLM, Swissair, tourist offices, recent productions: Bicentennial films for state of Virginia, city of Charleston, NY state; winner, Atlanta Film Festival, Sunset Travel Film Festival; Burton Holmes Travelogue subjects; Corporate Incentive Videos, V-P-R Educational Films; prod., director, lecturer, narrator.

DEL BELSO, RICHARD
Marketing Executive. b. Albany, NY, Aug. 9, 1939. e. Fordham U, 1961, NYU, 1965. Began career in adv./research dept. at Benton & Bowles Advertising, NY. Served as research dept. group head for Kenyon and Eckhart; group head for Grudin/Appell/Haley Research Co. (now known as A/H/F/ Marketing Research, Inc.). Two years as assoc. dir. of mktg., research for Grey Advertising (N.Y.). Joined MCA/Universal in 1976 as assoc. dir., mktg. research. In 1980 named v.p. & dir. of mktg. research for Warner Bros; became worldwide v.p. of mktg. research, 1984; named sr. v.p. worldwide theatrical film market research, 1990. In 1998, promoted to Sr. V.P. Market Strategy, Worldwide Theatrical Films.

DELON, ALAIN
Actor. b. Sceaux, France, Nov. 8, 1935. Discovered by Yves Allegret. Served in French Navy as a Marine.
PICTURES: When a Woman Gets Involved (debut, 1957), Be Beautiful and Keep Quiet, 3 Murderesses, Christine, Le Chemin Des Ecoliers, Plein Soleil (Purple Noon), Quelle Joie de Vivre!, Rocco and His Brothers, Famous Loves, Eclipse, The Leopard, The Devil and the 10 Commandments, Any Number Can Win, The Black Tulip, The Felines (Joy House), L'Insoumis (also prod., co-s.p.), The Yellow Rolls Royce, Once a Thief, Lost Command, Is Paris Burning?, Texas Across the River, The Adventurers, Spirits of the Dead, Samaurai, Diabolically Yours, Girl on a Motorcycle, Goodbye Friend, The Swimming Pool, Jeff (also prod.), The Sicilian Clan, Borsalino, The Red Circle, Madly (also prod.), Doucement Les Basses, Red Sun, The Widow Cuderc, Assassination of Trotsky, Dirty Money, The Teacher, Scorpio, Shock Treatment, The Burning Barn, Big Guns, Two Men in the City, La Race des Seigneurs, Les Seins de Glace, Borsalino & Company (also prod.), Zorro, Police Story, The Gypsy, Mr. Klein (also prod.), Like a Boomerang (also prod., s.p.), The Gang (also exec. prod.), Armaggedon, L'Homme Presse, Mort d'un Pourri (also s.p.), Attention Les Enfants Regardent, The Concorde - Airport 79, The Doctor, Teheran 43, Three Men to Destroy (also prod.), For a Cop's Honor (also dir, s.p., prod.), The Shock (also s.p.), The Cache (also prod., dir., s.p.), Swann in Love, Our Story, Military Police (also exec. prod., s.p.), The Passage (also prod.), Let Sleeping Cops Lie (also prod., co-s.p.), New Wave, Dancing Machine, The Return of Casanova, Un Crime... L'Ours en Peluche.

DELPY, JULIE
Actress. b. Paris, France, 1970. Made acting debut as teenager for dir. Jean-Luc Godard.
PICTURES: Detective (debut, 1985) Bad Blood, King Lear, Beatrice, The Dark Night, Europa Europa, Voyager, The Three Musketeers, White, Killing Zoe, Younger and Younger, Before Sunrise, An American Werewolf in Paris, The Treat, LA Without a Map, The Treat, The Passion of Ayn Rand, But I'm A Cheerleader, Villa des roses, Tell Me, Sand, Investigating Sex. *Director:* Blah Blah Blah.
TELEVISION: *Movies:* The Passion of Ayn Rand, Crime and Punishment.

DEL ROSSI, PAUL R.
Executive. b. Winchester, MA, Oct. 19, 1942. e. Harvard Coll, 1964; Harvard Business Sch., 1967. Sr. v.p., The Boston Co., 1977-1980; sr. consultant, Arthur D. Little, Inc.; presently pres. & CEO, General Cinema Theatres.

DELORA, JENNIFER
Actress, Writer, Producer. b. Kingston, NY, March 2, 1962. e. Amer. Acad. Dramatic Arts, 1982. Antioch U., BA, 1993. CA Coast U., MA, 1995; PhD, 1997. Artistic Dir., LA Bridges Theatre Co. of the Deaf, 1993-present. Top industry technical advisor for projects involving deafness, 1995-present. Member AFTRA, SAG, ATAS, Amer. Bd. of Disability Analysts, Nat'l Assoc. of the Deaf, Deaf Artists of Amer., Deaf Entertainment Guild, Amer. Psych. Assoc.
PICTURES: *Actor*: Bad Girls' Dormitory, Young Nurses in Love, Robot Holocaust, New York's Finest, Deranged, Sexpot, Cleo/Leo, Frankenhooker, Deadly Manor, Bedroom Eyes II, Suburban Commando. *Tech. Advisor:* 413 Hope Street, His Bodyguard, Copland, Tango & Flush.
TELEVISION: *Movies*: Breaking Through, Blue Rodeo. *Tech. Advisor:* 7th Heaven.

DeLUCA, MICHAEL
Executive, Writer. b. Brooklyn, Aug., 1965. Left NYU to take intern job at New Line Cinema; became story editor before becoming production exec. in 1989. 1993 named pres. of production of New Line.
PICTURES: *Writer*: Freddy's Dead: The Final Nightmare, In the Mouth of Madness, Judge Dredd (story), B.A.P.S. (exec. prod.).

De LUISE, DOM
Comedian, Actor. b. Brooklyn, NY, Aug. 1, 1933. e. Tufts Coll. m. actress Carol Arthur. Sons: Peter, Michael, David. Spent two seasons with Cleveland Playhouse. Launched TV career on The Garry Moore Show with character, Dominick the Great.
THEATER: Little Mary Sunshine, Another Evening With Harry Stoones, All in Love, Half-Past Wednesday, Too Much Johnson, The Student Gypsy, Last of the Red Hot Lovers, Here's Love, Little Shop of Horrors, Die Fledermus (NY Met. Opera: 2 seasons), Peter and the Wolf.
PICTURES: Fail Safe (debut, 1964), Diary of a Bachelor, The Glass Bottom Boat, The Busy Body, What's So Bad About Feeling Good?, Norwood, The Twelve Chairs, Who Is Harry Kellerman...?, Every Little Crook and Nanny, Blazing Saddles, The Adventure of Sherlock Holmes' Smarter Brother, Silent Movie, The World's Greatest Lover, The End, The Cheap Detective, Sextette, The Muppet Movie, Hot Stuff (also dir.), The Last Married Couple in America, Fatso, Wholly Moses, Smokey and the Bandit II, History of the World Part I, The Cannonball Run, The Best Little Whorehouse in Texas, The Secret of NIMH (voice), Cannonball Run II, Johnny Dangerously, Haunted Honeymoon, An American Tail (voice), Spaceballs (voice), A Taxi Driver in New York, Going Bananas, Oliver & Company (voice), All Dogs Go To Heaven (voice), Loose Cannons, Driving Me Crazy, Fievel Goes West (voice), Munchie (voice), The Skateboard Kid (voice), Happily Ever After (voice), Robin Hood: Men in Tights, The Silence of the Hams, A Troll in Central Park (voice), All Dogs Go to Heaven 2 (voice), Boys Will Be Boys, The Good Bad Guys, The Godson, An All Dogs Christmas Carol, Wedding Band, Baby Geniuses.
TELEVISION: *Series*: The Entertainers, The Dean Martin Summer Show, Dom DeLuise Show, The Barrum-Bump Show, The Glenn Campbell Goodtime Hour, The Dean Martin Show, Lotsa Luck, Dom DeLuise Show (synd.), The New Candid Camera, Fievel's American Tails (voice), All Dogs Go To Heaven: The Series, Burke's Law. *Movies*: Evil Roy Slade, Only With Married Men, Happy (also exec. prod.), Don't Drink the Water, The Tin Soldier. *Guest*: The Munsters, Please Don't Eat the Daises, Ghost and Mrs. Muir, Medical Center, Amazing Stories, Easy Street, B.L. Stryker, Burke's Law, Murphy Brown, Beverly Hills 90210.

DEMME, JONATHAN
Director, Writer, Producer. b. Rockville Centre, NY, Feb. 22, 1944. e. U. of Florida. First job in industry as usher; was film critic for college paper, The Florida Alligator and the Coral Gable Times. Did publicity work for United Artists, Avco Embassy; sold films for Pathe Contemporary Films; wrote for trade paper, Film Daily, 1966-68. Moved to England in 1969; musical co-ordinator on Irving Allen's EyeWitness in 1970. In 1972 co-prod and co-wrote first film, Angels Hard As They Come. Appeared in film Into the Night.

PICTURES: Hot Box (prod., co-s.p.), Black Mama White Mama (story). Director: Caged Heat (also s.p.), Crazy Mama (also s.p.), Fighting Mad (also s.p.), Citizen's Band (Handle With Care), Last Embrace, Melvin and Howard, Swing Shift, Stop Making Sense, Something Wild (also co-prod.), Swimming to Cambodia, Married to the Mob, Miami Blues (prod. only), The Silence of the Lambs (Acad. Award, 1991), Cousin Bobby, Philadelphia (also co-prod.), Devil in a Blue Dress (exec. prod. only), That Thing You Do! (prod. only), Beloved (also prod.).
TELEVISION: *Specials*: Who Am I This Time?, Accumation With Talking plus Water Motor, Survival Guides, A Family Tree (Trying Times series, PBS), Haiti: Dreams of Democracy. *Movie*: Women & Men 2 (A Domestic Dilemma; prod. only), Subway Stories: Tales from the Underground.

DEMME, TED
Director. b. New York, NY, Oct. 26, 1964.
PICTURES: Who's the Man, The Ref, Beautiful Girls, Snitch (also prod.), Rounders (prod. only), Tumbleweeds (exec. prod. only), Life, Blow.
TELEVISION: *Movies:* Subway Stories: Tales from the Underground (also actor), A Lesson Before Dying (exec. prod. only). *Series:* Yo! MTV Raps (prod. only), Homicide: Life on the Streets, Robert Altman's Gun, Action.

DE MORNAY, REBECCA
Actress. b. Santa Rosa, CA, Aug. 29, 1962. Spent childhood in Europe, graduating from high school in Austria. Returned to America, enrolling at Lee Strasberg's Los Angeles Institute; apprenticed at Zoetrope Studios.
THEATER: Born Yesterday (Pasadena Playhouse), Marat/Sade (Williamstown Fest.).
PICTURES: Risky Business, Testament, The Slugger's Wife, Runaway Train, The Trip to Bountiful, Beauty and the Beast, And God Created Woman, Feds, Dealers, Backdraft, The Hand That Rocks the Cradle, Guilty as Sin, The Three Musketeers, Never Talk to Strangers (also exec. prod.), The Winner (also exec. prod.), Thick As Thieves, A Table for One.
TELEVISION: *Movies*: The Murders in the Rue Morgue, By Dawn's Early Light, An Inconvenient Woman, Blindside, Getting Out, The Shining, The Con, Night Ride Home.

DEMPSEY, PATRICK
Actor. b. Lewiston, ME, Jan. 13, 1966. e. St. Dominic Regional h.s. in Lewiston where he became State downhill skiing champion. Juggling, magic and puppetry led to performances before Elks clubs and community orgs. Cast by Maine Acting Co. in On Golden Pond. In 1983 acted in Torch Song Trilogy in San Francisco and toured in Brighton Beach Memoirs. NY Theatre debut, 1991 in The Subject Was Roses.
PICTURES: Heaven Help Us (debut, 1985), Meatballs III, Can't Buy Me Love, In the Mood, In a Shallow Grave, Some Girls, Loverboy, Coupe de Ville, Happy Together, Run, Mobsters, For Better and For Worse, Face the Music, Bank Robber, With Honors, Outbreak, Hugo Pool, The Treat, There 's No Fish Food in Heaven, Me and Will, Denial, Scream 3.
TELEVISION: *Movies*: A Fighting Choice, JFK: Reckless Youth, Bloodknot, Jeremiah, Crime and Punishment, 2000 Leagues Under the Sea. *Series*: Fast Times at Ridgemont High. *Special*: Merry Christmas Baby.

De MUNN, JEFFREY
Actor. b. Buffalo, NY, April 25, 1947. e. Union Col. Studied acting at Old Vic Theatre in Bristol, Eng.
THEATER: *NY*: Comedians, A Prayer for My Daughter, Modigliani, Augusta, Hands of Its Enemy, Chekhov Sketchbook, A Midsummer Night's Dream, Total Abandon, Country Girl, Bent, K-2, Sleight of Hand, Spoils of War, One Shoe Off, Hedda Gabler, Gunshy.
PICTURES: You Better Watch Out (Christmas Evil), The First Deadly Sin, Resurrection, Ragtime, I'm Dancing as Fast as I Can, Frances, Windy City, Enormous Changes at the Last Minute, Warning Sign, The Hitcher, The Blob, Betrayed, Blaze, Newsies, Eyes of an Angel, The Shawshank Redemption, Safe Passage, Killer, Phenomenon, Turbulence, Rocket Man, Harvest, The X-Files.
TELEVISION: *Movies*: The Last Tenant, Sanctuary of Fear, King Crab, Word of Honor, I Married Wyatt Earp, The Face of Rage, Sessions, When She Says No, Windmills of the Gods, Lincoln, Doubletake, A Time to Live, Who Is Julia?, Young Harry Houdini, Price of Justice, Switch, Elysian Fields, The Haunted, Treacherous Crossing, Jonathan: The Boy Nobody Wanted, Barbarians at the Gate, Crash: The Fate of Flight 1502, Settle the Score, Under the Influence, Betrayal of Trust, Citizen X, Down Came a Blackbird, Hiroshima, Almost Golden: The Jessica Savitch Story, A Christmas Memory, Path to Paradise, Black Cat Run, Storm of the Century. *Specials*: Mourning Becomes Electra, Peacemaker (Triple Play II), Sensiblity and Sense, The Joy That Kills, Teacher, Pigeon Feathers, Many Mansions, Wild Jackasses, Ebbie. *Mini-series*: Night Sins, Liberty! The American Revolution.

DENCH, DAME JUDI
Actress. b. York, England, Dec. 9, 1934. Studied for stage at Central Sch. of Speech and Drama. Theatre debut Old Vic, 1957. Created a Dame in 1988 Honours List. Recent Theatre: Cymbeline, Juno and the Paycock, A Kind of Alaska, The Cherry Orchard, The Plough and the Stars, Importance of Being Earnest, Pack of Lies, Mr. and Mrs. Nobody, Antony and Cleopatra, The Sea, Coriolanus, The Gift of the Gorgon, The Seagull. Director: Much Ado About Nothing, Look Back in Anger, Boys from Syracuse, Romeo and Juliet, Absolute Hell, A Little Night Music.
PICTURES: The Third Secret (debut, 1964), He Who Rides a Tiger, A Study in Terror, Four in the Morning, A Midsummer Night's Dream (RSC Prod.), Luther, Dead Cert, Wetherby, A Room With a View, 84 Charing Cross Road, A Handful of Dust, Henry V, Jack and Sarah, Goldeneye, Hamlet, Mrs. Brown (BAFTA Award, Golden Globe Award, Chicago Film Crits. Award, Best Actress, 1997), Tomorrow Never Dies, Shakespeare in Love (Acad. Award Best Supp. Actress), Tea with Mussolini, The World is Not Enough, Into the Arms of Strangers: Stories of the Kindertransport, Chocolat, Therese Raquin.
TELEVISION: Major Barbara, Pink String and Sealing Wax, Talking to a Stranger, The Funambulists, Age of Kings, Jackanory, Hilda Lessways, Luther, Neighbours, Parade's End, Marching Song, On Approval, Days to Come, Emilie, The Comedy of Errors (RSC Prod.), Macbeth (RSC Prod.), Langrishe Go Down, On Giant's Shoulders, Love in a Cold Climate, Village Wooing, A Fine Romance (series), The Cherry Orchard, Going Gently, Saigon—Year of the Cat, Ghosts, Behaving Badly, Torch, Can You Hear Me Thinking?, Absolute Hell, As Time Goes By (series).

DENEUVE, CATHERINE
Actress. r.n. Catherine Dorleac. b. Paris, France, Oct. 22, 1943. Sister was the late Francoise Dorleac. Made screen debut as teen using adopting mother's maiden name.
PICTURES: Les Collegiennes (debut, 1956), Wild Roots of Love, L'homme a Femmes, The Doors Slam, La Parisiennes (segment: Sophie), Vice and Virtue, Satan Leads the Dance, Vacances Portugaises, Les Plus Belles Escroqueries du Monde, The Umbrellas of Cherbourg (Cannes Film Fest. Award, 1964), Male Hunt (La Chasse a l'Homme), Male Companion, La Costanza della Ragione, Repulsion, Le Chant du Monde, La Vie de Chateau (A Matter of Resistance), Who Wants to Sleep?, Les Creatures, The Young Girls of Rochefort, Belle de Jour (Venice Film Fest. Award, 1967), Benjamin, Manon 70, Mayerling, La Chamade (Heartbeat), The April Fools, Mississippi Mermaid, Don't Be Blue, Tristana, Donkey Skin, Henri Langolis, Liza, It Only Happens to Others, Dirty Money, Melampo, The Slightly Pregnant Man, Touche Pas a la Femme Blanche, La Grande Bourgeoise, Zig-Zag, La Femme aux Bottes Rouges, Hustle, Lovers Like Us, Act of Agression, The Beach Hut, Second Chance, March or Die, Ecoute voir, L'Argent des Autres, When I Was a Kid I Didn't Dare, Anima Persa, An Adventure for Two, Ils Sont Grandes ces Petits, Courage--Let's Run, The Last Metro, Je vous Aime, Choice of Arms, Hotel des Ameriques, Reporters, Daisy Chain, Le Choc, The African, The Hunger, Le Bon Plaisir, Fort Saganne, Love Songs, Let's Hope It's a Girl, Le Mauvaise Herbe, Scene of the Crime, Agent Trouble, A Strange Place to Meet (also prod.), Hotel Panique, The Man Who Loved Zoos, Frequency Murder, Helmut Newton: Frames From the Edge (doc.), The White Queen, Indochine (Acad. Award nom.), Ma Saison Preferee (My Favorite Season), The Chess Game, The Convent, The Child of the Night, Genealogies of a Crime, Place Vendome, Time Regained, The Last Napoleon, East-West, The Letter, Belle Maman, Pola X, Dancer in the Dark, Tom Thumb, D'Artagnan.

DENHAM, MAURICE
O.B.E., 1992: Actor. b. Beckenham, Kent, England, Dec. 23, 1909. e. Tonbridge Sch. Started theatrical career with repertory com. 1934. Served in W.W.II. In numerous plays, films & radio shows.
PICTURES: Blanche Fury, London Belongs To Me, It's Not Cricket, Traveller's Joy, Landfall, Spider and the Fly, No Highway in the Sky, The Net, Time Bomb, Street Corner (Both Sides of the Law), Million Pound Note (Man With a Million), Eight O'Clock Walk, Purple Plain, Simon and Laura, 23 Paces to Baker Street, Checkpoint, Carrington V.C. (Court Martial), Doctor at Sea, Night of the Demon, Man With a Dog, Barnacle Bill, The Captain's Table, Our Man in Havana, Sink the Bismark, Two-Way Stretch, Greengage Summer, Invasion, Quartette, The Mark, HMS Defiant, The Very Edge, Paranoiac, The Set Up, Penang, The King's Breakfast, Downfall, Hysteria, The Uncle, Operation Crossbow, Legend of Dick Turpin, The Alphabet Murders, The Night Callers, The Nanny, Those Magnificent Men in Their Flying Machines, Heroes of Telemark, After the Fox, The Torture Garden, The Long Duel, The Eliminator, Danger Route, Attack on the Iron Coast, The Best House in London, Negatives, The Midas Run, Some Girls Do, The Touch of Love, The Virgin and the Gypsy, Bloody Sunday, Countess Dracula, Nicholas and Alexandra, The Day of the Jackal, Luther, Shout at the Devil, Julia, The Recluse, From a Far Country, Mr. Love, The Chain, Monsignor Quixote, Murder on the Orient Express, 84 Charing Cross Road.

TELEVISION: Uncle Harry, Day of the Monkey, Miss Mabel, Angel Pavement, The Paraguayan Harp, The Wild Bird, Soldier Soldier, Changing Values, Maigret, The Assassins, Saturday Spectacular, Vanishing Act, A Chance in Life, Virtue, Somerset Maugham, Three of a Kind, Sapper, Pig in the Middle, Their Obedient Servants, Long Past Glory, Devil in The Wind, Any Other Business, The Retired Colourman, Sherlock Holmes (series), Blackmail, Knock on Any Door, Danger Man, Dr. Finley's Casebook, How to Get Rid of Your Husband, Talking to a Stranger, A Slight Ache, From Chekhov with Love, Home Sweet Honeycomb, St. Joan, Julius Caesar, Golden Days, Marshall Petain, The Lotus Eaters, Fall of Eagles, Carnforth Practice. The Unofficial Rose, Omnibus, Balzac, Loves Labour Lost, Angels, Huggy Bear, The Portrait, The Crumbles Murder, A Chink In The Wall, Porridge, For God's Sake, Bosch, Marie Curie, Upchat Line, Secret Army, My Son, My Son, Edward and Mrs. Simpson, Gate of Eden, Potting Shed, Double Dealer, Minder, Agatha Christie Hour, Chinese Detective, The Old Men at the Zoo, The Hope and the Glory, Luther, Love Song, Mr. Palfrey, The Black Tower, Boon, Rumpole, All Passions Spent, Trial of Klaus Barbie, Miss Marple, Tears in the Rain, Behaving Badly, Seeing in the Dark, Inspector Morse: Fat Chance, La Nonna, Lovejoy, Memento Mori, Sherlock Holmes, The Last Vampire, Peak Pratice, Bed, The Bill, Prisoner In Time, Pie In The Sky.

De NIRO, ROBERT
Actor. b. New York, NY, Aug. 17, 1943. Studied acting with Stella Adler and Lee Strasberg; 1988, formed Tribeca Film Center in NY. Co-Prod. of film Thunderheart.
THEATER: One Night Stand of a Noisy Passenger (Off-B'way), Cuba and His Teddy Bear (Public Theater and B'way; Theatre World Award).
PICTURES: The Wedding Party (debut, 1969), Greetings, Sam's Song (The Swap), Bloody Mama, Hi Mom, Born to Win, Jennifer on My Mind, The Gang That Couldn't Shoot Straight, Bang the Drum Slowly, Mean Streets, The Godfather Part II (Acad. Award, best supporting actor, 1974), Taxi Driver, The Last Tycoon, New York New York, 1900, The Deer Hunter, Raging Bull (Acad. Award, 1980), True Confessions, The King of Comedy, Once Upon a Time in America, Falling in Love, Brazil, The Mission, Angel Heart, The Untouchables, Midnight Run, Jacknife, We're No Angels, Stanley and Iris, GoodFellas, Awakenings, Guilty by Suspicion, Backdraft, Cape Fear, Mistress (also co-prod.), Night and the City, Mad Dog and Glory, This Boy's Life, A Bronx Tale (also dir., co-prod.), Mary Shelley's Frankenstein, Casino, Heat, Marvin's Room (also exec. prod.), The Fan, Sleepers, Stolen Flower, Cop Land, Jackie Brown, Wag the Dog (also prod.), Great Expectations, Ronin, Analyze This, Flawless, Adventures of Rocky and Bullwinkle, Men of Honor, Meet the Parents, Fifteen Minutes, The Score.
TELEVISION: *Specials*: Night of 100 Stars, Dear America: Letters Home From Vietnam (reader), Lenny Bruce: Swear to Tell the Truth.

DENNEHY, BRIAN
Actor. b. Bridgeport, CT, July 9, 1939. e. Columbia U. In Marine Corps five years, including Vietnam. After discharge in 1965 studied with acting coaches in N.Y., while working at part time jobs as a salesman, bartender, truck driver.
THEATER: Streamers, Galileo (Goodman Th.), The Cherry Orchard, Translations, Death of a Salesman.
PICTURES: Looking for Mr. Goodbar, Semi-Tough, F.I.S.T., Foul Play, 10, Butch and Sundance: The Early Days, Little Miss Marker, Split Image, First Blood, Never Cry Wolf, Gorky Park, Finders Keepers, River Rat, Cocoon, Silverado, Twice in a Lifetime, F/X, Legal Eagles, The Check Is in the Mail, Best Seller, The Belly of an Architect, Return to Snowy River Part II, Miles From Home, Cocoon: The Return, The Last of the Finest, Presumed Innocent, FX2, Gladiator, Seven Minutes, Tommy Boy, The Stars Fell on Henrietta, Midnight Movie, Romeo and Juliet, Gilligan's Island.
TELEVISION: *Series:* Big Shamus Little Shamus, Star of the Family, Birdland. *Movies*: Johnny We Hardly Knew Ye, It Happened at Lake Wood Manor, Ruby and Oswald, A Death in Canaan, A Real American Hero, Silent Victory: The Kitty O'Neil Story, The Jericho Mile, Dummy, The Seduction of Miss Leona, A Rumor of War, Fly Away Home, Skokie, I Take These Men, Blood Feud, Off Sides, Acceptable Risks, Private Sessions, The Lion of Africa, A Father's Revenge, Day One, Perfect Witness, Pride and Extreme Prejudice, Rising Son, A Killing in a Small Town, In Broad Daylight, The Burden of Proof, To Catch a Killer, Diamond Fleece, Teamster: The Jackie Presser Story, Deadly Matrimony, Foreign Affairs, Murder in the Heartland, Prophet of Evil: The Ervil LeBaron Story, Final Appeal, Jack Reed: Badge of Honor (also co-exec. prod.), Leave of Absence, Jack Reed: Search for Justice (also dir., co-writer), Contagious, Indefensible: The Truth About Edward Brannigan (also dir.), Voyage of Terror. *Mini-Series:* Evergreen, Thanks of a Grateful Nation, Too Rich: The Secret Life of Doris Duke, Netforce. *Guest*: M*A*S*H, Lou Grant, Cagney and Lacey, Hunter, Tall Tales (Annie Oakley), Just Shoot Me. *Special*: Dear America: Letter Home From Vietnam (reader).

DENVER, BOB
Actor. b. New Rochelle, NY, Jan. 9, 1935. e. Loyola U.
PICTURES: A Private's Affair, Take Her She's Mine, For Those Who Think Young, Who's Minding the Mint? The Sweet Ride, Did You Hear the One About the Travelling Saleslady?, Back to the Beach.
TELEVISION: *Series*: The Many Loves of Dobie Gillis, Gilligan's Island, The Good Guys, Dusty's Trail. *Movies*: Rescue from Gilligan's Island, The Castaways on Gilligan's Island, The Harlem Globetrotters on Gilligans Island, The Invisible Woman, High School USA, Bring Me the Head of Dobie Gillis. Also: Far Out Space Nuts, Scamps.

De PALMA, BRIAN
Director, Writer, Producer. b. Newark, NJ, Sept. 11, 1940. e. Columbia U.,B.A.; Sarah Lawrence, M.A. While in college made series of shorts, including Wotan's Wake, winner of Rosenthal Foundation Award for best film made by American under 25. Also judged most popular film of Midwest Film Festival (1963); later shown at San Francisco Film Festival. Dir.: The Responsive Eye (doc., 1966).
PICTURES: *Director*: Murder a La Mod (also s.p., edit.), Greetings (also co-s.p. ed.), The Wedding Party (also co-s.p., co-prod., ed.), Hi Mom (also co-story, s.p.), Dionysus in '69 (also co-prod., co-photog., co-ed.), Get To Know Your Rabbit, Sisters (also co-s.p.), Phantom of the Paradise (also co-s.p.), Obsession (also co-story), Carrie, The Fury, Home Movies (also s.p., co-prod.), Dressed to Kill (also s.p.), Blow Out (also s.p.), Scarface, Body Double (also prod., s.p.), Wiseguys, The Untouchables, Casualties of War, The Bonfire of the Vanities (also prod.), Raising Cain (also s.p.), Carlito's Way, Mission: Impossible, Snake Eyes (also prod., story), Mission to Mars, Mr. Hughes.

DEPARDIEU, GÉRARD
Actor. b. Chateauroux, France, Dec. 27, 1948. Studied acting at Theatre National Populaire in Paris. Made film debut at 16 in short by Roger Leenhardt (Le Beatnik et Le Minet). Acted in feature film by Agnes Varda (uncompleted).
PICTURES: Le Cri du Cormoran le Soir au-dessis des Jonques, Nathalie Granger, A Little Sun in Cold Water, Le Tueur, L'Affaire Dominici, Au Renedez-vous de la mort joyeuse, La Scoumone, Rude Journee our la Reine, Deux Hommes dans la Ville, The Holes, Going Places, Stavisky, Woman of the Granges, Vincent Francois Paul and the Others, The Wonderful Crook, 7 Morts sur ordonnance, Maitresse, Je t'Aime Moi Non Plus, The Last Woman, 1900, Barocco, Rene la Canne, Baxter Vera Baxter, The Truck, Tell Him I Love Him, At Night All Cats Are Gray, Get Out Your Handkerchiefs, The Left-Handed Woman, Bye Bye Monkey, Violanta, Le Sucre, Les Chiens, L'Ingorgo, Buffet Froid, Temporale Rosy, Mon Oncle d'Amerique, Loulou, The Last Metro, Inspector Blunder, I Love You, Choice of Arms, The Woman Next Door, Le Chevre. The Return of Martin Guerre, The Big Brother, Danton, The Moon in the Gutter, Les Comperes (also co-prod.), Fort Saganne, Le Tartuffe (also dir., co-s.p), Rive Droie Rive Gauche, Police, One Woman or Two, Menage, Ru du depart, Jean De Florette (also co-prod.), Under Satan's Sun (also co-prod.), A Strange Place for an Enounter (also co-prod.), Camille Claudel (also co-prod.), Dreux, Too Beautiful for You (also co-prod.), I Want to Go Home, Cyrano de Bergerac (also co-prod), Green Card, Uranus, Thanks for Life, Mon Pere ce Heros (My Father the Hero), 1492: Conquest of Paradise, Tous les Matins du Monde (All the Mornings of the World), Helas Pour Moi (Oh Woe is Me), Une Pure Formalite (A Pure Formality), Germinal, My Father the Hero, Colonel Chabert, La Machine, Elisa, Les Anges Gardiens, The Horseman on the Roof, Bogus, Le Garcu, She's So Lovely (exec.prod. only), Hamlet, XXL, The Man in the Iron Mask, La Parola Amore Esiste, Bimboland, Vidocq, Vatel, Mirka, Asterix and Obelix vs. Caesar, Un Pont Entre Deux Rives (also prod., dir.).

DEPP, JOHNNY
Actor. b. Owensboro, KY, June 9, 1963. Raised in Miramar, FL. Played lead guitar with band The Kids, with whom he moved to L.A. in 1983. With no prior acting experience made film debut in A Nightmare on Elm Street.
PICTURES: A Nightmare on Elm Street (debut, 1984), Private Resort, Platoon, Cry-Baby, Edward Scissorhands, Freddy's Dead: The Final Nightmare (cameo), Benny & Joon, What's Eating Gilbert Grape?, Ed Wood, Don Juan DeMarco, Dead Man, Nick of Time, Donnie Brasco, The Brave (also dir.),L.A. Without A Map, Just to Be Together, Fear and Loathing in Las Vegas, The Source, The Libertine, The Ninth Gate, The Astronauts Wife, Sleepy Hollow, The Man Who Cried, Chocolat, Blow, The Man Who Killed Don Quixote, From Hell.
TELEVISION: *Series*: 21 Jump Street. *Movie*: Slow Burn. *Guest*: Lady Blue.

DEPREZ, THERESE
Production Designer. b. 1966.
PICTURES: The Refrigerator, Swoon, The Outfit, Postcards from America, Living in Oblivion, Stonewall, The Doom Generation, I Shot Andy Warhol, Box of Moonlight, Grind, Going All the Way, No Looking Back, Happiness, Arlington Road, Summer of Sam, High Fidelity, Hedwig and the Angry Inch, Caveman's Valentine.
TELEVISION: *Movies*: Dottie Gets Spanked, Path to Paradise: The Untold Story of the World Trade Center Bombing.

DEREK, BO
Actress. r.n. Mary Cathleen Collins. b. Torrance, CA., Nov. 20, 1956. Discovered by actor-turned-filmmaker John Derek, whom she married.
PICTURES: Orca (debut, 1977), 10, A Change of Seasons, Fantasies (And Once Upon a Time), Tarzan the Ape Man (also prod.), Bolero (also prod.), Ghosts Can't Do It (also prod.), Hot Chocolate, Sognando la California (California Dreaming), Woman of Desire, Tommy Boy.
TELEVISION: *Movie*: Shattered Image, Wind on Water.

DERN, BRUCE
Actor. b. Chicago, IL, June 4, 1936. e. U. of Pennsylvania. Daughter is actress Laura Dern. Studied acting with Gordon Phillips, member, Actor's Studio, 1959 after N.Y. debut in Shadow of a Gunman. Broadway: Sweet Bird of Youth, Orpheus Descending, Strangers. Film Awards: Natl. Society of Film Critics (Drive He Said, 1971), People's Choice (Coming Home, 1978), Genie (Middle Age Crazy, 1980), Silver Bear (That Championship Season, 1982).
PICTURES: Wild River (debut, 1960), Marnie, Hush...Hush Sweet Charlotte, The Wild Angels, The St. Valentine's Day Massacre, Waterhole No. 3, The Trip, The War Wagon, Psych-Out, Rebel Rousers, Hang 'Em High, Will Penny, Number One, Castle Keep, Support Your Local Sheriff, They Shoot Horses Don't They?, Cycle Savages, Bloody Mama, The Incredible Two-Headed Transplant, Drive He Said, Silent Running, Thumb Tripping, The Cowboys, The King of Marvin Gardens, The Laughing Policeman, The Great Gatsby, Smile, Posse, Family Plot, Won Ton Ton the Dog Who Saved Hollywood, The Twist (Folies Bourgeoises), Black Sunday, Coming Home (Acad. Award nom.), The Driver, Middle Age Crazy, Tattoo, Harry Tracy: Desperado, That Championship Season, On the Edge, The Big Town, World Gone Wild, 1969, The 'burbs, After Dark My Sweet, Diggstown, Wild Bill, Down Periscope, Mulholland Falls, Last Man Standing, Small Soldiers (voice), If...Dog...Rabbit, The Haunting, All the Pretty Horses.
TELEVISION: *Series*: Stoney Burke. *Mini-Series*: Space. *Movies*: Sam Hill: Who Killed the Mysterious Mr. Foster?, Toughlove, Roses Are for the Rich, Uncle Tom's Cabin, Trenchcoat in Paradise, The Court-Martial of Jackie Robinson, Into the Badlands, Carolina Skeletons, It's Nothing Personal, Deadman's Revenge, Amelia Earhart: The Final Flight, A Mother's Prayer, Comfort Texas, Perfect Prey, Hard Time. *Guest:* Naked City, Ben Casey, The Virginian, Twelve O'Clock High, The Big Valley, Gunsmoke, The FBI, Land of the Giants, Fallen Angels.

DERN, LAURA
Actress. b. Los Angeles, CA, Feb. 10, 1967. Daughter of actors Diane Ladd and Bruce Dern. At age 5 appeared with mother on daytime serial The Secret Storm. Was an extra in several of her father's films and her mother's Alice Doesn't Live Here Anymore. Studied acting at RADA appearing on stage in Hamlet, A Midsummer Night's Dream.
THEATER: *NY*: The Palace of Amateurs. *LA*: Brooklyn Laundry.
PICTURES: White Lightning (debut, 1973), Alice Doesn't Live Here Anymore, Foxes, Ladies and Gentlemen: The Fabulous Stains, Teachers, Mask, Smooth Talk, Blue Velvet, Haunted Summer, Fat Man and Little Boy, Wild at Heart, Rambling Rose (Acad. Award nom.), Jurassic Park, A Perfect World, Bastard Out of Carolina, Citizen Ruth, October Sky, Dr. T and the Women, Novocaine, Daddy and Them, Jurassic Park III, Focus.
TELEVISION: *Movies*: Happy Endings, Three Wishes of Billy Greer, Afterburn (Golden Globe Award), Down Came a Blackbird, Ruby Ridge: An American Tragedy, The Baby Dance. *Special*: The Gift (dir., co-story only). *Guest*: Fallen Angels, Frasier, Ellen.

DE SANTIS, GREGORY JOSEPH
Producer, Writer, Director. b. Los Angeles, CA, July 12, 1955. e. Durham Univ.; Canaan Coll. Pres., Millennium Mulitmedia.
PICTURES: *Prod.*: The Companion, Car Trouble, Pass the Buck, Die Sister Die!, Diary of a Surfing Film, Firepower, The Forest.
TELEVISION: *Prod.*: Volleyball: A Sport Come of Age, The Nature Series, Caribou Crossing, California Day, Midnight Son, Lightning, Mysterious River.

DESCHANEL, CALEB
Cinematographer, Director. b. Philadelphia, PA, Sept. 21, 1944. m. actress Mary Jo Deschanel. e. Johns Hopkins U., U. of Southern California Film Sch. Studied at AFI, interned under Gordon Willis then made commercials, short subjects, docs.
PICTURES: *Cinematographer*: More American Graffiti, Being There, The Black Stallion, Apocalypse Now (2nd unit photog.), The Right Stuff, Let's Spend the Night Together (co-cinematographer), The Natural, The Slugger's Wife, It Could Happen to You, Flying Wild. *Director:* The Escape Artist, Crusoe.

De TOTH, ANDRE
Writer, Director, Producer. b. Hungary. Dir.-writer European films, 1931-39; U.S. assoc. Alexander Korda prod., 1940; dir. Columbia, 1943; assoc. David Selznick, 1943; assoc. Hunt Stromberg-UA, 1944-45; staff dir., Enterprise 1946-47; dir., 20th-Fox, 1948-49; collab. story, The Gunfighter; assoc., Sam Spiegel, Horizon Pictures, Columbia, 1962; Harry Saltzman, Lowndes Prod., U.A. 1966-68; National General, 1969-70.
PICTURES: Passport to Suez, None Shall Escape, Pitfall, Slattery's Hurricane, Springfield Rifle, Thunder Over the Plains, House of Wax, The Stranger Wore a Gun, Bounty Hunter, Tanganyika, The Indian Fighter, Monkey on My Back, Two Headed Spy, Day of the Outlaw, Man on a String, Morgan The Pirate, The Mongols, Gold for the Caesars, Billion Dollar Brain (exec. prod. only), Play Dirty (also exec. prod.), El Condor (prod. only), The Dangerous Game.

DEUTCH, HOWARD
Director. b. New York, NY. e. Ohio State U. m. actress Lea Thompson. Son of music publisher Murray Deutch. Spent 10 yrs. working in various film media, including music videos and film trailer advertising, before feature debut with Pretty in Pink, 1986.
PICTURES: Pretty in Pink, Some Kind of Wonderful, The Great Outdoors, Article 99, Getting Even With Dad, Grumpier Old Men, The Odd Couple II.
TELEVISION: *Series*: Tales from the Crypt (2 episodes; ACE Award for Dead Right), Caroline in the City.

DEUTCHMAN, IRA J.
Executive. b. Cherry Point, NC, March 24, 1953. e. Northwestern U., B.S., majoring in film. Began career with Cinema 5, Ltd. serving, 1975-79, as non-theatrical sls. mgr.; dir. theatrical adv./pub./dir. acquisitions. Joined United Artists Classics, 1981 as dir. of adv./pub. 1982, left to become one of the founding partners in Cinecom Intl. Films, where headed mktg./dist. div. from inception. In Jan. 1989 formed the Deutchman Company, Inc., a production company and marketing consultancy firm. Founded and served as pres. of Fine Line Features, a division of New Line Cinema, and sr. v.p. of parent corp, 1991-95. Currenly, pres. of Redeemable Features, a New York-based prod. company. Adjunct prof. Columbia U. film dept. On advisory board Sundance Film Festival.
PICTURES: *Exec. Prod.*: Swimming to Cambodia, Matewan (assoc. prod.), Miles From Home (co-exec. prod.), Scenes from the Class Struggle in Beverly Hills, Straight Out of Brooklyn, Waterland, The Ballad of Little Jo, Mrs. Parker and the Vicious Circle, Lulu on the Bridge. *Producer*: Kiss Me Guido, 54, The Hairy Bird a.k.a. Strike!, Way Past Cool.

DEUTCHMAN, LAWRENCE SCOT
Executive. b. Bronx, NY, Dec. 10, 1960. e. Rutgers U. Wrote, prod. & dir. Mythbusters campaign. 1986-92, various positions: Entertainment Industries Council, Inc.; wrote, prod., co-dir. That's a Wrap campaign. 1986-88, board member, Public Interest Radio & Television Educational Society. 1987-88, wrote, exec. prod., post-prod. sprv., Buckle Up educational & music video (CINE Golden Eagle). 1989: EIC: An Industry in Action (writer, prod., dir.); Campaigns: Natl. Red Ribbon, Office for Substance Abuse Prevention (writer, dir., exec. prod.), Stop the Madness (co-writer, prod.). 1990, developed: Vince & Larry: The Amazing Crash Test Dummies (series, NBC), Drug Proofing Your Kids (TV special); Campaigns: Alcoholism Runs in Families, Texas Prevention Partnership (dir., exec. prod.), They Do as You Do (writer, exec. prod.). 1991: The Inhalant Problem in Texas docum. (co-exec. prod.), Inhalants: The Silent Epidemic award-winning drama (writer, co-exec. prod.), KBVO Fox Kids Club segments (writer, prod., set designer), The Incredible Crash Dummies toy property (co-creator), Ollie Odorfree property (creator). 1992-present: Pres., Dynamic Comm. Intl. Inc.; v.p. prod. & mktg., EIC. 1993: Hollywood Gets M.A.D.D. TV special (co-prod., TBS, TNT, synd.). 1994: Dinorock Time TV series (exec. prod., writer.); 1994-present, s.r., vp. prod. & mktg, EIC.

DEUTSCH, STEPHEN
Producer. b. Los Angeles, CA, June 30, 1946. e. UCLA, B.A.; Loyola Law Sch., 1974. Son of late S. Sylvan Simon. Stepson of Armand Deutsch. Private law practice before joining Rastar 1976 as asst. to Ray Stark; 1977, sr. v.p., Rastar; prod. head for SLM Inc. Film Co. entered independent prod. 1978.
PICTURES: Somewhere in Time, All the Right Moves, Russkies (co-exec. prod.), She's Out of Control, Bill & Ted's Excellent Adventure (exec. prod.), Lucky Stiff, Bill and Ted's Bogus Journey (co-exec. prod.), Body of Evidence (exec. prod.).

DEVANE, WILLIAM
Actor. b. Albany, NY, Sept. 5, 1939. Appeared in some 15 productions with N.Y. Shakespeare Festival, also B'way & off-B'way shows before heading to California for films and TV.
PICTURES: The Pursuit of Happiness (debut, 1970), The 300 Hundred Year Weekend, Lady Liberty, McCabe and Mrs. Miller, Glory Boy (My Old Man's Place), Irish Whiskey Rebellion, Report to the Commissioner, Family Plot, Marathon Man, Bad News Bears in Breaking Training, Rolling Thunder, The Dark, Yanks, Honky Tonk Freeway, Testament, Hadley's Rebellion, Vital Signs, Exception to the Rule, Payback.
TELEVISION: *Series*: From Here to Eternity, Knots Landing, Phenom, The Monroes, Turks, Titans. *Movies*: Crime Club, The Bait, Fear on Trial, Red Alert, Black Beauty, Red Flag: The Ultimate Game, The Other Victim, Jane Doe, With Intent to Kill, Timestalker, Murder C.O.D., Nightmare in Columbia County, Obsessed, The President's Child. Prophet of Evil: The Ervil LeBaron Story, Rubdown, For the Love of Nancy, Falling From the Sky!: Flight 174, Robin Cook's Virus, Alistair MacLean's Night Watch. *Special:* The Missiles of October. *Mini-Series*: A Woman Named Jackie, Knot's Landing: Back to the Cul-de-Sac, Doomsday Rock.

De VITO, DANNY
Actor, Director, Producer. b. Asbury Park, NJ, Nov. 17, 1944. m. actress Rhea Perlman. e. Oratory Prep Sch. Studied at American Acad. of Dramatic Arts. Wilfred Acad. of Hair and Beauty Culture. At 18 worked as hair dresser for 1 yr. at his sister's shop. NY stage in The Man With a Flower in His Mouth (debut, 1969), Down the Morning Line, The Line of Least Existence, The Shrinking Bride, Call Me Charlie, Comedy of Errors, Merry Wives of Windsor (NYSF). Three By Pirandello. Performance in One Flew Over the Cuckoo's Nest led to casting in the film version. Prod. short films: The Sound Sleeper (1973), Minestrone (1975).
PICTURES: Lady Liberty (debut, 1971), Hurry Up or I'll Be 30, Scalawag, One Flew Over the Cuckoo's Nest, Deadly Hero, The Van, The World's Greatest Lover, Goin' South, Going Ape, Terms of Endearment, Romancing the Stone, Johnny Dangerously, The Jewel of the Nile, Head Office, Wiseguys, Ruthless People, My Little Pony (voice), Tin Men, Throw Momma from the Train (also dir.), Twins, The War of the Roses (also dir.), Other People's Money, Batman Returns, Hoffa (also dir., co-prod.), Jack the Bear, Last Action Hero (voice), Look Who's Talking Now (voice), Reality Bites (co-prod. only), Renaissance Man, Pulp Fiction (co-exec. prod. only), Junior, Get Shorty (also co-prod.), Sunset Park (prod.), Matilda (also dir., co-prod.), Mars Attacks, Hercules (voice), L.A. Confidential, Space Jam. (voice), The Rainmaker, Living Out Loud, Stretch Armstrong, Foolproof, Out of Sight (prod. only), Gattaca (prod. only), Man on the Moon (also prod.), The Virgin Suicides, Drowning Mona (also prod.), Screwed, What's The Worst That Could Happen?, The Heist.
TELEVISION: *Series*: Taxi (Emmy & Golden Globe Awards, 1981; also dir. episodes), Mary (dir. only). Movies: Valentine, The Ratings Game (also dir.). Specials: All the Kids Do It (Afterschool Special), A Very Special Christmas Party, Two Daddies? (voice), What a Lovely Way to Spend an Evening (dir.), The Selling of Vince DeAngelo (dir.). Guest: Police Woman, Amazing Stories (also dir.), The Simpsons (voice).

DEVLIN, DEAN
Actor, Writer, Producer. b. Aug. 27, 1962. Began career as an actor, appearing in numerous film and television projects, as well as B'way production of There Must Be a Pony. Met Roland Emmerich while acting in Moon 44. Joined Emmerich as a partner at Centropolis Films. Prod. TV series, The Visitor, 1997.
PICTURES: *Actor*: My Bodyguard, The Wild Life, Real Genius, City Limits, Moon 44, Martians Go Home, Total Exposure. *Writer/Producer*: Stargate, Independence Day, Godzilla, The Mark, Patriot. *Writer*: Universal Soldier, Gargoyles.
TELEVISION: *Series creator*: The Visitor. *Series actor*: Hard Copy, Generations.

De WITT, JOYCE
Actress. b. Wheeling, WV, April 23, 1949. e. Ball State U., B.A., theatre; UCLA, MFA in acting. Classically trained, worked in theater since 13 as actress and dir.
TELEVISION: *Series*: Three's Company. *Guest*: Baretta, The Tony Randall Show, Most Wanted, Risko, Finder of Lost Loves. *Movies*: With This Ring, Spring Fling.

DEY, SUSAN
Actress. b. Pekin, IL, Dec. 10, 1952. Signed as magazine teen model at age 15. Made professional TV debut at 17, appearing in The Partridge Family 1970.
PICTURES: Skyjacked (debut, 1972), First Love, Looker, Echo Park, That's Adequate.
TELEVISION: *Series*: The Partridge Family, Loves Me Loves Me Not, Emerald Point N.A.S., L.A. Law, Love and War. *Movies*: Terror on the Beach, Cage Without a Key, Mary Jane Harper Cried Last Night, Little Women, The Comeback Kid, The Gift of Life, Malibu, Sunset Limousine, I Love You Perfect, Bed of Lies, Lies and Lullabies (also co-prod.), Whose Child Is This? The War for Baby Jessica, Beyond Betrayal, Deadly Love.

DE YOUNG, CLIFF
Actor. b. Inglewood, CA, Feb. 12, 1947. e. California State Coll., Illinois State U. On stage in Hair, Sticks and Bones, Two By South, The Three Sisters, The Orphan.
PICTURES: Harry and Tonto, Blue Collar, Shock Treatment, Independence Day, The Hunger, Reckless, Protocol, Secret Admirer, F/X, Flight of the Navigator, Fear, Pulse, Rude Awakening, Glory, Flashback, Crackdown, Dr. Giggles, Carnosaur II, Final Frontier, The Craft, The Substitute, Suicide Kings.
TELEVISION: *Series*: Sunshine, Robocop, Relativity. *Special*: Sticks and Bones. *Mini-Series*: Centennial, Master of the Game, Captains and the Kings, King, Robert Kennedy and His Times, Andersonville, Seduced By Madness, The Last Don. *Movies*: Sunshine, The 3000 Mile Chase, The Lindbergh Kidnapping Case, Scared Straight: Another Story, Invasion of Privacy, The Seeding of Sarah Burns, The Night That Panicked America, This Girl for Hire, The Awakening of Candra, Deadly Intentions, Sunshine Christmas, Fun and Games, Where Pigeons Go to Die, Fourth Story, Criminal Behavior, Love Can Be Murder, The Tommyknockers, Precious Victims, Heaven & Hell: North and South Book III, JAG, Element of Truth, The Westing Game, Nails, George Wallace, The Westing Game.

DIAMANT, LINCOLN
Executive, Biographer, Historian. b. New York, NY, Jan. 25, 1923. e. Columbia Coll., A.B. cum laude 1943. Cofounder, Columbia U. radio station. WKCR-FM; served in Wash. as prod., Blue Network (NBC), then in NY as CBS newswriter; 1949 joined World Pub. Co. as adv. and promo. dir.; 1952-69 worked in creative/TV dept. McCann-Erickson, Grey, then Ogilvy & Mather ad agencies (winning 6 Clio Awards). Prod. Lend Us Your Ears (Met. Museum Art broadcast series); founder, pres., Spots Alive, Inc., broadcast adv. consultants, 1969; Author, The Broadcast Communications Dictionary, Anatomy of a Television Commercial, Television's Classic Commercials, biography of Bernard Romans, Chaining the Hudson (Sons of Revolution Book Award), Stamping Our History, Yankee Doodle Days. Contrib., to Effective Advertising, to Messages and Meaning; New Routes to English; columnist Back Stage/Shoot. Member, Broadcast Pioneers, Acad. TV Arts & Sciences; v.p. Broadcast Advertising Producer's Society of America. Adjunct faculty member, Pace U., Hofstra U. Fellow, Royal Society of Arts.

DIAMOND, NEIL
Singer, Songwriter. b. Brooklyn, NY, Jan. 24, 1941. Many concert tours.
PICTURES: Jonathan Livingston Seagull (music), Every Which Way But Loose (music), The Last Waltz (actor), The Jazz Singer (actor, music).
TELEVISION: *Specials*: Neil Diamond... Hello Again, I Never Cared for the Sound of Being Alone, I'm Glad You're Here With Me Tonight, Greatest Hits Live, Neil Diamond's Christmas Special, Neil Diamond... Under a Tennessee Moon.

DIAZ, CAMERON
Actress. Began career as model for Elite. Feature debut was in The Mask. Received ShoWest 1996 Female Star of Tomorrow Award.
PICTURES: The Mask, The Last Supper, Keys to Tulsa, Feeling Minnesota, Head Above Water, She's the One, Head Above Water, My Best Friend's Wedding, A Life Less Ordinary, There's Something About Mary, Very Bad Things, Invisible Circus, Fear and Loathing in Las Vegas, Being John Malkovich, Any Given Sunday, Things You Can Tell Just By Looking At Her, Invisible Circus, Shrek, Vanilla Sky, The Gangs of New York.

DI BONAVENTURA, LORENZO
Executive. b. New York, NY. e. B.A., intellectual history, Harvard College, M.B.A., Wharton School of Business, U. of Pennsylvania. After running a river-rafting company following college, held a number of creative, production, and distribution positions at Columbia Pictures, including manager, Pay Cable & Home Entertainment. Joined Warner Bros. Pictures as production exec., 1989; promoted to v.p., production, then named senior v.p., production, 1993; exec. v.p., production, 1995; co-head, theatrical production, 1996. Currently president, worldwide theatrical production, Warner Bros. Pictures, (since 1998), where he is responsible for overseeing the development and production of all feature films, live-action and animation.

DI CAPRIO, LEONARDO
Actor. b. Hollywood, CA, Nov. 11, 1974. Started acting at age 15 in commercials and educational films. Appeared in short film The Foot Shooting Party.
PICTURES: Critters III (debut, 1991), Poison Ivy, This Boy's Life, What's Eating Gilbert Grape? (Natl. Board of Review, Chicago Film Critics & LA Film Critics Awards, Acad. Award nom.), The Quick and the Dead, The Basketball Diaries, Total Eclipse, Marvin's Room, Romeo + Juliet, Titanic, Don's Plum, Celebrity, The Man in the Iron Mask, The Beach, Johnny Eck, The Gangs of New York.
TELEVISION: *Series*: Growing Pains, Parenthood.

DICK, ANDY
Actor. b. Charleston, SC, Dec. 21, 1965.
PICTURES: Elvis Stories, Double Dragon, Reality Bites, In the Army Now, Hotel Oasis, The Cable Guy, Best Men, Ted, Bongwater, Picking up the Pieces, Inspector Gadget.
TELEVISION: *Movies:* Earth Angel, The Lion King II: Simba's Pride. *Series:* The Ben Stiller Show, Get Smart, NewsRadio. *Guest:* Anything But Love, Talk Soup (host), Flying Blind, The Building, The Nanny, Star Trek: Voyager.

DICKERSON, ERNEST
(A.S.C.): Cinematographer, Director. b. Newark, NJ, 1952. e. Howard U., architecture, NYU, grad. film school. First job, filming surgical procedures for Howard U. medical school. At NYU film school shot classmate Spike Lee's student films Sarah, and Joe's Bed Stuy Barbershop: We Cut Heads. Also shot Nike commercial and several music videos including Bruce Springsteen's Born in the U.S.A., Patti LaBelle's Stir It Up and Miles Davis' Tutu; and Branford Marsalis' Royal Garden Blues directed by Spike Lee. Admitted into Amer. Soc. of Cinematographers in 1989.
PICTURES: *Cinematographer:* The Brother From Another Planet, She's Gotta Have It (also cameo), Krush Groove, School Daze, Raw, Do the Right Thing, Def By Temptation, The Laser Man, Mo' Better Blues, Jungle Fever, Sex Drugs Rock & Roll, Cousin Bobby (co-photog.), Malcolm X. *Director:* Juice (also co-s.p., story), Surviving the Game, Tales Fromt he Crypt Presents Demon Knight.
TELEVISION: Do it Acapella (dir.; PBS).

DICKINSON, ANGIE
Actress. r.n. Angeline Brown. b. Kulm, ND, Sept. 30, 1931. e. Immaculate Heart Coll., Glendale Coll., secretarial course. Beauty contest winner.
PICTURES: Lucky Me (debut in bit part, 1954), Man With the Gun, The Return of Jack Slade, Tennessee's Partner, The Black Whip, Hidden Guns, Tension at Table Rock, Gun the Man Down, Calypso Joe, China Gate, Shoot Out at Medicine Bend, Cry Terror, I Married a Woman, Rio Bravo, The Bramble Bush, Ocean's 11, A Fever in the Blood, The Sins of Rachel Cade, Jessica, Rome Adventure, Captain Newman M.D., The Killers, The Art of Love, Cast a Giant Shadow, The Chase, The Poppy is Also a Flower, The Last Challenge, Point Blank, Sam Whiskey, Some Kind of a Nut, Young Billy Young, Pretty Maids All in a Row, The Resurrection of Zachary Wheeler, The Outside Man, Big Bad Mama, Klondike Fever, Dressed to Kill, Charlie Chan and the Curse of the Dragon Queen, Death Hunt, Big Bad Mama II, Even Cowgirls Get the Blues, The Maddening, Sabrina, The Sun—The Moon and The Stars.
TELEVISION: *Series*: Police Woman, Cassie & Co. *Movies*: The Love War, Thief, See the Man Run, The Norliss Tapes, Pray for the Wildcats, A Sensitive Passionate Man, Overboard, The Suicide's Wife, Dial M for Murder, One Shoe Makes It Murder, Jealousy, A Touch of Scandal, Stillwatch, Police Story: The Freeway Killings, Once Upon a Texas Train, Prime Target, Treacherous Crossing, Danielle Steel's Remembrance, Deep Family Secrets. *Mini-Series*: Pearl, Hollywood Wives, Wild Palms. *Special*: Ira Geshwin at 100.

DICKINSON, WOOD
Executive, Exhibitor. r.n. Glen Wood Dickinson III. b. Fairway, KS, Sept. 14, 1952. e. Texas Christian U (BFA Communications, MA Film). Chairman and CEO of Dickinson Theatres, Inc.

DIESEL, VIN
Actor. b. New York, NY, July 18, 1967.
PICTURES: Multi-Facial (also dir.), Strays (also dir.), Saving Private Ryan, The Iron Giant, Boiler Room, Pitch Black, Knockaround Guys, Redline.

DILLER, BARRY
Executive. b. San Francisco, CA, Feb. 2, 1942. Joined ABC in April, 1966, as asst. to v.p. in chg. programming. In 1968, made exec. asst. to v.p. in chg. programming and dir. of feature films. In 1969, named v.p., feature films and program dev., east coast. In 1971, made v.p., Feature Films and Circle Entertainment, a unit of ABC Entertainment, responsible for selecting, producing and scheduling The Tuesday Movie of the Week, The Wednesday Movie of the Week, and Circle Film original features for airing on ABC-TV, as well as for acquisition and scheduling of theatrical features for telecasting on ABC Sunday Night Movie and ABC Monday Night Movie. In 1973, named v.p. in chg. of prime time TV for ABC Entertainment. In 1974 joined Paramount Pictures as bd. chmn. and chief exec. officer. 1983, named pres. of Gulf & Western Entertainment and Communications Group, while retaining Paramount titles. Resigned from Paramount in 1984 to join 20th Century-Fox as bd. chmn. and chief. exec. officer. Named chmn. & CEO of Fox, Inc. (comprising 20th Fox Film Corp., Fox TV Stations & Fox Bdcstg. Co.), Oct., 1985. Named to bd., News Corp. Ltd., June, 1987. Resigned from Fox in Feb., 1992. Named CEO of QVC Network Inc. TV shopping concern. Resigned QVC in 1995. CEO and bd. chair, Silver King Communications, Inc, Aug. 1995. Bd. chairman, Home Shopping Network, Nov. 1995.

DILLER, PHYLLIS
Comedienne, Actress. b. Lima, OH, July 17, 1917. r.n. Phyllis Ada Driver. e. Sherwood Music Sch., 1935-37; Bluffton Coll., OH, 1938-39. Started as publicist at San Francisco radio station before becoming nightclub comic at the age of 37. Recordings: Phyllis Diller Laughs, Are You Ready for Phyllis Diller?, Great Moments of Comedy, Born to Sing. Performed with many U.S. symphonies, 1971-90.
AUTHOR: Phyllis Diller's Housekeeping Hints, Phyllis Diller's Marriage Manual, Phyllis Diller's The Complete Mother, The Joys of Aging and How to Avoid Them.
THEATER: Hello Dolly! (B'way), Everybody Loves Opal, Happy Birthday, The Dark at the Top of the Stairs, Subject to Change, The Wizard of Oz, Nunsense, Cinderella.
PICTURES: Splendor in the Grass (debut, 1961), Boy Did I Get a Wrong Number!, The Fat Spy, Mad Monster Party (voice), Eight on the Lam, Did You Hear the One About the Traveling Saleslady?, The Private Navy of Sgt. O'Farrell, The Adding Machine, The Sunshine Boys (cameo), A Pleasure Doing Business, Pink Motel, Pucker Up and Bark Like a Dog, Dr. Hackenstein, Friend to Friend, The Nutcracker Prince (voice), The Boneyard, Wisecracks, Happily Ever After (voice), The Perfect Man, The Silence of the Hams.
TELEVISION: *Series*: Showstreet, The Pruitts of Southampton, The Beautiful Phyllis Diller Show. Specials: The Phyllis Diller Special, An Evening With Phyllis Diller, Phyllis Diller's 102nd Birthday Party. *Guest*: Laugh In, Love American Style, The Muppet Show, The Love Boat, CHiPs, etc.

DILLMAN, BRADFORD
Actor. b. San Francisco, CA, April 14, 1930. m. actress-model Suzy Parker. e. Yale U., 1951. Studied at Actors Studio. Author: Inside the New York Giants, Are You Anybody?
THEATER: The Scarecrow (1953), Third Person, Long Day's Journey into Night (premiere; Theatre World Award), The Fun Couple.
PICTURES: A Certain Smile (debut, 1958), In Love and War, Compulsion, Crack in the Mirror, Circle of Deception, Sanctuary, Francis of Assisi, A Rage to Live, The Plainsman, Sergeant Ryker, Helicopter Spies, Jigsaw, The Bridge at Remagen, Suppose They Gave a War and Nobody Came, Brother John, The Mephisto Waltz, Escape from the Planet of the Apes, The Resurrection of Zachary Wheeler, The Iceman Cometh, The Way We Were, Chosen Survivors, 99 and 44/100% Dead, Gold, Bug, Mastermind, The Enforcer, The Lincoln Conspiracy, Amsterdam Kill, The Swarm, Piranha, Love and Bullets, Guyana: Cult of the Damned, Sudden Impact, Treasure of the Amazon, Man Outside, Lords of the Deep, Heroes Stand Alone.
TELEVISION: *Series*: Court-Martial, King's Crossing, Dynasty. *Movies*: Fear No Evil, Black Water Gold, Longstreet, Five Desperate Women, Revenge, Eyes of Charles Sand, The Delphi Bureau, Moon of the Wolf, Deliver Us From Evil, Murder or Mercy, Disappearance of Flight 412, Adventures of the Queen, Force Five, Widow, Street Killing, Kingston: The Power Play, The Hostage Heart, Jennifer: A Woman's Story, Before and After, The Memory of Eva Ryker, Tourist, The Legend of Walks Far Woman, Covenant, Heart of Justice.

DILLON, KEVIN
Actor. b. Mamaroneck, NY, Aug. 19, 1965. Younger brother of actor Matt Dillon. Stage work includes Dark at the Top of the Stairs, The Indian Wants the Bronx.
PICTURES: No Big Deal, Heaven Help Us, Platoon, Remote Control, The Rescue, The Blob, War Party, Immediate Family, The Doors, A Midnight Clear, No Escape, True Crime, Criminal Hearts, Misbegotten, Stag, Hidden Agenda.
TELEVISION: *Movie*: When He's Not a Stranger, Frankie's House, The Pathfinder, Gone in the Night, Medusa's Child. *Series:* St. Michael's Crossing. *Special*: Dear America: Letters Home from Vietnam (reader). *Guest*: Tales From the Crypt, NYPD Blue.

DILLON, MATT
Actor. b. New Rochelle, NY, Feb. 18, 1964. Brother is actor Kevin Dillon. Discovered at age 14 in junior high school by casting dir. who cast him in Over the Edge.
THEATER: *NY*: The Boys of Winter (B'way debut, 1985).
PICTURES: Over the Edge (debut, 1979), Little Darlings, My Bodyguard, Liar's Moon, Tex, The Outsiders, Rumble Fish, The Flamingo Kid, Target, Rebel, Native Son, The Big Town, Kansas, Bloodhounds of Broadway, Drugstore Cowboy, A Kiss Before Dying, Singles, Mr. Wonderful, The Saint of Fort Washington, Golden Gate, To Die For, Frankie Starlight, Beautiful Girls, Grace of My Heart, Albino Alligator, In & Out, Wild Things, There's Something About Mary, One Night At McCool's, Deuces Wild.
TELEVISION: *Movie*: Women & Men 2: In Love There Are No Rules (Return to Kansas City). *Specials*: The Great American Fourth of July and Other Disasters, Dear America: Letters Home From Vietnam (reader).

DILLON, MELINDA
Actress. b. Hope, AR, Oct. 13, 1939. e. Chicago Sch. of Drama, Art Inst., Goodman Theatre. Launched career on Broadway in original prod. of Who's Afraid of Virginia Woolf? (Theatre World Award, Tony Award nom., Drama Critics Award).
THEATER: Story Theater, You Know I Can't Hear You When The Water's Running, A Way of Life, Our Town
PICTURES: The April Fools (debut, 1969), Bound for Glory (People's Choice Award), Slap Shot, Close Encounters of the Third Kind (Acad. Award nom.), F.I.S.T., Absence of Malice (Acad. Award nom.), A Christmas Story, Songwriter, Harry and the Hendersons, Staying Together, Spontaneous Combustion, Capt. America, The Prince of Tides, Sioux City, To Fong Woo–Thanks for Everything Julie Newmar, How to Make an American Quilt, Dorothy Day, The Effects of Magic.
TELEVISION: *Series*: Paul Sills Story Theatre. *Guest*: Twilight Zone, The Defenders, Bonanza, East Side West Side, The Paul Sand Show, The Jeffersons, Good Morning America, The Today Show, Dick Cavett Show, Dinah Shore Show, Picket Fences, The Client, Texarkana. *Mini-Series*: Space. *Movies*: Critical List, Transplant, Marriage is Alive and Well, The Shadow Box, Fallen Angel, Hellinger's Law, Right of Way, Shattered Spirits, Shattered Innocence, Nightbreaker, Judgment Day: The John List Story, State of Emergency, Confessions: Two Faces of Evil, Naomi & Wynonna: Love Can Build a Bridge.

DINDAL, MARK
Animator, director. b. Columbus, OH.
PICTURES: The Fox and the Hound, Mickey's Christmas Carol, The Black Cauldron, The Great Mouse Detective, Oliver & Company, The Little Mermaid, The Rocketeer, Cats Don't Dance (voice, dir., writer), Kingdom of the Sun (dir.).

DiNOVI, DENISE
Producer. b. Canada. Started as journalist, reporter, film critic in Toronto before entering film industry as unit publicist. 1980, joined Montreal's Film Plan production co. as co-prod., assoc. prod. and exec. in charge of prod. working on such movies as Visiting Hours, Going Berserk, Videodrome. Became exec. v.p. of prod. at New World, then head of Tim Burton Prods., 1989-92.
PICTURES: Heathers, Edward Scissorhands, Meet the Applegates, Batman Returns, The Nightmare Before Christmas, Cabin Boy, Little Women, Ed Wood, James and the Giant Peach, Practical Magic, Almost Heroes, Messge in a Bottle.

Di PIETRA, ROSEMARY
Executive. Joined Paramount Pictures in 1976, rising through ranks to become director-corporate administration. 1985, promoted to exec. dir.-corporate administration.

DISHY, BOB
Actor. b. Brooklyn, NY. e. Syracuse U.
THEATER: Damn Yankees, From A to Z, Second City, Flora the Red Menace, By Jupiter, Something Different, The Goodbye People, The Good Doctor, The Unknown Soldier at His Wife, The Creation of the World and Other Business, An American Millionaire, Sly Fox, Murder at Howard Johnson's, Grown Ups, Cafe Crown.
PICTURES: The Tiger Makes Out, Lovers and Other Strangers, The Big Bus, I Wonder Who's Killing Her Now?, The Last Married Couple in America, First Family, Author! Author!, Brighton Beach Memoirs, Critical Condition, Stay Tuned, Used People, My Boyfriend's Back, Don Juan DeMarco, Jungle to Jungle.
TELEVISION: *Series*: That Was the Week That Was. *Specials*: Story Theatre (dir.), The Cafeteria. *Guest*: The Comedy Zone. *Movies*: It Couldn't Happen to a Nicer Guy, Thicker Than Blood: The Larry McLinden Story.

DISNEY, ROY E.
Producer, Director, Writer, Cameraman, Film editor. b. Los Angeles, CA, Jan. 10, 1930. e. Pomona Coll., CA. 1951 started as page, NBC-TV. Asst. film editor Dragnet TV series. 1952-78, Walt Disney Prods., Burbank, Calif., various capacities; vice chmn. of the board, The Walt Disney Co.; bd. chmn., Shamrock Holdings, Inc., bd. dir., Walt Disney Co.
PICTURES: Perri, Mysteries of the Deep, Mustang (dir.), Pacific High, The Fantasy Film Worlds of George Pal (actor), The Wonderful Ice Cream Suit (prod.).
TELEVISION: Walt Disney's Wonderful World of Color, The Hound That Thought He Was A Raccoon, Sancho, The Homing Steer, The Silver Fox and Sam Davenport, Wonders of the Water World, Legend of Two Gypsy Dogs, Adventure in Wildwood Heart, The Postponed Wedding, Zorro series, An Otter in the Family, My Family is a Menagerie, Legend of El Blanco, Pancho, The Fastest Paw in the West, The Owl That Didn't Give A Hoot, Varda the Peregrine Falcon, Cristobalito, The Calypso Colt, Three Without Fear, Hamade and the Pirates, Chango, Guardian of the Mayan Treasure, Nosey the Sweetest Skunk in the World, Mustang!, Call It Courage, Ringo the Refugee Raccoon, Shokee the Everglades Panther, Deacon the High-Noon Dog, Wise One, Whale's Tooth, Track of African Bongo, Dorsey the Mail-Carrying Dog.

DIXON, BARBARA
Executive. b. Pasadena CA. e. USC, grad. degree from Johns Hopkins U. Served as staff member of Senate Judiciary Committee and was dir. of legislation for Sen. Birch Bayh, 1974-79. Left to become dir. of Office of Government & Public Affairs of Natl. Transportation Safety Board. Named v.p., Fratelli Group, p.r. firm in Washington; took leave of absence in 1984 to serve as deputy press secty. to Democratic V.P. candidate, Geraldine Ferraro. In 1985 joined Motion Picture Assn. of America as v.p. for public affairs. Moved to Columbia/Tristar.

DIXON, DONNA
Actress. b. Alexandria, VA, July 20, 1957. m. actor-writer Dan Aykroyd. e. Studied anthropology and medicine, Mary Washington U. Left to become a model, both on magazine covers and in TV commercials (Vitalis, Max Factor, Gillette).
PICTURES: Dr. Detroit, Twilight Zone--The Movie, Spies Like Us, The Couch Trip, It Had To Be You, Speed Zone!, Lucky Stiff, Wayne's World, Exit to Eden, Nixon.
TELEVISION: *Series*: Bosom Buddies, Berrenger's. *Movies*: Mickey Spillane's Margin for Murder, No Man's Land, Beverly Hills Madam. *Specials*: Women Who Rate a "10," The Shape of Things, The Rodney Dangerfield Show: I Can't Take it No More.

DIXON, WHEELER WINSTON
Educator, Writer, Filmmaker. b. New Brunswick, NJ, March 12, 1950. e. Rutgers U. In 1960s asst. writer for Time/Life publications; also writer for Interview magazine. 1976, directed TV commercials in NY. One season with TVTV, Los Angeles, as post-prod. suprv. 1978, formed Deliniator Films, Inc., serving as exec. prod./dir. Since 1988 has directed film program at Univ. of Nebraska, where holds rank of tenured full prof. and chair, Film Studies Prog.; received Rockefeller Foundation grant. Prod., dir. with Gwendolyn Audrey-Foster: Women Who Made the Movies (video). Prod/Dir: What Can I Do?, Squatters. 1992, guest prog. at the Brit. Film Inst./ Natl. Film Theatre. 1993, Distinguished Teaching Award. Invited lecturer at Yale, 1995; Series ed. for SUNY Press Cultural Studies in Cinema/Video (20 vol.)
AUTHOR: The `B' Directors, 1985; The Cinematic Vision of F. Scott Fitzgerald, 1986; PRC: A History of Producer's Releasing Corp., 1986; books on Freddie Francis, Terence Fisher, Reginald Le Borg, 1992-93; The Early Film Criticism of Francois Truffaut; Re-Viewing British Cinema, 1900-92; It Looks at You: The Returned Gaze of Cinema, 1995; The Films of Jean-Luc Godard, 1997; The Exploding Eye: A Revisionary History of 1960s American Experimental Cinema, 1997.

DOBSON, KEVIN
Actor. b. New York, NY, March 18, 1943.
PICTURES: Love Story, Bananas, Klute, The Anderson Tapes, The French Connection, Carnal Knowledge, Midway, All Night Long.
TELEVISION: *Series*: Kojak, Shannon, Knots Landing (also dir. 9 episodes), F/X: The Series. *Movies*: The Immigrants, Transplant, Orphan Train, Hardhat and Legs, Reunion, Mark I Love You, Mickey Splillane's Margin for Murder, Money Power Murder (also prod.), Casey's Gift: For Love of a Child, Sweet Revenge, Fatal Frienship, Dirty Work, House of Secrets and Lies, The Conviction of Kitty Dodds, If Someone Had Known, Crimes of Passion: Voice from the Grave, Nobody Lives Forever. *Mini-series*: Knots Landing: Back to the Cul-de-Sac. *Guest*: The Nurses, The Doctors, Greatest Heroes of the Bible.

DOERFLER, RONALD J.
Executive. e. Fairleigh Dickinson Univ. Became CPA in 1967. 1972, received M.B.A. from Fairleigh Dickinson. Joined Capital Cities 1969 as asst. controller. Became treas. in 1977; v.p. & CFO, 1980. 1983, named sr. v.p.,.then sr. v.p. & CFO.

DOHERTY, SHANNEN
Actress. b. Memphis, TN, April 12, 1971. On stage in The Mound Builders.
PICTURES: Night Shift, The Secret of NIMH (voice), Girls Just Want to Have Fun, Heathers, Freeze Frame, Mallrats, Nowhere, Striking Poses.
TELEVISION: *Series*: Little House on the Prairie, Our House, Beverly Hills 90210, Charmed. *Movies*: The Other Lover, Obsessed, Blindfold, Jailbreakers, A Burning Passion: The Margaret Mitchell Story, Gone in the Night, Friends 'Til the End, Sleeping with the Devil. *Mini-Series*: Robert Kennedy and His Times. *Pilot:* His and Hers. *Guest:* 21 Jump Street, Cagney and Lacey, Highway to Heaven, Life Goes On, The Dennis Miller Show, Parker Lewis Can't Lose.

DOLAN, CHARLES F.
Executive. b. Cleveland, OH, Oct. 16, 1926. e. John Carroll U. Established Teleguide Inc., early 1960s. Found. Sterling Manhattan Cable, mid 1960s. Found. Home Box Office Inc., early 1970s; after sale of HBO to Time Life Inc., organized Cablevision Systems Corp., 1973; presently, chmn. Chmn., Natl Acad. of TV Arts & Sci. Bd. govs., Natl Hockey League. Bd. dirs.: Madison Square Garden Prop.; St. Francis Hospital, NY. Mng. dir., Metropolitan Opera of NY. Trustee, Fairfield U, CT.

DOLAN, JAMES L.
Executive. Began working at Cablevision in the 1970s, in construction, field sales & collections depts.; named asst. gen mngr. of Cablevision of Chicago, late 1970's. Early 1980s, as Cablevision v.p., found. & mngd. WKNR-AM, Cleveland; also oversaw weekly TV mag. Total. During the 1980s, corp. dir. advt., at Rainbow, & v.p. for advt. sales at Cablevision. CEO, Rainbow Media Holdings, Inc., 1993-1995. CEO, Cablevision Systems Corp., 1995-; also on bd. dirs., & exec. com. On bd. & exec. com., Natl Cable TV Assn., & chair., music licensing com. On bd. dirs., Hazelden NY & Cable Labs, CO. Hon. co-chair, LI Film & TV Found.

DOLGEN, JONATHAN L.
Executive. b. New York, NY, April 27, 1945. e. Cornell U., NYU Sch. of Law. Began career with Wall Street law firm, Fried, Frank, Harris, Shriver & Jacobson. In 1976 joined Columbia Pictures Industries as asst. gen. counsel and deputy gen. counsel. 1979, named sr. v.p. in chg. of worldwide business affairs; 1980, named exec. v.p. Joined Columbia m.p. div., 1981; named pres. of Columbia Pay-Cable & Home Entertainment Group. Also pres. Columbia Pictures domestic operations, overseeing Music Group. 1985, joined 20th-Fox in newly created position of sr. exec. v.p. for telecommunications. Became pres. of Sony Motion Picture Group, 1991. Appointed chmn. Viacom Entertainment Group, 1994 where he oversees the operations of Paramount Motion Picture Group (Motion Picture Production & Distribution, Famous Music Publishing, Theatrical Exhibition) and Paramount Television Group (prod. & dist. of TV product and ownership of TV stations and interests in the United Paramount Network).

DONAHUE, ELINOR
Actress. b. Tacoma, WA, April 19, 1937.
PICTURES: Mr. Big, Tenth Avenue Angel, Unfinished Dance, Three Daring Daughters, Love is Better Than Ever, Girls Town, Pretty Woman, Freddy's Dead: The Final Nightmare.

TELEVISION: *Series*: Father Knows Best, The Andy Griffith Show, Many Happy Returns, The Odd Couple, Mulligan's Stew, Please Stand By, Days of Our Lives,The New Adventures of Beans Baxter, Get a Life. Pilot: The Grady Nutt Show. *Guest*: One Day at a Time, Sweepstakes$, The Golden Girls. *Movies*: In Name Only, Gidget Gets Married, Mulligan's Stew (pilot), Doctors' Private Lives, Condominium, High School U.S.A. Special: Father Knows Best Reunion.

DONAHUE, PHIL
Television Host. b. Cleveland, OH, Dec. 21, 1935. e. Notre Dame, BBA. m. actress Marlo Thomas. Worked as check sorter, Albuquerque Natl. Bank, 1957, then as announcer at KYW-TV & AM, Cleveland; news dir. WABJ radio, Adrian, MI; morning newscaster WHIO-TV. Interviews with Jimmy Hoffa and Billy Sol Estes picked up nationally by CBS. Host of Conversation Piece, phone-in talk show. Debuted The Phil Donahue Show, daytime talk show in Dayton, Ohio, 1967. Syndicated 2 years later. Moved to Chicago, 1974. Host, Donahue, now in 165 outlets in U.S. In 1979 a mini-version of show became 3-times-a-week segment on NBC's Today Show. Winner of several Emmys. *Books:* Donahue: My Own Story (1980), The Human Animal (1985).

DONAHUE, TROY
Actor. r.n. Merle Johnson, Jr. b. New York, NY, Jan. 27, 1937. e. Bayport H.S., N.Y. Military Acad. Columbia U., Journalism. Directed, wrote, acted in school plays. Summer stock, Bucks County Playhouse, Sayville Playhouse; contract, Warner Brothers, 1959.
PICTURES: Man Afraid (debut, 1957), The Tarnished Angels, This Happy Feeling, The Voice in the Mirror, Live Fast Die Young, Monster on the Campus, Summer Love, Wild Heritage, The Perfect Furlough, Imitation of Life, A Summer Place, The Crowded Sky, Parrish, Susan Slade, Rome Adventure, Palm Springs Weekend, A Distant Trumpet, My Blood Runs Cold, Blast-Off! (Those Fantastic Flying Fools), Come Spy With Me, Sweet Savior, Cockfighter, Seizure, The Godfather Part II, Tin Man, Grandview U.S.A., Low Blow, Cyclone, Deadly Prey, American Revenge, Dr. Alien (I Was a Teenage Sex Mutant), Sexpot, Hard Rock Nightmare, Bad Blood, John Travis, Solar Survivor, The Chilling, The Housewarming, Deadly Spy Games, Assault of the Party Nerds, Deadly Diamonds, Deadly Embrace, Cry-Baby, Double Trouble.
TELEVISION: *Series*: Hawaiian Eye, Surfside 6. *Guest*: Matt Houston. *Movies*: Split Second to an Epitaph, The Loneliest Profession, Malibu.

DONALDSON, ROGER
Director. b. Ballarat, Australia, Nov. 15, 1943. Emigrated to New Zealand at 19. Established still photography business; then began making documentaries. Directed Winners and Losers, a series of short dramas for NZ-TV.
PICTURES: Sleeping Dogs (also prod.), Smash Palace (also s.p. prod.), The Bounty, Marie, No Way Out, Cocktail, Cadillac Man (also prod.), White Sands, The Getaway, Species, Dante's Peak, The Guide.

DONEN, STANLEY
Director, Producer, Choreographer. b. Columbia, SC, April 13, 1924. e. USC. Former dancer, B'way debut 1940 in chorus of Pal Joey starring Gene Kelly. Assisted Kelly as choreog. on stage prod. of Best Foot Forward; hired by MGM to repeat duties in film version. Choreographer on such films as Cover Girl, Holiday in Mexico, This Time for Keeps, A Date With Judy, Take Me Out to the Ballgame (also co-story credit). Honorary Acad. Award, 1997.
PICTURES: *Director*: On the Town (debut, 1949; co-dir. with Gene Kelly), Royal Wedding, Singin' in the Rain (co-dir., co-choreog. with Gene Kelly), Fearless Fagan, Love Is Better Than Ever, Give a Girl a Break (also co-choreog.), Seven Brides for Seven Brothers, Deep in My Heart (also co-choreog.), It's Always Fair Weather (co-dir., co-choreog. with Gene Kelly), Funny Face, The Pajama Game (co-dir., co-prod. with George Abbott), Kiss Them for Me. *Director-Producer:* Indiscreet, Damn Yankees (co-dir., co-prod. with George Abbott), Once More With Feeling, Surprise Package, The Grass Is Greener, Charade, Arabesque, Two for the Road, Bedazzled, Staircase, The Little Prince, Lucky Lady (dir. only), Movie Movie, Saturn 3, Blame It on Rio, Love Letters.TELEVISION: *Actor:* The Making of Seven Brides for Seven Brothers, The Hollywood Fashion Machine.

DONIGER, WALTER
Writer, Director, Producer. b. New York NY. e. Duke U., Harvard U. Graduate Business Sch. Entered m.p. business as writer later writer-prod-dir. Wrote documentaries in Army Air Forces M.P. Unit in W.W.II. WGA award nominee and other awards.
PICTURES: Rope of Sand, Desperate Search, Cease Fire, Safe At Home (dir.), House of Women (dir.), Duffy of San Quentin (dir.), Along the Great Divide, Tokyo Joe, Alaska Seas, Steel Cage (dir.), Steel Jungle (dir.), Hold Back the Night, Guns of Fort Petticoat, Unwed Mother (dir.), Stone Cold (exec. prod., s.p.).
TELEVISION: *Series*: Delvecchio, Mad Bull, Switch, Moving On, Baa Baa Blacksheep, McCloud, The Man and the City, Sarge, Owen Marshall, Peyton Place, Mr. Novak, The Greatest Show on Earth, Travels of Jaimie McPheeters, Outlaws, Hong Kong, Checkmate, Bat Masterson, The Web, Bold Venture, Tombstone Territory, Maverick, Rough Riders, Lockup, Dick Powell, The Survivors, Bracken's World, Bold Ones, Kung Fu, Barnaby Jones, Marcus Welby, Lucas Tanner.

DONNELLY, DONAL
Actor. b. Bradford, England, July 6, 1931. Studied for theatre at the Dublin Gate Theatre.
THEATER: *NY Theatre*: Philadelphia Here I Come (B'way debut, 1966), Joe Egg, Sleuth (NY and U.S. tour), The Elephant Man, The Faith-Healer, The Chalk Garden, My Astonishing Self, Big Maggie, Execution of Justice, Sherlock's Last Case, Ghetto, Dancing at Lughnasa, Translations.
PICTURES: Rising of the Moon (1957), Gideon's Day, Shake Hands With the Devil, Young Cassidy, The Knack, Up Jumped a Swagman, The Mind of Mr. Soames, Waterloo, The Dead, The Godfather Part III, Squanto: A Warrior's Tale, Korea.
TELEVISION: Juno and the Paycock (BBC, 1958), Home Is the Hero, The Venetian Twins, The Plough and the Stars, Playboy of the Western World, Sergeant Musgrave's Dance, Yes-Honestly (series).

DONNELLY, RALPH E.
Executive. b. Lynbrook, NY, Jan. 20, 1932. e. Bellmore, NY public school; W. C. Mepham H.S., 1949. Worked for Variety (publication) as writer, 1950; Long Island Press as daily columnist, 1951; joined Associated Independent Theatres, 1953, as gen. mgr.; later film buyer; in 1973 left to become independent buyer and booker for Creative Films; film buyer and v.p., RKO/Stanley Warner Theatres, 1976-79; pres. & gen. mgr. for Cinema 5 Ltd. circuit, N.Y., 1980-87; 1987-93, exec. v.p. City Cinemas, N.Y. Now chmn. of Cinema Connection.

DONNER, CLIVE
Director. b. London, England,, Jan 21, 1926. Ent. m.p. ind. 1942. Asst. film ed. Denhem Studios, 1942. Dir. London stage: The Formation Dancers, The Front Room Boys, Kennedy's Children (also NY). *Film editor:* A Christmas Carol (Scrooge), The Card (The Promoter), Genevieve, Man With a Million (The Million Pound Note), The Purple Plain, I Am a Camera.
PICTURES: The Secret Place (debut, 1957), Heart of a Child, Marriage of Convenience, The Sinister Man, Some People, The Caretaker (The Guest), Nothing But the Best, What's New Pussycat?, Luv, Here We Go Round the Mulberry Bush (also prod.), Alfred the Great, Old Dracula (Vampira), The Nude Bomb, Charlie Chan and the Curse of the Dragon Queen, Stealing Heaven.
TELEVISION: Danger Man, Sir Francis Drake, Mighty and Mystical, British Institutions, Tempo, Spectre, The Thief of Baghdad, Oliver Twist, Rogue Male, The Scarlet Pimpernel, Arthur the King, To Catch a King, Three Hostages, She Fell Among Thieves, A Christmas Carol, Dead Man's Folly, Babes in Toyland, Not a Penny More Not a Penny Less, Coup de Foudre (Love at First Sight), Terror Strikes the Class Reunion (For Better or Worse), Charlemagne.

DONNER, RICHARD
Director. b. New York, NY, 1939. Began career as actor off-B'way. Worked with director Martin Ritt on TV production of Maugham's Of Human Bondage. Moved to California 1958, directing commercials, industrial films and documentaries. First TV drama: Wanted: Dead or Alive.
PICTURES: X-15 (debut, 1961), Salt and Pepper, Twinky (Lola), The Omen, Superman, Inside Moves, The Final Conflict (exec. prod. only), The Toy (also exec. prod.), Ladyhawke (also prod.), The Goonies (also prod.), Lethal Weapon (also prod.), The Lost Boys (exec. prod. only), Scrooged (also prod.), Lethal Weapon 2 (also prod.), Delirious (exec. prod. only), Radio Flyer, Lethal Weapon 3 (also prod.), Free Willy (co-exec. prod. only), Maverick (also prod.), Tales From the Crypt Presents Demon Knight (co-exec. prod. only), Assassins (also prod.), Conspiracy Theory (also prod.), Free Willy 3: The Rescue (exec. prod.), Lethal Weapon 4.
TELEVISION: *Series episodes:* Have Gun Will Travel, Perry Mason, Cannon, Get Smart, The Fugitive, Kojak, Bronk, Gilligan's Island, Man From U.N.C.L.E., Wild Wild West, Tales From the Crypt, Two Fisted Tales, Twilight Zone, The Banana Splits, Combat. *Movies*: Lucas Tanner (pilot), Sarah T.: Portrait of a Teen-Age Alcoholic, Senior Year, A Shadow in the Streets, Tales From the Crypt (exec. prod.; also dir. episode: Dig That Cat... He's Real Gone).

D'ONOFRIO, VINCENT PHILLIP
Actor. b. Brooklyn, NY, 1960. Studied acting with the American Stanislavsky Theatre in NY, appearing in Of Mice and Men, The Petrified Forest, Sexual Perversity in Chicago, and The Indian Wants the Bronx.
THEATER: *B'way*: Open Admissions.
PICTURES: The First Turn On! (debut, 1984), Full Metal Jacket, Adventures in Babysitting, Mystic Pizza, Signs of Life, The Blood of Heroes, Crooked Hearts, Dying Young, Fires Within, Naked Tango, JFK, The Player, Desire, Household Saints, Mr. Wonderful, Being Human, Ed Wood, Imaginary Crimes, Stuart Saves His Family, Strange Days, Feeling Minnesota, Men in Black, The Velocity of Gary, The Whole Wide World (also prod.), The Newton Boys, Claire Dolan, Steal This Movie (also exec. prod.), Imposter, The Thirteenth Floor, The Cell, The Salton Sea, Happy Accidents, Spanish Judges, The Dangerous Lives of Altar Boys.
TELEVISION: *Movies:* The Taking of Pelham One Two Three, That Championship Season.

DONOHOE, AMANDA
Actress. b. London, England, June 29, 1962. e. Francis Holland Sch. for Girls, Central Sch. of Speech & Drama. Member of Royal Exchange Theatre in Manchester. B'way debut 1995 in Uncle Vanya.
PICTURES: Foreign Body (debut, 1986), Castaway, The Lair of the White Worm, The Rainbow, Tank Malling, Diamond Skulls (Dark Obsession), Paper Mask, The Madness of King George, Liar Liar, Writer's Block, I'm Losing You, The Real Howard Spitz, Circus.
TELEVISION: *Series*: L.A. Law (Golden Globe Award). *Movies*: Married to Murder, Shame, It's Nothing Personal (also co-exec. prod.), The Substitute, Shame II: The Secret (also co-exec. prod.), A Knight in Camelot. *Special*: Game Set and Match (Mystery!). *Guest:* The Hidden Room, Murder Most Horrid, Frasier.

DONOVAN, ARLENE
Producer. b. Kentucky. e. Stratford Coll., VA. Worked in publishing before entering industry as asst. to late dir. Robert Rosen on Cocoa Beach, uncompleted at his death. Worked as story editor, Columbia Pictures. 1969-82, literary head of m.p. dept. for ICM; involved in book publishing as well as stage and screen projects.
PICTURES: Still of the Night, Places in the Heart, Nadine, The House on Carroll Street (co-exec. prod.), Billy Bathgate, Nobody's Fool, Twilight.

DONOVAN, HENRY B.
Executive, Producer. b. Boston, MA. Entered m.p. ind. for RKO Pathe Studios, property master, special effects dir., unit mgr., asst. dir., prod. mgr.; worked on over 320 pictures; Harry Sherman, Hopalong Cassidy features (for Paramount). 10 yrs., U.S. Army Signal Corps, as head of dept. of California studios prod. training m.p.; pres.: Telemount Pictures, Inc. Prod., dir., writer Cowboy G Men (TV series). Wrote: Corkscrewed (novel), 7 Zane Grey westerns for Paramount. Founder and chair of SCOA & SCOW Corp.
PICTURES: Hopalong Cassidy Features, Gone with the Wind, Becky Sharp, Our Flag (dir.), Magic Lady (13 one-reel features), others. Cowboy G Men (prod., writer; 39 films).
TELEVISION: programming, financing, distribution. Global Scope; International TV; Dist., Financing, programming; sls. consultant, Intl. TV & motion pictures. Cable TV & distribution & program development, collector of movie memorabilia; DBS TV programming & financing: production software. Worldwide TV consultant. Created Silicon Valley for satellite B.D. Frontier Lawyer: Historical United States of America.

DONOVAN, TATE
Actor. b. New York, NY, Sept. 25, 1963. Raised in New Jersey. Studied acting at USC. Worked as still photographer for two Mutual of Omaha documentaries.
THEATER: Ruffian on the Stair, The American Plan, The Rhythm of Torn Stars, Bent. B'way: Picnic.
PICTURES: SpaceCamp, Clean and Sober, Dead Bang, Memphis Belle, Love Potion No. 9, Ethan Frome, Equinox, Holy Matrimony, Murder at 1600, Hercules (voice), Waiting for Woody, The Only Thrill.
TELEVISION: *Series:* Partners, Hercules (voice), Trinity. *Movies*: Not My Kid, Into Thin Air, A Case of Deadly Force, Nutcracker: Money Madness Murder. *HBO Special*: Vietnam War Stories. *Guest:* Friends.

DOOHAN, JAMES
Actor. b. Vancouver, B.C., Canada, March 3, 1920. WWII capt. in Royal Canadian Artillery. 1946 won scholarship to Neighborhood Playhouse in NY and later taught there. 1953, returned to Canada to live in Toronto, becoming engaged in acting career on radio, TV and in film. Then to Hollywood and chief fame as Chief Engineer Scott in TV series, Star Trek.
PICTURES: The Wheeler Dealers, The Satan Bug, Bus Riley's Back in Town, Pretty Maids All in a Row, Star Trek—The Motion Picture, Star Trek II: The Wrath of Khan, Star Trek III: The Search for Spock, Star Trek IV: The Voyage Home, Star Trek V: The Final Frontier, Star Trek VI: The Undiscovered Country, Double Trouble, National Lampoon's Loaded Weapon 1, Star Trek: Generations, Storybook, Trekkies, The Duke.
TELEVISION: *Series*: Star Trek. *Guest*: Hazel, Bonanza, The Virginia, Gunsmoke, Peyton Place, The Fugitive, Marcus Welby MD, Ben Casey, Bewitched, Fantasy Island. *Movie:* Scalplock.

DOOLEY, PAUL
Actor. r.n. Paul Brown. b. Parkersburg, WV, Feb. 22, 1928. Began career on NY stage in Threepenny Opera. Later member of Second City. B'way credits include The Odd Couple, Adaptation/Next, The White House Murder Case, Hold Me. Co-creator and writer for The Electric Company on PBS.
PICTURES: What's So Bad About Feeling Good? (debut, 1968), The Out-of-Towners, Death Wish, The Gravy Train, Slap Shot, A Wedding, A Perfect Couple, Breaking Away, Rich Kids, Popeye, Health (also co-s.p.), Paternity, Endangered Species, Kiss Me Goodbye, Strange Brew, Going Berserk, Sixteen Candles, Big Trouble, O.C. and Stiggs, Monster in the Closet, Last Rites, Flashback, Shakes the Clown, The Player, My Boyfriend's Back, A Dangerous Woman, The Underneath, God's Lonely Man, Loved, Clockwatchers, Telling Lies in America, Runaway Bride, I'll Remember April, Guinevere, Happy Texas.
TELEVISION: *Specials*: Faerie Tale Theater, The Firm, Traveler's Rest, Tales of the City. *Movies*: The Murder of Mary Phagan, Lip Service, Guts and Glory: The Rise and Fall of Oliver North, When He's Not a Stranger, The Court Martial of Jackie Robinson, Guess Who's Coming for Christmas?, White Hot: The Mysterious Murder of Thelma Todd, Cooperstown, Mother of the Bride, State of Emergency, The Computer Wore Tennis Shoes. *Series*: The Dom DeLuise Show, Coming of Age. *Guest:* Dream On, ALF, The Golden Girls, thirtysomething, Mad About You, Evening Shade, Coach, Wonder Years, The Boys, L.A. Law, The Mommies, Star Trek: Deep Space Nine, The Practice, ER, Dharma & Greg, My So-Called Life.

DORAN, LINDSAY
Executive. b. Los Angeles, CA. e. U. of California at Santa Cruz. Moved to London where was contributing author to The Oxford Companion to Film and the World Encyclopedia of Film. Returned to U.S. to write and produce documentaries and children's programs for Pennsylvania public affairs station WPSX-TV. Career in m.p. industry began in story dept. at Embassy Pictures which she joined in 1979; 1982 promoted to dir. of development; then v.p., creative affairs. 1985, joined Paramount Pictures as v.p., production, for MP Group. 1987, promoted to senior v.p., production. 1989, appointed pres., Mirage Productions. Pres. and COO, United Artists Pictures, 1996-.

DORFF, STEPHEN
Actor. b. July 29, 1973. Started acting at age 9.
PICTURES: The Gate (debut, 1987), The Power of One, An Ambush of Ghosts, Judgment Night, Rescue Me, Backbeat, S.F.W., Reckless, Halcyon Days, Innocent Lies, I Shot Andy Warhol, The Audition, Star Truckers, City of Industry, Blade, Entropy, Blood and Wine, Earthly Possessions, Quantum Project, Cecil B. Demented, Deuces Wild.
TELEVISION: *Series*: What a Dummy. *Movies*: I Know My First Name Is Steven, Always Remember I Love You, Do You Know the Muffin Man?, A Son's Promise, Earthly Possessions. *Guest*: Empty Nest, Roseanne, The Outsiders, Married...With Children, Blossom.

DORTORT, DAVID
Executive Producer. b. New York, NY, Oct. 23, 1916. e. City Coll. of New York. Served U.S. Army, 1943-46. Novelist and short story writer, 1943-49. Also TV writer. Now pres. of Xanadu Prods., Aurora Enterprises, Inc., and Bonanza Ventures, Inc. & Pres. TV branch, WGA, West, 1954-55; TV-radio branch, 1955-57; v.p. PGA, 1967; pres. 1968. Chmn., Caucus for Producers, Writers and Directors, 1973-75. Pres., PGA, 1980-81; campaign dir., Permanent Charities Comm., 1980-81; chmn., Interguild Council 1980-81. Received WGA/West noms. for TV work on An Error in Chemistry (Climax), and The Ox-Bow Incident (20th Century Fox Hour). Author: novels include Burial of the Fruit, The Post of Honor.
PICTURES: The Lusty Men, Reprisal, The Big Land, Cry in the Night, Clash by Night, Going Bananas (exec. prod.).
TELEVISION: *Creator and exec. prod.*: Bonanza, High Chaparral, The Chisholms, Hunter's Moon, Bonanza: Legends of the Ponderosa. *Producer:* The Restless Gun, The Cowboys. *Creator, story and exec. prod.*: Bonanza: The Next Generation. *Exec. prod.*: Bonanza: The Return, Bonanza: Under Attack.

DOUGHERTY, MARION
Executive. e. Penn St. U. Gained fame as casting director. Casting dir. on series Naked City, Route 66. Formed own co. in 1965. Acted as co-exec. prod. on Smile, 1975. In 1977 named v.p. in chg. talent for Paramount Pictures. In 1979 joined Warner Bros. as sr. v.p. in chg. talent to work with production dept. and producers and directors.
CASTING: A Little Romance, Urban Cowboy, Honky Tonk Freeway, Reds, Firefox, Honkytonk Man, The World According to Garp, Sudden Impact, The Man With Two Brains, The Killing Fields, Swing Shift, The Little Drummer Girl, Lethal Weapon (also 2 & 3), Batman, Batman Returns, Forever Young, Falling Down.

DOUGLAS, ILLEANA
Actress. Grandfather was actor Melvyn Douglas. Directed short films The Perfect Woman (Aspen Film Fest. prize, 1994), Boy Crazy—Girl Crazier.
THEATER: *NY*: Takes on Women, As Sure as You Live, Black Eagles.
PICTURES: Hello Again, New York Stories, GoodFellas, Guilty By Suspicion, Cape Fear, Alive, Household Saints, Grief, Quiz Show, Search and Destroy, To Die For, Grace of My Heart, Picture Perfect, Hacks, Flypaper, Wedding Bell Blues, Stir of Echoes, Can't Stop Dancing, Message in a Bottle, Happy Texas
TELEVISION: *Movies:* Weapons of Mass Distraction, Rough Riders, Bella Mafia. *Series:* Action.

DOUGLAS, KIRK
Actor, Producer, Director. r.n. Issur Danielovitch (changed to Demsky). b. Amsterdam, NY, Dec. 9, 1916. m. Anne Buydens, pres. of Bryna Prod. Co. Father of Michael, Joel, Peter, Eric. e. St. Lawrence U, B.A, AADA. Stage debut in New York: Spring Again. U.S. Navy during W.W.II; resumed stage work. Did radio soap operas. Signed by Hal B. Wallis for film debut. Autobiography: The Ragman's Son (1988). Novels: Dance With the Devil, The Secret, Last Tango in Brooklyn. Recipient of U.S. Presidential Medal of Freedom, 1981. Career achievement award, National Board of Review, 1989. Received AFI Lifetime Achievement Award, 1991.

THEATER: Spring Again, Three Sisters, Kiss and Tell, Trio, The Wind is Ninetry, Star in the Window, Man Bites Dog, One Flew Over the Cuckoo's Nest, The Boys of Autumn.
PICTURES: The Strange Love of Martha Ivers (debut, 1946), Out of the Past, I Walk Alone, Mourning Becomes Electra, The Walls of Jericho, My Dear Secretary, Letter to Three Wives, Champion, Young Man with a Horn, The Glass Menagerie, Ace in the Hole (The Big Carnival), Along the Great Divide, Detective Story, The Big Trees, The Big Sky, Bad and the Beautiful, Story of Three Loves, The Juggler, Act of Love, 20,000 Leagues Under the Sea, Ulysses, Man Without a Star, The Racers, The Indian Fighter (also prod.), Lust for Life, Top Secret Affair, Gunfight at the OK Corral, Paths of Glory, The Vikings (also prod.), Last Train from Gun Hill, The Devil's Disciple, Strangers When We Meet, Spartacus (also prod.), The Last Sunset, Town Without Pity, Lonely Are the Brave (also prod.), Two Weeks in Another Town, The Hook, List of Adrian Messenger (also prod.), For Love or Money, Seven Days in May (also prod.), In Harm's Way, The Heroes of Telemark, Cast a Giant Shadow, Is Paris Burning?, The Way West, The War Wagon, A Lovely Way to Die, The Brotherhood (also prod.), The Arrangement, There Was a Crooked Man, A Gunfight, Summertree (prod. only), The Light at the Edge of the World (also prod.), Catch Me a Spy, Scalawag (also dir., prod.), Master Touch, Once is Not Enough, Posse (also dir., prod.), The Chosen, The Fury, The Villain, Saturn III, Home Movies, The Final Countdown, The Man from Snowy River, Eddie Macon's Run, Tough Guys, Oscar, Welcome to Veraz, Greedy, A Century of Cinema, The Films of John Frankenheimer.
TELEVISION: *Movies*: Mousey, The Money Changers, Draw! (HBO), Victory at Entebbe, Remembrance of Love, Amos, Queenie, Inherit the Wind, The Secret, Take Me Home Again. *Guest*: The Lucy Show, Tales From the Crypt (Yellow) The Simpsons (voice). *Specials*: Legend of Silent Night, Dr. Jekyll & Mr. Hyde.

DOUGLAS, MICHAEL
Actor, Producer. b. New Brunswick, NJ, Sept 25, 1944. p. Kirk Douglas and Diana Dill. e. Black Fox Military Acad., Choate, U. of California. Worked as asst. director on Lonely Are the Brave, Heroes of Telemark, Cast a Giant Shadow; after TV debut in The Experiment (CBS Playhouse), appeared off-Broadway in City Scene, Pinkville (Theatre World Award). Produced 1993 Off-B'way show The Best of Friends.
PICTURES: Hail Hero (debut, 1969), Adam at 6 A.M., Summertree, Napoleon and Samantha, One Flew Over the Cuckoo's Nest (co-prod. only; Acad. Award for Best Picture, 1975), Coma, The China Syndrome (also prod.), Running (also exec. prod.), It's My Turn, The Star Chamber, Romancing the Stone (also prod.), Starman (exec. prod. only), A Chorus Line, The Jewel of the Nile (also prod.), Fatal Attraction, Wall Street (Acad. Award; Natl. Board of Review Award, 1987), Black Rain, The War of the Roses, Flatliners (co-exec. prod. only), Shining Through, Radio Flyer (co-exec. prod. only), Basic Instinct, Falling Down, Made in America (co-exec. prod. only), Disclosure, The American President, The Ghost and the Darkness, Face/Off (exec. prod. only), The Game, The Rainmaker (prod. only), A Perfect Murder, Wonder Boys, One Night At McCool's, Traffic, Don't Say A Word.
TELEVISION: *Series*: Streets of San Francisco. *Guest*: The FBI, Medical Center. *Movies*: Streets of San Francisco (pilot), When Michael Calls.

DOUGLAS, MIKE
TV host. r.n. Michael Delaney Dowd, Jr. b. Chicago, IL, Aug. 11, 1925. Started career singing with bands in and around Chicago. 1950-54 featured singer with Kay Kyser's band. In 1953 became host of WGN-TV's Hi Ladies in Chicago; also featured on WMAQ-TV, NBC, Chicago, as singer and host. Moved to Hollywood in late '50s, working as piano bar singer. In 1961 hired as host for new show on station KYW-TV in Cleveland, owned by Westinghouse Bdg. Co., featuring celebrity guests. This became the Mike Douglas Show which was later nationally syndicated and moved base of operations to Philadelphia, then Los Angeles. Ran 21 years til Mid-1982. Books: The Mike Douglas Cookbook (1969), Mike Douglas My Story (1978), When the Going Gets Tough.
PICTURES: Gator, Nasty Habits, The Incredible Shrinking Woman.

DOUMANIAN, JEAN
Producer.
PICTURES: Oxen, Bullets Over Broadway (exec. prod.), Mighty Aphrodite (exec. prod.), Everyone Says I Love You (exec. prod.), Deconstructing Harry, Story of a Bad Boy, Elements, Wild Man Blues.

DOURIF, BRAD
Actor. b. Huntington, WV, March 18, 1950. Studied with Stanford Meisner. Stage actor, three years with Circle Repertory Co., NY (When You Comin' Back Red Ryder?), before films and TV.
PICTURES: Split, One Flew Over the Cuckoo's Nest (Acad. Award nom., Golden Globe & BAFTA Awards, 1975), Group Portrait with Lady, Eyes of Laura Mars, Wise Blood, Heaven's Gate, Ragtime, Dune, Impure Thoughts, Istanbul, Blue Velvet, Fatal Beauty, Child's Play, Mississippi Burning, Medium Rare, The Exorcist: 1990, Spontaneous Combustion, Grim Prairie Tales, Sonny Boy, Graveyard Shift, Child's Play II, Hidden Agenda, Dead Certain, Jungle Fever, The Horseplayer, Body Parts, Child's Play 3, Common Bonds, Scream of Stone, Critters 4, London Kills Me, Diary of the Hurdy Gurdy Man, Murder Blues, Final Judgment, Amos & Andrew, Trauma, Color of Night, Murder in the First, Alien: Resurrection, Best Men, Brown's Requiem, Bride of Chucky (voice), Senseless, Nightwatch, Urban Legend, The Progeny, Son of Chucky (voice).
TELEVISION: *Movies*: Sgt. Matlovitch vs. the U.S. Air Force, Guyana Tragedy—The Story of Jim Jones, I Desire, Vengeance: The Story of Tony Cimo, Rage of Angels: The Story Continues, Desperado: The Outlaw Wars, Class of '61, Escape From Terror: The Teresa Stamper Story, Escape to Witch Mountain. *Mini-Series*: Studs Lonigan, Wild Palms. *Specials*: Mound Builders, The Gardener's Son. *Guest:* Miami Vice, The Hitchhiker, Spencer for Hire, Tales of the Unexpected, Moonlighting, The Equalizer, Murder She Wrote, Babylon 5, Voyager, The X Files.

DOWN, LESLEY-ANNE
Actress. b. London, England, March 17, 1954. At age of 10 modeled for TV and film commercials, leading to roles in features. Film debut at 14 in The Smashing Bird I Used to Know (billed as Lesley Down).
THEATER: Great Expectations, Hamlet, etc.
PICTURES: The Smashing Bird I Used to Know (debut, 1969), All the Right Noises, Countess Dracula, Assault, Pope Joan, Scalawag, From Beyond the Grave, Brannigan, The Pink Panther Strikes Again, The Betsy, A Little Night Music, The Great Train Robbery, Hanover Street, Rough Cut, Sphinx, Nomads, Scenes from the Goldmine, Mardi Gras for the Devil, Death Wish V: The Face of Death, Munchie Stikes Back, The Unfaithful, Beastmaster III, The Secret Agent Club, Meet Wally Sparks.
TELEVISION: *Series*: Upstairs, Downstairs, Dallas, Sunset Beach. *Movies*: Agatha Christie's Murder is Easy, Hunchback of Notre Dame, The One and Only Phyllis Dixey, Arch of Triumph, Indiscreet, Lady Killers, Night Walk, Family of Cops. *Mini-Series*: North and South Books I & II & III, Last Days of Pompeii. *Specials*: Unity Mitford,. Heartbreak House. *Pilots:* Shivers, 1775.

DOWNEY, ROBERT, JR.
Actor. b. New York, NY, April 4, 1965. Father is indep. filmmaker Robert Downey. Film debut at age 5 in his father's film Pound.
PICTURES: Pound (debut, 1970), Greaser's Palace, Jive, Up the Academy, Baby Its You, Firstborn, Tuff Turf, Weird Science, To Live and Die in L.A., Back to School, America, The Pick-Up Artist, Less Than Zero, Johnny B. Good, Rented Lips, 1969, True Believer, Chances Are, That's Adequate, Air America, Too Much Sun, Soapdish, Chaplin (Acad. Award nom., BAFTA Award), Hail Caesar, Heart and Souls, The Last Party (also writer), Short Cuts, Natural Born Killers, Only You, Restoration, Danger Zone, Home for the Holidays, Richard III, Two Girls & A Guy, One Night Stand, Hugo Pool, Blue Vision, The Gingerbread Man, U.S. Marshals, Wonder Boys, In Dreams, Friends & Lovers, Bowfinger, Last Party 2000.
TELEVISION: *Series*: Saturday Night Live, Ally McBeal. *Mini-Series*: Mussolini: The Untold Story. *Special*: Dear America (reader). *Movie*: Mr. Willowby's Christmas Tree.

DOWNS, HUGH
Broadcaster. b. Akron, OH, Feb. 14, 1921. e. Bluffton Coll., 1938. Wayne U., 1941. Col. U., N.Y., 1955; Supervisor of Science Programming, NBC's Science Dept. one yr.; science consultant for Westinghouse Labs., Ford Foundation, etc.; chmn. of bd., Raylin Prods., Inc. Today, Chairman, U.S. Committee for UNICEF. Chm. of bd. of governors, National Space Society. Books: Thirty Dirty Lies About Old, Rings Around Tomorrow, School of Stars, Yours Truly Hugh Downs, On Camera: My Ten Thousand Hours on Television, Perspectives, Fifty to Forever.
TELEVISION: *Series*: Kukla Fran & Ollie (announcer), Home, Sid Caesar (announcer), The Jack Paar Show, Concentration, The Tonight Show (announcer, 1962), Today. *Host*: 20/20, Over-Easy (Emmy Award, 1981), Live From Lincoln Center.
RADIO: NBC's Monitor, ABC's Perspectives.

DOYLE, KEVIN
Executive. b. Sydney, Australia, June 21, 1933. e. N. Sydney Tech. HS., Aust. Jr. exec., asst. adv. & pub. div., 20th Century-Fox, Aust., 1947-59; adv. & pub. dir., Columbia Pictures Aust., 1960-66; international ad/pub. mgr.; Columbia Pictures Int'l, N.Y. 1966; intl. pub./promo. mgr., 1980; 1987, Columbia Int'l. rep., Coca-Cola promotions/mktg. sub-committee; int'l pub./promo. mgr. Columbia Tri-Star Film Distributors Inc., 1988; int'l pub./promo. dir. Columbia/Tri-Star Film distrib. Inc. 1990. Retired 1992.

DOYLE-MURRAY, BRIAN
Actor, Writer. b. Chicago, IL., Oct. 31. Brother is comedian Bill Murray. Started as member of Chicago's Second City improv. troupe, before joining the Organic Theatre of Chicago and the Boston Shakespeare Co. Appeared Off-B'way in The National Lampoon Show and on radio on weekly National Lampoon Show.
PICTURES: Caddyshack (also co-s.p.), Modern Problems, National Lampoon's Vacation, Sixteen Candles, The Razor's Edge, Legal Eagles, Club Paradise (also co-s.p.), Scrooged, The Experts, How I Got Into College, Ghostbusters II, National Lampoon's Christmas Vacation, Nothing But Trouble, JFK, Wayne's World, Groundhog Day, Cabin Boy, Jury Duty, Multiplicity, Waiting for Guffman, As Good As It Gets, Casper: A Spirited Beginning, Dennis the Menace 2, Doctor Dolittle (voice), Kill the Man.

TELEVISION: *Series*: Saturday Night Live (also writer), Get a Life, Good Sports, Bakersfield P.D., The Martin Short Show, The George Wendt Show, Recess, Love & Money. *Movies*: Babe Ruth, My Brother's Keeper, Frosty Returns (voice). *Special*: Texan.

DRAGOTI, STAN
Director. b. New York, NY, Oct. 4, 1932. e. Cooper Union and Sch. of Visual Arts. 1959 hired as sketch at ad agency, promoted to sr. art dir., later TV dept. and art dir. of Young & Rubicam. Studied acting HB Studios. Directed Clio awarding-winning TV commercials (including I Love New York campaign).
PICTURES: Dirty Little Billy (debut, 1972; also co-prod., co-s.p.), Love at First Bite, Mr. Mom, The Man With One Red Shoe, She's Out of Control, Necessary Roughness.

DRAI, VICTOR
Producer. b. Casablanca, Morocco, July 25, 1947. e. Lycee de Port Lyautey, 1957-63. In real estate in Los Angeles 1976-82; clothing designer/mfg. in Paris, France, 1969-76. Began producing features in 1984, The Woman in Red.
PICTURES: The Man with One Red Shoe, The Bride, Weekend at Bernie's, Folks!, Weekend at Bernie's II.

DRAZEN, LORI
Executive. Began career as asst. to dir. of adv. for Orion Pictures; creative dept. mgr., Kenyon & Eckhardt; gen. mgr., Seiniger Advertising; joined Warner Bros. 1985 as v.p., worldwide adv. & pub. services.

DREYFUSS, RICHARD
Actor. b. Brooklyn, NY, Oct. 29, 1947. e. Beverly Hills H.S.; San Fernando Valley State Coll. 1965-67. Prof. career began at Gallery Theatre (L.A.) in In Mama's House. Co-Exec. Prod. of film Quiz Show.
THEATER: Journey to the Day, Incident at Vichy, People Need People, Enemy Line, Whose Little Boy Are You, But Seriously, Major Barbara, The Time of Your Life, The Hands of Its Enemy (L.A.), The Normal Heart, Death and the Maiden, others.
PICTURES: The Graduate, Valley of the Dolls, The Young Runaways, Hello Down There, Dillinger, American Graffiti, The Second Coming of Suzanne, The Apprenticeship of Duddy Kravitz, Jaws, Inserts, Close Encounters of the Third Kind, The Goodbye Girl (Acad. Award, 1977), The Big Fix (also co-prod.) The Competition, Whose Life Is It Anyway?, The Buddy System, Down and Out in Beverly Hills, Stand by Me, Tin Men, Stakeout, Nuts, Moon Over Parador, Let It Ride, Always, Postcards from the Edge, Once Around, Rosencrantz and Guildenstern Are Dead, What About Bob?, Lost in Yonkers, Another Stakeout, Silent Fall, The Last Word, The American President, Mr. Holland's Opus, James and the Giant Peach, Night Falls on Manhattan, Mad Dog Time, The Call of the Wild (narr.), A Fine and Private Place, Krippendorf's Tribe.
TELEVISION: *Series*: Karen. *Host*: American Chronicles. *Guest*: Love on a Rooftop, Occasional Wife, The Big Valley, Room 222, Judd for the Defense, Mod Squad, The Bold Ones. *Special*: Funny You Don't Look 200 (host, co-prod., co-writer). *Movies*: Two for the Money, Victory at Entebbe, Prisoner of Honor (also prod.), Lincoln (voice), The Universal Story, Frank Capra's American Dream, Oliver Twist, Lansky.

DRESCHER, FRAN
Actress. b. Queens, NY, Sept. 30, 1957. e. Queen's College.
PICTURES: Saturday Night Fever (debut), American Hot Wax, Gorp, The Hollywood Knights, Ragtime, Cadillac Man, Serious Money, UHF, This is Spinal Tap, The Big Picture, Car 54, Where Are You?, Jack, The Beautician and the Beast, Picking up the Pieces.
TELEVISION: *Series*: Princesses, The Nanny (Golden Globe nom., also co-creator, writer. prod.). Movies: Stranger In Our House, Rock 'n' Roll Mom, Love & Betrayal, Wedding Band, Without Warning: Terror In the Towers.

DRIVER, MINNIE
Actress. r. n. Amelia Driver. b. England, Jan. 31, 1970. e. Bedales School, Petersfield, Hants.
PICTURES: Circle of Friends, GoldenEye, Baggage, Big Night, Sleepers, Grosse Pointe Blank, Good Will Hunting, Tarzan (voice), The Governess, Hard Rain, Slow Burn, An Ideal Husband, South Park: Bigger Longer and Uncut (voice), Return to Me.
TELEVISION: *Series*: God on the Rocks, Mr. Wroe's Virgins. *Mini-Series*: The Politician's Wife. *Guest*: Lovejoy. *Movies*: Merry Christmas George Bailey, That Sunday.

DROMGOOLE, PATRICK
Director, Producer, Executive. b. Iqueque, Chile, Aug. 30, 1930; e. Dulwich Coll., University Coll., Oxford. Joined BBC Radio as dir. 1954, later directing TV plays for BBC and ABC, incl. Armchair Theatre, Frontier, Dracula, Mystery Imagination. Joined HTV as West Country Programme Controller, 1968; dir. award-winning dramas; Thick as Thieves, Machine Gunner. Developed Company's drama output and promoted policy of int'l pre-sales with such dramas as Jamaica Inn, Separate Tables, Catholics, Smuggler, Into the Labyrinth, Kidnapped, Robin of Sherwood, Arch of Triumph, Mr. Halpern and Mr. Johnson, Jenny's War, Codename Kyril, The Diamond Trap, Wall of Tyranny, Strange Interlude, The Woman He Loved, Grand Larceny, Suspicion, Maigret, September. Made Fellow of RTS, 1978; chief exec. HTV Group since 1988.
THEATER: *Director*: incl. first plays of Charles Wood, Joe Orton, David Halliwell, Colin Welland; Peter O'Toole in Man and Superman.
PICTURES: Two Vale South, Hidden Face, Dead Man's Chest, Anthony Purdy Esq., Point of Dissent, The Actors, King of the Wind (exec. prod.), Visage du Passe (dir.), Meutres en Douce, The Canterville Ghost, The Little Match Girl (exec. prod.), Sunday Pursuit (exec, prod.), The Last Butterfly (assoc. prod.).
TELEVISION: *Movie*: Machine Gunner. *Mini-series*: Kidnapped, Return to Treasure Island. *Series*: Smuggler, Into the Labyrinth, Public Eye.

DRURY, JAMES
Actor. b. New York, NY, April 18, 1934. e. New York U. Acting debut at age 8 in biblical play for children at Greenwich Settlement Playhouse. Performed on stage while youngster. Signed by MGM in 1955, working one day in each of seven movies that year, including Blackboard Jungle. Then got two-year contract at 20th-Fox. Gained fame as hero of TV series, The Virginian, which had nine-year run.
PICTURES: Forbidden Planet, Love Me Tender, Bernardine, Toby Tyler, Pollyana, Ten Who Dared, Ride the High Country, The Young Warriors.
TELEVISION: *Series*: The Virginian, Firehouse. *Movies*: Breakout, Alias Smith and Jones, The Devil and Miss Sarah, The Gambler Returns: Luck of the Draw.

DUBAND, WAYNE
Executive. b. Sydney, Australia, Feb. 13, 1947. Joined Warner Bros. 1969 as mgr. trainee in Australia. 1973, transferred to South Africa as mgr. dir.; 1977 gen. mgr. of CIC/Warner Bros. joint venture, also managing the CIC theatre operation there. 1980, named exec. asst. to Myron D. Karlin, pres. WB Intl., in Burbank. 1981, mgr. dir. of Warner/Columbia joint venture in France. 1985, appt. v.p. of sls. for WB Intl. division. 1987, appt. senior v.p. for Warner Bros. Intl. division. 1992, appt. pres. Intl. Theatrical div., WB Intl.

DUBE, JACKSON E.
Executive. b. New York, NY. e. U. of North Carolina. m. Pat Lavelle, actress. USAF 1942-45 Radar-Gunner, AAF, Italy. Writer: Television and Sponsor Magazine 1947-48; reviews of recorded music. 1947-51, Consol Film Inds. Penthouse Prods. Dist.: E. sales mgr. Atlas Tel. Corp. 1951-54; vp & gen. mgr., Craftsman Film Greatest Fights of the Century 1954; vp, Conquest Prods. CBS Net. Docus. 1954-57. TV and radio dir. Cote Fischer & Rogow Adv., 1957-59; exec. vp, Bon Ami Film; dist.: UA Feats. abroad 1959-63; prod's rep. Le Vien Prods.— Finest Hours King's Story; Eastern sales mgr. Desilu, 1964-67; exec. vp, UCC Films; dist. RKO feature Library abroad, 1969-70; pres. JED Rrns. Corp. Dist. London Films, Rank chidren's features, 1967-88. Consultant: New Century Ent., Windsor Pdns., Rurner Program Services, 1985-88. Agent for Weiss Global, Medallion TV Enterprises, Turner International, Morin International, 1988-92. Agent for Aries S.A. and Sidney Beckerman Prods. Agent for Otto Preminger Films Ltd. JED Productions Corp. owner or partner in remake rights to 125 US feature motion pictures 1992 to present.

DUBS, ARTHUR R.
Executive, Producer, Director, Writer, President and Owner of Pacific International Enterprises, b. Medford, OR, Feb. 26, 1930. e. Southern Oregon State Coll. Founded Pacific International Enterprises, 1969.
PICTURES: *Producer-Director*: American Wilderness, Vanishing Wilderness, Wonder of It All. *Exec. Prod.:* Challenge to Be Free. *Prod.*: Adventures of the Wilderness Family, Wilderness Family Part 2 (also s.p.), Mountain Family Robinson (also s.p.), Across the Great Divide, Sacred Ground, Mystery Mansion, Dream Chasers (also co-dir.). *Co-Prod.:* Windwalker.

DUCHOVNY, DAVID
Actor. b. New York, NY, Aug. 7, 1960. e. Yale. Was teaching asst. at Yale before landing first acting job in beer commercial. m. actress Tea Leoni
PICTURES: Working Girl (debut, 1988), New Year's Day, Bad Influence, Julia Has Two Lovers, Don't Tell Mom the Babysitter's Dead, The Rapture, Ruby, Venice/Venice, Chaplin, Kalifornia, Playing God, The X Files: Fight the Future, Return to Me, Evolution.
TELEVISION: *Series:* Twin Peaks, The X Files (Golden Globe Award, 1997). *Movies*: Red Shoe Diaries, Red Shoe Diaries 2: Double Dare, Baby Snatcher, Red Shoe Diaries 3: Another Woman's Lipstick, Red Shoe Diaries 6: How I Met My Husband, Red Shoe Diaries 7: Burning Up, Red Shoe Diaries 8: Night of Abandon. Guest: The Simpsons (voice).

DUDELHEIM, HANS RUDOLF
Communications Executive. b. Berlin, Germany, June 17, 1927. e. Sch. of Photography Berlin, School of Radio & TV NY. Film editor, ABC, 1951-66. Prod/Dir/Edit.: Cinema Arts Assn. 1966-90; served as pres. Founder, 1961, Cinema Arts Film Soc. Editor of documentaries: Saga of Western Man, Comrade Student, Sublimated Birth (also prod.), Kent State, Sigmund Freud, IBM Motivation Project, The Forgotten Pioneers of Hollywood, Painting With Love. *Producer*: Sesame Street, 60 Minutes: Ranaissance Community, American Dream Machine, Voyage of the Barba Negra. Presently film and video consultant. Instructor at New School For Social Reserach.

DUDLEY, ANNE
Composer. b. Chatham, Kent, England, May 7, 1956.
PICTURES: Hiding Out, Buster, The Misadventures of Mr. Wilt, The Mighty Quinn, Zwei Frauen, Say Anything..., The Pope Must Die, The Miracle, Knight Moves, The Crying Game, Felidae, When Saturday Comes, The Grotesque, Hollow Reed, The Full Monty (Acad. Award, 1997), American History X.
TELEVISION: *Series*: Jeeves and Wooster, Ngaio Marsh's Alleyn Mysteries, Anna Lee.

DUDIKOFF, MICHAEL
Actor. b. Torrance, CA, Oct. 8, 1954.
PICTURES: Making Love, I Ought to Be in Pictures, Tron, Bachelor Party, Bloody Birthday, American Ninja, Radioactive Dreams, Avenging Force, American Ninja II: The Confrontation, Platoon Leader, River of Death, American Ninja 4: The Annihilation, Midnight Ride, Human Shield, Rescue Me, Virtual Assassin, Shooter, Executive Command, Bounty Hunters II, Crash Dive, Moving Target, Soldier Boyz, Cyberjack, Chain of Command, Strategic Command, In Her Defense, Freedom Strike, Ringmaster
TELEVISION: *Mini-Series*: North and South Book II. *Movie*: The Woman Who Sinned. *Series*: Star of the Family, Cobra. *Pilot*: Sawyer and Finn. *Guest*: Happy Days, Dallas.

DUFFY, JAMES E.
Executive. b. Decatur, IL, April 2, 1926. e. Beloit Coll. Radio announcer, then reporter; joined publicity dept., ABC in 1949; named dir. of adv. & promo., then account exec. for Central division of ABC Radio Network; dir. of sales ABC Radio, 1957; central div. account exec., ABC TV Network, 1955; natl. dir. of Sales, ABC Radio central division, 1960; v.p., ABC Radio Network, 1961; exec. v.p. & natl. dir. of sales, 1962; v.p. in charge of sales, ABC TV Network, 1963; pres., ABC TV Network, 1970-85; pres., communications, 1985-86; v.p. Capital Cities/ABC, Inc.; pres., communications, ABC Network & Bdgst. Divisions.

DUFFY, PATRICK
Actor. b. Townsend, MT, March 17, 1949. e. U. of Washington. Became actor-in-residence in state of Washington, where performed with various statefunded groups. Acted off-B'way Taught mime and movement classes in summer camp in Seattle. Moved to L.A. and began TV acting career.
PICTURE: Vamping (also co-exec prod.), Perfect Game.
TELEVISION: *Specials*: The Last of Mrs. Lincoln, Freedom Festival '89 (host). *Movies*: The Stranger Who Looks Like Me, Hurricane, Man From Atlantis, Enola Gay, Cry for the Strangers, Strong Medicine, Alice in Wonderland, Too Good to Be True, Unholy Matrimony, Murder C.O.D, Children of the Bride, Danielle Steel's Daddy, Texas, Dallas: J.R. Returns, Heart of Fire, Dallas: War of the Ewings, Don't Look Behind You. *Series*: Man from Atlantis, Dallas, Step By Step. *Guest*: Switch, George Burns' Comedy Week.

DUGAN, DENNIS
Actor, Director. b. Wheaton, IL, Sept. 5, 1946. Studied acting at Goodman Theatre School.
THEATER: *NY*: A Man's Man, The House of Blue Leaves. *LA*: Once in a Lifetime, Rainbows for Sales, Estonia, The Dining Room, The Kitchen.
PICTURES: Night Call Nurses, The Day of the Locust, Night Moves, Smile, Harry and Walter Go to New York, Norman ... Is That You?, Unidentified Flying Oddball, The Howling, Water, Can't Buy Me Love, She's Having a Baby, The New Adventures of Pippi Longstocking, Parenthood, Problem Child (also dir.), Brain Donors (also dir.), Happy Gilmore (also dir.), Beverly Hills Ninja (dir. only), Big Daddy (also dir.).
TELEVISION: *Series*: Richie Brockelman: Private Eye, Empire, Shadow Chasers. *Movies*: Death Race, The Girl Most Likely To..., Last of the Good Guys, Country Gold, The Toughest Man in the World, Columbo: Butterfly in Shades of Grey. *Mini-Series*: Rich man Poor Man. *Guest*: Hooperman, Moonlighting, M*A*S*H, The Rockford Files, Scene of the Crime, Making a Living, Hill Street Blues. *Pilots*: Alice, Father O Father, Did You Hear About Josh and Kelly?, Full House, Channel 99. *Director*: Hunter, Sonny Spoon, Wiseguy, Moonlighting, The Shaggy Dog (movie), L.A. Law, Columbo, Picket Fences, NYPD Blue, Chicago Hope, Ally McBeal.

DUGGAN, ERVIN S.
Executive. Started as reporter for the Washington Post in early 1960's. As member of President Lydon Johnson's staff helped define government's role in supporting public broadcasting with the Public Broadcasting Act of 1967. Served as special asst. to Senators Lloyd Bentsen and Adlai Stevenson III, Health Education and Welfare Secretary Joseph Califano; and as member of the State Dept. Policy Planning Staff. 1981-90, managed communications and consulting firm. Served 4 years as Commissioner of the Federal Communications Commission. Feb. 1994 joined PBS as pres. and CEO.

DUIGAN, JOHN
Director, Writer. b. Hartley Wintney, Hampshire, England, June 19, 1949. Lived in England and Malaysia before moving to Sydney, Australia. e. Univ. of Melbourne, philosophy, M.A. Taught for several years at Univ. of Melbourne and Latrobe U. before entering films. Directed and wrote experimental short, The Firm Man (1974). Novels: Badge, Players, Room to Move.
PICTURES: *Dir.-Writer*: Trespassers, Mouth to Mouth, Winter of Our Dreams (Australian Writers Guild Award), Far East, The Year My Voice Broke (Australian Acad. Award for best dir., s.p.) Romero (dir. only), Flirting, Wide Sargasso Sea, Sirens (also actor), The Journey of August King, The Leading Man, Lawn Dogs, Molly.
TELEVISION: *Mini-Series*: Vietnam (co-dir.). *Movie*: Fragments of War: The Story of Damien Parer.

DUKAKIS, OLYMPIA
Actress. b. Lowell, MA, June 20, 1931. m. actor Louis Zorich. e. Boston U., B.A., M.F.A. Founding mem. of The Charles Playhouse, Boston, establishing summer theatre 1957-60. Taught acting at NYU: 1967-70 as instructor, 1974-83 as master teacher, and at Yale U. 1976. With husband conceived and guided artistic dev. of Whole Theatre of Monclair, NJ, 1977-90; producing artistic dir. Adapted plays for her co. and dir. theater there; also at Williamstown Theatre Fest. and Delaware Summer Fest. Appeared in more than 100 plays on B'way, Off-B'way and in regional and summer theater.
THEATER: Who's Who in Hell, The Aspern Papers, Night of the Iguana, The Breaking Wall, Curse of the Starving Class, Snow Orchid, The Marriage of Bette and Boo (Obie Award), Social Security.
PICTURES: Lilith, Twice a Man, John and Mary, Made for Each Other, Death Wish, Rich Kids, The Wanderers, The Idolmaker, National Lampoon Goes to the Movies, Flanagan, Moonstruck (Acad. Award, best supporting actress, 1987), Working Girl, Look Who's Talking, Steel Magnolias, Dad, In the Spirit, Look Who's Talking Too, The Cemetery Club, Over the Hill, Look Who's Talking Now, Naked Gun 33 1/3: The Final Insult (cameo), I Love Trouble, Jeffrey, Mighty Aphrodite, Mr. Holland's Opus, Picture Perfect, Never Too Late, Milk and Money, Better Living, Jane Austen's Mafia, Brooklyn Sonnet.
TELEVISION: *Specials*: The Rehearsal, Sisters, Last Act is a Solo, A Century of Women. *Series*: Search for Tomorrow, One of the Boys. *Movies*: Nicky's World, The Neighborhood, FDR-The Last Year, King of America, Lucky Day, Fire in the Dark, Sinatra, Young at Heart. *Mini-Series*: Tales of the City, More Tales of the City, Joan of Arc.

DUKE, BILL
Actor, Director. b. Poughkeepsie, NY, Feb. 26, 1943. e. Boston Univ., NY Univ. Sch. of the Arts. Recieved AFI Best Young Director Award for short The Hero (Gold Award, Houston Film Festival). Has written poetry, short stories for children. Member bd. of dirs. American Film Institute.
PICTURES: *Actor*: Car Wash, American Gigolo, Commando, Predator, No Man's Land, Action Jackson, Bird on a Wire, Street of No Return, Menace II Society, Payback. *Director:* A Rage in Harlem, Deep Cover, The Cemetery Club, Sister Act 2: Back in the Habit, America's Dream, Hoodlums (also exec. prod.).
TELEVISION: *Actor: Movies*: Love is Not Enough, Sgt. Matlovich Vs. the U.S. Air Force. *Series*: Palmerstown U.S.A. *Director: Series*: A Man Called Hawk, Cagney & Lacey, Hill Street Blues, Miami Vice, Dallas. *Specials*: The Killing Floor, A Raisin in the Sun, The Meeting. *Movie*: Johnnie Mae Gibson.

DUKE, PATTY
Actress. r.n. Anna Marie Duke. b. New York, NY, Dec. 14, 1946. e. Quintano Sch. for Young Professionals. Mother of actors Sean and Mackenzie Astin. Pres., Screen Actors Guild, 1985-88. *Author*: Surviving Sexual Assault (1983), Call Me Anna (1987).
THEATER: The Miracle Worker (Theatre World Award), Isle of Children.
PICTURES: I'll Cry Tomorrow (debut as extra 1955), The Goddess, Happy Anniversary, The 4-D Man, The Miracle Worker (Acad. Award, best supporting actress, 1962), Billie, Valley of the Dolls, Me Natalie, The Swarm, By Design, Something Special, Prelude to a Kiss, Harvest of Fire, Kimberly.
TELEVISION: *Series*: The Brighter Day, The Patty Duke Show, It Takes Two, Hail to the Chief, Karen's Song, Amazing Grace. *Guest*: Armstrong Circle Theatre, The SS Andrea Doria, U.S. Steel Hour, All's Fair. *Specials*: The Prince and the Pauper, Wuthering Heights, Swiss Family Robinson, Meet Me in St. Louis, The Power and the Glory. *Movies*: My Sweet Charlie (Emmy Award, 1970), Two on a Bench, If Tomorrow Comes, She Waits, Deadly Harvest, Nightmare, Look What's Happened to Rosemary's Baby, Fire!, Rosetti & Ryan: Men Who Love Women, Curse of the Black Widow, Killer on Board, The Storyteller, Having Babies III, A Family Upside Down, Women in White, Hanging by a Thread, Before and After, The Miracle Worker (Emmy Award, 1980), The Women's Room, Mom The Wolfman and Me, The Babysitter, Violation of Sarah McDavid, Something So Right, September Gun, Best Kept Secrets, Fight for Life, Perry Mason: The Case of the Avenging Angel, A Time to Triumph, Fatal Judgment, Everybody's Baby: The Rescue of Jessica McClure, Amityville: The Evil Escapes, Call Me Anna, Always Remember I Love You, Absolute Strangers, Last Wish, Grave Secrets: The Legacy of Hilltop Drive, A Killer Among Friends, Family of Strangers, No Child of Mine, A Matter of Justice, One Woman's Courage, Cries From the Heart, When the Vows Break, Race Against Time: The Search for Sarah, The Disappearing Act, A Christmas Memory, When He Didn't Come Home. *Mini-Series*: Captains and the Kings (Emmy Award, 1977), George Washington.

DUKES, DAVID
Actor. b. San Francisco, CA, June 6, 1945. With The American Consevatory Theatre in San Francisco, The CA Shakespeare Festival in Los Gatos, The Alley Theater in Houston, The San Diego Shakespeare Festival, The Matrix Theatre Co. in L.A., and many others.
THEATER: *B'way*: The School for Wives, Don Juan, The Great God Brown, Chemin de Fer, The Visit, Holiday, The Play's the Thing, Love for Love, Rules of the Game, Travesties, Dracula, Bent, Frankenstein, Amadeus, M. Butterfly, Love Letters, Someone Who'll Watch Over Me, Broken Glass.
PICTURES: The Strawberry Statement, Call Me Mister Tibbs!, The Wild Party, A Little Romance, The First Deadly Sin, Only When I Laugh, Without a Trace, The Men's Club, Rawhead Rex, Catch the Heat, Date With an Angel, Deadly Intent, See You in the Morning, Under Surveillance, The Rutanga Tapes, The Handmaid's Tale, Me and the Kid, Slappy and the Stinkers, Fled.
TELEVISION: *Series*: Beacon Hill, All That Glitters, Sisters, The Mommies, Pauly. *Mini-Series*: 79 Park Avenue, George Washington, Kane & Abel, Space, The Winds of War, War and Remembrance, Look at it This Way. *Specials*: Strange Interlude, Cat on a Hot Tin Roof. *Movies*: Valley Forge, The Norming of Jack 243, A Fire in the Sky, The Triangle Factory Fire, How the West Was Won, Some Kind of Miracle, Mayflower—The Pilgrim Adventure, Margaret Sanger— Portrait of a Rebel, Miss All-American Beauty, Sentimental Journey, Darlin' Clementine, Snowkill, Held Hostage: The Sis and Jerry Levin Story, The Josephine Baker Story, Turn Back the Clock, Wife—Mother—Murderer, She Woke Up, Spies Look at It This Way (BBC), And The Band Played On, The Surrogate, Norma Jean & Marilyn, Last Stand at Saber River, The Love Letter. *Guest*: All in the Family, The Jeffersons, Once Day at a Time, Barney Miller, Hawaii 5-0, Police Story, Police Woman, Cannon, etc.

DULLEA, KEIR
Actor. b. Cleveland, OH, May 30, 1936. e. Rutgers Univ., San Francisco State Coll., Sanford Meisner's Neighborhood Playhouse. Acted as resident juvenile at the Totem Pole Playhouse in PA. NY theatre debut in the revue Sticks and Stones, 1956; appeared in stock co. prods. at the Berkshire Playhouse and Philadelphia's Hedgerow Theatre, 1959; off-Broadway debut in Season of Choice, 1969. Won San Francisco Film Festival Award for performance in film David and Lisa, 1963.
THEATER: Dr. Cook's Garden, Butterflies Are Free, Cat on a Hot Tin Roof, P.S. Your Cat is Dead, The Other Side of Paradise.
PICTURES: The Hoodlum Priest (debut, 1961), David and Lisa, The Thin Red Line, Mail Order Bride, The Naked Hours, Bunny Lake Is Missing, Madame X, The Fox, 2001: A Space Odyssey, De Sade, Pope Joan, Paperback Hero, Il Diavolo nel Cervello, Paul and Michelle, Black Christmas (Silent Night Evil Night), Leopard in the Snow, Welcome to Blood City, The Haunting of Julia (Full Circle), Because He's My Friend, The Next One, Brainwaves, Blind Date, 2010, Oh What a Night.
TELEVISION: *Movies*: Black Water Gold, Law and Order, Legend of the Golden Gun, Brave New World, The Hostage Tower, No Place to Hide. *Special:* Mrs. Miniver.

DUNAWAY, FAYE
Actress. b. Bascom, FL, Jan. 14, 1941. e. Texas, Arkansas, Utah, Germany, U. of Florida. Awarded a Fulbright scholarship in theatre. Boston U. of Fine Applied Arts. With Lincoln Center Rep. Co. for 3 years. NY Stage: A Man for All Seasons, After the Fall, Hogan's Goat (Theatre World Award), The Curse of an Aching Heart.
PICTURES: Hurry Sundown (debut, 1967), The Happening, Bonnie and Clyde, The Thomas Crown Affair, The Extraordinary Seaman, A Place for Lovers, The Arrangement, Puzzle of a Downfall Child, Little Big Man, The Deadly Trap, Doc, Oklahoma Crude, The Three Musketeers, Chinatown, The Towering Inferno, The Four Musketeers, Three Days of the Condor, Network (Acad. Award, 1976), Voyage of the Damned, Eyes of Laura Mars, The Champ, The First Deadly Sin, Mommie Dearest, The Wicked Lady, Ordeal by Innocence, Supergirl, Barfly, Midnight Crossing, Burning Secret, The Handmaid's Tale, Wait Until Spring Bandini, The Gamble, On a Moonlit Night, Scorchers, Double Edge, The Temp, Arizona Dream, Don Juan DeMarco, Drunks, Dunston Checks In, Albino Alligator, The Chamber, The Yards, The Thomas Crown Affair, The Messenger: The Story of Joan of Arc, Stanley's Gig.
TELEVISION: *Movies*: The Woman I Love, The Disappearance of Aimee, Evita, Peron, 13 at Dinner, Beverly Hills Madam, The Country Girl, Casanova, The Raspberry Ripple, Cold Sassy Tree, Silhouette, Columbo: It's All in the Game (Emmy Award, 1994), A Family Divided, Rebecca, Gia. *Mini-Series*: Ellis Island, Christopher Columbus. *Specials*: Hogan's Goat, After the Fall, Supergirl: The Making of the Movie (host), Inside the Dream Factory (host). *Series*: It Had to Be You.

DUNCAN, LINDSAY
Actress. Stage actress with National Theatre, Royal Shakespeare Company.
THEATER: Plenty, The Provok'd Wife, The Prince of Homburg, Top Girls, Progress, The Merry Wives of Windsor, Les Liaisons Dangereuses (RSC, West End, Broadway; Theatre World Award), Cat On A Hot Tin Roof, Hedda Gabler, A Midsummer Night's Dream, Cryptogram.
PICTURES: Loose Connections, Samson & Delilah, Prick Up Your Ears, Manifesto, The Reflecting Skin, Body Parts, City Hall, A Midsummer Night's Dream.
TELEVISION: *Movies*: Reilly, Ace of Spies, A Year in Provence, The Rector's Wife. *Mini-series*: Dead Head, Traffik, A Year in Provence, G.B.H., Jake's Progress, The History of Tom Jones A Foundling. *Guest*: The Storyteller: Greek Myths, The New Avengers, Colin's Sandwich, Tecx.

DUNCAN, MICHAEL
Actor. b. 1964.
PICTURES: Back in Business, A Night at the Roxbury, Caught Up, The Players Club, Bulworth, Armageddon, The Green Mile.

DUNCAN, SANDY
Actress. b. Henderson, TX, Feb. 20, 1946. m. singer-dancer Don Correia. e. Len Morris Coll.
THEATER: The Music Man (NY debut, 1965); The Boyfriend, Ceremony of Innocence (Theatre World Award), Your Own Thing, Canterbury Tales, Peter Pan, Five Six Seven Eight Dance!, My One and Only.
PICTURES: $1,000,000 Duck, Star Spangled Girl, The Cat from Outer Space, Rock a Doodle (voice), The Swan Princess (voice).
TELEVISION: *Series*: Funny Face, The Sandy Duncan Show, Valerie's Family. *Movies*: My Boyfriend's Back, Miracle on Interstate 880. *Mini-Series*: Roots. *Specials*: Pinocchio, Sandy in Disneyland, The Sandy Duncan Special.

DUNING, GEORGE
Composer, Conductor, Arranger. b. Richmond, IN, Feb. 25, 1908. e. Cincinnati Conservatory of Music, U. of Cincinnati. Music dir. Aaron Spelling Prods., 1970-71, Bobby Sherman Show, Movies of the Week. Board of Directors, ASCAP, 1969-83. V.P. ASCAP, 1977-79. Society for Preservation of Film Music Career Achievement Award, 1987; Indiana Composer of the Year, 1993.
PICTURES: Down to Earth, The Guilt of Janet Ames, Johnny O'Clock, To the Ends of the Earth, Jolson Sings Again, The Eddy Duchin Story, From Here to Eternity, Picnic, Pal Joey, Cowboy, The Last Angry Man, The World of Susie Wong, Devil at 4 O'Clock, The Notorious Landlady, Toys in the Attic, Ensign Pulver, Dear Brigitte, Any Wednesday, Terror in the Wax Museum, The Man with Bogart's Face.
TELEVISION: No Time for Sergeants, Wendy and Me, The Farmer's Daughter, Big Valley, The Long Hot Summer, The Second Hundred Years, Star Trek, Mannix, Then Came Bronson.

DUNLAP, RICHARD D.
Producer, Director. b. Pomona, CA, Jan. 30, 1923. e. Yale U., B.A., 1944; M.F.A., 1948. U.S. Navy 1943-46; Instructor, English dept., Yale U., 1947-48; Prod.-dir., Kraft TV Theatre, 3 years; Dir, Assoc. Prod., Omnibus, 3 seasons; Dir., 25 half-hr. Dramatic Film Shows. Frank Sinatra Specials, Prod.-Dir., 11 Academy Award Shows, 4 Emmy Award Shows.

DUNNE, DOMINICK
Producer. Writer. b. Hartford, CT, Oct. 29, 1925. e. Canterbury Sch., 1944; Williams Col., 1949. Son is actor-prod. Griffin Dunne. Began career as stage manager at NBC-TV; then produced shows for CBS Studio One. Later exec. prod. at 20th-Fox TV, v.p. at Four Star. Novels: The Winners, The Two Mrs. Grenvilles, People Like Us, An Inconvenient Woman, A Season in Purgatory, Fatal Charms, The Mansions of Limbo.
PICTURES: The Boys in the Band (exec. prod.), The Panic in Needle Park, Play It as It Lays, Ash Wednesday.

DUNN, KEVIN
Actor. b. Chicago, IL, 1956.
PICTURES: Mississippi Burning, Ghostbusters II (uncredited), Taken Away, Marked for Death, Blue Steel, The Bonfire of the Vanities, Hot Shots!, Only the Lonely, Chaplin, 1492: Conquest of Paradise, Dave, Little Big League, Mad Love, Nixon, Commandments, Chain Reaction, Edwards and Hunt, The Sixth Man, Picture Perfect, Almost Heroes, Godzilla, Snake Eyes, Small Soldiers, Stir of Echoes.
TELEVISION: *Series*: Jack & Mike, Arsenio. *Movies*: Night of Courage, Blind Faith, Double Edge, Shadow of a Doubt, The Four Diamonds, Unforgivable, The Second Civil War, On the Edge of Innocence. *Guest*: Cheers, Roseanne, 21 Jump Street, Seinfeld.

DUNNE, GRIFFIN
Actor, Producer. b. New York, NY, June 8, 1955. Son of prod.-writer Dominick Dunne. foremerly m. actress Carey Lowell. Formed Double Play Prods. with Amy Robinson. Studied at Neighborhood Playhouse and with Uta Hagen. On Stage in Album, Marie and Bruce, Coming Attractions, Hotel Play, Search and Destroy (B'way debut; Theatre World Award).
PICTURES: *Actor*: The Other Side of the Mountain (debut, 1975), Chilly Scenes of Winter (also prod.), The Fan, American Werewolf in London, Cold Feet, Almost You, Johnny Dangerously, After Hours (also co-prod., Golden Globe nom.), Who's That Girl, Amazon Women on the Moon, Big Blue, Me and Him, Once Around (also co-prod.), My Girl, Straight Talk, Big Girls Don't Cry... They Get Even, The Pickle, Naked in New York, Quiz Show, I Like It Like That, Search and Destroy. *Producer only*: Baby It's You, Running on Empty, White Palace, Once Around, Joe's Apartment (exec.). *Director/Writer*: Duke of Groove (short, Oscar nom.), Addicted to Love, Practical Magic.

TELEVISION: *Movies*: The Wall, Secret Weapon, Love Matters, The Android Affair, Love Matters (Ace nom.). *Specials*: Lip Service, Trying Times: Hunger Chic, Partners. *Pilot*: Graham.

DUNST, KIRSTEN
Actress. b. Point Pleasant, NJ, April 30, 1982
PICTURES: New York Stories, The Bonfire of the Vanities, Little Women, High Strung, Greedy, Interview with the Vampire, Jumanji, Mother Night, Anastasia (voice), Wag the Dog, Strike, Small Soldiers, The Virgin Suicides, Drop Dead Gorgeous, Dick, The Crow: Salvation, Luckytown Blues, Bring It On, Deeply, All Forgotten, Getting Over Allison, At Seventeen..
TELEVISION: *Movies:* Darkness Before Dawn, Children Remember the Holocaust (voice), Ruby Ridge: An American Tragedy, Tower of Terror, Fifteen and Pregnant, The Animated Adventures of Tom Sawyer (voice), Devil's Arithmetic. *Series:* Stories from My Childhood. *Guest:* Sisters, Star Trek: The Next Generation, Touched by an Angel, Gun, ER.

DURNING, CHARLES
Actor. b. Highland Falls, NY, Feb. 28, 1923. e. NYU. Studied acting on the G.I. Bill. Prof. stage debut, 1960. Made several appearances with Joseph Papp's NY Shakespeare Festival.
THEATER: That Championship Season, Knock Knock, Au Pair Man, In the Boom Boom Room, The Happy Time, Indians, Cat on a Hot Tin Roof (Tony Award, 1990), Queen of the Stardust Ballroom, Inherit the Wind.
PICTURES: Harvey Middleman—Fireman (debut, 1965), I Walk the Line, Hi Mom!, The Pursuit of Happiness, Dealing: or the Berkeley-to- Boston Forty-Brick Lost-Bag Blues, Deadhead Miles, Sisters, The Sting, The Front Page, Dog Day Afternoon, The Hindenburg, Breakheart Pass, Harry and Walter Go to New York, Twilight's Last Gleaming, The Choirboys, An Enemy of the People, The Fury, The Greek Tycoon, Tilt, The Muppet Movie, North Dallas Forty, Starting Over, When a Stranger Calls, Die Laughing, The Final Countdown, True Confessions, Sharky's Machine, The Best Little Whorehouse in Texas (Acad. Award nom.), Tootsie, To Be or Not to Be (Acad. Award nom.), Two of a Kind, Hadley's Rebellion, Mass Appeal, Stick, The Man With One Red Shoe, Stand Alone, Big Trouble, Tough Guys, Where the River Runs Black, Solarbabies, Happy New Year, The Rosary Murders, A Tiger's Tail, Cop, Far North, Cat Chaser, Dick Tracy, V. I. Warshawski, Brenda Starr, Etolie, Fatal Sky, The Music of Chance, The Hudsucker Proxy, I.Q., Home for the Holidays, The Last Supper, The Grass Harp, Spy Hard, One Fine Day, Shelter, Secret Life of Algernon, Justice, Jerry & Tom, Hi-Life, The Last Producer.
TELEVISION: *Series*: Another World (1972), The Cop and the Kid, Eye to Eye, Evening Shade. *Mini-Series*: Captains and the Kings, Studs Lonigan, The Kennedys of Massachusetts, A Woman of Independent Means. *Specials*: The Rivalry, The Dancing Bear, Working, Mr. Roberts, Side by Side (pilot), P.O.P. (pilot), Eye to Eye, Tales from Hollywood, Normandy (narrator), Texan, Leslie's Folly. *Movies*: The Connection, The Trial of Chaplain Jensen, Queen of the Stardust Ballroom, Switch, Special Olympics, Attica, Perfect Match, Crisis at Central High, The Best Little Girl in the World, Dark Night of the Scarecrow, Death of a Salesman, Kenny Rogers as The Gambler III—The Legend Continues, The Man Who Broke 1000 Chains, Case Closed, Unholy Matrimony, Prime Target, It Nearly Wasn't Christmas, Dinner at Eight, The Return of Eliot Ness, The Story Lady, The Water Engine, Roommates, Mrs. Santa Claus, Hard Time. *Guest*: Madigan, All in the Family, Barnaby Jones, Hawaii Five-O, Amazing Stories, Everybody Loves Raymond.

DURWOOD, RICHARD M.
Executive. b. Kansas City, MO, Aug. 18, 1929. e. Brown U., A.B. Pres. Crown Cinema Corp. Member: Motion Picture Assn. of Kansas City (pres.), United Motion Pictures Assn. (pres. 1972-73), Young NATO (chmn., 1968-69), Past Chief Barker, Tent No. 8. Past mem., exec. comm., National NATO. Sr. v.p., and on bd. of dirs. of American Movie Classics, 1952-1976. 1996, sold Crown Cinema Corp. to Hollywood, Inc.

DUSSAULT, NANCY
Actress. b. Pensacola, FL, Jun. 30, 1936. e. Northwestern U.
THEATER: *B'way:* Street Scene, The Mikado, The Cradle Will Rock, Do Re Mi (Theatre World Award), Sound of Music, Carousel, Fiorello, The Gershwin Years, Into the Woods. *L.A. stage:* Next in Line.
PICTURE: The In-Laws, The Nurse.
TELEVISION: *Special*: The Beggars Opera. *Host*: Good Morning America. *Series*: The New Dick Van Dyke Show, Too Close for Comfort (The Ted Knight Show).

DUTTON, CHARLES S.
Actor. b. Baltimore, MD, Jan. 30, 1951. e. Towson St., Yale Sch. of Drama.
THEATER: *Yale Rep:* The Works, Beef No Chicken, Astopovo, Othello. *NY*: Ma Rainey's Black Bottom (Theatre World Award, 1983), Joe Turner's Come and Gone, The Piano Lesson.
PICTURES: No Mercy, Crocodile Dundee II, Jacknife, An Unremarkable Life, Q & A, Mississippi Masala, Alien3, The Distinguished Gentleman, Menace II Society, Rudy, Foreign Student, A Low Down Dirty Shame, Cry the Beloved Country, Nick of Time, Last Dance, A Time to Kill, Get on the Bus, Mimic, Blind Faith, Black Dog, Cookie's Fortune, Random Hearts, Detox.
TELEVISION: *Series*: Roc (also prod.). *Guest*: Miami Vice, The Equalizer, Cagney and Lacey, Oz. *Movies*: Apology, The Murder of Mary Phagan, Jack Reed: Search for Justice, The Piano Lesson, Zooman, Aftershock, The '60s. *Special*: Runaway.

DUVAL, JAMES
Actor. b. Detroit, MI, Sept. 10, 1973.
PICTURES: Totally F***ed Up, An Ambush of Ghosts, Mod Fuck Explosion, The Doom Generation, Independence Day, River Made to Drown In, Nowhere, The Clown at Midnight, S.L.C. Punk!, How to Make the Cruelest Month, Go, The Weekend.

DUVALL, ROBERT
Actor. b. San Diego, CA, Jan. 5, 1931. e. Principia College, IL. Studied at the Neighborhood Playhouse, NY.
THEATER: *Off-B'way*: The Days and Nights of Bee Bee Fenstermaker, Call Me By My Rightful Name, A View From the Bridge (Obie Award, 1965). *B'way*: Wait Until Dark, American Buffalo.
PICTURES: To Kill a Mockingbird (debut, 1962), Captain Newman M.D., Nightmare in the Sun, The Chase, Countdown, The Detective, Bullitt, True Grit, The Rain People, M*A*S*H, The Revolutionary, THX-1138, Lawman, The Godfather, Tomorrow, The Great Northfield Minnesota Raid, Joe Kidd, Lady Ice, Badge 373, The Outfit, The Conversation, The Godfather Part II, Breakout, The Killer Elite, The Seven Percent Solution, Network, We're Not the Jet Set (dir., co-prod. only), The Eagle Has Landed, The Greatest, The Betsy, Invasion of the Body Snatchers (cameo), Apocalypse Now, The Great Santini, True Confessions, The Pursuit of D.B. Cooper, Tender Mercies (Acad. Award, 1983; also co-prod, songwriter), Angelo My Love (dir., prod., s.p. only), The Stone Boy, The Natural, Bellizaire the Cajun (cameo; also creative consultant), The Lightship, Let's Get Harry, Hotel Colonial, Colors, The Handmaid's Tale, A Show of Force, Days of Thunder, Rambling Rose, Convicts, Newsies, Falling Down, The Plague, Geronimo: An American Legend, Wrestling Ernest Hemingway, The Paper, Something to Talk About, The Stars Fell on Henrietta, The Scarlet Letter, A Family Thing (also co-prod.), Sling Blade, Phenomenon, The Apostle (also s.p., dir., exec. prod., Chicago Film Crits. Award, LA Film Crits. Award, Best Actor, 1997), Deep Impact, The Gingerbread Man, A Civil Action (Acad. Award nom.), Gone in Sixty Seconds, A Shot At Glory (also prod.), The 6th Day, John Q.
TELEVISION: *Movies*: Fame Is the Name of the Game, The Terry Fox Story, Stalin. *Mini-Series*: Ike, Lonesome Dove. *Guest*: Great Ghost Tales, The Outer Limits, Naked City, Route 66, The Defenders, Alfred Hitchcock Presents, Twilight Zone, Combat, Wild Wild West, The FBI, Mod Squad.

DUVALL, SHELLEY
Actress, Producer. b. Houston, TX, July 7, 1949. Founded Think Entertainment, TV prod. co. Appeared in 1984 short film Frankenweenie.
PICTURES: Brewster McCloud (debut, 1970), McCabe and Mrs. Miller, Thieves Like Us, Nashville, Buffalo Bill and the Indians, Three Women (Cannes Fest. Award, 1977), Annie Hall, The Shining, Popeye, Time Bandits, Roxanne, Suburban Commando, The Underneath, Portrait of a Lady, Changing Habits, Rocket Man, Russell Mulcahy's Tale of the Mummy, Home Fries, The 4th Floor.
TELEVISION: *Actress*: Bernice Bobs Her Hair, Lily, Twilight Zone, Mother Goose Rock 'n' Rhyme, Faerie Tale Theatre (Rumpelstiltskin, Rapunzel), Tall Tales and Legends (Darlin' Clementine), Alone. *Exec. Producer*: Faerie Tale Theatre, Tall Tales and Legends, Nightmare Classics, Dinner at Eight (movie), Mother Goose Rock 'n' Rhyme, Stories from Growing Up, Backfield in Motion (movie), Bedtime Stories, Mrs. Piggle-Wiggle.

DYSART, RICHARD A.
Actor. b. Brighton, MA, March 30, 1929. e. Emerson Coll., B.S., M.S., L.L.D.(honorary). Univ. of Maine, PhD (honorary). Trustee Gallaudet Univ, DC. Bd. of Dir, American Judicature Society.
THEATER: *B'way*: in A Man for All Seasons, All in Good Time, The Little Foxes, A Place without Doors, That Championship Season, Another Part of the Forest. *Off-B'way*: in The Quare Fellow, Our Town, Epitaph for George Dillon, Six Characters in Search of an Author.
PICTURES: Petulia, The Lost Man, The Sporting Club, The Hospital, The Terminal Man, The Crazy World of Julius Vrooder, The Day of the Locust, The Hindenberg, Prophecy, Meteor, Being There, An Enemy of the People, The Thing, The Falcon and the Snowman, Mask, Warning Signs, Pale Rider, Wall Street, Back to the Future Part III, Hard Rain.
TELEVISION: *Movies*: The Autobiography of Miss Jane Pittman, Gemini Man, It Happened One Christmas, First You Cry, Bogie, The Ordeal of Dr. Mudd, Churchill and the Generals (BBC), People Vs. Jean Harris, Bitter Harvest, Missing, Last Days of Patton, Children--A Mother's Story, Malice in Wonderland, Day One, Bobby and Marilyn: Her Final Affair, Truman, A Child Is Missing, Spawn. *Specials*: Sandburg's Lincoln, Jay Leno's Family Comedy Hour, Concealed Enemies, Charlie Smith and the Fritter Tree, Moving Target. *Mini-Series*: War and Rememberance. *Series*: L.A. Law (Emmy Award, 1992).

DZUNDZA, GEORGE
Actor. b. Rosenheim, Germany, 1945. Spent part of childhood in displaced-persons camps before he was moved to Amsterdam in 1949. Came to NY in 1956 where he attended St. John's U. as speech and theater major.
THEATER: King Lear (NY Shakespeare Fest., debut, 1973), That Championship Season (tour, 1973), Mert and Phil, The Ritz, Legend, A Prayer for My Daughter.
PICTURES: The Happy Hooker, The Deer Hunter, Honky Tonk Freeway, Streamers, Best Defense, No Mercy, No Way Out, The Beast, Impulse, White Hunter Black Heart, The Butcher's Wife, Basic Instinct, Crimson Tide, Dangerous Minds, That Darn Cat, Species II, Instinct, Above Suspicion.
TELEVISION: *Series*: Open All Night, Road Rovers (voice), Superman (voice), Law and Order, Batman: Gotham Knights (voice), Jesse. *Movies*: The Defection of Simas Kudirka, Salem's Lot, Skokie, A Long Way Home, The Face of Rage, The Last Honor of Kathryn Beck, When She Says No, The Rape of Richard Beck, Brotherly Love, The Execution of Raymond Graham, Something is Out There, The Ryan White Story, Terror on Highway 91, What She Doesn't Know, The Enemy Within, The Babymaker: The Dr. Cecil Jacobson Story, The Limbic Region, The Batman/Superman Movie. *Guest*: Starsky and Hutch, The Waltons.

E

EASTWOOD, ALISON
Actress. b. May 22, 1972. Father is actor-director Clint Eastwood.
PICTURES: Tightrope, Absolute Power, Midnight in the Garden of Good and Evil, Suicide: the Comedy, Black & White, Just a Little Harmless Sex, Breakfast of Champions, Friends & Lovers, The Spring, If You Only Knew.

EASTWOOD, CLINT
Actor, Producer, Director. b. San Francisco, CA, May 31, 1930; e. Oakland Technical H.S., Los Angeles City Coll. Daughter is actress Alison Eastwood. Worked as a lumberjack in Oregon before being drafted into the Army, Special Services 1950-54. Then contract player at Universal Studios. Starred in TV series Rawhide, 1958-65. Formed Malpaso Productions, 1969. Made a Chevalier des Lettres by French gov., 1985. Mayor, Carmel, CA, 1986-88. Best Director for Bird: Hollywood Foreign Press Assoc., Orson Award. Made Commandeur de Ordre des Arts & Lettres by French Government, 1994. Received Irving G. Thalberg Award, 1995. Received American Film Institute Life Achievement Award, 1996.
PICTURES: Revenge of the Creature (debut, 1955), Francis in the Navy, Lady Godiva, Tarantula, Never Say Goodbye, Away All Boats, The First Traveling Saleslady, Star in the Dust, Escapade in Japan, Ambush at Cimarron Pass, Lafayette Escadrille, A Fistful of Dollars, For a Few Dollars More, The Witches, The Good The Bad and The Ugly, Hang 'Em High, Coogan's Bluff, Where Eagles Dare, Paint Your Wagon, Kelly's Heroes, Two Mules For Sister Sara, Beguiled, Play Misty For Me (also dir.), Dirty Harry, Joe Kidd, Breezy (dir. only), High Plains Drifter (also dir.), Magnum Force, Thunderbolt & Lightfoot, The Eiger Sanction (also dir.), The Outlaw Josey Wales (also dir.), The Enforcer, The Gauntlet (also dir.), Every Which Way But Loose, Escape from Alcatraz, Bronco Billy (also dir.), Any Which Way You Can, Firefox (also dir., prod.), Honky Tonk Man (also dir., prod.), Sudden Impact (also dir., prod.), Tightrope (also prod.), City Heat, Pale Rider (also dir., prod.), Heartbreak Ridge (also dir., prod.), The Dead Pool (also prod.), Bird (dir. only), Thelonius Monk: Straight, No Chaser (exec. prod. only), Pink Cadillac, White Hunter Black Heart (also dir., prod.), The Rookie (also dir.), Unforgiven (also dir., prod.; Acad. Awards for Best Picture & Director; L.A. Film Critics Awards for Best Actor, Director & Picture; Natl. Society of Film Critics Awards for Best Director & Picture; Golden Globe Award for Best Director; DGA Award, 1992), In the Line of Fire, A Perfect World (also dir.), Casper (cameo), The Bridges of Madison County (also dir., prod.), The Stars Fell on Henrietta (co-prod. only), Absolute Power (also dir., prod., comp.), Midnight in the Garden of Good &Evil (also dir., prod.), True Crime (also, dir., prod.), Space Cowboys (also dir, prod.).
TELEVISION: *Series*: Rawhide. *Specials*: Fame Fortune and Romance, Happy Birthday Hollywood, Clint Eastwood: The Man From Malpaso, Don't Pave Main Street: Carmel's Heritage, Salute to Martin Scorcese, Big Guns Talk: Story of the Western, Eastwood on Eastwood. *Dir.*: Amazing Stories (Vanessa in the Garden). *Guest*: Navy Log, Maverick, Mr. Ed, Danny Kaye Show.

EBERSOL, DICK
Executive. 1968, started at ABC as Olympic Television researcher; 1974, joined NBC as dir. of weekend late- night programming; named v.p. late night programming; 1977, became v.p. of Comedy Variety and Event Programming; 1981-85, served as exec. prod. of series Saturday Night Live; 1983, formed his own production company, No Sleep Productions, creating Friday Night Videos, Saturday Night's Main Event, Later With Bob Costas; 1989, named pres. of NBC Sports; served as exec. prod. of NBC's coverage of the 1992 Barcelona Summer Olympics, and the 1996 Atlanta Summer Olympics.

EBERTS, JOHN DAVID (JAKE)
Producer, Financier. b. Montreal, Canada, July 10, 1941. e. McGill Univ, Harvard. President Goldcrest, founder & CEO 1976-83, 1985-6; 1984 joined Embassy Communications Intl. 1985 founded and chief exec. of Allied Filmmakers. Film Prods. Award of Merit 1986; Evening Standard Special Award 1987. Publication: My Indecision Is Final (1990).
PICTURES: Chariots of Fire, Gandhi, Another Country, Local Hero, The Dresser, Cal, The Emerald Forest, The Name of the Rose, Hope and Glory, Cry Freedom, The Adventures of Baron Munchausen, Driving Miss Daisy, Dances With Wolves, Black Robe, Get Back, City of Joy, A River Runs Through It, Super Mario Bros., No Escape, Arabian Knight.

EBSEN, BUDDY
Actor. r.n. Christian Ebsen, Jr. b. Belleville, IL, April 2, 1908. e. U. of Florida, Rollins Coll. Won first Broadway role as dancer in Ziegfeld's Whoopee in 1928. Sister, Vilma, became dancing partner. Went to Hollywood and appeared in Broadway Melody of 1936 with Vilma then in many musicals as single. Later became dramatic actor and appeared on TV. Co-wrote title song for film Behave Yourself.
PICTURES: Broadway Melody of 1936 (debut, 1935), Born to Dance, Captain January, Banjo on My Knee, Yellow Jack, Girl of the Golden West, My Lucky Star, Broadway Melody of 1938, Four Girls in White, Parachute Battalion, They Met in Argentina, Sing Your Worries Away, Thunder in God's Country, Night People, Red Garters, Davy Crockett--King of the Wild Frontier, Davy Crockett and the River Pirates, Between Heaven and Hell, Attack!, Breakfast at Tiffany's, The Interns, Mail Order Bride, The One and Only Genuine Original Family Band, The Beverly Hillbillies.
TELEVISION: *Series*: Davy Crockett, Northwest Passage, The Beverly Hillbillies, Barnaby Jones, Matt Houston. *Guest*: Hawaii Five-O, Gunsmoke. *Movies*: Stone Fox, The Daughters of Joshua Cabe, Horror at 37000 Feet, Smash-Up on Interstate 5, The President's Plane is Missing, Leave Yesterday Behind, The Paradise Connection, Fire on the Mountain, The Return of the Beverly Hillbillies, The Bastard, Tom Sawyer, Stone Fox, Working Trash. *Special*: The Legend of the Beverly Hillbillies.
THEATER: Flying Colors, Yokel Boy, The Male Animal, Ziegfeld Follies, Take Her She's Mine, Our Town, The Best Man.

ECKERT, JOHN M.
Producer, Production Executive. b. Chatham, Ontario, Canada, e. Ryerson Poly. Inst., 1968-71 (film major). Member: DGA, DGC.
PICTURES: Power Play (assoc. prod.), Running (co-prod.), Middle Age Crazy (co-prod.), Dead Zone (unit prod. mgr.), Cats Eye (exec. in charge of prod.), Silver Bullet (assoc. prod.), The Incubus, Home Is Where the Heart Is (prod.), Millenium (suprv. prod.), Deep Sleep (prod.), Car 54 Where Are You? (s.p., prod.), Legends of the Fall (unit prod. mngr.), The Scarlet Letter (unit prod. mngr.), Flying Wild (assoc. prod.), Booty Call (co-prod.), The Big Hit (exec. prod), The Big Hit.
TELEVISION: Terry Fox Story (assoc. prod.), Special People (prod., Christopher Award), Danger Bay (series supv. prod., 1985-87), Family Pictures (unit prod. mngr.), Getting Gotti (prod.).

EDELMAN, RANDY
Composer. b. Patterson, NJ, June 10, 1947.
PICTURES: Feds, Twins, Troop Beverly Hills, Ghostbusters II, Quick Change, Come See the Paradise, Kindergarten Cop, V.I. Warshawski, Drop Dead Fred, Eyes of an Angel, The Distinguished Gentleman, Beethoven, My Cousin Vinny, The Last of the Mohicans (Golden Globe nom.), Gettysburg, Dragon: The Bruce Lee Story, Beethoven's 2nd, Tall Tale, Pontiac Moon, Greedy, Angels in the Outfield, The mas, Billy Madison, While you Were Sleeping, The Indian in the Cupboard, The Big Green, Down Periscope, Diabolique, The Quest, Dragonheart, Dayllight, Anaconda, Gone Fishin', The Chipmunk Adventure, Executive Action, The Big Green, Leave It To Beaver, For Richer or Poorer, Six Days Seven Nights.
TELEVISION: A Doctor's Story, Dennis the Menace, Citizen X. Series: MacGyver, The Adventures of Brisco County Jr.

EDEN, BARBARA
Actress. b. Tucson, AZ, Aug. 23, 1934. r.n. Barbara Jean Huffman. e. San Francisco Conservatory of Music. Pres. Mi-Bar Productions. Dir. Security National Bank of Chicago.
PICTURES: Back From Eternity (debut, 1956), The Wayward Girl, A Private's Affair, From the Terrace, Twelve Hours to Kill, Flaming Star, All Hands on Deck, Voyage to the Bottom of the Sea, Five Weeks in a Balloon, Swingin' Along (Double Trouble), The Wonderful World of the Brothers Grimm, The Yellow Canary, The Brass Bottle, The New Interns, Ride the Wild Surf, 7 Faces of Dr. Lao, Quick Let's Get Married, The Amazing Dobermans, Harper Valley PTA, Chattanooga Choo Choo, A Very Brady Sequel.
TELEVISION: *Series*: How to Marry a Millionaire, I Dream of Jeannie, Harper Valley P.T.A., A Brand New Life, Dallas. *Movies*: The Feminist and the Fuzz, A Howling in the Woods, The Woman Hunter, Guess Who's Sleeping in My Bed, The Stranger Within, Let's Switch, How to Break Up a Happy Divorce, Stonestreet: Who Killed the Centerfold Model?, The Girls in the Office, Condominium, Return of the Rebels, I Dream of Jeannie: 15 Years Later, The Stepford Children, The Secret Life of Kathy McCormick (also co-prod.), Your Mother Wears Combat Boots, Opposites Attract, Her Wicked Ways, Hell Hath No Fury, I Still Dream of Jeannie, Visions of Murder I & II, Eyes of Terror, Dean Man's Island (also co-prod.).

EDWARDS, ANTHONY
Actor. b. Santa Barbara, CA, July 19, 1962. Grandfather designed Walt Disney Studios in the 1930s and worked for Cecil B. De Mille as conceptual artist. Joined Santa Barbara Youth Theatre; acted in 30 plays from age 12 to 17. At 16 worked professionally in TV commercials. 1980 attended Royal Acad. of Dramatic Arts, London, and studied drama at USC. On NY stage 1993 in Ten Below.
PICTURES: Fast Times at Ridgemont High (debut, 1982), Heart Like a Wheel, Revenge of the Nerds, The Sure Thing, Gotcha!, Top Gun, Summer Heat, Revenge of the Nerds II (cameo), Mr. North, Miracle Mile, How I Got Into College, Hawks, Downtown, Delta Heat, Pet Sematary II, The Client, Charlie's Ghost story, Us Begins with You (also prod.), Playing by Heart, Jacpot.
TELEVISION: *Series*: It Takes Two, Northern Exposure, ER (Emmy Award, 1998), Soul Man, Rock Story. *Movies*: The Killing of Randy Webster, High School U.S.A., Going for the Gold: The Bill Johnson Story, El Diablo, Hometown Boy Makes Good. *Specials*: Unpublished Letters, Sexual Healing.

EDWARDS, BLAKE
Director, Writer, Producer. r.n. William Blake McEdwards. b. Tulsa, OK, July 26, 1922. m. actress Julie Andrews. e. Beverly Hills H.S. Coast Guard during war. Film acting debut, Ten Gentlemen from West Point (1942).
RADIO: Johnny Dollar, Line-up; *writer-creator*: Richard Diamond.
PICTURES: *Writer*: Panhandle, Stampede, Sound Off, All Ashore, Cruising Down the River, Rainbow Round My Shoulder, Drive a Crooked Road, The Atomic Kid (story), My Sister Eileen, Operation Mad Ball, Notorious Landlady, Soldier in the Rain. *Producer*: Waterhole *Director*: Bring Your Smile Along (also s.p.), He Laughed Last (also s.p.), Mister Cory (also s.p.), This Happy Feeling (also s.p.), The Perfect Furlough (also s.p.), Operation Petticoat, High Time, Breakfast at Tiffany's, Experiment in Terror, Days of Wine and Roses, The Pink Panther (also s.p.), A Shot in the Dark (also s.p., prod.), The Great Race (also s.p., prod.), What Did You Do in the War Daddy? (also s.p., prod.), Gunn (also prod.), The Party (also s.p., prod.), Darling Lili (also s.p., prod.), Wild Rovers (also s.p., prod.), The Carey Treatment (also s.p., prod.), The Tamarind Seed (also s.p.), The Return of the Pink Panther (also s.p., prod.), The Pink Panther Strikes Again (also s.p., prod.), Revenge of the Pink Panther (also s.p., prod.), "10" (also co-prod., s.p.), S.O.B. (also co-prod., s.p.), Victor/Victoria (also co-prod., s.p.), Trail of the Pink Panther (also co-prod., co-s.p.), The Curse of the Pink Panther (also co-prod., s.p.), The Man Who Loved Women (also prod., co-s.p.), Micki and Maude, A Fine Mess (also s.p.), That's Life (also co-prod.), Blind Date, Sunset (also s.p.), Skin Deep (also s.p.), Switch (also s.p.), Son of the Pink Panther (also s.p.).
TELEVISION: City Detective (prod., 1953), The Dick Powell Show (dir.), Creator: Dante's Inferno, Mr. Lucky, Justin Case (exec. prod., dir., writer), Peter Gunn (exec. prod., dir., writer), Julie (exec. prod., dir.). *Specials*: Julie! (prod., dir.), Julie on Sesame St. (exec. prod.), Julie and Dick in Covent Garden (dir.).

EDWARDS, JAMES H.
Executive. President & CEO, Storey Theatres, Inc. b. Cedartown, GA, Aug. 14, 1927. e. Georgia State. U.S. Navy, 1948-50. With Ga. Theatre Co., 1950-1952; Storey Theatres, 1952-present. Formerly pres. & chmn., NATO of GA; formerly pres., Variety Club of Atlanta. Former dir. at large, Nat'l. NATO. Director, numerous theatre cos.

EDWARDS, RALPH
Producer, Emcee. b. Merino, CO, June 13, 1913. e. U. of California, Berkeley. Began career in radio in 1929 as writer-actor-prod.-announcer at station KROW, Oakland. Later joined CBS & NBC Radio in New York as announcer. Originated, produced and emceed Truth or Consequences, This Is Your Life and The Ralph Edwards Show for both radio & TV.
PICTURES: Seven Days Leave, Radio Stars on Parade, Bamboo Blonde, Beat the Band, I'll Cry Tomorrow, Manhattan Merry-go-round, Radio Stars of 1937.
TELEVISION: *Producer/Creator*: It Could Be You, Place the Face, About Faces, Funny Boners, End of the Rainbow, Who in the World, The Woody Woodbury Show, This is Your Life (specials for NBC; host). *Producers*: Wide Country, Name That Tune, Cross Wits, Knockout, Annabelle's Wish. *Producer* (with partner, Stu Billett): The People's Court, So You Think You Got Troubles?, Family Medical Center, Love Stories, Superior Court, Bzzz.

EGGAR, SAMANTHA
Actress. b. London, England,, March 5, 1939. e. student Webber-Douglas Dramatic Sch., London; Slade Sch. of Art.
PICTURES: The Wild and the Willing, Dr. Crippen, Doctor in Distress, Psyche '59, The Collector (Acad. Award nom.), Return From the Ashes, Walk Don't Run, Doctor Dolittle, The Molly Maguires, The Lady in the Car With Glasses and a Gun, The Walking Stick, The Grove, The Light at the Edge of the World, The Dead Are Alive, The Seven Percent Solution, The Uncanny, Welcome to Blood City, The Brood, The Exterminator, Demonoid, Why Shoot the Teacher?, Curtains, Hot Touch, Loner, Ragin' Cajun, Dark Horse, Inevitable Grace, The Phantom, Hercules.
TELEVISION: *Series*: Anna and the King. *Movies*: Double Indemnity, All The Kind Strangers, The Killer Who Wouldn't Die, Ziegfeld: the Man and His Women, The Hope Diamond, Love Among Thieves, A Ghost in Monte Carlo. A Case for Murder. *Mini-Series*: For the Term of His Natural Life, Davy Crockett, Great Escapes: Secrets of Lake Success. *Guest*: Columbo, Baretta, Love Story, Kojak, McMillan & Wife, Streets of San Francisco, Starsky and Hutch, Hart to Hart, Murder She Wrote, Finder of Lost Loves, George Burns Comedy Week, Lucas Tanner, Hotel, Fantasy Island, Magnum P.I., Stingray, Tales of the Unexpected, Heartbeat, Love Boat, 1st & Ten, Outlaws, Alfred Hitchcock Presents, Matlock, L.A. Law, Star Trek: The Next Generation. *Specials*: Man of Destiny, Hemingway Play.

EGOYAN, ATOM
Director, Writer, Producer, Editor, Actor, Cinematographer. b. Cairo, Egypt, July 19, 1960. Raised in Victoria, British Columbia, Canada. e. Univ. of Toronto. Made short films, one of which, Open House appeared on TV series Canadian Reflections.
PICTURES: *Various credits*: Howard in Particular, After Grad with Dad, Peep Show, Open House, Next of Kin, Men: A Passion Playground, Family Viewing, Speaking Parts, The Adjuster, Montreal Sextet, Calendar, Exotica, Curtis's Charm, A Portrait of Arshile, The Sweet Hereafter, Vinyl, Bach Cello Suite #4: Sarabande, Felicia's Journey (dir., s.p.).
TELEVISION: *Movies*: In This Corner, Looking for Nothing, Gross Misconduct: The Life of Brian Spencer, Krapp's Last Tape. *Series*: Alfred Hitchcock Presents, Twilight Zone, Friday the 13th.

EICHHORN, LISA
Actress. b. Reading, PA, Feb. 4, 1952. e. Queen's U. Kingston, Canada and Eng. for literature studies at Oxford. Studied at Royal Acad. of Dramatic Art.
THEATER: The Hasty Heart (debut, LA). NY: The Common Pursuit, The Summer Winds, The Speed of Darkness, Down the Road, Any Given Day.
PICTURES: Yanks, The Europeans, Why Would I Lie?, Cutter and Bone, Weather in the Streets, Wild Rose; Opposing Force, Moon 44, Grim Prairie Tales, The Vanishing, King of the Hill, Sticks and Stones, First Kid, A Modern Affair, Judas Kiss.
TELEVISION: *Series*: All My Children (1987). *Movies*: The Wall, Blind Justice, Devlin. *Mini-Series*: A Woman Named Jackie.

EIKENBERRY, JILL
Actress. b. New Haven, CT, Jan. 21, 1947. e. Yale U. Drama Sch. m. actor Michael Tucker.
THEATER: B'way: All Over Town, Watch on the Rhine, Onward Victoria, Summer Brave, Moonchildren. Off-B'way: Lemon Sky, Life Under Water, Uncommon Women and Others, Porch, The Primary English Class.
PICTURES: Between the Lines, The End of the World in Our Usual Bed in a Night Full of Rain, An Unmarried Woman, Butch and Sundance: The Early Days, Rich Kids, Hide in Plain Sight, Arthur, The Manhattan Project.
TELEVISION: *Movies*: The Deadliest Season, Orphan Train, Swan Song, Sessions, Kane & Abel, Assault and Matrimony, Family Sins, A Stoning in Fulham Country, My Boyfriend's Back, The Diane Martin Story, The Secret Life of Archie's Wife, An Inconvenient Woman, Living a Lie, A Town Torn Apart, Chantilly Lace, Parallel Lives, Without Consent, Rugged Gold, The Other Woman, Dare to Love. *Series*: L.A. Law, The Best of Families (PBS). *Specials*: Uncommon Women & Others, Destined to Live (prod., host), A Family Again, On Hope.

EILBACHER, LISA
Actress. b. Dharan, Saudi Arabia, May 5, 1957. Moved to California at age 7; acted on TV as child.
PICTURES: The War Between Men and Women (debut, 1972), Run for the Roses (Thoroughbred), On the Right Track, An Officer and a Gentleman, Ten to Midnight, Beverly Hills Cop, Deadly Intent, Leviathan, Never Say Die, The Last Samurai.
TELEVISION: *Series*: The Texas Wheelers, The Hardy Boys Mysteries, Ryan's Four, Me and Mom. *Movies*: Bad Ronald, Panache, Spider Man, The Ordeal of Patty Hearst, Love for Rent, To Race the Wind, This House Possessed, Monte Carlo, Deadly Deception, Joshua's Heart, Blind Man's Bluff, Deadly Matrimony, The Return of Hunter, Dazzle, 919 Fifth Avenue. *Mini-Series*: Wheels, The Winds of War. *Guest*: Wagon Train, Laredo, My Three Sons, Gunsmoke, Combat.

EISNER, MICHAEL D.
Executive. b. Mt. Kisco, NY, March 7, 1942. e. Denison U., B.A. Started career with programming dept. of CBS TV network. Joined ABC in 1966 as mgr. talent and specials. Dec., 1968 became dir. of program dev., east coast. 1968, named v.p., daytime programming, ABC-TV. 1975 made v.p., prog. planning and dev. 1976 named sr. v.p., prime time production and dev., ABC Entertainment. 1976, left ABC to join Paramount Pictures as pres. & chief operating officer. 1984, joined The Walt Disney Company as chmn. & CEO. Host of TV series, The Wonderful World of Disney, 1997.

EKBERG, ANITA
Actress. b. Malmo, Sweden, Sept. 29, 1931. Came to U.S. in 1951 as Miss Universe contestant. Worked as model before becoming actress appearing in small roles at Universal.

PICTURES: Mississippi Gambler, Abbott & Costello Go to Mars, Take Me to Town, The Golden Blade, Blood Alley, Artists and Models, Man in the Vault, War and Peace, Back from Eternity, Hollywood or Bust, Zarak, Pickup Alley, Valerie, Paris Holiday, The Man Inside, Screaming Mimi, Sign of the Gladiator, La Dolce Vita, The Dam on the Yellow River (Last Train to Shanghai), Little Girls and High Finance, Behind Locked Doors, The Last Judgment, The Mongols, Boccaccio '70, Call Me Bwana, 4 for Texas, L'Incastro, Who Wants to Sleep?, The Alphabet Murders, Way Way Out, How I Learned to Love Women, Woman Times Seven, The Glass Sphinx, The Cobra, Malenka the Vampire (Fangs of the Living Dead), If It's Tuesday This Must Be Belgium, The Clowns, Valley of the Widows, Killer Nun, Daisy Chain, Intervista, The Count.
TELEVISION: *Movies*: Gold of the Amazon Women, S*H*E.

EKLAND, BRITT
Actress. b. Stockholm, Sweden, Oct. 6, 1942. Was model before debuting in European films.
PICTURES: Short Is the Summer (debut, 1962), Il Commandante, After the Fox, The Double Man, The Bobo, The Night They Raided Minsky's, Stiletto, Cannibals, Machine Gun McCain, Tintomara, Percy, Get Carter, A Time for Loving, Endless Night, Baxter, Asylum, The Wicker Man, Ultimate Thrill, The Man With the Golden Gun, Royal Flash, Casanova & Co., High Velocity, Slavers, King Solomon's Treasure, The Monster Club, Satan's Mistress (Demon Rage), Hellhole, Fraternity Vacation, Marbella, Moon in Scorpio, Scandal, Beverly Hills Vamp, The Children.
TELEVISION: *England*: Carol for Another Christmas, Too Many Thieves, A Cold Peace. *USA: Guest*: Trials of O'Brien, McCloud, Six Million Dollar Man. *Movies*: Ring of Passion, The Great Wallendas, The Hostage Tower, Valley of the Dolls 1981, Dead Wrong.

ELAM, JACK
Actor. b. Miami, AZ, Nov. 13, 1916. e. Santa Monica Jr. Coll., Modesto Jr. Coll. Worked in Los Angeles as bookkeeper and theatre mgr.; civilian employee of Navy in W.W.II; Introduction to show business was as bookkeeper for Sam Goldwyn. Later worked as controller for other film producers. Given first acting job by prod. George Templeton in 1948; has since appeared in over 100 films.
PICTURES: Wild Weed (debut, 1949), Rawhide, Kansas City Confidential, Rancho Notorious, Ride Vaquero, Appointment in Honduras, The Moonlighter, Vera Cruz, Cattle Queen of Montana, The Far Country, Moonfleet, Kiss Me Deadly, Artists and Models, Gunfight at the OK Corral, Baby Face Nelson, Edge of Eternity, Girl in Lovers Lane, The Last Sunset, The Comancheros, The Rare Breed, The Way West, Firecreek, Never a Dull Moment, Once Upon a Time in the West, Support Your Local Sheriff, Rio Lobo, Dirty Dingus Magee, Support Your Local Gunfighter, The Wild Country, Hannie Caulder, Last Rebel, Pat Garrett and Billy the Kid, Hawmps, Grayeagle, Hot Lead Cold Feet, The Norsemen, The Villain, The Apple Dumpling Gang Rides Again, The Cannonball Run, Jinxed, Cannonball Run II, The Aurora Encounter, Big Bad John, Suburban Commando.
TELEVISION: *Series*: The Dakotas, Temple Houston, The Texas Wheelers, Struck by Lightning, Detective in the House, Easy Street. *Movies*: The Over-the-Hill Gang, The Daughters of Joshua Cabe, Black Beauty, Once Upon a Texas Train, Where the Hell's That Gold!!!?.

ELEFANTE, TOM
Executive. Began career as usher at Loews Riviera in Coral Gables, FL; progressed through ranks to asst. mgr., mgr. & Florida division mgr. 1972, joined Wometco Theatres as gen. mgr. 1975, returned to Loews Theatres as southeast div. mgr.; 1979, named natl. dir. of concessions, moving to h.o. in New York. 1987, appt. sr. v.p. & gen. mgr., Loews. Served as pres. and chmn. of NATO of Florida. 1990, then pres. of NATO of NY. Joined Warner Bros. Int'l Theatres as sr. v.p., 1992. Founded T.P. Consulting Co., 1997.

ELFAND, MARTIN
Executive. b. Los Angeles, CA, 1937. Was talent agent for ten years with top agencies; joined Artists Entertainment Complex in 1972. First film project as prod.: Kansas City Bomber, first venture of AEC, of which he was sr. v.p. In 1977 joined Warner Bros. as production chief.T
PICTURES: *Prod.*: Dog Day Afternoon, It's My Turn, An Officer and a Gentleman, King David, Clara's Heart. *Exec. prod.*: Her Alibi, Talent for the Game.

ELFMAN, DANNY
Composer. b. Los Angeles, CA, May 29, 1953. Member of rock band Oingo Boingo, recorded songs for such films as The Tempest, Fast Times at Ridgemont High, 16 Candles, Beverly Hills Cop, Weird Science, Texas Chainsaw Massacre 2, Something Wild. Appeared in Hot Tomorrows, Back to School.
PICTURES: Forbidden Zone, Pee-wee's Big Adventure, Back to School, Wisdom, Summer School, Beetlejuice, Midnight Run, Big Top Pee-wee, Hot to Trot, Scrooged, Batman, Nightbreed, Dick Tracy, Darkman, Edward Scissorhands, Pure Luck, Article 99, Batman Returns, Sommersby, The Nightmare Before Christmas (also vocalist), Black Beauty, Dolores Claiborne, To Die For, Dead Presidents, Mission: Impossible, The Frighteners, Mars Attacks!, Men in Black, Flubber, Godd Will Hunting, Scream 2, A Simple Plan, A Civil Action, Modern Vampyres, My Favorite Martian, Psycho, Instinct, Anywhere But Here, Sleepy Hollow.
TELEVISION: *Series*: Pee-wee's Playhouse, Sledgehammer, Fast Times, Tales from the Crypt, The Simpsons, The Flash, Beetlejuice, Perversions of Science, Dilbert. Segments of Amazing Stories, Alfred Hitchcock Presents (The Jar).

ELFMAN, JENNA
Actress. b. Los Angeles, CA, Sept. 30, 1971.
PICTURES: Grosse Pointe Blank, Doctor Dolittle (voice) Krippendorf's Tribe, Can't Hardly Wait, Venus, Edtv, Keeping the Faith, CyberWorld (voice), Town and Country.
TELEVISION: *Movies:* Her Last Chance. *Series:* Townies, Dharma & Greg. *Guest:* Roseanne, NYPD Blue, Murder One, Almost Perfect, The Single Guy.

ELG, TAINA
Actress, Dancer. b. Helsinki, Finland, March 9, 1930. Trained and performed with Natl. Opera of Finland. Toured with Swedish Dance Theatre, then Marquis de Cuevas Ballet.
THEATER: Look to the Lilies, Where's Charley?, The Utter Glory of Morrissey Hall, Strider, Nine, O! Pioneers.
PICTURES: The Prodigal (debut, 1955), Diane, Gaby, Les Girls, Watusi, Imitation General, The 39 Steps, The Bacchae, Liebestraum, The Mirror Has Two Faces.
TELEVISION: *Movie*: The Great Wallendas. *Mini-Series*: Blood and Honor: Youth Under Hitler (narrator).

ELIAS, HAL
Executive. b. Brooklyn, NY, Dec. 23, 1899. Publicity dir., State Theatre, Denver; western exploitation mgr., MGM; adv. dept., pub. dept., MGM, Culver City studios; Head, MGM cartoon studio (Tom and Jerry); UPA Pictures, Inc., vice-pres. studio mgr.: Hollywood Museum; bd. dir., Academy of Motion Picture Arts & Sciences, 35 years; treasurer, AMPAS 1976-1979. Academy Oscar, 1979, for dedicated and distinguished service to AMPAS.

ELIZONDO, HECTOR
Actor. b. New York, NY, Dec. 22, 1936. m. actress Carolee Campbell. Studied with Ballet Arts Co. of Carnegie Hall and Actors Studio. Many stage credits in N.Y. and Boston.
THEATER: The Prisoner of Second Avenue, Dance of Death, Steambath (Obie Award), The Great White Hope, Sly Fox, The Price.
PICTURES: The Fat Black Pussycat, Valdez Is Coming, Born to Win, Pocket Money, Deadhead Miles, Stand Up and Be Counted, The Taking of Pelham One Two Three, Report to the Commissioner, Thieves, Cuba, American Gigolo, The Fan, Young Doctors in Love, The Flamingo Kid, Private Resort, Nothing in Common, Overboard, Beaches, Leviathan, Pretty Woman (Golden Globe nom.), Taking Care of Business, Necessary Roughness, Frankie and Johnny, Final Approach, Samantha, There Goes the Neighborhood, Being Human, Beverly Hills Cop III, Getting Even With Dad, Exit to Eden, Perfect Alibi, Dear God, Turbulence, Runaway Bride, Entropy, Safe House, The Other Sister.
TELEVISION: *Series*: Popi (1976), Casablanca, Freebie and the Bean; A.K.A. Pablo (also dir.), Foley Sq, Down and Out in Bevery Hills, Fish Police (voice), Chicago Hope (Emmy Award, 1997). *Guest*: The Wendie Barrie Show (1947), The Impatient Heart, Kojack, the Jackie Gleason Show, All in the Family, The Pirates of Dark Water (voice), Tales from the Crypt. *Movies*: The Impatient Heart, Wanted: The Sundance Woman, Honeyboy, Women of San Quentin, Courage, Out of the Darkness, Addicted to His Love, Your Mother Wears Combat Boots, Forgotten Prisoners: The Amnesty Files, Finding the Way Home, Chains of Gold, The Burden of Proof, Borrowed Hearts. *Mini-Series*: The Dain Curse. *Specials:* Medal of Honor Rag, Mrs. Cage.

ELKINS, HILLARD
Producer. b. New York, NY, Oct. 18, 1929. e. NYU, B.A., 1951. Exec., William Morris Agy., 1949-51; exec. v.p., Gen. Artists Corp., 1952-53; pres., Hillard Elkins Mgmt., 1953-60; Elkins Prods. Intl. Corp., N.Y., 1960-71; Elkins Prods. Ltd., 1972-; Hillard Elkins Entertainment Corp., 1974; Media Mix Prods., Inc., 1979-82.
MEMBER: Academy of Motion Picture Arts & Sciences, Acad. of TV Arts & Sciences, Dramatists Guild, League of New York Theatres, American Fed. of TV & Radio Artists.
THEATER: Come On Strong, Golden Boy, Oh Calcutta!, The Rothschilds, A Doll's House, An Evening with Richard Nixon, Sizwe Banzi Is Dead, etc.
PICTURES: Alice's Restaurant, A New Leaf, Oh Calcutta!, A Doll's House, Richard Pryor Live in Concert, Sellers on Sellers, Inside.
TELEVISION: The Importance of Being Earnest, The Deadly Game, Princess Daisy, The Meeting (exec. prod.), Father & Son: Dangerous Relationsm A Father for Charlie, In His Father's Shoes.

ELKINS, KEN JOE
Broadcasting Executive. b. Prenter, WV, Oct. 12, 1937. e. Nebraska U., 1966-69. Eng. sta. KETV-TV, NE, 1960-67; asst. chief engr., 1967-70; ops. mgr., nat. sales, gen. sales mgr., 1972-75; gen. mgr., 1975-80. Chief engr. sta. KOUB-TV, IA, 1970-71; gen mgr., 1871-72. Gen. mgr. sta. KSDK-TV, MO, 1980-81. V.P., CEO Pulitzer B'casting Co., St. Louis, 1981-84; pres., CEO, 1984-. Bd. Dirs.: Commerce Bank St. Louis; Maximum Svc. Telecasters, WA; BMI; BJC Health Sys. Pres., NE B'casters, 1979-80. Chmn., NBC Affiliate Bd. Govs. With USAF, 1957-61. Inducted into NE Broadcasters Hall of Fame, 1990. Mem.: Nat. Assn. B'casters; Found. B'casters Hall of Fame (bd. dirs., trustee 1990); TV Operators Caucus; Algonquin Club.

ELKINS, SAUL
Producer. b. New York, NY, June 22, 1907. e. City Coll. of New York, B.S., 1927. Radio writer, dir., prod. 1930-2; dir., prod. stock co. touring Latin America 1932-34; writer Fox Films, 20th Century-Fox; writer RKO, Columbia 1937-42; writer, dial-dir., dir. Warner Bros. 1943-7; prod. Warner Bros. since 1947. Member: AMPAS, Screen Writer's Guild. Exec. prod., Comprenetics, Inc. Dir., Pioneer Prods., 1982.
PICTURES: Younger Brothers, One Last Fling, Homicide, House Across the Street, Flaxy Martin, Barricade, Return of the Frontiersmen, This Side of the Law, Colt .45, Sugarfoot, Raton Pass, The Big Punch, Smart Girls Don't Talk, Embraceable You.

ELLIOTT, CHRIS
Actor, Writer. b. New York, NY, May 31, 1960. Father is comedian Bob Elliott. Was performer in improv. theatres, summer stock; also tour guide at Rockefeller Center. Became writer/performer for David Letterman starting in 1982. *Author:* Daddy's Boy: A Son's Shocking Account of Life With a Famous Father (1989).
PICTURES: Manhunter (debut, 1986), The Abyss, Hyperspace, Groundhog Day, CB4, Cabin Boy (also co-story), Kingpin, The Sky Is Falling, There's Something About Mary, Snow Day.
TELEVISION: *Series*: Late Night With David Letterman (also co-writer; 2 Emmy Awards for writing: 1984, 1985), Nick and Hillary, Get a Life (also creator, co-writer, prod.), The Naked Truth, Dilbert (voice). *Specials*: Late Night With David Letterman Anniversary Specials (also co-writer; 2 Emmy Awards for writing: 1986, 1987), Chris Elliott's FDR: One-Man Show (also writer, prod.).

ELLIOTT, LANG
Producer, Director. b. Los Angeles, CA, Oct. 18, 1949. Began acting in films at an early age, influenced by his uncle, the late actor William Elliott (known as Wild Bill Elliott). Employed by, among others the McGowan Brothers. Turned to film production; co-founded distribution co., The International Picture Show Co., serving as exec. v.p. in chg. of financing, production & distribution. In 1976 formed TriStar Pictures, Inc. to finance and distribute product. In 1980 sold TriStar to Columbia, HBO and CBS. 1982, formed Lang Elliott Productions, Inc. Co-founded Longshot Enterprises with actor Tim Conway to prod. films and home videos, 1985. Videos include Dorf on Golf (the first made-for-home-video comedy), 'Scuse Me!, Dorf and the First Olympic Games. Formed Performance Pictures, Inc., in 1989, a prod. & distrib. company. Received Academy Award nom. for Soldier of Orange and The Magic of Lassie.
PICTURES: *Prod:* Ride the Hot Wind, Where Time Began, The Farmer, The Billion Dollar Hobo, They Went That-a-Way & That-a-Way, The Prize Fighter. *Prod.-dir.:* The Private Eyes, Cage, Cage II.
TELEVISION: Experiment in Love (prod.), Boys Will Be Boys (writer).

ELLIOTT, SAM
Actor. b. Sacramento, CA, Aug. 9, 1944. m. actress Katharine Ross. e. U. of Oregon.
PICTURES: Butch Cassidy and the Sundance Kid (debut in bit, 1969), The Games, Frogs, Molly and Lawless John, Lifeguard, The Legacy, Mask, Fatal Beauty, Shakedown, Road House, Prancer, Sibling Rivalry, Rush, Gettysburg, Tombstone, The Desperate Trail, The Final Cut, Dog Watch, The Hi-Lo Country, The Big Lebowski.
TELEVISION: *Movies*: The Challenge, Assault on the Wayne, The Blue Knight, I Will Fight No More Forever, The Sacketts, Wild Times, Murder in Texas, Shadow Riders, Travis McGee, A Death in California. The Blue Lightning, Houston: The Legend of Texas, The Quick and the Dead, Conagher (also co-writer, exec. prod.), Fugitive Nights: Danger in the Desert, Buffalo Girls, The Ranger the Cook and a Hole in the Sky, Woman Undone, Rough Riders, You Know My Name. *Series*: Mission: Impossible, The Yellow Rose. *Mini-Series*: Once and Eagle, Aspen (The Innocent and the Damned). *Guest*: Lancer, The FBI, Gunsmoke, Streets of San Francisco, Hawaii 5-0, Police Woman. *Pilot*: Evel Knievel.

ELWES, CARY
Actor. b. London, England, Oct. 26, 1962. e. Harrow. Studied for stage with Julie Bovasso at Sarah Lawrence, Bronxville, NY.
PICTURES: Another Country (debut 1984), Oxford Blues, The Bride, Lady Jane, The Princess Bride, Glory, Days of Thunder, Leather Jackets, Hot Shots!, Bram Stoker's Dracula, The Crush, Robin Hood: Men in Tights, Rudyard Kipling's The Jungle Book, Twister, Kiss the Girls, The Informant, Liar Liar, Quest for Camelot (voice), The Cradle Will Rock.

EMMERICH, ROLAND
Director, Writer, Exec. Producer. b. Stuttgart, Germany, Nov. 10, 1955. Studied production design in film school in Munich. First film was student production, The Noah's Ark Principle, which opened the 1984 Berlin Film Festival and was sold to more than 20 countries. Formed Centropolis Film Productions. Prod. TV series, The Visitor, 1997.
PICTURES: *Co-s.p./Dir.*:Making Contact (a.k.a. Joey; dir. only), Ghost Chase, Moon 44, Universal Soldier, Stargate, Independence Day, Godzilla, The Patriot (also exec. prod.). *Prod:* Eye of the Storm, The Thirteenth Floor, The Mark.

ENGEL, CHARLES F.
Executive. b. Los Angeles, CA, Aug. 30. e. Michigan State U., UCLA. Son of writer-prod. Samuel G. Engel. Pgm. devel., ABC-TV, 1964-68; v.p. Univ.-TV, 1972; sr. v.p., 1977; exec. v.p., 1980; pres., MCA Pay-TV Programming, 1981. ACE Award, 1988 for outstanding contribution to cable; v.p. Universal TV, exec. in chg. ABC Mystery Movie, 1989. Sr. v.p. 1992 in chg. Columbo, Murder She Wrote, SeaQuest, The Rockford Files. Founding member board of governors, the National Academy of Cable Programming. Member, Television Academy. Exec. v.p. of Programming Universal Television, 1997.
TELEVISION: The Aquarians (exec. prod.), Run a Crooked Mile (exec. prod.), Road Raiders (prod.), ABC Mystery Movie (exec. in chg. of prod.).

ENGELBERG, MORT
Producer. b. Memphis, TN. e. U. of Illinois, U. of Missouri. Taught journalism; worked as reporter for UPI, AP. Worked for US government, including USIA, Peace Corps., Office of Economic Opportunity; President's Task Force on War on Poverty. Left gov. service in 1967 to become film unit publicist, working on three films in Europe: Dirty Dozen, Far From the Madding Crowd, The Comedians. Returned to U.S.; appt. pub. mgr. for United Artists. Sent to Hollywood as asst. to Herb Jaffe, UA head of west coast prod., which post he assumed when Jaffe left. Left to join indep. prod., Ray Stark.
PICTURES: Smokey and the Bandit, Hot Stuff, The Villain, The Hunter, Smokey and the Bandit II, Smokey and the Bandit III, Nobody's Perfekt, The Heavenly Kid, The Big Easy, Maid to Order, Dudes, Three For the Road, Russkies, Pass the Ammo, Trading Hearts, Fright Night Part 2, Rented Lips, Remote Control.

ENGLANDER, MORRIS K.
Executive. b. New York, NY, July 5, 1934. e. Wharton Sch., U. of Pennsylvania. With General Cinema Corp. circuit before joining RKO Century Warner Theatres 1984 as exec. v.p., develp.; later co-vice chmn. of circuit. 1986, sr. real estate advisor, American Multi-Cinema. 1988: v.p. real estate Hoyts Cinemas Corp.; 1990 COO of Hoyts; pres. & COO of Hoyts. 1991.

ENGLUND, ROBERT
Actor. b. Glendale, CA, June 6, 1949. e. UCLA, RADA. First role was in the Cleveland stage production of Godspell, 1971.
PICTURES: Buster and Billie, Hustle, Stay Hungry, Death Trap (Eaten Alive), The Last of the Cowboys, St. Ives, A Star is Born, Big Wednesday, Bloodbrothers, The Fifth Floor, Dead and Buried, Galaxy of Terror, Don't Cry It's Only Thunder, A Nightmare on Elm Street, A Nightmare on Elm Street Part 2: Freddy's Revenge, Never Too Young to Die, A Nightmare on Elm Street 3: Dream Warriors, A Nightmare on Elm Street 4: The Dream Master, 976-EVIL (dir. only), A Nightmare on Elm Street: The Dream Child, Phantom of the Opera, The Adventures of Ford Fairlane, Danse Macabre, Freddy's Dead: The Final Nightmare, Eugenie, Wes Craven's New Nightmare, The Mangler, The Paper Route, Vampyre Wars, Killer Tongue, Regeneration, Wishmaster, Meet the Deedles, Urban Legend, Strangeland, The Prince and the Surfer, Freddy vs. Jason.
TELEVISION: *Series*: Downtown, V, Freddy's Nightmares, Nightmare Cafe. *Specials and Movies*: Hobson's Choice, Young Joe: The Forgotten Kennedy, The Ordeal of Patty Hearst, The Courage and the Passion, Mind Over Murder, Thou Shalt Not Kill, The Fighter, Journey's End, Starflight: The Plane That Couldn't Land, I Want to Live, Infidelity, A Perry Mason Mystery: The Case of the Lethal Lifestyle, Robin Cook's Mortal Fear, The Unspoken Truth. *Mini-Series*: V, North and South Book II. *Host*: Horror Hall of Fame, Sci-Fi Channel. *Guest:* The Simpsons (voice).

EPHRON, NORA
Writer, Director. b. New York, NY, May 19, 1941. e. Wellesley Col. Daughter of writers Henry and Phoebe Ephron. m. writer Nicholas Pileggi. *Author:* Heartburn, Crazy Salad, Scribble Scribble. Appeared in Crimes and Misdemeanors, Husbands and Wives.
PICTURES: *Writer*: Silkwood, Heartburn, When Harry Met Sally... (also assoc. prod.), Cookie (also exec. prod.), My Blue Heaven (also exec. prod.), This is My Life (also dir.), Sleepless in Seattle (also dir.), Mixed Nuts (also dir.), Michael (also dir., prod., exec. prod.), You've Got Mail (also prod.), Hanging Up (also prod.).
TELEVISION: *Movie (writer):* Perfect Gentlemen, Red Tails in Love: A Wildlife Drama in Central Park (also prod., dir.).

EPSTEIN, JULIUS J
Screenwriter. b. New York, NY, Aug. 22, 1909. e. Pennsylvania State U. Worked as publicist before going to Hollywood where began writing. Had long collaboration with twin brother, Philip G. Epstein. Under contract with Warner Bros. over 17 years.
PICTURES: In Caliente, Broadway Gondolier, Four Daughters, Daughters Courageous, Four Wives, Saturday's Children, No Time for Comedy, The Strawberry Blonde, The Bride Came C.O.D., The Man Who Came to Dinner, The Male Animal, Casablanca (Acad. Award, 1943), Arsenic and Old Lace, Mr. Skeffington (also co-prod.), Romanc on the High Seas, My Foolish Heart, Forever Female, The Last Time I Saw Paris, Young at Heart, The Tender Trap, Kiss Them for Me, Take a Giant Step (also prod.), Tall Story, Fanny, Light in the Piazza, Send Me No Flowers, Return From the Ashes, Any Wednesday (also prod.), Pete n' Tillie (also prod.), Jacqueline Susann's Once Is Not Enough, Cross of Iron, House Calls, Reuben Reuben (also co-prod.).

ERDMAN, RICHARD
Actor, Director. b. Enid, OK, June 1, 1925. e. Hollywood H.S.
PICTURES: *Actor*: Janie, Objective Burma, Time of Your Life, Four Days Leave, The Men, Cry Danger, Jumping Jacks, Happy Time, The Stooge, Stalag 17, The Power and the Prize, Saddle the Wind, Namu The Killer Whale. *Director*: Bleep, The Brothers O'Toole, Oscar In Limbo (also writer). *Writer-Prod.*: The Hillerman Project.
TELEVISION: Ray Bolger Show, Perry Mason, Police Story, Tab Hunter Show, Alice, Bionic Woman, One Day at a Time, Playhouse of Stars, Twilight Zone, The Lucy Show, Lou Grant, Cheers, Wings, Picket Fences. *Movie*: Jesse. *Director:* The Dick Van Dyke Show, Mooch (special). *Writer-Prod.*: More Than a Scarecrow.

ERICE, VICTOR
Writer, Director. b. San Sebastian, Spain, June 1940.
PICTURES: En la terraza, Paginas de un diario perdido, Los dias perdidos, Entre Vias, Los Desafios, The Spirit of the Beehive, Obscure August Dreams (sp. only), El Proximo otono (s.p. only), The South, The Dream of Light, The Shanghai Gesture (dir. only).

ERICSON, JOHN
Actor. b. Detroit, MI, Sept. 25, 1926. e. American Acad. of Dramatic Arts. Appeared in stock; then Stalag 17 on Broadway.
PICTURES: Teresa (debut, 1951), Rhapsody, The Student Prince, Green Fire, Bad Day at Black Rock, The Return of Jack Slade, The Cruel Tower, Oregon Passage, Forty Guns, Day of the Bad Man, Pretty Boy Floyd, Under Ten Flags, Slave Queen of Babylon, 7 Faces of Dr. Lao, Operation Atlantis, The Money Jungle, The Destructors, Treasure of Pancho Villa, The Bamboo Saucer (Collision Course), Heads or Tails, Bedknobs and Broomsticks, Hustle Squad, Crash, Final Mission, Alien Zone, Project Saucer, Golden Triangle, Queens Are Wild, Hustler Squad, $10,000 Caper, Primary Target.
TELEVISION: *Series*: Honey West, General Hospital. *Movies*: The Bounty Man, Hog Wild, Hunter's Moon, House on the Rue Riviera, Tenafly. *Mini-Series*: Robert Kennedy and His Times, Space. *Specials*: Saturday's Children, Heritage of Anger, The Innocent Sleep. *Guest*: Marcus Welby, Mannix, Streets of San Francisco, Fantasy Island, Bonanza, Medical Center, Route 66, Murder She Wrote, Police Story, General Hospital, Air Wolf, Gunsmoke, Police Woman, The FBI, One Day at a Time, Magnum P.I.

ERMAN, JOHN
Director. b. Chicago, IL, Aug. 3, 1935. e. U. of California. Debut as TV director, Stoney Burke, 1962.
PICTURES: Making It, Ace Eli and Rodger of the Skies, Stella.
TELEVISION: *Movies*: Letters From Three Lovers, Green Eyes, Alexander the Other Side of Dawn, Just Me and You, My Old Man, Moviola (This Year's Blonde; Scarlett O'Hara War; The Silent Lovers), The Letter, Eleanor: First Lady of the World, Who Will Love My Children? (Emmy Award, 1983), Another Woman's Child, A Streetcar Named Desire, Right to Kill?, The Atlanta Child Murders, An Early Frost, The Two Mrs. Grenvilles (also sprv. prod.), When the Time Comes, The Attic: The Hiding of Anne Frank (also prod.), David (also sprv. prod.), The Last Best Year (also sprv. prod.), The Last to Go (also prod.), Our Sons, Carolina Skeletons, Breathing Lessons (also prod.), The Sunshine Boys (also prod.). Mini-Series: Roots: The Next Generations (co-dir.), Queen (also co-prod.), Scarlett (also prod.), The Boys Next Door (also prod.), Ellen Foster, (also prod.), Only Love.

ESBIN, JERRY
Executive. b. Brooklyn, NY, 1931. Started in mailroom at Columbia at 17 and worked for co. nearly 25 years. Then joined American Multi Cinema. Joined Paramount Pictures in 1975 as mgr. of branch operations; later named v.p., asst. sls. mgr. In 1980 named v.p., gen. sls. mgr. 1981, sr. v.p., domestic sls. & mktg. 1981, joined United Artists as sr. v.p., mktg. & dist.; 1982, named pres., MGM/UA m.p. dist. & mktg. div; 1983, sr. v.p., domestic dist., Tri-Star Pictures; 1985, promoted to exec. v.p.; 1989, joined Loews Theaters as sr. exec. v.p. and chief oper. officer, also in 1989 named pres. as well as chief operating officer, Loews Theater Management Corp. Consultant for Conehco Pictures 1991 to 1992. Consultant for American Multi Cinema 1993 to present.

ESMOND, CARL
Actor. b. Vienna, Austria, June 14, 1906. e. U. of Vienna. On stage Vienna, Berlin, London (Shakespeare, Shaw, German modern classics). Acted in many European films under the name Willy Eichberger. Originated part of Prince Albert in Victoria Regina (London). On screen in Brit. prod. incl. Blossom Time, Even Song, Invitation to the Waltz. To U.S. in 1938. Guest star on many live and filmed TV shows. US stage incl. The Woman I Love, Four Winds. Appeared in Oscar nom. docum. Resisting Enemy Interrogation.
PICTURES: Dawn Patrol, First Comes Courage, Little Men, Sergeant York, Panama Hattie, Seven Sweethearts, Address Unknown, Margin for Error, Master Race, Ministry of Fear, Experiment Perilous, Story of Dr. Wassell. The Catman of Paris, Smash-up, Story of a Woman, Casablanca, Climax, Slave Girl, Walk a Crooked Mile, The Navy Comes Through, Sundown, Lover Come Back, This Love of Ours, Without Love, Mystery Submarine, The Desert Hawk, The World in His Arms, Thunder in the Sun, From the Earth to the Moon, Brushfire, Kiss of Evil, Agent for H.A.R.M., Morituri.
TELEVISION: My Wicked Wicked Ways. *Guest*: The Man From Uncle, Lassie, The Big Valley, Treasury Agent, etc.

ESPOSITO, GIANCARLO
Actor. b. Copenhagen, Denmark, April 26, 1958. Made B'way debut as child in 1968 musical Maggie Flynn.
THEATER: *B'way*: Maggie Flynn, The Me Nobody Knows, Lost in the Stars, Seesaw, Merrily We Roll Along, Don't Get God Started, Sacrilege. *Off-B'way*: Zooman and the Sign (Theatre World Award, Obie Award), Keyboard, Who Loves the Dancer, House of Ramon Iglesias, Do Lord Remember Me, Balm in Gilead, Anchorman, Distant Fires, Trafficking in Broken Hearts.
PICTURES: Running, Taps, Trading Places, The Cotton Club, Desperately Seeking Susan, Maximum Overdrive, Sweet Lorraine, School Daze, Do the Right Thing, Mo'Better Blues, King of New York, Harley Davidson and the Marlboro Man, Night on Earth, Bob Roberts, Malcolm X, Amos & Andrew, Fresh, Smoke, The Keeper (co-prod. only), The Usual Suspects, Kla$h, Blue in the Face, The Keeper, Reckless, Loose Women, Nothing to Lose, The Maze, The People, Trouble on the Corner, Twilight, Phoenix.
TELEVISION: *Series*: Bakersfield P.D. *Movies*: The Gentleman Bandit, Go Tell It on the Mountain, Relentless: Mind of a Killer, The Tomorrow Man, Five Desperate Hours . *Special*: Roanok. *Guest*: Miami Vice, Spencer: For Hire, Legwork, NYPD Blue, Nash Bridges, Living Single, Chicago Hope.

ESSEX, DAVID
Actor, Singer, Composer. b. Plaistow, London, England, July 23, 1947. e. Shipman Sch., Custom House. Started as a singer-drummer in East London band. 1967: Joined touring Repertory Co. in The Fantasticks, Oh, Kay, etc. 1970: West End debut in Ten Years Hard, 1972: Jesus Christ in Godspell, Che in Evita; Lord Byron in Childe Byron, 1983-84: Fletcher Christian in own musical Mutiny! on album and stage. International recording artist. Variety Club of Great Britain show business personality of 1978. Many gold & silver disc intl. awards. 1989, Royal Variety performance. World concerts since 1974.
PICTURES: Assault, All Coppers Are..., That'll Be the Day, Stardust, Silver Dream Racer (also wrote score), Shogun Mayeda.
TELEVISION: Top of the Pops, Own Specials, The River (also composed music), BBC series. U.S.: Merv Griffin, Johnny Carson, Dinah Shore, American Bandstand, Midnight Special, Grammy Awards, Salute To The Beatles, Don Kirshner's Rock Concert, A.M. America, Phil Everly in Session, Paul Ryan Show, The David Essex Showcase.

ESTEVEZ, EMILIO
Actor, Director, Writer. b. New York, NY, May 12, 1962. Father is actor Martin Sheen; brother is actor Charlie Sheen. Made prof. debut at age 20 in TV movie starring his father, In the Custody of Strangers.
PICTURES: Tex (debut, 1982), The Outsiders, Nightmares, Repo Man, The Breakfast Club, St. Elmo's Fire, That Was Then This is Now (also s.p.), Maximum Overdrive, Wisdom (also dir., s.p.), Stakeout, Young Guns. Men at Work (also dir., s.p.), Young Guns II, Freejack, The Mighty Ducks, National Lampoon's Loaded Weapon 1, Another Stakeout, Judgment Night, D2: The Mighty Ducks, The Jerky Boys (co- exec. prod. only), The War at Home (also dir. and prod.), Mighty Ducks 3, Mission: Impossible, The Bang Bang Club (dir., prod. only), Killer's Head, Rated X, Sand.
TELEVISION: *Movies*: In the Custody of Strangers. Nightbreaker, Dollar for the Dead, Late Last Night.

ESTRADA, ERIK
Actor. r.n. Enrique Estrada. m. actress Peggy Rowe. b. New York, NY, March 16, 1949. Began professional career in Mayor John Lindsay's Cultural Program, performing in public parks. Joined American Musical Dramatic Acad. for training. Feature film debut in The Cross and the Switchblade (1970).
PICTURES: The New Centurions, Airport '75, Midway, Trackdown, Where Is Parsifal?, Lightblast, The Repentant, Hour of the Assassin, The Lost Idol, A Show of Force, Night of the Wilding, Twisted Justice, Caged Fury, Guns, Spirits, Do or Die, The Divine Enforcer, Alien Seed, Night of the Wilding, National Lampoon's Loaded Weapon 1, The Last Riders, Gang Justice, Visions, Tom Sawyer, Seth.
TELEVISION: *Series*: CHiPS. *Guest*: Hawaii Five-0, Six Million Dollar Man, Police Woman, Kojak, Medical Center, Hunter, Alfred Hitchcock Presents (1988), Cybill, Family Guy (voice), King of the Hill (voice). *Movies*: Fire!, Honeyboy, The Dirty Dozen: The Fatal Mission, She Knows Too Much, Earth Angel, Angel Eyes, Panic in the Skies!, We're No Angels, CHiPs '99.

ESZTERHAS, JOE
Writer. Author of novel Charlie Simpson's Apocalypse (nom. National Book Award, 1974), Nark!, and novelization of F.I.S.T.,
PICTURES: F.I.S.T., Flashdance, Jagged Edge, Big Shots, Betrayed, Checking Out, Music Box (also co-exec. prod.), Basic Instinct, Nowhere to Run (co-sp., co-exec. prod.), Sliver (also co-exec. prod.), Jade (exec. prod. only), Hearts of Fire, Original Sin, Showgirls, One Night Stand, Telling Lies in America, Male Pattern Baldness, An Alan Smithee Film: Burn Hollywood Burn (also actor).

ETTINGER, EDWIN D.
Publicist. b. New York, NY, 1921. Entered m.p. ind. as office boy, MGM; pub. rel. and publ. for industrial, comm. clients, 1946-52; joined Ettinger Co., pub. rel., 1952; pub. rel. dir., Disneyland Inc., 1955; marketing dir., Disneyland, 1955-65; v.p., M.C.A. Enterprises, Inc., 1965-66; Board chmn. & CEO, Recreation Environments, Inc., 1967-70; Board chmn. & CEO Recreations Inc., 1967-70; Pres., Ettinger, Inc., 1975-85; semi-retired in 1985.

ETTLINGER, JOHN A.
Producer, Director, Distributor. b. Chicago, IL, Oct. 14, 1924. e. Peddie Inst., Cheshire Acad. Signal Corps Photog. Center, 1942-45; with Paramount Theatres Corp., 1945-47; dir., KTLA, Paramount TV Prod., Inc., Los Angeles, 1948-50; radio-TV dir., Nat. C. Goldstone Agency, 1950-53; pres. Medallion TV Enterprises, Inc.; TV prod., View the Clue, Greenwich Village, High Road to Danger, Sur Demande, Star Route, Las Vegas Fights, Celebrity Billiards; Pres., KUDO-FM, Las Vegas.

EVANS, HARRY KENT
Executive. b. Long Beach, CA, July 16, 1935. Intl. representative, UAW, 1960-76. Exec. dir., International Photographers Guild, 1976-90. CEO of the ASC, 1990-94. Exec. VP, Meier Entertainment Group, Vancouver, BC, 1994-96. Exec. VP. Meier Worldwide Intermedia, 1996-.

EVANS, LINDA
Actress. b. Hartford, CT, Nov. 18, 1942. e. Hollywood H.S., L.A. TV commercials led to contract with MGM.
PICTURES: Twilight of Honor (debut, 1963), Those Calloways, Beach Blanket Bingo, The Klansman, Mitchell, Avalanche Express, Tom Horn.
TELEVISION: *Series*: The Big Valley, Hunter, Dynasty. *Movies*: Nakia, Nowhere to Run, Standing Tall, The Last Frontier, I'll Take Romance, Dynasty: The Reunion, Step Sister. *Mini-Series*: North & South Book II, Dazzle, Bare Essence, The Gambler Returns: Luck of the Draw, Gambler: The Adventure Continues.

EVANS, RAY
Songwriter. b. Salamanca, NY, Feb. 4, 1915. e. Wharton Sch. of U. of Pennsylvania. Musician on cruise ships, radio writer spec. material. Hellzapoppin', Sons o' Fun. Member: exec. bd. Songwriters Guild of America, Dramatists Guild, West Coast advisory bd. ASCAP., bd., Myasthenia Gravis Fdn. CA chap., Songwriters Hall of Fame, Motion Picture Acad. Received star on Hollywood Blvd. Walk of Fame. Songs included on Great Composer Series, by Columbia Records.
SONGS: To Each His Own, Golden Earrings, Buttons and Bows (Acad. Award, 1948), Mona Lisa (Acad. Award, 1950), Whatever Will Be Will Be (Acad. Award, 1956), A Thousand Violins, I'll Always Love You, Dreamsville, Love Song from Houseboat, Tammy, Silver Bells, Dear Heart, Angel, Never Let Me Go, Almost in Your Arms, As I Love You, In the Arms of Love, Wish Me a Rainbow.
PICTURES: The Paleface, Sorrowful Jones, Fancy Pants, My Friend Irma, Aaron Slick From Punkin Crick, Son of the Paleface, My Friend Irma Goes West, The Night of Grizzly, Saddle the Wind, Isn't It Romantic, Capt. Carey U.S.A., Off Limits, Here Come the Girls, Red Garters, Man Who Knew Too Much, Stars Are Singing, Tammy, Houseboat, Blue Angel, A Private's Affair, All Hands on Deck, Dear Heart, The Third Day, What Did You Do in the War Daddy?, This Property Is Condemned.
TELEVISION THEMES: Bonanza, Mr. Ed, Mr. Lucky, To Rome With Love.

EVANS, ROBERT
Producer. r.n. Robert J. Shapera. b. New York, NY, June 29, 1930. Son is actor Josh Evans. Radio actor at age 11; went on to appear in more than 300 radio prog. (incl. Let's Pretend, Archie Andrews, The Aldrich Family, Gangbusters) on major networks. Also appeared on early TV. At 20 joined brother, Charles, and Joseph Picone, as partner in women's clothing firm of Evan-Picone, Inc., 1952-67. In 1957 signed by Universal to play Irving Thalberg in Man of a Thousand Faces after recommendation by Norma Shearer, Thalberg's widow. Guest columnist NY Journal American, 1958. Independent prod. at 20th Century-Fox. 1966-76, with Paramount Pictures as head of prod., then exec. v.p. worldwide prod. (supervising Barefoot in the Park, Rosemary's Baby, Barbarella, Goodbye Columbus, Love Story, The Godfather I & II, The Great Gatsby, etc.). Resigned to become indep. prod. again; with exclusive contract with Paramount. *Autobiography:* The Kid Stays in the Picture (1994).
PICTURES: *Actor*. Man of a Thousand Faces, The Sun Also Rises, The Fiend Who Walked the West, The Best of Everything. *Producer*. Chinatown, Marathon Man, Black Sunday, Players, Urban Cowboy, Popeye, The Cotton Club, The Two Jakes, Sliver, Jade, The Phantom, The Saint, The Out of Towners.
TELEVISION: *Actor*. Elizabeth and Essex (1947), Young Widow Brown, The Right to Happiness. *Prod.*: Get High on Yourself.

EVERETT, CHAD
Actor. r.n. Raymond Lee Cramton. b. South Bend, IN, June 11, 1937. e. Wayne State U., Detroit. Signed by William T. Orr, head of TV prod. for Warner Bros. to 7-year contract. Appeared in many TV series as well as films. Next became contract player at MGM (1963-67). Received star on Hollywood Walk of Fame.
PICTURES: Claudelle Inglish (debut, 1961), The Chapman Report, Rome Adventure, Get Yourself a College Girl, The Singing Nun, Made in Paris, Johnny Tiger, The Last Challenge, Return of the Gunfighter, First to Fight, The Impossible Years, Firechasers, Airplane II: The Sequel, Fever Pitch, Jigsaw, Heroes Stand Alone, Official Denial, Hard to Forget.
TELEVISION: *Series*: The Dakotas, Medical Center, Hagen, The Rousters, McKenna, Dark Skies (narr. of pilot). *Guest*: Hawaiian Eye, 77 Sunset Strip, Surfside Six, Lawman, Bronco, The Lieutenant, Redigo, Route 66, Ironside, Hotel, Murder She Wrote, Shades of L.A., Cybil. *Movies*: Intruder, The Love Boat, Police Story, Thunderboat Row, Malibu, The French Atlantic Affair, Mistress in Paradise, Journey to the Unknown, In the Glitter Palace. *Mini-Series*: Centennial, McKenna, Star Command, When Time Expires.

EVERETT, RUPERT
Actor. b. Norfolk, England, 1959. e. Ampleforth Central School for Speech & Drama. Apprenticed with Glasgow's Citizen's Theatre. Originated role of Guy Bennett in Another Country on London stage in 1982 and made feature film debut in screen version in 1984. Author: Are You Working Darling?
PICTURES: Another Country, Real Life, Dance with a Stranger, Duet for One, Chronicle of a Death Foretold, The Right Hand Man, Hearts of Fire, The Gold-Rimmed Glasses, Jigsaw, The Comfort of Strangers, Inside Monkey Zetterland, Ready to Wear (Pret-a-Porter), The Madness of King George, Dunston Checks In, Cemetary Man, My Best Friend's Wedding, Shakespeare in Love, B. Monkey, A Midsummer Night's Dream, Inspector Gadget, An Ideal Husband, The Next Best Thing, Unconditional Love.
TELEVISION: Arthur the King, The Far Pavilions, Princess Daisy.

EVIGAN, GREG
Actor. b. South Amboy, NJ, Oct. 14, 1953. Appeared on NY stage in Jesus Christ Superstar and Grease.
PICTURES: Stripped to Kill, DeepStar Six, House of the Damned, Mel.
TELEVISION: *Series*: A Year at the Top, B.J. and the Bear, Masquerade, My Two Dads, P.S. I Luv U, TekWar, Melrose Place, Pacific Palisades, Family Rules. *Movies*: B.J. and the Bear (pilot), Private Sessions, The Lady Forgets, Lies Before Kisses, TekWar, TekJustice, TekLab, TekLords, One of Her Own, Deadly Family Secrets, Nobody Lives Forever, Survivor. *Guest*: One Day at a Time, Barnaby Jones, Murder She Wrote, New Mike Hammer, Matlock.

F

FABARES, SHELLEY
Actress. r.n. Michele Marie Fabares. b. Los Angeles, CA, Jan. 19, 1944. . m. actor Mike Farrell. Earned gold record for 1962 single Johnny Angel.
PICTURES: Never Say Goodbye, Rock Pretty Baby, Marjorie Morningstar, Summer Love, Annette, Ride the Wild Surf, Girl Happy, Hold On!, Spinout, Clambake, A Time to Sing, Hot Pursuit, Love or Money.
TELEVISION: *Series*: Annie Oakley, The Donna Reed Show, The Little People, The Practice, Mary Hartman Mary Hartman, Forever Fernwood, Highcliffe Manor, One Day at a Time, Coach, Superman (voice). *Guest*: Twilight Zone, Mr. Novak, Love American Style, The Rookies, Marcus Welby, Hello Larry. *Movies*: U.M.C., Brian's Song, Two for the Money, Sky Heist, Pleasure Cove, Friendships Secrets & Lies, Donovan's Kid, The Great American Traffic Jam (Gridlock), Memorial Day, Run Till You Fall, Class Cruise, Deadly Relations, The Great Mom Swap, Dream Is a Wish Your Heart Makes: The Annette Funicello Story, A Nightmare Come True, Playing to Win: A Moment of Truth Movie.

FAHEY, JEFF
Actor. b. Olean, NY, Nov. 29, 1956. Family moved to Buffalo when he was 10 years old. Was member of Joffrey Ballet for 3 years. Appeared on B'way in Brigadoon (1980), tour of Oklahoma!, Paris prod. of West Side Story, and London prod. of Orphans.
PICTURES: Silverado (debut, 1985), Psycho III, Riot on 42nd Street, The Serpent of Death, Wrangler, Split Decisions, Backfire, Outback, True Blood, Out of Time, Last of the Finest, Impulse, White Hunter Black Heart, Body Parts, Iron Maze, The Lawnmower Man, Woman of Desire, Freefall, Wyatt Earp, Temptation, Quick, The Sweeper (also asst. prod.), Serpent's Liar, Eye of the Wolf, Darkman III: Die Darkman Die, When Justice Fails, Waiting for the Man, Operation Delta Force, Johnny 2.0, Catherine's Grove, Lethal Tender, The Underground (also co-prod), Small Time, Detour, Spoken in Silence, Revelation.
TELEVISION: *Series*: One Life to Live, The Marshal. *Movies*: Execution of Raymond Graham, Parker Kane, Curiosity Kills, Iran: Days of Crisis, Sketch Artist, In the Company of Darkness, The Hit List, Blindsided, Baree, Sketch Artist II: Hands That See, Virtual Seduction, Every Woman's Dream, On the Line.

FAIMAN, PETER
Director. b. Australia. Entered entertainment business through TV, involved early in production-direction of major variety series in Australia. Assoc. prod.-dir. of over 20 programs for The Paul Hogan Show and two Hogan specials filmed in England (1983). Developed Australia's most popular and longest-running national variety program, The Don Lane Show. Responsible for creative development of the TV Week Logie Awards on the Nine Network. For 4 years headed Special Projects Division of the Nine Network Australia. Resigned to establish own prod. co., Peter Faiman Prods. Pty Ltd. 1984. Made m.p. theatrical film debut as director of Crocodile Dundee, followed by Dutch.

FAIRBANKS, DOUGLAS, JR.
K.B.E., (Hon.) D.S.C., M.A., (Oxon), (Hon.) D.F.I., Westminster (Fulton, MO), (Hon.) LL.D (Denver). **Actor, Producer, Executive**. b. New York, NY, Dec. 9, 1909. e. Pasadena (CA) Polytech. Sch.; Harvard Mil. Acad., Los Angeles; Bovee and Collegiate Sch., N.Y.; was also tutored in Paris, London. Son of late Douglas Fairbanks. Began as screen actor 1923 in Stephen Steps Out; thereafter in more than 80 pictures. On U.S. stage from 1926. Formed own film prod. co. 1935; commissioned Lieut. (j.g.) USNR, 1940; Appt. Presidential envoy to certain South Amer. nations by Pres. Roosevelt. Helped org. British War Relief and was natl. chmn., Committee for CARE. W.A. White Committee to Defend America 1939-41. Promoted through ranks to Capt., USNR, Now retired. Awarded U.S. Silver Star, Combat Legion of Merit with "V" Attachment; Knight Commander of Order of British Empire, 1949. Distinguished Service Cross, Knight of Justice of Order of St. John of Jerusalem; French Legion of Honor, Croix de Guerre with Palm, etc. Chairman, American Relief for Korea. Entered TV film prod., 1952. Autobiographies: The Fairbanks Album (1975; with Richard Schickel), The Salad Days (1988), A Hell of a War (1993). FYI: republished in England, 1995.
THEATER: U.S.: Young Woodley, Saturday's Children, Present Laughter, Out on a Limb, Sleuth, The Pleasure of His Company (also U.K., Ireland, Canada, Australia, Hong Kong), The Winding Journey, Moonlight in Silver, My Fair Lady, The Secretary Bird.
PICTURES: (since sound): The Forward Pass, The Careless Age, The Show of Shows, Party Girl, Loose Ankles, The Little Accident, The Dawn Patrol, Little Caesar, Outward Bound, One Night at Susie's, Chances, I Like Your Nerve, Union Depot, It's Tough to Be Famous, Love is a Racket, Parachute Jumper, Morning Glory, Life of Jimmy Dolan, The Narrow Corner, Captured, Catherine the Great, Success at Any Price, Mimi, The Amateur Gentleman (also prod.), Man of the Moment, Accused, When Thief Meets Thief, The Prisoner of Zenda, Joy of Living, Having Wonderful Time, The Rage of Paris, The Young in Heart, Gunga Din, The Sun Never Sets, Rulers of the Sea, Green Hell, Safari, Angels Over Broadway, The Corsican Brothers, Sinbad the Sailor, That Lady in Ermine, The Exile, The Fighting O'Flynn, State Secret, Mr. Drake's Duck, Another Man's Poison (prod. only), Chase a Crooked Shadow (prod. only), Ghost Story.
TELEVISION: *Series*: Douglas Fairbanks Presents (also prod.). *Guest*: The Rheingold Theatre (also prod.), The Chevy Show, Route 66, Dr. Kildare, The Love Boat, B.L. Stryker. *Special*: The Canterville Ghost (ABC Stage '67). *Movies*: The Crooked Hearts, The Hostage Tower.

FAIRBANKS, JERRY
Executive Producer. b. San Francisco, CA, Nov. 1, 1904. Cameraman, 1924-29; prod., shorts, Universal, 1929-34; prod., Popular Science, Unusual Occupations, Speaking of Animals Series, Para., 1935-49; Winner two Acad. Awards; set up film div., NBC, 1948; formed, NBC Newsreel, 1949; devel. Zoomar Lens and Multicam System; formed Jerry Fairbanks Prods., 1950.
PICTURES: The Last Wilderness, Down Liberty Road, With This Ring, Counterattack, Collision Course, Land of the Sea, Brink of Disaster, The Legend of Amaluk, North of the Yukon, Damage Report, The Boundless Seas.
TELEVISION: Public Prosecutor (first film series for TV); other series: Silver Theatre, Front Page Detective, Jackson and Jill, Hollywood Theatre, Crusader Rabbit.

FAIRCHILD, MORGAN
Actress. b. Dallas, TX, Feb. 3, 1950. e. Southern Methodist U.
PICTURES: Bullet for Pretty Boy, The Seduction, Pee-wee's Big Adventure, Red-Headed Stranger, Campus Man, Sleeping Beauty, Midnight Cop, Deadly Illusion, Phantom of the Mall, Body Chemistry 3: Point of Seduction, Freaked, Virgin Hunters, Naked Gun 33 1/3: The Final Insult, Gospa, Venus Rising, Criminal Hearts, Holy Man, Nice Guys Sleep Alone, Held For Ransom, Unshackled, Peril, Call O' The Glen.
TELEVISION: *Series*: Search for Tomorrow, Flamingo Road, Paper Dolls, Falcon Crest, Roseanne, The City. *Movies*: The Initiation of Sarah, Murder in Music City, Concrete Cowboys, The Memory of Eva Ryker, Flamingo Road (pilot), The Dream Merchants, The Girl the Gold Watch and Dynamite, Honeyboy, The Zany Adventures of Robin Hood, Time Bomb, Street of Dreams, The Haunting of Sarah Harding, How to Murder a Millionare, Menu for Murder, Writer's Block. Perry Mason: The Case of the Skin-Deep Scandal, Based on an Untrue Story, Dead Man's Island, Star Command, Into the Arms of Danger. *Mini-Series*: 79 Park Avenue, North and South Book II.

FAIRCHILD, WILLIAM
Writer, Director. b. Cornwall, England, 1918. e. Royal Naval Coll., Dartmouth. Early career Royal Navy.
AUTHOR: A Matter of Duty, The Swiss Arrangement, Astrology for Dogs, Astrology for Cats, Catsigns (U.S.), The Poppy Factory, No Man's Land (U.S.), Tierra de Nadie (Spain).
THEATER: Sound of Murder, Breaking Point, Poor Horace, The Pay-Off, The Flight of the Bumble B.
PICTURES: *Writer:* Morning Departure, Outcast of the Islands, The Gift Horse, The Net, Newspaper Story, Malta Story, The Seekers, Passage Home, Value For Money, John and Julie (also dir.), The Extra Day (also dir.), The Silent Enemy (also dir.), Star!, Embassy, The Darwin Adventure, Invitation to the Wedding, Bruno Rising, The Promise, Statues in a Garden. *Director only:* The Horsemasters (tv in U.S.).
TELEVISION: The Man with the Gun, No Man's Land, The Signal, Four Just Men, Some Other Love, Cunningham 5101, The Break, The Zoo Gang, Lady with a Past.

FALK, PETER
Actor. b. New York, NY, Sept. 16, 1927. e. New Sch. for Social Research, B.A., 1951; Syracuse U. M.F.A. Studied with Eva Le Galliene and Sanford Meisner. Worked as efficiency expert for Budget Bureau State of CT.
THEATER: *Off-B'way*: Don Juan (debut, 1956), The Iceman Cometh, Comic Strip, Purple Dust, Bonds of Interest, The Lady's Not for Burning, Diary of a Scoundrel. *On Broadway*: Saint Joan, The Passion of Josef D., The Prisoner of Second Avenue. Regional: Light Up the Sky (L.A.), Glengarry Glen Ross (tour).
PICTURES: Wind Across the Everglades (debut, 1958), The Bloody Brood, Pretty Boy Floyd, The Secret of the Purple Reef, Murder Inc. (Acad. Award nom.), Pocketful of Miracles (Acad. Award nom.), Pressure Point, The Balcony, It's a Mad Mad Mad Mad World, Robin and the 7 Hoods, Italiano Brava Gente (Attack and Retreat), The Great Race, Penelope, Luv, Anzio, Castle Keep, Machine Gun McCann, Operation Snafu, Husbands, A Woman Under the Influence, Murder by Death, Mikey and Nicky, The Cheap Detective, The Brink's Job, Opening Night, The In-Laws, The Great Muppet Caper, All the Marbles, Big Trouble, Happy New Year, The Princess Bride, Wings of Desire, Vibes, Cookie, In the Spirit, Tune in Tomorrow, The Player, Faraway So Close!, Roommates.
TELEVISION: *Series*: The Trials of O'Brien, Columbo (1971-77; Emmy Awards: 1972, 1975, 1976), Columbo (1989, also co-exec. prod.; Emmy Award, 1990). *Guest*: Studio One, Kraft Theatre, Alcoa Theatre, N.T.A. Play of the Week, Armstrong Circle Theatre, Omnibus, Robert Montgomery Presents, Brenner, Deadline, Kraft Mystery Theatre, Rendezvous, Sunday Showcase, The Untouchables, Dick Powell Show (The Price of Tomatoes; Emmy Award, 1962), Danny Kaye Show, Edie Adams Show, Bob Hope Chrysler Theatre. *Movies:* Prescription: Murder, A Step Out of Line, Ransom for a Dead Man, Griffin and Phoenix: A Love Story, Columbo Goes to College, Caution: Murder Can Be Hazardous to Your Health, Columbo and the Murder of a Rock Star, Death Hits the Jackpot, Columbo: No Time to Die, Columbo: A Bird in the Hand (also exec. prod.), Columbo: It's All in the Game (also writer, exec. prod.), Columbo: Butterfly in Shades of Grey (also exec. prod.), Columbo: Undercover, Columbo: Strange Bedfellows (also exec. prod.), Pronto, Columbo: A Trace of Murder, Columbo: Ashes to Ashes, Vig, Columbo: Murder with Too Many Notes. *Specials:* The Sacco-Vanzetti Story, The Million Dollar Incident, Brigadoon, A Hatful of Rain, Clue: Movies Murder and Mystery.

FANGMEIER, STEFEN
Special Effects.
PICTURES: Terminator 2: Judgment Day (comp. graph. super.), Hook (comp. graph. super.), Jurassic Park (lead comp. graph. super.), Casper (dig. char. co-super). *Visual Effects Supervisor:* Twister, The Trigger Effect, Speed 2: Cruise Control, Small Soldiers, Saving Private Ryan, Galaxy Quest (co-super.).

FARBER, BART
Executive. Joined United Artists Corp. in early 1960s when UA acquired ZIV TV Programs. Served as v.p. United Artists Television and United Artists Broadcasting. 1971 named v.p. in charge of legal affairs of the cos. 1978, named sr. v.p.—TV, video and special markets; indep. consultant, TV, Pay TV, home video. 1982, joined Cable Health Network as v.p., legal & business affairs; 1984, v.p., business & legal affairs, Lifetime Network; 1986, independent communications consultant.

FARENTINO, JAMES
Actor. b. Brooklyn, NY, Feb. 24, 1938. e. American Acad. of Dramatic Arts.
THEATER: *B'way*: Death of a Salesman, A Streetcar Named Desire (revival, 1973; Theatre World Award). *Off-B'way*: The Days and Nights of Bebe Fenstermaker, In the Summerhouse. *Regional*: One Flew Over the Cuckoo's Nest (Jos. Jefferson, Chas. MacArthur & Chicago Drama Critics League Awards), California Suite, The Best Man, The Big Knife, Good-Bye Charlie, A Thousand Clowns, Love Letters.
PICTURES: Psychomania (Violent Midnight), Engine Pulver, The War Lord, The Pad... And How to Use It (Golden Globe Award, 1966), The Ride to Hangman's Tree, Banning, Rosie!, Me Natalie, The Story of a Woman, The Final Countdown, Dead and Buried, Her Alibi, Bulletproof, Termination Man, Radio Silence.

TELEVISION: *Series*: The Lawyers (The Bold Ones), Cool Million, Dynasty, Blue Thunder, Mary Tyler Moore, Julie Andrews Show. *Guest*: Naked City, daytime soap operas, Laredo, Route 66, The Alfred Hitchcock Hour, Ben Casey, Twelve O'Clock High, Melrose Place, ER. *Special*: DOS Pasos USA. *Mini-Series*: Sins, Jesus of Nazareth (Emmy nom.), Dazzled, On Common Ground, Death of a Salesman, Vanished, Evita Peron, Secrets of the Sahara (Italy). *Movies*: Wings of Fire, The Whole World is Watching, The Sound of Anger, Longest Night, Family Rico, Cool Million, The Elevator, Crossfire, Possessed, Silent Victory: Undercover Cop, The Kitty O'Neil Story, Son Rise: A Miracle of Love, That Secret Sunday, Something So Right (Emmy nom.), The Cradle Will Fall, License to Kill, A Summer to Remember, That Secret Sunday, Family Sins, Naked Lies, The Red Spider, Who Gets the Friends?, Picking Up the Pieces, In the Line of Duty: A Cop for the Killing, Miles From Nowhere, When No One Would Listen, One Woman's Courage, Honor Thy Father and Mother: The True Story of the Menendez Murders. *Pilot*: American Nuclear.

FARGAS, ANTONIO
Actor. b. Bronx, NY, Aug. 14, 1946. Studied acting at Negro Ensemble Co. and Actor's Studio.
THEATER: The Great White Hope, The Glass Menagerie, Mod Hamlet, Romeo and Juliet, The Slave, Toilet, The Amen Corner.
PICTURES: The Cool World (debut, 1964), Putney Swope, Pound, Believe in Me, Shaft, Cisco Pike, Across 110th Street, Cleopatra Jones, Busting, Foxy Brown, Conrack, The Gambler, Cornbread Earl and Me, Next Stop Greenwich Village, Car Wash, Pretty Baby, Up the Academy, Firestarter, Streetwalkin', Night of the Sharks, Shakedown, I'm Gonna Git You Sucka, The Borrower, Howling VI: The Freaks, Whore.
TELEVISION: *Series*: Starsky and Hutch, All My Children. *Movies*: Starsky and Hutch (pilot), Huckleberry Finn, Escape, Nurse, The Ambush Murders, A Good Sport, Florida Straits, Maid for Each Other, Percy and Thunder. *Guest*: Ironside, The Bill Cosby Show, Sanford and Son, Police Story, Kolchak The Night Stalker, Miami Vice, Kojak.

FARGO, JAMES
Director. b. Republic, WA, Aug. 14, 1938. e. U. of Washington, B.A.
PICTURES: The Enforcer, Caravans, Every Which Way But Loose, A Game for Vultures, Forced Vengeance, Born to Race, Voyage of the Rock Aliens, Riding the Edge (also actor).
TELEVISION: *Movies*: Gus Brown and Midnight Brewster, The Last Electric Knight, Hunter, Snoops, Sky High. *Series*: Tales of the Gold Monkey, Sidekicks.

FARINA, DENNIS
Actor. b. Chicago, IL, Feb. 29, 1944. Served 18 years with Chicago police before being introduced to producer-director Michael Mann who cast him in film Thief. Celebrity Chmn. of Natl. Law Enforcement Officers Memorial in Washington, D.C.
THEATER: A Prayer for My Daughter, Streamers, Tracers, Bleacher Bums, Some Men Need Help, The Time of Your Life.
PICTURES: Thief (debut, 1981), Jo Jo Dancer Your Life Is Calling, Manhunter, Midnight Run, Men of Respect, We're Talkin' Serious Money, Mac, Another Stakeout, Striking Distance, Romeo Is Bleeding, Little Big League, Get Shorty, Eddie, That Old Feeling, Out of Sight, Saving Private Ryan, The Mod Squad.
TELEVISION: *Series*: Crime Story, Buddy Faro (also co-exec. prod.). *Mini-Series*: Drug Wars: Columbia. *Movies*: Six Against the Rock, Open Admissions, The Hillside Stranglers, People Like Us, Blind Faith, Cruel Doubt, The Disappearance of Nora, One Woman's Courage, The Corpse Had a Familiar Face, Bonanza: Under Attack, Out of Annie's Past, Bella Mafia. *Guest*: Miami Vice, Hunter, Tales from the Crypt. Special: The Killing Floor.

FARNSWORTH, RICHARD
Actor. b. Los Angeles, CA, Sept. 1, 1920. Active as stuntman for 40 years before turning to acting.
PICTURES: Comes a Horseman, Tom Horn, Resurrection, The Legend of the Lone Ranger, Ruckus, Waltz Across Texas, The Grey Fox, The Natural, Rhinestone, Into the Night, Sylvester, Space Rage, The Two Jakes, Misery, Highway to Hell, The Getaway, Lassie, The Straight Story.
TELEVISION: *Series*: Boys of Twilight. *Movies*: Strange New World, A Few Days in Weasel Creek, Travis McGee, Ghost Dancing, Anne of Green Gables, Chase, Wild Horses, Red Earth White Earth, Good Old Boy, The Fire Next Time, Best Friends for Life.
(d. Oct. 6 2000)

FARR, FELICIA
Actress. b. Westchester, NY, Oct. 4, 1932. e. Pennsylvania State Coll. m. Jack Lemmon. Stage debut: Picnic (Players Ring Theatre). In Memorandum for a Spy, 1965 tv movie.
PICTURES: Timetable, Jubal, Reprisal!, The First Texan, The Last Wagon, 3:10 to Yuma, Onionhead, Hell Bent for Leather, Kiss Me Stupid, The Venetian Affair, Kotch, Charley Varrick, That's Life!, The Player.

FARR, JAMIE
Actor. r.n. Jameel Joseph Farah. b. Toledo, OH, July 1, 1934. e. Columbia Coll. Trained for stage at Pasadena Playhouse.
PICTURES: Blackboard Jungle (debut, 1955), The Greatest Story Ever Told, Ride Beyond Vengeance, Who's Minding the Mint?, With Six You Get Eggroll, The Gong Show Movie, Cannonball Run, Cannonball Run II, Happy Hour, Scrooged, Speed Zone!, Curse II: The Bite, Scrooged.
TELEVISION: *Series*: The Chicago Teddy Bears, M*A*S*H (also dir. episodes), The Gong Show (panelist), The $1.98 Beauty Show (panelist), After M*A*S*H (also dir. episodes), Port Charles. *Guest*: Dear Phoebe, The Red Skelton Show, The Dick Van Dyke Show, The Danny Kaye Show, The Love Boat, The New Love American Style, Murder She Wrote. *Movies*: The Blue Knight, Amateur Night at the Dixie Bar and Grill, Murder Can Hurt You!, Return of the Rebels, For Love or Money, Run Till You Fall.

FARRELL, HENRY
Writer. Author of novels and screenplays
PICTURES: Whatever Happened to Baby Jane? Hush ... Hush Sweet Charlotte, What's the Matter with Helen?
TELEVISION: *Movies*: How Awful About Allan, The House That Would Not Die, The Eyes of Charles Sand.

FARRELL, MIKE
Actor, Producer. b. St. Paul, MN, Feb. 6, 1939. m. actress Shelley Fabares. Currently co-chair of Human Rights Watch in CA.; pres. of Death Penalty Focus; member of the adv. bd. of the Natl Coalition to Abolish the Death Penalty; member of the adv. bd. of the Cult Awareness Network; founding bd. member of Peace Studies, ATV, at Augusta Correctional Ctr in Virginia.
PICTURES: Captain Newman M.D., The Americanization of Emily, The Graduate, Targets. *Prod.*: Dominick and Eugene, Patch Adams.
TELEVISION: *Series*: Days of Our Lives, The Interns, The Man and the City, M*A*S*H, Providence. *Specials*: JFK: One Man Show (PBS), The Best of Natl. Geographic Specials (host/narrator), Saving the Wildlife (co-host). *Movies*: The Longest Night, She Cried Murder!, The Questor Tapes, Live Again Die Again, McNaughton's Daughter, Battered, Sex and the Single Parent, Letters from Frank, Damien: The Leper Priest, Prime Suspect, Memorial Day (also prod.), Choices of the Heart, Private Sessions, Vanishing Act, A Deadly Silence, Price of the Bride, Incident at Dark River (also prod.), The Whereabouts of Jenny, Silent Motive (also prod.), Hart Attack, The Enemy Inside, Vows of Seduction, Twisted Path, Hart to Hart: Old Friends Never Die, Superman, Sins of the Mind. *Director*: Run Till You Fall. *Guest*: The Monroes.

FARRELLY, BOBBY
Writer, Director. b. Cumberland, RI, 1958. Collaborates with brother Peter.
PICTURES: Dumb & Dumber (also prod.), Bushwhacked (co-s.p. only), There's Something About Mary (also co-exec. prod.), Outside Providence (s.p., co-prod. only), Me Myself and Irene (also co-prod.), Osmosis Jones (also prod.), Say It Isn't So (prod. only), Shallow Hal.

FARRELLY, PETER
Director, Writer. b. Cumberland, RI, 1957. Collaborates with brother Bobby.
PICTURES: Dumb & Dumber, Bushwhacked (co-s.p. only), Kingpin (dir. only), There's Something About Mary (also co-exec. prod.), Outside Providence (novel, co-prod. only), Me Myself and I (also co-prod.), Say It Isn't So (prod. only), Osmosis Jones (also prod.), Shallow Hal.

FARROW, MIA
Actress. b. Los Angeles, CA, Feb. 9. 1945. r.n. Maria de Lourdes Villiers Farrow. d. of actress Maureen O'Sullivan and late dir. John Farrow. e. Marymount, Los Angeles, Cygnet House, London.
THEATER: The Importance of Being Earnest (debut, Madison Ave. Playhouse, NY, 1963); Royal Shakespeare Co. (Twelfth Night, A Midsummer Night's Dream, Ivanov, Three Sisters, The Seagull, A Doll's House), Mary Rose (London), Romantic Comedy (B'way debut, 1979).
PICTURES: Guns at Batasi (debut, 1964), A Dandy in Aspic, Rosemary's Baby, Secret Ceremony, John and Mary, See No Evil, The Public Eye, Dr. Popaul (High Heels), The Great Gatsby, Full Circle (The Haunting of Julia), Avalanche, A Wedding, Death on the Nile, Hurricane, A Midsummer Night's Sex Comedy, The Last Unicorn (voice), Zelig, Broadway Danny Rose, Supergirl, The Purple Rose of Cairo, Hannah and Her Sisters, Radio Days, September, Another Woman, New York Stories (Oedipus Wrecks), Crimes and Misde-meanors, Alice (Natl. Board of Review Award, 1990), Shadows and Fog, Husbands and Wives, Widow's Peak, Miami Rhapsody, Reckless, Redux Riding Hood (voice), Private Parts, Coming Soon, Purpose.
TELEVISION: *Series*: Peyton Place. *Specials*: Johnny Belinda, Peter Pan. *Movie*: Goodbye Raggedy Ann, Miracle at Midnight.

FAWCETT, FARRAH
Actress. b. Corpus Christi, TX, Feb. 2, 1947. e. U. of Texas. Picked as one of the ten most beautiful girls while a freshman; went to Hollywood and signed by Screen Gems. Did films, TV shows, and made over 100 TV commercials. Off B'way debut: Extremities (1983).

PICTURES: Love Is a Funny Thing, Myra Breckinridge, Logan's Run, Somebody Killed Her Husband, Sunburn, Saturn 3, Cannonball Run, Extremities, See You in the Morning, Man of the House, The Apostle, Dr. T and the Women.
TELEVISION: *Series*: Charlie's Angels, Good Sports. *Guest*: Owen Marshall Counselor at Law, The Six Million Dollar Man, Rockford Files, Harry-O. *Movies:* Three's a Crowd, The Feminist and the Fuzz, The Great American Beauty Contest, The Girl Who Came Gift-Wrapped, Murder on Flight 502, Murder in Texas, The Burning Bed, Red Light Sting, Between Two Women, Nazi Hunter: The Beate Klarsfeld Story, Poor Little Rich Girl: The Barbara Hutton Story, Margaret Bourke-White, Small Sacrifices, Criminal Behavior, The Substitute Wife, Children of the Dust.

FAVREAU, JON
Actor. b. Queens, NY, October 19, 1966. Alumnus of Chicago's Improv Olympia improvisational acting troupe.
PICTURES: Folks!, Rudy, Mrs. Parker and the Vicious Circle, PCU, Batman Forever, Notes from Underground, Swingers (also s.p.), Just Your Luck, Persons Unknown, Dogtown, Deep Impact, Very Bad Things, Love & Sex, The Replacements, Made (also dir., s.p., prod.).
TELEVISION: *Movies:* Grandpa's Funeral, Smog (s.p. and dir.), Rocky Marciano. *Guest:* Seinfeld, Chicago Hope, Friends, Dilbert (voice), The Larry Sanders Show, The Sopranos.

FAY, PATRICK J.
Director, Producer. b. June 7, 1916. e. Carnegie Tech. Dumont TV Network, 10 years. Director of over 100 Army training films; also dir. IBM Industrials.
AUTHOR: Melba, The Toast of Pithole, The Last Family Portrait in Oil, Coal Oil Johnny, French Kate, No Pardon in Heaven, An Ill Wind, Tighten Your G-String, As It Was in the Beginning (Television 50 Yrs. Ago).
PICTURES: Director for RCA, General Electric H.G. Peters Company, Bransby Films. *Screenplays:* Sanctuary, The Burning of New York City, Johnson's Island.
TELEVISION: Bishop Sheen, Broadway to Hollywood, Cavalcade of Stars, Manhattan Spotlight, Life is Worth Living, Front Row Center, Ilona Massey Show, Alec Templeton Show, Maggi McNellis Show, Key to Missing Persons, Kids and Company, Confession (also prod.), The Big Picture.

FEINSTEIN, ALAN
Actor. b. New York, NY, Sept. 8, 1941.
THEATER: *NY:* Malcolm, Zelda, A View from the Bridge (NY Drama Desk Award), As Is, A Streetcar Named Desire.
PICTURE: Looking for Mr. Goodbar.
TELEVISION: *Series*: Edge of Night, Love Of Life, Search for Tomorrow, Jigsaw John, The Runaways, The Family Tree, Berrenger's. *Movies*: Alexander: The Other Side of Dawn, Visions, The Hunted Lady, The Users, The Two Worlds of Jenny Logan, On Fire. *Mini-Series:* Masada.

FEITSHANS, BUZZ
Executive. b. Los Angeles, CA. e. USC. Started in film business as editor. Worked for 10 years at American-International as supvr. of prod. In 1975 formed A-Team Productions with John Milius. With Carolco Pictures: producer, 1981-6; exec. v.p. for mo. pic. production, member bd. dir. 1986-90. 1990\-, v.p. for Cinergi Prods.; 1994, pres. of Cinergi.
PICTURES: *Producer*: Dillinger, Act of Vengeance, Foxy Brown, Big Wednesday, Hardcore, 1941, Extreme Prejudice (exec. prod.), Conan the Barbarian, First Blood, Uncommon Valor, Rambo II, Red Dawn, Rambo III, Total Recall, Tombstone (exec. prod.), Color of Night, Shadow Conspiracy (exec. prod.).

FELDMAN, COREY
Actor. b. Reseda, CA, July 16, 1971. Has been performing since the age of 3 in commercials, television (Love Boat, Father Murphy, Foul Play, Mork and Mindy, Eight Is Enough, Alice, Gloria) and films.
PICTURES: Time After Time, The Fox and the Hound (voice), Friday the 13th—The Final Chapter, Gremlins, Friday the 13th—A New Beginning, The Goonies, Stand by Me, Lost Boys, License to Drive, The 'burbs, Dream a Little Dream, Teenage Mutant Ninja Turtles (voice only), Rock 'n' Roll High School Forever, Edge of Honor, Meatballs 4, Round Trip to Heaven, Stepmonster, Blown Away, National Lampoon's Loaded Weapon 1, Lipstick Camera, National Lampoon's Last Resort, Maverick, Dream a Little Dream 2, A Dangerous Place, Evil Obsession, Tales From the Crypt: Bordello of Blood, Mr. Atlas, Born Bad, The Thief and the Stripper, She's Too Tall (assoc. prod.), Fortune Hunters.
TELEVISION: *Series*: The Bad News Bears, Madame's Place, Dweebs. *Movies*: Willa, Father Figure, Kid with a Broken Halo, Still the Beaver, Out of the Blue, When the Whistle Blows, I'm a Big Girl Now, Exile, Legion. *Specials*: 15 & Getting Straight, How to Eat Like a Child.

FELDMAN, EDWARD S.
Producer. b. New York, NY, Sept. 5, 1929. e. Michigan State U. Trade press contact, newspaper and mag. contact, 20th Century Fox, 1950; dir. info. services, Dover Air Force Base. 1954-56; publ. coordinator, The World of Suzie Wong, 1960; joined Embassy, dir. of publicity, 1969; v.p. in chg., adv. & pub, 7 Arts Prods., 1962; v.p. exec. asst. to head prod. Warner-7 Arts Studio 1967; pres., m.p. dept., Filmways, 1970; Formed Edward S. Feldman Co., 1978.

PICTURES: *Prod./exec. prod.*: What's the Matter With Helen?, Fuzz, Save the Tiger, The Other Side of the Mountain, Two-Minute Warning, The Other Side of the Mountain Part 2, The Last Married Couple in America, Six Pack, The Sender, Hot Dog ... The Movie! (co-prod.), Witness, Explorers, The Golden Child, The Hitcher, Near Dark, Wired, Green Card, The Doctor, Honey I Blew Up the Kid, Forever Young, My Father the Hero, The Jungle Book, The Truman Show, 101 Dalmations.
TELEVISION: *Exec. Prod.*: Moon of the Wolf, My Father's House, Valentine, 300 Miles for Stephanie, Charles and Diana: A Royal Love Story, 21 Hours at Munich, King, Not in Front of the Children, Obsessed with a Married Woman.

FELDON, BARBARA
Actress. b. Pittsburgh, PA, Mar. 12, 1941. e. Carnegie Tech. Former fashion model, also appeared in many commercials. On NY stage in Past Tense, Cut the Ribbons.
PICTURES: Fitzwilly, Smile, No Deposit No Return.
TELEVISION: *Series*: Get Smart, The Marty Feldman Comedy Machine, The Dean Martin Comedy Hour (host), Special Edition (host), The 80's Woman (synd.; host), Get Smart (1995). *Movies*: Getting Away From It All, Playmates, What Are Best Friends For?, Let's Switch, A Guide for the Married Woman, Sooner or Later, A Vacation in Hell, Before and After, Children of Divorce, Get Smart Again!

FELDSHUH, TOVAH
Actress. b. New York, NY, Dec. 27, 1953. e. Sarah Lawrence Col., Univ. of MN. For humanitarian work received the Israel Peace Medal and the Eleanor Roosevelt Humanitarian Award.
THEATER: *NY*: Cyrano, Straws in the Wind, Three Sisters, Rodgers and Hart, Yentl (Theatre World Award), Sarava, The Mistress of the Inn, Springtime for Henry, She Stoops to Conquer, Lend Me a Tenor, A Fierce Attachment, Sarah and Abraham, Six Wives, Hello Muddah! Hello Fadduh!
PICTURES: White Lies, Nunzio, The Idolmaker, Cheaper to Keep Her, Daniel, Brewster's Millions, The Blue Iguana, A Day in October, Comfortably Numb.
TELEVISION: *Series*: As the World Turns, Mariah. *Movies*: Scream Pretty Peggy, The Amazing Howard Hughes, Terror Out of the Sky, The Triangle Factory Fire Scandal, Beggarman Thief, The Women's Room, Citizen Cohn, Sexual Considerations. *Specials*: Dosvedanya Mean Goodbye, Saying Kaddish. *Mini-Series*: Holocaust. Guest: LA Law, Law and Order, etc.

FELLMAN, DANIEL R.
Executive. b. Cleveland, OH, March 14, 1943. e. Rider Coll., B.S., 1964. Paramount Pictures, 1964-69; Loews Theatres, 1969-71; Cinema National Theatres, 1971-76; 1976-78, pres., American Theatre Mgmt. Joined Warner Bros. in 1978, named exec. v.p. Warner Bros. domestic distribution, Jan. 1993. Named pres. Warner Bros. theatrical distribution, March 1999. President Variety Club Tent 35, 1977-78. Member exec. comm., Will Rogers Foundation; Past Chmn, Foundation of Motion Picture Pioneers.

FELLMAN, NAT D.
Executive. b. New York, NY, Feb. 19, 1910. Started as office boy, Warner Bros. Pictures, 1928; transferred to Warner Bros. Theatres, asst. to chief booker; handled pool, partnership operations; head buyer, booker for Ohio zone, 1941; asst. to chief film buyer in New York, 1943; apptd. chief film buyer, 1952; exec. asst. to v.p. and gen. mgr., Stanley Warner Theatres, 1955; asst. gen. mgr., Stanley Warner Theatres, 1962; acting gen. mgr., Stanley Warner Theatres, July, 1964; Stanley Warner Theatres, v.p. and gen. mgr., 1965; v.p., NGC Theatre Corp. and division mgr. Fox Eastern Theatres, 1968; v.p. National General Corp., and pres., National General Theatres, 1969; 1974, formed Exhibitor Relations Co., operations consultant; sold it and retired in 1982. Served as vice pres., Variety Clubs International and NATO, Chmn., presidents' advisory comm.

FENADY, ANDREW J.
Producer, Writer. b. Toledo, OH, Oct. 4, 1928. e. U. of Toledo, 1946-50. Radio-prod.-actor-writer. *Novels:* The Man With Bogart's Face, The Secret of Sam Marlow, The Claws of the Eagle, The Summer of Jack London, Mulligan, Runaways.
PICTURES: Stakeout on Dope Street, The Young Captives, Ride Beyond Vengeance, Chisum, Terror in the Wax Museum, Arnold, The Man with Bogart's Face.
TELEVISION: *Series*: Confidential File, The Rebel, Branded, Hondo. *Movies*: The Woman Hunter, Voyage of the Yes, The Stranger, The Hanged Man, Black Noon, Sky Heist, Mayday 40,000 Ft., The Hostage Heart, Mask of Alexander, Masterpiece of Murder, Who Is Julia?, Jake Spanner—Private Eye, The Love She Sought, Yes Virginia There Is a Santa Claus, The Sea Wolf.

FENN, SHERILYN
Actress. b. Detroit, MI, Feb. 1, 1965.
PICTURES: The Wild Life (debut, 1984), Just One of the Guys, Out of Control, Thrashin', The Wraith, Zombie High, Two Moon Junction, Crime Zone, True Blood, Meridian: Kiss of the Beast, Wild at Heart, Backstreet Dreams, Ruby, Desire and Hell at Sunset Motel, Diary of a Hit Man, Of Mice and Men, Three of Hearts, Boxing Helena, Fatal Instinct, The Shadow Men, Lovelife, Johnny Hit and Run Pauline, Just Write, Darkness Falls, Outside Ozona, Cement.

TELEVISION: *Series*: Twin Peaks, Rude Awakening. *Movies*: Silence of the Heart, Dillinger, Spring Awakening, Liz: The Elizabeth Taylor Story, Slave of Dreams, The Assassination File, The Don's Analyst, Nightmare Street. *Guest*: Cheers, 21 Jump Street, Heart of the City, Friends. *Specials*: Tales From the Hollywood Hills (A Table at Ciro's), Divided We Stand, A Family Again. *Mini-series*: A Season in Purgatory.

FERRARA, ABEL
Director, Writer. b. Bronx, NY, 1951. Moved to Peekskill, NY, as teenager where he made short films with future writer Nicholas St. John. Traveled to England, worked for the BBC. Returned to U.S. to attended SUNY/Purchase, making short Could This Be Love, which received some theatrical distribution. Has used the pseudonymn Jimmy Laine.
PICTURES: Driller Killer (also actor, s.p. songs), Ms. 45 (also actor), Fear City, China Girl (also songs), Cat Chaser, King of New York, Bad Lieutenant (also co-s.p.), Dangerous Game, Body Snatchers, The Addiction, The Funeral, The Blackout, New Rose Hotel, R-Xmas.
TELEVISION: Miami Vice, Crime Story(pilot), Subway Stories: Tales from the Underground.

FERRARO, JOHN E.
Executive. b. Greenwich, CT, July 20, 1958. e. Emerson College, B.S. in Mass Communications, 1980. Joined Paramount Pictures Corp. 1980. 1983-84, story analyst, Paramount TV; 1984-85 supervisor, Drama Development; 1985-87 manager, Current Programs & Special Projects; 1987-88, dir. Drama Development. 1988, exec. dir., Acquisitions, Paramount Pictures; 1990, v.p., acquisitions; 1997, sr. v.p., acquisitions & co-productions.

FERRAZZA, CARL J.
Executive. b. Cleveland, OH, Aug. 29, 1920. e. Catholic U. of America, Washington, DC. Started career 1945: as asst. mgr. & mgr. for Loews Theatres. 1952, joined Cincinnati Theatre Co., first as mgr. for Keith's Theatre, Cincinnati, and after prom. dir. for circuit. 1963, field rep. for United Artists, covering midwest. 1968, UA prom. mgr., N.Y. 1975-83, dir. of field activities, MGM/UA; 1984, joined Orion Pictures Distributing Corp. as v.p. promotional and field activities.

FERRELL, CONCHATA
Actress. b. Charleston, WV, Mar. 28, 1943. e. Marshall Univ.
THEATER: *NY*: The Three Sisters, Hot L Baltimore, Battle of Angels, The Sea Horse (Theatre World, Obie & Vernon Rice Drama Desk Awards), Wine Untouched. *LA*: Getting Out, Picnic.
PICTURES: Deadly Hero, Network, Heartland, Where the River Runs Black, For Keeps?, Mystic Pizza, Edward Scissorhands, Family Prayers, True Romance, Samuari Cowboy, Heaven and Earth, Freeway, My Fellow Americans, Touch.
TELEVISION: *Series*: Hot L Baltimore, B.J. and the Bear, McClain's Law, E/R, Peaceable Kingdom, L. A. Law, Hearts Afire, Townies, Teen Angel. *Movies*: The Girl Called Hatter Fox, A Death in Canaan, Who'll Save My Children?, Before and After, The Seduction of Miss Leona, Reunion, Rape and Marriage: The Rideout Case, Life of the Party: The Story of Beatrice, Emergency Room, Nadia, The Three Wishes of Billy Grier, North Beach and Rawhide, Samaritan: The Mitch Snyder Story, Eye on the Sparrow, Your Mother Wears Combat Boots, Goodbye Miss 4th of July, Opposites Attract, Deadly Intentions... Again?, Backfield in Motion, The Buccaneers. *Guest*: Good Times, Love Boat, Lou Grant, St. Elsewhere, Frank's Place, Murder She Wrote, Who's the Boss?, Matlock, Buffy the Vampire Slayer. *Specials:* The Great Gilly Hopkins, Portrait of a White Marriage, Runaway Ralph, Picnic.

FERRER, MEL
Actor, Producer, Director. r.n. Melchor Ferrer. b. Elberon, NJ, Aug. 25, 1917. e. Princeton U. During coll. and early career worked summers at Cape Cod Playhouse, Dennis, MA; then writer in Mexico, authored juvenile book, Tito's Hats; later ed. Stephen Daye Press, VT. Left publishing upon reaching leading-man status at Dennis; on B'way as dancer in You Never Know, Everywhere I Roam, others; also in Kind Lady, Cue For Passion; then to radio, serving apprenticeship in small towns; prod.-dir. for NBC Land of the Free, The Hit Parade, and Hildegarde program. Entered m.p. ind., 1945, when signed by Columbia as dial. dir.; then directed The Girl of the Limberlost; later, returned to Broadway, leading role, Strange Fruit; signed by David Selznick as producer-actor, on loan to John Ford as prod. asst. on The Fugitive; then to Howard Hughes-RKO for Vendetta.
THEATER: Kind Lady, Cue for Passion, Strange Fruit, Ondine, Gore Vidal's "The Best Man" (L.A., 1987), Cyrano (director).
PICTURES: *Actor*: Lost Boundaries (debut, 1949), Born to Be Bad, The Brave Bulls, Rancho Notorious, Scaramouche, Lili, Saadia, Knights of the Round Table, Oh Rosalinda!, Proibito (Forbidden), War and Peace, Paris Does Strange Things, The Sun Also Rises, The Vintage, Fraulein, The World the Flesh and the Devil, L'Homme a Femmes, The Hands of Orlac, Blood and Roses, Legge di Guerra, Devil and the 10 Commandments, The Longest Day, The Fall of the Roman Empire, Paris When It Sizzles (cameo), Sex and the Single Girl, El Greco (also prod.), El Senor de la Salle, The Black Pirate, The Girl From the Red Cabaret, Brannigan, The Tempter (The Antichrist), Death Trap (Eaten Alive), Hi-Riders, Pyjama Girl, Island of the Fish Men, The Norsemen, Yesterday's Tomorrow, The Visitor, The Fifth Floor, Nightmare City, Lili Marleen, Deadly Game, Screamers, Mad Dog Anderson. *Director*: The Girl of the Limberlost (debut, 1945), The Secret Fury, Vendetta (co-dir.), Green Mansions, Cabriola (Every Day Is a Holiday; also exec. prod., co-s.p.). *Producer*: Wait Until Dark, The Night Visitor, A Time for Loving, Embassy, W.
TELEVISION: *Series*: Behind the Screen, Falcon Crest. *Movies*: One Shoe Makes It Murder, Seduced, Outrage, Dream West, Peter the Great, Christine Cromwell, A Thanksgiving Promise (prod.). *Special*: Mayerling.

FERRER, MIGUEL
Actor. b. Santa Monica, CA, Feb. 7, 1954. m. actress Leilani Sarelle. Son of actor Jose Ferrer and singer Rosemary Clooney. Began performing as a drummer. With actor Bill Mumy created comic book The Comet Man.
PICTURES: Heartbreaker (debut, 1983), Lovelines, Star Trek III: The Search for Spock, Flashpoint, Robocop, Deepstar Six, Valentino Returns, Revenge, The Guardian, Twin Peaks: Fire Walk With Me, Point of No Return, Hot Shots! Part Deux, Another Stakeout, It's All True (narrator), The Harvest, Blank Check, Death in Granada, Night Flier, Mr. Magoo, Where's Marlowe?, Mulan (voice).
TELEVISION: *Series*: Twin Peaks, Broken Badges, On the Air, Lateline. *Guest*: Miami Vice, Hill Street Blues, Cagney & Lacey, Shannon's Deal, Will & Grace. *Pilot*: Badlands 2005. *Mini-Series*: Drug Wars: The Camarena Story, The Stand, The Shining. *Movies*: Downpayment on Murder, C.A.T. Squad, Guts & Glory: The Rise and Fall of Oliver North, Murder in High Places, In the Shadow of a Killer, Cruel Doubt, Scam, Royce, Incident at Deception Ridge, Jack Reed: Search for Justice, A Promise Kept: The Oksana Baiul Story, The Return of Hunter, In the Line of Duty: Hunt for Justice, Project: ALF, Justice League of America, Brave New World.

FERRETTI, DANTE
Production Designer. b. Macerata, Italy, February 26, 1943.
PICTURES: Medea, The Decameron, The Canterbury Tales, Io non vedo, tu non parli, lui non sente, Lulu the Tool, Bawdy Tales, Slap the Monster on Page One, Arabian Nights, How Long Can You Fall?, Salo, or the 120 Days of Sodom, Somewhere Beyond Love, The Beach Hut, La Presidentessa, Il Mostro, Bye Bye Monkey, Orchestra Rehersal, City of Women, The Skin, Il Minestrone, Tales of Ordinary Madness, That Night in Varennes, And the Ship Sails On, The Adventures of Baron von Munchausen, Ginger and Fred, The Name of the Rose, Hamlet, Dr. M, La traviata, The Age of Innocence, Interview with the Vampire, Casino, Kundun, Meet Joe Black, Bringing Out the Dead, Titus, The Gangs of New York.

FIEDLER, JOHN
Executive. Launched m.p. career in 1975 working in commercials and industrial and ed. films. Joined Technicolor as sr. exec. in prod. svcs. in mktg. Joined Rastar 1980 as v.p., prod. dev. and asst. to Guy McElwaine, pres. & CEO. Joined Paramount as v.p. in prod.; then to Tri-Star Pictures in same post. Resigned to join Columbia Pictures as exec. v.p., worldwide prod., 1984, then pres. of prod. 1986. 1987, left to become independent prod. 1989 named pres. of prod., Rastar IndieProd.
PICTURES: *Producer*: The Beast, Tune in Tomorrow, Mortal Thoughts, Serial Mom, A Good Man in Africa, Radio Inside, I Love You —I Love You Not. *Exec. prod.*: Copycat.
TELEVISION: *Producer*: Beyond the Law.

FIELD, DAVID M.
Executive, Writer. b. Kansas City, MO, Apr. 22, 1944. e. Princeton U. Worked as reporter on city desk at Hartford (CT) Courant. In 1968 with NBC News in N.Y. and Washington, DC. Entered film school at U. of Southern California (L.A.) after which joined Columbia Pictures as west coast story editor. In 1973 went to ABC-TV Network as mgr., movies of the week. 1975, moved to 20th-Fox as v.p., creative affairs. Joined United Artists in 1978; named sr. v.p.—west coast production. Left in 1980 to become 20th-Fox exec. v.p. in chg. of worldwide production 1983, resigned to enter independent production deal with 20th-Fox, Consultant, Tri-Star Pictures. Wrote and produced Amazing Grace and Chuck, 1987.

FIELD, SALLY
Actress. b. Pasadena, CA, Nov. 6, 1946. m. Daughter of Paramount contract actress Maggie Field Mahoney. Stepdaughter of actor Jock Mahoney. e. Actor's Studio 1973-75. Acting classes at Columbia studios. Picked over 150 finalists to star as lead in TV series, Gidget, 1965.
PICTURES: The Way West (debut, 1967), Stay Hungry, Smokey and the Bandit, Heroes, The End, Hooper, Norma Rae (Academy Award, 1979), Beyond the Poseidon Adventure, Smokey and the Bandit II, Back Roads, Absence of Malice, Kiss Me Goodbye, Places in the Heart (Academy Award, 1984), Murphy's Romance (also exec. prod.), Surrender, Punchline (also prod.), Steel Magnolias, Not Without My Daughter, Soapdish, Dying Young (co-prod. only), Homeward Bound: The Incredible Journey (voice), Mrs. Doubtfire, Forrest Gump, Eye for an Eye, Homeward Bound II: Lost in San Francisco (voice), A Cooler Climate. Beautiful (dir. only), Where the Heart Is.

TELEVISION: *Series*: Gidget, The Flying Nun, Alias Smith and Jones, The Girl With Something Extra, ER. *Movies*: Maybe I'll Come Home in the Spring, Marriage Year One, Mongo's Back in Town, Home for the Holidays, Hitched, Bridger, Sybil (Emmy Award, 1977), The Christmas Tree (also prod., dir., co-s.p.), Merry Christmas George Bailey, From the Earth to the Moon, David Copperfield. *Mini-Series*: A Woman of Independent Means (also co-exec. prod.). *Host*: Barbara Stanwyck: Fire and Desire. *Guest*: Hey Landlord, Marcus Welby M.D., Bracken's World, King of the Hill (voice). *Special*: All the Way Home.

FIELD, SHIRLEY-ANNE
Actress. b. London, Eng., June 27. Ent. films after repertory experience. Under contract to Ealing-M.G.M. 1958.
THEATER: The Lily White Boys, Kennedy's Children, Wait Until Dark, The Life and Death of Marilyn Monroe, How the Other Half Loves.
PICTURES: It's Never Too Late, The Silken Affair, The Good Companions, Horrors of the Black Museum, Upstairs and Downstairs, Beat Girl, The Entertainer, Man in the Moon, Once More With Feeling, Peeping Tom, Saturday Night and Sunday Morning, These Are the Damned, The War Lover, Kings of the Sun, Alfie, Doctor in Clover, Hell Is Empty, With Love in Mind, House of the Living Dead (Doctor Maniac), My Beautiful Laundrette, Getting It Right, The Rachel Papers, Shag, Hear My Song, At Risk, Carrington.
TELEVISION: *U.S.:* Bramwell, Santa Barbara, Anna Lees, Lady Chatterly.

FIELD, TED
Producer. r.n. Frederick W. Field. e. U. of Chicago, Pomona Coll. Started career as one of owners of Field Enterprises of Chicago; transferred to west coast, concentrating on movies and records. Founded Interscope Communications, diversified co., which develops and produces theatrical films; Interscope Records, 1990; Radar Pictures, 1999.
PICTURES: Revenge of the Nerds, Turk 182, Critical Condition, Outrageous Fortune, Three Men and a Baby, The Seventh Sign, Cocktail, Bill & Ted's Excellent Adventure (exec.), Renegades (exec.), Innocent Man, The First Power (exec. prod.), Bird on a Wire, Three Men and a Little Lady, Paradise, The Hand That Rocks the Cradle, The Cutting Edge, FernGully, The Gun in Betty Lou's Handbag, Out on a Limb, Jersey Girl, Holy Matrimony, Imaginary Crimes, Operation Dumbo Drop, The Tie That Binds, Jumanji, Mr. Holland's Opus, The Arrival (exec.), Kazaam (exec.), The Associate, Gridlock'd (exec), Snow White (exec.), What Dreams May Come (exec.), Very Bad Things (exec.), Earl Watt, The 59-Story Crisis (exec.), The Proposition, Teaching Mrs. Tingle (exec.), Runaway Bride, Pitch Black (exec.).
TELEVISION: The Father Clements Story (co-exec.). Everybody's Baby: The Rescue of Jessica McClure (co-exec.), My Boyfriend's Back, A Mother's Courage: The Mary Thomas Story (co-exec.), Crossing the Mob, Murder Ordained, Foreign Affairs (co-exec.), A Part of the Family (co-exec.), Body Language (co-exec.).

FIELD, TODD
Actor. r.n. William Todd Field. b. Pomona, CA, Feb. 24, 1964. Extensive behind the scenes work in film. *Dir./Writer:* Too Romantic, When I Was a Boy (also cam. op.), Delivering, Nonnie & Alex (also cam. op.), If...Dog...Rabbit (s.p. only)
PICTURES: Radio Days, The Allnighter, Gross Anatomy (also comp.), Fat Man and Little Boy, Eye of the Eagle 2: Inside the Enemy, Full Fathom Five, Back to Back, Queens Logic, The End of Innocence, The Dog (also dir, comp., Ruby in Paradise (also comp.), Sleep with Me, Frank and Jesse, Twister, Walking and Talking, Farmer & Chase, Broken Vessels (also co-prod., comp.), Stranger Than Fiction, Net Worth, The Haunting, Eyes Wide Shut.
TELEVISION: *Movies:* Student Exchange. *Series:* Take Five, Danger Theatre, Once and Again. *Guest:* Roseanne, Tales from the Crypt, Chicago Hope.

FIELDS, ALAN
Executive. Spent five years with Madison Square Garden before joining Paramount Pictures. Career there included various positions: v.p. for pay-TV and Home Video TV. Spent two years at studio lot in L.A. as part of network TV organization. 1981, named bd. director for Paramount Pictures (U.K.) in London, serving as liaison to United Intl. Pictures and Cinema Intl. Corp., serving on operating committees of both. 1985, appt. v.p., Entertainment & Communications Group of Gulf & Western Industries, Inc., parent co. of Paramount; C.O.O., exec. v.p. Madison Square Garden Corp.

FIELDS, FREDDIE
Executive. b. Ferndale, NY, July 12, 1923. Vice-pres., member of bd. of directors, MCA-TV, MCA Canada Ltd., MCA Corp.; mem., Pres. Club, Wash., D.C.; pres., Freddie Fields Associates Ltd., 1960; founder pres., chief exec. officer Creative Management Assoc. Ltd. Agency, Chicago, Las Vegas, Miami, Paris, Los Angeles, N.Y., London, Rome, 1961. Was exclusive agent of Henry Fonda, Phil Silvers, Judy Garland, Paul Newman, Peter Sellers, Barbra Streisand, Steve McQueen, Woody Allen, Robert Redford, Mick Jagger, Liza Minnelli and others. In 1975 sold interest in CMA (now International Creative Mgt.) but continued as consultant. Produced for Paramount Pictures. 1977: Looking for Mr. Goodbar. American Gigolo, Citizen's Band; Victory. In 1983 named pres. and COO, MGM Film Co. and UA Pictures. Resigned 1985 to become independent producer for MGM/UA. Chairman, The Fields & Hellman Co; dir., Network Event Theater, Inc.; chairman, Net Programming Ltd.; dir., LA Sports and Entertainment Comm.
PICTURES: Fever Pitch. Poltergeist II, Crimes of the Heart, Millenium, Glory, The Year of Living Dangerously. *Exec. Prod.*: The Montel Williams Show.

FIENNES, JOSEPH
Actor. b. Salisbury, England, May 27, 1970.
PICTURES: Stealing Beauty, Shakespeare in Love, Elizabeth, The Very Thought of You, Forever Mine, Rancid Aluminium, Enemy at the Gates, Killing Me Softly, Dust.
TELEVISION: The Vacillations of Poppy Carew.

FIENNES, RALPH
Actor. b. Suffolk, England, Dec. 22, 1962. e. Chelsea College of Art & Design, RADA. Stage work with the Royal Shakespeare Co. includes King Lear, Troilus and Cressida, Love's Labour's Lost. B'way debut in Hamlet (Tony & Theatre World Awards, 1995).
PICTURES: Wuthering Heights (tv in U.S.), The Baby of Macon, Schindler's List (Acad. Award nom.; Natl. Society of Film Critics, NY Film Critics & BAFTA Awards), Quiz Show, Strange Days, The English Patient, Oscar and Lucinda, The Avengers, The Prince of Egypt (voice), The Avengers, Onegin (also prod.), The Taste of Sunshine, The End of the Affair.
TELEVISION: Prime Suspect, A Dangerous Man: Lawrence After Arabia, The Cormorant (theatrical release in U.S.), The Great War (voice), The Miracle Maker (voice).

FIERSTEIN, HARVEY
Actor, Writer. b. New York, NY, June 6, 1954. e. Pratt Inst.
THEATER: Actor: Andy Warhol's Pork, The Haunted Host, Pouf Positive. Actor-Writer: Torch Song Trilogy (NY & London; Tony Awards for best actor & play; Theatre World Award), Safe Sex. Writer: Spookhouse, La Cage Aux Folles (Tony Award), Legs Diamond.
PICTURES: Garbo Talks, The Times of Harvey Milk (narrator), Torch Song Trilogy (also s.p.), The Harvest, Mrs. Doubtfire, Bullets Over Broadway, The Celluloid Closet, Dr. Jekyll & Ms. Hyde, Independence Day, Everything Relative, Kull the Conqueror, Mulan (voice), Safe Men, Hookers in a Haunted House.
TELEVISION: *Movies*: The Demon Murder Case (voice), Apology, Double Platinum. *Series*: Daddy's Girls. *Guest*: Miami Vice, The Simpsons (voice), Cheers, Murder She Wrote. *Specials*: Tidy Endings, In the Shadow of Love.

FIGGIS, MIKE
Director, Writer, Musician. b. Kenya, 1949. At age 8 family moved to Newcastle, England. Studied music before performing with band Gas Boad; joined experimental theatre group The People Show in early 70's as musician. Began making indept. films including Redheugh, Slow Fade, Animals of the City. Made 1-hr. film The House for U.K.'s Channel 4.
PICTURES: *Director*: Stormy Monday (debut, 1988; also s.p., music), Internal Affairs (also music), Liebestraum (also s.p., music), Mr. Jones, Leaving Las Vegas (also s.p., music; IFP Independent Spirit Award, 1996; Nat'l Society of Film Critics Award), One Night Stand (also s.p., comp., prod., actor), Flamenco Women, Miss Julie (also prod.), The Loss of Sexual Innocence (also comp., s.p., prod.), Timecode (also. comp. & prod.).

FINCH, JON
Actor. b. London, England, Mar. 2, 1943. Came to acting via backstage activities, working for five years as company manager and director.
PICTURES: The Vampire Lovers (debut, 1970), The Horror of Frankenstein, Sunday Bloody Sunday, L'affaire Martine Desclos, Macbeth, Frenzy, Lady Caroline Lamb, The Final Programme (The Last Days of Man on Earth), Diagnosis: Murder, Une Femme Fidele, The Man With the Green Cross, El Segundo Poder, Battle Flag, El Mister, Death on the Nile, La Sabina, Gary Cooper Which Art in Heaven, Breaking Glass, The Threat, Giro City (And Nothing But the Truth), Plaza Real, Streets of Yesterday, Game of Seduction, The Voice, Beautiful in the Kingdom, Mirror Mirror, Darklands, Lucan.
TELEVISION: The Martian Chronicles (U.S.), Peter and Paul, The Rainbow, Unexplained Laughter, Dangerous Curves, Maigret, Beautiful Lies, Make or Break, The Oddjob Man (series), Sherlock Homes, Counterstrike (series), Mary Queen of Scots, Riviera, White Men Are Cracking Up, A Love Renewed, Merlin of the Crystal Cave, Richard II, Henry IV, Much Ado About Nothing, South of the Border, Hammer House of Horrors, Ben Hall (series).

FINCHER, DAVID
Director. b. 1963. Ent. ind. at 18, working at Lucas' Industrial Light and Magic for 4 yrs; left to make TV commercials & dir. pop videos for Madonna, Paula Abdul & Aerosmith.
PICTURES: The Beat of the Live Drum, Alien 3, Se7en, The Game, Fight Club, The Panic Room.

FINESHRIBER, WILLIAM H., JR.
Executive. b. Davenport, IA, Nov. 4, 1909. e. Princeton U., B.A., 1931. Pub., CBS, 1931-34; mgr. Carnegie Hall, N.Y., 1934-37; script writer, dir., music comm., dir. of music dept., CBS, 1937-40; dir. of short wave programs, CBS, 1940-43; gen. mgr. CBS program dept. 1943-49; v.p. in charge of programs MBS, 1949-51; exec. v.p. & dir., MBS, 1951-53; v.p. & gen. mgr. of networks, NBC, 1953-54; v.p. in charge of Radio Network, NBC, 1955; v.p. Television Programs of America, 1956; director International operations, Screen Gems, 1957; v.p., Motion Picture Assoc. of America and Motion Picture Export Assoc. of America, 1960; bd. of dir., NARTB: exec. comm., bd. of dir., R.A.B; v.p. Radio Pioneers. Author, Stendhal the Romantic Rationalist.

FINLAY, FRANK
Actor. C.B.E. b. Farnworth, Eng., Aug. 6, 1926. Rep. in Troon, 1951, Halifax and Sunderland, 1952-3, before winning Sir James Knott Scholarship to RADA. e. Studied acting at RADA. Appeared with Guildford Repertory Theatre Co. 1957. London stage debut: The Queen and the Welshman, 1957. Broadway debut, Epitaph for George Dillon, 1958.
THEATER: Work with Royal Court, Chichester Fest., National Theatre includes: Sergeant Musgrave's Dance, Chicken Soup with Barley, Roots, Platonov, Chips with Everything, Saint Joan, Hamlet, Othello, Saturday Sunday Monday, Plunder, Watch It Come Down, Weapons of Happiness, Tribute to a Lady, Filumena (and N.Y.), Amadeus, The Cherry Orchard, Mutiny, Beyond Reasonable Doubt, Black Angel, A Slight Hangover.
PICTURES: The Loneliness of the Long Distance Runner (debut, 1962), The Longest Day, Life for Ruth (Walk in the Shadow), Private Potter, Doctor in Distress, Underworld Informers, The Comedy Man, Agent 8 3/4 (Hot Enough for June), The Wild Affair, A Study in Terror, Othello (Acad. Award nom.), The Sandwich Man, The Jokers, The Deadly Bees, Robbery, I'll Never Forget What's 'is Name, The Shoes of the Fisherman, Inspector Clouseau, Twisted Nerve, The Molly Maguires, Cromwell, The Body (narrator), Assault (The Devil's Garden), Gumshoe, Danny Jones, Sitting Target, Neither the Sea Nor the Sand, Shaft in Africa, The Three Musketeers, The Four Musketeers, The Wild Geese, Murder by Decree, Enigma, The Ploughman's Lunch, The Return of the Soldier, The Key, 1919, Lifeforce, The Return of the Musketeers (tv in U.S.), King of the Wind, Cthulhu Mansion.
TELEVISION: The Adventures of Don Quixote, Casanova, Candide, Julius Caesar, Les Miserables, This Happy Breed, The Lie, The Death of Adolph Hitler, Voltaire, The Merchant of Venice, Bouquet of Barbed Wire, 84 Charing Cross Road, Saturday Sunday Monday, Count Dracula, The Last Campaign, Thief of Bagdad, Betzi, Sakharov, A Christmas Carol, Arch of Triumph, The Burning Shore, In the Secret State, Verdict of Erebus, Mountain of Diamonds, Encounter, Stalin.

FINNEY, ALBERT
Actor. b. Salford, England, May 9, 1936. Studied for stage at Royal Acad. Dramatic Art making his West End debut 1958 in The Party. Appeared at Stratford-Upon-Avon 1959, playing title role in Coriolanus, etc.
THEATER: The Lily White Boys, Billy Liar, Luther (also NY), Much Ado About Nothing, Armstrong's Last Goodnight, Love for Love, Miss Julie, Black Comedy, A Flea in Her Ear, Joe Egg (NY), Alpha Beta, Krapp's Last Tape, Cromwell, Chez Nous, Hamlet, Tamburlaine, Uncle Vanya, Present Laughter. National Theatre, The Country Wife, The Cherry Orchard, Macbeth, The Biko Inquest, Sergeant Musgrave's Dance (also dir.), Orphans, Another Time (also Chicago), Reflected Glory.
PICTURES: The Entertainer (debut, 1960), Saturday Night and Sunday Morning, Tom Jones, The Victors, Night Must Fall (also co-prod.), Two for the Road, Charlie Bubbles (also dir.), The Picasso Summer (tv in U.K.), Scrooge, Gumshoe, Alpha Beta (tv in U.K.), Murder on the Orient Express, The Adventure of Sherlock Holmes' Smarter Brother (cameo), The Duellists, Wolfen, Looker, Loophole, Shoot the Moon, Annie, The Dresser, Under the Volcano, Orphans, Miller's Crossing, The Playboys, Rich in Love, The Browning Version, A Man of No Importance, The Run of the Country, Washington Square, Breakfast of Champions.
TELEVISION: The Claverdon Road Job, The Miser, Pope John Paul II, Endless Game, The Image, The Green Man, Joan of Arc: The Virgin Warrior.

FIORENTINO, LINDA
Actress. b. Philadelphia, PA, 1960. e. Rosmont Col. To New York, 1980, studied acting at Circle in the Square Theatre School.
PICTURES: Vision Quest (debut, 1985), Gotcha!, After Hours, The Modrens, Queens Logic, Shout, Chain of Desire, The Last Seduction, Bodily Harm, Jade, Unforgettable, Men in Black, Where the Money Is, Killer Kiss, Dogma, Ordinary Decent Criminal, What Planet Are You From?, Where The Money Is.
TELEVISION: *Movies*: The Neon Empire, Acting on Impulse, The Desperate Trail.

FIRTH, COLIN
Actor. b. Grayshott, Hampshire, Eng., Sept. 10, 1960. Studied acting at the Drama Centre at Chalk Farm. Author of A Month in the Country (screenplay), Making of Pride and Prejudice.
THEATRES: *London*: in Tartuffe, King Lear, Hamlet, Another Country, Doctor's Dilemma, The Lonely Road, Desire Under the Elms, The Caretaker, Chatsky.
PICTURES: Another Country, 1919, A Month in the Country, Apartment Zero, Valmont, Wings of Fame, The Hour of the Pig, The Pleasure Principle, Femme Fatale, Playmaker, The Advocate, Circle of Friends, The English Patient, Fever Pitch, A Thousand Acres, The World of Moss, Shakespeare in Love.
TELEVISION: *Movies*: Camille, Crown Court, Dutch Girls, Tumbledown, Hostages, Master of the Moor, The Deep Blue Sea, Pride and Prejudice, The Widowing of Mrs. Holroyd, Nostromo. *Series*: Lost Empires. *Specials*: Tales from the Hollywood Hills (Pat Hobby Teamed With Genius).

FIRTH, PETER
Actor. b. Bradford, Yorkshire, Oct. 27, 1953. Appeared in local TV children's show where casting director spotted him and got him role in series, The Flaxton Boys. Moved to London and worked in TV, first in children's show, later on dramas for BBC. Breakthrough role in Equus at National Theatre, 1973 which he repeated in film.
THEATER: Equus (Theatre World Award), Romeo and Juliet, Spring Awakening, Amadeus.
PICTURES: Diamonds on Wheels (debut, 1972; tv in U.S.), Brother Sun Sister Moon, Daniel and Maria, Equus (Acad. Award nom.), Joseph Andrews, Aces High, When You Comin' Back Red Ryder, Tess, Lifeforce, Letter to Brezhnev, Trouble in Paradise, White Elephant, A State of Emergency, Born of Fire, The Tree of Hands, Prisoner of Rio, Burndown, The Hunt for Red October, The Rescuers Down Under (voice), The Perfect Husband, White Angel, Shadowlands, An Awfully Big Adventure, The Garden of Redemption, Marco Polo, Amistad.
TELEVISION: *Series*: The Flaxon Boys, Home and Away, Country Matters. *Movies and specials*: Here Comes the Doubledeckers, Castlehaven, The Sullen Sisters, The Simple Life, The Magistrate, The Protectors, Black Beauty, Arthur, Her Majesty's Pleasure, the Picture of Dorian Gray, Lady of the Camillias, The Flip Side of Domenic Hide, Blood Royal, Northanger Abbey, The Way, The Truth: the Video, The Incident, Children Crossing, Prisoner of Honor, Married to Murder, The Laughter of God, Murder in Eden, Brighton Boy, The Broker's Man, Holding On.

FISHBURNE, LAURENCE
Actor. b. Augusta, GA, July 30, 1961. Raised in Brooklyn. Landed role on daytime serial One Life to Live at age 11. On NY stage in Short Eyes, Two Trains Running (Tony and Theatre World Awards), Riff Raff (also wrote and directed).
PICTURES: Cornbread Earl and Me (debut, 1975), Fast Break, Apocalypse Now, Willie and Phil, Death Wish II, Rumble Fish, The Cotton Club, The Color Purple, Quicksilver, Band of the Hand, A Nightmare on Elm Street 3: Dream Warriors, Gardens of Stone, School Daze, Red Heat, King of New York, Cadence, Class Action, Boyz N the Hood, Deep Cover, What's Love Got to Do With It (Acad. Award nom.), Searching for Bobby Fischer, Higher Learning, Bad Company, Just Cause, Othello, Fled, Hoodlums (also exec. prod.), Event Horizon, The Matrix, Michael Jordan to the Max (voice), Osmosis Jones (voice), Once in the Life.
TELEVISION: *Series*: One Life to Live, Pee-wee's Playhouse. *Guest*: M*A*S*H, Trapper John, M.D., Spenser: For Hire, Tribeca (Emmy Award, 1993). *Movies*: A Rumor of War, I Take These Men, Decoration Day, The Tuskegee Airmen, Miss Ever's Boys, Always Outnumbered.

FISHER, AL
Executive. b. Brooklyn, NY. Entered m.p. industry as office boy, Fox Metropolitan Theatres; U.S. Army Provost Marshal General's Office, 1942-46; Universal Pictures, mgr., Park Avenue Theatre, N.Y. & Copley Plaza Theatre, Boston, 1946; Eagle Lion Film Co., mgr., Red Shoe's Bijou Theatre, N.Y., 1947; Stanley Kramer Prods., exploitation, Cyrano de Bergerac, 1951; press agent, 1951; prod., Bway show, Daphine, 1952; joined United Artists Corporation, 1952, named dir. of exploitation; now freelancing as producer's repr.

FISHER, CARRIE
Actress, Writer. b. Beverly Hills, CA, Oct. 21, 1956. e. London Central Sch. of Speech & Drama. Daughter of actress Debbie Reynolds and singer Eddie Fisher. On Broadway in the chorus of revival of Irene (1972; with mother); later in Censored Scenes from King Kong. *Author:* Postcards From the Edge (1987), Surrender the Pink (1990), Delusions of Grandma (1994).
PICTURES: Shampoo (debut, 1975), Star Wars: A New Hope, Mr. Mike's Mondo Video, Star Wars: The Empire Strikes Back, The Blues Brothers, Under the Rainbow, Star Wars: Return of the Jedi, Garbo Talks, The Man with One Red Shoe, Hannah and Her Sisters, Hollywood Vice Squad, Amazon Women on the Moon, Appointment with Death, The 'Burbs, Loverboy, She's Back, When Harry Met Sally..., The Time Guardian, Postcards From the Edge (s.p. only), Sibling Rivalry, Drop Dead Fred, Soapdish, This Is My Life.
TELEVISION: *Movies*: Leave Yesterday Behind, Liberty, Sunday Drive, Sweet Revenge. *Specials*: Come Back Little Sheba, Classic Creatures: Return of the Jedi, Thumbelina (Faerie Tale Theatre), Paul Reiser: Out on a Whim, Two Daddies? (voice), Trying Times (Hunger Chic), Carrie Fisher: The Hollywood Family (also writer). *Guest*: Laverne and Shirley, George Burns' Comedy Week, Sex in the City.

FISHER, EDDIE
Singer. b. Philadelphia, PA, Aug. 10, 1928. Daughter is actress Carrie Fisher. Band, nightclub, hotel singer; discovered by Eddie Cantor, 1949; U.S. Army, 1951-53; many hit records include Wish You Were Here, Lady of Spain and Oh My Papa; radio & TV shows, NBC.
PICTURES: Bundle of Joy, Butterfield 8, Nothing Lasts Forever.
TELEVISION: *Series*: Coke Time With Eddie Fisher (1953-57), The Eddie Fisher Show (1957-59).

FISHER, FRANCES
Actress. b. Milford-on-Sea, England, May 11. Father was intl. construction supervisor. Raised in Colombia, Canada, France, Brazil, Turkey. Made stage debut in Texas in Summer and Smoke.
THEATER: *NY:* Fool for Love, Desire Under the Elms, Cat on a Hot Tin Roof, The Hitch-Hikers, Orpheus Descending, A Midsummer Night's Dream, Jammed.
PICTURES: Can She Bake a Cherry Pie? (debut, 1983), Tough Guys Don't Dance, The Principal, Patty Hearst, Bum Rap, Heavy Petting, Pink Cadillac, Lost Angels, Welcome Home Roxy Carmichael, L.A. Story, Unforgiven, Babyfever, The Stars Fell on Henrietta, Waiting for Guffman, Female Perversion, Wild America, Titanic.
TELEVISION: *Series:* The Edge of Night (1976-81), The Guiding Light (1985), Strange Luck. *Movies:* Broken Vows, Devlin, Lucy & Desi: Before the Laughter, The Other Mother. *Pilots*: Elysian Fields. *Guest:* The Equalizer, Matlock, Newhart.

FISHER, GEORGE M.C.
Executive. b. Anna, IL. e. Univ. of IL, Brown Univ. Worked in research and devlop. at Bell Labs before joining Motorola in 1976, eventually becoming pres. & CEO in 1988. 1990, elected chmn. & CEO. Named chmn., pres. & CEO of Eastman Kodak Company, Dec. 1993. Currently, Chairman and CEO.

FISHER, LUCY
Executive. b. Oct. 2, 1949. e. Harvard U., B.A. Exec. chg. creative affairs, MGM; v.p., creative affairs, 20th Century Fox; v.p., prod., Fox. 1980, head of prod., Zoetrope Studios; 1980-82, v.p., sr. prod. exec., Warner Bros.; 1983, sr. v.p. prod., WB. Joined Columbia TriStar in March, 1996 as vice chmn.

FISHER, THOMAS L.
Special Effects.
PICTURES: The Devil's Rain, City on Fire, First Blood, Legal Eagles, Desperate Hours, Terminator 2: Judgment Day, The Taking of Beverly Hills, Under Siege, On Deadly Ground, True Lies, Batman Forever, Titanic (Acad. Award, Best Visual Effects, 1997), Supernova.

FISK, JACK
Director. b. Ipava, IL. e. Cooper Union-Pa. Acad. of the Fine Arts. m. actress Sissy Spacek. Began in films as designer; turning to direction with Raggedy Man (1981).
PICTURES: *Director*: Raggedy Man, Violets Are Blue, Daddy's Dyin', ... Who's Got the Will? *Art Director*: Badlands, Phantom of the Paradise, Carrie, Days of Heaven, Heart Beat.

FITZGERALD, GERALDINE
Actress. b. Dublin, Ireland, Nov. 24, 1914. e. Dublin Art Sch. Mother of director Michael Lindsay-Hogg. On stage Gate Theat., Dublin; then in number of Brit. screen prod. including Turn of the Tide, Mill on the Floss. On N.Y. stage in Heartbreak House. Founded Everyman Street Theatre with Brother Jonathan Ringkamp.
THEATER: Sons and Soldiers, Portrait in Black, The Doctor's Dilemma, King Lear, Hide and Seek, A Long Day's Journey Into Night, (1971), Ah, Wilderness, The Shadow Box, A Touch of the Poet, Songs of the Streets (one woman show), Mass Appeal (dir. only), The Lunch Girls (dir.).
PICTURES: Blind Justice (debut, 1934), Open All Night, The Lad, The Aces of Spades, Three Witnesses, Lieutenant Daring RN, Turn of the Tide, Radio Parade of 1935, Bargain Basement (Department Store), Debt of Honor, Cafe Mascot, The Mill on the Floss, Wuthering Heights (U.S. debut, 1939; Acad. Award nom.), Dark Victory, A Child Is Born, 'Til We Meet Again, Flight from Destiny, Shining Victory, The Gay Sisters, Watch on the Rhine, Ladies Courageous, Wilson, The Strange Affair of Uncle Harry, Three Strangers, O.S.S., Nobody Lives Forever, So Evil My Love, The Late Edwina Black (The Obsessed), 10 North Frederick, The Fiercest Heart, The Pawnbroker, Rachel Rachel, The Last American Hero, Harry and Tonto, Cold Sweat, Echoes of a Summer, The Mango Tree, Bye Bye Monkey, Lovespell (Tristan and Isolde), Arthur, Blood Link, Easy Money, Poltergeist II, Arthur 2: On the Rocks.
TELEVISION: *Series*: Our Private World, The Best of Everything. *Movies*: Yesterday's Child, The Quinns, Dixie: Changing Habits, Do You Remember Love?, Circle of Violence, Night of Courage, Bump in the Night. *Mini-Series*: Kennedy. *Specials*: The Moon and Sixpence, Street Songs.

FITZGERALD, TARA
Actress. b. England, 1968. e. London's Drama Centre, 1990.
THEATER: *London*: Our Song. *NY*: Hamlet.
PICTURES: Hear My Song (debut, 1991), Sirens, A Man of No Importance, The Englishman Who Went Up a Hill But Came Down a Mountain, Brassed Off!
TELEVISION: The Black Candle, The Camomille Lawn, Anglo-Saxon Attitudes, Six Characters in Search of an Author, Fall From Grace, The Tenants of Wildfell Hall, The Woman in White, The Student Prince.

FLAGG, FANNIE
Actress, Writer. b. Birmingham, AL, Sept. 21, 1944. e. Univ. of AL. Studied acting at Pittsburgh Playhouse, Town & Gown Theatre. Had her own live 90 minute tv show in Birmingham. To NY where she wrote and appeared in revues for Upstairs at the Downstairs Club. *Comedy albums:* Rally 'Round the Flagg, My Husband Doesn't Know I'm Making This Phone Call. *Author:* Coming Attractions: A Wonderful Novel (Daisy Fay and the Miracle Man), Fried Green Tomatoes at the Whistle Stop Cafe, Fannie Flagg's Original Whistle Stop Cafe Cookbook.
THEATER: *B'way*: Patio Porch, Come Back to the Five and Dime Jimmy Dean Jimmy Dean, The Best Little Whorehouse in Texas. Regional: Private Lives, Gypsy, Mary Mary, Tobacco Road, Old Acquaintance, etc.
PICTURES: Five Easy Pieces (debut, 1970), Some of My Best Friends Are..., Stay Hungry, Grease, Rabbit Test, My Best Friend Is a Vampire, Fried Green Tomatoes (also co-s.p.; Acad. Award nom. for s.p.).
TELEVISION: *Series*: The New Dick Van Dyke Show, Match Game P.M., Liar's Club, Harper Valley P.T.A. *Movies*: The New Original Wonder Woman, Sex and the Married Woman. *Pilots*: Comedy News, Home Cookin'. *Producer*: Morning Show.

FLANERY, SEAN PATRICK
Actor. b. Lake Charles, LA
PICTURES: A Tiger's Tale, Frank and Jesse, The Grass Harp, Powder, Raging Angels, Suicide Kings, Eden, Best Men, Run the Wild Fields, Girl, Simply Irresistible.
TELEVISION: *Movies:* Guinevere, Young Indiana Jones and the Hollywood Follies, Young Indiana Jones and the Attack of the Hawkmen, Young Indiana Jones and the Treasure of the Peacock's Eye, Young Indiana Jones Travels with Father, Just Your Luck. *Series:* The Young Indiana Jones Chronicles.

FLATTERY, THOMAS L.
Executive-Lawyer b. Detroit, MI, Nov. 14, 1922. e. U.S. Military Acad., West Point, B.S., 1944-47; UCLA, J.D., 1952-55; USC, LL.M. 1955-65. Radioplane Company, staff counsel and asst. contract admin. 1955-7. Gen'l counsel and asst. sec'y, McCulloch Corp., CA, 1957-64; sec. & corp. counsel, Technicolor, Inc., 1964-70; v.p., sec. & gen. counsel, Amcord, Inc. 1970-72; v.p., sec. & gen. counsel, Schick Inc., 1972-75; counsel asst. sec., C.F. Braun & Co., 1975-76; sr. v.p., sec. & gen. counsel PCC Technical Industries, Inc. 1976-86; v.p., gen. counsel & sec., G & H Technology, Inc. 1986.-93. Attorney at law, 1993.

FLAXMAN, JOHN P.
Producer. b. New York, NY, March 3, 1934. e. Dartmouth U., B.A. 1956. 1st Lt. U.S. Army, 1956-58. Ent. m.p. industry in executive training program, Columbia Pictures Corp., 1958-63; exec. story consultant, Profiles in Courage, 1964-65; head of Eastern Literary Dept., Universal Pictures, 1965; writer's agent, William Morris Agency, 1966; partner with Harold Prince in Media Productions, Inc. 1967; founded Flaxman Film Corp., 1975. President-Tricorn Productions 1977; pres. Filmworks Capital Corp., 1979-83; Becker/Flaxman & Associates, 1979-83; pres., Cine Communications, 1983-present. Producer Off-Broadway, Yours, Anne (1985). Co-prod. with NY Shakespeare Fest., The Petrified Prince.
PICTURES: Something for Everyone, Jacob Two-Two Meets the Hooded Fang.
TELEVISION: The Caine Mutiny Court-Martial (prod.).

FLEDER, GARY
Director.
PICTURES: Things to Do in Denver when You're Dead, Kiss the Girls, Imposter.
TELEVISION: *Movies*: Air Time (also prod.), The Companion. *Series*: Homicide: Life on the Street, L.A. Doctors. *Mini-series*: From the Earth to the Moon.

FLEISCHER, RICHARD
Director. b. Brooklyn, NY, Dec. 8, 1916. e. Brown U., B.A.; Yale U., M.F.A. Son of animator Max Fleischer. Stage dir.; joined RKO Pathe 1942. Dir. and wrote This Is America shorts, prod./dir. Flicker Flashbacks. Author: Just Tell Me When to Cry.
PICTURES: Child of Divorce (debut, 1946), Banjo, Design for Death (also co-prod.; Academy Award for Best Feature-Length Documentary, 1948), So This Is New York, Bodyguard, Follow Me Quietly, Make Mine Laughs, The Clay Pigeon, Trapped, Armored Car Robbery, The Narrow Margin, The Happy Time, Arena, 20000 Leagues Under the Sea, Violent Saturday, Girl in the Red Velvet Swing, Bandido, Between Heaven and Hell, The Vikings, These Thousand Hills, Compulsion, Crack in the Mirror, The Big Gamble, Barabbas, Fantastic Voyage, Doctor Dolittle, The Boston Strangler, Che!, Tora! Tora! Tora!, 10 Rillington Place, The Last Run, See No Evil, The New Centurions, Soylent Green, The Don Is Dead, The Spikes Gang, Mr. Majestyk, Mandingo, The Incredible Sarah, Crossed Swords (The Prince and the Paupre), Ashanti, The Jazz Singer, Tough Enough, Amityville 3-D, Conan the Destroyer, Red Sonja, Million Dollar Mystery, Call From Space (Showcan).

FLEMING, JANET BLAIR
Executive. b. Ottawa, Canada, November 29, 1944. e. Carlton U., Ottawa, Canada, B.A. Secretary to Canada's Federal Minister of Transport 1967-72; 1973-77, asst. to Sandy Howard—business affairs; 1977, co-founder and v.p./sales & admin. of Producers Sales Organization; 1981, named sr. v.p., admin.; 1982, sr. v.p., acquisitions; 1983, exec. v.p., Skouras Pictures; 1985 promoted to pres., intl. div.; 1987-88 mgr. Lift Haven Inn, Sun Valley, ID; 1989-present, owner/partner Premiere Properties (prop. management, Sun Valley, ID).

FLEMING, RHONDA
Actress. r.n. Marilyn Louis. b. Los Angeles, CA, Aug. 10. m. Ted Mann (Mann Theatres). e. Beverly Hills H.S. Member, several charity orgs. Bd. of Dir. trustee of World Opportunities Intl. (Help the Children). Alzheimer Rsch., Childhelp USA, bd. of trustees of the UCLA Foundation. Opened Rhonda Fleming Mann Resource Center for Women with Cancer at UCLA Medical Center, 1994. Many awards incl. Woman of the Year Award from City of Hope 1986 & 1991; Woman of the World Award from Childhelp USA; Excellence in Media, Gold Angel Award; The Mannequins of Assistance of Southern Califronia, Golden Eve Award. Stage incl. The Women (B'way), Kismet (LA), The Boyfriend (tour), one woman concerts.
PICTURES: Spellbound, Abiline Town, Spiral Staircase, Adventure Island, Out of the Past, A Connecticut Yankee in King Arthur's Court, The Great Lover, The Eagle and the Hawk, The Redhead and the Cowboy, The Last Outpost, Cry Danger, Crosswinds, Little Egypt, Hong Kong, Golden Hawk, Tropic Zone, Pony Express, Serpent of the Nile, Inferno, Those Redheads from Seattle, Jivaro, Yankee Pasha, Tennessee's Partner, While the City Sleeps, Killer Is Loose, Slightly Scarlet, Odongo, Queen of Babylon, Gunfight at the OK Corral, Buster Keaton Story, Gun Glory, Bullwhip, Home Before Dark, Alias Jesse James, The Big Circus, The Crowded Sky, The Patsy (cameo), Won Ton Ton The Dog Who Saved Hollywood, The Nude Bomb.
TELEVISION: *Guest*: Wagon Train, Police Woman, Love Boat, McMillian and Wife, Legends of the Screen, Road to Hollywood, Wildest West Show of Stars. *Movies*: The Last Hours Before Morning, Love for Rent, Waiting for the Wind.

FLETCHER, LOUISE
Actress. b. Birmingham, AL, July 22, 1934. e. U. of North Carolina, B.A. Came to Hollywood at age 21; studied with Jeff Corey. Worked on TV shows (including Playhouse 90, Maverick). Gave up career to be a mother for 10 yrs.; returned to acting in 1973. Board of Directors: Deafness Research Foundation, 1980-. Honorary Degrees: Doctor of Humane Letters from Gallaudet U. and West Maryland Col. Advisory board: The Caption Center, The Nat'l Institute on Deafness and Other Communication Disorders.
PICTURES: Thieves Like Us, Russian Roulette, One Flew Over the Cuckoo's Nest (Academy Award, 1975), Exorcist II: The Heretic, The Cheap Detective, Natural Enemies, The Magician of Lublin, The Lucky Star, The Lady in Red, Strange Behavior, Mamma Dracula, Brainstorm, Strange Invaders, Firestarter, Once Upon a Time in America, Overnight Sensation, Invaders from Mars, The Boy Who Could Fly, Nobody's Fool, Flowers in the Attic, Two Moon Junction, Best of the Best, Shadow Zone, Blue Steel, Blind Vision, The Player, Georgino, Tollbooth, Return to Two Moon Junction, Virtuosity, High School High, 2 Days in the Valley, Mulholland Falls, Mojave Frankenstein, Edie and Pen, Gone Fishing, High School High, Girl Gets Moe, Love Kills, Cruel Intentions.
TELEVISION: *Series*: Boys of Twilight, Deep Space Nine, Picket Fences, VR 5, Profiler. *Movies*: Can Ellen Be Saved?, Thou Shalt Not Commit Adultery, A Summer to Remember, Island, Second Serve, J. Edgar Hoover, The Karen Carpenter Story, Final Notice, Nightmare on the 13th Floor, In a Child's Name, The Fire Next Time, The Haunting of Seacliff Inn, Someone Else's Child, Stepford Husbands, Twisted Path, Breastmen, Married to a Stranger, Heartless, The Devil's Arithmetic. *Guest:* Twilight Zone, Tales from the Crypt, Civil Wars, Dream On.

FLINN, JOHN C.
Publicist. b. Yonkers, NY, May 4, 1917. e. U. of California. p. late John C. Flinn, pioneer m.p. executive. In pub. dept. David O. Selznick, 1936-39; unit publicist, then head planter, Warner, 1936-46; joined Monogram as asst. to nat'l adv. & pub. head & pub. mgr. 1946; apptd. nat'l dir. of pub. & adv. of Allied Artists Pictures, 1951; appt'd studio dir. adv. & pub., Columbia, 1959; v.p., Jim Mahoney & Assocs. (p.r. firm) 1971. Joined MGM West Coast publ. dept. as publ. coordinator, 1973; rejoined Columbia Pictures in 1974 as studio publ. dir.; 1979, promoted to dir. industry relations. Joined MGM/UA publ. staff, 1988 to work on m.p. academy campaign for Moonstruck. Engaged by Paramount 1988-89 to assist in Acad. Award campaigns. Retired.

FLOCKHART, CALISTA
Actress. b. Freeport, IL, Nov. 11, 1964. e. Rutgers College, NJ.
THEATER: *B'way*: The Glass Menagerie. *Off B'way*: The Loop, All for One, Sophistry, Wrong Turn at Lungfish, Beside Herself, Bovver Boys. *Regional*: The Three Sisters, Our Town, Death Takes a Holiday, Bash: Latter Day Plays.
PICTURES: Quiz Show, Getting In, Naked in New York, Drunks, The Birdcage, Milk and Money, Telling Lies in America, A Midsummer's Night's Dream, Like A Hole in the Head, Things You Can Tell Just By Looking At Her.
TELEVISION: *Series*: Ally McBeal (Golden Globe Award, 1998), Ally. *Movie*: Darrow. *Guest*: The Practice.

FLOREA, JOHN
Producer, Director, Writer. b. Alliance, OH, May 28, 1916. Served as photo journalist with Life magazine, 1940-50; assoc. editor Colliers magazine, 1950-53. Prod.-dir. with David Gerber 1979-84.
PICTURES: A Time to Every Purpose, The Astral Factor, The Invisible Strangler, Hot Child in the City.
TELEVISION: *Dir. several episodes*: Sea Hunt series, 1957-60; Bonanza, Outlaws, Outpost (pilot), The Virginian, Honey West, Daktari, Gentle Ben, Cowboy in Africa, High Chapparal, Flipper, Destry Rides Again, Not For Hire, Ironside, Highway Patrol, V, Target, Everglades, (also prod.), CHiPS, MacGyver. Prod.-dir. of film Islands of the Lost. With Ivon Tors Films. Nominated as one of the Top 10 directors in America by DGA for 1968 Mission Impossible episode. Dir. several Ironside episodes. Doc: Kammikazi, Attack Hawaiian Hospitality, Million Dollar Question, Marineland, Brink of Disaster. (Valley Freedom Award), Dangerous Report, (for CIA), The Runaways (Emmy Award), Down the Long Hills, Dark Canyon.

FLYNN, BEAU
Producer.
PICTURES: I.Q. (asst. prod.), Johns, Life During Wartime (exec. prod), The House of Yes, Dust & Stardust, Little City.

FLYNN, JOHN
Director, Writer. b. Chicago IL. e. George Washington U, Stanford, UCLA, B.A. (Eng.). Worked in mailroom at MCA then with p.r. firm. Began career as trainee script supvr. for dir. Robert Wise on West Side Story. Soon working as ass't. dir. on MGM-TV shows. Made dir. debut with The Sergeant, 1969.
PICTURES: The Jerusalem File, The Outfit (also s.p.), Rolling Thunder, Defiance, Touched, Best Seller, Lock Up, Brainscan.
TELEVISION: Marilyn—The Untold Story (dir.).

FOCH, NINA
Actress. b. Leyden, Holland, April 20, 1924. Daughter of Consuelo Flowerton, actress, & Dirk Foch, symphony orch. conductor. Adjunct Prof., USC, 1966-67; 1978-80, Adjunct professor, USC Cinema-TV grad. sch. 1986-; sr. faculty, American Film Inst,, 1974-77; bd. of Governors, Hollywood Acad. of Television Arts & Sciences, 1976-77; exec. Comm. Foreign Language Film Award, Acad. of Motion Picture Arts & Sciences, 1970-. Co-chmn., exec. comm. Foreign Language Film Award 1983-.
PICTURES: The Return of the Vampire (debut, 1943), Nine Girls, Cry of the Werewolf, She's a Soldier Too, She's a Sweetheart, Shadows in the Night, I Love a Mystery, Prison Ship, Song to Remember, My Name is Julia Ross, Boston Blackie's Rendezvous, Escape in the Fog, The Guilt of Jane Ames, Johnny O'Clock, The Dark Past, Johnny Allegro, Undercover Man, St. Benny the Dip, An American in Paris, Young Man With Ideas, Scaramouche, Sombrero, Fast Company, Executive Suite (Acad. Award nom.), Four Guns to the Border, The Ten Commandments, Illegal, You're Never Too Young, Three Brave Men, Cash McCall, Spartacus, Such Good Friends, Salty, Mahogany, Jennifer, Rich and Famous, Skin Deep, Sliver, Morning Glory, It's My Party, 'Til There Was You, Kilronan, Hush, Reasonable Doubt.
TELEVISION: *Series*: Q.E.D. (panelist), It's News to Me (panelist), Shadow Chasers. *Movies*: Outback Bound, In the Arms of a Killer, The Sands of Time. *Mini-series*: War and Remembrance. *Special*: Tales of the City. Guest star, most major series incl. Studio One, Playhouse 90, US Steel Hour, L.A. Law, Dear John, Hunter; talk shows, specials.

FOGARTY, JACK V.
Executive, Producer, Writer. b. Los Angeles, CA. e. UCLA. Management, MGM, 1960-62; exec. prod. mgr., Cinerama, Inc., 1962-64; assoc. prod., The Best of Cinerama, 1963; est. own p.r. firm, 1965; pres., AstroScope, Inc., 1969-74.
TELEVISION: *Writer/prod.*: The Rookies, S.W.A.T., Charlie's Angels, Most Wanted, Barnaby Jones, A Man Called Sloane, Trapper John, T.J. Hooker, Crazy Like a Fox, The Equalizer, Jake and the Fatman, Murder She Wrote, Charlie's Angels (story edit.). *Exec. Story consultant:* Most Wanted, A Man Called Sloane, Sheriff Lobo, T.J. Hooker. *Producer:* T.J. Hooker, Jessie.

FOLEY, DAVE
Actor. b. Toronto, Canada, Jan. 4, 1963.
PICTURES: High Stakes, Three Men and a Baby, It's Pat, Kids in the Hall: Brain Candy, Hacks, A Bug's Life (voice), The Wrong Guy (also s.p.), Dick, Blast from the Past, South Park: Bigger, Longer and Uncut (voice)
TELEVISION: *Movies/Specials:* Anne of Avonlea, The Lawrenceville Stories, From the Earth to the Moon, It's Tough to Be a Bug (voice). *Series:* The Kids in the Hall (also dir.), NewsRadio (also dir.).

FOLEY, JAMES
Director. b. New York, NY. E. NYU, USC. While at USC directed two short films, Silent Night and November which brought him attention. Directed two Madonna videos.
PICTURES: Reckless, At Close Range, Who's That Girl, After Dark My Sweet, Glengarry Glen Ross, A Day to Remember, Fear, Two Bits, The Chamber, The Corrupter.

FOLSEY, GEORGE, JR
Producer, Editor. b. Los Angeles, CA, Jan. 17, 1939. Son of late cinematographer George Folsey Sr. e. Pomona Coll., B.A., 1961. Chairman, Q Sound Labs, Canadian sound localization and Tech. Co., 1988-1992.
PICTURES: *Editor*: Glass Houses, Bone, Hammer, Black Caesar, Schlock, Trader Horn, Bucktown, J.D.'s Revenge, Norman... Is That You?, Tracks, The Chicken Chronicles, The Kentucky Fried Movie, National Lampoon's Animal House, Freedom Road, The Great Santini (addt'l editing), The Blues Brothers (also assoc. prod.), Bullet Proof. *Producer*: An American Werewolf in London, Twilight Zone—The Movie (assoc. prod.); Trading Places (exec. prod. & 2nd unit dir.), Into the Night (co-prod.), Spies Like Us (co-prod.), Clue (co-exec. prod.), Three Amigos, Coming to America (co-prod., co-editor), Greedy (co-exec. prod.), Grumpier Old Men.
VIDEO: Michael Jackson's Thriller (co-prod., editor).

FONDA, BRIDGET
Actress. b. Los Angeles, CA, Jan. 27, 1964. Daughter of actor Peter Fonda. Grew up in Los Angeles and Montana. e. NYU theater prog. Studied acting at Lee Strasberg Inst., and with Harold Guskin. Starred in grad. student film PPT. Workshop stage performances include Confession and Pastels.
PICTURES: Aria (Tristan and Isolde; debut, 1987), You Can't Hurry Love, Light Years (voice), Scandal, Shag, Strapless, Frankenstein Unbound, The Godfather Part III, Drop Dead Fred (unbilled), Doc Hollywood, Leather Jackets, Out of the Rain, Iron Maze, Single White Female, Singles, Army of Darkness, Point of No Return, Bodies Rest and Motion, Little Buddha, It Could Happen to You, The Road to Wellville, Camilla, Rough Magic, Balto (voice), City Hall, Touch, Mr. Jealousy, The Road to Graceland, Jackie Brown, The Break-Up, A Simple Plan, Lake Placid, South of Heaven West of Hell, The Whole Shebang.
TELEVISION: *Specials*: Jacob Have I Loved (Wonderworks), The Edge (The Professional Man). *Guest*: 21 Jump Street, In the Gloaming.

FONDA, JANE
Actress. b. New York, NY, Dec. 21, 1937. e. Emma Willard Sch., Troy, NY. Active in dramatics, Vassar. Father was late actor Henry Fonda. Brother is actor Peter Fonda. m. executive Ted Turner. Appeared with father in summer stock production, The Country Girl, Omaha, NB. Studied painting, languages, Paris. Art Students League, N.Y. Appeared in The Male Animal, Dennis, MA. Modeled, appeared on covers, Esquire, Vogue, The Ladies Home Journal, Glamour, and McCall's, 1959. Appeared in documentaries: Introduction to the Enemy, No Nukes.
THEATER: There Was A Little Girl (Theatre World Award), Invitation to a March, The Fun Couple, Strange Interlude.
PICTURES: Tall Story (debut, 1960), Walk on the Wild Side, The Chapman Report, Period of Adjustment, In the Cool of The Day, Sunday in New York, The Love Cage (Joy House), La Ronde (Circle of Love), Cat Ballou, The Chase, La Curee (The Game is Over), Any Wednesday, Hurry Sundown, Barefoot in the Park, Barbarella, Spirits of the Dead, They Shoot Horses Don't They? (Acad. Award nom.), Klute (Academy Award, 1971), F.T.A. (also prod.), Tout va Bien, Steelyard Blues, A Doll's House, The Bluebird, Fun With Dick and Jane, Julia (Acad. Award nom.), Coming Home (Academy Award, 1978), Comes a Horseman, California Suite, The China Syndrome (Acad. Award nom.), The Electric Horseman, Nine To Five, On Golden Pond (Acad. Award nom.), Rollover, Agnes of God, The Morning After (Acad. Award nom.), Leonard Part 6 (cameo), Old Gringo, Stanley and Iris.
TELEVISION: *Specials*: A String of Beads, Lily--Sold Out, The Helen Reddy Special, I Love Liberty, Tell Them I'm a Mermaid, Fonda on Fonda (host), A Century of Women (narrator). *Movie*: The Dollmaker (Emmy Award, 1984). *Series*: 9 to 5 (exec. prod. only).

FONDA, PETER
Actor, Director. b. New York, NY, Feb. 23, 1939. e. studied at U. of Omaha. Son of late actor Henry Fonda. Sister is actress Jane Fonda; daughter is actress Bridget Fonda.
PICTURES: Tammy and the Doctor (debut, 1963), The Victors, Lilith, The Young Lovers, The Wild Angels, The Trip, Spirits of the Dead, Easy Rider (also co-s.p., prod.), Idaho Transfer (dir.), The Last Movie, The Hired Hand (also dir.), Two People, Dirty Mary Crazy Larry, Open Season, Race With the Devil, 92 in the Shade, Killer Force, Fighting Mad, Futureworld, Outlaw Blues, High Ballin!, Wanda Nevada (also dir.), Cannonball Run (cameo), Split Image, Certain Fury, Dance of the Dwarfs, Mercenary Fighters, Jungle Heat, Diajobu My Friend, Peppermint Frieden, Spasm, The Rose Garden, Fatal Mission, Family Spirit, Reckless, South Beach, Bodies Rest & Motion, DeadFall, Molly & Gina, Love and a .45, Painted Hero, Nadja, John Carpenter's Escape from L.A., Grace of My Heart, Ulee's Gold (NY Film Crits. Circle Award, Golden Globe Award, Best Actor, 1997), The Passion of Ayn Rand, The Limey, Thomas and the Magic Railroad.
TELEVISION: *Movies*: A Reason to Live, The Hostage Tower, A Time of Indifference, Sound, Certain Honorable Men, Montana, The Tempest, Don't Look Back.

FONER, NAOMI
Writer, Producer. b. New York, NY. e. Barnard Col., Columbia U. m. dir. Stephen Gyllenhaal. Was media dir. of Eugene McCarthy's 1968 political campaign, then prod. asst. & researcher at PBS. 1968 joined Children's Television Workshop on staff of Sesame Street. Later helped develop series The Electric Company, 3-2-1 Contact. Creator and co-prod. of series The Best of Families. Wrote teleplay Blackout for PBS series Visions.
PICTURES: *Writer:* Violets Are Blue, Running on Empty (Golden Globe Award, Acad. Award nom.; also exec. prod.), A Dangerous Woman (also prod.), Losing Isaiah (also prod.).

FONTAINE, JOAN
Actress. b. Tokyo, Oct. 22, 1917. r.n. Joan de Beauvior de Havilland. e. American School in Japan. Sister is actress Olivia de Havilland. Started on stage in L.A., Santa Barbara and San Francisco in Kind Lady; then as Joan Fontaine in Call it a Day (L.A.), where she was spotted and signed to contract by prod. Jesse Lasky. Sold contract to RKO. On B'way in Tea and Sympathy (1954). *Author:* No Bed of Roses (1978) Appeared in The Lion in Winter at Vienna's English Speaking Theatre 1979.
PICTURES: No More Ladies (debut, 1935), Quality Street, You Can't Beat Love, Music for Madame, Maid's Night Out, A Damsel in Distress, Blonde Cheat, The Man Who Found Himself, The Duke of West Point, Sky Giant, Gunga Din, Man of Conquest, The Women, Rebecca (Acad. Award nom.), Suspicion (Academy Award, 1941), This Above All, The Constant Nymph (Acad. Award nom.), Jane Eyre, Frenchman's Creek, Affairs of Susan, From This Day Forward, Ivy, The Emperor Waltz, Letter From an Unknown Woman, Kiss the Blood Off My Hands, You Gotta Stay Happy, Born to Be Bad, September Affair, Darling How Could You?, Something to Live For, Othello (cameo), Ivanhoe, Decameron Nights, Flight to Tangier, The Bigamist, Casanova's Big Night, Serenade, Beyond a Reasonable Doubt, Island in the Sun, Until They Sail, A Certain Smile, Voyage to the Bottom of the Sea, Tender Is the Night, The Devil's Own.
TELEVISION: Crossings, Dark Mansions, Cannon, The Users, Bare Essence, Good King Wenceslas.

FOOTE, HORTON
Writer. b. Wharton, TX, March 14, 1916. Actor before becoming playwright.
THEATER: Only the Heart, The Chase, The Trip to Bountiful, Traveling Lady, Courtship, 1918, The Widow Claire, The Habitation of Dragons, Lily Dale, Valentine's Day, Dividing the Estate, Talking Pictures, The Roads to Home, Night Seasons, The Young Man From Atlanta (Pulitzer prize), Cousins, The Death of Papa, Convicts, Roots In a Parched Ground, A Coffin In Egypt, Tomorrow, Getting Frankie Married and Afterwards, Laura Dennis, Vernon Early.
PICTURES: Storm Fear, To Kill a Mockingbird (Acad. Award, 1962), Baby the Rain Must Fall, The Chase, Hurry Sundown, Tomorrow, Tender Mercies (Acad. Award, 1983), 1918 (also co-prod.), The Trip to Bountiful (also co-prod.), On Valentine's Day, Convicts, Of Mice and Men.
TELEVISION: Only the Heart, Ludie Brooks, The Travelers, The Old Beginning, Trip to Bountiful, Young Lady of Property, Death of the Old Man, Flight, The Night of the Storm, The Roads to Home, Drugstore: Sunday Night, Member of the Family, Traveling Lady, Old Man (Emmy Award, 1997), Tomorrow, The Shape of the River, The Displaced Person, Barn Burning, The Habitation of Dragons.

FORBES, BRYAN
Actor, Writer, Producer, Director. b. Stratford (London), July 22, 1926. m. actress Nanette Newman. Former head of prod., man. dir., Associated British Prods. (EMI). Stage debut, The Corn Is Green (London), 1942; screen debut, The Small Back Room, 1948. Pres.: National Youth Theatre of Great Britain, 1985-; Pres.: Writers Guild of Great Britain, 1988-91.
AUTHOR: Short stories: Truth Lies Sleeping. Novels: The Distant Laughter, Familiar Strangers (U.S.: Stranger), The Rewrite Man, The Endless Game, A Song at Twilight (U.S.: A Spy at Twlight), The Twisted Playground, Partly Cloudy, Quicksand. Novelizations: The Slipper and the Rose, International Velvet. Non-Fiction: Ned's Girl (bio. of Dame Edith Evans) That Despicable Race (history of the British acting tradition). Autobiographies: Notes for a Life, A Divided Life.
THEATER: *Director*: Macbeth, Star Quality, Killing Jessica, The Living Room.
PICTURES: *Actor*: Tired Men, The Small Back Room All Over the Town, Dear Mr. Prohack, Green Grow The Rushes, The Million Pound Note (Man With a Million), An Inspector Calls, The Colditz Story, Passage Home, Appointment in London, Sea Devils, The Extra Day, Quatermass II, It's Great To be Young, Satellite in The Sky, The Baby and The Battleship, Yesterday's Enemy, The Guns of Navarone, A Shot in The Dark, Of Human Bondage, Restless Natives. Writer: The Cockleshell Heroes, The Black Tent, Danger Within, I Was Monty's Double (also actor), The League of Gentlemen (also actor), The Angry Silence (also prod., actor), Man in the Moon, Only Two Can Play, Station Six Sahara, Of Human Bondage (also actor), Hopscotch, Chaplin.

Director-Writer: Whistle Down the Wind (dir. only), The L-Shaped Room (also actor), Seance on a Wet Afternoon (also prod.), King Rat, The Wrong Box, The Whisperers, Deadfall, The Madwoman of Chaillot (dir. only), The Raging Moon (Long Ago Tomorrow; also actor), The Stepford Wives (dir., actor), The Slipper and the Rose (also actor), International Velvet (also actor), Sunday Lovers (co-dir. only), Better Late Than Never (Menage a Trois), The Naked Face. *Exec. Prod.:* Hoffman, Forbush and the Penguins, The Railway Children, Peter Rabbit and the Tales of Beatrix Potter, The Go-Between, And Soon The Darkness, On The Buses, Dulcima.
TELEVISION: *Actor:* Johnnie Was a Hero, The Breadwinner, French Without Tears, Journey's End, The Gift, The Road, The Heiress, December Flower, First Amongst Equals. *Writer/Dir.:* I Caught Acting Like The Measles (documentary on the life of Dame Edith Evans) Goodbye Norma Jean and Other Things (documentary on the life of Elton John) Jessie, The Endless Game.

FORD, GLENN
Actor. r.n. Gwylin Ford. b. Quebec, Canada, May 1, 1916. Moved to Southern California as child. On stage with various West Coast theatre cos.; featured in The Children's Hour 1935; Broadway in Broom for a Bride, Soliloquy. Signed contract for film career with Columbia Pictures, 1939. Served in U.S. Marine Corps 1942-45.
PICTURES: Heaven With a Barbed Wire Fence (debut, 1940), My Son Is Guilty, Convicted Women, Men Without Souls, Babies for Sale, Blondie Play Cupid, The Lady in Question, So Ends Our Night, Texas, Go West Young Lady, The Adventures of Martin Eden, Flight Lieutenant, Destroyer, The Desperadoes, A Stolen Life, Gilda, Gallant Journey, Framed, The Mating of Millie, The Return of October, The Loves of Carmen, The Man from Colorado, Mr. Soft Touch, The Undercover Man, Lust for Gold, The Doctor and the Girl, The White Tower, Convicted, The Flying Missile, The Redhead and the Cowboy, Follow the Sun, The Secret of Convict Lake, Green Glove, Young Man with Ideas, Affair in Trinidad, Time Bomb (Terror on a Train), The Man from the Alamo, Plunder of the Sun, The Big Heat, Appointment in Honduras, Human Desire, The Americano, The Violent Men, Blackboard Jungle, Interrupted Melody, Trial, Ransom, The Fastest Gun Alive, Jubal, The Teahouse of the August Moon, 3:10 to Yuma, Don't Go Near the Water, Cowboy, The Sheepman, Imitation General, Torpedo Run, It Started With a Kiss, The Gazebo, Cimarron, Cry for Happy, Pocketful or Miracles, The Four Horsemen of The Apocalypse, Experiment in Terror, Love Is a Ball, The Courtship of Eddie's Father, Advance to the Rear, Fate Is the Hunter, Dear Heart, The Rounders, The Money Trap, Is Paris Burning?, Rage, A Time for Killing, The Last Challenge, Day of the Evil Gun, Heaven With a Gun, Smith!, Santee, Midway, Superman, The Visitor, Virus, Happy Birthday to Me, Border Shootout, Raw Nerve.
TELEVISION: *Series*: Cade's County, Friends of Man (narrator), The Family Holvak, When Havoc Struck (narrator). *Movies*: Brotherhood of the Bell, The Greatest Gift, Punch and Jody, The 3000 Mile Chase, Evening in Byzantium, The Sacketts, Beggarman Thief, The Gift, Final Verdict. *Mini-Series*: Once an Eagle.

FORD, HARRISON
Actor. b. Chicago, IL, July 13, 1942. e. Ripon Coll. Started acting in summer stock at Williams Bay, WI, in Damn Yankees, Little Mary Sunshine. Moved to L.A. where he acted in John Brown's Body. Signed by Columbia Studios under seven-year contract. Took break from acting to undertake carpentry work which included building Sergio Mendes' recording studio. Returned to acting in American Graffiti.
PICTURES: Dead Heat on a Merry-Go-Round (debut, 1966), Luv, A Time for Killing, Journey to Shiloh, Zabriskie Point, Getting Straight, American Graffiti, The Conversation, Star Wars, Heroes, Force 10 from Navarone, Hanover Street, The Frisco Kid, More American Graffiti (cameo), Apocalypse Now, The Empire Strikes Back, Raiders of the Lost Ark, Blade Runner, Return of the Jedi, Indiana Jones and the Temple of Doom, Witness (Acad. Award nom.), The Mosquito Coast, Frantic, Working Girl, Indiana Jones and the Last Crusade, Presumed Innocent, Regarding Henry, Patriot Games, The Fugitive, Jimmy Hollywood (cameo), Clear and Present Danger, Sabrina, The Devil's Own, Air Force One, Six Days Seven Nights, Random Hearts, What Lies Beneath.
TELEVISION: *Movies*: The Intruders, James A. Michener's Dynasty, The Possessed. *Guest*: The Virginian, Ironside, The FBI, Love American Style, Gunsmoke, The Young Indiana Jones Chronicles. *Special*: Trial of Lt. Calley.

FORD, MICHAEL
Set decorator, Sound, Actor.
PICTURES: Voyage to the Bottom of the Sea, Don't Worry We'll Think of a Title, Machismo-40 Graves for 40 Guns, The Empire Strikes Back, Raiders of the Lost Ark, Jinxed!, Return of the Jedi, Return of Oz, Empire of the Sun, The Living Daylights, Jaws: The Revenge, Back Street Jane, Licence to Kill, Kill Line, The Taking of Beverly Hills, Nostradamus, GoldenEye, Titanic (Acad. Award, Best Set. Decoration, 1997), Wing Commander.
TELEVISION: *Movies, actor*: Giving Tongue, September.

FORLANI, CLAIR
Actress.
PICTURES: Gypsy Eyes, Police Academy: Mission to Moscow, Mallrats, The Rock, Garage Sale, Basquiat, Basil, The Last Time I Commited Suicide, Meet Joe Black, Into My Heart, Mystery Men, Boys & Girls, Magicians, Anti-Trust.
TELEVISION: *Mini-series*: JFK: Reckless Youth.

FORMAN, SIR DENIS
O.B.E., M.A.: Executive. b. Moffat, Dumfriesshire, Scot., Oct. 13, 1917. e. Loretto Sch., Musselburgh, Pembroke Coll., Cambridge. Served in Argyll & Sutherland Highlanders, W.W.II. Entered film business 1946, production staff Central Office of Information, 1947; Chief Production Officer C.O.I. 1948; appointed dir. of the British Film Inst., 1949; joined Granada Television Ltd., 1955. Jnt. Mng. Dir., 1965 chmn., British Film Inst., bd. of Gov., 1971-73. Chmn. Granada T.V. 1975-87. Chmn. Novello & Co. 1972. Fellow, British Acad. Film & TV Arts, 1976. Dep. chmn. Granada Group, 1984-90, consultant, 1990-96. Deputy chmn. Royal Opera House, 1983-92.

FORMAN, JEROME A.
Executive. b. Hood River, Oregon, June 20, 1934. e. U Arizona. 1966, became gen. mgr. Forman and United Theatres of the Northwest. 1971, joined Pacific Theatres; 1972, appointed v.p. & gen. mgr.; 1978-87, exec. v.p.; 1987-present, pres. One of the original founders of the ShoWest Convention. Currently chmn. emeritus, NATO of Calif.; 1991, chmn. NATO. 1991 elected chmn. bd. of Will Rogers Memorial Fund. Board member of the Foundation of the Motion Picture Pioneers.

FORMAN, MILOS
Director. b. Caslav, Czechoslovakia, Feb. 18, 1932. Trained as writer at Czech Film Sch. and as director at Laterna Magika. Directed short films Audition (Competition), If There Were No Music. Won Int'l. attention with first feature length film Black Peter, 1963. Emigrated to U.S. after collapse of Dubcek govt. in Czechoslovakia, 1969. Appeared as actor in films Heartburn, New Year's Day.
PICTURES: Peter and Pavla/Black Peter (also co-s.p.; Czech Film Critics & Grand Prix Locarno Awards), Loves of a Blonde (also co- s.p.), The Firemen's Ball (also co-s.p.), Taking Off (U.S. debut, 1971), Visions of Eight (Decathalon segment), One Flew Over the Cuckoo's Nest (Academy Award, 1975), Hair, Ragtime, Amadeus (Acad. Award, 1984), Valmont, The People vs. Larry Flynt (Golden Globe Award, 1997), Man on the Moon.

FORREST, FREDERIC
Actor. b. Waxahachie, TX, Dec. 23, 1936. e. Texas Christian U., U. of Oklahoma, B.A. Studied with Sanford Meisner and Lee Strasberg. Began career off-off B'way at Caffe Cino in The Madness of Lady Bright then off-B'way in Futz, Massachusetts Trust and Tom Paine, all with La Mama Troupe under direction of Tom O'Horgan. Moved to Hollywood in 1970.
PICTURES: Futz (debut, 1969), When the Legends Die, The Don Is Dead, The Conversation, The Gravy Train, Permission to Kill, The Missouri Breaks, It Lives Again!, Apocalypse Now, The Rose (Acad. Award nom.), One From the Heart, Hammett, Valley Girl, The Stone Boy, Return, Where Are the Children?, Stacking, Tucker: The Man and His Dream, Valentino Returns, Music Box, The Two Jakes, Cat Chaser, Rain Without Thunder, Falling Down, Trauma, Chasers, One Night Stand
TELEVISION: *Movies*: Larry, Promise Him Anything, Ruby and Oswald, Calamity Jane, Right to Kill?, The Deliberate Stranger, Quo Vadis, Little Girl Lost, Saigon: Year of the Cat (U.K.), Best Kept Secrets, Who Will Love My Children? A Shadow on the Sun, Margaret Bourke-White, Citizen Cohn, The Habitation of Dragons, Against the Wall. *Mini-Series*: Die Kinder.

FORREST, STEVE
Actor. r.n. William Forrest Andrews. b. Huntsville, TX, Sept. 29, 1925. Brother of late actor Dana Andrews. e. UCLA, 1950. Acted at La Jolla Playhouse; appeared on radio, TV; m.p. debut in Crash Dive billed as William Andrews.
PICTURES: Crash Dive (debut, 1942), The Ghost Ship, Geisha Girl, Sealed Cargo, Last of the Comanches, The Bad and the Beautiful (1st billing as Steve Forrest), Dream Wife, Battle Circus, The Clown, The Band Wagon, So Big, Take the High Ground, Phantom of the Rue Morgue, Prisoner of War, Rogue Cop, Bedevilled, The Living Idol, It Happened to Jane, Heller in Pink Tights, Five Branded Women, Flaming Star, The Second Time Around, The Longest Day, The Yellow Canary, Rascal, The Wild Country, The Late Liz, North Dallas Forty, Mommie Dearest, Sahara, Spies Like Us, Amazon Women on the Moon.
TELEVISION: *Movies*: The Hatfields and the McCoys, Wanted: The Sundance Women, The Last of the Mohicans, Testimony of Two Men, Maneaters are Loose, Hollywood Wives, Gunsmoke: Return to Dodge, Columbo: A Bird in the Hand. *Series*: The Baron, S.W.A.T., Dallas.

FORSTER, ROBERT
Actor. b. Rochester, NY, July 13, 1941. e. Heidelberg Coll., Alfred U., Rochester U., B.S.
THEATER: Mrs. Dally Has a Lover, A Streetcar Named Desire, The Glass Menagerie, 12 Angry Men, The Sea Horse, One Flew Over the Cuckoo's Nest, The Big Knife, In the Moonlight Eddie.

PICTURES: Reflections in a Golden Eye (debut, 1967), The Stalking Moon, Medium Cool, Justine, Cover Me Babe, Pieces of Dreams, Journey Through Rosebud, The Don is Dead, Stunts, Avalanche, The Black Hole, Lady in Red (unbilled), Crunch, Alligator, Vigilante, Walking the Edge, Hollywood Harry (also prod., dir.), The Delta Force, Committed, Esmeralda Bay, Heat from Another Sun, The Banker, Peacemaker, Diplomatic Immunity, 29th Street, In Between, Maniac Cop 3: Badge of Silence, South Beach, Cover Story, Body Chemistry 3: Point of Seduction, Demo University, American Perfekt, Original Gangstas, Jackie Brown, Outside Ozona, Psycho, Kiss Toledo Goodbye, Night Vision, Family Tree, Great Sex.
TELEVISION: *Series*: Banyon, Nakia, Once a Hero, Spawn (voice), Mulholland Drive. *Movies*: Banyon, The Death Squad, Nakia, The City, Standing Tall, The Darker Side of Terror, Goliath Awaits, In the Shadow of a Killer, Sex Love and Cold Hard Cash, Rear Window. *Pilots*: Checkered Flag, Mickie & Frankie.

FORSYTH, BILL
Director. Writer. b. Glasgow, Scotland, July 29, 1946. At 16 joined film co. For next 10 years made industrial films, then documentaries. Joined Glasgow Youth Theater.
PICTURES: *Director-Writer:* That Sinking Feeling (debut, 1979; also prod.), Gregory's Girl, Local Hero, Comfort and Joy, Housekeeping, Breaking In, Rebecca's Daughters, Being Human.
TELEVISION: Andrina.

FORSYTHE, JOHN
Actor. b. Penn's Grove, NJ, Jan. 29, 1918. r.n. John Freund. Former commentator for Brooklyn Dodgers, prior to becoming actor. Debuted on tv in 1947.
THEATER: Mr. Roberts, All My Sons, Yellow Jack, Teahouse of the August Moon and others.
PICTURES: Destination Tokyo (debut, 1943), The Captive City, It Happens Every Thursday, The Glass Web, Escape From Fort Bravo, The Trouble With Harry, The Ambassador's Daughter, Everything But the Truth, Kitten With a Whip, Madame X, In Cold Blood, The Happy Ending, Topaze, Goodbye and Amen, And Justice for All, Scrooged, Hotel de Love.
TELEVISION: *Series*: Bachelor Father, The John Forsythe Show, To Rome With Love, Charlie's Angels (voice only), Dynasty, The Powers That Be. *Movies*: See How They Run, Shadow on the Land, Murder Once Removed, The Letters, Lisa—Bright and Dark, Cry Panic, Healers, Terror on the 40th Floor, The Deadly Tower, Amelia Earhart, Tail Gunner Joe, Never Con a Killer, Cruise Into Terror, With This Ring, The Users, A Time for Miracles, Sizzle, The Mysterious Two, On Fire, Opposites Attract, Dynasty: The Reunion. *Guest:* Studio One, Kraft Theatre, Robert Montgomery Presents, I Witness Video, Kings of the Court.

FORSYTHE, WILLIAM
Actor. b. Brooklyn, NY.
THEATER: A Streetcar Named Desire, A Hatful of Rain, Othello, Julius Caesar, 1776, Hair, Godspell, Vox Humana #3, If You Don't Like It—You Can Leave.
PICTURES: King of the Mountain, Smokey Bites the Dust, The Man Who Wasn't There, Sons, Dead Bang, Torrents of Spring, Patty Hearst, Savage Dawn, Cloak and Dagger, The Lightship, Once Upon a Time in America, Raising Arizona, Extreme Prejudice, Weeds, Dick Tracy, Career Opportunities, Out for Justice, Stone Cold, The Waterdance, American Me, The Gun in Betty Lou's Handbag, Relentless 3, Direct Hit, Beyond Desire, The Immortals, Virtuosity, Don't Ask Too Much of love, Things to Do in Denver When You're Dead, The Substitute, The Rock, Palookaville, For Which He Stands, Firestorm, Hell's Kitchen.
TELEVISION: *Series*: The Untouchables (1993). *Movies*: The Miracle of Kathy Miller, The Long Hot Summer, Baja Oklahoma, Cruel Doubt, A Kiss to Die For, Bedroom Eyes, Willing to Kill: The Texas Cheerleader Story, Peacock Blues, Gotti. *Guest*: CHiPs, Fame, Hill Street Blues. *Mini-Series:* Blind Faith.

FORTE, FABIAN
Singer, Actor. b. Philadelphia, PA, Feb. 6, 1943. e. South Philadelphia H.S. At 14, signed contract with Chancellor Records. Studied with Carlo Menotti. Formerly billed simply as Fabian.
RECORDS: Turn Me Loose, Tiger, I'm a Man, Hound Dog Man, The Fabulous Fabian (gold album).
PICTURES: Hound Dog Man (debut, 1959), High Time, North to Alaska, Love in a Goldfish Bowl, Five Weeks in a Balloon, Mr. Hobbs Takes a Vacation, The Longest Day, Ride the Wild Surf, Dear Brigitte, Ten Little Indians, Fireball 500, Dr. Goldfoot and the Girl Bombs, Thunder Alley, Maryjane, The Wild Racers, The Devil's Eight, A Bullet for Pretty Boy, Lovin' Man, Little Laura and Big John, Disco Fever, Kiss Daddy Goodbye, Get Crazy.
TELEVISION: *Movies*: Getting Married, Katie: Portrait of a Centerfold, Crisis in Mid-Air. *Guest*: Bus Stop, Love American Style, Laverne & Shirley, The Love Boat.

FOSSEY, BRIGITTE
Actress. b. Tourcoing, France, Mar. 11, 1947. After debut at the age of 5 in Rene Clement's Forbidden Games (1952) returned to school, studying philosophy and translating. Rediscovered by director Jean-Gabriel Albicocco and cast in Le Grand Meaulnes (1967).
PICTURES: Forbidden Games (debut, 1952), The Happy Road, Le Grand Meaulnes (The Wanderer), Adieu l'Ami, M Comme Mathieu, Raphael ou le DeBauche, Going Places, La Brigade, The Blue Country, Femme Fetales, The Good and the Bad, The Man Who Loved Women, The Swiss Affair, Quintet, Mais ou et donc Orincar, The Triple Death of the Third Character, A Bad Son, The Party, Chanel Solitaire, A Bite of Living, Imperativ, The Party-2, Enigma, Au nom de tous les Meins, Scarlet Fever, A Strange Passion, A Case of Irresponsibility, The Future of Emily, The False Confidences, Cinema Paradiso.

FOSTER, CHRISTINE
Executive. r.n. Mary Christine Foster. b. Los Angeles, CA, March 19, 1943. e. Immaculate Heart Coll, B.A. 1967. UCLA MJ, 1968. Teacher while member of Immaculate Heart Community, 1962-65. Teacher, Pacific U., Tokyo, 1968; dir., research and dev. Metromedia Producers Corp., 1968-71; dir., dev. & prod. services, Wolper Org. 1971-76; mgr., film progs. NBC TV 1976-77; v.p. movies for TV & mini-series, Columbia Pictures TV, 1977-81; v.p. series programs, Columbia TV, 1981; v.p. prog. dev., Group W. Prods. 1981-87; v.p., The Agency, 1988-90; agent, Shapiro-Lichtman-Stein Talent Agency, 1990-. Member: exec. comm. Humanitas Awards, 1986-; exec. comm. Catholics in Media, 1993-; Activities Committee, Acad. of TV Arts & Sciences, 1989-91; L.A. Roman Catholic Archdiocesan Communications Comm., 1986-89; Women in Film, bd. of dirs., 1977-78; teacher UCLA Extension, 1987-. Foreign and domestic university and public group lecturer and speaker.

FOSTER, DAVID
Producer. b. New York, NY, Nov. 25, 1929. e. Dorsey H.S., U. of Southern California Sch. of Journalism. U.S. Army, 1952-54; entered public relations field in 1952 with Rogers, Cowan & Brenner; Jim Mahoney, 1956; Allan, Foster, Ingersoll & Weber, 1958; left field in 1968 to enter independent m.p. production. Was partner in Turman-Foster Co.
PICTURES: *Producer* (with Mitchell Brower): McCabe and Mrs. Miller, The Getaway. Produced (with Lawrence Turman): The Nickel Ride (exec. prod.), The Drowning Pool, The Legacy, Tribute (exec. prod.), Caveman, The Thing, Second Thoughts, Mass Appeal, The Mean Season, Short Circuit, Running Scared, Full Moon in Blue Water, Short Circuit II, Gleaming the Cube, The Getaway (1993), The River Wild, The Mask of Zorro.
TELEVISION: Jesse (co-exec. prod), Between Two Brothers, Surrogate Mother.

FOSTER, JODIE
Actress. r.n. Alicia Christian Foster. b. Los Angeles, CA, Nov. 19, 1962. e. Yale U. Started acting in commercials including famous Coppertone ad. Acting debut on Mayberry, R.F.D. TV series (1968). Followed with many TV appearances, from series to movies of the week.
PICTURES: Napoleon and Samantha (debut, 1972), Kansas City Bomber, Tom Sawyer, One Little Indian, Alice Doesn't Live Here Anymore, Taxi Driver (Acad. Award nom.), Echoes of a Summer, Bugsy Malone, Freaky Friday, The Little Girl Who Lives Down the Lane, Il Casotto (The Beach Hut), Moi fleur bleue (Stop Calling Me Baby!), Candleshoe, Foxes, Carny, O'Hara's Wife, The Hotel New Hampshire, Mesmerized (also co-prod.), Siesta, Five Corners, Stealing Home, The Accused (Academy Award, 1988), The Silence of the Lambs (Academy Award, 1991), Little Man Tate (also dir.), Shadows and Fog, Sommersby, Maverick, Nell (Acad. Award nom.; also co-prod.), Home for the Holidays (dir., co-prod. only), Contact, Anna and the King, The Dangerous Lives of Altar Boys, Flora Plum (dir. and prod. only).
TELEVISION: *Series*: Bob & Carol & Ted & Alice, Paper Moon. *Guest*: The Courtship of Eddie's Father, Gunsmoke, Julia, Mayberry R.F.D., Ironside, My Three Sons. *Specials*: Alexander, Rookie of the Year, Menace on the Mountain, The Secret Life of T.K. Dearing, The Fisherman's Wife. *Movies*: Smile Jenny--You're Dead, The Blood of Others, Svengali, Backtrack.

FOSTER, JULIA
Actress. b. Lewes, Sussex, England, 1941. First acted with the Brighton Repertory Company, then two years with the Worthing, Harrogate and Richmond companies. 1956, TV debut as Ann Carson in Emergency Ward 10.
THEATER: The Country Wife, What the Butler Saw.
PICTURES: Term of Trial (debut, 1962), The Loneliness of the Long Distance Runner, Two Left Feet, The Small World of Sammy Lee, The System (The Gir Getters), The Bargee, One Way Pendulum, Alfie, Half a Sixpence, All Coppers Are..., The Great McGonagall.
TELEVISION: A Cosy Little Arrangement, The Planemakers, Love Story, Taxi, Consequences, They Throw It at You, Crime and Punishment, The Image, Henry VI Pt. 1 of 3, Cabbage Patch, The Tragedy of Richard III.

FOSTER, MEG
Actress. b. Reading, PA, May 14, 1948.
PICTURES: Adam at 6 A.M. (debut, 1970), Thumb Tripping, Welcome to Arrow Beach (Tender Flesh), A Different Story, Once in Paris, Carny, Ticket to Heaven, The Osterman Weekend, The Emerald Forest, Masters of the Universe, The Wind, They Live, Leviathan, Relentless, Stepfather 2, Blind Fury, Tripwire, Jezebel's Kiss, Diplomatic Immunity, Dead One: Relentless II, Project Shadowchaser, Immortal Combat.

TELEVISION: *Movies*: The Death of Me Yet, Sunshine, Things In This Season, Promise Him Anything, James Dean, Sunshine Christmas, Guyana Tragedy, Legend of Sleepy Hollow, Desperate Intruder, Best Kept Secrets, Desperate, Back Stab, To Catch a Killer. *Series*: Sunshine, Cagney & Lacey. *Guest*: Here Come the Brides, Mod Squad, Men at Law, Hawaii Five-O, Murder She Wrote, Miami Vice. Mini-*Series*: Washington: Behind Closed Doors. *Special*: The Scarlet Letter.

FOWKES, RICHARD O.
Executive. b. Yonkers, NY, April 15, 1946. e. NYU, Geo. Washington U. Staff attorney for The Dramatists Guild, 1973-77; joined Paramount as assoc. counsel, 1977-80; moved to UA (NYC) as prod. attorney from 1980-82; returned to Paramount as v.p., legal & bus. affairs., MoPic division (LA) 1983; promoted to sr. v.p., bus. affairs & acquisitions, 1989; promoted to sr. v.p. in charge of bus. affairs, 1994.

FOWLER, HARRY
Actor. b. London, England, Dec. 10, 1926. e. West Central Sch., London. Stage debut, Nothing Up My Sleeve (London) 1950; Screen debut, 1941.
PICTURES: Demi-Paradise, Don't Take It to Heart, Champaigne Charlie, Painted Boats, Hue and Cry, Now Barabbas, The Dark Man, She Shall Have Murder, The Scarlet Thread, High Treason, The Last Page, I Believe in You, Pickwick Papers, Top of the Form, Angels One Five, Conflict of Wings (Fuss Over Feathers), A Day to Remember, Blue Peter, Home and Away, Booby Trap, Town on Trial, Lucky Jim, Birthday Present, Idle on Parade, Don't Panic Chaps, Heart of a Man, Crooks Anonymous, The Longest Day, Lawrence of Arabia, Flight from Singapore, The Golliwog, Ladies Who Do, Clash By Night, The Nanny, Life at the Top, Start the Revolution Without Me, The Prince and The Pauper, Fanny Hill, Chicago Joe and the Showgirl.
TELEVISION: Stalingrad, I Remember the Battle, Gideon's Way, That's for Me, Our Man at St. Mark's, Dixon of Dock Green, Dr. Finlay's Case Book, I Was There, Cruffs Dog Show, The Londoners, Jackanory, Get This, Movie Quiz, Get This (series), Going a Bundle, Ask a Silly Answer, London Scene, Flockton Flyer, Sun Trap, The Little World of Don Camillo, World's End, Minder, Dead Ernest, Morecambe Wise Show, Gossip, Entertainment Express, Fresh Fields, Supergram, A Roller Next Year, Harry's Kingdom, Body Contact, Davro's Sketch Pad, The Bill, In Sickness and in Health, Casualty, Leaves on the Line, Young Indiana Jones Chronicles, Southside Party, London Tonight.

FOX, EDWARD
Actor. b. London, England, April 13, 1937. Comes from theatrical family; father was agent for leading London actors; brother is actor James Fox.
PICTURES: The Mind Benders (debut, 1962), Morgan!, The Frozen Dead, The Long Duel, The Naked Runner, The Jokers, I'll Never Forget What's 'is Name, The Battle of Britain, Oh! What a Lovely War, Skullduggery, The Go-Between, The Day of The Jackal, A Doll's House, Galileo, The Squeeze, A Bridge Too Far, The Duellists, The Big Sleep, Force 10 from Navarone, The Cat and the Canary, Soldier of Orange, The Mirror Crack'd, Gandhi, Never Say Never Again, The Dresser, The Bounty, Wild Geese II, The Shooting Party, Return From the River Kwai, A Feast at Midnight, A Month by the Lake, Prince Valiant, Lost in Space.
TELEVISION: Edward and Mrs. Simpson, A Hazard of Hearts, Anastasia: The Mystery of Anna, Quartermaine's Terms, They Never Slept, Shaka Zulu, Robin Hood, The Crucifer of Blood, Forbidden Territory.

FOX, JAMES
Actor. b. London, England, May 19, 1939. Brother is actor Edward Fox. Ent. films as child actor in 1950 as William Fox. Left acting in 1973 to follow spiritual vocation. Returned to mainsteam films in 1982. B'way debut 1995 in Uncle Vanya.
PICTURES: The Miniver Story (debut, 1950; as William Fox), The Magnet, One Wild Oat, The Lavender Hill Mob, Timbuktu, The Queen's Guards, The Secret Partner, She Always Gets Their Man, What Every Woman Wants, The Loneliness of the Long-Distance Runner; Tamahine (1st film billed as James Fox), The Servant, Those Magnificent Men in Their Flying Machines, King Rat, The Chase, Thoroughly Modern Millie, Arabella, Duffy, Isadora, Performance, No Longer Alone, Runners, Greystoke: The Legend of Tarzan, A Passage to India, Pavlova, Absolute Beginners, The Whistle Blower, Comrades, High Season, The Mighty Quinn, Farewell to the King, The Boys in the Island, The Russia House, Patriot Games, Afraid of the Dark, The Remains of the Day, Anna Karenina, Up at the Villa, Shadow Run, Mickey Blue Eyes.
TELEVISION: The Door, Espionage, Love Is Old, Love Is New, Nancy Astor, Country, New World, Beryl Markham: A Shadow on the Sun, Sun Child, She's Been Away (BBC; shown theatrically in U.S.), Never Come Back, Slowly Slowly in the Wind, Patricia Highsmith Series, As You Like It, A Question of Attribution, Heart of Darkness, Fall from Grace, Hostage, Doomsday Gun, Headhunters, The Old Curiosity Shop, Fall From Grace, The Choir, Gulliver's Travels.

FOX, MICHAEL J.
Actor. b. Edmonton, Alberta, Canada, June 9, 1961. r.n. Michael Andrew Fox. m. actress Tracy Pollan. Appeared in Vancouver TV series Leo and Me, and on stage there in The Shadow Box. Moved to Los Angeles at age 18.
PICTURES: Midnight Madness (debut, 1980), The Class of 1984, Back to the Future, Teen Wolf, Light of Day, The Secret of My Success, Bright Lights Big City, Casualties of War, Back to the Future Part II, Back to the Future Part III, The Hard Way, Doc Hollywood, Homeward Bound: The Incredible Journey (voice), Life With Mikey, For Love or Money, Where the Rivers Flow North, Greedy, Coldblooded (also co-prod.), Blue in the Face, The American President, Homeward Bound II: Lost in San Francisco (voice), The Frighteners, Mars Attacks!, Stuart Little (voice).
TELEVISION: *Series*: Palmerstown U.S.A., Family Ties (3 Emmy Awards), Spin City (Golden Globe Award, 1998; Emmy award, 2000). *Guest*: Lou Grant, The Love Boat, Night Court, Trapper John M.D., Tales from the Crypt (The Trap; also dir.). *Specials*: Teachers Only, Time Travel: Fact Fiction and Fantasy, Dear America: Letters Home From Vietnam (reader), James Cagney: Top of the World (host). *Movies*: Letters From Frank, High School USA, Poison Ivy, Family Ties Vacation, Don't Drink the Water, I Am Your Child. *Director*: Brooklyn Bridge (episode).

FOX, RICHARD
Executive. b. New York, NY, Feb. 24, 1947. Joined Warner Bros. Intl. as mgt. trainee in October 1975, working in Australia and Japan. 1977, named gen. mgr. of Columbia-Warner Dist., New Zealand. Served as gen. mgr. of WB in Tokyo, 1978\-1981. Joined WB in L.A. as exec. asst. to Myron D. Karlin, pres. of WB Intl., 1981; appt. v.p., sls. 1982; 1983, promoted to exec. v.p. of intl. arm; 1985, named pres. of WB Intl., assuming post vacated by Karlin. 1992, promoted to exec. v.p., Intl. Theatrical Enterprises, WB.

FOX, RICHARD A.
Executive. b. Buffalo, NY, Jan 5, 1929. e. U. of Buffalo, 1950. Chmn., Fox Theatres Management Corp. Pres., Nat'l NATO 1984-86; chmn., Nat'l NATO 1986-1988.

FOX, VIVICA A.
Actress. b. July 30, 1964.
PICTURES: Born on the Fourth of July, Don't Be a Menace to South Central While Drinking Your Juice in the Hood, Independence Day, Set It Off, Booty Call, Batman & Robin, Soul Food, Teaching Mrs. Tingle, Why Do Fools Fall in Love?, Idle Hands.
TELEVISION: *Series*: The Young and the Restless, Generations, Getting Personal, Arsenio. *Movies:* Out All Night, The Tuskegee Airmen, Solomon, A Saintly Switch. *Guest*: Who's the Boss, The Fresh Prince of Bel-Air, Beverly Hills 90210.

FOXWELL, IVAN
Producer, Writer. b. London, Eng., Feb. 22, 1914. Entered m.p. ind. 1933 as technician with British & Dominions Film Corp., subsequently with Paramount British & London Films; Assoc. with Curtis Bernhardt in Paris 1937 becoming producer & collaborating on story, s.p. of Carefour, Le Train pour Venise, De Mayerling Sarajevo, others. WWII with BEF and AEF 1939-46. Returned to British films 1947. Director, Foxwell Film Prods. Ltd.
PICTURES: *Producer*: No Room at the Inn (also co-s.p.), Guilt Is My Shadow (also co-s.p.), Twenty-Four Hours of a Woman's Life, The Intruder (also co-s.p.), Manuela, A Touch of Larceny, Tiara Tahiti, The Quiller Memorandum, Decline and Fall (also s.p.).
TELEVISION: The Intruder (co-writer), The Colditz Story (prod.).

FOXWORTH, ROBERT
Actor. b. Houston, TX, Nov. 1, 1941. e. Carnegie-Mellon U. Began acting at age 10 at Houston Alley Theatre and stayed with stage part-time while completing formal education. Returned to theatre on full-time basis after graduation. Made TV debut in Sadbird, 1969.
THEATER: *NY*: Henry V, Terra Nova, The Crucible (Theatre World Award), Love Letters, Candida. *Regional:* Antony & Cleopatra, Uncle Vanya, Cyrano de Bergerac, Who's Afraid of Virginia Woolf?, Othello, Habeus Corpus, The Seagull, Macbeth.
PICTURES: Treasure of Matecumbe (debut, 1976), The Astral Factor, Airport '77, Damien: Omen II, Prophecy, The Black Marble, Beyond the Stars.
TELEVISION: *Series*: The Storefront Lawyers, Falcon Crest. *Movies*: The Devil's Daughter, Frankenstein, Mrs. Sundance, The Questor Tapes (pilot), The FBI Story: The FBI Vs. Alvin Karpis, James Dean, It Happened at Lakewood Manor, Death Moon, The Memory of Eva Ryker, Act of Love, Peter and Paul, The Return of the Desperado, Double Standard, Face to Face, The Price of the Bride, With Murder in Mind, For Love and Glory. *Specials*: Hogan's Goat, Another Part of the Forest.

FOXX, JAMIE
Actor. b. Terrell, TX, December 13, 1967.
PICTURES: Toys, The Truth About Cats & Dogs, The Great White Hype, The Player's Club, Booty Call, Any Given Sunday.
TELEVISION: *Series*: In Living Color, The Jamie Foxx Show (also prod.), C Bear and Jamal (voice).

FRAKER, WILLIAM A.
Cinematographer, Director. b. Los Angeles, CA, 1923. e. U. of Southern California Film Sch. Worked as camera operator with Conrad Hall; moved to TV before feature films. Photographed and co-prod. doc. Forbid Them Not.
PICTURES: *Cinematographer:* Games, The Fox, The President's Analyst, Fade In, Rosemary's Baby, Bullitt, Paint Your Wagon, Dusty and Sweets McGee, The Day of the Dolphin, Rancho Deluxe, Aloha Bobby and Rose, Lipstick, The Killer Inside Me, Gator, Exorcist II--The Heretic, Looking for Mr. Goodbar, American Hot Wax, Heaven Can Wait, Old Boyfriends, 1941, The Hollywood Knights, Divine Madness, Sharky's Machine, The Best Little Whorehouse in Texas, WarGames, Irreconcilable Differences, Protocol, Fever Pitch, Murphy's Romance, SpaceCamp, Burglar, Baby Boom, Chances Are, An Innocent Man, The Freshman, Memoirs of an Invisible Man, Honeymoon in Vegas, Tombstone (also co-assoc. prod.), Street Fighter, Father of the Bride II. *Director:* Monte Walsh, Reflection of Fear, Legend of the Lone Ranger.
TELEVISION: Stony Burke, Outer Limits, Ozzie and Harriet, Daktari, B.L. Stryker: The Dancer's Touch (dir.).

FRAKES, JONATHAN
Actor, Director. b. Bethlehem, PA, Aug. 19, 1952. m. Actress Gennie Francis.
PICTURES: Gargoyles: The Heroes Awaken (voice), Star Trek: Generations, Star Trek: First Contact (also dir.), Trekkies, Star Trek: Insurrection (also dir.).
TELEVISION: *Movies*: Beach Patrol, The Night the City Screamed, Star Trek: The Next Generation (pilot), The Cover Girl and the Cop, Dying to Live. *Series*: The Doctors, Bare Essence, Paper Dolls, Star Trek: The Next Generation (also dir.), Gargoyles (voice), University Hospital (dir. only), Gargoyles: The Goliath Chronicles (voice) Beyond Belief: Fact or Fiction. *Mini-series*: Beulah Land, North & South, North & South II, Dream West, Nutcracker: Money—Madness & Murder, North & South III, The Lot. *Guest*: Voyagers, Remington Steele, Highway to Heaven, Matlock, Married... With Children, The New Twilight Zone, Star Trek: Deep Space Nine (also dir.), Wings, Lois & Clark, Star Trek: Voyager (also dir.), Cybill.

FRANCIOSA, ANTHONY
Actor. b. New York, NY, Oct. 25, 1928. e. Ben Franklin h.s. in NY. Erwin Piscator's Dramatic Workshop (4-year scholarship). First stage part in YWCA play; joined Off-Broadway stage group; stock at Lake Tahoe, CA, Chicago and Boston.
THEATER: *B'way*: End as a Man, The Wedding Breakfast, A Hatful of Rain (Theatre World Award, Tony nom.), Rocket to the Moon, Grand Hotel. Tour: Love Letters.
PICTURES: A Face in the Crowd (debut, 1957), This Could Be The Night, A Hatful of Rain (Acad. Award nom.), Wild Is The Wind, The Long Hot Summer, The Naked Maja, Career, The Story on Page One, Go Naked in the World, Senilita (Carless), Period of Adjustment, Rio Conchos, The Pleasure Seekers, A Man Could Get Killed, Assault on a Queen, The Swinger, Fathom, In Enemy Country, The Sweet Ride, A Man Called Gannon, Ghost in the Noonday Sun, Across 110th Street, The Drowning Pool, Firepower, The World is Full of Married Men, Death Wish II, Julie Darling, Ghost in the Noonday Sun, Death Is in Fashion, Tenebrae, Help Me Dream, The Cricket, A Texas Legend, Backstreet Dreams, Death House, Brothers in Arms, Double Threat, City Hall.
TELEVISION: *Series*: Valentine's Day, The Name of the Game, Search, Matt Helm, Finder of Lost Loves. *Movies*: Fame is the Name of the Game, Deadly Hunt, Earth II, The Catcher, This is the West That Was, Matt Helm, Curse of the Black Widow, Side Show, Till Death Do Us Part, Ghost Writer. *Mini-Series*: Aspen, Wheels. *Guest*: Kraft Theatre, Philco Playhouse, Danger, Naked City, Arrest & Trial, Playhouse 90, etc *Specials:* A Lincoln Portrait, (narrator).

FRANCIS, ANNE
Actress b. Ossining, NY, Sept. 16, 1932. Child model; radio, TV shows as child & adult; on B'way in Lady in the Dark.
PICTURES: Summer Holiday (debut, 1948), So Young So Bad, Whistle at Eaton Falls, Elopement, Lydia Bailey, Dream Boat, A Lion Is in the Streets, Rocket Man, Susan Slept Here, Rogue Cop, Bad Day at Black Rock, Battle Cry, Blackboard Jungle, The Scarlet Coat, Forbidden Planet, The Rack, The Great American Pastime, The Hired Gun, Don't Go Near the Water, Crowded Sky, Girl of the Night, Satan Bug, Brainstorm, Funny Girl, Hook Line and Sinker, More Dead Than Alive, The Love God?, Impasse, Pancho Villa, Survival, Born Again, The High Fashion Murders, The Return, Little Vegas.
TELEVISION: *Series*: Honey West, My Three Sons, Dallas, Riptide. *Guest:* Partners in Crime, Crazy Like a Fox, Jake and the Fatman, Twilight Zone, Finder of Lost Loves, Golden Girls, Matlock, Murder She Wrote, Burke's Law. *Movies*: Wild Women, The Intruders, The Forgotten Man, Mongo's Back in Town, Fireball Forward, Haunts of the Very Rich, Cry Panic, FBI Vs. Alvin Karpis, The Last Survivors, A Girl Named Sooner, Banjo Hackett, Little Mo, The Rebels, Beggarman Thief, Detour to Terror, Rona Jaffe's Mazes and Monsters, Poor Little Rich Girl: The Barbara Hutton Story, Laguna Heat, My First Love, Love Can Be Murder, Fortune Hunter.

FRANCIS, ARLENE
Actress. r.n. Arlene Francis Kazanjian; b. Boston, MA, Oct. 20, 1908. e. Convent of Mount St. Vincent Acad., Riverdale, NY, Finch Finishing Sch., Theatre Guild Sch., NY. m. Martin Gabel, late actor. *Author:* That Certain Something (1960); Arlene Francis--A Memoir (1978).
THEATER: The Women (1937), Horse Eats Hat (Mercury Theater), Danton's Death, All That Glitters, Doughgirls, The Overtons, Once More With Feeling, Tchin-Tchin, Beekman Place, Mrs. Dally, Dinner at Eight, Kind Sir, Lion in Winter, Pal Joey, Who Killed Santa Claus?, Gigi, Social Security.
PICTURES: Murders in the Rue Morgue, Stage Door Canteen, All My Sons, One Two Three, The Thrill of It All, Fedora.
TELEVISION: Soldier Parade 1949-55, Blind Date, What's My Line; Home, Arlene Francis Show, Talent Patrol, etc.
RADIO: Arlene Francis Show, Emphasis, Monitor, Luncheon at Sardis.

FRANCIS, CONNIE
Singer. r.n. Constance Franconero. b. Newark, NJ, Dec. 12, 1938. Appeared, Star Time when 12 years old; won Arthur Godfrey's Talent Scout Show, 12 years old. Autobiography: Who's Sorry Now (1984). Regular on series The Jimmie Rodgers Show, 1959. Gold Records: Who's Sorry Now, My Happiness. Numerous vocalist awards.
PICTURES: Where the Boys Are, Follow the Boys, Looking For Love.

FRANCIS, FREDDIE
Producer, Director, Cinematographer. b. London, 1917. Joined Gaumont British Studios as apprentice to stills photographer; then clapper boy at B.I.P. Studios, Elstree; camera asst. at British Dominion. After W.W.II returned to Shepperton Studios to work for Korda and with Powell and Pressburger as cameraman.
PICTURES: *Director*: Two and Two Make Six (A Change of Heart/The Girl Swappers; debut, 1962), Paranoiac, Vengeance, The Evil of Frankenstein, Nightmare, Traitor's Gate, Hysteria, Dr. Terror's House of Horrors, The Skull, The Psychopath, The Deadly Bees, They Came from Beyond Space, Torture Garden, Dracula Has Risen from the Grave, Mumsy Nanny Sonny and Girly, Trog, Tales from the Crypt, The Creeping Flesh, Tales That Witness Madness, Son of Dracula, Craze, The Ghoul, Legend of the Werewolf, The Doctor and the Devils, Dark Tower. *Cinematographer:* Moby Dick (second unit photo., special effects), A Hill in Korea (Hell in Korea), Time Without Pity, Room at the Top, The Battle of the Sexes, Saturday Night and Sunday Morning, Sons and Lovers (Academy Award, 1960), The Innocents, Night Must Fall, The Elephant Man, The French Lieutenant's Woman, Dune, Memed My Hawk, Clara's Heart, Her Alibi, Brenda Starr, Glory (Academy Award, 1989), Man in the Moon, Cape Fear, School Ties, Princess Caraboo, Rainbow.
TELEVISION: *Movie:* A Life in the Theatre.

FRANCIS, KEVIN
Producer, Executive. b. London, England, 1949. Produced It's Life, Passport, Troubl with Canada, Persecution, The Ghoul, Legend of the Werewolf, etc. Executive produ. The Masks of Death, Murder Elite, A One-Way Ticket to Hollywood, etc. 1976, prod. Film Technique Educational course for BFI. 1972-94, CEO Tyburn Prods. Ltd. 1994-present, Ar;ington Productions Ltd.

FRANK, SCOTT
Writer. b. 1960.
PICTURES: Plain Clothes (story), The Walter Ego, Little Man Tate, Dead Again, Malice, Get Shorty, Heaven's Prisoners, Out of Sight (Acad. Award nom.), Caveman's Valentine..

FRANKENHEIMER, JOHN
Director. b. Malba, NY, Feb. 19, 1930. e. Williams Coll. Actor, dir., summer stock; radio-TV actor, dir., Washington, DC; then joined CBS network in 1953. Theater: The Midnight Sun (1959).
PICTURES: The Young Stranger (debut, 1957), The Young Savages, Birdman of Alcatraz, All Fall Down, The Manchurian Candidate (also co-prod.), Seven Days in May, The Train, Seconds, Grand Prix, The Fixer, The Extraordinary Seaman, The Gypsy Moths, I Walk the Line, The Horsemen, The Impossible Object (Story of a Love Story), The Iceman Cometh, 99 and 44/100% Dead, French Connection II, Black Sunday, Prophecy, The Challenge, The Holcroft Covenant, 52 Pick-Up, Dead-Bang, The Fourth War, Year of the Gun, The Island of Dr. Moreau, Ronin, Reindeer Games.
TELEVISION: *Series dir.*: I Remember Mama, You Are There, Danger, Climax, Studio One, Playhouse 90, Du Pont Show of the Month, Ford Startime, Sunday Showcase. *Specials*: The Comedian, For Whom the Bell Tolls, The Days of Wine and Roses, Old Man, The Turn of the Screw, The Browning Version, The Rainmaker. *Movies*: Against the Wall (Emmy Award, 1994), The Burning Season (Emmy Award, 1995; also co-prod.), George Wallace (Emmy Award, 1998; also prod.). *Mini-Series:* Andersonville (Emmy Award, 1996).

FRANKLIN, BONNIE
Actress. b. Santa Monica, CA, Jan. 6, 1944. e. Smith & UCLA.
THEATRE: *B'way.*: Applause (Theatre World Award, Tony nom. Outer Critics Circle award). *Off-B'way.*: Frankie and Johnny in the Claire de Lune. Grace & Glory, Dames at Sea, Your Own Thing.

TELEVISION: *Series*: One Day at a Time. *Movies*: The Law, A Guide for the Married Woman, Breaking Up Is Hard to Do, Portrait of a Rebel: Margaret Sanger, Your Place or Mine, Sister Margaret and Saturday Night Ladies, Shalom Sesame.

FRANKLIN, MICHAEL HAROLD
Executive. b. Los Angeles, CA, Dec. 25, 1923. e. U. of California, A.B., USC, LL.B. Admitted to CA bar, 1951; pvt. practice in L.A. 1951-52; atty. CBS, 1952-54; atty. Paramount, 1954-58; exec. dir. Writers Guild Am. West, Inc. 1958-78; natl exec. dir., Directors Guild of America 1978-. Mem. Am. Civil Liberties Union, Los Angeles Copyright Soc.

FRANKLIN, PAMELA
Actress. b. Tokyo, Japan, Feb. 4, 1950. Attended Elmshurst Ballet Sch., Camberley, Surrey.
PICTURES: The Innocents (debut, 1961), The Lion, The Third Secret, Flipper's New Adventure, The Nanny, Our Mother's House, The Prime of Miss Jean Brodie, The Night of the Following Day, And Soon the Darkness, Necromancy, Ace Eli and Rodger of the Skies, The Legend of Hell House, The Food of the Gods.
TELEVISION: *Movies*: The Horse Without a Head (theatrical in U.K.), See How They Run, David Copperfield (theatrical in U.K.), The Letters, Satan's School for Girls, Crossfire, Eleanor and Franklin.

FRANKLIN, RICHARD
Director, Producer, Writer. b. Melbourne, Australia, July 15, 1948. e. USC (Cinema, 1967).
PICTURES: *Director:* The True Story of Eskimo Nell (also co-prod., co-s.p.), Patrick (also co-prod., co-s.p.), The Blue Lagoon (co-prod. only), Road Games (also prod., co-s.p.), Psycho II, Cloak and Dagger, Into the Night (actor only), Link (also prod.), FX2, Hotel Sorrento (also prod.).
TELEVISION: *Pilots:* Beauty and the Beast, A Fine Romance. *Movie:* Running Delilah.

FRANKLIN, ROBERT A.
Executive. b. New York, NY, April 15. e. U. of Miami, B.B.A., 1958; Columbia Pacific U., M.B.A., 1979; Ph.D., 1980 majoring in marketing. Before entering film industry worked with House of Seagram, Canada Dry Corp., J. M. Mathes Adv. 1967, joined 20th Century-Fox as dir. of mkt. planning. Formed RP Marketing Intl. (entertainment consulting firm) in 1976 and World Research Systems (computer software marketer). 1981 joined MPAA; 1983, named v.p., admin. & info. services. 1986, named v.p. worldwide market research. Chmn., MPAA research comm.; member, AMA and ESOMAR.

FRANZ, ARTHUR
Actor. b. Perth Amboy, NJ, Feb. 29, 1920. e. Blue Ridge Coll., MD. U.S. Air Force. Radio, TV shows.
THEATER: A Streetcar Named Desire, Second Threshold.
PICTURES: Jungle Patrol (debut, 1948), Roseanna McCoy, The Red Light, The Doctor and the Girl, Sands of Iwo Jima, Red Stallion in the Rockies, Three Secrets, Tarnished, Abbott and Costello Meet the Invisible Man, Flight to Mars, Submarine Command, Strictly Dishonorable, The Sniper, Rainbow 'Round My Shoulder, The Member of the Wedding, Eight Iron Men, Invaders From Mars, Bad for Each Other, The Eddie Cantor Story, Flight Nurse, The Caine Mutiny, Steel Cage, Battle Taxi, New Orleans Uncensored, Bobby Ware Is Missing, Beyond a Reasonable Doubt, The Wild Party, Running Target, The Devil's Hairpin, Back From the Dead, The Unholy Wife, Hellcats of the Navy, The Young Lions, The Flame Barrier, Monster on the Campus, Atomic Submarine, The Carpetbaggers, Alvarez Kelly, Anzio, The Sweet Ride, The Human Factor, Sister of Death, That Championship Season.
TELEVISION: *Movies*: Murder or Mercy, Jennifer: A Woman's Story, Bogie.

FRANZ, DENNIS
Actor. b. Chicago, IL, Oct. 28, 1944. Started in Chicago Theatre.
PICTURES: Stony Island, Dressed to Kill, Blow Out, Psycho II, Body Double, A Fine Mess, The Package, Die Hard 2, The Player, American Buffalo, City of Angels.
TELEVISION: *Series*: Chicago Story, Bay City Blues, Hill Street Blues, Beverly Hills Buntz, Nasty Boys, N.Y.P.D. Blue (Emmy Award, 1994, 1996, 1997, 1999), Mighty Ducks (voice). *Movies*: Chicago Story (pilot), Deadly Messages, Kiss Shot, Moment of Truth: Caught in the Crossfire (also co-prod.), Texas Justice. *Guest:* The Simpsons (voice).

FRASER, BRENDAN
Actor. b. Indianapolis, IN, 1968. Raised in Holland, Switzerland, Canada. e. Actors' Conservatory, Cornish College of the Arts, Seattle. Member of Laughing Horse Summer Theatre in Ellensberg, WA.
THEATER: Waiting for Godot, Arms and the Man, Romeo and Juliet, A Midsummer Night's Dream, Moonchildren, Four Dogs and a Bone.
PICTURES: Dogfight (debut, 1991), Encino Man, School Ties, Twenty Bucks, Younger and Younger, With Honors, Airheads, The Scout, Now and Then, The Passion of Darkly Noon, Mrs. Winterbourne, Glory Daze, George of the Jungle, Still Breathing, Gods and Monsters, Dudley Do-Right, Blast from the Past, The Mummy, Bedazzled.
TELEVSION: *Movie*: Guilty Until Proven Innocent, The Twilight of the Golds. *Pilot*: My Old School. *Guest:* The Simpsons (voice).

FRAZIER, SHEILA E.
Actress, Producer. b. Bronx, NY, Nov. 13. e. Englewood, NJ. Was exec. sect'y. and high-fashion model. Steered to acting career by friend Richard Roundtree. Studied drama with N.Y. Negro Ensemble Co. and New Federal Theatre, N.Y., also with Bob Hickey at H.B. Studios, N.Y. Currently working as a TV producer.
PICTURES: Super Fly (debut), Superfly T.N.T., The Super Cops, California Suite, What Does It Take?, Three the Hard Way, The Hitter, I'm Gonna Git You Sucker.
TELEVISION: *Movie:* Firehouse. *Mini-Series*: King. *Series*: The Lazarus Syndrome.

FREARS, STEPHEN
Director. b. Leicester, Eng., June 20, 1941. e. Cambridge, B.A in law. Joined Royal Court Theatre, working with Lindsay Anderson on plays. Later assisted Karel Reisz on Morgan: A Suitable Case for Treatment, Albert Finney on Charlie Bubbles, and Lindsay Anderson on If ... Worked afterwards mostly in TV, directing and producing. First directorial credit was 30-minute film The Burning, 1967.
PICTURES: Gumshoe (dir. debut 1971), Bloody Kids, The Hit, My Beautiful Laundrette, Prick Up Your Ears, Sammy and Rosie Get Laid, Dangerous Liaisons, The Grifters, Hero (GB: Accidental Hero), The Snapper, Mary Reilly, The Van, The Hi-Lo Country, High Fidelity, Liam.
TELEVISION: A Day Out (1971), England Their England, Match of the Day, Sunset Across the Bay, Three Men in a Boat, Daft as a Brush, Playthings, Early Struggles, Last Summer, 18 Months to Balcomb Street, A Visit from Miss Protheroe, Abel's Will, Cold Harbour, Song of Experience; series of six Alan Bennett plays; Long Distance Information, Going Gently, Loving Walter, Saigon: Year of the Cat, December Flower.

FREDERICKSON, H. GRAY, JR.
Producer. b. Oklahoma City, OK, July 21, 1937. e. U. of Lausanne, Switzerland, 1958\-59; U. of Oklahoma. B.A., 1960. Worked one yr. with Panero, Weidlinger & Salvatori Engineering Co., Rome Italy. In 1979 named v.p. of feature films, Lorimar Films.
PICTURES: Candy, Inspector Sterling, Gospel 70, An Italian in America, The Man Who Wouldn't Die, The Good, the Bad and the Ugly, Intrigue in Suez, How to Learn to Love Women, God's Own Country, Wedding March, An American Wife, Natika, Echo in the Village, Little Fauss and Big Halsey, Making It, The Godfather (assoc. prod.), The Godfather Part II (co-prod; Academy Award for Best Picture, 1974), Hit (exec. prod.), Apocalypse Now (co.-prod.; Acad. Award nom.), One From the Heart, The Outsiders, UHF, The Godfather Part III (co-prod.), Ladybugs (exec. prod.), Bad Girls (story), Heaven's Prisoners.
TELEVISION: *Producer*: The Return of Mickey Spillane's Mike Hammer, Houston Nights, Staying Afloat.

FREEBORN, STUART
Make-up. London, England, September 5, 1914.
PICTURES: I See A Dark Stranger, Captain Boycott, Oliver Twist, Silent Dust, Obsession, The Man Who Watched The Trains Go By, His MajestyO'Keefe, The Bridge on the River Kwai, The Naked Truth, I Was Monty's Double, Kidnapped, Mr.Topaze, The Hands of Orlac, The Devil's Daffodil, Foxhole in Cairo, Tarzan Goes to India, The Wrong Arm of the Law, Private Potter, Heaven's Above, Dr.Strangelove: Or How I Learned to Stop Worrying and Love the Bomb, Seance on a Wet Afternoon, 2001: A Space Odyssey, Oh! What A Lovely War, 10 Rillington Place, See No Evil, Young Winston, Alice's Adventures in Wonderland, Murder on the Orient Express, The Adventures of Sherlock Holmes' Smarter Brother, The Omen, Star Wars, Superman, The Empire Strikes Back, Superman II, The Great Muppet Caper, Return of the Jedi, Top Secret!, Santa Claus, Haunted Honeymoon.

FREEDMAN, JERROLD
Director, Writer. b. Philadelphia, PA, Oct.29, 1942. e. Univ. of PA. Novel: Against the Wind.
PICTURES: Kansas City Bomber, Borderline, Native Son.
TELEVISION: *Director-Writer*: Blood Sport, Betrayal, Some Kind of Miracle, Legs, This Man Stands Alone. *Director*: The Streets of L.A., The Boy Who Drank Too Much, Victims, The Seduction of Gina, Best Kept Secrets, Seduced, Family Sins, Unholy Matrimony, The Comeback, Night Walk, A Cold Night's Death, The Last Angry Man, Goodnight Sweet Wife: A Murder in Boston, Condition: Critical.

FREEMAN, AL, JR.
Actor. b. San Antonio, TX, March 21, 1934. e. LA City Coll.
THEATER: The Long Dream (1960), Kicks and Co., Tiger Tiger Burning Bright, Trumpets of the Lord, Blues for Mister Charlie, Conversation at Midnight, Look to the Lilies, Are You Now or Have You Ever Been?, The Poison Tree.
PICTURES: Torpedo Run, Black Like Me, Dutchman, Finian's Rainbow, The Detective, Castle Keep, The Lost Man, A Fable (also dir.), Seven Hours to Judgement, Malcolm X.
TELEVISION: *Movies*: My Sweet Charlie, Assault at West Point. *Mini-Series*: Roots: The Next Generations, King. *Series*: Hot L Baltimore, One Life to Live (Emmy Award, 1979).

FREEMAN, JOEL
Producer. b. Newark, NJ, June 12, 1922. e. Upsala Coll. Began career at MGM studios, 1941. Air Force Mot. Pic. Unit 1942-46. Became assist. dir. at RKO, 1946. 1948 returned to MGM as asst. dir.; later assoc. prod. 1956 entered indep. field as prod. Supv. on various features and TV series. 1960 to Warner Bros., assoc. producing Sunrise at Campobello, The Music Man and Act One. After such films as Camelot and Finian's Rainbow, became studio exec. at Warners. Presently senior v.p. prod., New Century Entertainment Corp.
PICTURES: *Producer*: The Heart Is a Lonely Hunter, Shaft, Trouble Man, Love at First Bite, Octagon, The Kindred, Soapdish (co-prod.).

FREEMAN, KATHLEEN
Actress. b. Chicago, IL, Feb. 17, 1919.
PICTURES: Casbah (debut, 1948), The Saxon Charm, The Naked City, Behind Locked Doors, Mr. Belvedere Goes to College, The Reformer and the Redhead, A Life of Her Own, The House by the River, Lonely Hearts Bandits, Appointment With Danger, A Place in the Sun, The Company She Keeps, O. Henry's Full House, Singin' in the Rain, Talk About a Stranger, Love Is Better Than Ever, She's Back on Broadway, The Affairs of Dobie Gillis, Half a Hero, Athena, Artists and Models, The Far Country, The Midnight Story, Kiss Them for Me, Houseboat, The Fly, The Missouri Traveler, The Buccaneer, North to Alaska, The Ladies Man, The Errand Boy, Madison Avenue, The Nutty Professor, The Disorderly Orderly, Mail Order Bride, The Rounders, Marriage on the Rocks, Three on a Couch, Point Blank, Hook Line and Sinker, The Good Guys and the Bad Guys, Myra Breckinridge, The Ballad of Cable Hogue, Which Way to the Front?, Support Your Local Gunfighter, Stand Up and Be Counted, Where Does It Hurt?, Unholy Rollers, Your Three Minutes Are Up, The Strongest Man in the World, The Norsemen, The Blues Brothers, Heartbeeps, The Best of Times, Malibu Bikini Shop, Dragnet, Innerspace, In the Mood, The Willies, Gremlins 2: The New Batch, Joey Takes a Cab, Dutch, FernGully ... The Last Rainforest (voice), Little Nemo: Adventures in Slumberland (voice), Hocus Pocus, Naked Gun 33 1/3: The Final Insult, At First Sight.
TELEVISION: *Series*: Topper, Mayor of the Town, It's About Time, Funny Face, Lotsa Luck. *Movies*: But I Don't Want to Get Married!, Call Her Mom, Hitched, The Daughters of Joshua Cabe Return, The Last Ride of the Dalton Gang.

FREEMAN, MORGAN
Actor. b. Memphis, TN, June 1, 1937. e. LA City Coll. Served in Air Force 1955-59 before studying acting. Worked as dancer at NY's 1964 World's Fair. Broadway debut in Hello Dolly! with Pearl Bailey. Took over lead role in Purlie. Became known nationally when he played Easy Reader on TV's The Electric Company (1971-76).
THEATER: *NY*: Ostrich Feathers, The Nigger Lovers, Hello Dolly!, Scuba Duba, Purlie, Cockfight, The Last Street Play, The Mighty Gents (Drama Desk & Clarence Derwent Awards), Coriolanus (Obie Award), Julius Caesar, Mother Courage, Buck, Driving Miss Daisy (Obie Award), The Gospel at Colonus (Obie Award), The Taming of the Shrew.
PICTURES: Who Says I Can't Ride a Rainbow? (debut, 1972), Brubaker, Eyewitness, Death of a Prophet, Harry and Son, Teachers, Marie, That Was Then...This Is Now, Street Smart (NY & LA Film Critics & Natl. Board of Review Awards; Acad. Award nom., 1987), Clean and Sober, Lean on Me, Johnny Handsome, Glory, Driving Miss Daisy (Natl. Board of Review & Golden Globe Awards; Acad. Award nom., 1989), The Bonfire of the Vanities, Robin Hood: Prince of Thieves, The Power of One, Unforgiven, Bopha (dir. only), The Shawshank Redemption (Acad. Award nom.), Outbreak, Seven, Moll Flanders, Chain Reaction, Hurricane (dir., prod., s.p., only), Kiss the Girls, Under Suspicion, Long Walk to Freedom, High Crimes, Along Came a Spider.
TELEVISION: *Movies*: Hollow Image, Attica, The Marva Collins Story, The Atlanta Child Murders, Resting Place, Flight For Life, Roll of Thunder Hear My Cry, Charlie Smith and the Fritter Tree, Clinton and Nadine. *Series*: The Electric Company, Another World (1982-4). *Specials* (narrator): The Civil War, Follow the Drinking Gourd, The Promised Land.

FRESCO, ROBERT M.
Writer. b. Burbank, CA, Oct. 18, 1928. e. Los Angeles City Coll. Newspaperman. Los Angeles, 1946-47; U.S. Army, 1948-49; staff writer, Hakim Prod., 1950-51; various screenplays, 1951-56.
PICTURES: Tarantula, They Came to Destroy the Earth, Monolith.
TELEVISION: Scripts for Science Fiction Theatre, Highway Patrol.

FREWER, MATT
Actor. b. Washington, D. C., Jan. 4, 1958. Raised in Victoria, British Columbia. Studied drama at the Bristol Old Vic Theatre, appearing in Romeo and Juliet, Macbeth, Waiting for Godot, Deathtrap.
PICTURES: The Lords of Discipline (debut, 1983), Supergirl, Spies Like Us, Ishtar, The Fourth Protocol, Far From Home, Speed Zone, Honey I Shrunk the Kids, Short Time, The Taking of Beverly Hills, Twenty Bucks, National Lampoon's Senior Trip, Lawnmower Man II.
TELEVISION: *BBC*: Tender is the Night, Robin of Sherwood; U.S. *Series*: Max Headroom, Doctor Doctor, Shaky Ground, The Pink Panther (voice), Outer Limits. *Movie*: The Positively True Adventures of the Alleged Texas Cheerleader-Murdering Mom, The Day My Parents Ran Away, Kissinger and Nixon. *Mini-Series*: The Stand. *Guest*: Miami Vice. Specials: Long Shadows, In Search of Dr. Seuss.

FRICKER, BRENDA
Actress. b. Dublin, Ireland, Feb. 17, 1945. Appeared in short film The Woman Who Married Clark Gable. Theatre work with the RSC, Royal Court Theatre, and The National Theatre.
PICTURES: Quatermass Conclusion, Bloody Kids, Our Exploits at West Poley, My Left Foot (Academy Award, best supporting actress, 1989), The Field, Utz, Home Alone 2: Lost in New York, So I Married an Axe Murderer, Angels in the Outfield, A Man of No Importance, Moll Flanders, A Time to Kill.
TELEVISION: *Series*: Casualty. *Specials*: Licking Hitler, The House of Bernarda Alba, The Ballroom Romance. *Mini-Series*: Brides of Christ, The Sound and the Silence, A Woman of Independent Means.

FRIEDBERG, A. ALAN
Executive. b. New York, NY, Apr. 13, 1932. e. Columbia Coll., B.A. 1952, Junior Phi Beta Kappa, Summa Cum Laude; Harvard Law School 1955. Past pres. and chmn. of bd. NATO. 1990, named chmn. Loews Theatre Mgmt. Co. Chairman of the Board National Center of Jewish Film Brandeis University, Board of Visitor Columbia College, Board of Overseers Boston Symphony Orchestra, Board of Overseers Museum of Fine Arts Boston, Board of Advisors American Repertory Theatre at Harvard University. Retired, 1993.

FRIEDKIN, JOHN
Executive. b. New York, NY, Dec. 9, 1926. e. Columbia Univ. Entered industry in New York as publicist for Columbia Pictures; spent eight years at Young & Rubicam adv. agency. Formed Sumner & Friedkin with Gabe Sumner as partner; left to join Rogers & Cowan, where named v.p. In 1967 resigned to join 20th-Fox, moving to California in 1972 when home offices were transferred. Appointed Fox v.p. worldwide publ. & promo. In 1979 joined Warner Bros. as v.p., adv. pub. for intl. div; 1988, joined Odyssey Distributors Ltd. as sr. v.p., intl. marketing. 1990, formed indept. marketing firm. 1995, rep. for Australia's Kennedy Miller Ent.

FRIEDKIN, WILLIAM
Director, Writer. b. Chicago, IL, Aug. 29, 1939. m. producer Sherry Lansing. Joined WGN-TV, 1957, worked for National Education TV, did TV documentaries before feature films. Dir. B'way play Duet for One.
PICTURES: *Director:* Good Times (debut, 1967), The Night They Raided Minsky's, The Birthday Party, The Boys in the Band, The French Connection (Academy Award, 1971), The Exorcist, Sorcerer (also prod.), The Brink's Job, Cruising (also s.p.), Deal of the Century, To Live and Die in L.A. (also co-s.p.), Rampage (also s.p.), The Guardian (also co-s.p.), Blue Chips, Jade, Rules of Engagement.
TELEVISION: *Movies*: C.A.T. Squad (also exec. prod.), C.A.T. Squad: Python Wolf, Jailbreakers, 12 Angry Men. *Special*: Barbra Streisand: Putting It Together. *Series*: Tales From the Crypt (On a Dead Man's Chest).

FRIEDMAN, JOSEPH
Executive. b. New York, NY. e. City Coll. of New York, 1940-42, NYU, 1946-47. U.S. Navy 3 yrs. Asst. to nat'l dir. field exploitation, Warner Bros. Pictures, 1946-58; nat'l exploitation mgr., Paramount 1958-60; exec. asst. to dir. of adv., publicity & exploitation, Para., 1961; dir. adv. & pub., Paramount 1964; v.p., Para., 1966; v.p. in charge of mktg., 1968; v.p., adv., and p.r., Avco Embassy, 1969; v.p., p.r. American Film Theatre, 1973; v.p., adv. and p.r., ITC, motion picture div., 1976, pres., Joseph Friedman Mktg. & Adv., Inc., 1977. Exec. dir. New Jersey M.P. & T.V. Commission, 1978; v.p. worldwide adv./pub. /promo., Edie & Ely Landau, Inc., 1980; exec. dir., NJ Motion Picture & Television Commission, 1981.

FRIEDMAN, PAUL
Executive. e. Princeton U. Woodrow Wilson Sch. of Public & Intl. Affairs, Columbia Sch. of Journalism. 1967, joined NBC News as newswriter in NY; 1970-75, served as reporter for WRC-TV in D.C., field prod. for The Huntley-Brinkley Report, sr. prod. for NBC Weekend Nightly News, exec. prod. of News 4 New York, sr. prod. NBC Nightly News; 1976-79, was exec. prod. of Today; 1982, joined ABC News as sr, prod. in London; there became dir. of news coverage for Europe, Africa, Middle East; 1988-92, exec. prod. of World News Tonight With Peter Jennings; Jan. 1993 named exec. v.p. of ABC News.

FRIEDMAN, ROBERT G.
Executive. Began in the mailroom of Warner Bros. and moved up to president of Worldwide Advertising & Publicity. Currently vice chairman, Paramount Pictures Motion Picture Grp., (since 1996). Also currently a faculty member of the Independent Producers' Program, UCLA Dept. of Theater, Film and Television; member, Next Generation Council for the Motion Picture & Television Fund Found., member of the board of directors, Motion Picture Pioneers, and Southern Calif. Special Olympics.

FRIEDMAN, ROBERT L.
Executive. b. Bronx, NY, March 1, 1930. e. DeWitt Clinton H.S, Bronx. Started as radio announcer and commentator with Armed Forces Radio Service in Europe and U.S. sr. v.p., distrib. & mktg., United Artists Corp.; pres. domestic distribution, Columbia Pictures. 1984, named pres., AMC Entertainment Int'l Inc. 1992, named pres. of AMC Entertainment - the Motion Picture Group. On Century City bd. of dirs.; chmn. of Entertainment Industry Council. Member: M.P. Associates Foundation, Phila., pres. 2 yrs.; Variety Club (on board) M.P. Pioneers; (on board) area chmn. Distrib., chmn., Will Rogers Hospital Foundation, American Film Inst., Academy of M.P. Arts & Sciences. Member on DARE bd. of dirs.

FRIEDMAN, SEYMOUR MARK
Director. b. Detroit, MI, Aug. 17, 1917. e. Magdalene Coll., Cambridge, B.S. 1936; St. Mary's Hospital Medical Sch., London. Entered m.p. ind. as asst. film ed. 1937; 2nd asst. dir. 1938; 1st asst. dir. 1939, on budget pictures; entered U.S. Army 1942; returned to ind. 1946; dir. Columbia Pictures 1947. Vice president & executive production for Columbia Pictures Television, division of Columbia Pictures Industries, 1955. Member: Screen Directors Guild.
PICTURES: To the Ends of the Earth, Rusty's Birthday, Prison Warden, Her First Romance, Rookie Fireman, Son of Dr. Jekyll, Loan Shark, Flame of Calcutta, I'll Get You, Saint's Girl Friday, Khyber Patrol, African Manhunt, Secret of Treasure Mountain.

FRIELS, COLIN
Actor. b. Scotland, e. Australia Natl. Inst. of Dramatic Art. m. actress Judy Davis. First began acting with the State Theatre Co. of So. Australia and the Sydney Theatre Co. Theatre includes Sweet Bird of Youth and Hedda Gabler. TV includes special Stark.
PICTURES: Buddies, Monkey Grip, For the Term of His Natural Life, Kangaroo, Malcolm, High Tide, Ground Zero, Grievous Bodily Harm, Warm Nights on a Slow Moving Train, Darkman, Class Action, Dingo, A Good Man in Africa., Angel Baby, Back of Beyond.

FRIES, CHARLES W.
Executive, Producer. b. Cincinnati, OH. e. Ohio State U., B.S. Exec.-prod., Ziv Television; v.p., prod., Screen Gems; v.p., prod., Columbia Pictures; exec. v.p., prod. and exec. prod., Metromedia Prod. Corp., 1970-74; pres., exec. prod., Alpine Prods. and Charles Fries Prods. 1974-83; chmn. & pres., Fries Entertainment, 1984-1995; pres., Charles Fries Prods., 1996. Nat'l. treas., TV Academy; pres., Alliance TV Film Producers; exec. comm., MPPA. Chmn., Caucus of Producers, Writers and Directors, board of governors and exec. comm. of Academy of TV Arts and Sciences. Bd. trustees, secretary, Exec. committee & vice-chmn., American Film Institute. V.P. & dir. of the Center Theatre Group.
PICTURES: *Prod.*: Cat People, Flowers in the Attic, Troop Beverly Hills, Screamers.
TELEVISION: *Movies*: Toughlove, The Right of the People, Intimate Strangers, Bitter Harvest, A Rumor of War, Blood Vows: The Story of a Mafia Wife, The Alamo: 13 Days to Glory, Intimate Betrayal, Drop Out Mother, Crash Course, Supercarrier, Bridge to Silence, The Case of the Hillside Strangler, Deadly Web. Small Sacrifices, The Martian Chronicles. *Specials:* It's Howdy Doody Time: A 40 Year Celebration.

FRONTIERE, DOMINIC
Executive, Composer. b. New Haven, CT, June 17, 1931. e. Yale School of Music. Studied composing, arranging and conducting; concert accordionist, World's Champion Accordionist, 1943; An Hour with Dominic Frontiere, WNHC-TV, New Haven, 3 years, 1947; exec. vice-pres., musical dir., Daystar Prods. Composer or arranger over 75 films.
PICTURES: Giant, Gentlemen Prefer Blondes, Let's Make Love, High Noon, Meet Me in Las Vegas, 10,000 Bedrooms, Hit the Deck, Marriage-Go-Round, The Right Approach, One Foot in Hell, Hero's Island, Hang 'Em High, Popi, Barquero, Chisum, A for Alpha, Cancel My Reservation, Hammersmith is Out, Freebie and the Bean, Brannigan, The Gumball Rally, Cleopatra Jones and the Casino of Gold, The Stunt Man, Modern Problems, The Aviator.
TELEVISION: *Composer-conductor*: The New Breed, Stoney Burke, Bankamericard commercials (Venice Film Fest. Award for best use of original classical music for filmed TV commercials), Outer Limits, Branded, Iron Horse, Rat Patrol, Flying Nun, The Invaders, Name of the Game, That Girl, Twelve O'Clock High, Zig Zag, The Young Rebel, The Immortal, Fugitive, The Love War. *Movie*: Washington Behind Closed Doors.

FRUMKES, EDWARD E.
Executive. b. New York, May 1, 1958. e. George Washington University. BA intl finance, MBA intl marketing. Joined Columbia Pictures as Intl. Financial Analyst, then became mgr. special projects. Moved to London as Columbia's Dir., ad-pub., Europe, Africa, Middle East. Returned to NY as v.p. ad-pub. Joined Warner Bros. in 1988 as Dir., intl. thearical dist; v.p., 1989; sr. v.p., 1992; exec. v.p., 1993; pres., WB Intl. theatrical dist., 1996

FUCHS, FRED
Producer.
PICTURES: *Exec. Prod.*: Vietnam War Story: The Last Days, The Spirit of '76, The Godfather: Part III, The Secret Garden, Mary Shelley's Frankenstein, Don Juan DeMarco, Haunted, Jack, Buddy, The Rainmaker. Producer: New York Stories (segment 2), Tucker: The Man and His Dream, Bram Stoker's Dracula
TELEVISION: *Series*: Faerie Tale Theater. *Mini-Series*: The Odyssey. *Movies*: Dark Angel.

FUCHS, LEO L.
Independent producer. b. Vienna, June 14, 1929. Moved to U.S., 1939. e. Vienna and New York. U.S. Army cameraman 1951-53; int'l. mag. photographer until entered motion pictures as producer with Universal in Hollywood in 1961.
PICTURES: Gambit, A Fine Pair, Sunday Lovers, Just the Way You Are.

FUCHS, MICHAEL
Executive. b. New York, NY, March 9, 1946. e. Union Coll., NYU Law School (J.D. degree). Show business lawyer before joining Home Box Office in 1976, developing original and sports programming. Named chmn. and CEO of HBO in 1984. 1982-87, v.p. Time Inc. in NY; 1987-1995, exec. v.p. Time Inc.

FUEST, ROBERT
Director. b. London, 1927. Early career as painter, graphic designer. Ent. TV industry as designer with ABC-TV, 1958. 1962: directing doc., commercials. 1966: Wrote and dir. Just Like a Woman, 1967-68; dir. 7 episodes of The Avengers, 1969: wrote and directed 6 episodes of The Optimists.
PICTURES: And Soon the Darkness, Wuthering Heights, Doctor Phibes, Doctor Phibes Rides Again (also s.p.), The Final Programme (also s.p., design), The Devil's Rain, The Geller Effect (s.p. only), The New Avengers, The Gold Bug, Revenge of the Stepford Wives, The Big Stuffed Dog, Mystery on Fire Island, Aphrodite, Worlds Beyond, Cat's Eyes.

FURIE, SIDNEY J.
Director, Writer, Producer. b. Toronto, Canada, Feb. 28, 1933. Ent. TV and films 1954. Canadian features include: Dangerous Age, A Cool Sound from Hell. Also dir. many Hudson Bay TV series. To England 1960. 1961 appt. exec. dir. Galaworldfilm Productions, Ltd.
PICTURES: The Snake Woman, Doctor Blood's Coffin, Wonderful to Be Young, Night of Passion (also prod., s.p.), The Young Ones, The Leather Boys, Wonderful Life, The Ipcress File, The Appaloosa, The Naked Runner, The Lawyer, Little Fauss and Big Halsy, Lady Sings the Blues, Hit!, Sheila Levine Is Dead and Living in New York, Gable and Lombard, The Boys in Company C, The Entity, Purple Hearts (also prod., s.p.), Iron Eagle, Superman IV: The Quest For Peace, Iron Eagle II (also co-s.p.), The Taking of Beverly Hills, Ladybugs, Hollow Point, Iron Eagle IV, The Rage, Top of the World.

FURLONG, EDWARD
Actor. b. Glendale, CA, Aug. 2, 1977. Discovered by casting agent for Terminator 2, having no previous acting experience. Appeared in Aerosmith video Livin' on the Edge.
PICTURES: Terminator 2: Judgment Day (debut, 1991), Pet Sematary 2, American Heart, A Home of Our Own, Brainscan, Little Odessa, The Grass Harp, Before and After, Pecker, American History X, Detroit Rock City, The Animal Factory, The Knights of the Quest, Terminator 3.

FURMAN, ROY L.
Attorney, Executive. b. New York, NY, April 19, 1939. e. Brooklyn Coll., A.B. 1960; Harvard U., L.L.B. 1963. Pres., Furman Selz. Chmn., Film Society of Lincoln Center.

FURST, AUSTIN O.
Executive. e. Lehigh U., B.S. in economics/marketing. Began career in mktg. dept., Proctor and Gamble; 1972, joined Time Inc. as dir., new subscription sales for Time magazine; later joined Time Inc.'s new magazine dev. staff for People magazine; named circulation mgr., People magazine, 1974; 1975 named pres., Time Inc.'s Computer Television Inc., a pay-per-view hotel operation and was responsible for successful turnaround and sale of co.; 1976, v.p., programming, Home Box Office; named exec. v.p. HBO, 1979; appointed pres. and CEO, Time-Life Films, Inc., 1980; 1981 established Vestron after acquiring home video rights to Time/Life Video Library; chmn. and CEO, Vestron, Inc.

G

GABLER, ELIZABETH
Executive. Began career as literary agent at ICM and creative exec., Columbia Pictures; v.p. of production, United Artists; exec. v.p. of production, Twentieth Century Fox, 1988. Currently president, Fox 2000 Pictures, 1999.

GABOR, ZSA ZSA
Actress. r.n. Sari Gabor. b. Hungary, Feb. 6, 1918. e. Lausanne, Switzerland. Stage debut in Europe. *Author*: Zsa Zsa's Complete Guide to Men (1969), How to Get a Man How to Keep a Man and How to Get Rid of a Man (1971), One Lifetime is Not Enough (1991). As accomplished horsewoman has won many prizes in various intl. horse shows. Stage work incl. 40 Carats, Blithe Spirit.

PICTURES: Lovely to Look At, We're Not Married, Moulin Rouge, The Story of Three Loves, Lili, Three Ring Circus, The Most Wanted Man in the World, Death of a Scoundrel, Girl in the Kremlin, The Man Who Wouldn't Talk, Touch of Evil, Queen of Outer Space, Country Music Holiday, For the First Time, Pepe, Boys' Night Out, Picture Mommy Dead, Arrivederci Baby, Jack of Diamonds, Won Ton Ton the Dog Who Saved Hollywood, Frankenstein's Great Aunt Tillie, A Nightmare on Elm Street 3, The Naked Gun 2 1/2: The Smell of Fear, Happily Ever After (voice).

GAIL, MAX
Actor. b. Grosse Ile, MI, Apr. 5, 1943. e. William Coll. B.A. Economics, Univ. of Mich M.B.A.
THEATER: *NY*: The Babe, One Flew Over the Cuckoo's Nest (also S.F.). *LA*: Visions of Kerouac.
PICTURES: The Organization, Dirty Harry, D.C. Cab, Heartbreakers, Pontiac Moon, Mind Lies, Sodbusters, Ox and the Eye, Lords of Tanglewood.
TELEVISION: *Series*: Barney Miller, Whiz Kids, Normal Life. *Mini-Series*: Pearl. *Movies*: The Priest Killer, Like Mom Like Me, Desperate Women, The 11th Victim, The Aliens Are Coming, Fun and Games, Letting Go, The Other Lover, Killer in the Mirror, Intimate Strangers, Can You Feel Me Dancing?, Tonight's the Night, Man Against the Mob, The Outside Woman, Ride With the Wind, Robin Cook's Mortal Fear, Naomi & Winona: Love Can Build a Bridge, Secret Agent (prod.), Wrong Side of the Fence (prod.).

GALE, BOB
Writer, Producer. b. St. Louis, MO, May 25, 1951. e. USC Sch. of Cinema. Joined with friend Robert Zemeckis to write screenplays, starting with episode for TV series, McCloud. Also co-wrote story for The Nightstalker series. Turned to feature films, co-writing with Zemeckis script for I Wanna Hold Your Hand, on which Gale also acted as associate producer. Exec. prod. of CBS animated series Back to the Future. Wrote and directed interactive feature Mr. Payback.
PICTURES: I Wanna Hold Your Hand (co-s.p., co-assoc. prod.), 1941 (co-s.p.), Used Cars (prod., co-s.p.), Back to the Future (co.-prod., s.p.), Back to the Future Part II (prod., co-s.p.), Back to the Future Part III (prod., s.p.), Trespass (co-exec. prod., co-s.p.), Tales From the Crypt: Bordello of Blood (co-s.p.).
TELEVISION: *Series:* Back to the Future (animated; exec. prod.), Tales From the Crypt (wrote, dir. House of Horror).

GALE, GEORGE
Executive. b. Budapest, Hungary, May 26, 1919. e. Sorbonne U., Paris, France. Feature editor, Budapest Ed., U.S. Army Pictorial Service. Feature and TV editor MGM, Hal Roach, Disney Studios; prod. and prod. exec. Ivan Tors; American National Enterprises, Inc. Producer and director. Supervised the production of over 30 features for tv syndication and numerous theatrical features. Member ACE and Academy of Motion Picture Arts and Sciences. Formed George Gale Productions, Inc. in 1976. Currently V.P. Post Production for N.U. Image Beverly Hills, CA.

GALLAGHER, PETER
Actor. b. New York, NY, Aug. 19, 1955. e. Tufts Univ.
THEATER: *NY*: Hair (1977 revival), Grease, A Doll's Life (Theatre World Award), The Corn is Green, The Real Thing (Clarence Derwent Award), Long Day's Journey Into Night (Tony Award nom.; also London), Guys & Dolls. Also: Another Country, Pride & Prejudice (both Long Wharf), Pal Joey.
PICTURES: The Idolmaker (debut, 1980), Summer Lovers, Dream Child, My Little Girl, High Spirits, Sex Lies and Videotape, Tune in Tomorrow, Late for Dinner, The Cabinet of Dr. Ramirez, The Player, Bob Roberts, Watch It, Malice, Short Cuts, Mother's Boys, The Hudsucker Proxy, Mrs. Parker and the Vicious Circle, While You Were Sleeping, The Underneath, Cafe Society, The Last Dance, To Gillian on Her 37th Birthday, The Man Who Knew Too Little, Johnny Skidmarks, American Beauty.
TELEVISION: *Series*: Skag, The Secret Lives of Men. *Movies*: Skag, Terrible Joe Moran, The Caine Mutiny Court-Martial, The Murder of Mary Phagan, I'll Be Home for Christmas, Love and Lies, An Inconvenient Woman, White Mile, Titanic, Path to Paradise, The Frightening Frammis, The Quiet Room, The Cabinet of Dr. Ramirez, Virtual Obsession, Host. *Specials*: The Big Knife, Long Day's Journey Into Night, Private Contentment, Guys & Dolls: Off the Record. *Mini-series*: Brave New World.

GALLIGAN, ZACH
Actor. b. New York, NY, Feb. 14, 1964. e. Columbia U.
PICTURES: Gremlins, Nothing Lasts Forever, Waxwork, Mortal Passions, Rising Storm, Gremlins II, Zandalee, Waxwork II: Lost in Time, Round Trip to Heaven, All Tied Up, Warlock: The Armageddon, Ice, Caroline at Midnight, The First to Go, Prince Valiant, Cupid.
TELEVISION: *Movies*: Jacobo Timerman: Prisoner Without a Name Cell Without a Number, Surviving, Psychic, For Love and Glory. *Specials*: The Prodigious Hickey, The Return of Hickey, The Beginning of the Firm, A Very Delicate Matter, The Hitchhiker: Toxic Shock. *Mini-Series*: Crossings. *Pilot*: Interns in Heat. *Guest:* Tales From the Crypt (Strung Along), Melrose Place, Extreme.

GAMBON, MICHAEL
Actor. b. Dublin, Ireland, Oct. 19, 1940. Ent. ind. 1966. Early experience in theatre. 1985-87 Acting at National Theatre and London's West End. 1988: in Harold Pinter's Mountain Language.
PICTURES: Othello, The Beast Must Die, Turtle Diary, Paris By Night, The Rachel Papers, A Dry White Season, The Cook the Thief His Wife and Her Lover, Mobsters, Toys, Clean Slate, The Browning Version, Squanto: A Warrior's Tale, A Man of No Importance, Midnight in St. Petersberg, Bullet to Beijing, The Innocent Sleep, Nothing Personal, Mary Reilly, The Wings of the Dove, The Gambler, Plunkett & MacLeane, Dancing at Lughnasa.
TELEVISION: Uncle Vanya, Ghosts, Oscar Wilde, The Holy Experiment, Absurd Person Singular, The Singing Detective (serial), The Heat of the Day, The Storyteller, Maigret Sets a Trap, Samson & Delilah.

GAMMON, JAMES
Actor. b. Newman, IL, Apr. 20. e. Boone H.S., Orlando, FL. Former television cameraman. First acting role was small part on Gunsmoke. Head of Los Angeles' Met Theatre for 10 years.
THEATER: The Dark at the Top of the Stairs (L.A. Critics Circle Award, best actor), Bus Stop (L.A. Drama Critics award, best director), Curse of the Starving Class (NY, L.A.), A Lie of the Mind (NY, L.A.).
PICTURES: Cool Hand Luke (debut, 1967), Journey to Shiloh, Macho Callahan, A Man Called Horse, Macon County Line, Black Oak Conspiracy, Urban Cowboy, Any Which Way You Can, Smithereens, Vision Quest, Sylvester, Silverado, Silver Bullet, Made in Heaven, Ironweed, The Milagro Beanfield War, Major League, Revenge, Coupe de Ville, I Love You to Death, Leaving Normal, Crisscross, The Painted Desert, Running Cool, Cabin Boy, Vegas Vice, Natural Born Killers, Wild Bill.
TELEVISION: *Series*: Bagdad Cafe. *Guest*: Bonanza, The Wild Wild West, Cagney & Lacey, The Equalizer, Crime Story, Midnight Caller. *Movies*: Kansas City Massacre, Rage, Women of San Quentin, M.A.D.D.: Mothers Against Drunk Drivers, Hell Town, The Long Hot Summer, Roe vs. Wade, Dead Aim, Conagher, Stranger at My Door, Men Don't Tell, Truman. *Mini-Series*: Lincoln.

GANDOLFINI, JAMES
Actor. b. NJ, 1961.
PICTURES: A Stranger Among Us, True Romance, Mr Wonderful, Money for Nothing, Angie, Terminal Velocity, The New World, Crimson Tide, Get Shorty, The Juror, She's So Lovely, Night Falls on Manhattan, Perdita Durango, The Mighty, A Civil Action, Fallen, 8MM, The Mexican, The Barber Project.
TELEVISION: *Movies:* 12 Angry Men. *Series:* The Sopranos.

GANIS, SIDNEY M.
Executive. b. New York, NY, Jan. 8, 1940. e. Brooklyn Coll. Staff writer, newspaper and wire service contact, 20th Century-Fox 1961-62; radio, TV contact and special projects, Columbia Pictures 1963-64. Joined Seven Arts Prod. 1965 as publicity mgr.; 1967, appt. prod. publicity mgr. Warner-7 Arts, Ass't prod., There Was a Crooked Man, 1969. Studio publicity dir., Cinema Center Films, 1970. Director of Ad-Pub for Mame, Warner Bros., 1973; Director of Advertising, Warner Bros., 1974; named WB v.p., worldwide adv. & pub., 1977; 1979, sr. v.p., Lucasfilm, Ltd.; 1982 Emmy winner, exec. prod., best documentary, The Making of Raiders of the Lost Ark. 1986, joined Paramount Pictures as pres., worldwide mktg; 1986, named pres., Paramount Motion Picture Group. 1988, elected trustee University Art Museum, Berkeley, CA. 1991, appointed exec. v.p., Sony Pictures Ent. Exec. v.p., pres. mktg. & distrib., Columbia Pictures, 1992. Elected to bd. of govs. AMPAS, 1992. Vice chmn., Columbia Pictures, 1994. Pres., worldwide mktg., Columbia TriStar. Pres. Out of the Blue... Ent., 1997.

GANZ, BRUNO
Actor. b. Zurich, Switzerland, March 22, 1941. Theatre debut in 1961. Founded the Berlin Theatre troupe, Schaubuehne, with Peter Stein in 1970.
THEATER: Hamlet (1967), Dans La Jungle Des Villes, Torquato Tasso, La Chevauchee Sur Le Lac de Constance, Peer Gynt.
PICTURES: Der Sanfte Lauf (1967), Sommergaste, The Marquise of O, Lumiere, The Wild Duck, The American Friend, The Lefthanded Woman, The Boys from Brazil, Black and White Like Day and Night, Knife in the Head, Nosferatu the Vampyre, Return of a Good Friend, 5% Risk, An Italian Woman, Polenta, La Provinciale, La Dame Aux Camelias, Der Erfinder, Etwas Wird Sichtbar, Circle of Deceit, Hande Hoch, Logik Der Gerfuhls, War and Peace, In the White City, System Ohne Schatten, Der Pendler, Wings of Desire, Bankomatt, Strapless, The Last Days of Chez Nous, Especially on Sunday, Faraway So Close!, Heller Tag, Lumiere & Company, Saint-Ex, Eternity and a Day.
TELEVISION: Father and Son, Todliches Schweigen, Ein Richter In Angst, Tatort — Schattenwelt (German TV), Gegen Ende der Nacht. *Mini-series*: Grande Fausto II.

GANZ, LOWELL
Writer, Producer, Director. b. New York, NY, Aug. 31, 1948. e. Queens Col. Worked as staff writer on tv series The Odd Couple. Met writing partner Babaloo Mandel at The Comedy Store in the early 1970s. Was co-creator Laverne & Shirley. First teamed with Mandel on script for 1982 comedy Night Shift.
PICTURES: *Writer*: Night Shift, Splash (Acad. Award nom.; also actor), Spies Likes Us, Gung Ho, Vibes, Parenthood (also actor), City Slickers, A League of Their Own (also actor), Mr. Saturday Night (also actor), Greedy (also actor), City Slickers II: The Legend of Curly's Gold, Forget Paris, Multiplicity, Father's Day, The Secret Life of Walter Mitty, Doctor Dolittle.
TELEVISION: *Writer-Exec. Prod* (series): The Odd Couple, Happy Days, Busting Loose, The Ted Knight Show, Makin' It, Joanie Loves Chachi, Gung Ho, Knight and Dave, Parenthood. *Producer*: Laverne & Shirley (also writer).

GANZ, TONY
Producer. b. New York, NY. e. studied film at Harvard U. Produced documentaries for PBS in N.Y. Moved to L.A. 1973 where in charge of dev., Charles Fries Productions. Then joined Ron Howard Productions 1980. Left to form own prod. co. with Deborah Blum.
PICTURES: Gung Ho, Clean and Sober, Vibes.
TELEVISION: *Series*: American Dream Machine, Maximum Security (exec. prod.). *Movies*: Bitter Harvest, Into Thin Air.

GARCIA, ANDY
Actor. r.n. Andres Arturo Garcia Menendez. b. Havana, Cuba, Apr. 12, 1956. Family moved to Miami Beach in 1961. e. Florida International U, Miami. Spent several years acting with regional theaters in Florida; also part of improv. group. Music producer of album: Cachao Master Sessions Vol. I (Grammy Award), Chachao Master Sessions Vol II (Grammy nom.).
PICTURES: The Mean Season, 8 Million Ways to Die, The Untouchables, Stand and Deliver, American Roulette, Black Rain, Internal Affairs, A Show of Force, The Godfather Part III (Acad. Award nom.), Dead Again, Hero, Jennifer Eight, Cachao... Como Su Ritmo No Hay Dos (Like His Rhythm There Is No Other; also dir., co-prod.), When a Man Loves a Woman, Steal Big Steal Little, Things to Do in Denver When You're Dead, Night Falls on Manhattan, The Disappearance of Garcia Lorca, Hoodlum, Desperate Measures, Just the Ticket (also prod.), Sins of the Father, Just to Be Together, Just Like Mona.
TELEVISION: *Movie*: Clinton and Nadine, Swing Vote (also co-exec. prod.).

GARDINER, PETER R.
Executive. b. Santa Monica, CA, Apr. 25, 1949. Independent still photographer and industrial filmmaker before joining Paramount, 1973, in feature post-prod. 1979, joined Warner Bros. as asst. dir., corporate services. 1987, promoted to v.p., opns., WB corporate film-video services. 1993, promoted to v.p. Warner Bros. corp. film & video services.

GARDNER, ARTHUR
Producer. b. Marinette, WI, June 7. e. Marinette h.s. Entered m.p. ind. as actor, in orig. cast All Quiet on the Western Front, 1929. Juvenile leads in: Waterfront, Heart of the North, Assassin of Youth, Religious Racketeer; production, asst. dir. King Bros. 1941, then asst. prod. U.S. Air Force 1st Motion Picture Unit, 1943-45. Formed Levy-Gardner-Laven Prods. with Jules Levy, Arnold Laven, 1951.
PICTURES: (Asst. dir.): Paper Bullets, I Killed That Man, Rubber Racketeers, Klondike Fury, I Escaped From the Gestapo, Suspense; *Asst. prod.*: Gangster, Dude Goes West, Badmen of Tombstone, Gun Crazy, Mutiny, Southside 1-1000. *Prod.*: Without Warning, Vice Squad, Down Three Dark Streets, Return of Dracula, The Flame Barrier, The Vampire, The Monster that Challenged the World. Geronimo, The Glory Guys, Clambake, Scalphunters, Sam Whiskey, Underground, McKenzie Break, The Honkers, Hunting Party, Kansas City Bomber, White Lightning, McQ, Brannigan, Gator, Safari 3000.
TELEVISION: The Rifleman, Robert Taylor's Detectives, Law of the Plainsman, The Big Valley.

GARFIELD, ALLEN
Actor. r.n. Allen Goorwitz. b. Newark, NJ, Nov. 22, 1939. e. Upsala Col, Actors Studio. Worked as journalist for Newark Star Ledger and Sydney Morning Herald (Australia) prior to becoming an actor. Has also acted as Allen Goorwitz. Life Member of the Actors Studio, NYC.
PICTURES: Greetings, Putney Swope, Hi Mom!, The Owl and the Pussycat, Bananas, Believe in Me, Roommates, The Organization, Taking Off, Cry Uncle!, You've Got to Walk it Like You Talk It or You'll Lose That Beat, Get to Know Your Rabbit, The Candidate, Top of the Heap, Deadhead Miles, Slither, Busting, The Conversation, The Front Page, Nashville, Gable and Lombard, Mother Jugs & Speed, The Brink's Job, Skateboard, Paco, One-Trick Pony, The Stunt Man, Continental Divide, One from the Heart, The State of Things, The Black Stallion Returns, Get Crazy, Irreconcilable Differences, Teachers, The Cotton Club, Desert Bloom, Beverly Hills Cop II, Rich Boys, Let it Ride, Night Visitor, Dick Tracy, Club Fed, Until the End of the World, Jack and His Friends, Family Prayers, The Patriots, The Glass Shadow, Miracle Beach, Sketches of a Strangler, Destiny Turns on the Radio, Diabolique.
TELEVISION: *Movies*: Footsteps, The Marcus-Nelson Murders, The Virginia Hill Story, Serpico: The Deadly Game, The Million Dollar Rip-Off, Nowhere to Run, Ring of Passion, Leave 'Em Laughing, Citizen Cohn, Killer in the Mirror, Incident at Vichy, Judgment: The Trial of Julius and Ethel Rosenberg. *Guest*: Law and Order, Equal Justice, Eddie Dodd, Jack's Place, Taxi.

GARFINKLE, LOUIS
Writer, Director, Producer. b. Seattle, WA, February 11, 1928. e. U. of California, U. of Washington, U. of Southern California (B.A., 1948). Writer KOMO, Seattle, 1945; Executive Research, Inc., 1948; writer, educ. doc. screenplays, Emerson Films, EBF. 1948-50; s.p. You Can Beat the A-Bomb (RKO), 1950; writer-dir. training films, info. films, Signal Photo, 1950-53; copy, Weinberg Adv., 1953; head of doc. research in TV, U. of California, Berkeley, 1954-55; staff, Sheilah Graham Show, 1955; formed Maxim Prod. Inc. with Albert Band, 1956. Co-creator Collaborator Interactive Computer Software to asst. in writing stories for screen & TV, 1990; formed Collaborator Systems Inc. with Cary Brown and Francis X. Feighan, 1991. Received Best Screenwriting Tool Award from Screen Writers Forum, 1991. Member: AMPAS, WGA West, ATAS, Dramatists Guild, Board of Advisers Filmic Writing Major, USC School of Cinema & TV.
PICTURES: *Screenplay*: The Young Guns (also story), I Bury the Living (also story, co-prod.), Face of Fire (also co-prod.), Hellbenders, A Minute to Pray A Second to Die, The Love Doctors (also story, prod.), Beautiful People, The Models (also story), The Doberman Gang (also story), Little Cigars (also story), The Deer Hunter (story collab.; Acad. Award nom.), Milena.
TELEVISION: *Writer*: 712 teleplays for Day in Court, Morning Court, Accused, 1959-66. *Co-writer-creator*: Direct Line (pilot), June Allyson Show, Threat of Evil, Death Valley Days, Crullers At Sundown, Captain Dick Mine, No. 3 Peanut Place (pilot).

GARFUNKEL, ART
Singer, Actor. b. New York, NY, Nov. 5, 1942. e. Columbia Coll. Began singing at age 4. Long partnership with Paul Simon began in grade school at 13 in Queens, NY; first big success in 1965 with hit single, Sound of Silence. Partnership dissolved in 1970. Winner of 4 Grammy Awards.
PICTURES: Catch-22 (debut, 1970), Carnal Knowledge, Bad Timing/A Sensual Obsession, Good to Go, Boxing Helena.

GARLAND, BEVERLY
Actress. r.n. Beverly Fessenden. b. Santa Cruz, CA, Oct. 17, 1930. e. Glendale Coll., 1945-47.
PICTURES: D.O.A., The Glass Web, Miami Story, Bittercreek, Two Guns and a Badge, Killer Leopard, The Rocket Man, Sudden Danger, Desperate Hours, Curucu: Beast of the Amazon, Gunslinger, Swamp Woman, The Steel Jungle, It Conquered the World, Not of This Earth, Naked Paradise, The Joker is Wild, Chicago Confidential, Badlands of Montana, The Saga of Hemp Brown, Alligator People, Stark Fever, Twice Told Tales, Pretty Poison, The Mad Room, Where the Red Fern Grows, Airport 1975, Roller Boogie, It's My Turn, Death Falls, Haunted Symphony.
TELEVISION: *Series*: Mama Rosa, Pantomime Quiz, The Bing Crosby Show, My Three Sons, Scarecrow & Mrs. King, Decoy. *Guest*: Twilight Zone, Dr. Kildare, Medic (Emmy nom.), Magnum P.I., Remington Steele, Lois and Clark. *Movies*: Cutter's Trail, Say Goodbye Maggie Cole, Weekend Nun, Voyage of the Yes, Unwed Father, Healers, Day the Earth Moved, This Girl for Hire, The World's Oldest Living Bridesmaid, Finding the Way Home.

GARNER, JAMES
Actor. r.n. James Baumgarner. b. Norman, OK, April 7, 1928. e. Norman H.S. Joined Merchant Marine, U.S. Army, served in Korean War. Prod. Paul Gregory suggested acting career. Studied drama at N.Y. Berghof School. Toured with road companies; Warner Bros. studio contract followed.
PICTURES: Toward the Unknown (debut, 1956), The Girl He Left Behind, Shoot Out at Medicine Bend, Sayonara, Darby's Rangers, Up Periscope, Alias Jesse James (cameo), Cash McCall, The Children's Hour, Boys' Night Out, The Great Escape, The Thrill of It All, The Wheeler Dealers, Move Over Darling, The Americanization of Emily, 36 Hours, The Art of Love, Mister Buddwing, A Man Could Get Killed, Duel at Diablo, Grand Prix, Hour of the Gun, The Pink Jungle, How Sweet It Is, Support Your Local Sheriff, Marlowe, A Man Called Sledge, Support Your Local Gunfighter, Skin Game, They Only Kill Their Masters, One Little Indian, The Castaway Cowboy, Health, The Fan, Victor/Victoria, Tank, Murphy's Romance (Acad. Award nom.), Sunset, The Distinguished Gentleman, Fire in the Sky, Maverick, My Fellow Americans, The Hidden Dimension, Twilight.
TELEVISION: *Series*: Maverick, Nichols, The Rockford Files, Bret Maverick, Man of the People. *Movies*: The Rockford Files (pilot), The New Maverick (pilot), The Long Summer of George Adams, The Glitter Dome, Heartsounds, Promise (also exec. prod.), Obsessive Love, My Name Is Bill W. (also exec. prod.), Decoration Day, Barbarians at the Gate, The Rockford Files: I Still Love L.A. (also co-exec. prod.), The Rockford Files: A Blessing in Disguise (also co-exec. prod.), The Rockford Files: Godfather Knows Best, The Rockford Files: Friends and Foul Play, The Rockford Files: Crime and Punishment, Dead Silence, The Rockford Files: Murder and Misdemeanors, Legalese, The Rockford Files: If It Bleeds...It Leeds. *Mini-Series*: Space. *Specials:* Sixty Years of Seduction, Lily for President.

GAROFALO, JANEANE
Actress. b. Newton, NJ, Sept. 28, 1964. Created I Hate Myself Productions.
PICTURES: Late for Dinner, Reality Bites, Suspicious, I Shot a Man in Vegas, Bye Bye Love, Coldblooded, Now and Then, Kids in the Hall: Brian Candy, The Truth About Cats and Dogs, The Cable Guy, Larger than Life, Sweethearts, Touch, Romy and Michele's High School Reunion, Cop Land, The Matchmaker, Clay Pigeons, Dog Park, Thick as Thieves, Steal This Movie, 200 Cigarettes, Half Baked, Permanent Midnight, Mystery Men, The Minus Man, Dogma, Can't Stop Dancing, The Bumblebee Flies Anyway, The Adventures of Rocky and Bullwinkle, Titan A.E. (voice), Wet Hot Summer, Nobody Knows Anything, The Search for John Gissing, Big Trouble.
TELEVISION: *Series*: Saturday Night Live, The Larry Sanders Show, The Ben Stiller Show, TV Nation. *Mini-series*: Tales of the City. *Guest*: Law & Order, Seinfeld, Home Improvement, Felicity (voice), Ellen, NewsRadio, Dr. Katz— Professional Therapist (voice), Mad About You (voice), The Simpsons (voice).

GARR, TERI
Actress. b. Lakewood, OH, Dec. 11, 1949. Began career as dancer, performing S.F. Ballet at 13. Later appeared with L.S. Ballet and in original road show co. of West Side Story. Several film appearances as a dancer incl. Fun in Acapulco, Viva Las Vegas, What a Way to Go, Roustabout, etc. Did commercials; appeared in film Head written by a fellow acting student, Jack Nicholson. Career boosted by appearance on TV as semi-regular on The Sonny and Cher Show.
PICTURES: Maryjane, Head, The Moonshine War, The Conversation, Young Frankenstein, Won Ton Ton the Dog Who Saved Hollywood, Oh God!, Close Encounters of the Third Kind, Mr. Mike's Mondo Video, The Black Stallion, Witches' Brew, Honky Tonk Freeway, One from the Heart, The Escape Artist, Tootsie (Acad. Award nom.), The Sting II, The Black Stallion Returns, Mr. Mom, Firstborn, Miracles, After Hours, Full Moon in Blue Water, Out Cold, Let It Ride, Short Time, Waiting for the Light, The Player, Mom and Dad Save the World, Dumb & Dumber, Ready to Wear (Pret-a-Porter), Michael, A Simple Wish, The Definite Maybe, Changing Habits, The Sky is Falling, Kill the Man, Dick.
TELEVISION: *Series regular*: Shindig, The Ken Berry "Wow" Show, (1972), Burns and Schreiber Comedy Hour, Girl With Something Extra, The Sonny and Cher Comedy Hour, The Sonny Comedy Revue, Good and Evil, Good Advice, Women of the House. *Movies*: Law and Order, Doctor Franken, Prime Suspect, Winter of Our Discontent, To Catch a King, Intimate Strangers, Pack of Lies, A Quiet Little Neighborhood A Perfect Little Murder, Stranger in the Family, Deliver Them From Evil: The Taking of Alta View, Fugitive Nights: Danger in the Desert, Murder Live!, Nightscream, Half a Dozen Babies. *Specials*: The Frog Prince (Faerie Tale Theatre), Drive She Said (Trying Times), Paul Reiser: Out on a Whim, Mother Goose Rock 'n' Rhyme, The Whole Shebang, Aliens for Breakfast. *Mini-Series*: Fresno. *Guest*: Tales from the Crypt (The Trap), The Larry Sanders Show.

GARRETT, BETTY
Singer, Actress. b. St. Joseph, MO, May 23, 1919. e. scholarships: Annie Wright Seminary, Tacoma, WA; Neighborhood Playhouse, N.Y. Sang in night clubs, hotels, Broadway shows: Call Me Mister (Donaldson Award, 1946), Spoon River Anthology, A Girl Could Get Lucky, Meet Me in St. Louis (1989). Motion Picture Herald, Star of Tomorrow, 1949. Starred in one woman show, Betty Garrett and Other Songs, beginning in 1974 and touring through 1993 (Bay Area Critics & LA Drama Critics Awards); also in autobiographical show, No Dogs or Actors Allowed (Pasadena Playhouse, 1989), So There! (with Dale Gonyear; Pasadena Playhouse, 1993). Given Life Achievement Award by Los Angeles Drama Critics Circle, 1995. With Ron Rapaport author of Betty Garrett and Other Songs—A Life on Stage & Screen, 1998.
PICTURES: The Big City (debut, 1948), Words and Music, Take Me Out to the Ball Game, Neptune's Daughter, On the Town, My Sister Eileen, Shadow on the Window.
TELEVISION: *Series*: All in the Family, Laverne and Shirley. *Guest*: Love Boat, Black's Magic, Somerset Gardens, Murder She Wrote, Harts of the West, The Good Life. Movies: All the Way Home, Who's Happy Now, Golden Girls, Townies..

GARY, LORRAINE
Actress. b. New York, NY, Aug. 16, 1937. r.n. Lorraine Gottfried. m. executive Sidney J. Scheinberg. e. Columbia Univ.
PICTURES: Jaws, Car Wash, I Never Promised You a Rose Garden, Jaws 2, Just You and Me Kid, 1941, Jaws-The Revenge.
TELEVSION: *Movies*: The City, The Marcus-Nelson Murders, Partners in Crime, Pray for the Wildcats, Man on the Outside, Lanigan's Rabbi, Crash.

GASSMAN, VITTORIO
Actor. b. Genoa, Italy, Sept. 1, 1922. e. Acad. of Dramatic Art, Rome. Stage actor, 1943; m.p. debut, 1946.
PICTURES: Daniele Cortis, Mysterious Rider, Bitter Rice, Lure of Sila, The Outlaws, Anna, Streets of Sorrow; to U.S., Cry of the Hunted, Sombrero, The Glass Wall, Rhapsody, Girls Marked Danger, Mambo, War and Peace, World's Most Beautiful Woman, Tempest, The Love Specialist, The Great War, Let's Talk About Women, Il Successo, The Tiger, Woman Times Seven, Ghosts-Italian Style, Scent of a Woman, Viva Italia!, A Wedding, Quintet, Immortal Bachelor, The Nude Bomb, Sharky's Machine, Tempest, I Picari, The Family, The Sleazy Uncle, The House of the Lord, The Hateful Dead, To Forget Palermo, Los Alegres Picaro, Scheherzade, The Long Winter, Sleepers.

GATES, WILLIAM H.
Executive. b. 1957. Started computer programming at age 13. 1974, developed BASIC for the first microcomputer, MITS Altair. 1975, with Paul Allen formed Microsoft to develop software for personal computers. Chmn. & CEO of Microsoft Corp. leading provider of worldwide software for personal computers.

GATWARD, JAMES
Executive. b. London, England. Ent. Ind. 1957. Early career as freelance drama prod. dir. in Canada, USA, UK (with ITV & BBC). Prod. dir. various intern. co-productions in UK, Ceylond, Australia, Germany. Currently chief executive and Dep. chmn. TVS Television Ltd., chmn. Telso Communications Ltd., dir. of ITN, Channel Four, Super Channel, Oracle Teletext.

GAVIN, JOHN
Executive, Diplomat, Former Actor. b. Los Angeles, CA, April 8, 1932. m. actress Constance Towers. e. St. John's Military Acad., Villanova Prep at Ojai, Stanford Univ., Naval service: air intelligence officer in Korean War. Broadway stage debut: Seesaw, 1973. 1961-73 public service experience as spec. advisor to Secretary Gen. of OAS, performed gp. task work for Dept. of State and Exec. Office of the President. Pres. Screen Actors Guild, 1971-73. Named U.S. Ambassador to Mexico, 1981-86. Partner in Gavin & Dailey, a venture capital firm; Pres., Gamma Services Corp. (Intl. Consultants); dir., Atlantic Richfield Co., Dresser Industries, Pinkerton, Inc., The Hotchkiss and Wiley Funds, International Wire Group Co. Consultant to Dept. of State and serves pro-bono on several boards.
PICTURES: Behind the High Wall (debut, 1956), Four Girls in Town, Quantez, A Time to Love and a Time to Die, Imitation of Life, Psycho, Midnight Lace, Spartacus, A Breath of Scandal, Romanoff and Juliet, Tammy Tell Me True, Back Street, Thoroughly Modern Millie, The Madwoman of Chaillot, Pussycat Pussycat I Love You.
TELEVISION: *Movies*: Cutler's Trail, The New Adventures of Heidi, Sophia Loren: Her Own Story. *Series*: Destry, Convoy. *Mini-Series*: Doctors' Private Lives.

GAY, JOHN
Writer. b. Whittier, CA, April 1, 1924. e. LA City Coll.
PICTURES: Run Silent, Run Deep, Separate Tables, The Happy Thieves, Four Horsemen, The Courtship of Eddie's Father, The Hallelujah Trail, The Last Safari, The Power, No Way to Treat a Lady, Soldier Blue, Sometimes a Great Notion, Hennessey, A Matter of Time.
TELEVISION: Amazing Howard Hughes, Kill Me If You Can, Captains Courageous, Red Badge of Courage, All My Darling Daughters, Les Miserables, Transplant, A Private Battle, A Tale of Two Cities, The Bunker, Berlin Tunnel 21, Stand By Your Man, Dial "M" For Murder, The Long Summer of George Adams, A Piano for Mrs. Cimino, The Hunchback of Notre Dame, Ivanhoe, Witness for the Prosecution, Samson and Delilah, Fatal Vision, Doubletake, Uncle Tom's Cabin, Outlaw, Six Against the Rock, Around the World in 80 Days, Blind Faith, Cruel Doubt.

GAYNOR, MITZI
Actress. r.n. Francisca Mitzi Von Gerber. b. Chicago, IL, Sept. 4, 1931. e. Powers Professional H.S., Hollywood. Studied ballet since age four; was in L.A. Light Opera prod. Roberta. Stage: Anything Goes (natl. co., 1989).
OPERA: Fortune Teller, Song of Norway, Louisiana Purchase, Naughty Marietta, The Great Waltz.
PICTURES: My Blue Heaven (debut, 1950), Take Care of My Little Girl, Golden Girl, We're Not Married, Bloodhounds of Broadway, The I Don't Care Girl, Down Among the Sheltering Palms, There's No Business Like Show Business, Three Young Texans, Anything Goes, The Birds and the Bees, The Joker Is Wild, Les Girls, South Pacific, Happy Anniversary, Surprise Package, For Love or Money.
TELEVISION: *Specials:* Mitzi, Mitzi's Second Special, The First Time, A Tribute to the American Housewife, Mitzi and a Hundred Guys, Roarin' in the 20s, Mitzi...Zings Into Spring, What's Hot What's Not.

GAZZARA, BEN
Actor. b. New York, NY, Aug. 28, 1930. e. Studied at CCNY 1947-49. Won scholarship to study with Erwin Piscator; joined Actor's Studio, where students improvised a play, End as a Man, which then was performed on Broadway with him in lead. Screen debut (1957) in film version of that play retitled The Strange One.
THEATER: Jezebel's Husband, End as a Man, Cat on a Hot Tin Roof, A Hatful of Rain, The Night Circus, Epitaph for George Dillon, Two for the Seesaw, Strange Interlude, Traveler Without Luggage, Hughie, Who's Afraid of Virginia Woolf, Dance of Death, Thornhill, Shimada.

PICTURES: The Strange One (debut, 1957), Anatomy of a Murder, The Passionate Thief, The Young Doctors, Convicts Four, Conquered City, A Rage to Live, The Bridge at Remagen, Husbands, The Neptune Factor, Capone, Killing of a Chinese Bookie, Voyage of the Damned, High Velocity, Opening Night, Saint Jack, Bloodline, They All Laughed, Inchon, Tales of Ordinary Madness, Road House, Quicker Than the Eye, Don Bosco, A Lovely Scandal, Girl from Trieste, Il Camorrista, Tattooed Memory, Beyond the Ocean (also dir., s.p.), Forever, Farmer & Chase, The Shadow Conspiracy, The Big Lebowski, The Spanish Prisoner, Buffalo 66, Illuminata, Happiness, The Thomas Crown Affair, Summer of Sam, Believe.
TELEVISION: *Series*: Arrest and Trial, Run for Your Life. *Movies*: When Michael Calls, Maneater, QB VII, The Death of Ritchie, A Question of Honor, An Early Frost, A Letter to Three Wives, Police Story: The Freeway Killings, Downpayment on Murder, People Like Us, Lies Before Kisses, Blindsided, Love Honor & Obey: The Last Mafia Marriage, Parallel Lives, Fatal Vows: The Alexandria O'Hara Story, Valentine's Day, Angelo Nero, Tre Stelle.

GEARY, ANTHONY
Actor. b. Coalville, UT, May 29, 1947. e. U. of Utah.
THEATRE: The Inspector General, The Glass Menagerie, The Wild Duck, Barabbas.
PICTURES: Blood Sabbath (debut, 1969), Johnny Got His Gun, Private Investigations, Disorderlies, Penitentiary III, You Can't Hurry Love, Pass the Ammo, Dangerous Love, It Takes Two, UHF, Night Life, Crack House, Night of the Warrior, Scorchers.
TELEVISION: *Series*: Bright Promise, General Hospital (1978-83; 1990-). *Guest*: The Young and the Restless, Osmond Family Holiday Special, Sunset Beat, Murder She Wrote, Hotel, All in the Family, Streets of San Francisco. *Movies*: Intimate Agony, Sins of the Past, The Imposter, Kicks, Perry Mason: The Case of the Murdered Madam, Do You Know the Muffin Man?

GEBHARDT, FRED
Producer, Writer, Exhibitor. b. Vienna, Austria, Mar. 16, 1925. e. Schotten Gymnasium, Vienna, UCLA, 1939. Usher Boyd Theatre, Bethlehem, PA; Mgr., Rivoli Thea. L.A., 1944; 18 yrs. mgr. many theatres. Fox West Coast, then Fine Arts Theatre. Writer, prod.: 12 To the Moon, The Phantom Planet; prod., Assignment Outer Space, Operation M; s.p., All But Glory, The Starmaker, Shed No Blood, Fortress in Heaven, Eternal Woman. Pres., Four Crown Prods., Inc.; recipient of Medal of Americanism, D.A.R., 1963; Honorary Lifetime Member, P.T.A., Young Man of The Year Award, 1956, 24 Showmanship Awards; Mem. Acad. M.P. Arts and Sciences, Ind. M.P. Prod. Assoc.
AUTHOR: Mental Disarmament, All But Glory, Starmaker, Shed No Blood, The Last of the Templars.

GEDRICK, JASON
Actor. b. Chicago, IL, Feb. 7, 1965.
PICTURES: Massive Retaliation (debut, 1984), The Zoo Gang, The Heavenly Kid, Iron Eagle, Stacking, Promised Land, Rooftops, Born on the Fourth of July, Backdraft, Crossing the Bridge, The Force, Power 98.
TELEVISION: *Series:* Class of 96, Murder One, Sweet Justice, EZ Streets. Movies/Specials: Dare to Love, EZ Streets (pilot), The Last Don, The Third Twin, The Last Don II.

GEESON, JUDY
Actress. b. Arundel, Sussex, England, Sept. 10, 1948. e. Corona Stage Sch. Began professional career on British TV, 1960.
THEATER: Othello, Titus Andronicus, Two Gentlemen of Verona, Section Nine, An Ideal Husband.
PICTURES: To Sir with Love, Berserk, Here We Go Round the Mulberry Bush, Prudence and the Pill, Hammerhead, Three into Two Won't Go, The Oblong Box, Two Gentlemen Sharing, The Executioner, Nightmare Hotel, 10 Rillington Place, Doomwatch, Fear in the Night, It's Not the Size That Counts, Brannigan, Diagnosis Murder, The Eagle Has Landed, Carry On England, Dominique, Horror Planet, The Plague Dogs (voice).
TELEVISION: Dance of Death, Lady Windermere's Fan, Room with a View, The Skin Game, Star Maidens, Poldark, She, The Coronation, Murder She Wrote, Astronomy (Triple Play II). Movie: The Secret Life of Kathy McCormick.

GEFFEN, DAVID
Executive, Producer. b. Brooklyn, NY, Feb. 21, 1943. Began in mailroom of William Morris Agency before becoming agent there and later at Ashley Famous. With Elliott Roberts founded own talent management co. for musicians. Founded Asylum Records, 1970. Pres. then chmn. Elektra-Asylum Records 1973-76. Sold co. to Warner Communications for whom he headed film prod. unit. Vice-chmn. Warner Bros. Pictures, 1975; exec. asst. to chmn., Warner Communications, 1977; Member music faculty Yale U., 1978. Formed Geffen Records 1980 and Geffen Film Co. Producer of Broadway shows Master Harold... and the Boys, Cats, Good, Dreamgirls, Social Security, Chess. 1990, sold record co. to MCA, Inc. With Steven Spielberg and Jeffrey Katzenberg formed Dreamworks entertainment company, 1995.
PICTURES: Personal Best, Risky Business, Lost in America, After Hours, Little Shop of Horrors, Beetlejuice (exec. prod.), Men Don't Leave, Defending Your Life, M. Butterfly, Interview With the Vampire.

GELBART, LARRY
Writer. b. Chicago, IL, Feb. 25, 1928. Began at age 16 writing for Danny Thomas on Fanny Brice Show. Followed by Duffy's Tavern, Bob Hope and Jack Paar radio shows. Author of Laughing Matters, 1998.
THEATER: The Conquering Hero, A Funny Thing Happened on the Way to the Forum (with Burt Shevlove; Tony Award, 1962), Sly Fox, Mastergate, City of Angels (Tony Award, 1990), Power Failure.
PICTURES: The Notorious Landlady, The Thrill of It All, The Wrong Box, Not With My Wife You Don't, The Chastity Belt, A Fine Pair, Oh God!, Movie Movie, Neighbors, Tootsie, Blame It on Rio.
TELEVISION: *Series*: Caesar's Hour, M*A*S*H (Emmy Award, 1974; also co-prod.), United States. *Movie*: Barbarians at the Gate (Cable Ace Award, 1993), Weapons of Mass Distraction. *Special*: Mastergate.

GELFAN, GREGORY
Executive. b. Los Angeles, CA, Aug. 7, 1950. Was entertainment atty. with Kaplan, Livingston et. al., and Weissmann, Wolff et. al. before joining Paramount Pictures in 1983 as dir. of business affairs. 1985, named v.p., business affairs, for M.P. Group of Paramount; 1989 promoted to sr. v.p. in chg. of business affairs. 1994, named exec. v.p. in chg. of business & legal affairs, 20th Century Fox.

GELLAR, SARAH MICHELLE
Actress. b. New York, NY, April 14, 1977.
PICTURES: Over the Brooklyn Bridge, Funny Farm, High Stakes, I Know What You Did Last Summer, Scream 2, Small Soldiers (voice), She's All That (cameo), Simply Irresistible, Cruel Intentions, The It Girl, Harvard Man.
TELEVISION: *Movies:* An Invasion of Privacy, A Woman Named Jackie. *Series:* Girl Talk, Swans Crossing, All My Children, Buffy the Vampire Slayer. *Guest:* Love Sydney, The Guiding Light, Spenser: For Hire, King of the Hill (voice).

GELLER, BRIAN L.
Executive. b. New York, NY, Feb. 3, 1948. e. Queens Coll. Entered industry with Columbia Pictures as sls. trainee in 1966, leaving in 1968 to go with American Intl. Pictures as asst. branch mgr. In 1969 joined Cinemation Industries as eastern div. sls. mgr.; 1978, left to become gen. sls. mr. of NMD Film Distributing Co. 1982, named dir. of dist., Mature Pictures Corp. 1983, gen. sls. mgr., Export Pix.; with Cinema Group as east. sls. mgr.; joined Scotti Brothers Pictures as national sales, mgr. Joined 20th Century Fox sls. dep't. Member of Motion Picture Bookers Club of N.Y.; Variety Tent 35, Motion Picture Pioneers.

GENDECE, BRIAN
Producer, Executive. b. St. Louis, MO, Dec. 3, 1956. e. Drury Coll., Springfield, MO. 1981-85, Director of Business Affairs, Weinstein/Skyfield Productions and Skyfield Management. 1986-87, dir. of business affairs, Cannon Films; 1987-89, dir. creative affairs, Cannon Films; 1989 co-pres., Sheer Entertainment; indie first look Epic Prods.; 1991 owner The Gendece Film Co.; 1991-93, prod./dir., 21st Century Film; 1993-96, dir. of mktg., Raleigh Film and Television Studios. 1997-98, pres., G & G Prods.
THEATER: Jack Klugman as Lyndon, The Bob Fosse Awards.
PICTURES: Runaway Train, Salsa, Rope Dancin', The Hunters, The American Samurai, Ceremony.
VIDEO: Bad Habits, Shape Up with Arnold, Laura Branigan's Your Love, How to Become a Teenage Ninja, L.A. Raiders' Wild Wild West, The Making of Crime and Punishment.

GEORGE, GEORGE W.
Writer, Producer. b. New York, NY, Feb.8, 1920. e. Williams Coll. U.S. Navy, 1941-44; screen-writer since 1948. President, Jengo Enterprises, dev. theatrical and m.p. projects.
THEATER: *Prod.*: Dylan, Any Wednesday, Ben Franklin in Paris, The Great Indoors, Happily Never After, Night Watch, Via Galactica, Bedroom Farce, Program for Murder (also co-author).
PICTURES: *Writer*: Bodyguard, The Nevadan, Woman on Pier 13, Peggy, Mystery Submarine, Red Mountain Experiment, Alcatraz, Fight Town, Smoke Signal, Desert Sands, Uranium Boom, Halliday Brand, Doc, The James Dean Story, The Two Little Bears. *Prod.*: The James Dean Story, A Matter of Innocence, Twisted Nerve, Hello-Goodbye, Night Watch, Rich Kids, My Dinner With Andre.
TELEVISION: Climax, Screen Gems, Loretta Young Show, The Rifleman, Peter Gunn, The Real McCoys, Adventures in Paradise, Hong Kong, Follow the Sun, Bonanza.

GEORGE, LOUIS
Executive. b. Karavas, Kyrenia, Cyprus, June 7, 1935. e. Kyrenia Business Acad., Cyprus (honored 1951). Emigrated to U.S. in 1952. After brief stint in Foreign Exchange Dept. of City National Bank, New York, served in U.S. Army, 1953-55. Entered industry in 1956 as theatre manager with Loew's Theatres in N.Y. metro area, managing Metropolitan, Triboro, New Rochelle, between 1958-66. 1966 joined MGM as dir. of intl. theatre dept. 1969 promoted to dir. of world-wide non-theatrical sales. 1972-74 served as regional dir. of MGM Far East operations. 1974 left MGM to establish Arista Films, Inc., an indep. prod./dist. co. Pres. & CEO, Arista Films, Inc. Also bd. member, American Film Marketing Assn., chmn. Copywright and Film Security Committee of the Assn.

PICTURES: Slaughterhouse Rock, Buying Time, Violent Zone (exec. prod.), Angels Brigade, Final Justice, Surf II, Crackdown.

GEORGE, SUSAN
Actress, Producer. b. Surrey, England, July 26, 1950. m. actor-prod. Simon MacCorkindale. e. Corona Acad.
PICTURES: Billion Dollar Brain, The Sorcerers, Up the Junction, The Strange Affair, The Looking Glass War, All Neat in Black Stockings, Twinky (Lola), Spring and Port Wine, Eye Witness (Sudden Terror), Die Screaming Marianne, Fright, Straw Dogs, Sonny and Jed, Dirty Mary Crazy Larry, Mandingo, Out of Season, A Small Town in Texas, Tintorera, Tomorrow Never Comes, Enter the Ninja, Venom, The House Where Evil Dwells, Jigsaw Man, Lightning: The White Stallion, Stealing Heaven (exec. prod. only), That Summer of White Roses (also exec. prod.), The House That Mary Bought (also exec. prod.).
TELEVISION: Swallows and Amazons, Adam's Apple, Weaver's Green, Compensation Alice, The Right Attitude, Dracula, Lamb to the Slaughter, Royal Jelly, Masquerade, Czechmate, Hotel, Blacke's Magic, Jack the Ripper, Castle of Adventure, Cluedo, Stay Lucky.

GERALD, HELEN
Actress. b. New York, NY, Aug. 13. e. U. of Southern California, 1948. Stage: Italian Teatro D'Arte, Les Miserables, The Civil Death, Feudalism.
PICTURES: The Gay Cavalier, The Trap, Tarzan and the Leopard Woman, Cigarette Girl, Meet Miss Bobby Socks, G.I. War Brides, Gentleman's Agreement, A Bell for Adano, Tomorrow Is Forever, Janie, Grand Prix, The Sandpiper, Make Mine Mink, Best of Everything.
TELEVISION: Robert Montgomery Presents, Frontiers of Faith, Valiant Lady, Kraft Theatre, Gangbusters, Adventures of The Falcon, Schlitz Playhouse of Stars, This Is the Answer, Man from U.N.C.L.E., Run for Your Life, Perry Mason.

GERARD, GIL
Actor. b. Little Rock, AK, Jan. 23, 1943. e. Arkansas State Teachers Coll. Appeared in over 400 TV commercials. On stage in I Do! I Do!, Music Man, Stalag 17, Applause, etc.
PICTURES: Some of My Best Friends Are (1971), Man on a Swing, Hooch (also co-prod.), Airport '77, Buck Rogers in the 25th Century, Soldier's Fortune, Looking for Bruce.
TELEVISION: *Series*: The Doctors, Buck Rogers in the 25th Century, Nightingales, Sidekicks, E.A.R.T.H. Force, Fish Police, Code 3 (host). *Movies*: Ransom for Alice, Killing Stone, Help Wanted: Male, Not Just Another Affair, Hear No Evil, Johnny Blue (pilot), For Love or Money, Stormin' Home, International Airport, Final Notice, The Elite, Last Electric Knight.

GERARD, LILLIAN
Publicist, Writer b. New York, NY, Nov. 25, 1914. e. Baruch, CCNY, Columbia U. Publicity, Rialto Theatre, 1936; publicity-adv. Filmarte Theatre, 1938, Gerard Associates, 1938-47; V.P. and managing dir. of Paris Theatre, 1948-62; publicity-adv. dir., Rugoff Theatres, 1962. Film consultant to Times Films, Lopert Films, Landau Co., 1962-65. Adjunct Professor, Film, 1968-70, Columbia U., Sch. of the Arts, Special Projects Co-Ordinator, Museum of Modern Art, 1968-80. Now associated with Philip Gerard in Gerard Associates.

GERARD, PHILIP R.
Executive. b. New York, NY, Aug. 23, 1913. e. City Coll. of New York, B.B.A. 1935; Columbia U.. Publicity dir. Mayer-Burstyn 1936-39; Gerard Associates, 1939-41; in public relations U.S. War Dept. 1942-44; with MGM 1944-48; with Universal Pictures since 1948; Eastern pub. mgr., 1950-59; Eastern ad. and pub. dir., Dec. 1959-68; N.Y. Production Exec., 1968-76. As of Jan. 1, 1977 formed Gerard Associates, film consultants on marketing, production and acquisitions. N.Y.C. Board member of CSS/RSVP (Retired Seniors Volunteer Program); Community Service Society. Member: Visitor's Day Comm., New York Hospital; volunteer at the International Center.

GERBER, DAVID
Executive. b. Brooklyn, NY. e. U. of the Pacific. m. actress Laraine Stephens. Joined Batten, Barton, Durstine and Osborn ad agency in N.Y. as TV supvr. Left to become sr. v.p. of TV at General Artists Corp. 1956, named v.p. in chg. sales at 20th-Fox TV where sold and packaged over 50 prime-time series and specials. Entered indep. prod. with The Ghost and Mrs. Muir, followed by Nanny and the Professor. 1970 was exec. prod. of The Double Deckers, children's series made in England. 1972 joined Columbia Pictures Television as indep. prod.; 1974 was named exec. v.p. worldwide prod. for CPT. 1976 returned to indep. prod. 1985, joined MGM/UA TV broadcasting group in chg. world-wide prod. 1986 named president, MGM/UA Television. 1988-92, chmn & CEO, MGM/UA Television Prods. group.
TELEVISION: *Exec. prod.*: Cade's County, Police Story (Emmy, best dramatic series), Police Woman, The Lindbergh Kidnapping Case, Joe Forrester, The Quest and Gibbsville, To Kill a Cop, Power, Medical Story, Born Free, Beulah Land, The Night the City Screamed, Follow the North Star, Nothing Lasts Forever, Lady Blue, The Ghost and Mrs. Muir.

GERBER, MICHAEL H.
Executive. b. New York, NY, Feb. 6, 1944. e. St. Johns U., B.A., 1969; St. Johns U. School of Law, J.D., 1969. Atty. for Screen Gems, 1969-71; asst. secy. & asst. to gen. counsel, Columbia Pictures Industries, 1971-74; corporate counsel and secretary, Allied Artists Pictures, 1974, v.p. corporate affairs, Allied Artists, 1978; v.p., business affairs, Viacom Intl. 1980-86; 1986-89, sr. v.p.; 1989-93, pres., first run, intl. distrib. & acquisitions, Viacom Enterprises.

GERE, RICHARD
Actor. b. Philadelphia, PA, Aug. 29, 1949. e. U. of Massachusetts. Started acting in college; later joined Provincetown Playhouse and Seattle Repertory Theatre. Composed music for productions of these groups.
THEATER: *B'way*: Grease, Soon, Habeas Corpus, Bent (Theatre World Award), A Midsummer Night's Dream (Lincoln Center). *Off-B'way* in Killer's Head. *London*: Taming of the Shrew (with Young Vic).
PICTURES: Report to the Commissioner (debut, 1975), Baby Blue Marine, Looking for Mr. Goodbar, Days of Heaven, Bloodbrothers, Yanks, American Gigolo, An Officer and a Gentleman, Breathless, Beyond the Limit, The Cotton Club, King David, Power, No Mercy, Miles From Home, Internal Affairs, Pretty Woman, Rhapsody in August, Final Analysis (also co-exec. prod.), Sommersby (also co-exec. prod.), Mr. Jones (also co-exec. prod.), Intersection, First Knight, Primal Fear, Runaway Bride, Dr.T and the Women.
TELEVISION: *Movies*: Strike Force, And the Band Played On. *Guest:* Kojak. *Pilot*: D.H.P.

GERTZ, IRVING
Composer, Musical director. b. Providence, RI, May 19, 1915. e. Providence Coll. of Music, 1934-37. Assoc. with Providence Symph. Orch., comp. choral works for Catholic Choral Soc.; music dept., Columbia, 1939-41; U.S. Army, 1941-46; then comp. arranger, mus. dir. for many cos. incl. Columbia, Universal International, NBC, 20th Century Fox. Compositions: Leaves of Grass, Serenata for String Quartet, Divertimento for String Orchestra, Tableau for Orchestra.
PICTURES: Bandits of Corsica, Gun Belt, Long Wait, The Fiercest Heart, First Travelling Saleslady, Fluffy, Nobody's Perfect, Marines Let's Go!, It Came from Outer Space, The Man from Bitter Ridge, Posse from Hell, The Creature Walks Among Us, The Incredible Shrinking Man, Hell Bent for Leather, Seven Ways from Sundown, Francis Joins the WACS, Raw Edge, East of Sumatra, A Day of Fury, To Hell and Back, Cult of the Cobra, Plunder Road, Top Gun, Tombstone Express, The Alligator People, Khyber Patrol, The Wizard of Baghdad. Fluffy, Marines, Let's Go!
TELEVISION: *Orig. theme & scores:* America, The Golden Voyage, Across the Seven Seas, The Legend of Jesse James, Daniel Boone, Voyage to the Bottom of the Sea, Peyton Place, Land of the Giants, Lancer, Medical Center, Boutade for Wood-Wind Quartet, Salute to All Nations, A Village Fair, Liberty! Liberte! (for symphony orchestra).

GERTZ, JAMI
Actress. b. Chicago, IL, Oct. 28, 1965. e. NYU. Won a nationwide talent search competition headed by Norman Lear to cast TV comedy series Square Pegs. Following series studied at NYU drama school. Los Angeles theater includes Out of Gas on Lovers' Leap and Come Back Little Sheba. On NY stage in Wrong Turn at Lungfish. Also appeared in the Julian Lennon music video Stick Around.
PICTURES: Endless Love (debut, 1981), On the Right Track, Alphabet City, Sixteen Candles, Mischief, Quicksilver, Crossroads, Solarbabies, The Lost Boys, Less Than Zero, Listen to Me, Renegades, Silence Like Glass, Don't Tell Her It's Me, Sibling Rivalry, Jersey Girl, Twister, Seven Girlfriends.
TELEVISION: *Series*: Square Pegs, Dreams, Sibs, ER. *Guest:* Diff'rent Strokes, The Facts of Life. *Movie*: This Can't Be Love.

GETTY, BALTHAZAR
Actor. b. California, Jan. 22, 1975. Spotted by talent agent while at Bel Air Prep School, winning lead role in remake of Lord of the Flies.
PICTURES: Lord of the Flies (debut, 1990), Young Guns II, My Heroes Have Always Been Cowboys, The Pope Must Die, December, Where the Day Takes You, Halfway House, Red Hot, Dead Beat, Natural Born Killers, Don't Do It, Terrified, Judge Dredd, City Scrapers, White Squall, Habitat, Lost Highway, Four Dogs Playing Poker, Big City Blues, Center of the World, Deuces Wild.
TELEVISION: *Special*: The Turn of the Screw.

GETTY, ESTELLE
Actress. b. New York, NY, July 25, 1923. e. attended New School for Social Research. Trained for stage with Gerald Russak and at Herbert Berghof Studios. Worked as comedienne on Borscht Belt circuit and as actress with Yiddish theatre. Founder Fresh Meadows Community theater. Also worked as acting teacher and coach and secretary. Author, If I Knew What I Know Now... So What? (1988).

THEATER: The Divorce of Judy and Jane (off-B'way debut, 1971), Widows and Children First, Table Settings, Demolition of Hannah Fay, Never Too Old, A Box of Tears, Hidden Corners, I Don't Know Why I'm Screaming, Under the Bridge There's a Lonely Place, Light Up the Sky, Pocketful of Posies, Fits and Starts, Torch Song Trilogy (off-B'way, B'way and tour, Drama Desk nom., 1982, Helen Hayes Award, best supp. performer in a touring show).
PICTURES: The Chosen, Tootsie, Protocol, Mask, Mannequin, Stop Or My Mom Will Shoot.
TELEVISION: *Series*: The Golden Girls (Golden Globe Award, Emmy Award, 1988), The Golden Palace, Empty Nest. *Movies:* No Man's Land, Victims for Victims: The Teresa Saldana Story, Copacabana. *Guest*: Cagney and Lacey, Nurse, Baker's Dozen, One of the Boys, Fantasy Island.

GETZ, JOHN
Actor. e. Univ Iowa, Amer. Conservatory Theatre (SF). Appeared on B'way in They're Playing Our Song, M. Butterfly. LA stage: Money & Friends.
PICTURES: Tattoo, Thief of Hearts, Blood Simple, The Fly, The Fly II, Born on the Fourth of July, Men at Work, Don't Tell Mom the Babysitter's Dead, Curly Sue, A Passion to Kill, Painted Hero, Mojave Moon.
TELEVISION: *Series*: Rafferty, Suzanne Pleshette is Maggie Briggs, MacGruder & Loud, Mariah. *Movies*: Killer Bees, A Woman Called Moses, Kent State, Rivkin: Bounty Hunter, Muggable Mary: Street Cop, Not in Front of the Children, Concrete Beat, The Execution, In My Daughter's Name, Betrayal of Trust, Untamed Love, Awake to Murder, The Late Shift. *Mini-Series:* Loose Change.

GHOSTLEY, ALICE
Actress. b. Eve, MO, Aug. 14, 1926. e. Univ. of OK.
THEATER: New Faces of 1952, Sandhog, Trouble in Tahiti, Maybe Tuesday, A Thurber Carnival, The Sign in Sidney Brustein's Window (Tony Award, 1965), Stop Thief Stop, Annie, The Beauty Part, Livin' The Life, Nunsense, Come Blow Your Horn, Bye Bye Birdie, Arsenic and Old Lace, Shangri-La.
PICTURES: New Faces (debut, 1954), To Kill a Mockingbird, My Six Loves, Ace Eli and Rodger of the Skies, Gator, Rabbit Test, Grease, Not for Publication, Viva Ace, The Flim Flam Man, With Six You Get Egg Roll, The Graduate, Blue Sunshine, Record City, The Wrong Guys, Odd Couple II.
TELEVISION: *Series*: The Jackie Gleason Show (1962-64), Captain Nice, The Jonathan Winters Show, Bewitched, Mayberry R.F.D., Nichols, The Julie Andrews Hour, Temperatures Rising, Small Wonder, Designing Women. *Movie*: Two on a Bench, Perry Mason: The Case of the Silenced Singer. *Specials*: Cinderella, Twelfth Night, Shangri-La, Everybody's Doin' It. *Guest*: Please Don't Eat the Daisies, Get Smart, Love American Style, Hogan's Heroes, The Odd Couple, What's Happening!, Good Times, Gimme a Break, The Golden Girls, The Client, Cybill.

GIANNINI, GIANCARLO
Actor. b. Spezia, Italy, Aug. 1, 1942. Acquired degree in electronics but immediately after school enrolled at Acad. for Drama in Rome. Cast by Franco Zeffirelli as Romeo at age of 20. Subsequently appeared in a play also directed by Zeffirelli, Two Plus Two No Longer Make Four, written by Lina Wertmuller.
PICTURES: Rita la Zanzara, Arabella, Anzio, Fraulein Doktor, The Secret of Santa Vittoria, Love and Anarchy, The Seduction of Mimi, Swept Away by an Unusual Destiny in the Blue Sea of August, Seven Beauties, How Funny Can Sex Be?, A Night Full of Rain, The Innocent, Buone Notizie (also prod.), Revenge, Travels with Anita, Lili Marleen, Lovers and Liars, La Vita e Bella, Picone Sent Me, Immortal Bachelor, American Dreamer, Fever Pitch, Saving Grace, New York Stories (Life Without Zoe), I Picari, The Sleazy, Uncle, Snack Bar Budapest, Oh King, Blood Red, Brown Bread Sandwiches, Killing Time, Short Cut, Night Sun, Criminals, Once Upon a Crime, Giovanni Falcone, Colpo di Coda, Celluloide, A Walk in the Clouds, New York Crossing, Come Due Coccodrilli, La Frontiera, Broken Dreams, The Scirocco Room, The Last Target, Blood of a Poet, La Lupa, Heaven Before I Die, Lorca, Mimic, Vuoti o Perdere.
TELEVISION: Sins, Jacob, Nessuno Escluso, Voglia Di Volare, World Cup '98.

GIANNOLI, XAVIER
Director.
PICTURES: J'aime beaucoup ce que vous faites, Dialogue au sommet, L'Interview (Cannes Film Fest. Palme d'Or, 1998).

GIANOPULOUS, JIM
Executive. Pres., Fox International Theatrical Distribution, Twentieth Century Fox, Inc.

GIBBS, DAVID
Executive. b. 1944. Ent. motion picture industry 1961, Kodak research, worked as a photographer for Kodak 1963-66. Lectured at Harrow College of Technology and Kodak Photographic School until 1972. Left Kodak, 1975, after three years as a market specialist to join Filmatic Laboratories. Appt. asst. man. director, 1977, becoming chmn. and man. director, 1988. Member of RTS, SMPTE and IVCA. Past Chmn. BISFA 1988-90. Past president of the British Kinematograph, Sound and Television Society.

GIBBS, MARLA
Actress. b. Chicago, IL, June 14, 1931. e. Cortez Peters Business School, Chicago. Worked as receptionist, switchboard operator, travel consultant (1963-74) before co-starring as Florence Johnston on the Jeffersons (1974-85). Formed Marla Gibbs Enterprises, Los Angeles, 1978. Member of CA State Assembly, 1980. Image Award NAACP, 1979-83.
PICTURES: Black Belt Jones, Sweet Jesus Preacher Man, The Meteor Man, Border to Border, Foolish, Lost & Found.
TELEVISION: *Series*: The Jeffersons, Checking In, 227. *Movies*: The Missing Are Deadly, Tell Me Where It Hurts, Nobody's Child, Menu for Murder, Lily in Winter. *Mini-Series*: The Moneychangers. *Special*: You Can't Take It With You.

GIBSON, DEREK
Executive. b. Huyton, England, July 7, 1945. e. Wigan Col. Head of Prod. at Astral Bellevue Pathe, 1979-80; v.p. Sandy Howard Prods.; Pres. Hemdale Film Group., 1982-present.
PICTURES: *Prod./Exec.:* Death Ship, Savage Harvest, Triumphs of a Man Called Horse, The Terminator, River's Edge, Platoon, Hoosiers, Salvador, At Close Range, Scenes from a Goldmine, Best Seller, War Party, Vampire's Kiss, Staying Together, Out Cold, Shag, Miracle Mile, Criminal Law, Hidden Agenda, Don't Tell Her It's Me, Bright Angel.

GIBSON, HENRY
Actor. b. Germantown, PA, Sept. 21, 1935. e. Catholic U. of America. Appeared as child actor with stock companies, 1943-57; B'way debut in My Mother My Father and Me, 1962.
PICTURES: The Nutty Professor, Kiss Me Stupid, The Outlaws Is Coming, Charlotte's Web (voice), The Long Goodbye, Nashville (Nat'l Soc. Film Critics Award, 1975), The Last Remake of Beau Geste, Kentucky Fried Movie, A Perfect Couple, The Blues Brothers, Tulips, Health, The Incredible Shrinking Woman, Monster in the Closet, Brenda Starr, Inner Space, Switching Channels, The 'Burbs, Night Visitor, Gremlins II, Tune in Tomorrow, Tom and Jerry: The Movie (voice), A Sailor's Tattoo, Biodome, Color of a Brisk and Leaping Day, Mother Night (voice), Asylum, A Stranger in the Kingdom, Magnolia.
TELEVISION: *Series*: Rowan and Martin's Laugh-In (1968-72). *Movies*: Evil Roy Slade, Every Man Needs One, The New Original Wonder Woman (pilot), Escape from Bogen County, The Night They Took Miss Beautiful, Amateur Night at the Dixie Bar & Grill, For the Love of It, Nashville Grab, Long Gone, Slow Burn, Return to Green Acres, Return to Witch Mountain. *Mini-Series*: Around the World in 80 Days.

GIBSON, MEL
Actor. b. Peekskill, NY, Jan. 3, 1956. Emigrated in 1968 to Australia with family. Attended Nat'l Inst. of Dramatic Art in Sydney; in 2nd yr. was cast in his first film, Summer City. Graduated from NIDA, 1977. Joined South Australian Theatre Co. in 1978, appearing in Oedipus, Henry IV, Cedoona. Other plays include Romeo and Juliet, No Names No Pack Drill, On Our Selection, Waiting for Godot, Death of a Salesman.
PICTURES: Summer City (Coast of Terror; debut, 1977), Mad Max, Tim, Chain Reaction (unbilled), Attack Force Z, Gallipoli, The Road Warrior (Mad Max II), The Year of Living Dangerously, The Bounty, The River, Mrs. Soffel, Mad Max Beyond Thunderdome, Lethal Weapon, Tequila Sunrise, Lethal Weapon 2, Bird on a Wire, Air America, Hamlet, Lethal Weapon 3, Forever Young, The Man Without a Face (also dir.), Maverick, Braveheart (also dir., co-prod.; Academy Award, 1996; Golden Globe, 1996), Casper (cameo), Pocahontas (voice), Ransom, Father's Day (cameo), Conspiracy Theory, Lethal Weapon 4, Payback, The Million Dollar Hotel, The Patriot, What Women Want.
TELEVISION: *Series*: The Sullivans, The Oracle. *Specials*: The Ultimate Stuntman: A Tribute to Dar Robinson, Australia's Outback: The Vanishing Frontier (host), Wallace and Grommit Go Chicken. *Guest:* The Simpsons (voice).

GIBSON, THOMAS
Actor. b. Charleston, SC, July 3, 1962.
PICTURES: Far and Away, Love & Human Remains, The Age of Innocence, Sleep with Me, Men of War, Barcelona, To Love Honor and Deceive, The Next Step, The Flintstones in Viva Rock Vegas, Eyes Wide Shut, Psycho Beach Party, The Broken Hearts Club: A Romantic Comedy, Stardom.
TELEVISION: *Movies:* Lincoln, The Kennedys of Massachusetts, Tales of the City, Secrets, Night Visitors, Inheritance, The Devil's Child, Nightmare Street, More Tales of the City, A Will of Their Own. *Series:* As the World Turns, Another World, Chicago Hope, Dharma & Greg. *Guest:* Leg Work, Caroline in the City.

GIELGUD, SIR JOHN
Actor. b. London, England, Apr. 14, 1904. e. Westminster Sch., Lady Benson's Sch. (dram.), London; Royal Acad. of Dramatic Art. Knighted, 1953. Autobiography: Early Stages (1983). Honorary degress: Oxford, London, St. Andrews, Brandeis (U.S), Assoc. Legion of Honor.
THEATER: Began stage career in Shakespearean roles; on London stage also in the Constant Nymph, The Good Companions, Dear Octopus, The Importance of Being Earnest, Dear Brutus, etc., various Shakespearean seasons, London & N.Y. 1988: The Best of Friends.

PICTURES: Who is the Man? (debut, 1924), The Clue of the New Pin; Insult (sound debut, 1932), The Good Companions, Secret Agent, The Prime Minister, Julius Caesar (1953), Romeo and Juliet, Richard III, Around the World in 80 Days, The Barretts of Wimpole Street, Saint Joan, Hamlet, Becket (Acad. Award nom.), To Die in Madrid (narrator), The Loved One, Chimes at Midnight (Falstaff), Sebastian, Assignment to Kill, The Charge of the Light Brigade, The Shoes of the Fisherman, Oh What a Lovely War, Julius Caesar (1971), Eagle in a Cage, Lost Horizon, Galileo, 11 Harrowhouse, Gold, Murder on the Orient Express, Aces High, Providence, Portrait of the Artist as a Young Man, Joseph Andrews, Murder by Decree, Caligula, The Human Factor, The Elephant Man, The Formula, Sphinx, Lion of the Desert, Arthur (Academy Award , best supporting actor, 1981), Chariots of Fire, Priest of Love, Gandhi, The Wicked Lady, Invitation to the Wedding, Scandalous, The Shooting Party, Plenty, Time After Time, Whistle Blower, Appointment With Death, Bluebeard Bluebeard, Arthur 2 on the Rocks, Getting It Right, Strike It Rich, Prospero's Books, Shining Through, The Power of One, First Knight, Haunted, Shine, The Leopard Son (narrator), Hamlet.
TELEVISION: *Specials/Movies/Mini-Series*: A Day by the Sea, The Browning Version, The Rehearsal, Great Acting, Ages of Man, Mayfly and th Frog, Cherry Orchard, Ivanov, From Chekhov With Love, St. Joan, Good King Charles' Golden Days, Conversation at Night, Hassan, Deliver Us from Evil, Heartbreak House, Brideshead Revisited, The Canterville Ghost, The Hunchback of Notre Dame, Inside the Third Reich, Marco Polo, The Scarlet and the Black, The Master of Ballantrae, Wagner, The Far Pavillions, Camille, Romance on the Orient Express, Funny You Don't Look 200, Oedipus the King, A Man For All Seasons, War and Remembrance, Summer Lease (Emmy Award, 1991), The Best of Friends, Inspector Alleyn: Hand in Glove, Leave All Fair, Ages of Man, John Gielgud: An Actor's Life, Lovejoy: The Lost Colony, Scarlett.
(d. May 21, 2000)

GILBERT, ARTHUR N.
Producer. b. Detroit, MI, Oct. 17, 1920. Lt., U.S.M.C., 1941-45. e. U. of Chicago, 1946. Special Agent, FBI, 1946-53; world sales dir., Gen. Motors, Cadillac Div., 1953-59; investments in mot. pictures and hotel chains, 1959-64; exec. prod., Mondo Hollywood, 1965; exec. prod. Jeannie-Wife Child, 1966; assoc. prod., The Golden Breed, 1967; commissioned rank of Colonel U.S.M.C., 1968; 1970-80, exec. prod. Jaguar Pictures Corp; Columbia, 1981-86; Indi Pic. Corp. Also account exec. and v.p. Pacific Western Tours. v.p., Great Basion Corp. Bev. Hills 1987-9; v.p., Lawrence 3-D TV 1990-present; v.p. Cougar Prods. Co. 1990-91. Producer in development at Jonte Prods. of Paris/London, 1992-94.
PICTURES: The Glory Stompers, Fire Grass, Cycle Savages, Bigfoot, Incredible Transplant, Balance of Evil.

GILBERT, BRUCE
Producer. b. Los Angeles, CA, March 28, 1947. e. U. of California. Pursued film interests at Berkeley's Pacific Film Archive; in summer involved in production in film dept. of San Francisco State U. Founded progressive pre-school in Bay Area. Became story editor in feature film division of Cine-Artists; involved in several projects, including Aloha, Bobby and Rose. Formally partnered with Jane Fonda in IPC Films, Inc., then pres., American Filmworks.
PICTURES: Coming Home (assoc. prod.), The China Syndrome (exec. prod.). *Producer:* Nine to Five, On Golden Pond, Rollover, The Morning After, Man Trouble, Jack the Bear.
TELEVISION: *Series:* Nine to Five (exec. prod.). *Movies:* The Dollmaker (exec. prod.), By Dawn's Early Light (writer, exec. prod.).

GILBERT, LEWIS
Producer, Writer, Director, Former Actor. b. London, England, Mar. 6, 1920. In RAF, W.W.II. Screen debut, 1932; asst. dir. (1930-39) with London Films, Assoc. British, Mayflower, RKO-Radio; from 1939-44 attached U.S. Air Corps Film Unit (asst. dir., Target for Today). In 1944 joined G.B.I. as writer and dir. In 1948, Gainsborough Pictures as writer, dir., 1949; Argyle Prod. 1950; under contract Nettlefold Films, Ltd. as dir.
PICTURES: *Actor*: Under One Roof, I Want to Get Married, Haunting Melody. Director: The Little Ballerina, Marry Me (s.p. only), Once a Sinner, Scarlet Thread, There Is Another Sun, Time Gentlemen Please, Emergency Call, Cosh Boy, Johnny on the Run, Albert R.N., The Good Die Young, The Sea Shall Not Have Them, Reach for the Sky, Cast a Dark Shadow, The Admirable Crichton, Carve Her Name with Pride, A Cry from the Street, Ferry to Hong Kong, Sink the Bismarck, Light Up the Sky, The Greengage Summer, H.M.S. Defiant, The Patriots, Spare the Rod, The Seventh Dawn, Alfie, You Only Live Twice, The Adventurers, Friends (also prod., story), Paul & Michelle (also prod., story), Operation Daybreak, Seven Nights in Japan, The Spy Who Loved Me, Moonraker, Educating Rita (also prod.), Not Quite Paradise, Shirley Valentine (also prod.), Stepping Out (also co-prod.), Haunted (also s.p.).

GILBERT, MELISSA
Actress. b. Los Angeles, CA, May 8, 1964. m. actor Bruce Boxleitner. Made debut at age of 3 in TV commercial. Comes from show business family: father, late comedian Paul Gilbert; mother, former dancer-actress Barbara Crane. Grandfather, Harry Crane created The Honeymooners. NY Off-B'way debut A Shayna Madel (1987; Outer Critics Circle & Theatre World Awards).
PICTURES: Sylvester (debut, 1985), Ice House.
TELEVISION: *Series*: Little House on the Prairie, Stand By Your Man, Sweet Justice. *Guest*: Gunsmoke, Emergency, Tenafly, The Hanna-Barbera Happy Hour, Love Boat. *Movies*: Christmas Miracle in Caulfield U.S.A., The Miracle Worker, Splendor in the Grass, Choices of the Heart, Choices, Penalty Phase, Family Secrets, Killer Instincts, Without Her Consent, Forbidden Nights, Blood Vows: The Story of a Mafia Wife, Joshua's Heart, Donor, The Lookalike, With a Vengeance, Family of Strangers, With Hostile Intent, Shattered Trust: The Shari Karney Story, House of Secrets, Dying to Remember, Babymaker: The Dr. Cecil Jacobson Story, Against Her Will: The Carrie Buck Story, Cries From the Heart, A Touch of Truth, Danielle Steel's. Zoya, Seduction in a Small Town, Christmas in My Home Town, Childhood Sweetheart, Me & My Hormones (dir.).

GILER, DAVID
Producer, Writer, Director. b. New York, NY. Son of Bernie Giler, screen and TV writer. Began writing in teens; first work an episode for ABC series, The Gallant Men. Feature film career began as writer on Myra Breckenridge (1970).
PICTURES: *Writer*: The Parallax View, Fun with Dick and Jane, The Blackbird (also dir.), Southern Comfort (also prod.). *Prod.:* Aliens (story), Rustlers' Rhapsody, Let It Ride, Alien^3(ex. prod., also writer).
TELEVISION: *Writer*: The Kraft Theatre, Burke's Law, The Man from U.N.C.L.E., The Girl from U.N.C.L.E., Tales From the Crypt (exec. prod.).

GILLIAM, TERRY
Writer, Director, Actor, Animator. b. Minneapolis, MN, Nov. 22, 1940. e. Occidental Coll. Freelance writer and illustrator for various magazines and ad agencies before moving to London. Animator for BBC series Do Not Adjust Your Set, We Have Ways of Making You Laugh. Member, Monty Python's Flying Circus (1969-76). Books incl. numerous Monty Python publications. Honorary degrees: DFA Occidental Col. 1987, DFA Royal Col. of Art 1989.
PICTURES: And Now for Something Completely Different (animator, co-s.p., actor), Monty Python and the Holy Grail (co-dir., co-s.p., actor, animator), Jabberwocky (dir., co-s.p.), Life of Brian (actor, co-s.p., animator), The Do It Yourself Animation Film, Time Bandits (prod., dir., co-s.p.), Monty Python Live at the Hollywood Bowl (actor, co-s.p., animator, designer), The Miracle of Flight (animator, s.p.), Monty Python's The Meaning of Life (co-s.p., actor, animator), Spies Like Us (actor), Brazil (co-s.p., dir.), The Adventures of Baron Munchausen (dir., co-s.p.), The Fisher King (dir.), Twelve Monkeys (dir.), Fear and Loathing in Las Vegas (dir., s.p.), The Man Who Killed Don Quixote, Good Omens.
TELEVISION: *Series*: Monty Python's Flying Circus (also animator, dir.), Do Not Adjust Your Set, We Have Ways of Making You Laugh, The Mart Feldman Comedy Machine, The Last Machine (1995).

GILMORE, WILLIAM S.
Producer. b. Los Angeles, CA, March 10, 1934. e. U. of California at Berkeley. Started career in film editing before becoming asst. dir. and prod. mgr. at Universal Studios, where worked on 20 feature films. Headed prod. for Mirisch Co. in Europe; then to Zanuck/Brown Co. as exec. in chg. prod. Sr. v.p./prod. of Filmways Pictures, supervising literary development, prod. and post-prod.
PICTURES: Jaws (prod. exec.), The Sugarland Express (prod. exec.), The Last Remake of Beau Geste, Defiance, Deadly Blessing, Tough Enough, Against All Odds, White Nights, Little Shop of Horrors, The Man in the Moon, The Player, A Few Good Men, Watch It, The Sandlot, Curse of the Starving Class, Fire Down Below.
TELEVISION: Just Me and You, One in a Million--The Ron Leflore Story, The Legend of Walks Far Woman, S.O.S. Titanic, Another Woman's Child, Women and Men, Women and Men 2.

GILROY, FRANK D.
Writer, Director. b. New York, NY, Oct. 13, 1925. e. Dartmouth; postgrad. Yale School of Drama. TV writer: Playhouse 90, US Steel Hour, Omnibus, Kraft Theatre, Lux Video Theater, Studio One. B'way playwright.
AUTHOR: *Plays*: Who'll Save the Plowboy? (Obie award, 1962), The Subject Was Roses (Pulitzer Prize & Tony Award, 1965), The Only Game in Town, Present Tense, The Next Contestant, Dreams of Glory, Real to Reel, Match Point, A Way with Words, The Housekeeper, Last Licks, Any Given Day. *Novels:* Private, Little Ego (with Ruth Gilroy), From Noon to 3. *Book:* I Wake Up Screening!: Everything You Need to Know About Making Independent Films Including a Thousand Reasons Not To (1993).
PICTURES: *Writer*: The Fastest Gun Alive, The Gallant Hours, The Subject Was Roses, The Only Game in Town. *Dir.-Writer*: Desperate Characters (also prod.), From Noon Till Three, Once in Paris, The Gig, The Luckiest Man in the World.

TELEVISION: *Writer-Dir.*: The Doorbell Rang, Turning Point of Jim Malloy, Money Plays.

GILULA, STEPHEN
Executive. b. Herrin, IL, Aug. 20, 1950. e. Stanford U. UA Theatre Circuit, film booker for San Francisco area, 1973; Century Cinema Circuit, film buyer, LA, 1974. Co-founder, Landmark Theatre Corp., 1974; serving as pres., 1982-present. Landmark became a subsidiary of Metromedia Intl. Group Inc., in 1996. Chmn. NATO of California/Nevada, 1991-present; also on bd. of dirs. of NATO, 1992-present.

GIMBEL, ROGER
Producer, Executive. b. March 11, 1925. e. Yale. Began tv prod. career as creative chief of RCA Victor TV, then became assoc. prod. of the Tonight Show for NBC; named head of prog. dev. of NBC daytime programming; then prod. of the 90-minute NBC Tonight Specials, including The Jack Paar Show and the Ernie Kovacs Show. Became prod. and co-packager of the Glen Campbell Goodtime Hour for CBS, 1969; v.p. in chg. of prod. for Tomorrow Entertainment, 1971. Formed his own prod. co., Roger Gimbel's Tomorrow Enterprises, Inc., 1975; prod. Minstrel Man. Became U.S. pres. of EMI-TV, 1976. Received special personal Emmy as exec. prod. of War of the Children, 1975. Produced 33 movies for TV under the EMI banner and won 18 Emmys. In 1984, EMI-TV became The Peregrine Producers Group, Inc., of which he was pres. & COO. 1987, spun off Roger Gimbel Prods. as an independent film co; 1988-89, pres./exec. prod., Carolco/Gimbel Productions, Inc. 1989-1996, pres. & exec. prod. of Roger Gimbel Prods Inc. in association with Multimedia Motion Pictures Inc. 1997, pres. & exec. prod. of Roger Gimbel Prods Inc for independent film production.
TELEVISION: *Movies/Specials*: The Autobiography of Miss Jane Pittman, Born Innocent, Birds of Prey, Brand New Life, Gargoyles, Glass House, In This House of Brede, I Heard the Owl Call My Name, I Love You Goodbye, Larry, Miles to Go Before I Sleep, Queen of the Stardust Ballroom, Tell Me Where It Hurts, The Man Who Could Talk to Kids, Things in Their Season, A War of Children (Emmy Award), The Amazing Howard Hughes, Deadman's Curve, Steel Cowboy, Betrayal, The Cracker Factory, Survival of Diana, Can You Hear the Laughter?, S.O.S. Titanic, Walks-Far Woman, Sophia Loren: Her Own Sotory, Manions of America, A Question of Honor, The Killing of Randy Webster, Broken Promise, A Piano for Mrs. Cimino, Deadly Encounter, Aurora, Rockabye, Blackout, Apology, Montana, Shattered Dreams, Chernobyl: The Final Warning, Desperate Rescue: The Cathy Mahone Story, Murder Between Friends, The Perfect Mother.

GINNA, ROBERT EMMETT, JR.
Producer, Writer. b. New York, NY, Dec. 3, 1925. e. U. of Rochester, Harvard U., M.A. In U.S. Navy, WWII. Journalist for Life, Scientific American, Horizon, 1950-55; 1958-61, contributor to many magazines. Staff writer, producer, director NBC-TV, 1955-58; v.p., Sextant, Inc.; dir., Sextant Films Ltd., 1961-64. Founded Windward Productions, Inc., Windward Film Productions, Ltd., 1965. Active in publishing 1974-82; sr. ed. People; ed. in chief, Little Brown; asst. mgr., Life. Resumed pres., Windward Prods, Inc., 1982; publishing consultant.
PICTURES: Young Cassidy (co-prod.), The Last Challenge (co-s.p.), Before Winter Comes (prod.), Brotherly Love (prod.).

GINNANE, ANTHONY I.
Executive, Producer. e. Melbourne U (law), 1976. 1977 formed joint venture with financier William Fayman for Australian film production and distribution. 1981 established company Film and General Holdings Inc. for locating film projects/financing.
PICTURES: *Producer or Exec. Prod:* Sympathy in Summer (debut, 1970; also dir.), Fantasm, Patrick, Snapshot, Thirst, Harlequin, Race for the Yankee Zephyr, Strange Behavior, Turkey Shoot, Prisoners, Second Tim Lucky, Mesmerized, Dark Age, Slate Wyn & Me, Initiation, High Tide, The Lighthorsemen, Time Guardian, Incident at Raven's Gate, The Everlasting Secret Family, The Dreaming, Grievous Bodily Harm, Boundaries of the Heart, Killer Instinct, Savage Justice, Outback, A Case of Honor, Siege of Firebase Gloria, Driving Force, Demonstone, Fatal Sky, No Contest, Screamers, Bonjour Timothy.

GINSBURG, LEWIS S.
Distributor, Importer, Prod. b. New York, NY, May 16, 1914. e. City Coll. of New York, 1931-32. Columbia U., 1932-33. Ent. film industry, tabulating dept., United Artists, 1933; sls. contract dept. 1934; asst. to eastern district mgr., 1938; slsmn., New Haven exch., 1939. Army, 1943. Ret. to U.S., then formed first buying & booking service in Connecticut, 1945-55; in chg., New England Screen Guild Exchanges, 1955; TV film distr., 1955; Formed & org. International Film Assoc., Vid-EX Film Distr. Corp., 1961. Prod., TV half-hour series; vice-pres. in chg., dist., Desilu Film Dist. C., 1962; organized Carl Releasing Co., 1963; Walter Reade-Sterling Inc., 1964-65; formed L.G. Films Corp.; contract and playdate mgr., 20th Fox, 1965-68. Cinerama Releasing Corp. Adm. Ass't to sales mgr., 1968-69; 20th Cent.-Fox. Nat'l sales coordinator, 1969-present. 1970, 20th Century-Fox, Asst. to the Sales Mgr. 1971, Transnational Pictures Corp., v.p. in chg. of dist., pres., Stellar IV Film Corp., 1972.

GIRARDOT, ANNIE
Actress. b. Paris, France, Oct. 25, 1931. Studied nursing. Studied acting at the Paris Conservatory, made her acting debut with the Comedie Franccaise. Has acted on the French stage and in reviews in the Latin Quarter.
PICTURES: Trezie a Table (debut, 1955), Speaking of Murder, Inspector Maigret, Love and the Frenchwoman, Rocco and His Brothers, Le Rendezvous, Crime Does Not Pay, Vice and Virtue, The Organizer, La Bonne Soupe (Careless Love), Male Companion, The Dirty Game, The Witches, Live for Life, Les Galoises Bleues, Dillinger Is Dead, The Seed of Man, Trois Chambres a Manhattan (Venice Film Fest. Award), The Story of a Woman, Love Is a Funny Thing, Shock!, Where THere's Smoke, Juliette et Juliette, The Slap, It Is Raining in Santiago, No Time for Breakfast (Cesar Award), Dear Inspector, The Skirt Chaser, Traffic Jam, Jupiter's Thigh, Five Days in June, La Vie Continue, Prisonniers, Comedie D'Amour, Girls With Guns, Les Miserables.

GISH, ANNABETH
Actress. b. Albuquerque, NM, Mar. 13, 1971. e. Duke U ('93). Started acting at age 8; appeared in several TV commercials in Iowa.
PICTURES: Desert Bloom, Hiding Out, Mystic Pizza, Shag, Coupe de Ville, Wyatt Earp, The Red Coat, Nixon, The Last Supper, Beautiful Girls, Steel, S.L.C. Punk!, Double Jeopardy.
TELEVISION: *Series:* Courthouse. *Movies*: Hero in the Family, When He's Not a Stranger, The Last to Go, Lady Against the Odds, Silent Cries, Don't Look Back, to Live Again, God's New Plan, Different. *Mini-Series*: Scarlett, True Women.

GIVENS, ROBIN
Actress. b. New York, NY, Nov. 27, 1964. e. Sarah Lawrence Col., Harvard Univ. Graduate Sch. of Arts & Sciences. While at college became model, made appearances on daytime dramas The Guiding Light and Loving.
PICTURES: A Rage in Harlem (debut, 1991), Boomerang, Foreign Student, Blankman,.
TELEVISION: *Series*: Head of the Class, Angel Street, Courthouse, Sparks. *Movies*: Beverly Hills Madam, The Women of Brewster Place, The Penthouse, Dangerous Intentions, A Face to Die For.

GLASER, PAUL MICHAEL
Actor, Director. b. Cambridge, MA, March 25, 1943. e. Tulane U., Boston U., M.A. Did five seasons in summer stock before starting career in New York, making stage debut in Rockabye Hamlet in 1968. Appeared in numerous off-B'way plays and got early TV training as regular in daytime series, Love of Life and Love Is a Many Splendored Thing.
PICTURES: *Actor*: Fiddler on the Roof, Butterflies Are Free, Phobia. *Director*: Band of the Hand, The Running Man, The Cutting Edge, The Air Up There, Kazaam (also prod., story).
TELEVISION: *Series*: Starsky and Hutch. *Guest*: Kojak, Toma, The Streets of San Francisco, The Rockford Files, The Sixth Sense, The Waltons. *Movies*: Trapped Beneath the Sea, The Great Houdinis, Wail Till Your Mother Gets Home!, Princess Daisy, Jealousy, Attack on Fear, Single Bars Single Women, Amazons (dir. only).

GLASS, PHILIP
Composer, Actor, Writer. b. Baltimore, MD, Jan. 31, 1937.
PICTURES: Cenere, Chappaqua, Mark Di Suvero Sculptor, Four American Composers (also actor), Koyaanisqatsi, High Wire, Mishima: A Life in Four Chapters, Dead End Kids, Hamburger Hill, Einstein on the Beach: The Changing Image of Opera, The Thin Blue Line, Powaqqatsi, Le Chiesa, Mindwalk, Closet Land, Anima Mundi, Candyman, A Brief History of Time, Niki de Saint Phalle: Wer ist das Monster-du oder ich?, Jenipapo, Candyman: Farewell to the Flesh, The Secret Agent, Absence Stronger Than Presence, Bent, Kundun (LA Film Critics Award, Best Musical Score, 1997), The Truman Show (actor), Noyaqqatsi (also s.p.).

GLAZER, WILLIAM
Executive b. Cambridge, MA. e. State U. of New York, Entered m.p. ind. with Ralph Snider Theatres 1967-69; General Cinema Corp. 1969-71; Loews Theatres 1971-73; Joined Sack Theatres/USA Cinemas 1973 as Dist. mgr.; 1974 Exec. Asst. to Pres.; 1976 Gen. Mgr.; 1980 V.P. Gen. Mgr.; 1982-86 Exec. V.P. Joined Interstated Theatres 1987 (Pres.); Fox Theatres 1993-95. MP industry consultant, 1988-pres. Bd. of Dir. Member of SMPTE; NATO (Exec. Bd.); Theatre Owners of New England (Pres. and Chairman.)

GLEASON, LARRY
Executive. b. Boston, MA, Apr. 30, 1938. e. Boston Coll., M.A., 1960. Held various positions, western div., mgr., General Cinema Corp.; 1963-73; gen. mgr., Gulf States Theatres, New Orleans, 1973-74; pres., Mann Theatres, 1974-85; joined DeLaurentiis Entertainment Group as pres., mktg./dist., 1985. Named sr. v.p., Paramount Pictures Corp, theatrical exhibition group, 1989. Named pres. Paramount Pictures Corp. theatrical exhib. group, 1991. Joined MGM/UA as pres. of Worlwide Distrib., 1994. Foundation of Motion Picture Pioneers v.p. Member, Variety Club, Will Rogers Foundation.

GLEN, JOHN
Director. b. Sunbury on Thames, Eng., May 15, 1932. Entered industry in 1947. Second unit dir.: On Her Majesty's Secret Service, The Spy Who Loved Me, Wild Geese, Moonraker (also editor). Editor: The Sea Wolves.
PICTURES: For Your Eyes Only (dir. debut, 1981), Octopussy, A View to a Kill, The Living Daylights, Licence to Kill, Aces: Iron Eagle III, Christopher Columbus: The Discovery.
TELEVISION: *Series*: Space Precinct (7 episodes).

GLENN, CHARLES OWEN
Executive. b. Binghamton, NY, March 27, 1938. e. Syracuse U., B.A., U. of PA. Capt., U.S. Army, 1961-63. Asst. to dir. of adv., 20th Cent. Fox, 1966-67; asst. adv. mgr., Paramount, 1967-68; acct. spvsr. & exec., MGM record & m.p. div., 1968-69; nat'l adv. mgr., Paramount, 1969-70; nat'l. dir. of adv., Paramount, 1970-71; v.p. adv.-pub.-prom., 1971-73; v.p. marketing, 1974; v.p. prod. mktg., 1975; joined American Intl. Pictures as v.p. in chg. of adv./creative affairs, 1979. 1980, when Filmways took AIP over he was named their v.p. in chg. worldwide adv./pub./promo.; joined MCA/Universal in 1982 as exec. v.p., adv.-promo.; 1984, appt. Orion Pictures adv.-pub.-promo. exec. v.p.; 1987, appt. Orion mktg. exec. v.p. 1989 recipient Outstanding Performance Award Leukemia Society of Amer. for completing NYC Marathon. 1993, pres. mktg., Bregman/Baer Prods. Featured actor in 1993 film Philadelphia. Member: Exec. comm. public relations branch, Academy of M.P. Arts & Sciences. Holder of NATO mktg. exec. of year (1983) award, Clio Award for U.S. adv. of Platoon; Variety Club, Motion Picture Pioneers, Screen Actors Guild.

GLENN, SCOTT
Actor. b. Pittsburgh, PA, Jan. 26, 1942. e. William & Mary Coll. Worked as U.S. Marine, newspaper reporter before going to New York to study drama at Actors Studio in 1968.
THEATER: *Off-B'way*: Zoo Story, Fortune in Men's Eyes, Long Day's Jack Street, Journey into Night. *B'way:* The Impossible Years, Burn This, Dark Picture.
PICTURES: The Baby Maker (debut, 1970), Angels Hard as They Come, Hex, Nashville, Fighting Mad, More American Graffiti, Apocalypse Now, Urban Cowboy, Cattle Annie and Little Britches, Personal Best, The Challenge, The Right Stuff, The Keep, The River, Wild Geese II, Silverado, Verne Miller, Man on Fire, Off Limits, Miss Firecracker, The Hunt for Red October, The Silence of the Lambs, My Heroes Have Always Been Cowboys, Backdraft, The Player, Night of the Running Man, Tall Tale, Reckless, Edie and Pen, Courage Under Fire, Carla's Song, Lesser Prophets, Absolute Power, Larga Distancia, Firestorm, The Virgin Suicides.
TELEVISION: *Movies*: Gargoyles, As Summers Die, Intrigue, The Outside Woman, Women & Men 2, Shadowhunter, Slaughter of the Innocents, Past Tense, Naked City: Justice with a Bullet, Naked City: A Killer Christmas. *Series:* Mobile Suit Gundam.

GLENNON, JAMES M.
Cinematographer. b. Burbank, CA, Aug. 29, 1942. e. UCLA. m. actress Charmaine Glennon. Focus Awards judge 1985-; bd. or dirs., UCLA Theatre Arts Alumni Assoc. 1985-. ASC - member of American Society of Cinematographers, AMPAS.
PICTURES: Return of the Jedi, El Norte, The Wild Life, Smooth Talk, Flight of the Navigator, Time of Destiny, A Show of Force, December, The Gift, Citizen Ruth, Best Men.
TELEVISION: Lemon Sky (American Playhouse), Laurel Ave, DEA (pilot), Bakersfield (pilot), Judicial Consent.

GLESS, SHARON
Actress. b. Los Angeles, CA, May 31, 1943. m. producer Barney Rosenzweig. London stage: Misery.
PICTURES: Airport 1975, The Star Chamber.
TELEVISION: *Series*: Marcus Welby M.D., Faraday and Co., Switch, Turnabout, House Calls, Cagney and Lacey (2 Emmy Awards, Golden Globe Award), The Trials of Rosie O'Neill (Golden Globe Award). *Mini-Series*: Centennial, The Immigrants, The Last Convertible. *Movies*: The Longest Night, All My Darling Daughters, My Darling Daughters' Anniversary, Richie Brockelman: Missing 24 Hours, The Flying Misfits, The Islander, Crash, Whisper in the Gloom (Disney), Hardhat and Legs, Moviola: The Scarlett O'Hara War, Revenge of the Stepford Wives, The Miracle of Kathy Miller, Hobson's Choice, The Sky's No Limit, Letting Go, The Outside Woman, Honor Thy Mother, Separated by Murder, Cagney & Lacey: The Return, Cagney & Lacey: Together Again, Cagney & Lacey: True Convictions, Cagney & Lacey: The View Through the Glass Ceiling, The Girl Next Door.

GLICK, PHYLLIS
Executive. b. New York, NY. e. Queens Coll. of C.U.N.Y. Began career with Otto-Windsor Associates, as casting director; left to be independent. 1979, joined ABC-TV as mgr. of comedy series development; promoted 1980 to director, involved with all comedy series developed for network. 1985, joined Paramount Pictures as exec. dir., production, for M.P. Group; 1989, co-exec. prod., Living Dolls.

GLOBUS, YORAM
Producer. b. Israel, Came to U.S. 1979. Has co-produced many films with cousin and former partner Menahem Golan. Sr. exec. v.p., Cannon Group; Pres. and CEO Cannon Entertainment and Cannon Films; 1989 named chmn. and C.E.O Cannon Entertainment and officer of Cannon Group Inc.; then co-pres. Pathe Communications Corp. and chmn. and C.E.O. Pathe Intl. Left MGM/Pathe in 1991.
PICTURES: All as producer or exec. prod. with Menahem Golan: Sallah; Trunk to Cairo; My Margo; What's Good for the Goose; Escape to the Sun; I Love You, Rosa; The House on Chelouch Street; The Four Deuces; Kazablan; Diamonds; God's Gun; Kid Vengeance, Operation Thunderbolt, The Uranium Conspiracy, Savage Weekend, The Magician of Lublin, The Apple, The Happy Hooker Goes to Hollywood, Dr. Heckyl and Mr. Hype, The Godsend, New Year's Evil, Schizoid, Seed of Innocence, Body and Soul, Death Wish II, Enter the Ninja, Hospital Massacre, The Last American Virgin, Championship Season, Treasure of Four Crowns, 10 to Midnight, Nana, I'm Almost Not Crazy..., John Cassavetes: The Man and His Work, The House of Long Shadows, Revenge of the Ninja, Hercules, The Wicked Lady, Sahara, The Ambassador, Bolero, Exterminator 2, The Naked Face, Missing in Action, Hot Resort, Love Streams, Breakin', Grace Quigley, Making the Grade, Ninja III-The Domination, Breakin' 2: Electric Boogaloo, Lifeforce, Over the Brooklyn Bridge, The Delta Force, The Assisi Underground, Hot Chili, The Berlin Affair, Missing in Action 2-The Beginning, Rappin', Thunder Alley, American Ninja, Mata Hari, Death Wish 3, King Solomon's Mines, Runaway Train, Fool for Love, Invasion U.S.A., Maria's Lovers, Murphy's Law, The Naked Cage, P.O.W.: The Escape, The Texas Chainsaw Massacre, Part 2, Invaders from Mars, 52 Pick-Up, Link, Firewalker, Dumb Dicks, The Nutcracker: The Motion Picture, Avenging Force, Hashigaon Hagadol, Journey to the Center of the Earth, Prom Queen, Salome, Otello, Cobra, America 3000, American Ninja 2: The Confrontation, Allan Quartermain and the Lost City of Gold, Assassination, Beauty and the Beast, Down Twisted, Duet for One, The Emperor's New Clothes, The Hanoi Hilton, The Barbarians, Dutch Treat, Masters of the Universe, Number One with a Bullet, Rumpelstiltskin, Street Smart, UnderCover, The Assault, Hansel and Gretel, Going Bananas, Snow White, Sleeping Beauty, Tough Guys Don't Dance, Shy People, Dancers, Red Riding Hood, King Lear, Braddock: Missing in Action III, Too Much, Die Papierene Brucke, Field of Honor, Barfly (exec. prod.), Surrender (exec. prod.), Death Wish 4: The Crackdown (exec. prod.), Gor (exec. prod.), Business as Usual (exec. prod.), Over the Top, Superman IV: The Quest for Peace. Prod.: Delta Force, Operation Crackdown, Manifesto, Stranglehold, Delta Force II, Cyborg, Step By Step. Exec. prod.: The Kitchen Toto, Doin' Time on Planet Earth, Kickboxer, Kinjite, A Man Called Sarge, The Rose Garden, The Secret of the Ice Cave.

GLOVER, CRISPIN
Actor. b. New York, NY, 1964. e. Mirman School. Trained for stage with Dan Mason and Peggy Feury. Stage debut, as Friedrich Von Trapp, The Sound of Music, Los Angeles, 1977. Wrote books, Rat Catching (1987), Oak Mot (1990), Concrete Inspection (1992), What It Is and How It Is Done (1995). Recorded album The Big Problem Does Not Equal the Solution- The Solution Equals Let it Be.
PICTURES: My Tutor, Racing with the Moon, Friday the 13th-The Final Chapter, Teachers, Back to the Future, At Close Range, River's Edge, Twister, Where the Heart Is, Wild at Heart, The Doors, Little Noises, Rubin and Ed, Thirty Door Key, What's Eating Gilbert Grape, Chasers, Even Cowgirls Get the Blues, Crime and Punishment, Dead Man, What Is It? (dir. and wrote), The People vs. Larry Flynt, Nurse Betty, Charlie's Angels, What Is It?, Crime and Pusnishment, Beaver Trilogy, Bartleby.
TELEVISION: *Movie*: High School U.S.A. *Special*: Hotel Room (Blackout).

GLOVER, DANNY
Actor. b. San Francisco, CA, July 22, 1947. e. San Francisco State U. Trained at Black Actors Workshop of American Conservatory Theatre. Appeared in many stage productions (Island, Macbeth, Sizwe Banzi Is Dead, etc.). On N.Y. stage in Suicide in B Flat, The Blood Knot, Master Harold... and the Boys (Theatre World Award).
PICTURES: Escape from Alcatraz (debut, 1979), Chu Chu and the Philly Flash, Out (Deadly Drifter), Iceman, Places in the Heart, Witness, Silverado, The Color Purple, Lethal Weapon, Bat-21, Lethal Weapon 2, To Sleep with Anger (also co-exec. prod.), Predator 2, Flight of the Intruder, A Rage in Harlem, Pure Luck, Grand Canyon, Lethal Weapon 3, Bopha!, The Saint of Fort Washington, Maverick (cameo), Angels in the Outfield, Operation Dumbo Drop, Gone Fishin', Wild America (cameo), Switchback, The Rainmaker (cameo), The Prince of Egypt (voice), Beloved, Antz (voice), Lethal Weapon 4, The Monster.
TELEVISION: *Mini-Series*: Chiefs, Lonesome Dove, Queen. *Movies*: Face of Rage, Mandela, Dead Man Out, Buffalo Soldiers (also exec. prod.). *Series*: Storybook Classics (host), Civil War Journal (host). *Specials*: And the Children Shall Lead, How the Leopard Got Its Spots (narrator), A Place at the Table, A Raisin in the Sun, Override (dir. only), Shelley Duvall's Tall Tales and Legends: John Henry, Can't You hear the Wind Howl?: The Life & Music of Robert Johnson (voice), Scared Straight! 20 Years Later (voice). *Guest*: Lou Grant, Palmerstown U.S.A., Gimme a Break, Hill Street Blues, Many Mansions.

GLOVER, JOHN
Actor. b. Kingston, NY, Aug. 7, 1944. e. Towson State Coll., Baltimore.
THEATER: On regional theatre circuit; Off-B'way in A Scent of Flowers, Subject to Fits, The House of Blue Leaves, The Selling of the President, Love! Valour! Compassion! (also B'way; Tony Award, 1995). With APA Phoenix Co. in Great God Brown (Drama Desk Award), The Visit, Don Juan, Chermin de Fer, Holiday. Other NY stage: The Importance of Being Earnest, Hamlet, Frankenstein, Whodunnit, Digby. L.A.: The Traveler (L.A. Drama Critics Award), Lips Together Teeth Apart.
PICTURES: Shamus, Annie Hall, Julia, Somebody Killed Her Husband, Last Embrace, Success, Melvin and Howard, The Mountain Men, The Incredible Shrinking Woman, A Little Sex, The Evil That Men Do, A Flash of Green, 52 Pick-Up, White Nights, Something Special, Masquerade, A Killing Affair, Rocket Gibraltar, The Chocolate War, Scrooged, Meet the Hollowheads, Gremlins 2: The New Batch, Robocop 2, Ed and His Dead Mother, Night of the Running Man, In the Mouth of Madness, Schemes, Automatics, Batman and Robin, Love! Valour! Compassion!, Macbeth in Manhattan, Dead Broke, Payback, On Edge.
TELEVISION: *Movies*: A Rage of Angels, The Face of Rage, Ernie Kovacs-Between the Laughter, An Early Frost (Emmy nom.), Apology, Moving Target, Hot Paint, Nutcracker: Money Madness and Murder (Emmy nom.), David, The Traveling Man (ACE nom.), Twist of Fate, Breaking Point, El Diablo, What Ever Happened to Baby Jane?, Dead on the Money, Drug Wars: The Cocaine Cartel, Grass Roots, Majority Rule, Assault at West Point, Dead by Midnight, The Tempest. *Specials*: An Enemy of the People, Paul Reiser: Out on a Whim, Crime and Punishment (Emmy nom.). *Mini-Series*: Kennedy, George Washington, Medusa's Child. *Series*: South Beach, Brimstone. *Guest*: L.A. Law (Emmy nom.), Frasier (Emmy nom.)

GLYNN, CARLIN
Actress. b. Cleveland, OH, Feb. 19, 1940. m. actor-writer-dir. Peter Masterson. Daughter is actress Mary Stuart Masterson. e. Sophie Newcomb College, 1957-58. Studied acting with Stella Adler, Wynn Handman and Lee Strasberg in NY. Debut, Gigi, Alley Theatre, Houston, TX 1959. Adjunct professor at Columbia U film sch. Resource advisor at the Sundance Inst.
THEATRE: (NY debut, 1960) Waltz of The Toreadors, The Best Little Whorehouse in Texas (Tony, Eleanora Duse & Olivier Awards), Winterplay, Alterations, Pal Joey (Chicago; Jos. Jefferson Award), The Cover of Life, The Young Man From Atlanta (winner, Pulitzer Prize for Drama, 1995), Amazing Grace.
PICTURES: Three Days of the Condor, Continental Divide, Sixteen Candles, The Trip to Bountiful, Gardens of Stone, Blood Red, Night Game, Convicts, Blessing, Judy Berlin.
TELEVISION: *Series*: Mr. President. *Mini-Series*: A Woman Named Jackie.

GODARD, JEAN-LUC
Writer, Director. b. Paris, France, Dec. 3, 1930. e. Lycee Buffon, Paris. Journalist, film critic Cahiers du Cinema. Acted in and financed experimental film Quadrille by Jacques Rivette, 1951. 1954: dir. first short, Operation Beton, followed by Une Femme Coquette. 1956, was film editor. 1957: worked in publicity dept. 20th Century Fox.
PICTURES: *Director/Writer*: Breathless (A Bout de Souffle; feature debut, 1960), Le Petit Soldat, A Woman Is a Woman, My Life to Live, Les Carabiniers, Contempt, Band of Outsiders, The Married Woman, Alphaville, Pierrot le Fou, Masculine-Feminine, Made in USA, Two or Three Things I Know About Her, La Chinoise, Weekend, Sympathy for the Devil, Le Gai Savoir, Tout a Bien (co-dir.), Numero Deux, Every Man For Himself, First Name Carmen, Hail Mary, Aria (Armide segment), King Lear, Keep Up Your Right (also edit, actor), Nouvelle Vogue (New Wave), Helas Pour Moi (Oh Woe is Me). Germany Year, J.L.G. by J.L.G., The Kids Play Russian, Forever Mozart (also edit.), The Old Place, Eloge de l'Amour.

GOLAN, MENAHEM
Producer, Director, Writer. b. Tiberias, Israel, May 31, 1929. e. NYU. Studied theater dir. at Old Vic Theatre London, m.p. prod. at City Coll, NY. Co-founder and prod. with cousin Yoram Globus, Golan-Globus Prods., Israel, then L.A., 1962. Later Noah Films, Israel, 1963, Ameri-Euro Pictures Corp, before buying controlling share in Cannon Films, 1979. Sr. exec. v.p., Cannon Group; chmn. of bd., Cannon Entertainment and Cannon Films. 1988, dir. and sr. exec. v.p. Cannon Group, chmn. and head of creative affairs, Cannon Entertainment when it became div. of Giancarlo Parretti's Pathe Communications Corp. Resigned March, 1989 to form 21st Century Film Corp as chmn. and CEO.
PICTURES: *Director/co-writer*: Kasablan, Diamonds, Entebbe (Operation Thunderbolt), Teyve and His Seven Daughters, What's Good for the Goose? Lepke, The Magician of Lublin, The Goodsend, Happy Hooker Goes to Hollywood, Enter the Ninja. *Producer-Writer-Director*: Mack the Knife, Hanna's War. *Producer-Director*: The Uranium Conspiracy, Delta Force, Over the Brooklyn Bridge, Over the Top. *Producer/Exec. prod.*: Sallah, Runaway Train, Sallah, Fool For Love, Maria's Lovers, Cobra, Evil Angels, I Love You Rosa, Body and Soul, also: Deathwish II, The Last American Virgin, That Championship Season, House of Long Shadows, Revenge of the Ninja, Hercules, The Movie Tales (12 children's fairy tales films), The Wicked Lady, Cobra, Barfly (exec. prod.), Breakin', Missing in Action, Dancers (prod.), Surrender (exec. prod.), Death Wish 4: The Crackdown (exec. prod.), King Lear (prod.), Too Much (prod.), Powaqquatsi (exec. prod.), Mercenary Fighters (prod.), Doin' Time on Planet Earth (prod.), Manifesto (prod.), Kinjite (exec. prod.), Messenger of Death (exec. prod.), Alien From L.A. (prod.), Hero and the Terror (exec. prod.), Haunted Summer (exec. prod.), A Cry in the Dark (exec. prod.), Delta Force-Operation Crackdown (prod.), A Man Called Sarge (exec. prod.), Stranglehold: Delta Force II (prod.), Cyborg (prod.), The Rose Garden (exec. prod.), Rope Dancing (exec. prod.), The Phantom of the Opera.

GOLCHAN, FREDERIC
Producer. b. Neuilly sur Seine, France, Nov. 20, 1955. e. UCLA Film School, HEC in Paris, NYU Bus.Sch. Journalist/photographer for various European magazines. Worked for American Express, 1979-80. Started indept. investment banking firm, 1980-84. Started own production co., 1985. Directed Victory of the Deaf. V.P. French Hollywood Circle
PICTURES: Flagrant Desire, Quick Change, Intersection, The Associate.
TELEVISION: Freedom Fighter, Home by Midnight, In The Deep Woods.

GOLD, ERNEST
Composer, Conductor. b. Vienna, Austria, July 13, 1921. e. State Acad. for Music and Performing Arts, Austria 1937-38; private study, 1939-49 in U.S. Worked as song writer 1939-42 and taught in private schools, 1942. Composed first score for Columbia Pictures, 1945. Musical dir., Santa Barbara Symphony, 1958-59. Taught at UCLA, 1973 and 1983-90 (adult ed.). Gold record for soundtrack of Exodus, 1968. Received star on Walk of Fame on Hollywood Blvd., 1975. Elected to bd. of govs., AMPAS, 1984.
PICTURES: Smooth as Silk, Wyoming, Witness for the Prosecution, The Pride and the Passion, Too Much Too Soon, On the Beach (Acad. Award nom.), Exodus (Academy Award, 1960), Inherit the Wind, The Last Sunset, Judgment at Nuremberg, Pressure Point, A Child Is Waiting, It's a Mad Mad Mad Mad World (Acad. Award nom.), Ship of Fools, The Secret of Santa Vittoria (Acad. Award nom.), The Wild McCullochs, Cross of Iron, Fun With Dick and Jane, Good Luck Miss Wyckoff, The Runner Stumbles, Tom Horn.
TELEVISION: Small Miracle, Wallenberg: a Hero's Story.

GOLDBERG, FRED
Executive. b. New York, NY, Aug. 26, 1921. e. Pace Col., Sch. of Mktg. & Advt. Expl. Paramount, 1946; asst. expl. mgr. trade contact, syndicate contact, NY newspaper contact promotion mgr., 1946-52; asst. publ. mgr. RKO, 1952; natl. publ. mgr., IFE, 1953; v.p. Norton and Condon, pub., 1953; returned to IFE Sept. 1954 as natl. pub. mgr.; head of NY office, Arthur Jacobs, then Blowitz-Maskel, 1956; exec. asst. to dir. pub., adv. UA Corp., 1958; exec. dir., adv., pub. exploitation, UA Corp., 1961; named v.p., 1962; sr. v.p., 1972; sr. v.p., dir. of mrkt., 1977. Left in 1978 to be cons. with Diener, Hauser & Bates Agency. In 1979 joined Columbia Pics. as sr. v.p. in chg. of adv./pub. Left in 1981 to form new co. 1982, sr. v.p. mktg., Orion Pictures. Became teacher of M.P. Mktg. & Distrib. at Univ. of Miami's Sch. of Comm. Author: Motion Picture Marketing & Distribution.

GOLDBERG, LEONARD
Executive, Producer. b. Brooklyn, NY, Jan. 24, 1934. e. Wharton ch., U. of Pennsylvania. Began career in ABC-TV research dept.; moved to NBC-TV research div.; 1961 joined BBD&Q ad agency in charge of overall bdcst. coordinator. In 1963 rejoined ABC-TV as mgr. of program devel. 1964-66, v.p., Daytime programs. 1966 named VP in chg of network TV programming. Resigned in 1969 to join Screen Gems as VP in chg. of prod. Left for partnership with Aaron Spelling in Spelling/Goldberg Prods.; later produced TV and theatrical films under own banner, Mandy Prods. 1986, named pres., COO, 20th Century Fox. Resigned, 1989. Elected to the board of Spectradyne Inc.
PICTURES: *Prod.*: All Night Long, WarGames, Space Camp, Sleeping With the Enemy, The Distinguished Gentleman, Aspen Extreme, Double Jeopardy.
TELEVISION: *Series*: The Rookies, SWAT, Starsky and Hutch, Charlie's Angels, Family, Hart to Hart, T.J. Hooker, Fantasy Island, Paper Dolls, The Cavanaughs, Class of '96. *Movies*: Brian's Song (Peabody Award, Emmy Awards), Little Ladies of the Night, The Legend of Valentino, The Boy in the Plastic Bubble, Something About Amelia (Emmy Awards, 1984), Alex: The Life of a Child, She Woke Up, Love Letters.

GOLDBERG, WHOOPI
Actress. r.n. Caryn Johnson. b. New York, NY, Nov. 13, 1949. e. Sch. for the Performing Arts. Began performing at age 8 in N.Y. with children's program at Hudson Guild and Helena Rubenstein Children's Theatre. Moved to San Diego, CA, 1974, and helped found San Diego Rep. Theatre appearing in Mother Courage, Getting Out. Member: Spontaneous Combustion (improv. group). Joined Blake St. Hawkeyes Theatre in Berkeley, partnering with David Schein. Went solo to create The Spook Show,

working in San Francisco and later touring U.S. & Europe. 1983 performance caught attention of Mike Nichols which led to B'way show (for which she received a Theatre World Award) based on it and directed by him. Founding member of Comic Relief benefits. Theatrical film debut in The Color Purple (1985; Image Award NAACP, Golden Globe). Author of, Alice.
THEATER: small roles in B'way prods. of Pippin, Hair, Jesus Christ Superstar. Living on the Edge of Chaos (tour, 1988), A Funny Thing Happened on the Way to the Forum.
PICTURES: The Color Purple (debut, 1985; Acad. Award nom.), Jumpin' Jack Flash, Burglar, Fatal Beauty, The Telephone, Clara's Heart, Beverly Hills Brats (cameo), Homer and Eddie, Ghost (Academy Award, best supporting actress, 1990), The Long Walk Home, Soapdish, House Party 2 (cameo), The Player, Sister Act, Wisecracks, Sarafina!, The Magic World of Chuck Jones, National Lampoon's Loaded Weapon 1 (cameo), Made in America, Sister Act 2: Back in the Habit, Naked in New York (cameo), The Lion King (voice), The Little Rascals, Corrina Corrina, Star Trek: Generations, Theodore Rex, The Pagemaster (voice), Liberation (narrator), Boys on the Side, Moonlight and Valentino, The Celluloid Closet, Bogus, Eddie, The Associate, Ghosts of Mississippi, An Alan Smithee Film: Burn Hollywood Burn, How Stella Got Her Groove Back, The Rugrats Movie (voice), Monkey Bone, Get Bruce, The Deep End of the Ocean, Girl Interrupted.
TELEVISION: *Series*: Star Trek: The Next Generation, Bagdad Cafe, The Whoopi Goldberg Show (synd. talk show), Hollywood Squares. *Specials*: Whoopi Goldberg Direct From Broadway, Comic Relief, Carol Carl Whoopi and Robin, Scared Straight: 10 Years Later, Funny You Don't Look 200, Comedy Tonight (host), My Past is My Own (Schoolbreak Special), Free to Be... a Family, The Debbie Allen Special, Cool Like That Christmas (voice), 34th Annual Grammy Awards (host), A Gala for the President's at Ford's Theatre (host), The 66th Annual Academy Awards (host), The 68th Annual Academy Awards (host). *Guest*: Moonlighting (Emmy nom.), A Different World. *Movie*: Kiss Shot, In the Gloaming, Cinderella, A Knight in Camelot, Leprechauns, Jackie's Back!, Alice in Wonderland.

GOLDBLUM, JEFF
Actor. b. Pittsburgh, PA, Oct. 22, 1952. Studied at Sanford Meisner's Neighborhood Playhouse in New York. On B'way in Two Gentleman of Verona, The Moony Shapiro Songbook. Off-B'way: El Grande de Coca Cola, City Sugar, Twelfth Night.
PICTURES: Death Wish (debut, 1974), California Split, Nashville, Next Stop Greenwich Village, St. Ives, Special Delivery, The Sentinel, Annie Hall, Between the Lines, Remember My Name, Thank God It's Friday, Invasion of the Body Snatchers, Threshold, The Big Chill, The Right Stuff, The Adventures of Buckaroo Banzai, Into the Night, Silverado, Transylvania 6-5000, The Fly, Beyond Therapy, Vibes, Earth Girls Are Easy, Twisted Obsession, The Tall Guy, Mr. Frost, The Player, Deep Cover, The Favor the Watch and the Very Big Fish, Fathers and Sons, Jurassic Park, Hideaway, Nine Months, Powder, The Great White Hype, Independence Day, Mad Dog Time, The Lost World: Jurassic Park, Welcome to Hollywood, The Prince of Egypt (voice), Holy Man, The Prince of Egypt (voice), Playmate Pajama Party, Chain of Fools, One of the Hollywood Ten, Auggie Rose, Like Cats & Dogs, Perfume.
TELEVISION: *Movies*: The Legend of Sleepy Hollow, Rehearsal for Murder, Ernie Kovacs: Between the Laughter, The Double Helix (BBC), Framed, Lush Life, The Story of Bean. *Series*: Tenspeed and Brownshoe, Future Quest (host). *Guest*: The Blue Knight, It's Garry Shandling's Show.

GOLDEN, HERBERT L.
b. Philadelphia, PA, Feb. 12, 1914. e. Temple U., 1936, B.S. Reporter, rewrite man. asst. city ed., Philadelphia Record, 1933-38; joined Variety, 1938; on leave of absence, 1942-43, when asst. to John Hay Whitney and Francis Alstock, directors, M.P. Division, Coordinator of Inter-American Affairs (U.S.); in U.S. Navy, 1943-46; then returned to Variety. m.p. ed. Consultant on motion pictures, Good Housekeeping magazine McGraw-Hill Publications, American Yearbook. Ent. Ind. Div. Bankers Trust Co., NY, 1952; named v.p. 1954-56; v.p. & mem. of bd. United Artists Corp., 1958; member of board, MPAA, 1959; pres., Lexington Int., Inc. investments, 1962; mem. bd., chmn. exec. com., Perfect Photo Inc., 1962; 1965 sect. & mem. bd. Century Broadcasting Group; chmn. G & G Thea. Corp.; pres. Diversifax Corp., 1966; consult. Pathe Lab, 1967; Mem. bd. Childhood Prod. Inc., Music Makers Group, Inc., Cinecom Corp. pres., Vere/Swiss Corp., 1977; mem. bd., Coral Reef Publications, Inc., 1977. Returned to Bankers Trust, 1979, to head its Media Group (service to film and TV industries). Retired, 1992.

GOLDEN, JEROME B.
Executive, Attorney. b. New York, NY, Nov. 26, 1917. e. St. Lawrence U., LL.B., 1942. Member legal dept., Paramount Pictures, Inc., 1942-50; United Paramount Theatres, Inc., 1950-53; ABC, Inc., 1953; secy., ABC, 1958-86; v.p., ABC, 1959-86. Consultant.

GOLDEN, PAT
Casting Director, Director. b. Pittsburgh, PA, July 21, 1951. e. U Pittsburgh, Carnegie-Mellon U. Has directed plays for theatre incl. Homeboy at Perry St. Th. in NY. Was in casting dept. of NY Shakespeare Festival Public Th. Served as assoc. prod. on PBS series The Negro Ensemble Company's 20th Anniversary. Assoc. prod.: Hallelujah (PBS); dir.: House Party 2 documentary, My Secret Place (tv pilot).
PICTURES: Ragtime, Beat Street, Krush Groove, The Killing Fields, Blue Velvet, Platoon (Awarded Casting Society of America Award), Dear America, The Handmaid's Tale, House Party 2 (assoc. prod.), Voyager, Posse.

GOLDENSON, LEONARD H.
Executive. b. Scottsdale, PA, December 7, 1905. e. Harvard Coll., B.A., Harvard Law School, LL.B. Practiced law, NY; counsel in reorg. Paramount theatres in New England, 1933-37; 1937 apptd. asst. to v.p. Paramount in charge theat. operations; became head of theat. operations, 1938; elected pres. Paramount Theat. Service Corp., v.p. Paramount Pictures, 1938; dir. Paramount Pictures, 1942 (also pres. various Paramount theat. subsids) Pres., CEO & dir. United Paramount Theatres, Inc., 1950, and of American Broadcasting-Paramount Theatres, Inc., 1953, result of merger of ABC and United Paramount Theatres, Inc.; chmn. of bd. & CEO of ABC to 1986. Then chmn. of exec. comm. & dir. Capital Cities/ABC, Inc. 1972; mem., International Radio and TV Society, Natl. Acad. of TV Arts & Sciences, Broadcast Pioneers, Motion Picture Pioneers; founder/member of Hollywood Museum; grad. dir. of Advertising Council, Inc.; Trustee Emeritus Museum of TV & Radio; Hon. Chmn. Acad. of TV Arts & Sciences.

GOLDMAN, BO
Writer. b. New York, NY, Sept. 10, 1932. e. Princeton U., B.A., 1953. Wrote lyrics for B'way musical version of Pride and Prejudice entitled First Impressions (1959). Assoc. prod. & script editor for Playhouse 90 1958-60; writer-prod., NET Playhouse 1970-71, Theater in America 1972-74.
PICTURES: One Flew Over the Cuckoo's Nest (co-s.p.; WGA & Academy Awards, 1975), The Rose (co-s.p.), Melvin and Howard (NY Film Critics, WGA & Academy Awards, 1980), Shoot the Moon, Swing Shift (uncredited), Little Nikita (co-s.p.), Dick Tracy (uncredited), Scent of a Woman (Golden Globe Award, Acad. Award nom.), First Knight (co-s.p.), City Hall (co-s.p.).

GOLDMAN, EDMUND
Executive, Producer. b. Shanghai, China, Nov. 12, 1906. e. Shanghai and San Francisco. Entered ind. as asst. mgr., for Universal in Shanghai, 1935-36; named mgr. Columbia Pictures' Philippine office, 1937. 1951 named Far East. supvr. for Columbia, headquartering in Tokyo. 1953, co-founded Manson Intl. 1953-91 indep. m.p. dist., specializing in foreign mktg. representing indep. prods. and dist. Retired, 1991.
PICTURES: Surrender Hell (prod.), The Quick and the Dead (exec. prod.).

GOLDMAN, MICHAEL F.
Executive. b. Manila, Philippines, Sept. 28, 1939. e. UCLA, B.S. in acct., 1962 California C.P.A. certificate issued June, 1972. In 1962 incorporated Manson International, which was sold in 1986. Incorporated Quixote Prods., 1979. Also owner and sole proprietor Taurus Film co. of Hollywood, founded 1964. Co-founder and first chief financial officer of American Film Marketing Association, sponsor of First American Film Market in Los Angeles in 1981; v.p. of AFMA 1982 and 1983, President AFMA 1984 and 1985. Chmn. AFMA, 1992-3. AFMA bd. mbr., 1981-87, 1988-present; Co-founder, Cinema Consultants Group, 1988. Produced feature, Jessi's Girls in 1975. Founded Manson Interactive, 1995. Member A.M.P.A.S. since 1979. Director, Foundation of Motion Picture Pioneers.

GOLDMAN, STEVE
Executive. e. Univ. of IL. 1980, joined Paramount as Midwest division mngr., Chicago. Then served in NY as v.p. Eastern regional mngr. 1983, to Hollywood office. 1985, exec. v.p., sls. & mktg. 1989, exec. v.p. 1992, pres. Paramount Domestic Television. 1995, named exec. v.p. of Paramount Television Group.

GOLDMAN, WILLIAM
Writer. b. Chicago, IL, Aug. 12, 1931. e. Oberlin College, B.A., Columbia U., M.A.
WRITER: The Temple of Gold, Your Turn to Curtsy—My Turn to Bow, Soldier in the Rain (filmed), Boys and Girls Together, No Way to Treat a Lady (filmed), The Thing of It Is, Father's Day, The Princess Bride (filmed), Marathon Man (filmed), Magic (filmed), Tinsel, Control, Heat (filmed), The Silent Gondoliers, The Color of Light, Brothers, Absolute Power(filmed), Four Screenplays, Five Screenplays, The Ghost & The Darkness (filmed). *Non-fiction*: The Season: A Candid Look at Broadway, Adventures in the Screen Trade, Wait Until Next Year (w/Mike Lupica), Hype and Glory.

PICTURES: Harper, Butch Cassidy and the Sundance Kid (Academy Award, 1969), The Hot Rock, The Stepford Wives, The Great Waldo Pepper, All the President's Men (Academy Award, 1976), Marathon Man (based on his novel), A Bridge Too Far, Magic (based on his novel), Mr. Horn, Heat (based on his novel), The Princess Bride (based on his novel), Misery, Memoirs of an Invisible Man (co-s.p.), Year of the Comet, Chaplin (co-s.p.), Last Action Hero (co-s.p.), Maverick, The Chamber, The Ghost and the Darkness (based on his novel), Fierce Creatures (co-s.p.), Absolute Power (based.on his novel), The General's Daughter, Jurassic Park III.

GOLDSMITH, JERRY
Composer. b. Los Angeles, CA, Feb. 10, 1929. e. Los Angeles City Coll. Studied piano with Jakob Gimpel and music composition, harmony, theory with Mario Castelnuovo-Tedesco. With CBS radio first with own show (Romance) and then moved on to others (Suspense). Began scoring for TV, including Climax, Playhouse 90, Studio One, Gunsmoke. Emmy Awards for QB VIII, Masada, Babe, The Red Pony, Star Trek Voyager Theme.
PICTURES: Black Patch (debut, 1957), Lonely Are the Brave, Freud (Acad. Award nom.), The Stripper, The Prize, Seven Days in May, Lilies of the Field, In Harm's Way, Von Ryan's Express, Our Man Flint, A Patch of Blue (Acad. Award nom.), The Blue Max, Seconds, Stagecoach, The Sand Pebbles (Acad. Award nom.), In Like Flint, Planet of the Apes (Acad. Award nom.), The Ballad of Cable Hogue, Tora! Tora! Tora!, Patton (Acad. Award nom.), The Wild Rovers, The Other, Papillon (Acad. Award nom.), The Reincarnation of Peter Proud, Chinatown (Acad. Award nom.), Logan's Run, The Wind and the Lion (Acad. Award nom.), The Omen (Academy Award, 1976), Islands in the Stream, MacArthur, Coma, Damien: Omen II, The Boys From Brazil (Acad. Award nom.), The Great Train Robbery, Alien, Star Trek-The Motion Picture (Acad. Award nom.), The Final Conflict, Outland, Raggedy Man, The Secret of NIMH, Poltergeist (Acad. Award nom.), First Blood, Twilight Zone—The Movie, Psycho II, Under Fire (Acad. Award nom.), Gremlins, Legend (European ver.), Explorers, Rambo: First Blood II, Poltergeist II: The Other Side, Hoosiers (Acad. Award nom.), Extreme Prejudice, Innerspace, Lionheart, Rent-a-Cop, Rambo III, Criminal Law, The 'Burbs, Leviathan, Star Trek V: The Final Frontier, Total Recall, Gremlins 2: The New Batch (also cameo), The Russia House, Not Without My Daughter, Sleeping With the Enemy, Medicine Man, Basic Instinct (Acad. Award nom.), Mom and Dad Save the World, Mr. Baseball, Love Field, Forever Young, Matinee, The Vanishing, Dennis the Menace, Malice, Rudy, Six Degrees of Separation, Angie, Bad Girls, The Shadow, The River Wild, I.Q., Congo, First Knight, Powder, City Hall, Executive Decision, Powder, Chain Reaction, The Ghost and the Darkness, Star Trek: First Contact, Fierce Creatures, Air Force One, L.A. Confidential (Acad. Award nom.), Deep Rising, The Edge, U.S. Marshalls, Mulan, Small Soldiers, Star Trek: Insurrection, The Haunting, The Mummy, The 13th Warrior.

GOLDSMITH, MARVIN F.
Executive. b. Brooklyn, NY. e. NY Inst. of Tech. Started as page at CBS, eventually becoming film editor. Was tv group supervisor with Batten Barton Durstine & Osborne. 1973, joined ABC as mgr. nighttime sales proposals; 1976-78, account exec. in sports sales, then v.p. prime time sales proposals, then v.p. Eastern Sales. 1986, promoted to sr. v.p., natl. sls. mngr.; 1989, became sr. v.p. gen. sls. mngr. 1992, promoted to pres., sls. & marketing, ABC Television Network.

GOLDSTEIN, MILTON
Executive. b. New York, NY, Aug. 1, 1926. e. NYU, 1949. In exec. capac., Paramount; foreign sales coord., The Ten Commandments, Psycho; v.p. foreign sales, Samuel Bronston org.; asst. to Pres., Paramount Int'l, special prods., 1964; Foreign sales mgr., 1966; v.p., world wide sales, 1967, Cinerama; Sr. v.p. Cinema Center Films, 1969; pres., Cinema Center Films, 1971; v.p. Theatrical Mktg. & Sales, Metromedia Producers Corp., 1973; in March, 1974, formed Boasberg-Goldstein, Inc., consultants in prod. and dist. of m.p.; 1975, named exec. vice pres., Avco Embassy Pictures; 1978, named exec. v.p. & chief operating officer, Melvin Simon Prods. 1980, named pres.; 1985, pres. Milt Goldstein Enterprises, Inc.; 1990, chairman and ceo, HKM Films. 1991, pres., Introvision movies.

GOLDSTONE, JAMES
Director. b. Los Angeles, CA. June 8, 1931. e. Dartmouth Coll., B.A., Bennington Coll., M.A. Film editor from 1950. Writer, story editor from 1957. Dir. starting from 1958. Visiting professor, Columbia Univ., 1996-97.
PICTURES: Jigsaw (debut, 1968), A Man Called Gannon, Winning, Brother John, Red Sky at Morning, The Gang That Couldn't Shoot Straight, They Only Kill Their Masters, Swashbuckler, Rollercoaster, When Time Ran Out.
TELEVISION: Pilots: Star Trek, Ironside, Iron Horse, The Senator, etc. Specials-Movies: A Clear and Present Danger (Emmy nom.), Eric (Virgin Islands Int'l. Film Fest. Gold Medal). Journey from Darkness (Christopher Award). Studs Lonigan (miniseries 1978), Kent State, (Emmy, best dir., special), Things in Their Season, Calamity Jane, The Sun Also Rises, Dreams of Gold, Earthstar Voyager.

GOLDTHWAIT, BOBCAT (BOB)
Comedian, Actor. b. Syracuse, NY, May 1, 1962. Performed with The Generic Comics in early 1980's. Album: Meat Bob.
PICTURES: Police Academy 2: Their First Assignment (debut, 1985), One Crazy Summer, Police Academy 3: Back in Training, Burglar, Police Academy 4: Citizens on Patrol, Hot to Trot, Scrooged, Shakes the Clown (also dir., s.p.), Freaked, Radioland Murders, Destiny Turns on the Radio, Hercules (voice).
TELEVISION: *Series*: Capitol Critters (voice), Unhappily Ever After (voice), Bobcat's Big Ass Show, Hercules (voice). *Specials*: Bob Goldthwait: Don't Watch This Show, Share the Warmth, Is He Like That All the Time? (also dir., writer), Bob Saget: In the Dream Suite, Comic Relief, Medusa: Dare to Be Truthful. *Movies:* Out There, Encino Woman, Back to Back. *Guest*: Tales From the Crypt, Married... With Children, The Larry Sanders Show, E.R., Beavis and Butthead (voice), Comic Relief, The John Laroquette Show, The Simpsons (voice).

GOLDWATER, CHARLES
Executive, Exhibitor. b. New Orleans, LA. e. Boston U., B.S. Broadcasting & Film. Began career with Walter Reade Organization as usher in 1971-74, promoted to manager. Sack Theatres/USA Cinemas 1974-88, began as manager, promoted to s.v.p. & g.m. National Amusements, exec. dir. Project Development, 1988-90. Loews/Sony Theatres, sr. v.p. & general manager, 1990-1995. Pres. & CEO, Cinamerica/Mann Theatres, 1995-1998. March, 1998 became Pres., CEO and Chairman, I Works Entertainment. NATO bd. of dir. 1987-present. Chmn. CARA/Product Committee, 1991-1996; Exec Comm.,1995-. Gen. chmn. Showeast 1992-1995; chmn of the bd. Showeast, 1995-present. Bd. of directors, Motion Picture Pioneers, Will Rogers. Past pres./chmn. of bd., Theatre Owners of New England. Past bd. of directors, Variety Clubs of New England & New York.

GOLDWYN, JOHN
Executive. Grandson of Samuel Goldwyn. Began career as exec. story editor, The Ladd Co., 1982; later promoted to v.p., creative affairs, served as exec. producer on Police Academy II. Became senior v.p., motion picture production, MGM/UA Entertainment Co., 1985, and was named exec. v.p., motion picture production for MGM in 1988. Joined Paramount Pictures in 1990 as exec. v.p., production and was promoted to president, Motion Picture Grp./production, 1991. 1997 became president, Paramount Pictures.

GOLDWYN, SAMUEL, JR.
Producer, Director. b. Los Angeles, CA, Sept. 7, 1926. e. U. of Virginia. Father of actor Tony Goldwyn. U.S. Army, 1944; following war writer, assoc. prod., J. Arthur Rank Org.; prod. Gathering Storm on London stage; returned to U.S., 1948; assoc. prod., Universal; recalled to Army service, 1951; prod., dir., Army documentary films including Alliance for Peace (Edinburgh Film Festival prize); prod. TV shows, Adventure series for CBS, 1952-53; prod. TV series, The Unexpected, 1954; pres., The Samuel Goldwyn Company, 1955-. Also established Samuel Goldwyn Home Entertainment, and Goldwyn Pavilion Cinemas.
PICTURES: *Prod.*: Man With the Gun, The Sharkfighters, The Proud Rebel, The Adventures of Huckleberry Finn, The Young Lovers (also dir.), Cotton Comes to Harlem, Come Back Charleston Blue, The Golden Seal, Mystic Pizza (exec. prod.), Stella, The Preacher's Wife.
TELEVISION: The Academy Awards, 1987, 1988; April Morning (co-exec. prod.).

GOLDWYN, TONY
Actor. b. Los Angeles, CA, May 20, 1960. e. Brandeis U., London Acad. of Music & Dramatic Art.
THEATER: Digby, The Foreigner, The Real Thing, Pride and Prejudice, The Sum of Us, Spike Heels, Inherit the Wind.
PICTURES: Friday the 13th Part VI: Jason Live, Gaby-A True Story, Ghost, Kuffs, Traces of Red, The Pelican Brief, Reckless, The Substance of Fire, Nixon, The Substance of Fire, Kiss the Girls.
TELEVISION: *Movies*: Favorite Son, Dark Holiday, Iran: Days of Crisis, Taking the Heat, Love Matters, Doomsday Gun, The Last Word, The Boys Next Door, Truman. *Mini-Series*: A Woman of Independent Means. *Special*: The Last Mile. *Guest*: L.A. Law, Tales from the Crypt.

GOLINO, VALERIA
Actress. b. Naples, Italy, Oct. 22, 1966. Raised in Athens, Greece. Was model at age 14 before being discovered by dir. Lina Wertmuller for film debut.
PICTURES: A Joke of Destiny (debut, 1983), Blind Date, My Son Infinitely Beloved, Little Fires, Dumb Dicks, Storia d'Amore (Love Story), Last Summer in Tangiers, The Gold-Rimmed Glasses, Three Sisters, Big Top Pee-wee, Rain Man, Torrents of Spring, The King's Whore, Traces of an Amorous Life, Hot Shots!, The Indian Runner, Hot Shots! Part Deux, Clean Slate, Immortal Beloved, Leaving Las Vegas, Four Rooms, Escape From L.A., The Acrobats, Side Streets, Le Acrobate, The Pear Tree, Harem Suare.

GOMEZ, NICK
Director, Writer. b Sommerville, MA, 1963. Stunts in film Powder. Acted in films Mob War and Blue Vengeance.
PICTURES: Laws of Gravity, New Jersey Drive (also story), Illtown, Drowning Mona.
TELEVISION: *Series:* Homicide: Life on the Street, Oz.

GONZALEZ-GONZALEZ, PEDRO
Actor. r.n. Ramiro Gonzalez-Gonzalez. b. Aguilares, TX, May 24, 1925. Comedian in San Antonio Mexican theatres.
PICTURES: Wings of the Hawk, Ring of Fear, Ricochet Romance, The High and the Mighty, Strange Lady in Town, Bengazi, I Died a Thousand Times, Bottom of the Bottle, The Sheepman, Gun the Man Down, Rio Bravo, The Young Land, The Adventures of Bullwhip Griffin, The Love Bug, The Love God, Hellfighters, Hook Line and Sinker, Chisum, Support Your Local Gunfighter, Zachariah, Six-Pack Annie, Won Ton Ton the Dog Who Saved Hollywood, Dreamer, Lust in the Dust, Uphill All the Way, Deception.
TELEVISION: *Guest*: O'Henry Playhouse, Felix the Fourth, Ann Southern Show, No Time for Sergeants, Gunsmoke, Perry Mason, The Monkees, Love American Style, Adam 12, Farmer's Daughter, Danny Kaye Show, National Velvet, Bachelor Father, Bonanza, The Fall Guy, Moonlighting, many others. *Movies*: Donor, Ghost Writer, Bates Motel (pilot).

GOOD, CHARLES E.
Executive. b. 1922. Joined Buena Vista in 1957 in Chicago office; progressed from salesman to branch mgr. and then district mgr. Later moved to Burbank as domestic sales mgr. in 1975; 1978, named v.p. & general sales mgr.; 1980, appointed pres., BV Distribution Co. Resigned presidency 1984; became BV consultant until retirement, 1987.

GOODALL, CAROLINE
Actress. b. London, England, Nov. 13, 1959. e. Natl Youth Theatre of Great Britain; Bristol Univ. On stage with Royal Court Theatre, Royal Natl. Theatre, Royal Shakespeare Co. Toured Australia in Richard III for RSC, 1986.
PICTURES: Every Time We Say Goodbye (debut, 1986), Hook, The Silver Brumby, The Webbers' 15 Minutes, Cliffhanger, Schindler's List, Disclosure, Hotel Sorrento, White Squall.
TELEVISION: *Movies* (Australia): Cassidy, Ring of Scorpio, The Great Air Race, Diamond Swords (Fr.). *Mini-Series*: After the War. *Guest*: Remington Steele, Tales of the Unexpected, Quantum Leap, The Commish, Rumpole of the Bailey, Poirot: Curse of the Western Star.

GOODING, CUBA, JR.
Actor. b. Bronx, NY, Sept. 2, 1968. Son of rhythm and blues vocalist Cuba Gooding. Raised in California. Prof. debut as dancer backing up Lionel Richie at 1984 Olympic Games. Recipient of NAACP Image Awards for Boyz in the Hood and tv movie Murder Without Motive. Voted by NATO/Showest as Newcomer of the Year, 1992.
PICTURES: Coming to America (debut, 1988), Sing, Boyz in the Hood, Hitz, Gladiator, A Few Good Men, Judgment Night, Lightning Jack, Outbreak, Losing Isaiah, Jerry Maguire (Acad. Award, 1996; Chicago Film Critics Award; Screen Actors Guild Award), Do Me a Favor (cameo), As Good As It Gets, What Dreams May Come, Welcome to Hollywood, Chill Factor, A Murder of Crows (also prod.), Instinct, Men of Honor, Pearl Harbor, Rat Race, In the Shadows..
TELEVISION: *Movies*: Murder Without Motive: The Edmund Perry Story, Daybreak, The Tuskegee Airmen. *Special:* No Means No.

GOODMAN, DAVID Z.
Writer. e. Queens Coll., Yale School of Drama.
PICTURES: Lovers and Other Strangers, Straw Dogs, Farewell My Lovely, Logan's Run, Eyes of Laura Mars, Man Woman and Child (co.-s.p.).

GOODMAN, JOHN
Actor. b. Afton, MO, June 20, 1952. e. Southwest Missouri State U. Moved to NY in 1975 where he appeared on stage (incl. A Midsummer Night's Dream) and in commercials. On Broadway in Loose Ends, Big River. L.A. stage in Antony and Cleopatra.
PICTURES: Eddie Macon's Run (1983, debut), The Survivors, Revenge of the Nerds, C.H.U.D., Maria's Lovers, Sweet Dreams, True Stories, Raising Arizona, Burglar, The Big Easy, The Wrong Guys, Punchline, Everybody's All-American, Sea of Love, Always, Stella, Arachnophobia, King Ralph, Barton Fink, The Babe, Matinee, Born Yesterday, We're Back! A Dinosaur's Story (voice), The Flintstones, The Hudsucker Proxy (cameo), Pie in the Sky, Mother Night, The Borrowers, The Big Lebowski, Fallen, Blues Brothers 2000, Dirty Work (cameo), The Runner, Bringing Out the Dead, Coyote Ugly, What Planet Are You From, O Brother Where Art Thou? One Night at McCool's, The Emperor's New Groove.
TELEVISION: *Series*: Roseanne, Normal Ohio. *Movies*: The Face of Rage, Heart of Steel, The Mystery of Moro Castle, Murder Ordained, Kingfish: A Story of Huey P. Long (also co-prod.), A Streetcar Named Desire, The Jack Bull. *Mini-Series*: Chiefs. *Guest*: The Equalizer, Moonlighting.

GOODRICH, ROBERT EMMETT
Executive. b. Grand Rapids, MI, June 27, 1940. e. U. of Michigan, B.A., 1962; J.D., 1964; NYU. LL.M, 1966. Pres. & Secty., Goodrich Quality Theaters, Inc. 1967-present, developed circuit from father's one theater to 313 screens plus Wabash Landing at 38 locations in 17 Mich. cities, 4 Indiana cities, 4 Illinois cities, 2 Kansas cities, 4 Missouri cities. Owns and operates 2 AM radio stations in Grand Rapids, MI. NATO; Will Rogers Inst. advisory comm; bd. of dirs., Mich. Millers Mutual Insurance Co.; bd. of dirs., Western Migh. Branch ACLU. State of MI Bar Assn.

GOODWIN, RICHARD
Producer. b. Bombay, India, Sept. 13, 1934. e. Rugby. Entered film world by chance: while waiting to go to Cambridge U. took temporary job as tea boy at studio which led to 20-year-long association with producer Lord Brabourne.
PICTURES: *Prod. Mgr.*: The Sheriff of Fractured Jaw, Carve Her Name with Pride, The Grass Is Greener, Sink the Bismarck, HMS Defiant. *Prod.*: The Tales of Beatrix Potter. *Co-Prod.*: Murder on the Orient Express, Death on the Nile, The Mirror Crack'd, Evil Under the Sun, A Passage to India, Little Dorrit, Seven Years In Tiber (exec. prod.).

GOODWIN, RONALD
Composer, Arranger, Conductor. b. Plymouth, Eng., Feb. 17, 1925. e. Pinner County Grammar Sch. Early career: arranger for BBC dance orchestra; mus. dir., Parlophone Records; orchestra leader for radio, TV and records. Fut. m.p. ind., 1958. Many major film scores. Guest cond. R.P.O., B.S.O., Toronto Symph. Orch. New Zealand Symphony Orch., Sydney Symphony Orch. Royal Scottish Natl. Orch., BBC Scottish Symphony Orch., BBC Welsh Symphony Orch., BBC Radio Orch., BBC Concert Orch., London Philharmonic Orch., Gothenberg Symphony Orch., Norwegian Opera Orch. & Chorus, Halle Orchestra, Singapore Symphony Orch., Australian Pops Orch, Detroit Symphony Orchestra, Danish Radio Orchestra, Odense Symphony Orch., Norrkoping Symphony Orch.
PICTURES: Whirlpool, I'm All Right Jack, The Trials of Oscar Wilde, Johnny Nobody, Village of the Damned, Murder She Said, Follow the Boys, Murder at the Gallop, Children of the Damned, 633 Squadron, Murder Most Foul, Murder Ahoy, Operation Crossbow, The ABC Murders, Of Human Bondage, Those Magnificent Men in Their Flying Machines, The Trap, Mrs. Brown, You've Got a Lovely Daughter; Submarine X-1, Decline and Fall, Where Eagles Dare, Monte Carlo or Bust, Battle of Britain, The Executioner, The Selfish Giant, Frenzy, Diamonds on Wheels, The Little Mermaid, The Happy Prince, One of Our Dinosaurs Is Missing, Escape From the Dark, Born to Run, Beauty and the Beast, Candleshoe, Force Ten from Navarone, Spaceman and King Arthur, Clash of Loyalties, Valhalla.

GORDON, ALEX
Producer. b. London, Eng., Sept. 8, 1922. e. Canford Coll., Dorset, 1939. Writer, m.p. fan magazines, 1939-41; British Army, 1942-45; pub. dir. Renown Pictures Corp., 1946-47; P.R. and pub. rep. for Gene Autry, 1948-53; v.p. and prod. Golden State Productions, 1954-58; prod. Alex Gordon Prods., 1958-66; producer Twentieth Century-Fox Television, 1967-76; film archivist/preservationist, 1976-84; v.p., Gene Autry's Flying A Pictures, 1985.
PICTURES: Lawless Rider, Bride of the Monster, Apache Woman, Day the World Ended, Oklahoma Woman, Girls in Prison, The She-Creature, Runaway Daughters, Shake Rattle and Rock, Flesh and the Spur, Voodoo Woman, Dragstrip Girl, Motorcycle Gang, Jet Attack, Submarine Seahawk, Atomic Submarine, The Underwater City, The Bounty Killer, Requiem for a Gunfighter.
TELEVISION: Movie of the Year, Golden Century, Great Moments in Motion Pictures.

GORDON, BERT I.
Producer, Director, Writer. b. Kenosha, WI, Sept. 24, 1932. e. Univ. of WI. Started on tv as commercial prod.
PICTURES: *Dir./Prod.*: Serpent Island (debut, 1954), King Dinosaur, Beginning of the End, Cyclops (also s.p.), The Amazing Colossal Man (also co-s.p.), Attack of the Puppet People (also story), War of the Colossal Beast, The Spider, Tormented, The Boy and the Pirates, The Magic Sword (also story), Village of the Giants (also story), Picture Mommy Dead, How to Succeed With Sex (dir., s.p.), The Big Bet, Necromancy (also s.p.), The Mad Bomber (also s.p.), The Police Connection (also s.p.), The Food of the Gods (also s.p.), Empire of the Ants (also s.p.), The Coming (also s.p.), Satan's Princess, Malediction.

GORDON, BRUCE
Executive. b. Sidney, Australia, Feb. 4, 1929. Began career in Australian entertainment industry 1952 with Tivoli Circuit, live theatre chain; acted as advance man, front-of-house mgr., adv. dir.; promoted to busn. mgr., 1958. Named Tivoli membr. bd. of management, 1960-62. Joined Desilu Studios in 1962, developing Far East territories; promoted 1968 when Paramount acquired Desilu to mng. dir. Para. Far East opns. Named to bd. of TV Corp., 1969, operator of Channel 9 TV stns. & co.'s theatres in Sydney, Melbourne. Dir. on bd. of Academy Investments, operator of Perth theatre chain; responsible for building Perth Entertainment Centre. Named pres., Paramount TV Intl. Services, Ltd., 1974, in New York office. 1981, pres. Intl. Television of Paramount Pictures.

GORDON, CHARLES
Executive, Producer. b. Belzoni, MS. Began career as a talent agent with William Morris Agency. Left to write and develop television programming creating and producing 5 pilots and 3 series. Left TV to enter motion picture production in partnership with brother Lawrence Gordon. President and chief operating officer, The Gordon Company.

PICTURES: *Exec. prod.*: Die Hard, Leviathan. *Co-prod.*: Night of the Creeps, The Wrong Guys, Field of Dreams, K-9, Lock Up, The Rocketeer, The Super, Unlawful Entry, Waterworld, Trojan War (prod.), Rocket Boys (prod.).
TELEVISION: *Writer-creator*: When the Whistle Blows. *Exec. prod.*: The Renegades, Just Our Luck (also creator), Our Family Honor (also creator).

GORDON, DON
Actor. r.n. Donald Walter Guadagno. b. Los Angeles, CA, Nov. 13, 1926. Served, U.S. Navy, 1941-45. Studied acting with Michael Chekhov. e. Columbia U. Theatre includes On an Open Roof, Stockade.
PICTURES: Bullitt, The Lollipop Cover (best actor, Chicago Film Fest.), W.U.S.A., The Last Movie, Papillon, The Gambler, Out of the Blue, The Final Conflict, The Beast Within, Lethal Weapon, Skin Deep, The Exorcist III, The Borrower.
TELEVISION: *Series*: The Blue Angels, Lucan, The Contender. *Guest*: The Defenders, Remington Steele, Charlie's Angels, Twilight Zone, Simon & Simon, Outer Limits, MacGyver, etc. *Movies*: Happiness is a Warm Clue, Street Killing, Confessions of a Married Man.

GORDON, JEROME
Executive, Exhibitor. b. Newport News, VA, Mar. 1, 1915. Began movie career at age 10 as usher in father's theatre. At age 18, owned and operated two theatres. Spent one year in theater decorating business in Philadelphia. Worked for Fox West Coast circuit in Los Angeles, 1937-40. Returned to VA and developed small theater circuit with brothers. Served as pres. of Virginia NATO for 4 yrs. 1975-, exec. dir., Virginia NATO; 1976-, exec. dir., Maryland & D.C. NATO. Coordinated Mid-Atlantic NATO convention from 1975 until it merged with ShowEast in 1989. Currently exec. dir., Mid-Atlantic NATO. 1978-86, spec. asst. to pres., NATO; coordinated campaigns to pass Anti-Blind Bidding Laws in individual states. Edited Regional Presidents' NATO Handbook. Member, bd. of dirs., NATO; chmn., NATO Membership Development Committee; secretary NATO, 1996-. Exec. Committee, ShowEast. Recipient of Distinguished Service Award, ShowEast, 1992; B.V. Sturdivant Award, NATO/ShowEast, 1992.

GORDON, KEITH
Actor, Director, Writer. b. Bronx, NY, Feb. 3, 1961.
THEATRE: A Traveling Companion, Richard III, Album, Back to Back The Buddy System, Third Street.
PICTURES: *Actor*: Jaws 2 (debut, 1978), All That Jazz, Home Movies, Dressed to Kill, Christine, The Legend of Billie Jean, Static (also co-s.p., co-prod.), Back to School, I Love Trouble. *Director-Writer*: The Chocolate War, A Midnight Clear. Mother Night (also prod.), Waking the Dead (also prod.).
TELEVISION: *Mini-Series*: Studs Lonigan. *Movies*: Kent State, Single Bars Single Women, Combat High. *Special*: My Palikari (Amer. Playhouse). *Director*: Wild Palms, Homicide (1 episode), Fallen Angels: The Black Bargain.

GORDON, LAWRENCE
Producer, Executive. b. Yazoo City, MS, March 25, 1936. e. Tulane U. (business admin.). Assist. to prod. Aaron Spelling at Four Star Television, 1964. Writer and assoc. prod. on several Spelling shows. 1965, joined ABC-TV as head of west coast talent dev; 1966, TV and motion pictures exec. with Bob Banner Associates; 1968 joined AIP as v.p. in charge of project dev.; 1971 named v.p., Screen Gems (TV div. of Columbia Pictures) where he helped dev. Brian's Song and QB VII. Returned to AIP as v.p. worldwide prod. Formed Lawrence Gordon Prods. at Columbia Pictures; 1984-86, pres. and COO 20th Century Fox. Currently indep. prod. with 20th Century Fox. Producer of B'way musical Smile.
PICTURES: Dillinger (1973), Hard Times, Rolling Thunder, The Driver, The End, Hooper, The Warriors, Xanadu, Paternity, Jekyll and Hyde, Together Again, 48 Hours, Streets of Fire, Brewster's Millions, Lucas, Jumpin' Jack Flash, Predator, The Couch Trip, The Wrong Guys, Die Hard, Leviathan (exec. prod.), K-9, Field of Dreams, Lock Up, Family Business, Another 48 HRS, Die Hard 2, Predator 2, The Rocketeer, Used People, The Devil's Own, Boogie Nights, Event Horizon, Tomb Raider, Thieves, Mystery Men.
TELEVISION: *Co-creator and co-exec. prod.*: Dog and Cat, Matt Houston, Renegades, Just Our Luck, Our Family Honor, Timecop.

GORDON, RICHARD
Producer. b. London, Eng., Dec. 31, 1925. e. U. of London, 1943. Served in Brit. Royal Navy, 1944-46; ed. & writer on fan magazines & repr. independent American cos. 1946, with publicity dept. Assoc. Brit. Pathe 1947; org. export-import business for independent, British and American product; formed Gordon Films, Inc., 1949; formed Amalgamated prod., 1956; formed Grenadier Films, Ltd. 1971. 1992, prod. of A Tribute to Orson Welles.
PICTURES: The Counterfeit Plan, The Haunted Strangler, Fiend Without a Face, The Secret Man, First Man into Space, Corridors of Blood, Devil Doll, Curse of Simba, The Projected Man, Naked Evil, Island of Terror, Tales of the Bizarre, Tower of Evil, Horror Hospital, The Cat and the Canary, Inseminoid.

GORDON, STUART
Director, Writer. b. Chicago, IL, Aug. 11, 1947. e. Univ. of WI. Worked at commercial art studio prior to founding Broom Street Theater in Madison, WI. Later founder and prod. dir. of Organic Theater Co. in Madison, then Chicago, 1969-85. Was fight choreographer on 1976 film The Last Affair.
PICTURES: *Director*: Re-Animator (also co-s.p.), From Beyond (also co-s.p.), Dolls, Robot Jox (also wrote story), Honey I Shrunk the Kids (co-story only), The Pit and the Pendulum, Honey I Blew Up the Kid (exec. prod., co-story only), Fortress, Body Snatchers (co-s.p. only), Castle Freak (also co-story), Space Truckers (dir., prod., co-story).
TELEVISION: *Director*: Bleacher Bums (special), Daughter of Darkness (movie).

GORDY, BERRY
Executive. b. Detroit, MI, Nov. 28, 1929. Was working on auto assembly line in Detroit when decided to launch record co., Motown. In 1961 wrote song, Shop Around; recording by Smokey Robinson made it his first million dollar record. Expanded into music publishing, personal mgt., recording studios, film and TV, also backing stage shows. Former bd. chmn., Motown Industries. Chmn. The Gordy Co. Received Business Achievement Award, Interracial Council for Business Opportunity, 1967; Whitney M. Young Jr. Award, L.A. Urban League, 1980; Inducted into Rock and Roll Hall of Fame, 1988. Recipient of NARAS Trustee Award, 1991. Author of To Be Loved (1994). Member BMI, NAACP, A.M.P.A.S., DGI, NARAS.
PICTURES: Lady Sings the Blues (prod.), Bingo Long Traveling All-Stars and Motor Kings (exec. prod.), Mahogany (dir.), Almost Summer, The Last Dragon (exec. prod.).

GORE, MICHAEL
Composer, Producer. b. New York City, New York, March 5, 1951. e. Yale University and studied in Paris with composer Max Deustch. Began writing pop songs for his sister singer Lesley Gore; as a staff songwriter for Screen Gems-Columbia; and as a producer of classical recordings for CBS Records. Prod. for Philips Classics recording of The King and I (with Julie Andrews, Ben Kingsley). Wrote Whitney Houston's hit single All the Man That I Need.
PICTURES: Fame (2 Academy Awards for Best Score and Title Song, 1980), Terms of Endearment, Footloose, Pretty in Pink, Broadcast News, Defending Your Life, The Butcher's Wife, Mr. Wonderful.
TELEVISION: Generations (theme); Fame (theme).

GOROG, LASZLO
Writer. b. Hungary, Sept. 30, 1903. e. U. of Sciences, Budapest. Playwright, short story writer, asst. editor, Budapest, 1928-39.
PICTURES: Tales of Manhattan, The Affairs of Susan, She Wouldn't Say Yes, The Land Unknown, Mole People.
TELEVISION: 4 Star, Dupont, The Roaring Twenties, 77 Sunset Strip, Maverick, etc.

GORSHIN, FRANK
Actor. b. Pittsburgh, PA, Apr. 5, 1933. Also nightclub comic and impresionist. On B'way stage in Jimmy.
PICTURES: Hot Rod Girl, Dragstrip Girl, Invasion of the Saucer Men, Portland Exposse, Warlock, Bells Are Ringing, Studs Lonigan, Where the Boys Are, The Great Impostor, Ring of Fire, The George Raft Story, Sail a Crooked Ship, That Darn Cat, Ride Beyond Vengeance, Batman, Skidoo, Record City, Underground Aces, The Uppercrust, Hot Resort, Uphill All the Way, Hollywood Vice Squad, Midnight, Beverly Hills Bodysnatchers, Hail Caesar, The Meteor Man, Twelve Monkeys, From Hare to Eternity (voice), Twilight of the Ice Nymphs, Bloodmoon, After the Game, Pullet Surprise (voice), Man of the Century, Final Rinse, Everything's George, All Shook Up.
TELEVISION: *Series*: ABC Comedy Hour (The Kopycats), The Edge of Night, Black Scorpion, General Hospital, The Bold and the Beautiful. *Movies*: Sky Heist, Death on the Freeway, Goliath Awaits, A Masterpiece of Murder. *Guest*: Hennessey, The Detectives, Have Gun Will Travel, The Defenders, Naked City, The Munsters, Batman, Police Woman, SWAT, The Fall Guy, Murder She Wrote.

GORTNER, MARJOE
Actor, Producer. b. Long Beach, CA, Jan. 14, 1944. Was child evangelist, whose career as such was basis for Oscar-winning documentary film, Marjoe. Acted in films and TV; turned producer in 1978 for When You Comin' Back Red Ryder?
PICTURES: Earthquake, Bobbie Joe and the Outlaw, The Food of the Gods, Viva Knievel, Sidewinder One, Acapulco Gold, Starcrash, When You Comin' Back Red Ryder?, Mausoleum, Jungle Warriors, Hellhole, American Ninja III: Blood Hunt, Wild Bill.
TELEVISION: *Movies*: The Marcus-Nelson Murders, Pray for the Wildcats, The Gun and the Pulpit, Mayday at 40000 Feet. *Guest*: Police Story, Barnaby Jones, The A-Team. *Series*: Falcon Crest.

GOSSETT, LOUIS, JR.
Actor. b. Brooklyn, NY, May 27, 1936. e. NYU, B.S. Also nightclub singer during 1960s.

THEATER: Take a Giant Step (debut, 1953), The Desk Set, Lost in the Stars, A Raisin in the Sun, Golden Boy, The Blacks, Blood Knot, The Zulu and the Zayda, My Sweet Charlie, Carry Me Back to Morningside Heights, Murderous Angels (L.A. Drama Critics Award).
PICTURES: A Raisin in the Sun (debut, 1961), The Bushbaby, The Landlord, Skin Game, Travels With My Aunt, The Laughing Policeman, The White Dawn, The River Niger, J.D.'s Revenge, The Deep, The Choirboys, An Officer and a Gentleman (Academy Award, best supporting actor, 1982), Jaws 3-D, Finders Keepers, Enemy Mine, Iron Eagle, Firewalker, The Principal, Iron Eagle II, Toy Soldiers, The Punisher, Aces: Iron Eagle III, Diggstown, Monolith, Flashfire, Blue Chips (unbilled), A Good Man in Africa, Iron Eagle IV, Inside, Managua, Bram Stoker's Legend of the Mummy, Y2K.
TELEVISION: *Series*: The Young Rebels, The Lazarus Syndrome, The Powers of Matthew Star, Gideon Oliver, The Great War (voice). *Movies*: Companions in Nightmare, It's Good to Be Alive, Sidekicks, Delancey Street, The Crisis Within, Don't Look Back, Little Ladies of the Night, To Kill a Cop, The Critical List, This Man Stands Alone, Sadat, The Guardian, A Gathering of Old Men, The Father Clements Story, Roots: The Gift, El Diablo, Sudie and Simpson, The Josephine Baker Story, Carolina Skeletons, Father & Son: Dangerous Relations (also co-exec. prod.), Ray Alexander: A Taste for Justice, A Father for Charlie (also co-exec. prod.), Curse of the Starving Class, Zooman, Ray Alexander: A Menu for Murder, Captive Heart: The James Mink Story, to Dance with Olivia, The Inspectors, Love Songs. *Mini-Series*: Roots (Emmy Award, 1977), Backstairs at the White House. Return to Lonesome Dove. *Specials*: Welcome Home, A Triple Play: Sam Found Out, Zora Is My Name, The Century Collection Presents Ben Vereen: His Roots, In His Father's Shoes (Emmy Award, 1998). *Guest*: The Mod Squad, Bill Cosby Show, Partridge Family, The Rookies, Love American Style, Police Story, Rockford Files.

GOTTESMAN, STUART
Executive. b. New York, NY, June 11, 1949. Started career in mailroom of Warner Bros., 1972; later named promo. asst. to southwestern regional fieldman; promoted to that post which held for 10 years. 1987, named WB dir. field activities; 1990, appointed v.p. WB national field operations.

GOTTLIEB, CARL
Writer, Director, Actor. b. New York, NY, March 18. e. Syracuse U., B.S., 1960. Directed short film The Absent- Minded Waiter.
PICTURES: *Actor*: Maryjane, M*A*S*H, Up the Sandbox, Cannonball, The Sting II, Johnny Dangerously, The Committee, Into the Night, Clueless. *Director*: Caveman (also co-s.p.), Amazon Women on the Moon (co-dir.). *Co-Writer*: Jaws (also actor), Which Way Is Up?, Jaws II, The Jerk (also actor), Doctor Detroit, Jaws 3-D.
TELEVISION: *Writer*: Smothers Bros. Comedy Hour (Emmy Award, 1969), The Odd Couple, Flip Wilson, Bob Newhart Show, The Super, Crisis at Sun Valley, The Deadly Triangle. *Director*: Paul Reiser: Out on a Whim, Partners In Life, Campus Cops, Honey I Shrunk the Kids. *Director-Co-creator*: Leo & Liz in Beverly Hills. *Co-creator*: George Burns' Comedy Week.

GOUGH, MICHAEL
Actor. b. Malaya, Nov. 23, 1917. e. Rose Hill Sch., in Kent, England, and at Durham School. Studied at Old Vic School in London; first stage appearance in 1936 at Old Vic Theatre. N.Y. stage debut 1937 in Love of Women. London debut in 1938 in The Zeal of Thy House. Won 1979 Tony Award for Bedroom Farce.
PICTURES: Blanche Fury (debut, 1947), Anna Karenina, Saraband for Dead Lovers, The Small Back Room, The Man in the White Suit, Rob Roy, The Sword and the Rose, Richard III, Reach for the Sky, Horror of Dracula (Dracula), Horrors of the Black Museum, The Horse's Mouth, Konga, Candidate for Murder, I Like Money (Mr. Topaze), The Phantom of the Opera, Black Zoo, Dr. Terror's House of Horrors, The Skull, Berserk, They Came From Beyond Space, A Walk With Love and Death, Women in Love, Trog, Julius Caesar, The Go-Between, Savage Messiah, Legend of Hell House, Horror Hospital (Computer Killers), Galileo, The Boys from Brazil, Venom, The Dresser, Top Secret!, Oxford Blues, Out of Africa, Caravaggio, Memed My Hawk, The Fourth Protocol, The Serpent and the Rainbow, Batman, Strapless, Let Him Have It, Blackeyes, Batman Returns, Little Nemo (voice), The Age of Innocence, Wittgenstein, Uncovered, Batman Forever.
TELEVISION: The Search for the Nile, Six Wives of Henry VIII, QB VII, Shoulder to Shoulder, The Citadel, Smiley's People, Brideshead Revisited, Mistral's Daughter, Lace II, Inside the Third Reich, To the Lighthouse, Suez, Vincent the Dutchman, Heart Attack Hotel, After the War, The Shell Seekers, Children of the North, Dr. Who, Sleepers.

GOULD, ELLIOTT
Actor. r.n. Elliott Goldstein. b. Brooklyn, NY, August 29, 1938. e. Professional Children's Sch., NY 1955. Vaudeville: appeared at Palace Theater, 1950. Broadway debut in Rumple (1957). Son is actor Jason Gould.
THEATER: Say Darling, Irma La Douce, I Can Get It for You Wholesale, On the Town (London), Fantasticks (tour), Drat the Cat, Little Murders, Luv (tour), Hit the Deck (Jones Beach), Rumors, Breakfast With Les & Bess.
PICTURES: Quick Let's Get Married (debut, 1965), The Night They Raided Minsky's, Bob & Carol & Ted & Alice (Acad. Award nom.), M*A*S*H, Getting Straight, Move, I Love My Wife, Little Murders (also prod.), The Touch, The Long Goodbye, Busting, S*P*Y*S!, California Split, Who?, Nashville (cameo), Whiffs, I Will I Will... For Now, Harry and Walter Go to New York, Mean Johnny Barrows, A Bridge Too Far, Capricorn One, Matilda, The Silent Partner, Escape to Athena, The Muppet Movie, The Last Flight of Noah's Ark, The Lady Vanishes, Falling in Love Again, The Devil and Max Devlin, Dirty Tricks, The Naked Face, Over the Brooklyn Bridge, The Muppets Take Manhattan, Inside Out, My First 40 Years, Lethal Obsession, The Telephone, The Big Picture, Dangerous Love, Night Visitor, The Wounded King, The Lemon Sisters, Judgment, Dead Men Don't Die, Bugsy, Strawanser, The Player, Exchange Lifeguards, Wet and Wild Summer, Naked Gun 33 1/3: The Final Insult (cameo), White Man's Burden, The Glass Shield, Kicking and Screaming, A Boy Called Hate, Johns, City of Industry (cameo), Camp Stories, Michael Kael in Katango, The Big Hit, American History X, Picking up the Pieces.
TELEVISION: *Specials*: Once Upon A Mattress, Come Blow Your Horn, Jack and the Beanstalk (Faerie Tale Theater), Paul Reiser: Out on a Whim, Prime Time, Out to Lunch, Casey at the Bat (Tall Tales & Legends), *Guest*: Twilight Zone, Electric Company, Saturday Night Live, George Burns Comedy Week, Ray Bradbury Theatre, The Hitchhiker, Friends, It's Like You Know.... *Movies*: The Rules of Marriage, Vanishing Act, Conspiracy: The Trial of the Chicago 8, Stolen: One Husband, Somebody's Daughter, Bloodlines: Murder in the Family, The Shining. *Series*: E/R, Together We Stand, Sessions (HBO), Getting Personal.

GOULD, HAROLD
Actor. b. Schenectady, NY, Dec. 10, 1923. e. SUNY, Albany, B.A. Cornell U., MA., Ph.D. Instructor of theatre and speech, 1953-56, Randolph Macon's Woman's Col., Lynchburg, VA. Asst. prof. drama and speech, 1956-60, Univ. of Calif., Riverside. Acted with Ashland, OR Shakespeare Fest. in 1958 and Mark Taper Forum (The Miser, Once in a Lifetime). Won Obie Award for Off-B'way debut in The Increased Difficulty of Concentration, 1969. ACE Award for Ray Bradbury Theatre. L.A. Drama Critics Award, 1994.
THEATER: The House of Blue Leaves, Fools, Grown Ups, Artist Descending a Staircase, I Never Sang for My Father, Freud (one man show), Love Letters, Incommunicado, King Lear (Utah Shakespearean Fest.), Mixed Emotions, Old Business, The Tempest (Utah Shakespearean Fest.), Substance of Five (San Diego Olde Globe).
PICTURES: Two for the Seesaw, The Couch, Harper, Inside Daisy Clover, Marnie, An American Dream, The Arrangement, The Lawyer, Mrs. Pollifax: Spy, Where Does It Hurt?, The Sting, The Front Page, Love and Death, The Big Bus, Silent Movie, The One and Only, Seems Like Old Times, Playing for Keeps, Romero, Flesh Suitcase, Killer.
TELEVISION: *Series*: Rhoda (Emmy nom.), Park Place, Foot in the Door, Under One Roof, Singer and Sons, Golden Girls, Feather and Father Gang. *Movies*: To Catch a Star, Moviola (Emmy nom.), Washington Behind Closed Doors, Aunt Mary, Better Late Than Never, King Crab, Have I Got a Christmas for You, Man in the Santa Claus Suit, I Never Sang For My Father, Get Smart Again!, Mrs. Delafield Wants to Marry (Emmy nom.), Love Bug II, Fox Hope. *Special*: The Sunset Gang. *Guest*: Police Story (Emmy nom.), Tales from the Hollywood Hills: The Closed Set, Ray Bradbury Theater (Emmy nom.).

GOULET, ROBERT
Singer, Actor. b. Lawrence, MA., Nov. 26, 1933. e. Edmonton; scholarship, Royal Conservatory of Music. Sang in choirs, appeared with numerous orchestras; disk jockey, CKUA, Edmonton; pub. rel., Rogo & Rove,Inc.
THEATER: *NY*: Camelot (as Lancelot; Theatre World Award), The Happy Time (Tony Award, 1968), Camelot (as King Arthur; 1993 revival). *Regional:* numerous tours including I Do I Do, Carousel, On a Clear Day You Can See Forever, Kiss Me Kate, South Pacific, The Fantasticks, Camelot (as King Arthur).
PICTURES: Gay Purr-ee (voice), Honeymoon Hotel, I'd Rather Be Rich, I Deal in Danger, Atlantic City, Beetlejuice, Scrooged, The Naked Gun 2 1/2: The Smell of Fear, Mr. Wrong.
TELEVISION: *Series*: Robert Goulet Show, Blue Light. *Guest*: The Ed Sullivan Show, Garry Moore, The Enchanted Nutcracker, Omnibus, The Broadway of Lerner and Loewe, Rainbow of Stars, Judy Garland Show, Bob Hope Show, The Bell Telephone Hour, Granada-TV special (U.K.), Jack Benny, Dean Martin, Andy Williams, Jack Paar, Red Skelton, Hollywood Palace, Patty Duke Show, The Big Valley, Mission: Impossible, Police Woman, Cannon, Murder She Wrote, Mr. Belvedere, Fantasy Island, Matt Houston, Glitter, WKRP in Cincinnati, The Simpsons. *Pilot*: Make My Day. *Specials*: Brigadoon, Carousel, Kiss Me Kate. Movie: Based on an Untrue Story.

GOWDY, CURT
Sportscaster. b. Green River, WY, July 31, 1919. Basketball star at U. of Wyoming. All-Conference member; graduated U. of Wyoming. 1942. Officer in U.S. Air Force WWII, then became sportscaster. Voted Sportscaster of the Year, 1967, Nat'l Assn. of Sportswriters Broadcasters. Best Sportscaster, Fame, 1967. Did play-by-play telecasts for 16 World Series, 7 Super Bowls, 12 Rose Bowls, 8 Orange Bowls, 18 NCAA Final 4 college basketball championships. In 1970 was the first individual from the field of sports to receive the George Foster Peabody Award. Hosted the American Sportsman outdoor TV show on ABC for 20 years. (Received 8 Emmy Awards). Inducted into the Sportscasters Hall of Fame in 1981, the Fishing Hall of Fame in 1982, and the Baseball Hall of Fame in 1984, Pro Football Hall of Fame in 1992.

GRADE, LORD LEW
Executive. r.n. Louis Winogradsky. b. Tokmak, Russia, Dec. 25, 1906. Brother of Lord Bernard Delfont. Came to Eng. 1912. Was first a music hall dancer until 1934 when he became an agent with Joe Collins, founding Collins and Grade Co. Joint managing dir. Lew & Leslie Grade Ltd. theatrical agency until 1955; Chmn. & mng. dir., ITC Entertainment Ltd. 1958-82; chmn. & chief exec., Associated Communications Corp. Ltd., 1973-82; pres. ATV Network Ltd., 1977-82; chmn., Stoll Moss Theatres Ltd., 1969-82; chmn. & chief exec., Embassy Communications International Ltd., 1982-85; chmn. & chief exec., The Grade Co. 1985-; Dir. Euro Disney S.C.A. Paris 1988, v.p. British Olympic Assn. Fellow BAFTA, 1979, KCSS 1979. Chairman for Life Active–I.T.C., 1995. Consultant to Polygram Entertainment Group. *Autobiography:* Still Dancing (1988).
NY THEATER: *Prod.*: Merrily We Roll Along, Starlight Express, Sly Fox.
PICTURES: *Prod.*: The Cassandra Crossing, The Domino Principle, The Big Sleep, Escape to Athena, Raise the Titanic, Something to Believe In.
TELEVISION: *Movies*: Madame Sin, Destination Moonbase Alpha, Lady and the Highwayman, Duel of Hearts. *Series*: The Saint, The Return of the Saint, Root Into Europe (actor).

GRADE, MICHAEL
Executive. b. London, England, March 8, 1943. e. Stowe. Entered industry 1966. Early career as newspaper columnist, became an executive at London Weekend Television then Embassy Television in Hollywood. Joined BBC Television, 1983 as controller of BBC 1 and director of Programmes (TV), 1986. Joined Channel 4 as chief executive, 1988.

GRAFF, RICHARD B.
Executive. b. Milwaukee, WI, Nov. 9, 1924. e. U. of Illinois. Served U.S. Air Force; Universal Pictures 1946 to 1964 in Chicago, Detroit, Chicago and NY home office as asst. to genl. sales mgr.; 1964 joined National General in Los Angeles. 1967 became v.p. and general sales mgr. of National General Pictures, formed and operated company. 1968, exec. v.p. in charge of world-wide sales and marketing. 1968 made v.p. of parent company; v.p. general sales mgr. AIP in 1971; 1975, pres. Cine Artists Pictures; 1977, pres. Richard Graff Company Inc; 1983, pres. of domestic distribution, MGM/UA. 1987, pres., worldwide distribution, Weintraub Entertainment Group. 1990, pres. The Richard Graff Company, Inc.

GRAFF, TODD
Actor, Writer. b. New York, NY, Oct. 22, 1959. e. SUNY/Purchase.
THEATER: *NY*: Baby (Tony nom., Theatre World Award), Birds of Paradise. Author: The Grandma Plays, Sheila Levine.
PICTURES: *Actor*: Sweet Lorraine (also composed songs), Five Corners, Dominick & Eugene, The Abyss, An Innocent Man, Opportunity Knocks, City of Hope. *Writer:* Used People, The Vanishing (also co-prod.), Fly by Night (also actor), Angie (also co-prod., cameo), The Beautician and the Beast (prod. only).
TELEVISION: *Special*: Vietnam War Story.

GRAHAM, HEATHER
Actress. b. Milwaukee, WI. Jan. 29, 1970.
PICTURES: License to Drive, Twins, Drugstore Cowboy, I Love You to Death, Shout, Guilty as Charged, Twin Peaks: Fire Walk With Me, Diggstown, Six Degrees of Separation, Even Cowgirls Get the Blues, The Ballad of Little Jo, Mrs. Parker and the Vicious Circle, Don't Do It, Terrified, Desert Winds, Swingers, Entertaining Angels: The Dorothy Day Story, Two Girls and a Guy, Boogie Nights, Nowhere, Scream 2, Committed, Bowfinger, Lost in Space, Austin Powers: The Spy Who Shagged Me, Kiss & Tell, Committed, Sidewalks of New York, When the Cat's Away, Alien Love Triangle, Killing Me Softly, From Hell, .45, Say It Isn't So.
TELEVISION: *Movies*: Student Exchange, O Pioneers!. *Series*: Twin Peaks.

GRAMMER, KELSEY
Actor. b. St. Thomas, Virgin Islands, Feb. 20, 1955. e. Juilliard. Acting debut on tv in Another World. On B'way in Sunday in the Park With George. Supplied voice for Disney/Mickey Mouse short Runaway Brain.
PICTURE: Down Periscope, Star Trek: First Contact (cameo), Anastasia (voice), The Real Howard Spitz, Standing on Fishes, Toy Story 2 (voice).
TELEVISION: *Series*: Cheers, Frasier (5 Emmy Awards, 1994-98; Golden Globe, 1996), Fired Up (exec. prod. only). *Guest:* The Simpsons (voice), Just Shoot Me. *Movies*: Dance 'Til Dawn, Beyond Suspicion, The Innocent, London Suite, The Pentagon Wars, Animal Farm (voice).

GRANATH, HERBERT A.
Executive. e. Fordham U. Started with ABC TV in sales, marketing and production. 1979, became v.p. of Capital Cities/ABC Video Enterprises Inc.; 1982-93, served as pres. of same; Oct. 1993, named pres. ABC Cable and International Broadcast Group, sr. v.p. Capital Cities/ABC Inc.

GRANET, BERT
Producer, Writer. b. New York, NY, July 10, 1910. e. Yale U. Sch. of Fine Arts (47 workshop). From 1936 author s.p. orig. & adapt. numerous pictures. Exec. prod.: Universal, 1967-69, CBS, Desilu Studios.
PICTURES: Quick Money, The Affairs of Annabel, Mr. Doodle Kicks Off, Laddie, A Girl a Guy and a Gob, My Favorite Wife, Bride by Mistake, Sing Your Way Home, Those Endearing Young Charms, The Locket, Do You Love Me?, The Marrying Kind, Berlin Express, The Torch, Scarface Mob.
TELEVISION: Desilu (1957-61), Twilight Zone (pilot), The Untouchables (pilot), Scarface Mob; Loretta Young Show (1955-56), Walter Winchell File 1956-57, Lucille Ball-Desi Arnaz Show 1957-60, Westinghouse Desilu Playhouse, The Great Adventure.

GRANGER, FARLEY
Actor. b. San Jose, CA, July 1, 1925. e. Hollywood. U.S. Armed Forces 1944-46. Joined Eva Le Gallienne's National Rep. Co. in 1960s (The Sea Gull, The Crucible, Ring Round the Moon).
PICTURES: The North Star (debut, 1943), The Purple Heart, Rope, Enchantment, The Live By Night, Roseanna McCoy, Side Street, Our Very Own, Edge of Doom, Strangers on a Train, Behave Yourself, I Want You, O. Henry's Full House, Hans Christian Andersen, Story of Three Loves, Small Town Girl, Senso, Naked Street, Girl in the Red Velvet Swing, Rogue's Gallery, Something Creeping in the Dark, They Call Me Trinity, Replica of a Crime, Amuk, The Slasher, The Redhead with the Translucent Skin, Kill Me My Love, Planet Venus, Night Flight From Moscow, Man Called Neon, Arnold, Savage Lady, The Co-ed Murders, Deathmask, The Prowler, The Imagemaker.
TELEVISION: *Series*: One Life to Live (1976-7), As the World Turns (1986-8). *Movies*: The Challengers, The Lives of Jenny Dolan, Widow, Black Beauty. *Guest*: Playhouse of Stars, U.S. Steel Hour, Producer's Showcase, Climax, Ford Theatre, Playhouse 90, 20th Century Fox Hour, Robert Montgomery Presents, Arthur Murray Dance Party, Wagon Train, Masquerade Party, Kojak, 6 Million Dollar Man, Ellery Queen.

GRANT, DAVID MARSHALL
Actor. b. Westport, CT, June 21, 1955. e. Yale School of Drama.
THEATER: *NY*: Sganarelle, Table Settings, The Tempest, Bent, The Survivor, Making Movies, Angels in America: Millenium Approaches/Perestroika, Three Sisters. *Regional:* Bent (also dir.), Once in a Lifetime, Lake Boat, Free and Clear, True West, The Wager, Rat in the Skull, Snakebit (author), The End of the Day.
PICTURES: French Postcards (debut, 1979), Happy Birthday Gemini, The End of August, American Flyers, The Big Town, Bat 21, Air America, Strictly Business, Forever Young, The Rock, The Chamber, Remembering Sex.
TELEVISION: *Series*: thirtysomething. *Movies*: Kent State, Legs, Sessions, Dallas: The Early Years, What She Doesn't Know, Citizen Cohn, Through the Eyes of a Killer. *Special*: A Doonesbury Special (voice). *Pilot*: Graham. *Host*: The Legend of Billy the Kid, Night Sins.

GRANT, HUGH
Actor. b. London, England, Sept. 9, 1960. e. New Coll., Oxford U. Acted with OUDS before landing role in Oxford Film Foundation's Privileged. Acted at Nottingham Playhouse and formed revue group, The Jockeys of Norfolk.
PICTURES: Privileged (debut, 1982), Maurice, White Mischief, The Lair of the White Worm, The Dawning, Remando al Viento (Rowing With the Wind), Bengali Night, Impromptu, Crossing the Line, The Remains of the Day, Night Train to Venice, Sirens, Four Weddings and a Funeral (BAFTA & Golden Globe Awards), Bitter Moon, The Englishman Who Went Up a Hill But Came Down a Mountain, Nine Months, An Awfully Big Adventure, Restoration, Sense and Sensibility, Extreme Measures (also prod.), Notting Hill, Mickey Blue-Eyes, Small Time Crooks.
TELEVISION: *Mini-Series*: The Last Place on Earth. *Series*: The Demon Lover, Ladies in Charge. *Movies/Specials*: The Detective, Handel: Honour, Profit and Pleasure, Jenny's War, The Lady and the Highwayman, Champagne Charlie, 'Til We Meet Again, Our Sons (U.S.), The Changeling.

GRANT, LEE
Actress. r.n. Lyova Rosenthal. b. New York, NY, Oct. 31, 1931. m. producer Joseph Feury. Daughter is actress Dinah Manoff. At 4 was member of Metropolitan Opera Company; played princess in L'Orocolo. Member of the American Ballet at 11. e. Juilliard Sch. of Music, studied voice, violin and dance. At 18 with road co. Oklahoma as understudy. Acting debut: Joy to the World.
THEATER: acted in a series of one-acters at ANTA with Henry Fonda. Detective Story (Critics Circle Award, 1949), Lo and Behold, A Hole in the Head, Wedding Breakfast; road co. Two for the Seesaw, The Captains and the Kings; toured with Electra, Silk Stockings, St. Joan, Arms and the Man, The Maids (Obie Award), Prisoner of Second Avenue.
PICTURES: Detective Story (debut, 1951; Acad. Award nom.), Storm Fear, Middle of the Night, Affair of the Skin, The Balcony, Terror in the City, Divorce American Style, In the Heat of the Night, Valley of the Dolls, Buona Sera Mrs. Campbell, The Big Bounce, Marooned, The Landlord (Acad. Award nom.), There Was a Crooked Man, Plaza Suite, Portnoy's Complaint, The Internecine Project, Shampoo (Academy Award, best supporting actress, 1975), Voyage of the Damned (Acad. Award nom.), Airport '77, Damien: Omen II, The Swarm, The Mafu Cage, When You Comin' Back Red Ryder, Little Miss Marker, Charlie Chan and the Curse of the Dragon Queen, Visiting Hours, Teachers, The Big Town, Defending Your Life, Under Heat. *Dir.*: Tell Me a Riddle, Willmar Eight, Staying Together.
TELEVISION: *Series*: Search for Tomorrow (1953-4), Peyton Place (Emmy Award, 1965), Fay. *Guest*: Studio One, The Kraft Theatre, Slattery's People, The Fugitive, Ben Casey, The Nurses, The Defenders, East Side/West Side, One Day at a Time, Bob Hope Show (Emmy nom.). *Movies*: Night Slaves, The Love Song of Bernard Kempenski, BBC's The Respectful Prostitute, The Neon Ceiling (Emmy Award, 1971), Ransom for a Dead Man, Lt. Schuster's Wife, Partners in Crime, What Are Best Friends For?, Perilous Voyage, The Spell, Million Dollar Face, For Ladies Only, Thou Shalt Not Kill, Bare Essence, Will There Really Be A Morning?, The Hijacking of the Achille Lauro, She Said No, Something to Live For: The Alison Gertz Story, In My Daughter's Name, Citizen Cohn. *Mini-Series*: Backstairs at the White House, Mussolini--The Untold Story. *Special*: Plaza Suite. *Director*: Nobody's Child, Shape of Things, When Women Kill, A Matter of Sex, Down and Out in America, No Place Like Home, Following Her Heart.

GRANT, RICHARD E.
Actor. b. Mbabane, Swaziland, May 5, 1957. e. Cape Town U., South Africa (combined English and drama course). Co-founded multi-racial Troupe Theatre Company with fellow former students and members of Athol Fugard and Yvonne Bryceland's Space Theatre, acting in and directing contemporary and classic plays. Moved to London 1982 where performed in fringe and rep. theater. Nominated most promising newcomer in Plays and Players, 1985, for Tramway Road.
PICTURES: Withnail and I, Hidden City, How to Get Ahead in Advertising, Killing Dad, Mountains of the Moon, Henry and June, Warlock, L.A. Story, Hudson Hawk, The Player, Bram Stoker's Dracula, Franz Kafka's It's A Wonderful Life (short), The Age of Innocence, Ready to Wear (Pret-a-Porter), Jack and Sarah, Twelfth Night, The Portrait of a Lady, Spice World, Keep the Aspidstra Flying, The Serpent's Kiss, St. Ives, Cash in Hand, The Match.
TELEVISION: *Series*: Sweet Sixteen, Captain Star (voice). *Movies/Specials*: Honest Decent and True, Lizzie's Pictures, Codename Kyril, Thieves in the Night (also released theatrically), Here Is the News, Suddenly Last Summer, Hard Times, Bed, Karaoke, Cold Lazarus, The Scarlet Pimpernel, The Miracle Maker (voice) Moonshot-The Spirit of '69 (voice).

GRASGREEN, MARTIN
Executive. b. New York, NY, July 1, 1925. Entered m.p. ind. 1944, Columbia Pictures in contract dept. Promoted to travelling auditor 1947. Appt. office mgr. Omaha branch 1948; salesman Omaha, 1950. To Indianapolis, 1952, as city salesman; transferred to Cleveland as sales mgr., 1953. Left Columbia in 1960 to become 20th-Fox branch mgr. in Cleveland. Transferred to Philadelphia in 1965 as branch mgr.; transferred to NY in 1967 as Eastern dist. mgr. Resigned in 1970 to form Paragon Pictures, prod.-dist. co. 1975, formed Lanira Corp., representing producers for U.S. sales and dist. of films in U.S. Retired 1980.

GRASSHOFF, ALEX
Director. b. Boston, MA, Dec. 10, 1930. e. USC. 3 Acad. Award nominations for feature documentaries; Really Big Family; Journey to the Outer Limits; Young Americans (Acad. Award, 1968).
PICTURES: A Billion For Boris, J.D. and the Salt Flat Kid, The Last Dinosaur, The Jailbreakers.
TELEVISION: *Series*: The Rockford Files, Toma, Chips, Night Stalker, Barbary Coast, Movin' On. *Specials*: The Wave (Emmy Award), Future Shock (1973 Cannes Film Fest. Awards), Frank Sinatra, Family and Friends.

GRASSO, MARY ANN
Executive. b. Rome, NY, Nov. 3, 1952. e. U. of Calif., Riverside, B.A. art history, 1973; U. of Oregon, Eugene, Master of Library Science, 1974. Dir., Warner Research Collection, 1975-85; mgr., CBS-TV, docu-drama, 1985-88; Instructor 1980-88 UCLA Extension, American Film Institute. v.p. & exec. dir. National Association of Theater Owners, 1988-present. Theatre Arts instructor UCLA 1980-85. Amer. Film Inst., LA, 1985-88. Member: Acad. Motion Picture Arts & Sciences, Foundation of the Motion Picture Pioneers, American Society of Association Executives, Phi Beta Kappa. Woman of Achievement, BPOA Awarded 1984, Friend of Tripod 1999. TV credits: The Scarlet O'Hara Wars, This Year's Blonde, The Silent Lovers, A Bunnies Tale, Embassy. Member: NATO (VP); Business and Prof'l. Women's Assoc. ;AMPAS; Foundation Motion Picture Pioneer; Commissioner Burbank Heritage Commission; Board of Directors Burbank Historical Society; Board Center of Film and Television Design.

GRAVES, PETER
Actor. r.n. Peter Aurness. b. Minneapolis, MN, March 18, 1926. e. U. of Minnesota. Brother of actor James Arness. Played with bands, radio announcer, while at school; U.S. Air Force 2 yrs.; summer stock appearances.
PICTURES: Rogue River (debut, 1950), Fort Defiance, Red Planet Mars, Stalag 17, East of Sumatra, Beneath the 12-Mile Reef, Killers From Space, The Raid, Black Tuesday, Wichita, Long Gray Line, Night of the Hunter, Naked Street, Fort Yuma, Court Martial of Billy Mitchell, It Conquered the World, The Beginning of the End, Death in Small Doses, Poor White Trash (Bayou), Wolf Larsen, A Rage to Live, Texas Across the River, Valley of Mystery, The Ballad of Josie, Sergeant Ryker, The Five Man Army, Sidecar Racers, Parts: The Clonus Horror, Survival Run, Airplane!, Savannah Smiles, Airplane II: The Sequel, Number One With a Bullet, Addams Family Values.
TELEVISION: *Series*: Fury, Whiplash, Court-Martial, Mission Impossible, New Mission: Impossible. *Movies*: A Call to Danger, The President's Plane is Missing, Scream of the Wolf, The Underground Man, Where Have All the People Gone?, Dead Man on the Run, SST-Death Flight, The Rebels, Death on the Freeway, The Memory of Eva Ryker, 300 Miles for Stephanie, If It's Tuesday It Still Must Be Belgium. *Mini-Series*: Winds of War, War and Remembrance. *Host/narrator*: Discover! The World of Science, Biography, Tarzan the Legacy of Edgar Rice Burroughs.

GRAVES, RUPERT
Actor. b. Weston-Super-Mare, England, June 30, 1963. Before film debut worked as a clown with the Delta travelling circus in England.
THEATER: The Killing of Mr. Toad, 'Tis Pity She's a Whore, St. Ursula's in Danger, Sufficient Carbohydrates, Amadeus, Torch Song Trilogy, Candida, Pitchfork Disney, History of Tom Jones, A Madhouse in Goa, A Midsummer Night's Dream, Design for Living.
PICTURES: A Room with a View, Maurice, A Handful of Dust, The Children, Where Angels Fear to Tread, Damage, The Madness of King George, The Innocent Sleep, Different for Girls, Mrs. Dalloway, Bent, The Revengers Comedies, Dreaming of Joseph Lees.
TELEVISION: Vice Versa, All for Love, A Life of Puccini, Fortunes of War, The Plot to Kill Hitler, The Sheltering Desert, Union Matters, Starting Out, Royal Celebration, Good and Bad at Games, Inspector Morse, Doomsday Gun.

GRAY, COLEEN
Actress. r.n. Doris Jensen. b. Staplehurst, NB, Oct. 23, 1922. e. Hamline U., B.A. summa cum laude, 1943, Actor's Lab. m. Fritz Zeiser. Member: Nat'l Collegiate Players, Kappa Phi, a capella choir, little theatres, 1943-44.
PICTURES: State Fair (debut, 1945), Kiss of Death, Nightmare Alley, Fury at Furnace Creek, Red River, Sleeping City, Riding High, Father Is a Bachelor, Apache Drums, Lucky Nick Cain, Models Inc., Kansas City Confidential, Sabre Jet, Arrow in the Dust, The Fake, The Vanquished, Las Vegas Shakedown, Twinkle in God's Eye, Tennessee's Partner, The Killing, Wild Dakotas, Death of a Scoundrel, Frontier Gambler, Black Whip, Star in the Dust, The Vampire, Hell's Five Hours, Copper Sky, Johnny Rocco, The Leech Woman, The Phantom Planet, Town Tamer, P.J., The Late Liz, Cry from the Mountain.
TELEVISION: *Series*: Window on Main Street, Days of Our Lives, (1966-67), Bright Promise (1968-72). *Guest*: Family Affair, Ironside, Bonanza, Judd for the Defense, Name of the Game, The FBI, The Bold Ones, World Premiere, Mannix, Sixth Sense, McCloud, Tales from the Dark Side. *Movies*: Ellery Queen: Don't Look Behind You, The Best Place to Be.

GRAY, DULCIE
C.B.E., F.L.S., F.R.S.A. Actress b. Malaya, Nov. 20, 1919. e. Webber Douglas Sch. Stage debut 1939, Aberdeen, Hay Fever, Author: Love Affair (play), 18 detective novels, book of short stories. 8 radio plays; co-author with husband Michael Denison, An Actor and His World; Butterflies on My Mind, The Glanville Women, Anna Starr; Mirror Image, Looking Forward Looking Back.

THEATER: Over 50 West End plays including Little Foxes, Brighton Rock, Dear Ruth, Rain on the Just, Candida, An Ideal Husband (1965, 1962, 1996 London & NY), Where Angels Fear to Tread, Heartbreak House, On Approval, Happy Family, No. 10, Out of the Question, Village Wooing, Wild Duck, At The End of the Day, The Pay Off, A Murder Has Been Announced, Bedroom Farce, A Coat of Varnish, School for Scandal, The Living Room, Tartuffe, Cavell, Pygmalion, The School Mistress (Chicester), Two of a Kind.
PICTURES: Two Thousand Women, A Man About the House, Mine Own Executioner, My Brother Jonathan, The Glass Mountain, They Were Sisters Wanted for Murder, The Franchise Affair, Angels One Five, There Was a Young Lady, A Man Could Get Killed, The Trail of the Pink Panther, The Curse of the Pink Panther, The Black Crow.
TELEVISION: Milestones, The Will, Crime Passionel, Art and Opportunity, Fish in the Family, The Governess, What the Public Wants, Lesson in Love, The Happy McBaines, Winter Cruise, The Letter, Tribute to Maugham, Virtue, Beautiful Forever, East Lynne, Unexpectedly Vacant, The Importance of Being Earnest, This Is Your Life (1977; and with Michael Denison, 1995), Crown Court, Making Faces, Read All About It, The Voysey Inheritance, Life After Death, The Pink Pearl, Britain in the Thirties, Rumpole (The Old Boy Net.), Cold Warrior, Hook, Line and Sinker, Howard's Way (series; 6 yrs.), Three Up, Two Down, The Time and the Place.

GRAY, LINDA
Actress. b. Santa Monica, CA, Sept. 12, 1940.
PICTURES: Under the Yum Yum Tree, Palm Springs Weekend, Dogs, Fun With Dick and Jane, Oscar.
TELEVISION: *Series*: Dallas, Models Inc. *Guest:* Melrose Place, Touched By an Angel. *Movies*: The Big Ripoff, Murder in Peyton Place, The Grass is Always Greener Over the Septic Tank, Two Worlds of Jennie Logan, Haywire, The Wild and the Fire, Not in Front of the Children, The Entertainers, Highway Heartbreaker, Moment of Truth: Why My Daughter?, Bonanza: The Return, To My Daughter with Love, Accidental Meeting, Moment of Truth: Broken Pledges, When the Cradle Falls.

GRAY, SPALDING
Performance artist, Actor, Writer. b. Barrington, RI, June 5, 1941. Began career as actor in 1965 at Alley Theater, Housten, then off-B'way in Tom Paine at LaMama Co. In 1969 joined the Wooster Group, experimental performance group. Has written and performed autobiographical monologues (Three Places in Rhode Island, Sex and Death to the Age 14, Swimming to Cambodia, Monster in a Box, Gray's Anatomy) throughout U.S, Europe and Australia. Taught theater workshops for adults and children and is recipient of Guggenheim fellowship. Artist in residence Mark Taper Forum, 1986-87. B'way debut: Our Town (1988).
PICTURES: *Actor*: Almost You, The Killing Fields, Hard Choices, True Stories, Swimming to Cambodia (also s.p.), Stars and Bars, Clara's Heart, Beaches, Heavy Petting, Straight Talk, Monster in a Box (also s.p.), The Pickle, King of the Hill, Twenty Bucks, The Paper, Bad Company, Beyond Rangoon, Drunks, Diabolique, Gray's Anatomy, Bliss.
TELEVISION: *Special*: Terrors of Pleasure (HBO). *Movies*: The Image, To Save a Child, Zelda. *Guest*: The Nanny, Missing Links.

GRAY, THOMAS K.
Executive, producer. b. New York City, N. Y., July 1, 1945. e. U. of Arizona, B.A., post grad work at American Graduate School of Int'l Management, Phoenix. Began career as management trainee with United Atists film exchange in Spain, 1970, and year later became managing director, UA, Chile. Also managing director for UA, New Zealand, 1972; Columbia, 1973; South and East Africa, 1974. Joined Cinema Int'l Corp., London, as exec. assist. to co-chairman, 1974, and moved up to managing director of CIC/Warner, South Africa, 1976. Returned to UA as vice pres. Far East, Latin America, Africa and Australia, 1977. Joined Golden Communications Overseas Ltd., London, as vice pres. foreign sales, 1980. With Golden Harvest Films, Inc. since 1984 as sr. vice. pres., production. Executive in charge of prod. for Golden Harvest features: Flying, The Protector, China O'Brien, China O'Brien II, A Show of Force, Teenage Mutant Ninja Turtles, Best of Martial Arts (prod.), Teenage Mutant Ninja Turtles II: Secret of the Ooze (prod.), Teenage Mutant Ninja Turtles III. 1992, pres. and CEO of Rim Film Distribution Inc.

GRAYSON, KATHRYN
Actress, Singer. r.n. Zelma Hedrick. b. Winston-Salem, NC, Feb. 9, 1923. e. St. Louis schools.
THEATER: Camelot, Rosalinda, Merry Widow, Kiss Me Kate, Showboat.
PICTURES: Andy Hardy's Private Secretary (debut, 1941), The Vanishing Virginian, Rio Rita, Seven Sweethearts, Thousands Cheer; Anchors Aweigh, Ziegfeld Follies, Two Sisters from Boston, Till the Clouds Roll By, It Happened in Brooklyn, The Kissing Bandit, That Midnight Kiss, The Toast of New Orleans, Grounds for Marriage, Show Boat, Lovely to Look At, The Desert Song, So This Is Love, Kiss Me Kate, The Vagabond King.
TELEVISION: *Guest*: GE Theatre (Emmy nom.), Playhouse 90, Lux Playhouse, Murder She Wrote. *Special*: Die Fliedermaus.

GRAZER, BRIAN
Producer. b. Los Angeles, CA, July 12, 1951. e. U. of Southern California. Started as legal intern at Warner Bros.; later script reader (for Brut/Faberge) & talent agent. Joined Edgar J. Scherick-Daniel Blatt Co.; then with Ron Howard as partner in Imagine Films Entertainment. Received NATO/ShoWest Producer of the Year Award, 1992.
PICTURES: Night Shift, Splash (also co-story), Real Genius, Spies Like Us, Armed and Dangerous (also co-story), Like Father Like Son, Vibes, The 'burbs, Parenthood, Cry-Baby (co-exec. prod.), Kindergarten Cop, The Doors (co-exec. prod.), Closet Land (co-exec. prod.), Backdraft (exec. prod.), My Girl, Far and Away, Housesitter, Boomerang, CB4 (co-exec. prod.), Cop and a Half, For Love or Money, My Girl 2, Greedy, The Paper, The Cowboy Way, Apollo 13, Fear, Sgt. Bilko, The Nutty Professor, Ransom, Inventing the Abbotts, Liar Liar, Mercury Rising, Psycho, Life, Into thin Air, How to Eat Fried Worms, Edtv, Bowfinger, Sprockets, The Nutty Professor II, How the Grinch Stole Christmas, Curious George.
TELEVISION: *Movies*: Zuma Beach, Thou Shalt Not Commit Adultery, Splash Too, Student Affairs. *Series (executive prod.)*: Shadow Chasers, Take Five, Ohara, Parenthood, Hiller & Diller, Felicity, Sports Night, The PJs, Wonderland. *Special*: Poison (prod.), From Earth to the Moon.

GREATREX, RICHARD
Cinematographer.
PICTURES: Forbidden Sun, For Queen and Country, War Requiem, A Foreign Field, Deadly Advice, Blue Juice, Mrs. Brown, Shakespeare in Love (Acad. Award nom.).
TELEVISION: *Movies:* Aderyn Papur...and Pigs Might Fly, Truth or Dare, The Woman in White, Dalziel and Pascoe: Exit Lines, Tess of the D'Urbervilles, Getting Hurt.

GREEN, ADOLPH
Writer, Actor. b. New York, NY, Dec. 2, 1915. m. actress-singer Phyllis Newman. Began career in the cabaret act The Revuers with partner Betty Comden and Judy Holliday (1944).
THEATER: Wrote book, sketches and/or lyrics for many Broadway shows including: On the Town (also actor), Billion Dollar Baby, Bonanza Bound! (also actor), Two on the Aisle, Wonderful Town (Tony Award for lyrics, 1953), Peter Pan (Mary Martin), Say Darling, Bells Are Ringing, A Party with Comden and Green (1959 & 1977), Do Re Mi, Subways Are For Sleeping, Fade Out Fade In, Halleuljah Baby (Tony Awards for lyrics & best musical, 1968), Applause (Tony Award for book, 1970), Lorelei: Or Gentlemen Still Prefer Blondes (new lyrics), By Bernstein (book), On the Twentieth Century (Tony Awards for book & lyrics, 1978), A Doll's Life, The Will Rogers Follies (Tony Award for lyrics, 1991).
PICTURES: *Writer* (with Betty Comden): Good News, On the Town, The Barkleys of Broadway, Take Me Out to the Ball Game (co-lyrics), Singin' in the Rain, The Band Wagon, It's Always Fair Weather, Auntie Mame, What a Way to Go. *Actor:* Greenwich Village, Simon, My Favorite Year, Lily in Love, Garbo Talks, I Want to Go Home.

GREEN, GUY
Director. b. Somerset, Eng. Nov. 5, 1913. Joined Film Advertising Co. as projectionist & camera asst. 1933; camera asst., Elstree Studios (BIP) 1935; started as camera operator on films including One of Our Aircraft Is Missing, In Which We Serve, This Happy Breed. 1944: Director of Photography; Dir of Allied Film Makers Ltd.
PICTURES: *Dir. of Photography*: The Way Ahead, Great Expectations (Acad. Award, 1947), Oliver Twist, Captain Horatio Hornblower, I Am a Camera. *Director*: River Beat (debut, 1954), Portrait of Alison, Tears for Simon, House of Secrets, The Snorkel, Desert Patrol (Sea of Sand), The Angry Silence, The Mark, Light in the Piazza, Diamond Head, A Patch of Blue (also co-exec. prod., s.p.), Pretty Polly (A Matter of Innocence), The Magus, A Walk in the Spring Rain (also co-exec. prod.), Luther, Once Is Not Enough, The Devil's Advocate.
TELEVISION: (U.S.) Incredible Journey of Dr. Meg Laurel; Isabel's Choice; Jennifer: A Woman's Story; Arthur Hailey's Strong Medicine, Jimmy B. and Andre, Inmates.

GREEN, JACK N.
Cinematographer. b. San Francisco. Started as camera operator for Bruce Surtees.
PICTURES: *Camera operator*: Fighting Mad, Firefox, Honky Tonk Man, Risky Business, Sudden Impact, Tightrope, Beverly Hills Cop, City Heat, Pale Rider, Ratboy. *Cinematographer*: Heartbreak Ridge, Like Father Like Son, The Dead Pool, Bird, Pink Cadillac, Race for Glory, White Hunter Black Heart, The Rookie, Deceived, Unforgiven, Rookie of the Year, A Perfect World, Bad Company, The Bridges of Madison County, The Net, The Amazing Panda Adventure, Twister, Speed 2: Cruise Control.

GREEN, JOSEPH
Executive, Producer, Director. b. Baltimore, MD, Jan. 28, 1938. e. U. of Maryland, B.A. Since 1970 has headed own distribution co. Joseph Green Pictures and released its library of 150 features to theatres, TV and cable.
PICTURES: The Brain that Wouldn't Die (dir., s.p.), The Perils of P.K. (assoc. prod., dir.), Psychedelic Generation (prod., dir., s.p.).

GREEN, MALCOLM C.
Theatre Executive. b. Boston, MA, Mar. 1, 1925. e. Harvard Coll. Began career as asst. mgr., Translux Theatre, Boston & Revere Theatre, Revere, MA. Treas., Interstate Theatres, 1959-64. Film Buyer, Interstate, 1959-72. Formed Theatre Management Services in 1972 with H. Rifkin and P. Lowe and Cinema Centers Corp. with Rifkin and Lowe families in 1973. Treas., Cinema Center, & pres., Theatre Mgmt. Services. Cinema Center grew to 116 theatres in 6 Northeast states, sold to Hoyts Cinemas Corp., 1986. Sr. v.p., Hoyts Cinemas Corp. 1986-89. Pres., Theatre Owners of New England, 1964-65; chmn bd., 1965-69; treas., 1970-84. Pres., NATO, 1986-88, Chmn Bd, 1988-90. Dir., Natl. Assoc. Theatre Owners. Chmn., NATO of New York State. Director, Vision Foundation. Dir., The Lyric Stage, Boston 1990-94; dir. & v.p., New Hampshire Music Festival, 1988-1996.

GREEN, SETH
Actor. b. Philadelphia, PA, Feb. 8, 1974.
PICTURES: The Hotel New Hampshire, Willy/Milly, Radio Days, Can't Buy Me Love, My Stepmother is an Alien, Big Business, Pump Up the Volume, Ticks, The Double 0 Kid, Airborne, White Man's Burden, To Gillian on Her 37th Birthday, Austin Powers: International Man of Mystery, Enemy of the State, The Attic Expeditions, Can't Hardly Wait, Austin Powers: The Spy Who Shagged Me, Stonebrook, Idle Hands, The Attic Expeditions, The Trumpet of the Swan, Knockaround Guys, Diary of a Mad Freshman, Rat Race, Josie and the Pussycats..
TELEVISION: *Movies:* Stephen King's It, Our Shining Moment, Arcade, The Day My Parents Ran Away. *Series:* Good & Evil, The Byrds of Paradise, Buffy the Vampire Slayer, Temporarily Yours, Batman Beyond (voice), Family Guy (voice). *Guest:* Amazing Stories, Life Goes On, The Wonder Years, Beverly Hills 90210, The X Files, SeaQuest DSV, Mad About You, The Drew Carey Show, Angel.

GREENAWAY, PETER
Director, Writer. b. Newport, Wales, Apr. 5, 1942. Trained as a painter, first exhibition was at Lord's Gallery in 1964. Started making short films and documentaries in 1966, including: A Walk Through H, The Falls, Act of God, Vertical Features Remake. Directorial feature debut in 1982. Author of numerous books including, 100 Objects to Represent the World, The Physical Self, Les Bruits des Nuages.
PICTURES: The Draughtsman's Contract, A Zed and Two Noughts, The Belly of an Architect, Drowning By Numbers, The Cook The Thief His Wife and Her Lover, Prospero's Books, The Baby of Macon, The Pillow Book (also ed.), The Bridge, Death of a Composer (also act.), 8 1/2 Women.
TELEVISION: Death in the Seine, series of 9 Cantos from Dante's Inferno in collaboration with painter Tom Phillips, M Is for Man Music Mozart, Darwin.

GREENE, DAVID
Director, Writer. b. Manchester, Eng., Feb. 22, 1921. Early career as actor. To U.S. with Shakespeare company early 1950's; remained to direct TV in Canada, New York and Hollywood.
PICTURES: The Shuttered Room, Sebastian, The Strange Affair, I Start Counting, Godspell, Gray Lady Down, Hard Country (prod., dir.).
TELEVISION: The Defenders. *Movies*: The People Next Door, Mdame Sin, Count of Monte Cristo, Friendly Fire, The Trial of Lee Harvey Oswald, A Vacation in Hell, The Choice, World War III, Rehearsal For Murder, Take Your Best Shot, Ghost Dancing, Prototype, Sweet Revenge, The Guardian, Fatal Vision (Emmy nom.), Guilty Conscience, This Child Is Mine, Vanishing Act, Miles to Go, Circle of Violence, The Betty Ford Story, After the Promise; Inherit the Wind, Liberace: Behind the Music, Red Earth, White Earth; The Penthouse (dir., exec. prod.), Small Sacrifices (Peabody Award), Honor Thy Mother.

GREENE, ELLEN
Actress, Singer. b. Brooklyn, NY, Feb. 22. e. Ryder Coll. After coll. joined musical road show. Appeared in cabaret act at The Brothers & the Sisters Club and Reno Sweeney's, NY. Off-B'way debut, Rachel Lily Rosenbloom. B'way in the The Little Prince and The Aviator. With NY Shakespeare Fest. in In the Boom Boom Room, The Sorrows of Steven, The Threepenny Opera (Tony nom.). Film debut Next Stop, Greenwich Village (1976). Off B'way co-starred in musical Little Shop of Horrors 1982, repeated role in film. Also Off-B'way in Weird Romance. L.A. stage: David's Mother.
PICTURES: Next Stop Greenwich Village (debut, 1976), I'm Dancing as Fast as I Can, Little Shop of Horrors, Me and Him, Talk Radio, Pump Up the Volume, Stepping Out, Rock a Doodle (voice), Fathers and Sons, Naked Gun 33 1/3: The Final Insult, Wagons East!, The Professional, A Journal of Murder, Jaded, One Fine Day, States of Control.
TELEVISION: *Special*: Rock Follies. *Movie*: Glory Glory. *Mini-Series*: Seventh Avenue. Pilot: Road Show.

GREENE, GRAHAM
Actor. b. Six Nations Reserve, Ontario, Canada, June 22, 1952. Member of the Oneida tribe. First show business job as audio technician for several rock bands. Began acting in theater in England.
THEATER: Diary of a Crazy Boy, Coming Through Slaughter, Crackwalker, Jessica, Dry Lips Oughta Move to Kapuskasing.
PICTURES: Running Brave, Revolution, Powwow Highway, Dances With Wolves (Acad. Award nom.), Thunderheart, Clearcut, Savage Land, Rain Without Thunder, Benefit of the Doubt, Maverick, North, Camilla, Die Hard With a Vengeance, Sabotage, The Pathfinder, Dead Innocent, Song of Hiawatha, Wounded, The Education of the Little Tree, Shattered Image, Bad Money, Grey Owl, The Green Mile.
TELEVISION: *U.S.*: *Series*: Northern Exposure, 500 Nations. *Movies*: Unnatural Causes, The Last of His Tribe, Cooperstown, Huck and the King of Hearts, Rugged Gold, The Pathfinder, Stranger in Town. *Guest*: Adderly, L.A. Law. *Canada: Series*: 9B, Spirit Bay. *Movies:* Murder Sees the Light, The Great Detective, Street Legal.

GREENHUT, ROBERT
Producer. b. New York, NY. e. Univ. of Miami. Began career as prod. asst. on Arthur Hiller's The Tiger Makes Out, 1967. Worked as prod. manager and asst. director on such films as Pretty Poison, The Night They Raided Minsky's, Where's Poppa?, The Owl and the Pussycat, Husbands, Born to Win, Panic in Needle Park, The Last of the Red Hot Lovers. Received Crystal Apple from city of NY and Eastman Kodak Award for lifetime achievement.
PICTURES: *Prod./assoc. prod./exec. prod.*: Huckleberry Finn, Lenny, Dog Day Afternoon, The Front, Annie Hall, Interiors, Hair, Manhattan, Stardust Memories, Arthur, A Midsummer Night's Sex Comedy, The King of Comedy, Zelig, Broadway Danny Rose, The Purple Rose of Cairo, Hannah and Her Sisters, Heartburn, Radio Days, September, Big, Another Woman, Working Girl, New York Stories, Crimes and Misdemeanors, Quick Change, Postcards From the Edge, Alice, Regarding Henry, Shadows and Fog, A League of Their Own, Husbands and Wives, Manhattan Murder Mystery, Renaissance Man, Wolf, Bullets Over Broadway, Mighty Aphrodite, Everyone Says I Love You, The Preacher's Wife, Mom's On the Roof, With Friends Like These, Siegfried and Roy: The Magic Box, White River Kid, Company Man.
TELEVISION: *Movie*: Don't Drink the Water.

GREENSPAN, ALAN
Producer.
PICTURES: *Exec. Prod.*: Photographing Fairies, Donnie Brasco, Best Laid Plans.

GREENWALD, ROBERT
Director, Producer, Teacher. b. New York, NY, Aug. 28, 1948. e. Antioch Coll., New School for Social Research. Teaches film and theatre at NYU, New Lincoln, New School. Formed Robert Greenwald Prods.
THEATER: A Sense of Humor, I Have a Dream, Me and Bessie.
PICTURES: *Director*: Xanadu, Sweet Hearts Dance (also exec. prod.), Hear No Evil, Breaking Up (also prod.), Steal This Movie (also prod.).
TELEVISION: *Prod.*: The Desperate Miles, 21 Hours at Munich, Delta Country USA, Escape From Bogen County, Getting Married, Portrait of a Stripper, Miracle on Ice, The Texas Rangers, The First Time. *Exec. prod.*: My Brother's Wife, Hiroshima, Zelda, The Portrait, Daddy, Scattered Dreams, Murder in New Hampshire, Death in Small Doses, Blood on Her Hands, The Day Lincoln Was Shot, The Secret Path, Our Guys: Outrage at Glen Ridge. *Director*: Sharon: Portrait of a Mistress, In the Custody of Strangers, The Burning Bed, Katie: Portrait of a Centerfold, Flatbed Annie and Sweetpie: Lady Truckers, Shattered Spirits (also exec. prod.), Forgotten Prisoners, A Woman of Independent Means (also co-exec. prod.).

GREENWOOD, BRUCE
Actor. b. Noranda, Quebec, Canada, Aug. 14, 1956. e. Univ. of British Columbia, London Sch. of Speech and Learning, AADA. Worked in Canadian theater and as lead singer/guitarist with blues/rock band in Vancouver before arriving in LA in 1983.
PICTURES: Bear Island (debut, 1980), First Blood, Malibu Bikini Shop, Another Chance, Wild Orchid, Passenger 57, Exotica, Paint Cans, Dream Man, Father's Day.
TELEVISION: *Series*: Legmen, St. Elsewhere, Knots Landing, Hardball, Nowhere Man, Sleepwalkers. *Movies:* Peyton Place: The Next Generation, Destination: America, In the Line of Duty: The FBI Murders, Perry Mason: The Case of the All-Star Assassin, Spy, Summer Dreams: The Story of the Beach Boys, The Great Pretender, Rio Diablo, Adrift, The Heart of a Child, Bitter Vengeance, Treacherous Beauties, The Companion, Servants of Twilight, Little Kindappers, Twist of Fate, Woman on the Run: The Lawrencia Bembenek Story, Jazzle, The Judds: Love Can Build a Bridge. *Guest*: Hitchhiker, Jake and the Fatman, Road to Avonlea.

GREER, JANE
Actress. r.n. Bettyjane Greer. b. Washington, DC, Sept. 9, 1924. Orchestra singer; photograph as WAC on Life Magazine cover won screen debut in Pan-Americana (as Bettejane Greer).

PICTURES: Pan American (debut, 1945), Two O'Clock Courage, George White's Scandals; Dick Tracy (1st film as Jane Greer), Falcon's Alibi, Bamboo Blonde, Sunset Pass, Sinbad the Sailor, They Won't Believe Me, Out of the Past, Station West, Big Steal, You're in the Navy Now, The Company She Keeps, You For Me, The Prisoner of Zenda, Desperate Search, The Clown, Down Among the Sheltering Palms, Run for the Sun, Man of a Thousand Faces, Where Love Has Gone, Billie, The Outfit, Against All Odds, Just Between Friends, Immediate Family.
TELEVISION: *Movie*: Louis L'Amour's The Shadow Riders. *Guest*: Murder She Wrote, Twin Peaks.

GREGORY, JOHN R.
Executive, Producer, Writer. b. Brooklyn, NY, Nov. 19, 1918. e. Grover Cleveland H.S., 1935, New Inst. of M.P. & Telev., 1952; Sls., adv. dept. Fotoshop, Inc., N.Y., 1938-42; Spec. Serv., Photo. instructor, chief projectionist, supv., war dept. theatres, U.S. Army, 1942-46; sls. mgr., J. L. Galef & Son, N.Y.; 1948-49, gen. mgr., Camera Corner Co.; 1949-58, pres.; City Film Center, Inc., 1957; exec. v.p., Talent Guild of New York, 1958; pres., Teleview Prods., Inc., 1961; executive producer, City Film Productions, 1970. Executive post-production supervisor, Jerry Liotta Films, 1977. Author of many articles in nat'l publications dealing with m.p. practices and techniques; tech. editor, Better Movie-Making magazine, 1962; editor, pub., National Directory of Movie-Making Information, 1963; assoc. ed., Photographic Product News, 1964; contrib. editor, U.S. Camera. M.P. columnist, contributing ed. Travel and Camera magazine, 1969; Advisory panelist, Photo-methods (N.Y.), 1975. Consultant, Photographic Guidance Council, 1957, assoc. Society of M.P. & Television-Engineers, 1952.

GREIST, KIM
Actress. b. Stamford, CT, May 12, 1958. e. New Sch. for Social Research.
THEATER: Second Prize: Two Months in Leningrad, Twelfth Night (NY Shakespeare Fest.).
PICTURES: C.H.U.D. (debut, 1984), Brazil, Manhunter, Throw Momma from the Train, Punchline, Why Me?, Homeward Bound: The Incredible Journey, Houseguest, Homeward Bound II: Lost in San Francisco.
TELEVISION: *Guest*: Miami Vice, Tales From the Darkside, Chicago Hope (recurring). *Movies*: Payoff, Duplicates, Roswell.

GREY, BRAD
Producer. e. SUNY Buffalo. Managed comedians and signed first client, Bob Saget, while still an undergraduate; mngr., for Garry Shandling, Dana Carvey, Dennis Miller. With manager, Bernie Brillstein, formed the prod. co., Brillstein-Grey; later bought out Brillstein's share, and currently runs the co.
PICTURES: The Burning, Opportunity Knocks, The Celluloid Closet, Cat and Mouse, Happy Gilmore, The Cable Guy, Bulletproof, Dirty Work, What Planet Are You From? Screwed, Scary Movie.
TELEVISION: The Larry Sanders Show, Mr. Show, The Naked Truth, The Steve Harvey Show, Just Shoot Me, Alright Already, C-16: FBI, The Sopranos, Sammy.

GREY, JENNIFER
Actress. b. New York, NY, Mar. 26, 1960. Father is actor Joel Grey. Appeared as dancer in Dr. Pepper commercial before making NY stage debut in Off-B'way play Album. B'way in The Twilight of the Golds.
PICTURES: Reckless (debut, 1984), Red Dawn, The Cotton Club, American Flyers, Ferris Bueller's Day Off, Dirty Dancing, Bloodhounds of Broadway, Stroke of Midnight (If the Shoe Fits), Wind, Portraits of a Killer, Lover's Knot, Red Meat.
TELEVISION: *Movies*: Murder in Mississippi, Criminal Justice, Eyes of a Witness, A Case for Murder, The West Side, Waltz, Outrage, Since You've Been Gone. *Series:* It's Like You Know....

GREY, JOEL
Actor, Singer, Dancer. r.n. Joel Katz. b. Cleveland, OH, April 11, 1932. Father was performer Mickey Katz; daughter is actress Jennifer Grey. e. Alexander Hamilton H.S., L.A. Acting debut at 9 years in On Borrowed Time at Cleveland Playhouse. Extensive nightclub appearances before returning to theatre and TV. Performed Silverlake in NY.
THEATER: *NY:* Come Blow Your Horn, Stop the World—I Want to Get Off, Half a Sixpence, Harry: Noon and Night, Littlest Revue, Cabaret (Tony Award, 1967), George M!, Goodtime Charley, The Grand Tour, Cabaret (1987, B'way revival), Chicago. *Regional:* Herringbone.
PICTURES: About Face (debut, 1952), Calypso Heat Wave, Come September, Cabaret (Academy Award, best supporting actor, 1972), Man on a Swing, Buffalo Bill and the Indians or Sitting Bull's History Lesson, The Seven Percent Solution, Remo Williams: The Adventure Begins..., Kafka, The Player, The Music of Chance, The Fantasticks.
TELEVISION: *Specials*: Jack and the Beanstalk, George M!, The Wizard of Oz in Concert. *Guest*: Maverick, December Bride, Ironside, Night Gallery, The Burt Bacharach Show, The Tom Jones Show, The Englebert Humperdinck Show, The Carol Burnett Show, The Julie Andrews Hour, Dallas, Brooklyn Bridge, Star Trek Voyager. *Movies*: Man on a String, Queenie.

GREY, VIRGINIA
Actress. b. Los Angeles, CA, March 22, 1917. Screen career started 1927 with Uncle Tom's Cabin.
PICTURES: Misbehaving Ladies, Secrets, Dames, The Firebird, The Great Ziegfeld, Rosalie, Test Pilot, The Hardys Ride High, Hullaballoo, Blonde Inspiration, The Big Store, Grand Central Murder, Idaho, Strangers in the Night, Blonde Ranson, Unconquered, Who Killed Doc Robbin, The Bullfighter and the Lady, Highway 301, Slaughter Trail, Desert Pursuit, Perilous Journey, Forty-Niners, Target Earth, Eternal Sea, Last Command, Rose Tattoo, All That Heaven Allows, Crime of Passion, Jeanne Eagles, The Restless Years, No Name on the Bullet, Portrait in Black, Tammy Tell Me True, Back Street, Bachelor In Paradise, Black Zoo, The Naked Kiss, Love Has Many Faces, Madame X, Rosie, Airport.

GREYSON, JOHN
Director, Writer. b. Canada, 1960.
PICTURES: Kipling Meets the Cowboy (dir. only), The Jungle Boy (dir. only), Moscow Does Not Believe in Queers (dir. only), A Moffie Called Simon (dir. only), Pissoir, Zero Patience, Lilies (dir. only), Uncut (also prod.), The Making of Monsters.

GRIECO, RICHARD
Actor. b. Watertown, NY, 1966. Started with Elite Modeling Agency. Studied acting at Warren Robertson Theatre Workshop appearing in prods. of Orphans, Golden Boy. As musician released album Waiting for the Sky to Fall.
PICTURES: Born to Ride, If Looks Could Kill, Mobsters, Tomcat: Dangerous Desires, Bolt, The Demolitionist, Mutual Needs, Heaven or Vegas, Against the Law, A Night at the Roxbury, Blackheart.
TELEVISION: *Series*: One Life to Live, 21 Jump Street, Booker, Marker. *Movies*: Sin and Redemption, A Vow to Kill, It Was Him or Us, When Time Expires, Sinbad: Battle of the Dark Knights Ultimate Deception.

GRIEM, HELMUT
Actor. b. Hamburg, Germany, 1940. e. Hamburg U.
PICTURES: The Girl From Hong Kong, The Damned, The Mackenzie Break, Cabaret, Ludwig, Children of Rage, Desert of the Tartars, Voyage of the Damned, Germany in Autumn, The Glass Cell, Sgt. Steiner (Breakthrough), Berlin Alexanderplatz, Malou, La Passante, The Second Victory.
TELEVISION: *Mini-Series*: Peter the Great.

GRIER, DAVID ALAN
Actor. b. Detroit, MI, June 30, 1955. e. U. of MI, Yale. Acted with Yale Rep.
THEATER: *NY:* A Soldier's Play, The First (Theatre World Award), Richard III, Dreamgirls, The Merry Wives of Windsor.
PICTURES: Streamers (debut, 1983), A Soldier's Story, Beer, From the Hip, Amazon Women on the Moon, Off Limits, I'm Gonna Git You Sucka, Me and Him, Loose Cannons, Almost an Angel, The Player, Boomerang, In the Army Now, Blankman, Tales From the Hood, Jumanji, Top of the World, McHale's Navy, Return to Me.
TELEVISION: *Series*: All Is Forgiven, In Living Color, The Preston Episodes (also co-exec. prod.), Damon. *Movies:* A Saintly Switch, The '60s.

GRIER, PAM
Actress. b. Winston-Salem, NC, 1949.
PICTURES: The Big Doll House, Big Bird Cage, Black Mama White Mama, Cool Breeze, Hit Man, Women in Cages, Coffy, Scream Blacula Scream, Twilight People, The Arena, Foxy Brown, Bucktown, Friday Foster, Sheba Baby, Drum, Greased Lightning, Fort Apache The Bronx, Tough Enough, Something Wicked This Way Comes, The Vindicator, On the Edge, Stand Alone, The Allnighter, Above the Law, The Package, Class of 1999, Bill & Ted's Bogus Journey, Posse, Original Gangstas, Mars Attacks!, Jackie Brown, Jawbreaker, Holy Smoke, Fortress 2, In Too Deep.
TELEVISION: *Mini-Series*: Roots: The Next Generations. *Movie*: A Mother's Right: The Elizabeth Morgan Story, family Blessings. *Guest*: Miami Vice, Crime Story, Pacific Station, Frank's Place, The Cosby Show, Night Court, In Living Color, Sinbad Show, Fresh Prince of Bel Air. *Series:* Linc's.

GRIFFIN, MERV
Executive, Singer, Emcee. b. San Mateo, CA, July 6, 1925. e. U. of San Francisco, Stanford U. Host of The Merv Griffin Show, KFRC-Radio, 1945-48; vocalist, Freddy Martin's orch., 1948-52; recorded hit song I've Got a Lovely Bunch of Coconuts; contract Warner Bros., 1952-54; Prod. Finian's Rainbow, City Center, NY, 1955. Chairman, Merv Griffin Prods.
PICTURES: By the Light of the Silvery Moon, So This Is Love, Boy From Oklahoma, Phantom of the Rue Morgue, Hello Down There, Two Minute Warning, The Seduction of Joe Tynan, The Man With Two Brains, The Lonely Guy, Slapstick of Another Kind.
TELEVISION: *Series*: The Freddy Martin Show (vocalist), Summer Holiday, Morning Show, The Robert Q. Lewis Show, Keep Talking (emcee), Play Your Hunch (emcee), Saturday Prom, The Merv Griffin Show (1962-63), Talent Scouts, Word for Word, The Merv Griffin Show (1965-86; Emmy Award for writing, 2 Emmy Awards for hosting), Secrets Women Never Share (exec. prod., host, 1987). *Creator*: Jeopardy (Emmy Award, 1998), Wheel of Fortune.

GRIFFITH, ANDY
Actor. b. Mount Airy, NC, June 1, 1926. e. U. of North Carolina. Began career as standup comedian, monologist, recording artist (What It Was Was Football, 1954). TV acting debut in U.S. Steel Hour production of No Time for Sergeants, which he later played on Broadway and film.
THEATER: *B'way*: No Time for Sergeants (Theatre World Award), Destry Rides Again.
PICTURES: A Face in the Crowd (debut, 1957), No Time for Sergeants, Onionhead, The Second Time Around, Angel in My Pocket, Hearts of the West, Rustler's Rhapsody, Spy Hard.
TELEVISION: *Series*: The Andy Griffith Show, The Headmaster, The New Andy Griffith Show, Salvage One, Matlock. *Movies*: Strangers in 7A, Go Ask Alice, Pray for the Wildcats, Winter Kill, Savages, Street Killing, Girl in the Empty Grave, Deadly Games, Salvage, Murder in Texas, For Lovers Only, Murder in Coweta County, The Demon Murder Case, Fatal Vision, Crime of Innocence, Diary of a Perfect Murder, Return to Mayberry, Under the Influence, Matlock: The Vacation (also co-exec. prod.), The Gift of Love, Gramps. *Mini-Series*: Washington Behind Closed Doors, Centennial, From Here to Eternity, Roots: The Next Generations.

GRIFFITH, MELANIE
Actress. b. New York, NY, Aug. 9, 1957. m. Anotnio Banderas. Mother is actress Tippi Hedren. Moved to Los Angeles at 4. e. Catholic academies until Hollywood Prof. Sch., 1974. Did some modeling before being cast in Night Moves at 16. Studied acting with Stella Adler, Harry Mastrogeorge and Sandra Seacat.
PICTURES: The Harrad Experiment (debut, 1973), Smile, Night Moves, The Drowning Pool, One on One, Joyride, Underground Aces, Roar, Fear City, Body Double, Something Wild, Cherry 2000, The Milagro Beanfield War, Stormy Monday, Working Girl (Acad. Award nom.), In the Spirit, Pacific Heights, The Bonfire of the Vanities, Paradise, Shining Through, A Stranger Among Us, Born Yesterday, Milk Money, Nobody's Fool, Now and Then, Two Much, Mulholland Falls, Lolita, Celebrity, Another Day in Paradise, Shadow of a Doubt, RKO 281, Crazy in Alabama, Loving Lulu.
TELEVISION: *Series*: Carter Country. *Mini-Series*: Once an Eagle. *Movies*: Daddy I Don't Like It Like This, Steel Cowboy, The Star Maker, She's in the Army Now, Golden Gate, Women & Men: Stories of Seduction (Hills Like White Elephants), Buffalo Girls. *Guest*: Vega$, Miami Vice, Alfred Hitchcock Presents.

GRIFFITHS, RACHEL
Actress. b. Melbourne, Australia, 1968.
PICTURES: Muriel's Wedding, Jude, Cosi, Children of the Revolution, Welcome to Woop Woop, To Have and to Hold, My Best Friend's Wedding, Hilary and Jackie, Among Giants, Amy.
TELEVISION: *Movies:* Since You've Been Gone. *Series:* Jimeoin.

GRILLO, BASIL F.
Executive. b. Angel's Camp, CA, Oct. 8, 1910. e. U. of California, Berkeley, A.B. Certified public accountant, exec. v.p., dir., Bing Crosby Ent., Inc., 1948-57; bus. mgr., Bing Crosby, 1945; co-organizer, dir., 3rd pres., & treas., Alliance of T.V. Film Producers, 1950-54; exec. prod., BCE, Inc., shows incl. Fireside Thea., Rebound, Royal Playhouse, The Chimps; dir., KCOP, Inc., 1957-60; dir. KFOX, Inc., 1958-62; pres., dir., Bing Crosby Prods., 1955-72; dir., Seven Leagues Ent., Inc., 1958; dir. Electrovision Prods., 1970, CEO, Bing Crosby Enterprises.

GRIMALDI, ALBERTO
Producer. b. Naples, Italy, Mar. 28, 1925. Studied law, serving as counsel to Italian film companies, before turning to production with Italian westerns starring Clint Eastwood and Lee Van Cleef. Is owner of P.E.A. (Produzioni Europee Associate, s.r.l.).
PICTURES: For a Few Dollars More, The Good the Bad and the Ugly, The Big Gundown, Three Steps in Delirium, A Quiet Place in the Country, The Mercenary, Satyricon, Burn!, The Decameron, Man of the East, The Canterbury Tales, Last Tango in Paris, Bawdy Tales, Arabian Nights, Salo or the 100 Days of Sodom, Burnt Offerings, Fellini's Casanova, 1900, Illustrious Corpses, Lovers and Liars, Hurricane Rosy, Ginger and Fred.

GRIMES, GARY
Actor. b. San Francisco, CA, June 2, 1955. Family moved to L.A. when he was nine. Made film debut at 15 in Summer of '42, 1971. Voted Star of Tomorrow in QP poll, 1971.
PICTURES: Summer of '42, The Culpepper Cattle Company, Cahill: U.S. Marshal, Class of '44, The Spikes Gang, Gus, Concrete Angels.
TELEVISION: *Mini-Series*: Once an Eagle.

GRIMES, TAMMY
Actress. b. Boston, MA, Jan. 30, 1934. Daughter is actress Amanda Plummer. e. Stephens Coll, The Neighborhood Playhouse. Recipient: Woman of Achievment Award (ADL), Mother of the Year Award, Mayor's Outstanding Contribution to the Arts Award (NYC). Member: bd. dirs. & v.p. of the Upper East-Side Historic Preservation District (NYC).
THEATER: Look After Lulu (Theatre World Award, 1959), Clerambard, The Littlest Revue, Stratford (Ont.) Shakespeare Fest., Bus Stop, The Cradle Will Rock, The Unsinkable Molly Brown (Tony Award, 1961), Rattle of a Simple Man, High Spirits, Private Lives (Tony Award, 1970), Trick, California Suite, 42nd Street, Tartuffe, A Month in the Country, The Guardsman, The Millionairess, Imaginary Invalid, The Importance of Being Earnest, Mademoiselle Columbe, Blythe Spirit, Waltz of the Toreadors, Molly, Taming of the Shrew, Orpheus Descending, Tammy Grimes: A Concert in Words and Music, A Little Night Music, Pygmalion.
PICTURES: Three Bites of the Apple (debut, 1967), Play It as It Lays, Somebody Killed Her Husband, The Runner Stumbles, Can't Stop the Music, The Last Unicorn (voice), The Stuff, No Big Deal, America, Mr. North, Slaves of New York, A Modern Affair.
TELEVISION: *Specials*: Omnibus, Hollywood Sings, Hour of Great Mysteries, Four Poster. *Guest*: St. Elsewhere, The Young Riders. Series: The Tammy Grimes Show. *Movies*: The Other Man, The Horror at 37,000 Feet, The Borrowers, You Can't Go Home Again, An Invasion of Privacy.

GRISSMER, JOHN
Executive, Producer, Director. b. Houston, TX, Aug. 28, 1933. e. Xavier U., B.S., 1955; Catholic U., M.F.A., dramatic writing, 1959. Taught drama courses, directed student productions at U. of CT & American U., Washington, DC. Produced and co-wrote House That Cried Murder, 1973; co-produced, wrote and directed Scalpel; directed Nightmare at Shadow Woods. Partner in P.J. Productions Co. & North Salem Prods., Inc. Guest Director, Xavier Univ. Theatre.

GRIZZARD, GEORGE
Actor. b. Roanoke Rapids, NC, April 1, 1928. e. U. of North Carolina, B.A., 1949. Has been member of Arena Stage, Washington, D.C., APA repertory company and Tyrone Guthrie resident company in Minneapolis.
THEATER: The Desperate Hours. (B'way debut, 1955), The Happiest Millionaire (Theatre World Award), The Disenchanted, Face of a Hero, Big Fish, Little Fish, Who's Afraid of Virginia Woolf?, The Glass Menagerie, You Know I Can't Hear You When the Water's Running, The Gingham Dog, Inquest, The Country Girl, The Creation of the World and Other Business, Crown Matrimonial, The Royal Family, California Suite, Man and Superman, Another Antiqone, Show Boat, A Delicate Balance (Tony Award, 1996).
PICTURES: From the Terrace, Advise and Consent, Warning Shot, Happy Birthday Wanda June, Comes a Horseman, Firepower, Seems Like Old Times, Wrong Is Right, Bachelor Party.
TELEVISION: *Movies*: Travis Logan D.A., Indict & Convict, The Stranger Within, Attack on Terror: The FBI vs. the Ku Klux Klan, The Lives of Jenny Dolan, The Night Rider, Attica, Not In Front of the Children, The Deliberate Stranger, Underseige, That Secret Sunday, International Airport, Embassy, The Shady Hill Kidnapping, Oldest Living Graduate (Emmy Award, 1980), Perry Mason: The Case of the Scandalous Scoundrel, David, Caroline?, Iran: Days of Crisis, Not in My Family, Triumph Over Disaster: The Hurricane Andrew Story, Suspicion of Innocence. *Specials*: Enemy of the People. *Mini-Series*: The Adams Chronicles, Robert Kennedy and His Times, Queen, Scarlett.

GRODIN, CHARLES
Actor, Director, Writer. b. Pittsburgh, PA, April 21, 1935. e. U. of Miami. After time with Pittsburgh Playhouse studied acting with Uta Hagen and Lee Strasberg; began directing career in New York 1965 as asst. to Gene Saks. Has appeared in some 75 plays all over the country. Has also written scripts, produced plays. *Books:* It Would Be So Nice If You Weren't Here, How I Get Through Life, We're Ready for You Mr. Grodin.
THEATER: Tchin-Tchin (B'way debut, 1962), Absence of a Cello, Same Time Next Year, It's a Glorious Day... And All That (dir., co-author), Lovers and Other Strangers (dir.), Thieves (prod., dir.), Unexpected Guests (prod., dir.), Price of Fame (also author), One of the All-Time Greats (author).
PICTURES: Sex and the College Girl (debut, 1964), Rosemary's Baby, Catch-22, The Heartbreak Kid, 11 Harrowhouse (also adapt.), King Kong, Thieves, Heaven Can Wait, Real Life, Sunburn, It's My Turn, Seems Like Old Times, The Incredible Shrinking Woman, The Great Muppet Caper, The Lonely Guy, The Woman in Red, Movers and Shakers (also s.p., co-prod.), Last Resort, Ishtar, The Couch Trip, You Can't Hurry Love, Midnight Run, Taking Care of Business, Beethoven, Dave, So I Married an Axe Murderer, Heart and Souls, Beethoven's 2nd, Clifford, It Runs in the Family (My Summer Story).
TELEVISION: *Specials* (writer): Candid Camera (also dir.), The Simon & Garfunkel Special, Paul Simon Special (also dir.; Emmy Award for writing, 1978). *Specials* (dir.): Acts of Love and Other Comedies, Paradise (also prod.). *Actor: Guest*: The Defenders, My Mother the Car, The FBI, Guns of Will Sonnett, The Big Valley. *Specials*: Grown Ups, Love Sex and Marriage (also writer), Charley's Aunt. *Movies*: Just Me and You, The Grass Is Always Greener Over the Septic Tank. *Mini-Series*: Fresno. *Series*: Charles Grodin (talk).

GROENING, MATT
Animator, Cartoonist. b. Portland, OR, Feb. 14, 1954. Moved to LA in mid 1980s, started drawing comic strip named "Life in Hell". In 1988 created The Simpsons, originally filler in The Tracy Ullman show, later TV series. Author of Kevin Newcombe (bio.).

TELEVISION: Series: The Simpsons (exec. prod., creator), Futurama (exec. prod., creator).
PICTURES: The Simpsons Movie (exec. prod.).

GROSBARD, ULU
Director. b. Antwerp, Belgium. Jan. 9, 1929. e. U. of Chicago, B.A. 1950, M.A. 1952. Trained at Yale Sch. of Drama 1952-53. Asst. dir. to Eliza Kazan on Splendor in the Grass, 1961; asst. dir.: West Side Story, The Hustler, The Miracle Worker. Unit mgr.: The Pawnbroker.
THEATER: The Days and Nights of Beebee Fenstermaker, The Subject Was Roses, A View From the Bridge, The Investigation, That Summer—That Fall, The Price, American Buffalo, The Woods, The Wake of Jamie Foster, The Tenth Man.
PICTURES: The Subject Was Roses (debut, 1968), Who Is Harry Kellerman and Why Is He Saying Those Terrible Things About Me? (also co-prod.), Straight Time, True Confessions, Falling in Love, Georgia (also co-prod.), The Deep End of the Ocean.

GROSS, KENNETH H.
Executive. b. Columbus, OH, Feb. 12, 1949. e. New School for Social Research, U. of London. Conducted film seminars at New School and active in several indep. film projects. Published film criticism in various journals and magazines. Joined ABC Ent. 1971. Named supvr. of feature films for ABC-TV. Appt. mgr. of feature films, 1974. Promoted 1975 to program exec., ABC Ent. Prime Time/West Coast. Promoted to exec. prod., movies for TV, ABC Ent. 1976 in L.A.; 1978, with literary agency F.C.A. as partner in L.A.; 1979 prod. for Lorimar; then with Intl. Creative Mgt; 1982, formed own literary talent agency, The Literary Group; 1985, merged agency with Robinson-Weintraub & Assoc. to become Robinson-Weintraub-Gross & Assoc. 1993, founding partner of Paradigm, a talent and literary agency. 1997, formed Ken Gross Management, mgmt. and prod. co.

GROSS, MARY
Actress. b. Chicago, IL, March 25, 1953. Brother is actor Michael Gross. e. Loyola U. Is also student of the harp. In 1980 discovered by John Belushi who saw her perform as resident member of Chicago's Second City comedy troupe, where she won Chicago's Joseph Jefferson Award as best actress for the revue, Well, I'm Off to the Thirty Years War. First came to national attention as regular on Saturday Night Live, 1981-85.
PICTURES: Club Paradise, The Couch Trip, Casual Sex?, Baby Boom, Big Business, Feds, Troop Beverly Hills, The Santa Clause, The Evening Star, Mixed Nuts (voice), Practical Magic, The Rugrats Movie (voice).
TELEVISION: *Series*: Saturday Night Live, The People Next Door, Billy, Sabrina the Teenage Witch, Animaniacs (voice). *Specials*: Comic Relief I, The Second City 25th Anniversary Reunion.

GROSS, MICHAEL
Actor. b. Chicago, IL, June 21, 1947. m. casting dir. Elza Bergeron. Sister is actress Mary Gross. e. U. Illinois, B.A., Yale School of Drama, M.F.A.
THEATER: NY Shakespeare Fest. (Sganarelle, An Evening of Moliere Farces, Othello). *Off-B'way:* Endgame, No End of Blame (Obie Award), Put Them All Together, Geniuses, Territorial Rites. *B'way:* Bent, The Philadelphia Story. L.A. stage: Hedda Gabler, The Real Thing, Love Letters, Money & Friends.
PICTURES: Just Tell Me What You Want, Big Business, Tremors, Midnight Murders, Cool as Ice, Alan & Naomi, Tremors II: Aftershocks, Ground Control.
TELEVISION: *Series*: Family Ties. *Movies*: A Girl Named Sooner, FDR: The Last Year, Dream House, The Neighborhood, Little Gloria Happy at Last, Cook and Peary-The Race to the Pole, Summer Fantasy, Family Ties Vacation, A Letter to Three Wives, Right to Die, In the Line of Duty: The FBI Murders, A Connecticut Yankee in King Arthur's Court, Vestige of Honor, In the Line of Duty: Manhunt in the Dakotas, With a Vengeance, Snowbound: The Jim and Jennifer Stolpa Story, In the Line of Duty: The Price of Vengeance, Avalanche, Awake to Danger, Deceived by Trust.

GROSSBART, JACK
Producer. b. Newark, NJ, Apr. 18, 1948. e. Rutgers Univ. Was agent, 1975-80, then personal manager, Litke-Grossbart Mgmt., 1980-87. Became tv prod., Jack Grossbart Prods., 1987.
TELEVISION: *Movies: Exec. prod./prod.:* Shattered Vows, The Seduction of Gina, Rockabye, Killer in the Mirror, Something in Common, Dangerous Affection, Echoes in the Darkness, She Was Marked for Murder, The Preppie Murder, Joshua's Heart, Lies Before Kisses, Honor Bright, Last Wish, Something to Live For: The Alison Gertz Story, A Jury of One, Comrades of Summer, The Woman Who Loved Elvis, One of Her Own, Leave of Absence, Between Love & Honor, Rage Against Time: A Search for Sara, Unforgivable, Breaking Through. *Series: Exec. prod.:* Sydney, Cafe Americain.

GROSSBERG, JACK
Producer, Executive. b. Brooklyn, NY, June 5, 1927.
PICTURES: Requiem for a Heavyweight, Pretty Poison, The Producers, Don't Drink the Water, Take the Money and Run, Bananas, Everything You Always Wanted To Know About Sex, Sleeper, A Delicate Balance, Luther, Rhinoceros, Leadbelly, King Kong, The Betsy, Fast Break, A Stranger is Watching, Brainstorm, Strange Brew, Touch and Go, The Experts, Little Monsters.

GROSSMAN, ERNIE
Executive. b. New York, NY, Sept. 19, 1924. Still dept., pressbook edit., asst. field mgr., Warner Bros., 1940-58; Studio publicist, 1958-60; exploitation, promo. mgr. field dept., 1960-64; nat'l mgr., pub., exploit., promo.; 1964-67 exec. co-ord. advt., pub. & promo., Warner-7 Arts, 1967; WB nat'l supv. ad.-pub., 1970. exec. assist. to Richard Lederer, 1971-72; 1973 nat'l dir. of Pub. & Promotion, Warner Bros. Inc.; 1977, natl. dir. of adv.-pub.; 1980-85, natl. dir. promo. 1987, named south-west special events dir. Retired, 1994.

GRUEN, ROBERT
Executive. b. New York, NY, Apr. 2, 1913, e. Carnegie Mellon U., B.A. Stage designer, 1934-35; designer, 20th-Fox, 1936; prod. exec., National Screen Service Corp., 1936; head, Robert Gruen Associates, ind. design org., 1940; nat. pres. Industrial Designers Inst., 1954-55; dir. and v.p., National Screen Service Corp. since 1951; senior v.p. 1975-78; dir., NSS Corp., Continental Lithograph and NSS, Ltd., 1978-85. Retired 1985.

GRUENBERG, ANDY
Executive. b. Minneapolis, MN, March 10, 1950. e. University of Wisconsin. Held various sales positions with 20th Century Fox and Warner Bros. from 1976 to 1984. Joined Columbia Pictures as asst. general sales mgr. Lorimar Pictures s.v.p. and general sales mgr. 1985-89. Hemdale Prods. pres. of distribution, 1989-91. Joined MGM/UA in 1991, currently exec. v.p. of distribution.

GRUENBERG, LEONARD S.
Executive. b. Minneapolis, MN, Sept. 10, 1913, e. U. of Minnesota. Began as salesman Republic Pictures, Minneapolis, 1935; with RKO in same capacity, 1936; promoted to city sales mgr., St. Louis, 1937, then branch mgr., Salt Lake City, 1941; later that year apptd. Rocky Mt. Dist. Mgr. (hqts., Denver, CO); 1946 Metropolitan, div. mgr., v.p. NTA, v.p. Cinemiracle Prods.; Pres., Chmn. of bd., Sigma III Corp., 1962. Chmn. of bd., Filmways, 1967. Chmn. of bd. Gamma III Dist. Co. & Chmn of bd. and Pres. Great Owl Corp., 1976. Member Variety Club, Sigma Alpha Mu Fraternity; Lieut. Civil Air Patrol, Lieut. Comdr., U.S.N.R.

GRUSIN, DAVID
Composer, Conductor, Performer. b. Littleton, CO, June 26, 1934. Directed music for the Andy Williams Show on TV for 7 yrs in the 1960s, where met Norman Lear and Bud Yorkin, producers of the series, who signed him to score their first feature film, Divorce, American Style (1967).
PICTURES: Waterhole No. 3, The Graduate, Candy, The Heart Is a Lonely Hunter, Winning, Where Were You When the Lights Went Out?, Generation, A Man Called Gannon, Tell Them Willie Boy Is Here, Adam at 6 A.M., Halls of Anger, The Gang That Couldn't Shoot Straight, The Pursuit of Happiness, Shoot Out, Fuzz, The Great Northfield Minnesota Raid, The Friends of Eddie Coyle, The Midnight Ride, W.W. and the Dixie Dancekings, The Yakuza, Three Days of the Condor, Murder By Death, The Front, Fire Sale, Mr. Billion, Bobby Deerfield, The Goodbye Girl, Heaven Can Wait, And Justice for All, The Champ, The Electric Horseman, My Bodyguard, Absence of Malice, On Golden Pond, Reds, Author! Author!, Tootsie, Scandalous, Racing with the Moon, The Pope of Greenwich Village, The Little Drummer Girl, Falling in Love, Lucas, The Goonies, The Milagro Beanfield War (Acad. Award, 1988), Clara's Heart, Tequila Sunrise, A Dry White Season, Havana, The Bonfire of the Vanities, For the Boys, The Cure, The Firm, Mulholland Falls, Selena, Hope Floats, Random Hearts.
TELEVISION: *Movies*: Deadly Dream, Prescription: Murder, Scorpio Letters, Eric, The Family Rico, The Death Squad. *Series*: Maude, Good Times, Baretta, The Name of the Game, It Takes a Thief, The Girl From Uncle, St. Elsewhere, In the Gloaming, Hope.

GUBER, PETER
Producer. b. 1942. e. Syracuse U., B.A.; U. at Florence (Italy), S.S.P.; Sch. of Law, J.D., L.L.M. Recruited by Columbia Pictures as exec. asst. in 1968 while at NYU. Graduate Sch. of Business Adm. With Col. seven yrs. in key prod. exec. capacities, serving last three as studio chief. Formed own company, Peter Guber's Filmworks, which in 1976 was merged with his Casablanca Records to become Casablanca Record and Filmworks where he was co-owner & chmn. bd. 1980 formed Polygram Pictures later bringing in Jon Peters as partner. 1983 sold Polygram and formed Guber-Peters. 1988 merged co. with Burt Sugarman's Barris Industries to form Guber-Peters-Barris Entertainment Co. Co-chmn. & man. dir. 1989 took full control of co. with Sugarman's exit and addition of Australia's Frank Lowy as new partner. 1989 became CEO of Columbia Pictures Ent.; 1992 became chairman and CEo of Sony Pictures Ent. Awards: Producer of Year, NATO, 1979; NYU Albert Gallatin Fellowship; Syracuse U Ardent Award. Visiting prof., & chmn. producer's dept., UCLA Sch. of Theatre Arts. Member of NY, CA and Wash. DC Bars. *Books:* Inside the Deep, Above the Title.
PICTURES: The Deep (first under own banner), Midnight Express. Co-Prod. with Jon Peters: An American Werewolf in London, Missing, Flashdance (exec. prod.), D.C. Cab (exec. prod.), Endless Love, Vision Quest (exec. prod.), The Legend of Billie Jean, Head Office, Clan of the Cave Bear, Six Weeks (exec. prod.), The Pursuit of D.B. Cooper (exec. prod.),

Clue (exec. prod.), The Color Purple (exec. prod.), The Witches of Eastwick (prod.), Innerspace (exec. prod.), Who's That Girl (exec. prod.), Gorillas in the Mist (exec. prod.), Caddyshack II, Rain Man (exec. prod), Batman (prod.), Johnny Handsome, Tango and Cash (prod.), Batman Returns, This Boy's Life (exec. prod.), With Honors (exec. prod.).
TELEVISION: Mysteries of the Sea (doc. Emmy Award). *Exec. prod.:* Television and the Presidency, Double Platinum, Dreams (series). *Movies:* Stand By Your Man, The Toughest Man in the World (exec. prod.), Bay Coven, Oceanquest, Brotherhood of Justice, Nightmare at Bitter Creek, Finish Line.

GUEST, CHRISTOPHER
Actor, Writer, Composer, Director. b. New York, NY, Feb. 5, 1948. m. actress Jamie Lee Curtis. Brother is actor Nicholas Guest. Wrote the musical score and acted in National Lampoon's Lemmings off-B'way. On B'way in Room Service, Moonchildren.
PICTURES: *Actor:* The Hospital (debut, 1971), The Hot Rock, Death Wish, The Fortune, Girlfriends, The Last Word, The Long Riders, Heartbeeps, This Is Spinal Tap (also co-s.p.), Little Shop of Horrors, Beyond Therapy, The Princess Bride, Sticky Fingers, The Big Picture (also dir. co-s.p., story), A Few Good Men, Waiting for Guffman (also dir.), Edwards and Hunt (also dir.), Small Soldiers (voice).
TELEVISION: *Series*: Saturday Night Live (1984-5). *Movies*: It Happened One Christmas, Haywire, Million Dollar Infield, A Piano for Mrs. Cimino, Attack of the 50 Ft. Woman (dir.). *Specials*: The TV Show, The Chevy Chase Special (also writer), The Billion Dollar Bubble, Lily Tomlin (also writer, Emmy Award, 1976), A Nice Place to Visit (writer only), Spinal Tap Reunion (also co-writer). *Mini-Series*: Blind Ambition.

GUEST, LANCE
Actor. b. Saratoga, CA, July 21, 1960. e. UCLA.
PICTURES: Halloween II, I Ought To Be in Pictures, The Last Starfighter, Jaws-The Revenge, The Wizard of Loneliness, Plan B.
TELEVISION: *Series*: Lou Grant, Knots Landing, Life Goes On. *Guest*: St. Elsewhere. *Movies*: Confessions of a Married Man. *Specials*: One Too Many, My Father My Rival, The Roommate. *Mini-Series*: Favorite Son.

GUEST, VAL
Writer, Director, Producer. b. London, England, 1911. e. England and America. Journalist with Hollywood Reporter, Zit's Los Angeles Examiner and Walter Winchell. Debuted as dir. & writer of 1942 short film The Nose Has It.
PICTURES: *Director/Writer*: Miss London Ltd. (feature debut, 1943), Murder at the Windmill, Miss Pilgrim's Progress, The Body Said No, Mr. Drake's Duck, Happy Go Lovely, Another Man's Poison, Penny Princess, The Runaway Bus, Life With the Lyons, Dance Little Lady, Men of Sherwood Forest, Lyons in Paris, Break in the Circle, It's A Great Life, The Quatermass Experiment (The Creeping Unknown), They Can't Hang Me, The Weapon, It's a Wonderful World, Quatermass II (Enemy From Space), The Abominable Snowman, Carry on Admiral, The Camp on Blood Island, Up the Creek, Further Up the Creek, Yesterday's Enemy, Expresso Bongo (also prod.), Life Is a Circus, Hell Is a City, Full Treatment (Stop Me Before I Kill; also prod.), The Day the Earth Caught Fire (also prod.), Jigsaw (also prod.), 80,000 Suspects (also prod.), The Beauty Jungle (Contest Girl; also co-prod.), Where the Spies Are (also co-prod.), Casino Royale (co-dir.), Assignment K, When Dinosaurs Ruled the Earth, Tomorrow, The Persuaders, Au Pair Girls, Confessions of a Window Cleaner, Killer Force (Diamond Mercenaries; dir. only), The Boys in Blue.
TELEVISION: Space 1999, The Persuaders, The Adventurer, The Shillingbury Blowers, The Band Played On, Sherlock Holmes & Dr. Watson, Shillingbury Tales, Dangerous Davies, The Last Detective, In Possession, Mark of the Devil, Child's Play, Scent of Fear.

GUILLAUME, ROBERT
Actor. b. St. Louis, MO, Nov. 30, 1937. e. St. Louis U., Washington U. Scholarship for musical fest. in Aspen, CO. Then apprenticed with Karamu Theatre where performed in operas and musicals. B'way plays and musicals include Fly Blackbird, Kwamina, Guys and Dolls, Purlie, Jacques Brel is Alive and Well and Living in Paris, Cyrano. In L.A. in Phantom of the Opera.
PICTURES: Super Fly T.N.T. (debut, 1973), Seems Like Old Times, Prince Jack, They Still Call Me Bruce, Wanted Dead or Alive, Lean On Me, Death Warrant, The Meteor Man, The Lion King (voice), First Kid, Spy Hard.
TELEVISION: *Series*: Soap (Emmy Award, 1979), Benson (Emmy Award, 1985), The Robert Guillaume Show, Saturdays, Pacific Station, Fish Police (voice), Happily Ever After... Fairytales for Every Child, Sports Night. *Guest*: Dinah, Mel and Susan Together, Rich Little's Washington Follies, Jim Nabors, All in the Family, Sanford and Son, The Jeffersons, Marcus Welby, M.D., Carol & Company, Sister Kate, A Different World. *Mini-Series*: North and South, Pandora's Clock. *Movies*: The Kid From Left Field, The Kid with the Broken Halo, You Must Remember This, The Kid with the 100 I.Q. (also exec. prod.), Perry Mason: The Case of the Scandalous Scoundrel, The Penthouse, Fire and Rain, Greyhounds, Children of the Dust, A Good Day to Die, Panic in the Skies!, Merry Christmas George Bailey, His Bodyguard. *Specials*: Purlie, 'S Wonderful 'S Marvellous 'S Gershwin, John Grin's Christmas, Martin Luther King: A Look Back A Look Forward, Living the Dream: A Tribute to Dr. Martin Luther King Jr. (host), The Debbie Allen Special, Carol & Company, Sister Kate, Story of a People (host), Mastergate, Cosmic Slop. *Pilot*: Driving Miss Daisy.

GUILLERMIN, JOHN
Director, Producer, Writer. b. London, England, Nov. 11, 1925. e. City of London Sch., Cambridge U. RAF pilot prior to entering film industry.
PICTURES: *Director*: Torment (debut, 1949; also co-prod., s.p.), Smart Alec, Two on the Tiles, Four Days, Song of Paris, Miss Robin Hood, Operation Diplomat (also co-s.p.), Adventure in the Hopfields, The Crowded Day, Dust and Gold, Thunderstorm, Town on Trial, The Whole Truth, I Was Monty's Double, Tarzan's Greatest Adventure (also co-s.p.), The Day They Robbed the Bank of England, Never Let Go (also co-story), Waltz of the Torreadors, Tarzan Goes to India (also co-s.p.), Guns at Batasi, Rapture, The Blue Max. P.J. (U.S. debut, 1968), House of Cards, The Bridge of Remagen, El Condor, Skyjacked, Shaft in Africa, The Towering Inferno, King Kong, Death on the Nile, Mr. Patman, Sheena, King Kong Lives, The Favorite.
TELEVISION: *Movie*: The Tracker.

GUINNESS, SIR ALEC
Actor. b. London, Eng., April 2, 1914. e. Pembroke Lodge, Southbourne & Roborough Sch., Eastbourne. Studied acting at Fay Compton Studio of Dramatic Art. Created C.B.E. 1955; Knighted 1959. C.H., 1994. Honorary degrees in literature: Oxford, 1977; Canterbury, 1991. Stage debut: London, 1934. First film appearance was extra in 1934 in Evensong. Special Academy Award, 1980, for services to film. *Autobiography:* Blessings in Disguise (1985). Also author of Blessings in Disguise, and My Name Escapes Me.
THEATER: Libel! (walk-on debut, 1934), Queer Cargo, Hamlet (1934), Noah, Romeo & Juliet (1935), The Seagull, Love's Labour's Lost, As You Like It, The Witch of Edmonton, Hamlet (1937), Twelfth Night (1937), Henry V, Richard III, School for Scandal, The Three Sisters, The Merchant of Venice (1937), The Doctor's Dilemma, Trelawny of the Wells, Hamlet (1938), Henry V, The Rivals, The Ascent of F.6, Romeo and Juliet (1939), Great Expectations (also adapt.), Cousin Muriel, The Tempest, Thunder Rock, Flare Path (B'way), Heart of Oak, The Brothers Karamozov, Vicious Circle, King Lear, An Inspector Calls, Cyrano de Bergerac, The Alchemist, Richard II, Saint Joan, The Government Inspector, Coriolanus, Twelfth Night (1948; also dir.), The Human Touch, The Cocktail Party (Edinburgh; B'way), Hamlet (1951; also dir.), Under the Sycamore Tree, All's Well That Ends Well, Richard III, The Prisoner, Hotel Paradiso, Ross, Exit the King, Dylan (B'way; Tony Award, 1964), Time Out of Mind, Voyage Round My Father, Habeas Corpus, A Family and a Fortune, Yahoo (also author), The Old Country, The Merchant of Venice (1984), A Walk in the Woods.
PICTURES: Great Expectations (debut, 1946), Oliver Twist, Kind Hearts and Coronets, A Run for Your Money, Last Holiday, The Mudlark, The Lavender Hill Mob (Acad. Award nom.), The Man in the White Suit, The Card (The Promoter), Malta Story, The Captain's Paradise, Father Brown (The Detective), To Paris With Love, The Prisoner, The Ladykillers, The Swan, The Bridge on the River Kwai (Academy Award, 1957), Barnacle Bill (All at Sea), The Horse's Mouth (also s.p.; Acad. Award nom. for s.p.), The Scapegoat (also co-prod.), Our Man in Havana, Tunes of Glory, A Majority of One, H.M.S. Defiant (Damn the Defiant!), Lawrence of Arabia, The Fall of the Roman Empire, Situation Hopeless But Not Serious, Doctor Zhivago, Hotel Paradiso, The Quiller Memorandum, The Comedians, Cromwell, Scrooge, Brother Sun Sister Moon, Hitler: The Last Ten Days, Murder by Death, Star Wars: A New Hope (Acad. Award nom.), Star Wars: The Empire Strikes Back, Raise the Titanic!, Lovesick, Star Wars: Return of the Jedi, A Passage to India, A Handful of Dust, Little Dorrit (Acad. Award nom.), Kafka.
TELEVISION: *Movies/Specials/Mini-Series*: The Wicked Scheme of Jebel Deeks, Twelfth Night, Conversation at Night, Solo, Little Gidding, The Gift of Friendship, Caesar and Cleopatra, Little Lord Fauntleroy, Tinker Tailor Soldier Spy (mini-series; BAFTA Award), Smiley's People (mini-series; BAFTA Award), Edwin, Monsignor Quixote, Tales From Hollywood, A Foreign Field, Eskimo Day.

GULAGER, CLU
Actor. b. Holdenville, OK, Nov. 16, 1928. Father, John Gulager, cowboy entertainer. e. Baylor U. Starred at school in original play, A Different Drummer, where spotted by prod. of TV's Omnibus; invited to New York to recreate role on TV.
PICTURES: The Killers, Winning, The Last Picture Show, Company of Killers, McQ, The Other Side of Midnight, A Force of One, Touched by Love, The Initiation, Lies, Into the Night, Prime Risk, The Return of the Living Dead, Hunter's Blood, The Hidden, Tapeheads, Uninvited, I'm Gonna Git You Sucka, Teen Vamp, My Heroes Have Always Been Cowboys, The Killing Device, Eddie Pressley, Puppet Master, Gunfighter.

TELEVISION: *Series*: The Tall Man, The Virginian, The Survivors, San Francisco International Airport, MacKenzies of Paradise Cove. *Movies*: San Francisco International, Glass House, Footsteps, Smile Jenny You're Dead, Houston We've Got a Problem, Hit Lady, Killer Who Wouldn't Die, Charlie Cobb: Nice Night for a Hanging, Ski Lift to Death, Sticking Together, A Question of Love, Willa, This Man Stands Alone, Kenny Rogers as The Gambler, Skyward, Living Proof: The Hank Williams Jr. Story, Bridge Across Time. *Mini-Series*: Once an Eagle, Black Beauty, King, North and South II, Space, Dan Turner Hollywood Detective, In the Line of Duty (Ambush in Waco).

GUMBEL, BRYANT
Announcer, News Show Host. b. New Orleans, LA, Sept. 29, 1948. e. Bates Coll. Started as writer for Black Sports Magazine, NY, 1971; sportscaster, then sports dir., KNBC, Los Angeles. Sports host NBC Sports NY 1975-82. Now host on Today Show, New York (Emmy Awards, 1976, 1977).
TELEVISION: Super Bowl games, '88 Olympics, Games People Play, The R.A.C.E, Public Eye With Bryant Gumbel.

GUMPERT, JON
Executive. e. Cornell U. Law Sch. Sr. v.p., business affairs, MGM/UA Entertainment; pres., World Film Services, Inc., indep. prod. co. in N.Y. 1985, named v.p., business affairs, Warner Bros; 1986 sr. v.p. Vista Films. Named sr. v.p. legal bus. affairs, Universal Pictures 1990. Named exec. v.p., legal business affairs, Universal Pictures, 1994. Group ex. v.p., Universal Pictures, 1996-.

GUNTON, BOB
Actor. b. Santa Monica, CA, Nov. 15, 1945. e. U. of Cal. Served in army during Vietnam War. Prof. acting debut at Cumberland County Playhouse in Tennesse U.S.A.
THEATER: *Off-B'way:* Who Am I? (debut, 1971), How I Got That Story (Obie Award), Tip Toes, The Death of Von Richtofen. *B'way:* Happy End (debut, 1977), Working, Evita (Drama Desk Award; Tony nom.), Passion, King of Hearts, Big River, Rozsa, Sweeney Todd (Drama Desk Award; Tony nom.).
PICTURES: Rollerover (debut, 1981), Static, Matewan, The Pick-Up Artist, Cookie, Born on the Fourth of July, Glory, JFK, Patriot Games, The Public Eye, Jennifer Eight, Demolition Man, The Shawshank Redemption, Dolores Claiborne, Ace Ventura: When Nature Calls, Broken Arrow, The Glimmer Man, Changing Habits, Midnight in the Garden of Good and Evil, Patch Adams, Bats.
TELEVISION: *Series:* Comedy Zone, Hot House, Courthouse. *Movies:* Lois Gibbs and the Love Canal, A Woman Named Jackie, Finnegan Begin Again, Ned Blessing, Dead Ahead: The Exxon Valdez Disaster, Murder in the Heartland, Sinatra, Ruby Ridge: An American Tragedy, Elvis Meets Nixon, Buffalo Soldiers. *Mini-Series:* Wild Palms.

GURIAN, PAUL R.
Executive, Producer. b. New Haven, CT, Oct.18, 1946. e. Lake Forest Coll., U. of Vienna, NYU. Started producing films in 1971 with Cats and Dogs, a dramatic short which won prizes at Chicago Int. Film Fest and Edinburgh Fest. In 1977 formed Gurian Entertainment Corp., to acquire film properties for production.
PICTURES: Cutter and Bone, Peggy Sue Got Married, The Seventh Sign (exec. prod.).
TELEVISION: The Garden Party (PBS program), Profile Ricardo Alegria (short), Bernice Bobs Her Hair (shown at 1977 N.Y. Film Festival)

GUTTENBERG, STEVE
Actor. b. Brooklyn, NY, Aug. 24, 1958. e. Sch. of Performing Arts, N.Y. Off-B'way in The Lion in Winter; studied under John Houseman at Juilliard; classes with Lee Strasberg and Uta Hagen. Moved to West Coast in 1976; landed first TV role in movie, Something for Joey. B'way debut 1991 in Prelude to a Kiss.
PICTURES: Rollercoaster, The Chicken Chronicles, The Boys from Brazil, Players, Can't Stop the Music, Diner, The Man Who Wasn't There, Police Academy, Police Academy 2: Their First Assignment, Cocoon, Bad Medicine, Police Academy 3: Back in Training, Short Circuit, The Bedroom Window, Police Academy 4: Citizens on Patrol (also prod. assoc.), Amazon Women on the Moon, Surrender, Three Men and a Baby, High Spirits, Cocoon: The Return, Don't Tell Her It's Me, Three Men and a Little Lady, The Big Green, Home for the Holidays, It Takes Two, Zeus and Roxanne, Casper, Airborne.
TELEVISION: *Guest*: Police Story, Doc. *Series*: Billy, No Soap Radio. *Movies*: Something for Joey, To Race the Wind, Miracle on Ice, The Day After. *Specials*: Gangs (co-prod.), Pecos Bill: King of the Cowboys.

GUY, JASMINE
Actress. b. Boston, MA, March 10, 1964. Toured with Grease!, 1996-97.
PICTURES: School Daze, Harlem Nights, Kla$h, America's Dream, Cats Don't Dance (voice), Lillie, Guinevere.
TELEVISION: *Movies*: At Mother's Request, A Killer Among Us, Stomping at the Savoy, Perfect Crime. *Series*: A Different World. *Mini-series*: Alex Haley's Queen, A Century of Women. *Guest*: Melrose Place, Lois & Clark, Touched by an Angel, The Outer Limits.

GYLLENHAAL, STEPHEN
Director. b. Pennsylvania. e. Trinity Col, CT. Started career in NYC making industrial films. Directed short film Exit 10.m.. writer-producer Naomi Foner.
PICTURES: Waterland, A Dangerous Woman, Losing Isaiah, Piece of My Heart, Homegrown.
TELEVISION: *Movies:* The Abduction of Kari Swenson, Promised a Miracle, Leap of Faith, Family of Spies, A Killing in a Small Town, Paris Trout, Shattered Mind.

H

HAAS, LUKAS
Actor. b. West Hollywood, CA, Apr. 16, 1976. Kindergarten school principal told casting dir. about him which resulted in film debut in Testament. NY theater debut in Mike Nichols' Lincoln Center production of Waiting for Godot (1988). Appeared in AFI film The Doctor.
PICTURES: Testament (debut, 1983), Witness, Solarbabies, Lady in White, The Wizard of Loneliness, See You in the Morning, Music Box, Rambling Rose, Convicts, Alan and Naomi, Leap of Faith, Warrior Spirit, Boys, Johns, Palookaville, Mars Attacks!, Everyone Says I Love You, Boys, Mars Attacks!, Johns, In the Quiet Night, Breakfast of Champions.
TELEVISION: *Movies*: Love Thy Neighbor, Shattered Spirits, The Ryan White Story, The Perfect Tribute, Kiss and Tell, David and Lisa. *Guest*: Amazing Stories (Ghost Train), Twilight Zone, The Young Indiana Jones Chronicles. *Pilot*: Brothers-in-Law. *Specials*: A Place at the Table, My Dissident Mom, Peacemaker (Triple Play II).

HACK, SHELLEY
Actress. b. Greenwich, CT, July 6, 1952. e. Smith Coll. and U. of Sydney, Australia. Made modeling debut at 14 on cover of Glamour Magazine. Gained fame as Revlon's Charlie Girl on TV commercials.
PICTURES: Annie Hall, If Ever I See You Again, Time After Time, The King of Comedy, Troll, The Stepfather, Blind Fear, Me Myself and I, The Finishing Touch.
TELEVISION: *Series*: Charlie's Angels, Cutter to Houston, Jack and Mike. *Movies*: Death on the Freeway, Trackdown: Finding the Goodbar Killer, Found Money, Single Bars Single Women, Bridesmaids, Casualty of War, Taking Back My Life: The Nancy Ziegenmeyer Story, Not in My Family, The Case of the Wicked Wives, Falling From the Sky: Flight 174, Freefall, Frequent Flyer.

HACKER, CHARLES R.
Executive. b. Milwaukee, WI, Oct. 8, 1920. e. U. of Wisconsin. Thea. mgr., Fox Wisc. Amuse. Corp., 1940; served in U.S.A.F., 1943-45; rejoined Fox Wisconsin Amusement Corp.; joined Standard Theatres Management Corp. 1947, on special assignments; apptd. district mgr. of Milwaukee & Waukesha theatres 1948; joined Radio City Music Hall Corp. as administrative asst. July, 1948; mgr. of oper., 1952; asst. to the pres., Feb. 1957; v.p., Radio City Music Hall Corp., 1964; appointed executive vice president and chief operating officer, February 1, 1973. Pres., Landmark Pictures, May, 1979. Treas. Will Rogers Memorial Fund, 1978-95. Award: Quigley Silver Grand Award for Showmanship, 1947. Member: U.S. Small Business Admin. Region 1, Hartford Advisory Council 1983-93.

HACKETT, BUDDY
Actor. r.n. Leonard Hacker. b. Brooklyn, NY, Aug. 31, 1924. Prof. debut, borscht circuit.
THEATER: *B'way*: Call Me Mister, Lunatics and Lovers, I Had a Ball.
PICTURES: Walking My Baby Back Home (debut, 1953), Fireman Save My Child, God's Little Acre, Everything's Ducky, All Hands on Deck, The Music Man, The Wonderful World of the Brothers Grimm, It's a Mad Mad Mad Mad World, Muscle Beach Party, The Golden Head, The Good Guys and the Bad Guys (cameo), The Love Bug, Loose Shoes, Hey Babe!, Scrooged, The Little Mermaid (voice), Paulie.
TELEVISION: *Series*: School House, Stanley, Jackie Gleason Show, Jack Paar Show, You Bet Your Life (1980), Fish Police (voice), Action. *Movie:* Bud and Lou. *Specials:* Entertainment 55, Variety, The Mama Cass TV Program, Plimpton: Did You Hear the One About...?, Jack Frost (voice), Circus of the Stars, Buddy Hackett—Live and Uncensored.

HACKFORD, TAYLOR
Director, Producer. b. Santa Barbara, CA, Dec. 31, 1944. e. USC, B.A., int'l. relations. Was Peace Corps volunteer in Bolivia 1968-69. Began career with KCET in Los Angeles 1970-77. As prod.-dir. won Oscar for short, Teenage Father, 1978. Theatrical film debut as dir. with The Idolmaker (1980).
PICTURES: *Dir. &/or Prod.*: The Idolmaker, An Officer and a Gentleman, Against All Odds, White Nights, Chuck Berry: Hail! Hail! Rock 'n' Roll, Everyone's All-American, Bound By Honor/Blood In Blood Out, Dolores Claiborne, The Devil's Advocate, Proof of Life (also. prod) *Prod.*: Rooftops, La Bamba, The Long Walk Home, Sweet Talker, Queens Logic, Defenseless, Mortal Thoughts, When We Were Kings.

HACKMAN, GENE
Actor. b. San Bernardino, CA, Jan. 30, 1930. First major broadway role in Any Wednesday. Other stage productions include: Poor Richard, Children from Their Games, A Rainy Day in Newark, The Natural Look, Death and the Maiden. Formed own production co., Chelly Ltd.
PICTURES: Mad Dog Coll (debut, 1961), Lilith, Hawaii, A Covenant With Death, Bonnie and Clyde (Acad. Award nom.), First to Fight, Banning, The Split, Riot, The Gypsy Moths, Downhill Racer, Marooned, I Never Sang for My Father (Acad. Award nom.), Doctors' Wives, The Hunting Party, The French Connection (Acad. Award, 1971), Cisco Pike, Prime Cut, The Poseidon Adventure, Scarecrow, The Conversation, Zandy's Bride, Young Frankenstein, Night Moves, Bite the Bullet, French Connection II, Lucky Lady, The Domino Principle, A Bridge Too Far, March or Die, Superman, All Night Long, Superman II, Reds, Eureka, Under Fire, Uncommon Valor, Misunderstood, Target, Twice in a Lifetime, Power, Hoosiers, Superman IV, No Way Out, Another Woman, Bat-21, Split Decisions, Full Moon in Blue Water, Mississippi Burning (Acad. Award nom.), The Package, Loose Cannons, Postcards From the Edge, Narrow Margin, Class Action, Company Business, Unforgiven (Acad. Award, Natl. Soc. of Film Critics, NY Film Critics, BAFTA, LA Film Critics & Golden Globe Awards, best supporting actor, 1992), The Firm, Geronimo: An American Legend, The Quick and the Dead, Crimson Tide, Get Shorty, Birdcage, Extreme Measures, The Chamber, Absolute Power, Antz (voice), Twilight, Enemy of the State, Under Suspicion, The Replacements, The Heist, Breakers, Behind Enemy Lines.
TELEVISION: *Guest*: U.S. Steel Hour, The Defenders, Trials of O'Brien, Hawk, CBS Playhouse's My Father My Mother, The F.B.I., The Invaders, The Iron Horse. *Movie*: Shadow on the Land.

HADLOCK, CHANNING M.
Marketing. TV Executive. b. Mason City, IA. e. Duke U., U. of North Carolina. Newspaperman, Durham, NC Herald, war corr., Yank; NBC, Hollywood; television prod.-writer, Cunning-ham & Walsh Adv.; v.p. account supr. Chirug & Cairns Adv.; v.p. Marketing Innovations; dir. mktg. Paramount Pictures; mktg. svcs, Ogilvy & Mather; mktg, Time Life Books.

HAGERTY, JULIE
Actress. b. Cincinnati, OH, June 15, 1955. Studied drama for six years before leaving for NY where studied with William Hickey. Made acting debut in her brother Michael's theatre group in Greenwich Village called the Production Company.
THEATER: The Front Page (Lincoln Center), The House of Blue Leaves (Theatre World Award, 1986), Wild Life, Born Yesterday (Phil. Drama Guild), The Years, Three Men on a Horse, Wifey, A Cheever Evening, Raised in Captivity.
PICTURES: Airplane! (debut, 1980), A Midsummer Night's Sex Comedy, Airplane II: The Sequel, Lost in America, Goodbye New York, Bad Medicine, Beyond Therapy, Aria, Bloodhounds of Broadway, Rude Awakening, Reversal of Fortune, What About Bob?, Noises Off, The Wife, U Turn, Mel.
TELEVISION: *Series*: Princesses, Women of the House, Reunited. *Specials:* The Visit (Trying Times). House of Blue Leaves, Necessary Parties. *Movie*: The Day the Women Got Even, Jackie's Back!, London Suite.

HAGGAR, PAUL JOHN
Executive. b. Brooklyn, NY, Aug. 5, 1928. e. LA h.s. Veteran of over 40 yrs. with Paramount Pictures, working way up from studio mail room to become apprentice editor in 1953; promoted to asst. editor 1955; music editor, 1957. 1968, named head of post-prod. for all films and TV made by Paramount. 1985, named sr. v.p., post-prod. for the Motion Picture Group.

HAGGARD, PIERS
Director. b. London, 1939. e. U. of Edinburgh. Son of actor Stephen Haggard; great grandnephew of author Rider Haggard. Began career in theatre in 1960 as asst. to artistic dir. at London's Royal Court. Named dir. of Glasgow Citizens' Theatre, 1962. 1963-65 worked with the National Theatre, where co-directed Hobson's Choice and The Dutch Courtesan. Has directed many prize winning TV commercials.
PICTURES: Wedding Night (debut, 1969; also co-s.p.), Blood on Satan's Claw (Satan's Skin), The Fiendish Plot of Dr. Fu Manchu, Venom, A Summer Story.
TELEVISION: *Specials/Movies*: A Triple Play: Sam Found Out (Liza Minnelli special), The Fulfillment of Mary Gray, Back Home, Quatermass Conclusion, Chester Cycle of Mystery Plays, Mrs. Reinhardt, Knockback, Visitors, Heartstones, I'll Take Romance, Four Eyes and Six-Guns, Eskimo Day, The Double (s.p.), Cold Enough for Snow. *Series*: Pennies from Heaven, Quatermass, Return to Treasure Island, Centrepoint, Space Precinct.

HAGMAN, LARRY
Actor. b. Fort Worth, TX, Sept. 21, 1931. e. Bard Coll. Son of late actress Mary Martin. First stage experience with Margo Jones Theatre in the Round in Dallas. Appeared in N.Y. in Taming of the Shrew; one year with London production of South Pacific. 1952-56 was in London with US Air Force where produced and directed show for servicemen. Returned to N.Y. for plays on and off B'way: God and Kate Murphy (Theatre World Award), The Nervous Set, The Warm Peninsula, The Beauty Part.
PICTURES: Ensign Pulver, Fail Safe, In Harm's Way, The Group, The Cavern, Up in the Cellar, Son of Blob (aka: Beware! The Blob; also dir.), Harry and Tonto, Stardust, Mother Jugs and Speed, The Big Bus, The Eagle Has Landed, Checkered Flag or Crash, Superman, S.O.B., Nixon, Primary Colors.
TELEVISION: *Series*: The Edge of Night, I Dream of Jeannie, The Good Life, Here We Go Again, Orleans, Dallas. *Movies*: Three's a Crowd, Vanished, A Howling in the Woods, Getting Away from It All, No Place to Run, The Alpha Caper, Blood Sport, What Are Best Friends For?, Sidekicks, Hurricane, Sarah T.-Portrait of a Teenage Alcoholic, The Big Rip-Off, Return of the World's Greatest Detective, Intimate Strangers, The President's Mistress, Last of the Good Guys, A Double Life, Deadly Encounter, Dallas: The Early Years, Staying Afloat, In the Heat of the Night: Who Was Geli Bendl? (dir. only), Dallas: War of the Ewings, Dallas: Who Killed J.R.?, Dallas: J.R. Returns. *Special*: Applause, Lone Star. *Mini-series*: The Third Twin, The Rhinemann Exchange.

HAHN, HELENE
Executive. b. New York, NY. e. Loyola U. Sch. of Law. Instructor of entertainment law at Loyola. Attorney for ABC before joining Paramount in 1977 in studio legal dept. 1979, moved to business affairs; promoted to dir. 1980, v.p., 1981; sr. v.p., 1983. Left in 1985 to join Walt Disney Pictures as sr. v.p., business & legal affairs for m.p. division. 1987, promoted to exec. v.p., Walt Disney Studios.

HAID, CHARLES
Actor, Director, Producer. b. San Francisco, CA, June 2, 1943. e. Carnegie Tech. Appeared on NY stage in Elizabeth the First. Co-produced Godspell. Prod. & dir. short film The Last Supper.
PICTURES: *Actor*: The Choirboys, Who'll Stop the Rain, Oliver's Story, House of God, Altered States, Square Dance (co-exec. prod. only), Cop, The Rescue, Nightbreed, Storyville. *Director:* Iron Will.
TELEVISION: *Series*: Kate McShane, Delvecchio, Hill Street Blues, Cop Rock (prod. only). *Movies*: The Execution of Private Slovik, Remember When, Things in Their Season, Kate McShane (pilot), Foster and Laurie, A Death in Canaan, The Bastard, Death Moon, Twirl, Divorce Wars, Children in the Crossfire (also co-prod.), Code of Vengeance, Six Against the Rock, Weekend War, The Great Escape II: The Untold Story, A Deadly Silence, Fire and Rain, Man Against the Mob: The Chinatown Murders, In the Line of Duty: A Cop for the Killing (also co-prod.), In the Line of Duty: Siege at Marion (dir. only), The Nightman (dir., prod. only), Cooperstown (also dir.), For Their Own Good, The Fire Next Time, Broken Trust.

HAIM, COREY
Actor. b. Toronto, Canada, Dec. 23, 1972. Performed in TV commercials at 10; regular on children's show, The Edison Twins.
PICTURES: Firstborn (debut, 1984), Secret Admirer, Silver Bullet, Murphy's Romance, Lucas, The Lost Boys, License to Drive, Watchers, Dream a Little Dream, Fast Getaway (also assoc. prod.), Prayer of the Roller Boys, The Dream Machine, Oh What a Night, Blown Away, The Double-O Kid, National Lampoon's Last Resort, Fast Getaway 2, Dream a Little Dream 2, Life 101 (also assoc. prod.), Snowboard Academy, Fever Lake, Demolition High, Busted, Never Too Late, Tales From the Crypt: Bordello of Blood.
TELEVISION: *Movies*: A Time to Live, Just One of the Girls. *Series*: Roomies.

HAINES, RANDA
Director. b. Los Angeles, CA, Feb. 20, 1945. Raised in NYC. Studied acting with Lee Strasberg. e. School of Visual Arts. 1975 accepted into AFI's Directing Workshop for Women. Dir. & co-wrote short film August/September, which led to work as writer for series Family. Appeared in documentary Calling the Shots.
PICTURES: Children of a Lesser God, The Doctor, Wrestling Ernest Hemingway, A Family Thing (co-prod. only).
TELEVISION: *Series*: Family (writer), Hill Street Blues (dir. of 4 episodes), Alfred Hitchcock Presents (Bang You're Dead), Tales from the Crypt (Judy You're Not Yourself Today). *Movie*: Something About Amelia. *Specials*: Under This Sky, The Jilting of Granny Weatherall, Just Pals.

HALE, BARBARA
Actress. b. DeKalb, IL, Feb. 18, 1922. Was married to late actor Bill Williams. Son is actor William Katt. e. Chicago Acad. of Fine Arts. Beauty contest winner, Little Theatre actress. Screen debut, 1943.
PICTURES: Gildersleeve's Bad Day, The Seventh Victim, Higher and Higher, Belle of the Yukon, The Falcon Out West, Falcon in Hollywood, Heavenly Days, West of the Pecos, First Yank in Tokyo, Lady Luck, A Likely Story, Boy with Green Hair, The Clay Pigeon, Window, Jolson Sings Again, And Baby Makes Three, Emergency Wedding, Jackpot, Lorna Doone, First Time, Last of the Comanches, Seminole, Lone Hand, A Lion Is in the Streets, Unchained, Far Horizons, Houston Story, 7th Cavalry, Oklahoman, Slim Carter, Desert Hell, Buckskin, Airport, Soul Soldier, Giant Spider Invasion, Big Wednesday.
TELEVISION: *Series*: Perry Mason (Emmy Award, 1959). *Movies*: Flight of the Grey Wolf, Perry Mason Returns (1985) and 29 other Perry Mason's incl. The Case of the... Murdered Madam, Avenging Ace, Lady in the Lake, Scandalous Scoundrel, Lethal Lesson, Poisoned Pen, Fatal Fashion, Reckless Romeo.

HALEY, JR., JACK
Executive, Director. b. Los Angeles, CA, Oct.25, 1933. e. Loyola U. Son of late actor Jack Haley. 1959-67 Wolper Prods., 1967-73. sr. v.p. at Wolper before joining MGM. Named dir. of creative affairs. Left in 1974, to join 20th Century-Fox as pres. of TV div. and v.p., TV for 20th-Fox Film Corp. Winner of 2 Peabody Awards, best prod. at Int'l. TV Festival at Monte Carlo and 3 Silver Lion Awards at Venice Film Festival. Won Emmy for best dir. in music or variety shows for Movin' On with Nancy. Directed Academy Awards Show in 1970; prod. it in 1974 and 1979. Left Fox 1976 to be indep. prod.
PICTURES: *Director*: Norwood, The Love Machine, That's Entertainment (also prod, s.p.), Better Late Than Never (prod. only), That's Dancing (also co-prod., s.p.).
TELEVISION: The Incredible World of James Bond, The Legend of Marilyn Monroe, The Supremes, The Hidden World, Movin' with Nancy (Emmy Award, dir., 1968), With Love Sophia, Monte Carlo, Life Goes to War: Hollywood and the Homefront; Heroes of Rock n' Roll (exec. prod.), 51st Academy Awards (Emmy Award, 1979), Hollywood, the Golden Years (with David Wolper), Ripley's Believe It or Not, The Night They Saved Christmas, Cary Grant: A Celebration (exec. prod.).

HALL, ANTHONY MICHAEL
Actor. r.n. Michael Anthony Hall. b. Boston, MA, Apr. 14, 1968.
PICTURES: Six Pack (debut, 1982), National Lampoon's Vacation, Sixteen Candles, The Breakfast Club, Weird Science, Out of Bounds, Johnny Be Good, Edward Scissorhands, A Gnome Named Gnorm, Into the Sun, Hail Caesar (also dir.), Six Degrees of Separation, Me and the Mob, The Grave, Exit in Red, Trojan War, The Killing Grounds.
TELEVISION: *Series*: Saturday Night Live (1985-86). *Mini-Series*: Texas. *Movies*: Rascals and Robbers: The Secret Adventures of Tom Sawyer and Huck Finn, Running Out, A Bucket of Blood, Hijacked: Flight 285, A Touch of Hope, Pirates of Silicon Valley. *Guest*: NYPD Blue, Tales from the Crypt, Boys and Girls.

HALL, ARSENIO
Actor, Comedian. b. Cleveland, OH. Feb. 12, 1959. e. Kent State U. Became interested in magic at 7, which later led to own local TV special, The Magic of Christmas. Switched from advertising career to stand-up comedy, 1979. Discovered at Chicago night-club by singer Nancy Wilson.
PICTURES: Amazon Women on the Moon (debut, 1987), Coming to America, Harlem Nights, Bopha! (exec. prod. only), Blankman (cameo).
TELEVISION: *Series*: The 1/2 Hour Comedy Hour (1983, co-host), Thicke of the Night, Motown Revue, The Late Show (1987, host), The Arsenio Hall Show, The Party Machine With Nia Peeples (prod. only), Arsenio, Martial Law. *Special*: Happy Birthday Elizabeth: A Celebration of Life.

HALL, CONRAD
Cinematographer. b. Papeete, Tahiti, June 21, 1926. Worked as camera operator with Robert Surtees, Ted McCord, Ernest Haller; moved to TV as dir. of photography before feature films.
PICTURES: Wild Seed, The Saboteur–Code Name: Morituri, Harper, The Professionals, Rogue's Gallery, Incubus, Divorce American Style, In Cold Blood, Cool Hand Luke, Hell in the Pacific, Butch Cassidy and the Sundance Kid (Academy Award, 1969), Tell Them Willie Boy Is Here, The Happy Ending, Fat City, Electra Glide in Blue, The Day of the Locust, Smile, Marathon Man, Black Widow, Tequila Sunrise, Class Action, Jennifer Eight, Searching for Bobby Fischer, Love Affair, A Civil Action (Acad. Award nom.), Without Limits, American Beauty.
TELEVISION: *Movie*: It Happened One Christmas, Stoney Burke. *Series*: Outer Limits.

HALL, KURT C.
Executive. b. Burlington, VT. e. Univ. of VT. Served as dir. of financial reporting, dir. of finance, and v.p. & treas. of UA Entertainment before becoming v.p. & treas. of United Artists Theatre Circuit, 1990-91. Named exec. v.p. and CFO of United Artists Theatre Circuit, Inc.

HALL, MONTY; O.C.
Actor. b. Winnipeg, Manitoba, Canada, Aug. 25, 1925. e. U. of Manitoba, B.S. Host of Keep Talking, 1958. Host of Let's Make a Deal, 1964-86. International chmn., Variety Clubs International. Appeared in tv movie The Courage & The Passion, 1978.

HALL, PHILIP BAKER
Actor. b. Toldeo, Ohio, September 10, 1931. e. University of Toldeo.
PICTURES: Cowards, The Man With Bogart's Face, The Last Reunion, Dream On, Secret Honor, Three O'Clock High, Midnight Run, Ghostbusters II, Say Anything, An Innocent Man, How I Got Into College, Blue Desert, Live Wire, Cigarettes and Coffee, Kiss of Death, The Little Death, Eye for an Eye, Hit Me, Hard Eight, The Rock, Buddy, Air Force One, Boogie Nights, Sour Grapes, The Truman Show, Judas Kiss, Rush Hour, Enemy of the State, Psycho, Implicated, Cradle Will Rock, The Insider, Magnolia, The Talented Mr. Ripley, Let the Devil Wear Black, Rules of Engagement, The Contender, Lost Souls.
TELEVISION: *Movies:* The Last Survivors, Mayday at 40000 Feet, Man from Atlantis, Kill Me If You Can, The Bastard, Terror Out of the Sky, Samurai, The Night the Bridge Fell Down, This House Possessed, Games Mother Never Taught You, Who is Julia?, Goddess of Love, A Cry for Help: The Tracey Thurman Story, Incident at Dark River, Crash Landing; The Rescue of of Flight 232, Stormy Weathers, M.A.N.T.I.S, Roswell, Without Warning, Tempting Fate, Witness to the Mob. *Series:* Mariah, Falcon Crest. *Guest:* Good Times, Emergency!, MASH, The Waltons, Quincy, Cheers, Matlock, T.J. Hooker, Bagdad Cafe, Murder, She Wrote, Seinfeld, Life's Work, Hardball, The Good Life, Chicago Hope, Third Rock from the Sun, The Practice, Millenium.

HALLSTROM, LASSE
Director. b. Stockholm, Sweden, 1946. m. actress Lena Olin. As teenager made 16mm film which was eventually screened on Swedish tv. Began professional career filming and editing inserts for Swedish TV. Directed program Shall We Dance? for Danish TV, followed by TV prod. on The Love Seeker, dir. of program Shall We Got to My or to Your Place or Each Go Home Alone?.
PICTURES: A Love and His Lass (debut, 1974), ABBA: The Movie, Father-to-Be, The Rooster, Happy We, The Children of Bullerby Village, More About the Children of Bullerby Village, My Life as a Dog (also co-s.p.; Acad. Award noms. for dir. & s.p.), Once Around (U.S. debut, 1991), What's Eating Gilbert Grape (also co-exec. prod.), Lumiere & Company, Something to Talk About, The Golden Hour, The Shipping News.

HALMI, ROBERT SR.
Producer. b. Budapest, Hungary, Jan 22, 1924. Originally writer-photographer under contract to Life Magazine.
PICTURES: Created documentaries for U.N. Features include: Hugo the Hippo, Visit to a Chief's Son, The One and Only, Brady's Escape, Cheetah, Mr. and Mrs. Bridge.
TELEVISION: Bold Journey (dir.-cin.), American Sportsman, The Oriental Sportsman, The Flying Doctor, The Outdoorsman, Julius Boros Series, Rexford, Who Needs Elephants, Calloway's Climb, Oberndorf Revisited, True Position, Wilson's Reward, Nurse, Buckley Sails, A Private Battle, My Old Man, Mr. Griffin and Me, When the Circus Came to Town, Best of Friends, Bush Doctor, Peking Encounter, Svengali, China Rose, Cook and Peary-The Race to the Pole, Terrible Joe Moran, Nairobi Affair, The Night They Saved Christmas, Spies, Lies and Naked Thighs. *Exec. prod.*: The Prize Pulitzer, Paradise, Bridesmaids, Face to Face, Margaret Bourke-White, The Incident, Josephine Baker Story, The Secret, An American Story, Call of the Wild, Blind Spot, Incident in a Small Town, Spoils of War, The Yearling, A Promise Kept: The Oksana Baiul Story, A Mother's Gift, Scarlett, Reunion, My Brother's Keeper, White Dwarf, Secrets, Bye Bye Birdie, Kidnapped, Gulliver's Travels (Emmy Award, 1996), Captains Courageous, Dead Man's Walk, The Oddysey, In Cold Blood, Mrs. Santa Claus, Forbidden Territory: Stanley's Search for Livingstone, A Christmas Memory, Mary and Tim, Moby Dick, Merlin, The Long Way Home.

HAMADY, RON
Producer. b. Flint, MI, June 16, 1947. e. U. of California, B.A. 1971. Co-founder of The Crystal Jukebox, record prod's., music mgmt. and music pub. co. Prod. 12 hit albums for Decca Records of England and London Records, U.S. Entered m.p. industry in 1975, producing Train Ride to Hollywood for Taylor-Laughlin dist. Co.
PICTURES: Fade to Black, Surf II, And God Created Woman (1987), Out Cold, Don't Tell Her It's Me, Meltdown.

HAMEL, VERONICA
Actress. b. Philadelphia, PA, Nov. 20, 1943. e. Temple U. Moved to NY and began a modelling career with Eileen Ford Agency. Off B'way debut: The Big Knife. Acted in dinner theater prods. Moved to L.A. 1975.
THEATER: *B'way*: Rumors. *Off B'way*: The Big Knife, The Ballad of Boris K.
PICTURES: Cannonball, Beyond the Poseidon Adventure, When Time Ran Out, A New Life, Taking Care of Business.
TELEVISION: *Movies*: The Gathering, Ski Lift to Death, The Gathering II, The Hustler of Muscle Beach, Valley of the Dolls, Sessions, Twist of Fate, She Said No, Stop at Nothing, Deadly Medicine (also co-exec. prod.), Baby Snatcher (also co-exec. prod.), The Disappearance of Nora, The Conviction of Kitty Dodds, Shadow of Obsession, A Child's Cry for Help, Intensive Care, Secrets, Here Come the Munsters, Blink of an Eye, Brother's Keeper. *Mini-Series*: 79 Park Avenue, Kane & Abel. *Series*: Hill Street Blues. *Guest*: Kojak, Rockford Files, Bob Newhart Show, Switch.

HAMILL, MARK
Actor. b. Oakland, CA, Sept. 25, 1951. While studying acting at LA City Col. made prof. debut in episode of The Bill Cosby Show, 1970. Featured in CD-ROM interactive game Wing Commander III.
THEATER: *NY*: The Elephant Man (B'way debut), Amadeus (also Natl. tour), Harrigan 'n' Hart, Room Service (off-B'way), The Nerd.

PICTURES: Star Wars (debut, 1977), Wizards (voice), Corvette Summer, The Empire Strikes Back, The Big Red One, The Night the Lights Went Out in Georgia, Britannia Hospital, Return of the Jedi, Slipstream, Midnight Ride, Black Magic Woman, Sleepwalkers (cameo), Time Runner, The Guyver, Batman: Mask of the Phantasm (voice), Village of the Damned, Laserhawk, Gen 13 (voice), Hamilton, Wing Commander (cameo, voice).
TELEVISION: *Series*: General Hospital, The Texas Wheelers, Batman (voice), The Incredible Hulk (voice), Bruno the Kid (voice), Wing Commander Academy (voice), Cow and Chicken. *Movies*: Sarah T.-Portrait of a Teenage Alcoholic, Eric, Delancey Street: The Crisis Within, Mallory: Circumstantial Evidence, The City, Earth Angel, Body Bags, Hollyrock-a-Bye Baby (voice), When Time Expires, Sinbad: Beyond the Veil of Mists. *Guest*: Room 222, The Partridge Family, Headmaster, Medical Center, Owen Marshall, The FBI, Streets of San Francisco, One Day at a Time, Manhunter, Hooperman, Alfred Hitchcock Presents, Amazing Stories, The Flash, seaQuest DSV, The Simpsons (voice), Just Shoot Me. *Specials:* Get High on Yourself, Night of 100 Stars.

HAMILTON, GEORGE
Actor. b. Memphis, TN, Aug. 12, 1939. e. grammar, Hawthorne, CA; military sch., Gulfport, MS, N.Y. Hackley Prep Sch., FL, Palm Beach H.S. Won best actor award in Florida, high sch. contest.
PICTURES: Crime and Punishment USA (debut, 1959), Home From the Hill, All the Fine Young Cannibals, Where the Boys Are, Angel Baby, By Love Possessed, A Thunder of Drums, Light in the Piazza, Two Weeks in Another Town, Act One, The Victors, Looking for Love, Your Cheatin' Heart, Viva Maria, That Man George, Doctor You've Got to Be Kidding!, Jack of Diamonds, A Time for Killing, The Power, Togetherness, Evel Knievel (also co-p), Medusa (also exec. prod.), The Man Who Loved Cat Dancing, Once Is Not Enough, The Happy Hooker Goes to Washington, Love at First Bite (also co-exec. prod.), Sextette, From Hell to Victory, Zorro the Gay Blade (also co-prod.), The Godfather Part III, Doc Hollywood, Once Upon a Crime, Double Dragon, Amore!, Playback, Meet Wally Sparks, 8 Heads in a Duffel Bag, She's Too Tall, Bulworth (cameo).
TELEVISION: *Mini-Series*: Roots. *Movies*: Two Fathers' Justice, Monte Carlo, Poker Alice, Caution: Murder Can Be Hazardous to Your Health, The House on Sycamore Street, Two Fathers: Justice for the Innocent, Danielle Steel's Vanished, Rough Riders. *Series*: The Survivors, Paris 7000, Dynasty, Spies, The Bold & the Beautiful, The George and Alana Show (also prod.), The Guilt, Jenny, Match Game. *Guest*: Rin Tin Tin, The Donna Reed Show, Dream On, The John Laroquette Show, The Bonnie Hunt Show, The Naked Truth. *Special*: The Veil.

HAMILTON, GUY
Director. b. Paris, France, Sept. 24, 1922. Ent. m.p. industry 1939 as apprentice at Victorine Studio, Nice; Royal Navy, 1940-45, in England asst. dir., Fallen Idol, Third Man, Outcast of the Islands, African Queen.
PICTURES: The Ringer, The Intruder, An Inspector Calls, Dragnet (actor only), Colditz Story, Manuela, The Devil's Disciple, A Touch of Larceny, The Best of Enemies, The Party's Over, Man in the Middle, Goldfinger, Funeral in Berlin, Battle of Britain, Diamonds Are Forever, Live and Let Die, The Man with the Golden Gun, Force Ten from Navarone, The Mirror Crack'd, Evil Under the Sun, Remo Williams, Try This One For Size.

HAMILTON, LINDA
Actress. b. Salisbury, MD, Sept. 26, 1956. Appeared on NY stage in Looice and Richard III.
PICTURES: Tag: The Assassination Game, Children of the Corn, The Stone Boy, The Terminator, Black Moon Rising, King Kong Lives!, Mr. Destiny, Terminator 2: Judgment Day, Silent Fall, The Shadow Conspiracy, Dante's Peak, Unglued.
TELEVISION: *Series*: Secrets of Midland Heights, King's Crossing, Beauty and the Beast. *Movies*: Reunion, Rape and Marriage-The Rideout Case, Country Gold, Secrets of a Mother and Daughter, Secret Weapons, Club Med, Go Toward the Light, A Mother's Prayer, Rescuers: Stories of Courage: Two Couples, On the Line, Point Last Seen, The Color of Courage. *Guest*: Hill Street Blues, Murder She Wrote.

HAMLIN, HARRY
Actor. b. Pasadena, CA, Oct. 30, 1951. e. U. of California, Yale U., 1974 in theatre, psychology. Awarded IT&T Fulbright Grant, 1977. 1974-1976 with the American Conservatory Theatre, San Francisco, then joined McCarter Theatre, Princeton (Hamlet, Faustus in Hell, Equus). B'way debut Awake and Sing! (1984). Also performed in Henry V, Smoke.
PICTURES: Movie Movie (debut, 1978), King of the Mountain, Clash of the Titans, Making Love, Blue Skies Again Maxie, Ebbtide, Save Me, The Celluloid Closet, Badge of Bertrayal, Allie & Me, Frogs for Snakes, Perfume.
TELEVISION: *Mini-series*: Studs Lonigan, Master of the Game, Space, Favorite Son, Night Sins. *Movies*: Laguna Heat, Deceptions, Deadly Intentions... Again?, Deliver Them From Evil: The Taking of Alta View, Poisoned By Love: The Kern County Murders, In the Best of Families: Marriage Pride & Madness, Tom Clancy's Op Center, Her Deadly Rival, The Hunted, Like Father Like Santa, Silent Predators. *Series*: L.A. Law, Ink, Movie Stars.

HAMLISCH, MARVIN
Composer. b. New York, NY, June 2, 1944. e. Juilliard. Accompanist and straight man on tour with Groucho Marx 1974-75; debut as concert pianist 1975 with Minn. Orch. Scores of B'way shows: A Chorus Line (Tony Award & Pulitzer Prize); They're Playing Our Song, Smile, The Goodbye Girl. Composer of popular songs: Sunshine Lollipops and Rainbows, Nobody Does it Better. Winner 4 Grammy awards, 3 Oscars, 2 Emmys, 1 Tony, 3 Golden Globe awards. Autobiography, The Way I Was, 1992. Conductor for the Pittsburgh Symphony Orchestra, 1995-; Baltimore Symphony Orchestra, 1996-.
PICTURES: The Swimmer, Take the Money and Run, Bananas, Save the Tiger, Kotch, The Way We Were (2 Acad. Awards for orig. score and title song, 1973), The Sting (Acad. Award for music adapt., 1973), The Spy Who Loved Me, Same Time Next Year, Ice Castles, Chapter Two, Seems Like Old Times, Starting Over, Ordinary People, The Fan, Sophie's Choice, I Ought to Be in Pictures, Romantic Comedy, D.A.R.Y.L., Three Men and a Baby, Little Nikita, The January Man, The Experts, Frankie and Johnny, Open Season, The Mirror Has Two Faces.
TELEVISION: *Series*: Good Morning America (theme), Brooklyn Bridge. *Movies*: The Entertainer (also prod.), A Streetcar Named Desire, The Two Mrs. Grenvilles, Women & Men: Stories of Seduction, Switched at Birth, Seasons of the Heart.

HAMMOND, PETER
Actor, Writer, Director. b. London, England,, Nov.15, 1923. e. Harrow Sch. of Art. Stage debut: Landslide, Westminster Theatre. Screen debut: Holiday Camp. Dir./writer, 1959-61, tv plays.
PICTURES: The Huggetts, Helter Skelter, Fools Rush In, The Reluctant Widow, Fly Away Peter, The Adventurers, Operation Disaster, Come Back, Peter, Little Lambs Eat Ivy, Its Never Too Late, The Unknown, Morning Departure, Confession. *Dir.:* Spring and Port Wine.
TELEVISION: *Series:* William Tell, Robin Hood, The Buccaneers. *Dir.:* Avengers, 4 Armchair Theatres, Theatre 625, BBC classic serials Count of Monte Cristo, Three Musketeers, Hereward the Wake, Treasure Island, Lord Raingo, Cold Comfort Farm, The White Rabbit, Out of the Unknown, Follyfoot; Lukes Kingdom, Time to Think, Franklin's Farm, Sea Song, Shades of Greene, Our Mutual Friend, The House that Jack Built, The King of the Castle, The Black Knight, Kilvert's Diary, Turgenev's Liza, Wuthering Heights, Funnyman, Little World of Don Camillo, Rumpole of the Bailey, Bring on the Girls, Hallelujah Mary Plum, Aubrey Beardsley, The Happy Autumn Fields, The Combination, Tales of the Unexpected, The Glory Hole, The Hard Word, Shades of Darkness-The Maze, The Blue Dress.

HAMNER, EARL
Producer, Writer. b. Schuyler, VA, July 10, 1923. e. U. of Richmond 1940-43, Northwestern U.; U of Cincinnati, Coll. Conservatory of Music, B.F.A., 1958. With WLW, Cincinnati, as radio writer-prod.; joined NBC 1949 as writer; (The Georgia Gibbs Show, The Helen O'Connell Show); freelance 1961-71; writer, prod. Lorimar Prods. 1971-86; writer prod. Taft Entertainment 1986-; Pres. Amanda Prods.
PICTURES: Palm Springs Weekend, Spencer's Mountain, The Tamarind Seed, Charlotte's Web (adaptor), Where the Lilies Bloom.
TELEVISION: *Exec. prod.*: *Series*: The Waltons (creator, co-prod., narrator), Apple's Way (creator), The Young Pioneers (creator), Joshua's World, Falcon Crest, Boone (also creator), Morning Star/Evening Star (also narrator), *Movies*: The Homecoming: A Christmas Story (writer only), You Can't Get There From Here (writer only), A Wedding on Walton's Mountain, Mother's Day on Walton's Mountain, A Day of Thanks on Walton's Mountain (also actor), The Gift of Love--A Christmas Story (also writer).

HAMPSHIRE, SUSAN
O.B.E., 1995. Actress. b. London, England,, May 12, 1941.
THEATER: Expresso Bongo, Follow That Girl, Fairy Tales of New York, Ginger Man, Past Imperfect, She Stoops to Conquer, On Approval, The Sleeping Prince, A Doll's House, Taming of the Shrew, Peter Pan, Romeo & Jeanette, As You Like It, Miss Julie, The Circle, Arms and the Man, Man and Superman, Tribades, An Audience Called Edward, The Crucifer of Blood, Night and Day, The Revolt, House Guest, Blithe Spirit, Married Love, A Little Night Music, The King and I, Noel & Gertie, Relative Values, Susanna Andler, Black Chiffon.
PICTURES: The Three Lives of Thomasina, Night Must Fall, Wonderful Life, Paris Au Mois d'Aout, The Fighting Prince of Donegal, The Trygon Factor, Monte Carlo or Bust, Rogan, David Copperfield, A Room in Paris, Living Free, Time for Loving, Malpertius, Baffled, Neither the Sea nor the Sand, Roses and Green Peppers, David the King, Bang.
TELEVISION: Andromeda, The Forsyte Saga, Vanity Fair, Katy, The First Churchills; An Ideal Husband, The Lady Is a Liar, The Improbable Mr. Clayville, Dr. Jekyll and Mr. Hyde (musical), The Pallisers, Barchester Chronicles, Leaving, Leaving II, Going to Pot (I, II, and III), Don't Tell Father, The Grand I & II, Coming Home.

HAMPTON, JAMES
Actor. b. Oklahoma City, OK, July 9, 1936. e. N. Texas St. Univ.
PICTURES: Fade In, Soldier Blue, The Man Who Loved Cat Dancing, The Longest Yard, W.W. & The Dixie Dancekings, Hustle, Hawmps!, The Cat from Outer Space, Mackintosh & T.J., The China Syndrome, Hangar 18, Condorman, Teen Wolf, Teen Wolf Too, Police Academy 5, Pump Up the Volume, The Giant of Thunder Mountain.
TELEVISION: *Series*: F Troop, The Doris Day Show, Love—American Style, Mary, Maggie. *Movies:* Attack on Terror: The FBI Versus the Ku Klux Klan, Force Five, The Amazing Howard Hughes, Three on a Date, Thaddeus Rose and Eddie, Stand By Your Man, Through the Magic Pyramid, World War III, The Burning Bed. *Mini-Series*: Centennial.

HANCOCK, JOHN
Director. b. Kansas City, MO, Feb. 12, 1939. e. Harvard. Was musician and theatre dir. before turning to films. Dir. play A Man's a Man, NY 1962. Artistic dir. San Francisco Actors Workshop 1965-66, Pittsburgh Playhouse 1966-67. Obie for dir. Midsummer Night's Dream, NY 1968. Nominated for AA for short, Sticky My Fingers, Fleet My Feet.
PICTURES: Let's Scare Jessica to Death, Bang the Drum Slowly, Baby Blue Marine, California Dreaming, Weeds (also co-s.p.), Prancer, Steal the Sky.
TELEVISION: The Twilight Zone (1986), Hill Street Blues.

HAND, BETHLYN J.
Executive. b. Alton, IL. e. U. of Texas. Entered motion picture industry in 1966 as administrative assistant to president of Motion Picture Association of America, Inc. In 1975 became associate dir. of advertising administration of MPAA. In 1976 became dir. of advertising administration; in 1979 became; v.p.-west coast activities, board of directors, Los Angeles. S.P.C.A. 1981, appointed by Governor to Calif. Motion Picture Council 1983, elected vice chmn., California Motion Picture Council. 1990, named sr. v.p. MPAA.

HANDEL, LEO A.
Producer, Director. b. Vienna, Austria, Mar. 7, 1924. e. Univ. of Vienna (Ph.D. economics). Dir. audience research, MGM, 1942-51; organized Meteor Prod., 1951; organized Leo A. Handel Prod., for TV films, 1953; author, Hollywood Looks at Its Audience, also TV plays; pres., Handel Film Corp. Exec. prod. & v.p., Four Crown Prods., Inc. Prod.-writer-dir., feature film, The Case of Patty Smith, 1961; book, A Dog Named Duke, 1965.
TELEVISION: prod. TV series including Everyday Adventures, Magic of the Atom. exec. prod., Phantom Planet, Americana Series. Also produced numerous educational specials and videos.

HANEKE, MICHAEL
Director, Writer. b. Munich, Germany, 1942.
PICTURES: The Seventh Continent, Benny's Video, 71 Fragments of a Chronology of Chance, The Age of the Wolves, Lumiere and Company (dir. only), The Moor's Head (s.p. only), The Castle, Funny Games.
TELEVISION: *Movies:* After Liverpool, Sperrmull (dir. only), Drei Wege zum See, Variation, Wer war Edgar Allan?, Fraulein, Nachruf fur einen Morder, Die Rebellion.

HANKS, TOM
Actor. b. Concord, CA, July 9, 1956. m. actress Rita Wilson. Traveled around Northern CA. with family before settling in Oakland, CA. e. Chabot Jr. Col., California State U. Began career with Great Lakes Shakespeare Festival, Cleveland (3 seasons) and NY's Riverside Theater (Taming of the Shrew).
PICTURES: He Knows You're Alone (debut, 1980), Splash, Bachelor Party, The Man With One Red Shoe, Volunteers, The Money Pit, Nothing in Common, Every Time We Say Goodbye, Dragnet, Big (Acad. Award nom.), Punchline, The 'Burbs, Turner and Hooch, Joe Versus the Volcano, The Bonfire of the Vanities, Radio Flyer, A League of Their Own, Sleepless in Seattle, Philadelphia (Academy Award, 1993; Golden Globe Award), Forrest Gump (Academy Award, 1994; Golden Globe Award),The Celluloid Closet, Apollo 13, Toy Story (voice), That Thing You Do! (also dir.), Saving Private Ryan (Acad. Award nom.), You've Got Mail, Toy Story 2 (voice), The Green Mile, Cast Away, Road to Perdition.
TELEVISION: *Series*: Bosom Buddies. *Guest*: The Love Boat, Taxi, Happy Days, Family Ties, Tales From the Crypt (None but the Lonely Heart; also dir.), Fallen Angels (I'll Be Waiting; also dir.), The Naked Truth. *Movie*: Rona Jaffe's Mazes and Monsters, From the Earth to the Moon (also dir., co-s.p., co-exec. prod.). *Episode Dir.*: A League of Their Own.

HANN-BYRD, ADAM
Actor.
PICTURES: Little Man Tate, Digger, Jumanji, Diabolique, The Ice Storm, Souvenir (voice), Halloween: H20, The Uninvited.
TELEVISION: *Guest*: NYPD Blue.

HANNA, WILLIAM
Executive. b. Melrose, NM, July 14, 1910 e. Compton Coll. Studied engineering and journalism. Joined firm in CA as structural engineer; turned to cartooning with Leon Schlessinger's company in Hollywood. In 1937 hired by MGM as dir. and story man in cartoon dept. There met Joseph R. Barbera and created famous cartoon series Tom & Jerry, continuing to produce it from 1938 to 1957. Left MGM in 1957 to form Hanna-Barbera Productions to make cartoons for TV. Series have included Yogi Bear, Huckleberry Hound, The Flintstones, The Jetsons. Hanna-Barbera became a subsidiary of Taft Broadcasting Co. in 1968 with both men operating studio under long-term agreements with Taft (which became Great American Broadcasting, 1987). Received Governor's Award from Academy of Television Arts & Sciences, 1988.
PICTURES: Hey There It's Yogi Bear, A Man Called Flintstone, Charlotte's Web, C.H.O.M.P.S., Heidi's Song, Once Upon a Forest, The Flintstones (co-exec. prod. of live-action film; also cameo appearance).
TELEVISION: *Series*: The Huckleberry Hound Show (Emmy Award), Quick Draw McGraw, The Flintstones, The Jetsons, Jonny Quest, Top Cat, Scooby-Doo, Smurfs (2 Emmy Awards). *Movies*: I Yabba Dabba Do!, Hollyrock-a-Bye Baby.

HANNAH, DARYL
Actress. b. Chicago, IL, Dec. 3, 1960. Niece of cinematographer Haskell Wexler. e. UCLA. Studied ballet with Maria Tallchief. Studied acting with Stella Adler.
PICTURES: The Fury (debut, 1978), The Final Terror, Hard Country, Blade Runner, Summer Lovers, Reckless, Splash, The Pope of Greenwich Village, Clan of the Cave Bear, Legal Eagles, Roxanne, Wall Street, High Spirits, Crimes and Misdemeanors, Steel Magnolias, Crazy People, At Play in the Fields of the Lord, Memoirs of an Invisible Man, Grumpy Old Men, The Little Rascals, The Tie That Binds, Two Much, Grumpier Old Men, The Real Blonde, The Gingerbread Man, Hi-Life, Wild Flowers, Speedway Junky, Enemy of My Enemy, Diplomatic Siege, My Favorite Martian.
TELEVISION: *Movies*: Paper Dolls, Attack of the 50 Ft. Woman (also co-prod.), The Last Don, Rear Window. *Series:* Robert Altman's Gun.

HANNAH, JOHN
Actor. b. Kilbride, Scotland, UK, 1962. Was an apprentice electrician before entering mp industry.
PICTURES: Harbour Beat, Four Weddings and a Funeral, Madagascar Skin, The Innocent Sleep, The Final Cut, The James Gang, Sliding Doors, The Mummy.
TELEVISION: *Movies*: Paul Calf's Video Diary, Pauline Calf's Wedding Video, Truth or Dare, Romance and Rejection, Circles of Deceit: Kalon, The Love Bug. *Series*: Out of the Blue, McCallum. *Guest*: Taggart.

HANNEMANN, WALTER A.
Film editor. b. Atlanta, GA, May 2, 1914. e. USC, 1935. Editorial training, RKO 1936-40; edit. supvr., Universal, 1941-42; consultant 1970-75 national educational media. Bd. of govs., TV Academy (2 terms, 1960 & 1970); bd. of govs., AMPAS. 1983-86; board of dir., Motion Picture Film Editors, 1944-48, 1981-88, past v.p., American Cinema Editors.
PICTURES: Interval, The Revengers, Dream of Kings, Guns of the Magnificent Seven, Krakatoa: East of Java, The Bob Mathias Story, Pay or Die, Al Capone, (Amer. Cinema Editor's nom., 1959), Hell's Five Hours, Armoured Command, Only the Valiant, Time of Your Life, Kiss Tomorrow Goodbye, Blood on the Sun, Guest in the House, Texas Masquerade, Cannon for Cardoba, El Condor, Maurie, Lost in the Stars, Big Mo, Two Minute Warning (Acad. Award nom.) Smokey and the Bandit (Acad. Award nom.), The Other Side of the Mountain-Part II, The Visitor, The Villain, The Nude Bomb, Charlie Chan and the Curse of the Dragon Queen.
TELEVISION: *Series:* Death Valley Days, Reader's Digest, Rosemary Clooney Show, 77 Sunset Strip, June Allison Show, Stagecoach West, The Rifleman, Ben Casey, The New Breed, The Fugitive, Twelve O'Clock High, The Invaders, Storefront Lawyers, Hawaii Five-O, Streets of San Francisco, Cannon, Barnaby Jones, The F.B.I. on T.V., Caribe. *Movies*: The Abduction of Saine Anne, Intimate Strangers, The Day the Loving Stopped, The Man Who Broke a 1000 Chains, Sooner

HANNIGAN, ALYSON
Actress. r.n. Allison Lee Hannigan. b. Washington, DC, March 24, 1974.
PICTURES: My Stepmother Is an Alien, Dead Man on Campus, American Pie, Boys and Girls, Beyond City Limits.
TELEVISION: *Movies:* Switched at Birth, The Stranger Beside Me, Indecent Seduction. *Series:* Free Spirit, Buffy the Vampire Slayer. *Guest:* Roseanne, Almost Home, Touched by an Angel, Picket Fences.

HANSON, CURTIS
Director, Writer. b. Reno, NV, March 24, 1945. Editor of Cinema magazine before becoming screenwriter.

PICTURES: *Writer.* The Silent Partner, White Dog, Never Cry Wolf. *Director.* Sweet Kill, Little Dragons, Losin' It, The Bedroom Window (also s.p.), Bad Influence, The Hand That Rocks the Cradle, The River Wild, L.A. Confidential (also co-s.p., prod., Acad. Award, Best Adapted Screenplay, Chicago Film Crits. Award, LA Film Crits. Award, NY Film Crits. Award, Best Director, Best Screenplay, 1997), Wonder Boys (also prod.). *Actor:* The Goonies.
TELEVISION: *Movie*: Killing at Hell's Gate, The Children of Times Square.

HARBACH, WILLIAM O.
Producer. b. Yonkers, NY, Oct. 12, 1919, e. Brown U. Father was lyricst Otto Harbach. Served with U.S. Coast Guard, 1940-45; actor, MGM, 1945-47; broadcast co-ordinator. NBC, 1947-49; stage mgr., 1949-50; dir., NBC, 1950-53
TELEVISION: *Producer.* Tonight, Steve Allen Show, Bing Crosby shows (also dir.), Milton Berle Special, Hollywood Palace, The Julie Andrews Show (Emmy Award, 1973), Shirley MacLaine's Gypsy in My Soul (Emmy Award, 1976), Bob Hope Specials.

HARBERT, TED
Executive. e. Boston Univ. 1976-77, prod. of new dept. at WHDH radio in Boston. Joined ABC, 1977 as feature film coordinator; 1979, named supervisor, feature film and late-night program planning, then assst. to v.p., program planning & scheduling; 1981, became dir. program planning & scheduling; 1984, promoted to v.p. program planning & scheduling; 1987, named v.p. motion pictures and scheduling, ABC Entertainment; 1988, v.p., prime time, ABC Entertainment; 1989, became exec. v.p., Prime Time, ABC Entertainment; 1993, promoted to pres. of ABC Entertainment.

HARDEN, MARCIA GAY
Actress. b. La Jolla, CA, Aug. 14, 1959.
Father was naval captain. Schooled in Athens, Munich, then returned to states attending Univ. of TX, NYU. Stage work in Washington D.C. in Crimes of the Heart, The Miss Firecracker Contest.
THEATER: *Off-B'way:* The Man Who Shot Lincoln (debut, 1989), Those the River Keeps, The Skin of Our Teeth, The Years, Simpatico. *B'way:* Angels in America: Millenium Approaches/ Perestroika (Theatre World Award; Tony nom.)
PICTURES: Miller's Crossing (debut, 1990), Late for Dinner, Used People, Crush, Safe Passage, The Spitfire Grill, The Daytrippers, The First Wives Club, Spy Hard, Desperate Measures, Flubber, Meet Joe Black, Labor of Love, Curtain Call, Pollock.
TELEVISION: *Mini-Series:* Sinatra. *Movie:* Fever, Path to Paradise, Spenser: Small Vices.

HARDISON, KADEEM
Actor. b. Brooklyn, NY, July 24, 1966. Studied acting with Earl Hyman and at H.B.Studios.
PICTURES: Beat Street (debut, 1984), Rappin', School Daze, I'm Gonna Git You Sucka, Def by Temptation, White Men Can't Jump, Gunmen, Renaissance Man, Panther, Vampire in Brooklyn, Drive, The Sixth Man, Blind Faith.
TELEVISION: *Series:* A Different World, Between Brothers. *Specials:* The Color of Friendship, Amazing Grace, Don't Touch, Go Tell It on the Mountain. *Movie:* Dream Date. *Guest:* The Cosby Show, Spenser for Hire.

HARE, DAVID
Writer, Director. b. St. Leonards, Sussex, England, June 5, 1947. e. Lancing Coll., Jesus Coll., Cambridge. After leaving univ. in 1968 formed Portable Theatre Company, experimental touring group. Hired by Royal Court Theater as literary manager, 1969. 1970, first full-length play, Slag, prod. at Hampstead Theatre Club. Resident dramatist, Royal Court (1970-71), and Nottingham Playhouse (1973). Assoc. dir., National Theatre. West End debut, Knuckle.
THEATER: Slag, The Great Exhibition, Brassneck, Knuckle, Fanshen, Teeth 'n' Smiles, Plenty, A Map of the World, Pravda, The Bay at Nice, Secret Rapture, Racing Demon, Murmuring Judges, Rules of the Game (new version of Pirandello Play), Brecht's The Absence of War, Skylight, Galileo, Mother Courage.
PICTURES: *Writer.* Plenty, Wetherby (also dir.), Paris by Night (also dir.), Strapless (also dir.), Damage.
TELEVISION: *Writer.* Licking Hitler (also dir.), Dreams of Leaving (also dir.), Saigon: Year of the Cat, Knuckle, Heading Home (also dir.).

HAREWOOD, DORIAN
Actor. b. Dayton, OH, Aug. 6, 1950. m. actress Ann McCurry. e. U. of Cincinnati.
THEATER: Jesus Christ Superstar (road co.), Two Gentlemen of Verona, Miss Moffat, Streamers, Over Here, Don't Call Back (Theatre World Award), The Mighty Gents, Kiss of the Spider Woman.
PICTURES: Sparkle (debut, 1976), Gray Lady Down, Looker, Tank, Against All Odds, The Falcon and the Snowman, Full Metal Jacket, Pacific Heights, Solar Crisis, The Pagemaster (voice), Sudden Death, Space Jam (voice), Archibald the Rainbow Painter.

TELEVISION: *Series*: Strike Force, Trauma Center, Glitter, The Trials of Rosie O'Neill, Viper, The Tick (voice), Mortal Kombat: The Animated Series (voice), The Hoop Life. *Mini-Series*: Roots: The Next Generations, Amerika. *Movies*: Foster and Laurie, Panic in Echo Park, Siege, An American Christmas Carol, High Ice, Beulah Land, The Ambush Murders, I Desire, The Jesse Owens Story, Guilty of Innocence, God Bless the Child, Kiss Shot, Polly, Polly-Comin' Home!, Getting Up and Going Home, Bermuda Grace, Shattered Image, When the Cradle Falls, 12 Angry Men, A Change of Heart. *Pilot*: Half 'n' Half.

HARGREAVES, JOHN
Executive. b. Freckleton, Lancashire, England,, July 1921. Joined Gainsborough Pictures 1945. Transferred to Denham Studios 1946 and later Pinewood Studios. Joined Allied Film Makers 1960, then Salamander Film Productions as Bryan Forbes' financial controller and asst. prod. 1965. Joined EMI Film Prods. Ltd. as asst. man. dir. and prod. controller 1969-72. 1983-, U.K. dir. and production executive for Completion Bond Company, Inc. Cal. USA.
PICTURES: Don Quixote (prod.), The Slipper and the Rose (prod. asst.), International Velvet (assoc. prod.), The Awakening (prod. rep.), The Fiendish Plot of Dr. Fu Manchu (post-prod. exec.), Excalibur (prod. rep.), The Year of Living Dangerously, Carrington (financial consultant).

HARK, TSUI
Director, Producer. b. Vietnam, Jan. 2, 1951. e. University of Texas. Started filming 8mm movies at 13. Moved to Hong Kong in 1966, then in 1975 relocated to NY where he became editor for a local Chinese newspaper. Returned to Hong Kong in 1977 and made his directorial debut with The Butterfly Murders. In the 1990's played a major part in reviving "swordsfighting" and "kung-fu" movies.
PICTURES: *Director.* Dangerous Encounter, Hell Has No Door, All the Wrong Clues, Zu: Warriors From the Magic Mountain, Aces go Places III, Shanghai Blues, Working Class, Peking Opera Blues, A Better Tomorrow III, Once Upon A Time in China (also II, III, V), The Master, Green Snake, The Lovers, A Chinese Feast, Love In a Time of Twilight, Tri-Star, Blade, Double Team. *Co-director.* Swordsman, The Banquet, Chess King, Twin Dragons. *Producer.* A Chinese Ghost Story (also II, III) A Better Tomorrow, I Love Maria, Deception, Gunmen, Diary of a Big Man, The Big Heat, The Killer, Spy Games, The Raid, The Wicked City, Swordsman II, Dragon Inn, The East is Red, Once Upon a Time in China (also IV), The Magic Crane, Burning Paradise, Shanghai Grand, Black Mask, Once Upon a Time in China & America, Chinese Ghost Story: The Tsui Hark Animation.

HARKINS, DANIEL E.
Executive, Exhibitor. b. Mesa, AZ, Feb. 6, 1953. e. Arizona State U. Joined Harkins Theatres in 1968. Acquired company in 1975. President and CEO Harkins Amusement Enterprises, Inc. National NATO bd. member. Pres., Arizona Theatre Assoc. V.P., Governor's Film Commission. Recipient of United Motion Picture Assoc. National Showman of the Year award 1976, 1980, 1981. Hollywood Reported Marketing Concept award, 1983. Box Office Showmandizer award, 1976, 1978. Phoenix Artistic Achievement award, 1989. American Institute of Architects award. 1996. Arizona Best awards, 1991-1995.

HARLIN, RENNY
Director. r.n. Lauri Mauritz Harjola. b. Helsinki, Finland, March 15, 1959. e. Univ. of Helsinki film school. Formed prod. co. The Forge with actress Geena Davis.
PICTURES: Born American (debut, 1986), Arctic Heat (also s.p.), Prison, A Nightmare on Elm Street IV: The Dream Master, Die Hard 2, The Adventures of Ford Fairlane, Rambling Rose (prod. only), Cliffhanger, Speechless (co-prod. only), Cutthroat Island (also prod.), Exit Zero, The Long Kiss Goodnight (also prod.), Blast From the Past (prod. only), Deep Blue Sea, Driven.
TELEVISION: *Movie*: Mistrial, T.R.A.X.

HARMON, MARK
Actor. b. Burbank, CA, Sept. 2, 1951. Son of actress Elyse Knox and football star Tom Harmon. m. actress Pam Dawber. Brother of actresses Kelly and Kristin Harmon. On stage in Wrestlers, The Wager (both L.A.), Key Exchange (Toronto).
PICTURES: Comes a Horseman, Beyond the Poseidon Adventure, Let's Get Harry, Summer School, The Presidio, Stealing Home, Worth Winning, Till There Was You, Cold Heaven, Wyatt Earp, Natural Born Killers (cameo), Magic in the Water, The Last Supper, Casualties, Fear and Loathing in Las Vegas (cameo), I'll Remember April.
TELEVISION: *Series*: Sam, 240-Robert, Flamingo Road, St. Elsewhere, Reasonable Doubts, Charlie Grace, Chicago Hope. *Movies*: Eleanor and Franklin: The White House Years, Getting Married, Little Mo, Flamingo Road (pilot), The Dream Merchants, Goliath Awaits, Intimate Agony, The Deliberate Stranger, Prince of Bel Air, Sweet Bird of Youth, Dillinger, Fourth Story, Long Road Home, Shadow of a Doubt. *Guest*: Adam-12, Laverne & Shirley, Nancy Drew, Police Story, Moonlighting. *Mini-Series*: Centennial, From the Earth to the Moon.

HARNELL, STEWART D.
Executive. b. New York, NY, Aug. 18, 1938. e. U. of Miami, UCLA, New School for Social Research. Entertainer with Youth Parade in Coral Gables, FL, 1948-55, performing for handicapped children, Variety Club, etc. as singer, dancer, musician. Had own bands, Teen Aces & Rhythm Rascals, 1950-56; performed on Cactus Jim TV show and Wood & Ivory, 1953-54, WTVJ, Miami. Catskills, Sand Lake, NY, 1954-55. Joined National Screen Service as exec. trainee in 1960 in Chicago; worked as booker & salesman. Transferred to NY home office, 1963; worked in special trailer production. Promoted to asst. gen. sls. mgr., 1964-66; New Orleans branch mgr., 1966-67; Atlanta division mgr., 1967-70. Formed own distribution co., 1970-77 Harnell Independent Productions. Resumed post as gen. sls. mgr. of NSS, New York, 1977-78; In 1986, founded Cinema Concepts. In 1995, founded Silver Screen Signs & Display, Inc. Chief barker of Variety Club of Atlanta, Tent 21, 1972, 1976, 1979, 1988, 1989, 1993, 1994. In 1986 formed Cinema Concepts Communications, film-video animation studio in Atlanta. Motion Picture Pioneers Bd. of Directors (1990-97).

HARPER, JESSICA
Actress. b. Chicago, IL, Oct. 10, 1949. m. prod. exec. Thomas E. Rothman. e. Sarah Lawrence Coll. Understudied on Broadway for Hair for one year. Appeared in summer stock and off-B'way shows (Richard Farina: Long Time Coming Longtime Gone, Doctor Selavy's Magic Theatre.)
PICTURES: Taking Off, Phantom of the Paradise, Love and Death, Inserts, Suspiria, The Evictors, Stardust Memories, Shock Treatment, Pennies from Heaven, My Favorite Year, The Imagemaker, Dario Argento's World of Horror, The Blue Iguana, Big Man on Campus, Mr. Wonderful, Safe, Boys.
TELEVISION: *Series*: Little Women, It's Garry Shandling's Show. *Mini-Series*: Studs Lonigan, Aspen (The Innocent and the Damned), When Dreams Come True. *Special*: The Garden Party. *Guest*: Tales from the Darkside, The Equalizer, Trying Times (Bedtime Story), Wiseguy, Chicago Hope, Moonlighting.

HARPER, TESS
Actress. b. Mammoth Springs, AR, 1952. e. Southwest Missouri State Coll., Springfield. Worked in Houston, then Dallas in children's theater, dinner theater, and commercials.
PICTURES: Tender Mercies (debut, 1983), Amityville 3-D, Silkwood, Flashpoint, Crimes of the Heart (Acad. Award nom.), Ishtar, Far North, Her Alibi, Criminal Law, Daddy's Dyin'... Who's Got the Will?, My Heroes Have Always Been Cowboys, The Man in the Moon, My New Gun, Dirty Laundry.
TELEVISION: *Mini-Series*: Chiefs, Celebrity. *Movies*: Kentucky Woman, Starflight: The Plane That Couldn't Land, A Summer to Remember, Promises to Keep, Little Girl Lost, Unconquered, In the Line of Duty: Siege at Marion, Willing to Kill: The Texas Cheerleader Story, Death in Small Doses.

HARPER, VALERIE
Actress. b. Suffern, NY. Aug. 22, 1940. e. Hunter Coll, New Sch. for Social Research. Started as dancer in stage shows at Radio City Music Hall. First professional acting in summer stock in Conn.; actress with Second City Chicago 1964-69; Appeared on B'way. in Lil' Abner, Take Me Along, Wildcat, Subways Are for Sleeping, Something Different, Story Theatre, Metamorphoses. Won 3 Emmys for best performance in supporting role in comedy for portrayal of Rhoda on The Mary Tyler Moore Show and 1 for best leading actress on Rhoda. Off B'way, Death Defying Acts (1995-96).
PICTURES: Rock Rock Rock, Lil Abner, Freebie and the Bean, Chapter Two, The Last Married Couple in America, Blame It on Rio.
TELEVISION: *Series*: The Mary Tyler Show, Rhoda, Valerie, City, The Office, Melrose Place. *Movies*: Thursday's Game, Night Terror, Fun and Games, The Shadow Box, The Day the Loving Stopped, Farrell for the People (pilot), Don't Go to Sleep, An Invasion of Privacy, Execution, Strange Voices, Drop Out Mother, The People Across the Lake, Stolen: One Husband, A Friend To Die For, The Great Mom Swap, Dog's Best Friend (voice), Mary & Rhoda.

HARRINGTON, CURTIS
Director, Writer. b. Los Angeles, CA, Sept. 17, 1928. e. U. of Southern California, B.A. Exec. asst. to Jerry Wald, 1955-61 Associate prod. at 20th Cent. Fox.
PICTURES: Assoc. Prod.: Mardi Gras (also story), Hound Dog Man, Return to Peyton Place, The Stripper. Director: Night Tide (also s.p.), Queen of Blood (Planet of Blood; also s.p.), Games (also co-story), What's the Matter with Helen?, Who Slew Auntie Roo?, The Killing Kind, Ruby, Mata Hari.
TELEVISION: *Series episodes*: Hotel, Dynasty, The Colby's, Tales of the Unexpected, Twilight Zone, Baretta, Vega$, Glitter, Logan's Run. *Movies*: How Awful About Allan, The Cat Creature, Killer Bees, The Dead Don't Die, Devil Dog: The Hound of Hell.

HARRINGTON, PAT
Actor. b. New York, NY, Aug. 13, 1929. e. Fordham U. Served USAF as 1st Lt., 1952-54. Time salesman for NBC, 1954-58.
PICTURES: The Wheeler Dealers, Move Over Darling, Easy Come Easy Go, The President's Analyst, 2000 Years Later, The Candidate.
TELEVISION: *Series*: The Steve Allen Show, The Danny Thomas Show, The Jack Paar Show, Stump the Stars (host), Mr. Deeds Goes to Town, One Day at a Time (Emmy Award, 1984).

HARRIS, BARBARA
Actress. r.n. Sandra Markowitz. b. Evanston, IL, July 25, 1935. e. Wright Junior Coll., Chicago; Goodman Sch. of the Theatre; U. of Chicago. Joined acting troup, The Compass. Founding member, Second City Players, 1960. Came to NY where first role was in Oh Dad Poor Dad Mama's Hung You in the Closet and I'm Feeling So Sad (Theatre World Award), repeating role in film version.
THEATER: Mother Courage and Her Children, Dynamite Tonight, On a Clear Day You Can See Forever, The Apple Tree (Tony Award, 1967), Mahogany.
PICTURES: A Thousand Clowns (debut, 1965), Oh Dad Poor Dad Mama's Hung You in the Closet and I'm Feeling So Sad, Plaza Suite, Who Is Harry Kellerman and Why Is He Saying Those Terrible Things About Me? (Acad. Award nom.), The War Between Men and Women, The Manchu Eagle Murder Caper Mystery, Mixed Company, Nashville, Family Plot, Freaky Friday, Movie Movie, The North Avenue Irregulars, The Seduction of Joe Tynan, Second Hand Hearts, Peggy Sue Got Married, Nice Girls Don't Explode, Dirty Rotten Scoundrels.
TELEVISION: *Guest*: Alfred Hitchcock Presents, Naked City, The Defenders.

HARRIS, BURTT
Producer, Actor. Began career as actor; later worked with Elia Kazan as prod. asst. and asst. dir. on America America, Splendor in the Grass, and The Arrangement. Worked as second unit dir. and asst. dir. on many films as well as prod. and actor.
PICTURES: *Exec. prod./line prod./assoc. prod.*: The Wiz, Just Tell Me What You Want, Cruising, Prince of the City, The Verdict (also actor), Deathtrap, Garbo Talks, D.A.R.Y.L. (co-prod., actor), The Glass Menagerie, See No Evil Hear No Evil, Q & A (also actor), A Stranger Among Us (also actor), Drunks (also actor), The Last Good Time. *Assoc. prod.*: Little Murders, Gilda Live, Family Business. *Actor*: Splendor in the Grass, Fail Safe, The Taking of Pelham 1-2-3, The Wanderers, Undertow, Hudson Hawk, The Last Good Time. *Asst. dir.*: Illtown, Grace of My Heart, Affliction, The Devil's Advocate.
TELEVISION: *Movies*: Zoya.

HARRIS, ED
Actor. b. Tenafly, NJ, Nov. 28, 1950. m. actress Amy Madigan. Played football 2 years at Columbia U. prior to enrolling in acting classes at OK State U. Summer stock. Grad. CA Institute of the Arts, B.F.A, 1975. Worked in West Coast Theater.
THEATER: *NY*: Fool For Love (Off-B'way debut; Obie Award), Precious Sons (B'way debut; Theatre World Award), Simpatico, Taking Sides. *LA*: Scar.
PICTURES: Coma (debut, 1978), Borderline, Knightriders, Dream On, Creepshow, The Right Stuff, Under Fire, Swing Shift, Places in the Heart, Alamo Bay, A Flash of Green, Sweet Dreams, Code Name: Emerald, Walker, To Kill a Priest, Jacknife, The Abyss, State of Grace, Glengarry Glen Ross, The Firm, Needful Things, China Moon, Milk Money, Just Cause, Apollo 13, Eye for an Eye, Nixon, The Rock, Absolute Power, The Truman Show (Acad. Award nom.), Stepmom, The Third Miracle, Waking the Dead, The Prime Gig, Pollock, Enemy at the Gates, Absolute Zero.
TELEVISION: *Movies*: The Amazing Howard Hughes, The Seekers, The Aliens Are Coming (Alien Force), The Last Innocent Man, Paris Trout, Running Mates, Riders of the Purple Sage. *Mini-Series*: The Stand, Baseball (voice).

HARRIS, JAMES B.
Producer, Director, Writer. b. New York, NY, Aug. 3, 1928. e. Juilliard Sch. U.S. film export, 1947; Realart Pictures, 1948; formed Flamingo Films, 1949; formed Harris-Kubrick Productions, 1954. formed James B. Harris Prods., Inc., 1963.
PICTURES: *Producer*: The Killing, Paths of Glory, Lolita, The Bedford Incident (also dir.), Some Call It Loving (also dir., s.p.), Telefon, Fast-Walking (also dir., s.p.), Cop (also dir., s.p.), Boiling Point (dir., s.p.).

HARRIS, JULIE
Designer. b. London, England. e. Chelsea Arts Sch. Entered industry in 1945 designing for Gainsborough Studios. First film, Holiday Camp.
PICTURES: Greengage Summer, Naked Edge, The War Lover, Fast Lady, Chalk Garden, Psyche 59, A Hard Day's Night, Darling, Help!, The Wrong Box, Casino Royale, Deadfall, Prudence and the Pill, Decline and Fall, Goodbye Mr. Chips, Sherlock Holmes, Follow Me!, Live and Let Die, Rollerball, Slipper and The Rose, Dracula.
TELEVISION: Laura (with Lee Radziwill), Candleshoe, The Sailor's Return, Lost and Found, The Kingfisher, Arch of Triumph, Sign of Four, Hound of the Baskervilles, A Hazard of Hearts, A Perfect Hero.

HARRIS, JULIE
Actress. b. Grosse Pointe, MI, Dec. 2, 1925. e. Yale Drama Sch.
THEATER: Sundown Beach, Playboy of the Western World, Macbeth, Young and the Fair, Magnolia Alley, Monserrat, Member of the Wedding, I Am a Camera (Tony Award, 1952), Colombe, The Lark (Tony Award, 1956), A Shot in the Dark, Marathon 33, Ready When You Are, C.B., Break a Leg, Skyscraper, Voices,

And Miss Reardon Drinks a Little, 40 Carats (Tony Award, 1969), The Last of Mrs. Lincoln (Tony Award, 1973), In Praise of Love, The Belle of Amherst (Tony Award, 1973), Driving Miss Daisy (Natl. co.), Lucifer's Child, Lettice & Lovage (tour), The Fiery Furnace (Off-B'way debut, 1993), The Glass Menagerie.
PICTURES: The Member of the Wedding (debut, 1952; Acad. Award nom.), East of Eden, I Am a Camera, The Truth About Women, The Poacher's Daughter, Requiem for a Heavyweight, The Haunting, Harper, You're a Big Boy Now, Reflections in a Golden Eye, The Split, The People Next Door, The Hiding Place, Voyage of the Damned, The Bell Jar, Nutcracker: The Motion Picture (voice), Gorillas in the Mist, Housesitter, The Dark Half, Carried Away.
TELEVISION: *Specials*: Little Moon of Alban (Emmy Award, 1959), Johnny Belinda, A Doll's House, Ethan Frome, The Good Fairy, The Lark, He Who Gets Slapped, The Heiress, Victoria Regina (Emmy Award, 1962), Pygmalion, Anastasia, The Holy Terror, The Power and The Glory, The Woman He Loved. *Movies*: The House on Greenapple Road, How Awful About Alan, Home for the Holidays, The Greatest Gift, The Gift, Too Good To Be True, The Christmas Wife, They've Taken Our Children: The Chowchilla Kidnapping, When Love Kills: The Seduction of John Hearn, One Christmas. *Series*: Thicker Than Water, The Family Holvak, Knots Landing. *Mini-Series*: Backstairs at the White House, Scarlett.

HARRIS, MEL
Executive. b. Arkansas City, Kansas, 1942. e. Ph.D., mass comm., Ohio U. Broadcaster, Kaiser and Metromedia; pres., TV Group, Paramount Pictures, 1978-92, where he co-founded Paramount Home Video and CIC Home Video, engineered the formation of USA Cable Network and the introduction of satellite distribution for first-run programming, launching Entertainment Tonight; president, Sony Pictures Entertainment (SPE) Television Group, 1992-95, Currently co-president and CEO, SPE, 1999.

HARRIS, MEL
Actress. r.n. Mary Ellen Harris. b. Bethlehem, PA, July 12, 1957. e. Columbia. Career as model before turning to acting in 1984. NY theatre debut in Empty Hearts, 1992 (Theatre World Award).
PICTURES: Wanted: Dead or Alive, Cameron's Closet, K-9, Raising Cain, Desperate Motive (Distant Cousins), Suture, The Pagemaster, Sonic Impact.
TELEVISION: *Series*: thirtysomething, Something So Right. *Guest*: M*A*S*H, Alfred Hitchcock Presents, Rags to Riches, Heart of the City, The Wizard. *Movies*: Seduced, Harry's Hong Kong, Cross of Fire, My Brother's Wife, The Burden of Proof, Grass Roots, Child of Rage, With Hostile Intent, Desperate Journey: The Allison Wilcox Story, Ultimate Betrayal, The Spider and the Fly, The Women of Spring Break, Sharon's Secret, The Secretary, A Case for Life, Murder She Wrote: South by Southwest.

HARRIS, NEIL PATRICK
Actor. b. Albuquerque, NM, June 15, 1973. While attending week-long theatre camp at New Mexico St. Univ. met writer Mark Medoff who suggested him for co-starring role in Clara's Heart.
THEATER: Luck Pluck and Virtue (Off-B'way debut, 1995).
PICTURES: Clara's Heart (debut, 1988), Purple People Eater, Hairspray, Starship Troopers, The Proposition.
TELEVISION: *Series*: Doogie Howser M.D., Capitol Critters (voice), Stark Raving Mad. *Movies*: Too Good to Be True, Home Fires Burning, Cold Sassy Tree, Stranger in the Family, A Family Torn Apart, Snowbound: The Jim and Jennifer Stolpa Story, Not Our Son, My Antonia, The Man in the Attic, Legacy of Sin: The William Coit Story, The Christmas Wish, Joan of Arc. *Guest*: B. J. Stryker, Carol & Company, Roseanne, Quantum Leap, Murder She Wrote, The Simpsons (voice).

HARRIS, RICHARD
Actor. b. Limerick, Ireland, Oct. 1, 1930. Attended London Acad. of Music and Dramatic Arts. Prod.-dir. Winter Journey 1956. Prof. acting debut in Joan Littlewood's prod. of The Quare Fellow, Royal Stratford, 1956. Recorded hit song MacArthur's Park, 1968. Author of novel Honor Bound (1982) and poetry compilation: I in the Membership of My Days (1973).
THEATER: *London*: A View from the Bridge, Man Beast and Virtue, The Ginger Man. *B'way*: Camelot.
PICTURES: Alive and Kicking (debut, 1958), Shake Hands With the Devil, The Wreck of the Mary Deare, A Terrible Beauty (Night Fighters), The Long The Short and The Tall (Jungle Fighters), The Guns of Navarone, Mutiny on the Bounty, This Sporting Life (Acad. Award nom.), Red Desert, Major Dundee, The Heroes of Telemark, The Bible, Hawaii, Caprice, Camelot, The Molly Maguires, A Man Called Horse, Cromwell, The Hero (Bloomfield; also dir., s.p.), Man in the Wilderness, The Deadly Trackers, 99 and 44/100% Dead, Juggernaut, Echoes of a Summer (also co-exec. prod.), Robin and Marian, Return of a Man Called Horse (also co-exec. prod.), The Cassandra Crossing, Gulliver's Travels, Orca, Golden Rendezvous, The Wild Geese, Ravagers, The Last Word, Game for Vultures, Your Ticket Is No Longer Valid, Highpoint, Tarzan the Ape Man, Martin's Day, Triumphs of a Man Called Horse, Mack the Knife, The Field (Acad. Award nom.), Patriot Games, Unforgiven, Wrestling Ernest Hemingway, Silent Tongue, Savage Hearts, Cry the Beloved Country, Trojan Eddie, Smilla's Sense of Snow, The Barber of Siberia, This is the Sea, To Walk with Lions.
TELEVISION: *Specials*: Ricardo, The Iron Harp, The Snow Goose, Camelot. *Movies*: Maigret, The Return, The Hunchback.

HARRIS, RICHARD A.
Editor.
PICTURES: The Bamboo Saucer, Downhill Racer, The Christian Licorice Store, Chandler, The Candidate, Catch My Soul, Smile, The Bad News Bears, Semi-Tough, The Bad News Bears Go to Japan, An Almost Perfect Affair, The Island, The Toy, The Survivors, Fletch, The Golden Child, Wildcats, The Couch Trip, Fletch Lives, L.A. Story, Terminator 2: Judgment Day, The Bodyguard, Last Action Hero, True Lies, Titanic (Acad. Award, 1997).
TELEVISION: *Movies*: Dracula, The Kansas City Massacre, Murder at the World Series, The Executioner's Song, Tiger Town, 14 Going on 30, My Boyfriend's Back, A Mother's Courage: The Mary Thomas Story, Indictment: The McMartin Trial.

HARRIS, ROBERT A.
Archivist, Producer. b. New York, NY, Dec. 27, 1945. e. NYU, Sch. of Commerce and Sch. of Arts, 1968. Worked as exec. trainee with 7 Arts assoc., NY while in school, 1960-68; worked in corp. communications, Pepsico, 1970-71; formed Center for Instructional Resources, SUNY Purchase, 1971-73; organized Images Film Archive, dist. of classic theatrical and non theat. films, 1974; pres., Images Video and Film Archive, 1985; formed Davnor Prods., pres., 1986; formed The Film Preserve, Ltd. pres. 1989-. 1975-80: restored Abel Gance films Beethoven, J'Accuse, Lucretia Borgia; 1974-79: worked with Kevin Brownlow to complete restoration of Abel Gance's Napoleon. Partnered with Francis Coppola/Zoetrope Studios to present Napoleon at Radio City Music Hall, 1981 and worldwide tour; 1986-89; reconstruction and restoration of David Lean's Lawrence of Arabia for Columbia Pictures, released 1989; The Grifters (prod.); restoration and reconstruction of Stanley Kubrick's Spartacus for Univ. Pictures, 1991; restoration of George Cukor's My Fair Lady for CBS Video, 1994, restoration in SuperVistaVision 70 of Alfred Hitchcock's Vertigo, 1996.

HARRIS, ROSEMARY
Actress. b. Ashby, Suffolk, Sept. 19, 1930. e. India and England. Early career, nursing; studied Royal Acad. of Dramatic Art, 1951-52.
THEATER: Climate of Eden (NY debut 1952), Seven Year Itch, Confidential Clerk (Paris Festival), and with Bristol Old Vic in The Crucible, Much Ado About Nothing, Merchant of Venice. With Old Vic, 1955-56; U.S. tour, 1956-57; U.S. stage, 1958-63. Chichester Festivals 1962 and 63; Nat'l Theatre 1963-64; You Can't Take It With You, 1965; The Lion in Winter (Tony Award, 1966), 1967, APA Repertory Co., Heartbreak House, The Royal Family, The New York Idea (Obie Award), Pack of Lies, Hay Fever, Lost in Yonkers, An Inspector Calls, A Delicate Balance.
PICTURES: Beau Brummell, The Shiralee, A Flea in Her Ear, The Boys from Brazil, The Ploughman's Lunch, Heartbreak House, Crossing Delancey, The Delinquents, The Bridge, Tom and Viv (Acad. Award nom.), Looking for Richard, Hamlet, World of Moses.
TELEVISION: *Series*: The Chisholms. *Specials*: Cradle of Willow (debut, 1951), Othello, The Prince and the Pauper, Twelfth Night, Wuthering Heights, Blithe Spirit, Profiles in Courage, To the Lighthouse, Strange Interlude, Tales From the Hollywood Hills: The Old Reliable. *Mini-Series*: Notorious Woman (Emmy Award, 1976), Holocaust (Golden Globe Award), The Chisholms, The Camomille Lawn. *Movie*: The Little Riders.

HARRIS, TIMOTHY
Writer, Producer. b. Los Angeles, CA, July 21, 1946. e. Charterhouse, 1963-65; Peterhouse Coll., Cambridge, 1966-69, M.A. Honors Degree, Eng. lit. Author of novels, Knonski/McSmash, Kyd For Hire, Goodnight and Goodbye; author of novelizations, Steelyard Blues, Hit, Heatwave, American Gigolo.
PICTURES: *Co-writer with Herschel Weingrod*: Cheaper to Keep Her, Trading Places (BAFTA nom., orig. s.p.; NAACP Image Awards, best m.p. 1983), Brewster's Millions, My Stepmother is an Alien, Paint It Black, Twins (People's Choice Award, best comedy, 1988), Kindergarten Cop, Pure Luck. *Co-Prod.*: Falling Down, Space Jam (s.p. only).
TELEVISION: Street of Dreams (based on his novel Goodnight and Goodbye; also exec. prod.).

HARRISON, GEORGE
Singer, Composer, Producer. b. Liverpool, England, Feb. 25, 1943. Former member, The Beatles. Winner of 2 Grammys on own in addition to Beatles' group awards. Founder of Handmade Films.
PICTURES: *Performer*: A Hard Day's Night (debut, 1964), What's Happening! The Beatles in the U.S.A., The Beatles at Shea Stadium, Help!, The Magical Mystery Tour (also prod., dir., composer), Yellow Submarine (cameo), Let It Be, The Concert for Bangladesh (also prod.), The Compleat Beatles, Ready Steady Go—Volume 1, Ready Steady Go—Volume 2, Rolling Stone: The First 20 Years, It Was 20 Years Ago Today, Imagine: John Lennon. *Exec. Prod.:* Little Malcolm. *Exec. Prod.* (for Handmade Films): Life of Brian (also cameo), Time Bandits, Monty Python Live at the Hollywood Bowl, The Missionary, Privates on Parade, Scrubbers, Bullshot, A Private Function, Water (also cameo), Mona Lisa, Shanghai Surprise (also songs, cameo), Withnail and I, Five Corners, Bellman and True, The Lonely Passion of Judith Hearne, Track 29, How to Get Ahead in Advertising, Powwow Highway, Checking Out, Cold Dog Soup, Nuns on the Run, The Raggedy Rawney, Everest (composer only).

TELEVISION: All You Need Is Cash. *Mini-series*: The Beatles Anthology. *Guest*: Morecambe & Wise, Rutland Weekend Television, The Simpsons.

HARRISON, GREGORY
Actor, Producer, Director. b. Avalon, CA, May 31, 1950. Started acting in school plays; then joined Army (1969-71). Studied at Estelle Harman Actors Workshop; later with Lee Strasberg and Stella Adler. Formed Catalina Productions with Franklin Levy, 1981.
THEATER: Child's Play, Carnal Knowledge, Picnic, The Hasty Heart, Love Letters, Festival, Billy Budd, The Subject Was Roses, The Promise, The Music Man, Paper Moon—The Musical.
PICTURES: Jim: the World's Greatest (debut, 1976), Fraternity Row, Razorback, North Shore (also 2nd unit dir.), Voice of a Stranger (also 2nd unit dir.), Cadillac Girls, It's My Party, Hard Evidence, Air Bud 2: Golden Retriever.
TELEVISION: *Series*: Logan's Run, Trapper John M.D. (also dir. 6 episodes), Falcon Crest, The Family Man, True Detectives, New York News. *Guest*: M*A*S*H, Barnaby Jones, Sisters. *Movies* (actor): The Gathering, Enola Gay, Trilogy in Terror, The Best Place To Be, The Women's Room, For Ladies Only (also co-prod.), The Fighter, Seduced (also exec. prod.), Oceans of Fire, Spot Marks the X (exec. prod. only), Hot Paint, Red River, Dangerous Pursuit, Angel of Death, Bare Essentials, Breaking the Silence, Duplicates, Split Images, Caught in the Act, The Tower (exec. prod. only), A Family Torn Apart, Lies of the Heart: The Story of Laurie Kellogg, Robin Cook's Mortal Fear, A Christmas Romance, A Dangerous Affair, When Secrets Kill. *Mini-series*: Centennial, Fresno, 500 Nations (narrator), Nothing Lasts Forever. *Movies (exec. prod. only)*: Thursday's Child, Legs, Samson & Delilah.

HARROLD, KATHRYN
Actress. b. Tazewell, VA, Aug. 2, 1950. e. Mills Coll. Studied acting at Neighborhood Playhouse in N.Y., also with Uta Hagen. Appeared in Off-Off-B'way. plays for year; then joined experimental theatre group, Section Ten, touring East, performing and teaching at Connecticut Coll. and NYU. Cast in TV daytime serial, The Doctors.
PICTURES: Nightwing (debut, 1979), The Hunter, Modern Romance, The Pursuit of D.B. Cooper, Yes Gorgio, The Sender, Heartbreakers, Into the Night, Raw Deal, Someone to Love, The Companion.
TELEVISION: *Movies*: Son-Rise: A Miracle of Love, Vampire, The Women's Room, Bogie, An Uncommon Love, Women in White, Man Against the Mob, Dead Solid Perfect, Capital News, Rainbow Drive, Deadly Desire, The Companion, Rockford Files: The Crime & Punishment, Outrage. *Series*: The Doctors (1976-78), MacGruder and Loud, Bronx Zoo, I'll Fly Away, The Larry Sanders Show, Chicago Hope

HARRYHAUSEN, RAY
Special Effects Expert, Producer, Writer. b. Los Angeles, CA, June 29, 1920. e. Los Angeles City Coll. While at coll. made 16mm animated film, Evolution, which got him job as model animator for George Pal's Puppetoons in early '40s. Served in U.S. Signal Corps; then made series of filmed fairy tales with animated puppets for schools and churches. In 1946 worked on Mighty Joe Young as ass't. to Willis O'Brien. Designed and created special visual effects for The Beast from 20,000 Fathoms; then began evolving own model animation system called Dynarama. In 1952 joined forces with prod. Charles H. Schneer, using new process for first time in It Came from Beneath the Sea. Subsequently made many films with Schneer in Dynamation. Received Gordon E. Sawyer Award for Acad. of Motion Picture Arts & Sciences, 1992. Appeared in films Spies Like Us, Beverly Hills Cop III.
PICTURES: Mighty Joe Young, The Beast From 20000 Fathoms, It Came From Beneath the Sea, Earth Vs. the Flying Saucers, Animal World, Twenty Million Miles to Earth, 7th Voyage of Sinbad, The Three Worlds of Gulliver, Mysterious Island, Jason and the Argonauts, First Men in the Moon, One Million Years B.C., The Valley of Gwangi, The Golden Voyage of Sinbad, Sinbad and the Eye of the Tiger (also co-prod.), Clash of the Titans (also co. prod.).

HART, GARRETT S.
Executive. e. Univ. of MA, Amherst; Queens Col/CUNY. 1979, joined Paramount as mngr. then v.p. of research; 1982, became dir. of comedy develp. Served as sr. v.p., research for Lorimar-Telepictures Corp. before joining Universal 1987; 1990, became sr. v.p., current programs. 1993, named pres. of the network tv division of the Paramount Television Group.

HART, MELISSA JOAN
Actress. b. Smithtown, NY, April 18, 1976.
PICTURES: Can't Hardly Wait (cameo), The Specials, Drive Me Crazy, The Bachelor and the Bobby-Soxer, Backflash Blues..
TELEVISION: *Movies:* Family Reunion: A Relative Nightmare, Sabrina the Teenage Witch (pilot), Twisted Desire, The Right Connections, Two Came Back, Silencing Mary, Sabrina Goes to Rome (also prod.), Sabrina Down Under. *Mini-Series:* Kane & Abel. *Series:* Clarissa Explains It All. Sabrina the Teenage Witch. *Guest:* The Equalizer, Are You Afraid of the Dark?, Touched by an Angel, Clueless, Boy Meets World, Teen Angel, You Wish.

HARTLEY, HAL
Director, Writer. b. Long Island, NY, 1959. e. SUNY/Purchase (film). Following graduation made 3 short movies: Kid, The Cartographer's Girlfriend, Dogs. For PBS made the shorts Theory of Achievement, Ambition, Surviving Desire; also NYC 3/94, Opera No. 1. *Music videos:* The Only Living Boy in New York (Everything But the Girl), From a Motel 6 (Yo La Tengo), Iris.
PICTURES: *Director/Writer*: The Unbelievable Truth (debut, 1990), Trust, Simple Men, Amateur, Flirt (also actor, editor), Henry Fool (Cannes Film Festival Award, Best Screenplay, 1998), The Book of Life, Kimono, Monster.

HARTLEY, MARIETTE
Actress. b. New York, NY, June 21, 1940. Student Carnegie Tech. Inst. 1956-57; studied with Eva Le Gallienne. Appeared with Shakespeare Festival, Stratford 1957-60. Co-host Today Show, 1980. Co-host on CBS Morning Show, 1987. Returned to stage in King John (NYSF in Central Park), 1989. Nominated for 6 Emmys for Best Actress. Received 3 Clio Awards, 1979, 1980, and 1981, for acting in commercials. Autobiography: Breaking the Silence.
THEATRE: The Sisters Rosenweig, Deathtrap, Sylvia.
PICTURES: Ride the High Country (debut, 1962), Drums of Africa, Marnie, Marooned, Barquero, The Return of Count Yorga, Skyjacked, The Magnificent Seven Ride!, Improper Channels, O'Hara's Wife, 1969, Encino Man, Snitch.
TELEVISION: *Series*: Peyton Place, The Hero, Good Night Beantown, WIOU. *Guest*: The Rockford Files, The Incredible Hulk (Emmy Award, 1979), Stone, Caroline in the City. *Movies*: Earth II, Sandcastles, Genesis II, Killer Who Wouldn't Die, Last Hurrah, M.A.D.D.: Mothers Against Drunk Drivers, Drop-Out Father, One Terrific Guy, Silence of the Heart, My Two Loves, Murder C.O.D., Diagnosis of Murder, The House on Sycamore Street, Child of Rage, Heaven & Hell: North and South Book III, Falling From the Sky!: Flight 174. *Mini-Series*: Passion and Paradise. *Specials*: The Halloween That Almost Wasn't, Wild About Animals (host).

HARTMAN BLACK, LISA
Actress. Houston, TX, June 1, 1956. m. musician Clint Black. Attended NYC's H.S. of Performing Arts prior to becoming a nightclub performer.
PICTURES: Deadly Blessing, Where the Boys Are.
TELEVISION: *Series*: Tabitha, Knots Landing, High Performance, 2000 Malibu Road. *Movies*: Murder at the World Series, Valentine Magic on Love Island, Where the Ladies Go, Gridlock, Jacqueline Susann's Valley of the Dolls 1981, Beverly Hills Cowgirl Blues, Full Exposure: The Sex Tapes Scandal, The Operation, The Take, Bare Essentials, Fire: Trapped on the 39th Floor, Not of This World, Red Wind, The Return of Eliot Ness, Without a Kiss Goodbye, Search for Grace, Dazzle, Someone Else's Child, Have You Seen My Son?, Out of Nowhere.

HARTZ, JIM
TV Newsman, Panelist. b. Tulsa, OK, Feb. 3, 1940. Pre-med student at U. of Tulsa, where worked in spare time as reporter for radio station KRMG. 1963 left studies for career as newsman and joined KOTV in Tulsa. 1964 moved to NBC News in New York, acting as reporter and anchorman. 1974 became co-host of Today Show, joined Barbara Walters.

HARVEY, ANTHONY
Director, Editor. b. London, England,, June 3, 1931. Royal Acad. of Dramatic Art. Two yrs. as actor. Ent. m.p. ind. 1949 with Crown Film Unit.
PICTURES: *Editor*: Private's Progress, Brothers-in-Law, Man in a Cocked Hat (Carlton Brown of the F.O.), I'm Alright Jack, The Angry Silence, The Millionairess, Lolita, The L-Shaped Room, Dr. Strangelove, The Spy Who Came In From the Cold, The Whisperers. *Director:* Dutchman (debut, 1966), The Lion in Winter, They Might Be Giants, Eagles' Wing, Players, The Abdication, Richard's Things, Grace Quigley.
TELEVISION: *Movies*: The Disappearance of Aimee, Svengali, The Patricia Neal Story, The Glass Menagerie, This Can't Be Love.

HARVEY, TIM
Production Designer
PICTURES: Henry V, Dead Again, Peter's Friends, Much Ado About Nothing, Frankenstein, A Midwinter's Tale, Othello, Hamlet, Love's Labour's Lost.
TELEVISION: *Series:* Out of the Unknown, The Pallisers. *Movies:* The Aerodome, The Secret Life of Ian Fleming, Voice of the Heart. *Mini-Series:* Emma, I, Claudius, The Borgias, Fortunes of War, Nancy Astor, Bleak House, Summer's Lease.

HARWOOD, RONALD
Writer. b. Cape Town, South Africa, 1934. e. Royal Acad. of Dramatic Art.
THEATER: The Dresser, Interpreters, J.J. Farr, Another Time, Reflected Glory, Poison Pen, Taking Sides.
PICTURES: Barber of Stamford Hill, Private Potter, High Wind in Jamaica, Arrivederci Baby, Diamonds for Breakfast, Sudden Terror (Eye Witness), One Day in the Life of Ivan Denisovich, Operation Daybreak (Price of Freedom), The Dresser (also prod.), The Doctor and the Devils, Tchin-Tchin, The Browning Version, Cry the Beloved Country.

TELEVISION: The Barber of Stamford Hill, Private Potter, Take a Fellow Like Me, The Lads, Convalescence, Guests of Honor, The Guests. Adapted several of the Tales of the Unexpected, The Deliberate Death of a Polish Priest, Mandela, Breakthrough at Rykjavik, Countdown to War, All the World's a Stage (series).

HASSANEIN, RICHARD C.
Executive. b. New York, NY, Aug. 13, 1951; e. Staunton Military Acad., 1966-70; American U., 1970-74. Booker/real estate dept. opns., United Artists Theater Circuit, 1974-77; joined United Film Distribution Co., 1977; 1978-88, pres. of UFD. 1988-91 served as pres., prod.s' rep., foreign & U.S. sls., of Myriad Enterprises. Joined Todd-AO Glen Glenn Studios in 1991 as v.p. of new bus. ventures. 1991 appointed exec. v.p. of Todd-AO Studios East, NY. 1993, elected to bd. of dirs. of Todd-AO Corp. 1995, appointed v.p. of Todd-AO Studios West, Los Angeles; 1996, pres. and COO of Todd-AO Studios West. 1999, Executive Vice President of Todd-AO Studios

HASSANEIN, SALAH M.
Executive. b. Suez, Egypt, May 31, 1921. e. British Sch., Alexandria, Egypt. Nat'l Bank of Egypt, Cairo, 1939-42. Asst. division mgr. Middle East, 20th-Fox, Cairo, Egypt, 1942-44: U.S. armed forces, 1945-47; usher, asst. mgr., Rivoli Theatre, N.Y., 1947-48. Film buyer, booker, oper. v.p. U.A. Eastern Theas., 1948-59; pres. 1960; exec. v.p. U.A. Communications, Inc. 1960; v.p. United Artists Cable Corp., 1963. Exec. v.p., Todd-AO Corp., 1980. President, Warner Bros. International Theaters, 1988. President, Todd AO Corp., 1994.
PICTURES: *Exec. prod.*: Knightriders, Creepshow, Hello Again, Love or Money.

HASSELHOFF, DAVID
Actor. b. Baltimore, MD, July 17, 1952.
PICTURES: Starcrash, Starke Zeiten, Witchery, W.B. Blue and the Bean, The Final Alliance, Ring of the Musketeers, Dear God (cameo), The Big Tease.
TELEVISION: *Series*: The Young and the Restless, Knight Rider, Baywatch, Baywatch Nights. *Movies*: Griffin and Phoenix, Semi Tough, The Cartier Affair, Bridge Across Time, Perry Mason: The Case of the Lady in the Lake, Baywatch: Panic at Malibu Pier, Fire & Rain, Knight Rider 2000, Avalanche, Baywatch: Forbidden Paradise, Gridlock, Nick Fury, Baywatch: White Thunder at Glacier Bay.

HASTINGS, DON
Actor. b. Brooklyn, NY, Apr. 1, 1934. e. Professional Children's Sch., Lodge H.S. On B'way in I Remember Mama, Summer and Smoke, etc.; Natl. co. of Life With Father; on various radio shows. Also wrote scripts for tv series The Guiding Light.
TELEVISION: *Series*: Captain Video, The Edge of Night, As the World Turns (also writer).

HATFIELD, TED
Executive. b. Wilton Junction, IA. e. Hot Springs, AR. Started in industry ABC Paramount Theatres, advancing from usher to district mgr. 1970-1991, MGM/UA V.P. Field Operations, then V.P. Exhibitor Relations. 1991-1997, Sony Pictures V.P. Exhibitor Relations. 1998, Regal Cinemas Nationwide Promotion Director.

HATOSY, SHAWN
Actor. b. Fredrick, MD, Dec. 29, 1975.
PICTURES: Home for the Holidays, In & Out, No Way Home, Inventing the Abbotts, All Over Me, The Postman, The Faculty, Simpatico, The Joyriders, Anywhere But Here, Outside Providence.
TELEVISION: *Guest:* Homicide: Life on the Street, Law & Order.

HAUER, RUTGER
Actor. b. Breukelen, Netherlands, Jan. 23, 1944. Stage actor in Amsterdam for six years.
PICTURES: Repelsteeltje (debut, 1973), Turkish Delight, Pusteblume, The Wilby Conspiracy, Keetje Tippel, Het Jaar van de Kreeft, Max Havelaar, Griechische Feigen, Soldier of Orange, Pastorale 1943, Femme Entre Chien et Loup, Mysteries (also co-prod.), Gripsta en de Gier, Spetters, Nighthawks, Chanel Solitaire, Blade Runner, Eureka, The Osterman Weekend, A Breed Apart, Ladyhawke, Flesh and Blood, The Hitcher, Wanted: Dead or Alive, The Legend of the Holy Drinker, Bloodhounds of Broadway, The Blood of Heroes, Blind Fury, Ocean Point, On a Moonlit Night, Past Midnight, Split Second, Buffy the Vampire Slayer, Arctic Blue, Beyond Forgiveness, Surviving the Game, Nostradamus, The Beans of Egypt Maine, Angel of Death, Hemoglobin, Deathline, Tactical Assault, Bone Daddy, New World Disorder, Partners in Crime.
TELEVISION: *Movies*: Escape from Sobibor, Inside The Third Reich, Deadlock, Blind Side, Voyage, Amelia Earhart: The Final Flight, Fatherland, Hostile Waters, Merlin. *Series*: Floris (Netherlands TV). *Mini-Series*: Maketub: The Law of the Desert (Italy).

HAUSER, WINGS
Actor. b. Hollywood, CA, 1947. Nickname derived from playing wing back on h.s. football team. Began studying acting in 1975.
PICTURES: First to Fight, Who'll Stop the Rain, Homework, Vice Squad, Deadly Force, Uncommon Valor (assoc. prod., story only), Night Shadows, A Soldier's Story, Jo Jo Dancer Your Life is Calling, 3:15, Tough Guys Don't Dance, Nightmare at Noon, The Wind, Hostage, Dead Man Walking, The Carpenter, The Siege of Firebase Gloria, No Safe Haven (also co-s.p.), Reason to Die, L.A. Bounty, Street Asylum, Pale Blood, Out of Sight Out of Mind, Nightmare at Noon, Living to Die, Exiled in America, Bedroom Eyes II, Wilding, The Killer's Edge, In Between, Frame Up, Cold Fire, Beastmaster 2: Through the Portal of Time, The Art of Dying, Mind Body & Soul, Frame-up III: The Cover Up, Watchers 3, Tales From the Hood, Victim of Desire, Life Among the Cannibals, Original Gangstas.
TELEVISION: *Series*: The Young and the Restless, The Last Precinct, Lightning Force, Command 5, Roseanne, Beverly Hills 90210. *Movies*: Hear No Evil, Ghost Dancing, Sweet Revenge, The Long Hot Summer, Perry Mason: The Case of the Scandalous Scoundrel, Highway Man, Bump In the Night. *Guest*: Murder She Wrote, China Beach, Hard Ball, The Young Riders, Space Rangers, Walker Texas Ranger, Jag.

HAUSMAN, MICHAEL
Producer. Former stockbroker and still photographer. Entered film industry as assoc. prod. and prod. mgr. on The Heartbreak Kid and Taking Off. Worked as head of prod. for Robert Stigwood on Saturday Night Fever.
PICTURES: I Never Promised You a Rose Garden, Alambrista!, Heartland, Rich Kids, One-Trick Pony, Ragtime (exec. prod., 1st asst. dir.), The Ballad of Gregorio Cortez, Silkwood, Amadeus (exec. prod.), Places in the Heart (exec. prod.), Desert Bloom, Flight of the Spruce Goose, No Mercy, House of Games, Things Change, Valmont, State of Grace, Homicide, Nobody's Fool, A Family Thing, Twilight.
TELEVISION: Lip Service (exec. prod.).

HAVERS, NIGEL
Actor. b. London, England,, Nov. 6, 1949. e. Leicester U., trained for stage at Arts Educational Trust. Father, Sir Michael Havers, was Attorney General of Britain. As child played Billy Owen on British radio series, Mrs. Dale's Diary. Records voice overs and books for the blind.
THEATER: Conduct Unbecoming, Richard II, Man and , Superman (RSC), Family Voices, Season's Greetings, The Importance of Being Earnest.
PICTURES: Pope Joan (debut, 1972), Full Circle, Who is Killing the Great Chefs of Europe?, Chariots of Fire, A Passage to India, Burke and Wills, The Whistle Blower, Empire of the Sun, Farewell to the King, Clichy Days.
TELEVISION: *Series*: A Horseman Riding By, Don't Wait Up. *Mini-Series*: The Glittering Prizes, Nicholas Nickleby, Pennies From Heaven, Winston Churchill: The Wilderness Years, Nancy Astor, The Little Princess, Death of the Heart, Naked Under Capricorn, Sleepers. *Movies*: The Charmer, Private War of Lucina Smith, Lie Down With Lions, The Burning Season. *Guest*: Thriller, Star Quality: Noel Coward Stories (Bon Voyage), A Question of Guilt, Aspects of Love, Upstairs Downstairs, Edward VII, Liz: The Elizabeth Taylor Story.

HAVOC, JUNE
Actress. r.n. Hovick. b. Seattle, WA, Nov. 8, 1916. Sister was late Gypsy Rose Lee. Made film bow at 2 yrs. old in Hal Roach/Harold Lloyd productions billed as Baby June. Danced with Anna Pavlova troupe, then entered vaudeville in own act. Later, joined Municipal Opera Company, St. Louis, and appeared in Shubert shows. Musical comedy debut: Forbidden Melody (1936). To Hollywood, 1942. Author: Early Havoc (1959), More Havoc (1980).
THEATER: Pal Joey, Sadie Thompson, Mexican Hayride, Dunnigan's Daughter, Dream Girl, Affairs of State, The Skin of Our Teeth, A Midsummer Night's Dream (Stratford, CT. American Shakespeare Fest., 1958), Tour for U.S. Dept. of St., 1961; wrote Marathon 33. The Ryan Girl, The Infernal Machine, The Beaux Strategem, A Warm Peninsula, Dinner at Eight, Habeas Corpus. An Unexpected Evening with June Havoc (one woman show, London 1985), The Gift (tour), Eleemosynary, The Old Lady's Guide to Survival, Do Not Go Gently.
PICTURES: Four Jacks and a Jill (debut, 1941), Powder Town, My Sister Eileen, Sing Your Worries Away, Hi Diddle Diddle, Hello Frisco Hello, No Time for Love, Casanova Burlesque, Timber Queen, Sweet and Low Down, Brewster's Millions, Intrigue, Gentleman's Agreement, When My Baby Smiles at Me, The Iron Curtain, The Story of Molly X, Red Hot and Blue, Chicago Deadline, Mother Didn't Tell Me, Once a Thief, Follow the Sun, Lady Possessed, Three for Jamie Dawn, The Private Files of J. Edgar Hoover, Can't Stop the Music, Return to Salem's Lot.
TELEVISION: Anna Christie, The Bear, Cakes and Ale, Daisy Mayme, The Untouchables, Willy, MacMillan & Wife, The Paper Chase, Murder She Wrote. *Series*: More Havoc (1964-65), Search for Tomorrow, General Hospital.

HAWKE, ETHAN
Actor. b. Austin, TX, Nov. 6, 1970. Attended NYU. Studied acting at McCarter Theatre in Princeton, NJ, the British Theatre Assn., Carnegie Mellon U. Stage debut in St. Joan. Co-founder of Malaparte Theatre Co. in NYC. Dir. & wrote short film Straight to One. Author of novel The Hottest State, 1996.
THEATER: *NY*: Casanova (Off-B'way debut, 1991), A Joke, The Seagull (B'way debut, 1992), Sophistry, Hesh, The Great Unwashed.

PICTURES: Explorers (debut, 1985), Dead Poets Society, Dad, White Fang, Mystery Date, A Midnight Clear, Waterland, Alive, Rich in Love, Reality Bites, White Fang 2: Myth of the White Wolf (cameo), Quiz Show (cameo), Floundering, Before Sunrise, Search and Destroy, Gattaca, Snow Falling on Cedars, The Newton Boys, Great Expectations, Hamlet, Joe the King, Waking Life, Training Day.

HAWN, GOLDIE
Actress, Producer. b. Washington, DC, November 21, 1945. Started as professional dancer (performed in Can-Can at the N.Y. World's Fair, 1964), and made TV debut dancing on an Andy Griffith Special.
PICTURES: The One and Only Genuine Original Family Band (debut, 1968), Cactus Flower (Academy Award, best supporting actress, 1969), There's a Girl in My Soup, $ (Dollars), Butterflies Are Free, The Sugarland Express, The Girl From Petrovka, Shampoo, The Duchess and the Dirtwater Fox, Foul Play, Private Benjamin (Acad. Award nom.; also exec. prod.), Seems Like Old Times, Lovers and Liars (Travels With Anita), Best Friends, Swing Shift, Protocol (also exec. prod.), Wildcats (also exec. prod.), Overboard (also exec. prod.), Bird on a Wire, My Blue Heaven (co-exec. prod. only), Deceived, Crisscross (also co-exec. prod.), Housesitter, Death Becomes Her, Something to Talk About (exec. prod. only), The First Wives Club, Everyone Says I Love You, The Out-of-Towners, Town and Country.
TELEVISION: *Series*: Good Morning World, Rowan & Martin's Laugh-In (1968-70). *Specials*: The Goldie Hawn Special, Goldie & Liza Together, Goldie and the Kids: Listen to Us.

HAWTHORNE, NIGEL
Actor. b. Coventry, England, Apr. 5, 1929. Extensive career on stage. Ent. TV ind. 1953. Films, 1957. Won 1991 Tony Award for best actor for Shadowlands; Olivier & Evening Standard Awards for The Madness of George III (Natl. Th.).
PICTURES: Young Winston, The Hiding Place, Watership Down (voice), History of the World Part 1, Plague Dogs (voice), Firefox, Gandhi, The Black Cauldron (voice), The Chain, Turtle Diary, Freddie as F.R.O.7 (voice), Demolition Man, The Madness of King George (Acad. Award nom., BAFTA Award), Richard III, Inside, Twelfth Night, The Fragile Heart (BAFTA Award).
TELEVISION: Mapp and Lucia, The Knowledge, The Miser, The Critic, Barchester Chronicles, Marie Curie, Edward and Mrs. Simpson, Yes Minister, Yes Prime Minister (series), The Oz Trials, Flea-Bites. The Shawl, Relatively Speaking, Late Flowering Lust.

HAYEK, SALMA
Actress. b. Coatzacoalcos, Veracruz, Mexico, Sept. 2, 1968. Began her acting career in the 1980's in Mexican TV soap operas. Was first noticed in 1995 for her role in Desperado.
PICTURES: My Crazy Life, Midaq Alley, Desperado, Fair Game, Four Rooms, From Dusk Till Dawn, Fled, Fools Rush In, Breaking Up, The Velocity of Gary, The Faculty, Dogma, 54, Wild Wild West, Forever Hollywood, Timecode, Chain of Fools, Traffic, La Gran Vida, Frida Kahlo.
TELEVISION: *Movies*: Roadracers, The Hunchback. *Series*: Teresa, The Sinbad Show. *Guest*: Dream On, Nurses.

HAYES, ISAAC
Musician, Actor. b. Covington, TN, Aug. 20, 1942. Was session musician with Stax Records in Memphis, eventually working as composer, prod.. Debuted with solo album Presenting Isaac Hayes in 1968.
PICTURES: *Music:* Shaft (Academy Award for best song: Theme from Shaft, 1971), Shaft's Big Score. *Actor:* Wattstax, Save the Children, Three Tough Guys (also music), Truck Turner (also music), Escape From New York, I'm Gonna Git You Sucka, Guilty as Charged, Posse, Robin Hood: Men in Tights, It Could Happen to You, Illtown, Once Upon a Time...When We Were Colored, Flipper, Six Ways to Sunday, Blues Brothers 2000, Ninth Street (also comp.).
TELEVISION: *Series theme:* The Men.

HAYES, JOHN EDWARD
Broadcasting Executive. b. Niagara Falls, NY, Sept. 14, 1941. e. U. FL, BS broadcasting, 1963. State capital bur. chief Sta. WTVJ-TV, FL, 1963-67. Exec. asst. FL, Dept. Comsumer Svcs., 1967-71. State capitol bur. chief Sta. WTVT-TV, Tallahassee, 1971-77. Asst. news dir. Sta. WTVT-TV, FL, 1977-79. News dir:. Sta. WBRC-TV, AL 1979-82; Sta. KNTV-TV, CA, 1982-83. V.p. gen. mgr. Sta. KLAS-TV, NV, 1983-87. Gen mgr. Sta. WIVB-TV, NY 1987-89. Pres. Jour. Broadcasting of Charlotte Co., 1989-92. V.p. TV Providence Jour. Co., 1992-. Recipient of: Nat. Headliners award Headliner Club, 1973; Emmy award TV Acad. Arts & Sci., 1982. Mem.: Nat. Assn. Broadcasters; TV Bur. Advertisers & NBC Affiliates.

HAYES, JOHN MICHAEL
Writer. b. Worcester, MA, May 11, 1919. e. U. of Mass., 1941.
PICTURES: Red Ball Express, Thunder Bay, Torch Song, War Arrow, Rear Window, To Catch a Thief, The Trouble with Harry, It's a Dog's Life, The Man Who Knew Too Much, The Matchmaker, Peyton Place, But Not for Me, Butterfield 8, The Children's Hour, Where Love Has Gone, The Chalk Garden, Judith, Iron Will.
TELEVISION: *Movie*: Winter Kill, Nevada Smith, Pancho Barnes.

HAYNES, TODD
Director, Writer, Producer, Editor, Actor.
PICTURES: Superstar: The Karen Carpenter Story, He Was Once, Poison (Sundance Film Fest. Grand Jury Prize, 1991), Swoon, Safe (Seattle Int'l. Film Fest. Amer. Indep. Award, 1995), Velvet Goldmine (Cannes Film Fest., Best Art. Contribution, 1998).
TELEVISION: *Movies*: Dottie Gets Spanked.

HAYS, ROBERT
Actor. b. Bethesda, MD, July 24, 1947. e. Grossmont Coll., San Diego State U. Left school to join San Diego's Old Globe Theatre five years, appearing in such plays as The Glass Menagerie, The Man in the Glass Booth, Richard III.
PICTURES: Airplane! (debut, 1980), Take This Job and Shove It!, Utilities, Airplane II: The Sequel, Trenchcoat, Touched, Scandalous, Cat's Eye, Honeymoon Academy, Hot Chocolate, Homeward Bound: The Incredible Journey, Fifty Fifty, Raw Justice, Homeward Bound II: Lost in San Francisco.
TELEVISION: *Series*: Angie, Starman, FM, Cutters, Kelly Kelly. *Movies*: Young Pioneers, Young Pioneers' Christmas, Delta County U.S.A., The Initiation of Sarah, The Girl The Gold Watch and Everything, California Gold Rush, The Fall of the House of Usher, The Day the Bubble Burst, Murder by the Book, Running Against Time, No Dessert Dad 'Til You Mow the Lawn, Deadly Invasion: The Killer Bee Nightmare, Danielle Steel's Vanished. *Mini-Series*: Will Rogers: Champion of the People. *Specials*: Mr. Roberts, Partners. *Guest*: Love Boat, Harry O, Laverne and Shirley.

HAYSBERT, DENNIS
Actor. b. San Mateo, CA, June 2.
THEATER: Wedding Band, Yanks-3 Detroit-0 Top of the Seventh, Diplomacy, Othello, On the Death of, All Over Town, Blood Knot, No Place to Be Somebody, Jimmy Shine, The Time of Your Life, Ten Little Indians.
PICTURES: Major League, Navy SEALS, Mr. Baseball, Love Field, Suture, Major League 2, Amanda, Waiting to Exhale, Absolute Power, Heat, Prairie Fire.
TELEVISION: *Series*: Code Red, Off the Rack. *Mini-Series*: Queen. Movies: A Summer to Remember, Grambling's White Tiger, K-9000. *Specials*: The Upper Room, Hallelujah.

HEAD, ANTHONY
Actor. b. Camden, London, England, February 20, 1954.
PICTURES: Lady Chatterly's Lover, A Prayer for the Dying, Woof Again! Why Me?.
TELEVISION: *Movies:* Royce, Roger Roger, Best Actress. *Series:* VR 5, Buffy the Vampire Slayer *Mini:* Lillie. *Guest:* The Comic Strip Presents, Spenser for Hire, Boon, Woof!, The Detectives, Highlander, Ghostbusters of East Finchley, NYPD Blue, Jonathan Creek, Bergerace, Two Guys, a Girl, and a Pizza Place.

HEADLY, GLENNE
Actress. b. New London, CT, March 13, 1957. e. High Sch. of Performing Arts. Studied at HB Studios. In Chicago joined St. Nicholas New Works Ensemble. Won 3 Joseph Jefferson awards for work with Steppenwolf Ensemble in Say Goodnight Gracie, Miss Firecracker Contest, Balm in Gilead, Coyote Ugly, Loose Ends. Directed Canadian Gothic.
THEATER: *NY*: Balm in Gilead, Arms and the Man, Extremities, The Philanthropist (Theatre World Award).
PICTURES: Four Friends (debut, 1981), Dr. Detroit, Fandango, The Purple Rose of Cairo, Eleni, Making Mr. Right, Nadine, Stars and Bars, Dirty Rotten Scoundrels, Paperhouse, Dick Tracy, Mortal Thoughts, Grand Isle, Ordinary Magic, Getting Even With Dad, Mr. Holland's Opus, Bastard Out of Carolina, Sgt. Bilko, 2 Days in the Valley, The X Files: Fight the Future, Babe: Pig in the City (voice), Breakfast of Champions.
TELEVISION: *Movies*: Say Goodnight Gracie, Seize the Day, Grand Isle, And the Band Played On, Pronto, Winchell, My Own Country. *Mini-Series*: Lonesome Dove (Emmy nom.). *Series:* David Lynch's Hotel Room, Encore! Encore!. *Guest*: Frasier, ER.

HEALD, ANTHONY
Actor. b. New Rochelle, NY, Aug. 25, 1944. e. Michigan St. Univ.
THEATER: *B'way*: The Wake of Jamey Foster, The Marriage of Figaro, Anything Goes, A Small Family Business, Love! Valour! Compassion!, Inherit the Wind. *Off-B'way*: The Glass Menagerie, The Electra Myth, Inadmissible Evidence, Misalliance (Theatre World Award), The Caretaker, The Fox, The Philanthropist, Henry V, The Foreigner, Digby, Principia Scriptoriae, The Lisbon Traviata, Elliot Loves, Lips Together Teeth Apart, Pygmalion, Later Life, Love! Valour! Compassion! *Regional:* Quartermaine's Terms, J.B., Look Back in Anger, The Rose Tattoo, Bonjour la Bonjour, The Matchmaker.
PICTURES: Silkwood (debut, 1983), Teachers, Outrageous Fortune, Happy New Year, Orphans, Postcards From the Edge, The Silence of the Lambs, The Super, Whispers in the Dark, Searching for Bobby Fisher, The Ballad of Little Jo, The Pelican Brief, The Client, Kiss of Death, Bushwacked, A Time to Kill, Deep Rising.

TELEVISION: *Movies*: A Case of Deadly Force, Royce. *Mini-Series*: Fresno. Pilot: After Midnight. *Special*: Abby My Love. *Guest*: Hard Copy, Crime Story, Spenser for Hire, Miami Vice, Tales From the Darkside, Against the Law, Law and Order, Class of '96, Cheers, Murder She Wrote, Under Suspicion.

HEARD, JOHN
Actor. b. Washington, D.C., Mar. 7, 1947. e. Catholic U. Career began at Organic Theatre, starring in Chicago & N.Y. productions of Warp. Other stage roles include Streamers, G.R. Point (Theatre World Award), Othello, Split, The Glass Menagerie, Total Abandon, The Last Yankee.
PICTURES: Between the Lines (debut, 1977), First Love, On the Yard, Head Over Heels (Chilly Scenes of Winter), Heart Beat, Cutter and Bone (Cutter's Way), Cat People, Best Revenge, Violated, Heaven Help Us, Lies, C.H.U.D., Too Scared to Scream, After Hours, The Trip to Bountiful, The Telephone, The Milagro Beanfield War, The Seventh Sign, Big, Betrayed, Beaches, The Package, Home Alone, End of Innocence, Awakenings, Rambling Rose, Deceived, Mindwalk, Radio Flyer, Gladiator, Waterland, Home Alone 2: Lost in New York, In the Line of Fire, Me and Veronica, The Pelican Brief, Before and After, My Fellow Americans, 187, Executive Power, Men, Snake Eyes.
TELEVISION: *Series*: John Grisham's The Client. *Specials*: The Scarlet Letter, Edgar Allan Poe: Terror of the Soul. *Mini-Series*: Tender Is the Night. *Movies*: Will There Really Be a Morning?, Legs, Out on a Limb, Necessity, Cross of Fire, Dead Ahead: The Exxon Valdez Disaster, There Was a Little Boy, Spoils of War, Because Mommy Works.

HECHE, ANNE
Actress. b. Aurora, OH, May 25, 1969.
PICTURES: An Ambush of Ghosts, The Adventures of Huck Finn, A Simple Twist of Fate, Milk Money, I'll Do Anything, The Wild Side, Pie in the Sky, The Juror, Walking and Talking, Donnie Brasco, Volcano, I Know What You Did Last Summer, Six Days Seven Nights, Wag the Dog, Return to Paradise, Psycho.
TELEVISION: *Series*: Another World. *Movies*: O Pioneers!, Against the Wall, Girls in Prison, Kingfish: A Story of Huey P. Long, If These Walls Could Talk, Subway Stories,. *Guest*: Murphy Brown, Ellen.

HECHT, ALBIE
Producer, Executive. b. Queens, NY. e. B.A., Columbia U. Exec. producer and founding principal, Chauncey Street Prods. Currently president, Film and TV Entertainment for Nickelodeon. Exec. producer, Snow Day, The Rugrats Movie, and Rugrats in Paris–The Movie. Recipient of three CableACE Awards and an ACT Award for excellence in children's television; also the first recipient of the Children's Museum of Los Angeles Freedom Award.

HECKART, EILEEN
Actress. b. Columbia, OH, Mar. 29, 1919. e. Ohio State U., American Theatre Wing. m. Jack Yankee.Inducted into Theatre Hall of Fame, 1995. Awards: Foreign Press, and Donaldson, Oscar nom. and Film Daily Citation (Bad Seed), TV Sylvania for the Haven, Variety Poll of N.Y. and Drama Critics (Dark at The Top of the Stairs); Emmy (Save Me a Place at Forest Lawn). Also 5 Tony noms., 5 Emmy noms. Honorary Doctorates from: Ohio St. Univ., Sacred Heart, Niagara Univ.
THEATER: Voice of the Turtle, Brighten the Corner, They Knew What They Wanted, Hilda Crane, Picnic (Theatre World & Outer Critics Circle Awards), The Bad Seed, A View From the Bridge, Family Affair, Pal Joey, Invitation to a March, Everybody Loves Opal, The Dark at the Top of the Stairs, And Things That Go Bump in the Night, You Know I Can't Hear You When the Water's Running, Too True to Be Good, Barefoot in the Park, Butterflies Are Free, Veronica's Room, The Effect of Gamma Rays on Man in the Moon Marigolds, Eleemosynary, The Cemetery Club, Love Letters, Driving Miss Daisy.
PICTURES: Miracle in the Rain (debut, 1956), Somebody Up There Likes Me, The Bad Seed, Bus Stop, Hot Spell, Heller in Pink Tights, My Six Loves, Up the Down Staircase, No Way to Treat a Lady, The Tree, Butterflies Are Free (Academy Award, best supporting actress, 1972), Zandy's Bride, The Hiding Place, Burnt Offerings, Heartbreak Ridge, The First Wives' Club.
TELEVISION: *Series*: The Five Mrs. Buchanans. *Guest*: Kraft, Suspense, Philco Playhouse, The Web, Mary Tyler Moore, Annie McGuire, Love and War (Emmy Award, 1994), The Five Mrs. Buchanans, Murder One. *Movies*: The Victim, FBI Story: The FBI Versus Alvin Karpis, Sunshine Christmas, Suddenly Love, White Mama, FDR: The Last Year, The Big Black Pill, Games Mother Never Taught You, Seize the Day, Ultimate Betrayal, A Doll's House, Stuck with Each Other, Triumph Over Disaster: The Hurricane Andrew Story, Breathing Lessons, Ultimate Betrayal. *Mini-Series*: Backstairs at the Whitehouse.

HECKERLING, AMY
Director. b. New York, NY, May 7, 1954. e. Art & Design H.S., NYU, (film and TV), American Film Institute. Made shorts (Modern Times, High Finance, Getting It Over With), before turning to features.
PICTURES: Fast Times at Ridgemont High, Johnny Dangerously, Into the Night (actor only), National Lampoon's European Vacation, Look Who's Talking, Look Who's Talking Too, Look Who's Talking 3 (co-exec. prod. only), Clueless, A Night at the Roxbury (prod.,s.p.), Molly (prod. only), Loser. (also prod.).
TELEVISION: George Burns Comedy Hour, Fast Times, They Came From Queens. *Series*: Clueless.

HEDAYA, DAN
Actor. b. Brooklyn, NY, July 24, 1940. e. Tufts Univ. Taught junior high school for seven yrs. before turning to acting. Joined NY Shakespeare Fest. in 1973.
THEATER: *NY*: Last Days of British Honduras, Golden Boy, Museum, The Basic Training of Pavlo Hummel, Conjuring an Event, Survivors, Henry V.
PICTURES: The Passover Plot (debut, 1976), The Seduction of Joe Tynan, Night of the Juggler, True Confessions, I'm Dancing As Fast As I Can, Endangered Species, The Hunger, The Adventures of Buckaroo Banzai, Blood Simple, Reckless, Tightrope, Commando, Wise Guys, Running Scared, Joe Vs. the Volcano, Pacific Heights, Tune in Tomorrow, The Addams Family, Boiling Point, Benny & Joon, Rookie of the Year, For Love or Money, Mr. Wonderful, Maverick, Search and Destroy, Clueless, Nixon, The Usual Suspects, To Die For, Marvin's Room, Freeway, Ransom, Daylight, In & Out, Alien: Resurrection, A Life Less Ordinary, A Night at the Roxbury, A Civil Action, Dick.
TELEVISION: *Series*: The Tortellis, One of the Boys, ER. *Movies*: The Prince of Central Park, Death Penalty, The Dollmaker, Courage, Slow Burn, A Smoky Mountain Christmas, Betrayal of Trust, Reluctant Agent, The Whereabouts of Jenny, The Garden of Redemption. *Guest*: Hill Street Blues, Cheers, L.A. Law. *Pilots*: The Earthlings, The Flamingo Kid, The Rock. *Special*: Just Like Family, Mama's Boy, Veronica Clare, The Second Civil War.

HEDLUND, DENNIS
Executive. b. Hedley, TX, Sept. 3, 1946. e. U. of Texas, Austin, B.A., business admin., 1968. Captain U.S. Marine Corp, 1966-72. 1970-74, newscaster and disc jockey, KGNC Amarillo, TX; KOMA Oklahoma City, OK; WTIX New Orleans, LA; WFLA Tampa, FL. 1974-77, nat'l sales mgr., Ampex Corp., NY. 1977-80, v.p., Allied Artists Video Corp., NY. 1980-present, founder and pres., Kultur International Films Ltd., distributor of over 800 performing arts programs on home video. 1990, created White Star Entertainment, prod. of original programs for tv, and marketer of over 400 non-theatrical home video titles. Recently acquired Duke USA, 1200 motorsports programs for tv and home video.
TELEVISION: Roger Miller: King of the Road, Jackie Mason: An Equal Opportunity Offender, Merle Haggard: A Portrait of a Proud Man, History of Talk Radio, George Jones: Golden Hits, Raised Catholic: Still Catholic After All These Fears.

HEDREN, TIPPI
Actress. r.n. Nathalie Hedren. b. Lafayette, MN, Jan. 18, 1935. Daughter is actress Melanie Griffith. Was hired by Alfred Hitchcock for leading role in The Birds after being spotted on a commercial on the Today Show. Author of The Cats of Shambala. Founder and pres. of The Roar Foundation. Founder of the Shambala preserve. Bd. member, The Wildlife Safari, The Elsa Wild Animal Appeal, The ASPCA, The American Heart Assoc., etc.
THEATRE: Black Comedy, A Hatful of Rain, Love Letters.
PICTURES: The Birds (debut, 1963), Marnie, A Countess From Hong Kong, The Man and the Albatross, Satan's Harvest, Tiger By the Tail, Mr. Kingstreet's War, The Harrad Experiment, Where the Wind Dies, Roar (also prod.), Foxfire Light, Deadly Spygames, Pacific Heights, In the Cold of the Night, Inevitable Grace, Theresa's Tattoo, Mind Lies, The Devil Inside, Citizen Ruth, I Woke Up Early the Day I Died, The Breakup.
TELEVISION: *Series*: The Bold and the Beautiful, Dream On. *Guest*: Run for Your Life, The Courtship of Eddie's Father, Alfred Hitchcock Presents (1985), Baby Boom, Hart to Hart, In the Heat of the Night, Hotel, Improv (guest host), Tales From the Darkside, Murder She Wrote, Capitol News, The Guardian, Heroes Die Hard, Our Time. *Movies*: Alfred Hitchcock Presents..., Through the Eyes of a Killer, Shadow of a Doubt, Perry Mason: The Case of the Skin-Deep Scandal, The Birds II: Land's End, Treacherous Beauties, Return to Green Acres, Kraft Suspense Theatre: The Trains of Silence, The Book of Virtues (voice), Freakazoid! (voice), Sixth Sense (short), Mulligans(short).*Special*: Inside The Birds.

HEFFNER, RICHARD D.
Executive. b. New York, NY, Aug. 5, 1925. e. Columbia U. Instrumental in acquisition of Channel 13 (WNET) as New York's educational tv station; served as its first gen. mngr. Previously had produced and moderated Man of the Year, The Open Mind, etc. for commercial and public TV. Served as dir. of public affairs programs for WNBC-TV in NY. Was also dir. of special projects for CBS TV Network and editorial consultant to CBS, Inc. Editorial Board. Was radio newsman for ABC. Exec. editor of From The Editor's Desk on WPIX-TV in NY. Taught history at U. of California at Berkeley, Sarah Lawrence Coll., Columbia U. and New School for Social Research, NY. Served as American specialist in communications for U.S. Dept. of State in Japan, Soviet Union, Germany, Yugoslavia, Israel, etc. Prof. of Communications and Public Policy at Rutgers U. 1974-94, chmn. of classification and rating admin. rating board. 1994-95, sr. fellow, Freedom Forum Media Studies Center at Columbia Univ.

HEFFRON, RICHARD T.
Director. b. Chicago, Oct. 6, 1930.
PICTURES: Fillmore, Newman's Law, Trackdown, Futureworld, Outlaw Blues, I the Jury, The French Revolution.
TELEVISION: The Morning After, Dick Van Dyke Special, I Will Fight No More Forever, Toma (pilot), Rockford Files (pilot), North and South (mini-series). *Movies*: The California Kid, Young Joe Kennedy, A Rumor of War, A Whale for the Killing, The Mystic Warrior, V: The Final Battle, Anatomy of an Illness, Convicted: A Mother's Story, Guilty of Innocence, Samaritan, Napoleon and Josephine: A Love Story, Broken Angel, Pancho Barnes, Tagget, Deadly Family Secrets, No Greater Love.

HEIDER, FREDERICK
Producer. b. Milwaukee, WI, Apr. 9, 1917. e. Notre Dame U.Actor in Globe Theatre, Orson Welles' Mercury Theatre.
TELEVISION & RADIO: Chesterfield Supper Club, Sammy Kaye's So You Want to Lead a Band, Frankie Carle Show, Jo Stafford Show, Paul Whiteman Goodyear Revue, Billy Daniels Show, Martha Wright Show, Earl Wrightson Show, Club Seven, Mindy Carson Show; Ted Mack Family Hour, Dr. I.Q., Miss America Pageant, Bishop Sheen's Life Is Worth Living, Voice of Firestone, Music for a Summer Night. Music for a Spring Night, The Bell Telephone Hour. Publisher, Television Quarterly, National Academy of Television Arts and Sciences. Became columnist, The Desert Sun, Palm Springs, CA.

HEILMAN, CLAUDE
Executive. b. Cologne, Germany, June 27, 1927. Early career in Europe in prod. and distribution. In U.S. joined Fox in Hollywood and NY; incl. mgmt. of Grauman's Chinese and other Fox theaters. Formed Vintage Prods. Inc., United Film Associates Intlo., Inter Road Shows. Currently pres./chief. exec. GEM Communications and Islandia Enterprises.
PICTURES: This Earth Is Mine, Odyssey of Justice Lee, The Adventures of Gulliver, Desamor, Sound General Quarters, Islandia.

HELGELAND, BRIAN
Writer, Director, Producer. b. Providence, RI, 1961.
PICTURES: *Writer*: A Nightmare on Elm Street 4: The Dream Master, 976-EVIL, Highway to Hell, Assassins, L.A. Confidential (also co-prod., Acad. Award, Best Adapted Screenplay, Chicago Film Crits. Award, LA Film Crits. Award, NY Film Crits. Awards Best Screenplay, 1997), Conspiracy Theory, The Postman, Payback.
TELEVISION: *Series*: Tales from the Crypt (dir.).

HELGENBERGER, MARG
Actress. b. North Bend, NE, Nov. 16, 1958. e. Northwestern U. Came to NY where she landed first professional job as regular on daytime serial Ryan's Hope.
PICTURES: After Midnight (debut, 1989), Always, Crooked Hearts, Distant Cousins, The Cowboy Way, Bad Boys, Species, My Fellow Americans, Fire Down Below, Species II.
TELEVISION: *Series*: Ryan's Hope, Shell Game, China Beach (Emmy Award, 1990). *Movies*: Blind Vengeance, Death Dreams, The Hidden Room, Deadline (pilot), Through the Eyes of a Killer, The Tommyknockers, When Love Kills: The Seduction of John Hearn, Where Are My Children?, Red Eagle, Partners, Inflammable, Conundrum, Murder Live!, The Last Time I Commited Suicide, Gold Coast. *Special:* Fallen Angels. *Guest:* Spenser for Hire, thirtysomething, Tales From the Crypt, The Larry Sanders Show, ER. *Mini-series*: When Love Kills: The Seduction of John Hearn.

HELLER, PAUL M.
Producer. b. New York, NY, Sept. 25, 1927. e. Hunter Coll., Drexel Inst. of Technology. President, Intrepid Productions. Studied engineering until entry into U.S. Army as member of security agency, special branch of signal corps. Worked as set designer (Westport, East Hampton, Palm Beach) and in live TV and then on theatrical films. Produced the NY Experience and South Street Venture. Debut as film prod., David and Lisa, 1963. From 1964 to 1969 was president of MPO Pictures Inc. Joined Warner Bros. as prod. exec., 1970. Founded the Community Film Workshop Council for the American Film Institute. In 1972 founded Sequoia Pictures, Inc. with Fred Weintraub. Pres. of Paul Heller Prods. Inc. formed in 1978. Founded the Audrey Skirball-Kenis Theatre. Bd of dirs., the British Academy of Film and Television - Los Angeles, The Hearst Monument Foundation, The Geffen Theatre.
PICTURES: David and Lisa, The Eavesdropper, Secret Ceremony, Enter the Dragon, Truck Turner, Golden Needles, Dirty Knight's Work, Outlaw Blues, The Pack, The Promise, First Monday in October, Withnail and I, My Left Foot (exec. prod.), The Lunatic, Fatal Inheritance.
TELEVISION: Pygmalion, Falcon's Gold.

HELLMAN, JEROME
Producer. b. New York, NY, Sept. 4, 1928. e. NYU. Joined ad dept. of New York Times then went to William Morris Agency as apprentice. Made asst. in TV dept. Worked as agent for Jaffe Agency. After hiatus in Europe joined Ashley-Steiner Agency (later IFA) where clients included Franklin Schaffner, Sidney Lumet, George Roy Hill, John Frankenheimer. Functioned as TV prod., inc. Kaiser Aluminum Hour. Left to form own agency, Ziegler, Hellman and Ross. Switched to feature prod. with The World of Henry Orient in 1964.
PICTURES: The World of Henry Orient, A Fine Madness, Midnight Cowboy (Academy Award for Best Picture, 1969), The Day of the Locust, Coming Home, Promises in the Dark (also dir.), The Mosquito Coast.

HELLMAN, MONTE
Director, Editor. b. New York, NY, 1932. e. Stanford Univ., UCLA. Started by working for Roger Corman's company as dir., editor, 2nd Unit dir. Replaced deceased directors on the films The Greatest, Avalanche Express. Dialogue Director: St. Valentine's Day Massacre. Acted in The Christian Licorice Store, Someone to Love.
PICTURES: *Director*: Beast from Haunted Cave, Back Door to Hell, Flight to Fury (also story) , Ride in the Whirlwind (also edit., prod.), The Shooting (also edit., prod.), Two-Lane Blacktop (also edit.), Cockfighter, China 9 Liberty 37 (also prod.), Iguana (also s.p., edit.), Silent Night Deadly Night 3 (also story). *Editor*: The Wild Angels, The Long Ride Home, How to Make It, The Killer Elite. *Second Unit Director*: Last Woman on Earth, Ski Troop Attack, Creature from the Haunted Sea, The Terror. *Exec. Prod.*: Reservoir Dogs.

HELMOND, KATHERINE
Actress. b. Galveston, TX, July 5, 1934. Initial stage work with Houston Playhouse and Margo Jones Theatre, Dallas. Joined APA Theatre, NY, and Trinity Square Rep. Co., RI, Hartford Stage, CT and Phoenix Rep. NY. In 1950s opened summer stock theatre in the Catskills. Taught acting at American Musical and Dramatic Acad., Brown U. and Carnegie-Mellon U. 1983, accepted into AFI's Directing Workshop for Women. Directed Bankrupt.
THEATER: The Great God Brown, House of Blue Leaves (Clarence Derwent, NY and LA Drama Critics Awards, 1972), Mixed Emotions.
PICTURES: The Hindenberg, Baby Blue Marine, Family Plot, Time Bandits, Brazil, Shadey, Overboard, Lady in White, Inside Monkey Zetterland, Amore!, The Flight of the Dove, Fear & Loathing in Las Vegas.
TELEVISION: *Series*: Soap, Who's The Boss? (also episode dir), Benson (episode dir. only), Coach. *Movies*: Dr. Max, Larry, Locusts, The Autobiography of Miss Jane Pittman, The Legend of Lizzie Borden, The Family Nobody Wanted, Cage Without a Key, The First 36 Hours of Dr. Durant, James Dean, Wanted: The Sundance Woman, Little Ladies of the Night, Getting Married, Diary of a Teenage Hitchhiker, Scout's Honor, World War III, For Lovers Only, Rosie: The Rosemary Clooney Story, Meeting of the Minds, Save the Dog, When Will I Be Loved?, The Perfect Tribute, Deception: A Mother's Secret, Grass Roots, Liz: The Elizabeth Taylor Story, Ms. Scrooge. *Special:* Christmas Snow.

HEMINGWAY, MARIEL
Actress. b. Ketchum, ID, Nov. 22, 1961. Granddaughter of writer Ernest Hemingway. Sister of late actress-model Margaux Hemingway.
PICTURES: Lipstick (debut, 1976), Manhattan (Acad. Award nom.), Personal Best, Star 80, The Mean Season, Creator, Superman IV: The Quest for Peace, Sunset, The Suicide Club (also co-prod.), Delirious, Falling From Grace, Naked Gun 33 1/3: The Final Insult, Deceptions II: Edge of Deception, Bad Moon, Road Ends, Little Men, Deconstructing Harry, Drop-Dead, American Reel.
TELEVISION: *Series*: Civil Wars, Central Park West. *Movies*: I Want to Keep My Baby, Steal the Sky, Into the Badlands, Desperate Rescue: The Cathy Mahone Story, September, The Crying Child. *Mini-Series*: Amerika. *Guest*: Tales From the Crypt, Roseanne.

HEMMINGS, DAVID
Actor, Director. b. Guildford, England, Nov.18, 1941. Early career in opera. Ent. m.p. ind. 1956. Former co-partner in Hemdale Company.
THEATER: Adventures in the Skin Trade, Jeeves.
PICTURES: Five Clues to Fortune, Saint Joan, The Heart Within, In the Wake of a Stranger, No Trees in the Street, Men of Tomorrow, The Wind of Change, The Painted Smile (Murder Can Be Deadly), Some People, Play It Cool, Two Left Feet, West 11, Live It Up (Sing and Swing), The System (The Girl-Getters), Be My Guest, Dateline Diamonds, Eye of the Devil, Blow-Up, Camelot, The Charge of the Light Brigade, Only When I Larf, Barbarella, The Long Day's Dying, The Best House in London, Alfred the Great, The Walking Stick, Fragment of Fear, The Love Machine, Unman Wittering and Zigo, Voices, Juggernaut, Running Scared (dir.only), The 14 (dir. only), Mr. Quilp, Deep Red, Islands in the Stream, The Squeeze, The Disappearance, Blood Relatives, Crossed Swords, Power Play, Murder by Decree, Just a Gigolo (also dir.), Thirst, Beyond Reasonable Doubt, The Survivor (dir. only), Harlequin, Race to the Yankee Zephyr (dir., prod. only), Man Woman and Child, Prisoners (also exec. prod.), Coup D'Grat (also prod.), The Rainbow, Dark Horse (dir. only).
TELEVISION: Auto Stop, The Big Toe, Out of the Unknown, Beverly Hills Cowgirl Blues, Clouds of Glory, Davy Crockett: Rainbow in the Thunder (also dir.). *Director only*: Hardball, Magnum PI, A-Team, Airwolf, Murder She Wrote, In the Heat of the Night, Quantum Leap, The Turn of the Screw, Tales From the Crypt, Passport to Murder (movie). *Guest*: Northern Exposure, The Raven, Ned Blessing.

HEMSLEY, SHERMAN
Actor. b. Philadelphia, PA, Feb. 1, 1938. On NY stage in Purlie.
PICTURES: Love at First Bite, Stewardess School, Ghost Fever, Mr. Nanny, Home Angels, Casper: A Spirited Beginning, Sprung.
TELEVISION: *Series*: All in the Family, The Jeffersons, Amen, Dinosaurs (voice), Townsend Television, Goode Behavior. *Guest*: The Rich Little Show, Love Boat, E/R, 227, Family Matters, Lois & Clark, Fresh Prince of Bel Air, Sister Sister. *Movies*: Alice in Wonderland, Combat High, Camp Cucamonga.

HENDERSON, FLORENCE
Actress, Singer. b. Dale, IN, Feb. 14, 1934. e. AADA. Made B'way debut while teenager in musical Wish You Were Here.
THEATER: Oklahoma!, The Great Waltz, Fanny, The Sound of Music, The Girl Who Came to Supper, South Pacific. *Tour:* Annie Get Your Gun.
PICTURES: Song of Norway, Shakes the Clown, Naked Gun 33 1/3: The Final Insult, The Brady Bunch Movie, Holy Man (cameo), Get Bruce (cameo).
TELEVISION: *Series:* Sing Along, The Jack Paar Show, Oldsmobile Music Theatre, The Brady Bunch, The Brady Bunch Hour, The Brady Brides, Florence Henderson's Home Cooking, The Bradys. *Movies:* The Love Boat (pilot), The Brady Girls Get Married, A Very Brady Christmas, Fudge-A-Mania. *Guest:* Car 54 Where Are You?, Garry Moore Show, Ed Sullivan Show, Medical Center, The Love Boat, Fantasy Island, It's Garry Shandling's Show, Police Squad, many others. *Specials:* Huck Finn, Little Women, An Evening With Richard Rodgers.

HENDERSON, SKITCH
Music Director. r.n. Lyle Cedric Henderson. b. Birmingham, England, Jan. 27, 1918. e. U. of California. Began as pianist in dance bands, then theatre orchestras, films and radio on West Coast. Accompanist to Judy Garland on tour. Served, USAF, WW II. Music dir. radio, Bing Crosby. Toured with own dance band, 47-49. Music Dir. for NBC Network, Steve Allen Show, Tonight Show, Today Show, Street Scene (NY Opera). Guest conductor, symphony orchestras including NY Philharmonic, London Philharmonic. Founder and Music Dir., NY Pops Orchestra. Music Dir., Florida Orchestra Pops, Virginia Symphony Pops, Louisville Orchestra Pops. Grammy Award for RCA album NY Philharmonic with Leontyne Price and William Warfield, highlights from Porgy and Bess. Instrumental works: Skitch's Blues, Minuet on the Rocks, Skitch in Time, Come Thursday, Curacao. Scores: American Fantasy, Act One (film).

HENNER, MARILU
Actress. b. Chicago, IL, Apr. 6, 1952. e. U. of Chicago. Studied singing and dancing, appearing in musicals in Chicago and on Broadway in Over Here and Pal Joey. Autobiography: By All Means Keep on Moving (1994).
PICTURES: Between the Lines (debut, 1977), Blood Brothers, Hammett, The Man Who Loved Women, Cannonball Run II, Johnny Dangerously, Rustler's Rhapsody, Perfect, L.A. Story, Noises Off, Chasers, Grease, Social Security, Chicago, Man on the Moon.
TELEVISION: *Series*: Taxi, Evening Shade, Marilu. *Movies*: Dream House, Stark, Love with a Perfect Stranger, Ladykillers, Chains of Gold, Abandoned and Deceived (co-exec. prod. only), Fight for Justice, Grand Larceny, My Son Is Innocent, For the Future: The Irvine Fertility Scandal. *Mini-series*: Titanic.

HENNING, LINDA
Actress, Singer. b. Toluca Lake, CA, Sept. 16, 1944. Daughter of prod. Paul Henning. e. Cal State Northridge, UCLA. Member of California Artists Radio Theatre.
THEATER: Gypsy, Applause, Damn Yankees, I Do, I Do, Pajama Game, Sugar, Wonderful Town, Fiddler on the Roof, Sound of Music, Vanities, Born Yesterday, Mary, Mary, Bus Stop, etc.
PICTURES: Bye Bye Birdie, Mad About You.
TELEVISION: *Series*: Petticoat Junction, Sliders. *Guest*: Beverly Hillbillies, Happy Days, Mork & Mindy, Double Trouble, Barnaby Jones, The New Gidget, Hunter. *Pilots*: Kudzu, The Circle, Family. *Movie*: The Return of the Beverly Hillbillies.

HENNING, PAUL
Producer, Writer. b. Independence, MO, Sept. 16, 1911. e. Kansas City Sch. of Law, grad. 1932. Radio singer and disc jockey. Also acted, ran sound effects, sang, wrote scripts. To Chicago 1937-38, to write for Fibber McGee and Molly. To Hollywood as writer for Rudy Vallee, 1939. Wrote scripts for Burns and Allen 10 years, including transition radio to TV.
PICTURES: *Writer*: Lover Come Back, Bedtime Story, Dirty Rotten Scoundrels.
TELEVISION: *Series* (creator, writer, prod.): The Bob Cummings Show, The Beverly Hillbillies, Petticoat Junction, Green Acres (exec. prod.)

HENRIKSEN, LANCE
Actor. b. New York, NY, May 5, 1943. Appeared on B'way in The Basic Training of Pavo Hummel, Richard III.
PICTURES: It Ain't Easy (debut, 1972), Dog Day Afternoon, The Next Man, Mansion of the Doomed, Close Encounters of the Third Kind, Damien: Omen II, The Visitor, The Dark End of the Street, Prince of the City, Piranha II: The Spawning, Nightmares, The Right Stuff, Savage Dawn, The Terminator, Jagged Edge, Choke Canyon, Aliens, Near Dark, Deadly Intent, Pumpkinhead, Hit List, The Horror Show, Johnny Handsome, Survival Quest, The Last Samurai, Stone Cold, Comrades in Arms, Delta Heat, Alien^3, Jennifer Eight, Excessive Force, The Outfit, Super Mario Bros., Hard Target, Man's Best Friend, No Escape, Color of Night, The Quick and the Dead, Powder, The Criminal Mind, Profile for Murder, No Contest II, Tarzan (voice), Scream 3.
TELEVISION: *Series*: Millenium. *Guest*: Scene of the Crime, Paul Reiser: Out on a Whim, Tales From the Crypt (Cutting Cards). *Movies*: Return to Earth, Question of Honor, Blood Feud, Reason for Living: The Jill Ireland Story, Wes Craven Presents Mind Ripper, The Day Lincoln Was Shot.

HENRY, BUCK
Actor, Writer. r.n. Henry Zuckerman. b. New York, NY, Dec. 9, 1930. e. Dartmouth Coll. Acted in Life with Father, (tour, 1948), Fortress of Glass, Bernardine, B'way; 1952-54, U.S. Army; No Time for Sergeants (Nat'l. Co.), The Premise, improvisational theatre, off-B'way.
PICTURES: *Actor*: The Secret War of Harry Frigg, Taking Off, The Man Who Fell to Earth, Old Boyfriends, Gloria, Eating Raoul, Aria, Dark Before Dawn, Rude Awakening, Tune in Tomorrow, Defending Your Life, The Player, The Linguini Incident, Short Cuts, Even Cowgirls Get the Blues, Grumpy Old Men Shotgun Freeway: Drives Through Lost L.A., The Real Blonde, Later Life, I'm Losing You, 1999, Curtain Call, Breakfast of Champions. *Actor-Writer*: The Troublemaker, The Graduate, Is There Sex After Death?,Catch-22, Heaven Can Wait (also dir.), First Family (also dir.), To Die For. *Writer*: Candy, The Owl and the Pussycat, What's Up Doc?, The Day of the Dolphin, Protocol.
TELEVISION: *Series (writer)*: Garry Moore Show, Steve Allen Show (also performer), The Bean Show, That Was the Week That Was (also performer), Get Smart (co-creator, story ed.), Captain Nice (also exec. prod.), Alfred Hitchcock Presents (1985, also actor), Quark, The New Show (also performer), Falcon Crest (actor only), Trying Times: Hunger Chic (dir. only), Saturday Night Live. *Guest:* Murphy Brown. *Movies:* Keep the Change, Harrison Bergeron. *Special:* Mastergate.

HENRY, JUSTIN
Actor. b. Rye, NY, May 25, 1971. Debut at age 8 in Kramer vs. Kramer, 1979 for which he received an Academy Award nom.
PICTURES: Kramer vs Kramer, Sixteen Candles, Martin's Day, Sweet Hearts Dance.
TELEVISION: *Movies*: Tiger Town, Andersonville.

HENSON, LISA
Executive. b. 1960. e. Harvard U. Father was performer-puppeteer-director Jim Henson. Joined Warner Bros., 1983, as exec. asst. to head of prod. 1985, named dir. of creative affairs. 1985, promoted to v.p., prod. 1992, became exec. v.p., production. 1993, named pres. of worldwide prod. of Columbia Pictures. 1994, named pres. of Columbia Pictures. Resigned in 1996 to form own production company.

HEPBURN, KATHARINE
Actress. b. Hartford, CT, May 12, 1907. *Author*: The Making of the African Queen (1987), Me: Stories of My Life (1991). Received a record 12 Academy Award nominations for acting.
THEATER: Death Takes a Holiday, The Warrior's Husband, The Lake, The Philadelphia Story, As You Like It, The Millionairess, The Merchant of Venice, The Taming of the Shrew, Measure for Measure, Coco, A Matter of Gravity, West Side Waltz.
PICTURES: A Bill of Divorcement (debut, 1932), Christopher Strong, Morning Glory (Academy Award, 1933). Little Women, Spitfire, The Little Minister, Break of Hearts, Alice Adams, Sylvia Scarlett, Mary of Scotland, A Woman Rebels, Quality Street, Stage Door, Bringing Up Baby, Holiday, The Philadelphia Story, Woman of the Year, Keeper of the Flame, Stage Door Canteen, Dragon Seed, Without Love, Undercurrent, The Sea of Grass, Song of Love, State of the Union, Adam's Rib, The African Queen, Pat and Mike, Summertime, The Iron Petticoat, The Rainmaker, The Desk Set, Suddenly Last Summer, Long Day's Journey Into Night, Guess Who's Coming to Dinner (Academy Award, 1967), The Lion in Winter (Academy Award, 1968), The Madwoman of Chaillot, The Trojan Women, A Delicate Balance, Rooster Cogburn, Olly Olly Oxen Free, On Golden Pond (Academy Award, 1981), Grace Quigley, Love Affair.
TELEVISION: *Movies*: The Glass Menagerie, Love Among the Ruins (Emmy Award, 1975), The Corn Is Green, Mrs. Delafield Wants To Marry, Laura Lansing Slept Here, The Man Upstairs, This Can't Be Love, One Christmas. *Special*: Katharine Hepburn: All About Me (host, co-writer).

HERALD, PETER
Executive. b. Berlin, Germany, Dec. 20, 1930. e. UCLA, B.A. US Gov't. film officer in Europe 8 years. In charge of continental European prod. operation for Walt Disney Prods., 6 years. Supervisory prod. manager, Columbia Pictures, 3 years. Corporate Prod. mgr. Universal 3 years.
PICTURES: *Executive-, Co-, Assoc.-, Line Producer and/or Production Mgr.*: Almost Angels, Magnificent Rebel, Miracle of the White Stallions, Emil and the Detectives, There Was a Crooked Man, Outrageous Fortune, National Lampoon's Class Reunion, Doctor Detroit, D. C. Cab; The Great Waltz, Foul Play, Nightwing, W. W. and the Dixie Dancekings, Mandingo, W. C. Fields and Me, Alex and the Gypsy, Silver Streak, Star Wars, Stick, Married to It, others.

HEREK, STEPHEN
Director. b. San Antonio, TX, Nov. 10, 1958.
PICTURES: Critters (debut, 1986), Bill & Ted's Excellent Adventure, Don't Tell Mom the Babysitter's Dead, The Mighty Ducks, The Three Musketeers, Mr. Holland's Opus, 101 Dalmatians, Holy Man, Tomb Raider.

HERMAN, NORMAN
Producer, Director. b. Newark, NJ. e. Rutgers U., NYU. Was accountant in California; in 1955 switched to film ind., joining American Int'l Pictures. Headed AIP prod. dept. 4 years, incl. prod., post-prod., labor negotiations, supervising story dept., etc. Pres. of Century Plaza Prods. for 9 yrs. Sr. v.p./staff writer DEG, 1986-9; Pres. No. Carolina Studios, 1989-90.
PICTURES: *Prod. except as noted*: Sierra Stranger, Hot Rod Girl, Hot Rod Rumble, Crime Beneath Seas, Look in any Window (exec. prod. mgr.), Tokyo After Dark (also dir., s.p.), Everybody Loves It (dir.), Mondy Teeno (also dir. co-s.p.), Glory Stompers, Three in the Attic (assoc. prod.), Pretty Boy Floyd, Dunwich Horror, Three in the Cellar, Angel Unchained, Psych-Out, Sadismo (s.p.), Bloody Mama, Bunny O'Hare, Killers Three, Frogs (exec. prod.), Planet of Life (s.p.), Blacula, Dillinger (s.p.), Legend of Hell House, Dirty Mary Crazy Larry, Rolling Thunder, In God We Trust (exec. prod.).
TELEVISION: *Writer*: Robert Taylor Detective, Iron Horse, Invaders, Adam 12, Lancer. *Dir.-Prod.*: Hannibal Cobb, You Are the Judge.

HEROUX, CLAUDE
Producer. b. Montreal, Canada, Jan. 26, 1942. e. U. of Montreal. 1979, prod. v.p., Film Plan Intl., Montreal.
PICTURES: Valerie, L'Initiation, L'Amour Humain, Je t'aime, Echoes of a Summer, Jacques Brel Is Alive and Well and Living in Paris, Breaking Point,Born for Hell, Hog Wild, City of Fire, Dirty Tricks, Gas, Visiting Hours, Videodrome, The Funny Farm, Going Berserk, Of Unknown Origin, Covergirl.
TELEVISION: The Park is Mine, Popeye Doyle, Desjardins.

HERRMANN, EDWARD
Actor. b. Washington, DC, July 21, 1943. Raised in Grosse Pointe, MI. e. Bucknell U. Postgrad. Fulbright scholar, London Acad. Music and Dramatic Art 1968-69. Acted with Dallas Theater Center for 4 years.
THEATER: *NY*: The Basic Training of Pavlo Hummel, Moonchildren, Mrs. Warren's Profession (Tony Award, 1976), Journey's End, The Beach House, The Philadelphia Story, Plenty, Tom and Viv, Julius Caesar, Not About Heroes, Life Sentences. London: A Walk in the Woods. Regional: many prods. with Williamstown Playhouse; Harvey, Twelfth Night, Love Letters, Three Sisters, Life Sentences, Psychopathia Sexualis.
PICTURES: Lady Liberty, The Paper Chase, The Day of the Dolphin, The Great Gatsby, The Great Waldo Pepper, The Betsy, Brass Target, Take Down, The North Avenue Irregulars, Harry's War, Reds, Death Valley, A Little Sex, Annie, Mrs. Soffel, The Purple Rose of Cairo, The Man With One Red Shoe, Compromising Positions, The Lost Boys, Overboard, Big Business, Hero (unbilled), Born Yesterday, My Boyfriend's Back, Foreign Student, Richie Rich, Critical Care, Frank Lloyd Wright, A Civil Action, Better Living.
TELEVISION: *Series*: Beacon Hill, Our Century (host), The Practice. *Guest*: M*A*S*H, St. Elsewhere. *Mini-Series*: Freedom Road. *Movies*: Eleanor and Franklin, Eleanor and Franklin: The White House Years, A Love Affair: The Eleanor and Lou Gehrig Story, Portrait of a Stripper, The Gift of Life, Memorial Day, So Proudly We Hail, Sweet Poison, Fire in the Dark, The Face on the Milk Carton, Hostile Waters, The Soul of the Game, Pandora's Clock, Liberty! The American Revolution. *Specials*: Sorrows of Gin, The Private History of The Campaign That Failed, Murrow, Dear Liar, Concealed Enemies, The Return of Hickey, The Beginning of the Firm, Last Act is a Solo, The End of a Sentence, A Foreign Field.

HERSHEY, BARBARA
Actress. r.n. Barbara Herzstein. b. Los Angeles, CA, Feb. 5, 1948. e. Hollywood H.S. m. painter Stephen Douglas. Briefly, in the mid-1970's, acted under the name Barbara Seagull.
PICTURES: With Six You Get Eggroll (debut, 1968), Heaven With a Gun, Last Summer, The Liberation of L.B. Jones, The Baby Maker, The Pursuit of Happiness, Dealing, Boxcar Bertha, Angela (Love Comes Quietly), The Crazy World of Julius Vrooder, Diamonds, You and Me, The Last Hard Men, Dirty Knights' Work, The Stunt Man, Americana, Take This Job and Shove It, The Entity, The Right Stuff, The Natural, Hannah and Her Sisters, Hoosiers, Tin Men, Shy People (Cannes Film Fest. Award, 1987), A World Apart (Cannes Film Fest. Award, 1988), The Last Temptation of Christ, Beaches, Tune in Tomorrow, Defenseless, The Public Eye, Falling Down, Swing Kids, Splitting Heirs, A Dangerous Woman, Last of the Dogmen, Portrait of a Lady (LA Film Critics Award; Natl Society of Film Critics Award) , The Pallbearer, A Soldier's Daughter Never Cries, Frogs for Snakes, Breakfast of Champions, Passion.
TELEVISION: *Series*: The Monroes, From Here to Eternity. *Guest*: Gidget, The Farmer's Daughter, Run for Your Life, The Invaders, Daniel Boone, CBS Playhouse, Chrysler Theatre, Kung Fu, Alfred Hitchcock Presents (1985). *Movies*: Flood, In the Glitter Palace, Just a Little Inconvenience, Sunshine Christmas, Angel on My Shoulder, My Wicked Wicked Ways... The Legend of Errol Flynn, Passion Flower, A Killing in a Small Town (Emmy & Golden Globe Awards, 1990), Paris Trout, Stay the Night, Abraham, The Staircase. *Mini-Series*: A Man Called Intrepid, Return to Lonesome Dove. *Special*: Working.

HERSKOVITZ, MARSHALL
Producer, Director, Writer. b. Philadelphia, PA, Feb. 23, 1952. e. Brandeis U., BA, 1973; American Film Inst., MFA. 1975. Worked as freelance writer, dir., and prod. on several TV shows. Received Humanitas Award, 1983 and Writers Guild award, 1984.
PICTURE: Jack the Bear (dir.), Legends of the Fall (co-prod.), Dangerous Beauty, Executive Search.
TELEVISION: Family (writer, dir.), White Shadow (writer), Special Bulletin (prod., writer, 2 Emmys for writing and dramatic special), thirtysomething (exec. prod., co-writer, dir; 2 Emmy awards for writing and dramatic series, 1988; Also Humanitas Award and Directors Guild Award, 1988 & 1989, Peabody Award, 1989.), My So-Called Life, Relativity, Once and Again.

HERTZ, WILLIAM
Executive. b. Wishek, ND, Dec. 5, 1923. Began theatre career in 1939 with Minnesota Amusement in Minneapolis; 1946 joined Fox West Coast Theatres; theatre mgr., booking dept.; 1965 appointed Los Angeles first-run district mgr.; promoted to Pacific Coast Division Mgr., National General Corp., 1967; v.p. Southern Pacific Div. Mgr., National General Theatres, Inc. 1971. Joined Mann Theatres as dir. of marketing, public relations, 1973-.

HERZFELD, JOHN
Writer, Director, Actor, Producer.
PICTURES: *Writer*: Voices, Hard Feelings, Two of a Kind (also dir.), The Last Winter, Ha-Kala, 2 Days in the Valley, Turbulence.
TELEVISION: *Movies*: Lieutenant Schuster's Wife (actor only), Cannonball (actor only), Shattered Spirits (actor only), Cobra (actor only), On Fire (also actor), Daddy (also dir.), The Ryan White Story (also actor, dir.), The Preppie Murder (also dir.), Casualties of Love: The Long Island Lolita Story (also dir., prod.), Barbara Taylor Bradford's 'Remember,' (also dir.), Don King: Only in America (dir. only, Directors' Guild Award, 1998). *Series*: Tales from the Crypt (dir.)

HERZOG, WERNER
Director, Producer, Writer. r.n. Werner Stipetic. b. Sachrang, Germany, September 5, 1942. e. U. of Munich, Duquesne U., Pittsburgh. Wrote first s.p. 1957; 1961 worked nights in steel factory to raise money for films; 1966, worked for U.S. National Aeronautics and Space Admin.
PICTURES: Signs of Life (debut, 1968), Precautions Against Fanatics, Even Dwarfs Started Small (also composer), Fata Morgana, The Land of Silence and Darkness, Aguirre—Wrath of God, The Great Ecstasy of Woodcarver Steiner, The Mysery of Kasper Hauser, Nobody Wants to Play With Me, How Much Wood Would a Woodchuck Chuck, Heart of Glass, Stroszek, La Soufriere, Nosferatu: The Vampyre (also cameo), Woyzeck, Garlic Is As Good As Ten Mothers (actor), Werner Herzog Eats His Shoe (actor), Fitzcarraldo, Burden of Dreams (actor), Man of Flowers (actor), Tokyo-Ga (actor), Where the Green Ants Dream, Les Gauloises, Cobra Verde, Scream of Stone, Lessons in Darkness, Bride of the Orient (actor), It Isn't Easy Being God (actor), Echoes of a Somber Empire, Burning Heart (actor), Little Dieter Needs to Fly, Mexico, My Best Friend.
TELEVISION: *Movies*: Huie's Sermon, God's Angry Man, Chambre 666, The Dark Glow of the Mountains, Ballad of the Little Soldier, Herdsmen of the Sun, The Transformation of the World Into Music (actor), Death for Five Voices, and many others.

HESSEMAN, HOWARD
Actor. b. Salem, OR, Feb. 27, 1940. Started with the San Francisco group, The Committee and worked as a disc jockey in San Francisco in the late 1960s.
PICTURES: Petulia, Billy Jack, Steelyard Blues, Shampoo, The Sunshine Boys, Jackson County Jail, The Big Bus, The Other Side of Midnight, Silent Movie, Honky Tonk Freeway, Private Lessons, Loose Shoes, Doctor Detroit, This is Spinal Tap, Police Academy 2: Their First Assignment, Clue, My Chauffeur, Flight of the Navigator, Heat, Amazon Women on the Moon, Rubin and Ed, Little Miss Millions, Munchie Strikes Back (voice), Out of Sync, Boys Night Out, Gridlock'd, The Sky is Falling.
TELEVISION: *Series*: WKRP in Cincinnati, One Day at a Time, Head of the Class. *Guest*: Mary Hartman Mary Hartman, Fernwood 2night, George Burns Comedy Week. *Movies*: Hustling, The Blue Knight (pilot), Tail Gunner Joe, The Amazing Howard Hughes, Tarantulas: The Deadly Cargo, The Ghost on Flight 401, The Comedy Company, More Than Friends, Outside Chance, The Great American Traffic Jam, Victims, One Shoe Makes It Murder, Best Kept Secrets, The Diamond Trap, Call Me Anna, Murder in New Hampshire: The Pamela Smart Story, Quiet Killer, Lethal Exposure, High Stakes, On the 2nd Day of Christmas.

HESSLER, GORDON
Producer, Director. b. Berlin, Germany, 1930. e. Reading U., England. Dir., vice pres., Fordel Films, Inc., 1950-58; dir., St. John's Story (Edinborough Film Festival), March of Medicine Series, Dr. Albert Lasker Award; story edit., Alfred Hitchcock Presents 1960-62; assoc. prod., dir., Alfred Hitchcock Hour, 1962; prod., Alfred Hitchcock Hour; prod., dir., Universal TV 1964-66.

PICTURES: The Woman Who Wouldn't Die, The Last Shot You Hear, The Oblong Box, Scream and Scream Again, Cry of the Banshee, Murders of the Rue Morgue, Sinbad's Golden Voyage, Medusa, Embassy, Puzzle, Pray for Death, Rage of Honour, The Misfit Brigade, The Girl in a Swing (also s.p.), Out on Bail, Mayeda, Journey of Honor.
TELEVISION: *Series*: Alfred Hitchcock Presents (1960-62), Alfred Hitchcock Hour, Run for Your Life, Convoy, Bob Hope Chrysler Show, ABC Suspense Movies of the Week, ABC Movies of the Week, Lucas Tanner, Night Stalker, Amy Prentiss, Switch, Kung Fu, Sara, Hawaii Five-O, Blue Knight, Wonder Woman, Master, CHiPs, Tales of the Unexpected, Equilizer. *Pilots*: Tender Warriors.

HESTON, CHARLTON
Actor. b. Evanston, IL, Oct. 4, 1924. e. Northwestern U. Sch. of Speech. Radio, stage, TV experience. Following coll. served 8 yrs. 11th Air Force, Aleutians. After war, dir. and co-starred with wife at Thomas Wolfe Memorial Theatre, Asheville, NC in State of the Union, Glass Menagerie; member, Katharine Cornell's Co., during first year on Broadway; Anthony and Cleopatra, other Bway. plays, Leaf and Bough, Cockadoodle Doo; Studio One (TV): Macbeth, Taming of the Shrew, Of Human Bondage, Julius Caesar. Pres. Screen Actors Guild 1966-71; Member, Natl. Council on the Arts, 1967-72; Trustee: Los Angeles Center Theater Group, American Film Inst. 1971, chmn. 1981-; Received Jean Hersholt Humanitarian award, 1978. Pres., Nat'l Rifle Assoc., 1998-. *Autobiographies:* The Actor's Life (1978), In the Arena (1995).
RECENT THEATER: A Man for All Seasons, The Caine Mutiny (dir., in China).
PICTURES: Dark City (debut, 1950), The Greatest Show on Earth, The Savage, Ruby Gentry, The President's Lady, Pony Express, Arrowhead, Bad for Each Other, The Naked Jungle, The Secret of the Incas, The Far Horizons, Lucy Gallant, The Private War of Major Benson, The Ten Commandments, Three Violent People, Touch of Evil, The Big Country, The Buccaneer, Ben-Hur (Academy Award, 1959), The Wreck of the Mary Deare, El Cid, The Pigeon That Took Rome, 55 Days at Peking, Major Dundee, The Agony and the Ecstasy, The War Lord, The Greatest Story Ever Told, Khartoum, Counterpoint, Planet of the Apes, Will Penny, Number One, Beneath the Planet of the Apes, Julius Caesar, The Hawaiians, The Omega Man, Antony and Cleopatra (also dir.), Skyjacked, Soylent Green, The Three Musketeers, Airport 1975, Earthquake, The Four Musketeers, The Last Hard Men, Midway, Two Minute Warning, Crossed Swords (The Prince and the Pauper), Gray Lady Down, Mountain Men, The Awakening, Mother Lode (also dir.), Almost an Angel (cameo), Solar Crisis, Wayne's World 2 (cameo), Tombstone, True Lies, In the Mouth of Madness, Alaska, Hamlet, Hercules (voice), Alaska: Spirit of the Wild (voice), Illusion Infinity, Gideon's Webb, Armageddon (voice), Any Give Sunday.
TELEVISION: *Series:* The Colbys. *Mini-Series*: Chiefs. *Movies*: The Nairobi Affair, The Proud Men, A Man For All Seasons (also dir.), Original Sin, Treasure Island, The Little Kidnappers, The Crucifer of Blood, Crash Landing: The Rescue of Flight 232, The Avenging Angel, Texas (narrator). *Special*: Charlton Heston Presents the Bible (also writer).

HEWITT, JENNIFER LOVE
Actress. b. Waco, TX, Feb. 21, 1979.
PICTURES: Munchie, Little Miss Millions, Sister Act 2: Back in the Habit, House Arrest, Trojan War, I Know What You Did Last Summer, Telling You, Can't Hardly Wait, I Still Know What You Did Last Summer, The Suburbans, The Adventures of Tom Thumb and Thumbelina (voice), The Hunchback of Notre Dame II, Bunny, Breakers.
TELEVISION: *Movies:* Audrey Hepburn. *Series:* Kids Incorporated, Shaky Ground, The Byrds of Paradise, McKenna, Party of Five, Time of Your Life. *Guest:* Boy Meets World.

HEYER, STEVEN
Executive. b. New York, NY, June 13, 1952. e. Cornell U., BS industrial relations, 1974; Stern Sch. of Business at NYU, MBA, 1976. Various positions with Booz, Allen & Hamilton, finally SVP/managing partner, 1976-92. Pres./COO Young & Rubicam Adv. Worldwide and exec. VP Young & Rubicam, Inc., 1992-94. Pres., Turner Broadcasting Sales Inc., 1994-98. Pres., worldwide sales/mktng./distribution/int'l. networks, Turner Broadcasting System, 1996-98. Pres/COO Turner Broadcasting System Inc., 1998-.

HEYMAN, JOHN
Producer. b. Germany, 1933. e. Oxford U. Started with Independent British Television creating,. writing and producing entertainment and documentary programs. Had 5 top-ten programs 1955-57. Expanded into personal management, forming International Artists, representing Elizabeth Taylor, Richard Burton, Richard Harris, Shirley Bassey, Laurence Harvey, Trevor Howard, among others. In 1963, formed World Film Services Ltd. to produce package and finance films and World Film Sales Ltd., the first major independent film sales co. Co-financed 250 major studio films 1969-91. In 1973, formed Genesis Project. In 1989 co-founded Island World and Islet. Island sold to Polygram, and in 1994, formed World Group of Companies Ltd., parent co. to World Production Ltd.

PICTURES: Privilege, Boom!, Secret Ceremony, Twinky, Bloomfield, The Go-Between (Grand Prix, Cannes 1971), Superstars, Hitler: The Last Ten Days, Black Gunn, Divorce His, Divorce Hers, The Hireling (Grand Prix, Cannes 1973), A Doll's House, Daniel, Beyond the Limit, The Dresser, A Passage to India (co-prod.), Martin's Day, Steaming, D.A.R.Y.L., Saturday Night Fever, Grease, Heaven Can Wait, Home Alone, Reds.

HICKS, CATHERINE
Actress. b. New York NY, Aug. 6, 1951. e. St. Mary's Notre Dame; Cornell U. (2 year classical acting prog.). On B'way. in Tribute, Present Laughter.
PICTURES: Death Valley, Better Late Than Never, Garbo Talks, The Razor's Edge, Fever Pitch, Peggy Sue Got Married, Star Trek IV: The Voyage Home, Like Father Like Son, Child's Play, She's Out of Control, Cognac, Liebestraum, Dillinger and Capone, Eight Days a Week, Turbulence.
TELEVISION: *Series*: Ryan's Hope (1976-8), The Bad News Bears, Tucker's Witch, Winnetka Road, 7th Heaven. *Movies*: Love for Rent, To Race the Wind, Marilyn- the Untold Story, Valley of the Dolls 1981, Happy Endings, Laguna Heat, Spy, Hi Honey I'm Dead, Redwood Curtain. *Pilot*: The Circle Game.

HICKS, SCOTT
Director, Writer, Producer. b. Australia, March 4, 1953.
PICTURES: *Director*: Down the Wind (also prodr.), Freedom, Call Me Mr. Brown (also writer), Sebastian and the Sparrow (also writer & prodr.), Shine (also writer; Golden Globe nom., Acad. Award nom), Snow Falling on Cedars, Arkansas.

HILL, ARTHUR
Actor. b. Melfort, Saskatchewan, Canada, Aug. 1, 1922. e. U. of British Columbia. Moved to England in 1948, spending ten years in varied stage & screen pursuits
THEATER: *B'way*: The Matchmaker, Home of the Brave, The Male Animal, Look Homeward Angel, All the Way Home, Who's Afraid of Virginia Woolf? (Tony Award, 1963), More Stately Mansions.
PICTURES: Miss Pilgrim's Progress, Scarlet Thread, Mr. Drake's Duck, A Day to Remember, Life With the Lyons, The Crowded Day, The Deep Blue Sea, Raising a Riot, The Young Doctors, The Ugly American, In the Cool of the Day, Moment to Moment, Harper, Petulia, The Chairman, Rabbit Run, The Pursuit of Happiness, The Andromeda Strain, The Killer Elite, Futureworld, A Bridge Too Far, A Little Romance, Butch and Sundance: The Early Days, The Champ, Dirty Tricks, Making Love, The Amateur, Something Wicked This Way Comes (narrator), One Magic Christmas.
TELEVISION: *Series*: Owen Marshall: Counselor-At-Law, Hagen, Glitter. *Movies*: The Other Man, Vanished, Ordeal, Owen Marshall: Counselor at Law (pilot; a.k.a. A Pattern of Morality), Death Be Not Proud, Judge Horton and the Scottsboro Boys, Tell Me My Name, The Ordeal of Dr. Mudd, Revenge of the Stepford Wives, The Return of Frank Cannon, Angel Dusted, Tomorrow's Child, Intimate Agony, Prototype, Love Leads the Way, Murder in Space, Churchill and the Generals, The Guardian, Perry Mason: The Case of the Notorious Nun.

HILL, BERNARD
Actor: b. Manchester, England,, Dec. 17, 1944. Joined amateur dramatic society in Manchester then studied drama at Manchester Art Coll. Joined Liverpool Everyman rep. co. West End debut as John Lennon in John, Paul, George, Ringo... and Burt. Also in Normal Service, Shortlist, Twelfth Night, Macbeth, Cherry Orchard, Gasping, A View From the Bridge.
PICTURES: Gandhi, The Bounty, The Chain, Restless Natives, No Surrender, Bellman and True, Drowning by Numbers, Shirley Valentine, Mountains of the Moon, Double X: The Name of the Game, Skallagrigg, Madagascar Skin, The Ghost and the Darkness, The Wind in the Willows, Titanic, The Mill on the Floss, A Midsummer Night's Dream, Blessed Art Thou, True Crime, The Loss of Sexual Innocence, The Red Door.
TELEVISION: I Claudius, Squaring the Circle, John Lennon: A Journey in the Life, New World, St. Luke's Gospel, Boys from the Blackstuff, Burston Rebellion, Great Expectations.

HILL, DEBRA
Producer, Director, Writer. b. Philadelphia, PA. Career on feature films started with work as script supvr., asst. dir. and 2nd unit dir. of 13 pictures. Producer's debut with Halloween, 1980, for which also co-wrote script with dir. John Carpenter.
PICTURES: Halloween (also co-s.p.), The Fog (and co-s.p.), Escape from New York, Halloween II (and co-s.p.), Halloween III: Season of the Witch, The Dead Zone, Clue, Head Office, Adventures in Babysitting, Big Top Pee-wee, Heartbreak Hotel, The Fisher King, Escape From L.A., The Replacement Killers, Crazy in Alabama.
TELEVISION: Adventures in Babysitting (pilot, exec. prod.), Monsters (dir. episodes), Dream On (dir. episodes). *Movies*: El Diablo, Attack of the 50 Ft. Woman. *Rebel Highway Film Series*: Roadracers, Confessions of a Sorority Girl (also co-writer), Dragstrip Girl, Shake Rattle and Roll, The Cool and the Crazy, Runaway Daughters, Motocycle Gang, Drag Strip Girl, Reform School Girl, Jailbreakers (also co-writer), Girls in Prison.

HILL, GEORGE ROY
Director. b. Minneapolis, MN, Dec. 20, 1921. e. Yale U., Trinity Coll., Dublin. Started as actor, Irish theatres and U.S. Margaret Webster's Shakespeare Repertory Co., also off-B'way. Served as Marine pilot in WWII and Korean War. Wrote TV play, My Brother's Keeper, for Kraft Theatre, later rose to dir. with show.
THEATER: Look Homeward Angel (B'way debut, 1957), The Gang's All Here, Greenwillow, Period of Adjustment, Moon on a Rainbow Shawl (also prod.), Henry Sweet Henry.
PICTURES: Period of Adjustment (debut, 1962), Toys in the Attic, The World of Henry Orient, Hawaii, Thoroughly Modern Millie, Butch Cassidy and the Sundance Kid, Slaughterhouse Five, The Sting (Academy Award, 1973), The Great Waldo Pepper (also prod., story), Slap Shot, A Little Romance (also co-exec. prod.), The World According to Garp (also co-prod., cameo), The Little Drummer Girl, Funny Farm.
TELEVISION: *Writer-Dir.*: A Night to Remember, The Helen Morgan Story, Judgment at Nuremberg, Child of Our Time.

HILL, TERENCE
Actor, Director. r.n. Mario Girotti. b. Venice, March 29, 1939. Debuted as actor under his real name. First attracted attention as actor in Visconti's The Leopard, 1963. Gained fame in European-made westerns. Formed Paloma Films.
PICTURES: *as Mario Girotti:* Vacanze col Gangster (debut, 1951), Villa Borghese, Il Viale della speranza, La Vena d'oro, The Wide Blue Road, Mary Magdalene, Anna of Brooklyn, Hannibal, Pecado de amor, Carthage in Flames, Joseph and His Brethren, The Wonders of Aladdin, Seven Seas to Calais, The Leopard, Games of Desire, Last of the Renegades, Arizona Wildcat, Duell vor Sonnenuntergang, Ruf de Walder, Rampage at Apache Wells, Flaming Frontier, Whom the Gods Destroy, Blood River; *as Terence Hill:* The Crazy Kids of the War, Io non protesto io amo, Preparati la bara!, Rita in the West, God Forgives I Don't, Viva Django, Boot Hill, Ace High, Barbagia, Blackie the Pirate, Anger of the Wind, They Call Me Trinity, The True and the False, A Reason to Live a Reason to Die, Trinity Is Still My Name, Man of the East, Baron Blood, All the Way Boys!, My Name Is Nobody, The Two Missionaries, The Genius, Crime Busters, Mr. Billion, March or Die, Odds & Evens, I'm for the Hippopotamus, Super Fuzz, Watch Out We're Mad, Double Trouble, Don Camillo (also dir.), Miami Supercops, Renegade Luke (also exec. prod.), Go for It!, Lucky Luke (also dir.), The F(N)ight Before Christmas (also dir.), Botte di Natale, Troublemakers.

HILL, WALTER
Director, Writer, Producer. b. Long Beach, CA, Jan. 10, 1942. e. Michigan State U.; Mexico City College; U. of the Americas.
PICTURES: *Writer*: Hickey and Boggs, Thief Who Came to Dinner, The Getaway (1972), The Mackintosh Man, The Drowning Pool, Blue City (also prod.), Alien 3 (also prod.), The Getaway (1993; co-s.p.). *Writer/Dir.*: Hard Times, The Driver, The Warriors, Southern Comfort, 48 HRS, Streets of Fire (also exec. prod.), Red Heat (also prod.). *Director*: The Long Riders, Brewster's Millions, Crossroads, Extreme Prejudice, Johnny Handsome, Another 48 HRS, Trespass, Geronimo: An American Legend (also co-prod.), Wild Bill, Last Man Standing. *Other*: Alien (prod.), Aliens (exec. prod., story), Tales From the Crypt Presents Demon Knight (co-exec. prod.).
TELEVISION: *Series*: Dog and Cat (creator, writer), Tales From the Crypt (exec. prod.; also dir. & writer of episodes: The Man Who Was Death, Cutting Cards, Deadline (Cable ACE Award, Best Dir.).

HILLER, ARTHUR
Director. b. Edmonton, Alberta, Can., Nov. 22, 1923. e. U. of Alberta, U. of Toronto, U. of British Columbia. Worked for Canadian Broadcasting Corp. as dir. of live tv before moving to L.A. Pres. of DGA. 1993, became pres. of AMPAS. Appeared in Beverly Hills Cop III.
PICTURES: The Careless Years (debut, 1957), Miracle of the White Stallions, The Wheeler Dealers, The Americanization of Emily, Promise Her Anything, Penelope, Tobruk, The Tiger Makes Out, Popi, The Out-of-Towners, Love Story, Plaza Suite, The Hospital, Man of La Mancha, The Crazy World of Julius Vrooder (also co-prod.), The Man in the Glass Booth, W. C. Fields and Me, Silver Streak, Nightwing, The In-Laws (also co-prod.), Making Love, Author Author, Romantic Comedy, The Lonely Guy (also prod.), Teachers, Outrageous Fortune, See No Evil Hear No Evil, Taking Care of Business, The Babe, Married to It, Beverly Hills Cop III (actor only), Wild Bill: A Hollywood Maverick (actor only), Carpool, An Alan Smithee Film: Burn Hollywood Burn.
TELEVISION: Matinee Theatre, Playhouse 90, Climax, Alfred Hitchcock Presents, Gunsmoke, Ben Casey, Rte. 66, Naked City, The Dick Powell Show, Roswell (actor only), Frank Capra's American Dream (actor only).

HILLER, DAME WENDY
Actress. D.B.E., 1975, O.B.E., 1971, Hon. LLD, Manchester, 1984. b. Bramhall, Cheshire, Eng., Aug. 15, 1912. e. Winceby House Sch., Bexhill. On stage 1930, Manchester Repertory Theatre, England; then on British tour. London debut 1935 in Love On the Dole; to N.Y., same role 1936. m.p. debut in Lancashire Luck, 1937.
THEATER: First Gentleman, Cradle Song, Tess of the D'Urbervilles, Heiress (NY & London), Ann Veronica, Waters of the Moon, Night of the Ball, Old Vic Theatre, Wings of the Dove, Sacred Flame, Battle of Shrivings, Crown Matrimonial, John Gabriel Borkman, Waters of the Moon (revival), Aspern Papers (revival), The Importance of Being Earnest, Driving Miss Daisy.
PICTURES: Lancashire Luck (debut, 1937), Pygmalion, Major Barbara, I Know Where I'm Going, Outcast of the Islands, Single Handed (Sailor of the King), Something of Value, How to Murder a Rich Uncle, Separate Tables (Academy Award, best supporting actress, 1958) Sons and Lovers, Toys in the Attic, A Man For All Seasons, Murder on the Orient Express, Voyage of the Damned, The Cat and the Canary, The Elephant Man, Making Love, The Lonely Passion of Judith Hearne.
TELEVISION: The Curse of King Tut's Tomb, David Copperfield (theatrical in U.K.), Witness for the Prosecution, Anne of Green Gables-The Sequel, Peer Gynt, The Kingfisher, All Passion Spent, A Taste for Death, Ending Up, The Best of Friends, The Countess Alice.

HILLERMAN, JOHN
Actor. b. Denison, TX, Dec. 20, 1932. e. U. of Texas. While in U.S. Air Force joined community theatre group and went to New York after completing military service. Studied at American Theatre Wing, leading to summer stock and off-B'way.
PICTURES: The Last Picture Show, Lawman, The Carey Treatment, What's Up Doc?, Skyjacked, High Plains Drifter, The Outside Man, The Thief Who Came to Dinner, Paper Moon, Blazing Saddles, Chinatown, At Long Last Love, The Nickel Ride, The Day of the Locust, Lucky Lady, Audrey Rose, Sunburn, History of the World Part I, Up the Creek, A Very Brady Sequel.
TELEVISION: *Series*: Ellery Queen, The Betty White Show, Magnum P.I. (Emmy Award, 1987), The Hogan Family, Berlin Break. *Movies*: Sweet Sweet Rachel, The Great Man's Whiskers, The Law, Ellery Queen, The Invasion of Johnson County, Relentless, Kill Me If You Can, A Guide for the Married Woman, Betrayal, Marathon, The Murder That Wouldn't Die, Little Gloria... Happy at Last, Assault and Matrimony, Street of Dreams, Hands of a Murderer. *Mini-Series*: Around the World in 80 Days.

HILLMAN, WILLIAM BRYON
Writer, Director, Producer. b. Chicago, IL, Feb. 3, 1951. e. Oklahoma Military Acad., UCLA. Head of production at Intro-Media Prod.; Fairchild Ent.; Spectro Prod.; Double Eagle Ent. Corp; Excellent Films Inc.; Creative consultant for The Hit 'Em Corp. Presently head of SpectroMedia Ent.
AUTHOR: *Novels:* Silent Changes, The Combination, The Liar, Additives The Perfect Crime, Why Me, The Loner.
PICTURES: *Dir.-Writer*: His Name is Joey (also exec. prod.), Tis the Season (also co-prod.), Strangers (also co-prod.), Back on the Street (also co-prod.), Loner (also co-prod.), Fast & Furious, The Master, Lovelines (s.p. only), Double Exposure (also co-prod.), The Passage, Campus, The Photographer (also prod.), The Man From Clover Grove (also co-prod.), Thetus, The Trail Ride (also co-prod.), Betta Betta (also prod.), Ragin' Cajun (also co-prod.).
TELEVISION: Working Together (pilot writer), Disco-Theque Pilot (dir., writer), Everything Will Be Alright (writer), Money (dir., writer), RIPA (writer).

HINDERY, LEO JOSEPH , JR.
Media Co. Executive. b. Springfield, Ill, Oct. 31, 1947. e. Seattle U, BA 1969; Stanford U, MBA 1971. With US army, 1968-70. Asst. treas., Utah Internat, 1971-80. Treas. Natomas Co., 1980-82. Exec. v.p. fin. Jefferies & Co., 1982-83. Chief fin. officer A.G. Becker Paribas, 1983-85. Chief officer. planning & fin. Chronicle Pub. Co., 1985-88. Mng. gen. ptnr. Intermedia Ptnrs., 1988-. Bd. dirs.: Certus Fin. Corp.; Trustee Seattle U. Mem., Olympic club.

HINES, GREGORY
Actor, Dancer. b. NY, Feb. 14, 1946. Early career as junior member of family dancing act starting at age 2. Nightclub debut at 5 as Hines Kids with brother Maurice (later renamed Hines Brothers as teenagers) and joined by father as Hines, Hines and Dad. B'way debut at 8 in The Girl in Pink Tights. Continued dancing with brother until 1973. Formed and performed with jazz-rock band, Severance. Solo album, Gregory Hines (1988).
THEATER: The Last Minstral Show (closed out of town). B'way: Eubie (Theatre World Award), Comin' Uptown (Tony nom.), Sophisticated Ladies (Tony nom.), Twelfth Night, Jelly's Last Jam (Tony Award, 1992).
PICTURES: History of the World Part 1 (debut, 1981), Wolfen, Deal of the Century, The Muppets Take Manhattan, The Cotton Club (also choreog.), White Nights, Running Scared, Off Limits, Tap (also choreog.), Eve of Destruction, A Rage in Harlem, Renaissance Man, Waiting to Exhale, Mad Dog Time, The Preacher's Wife., Good Luck, The Tic Code
TELEVISION: *Movies*: White Lie, T Bone N Weasel, Dead Air, A Stranger in Town, The Cherokee Kid, Subway Stories: Tales from the Underground, Color of Justice. *Guest*: Motown Returns to the Apollo. *Series*: The Gregory Hines Show.

HINGLE, PAT
Actor. b. Miami, FL, July 19, 1924. e. U. of Texas, 1949. Studied at Herbert Berghof Studio, American Theatre Wing, Actor's Studio.
THEATER: End as a Man (N.Y. debut, 1953), The Rainmaker, Festival, Cat on a Hot Tin Roof, Girls of Summer, Dark at the Top of the Stairs, J.B., The Deadly Game, Macbeth and Troilus and Cresida (with American Shakespeare Festival, Stratford, CT), Strange Interlude, Blues for Mr. Charlie, A Girl Could Get Lucky, The Glass Menagerie, The Odd Couple, Johnny No-Trump, The Price, Child's Play, The Selling of the President, That Championship Season, The Lady from the Sea, A Life, Thomas Edison: Reflections of a Genius (one man show).
RADIO: Voice of America.
PICTURES: On the Waterfront (debut, 1954), The Strange One, No Down Payment, Splendor in the Grass, All the Way Home, The Ugly American, Invitation to a Gunfighter, Nevada Smith, Sol Madrid, Hang 'em High, Jigsaw, Norwood, Bloody Mama, WUSA, The Carey Treatment, One Little Indian, Running Wild, Nightmare Honeymoon, The Super Cops, The Gauntlet, When You Comin' Back Red Ryder?, Norma Rae, America: Lost and Found (narrator), Sudden Impact, Running Brave, Going Berserk, The Falcon and the Snowman, Brewster's Millions, Maximum Overdrive, Baby Boom, The Land Before Time (voice), Batman, The Grifters, Batman Returns, Lightning Jack, The Quick and the Dead, Batman Forever, Larger Than Life, Batman & Robin, A Thousand Acres.
TELEVISION: *Series*: Stone. *Guest*: Gunsmoke, MASH, Blue Skies, Matlock, Twilight Zone, The Untouchables, Trapper John M.D., Murder She Wrote, In the Heat of the Night, Cheers, Wings, American Gothic. *Movies*: The Ballad of Andy Crocker, A Clear and Present Danger, The City, Sweet Sweet Rachel, If Tomorrow Comes, Trouble Comes to Town, The Last Angry Man, The Secret Life of John Chapman, Escape from Bogen County, Sunshine Christmas, Tarantulas, Elvis, Stone (pilot), Disaster at the Coastliner, Wild Times, Of Mice and Men, Washington Mistress, The Fighter, Stranger on My Land, The Town Bully, Everybody's Baby: The Rescue of Jessica McClure, Not of This World, Gunsmoke: To the Last Man, Citizen Cohn, The Habitation of Dragons, Simple Justice, Against Her Will: The Carrie Buck Story, Truman. *Mini-Series*: War and Remembrance, The Kennedy's of Massachusetts, The Shining.

HINKLE, ROBERT
Actor, Producer, Director. b. Brownfield, TX, July 25, 1930. e. Texas Tech. U. Joined Rodeo Cowboys Association, 1950 and rodeoed professionally until 1953 when began acting career in Outlaw Treasure. Pres. Cinema Pictures, Inc.
PICTURES: *Actor*: Giant, All the Fine Young Cannibals, Hud, The First Texan, Dakota Incident, Gun the Man Down, The Oklahoman, First Traveling Saleslady, No Place to Land, Under Fire, Speed Crazy, The Gunfight at Dodge City, Broken Land, Law in Silver City, *Producer-Director*: Ole Rex, Born Hunter, Trauma, Something Can Be Done, Mr. Chat, Stuntman, Jumping Frog Jubilee, Mr. Chat-Mexico Safari, Trail Ride, Virginia City Cent., Texas Today, Texas Long Horns, Kentucky Thoroughbred Racing, Country Music, Guns of a Stranger.
TELEVISION: *Prod. & Dir.*: Test Pilot, Dial 111, Juvenile Squad, X13 Vertijet, Cellist Extraordinary, Sunday Challenge, The Drifter, Country Music Tribute, World of Horses, Country Music Videos.

HIRD, DAME THORA
Actress. b. Morecambe, Lancashire, England,, May 28, 1911. e. The Nelson Sch., Morecambe.
PICTURES: (Screen debut, 1940) The Black Sheep of Whitehall; Street Corner, Turn the Key Softly, Personal Affair, The Great Game, Storks Don't Talk, Shop Soiled, For Better or Worse; Love Match, One Good Turn, Quatermass Experiment, Simon and Laura, Lost, Sailor Beware, Home and Away, Good Companions, The Entertainer, A Kind of Loving, Term of Trial, Bitter Harvest, Rattle of a Simple Man, Some Will Some Won't, The Nightcomers, Consuming Passions.
TELEVISION: The Winslow Boy, The Bachelor, What Happens to Love, The Witching Hour, So Many Children, The Queen Came By, Albert Hope, All Things Bright and Beautiful, Say Nothing, Meet the Wife, Who's a Good Boy Then? I AM! Dixon of Dock Green, Romeo and Juliet, The First Lady, Ours Is a Nice House, The Foxtrot, Seasons, She Stoops to Conquer, Villa Maroc, When We Are Married, In Loving Memory, Flesh and Blood, Your Songs of Praise Choice, Hallelujah, Happiness, That's the Main Thing, Intensive Care, In Loving Memory, Praise Be, Last of the Summer Wine, The Fall, Cream Cracker Under the Settee (Talking Heads), Perfect Scoundrels, Wide Eyed and Legless... It's a Girl, Pat & Margaret, Thora on the Broad 'n' Narrow... South Bank Show.

HIRSCH, JUDD
Actor. b. New York, NY, March 15, 1935. e. City Coll. of New York. Studied physics but turned to acting; studied at Amer. Acad. of Dramatic Arts., HB Studios. First acting job in 1962 in Crisis in the Old Sawmill in Estes, Colorado; then to Woodstock Playhouse, before returning to N.Y.C.
THEATER: *NY*: On the Necessity of Being Polygamous, Barefoot in the Park, Scuba Duba, Mystery Play, HotL Baltimore, King of the United States, Prodigal, Knock Knock, Chapter Two, Talley's Folly (Obie Award), I'm Not Rappaport (Tony Award), Conversations With My Father (Tony Award).
PICTURES: Serpico (debut, 1973), King of the Gypsies, Ordinary People (Acad. Award nom.), Without a Trace, The Goodbye People, Teachers, Running on Empty, Independence Day, Man on the Moon.
TELEVISION: *Series*: Delvecchio, Taxi (2 Emmy Awards: 1981, 1983), Detective in the House, Dear John, George & Leo. *Movies*: The Law, Fear on Trial, Legend of Valentino, The Keegans, Sooner or Later, Marriage is Alive and Well, Brotherly Love, First Steps, The Great Escape II: The Untold Story, She Said No, Betrayal of Trust, Color of Justice, Rocky Marciano. *Special:* The Halloween That Almost Wasn't.

HIRSCHFIELD, ALAN J.
Executive. b. Oklahoma City, OK; Oct.10, 1935. e. U. of Oklahoma, B.A.; Harvard Business School, M.B.A. V.P., Allen & Co., 1959-66; Financial v.p. & dir. Warner/7 Arts, 1967-68; v.p. & dir., American Diversified Enterprises, 1969-73; pres. & chief exec. officer, Columbia Pictures Industries, 1973-78; consultant, Warner Communications, 1979, 1980-85, chmn. and chief exec. officer, 20th Century-Fox. Current: Co-CEO Data Broadcasting Corp. Dir., Cantel Inc., Chyron Corp.

HIRSHAN, LEONARD
Theatrical Agent. b. New York, NY, Dec.27, 1927. e. NYU. Joined William Morris Agency as agent trainee, New York, 1951. Agent legit theatre & TV dept. 1952-54. Sr. exec. agent M.P. dept., California office, 1955; sr. v.p., 1983; head of m.p. dept., west coast, 1986; named exec. v.p. and mem. bd. of dir., William Morris Agency, 1989; mem. bd. of dir., Center Theater Group, 1988; bd. governors Cedars-Sinai Hospital in L.A. 1987.

HIRSCHHORN, JOEL
Composer. b. Bronx, NY, Dec. 18, 1937. e. HS for the Performing Arts, Hunter Col.
PICTURES: *Songs* (with collaborator Al Kasha): The Fat Spy, The Cheyenne Social Club, The Poseidon Adventure (Academy Award for best song: The Morning After, 1972), The Towering Inferno (Acad. Award for best song: We May Never Love Like This Again, 1974), Freaky Friday, Pete's Dragon, Hot Lead Cold Feet, The North Avenue Irregulars, All Dogs Go to Heaven, Rescue Me, Hungry For You
TELEVISION: *Series:* Kids Inc., First and Ten, Getting in Touch, The Challengers. *Specials:* Kingdom Chums, A Precious Moments Christmas, The Magic Paintbrush, Caddie Woodlawn. *Movies:* Trapped Beneath the Sea, Someone I Touch, Charles Dickens' David Copperfield.

HITZIG, RUPERT
Producer, Director. b. New York, NY, Aug. 15, 1942. e. Harvard. At CBS as doc. writer-prod.-dir.; later moved into dramas and comedy. Alan King's partner in King-Hitzig Prods.
PICTURES: *Prod.*: Electra Glide in Blue, Happy Birthday Gemini, Cattle Annie and Little Britches, Wolfen (also 2nd unit dir.), Jaws 3-D, The Last Dragon, The Squeeze. Dir.: Night Visitor, Backstreet Dreams, The Legend of O.B. Taggart, Last Lives (dir.), Nowhere Land.
TELEVISION: Much Ado About Nothing, The Wonderful World of Jonathan Winters, Playboy After Dark, How to Pick Up Girls, Return to Earth, Saturday Night Live, Birds of Prey, Date My Dad, Save Our Streets, Snakes and Ladders (prod., dir.), annual comedy awards, television series and numerous specials.

HOBERMAN, DAVID
Executive. b. 1953. Started career as prod. exec. with TAT Communications for five years. 1982-85, worked as m.p. agent with Writers and Artists Agency and later at Ziegler Associates and ICM. 1985, named v.p. of prod. for Walt Disney Pictures based at studio. 1987, promoted to sr. v.p., prod. 1988, named president, production. 1989, pres. Touchstone Pictures. 1994, appointed head of all motion pictures produced by Walt Disney. Resigned from Disney, 1995, to form Mandeville Films. Produced George of the Jungle, 1997. Produced The 6th Man, 1997.

HOCK, MORT
Executive. Blaine-Thompson Agency; A. E. Warner Bros., 1948; David Merrick B'way Prod., 1958; asst. adv. mgr., Paramount Pictures Corp., 1960; adv. mgr., United Artists Corp., 1962; dir. adv., UA Corp., 1964; adv. dir., Paramount, 1965; v.p. adv. & public rltns., Paramount, 1968-71; v.p., marketing, Rastar Prods., 1971; exec. v.p., Charles Schlaifer & Co., 1974; sr. v.p. entertainment div., DDB Needham Worldwide, 1983; exec. v.p. DDB, 1994.

HODGE, PATRICIA
Actress. b. Cleethorpes, Lincolnshire, England, Sept. 29, 1946. Studied at London Acad. of Music and Dramatic Arts.
THEATER: Popkiss, Two Gentlemen of Verona, Pippin, The Mitford Girls, Benefactors, Noel and Gertie, Separate Tables, The Prime of Miss Jean Brodie.
PICTURES: The Elephant Man, Betrayal, Sunset, Thieves in the Night, Diamond's Edge.

TELEVISION: The Naked Civil Servant, Rumpole of the Bailey, Edward and Mrs. Simpson, Holding the Fort, Jemima Shore Investigates, Hay Fever, Hotel Du Lac, The Life and Loves of a She-Devil, Exclusive Yarns, Let's Face the Music of..., Inspector Morse, The Shell Seekers, The Secret Life of Ian Fleming, The Heat of the Day, Rich Tea and Sympathy, The Cloning of Joanna May.

HOFFMAN, DUSTIN
Actor. b. Los Angeles, CA, Aug. 8, 1937. m. Lisa Hoffman. e. Los Angeles Conservatory of Music, Santa Monica Coll., Pasadena Playhouse, 1958. Worked as an attendant at a psychiatric institution, a demonstrator in Macy's toy dept., and a waiter. First stage role 1960 in Yes Is for a Very Young Man at Sarah Lawrence Coll. Acted in summer stock, television and dir. at community theatre. Asst. dir. Off-B'way of A View From the Bridge. Recipient of the Golden Globe Cecil B. DeMille Award, 1997.
THEATER: *B'way and Off B'way*: A Cook for Mr. General (bit part, B'way debut), Harry Noon and Night, Journey of the Fifth Horse (Obie Award), Eh? (Vernon Rice & Theatre World Awards), Jimmy Shine, All Over Town (dir. only), Death of a Salesman (Drama Desk Award), The Merchant of Venice (also London).
PICTURES: The Tiger Makes Out (debut, 1967), Madigan's Millions, The Graduate, Midnight Cowboy, John and Mary, Little Big Man, Who Is Harry Kellerman and Why Is He Saying Those Terrible Things About Me?, Straw Dogs, Alfredo Alfredo, Papillon, Lenny, All the President's Men, Marathon Man, Straight Time, Agatha, Kramer vs. Kramer (Academy Award, 1979), Tootsie, Ishtar, Rain Man (Academy Award, 1988), Family Business, Dick Tracy, Billy Bathgate, Hook, Hero, Outbreak, American Buffalo, Sleepers, Mad City, Wag the Dog, Sphere, Being John Malkovich, The Messenger: The Story of Joan of Arc, Cosm.
TELEVISION: *Specials*: Journey of the Fifth Horse, The Star Wagons, Free to Be You and Me, Bette Midler: Old Red Hair Is Back, Common Threads: Stories from the Quilt (narrator), The Earth Day Special. Movies: The Point (narrator), Death of a Salesman (Emmy Award, 1985). *Guest*: Naked City, The Defenders, The Simpsons (voice).

HOFFMAN, PHILIP SEYMOUR
Actor. b. Fairport, NY, July 23, 1967.
PICTURES: Triple Bogey On A Par Five Hole, My New Gun, Szuler, Scent of a Woman, Leap of Faith, My Boyfriend's Back, Money for Nothing, Joey Breaker The Getaway, The Yearling, Nobody's Fool, When A Man Loves A Woman, The Fifteen Minute Hamlet, Twister, Hard Eight, Boogie Nights, Montana, Next Stop Wonderland, The Big Lebowski, Happiness, Patch Adams, Culture, Flawless, Magnolia, The Talented Mr. Ripley, State And Main, Almost Famous, Last Party 2000.

HOGAN, HULK
Actor. r.n. Terry Gene Bollea. b. Augusta, GA, Aug. 11, 1953. Former bodyguard then prof. wrestler using names Sterling Golden, Terry Boulder, Hulk Hogan, finally Hollywood Hogan.
PICTURES: Rocky III (debut, 1982), No Holds Barred, Gremlins 2: The New Batch, Suburban Commado, Mr. Nanny, Spy Hard, The Secret Agent Club, Santa with Muscles, McCinsey's Island, 3 Ninjas: High Noon at Mega Mountain, Muppets From Space.
TELEVISION: *Series:* Hulk Hogan's Rock 'n' Wrestling (voice), Thunder in Paradise (also exec. prod.). *Pilot:* Goldie and the Bears. *Guest:* The A-Team, The Love Boat.

HOGAN, PAUL
Actor, Writer. b. Lightning Ridge, New South Wales, Australia, Oct. 8, 1939. m. actress Linda Kozlowski. Worked as rigger before gaining fame on Australian TV as host of nightly current affairs show (A Current Affair) and The Paul Hogan Show. Shows now syndicated in 26 countries. In U.S. gained attention with commercials for Australian Tourist Commission. 1985, starred in dramatic role on Australian TV in series, Anzacs. Live one-man show, Paul Hogan's America, 1991.
PICTURES: Fatty Finn (debut, 1980), Crocodile Dundee (also co-s.p.), Crocodile Dundee II (also exec. prod., co-s.p.), Almost an Angel (also exec. prod., s.p.), Lightning Jack (also s.p., co-prod.), Flipper.
TELEVISION: Anzacs: The War Down Under.

HOLBROOK, HAL
Actor. r.n. Harold Rowe Holbrook Jr. b. Cleveland, OH, Feb. 17, 1925. m. actress Dixie Carter. e. Denison U., 1948. Summer stock 1947-53. Gained fame and several awards for performance as Mark Twain on stage in Mark Twain Tonight over a period of years throughout the US and abroad.
THEATER: Mark Twain Tonight (Tony Award, 1966), Do You Know the Milky Way?, Abe Lincoln in Illinois, American Shakespeare Fest., Lincoln Center Repertory (After the Fall, Marco Millions, Incident at Vichy, Tartuffe), The Glass Menagerie, The Apple Tree, I Never Sang For My Father, Man of La Mancha, Does a Tiger Wear a Necktie?, Lake of the Woods, Buried Inside Extra, The Country Girl, King Lear. Regional: Our Town, The Merchant of Venice, Uncle Vanya, Eye of God.
PICTURES: The Group (debut, 1966), Wild in the Streets, The People Next Door, The Great White Hope, They Only Kill Their Masters, Jonathan Livingston Seagull (voice), Magnum Force, The Girl From Petrovka, All the President's Men, Midway, Julia, Rituals (The Creeper), Capricorn One, Natural Enemies, The Fog, The Kidnapping of the President, Creepshow, The Star Chamber, Girls Night Out (The Scaremaker), Wall Street, The Unholy, Fletch Lives, The Firm, Carried Away, Hercules (voice), Cats Don't Dance, Eye of God, Judas Kiss, Hush, The Florentine, Navy Diver.
TELEVISION: *Series*: The Bold Ones: The Senator (Emmy Award, 1971), Designing Women, Portrait of America (4 annual ACE Awards, 2 Emmy Awards, 1988, 1989), Evening Shade, Hercules (voice). *Movies*: Coronet Blue, The Whole World is Watching, A Clear and Present Danger, Travis Logan, Suddenly Single, Goodbye Raggedy Ann, That Certain Summer, Murder by Natural Causes, Legend of the Golden Gun, When Hell Was in Session, Off the Minnesota Strip, The Killing of Randy Webster, Under Siege, Behind Enemy Lines, Dress Gray, The Fortunate Pilgrim, Three Wishes for Billy Grier, Emma, Queen of the South Seas, Day One, Sorry Wrong Number, A Killing in a Small Town, Bonds of Love, A Perry Mason Mystery: The Case of the Lethal Lifestyle, A Perry Mason Mystery: The Case of the Grimacing Governor, A Perry Mason Mystery: The Case of the Jealous Jokester, She Stood Alone: The Tailhook Scandal, Beauty. *Specials*: Mark Twain Tonight, Pueblo (Emmy Award, 1974), Sandburg's Lincoln (Emmy Award, 1976), Our Town, Plaza Suite, The Glass Menagerie, The Awakening Land, The Oath: 33 Hours in the Life of God, Omnibus. *Mini-Series*: North and South Books I & II, Celebrity, George Washington, Rockport Christmas, Lewis & Clark: The Journey of the Corps of Discovery, The Third Twin.

HOLDRIDGE, LEE
Composer. b. Port-au-Prince, Haiti, March 3, 1944. e. Manhattan School of Music. Music arranger for Neil Diamond, 1969-73, with whom he collaborated on the score for Jonathan Livingston Seagull. Wrote score for B'way musical Into the Light (1986). With Alan Raph wrote score for the Joffrey Ballet's Trinity. One-act opera for L.A. Opera commission: Journey to Cordoba.
PICTURES: Jeremy, Jonathan Livingston Seagull, Forever Young Forever Free, Mustang Country, The Other Side of the Mountain—Part 2, The Pack, Moment By Moment, Oliver's Story, French Postcards, Tilt, American Pop, The Beastmaster, Mr. Mom, Micki and Maude, Splash, Sylvester, 16 Days of Glory, Transylvania 6-5000, The Men's Club, Big Business, Old Gringo, Pastime, Freefall, The Long Way Home.
TELEVISION: *Series*: One Life to Live, Hec Ramsey, Moonlighting, Beauty and the Beast, Bob. *Movies*: East of Eden, Fly Away Home, The Day the Loving Stopped, For Ladies Only, The Sharks, The Story Lady, One Against the Wind, In Love With an Older Woman, Running Out, Thursday's Child, Wizards and Warriors, The Mississippi, Legs, I Want to Live, Letting Go, Fatal Judgment, The Tenth Man, I'll Take Manhattan, Do You Know the Muffin Man?, Incident at Dark River, A Mother's Courage, In the Arms of a Killer, Face of a Stranger, Deadly Matrimony, Killer Rules, One Against the Wind, Call of the Wild, Torch Song, Barcelona '92: 16 Days of Glory, Jack Reed: Badge of Honor, Incident in a Small Town, The Yearling, Heidi, Texas, Buffalo Girls, The Tuskegee Airmen, Nothing Lasts Forever, Twilight of the Golds, Into Thin Air.

HOLLAND, AGNIESZKA
Director, Writer. b. Warsaw, Poland, Nov. 28, 1948. e. FAMU, Prague. m. dir. Laco Adamik. Studied filmmaking in Czechoslovakia. Worked in Poland with dir. Andrzej Wajda. Moved to Paris in 1981.
PICTURES: *Dir./s.p.*: Screen Tests, Provincial Actors, Bez Znieczulenia (s.p. only), A Woman Alone (co-s.p.), Danton (co-s.p.), Interrogation (actor only), A Love in Germany (co-s.p.), Angry Harvest (co-s.p.), Anna (only s.p., story), Les Possedes (only co-s.p.), La Amiga (only co-s.p.), To Kill a Priest (co-s.p.), Korczak (s.p. only), Europa Europa, Olivier Olivier, Three Colors: Blue (s.p. only)The Secret Garden (dir. only), Total Eclipse (dir. only), Washington Square (dir. only).
TELEVISION: *Movies*: Evening With Abdon, The Children of Sunday, Something for Something, Lorenzaccio, The Trial, Largo Desolato. *Series*: Fallen Angels (dir. only).

HOLLAND, TODD
Director.
PICTURES: The Wizard, Krippendorf's Tribe.
TELEVISION: *Series*: Amazing Stories, Vietman War Story, Max Headroom, Tales from the Crypt, Twin Peaks, Eerie Indiana, Bill & Ted's Excellent Adventures, The Larry Sanders Show (Emmy Award, 1998), My So-Called Life, Friends, Maximum Bob, Felicity.

HOLLAND, TOM
Director, Writer. b. Highland, NY, July 11, 1945. e. Northwestern U. Started as actor, working at Bucks County Playhouse in PA and HB Studios in NY. Appeared on daytime serials Love of Life, Love is a Many-Splendored Thing. Turned to commercial prod. while attended UCLA law school, then took up screenwriting.

PICTURES: *Writer*: The Beast Within, The Class of 1984, Pyscho II (also actor), Scream for Help, Cloak and Dagger. *Director*: Fright Night (also s.p.), Fatal Beauty, Child's Play (also co-s.p.), The Temp, Stephen King's Thinner (also s.p.).
TELEVISION: *Movie*: The Stranger Within. *Series*: Tales From the Crypt (dir. 3 episodes: Love Come Hack to Me-also co-writer, Four-Sided Triangle-also co-writer, King of the Road). *Mini-Series*: Stephen King's The Langoliers (also writer, actor).

HOLLIMAN, EARL
Actor. b. Delhi, LA, Sept. 11, 1928. e. U. of Southern California, Pasadena Playhouse. Pres., Actors and Others for Animals.
THEATER: Camino Real (Mark Taper Forum), A Streetcar Named Desire (Ahmanson).
PICTURES: Scared Stiff, The Girls of Pleasure Island, Destination Gobi, East of Sumatra, Devil's Canyon, Tennessee Champ, The Bridges at Toko-Ri, Broken Lance, The Big Combo, I Died a Thousand Times, Forbidden Planet, Giant, The Burning Hills, The Rainmaker, Gunfight at the OK Corral, Trooper Hook, Don't Go Near the Water, Hot Spell, The Trap, Last Train From Gun Hill, Visit to a Small Planet, Armored Command, Summer and Smoke, The Sons of Katie Elder, A Covenant With Death, The Power, Anzio, The Biscuit Eater, Good Luck Miss Wyckoff, Sharky's Machine.
TELEVISION: *Series*: Hotel de Paree, Wide Country, Police Woman, P.S. I Luv You, Delta. *Pilot*: Twilight Zone. *Movies*: Tribes, Alias Smith and Jones, Cannon, The Desperate Mission, Trapped, Cry Panic, I Love You... Goodbye, Alexander: The Other Side of Down, The Solitary Man, Where the Ladies Go, Country Gold, Gunsmoke: Return to Dodge, American Harvest, P.S. I Luv You (pilot). *Mini-Series*: The Thorn Birds. *Specials*: The Dark Side of the Earth, The Return of Ansel Gibbs.

HOLLOWOOD, ANN
Costume Designer.
PICTURES: Nightbreed, The Second Jungle Book: Mowgli & Baloo.
TELEVISION: *Movies*: Tears in the Rain, The Old Man and the Sea. *Mini-series*: The Storyteller, The Storyteller: Greek Myths, Merlin (Emmy Award, 1998).

HOLLY, LAUREN
Actress. b. Bristol, PA, October 28, 1963.
PICTURES: Seven Minutes in Heaven, Band of the Hand, The Adventures of Ford Fairlane, Dragon: The Bruce Lee Story, Dumb & Dumber, Sabrina, Beautiful Girls,Down Periscope, Turbulence, A Smile Like Yours, No Looking Back, Entropy, Any Given Sunday
TELEVISION: *Series*: All My Children, The Antagonists, Picket Fences. *Movies*: Archie: To Riverdale and Back Again, Fugitive Among Us, Dangerous Heart, Vig. *Guest:* Spenser For Hire.

HOLM, CELESTE
Actress. b. New York, NY, Apr. 29, 1919. e. Univ. Sch. for Girls, Chicago, Francis W. Parker, Chicago, Lyceae Victor Durui (Paris), U. of Chicago, UCLA. p. Theodor Holm and Jean Parke Holm. m. actor Wesley Addy.
THEATER: *B'way*: Gloriana, The Time of Your Life, 8 O'Clock Tuesday, Another Sun, Return of the Vagabond, My Fair Ladies, Papa Is All, All the Comforts of Home, The Damask Cheek, Oklahoma!, Bloomer Girl, She Stoops to Conquer, Affairs of State, Anna Christie, The King and I, Interlock, Third Best Sport, Invitation to a March, Mame, Candida, Habeas Corpus, The Utter Glory of Morrissey Hall, I Hate Hamlet. *Off-B'way*: A Month in the Country. Theatre-in-Concert for the U.S. State Department in 8 countries May-July 1966. *Regional*: Janet Flanner's Paris Was Yesterday. Natl. Tour: Mame (Sarah Siddons Award), Hay Fever, Road to Mecca, Cocktail Hour.
PICTURES: Three Little Girls in Blue (debut, 1946), Carnival in Costa Rica, Gentleman's Agreement (Academy Award, best supporting actress, 1947), Road House, The Snake Pit, Chicken Every Sunday, Come to the Stable (Acad. Award nom.), A Letter to Three Wives (voice), Everybody Does It, Champagne for Caesar, All About Eve (Acad. Award nom.), The Tender Trap, High Society, Bachelor Flat, Doctor You've Got To Be Kidding, Tom Sawyer, Bittersweet Love, The Private Files of J. Edgar Hoover, Three Men and a Baby.
TELEVISION: *Specials*: A Clearing in the Wood, Play of the Week, Cinderella, Nora's Christmas Gift. *Mini-Series*: Backstairs at the White House (Emmy nom.). *Movies*: Underground Man, Death Cruise, Love Boat II, Midnight Lace, The Shady Hill Kidnapping, This Girl for Hire, Murder by the Book, Polly, Polly-Comin' Home! *Pilot*: Road Show. *Series*: Honestly Celeste, Who Pays, Nancy, Jessie, Falcon Crest, Christine Cromwell, Loving, Promised Land. *Guest*: Love Boat, Trapper John M.D., Magnum P.I.

HOLM, IAN
C.B.E. Actor. r.n. Ian Holm Cuthbert. b. Ilford, Essex, England, Sept. 12, 1931. e. RADA. On British stage in Love Affair, Titus Andronicus, Henry IV, Ondine, Becket, The Homecoming (B'way: Tony Award, 1967), Henry V, Richard III, Romeo and Juliet, The Sea.
PICTURES: The Bofors Gun (debut, 1968), A Midsummer Night's Dream, The Fixer, Oh! What a Lovely War, A Severed Head, Nicholas and Alexandra, Mary Queen of Scots, Young Winston, The Homecoming, Juggernaut, Robin and Marian, Shout at the Devil, March or Die, Alien, Chariots of Fire (Acad. Award nom.), Time Bandits, Return of the Soldier, Greystoke: The Legend of Tarzan Lord of the Apes, Dance With a Stranger, Wetherby, Dreamchild, Brazil, Laughterhouse, Another Woman, Henry V, Hamlet, Kafka, Naked Lunch, The Advocate, Mary Shelley's Frankenstein, The Madness of King George, Big Night, Night Falls On Manhattan, The Fifth Element, The Sweet Hereafter, A Life Less Ordinary, Joe Gould's Secret, eXistenZ, The Match, The Lord of the Rings: The Fellowship of the Ring.
TELEVISION: *Mini-Series/Movies*: Les Miserables, S.O.S. Titanic, Napoleon, We the Accused, All Quiet on the Western Front, Holocaust, Man in the Iron Mask, Jesus of Nazareth, Thief of Bagdad, Game Set and Match, A Season of Giants, The Borrowers, The Miracle Maker (voice), Alice Through the Looking Glass, Animal Farm (voice). *Specials*: The Browning Version, Murder By the Book, Uncle Vanya, Tailor of Gloucester, The Lost Boys, The Last Romantics.

HOLMES, KATIE
Actress. r.n. Kate Noelle Holmes. b. Toledo, OH, Dec. 18, 1978.
PICTURES: The Ice Storm, Disturbing Behavior, Wonder Boys, Go, Muppets From Space, Teaching Mrs. Tingle.
TELEVISION: *Series:* Dawson's Creek. *Guest:* Fanatic.

HOMEIER, SKIP
Actor. r.n. George Vincent Homeier. b. Chicago, IL, Oct. 5, 1930. e. UCLA. Started in radio, 1936-43; on B'way stage, Tomorrow the World, 1943-44 which led to film debut in adaptation of same (billed as Skippy Homeier).
PICTURES: Tomorrow the World (debut, 1944), Boys' Ranch, Mickey, Arthur Takes Over, The Big Cat, The Gunfighter, Halls of Montezuma, Fixed Bayonets, Sealed Cargo, Sailor Beware, Has Anybody Seem My Gal?, The Last Posse, The Lone Gun, Beachhead, Black Widow, Dawn at Socorro, Ten Wanted Men, The Road to Denver, At Gunpoint, Cry Vengeance, The Burning Hills, Between Heaven and Hell, Dakota Incident, No Road Back, Stranger at My Door, Thunder Over Arizona, The Tall T, Lure of the Swamp, Decision at Durango, Day of the Badman, Journey Into Darkness, The Punderers of Painted Flats, Commanche Station, Showdown, Bullet for a Badman, Stark Fear, The Ghost and Mr. Chicken, Dead Heat on a Merry-Go-Round, Tiger By the Tail, The Greatest.
TELEVISION: *Series*: Dan Raven, The Interns. *Guest*: Playhouse 90, Alcoa Hour, Kraft Theatre, Studio 1, Armstrong Circle Theatre, Alfred Hitchcock. *Movies*: The Challenge, Two for the Money, Voyage of the Yes, Helter Skelter, Overboard, The Wild Wild West Revisited. *Mini-Series*: Washington: Behind Closed Doors.

HOOKS, KEVIN
Actor, Director. b. Philadelphia, PA, Sept. 19, 1958. Son of actor-dir. Robert Hooks.
PICTURES: Sounder, Aaron Loves Angela, A Hero Ain't Nothin' But a Sandwich, Take Down, Innerspace, Strictly Business (also dir.), Passenger 57 (dir. only), Fled, Glory & Honor (also dir.), Black Dog (dir. only).
TELEVISION: *Series*: The White Shadow, He's the Mayor. *Movies*: Just an Old Sweet Song, The Greatest Thing That Almost Happened, Friendly Fire, Can You Hear the Laughter?-The Story of Freddie Prinze, Roots: The Gift (dir.), Murder Without Motive: The Edmund Perry Story (dir.). *Mini-Series*: Backstairs at the White House. *Special*: Home Sweet Homeless (dir.).

HOOKS, ROBERT
Actor, Director, Producer. b. Washington, D.C., April 18, 1937. Father of actor-dir. Kevin Hooks. Co-founder and exec. dir. Negro Ensemble Co. NY 1967-present. Founder DC Black Repertory Company, 1970-77. Co-star of TV series NYPD, 1967-69.
THEATER: *B'way*: A Raisin In the Sun (B'way debut, 1960), A Taste of Honey, Tiger Tiger Burning Bright, Arturo Ui, The Milktrain Doesn't Stop Here Anymore, Where's Daddy? (Theatre World Award for last two), Hallelujah, Baby?. *Off B'way.*: The Blacks, Dutchman, Happy Ending, Day of Absence, Henry V, Ballad for Bimshire, Kongi's Harvest. A Soldier's Play (Mark Taper Forum, LA). *Co-prod.* (with Gerald S. Krone): Song of the Lusitanian Bogey, Daddy Goodness, Ceremonies in Dark Old Men, Day of Absence, The Sty of the Blind Pig, The River Niger, The First Breeze of Summer.
PICTURES: Sweet Love Bitter, Hurry Sundown, The Last of the Mobile Hot-Shots, Trouble Man, Aaron Loves Angela, Airport '77, Fast-Walking, Star Trek III: The Search For Spock, Passenger 57, Posse, Fled, Glory and Honor, Free of Eden.
TELEVISION: *Series*: N.Y.P.D., Supercarrier, Seinfeld, Parenthood, Family Matters, Different World, Murder She Wrote. *Pilots*: The Cliff Dweller, Two for the Money, Down Home. *Movies*: Carter's Army, Vanished, The Cable Car Murder, Crosscurrent, Trapped, Ceremonies in Dark Old Men, Just an Old Sweet Song, The Killer Who Wouldn't Die, The Courage and the Passion, To Kill a Cop, A Woman Called Moses, Hollow Image, Madame X, The Oklahoma City Dolls, The Sophisticated Gents, Cassie and Co., Starflight-The Plane that Couldn't Land, Feel the Heat, Sister Sister, The Execution.

HOOL, LANCE
Producer, Director. b. Mexico City, Mex., May 11, 1948. e. Univ. of the Americas.
PICTURES: *Producer*: Cabo Blanco, Ten to Midnight, The Evil That Men Do, Missing in Action (also s.p.), Missing in Action 2 (dir.), Steel Dawn (also dir.), Options, Damned River, Pure Luck, The Air Up There, Gunmen, Road Flower, Flipper, McHale's Navy, One Man's Hero.
TELEVISION: The Tracker, Born To Run, Cover Girl Murders, Flashfire.

HOOPER, TOBE
Director. b. Austin, Texas, Jan. 25, 1943. e. Univ. of TX. Began film career making documentary and industrial films and commercials in Texas. Was asst. dir. of U. of Texas film program, continuing filmmaking while working with students. First feature film: documentary Peter Paul & Mary, followed by Eggshells. Directed Billy Idol video Dancing With Myself.
PICTURES: The Texas Chainsaw Massacre (also prod., co-s.p.), Eaten Alive (Death Trap), The Funhouse, Poltergeist, Lifeforce, Invaders from Mars, The Texas Chainsaw Massacre Part 2 (also co-prod., co- music), Spontaneous Combustion, Sleepwalkers (actor only), Night Terrors, The Mangler (also co-s.p.).
TELEVISION: *Movie*: I'm Dangerous Tonight. *Mini-Series*: Salem's Lot. *Series episodes*: Amazing Stories, Freddy's Nightmares (No More Mr. Nice Guy-1st episode), Equalizer (No Place Like Home), Tales from the Crypt (Dead Wait), Nowhere Man, Dark Skies. *Pilots*: Haunted Lives, Body Bags.

HOPE, BOB
Actor. r.n. Leslie Townes Hope. b. Eltham, England, May 29, 1903. To U.S. at age 4; raised in Cleveland, OH. Became American citizen in 1920. Was amateur boxer before appearing in vaudeville as comedian/song and dance man. Debuted on B'way 1933 in Roberta, followed by stage work in Ziegfeld Follies, Red Hot & Blue. Began film career 1934, appearing in 8 short films made in NY, before going to Hollywood for feature debut, 1938, signing contract with Paramount. Starred on radio, 1938-56; made countless trips overseas to entertain U.S. troops during wartime; lent name to Bob Hope Desert Classic golf tournament. Voted one of top ten Money-Making Stars in M.P. Herald-Fame Poll: 1941-47, 1949-53. Recipient: 5 special Academy Awards (1940, 1944, 1952, 1959, 1965); special Emmy Awards: Trustees Award (1959), Governors Award (1984); Kennedy Center Honors (1985); Presidential Medal of Freedom, and many other awards. Author (or-co-author): They Got Me Covered, I Never Left Home, So This Is Peace, Have Tux Will Travel, I Owe Russia $1,200, Five Women I Love: Obit Hope's Vietnam Story, The Last Christmas Show, The Road to Hollywood: My 40-Year Love Affair With the Movies, Confessions of a Hooker: My Lifelong Love Affair With Golf, Don't Shoot It's Only Me.
PICTURES: The Big Broadcast of 1938 (feature debut, 1938), College Swing, Give Me a Sailor, Thanks for the Memory, Never Say Die, Some Like It Hot, The Cat and the Canary, Road to Singapore, The Ghost Breakers, Road to Zanzibar, Caught in the Draft, Louisiana Purchase, My Favorite Blonde, Road to Morocco, Nothing But the Truth, They Got Me Covered, Star Spangled Rhythm, Let's Face It, Road to Utopia, The Princess and the Pirate, Monsieur Beaucaire, My Favorite Brunette, Where There's Life, Road to Rio, The Paleface, Sorrowful Jones, The Great Lover, Fancy Pants, The Lemon Drop Kid, My Favorite Spy, Son of Paleface, Road to Bali, Off Limits, Scared Stiff (cameo), Here Come the Girls, Casanova's Big Night, The Seven Little Foys, That Certain Feeling, The Iron Petticoat, Beau James, Paris Holiday (also prod., story), Alias Jesse James (also prod.), The Five Pennies (cameo), The Facts of Life, Bachelor in Paradise, The Road to Hong Kong, Call Me Bwana, A Global Affair, I'll Take Sweden, The Oscar (cameo), Boy Did I Get a Wrong Number!, Not With My Wife You Don't (cameo), Eight on the Lam, The Private Navy of Sgt. O'Farrell, How to Commit Marriage, Cancel My Reservation (also exec. prod.), The Muppet Movie (cameo), Spies Like Us (cameo).
TELEVISION: *Series*: Chesterfield Sound Off Time, Colgate Comedy Hour (rotating host), Bob Hope Presents the Chrysler Theatre (Emmy Award as exec. prod. and host, 1966). *Movie*: A Masterpiece of Murder. Many specials incl. prod. of Roberta, annual variety shows; also was frequent host of annual Academy Award telecast.

HOPE, TED
Producer. b. 1962.
PICTURES: Tiger Warsaw (assoc.), The Unbelievable Truth, (1st asst. dir.), Theory of Achievement, Surviving Desire, Ambition, Pushing Hands (Tui Shou), I Was on Mars (also actor), Simple Men, The Wedding Banquet, Roy Cohn/Jack Smith, Eat Drink Man Woman, (assoc.), Amateur, Safe (exec.), The Brothers McMullen (exec.), Flirt, Walking and Talking, She's the One, Little Cobras, Arresting Gena, The Myth of Fingerprints (exec. prod.), The Ice Storm, Office Killer, Love God, No Looking Back, The Lifestyle (exec.), Ride with the Devil.
TELEVISION: Punch and Judy Get Divorced.

HOPKINS, SIR ANTHONY
C.B.E.: Actor. r.n. Philip Anthony Hopkins. b. Port Talbot, South Wales, Dec. 31, 1937. Trained at Royal Acad. of Dramatic Art; Welsh Coll. of Music & Drama. Joined National Theatre, gaining fame on stage in England, then TV and films. Appeared in short The White Bus. Recordings: Under Milk Wood (1988), Shostakovich Symphony No. 13 Babi Yar (reciting Yevtushenko's poem, 1994). Dir. An Evening With Dylan Thomas, 1993. Received special award at Montreal Film Festival for Career Excellence, 1992; Evening Standard Film Awards Special Award for Body of Work, 1994; BAFTA Britannia Award for Outstanding Contribution to the International Film and TV Industry, 1995.
THEATER: Julius Caesar (debut, 1964), Juno and the Paycock, A Flea in Her Ear, The Three Sisters, Dance of Death, As You Like It, The Architect and the Emperor of Assyria, A Woman Killed With Kindness, Coriolanus, The Taming of the Shrew, Macbeth, Equus (NY, 1974-75; Outer Critics Circle, NY Drama Desk, US Authors & Celebrities Forum Awards), Equus (LA 1977, also dir.; LA Drama Critics Award), The Tempest, Old Times, The Lonely Road, Pravda (Variety Club Stage Actor Award, 1985; British Theatre Association Best Actor, Laurence Olivier & Observer Awards), King Lear, Antony and Cleopatra, M. Butterfly, August (also dir.).
PICTURES: The Lion in Winter (debut, 1967), The Looking Glass War, Hamlet, When Eight Bells Toll, Young Winston, A Doll's House, The Girl from Petrovka, Juggernaut, Audrey Rose, A Bridge Too Far, International Velvet, Magic, The Elephant Man, A Change of Seasons, The Bounty (Variety Club UK Film Actor Award, 1983), 84 Charing Cross Road (Moscow Film Fest. Award, 1987), The Good Father, The Dawning, A Chorus of Disapproval, Desperate Hours, The Silence of the Lambs (Academy Award, Natl. Board of Review, NY Film Critics, Boston Film Critics & BAFTA Awards, 1991), Freejack, One Man's War, Howards End, The Efficiency Expert (Spotswood), Bram Stoker's Dracula, Chaplin, The Remains of the Day (BAFTA, Variety Club UK Film Actor, LA Film Critics, Japan Critics Awards, 1993), The Trial, Shadowlands (Natl. Board of Review & LA Film Critics Award, 1993), The Road to Wellville, Legends of The Fall, The Innocent, August (also dir.), Nixon, Surviving Picasso, The Edge, Amistad, Meet Joe Black, The Mask of Zorro, Instinct, Titus.
TELEVISION: A Heritage and Its History, Vanya, Hearts and Flowers, Decision to Burn, War & Peace, Cuculus Canorus, Lloyd George, QB VII, Find Me, A Childhood Friend, Possessions, All Creatures Great and Small, The Arcata Promise, Dark Victory, The Lindbergh Kidnapping Case (Emmy Award, 1976), Victory at Entebbe, Kean, Mayflower: The Pilgrim's Adventure, The Bunker (Emmy Award, 1981), Peter and Paul, Othello, Little Eyolf, The Hunchback of Notre Dame, A Married Man, Corridors of Power, Strangers and Brothers, Arch of Triumph, Mussolini and I / Mussolini: The Rise and Fall of Il Duce (ACE Award), Hollywood Wives, Guilty Conscience, Blunt, The Dawning, Across the Lake, Heartland, The Tenth Man, Great Expectations, One Man's War, To Be the Best, A Few Selected Exits, Big Cats.

HOPKINS, BO
Actor. b. Greenwood, SC, Feb. 2, 1942. Studied with Uta Hagen in N.Y. then with Desilu Playhouse training school in Hollywood. Parts in several prods. for that group won him an agent, an audition with dir. Sam Peckinpah and his first role in latter's The Wild Bunch.
PICTURES: The Wild Bunch (debut, 1969), Monte Walsh, The Moonshine War, The Culpepper Cattle Co., The Getaway, White Lightning, The Man Who Loved Cat Dancing, American Graffiti, The Nickel Ride, The Day of the Locust, Posse, The Killer Elite, A Small Town in Texas, Tentacles, Midnight Express, More American Graffiti, The Fifth Floor, Sweet Sixteen, Night Shadows, Trapper Country, What Comes Around, War, The Bounty Hunter, The Stalker, Nightmare at Noon, The Tenth Man, Big Bad John, Center of the Web, Inside Monkey Zetterland, The Ballad of Little Jo, Cheyenne Warrior, Radioland Murders, Riders in the Storm, The Feminine Touch.
TELEVISION: *Series*: Doc Elliott, The Rockford Files, Dynasty. *Movies*: The Runaway Barge, Kansas City Massacre, Charlie's Angels (pilot), The Invasion of Johnson County, Dawn: Portrait of a Teenage Runaway, Thaddeus Rose and Eddie, Crisis in Sun Valley, Plutonium Incident, A Smoky Mountain Christmas, Beggerman Thief, Down the Long Hills, Last Ride of the Dalton Gang, Casino, Rodeo Girl, Ghost Dancing, Blood Ties. *Special*: Wyatt Earp: Return to Tombstone.

HOPPER, DENNIS
Actor, Director. b. Dodge City, KS, May 17, 1936. e. San Diego, CA, public schools. *Author:* Out of the Sixties (1988; book of his photographs).
PICTURES: Rebel Without a Cause, I Died a Thousand Times, Giant, The Steel Jungle, The Story of Mankind, Gunfight at the OK Corral, From Hell to Texas, The Young Land, Key Witness, Night Tide, Tarzan and Jane Regained Sort Of, The Sons of Katie Elder, Queen of Blood, Cool Hand Luke, Glory Stompers, The Trip, Panic in the City, Hang 'Em High, True Grit, Easy Rider (also dir., co-s.p.), The Last Movie (also dir., s.p.), Kid Blue, James Dean-The First American Teenager, Bloodbath (The Sky Is Falling), Mad Dog Morgan, Tracks, The American Friend,

Douleur Chair, The Sorcerer's Appentices, L'Ordre et la Securite du Monde, Resurrection, Apocalypse Now, Out of the Blue (also dir.), King of the Mountain, Renacida, White Star, Human Highway, Rumble Fish, The Osterman Weekend, My Science Project, The Texas Chainsaw Massacre Part 2, Hoosiers (Acad. Award nom.), Blue Velvet, Black Widow, River's Edge, Straight to Hell, The Pick Up Artist, O.C. and Stiggs, Riders of the Storm, Blood Red, Colors (dir. only), Flashback, Chattachoochee, The Hot Spot (dir. only), Superstar: The Life and Times of Andy Warhol, The Indian Runner, Hearts of Darkness: A Filmmaker's Apocalypse, Midnight Heat, Eye of the Storm, Boiling Point, Super Mario Bros., True Romance, Red Rock West, Chasers (also dir.), Speed, Search and Destroy, Waterworld, Acts of Love, Basquiat, Carried Away, Star Truckers, The Blackout, Tycus, Meet the Deedles, The Source, The Prophet's Game, Lured Innocence, Jesus' Son, Bad City Blues, EDtv, Straight Shooter.
TELEVISION: *Movies*: Wild Times, Stark, Paris Trout, Doublecrossed, Backtrack (also dir.), Nails, The Heart of Justice, Witch Hunt. *Guest*: Pursuit, Espionage, Medic, Loretta Young Show, King of the Hill (voice).

HORN, ALAN
Executive. b. 1944. e. M.B.A., Harvard Bus. Sch. Began career in brand management with Proctor & Gamble, then five years in the U.S. Air Force, rank of Captain. Entered entertainment as an executive for Tandem Prods., T.A.T. Communications, and as CEO for Embassy Communications (with Norman Lear and Jerry Perenchio), 1973-87. Co-founder, chairman & CEO, Castle Rock Entertainment, 1987-99. Named president & CEO, Warner Bros. Pictures, 1999.

HORNE, LENA
Singer, Actress. b. Brooklyn, NY, June 30, 1917. Radio with Noble Sissle, Charlie Barnet, other bands. Floor shows at Cotton Club, Cafe Society, Little Troc. Started screen career 1942. Appeared in short subjects Harlem Hotshots, Boogie Woogie Dream. Autobiographies: In Person (1950), Lena (1965) Recipient Kennedy Center Honors for Lifetime contribution to the Arts, 1984. Spingarn Award, NAACP, 1983; Paul Robeson Award, Actors Equity Assn., 1985.
THEATER: Blackbirds, Dance With Your Gods, Jamaica, Pal Joey (L.A. Music Center), Lena Horne: The Lady and Her Music (Tony Award).
PICTURES: The Duke Is Tops (debut, 1938), Panama Hattie, Cabin in the Sky, Stormy Weather, I Dood It, Thousands Cheer, Broadway Rhythm, Swing Fever, Two Girls and a Sailor, Ziegfeld Follies, Till the Clouds Roll By, Words and Music, Duchess of Idaho, Meet Me in Las Vegas, Death of a Gunfighter, The Wiz, That's Entertainment III.
TELEVISION: *Guest*: Music '55, Perry Como Show, Here's to the Ladies, The Flip Wilson Show, Dean Martin Show, Sesame Street, Ed Sullivan Show, Sanford & Sons, Laugh-In, Hollywood Palace, The Cosby Show. *Specials*: The Lena Horne Show (1959), The Frank Sinatra Timex Show, Lena in Concert, Harry and Lena, The Tony & Lena Show, Lena Horne: The Lady and Her Music.

HORNER, JAMES
Composer. b. Los Angeles, CA, Aug. 14, 1953. e. Royal Col. of Music: London, USC, UCLA. Received Grammy Awards for the song Somewhere Out There (from the film An American Tail), and for instrumental composition from Glory.
PICTURES: The Lady in Red, Battle Beyond the Stars, Humanoids From the Deep, Deadly Blessing, The Hand, Wolfen, The Pursuit of D.B. Cooper, 48 HRS, Star Trek II: The Wrath of Khan, Something Wicked This Way Comes, Krull, Brainstorm, Testament, Gorky Park, The Dresser, Uncommon Valor, The Stone Boy, Star Trek III: The Search for Spock, Heaven Help Us, Cocoon, Volunteers, Journey of Natty Gann, Commando, Aliens, Where the River Runs Black, The Name of the Rose, An American Tail, P.K. and the Kid, Project X, Batteries Not Included, Willow, Red Heat, Vibes, Cocoon: The Return, The Land Before Time, Field of Dreams, Honey I Shrunk the Kids, Dad, Glory, I Love You to Death, Another 48 HRS., Once Around, My Heroes Have Always Been Cowboys, Class Action, The Rocketeer, An American Tail: Fievel Goes West, Thunderheart, Patriot Games, Unlawful Entry, Sneakers, Swing Kids, A Far Off Place, Jack the Bear, Once Upon a Forest, Searching for Bobby Fischer, The Man Without a Face, Bopha!, The Pelican Brief, Clear and Present Danger, Legends of the Fall, Braveheart, Casper, Apollo 13 (Acad. Award nom.), Jumanji, Courage Under Fire, Ransom, To Gillian on Her 37th Birthday, Titanic (Acad. Award, Best Dramatic Score, Best Orig. Song, Golden Globe Award, Best Orig. Score, Best Orig. Song, Chicago Film Crits. Award, Best Musical Score, 1997), The Devil's Own, Deep Impact, The Mask of Zorro, Mighty Joe Young, Bicentennial Man.

HORSLEY, LEE
Actor. b. Muleshoe, TX, May 15, 1955. e. U. of No. Colorado. On stage in Mack and Mabel, West Side Story, Sound of Music, Oklahoma!, Forty Carats, 1776, Damn Yankees.
PICTURE: The Sword and the Sorcerer, Unlawful Passage.
TELEVISION: *Series*: Nero Wolfe, Matt Houston, Guns of Paradise, Bodies of Evidence, Hawkeye. *Mini-series*: Crossings, North and South Book II. *Movies*: The Wild Women of Chastity Gulch, Infidelity, When Dreams Come True, Thirteen at Dinner, Single Women Married Men, The Face of Fear, Danielle Steel's Palomino, French Silk, The Corpse Had a Familiar Face, Home Song, The Care and Handling of Roses, Nightmare Man. *Documentary*: Western Ranching Culture In Crisis, The Forest Wars.

HORTON, PETER
Actor. b. Bellevue, DC, Aug. 20, 1953. e. Univ. of CA, Santa Barbara. Stage work includes appearances with Lobero Rep. Co. Theatre in Santa Barbara, Butterflies Are Free in L.A.
PICTURES: Serial, Fade to Black, Split Image, Children of the Corn, Where the River Runs Black, Amazon Women on the Moon (also co-dir.), Sideout, Singles, The Cure (dir. only), The Baby-sitters Club, 2 Days in the Valley, Death Benefit, T-Rex: Back to the Cretaceous.
TELEVISION: *Series*: Seven Brides for Seven Brothers, thirtysomething (also dir.), The Wonder Years (dir. only), Class of '96 (dir., actor), Brimstone(also prod.). *Pilot*: Sawyer and Finn. *Movies*: She's Dressed to Kill, Miracle on Ice, Freedom, Choices of the Heart, Children of the Dark, Crazy Horse, One Too Many (dir. only), Murder Live!, Into Thin Air: Death on Everest, From the Earth to the Moon. *Special*: The Gift. *Guest*: The White Shadow, St. Elsewhere.

HORTON, ROBERT
Actor. b. Los Angeles, CA, July 29, 1924. e. U. of Miami. UCLA, B.A. Cum Laude, 1949. Yale Grad School, 1949-50. With U.S. Coast Guard; many legit. plays; many radio & TV appearances. Star of Broadway musical 110 in the Shade.
PICTURES: A Walk in the Sun, The Tanks Are Coming, Return of the Texan, Pony Soldier, Apache War Smoke, Bright Road, The Story of Three Loves, Code Two, Arena, Prisoner of War, Men of the Fighting Lady, The Green Slime, The Dangerous Days of Kiowa Jones, The Spy Killer, Foreign Exchange.
TELEVISION: *Series*: Kings Row, Wagon Train, A Man Called Shenandoah, As the World Turns. *Movie*: Red River. *Guest*: Alfred Hitchcock Presents, Suspense, Houston Knights, Murder She Wrote.

HOSKINS, BOB
Actor. b. Bury St. Edmunds, Suffolk, England, Oct. 26, 1942. Porter and steeplejack before becoming actor at 25. Veteran of Royal Shakespeare Co. Appeared with Britain's National Theatre (Man Is Man, King Lear, Guys and Dolls.)
PICTURES: The National Health (debut, 1973), Royal Flash, Inserts, Zulu Dawn, The Long Good Friday, Pink Floyd: The Wall, Beyond the Limit, Lassiter, The Cotton Club, Brazil, Sweet Liberty, Mona Lisa (Acad. Award nom.), A Prayer for the Dying, The Lonely Passion of Judith Hearne, Who Framed Roger Rabbit, The Raggedy Rawney (also dir., co-s.p.), Heart Condition, Mermaids, Shattered, The Inner Circle, The Favor the Watch and the Very Big Fish, Hook, Passed Away, Super Mario Bros., The Rainbow, The Secret Agent, Nixon, Balto (voice), Joseph Conrad's The Secret Agent, Michael, Spice World (cameo), Twenty Four Seven, Parting Shots, Captain Jack, Cousin Bette, The White River Kid, A Room for Romeo Bass, Live Virgin, Felicia's Journey.
TELEVISION: Villains on the High Road (debut, 1972), New Scotland Yard, On the Move, Rock Follies, In the Looking Glass, Napoleon, Flickers, Pennies from Heaven, Othello, Mussolini, The Dunera Boys, World War II: When Lions Roar, The Changeling, The Forgotten Toys, David Copperfield, Don Quixote.

HOU, HSIAO-HSIEN
Director. b. Meixian, China, April 8, 1947.
PICTURES: Cute Girl, Cheerful Wind, Six is Company (s.p. only), Growing Up (s.p., prod. only), The Green Green Grass of Home, All the Youthful Days, The Sandwich Man, A Summer at Grandpa's, The Time to Live and the Time to Die (also s.p.), Dust in the Wind, Daughter of the Nile, City of Sadness, Raise the Red Lantern (exec. prod. only), Dust of Angels (exec. prod. only), The Puppetmaster, A Borrowed Life (exec. prod. only), Good Men Good Women, Heartbreak Island (s.p., exec. prod. only), Goodbye South Goodbye, Flowers of Shanghai, Borderline (prod. only).

HOUGH, JOHN
Director. b. London, England,, Nov. 21, 1941. Worked in British film prod. in various capacities; impressed execs. at EMI-MGM Studios, Elstree, London, so was given chance to direct The Avengers series for TV. Began theatrical films with Sudden Terror for prod. Irving Allen, 1971.
PICTURES: Sudden Terror, The Practice, Twins of Evil, Treasure Island, The Legend of Hell House, Dirty Mary Crazy Larry, Escape to Witch Mountain, Return From Witch Mountain, Brass Target, The Watcher in the Woods, The Incubus, Triumphs of a Man Called Horse, Biggles: Adventures in Time, American Gothic, Howling IV—The Original Nightmare.
TELEVISION: A Hazard of Hearts (also co-prod.), The Lady and the Highwayman (also prod.), A Ghost in Monte Carlo (also prod.), Duel of Hearts (also prod.), Distant Scream, Black Carrion, Check-Mate.

HOUNSOU, DJIMON
Actor. b. Benin, West Africa. Was model before he began acting.
PICTURES: Without You I'm Nothing, Unlawful Entry, Stargate, Amistad, Ill Gotten Gains, Deep Rising.

HOWARD, ARLISS
Actor. b. Independence, MO, 1955. e. Columbia Col., MO. m. actress Debra Winger.
THEATER: American Buffalo, Lie of the Mind.
PICTURES: The Prodigal, Sylvester, Door to Door, The Ladies Club, The Lightship, Full Metal Jacket, Plain Clothes, Tequila Sunrise, Men Don't Leave, For the Boys, Ruby, Crisscross, The Sandlot, Wilder Napalm, Natural Born Killers, Wet, To Wong Foo—Thanks for Everything—Julie Newmar, Johns, Beyond the Call, The Lost World: Jurassic Park, Amistad.
TELEVISION: *Movies*: Hands of a Stranger, I Know My First Name is Steven, Somebody Has to Shoot the Picture, Iran: Days of Crisis, Till Death Us Do Part, Those Secrets, The Infiltrator, The Man Who Captured Eichmann, Old Man.

HOWARD, CLINT
Actor. b. Burbank, CA, Apr. 20, 1959. Brother is dir. Ron Howard; father is actor Rance Howard.
PICTURES: An Eye for an Eye, Gentle Giant, The Jungle Book (voice), Winnie the Pooh and the Blustery Day (voice), The Wild Country, The Grand Auto Theft, The Many Adventures of Winnie the Pooh (voice), Harper Valley P.T.A., Rock 'n' Roll High School, Evil Speak, Night Shift, Flip Out, Spalsh, Cocoon, Gung Ho, The Wraith, End of the Line, Freeway, B.O.R.N., An Innocent Man, Parenthood, Tango and Cash, Silent Night Deadly Night 4: Inititation, Disturbed, Backdraft, The Rocketeer, Silent Night Deadly Night 5: The Toy Maker, Voice of a Stranger, Far and Away, Ticks, Forced to Kill, Carnosaur, Leprechaun 2, The Paper, Bigfoot: The Unforgettable Encounter, Not Like Us, The Ice Cream Man, Fist of the North Star, Dillinger and Capone, Digital Man, Baby Face Nelson, Forget Paris, Apollo 13, Twisted Love, That Thing You Do!, Rattled, Barb Wire, Unhook the Stars, Santa with Muscles, The Protector, Austin Powers: International Man of Mystery, Telling You, Twilight, The Dentist II, The Waterboy, Sparkle and Charm, My Dog Skip, Fortune Hunters, Austin Powers: The Spy Who Shagged Me, Arthur's Quest, Edtv.
TELEVISION: *Series*: The Andy Griffith Show, The Baileys of Balboa, Gentle Ben, Salty, The Cowboys, Gung Ho, Space Rangers. *Movies*: The Red Pony, Huckleberry Finn, The Death of Richie, Cotton Candy (also writer), Skyward, Little White Lies, Cheyenne Warrior, Sawbones, Humanoids from the Deep. *Guest*: The Streets of San Francisco, Happy Days, Star Trek, Night Gallery, Seinfeld, Star Trek: Deep Space Nine, Silk Stalkings, The Outer Limits, Gun.

HOWARD, JAMES NEWTON
Composer. m. actress Rosanna Arquette. Started as keyboard player for Elton John, before composing and producing for such artists as Cher, Diana Ross, Barbra Streisand, Chaka Khan, Randy Newman.
PICTURES: Tough Guys, Nobody's Fool, Head Office, Wildcats, 8 Million Ways to Die, Five Corners, Campus Man, Promised Land, Off Limits, Tap, Some Girls, Everybody's All-American, Major League, The Package, Marked for Death, Pretty Woman, Coupe de Ville, Flatliners, Three Men and a Little Lady, Dying Young, The Man in the Moon, My Girl, The Prince of Tides (Acad. Award nom.), Grand Canyon, Guilty by Suspicion, King Ralph, Dying Young, The Man in the Moon, Glengarry Glen Ross, Night and the City, American Heart, Diggstown, Alive, Falling Down, Dave, The Fugitive (Acad. Award nom.), The Saint of Fort Washington, Intersection, Wyatt Earp, Junior (Acad. Award nom; Golden Globe nom.), Restoration, Just Cause, Outbreak, Eye for an Eye, The Juror, Primal Fear, The Trigger Effect, The Rich Man's Wife, Space Jam, One Fine Day (Acad. Award nom.), Dante's Peak, Liar Liar, Fathers' Day, My Best Friend's Wedding, The Devil's Advocate, The Postman, Snow Falling on Cedars, A Perfect Murder.
TELEVISION: *Movies*: The Image, Revealing Evidence: Stalking the Honolulu Stangler, Somebody Has to Shoot the Picture, Descending Angel, A Private Matter. *Series*: ER (Emmy nom.).

HOWARD, KEN
Actor. b. El Centro, CA, March 28, 1944. e. Yale Drama Sch. Left studies to do walk-on in B'way. musical, Promises Promises.
THEATER: Promises Promises, 1776 (Theatre World Award), Child's Play (Tony Award, 1970), Seesaw, 1600 Pennsylvania Avenue, The Norman Conquests, Equus, Rumors, Camping With Henry and Tom.PICTURES: Tell Me That You Love Me Junie Moon (debut, 1970), Such Good Friends, The Strange Vengeance of Rosalie, 1776, Second Thoughts, Oscar, Clear and Present Danger, The Net.
TELEVISION: *Series*: Adam's Rib, The Manhunter, The White Shadow, It's Not Easy, The Colbys, Dynasty, Dream Girl U.S.A., What Happened? (host). Guest: Bonanza, Medical Center. *Movies*: Manhunter, Superdome, Critical List, A Real American Hero, Damien: The Leper Priest, Victims, Rage of Angels, The Trial of George Armstrong Custer, He's Not Your Son, Rage of Angels: The Story Continues, Murder in New Hampshire: The Pamela Smart Story, Memories of Midnight, Hart to Hart Returns, Moment of Truth: To Walk Again, Tom Clancy's Op Center. Specials: Strange Interlude, The Man in the Brown Suit, Mastergate. *Mini-Series*: The Thorn Birds.

HOWARD, RON
Actor, Director, Producer. b. Duncan, OK, March 1, 1954. e. Univ. of So. Calif. Los Angeles Valley Col. Acting debut as Ronny Howard at age of 2 with parents, Rance and Jean Howard, in The Seven Year Itch at Baltimore's Hilltop Theatre. Two years later traveled to Vienna to appear in first film, The Journey. Brother is actor Clint Howard, also former child actor. Co-Chairman of Imagine Films Entertainment.
PICTURES: *Actor*. The Journey (debut, 1959), Door-to-Door Maniac, The Music Man, The Courtship of Eddie's Father, Village of the Giants, The Wild Country, American Graffiti, Happy Mother's Day... Love George, The Spikes Gang, Eat My Dust!, I'm a Fool, The Shootist, The First Nudie Musical (cameo), More American Graffiti, The Magical World of Chuck Jones. *Director:* Grand Theft Auto (dir. debut, 1977; also actor, co-s.p.),Night Shift, Splash, Cocoon, Gung Ho (also exec. prod.), Willow, Parenthood (also co-story), Backdraft, Far and Away (also co-prod., co-story), The Paper, Apollo 13, Ransom, Edtv (also prod.). *Exec. prod/prod.:* Leo & Loree, No Man's Land, Vibes, Clean and Sober, Closet Land, Far and Away, The Chamber, Inventing the Abbotts.
TELEVISION: *Series*: The Andy Griffith Show, The Smith Family, Happy Days, Fonz and the Happy Days Gang (voice), Parenthood, Hiller & Diller (exec. prod), Felicity (prod.), The PJs (exec. prod.). *Movies*: The Migrants, Locusts, Huckleberry Finn, Cotton Candy (dir., co-writer), Act of Love, Bitter Harvest, Fire on the Mountain, When Your Lover Leaves (also co.exec. prod.), Through the Magic Pyramid (exec. prod., dir.), Splash Too, Skyward (co-exec. prod., dir.), Into Thin Air (exec. prod.), Return to Mayberry, Frank Capra's American Dream. *Mini-series*: From the Earth to the Moon. *Guest*: Red Skelton Hour, Playhouse 90, Dennis the Menace, Many Loves of Dobie Gillis, Five Fingers, Twilight Zone, Dinah Shore Show, The Fugitive, Dr. Kildare, The Big Valley, I Spy, Danny Kaye Show, Gomer Pyle USMC, The Monroes, Love American Style, Gentle Ben, Gunsmoke; Disney TV films (incl. A Boy Called Nuthin', Smoke), The Simpsons (voice).

HOWARD, SANDY
Producer. b. Aug. 1, 1927. e. Florida So. Coll. Ent. m.p. ind. 1946.
PICTURES: Tarzan and the Trappers (dir. only), Perils of the Deep, Diary of a Bachelor (dir. only), Gamera the Invincible (dir. only), One Step to Hell (also dir. & s.p.), Jack of Diamonds (s.p. only), A Man Called Horse, Man in the Wilderness, Together Brothers, Neptune Factor, The Devil's Rain (exec. prod.), Sky Riders, The Last Castle, Embryo, Magna I-Beyond the Barrier Reef, The Battle, Island of Dr. Moreau, City on Fire, Death Ship (exec. prod.), Avenging Angel, Vice Squad (s.p. only), Kidnapped, The Boys Next Door, Street Justice (exec. prod.), Nightstick, Dark Tower (exec. prod.), Truk Lagoon (exec. prod.).

HOWELL, C. THOMAS
Actor. r.n. Christopher Thomas Howell. b. Los Angeles, CA, Dec. 7, 1966. Former junior rodeo circuit champion.
PICTURES: E.T.: The Extra Terrestrial (debut, 1982), The Outsiders, Tank, Grandview U.S.A., Red Dawn, Secret Admirer, The Hitcher, Soul Man, A Tiger's Tale, Young Toscanini, Side Out, Far Out Man, The Return of the Musketeers, Kid, Nickel and Dime, Breaking the Rules, First Force, That Night, Tattle Tale, Streetwise, To Protect and Serve, Gettysburg, Jail Bate, Teresa's Tattoo, Power Play, Treacherous, Payback, Dangerous Indiscretion, Hourglass (also dir.), Baby Face Nelson, Mad Dogs and Englishmen, Pure Danger (also dir.), The Big Fall (also dir.), Sleeping Dogs, Last Lives, Dilemma, The Prince and the Surfer, The Glass Jar, Felons, Fortune Hunters.
TELEVISION: *Series*: Little People (only 4 yrs. old), Two Marriages, Kindred: The Embraced. *Movies*: It Happened One Christmas, Into the Homeland, Curiosity Kills, Acting on Impulse, Dark Reflection, Suspect Device, Dead. Fire. *Guest*: Nightmare Classics (Eye of the Panther).

HOWELLS, URSULA
Actress. b. Sept. 17, 1922. e. St. Paul's Sch., London. Stage debut, 1939, at Dundee Repertory with Bird in Hand followed by several plays inc. Springtime for Henry in N.Y., 1951; m.p. debut in Flesh and Blood, 1950; TV debut in Case of the Frightened Lady for BBC, 1948.
PICTURES: Lolly Madonna XXX, Catch My Soul, Hardcore, Escape from New York, Vice Squad, Total Exposure, Twist of Fate, I Believe in You, The Weak and the Wicked, The Horse's Mouth, Track the Man Down, Handcuffs London, The Constant Husband, The Third Key, Keep It Clean, Account Rendered, The Sicilians, The Blood Suckers, Torture Garden, Assignment K, Girly, Crossplot, Time After Time, The Tichborne Claimant.
TELEVISION: *Movies*: King Lear, The Small Back Room, A Woman Comes Home, For Services Rendered, Mine Own Executioner, The Cocktail Party, Father Dear Father, A Murder is Announced, The Cold Room, Jewels. *Series*: The Forsyte Saga, The Many Wives of Patrick. *Mini-series*: Cousin Bette.

HUBBARD, STANLEY
Satellite Broadcast Executive. b. St. Paul, MN, May 28, 1933. B.A. Univ. MN 1955. With Hubbard Broadcasting from 1950, named president 1967, chmn. & CEO 1983. Chairman & CEO U.S. Satellite Broadcasting Corp. Bd. dir. Fingerhut Corp. Broadcasting & Cable Hall of Fame 1991, Dist. Service Award , NAB 1995.

HUBLEY, SEASON
Actress. b. New York, NY, Mar. 14, 1951. Studied acting with Herbert Berghoff.
THEATER: *LA*: Heat, Triplet Collection, Rhythm of Torn Stars.
PICTURES: The Oracle (Horse's Mouth), Track the Man Down, They Can't Hang Me, Keep It Clean, Long Arm (Third Key), Death and The Sky Above, Mumsy Nanny Sonny and Girly, Crossplot.
TELEVISION: *Series*: Kung Fu, Family, All My Children, *Pilots*: Lond and Davis in New York, Blues Skies, The City. *Movies/Specials*: She Lives, The Healers, SST—Death Flight, Loose Change, Elvis, Mrs. R's Daughter, Three Wishes of Billy Grier, Under the Influence, Christmas Eve, Shakedown on Sunset Strip, Unspeakable Acts, Child of the Night, Steel Justice, Key to Rebecca, All I Could See From Where I Stood, Stepfather III, Caribbean Mystery, Black Carrion, Vestige of Honor, Humanoids From the Deep. *Guest*: The Partridge Family, The Rookies, Kojak, Twilight Zone, Alfred Hitchcock Presents, Twilight Zone, Hitchhiker.

HUDDLESTON, DAVID
Actor, Producer. b. Vinton, VA, Sept. 17, 1930. e. American Acad. of Dramatic Arts. Son is actor Michael Huddleston.
THEATER: A Man for All Seasons, Front Page, Everybody Loves Opal, Ten Little Indians, Silk Stockings, Fanny, Guys and Dolls, The Music Man, Desert Song, Mame. Broadway: The First, Death of a Salesman.
PICTURES: All the Way Home (debut, 1963), A Lovely Way to Die, Slaves, Norwood, Rio Lobo, Fools, Parade, Bad Company, Blazing Saddles, McQ, The World's Greatest Lover, Capricorn One, Gorp, Smokey and the Bandit II, The Act, Santa Claus, Frantic, Life With Mikey, Cultivating Charlie. Something to Talk About (unbilled), Joe's Apartment, The Big Lebowski.
TELEVISION: *Series*: Tenafly, Petrocelli, The Kallikaks, Hizzoner. *Movies*: Sarge: The Badge or the Cross, The Priest Killer, Suddenly Single, The Homecoming, Brian's Song, Tenafly (pilot), Brock's Last Case, Hawkins on Murder, Heatwave, The Gun and the Pulpit, The Oregon Trail, Shark Kill, Sherlock Holmes in New York, Kate Bliss and the Ticker Tape Kid, Oklahoma City Dolls, Family Reunion, Computerside, M.A.D.D.: Mothers Against Drunk Drivers, Finnegan Begin Again, Family Reunion, Spot Marks the X, The Tracker, Margaret Bourke-White, In a Child's Name. *Mini-Series*: Once an Eagle.

HUDSON, ERNIE
Actor. b. Benton Harbor, MI, Dec. 17, 1945. e. Wayne St. Univ., Yale Sch. of Drama. Former Actors Ensemble Theater while in Detroit. Professional stage debut in L.A. production of Daddy Goodness.
PICTURES: Leadbelly (debut, 1976), The Main Event, The Jazz Singer, Penitentiary II, Spacehunter: Adventures in the Forbidden Zone, Going Berserk, Ghostbusters, The Joy of Sex, Weeds, Leviathan, Ghostbusters II, The Hand That Rocks the Cradle, Sugar Hill, No Escape, The Crow, The Cowboy Way, Airheads, Speechless, The Basketball Diaries, Congo, The Substitute, Operation Delta Force, Levitation, Fakin' Da Funk, Mr Magoo, Stranger in the Kingdom, Butter, Lillie, Shark Attack.
TELEVISION: *Series*: Highcliffe Manor, The Last Precinct, Broken Badges, Oz. *Mini-Series*: Roots: The Next Generations, Wild Palms. *Movies*: White Mama, Dirty Dozen: The Fatal Mission, Love on the Run, Clover, Tornado!, The Cherokee Kid. *Guest*: Fantasy Island, Little House on the Praire, One Day at a Time, Diff'rent Strokes, St. Elsewhere.

HUDSON, HUGH
Producer, Director. b. England. e. Eton. Began career as head of casting dept. with ad agency in London; left for Paris to work as editor for small film co. Returned to London to form Cammell-Hudson-Brownjohn Film Co., production house., turning out award-winning documentaries (Tortoise and Hare, A is for Apple). 1970, joined Ridley Scott to make TV commercials. 1975, formed Hudson Films to produce.
PICTURES: *Director*: Chariots of Fire, Greystoke: The Legend of Tarzan Lord of the Apes (also prod.), Revolution, Lost Angels, Lumiere and Company, My Life So Far, I Dreamed of Africa.

HUEY, WARD L. JR.,
Media Executive. b. Dallas, TX, Apr. 26, 1938. e. So. Meth. U, BA, 1960. With dept. prodn., sales svc. mgr., regional sales mgr., gen sales mgr. Sta. WFAA-TV, TX 1970-67; sta. mgr., 1972-75. V.p. gen. mgr. Belo Broadcasting Corp., 1975; vice chmn. bd. dirs., pres. broadcast div, A. H. Belo Corp., 1987-. Chmn. affiliate bd. govs. ABC-TV, 1981-82. Chmn. bd. TV Operators Caucus, 1989. Mem.: exec. com., So. Meth. U. Meadows Sch. Arts, 1986-; Goodwill Industries Dallas, 1978-79; State Fair Tex., 1992. Bd. Dirs.: Children's Med. Found., 1985-94; Dallas Found, 1993-. Mem.: Maximum Svc TV Assn. (vice chmn., 1988-94); TV Bur. ADvt. (bd. dirs., exec. com., 1984-88); Assn. Broadast Execs. Tex. (bd. dirs., 1977-78); Dallas Advt. league (bd. dirs. 1975-76); Salesman Club Dallas (pres. 1992-93); Dallas Country Club.

HUGH KELLY, DANIEL
Actor. b. Hoboken, NJ, Aug. 10, 1949. Began acting with the National Players touring U.S. in such plays as Henry IV Part 1, Charlie's Aunt, School for Wives.
THEATER: Arena Stage (DC): An Enemy of the People, Once in a Lifetime, Long Day's Journey Into Night. Actors Theatre (Louisville): Much Ado About Nothing, The Best Man, The Taming of the Shrew, The Rainmaker. *Off-B'way*: Hunchback of Notre Dame, Miss Margarita's Way, Juno's Swans, Fishing, Short-Changed Revue. *B'way*: Born Yesterday, Cat on a Hot Tin Roof.
PICTURES: Cujo, Nowhere to Hide, Someone to Watch Over Me, The Good Son, Bad Company.
TELEVISION: *Series*: Chicago Story, Hardcastle and McCormick, Second Noah. *Movies*: Nutcracker, Thin Ice, Murder Ink, Night of Courage, Citizen Cohn, Moment of Truth: A Mother's Deception, A Child's Cry for Help, The Tuskegee Airmen, Never Say Never: The Deidre Hall Story, No Greater Love, Stranger in My Home, Five Desperate Hours, Bad As I Wanna Be: The Dennis Rodman Story.

HUGHES, BARNARD
Actor. b. Bedford Hills, NY, July 16, 1915. Winner of Emmy for role as Judge in Lou Grant series (1978) and Tony Award for Da (1978). Inducted into Theatre Hall of Fame (1993).
PICTURES: Midnight Cowboy, Where's Poppa?, Cold Turkey, The Pursuit of Happiness, The Hospital, Rage, Sisters, Deadhead Miles, Oh God!, First Monday in October, Tron, Best Friends, Maxie, Where Are the Children?, The Lost Boys, Da, Doc Hollywood, Sister Act 2: Back in the Habit, The Fantasticks, The Odd Couple II.
TELEVISION: *Series*: Doc, Mr. Merlin, The Cavanaughs, Blossom. *Movies*: Guilty or Innocent, The Sam Sheppard Murder Case, See How She Runs, The Caryl Chessman Story, Tell Me My Name, Look Homeward, Angel, Father Brown: Detective, Nova, Homeward Bound, The Sky's No Limit, A Caribbean Mystery, Night of Courage, A Hobo's Christmas, Day One, Home Fires Burning, Guts and Glory: The Rise and Fall of Oliver North, The Incident, Miracle Child, Trick of the Eye, Past the Bleachers. *Guest*: Homicide, The Marshal.

HUGHES, JOHN
Writer, Director, Producer. b. Detroit, MI, Feb. 18, 1950. e. Univ. of AZ. Editor of National Lampoon before writing film script of National Lampoon's Class Reunion (1982). Made directorial debut with Sixteen Candles in 1984 which also wrote. In 1985 entered into deal with Paramount Pictures to write, direct and produce films with his own production unit, The John Hughes Co.
PICTURES: *Writer*: National Lampoon's Class Reunion, National Lampoon's Vacation, Mr. Mom, Nate and Hayes, Sixteen Candles (also dir.), The Breakfast Club (also dir., co-prod.), National Lampoon's European Vacation, Weird Science (also dir.), Pretty in Pink (also co-exec. prod.). *Writer/Prod.*: Ferris Bueller's Day Off (also dir.), Some Kind of Wonderful, Planes Trains & Automobiles (also dir.), She's Having a Baby (also dir.), The Great Outdoors (exec. prod., s.p.), Uncle Buck (also dir.), National Lampoon's Christmas Vacation, Home Alone, Career Opportunities (exec. prod., co-s.p.), Only the Lonely (co-prod. only), Dutch, Curly Sue (also dir.), Home Alone 2: Lost in New York, Dennis the Menace, Baby's Day Out, Miracle on 34th Street, 101 Dalmations, Reach the Rock, Flubber, Home Alone 3.

HUGHES, KATHLEEN
Actress. r.n. Betty von Gerkan; b. Hollywood, CA, Nov. 14, 1928. e. Los Angeles City Coll., UCLA. m. Stanley Rubin, prod., mother of 4, Michael played Baby Matthew on Peyton Place. Studied drama; under contract, 20th-Fox, 1948-51; starred in Seven Year Itch 1954, La Jolla Playhouse; signed by UI, 1952. Theatre includes You Can't Take It With You, An Evening With Tennessee Williams, The Bar Off Melrose.
PICTURES: Road House, Mother is a Freshman, Mr. Belvedere Goes to College, Take Care of My Little Girl, It Happens Every Spring, When Willie Comes Marching Home, My Blue Heaven, Mister 880, No Way Out, I'll See You in My Dreams, Thy Neighbor's Wife, For Men Only (The Tall Lie), Sally and Saint Anne, Golden Blade, It Came From Outer Space, Dawn at Socorro, Glass Web, Cult of the Cobra, Three Bad Sisters, Promise Her Anything, The President's Analyst, The Take, Pete and Tillie, Ironweed, The Couch Trip, Revenge.
TELEVISION: *Guest*: Bob Cummings Show, Hitchcock, 77 Sunset Strip, G.E. Theatre, Bachelor Father, Frank Sinatra Show, Ed Wynn Show, Alan Young Show, The Tall Man, Dante, Tightrope, Markham, I Dream of Jeannie, Peyton Place, Gomer Pyle, Kismet, Ghost and Mrs. Muir, Bracken's World, The Survivors, Julia, Here's Lucy, To Rome with Love, The Interns, The Man and the City, Mission Impossible, The Bold Ones, Lucas Tanner, Marcus Welby, Barnaby Jones, Medical Center, M.A.S.H., General Hospital, Quincy, Finder of Lost Loves, The Young and the Restless. *Movies*: Babe, Forbidden Love, The Spell, Portrait of an Escort, Capitol, Mirror, Mirror, And Your Name is Jonah.

HUGHES, KEN
Director, Writer. b. Liverpool, England,, 1922. Ent. ind. as sound engineer with BBC, 1940; Doc. films, Army training films. Wrote book and lyrics for stage musical Oscar. Member: Assn. Cine Technicians, Writers' Guild of Great Britain.

AUTHOR: High Wray, The Long Echo, An Enemy of the State. Scripts: The Matarese Circle, Tussy is Me, The Queen's Own, RatsHallo Berlin.
PICTURES: *Dir./Writer*: Wide Boy, The House Across the Lake, Black 13 (dir. only), The Brain Machine, Case of the Red Monkey, Confession (The Deadliest Sin), Timeslip (The Atomic Man), Joe Macbeth, Wicked as They Come, The Long Haul, Jazz Boat, In the Nick, The Trials of Oscar Wilde, The Small World of Sammy Lee, Of Human Bondage (dir. only), Arrivederci Baby (also prod.), Casino Royale (co-dir.), Chitty Chitty Bang Bang, Cromwell, The Internecine Project, Alfie Darling (Oh Alfie!), Sextette (dir. only), Night School.
TELEVISION: Eddie (Emmy Award for writing, 1959), Sammy (Brit. Acad. Award). *Serials*: Solo for Canary, Enemy of the State. *Series*: Lenin 1917 (The Fall of Eagles), The Haunting, The Voice, Oil Strike North, Colditz, Churchill (BBC).
AWARDS: Golden Globe, Emmy, British TV Acad. Award (Script Writer of Year), Avorias Festival Merit Award, British Writer's Guild Award, British Critics Award (best serial).

HUGHES, WENDY
Actress. b. Melbourne, Australia, July 29, 1952. Studied acting at National Institute of Dramatic Art, Sydney.
PICTURES: Petersen, Sidecar Racers, High Rolling, Newsfront, My Brilliant Career, Kostas, Lucinda Brayford, Touch and Go, Hoodwink, A Dangerous Summer, Partners, Duet for Four, Lonely Hearts, Careful He Might Hear You, My First Wife, Remember Me, An Indecent Obsession, Happy New Year, Echoes of Paradise, Warm Nights on a Slow Moving Train, Boundaries of the Heart, Luigi's Ladies (also co-s.p.), Wild Orchid II, Princess Caraboo, Lust & Revenge, Paradise Road.
TELEVISION: *Movies*: Coralie Landsdowne Says No, Puzzle, Promises to Keep, Can't Get Started, The Heist, Donor. *Mini-series*: Power Without Glory, Return to Eden, Amerika, A Woman Named Jackie, *Series*: Rush, Snowy River: The McGregor Saga, State Coroner. *Guest*: Star Trek: The Next Generation, Homicide: Life on the Street.

HUIZENGA, HARRY WAYNE
Entrepreneur, Entertainment Executive. b. Evergreen Park, IL, Dec 29, 1939. e. Calvin College, 1957-58. m. Martha Jean Pike, Apr. 17, 1972. Vice chmn., pres., chief operating officer Waste Mgmt. Inc., Oak Brook, IL, 1968-84; prin. Huizenga Holdings, Inc., Ft. Lauderdale, FL, 1984–; chmn., chief exec. officer Blockbuster Entertainment Corp., Ft. Lauderdale, 1987-1995; owner Florida Marlins, Miami, 1992–; co-owner Miami Dolphins, Joe Robbie Stadium. Mem. Florida Victory Com., 1988-89, Team Repub. Nat. com., Washington, 1988-90. Recipient Entrepeneur of Yr. award Wharton Sch. U. Pa., 1989, Excalibur award Bus. Leader of Yr. News/Sun Sentinel, 1990, Silver Medallion Brotherhood award Broward Region Nat. Conf. Christians and Jews, 1990, Laureates award Jr. Achievement Broward and Palm Beach Counties, 1990, Jim Murphy Humanitarian Award The Emerald Soc., 1990, Entrepreneur of Yr. award Disting. Panel Judges Fla., 1990, Man of Yr. Billboard/Time Mag., 1990, Man of Yr. Juvenile Diabetes Found., 1990, Florida Free Enterpriser of Yr. award Fla. Coun. on Econ. Edn., 1990, commendation for youth restricted video State of Fla. Office of Gov., 1989, Hon. Mem. Appreciation award Bond Club Ft. Lauderdale, 1989, honored with endowed teaching chair Broward Community Coll., 1990. Mem. Lauderdale Yacht Club, Tournament Players Club, Coral Ridge Country Club, Fisher Island Club, Ocean Reef Club, Cat Cay Yacht Club, Linville Ridge Country Club. Avocations: golf, collecting antique cars. Sold Blockbuster Entertainment Corp. to Viacom, 1994. Retired.

HULCE, TOM
Actor. b. White Water, WI, Dec. 6, 1953. e. NC School of the Arts. Understudied and then co-starred in Equus on Broadway. Directorial stage debut Sleep Around Town. Appeared in IMAX film Wings of Courage. Recipient of Emmy Award, 1996.
THEATER: A Memory of Two Mondays, Julius Caesar, Candida, The Sea Gull, The Rise and Rise of Daniel Rocket, Eastern Standard, A Few Good Men (Tony nom.), Hamlet.
PICTURES: September 30, 1955 (debut, 1978), National Lampoon's Animal House, Those Lips Those Eyes, Amadeus (Acad. Award nom.), Echo Park, Slamdance, Dominick and Eugene, Parenthood, Shadowman, The Inner Circle, Fearless, Mary Shelley's Frankenstein, Wings of Courage, The Hunchback of Notre Dame (voice).
TELEVISION: *Movies*: Murder in Mississippi, Black Rainbow, The Heidi Chronicles. *Mini-Series*: The Adams Chronicles. *Specials*: Emily Emily, The Rise and Rise of Daniel Rocket, Song of Myself, Forget-Me-Not Lane, Tall Tales and Legends (John Henry).

HUNDT, REED
Federal Official. b. Ann Arbor, MI, March 3, 1948. B.A. Yale 1969, J.D. 1974. Served on various U.S. circuit courts 1975-80. Associate Latham & Watkins 1975, partner 1982. Named to FCC 1994 as Chairman. Resigned 1997.

HUNNICUT, GAYLE
Actress. b. Fort Worth, TX, February 6, 1943. e. UCLA, B.A., with honors, theater arts & English major. Early career, community theatres in Los Angeles.
THEATER: The Ride Across Lake Constance, Twelfth Night, The Tempest, Dog Days, The Admirable Crichton, A Woman of No Importance, Hedda Gabler, Peter Pan, Macbeth, Uncle Vanya, The Philadelphia Story, Miss Firecracker Contest, Exit The King, The Doctor's Dilemma, So Long on Lonely Street, The Big Knife, Edith Wharton at Home, The Little Foxes, Dangerous Corner.
PICTURES: The Wild Angels (debut, 1966), P.J., Eye of the Cat, Marlowe, Fragment of Fear, The Freelance, Voices, Running Scared, Legend of Hell House, Scorpio, L'Homme Sans Visage, The Spiral Staircase, The Sell Out, Strange Shadows in an Empty Room, Once in Paris, One Take Two, Fantomas, Privilege, Sherlock Holmes, Target, Dream Lover, Turnaround, Silence Like Glass.
TELEVISION: *Series*: Dallas (1989-91). *Movies*: The Smugglers, The Million Dollar Face, The Return of the Man From U.N.C.L.E., The First Olympics: Athens 1896. *Specials*: Man and Boy, The Golden Bowl, The Ambassadors, The Ripening Seed, Fall of Eagles, The Switch, Humboldt's Gift, The Life and Death of Dylan Thomas, Return of the Saint, The Lady Killers, Savage in the Orient, Strong Medicine. *Mini-Series*: A Man Called Intrepid, The Martian Chronicles, Dream West. *Guest*: Taxi.

HUNT, HELEN
Actress. b. Los Angeles, CA, June 15, 1963. Daughter of dir. Gordon Hunt. m. actor Hank Azaria.
THEATER: Been Taken, Our Town, The Taming of the Shrew, Methusalem.
PICTURES: Rollercoaster, Girls Just Want to Have Fun, Peggy Sue Got Married, Project X, Miles From Home, Trancers, Stealing Home, Next of Kin, The Waterdance, Only You, Bob Roberts, Mr. Saturday Night, Kiss of Death, Twister, As Good as It Gets (Acad. Award, Golden Globe Award, Best Actress, 1997).
TELEVISION: *Series*: Swiss Family Robinson, Amy Prentiss, The Fitzpatricks, It Takes Two, Mad About You (Emmy Award, 1996, 1997, 1999; Golden Globe Award, 1997). *Movies*: Pioneer Woman, All Together Now, Death Scream, The Spell, Transplant, Angel Dusted, Child Bride of Short Creek, The Miracle of Kathy Miller, Quarterback Princess, Bill: On His Own, Sweet Revenge, Incident at Dark River, Into the Badlands, Murder in New Hampshire: The Pamela Smart Story, In the Company of Darkness. Specials: Weekend, Land of Little Rain. *Special*: Sexual Healing. *Guest*: St. Elsewhere, Family, Mary Tyler Moore Show, The Hitchhiker, The Simpsons (voice).

HUNT, LINDA
Actress. b. Morristown, NJ, Apr. 2, 1945. e. Interlochen Arts Acad., MI, and Chicago's Goodman Theatre & Sch. of Drama. Narrated documentary Ecological Design: Inventing the Future.
THEATER: *Long Wharf (New Haven)*:Hamlet, The Rose Tattoo, Ah Wilderness. *NY*: Mother Courage, End of the World (Tony nom.), A Metamorphosis in Miniature (Obie Award), Top Girls (Obie Award), Aunt Dan and Lemon, The Cherry Orchard. *Regional*: The Three Sisters.
PICTURES: Popeye (debut, 1980) The Year of Living Dangerously (Academy Award, best supporting actress, 1983), The Bostonians, Dune, Silverado, Eleni, Waiting for the Moon, She-Devil, Kindergarten Cop, If Looks Could Kill, Rain Without Thunder, Twenty Bucks, Younger and Younger, Ready to Wear (Pret-a-Porter), Pocahontas (voice), The Relic, Eat Your Heart Out, Amazon, Paul Monette: The Brink of Summer's End.
TELEVISION: *Series*: Space Rangers. *Movie*: The Room Upstairs. *Specials*: Ah Wilderness, The Room. *Guest*: Fame.

HUNT, MARSHA
Actress. b. Chicago, IL, Oct. 17, 1917.
THEATER: *B'way*: Joy to the World, Devils Disciple, Legend of Sarah, Borned in Texas, Tunnel of Love, The Paisley Convertible.
PICTURES: The Virginia Judge (debut, 1935), College Holiday, Easy to Take, Blossoms in the Dust, Panama Hattie, Joe Smith American, These Glamour Girls, Winter Carnival, Irene, Pride and Prejudice, Flight Command, The Affairs of Martha, Kid Glove Killer, Seven Sweethearts, Cheers for Miss Bishop, Trial of Mary Dugan, Thou•ands Cheer, The Human Comedy, None Shall Escape, Lost Angel, Cry Havoc, Bride by Mistake, Music for Millions, Valley of Decision, A Letter for Evie, Smash-Up, Carnegie Hall, The Inside Story, Raw Deal, Jigsaw, Take One False Step, Actors and Sin, Happy Time, No Place to Hide, Back from the Dead, Bombers B-52, Blue Denim, The Plunderers, Johnny Got His Gun.
TELEVISION: *Series*: Peck's Bad Girl. *Guest*: Philco, Studio One, Ford Theatre, Show of Shows, G.E. Theatre, Climax, Hitchcock, The Defenders, Twilight Zone, Cains Hundred, Gunsmoke, The Breaking Point, Outer Limits, Profiles in Courage, Ben Casey, Accidental Family, Run For Your Life, My Three Sons, The Outsiders, Name of the Game, Univ.'s 120, Ironside, Marcus Welby, M.D., Police Story, The Young Lawyers, Harry-O, The Mississippi, Hot Pursuit, Shadow Chaser, Matlock, Murder She Wrote, Star Trek: The Next Generation.

HUNT, PETER R.
Director, Editor. b. London, England,, March 11, 1928. e. Romford, England and Rome, Italy, London Sch. of Music. Actor English Rep. Entered film as camera asst. documentary, later asst film editor documentary, then asst editor features, London Films.

PICTURES: *Editor*: Stranger from Venus (Immediate Decision), Doublecross, A Hill in Korea, Secret Tent, Admirable Crichton, A Cry From the Streets, Next to No Time, Ferry to Hong Kong, Sink the Bismark!, There was a Crooked Man, The Greengage Summer (Loss of Innocence), On the Fiddle (Operation Snafu) H.M.S. Defiant (Damn the Defiant). *Supervising editor/2nd Unit Director*: Dr. No, Call Me Bwana, From Russia With Love, Goldfinger, The Ipcress File, Thunderball, You Only Live Twice. *Assoc. Prod.*: Chitty Chitty Bang Bang. *Director*: On Her Majesty's Secret Service, Gullivers Travels, Gold, Shout at the Devil, Death Hunt, Wild Geese II, Hyper Sapien, Assassination.
TELEVISION: *Director: Series*: The Persuaders, Shirley's World, The Pencil, Smart Alec Kill (Philip Marlowe). *Movies*: The Beasts Are in the Streets, Eyes of a Witness. *Mini-Series*: Last Days of Pompeii.

HUNT, PETER H.
Director. b. Pasadena, CA, Dec. 16, 1938. e. Hotchkiss, Yale U., Yale Drama Sch. m. actress Barbette Tweed. Dir. for Williamston Theatre since 1957. Lighting designer on B'way. (1963-69) Awards: Tony, Ace, Peabody (twice), N.Y. Drama Critics, London Drama Critics, Edgar Allan Poe, Christopher.
THEATER: 1776 (London & B'way.), Georgy (B'way.), Scratch (B'way.), Goodtime Charley (B'way.), Give 'Em Hell Harry, Magnificent Yankee (Kennedy Center). *Tours*: Bully, Three Penny Opera, Sherlock Holmes, Bus Stop.
PICTURES: 1776, Give 'Em Hell Harry.
TELEVISION: *Specials*: Adventures of Huckleberry Finn, Life on the Mississippi, A Private History of a Campaign That Failed, A New Start, Mysterious Stranger, Sherlock Holmes (cable), Bus Stop (cable). *Movies*: Flying High, Rendezvous Motel, When She Was Bad, Skeezer, The Parade, Sins of the Past, It Came Upon the Midnight Clear, Charley Hannah, Danielle Steel's Secrets, Sworn to Vengeance. *Pilots*: Adam's Rib, Hello Mother Goodbye, Ivan the Terrible, Quark, Mixed Nuts, Wilder and Wilder, The Main Event, Nuts and Bolts, The Good Witch of Laurel Canyon, Masquerade, Stir Crazy, The Wizard of Elm Street, Travelling Man, My Africa.

HUNT, WILLIE
Executive Producer. b. Van Nuys, CA, Oct. 1, 1941. e. Utah State U., B.A., 1963. m. writer Tim Considine. Started in industry as secretary at Warner Bros., 1965; named exec. secty. to Ted Ashley, WB, 1969; story analyst, WB, 1974; story editor, WB, 1975; named West Coast story editor for WB, 1978; joined MGM in 1979 as v.p., motion picture development. Moved to United Artists as v.p.-prod., 1982. 1983 sr. v.p. of prod. at Rastar Prods.; 1984, indep. prod., Tri-Star; 1986, sr. v.p., Freddie Fields Prods. 1988: Loverboy (co-prod.) 1989, sr. v.p. Considine Prods. 1993, partner, Creative Entertainment Group.

HUNTER, HOLLY
Actress. b. Conyers, GA. March 20, 1958. e. studied acting, Carnegie-Mellon Univ. Appeared Off-B'way in Battery (1981) and Weekend Near Madison. Appeared in 5 Beth Henley plays: The Miss Firecracker Contest (Off-B'way), as a replacement in Crimes of the Heart (B'way) The Wake of Jamey Foster (B'way), Lucky Spot (Williamstown Theater Festival), and Control Freaks (L.A.; also co-prod.). Also: A Lie of the Mind (L.A.).
PICTURES: The Burning (debut, 1981), Swing Shift, Raising Arizona, Broadcast News (NY Film Critics, LA Film Critics and Natl. Board of Review Awards, Acad. Award nom., 1987), End of the Line, Miss Firecracker, Animal Behavior, Always, Once Around, The Firm (Acad. Award nom.), The Piano (Academy Award, Cannes Film Fest., LA Film Critics, NY Film Critics, Natl. Board of Review, Natl. Society of Film Critics & Golden Globe Awards, 1993), Home for the Holidays, Copycat, Crash, A Life Less Ordinary, Living Out Loud, Woman Wanted, Jesus' Son.
TELEVISION: *Movies*: Svengali, An Uncommon Love, With Intent to Kill, A Gathering of Old Men, Roe vs. Wade (Emmy Award, 1989), Crazy in Love, The Positively True Adventures of the Alleged Texas Cheerleader-Murdering Mom (Emmy Award, 1993). *Guest*: Fame (pilot).

HUNTER, KIM
Actress. r.n. Janet Cole. b. Detroit, MI, Nov. 12, 1922. e. public schools. d. Donald and Grace Mabel (Lind) Cole. Studied acting with Charmine Lantaff Camine, 1938-40, Actors Studio; First stage appearance, 1939; played in stock, 1940-42; Broadway debut in A Streetcar Named Desire, 1947; frequent appearances in summer stock and repertory theater, 1940-; appeared Am. Shakespeare Festival, Stratford, CT, 1961. Autobiography-cookbook: Loose in the Kitchen (1975).
THEATER: *NY*: Darkness at Noon, The Chase, The Children's Hour (revival), The Tender Trap, Write Me a Murder, Weekend, The Penny Wars, The Women, The Cherry Orchard, To Grandmother's House We Go, When We Dead Awaken, Territorial Rites, Man and Superman, A Murder of Crows, Eye of the Beholder, An Ideal Husband. *Tours:* Two Blind Mice, They Knew What They Wanted, And Miss Reardon Drinks a Little, In Praise of Love, The Gin Game. *Regional:* The Glass Menagerie, The Lion in Winter, The Chalk Garden, Elizabeth the Queen, Semmelweiss, The Belle of Amherst, The Little Foxes, Another Part of the Forest, Ghosts, Death of a Salesman, Cat on a Hot Tin Roof, Life With Father, Sabrina Fair, Faulkner's Bicycle, Antique Pink, The Belle of Amherst, Painting Churches, A Delicate Balance, Jokers, Remembrance, The Gin Game, A Murder of Crows, Watch on the Rhine, Suddenly Last Summer, A Smaller Place, Open Window, The Cocktail Hour, The Belle of Amherst, Love Letters, Do Not Go Gentle, All The Way Home, Driving Miss Daisy, Greytop in Love.
PICTURES: The Seventh Victim (debut, 1943), Tender Comrade, When Strangers Marry (Betrayed), You Came Along, Stairway to Heaven (A Matter of Life and Death), A Canterbury Tale, A Streetcar Named Desire (Academy Award, best supporting actress, 1951), Anything Can Happen, Deadline: U.S.A., The Young Stranger, Bermuda Affair, Storm Center, Money Women and Guns, Lilith, Planet of the Apes, The Swimmer, Beneath the Planet of the Apes, Escape from the Planet of the Apes, Dark August, The Kindred, Two Evil Eyes, Midnight in the Garden of Good and Evil, A Price Below Rubies, A Smaller Place.
TELEVISION: Made TV debut on Actors Studio Program, 1948. *Series:* The Edge of Night (1979-80). *Specials*: Requiem for a Heavyweight, The Comedian (both on Playhouse 90); Give Us Barabbas, Stubby Pringle's Christmas, Project: U.F.O., Three Sovereigns for Sarah, Vivien Leigh: Scarlett and Beyond, Martin Luther King: The Dream and the Drum, Hurricane Andrew Project. *Guest*: Love American Style, Columbo, Cannon, Night Gallery, Mission Impossible, Marcus Welby, Hec Ramsey, Griff, Police Story, Ironside, Medical Center, Baretta, Gibbsville, The Oregon Trail, Scene of the Crime, Hunter, Murder She Wrote, Class of '96, Mad About You, L.A. Law, All My Children, As the World Turns. *Movies*: Dial Hot Line, In Search of America, The Magician (pilot), Unwed Father, Born Innocent, Bad Ronald, Ellery Queen (Too Many Suspects), The Dark Side of Innocence, The Golden Gate Murders, F.D.R.: The Last Year, Skokie, Private Sessions, Drop-Out Mother, Cross of Fire, Bloodlines: Murder in the Family, Hurricane Andrew. *Mini-Series*: Once an Eagle, Backstairs at the White House.

HUNTER, TAB
Actor. r.n. Arthur Gelien. b. New York, NY, July 11, 1931. Served with U.S. Coast Guard. Entered industry in 1948.
PICTURES: The Lawless (debut, 1950), Island of Desire, Gun Belt, Steel Lady, Return to Treasure Island, Track of the Cat, Battle Cry, Sea Chase, The Burning Hills, The Girl He Left Behind, Lafayette Escadrille, Gunman's Walk, Damn Yankees, That Kind of Woman, They Came to Cordura, The Pleasure of His Company, Operation Bikini, The Golden Arrow, Ride the Wild Surf, The Loved One, War Gods of the Deep, Birds Do It, Fickle Finger of Fate, Hostile Guns, The Arousers (Sweet Kill), Life and Times of Judge Roy Bean, Timber Tramp, Won Ton Ton the Dog Who Saved Hollywood, Polyester, Pandemonium, Grease 2, Lust in the Dust (also co-prod.), Cameron's Closet, Grotesque, Out of the Dark, Dark Horse (also story).
TELEVISION: *Movies*: San Francisco International, Katie: Portrait of a Centerfold. *Series*: The Tab Hunter Show, Mary Hartman Mary Hartman.

HUNTER, TIM
Director. e. Harvard, AFI.
PICTURES: Over the Edge (co-s.p.). Dir.: Tex (also s.p.), Sylvester, River's Edge, Paint It Black, The Saint of Fort Washington, The Maker .
TELEVISION: *Movie*: Lies of the Twins, People Next Door. *Series*: Homicide: Life on the Street, Chicago Hope, Nowhere Man.

HUPPERT, ISABELLE
Actress. b. Paris, France, March 16, 1955. e. Conservatoire National d'Art Dramatique.
PICTURES: Faustine and the Beautiful Summer (Growing Up; debut, 1971), Cesar and Rosalie, Going Places, Rosebud, The Rape of Innocence, The Judge and the Assassin, The Lacemaker, Violette (Cannes Fest. Award, 1977), The Bronte Sisters, Loulou, Heaven's Gate, Coup de Torchon, Every Man for Himself, The True Story of Camille, Wings of the Dove, Deep Water, Entre Nous, The Trout, Cactus, Signed Charlotte, The Bedroom Window, The Possessed, Story of Women (Venice Fest Award, 1988), Milan Noir, Madame Bovary, Revenge of a Woman, Malina, Apres l'Amour (After Love), Amateur, The Separation, A Judgment in Stone, Love's Debris, The Elective Affinities, Les Palmes de M. Schultz, Rien ne va Plus.
TELEVISION: Gulliver's Travels (voice). *Mini-series*: Seobe.

HURD, GALE ANNE
Producer. b. Los Angeles, CA, Oct. 25, 1955. e. Stanford U., Phi Beta Kappa, 1977. Joined New World Pictures in 1977 as exec. asst. to pres. Roger Corman, then named dir. of advertising and pub. and moved into prod. management capacities on several New World films. Left in 1982 to form own co., Pacific Western Productions. Honored by NATO with special merit award for Aliens. Served as juror, U.S. Film Fest., Utah, 1988 and for 1989 Focus Student Film Awards. Member, Hollywood Women's Political Committee. Board of Trustees, AFI. The Amer. Film Inst. created Gale Anne Hurd production grants for Institute's Directing Workshop for Women. Bd. of dir. The Independent Feature Project/West.

PICTURES: Smokey Bites the Dust (co-prod. with Roger Corman, 1981), The Terminator (Grand Prix, Avoriaz Film Fest., France), Aliens (Hugo Award) Alien Nation (Saturn nom.), The Abyss, Downtown (exec. prod.), Tremors (exec. prod.), Terminator 2 (exec. prod.), The Waterdance, Raising Cain, No Escape, Safe Passage, The Relic, The Ghost and The Darkness, Dante's Peak, Switchback, Snake Eyes, Armageddon, Dead Man on Campus, Virus, Dick.
TELEVISION: *Movies*: Cast a Deadly Spell, Witch Hunt, Sugartime.

HURLEY, ELIZABETH
Actress. b. Hampshire, England, June 10, 1965.
PICTURE: Rowing In the Wind, Aria, Kill Cruise, The Long Winter of '39, Passenger 57, Beyond Bedlam, Mad Dogs and Englishmen, Extreme Measures (prod. only), Dangerous Ground, Austin Powers: International Man of Mystery, Permanent Midnight, Austin Powers: The Spy Who Shagged Me, My Favorite Martian, Edtv, Mickey Blue Eyes (prod. only).
TELEVISION: *Movies/Specials:* Christabel, Act of Will, Death Has a Bad Reputation, Orchid House, Sharpe's Enemy, The World of 007 (host), Samson and Delilah. *Guest:* The Young Indiana Jones Chronicles.

HURLOCK, ROGER W.
Pres. Hurlock Cine-World. b. Cambridge, MD, May 30, 1912. e. Baltimore City Coll. Ent. m.p. ind. as publicist, Hippodrome Theatre, Balt.; asst. mgr., Lessor-operator Imperial and Majestic Theatres, Balt., 1931-35; real estate, bldg., farming, Maryland and Alaska, 1936-58; elected bd. mem., Allied Artists, 1958; asst. to pres., 1961-63; chmn. budget comm., 1963; chmn. policy comm., 1964; c.p. exec. comm. member, 1964; v.p., chf. operating officer 1965; chmn. exec. comm., 1966; pres., 1967. pres., Hurlock Cine-World, 1969.

HURT, JOHN
Actor. b. Shirebrook, Derbyshire, Jan. 22, 1940. e. St. Martin's Sch. for Art, London, RADA.
THEATER: The Dwarfs, Little Malcolm and His Struggle Against the Eunuchs, Man and Superman, Belcher's Luck, Ride a Cock Horse, The Caretaker, Romeo and Juliet, Ruffian on the Streets, The Dumb Waiter, Travesties, The Arrest, The Seagull, The London Vertigo, A Month in the Country.
PICTURES: The Wild and the Willing (debut, 1962), This is My Street, A Man for All Seasons, The Sailor from Gibraltar, Before Winter Comes, Sinful Davey, In Search of Gregory, 10 Rillington Place, Mr. Forbush and the Penguins, The Pied Piper, Little Malcolm, The Naked Civil Servant, La Linea del Fiume, The Ghoul, East of Elephant Rock, The Disappearance, Midnight Express (Acad. Award nom.), Watership Down (voice), The Lord of the Rings (voice), The Shout, Alien, The Elephant Man (Acad. Award nom.), Heaven's Gate, History of the World Part I, Night Crossing, Partners, The Plague Dogs (voice), The Osterman Weekend, Champions, The Hit, Success Is the Best Revenge, 1984, After Darkness, The Black Cauldron (voice), Jake Speed, From the Hip, Spaceballs, Aria, Vincent (voice), White Mischief, Little Sweetheart, Poison Candy, Bengali Night, Scandal, Frankenstein Unbound, The Field, King Ralph, Romeo-Juliet, Resident Alien, Windprints, I Dreamt I Woke Up, Lapse of Memory, Dark at Noon or Eyes and Lies, Monolith, Hans Christian Andersen's Thumbelina (voice), Even Cowgirls Get the Blues, Crime and Punishment, Great Moments in Aviation, Second Best, Betrayal (voice), Rob Roy, Wild Bill, Two Nudes Bathing, Saigon Baby, Dead Man, Love & Death on Long Island, Contact, The Climb, Bandyta, If... Dog... Rabbit, Desert Blue, The Commissioner, All the Little Animals.
TELEVISION: Playboy of the Western World, A Tragedy of Two Ambitions, Green Julia, Nijinsky, Ten from the Twenties, The Peddler, The Naked Civil Servant, Spectre, Deadline, The Jim Henson Hour, King Lear, The Investigation: Inside a Terrorist Bombing, Six Characters in Search of an Author, Shades of Fear, Prisoners in Time. *Mini-series*: Crime and Punishment, I Claudius, The Storyteller, Red Fox.

HURT, MARY BETH
Actress. r.n. Mary Beth Supinger. b. Marshalltown, IA, Sept. 26, 1946. m. writer-dir. Paul Schrader. e. U. of Iowa, NYU Sch. of Arts. Stage debut in 1973 with N.Y. Shakespeare Fest. (More Than You Deserve, Pericles, The Cherry Orchard).
THEATER: As You Like It (Central Park), 2 seasons with Phoenix Theater, Love For Love, Tralawny of the Wells, Secret Service, Boy Meets Girl, Father's Day, Crimes of the Heart, The Misanthrope, Benefactors, The Nest of the Wood Grouse, The Day Room, Othello, A Delicate Balance.
PICTURES: Interiors (debut, 1978), Head Over Heels (Chilly Scenes of Winter), A Change of Seasons, The World According to Garp, D.A.R.Y.L., Compromising Positions, Parents, Slaves of New York, Defenseless, Light Sleeper, My Boyfriend's Back, The Age of Innocence, Six Degrees of Separation, From the Journals of Jean Seberg, Alkali Iowa, Affliction, Boy's Life 2, Bringing Out the Dead.
TELEVISION: *Series*: Nick and Hillary, Working It Out. *Movies*: Baby Girl Scott, Shimmer. *Specials*: The Five-Forty-Eight, Secret Service (NET Theatre). *Guest*: Kojak.

HURT, WILLIAM
Actor. b. Washington, DC, Mar. 20, 1950. Lived as child in South Pacific when father was dir. of Trust Territories for U.S. State Dept. e. Tufts as theology major, switched to drama in jr. year, Juilliard. Acted with Oregon Shakespearean Fest. Leading actor with New York's Circle Repertory Company (Theatre World Award), since 1976,
THEATER: *NY*: The Fifth of July, My Life (Obie Award), Ulysses in Traction, The Runner Stumbles, Hamlet, Childe Byron, Beside Herself. *NY Shakespeare Festival:* Henry V, A Midsummer's Night's Dream, Hurlyburly (off-B'way and B'way). *Regional:* Good (S.F.), Ivanov (Yale).
PICTURES: Altered States (debut, 1980), Eyewitness, Body Heat, The Big Chill, Gorky Park, Kiss of the Spider Woman (Academy Award, 1985), Children of a Lesser God, Broadcast News, A Time of Destiny, The Accidental Tourist, I Love You to Death, Alice, The Doctor, Until the End of the World, Mr. Wonderful, The Plague, Trial by Jury, Second Best, Smoke, Jane Eyre, A Couch in New York, Michael, Loved, Dark City, The Proposition, Lost in Space, One True Thing, The Taste of Sunshine, The Big Brass Ring, The 4th Floor.
TELEVISION: *Specials*: Verna: USO Girl, Best of Families, All the Way Home, The Odyssey of John Dos Passos (voice).

HUSSEY, OLIVIA
Actress. b. Buenos Aires, Apr. 17, 1951. Attended Italia Conti Stage School, London. Began acting at age 8.
PICTURES: The Battle of the Villa Fiorita (debut, 1965), Cup Fever, All the Right Noises, Romeo and Juliet, Summertime Killer, Lost Horizon, Black Christmas, Death on the Nile, The Cat and the Canary, Virus, The Man With Bogart's Face, Escape 2000, Distortions, The Jeweler's Shop, The Undeclared War, Save Me, Ice Cream Man.
TELEVISION: *Movies/Mini-Series:* Jesus of Nazareth, The Pirate, The Bastard, Ivanhoe, Last Days of Pompeii, The Corsican Brothers, Psycho IV: The Beginning, Stephen King's IT, Save Me, Quest of the Delta Knights, H-Bomb, Dead Man's Island, Lonesome Dove, Shame, The Gardener. *Guest*: Murder She Wrote, Boy Meets World.

HUSTON, ANJELICA
Actress. b. Santa Monica, CA, July 8, 1951. Father is late writer-dir.-actor, John Huston. Brother is dir. Danny Huston. Raised in St. Clerans, Ireland. Studied acting at the Loft Studio and with Peggy Furey, Martin Landau. Appeared in 3-D Disney short Captain Eo.
PICTURES: A Walk With Love and Death (debut, 1969), Sinful Davey, Swashbuckler, The Last Tycoon, The Postman Always Rings Twice, Frances, The Ice Pirates, This is Spinal Tap, Prizzi's Honor (Academy Award, best supporting actress, 1985), Good to Go (Short Fuse), Gardens of Stone, The Dead, A Handful of Dust, Mr. North, Crimes and Misdemeanors, Enemies a Love Story (Acad. Award nom.), The Witches, The Grifters (Acad. Award nom.), The Addams Family, The Player (cameo), Manhattan Murder Mystery, Addams Family Values, The Perez Family, The Crossing Guard, Bastard Out of Carolina (dir.), Buffalo `66, Phoenix, Ever After: A Cinderella Story, Agnes Browne (also dir., prod.).
TELEVISION: *Movies*: The Cowboy and the Ballerina, Family Pictures, And the Band Played On. *Specials*: Faerie Tale Theatre, A Rose for Miss Emily. *Mini-Series*: Lonesome Dove, Buffalo Girls.

HUSTON, DANNY
Director. b. Rome, Italy, May 14, 1962. Youngest son of dir.-actor John Huston and actress Zoe Sallis. Brother of actress Anjelica and screenwriter Tony Huston. e. Overseas School, Rome; Intl branch of Milfield School in Exeter, London Film School. A constant visitor to his father's sets throughout the world, he began working on his father's films, beginning in Cuernavaca, Mexico as second-unit dir. on Under the Volcano. Directed TV doc. on Peru and on making of Santa Claus: The Movie; and TV features Bigfoot and Mr. Corbett's Ghost.
PICTURES: Mr. North (debut, 1988), Becoming Colette, The Maddening. *Actor:* Leaving Las Vegas, Ana Karenina, Susan's Plan, Spanish Fly, Rockin' Good Times.
TELEVISION: *Movie*: Ice Princess.

HUTTE, ROBERT E.
Exhibitor. b. Escanaba, MI, Oct. 22, 1917. e. Wisc. Inst. of Technology. Mgr. insp. lab. Iowa Ord. Plant 1940-42, Army Artil. 1942, Entered business as exhibitor in Southern Iowa 1943; then theatre owner and manager there. Elected board of directors, Allied Theatre Owners of Iowa, Nebraska & Missouri 1948, 1950, 1952. Democratic candidate Iowa State Auditor 1960; Pres. Insurance Advisors, Des Moines, IA; pres Leisure Homes, Nursing Homes; pres., Leisure Homes of Texas; pres. Wodon & Romar Prods., Austin, TX 1970-75. Real estate broker & pres Leisure Mor, theatres in West TX; elected board of dir. National Independent Theatre Exhibitors 1979; Pres. Southwestern Indep. Theatre Exhibitors Assn. of TX, OK, AR, LA & NM; 1979 elected pres. Natl. Independent Theatre Exhibitors Assn. 1980-present. Lifetime member, Foundation of Motion Picture Pioneers.

HUTTON, BETTY
Actress. r.n. Betty June Thornburg. b. Battle Creek, MI, Feb. 26, 1921. Sister was singer-actress Marion Hutton. Was vocalist for Vincent Lopez orchestra earning nickname the Blonde Bombshell. Debuted on B'way 1940 in Two for the Show, followed by Panama Hattie. Signed by Paramount in 1941. Returned to stage in Fade Out Fade In, Annie.
PICTURES: The Fleet's In (debut, 1942), Star Spangled Rhythm, Happy Go Lucky, Let's Face It, The Miracle of Morgan's Creek, And the Angels Sing, Here Come the Waves, Incendiary Blonde, Duffy's Tavern, The Stork Club, Cross My Heart, The Perils of Pauline, Dream Girl, Red Hot and Blue, Annie Get Your Gun, Let's Dance, Sailor Beware (cameo), The Greatest Show on Earth, Somebody Loves Me, Spring Reunion.
TELEVISION: *Series*: The Betty Hutton Show (1959-60). *Special*: Satins and Spurs. *Guest*: Dinah Shore Chevy Show, Greatest Show on Earth, Burke's Law, Gunsmoke.

HUTTON, BRIAN, G.
Director. b. New York, NY, 1935. Started as bit player in films (incl. Fear Strikes Out, Gunfight at the O.K. Corral) before dir. for tv, then features.
PICTURES: The Wild Seed (debut, 1965), The Pad and How to Use It, Sol Madrid, Where Eagles Dare, Kelly's Heroes, X Y and Zee (Zee & Company), Night Watch, The First Deadly Sin, High Road to China, Hostile Takeover.
TELEVISION: Institute For Revenge.

HUTTON, LAUREN
Actress. r.n. Mary Laurence Hutton. b. Charleston, SC, Nov. 17, 1943. e. U. of South Florida, Sophie Newcombe Coll. As model featured on more covers than any other American. Stage debut at LA Public Theatre in Extremities.
PICTURES: Paper Lion (debut, 1968), Pieces of Dreams, Little Fauss and Big Halsy, Rocco Papaleo, The Gambler, Gator, Welcome to L.A., Viva Knievel!, A Wedding, American Gigolo, Paternity, Zorro the Gay Blade, Tout Feu tout Flamme (Hecate), Lassiter, Once Bitten, Flagrant Desire, Malone, Blue Blood, Bulldance (Forbidden Sun), Run For Your Life, Billions, Guilty as Charged, Missing Pieces, My Father the Hero, A Rat's Tale, 54, Loser Love, Just a Little Harmless Sex.
TELEVISION: *Mini-Series*: The Rhinemann Exchange, Sins. *Movies*: Someone Is Watching Me, Institute for Revenge, Starflight, The Cradle Will Fall, Scandal Sheet, The Return of Mike Hammer, Time Stalker, Monte Carlo, Perfect People, Fear, We the Jury. *Series*: Paper Dolls, Falcon Crest, Lauren Hutton and... (talk show), Central Park West.

HUTTON, TIMOTHY
Actor. b. Malibu, CA, Aug. 16, 1960. Father was late actor Jim Hutton. Debut in bit part in father's film Never Too Late. Acted in high school plays; toured with father in Harvey during vacation. Directed Cars video Drive (1984).
THEATER: *NY*: Love Letters (B'way debut, 1989), Prelude to a Kiss, Babylon Gardens.
PICTURES: Never Too Late (debut, 1965), Ordinary People (Academy Award, best supporting actor, 1980; also Golden Globe & LA Film Critics Awards), Taps, Daniel, Iceman, The Falcon and The Snowman, Turk 182, Made in Heaven, A Time of Destiny, Betrayed (cameo), Everybody's All American, Torrents of Spring, Q&A, Strangers, The Temp, The Dark Half, French Kiss, Beautiful Girls, The Substance of Fire, City of Industry, City of Industry, Playing God, Deterrence, The General's Daughter.
TELEVISION: *Movies*: Zuma Beach, Friendly Fire, The Best Place to Be, And Baby Makes Six, Young Love First Love, Father Figure, A Long Way Home, Zelda, The Last Word, Mr. & Mrs. Loving, Dead by Midnight, Vig, Aldrich Ames: Traitor Within. *Director*: Amazing Stories (Grandpa's Ghost).

HUYCK, WILLARD
Writer, Director. e. U. of Southern California. Worked as reader for Larry Gordon, executive at American-International Pictures; named Gordon's asst., working on scene rewrites for AIP films. First screen credit on The Devil's Eight as co-writer with John Milius.
PICTURES: *Writer*: French Postcards (also dir.), Indiana Jones and the Temple of Doom, Best Defense (also dir.), Howard the Duck (also dir.), Radioland Murders, Mission: Impossible.
TELEVISION: A Father's Homecoming (co-exec. prod., co-s.p.), American River (co-exec. prod., co-s.p.).

HYAMS, JOSEPH
Advertising & Publicity Executive. b. New York, NY, Sept. 21, 1926. e. NYU Ent. industry, 1947. Various publicity posts, 20th Century-Fox, Columbia Pictures, 1947-55; eastern pub. mgr., Figaro Prods., 1955-56; West Coast pub. mgr., Hecht-Hill-Lancaster, 1955-58; pub. adv. dir., Batjac Prods. 1959-60 national adv. & pub. dir., Warner Bros.-7 Arts, 1960. v.p., worldwide pub., Warner Bros., Inc., 1970-87; sr. v.p., special projects, 1987.

HYAMS, PETER
Director, Writer, Cinematographer. b. New York, NY, July 26, 1943. e. Hunter Coll., Syracuse U. Joined CBS news staff N.Y. and made anchor man. Filmed documentary on Vietnam in 1966. Left CBS in 1970 and joined Paramount in Hollywood as writer. Hired by ABC to direct TV features.
PICTURES: *Writer:* T.R. Baskin (also prod.), Telefon, The Hunter. *Exec. Prod.:* The Monster Squad. *Director:* Busting (dir. debut 1974; also s.p.), Our Time (also s.p.), Peeper, Capricorn One (also s.p..), Hanover Street (also s.p)., Outland (also s.p.), The Star Chamber (also s.p.), 2010 (also prod., s.p., photog.), Running Scared (also exec. prod., photog.), The Presidio (also photog.), Narrow Margin (also s.p., photog.), Stay Tuned (also photog.), Timecop (also photog.), Sudden Death (also photog.), The Relic (also photog.) .
TELEVISION: *Movies* (dir., writer): The Rolling Man, Goodnight My Love.

HYDE, TOMMY
Executive. r.n. Thomas L. b. Meridian, MS, June 29, 1916. e. Lakeland H.S., grad., 1935. Worked E.J. Sparks Theatres, 1932-41. Florida State Theatres, 1941-42. U.S. Navy, 1942-46. Florida State Theatres, 1946-47; city mgr. (Tallahassee). Talgar Theatres, 1947-58; v.p. and gen. mgr. Kent Theatres, 1958-86; vice-pres. Motion Picture Films, Inc.; pres., NATO of Florida, 1961-62; chmn. bd. 1963-70; 1987-, theatre consultant.

HYER, MARTHA
Actress. b. Fort Worth, TX, Aug. 10, 1924. e. Northwestern U., Pasadena Playhouse.
PICTURES: The Locket (debut, 1946), Thunder Mountain, Born to Kill, Woman on the Beach, The Velvet Touch, Gun Smugglers, The Judge Steps Out, Clay Pigeon, Roughshod, The Rustlers, The Lawless, Outcast of Black Mesa, Salt Lake Raiders, Frisco Tornado, Geisha Girl, The Kangaroo Kid, The Invisible Mr. Unmei, Wild Stallion, Yukon Gold, Abbott and Costello Go to Mars, So Big, Riders to the Stars, Scarlet Spear, Battle of Rogue River, Lucky Me, Down Three Dark Streets, Sabrina, Cry Vengeance, Wyoming Renegades, Kiss of Fire, Paris Follies of 1956, Francis in the Navy, Red Sundown, Showdown at Abilene, Battle Hymn, Kelly and Me, Mister Cory, The Delicate Delinquent, My Man Godfrey, Paris Holiday, Once Upon a Horse, Houseboat, Some Came Running (Acad. Award nom.), The Big Fisherman, The Best of Everything, Ice Palace, Desire in the Dust, Mistress of the World, The Right Approach, The Last Time I Saw Archie, Girl Named Tamiko, The Man from the Diner's Club, Wives and Lovers, Pyro, The Carpetbaggers, First Men in the Moon, Blood on the Arrow, Bikini Beach, The Sons of Katie Elder, The Chase, Night of the Grizzly, Picture Mommy Dead, War Italian Style, The Happening, Some May Live, Lo Scatenato (Catch as Catch Can), House of 1000 Dolls, Once You Kiss a Stranger, Crossplot, Day of the Wolves.
TELEVISION: *Guest*: Adventures of Wild Bill Hickock, Zane Greay Theatre, The Virginian, The Alfred Hitchcock Hour, Bewitched, The Young Lawyers.

HYMAN, DICK
Composer. b. New York, NY, March 8, 1927.
PICTURES: Erased Off, French Quarter, Stardust Memories, Zelig, Broadway Danny Rose (also mus. supv.), The Purple Rose of Cairo, Moonstruck, Thelonious Monk: Straight—No Chaser, Radio Days (mus. supv.), The Lemon Sisters, Alan & Naomi, Mighty Aphrodite, Everyone Says I Love You.
TELEVISION: Bernice Bobs Her Hair, The Last Tenant, Natica Jackson, Ask Me Again.

I

IANNUCCI, SALVATORE J.
Executive. b. Brooklyn, NY, Sept. 24, 1927. e. NYU, B.A., 1949; Harvard Law School, J.D., 1952. 2 yrs. legal departments RCA and American Broadcasting Companies, Inc.; 14 yrs. with CBS Television Network: asst. dir. of bus. affairs, dir. of bus. affairs, v.p. of bus. affairs; 2 yrs. v.p. admin. National General Corp.; 2-1/2 yrs. pres. of Capital Records; 4-1/2 yrs. Corp. v.p. and dir. of Entertainment Div. of Playboy Enterprises, Inc.; 4 yrs. partner with Jones, Day Reavis & Pogue in Los Angeles office, handling entertainment legal work; Pres., Filmways Entertainment, and sr. v.p., Filmways, Inc.; exec. v.p., Embassy Communications; COO, Aaron Spelling Prods.; sr. partner Bushkin, Gaims, Gaines, & Jonas; pres. and chief operating officer, Brad Marks International; prod. of features, tv movies and infomercials.

IBERT, LLOYD
Executive. Began career as mgng. editor, Independent Film Journal. 1973, joined Paramount Pictures pub. dept.; named sr. publicist. 1985, appointed dir., natl. pub. for M.P. Group.

ICE CUBE
Actor, Singer. r.n. O'Shea Jackson. b. Los Angeles, CA, June 15, 1969. e. Phoenix Inst. of Tech. Debuted as rap performer with group N.W.A. Solo debut 1990 with album Amerikkka's Most Wanted.
PICTURES: Boyz N the Hood (debut, 1991), Trespass, CB4 (cameo), Higher Learning, Friday (also co-s.p., co-exec. prod.), The Glass Shield, Anaconda, Dangerous Ground (also exec. prod.), The Players' Club (also co-s.p., co-exec. prod., dir.), I Got the Hook-up, Three Kings, Next Friday (also co-s.p., co-exec. prod.).

ICE-T
Actor, Singer. r.n. Tracy Marrow. b. Newark, NJ, February 16, 1958. Raised in Los Angeles. Served 4 yrs. as ranger in U.S. Army. Made debut as rap performer with 1982 single The Coldest Rap. Received Grammy Award 1990 for Back on the Block.
PICTURES: Breakin' (debut, 1984), Breakin' 2: Electric Boogaloo, New Jack City, Ricochet, Trespass, Who's the Man?, Surviving the Game, Tank Girl, Johnny Mnemonic, Below Utopia, Rhyme & Reason (cameo), The Deli, Crazy Six, The Replacement, Jacob Two Two Meets the Hooded Fang, Final Voyage.
TELEVISION: *Movies:* Exiled. *Series*: Players. *Guest*: New York Undercover.

IDLE, ERIC
Actor, Writer. b. South Shields, England, March 29, 1943. e. Pembroke Coll., Cambridge, 1962-65. Pres. Cambridge's Footlights appearing at Edinburgh Fest. 1963-64. Member Monty Python's Flying Circus appearing on BBC, 1969-74.
THEATER: Oh What a Lovely War, Monty Python Live at the Hollywood Bowl, Monty Python Live, The Mikado (English Natl. Opera, 1986).
BOOKS: Hello Sailor, The Rutland Dirty Weekend Book, Pass the Bulter; as well as co-author of Monty Python books: Monty Python's Big Red Book, The Brand New Monty Python Book, Monty Python and the Holy Grail, The Complete Works of Shakespeare and Monty Python.
PICTURES: And Now for Something Completely Different (also co-s.p.), Monty Python and the Holy Grail (also co-s.p.), Monty Python's Life of Brian (also co-s.p.), Monty Python Live at the Hollywood Bowl (also co-s.p.), Monty Python's The Meaning of Life (also co-s.p.), Yellowbeard, National Lampoon's European Vacation, Transformers (voice), The Adventures of Baron Munchausen, Nuns on the Run, Too Much Sun, Missing Pieces, Mom & Dad Save the World, Splitting Heirs (also s.p., exec. prod.), Casper, The Wind and the Willows, An Alan Smithee Film: Burn Hollywood Burn, Quest for Camelot, Dudley Do-Right, South Park: Bigger Longer and Uncut (voice).
TELEVISION: Isadora (debut, 1965), The Frost Report (writer), Do Not Adjust Your Set, Monty Python's Flying Circus, Rutland Weekend Television (series), All You Need is Cash (The Rutles), Faerie Tale Theater (The Frog Prince; dir., writer ACE Award, 1982; The Pied Piper), Saturday Night Live, The Mikado, Around the World in 80 Days, Nearly Departed (series).

IDZIAK, SLAVOMIR
Cinematogrpaher.
PICTURES: A Woman's Decision, The Scar, Partita for a Wooden Instrument, The Conductor, Constancy, The Contract, Imperative, The Year of the Quiet Sun, Power of Evil, Harmagedon, A Short Film About Killing, Yasemin, Wherever You Are, Inventory, The Double Life of Veronique, Blue, Weltmesiter, The Journey of August King, Lilian's Story, Mannerpension, Tears of Stone, Men With Guns, Gattaca, Commandments, I Want You, Love and Rage, The Last September, Paranoid, LiebesLuder, Proof of Life.
TELEVISION: *Movies:* Podrozni jak inni, Gory o zmierzchu, Pizama, The Underground Passage, From A Far Country: Pope John Paul, The Unapproachable, The Decalogue, Long Conversation with a Bird.

IGER, ROBERT
Executive. b. New York, NY, 1951. e. Ithaca Col. Joined ABC in 1974 as studio supervisor. 1976 moved to ABC Sports. 1985, named v.p. in charge of program plan. & dev. as well as scheduling and rights acquisitions for all ABC Sports properties. 1987, named v.p. program. for ABC Sports and mgr. & dir. for ABC's Wide World of Sports; 1988, appt. exec. v.p., ABC Network Group. 1989 named pres., ABC Entertainment. 1992 became pres. of ABC TV Network Group.; 1993, sr. v.p. CC/ABC Inc., exec. v.p. of Capital Cities/ABC Inc. Sept., 1994, elected pres. & COO.

IMAMURA, SHOHEI
Director, Producer, Writer. b. Tokyo, Japan, Sept. 15, 1926. e. Waseda U. Joined Shochiku Ofuna Studio 1951 asst. dir., transferred Nikkatsu in 1954 as asst. dir., director Stolen Desire 1958 then 4 more films before refusing to work on any film distasteful to him; and wrote play later made into film directed by him in 1968; later turned to documentaries and from 1976 onward as independent; Ballad of Narayama awarded Golden Palm Prize, Cannes Festival, 1983.
PICTURES: *Director*: Bakumatsu Taiyoden (writer, asst. dir. only), Stolen Desire, Lights of Night, Endless Desire, Nianchan, Big Brother, Pigs and Battleships, Insect Woman, Intentions of Murder, The Pornographers, A Man Vanishes, The Profound Desire of the Gods, Human Evaporation, History of Postwar Japan, Karayuki-san—the Making of a Prostitue, Vengeance Is Mine, Why Not?, The Ballad of Narayama (also writer), Zegen, Black Rain (also writer), Unagi (The Eel, also writer; Palme d'Or).

IMI, TONY
Cinematographer. b. London, March 27, 1937. Ent. ind. 1959.
PICTURES: The Raging Moon, Dulcima, The Slipper and the Rose, International Velvet, Brass Target, Ffolkes, The Sea Wolves, Night Crossing, Nate and Hayes, Not Quite Jerusalem, Enemy Mine, Empire State, American Roulette, Buster, Options, Wired, Fire Birds, Pretty Hattie's Baby, Shopping, Downtime, Aimee and Jaguar.
TELEVISION: Queenie, The Return of Sherlock Holmes, Oceans of Fire, The Last Days of Frank and Jesse James, Reunion at Fairborough, A Christmas Carol, Sakharov, Princess Daisy, John Paul II, Little Gloria–Happy at Last, Inside the Third Reich, Dreams Don't Die, For Ladies Only, Nicholas Nickleby, A Tale of Two Cities, Babycakes, Old Man and the Sea, Fourth Story, The Last to Go, Our Sons, Carolina Skeletons, Child of Rage, Queen, Cobb's Law, For the Love of My Child: The Anissa Ayala Story, Blind Angel, Scarlett, The Sunshine Boys, The Turn of the Screw, Dalva, The Abduction, Desperate Justice.

IMMERMAN, WILLIAM J.
Producer, Attorney, Executive. b. New York, NY, Dec. 29, 1937. e. Univ. Wisconsin, BS, 1959; Stanford Law, J.D., 1963. 1963-65, served as deputy district attorney, LA County. 1965-72, assoc. counsel, v.p.-bus. affairs, American Intl. Pictures. 1972-77, v.p., business affairs, sr. v.p. feature film division 20th Century-Fox. 1977-1979, producer at Warner Bros. 1979-82, founder and chmn. of bd. of Cinema Group Inc. 1978-present, pres. Salem Productions. 1988-94, pres. Distribution Expense Co. 1988-present, pres., ImmKirk Financial Corp. 1988-89, spec. consultant to office of pres., Pathe Communications. 1989-90, vice chmn. Cannon Pictures. 1986-90, dir. Heritage Ent., Inc. 1991-present, v.p. The Crime Channel, 1983-93, of counsel to law firm of Barash and Hill. 1993-present, of Counsel to law firm of Kenoff and Machtinger (LA). 1990-present, Regional Adjudicator (Southwest). Member of AFMA Arbitration Panel. Member of AMPAS. Stage Productions: Berlin to Broadway (LA), The Knife Thrower's Assistant (LA, tour), The Wiz (B'way).
PICTURES: *Exec. prod.*: Highpoint, Southern Comfort, Hysterical, Mind Games, Take this Job and Shove It, Where the Red Ferns Grows Part II, The St. Tammany Miracle. *Prod.*: Primal Rage, Nightmare Beach (Welcome to Spring Break).

INDELLI, JOSEPH
Executive. e. Vanderbilt U., 1948. Began TV career at MGM/Chicago in sales, 1968-80, Regional Sales Mgr.; Pres., Columbia Pictures Television Dist., 1980-86; Pres., MTM Television Dist. Grp., 1986-89; Exec. VP, Orion Pictures Television, 1989-97.

INGALLS, DON
Producer, Writer. b. Humboldt, NE, July 29, 1928. e. George Washington U., 1948. Columnist, Washington Post; producer-writer, ATV England and Australia; writer-prod., Have Gun Will Travel, also prod. for TV: The Travels of Jamie McPheeters, The Virginian, Honey West, Serpico, Kingston: Confidential. Exec. story consultant The Sixth Sense; prod.: Fantasy Island, T.J. Hooker, Duel at Shiloh, Smile of the Dragon, In Preparation: Watchers on the Mountain, Hearts & Diamonds, Motherwit, Funny Man, Beaumaris.
PICTURES: Airport—1975, Who's Got the Body?
TELEVISION: *Writer*: Gunsmoke, Have Gun Will Travel, The Bold Ones, Marcus Welby M.D., Mod Squad, Star Trek, Honey West, Bonanza, The Sixth Sense, Then Came Bronson, Police Story, World Premier Movie, Shamus, Flood, Capt. America, The Initiation of Sarah, Blood Sport, Fantasy Island.

INGELS, MARTY
Actor, Former Comedian, Executive. b. Brooklyn, NY, Mar. 9, 1936. m actress-singer Shirley Jones. U.S. Infantry 1954-58. Ent. show business representing Army, Name That Tune. Stage: Sketchbook revue, Las Vegas. Pres., Celebrity Brokerage, packaging celebrity events and endorsements. Active in community affairs and charity funding.
PICTURES: The Ladies Man, Armored Command, The Horizontal Lieutenant, The Busy Body, Wild and Wonderful, A Guide for the Married Man, If It's Tuesday It Must be Belgium, For Singles Only, Instant Karma, Round Numbers, The Opposite Sex, How to Live with Them, Cops and Robertsons.
TELEVISION: *Series*: I'm Dickens... He's Fenster, The Phyllis Diller Show. *Guest*: Phil Silvers Show, Steve Allen, Jack Paar, Playboy Penthouse, Bell Telephone Hour, Manhunt, Ann Sothern Show, Peter Loves Mary, The Detectives, Joey Bishop Show, Hennessey, Dick Van Dyke Show, Burke's Law, Hollywood Palace, Family, Murder She Wrote.

INMAN, ROBERT
Writer.
TELEVISION: *Movies*: Home Fires Burning, My Son Is Innocent, The Summer of Ben Tyler (also prod., Writers' Guild Award, 1998), Family Blessings.

INSDORF, ANNETTE
Film Professor, Critic, Translator, TV Host. b. Paris, France. e. 1963-68 studied voice, Juilliard Sch. of Music and performed as singer; Queens Coll. (summa cum laude), B.A. 1972; Yale U., M.A., 1973; Yale U., Ph.D., 1975. 1973: soloist in Leonard Bernstein's Mass (European premiere in Vienna and BBC/WNET TV). 1975-87: professor of film, Yale U. Author of Francois Truffaut (1979; updated 1989), Indelible Shadows: Film and the Holocaust (1983, updated 1989). Since 1979: frequent contributor to NY Times (Arts and Leisure), Los Angeles Times, San Francisco Chronicle, Film Comment, and Premiere. Named Chevalier dans l'ordre des arts et lettres by French Ministry of Culture, 1986. Since 1987, dir. of Undergrad. Film Studies, Columbia U., and prof. Graduate Film Div. 1990 named chmn. of Film Div. 1987: exec.-prod. Shoeshine (short film nom. for Oscar). 1989: exec. prod., Tom Abrams' Performance Pieces (named best fiction short, Cannes Fest).

IRELAND, SIMONE
Casting Director.
PICTURES: Circle of Friends, Madagascar Skin, Jude, Hamlet, Welcome to Sarajevo, Under the Skin, Spice World, My Son the Fanatic, Resurrection Man, I Want You, What Rat's Won't Do, Appetite, Elizabeth, Hilary and Jackie, Alegria, The Lost Son.

IRONS, JEREMY
Actor. b. Isle of Wight, UK, Sept. 19, 1948. m. actress Sinead Cusack. e. Sherborne Sch., Dorset. Stage career began at Marlowe Theatre, Canterbury, where he was student asst. stage manager. Accepted at Bristol Old Vic Theatre Sch. for two-yr. course; then joined Bristol Old Vic Co. In London played in Godspell, Much Ado About Nothing, The Caretaker, Taming of the Shrew, Wild Oats, Rear Column, An Audience Called Edouard, etc. N.Y. stage debut, The Real Thing (Tony Award, 1984).
PICTURES: Nijinsky (debut, 1980), The French Lieutenant's Woman, Moonlighting, Betrayal, The Wild Duck, Swann in Love, The Mission, Dead Ringers, A Chorus of Disapproval, Danny the Champion of the World (tv in U.S.), Australia, Reversal of Fortune (Academy Award, 1990), Kafka, Waterland, Damage, M. Butterfly, The House of the Spirits, The Lion King (voice), Die Hard With a Vengeance,Stealing Beauty, Lolita, The Man in the Iron Mask, Chinese Box, Longitude, Dungeons & Dragons.
TELEVISION: The Pallisers, Notorious Woman, Love for Lydia, Langrishe Go Down, Brideshead Revisited, The Captain's Doll, Autogeddon, Tales From Hollywood, The Dream of a Ridiculous Man, The Great War (voice).

IRONSIDE, MICHAEL
Actor. b. Toronto, Ontario, Canada, Feb. 12, 1950. e. Ontario Col. of Art.
PICTURES: Scanners, Visiting Hours, Spacehunter: Adventures in the Forbidden Zone, The Falcon and the Snowman, Jo Jo Dancer Your Life Is Calling, Top Gun, Extreme Prejudice, Nowhere to Hide, Hello Mary Lou: Prom Night II, Watchers, Total Recall, McBain, Highlander II: The Quickening, The Vagrant, Fortunes of War, The Killing Man, Free Willy, The Next Karate Kid, Major Payne, The Glass Shield, Starship Troopers, Desert Blue, Chicago Cab, Captive, Black Light, Going to Kansas City, One of Our Own, Ivory Tower, The Omega Code.
TELEVISION: *Series*: V, ER, seaQuest DSV. *Movie*: Probable Cause (also co-exec. prod.), The Arrow, Voyage of Terror, Nuremberg.

IRVIN, JOHN
Director. b. Cheshire, England, May 7, 1940. In cutting rooms at Rank Organisation before making first film documentary, Gala Day, on grant from British Film Inst.; made other award-winning documentaries before turning to features.
PICTURES: The Dogs of War (debut, 1981), Ghost Story, Champions, Turtle Diary, Raw Deal, Hamburger Hill, Next of Kin, Eminent Domain, Widow's Peak, A Month by the Lake, City of Industry, Wisegirls.
TELEVISION: The Nearly Man, Hard Times, Tinker Tailor Soldier Spy, Robin Hood (foreign theatrical), Crazy Horse, When Trumphets Fade, Noah's Ark.

IRVING, AMY
Actress. b. Palo Alto, CA, Sept. 10, 1953. e. American Conservatory Theatre, London Acad. of Dramatic Art. Daughter of late theatre dir. Jules Irving and actress Priscilla Pointer. m. director Bruno Barreto.
THEATER: *NY*: Amadeus, Heartbreak House, Road to Mecca, Broken Glass. *LA*: The Heidi Chronicles.
PICTURES: Carrie (debut, 1976), The Fury, Voices, Honeysuckle Rose, The Competition, Yentl (Acad. Award nom.), Micki and Maude, Rumpelstiltskin, Who Framed Roger Rabbit (voice), Crossing Delancey, A Show of Force, An American Tail: Fievel Goes West (voice), Benefit of the Doubt, Kleptomania, Acts of Love (also co- exec. prod.), I'm Not Rappaport, Carried Away, Deconstructing Harry, One Tough Cop, Blue Ridge Fall, The Confession, The Rage: Carrie 2.
TELEVISION: *Movies*: James Dean, James A. Michener's Dynasty, Panache, Anastasia: The Mystery of Anna. Mini-*Series*: Once an Eagle, The Far Pavilions. *Specials*: I'm a Fool, Turn of the Screw, Heartbreak House, Twilight Zone: Rod Serling's Lost Classics: The Theater. *Guest*: The Rookies, Police Woman.

IRWIN, BILL
Actor. b. Santa Monica, CA, April 11, 1950.
THEATER: *B'way*: Accidental Death of an Anarchist, 5-6-7-8 Dance, Largely New York, Fool Moon. *Off-B'way*: The Regard of Flight, The Courtroom, Not Quite New York, Waiting for Godot. Regional: Scapin (also dir., adaptation).
PICTURES: Popeye (debut, 1980), A New Life, Eight Men Out, My Blue Heaven, Scenes From a Mall, Hot Shots!, Stepping Out, Silent Tongue, Manhattan by Numbers, Water Ride.
TELEVISION: *Movies*: Subway Stories: Tales from the Underground. *Specials*: The Regard of Flight, Bette Midler—Mondo Beyondo, The Paul Daniels Magic Show (BBC), The Last Mile. *Guest*: Cosby Show, Northern Exposure.

ISAACS, CHERYL BOONE
Executive. b. Springfield, MA. Entered m.p. industry 1977 as staff publicist for Columbia Pictures. Worked five years after that for Melvin Simon Prods., named v.p. Left to become dir. of adv./pub. for The Ladd Co. 1984, named dir., pub. & promo., West Coast, for Paramount Pictures. Promoted to vice pres., Worldwide Publicity, Paramount, 1986; sr. v.p., Worldwide Publicity, Paramount, 1991; exec. v.p., Worldwide Publicity, Paramount, 1994. Member A.M.P.A.S. Board of Governors since 1988.

ISAACS, PHIL
Executive. b. New York, NY, May 20, 1922. e. City Coll. of New York. In U.S. Navy, 1943-46. Joined Paramount Pictures in 1946 as bookers asst., N.Y. exch. Branch mgr. in Washington; then mgr. Rocky Mt. div. In 1966 was Eastern-Southern sls. mgr.; 1967 joined Cinema Center Films as v.p. domestic dist. In 1972 named v.p., marketing, for Tomorrow Entertainment; Joined Avco-Embassy 1975 as v.p., gen. sls. mgr., named exec. v.p., 1977. 1978 joined General Cinema Corp. as v.p. 1980 v.p., gen. sls. mgr., Orion Pictures. 1983, formed Phil Isaacs Co; 1988, v.p., general sales mgr., TWE Theatrical; 1989, appointed pres. Became pres. South Gate Entertainment 1989.

ISRAEL, NEAL
Writer, Director, Producer.
PICTURES: Tunnelvision (exec. prod., s.p., actor), Cracking Up (s.p., actor), Americathon (dir., s.p.), Police Academy (s.p.), Bachelor Party (dir., s.p.), Johnny Dangerously (actor), Moving Violations (dir., s.p.), Real Genius (s.p.), It's Alive III (s.p.), Buy and Cell (co-s.p.), Look Who's Talking Too (co-prod., actor), Spurting Blood (exec. prod., s.p.), All I Want for Christmas (co-s.p.), Breaking the Rules (dir.), Surf Ninjas (dir., actor), Tunnelvision (co-dir.),Three O'clock High (prod.).
TELEVISION: Lola Falana Special (writer), Mac Davis Show, Ringo, Marie (prod.), Twilight Theatre (writer, prod.), Man of the People (co-prod.), The Wonder Years (dir.), Hearts of the West (dir.). Movies: The Cover Girl and the Cop (dir.), Woman With a Past (co-exec. prod.), Combat High (dir.), Taking the Heat (co-prod.), Dream Date (prod.), Bonnie and Clyde: The True Story (co-prod.), A Quiet Little Neighborhood (co-prod.), Foster's Field Trip (dir., writer), Family Reunion: A Relative Nightmare (dir., co-writer, co-prod.), National Lampoon's Dad's Week Off (dir., writer), Nash Bridges (dir.) Clueless (dir.).

IVANEK, ZELJKO
Actor. b. Ljubljana, Yugoslavia, Aug. 15, 1957. Came to U.S. with family in 1960 and returned to homeland before settling in Palo Alto, CA, in 1967. Studied at Yale, majoring in theatre studies: graduated in 1978. Also graduate of London Acad. of Music and Dramatic Arts. Was member of Williamstown Theatre Festival, appearing in Hay Fever, Charley's Aunt, Front Page. B'way debut in The Survivor.
THEATER: *B'way*: The Survivor, Brighton Beach Memoirs, Loot, Two Shakespearean Actors, The Glass Menagerie. Regional: Master Harold... and the Boys (Yale Rep. premiere prod.), Hamlet (Guthrie), Ivanov (Yale Rep.). *Off B'way*: Cloud 9, A Map of the World, The Cherry Orchard.
PICTURES: Tex, The Sender, The Soldier, Mass Appeal, Rachel River, School Ties.
TELEVISION: *Movies*: The Sun Also Rises, Echoes in the Darkness, Aftermath: A Test of Love, Our Sons, My Brother's Keeper, Truman. *Special*: All My Sons. *Guest*: Homicide: Life on the Street.

IVANY, PETER
Executive. b. Melbourne, Australia, Aug. 23, 1954. e. Monash U. Melbourne, B.A. Victoria Health Commission as strategic planning analyst, 1978-80. Kodak Australia, estimating and planning analyst, 1980-81. Joined Hoyts Corporation Pty Ltd. in 1982 as cinema mgr., then general mgr., Hoyts Video; general mgr., corporate development, 1988. Presently, CEO Hoyts Corp.

IVEY, JUDITH
Actress. b. El Paso, TX, Sept. 4, 1951. m. ind. prod., Tim Braine. e. Illinois State U. Stage debut in The Sea in Chicago, 1974.
THEATER: Bedroom Farce, The Goodbye People, Oh Coward!, Design for Living, Piaf, Romeo and Juliet, Pastorale, Two Small Bodies, Steaming (Tony & Drama Desk Awards), Second Lady (off-B'way work she helped develop), Hurlyburly (Tony & Drama Desk Awards), Precious Sons (Drama Desk nom.), Blithe Spirit, Mrs. Dally Has a Lover, Park Your Car in Harvard Yard (Tony nom.), The Moonshot Tape (Obie Award), A Fair Country, A Madhouse in Goa.

PICTURES: Harry and Son (debut, 1984), The Lonely Guy, The Woman in Red, Compromising Positions, Brighton Beach Memoirs, Hello Again, Sister Sister, Miles from Home, In Country, Everybody Wins, Alice, Love Hurts, There Goes the Neighborhood, Washington Square, The Devil's Advocate, Without Limits, Mystery Alaska.
TELEVISION: *Series*: Down Home, Designing Women, The Critic (voice), The Five Mrs. Buchanans, Buddies. *Movies*: The Shady Hill Kidnapping, Dixie: Changing Habits, We Are the Children, The Long Hot Summer, Jesse and the Bandit Queen, Decoration Day, Her Final Fury: Betty Broderick—The Last Chapter, On Promised Land, Almost Golden: The Jessica Savitch Story, What the Deaf Man Saw. *Special*: Other Mothers (Afterschool Special).

IVORY, JAMES
Director. b. Berkeley, CA, June 7, 1928. e. U. of Oregon, B.F.A., 1951; U. of Southern California, M.A. (cinema) 1956. First film Venice: Theme and Variations (doc. made as M.A. thesis, 1957). Early work: The Sword and the Flute, The Delhi Way. Formed Merchant Ivory Productions with prod. Ismail Merchant and script writer Ruth Prawer Jhabvala. Received D.W. Griffith Lifetime Achievement Award from DGA, 1995, Commandeur Des Arts et Des Lettres, France 1996.
PICTURES: The Householder, Shakespeare Wallah (also co-s.p.), The Guru (also co-s.p.), Bombay Talkie (also co-s.p.), Savages, The Wild Party, Roseland, The Europeans (also cameo), Quartet, Heat and Dust, The Bostonians, A Room With a View, Maurice (also co-s.p.), Slaves of New York, Mr. and Mrs. Bridge, Howards End, The Remains of the Day, Jefferson in Paris, Surviving Picasso, A Soldier's Daughter Never Cries (also s.p.), The Golden Bowl.
TELEVISION: Noon Wine (exec. prod.). Dir: Adventures of a Brown Man in Search of Civilization, Autobiography of a Princess (also released theatrically), Hullabaloo Over George and Bonnie's Pictures, Jane Austen in Manhattan (also released theatrically), The Five Forty Eight.

J

JACKSON, ANNE
Actress. b. Allegheny, PA, Sept. 3, 1926. e. Neighborhood Playhouse, Actors Studio. Married to actor Eli Wallach. Stage debut in The Cherry Orchard, 1944. Autobiography: Early Stages.
THEATER: Major Barbara, Middle of the Night, The Typist and the Tiger, Luv, Waltz of the Toreadors, Twice Around the Park, Summer and Smoke, Nest of the Woodgrouse, Marco Polo Sings a Solo, The Mad Woman of Chaillot, Cafe Crown, Lost in Yonkers, In Persons, The Flowering Peach, Love Letters.
PICTURES: So Young So Bad (debut, 1950), The Journey, Tall Story, The Tiger Makes Out, How to Save a Marriage and Ruin Your Life, The Secret Life of an American Wife, The Angel Levine, Zig Zag, Lovers and Other Strangers, Dirty Dingus Magee, Nasty Habits, The Bell Jar, The Shining, Sam's Son, Funny About Love, Folks!
TELEVISION: *Series*: Everything's Relative. *Special*: 84 Charing Cross Road. *Movies*: The Family Man, A Woman Called Golda, Private Battle, Blinded By the Light, Leave 'em Laughing, Baby M.

JACKSON, BRIAN
Actor, Film & Theatre Producer. b. Bolton, England, 1931. Early career in photography then numerous stage performances incl. Old Vic, Royal Shakespeare. Ent. film/TV industry 1958. Formed Quintus Plays, 1965; formed Brian Jackson Productions 1966; formed Hampden Gurney Studios Ltd. 1970. Co-produced The Others 1967; presented The Button, 1969; co-produced the documentary film Village in Mayfair, 1970; 1971: Formed Brian Jackson Films Ltd.; produced Yesterday, The Red Deer, The Story of Tutankhamen.
THEATER: Mame, Drury Lane, Fallen Angels, In Praise of Love.
PICTURES: Incident in Karandi, Carry On Sergeant, Gorgo, Jack the Ripper, Taste of Fear, Heroes of Telemark, Only the Lonely, The Deadly Females, The Revenge of the Pink Panther, Deceptions, Shadow Chasers.
TELEVISION: Moon Fleet, Private Investigator, Life of Lord Lister, Z Cars, Vendetta, Sherlock Holmes, Mr. Rose, Hardy Heating International, Nearest & Dearest, The Persuaders, The Paradise Makers, The New Avengers, Smugglers Bay, The Tomorrow People, Secret Army, Last Visitor for Hugh Peters, Six Men of Dorset, Commercials: featured as the man from Delmonte for 5 years.

JACKSON, GLENDA
Actress. b. Birkenhead, England, May 9, 1936. Stage debut: Separate Tales (Worthing, England, 1957). 1964 joined Peter Brooks' Theatre of Cruelty which led to film debut. Became Member of Parliament, 1992.
THEATER: (Eng.): All Kinds of Men, Hammersmith, The Idiot, Alfie. Joined Royal Shakespeare Co in experimental Theatre of Cruelty season. Marat Sade (London, N.Y.), Three Sisters, The Maids, Hedda Gabler, The White Devil, Rose, Strange Interlude (N.Y.), Macbeth (N.Y.), Who's Afraid of Virginia Woolf? (L.A.).
PICTURES: The Persecution and Assassination of Jean-Paul Marat as Performed by the Inmates of the Asylum at Charenton Under the Direction of the Marquis de Sade (debut, 1967), Tell Me Lies, Negatives, Women in Love (Academy Award, 1970), The Music Lovers, Sunday Bloody Sunday, Mary Queen of Scots, The Boy Friend, Triple Echo, The Nelson Affair, A Touch of Class (Academy Award, 1973), The Maids, The Temptress, The Romantic Englishwoman, The Devil is a Woman, Hedda, The Incredible Sarah, Nasty Habits, House Calls, Stevie, The Class of Miss McMichael, Lost and Found, Health, Hopscotch, Giro City, The Return of the Soldier, Turtle Diary, Beyond Therapy, Business as Usual, Salome's Last Dance, The Rainbow, The Visit, King of the Wind.
TELEVISION: *Movies*: The Patricia Neal Story, Sakharov. *Mini-Series*: Elizabeth R (2 Emmy Awards, 1972). *Special*: Strange Interlude, A Murder of Quality, The House of Bernarda Alba, Secret Life of Sir Arnold Bax.

JACKSON, JOSHUA
Actor. b. Vancouver, Canada, June 11, 1978.
PICTURES: Crooked Hearts, The Mighty Ducks, Digger, Andre, D2: The Mighty Ducks, Magic in the Water, Robin of Locksley, D3: The Mighty Ducks, Scream 2, Apt Pupil, Urban Legend, Cruel Intentions, Muppets From Space, Skulls.
TELEVISION: *Movies:* Ronnie & Julie. *Series:* Dawson's Creek. *Guest:* The Outer Limits.

JACKSON, KATE
Actress. b. Birmingham, AL, Oct. 29, 1949. e. U. of Miss., Birmingham Southern U. Did stock before going to N.Y. to enter American Acad. of Dramatic Arts, appearing in Night Must Fall, The Constant Wife, Little Moon of Alban. Worked as model and became tour guide at NBC. First role on TV in Dark Shadows (series).
PICTURES: Night of Dark Shadows, Limbo, Thunder and Lightning, Dirty Tricks, Making Love, Loverboy.
TELEVISION: *Movies*: Satan's School for Girls, Killer Bees, Death Cruise, Death Scream, Charlie's Angels (pilot), Death at Love House, James at 15 (pilot), Topper, Inmates: A Love Story, Thin Ice, Listen to Your Heart, The Stranger Within, Quiet Killer, Homewrecker (voice), Adrift, Empty Cradle, Armed and Innocent, Justice in a Small Town. *Series*: Dark Shadows, The Rookies, Charlie's Angels, Scarecrow and Mrs. King, Baby Boom. *Guest*: The Jimmy Stewart Show.

JACKSON, MICHAEL
Singer, Composer. b. Gary, IN, Aug. 29, 1958. Musical recording artist with family group known as Jackson 5: all brothers, Jackie, Jermaine, Tito, Marlon, and Michael. Sister is singer Janet Jackson.
PICTURES: Save the Children, The Wiz, Moonwalker (also exec. prod., story).
TELEVISION: *Series*: The Jacksons (1976-77). *Specials*: Free to Be You and Me, Sandy in Disneyland, Motown on Showtime: Michael Jackson.

JACKSON, MICK
Director. b. Grays, England. e. Bristol Univ. Joined BBC as film editor, following post-grad work in film & tv. Produced and directed many documentaries for the BBC.
PICTURES: Chattahoochee, L.A. Story, The Bodyguard, Clean Slate, Volcano, Josiah's Canon.
TELEVISION: *Documentaries*: The Ascent of Man, Connections, The Age of Uncertainty. *Movies/Specials*: Threads, The Race for the Double Helix, Yuri Nosenko KGB (HBO), Indictment: The McMartin Trial. *Mini-Series*: A Very British Coup.

JACKSON, PETER
Director, Writer, Producer. b. New Zealand, Oct. 31, 1961.
PICTURES: Bad Taste, Meet the Feebles, Dead Alive, Heavenly Creatures, Forgotten Silver, The Frighteners, Contact (special effects only), The Lord of the Rings: The Fellowship of the Ring, The Lord of the Rings: The Two Towers, The Lord of the Rings: The Return of the King .

JACKSON, SAMUEL L.
Actor. b. Washington, D.C., Dec. 21, 1948. e. Morehouse Col. m. actress LaTanya Richardson. Co-founder, member of the Just Us Theatre Co. in Atlanta.
THEATER: *Negro Ensemble Company*: Home, A Soldier's Story, Sally/Prince, Colored People's Time. *NY Shakespeare Fest*: Mother Courage, Spell No. 7, The Mighty Gents. *Yale Rep*: The Piano Lesson, Two Trains Running. *Seattle Rep*: Fences.
PICTURES: Ragtime (debut, 1981), Eddie Murphy Raw, School Daze, Coming to America, Do the Right Thing, Sea of Love, A Shock to the System, Def by Temptation, Betsy's Wedding, Mo' Better Blues, The Exorcist III, GoodFellas, Mob Justice, Jungle Fever (Cannes Film Fest. & NY Film Critics Awards, 1991), Strictly Business, Juice, White Sands, Patriot Games, Johnny Suede, Jumpin at the Boneyard, Fathers and Sons, National Lampoon's Loaded Weapon 1, Amos & Andrew, Menace II Society, Jurassic Park, True Romance, Hail Caesar, Fresh, The New Age, Pulp Fiction (Acad. Award nom.), Losing Isaiah, Kiss of Death, Die Hard With a Vengeance, Fluke (voice), The Great White Hype, A Time to Kill, The Long Kiss Goodnight, 187, Eve's Bayou (also prod.), Jackie Brown, The Red Violin, Sphere, Out of Sight (cameo), The Negotiator, Rules of Engagement, Deep Blue Sea, Star Wars: Episode I-The Phantom Menace.

TELEVISION: *Movies*: Assault at West Point: The Court-Martial of Johnson Whittaker, Against the Wall.

JACOBI, DEREK
O.B.E. Actor. b. London, England, Oct. 22, 1938. e. Cambridge. On stage in Pericles, The Hollow Crown, Hobson's Choice, The Suicide, Breaking the Code (London, NY).
PICTURES: Othello (debut, 1965), Interlude, The Three Sisters, The Day of the Jackal, Blue Blood, The Odessa File, The Medusa Touch, The Human Factor, Enigma, The Secret of NIMH (voice), Little Dorrit, Henry V, Dead Again, Hamlet, Basil, Up at the Villa, Love Is the Devil.
TELEVISION: She Stoops to Conquer, Man of Straw, The Pallisers; I, Claudius; Philby, Burgess and MacLean, Hamlet. Movies: Othello, Three Sisters, Interlude, Charlotte, The Man Who Went Up in Smoke, The Hunchback of Notre Dame, Inside the Third Reich, The Secret Garden, The Tenth Man (Emmy Award). *Series*: Minder, Tales of the Unexpected, Mr. Pye, The Leper of St. Giles.

JACOBS, JOHN
Executive. b. New York, NY. e. Syracuse U.'s Newhouse Communications Sch. Full-service agency background, including 13 years with Grey Advertising agency, where handled Warner Bros. & Warner Home Video accts. Supvr. media on RCA, ABC-TV, Murdoch Publishing, Radio City Musical Hall, etc. Named v.p. & group media dir. for Grey. 1986, left to join Warner Bros. as v.p., media; then sr. v.p. worldwide media.

JACOBS, MICHAEL
Producer, Writer. b. New Brunswick, NJ. Studied at Neighborhood Playhouse in NY. Had first play, Cheaters, prod. on B'way when he was only 22 yrs. old, followed by Getting Along Famously.
PICTURE: 3:15 (writer only), Halloween 5 (writer only) Quiz Show.
TELEVISION: *Series: Creator/prod.:* Charles in Charge, No Soap Radio, Together We Stand, Singer and Songs, My Two Dads (also dir.), Dinosaurs, The Torkelsons (Almost Home), Boy Meets World, Where I Live, You Wish.

JACOBSEN, JOHN M.
Producer, Executive. b. Oslo, Norway, Dec. 27, 1944. Produced number of feature films incl. Pathfinder (Acad. Award nom.), Shipwrecked, Head Above Water. Pres., Norwegian Film and HTV Producers Assn.; Pres. AB Svensk Filmindustri Norwegian Operation. Produced Head Above Water, 1996.

JACOBY, FRANK DAVID
Director, Producer. b. New York, NY, July 15, 1925. e. Hunter Coll., Brooklyn Coll. m. Doris Storm, producer/director educational films, actress. 1949-52, NBC network tv dir.; 1952-56, B.B.D.O., Biow Co., tv prod./dir.; 1956-58 Metropolitan Educational TV Assn., dir. of prod.; 1958-65, United Nation, film prod./dir.; 1965 to present, pres., Jacoby/Storm Prods., Inc., Westport, CT—documentary, industrial, educational films and filmstrips. Clients include Xerox Corp., Random House, Publ., Lippincott Co., IBM, Heublein, G.E., and Pitney Bowes. Winner, Sherwood Award, Peabody Award. Member, Director's Guild of America; winner, Int'l TV & Film Festival, National Educational Film Festival, American Film Festival.

JACOBY, JOSEPH
Producer, Director, Writer. b. Brooklyn, NY, Sept. 22, 1942. e. NYU. Sch. of Arts and Sciences, majoring in m.p. As undergraduate worked part-time as prod. asst. on daytime network TV shows and as puppeteer for Bunin Puppets. 1964 joined Bil Baird Marionettes as full-time puppeteer, working also on Baird film commercials. Made feature m.p. debut as prod.-dir of Shame Shame Everybody Knows Her Name, 1968. Contributing essayist, NY Woman Magazine. Founder/Dir.-Prod., Children's Video Theatre starring The Bil Baird Marionettes. Adjunct professor, New School for Social Reserach, NY.
PICTURES: *Dir./Prod./Writer*. Hurry Up or I'll Be 30, The Great Bank Hoax, Davy Jones' Locker.

JACOBY, SCOTT
Actor. b. Chicago, IL, Nov. 26, 1956.
PICTURES: The Little Girl Who Lives Down the Lane, Love and the Midnight Auto Supply, Our Winning Season, Return to Horror High, To Die For, To Die For II.
TELEVISION: *Movies*: No Place to Run, That Certain Summer (Emmy Award, 1973), The Man Who Could Talk to Kids, Bad Ronald, Smash-Up on I 5, No Other Love, The Diary of Anne Frank. *Mini-Series*: 79 Park Avenue. *Series*: One Life to Live (73-74). *Guest*: Medical Center, Marcus Welby M.D., The Golden Girls.

JAFFE, STANLEY R.
Producer. b. New York, NY, July, 31, 1940. Graduate of U. of Pennsylvania Wharton Sch. of Finance. Joined Seven Arts Associates, 1962; named exec. ass't to pres., 1964; later, head of East Coast TV programming. Produced Goodbye, Columbus, in 1968 for Paramount; joined that company as exec. v.p., 1969. Named pres. of Paramount in 1970; resigned 1971 to form own prod. unit. Joined Columbia as exec. v.p. of global prod. in 1976, but resigned to be independent prod. Named pres. & COO of Paramount Communications in 1991-1994. Owner of Jaffilms LLC, 1994-.
PICTURES: Goodbye Columbus, A New Leaf, Bad Company, Man on a Swing, The Bad News Bears, Kramer vs. Kramer (Academy Award for Best Picture, 1979), Taps, Without a Trace (also dir.), Madeline (exec.). *Co-prod.*(with Sherry Lansing): Racing with the Moon, Firstborn, Fatal Attraction, The Accused, Black Rain, School Ties, I Dreamed of Africa.

JAFFE, STEVEN-CHARLES
Producer. b. Brooklyn, NY, 1954. e. U. of Southern California, cinema. First professional job as documentary prod. on John Huston's Fat City. Served as prod. asst. on The Wind and the Lion in Spain. Assoc. prod. on Demon Seed (written by brother Robert); served as location mgr. on Who'll Stop the Rain; assoc. prod. on Time After Time. On tv worked as 2nd unit dir. on The Day After.
PICTURES: Those Lips Those Eyes, Motel Hell (also co-s.p.), Scarab (dir.), Flesh + Blood (2nd unit. dir.), Near Dark, Plain Clothes (exec. prod.), The Fly II, Ghost (exec. prod., 2nd unit dir.), Company Business, Star Trek VI: The Undiscovered Country, Strange Days, The Informant.

JAGGER, MICK
Singer, Composer, Actor. b. Dartford, Kent, England, July 26, 1943. Lead singer with the Rolling Stones.
PICTURES: The Rolling Stones Rock and Roll Circus, Performance, Ned Kelly, Popcorn, Gimme Shelter, Sympathy for the Devil, Ladies and Gentlemen: The Rolling Stones, The London Rock 'n' Roll Show, Let's Spend the Night Together, At the Max, Freejack, Bent.
TELEVISION: *Special*: The Nightingale (Faerie Tale Theatre), History of Rock 'N' Roll Pt. 3, 5 and 6.

JAGGS, STEVE
Executive. b. London, England, June 29, 1946. Ent. motion picture industry, 1964. Gained experience in the film production and laboratory areas with Colour Film Service and Universal Laboratories. Joined Agfa-Gevaert Ltd., Motion Picture Division, 1976. Appt. sales manager, 1979; divisional manager, 1989. Joined Rank Organisation, 1992. Appoint. mng. dir. of Pinewood Studios, 1993.

JAGLOM, HENRY
Director, Writer, Editor, Actor. b. London, Eng., Jan. 26, 1943. Studied acting, writing and directing with Lee Strasberg and at Actors Studio. Did off-B'way. shows; went to West Coast where guest-starred in TV series (Gidget, The Flying Nun, etc.). Shot documentary film in Israel during Six Day War. Hired as edit consultant for Easy Rider by producer Bert Schneider. Acted in Psych Out, Drive He Said, The Last Movie, Thousand Plane Raid, Lili Aime Moi, The Other Side of the Wind (Orson Welles' unreleased last film). Wrote and dir. first feature, A Safe Place, in 1971. Created The Women's Film Co. (to prod. and distrib. motion pictures by women filmmakers), and Jagfilms Inc., Rainbow Film Company, and Rainbow Releasing. Presented Academy Award winning documentary Hearts and Minds, 1974.
PICTURES: *Dir.-Writer-Prod.-Editor*: A Safe Place, Tracks, Sitting Ducks (also actor), National Lampoon Goes to the Movies (co-dir. only), Can She Bake A Cherry Pie?, Always (also actor), Someone To Love (also actor), New Year's Day (also actor), Eating, Venice Venice (also actor), Babyfever, Last Summer in the Hamptons (dir., co-s.p., edit., actor), Deja Vu (dir., s.p., edit.).

JALBERT, JOE JAY
Executive. e. U. of Washington. Was ski captain in school and began film career as technical director on Downhill Racer, 1969, also cinematographer and double for Robert Redford. 1970, produced Impressions of Utah, documentary, with Redford. Won Emmy for cinematography on TV's Peggy Fleming Special. In 1970 formed Jalbert Productions, Inc., to make feature films, TV sports, specials, commercials, etc. Co. has prod. Winter Sportscast and 9 official films at Innsbruck Winter Olympics (1976), Lake Placid (1980), Sarajevo (1984). Albertville Winter Olympic Games official film, One Light One World, 1992. Ten years as the official film prod. for the U.S. ski team.

JAMES, CLIFTON
Actor. b. Portland, OR, May 29, 1925. e. U. of Oregon. Studied at Actors Studio. Made numerous appearances on stage and TV, as well as theatrical films.
THEATER: *NY: B'way*: J.B., All the Way Home, The Shadow Box, American Buffalo. *Off-B'way*: All the King's Men.
PICTURES: On The Waterfront, The Strange One, The Last Mile, Something Wild, Experiment in Terror, David and Lisa, Black Like Me, The Chase, The Happening, Cool Hand Luke, Will Penny, The Reivers, ...tick...tick...tick..., WUSA, The Biscuit Eater, The New Centurions, Kid Blue, Live and Let Die, The Iceman Cometh, Werewolf of Washington, The Last Detail, Bank Shot, Juggernaut, The Man with the Golden Gun, Rancho DeLuxe, Silver Streak, The Bad News Bears in Breaking Training, Superman II, Where Are the Children?, Whoops Apocalypse, Eight Men Out, The Bonfire of the Vanities, Lone Star.
TELEVISION: *Series*: City of Angels, Lewis and Clark. *Movies*: Runaway Barge, Friendly Persuasion, The Deadly Tower, Hart to Hart (pilot), Undercover With the KKK, Guyana Tragedy: The Story of Jim Jones, Carolina Skeletons, The John Vernon Story. *Mini-Series*: Captains and the Kings.

JAMES, FRANCESCA.
Actress, Director.
TELEVISION: *Series*: One Life to Live, All My Children (also dir., Emmy Awards, 1980, 1998), Loving (also dir.).

JAMES, POLLY
Writer. b. Ancon, Canal Zone. e. Smith Coll. Newspaper work, Panama; with trade mag., N.Y.; screenwriter since 1942.
PICTURES: Mrs. Parkington, The Raiders, Redhead from Wyoming, Quantrill's Raiders.

JAMESON, JERRY
Director. b. Hollywood, CA. Started as editorial asst.; then editor and supv. editor for Danny Thomas Prods. Turned to directing.
PICTURES: Dirt Gang, The Bat People, Brute Core, Airport '77, Raise the Titanic.
TELEVISION: *Movies*: Heatwave!, The Elevator, Hurricane, Terror on the 40th Floor, The Secret Night Caller, The Deadly Tower, The Lives of Jenny Dolan, The Call of the Wild, The Invasion of Johnson County, Superdome, A Fire in the Sky, High Noon--Part II, The Return of Will Kane, Stand By Your Man, Killing at Hell's Gate, Hotline, Starflight: The Plane That Couldn't Land, Cowboy, This Girl for Hire, Last of the Great Survivors, The Cowboy and the Ballerina, Stormin' Home, One Police Plaza, The Red Spider, Terror on Highway 91, Fire and Rain, Gunsmoke: The Last Ride.

JANKOWSKI, GENE F.
Executive. b. Buffalo, NY, May 21, 1934. e. Canisius Coll., B.S., Michigan State U., M.A. in radio, TV and film. Joined CBS radio network sls, 1961 as acct. exec.; eastern sls. mgr., 1966; moved to CBS-TV as acct. exec. 1969; gen. sls. mgr. WCBS-TV, 1970; dir. sls, 1971; v.p. sls., CBS-TV Stations Divisions, 1973; v.p., finance & planning, 1974; v.p., controller, CBS Inc. 1976; v.p. adm., 1977; exec. v.p. CBS/Broadcast Group, 1977; pres., CBS/Broadcast Group, 1977; chmn. CBS/Broadcast Group, 1988-89; chmn. Jankowski Communications Systems, Inc. 1989-. Member: pres., Intl. Council of National Acad. of Television Arts & Sciences; chmn. & trustee Amer. Film Institute; trustee, Catholic U. of Amer.; director, Georgetown U.; bd. of gov. American Red Cross; vice chmn., business comm. Metropolitan Museum of Art. Member, Library of Congress Film Preservation Board; adjunct prof. telecommunications, Michigan St. U.AWARDS: Received Distinguished Communications Medal from South Baptist Radio & Television Commission; honorary Doctorate of Humanities, Michigan State U.; Humanitarian Award, National Conference of Christians and Jews.

JARMAN, CLAUDE, JR.
Actor. b. Nashville, TN, Sept. 27, 1934. e. MGM Sch. Received special Oscar for The Yearling. Exec. prod. of concert film Fillmore.
PICTURES: The Yearling (debut, 1946), High Barbaree, The Sun Comes Up, Intruder in the Dust, Roughshod, The Outriders, Inside Straight, Rio Grande, Hangman's Knot, Fair Wind to Java, The Great Locomotive Chase.
TELEVISION: *Mini-Series*: Centennial.

JARMUSCH, JIM
Director, Writer, Composer, Actor. b. Akron, OH, 1953. e. attended Columbia U., went to Paris in senior year. NYU Film Sch., studied with Nicholas Ray and became his teaching asst. Appeared as an actor in Red Italy and Fraulein Berlin. Composed scores for The State of Things and Reverse Angle. Wrote and directed The New World using 30 minutes of leftover, unused film from another director. (Won International Critics Prize, Rotterdam Film Festival). Expanded it into Stranger Than Paradise.
PICTURES: *Director-Writer*: Permanent Vacation (dir. debut, 1980; also prod., music, edit.), Stranger Than Paradise (also edit., Golden Leopard, Locarno Film Festival; Camera d'Or best new director, Cannes), Down by Law, Mystery Train (also actor) Night on Earth (also prod.), When Pigs Fly (prod. only), Coffee and Cigarettes (also II & III), Dead Man, Year of the Horse, Ghost Dog: The Way of the Samurai (also prod.). *Actor*: American Autobahn, Straight to Hell, Running Out of Luck, Helsinki Napoli All Night Long, Candy Mountain, Leningrad Cowboys Go America, The Golden Boat, Iron Horsemen, In the Soup, Tigrero: A Film That Was Never Made, Blue in the Face, The Typewriter the Rifle & the Movie Camera, Cannes Man, Sling Blade, Divine Trash, .

JARRE, MAURICE
Composer. b. Lyons, France, Sept. 13, 1924. Studied at Paris Cons. Was orchestra conductor for Jean Louis Barrault's theatre company four years. 1951 joined Jean Vilar's nat'l theatre co., composing for plays. Musical dir., French National Theatre for 12 years before scoring films. Also has written ballets (Masques de Femmes, Facheuse Rencontre, The Murdered Poet, Maldroros, The Hunchback of Notre Dame) and served as cond. with Royal Phil. Orch, London, Japan Phil. Orch, Osaka Symph. Orch., Quebec Symp. Orch, Central Orchestra of People's Republic of China.
PICTURES: La Tete contre les Murs (The Keepers; feature debut, 1959), Eyes Without a Face, Crack in the Mirror, The Big Gamble, Sundays and Cybele, The Longest Day, Lawrence of Arabia (Academy Award, 1962), To Die in Madrid, Behold a Pale Horse, The Train, The Collector, Is Paris Burning?, Weekend at Dunkirk, Doctor Zhivago (Academy Award, 1965), The Professionals, Grand Prix, Gambit, The Night of the Generals, Villa Rides!, Five Card Stud, Barbarella, Isadora, The Extraordinary Seaman, The Damned, Topaz, The Only Game in Town, El Condor, Ryan's Daughter, Plaza Suite, Red Sun, Pope Joan, The Life and Times of Judge Roy Bean, The Effect of Gamma Rays on Man-in-the-Moon Marigolds, The Mackintosh Man, Ash Wednesday, Island at the Top of the World, Mandingo, Posse, The Man Who Would Be King, Shout at the Devil, The Last Tycoon, Crossed Swords, Winter Kills, The Magician of Lublin, Resurrection, The American Success Company, The Black Marble, Taps, Firefox, Young Doctors in Love, Don't Cry It's Only Thunder, The Year of Living Dangerously, Dreamscape, A Passage to India (Academy Award, 1984), Top Secret!, Witness (BAFTA Award, 1985), Mad Max Beyond Thunderdome, Solarbabies, The Mosquito Coast, Tai-Pan, No Way Out, Fatal Attraction, Gaby--A True Story, Julia and Julia, Moon Over Parador, Gorillas in the Mist, Wildfire, Distant Thunder, Chances Are, Dead Poets Society (BAFTA Award, 1989), Prancer, Enemies a Love Story, Ghost, After Dark My Sweet, Jacob's Ladder, Almost an Angel, Only the Lonely, Fires Within, School Ties, Shadow of the Wolf, Mr. Jones, Fearless, A Walk in the Clouds (Golden Globe, 1996).

JARROTT, CHARLES
Director. b. London, England, June 16, 1927. Joined British Navy; wartime service in Far East. After military service turned to theatre as asst. stage mgr. with Arts Council touring co. 1949 joined Nottingham Repertory Theatre as stage dir. and juvenile acting lead. 1953 joined new co. formed to tour Canada; was leading man and became resident leading actor for Ottawa Theatre. 1955 moved to Toronto and made TV acting debut opposite Katharine Blake whom he later wed. 1957 dir. debut in TV for Canadian Bdcstg. Co. Became CBC resident dir. Moved to London to direct for Armchair Theatre for ABC-TV. Then became freelance dir., doing stage work, films, TV. Received BAFTA Best Director Award, 1962. Golden Globe Awards, 1969, 1987.
THEATER: The Duel, Galileo, The Basement, Tea Party, The Dutchman, etc.
PICTURES: Time to Remember (debut, 1962), Anne of the Thousand Days, Mary Queen of Scots, Lost Horizon, The Dove, The Littlest Horse Thieves, The Other Side of Midnight, The Last Flight of Noah's Ark, Condorman, The Amateur, The Boy in Blue, Morning Glory (co-s.p. only), The Secret Life of Algernon, Byron (s.p., dir.).
TELEVISION: The Hot Potato Boys, Roll On, Bloomin' Death, Girl in a Birdcage, The Picture of Dorian Gray, Rain, The Rose Affair, Roman Gesture, Silent Song, The Male of the Species, The Young Elizabeth, A Case of Libel, Dr. Jekyll and Mr. Hyde. U.S. *Movies/Mini-Series*: A Married Man, Poor Little Rich Girl: The Barbara Hutton Story, The Woman He Loved, Till We Meet Again (mini-series), Night of the Fox (mini-series), Lucy & Desi: Before the Laughter, Changes, Yes Virginia There is a Santa Claus, Stranger in the Mirror, Jackie Collins' Lady Boss, Treacherous Beauties, Trade Winds, A Promise Kept: The Oksana Baiul Story (Emmy Award for dir.), At The Midnight Hour, The Christmas List.

JASON, RICK
Actor. b. New York, NY, May 21, 1923. e. American Acad. of Dramatic Arts. B'way debut in Now I Lfay Me Down To Sleep (Theatre World Award). Has acted in over 400 TV shows, beginning with Live TV (1945) and over 40 feature films.
PICTURES: Sombrero, Saracen Blade, This Is My Love, Lieutenant Wore Skirts, Wayward Bus, Partners, Illegally Yours.
TELEVISION: *Series*: The Case of the Dangerous Robin, Combat. *Mini-Series*: Around the World in 80 Days. *Movies*: The Monk, Who is the Black Dahlia?, The Best Place to Be.

JAYSTON, MICHAEL
Actor. b. Nottingham, England, Oct. 28, 1935. Member of Old Vic theatre Co. & Bristol Old Vic.
PICTURES: A Midsummer Night's Dream, Cromwell, Nicholas and Alexandra, The Public Eye, Alice's Adventures in Wonderland, The Nelson Affair, Tales That Witness Madness, The Homecoming, Craze, The Internecine Project, Dominique, Zulu Dawn.
TELEVISION: She Fell Among Thieves, Tinker Tailor Soldier Spy.

JEFFREYS, ANNE
Actress. b. Goldsboro, NC, Jan. 26. m. actor Robert Sterling. Named by Theatre Arts Magazine as one of the 10 outstanding beauties of the stage. Trained for operatic career. Sang with NY's Municipal Opera Co. while supplementing income as a Powers model. Appeared as Tess Trueheart in Dick Tracy features.
THEATER: *B'way*: in Street Scene, Kiss Me Kate, Romance, Three Wishes for Jamie, Kismet. Stock: Camelot, King & I, Kismet, Song of Norway, Bells Are Ringing, Marriage Go Round, No Sex Please, We're British, Take Me Along, Carousel, Anniversary Waltz, Do I Hear a Waltz, Ninotchka, Pal Joey, Name of the Game, Destry Rides Again, The Merry Widow, Bitter Sweet, Desert Song, High Button Shoes, Sound of Music.

PICTURES: I Married an Angel, Billy the Kid, Trapped, Joan of Ozark, The Old Homestead, Tarzan's New York Adventure, X Marks the Spot, Yokel Boy, Catterbox, Man from Thunder River, Nevada, Step Lively, Dillinger, Sing Your Way Home, Those Endearing Young Charms, Zombies on Broadway, Dick Tracy Vs. Cueball, Genius at Work, Step By Step, Vacation in Reno, Trail Street, Riffraff, Return of the Bad Men, Boys' Night Out, Panic in the City, Southern Double Cross, Clifford.
TELEVISION: *Series*: Topper, Love That Jill, Bright Promise, Delphi Bureau, General Hospital, Finder of Lost Loves. *Guest*: Falcon Crest, Hotel, Murder She Wrote, L.A. Law, Baywatch. *Movies*: Beggarman Thief, A Message From Holly, American Movie Classics (host).

JEFFRIES, LIONEL
Actor, Director. b. Forest Hill, London, England, 1926. e. Queens Elizabeth's Grammar Sch, Wimbone Dorset. Ent. m.p. ind. 1952.
THEATER: Hello, Dolly!, See How They Run, Two Into One, Pygmalion (U.S.), The Wild Duck.
PICTURES: The Black Rider, The Colditz Story, No Smoking, Will Any Gentleman?, Windfall, All for Mary, Bhowani Junction, Eyewitness, Jumping for Joy, Lust for Life, Creeping Unknown (Quatermass Experiment), Baby and the Battleship, Decision Against Time, Doctor at Large, High Terrace, Hour of Decision, Up in the World, Behind the Mask, Blue Murder at St. Trinian's, Dunkirk, Girls at Sea, Law and Disorder, Orders to Kill, Revenge of Frankenstein, Up the Creek, Bobbikins, The Vicious Circle, Idol on Parade, Nowhere to Go, The Nun's Story, Jazzboat, Let's Get Married, Trials of Oscar Wilde, Please Turn Over, Tarzan the Magnificent, Two-Way Stretch, Fanny, The Hellions, Life is a Circus, Kill or Cure, Mrs. Gibbons' Boys, Operation Snatch, The Notorious Landlady, The Wrong Arm of the Law, Call Me Bwana, The Crimson Blade, First Men in the Moon, The Long Ships, Murder Ahoy, The Secret of My Success, The Truth About Spring, You Must Be Joking!, Arrivederci Baby!, The Spy With a Cold Nose, Oh Dad Poor Dad, Blast Off!, Camelot, Chitty Chitty Bang Bang, Sudden Terror, The Railway Children (dir., s.p. only), Lola, Who Slew Auntie Roo?, The Amazing Mr. Blunden (dir., s.p. only), Baxter (dir. only), Royal Flash, Wombling Free (voice, also dir., s.p.), The Water Babies (dir. only), The Prisoner of Zenda, Better Late Than Never, A Chorus of Disapproval.
TELEVISION: Father Charlie, Tom Dick and Harriet, Cream in My Coffee, Minder, Danny: the Champion of the World, Jekyll and Hyde, Boon Morse, Ending Up, Look at It This Way, Bed.

JENKINS, DAN
Public Relations Consultant. b. Montclair, NJ, Dec. 5, 1916. e. U. of Virginia. 1938. U.S. Army, 1940-45; major, infantry. P.R. officer, Hq. Eighth Army. Mng. ed., Motion Picture Magazine, 1946-48; editor, Tele-Views Magazine, 1949-50; TV editor, columnist, Hollywood Reporter, 1950-53; Hollywood bureau chief, TV Guide, 1953-63; v.p., exec. dir. TV dept., Rogers, Cowan & Brenner, Inc., 1963-71. Formed Dan Jenkins Public Relations, Inc. 1971. Joined Charles A. Pomerantz Public Relations, Ltd. as v.p., 1975, while retaining own firm. Sr. associate, Porter, Novelli, Assocs., 1981. Mem. bd. trustees, Natl. Academy of TV Arts & Sciences; bd. gov., Hollywood chapter, Natl. Academy of TV Arts & Sciences, 1967-71. Rejoined Rogers & Cowan, 1983, v.p., TV dept. Retired, 1988.

JENKINS, GEORGE
Art Director. b. Baltimore, MD, Nov. 19, 1908. e. U. of Pennsylvania. Hollywood-New York art dir. since 1946; TV pictures for Four Star Playhouse and Revue productions; NBC-TV opera, Carmen; color dir., CBS-TV, 1954; NBC color spec. Annie Get Your Gun, 1957; TV music with Mary Martin, 1959. Professor, Motion Picture Design, UCLA, 1985-88.
THEATER: Mexican Hayride, I Remember Mama, Dark of the Moon, Lost in the Stars, Bell Book and Candle, The Bad Seed, The Happiest Millionaire, Two for the Seesaw, Ice Capades, Song of Norway, Paradise Island, Around the World in 80 Days, Mardi Gras, The Miracle Worker, Critic's Choice, A Thousand Clowns, Jennie, Generation, Wait Until Dark, Only Game in Town, Night Watch, Sly Fox.
PICTURES: The Best Years of Our Lives, The Secret Life of Walter Mitty, A Song Is Born, Rosanna McCoy, The Miracle Worker, Mickey One, Up the Down Staircase, Wait Until Dark, The Subject Was Roses, Klute, 1776, The Paper Chase, The Parallax View, Night Moves, Funny Lady, All the President's Men (Academy Award, 1976), Comes a Horseman, The China Syndrome (Acad. Award nom.), Starting Over, The Postman Always Rings Twice, Rollover, Sophie's Choice, Orphans, See You in the Morning, Presumed Innocent.
TELEVISION: *Movie*: The Dollmaker.

JENNINGS, PETER
TV News Anchor. b. Toronto, Canada, July 29, 1938. Son of Canadian b'caster Charles Jennings. e. Carleton U.; Rider Coll. Worked as a bank teller and late night radio host in Canada. Started career as host of Club 13, a Canadian American Bandstand-like dance prog., then as a newsman on CFJR (radio), Ottawa; then with CJOH-TV and CBC. Joined ABC in 1964 as NY corr.; 1965, anchor, Peter Jennings with the News; 1969, overseas assignments for ABC news; 1975, Washington corr. and anchor for AM America; 1977, chief foreign corr.; 1978, foreign desk anchor, World News Tonight; 1983-, anchor, sr. editor, World News Tonight.

JENS, SALOME
Actress. b. Milwaukee, WI, May 8, 1935. e. Northwestern U. Member Actors Studio.
THEATER: The Disenchanted, Far Country, Night Life, Winter's Tale, Mary Stuart, Antony and Cleopatra, After the Fall, Moon For the Misbegotten, The Balcony.
PICTURES: Angel Baby (debut, 1961), The Fool Killer, Seconds, Me Natalie, Cloud Dancer, Harry's War, Just Between Friends, Coming Out Under Fire (narrator).
TELEVISION: *Movies*: In the Glitter Palace, Sharon: Portrait of a Mistress, The Golden Moment: An Olympic Love Story, A Killer in the Family, Playing with Fire, Uncommon Valor. *Guest*: Mary Hartman, Mary Hartman. *Series*: Falcon Crest. *Mini-Series*: From Here to Eternity.

JERGENS, ADELE
Actress. b. Brooklyn, NY, Nov. 26, 1917. Began career in musical shows during summer vacation at 15; won contest, New York's World Fair, as model; appeared on New York stage; night clubs, U.S. and abroad.
PICTURES: A Thousand and One Nights, She Wouldn't Say Yes, The Corpse Came C.O.D., Dwon to Earth, Woman From Tangier, The Fuller Brush Man, The Dark Past, Treasure of Monte Cristo, SLightly French, Edge of Doom, Side Street, Abbott and Costello Meet the Invisible Man, Sugarfoot, Try and Get Me, Show Boat, Somebody Loves Me, Aaron Slick from Punkin' Crick, Overland Pacific, Miami Story, Fireman Save My Child, Big Chase, Strange Lady in Town, The Cobweb, Girls in Prison, The Lonesome Trail, Treasure of Monte Cristo, Runaway Daughters, Fighting Trouble, The Day the World Ended.

JETER, MICHAEL
Actor. b. Lawrenceberg, TN, Aug. 20, 1952.e. Memphis State U.
THEATER: Alice, G.R. Point (Theatre World Award), Cloud 9, Greater Tuna, Once in a Lifetime, Zoo Story, Waiting for Godot, Only Kidding, The Boys Next Door, Grand Hotel (Tony Award, 1990).
PICTURES: Hair, Ragtime, Soup for One, Zelig, The Money Pit, Dead-Bang, Tango & Cash, Just Like in the Movies, Miller's Crossing, The Fisher King, Bank Robber, Sister Act 2: Back in the Habit, Drop Zone, Waterworld, Air Bud.
TELEVISION: *Series*: One Life to Live, Hothouse, Evening Shade (Emmy Award, 1992). *Movies*: My Old Man, Sentimental Journey, When Love Kills: The Seduction of John Hearn, Gypsy. *Mini-Series*: From Here to Eternity. Guest: Lou Grant, Designing Women.

JEWISON, NORMAN
Producer, Director. b. Toronto, Canada, July 21, 1926. e. Malvern Collegiate Inst., Toronto, 1940-44; Victoria Coll., U. of Toronto, 1946-50, B.A. Stage and TV actor 1950-52. Director, Canadian Broadcasting Corp 1953-58. Awarded 1988 Acad. of Canadian Cinema and Television Special Achievement Award. Made Companion Order of Canada, 1992. Thalberg Award, 1998.
PICTURES: *Director*: 40 Pounds of Trouble (debut, 1962), The Thrill of It All, Send Me No Flowers, The Art of Love, The Cincinnati Kid. *Director-Producer*: The Russians Are Coming! The Russians Are Coming! (Acad. Award nom. for picture), In the Heat of the Night (dir. only; Acad. Award nom.), The Thomas Crown Affair, Gaily Gaily, Fiddler on the Roof (Acad. Award nom. for dir. & picture), Jesus Christ Superstar (also co-s.p.), Rollerball, F.I.S.T., ... And Justice for All, Best Friends, A Soldier's Story (Acad. Award nom. for picture), Agnes of God, Moonstruck (Acad. Award noms. for dir. & picture), In Country, Other People's Money, Only You, Bogus, The Hurricane. *Producer:* The Landlord, Billy Two Hats, The Dogs of War (exec.), Iceman, The January Man, Dance Me Outside (exec.), A Brother's Kiss (exec.), The Incredible Mr. Limpet.
TELEVISION: *Exec. prod.* of 8 episodes of The Judy Garland Show. *Prod.-Dir.*: Judy Garland specials, The Andy Williams Show. *Dir. of Specials*: Tonight with Harry Belafonte, The Broadway of Lerner and Loewe.

JEUNET, JEAN-PIERRE
Director.
PICTURES: The Escape, Le Manege, The Bunker of the Last Gunshots, Pas du repos pour Billy Brakko, Things I Like, Things I Don't Like, Delicatessen (also s.p.), The City of Lost Children (also s.p.), Alien: Resurrection, Amelie (also s.p.).

JHABVALA, RUTH PRAWER
Writer. b. Cologne, Germany, May 7, 1927. Emigrated with her family to England, 1939. e. Hendon County Sch., Queen Mary Coll., London U. (degree in English). m. architect C.S.H. Jhabvala, 1951 and moved to Delhi. Has written most of the screenplays for the films of Ismail Merchant and James Ivory.
AUTHOR: To Whom She Will, Esmond in India, The Nature of Passion, The Householder, Get Ready for Battle, Heat and Dust, In Search of Love and Beauty, Three Continents, Poet and Dancer, Shards of Memory.
PICTURES: The Householder (debut, 1963; based on her novel), Shakespeare Wallah (with Ivory), The Guru (with Ivory), Bombay Talkie (with Ivory), Roseland, The Europeans, Quartet, Heat and Dust (based on her own novel; BAFTA Award), The Bostonians, A Room with a View (Academy Award, 1986), Madame Sousatzka (co.-s.p. with John Schlesinger), Mr. and Mrs. Bridge (NY Film Critics Award), Howards End (Academy Award, 1992), The Remains of the Day, Jefferson in Paris, Surviving Picasso.

TELEVISION: Hullabaloo Over Georgie and Bonnie's Pictures, Autobiography of a Princess, Jane Austen in Manhattan.

JILLIAN, ANN
Actress. b. Cambridge, MA, Jan. 29, 1951. Began career at age 10 in Disney's Babes in Toyland; in film version of Gypsy at age 12. Broadway debut in musical, Sugar Babies, 1979. Formed own company: 9-J Productions, developing TV movies and series.
PICTURES: Babes in Toyland, Gypsy, Mr. Mom, Sammy the Way Out Seal.
TELEVISION: *Series*: Hazel, It's a Living, Jennifer Slept Here, Ann Jillian. *Guest*: Love Boat, Fantasy Island, Twilight Zone, Ben Casey, etc. *Mini-Series*: Ellis Island (Emmy & Golden Globe nom.), Alice in Wonderland, Malibu. *Movies*: Mae West (Emmy & Golden Globe nom.), Death Ride to Osaka, Killer in the Mirror, Convicted: A Mother's Story, Perry Mason: The Case of the Murdered Madam, The Ann Jillian Story (Golden Globe Award; Emmy nom.), Original Sin, This Wife for Hire, Little White Lies, Mario and the Mob, Labor of Love: The Arlette Schweitzer Story, Heart of a Child, The Disappearance of Vonnie, Fast Company, It's Him Or Us, My Son The Match Maker, The Care and Handling of Roses, I'll Be Home for Christmas.

JOANOU, PHIL
Director. b. La Canada, CA, Nov. 20, 1961. e. UCLA, USC. Student film The Last Chance Dance won him first professional job directing 2 episodes of tv's Amazing Stories.
PICTURES: Three O'Clock High (debut, 1987), U2: Rattle and Hum (also edit., camera operator), State of Grace, Final Analysis, Heaven's Prisoners, Entropy.
TELEVISION: *Mini-Series*: Wild Palms (co-dir.). *Series*: Fallen Angels (Dead-End for Delia).

JOFFE, CHARLES H.
Executive. b. Brooklyn, NY, July 16, 1929. e. Syracuse U. Joined with Jack Rollins to set up management-production org., clients including Woody Allen, Ted Bessell, Billy Crystal, David Letterman, Tom Poston, Robin Williams.
PICTURES: *Producer*: Don't Drink the Water, Take the Money and Run, Everything You Always Wanted to Know About Sex but Were Afraid To Ask, Love and Death, Annie Hall (Academy Award for Best Picture, 1977), House of God. *Exec. prod.*: Play It Again Sam, Bananas, Sleeper, Manhattan, Interiors, Stardust Memories, Arthur, A Midsummer Nights' Sex Comedy, Zelig, Broadway Danny Rose, The Purple Rose of Cairo, Hannah and Her Sisters, Radio Days, September, Another Woman, New York Stories (Oedipus Wrecks), Crimes and Misdemeanors, Alice, Shadows and Fog, Husbands and Wives, Manhattan Murder Mystery, Bullets Over Broadway, Everyone Says I Love You (co-exec. prod.).
TELEVISION: Woody Allen specials. Star of the Family, Good Time Harry, Triplecross.

JOFFE, EDWARD
Producer, Director, Writer, Production Consultant. Worked in m.p., theatre, commercial radio and as journalist before ent. TV ind. in Britain as writer/prod with ATV. 1959-61 staff prod. Granada TV. 1962, dir., Traitor's Gate & Traveling Light for Robt Stigwood; prod. dir., numerous series for Grampian TV; 1967, dir. film The Price of a Record—Emmy finalist; 1967-68 films, Columba's Folk & So Many Partings ITV entries in Golden Harp Fest.; 1968, prod., dir. Tony Hancock Down Under in Australia, prod. dir. Up At The Cross; prod. dir. ind. film, Will Ye No' Come Back Again; dir., This Is... Tom Jones; prod. dir., The Golden Shot; 1971, senior production lecturer, Thomson TV College; dir., films for U.S. for London Television Service; Evening Standard Commercials for Thames TV. Co. prod. dir.,ind. film Sound Scene, 1972-8, Contract prod. dir. Thames TV various series: Magpie, Today, Opportunity Knocks, The David Nixon Show, Seven Ages of Man, Problems, Finding Out; 1980 production consultant, CBC-TV; 1978-82, prod. dir. series Writers' Workshop, About Books; 1978, film, Places & Things (British Academy Award nom.) film, Who Do You Think You Are? (British Academy Award nom., ITV's Japan Prize entry, Special Jury Award San Francisco Intl. Film Fest), 1981, Film Images, (British Academy Award nom.; Gold Plaque Chicago Intl. Film Fest.); The Protectors (medal winner Intl. Film & TV Festival, N.Y.). 1982-86: film Rainbow Coloured Disco Dancer. Various Series: Taste of China, Jobs Ltd., Spin-Offs, The Buzz. Doc.: War Games in Italy. 1989-95, devised, prod., dir. Video View for ITV Network; Co-prod. & dir. 2 series Sprockets; dir. Challenge. Dir. Screen Scene Prods, String of Pearls, PLC, String of Pearls 2 PLC. Companies produced mopics Double X, Little Devils - The Birth, To Catch a Yeti, Big Game, Shepherd on the Rock.

JOFFE, ROLAND
Director, Producer. b. London, England, Nov. 17, 1945. e. Lycee Francaise, Carmel Col. Manchester U., England. Worked in British theatre with the Young Vic, the National Theatre and the Old Vic. 1973 became youngest director at National Theatre. 1978, moved into directing TV for Granada TV, then Thames and B.B.C. before feature debut in 1984 with The Killing Fields.
PICTURES: *Director*: The Killing Fields (debut, 1984), The Mission, Fat Man and Little Boy (also co-s.p.), City of Joy (also co-prod.), The Scarlett Letter. *Producer*: Made in Bangkok, Super Mario Bros, Goodbye Lover.
TELEVISION: *Documentaries*: Rope, Ann, No Mama No. Plays: The Spongers, Tis Pity She's a Whore, The Legion Hall Bombing, United Kingdom (also co-wrote). *Series*: Coronation Street, Bill Brand, The Stars Look Down.

JOHNS, GLYNIS
Actress. b. Durban, South Africa, Oct. 5, 1923. e. in England. Daughter of Mervyn Johns, actor, and Alys Steele, pianist. On London stage from 1935 (Buckie's Bears, The Children's Hour, A Kiss for Cinderella, Quiet Week-End; Gertie, N.Y. stage, 1952; Major Barbara, N.Y., 1956-57.) Voted one of top ten British Money-making stars in Motion Picture Herald-Pathe poll, 1951-54.
THEATER: Too Good to Be True (NY), The King's Mare, Come as You Are, The Marquise (tour), A Little Night Music (NY; Tony Award), Cause Celebre, Harold and Maude (Canada, Hay Fever (U.K. tour), The Boy Friend (Toronto), The Circle (NY).
PICTURES: South Riding (debut, 1938), Murder in the Family, Prison Without Bars, On the Night of the Fire, Mr. Brigg's Family, Under Your Hat, The Prime Minister, 49th Parallel, Adventures of Tartu, Half-Way House, Perfect Strangers, This Man Is Mine, Frieda, An Ideal Husband, Miranda, Third Time Lucky, Dear Mr. Prohack, State Secret, Flesh and Blood, No Highway in the Sky, Appointment With Venus (Island Rescue), Encore, The Magic Box, The Card (The Promoter), The Sword and the Rose, Rob Roy the Highland Rogue, Personal Affair, The Weak and the Wicked, The Seekers (Land of Fury), The Beachcomber, Mad About Men, Court Jester, Josephine and Men, Loser Takes All, All Mine to Give, Around the World in 80 Days, Another Time Another Place, Shake Hands with the Devil, The Sundowners, The Spider's Web, The Cabinet of Caligari, The Chapman Report, Papa's Delicate Condition, Mary Poppins, Dear Brigette, Don't Just Stand There, Lock Up Your Daughters, Under Milk Wood, Vault of Horror, Zelly and Me, Nukie, The Ref, While You Were Sleeping.
TELEVISION: *Series*: Glynis, Coming of Age. *Guest*: Dr. Kildare, Roaring Twenties, Naked City, The Defenders, Danny Kaye Show. Also: Noel Coward's Star Quality, Mrs. Amworth, All You Need Is Love, Across a Crowded Room, Little Gloria... Happy at Last, Skagg.

JOHNSON, ARTE
Actor. b. Chicago, IL, Jan. 20, 1934. e. Univ. of IL. To NY in 1950's where he landed role on B'way in Gentlemen Prefer Blondes. Also worked in nightclubs, summer stock, tv commercials. Gained fame on Rowan and Martin's Laugh-In in late 1960's. Much voice work on tv cartoons.
PICTURES: Miracle in the Rain, The Subterraneans, The Third Day, The President's Analyst, Love at First Bite, A Night at the Magic Castle, What Comes Around, Tax Season, Evil Spirits, Munchie, Second Chance, Captiva.
TELEVISION: *Series*: It's Always Jan, Sally, Hennesey, Don't Call Me Charlie, Rowan & Martin's Laugh-In (Emmy Award, 1969), Ben Vereen... Comin' at Ya!, The Gong Show (panelist), Games People Play, Glitter, General Hospital. *Movies*: Twice in a Lifetime, Bud and Lou, If Things Were Different, Detour to Terror, The Love Tapes, Condominium, Making of a Male Model, Alice in Wonderland, Dan Turner--Hollywood Detective.

JOHNSON, DON
Actor. b. Flatt Creek, MO, Dec. 15, 1949. Worked at ACT (Amer. Conservatory Th.), San Francisco. On stage in Your Own Thing. In L.A. in Fortune and Men's Eyes. Recording: Heartbeat (1986).
PICTURES: The Magic Garden of Stanley Sweetheart (debut, 1970), Zachariah, The Harrad Experiment, A Boy and His Dog, Return to Macon County, Soggy Bottom USA, Cease Fire, Sweet Hearts Dance, Dead-Bang, The Hot Spot, Harley Davidson and the Marlboro Man, Paradise, Born Yesterday, Guilty as Sin, Tin Cup, Goodbye Lover.
TELEVISION: *Series*: From Here to Eternity, Miami Vice, Nash Bridges (also prod.). *Mini-Series*: The Rebels, Beulah Land, The Long Hot Summer. *Movies*: First You Cry, Ski Lift to Death, Katie: Portrait of a Centerfold, Revenge of the Stepford Wives, Amateur Night at the Dixie Bar and Grill, Elvis and the Beauty Queen, The Two Lives of Carol Letner, In Pursuit of Honor. *Special*: Don Johnson's Heartbeat (music video, also exec. prod.). *Guest*: Kung Fu, The Bold Ones, Police Story.

JOHNSON, G. GRIFFITH
Executive. b. New York, NY, Aug. 15, 1912. e. Harvard U., 1934, A.M. 1936, Ph.D. 1938. U.S. Treasury Dept. 1936-39; Dept. of Comm., 1939-40; O.P.A. & predecessor agencies, 1940-46; consulting economist, 1946-47; dir., Econ. Stab. Div., Nat'l. Security Resources Bd., 1948-49; chief econ., U.S. Bur. of Budget, 1949-50; econ. advisor to Econ. Stab. Admin. 1950-52; Exec. v.p. MPEAA, 1965, MPAA, 1971; Asst. Sec'y of State for Economic Affairs, 1962-65; v.p. MPAA, 1953-62. Author of several books & articles.

JOHNSON, J. BOND
Producer, Executive. b. Fort Worth, TX, June 18, 1926. e. Texas Wesleyan Univ., B.S., 1947; Texas Christian U., M.Ed., 1948; Southern Methodist U., B.D., 1952; USC, Ph.D., 1967. Army Air Forces, WWII; public info. officer, captain, U.S. Marine Corps, Korean War. Formerly member Marine Corps Reserve, Motion Picture Prod. Unit, Hollywood. Was Col. U.S. Army; now retired. Newspaper reporter, Fort Worth Star-Telegram, 1942-48; pres., West Coast News Service, 1960; pres., exec. prod., Bonjo Prods., Inc., 1960, President, CEO, Cine-Media International, 1975 managing partner, Capra-Johnson Productions, Ltd., 1978.

PICTURES: Sands of Iwo Jima, Retreat Hell, Flying Leathernecks; photographed aerial portions, Jamboree 53, Norfleet, Devil at My Heels, Kingdom of the Spiders, Ordeal at Donner Pass, Place of the Dawn, Lies I Told Myself, Backstretch, Airs Above The Ground, The Jerusalem Concert, The Berkshire Terror, The Seventh Gate.
TELEVISION: *Series*: Creator, story consultant, tech. advisor, Whirlpool. *Exec. producer, creator*: On The Go (TV News-Sports), Coasties, Desert Rangers. *Producer*: Fandango.

JOHNSON, LAMONT
Director, Producer. b. Stockton, CA, Sept. 30, 1922. e. UCLA. 4 time winner of Director's Guild Award for TV work. Directed plays The Egg, Yes Is For a Very Young Man. Dir. two operas, L.A. Philharmonic, 1964; founder, dir., UCLA Professional Theatre Group.
PICTURES: A Covenant With Death (debut, 1967), Kona Coast, The McKenzie Break, A Gunfight, The Groundstar Conspiracy, You'll Like My Mother, The Last American Hero, Visit to a Chief's Son, Lipstick, One on One (also actor), Somebody Killed Her Husband, Cattle Annie and Little Britches, Spacehunter: Adventures in the Forbidden Zone.
TELEVISION: *Series*: The Defenders, Profiles in Courage, Twilight Zone. *Movies/Mini-Series*: Deadlock, My Sweet Charlie, That Certain Summer, The Execution of Pvt. Slovik, Fear on Trial, Off the Minnesota Strip, Crisis at Central High, Escape from Iran, Dangerous Company, Life of the Party: The Story of Beatrice, Ernie Kovacs: Between the Laughter, Wallenberg: A Hero's Story (also co-prod.; Emmy Award, 1985), Unnatural Causes, Gore Vidal's Lincoln (Emmy Award, 1988), The Kennedys of Massachusetts, Voices Within: The Lives of Truddi Chase, Crash Landing: The Rescue of Flight 232, The Broken Chain (also prod.).

JOHNSON, MARK
Producer. b. Washington, DC, Dec. 27, 1945. Moved to Spain at age 7, lived there for eleven years before returning to America. e. Univ. of VA, Univ. of IA. Joined Directors Guild training program receiving first credit on Next Stop Greenwich Village. Worked as prod. asst., then asst. dir. on High Anxiety, Movie Movie, The Brink's Job, and Escape From Alcatraz. Starting with Diner in 1982 served as executive prod. or prod. on all Barry Levinson films. With Levinson formed Baltimore Pictures in 1989.
PICTURES: Diner (exec. prod.), Kafka (co-exec. prod.), The Astronaut's Wife (exec. prod.), My Dog Skip (exec. prod.), Mouse Hunt (exec. prod.). *Producer*: The Natural, Young Sherlock Holmes, Tin Men, Good Morning Vietnam, Rain Man (Academy Award for Best Picture of 1988), Avalon, Bugsy (L.A. Film Critics & Golden Globe Awards for Best Picture of 1991), Toys, Sniper, Wilder Napalm, A Perfect World, A Little Princess, Donnie Brasco, Home Fries.

JOHNSON, RICHARD
Actor. b. Upminster, Essex, England, July 30, 1927. Studied at Royal Acad. of Dramatic Art. First stage appearance Opera House, Manchester, then with John Gielgud's repertory season, 1944. Served in Royal Navy 1945-48. Subsequent stage appearances incl. The Madwoman of Chaillot, The Lark. Visited Moscow with Peter Brook's production of Hamlet. Royal Shakespeare Thea.: Stratford, London, 1957-62. Royal Shakespeare Co. 1972-73. National Theatre, 1976-77. Founded United British Artists, 1983.
PICTURES: Captain Horatio Hornblower (debut, 1951), Calling Bulldog Drummond, Scotland Yard Inspector (Lady in the Fog), Saadia, Never So Few, Cairo, The Haunting, 80,000 Suspects, The Pumpkin Eater, The Amorous Adventures of Moll Flanders, Operation Crossbow, Khartoum, The Witch in Love, Deadlier Than the Male, The Rover, Danger Route, A Twist of Sand, Oedipus the King, Lady Hamilton, Some Girls Do, Julius Caesar, The Tyrant, The Beloved, Behind the Door, Hennessy, Night Child, The Cursed Medallion, Aces High, The Last Day of Spring, The Comeback, Zombie, The Monster Club, Screamers, What Waits Below, Lady Jane, Turtle Diary, Foreign Student, Diving In. Producer: Turtle Diary, Castaway, The Lonely Passion of Judith Hearne, The Secret Life of Ian Fleming, The Camomile Lawn, Duel of Hearts, Heavy Weather, Breaking the Code.
TELEVISION: The Flame is Love, Haywire, The Four Feathers, Portrait of a Rebel: Margaret Sanger, A Man For All Seasons, Voice of the Heart, The Crucifer of Blood, Duel of Hearts. Guest: Wagon Train, Lou Grant, Ironside, Knots Landing, That Girl, MacGyver, Police Story, Route 66, many others. Live TV incl. Lux Video Theatre, Front Row Center, Hallmark Hall of Fame.

JOHNSON, RUSSELL
Actor. b. Ashley, PA, Nov. 10, 1924. e. Girard Coll, Actors Laboratory, L.A. W.W.II, Army Air Corps. Author: Here on Gilligan's Isle (1993).
PICTURES: A Town of the 80's, Stand at Apache Landing, A Distant Trumpet, Ma & Pa Kettle at Waikiki, Rogue Cop, Loan Shark, Seminole, Tumbleweed, Blue Movies, It Came From Outer Space, Many Rivers to Cross, Law and Order, Black Tuesday, This Island Earth, Rock All Night, Attack of the Crab Monsters, The Space Children, For Men Only, The Greatest Story Ever Told, Hitchhike to Hell, MacArthur.
TELEVISION: *Series*: Black Saddle, Gilligan's Island. *Guest*: Studio One, Front Row Center, Playhouse 90, Lux Video Theatre, Mobile One, The Great Adventure Jane Powell Show, Climax, You Are There, Rawhide, Twilight Zone, Gunsmoke, Outer Limits, Cannon, Marcus Welby, That Girl, The FBI, Dallas, Fame, Dynasty, My Two Dads, Bosom Buddies, Buffalo Bill, Vanished, Harry Truman Biography, Truman vs. MacArthur, Knots Landing, Santa Barbara, Roseanne. *Movie:* With a Vengeance.

JOHNSON, TOM
Sound.
PICTURES: Star Wars: Return of the Jedi, Indiana Jones and the Temple of Doom, Seize the Day, Howard the Duck, Dirty Rotten Scoundrels, Colors, The Couch Trip, Tucker: The Man and His Dream, The Karate Kid III, To Cross the Rubicon, The Five Heartbeats, Terminator II: Judgment Day, F/X2, Single White Female, Quiz Show, Forrest Gump, Nine Months, Strange Days, Stealing Beauty, Jack, One Fine Day, Titanic (Acad. Award, Best Sound, 1997), Beverly Hills Ninja, Contact, Wag the Dog.
TELEVISION: *Movies*: The Dreamer of Oz.

JOHNSON, VAN
Actor. b. Newport, RI, Aug. 25, 1916. Began in vaudeville; then on N.Y. stage New Faces of 1937, Eight Men of Manhattan, Too Many Girls, Pal Joey. Voted one of the top ten Money Making Stars in Motion Picture Herald-Fame Poll 1945-46. Stage includes The Music Man (London), La Cage aux Folles (NY) and numerous tours.
PICTURES: Too Many Girls (debut, 1940), Murder in the Big House, Somewhere I'll Find You, War Against Mrs. Hadley, Dr. Gillespie's New Assistant, The Human Comedy, Pilot No. 5, Dr. Gillespies's Criminal Case, Guy Named Joe, White Cliffs of Dover, Three Men in White, Two Girls and a Sailor, Thirty Seconds Over Tokyo, Between Two Women, Thrill of Romance, Weekend at the Waldorf, Easy to Wed, No Leave No Love, Till the Clouds Roll By, High Barbaree, Romance of Rosy Ridge, Bride Goes Wild, State of the Union, Command Decision, Mother is a Freshman, In the Good Old Summertime, Scene of the Crime, Battleground, Big Hangover, Duchess of Idaho, Three Guys Named Mike, Grounds for Marriage, Go For Broke, Too Young to Kiss, It's a Big Country, Invitation, When in Rome, Washington Story, Plymouth Adventure, Confidentially Connie, Remains to Be Seen, Easy to Love, Caine Mutiny, Siege at Red River, Men of the Fighting Lady, Brigadoon, Last Time I Saw Paris, End of the Affair, Bottom of the Bottle, Miracle in the Rain, 23 Paces to Baker Street, Slander, Kelly and Me, Action of the Tiger, The Last Blitzkreig, Subway in the Sky, Beyond This Place, Enemy General, Wives and Lovers, Divorce American Style, Yours Mine and Ours, Where Angels Go... Trouble Follows, Company of Killers, Eagles Over London, The Kidnapping of the President, The Purple Rose of Cairo, Down There in the Jungle, Escape From Paradise, Three Days to a Kill.
TELEVISION: *Special*: Pied Piper of Hamelin. *Mini-Series*: Rich Man Poor Man, Black Beauty. *Movies*: Doomsday Flight, San Francisco International, Call Her Mom, The Girl on the Late Late Show, Superdome. *Guest*: I Love Lucy, G.E. Theatre, Batman, Love American Style, The Love Boat, Murder She Wrote.

JOHNSTON, JOANNA
Costume Designer.
PICTURES: Hellraiser, Who Framed Roger Rabbit, Indiana Jones and the Last Crusade, Back to the Future Part II, Back to the Future Part III, Far and Away, Death Becomes, Forrest Gump, French Kiss, Contact, Saving Private Ryan, The Sixth Sense, Unbreakable.

JOHNSTON, MARGARET
Actress. b. Sydney, Australia, Aug. 10, 1918. e. Sydney U., Australia; RADA. London stage debut: Murder Without Crime.
THEATER: Ring of Truth, The Masterpiece, Lady Macbeth, Merchant of Venice, Measure for Measure, Othello.
PICTURES: The Prime Minister, The Rake's Progress (The Notorious Gentleman), A Man About the House, Portrait of Clare, The Magic Box, Knave of Hearts, Touch and Go, Burn With Burn (Night of the Eagle), The Nose on My Face, Girl in the Headlines (The Model Murder Case), Life at the Top, The Psychopath, Schizo, Sebastian.
TELEVISION: Always Juliet, Taming of the Shrew, Man with a Load of Mischief, Light of Heart, Autumn Crocus, Androcles and the Lion, Sulky Five, Windmill Near a Frontier, The Shrike, The Out of Towners, Looking for Garrow, The Typewriter, The Glass Menagerie, That's Where the Town's Going, The Vortex.

JOLIE, ANGELINA
Actress. b. Los Angeles, CA, June 4, 1975. m. actor Billy Bob Thornton.
PICTURES: Cyborg 2: Glass Shadow, Hackers, Mojave Moon, Foxfire, Love Is All There Is, Playing God, Pushing Tin, Hell's Kitchen, Dancing About Architecture, Girl Interrupted, The Bone Collector, Gone in Sixty Seconds, Original Sin, Tomb Raider, Beyond Borders..
TELEVISION: *Movies*: George Wallace (Golden Globe Award, 1998), Gia. *Mini-series*: True Women.

JOLLEY, STAN
Producer, Director, Production Designer, Art Director. b. New York, NY, May 17, 1926. e. U. of Southern California, col. of architecture. Son of actor I. Stanford Jolley. In Navy in W.W.II. Has acted in capacities listed for many feature films and TV series. One of orig. designers of Disneyland.
PICTURES: *Prod./Prod. Designer*: Knife for the Ladies. *Assoc. Prod./ Prod. Designer*: The Good Guys and the Bad Guys. 2nd Unit Dir.: Superman. *Prod. Designer*: Dutch, The Good Mother, Witness (Acad. Award nom.), Taps, Caddyshack, Cattle Annie and Little Britches, Americathon (also second unit director), The Swarm, Drum, Framed, Dion Brothers, Mixed Company, Walking Tall, Terror in the Wax Museum, Night of the Lepus (also second unit director), War Between Men and Women, Law Man, The Phynx. *Art Director:* Young Billy Young, Ride Beyond Vengeance, Broken Saber, The Restless Ones, Mail Order Bride, Toby Tyler, The Grass Harp. *Assoc. Prod./Prod. designer & 2nd unit dir.*: Happily Ever After.
TELEVISION: *Movies: 2nd Unit Dir./Prod. Designer*: Swiss Family Robinson, Adventures of the Queen, Woman Hunter, Abduction of Carrie Swenson, Eagle One, No Man's Land, Last of the Great Survivors, Like Normal People, Rescue From Gilligan's Island, Flood, Voyage of the Yes, The Stranger, Punch & Jody, City Beneath the Sea, Women of San Quentin. *Mini-series*: Howards, The Amazing Mr. Hughes. *Series*: *Dir./Prod. Designer*: MacGuyver, Today's FBI. *Assoc. Prod./Prod. Designer*: Jessie. *Prod. Designer:* Walking Tall, For Love and Honor. *Art Dir.*: Walt Disney Presents, Pete and Gladys, Gunsmoke, Mr. Ed, Branded, Voyage to the Bottom of the Sea, Land of the Giants, O'Hara Shane, Acapulco, The Racers, *Docu-drama*: Under Fire. *Pilots*: Get Smart, Some Like It Hot. *Cartoon*: Donald in Mathmagic Land. *Documentary*: Crisis in the Wetlands (prod./dir.).

JONES, AMY HOLDEN
Director, Writer. b. Philadelphia, PA, Sept. 17, 1953. m. cinematographer, Michael Chapman. e. Wellesley Coll., B.A., 1974; film and photography courses, Massachusetts Inst. of Technology. Winner, first place, Washington National Student Film Festival, 1973.
PICTURES: *Editor*: Hollywood Boulevard (debut, 1976), American Boy, Corvette Summer, Second Hand Hearts. *Director*: Slumber Party Massacre, Love Letters (also s.p.), Mystic Pizza (s.p. only), Maid to Order (also co-s.p.), Rich Man's Wife (also s.p.). *Writer*: Beethoven, Indecent Proposal, The Getaway, It Had to Be Steve (co-s.p.), The Relic (co-s.p.).
TELEVISION: *Pilot* (writer): Jack's Place.

JONES, CHUCK
Producer, Director, Writer, Animator. b. Spokane, WA, Sept. 21, 1912. e. Chouinard Art Inst. Dir., Warner Bros. Animation until 1962 where he created and directed Road Runner & Wile E. Coyote, Pepe le Pew; directed and helped create Bugs Bunny, Porky Pig, Daffy Duck etc. Created Snafu character, U.S. Armed Service. Later headed MGM Animation Dept. Lecturer at many Universities. Establisehd indept. co. Chuck Jones Enterprises. Academy Awards for best animated short subjects: For Scentmental Reasons (1950), The Dot and the Line (1965), best documentary short subject: So Much for So Little (1950). 1989, published Chuck Amuck: The Life and Times of an Animated Cartoonist. 1990, chmn. Chuck Jones Prods.; currently consultant and good-will representative to Warner Bros.
PICTURES: The Phantom Tollbooth, The Bugs Bunny/Road Runner Movie, The Magical World of Chuck Jones; created animated sequences for live-action features Stay Tuned, Mrs. Doubtfire.
TELEVISION: The Bugs Bunny Show (co-prod., writer, dir.). *Dir.*: How the Grinch Stole Christmas, Horton Hears a Who, Pogo. *Producer- Director-Writer*: The Cricket in Times Square, A Very Merry Cricket, Yankee Doodle Cricket, Rikki-Tikki-Tavi, The White Seal, Mowgli's Brothers, The Carnival of the Animals, A Connecticut Rabbit in King Arthur's Court, Raggedy Ann and Andy in The Great Santa Claus Caper, The Pumpkin Who Couldn't Smile, Daffy Duck's Thanks-for-Giving Special, Bugs Bunny's Bustin' Out All Over.

JONES, DAVID
Director, Producer. b. Poole, Eng., Feb. 19, 1934. e. Christ's Coll., Cambridge U., B.A., 1954, M.A., 1957. Immigrated to U.S. in 1979. Artistic controller, then assoc. dir., Royal Shakespeare Co., 1964-75; artistic dir, RSC at Aldwych Theatre 1975-78; artistic dir, Brooklyn Acad. of Music Theatre Co., NY 1979-81; prof. Yale Sch. of Drama, 1981.
THEATER: Sweeney Agonistes (debut, 1961); *U.S.*: Summerfolk, Loves Labour's Lost, Winter's Tale, Barbarians, Jungle of Cities.
PICTURES: Betrayal, Jacknife, The Trial.
TELEVISION: *Prod.*: Monitor 1958-64 (BBC series), Play of the Month, The Beaux' Stratagem, Langrishe Go Down, Ice Age. *Dir.*: Shakespeare series, BBC 1982-83, Devil's Disciple, The Christmas Wife, Sensibility and Sense, Is There Life Out There?

JONES, DEAN
Actor. b. Decatur, AL, Jan. 25, 1931. e. Asbury Coll., Wilmore, KY. Prof. debut as blues singer, New Orleans; U.S. Navy, 1950-54. Author: Under Running Laughter.
THEATER: There Was a Little Girl, Under the Yum-Yum Tree, Company, Into the Light, Show Boat.
PICTURES: Tea and Sympathy (debut, 1956), The Rack, The Opposite Sex, These Wilder Years, The Great American Pastime, Designing Woman, Ten Thousand Bedrooms, Jailhouse Rock, Until They Sail, Imitation General, Torpedo Run, Handle with Care, Night of the Quarter Moon, Never So Few, Under the Yum-Yum Tree, The New Interns, That Darn Cat, Two on a Guillotine, Any Wednesday, The Ugly Dachshund, Monkeys Go Home, Blackbeard's Ghost, The Horse in the Grey Flannel Suit, The Love Bug, $1,000,000 Duck, Snowball Express, Mr. Super Invisible, The Shaggy D.A., Herbie Goes to Monte Carlo, Born Again, Other People's Money, Beethoven, Clear and Present Danger, That Darn Cat II.
TELEVISION: *Series*: Ensign O'Toole, The Chicago Teddy Bears, What's It All About World?, Herbie the Love Bug, Beethoven (animated; voice). *Movies*: Guess Who's Sleeping in My Bed?, When Every Day Was the 4th of July, Long Days of Summer, Fire and Rain, The Great Man's Whiskers, Saved By the Bell: Hawaiian Style, The Computer Wore Tennis Shoes, The Love Bug Reunion. *Specials*: Journey to Mars, Out of Jerusalem.

JONES, GEMMA
Actress. b. London, Eng., Dec. 4, 1942. e. Royal Acad. of Dramatic Art.
THEATER: Baal, Alfie, The Cavern, The Pastime of M Robert, Portrait of a Queen, Next of Kin, The Marriage of Figaro, And A Nightingale Sang, reaking the Silence, Howards End, A Midsummer Night's Dream, The Homecoming, Mount Morgan, The Winter's Tale.
PICTURES: The Devils, The Paper House, On the Black Hill, The Devils Feast of July, Sense and Sensibility, Wilde, The Winslow Boy, O.K. Garage.
TELEVISION: The Lie, The Way of the World, The Merchant of Venice, The Duchess of Duke Street (series), The Jim Henson Hour, Forget Me Not Lane,Call My Bluff, Dial M For Murder, The Way of the World, Churchill's People, The Cherry Orchard, The Lie, Man In A Sidecar, Shadows of Fear, Crimes of Passion, The Spoils of Poynton, The Duchess of Duke Street, The Importance of Being Earnest, Chelworth, After The Dance, Inspector Morse, The Storyteller, Sevises and Desires, Some Lie Some Die, Wycliffe, The Borrowers, Faith, Wilderness, Jane Eyre, The Phoenix and the Carpet, An Unsuitable Job for a Woman.

JONES, GLENN R.
Executive. Began career in law, representing cable TV cos. in acquisition efforts. Purchased his first cable TV system in 1967 which became part of Jones Intercable, Inc., founded 1970. Pres. and CEO of the corp. since its inception.

JONES, GRACE
Singer, Actress. r.n. Grace Mendoza. b. Spanishtown, Jamaica, May 19, 1948. e. Syracuse U. Modelled and appeared in several Italian pictures before career as singer.
PICTURES: Conan the Destroyer, A View to a Kill, Vamp, Straight to Hell, Siesta, Boomerang, Cyber Bandits, McCinsey's Island, Palmer's Pick Up.

JONES, JAMES EARL
Actor. r.n. Todd Jones. b. Arkabutla, MS, Jan. 17, 1931. e. U. of Michigan. Son of actor Robert Earl Jones. Awarded Hon. Doctor of Fine Arts (Yale, Princeton); Medal for Spoken Language (Amer. Acad. and Inst. of Arts and Letter; Hon. Doctor of Humane Letters (Columbia Coll. & U. of Mich.).
THEATER: Moon on a Rainbow Shawl (Theatre World Award), The Cool World, Othello, Paul Robeson, Les Blancs, The Great White Hope (Tony Award, 1969), The Iceman Cometh, Of Mice and Men, A Lesson from Aloes, Master Harold ... and the Boys, Fences (Tony Award, 1986).
PICTURES: Dr. Strangelove, or: How I Learned to Stop Worrying and Love the Bomb (debut, 1964), The Comedians, King: A Filmed Record ... Montgomery to Memphis, End of the Road, The Great White Hope (Acad. Award nom.), Malcolm X (narrator), The Man, Claudine, Deadly Hero, Swashbuckler, The Bingo Long Travelling All-Stars and Motor Kings, The River Niger, The Greatest, Star Wars (voice), Exorcist II: The Heretic, The Last Remake of Beau Geste, A Piece of the Action, The Bushido Blade, The Empire Strikes Back (voice), Conan the Barbarian, Blood Tide (The Red Tide), Return of the Jedi (voice), City Limits, My Little Girl, Soul Man, Allan Quartermain and the Lost City of Gold, Gardens of Stone, Matewan, Pinocchio and the Emperor of the Night (voice), Coming to America, Three Fugitives, Field of Dreams, Best of the Best, The Hunt for Red October, Grim Prairie Tales, The Ambulance, True Identity, Convicts, Patriot Games, Sneakers, Sommersby, The Sandlot, The Meteor Man, Naked Gun 33 1/3: The Final Insult, Clean Slate, The Lion King (voice), Clear and Present Danger, Jefferson in Paris, Judge Dredd (voice), Cry the Beloved Country, Lone Star, A Family Thing, Good Luck (cameo), Gang Related, Summer's End, The Lion King II: Simba's Pride (voice).
TELEVISION: *Series*: As the World Turns, The Guiding Light, Paris, Me and Mom, Gabriel's Fire (Emmy Award, 1991), Pros & Cons, Under One Roof. *Movies*: The UFO Incident, Jesus of Nazareth, The Greatest Thing That Almost Happened, Guyana Tragedy—The Story of Jim Jones, Golden Moment: An Olympic Love Story, Philby, Burgess and MacLean, The Atlanta Child Murders, The Vegas Strip War, By Dawn's Early Light,

Heat Wave (Emmy Award, 1991), Last Flight Out, The Last Elephant, Percy & Thunder, The Vernon Johns Story, Confessions: Two Faces of Evil, Alone, The Second Civil War, What the Deaf Man heard, Merlin. *Mini-Series*: Roots: The Next Generations. *Specials:* King Lear, Soldier Boy, Mathnet, Bailey's Bridge, Third and Oak: The Pool Hall, Teach 109, Hallelujah. *Host:* Black Omnibus, Vegetable Soup, Summer Show, Long Ago and Far Away.

JONES, JEFFREY
Actor. b. Buffalo, NY, Sept. 28, 1947. e. Lawrence U., Wisconsin. While pre-med student, performed in 1967 prod. of Hobson's Choice and was invited by Sir Tyrone Guthrie to join Guthrie Theatre in Minneapolis. After short time in South America, studied at London Acad. of Music and Dramatic Arts before joining Stratford Theater in Ontario. 1973-74 worked with Vancouver touring children's theater co. Playhouse Holiday. Moved to N.Y. where performed on stage.
THEATER: The Elephant Man (B'way debut), Trelawney of the Wells, Secret Service, Boy Meets Girl, Cloud Nine, Comedy of Errors, The Tempest, The Death of Von Richtoven, London Suite.
PICTURES: The Revolutionary, The Soldier, Easy Money, Amadeus, Transylvania 6-5000, Ferris Bueller's Day Off, Howard the Duck, The Hanoi Hilton, Beetlejuice, Without a Clue, Who Is Harry Crumb?, Valmont, The Hunt for Red October, Over Her Dead Body, Mom and Dad Save the World, Stay Tuned, Out on a Limb, Heaven and Earth (cameo), Ed Wood, Houseguest, The Pest, The Crucible, Sante Fe, Flypaper, The Pest, The Devil's Advocate, There Is No Fish Food in Heaven, Ravenous, Sleepy Hollow.
TELEVISION: *Mini-Series*: George Washington: The Forging of a Nation, Fresno. *Movies*: Kenny Rogers as The Gambler III—The Legend Continues, The Avenging Angel. *Guest*: Amazing Stories, Twilight Zone, Remington Steele. *Series*: The People Next Door.

JONES, JENNIFER
Actress. r.n. Phyllis Isley. b. Tulsa, OK, Mar. 2, 1919. e. Northwestern U., American Acad. of Dramatic Arts. Daughter of Phil R., Flora Mae (Suber) Isley, exhib. m. industrialist Norton Simon. Son is actor Robert Walker Jr. Toured with parents stock company as child; in summer stock in East; little theat. East & West. Began screen career as Phyllis Isley. Pres., Norton Simon Museum.
PICTURES: Dick Tracy's G-Men (debut, 1939), The New Frontier, The Song of Bernadette (Academy Award, 1943; first film billed as Jennifer Jones), Since You Went Away, Love Letters, Cluny Brown, Duel in the Sun, Portrait of Jennie, We Were Strangers, Madame Bovary, Carrie, Wild Heart (Gone to Earth), Ruby Gentry, Indiscretion of an American Wife (Terminal Station), Beat the Devil, Love Is a Many-Splendored Thing, Good Morning Miss Dove, The Man in the Gray Flannel Suit, The Barretts of Wimpole Street, A Farewell to Arms, Tender Is the Night, The Idol, Angel Angel Down We Go (Cult of the Damned), The Towering Inferno.

JONES, KATHY
Executive. b. Aug. 27, 1949. Began career as acct. exec. for m.p. clients, Stan Levinson assoc., Dallas. Joined Paramount Pictures in 1977 as sr. publicist in field marketing then exec. dir., field mktg. Left to join Time-Life Films as v.p., domestic mktg., for m.p. div. Returned to Paramount 1981 as v.p., domestic pub. & promo. 1984, appt. sr. v.p., domestic pub. & promo. for Motion Picture Group, Paramount. Formed m.p. consultancy with Buffy Shutt, 1987. 1989, appt. exec. v.p., marketing, Columbia Pictures. 1991, appt. exec. v.p. marketing, TriStar Pictures.

JONES, QUINCY
Producer, Composer, Arranger, Recording Artist. b. Chicago, IL, March 14, 1933. e. Seattle U., Berklee Sch. Music, Boston Conservatory, Trumpeter and arranger for Lionel Hampton's orch. 1950-53, played with Dizzy Gillespie, Count Basie and arranged for orchs., singers-Frank Sinatra, Sarah Vaughn, Peggy Lee, Dinah Washington and led own orch. for European tours, and recordings. Prod. recordings for Michael Jackson, Tevin Campbell, Barbra Streisand, Donna Summer. Music dir. and v.p., Mercury Records 1961-64 before scoring films. Prod. & arranged We Are the World recording. Owns own Qwest Records record company. Received Jean Hersholt Humanitarian Award, 1995.
PICTURES: The Pawnbroker, Mirage, The Slender Thread, Made in Paris, Walk Don't Run, Banning, The Deadly Affair, In the Heat of the Night, In Cold Blood (Acad. Award nom.), Enter Laughing, A Dandy in Aspic, For Love of Ivy, The Hell With Heroes, The Split, Up Your Teddy Bear, Jocelyn, McKenna's Gold, The Italian Job, Bob & Carol & Ted & Alice, The Lost Man, Cactus Flower, John and Mary, The Last of the Mobile Hotshots, The Out-of-Towners, They Call Me Mister Tibbs, Brother John, $ (Dollars), The Anderson Tapes, Yao of the Jungle, The Hot Rock, The New Centurions, Come Back Charleston Blue, The Getaway, The Wiz (also cameo), The Color Purple (also co-prod.; Acad. Award nom.), Listen Up, Steel.
TELEVISION: *Mini-Series*: Roots (Emmy, 1977). *Special*: An American Reunion (exec. prod.). *Series*: Fresh Prince of Bel Air, In the House (prod.).

JONES, SAM J.
Actor. b. Chicago, IL, Aug. 12, 1954.
PICTURES: "10," Davinci's War, One Man Force, Night Rhythms, South Beach, Iron Fist, Where the Truth Lies, Evasive Action, Flash Gordon, Lady Dragon II, Last Breath, My Chauffeur, Under the Gun, Silent Assassins, Jane & the Lost City, White Fire, Trigon Factor, Driving Force, In Gold We Trust, Human Shields, Fists of Honor, Ballistic, American Strays, Texas Payback, Hard Vice, R.I.O.T., American Tigers, Baja Run, Earth Minus Zero.
TELEVISION: *Series*: Training Camp, Code Red, The Highwayman, Hollywood Safari. *Movies*: This Wife for Hire, Ray Alexander. *Pilot*: Hat Squad, Cobra, Thunder in Paradise,Stunts Unlimited, No Man's Land, The Spirit. *Guest*: Co-ed Fever, A-Team, Riptide, Hunter, Baywatch, Diagnosis Murder, Pacific Blue.

JONES, SHIRLEY
Actress. b. Smithton, PA, March 31, 1934. m. agent-prod. Marty Ingels. Mother of actors Shaun and Patrick Cassidy. Former Miss Pittsburgh. Natl. chair, Leukemia Foundation. Book: Shirley & Marty: An Unlikely Love Story (Wm. Morrow, 1990). Received hom. Doctor of Humane Letters degree from Point Park Col. 1991.
THEATER: Appeared with Pittsburgh Civic Light Opera in Lady in the Dark, Call Me Madam. *B'way:* South Pacific, Me and Juliet, Maggie Flynn.
PICTURES: Oklahoma! (debut, 1955), Carousel, April Love, Never Steal Anything Small, Bobbikins, Elmer Gantry (Academy Award, best supporting actress, 1960), Pepe, Two Rode Together, The Music Man, The Courtship of Eddie's Father, A Ticklish Affair, Dark Purpose, Bedtime Story, Fluffy, The Secret of My Success, The Happy Ending, El Golfo, Oddly Coupled, The Cheyenne Social Club, Beyond the Poseidon Adventure, Tank, There Were Times Dear, Jack L. Warner: The Last Mogul, Cops n' Roberts, Gideon's Webb
TELEVISION: *Movies*: Silent Night Lonely Night, But I Don't Want to Get Married, The Girls of Huntington House, The Family Nobody Wanted, Winner Take All, The Lives of Jenny Dolan, Yesterday's Child, Evening in Byzantium, Who'll Save Our Children? A Last Cry For Help, Children of An Lac, Intimates: A Love Story, Widow, Charlie, Dog's Best Friend. *Series*: The Partridge Family, Shirley, The Slap Maxwell Story. *Guest*: McMillan and Wife, The Love Boat, Hotel, Murder She Wrote, Empty Nest.

JONES, TERRY
Writer, Actor, Director. b. Colwyn Bay, North Wales, Feb. 1, 1942. Worked with various rep. groups before joining BBC script dept. Was member of Monty Python's Flying Circus.
PICTURES: *Actor*: And Now for Something Completely Different (also co-s.p.), Monty Python and the Holy Grail (also co-dir., co-s.p.), Monty Python's Life of Brian (also dir., co-s.p.), Monty Python's The Meaning of Life (also co-s.p., dir., music), Labyrinth (s.p. only), Personal Services (dir. only), Erik the Viking (also dir., s.p.), LA Story, The Wind and the Willows, Starship, Titanic.
TELEVISION: Late Night Lineup, The Late Show, A Series of Birds, Do Not Adjust Your Set, The Complete and Utter History of Britain, Monty Python's Flying Circus, Secrets, The Crusades (also dir., writer), So This Is Progress.

JONES, TOMMY LEE
Actor. b. San Saba, TX, Sept. 15, 1946. Worked in oil fields; graduated Harvard, where earned a degree, cum laude, in English. Broadway debut in A Patriot for Me; appeared on stage in Four in a Garden, Ulysses in Nighttown, Fortune and Men's Eyes.
PICTURES: Love Story (debut, 1970), Eliza's Horoscope Jackson County Jail, Rolling Thunder, The Betsy, Eyes of Laura Mars, Coal Miner's Daughter, Back Roads, Nate and Hayes, The River Rat, Black Moon Rising, The Big Town, Stormy Monday, The Package, Firebirds, JFK (Acad. Award nom.), Under Siege, House of Cards, The Fugitive (Acad. Award, best supporting actor, 1993; LA Film Critics & Golden Globe Awards), Heaven and Earth Blown Away, The Client, Natural Born Killers, Blue Sky, Cobb, Batman Forever, Men in Black, Volcano, U.S. Marshalls, Small Soldiers (voice), Rules of Engagement, Double Jeopardy.
TELEVISION: *Movies*: Charlie's Angels (pilot), Smash-Up on Interstate 5, The Amazing Howard Hughes, The Executioner's Song (Emmy Award, 1983), Broken Vows, The Park is Mine, Yuri Nosenko: KGB, Gotham, Stranger on My Land, April Morning, The Good Old Boys (also dir., co-writer). *Mini-Series*: Lonesome Dove. *Specials*: The Rainmaker, Cat on a Hot Tin Roof.

JONES, TREVOR
Composer, conductor. b. Cape Town, S. Africa, March 23, 1949.
PICTURES: The Dollar Bottom, Brothers and Sisters, The Beneficiary, The Appointment, Excalibur, The Sender, The Dark Crystal, Nate and Hayes, Runaway Train, From an Immigrant's Diary, Labyrinth, Angel Heart, Sweet Lies, A Private Life Mississippi Burning, Just Ask For Diamond, Dominick and Eugene, Sea of Love, Bad Influence, Arachnophobia, True Colors, CrissCross, Blame It on the Bellboy, Freejack, The Last of the Mohicans (Golden Globe nom.), In the Name of the Father, Cliffhanger, De Baby huilt, LochNess, Hideaway, Kiss of Death, Richard III, Brassed Off, Lawn Dogs, Roseanna's Grave Talk of Angels, Desperate Measures, G.I. Jane, Titanic Town Plunkett & MacLeane, Analyse This, Dark City, The Mighty Notting Hill, Molly, From Hell, Frederic Wilde.

TELEVISION: *Movies*: Those Glory Glory Days, One of Ourselves, Aderyn Papur.. and Pigs Might Fly, Dr. Fischer of Geneva, A Private Life, Murder by Moonlight, By Dawn's Early Light, Chains of Gold, Guns... A Day In the Death of America, Death Train, *Mini-series*: Joni Jones, The Last Days of Pompeii, Jim Henson Presents the World of International Puppeteering, The Last Place on Earth, Gulliver's Travels, Merlin, Cleopatra.

JONZE, SPIKE
Actor, Director. b. Rockville, Maryland, 1969. r.n. Adam Speigel. Has directed many television commercials and music videos for artists. Is heir to the Spiegel mail order catalog.
PICTURES: Mi Vida Loca (actor), The Game (actor only), Being John Malkovich, Three Kings (actor only), Hannibal (actor only).

JORDAN, GLENN
Director, Producer, b. San Antonio, TX, April 5, 1936. e. Harvard, B.A.; Yale Drama Sch. Directed plays off-B'way and on tour.
PICTURES: *Director*: Only When I Laugh, The Buddy System, Mass Appea, Mary & Tim.
TELEVISION: *Specials*: Hogan's Goat, Paradise Lost, Benjamin Franklin (prod.; Emmy Award), Eccentricities of a Nightingale, The Oath, The Court Martial of Gen. George Armstrong Custer. *Movies*: *Director*: Frankenstein, The Picture of Dorian Gray, Shell Game, One of My Wives is Missing, The Displaced Person, Delta County U.S.A., In the Matter of Karen Ann Quinlan, Sunshine Christmas, Les Miserables, Son Rise: A Miracle of Love, The Family Man, The , The Princess and the Cabbie, Lois Gibbs and the Love Canal, Heartsounds, Dress Grey (also prod.). *Series*: Family. *Dir./Prod.*: Women's Room, Promise (2 Emmy Awards), Something in Common, Echoes in the Darkness, Jesse, Home Fires Burning, Challenger, Sarah: Plain and Tall, Aftermath: A Test of Love, The Boys, O Pioneers!, Barbarians at the Gate (Emmy Award; co-exec. prod.), To Dance With the White Dog, Jane's House, My Brother's Keeper, A Streetcar Named Desire, Jake's Women, After Jimmy, A Christmas Memory.

JORDAN, HENRIETTA
Executive. b. New York, NY. Ent. m.p. ind. as ass't to exec. v.p. UPA Pictures, 1950. V.p. in charge of sales, Format Prods., Inc.; v.p. and assoc. prod., 1962-71. Assoc. prod. Levitow-Hanson Films, Inc., 1972. Prod., Image West, Ltd., 1975-84. Dir. sales., Cause & EFX, 1984-85. Dir. sales Modern Videofilm Braphics, 1986-88. Personal comm., Hank Jordan Enterprises, 1988-.

JORDAN, NEIL
Director, Writer. b. Sligo, Ireland, Feb. 25, 1950. e. University Coll, B.A., 1972. Novels: The Past, Night in Tunisia, Dream of a Beast.
PICTURES: Traveller (s.p.), The Courier (co-exec. prod.). *Dir.-Writer:* Angel, The Company of Wolves, Mona Lisa (LA Film Critics Award for s.p., 1986), High Spirits, We're No Angels (dir. only), The Miracle, The Crying Game (Academy Award, WGA & NY Film Critics Awards for s.p., 1992), Interview With the Vampire, Michael Collins, The Butcher Boy, In Dreams, The End of the Affair.
TELEVISION: Mr. Solomon Wept (BBC), RTE (Ireland), Seduction, Tree, Miracles and Miss Langan.

JOSEPHSON, ERLAND
Actor, Director, Writer. b. Stockholm, Sweden, June 15, 1923. Acted in over 100 plays in Sweden. Joined Sweden's Royal Dramatic Theatre in 1956 replacing Ingmar Bergman as head of the theater, 1966-76. Closely associated with Bergman, with whom he staged plays in his late teens. Co-authored s.p. The Pleasure Garden and Now About These Women. Also has pub. poetry, six novels, and scripts for stage, screen and radio. American stage debut: The Cherry Orchard, 1988. In numerous movies on Swedish television.
PICTURES: It Rains on Our Love, To Joy (uncredited), Sceningang, Som man baddar, Brink of Life, The Magician, Hour of the Wolf, The Girls, Eva: Diary of Half Virgin, The Passion of Anna, Cries and Whispers, Scenes from a Marriage, Monismanien, Face to Face, A Look at Liv, Io ho paura, Beyond Good and Evil, Games of Love and Loneliness, I'm Afraid, Autumn Sonata, Die Erste Polka, To Forget Venice, One and One (also dir.), The Marmalade Revolution (also dir., s.p.), Karleken, Victor Sjostrom (voice), You Love Only Once, Montenegro, Sezona Mira u Parizu, Fanny and Alexander, Bella Donna, Nostalgia, House of the Yellow Carpet, After the Rehearsal, Angela's War, Bakom jalusin, Behind the Shutters, A Case of Irresponsibility, Dirty Story, Amorosa, The Flying Devils, Garibaldi, The General, The Last Mazurka, The Sacrifice, The Malady of Love, Saving Grace, Le Testament d'un poete juif assassine, Unbearable Lightness of Being, Directed by Andrei Tarkovsky, Hanussen, Good Evening Mr. Wallenberg, The Wicked, Meeting Venus, Prospero's Books, The Ox, The Accidental Golfer, Sofie, Holozan, The Dancer, Dreamplay, Ulysses' Gaze, Vendetta, Waiting for Sunset, Kristin Lavransdatter.

JOSEPHSON, MARVIN
Executive. b. Atlantic City, NJ, March 6, 1927. e. Cornell U., B.A., 1949; L.L.B. NYU, 1952. Lawyer at CBS Television 1952-55; founded company which today is ICM Holdings Inc. in 1955. ICM Holdings Inc. is the parent company of Intl. Creative Management Inc. and ICM Artists Ltd.

JOSIAH, JR., WALTER J.
Executive. b. New York, NY, Nov. 9, 1933. e. Fordham U., B.S., 1955: Harvard Law, LL.B., 1962. U.S.A.F., 1955-58, First Lt. and Pilot. Assoc., Simpson Thacher & Bartlett, 1962-67. Legal staff, Paramount, 1967-69. Asst. resident counsel, 1969; chief resident counsel, 1970 and v.p. & chief resident counsel, 1971-82. ex.-v.p. & general counsel, MPAA, 1983-93. Prof. Assoc.: Chmn., Committee 307, Authors Rights, 1981-82, Patent, Trademark & Copyright Law Section of the American Bar Assn.; NY Bar Assoc.(Committee on Copyright and Literary Property, 1976-79, 1982-85, chmn. 1986-89): Copyright Society of the U.S.A.—Member of the Board of Trustees commencing 1981; v.p., from 1988; pres. 1990-; member, AMPAS; Copyright Office Advisory Committee, 1981-82; National Sculpture Society advisor to the president; Advisory Board, Publication: Communications and the Law; Member, President's Club Exec. Committee and Annual Fund Council, Fordham U.

JOST, JON
Director, Writer, Cinematographer, Editor. b. May 16, 1943.
PICTURES: Speaking Directly, Angel City, Last Chants for a Slow Dance, Chameleon (also prod.), Stagefright, Psalm, Slow Moves, Bell Diamond, Rembrandt Laughing, Plain Talk & Common Sense, Blood Orgy of the Leather Girls (assoc. prod. only), All the Vermeers in New York, The Living End (exec. prod. only), Sure Fire, Frame Up, The Bed You Sleep In, One for You One for Me and One for Raphael, Albrecht's Wings.

JOURDAN, LOUIS
Actor, r.n. Louis Gendre. b. Marseille, France, June 19, 1921. Stage actor prior to m.p.
PICTURES: Le Corsaire (debut, 1940), Her First Affair, La Boheme, L'Arlesienne, La Belle, Adventure, Felicie Nanteuil, The Paradine Case, Letter from an Unknown Woman, No Minor Vices, Madame Bovary, Bird of Paradise, Anne of the Indies, The Happy Time, Decameron Nights, Three Coins in the Fountain, The Swan, Julie, The Bride is Much Too Beautiful, Dangerous Exile, Gigi, The Best of Everything, Can-Can, Leviathan, Streets of Montmartre, Story of the Count of Monte Cristo, Mathias Sandorf, The VIPs, Made in Paris, To Commit a Murder, A Flea in Her Ear, Young Rebel (Cervantes), The Silver Bears, Double Deal, Swamp Thing, Octopussy, The Return of Swamp Thing, Counterforce, Year of the Comet.
TELEVISION: *Series*: Paris Precinct, Romance Theatre (host). *Mini-Series*: The French Atlantic Affair, Dracula. *Movies*: Run a Crooked Mile, Fear No Evil, Ritual of Evil, The Great American Beauty Contest, The Count of Monte Cristo, The Man in the Iron Mask, The First Olympics-Athens, Beverly Hills Madam. *Guest*: Ford Theatre, The FBI, Name of the Game, Charlie's Angels.

JOY, ROBERT
Actor. b. Montreal, Canada, Aug. 17, 1951. e. Memorial Univ. of Newfoundland; Rhodes Scholar. Acted in regional and off-Broadway theatre. Off-B'way debut The Diary of Anne Frank (1978). Has composed music for stage, radio and film.
THEATER: NY Shakespeare Fest. (Found a Peanut, Lenny and the Heartbreakers, The Death of von Richtofen), Life and Limb, Fables for Friends, Welcome to the Moon, What I Did Last Summer, Lydie Breeze, Romeo and Juliet (La Jolla Playhouse; Drama-Logue Award), Hay Fever (B'way debut), Big River (premiere), The Nerd, Hyde in Hollywood, The Taming of the Shrew, Shimada, Goodnight Desdemona (Good Morning Juliet), Abe Lincoln in Illinois, No One Will Be Immune, June Moon.
PICTURES: Atlantic City, Ragtime, Ticket to Heaven, Threshold, Terminal Choice, Amityville 3-D, Desperately Seeking Susan, Joshua Then and Now, Adventure of Faustus Bidgood (also co-prod. music), Radio Days, Big Shots, The Suicide Club, She's Back!, Millenium, Longtime Companion, Shadows and Fog, The Dark Half, Death Wish 5: The Face of Death, I'll Do Anything, Henry & Verlin, Waterworld, A Modern Affair, Pharoah's Army, Dangerous Offender, Harriet the Spy, The Divine Ryans, Fallen.
TELEVISION: *Series*: One Life to Live, The High Life. *Guest*: The Equalizer, Moonlighting, Law and Order, The Marshal, New York Undercover, Wings. *Specials*: The Prodigious Hickey, The Return of Hickey, The Beginning of the Firm, Hyde in Hollywood. *Movies*: Escape from Iran: The Canadian Caper, Gregory K, Woman on the Run: The Lawrencia Bembenek Story, The High Life.

JUDD, ASHLEY
Actress. b. Los Angeles, CA, April 19, 1968. Mother and sister are country singers, Naomi and Wynona Judd.
PICTURES: Kuffs, Ruby in Paradise, The Passion of Darkly Noon, Smoke, Heat, A Time to Kill, Normal Life, The Locusts, Kiss the Girls, Simon Birch, Eye of the Beholder, Double Jeopardy, Where the Heart Is, High Crimes, Frida Kahlo, Animals Husbandry.
TELEVISION: *Series*: Sisters. *Movies*: Till Death Us Do Part, Norma Jean and Marilyn. *Special*: Naomi & Wynona: Love Can Build a Bridge. *Guest*: Star Trek: The Next Generation.

JUDGE, MIKE
Animator, actor, director, producer. b. Guayaquil, Ecuador, Oct. 17, 1962. e. UC San Diego. *Shorts:* Frog Baseball (also voices, dir., prod., s.p.), Inbred Jed (also voices, dir., prod., s.p.), Office Space (voice, composer, dir.).
PICTURES: Airheads (voice), Beavis & Butt-head Do America (also dir., prod., composer, voices), Mene Tekel (voices), Office Space (dir., s.p., act.), South Park: Bigger Longer and Uncut (voice).

TELEVISION: *Series*: Beavis and Butt-head, (also dir., prod., composer, voices), King of the Hill (also prod., voices). *Guest:* The Simpsons (voice).

JURADO, KATY
Actress. r.n. Maria Christina Jurado Garcia. b. Guadalajara, Mexico, Jan. 16, 1927. Appeared in numerous Mexican films beginning in 1943. Also m.p. columnist for Mexican publications.
PICTURES: No Maturas (debut, 1943), El Museo del Crimen, Rosa del Caribe, The Bullfighter and the Lady (U.S. debut, 1951), High Noon, San Antone, Arrowhead, Broken Lance (Acad. Award nom.), The Sword of Granada, The Racers, Trial, Trapeze, Man from Del Rio, Dragoon Wells Massacre, Badlanders, One Eyed Jacks, Barabbas, Seduction of the South, Target for Killing, Smoky, A Covenant With Death, Stay Away Joe, Bridge in the Jungle, Pat Garrett and Billy the Kid, Once Upon a Scoundrel, The Children of Sanchez, Reasons of State, Under the Volcano, La Nueva Jerusalem.
TELEVISION: *Movies*: Any Second Now, A Little Game, Evita Peron, Lady Blue. *Series*: A.K.A. Pablo.

K

KAGAN, JEREMY
Director, Writer. b. Mt. Vernon, NY, Dec. 14, 1945. e. Harvard; NYU, MFA; student Amer. Film Inst. 1971. Film animator, 1968; multi-media show designer White House Conf. on Youth and Ed. Previously credited as Jeremy Paul Kagan.
PICTURES: Scott Joplin, Heroes, The Big Fix, The Chosen (Montreal World Film Fest. Prize, 1981), The Sting II, The Journey of Natty Gann (Gold Prize, Moscow Film Fest., 1987), Big Man on Campus, By the Sword.
TELEVISION: *Series*: Columbo, The Bold Ones, Chicago Hope (Emmy Award, 1996). *Movies*: Unwed Father, Judge Dee and the Monastery Murders, Katherine (also writer), Courage, Roswell (also co-prod., co-story). *Specials*: My Dad Lives in a Downtown Hotel, Conspiracy: The Trial of the Chicago 8 (also writer; ACE Award, 1988).

KAHN, MADELINE
Actress, Singer. b. Boston, MA., Sept. 29, 1942. e. Hofstra U. Broadway bow in New Faces of '68. Trained as opera singer and appeared in La Boheme, Showboat, Two by Two, Candide. Appeared in short film The Dove.
THEATER: Promenade, Two by Two, In the Boom Boom Room, On the Twentieth Century, Born Yesterday, The Sisters Rosensweig (Tony Award, 1993).
PICTURES: What's Up Doc? (debut, 1972), Paper Moon (Acad. Award nom.), From the Mixed-Up Files of Mrs. Basil E. Frankweiler (The Hideaways), Blazing Saddles (Acad. Award nom.), Young Frankenstein, At Long Last Love, The Adventures of Sherlock Holmes' Smarter Brother, Won Ton Ton the Dog Who Saved Hollywood, High Anxiety, The Cheap Detective, The Muppet Movie, Simon, Happy Birthday Gemini, Wholly Moses, First Family, History of the World—Part 1, Yellowbeard, Slapstick of Another Kind, City Heat, Clue, My Little Pony (voice), An American Tail (voice), Betsy's Wedding, Mixed Nuts, Nixon, A Bug's Life (voice), Judy Berlin.
TELEVISION: *Series*: Comedy Tonight, Oh Madeline! (People's Choice award), Mr. President, New York News, Cosby. *Specials*: Harvey, The Perfect Guy (afterschool special, Emmy award), Celebrating Gershwin: The Jazz Age, Irving Berlin Gala, Stephen Sondheim Gala, Danny Kaye: A Legacy of Laughter. *Movies*: For Richer For Poorer, London Suite.

KAHN, MILTON
Publicist. b. Brooklyn, NY, May 3, 1934. e. Syracuse U., Ohio U., B.S.J. 1957. Formed Milton Kahn Associates, Inc. in 1958. Represented: Gregory Peck, Joan Crawford, Steve Allen, Glenn Ford, Lee Grant, Herb Alpert, Roger Corman, Robert Aldrich, Arthur Hiller, Chuck Norris, Bob Cousy, Gordie Howe, Michael Landon, Dean Hargrove, Bill Conti, etc. and New World Pictures (1970-83), Avco-Embassy, Vista Films, Roger Corman's Concorde (1983-), Electric Shadow Prods. Named Publicist of the Year by Book Pub. of So. CA, 1996.

KAHN, RICHARD
Executive. b. New Rochelle, NY, Aug. 19, 1929. e. Wharton Sch. of Finance and Commerce, U. of Pennsylvania, B.S., 1951; U.S. Navy, 3 yrs.; joined Buchanan & Co., 1954; ent. m.p. ind. as pressbook writer, Columbia Pictures, 1955; exploitation mgr., 1958; natl. coord. adv. and pub., 1963; natl. dir. of adv., pub. and exploitation, 1968; v.p., 1969; 1974 v.p. in chg. of special marketing projects; 1975; moved to MGM as v.p. in chg. of worldwide advertising, publicity and exploitation; 1978, named sr. v.p. in chg. worldwide mktg. & pres., MGM Intl. 1980, elected bd. of govs., Academy of M.P. Arts & Sciences. 1982, named exec. v.p. of adv., pub., promo. for MGM/UA; 1983, formed the Richard Kahn Co., dist. & mktg. consultancy, 1984-88. Faculty mem. Peter Stark m.p. producing prog., USC Sch. of Cinema & TV. Exec. chmn., Film Inf. Council. 1982-95 elected secretary Acad. of Motion Picture Arts & Sciences; elected v.p. 1983-87; elected pres. 1988.

KALB, MARVIN
TV news reporter. e. City Coll. of NY; Harvard, M.A., 1953, Russian Language Sch., Middlebury Coll. Worked for U.S. State Dept., American Embassy, Moscow; CBS News, 1957; writer, reporter-researcher. Where We Stand: reporter-assignment editor; Moscow Bureau Chief, 1960-63; first diplomatic corresp., Washington Bureau, 1963. Chief diplomatic corresp. CBS News and NBC News, moderator Meet the Press; Teacher and lecturer; first dir. Joan Shorenstein Barone Center on the Press, Politics and Public Policy at J.F.K. Sch. of Govt. of Harvard U., since 1987. Host of PBS series, Candidates '88. Author: Eastern Exposure, Kissinger, Dragon in the Kremlin, Roots of Involvement, The U.S. in Asia 1784-1971, Candidates '88 (with Hendrik Hertzberg).

KALISH, EDDIE
Executive. b. New York, NY, April 27, 1939. Reporter/reviewer, Variety, 1959-64; sr. publicist, Paramount, 1964-65; adv./pub./promo dir., Ken Greengras Personal Management, 1965-66; pub. dir., Harold Rand & Co., 1966-67; indept. publicist overseas, 1967-75; rejoined Paramount in 1975 as dir. of intl. mktg.; later named v.p.; 1978, v.p., worldwide pub. & promo. 1979 appt. sr. v.p., worldwide mktg. 1980 joined UA as v.p. domestic mktg.; sr. v.p., adv., pub., promo, for MGM/UA 1981-82; became sr. v.p., worldwide mkt., PSO, 1982-1986. Now pres., Kalish/Davidson Marketing, Inc.

KAMBER, BERNARD M.
Executive. e. U. of Pennsylvania. New England exploitation rep. U.A. 1940; Army service 1941-43; dir. special events dept. U.A., 1943; asst. to Gradwell L. Sears, nat'l distrib. chmn. 6th War Loan Drive; dir. pub. 7th War Loan Drive, 1943-47; dir. pub. & prom. Eagle Lion Classics, 1951; org. Kamber Org., pub. rel. rep. for ind. prod. v.p. sales, adv. pub. Ivan Tors Prod. Greene-Rouse Prods. 1953; exec. asst. Hecht-Hill-Lancaster, chg. of N.Y. off., 1957; v.p. Hecht-Hill-Lancaster Companies, 1958; formed Cinex Distr. Corp., 1962; Pres. Cinex and Posfilm, Inc.; 1967, v.p. in chg. sls. Du Art Film Lab. Inc; 1975 joined Technicolor, Inc.

KAMEN, MICHAEL
Composer, conductor, arranger. b. New York, NY, 1948. Began career composing music for the Joffrey Ballet and the La Scala Opera Co. Wrote his first film score in 1970 for The Next Man. Has also written for David Bowie, Eric Clapton and the Eurythmics.
PICTURES: *Scores*: The Next Man (debut), Stunts, Between the Lines, Polyester, Venom, Pink Floyd—The Wall, Angelo My Love, The Dead Zone, Brazil, Lifeforce, Shoot for the Sun, Rita—Sue and Bob Too, Highlander, Mona Lisa, Shanghai Surprise, Suspect, Someone to Watch Over Me, Adventures in Babysitting, Lethal Weapon, The Raggedy Rawney, Crusoe, Action Jackson, Homeboy, Die Hard, Rooftops, For Queen and Country, The Adventures of Baron Munchausen, Road House, License to Kill, Dead-Bang, Lethal Weapon, Renegades, The Krays, Cold Dog Soup, Die Hard 2, Nothing But Trouble, Let Him Have It, Company Business, Robin Hood: Prince of Thieves (Acad. award nom., Golden Globe nom.), Hudson Hawk, The Last Boy Scout, Blue Ice, Shining Through, Lethal Weapon 3, Wilder Napalm, Splitting Hairs, Last Action Hero, The Three Musketeers, Stonewall, Mr Holland's Opus, Circle of Friends, Don Juan DeMarco, Die Hard: With a Vengeance, Jack, 101 Dalmations, Remember Me?, Inventing the Abbotts, Event Horizon, The Winter Guest, Lethal Weapon 4, The Avengers.
TELEVISION: *Scores*: Liza's Pioneer Diary, S*H*E, Amazing Stories, Edge of Darkness, Tales from the Crypt, The Heart Surgeon.

KAMINSKI, JANUSZ
Cinematographer. b. Ziembice, Poland, June 27, 1959. Second unit work on films: Watchers II, To Die Standing, One False Move.
PICTURES: The Terror Within II (debut, 1990), Grim Prairie Tales, The Rain Killer, Pyrates, Cool as Ice, Trouble Bound, Mad Dog Coll, The Adventures of Huck Finn, Schindler's List, Little Giants, Tall Tale, How to Make an American Quilt, Jerry Maguire, Amistad, The Lost World: Jurassic Park, Armageddon (addt'l), Saving Private Ryan (Acad. Award), Memoirs of a Geisha, A.I., Minority Report. *Director:* Lost Souls.
TELEVISION: *Movies:* Wildflower, Class of '61.

KANAKAREDES, MELINA
Actress. b. Akron, OH, April 23, 1967.
PICTURES: White Man's Burden, The Long Kiss Goodnight, Rounders, Dangerous Beauty, 15 Minutes.
TELEVISION: *Movies:* Saint Maybe. *Series:* The Guiding Light, NYPD Blue, New York News, Leaving L.A., Providence. *Guest:* Due South, The Practice, Oz.

KANE, CAROL
Actress. b. Cleveland, OH, June 18, 1952. e. Professional Children's Sch., NY. Began professional acting career at age 14, touring, then on B'way in The Prime of Miss Jean Brodie.
THEATER: The Tempest, The Effect of Gamma Rays on Man-in-the-Moon Marigolds, Are You Now or Have You Ever Been? Arturo Ui, The Enchanted, The Tempest, Macbeth, Tales of the Vienna Woods, Frankie and Johnny in the Claire de Lune, Control Freaks.

PICTURES: Carnal Knowledge (debut, 1971), Desperate Characters, Wedding in White, The Last Detail, Dog Day Afternoon, Hester Street, Harry and Walter Go to New York, Annie Hall, Valentino, The World's Greatest Lover, The Mafu Cage, The Muppet Movie, When a Stranger Calls, Pandemonium, Norman Loves Rose, Over the Brooklyn Bridge, Racing With the Moon, The Secret Diary of Sigmund Freud, Transylvania 6-5000, Jumpin' Jack Flash, Ishtar, The Princess Bride, Sticky Fingers, License to Drive, Scrooged, Flashback, Joe Vs. the Volcano, My Blue Heaven, The Lemon Sisters, Ted and Venus, In the Soup, Addams Family Values, Even Cowgirls Get the Blues, Big Bully, The Pallbearer, Sunset Park, The Pallbearer, American Strays, Office Killer, Gone Fishin', The Tic Code, Jawbreaker, Man on the Moon.
TELEVISION: *Series*: Taxi (2 Emmy Awards: 1982, 1983), All Is Forgiven, American Dreamer, Pearl, Beggars and Choosers. *Movies*: An Invasion of Privacy, Burning Rage, Drop Out Mother, Dad the Angel and Me, Freaky Friday, Merry Christmas George Bailey. *Specials*: Faerie Tale Theatre, Paul Reiser: Out on a Whim, Tales From the Crypt (Judy, You're Not Yourself Today), Noah's Ark.

KANE, JOHN
Publicity Manager. b. New York, NY. e. Rutgers, B.A.; NYU, M.A. Publicist, Solters & Roskin, 1976-80. Unit publicist: Fame, Tender Mercies, Prince of the City, 1980-82. 1982-90, Home Box Office, unit publicist, manager. 1991, unit publ. for Ricochet, Arizona Dream.

KANE, STANLEY D.
Judge. b. Minneapolis, MN, Dec. 21, 1907. e. U of MN, B.A. (magna cum laude), 1930;, M.A., 1931; MN Coll. of Law, LL.B., 1940. Instructor, U. of Minnesota, 1930-33. Exec. sec. Allied Theatre Owners of the Northwest, 1933-37; city attorney, 1940-60; exec. v.p. & gen. counsel, North Central Allied Independent Theatre Owners, 1946-63; dist. court judge, then sr. judge, Hennepin County, 1963-90.

KANEW, JEFF
Director.
PICTURES: Black Rodeo (also prod., edit.), Natural Enemies (also s.p., edit.), Eddie Macon's Run (also s.p., edit.), Revenge of the Nerds, Gotcha!, Tough Guys, Troop Beverly Hills, V. I. Warshawski.
TELEVISION: Alfred Hitchcock Presents (1985).

KANFER, MICHAEL
Special Effects.
PICTURES: Apollo 13, Titanic (Acad. Award, Best Visual Effects, 1997).

KANIN, FAY
Writer. b. New York, NY, May 9. e. Elmira Coll., U. of Southern California, 1937. m. Michael Kanin, writer. Contrib. fiction to mags., Writers Guild of Amer. pres. screen branch, 1971-73; Acad. Motion Picture Arts & Sciences 1983-88. also bd. mem. of latter. Co-chair, National Center for Film and Video Preservation; Bd. of trustees, Amer. Film Institute; Chair, Natl. Film Preservation Board.
THEATER: Goodbye My Fancy, His and Hers, Rashomon, The High Life, Grind (1985).
PICTURES: My Pal Gus, Rhapsody, The Opposite Sex, Teacher's Pet, Swordsman of Siena, The Right Approach.
TELEVISION: Heat of Anger, Tell Me Where It Hurts (Emmy Award, 1974), Hustling (also co-prod.), Friendly Fire (also co-prod., Emmy Award, San Francisco Film Fest. Award, Peabody Award), Heartsounds (Peabody Award; also co-prod.).

KANTER, HAL
Writer, Director, Producer. b. Savannah, GA, Dec. 18, 1918. On B'way contributor to Hellzapoppin. Then began writing radio dramas before mil. service, WW II. Served as combat corresp. Armed Forces Radio; writer, Paramount, 1951-54; dir., RKO, 1956; writer, prod. for Lucille Ball Prods., 1979-80. Savannah Prods., 1982-86. Received Writers Guild Paddy Chayefsky Laurel Award, 1989. Writer (radio): Danny Kaye Show, Amos 'n Andy, Bing Crosby Show, Jack Paar, Beulah. Winner 3 Emmy Awards for writing, 1954, 1991, 1992; W.G.A.W. Valentine Davies award. Was member: bd. of dir., WGAW; bd. of govs. AMPAS; v.p. Writers Guild Foundation.
PICTURES: *Writer*: My Favorite Spy, Off Limits, Road to Bali, Casanova's Big Night, About Mrs. Leslie, Money from Home, Artists and Models, The Rose Tattoo, I Married a Woman (dir. only), Loving You (also dir.), Mardi Gras, Once Upon a Horse (also dir., prod.), Blue Hawaii, Pocketful of Miracles, Bachelor in Paradise, Move Over Darling, Dear Brigitte.
TELEVISION: *Writer*: Ed Wynn Show, George Gobel Show (also creator, prod.), Kraft Music Hall (also dir., prod.; 1958-59), Chrysler Theatre (also prod., dir.; 1966-67), Julia (also dir., prod., creator), Jimmy Stewart Show (also prod., dir., creator), All In The Family (exec. prod.: 1975-76), Chico & The Man (spv. prod., 1976-77), You Can't Take It With You. *Specials (writer)*: AFI Life Achievement Awards for Henry Fonda & Alfred Hitchcock, 26 & 28 Annual Academy Awards and many others.

KANTER, JAY
Executive. b. Chicago, IL, Dec. 12, 1926. Entered industry with MCA, Inc., where was v.p. Left after more than 20 yrs. to become indep. prod., then pres. of First Artists Production Co., Ltd. 1975 joined 20th-Fox as v.p. prod.; 1976, named sr. v.p., worldwide prod. Named v.p., The Ladd Co., 1979. Joined MGM/UA Entertainment Co. as pres., worldwide prod., Motion Picture Division, 1984. 1985, named pres., worldwide prod., UA Corp.; then pres., production MGM Pictures Inc.; 1989, named chmn. of prod. of Pathe Entertainment Co. 1991, became COO & chmn. of prod., MGM-Pathe Commun. Co. (MGM Communications, 1992). 1994-95, MGM consultant. March, 1995, independent prod.

KANTOR, IGO
Producer, Film Editor. b. Vienna, Austria, Aug. 18, 1930. e. UCLA, A.A. 1950; B.S., 1952; M.S., 1954. Foreign corres., Portugal magazine, FLAMA, 1949-57, music supvr., Screen Gems, Columbia 1954-63; post-prod. supvr., film ed., features, TV; assoc. prod., 1963-64; prod., exec., International Entertainment Corp., 1965; pres., Synchrofilm, Inc., post-production co. and Duque Films Inc., production co. 1968-74. 1975-present, produced and edited films. 1982, pres., Laurelwood Prods; 1988, pres. Major Arts Corp.
PICTURES: *Assoc. Producer*: Bye Bye Birdie, Under the Yum Yum Tree, Gidget Goes to Rome, A House Is Not a Home, Pattern for Murder, Willy. *Producer*: Assault on Agathon (also edit.), FTA, Dixie Dynamite (assoc. prod., edit.), Kingdom of the Spiders (also edit., music spvr.), The Dark (assoc. prod.), Good Luck Miss Wyckoff (prod. spvr.), Hardly Working, Kill and Kill Again, Mutant, Shaker Run, Act of Piracy, They Call Me Bruce Levy, Twirpy.
TELEVISION: From Hawaii with Love (1984), The Grand Tour, It's a Wonderful World (prod.-dir.), Nosotros Golden Eagle Awards (prod.), United We Stand (pre-Olympic special), Legends of the West With Jack Palance, Mom U.S.A., A Desperate Affair, Holiday Classics Cartoons (special).

KAPLAN, GABRIEL
Actor, Comedian. b. Brooklyn, NY, March 31, 1945. After high school worked as bellboy at Lakewood, NJ hotel, spending free time studying comedians doing routines. Put together a comedy act, landing engagements in small clubs and coffee houses all over U.S. Made several appearances on Tonight Show, Merv Griffin Show, Mike Douglas Show, etc. Has played Las Vegas clubs.
PICTURES: Fast Break, Tulips, Nobody's Perfekt.
TELEVISION: *Series*: Welcome Back Kotter, Gabriel Kaplan Presents Future Stars, Lewis and Clark. *Movie*: Love Boat (pilot).

KAPLAN, JONATHAN
Director, Writer. b. Paris, France, Nov. 25, 1947. Son of composer Sol Kaplan. e. U. of Chicago, B.A.; NYU, M.F.A. Made short film Stanley Stanley. Member of tech. staff Fillmore East, NY 1969-71. New World Pictures' Roger Corman post-grad. sch. of filmmaking, Hollywood, 1971-73. As actor on B'way in Dark at the Top of the Stairs. Appeared in films: Cannonball, Hollywood Boulevard.
PICTURES: *Director*: Night Call Nurses, Student Teachers, The Slams, Truck Turner, White Line Fever (also co-s.p.), Mr. Billion, Over the Edge, Heart Like a Wheel, Project X, The Accused, Immediate Family, Unlawful Entry, Love Field, Bad Girls, Brokedown Palace.
TELEVISION: *Movies*: The 11th Victim, The Hustler of Muscle Beach, The Gentleman Bandit, Girls of the White Orchid, Reform School Girl, In Cold Blood. *Series*: Fallen Angels, ER.

KAPOOR, SHASHI
Actor. b. Calcutta, India, March 18, 1938. Son of late Prithviraj Kapoor, Indian film and stage actor. As child worked in Prithvi Theatre and in brother, Raj's films. Toured with father's co. at 18 and joined the Kendals' Shakespeareana Co. in India. Starred in over 200 Indian films as well as several Merchant-Ivory Prods.
PICTURES: Aag, Awara, Prem Patra, The Householder, Waqt, Shakespeare Wallah, A Matter of Innocence, Pretty Polly, Bombay Talkie, Sharmilee, Siddhartha, Roti Kapda Aur Makaan, Deewar, Kabhie Kabhie, Imaan Dharam, Trishul; Satyam, Shivam, Sundaram; Junoon (also prod.), Suhaag, Kaala Pathar, Shaan, Kalyug (also prod.), Do Aur do Paanch, 36 Chowringhee Lane (prod. only), Silsila, Bezubaan, Namak Halal, Heat and Dust, Door-desh, Utsav (also prod.), New Delhi Times, Abodh, Sammy and Rosie Get Laid, Ijaazat, The Deceivers, Nomads, Akayla, Ajooba (dir. only), In Custody, Side Streets.
TELEVISION: *Movie*: Gulliver's Travels.

KAPUR, SHEKHAR
Director. b. Lahore, Pakistan, 1945.
PICTURES: Masoom, Joshilar, Mr. India, Time Machine, Bandit Queen, Dushmani, Elizabeth, Long Walk to Freedom, Four Feathers.
TELEVISION: Tahqiqat.

KARANOVIC, SRDJAN
Director. b. Belgrade, Yugoslavia, November 17, 1945. 1994-1996, Guest Instructor, Boston University.
PICTURES: Stvar Srca, Pani Vratna, Neblbni, Drustvena Igra, If It Kills Me (s.p. only), Miris Poljskog Cveca, Bravo Maestro (s.p. only), Nesto Izmedju (also s.p.), Jagode U Grlu, A Film with No Name, Virdzina.

TELEVISION: *Movies:* Apotekarica, Dom, Pogledaj Me Nevernice. *Series:* Grlom U Jagode, Petria's Wreath (also s.p.).

KARDISH, LAURENCE
Curator, Dept. of Film, Museum of Modern Art. b. Ottawa, Ontario, Canada, Jan. 5, 1945. e. Carlton U. Ottawa, Canada, 1966, Honors B.A. in philosophy; Columbia U., Sch. of the Arts, 1968, M.F.A. in film, radio, and television. 1965-66: Canadian Film Inst., programmer for National Film Theatre, Ottawa; researched a history of Canadian filmmaking. 1965: founded first film society in Canada to exhibit Amer. avant-garde films (Carleton U. Cine Club); directed summer seminar on film, Carleton U., 1966. 1966-68: New American Cinema Group, Inc., NY, worked for the Film-Makers' Distribution Center. 1968: joined Dept. of Film, MOMA; made curator 1984. Since 1968 involved with Cineprobe prog. Since 1972 participated in selection of films for New Directors/New Films series; dir. exhibitions of surveys of national cinemas (Senegal, Scandinavia, French-speaking Canada) and retrospectives of ind. Amer. filmmakers (includ. Rudolph Burkhardt, Stan Brakhage, Shirley Clarke), The Lubitsch Touch, Columbia Pictures, Warner Bros., MGM, Universal, RKO, and directors. 1980: toured Europe with prog. of indep. Amer. films. Author: Reel Plastic Magic (1972); also essays and monographs. Dir.feature Slow Run (1968). On jury for Channel 13's Indep. Focus series and on Board of Advisors, Collective for Living Cinema, NY. 1982-82: bd. of dirs. of National Alliance of Media Arts Centers; 1987-89: on Jerome Foundation panel. 1986 on Camera d'Or jury, Cannes Film Fest.

KARLIN, FRED
Composer, Conductor. b. Chicago, IL, June 16, 1936. e. Amherst Coll., B.A. Composer and arranger for Benny Goodman. Won Academy Award for Best Song for For All We Know (from Lovers and Other Strangers) and Emmy for original music in The Autobiography of Miss Jane Pittman. 4 Acad. Award noms., 11 Emmy Award noms.; Image Award for score to Minstrel Man. Author: On the Track: A Guide to Contemporary Film Scoring (with Rayburn Wright), Listening to Movies. Creator and instructor of the ASCAP/Fred Karlin Film Scoring Workshop, since 1988.
PICTURES: Up the Down Staircase, Yours Mine and Ours, The Sterile Cuckoo (including music for song, Come Saturday Morning; Acad. Award nom.), The Stalking Moon, Westworld, Futureworld, Lovers and Other Strangers, Leadbelly, Loving Couples.
TELEVISION: The Autobiography of Miss Jane Pittman, The Awakening Land, The Plutonium Incident, Minstrel Man, Sophia Loren—Her Own Story, Green Eyes, Strangers: The Story of a Mother and Daughter, Calamity Jane, Ike: the War Years, Inside the Third Reich, Hollywood—The Gift of Laughter, Homeward Bound, Dream West, Hostage Flight, A Place to Call Home, Robert Kennedy and His Times, Dadah is Death, Bridge to Silence, The Secret, Film Music Masters: Jerry Goldsmith (prod. and dir.), Film Music Masters: Elmer Bernstein (prod. and dir.).

KARLIN, MYRON D.
Executive. b. Revere, MA, Sept. 21, 1918. e. UCLA. Joined m.p. business in 1946 as gen. mgr. for MGM in Ecuador. Two yrs. later assigned same spot for MGM in Venezuela. 1952-53 was gen. sales mgr. for MGM in Germany, after which managing dir. in Argentina, returning to Germany as mgr. dir. in 1956. Named mgr. dir. for United Artists in Italy. 1960-68 was pres. of Brunswick Int'l., while also serving as advisor to World Health Organization and UNESCO. 1969 was European mgr. for MGM and mgn. dir. in Italy. Joined Warner Bros. Int'l. in 1970 as v.p. of European dist. 1972 appt. v.p. in chg. of int'l. operations for WB; 1977, appt. pres., WB Intl. & exec. v.p., Warner Bros., Inc; 1985, named exec. v.p., intl. affairs, WB, Inc. Pres. & COO, Motion Picture Export Assn. July, 1994, sr. consultant, Motion Picture Assoc. Decorations: Commander of the Italian Republic; Office of Order of Arts and Letters (France); Commander of Order of King Leopold (Belgium).

KARMAZIN, MELVIN ALLEN
Executive. b. 1944, New York. e. Pace University, BA in business administration, 1965. Station Mgr., CBS Radio, NY, 1960-70. VP and Gen'l Mgr. Metromedia Inc., 1970-81. Pres. Infinity Broadcast Corp., 1981-96. CEO Infinity Broadcast Corp., 1988-96. Chairman, CEO CBS Station Group, 1996-1998. 1999, Chairman & CEO, CBS, Inc.

KARP, ALLEN
Executive. b. Toronto, Ontario, Canada, Sept. 18, 1940. e. Univ. of Toronto, law degree, 1964; called to Ontario bar in 1966; masters of business law degree 1975, from Osgoode Hall Law School, York Univ. Upon graduation joined the firm of Goodman & Carr, became a partner in 1970. Served as business lawyer and sr. legal advisor, becoming dir. of Odeon Theatre Film circuit, 1977. 1986, named sr. exec. v.p. of Cineplex Odeon Corp; 1988, became pres. North American Theatres Division; 1989, pres. & COO; 1990, elected pres. & CEO. Chmn., CEO & dir., Cineplex Odeon Canada (Loews Cineplex Ent. Corp.), 1998-. On the bds. of Speedy Muffler King Inc., Alliance Communications Co. Member of the Canadian Civil Liberties Assn., New York City Partnership of CEO's.

KARRAS, ALEX
Actor. b. Gary, IN, July 15, 1935. e. Univ. of Iowa. As football player with Iowa State U., picked for All Amer. team. Received Outland Trophy, 1957. Former professional football player with Detroit Lions, 1958-62, and 1964-71. Sportswriter, Detroit Free Press, 1972-73. Also worked as prof. wrestler, salesman, steel worker and lecturer. m. actress Susan Clark. With her formed Georgian Bay Prods., 1979. Books: Even Big Guys Cry (with Herb Gluck, 1977), Alex Karras: My Life in Football Television and Movies (1979), Tuesday Night Football (1991).
PICTURES: Paper Lion (as himself; debut, 1968), Blazing Saddles, FM, Win Place or Steal, Jacob Two-Two Meets the Hooded Fang, When Time Ran Out, Nobody's Perfekt, Porky's, Victor/Victoria, Against All Odds.
TELEVISION: *Commentator and host*: Monday Night Football (1974-76). *Mini-Series*: Centennial. *Movies*: Hardcase, The 500-Pound Jerk, Babe, Mulligan's Stew, Mad Bull, Jimmy B. & Andre (also exec. prod.), Alcatraz: The Whole Shocking Story, Word of Honor (also exec. prod.), Maid in America (also exec. prod.), Fudge-a-Mania, Tracy Takes On.... *Series*: Webster (also co-prod.), The Tom Show.

KARTOZIAN, WILLIAM F.
Executive. b. San Francisco, CA, July 27, 1938. e. Stanford U., 1960; Harvard Law Sch., 1963. Deputy Attorney General State of CA, 1963-64; assoc. in law firm of Lillick, McHose Wheat Adams & Charles, San Francisco, 1964-65; corp. counsel and dir., Natl. Convenience Stores, Houston, 1965-67; v.p. and corp. counsel, UA Theatres, 1967-75; owner, Festival Enterprises, Inc., 1970-86; chmn. San Francisco Theatre Employers Assoc., 1973-76; Theatre Assoc. of CA, Inc., dir. 1972-86, v.p. 1974-75, pres. 1975-79, chmn. of bd. 1979-81; member, State of CA Industrial Welfare Comm. Amusement and Recreation Industries Wage Board, 1975-76; Natl Assoc. of Theatre Owners: dir. 1976-86, v.p. 1980-86, president 1988-present. Owner, Regency Enterprises, Inc., 1986-present; chmn. of bd., Lakeside Inn & Casino, Stateline, NV 1985-present. Member: Calif. Film Commission, 1988-present.

KAR-WAI, WONG
Director. b. Shanghai, 1959. e. B.A. in graphic design, Hong Kong, 1980.
PICTURES: *Dir.:* As Tears Go By (also s.p.), The True Story of Ah Fei (also s.p.), Let's Go Slam Dunk, Fallen Angels (also prod., s.p.), Ashes of Time (also s.p.), Chunking Express (also s.p.), Happy Together (also prod., s.p.). *Writer:* Intellectual Trio, The Final Test, The Final Victory, The Haunted Copshop, Dragon and Tiger Fight, The Haunted Copshop II, Saviour of Souls, Beijing Summer. *Prod.:* The Eagle Shooting Heroes, First Love: A Litter on the Breeze.

KARYO, TCHEKY
Actor. b. Istanbul, Turkey. Studied drama at the Cyrano Theatre and became a member of the Daniel Sorano Company, National Theatre of Strasbourg. Received the Jean Gabin Prize, 1986.
PICTURES: Vincent and Me, La Balance, The Return of Martin Guerre, All Night Long, La Java des ombres, The Outsider, Full Moon in Paris, Amour braque, L' Actor, États d'âme, Bleu comme l'enfer, L' Unique, Spirale, Sorceress, The Bear, Australia, La Fille des Collines, La Femme Nikita, Corps Perdus, Exposure, Isabelle Eberhardt, 1492: Conquest of Paradise, Sketch Artist, On Guard, Husbands and Lovers, And the Band Played On, The Black Angel, Nostradamus, Fear City: A Family-Style Comedy, Zadoc et le bonheur, GoldenEye, Operation Dumbo Drop, Bad Boys, Colpo di luna, Crying Freeman, Foreign Land, Albergo Roma, Gentle Into the Night, To Have and to Hold, Follow Your Heart, Les Mille merveilles de l'univers, Dobermann, Addicted to Love, Habitat, Que la lumière soit, World of Moss, Wing Commander.

KASDAN, LAWRENCE
Writer, Director, Producer. b. West Virginia, Jan. 14, 1949. e. U. of Michigan. Clio award-winning adv. copywriter, Detroit and LA before becoming screen writer. Became dir. with Body Heat (1981).
PICTURES: *Dir./s.p./co-s.p.*: The Empire Strikes Back, Raiders of the Lost Ark, Continental Divide, Body Heat, Return of the Jedi, The Big Chill (also co-exec. prod.), Into the Night (actor), Silverado (also prod), Cross My Heart (prod.), The Accidental Tourist (also co-prod.), Immediate Family (exec. prod.), I Love You to Death (also actor), Grand Canyon (also co-prod., actor), Jumpin at the Boneyard (exec. prod.), The Bodyguard (also co-prod.), Wyatt Earp (also co-prod.), French Kiss, Home Fires (prod.), Mumford.

KASLOFF, STEVE
Writer. b. New York, NY, Nov. 13, 1952. e. Pratt Institute, 1974, cum laude. Writer/supvr., Young & Rubicam, 1974-76; writer/sprv., Ally & Gargano, 1976; writer/supvr., Marsteller Inc., 1976-79; writer/creative supvr., Scali, McCabe, Sloves, 1979-82. hired as youngest v.p., Columbia Pictures, 1982; promoted to sr. v.p., creative dir., Columbia, 1983. Sr. v.p. creative dir., 20th Century Fox, 1992. Member, WGA. Winner of numerous Clio and Key Arts Awards and over 200 others for creative work (trailers, TV commercials, posters, etc.) on such films as Tootsie, Ghostbusters, Total Recall, Home Alone, Dances With Wolves, Terminator 2, Home Alone 2, Last Action Hero, Jurassic Park, Schindler's List, Dumb and Dumber, etc. Has directed stage productions, commercials & special teaser trailers. Screen-writing/Production deal with Columbia Pictures, 1988; 20th Century Fox Films, 1993-present.

KASSAR, MARIO
Executive, Producer. b. Lebanon, Oct. 10, 1951. At age of 18 formed own foreign distribution co. Kassar Films International, specializing in sale, dist. and exhibition of films in Asia and Europe. In 1976 became partners with Andrew Vajna who had own dist. co., forming Carolco. First prod. First Blood, followed by Rambo: First Blood Part II. Became sole chmn. of Carolco in 1989. Formed own production co. in 1996.
PICTURES: *Exec. Prod.*: Angel Heart, Extreme Prejudice, Rambo III, Red Heat, Iron Eagle II, Deep Star Six, Johnny Handsome, Mountains of the Moon, Total Recall, Air America, Jacob's Ladder, L.A. Story, The Doors, Terminator 2: Judgment Day, Rambling Rose, Basic Instinct, Universal Soldier, Light Sleeper, Chaplin, Cliffhanger, Heaven & Earth, Stargate, Last of the Dogmen, Showgirls, Cutthroat Island, Lolita (prod.), Icarus (prod.).

KASTNER, ELLIOTT
Producer. b. New York, NY, Jan. 7, 1933. e. U. of Miami, Columbia U. Was agent then v.p. with MCA, before becoming indep. prod., financing and personally producing 65 feature films in 25 yrs. Based in London, NY & LA.
PICTURES: Bus Riley's Back in Town, Harper, Kaleidoscope, The Bobo, Sweet November, Sol Madrid, Michael Kohlaas, Laughter in the Dark, Night of the Following Day, Where Eagles Dare, A Severed Head, Tam Lin, The Walking Stick, X Y and Zee (Zee & Company), The Nightcomers, Big Truck and Poor Clare, Face to the Wind, Fear Is the Key, The Long Goodbye, Cops and Robbers, Jeremy, 11 Harrowhouse, Spot, Rancho Deluxe, 92 in the Shade, Farewell My Lovely, Russian Roulette, Breakheart Pass, The Missouri Breaks, Swashbuckler, Equus, A Little Night Music, The Medusa Touch, The Big Sleep, Absolution, Goldengirl, Yesterday's Hero, Ffolkes, The First Deadly Sin, Death Valley, Man Woman and Child, Garbo Talks, Oxford Blues, Nomads, Heat, Angel Heart, Black Joy, Spy Trap, Jack's Back, The Blob, White of the Eye, Zombie High, Never on Tuesday, Homeboy, A Chorus of Disapproval, The Last Party, Love is All There is.
TELEVISION: *Movie*: Frank and Jesse.

KATLEMAN, HARRIS L.
Executive. b. Omaha, NB, Aug. 19, 1928. e. UCLA. Joined MCA in 1949; 1952 transferred to NY as head of TV Packaging Dept. Left to join Goodson-Todman Prods. in 1955, where named v.p., 1956; exec. v.p., 1958; sr. exec. v.p., 1968. Was directly responsible for all programs prod. in L.A., including The Rebel, Branded, The Richard Boone Show, and Don Rickles Show, on which was exec. prod. Joined M-G-M in 1972 as v.p. of MGM-TV; promoted following year to pres., MGM-TV and sr. v.p. of MGM, Inc. Resigned as pres., MGM-TV, 1977. Formed Bennett/Katleman Productions under contract to Columbia Pictures. Exec. prod.: From Here to Eternity, Salvage 1; 1980, named bd. chmn. 20th-Fox Television. Appointed pres. & CEO, Twentieth TV, 1982. Oversaw prod. of final years of M*A*S*H, as well as Mr. Belvedere, The Fall Guy, Trapper John M.D., L.A. Law, Hooperman, Anything But Love, Tracey Ullman Show, Alien Nation, The Simpsons, In Living Color. Resigned, 1992. Formed Shadow Hill Prods. under contract to Twentieth TV. Joined Mark Goodson Prods., 1993, as COO.

KATSELAS, MILTON GEORGE
Director, Writer, Teacher, Painter. b. Pittsburgh, PA, Feb. 22, 1933. e. drama dept., Carnegie Inst. of Technology (now Carnegie-Mellon U.). Acting teacher-owner, Beverly Hills Playhouse. Has exhibited paintings in several major solo exhibitions. Awards: 3 time recipient of the L.A. Drama Critics Circle Award, Drama Logue Best Director Award, NAACP and Tony Nominations for Best Director.
THEATER: *B'way*: The Rose Tattoo, Butterflies are Free, Camino Real. *Off-B'way*: Call Me By My Rightful Name, The Zoo Story.
PICTURES: Butterflies Are Free, 40 Carats, Report to the Commissioner, When You Comin' Back Red Ryder?
TELEVISION: *Movies*: The Rules of Marriage, Strangers—The Story of a Mother and Daughter.

KATT, WILLIAM
Actor. b. Los Angeles, CA, Feb. 16, 1955. Son of actors Barbara Hale and Bill Williams. e. Orange Coast Coll. Majored in music, playing piano and guitar. Acted with South Coast Repertory Theatre, later working in productions at the Ahmanson and Mark Taper Theatres in L.A. Phoenix Rep (N.Y.): Bonjour La Bonjour. Regional: Sarah and Abraham, Days of Wine and Roses.
PICTURES: Carrie (debut, 1976), First Love, Big Wednesday, Butch and Sundance: The Early Days, Baby, Rising Storm, House, White Ghost, Wedding Band, Naked Obsession, Double X: The Name of the Game, House IV: Home Deadly Home, Desperate Motive (Distant Cousins), Tollbooth, The Paperboy, Stranger by Night, Cyborg 3: The Recycler, Rattled, Devil's Food.
TELEVISION: *Series*: The Greatest American Hero, Top of the Hill, Good Sports, Models Inc.. *Movies*: Night Chase, The Daughters of Joshua Cabe, Can Ellen Be Saved?, Perry Mason Returns and several Perry Mason follow-ups (Case of the... Murdered Madam, Avenging Ace, Scandalous Scoundrel, Lady in the Lake, Notorious Nun, Shooting Star, Lost Love, Sinister Spirit), Swim Suit, Americanski Blues, Problem Child 3: Junior in Love, Piranha, Rough Riders. *Specials*: Pippin, The Rainmaker.

KATZ, GLORIA
Producer, Writer. e. UCLA. Film Sch. Joined Universal Pictures as editor, cutting educational films. Later joined forces with Willard Huyck, whom she had met at U.C.L.A. Pair signed by Francis Ford Coppola to write and direct for his newly created company, American Zoetrope.
PICTURES: *Writer*: American Graffiti, Lucky Lady, French Postcards (also prod.), Indiana Jones and the Temple of Doom, Best Defense (also prod.), Howard the Duck (also prod.), Radioland Murders.
TELEVISION: *Co-Producer, Co-Writer*: A Father's Homecoming, Mothers Daughters and Lovers.

KATZ, JAMES C.
Producer, Executive. b. New York, NY, March 17, 1939. e. Ohio St. U. Started in publicity dept. of United Artists, 1963, eventually serving as v.p. of publicity for UA, 1966-68. Publicity co-ord. on film Khartoum, 1964. To London, 1968 as unit publicist for The Charge of the Light Brigade, Joanna. Prod. & dir. for C.I.C. special shorts and documentaries. 1973-78, prod./dir. commercials for own company in London. 1980, pres. Universal Classics Dept.; 1984, v.p. prod, Universal Pictures. With Robert A. Harris worked on restoration of Spartacus, My Fair Lady.
PICTURES: Three Sisters (co-prod.), Lust in the Dust (exec. prod.), Nobody's Fool (prod.), Scenes From the Class Struggle in Beverly Hills (prod.).

KATZ, MARTY
Producer. b. Landsburg, West Germany, Sept. 2, 1947. e. UCLA, U. of Maryland. Served in Vietnam War as U.S. Army first lieut.; awarded Bronze Star as combat pictorial unit director. 1971, dir. of film prod., ABC Circle Films; 1976, exec. v.p., prod., Quinn Martin Prods; 1978-80, producer and consultant, Paramount Pictures' 1981-85, independent producer (Lost in America, Heart Like a Wheel). 1985, joined Walt Disney Prods. as sr. v.p., motion picture & TV prod. Named exec. v.p. motion picture and TV production, 1988-92. 1992-present, prod. Marty Katz Prods./Walt Disney Studios. Producer of Mr. Wrong.

KATZ, NORMAN B.
Executive. b. Scranton, PA, Aug. 23, 1919. e. Columbia U. In U.S. Army 1941-46 as intelligence officer, airborne forces. Entered m.p. industry in 1947 with Discina Films, Paris, France, as prod. asst. Named exec. asst. to head of prod. in 1948. 1950 named v.p. Discina Int'l. Films and in 1952 exec. v.p. 1954 joined Associated Artists Prods. as foreign mgr.; named dir. of foreign operation in 1958. 1959 became dir. of foreign operations for United Artists Associated. 1961 joined 7 Arts Associated Corp. as v.p. in chg. of foreign optns.; 1964, named exec. v.p., 7 Arts Prods. Int'l.; 1967, exec. v.p. Warner Bros.-7 Arts Int'l. 1969 appt. exec. v.p. & CEO WB Intl. & bd. mem. of WB Inc. 1974 named sr. v.p. int'l. div. of American Film Theatre. Pres. of Cinema Arts Assoc. Corp. 1979, exec. v.p. and bd. member, American Communications Industries and pres., CEO of ACI subsidiary, American Cinema; 1983, pres., The Norkat Co., Also, bd. chmn., CEO, American Film Mktg. Assoc., 1985-87; chmn. Amer. Film Export Assn. 1988-92.

KATZENBERG, JEFFREY
Executive, Executive Producer. b. 1950. Entered motion picture industry in 1975 as asst. to Paramount Pictures chmn. and CEO Barry Diller in NY. In 1977, became exec. dir. of mktg.; later same year moved to west coast as v.p. of programming for Paramount TV. Promoted to v.p., feature production for Paramount Pictures 1978; 2 years later assumed role of sr. v.p. prod. of m.p. div; 1982, pres. of prod., m.p. and TV, Paramount Pictures. Left to join The Walt Disney Company, 1984; chairman of The Walt Disney Studios, 1984-94. With Steven Spielberg and David Geffen formed DreamWorks entertainment company, 1995.
PICTURES: *Exec. Prod:* The Prince of Egypt, Road to El Dorado, Chicken Run.

KAUFFMAN, MARTA
Producer. b. 1956. Partner in Kauffman-Crane Prods.
TELEVISION: *Series:* Dream On (co-creator), Friends (exec., co-creator), Veronica's Closet (exec., co-creator), Jesse (exec.).

KAUFMAN, AVY
Casting Director.
PICTURES: Little Man Tate, The Super, The Basketball Diaries, Home for the Holidays, Across thr Sea of Time, Lone Star, Gotti, Boys Life 2, The Ice Storm, The Real Blonde, Critical Care, Snitch, Wide Awake, Rounders, Claire Dolan, A Civil Action, The Sixth Sense, Music of the Heart, Ride With the Devil, A Map of the World, The Hurricane, O, Keeping the Faith, Dancer in the Dark, Blow, Save the Last Dance, The Heist

KAUFMAN, CHARLIE
Producer, Writer.
PICTURES: Being John Malkovich, Human Nature
TELEVISION ; *Series:* Get A Life, Ned and Stacey.

KAUFMAN, HAL
Creative Director, TV Writer, Producer. b. New York, NY, Dec. 16, 1924. e. U. of TX, 1943-44; U. of MI, 1944-47. Started career as petroleum geologist, Western Geophysical Co., 1947-48; TV writer-prod-dir., KDYL-TV, Salt Lake City, 1948-49; prog. dir.,

LAV-TV, Grand Rapids, 1949-51; prod. mgr., WOOD-TV, Grand Rapids, 1951-54; TV writer-prod., Leo Burnett Co., Chicago, 1954-56; TV writer-prod., Gordon Best Company, Chicago, 1957-58; with Needham Louis & Brorby Inc.: 1959, sr. writer, TV/Radio creative dept.; 1962, v.p., asst. copy dir.; 1963, dir., tv, radio prod.; 1964, dir., b'cast design, production; assoc. creat. dir., asst. exec. v.p., Needham, Harper & Steers, Inc., 1965; creat. dir. L.A., 1966; sr. v.p. and mem. bd. of dir., 1966. 1969, creative & mktg consultant in Beverly Hills. 1970, exec. v.p., principle, Kaufman, Lansky Inc., Beverly Hills and San Diego; 1974 editor and publisher Z Magazine; prog. dir., Z Channel, Theta Cable TV. 1979, sr. v.p./adv. & p.r. & asst. to pres. & bd. chmn., World Airways, Inc. 1982, v.p., creative dir., Admarketing, Inc., Los Angeles. 1985, mktg. & adv. consultant copy dir., Teleflora, Inc.; pres. Hal Kaufman Inc., mktg. & adv. consultant; pres. Brochures on Video, library division, creators and prods. of promotional videos, distribs. religious videos to libraries; pres. Pious Publications, prods. and distribs. of religious videos. Member, Directors Guild of America, SAG, AFTRA. 1974.

KAUFMAN, LEONARD B.
Producer, Writer, Director. b. Newark, NJ, Aug. 31, 1927. e. NYU. In W.W.II served with Army Special Services writing and directing camp shows. Nat'l magazine writer, 1945-48; radio writer, including Errol Flynn Show, 1948-50; radio and TV writer, 1950-52. Headed own public relations firm: Kaufman, Schwartz, and Associates, 1952-64. Joined Ivan Tors Films as writer-prod., 1964. Films Corp., 1958.
PICTURES: Clarence the Cross-eyed Lion, Birds Do It (story).
TELEVISION: Daktari, Ivan Tors' Jambo, O'Hara U.S. Treasury (pilot feature and series). Producer: Hawaii-Five O, The New Sea Hunt, Scruples (mini-series), The Hawaiian (pilot), Writer: Knightrider, Dukes of Hazzard, Hawaii-Five O, Wet Heat (pilot), Hawaiian Heat, Island Sons (movie).

KAUFMAN, LLOYD
Executive. e. Yale Univ., 1969. From 1974-present, pres. of Troma, Inc. Co-writer of book, All I Need To Know About Filmmaking I Learned from the Toxic Avenger.
PICTURES: The Girl Who Returned (prod., dir., s.p.), Cry Uncle (prod. mgr.), Joe (prod. asst.), Sugar Cookie (exec. prod., s.p.), Silent Night Bloody Night (assoc. prod.), Battle of Love's Return (dir., prod., s.p., actor), Big Gus What's the Fuss (dir., prod.), Sweet Savior (prod. mgr.), Mother's Day (assoc. prod.), Rocky (pre-prod. spvr.), Slow Dancing in the Big City (prod. spvr.), The Final Countdown (assoc. prod.), Squeeze Play (dir., prod.), Waitress (Co-dir., prod.), Stuck on You (co-dir., co-prod., co-s.p.), The First Turn-On (co-dir., co-prod.), Screamplay (exec. prod.), When Nature Calls (assoc. prod.), The Toxic Avenger (co-dir., co-prod., co-s.p., story), Blood Hook (exec. prod.), Girl School Screams (exec. prod.), Class of Nuke 'Em High (co-dir., co-prod.), Lust for Freedom (exec. prod.), Monster in the Closet (exec. prod.), Troma's War (Co-dir., co-prod., co-s.p., story), Toxic Avenger Part II (co-dir., co-prod., co-s.p., story), Fortress of Amerikkka (prod.), Toxic Avenger III: The Last Temptation of Toxie (co-dir., co-s.p., co-prod.), Class of Nuke 'Em High Part II: Subhumanoid Meltdown (co-s.p., co-prod., story), Sgt. Kabukiman N.Y.P.D. (co-dir., co-prod., co-s.p.), The Good the Bad and the Subhumanoid (co-s.p., co-prod., co-story), Tromeo and Juliet (dir., co-s.p., co-prod.), Rowdy Girls (prod.), Terror Firmer (co-s.p., prod., dir.).

KAUFMAN, PHILIP
Writer, Director, Producer. b. Chicago, IL, Oct. 23, 1936. e. U. of Chicago, Harvard Law Sch. Was teacher in Italy and Greece before turning to film medium.
PICTURES: *Co-Writer*: The Outlaw Josey Wales, Raiders of the Lost Ark. *Director*: Goldstein (co-dir., co-s.p., co-prod.), Fearless Frank (also s.p., prod.), The Great Northfield Minnesota Raid (also s.p., prod.), The White Dawn, Invasion of the Body Snatchers, The Wanderers (also co-s.p.), The Right Stuff (also s.p.), The Unbearable Lightness of Being (also co-s.p.), Henry & June (also co-s.p.), Rising Sun (also co-s.p.).

KAUFMAN, VICTOR
Executive. b. New York, NY, June 21, 1943. e. Queens Coll.; NYU Sch. of Law, J.D., 1967. Taught criminal law at UCLA before joining Wall St. law firm, Simpson Thacher & Bartlett. Joined Columbia Pictures as asst. general counsel, 1974. Named chief counsel, 1975; then made vice chmn. Columbia Pictures. Later exec. v.p. Columbia Pictures Industries and vice chmn. Columbia Pictures motion picture div. when conceived a new studio as a joint venture between Coca-Cola, Time Inc.'s Home Box Office and CBS, Inc. forming Tri-Star Pictures. Named chmn. and CEO Tri-Star, 1983. When Columbia Pictures and Tri-Star merged in late 1987, became pres. and CEO of new entity, Columbia Pictures Entertainment. In June 1988, dropped title of chmn. of Tri-Star. 1993 became head of Savoy Pictures.

KAUFMANN, CHRISTINE
Actress. b. Lansdorf, Graz, Austria, Jan. 11, 1945. e. school in Munich, Germany. Film debut as a dancer. Salto Mortale at age 7.
PICTURES: The White Horse Inn, Salto Mortale, Der Klosterjager, Staatsanwaltin Corda, Rosenrosli (Little Rosie), Schweigende Engel (Silent Angel), Wenn die Alpenrosen Bluh'n, Ein Herz Schlagt fur Erika, Stimme der Sehnsucht, Witwer mit 5 Tochtern, Die Winzerin von Langenlois, Sag ja Mutti!, First Love, Madchen in Uniform, Embezzled Heaven, Winter Vacation, Madchen von denen man spricht, Everybody Loves Peter, Toto Fabrizio e i Giovani D'oggi, Der Letzte Fubganger, The Last Days of Pompeii, Red Lips, Un Trono Para Cristy, A Man Named Rocca, Town Without Pity, Via Mala, The Phony American, Swordsman of Siena, Taras Bulba (U.S debut), Escape from East Berlin, Constantine the Great, Neunzig Minuten nach Mitternacht, Wild & Wonderful, Love Birds, The Death of Maria Malibran, Murder in the Rue Morgue, Willow Springs, Goodbye with Mums, Auf Biegen oder Brechen, Goldflocken, Rich and Respectable, Orgie des Todes, It Can only Get Worse, Day of the Idiots, Egon Schiele - Exzesse, Lili Marleen, Lola, Ziemlich weit Weg, The Wild Fifties, The Excluded, Pankow '95, The Swing, Bagdad Cafe, Hard to Be a God, Der Geschichtenerzahler, The Talking Grave, War of Neighbours.
TELEVISION: *Movies*: World on a Wire, Immobilien, Inflation im Paradies, Birkenhof & Kirchenau, Weihnachten mit Willy Wuff II - Eine Mama fur Lieschen, Ein Flotter Dreier. *Mini-series*: Wie ein Blitz, Lockruf des Goldes, Monaco Franze - Der Ewige Stenz.

KAURISMAKI, AKI
Director, Writer. b. Finland, April 4, 1957. Brother is filmmaker Mika Kaurismaki. First film credit was acting and writing his brother's The Liar in 1980. Directed short subjects: Rocky VI, Thru the Wire, Those Were the Days, These Boots. Served as writer on brother's features: Jackpot 2, The Worthless (also actor), The Clan: The Tale of the Frogs, Rosso.
PICTURES: *Director*: The Saimaa Gesture (co-dir., with Mika), Crime and Punishment, Calamari Union, Shadows in Paradise, Hamlet Goes Business, Ariel, Leningrad Cowboys Go America, The Match Factory Girl, I Hired a Contract Killer, La Vie de Boheme (The Bohemian Life), Leningrad Cowboys Meet Moses (also s.p., prod., edit.), Total Balalaika Show (also s.p.), Take Care of Your Scarf Tatiana (also s.p., prod., edit.), Drifting Clouds (also s.p.).

KAVNER, JULIE
Actress. b. Los Angeles, CA, Sept. 7, 1951. e. San Diego State U. Professional debut as Brenda Morgenstern on TV's Rhoda, 1974.
THEATER: Particular Friendships (Off-B'way), Two for the Seesaw (Jupiter, FLA), It Had to Be You (Canada).
PICTURES: National Lampoon Goes to the Movies, Bad Medicine, Hannah and Her Sisters, Radio Days, Surrender, New York Stories (Oedipus Wrecks), Awakenings, Alice, This Is My Life, Shadows and Fog, I'll Do Anything, Forget Paris, Deconstructin Harry, Doctor Dolittle (voice), A Walk on the Moon, Judy Berlin.
TELEVISION: *Series*: Rhoda (Emmy Award, 1978), The Tracey Ullman Show, The Simpsons (voice), Tracey Takes On.... *Special*: The Girl Who Couldn't Lose (Afternoon Playbreak). *Movies*: Katherine, No Other Love, The Revenge of the Stepford Wives, Don't Drink the Water. *Pilot*: A Fine Romance. *Guest*: Lou Grant, Petrocelli, Taxi.

KAYLOR, ROBERT
Director. b. Plains, MT, Aug. 1, 1934. e. Art Center Sch. of Design. Received awards at Cannes, San Francisco and Dallas Film Festivals, Guggenheim Fellow, Amer. Film Inst.
PICTURES: Derby, Carny, Nobody's Perfect.

KAZAN, ELIA
Director. b. Constantinople, Turkey, Sept. 7, 1909. e. Williams Coll., Yale Dramatic Sch. With Group Theatre as apprentice & stage mgr.; on stage, 1934-41; plays include: Waiting for Lefty, Golden Boy, Gentle People, Five-Alarm, Lilliom. Author (novels): The Arrangement, The Assassins, The Understudy, Acts of Love, The Anatolian, A Life (autobiography, 1988), Beyond the Aegean (1994).Honorary Oscar Award, 1998.
THEATER: *Director*: Skin of Our Teeth, All My Sons, Streetcar Named Desire, Death of a Salesman, Cat on a Hot Tin Roof (co-dir.), One Touch of Venus, Harriet, Jocobowsky and the Colonel, Tea and Sympathy, Dark at the Top of the Stairs, J.B., Sweet Bird of Youth, Lincoln Center Repertory Theatre (co-dir., prod.), After The Fall, But For Whom Charlie.
PICTURES: *Actor*: City for Conquest, Blues in the Night. *Director*: A Tree Grows in Brooklyn (debut, 1945), Boomerang!, The Sea of Grass, Gentleman's Agreement (Acad. Award, 1947), Pinky, Panic in the Streets, A Streetcar Named Desire, Viva Zapata!, Man on a Tightrope, On the Waterfront (Academy Award, 1954). *Producer/Director*: East of Eden, Baby Doll, A Face in the Crowd, Wild River, Splendor in the Grass, America America (also s.p.), The Arrangement (also s.p.), The Visitors, The Last Tycoon.

KAZAN, LAINIE
Singer, Actress. b. New York, NY, May 15, 1942. e. Hofstra U.
PICTURES: Dayton's Devils, Lady in Cement, Romance of a Horse Thief, One from the Heart, My Favorite Year, Lust in the Dust, The Delta Force, The Journey of Natty Gann, Harry and the Hendersons, Beaches, Eternity, 29th Street, I Don't Buy Kisses Anymore, The Cemetery Club.
TELEVISION: *Series*: The Dean Martin Summer Show, Tough Cookies, Karen's Song. *Pilot*: Family Business, The Lainie Kazan Show. *Movies*: A Love Affair: The Eleanor and Lou Gehrig Story, A Cry for Love, Sunset Limousine, The Jerk Too, Obsessive Love, Prince for a Day. *Guest*: Too Close for Comfort, Dick Van Dyke Show, Beverly Hills 90210, Tales From the Crypt, Faerie Tale Theatre (Pinocchio), Hotel, Johnny Carson Show, Dean Martin, Merv Griffin, Joan Rivers, Amazing Stories, Pat Sajak Show, The Famous Teddy Z, Murder She Wrote.

KAZANJIAN, HOWARD G.
Producer. b. Pasadena, CA, July 26, 1943. e. U. of Southern California Film Sch.; DGA Training Program.
PICTURES: *Asst. dir.*: Cool Hand Luke, Camelot, Finian's Rainbow, The Wild Bunch, The Great Bank Robbery, I Love You Alice B. Toklas, Christine, The Arrangement, The Girl From Petrovka, The Front Page, The Hindenberg, Family Plot. *Producer*: Rollercoaster (assoc. prod.) More American Graffiti, Raiders of the Lost Ark, Return of the Jedi, The Rookie, Demolition Man, One Dozen.
TELEVISION: The Making of More American Graffiti, The Making of Raiders of the Lost Ark (Emmy award), The Making of Return of the Jedi, Rattled, JAG.

KAZURINSKY, TIM
Actor, Writer. b. Johnstown, PA, March 3, 1950. Raised in Australia. Worked as copywriter for Chicago ad agency. Took acting class at Second City and quit job to become actor and head writer for Second City Comedy Troupe. Co-starred with John Candy in CTV/NBC's series Big City Comedy, 1980. Joined cast of Saturday Night Live as writer-actor 1981-84.
PICTURES: *Actor*: My Bodyguard, Somewhere in Time, Continental Divide, Neighbors, Police Academy II: Their First Assignment, Police Academy III: Back in Training, About Last Night (also co-s.p.), Police Academy IV: Citizens on Patrol, For Keeps (s.p. only), Road to Ruin (also s.p.), Hot to Trot, Wedding Band, A Billion for Boris, Shakes the Clown, Plump Fiction.
TELEVISION: *Movies*: This Wife for Hire, Dinner at Eight, The Cherokee Kid (also s.p.).

KEACH, STACY
Actor, Director, Producer. b. Savannah, GA, June 2, 1942. Brother is actor James Keach. Began professional acting career in Joseph Papp's 1964 Central Park prod. of Hamlet.
THEATER: Long Day's Journey into Night (Obie Award), Macbird (Drama Desk & Obie Awards), Indians (Drama Desk Award & Tony nom.), Hamlet, Deathtrap, Hughie, Barnum, Cyrano de Bergerac, Peer Gynt, Henry IV Parts I & II, Idiot's Delight, Solitary Confinement, Richard III, The Kentucky Cycle (Helen Hayes Award), Steiglitz Loves O'Keefe.
PICTURES: The Heart Is a Lonely Hunter (debut, 1968), End of the Road, The Traveling Executioner, Brewster McCloud, Doc, The New Centurions, Fat City, Watched!, The Life and Times of Judge Roy Bean, Luther, The Gravy Train, The Killer Inside Me, Conduct Unbecoming, Street People, The Squeeze, The Duellists (narrator), Slave of the Cannibal God, The Great Battle, Gray Lady Down, Up in Smoke, The Ninth Configuration (Twinkle Twinkle Killer Kane), The Long Riders (also exec. prod., co-s.p.), Nice Dreams, Road Games, Butterfly, That Championship Season, Class of 1999, False Identity, Milena, Raw Justice, Batman: Mask of the Phantasm (voice), New Crime City, Escape from L.A., Prey of the Jaguar.
TELEVISION: *Series*: Caribe, Mickey Spillane's Mike Hammer, Case Closed (host). *Movies*: All the Kind Strangers, Caribe, The Blue and the Gray, Princess Daisy, Murder Me Murder You, More Than Murder, Wait Until Dark, Mistral's Daughter, Hemingway, Mickey Spillane's Mike Hammer: Murder Takes All, The Forgotten, Mission of the Shark, Revenge on the Highway, Rio Diablo, Body Bags, Against Their Will: Women in Prison, Texas, Amanda & the Alien. *Director:* Incident at Vichy, Six Characters in Search of an Author.

KEACH, SR., STACY
Executive. b. Chicago, IL, May 29, 1914. Father of actors, Stacy and James. e. Northwestern U., B.S. & M.A. Was instructor in theatre arts at Northwestern and Armstrong Coll. and dir. at Pasadena Playhouse before entering industry. For 4-1/2 yrs. was under contract at Universal Pictures; 3 yrs. at RKO; had own prod. on NBC, CBS. In 1946 began producing and directing industrial stage presentations for Union Oil Co. and from then on became full-time prod. of m.p. and stage industrial shows. In 1946 formed Stacy Keach Productions, of which he is pres. In addition to directing, producing and writing occasionally appears as actor in films. Created radio show, Tales of the Texas Rangers, 1950-53. Played Clarence Birds Eye on TV commercials as well as other commercials. Voiceovers/ spokesman for many major American Cos. Autobiography: Stacy Keach, Go Home! (1996). Received Man of the Year Award from Pasadena Playhouse Alumni in 1995. Recipient of the Diamond Circle Award from the Pacific Pioneers Broadcasters Assoc., 1996.

KEATON, DIANE
Actress, Director. r.n. Diane Hall. b. Santa Ana, CA, Jan. 5, 1946. e. Santa Ana Coll. Appeared in summer stock and studied at Neighborhood Playhouse in N.Y. Made prof. debut in B'way prod. of Hair (1968); then co-starred with Woody Allen in Play It Again Sam, repeating role for film version. Off-B'way: The Primary English Class. Author: photography books: Reservations (co-ed.), Still Life. Directed 1982 short What Does Dorrie Want?
PICTURES: Lovers and Other Strangers (debut, 1970), The Godfather, Play It Again Sam, Sleeper, The Godfather Part II, Love and Death, I Will I Will... for Now, Harry and Walter Go to New York, Annie Hall (Acad. Award, 1977), Looking for Mr. Goodbar, Interiors, Manhattan, Reds, Shoot the Moon, The Little Drummer Girl, Mrs. Soffel, Crimes of the Heart, Radio Days, Heaven (dir. only), Baby Boom, The Good Mother, The Lemon Sisters (also prod.), The Godfather Part III, Father of the Bride, Manhattan Murder Mystery, Look Who's Talking Now (voice), Unstrung Heroes (dir. only), Father of the Bride 2, Marvin's Room, The First Wives Club, The Only Thrill, Northern Lights, Town and Country, The Other Sister, Hanging Up.
TELEVISION: *Movies*: Running Mates, Amelia Earhart: The Final Flight, Northern Lights. *Guest*: Love American Style, The FBI, Mannix. *Director*: The Girl With the Crazy Brother, Twin Peaks, Wildflower (movie).

KEATON, MICHAEL
Actor. r.n. Michael Douglas. b. Coraopolis, PA, Sept. 5, 1951. Speech major, Kent State U, 2 years. Drove cab and ice-cream truck, worked for PBS station in Pittsburgh and appeared in regional theatre prods. while performing in local coffeehouses. Became memb. of improvisational troupe Jerry Vale. Moved to L.A. where honed craft at Comedy Store and Second City Improv. Workshops as stand-up comic.
PICTURES: Night Shift (debut, 1982), Mr. Mom, Johnny Dangerously, Gung Ho, Touch and Go, The Squeeze, Beetlejuice, Clean and Sober, The Dream Team, Batman, Pacific Heights, One Good Cop, Batman Returns, Much Ado About Nothing, My Life, The Paper, Speechless, Multiplicity, Inventing the Abbotts (narrator), Jackie Brown, Desperate Measures, Out of Sight (cameo), Jack Frost, A Shot At Glory.
TELEVISION: *Series*: All's Fair, Mary, The Mary Tyler Moore Hour, Working Stiffs, Report to Murphy. *Movie*: Roosevelt and Truman. *Special*: Frank Capra's American Dream.

KEENER, CATHERINE
Actress. b. Miami, FL 1961. m. actor Dermot Mulroney
PICTURES: About Last Night, The Education of Allison Tate, Survival Quest, Catchfire, Switch, Johnny Suede, The Gun in Betty Lou's Handbag, Living in Oblivion, Boys, Walking and Talking, Box of Moonlight, The Destiny of Marty Fine, The Real Blonde, Out of Sight, Your Friends & Neighbors, 8MM, Being John Malkovich, Simpatico, Simone.
TELEVISION: *Series:* Seinfeld, L.A. Law, Ohara.

KEEL, HOWARD
Actor. r.n. Harold Keel. b. Gillespie, IL, April 13, 1919. e. high school, Fallbrook, CA. Began career following George Walker scholarship award for singing, L.A.; appeared in plays, Pasadena Auditorium, concerts; won awards, Mississippi Valley and Chicago Musical Festivals. Stage debut: Carousel, 1945; followed by London prod. of Oklahoma! which led to contract with MGM.
THEATER: Carousel, Oklahoma!, Saratoga, No Strings, The Ambassador, Man of La Mancha.
PICTURES: The Small Voice (debut, 1948), Annie Get Your Gun, Pagan Love Song, Three Guys Named Mike, Show Boat, Texas Carnival, Callaway Went Thataway, Lovely to Look At, Desperate Search, I Love Melvin (cameo), Ride Vaquero!, Fast Company, Kiss Me Kate, Calamity Jane, Rose Marie, Seven Brides for Seven Brothers, Deep in My Heart, Jupiter's Darling, Kismet, Floods of Fear, The Big Fisherman, Armored Command, The Day of the Triffids, The Man From Button Willow (voice), Waco, Red Tomahawk, The War Wagon, Arizona Bushwhackers, That's Entertainment III.
TELEVISION: *Series*: Dallas. *Movie*: Hart to Hart: Home Is Where the Hart Is. *Guest*: Zane Grey Theatre, Bell Telephone Hour, Tales of Wells Fargo, Death Valley Days, Here's Lucy, Sonny and Cher, The Love Boat, etc. *Specials*: A Toast to Jerome Kern, Roberta, Music of Richard Rodgers.

KEESHAN, BOB
Performer. b. Lynbrook, NY, June 27, 1927. e. Fordham U. As network page boy became assistant to Howdy Doody's Bob Smith and originated role of Clarabelle the Clown; created children's programs Time for Fun, Tinker's Workshop, Mister Mayor, Captain Kangaroo (1955-85).

KEITEL, HARVEY
Actor. b. Brooklyn, NY, May 13, 1939. Served in U.S. Marine Corps. Studied with Frank Corsaro, Lee Strasberg, Stella Adler. Member of the Actors' Studio. Debuted in Martin Scorsese's student film Who's That Knocking at My Door?
THEATER: *NY*: Up to Thursday, Death of a Salesman, Hurlyburly, A Lie of the Mind.

PICTURES: Who's That Knocking at My Door? (debut, 1968), Mean Streets, Alice Doesn't Live Here Anymore, That's the Way of the World, Taxi Driver, Mother Jugs and Speed, Buffalo Bill and the Indians or: Sitting Bull's History Lesson, Welcome to L.A., The Duellists, Fingers, Blue Collar, Eagle's Wing, Deathwatch, Saturn 3, Bad Timing, The Border, Exposed, La Nuit de Varennes, Corrupt, Falling in Love, Knight of the Dragon (Star Knight), Camorra, Off Beat, Wise Guys, The Men's Club, The Investigation (The Inquiry), The Pick-Up Artist, The Last Temptation of Christ, The January Man, The Two Jakes, Mortal Thoughts, Thelma & Louise, Two Evil Eyes, Bugsy (Acad. Award nom.), Sister Act, Reservoir Dogs (also co-prod.), Bad Lieutenant, Point of No Return, Rising Sun, The Piano, Dangerous Game, The Young Americans, Monkey Trouble, Pulp Fiction, Imaginary Crimes, Somebody to Love, Smoke, Clockers, Blue in the Face, Ulysses' Gaze, From Dusk Till Dawn, Head Above Water, Somebody to Love, City of Industry, Cop Land, Shadrach, Finding Graceland, Lulu on the Bridge, My West, Three Seasons, Prince of Central Park, Holy Smoke, U-571, Little Nicky, Taking Sides, La Soutane Tourquoise, Nailed, Je Viens Apres La Pluie, Jack Shepard and Jonathan Wild, The Grey Zone, Dreaming of Julia.
TELEVISION: *Movie*: The Virginia Hill Story. *Special*: This Ain't Bebop (Amer. Playhouse).

KEITH, DAVID
Actor, Director. b. Knoxville, TN, May 8, 1954. e. U. of Tennessee, B.A., speech and theater. Appearance at Goodspeed Opera House in musical led to role in CBS sitcom pilot, Co-Ed Fever.
PICTURES: The Rose (debut, 1979), The Great Santini, Brubaker, Back Roads, Take This Job and Shove It, An Officer and a Gentleman, Independence Day, The Lords of Discipline, Firestarter, The Curse (dir. only), White of the Eye, The Further Adventures of Tennessee Buck (also dir.), Heartbreak Hotel, The Two Jakes, Off and Running, Desperate Motive, Caged Fear, Raw Justice, Temptation, Major League II, Liar's Edge, Till the End of the Night, Born Wild, Gold Diggers: The Secret of Bear Mountain, Deadly Sins, The Indian in the Cupboard, A Family Thing, Invasion of Privacy, Secret of the Andes, Ambushed, Judge & Jury, Red Blooded American Girl II, If... Dog... Rabbit, U-571.
TELEVISION: *Series*: Co-ed Fever, Flesh 'N' Blood, Strangers, High Incident, Local Heroes. *Movies*: Are You in the House Alone?, Friendly Fire, Gulag, Whose Child Is This?: The War for Baby Jessica, XXX's & OOO's (pilot), James Michener's Texas, If Looks Could Kill: From the Files of America's Most Wanted, Poodle Springs. *Mini-Series*: If Tomorrow Comes, Golden Moment: An Olympic Love Story, Guts and Glory: The Rise and Fall of Oliver North, The Great War (voice). *Guest:* Happy Days, Runaways.

KEITH, PENELOPE
O.B.E. Actress. b. Sutton, Surrey, Eng., 1939. London stage debut, The Wars of the Roses (RSC, 1964). Extensive theater work including The Norman Conquests, Donkey's Years, The Apple Cart, Hobson's Choice, Captain Brassbound's Conversion, Hay Fever.
PICTURES: Think Dirty (Every Home Should Have One), Take a Girl Like You, Penny Gold, Priest of Love.
TELEVISION: *Series*: Kate, The Good Life, To the Manor Born, Executive Stress. *Movies-Specials*: Private Lives, The Norman Conquests, Donkey's Years.

KELLER, MARTHE
Actress. b. Basel, Switzerland, 1945. e. Stanislavsky Sch., Munich. Joined a Heidelberg repertory group and Schiller Rep. in Berlin. Started acting in France and attracted attention of U.S. directors after appearing in Claude Lelouch's And Now My Love. Has acted in over 50 plays in French, German, Eng. & Italian.
PICTURES: Funeral in Berlin (debut, 1967), The Devil by the Tail, Give Her the Moon, La Vieille Fille, The Loser, Elle Court (Love in the Suburbs), And Now My Love, Down the Ancient Staircase, Le Guepier, Marathon Man, Black Sunday, Bobby Deerfield, Fedora, The Formula, Les Uns et les Autres, The Amateur, Wagner, Femmes de Personne, Joan Lui, I Come on Monday, Dark Eyes, Rouge Basier, The Artisan, Una Vittoria, Lapse of Memory, Mon Amie Max, According to Pereira, Nuits Blanches, K, Elles.
TELEVISION: Liberez mon Fils, Mein oder Dein, The Charthouse of Parma, Wagner, Die Frau des Reporters, La Ruelle de Clair de Lune, The Nightmare Years, Young Catherine, Turbulences, Im Kreis der Iris.

KELLERMAN, SALLY
Actress. b. Long Beach, CA, June 2, 1936. e. Hollywood H.S. Studied acting in N.Y. at the Actors Studio and in Hollywood with Jeff Corey. Recorded album Roll With the Feeling. Has done voice-overs for many commercials. m. Jonathan Krane.
THEATRE: Women Behind Bars, Holiday.
PICTURES: Reform School Girl (debut, 1959), Hands of a Stranger, The Third Day, The Boston Strangler, The April Fools, M*A*S*H (Acad. Award nom.), Brewster McCloud, Last of the Red Hot Lovers, Lost Horizon, Slither, Reflection of Fear, Rafferty and the Gold Dust Twins, The Big Bus, Welcome to L.A., The Mouse and His Child (voice), Magee and the Lady, A Little Romance, Serial, Head On (Fatal Attraction), Foxes, Loving Couples, Moving Violations, Lethal (KGB: The Secret War), Back to School, That's Life!, Meatballs III, Three For the Road, Someone to Love, You Can't Hurry Love, Paramedics (voice), All's Fair, Limit Up, The Secret of the Ice Cave, The Player, Doppelganger, Happily Ever After (voice), Younger and Younger, Ready to Wear (Pret-a-Porter), Mirror Mirror 2: Raven Dance, It's My Party, The Maze, The Lay of the Land (also prod.), Live Virgin, Bar Hopping.
TELEVISION: *Mini-Series*: Centennial. *Movies*: For Lovers Only, Dempsey, Secret Weapons, September Gun, Drop Dead Gorgeous, Boris and Natasha (also assoc. prod.), Columbo: Ashes to Ashes. *Specials*: Big Blonde, Verna: USO Girl, Elena, Faerie Tale Theatre, Dr. Paradise. *Guest*: Mannix, It Takes a Thief, Chrysler Theatre, Robert Altman's Gun.

KELLEY, DAVID E.
Producer, Writer.
PICTURES: *Writer*: From the Hip, To Gillian on Her 37th Birthday (also prod.), Lake Placid, Mystery Alaska (also prod.).
TELEVISION: *Movies*: Annie O (cam.). *Series prod.:* Doogie Howser M.D., Picket Fences, Chicago Hope, The Practice (Emmy Award, 1999), Ally McBeal (Emmy Award, 1999), Boston Public.

KELLEY, SHEILA
Actress. b. Philadelphia, PA, Sept. 9, 1963.
PICTURES: Wish You Were Here, Hostile Witness, Staying Together, Some Girls, Breaking In, Mortal Passions, Where the Heart Is, Wild Blade, Soapdish, Pure Luck, Singles, Passion Fish, Passion to Kill, Mona Must Die, One Fine Day, Sante Fe.
TELEVISION: *Series:* L.A. Law, Sisters, Moving Story. *Movie:* Tonight's the Night, The Betty Ford Story, Terrorist on Trial: The United States vs. Salim Ajami, Fulfillment, The Chase, Deconstructing Sarah, The Secretary. *Guest*: Wings.

KELLOGG, PHILIP M.
Executive. b. Provo, WA, March 17, 1912. e. UCLA. Special feature writer for Hearst papers and magazines, 1933-34; MGM story dept., production dept., Irving Thalberg unit, 1934-35; Warner Bros. film editor, 1935-41; Berg-Allenberg Agency, 1941-50; U.S. Naval Reserve officer, 1941-46; William Morris Agency, 1950-present, co-head of m.p. dept., dir. WMA, Ltd., London.

KELLY, FRANK
Executive. Was assoc. prod. of AM Los Angeles, then exec. prod./program dir. for KABC-TV prior to joining Paramount. 1983, named v.p. programming for Paramount domestic tv division; 1985, promoted to sr. v.p. 1989, became exec. v.p. programming. 1995, named pres. of creative affairs for domestic tv division of Paramount Television Group.

KELLY, MOIRA
Actress. b. Queens, NY, March 6, 1968. e. Marymount Col. In addition to acting also trained as violinist, operatic soprano.
PICTURES: The Boy Who Cried Bitch (debut, 1991), Billy Bathgate, The Cutting Edge, Twin Peaks: Fire Walk With Me, Chaplin, With Honors, The Lion King (voice), Little Odessa, The Tie That Binds, Entertaing Angels: The Doroth Day Story, Unhook the Stars, Henry Hill, Drive She Said, Changing Habits, The Lion King II: Simba's Pride, Love Walked In, Dangerous Beauty, Hi-Life.
TELEVISION: *Movies*: Love Lies and Murder, Daybreak, Monday After the Miracle. *Series:* To Have & To Hold, The West Wing.

KELSEY, LINDA
Actress. b. Minneapolis, MN, July 28, 1946. e. U. of Minnesota, B.A.
TELEVISION: *Series*: Lou Grant, Day by Day, Sessions. *Movies*: The Picture of Dorian Gray, Something for Joey; Eleanor and Franklin: The White House Years, The Last of Mrs. Lincoln, A Perfect Match, Attack on Fear, His Mistress, Nutcracker, Baby Girl Scott, A Place to Be Loved, A Family Torn Apart, If Someone Had Known. *Special*: Home Sweet Homeless. *Mini-Series*: Captains and the Kings.

KEMENY, JOHN
Producer. b. Budapest, Hungary. Producer for National Film Board of Canada, 1957-69. Formed International Cinemedia Center, Ltd. in 1969 in Montreal, as partner.
PICTURES: Ladies and Gentlemen... Mr. Leonard Cohen, Don't Let the Angels Fall, Seven Times a Day, The Apprenticeship of Duddy Kravitz, White Line Fever, Shadow of the Hawk, Ice Castles, The Plouffe Family (exec. prod.), Quest for Fire (co-prod.), The Bad Boy, Murder in the Family (exec. prod.), The Wraith, The Boy in Blue, The Gate, Iron Eagle II, Gate II.
TELEVISION: Louisiane, The Blood of Others, Sword of Gideon (exec. prod.), The Park is Mine, Murderers Among Us: The Simon Wiesenthal Story (co-prod.), Red King White King, The Josephine Baker Story, The Teamster Boss: The Jackie Presser Story, Dead Silence.

KEMP, JEREMY
Actor. b. Chesterfield, England, Feb. 3, 1935. e. Abbottsholme Sch., Central Sch. of Speech and Drama. Service with Gordon Highlanders. Early career on stage incl. Old Vic Theatre Company, 1959-61. Recent theatre: Celebration, Incident at Vichy, Spoiled, The Caretaker. National Theatre, 1979-80.
PICTURES: Cleopatra (debut, 1963), Dr. Terror's House of Horrors, Face of a Stanger, Operation Crossbow (The Great Spy Mission), Cast a Giant Shadow, The Blue Max, Assignment K, Twist of Sand, The Strange Affair, Darling Lili, The Games, Sudden Terror (Eye Witness), Pope Joan, The Bellstone Fox, The Blockhouse, The Seven Percent Solution, East of Elephant Rock, Queen of Diamonds, A Bridge Too Far, The Thoroughbreds (Treasure Seekers), Leopard in the Snow, Caravans, The Prisoner of Zenda, The Return of the Soldier, Top Secret!, When the Whales Came, Angels and Insects, Four Weddings and a Funeral.
TELEVISION: Z Cars, The Lovers of Florence, The Last Reunion, Colditz, Brassneck, Rhinemann Exchange, Lisa, Goodbye, Henry VIII, St. Joan, The Winter's Tale, Unity, The Contract, Sadat, King Lear, Sherlock Holmes, George Washington, Peter the Great, The Winds of War, War and Remembrance, Slip-Up (The Great Paper Chase), Cop-out, Summers Lease, Prisoner of Honor, Duel of Hearts, The Magician, Conan: The Adventurer. *Series*: Star Trek: The Next Generation (guest).

KEMPER, VICTOR J.
Cinematographer. b. Newark, NJ, April 14, 1927. e. Seton Hall, B.S./Engineer. Channel 13, Newark 1949-54; Tech. supervisor EUE Screen Gems NY 1954-56; v.p. engineering General TV Network. Pres. VJK Prods.
PICTURES: Husbands, The Magic Garden of Stanley Sweetheart, They Might Be Giants, Who is Harry Kellerman?, The Hospital, The Candidate, Last of the Red Hot Lovers, Shamus, The Friends of Eddie Coyle, Gordon's War, The Hideaways, The Gambler, The Reincarnation of Peter Proud, Dog Day Afternoon, Stay Hungry, The Last Tycoon, Mikey and Nicky, Slapshot, Audrey Rose, Oh God!, The One and Only, Coma, Eyes of Laura Mars, Magic, Night of the Juggler, And Justice for All, The Jerk, The Final Countdown, Xanadu, The Four Seasons, Chu Chu and the Philly Flash, Partner, Author! Author!, National Lampoon's Vacation, Mr. Mom, The Lonely Guy, Cloak and Dagger, Secret Admirer, Pee-wee's Big Adventure, Clue, Bobo, Hot to Trot, Cohen and Tate, See No Evil, Hear No Evil, Crazy People, FX2, Another You, Married to It, Beethoven, Tommy Boy, Eddie, Jingle All the Way.

KENNEDY, BURT
Director, Writer. b. Muskegon, MI, Sept. 3, 1922. e. Ravenna H.S. U.S. Army 1942-46; awarded Silver Star, Bronze Star and Purple Heart with Oak Leaf Cluster. Began as writer of TV and film scripts, and was writer, producer and director of Combat series and many TV and theatrical westerns.
PICTURES: *Writer*: Seven Men From Now, Gun the Man Down, Man in the Vault, the Tall T, Fort Dobbs, Ride Lonesome, Yellostone Kelly, Comanche Station, Six Black Horses, Stary Away Joe, The Littlest Horse Thiefs, White Hunter Black Heart. *Director*: The Canadians (debut, 1961; also s.p.), Mail Order Bride (also s.p.), The Rounders (also s.p.), The Money Trap, Return of the Seven, The War Wagon, Welcome to Hard Times (also s.p.), Support Your Local Sheriff, The Good Guys and the Bad Guys, Young Billy Young (also s.p.), Dirty Dingus Magee, Support Your Local Gunfighter (also exec. prod.), Hannie Caulder (also s.p. as Z.X. Jones), The Deserter, The Train Robbers (also s.p.), The Killer Inside Me, Wolf Lake (also s.p.), The Trouble with Spies (also prod., s.p.), Big Bad John (also s.p.), Suburban Commando.
TELEVISION: *Series*: Combat (prod., writer) The Rounders (also writer), How the West Was Won, The Yellow Rose, Simon & Simon, Magnum P.I. *Mini-Series*: The Rhinemann Exchange. *Movies*: Shoot out in a One-Dog Town, Side kicks (also prod.), All the Kind Strangers, Kate Bliss and the Ticker Tape Kid, The Wild Wild West Revisted, The Concrete Cowboys, More Wild Wild West, The Alamo-Thirteen Days to Glory, Down the Long Hills, Once Upon a Texas Train (also prod., writer), Where the Hell's That Gold?!!? (also prod., writer).

KENNEDY, GEORGE
Actor. b. New York, NY, Feb. 18, 1925. At 2 acted in touring co. of Bringing Up Father. At 7, disc jockey with his own radio show for children. Served in Army during WWII, earning two Bronze Stars and combat and service ribbons. In Army 16 years, became Capt. and Armed Forces Radio and TV officer. 1957, opened first Army Information Office, N.Y. Served as technical advisor to Phil Silvers's Sergeant Bilko TV series. Began acting in 1959 when discharged from Army.
PICTURES: The Little Shepard of Kingdom Come (debut, 1961), Lonely Are the Brave, The Man From the Diner's Club, Charade, Strait- Jacket, Island of the Blue Dolphins, McHale's Navy, Hush... Hush... Sweet Charlotte, Mirage, In Harm's Way, The Sons of Katie Elder, The Flight of the Phoenix, Shenandoah, Hurry Sundown, The Dirty Dozen, Cool Hand Luke (Acad. Award, best supporting actor, 1967), The Ballad of Josie, The Pink Jungle, Bandolero!, The Boston Strangler, The Legend of Lylah Claire, Guns of the Magnificent Seven, Gaily Gaily, The Good Guys and the Bad Guys, Airport, ... tick ... tick ... tick ..., Zigzag, Dirty Dingus Magee, Fool's Parade, Lost Horizon, Cahill: U.S. Marshal, Thunderbolt and Lightfoot, Airport 1975, Earthquake, The Human Factor, The Eiger Sanction, Airport '77, Ningen no Shomei (Proof of the Man), Mean Dog Blues, Death on the Nile, Brass Target, The Concorde—Airport '79, Death Ship, The Double McGuffin, Steel, Virus, Just Before Dawn, Modern Romance, A Rare Breed, Search and Destroy, Wacko, The Jupiter Menace, Bolero, Chattanooga Choo Choo, Hit and Run, Savage Dawn, The Delta Force, Radioactive Dreams, Creepshow 2, Born to Race, Demonwarp, Counterforce, Nightmare at Noon, Private Roads, Uninvited, The Terror Within, The Naked Gun: From the Files of Police Squad, Esmeralda Bay, Ministry of Vengeance, Brain Dead, Hangfire, The Naked Gun 2 1/2: The Smell of Fear, Driving Me Crazy, Distant Justice, Naked Gun 33 1/3: The Final Insult, Cats Don't Dance (voice), Dennis the Menace 2 .
TELEVISION: *Series*: The Blue Knight, Sarge, Counterattack: Crime in America, Dallas, Santo Bugito (voice). *Guest*: Sugarfoot, Cheyenne. *Movies*: See How They Run, Sarge: The Badge or the Cross, Priest Killer, A Great American Tragedy, Deliver Us From Evil, A Cry in the Wilderness, The Blue Knight, The Archer: Fugitive from the Empire, Jesse Owens Story, Liberty, International Airport, Kenny Rogers as the Gambler III, The Gunfighters, What Price Victory, Good Cops Bad Cops, Final Shot: The Hank Gathers Story, Dallas: J.R. Returns. *Mini-Series*: Backstairs at the White House.

KENNEDY, JAMES C.
Publishing & Media Executive. b. 1947. e. U. Denver, BBA, 1970. Prodn. asst. with Atlanta Newspapers, 1972-76, then exec. v.p. gen. mgr. 1976-79. Pres. Grand Junction newpapers, 1979-80. Pub. Grand Junction Daily Sentinel, 1980-85. V.p. Cox newspapers div. Cox Enterprises, Inc., 1985-86; exec. v.p. 1986-87; pres., COO, Exec. v.p., 1986-87; chmn., 1987-; chmn., CEO, Cox Ent. Inc., 1988-.

KENNEDY, JOSEPH W.
Executive. a.k.a. Scott Kennedy. b. New York, NY, Feb. 11, 1934. e. La Salle, NYU. Started as office boy at NBC in 1950, before studying acting in NY. Appeared on TV in The Defenders and The Naked City, in film Advise and Consent. Host of Scott Kennedy Luncheon radio show in 1964. Joined United Artists in Boston in 1967 as salesman. UA Chicago sls. mgr. 1969-72; Jacksonville branch mgr. 1972-78; southern div. mgr. 1978-79. 1980 named v.p. & asst. gen. sls. mgr. responsible for UA eastern sls. territories. 1983 joined Tri-Star Pictures as v.p. southern div. mgr. Dallas.

KENNEDY, KATHLEEN
Producer. b. 1954. Raised in Weaverville and Redding in No. Calif. e. San Diego State U. Early TV experience on KCST, San Diego, working as camera operator, video editor, floor director and news production coordinator. Produced talk show, You're On. Left to enter m.p. industry as prod. asst. on Steven Spielberg's 1941. Founding member and pres. of Amblin Entertainment. 1992, with husband and partner Frank Marshall formed the Kennedy/Marshall Company.
PICTURES: Raiders of the Lost Ark (prod. assoc.), Poltergeist (assoc. prod.), E.T.: The Extra-Terrestrial (prod.), Twilight Zone: The Movie (co-assoc. prod.), Indiana Jones and the Temple of Doom (assoc. prod.). *Exec. prod.* (with Frank Marshall): Gremlins, The Goonies, Back to the Future, The Color Purple (prod.), Young Sherlock Holmes (co-prod.), An American Tail, Innerspace, Empire of the Sun, Batteries Not Included, Who Framed Roger Rabbit, The Land Before Time, Indiana Jones and the Last Crusade, (prod. exec.), Dad, Always (prod.), Joe Versus the Volcano, Gremlins II, Hook (co-prod.), Noises Off, Alive, A Far Off Place, Jurassic Park, Milk Money, The Bridges of Madison County, Congo, The Indian in the Cupboard, Twister, The Thief of Always, The Sixth Sense, Snow Falling on Cedars. *Exec. Prod:* Schindler's List, A Dangerous Woman, The Flintstones, The Lost World: Jurassic Park, Olympic Glory.
TELEVISION: Amazing Stories (spv. prod.), You're On (prod.), Roger Rabbit & the Secrets of Toontown (exec. prod.).

KENNEY, H. WESLEY
Producer, Director. b. Dayton, OH, Jan. 3, 1926. e. Carnegie Inst. of Tech. Guest Instructor, UCLA; guest lecturer, Televisia: Mexico City.
THEATER: *Dir.* Ten Little Indians (Advent Th., L.A.), The Best Christmas Pageant Ever, Love Letters (WV State Theatre), Shadowlands (Tracey Roberts Theatre).
TELEVISION: *Series*: All in the Family (dir.), The Jefferson (pilot dir.), Days of Our Lives (exec. prod. 1979-81), Ladies Man (dir.), Filthy Rich (dir.), Flo (dir.), The Young and the Restless (exec. prod. 1981-86), General Hospital (exec. prod. 1986-89). Dir. Sopa Break. Infomercials (dir.): Elements of Beauty, Merle Norman Experience,

KENSIT, PATSY
Actress. b. London, England, March 4, 1968. Made film debut at the age of 4 in The Great Gatsby. Later appeared in commercials directed by Tony Scott and Adrian Lyne.

PICTURES: The Great Gatsby (debut, 1974), Alfie Darling, The Blue Bird, Hanover Street, Absolute Beginners, Lethal Weapon 2, A Chorus of Disapproval, Chicago Joe and the Showgirl, Timebomb, Twenty-One, Blue Tornado, Blame It on the Bellboy, Beltenebros, Kleptomania, The Turn of the Screw, Bitter Harvest, Angels and Insects, Grace of My Heart, Speedway Junky, Best, Janice Beard: 45 Words Per Minute, The Pavilion.
TELEVISION: *BBC*: Great Expectations, Silas Marner, Tycoon: The Story of a Woman, Adam Bede, French & Saunders. *U.S.*: The Corsican Brothers, Fall from Grace, Love and Betrayal: The Mia Farrow Story, Human Bomb, The Last Don, The Last Don II.

KENT, JEAN
Actress. r.n. Joan Summerfield. b. London, England, June 29, 1921. e. Marist Coll., Peekham, London. First stage appearance at 3; at age 10 played in parents' act; chorus girl at Windmill Theatre, London, 1935; 2 yrs. repertory before debuting on screen under real name.
PICTURES: The Rocks of Valpre (High Treason; debut, 1934), It's That Man Again (first film as Jean Kent, 1943), Fanny by Gaslight (Man of Evil), Champagne Charlie, 2000 Women, Madonna of the Seven Moons, The Wicked Lady, The Rake's Progress (The Notorious Gentleman), Caravan, The Magic Bow, The Man Within (The Smugglers), Good Time Girl, Bond Street, Sleeping Car to Trieste, Trottie True (Gay Lady), Her Favorite Husband, The Woman in Question, The Browning Version, The Big Frame (The Lost Hours), Before I Wake (Shadow of Fear), The Prince and the Showgirl, Bonjour Tristesse, Grip of the Strangler (The Haunted Strangler), Beyond This Place (Web of Evidence), Please Turn Over, Bluebeard's Ten Honeymoons, Shout at the Devil, The Saving of Aunt Esther.
TELEVISION: A Call on the Widow, The Lovebird, The Morning Star, November Voyage, Love Her to Death, The Lion and the Mouse, The Web, Sir Francis Drake series, Yvette, Emergency Ward 10, County Policy, Coach 7, Smile on the Face of the Tiger, No Hiding Place, Kipling, This Man Craig, The Killers, Vanity Fair, A Night with Mrs. Da Tanka, United serial. The Family of Fred, After Dark, Thicker than Water series, The Young Doctors, Brother and Sister, Up Pompei, Steptoe and Son, Doctor at Large, Family at War, K is for Killing, Night School, Tycoon series, Crossroads (series), Lyttons Diary, Lovejoy (series), Missing Persons, After Henry (series), Shrinks (series).

KENT, JOHN B.
Theatre executive, Attorney. b. Jacksonville, FL, Sept. 5, 1939. e. Yale U., U. of FL, Law Sch., NYU grad. sch. of law (L.L.M. in taxation, 1964). Partner in Kent Ridge & Crawford, P.A.; pres. & dir, Kent Investments, Inc. 1977-; dir., v.p. & gen. counsel, Kent Theatres, Inc. 1970-; dir. & v.p., Kent Enterprises, Inc. 1961-; dir. & v.p. Kent Cinemas Inc. 1993-. Was pres. of Kent Theatres Inc. 1967-70; resigned to devote full time to law practice. NATO dir. 1972 and Presidents' Advisory Cabinet, 1979-; v.p./dir. NATO of FL, 1968-. Member of Rotary Club ofJacksonville, Fla. Bar Ass'n., American Bar Ass'n.

KENYON, CURTIS
Writer. b. New York, NY, March 12, 1914.
PICTURES: Woman Who Dared, Lloyds of London, Wake Up and Live, Love and Hisses, She Knew All the Answers, Twin Beds, Seven Days' Leave, Thanks for Everything, Bathing Beauty, Fabulous Dorseys, Tulsa, Two Flags West, Mr. Ricco.
TELEVISION: Cavalcade of America, Fireside Theatre, Schlitz Playhouse, U.S. Steel Hour, 20th Century-Fox Hour. Series: Hawaii 5-O.

KERASOTES, GEORGE G.
Exhibitor. b. Springfield, IL. e. U. of IL, 1929-33; Lincoln Coll. of Law 1935-37. Past pres. & chmn., Kerasotes Theatres, 1935-85; Pres. & chmn., George Kerasotes Corp. & GKC Theatres, Inc., 1984-. Past pres. Theatre Owners of Illinois. Past pres. & chmn. Kerasotes Theatres, 1935-85. Past pres., Theatre Owners of America, 1959-60. Chmn. of board of TOA 1960-62; chmn. ACE Toll TV com.; bd. mem. NATO; treas., bd. of dirs., memebr, exec. comm., chmn., insurance comm. Director, St. Anthony's Hellenic Church, Hellenic Golf Classic. Director, Will Rogers Hospitals; Director, Pioneers. Robert W. Selig ShoWester of the Year, NATO, Las Vegas, 1992.

KERKORIAN, KIRK
Executive. b. Fresno, CA, June 6, 1917. e. Los Angeles public schools. Served as capt., transport command, RAF, 1942-44. Commercial air line pilot from 1940; founder Los Angeles Air Service (later Trans Intl. Airlines Corp.), 1948; Intl. Leisure Corp., 1968; controlling stockholder, Western Airlines, 1970; chief exec. officer, MGM, Inc., 1973-74; chmn. exec. com., vice-chmn. bd., 1974-1978. Stepped down from exec. positions while retaining financial interest in MGM/UA. Repurchased MGM in the summer of 1996.

KERNER, JORDAN
Producer. e. Stanford U, A.B. Political Science & Comm.; U.C. Berkely, J.D.-M.B.A.. Bgean career in entertainment working for CBS affiliate KPIX-TV. Joined law firm of Ball, Hunt, Brown & Baerwitz. Talent & Program Negotiator for CBS. Worked for Universal Pictures & QM Prods., 1978-81. Joined ABC Entertainment as dir., Dramatic Series Development. Promoted to v.p., 1983. While at ABC, placed Moonlighting, MacGyver, Dynasty, Spencer for Hire, Call To Glory. Founded the Avnet/Kerner Co. in 1986 with Jordan Kerner. Currently dir., Allied Communications, Inc. Member, bd. of dirs., The Starbright Foundation, The Chrysalis Foundation. Member, President's Advisory Council for the City of Hope, Sen. Dianne Feinstein's California Cabinet, Planned Parenthood, Earth Communications Office, A.M.P.A.S., A.F.I. Former gov., Academy of Television Arts & Sciences. Founder and former co-chmn., Committee for the Arts of the Beverly Hills Bar Asoc. Founder, COMM/ENT, the Journal of Communications & Entertainment Law.
PICTURES: Less Than Zero, Funny About Love, The Mighty Ducks, Fried Green Tomatoes, The War, The Three Musketeers, When A Man Loves A Woman, D2: The Mighty Ducks, Miami Rhapsody (exec. prod.), Up Close and Personal, Swiss Family Robinson, Dinner For Two at the El Cortez, To Live For, Friday Night Lights, Blaze of Glory, D3: The Mighty Ducks, Red Corner, George of the Jungle, Thirty Wishes, Inspector Gadget.
TELEVISION: Breaking Point, Do You Know the Muffin Man?, Heat Wave, Backfield in Motion, The Watchman, The Switch, For Their Own Good, The War, Love Can Build a Bridge, Side By Side, My First Love.

KERNS, JOANNA
Actress. r.n. Joanna de Varona. b. San Francisco, CA, Feb. 12, 1953. Former gymnast, became dancer, appeared on tv commercials. Sister is Olympic swimmer and tv commentator Donna de Varona. NY stage: Ulysses in Nighttown.
PICTURES: Coma, Cross My Heart, Street Justice, An American Summer.
TELEVISION: *Series*: The Four Seasons, Growing Pains (also wrote one episode). *Guest*: Three's Company, Magnum P.I., Hill Street Blues, Hunter, etc. *Movies*: The Million Dollar Rip-Off, Marriage Is Alive and Well, Mother's Day on Walton's Mountain, A Wedding on Walton's Mountain, A Day of Thanks on Walton's Mountain, The Return of Marcus Welby M.D., A Bunny's Tale, The Rape of Richard Beck, Stormin' Home, Mistress, Those She Left Behind, Like Mother Like Daughter, The Preppie Murder, Blind Faith, Captive, The Nightman, Not in My Family, The Man With 3 Wives, Shameful Secrets, No Dessert Dad 'Til You Mow the Lawn, Robin Cook's Mortal Fear, See Jane Run, Whose Daughter Is She?, Sisters and Other Strangers, Mother Knows Best, Morning Glory, Terror In the Family.

KERR, DEBORAH
Actress. b. Helensburgh, Scotland, Sept. 30, 1921; e. Phyllis Smale Ballet Sch. On stage 1939 in repertory before Brit. screen career began the following year. Voted Star of Tomorrow by Motion Picture Herald-Fame Poll, 1942. Voted one of top ten British money-making stars in Motion Picture Herald-Fame Poll, 1947. B'way debut in Tea and Sympathy, 1953. Received special Academy Award, 1994.
PICTURES: Major Barbara (debut, 1940), Love on the Dole, Penn of Pennsylvania, Hatter's Castle, The Day Will Dawn (The Avengers), The Life and Death of Colonel Blimp, Perfect Strangers (Vacation From Marriage), I See a Dark Stranger (The Adventuress), Black Narcissus (Acad. Award nom.), The Hucksters (U.S. debut), If Winter Comes, Edward My Son, Please Believe Me, King Solomon's Mines, Quo Vadis, The Prisoner of Zenda, Thunder in the East, Dream Wife, Julius Caesar, Young Bess, From Here to Eternity (Acad. Award nom.), End of the Affair, The King and I (Acad. Award nom.), The Proud and the Profane, Tea and Sympathy, Heaven Knows Mr. Allison (Acad. Award nom.), An Affair to Remember, Bonjour Tristesse, Separate Tables (Acad. Award nom.), The Journey, Count Your Blessings, Beloved Infidel, The Sundowners (Acad. Award nom.), The Grass Is Greener, The Innocents, The Naked Edge, The Chalk Garden, The Night of the Iguana, Marriage On the Rocks, Casino Royale, Eye of the Devil, Prudence and the Pill, The Gypsy Moths, The Arrangement, The Assam Garden.
TELEVISION: *Movies*: A Woman of Substance, Reunion at Fairborough, Hold the Dream, Witness for the Prosecution.

KERR, FRASER
Actor. b. Glasgow, Scotland, Feb. 25, 1931. Early career in repertory. Tours of Canada and America. Ent. TV 1956. Series incl. Emergency Ward 10, Dixon of Deck Green, Murder Bag. Many Shakespeare plays. Radio: BBC Drama Rep. Co., 39 Steps, The Ringer, The Bible, What Every Woman Knows, The Ruling Class.
THEATER & TELEVISION: Night Must Fall, Never a Cross Word, The Inside Man, On the Buses, Dr. Finlay's Casebook, Wicked Woman, Madelaine July, Doctor in the House, Counterstrike, Waggoner's Walk, Juno and the Paycock, Aquarius, Ev, Upstairs and Downstairs, Cover to Cover, Janine, Robert the Bruce, Caliph of Bagdad, Watch it, Sailor!, The Fosters, Weekend World, Doctor at Sea, Dads Army, Algernon Blackwood, Waiting for Sheila, Weekend Show, Mind Your Language, Yes, Minister, Dick Emery Show, Bottle Boys, The Hard Man, Brigadoon, Hair of the Dog.
PICTURES: What a Whopper, Carry on Regardless, Way of McEagle, Thomasina, Theatre of Death, Tom, Dick and Harriet, Granny Gets the Point, Nothing but the Night, The Lord of the Rings, Kidnapped, The Derelict, Bloomfield, Ace of Diamonds, Andy Robson, It's a Deal!, Howard's Way, One Step Beyond, The Trawler.

KERSHNER, IRVIN
Director. b. Philadelphia, PA, April 29, 1923. e. Tyler Sch. of Fine Arts of Temple U., 1946; Art Center Sch., U. of Southern California. Designer, photography, adv., documentary, architectural; doc. filmmaker, U.S.I.S., Middle East, 1950-52; dir., cameraman, TV doc., Confidential File, 1953-55; dir.-prod.-writer, Ophite Prod. Appeared as actor in film The Last Temptation of Christ.
PICTURES: Stakeout on Dope Street (debut, 1958; also co-s.p.), The Young Captives, The Hoodlum Priest, A Face in the Rain, The Luck of Ginger Coffey, A Fine Madness, The Flim-Flam Man, Loving, Up the Sandbox, S*P*Y*S, The Return of a Man Called Horse, Eyes of Laura Mars, The Empire Strikes Back, Never Say Never Again, Robocop 2, American Perkect (prod.).
TELEVISION: *Series*: The Rebel, Naked City, numerous pilots and other nat'l. shows. *Movies*: Raid on Entebbe (theatrical in Europe), The Traveling Man. *Pilot*: seaQuest dsv.

KERWIN, BRIAN
Actor. b. Chicago, IL, Oct. 25, 1949. e. USC.
THEATRE: *NY*: Emily (Theatre World Award), Lips Together Teeth Apart, Raised in Captivity. LA: Strange Snow (LA Drama Critics Award), Who's Afraid of Virginia Woolf?, A Loss of Roses, Torch Song Trilogy.
PICTURES: Hometown USA (debut, 1979), Nickel Mountain, Murphy's Romance, King Kong Lives, Torch Song Trilogy, S.P.O.O.K.S., Hard Promises, Love Field, Gold Diggers: The Secret of Bear Mountain, Getting Away With Murder, Jack, The Myth of Fingerprints, Mr. Jealousy, Flash.
TELEVISION: *Series*: The Young and the Restless (1976-77), The Misadventures of Sheriff Lobo, Angel Falls. *Mini-Series*: The Chisholms, The Blue and the Gray, Bluegrass. *Movies*: A Real American Hero, Power, Miss All-American Beauty, Intimate Agony, Wet Gold, The Greatest Thing That Almost Happened, Challenger, Switched at Birth, Against Her Will: An Incident in Baltimore, Abandoned and Deceived, It Came From Outer Space, Sins of Silence, Critical Choices, Volcano: Fire on the Mountain. *Special*: Natica Jackson. *Guest*: St. Elsewhere, The Love Boat, B.J. and the Bear, Roseanne, Murder She Wrote, Simon & Simon, Highway to Heaven.

KEYES, EVELYN
Actress. b. Port Arthur, TX, Nov. 20, 1919. e. high school. Began career as a dancer in night clubs.
AUTHOR: *Novel*: I Am a Billboard (1971). *Autobiographies*: Scarlett O'Hara's Younger Sister (1977), I'll Think About That Tomorrow (1991).
PICTURES: Artists and Models (debut, 1937), The Buccaneer, Men With Wings, Artists and Models Abroad, Sons of the Legion, Dangerous to Know, Paris Honeymoon, Union Pacific, Sudden Money, Gone with the Wind, Slightly Honorable, Before I Hang, Beyond Sacramento, The Lady in Question, The Face Behind the Mask, Here Comes Mr. Jordan, Ladies in Retirement, The Adventures of Martin Eden, Flight Lieutenant, There's Something About a Soldier, Dangerous Blondes, The Desperadoes, Nine Girls, Strange Affair, A Thousand and One Nights, The Jolson Story, Renegades, The Thrill of Brazil, The Mating of Millie, Johnny O'Clock, Enchantment, Mrs. Mike, Mr. Soft Touch, The Killer That Stalked New York, Smuggler's Island, The Iron Man, The Prowler, One Big Affair, Shoot First, 99 River Street, Hell's Half Acre, It Happend in Paris, Top of the World, The Seven Year Itch, Around the World in 80 Days, Across 110th Street, Return to Salem's Lot, Wicked Stepmother.
TELEVISION: *Guest*: Murder She Wrote.

KEYLOUN, MARK
Actor. b. Dec. 20, 1960. e. Georgetown U. Worked in New York theatre.
PICTURES: Those Lips Those Eyes, Sudden Impact, Forty-Deuce, Mike's Murder.
TELEVISION: Evergreen, War Stories: The Mine.

KHONDJI, DARIUS
Cinematographer.
PICTURES: Rive droite, rive gauche (first assistant cameraman), Le Tresor des chiennes, Delicatessen, Prague, Shadow of a Doubt, Before the Rain, Marie-Lousie ou la permission, City of Lost Children, Seven, Stealing Beauty, Evita (Academy Award nom.), Alien: Resurrection, In Dreams, The Ninth Gate, The Beach.

KIAROSTAMI, ABBAS
Director, Producer, Writer, Editor. b. Teheran, Iran, June 22, 1940. Recipient of the 1997 UNESCO Fellini-Medal in Gold for achievement in film, freedem, peace & tolerance.
PICTURES: The Window, The Bread & Alley, The Breaktime, The Experience, The Traveller, So I Can, Two Solutions for One Problem, The Colours, Suit for Wedding, The Report (Gozaresh), Tribute to the Teachers, How to Make Use of Our Leisure Time?, Solution No. 1, First Case—Second Case, Dental Hygiene, Orderly or Unorderly, The Chorus, Fellow Citizen, Toothache, First Graders, Where is the Friend's Home, The Key, Homework, Close Up, And Life Goes on..., Journey to the Land of the Traveller, Under the Olive Trees, The Journey, Lumiere & Company, The White Balloon, The Taste of Cherry (Cannes Film Festival Palme d'Or, 1997).

KIDD, MICHAEL
Choreographer, Dancer, Actor. r.n. Milton Greenwald. b. Brooklyn, NY, Aug. 12, 1919. e. CCNY. Studied dance at School of the American Ballet. Was dancer with Lincoln Kirstein's Ballet Caravan, Eugene Loring's Dance Players, Ballet Theatre. Became stage choreographer starting in 1945. Recipient of the Academy Award for Career Achievement, 1997.
THEATER: *B'way (choreographer):* Finian's Rainbow (Tony Award, 1947), Love Life, Arms and the Girl, Guys and Dolls (Tony Award, 1951), Can-Can (Tony Award, 1954), Li'l Abner (Tony Award, 1957; also dir., prod.), Destry Rides Again (Tony Award, 1960; also dir.), Wildcat (also dir., co-prod.), Subways Are for Sleeping (also dir.), Here's Love, Ben Franklin in Paris, Skyscraper, The Rothschilds (also dir.). *B'way (dir.):* Cyrano, Good News, Pal Joey, The Music Man, The Goodbye Girl.
PICTURES: *Choreographer:* Where's Charley?, The Band Wagon, Knock on Wood, Seven Brides for Seven Brothers, Guys and Dolls, Merry Andrew (also dir.), Li'l Abner, Star!, Hello Dolly!, Movie Movie (also actor). *Actor*: It's Always Fair Weather, Smile, Skin Deep.
TELEVISION: *Specials (choreographer):* Baryshnikov in Hollywood, Academy Awards. *Movie (actor):* For the Love of It.

KIDDER, MARGOT
Actress. r.n. Margaret Kidder. b. Yellowknife, Ca., Oct. 17, 1948.
PICTURES: The Best Damned Fiddler From Calabogie to Kaladar (debut, 1968), Gaily Gaily, Quackser Fortune Has a Cousin in the Bronx, Sisters, A Quiet Day in Belfast, The Gravy Train, Black Christmas, The Great Waldo Pepper, 92 in the Shade, The Reincarnation of Peter Proud, Superman, Mr. Mike's Mondo Video, The Amityville Horror, Willie and Phil, Superman II, Heartaches, Shoot the Sun Down, Some Kind of Hero, Trenchcoat, Superman III, Little Treasure, GoBots (voice), Superman IV: The Quest for Peace, Miss Right, Mob Story, White Room, Crime and Punishment, Maverick, Henry & Verlin, Beanstalk, The Pornographer, La Florida, Aaron Sent Me, Windrunner, Never Met Picasso, The Planet of Junior Brown .
TELEVISION: *Series*: Nichols, Shell Game. *Movies*: Suddenly Single, The Bounty Man, Honky Tonk, Louisiana, The Glitter Dome, Picking Up the Pieces, Vanishing Act, Body of Evidence, To Catch a Killer, One Woman's Courage, Bloodknot, Phantom 2040: The Ghost Who Walks, Young Ivanhoe, The Return of Alex Kelly. *Specials*: Bus Stop, Pygmalion. *Guest*: Murder She Wrote, Bostom Common. *Director*: White People, Love 40.

KIDMAN, NICOLE
Actress. b. Hawaii, June 20, 1967. m. actor Tom Cruise. Raised in Australia. Made acting debut at 14 in Australian film Bush Christmas. On Australian stage in Steel Magnolias (Sydney Theatre Critics Award for Best Newcomer).
PICTURES: Bush Christmas (debut, 1982), BMZ Bandits, Windrider, Dead Calm, Emerald City, Days of Thunder, Billy Bathgate, Far and Away, Flirting, Malice, My Life, Batman Forever, To Die For (Golden Globe, 1996), Portrait of a Lady, The Peacemaker, Practical Magic, Eyes Wide Shut, Birthday Girl, Moulin Rouge, The Panic Room, The Others, In the Cut..
TELEVISION: *Mini-Series* (Australia): Five-Mile Creek, Vietnam, Bangkok Hilton.

KIDRON, BEEBAN
Director. b. London, England. e. National Film School.
Made co-dir. debut (with Amanda Richardson) with documentary Carry Greenham Home (Chicago Film Fest. Hugo Award, 1983).
PICTURES: Antonia and Jane, Used People, Great Moments in Aviation, To Wong Foo—Thanks for Everything—Julie Newmar, Swept from the Sea (prod. only).
TELEVISION: The Global Gamble, Vroom, Oranges Are Not the Only Fruit.

KIEL, RICHARD
Actor. b. Detroit, MI, Sept. 13, 1939. Former nightclub bouncer.
PICTURES: The Phantom Planet (debut, 1961), Eegah!, House of the Damned, The Magic Sword, Roustabout, The Human Duplicators, Las Vegas Hillbillies, A Man Called Dagger, Skidoo, The Longest Yard, Flash and the Firecat, Silver Streak, The Spy Who Loved Me, Force 10 from Navarone, They Went Thataway and Thataway, Moonraker, The Humanoid, So Fine, Hysterical, Cannonball Run II, Pale Rider, Think Big, The Giant of Thunder Mountain (also co-s.p., co-exec. prod.), Happy Gilmore, Inspector Gadget (cameo).
TELEVISION: *Series*: The Barbary Coast, Van Dyke & Company. *Movies*: Now You See It Now You Don't, The Barbary Coast (pilot).

KIER, UDO
Actor. b. Cologne, Germany, October 14, 1944.
PICTURES: Road to St. Tropez, Season of the Senses, Schamlos, La Horse, Satan, Provocation, Erotomaneis, The Salzburg Connection, Sexual Eroticism, Pan, Olifant, Andy Warhol's Frankenstein, Andy Warhol's Dracula, The Last Word, The Story of O, Trauma, Goldflocken, Spermula, Suspiria, Bolweiser, Belcanto oder Darf eine Nutte schluchzen?, Counterfeit Commandos, Das Funfte Gebot, Kretakor, The Third Generation, Hungarian Rhapsody, Lulu, Psyche, Deutschland privat, Lili Marleen, Lola, The Blood of Dr. Jekyll, Escape from Blood Plantation, The Wild Fifties, Pankow '95, Hur und Heilig,

Seduction: The Cruel Woman, Der Unbesiegbare, Die Einsteiger, Egomania - Insel ohne Hoffmung, Die Schlacht der Idioten, Am nachsten Morgen kehrte der Minister nicht an seinen Arbeitsplatz zuruck, Mutters Mask, Epidemic, 100 Jahre Adolf Hitler- Die letzte Stunde im Fuhrerbunker, Blackest Heart, Europa, My Own Private Idaho, Der Unbekannte Deserteur, Terror 2000 - Intesivstation Deutschland, Even Cowgirls Get The Blues, Three Shake-A-Leg Steps to Heaven, Plotzlich und unerwarten, Josn and S.A.M, Ace Ventura: Pet Detective, For Love or Money, The Kingdom, Rotwang Must Go, Johnny Mnemonic, Over My Dead Body, Unter Druck, Paradise Framed, A Trick of the Light, Duke of Groove, Dog Daze, Ausgerstoben, United Trash, Barb Wire, Breaking the Waves, Pinocchio, Lea, The End of Violence, Prince Valiant, The Kingdom 2, Betty, Die 120 Tage von Bottrop, Armageddon, Blade, Modern Vampires, Ice, Simon Says, Guilty, Killer Deal, Besat, Spy Games, History is Made at Night, The Debtors, Under the Palms, The New Adventures of Pinocchio, End of Days, The Last Call, Doomsdayer, Shadow of the Vamprie, Dancer in the Dark, Just One Night, Red Letters, There's No Fish Food in Heaven, Invincible, Black Widow, Final Payback, Broken Cookies, Critical Mass, Citizens of Perpetual Indulgence, Cadillac Tramps, The Bloodcountess, Auf Herz und Nieren, All the Queen's Men.

KIERZEK, TERRY
Executive. b. Chicago, IL, Feb. 15, 1951. e. U. of Il. Joined Paramount Pictures Domestic Distrib., as booker in Chicago, 1974. Promoted to Sales in 1976, Dallas, TX. Named branch mgr., Dallas/OK City, 1978. V.P., Eastern Division in Washington, D.C., 1982-84. V.P., Southern Division, Dallas, TX., 1984-86. V.P., Western Division, Los Angeles, 1986-89. Orion Pictures v.p., Western Division, 1990-92. Joined National Film Service in 1993 as v.p., sales & mktg. Named exec. v.p., 1995. Appointed pres., National Film Service in 1996.

KILMER, VAL
Actor. b. Los Angeles, CA, Dec. 31, 1959. e. Hollywood Professional Sch., Juilliard, NY. Appeared in IMAX film Wings of Courage.
THEATRE: *NY*: Electra and Orestes, How It All Began (also co-writer), Henry IV Part One, Slab Boys (B'way debut), 'Tis Pity She's a Whore. *Also:* As You Like It (Guthrie MN), Hamlet (Colorado Shakespeare Fest.).
PICTURES: Top Secret! (debut, 1984), Real Genius, Top Gun, Willow, Kill Me Again, The Doors, Thunderheart, True Romance, The Real McCoy, Tombstone, Batman Forever, Heat, The Island of Dr. Moreau, The Ghost and the Darkness, The Saint, The Prince of Egypt (voice), Joe the King, At First Sight, Pollock, Red Planet, The Salton Sea.
TELEVISION: *Movies*: Murders in the Rue Morgue, The Man Who Broke 1000 Chains, Gore Vidal's Billy the Kid.

KIMBLEY, DENNIS
Executive. Early career in Kodak Testing Dept. responsible for quality control motion picture films. Joined Marketing Division 1966. Chairman BKSTS FILM 75 and FILM 79 Conference Committee. President BKSTS 1976-78. Governor, London International Film School, 1983. Bd. member, British Board of Film Classification; dir. of Children's Film Unit.

KIMBROUGH, CHARLES
Actor. b. St. Paul, MN, May 23, 1936. e. Indiana U., Yale U.
THEATER: *NY*: All in Love (debut, 1961), Cop-Out (B'way debut, 1969), Company (Tony nom.), Candide, Love for Love, The Rules of the Game, Secret Service, Mr. Happiness, Same Time Next Year, Drinks Before Dinner, The Dining Room, Sunday in the Park With George, Hay Fever. Several prods. with Milwaukee Rep. Theatre (1966-73).
PICTURES: The Front (debut, 1976), The Seduction of Joe Tynan, Starting Over, It's My Turn, Switching Channels, The Good Mother, The Hunchback of Notre Dame (voice).
TELEVISION: *Series*: Murphy Brown (Emmy nom.). *Movies*: For Ladies Only, A Doctor's Story, Weekend War, Cast the First Stone. Pilot: The Recovery Room. *Special*: Sunday in the Park With George.

KIMMELMAN, KEN
Producer, Director, Animator. b. New York, NY. Aug. 6, 1940. e. School of Visual Arts. Has produced tv programs, political films, theatricals, TV commercials, and many films for Sesame Street. Consultant on the faculty of the Aesthetic Realism Roundation. Pres. of Imagery Film Ltd; prod. films for UN. Recipient of: National Emmy Award 1995 (The Heart Knows Better), Newark Black Film Festival's Paul Robeson Award; Atlanta Film Festival's Dir's. Choice Award; Cindy Award; ASIFA East's Best Children's Film Award. Taught and lectured at NYU, presently at School of Visual Arts, NY. Published numerous articles & letters.
TELEVISION: *Director/Producer*: People Are Trying to Put Opposites Together (documentary). *Series*: Doug (Emmy nom., 1992, 93), The Head, Daria, Mr. Hiccup.

KING, ALAN
Actor, Producer. r.n. Irwin Alan Kingberg. b. Brooklyn, NY, Dec. 26, 1927. Started as musician, stand-up comedian in Catskills, then nightclubs. Author: Anybody Who Owns His Own Home Deserves It, Help I'm a Prisoner in a Chinese Bakery.
THEATER: The Impossible Years, The Investigation, Dinner at Eight, The Lion in Winter, Something Different.
PICTURES: *Actor*: Hit the Deck (debut, 1955), Miracle in the Rain, The Girl He Left Behind, The Helen Morgan Story, On the Fiddle (Operation Snafu), Bye Bye Braverman, The Anderson Tapes, Just Tell Me What You Want, Prince of the City (cameo), Author! Author!, I the Jury, Lovesick, Cat's Eye, You Talkin' to Me?, Memories of Me (also co-prod.), Enemies a Love Story, The Bonfire of the Vanities, Night and the City, Casino. *Producer:* Happy Birthday Gemini, Cattle Annie and Little Britches (co-prod.), Wolfen (exec. prod.).
TELEVISION: *Guest/Host*: The Tonight Show, Kraft Music Hall. *Prod-star NBC-TV specials*: Comedy is King, On Location: An Evening With Alan King at Carnegie Hall, etc. *Mini-Series*: Seventh Avenue. Movies: Return to Earth (co-exec. prod. only), How to Pick Up Girls (also exec. prod.), Pleasure Palace, Dad the Angel and Me, The Infiltrator. *Host*: Alan King: Inside the Comic Mind (Comedy Central).

KING, ANDREA
Actress. r.n. Georgette Barry. b. Paris, France, Feb. 1, 1919. e. Edgewood H.S., Greenwich, CT. m. N.H. Willis, attorney. Started career on NY stage, following high school; in Growing Pains & Fly Away Home, Boy Meets Girl, Angel Street (Boston); Life with Father (Chicago); signed by Warner, 1943. Screen debut as Georgette McKee in The Ramparts We Watch, 1940.
PICTURES: Hotel Berlin, God is My Co-Pilot, The Very Thought of You, The Man I Love, The Beast With Five Fingers, Shadow of a Woman, Roughly Speaking, My Wild Irish Rose, Ride the Pink Horse, Mr. Peabody and the Mermaid, Song of Surrender, Southside 1-10001, I Was a Shoplifter, Dial 1119, The Lemon Drop Kid, Mark of the Renegade, World in His Arms, Red Planet Mars, Darby's Rangers, Band of Angels, Daddy's Gone A-Hunting, The Linguini Incident, The Color of Evening.
TELEVISION: *Movie*: Prescription Murder. *Specials*: Dream Girl, Officer and the Lady, Witness for the Prosecution. *Guest*: Fireside Theatre, Maya.

KING, LARRY
Talk Show Host, Writer. b. Brooklyn, NY, Nov. 19, 1933. Started as disc jockey on various Miami radio stations from 1958-64. Became host of radio talk show, broadcast from Miami before moving to Arlington, VA, in 1978. Show has run since then on Mutual Broadcasting System. Host of CNN tv talk show since 1985, Larry King Live. Starred in tv special Larry King Extra. Columnist for Miami Beach Sun-Reporter, Sporting News, USA Today. Appeared in films Ghostbusters, Eddie and the Cruisers II: Eddie Lives, The Exorcist III.
AUTHOR: Larry King by Larry King, Tell It to the King, Mr. King You're Having a Heart Attack, Tell Me More, How to Talk to Anyone Anytime Anywhere: The Secrets of Good Conversation.

KING, PERRY
Actor. b. Alliance, OH, April 30, 1948. e. Yale. Studied with John Houseman at Juilliard. B'way debut 1990 in A Few Good Men.
PICTURES: Slaughterhouse-Five (debut, 1972), The Possession of Joel Delaney, The Lords of Flatbush, Mandingo, The Wild Party, Lipstick, Andy Warhol's Bad, The Choirboys, A Different Story, Search and Destroy (Striking Back), Class of 1984, Killing Hour (The Clairvoyant), Switch, A Cry in the Night.
TELEVISION: *Series*: The Quest, Riptide, Almost Home, The Trouble With Larry. *Guest*: Medical Center, Hawaii Five-O, Apple's Way, Cannon. Mini-Series: Aspen, The Last Convertible, Captain and the Kings. *Movies*: Foster and Laurie, The Cracker Factory, Love's Savage Fury, City in Fear, Inmates: A Love Story, Golden Gate, Helen Keller: The Miracle Continues, Stranded, Perfect People, Shakedown on Sunset Strip, The Man Who Lived at the Ritz, Disaster at Silo 7, The Prize Pulitzer, Danielle Steel's Kaleidoscope, Only One Survived, Something to Live For, Sidney Sheldon's A Stranger in the Mirror, Jericho Fever, Good King Wenceslas, She Led Two Lives. *Pilot:* Half 'n' Half.

KING, PETER
Executive, Barrister-at-law. b. London, England, March 22, 1928. e. Marlborough, Oxford U. (MA, honors). Bd., Shipman & King Cinemas Ltd., 1956; borough councillor, 1959-61; chmn., London & Home counties branch, CEA, 1962-63; pres., CEA, 1964; mang. dir. Shipman & King Cinemas Ltd., 1959-68; chmn. & mang. dir. Paramount Pictures (U.K.) Ltd. Britain, 1968-70; mang. dir., EMI Cinemas and Leisure Ltd., 1970-74; chmn. & mang. dir. King Publications/pub. Screen Intl., 1974-89; pres., Screen Intl., 1989-90; chmn. & mang. dir., Rex Publications Ltd., 1990-; pub., Majesty, 1990-; pub. Preview.

KING, STEPHEN
Writer. b. Portland, ME, Sept. 21, 1947. e. Univ. of Maine at Orono (B.S.). Best-selling novelist specializing in thrillers many of which have been adapted to film by others. *Movie adaptations:* Carrie, The Shining, The Dead Zone, Christine, Cujo, Children of the Corn, Firestarter, Cat's Eye, Stand By Me (The Body), The Running Man, Pet Sematary, Misery, Apt Pupil, The Lawnmower Man, The Dark Half, Needful Things, The Shawshank Redemption, The Mangler, Dolores Claiborne, Thinner, Night Flier, Apt Pupil, The Green Mile, Stud City (The Body), Desperation. *TV adaptations:* Salem's Lot, It, The Stand, Trucks, The Tommyknockers, The Langoliers, The Shining, Rose Madder.

PICTURES: Knightriders (actor), Creepshow (s.p., actor), Children of the Corn (s.p.), Silver Bullet (s.p.), Maximum Overdrive (dir., s.p., actor), Creepshow II (actor), Pet Sematary (s.p., actor), Sleepwalkers (s.p., actor).
TELEVISION: *Series*: Golden Years (creator, writer). *Movies/Mini-Series:* Sometimes They Come Back (s.p.), The Stand (actor), The Langoliers (actor), Sometimes They Come Back...Again (s.p.),Quicksilver Highway, Sometimes They Come Back..For More (s.p.), Storm of the Century (also prod.).

KING, ZALMAN
Actor, Director, Writer. r.n. Zalman King Lefkowitz. b. Trenton, NJ, 1941. m. writer Patricia Knop.
PICTURES: *Actor*: The Ski Bum, You've Got to Walk It Like You Talk It or You'll Lose the Beat, Neither by Day Nor Night, Some Call It Loving, Trip with the Teacher, Sammy Somebody, The Passover Plot, Blue Sunshine, Tell Me a Riddle, Galaxy of Terror. *Exec. Prod.*: Roadie (also co-story), Endangered Species, Siesta. *Prod./Writer*: 9 1/2 Weeks. *Director-Writer*: Wildfire, Two Moon Junction, Wild Orchid, Wild Orchid II: Two Shades of Blue, Delta of Venus.
TELEVISION: *Series*: The Young Lawyers, Red Shoe Diaries (exec. prod., creator, dir. episodes). *Guest*: Alfred Hitchcock Presents, Land of the Giants, Gunsmoke, Adam 12, Charlie's Angels, etc. *Movies*: The Dangerous Days of Kiowa Jones, Stranger on the Run, The Young Lawyers (pilot), The Intruders, Smile Jenny You're Dead, Like Normal People, Lake Consequence (co-prod., co-writer).

KINGMAN, DONG
Fine Artist. b. Oakland, CA, March 31, 1911. e. Hong Kong 1916-1920. 1928, mem. motion picture co., Hong Kong branch; 1935; began to exhibit as fine artist in San Francisco; promotional, advertising or main title artwork for following films: World of Suzie Wong, Flower Drum Song, 55 Days of Peking, Circus World, King Rat, The Desperados, The Sand Pebbles, Lost Horizon. 1966-67, created 12 paintings for Universal Studio Tour for posters and promotion; 1968, cover painting for souvenir program for Ringling Bros.,Barnum and Bailey Circus; treasurer for Living Artist Production since 1954; Exec. V.P. 22nd-Century Films, Inc. since 1968, Prod. & dir. short, Hongkong Dong. Also short subject film Dong Kingman, filmed and directed by James Wong Howe. 1993 Chinese-American Arts Council exhibition of all motion picture work. 1996, created official poster for Olympic Games.

KINGSLEY, BEN
Actor. r.n. Krishna Banji. b. Snaiton, Yorkshire, England, Dec. 31, 1943. Started career with Salford Players, amateur co. in Manchester. Turned pro in 1966 and appeared on London stage at a Chichester Festival Theatre. 1967, joined Royal Shakespeare Co., appearing in A Midsummer Night's Dream, Tempest, Measure for Measure, Merry Wives of Windsor, Volpone, Cherry Orchard, Hamlet, Othello, Judgement. On NY stage in Kean. Played Squeers in Nicholas Nickleby in 1980 in London.
PICTURES: Fear Is the Key (debut, 1972), Gandhi (Acad. Award, 1982), Betrayal, Turtle Diary, Harem, Maurice, Testimony, Pascali's Island, Without a Clue, Bugsy (Acad. Award nom.), Sneakers, Dave, Searching for Bobby Fisher (Innocent Moves), Schindler's List, Death and the Maiden, Species, Twelfth Night, The Assignment, Photographing Fairies, Parting Shots, Spooky House, Sexy Beast, Rules of Engagement, The Confession.
TELEVISION: *Movies/Specials*: Silas Marner, Kean, Oxbridge Blues, Camille, Murderers Among Us: The Simon Wiesenthal Story, Joseph, Moses, The Tale of Sweeney Todd, Crime and Punishment, Alice in Wonderland.

KINGSLEY, WALTER
Executive. b New York, NY, Oct. 20, 1923. e. Phillips Acad., Andover; Amherst Coll., B.A., 1947. Charter member Big Brothers of Los Angeles. WCOP, Boston, 1948-50; Ziv Television Programs, Inc., 1950-58; pres., Independent Television Corp. (ITC), 1958-62; member bd. dir Big Brothers of Amer.; pres. Kingsley Co., 1962-66; exec. v.p. Wolper Prods. Metromedia Prods. Corp., 1966-72; faculty, Inter-Racial Council of Business Opportunity, N.Y.; 1972-82, pres., Kingsley Company, Commercial Real Estate; 1983-present, special consultant, American Film Inst.; bd. mem.: Big Brothers/Big Sisters of America; Big Brothers of Greater Los Angeles.

KINOY, ERNEST
Writer. Started career in radio writing sci. fic. programs (X Minus One, Dimension X). Wrote for nearly all early dramatic shows, including Studio One, Philco Playhouse, Playhouse 90.
PICTURES: Brother John, Buck and the Preacher, Leadbelly, White Water Summer (co-s.p.).
TELEVISION: The Defenders (Emmy Award, 1964), Naked City, Dr. Kildare, Jacob and Joseph, David the King, Roots I & II, Victory at Entebbe, Skokie, Murrow, The President's Plane is Missing, Stones for Ibarra, Gore Vidal's Lincoln, The Fatal Shore, White Water Summer, Tad.

KINSKI, NASTASSJA
Actress. r.n. Nastassja Nakszynski. b. Berlin, Germany, Jan. 24, 1960. Daughter of late actor Klaus Kinski.
PICTURE: Falsche Bewegung (The Wrong Move; debut, 1975), To the Devil a Daughter, Passion Flower Hotel, Stay as You Are, Tess, One From the Heart, Cat People, For Your Love Only, Exposed, The Moon in the Gutter, Unfaithfully Yours, The Hotel New Hampshire, Maria's Lovers, Paris Texas, Revolution, Symphony of Love, Harem, Malady of Love, Silent Night, Torrents of Spring, On a Moonlit Night, Magdalene, The Secret, Night Sun, Faraway So Close!, Crackerjack, Terminal Velocity, The Blonde, The Ring, One Night Stand, Little Boy Blue, Your Friends and Neighbors, Fathers' Day, The Magic of Marciano, Timeshare, Town and Country, The Claim, Beyond City Limits, American Rhapsody.

KIRBY, BRUNO
Actor. b. New York, NY, April 28, 1949. Also acted as B. Kirby Jr., and Bruce Kirby Jr. Father is actor Bruce Kirby. On B'way 1991 in Lost in Yonkers.
PICTURES: The Harrad Experiment (debut, 1973), Cinderella Liberty, Superdad, The Godfather Part 2, Baby Blue Marine, Between the Lines, Almost Summer, Where the Buffalo Roam, Borderline, Modern Romance, This Is Spinal Tap, Birdy, Flesh + Blood, Tin Men, Good Morning Vietnam, Bert Rigby You're a Fool, When Harry Met Sally ..., We're No Angels, The Freshman, City Slickers, Hoffa (cameo), Golden Gate, The Basketball Diaries, Donnie Brasco, A Slipping Down Life, Stuart Little (voice).
TELEVISION: *Series*: The Super. *Movies*: All My Darling Daughters, A Summer Without Boys, Some Kind of Miracle, Million Dollar Infield. *Specials*: Run Don't Walk, The Trap, Mastergate. *Guest*: Room 222, Columbo, Kojak, Emergency, It's Garry Shandling's Show, Tales From the Crypt, The Larry Sanders Show, Fallen Angels.

KIRK (BUSH), PHYLLIS
Actress. r.n. Phyllis Kirkegaard. b. Syracuse, NY, Sept. 18, 1926. Perfume repr. model, Conover Agcy.; B'way debut in My Name Is Aquilon followed by Point of No Return. Worked as interviewer-host on all three major networks Executive with ICPR and Stone Associates. Joined CBS News in Los Angeles, 1978; 1988 named v.p. media relations Stone/Hallinan Associates.
PICTURES: Our Very Own (debut, 1950), A Life of Her Own, Two Weeks with Love, Mrs. O'Malley and Mr. Malone, Three Guys Named Mike, About Face, The Iron Mistress, Thunder Over the Plains, House of Wax, Crime Wave, River Beat, Canyon Crossroads, Johnny Concho, Back From Eternity, City After Midnight, The Sad Sack.
TELEVISION: *Series*: The Red Buttons Show, The Thin Man.

KIRKLAND, SALLY
Actress. b. NY, NY, Oct. 31, 1944. e. Actors Studio, studied acting with Uta Hagen and Lee Strasberg. Achieved notoriety in the 1960s for on-stage nudity (Sweet Eros, Futz), for work in experimental off-off B'way theater and as part of Andy Warhol's inner circle. Appeared as featured actress in over 25 films and countless avant-garde shows, before winning acclaim (and Acad. Award nom.) as the star of Anna (1987). 1983 founded Sally Kirkland Acting Workshop, a traveling transcendental meditation, yoga and theatrical seminar. Formed Artists Alliance Prods. with Mark and David Buntzman, 1988.
THEATER: The Love Nest, Futz, Tom Paine, Sweet Eros, Witness, One Night Stand of a Noisy Passenger, The Justice Box, Where Has Tommy Flowers Gone?, In the Boom Boom Room (L.A., Drama-Logue's best actress award, 1981), Largo Desolato.
PICTURES: The Thirteen Most Beautiful Woman (1964), Blue, Futz!, Coming Apart, Going Home, The Young Nurses, The Way We Were, Cinderella Liberty, The Sting, Candy Stripe Nurses, Big Bad Mama, Bite the Bullet, Crazy Mama, Breakheart Pass, A Star is Born, Pipe Dreams, Hometown U.S.A., Private Benjamin, The Incredible Shrinking Woman, Human Highway, Love Letters, Fatal Games, Talking Walls, Anna, Melanie Rose (High Stakes), Crack in the Mirror (White Hot), Paint It Black, Cold Feet, Best of the Best, Revenge, Bullseye, Two Evil Eyes, JFK, In the Heat of Passion, The Player, Blast 'Em, Primary Motive, Double Threat, Forever, Paper Hearts (also co-exec. prod.), Eye of the Stranger, Gunmen, Little Ghost, Amnesia, Excess Baggage, Wilbur Falls, Paranoia, It's All About You (cameo), The Island, Edtv.
TELEVISION: *Movies*: Kansas City Massacre, Death Scream, Stonestreet: Who Killed the Centerfold Model?, Georgia Peaches, Heat Wave, The Haunted. Double Jeopardy, The Woman Who Loved Elvis, Double Deception. *Specials*: Willow B—Women in Prison, Summer, Largo Desolato, The Westing Game, Brave New World. *Series*: Falcon Crest, Valley of the Dolls, Days of Our Lives. *Guest*: Roseanne.

KIRKWOOD, GENE
Producer. The Kirkwood Company.
PICTURES: Rocky, New York New York (assoc. prod.), Comes a Horseman, Uncle Joe Shannon, The Idolmaker, A Night in Heaven, Gorky Park, The Keep, The Pope of Greenwich Village, Ironweed, UHF (co-prod.), What Makes Sammy Run, Gia a Thing of Beauty, The Duke of Deception.

KIRKWOOD, PAT
Actress, Singer. r.n. Patricia Kirkwood. b. Pendleton, Manchester, England, Feb. 24, 1921. British stage debut 1936. US cabaret debut 1954. Autobiography The Time of My Life (1999). Recorded CD Miss Show Business (1999).

THEATRE: *LONDON:* Cinderella, Black Velvet, Top of the World, Lady Behave, Let's Face It, Happidrome, Starlight Roof, Roundabout, Ace of Clubs, Fancy Free, Peter Pan, Wonderful Town, Chrysanthemum, Pools Paradise, Villa Sleeps Four, Lock Up Your Daughters, The Constant Wife, The Rumpus, Hay Fever, Lady Frederick, A Chorus of Murder, Move Over Mrs. Markham, Pal Joey, The Cabinet Minister, An Evening with Pat Kirkwood, A Talent to Amuse, A Glamorous Night with Evelyn Laye and Friends, Glamorous Nights of Music, Noel/Cole-Let's Do It.
PICTURES: Save A Little Sunshine, Me and My Pal, Band Waggon, Come On George, Flight from Folly, No Leave No Love, Once A Sinner, Stars in Your Eyes, After the Ball, To See Such Fun.
TELEVISION: Starlight, Two of Everything, What's My Line?, The Pat Kirkwood Show, Our Marie, Pygmalion, The Great Little Tilley, From Me To You, Pat, Looks Familiar, Pebble Mill, Paul Merton's Palladium Story, This Is Your Life (subject).

KITANO, TAKESHI
Director, Writer. b. Tokyo, Japan, Jan. 18, 1948.
PICTURES: Merry Christmas Mr. Lawrence (actor only), Yasha (actor only), Comic Magazine (actor only), Violent Cop (also actor), Boiling Point (also actor), A Scene at the Sea (also ed.), Sonatine (also ed., actor), Many Happy Returns (actor, novel only), Getting Any? (also actor, ed.), Johnny Mnemonic (actor only), The Five (actor only), Kids Return (also ed.), Fireworks (also actor, ed.), Tokyo Eyes (actor only), Kikujiro no natsu.

KITT, EARTHA
Actress, Singer. b. Columbia, SC, Jan. 26, 1928. Professional career started as dancer in Katherine Dunham group; toured U.S., Mexico & Europe with group, then opened night club in Paris; in Orson Welles stage prod. of Faust (European tour); N.Y. night clubs before B'way debut in New Faces of 1952. Author: Thursday's Child, A Tart Is Not a Sweet, Alone with Me, Confessions of a Sex Kitten.
THEATRE: *NY:* New Faces of 1952, Shinbone Alley, Mrs. Patterson, The Skin of Our Teeth, The Owl and the Pussycat, Timbuktu.
PICTURES: New Faces (debut, 1954), The Mark of the Hawk (Accused), St. Louis Blues, Anna Lucasta, Saint of Devil's Island, Synanon, Uncle Tom's Cabin, Up the Chastity Belt, Friday Foster, The Last Resort, The Serpent Warriors, The Pink Chiquitas (voice), Master of Dragonard Hill, Erik the Viking, Ernest Scared Stupid, Boomerang, Fatal Instinct, Unzipped, Harriet the Spy, Ill Gotten Gains, I Woke Up Early the Day I Died, Kingdom of the Sun.
TELEVISION: *Movies*: Lt. Schuster's Wife, To Kill a Cop. *Guest*: Batman (as Catwoman), I Spy, Miami Vice.

KLEES, ROBERT E.
Executive. b. New York, NY, Feb. 21, 1927. e. Duke U., 1947-51. Univ. of CA Graduate Sch. of Mgt., 1973-75. U.S. Navy, 1944-46; Union Carbide Corp., 1951-57; Beckman Instruments Inc., 1957-69; International Biophysics Corp, 1969-73; sr. v.p., mktg., Deluxe Laboratories Inc., div. of 20th Century Fox, 1975-83. Retired member of AMPAS, ACE, AFI, ASC, SMPTE.

KLEIN, ALLEN
Producer. b. New Jersey, Dec. 18, 1931. e. Upsala. Pres. ABKCO Films, a division of ABKCO Music & Records, Inc.
PICTURES: Force of Impulse, Pity Me Not, Charlie is My Darling, Stranger in Town, Sympathy for the Devil, Mrs. Brown You've Got a Lovely Daughter, The Stranger Returns, The Silent Stranger, Come Together, Pearl & The Pole, Let It Be, Gimme Shelter, El Topo, Blind Man, The Concert for Bangladesh, The Holy Mountain, The Greek Tycoon, Personal Best, It Had to Be You, The Rolling Stones Rock and Roll Circus.

KLEIN, HAROLD J.
Executive. b. New York, NY, e. U. of West Virginia, New York Law Sch. Reviewer, sales staff. Showman's Trade Review; booker, Brandt Theatres; booker, later vice-pres., gen. mgr., JJ Theatres, 1941-59; account exec., exec. v.p., dir. of world-wide sales, ABC Films, Inc., N.Y., Pres., Klein Film Assn.; exec. v.p., Plitt Theatres, Inc. to Nov., 1985; pres., H.J.K. Film Associates, also acting consultant to P.E.G. (Plitt Entertainment Gp.). Retired.

KLEIN, MALCOLM C.
Executive. b. Los Angeles, CA, Nov. 22, 1927. e. UCLA, grad., 1948; U. of Denver. Prod. dir. management, KLAC-TV (KCOP), L.A., 1948-52; acct. exec., KABC-TV, 1952-56; asst. gen. sales mgr., KABC-TV, 1956-59; exec. v.p. gen. mgr., NTA Broadcasting, N.Y., 1959; v.p., gen. mgr., RKO-General-KHJ-TV, 1960. Joined National General Corp. 1968, v.p. creative services and marketing; pres. Nat. Gen. TV Prods. Inc.; pres. NGC Broadcasting Corp. 1971, pres. Filmways TV Presentations. 1972, pres. Malcolm C. Klein & Assoc. mgmt. & mktg. consultants. 1973, gen'l. exec. Sterling Recreation Org. & Gen'l Mgr. B'cast Division. 1976, pres., American Song Festival. Member of faculty, UCLA, USC. Exec. v.p., Telease Inc. & American Subscription Television. 1981, sr. v.p., mng. dir., STAR-TV (subscription TV). 1982, sr. v.p., InterAmerican Satellite TV Network. 1983, pres. Malcolm C. Klein & Assoc., management consultant. Exec. dir. prog., Interactive Network Inc; v.p., bus. development, Interactive Network Inc. 1995, exec. v.p., Vivid Travel Network. Consultant, Central European Media. Member of bd., Media Shower Inc.

KLEIN, ROBERT
Actor, Comedian. b. New York, NY, Feb. 8, 1942. e. Alfred U, Yale Drama School. Was member of Chicago's Second City comedy group. Comedy albums: Child of the '50s (Grammy nom.), Mind Over Matter, New Teeth, Let's Not Make Love.
THEATRE: *NY:* The Apple Tree, Morning Noon and Night, New Faces of 1968, They're Playing Our Song (Tony Award nom.), The Sisters Rosensweig.
PICTURES: The Landlord, The Owl and the Pussycat, Rivals, The Bell Jar, Hooper, Nobody's Perfekt, The Last Unicorn (voice), Tales from the Darkside—The Movie, Radioland Murders, Mixed Nuts, Jeffrey, One Fine Day, Next Stop Wonderland, Primary Colors, Suits, Labor Pains.
TELEVISION: *Series*: Comedy Tonight, Robert Klein Time, TV's Bloopers and Practical Jokes, Sisters. *Movies*: Your Place or Mine, Poison Ivy, This Wife for Hire. *Guest*: The Tonight Show, ABC Comedy Special, George Burns Comedy Week, Twilight Zone, Late Night With David Letterman. Also appeared in HBO comedy specials.

KLEINER, HARRY
Writer, Producer. b. Philadelphia, PA, Sept. 10, 1916. e. Temple U., B.S.; Yale U., M.F.A.
PICTURES: Fallen Angel, The Street With No Name, Red Skies of Mountain, Kangaroo, Miss Sadie Thompson, Salome, Carmen Jones, The Violent Men, The Garment Jungle (also prod.), Cry Tough (also prod.), The Rabbit Trap (prod. only), Ice Palace, Fever in the Blood, Fantastic Voyage, Bullitt, Le Mans, Extreme Prejudice, Red Heat.
TELEVISION: *Writer*: Rosenberg Trial.

KLEISER, RANDAL
Director, Producer. b. Lebanon, PA, July 20, 1946. e. U. of Southern California. For Disney Theme Parks dir. 70mm 3-D film Honey I Shrunk the Audience.
PICTURES: Street People (s.p.). *Director:* Grease, The Blue Lagoon, Summer Lovers (also s.p.), Grandview U.S.A., Flight of the Navigator, North Shore (exec. prod., co-story only), Big Top Pee-Wee, Getting it Right (also co-prod.), White Fang, Return to the Blue Lagoon (exec. prod. only), Honey I Blew Up the Kid, It's My Party, Shadow of Doubt.
TELEVISION: *Movies*: All Together Now, Dawn: Portrait of a Teenage Runaway, The Boy in the Plastic Bubble, The Gathering. *Series*: Marcus Welby, M.D., The Rookies, Starsky and Hutch, Family.

KLINE, FRED W.
Publicist. b. Oakland, CA, May 17, 1918. e. U. of California, Berkeley. M.P. pub. rel. since 1934; pres. & owner The Fred Kline Agency; pres. Kline Communications Corp.; Kline Communications Corp.; Fred W. Kline Prod., Inc.; Capitol News Service, Sacramento; L.A. News Bureau; Capitol Radio News Service, Inc.; Advisor, Calif. Film Commission. Member, Regional Filming Task Force Committee, Los Angeles City Council.

KLINE, KEVIN
Actor. b. St. Louis, MO, Oct. 24, 1947.e. Indiana U, School of Music. Studied at Juilliard Drama Center (1970-72), and became founding member of John Houseman's The Acting Company, touring in classics, incl. The School for Scandal, She Stoops to Conquer, The Lower Depths, The Way of the World. Associate prod., NY Shakespeare Festival, 1993-1997.
THEATER: Understudied Raul Julia in Lincoln Center's The Threepenny Opera; The Three Sisters (B'way debut, 1973), On the Twentieth Century (Tony Award, 1978), Loose Ends, The Pirates of Penzance (Tony Award, 1981), Richard III, Henry V (Central Park), Arms and the Man, Hamlet, Much Ado About Nothing, Hamlet (1990, also dir.), Measure for Measure.
PICTURES: Sophie's Choice (debut, 1982), The Pirates of Penzance, The Big Chill, Silverado, Violets Are Blue, Cry Freedom, A Fish Called Wanda (Acad. Award for Best Supporting Actor, 1988), The January Man, I Love You to Death, Soapdish, Grand Canyon, Consenting Adults, Chaplin, Dave, George Balanchine's The Nutcracker (narrator), Princess Caraboo, French Kiss, Fierce Creatures, The Hunchback of Notre Dame (voice), The Ice Storm, In & Out, Looking for Richard, Wild Wild West, A Midsummer Night's Dream, The Road to El Dorado, The Huncback of Notre Dame II (voice), The Anniversary Party.
TELEVISION: *Series*: Search For Tomorrow (1976-77). *Specials*: The Time of Your Life, Hamlet (also co-dir.).

KLUGMAN, JACK
Actor. b. Philadelphia, PA, April 27, 1922. e. Carnegie Tech. Much tv work in 1950's incl. Captain Video, Tom Corbett—Space Cadet, U.S. Steel Hour, Kraft Television Theatre, Playhouse 90.
THEATRE: *B'way*: Saint Joan, Stevedore, Mister Roberts, Gypsy, I'm Not Rappaport, Three Men on a Horse. *Tour/Stock*: The Odd Couple.
PICTURES: Timetable (debut, 1956), Twelve Angry Men, Cry Terror, The Scarface Mob, Days of Wine and Roses, I Could Go on Singing, The Yellow Canary, Act One, Hail Mafia, The Detective, The Split, Goodbye Columbus, Who Says I Can't Ride a Rainbow?, Two Minute Warning, Dear God.

TELEVISION: *Series*: The Greatest Gift (daytime serial; 1954-55), Harris Against the World, The Odd Couple (2 Emmy Awards: 1971, 1973), Quincy M.E., You Again? *Guest*: The Defenders (Emmy Award, 1964), The Twilight Zone, The FBI, Ben Casey, 90 Bristol Court. *Movies*: Fame Is the Name of the Game, Poor Devil, The Underground Man, One of My Wives Is Missing, The Odd Couple: Together Again, Parallel Lives. *Mini-Series*: Around the World in 80 Days.

KNIGHT, SHIRLEY
Actress. b. Goessell, KS, July 5, 1936. e. Lake Forest Coll., D.F.A., 1978. Won 1976 Tony Award for Kennedy's Children; Joseph Jefferson Award for Landscape of the Body, 1977; New Jersey Drama Critics Awards for A Streetcar Named Desire, 1979.
PICTURES: Five Gates to Hell (debut, 1959), Ice Palace, The Dark at the Top of the Stairs (Acad. Award nom.) The Couch, Sweet Bird of Youth (Acad. Award nom.), House of Women, Flight from Ashiya, The Group, Dutchman (Venice Film Fest. Award), Petulia, The Counterfeit Killer, The Rain People, Juggernaut, Secrets, Beyond the Poseidon Adventure, Endless Love, The Sender, Prisoners, Color of Night, Stuart Saves His Family, Diabolique, Somebody Is Waiting, The Man Who Counted, As Good as It Gets, Little Boy Blue.
TELEVISION: *Movies*: The Outsider, Shadow Over Elveron, Friendly Persuasion, Medical Story, Return to Earth, 21 Hours at Munich, The Defection of Simas Kudirka, Champions: A Love Story, Playing for Time (Emmy nom.), Billionaire Boys Club, Bump in the Night, Shadow of a Doubt, To Save a Child, When Love Kills: The Seduction of John Hearn, A Mother's Revenge, Baby Brokers, The Yarn Princess, A Part of the Family, Children of the Dust, Indictment: The McMartin Trial (Emmy Award, 1995; Golden Glove Award, 1996), Ties That Bind, Tim, The Haunting of Patricia Johnson. *Specials*: The Country Girl, The Lie. *Guest*: The Equalizer (Emmy nom.), thirtysomething (Emmy Award), Law and Order (Emmy nom.), NYPD Blue (Emmy Award, 1995), Cybill, Outer Limits Tribute.

KNOTTS, DON
Actor. b. Morgantown, WV, July 21, 1924. e. WV U., U. of AZ. Drafted into U.S. Army where became part of show called Stars and Gripes, teamed with comedian Mickey Shaughnessy. After schooling resumed was offered teaching fellowship but went to New York to try acting instead. Started out in radio show Bobby Benson and the B Bar B's. Appeared on TV, leading to role in No Time for Sergeants on B'way; appeared in film version.
PICTURES: No Time for Sergeants (debut, 1958), Wake Me When It's Over, The Last Time I Saw Archie, It's a Mad Mad Mad Mad World, Move Over Darling, The Incredible Mr. Limpet, The Ghost and Mr. Chicken, The Reluctant Astronaut, The Shakiest Gun in the West, The Love God?, How to Frame a Figg (also co-story), The Apple Dumpling Gang, No Deposit No Return, Gus, Herbie Goes to Monte Carlo, Hot Lead and Cold Feet, The Apple Dumpling Gang Rides Again, The Prize Fighter, Ther Private Eyes, Cannonball Run II, Pinocchio and the Emperor of the Night (voice), Big Bully.
TELEVISION: *Series*: Search for Tomorrow (1953-55), The Steve Allen Show, The Andy Griffith Show (5 Emmy Awards: 1961, 1962, 1963, 1966, 1967), The Don Knotts Show, Three's Company, What a Country, Matlock. *Movies*: I Love a Mystery, Return to Mayberry.

KOCH, HOWARD W.
Producer, Director. b. New York, NY, April 11, 1916. Runner on Wall St. Began film career in Universal's contracts and playdate dept. in NY; asst. cutter, 20th-Fox; asst. dir., 20th-Fox, Eagle Lion, MGM; 2nd unit dir., freelance; In 1953, joined Aubrey Schenck Prod. forming Bel Air Prods., made films for U.A.; 1961-64, prod. Frank Sinatra Enterprises; v.p., chg. prod., Paramount Pictures Corp., 1964-66, Past pres. of the Academy of Motion Picture Arts and Sciences, 1977-79. 1977, elected to the National Board of Directors Guild of America for two year term. 1980 honored by NATO as prod. of year. 1985 Silver Medallion Award of Honor, Motion Picture Television Fund. Produced eight Academy Award shows, 1972-1983. Has 24 year relationship with Paramount as exec., prod., and dir. 1990, received Jean Hersholt Humanitarian Award, honored by Amer. Society of Cinematographers. 1991: Frank Capra Award from Directors Guild, Motion Picture Showmanship Award from the Publicists Guild; 1995: David O. Selznick Lifetime Achievement Award from the Producers Guild.
PICTURES: *Exec. Prod.*: Sergeants 3, The Manchurian Candidate, Come Blow Your Horn, X-15, Robin and the 7 Hoods, None But the Brave, The President's Analyst, For Those Who Think Young, Dragonslayer. *Producer*: War Paint, Beachhead, Yellow Tomahawk, Desert Sands, Fort Yuma, Frontier Scout, Ghost Town, Broken Star, Crimes Against Joe, Three Bad Sisters, Emergency Hospital, Rebel in Town, The Black Sheep, Pharaoh's Curse, Tomahawk Trail, Revolt at Fort Laramie, War Drums, Voodoo Island, Hellbound, The Dalton Girls, The Odd Couple, On a Clear Day You Can See Forever, Plaza Suite, Star Spangled Girl, Last of the Red Hot Lovers, Jacqueline Susann's Once Is Not Enough, Some Kind of Hero, Airplane II: The Sequel, Collision Course. A Howard W. Koch *Production*: A New Leaf, Airplane!, Ghost. Director: Jungle Heat, Shield for Murder, Big House USA, Fort Bowie, Violent Road, Untamed Youth, Born Reckless, Frankenstein 1970, Andy Hardy Comes Home, The Last Mile, Girl in Black Stockings, Badge 373 (also prod.), The Beautician & the Beast.
TELEVISION: *Director*: Miami Undercover, The Untouchables, Maverick, Cheyenne, Hawaiian Eye. *Mini-Series: Prod.*: The Pirate, Hollywood Wives, Crossings. *Movie*: The Odd Couple: Together Again (prod.). *Specials: Prod.*: Ol' Blue Eyes Is Back, Oscar's Best Actors, Oscar's Best Movies (also dir.), Who Loves Ya Baby, On the Road with Bing (also dir.), The Stars Salute the Olympics.

KOCH, HOWARD W., JR.
Producer. b. Los Angeles, CA, Dec. 14, 1945. Was asst. dir. and in other industry posts before turning to production. Pres. & chief exec. off., Rastar (Peggy Sue Got Married, The Secret of My Success, Nothing in Common, Violets Are Blue, Amazing Chuck and Grace prod. under presidency); 1987, set up own prod. co. at De Laurentiis Entertainment Group. Oct. 1987: named president of the De Laurentiis Entertainment Group, Resigned April 1988 to produce independently.
PICTURES: Heaven Can Wait, The Other Side of Midnight, The Frisco Kid (exec.). *Co-prod./prod.*: The Idolmaker, Gorky Park, Honky Tonk Freeway, The Keep, A Night in Heaven, The Pope of Greenwich Village, Rooftops, The Long Walk Home, Necessary Roughness, Wayne's World, The Temp, Sliver, Wayne's World 2, Losing Isaiah, Virtuosity, Primal Fear (exec.), The Beautician and the Beast, Keeping the Faith.

KOCH, JOANNE
Executive Director, The Film Society of Lincoln Center. b. NY, NY, Oct. 7, 1929. e. Goddard College, B.A. political science, 1950. Dept. of Film, Museum of Modern Art, as circulation asst., film researcher, motion picture stills archivist, 1950. Early 1960s, technical dir., film dept. MOMA, supervised the implementation of MOMA's film preservation program. 1967, asst. to publisher of Grove Press, active in preparation of Grove's case in I Am Curious Yellow censorship trial. Joined film div., Grove, first in distribution then as tech. dir. and prod. coord. 1971 joined Film Society of Lincoln Center as prog. dir. of Movies-in-the-Parks. 1971 made admin. dir. Exec. dir. of N.Y. Film Festival, Film Comment magazine, Film-in-Education, New Directors/New Films, annual Film Society Tribute and Walter Reade Theater at Lincoln Center.

KOENEKAMP, FRED J.
Cinematographer. b. Los Angeles, CA, Nov. 11, 1922. Father was special effects cinematographer Hans F. Koenekamp. Member of American Society of Cinematographers.
PICTURES: Doctor You've Got to Be Kidding, Sol Madrid, Stay Away Joe, Live a Little Love a Little, Heaven With a Gun, The Great Bank Robbery, Patton (Acad. Award nom.), Beyond the Valley of the Dolls, Flap, Skin Game, Billy Jack, Happy Birthday Wanda June, Stand Up and Be Counted, Kansas City Bomber, The Magnificent Seven Ride, Rage, Harry in Your Pocket, Papillon, Uptown Saturday Night, The Towering Inferno (Acad. Award, 1974), The Wild McCullochs, Doc Savage, Posse, Embryo, Fun With Dick and Jane, The Other Side of Midnight, Islands in the Streams (Acad. Award nom.), The Bad News Bears in Breaking Training, The Dominic Principle, White Line Fever, The Swarm, The Champ, The Amityville Horror, Love and Bullets, When Time Ran Out, The Hunter, First Family, First Monday in October, Carbon Copy, Yes Giorgio, It Came From Hollywood, Two of a Kind, The Adventures of Buckaroo Banzai: Across the 8th Dimension, Stewardess School, Listen to Me, Welcome Home, Flight of the Intruder.
TELEVISION: *Movies*: Disaster on the Coastline, Tales of the Gold Monkey, Money on the Side, Return of the Man from U.N.C.L.E., Summer Fantasies, Whiz Kids, Flight 90—Disaster on the Potomac, Obsessive Love, City Killer, Las Vegas Strip War, A Touch of Scandal, Not My Kid, Hard Time on Planet Earth (pilot), Return of the Shaggy Dog, Foreign Exchange, Splash Too, Hard Times. *Series*: The Man From U.N.C.L.E. (Emmy nom.)

KOENIG, WALTER
Actor, Writer. b. Chicago, IL, Sept. 14, 1936. e. Grinnell Coll. (IA), U. of California. Performed in summer stock; after college enrolled at Neighborhood Playhouse, N.Y.; first acting job in TV's Day in Court. *Books*: Chekov's Enterprise, Buck Alice and the Actor Robot. Creator and writer of comic book series Raver.
PICTURES: Strange Lovers, The Deadly Honeymoon, Star Trek—The Motion Picture, Star Trek II: The Wrath of Khan, Star Trek III: The Search for Spock, Star Trek IV: the Voyage Home, Star Trek V: the Final Frontier, Moontrap, Star Trek VI: The Undiscovered Country, Star Trek: Generations, Drawing Down the Moon, Trekkies.
TELEVISION: *Series*: Star Trek. *Guest*: Colombo, Medical Center, Ironside, Mannix, Alfred Hitchcock Presents, Mr. Novak, Ben Casey, The Untouchables, Combat, Babylon V. *Movies*: The Questor Tapes, Goodbye Raggedy Ann. *Writer*: Family, The Class of '65, The Powers of Matthew Starr.

KOHN, HOWARD EDWARD, II
Executive. b. McKeesport, PA, Oct. 25, 1920. e. NYU. National dir. of adv., publicity, roadshow dept., UA; indep. prod., Hidden Fear, 1957; pres. Lioni-Warren-Kohn, Inc., 1958; national roadshow dir., Columbia Pictures, Porgy and Bess, 1959; World wide co-ordinator, co-ordinator adv. & pub. for El Cid, 1961; named world wide co-ordinator adv., pub. all Samuel Bronston Prods, 1962; pres., Starpower Inc., 1968; exec. v.p., Avanti Films, 1970; v.p. Avariac Prods., 1971; pres., Blossom Films, 1973. Elected member of ASCAP, 1975. Pres., Avanti Associates, 1976. Pres. Channel Television Prods., Inc., 1985; pres. Search Television Prods. 1988. Pres. Avanti Music Co. 1991. Exec. v.p., Petard TV and Video.

KOHNER, PANCHO
Producer. b. Los Angeles, CA, Jan. 7, 1939. e. U. of Southern California, U. of Mexico, Sorbonne.
PICTURES: The Bridge in the Jungle (also dir., s.p.), The Lie, Victoria (also s.p.), Mr. Sycamore (also dir., s.p.), St. Ives, The White Buffalo, Love and Bullets, Why Would I Lie?, 10 to Midnight, The Evil That Men Do, Murphy's Law, Assassination, Death Wish IV, Messenger of Death, Kinjite.

KOHNER, SUSAN
Actress, b. Los Angeles, CA. Nov. 11, 1936. m. designer & author John Weitz. Sons Paul and Christopher Weitz are screenwriters. Mother, Lupita Tovar, was one of Mexico's leading film actresses. Father was talent rep. Paul Kohner. e. U. of California, 1954-55. Received Golden Globe Awards, 1959 and 1960. Retired from acting in 1964. Co-chair, Juilliard Council, Juilliard Sch. NY.
THEATER: Love Me Little, He Who Gets Slapped, A Quiet Place, Rose Tatoo, Bus Stop, St. Joan, Sunday in New York, Take Her She's Mine, Pullman Car, Hiawatha, as well as summer stock.
PICTURES: To Hell and Back (debut, 1955), The Last Wagon, Trooper Hook, Dino, Imitation of Life (Acad. Award nom.), The Big Fisherman, The Gene Krupa Story, All the Fine Young Cannibals, By Love Possessed, Freud.
TELEVISION: Alcoa Hour, Schlitz Playhouse, Four Star Theatre, Matinee Theatre, Climax, Suspicion, Playhouse 90, Route 66, Dick Powell Theatre.

KONCHALOVSKY, ANDREI
Director, Writer. a.k.a. Mikhalkov Konchalovski. b. Moscow, Soviet Union, Aug. 20, 1937. Great grandfather: painter Sourikov; grandfather: painter Konchalovski; father is a writer; mother poet Natalia Konchalovskaia; brother is director Nikita Mikhalkov. e. as pianist Moscow Conservatoire, 1947-57; State Film Sch. (VGIK) under Mikhail Romm (1964). Dir. debut with 1961 short film The Boy and the Pigeon. Worked as scriptwriter during 1960s especially with Andrei Tarkovsky. 1962: asst. to Tarkovsky on Ivan's Childhood. In 1980, moved to US. In 1991, moved back to Russia.
THEATRE/OPERA: The Seagull (Theatre de L'Odeon, Paris), Eugene Onegin (La Scala, Milan), La Pique Dame (La Scala, Milan & Bastille Opera, Pairs).
PICTURES: *Writer*: The Steamroller and the Violin, Andrey Rublev, Tashkent City of Bread, The Song of Manshuk, The End of Chieftain. *Director*: The First Teacher (feature debut, 1965), Asya's Happiness, A Nest of Gentlefolk, Uncle Vanya, Romance for Lovers, Siberiade (Cannes Film Fest. Award, 1979), Maria's Lovers, Runaway Train, Duet for One, Shy People (also co-s.p.), Tango and Cash, Homer and Eddie, Ryaba, My Chicken (writer, dir.), The Inner Circle (also co-s.p.), Asia and the Hen with the Golden Eyes, Lumiere & Company..
TELEVISION: Split Cherry Terry (short). *Mini-series*: The Odyssey (Part I & II, Emmy Award, 1996).

KONIGSBERG, FRANK
Executive. b. Kew Gardens, NY, March 10, 1933. e. Yale, Yale Law Sch. Worked as lawyer at CBS for six years; moved to NBC 1960-65 in legal dept. as dir. prog. and talent administration. Left to package TV special for Artists Agency Rep. (later AFA) in Los Angeles; sr. v.p. of West Coast office seven years. Executive producer of many TV series, pilots, variety specials and made-for-TV movies. Formed own Konigsberg Company. Theatrical film debut as prod., Joy of Sex (1984).
TELEVISION: *Movies* (all exec. prod.): Pearl, Ellis Island, Bing Crosby: His Life and Legend, Dummy, Before and After, Guyana Tragedy, A Christmas Without Snow, The Pride of Jesse Hallam, Hard Case, Divorce Wars, Coming Out of the Ice, Onassis: The Richest Man in the World, Where the Hell's That Gold?!!?, Senior Prom, Babycakes. *Series* (exec. prod.): It's Not Easy, Breaking Away, Dorothy.

KOPELSON, ANNE
Producer. m. Producer, Arnold Kopelson.
PICTURES: *Exec. prod.*: Outbreak, Seven, Eraser, Murder at 1600, Mad City, Devil's Advocate, A Perfect Murder, U.S. Marshals, Hindenberg, Riptide.
TELEVISION: *Movies*: Past Tense.

KOPELSON, ARNOLD
Producer, Financier, Intl. Distributor. b. New York, NY, Feb. 14, 1935. e. New York Law Sch., J.D., 1959; NYU, B.S. 1956. Has executive-produced, produced, packaged, developed or distributed with wife, Anne Kopelson over 100 films. Handled intl. dist. of Twice in a Lifetime, Salvador, Warlock, Triumph of the Spirit and prod. Platoon. Chmn. Arnold Kopelson Prods., Co-chmn. Inter-Ocean Film Sales, Ltd. Named NATO/ShoWest Producer of the Year, 1994.
PICTURES: *Exec. Prod.*: The Legacy, Lost and Found, Night of the Juggler, Dirty Tricks, Final Assignment, Gimme an "F", Fire Birds, Warlock. *Producer*: Foolin' Around, Platoon (Acad. Award for Best Picture, 1986), Triumph of the Spirit, Out for Justice, Falling Down, The Fugitive (Acad. Award nom.), Outbreak, Seven, Eraser, Murder at 1600, Mad City, The Devil's Advocate, A Perfect Murder, U.S. Marshals, Hindenberg, Riptide.
TELEVISION: *Movie*: Past Tense.

KOPLOVITZ, KAY
Executive. b. Milwaukee, WI, April 11, 1945. e. U. Wis., 1967, BA, Mich. State U., MA, Communications, 1968. Radio/TV prod., WTMJ-TV, Milwaukee 1967. Ed. Comm. Satellite Corp. 1968-72. Dir. Community Svcs. UA Columbia Cablevision 1973-75. VP, Exec. dir. UA Columbia Satellite Services, Inc. 1977-80. Founder, pres., CEO USA Network and Sci-Fi Channel 1980-1998. Member Nat'l Cable TV Assn. 1984-. Nat'l Acad. TV Arts and Scis. 1984-95. Women in Cable 1979-83.

KOPPEL, TED
TV News Correspondent, Anchor, Host. b. Lancashire, England, Feb. 8, 1940. To U.S. in 1953; became citizen, 1963. e. Syracuse U, Stanford U. Started as writer and news correspondent for WMCA radio in NYC. Joined ABC News in New York, 1963, serving as correspondent in Vietnam, 1967, 1969-71; Miami Bureau chief, 1968; Hong Kong Bureau chief, 1969-71; diplomatic correspondent, 1971-76, 1977-79. Anchor of NBC Saturday Night News, 1976-77. Host of Nightline, beginning in 1980. Author: The Wit and Wisdom of Adlai Stevenson, In the National Interest.
TELEVISION: *Series*: ABC News (1971-80), ABC Saturday Night News (1975-77); Nightline (1980-), 20/20 (1986). Host/anchor/writer of many ABC news specials.

KOPPLE, BARBARA
Director, Producer.
PICTURES: *Dir.*: Harlan County USA (also prod., Acad. Award, Best Doc., LA Film Crits. Special Award, 1976), American Dream (Acad. Award, Best Doc., 1990, Directors' Guild Award, 1992, Cannes Film Festival Grand Jury Prize, 1991), Beyond JFK: The Question of Conspiracy, Woodstock '94 (also prod.), Wild Man Blues, In the Boom Boom Room. *Prod.*: Fallen Champ: The Mike Tyson Story (Directors' Guild Award, 1994).
TELEVISION: *Movies, dir.*: Keeping On. *Series, dir.*: Homicide: Life in the Street (Directors' Guild Award, 1998). *Mini-series, dir.*: A Century of Women.

KORMAN, HARVEY
Actor, Director. b. Chicago, IL, Feb. 15, 1927. e. Wright Junior Coll. Began dramatic studies at Chicago's Goodman Sch. of Drama at the Arts Inst. Acted in small roles in Broadway plays and did TV commercials until break came as comedian for Danny Kaye Show on TV. Staged comedy sketches for Steve Allen variety series in 1967. Became Carol Burnett's leading man on her show 1967-77. Directed two episodes of The New Dick Van Dyke Show.
PICTURES: Living Venus (debut, 1961), Gypsy, Lord Love a Duck, The Last of the Secret Agents?, The Man Called Flintstone (voice), Three Bites of the Apple, Don't Just Stand There, The April Fools, Blazing Saddles, Huckleberry Finn, High Anxiety, Americathon, Herbie Goes Bananas, First Family, History of the World Part I, Trail of the Pink Panther, Curse of the Pink Panther, The Longshot, Munchie, The Flintstones (voice), Radioland Murders, Dracula: Dead and Loving It, Jingle All the Way, Gideon's Webb, The Flintstones in Viva Rock Vegas.
TELEVISION: *Series*: The Danny Kaye Show, The Carol Burnett Show (4 Emmy Awards: 1969, 1971, 1972, 1974), The Tim Conway Show, Mama's Family, Leo and Liz in Beverly Hills, The Nutt House. Movies: Three's a Crowd, Suddenly Single, The Love Boat (pilot), Bud and Lou, The Invisible Woman, Carpool, Crash Course, Based on an Untrue Story. *Special*: The Carol Burnett Show: A Reunion (also co-exec. prod.).

KORMAN, LEWIS J.
Executive. b. 1945. Partner, Kaye, Scholer, Fierman, Hays & Handler 1978; founding partner, Gelberg & Abrams where pioneered dev. of public limited partnerships, Delphi Partners, to help finance Columbia Pictures' and Tri-Star Pictures' films. 1986, became consultant to Tri-Star involved in negotiations that led to acquisition of Loews Theatre Corp. that year. Joined Tri-Star, 1987, as sr. exec. v.p. 1988 appt. to additional post of COO and named dir. of Columbia Pictures Entertainment Inc.; 1989 also became chmn, Motion Picture Group. 1990, resigned his positions after Columbia sale to Sony. Co-founder, pres. & COO of Savoy Pictures Ent., Inc., 1992.

KORTY, JOHN
Director, Producer, Writer, Animator. b. Lafayette, IN, June 22, 1936. e. Antioch Coll, B.A. 1959. President, Korty Films. Documentary: Who Are the DeBolts? And Where Did They Get Nineteen Kids? (Acad. Award: 1977; Emmy & DGA Awards: 1978-79). Short Films: The Language of Faces (AFSC, 1961), Imogen Cunningham: Photographer (AFI grant, 1970), The Music School. Animation: Breaking the Habit (Oscar nom.), Twice Upon a Time.
PICTURES: Crazy Quilt (1966), Funnyman, Riverrun, Alex and the Gypsy, Oliver's Story, Twice Upon a Time.
TELEVISION: *Movies*: The People, Go Ask Alice, Class of '63, The Autobiography of Miss Jane Pittman (Emmy & DGA Awards, 1974), Farewell to Manzanar (Humanitas, Christopher Awards), Forever, A Christmas Without Snow (also writer, prod.), The Haunting Passion, Second Sight: A Love Story, The Ewok Adventure, Resting Place, Baby Girl Scott, Eye on the Sparrow, Winnie, Cast the First Stone, A Son's Promise, Line of Fire: The Morris Dees Story, Long Road Home, Deadly Matrimony, They, Getting Out, Redwood Curtain, Scrooge, Oklahoma City: A Survivor's Story.

KOTCHEFF, TED
Director. r.n. William Theodore Kotcheff. b. Toronto, Canada, April 7, 1931. Ent. TV ind. 1952. After five years with Canadian Broadcasting Corp. joined ABC-TV in London, 1957.
THEATER: *London*: Progress the Park, Play with a Tiger, Luv, Maggie May, The Au Pair Man, Have You Any Dirty Washing, Mother Dear?
PICTURES: Tiara Tahiti (debut, 1963), Life at the Top, Two Gentlemen Sharing, Wake in Fright, Outback, Billy Two Hats, The Apprenticeship of Duddy Kravitz, Fun with Dick and Jane, Who Is Killing the Great Chefs of Europe?, North Dallas Forty (also co-s.p.), First Blood, Split Image (also prod.), Uncommon Valor (also exec. prod.), Joshua Then and Now, The Check is in the Mail (prod. only), Switching Channels, Winter People, Weekend at Bernie's (also actor), Folks!, The Shooter, The Populist.
TELEVISION: *Movies*: A Family of Cops, A Husband a Wife and a Lover, Borrowed Hearts, The Return of Alex Kelly. *Specials*: Of Mice and Men, Desperate Hours, The Human Voice.

KOTEAS, ELIAS
Actor. b. Montreal, Quebec, Canada, 1961. e. AADA.
PICTURES: One Magic Christmas, Some Kind of Wonderful, Gardens of Stone, Tucker: The Man and His Dream, Full Moon in Blue Water, Malarek, Blood Red, Friends Lovers and Lunatics, Teenage Mutant Ninja Turtles, Backstreet Dreams, Desperate Hours, Look Who's Talking Too, Almost an Angel, The Adjuster, Teenage Mutant Ninja Turtles III, Chain of Desire, Camilla, Exotica, The Prophecy, Hit Me, Crash, Gattaca, The Thin Red Line, Fallen, Apt Pupil.

KOTTO, YAPHET
Actor. b. New York, NY, Nov. 15, 1937. Has many stage credits, including starring roles on Broadway in The Great White Hope, The Zulu and the Zayda. Off-B'way: Blood Knot, Black Monday, In White America, A Good Place To Raise a Boy.
PICTURES: The Limit (also prod.), 4 for Texas, Nothing But a Man, 5 Card Stud, Thomas Crown Affair, The Liberation of L. B. Jones, Man and Boy, Across 110th Street, Bone, Live and Let Die, Truck Turner, Report to the Commissioner, Sharks' Treasure, Friday Foster, Drum, Monkey Hustle, Blue Collar, Alien, Brubaker, Fighting Back, Star Chamber, Eye of the Tiger, Warning Sign, Prettykill, The Running Man, Midnight Run, Nightmare of the Devil (also prod., dir.), Terminal Entry, Jigsaw, A Whisper to a Scream, Tripwire, Ministry of Vengeance, Hangfire, Freddy's Dead, Almost Blue, Intent to Kill, The Puppet Masters, Two If By Sea.
TELEVISION: *Series*: Homicide. *Movies*: Night Chase, Raid on Entebbe, Rage, Playing With Fire, The Park Is Mine, Women of San Quentin, Badge of the Assassin, Harem, Desperado, Perry Mason: The Case of the Scandalous Scoundrel, Prime Target, After the Shock, Chrome Soldiers, It's Nothing Personal, Extreme Justice, The American Clock, The Corpse Had a Familiar Face, Deadline for Murder: From the Files of Edna Buchanan. *Guest*: Alfred Hitchcock Presents.

KOVACS, LASZLO
Cinematographer. b. Hungary, May 14, 1933. Came to U.S. 1957; naturalized 1963. e. Acad. Drama and M.P. Arts, Budapest, MA 1956.
PICTURES: Hell's Angels on Wheels, Hell's Bloody Devils, Psych Out, The Savage Seven, Targets, A Man Called Dagger, Single Room Furnished, Easy Rider, That Cold Day in the Park, Getting Straight, Alex in Wonderland, Five Easy Pieces, The Last Movie, Marriage of a Young Stockbroker, The King of Marvin Gardens, Pocket Money, What's Up Doc?, Steelyard Blues, Paper Moon, Slither, A Reflection of Fear, Huckleberry Finn, For Pete's Sake, Freebie and the Bean, Shampoo, At Long Last Love, Baby Blue Marine, Nickelodeon, Close Encounters of the Third Kind (addl. photog. only), Harry and Walter Go to New York, New York New York, F.I.S.T., The Last Waltz, Paradise Alley, Butch and Sundance: The Early Days, The Runner Stumbles, Heart Beat, Inside Moves, The Legend of the Lone Ranger, Frances, The Toy, Crackers, Ghostbusters, Mask, Legal Eagles, Little Nikita, Say Anything..., Shattered, Radio Flyer, Life With Mikey, Deception, The Next Karate Kid, The Scout, Free Willy 2: The Adventure Home, Copycat, Multiplicity, My Best Friend's Wedding, Jack Frost, Return to Me.

KOZAK, HARLEY JANE
Actress. b. Wilkes-Barre, PA, Jan. 28, 1957. e. NYU's School of the Arts. Member of Nebraska Repertory Theatre.
PICTURES: House on Sorority Row, Clean and Sober, When Harry Met Sally..., Parenthood, Sideout, Arachnophobia, Necessary Roughness, The Taking of Beverly Hills, All I Want for Christmas, The Favor, Magic in the Water.
TELEVISION: *Series*: The Guiding Light, Santa Barbara, Texas, Harts of the West, Bringing Up Jack, You Wish. *Guest*: L.A. Law, Highway to Heaven. *Movies*: So Proudly We Hail, The Amy Fisher Story, The Android Affair, Dark Planet, Unforgivable, A Friend's Betrayal. *Mini-series*: Titanic.

KOZLOWSKI, LINDA
Actress. b. 1956. m. actor Paul Hogan. Began professional acting career soon after graduating from Juilliard Sch., N.Y., 1981. Stage debut in How It All Began at the Public Theatre. In regional theatre appeared in Requiem, Translations, Make and Break, as well as on Broadway and on tour with Dustin Hoffman in Death of a Salesman and the TV adaptation.
PICTURES: Crocodile Dundee, Crocodile Dundee II, Pass the Ammo, Helena, Almost an Angel, The Neighbor, Backstreet Justice, Zorn, Village of the Damned.
TELEVISION: *Mini-Series*: Favorite Son.

KRABBE, JEROEN
Actor. b. Amsterdam, The Netherlands, Dec. 5, 1944. Trained for stage at De Toneelschool, Acad. of Dramatic Art, Amsterdam, 1965. Also studied at painting at Acad. of Fine Arts, grad. 1981. Founded touring theater co. in the Netherlands and translated plays into Dutch. Also costume designer. As a painter, work has been widely exhibited (one-man show at Francis Kyle Galleries, London). Author: The Economy Cookbook. Theatre dir. debut, new stage adaptation of The Diary of Anne Frank, 1985 in Amsterdam.
PICTURES: Soldier of Orange, A Flight of Rainbirds, Spetters, The Fourth Man, Turtle Diary, Jumpin' Jack Flash, No Mercy, The Living Daylights, Shadow of Victory, A World Apart, Crossing Delancey, Shadowman, Scandal, The Punisher, Melancholia, Till There Was You, Kafka, The Prince of Tides, For a Lost Soldier, The Fugitive, King of the Hill, Immortal Beloved, Farinelli, Blood of a Poet, Business for Pleasure, Lorca, Dangerous Beauty, Left Luggage (dir. debut).
TELEVISION: Danton's Death (debut, 1966), William of Orange, World War III. *Movies*: One for the Dancer, Family of Spies, After the War, Secret Weapon, Robin Hood (theatrical in Europe), Murder East Murder West, Dynasty: The Reunion, Stalin. *Mini-series*: The Odyssey.

KRAMER, LARRY
Writer, Producer. b. Bridgeport, CT, June 25, 1935. e. Yale U., B.A. 1957. Ent. m.p. ind. 1958. Story edit. Columbia Pictures, N.Y. London 1960-65. Asst. to David Picker and Herb Jaffe, UA, 1965. Assoc. prod. and additional dialogue Here We Go Round the Mulberry Bush, 1968. Writ. prod. Women in Love (Acad. Award nom. for s.p., 1970). Lost Horizon, 1973 (s.p.). Novel: Faggots (1978). Theater: The Normal Heart (NY Shakespeare Festival and throughout the world), Just Say No, The Destiny of Me. Cofounder: Gay Men's Health Crisis, Inc. (community AIDS org.). Founder: ACT UP: AIDS Coalition to Unleash Power (AIDS activist and protest org.). Book of Essays: Reports from the Holocaust: The Story of an AIDS Activist (St. Martin's Press, 1995).

KRAMER, SIDNEY
Sales executive. b. New York, NY, Oct. 25, 1911. e. New York Law Sch., LL.B., City Coll. of New York. Gen. sales mgr., RKO Pathe, June 1953; dir. and v.p. Cellofilm Corp. 1941-56; foreign sales mgr., RKO Radio, 1954-59; v.p. Cinemiracle Intl. 1960-61; v.p. T.P.E.A., 1960-61; foreign sls. mgr., Cinerama, Inc., 1962-65; exec. Commonwealth Theatres, Puerto Rico, Inc., 1965-68; exec. v.p. Cobian Jr. Enterprises Inc. 1968; m.p. consultant, exhibition, dist., foreign and Caribbean area, 1968-70; pres. Coqui Int'l Inc.; 1970-80; v.p. of UAPR, Inc., Puerto Rico, U.A. Communications, Inc. 1981-91. Retired.

KRAMER, STANLEY E.
Producer, Director. b. New York, NY, Sept. 29, 1913. e. NYU, B.Sc., 1933. Entered m.p. ind. via backlot jobs; with MGM research dept.; film cutter 3 yrs.; film ed.; m.p. & radio writer; served in U.S Signal Corps, 1st Lt. during WWII. Recipient of Irving G. Thalberg Award, 1961. Autobiography, A Mad Mad Mad Mad World, 1997.
PICTURES: *Assoc. Prod.*: So Ends Our Night, The Moon and Sixpence. *Producer*: So This Is New York, Champion, Home of the Brave, The Men, Cyrano de Bergerac, Death of a Salesman, High Noon, My Six Convicts, The Sniper, The Four Poster, The Happy Time, Eight Iron Men, The 5000 Fingers of Dr. T, The Wild One, The Juggler, Caine Mutiny, Pressure Point, A Child Is Waiting, Invitation to a Gunfighter. *Dir./Prod.*: Not as a Stranger (dir. debut, 1955), The Pride and the Passion, The Defiant Ones, On the Beach, Inherit the Wind, Judgment at Nuremberg, It's a Mad Mad Mad Mad World, Ship of Fools, Guess Who's Coming to Dinner, The Secret of Santa Vittoria, R.P.M., Bless the Beasts and Children, Oklahoma Crude, The Domino Principle, The Runner Stumbles.
TELEVISION: Guess Who's Coming to Dinner? (pilot), The Rosenberge: The Trial of Lt. Calley, The Trial of General Yamashito.

KRANE, JONATHAN
Executive. b. 1952. m. actress Sally Kellerman. e. St. Johns Coll. grad. with honors, 1972; Yale Law Sch., 1976. Joined Blake Edwards Entertainment in 1981, becoming pres. Formed talent management co. Management Company Entertainment Group representing clients such as John Travolta, Sally Kellerman, Kathryn Harrold, Sandra Bernhard, Howie Mandel, Drew Barrymore, others. Began producing vehicles for clients and transformed co. into production, distribution, management and finance co. Chairman and chief exec. officer, Management Company Entertainment Group (MCEG).
PICTURES: *Exec. prod./prod.*: Boardwalk, Honeymoon, Fly Away Home, The Man Who Loved Women, Micki & Maude, A Fine Mess, That's Life, The Chocolate War, The Experts, Fatal Charm, Boris and Natasha, Look Who's Talking, Chud II: Bud the Chud, Without You I'm Nothing (prod.), Look Who's Talking Too, Convicts, Cold Heaven, Breaking the Rules, Look Who's Talking Now, Face/Off, Lay of the Land, Primary Colors, Mad City, The General's Daughter, Battlefield Earth, Lucky Numbers, Bar Hopping.

TELEVISION: *Prod.*: Howie Mandel Life at Carnegie Hall, Howie Mandel: The North American Watusi Tour.

KRANTZ, STEVE
Executive. b. New York, NY, May 20, 1923. m. novelist Judith Krantz. e. Columbia U., B.A. Dir. progs., NBC, New York, 1953; dir. prog. dev., Screen Gems, N.Y., 1955; v.p., gen. mgr. Screen Gems, Canada, 1958; dir. int. sls., 1960; formed Steve Krantz Productions, Inc. 1964.
PICTURES: *Producer*: Fritz the Cat, Heavy Traffic, The Nine Lives of Fritz the Cat, Cooley High, Ruby, Which Way Is Up?, Jennifer. Swap Meet (also writer).
TELEVISION: *Series*: Steve Allen Show, Kate Smith Show, Hazel, Dennis the Menace, Winston Churchill—The Valiant Years, Marvel Super Heroes, Rocket Robin Hood. *Mini-series*: Princess Daisy, Sins, Mistral's Daughter, I'll Take Manhattan. *Movies*: Dadah is Death (exec. prod.), Till We Meet Again, Deadly Medicine, Deadly Matrimony, Torch Song, Jack Reed: Badge of Honor, House of Secrets, Children of the Dark, Dazzle.

KREUGER, KURT
Actor. b. St. Moritz, Switzerland, July 23, 1917. e. U. of Lausanne, Polytechnic. London. Came to U.S. 1937, partner in travel bureau: acted in Wharf Theat. group. Cape Cod, 1939; Broadway debut in Candle in the Wind with Helen Hayes, 1941.
PICTURES: The Moon Is Down, Edge of Darkness, The Strange Death of Adolph Hitler, Sahara, Mademoiselle Fifi, None Shall Escape, Escape in the Desert, Hotel Berlin, Paris Underground, The Spider, Dark Corner, Unfaithfully Yours, Spy Hunt, Fear, The Enemy Below, Legion of the Doomed, What Did You Do in the War Daddy?, The St. Valentine's Day Massacre.

KRIGE, ALICE
Actress. b. Upington, South Africa. Moved to London at 21 and studied at Central School of Speech and Drama. Professional debut on British TV: The Happy Autumn Fields. In London prod. of Forever Yours, Maylou. West End debut, Arms and the Man, 1981. Two seasons with Royal Shakespeare Co. at Stratford and London (The Tempest, King Lear, The Taming of the Shrew, Cyrano de Bergerac, Bond's Lear.), Venice Preserved at the Almeida, 1995.
PICTURES: Chariots of Fire (debut, 1981), Ghost Story, King David, Barfly, Haunted Summer, See You in the Morning, S.P.O.O.K.S., Sleepwalkers, Habitat, Institute Benjamenta, Amanda, Star Trek: First Contact, Twilight of the Icenymphs, The Commissioner.
TELEVISION: *Movies*: Wallenberg: A Hero's Story, Dream West, A Tale of Two Cities, Second Serve, Baja Oklahoma, Max and Helen, Iran: Days of Crisis, Ladykiller, Judgment Day: The John List Story, Double Deception, Jack Reed: Badge of Honor, Scarlet & Black, Sharpes Honour, Summer, Devil's Advocate, Donor Unknown, Joseph, Hidden in America, Like Father Like Son, Indefensible: The Truth About Edward Brannigan. *Mini-Series*: Ellis Island, Close Relations.

KRISTOFFERSON, KRIS
Actor, Singer. b. Brownsville, TX, June 22, 1936. e. Pomona Coll., Oxford U. (Rhodes Scholar). Joined U.S. Army briefly and taught English literature at West Point. Started writing songs (country music), hits have included Me and Bobby McGee, Why Me, Lord, Sunday Mornin' Comin' Down.
PICTURES: The Last Movie (debut, 1971), Cisco Pike, Pat Garrett and Billy the Kid, Blume in Love, Bring Me the Head of Alfredo Garcia, Alice Doesn't Live Here Anymore, Vigilante Force, The Sailor Who Fell from Grace with the Sea, A Star Is Born, Semi-Tough, Convoy, Heaven's Gate, Rollover, Flashpoint, Songwriter, Trouble in Mind, Big Top Pee-wee, Millennium, Welcome Home, Original Intent, Night of the Cyclone, Sandino, No Place to Hide, Cheatin' Hearts, Lone Star, Fire Down Below, A Soldier's Daughter Never Cries, Girls' Night, Blade, Dance with Me, Limbo, The Joyriders, Payback, Molokai: The Story of Father Damien, Detox.
TELEVISION: *Movies/Mini-Series*: Freedom Road, The Lost Honor of Kathryn Beck, The Last Days of Frank and Jesse James, Blood and Orchids, Stagecoach, The Tracker, Dead or Alive, Pair of Aces, Another Pair of Aces, Miracle in the Wilderness, Christmas in Connecticut, Troubleshooters: Trapped Beneath the Earth, Big Dreams & Broken Hearts: The Dottie West Story, Tad, Outlaw Justice, Two for Texas. *Mini-Series*: Amerika, Netforce.

KRONICK, WILLIAM
Writer, Director. b. Amsterdam, NY. e. Columbia Coll., A.B. U.S. Navy photography; wrote, dir. featurette, A Bowl of Cherries.
PICTURES: Nights in White Satin (s.p.), Horowitz in Dublin (dir., s.p.), Flash Gordon and King Kong (2nd unit dir.).
TELEVISION: *Documentaries: Wrote, dir., prod.*: The Ultimate Stuntman: a Tribute to Dar Robinson, To the Ends of the Earth, Mysteries of the Great Pyramid; George Plimpton Specials; National Geographic, Ripley's Believe It or Not, The World's Greatest Stunts. *Prod.*: In Search of... Series. *Dir.*: (movie) The 500 Pound Jerk.

KRUEGER, RONALD P.
Executive. b. St. Louis, MO, Oct. 19, 1940. e. Westminister Coll., 1961. Began working in theatres as a teenager. Assumed presidency Wehrenberg Theatres, 1963. Member: NATO, bd. member; American Film Inst.; Motion Picture Pioneers; Demolay Legion of Honor; Mercantile Bank, bd. member; Big Game Hunters; World Presidents Org. Bd. trustees, Westminster Col. at Fulton, MO. Divan member. Moolah Temple Shrine. Past Master Tuscan Lodge 360 AF & AM. Scottish Rite 32 KCCH. Advisory bd. chmn., Salvation Army. Recipient of the NATO B.V. Sturdiviant award for Community Svc. Member & past pres. of Safari Club Intl.

KRUGER, HARDY
Actor, Writer. b. Berlin, Germany, April 12, 1928. Ent. m.p. ind. 1943; on stage since 1945. Starred in approx. 25 German films). Has published 11 books, novels, travelogues.
PICTURES: The One That Got Away, Bachelor of Hearts, The Rest Is Silence (German film of Hamlet), Blind Date, Taxi Pour Tobrouk, Sundays and Cybele, Hatari! (U.S. debut, 1963), Le Gros Coup, Les Pianos Mecaniques (The Uninhibited), Le Chant du Monde, Flight of the Phoenix, The Defector, La Grande Sauterelle, Le Franciscain de Bourges, The Nun of Monza, The Secret of Santa Vittoria, The Battle of Neretva, The Red Tent, Night Hair Child, Death of a Stranger, Barry Lyndon, Paper Tiger, Un Solitaire, Potato Fritz, A Bridge Too Far, L'Autopsie d'un Monstre, The Wild Geese, Society Limited, Wrong Is Right, The Inside Man.
TELEVISION: *Mini-Series*: War and Remembrance. Series: Globetrotter (writer, prod; 1986).

KUDROW, LISA
Actress. e. Vassar College, NY, B.S., in biology. Member of The Groundlings improvisational theatre group, 1989-.
PICTURES: L.A. on $5 a Day, The Unborn, Dance with Death, In the Heat of Passion, Unfaithful, Behind Closed Doors, The Crazysitter, Mother, Hacks, Romy and Michele's High School Reunion, Clockwatchers, The Opposite of Sex, I Dream of Jeannie, Analyze This.
TELEVISION: *Series*: Bob, Mad About You, Friends (Emmy Award, 1998), Hercules (voice). *Guest*: Cheers, Newhart, Life Goes On, Coach, Flying Blind, Hope & Gloria, The Simpsons (voice).

KUHN, THOMAS G.
Executive/Executive Producer. e. Northwestern U., B.A.; USC, M.B.A. KNBC-TV sales; NBC business affairs; dir. live night time progs. Warner Bros. TV, v.p. prod. TV *Exec. prod.*: Alice, The Awakening Land, Torn Between Two Lovers, The Jayne Mansfield Story, Long Way Home. Pres., RCA Video Prods. Pres., Lightyear Ent., 1987. *Exec. prod.*: Aria, The Return of Swamp Thing, Heaven, The Lemon Sisters, Stories to Remember. With partner Fred Weintraub: The JFK Assassination: The Jim Garrison Tapes, Trouble Bound, Gypsy Eyes, Backstreet Justice, Guinevere, Triplecross, Young Ivanhoe, Young Connecticut Yankee, Undertow, Playboy's Really Naked Truth, Iron Fist, Bruce Lee: Curse of the Dragon, Triplecross, The New Adventures of Robin Hood.

KUREISHI, HANIF
Writer. b. South London, Eng., Dec. 5, 1956. e. King's Coll. (philosophy). At 18, first play presented at Royal Court Theatre where he ushered before becoming writer in residence. Early in career, wrote pornography as Antonia French. Stage and TV plays include: The Mother Country, Outskirts, Borderline and adaptations (Mother Courage). The Rainbow Sign, With Your Tongue Down My Throat (novella) and short stories have been pub. Anglo-Pakistani writer's first s.p. My Beautiful Laundrette earned Acad. Award nom., 1986 and began creative relationship with dir. Stephen Frears.
PICTURES: My Beautiful Laundrette, Sammy and Rosie Get Laid, London Kills Me (also dir.).

KURI, EMILE
Set Decorator. b. Cuernavaca, Mex., June 11, 1907. e. Chaminade Coll., 1924-27. Career began with 50 Hopalong Cassidy episodes for Harry Sherman. Under contract to Selznick Intl., Liberty Films, and Walt Disney Prods., supv. all film and tv sets, and all decor for both Disneyland and Disney World.
PICTURES: 71 films incl.: The Silver Queen (Acad. Award nom.), I'll Be Seeing You, Spellbound, It's a Wonderful Life, Duel in the Sun, Paradine Case, The Heiress (Acad. Award, 1949), Fancy Pants, A Place in the Sun, Carrie (Acad. Award nom.), The War of the Worlds, Shane, The Actress, Executive Suite (Acad. Award nom.), 20,000 Leagues Under the Sea (Acad. Award, 1954), Old Yeller, The Absent-Minded Professor (Acad. Award nom.), The Parent Trap, Mary Poppins (Acad. Award nom.), Bedknobs & Broomsticks (Acad. Award nom.).
TELEVISION: 15 seasons of The Wonderful World of Disney (Emmy Award, 1963), The Academy Awards (1960-70).

KURI, JOHN A.
Producer, Writer. b. Los Angeles, CA, Feb. 16, 1945. Son of set decorator and Disneyland co-designer, Emile Kuri. Began 13 yr. employment with Disney at age 16 in construction and maintenance at Disneyland. Progressed through mgmt. in Park Operations. 1969 transferred to Disney Studios in set decorating. 1973 became art director. 1975 at 20th Century Fox as exec. asst. to prod. Irwin Allen. 1976, formed own co., wrote and prod. both television and motion picture projects. 1979 thru 1982 developed and prod. television in partnership with Ron Howard. 1988 thru 1990 as pres. of Sheffield Ent. developed master broadcasting plan for KCMY TV, Sacramento, CA. Published works: Determined to Live: An American Epic, Remember Wes.
PICTURES: Captive Hearts (prod., co-s.p. 2nd unit dir., co-lyrics.) *Set decorator*: Apple Dumpling Gang, Leadbelly, Report to the Commissioner, Castaway Cowboy, Superdad, Mad Mad Movie Makers.
TELEVISION: One More Mountain (prod., writer, 2nd unit dir.; Christopher Award, 1994), Conagher (prod.; Western Heritage Award from Cowboy Hall of Fame), O'Hara (co-creator of series), Airwolf (2nd unit prod., dir.), Skyward (prod., 2nd unit dir.; Golden Halo Award), Skyward Christmas (prod., 2nd unit dir.), Through the Magic Pyramid (assoc. prod., art dir.). Art dir.: The Plutonium Incident, Scared Straight Another Story, Young Love First Love, Marriage is Alive and Well, Little Shots, The Red Pony (and set decorator, Emmy nom., 1973). Set decorator: Michael O'Hara IV, The Mouse Factory (22 episodes).

KURTZ, GARY
Producer, Director. b. Los Angeles, CA, July 27, 1940. e. USC Cinema Sch. Began prof. career during college. Has worked as cameraman, soundman, editor, prod. supervisor and asst. dir. on documentaries and features. Worked on many low budget features for Roger Corman including: The Terror, Beach Ball, Track of the Vampire, Planet of Blood, The Shooting, Ride in the Whirlwind. Drafted into Marines. Spent 2 yrs. in photo field as cameraman, editor and still photo.
PICTURES: The Hostage (prod. spvr., ed.), Two-Lane Blacktop (line prod.), Chandler (line prod.), American Graffiti (co.-prod.); Star Wars (prod.), The Empire Strikes Back (prod.), The Dark Crystal (prod., 2nd unit dir.), Return to Oz (exec. prod.), Slipstream (prod.) The Steal (prod.), 5-25-77 (prod.).

KURTZ, SWOOSIE
Actress. b. Omaha, NE. e. Studied at U. Southern Calif., London Acad. of Music and Dramatic Art.
THEATER: A History of the American Film (Drama Desk Award), Ah Wilderness (Tony nom.), Who's Afraid of Virginia Woolf? (with Mike Nichols and Elaine May), The Effect of Gamma Rays on Man-in-the Moon Marigolds, Fifth of July (Tony, Outer Critics Circle & Drama Desk Awards), House of Blue Leaves (Tony and Obie Awards), Uncommon Women and Others (Obie & Drama Desk Awards), Hunting Cockroaches (Drama League nom.), Six Degrees of Separation, Lips Together Teeth Apart.
PICTURES: Slap Shot, First Love, Oliver's Story, The World According to Garp, Against All Odds, Wildcats, True Stories, Vice Versa, Bright Lights Big City, Dangerous Liaisons, Stanley and Iris, A Shock to the System, Reality Bites, Storybook, Citizen Ruth, Liar Liar, Outside Ozona, The White River Kid, Cruel Intentions.
TELEVISION: *Series*: As the World Turns (1971), Mary, Love Sidney (Emmy noms.), Sisters (Emmy & SAG noms), Suddenly Susan. *Movies*: Walking Through the Fire, Marriage Is Alive and Well, Mating Season, A Caribbean Mystery, Guilty Conscience, A Time to Live, Baja Oklahoma (Golden Globe nom.), The Image (Emmy & Cable ACE noms.), Terror on Track 9, The Positively True Adventures of the Alleged Texas Cheerleader-Murdering Mom, And the Band Played On (Emmy & Cable Ace noms.), One Christmas, Betrayed: A Story of Three Women, A Promise to Carolyn, Little Girls in Pretty Boxes, My Own Country, More Tales of the City. *Specials*: Uncommon Women, Fifth of July, House of Blue Leaves, The Visit (Trying Times). *Guest*: Kojak, Carol & Company (Emmy Award, 1990).

KURYS, DIANE
Director, Writer. b. Lyons, France, Dec. 3, 1948. In 1970 joined Jean-Louis Barrault's theatre group, acted for 8 years on stage, television and film. Adapted and translated staged plays. 1977, wrote screenplay for Dibolo Menthe (Peppermint Soda) which she also directed and co-prod. Film won Prix Louis Deluc, Best Picture. Co-prod. Alexandre Arcady's Coup de Sirocco and Le Grand Pardon.
PICTURES: *Dir./Writer*: Peppermint Soda (also co-prod.), Cocktail Molotov, Entre Nous, A Man in Love, C'est la vie, Apres L'amour, Six Days Six Nights.

KUSHNER, DONALD
Producer, Executive. Exec. producer, all programming produced by Kushner Locke; producer, Tron, 1982. Currently co-chairman, co-CEO, & secretary, Kushner-Locke, 1983.

KUSTURICA, EMIR
Director. b. Sarajevo, Yugoslavia, 1955. e. FAMU.
PICTURES: Do You Remember Dolly Bell? (debut, 1981; Golden Lion Award at Venice Film Fest.), When Father Was Away on Business (Golden Palme at Cannes Film Fest., 1985), Time of the Gypsies (also co-s.p.), Arizona Dream, Underground (Golden Palme at Cannes Film Fest., 1995), White Cat Black Cat.

KWAN, NANCY
Actress. b. Hong Kong, May 19, 1939. Trained as dancer at British Royal Ballet.
PICTURES: The World of Suzie Wong (debut, 1960), Flower Drum Song, The Main Attraction, Tamahine, Fate Is the Hunter, The Wild Affair, Honeymoon Hotel, Arrivederci Baby, Lt. Robin Crusoe USN, The Corrupt Ones, Nobody's Perfect, The Wrecking Crew, The Girl Who Knew Too Much, The McMasters, Girl From Peking, Supercock, The Pacific Connection, Project: Kill, Night Creature, Streets of Hong Kong, Angkor, Walking the Edge, Night Children, Cold Dog Soup, Dragon: The Bruce Lee Story, Mr. P's Dancing Sushi Bar.
TELEVISION: *Movies*: The Last Ninja, Blade in Hong Kong, Miracle Landing.

KWIETNIOWSKI, RICHARD
Director. b. London, England, March 17, 1957.
PICTURES: Alfalfa, Ballad of Reading Gaol, Flames of Passion, Proust's Favorite Fantasy, Cost of Love, Actions Speak Louder Than Words, I Was a Jewish Sex Work (D.P. only), Love and Death on Long Island (also s.p.).

KWIT, NATHANIEL TROY, JR.
Executive. b. New York, NY, May 29, 1941. e. Cornell U., B.A.; NYU, M.B.A. 1964-68, American Broadcasting Co., Inc., exec. asst. to pres. of ABC Films. 1968-71, National Screen Service Corp., New York branch mgr., asst. genl. sls. mgr. 1971, founder, CEO Audience Marketing, Inc., later acquired by Viacom International as operating subsidiary. 1974 named v.p. marketing services, Warner Bros., Inc. 1979, named v.p. in charge video and special markets division, United Artists Corp.; 1981, named sr. v.p. in chg. UA television, video, special market div. Following acquisition of UA Corp. by MGM in 1981 promoted to pres., dist. & mktg. for MGM/UA Entertainment Co. 1983, pres. & CEO, United Satellite Communications, direct broadcast TV co. 1986, founder, pres. Palladium Entertainment, Inc.

L

LaBUTE, NEIL
Director, Writer. b. Detroit, MI, March 19, 1963. Graduate of Brigham Young University Theatre and Film program.
PICTURES: In the Company of Men, Your Friends & Neighbors, Nurse Betty (dir. only), Possession.
TELEVISION: Bash: Latter Day Plays.

LACHMAN, ED
Cinematographer. b. 1948. Son of a Morristown, NJ movie theater owner. e. Ohio U., BFA. Filmed documentaries Ornette: Made in America, Strippers, Huie's Sermon. Assisted Sven Nykvist on King of the Gypsies, Hurricane; Vittorio Storaro on Luna; Robby Muller on The American Friend and They All Laughed. Co-director of photography on Werner Herzog's La Soufriere and Stroszek and Wim Wenders' Lightning Over Water and A Tokyo Story.
PICTURES: Scalpel, Union City, Say Amen Somebody, Little Wars, Split Cherry Tree, Strippers, The Little Sister, Insignificance (American sequences) Desperately Seeking Susan, True Stories, Making Mr. Right, Chuck Berry: Hail Hail Rock 'n' Roll, Less Than Zero, El Dia Que Me Quieras, Mississippi Masala, Light Sleeper, London Kills Me, My New Gun, My Family/Mi Familia, Selena, Why Do Fools Fall In Love, The Virgin Suicides, The Limey, Erin Brockovich.
TELEVISION: Get Your Kicks on Route 66 (dir., cinematography, American Playhouse.), A Gathering of Old Men, Backtrack.

LACK, ANDREW
Executive. b. New York, NY, May 16, 1947. e. Sorbonne, Boston Univ. School of Fine Arts (BFA). Starting in 1976, worked at CBS as prod. for Who's Who, 60 Minutes, CBS Reports. 1981, named sr. prod. of CBS Reports and CBS News correspondent, 1983 became exec. prod. Exec. prod. and creator of Face to Face with Connie Chung, West 57th, Crossroads, Our Times With Bill Moyers. Exec. prod. of Street Stories, specials The 20th Anniversary of Watergate, Malcolm X. 1993, appointed pres. of NBC News.

LADD, JR., ALAN
Executive. b. Los Angeles, CA, Oct. 22, 1937. Son of late actor Alan Ladd. M. P. agent, Creative Mgmt. Associates, 1963-69.; m.p. prod., 1969-73. Joined 20th Century-Fox in 1973 in chg. of creative affairs in feature div.; promoted to v.p., prod., 1974; 1975, named sr. v.p. for worldwide prod.; 1976, promoted to pres. of 20th Century-Fox Pictures. Resigned & formed The Ladd Co., 1979. 1985, appt. pres. & COO, MGM/UA Ent. Film Corp; appt. chmn. of bd., CEO, MGM Pictures Inc., 1986; resigned 1988. 1989, named co-chmn. Pathe Communications Corp. and chmn., CEO, Pathe Ent.; chmn., & CEO, MGM-Pathe Ent., 1989-92; chmn. & CEO MGM-Pathe Comm. Co., 1991-92; co-chmn. & co-CEO, MGM, 1992-93. Founded Ladd Pictures.
PICTURES: *Prod.*: Walking Stick, A Severed Head, Tam Lin, Villian, Zee and Co., Fear Is the Key, Braveheart (Acad. Award), The Phantom, A Very Brady Sequel. *Exec. prod.*: Nightcomers, Vice Versa, The Brady Bunch Movie.

LADD, CHERYL
Actress. r.n. Cheryl Stoppelmoor. b. Huron, S.D., July 12, 1951. Joined professional Music Shop Band while in high school; after graduation toured with group ending up in Los Angeles. Cast as voice of Melody character in animated Josie and the Pussycats. Studied acting with Milton Katselas. Did TV commercials, small parts in TV. Film debut 1972 in Jamaica Reef (unreleased).
PICTURES: Purple Hearts, Now and Forever, Millennium, Lisa, Poison Ivy, Permanent Midnight, Perfect Little Angels, A Dog of Flanders.
TELEVISION: *Series*: The Ken Berry "Wow" Show, Charlie's Angels, One West Waikiki. *Specials*: Ben Vereen... His Roots, General Electric's All-Star Anniversary, John Denver and the Ladies; The Cheryl Ladd Special, Looking Back: Souvenirs, Scenes From a Special. *Guest*: Police Woman, Happy Days, Switch. *Movies*: Satan's School for Girls, When She Was Bad, Grace Kelly Story, Romance on the Orient Express, A Death in California, Crossings, Deadly Care, Bluegrass, Kentucky Woman, Jekyll & Hyde, The Fulfillment of Mary Gray, The Girl Who Came Between Them, Crash: The Mystery of Flight 1501, Danielle Steel's Changes, Locked Up: A Mother's Rage, Dead Before Dawn, Broken Promises: Taking Emily Back, Dancing With Danger, The Haunting of Lisa, Kiss & Tell, Tangled Web, Kiss and Tell, Every Mother's Worst Fear, Michael Landon: The Father I Knew.

LADD, DAVID ALAN
Actor, Producer, Motion Picture Executive. b. Los Angeles, CA, Feb. 5, 1947. e. USC. Son of late actor Alan Ladd. Exec. v.p. motion picture prod. at Pathe Entertainment and MGM.
PICTURES: *Actor*: The Big Land, The Proud Rebel (Golden Globe Award), The Sad Horse, A Dog of Flanders, Raymie, Misty, R.P.M., Catlow, Deathline (Raw Meat), The Klansman, The Day of the Locust, Wild Geese. Producer: The Serpent and the Rainbow.
TELEVISION: *Guest*: Zane Gray Theatre, Wagon Train, Pursuit, Ben Casey, Gunsmoke, Love American Style (pilot), Kojak, Emergency, Tom Sawyer, Bonanza, Quest, Police Story, Medical Story, etc. *Producer*: When She Was Bad, ABC Variety specials.

LADD, DIANE
Actress. r.n. Diane Rose Lanier. b. Meridian, MS. Daughter is actress Laura Dern. e. St. Aloysius Acad.; trained for stage with Curt Conway and Frank Corsaro. Member of Actors Studio. Worked as model, singer and as Copacabana nightclub dancer. At 17 in touring co. of Hatful of Rain. NY debut: Orpheus Descending.
THEATER: Carry Me Back to Morningside Heights, One Night Stands of a Noisy Passenger. The Wall, The Goddess, The Fantastiks, Women Speak, Texas Trilogy; Lu Ann Hampton Laverty, Love Letters.
PICTURES: Wild Angels (debut, 1966), Rebel Rousers, The Reivers, Macho Calahan, WUSA, White Lightning, Chinatown, Alice Doesn't Live Here Anymore (Acad. Award nom.), Embryo, All Night Long, Sweetwater, The Reivers, Something Wicked This Way Comes, Black Widow, Plain Clothes, National Lampoon's Christmas Vacation, Wild at Heart (Acad. Award nom.), A Kiss Before Dying, Rambling Rose (Acad. Award nom.), The Cemetery Club, Forever, Carnosaur, Hold Me Thrill Me Kiss Me, Father Hood, Ghost of Mississippi, Primary Colors, Can't Be Heaven, 28 Days.
TELEVISION: *Movies*: The Devil's Daughter, Black Beauty, Thaddeus Rose and Eddie, Willa, Guyana Tragedy, Desperate Lives, Grace Kelly, Crime of Innocence, Bluegrass, Rock Hudson, The Lookalike, Shadow of a Doubt, Hush Little Baby, Mrs. Munck (also dir., writer), The Staircase, Late Last Night. *Guest*: Hazel, Gunsmoke, City of Angels, The Love Boat, Dr. Quinn Medicine Woman (pilot), Grace Under Fire, Touched By An Angel. *Series*: The Secret Storm, Alice (Golden Globe Award). *Special*: The Gift.

LAFFERTY, PERRY
Executive. b. Davenport, IA, Oct. 3, 1920. e. Yale U. With CBS-TV as v.p., programs, Hollywood, 1965-76. Sr. v.p., programs and talent, west coast, for NBC Entertainment, 1979-85.
TELEVISION: Maybe Baby (exec. prod.), Murder C.O.D. (exec. prod.), An Early Frost (prod.).

LaGRAVENESE, RICHARD
Writer. b. Brooklyn, NY, Oct.30, 1959.
PICTURES: Rude Awakening, The Fisher King (also actor, Acad. Award nom.), The Ref (also prod.), A Little Princess, The Bridges of Madison County, Unstrung Heroes, The Mirror has Two Faces, The Kiss (also dir.), The Horse Whisperer, Defective Detective.

LAHTI, CHRISTINE
Actress. b. Birmingham, MI, April 4, 1950. m. dir. Thomas Schlamme. e. U. of Michigan. Trained for stage at Herbert Berghof Studios with Uta Hagen. TV commercials. As a mime, performed with Edinburgh Scotland's Travis Theatre. N.Y. stage debut in The Woods, 1978.
THEATER: The Zinger, Hooter (Playwrights Horizon), Loose Ends, Division St., The Woods (Theatre World Award), Scenes and Revelations, Present Laughter, The Lucky Spot, Summer and Smoke (LA), The Heidi Chronicles, Three Hotels.
PICTURES: ...And Justice For All (debut, 1979), Whose Life Is It Anyway?, Ladies and Gentlemen the Fabulous Stains, Swing Shift (Acad. Award nom.), Just Between Friends, Housekeeping, Stacking, Running on Empty, Miss Firecracker (cameo), Gross Anatomy, Funny About Love, The Doctor, Leaving Normal, Hideaway, Pie in the Sky. *Director:* Lieberman In Love (short; Academy Award).
TELEVISION: *Series:* Chicago Hope (Golden Globe Award, Emmy Award, 1998). *Movies*: Dr. Scorpion, The Last Tenant, The Henderson Monster, The Executioner's Song, Love Lives On, Single Bars Single Women, No Place Like Home, Crazy From the Heart, The Fear Inside, The Good Fight, The Four Diamonds, A Weekend in the Country, Subway Stories: Tales from the Underground, Hope, Judgment Day: The Ellie Nesler Story, An American Daughter. *Mini-Series*: Amerika.

LAI, FRANCIS
Composer. b. France, April 26, 1932.
PICTURES: A Man and a Woman, I'll Never Forget What's 'is Name, The Bobo, Three Into Two Won't Go, Hello Goodbye, Hannibal Brooks, The Games, Mayerling, House of Cards, Rider on the Rain, Love Story (Academy Award, 1970), Le Petit Matin, Another Man, Another Chance, Wanted: Babysitter, Bilitis, The Good and the Bad, Widow's Nest, Cat and Mouse, The Body of My Enemy, Emmanuelle 2; The Forbidden Room, International Velvet, Oliver's Story, Passion Flower Hotel, Robert and Robert, The Small Timers, By the Blood Brothers, Beyond the Reef, Bolero, A Second Chance, Edith and Marcel, My New Partner, Marie, A Man and a Woman: 20 Years Later, Bernadette, Itinerary of a Spoiled Child., Der Aten (The Spirit), La Belle Histoire.
TELEVISION: The Berlin Affair, The Sex Symbol, Sins.

LAKE, RICKI
Actress. b. New York, NY, Sept. 21, 1968. e. Manhattan's Professional Children's School. Won role in Hairspray while attending Ithaca Col. Theatre in LA: A Girl's Guide to Chaos.
PICTURES: Hairspray (debut, 1988), Working Girl, Starlight: A Musical Movie, Cookie, Cry-Baby, Last Exit to Brooklyn, Where the Day Takes You, Inside Monkey Zetterland, Cabin Boy, Serial Mom, Skinner, Mrs. Winterbourne.
TELEVISION: *Series*: China Beach, Ricki Lake (synd. talk show). *Movies*: Babycakes, The Chase, Based on an Untrue Story, Jackie's Back!, Murder She Purred.

LAM, RINGO
Director. e. York University, Toronto. Started training as an actor in 1973 but switched to production as asst. until 1976, then as TV dir. until 1978. In 1981 he returned to Hong Kong and two years later made his dir. debut with Esprit D'Amour.
PICTURES: The Other Side of a Gentleman, Cupid One, Aces Go Places IV: Mad Mission, City on Fire, Prison on Fire, School on Fire, Wild Search, Undeclared War, Touch and Go, Prison on Fire II, Full Contact, Twin Dragons, Burning Paradise (Rape of the Red Temple), The Adventurers, The Exchange, Full Alert, The Suspect.

LAMARR, HEDY
Actress. r.n. Hedwig Kiesler. b. Vienna, Austria, Nov. 9, 1915. Started in films as script girl, bit player before gaining fame for role in 1933 Czech prod. Ecstasy. To Hollywood, 1938. Autobiography: Ecstasy and Me (1966).
PICTURES: Ecstasy, Algiers (U.S. debut, 1938), Lady of the Tropics, I Take This Woman, Boom Town, Comrade X, Come Live With Me, Ziegfeld Girl, H. M. Pulham Esq., Tortilla Flat, Crossroads, White Cargo, The Heavenly Body, The Conspirators, Experiment Perilous, Her Highness and the Bellboy, The Strange Woman, Dishonored Lady, Let's Live a Little, Samson and Delilah, A Lady Without a Passport, Copper Canyon, My Favorite Spy, Love of 3 Queens, The Story of Mankind, The Female Animal.
(d. January 19, 2000)

LAMAS, LORENZO
Actor. b. Los Angeles, CA, Jan. 20, 1958. e. Santa Monica City Coll. Son of the late actor Fernando Lamas and actress Arlene Dahl. Studied at Tony Barr's Film Actors Workshop (Burbank Studios). Appeared on commercials for Diet Coke, BVD, Coors (Hispanic).
PICTURES: Grease, Tilt, Take Down, Body Rock, Snakeater, Night of the Warrior, Snakeater II, Final Impact, Snakeater III: His Law, Killing Streets, The Swordsman, Bounty Tracker, Final Round, Bad Blood.
TELEVISION: *Series*: California Fever, Secrets of Midland Heights, Falcon Crest, Dancin' to the Hits (host), Renegade. *Guest*: The Love Boat, Switch, Sword of Justice, The Hitchhiker, Dear John. *Movies*: Detour to Terror, CIA: Code Name Alexa, C.I.A.: Target Alexa II.

LAMBERT, CHRISTOPHER (also CHRISTOPHE)
Actor, Producer. b. New York , NY, Mar. 29, 1957; reared in Geneva; parents French. Studied at Paris Conservatoire Drama Academy.

PICTURES: La Bar du Telephone (debut, 1981), Putain d'Historie d'Amour, Legitime Violence, Greystoke: The Legend of Tarzan Lord of the Apes, Love Songs, Subway (Cesar Award), Highlander, I Love You, The Sicilian, Love Dream, To Kill a Priest, Un Plan d'Enfer, Why Me?, Highlander 2: The Quickening, Priceless Beauty, Knight Moves, Fortress, Gunmen, Road Flower, Highlander III: The Sorcerer, The Hunted, Nine Months (exec. prod. only), Mortal Kombat, North Star (also exec. prod.), When Saturday Comes (exec. prod. only).

LAMBERT, MARY
Director. b. Arkansas. e. attended U. of Denver, Rhode Island Sch. of Design where began making short films. Worked in variety of prod. jobs before moving to L.A. and directing TV commercials and music videos (includ. Madonna's Material Girl, Like a Virgin, Like a Prayer, others for Sting, Janet Jackson and Mick Jagger).
PICTURES: Siesta, Pet Sematary, Pet Sematary 2.
TELEVISION: *Movie*: Dragstrip Girl, Face of Evil, My Stepson My Lover, Clubland.

LAMBERT, VERITY
Producer. b. London, England, Nov. 27. Ent. TV 1961; prod. Dr. Who, Adam Adamant Lives, Detective, Somerset Maugham (all BBC series). Since 1971: (series), Budgie, Between The Wars. 1974: Appt. controller of Drama, Thames Television. 1979: Chief exec. Euston Films. 1983: Director of Production Thorn EMI Films Ltd. Relinquished her position as controller of Drama Thames Television and retained position as chief exec., Euston Films. Became indep. prod. developing projects for film and TV incl. BBC. Founded own company, Cinema Verity Ltd., 1985.
PICTURES: Link, Morons from Outer Space, Restless Natives, Dreamchild, Not for Publication, Clockwise, A Cry in the Dark.
TELEVISION: May to December, The Boys from the Bush, Sleepers, GBH, So Haunt Me, Comics, Coasting, Sam Saturday, Running Late, Class Act, She's Out, Heavy Weather.

LAMONT, PETER
Production designer.
PICTURES: Watch Your Stern, Night of the Eagle, This Sporting Life, On Her Majesty's Secret Service, Daimonds Are Forever, Sleuth, Live and Let Die, The Dove, The Main with the Golden Gun, Inside Out, Seven-Per-Cent Solution, The Spy Who Loved Me, The Boys from Brazil, Moonraker, For Your Eyes Only, Octopussy, Top Secret!, A View to a Kill, Aliens, The Living Daylights, Consuming Passions, Licence to Kill, Eve of Destruction, The Taking of Beverly Hills, True Lies, GoldenEye, Titanic (Acad. Award, Best Art Dir., LA Film Crits. Award, Best Prod. Design, 1997), Wing Commander, Bond 19.

LANDAU, JON
Producer. b. New York, NY.
PICTURES: *Prod.*: Campus Man (also unit prod. mgr.), Honey I Shrunk the Kids, Dick Tracy (also unit prod. mgr.), Titanic (Acad. Award, Best Pic., 1997), Mr. Hughes. *Unit prod. mgr.*: Manhunter, F/X, Making Mr. Right.

LANDAU, JULIET
Actress. Father is actor Martin Landau.
PICTURES: The Grifters, Pump Up the Volume, Neon City, Direct Hit, Ed Wood, Theodore Rex, Ravager, Citizens of Perpetual Indulgence, Carlo's Wake.
TELEVISION: *Series:* Buffy the Vampire Slayer. *Guest:* Parker Lewis Can't Lose, Millennium, La Femme Nikita.

LANDAU, MARTIN
Actor. b. Brooklyn, NY, June 20, 1930. e. Pratt Inst., Art Students League, Was cartoon and staff artist on NY Daily News; studied at Actors Studio. Daughter is actress Juliet Landau. Recipient: Lifetime Achievement Awards from Houston Film Fest. and Charleston Film Fest. Spoken word recording, Harry Truman: The journey to Independence, 1997 (Grammy nom).
THEATER: Middle of the Night, Uncle Vanya, Stalag 17, Wedding Breakfast, First Love, The Goat Song.
PICTURES: Pork Chop Hill (debut, 1959), North by Northwest, The Gazebo, Stagecoach to Dancer's Rock, Cleopatra, The Hallelujah Trail, The Greatest Story Ever Told, Decision at Midnight, Alien Attack, Nevada Smith, They Call Me Mister Tibbs, Situation Normal But All Fouled Up, A Town Called Hell, Black Gunn, Strange Shadows in an Empty Room, Meteor, Destination Moonbase Alpha, Without Warning, Trial By Terror, Cosmic Princess, Journey Through the Black Sun, The Last Word, The Return, Alone in the Dark, The Being, Access Code, Treasure Island, Run ... If You Can, Death Blow, W.A.R.: Women Against Rape, Sweet Revenge, Cyclone, Real Bullets, Empire State, Delta Fever, Tucker: The Man and His Dream (Acad. Award nom.), Crimes and Misdemeanors (Golden Globe Award, Acad. Award nom.), Paint It Black, Firehead, Tipperary, The Color of Evening, Mistress, Eye of the Stranger, Sliver, Intersection, Time Is Money, Ed Wood (Academy Award, best supporting actor, 1994; also Golden Globe, SAG, American Comedy, NY Film Critics, LA Film Critics, Natl. Society of Film Critics, Boston Film Critics, Chicago Film Critics & Texas Film Critics Awards), City Hall, Pinocchio, B.A.P.S., The Elevator, The X Files: Fight the Future, Rounders, The Joy Riders, Edtv, The New Adventures of Pinocchio, Sleepy Hollow, Carlo's Wake, Ready to Rumble, Very Mean Men, Shiner.
TELEVISION: *Series*: Mission Impossible (1966-69; 3 Emmy noms., Golden Globe Award), Space 1999, In The Beginning, Haven. *Movies*: Welcome Home Johnny Bristol, Savage, The Death of Ocean View Park, Harlem Globetrotters on Gilligan's Island, Fall of the House of Usher, Max and Helen (ACE Award nom.), The Neon Empire, By Dawn's Early Light (ACE Award nom.), Something to Live For: The Alison Gertz Story, Legacy of Lies (ACE Award), 12:01, Bonanno: A Godfather's Story. Numerous guest appearances.

LANDES, MICHAEL
Executive, Producer.. b. Bronx, NY, Feb. 4, 1939. e. Fairleigh Dickinson, B.A., 1961; Rutgers, J.D., 1964; NYU, L.L.M., 1965. Bars passed: NJ 1965, NY 1966, US Supreme Ct. 1969. 17 years of corporate law and financing experience as sr. partner in law firm of Hahn and Hessen. Co-chmn of The ALMI Group formed, 1978. Co-chmn. & CEO of Almi Pictures Inc. formed, 1982. 1986, Almi sold its 97-screen RKO Century Warner Theatre chain to Cineplex Odeon. 1986, purchased Video Shack Inc. assets and formed RKO Warner Video, Inc.; Chmn since inception. 1988, became chmn, Damon Creations, Inc. which merged with Enro Holding Corp. and Enro Shirt Co. into Damon Creations. Sold Damon, 1988. Chmn./CEO, RKO Warner Intl. Ltd. a video franchisor and chmn./CEO of The Lexington Group Ltd., org. 1990. Member: World Presidents Organization (WPO). Chief Executives Organization (CEO); Association for a Better New York; bd. of dirs. Motion Picture Pioneers; Academy of Motion Picture Arts and Sciences; bd. of dirs. Periwinkle Theatre Productions.
PICTURES: Spaceship, The Big Score, I Am the Cheese, Rosebud Beach Hotel, Night Stalker, B. C. Roch, The Bostonians.

LANDIS, JOHN
Director, Producer, Writer, Actor. b. Chicago, IL, Aug. 3, 1950. Raised in Los Angeles. Started in mailroom at 20th Century-Fox, then worked in Europe as prod. asst. and stuntman before making first low-budget film, Schlock.
PICTURES: *Director &/or Actor*: Schlock (also writer), The Kentucky Fried Movie, National Lampoon's Animal House, The Blues Brothers (also co-s.p.), An American Werewolf in London (also s.p.), Trading Places, Twilight Zone—The Movie (sequence dir., also s.p., co-prod.), Into the Night, Spies Like Us, Clue (co-exec. prod., co-story only), Three Amigos!, Amazon Women on the Moon (sequence dir.; also co-exec. prod.), Coming to America, Oscar, Innocent Blood, Beverly Hills Cop III, The Stupids, Battle for the Planet of the Apes, Death Race 2000, 1941, The Muppets Take Manhattan, Spontaneous Combustion, Darkman, Diva Las Vegas, Voice of a Stranger, Sleepwalkers, Venice/Venice, The Silence of the Hams., Vampirella, Mad City, Susan's Plan, Blues Brothers 2000.
TELEVISION: *Series*: *Exec. prod.*: Dream On (also. dir., actor), Topper (also dir.), Weird Science, Sliders, Campus Cops. *Movie*: Psycho IV (actor), Quicksilver Highway. *Mini-series*: The Stand. *Specials*: B.B. King Into the Night, Disneyland's 35th Anniversary Celebration. *Videos*: Thriller, Black or White (both for Michael Jackson).

LANDRES, PAUL
Director. b. New York, NY, Aug. 21, 1912. e. UCLA. Started as asst. film editor at Universal 1931. Editor 1937 to 1949 of many feature films. Director of feature films and TV since 1949. Under directorial contract to Warner Bros. 1961-62. Director of 22 feature films for theatrical release.
PICTURES: Oregon Passage, A Modern Marriage, Mark of the Vampire, Navy Bound, The Curse of Dracula, Miracle of the Hills, 54 Washington Street, Son of a Gunfighter.
TELEVISION: *Series:* Bonanza, Daktari, The Rifleman, 77 Sunset Strip, Maverick Hawaiian Eye, The Plainsman, Readers Digest, Topper, Wyatt Earp, Blondie, and numerous others.

LANDSBURG, ALAN
Executive, Producer, Writer. b. New York, NY, May 10, 1933. e. NYU. Producer for NBC News Dept., 1951-59; producer-writer, CBS, 1959-60; exec. prod., Wolper Productions/ Metromedia Producers Corp., 1961-70; chairman, The Alan Landsburg Company, 1970-present.
PICTURES: *Co-exec. prod.*: Jaws 3-D, Porky's II: The Next Day.
TELEVISION: *Exec. prod.*: Biography, National Geographic Specials (1965-70): The Undersea World of Jacques Cousteau; In Search of..., That's Incredible. *Movies*: Adam, Fear on Trial, Parent Trap II, Adam: His Song Continues, The George McKenna Story, Long Gone, Strange Voices, Bluegrass, A Place at the Table, Too Young the Hero, A Stoning in Fulham County, High Risk, Destined to Live, Quiet Victory: The Charlie Wedemeyer Story, The Ryan White Story, Unspeakable Acts (co-exec. prod., writer), A Mother's Right: The Elizabeth Morgan Story (writer), The Hunter (writer).

LANE, DIANE
Actress. b. New York, NY, Jan. 2, 1965. Acted in stage classics (Medea, Electra, As You Like It) at La Mama Experimental Theatre Club, NY. Addtl. stage: The Cherry Orchard, Agamemnon, Runaways, Twelfth Night.

PICTURES: A Little Romance (debut, 1979), Touched by Love, National Lampoon Goes to the Movies, Cattle Annie and Little Britches, Six Pack, Ladies and Gentlemen the Fabulous Stains, The Outsiders, Rumble Fish, Streets of Fire, The Cotton Club, The Big Town, Lady Beware, Priceless Beauty, Vital Signs, My New Gun, Chaplin, Knight Moves, Indian Summer, Judge Dredd, Wild Bill, Mad Dog Time, Jack, Murder at 1600, The Only Thrill, A Walk on the Moon, The Virginian, My Dog Skip, The Perfect Storm.
TELEVISION: *Movies*: Child Bride of Short Creek, Miss All-American Beauty, Descending Angel, Oldest Living Confederate Widow Tells All, Grace and Glorie. *Special*: Edith Wharton's Summer. *Guest*: Fallen Angels. *Mini-Series*: Lonesome Dove.

LANE, NATHAN
Actor. r.n. Joseph Lane. b. Jersey City, NJ, Feb. 3, 1956. Received 1992 Obie Award for Sustained Excellence in Off-B'way Theatre.
THEATER: *B'way*: Present Laughter (Drama Desk nom.), Merlin, The Wind in the Willows, Some Americans Abroad, On Borrowed Time, Guys & Dolls (Drama Desk & Outer Critics Circle Awards; Tony nom.), Laughter on the 23rd Floor, Love! Valour! Compassion! (Drama Desk, Outer Critics Circle and Obie Awards; also Off-B'way), A Funny Thing Happened On The Way To The Forum (Tony Award). *Off-B'way*: A Midsummer Night's Dream, Measure for Measure, The Merry Wives of Windsor, She Stoops to Conquer, Claptrap, The Common Pursuit (Dramalogue Award), In a Pig's Valise, The Film Society, Uncounted Blessings, Hidden in This Picture, Love, The Lisbon Traviata (also L.A.; Drama Desk, Lucille Lortel, LA Drama Critics Circle & Dramalogue Awards), Bad Habits, Lips Together Teeth Apart (also L.A.).
PICTURES: Ironweed (debut, 1987), Joe Vs. the Volcano, The Lemon Sisters, He Said She Said, Frankie and Johnny, Life With Mikey, Addams Family Values, The Lion King (voice), Jeffrey (American Comedy Award nom.), The Birdcage (Golden Globe nom., American Comedy Award, SAG award), Mouse Hunt, Trixie, The Lion King II: Simba's Pride, Love's Labour's Lost, Isn't She Great, Get Bruce (cameo), At First Sight, Titan A.E. (voice).
TELEVISION: *Series*: One of the Boys, Encore! Encore!. *Guest*: The Days and Nights of Molly Dodd, Miami Vice, Frasier (Emmy nom., American Comedy Award nom.). *Movies*: Hallmark Hall of Fame's The Boys Next Door, Timon and Pumba (Emmy Award), Merry Christmas George Bailey. *Specials*: Alice in Wonderland, The Last Mile, Co-host 1995 Tony Awards, 1995 Kennedy Center Honors, Host 1996 Tony Awards (American Comedy Award nom.).

LANG, OTTO
Producer, Director. b. Tesanj, Austria (now Yugoslavia), Jan. 21, 1908. e. Salzburg, Austria. Four Academy Award nominations for Cinemascope Specials, Twentieth Century-Fox Film Corp.
PICTURES: *Dir.*: Search for Paradise. *Prod.*: Call Northside 777, Five Fingers, White Witch Doctor. *Assoc. prod*: Tora! Tora! Tora!
TELEVISION: Man from U.N.C.L.E., Daktari, Iron Horse, Cheyenne, Dick Powell Show, Zane Gray Theatre, Ann Sothern Show, Rifleman, Bat Masterson, Seahunt, The Deputy, Surfside 6, Hawaiian Eye. Prod. Twentieth Century Fox Hour. *Dir.*: Man and the Challenge, Aquanauts, World of Giants, The Legend of Cortez, Beethoven: Ordeal and Triumph, Saga of Western Man.

LANG, STEPHEN
Actor. b. Queens, NY, July 11, 1952. e. Swarthmore Col. Professional debut 1974 at Washington D.C.'s Folger Theatre.
THEATER: *NY*: Rosencrantz and Guildenstern Are Dead, Henry V, Bloomsday on Broadway, The Shadow of a Gun, Saint Joan, Hamlet, Johnny on the Spot, Death of a Salesman, Barbarians, The Winter's Tale, A Few Good Men, The Speed of Darkness.
PICTURES: Twice in a Lifetime (debut, 1985), Band of the Hand, Manhunter, Project X, Last Exit to Brooklyn, The Hard Way, Another You, Guilty As Sin, Gettysburg, Tombstone, Tall Tale, The Amazing Panda Adventure, The Shadow Conspiracy, An Occasional Hell, Fire Down Below, A Town Has Turned to Dust.
TELEVISION: *Series*: Crime Story. *Movies*: King of America, Death of a Salesman, Stone Pillow, Babe Ruth, Taking Back My Life: The Nancy Ziegenmeyer Story, Darkness Before Dawn, Murder Between Friends, A Season of Hope, The Possession of Michael D., The Phantoms, Strangers, Escape: Human Cargo. *Specials*: Anyone for Tennyson?, The Mother. *Guest*: Tribeca.

LANGE, HOPE
Actress. b. Redding Ridge, CT, Nov. 28, 1936. e. Reed Coll., Portland, OR; Barmore Jr. Coll., N.Y. Parents: John Lange, musician and Minnette Buddecke Lange, actress. Prof. stage debut in The Patriots on Broadway
THEATER: The Hot Corner, Same Time Next Year, The Supporting Cast.
PICTURES: Bus Stop (debut, 1956), The True Story of Jesse James, Peyton Place (Acad. Award nom.), The Young Lions, In Love and War, The Best of Everything, Wild in the Country, Pocketful of Miracles, Love Is a Ball, Jigsaw, Death Wish, I Am the Cheese, The Prodigal, A Nightmare on Elm Street Part 2, Blue Velvet, Tune in Tomorrow, Clear and Present Danger, Just Cause.
TELEVISION: *Series*: The Ghost and Mrs. Muir (2 Emmy Awards: 1969, 1970), The New Dick Van Dyke Show, Knight and Dave. *Movies*: Crowhaven Farm, That Certain Summer (Emmy nom.), The 500 Pound Jerk, I Love You— Goodbye, Fer-de-Lance, The Secret Night Caller, Love Boat II, Like Normal People, The Day Christ Died, Beulah Land, Pleasure Palace, Private Sessions, Dead Before Dawn, Cooperstown. Special: A Family Tree (Trying Times). *Mini-Series*: The Henry Ford Story: Man and the Machine, Message from Nam. Guest: Murder She Wrote.

LANGE, JESSICA
Actress. b. Cloquet, MN, Apr. 20, 1949. e. U. of Minnesota. Left to study mime 2 years under Etienne Decroux in Paris. Dancer, Opera Comique, Paris; model with Wilhelmina, NY. Worked in experimental theatre in New York. Broadway debut 1992 in A Streetcar Named Desire (Theatre World Award).
PICTURES: King Kong (debut, 1976), All That Jazz, How to Beat the High Cost of Living, The Postman Always Rings Twice, Frances, Tootsie (Academy Award, best supporting actress, 1982), Country (also co-prod.), Sweet Dreams, Crimes of the Heart, Far North, Everybody's All-American, Music Box, Men Don't Leave, Cape Fear, Night and the City, Blue Sky (Acad. Award, 1994), Losing Isaiah, Rob Roy, A Thousand Acres, Hush, Cousin Bette, Titus, Prozac Nation.
TELEVISION: *Special*: Cat on a Hot Tin Roof. *Movies*: O Pioneers!, A Streetcar Named Desire (Golden Globe, 1996).

LANGELLA, FRANK
Actor. b. Bayonne, NJ, Jan. 1, 1938. Studied acting at Syracuse U.; later in regional repertory, summer stock, and On- and Off-B'way. Joined Lincoln Ctr. Rep. Co., 1963.
THEATER: *NY*: The Immoralist (Off-B'way debut, 1963), Benito Cereno, The Old Glory (Obie Award), Good Day (Obie Award), The White Devil (Obie Award), Long Day's Journey Into Night, Yerma, Seascape (B'way debut, 1975; Tony Award), Dracula, A Cry of Players, Cyrano de Bergerac, The Tooth of the Crime, Ring Around the Moon, Amadeus, Passion, Design for Living, Sherlock's Last Case, The Tempest, Booth. *L.A.*: The Devils, Les Liaisons Dangereuses, My Fair Lady, Scenes From an Execution.
PICTURES: Diary of a Mad Housewife (debut, 1970), The Twelve Chairs, The Deadly Trap, The Wrath of God, Dracula, Those Lips Those Eyes, Sphinx, The Men's Club, Masters of the Universe, And God Created Woman, True Identity, 1492: Conquest of Paradise, Body of Evidence, Dave, Brainscan, Junior, Bad Company, Cutthroat Island, Eddie, Lolita, I'm Losing You, Small Soldiers, The Ninth Gate.
TELEVISION: *Specials*: Benito Cereno, The Good Day, The Ambassador, The Sea Gull, The American Woman: Portrait in Courage, Eccentricities of a Nightingale, Sherlock Holmes, Fortitude (Kurt Vonnegut's Monkey House). *Movies*: The Mark of Zorro, Liberty, Doomsday Gun.

LANGFORD, FRANCES
Singer, Actress. b. Lakeland, FL, April 4, 1913. e. Southern Coll. Stage experience in vaudeville, nightclubs, national radio programs.
PICTURES: Every Night at Eight, Collegiate, Broadway Melody of 1936, Palm Springs, Born to Dance, The Hit Parade, Hollywood Hotel, Dreaming Out Loud, Too Many Girls, The Hit Parade of 1941, All-American Coed, Mississippi Gambler, Yankee Doodle Dandy, Cowboy in Manhattan, This Is the Army, Never a Dull Moment, Career Girl, The Girl Rush, Dixie Jamboree, Radio Stars on Parade, Bamboo Blonde, Make Mine Laughs, People Are Funny, Deputy Marshall, Purple Heart Diary, The Glenn Miller Story.

LANGNER, PHILIP
Producer, b. New York, NY, Aug. 24, 1926. e. Yale U. President of The Theatre Guild and Theatre Guild Films, Inc. Producer the Westport Country Playhouse 1947-53. Joined The Theatre Guild 1954.
THEATER: The Matchmaker, Bells Are Ringing, The Tunnel of Love, Sunrise at Campobello, A Majority of One, The Unsinkable Molly Brown, A Passage to India, Seidman and Son, The Royal Hunt of the Sun, The Homecoming, Absurd Person Singular, Golda.
PICTURES: *Producer*: The Pawnbroker, Slaves, Born to Win. Associate Prod.: Judgment at Nuremberg, A Child Is Waiting.

LANSBURY, ANGELA
Actress. b. London, England, Oct. 16, 1925. Brothers are producers Bruce and Edgar Lansbury. e. South Hampstead Sch. for Girls, England; Acad. of Music, London; Feagin Dramatic Sch., N.Y. Mother was actress Moyna Macgill. To NY 1940 to study drama. Signed to contract by MGM, 1944. Exercise and lifestyle video: Positive Moves, 1988. *Book*: Positive Moves, 1990.
THEATER: *B'way*: Hotel Paradiso (NY debut, 1957), A Taste of Honey, Anyone Can Whistle, Mame (Tony Award, 1966), Dear World (Tony Award, 1969), Prettybelle (closed out of town), All Over, Gypsy (Tony Award, 1975), Hamlet, The King and I, Sweeney Todd: The Demon Barber of Fleet Street (Tony Award, 1979), A Little Family Business, Mame (1983 revival).

PICTURES: Gaslight (debut, 1944; Acad. Award nom.), National Velvet, The Picture of Dorian Gray (Acad. Award nom.), The Harvey Girls, The Hoodlum Saint, The Private Affairs of Bel Ami, Till the Clouds Roll By, If Winter Comes, Tenth Avenue Angel, State of the Union, The Three Musketeers, The Red Danube, Samson and Delilah, Kind Lady, Mutiny, Remains to Be Seen, The Purple Mask, A Lawless Street, The Court Jester, Please Murder Me, The Key Man (A Life at Stake), The Long Hot Summer, The Reluctant Debutante, The Summer of the 17th Doll (Season of Passion), The Dark at the Top of the Stairs, A Breath of Scandal, Blue Hawaii, All Fall Down, The Manchurian Candidate (Acad. Award nom.), In the Cool of the Day, The World of Henry Orient, Dear Heart, The Greatest Story Ever Told, Harlow, The Amorous Adventures of Moll Flanders, Mister Buddwing, Something for Everyone, Bedknobs and Broomsticks, Death on the Nile, The Lady Vanishes, The Mirror Crack'd, The Last Unicorn (voice), The Pirates of Penzance, The Company of Wolves, Beauty and the Beast (voice), Beauty and the Beast: The Enchanted Christmas (voice), Anastasia (voice).
TELEVISION: *Special*: Sweeney Todd. *Movies*: Little Gloria... Happy at Last, The Gift of Love: A Christmas Story, The First Olympics: Athens 1896, A Talent for Murder, Lace, Rage of Angels: The Story Continues, Shootdown, The Shell Seekers, The Love She Sought, Mrs. Harris Goes to Paris, Mrs. Santa Claus, Murder She Wrote: South by Southwest, The Unexpected Mrs. Pollifax. *Series*: Pantomime Quiz, Murder She Wrote (also exec. prod.). *Guest*: Robert Montgomery Presents, Four Star Playhouse, Studio 57, Playhouse 90, GE Theatre, Fireside Theatre, Lux Video Theatre, Revlon Mirror Theatre, Ford Theatre, Schlitz Playhouse of the Stars, Stage 7, Front Row Center, Screen Directors Playhouse, Eleventh Hour, The Man from U.N.C.L.E., Climax, The Perry Como Show, The Julie Andrews Hour.

LANSBURY, BRUCE
Executive. b. London, England, Jan. 12, 1930. Brother of Angela and twin Edgar. e. UCLA. Mother was actress Moyna Macgill. Writer, prod. KABC-TV, Los Angeles, 1957-59; joined CBS-TV, 1959, was ass't. dir., program dev., Hollywood, director for daytime and nighttime programs, and v.p., programs, New York; 1964-66, indep. prod., Broadway stage; 1966-69 producer, Wild Wild West, CBS series; 1969-72, prod. Mission: Impossible, Paramount Movies of Week; now v.p., creative affairs, Paramount TV.
TELEVISION: Great Adventure (series; prod.), Wings of the Water (exec. prod.), Murder She Wrote.

LANSBURY, EDGAR
Producer, Director, Designer. b. London, England, Jan. 12, 1930. e. UCLA. Brother of Angela and Bruce Lansbury. Started career as scenic designer and art dir. 1955-60, art dir., CBS; 1962-63, exec. art dir. prod. for WNDT-TV, educational station.
THEATER: *Producer–B'way*: The Subject Was Roses, That Summer That Fall, Promenade, Waiting for Godot, Long Day's Journey into Night, Godspell, Gypsy, The Night That Made America Famous, American Buffalo, Amphigorey: The Musical, Any Given Day, In Circles, As Bees in Honey Drown, June Moon, etc. *Director*: Without Apologies, Advice From a Caterpillar, The Country Club.
PICTURES: *Producer*: The Subject Was Roses, Godspell, The Wild Party, Squirm, Blue Sunshine, He Knows You're Alone, The Clairvoyant.
TELEVISION: The Defenders (art. dir.), Summer Girl (exec. prod.), Wings of the Water (exec. prod.), A Stranger Waits.

LANSING, SHERRY
Executive. b. Chicago, IL, July 31, 1944. e. B.S., science, Northwestern Univ, 1966 (cum laude). m. director William Friedkin. Taught math and English in Los Angeles city schools, 1966-69. Acted in films (Loving, Rio Lobo) and numerous TV shows. Exec. story editor, movies, Wagner Intl. Prod. Co, 1970-74; v.p., production, Heyday Prods., 1973-75; director, West Coast Develop., 1974-75; story editor, mgr., 1975-77, v.p., creative affairs, 1977, senior v.p., production, 1977-80, Columbia Pictures. Became president of production, 20th Century Fox, 1980-83, being the first woman to hold this position in the motion picture industry. Founded Jaffe-Lansing Prods. with Stanley Jaffe, 1983; indpt. producer, Jaffe-Lansing Prods., 1983-91. Named chairman, Paramount Motion Pictures Grp. in 1992 (now a unit of Viacom Entertainment Grp.), where three pictures have won the Academy Award for Best Picture within four years under her chairmanship. Recipient of a star on Hollywood Walk of Fame, 1996. Member, board of directors: Music Center of Los Angeles, American Film Institute, Teach for America, American Found. for AIDS Research (AMFAR), Cedars Sinai Hospital, Stop Cancer, Big Sisters of Los Angeles Endowment Fund (co-founder); member, board of governors, National Conference of Christians and Jews, member, advisory board, Revlon/UCLA Women's Health Research Prog.; member, board of trustees, American Museum of the Moving Image, Regents of the U. of Calif.
PICTURES: *Co-prod*: Racing with the Moon, Firstborn, Fatal Attraction, The Accused, Black Rain, School Ties, Indecent Proposal.
TELEVISION: *Exec. producer*: When the Time Comes, Mistress.

LaPAGLIA, ANTHONY
Actor. b. Adelaide, Australia, 1959. Former teacher, moved to U.S. in 1984. Made Off-B'way debut in Bouncers, followed by On the Open Road. *B'way*: The Rose Tattoo (Theatre World Award).
PICTURES: Slaves of New York (debut, 1989), Dangerous Obsession (Mortal Sins), Betsy's Wedding, He Said/She Said, One Good Cop, 29th Street, Whispers in the Dark, Innocent Blood, So I Married an Axe Murderer, The Client, The Custodian, Mixed Nuts, Bulletproof Heart, Lucky Break, Empire Records, The Funeral, Brilliant Lies, The Garden of Redemption, Phoenix, Summer of Sam, The House of Mirth, Sweet and Lowdown, Black and Blue, Company Man, Looking for Alibrandi, Autumn in New York, The Bank, The Salton Sea, Lantana .
TELEVISION: *Movies*: Criminal Justice, Keeper of the City, Black Magic, Past Tense, Nitti: The Enforcer, Lansky, The Other Side. *Series*: Murder One, Normal Ohio.

LARDNER, RING W., JR.
Writer. b. Chicago, IL, Aug. 19, 1915. p. writer-humorist Ring W. and Ellis A. e. Phillips Andover Acad, Princeton U. Was reporter on New York Daily Mirror. Publ. writer, Selznick International. 1947, member of "Hollywood 10." In collab. with Ian Hunter conceived and wrote under pseudonyms many episodes in 5 TV series while blacklisted. Uncredited writer of such films as A Breath of Scandal, The Cardinal. 1989, received Writers Guild Laurel Award. Author of novels: The Ecstacy of Owen Muir, All For Love, and memoir, The Lardners My Family Remembered. Also collab. on B'way musical Foxy. 1992, WGA Ian McLellan Hunter Memorial Award for Lifetime Achievement.
PICTURES: Woman of the Year (Academy Award, 1942), The Cross of Lorraine, Tomorrow the World, Forever Amber, Forbidden Street, Four Days Leave, Cloak and Dagger, The Cincinnati Kid, M*A*S*H (Academy Award, 1970), The Greatest.

LARKIN, JAMES J.
Executive. b. Brooklyn, NY, Nov. 2, 1925. e. Columbia U., 1947-52. U.S. Air Force, 1943-46; BOAC rep. to entertainment ind., 1948-60; pres., Transportation Counselors Inc., 1960-62; pres., Larkin Associates, Inc., 1962-65; exec. Radio N.Y. Worldwide, 1965-68; v.p. Grolier Educational Corp., 1968-69; v.p. Visual Informational Systems, 1969-73; pres., Business TV Services, Inc., 1973-; exec. prod., Madhouse Brigade, 1977-79; prod.-writer, All Those Beautiful Girls, 1979-80.

LARROQUETTE, JOHN
Actor. b. New Orleans, LA., Nov. 25, 1947. Disc jockey on FM radio during 1960s and early 70s. Acted on L.A. stage from 1973 (The Crucible, Enter Laughing, Endgame). Prof. debut, TV series Doctor's Hospital, 1976-78. Was narrator for film Texas Chainsaw Massacre.
PICTURES: Altered States, Heart Beat, Green Ice, Stripes, Cat People, Hysterical, Twilight Zone—The Movie, Choose Me, Meatballs Part II, Star Trek III: The Search for Spock, Summer Rental, Blind Date, Second Sight, Madhouse, Tune in Tomorrow, Richie Rich, Tales from the Crypt Presents: Demon Knight (cameo), Isn't She Great.
TELEVISION: *Series*: Doctor's Hospital, Baa Baa Black Sheep, Night Court (4 Emmy Awards, 1985-88), The John Larroquette Show, Payne. *Movies*: Bare Essence, The Last Ninja, Hot Paint, Convicted, One Special Victory (also co-exec. prod.), The Defenders: Payback, The Tenth Kingdom. *Guest*: The Practice (Emmy Award, 1997), The West Wing.

LASSALLY, WALTER
Cinematographer. b. Berlin, Germany, Dec. 18, 1926. Entered indust. as clapper-boy at Riverside Studios. During 1950s allied himself with Britain's Free Cinema filmmakers working for Lindsay Anderson, Gavin Lambert, Tony Richardson and Karel Reisz.
PICTURES: A Girl in Black (feature debut, 1956), Beat Girl, A Taste of Honey, Electra, The Loneliness of the Long Distance Runner, Tom Jones, Zorba the Greek (Academy Award, 1964), The Day the Fish Came Out, Joanna, Oedipus the King, The Adding Machine, Three Into Two Won't Go, Something for Everyone, Twinky (Lola), Savages, Happy Mother's Day... Love George, To Kill a Clown, The Wild Party, Pleasantville, The Great Bank Hoax, The Woman Across the Way, Hullabaloo Over George and Bonnie's Pictures, Something Short of Paradise, The Blood of Hussain, Angel of Iron, Memoirs of a Survivor, Too Far to Go, Heat and Dust, Private School, The Bostonians, The Deceivers, Fragments of Isabella, The Perfect Murder, Ballad of the Sad Cafe, The Little Dolphins.
TELEVISION: Mrs. Delafield Wants to Marry, The Man Upstairs.

LASSER, LOUISE
Actress. b. New York, NY, April 11, 1939. e. Brandeis U., New School for Social Research. Appeared on stage before theatrical film debut in 1965 with What's New Pussycat? Won first Clio Award for best actress in a commercial.
THEATER: I Can Get it For You Wholesale, The Third Ear, Henry Sweet Henry, Lime Green/Khaki Blue, The Chinese, Marie & Bruce, A Coupla White Chicks Sitting Around Talking.
PICTURES: What's Up Tiger Lily? (voice), Take the Money and Run, Bananas, Such Good Friends, Everything You Always Wanted to Know About Sex, Slither, Simon, In God We Trust, Stardust Memories, Crimewave, Nightmare at Shadow Woods (Blood Rage), Surrender, Sing, Rude Awakening, Modern Love, Frankenhooker, The Night We Never Met.
TELEVISION: *Series*: Mary Hartman Mary Hartman, It's a Living. *Movies*: Coffee Tea or Me?, Isn't It Shocking?, Just Me and You (also writer), For Ladies Only. *Guest*: Bob Newhart Show, Mary Tyler Moor Show, Taxi, St. Elsewhere, Empty Nest, many others.

LASZLO, ANDREW
Cinematographer. b. Papa, Hungary, Jan. 12, 1926. To U.S. in 1947, working as cameraman on tv before turning to feature films.
PICTURES: One Potato Two Potato, You're a Big Boy Now, The Night They Raided Minskys, Popi, The Out of Towners, Lovers and Other Strangers, The Owl and the Pussycat, Jennifer on My Mind, To Find a Man, The Effect of Gamma Rays on Man-in-the-Moon Marigolds, Class of '44, Countdown at Kusini, Thieves, Somebody Killed Her Husband, The Warriors, The Funhouse, Southern Comfort, I the Jury, First Blood, Streets of Fire, Thief of Hearts, Remo Williams: The Adventure Begins, Poltergeist II, Innerspace, Star Trek V: The Final Frontier, Ghost Dad, Newsies.
TELEVISION: *Documentaries*: High Adventure with Lowell Thomas, The Twentieth Century. *Series*: The Phil Silvers Show, Joe and Mabel, Mama, Brenner, Naked City, The Nurses, Doctors and Nurses, Coronet Blue. Specials: New York New York, The Beatles at Shea Stadium, Ed Sullivan *Specials. Movies and feature pilots*: The Happeners, The Cliffdwellers, Daphne, Teacher Teacher, Blue Water Gold, The Man Without a Country, The Unwanted, Spanner's Key, Thin Ice, Love is Forever. *Mini-series*: Washington Behind Closed Doors, The Dain Curse, Top of the Hill, Shogun, and numerous commericals.

LATSIS, PETER C.
Publicist. b. Chicago, IL, Mar. 9, 1919. e. Wright Jr. Coll., Chicago. Newspaper reporter, Chicago Herald-American, 1942-45; Army, 1943; joined Fox West Coast Theatres, Los Angeles, in theatre operations 1945; adv.-pub. dept. 1946; asst. dir. adv.-pub. 1955; press rep. National Theatres, 1958; press relations dir., National General Corp., 1963; home office special field pub. repr., American International Pictures, 1973; Filmways Pictures, 1980-82; Recipient of Publicists Guild's Robert Yeager Award, 1983. Member, Motion Picture Pioneers. Unit rep., Executive Bd. of Publicists Guild of America, 1993-95.

LATTANZI, MATT
Actor. m. actress-singer Olivia Newton-John.
PICTURES: Xanadu (1980), Rich and Famous, Grease 2, My Tutor, That's Life!, Roxanne, Blueberry Hill, Catch Me If You Can, Diving In.
TELEVISION: *Series*: Paradise Beach.

LATTUADA, ALBERTO
Director. b. Milan, Italy, 1914. Son of Felice Lattuada, musician, opera composer, and writer of scores of many of son's films, Studied architecture; founded the periodical Cominare. Later founded Italian Film Library of which he still pres. Also, pres., Cinema D'Essay, First screen work as scriptwriter and asst. dir. of two films, 1940.
PICTURES: Mill on the Po, Anna, The Overcoat, La Lupa, Love in the City, White Sister, Flesh Will Surrender, Without Pity, The She Wolf, Tempest, The Unexpected, Mafioso, The Mandrake, Matchless, The Betrayal, The Steppe, Oh Serafina, Stay as You Are.

LAUGHLIN, TOM
Actor, Producer, Director, Writer. b. Minneapolis, MN, 1938. e. U. of Indiana, U. of Minnesota where had athletic scholarships. m. actress Delores Taylor. Travelled around world, studying in Italy with Dr. Maria Montessori. Established, ran a Montessori school in Santa Monica for several yrs. Worked his way to Hollywood, where acted in bit parts until stardom came in Born Losers in 1967. Produced and starred in Billy Jack and The Trial of Billy Jack, also writing s.p. with wife under pseudonym Frank Christina. Heads own prod. co., Billy Jack Enterprises.
PICTURES: *Actor*: Tea and Sympathy, The Delinquents, South Pacific, Senior Prom, Lafayette Escadrille, Gidget, Battle of the Coral Sea, Tall Story, Born Losers, Callan, Brannigan, Voyage of the Damned, The Littlest Horse Thieves, The Big Sleep, The Legend of the Lone Ranger, Murder Elite, No Escape, Wild Bill: A Hollywood Maverick. *Actor-Dir.-Prod.-Writer*: The Proper Time, The Young Sinner, Born Losers, Billy Jack, The Trial of Billy Jack, The Master Gunfighter, Billy Jack Goes to Washington.
TELEVISION: *Movies*: The War That Never Ends, Zoya.

LAUNER, DALE
Writer. b. Cleveland, OH. E. Cal State Northridge. PICTURES: Ruthless People, Blind Date, Dirty Rotten Scoundrels, My Cousin Vinny, Love Potion #9 (also dir.).

LAURENTS, ARTHUR
Writer, Director. b. New York, NY, July 14, 1917. e. Cornell U., B.A., 1937. First Professional writing as radio script writer in 1939. In Army 1941-45. Member of the Council of the Dramatists Guild; Theatre Hall of Fame.
THEATER: *Author*: Home of the Brave (Sidney Howard Award), Heartsong, The Bird Cage, The Time of the Cuckoo, A Clearing in the Woods, Invitation to a March, West Side Story, Gypsy, Hallelujah, Baby! (Tony Award), Scream, The Enclave, Running Time, Jolson Sings Again, The Radical Mystique. Director: Invitation to a March, I Can Get It for You Wholesale, La Cage aux Folles (Tony Award), Birds of Paradise. *Author-Director*: Anyone Can Whistle, Do I Hear a Waltz?, The Madwoman of Central Park West, Gypsy (revival), Nick and Nora.
PICTURES: *Writer:* The Snake Pit, Rope, Caught, Anna Lucasta, Anastasia, Bonjour Tristesse, The Way We Were (from his own novel), The Turning Point (also co-prod.; Golden Globe, WGA Award).

LAURIA, DAN
Actor. b. Brooklyn, NY, April 12, 1947. e. So Conn. St. Col., Univ. of Conn. Served in U.S. Marine Corps., 1970-73.
PICTURES: Without a Trace, Stakeout, Another Stakeout, Excessive Force II: Force on Force, Dog Watch, Independence Day, Ricochet River, Justice, Rhapsody in Bloom, True Friends, Wide Awake, A Wake in Providence, Stranger in My House.
TELEVISION: *Series*: Love of Life, One Life to Live, Hooperman, The Wonder Years, Amazing Grace, Party of Five, The Hoop Life, Costello. *Movies*: Johnny Brass, Johnny Bull, Doing Life, At Mother's Request, Angel in Green, David, Howard Beach: Making the Case for Murder, The Big One: The Great Los Angeles Earthquake, Overexposed, Dead and Alive, From the Files of Joseph Wambaugh: A Jury of One, In the Line of Duty: Ambush in Waco, In the Line of Duty: Hunt for Justice, Between Mother and Daughter, Terror in the Family, The Bachelor's Baby, Prison of Secrets, Merry Christmas George Bailey, Mr. Murder, From the Earth to the Moon. *Guest*: Growing Pains, Mike Hammer, Moonlighting, Hill Street Blues, NYPD Blue, Chicago Hope. *Special*: Between Mother and Daughter.

LAURIE, PIPER
Actress. r.n. Rosetta Jacobs. b. Detroit, MI, Jan. 22, 1932. e. Los Angeles H.S. Acted in school plays, signed by U.I. in 1949.
THEATER: The Glass Menagerie (revival), Marco Polo Sings a Solo, The Innocents, Biography, Rosemary, The Alligators, The Last Flapper (tour), The Destiny of Me.
PICTURES: Louisa (debut, 1950), The Milkman, Francis Goes to the Races, The Prince Who Was a Thief, Son of Ali Baba, Has Anybody Seen My Gal, No Room for the Groom, Mississippi Gambler, Golden Blade, Dangerous Mission, Johnny Dark, Dawn at Socorro, Smoke Signal, Ain't Misbehavin', Kelly and Me, Until They Sail, The Hustler (Acad. Award nom.), Carrie (Acad. Award nom.), Ruby, The Boss's Son, Tim, Return to Oz, Children of a Lesser God (Acad. Award nom.), Distortions, Appointment with Death, Tiger Warsaw, Dream a Little Dream, Mother Mother, Other People's Money, Storyville, Rich in Love, Trauma, Wrestling Ernest Hemingway, The Crossing Guard, The Grass Harp, The Faculty, Palmer's Pick Up.
TELEVISION: *Specials*: Days of Wine and Roses (Emmy nom.), The Road That Led Afar (Emmy nom.), The Deaf Heart (Emmy nom.), The Secret Life of Margaret Sanger. *Movies*: In the Matter of Karen Ann Quinlan, Rainbow, Skag, The Bunker (Emmy nom.), Mae West, Love Mary, Toughlove, Promise (Emmy Award, 1987), Go To the Light, Rising Son, Poisoned By Love: The Kern County Murders, Lies and Lullabies, Shadows of Desire, Fighting for My Daughter, In the Blink of an Eye, Road to Galveston, Alone, Inherit the Wind. *Series*: Skag, Twin Peaks (Golden Globe Award, Emmy nom.), Partners. *Mini-Series*: The Thorn Birds (Emmy nom.), Tender is the Night, Intensity. *Guest*: St. Elsewhere (Emmy nom.)

LAUTER, ED
Actor. b. Long Beach, NY, Oct. 30, 1940.
PICTURES: The New Centurions, Hickey & Boggs, The Last American Hero, Executive Action, Lolly Madonna XXX, The Longest Yard, French Connection II, Breakheart Pass, Family Plot, King Kong, The Chicken Chronicles, Magic, The Amateur, Death Hunt, Timerider, The Big Score, Eureka, Lassiter, Cujo, Finders Keepers, Death Wish 3, Girls Just Want to Have Fun, Youngblood, 3:15, Raw Deal, Chief Zabu, Revenge of the Nerds II, Gleaming the Cube, Fat Man and Little Boy, Tennessee Waltz, School Ties, Wagons East!, Trial by Jury, Girl in the Cadillac, Digital Man, Crash, Rattled, Coyote Summer, Mulholland Falls, Top of the World, Allie & Me, The Day October Died.
TELEVISION: *Series*: B.J. and the Bear. *Movies*: Class of '63, The Migrants, The Godchild, Satan's Triangle, A Shadow in the Streets, Last Hours Before Morning, The Clone Master, The Jericho Mile, Love's Savage Fury, Undercover with the KKK, The Boy Who Drank Too Much, Guyana Tragedy—The Story of Jim Jones, AlcatrazThe Whole Shocking Story, In the Custody of Strangers, Rooster, The Seduction of Gina, Three Wishes of Billy Grier, The Last Days of Patton, The Thanksgiving Promise, Calendar Girl Cop Killer?: The Bambi Bembenek Story, Extreme Justice, The Return of Ironside, Secret Sins of the Father, Tuskegee Airmen, Ravenhawk, Under Wraps, Mercenary, A Bright Shining Lie.

LAVEN, ARNOLD
Director, Producer. b. Chicago, IL, Feb. 23, 1922.
PICTURES: Without Warning (debut, 1952), Vice Squad, Down Three Dark Streets, The Rack, The Monster That Challenged the World, Slaughter on Tenth Ave., Anna Lucasta, Geronimo (also prod.), The Glory Guys (also co-prod.), Clambake (co-prod. only), Rough Night in Jericho, Sam Whiskey (also co-prod.).
TELEVISION: Part creator and director TV pilots: The Rifleman, Robert Taylor's Detectives, The Plainsmen.

LAVIN, LINDA
Actress. b. Portland, ME, Oct. 15, 1937. e. Coll. of William & Mary. First professional job in chorus of Camden County (N.J.) Music Circus. Worked in plays both off and on Broadway before turning to TV, where guest-starred on such series as Family, Rhoda, Phyllis and Harry O.

THEATER: Oh Kay! (Off-B'way debut, 1960), A Family Affair (B'way debut), Revues: Wet Paint (Theatre World Award), The Game Is Up, The Mad Show, member acting co.: Eugene O'Neil Playwright's Unit, 1968; It's a Bird It's a Plane... It's Superman, Something Different, Little Murders (Outer Critics Circle & Sat. Review Awards), Cop Out, The Last of the Red Hot Lovers (Tony nom.), Story Theatre, Dynamite Tonight, Broadway Bound (Tony, Drama Desk, Outer Critics Circle & Helen Hayes Awards), Gypsy, The Sisters Rosensweig, Death Defying Acts.
PICTURES: The Muppets Take Manhattan, See You in the Morning, I Want to Go Home.
TELEVISION: *Series*: Barney Miller, Alice (2 Golden Globe Awards; 2 Emmy noms.), Room for Two (also co-exec. prod.). *Movies*: The Morning After, Like Mom and Me, The $5.20 an Hour Dream, A Matter of Life and Death (also exec. prod. & developed), Another Woman's Child, A Place to Call Home (also exec. prod. & developed), Lena: My Hundred Children, Room for Two, Stolen Moments, Secrets from the Rose Garden, A Dream Is a Wish Your Heart Makes, The Annette Funicello Story, The Ring, For the Children: The Irvine Fertility Scandal, Conrad Bloom, Best Friends for Life.

LAW, JOHN PHILLIP
Actor. b. Hollywood, CA, Sept. 7, 1937. e. Neighborhood Playhouse. B'way debut in Coming on Strong. Appeared at Lincoln Center in After the Fall, Marco Millions, The Changeling, and Tartuffe. Has made more than 50 films in more than 20 countries world wide.
PICTURES: High Infidelity, Three Nights of Love, The Russians Are Coming The Russians Are Coming the Russians Are Coming (U.S. debut), Hurry Sundown, Barbarella, Danger Diabolik, The Sergeant, Death Rides a Horse, Skidoo, Diary of a Telephone Operator, Von Richtofen and Brown, The Hawaiians, Michael Strogoff, The Love Machine, The Last Movie, The Golden Voyage of Sinbad, Stardust, Open Season, Your God My Hell, The Spiral Staircase, Dr. Justice, African Rage, Whisper in the Dark, Portrait of an Assassin, The Crystal Man, Death in November, Ring of Darkness, The Cassandra Crossing, Der Schimmelreiter, Attack Force Z, Tarzan the Ape Man, Night Train to Terror, The Tin Man, Rainy Day Friends (L.A. Bad), No Time to Die, American Commandos (Mr. Salvage), Johann Strauss, The Moon Under the Trees, Moon in Scorpio, Striker, The Overthrow, Mutiny in Space, Thunder Warrior III, A Case of Honor, Blood Delirium, Alienator, L.A. Heat, Gorilla, The Guest, Alaska Stories, Angel Eyes, Shining Blood, Marilyn Behind Bars, Day of the Pig, The Mountain of the Lord, Europa Mission.
TELEVISION: *Series*: The Young and the Restless (1989). *Movie*: The Best Place to Be, A Great Love Story (It.), Experiences (It.), The Fourth Man (Austrian), Little Women of Today (It.). *Guest*: The Love Boat, Murder She Wrote.

LAW, JUDE
Actor. b. London, England, Dec. 29, 1972.
PICTURES: Shopping, I Love You I Love You Not, Wilde, Gattaca, Bent, Midnight in the Garden of Good and Evil, Final Cut, Music From Another Room, The Wisdom of Crocodiles, The Talented Mr. Ripley, eXistenZ, Love, Honour and Obey, A.I., Enemy at the Gates.
TELEVISION: *Movies:* The Marshal. *Series:* The Casebook of Sherlock Holmes, Families.

LAW, LINDSAY
Producer. e. NYU School of the Arts. Producer of specials for Warner Bros. Television, head of drama for WNET/New York and prod. for Theatre in America before becoming exec. prod. of American Playhouse. Advisory Board of Independent Feature Project/West, Sundance Film Festival.
PICTURES: *Exec. prod.*: On Valentine's Day, Smooth Talk, Native Son, In a Shallow Grave, Stand and Deliver, The Thin Blue Line, El Norte, The Wizard of Loneliness, Signs of Life, Bloodhounds of Broadway, Big Time, Eat a Bowl of Tea, Longtime Companion, Thousand Pieces of Gold, Straight Out of Brooklyn, Daughters of the Dust, Thank You and Goodnight, All the Vermeers in New York, Brother's Keeper, Ethan Frome, The Music of Chance, Golden Gate, I Shot Andy Warhol, Fast Cheap and Out of Control.
TELEVISION: *Prod.*: The Girls in Their Summer Dresses, The Time of Your Life, You Can't Take It With You, The Good Doctor, The Most Happy Fella, The Eccentricities of a Nightingale, Cyrano de Bergerac (assoc. prod.). *Prod. for American Playhouse*: Working, for Colored Girls Who Have Considered Suicide/When the Rainbow Is Enuf, Private Contentment, *Exec. prod.*: Concealed Enemies (Emmy Award, 1984), Land of Little Rain, Ask Me Again, The Diaries of Adam and Eve, A Walk in the Woods, Fires in the Mirror.

LAWRENCE, BARBARA
Actress. b. Carnegie, OK, Feb. 24, 1930. e. UCLA. Mother Berenice Lawrence. Child model; successful screen try-out, 1944; screen debut in Billy Rose Diamond Horse Shoe (1945).
PICTURES: Margie, Captain from Castile, You Were Meant for Me, Give My Regards to Broadway, Street with No Name, Unfaithfully Yours, Letter to Three Wives, Mother Is a Freshman, Thieves Highway, Two Tickets to Broadway, Here Come the Nelsons, The Star, Arena, Paris Model, Her 12 Men, Oklahoma, Man with the Gun, Joe Dakota, Kronos.

LAWRENCE, JOEY
Actor. b. Montgomery, PA, Apr. 20, 1976. e. USC.
PICTURES: Summer Rental, Oliver and Company (voice), Pulse, Radioland Murders, Tequila Body Shots.
TELEVISION: *Series*: Gimme a Break, Blossom, Brotherly Love. *Pilots*: Scamps, Little Shots. *Specials*: Andy Williams and the NBC Kids, Don't Touch, Alvin Goes Back to School, Umbrella Jack, Adventures in Babysitting, Disney's Countdown to Kids' Day, All That, Blossom in Paris, Kids' Choice Awards (host). *Movies:* Chains of Gold, Prince for a Day, Brothers of the Frontier.

LAWRENCE, MARC
Actor. r.n. Max Goldsmith. b. New York, NY, Feb. 17, 1914. e. City Coll. of New York. On stage in The Tree (Eva La Galliene Rep. Theatre.), Sour Mountain, Waiting for Lefty, Golden Boy, View From the Bridge.
PICTURES: White Woman, Little Big Shot, Dr. Socrates, Road Gang, San Quentin, The Ox Bow Incident, I Am the Law, While New York Sleeps, Dillinger, Flame of Barbary Coast, Club Havana, Don't Fence Me In, The Virginian, Life with Blondie, Yankee Fakir, Captain from Castile, I Walk Alone, Calamity Jane and Sam Bass, The Asphalt Jungle, Hurricane Island, My Favorite Spy, Girls Marked Danger, Helen of Troy, Johnny Cool, Nightmare in the Sun, Savage Pampas, Johnny Tiger, Custer of the West, Nightmare in the Sun (dir. co- prod., co-story only), Krakatoa East of Java, The Kremlin Letter, Fraser: The Sensuous Lion, The Man With the Golden Gun, Marathon Man, A Piece of the Action, Foul Play, Goin' Cocoanuts, Hot Stuff, Night Train to Terror, The Big Easy, Ruby, Newsies, Marilyn I Love You, Four Rooms, From Dusk Till Dawn.

LAWRENCE, MARTIN
Actor, Comedian. b. Frankfurt, Germany, 1965. Started as stand-up comic in Washington D.C.
PICTURES: Do the Right Thing (debut, 1989), House Party, Talkin' Dirty After Dark, House Party 2, Boomerang, You So Crazy (also exec. prod.), Bad Boys, Nothing to Lose, A Thin Line Between Love and Hate (also, exec. prod., dir., s.p.), Life, Blue Streak.
TELEVISION: *Series*: What's Happening Now?, Kid 'n' Play (voice), Russell Simmons' Def Comedy Jam (host, prod. consultant), Martin (also creator, co-exec. prod.). *Pilots*: Hammer Slammer & Slade, A Little Bit Strange. *Guest*: Stand Up Spotlight, Yo! MTV Laffs, An Evening at the Improv.

LAWRENCE, STEVE
Actor. r.n. Sydney Leibowitz. b. Brooklyn, NY, July 8, 1935. m. singer Eydie Gorme. Singer in nightclubs and on TV.
THEATER: What Makes Sammy Run?, Golden Rainbow.
PICTURES: Stand Up and Be Counted, The Blues Brothers, The Lonely Guy, Blues Brothers 2000.
TELEVISION: *Specials*: Steve and Eydie Celebrate Irving Berlin (also co-exec. prod.; Emmy Award, 1979), many specials. *Series*: Tonight, The Steve Lawrence-Eydie Gorme Show (1958), The Steve Lawrence Show (1965), Foul-Ups Bleeps and Blunders (host). *Guest*: Police Story, Murder, She Wrote. *Movie*: Alice in Wonderland.

LAWRENCE, VICKI
Actress. b. Inglewood, CA, March 26, 1949. Singer and recording artist appearing with Young Americans (1965-67). Gained fame on The Carol Burnett Show as comedienne (1967-78), winning Emmy Award in 1976. Gold record for The Night the Lights Went Out in Georgia (1972). Author: *Vicki!: The True Life Adventures of Miss Fireball* (Simon & Schuster, 1995).
TELEVISION: *Movies*: Having Babies, Hart to Hart: Old Friends Never Die. *Series*: Carol Burnett Show, Jimmie Rodgers Show, Mama's Family. *Host*: Win Lose or Draw (1987-88), Vicki!, Fox After Breakfast (synd. talk shows).

LAWSON, SARAH
Actress. b. London, Eng., Aug. 6, 1928. e. Heron's Ghyll Sch., Sussex. Stage debut in Everyman (Edinburgh Festival) 1947.
PICTURES: The Browning Version (debut, 1951), The Night Won't Talk, Street Corner, Street Corner (Both Sides of the Law), Three Steps in the Dark, Meet Mr. Malcolm, You Know What Sailors Are, Blue Peter (Navy Heroes), It's Never Too Late, Links of Justice, Three Crooked Men, The Solitary Child, Night Without Pity, On the Run, The World Ten Times Over, Island of the Burning Doomed, The Devil's Bride (The Devil Rides Out), Battle of Britain, The Stud, The Dawning (prod.).
TELEVISION: Face to Face, River Line, Whole Truth, Lady From the Sea, Mrs. Moonlight, Silver Card, An Ideal Husband, Love and Money, Rendezvous, Invisible Man, Saber Buccaneers, White Hunter, Flying Doctor, On the Night of the Murder, Haven in Sunset, The Odd Man, Zero 1 (series), The Innocent Ceremony, Department S, The Marrying Kind, The Expert, The Persuaders, Trial, Starcast, The Midsummer of Colonel Blossum, Callen, Crime of Passion, Full House, Father Brown, Within These Walls These Walls Series, The Standard, The Purple Twilight, The Professionals, Bergerac, Cuffy, Lovejoy.

LAYBOURNE, GERALDINE
Executive. e. Vassar College, B.A.; U. Penn, M.S. Joined Nickelodeon in 1980. Was vice chmn., MTV Networks; pres., Nickelodeon/Nick at Nite. Bd. member Viacom exec. committee. Left Nickelodeon to join ABC as pres., Disney/ABC Cable Networks. Inducted into Broadcast and Cable Hall of Fame, 1996. Resigned ABC/Cable post in 1998 and started own network/cable/internet production company, Oxygen Media.

LAZARUS, PAUL N.
Executive. b. Brooklyn, NY, March 31, 1913. e. Cornell U., B.A., 1933. In U.S. Army, W.W. II. Entered m.p. ind. 1933 as gen. asst., press book dept., Warner Bros.; pres., AMPA, 1939-40. Joined Buchanan & Co., 1942 as m.p. account exec. To United Artists 1943 as dir. adv. & pub. Named asst. to pres., 1948; joined Columbia exec. staff, New York, 1950; elected v.p. Columbia, 1954-62; exec. v.p. Samuel Bronston Prods., 1962-64; v.p., chg. Motion Pictures, Subscription Television Inc., 1964; exec. officer and partner, Landau Releasing Organization, 1964-65; exec. v.p., member bd. of dir., Nat'l Screen Serv. Corp., 1965-75; lecturer and consultant, Film Studies Program, U. of CA at Santa Barbara, 1975-. Consultant to Kenya Film Corp., Nairobi, 1983. Director, Santa Barbara Intl. Film Festival, 1986-87. Chief of Staff, Santa Barbara Writers' Conference, 1976-. Vice-chmn. Santa Barbara County Film Council, 1989-92.

LAZARUS, PAUL N. III
Executive. b. New York, NY, May 25, 1938. e. Williams Coll., BA.; Yale Law Sch, L.L.B. Third generation film exec. Began career with Palomar Pictures Int'l. as exec. v.p.; joined ABC Pictures Corp. as v.p. in chg. of creative affairs. Mng. dir., CRM Productions, maker of educational films; v.p. for motion pictures. Marble Arch Productions; 1983, v.p. in chg. of prod., Home Box Office. 1985, Film Commissioner, New Mexico; 1987, Dir. of Film Program, U of Miami.
PICTURES: *Prod.:* Extreme Close-Up, Westworld, Futureworld, Capricorn One, Hanover Street, Barbarosa, Doubles.

LAZENBY, GEORGE
Actor. b. Gouburn, Australia, Sept. 5, 1939. Appeared in Australian and British tv commericals before being chosen to star as James Bond.
PICTURES: On Her Majesty's Secret Service (debut, 1969), Universal Soldier, Who Saw Her Die?, The Dragon Flies, Stoner, The Man From Hong Kong, The Kentucky Fried Movie, Death Dimension, The Falcon's Ultimatum, Saint Jack, L'ultimo Harem, Never Too Young to Die, Hell Hunters, Gettysburg, Eyes of the Beholder, Emmanuelle's Revenge, Emmanuelle's Love, Emmanuelle Forever, Death By Misadventure, .Twin Sitters, Gut Feeling, Four Dogs Playing Poker.
TELEVISION: *Series*: General Hospital, Rituals. *Movies*: Is Anybody There?, Cover Girls, The Newman Shame, Evening in Byzantium, The Return of the Man From U.N.C.L.E., Batman Beyond: The Movie *Guest*: Hawaii Five-O, Bring "Em Back Alive, The Master, Freddy's Nightmares, Aldred Hitchcock Presents, Superboy, Kung Fu: The Legend Continues, Diagnosis Murder, Batham Beyond, Baywatch, The Pretender.

LEACHMAN, CLORIS
Actress. b. Des Moines, IA, April 30, 1926. e. Northwestern U. Broadway stage, television, motion pictures.
PICTURES: Kiss Me Deadly (debut, 1955), The Rack, The Chapman Report, Butch Cassidy and the Sundance Kid, Lovers and Other Strangers, The People Next Door, W.U.S.A., The Steagle, The Last Picture Show (Acad. Award, best supporting actress, 1971), Dillinger, Charlie and the Angel, Happy Mother's Day... Love George, Daisy Miller, Young Frankenstein, Crazy Mama, High Anxiety, The Mouse and His Child (voice), The North Avenue Irregulars, The Muppet Movie, Scavenger Hunt, Foolin' Around, Yesterday, Herbie Goes Bananas, History of the World—Part I, My Little Pony (voice), Shadow Play, Walk Like a Man, Hansel and Gretel, Prancer, Texasville, Love Hurts, My Boyfriend's Back, The Beverly Hillbillies, A Troll in Central park (voice), Now and Then, Beavis and Butt-Head Do America (voice), Never Too Late, Gen 13, The Iron Giant, Music of the Heart, Hanging Up, The Amati Girls, Animal, Manna From Heaven. .
TELEVISION: *Series*: Hold It Please, Charlie Wild: Private Detective, Bob and Ray, Lassie, Mary Tyler Moore Show (Emmy Awards 1974, 1975), Phyllis (Golden Globe Award), The Facts of Life, The Nutt House, Walter & Emily. *Movies*: Silent Night Lonely Night, Suddenly Single, Haunts of the Very Rich, A Brand New Life (Emmy Award, 1973), Crime Club, Dying Room Only, The Migrants, Hitchhike!, Thursday's Game, Death Sentence, Someone I Touched, A Girl Named Sooner, Death Scream, The New Original Wonder Woman, The Love Boat (pilot), It Happened One Christmas, Long Journey Back, Willa, Mrs. R's Daughter, S.O.S. Titanic, The Acorn People, Advice to the Lovelorn, Miss All-American Beauty, Dixie: Changing Habits, Demon Murder Case, Ernie Kovacs: Between the Laughter, Deadly Intentions, Love Is Never Silent, Wedding Bell Blues, Danielle Steel's Fine Things, In Broad Daylight, A Little Piece of Heaven, Fade to Black, Without a Kiss Goodbye, Miracle Child, Double Double Toil and Trouble, Between Love and Honor, Annabella Wish. *Specials*: Oldest Living Graduate, Of Thee I Sing, Breakfast With Les and Bess, Screen Actors Guild 50th Anniversary Celebration (Emmy Award, 1984). *Guest*: Twilight Zone, Untouchables, Big Valley, That Girl, Marcus Welby, Night Gallery, Cher (Emmy Award, 1975), Love Boat, Promised Land (Emmy Award, 1997), The Simpsons, The Nanny, Touched By An Angel, The Norm Show, many others.

LEAR, NORMAN
Producer, Director, Writer. b. New Haven, CT, July 27, 1922. e. Emerson Coll. In public relations 1945-49. Began in TV as co-writer of weekly one-hour variety show, The Ford Star Revue in 1950. Followed as writer for Dean Martin and Jerry Lewis on the Colgate Comedy Hour and for the Martha Raye and George Gobel TV shows. With partner, Bud Yorkin, created and produced such specials as Another Evening with Fred Astaire, Henry Fonda and the Family, An Evening with Carol Channing, and The Many Sides of Don Rickles. In 1965 their company, Tandem Productions, also produced the original Andy Williams Show. Moved into motion pictures in 1963, writing and producing Come Blow Your Horn. Formed Act III Communications, 1987.
PICTURES: Come Blow Your Horn (co-prod., s.p.), Never Too Late (prod.), Divorce-American Style (prod., s.p.), The Night They Raided Minsky's (co.-prod., co-s.p.), Start the Revolution Without Me (exec. prod.), Cold Turkey (dir., s.p., prod.), The Princess Bride (exec. prod.), Fried Green Tomatoes (co-exec. prod.), Way Past Cool (exec. prod.).
TELEVISION: *Creator-dir.*: TV Guide Award Show (1962), Henry Fonda and the Family (1963), Andy Williams Specials, Robert Young and the Family. Exec. prod. and creator or developer: All in the Family (3 Emmy Awards), Maude, Good Times, Sanford and Son, The Jeffersons, Mary Hartman Mary Hartman, One Day at a Time, All's Fair, A Year at the Top, All that Glitters, Fernwood 2 Night, The Baxters, Palmerstown, I Love Liberty, Heartsounds, Sunday Dinner, The Powers That Be, 704 Hauser.

LEARNED, MICHAEL
Actress. b. Washington, DC, Apr. 9, 1939. Studied ballet and dramatics in school. Many stage credits include Under Milkwood, The Three Sisters, A God Slept Here, The Sisters Rosensweig, etc.; resident performances with Shakespeare festivals in Canada, Stratford, CT, and San Diego, CA. Gained fame on hit TV series, The Waltons, as the mother, Olivia.
PICTURES: Touched by Love, Shanghai Shadows (narrator), Power, Dragon: The Bruce Lee Story, Life During Wartime.
TELEVISION: *Series*: The Waltons (3 Emmy Awards: 1973, 1974, 1976), Nurse (Emmy Award, 1982), Hothouse, Living Dolls. *Guest*: Gunsmoke, Police Story, St. Elsewhere, Murder She Wrote, Who's the Boss?. *Movies*: Hurricane, It Couldn't Happen to a Nicer Guy, Widow, Little Mo, Nurse (pilot), Off the Minnesota Strip, A Christmas Without Snow, Mother's Day on Walton Mountain, The Parade, A Deadly Business, Mercy or Murder?, Roots: The Gift, Gunsmoke: The Last Apache, Aftermath: A Test of Love, Keeping Secrets, A Walton Thanksgiving Reunion, A Walton Wedding, A Father for Brittany. *Specials*: All My Sons, Picnic.

LEARY, DENIS
Actor. b.Boston, MA, Aug. 18, 1957. e. Emerson Coll. Performed with the New Voices Theater Company, Charlestown Working Theater. Debuted one-man stand-up show No Cure for Cancer at Edinburgh Intl. Arts Fest., then later in London, Off-B'way, and cable tv. Appeared in and dir. short film for Showtime, Thy Neighbor's Wife.
PICTURES: Strictly Business (debut), National Lampoon's Loaded Weapon 1, The Sandlot, Who's the Man?, Gunmen, Demolition Man, Judgment Night, The Ref, Operation Dumbo Drop, The Neon Bible, Two If by Sea (also co-s.p.), Suicide Kings, The Real Blonde, Underworld, The MatchMaker, Wag the Dog, Snitch, A Bug's Life (voice), Love Walked In, Wide Awake, Small Soldiers, The Thomas Crown Affair, Sand, Jesus' Son, True Crime.
TELEVISION: *Movies:* The Second Civil War, Subway Stories: Tales from the Underground.

LEAUD, JEAN-PIERRE
Actor. b. Paris, France, May 5, 1944. Parents were screenwriter Pierre Leaud and actress Jacqueline Pierreux. At 14 chosen to play Antoine Doinel in Truffaut's The 400 Blows and subsequent autobiographical films Love at 20, Stolen Kisses, Bed and Board, Love on the Run. Also closely identified with major films by Jean-Luc Godard.
PICTURES: The 400 Blows, Boulevard, The Testament of Orpheus, Love at Twenty, Masculine-Feminine, Made in USA, Le Depart, La Chinoise, Weekend, Stolen Kisses, Le Gai Savoir, Pigsty, The Oldest Profession, Bed and Board, Two English Girls, Last Tango in Paris, Day for Night, Lola's Lolos, Love on the Run, Rebelote, Detective, Just a Movie, Seen by... 20 Years After, Treasure Island, The Grandeur and Decadence of a Small-Time Filmmaker, With All Hands, Time to Aim, Jane B, par Agnes V.; 36 Fillete, La Femme de Paille (The Straw Woman), The Color of the Wind, Femme de Papier, Bunker Palace Hotel, Treasure Island, I Hired a Contract Killer, Paris at Dawn, The Birth of Love, Nobody Loves Me, The Seducer's Diary, A Hundred & One Nights, Irma Vep, Mon Homme, Pour Rire!, Elizabeth.

LeBLANC, MATT
Actor. b. Newton, MA, July 25, 1967.
PICTURES: The Killing Box, Lookin' Italian, Ed, Lost in Space.
TELEVISION: *Movies:* Anything to Survive, Reform School Girl. *Series:* TV 101, Top of the Heap, Vinnie & Bobby, Friends. *Guest:* Just the Ten of Us, Married...with Children, Red Shoe Diaries.

LEDER, HERBERT JAY
Writer, Director, Producer, b. New York, NY, Aug. 15, 1922. e. B.A., Ph.D. Play Doctor on Broadway; Director TV dept., Benton and Bowles Adv. chg. all T.V. & Film production, 13 yrs. Sponsored Films: Child Molester, Bank Robber, Shoplifter, Untouchables.
PICTURES: *Writer*: Fiend Without a Face, Pretty Boy Floyd (also dir., co-prod.), Nine Miles to Noon (also dir., co-prod.), Aquarius Mission, Love Keeps No Score of Wrongs, The Frozen Dead (also dir., prod.), It (also dir., prod.), Candyman (also dir.), The Winners, The Way It Is, The Cool Crazies.

LEDER, MIMI
Director, Script Supervisor. b. 1952. Daughter of late Producer.Director Paul Leder.
PICTURES: The Peacemaker, Deep Impact, Sentimental Journey, Pay It Forward, Still Life.
TELEVISION: *Script Supervisor*: Dummy, The Boy Who Drank too Much, A Long Way Home, A time to Live, L.A. Law. *Director*: L.A. Law, China Beach, Nightingales, Midnight Caller, A Little Piece of Heaven, A Woman with a Past, Marked for Muder, There Was a Little Boy, Rio Shannon, Baby Broker, ER, The Innocent.

LEDERER, RICHARD
Executive. b. New York, NY, Sept. 22, 1916. e. U. of Virginia, B.S., 1938. Freelance writer, 1939-41; U.S. Army. Cryptanalyst, Signal Intell. Serv 1941-45; Adv. copywriter, Columbia Pictures, 1946-50; Adv. copywriter, Warner Bros., 1950-53; copy chief, Warner Bros., 1950-53; copy chief, Warner Bros., 1953-57; Asst. Nat'l Adv. mgr., Warner Bros. studios, 1957-59; Prod., theatrical, TV. Warner Bros. studios, 1959-60; Dir. of adv., publicity, Warner Bros. Pictures, 1960; v.p. Warner Bros. Pictures, 1963. V.P. production, Warner Bros. Studio, 1969-70; indep. prod. to 1971, when returned to WB as adv.-pub., v.p. Independent producer. 1980: Hollywood Knights. Joined Orion Pictures as v.p., adv. Resigned, 1984.

LEDGER, HEATH
Actor. b. Perth, Australia, April 4, 1979.
PICTURES: Blackrock, Paws, Two Hands, 10 Things I Hate About You, Patriot.
TELEVISION: *Series:* Sweat, Roar.

LEE, ANG
Director, Producer, Writer. b. Pingtung, Taiwan, Oct. 23, 1954.
PICTURES: Joe's Bed-Stuy Barbershop: We Cut Heads, Pushing Hands, The Wedding Banquet, Eat Drink Man Woman, Siao Yu, Sense and Sensibility, The Ice Storm, Ride with the Devil, Crouching Tiger, Hidden Dragon, Berlin Diaries: 1940-1945.

LEE, ANNA
Actress. M.B.E. r.n. Joan Boniface Winnifrith. b. Kent, England, Jan. 2, 1913. e. Central School of Speech Training and Dramatic Art, Royal Albert Hall. With London Repertory Theatre; toured in the Constant Nymph and Jane Eyre. In 1930s known as Britain's Glamour Girl. 1939 came to US to star in My Life With Caroline. Entertained troops with U.S.O. during WWII. 1950 moved to N.Y. to appear in live TV.
PICTURES: Ebb Tide (debut, 1932), Yes Mr. Brown, Say It With Music, Mayfair Girl, King's Cup, Chelsea Life, Mannequin, Faces, The Bermondsey Kid, Lucky Loser, The Camels Are Coming, Rolling in Money, Heat Wave, Passing of the Third Floor Back, First a Girl, The Man Who Changed His Mind, O.H.M.S., King Solomon's Mines, Non-Stop New York, The Four Just Men, Return to Yesterday, Young Man's Fancy, Seven Sinners, My Life With Caroline, How Green Was My Valley, Flying Tigers, The Commandos Strike at Dawn, Hangmen Also Die, Flesh and Fantasy, Forever and a Day, Summer Storm, Abroad With Two Yanks, Bedlam, G.I. War Brides, High Conquest, The Ghost and Mrs. Muir, Best Man Wins, Fort Apache, Prison Warden, Wyoming Mail, Boots Malone, Daniel Boone—Trail Blazer, Gideon of Scotland Yard, The Last Hurrah, The Horse Soldiers, Jet Over the Atlantic, This Eath Is Mine, The Big Night, The Crimson Kimono, Jack the Giant Killer, Two Rode Together, The Man Who Shot Liberty Valance, What Ever Happend to Baby Jane?, The Prize, The Unsinkable Molly Brown, For Those Who Think Young, The Sound of Music, Torn Curtain, Seven Women, Picture Mommy Dead, In Like Flint, Star!, Clash.
TELEVISION: Guest on many major television shows from 1950-77. *Series*: General Hospital (1978-present). *Movies*: Eleanor and Franklin, The Night Rider, The Beasts are Loose, Scruples.

LEE, CHRISTOPHER
Actor. b. London, England, May 27, 1922. e. Wellington Coll. Served RAF 1940-46. Ent. m.p. ind. 1947. *Autobiography*: Tall, Dark and Gruesome (1977).
PICTURES: include: Corridor of Mirrors (debut, 1947), One Night With You, A Song for Tomorrow, Scott of the Antarctic, Hamlet, The Gay Lady, Capt. Horatio Hornblower, Valley of the Eagles, The Crimson Pirate, Babes in Bagdad, Moulin Rouge, Innocents of Paris, That Lady, The Warriors, Cockleshell Heroes, Storm Over the Nile, Port Afrique, Private's Progress, Beyond Mombasa, Battle of the River Plate, Night Ambush, She Played With Fire, The Traitors, Curse of Frankenstein, Bitter Victory, Truth About Women, Tale of Two Cities, Dracula, Man Who Could Cheat Death, The Mummy, Too Hot to Handle, Beat Girl, City of the Dead (Horror Hotel), Two Faces of Dr. Jekyll, The Terror of the Tongs, The Hands of Orlac, Taste of Fear, The Devil's Daffodil, Pirates of Blood River, Devil's Agent, Red Orchid, Valley of Fear, Katharsis, Faust '63, The Virgin of Nuremberg, The Whip and the Body, Carmilla, The Devil Ship Pirates, The Gorgon, The Sign of Satan, The House of Blood, Dr. Terror's House of Horrors, She, The Skull, The Mask of Fu Manchu, Dracula, Prince of Darkness, Rasputin, Theatre of Death, Circus of Fear, The Brides of Fu Manchu, Five Golden Dragons, Vengeance of Fu Manchu, Night of the Big Heat, The Pendulum, The Face of Eve, The Devil Rides Out, The Blood of Fu Manchu, The Crimson Altar, Dracula Has Risen from the Grave, The Oblong Box, De Sade 70, Scream and Scream Again, The Magic Christian, Julius Caesar, One More Time, Count Dracula, Bloody Judge, Taste the Blood of Dracula, The Private Life of Sherlock Holmes, El Umbragolo, Scars of Dracula, The House That Dripped Blood, I Monster, Hannie Caulder, Dracula A.D. 1972, Horror Express, Death Line (Raw Meat), Nothing But the Night (also co-exec. prod.), The Creeping Flesh, The Wicker Man, Poor Devil, Dark Places, Satanic Rites of Dracula, Eulalie Quitte les Champs, The Three Musketeers, Earthbound, The Man with the Golden Gun, The Four Musketeers, Killer Force, Diagnosis—Murder, Whispering Death, The Keeper, To the Devil a Daughter, Dracula and Son, Airport '77, Starship Invasions, The End of the World, Return from Witch Mountain, Caravans, The Passage, Arabian Adventure, Jaguar Lives, Circle of Iron, 1941, Bear Island, Serial, The Salamander, An Eye for an Eye, Safari 3000, House of Long Shadows, The Return of Captain Invincible, The Rosebud Beach Hotel, Roadtrip, Dark Mission, The Howling II: Your Sister is a Werewolf, Olympus Force, Jocks, Murder Story, Mio In the Land of Faraway, The Girl, The Return of the Musketeers, Honeymoon Academy, The French Revolution, Gremlins 2: The New Batch, Curse III: Blood Sacrifice, The Rainbow Thief, L'Avaro, Jackpot, Double Vision, Shogun Mayeda, Special Class, Journey of Honor, Cybereden, Funny Man, Police Academy: Mission to Moscow, A Feast at Midnight, The Stupids, Sorellina, Jinnah, Russell Mulcahy's Tale of the Mummy, Sleepy Hollow, The Lord of the Rings: The Fellowship of the Ring.
TELEVISION: The Disputation, Metier du Seigneur, Movies: Poor Devil, Harold Robbins' The Pirate, Captain America II, Once a Spy, Charles and Diana: A Royal Love Story, Far Pavilions, Shaka Zulu, Goliath Awaits, Massarati and the Brain, Around the World in 80 Days, Treasure Island, Young Indiana Jones, The Care of Time, Sherlock Holmes & the Leading Lady, Sherlock Holmes and the Incident at Victoria Falls, Death Train, The Tomorrow People, Tales of Mystery & Imagination, Moses, Ivanhoe.

LEE, JASON SCOTT
Actor. b. Los Angeles, CA, 1966. Raised in Hawaii. e. Fullerton Col., Organge County, CA.
PICTURES: Born in East L.A. (debut, 1987), Back to the Future II, Map of the Human Heart, Dragon: The Bruce Lee Story, Rapa Nui, Rudyard Kipling's The Jungle Book, Tale of the Mummy, Soldier, Arabian Nights (voice).
TELEVISION: *Movie*: Vestige of Honor. *Special*: American Eyes. *Guest*: Showtime's Hunger Series.

LEE, JOIE
Actress. b. 1968. e. Sarah Lawrence Col. Brother is director-writer Spike Lee. On NY stage in Mulebone. Appeared in short film Coffee and Cigarettes Part Two. Has also been billed as Joy Lee, Joie Susannah Lee.
PICTURES: She's Gotta Have It (debut, 1986), School Daze, Do the Right Thing, Bail Jumper, Mo' Better Blues, A Kiss Before Dying, Fathers and Sons, Crooklyn (also story, co-s.p., assoc. prod.), Losing Isaiah, Girl 6, Get on the Bus, Summer of Sam.

LEE, MICHELE
Actress. b. Los Angeles, CA, June 24, 1942. On Broadway in How to Succeed in Business Without Really Trying, Seesaw.
PICTURES: How to Succeed in Business Without Really Trying, The Love Bug, The Comic.
TELEVISION: *Series*: Knots Landing (also dir. several episodes). *Movies*: Dark Victory, Bud and Lou, Letter to Three Wives, Single Women Married Men (also exec. prod.), The Fatal Image, My Son Johnny, Broadway Bound, When No One Would Listen (also exec. prod.), Big Dreams & Broken Hearts: The Dottie West Story (also exec. prod.), Color Me Perfect (also dir., prod., co-s.p.).

LEE, PEGGY
Singer, Actress. r.n. Norma Egstrom. b. Jamestown, ND, May 26, 1920. Began career as night club vocalist in Fargo; became& radio singer, WDAY, then with bandleader Sev Olsen in Minneapolis, Will Osborne, Benny Goodman. Collabolrated with Dave Barbour on such songs as Manana, It's a Good Day, What More Can a Woman Do?, Fever, Johnny Guitar, So What's New. Also leading recording artist.
\PICTURES: Stage Door Canteen, Mr. Music, The Jazz Singer, Pete Kelly's Blues (Acad. Award nom.), Lady and the Tramp (voices, co- composer).
TELEVISION: *Series*: TV's Top Tunes, Songs for Sale. *Guest*: Jimmy Durante, Dean Martin, Ed Sullivan, The Andy Williams Show.

LEE, SHERYL
Actress. b. Augsburg, Germany, April 22, 1967.
PICTURES: Wild at Heart, I Love You to Death, Twin Peaks: Fire Walk With Me, Jersey Girl, Backbeat, Don't Do It, Fall Times, Notes From Underground, Homage, Mother Night, Bliss, This World, Then the Fireworks, The Blood Oranges, Vampires, Kiss the Sky, Dante's View, Angel's Dance.
TELEVISION: *Movies:* Love, Lies, and Murder, Guinevere, Follow the River, David. *Series:* Twin Peaks, L.A. Doctors. *Guest:* Red Shoe Diaries, Dr. Quinn, Medicine Woman.

LEE, SPIKE
Director, Producer, Writer, Actor. r.n. Shelton Jackson Lee. b. Atlanta, GA, Mar. 20, 1957. Son of jazz bass musician, composer Bill Lee. Sister is actress Joie Lee. e. Morehouse Coll B.A., Mass Comm., MFA NYU Film Sch. Completed 2 student features and hour-long thesis: Joe's Bed-Stuy Barbershop: We Cut Heads which won student Acad. Award from Acad. M.P. Arts & Sciences. Wrote, prod., dir., co-starred in indep. feature, She's Gotta Have It, budgeted at $175,000. Appeared in films Lonely in America, Hoop Dreams. Author of five books on his films. Director of numerous tv commercials for Nike, Levi's, ESPN and others. Director of over 35 music videos for Michael Jackson, Stevie Wonder, Miles Davis, and others.
PICTURES: Joe's Bed-Stuy Barbershop: We Cut Heads (co-prod., dir., s.p., editor). *Dir.-Prod.-Writer-Actor*: She's Gotta Have It (LA Film Critics Award for best new director, 1986), School Daze, Do the Right Thing (LA Film Critics Awards for best picture & dir., 1989), Mo' Better Blues, Jungle Fever, Malcolm X, Crooklyn, Clockers, Girl 6, Get On the Bus, 4 Little Girls, He Got Game, Summer of Sam, Michael Jordan to the Max (actor only), Famous (actor), The Original Kings of Comedy, Bamboozled . *Executive Producer*: Drop Squad (also actor), New Jersey Drive, Tales From the Hood, Subway Stories: Tales from the Underground, 3 AM.
TELEVISION: *Guest*: The Debbie Allen's Special, Spike & Co. Do It A Capella.

LEEDS, MARTIN N.
Film-TV Executive. b. New York, NY, Apr. 6, 1916. e. NYU, B.S., 1936; J.D., 1938. Admitted NY Bar, 1938, CA Bar, 1948; dir. ind. rltns. Wabash Appliance Corp., 1943-44; ind. bus. rltns. cons. Davis & Gilbert, 1944-45; dir. ind. rltns. Flying Tiger Lines, 1947; dir. bus. affairs CBS TV div., 1947-53; exec. v.p. Desilu Productions, Inc., 1953-60; v.p. Motion Picture Center Studios, Inc.: memb. Industry comm. War Manpower Comm., 1943; chmn. Comm. to form Television Code of Ethics: U.S. Army 1941. Exec. v.p. in chg. of West Coast oper. & member of bd. of dir. Talent Associates—Paramount Ltd., Hollywood, 1962; TV production consultant; exec. v.p., Electronovision Prods. Inc., 1964; TV prod. & MP prod. consultant, 1965; pres., CEO, memb. of bd., Beverly Hills Studios, Inc., 1969; sr. v.p., American Film Theatre, 1973; 1975, motion picture and TV attorney & consultant.

LEEWOOD, JACK
Producer. b. New York, NY. May 20, 1913. e. Upsala Coll., Newark U., NYU. 1926-31 with Gottesman-Stern circuit as usher, asst. and relief mgr.; 1931-43 Stanley-Warner, mgr. of Ritz, Capitol and Hollywood theatres 1943-47. Joined Warner Bros. field forces in Denver-Salt Lake; Seattle-Portland, 1947-48. Dir. pub. & adv. Screen Guild Prod.; 1948-52, Lippert Productions; prod. exec., 1953-56, Allied Artists; 1957-62 prod. 20th Cent. Fox; 1965-68, prod., Universal; 1976-78. Affiliated Theatre S.F. & HTN.; 1978-83. Hamner Prod.
PICTURES: Holiday Rhythm, Gunfire, Hi-Jacked, Roaring City, Danger Zone, Lost Continent, F.B.I. Girl, Pier 23, Train to Tombstone, I Shot Billy the Kid, Bandit Queen, Motor Patrol, Savage Drums, Three Desperate Men, Border Rangers, Western Pacific Agent, Thundering Jets, Lone Texan, Little Savage, Alligator People, 13 Fighting Men, Young Jesse James, Swingin' Along, We'll Bury You, 20,000 Eyes, Thunder Island, The Plainsman.
TELEVISION: Longest 100 Miles, Escape to Mindanao, Dallas Cowboys Cheerleaders, When Hell Was in Session, Fugitive Family, Dallas Cowboys Cheerleaders II, Million Dollar Face, Portrait of a Showgirl, Margin For Murder, Anatomy of an Illness, Malibu.

LEFFERTS, GEORGE
Producer, Writer, Director. b. Paterson, NJ. e. Univ. of MI. Dir., numerous award-winning TV series, films. Exec. prod.-Time-Life films prod./writer, Movie of the Week (NBC) Biog: Who's Who in America, Who's Who in the World. Exec. prod., Bing Crosby Productions, prod., NBC 10 yrs, Independent. Exec. prod. David Wolper prods. 4 Emmy Awards, 2 Golden Globe Awards, 2 New England Journalism Awards, 1 Cine Golden Eagle Award.
THEATER: Hey Everybody, The Boat.
PICTURES: The Stake, Mean Dog Blues, The Living End, The Boat, The Teenager.
TELEVISION: *Specials*: Teacher Teacher (Emmy Award, 1969), Benjamin Franklin (Emmy Award, 1975), Purex Specials for Women (Emmy Award, Producer's Guild Award; writer, prod. dir.), Our Group (writer), Jean Seberg Story. *Series*: Breaking Point (exec. prod.), The Bill Cosby Show, Studio One, Kraft Theatre, Chrysler Theatre, Sinatra Show, Lights Out, Alcoa, The Bold Ones, One Life to Live (WGA Award), Ryan's Hope (prod.). *Movies*: The Harness, She's Dressed to Kill, The Night They Took Miss Beautiful, Smithsonian Institution Specials (exec. prod.).

LEGATO, ROBERT
Special Effects, Director.
PICTURES: Interview with the Vampire, Apollo 13, Titanic (Acad. Award, Best Visual Effects, 1997).
TELEVISION: *Series*: Star Trek: The Next Generation (also dir.), Star Trek: Deep Space 9 (also dir.) *Movies*: Star Trek: Deep Space Nine-Emissary.

LEGRAND, MICHEL JEAN
Composer, Conductor. b. France, Feb. 24, 1932. Son of well-known arranger, composer and pianist, Raymond Legrand. At 11 Michel, a child prodigy, entered Paris Cons. and graduated nine years later with top honors in composition and as solo pianist. In late fifties turned to composing for films and has composed, orchestrated and conducted scores of more than 140 films.
PICTURES: Lola, Eva, Vivre Sa Vie, La Baie des Anges, The Umbrellas of Cherbourg, Banda a Part, Un Femme Mariee, Une Femme est une Femme, The Young Girls of Rochefort, Ice Station Zebra, The Thomas Crown Affair (Academy Award for best song: The Windmills of Your Mind, 1968), Pieces of Dreams, The Happy Ending, Picasso Summer, Wuthering Heights, The Go-Between, Summer of '42 (Academy Award, 1971), Lady Sings the Blues, The Nelson Affair, Breezy, The Three Musketeers, Sheila Levine, Gable and Lombard, Ode to Billy Joe, The Savage, The Other Side of Midnight, The Fabulous Adventures of the Legendary Baron Munchausen, The Roads of the South, The Hunter, The Mountain Men, Atlantic City, Falling in Love Again, Best Friends, A Love in Germany, Never Say Never Again, Yentl (Academy Award, 1983), Hell Train, Micki and Maude, Secret Places, Spirale, Parking, Switching Channels, Three Seats for the 26th Cinq jours en juin (dir. debut, s.p., music), Dingo, The Pickle, Ready to Wear (Pret-a-Porter), Les Miserables, The Children of Lumiere, Aaron's Magic Village, Madeline, Doggy Bag.
TELEVISION: *Movies*: Brian's Song, The Jesse Owens Story, A Woman Called Golda, As Summers Die, Crossings, Sins, Promises to Keep, Not a Penny More Not a Penny Less, The Burning Shore, The Ring.

LE GROS, JAMES
Actor. b. Minneapolis, MN, Apr. 27, 1962.
THEATER: The Cherry Orchard, Galileo, Ceremony of Innocence, Table Settings, Curse of the Starving Class, American Buffalo, Bits and Bytes, Becoming Memories, Slab Boys.
PICTURES: Solarbabies, Near Dark, Fatal Beauty, Phantasm II, Drugstore Cowboy, Point Break, Blood & Concrete, The Rapture, Where the Day Takes You, Singles, My New Gun, Bad Girls, Floundering, Mrs. Parker and the Vicious Circle, Destiny Turns on the Radio, Panther, Safe, Living in Oblivion, Infinity, The Low Life, Boys, The Destiny of Marty Fine.
TELEVISION: *Movie:* Gun Crazy.

LEGUIZAMO, JOHN
Actor. b. Bogota, Colombia, July 22, 1964. Moved to Queens, NY at age 5. e. NYU. Appeared in award-winning student film Five Out of Six, while in school. Studied acting with Lee Strasberg and Wynn Handman. Made professional debut on Miami Vice on tv.
THEATER: A Midsummer Night's Dream, La Puta Vida, Parting Gestures, Mambo Mouth (also writer; Obie & Outer Critics Circle Awards), Spic-O-Rama (also writer; Drama Desk & Theatre World Awards).
PICTURES: Casualties of War, Revenge, Die Hard 2, Gentile Alouette, Street Hunter, Out for Justice, Hangin' With the Homeboys, Regarding Henry, Whispers in the Dark, Super Mario Bros., Night Owl, Carlito's Way, A Pyromaniac's Love Story, To Wong Foo—Thanks for Everything—Julie Newmar, Executive Decision, Romeo and Juliet, The Pest, A Brother's Kiss, Spawn, Frogs for Snakes, Doctor Dolittle (voice), The Split, Summer of Sam, Joe the King (also exec. prod.), Moulin Rouge, Titan A.E. (voice), King of the Jungle, What's The Worst That Could Happen?, Collateral Damage, Empire.

TELEVISION: *Series*: House of Buggin', The Brothers Garcia (voice). *Specials*: Talent Pool Comedy Special (ACE Award), Mambo Mouth (also writer), Spic-O-Rama (also writer; 3 Cable ACE Awards).

LEHMAN, ERNEST
Writer, Producer, Director. b. New York, NY, 1923. e. City Coll. of New York. Began career as free-lance journalist and magazine fiction writer. First pub. books, The Comedian, The Sweet Smell of Success. First hardcover novel, The French Atlantic Affair followed by Farewell Performance, and first non-fiction book, Screening Sickness. Pres., WGAW, 1983-85.1987, 1988, 1990: Acad. Awards show (co-writer). The Ernest Lehman Collection is archived at the Humanities Research Center, Univ. of TX at Austin, and in part at USC Film Library and Margaret Herrick Library. Co-prod. of musical stage adaptation of Sweet Smell of Success. Laurel Award for Screen Achievement, WGAW, 1973. Five Best Screenplay Awards, WGAW.
PICTURES: *Writer*: Executive Suite, Sabrina (co-s.p.; Acad. Award nom.), The King and I, Somebody Up There Likes Me, Sweet Smell of Success (co-s.p.; based on his own novelette), North By Northwest (Acad. Award nom.), From the Terrace, West Side Story (Acad. Award nom.), The Prize, The Sound of Music, Who's Afraid of Virginia Woolf? (also prod.; 2 Acad. Award noms. for picture & s.p.), Hello Dolly! (also prod.; Acad. Award nom. for picture), Portnoy's Complaint (also dir., prod.), Family Plot, Black Sunday (co-s.p.).

LEHMANN, MICHAEL
Director. b. San Francisco, CA, March 30, 1957. e. U Cal, Berkeley, Columbia U. Started in industry supervising video systems used in the Francis Ford Coppola films One From the Heart, Rumble Fish, The Outsiders. Dir. short films for Saturday Night Live incl. Ed's Secret Life. Served as exec. prod. on Ed Wood.
PICTURES: Heathers (debut, 1989), Meet the Applegates, Hudson Hawk, Airheads, Ed Wood (exec. prod. only), The Truth About Cats and Dogs, My Giant.
TELEVISION: *Series*: The Larry Sanders Show, Homicide: Life on the Street.

LEHRER, JIM
News Anchor. b. Wichita, KS, 1934. e. Victoria Col., Univ. of MO. Served in US Marine Corps. 1959-66, reporter for Dallas Morning News, Dallas Times-Herald; 1968 became Times-Herald's city editor before moving into tv as exec. dir. of public affairs, host and editor of news program on KERA-TV in Dallas. To Washington where he became public affairs coord. for PBS, then corresp. for the Natl. Public Affairs Center for Television. 1973 first teamed with Robert MacNeil to cover Senate Watergate hearings. 1975, served as D.C. corresp. for the Robert MacNeil Report on PBS (showed was re-named The MacNeil/Lehrer Report in 1976). 1983, started The MacNeil/Lehrer NewsHour. 1995, became exec. editor and anchor of new version of series The NewsHour With Jim Lehrer.

LEIBMAN, RON
Actor. b. New York, NY, Oct. 11, 1937. m. actress Jessica Walter. e. Ohio Wesleyan U. Joined Actor's Studio in N.Y.; first professional appearance in summer theatre production of A View from the Bridge.
THEATER: The Premise, Dear Me, The Sky Is Falling, We Bombed in New Haven (Theatre World Award), Cop Out, Room Service, I Oughta Be in Pictures, The Deputy, Bicycle Ride to Nevada, Doubles, Rumors, Angels in America: Millenium Approaches (Tony & Drama Desk Awards).
PICTURES: Where's Poppa (debut, 1970), The Hot Rock, Slaughterhouse Five, Your Three Minutes Are Up, Super Cops, Won Ton Ton the Dog Who Saved Hollywood, Norma Rae, Up the Academy, Zorro the Gay Blade, Romantic Comedy, Phar Lap, Rhinestone, Door to Door, Seven Hours to Judgement, Night Falls on Manhattan.
TELEVISION: *Series*: Kaz (Emmy Award, 1979), Pacific Station, Central Park West. *Movies*: The Art of Crime, A Question of Guilt, Rivkin: Bounty Hunter, Many Happy Returns, Christmas Eve, Terrorist on Trial: The United States vs. Salim Ajami.

LEIDER, GERALD J.
Producer, Executive. b. Camden, NJ, May 28, 1931. e. Syracuse U., 1953; Bristol U., Eng., 1954, Fulbright Fellow-ship in drama. m. Susan Trustman. 1955 joined MCA, Inc., N.Y.; 1956-59 theatre producer in NY, London: Shinbone Alley, Garden District, and Sir John Gielgud's Ages of Man. 1960-61; director of special programs, CBS/TV; 1961-62, dir. of program sales, CBS-TV; 1962-69, v.p., tv optns., Ashley Famous Agency, Inc.; 1969-74, pres. Warner Bros. TV, Burbank; 1975-76, exec. v.p. foreign prod. Warner Bros. Pictures, Rome; 1977-82, indept. prod. under Jerry Leider Prods.; 1982-87, pres., ITC Prods., Inc; named pres. and CEO, ITC Entertain-ment Group, 1987-91.
PICTURES: Wild Horse Hank, The Jazz Singer, Trenchcoat.
TELEVISION: *Movies*: And I Alone Survived, Willa, The Hostage Tower, The Scarlet and the Black, Secrets of a Married Man, The Haunting Passion, Letting Go, A Time to Live, The Girl Who Spelled Freedom, Unnatural Causes, Poor Little Rich Girl.

LEIGH, JANET
Actress. r.n. Jeanette Helen Morrison. b. Merced, CA, July 6, 1927. Mother of actresses Jamie Lee Curtis and Kelly Curtis. e. Coll. of Pacific, music. Author: There Really Was a Hollywood (autobiography, 1984), Behind the Scenes of Psycho (1995), House of Destiny (novel; 1995).
THEATER: includes: Murder Among Friends, Love Letters (with Van Johnson).
PICTURES: The Romance of Rosy Ridge (debut, 1947), If Winter Comes, Hills of Home, Words and Music, Act of Violence, Little Women, That Forsyte Woman, Red Danube, Doctor and the Girl, Holiday Affair, Two Tickets to Broadway, Strictly Dishonorable, Angels in the Outfield, It's a Big Country, Just This Once, Scaramouche, Fearless Fagan, Naked Spur, Confidentially Connie, Houdini, Walking My Baby Back Home, Prince Valiant, Living It Up, Black Shield of Falworth, Rogue Cop, My Sister Eileen, Pete Kelly's Blues, Safari, Jet Pilot, Touch of Evil, The Vikings, The Perfect Furlough, Who Was That Lady?, Psycho (Acad. Award nom.), Pepe, The Manchurian Candidate, Bye Bye Birdie, Wives and Lovers, Three on a Couch, Harper, An American Dream, Kid Rodelo, Grand Slam, Hello Down There, One Is a Lonely Number, Night of the Lepus, Boardwalk, The Fog, Other Realms, Halloween H20: Twenty Years Later.
TELEVISION: *Movies*: Honeymoon With a Stranger, House on Green Apple Road, The Monk, Deadly Dream, Mirror Mirror, Telethon, Murder at the World Series, Carriage from Britain, Murder in the First, Dear Deductible, Catch Me If You Can, One for My Baby, My Wives, Jane, The Chairman, Death's Head, This Is Maggie Mulligan, Tales of the Unexpected, On the Road, In My Sister's Shadow, Hitchcock: Shadow of a Genius.
Guest: Matt Houston, Starman, Murder She Wrote.

LEIGH, JENNIFER JASON
Actress. r.n. Jennifer Leigh Morrow. b. Los Angeles, CA, Feb. 5, 1962. Daughter of late actor Vic Morrow and TV writer Barbara Turner. At age 14 debuted in Disney tv movie The Young Runaway. Won L.A. Valley Coll. best actress award for stage prod. The Shadow Box (1979).
PICTURES: Eyes of a Stranger (debut, 1981), Wrong Is Right, Fast Times at Ridgemont High, Easy Money, Grandview U.S.A., The Hitcher, Flesh + Blood, The Men's Club, Undercover, Sister Sister, Heart of Midnight, The Big Picture, Miami Blues (NY Film Critics Award, 1990), Last Exit to Brooklyn (NY Film Critics Award, 1990), Backdraft, Crooked Hearts, Rush, Single White Female, Short Cuts, The Hudsucker Proxy, Mrs. Parker and the Vicious Circle (Natl. Society of Film Critics & Chicago Film Critics Awards, 1994), Dolores Claiborne, Georgia (also co-prod.), Kansas City, A Thousand Acres, Washington Square, eXistenZ, The King is Alive, Skipped Parts, Beautiful View, The Quickie, The Anniversary Party.
TELEVISION: *Movies*: The Young Runaway, Angel City, The Killing of Randy Webster, The Best Little Girl in the World, The First Time, Girls of the White Orchid, Buried Alive, The Love Letter, Thanks of a Grateful Nation.

LEIGH, MIKE
Director, Writer. b. Salford, England, Feb. 20, 1943. e. RADA, Camberwell Art Sch., Central Sch. of Arts & Crafts, London Film Sch. m. actress Alison Steadman. Began career in experimental theatre. Plays include Waste Paper Guards, The Box Play, Neena, Individual Fruit Pies, Down Here and Up There, Big Basil, Epilogue, Bleak Moments, A Rancid Pong, Wholesome Glory, The Jaws of Death, Dick Whittington and His Cat, Babies Grow Old, The Silent Majority, Abigail's Party, Ecstacy, Goose-Pimples, Smelling the Rat, Greek Tragedy, It's a Great Big Shame. Directed 1977 TV drama Abigail's Party. 1987 short: The Short and Curlies. Recipient of 1995 BAFTA Award for Outstanding British Contribution to Cinema.
PICTURES: Bleak Moments, Hard Labour, Nuts in May, The Kiss of Death, Who's Who, Grown-Ups, Home Sweet Home, Meantime, Four Days in July, High Hopes, Life Is Sweet, Naked, Secrets & Lies (Palme d'Or, Cannes 1996; LA Film Critics Award; BAFTA for Best Original S.P.), Career Girls, Topsy-Turvy.
TELEVISION: A Mug's Game, Plays for Britain.

LEIGH, SUZANNA
Actress. b. Reading, England, 1945. Studied at the Arts Educational Sch. and Webber Douglas Sch. 1965-66, under contract to Hal Wallis and Paramount.
PICTURES: Oscar Wilde, Bomb in High Street, Boeing Boeing, Paradise Hawaiian Style, The Deadly Bees, Deadlier Than the Male, The Lost Continent, Subterfuge, Lust for a Vampire (To Love a Vampire), Beware My Brethren, Son of Dracula.
TELEVISION: *Series*: Three Stars (France), One on an Island (West Indies). *Special*: The Plastic People. *Guest*: The Persuaders.

LEITCH, DONOVAN
Actor. Son of folksinger Donovan. Brother of actress Ione Skye. Acted in jr. high sch. musical then had bit part in PBS. show K.I.D.S.
PICTURES: And God Created Women (1988), The Blob, The In Crowd, Cutting Class, Glory, Gas Food Lodging, Dark Horse, I Shot Andy Warhol, One Night Stand, Love Kills, Cherry, Big City Blues, Men Make Women Crazy.
TELEVISION: *Movie*: For the Very First Time, The '60s. *Guest*: Life Goes On, 21 Jump Street, Sex and the City.

LELAND, DAVID
Director, Writer, Actor. b. Cambridge, Eng., April 20, 1947. Began as actor at Nottingham Playhouse. Then joined newly formed company at Royal Court Theatre, London. Also appeared in films Time Bandits, The Missionary, and his own Personal Services (Peter Sellers Award for Comedy) and on TV in The Jewel in the Crown. As stage director specialized in complete seasons of new works at the Crucible in Sheffield and London venues. Wrote play Psy-Warriors.
PICTURES: Mona Lisa (co-s.p.), Personal Services (s.p.), Wish You Were Here (dir., s.p.; BAFTA Award for s.p.), Checking Out (dir.), The Big Man (dir.; a.k.a. Crossing the Line), Land Girls (co-s.p., dir.).
TELEVISION: Wrote Birth of a Nation, Flying Into the Wind, Rhino, Made in Britain, Beloved Enemy, Ligmalion, Psy-Warriors.

LELOUCH, CLAUDE
Director, Writer, Producer, Cinematographer, Editor. b. Paris, France, Oct. 30, 1937. Began m.p. career with short subjects, 1956; French military service, motion picture department, 1957-60; formed Films 13, 1960; publicity Films and Scopitones, 1961-62.
PICTURES: Le Propre de l'Homme (The Right of Man; debut, 1960; also s.p., prod., actor), L'amour avec des Si (Love With Ifs; aalso prod., s.p.), La Femme Spectacle (Night Women; also prod., photog.), Une Fille et des Fusils (To Be a Crook; also co-s.p., prod., edit.), Les Grands Moments (also co-prod.), A Man and A Woman (also co-s.p., story, prod., photog., edit.; Academy Awards for Best Foreign Language Film & Original Screenplay, 1966; also Acad. Award nom. for dir.), Live for Life (also co-s.p., co-photog. , edit.), Farm From Vietnam (segment), 13 Jours en France (Grenoble; co-dir., co-s.p.), Life Love Death (also co-s.p.), Love Is a Funny Thing (also photog., co-s.p.), The Crook (also co- photog., co-s.p.), Smic Smac Smoc (also prod., s.p., photog., actor), Money Money Money (also s.p., prod., photog.), La Bonne Annee (Happy New Year; also prod., s.p., co-photog.), Visions of Eight (segment: The Losers), And Now My Love (also s.p., prod.), Marriage (also co-s.p.), Cat and Mouse (also s.p.), The Good and Bad (also s.p., photog.), Second Chance (also s.p., prod.), Another Man Another Chance (also s.p.), Robert and Robert (also s.p.), Adventure for Two, Bolero (also s.p., prod.), Edith and Marcel (also prod., s.p.), Vive la Vie (also prod., s.p., photog.), Partier Revenir (also prod., co-s.p.), A Man and a Woman: 20 Years Later (also prod., co-s.p.), Bandits (also prod., s.p.), Itinerary of a Spoiled Child (also co-prod., s.p.), There Were Days and Moons (also prod., co-s.p.), Les Miserables.
TELEVISION: Moliere (prod. only).

LE MAT, PAUL
Actor. b. Rahway, NJ, Sept. 22, 1945. Studied with Milton Katselas, Herbert Berghof Studio, A.C.T., San Francisco, Mitchel Ryan-Actor's Studio.
PICTURES: American Graffiti (debut, 1973), Aloha—Bobby and Rose, Citizens Band (Handle With Care), More American Graffiti, Melvin and Howard, Death Valley, Jimmy the Kid, Strange Invaders, P.K. and the Kid, Rock & Rule (voice), The Hanoi Hilton, Private Investigations, Puppet Master, Easy Wheels, Deuce Coupe, Grave Secrets, Veiled Threat, Wishman, Caroline at Midnight, Sensation, Deep Down, The Outfitters.
TELEVISION: *Movies*: Firehouse, The Gift of Life, The Night They Saved Christmas, The Burning Bed, Long Time Gone, Secret Witness, On Wings of Eagles, Into the Homeland, Blind Witness, In the Line of Duty: Siege at Marion, Woman With a Past. *Series*: Lonesome Dove.

LEMBERGER, KEN
Executive. e. B.A., Queen's College, CUNY and J.D., NYU School of Law. Began tenure with Sony Pictures Entertainment (SPE) in the legal dept., 1979-81; senior v.p., Studio Legal Affairs, 1981-83; senior v.p. & gen. counsel, SPE, 1983; vice chairman, TriStar Pictures, 1992-94; corporate exec. v.p., SPE, 1994-97. Currently president, Columbia TriStar Motion Picture Group.

LEMMON, JACK
Actor. r.n. John Uhler Lemmon III. b. Boston, MA. Feb. 8, 1925. e. Harvard U. m. actress Felicia Farr. Father of actor Chris Lemmon. Stage debut as a child; radio actor on soap operas; stock companies; U.S. Navy, W.W.II; many TV shows. Narrated film Stowaway in the Sky. Appeared in AFI short Wednesday. Albums: A Twist of Lemmon, Jack Lemmon Plays and Sings Music From Some Like It Hot. Recipient: American Film Institute Life Achievement Award (1988), Lincoln Center Tribute (1993).
THEATER: *B'way*: Room Service (debut, 1953), Face of a Hero, Tribute (also L.A., Denver), Long Day's Journey into Night (also London, Israel, D.C.). *Off-B'way*: Power of Darkness. *L.A.*: Idiot's Delight, Juno and the Paycock, A Sense of Humor (also Denver, S.F.). *London:* Veterans Day.
PICTURES: It Should Happen to You (debut, 1953), Phffft!, Three for the Show, Mister Roberts (Academy Award, best supporting actor, 1955), My Sister Eileen, You Can't Run Away from It, Fire Down Below, Operation Mad Ball, Cowboy, Bell Book and Candle, Some Like It Hot (Acad. Award nom.), It Happened to Jane, The Apartment (Acad. Award nom.), Pepe, The Wackiest Ship in the Army, The Notorious Landlady, Days of Wine and Roses (Acad. Award nom.), Irma La Douce, Under the Yum Yum Tree, Good Neighbor Sam, How to Murder Your Wife, The Great Race, The Fortune Cookie, Luv, The Odd Couple, The April Fools, The Out-of-Towners, Kotch (dir. debut; also cameo), The War Between Men and Women, Avanti!, Save the Tiger (Academy Award, 1973), The Front Page, The Prisoner of Second Avenue, Alex and the Gypsy, Airport '77, The China Syndrome (Cannes Film Fest. Award; Acad. Award nom., 1979), Tribute (Acad. Award nom.), Buddy Buddy, Missing (Cannes Film Fest. Award; Acad. Award nom., 1982), Mass Appeal, Macaroni, That's Life, Dad, JFK, The Player, Glengarry Glen Ross, Short Cuts, Grumpy Old Men, Getting Away With Murder, The Grass Harp, Grumpier Old Men, A Weekend in the Country, Hamlet, My Fellow Americans, Out to Sea, The Long Way Home, The Odd Couple II.
TELEVISION: *Series*: That Wonderful Guy, Toni Twin Time (host), Ad Libbers, Heaven For Betsy, Alcoa Theatre. *Guest on numerous dramatic shows*: Studio One, Playhouse 90 (Face of a Hero), Kraft Theatre, The Web, Suspense, etc. *Specials*: The Day Lincoln Was Shot, 'S Wonderful 'S Marvelous 'S Gershwin, Get Happy, The Entertainer, Long Day's Journey into Night, The Wild West (narrator), A Life in the Theatre. *Movies*: The Murder of Mary Phagan, For Richer For Poorer, Twelve Angry Men, The Long Way Home, Tuesday's with Morrie, Inherit the Wind.
RADIO: *Serials*: The Brighter Day, Road of Life.

LENFEST, H. F. "GERRY"
Executive. b. Jacksonville, FL. e. Mercersburg Academy, Washington and Lee U. and Columbia Law School. Served in US Navy, retired Captain. Practiced law in NYC before joining Triangle Publications., Inc. in Philadelphia as assoc. counsel in 1965. Became head of Triangle's Communications Div., 1970. Formed new co. in 1974 and bought two cable cos. from Triangle. Owns with his children Lenfest Communications, Inc. Subsidiaries incl. Suburban Cable, StarNet and Micronet.

LENO, JAY
Comedian, Actor. r.n. James Leno. b. New Rochelle, NY, April 28, 1950. e. Emerson College, B.A. speech therapy, 1973. Raised in Andover, MA. Worked as Rolls Royce auto mechanic and deliveryman while seeking work as stand-up comedian. Performed in comedy clubs throughout the U.S. and as opening act for Perry Como, Johnny Mathis, John Denver and Tom Jones. Guest on numerous talk shows and specials.
PICTURES: Fun With Dick and Jane, The Silver Bears, American Hot Wax, Americathon, Collision Course, What's Up Hideous Sun Demon? (voice), Dave, We're Back! (voice), Wayne's World 2, Major League 2, The Flintstones, The Birdcage (cameo), Meet Wally Sparks, In & Out, Contact, Wag the Dog, EDtv.
TELEVISION: *Series*: The Marilyn McCoo & Billy Davis Jr. Show, The Tonight Show (guest host: 1987-92; host: 1992-; Emmy Award, 1995). *Specials*: Jay Leno and the American Dream (also prod.), The Jay Leno Show, Our Planet Tonight, Jay Leno's Family Comedy Hour. *Guest:* The Simpsons (voice).

LENZ, KAY
Actress. b. Los Angeles, CA, March 4, 1953.
PICTURES: Breezy (debut, 1973), White Line Fever, The Great Scout and Cathouse Thursday, Moving Violation, Mean Dog Blues, The Passage, Fast-Walking, House, Stripped to Kill, Death Wish IV: The Crackdown, Headhunter, Physical Evidence, Fear, Streets, Falling From Grace.
TELEVISION: *Series*: Reasonable Doubts. *Movies*: The Weekend Nun, Lisa, Bright and Dark, A Summer Without Boys, Unwed Father, The Underground Man, The FBI Story: The FBI Versus Alvin Karpis, Journey from Darkness, Rich Man, Poor Man, The Initiation of Sarah, The Seeding of Sarah Burns, Sanctuary of Fear, The Hustler of Muscle Beach, Murder by Night, Heart in Hiding, How the West Was Won, Traveling Man, Escape, Hitler's Daughter, Against Their Will: Women in Prison, Trapped in Space, Shame II: The Secret. *Guest*: Midnight Caller (Emmy Award, 1989), Moonlighting, Hill St. Blues, Hotel, Cannon, McGyver, Cagney & Lacey, McCloud, Riptide. *Mini-Series*: Rich Man Poor Man—Book II.

LEON, SOL
Executive. b. New York, NY, July 2, 1913. e. NYU, City Coll. of New York, Brooklyn Law Sch., B.B.L., master of law. Exec. v.p., William Morris Agency, L.A.

LEONARD, ROBERT SEAN
Actor. b. Westwood, NJ, Feb. 28, 1969. Raised in Ridgewood, NJ. Started acting at age 12 in local summer stock. Joined NY Shakespeare Festival at 15.
THEATER: *Off-B'way*: Coming of Age in Soho, Sally's Gone—She Left Her Name, The Beach House, When She Danced, Romeo and Juliet, Good Evening, The Great Unwashed. *B'way*: Brighton Beach Memoirs, Breaking the Code, The Speed of Darkness, Candida (Tony nom.), Philadelphia Here I Come!, Arcadia. Regional: Biloxi Blues (tour), Rocky and Diego, Long Day's Journey Into Night, King Lear, The Double Inconstancy.
PICTURES: The Manhattan Project (debut, 1986), My Best Friend Is a Vampire, Dead Poets Society, Mr. & Mrs. Bridge, Swing Kids, Married to It, Much Ado About Nothing, The Age of Innocence, Safe Passage, Killer: A Journal of Murder, I Love You—I Love You Not, Ground Control, Stand Off, The Last Days of Disco.
TELEVISION: *Movies*: My Two Loves, Bluffing It. *Pilot*: The Robert Klein Show, In the Gloaming.

LEONI, TEA
Actress. b. New York, NY Feb. 25, 1966. m. actor David Duchovny
PICTURES: Switch, A League of Their Own, Wyatt Earp, Bad Boys, Flirting with Disaster, Deep Impact, There's No Fish Food In Heaven (also exec. prod.).
TELEVISION: *Movies:* The Counterfeit Contessa. *Series:* Santa Barbara, Flying Blind, The Naked Truth. *Guest:* Frasier.

LERNER, JOSEPH
Producer, Director, Writer. m. Geraldine Lerner. Actor on Broadway; radio actor & dir.; with RKO, Columbia and Republic as dir., dial. dir., writer, 2nd unit dir., test dir.; dir.-writer & head of special productions U.S. Army Signal Corps Photographic Center; writer of commercial and educational films 1946-47; v.p. in chg. of prod. Visual Arts Productions 1947; v.p. in chg. prod. Laurel Films 1949; Girl on the Run, comm. ind. films; dir., prod., writer, many TV commercials, documentaries 1967-73; pres., The Place for Film Making, Inc.; pres., Astracor Associates Ltd.; writer & line prod. for Gold Shield Prods; also lecturer and instructor at NYU, Wm. Patterson Coll., Broward Community Coll. (FL), College at Boca Raton. Member: Eastern Council of the Directors Guild of America. Trip the Light Fantastic, musical play in collaboration with song writer Dan Costello
TELEVISION: *Dir./Prod.*: Gangbusters, Grand Tour, Three Musketeers, United Nations Case Book. *Dir./Prod./Writer*: C-Man, Guilty Bystander, Mr. Universe, Dark of the Day, The Fight Never Ends, etc. *Prod./Writer*: Olympic Cavalcade, King of The Olympics, and many other documentaries.

LERNER, MICHAEL
Actor. b. Brooklyn, NY, June 22, 1941. e. Brooklyn Col., Univ. of CA, Berkeley. Prior to acting was professor of dramatic literature at San Francisco St. Col., 1968-69. Studied acting in London on Fullbright Scholarship. Was member of San Francisco's American Conservatory Theatre. On NY stage in Twelfth Night; L.A. stage in The Women of Trachis, Hurlyburly.
PICTURES: Alex in Wonderland (debut, 1970), The Candidate, Busting, Newman's Law, Hangup (Superdude), St. Ives, The Other Side of Midnight, Outlaw Blues, Goldengirl, Borderline, Coast to Coast, The Baltimore Bullet, The Postman Always Rings Twice, National Lampoon's Class Reunion, Threshold, Strange Invaders, Movers and Shakers, Anguish, Vibes, Eight Men Out, Harlem Nights, Any Man's Death, The Closer, Barton Fink (Acad. Award nom.), Newsies, Amos & Andrew, Blank Check, No Escape, Radioland Murders, The Road to Wellville, Girl in the Cadillac, A Pyromaniac's Love Story, The Beautician and the Beast, for Richer or Poorer, Russell Mulcahy's Tale of the Mummy, Godzilla, Celebrity, Safe Men, The Mod Squad, My Favorite Martian.
TELEVISION: *Series:* Courthouse. *Movies*: Thief, Marriage Year One, What's a Nice Girl Like You...?, Magic Carpet, Firehouse (pilot), Reflections of Murder, The Rockford Files (pilot), The Death of Sammy, A Cry for Help, Starsky and Hutch (pilot), Sarah T: Portrait of a Teenage Alcoholic, Dark Victory, F. Scott Fitzgerald in Hollywood, Scott Free, Killer on Board, A Love Affair: The Eleanor and Lou Gehrig Story, Vega$ (pilot), Ruby & Oswald, Hart to Hart (pilot), Moviola: This Year's Blonde, Gridlock, Blood Feud, Rita Hayworth: Love Goddess, The Execution, This Child is Mine, Betrayal of Trust, Hands of a Stranger, King of Love, Framed, Omen IV: The Awakening, The Comrades of Summer. *Special:* The Missiles of October. *Guest*: Amazing Stories, Macgyver. *Pilots*: Grandpa Max, The Boys, I Gave at the Office.

LESLIE, ALEEN
Writer. b. Pittsburgh, PA, Feb. 5, 1908. e. Ohio State U. Contributor to magazines; columnist Pittsburgh Press; orig. & wrote radio series A Date with Judy 1941-50. B'way play Slightly Married, 1943; wrote, prod. Date with Judy, TV series; author, The Scent of the Roses, The Windfall.
PICTURES: Doctor Takes a Wife, Affectionately Yours, Henry Aldrich Plays Cupid, Stork Pays Off, Henry Aldrich Gets Glamour, It Comes Up Love, Rosie the Riveter, A Date With Judy, Father Was a Fullback, Father Is a Bachelor.

LESLIE, JOAN
Actress. r.n. Joan Brodell. b. Detroit, MI, January 26, 1925. e. St. Benedicts, Detroit; Our Lady of Lourdes, Toronto; St. Mary's Montreal; Immaculate Heart. H.S., L.A. Child performer on stage as part of The Three Brodels. Became model before going to Hollywood in 1936. Voted Star of Tomorrow, 1946. Now on bd. of dir., St. Anne's Maternity Home, Damon Runyon Foundation.
PICTURES: *(as Joan Brodel)*: Camille (debut, 1937), Men with Wings, Nancy Drew—Reporter, Love Affair, Winter Carnival, Two Thoroughbreds, High School, Young as You Feel, Star Dust, Susan and God, Military Academy, Foreign Correspondent, Laddie. *(as Joan Leslie)*: Thieves Fall Out, The Wagons Roll at Night, High Sierra, The Great Mr. Nobody, Sergeant York, The Hard Way, The Male Animal, Yankee Doodle Dandy, The Sky's the Limit, This Is the Army, Thank Your Lucky Stars, Hollywood Canteen, Rhapsody in Blue, Where Do We Go From Here?, Too Young to Know, Janie Gets Married, Cinderella Jones, Two Guys From Milwaukee, Repeat Performance, Northwest Stampede, Born To Be Bad, The Skipper Surprised His Wife, Man in the Saddle, Hellgate, Toughest Man in Arizona, The Woman They Almost Lynched, Flight Nurse, Hell's Outpost, Jubilee Trail, The Revolt of Mamie Stover.
TELEVISION: *Guest*: Ford Theatre, G.E. Theatre, Queen for a Day, Simon and Simon, Murder, She Wrote. *Movies*: Charley Hannah, The Keegans, Turn Back the Clock. Various commercials.

LESTER, MARK
Actor. b. Oxford, England, July 11, 1958. Ent. m.p. ind. 1963.
THEATER: The Murder Game, The Prince and the Pauper 1976.
PICTURES: Allez France (The Counterfeit Constable; debut, 1963), Spaceflight IC-1, Fahrenheit 451, Arrividerci Baby!, Our Mother's House, Oliver!, Run Wild Run Free, Sudden Terror (Eye Witness), Melody, Black Beauty, Who Slew Auntie Roo?, Redneck, Scalawag, Jungle Boy, Crossed Swords (The Prince and the Pauper).
TELEVISION: The Boy Who Stole the Elephants, Graduation Trip, Danza Alla Porto Gli Olmi (Italian Entry Berlin '75), Seen Dimly Before Dawn.

LESTER, MARK LESLIE
Director. b. Cleveland, OH, Nov. 26, 1949. e. Cal. State Univ. Northridge, B.A.
PICTURES: *Director and/or Producer*: Steel Arena (debut, 1973; also co-prod., s.p.), Truck Stop Women (also co-s.p.), Bobbie Jo and the Outlaw, Stunts, Roller Boogie, The Funhouse (co-exec. prod. only), The Class of 1984 (also co-exec. prod., co-s.p.), Firestarter, Commando, Armed and Dangerous, Class of 1999 (also story), Showdown in Little Tokyo, Night of the Running Man, The Ex, Public Enemy #1, Double Take, Misbegotten.
TELEVISION: Gold of the Amazon Women, Extreme Justice.

LESTER, RICHARD
Director. b. Philadelphia, PA, Jan. 19, 1932. e. Univ. of PA. Started as stagehand at tv studio before becoming dir. and music. dir. CBS-TV in Philadelphia, then CBC-TV, Toronto. To England in 1956 where he resumed work as tv dir. TV dir. The Goon Shows. Composed (with Reg. Owen) Sea War Series. Short Film: composer and dir., The Running Jumping and Standing Still Film. Directed sequences for Mondo Teeno/ Teenage Rebellion, Superman.
PICTURES: It's Trad Dad (debut, 1962; aka Ring-a-Ding Rhythm; also prod.), The Mouse on the Moon, A Hard Day's Night, The Knack... and How to Get It, Help!, A Funny Thing Happened on the Way to the Forum, How I Won the War (also prod.), Petulia, The Bed-Sitting Room (also co-prod.), The Three Musketeers, Juggernaut, The Four Musketeers, Royal Flash, Robin & Marian (also co-prod.), The Ritz, Butch and Sundance: The Early Days, Cuba, Superman II, Superman III, Finders Keepers (also exec. prod.), The Return of the Musketeers (tv in U.S.), Get Back.

LETTERMAN, DAVID
Performer, Writer. b. Indianapolis, IN, Apr. 12, 1947. e. Ball State U. Began career as weatherman and talk show host on Indianapolis TV before going to Hollywood. Cameo appearances in films Cabin Boy, Beavis and Butt-head Do America (voice), Private Parts, Man on the Moon.
TELEVISION: *Series Writer*: Good Times, Paul Lynde Comedy Hour. *Writer* (specials): John Denver Special, Bob Hope Special. *Series Performer*: The Starland Vocal Band (also writer), Mary (1978), Tonight Show (guest host 1978-82), The David Letterman Show (Daytime Emmy Award for writing, 1981), Late Night with David Letterman (1982-93, on NBC; 4 Emmy Awards for Writing), Late Show With David Letterman (1993-, on CBS, 1997 Emmy Award). *Guest*: An NBC Family Christmas, The Larry Sanders Show.

LEVIN, GERALD M.
Executive. b. Philadelphia, PA, May 6, 1939. e. Haverford Col., Univ. of PA Law Sch. Attorney, 1963-67. Gen. mgr. & COO of Development Sources Corp., 1969. IBEC rep. in Tehran, Iran, 1971. Joined HBO in 1972 as v.p. of programming, then pres. & CEO, 1973-76; promoted to chmn, 1976. Became v.p. Time Inc., 1975; group v.p., video, 1979; exec. v.p. in 1984; on bd. of dirs., 1983-87. Named vice-chmn, Time Warner, 1989; COO, 1991; pres. & co-CEO of Time Warner, Inc., 1992; chmn. & CEO of Time Warner Inc., 1993.

LEVIN, MARC
Director, Writer, Actor, Producer.
PICTURES: The Last Party, Slam (Cannes Film Fest. Awards, Camera d'Or, Grand Jury Prize, 1998).

LEVIN, ROBERT B.
Executive. b. Chicago, IL, May 31, 1943. e. U. of Illinois, BS Journalism, 1965. Copywriter Sears Roebuck & Co. 1965-66, PR Natural Gas Pipeline Co. of Amer. 1966-69. Acct. Exec. Hurvis Binzer & Churchill 1969-70. McCann-Erickson 1975-82 Acct. Super. 1975-79, Mgmt. Super. Needham Harper Worldwide 1982-85. Pres. Mktg. WD Co. 1985-94, Chief Corp. Mktg. & Comm. 1994-95. Pres. Worldwide Mktg. Savoy Pictures 1995-96, Sony Pictures Entertainment, 1996-.

LEVINSON, ART
Producer. Began film career as office boy at Universal Studios where he entered training program and rapidly rose from asst. director to production manager on Harry and Tonto.

PICTURES: Shampoo, The Killing of a Chinese Bookie, Brothers, Audrey Rose, Breaking Away, Mr. Mom, The Money Pit, Mannequin, My Stepmother Is an Alien, Lethal Charm, Teenage Mutant Ninja Turtles III, Teachers, Stop or My Mom Will Shoot!, My Favorite Year, Racing with the Moon, Great Balls of Fire, Lethal Charm, A Family Torn Apart.
TELEVISION: The Kansas City Massacre, Billionaire Boys Club, Curacao (prod.), Fear Stalk, Shoot First: A Cop's Vengeance, Exclusive, A Family Torn Apart, The Yearling, The Great Mom Swap, True Crime. *Mini-series*: Return to Lonesome Dove.

LEVINSON, BARRY
Director, Producer, Writer, Actor. b. Baltimore, MD, Apr. 6, 1942. e. American Univ. Wrote and acted in L.A. comedy show leading to work on network tv incl. writing and performing on The Carol Burnett Show. Co-wrote film scripts with Mel Brooks, and then-wife Valerie Curtin. Apppeared as actor in History of the World Part I, Quiz Show.
PICTURES: *Writer*: Silent Movie (also actor), High Anxiety (also actor), ... And Justice for All (Acad. Award nom.), Inside Moves, Best Friends, Unfaithfully Yours. *Director*: Diner (also s.p.; Acad. Award nom. for s.p.), The Natural, Young Sherlock Holmes, Tin Men (also s.p.), Good Morning Vietnam, Rain Man (also actor; Acad. Award for Best Director, 1988), Avalon (also s.p.; WGA Award, Acad. Award nom. for s.p.), Bugsy (Acad. Award nom.), Toys (also co-s.p.), Jimmy Hollywood (also s.p., co-prod.), Disclosure (also co-prod.), Sleepers (also s.p., co-prod.), Donnie Brasco (prod. only), Wag the Dog (also co-prod.), Sphere (also co-prod.), Liberty Heights (also prod.), The Perfect Storm (exec. prod.), Possession (prod. only), An Everlasting Piece, Bandits (dir. only).
TELEVISION: *Series*: The Tim Conway Comedy Hour (writer), The Marty Feldman Comedy Machine (writer), The Carol Burnett Show (writer; Emmy Awards: 1974, 1975), Harry (exec. prod.), Homicide: Life on the Streets (dir., co-exec. prod.; Emmy Award for directing, 1993). *Pilot*: Diner (exec. prod., dir.), Oz (exec. prod.). *Specials*: Stopwatch 30 Minutes of Investigative Ticking (exec. prod.), The Path to War.

LEVINSON, NORM
Executive. b. New Haven, CT, Mar. 17, 1925. Started theatre business as usher for Loew's Theatres, 1940. U.S. Army, 1943-46. Returned Loew's Theatres managerial positions New Haven and Hartford, CT. MGM press representative, Minneapolis, Jacksonville, Atlanta, Dallas. General Manager, Trans-Texas Theatres, Dallas. President, Academy Theatres, Inc., Dallas. Promoted World Championship Boxing, Dallas and Johannesburg, South Africa. Executive Vice President, Cobb Theatres, Birmingham, Alabama; v.p., world-wide mktg., Artists Releasing Corp., Encino, CA.; head film buyer, Chakeres Theatres, Ohio & Kentucky.

LEVITAN, STEVEN
Producer.
TELEVISION: Series: Frasier (consult.), Just Shoot Me (also dir., creator).

LEVY, BERNARD
Executive. b. Boca Raton, FL. e. Brooklyn Law Sch., L.L.B. Legal staff of Superintendent of Insurance of the state of New York in the rehabilitation and liquidation of guaranteed title and mortgage companies, 1934-36; private practice of law, 1936-46; legal staff, Paramount Pictures, Inc., 1946-50; legal staff, United Paramount Theatres, 1950-51; exec. asst. to Edward L. Hyman, v.p., ABC, Inc., in chg. of theatre administration, north, 1951-62; apptd. exec. liaison officer for southern motion picture theatres, ABC, Inc., 1962-64; exec. liaison officer, m.p. theas., ABC, Inc., 1965-72; v.p., ABC Theatre Division, 1973. Retired, 1976.

LEVY, BUD
Executive. b. Jackson Heights, NY, April 3, 1928. e. NYU. Member: Variety Clubs Int'l., M.P. Pioneers, President's Advisory Board-NATO. Director: NATO, TOP, CATO. Elected pres., Trans-Lux Corp., 1980; pres. Trans Lux Theatres, (a subsidiary of Paramount Pictures), 1986-1991. Will Rogers Memorial Fund; chmn., Cara Committee for NATO; chmn. ShowEast; v.p. NATO; dir. Motion Picture Pioneers.

LEVY, DAVID
Executive, Producer, Writer. b. Philadelphia, PA, Jan. 2. e. Wharton Sch., U. of PA, B.S. in Eco., M.B.A., as v.p. & assoc. dir., Young & Rubicam. Inc., 1938-59, acquisitions for clients include: People's Choice, Kate Smith Hour, Wagon Train, Four Star Playhouse, What's My Line, Father Knows Best, Goodyear Playhouse, Life of Riley, Gunsmoke, Arthur Godfrey's Talent Scouts, I Married Joan, The Web, Treasury Men in Action, Person to Person, Maverick, etc. Prod. We the People, Manhattan at Midnight. Writer: Kate Smith radio series, Manhattan at Midnight, Reunion, Robert Montgomery Presents, Grand Central Station, CBS Radio Workshop, Alcoa/Goodyear. With War Finance div. of U.S. Treasury Dept. on detached duty from U.S. Navy, 1944-46. Was v.p. in chg. of network TV progs. & talent, NBC, 1959-61. Acquisitions for network include: Sing-a-Long With Mitch, Peter Pan, Bonanza, Dr. Kildare, Bob Newhart Show, Thriller, Car 54 Where Are You?, Loretta Young Show, Sunday Showcase, Alfred Hitchcock Presents, Dick Powell Show, Saturday Night at the Movies, Hazel, Klondike, Victory at Sea, Joey Bishop Show, Shirley Temple Show, etc. Created: Bat Masterson, The Addams Family, Americans, Outlaws, Pruitts of Southampton, Sarge, Hollywood Screen Test, Face the Music, etc. Developed: Double Life of Henry Phyffe, Name That Tune, You Asked for It, etc. Assigned as writer, training film section, photographic div., Bureau of Aeronautics, U.S. Navy, 1944. Novels: The Chameleons, The Gods of Foxcroft, Network Jungle, Potomac Jungle, as well as numerous TV plays and short stories. Currently creative consultant to Mark Goodson Prods. Pres., Wilshire Prods. Exec. dir., Caucus for Prods., Writers and Dirs.

LEVY, EUGENE
Actor, Writer, Director. b. Hamilton, Canada, Dec. 17, 1946. e. McMaster U. Acted with coll. ensemble theater. Film debut in Ivan Reitman's Cannibal Girls, 1970, before joining Toronto's Second City troupe which eventually led to his work as writer-performer on Second City Television's various programs, 1977-83. *Canadian theater*: Godspell (1971), The Owl and the Pussycat, Love Times Four.
PICTURES: Cannibal Girls, Running, Heavy Metal (voice), National Lampoon's Vacation, Strange Brew, Going Berserk, Splash, Armed and Dangerous, The Canadian Conspiracy, Club Paradise, Speed Zone, Father of the Bride, Once Upon a Crime (also dir.), Stay Tuned, I Love Trouble, Multiplicity, Almost Heroes, Unglued, America Pie.
TELEVISION: *Series*: Second City TV, SCTV Network 90, SCTV Network (Emmy Award as writer, 1983), Hiller & Diller. *Movies*: Partners in Love, Sodbusters (dir., co-writer, co-exec. prod.), Harrison Bergeron.

LEVY, HERMAN M.
Attorney. b. New Haven, CT, Sept. 27, 1904. e. Yale, B.A., 1927, Yale Law Sch., LL.B., 1929; Phi Beta Kappa, was in legal dept. RCA Photophone; newspaper reporter; admitted to Connecticut bar, 1929. 1939 elected exec. secy. of MPTO of Connecticut. 1943 elected gen. counsel MPTOA. Gen. counsel, Theatre Owners of America, 1947-63. Pres., New Haven County Bar Assn., 1964; legislative agent, CT Assn. of Theatre Owners. Retired as legislative agent, 1981. Received Distinguished Service Award from ShowEast '93. *Author*: More Sinned Against, Natl. Bd. of Review Magazine, 1941. Proving the Death of a Non-Resident Alien, Conn. Bar Journal, 1950; Need for a System of Arbitration M.P. Ind., Arbitration Journal, 1950; reprint of Industry Case Digest, 20th Century-Fox vs. Boehm in the Journal (Screen Producers Guild); Book Review of Antitrust in the Motion Picture Industry, by Michael Conant (Univ. of Calif. Law Review).

LEVY, JULES
Producer. b. Los Angeles, CA, Feb. 12, 1923. e. USC. Started in property dept. of WB, 1941; first m.p. unit Army Air Force.
PICTURES: The Vampire, Return of Dracula, Vice Squad, Without Warning, Down Three Dark Streets, Geronimo, The Glory Guys, Clambake, The Scalphunters, Sam Whiskey, The McKenzie Break, The Hunting Party, Kansas City Bomber, The Honkers, McQ, Branningan, White Lightning, Gator, Safari 3000.
TELEVISION: *Series*: The Rifleman, Robert Taylor in The Detectives, Law of the Plainsman, The Big Valley.

LEVY, MICHAEL
Executive. b. Brooklyn, NY. e. Brown U. Started in industry in editorial dept. of trade-paper Variety; held posts in New York with ABC Motion Pictures and with Diener/Hauser/Bates Advertising. Worked for Lawrence Gordon Productions as exec. asst. to Gordon and as story editor. Joined 20th Century Fox in January, 1985, as dir. of creative affairs for studio. 1986, named v.p., production, m.p. div., Fox; appointed sr. v.p. production, 20th Century Fox, 1988; named pres., Silver Pictures, 1989.

LEVY, NORMAN
Executive. b. Bronx, NY, Jan. 3, 1935. e. City Coll. of New York. 1957 joined Universal Pictures, holding various sales positions; 1967, went to National General Pictures, ultimately being named v.p. and exec. asst. to pres.; 1974, Columbia Pictures, v.p., gen. sls. mgr. 1975 named Columbia exec. v.p. in chg. of domestic sls.; 1977, exec. v.p., mktg; 1978. pres., Columbia Pictures Domestic Distribution. 1980 joined 20th-Fox as pres. of Entertainment Group; 1981, vice-chmn., 20th Century-Fox Film Corp. Resigned 1985 to become chmn, ceo, New Century/Vista Film Co. 1991, chmn. and CEO, Creative Film Enterprises.

LEWELLEN, A. WAYNE
Executive. b. Dallas, TX, Feb. 16, 1944. e. U. of Texas. Joined Paramount Pictures 1973 as brch. mgr., Dallas-Oklahoma City territory; 1978, v.p. Southern div.; 1984, exec. v.p., gen. sls. mngr.; 1986, pres. domestic distrib.; 1993, pres. M.P. distrib. chairman, Will Rogers Memorial Fund Board, dir. for the Found. of the Motion Picture Pioneers.

LEWINE, JEFFREY G.
Executive. b. New York, NY, 1955. e. Syracuse U. Entered the industry while young, working as an usher, a ticker-take, a janitor, and eventually as a theatre manager while in high school and during summers in college. 1977, named general sl's. mng'r., of Cinema 5, responsible for marketing and distribution of notable Cinema 5 films such as Pumping Iron, Endless Summer, Swept Away and Monty Python and The Holy Grail; 1980, named v.p., managing company's theatre and distibution activities. 1981, became managing dir., Cinema Int'l. Corp.,

in Sydney, Australia; created a new division to manage merchandising and ancillary film sales which expanded to the Far East. 1987, returned to the U.S., and with his partners, the Edgar Bronfman family, acquired Cinemette, movie theatre circuit based in Pittsburgh; became pres. and CEO, of the renamed Cinema World; 1994, sold Cinema World to Carmike Cinemas, Inc. 1995-96, consultant for Coca-Cola USA in several divisions. 1997, founded JJL Consultants, Inc., agc'y. dealing with theatre and real estate negotiations. Nov. 1997, together with Warburg Pinctus Ventures, formed WestStar Cinemas to acquire Cinamerica Theatres which operates as Mann Theatres, and was named pres. and CEO of WestStar Cinemas. Resigned, 1999. On Bd. of Dir's.: NATO, Will Rogers Memorial Foundation.

LEWIS, ARTHUR
Producer, Director, Writer. b. New York, NY, Sept. 15, 1918. e. USC, Yale U. Began career as writer and assoc. prod. on the Jones Family TV series. Five years in U.S. Army; returned to screenwriting before producing Three Wishes for Jamie on Broadway and producing and directing Guys and Dolls in London's West End. In mid-60s and 70s produced over 25 plays with Bernard Delfont in the West End of London.
PICTURES: *Producer*: Loot, Baxter, The Killer Elite, Brass Target.
TELEVISION: Brenner, The Asphalt Jungle, The Nurses. *Movies*: The Diary of Anne Frank, Splendor in the Grass.

LEWIS, EDWARD
Producer. b. Camden, NJ, Dec. 16, 1922. e. Bucknell U. Began entertainment career as script writer, then co-produced The Admiral Was a Lady and teamed with Marion Parsonnet to bring the Faye Emerson Show to TV. Subsequently prod. first Schlitz Playhouse and China Smith series. Was v.p. of Kirk Douglas' indep. prod. co., where was assoc. prod. and writer-prod. Collaborated with John Frankenheimer on 8 films.
PICTURES: Lizzie (assoc. prod.), The Careless Years (prod., s.p.), Spartacus, The Last Sunset, Lonely Are the Brave, The List of Adrian Messenger, Seconds, Grand Prix, The Fixer (exec. prod.), The Gypsy Moths (exec.), I Walk the Line (exec.), The Horsemen, The Iceman Cometh (exec.), Executive Action, Rhinoceros, Lost in the Stars, Missing (co-prod.), Crackers, The River, Brothers (prod., s.p.).
TELEVISION: Ishi: The Last of His Tribe (exec. prod.), The Thorn Birds (exec. prod.).

LEWIS, GEOFFREY
Actor. b. San Diego, CA, 1935. Father of actress Juliette Lewis, actors Lightfield & Peter Lewis.
PICTURES: Welcome Home Soldier Boys, The Culpepper Cattle Company, Bad Company, High Plains Drifter, Dillinger, Thunderbolt and Lightfoot, Macon County Line, The Great Waldo Pepper, Smile, The Wind and the Lion, Lucky Lady, The Return of a Man Called Horse, Every Which Way But Loose, Tilt, Human Experiments, Tom Horn, Broncho Billy, Heaven's Gate, Any Which Way You Can, Shoot the Sun Down, I the Jury, Ten to Midnight, Night of the Comet, Lust in the Dust, Stitches, Fletch Lives, Out of the Dark, Pink Cadillac, Catch Me If You Can, Disturbed, Double Impact, The Lawnmower Man, Point of No Return, Wishman, The Man Without a Face, Only the Strong, Army of One, Maverick.
TELEVISION: *Series*: Flo, Gun Shy. *Movies*: Moon of the Wolf, Honky Tonk, The Great Ice Rip-Off, Attack on Terror: The FBI Versus the Ku Klux Klan, The New Daughters of Joshua Cabe, The Great Houndinis, The Deadly Triangle, The Hunted Lady, When Every Day Was the Fourth of July, The Jericho Mile, Samurai, Salem's Lot, Belle Starr, The Shadow Riders, Life of the Party: The Story of Beatrice, The Return of the Man From U.N.C.L.E., Travis McGee, September Gun, Stormin' Home, Dallas: The Early Years, Day of Reckoning, Gambler V: Playing for Keeps, When the Dark Man Calls, Kansas. *Guest*: Mannix, Barnaby Jones, Starsky and Hutch, Streets of San Francisco, Police Woman, Little House on the Prairie, Laverne & Shirley, Lou Grant, Magnum P.I., Amazing Stories, Murder She Wrote, Paradise.

LEWIS, HAROLD G.
Executive. b. New York, NY, Sept. 18, 1938. e. Union Coll., 1960, electrical engineer. Joined ATA Trading Corp. in 1960 and has been pres. since 1977. Producer of feature animation. Importer and exporter for theatrical and TV features, documentaries, series, classics. Pres., ATA Trading Corp., and Favorite TV, Inc.

LEWIS, JERRY
Actor, Director, Writer, Producer. r.n. Joseph Levitch. b. Newark, NJ, Mar. 16, 1926. e. Irvington H.S. Parents Danny and Rae Lewis, prof. entertainers. Debut at 5 at a NY Borscht Circuit hotel singing Brother Can You Spare a Dime? 1946 formed comedy-team with Dean Martin at 500 Club, Atlantic City, NJ; then appeared on NBC tv, performed many theatres before being signed by Hal Wallis for m.p. debut. Voted Most Promising Male Star in Television in m.p. Daily's 2nd annual TV poll, 1950. Voted (as team) one of top ten money making stars in m.p. Herald-Fame poll: 1951-56 (including no. 1 position in 1952), voted as solo performer: 1957-59, 1961-64; named best comedy team in m.p. Daily's 16th annual radio poll, 1951-53. 1956 formed Jerry Lewis Prods. Inc., functioning as prod., dir., writer & star. National Chairman & bd. member, Muscular Dystrophy Association. Full professor USC; taught grad. film dir. Book: The Total Filmmaker (1971) based on classroom lectures. *Autobiography*: Jerry Lewis In Person (1982).
THEATER: Hellzapoppin (regional), Damn Yankees (B'way debut, 1995).
PICTURES: My Friend Irma (debut, 1949), My Friend Irma Goes West, At War With the Army, That's My Boy, Sailor Beware, Jumping Jacks, Scared Stiff, The Stooge, Road to Bali (cameo), The Caddy, Money From Home, Living It Up, Three Ring Circus, You're Never Too Young, Artists and Models, Pardners, Hollywood or Bust, The Delicate Delinquent (also prod.), The Sad Sack, Rock-a-Bye Baby, The Geisha Boy (also prod.), Don't Give Up the Ship, Li'l Abner (cameo), Visit to a Small Planet, Cinderfella (also prod.), The Bellboy (also dir., prod., s.p.), The Ladies Man (also dir., prod., co-s.p.), The Errand Boy (also dir., co-s.p.), It's Only Money, The Nutty Professor (also dir., co-s.p.), Who's Minding the Store?, It's a Mad Mad Mad Mad World (cameo), The Patsy (also dir., co-s.p.), The Disorderly Orderly, Boeing-Boeing, The Family Jewels (also dir., prod., co-s.p.), Three on a Couch (also dir., prod.), Way... Way Out, The Big Mouth (also dir., prod., co-s.p.), Don't Raise the Bridge Lower the River, Hook Line and Sinker (also prod.), Which Way to the Front? (also dir., prod.), One More Time (dir. only), The Day the Clown Cried (also dir., co-s.p.), Hardly Working (also dir., co-s.p.), The King of Comedy, Smorgasbord (Cracking Up; also dir., co-s.p.), Slapstick of Another Kind, Cookie, Mr. Saturday Night (cameo), Arizona Dream, Funny Bones.
TELEVISION: *Movie*: Fight for Life. *Series*: Colgate Comedy Hour, The Jerry Lewis Show (1963), The Jerry Lewis Show (1967-69). *Guest*: Wiseguy (5 episodes).

LEWIS, JOSEPH H.
Director. b. New York, NY, Apr. 6, 1907. e. DeWitt Clinton H.S. Camera boy, MGM; then asst. film ed. in chge. film ed., Republic; dir. in chge. 2nd units; debuted as dir. at Universal; served in U.S. Signal Corps., WW II. Dir. musical numbers for The Jolson Story.
PICTURES: Navy Spy (co-dir. with Crane Wilbur; debut, 1937), Courage of the West, Singing Outlaw, The Spy Ring, Border Wolves, The Last Stand, Two-Fisted Rangers, The Return of Wild Bill, That Gang of Mine, The Invisible Ghost, Pride of the Bowery, Arizona Cyclone, Bombs Over Burma, The Silver Bullet, Secrets of a Co-Ed, The Boss of Hangtown Mesa, The Mad Doctor of Market Street, Minstrel Man, The Falcon in San Francisco, My Name is Julia Ross, So Dark the Night, The Swordsman, The Return of October, The Undercover Man, Gun Crazy, A Lady Without Passport, Retreat Hell!, Desperate Search, Cry of the Hunted, The Big Combo, A Lawless Street, The Seventh Cavalry, The Halliday Brand, Terror in a Texas Town.
TELEVISION: *Series*: The Rifleman, The Big Valley.

LEWIS, JULIETTE
Actress. b. California, June 21, 1973. Father is actor Geoffrey Lewis.
PICTURES: My Stepmother Is an Alien (debut, 1988), Meet the Hollowheads, National Lampoon's Christmas Vacation, Crooked Hearts, Cape Fear (Acad. Award nom.), Husbands and Wives, That Night, Kalifornia, What's Eating Gilbert Grape, Romeo Is Bleeding, Natural Born Killers, Mixed Nuts, The Basketball Diaries, Strange Days, From Dusk Till Dawn, The Evening Star, The Audition, Full Tilt Boogie, The Other Sister, Men.
TELEVISION: *Series*: Homefires, I Married Dora, A Family for Joe. *Movie*: Too Young to Die?

LEWIS, MICHAEL J.
Composer. b. Wales, 1939. First film score 1969, The Mad Woman of Chaillot, won Ivor Novello Award for best film score. 1973: first Broadway musical, Cyrano, Grammy nomination '74, Caesar and Cleopatra (T.V. '76), The Lion the Witch and the Wardrobe (Emmy, 1979).
PICTURES: The Man Who Haunted Himself, Julius Caesar. Upon This Rock, Unman Wittering and Zigo, Running Scared, Baxter, Theatre of Blood, 11 Harrowhouse, 92 in the Shade, Russian Roulette, The Stick-Up, The Medusa Touch, The Legacy, The Passage, The Unseen, Sphinx, Yes Giorgio, The Hound of the Baskervilles, On the Third Day, The Naked Face.

LEWIS, RICHARD
Comedian, Actor. b. Brooklyn, NY, June 29, 1949. e. Ohio St. Univ. (marketing degree). Was copywriter for adv. agency before becoming stand-up comic performing in nightclubs in NYC, Las Vegas, 1971.
PICTURES: The Wrong Guys (debut, 1988), That's Adequate, Once Upon a Crime, Robin Hood: Men in Tights, Wagons East!, Leaving Las Vegas, Drunks.
TELEVISION: *Series*: Harry, Anything But Love, Hiller & Diller. *Specials*: Richard Lewis: I'm in Pain, Richard Lewis: I'm Exhausted, Richard Lewis: I'm Doomed, Living Against the Odds (also writer). *Pilot*: King of the Building.

LI, GONG
Actress. b. Shenyang, Liaoning Province, China, Dec. 31, 1965.
PICTURES: Red Field, Red Sorghum, The Terracotta Warrior, Ju Dou, God of Gamblers III: Back to Shanghai, Raise the Red Lantern, The Story of Qiu Ju, Mary from Beijing, Farewell—My Concubine, Flirting Scholar, La Peintre, Semi-Gods and Semi-Devils, The Great Conqueror's Concubine, To Live, Shanghai Triad, Temptress Moon.

LIBERMAN, FRANK P.
Publicist, b. New York, NY, May 29, 1917. e. Cheshire Acad., CT, 1934; Lafayette Coll., Easton, PA, B.A. 1938. m. Patricia Harris, casting dir. Worked as copy boy, N.Y. Daily News, 1938-39. Began career as publicist at Warner Bros., home office as messenger, 1939, promoted to pressbooks dept., transferred to Warner's Chicago office as field exploitation man. U.S. Signal Corps, 1941, public relations officer, Army Pictorial Service, on temporary duty with War Dept., Bureau of Public Relations in Pentagon. Discharged as Capt., 1946. Rejoined Warner Bros. on coast 2 years, 1947, est. own public relations office, 1947. Owner, Frank Liberman and Associates, Inc.

LIBERTINI, RICHARD
Actor. b. Cambridge, MA, May 21. Original member of Second City troupe in Chicago. With MacIntyre Dixon appeared as the Stewed Prunes in cabaret performances.
THEATER: Three by Three (1961), Plays for Bleecker Street, The Cat's Pajamas, The Mad Show, . Bad Habits. Solo: The White House Murder Case, Don't Drink the Water, Paul Sill's Story Theatre, Ovid's Metamorphoses, The Primary English Class, Neopolitan Ghosts, Love's Labour's Lost, As You Like It.
PICTURES: The Night They Raided Minsky's, Don't Drink the Water, Catch-22, The Out-of-Towners, Lovers and Other Strangers, Lady Liberty, Fire Sale, Days of Heaven, The In-Laws, Popeye, Sharky's Machine, Soup for One, Best Friends, Deal of the Century, Going Berserk, Unfaithfully Yours, All of Me, Fletch, Big Trouble, Betrayed, Fletch Lives, Animal Behavior. Duck Tales: The Movie (voice), Lemon Sisters, Awakenings, The Bonfire of the Vanities, Cultivating Charlie, Nell.
TELEVISION: *Series*: Story Theatre, The Melba Moore-Clifton Davis Show, Soap, Family Man, The Fanelli Boys, Pacific Station. *Guest*: George Burns Comedy Week, Barney Miller, Bob Newhart. *Pilots*: Calling Dr. Storm, M.D., Fair Game. *Movies*: Three on a Date, Extreme Close-Up. *Specials*: Let's Celebrate, The Fourth Wise Man, Fame (Hallmark Hall of Fame), The Trial of Bernhard Goetz, Equal Justice, Murder She Wrote, Law and Order, L.A. Law.

LICCARDI, VINCENT G.
Executive. b. Brooklyn, NY. Started as messenger at Universal Pictures, asst. adv. mgr. on Around the World in 80 Days, asst. to exec. coord. of sales & Adv. on Spartacus; National Dir. of Adv. & Publ., Continental; Nat. Dir. Adv. & Publ., Braintree Prod., adv. pub. mgr. Allied Artists, ad. mgr. Paramount, National Dir. Adv.-Pub., UMC Pictures, Screen-writer, Playboy to Priest, The Rivals, The Rivals-Part II, The Greatest Disaster of All Time, The Lady on the 9:40, All That Heaven Allows, All Mine to Love, Twice Over, Lightly!, Mr. Jim, The Reluctant Corpse.

LIEBERFARB, WARREN N.
Executive. e. Wharton Sch. of Commerce and Finance, U. of PA, B.S., economics; U. of Michigan. Started career in industry at Paramount Pictures as dir. of mktg. and exec. asst. to Stanley Jaffe, then pres. Later joined 20th-Fox as v.p., special market dist. (cable, pay-TV, non-theatrical). Joined Warner Bros. as v.p., exec. asst. to Ted Ashley, bd. chmn.; later named v.p., intl. adv.-pub. In 1979 joined Lorimar as v.p., of Lorimar Productions, Inc., the parent company, based in New York, Promoted to sr. v.p. 1982, named v.p. mktg., Warner Home Video; named pres., 1984.

LIEBERMAN, ROBERT
Director, Producer. b. Buffalo, NY, July 16, 1947. e. Univ. of Buffalo. m. actress Marilu Henner. Moved to LA, became editor for Desort-Fisher commercial production house, which led to dir. tv ad spots. Formed own commercial company, Harmony Pictures.
PICTURES: Table for Five, All I Want for Christmas, Fire in the Sky, D3: The Mighty Ducks.
TELEVISION: *Movies*: Fighting Back: The Story of Rocky Blier, Will: G. Gordon Liddy, To Save a Child (also exec. prod.). *Series*: thirtysomething, Dream Street (pilot), The Young Riders (pilot), Gabriel's Fire (also exec. prod.), Pros and Cons (exec. consultant), Under Suspicion (also exec. prod.), Medicine Ball (also exec. prod.), Titanic.

LIEBERSON, SANFORD
Producer. b. Los Angeles, CA, 1936. Early career with William Morris Agency. 1961-62, agent in Rome for Grade Org. Returned to LA as Founding Member CMA agency then exec. in charge of European operations. 1979, named pres. of 20th-Fox Productions, which company he joined in 1977 as v.p. European production. Previously an independent producer forming Good Times. With David Putnam formed Visual Programming Systems to produce, acquire and consult in the Home Video area for CBS, Phillips, Time/Life, etc. As v.p. intl. prod. at Fox, spv. intl. release of such films as Star Wars, 1900, Alien, Chariots of Fire, Nine to Five, Quest for Fire. V.P. Intl. prod. for The Ladd Company. Outland, Body Heat, Blade Runner, The Right Stuff, Police Academy, etc. Chief of prod. at Goldcrest Harvest: Dance With a Stranger, Room With a View, Absolute Beginners, etc. Pres. intl. prod. MGM spv. Russia House, Thelma & Louise, Liebestraum, Not Without My Daughter, Criss Cross, etc. Currently head of prod. at the Natl. Film and Television School of Great Britain.
PICTURES: *Producer*: Melody, Pied Piper, Radio Wonderful, James Dean: First American Teenager, Bugsy Malone, Slade in Flame, Final Programme, Stardust, That'll Be the Day, Brother Can You Spare a Dime, Swastika, Double Headed Eagle, All This and World War II, Mahler, Lisztomania, Jabberwocky, Rita Sue and Bob Too, Stars and Bars, The Mighty Quinn, Performance.
TELEVISION: *Movie:* Frank & Jessie (exec. prod.).

LIGHT, JUDITH
Actress. b. Trenton, NJ, Feb. 9. e. Carnegie-Mellon Univ. (BFA). Toured with USO in prod. of Guys and Dolls during college. Acted with Milwaukee and Seattle rep. companies. Made B'way debut in 1975 prod. of A Doll's House with Liv Ullmann. Other stage work: A Streetcar Named Desire, As You Like It, Richard III. Landed role of Karen Wolek on daytime serial One Life to Live in 1977.
TELEVISION: *Series*: One Life to Live (2 Emmy Awards), Who's the Boss?, Phenom. *Movies*: Intimate Agony, Dangerous Affection, The Ryan White Story, My Boyfriend's Back, In Defense of a Married Man, Wife Mother Murderer, Men Don't Tell, Betrayal of Trust, Against Their Will: Women in Prison, Lady Killer, A Husband, A Wife and A Lover, Murder at My Door, A Step Toward Tomorrow, Too Close to Home. *Guest*: St. Elsewhere, Family Ties, Remington Steele.

LIGHTMAN, M. A.
Exhibitor. b. Nashville, TN, Apr. 21, 1915. e. Southwestern U., Vanderbilt U., 1936, B.A. Bd. chmn. Malco Theatres, Inc., Memphis, Tenn.

LILLARD, MATTHEW
Actor. b. Lansing, MI, Jan. 24, 1970.
PICTURES: Ghoulies 3: Ghoulies Go to College, Serial Mom, Ride for Your Life, Mad Love, Hackers, Tarantella, Scream, Telling You, Dish Dogs, The Curve, Senseless, Without Limits, S.L.C. Punk!, Love's Labour's Lost, She's All That, Wing Commander.
TELEVISION: *Movies:* Vanishing Son IV, If These Walls Could Talk, The Devil's Child. *Guest:* Nash Bridges.

LIMAN, DOUG
Director. e. Brown Univeristy.
PICTURES: Getting In, Swingers (also photog.), Go (also photog.), Sonny Bridges, The Bourne Identity.

LINDBLOM, GUNNEL
Actress, Director. b. Gothenburg, Sweden, 1931. Discovered by Ingmar Bergman while studying at drama school of Gothenburg Municipal Theatre, 1950-53; she moved to Malmo, where he was director of the local Municipal Theatre. Under Bergman's direction she played in Easter, Peer Gynt, Faust, etc. between 1954-59. Later appeared in many Bergman films. Since 1968 has been on staff of Stockholm's Royal Dramatic Theatre, assisting Bergman and then beginning to direct on her own. Made film debut as director with Summer Paradise in 1977.
PICTURES: *Actress*: Love, Girl in the Rain, Song of the Scarlet Flower, The Seventh Seal, Wild Strawberries, The Virgin Spring, Winter Light, The Silence, My Love Is a Rose, Rapture, Loving Couples, Hunger, Woman of Darkness, The Girls, The Father, Brother Carl, Scenes From a Marriage, Misfire, Bakom Jalusin. *Director*: Summer Paradise (also co-s.p.), Sally and Freedom, Summer Nights on Planet Earth (also s.p.).

LINDEN, HAL
Actor. b. Bronx, NY, March 20, 1931. e. City Coll. of New York. Began career as saxophone player and singer, playing with bands of Sammy Kaye, Bobby Sherwood, etc. Drafted and performed in revues for Special Services. After discharge enrolled at N.Y.'s American Theatre Wing; appeared on B'way in Bells Are Ringing, replacing Sydney Chaplin.
THEATER: Wildcat, Something More, Subways Are for Sleeping, Ilya Darling, The Apple Tree, The Education of H*Y*M*A*N K*A*P*L*A*N, On a Clear Day You Can See Forever, Three Men on a Horse, The Pajama Game, The Rothschilds (Tony Award, 1971), I'm Not Rappaport, Unfinished Stories, The Sisters Rosensweig.
PICTURES: Bells Are Ringing, When You Comin' Back Red Ryder?, A New Life, Out to Sea.
TELEVISION: *Series*: Animals Animals Animals (host), Barney Miller, Blacke's Magic, F.Y.I. (Emmy Awards, 1983, 1984), Jack's Place, The Boys Are Back. *Specials*: I Do! I Do!, The Best of Everything. *Movies*: Mr. Inside/Mr. Outside, The Love Boat (pilot), How to Break Up a Happy Divorce, Father Figure, Starflight: The Plane That Couldn't Land, The Other Woman, My Wicked Wicked Ways: The Legend of Errol Flynn, The O'Connors, Dream Breakers, The Colony.

LINDHEIM, RICHARD D.
Executive. b. New York, NY, May 28, 1939. e. Univ. of Redlands, USC. Admin. Asst. Story Dept., CBS, 1962-64. Project Dir. Entertainment Testing ASI Mkt. Research, 1964-69. VP Prog. Research NBC 1969-78, VP Dramatic Prog. 1978-79, Prod. Universal TV 1979-81, VP Current Prog. 1981-85, SVP Series Prog. 1986-87. Exec. VP Creative Affairs 1987-91, Exec. VP Prog. Strategy MCA TV Group 1991-92. Exec. VP Paramount TV 1992-Asst. Prof. CSU. Sr. Lecturer, USC, UCLA. Author: Primetime Network TV Programming (w/ Richard Blum) 1987, Inside TV Producing 1991.

LINDO, DELROY
Actor. b. London, England, Nov. 18, 1952. Received NAACP Image Awards for film Malcolm X and play A Raisin in the Sun.
THEATER: *B'way:* Joe Turner's Come and Gone (Tony nom.), Master Harold and the Boys. *Off-B'way:* District Line, As You Like It, Romeo and Juliet, Spell #7, The Heliotrope Bouquet. *Regional:* Othello, Mrs. Ever's Boys, Cobb, A Raisin in the Sun, My Mark My Name, Union Boys, Macbeth, Black Branch, Home.
PICTURES: The Blood of Heroes (Salute to the Jugger; debut, 1990), Mountains of the Moon, Perfect Witness, The Hard Way, Bright Angel, Malcolm X, Bound by Honor, Mr. Jones, Behanzin, Crooklyn, Congo, Clockers, Get Shorty, Feeling Minnesota, Broken Arrow, Ransom, The Devil's Advocate (cameo), A Life Less Ordinary, Glory & Honor, Romeo Must Die, The Cider House Rules, The Book of Stars.
TELEVISION: *Movies:* First-Time Felon, Strange Justice. *Guest:* Going to Extremes, Against the Law, Hawk, Beauty and the Beast.

LINDSAY, ROBERT
Actor. b. Ilkeston, Derbyshire, Eng., Dec. 13, 1949. e. GLadstone Boys School, Ilkeston, Royal Acad. of Dramatic Art. With Manchester's Royal Exchange Theatre Co. (Hamlet, The Cherry Orchard, The Lower Depths). Also in Godspell, The Three Musketeers, Me and My Girl, (London—Olivier Award, NY—Tony, Theatre World & Drama Desk Awards, 1987), Becket (Olivier & Variety Club Awards), Cyrano de Bergerac.
PICTURES: That'll Be the Day (debut, 1974), Bert Rigby You're a Fool, Strike It Rich, Fierce Creatures.
TELEVISION: *Series*: Citizen Smith, Give Us A Break. *Mini-series*: Confessional. *Specials*: King Lear, G.B.H. (BAFTA Award), Genghis Cohn, Jake's Progress.

LINDSAY-HOGG, MICHAEL
Director. b. England, 1940. Mother is actress Geraldine Fitzgerald.
PICTURES: Let It Be, Nasty Habits, The Object of Beauty (also s.p.), Frankie Starlight.
TELEVISION: Brideshead Revisted (co-dir.), Master Harold ... and the Boys, As Is.

LINK, WILLIAM
Writer, Producer. b. Philadelphia, PA, Dec. 15, 1933. e. U. of Pennsylvania, B.S., 1956. With partner, late Richard Levinson, wrote and created numerous TV series and movies, specializing in detective-mystery genre. *Books*: Fineman, Stay Tuned: An Inside Look at the Making of Prime-Time Television, Off Camera. *Stage incl.*: Prescription Murder, Guilty Conscience, Merlin.
PICTURES: The Hindenberg, Rollercoaster.
TELEVISION: *Series writer-creator*: Mannix, Ellery Queen, Tenafly, Columbo (Emmy Award as writer, 1972), Murder She Wrote. *Movies* writer-prod.: That Certain Summer, My Sweet Charlie (Emmy Award as writer, 1970), The Judge and Jake Wyler, Savage (exec. prod., writer), The Execution of Private Slovik, The Gun, A Cry for Help (prod. only), The Storyteller, Murder by Natural Causes, Stone, Crisis at Central High, Rehearsal For Murder (also exec. prod.), Take Your Best Shot, Prototype (also exec. prod.), The Guardian (also exec. prod.), Guilty Conscience (also exec. prod.), Vanishing Act (also exec. prod.), The United States Vs. Salim Ajami, The Boys (also co-exec. prod.).

LINKLATER, RICHARD
Director, Writer, Producer. b. Houston, TX, 1961. Founded Austin Film Society, serving as artistic director. Filmed several super 8 films incl. feature It's Impossible to Learn to Plow by Reading Books.
PICTURES: *Director/Writer:* Slacker (also actor & prod.), Dazed and Confused (also co-prod.), The Underneath (actor only), Beavis & Butt-Head Do America (voice), Before Sunrise, Suburbia (dir. only), The Newton Boys.

LINKLETTER, ART
Emcee, Producer, Author. b. Moose Jaw, Saskatchewan, Canada, July 17, 1912. Raised in San Diego. e. San Diego State Coll. Radio prg. mgr., San Diego Exposition, 1935; radio pgm. mgr. S.F. World's Fair, 1937-39; freelance radio announcer and m.c. 1939-42; m.c. series People Are Funny starting in 1942. Author: The Secret World of Kids, 1959; Kids Say the Darndest Things, 1957; Linkletter Down Under, 1969; Yes You Can, 1979; Old Age Is Not For Sissies, 1988; Cavalcade of the Golden West; Cavalcade of America. Recorded albums: Howls, Boners & Shockers and We Love You, Call Collect (Grammy Award winner, 1966). Bd. of dir., MGM, 1979-88.
PICTURES: People Are Funny, Champagne for Caesar, The Snow Queen.
TELEVISION: *Series*: Art Linkletter's House Party, Life With Linkletter, People Are Funny (emcee), The Art Linkletter Show (emcee), Hollywood Talent Scouts. *Specials*: Inside Salute to Baseball (exec. prod., host), Art Linkletter's Secret World of Kids (host), Ford Startime, Young Man With A Band, Linkletters Spend Christmas in the Holy Land, Kid's Eye View of Washington. *Movies*: Zane Grey Theatre, G.E. Theatre, Wagon Train: Kid at the Stick.

LINN-BAKER, MARK
Actor, Director. b. St. Louis, MO, June 17, 1954. e. Yale Univ., Yale Sch. of Drama (M.F.A., 1979). Founding memb. American Repertory Th. in Cambridge, MA; founding prod./dir. NY Stage & Film Co. in NYC & Poughkeepsie. Co-founder of True Pictures, 1990.
THEATER: *B'way*: Doonesbury, Laughter on the 23rd Floor, A Funny Thing Happened On The Way To The Forum.
PICTURES: Manhattan (bit), The End of August, My Favorite Year, Me and Him (voice only), Noises Off, Me and Veronica (co-prod. only).
TELEVISION: *Series*: Comedy Zone, Perfect Strangers, Hangin' With Mr. Cooper (dir. only). *Movies*: Wedding Bell Blues, Bare Essentials. *Specials*: Doonesbury (voice of Kirby), The Ghost Writer (Amer. Playhouse), The Whole Shebang. *Director*: episodes of Family Matters, Family Man, Going Places.

LINSON, ART
Producer, Director. b. Chicago, IL, 1942. e. UCLA; LLD. UCLA, 1967. Was rock music manager with record prod. Lou Adler and ran own record co., Spin Dizzy records before turning to film production. Debuted as director also with Where the Buffalo Roam.
PICTURES: *Prod. &/or dir.*: Rafferty and the Gold Dust Twins (co.-prod.), Car Wash, American Hot Wax (also co-s.p.), Where the Buffalo Roam, Melvin and Howard, Fast Times at Ridgemont High (co-prod.), The Wild Life, The Untouchables, Scrooged (co-prod.), Casualties of War, We're No Angels, Dick Tracy (exec. prod.), Singles, Point of No Return, This Boy's Life, Heat, The Edge, Pushing Tin, Great Expectations, Fight Club.

LIOTTA, RAY
Actor. b. Newark, NJ, Dec. 18, 1955. e. Univ. of Miami. First prof. job on tv commercial, followed by continuing role on daytime serial, Another World.
PICTURES: Something Wild (debut, 1983), The Lonely Lady, Dominick and Eugene, Field of Dreams, GoodFellas, Article 99, Unlawful Entry, No Escape, Corrina Corrina, Operation Dumbo Drop, Unforgettable, Turbulence, Cop Land, Phoenix, A Rumor of Angels, Forever Mine, Muppets from Space, Pilgrim, Blow, Hannibal, John Q, Breakers.
TELEVISION: *Series*: Another World, Casablanca, Our Family Honor. *Movies*: Hardhat and Legs, Crazy Times, Women and Men 2: In Love There Are No Rules, The Rat Pack.

LIPPERT, ROBERT L., JR.
Producer, Exhibitor. b. Alameda, CA, Feb. 28, 1928. e. St Mary's Coll., 1946; all conference football 1947. Career began in theatre exhibition. Entered m.p. production in 1951. Film editor of 45 "b" features. Produced 9 pictures for Lippert Features and 20th Century Fox Films. Returned in 1966 to theatre exhibition. Became pres. of Affiliated, Lippert, Transcontinental theatres (180 theatres nation-wide). Semi-retired as of 1994.

LIPSTONE, HOWARD H.
Executive, Producer. b. Chicago, IL, Apr. 28, 1928. e. UCLA, USC. Ass't to gen. mgr. at KLTA, 1950-55; program dir. at KABC-TV, 1955-65; exec. ass't to pres. at Selmur Prods., ABC subsidiary, 1965-69. Ivan Tors Films & Studios as exec. v.p., 1969-70; pres., Alan Landsburg Prods., 1970-1985; The Landsburg Co., 1985-. Co-exec. prod.: The Outer Space Connection, The Bermuda Triangle, Mysteries, The White Lions, Jaws 3-D.
TELEVISION: *Exec. in charge of prod.*: The Savage Bees, Ruby and Oswald, The Triangle Factory Fire Scandal, Strange Voices, A Place at the Table, Kate & Allie, Gimme a Break, A Stoning in Fulham County, The Ryan White Story, Quiet Victory, Unspeakable Acts, In Defense of a Married Man, Triumph of the Heart, Nightmare in Columbia County, A Mother's Right, The Elizabeth Morgan Story, The Diamond Fleece, Terror in the Night, If Someone Had Known.

LIPTON, PEGGY
Actress. b. New York, NY, Aug. 30, 1947. Former model. Co-wrote song L.A. is My Lady (recorded by Frank Sinatra). Recorded album Peggy Lipton.
PICTURES: The Purple People Eater, Kinjite (Forbidden Subjects), Twin Peaks: Fire Walk With Me, Justice for Annie, The Postman.
TELEVISION: *Series*: The John Forsythe Show, The Mod Squad (Golden Globe Award, 1971), Twin Peaks, Angel Falls. *Movies*: The Return of the Mod Squad, Addicted to His Love, Fatal Charm, The Spider and the Fly, Deadly Vows.

LISI, VIRNA
Actress. r.n. Virna Pieralisi. b. Ancona, Italy, Nov. 8, 1936.
PICTURES: Desiderio e Sole, Violenza sul Lago, The Doll That Took the Town, Luna Nova, Vendicatta, La Rossa, Caterina Sforza, Il Mondo dei Miracoli, Duel of the Titans, Eva, Don't Tempt the Devil, The Black Tulip, The Shortest Day, How To Murder Your Wife, Casanova 70, The Possessed, A Virgin for a Prince, Kiss the Other Sheik, The Birds the Bees and the Italians, Made in Italy, La Bambole (The Dolls), Not With My Wife You Don't, Assault on a Queen, The 25th Hour, Anyone Can Play, The Girl and the General, Arabella, Better a Widow, The Girl Who Couldn't Say No, The Christmas Tree, The Secret of Santa Vittoria, If It's Tuesday This Must Be Belgium, Roma Bene, The Statue, Bluebeard, The Serpent, Ernesto, I Love N.Y.,

I Ragazzi di Via Panisperna, Beyond Good and Evil, Merry Christmas Happy New Year, Miss Right, Queen Margot (Cannes Film Fest. Award, 1994).
TELEVISION: *US*: Christopher Columbus.

LITHGOW, JOHN
Actor. b. Rochester, NY, Oct. 19, 1945. Father was prod. of Shakespeare Fests. in midwest. e. Harvard. Fulbright fellowship to study at London Acad. of Music and Dramatic Art. Interned in London with Royal Shakespeare Co. and Royal Court Theatre.
THEATER: *NY*: The Changing Room (Tony & Drama Desk Awards, 1973), My Fat Friend, Trelawney of the Wells, Comedians, Anna Christie, A Memory of Two Mondays, Once in a Lifetime, Spokesong, Bedroom Farce, Salt Lake City Skyline, Division Street (also LA), Kaufman at Large (also dir., writer), Beyond Therapy, Requiem for a Heavyweight (Drama Desk Award), The Front Page, M Butterfly. Regional: The Beggar's Opera, Pygmalion, Of Mice and Men, Troilus and Cressida, The Roar of the Greasepaint, What Price Glory?, The Lady's Not for Burning, Who's Afraid of Virginia Woolf? (LA Drama Critics Circle Award).
PICTURES: Dealing or The Berkeley-to-Boston Forty-Brick Lost-Bag Blues (debut, 1972), Obsession, The Big Fix, Rich Kids, All That Jazz, Blow Out, I'm Dancing as Fast as I Can, The World According to Garp (Acad. Award nom.), Twilight Zone—The Movie, Terms of Endearment (Acad. Award nom.), Footloose, The Adventures of Buckaroo Banzai: Across the Eighth Dimension, 2010, Santa Claus, The Manhattan Project, Mesmerized, Harry and the Hendersons, Distant Thunder, Out Cold, Memphis Belle, Ricochet, At Play in the Fields of the Lord, Raising Cain, Cliffhanger, The Pelican Brief, A Good Man in Africa, Princess Caraboo, Silent Fall, Hollow Point, Officer Buckle and Gloria, Johnny Skidmarks, A Civil Action, Homegrown.
TELEVISION: *Series*: Third Rock From the Sun (Emmy Award, 1996, 1997, 1999; Golden Globe Award, 1997). *Guest*: Amazing Stories (Emmy Award, 1987). *Movies*: Mom The Wolfman and Me, Not in Front of the Children, The Day After, The Glitter Dome, Resting Place, Baby Girl Scott, The Traveling Man, The Last Elephant (Ivory Hunters), The Boys, The Wrong Man, Love Cheat and Steal, World War II: When Lions Roared, Redwood Curtain, The Tuskegee Airmen, Don Quixote. *Specials*: The Country Girl (TV debut, 1973), Secret Service, Big Blonde, The Oldest Living Graduate, Goldilocks and the Three Bears (Faerie Tale Theatre).

LITTLE, RICH
Actor. b. Ottawa, Canada, Nov. 26, 1938. Started as radio disc jockey, talk show host in Canada; then impressionist in night clubs.
PICTURES: Dirty Tricks, Happy Hour, Bebe's Kids (voice).
TELEVISION: *Series*: Love on a Rooftop, The John Davidson Show, ABC Comedy Hour (The Kopycats), The Julie Andrews Hour, The Rich Little Show, The New You Asked For It (host). *Specials*: The Rich Little Show, Rich Little's Christmas Carol (also writer), Rich Little's Washington Follies, The Rich Little Specials (HBO), Rich Little's Robin Hood, Come Laugh With Me, Night of 42 Stars, The Christmas Raccoons, Rich Little and Friends in New Orleans.

LITTLEFIELD, WARREN
Executive. b. Montclair, NJ. e. American Univ. in DC, School of Government and Public Admin.; Hobart Col. (psych. degree). 1975-79, Westfall Prods., developing prime-time specials and movies before being promoted to v.p., develop. & prod. 1979, served as WB TV dir., comedy develop. Joined NBC 1979, as mngr. comedy develop. 1981, v.p. current comedy programs at NBC. 1985, sr. v.p. series specials & variety progs., NBC Entertainment; 1987, exec. v.p., Prime-Time progs. NBC Entertainment. 1990, named pres. NBC Entertainment.

LITTMAN, LYNNE
Director, Producer. b. New York, NY, June 26. e. Sarah Lawrence. B.A., 1962; Student the Sorbonne 1960-61. Researcher for CBS News 1965; assoc. prod. Natl. Educational TV 1964-68; dir. NIMH film series on drug abuse UCLA Media Center 1970; prod., dir. documentary films, news and pub. affairs series KCET Community TV, So. Calif. 1971-77; dir. WNET non-fiction film, Once a Daughter 1979; exec. v.p., movies-for-TV, ABC, 1980-81; Received Ford Fdn. Grant 1978 and numerous awards. Acad. Award film tribute to women, 1993.
PICTURES: In the Matter of Kenneth (doc.), Wanted-Operadoras (doc.), Till Death Do Us Part (doc.), Number Our Days (doc. short; Acad. Award 1977), Testament (co-prod., dir.), In Her Own Time (doc.).
TELEVISION: *Movies*: Cagney & Lacey, Marie Taquet, Freak City.

LITTO, GEORGE
Producer. b. Philadelphia, PA. e. Temple U. Joined William Morris Agency in New York and then became indep. literary agent. Opened own office in Hollywood, 1965. Packaged film and TV productions, including M*A*S*H, Hang 'Em High, Hawaii Five-O for TV prior to entering indep. prod.; 1981-82, chmn. bd. & CEO, Filmways; 1983-85 indep. prod. 20th Century Fox.
PICTURES: Thieves Like Us (exec. prod.), Drive-In (exec. prod.), Obsession (prod.), Over the Edge (prod.), Dressed To Kill (prod.). Blow Out (prod.), Kansas (prod.), Night Game (prod.).

LITVINOFF, SI
Producer, Executive. b. New York, NY, April 5. e. Adelphi Coll., A.B.; NYU Sch. of Law, LL.B. Theatrical lawyer, personal and business manager in New York until 1967 when left firm of Barovick, Konecky & Litvinoff to produce plays and films. June, 1987: sr. v.p. for production and dev., Hawkeye Entertainment, Inc.
THEATER: Leonard Bernstein's Theatre Songs, Cry of the Raindrop, Girl of the Golden West, Little Malcolm and His Struggle Against the Eunuchs, I and Albert (London).
PICTURES: The Queen, All the Right Noises, Walkabout, A Clockwork Orange (exec. prod.), Glastonbury Fayre (exec. in chg. prod.), The Man Who Fell to Earth (exec. prod.)
TELEVISION: *Exec. prod.*: 15th Annual Saturn Awards, Doobie Brothers Retrospective, Listen to the Music 1989.

LIU, LUCY ALEXIS
Actress. b. Jackson Heights, NY, 1967.
PICTURES: The Big Bang Theory, Guy, Jerry Maguire, Flypaper, Gridlock'd, City of Industry, Payback.
TELEVISION: *Movies:* Riot. *Series:* Pearl, Ally McBeal. *Guest:* Beverly Hills 90210, L.A. Law, Coach, Home Improvement, Hercules: The Legendary Journeys, ER, The X Files, Nash Bridges, NYPD Blue.

LIVINGSTON, JAY
Composer, Lyricist. b. McDonald, PA, March 28, 1915. e. U. of PA, 1937, UCLA, 1964-65. Army, WWII. Accompanist and arranger for various NBC singers and singing groups 1940-42, NY; author music and special material for Olsen & Johnson, including various editions of Hellzapoppin', and Sons O'Fun: began composing m.p. songs, 1944. Under contract to Paramount, 1945-55; then freelanced. Cameo appearance in Sunset Boulevard. Writer of songs and special material for Bob Hope starting in 1945. Has written songs for over 100 pictures. Elected to Songwriters Hall of Fame, 1975. Received star on Hollywood Blvd. Walk of Fame, 1995.
SONGS INCLUDE: G'bye Now, Stuff Like That There, To Each His Own, Golden Earrings, Silver Bells, Buttons and Bows (Academy Award, 1949), Mona Lisa (Academy Award, 1951), Que Sera Sera/Whatever Will Be Will Be (Academy Award, 1957), Tammy (Acad. Award nom.), Almost In Your Arms (Acad. Award nom.), Dear Heart, (Acad. Award nom.), Wish Me a Rainbow, In the Arms of Love, Never Let Me Go, As I Love You, All the Time, Maybe September.
THEATER: *B'way*: Oh Captain!, Let It Ride, Sugar Babies (2 songs).
PICTURES: Monsieur Beaucaire, My Favorite Brunette, The Paleface, My Friend Irma, Sorrowful Jones, My Friend Irma Goes West, Streets of Laredo, Isn't It Romantic?, Fancy Pants, Here Comes the Groom, The Lemon-Drop Kid, Son of Paleface, The Stars Are Singing, Here Come the Girls, Somebody Loves Me, Aaron Slick from Punkin' Crick, Red Garters, The Man Who Knew Too Much, Houseboat, Tammy and the Bachelor, Dear Heart, The Night of the Grizzly, This Property Is Condemned, The Oscar, Never Too Late, Harlow, What Did You Do in the War Daddy?, Wait Until Dark.
TELEVISION: Series themes: Bonanza, Mister Ed.

LLOYD, CHRISTOPHER
Actor. b. Stamford, CT, Oct. 22, 1938. Studied at Neighborhood Playhouse, NY.
THEATER: *NY*: Kaspar (Drama Desk & Obie Awards, 1973), Happy End, Red White and Maddox. Regional: The Father, Hot L Baltimore, The Possessed, A Midsummer Night's Dream.
PICTURES: One Flew Over the Cuckoo's Nest (debut, 1975), Goin' South, Butch and Sundance: The Early Days, The Onion Field, The Lady in Red, Schizoid, The Black Marble, The Postman Always Rings Twice, The Legend of the Lone Ranger, National Lampoon Goes to the Movies, Mr. Mom, To Be or Not to Be, Star Trek III: The Search for Spock, The Adventures of Buckaroo Banzai Across the Eighth Dimension, Joy of Sex, Back to the Future, Clue, Legend of the White Horse, Miracles, Walk Like a Man, Who Framed Roger Rabbit, Track 29, Eight Men Out, The Dream Team, Back to the Future Part II, Why Me?, Back to the Future Part III, Duck Tales: The Movie (voice), White Dragon, Suburban Commando, The Addams Family, Dennis the Menace, Twenty Bucks, Addams Family Values, Angels in the Outfield, Camp Nowhere, Radioland Murders, The Pagemaster, Things to Do in Denver When You're Dead, Cadillac Ranch, Changing Habits, Anastasia, Tom Sawyer, It Came from the Sky, Dinner at Fred's, Convegence, Baby Geniuses, My Favorite Martian, Man on the Moon.
TELEVISION: *Series*: Taxi (Emmy Awards: 1982, 1983), Back to the Future (voice for animated series), Deadly Games. *Specials*: Pilgrim Farewell, The Penny Elf, Tales From Hollywood Hills: Pat Hobby—Teamed With Genius, In Search of Dr. Seuss. *Movies*: Lacy and the Mississippi Queen, The Word, Stunt Seven, Money on the Side, September Gun, The Cowboy and the Ballerina, T Bone N Weasel, Dead Ahead: The Exxon Valdez Disaster, It Came from the Sky. *Guest*: Barney Miller, Best of the West, Cheers, Amazing Stories, Avonlea (Emmy Award, 1992), Angels in the End Zone.

LLOYD, EMILY
Actress. r.n. Emily Lloyd Pack. b. North London, Eng., Sept. 29, 1970. Father is stage actor Roger Lloyd Pack, mother worked as Harold Pinter's secretary. Father's agent recommended that she audition for screenwriter David Leland's directorial debut Wish You Were Here when she was 15.
PICTURES: Wish You Were Here (Natl. Society of Film Critics & London Evening Standard Awards, 1987; BAFTA nom.), Cookie, In Country, Chicago Joe and the Showgirl, Scorchers, A River Runs Through It, Under the Hula Moon, When Saturday Comes.

LLOYD, EUAN
Producer. b. Rugby, Warwick, England, Dec. 6, 1923. e. Rugby. Entered m.p. ind. in 1939 as theatre manager, then pub. dir.; dir. of Publ. Rank, 1946; joined Associated British-Pathe, Ltd. in same capacity; 1952 asst. to prod., Warwick Film Prod. Ltd. v.p. Highroad Productions, 1962-64. Rep. Europe Goldwyn's Porgy & Bess 1959.
PICTURES: April in Portugal, Heart of Variety, Invitation to Monte Carlo, The Secret Ways, Genghis Khan, Poppy Is Also a Flower, Murderer's Row, Shalako, Catlow, The Man Called Noon, Paper Tiger, The Wild Geese, The Sea Wolves, Who Dares Wins, Wild Geese II, The Final Option.

LLOYD, NORMAN
Actor, Producer, Director. b. Jersey City, NJ, Nov. 8, 1914. e. NYU, 1932. Acted on B'way in: Noah, Liberty Jones, Everywhere I Roam, 1935-44; in various stock companies. Joined Orson Welles and John Houseman in the original company of Mercury Theatre, NY, 1937-38. Prod. asst. on films Arch of Triumph, The Red Pony. Produced film Up Above the World.
THEATER: *With the Civic Repertory Theatre, 1932-33 and The Living Newspapers of The Federal Theatre, 1936:* Triple a Plowed Under, Injunction Granted. *Regional*: Power, Medicine Show, Ask My Friend, Sandy, Volpone. *American Shakespeare Festival*: Measure for Measure, Taming of the Shrew (also dir.). *With La Jolla Playhouse, 1948-1955*: Village Green, King Lear, The Cocktail Party, The Lady's Not for Burning, Madame Will You Walk, The Golden Apple, Major Barbara, The Will & Bart Show, Quiet City
PICTURES: *Actor*: Saboteur, Spellbound, The Southerner, A Walk in the Sun, A Letter for Evie, The Unseen, Green Years, The Beginning or The End, Limelight, Young Widow, No Minor Vices, The Black Book, Scene of the Crime, Calamity Jane and Sam Bass, Buccaneer's Girl, The Flame and the Arrow, He Ran All the Way, The Light Touch, Audrey Rose, FM, The Nude Bomb, Jaws of Satan, Dead Poets Society, Journey of Honor (Shogun Mayeda), The Age of Innocence.
TELEVISION: *Assoc. prod./exec. prod.*: The Alfred Hitchcock Show. *Prod.-Dir.*: The Alfred Hitchcock Hour, The Name of the Game, Hollywood Television Theater, Tales of the Unexpected, Omnibus (dir. of The Lincoln Films, 1952), Journey to the Unknown (series). *Actor*: St. Elsewhere (series), Harvest Home. *Movies* (prod.-dir.): The Smugglers, Companions in Nightmare, What's a Nice Girl Like You (prod.), The Bravos (prod.), Amityville: The Evil Escapes.

LOACH, KEN
Director, Writer. b. Nuneaton, England, June 17, 1936. e. Oxford (studied law). Served in Royal Air Force; then became actor. Began dir. career on British tv in early 1960's.
PICTURES: Poor Cow (debut, 1968; also co-s.p.), Kes (also co-s.p.), Family Life, Black Jack (also co-s.p.), Looks and Smiles (also co- s.p.), Fatherland (Singing the Blues in Red), Hidden Agenda, Riff- Raff, Raining Stones, Land and Freedom.
TELEVISION: Diary of a Young Man, 3 Clear Sundays, The End of Arthur's Marriage, Up the Junction, Coming Out Party, Cathy Come Home, In Two Minds, The Golden Vision, The Big Flame, In Black and White, After a Lifetime, The Rank and the File, Days of Hope, The Price of Coal, Auditions: The Gamekeeper, A Question of Leadership, Which Side Are You On.

LOBELL, MICHAEL
Producer. b. Brooklyn, NY, May 7, 1941. e. Michigan State U. on athletic baseball scholarship. Worked briefly in garment indust. Entered film industry in 1974 by buying Danish distribution rights to The Apprenticeship of Duddy Kravitz. Formed Lobell/ Bergman Prods. with Andrew Bergman.
PICTURES: Dreamer, Windows, So Fine, The Journey of Natty Gann, Chances Are, The Freshman, White Fang, Honeymoon in Vegas, Undercover Blues, Little Big League, It Could Happen to You, Striptease.

Lo BIANCO, TONY
Actor. b. New York, NY. Oct. 19, 1936. Performed on N.Y. stage as well as in films and TV. Former artistic dir. Triangle Theatre, NY.
THEATER: Yanks 3—Detroit 0—Top of the Seventh (Obie Award), The Office, The Rose Tattoo, A View From the Bridge (Outer Critics Circle Award), The Royal Hunt of the Sun, Hizzoner, Other People's Money (tour).
PICTURES: The Honeymoon Killers (debut, 1970), The French Connection, The Seven Ups, Demon (God Told Me To), F.I.S.T., Bloodbrothers, Separate Ways, City Heat, Too Scared to Scream (dir. only), Mean Frankie and Crazy Tony, La Romana, City of Hope, The Spiders Web, Boiling Point, The Ascent, The Last Home Run (dir. only), The Juror.
TELEVISION: *Series*: Love of Life, Jessie, Palace Guard. *Guest*: Police Story. *Movies/Mini-Series*: Mr. Inside Mr. Outside, The Story of Joseph and Jacob, Magee and the Lady (She'll Be Sweet), Jesus of Nazareth, Hidden Faces, Legend of the Black Hand, Lady Blue, Marco Polo, Welcome Home Bobby, Blood Ties, A Last Cry for Help, Marciano, Another Woman's Child, The Last Tenant, Goldenrod, Shadow in the Streets, Eugene O'Neill's A Glory of Ghosts, Police Story: The Freeway Killings, The Ann Jillian Story, Body of Evidence, Off Duty, True Blue, Perry Mason: The Case of the Poisoned Pen, Malcolm Takes a Shot, In the Shadow of a Killer, Stormy Weathers, Teamster Boss: The Jackie Presser Story, The First Circle, The Maharajah's Daughter, Tyson. *Specials*: Hizzoner (Emmy Award), A Glory of Ghosts. *Director*: Police Story, Kaz, Cliffhangers, When the Whistle Blows, The Duke.

LOCKE, PETER
Producer, Executive. Exec. producer, all programming produced by Kushner Locke. Producer, Stockard Channing Show, The Star Maker, The Hills Have Eyes, Parts I & II. Co-founder and currently co-chairman & co-CEO, Kushner-Locke, 1983.

LOCKE, SONDRA
Actress, Director. b. Shelbyville, TN, May 28, 1947. Autobiography: The Good the Bad and the Very Ugly, 1997.
PICTURES: The Heart Is a Lonely Hunter (debut, 1968; Acad. Award nom.), Cover Me Babe, Willard, A Reflection of Fear, The Second Coming of Suzanne, Death Game (The Seducers), The Outlaw Josey Wales, The Gauntlet, Every Which Way But Loose, Bronco Billy, Any Which Way You Can, Sudden Impact, Ratboy (also dir.), Impulse (dir. only), Do Me a Favor (dir.).
TELEVISION: *Movies*: Friendships, Secrets and Lies, Rosie: The Rosemary Clooney Story. *Guest*: Amazing Stories. *Director*: Death in Small Doses (movie).

LOCKHART, JUNE
Actress. b. New York, NY, June 25, 1925. p. actors, Gene and Kathleen Lockhart. B'way debut For Love or Money, 1947.
PICTURES: A Christmas Carol (debut, 1938), All This and Heaven Too, Adam Had Four Sons, Sergeant York, Miss Annie Rooney, Forever and a Day, White Cliffs of Dover, Meet Me in St. Louis, Son of Lassie, Keep Your Powder Dry, Easy to Wed, She-Wolf of London, Bury Me Dead, The Yearling, T-Men, It's a Joke Son, Time Limit, Butterfly, Deadly Games, Strange Invaders, Troll, Rented Lips, The Big Picture, Dead Women in Lingerie, Tis the Season, Sleep With Me, Lost in Space.
TELEVISION: *Series*: Who Said That? (panelist), Lassie, Lost in Space, Petticoat Junction, General Hospital, Roseanne, Step By Step, Fired Up. *Movies*: But I Don't Want to Get Married, The Bait, Who is the Black Dahlia?, Curse of the Black Widow, The Gift of Love, Walking Through the Fire, The Night They Saved Christmas, Perfect People, A Whisper Kills, Danger Island. *Mini-Series*: Loose Change.

LOCKLEAR, HEATHER
Actress. b. Los Angeles, CA, Sept. 25, 1961. e. UCLA. Appeared in commercials while in college.
PICTURES: Firestarter (debut, 1984), The Return of Swamp Thing, The Big Slice, Illusions, Wayne's World 2, The First Wives Club, Money Talks, Double Tap.
TELEVISION: *Series*: Dynasty, T.J. Hooker, Fright Night Videos (host), Going Places, Melrose Place. *Movies*: Return of the Beverly Hillbillies, Twirl, City Killer, Blood Sport, Rich Men Single Women, Jury Duty: The Comedy, Her Wicked Ways, Dynasty: The Reunion, Body Language, Highway Heartbreaker, Fade to Black, Texas Justice. Specials: Battle of the Network Stars, Hollywood Starr, TV Guide 40th Anniversary Special (host). *Guest*: Fantasy Island, The Fall Guy, Matt Houston, Hotel, The Love Boat.

LOCKWOOD, GARY
Actor. r.n. John Gary Yusolfsky. b. Van Nuys, CA, Feb. 21, 1937. Began in Hollywood as stuntman.
PICTURES: Tall Story, Splendor in the Grass, Wild in the Country, The Magic Sword, It Happened at the World's Fair, Firecreek, 2001: A Space Odyssey, They Came to Rob Las Vegas, Model Shop, The Body, R.P.M., Stand Up and Be Counted, The Wild Pair, Night of the Scarecrow.
TELEVISION: *Series:* Follow the Sun, The Lieutenant. *Movies*: Earth II, Manhunter, The FBI Story: The FBI Versus Alvin Karpus—Public Enemy, The Ghost of Flight 401, The Incredible Journey of Dr. Meg Laurel, Top of the Hill, The Girl The Gold Watch & Dynamite, Emergency Room.

LOCKWOOD, ROGER
Executive. b. Middletown, CT, June 7, 1936. e. Ohio Wesleyan U. Sports writer for Akron Beacon Journal, 1960-62. On executive staff of Lockwood & Gordon Theatres; exec. v.p. SBC Theatres, 1969-73. 1974 asst. to exec. v.p., General Cinema Corp. 1975 formed Lockwood/Friedman Theatres, buying-booking and exhibition organization. Pres., Theatre Owners of New England, 1971-72; pres., Young NATO 1965-67; bd. of dir. NATO, 1962-1968. Board of dir. Tone, 1968-present; pres., Jimmy Fund, present; 1979-80, Variety Club of New England, pres. Director,

Dana-Farber Cancer Institute, 1983-present. 1988, formed Lockwood/McKinnon Company Inc. operating theatres and Taco Bell Restaurants.

LOEKS, BARRIE LAWSON
Executive. b. Pittsburgh, PA. e. Univ. of MI, Univ. of MI Law Sch., 1979. Began career as associate in Grand Rapids, MI, law firm of Warner Norcross & Judd before serving for 7 yrs. as v.p. and gen. counsel of Jack Loeks Theatres; promoted to pres. of Loeks Michigan Theatres and Loeks-Star joint venture, 1988; Nov. 1992 named co-chmn., with husband Jim Loeks, of Sony/Loews Theatres, a Sony Retail Entertainment Co. April 1998 resigned from Loews Cineplex Entertainment; remains president and co-owner of Loeks-Star Theatres; named president of Loeks and Loeks Entertainment, Inc. Recipient of Entrepreneur Award for the State of Michigan, 1998. November 1998, named Chairman National Association of Theatre Owners. Member: Board of Directors of Meijer, Inc. and Carlow College; Visitor's Committee of the University of Michigan.

LOEKS, JIM
Executive. b. Grand Rapids, MI. e. Univ. of MI. Started as gen. mgr. of John Ball Concessions Inc, becoming chmn. of bd. and owner, 1976-91. 1978, elected v.p. of Jack Loeks Theatres Inc.; named pres. of chain in 1983. 1988, became chmn. & co-owner of Loeks Michigan Theatres Inc., also gen. partner & operating agent of Loeks-Star joint venture with Sony Pictures Entertainment. Nov., 1992 named co-chmn., with wife Barrie Lawson Loeks, of Sony/Loews Theatres. April 1998, resigned from Loews Cineplex Entertainment; remains chairman and co-owner of Loeks-Star Theatres; named chairman of Loeks and Loeks Entertainment, Inc. Recipient of Entrepreneur Award for State of Michican, 1998.

LOEKS, JOHN D. Jr.
Executive. b. Grand Rapids, MI, Feb 24, 1945. e. Wheaton Coll., B.A. 1967; Wayne State U., J.D. 1970. Began own law practice in 1970 until 1990. President, Showspan Inc., Jack Loeks Theatres Inc. Bd. member, Ausable Institute, Grand Rapids Symphony Orchestra, InterVarsity Christian Fellowship.

LOESCH, MARGARET
Executive. e. U. of S. MS, B.A; grad. work at U. of New Orleans. President, Fox Children's Network.

LOEWY, VICTOR
Executive. e. B.A., economics and German, McGill U., 1970. Co-founded Vivafilm, 1972; after Vivafilm became Alliance Communications Corp. in 1985, led that company to a dominant position in Canada's independent film distribution industry. Currently board member, Canadian Film Centre, Toronto International Film Festival; chairman, National Assn. of Canadian Film Distributors; chairman, Alliance Atlantis Motion Picture Grp.; board member and member of Executive Committee, Alliance Atlantis Communications, Inc.

LOGAN, JEFF
Exhibitor. b. Mitchell, SD, Dec. 29, 1950. e. Dakota Wesleyan U. & U. of SD. Started working in family's Roxy Theatre at 9 yrs. old. Worked as announcer on KORN radio, 1969-70. Announcer, reporter & photgrapher KUSD-TV, 1970-71. Relief anchor KXON-TV, 1972-78. Took over management of family theatre. Built co. into present circuit, Logan Luxury Theatres. Member Bd. of trustess Dakota Wesleyan U., 1990-present. Bd. of trustees Queen of Peace Hospital, 1991-1997. V.P. Variety Club of SD, 1994-96. Dir. NATO/North Central, 1980-90. V.P. VSDA of SD, 1989-1994. Dir., NATO, 1997-present. Chairman NATO Theatre Operations Committee, 1999.

LOGGIA, ROBERT
Actor. b. New York, NY, Jan. 3, 1930. e. U. of Missouri, B.A. journalism, 1951. Studied with Stella Adler and at The Actors Studio. Broadway debut, The Man with the Golden Arm, 1955.
THEATER: Toys in the Attic, The Three Sisters, In the Boom Boom Room, Wedding Band.
PICTURES: Somebody Up There Likes Me (debut, 1956), The Garment Jungle, Cop Hater, The Lost Missile, Cattle King, The Greatest Story Ever Told, Che, First Love, Speed Trap, Revenge of the Pink Panther, The Ninth Configuration (Twinkle Twinkle Killer Kane), S.O.B., An Officer and a Gentleman, Trail of the Pink Panther, Psycho II, Curse of the Pink Panther, Scarface, Prizzi's Honor, Jagged Edge (Acad. Award nom.), Armed and Dangerous, That's Life, Over the Top, Hot Pursuit, The Believers, Gaby: A True Story, Big, Oliver & Company (voice), Relentless, S.P.O.O.K.S. (Code Name: Chaos), Triumph of the Spirit, Opportunity Knocks, The Marrying Man, Necessary Roughness, Gladiator, Innocent Blood, The Last Tattoo, Bad Girls, I Love Trouble, Man With a Gun, Independence Day, Lost Highway, Smilla's Sense of Snow, Wide Awake, The Proposition, Holy Man, Live Virgin, The Suburbans, Return to Me.
TELEVISION: *Series*: T.H.E. Cat, Emerald Point N.A.S., Mancuso FBI, Sunday Dinner. *Specials*: Miss Julie, The Nine Lives of Elfego Baca, Conspiracy: The Trial of the Chicago 8, Merry Christmas Baby. *Movies:* Mallory: Circumstantial Evidence, Street Killing, Scott Free, Raid on Entebbe, No Other Love, Casino, A Woman Called Golda, A Touch of Scandal, Streets of Justice, Intrigue, Dream Breakers, Afterburn, Lifepod, Nurses on the Line: The Crash of Flight 7, White Mile, Jake Lassiter: Justice on the Bayou, Between Love and Honor, Mercy Mission: The Rescue of Flight 771, Right to Remain Silent, Joe Torre: Curveballs Along the Way, Hard Time: The Premonition. *Mini-Series*: Arthur Hailey's The Moneychangers, Echoes in the Darkness, Favorite Son, Wild Palms, Joan of Arc.

LOLLOBRIGIDA, GINA
Actress. b. Subiaco, Italy, July 4, 1927. e. Acad. of Fine Arts, Rome. Film debut (Italy) L'aguila nera, 1946. Published several volumes of her photography incl. Italia Mia, The Wonder of Innocence.
PICTURES: Pagliacci, The City Defends Itself, The White Line, Fanfan the Tulip, Times Gone By, Beat the Devil, Crossed Swords, The Great Game, Beauties of the Night, Wayward Wife, Bread Love and Dreams, Bread Love and Jealousy, Young Caruso, World's Most Beautiful Woman, Trapeze, Hunchback of Notre Dame, Solomon and Sheba, Never So Few, The Unfaithfuls, Fast and Sexy, Where the Hot Wind Blows, Go Naked in the World, Come September, Imperial Venus, Woman of Straw, That Splendid November, Hotel Paradiso, Buona Sera Mrs. Campbell, Plucked, The Private Navy of Sgt. O'Farrell, Bad Man's River, King Queen Knave, The Lonely Woman, Bambole.
TELEVISION: *Movie*: Deceptions. *Series*: Falcon Crest.

LOMIS, ERIK
Executive. b. Philadelphia, PA, November 21, 1958. e. B.S. Philadelphia Textile. Began career in 1979 at Sameric Theatres, where he held numerous positions including head film buyer. 1988-1993 United Artists Theatre Circuit, Sr. V.P. National Film Dept. 1993 joined MGM Distribution Co. as Sr. V.P. and G.S.M. Currently, Exec. V.P. and G.S.M. at MGM. President, Will Rogers Foundation; Board Member, Variety Club and Foundation of Motion Picture Pioneers.

LOMITA, SOLOMON
Executive. b. New York, NY, April 23, 1937. Started industry career with United Artists Corp. as follows: adm., intl. dept., 1962; asst., intl. sales, same year. 1963, asst. intl. print mgr.; 1965, intl., print mgr. 1973 appt. dir. of film services. 1981, v.p., film services. 1985 named v.p., post-prod., Orion Pictures; 1989-92; then sr. v.p. post-prod.

LONDON, BARRY
Executive. Joined Paramount Pictures 1971 in L.A. branch office as booker; later salesman. 1973, sls. mgr., Kansas City-St. Louis; 1974, branch mgr. Transferred to San Francisco, first as branch mgr.; later as district mgr. 1977, eastern div. mgr. in Washington, DC, 1978-81, western div. mgr. 1981, named v.p., gen. sls. mgr. 1983, advanced to sr. v.p., domestic distrib.1984, named pres., domestic div., for Motion Picture Group of Paramount; 1985, named pres., marketing and domestic distrib.; 1988, named pres. worldwide distrib., Motion Picture Group. Producer, Barry London Co. Member: Variety Club NYC (VP, 1984-), Will Rogers Hospital Dist. Chmn., 1985-.

LONDON, JASON
Actor. b. San Diego, CA, Nov. 7, 1972. Twin brother of actor Jeremy London. Raised in Oklahoma and Texas. Appeared in Aerosmith video Amazing.
PICTURES: The Man in the Moon (debut, 1991), December, Dazed and Confused, Safe Passage, To Wong Foo—Thanks for Everything—Julie Newmar, My Generation, Learning Curves, The Barefoot Executive, Fall Time, Countdown, Mixed Signals, Frontline, Broken Vessels, The Rage: Carrie 2, Goodbye Sunrise.
TELEVISION: *Movie:* A Matter of Justice, Alien Cargo. *Guest:* I'll Fly Away, Tales From the Crypt, Friends Til the End.

LONDON, JEREMY
Actor. b. San Diego, CA, Nov. 7, 1972. Twin brother of actor Jason London. Raised in OK and TX.
PICTURES: Breaking Free, The Babysitter, Mallrats, Levitation, Happenstance.
TELEVISION: *Movies:* In Broad Daylight, A Seduction in Travis County, A Season of Hope, A Mother's Gift, Bad to the Bone, The Defenders: Taking the First. *Series:* I'll Fly Away, Angel Falls, Party of Five. *Guest:* Perversions of Science.

LONDON, JERRY
Director. b. Los Angeles, CA, Jan 21, 1937. Apprentice film editor, Desilu Prods., 1955; film ed., Daniel Boone, 1962; staged plays in local theater workshops; editor, assoc. prod., then dir. Hogan's Heroes. Formed Jerry London Prods., 1984.
PICTURE: Rent-a-Cop (feature debut, 1988).
TELEVISION: *Series*: Mary Tyler Moore Show, Love American Style, The Bob Newhart Show, Marcus Welby, M.D., Kojak, The Six Million Dollar Man, Police Story, Rockford Files. *Mini-series*: Wheels, Shogun (DGA, best dir., special award), Chiefs (also sprv. prod.), Ellis Island (also sprv. prod.), If Tomorrow Comes, A Long Way From Home. *Movies*: Killdozer, McNaughton's Daughter, Cover Girls, Evening in Byzantium, Women in White, Father Figure, The Chicago Story, The Ordeal of Bill Carney (also prod.), The Gift of Life (also prod.), The Scarlet and the Black, Arthur Hailey's Hotel (also prod.), With Intent to Kill (exec. prod. only), Dark Mansions, Manhunt For Claude Dallas,

Harry's Hong Kong, Family Sins (exec. prod. only), Macgruder and Loud (also prod.), Dadah Is Death (also prod.), Kiss Shot (also exec. prod.), The Haunting of Sarah Hardy (also exec. prod.), Vestige of Honor, A Season of Giants, Victim of Love, Grass Roots, Calendar Girl Cop Killer?: The Bambi Bembenek Story (also prod.), A Twist of the Knife, Labor of Love: The Arlette Schweitzer Story, A Mother's Gift.

LONDON, JULIE
Singer, Actress. r.n. Julie Peck. b. Santa Rosa, CA, Sept. 26, 1926. Launched as actress by agent Sue Carol (wife of Alan Ladd) who arranged screen test, followed by contract for 6 films. As singer has appeared in nightclubs and recorded.
PICTURES: Nabonga (Jungle Woman; debut, 1944), On Stage Everybody, Billy Rose's Diamond Horseshoe, Night in Paradise, The Red House, Tap Roots, Task Force, Return of the Frontiersman, The Fat Man, Fighting Chance, The Great Man, The Girl Can't Help It, Crime Against Joe, Drango, Saddle the Wind, Man of the West, Voice in the Mirror, A Question of Adultery, The Wonderful Country, Night of the Quarter Moon, The Third Voice, The George Raft Story.
TELEVISION: *Series*: Emergency. *Guest*: Perry Como Show, Steve Allen Show, Ed Sullivan Show. Movie: Emergency (pilot).

LONDON, MILTON H.
Executive. b. Detroit, MI, Jan. 12, 1916. e. U. of Michigan, B.A., 1937. Wayne U. Law Sch., 1938. U.S. Army 1943-46. Invented Ticograph system of positive admissions control for theatres, 1950; pres. Theatre Control Corp., 1950-62; secy-treas. Co-op. Theas. of Michigan Inc., 1956-63; exec. comm., Council of M.P. Organizations, 1957-66; dir. M.P. Investors, 1960-67; exec. dir. Allied States Assoc. of M.P. Exhib., 1961-66; exec. dir. National Assoc. of Theatre Owners, 1966-69; pres., NATO of Michigan, 1954-74; Chief Barker, Variety Club of Detroit, Tent No. 5. 1975-76; Life Patron and Lifeliner, Variety Clubs International; trustee, Variety Club Charity for Children; chmn., Variety Club Myoelectric Center; dir., Motion Picture Pioneers; dir., Will Rogers Inst.; trustee, Detroit Inst. for Children; pres., Metropolitan Adv. Co.; Intl. ambassador, Variety Clubs Int'l; Detroit News 1991 Michiganian of the Year.

LONE, JOHN
Actor. b. Hong Kong. Studied at Chin Ciu Academy of the Peking Opera in Hong Kong, Moved to LA where he studied acting at Pasadena's American Acad. of Dramatic Art, becoming member of the East-West Players.
THEATER: *NY*: F.O.B., The Dance and the Railroad (Obie Awards for both plays), Paper Angels (dir.), Sound and Beauty (also dir.).
PICTURES: Iceman (debut, 1984), Year of the Dragon, The Last Emperor, The Moderns, Echoes of Paradise, Shadow of China, Shanghai 1920, M. Butterfly, The Shadow, The Hunted.
TELEVISION: The Dance and the Railroad, Paper Angels (dir.).

LONG, SHELLEY
Actress. b. Ft. Wayne, IN, Aug. 23, 1949. e. Northwestern U. Was co-host, assoc. prod. of local tv show Sorting It Out.
PICTURES: A Small Circle of Friends (debut, 1980), Caveman, Night Shift, Losin' It, Irreconcilable Differences, The Money Pit, Outrageous Fortune, Hello Again, Troop Beverly Hills, Don't Tell Her It's Me, Frozen Assets, The Brady Bunch Movie, A Very Brady Sequel.
TELEVISION: *Series*: Cheers (Emmy Award, 1983), Good Advice. *Movies*: The Cracker Factory, Princess and the Cabbie, Promise of Love, Voices Within: The Lives of Truddi Chase, Fatal Memories, A Message From Holly, The Women of Spring Break, Freaky Friday. Special: Basic Values: Sex Shock & Censorship in the '90's.

LONGSTREET, STEPHEN
Writer, Painter. b. New York, NY, April 18, 1907. e. Rutgers U.; Parsons Coll.; Rand Sch., London, B.A. Humorist, cartoonist (New Yorker, Collier's, etc.) 1930-37; ed. Free World Theatre, radio plays; edit. film critic, Saturday Review of Literature, 1940, U.S. at War, Time 1942-43. On staff UCLA. Elected pres. Los Angeles Art Assoc. 1970. 1973, joined USC as prof. Film and book critic for Readers' Syndicate starting in 1970.
AUTHOR: Decade, Last Man Around the World, Chico Goes to the Wars, Pedlocks, Lion at Morning, Promoters, Sometimes I Wonder (with Hoagy Carmichael), Wind at My Back (with Pat O'Brien), Goodness Had Nothing to Do With It (with Mae West), The Young Men of Paris, The Wilder Shore, War Cries on Horseback, Yoshiwara, Geishas and Courtesans, Canvas Falcons, Men and Planes of World War I, We All Went to Paris. Chicago 1860-1919 (show business & society), Divorcing (a novel), The General (novel), All Star Cast (Hollywood), The Queen Bees, Our Father's House, Storyville to Harlem, Dictionary of Jazz, Dreams that Swallowed the World: The Movies, Jazz Solos (poems & images), My Three Nobel Prizes, Life With Faulkner/Hemingway/Lewis.
THEATER: High Button Shoes (book, revived in Jerome Robbins' Broadway, 1989).
PICTURES: The Gay Sisters, Golden Touch, Stallion Road, The Jolson Story, Silver River, Helen Morgan Story, The First Traveling Saleslady, Untamed Youth, The Crime, Uncle Harry, Rider on a Dead Horse, The Imposter.

TELEVISION: Casey Jones (series), Clipper Ship (Playhouse 90), Man Called X, The Sea, Press & Clergy, Viewpoint, Boy in the Model T, John Kennedy Young Man From Boston, Blue and the Grey.

LONSDALE, PAMELA
Producer and Executive Producer for Children's drama, Thames TV for 15 years. Now freelance. Prod. short feature film, Exploits at West Poley (for CFTF), Prod.:News at Twelve (Central TV comedy series). Exec. prod. for E.B.U.'s world drama exchange for 2 years. Winner British Acad. Award for Rainbow, 1975.
TELEVISION: Exploits at West Poley (prod.), Ace of Wands (series, dir., prod.).

LOPEZ, JENNIFER
Actress. b. Bronx, NY, July 24, 1970.
PICTURES: My Little Girl, My Family—Mi Familia, Money Train, Jack, Blood and Wine, Selena, Anaconda, U-Turn, Out of Sight, Antz (voice), Thieves, The Cell, The Wedding Planner.
TELEVISION: *Movies*: Nurses on the Line: The Crash of Flight 7. *Series*: Second Chances, Hotel Malibu, In Living Color.

LORD, PETER
Director, Producer. b. England, UK, 1953.
PICTURES: *Director:* On Probation, Late Edition, Early Bird, Babylon, My Baby Just Carres For Me, Going Equipped, War Story, Adam, Wat's Pig, Chicken Run. *Producer:* On Probation, Adam (exec.), Not Without My Handbag (exec.), Wallace & Gromit: The Wrong Trousers (exec.), Wat's Pig (exec.), Stage Fight (exec.), Chicken Run.

LOREN, SOPHIA
Actress. b. Rome, Italy, Sept. 20, 1934. e. Naples. m. producer Carlo Ponti. *Autobiography:* Sophia: Living and Loving (with A.E. Hotchner, 1979).
PICTURES: Africa Beneath the Seas, Village of the Bells, Good People's Sunday, Neapolitan Carousel, Day in the District Court, Pilgrim of Love, Aida, Two Nights with Cleopatra, Our Times, Attila, Scourge of God, Gold of Naples, Too Bad She's Bad, Scandal in Sorrento, Miller's Beautiful Wife, Lucky to Be a Woman, Boy on a Dolphin (U.S. debut, 1957), The Pride and the Passion, Legend of the Lost, Desire Under the Elms, The Key, Houseboat, The Black Orchid, That Kind of Woman, Heller in Pink Tights, It Started in Naples, A Breath of Scandal, The Millionairess, Two Women (Academy Award, 1961), El Cid, Boccaccio 70, Madame Sans-Gene, Five Miles to Midnight, The Condemned of Altona, Yesterday Today and Tomorrow, The Fall of the Roman Empire, Marriage Italian Style, Operation Crossbow, Lady L, Judith, Arabesque, A Countess from Hong Kong, More than a Miracle, Ghosts—Italian Style, Sunflower, The Priest's Wife, Lady Liberty, White Sister, Man of La Mancha, The Voyage, The Verdict, The Cassandra Crossing, A Special Day, Angela, Brass Target, Firepower, Blood Feud, Ready to Wear (Pret-a-Porter), Grumpier Old Men.
TELEVISION: *Movies/Specials*: Brief Encounter, Sophia Loren—Her Own Story, Softly Softly, Rivals of Sherlock Holmes, Fantasy Island, Aurora, Courage, Mario Puzo's The Fortunate Pilgrim.

LOUDON, DOROTHY
Actress. b. Boston, MA, Sept. 17, 1933.
THEATER: *B'way*: Nowhere to Go But Up (Theatre World Award), The Fig Leaves Are Falling, Sweet Potato, Three Men on a Horse, The Women, Annie (Tony Award, 1977), Ballroom, Sweeney Todd, West Side Waltz, Noises Off, Jerry's Girls, Comedy Tonight. *Off-B'way*: The Matchmaker. Regional: Driving Miss Daisy, Love Letters.
PICTURE: Garbo Talks.
TELEVISION: *Series:* It's a Business?, Laugh Line, The Garry Moore Show, Dorothy, The Thorns (sang opening song). *Specials:* Many appearances on the Tony Awards; also Carnegie Hall Salutes Stephen Sondheim.

LOUGHLIN, LORI
Actress. b. Long Island, NY, July 28, 1964. Started modeling at age 7 for catalogues, then tv commercials. First professional acting job at 18 as regular on daytime serial The Edge of Night.
THEATER: Grease.
PICTURES: Amityville 3-D (debut, 1983), The New Kids, Secret Admirer, Back to the Beach, The Night Before.
TELEVISION: *Series*: The Edge of Night, Full House, Hudson Street. *Movies*: North Beach and Rawhide, Brotherhood of Justice, A Place to Call Home, Doing Time on Maple Drive, A Stranger in the Mirror, Empty Cradle, One of Her Own, Abandoned and Deceived.

LOUIS-DREYFUS, JULIA
Actress. b. New York, NY, Jan. 13, 1961. e. Northwestern Univ. Member of Second City comedy troupe which resulted in casting on Saturday Night Live.
PICTURES: Troll (debut, 1986), Hannah and Her Sisters, Soul Man, National Lampoon's Christmas Vacation, Jack the Bear, North, Deconstructing Harry, Father's Day, A Bug's Life (voice), Gilligan's Island, Geppetto.

TELEVISION: *Series*: Saturday Night Live (1982-85), Day by Day, Seinfeld (Golden Globe, 1994; Emmy Award, 1996). *Specials*: The Art of Being Nick, Spy Magazine's Hit List (host), Sesame Street's All-Star 25th Birthday. *Movies*: London Suite, Animal Farm (voice). *Guest*: Dinosaurs (voice), Dr Katz Professional Therapist.

LOUISE, TINA
Actress. r.n. Tina Blacker. b. New York, NY, Feb. 11. e. Miami U., N.Y. Neighborhood Playhouse, Actors Studio. Author, Sunday, 1997.
THEATER: Two's Company, The Fifth Season, John Murray Anderson's Almanac, Li'l Abner, Fade Out Fade In, Come Back to the 5 and Dime Jimmy Dean Jimmy Dean.
PICTURES: God's Little Acre (debut), The Trap, The Hangman, Day of the Outlaw, The Warrior Empress, Siege of Syracuse, Armored Command, For Those Who Think Young, The Wrecking Crew, The Good Guys and the Bad Guys, How to Commit Marriage, The Happy Ending, The Stepford Wives, Mean Dog Blues, Dogsday, Hellriders, Evils of the Night, O.C. and Stiggs, Dixie Lanes, The Pool, Johnny Suede.
TELEVISION: *Series*: Jan Murray Time, Gilligan's Island, Dallas, Rituals. *Guest*: Mannix, Ironside, Kung Fu, Police Story, Kojak, Roseanne. *Movies*: But I Don't Want to Get Married, A Call to Danger, Death Scream, Look What's Happened to Rosemary's Baby, Nightmare in Badham Country, SST—Death Flight, Friendships Secrets and Lies, The Day the Women Got Even, Advice to the Lovelorn, The Woman Who Cried Murder.

LOVE, COURTNEY
Actress, Musician. r.n. Love Michelle Harrison. b. San Francisco, CA, July 9, 1965. Late husband was musician Kurt Cobain. Fronts music group Hole. Began career as punk rock extra in films, television before acting debut in Sid and Nancy, 1986.
PICTURES: Sid and Nancy, Straight to Hell, Tapeheads, Tank Girl (exec. music co-ord. only), Basquiat, Feeling Minnesota, Not Bad for a Girl (also co-prod.), The People vs. Larry Flint, 200 Cigarettes, Man on the Moon.

LOVITZ, JON
Actor, Comedian. b. Tarzana, CA, July 21, 1957. e. U. of California at Irvine. Studied acting at Film Actors Workshop. Took classes at the Groundlings, L.A. comedy improvisation studio, 1982. Performed with Groundling's Sunday Company, before joining main company in Chick Hazzard: Olympic Trials. Developed comedy character of pathological liar which he later performed when he became regular member of Saturday Night Live in 1985.
PICTURES: The Last Resort, Ratboy, Jumpin' Jack Flash, Three Amigos, Big, My Stepmother Is an Alien, The Brave Little Toaster (voice), Mr. Destiny, An American Tail: Fievel Goes West (voice), A League of Their Own, Mom and Dad Save the World, National Lampoon's Loaded Weapon 1, Coneheads, City Slickers II: The Legend of Curly's Gold, North, Trapped in Paradise, The Great White Hype, High School High, Happiness, The Wedding Singer.
TELEVISION: *Series*: Foley Square, Saturday Night Live (1985-90), The Critic (voice), NewsRadio. *Special*: The Please Watch the Jon Lovitz Special. *Guest:* The Paper Chase, The Simpsons (voice).

LOWE, CHAD
Actor. b. Dayton, OH, Jan. 15, 1968. Brother is actor Rob Lowe. Stage debut in L.A. production of Blue Denim. On NY stage in Grotesque Love Songs.
PICTURES: Oxford Blues (debut, 1984), Apprentice to Murder, True Blood, Nobody's Perfect, Highway to Hell, Driven, Floating, Do Me a Favor, The Way We Are, Suicide: The Comedy.
TELEVISION: *Movies*: Silence of the Heart, There Must Be a Pony, April Morning, So Proudly We Hail, An Inconvenient Woman, Captive, Candles in the Dark, Fighting for My Daughter, In the Presence of Mine Enemies, Target Earth. *Series*: Spencer, Life Goes On (Emmy Award, 1993), Melrose Place. *Special*: No Means No (Emmy nom.).

LOWE, PHILIP L.
Executive. b. Brookline, MA, Apr. 17, 1917. e. Harvard. Army 1943-46. Checker, Loew's 1937-39; treasurer, Theatre Candy Co., 1941-58; Pres., ITT Sheraton Corp., 1969-70; Principal, Philip L. Lowe and Assoc.

LOWE, PHILIP M.
Executive. b. New Rochelle, NY, May 9, 1944. e. Deerfield Acad., Harvard Coll., cum laude in psychology, 1966; Columbia Business Sch., 1968. Work experience includes major marketing positions at General Foods, Gillette, Gray Advertising, and Estee Lauder Cosmetics before co-founding Cinema Centers Corp. and Theatre Management Services in Boston. Pres. of Lowe Group of Companies (cable television, broadcasting, hotels, real estate and management consulting). Past pres. and chmn. of the bd; National Association of Concessionaires (NAC); past director, National Association of Theater Owners (NATO). Professor of Marketing, Bentley Coll., Waltham, MA.; Contributing Editor; The Movie Business Book, Prentice-Hall, Inc. 1983.

LOWE, ROB
Actor. r.n. robert Helper Lowe. b. Charlottesville, VA, Mar. 17, 1964. Brother is Chad Lowe. Raised in Dayton, OH. Started acting as child appearing in commercials, local tv spots, summer stock. Family moved to California when he was 13 yrs. old. Job in Coca Cola commercial was followed by role on series A New Kind of Family. In 1992 made B'way debut in, A Little Hotel on the Side.
PICTURES: The Outsiders (debut, 1983), Class, The Hotel New Hampshire, Oxford Blues, St. Elmo's Fire, Youngblood, About Last Night..., Square Dance, Home Is Where the Heart Is, Masquerade, Illegally Yours, Mulholland Falls, Bad Influence, Stroke of Midnight (If the Shoe Fits), Desert Shield, The Dark Backward, The Finest Hour, Wayne's World, Tommy Boy, For Hire, Contact, Hostile Intent, Crazy Six, The Specials, Austin Powers: The Spy Who Shagged Me, Statistics, Dead Silent, The Specials, Under Pressure, Proximity.
TELEVISION: *Movies*: Thursday's Child, Frank and Jesse (also co-prod.), First Degree, Desert's Edge (s.p. dir.), Outrage, Atomic Train. *Series*: A New Kind of Family, The West Wing. *Mini-Series*: Stephen King's The Stand. *Specials*: A Matter of Time, Schoolboy Father, Suddenly Last Summer, On Dangerous Ground, Midnight Man.

LOWRY, DICK
Director. b. Oklahoma City, OK. e. U. of Oklahoma. Commercial photographer before being accepted by AFI. Dir. short film The Drought.
PICTURE: Smokey and the Bandit Part 3.
TELEVISION: *Mini-Series*: Dream West, Texas Justice, Dean Koontz's Mr. Murder. *Movies*: OHMS, Kenny Rogers as the Gambler, The Jayne Mansfield Story, Angel Dusted, Coward of the County, A Few Days in Weasel Creek, Rascals and Robbers: The Secret Adventures of Tom Sawyer and Huck Finn, Missing Children—A Mother's Story, Living Proof: The Hank Williams Jr. Story, Kenny Rogers as the Gambler—The Adventure Continues (also prod.), Off Sides (Pigs Vs. Freaks), Wet Gold, The Toughest Man in the World, Murder with Mirrors, American Harvest, Kenny Rogers as The Gambler III (also co-exec. prod.), Case Closed, In the Line of Duty: The FBI Murders, Unconquered (also prod.), Howard Beach: Making the Case For Murder, Miracle Landing (also prod.), Archie: To Riverdale and Back, In the Line of Duty: A Cop for the Killing (also prod.), In the Line of Duty: Manhunt in the Dakotas (also prod.), A Woman Scorned: The Betty Broderick Story (also co-prod.), In the Line of Duty: Ambush in Waco (also prod.), In the Line of Duty: The Price of Vengeance, One More Mountain, A Horse for Danny, In The Line of Duty: Hunt for Justice (also prod.), Forgotten Sins, Project Alf, In The Line of Duty: Smoke Jumpers (also prod.), Last Stand at Saber River, Blaze of Glory (also prod.).

LOWRY, HUNT
Producer. b. Oklahoma City, OK, Aug. 21, 1954. e. Rollins Coll., & Wake Forest. Abandoned plans to study medicine to enter film-making industry; first job for New World Pictures where he met Jon Davison, with whom was later to co-produce. Next made TV commercials as prod. asst. and then producer. Left to go freelance as commercials producer. 1980, appt. assoc. prod. to Davison on Airplane!
PICTURES: Humanoids from the Deep, Get Crazy, Top Secret!, Revenge, Career Opportunities, Only the Lonely, Last of the Mohicans, Striking Distance, My Life, First Knight, A Time to Kill.
TELEVISION: *Movies* (exec. prod.): Rascals and Robbers: The Secret Adventures of Tom Sawyer and Huckleberry Finn, Baja Oklahoma. *Movies* (prod.): His Mistress, Surviving, Wild Horses. *Mini-Series*: Dream West (prod.).

LUCAS, GEORGE
Producer, Director, Writer. b. Modesto, CA, May 14, 1944. e. USC, cinema. Made short film called THX-1138 and won National Student Film Festival Grand Prize, 1967. Signed contract with WB. Ass't. to Francis Ford Coppola on The Rain People, during which Lucas made 2-hr. documentary on filming of that feature entitled Filmmaker. Appeared as actor in film Beverly Hills Cop III. *Novel:* Shadow Moon (1995). Pres., Lucas Films, Industrial Light & Magic.
PICTURES: *Director/Writer*: THX-1138, American Graffiti, Star Wars: Episode IV-A New Hope, Star Wars: Episode I-The Phantom Menace (also exec. prod.), Star Wars: Episode I (also prod.), Star Wars: Episode III (also prod.). *Executive Producer*: More American Graffiti, Star Wars: Episode V-The Empire Strikes Back (also story), Raiders of the Lost Ark (also co-story), Star Wars: Episode VI-Return of the Jedi (also co-s.p., story), Twice Upon a Time, Indiana Jones and the Temple of Doom (also story), Mishima, Labyrinth, Howard the Duck, Willow (also story), Tucker: The Man and His Dream, The Land Before Time, Indiana Jones and the Last Crusade (also co-story), Radioland Murders (also story), Indiana Jones and the Lost Continent.
TELEVISION: *Exec. Prod.*: The Ewok Adventure (movie), Ewoks: The Battle for Endor (movie); The Young Indiana Jones Chronicles (series).

LUCCHESI, GARY
Executive. b. San Francisco, CA, 1955. e. UCLA. Entered industry as a trainee with the William Morris Agency, 1977. Joined Tri-Star, 1983, as vice pres. of production, became sr. vice pres., 1985. Joined Paramount Pictures as exec. vice pres., April 1987; pres. of motion picture production division, 1987-92. Pres. of the Really Useful Film Company, Inc., 1994-1998. President LakeShore Entertainment, Oct. 1998-Present.
PICTURES: *Producer/Executive Producer*: Jennifer Eight, Three Wishes, Virtuosity, Primal Fear, Gotti, Runaway Bride.

LUCCI, SUSAN
Actress. b. Scarsdale, NY, Feb. 23, 1948. e. Marymount Col. Was semifinalist in NY State Miss Universe Pageant. First professional job as "color girl" for CBS, sitting for cameras as new lighting system for color tv was developed. Had bit parts in films Me Natalie and Goodbye Columbus. Performed on 1983 album Love in the Afternoon.
PICTURES: Daddy You Kill Me, Young Doctors in Love (cameo).
TELEVISION: *Series*: All My Children (1970-; Daytime Emmy 1999). *Movies*: Invitation to Hell, Mafia Princess, Anastasia: The Story of Anna, Haunted By Her Past, Lady Mobster, The Bride in Black, The Woman Who Sinned, Double Edge, Between Love and Hate, French Silk, Seduced and Betrayed.

LUCKINBILL, LAURENCE
Actor. b. Fort Smith, AR, Nov. 21, 1934. m. actress Lucie Arnaz. e. U. of Arkansas, Catholic U. of America.
THEATER: NY: A Man for All Seasons, Arms and the Man, The Boys in the Band, Alpha Beta, The Shadow Box, Poor Murderer, Chapter Two, Past Tense.
PICTURES: The Boys in the Band, Such Good Friends, The Promise, Not for Publication, Cocktail, Messenger of Death, Star Trek V: The Final Frontier.
TELEVISION: *Series*: The Secret Storm, Where the Heart Is, The Delphi Bureau. *Movies*: The Delphi Bureau (pilot), Death Sentence, Panic on the 5:22, Winner Take All, The Lindbergh Kidnapping Case, The Mating Season, To Heal a Nation. *Mini-Series*: Ike. *Specials*: Lyndon Johnson (one-man show), Voices and Visions (narrator), The 5:48, Lucy & Desi: A Home Movie (co-exec. prod., co-dir., writer).

LUDDY, TOM
Producer. e. U. of California at Berkeley where he operated student film societies and rep. cinemas. Entered industry via Brandon Films. 1972, prog. dir. and curator of Pacific Film Archives. 1979, joined Zoetrope Studios as dir. of special projects where dev. and supervised revival of Gance's Napoleon and Our Hitler—A Film From Germany. Coordinated Koyaanisqatsi, Every Man For Himself, Passion. A founder, Telluride Film Fest. Served on selection comm., N.Y. and pres. San Francisco Film Fest.
PICTURES: Mishima (co-prod.), Tough Guys Don't Dance (co-exec. prod.), Barfly, King Lear (assoc. prod.), Manifesto (exec. prod.), Powwaqatsi (assoc. prod.), Wait Until Spring Bandini, Wind, The Secret Garden (co-prod.), Mi Familia (exec. prod.)

LUDWIG, IRVING H.
Executive. b. Nov. 3. Rivoli Theatre, N.Y., mgr., theatre oper., Rugoff and Becker, 1938-39; opened first modern art type theatre, Greenwich Village, 1940. With Walt Disney Prod. in charge of theatre oper. on Fantasia, 1940-41; buyer-booker, Rugoff and Becker, 1942-45; film sales admin., Walt Disney Prod. home office, 1945-53; v.p. and domestic sales mgr., Buena Vista Dist. Co., 1953; pres. sales & mktg., 1959-80. Member of bd. of dirs., Will Rogers Memorial Fund, Foundation of M.P. Pioneers; Motion Picture Club; Academy of M.P. Arts & Sciences.

LUEDTKE, KURT
Writer. b. Grand Rapids, MI, Sept. 29, 1938. e. Brown U., B.A., 1961. Reporter Grand Rapids Press 1961-62. Miami Herald, 1963-65; Detroit Free Press (reporter, asst. photography dir., asst. mgr. ed., asst. exec. ed., exec. ed. 1965-78.).
PICTURES: Absence of Malice, Out of Africa (Academy Award, 1985), Walls.

LUFT, LORNA
Actress, Singer. b. Hollywood, CA, Nov. 21, 1952. Daughter of actress-singer Judy Garland and producer Sid Luft. Has sung in nightclubs. Appeared on 1990 recording of Girl Crazy.
THEATER: *NY*: Judy Garland at Home at the Palace, Promises Promises, Snoopy, Extremities. *Tours*: They're Playing Our Song, Grease, Little Shop of Horrors, Jerry Herman's Broadway, The Unsinkable Molly Brown, Guys and Dolls.
PICTURES: I Could Go on Singing (cameo), Grease 2, Where the Boys Are.
TELEVISION: *Series*: Trapper John. *Movie*: Fear Stalk. *Guest*: Twilight Zone, Hooperman, Murder She Wrote, Tales from the Dark Side, The Cosby Show.

LUHRMANN, BAZ
Director. r.n.Bazmark Luhrmann.
PICTURES: *Dir./Writer.*: Strictly Ballroom, Romeo + Juliet (also prod., BAFTA Award, Best Direction, Best Adapted Screenplay, 1997), Moulin Rouge. *Actor*: Winter of Our Dreams, The Dark Room.

LUKE, PETER
Writer, Director. b. England, Aug. 12, 1919. *Autobiography*: Sisyphus & Reilly.
THEATER: Hadrian VII, Bloomsbury.
TELEVISION: *Writer*: Small Fish Are Sweet, Pigs Ear with Flowers, Roll on Bloomin' Death, A Man on Her Back (with William Sansom), Devil a Monk Won't Be, Anach 'Cuan (also dir.), Black Sound—Deep Song (also dir.).

LUMET, SIDNEY
Director. b. Philadelphia, PA, June 25, 1924. e. Professional Children's Sch.; Columbia U. Child actor in plays: Dead End, George Washington Slept Here, My Heart's in the Highlands, and films: The 400 Million, One Third of a Nation. U.S. Armed Forces, WWII, 1942-46; dir. summer stock, 1947-49; taught acting, H.S. of Prof. Arts. Assoc. dir. CBS, 1950, dir. 1951. Appeared in documentary Listen Up: The Lives of Quincy Jones. Author: Making Movies (Alfred A. Knopf, 1995).
PICTURES: 12 Angry Men (debut, 1957), Stage Struck, That Kind of Woman, The Fugitive Kind, A View From the Bridge, Long Day's Journey Into Night, Fail-Safe, The Pawnbroker, The Hill, The Group, The Deadly Affair (also prod.), Bye Bye Braverman (also prod.), The Sea Gull (also prod.), The Appointment, The Last of the Mobile Hotshots (also prod.), King: A Filmed Record... Montgomery to Memphis (co-dir., prod.), The Anderson Tapes, Child's Play, The Offence, Serpico, Lovin' Molly, Murder on the Orient Express, Dog Day Afternoon, Network, Equus, The Wiz, Just Tell Me What You Want (also co-prod.), Prince of the City (also co-s.p.), Deathtrap, The Verdict, Daniel (also co-exec. prod.), Garbo Talks, Power, The Morning After, Running on Empty, Family Business, Q & A (also s.p.), A Stranger Among Us, Guilty As Sin, Night Falls On Manhattan (also s.p.), Critical Care, Gloria, Whistle.
TELEVISION: *Series episodes*: Mama, Danger, You Are There, Omnibus, Best of Broadway, Alcoa, Goodyear Playhouse, Kraft Television Theatre (Mooney's Kid Don't Cry, The Last of My Gold Watches, This Property is Condemned), Playhouse 90, Play of the Week (The Dybbuk, Rashomon, The Iceman Cometh—Emmy Award). *Specials*: The Sacco and Vanzetti Story, John Brown's Raid, Cry Vengeance.

LUNDGREN, DOLPH
Actor. r.n. Hans Lundren. b. Stockholm, Sweden, Nov. 3, 1959. e. Washington State U., won Fulbright to Massachusetts Inst. of Technology, Royal Inst. of Technology, Stockholm, M.S.C. Was doorman at Limelight disco in NY while studying acting. Full Contact Karate champion. Made workout video, Maximum Potential. On stage in Another Octopus.
PICTURES: A View to a Kill, Rocky IV, Masters of the Universe, Red Scorpion, The Punisher, I Come in Peace, Cover-Up, Showdown in Little Tokyo, Universal Soldier, Army of One, Pentathlon, Men of War, Johnny Mnemonic, The Shooter, The Algonquin Goodbye, The Peacekeeper, The Minion, Sweepers, Storm Catcher, Bridge of Dragons.
TELEVISION: Movies: John Woo's Blackjack.

LUPONE, PATTI
Actress. b. Northport, NY, Apr. 21, 1949. e. Juilliard.
THEATER: School for Scandal, Three Sisters, The Beggars Opera, The Robber Bridegroom, Meaure for Measure, Edward II, The Water Engine, Working, Evita (Tony Award, 1980), Oliver!, Anything Goes, Les Miserables (London), Sunset Boulevard (London), Master Class, The Old Neighborhood.
PICTURES: 1941, Fighting Back, Witness, Wise Guys, Driving Miss Daisy, Family Prayers, Summer of Sam, State and Maine, 24 Hour Woman.
TELEVISION: *Series*: Life Goes On. *Movies*: LBJ: The Early Years, The Water Engine, The Song Spinner, Her Last Chance.

LURIE, JOHN
Composer, Actor
PICTURES: *Composer:* The Offenders, The Loveless, Permanent Vacation, Stranger than Paradise, Variety, City Limits, Down By Law, Mystery Train, On the Beautiful Blue Danube, Blue in the Face, Get Shorty, Manny & Lo, Excess Baggage, Lulu on the Bridge, Clay Pigeons, The Animal Factory. *Actor:* The Offenders, Subway Rider, Permanent Vacation, Paris, Texas, Stranger than Paradise, Desperately Seeking Susan, Down by Law, The Last Temptation of Christ, The Little Devil, Wild at Heart, John Lurie and the Lounge Lizard Live in Berlin, Smoke, Blue in the Face, Just Your Luck, New Rose Hotel.

LYDON, JAMES
Actor. b. Harrington Park, NJ, May 30, 1923; e. St. Johns Mil. Sch. On N.Y. stage in Prologue to Glory, Sing Out the News. For 20th Century Fox tv was assoc. prod. of series Anna and the King, Roll Out. Prod./Writer/Dir. of special The Incredible 20th Century. Dir. for Universal TV: 6 Million Dollar Man, Simon & Simon, Beggarman Thief.
PICTURES: *Actor*: Back Door to Heaven (debut, 1939), Two Thoroughbreds, Racing Luck, Tom Brown's Schooldays, Little Men, Naval Academy, Bowery Boy, Henry Aldrich for President, Cadets on Parade, The Mad Martindales, Star Spangled Rhythm, Henry Aldrich— Editor, Henry Aldrich Gets Glamour, Henry Aldrich Swings It, Henry Aldrich Haunts a House, Henry Aldrich Plays Cupid, Aerial Gunner, Henry Aldrich—Boy Scout,

My Best Gal, The Town Went Wild, Henry Aldrich's Little Secret, When the Lights Go on Again, Out of the Night, Twice Blessed, The Affairs of Geraldine, Life With Father, Cynthia, Sweet Genevieve, The Time of Your Life, Out of the Storm, Joan of Arc, An Old-Fashioned Girl, Bad Boy, Miss Mink of 1949, Tucson, Gasoline Alley, Tarnished, When Willie Comes Marching Home, Destination Big House, Hot Rod, September Affair, The Magnificent Yankee, Island in the Sky, The Desperado, Battle Stations, Chain of Evidence, The Hypnotic Eye, I Passed for White, The Last Time I Saw Archie, Brainstorm, Death of a Gunfighter, Scandalous John, Bonnie's Kids, Vigilante Force. Assoc. Prod.: My Blood Runs Cold, An American Dream, A Covenant With Death, First to Fight, The Cool Ones, Chubasco, Countdown, Assignment to Kill, The Learning Tree.
TELEVISION: *Guest*: Frontier Circus (also assoc. prod.). *Co-ordin. Prod.*: Wagon Train, Alfred Hitchcock Hour. *Assoc. Prod.*: McHale's Navy, 77 Sunset Strip, Mr. Roberts. *Series* (actor): So This Is Hollywood, The First Hundred Years, Love That Jill. Movies: Ellery Queen, The New Daughters of Joshua Cabe, Peter Lundy and the Medicine Hat Stallion.

LYLES, A. C.
Producer. b. Jacksonville, FL. May 17, 1918. e. Andrew Jackson H.S. Paramount Publix's Florida Theatre, 1928; interviewed Hollywood celebrities, Jacksonville Journal, 1932; mail boy, Paramount Studios, Hollywood, 1937; publicity dept., 1938; hd. of adv., publ. dept., Pine-Thomas unit at Paramount, 1940; assoc. prod., The Mountain. President, A. C. Lyles Productions, Inc. (Paramount Pictures).
PICTURES: Short Cut to Hell, Raymie, The Young and the Brave, Law of the Lawless, Stage to Thunder Rock, Young Fury, Black Spurs, Hostile Guns, Arizona Bushwackers, Town Tamer, Apache Uprising, Johnny Reno, Waco, Red Tomahawk, Fort Utah, Buckskin, Rogue's Gallery, Night of the Lepus, The Last Day, Flight to Holocaust.
TELEVISION: Rawhide (series; assoc. prod.), A Christmas for Boomer, Here's Boomer (series), Dear Mr. President, Conversations With the Presidents.

LYNCH, DAVID
Director, Writer. b. Missoula, MT, Jan. 20, 1946. e. Pennsylvania Acad. of Fine Arts, where received an independent filmmaker grant from America Film Institute. Made 16mm film, The Grandmother. Accepted by Center for Advanced Film Studies in Los Angeles, 1970. Wrote and directed Eraserhead (with partial AFI financing). Acted in films Zelly & Me, Nadja (also exec. prod.). Daughter is director Jennifer Lynch.
PICTURES: *Director-Writer*: Eraserhead (also prod., edit., prod.-design, f/x), The Elephant Man, Dune, Blue Velvet, Wild at Heart, Twin Peaks: Fire Walk With Me (also co-exec. prod., actor), Lost Highway, The Straight Story (also s.p.), Mulholland Drive.
TELEVISION: *Series*: Twin Peaks (dir., exec. prod., writer), On the Air (exec. prod., dir., writer), Mulholland Drive (also exec. prod.). *Special*: Hotel Room (co-dir., co-exec. prod.).

LYNCH, KELLY
Actress. b. Minneapolis, MN, 1959. Former model.
PICTURES: Osa, Bright Lights Big City, Cocktail, Road House, Warm Summer Rain, Drugstore Cowboy, Desperate Hours, Curly Sue, For Better and For Worse, Three of Hearts, Imaginary Crimes, The Beans of Egypt Maine, Virtuosity, White Man's Burden, Heaven's Prisoners, Persons Unknown, Cold Around the Heart, Mr. Magoo, Homegrown.
TELEVISION: *Guest*: Miami Vice, The Equalizer, Spenser for Hire, The Hitcher, The Edge (Black Pudding). *Movie*: Something in Common. *Pilot*: San Berdoo.

LYNCH, PAUL M.
Director.
PICTURES: Hard Part Begins, Blood and Guts, Prom Night, Cross Country, Flying, Blindside, Bullies.
TELEVISION: *Series*: Voyagers, Blacke's Magic, Murder She Wrote, In the Heat of the Night, Tour of Duty, Beauty and the Beast, Twilight Zone (1987), Moonlighting, Star Trek: The Next Generation, Dark Shadows, Tour of Duty, Top Cops, Mike Hammer, Hooperman, Bronx Zoo. *Movies*: Cameo By Night, Going to the Chapel, She Knows Too Much, Murder by Night, Drop Dead Gorgeous.

LYNCH, RICHARD
Actor. b. Brooklyn, NY. Trained with Lee Strasberg at Carnegie Hall. In 1970 became life time member of the Actors Studio, NY.
THEATRE: *NY*: The Devils (On and Off-B'way debut), The Basic Training of Pavlo Hummel, Lion in Winter, The Orphan, Arturo-U, The Lady From the Sea, One Night Stands of a Noisy Passenger, Action, Richard III, Live Like Pigs, The Man with the Flower in His Mouth, A View from the Bridge.
PICTURES: Scarecrow (debut, 1973), The Seven Ups, The Delta Fox, The Premonition, Steel, Open Season, The Formula, The Sword and the Sorcerer, Little Nikita, Savage Dawn, Invasion U.S.A., Cut and Run, Night Force, The Barbarians, Bad Dreams, The Ninth Configuration, Melanie Rose (High Stakes), Spirit, Aftershock, Return to Justice, One Man Force, The Forbidden Dance, October 32nd, Alligator II: The Mutation, Double Threat, H.P. Lovecraft's Necromonicon, Scanner Cop, Crime & Punishment.

TELEVISION: *Series*: Battlestar Gallactica, The Phoenix. *Movies*: Starsky and Hutch (pilot), Roger & Harry: The Mitera Target, Good Against Evil, Dog and Cat, Vampire, Alcatraz—The Whole Shocking Story, Sizzle, White Water Rebels, The Last Ninja.

LYNDON, VICTOR
Producer, Writer. b. London. e. St. Paul's. Ent. m.p. ind. 1942 as asst. dir., Gainsborough Pictures. Novel: Bermuda Blue (1984).
PICTURES: *Prod. mgr.*: The African Queen. *Assoc. Prod.*: Dr. Strangelove, Darling, 2001: A Space Odyssey. *Prod.*: Spare The Rod, Station Six—Sahara, The Optimists.

LYNE, ADRIAN
Director. b. Peterborough, England, March 4, 1941. Started as director of commercials.
PICTURES: Foxes, Flashdance, Nine 1/2 Weeks, Fatal Attraction, Jacob's Ladder, Indecent Proposal, Lolita.

LYNLEY, CAROL
Actress. b. New York, NY, Feb. 13, 1942. Was model as teenager.
PICTURES: The Light in the Forest (debut, 1958), Holiday for Lovers, Blue Denim, Hound-Dog Man, Return to Peyton Place, The Last Sunset, The Stripper, Under the Yum-Yum Tree, The Cardinal, The Pleasure Seekers, Shock Treatment, Harlow, Bunny Lake Is Missing, The Shuttered Room, Danger Route, Once You Kiss a Stranger, The Maltese Bippy, Norwood, Beware the Blob!, The Poseidon Adventure, Cotter, The Four Deuces, The Washington Affair, The Cat and the Canary, The Shape of Things to Come, Vigilante, Dark Tower, Blackout, Howling VI: The Freaks.
TELEVISION: *Series*: The Immortal. *Movies*: Shadow on the Land, The Smugglers, The Immortal (pilot), Weekend of Terror, The Cable Car Murder, The Night Stalker, The Elevator, Death Stalk, Willow B, Women in Prison, Flood, Fantasy Island, Having Babies II, Cops and Robin, The Beasts Are on the Streets.

LYNN, ANN
Actress. b. London, England, 1934. Ent. films and TV, 1958.
PICTURES: Johnny You're Wanted (debut, 1955), Moment of Indiscretion, Naked Fury, Piccadilly Third Stop, The Wind of Change, Strip Tease Murder, Strongroom, Flame in the Streets, HMS Defiant (Damn the Defiant), The Party's Over, Doctor in Distress, The Black Torment, The System (The Girl Getters), A Shot in the Dark, The Uncle, Four in the Morning, Separation, I'll Never Forget What's 'is Name, Baby Love, Hitler—The Last Ten Days, Screamtime.
TELEVISION: *Specials/Movies:* After The Show, All Summer Long, Trump Card, Man at the Top, The Expert, Hine, The Intruders, Too Far, King Lear, The Zoo Gang, Morning Tide, Estuary, Who Pays the Ferryman, The Professionals, Zeticula, Westway, The Perfect House, Minder, To the Sound of Guns, Crown Court, Just Good Friends, Starting Out, Paradise Park. *Series*: The Cheaters, The Other Side of the Underneath.

LYNN, JONATHAN
Director, Writer, Actor. b. Bath, England, Apr. 3, 1943. Was artistic dir. of Cambridge Theatre Company, 1976-81; Company Director of Natl. Theatre, 1987. Playwright: Pig of the Month. Books: A Proper Man, The Complete Yes Prime Minister, Mayday. Appeared as actor in Into the Night, Three Men and a Little Lady.
PICTURES: The Internecine Project (s.p.). *Director*: Clue (also s.p.), Nuns on the Run (also s.p.), My Cousin Vinny, The Distinguished Gentleman, Greedy (also actor), Sgt. Bilko, Trial and Error (also prod.).
TELEVISION: Doctor on the Go, My Name is Harry Worth, My Brother's Keeper, Yes Minister, Yes Prime Minister.

LYONNE, NATASHA
Actress. r.n. Natasha Braunstein. b. NY, April 4, 1979.
PICTURES: Heartburn (debut, 1986), Dennis the Menace, Everyone Says I Love You, Slums of Beverly Hills, Krippendorf's Tribe, Modern Vampyres, Freeway II: Confessions of a Trickbaby, Detroit Rock City, But I'm a Cheerleader, American Pie, the Auteur Theory, When Autumn Leaves, Rat Girl, Plan B.
TELEVISION: *Movies/Specials:* If These Walls Could Talk 2. *Series:* Pee-Wee's Playhouse.

LYONS, S. DANIEL
Executive. b. Toronto, Canada, Sept., 9, 1955. e. Brandeis Univ., B.A. magna cum laude 1977. Univ. of Toronto, LL.B. 1981. 1985, joined Astral Films as a lawyer. Promoted to dir. of bus. affairs, then v.p., Dist. for the Astral Entertainment Group. 1997, became v.p., Dist & Mktg., Coscient/Astral Dist. Author of: Public Strategy and Motion Pictures, and Showman (play, Cubiculo Theatre, NY).

LYON, FRANCIS D. "PETE"
Director, Editor. b. Bowbells, ND, July 29, 1905. e. Hollywood H.S., UCLA. WWII: writer, prod., dir., OWI; assoc. with training, exploitation and information films. Maj. U.S. Army Signal Corps. Author: Twists of Fate: An Oscar Winner's International Career.

PICTURES: *Editor:* Things to Come (co-edit.), Knight Without Armour, Rembrandt, Intermezzo, Adam Had Four Sons, The Great Profile, Four Sons, Daytime Wife, Body and Soul (Academy Award, 1947), He Ran All the Way. Director: Crazylegs, The Bob Mathias Story (Christopher Award), The Great Locomotive Chase, Cult of the Cobra, The Oklahoman, Gunsight Ridge, Bailout at 43,000, Escort West, Cinerama South Seas Adventure (co-dir.), The Young and the Brave, Destination Inner Space, The Destructors, The Money Jungle, The Girl Who Knew Too Much. *Producer*: Tiger by the Tail.
TELEVISION: *Series*: Laramie, Perry Mason, Zane Grey Theatre, Bus Stop, M. Squad, Wells Fargo, Kraft Suspense Theatre, Death Valley Days, Follow the Sun, etc.

LYON, SUE
Actress. b. Davenport, IA, July 10, 1946. e. Hollywood Prof. Sch.
PICTURES: Lolita (debut, 1962), The Night of the Iguana, Seven Women, Tony Rome, The Flim Flam Man, Evel Knievel, Crash, End of the World, Alligator, Invisible Strangler.
TELEVISION: *Movies*: But I Don't Want to Get Married!, Smash-Up on Interstate 5, Don't Push—I'll Charge When I'm Ready.

M

MacARTHUR, JAMES
Actor. b. Los Angeles, CA, Dec. 8, 1937. e. Harvard. p. actress Helen Hayes, writer Charles MacArthur. Stage debut, summer stock; The Corn Is Green, Life with Father.
PICTURES: The Young Stranger (debut, 1957), The Light in the Forest, Third Man on the Mountain, Kidnapped, Swiss Family Robinson, The Interns, Spencer's Mountain, Cry of Battle, The Truth About Spring, The Battle of the Bulge, The Bedford Incident, Ride Beyond Vengeance, The Love-Ins, Hang 'em High, The Angry Breed.
TELEVISION: *Series*: Hawaii Five-0. *Movies*: Alcatraz—The Whole Shocking Story, The Night the Bridge Fell Down. *Special*: Willie and the Yank (Mosby's Marauders).

MACCHIO, RALPH
Actor. b. Long Island, NY, Nov. 4, 1962. Started in TV commercials at age 16 before winning role in series Eight Is Enough. Broadway debut in Cuba and His Teddy Bear, 1986; Off-B'way in Only Kidding.
PICTURES: Up the Academy (debut, 1980), The Outsiders, The Karate Kid, Teachers, Crossroads, The Karate Kid Part II, Distant Thunder, The Karate Kid Part III, Too Much Sun, My Cousin Vinny, Naked in New York.
TELEVISION: *Series*: Eight Is Enough. *Movies*: Journey to Survival, Dangerous Company, The Three Wishes of Billy Grier, The Last P.O.W.?: The Bobby Garwood Story.

MacCORKINDALE, SIMON
Actor, Producer, Director, Writer. b. Isle-of-Ely, England, Feb. 2, 1952. m. actress Susan George. On stage in Dark Lady of the Sonnets, Pygmalion, French Without Tears, etc.
PICTURES: *Actor*: Death on the Nile, Quatermass Conclusion, Caboblanco, Robbers of the Sacred Mountain, The Sword and the Sorcerer, Jaws 3-D, The Riddle of the Sands, Sincerely Violet. *Producer*: Stealing Heaven, That Summer of White Roses (also co-s.p.), The House That Mary Bought (also dir., co-s.p.).
TELEVISION: *Specials*: I Claudius, Romeo and Juliet, Quatermass. *Movies*: The Manions of America, Falcon's Gold, Jesus of Nazareth, Twist of Fate, Obsessive Love, No Greater Love, At The Midnight Hour, A Family of Cops, While My Pretty One Sleeps, The Sands of Eden. *Mini-Series*: Pursuit, The Way to Dusty Death. *Series*: Manimal, Falcon Crest, Counterstrike.

MacCURDY, JEAN
Executive. Began career in the Children's Prog. dept., NBC TV network. Joined Warner Bros. Cartoons in 1979, as dir. of Animation and Prog.; named v.p. & gen. mngr, WB Cartoons & served as prodn. exec., 1982. Named v.p., Children's Prog., 1983. Returned to WB Animation as v.p. & gen. mngr., 1988; named sr. v.p. & gen. mngr., 1991; became first pres., WB TV Animation, 1992-.

MacDOWELL, ANDIE
Actress. r.n. Rose Anderson MacDowell. b. Gaffney, SC, April 21, 1958. Started as model for Elite Agency in NY appearing for L'Ordeal Cosmetics, The Gap, Calvin Klein.
PICTURES: Greystoke: The Legend of Tarzan Lord of the Apes (debut, 1984), St. Elmo's Fire, Sex Lies and Videotape (L.A. Film Critics Award, 1989), Green Card, The Object of Beauty, Hudson Hawk, The Player, Groundhog Day, Short Cuts, Deception, Four Weddings and a Funeral, Bad Girls, Unstrung Heroes, Michael, Multiplicity, The End of Violence, Shadrach, Just the Ticket (also exec. prod.), Muppets from Space, The Muse.
TELEVISION: *Movie*: Women and Men 2: In Love There Are No Rules (Domestic Dilemma). *Mini-Series* (Italy): Sahara's Secret.

MACGILLIVRAY, GREG
Executive. President & co-founder, MacGillivray Freeman Films, which specializes in large format documentary films, 1965-present. Director/producer, To Fly!, 1976 (the highest grossing documentary film of all time, selected by the Library of Congress for inclusion in the National Film Registry), To the Limit, The Living Sea, Dolphins, Adventures in Wild California.

MacGRAW, ALI
Actress. b. Pound Ridge, NY, April 1, 1939. e. Wellesley Coll. Son is actor Josh Evans. Editorial asst. Harper's Bazaar Mag.; asst. to photographer Melvin Sokolsky. Was top fashion model. *Author*: Moving Pictures (autobiography, 1991), Yoga Mind & Body (1995).
PICTURES: A Lovely Way to Die (debut, 1968). Goodbye Columbus, Love Story (Acad. Award nom.), The Getaway, Convoy, Players, Just Tell Me What You Want, Natural Causes, Glam.
TELEVISION: *Mini-Series*: The Winds of War. *Movies*: China Rose, Survive the Savage Sea, Gunsmoke: The Long Ride, The Hollywood Fashion Machine. *Series*: Dynasty.

MacLACHLAN, KYLE
Actor. b. Yakima, WA, Feb. 22, 1959. e. Univ. of WA. Acted in high school and college, then in summer stock. Joined Oregon Shakespeare Festival (Romeo and Juliet, Julius Caesar, Henry V). Cast as lead in Dune by dir. David Lynch in a nationwide search.
THEATRE: *NY*: Palace of Amateurs (Off-B'way).
PICTURES: Dune (debut, 1984), Blue Velvet, The Hidden, Don't Tell Her It's Me, The Doors, Twin Peaks: Fire Walk With Me, Where the Day Takes You, Rich in Love, The Trial, The Flintstones, Showgirls, Trigger Effect, Mad Dog Time, One Night Stand, Hamlet.
TELEVISION: *Series*: Twin Peaks, Sex and the City. *Guest*: Tales From the Crypt (Carrion Death). *Movies*: Dream Breakers, Against the Wall, Roswell, Windsor Protocol, Route 9, The Spring.

MacLAINE, SHIRLEY
Actress. r.n. Shirley MacLean Beaty. b. Richmond, VA, April 24, 1934. Brother is actor-prod. Warren Beatty. e. Washington and Lee H.S., Arlington, VA. Started as dancer; on B'way as understudy for Carol Haney in The Pajama Game, which resulted in contract with film prod. Hal Wallis. Prod., writer and co- dir. of Oscar-nominated film documentary: The Other Half of The Sky: A China Memoir. Returned to stage in Gypsy in My Soul, Shirley MacLaine on Broadway. Videos: Shirley MacLaine's Inner Workout, Relaxing Within.
AUTHOR: Don't Fall off the Mountain, You Can Get There from Here, Out on a Limb, Dancing in the Light, It's All In the Playing, Going Within, Dance While You Can, My Lucky Stars. *Editor*: McGovern: The Man and His Beliefs (1972).
PICTURES: The Trouble With Harry (debut, 1955), Artists and Models, Around the World in 80 Days, Hot Spell, The Matchmaker, The Sheepman, Some Came Running (Acad. Award nom.), Ask Any Girl, Career, Can-Can, The Apartment (Acad. Award nom.), Ocean's Eleven (cameo), All in a Night's Work, Two Loves, My Geisha, The Children's Hour, Two for the Seesaw, Irma La Douce (Acad. Award nom.), What a Way to Go!, John Goldfarb Please Come Home, The Yellow Rolls Royce, Gambit, Woman Times Seven, The Bliss of Mrs. Blossom, Sweet Charity, Two Mules for Sister Sara, Desperate Characters, The Possession of Joel Delaney, The Turning Point (Acad. Award nom.), Being There, Loving Couples, A Change of Seasons, Terms of Endearment (Acad. Award, 1983), Cannonball Run II, Madame Sousatzka, Steel Magnolias, Postcards From the Edge, Waiting for the Light, Defending Your Life (cameo), Used People, Wrestling Ernest Hemingway, Guarding Tess, Mrs. Winterbourne, The Celluloid Closet, Evening Star, A Smile Like Yours (cameo), Looking for Lulu, Bet Bruce, Bruno (also dir.).
TELEVISION: *Series*: Shirley's World. Variety *Specials:* The Other Half of the Sky: A China Memoir (also prod., co-writer), If They Could See Me Now, Where Do We Go From Here?, Shirley MacLaine at the Lido, Every Little Movement (Emmy Award for co-writing, 1980), Illusions, The Shirley MacLaine Show. *Movies*: Out on a Limb (also co-writer), The West Side Waltz, Joan of Arc.

MacLEOD, GAVIN
Actor. b. Mt. Kisco, NY, Feb. 28, 1930. e. Ithaca Coll.
PICTURES: I Want to Live, Compulsion, Operation Petticoat, McHale's Navy, McHale's Navy Joins the Air Force, The Sand Pebbles, Deathwatch, The Party, Kelly's Heroes.
TELEVISION: *Series*: McHale's Navy, The Mary Tyler Moore Show, The Love Boat. *Movies*: The Intruders, Only with Married Men, Ransom for Alice, Murder Can Hurt You, Student Exchange, The Love Boat: The Valentine Voyage. *Mini-Series*: Scruples. *Specials*: Last Act Is a Solo, If I Die Before I Wake.

MACMILLAN, MICHAEL
Executive. b. Scarborough, Ontario, Canada, 1956. e. Queen's U., Ontario. Co-founded and served as first cinematographer for Atlantis Films Ltd.,1978; chairman and CEO, Alliance Atlantis Communications, Inc. Producer/exec. producer, Boys and Girls, The Painted Door, Curse of the Viking Grave, Lost in the Barrens. Currently on the board of directors, Canadian Stage Co., Toronto East General Hospital Foundation, and The Canadian Film and Television Production Assn. Also vice-chair Canadian Film Centre.

MacNAUGHTON, ROBERT
Actor. b. New York, NY, Dec. 19, 1966. Entered entertainment industry in 1979. Member Circle Rep. Co., N.Y.
THEATER: Critic's Choice, A Thousand Clowns, Camelot, The Diviners, The Adventures of Huckleberry Finn, Henry V, Tobacco Road, Master Harold... and the Boys, Tomorrow's Monday, Talley and Son.
PICTURES: E.T.: The Extra-Terrestrial, I Am the Cheese.
TELEVISION: *Movies*: Angel City, A Place to Call Home. *Specials*: Big Bend Country, The Electric Grandmother, Hear My Cry, Visitors.

MacNICOL PETER
Actor. b. Dallas, TX, April 10, 1954. e. U. of Minnesota.
THEATER: Manhattan Theatre Club: Crimes of the Heart. NY Shakespeare Fest: Found a Peanut, Rum and Coke, Twelfth Night, Richard II, Romeo & Juliet. Regional theatre includes Guthrie, Alaska Rep., Long Wharf, Dallas Theatre Center, Trinity Rep. B'way: Crimes of the Heart (Theatre World Award), The Nerd, Black Comedy/White Liars.
PICTURES: Dragonslayer (debut, 1981), Sophie's Choice, Heat, Ghostbusters II, American Blue Note, Hard Promises, Housesitter, Addams Family Values, Radioland Murders, Dracula: Dead and Loving It, Mojave Moon, Bean, Baby Geniuses.
TELEVISION: *Movies*: Johnny Bull, By Dawn's Early Light, Roswel, Olive, the Other Reindeer (voice). *Guest*: Faerie Tale Theatre, Days and Nights of Molly Dodd, Cheers. *Series*: Powers That Be, Chicago Hope, Abducted: A Father's Love, Silencing Mary.

MACY, WILLIAM H.
Actor. b. Miami, FL, March 13, 1950. e. Goddard Col.
THEATER: *NY*: The Man in 605 (debut, 1980), Twelfth Night, Beaurecrat, A Call From the East, The Dining Room, Speakeasy, Wild Life, Flirtations, Baby With the Bathwater, The Nice and the Nasty, Bodies Rest and Motion, Oh Hell!, Life During Wartime, Mr. Gogol and Mr. Preen, Oleanna, Our Town (B'way).
PICTURES: Without a Trace, The Last Dragon, Radio Days, House of Games, Things Change, Homicide, Shadows and Fog, Benny and Joon, Searching for Bobby Fischer, The Client, Oleanna, Murder in the First, Mr. Holland's Opus, Down Periscope, Fargo (Acad. Award nom.), Ghosts of Mississippi, Boogie Nights, Air Force One, Wag the Dog, Pleasantville, Jerry & Tom, A Civil Action, Psycho, Mystery Men, Happy Texas, Magnolia, State and Maine, Panic, Jurassic Park III, Focus.
TELEVISION: *Movies:* The Murder of Mary Phagan, Texan, A Murderous Affair, The Water Engine, Heart of Justice, A Private Matter, The Con, A Slight Case of Murder, Night of the Headless Horseman (voice). *Guest:* ER, Law and Order, Chicago Hope, King of the Hill (voice).

MADDEN, BILL
Executive. b. New York, NY, March 1, 1915. e. Boston U. Joined Metro-Goldwyn-Mayer as office boy, 1930; student salesman, 1938; asst. Eastern div. sales mgr., 1939; U.S. Navy, 1942-46; Boston sales rep., MGM, 1947-53; Philadelphia branch mgr., 1954-59; Midwest div. sales mgr., 1960-68; roadshow sales mgr., 1969; v.p., gen. sales mgr., 1969-74, MGM; corp., v.p. & gen. sls. mgr., MGM, 1974; retired from MGM, 1975; 1976-present, exec. consultant to motion picture industry; lecturer and instructor at UCLA. Member: AMPAS, Motion Picture Associates, American Film Institute. Motion Picture Pioneers.

MADDEN, DAVID
Executive, Producer, Director. b. Chicago, IL, July 25, 1955. e. Harvard U., 1976; UCLA, M.A., 1978. Joined 20th Century-Fox in 1978 as story analyst. Named story editor, 1980; exec. story editor, 1982. Appt. v.p., creative affairs for 20th-Fox Prods., 1983; v.p., prod., 20th Century-Fox Prods; 1984, v.p., prod., Paramount Pictures. 1987, joined Interscope Commun. as prod. 1996, Formed Cort Madden Co. at Paramount with Robert Cort
PICTURES: *Producer*: Renegades, Blind Fury (exec. prod.), The First Power, Eve of Destruction, Jersey Girls, The Hand That Rocks the Cradle, Holy Matrimony, Operation Dumbo Drop, The Tie That Binds, Separate Lives (dir only.) The Associate, Odd Couple II.
TELEVISION: *Movies*: A Part of the Family (dir., writer), Body Language (co-exec. prod.).

MADDEN, JOHN
Director. b. Portsmouth, NH, April 8, 1949.
PICTURES: Ethan Frome, Golden Gate, Mrs. Brown, Shakespeare in Love (Acad. Award nom.).
TELEVISION: *Movies:* Grown-ups, A Wreath of Roses, The Widowmaker, The Storyteller: Greek Myths, Meat, Prime Suspect 4: The Lost Child, Truth or Dare. *Series:* The Return of Sherlock Holmes, Inspector Morse, The Casebook of Sherlock Holmes.

MADDIN, GUY
Director, Writer. b. Winnipeg, Canada, Feb. 28, 1956.
PICTURES: The Dead Father, Tales from the Gimli Hospital (also ed., d.p.), Archangel (also ed., d.p.), Careful (also ed., d.p.), Odilon Redon, Twilight of the Ice Nymphs (dir. only).

MADIGAN, AMY
Actress. b. Chicago, IL, Sept. 11, 1951. m. actor Ed Harris. For 10 years traveled country performing in bars and clubs with band. Then studied at Lee Strasberg Inst., L.A. NY Stage: The Lucky Spot (Theatre World Award), A Streetcar Named Desire.
PICTURES: Love Child (debut, 1982), Love Letters, Streets of Fire, Places in the Heart, Alamo Bay, Twice in a Lifetime (Acad. Award nom.), Nowhere To Hide, The Prince of Pennsylvania, Field of Dreams, Uncle Buck, The Dark Half, Female Perversions, Loved, With Friends Like These.
TELEVISION: *Special*: The Laundromat. *Movies*: Crazy Times, The Ambush Murders, Victims, Travis McGee, The Day After, Roe vs. Wade, Lucky Day, And Then There Was One, Riders of the Purple Sage, Big Guns Talk: The Story of the Western, A Bright Shining Lie..

MADONNA
Singer, Actress. r.n. Madonna Louise Veronica Ciccone. b. Pontiac, MI, Aug. 16, 1958. e. U. of Michigan. Gained fame as rock & recording star before professional acting debut in Desperately Seeking Susan, 1985. NY stage debut: Speed-the-Plow, 1988. Author: Sex (1992).
PICTURES: A Certain Sacrifice (debut, 1983), Vision Quest, Desperately Seeking Susan, Shanghai Surprise, Who's That Girl?, Bloodhounds of Broadway, Dick Tracy, Truth or Dare (also exec. prod.), Shadows and Fog, A League of Their Own, Body of Evidence, Dangerous Game, Blue in the Face, Four Rooms, Girl 6, Evita (Golden Globe Award for Actress, 1997), The Next Best Thing.

MADSEN, MICHAEL
Actor. b. Chicago, IL, Sept. 25, 1958. Sister is actress Virginia Madsen. Started acting with Chicago's Steppenwolf Theatre appearing in such plays as Of Mice and Men, A Streetcar Named Desire. On B'way in A Streetcar Named Desire (1992).
PICTURES: WarGames (debut, 1983), Racing With the Moon, The Natural, The Killing Time, Shadows in the Storm, Blood Red, Kill Me Again, The End of Innocence, The Doors, Thelma & Louise, Straight Talk, Inside Edge, Reservoir Dogs, Trouble Bound, House in the Hills, Free Willy, Money for Nothing, Fixing the Shadow, The Getaway, Beyond the Law, Dead Connection, Wyatt Earp, Man With a Gun, Species, Free Willy 2: The Adventure Home, Mulholland Falls, Donnie Brasco, The Maker, The Thief & The Stripper, Detour, Species II, The Replacement, The Florentine.
TELEVISION: *Movies*: Our Family Honor, Montana, Baby Snatcher, Supreme Sanction. *Specials:* Steve McQueen: The King of Cool. *Pilot*: Diner. *Series:* Vengeance Unlimited.

MADSEN, VIRGINIA
Actress. b. Chicago, IL, Sept. 11, 1963. Mother is Emmy-winning Chicago filmmaker; brother is actor Michael Madsen. Studied with Chicago acting coach Ted Liss. Prof. debut, PBS, A Matter of Principle. Received Avoriaz & Saturn Awards for Best Actress for Candyman.
PICTURES: Class (debut, 1983), Electric Dreams, Dune, Creator, Fire With Fire, Modern Girls, Zombie High, Slam Dance, Mr. North, Hot to Trot, Heart of Dixie, The Hot Spot, Highlander 2: The Quickening, Candyman, Becoming Colette, Caroline at Midnight, Blue Tiger, The Prophecy, Ghosts of Mississippi, Suicide Kings, The Rainmaker, McClintocks Peach, The Florentine, Ballad of the Nightingale, Ambushed, The Haunting, All the Fine Lines.
TELEVISION: *Movies*: Mussolini: The Untold Story, The Hearst and Davies Affair, Long Gone, Gotham, Third Degree Burn, Ironclads, Victim of Love, Love Kills, Linda, A Murderous Affair: The Carolyn Warmus Story, Bitter Revenge, Robert Ludlum's The Apocalypse Watch. *Guest*: The Hitchhiker, Frasier.

MAGNOLI, ALBERT
Director, Writer, Editor.
PICTURES: Jazz (dir., editor, s.p.), Reckless (edit.), Purple Rain (dir., edit., s.p.), American Anthem (dir. only).
TELEVISION: *Movie*: Born to Run.

MAGNUSON, ANN
Actress, Writer, Performance Artist. b. Charleston, WV, Jan. 4, 1956. e. Denison U. Intern at Ensemble Studio Theatre when she came to NY in 1978. Ran Club 57, an East Village club, 1979. Has performed Off-B'way, in East Village clubs, downtown art spaces, on college campuses since 1980, and at Whitney Museum, Soguestu Hall (Tokyo), Walker Art Ctr. (Minn.), Lincoln Center, Serious Fun Festival, Joseph Papp's Public Theatre. Also performed with band Bongwater. Debut as solo recording artist on Geffen Records with The Luv Show, 1995.
PICTURES: Vortex, The Hunger, Perfect Strangers, Desperately Seeking Susan, Making Mr. Right, A Night in the Life of Jimmy Reardon, Sleepwalk, Mondo New York, Tequila Sunrise, Checking Out, Heavy Petting, Love at Large, Cabin Boy, Clear and Present Danger, Tank Girl, Before and After, Hugo Pool, Still Breathing, Levitation.
TELEVISION: *Movies/Specials:* Night Flight, Made for TV, Alive from Off Center (co-host), Vandemonium, Table at Ciro's (Tales From the Hollywood Hills), The Hidden Room, The Adventures of Pete and Pete, From the Earth to the Moon. *Guest*: The John Laroquette Show, Caroline in the City, The Drew Carey Show. *Series*: Anything But Love.

MAGUIRE, TOBEY
Actor. b. Santa Monica, CA, June 27, 1975.
PICTURES: This Boy's Life, S.F.W., Plane Fear, Duke of Groove, Joyride, The Ice Storm, Deconstructing Harry, Pleasantville, Fear and Loathing in Las Vegas, Wonder Boys, The Cider House Rules, Ride with the Devil, Like Cats & Dogs, Jack Sheppard and Jonathan Wild, Spider Man.
TELEVISION: *Movie*: Spoils of War. *Series*: Great Scott!. *Guest*: Roseanne, Walker Texas Ranger, Blossom.

MAHARIS, GEORGE
Actor. b. Astoria, NY, Sept. 1, 1928. Studied at The Actors Studio.
PICTURES: Exodus (debut, 1960), Quick Before It Melts, Sylvia, The Satan Bug, A Covenant With Death, The Happening, The Desperadoes, Last Day of the War, The Land Raiders, The Sword and the Sorcerer, Doppelganger.
TELEVISION: *Series*: Search for Tomorrow, Route 66, Most Deadly Game. Guest: Naked City. *Movies*: Escape to Mindanao, The Monk, The Victim, Murder on Flight 502, Look What's Happened to Rosemary's Baby, SST—Death Flight, Return to Fantasy Island, Crash, A Small Rebellion. *Mini-Series*: Rich Man Poor Man. *Special*: A Death of Princes.

MAHONEY, JOHN
Actor. b. Manchester, England, June 20, 1940. Mem. of Stratford Children's Theatre from age 10\-13. Moved to U.S. at 19, taught Eng. at Western Illinois U. Then freelance ed. of medical manuscripts; assoc. ed., Quality Review Bulletin. At 35 quit medical book editing to become an actor. Studied acting, Chicago's St. Nicholas Theatre. Prof. debut, The Water Engine, 1977. Joined Steppenwolf Theatre Co., 1979. (The Hothouse, Taking Steps, Death of a Salesman). Chicago Film Crits. Special "Commitment to Chicago" Award, 1997.
THEATER: Orphans (Theatre World Award), The House of Blue Leaves (Tony & Clarence Derwent Awards), The Subject Was Roses.
PICTURES: Mission Hill, Code of Silence, The Manhattan Project, Streets of Gold, Tin Men, Suspect, Moonstruck, Frantic, Betrayed, Eight Men Out, Say Anything..., Love Hurts, The Russia House, Barton Fink, Article 99, In the Line of Fire, Striking Distance, Reality Bites, The Hudsucker Proxy, The American President, Primal Fear, She's the One, Antz (voice), The Iron Giant (voice).
TELEVISION: *Series*: Lady Blue, H.E.L.P., The Human Factor, Frasier. *Movies*: The Killing Floor, Chicago Story, First Steps, Listen to Your Heart, Dance of the Phoenix, First Steps, Trapped in Silence, Favorite Son, The Image, Dinner at Eight, The 10 Million Dollar Getaway, The Secret Passion of Robert Clayton, Unnatural Pursuits. *Special*: The House of Blue Leaves.

MAJORS, LEE
Actor. r.n. Lee Yeary. b. Wyandotte, MI, April 23, 1939. Star athlete in high school; turned down offer from St. Louis Cardinals in final year at Eastern Kentucky State Coll. to pursue acting career. In L.A. got job as playground supervisor for park dept. while studying acting at MGM Studio. Debuted in films 1964 under his real name.
PICTURES: Strait-Jacket (debut, 1964), Will Penny, The Liberation of L. B. Jones, The Norsemen, Killer Fish, Steel, Agency, The Last Chase, Scrooged, Keaton's Cop, Trojan War.
TELEVISION: *Series*: The Big Valley, The Men From Shiloh, Owen Marshall-Counselor at Law, The Six Million Dollar Man, The Fall Guy, Tour of Duty, Raven. *Pilot*: Road Show (also exec. prod.). *Movies*: The Ballad of Andy Crocker, Weekend of Terror, The Gary Francis Powers Story, The Cowboy and the Ballerina, A Rocky Mountain Christmas, The Return of the Six Million Dollar Man and the Bionic Woman, Danger Down Under (exec. prod., actor), The Bionic Showdown: the Six Million Dollar Man and the Bionic Woman, Fire!, Trapped on the 37th Floor, The Cover Girl Murders, Bionic Ever After?, Lost Treasures of Dos Santos.

MAKAVEJEV, DUSAN
Director. b. Belgrade, Yugoslavia, Oct. 13, 1932.
PICTURES: Jatagan Mala, Pecat, Antonijevo Razbijeno Ogledalo, Spomenicima ne Treba Verovati, Slikovnica Pcelara, Prokleti Praznik, Boje Sanjaju, Sto je Radnicki Savjet?, Pedagoska Bajka, Osmjeh 61, Eci Pec Pec, Parada, Ljepotica 62, Film o Knjizi ABC, Dole Plotovi, Nova Igracka, Nova Domaca Zivotinja, Man is Not a Bird, An Affair of the Heart, Innocence Unprotected, Mystery of Body (also s.p.), I Miss Sonia Henie, Wet Dreams, Sweet Movie (also s.p.), Montenegro (also s.p.), The Coca-Cola Kid, Manifesto (also s.p.), Gorilla Bathes at Noon (also s.p.), A Hole in the Soul, Danish Girls Show Everything.

MAKEPEACE, CHRIS
Actor. b. Montreal, Canada, April 22, 1964. e. Jarvis Collegiate Institute. Trained for stage at Second City Workshop.
PICTURES: Meatballs (debut, 1979), My Bodyguard, The Last Chase, The Oasis, The Falcon and the Snowman, Vamp, Captive Hearts, Aloha Summer.
TELEVISION: *Movies*: The Terry Fox Story, The Mysterious Stranger, Mazes and Monsters, The Undergrads. *Series*: Going Great (host, 1982-84), Why On Earth?

MAKO
Actor. r.n. Makoto Iwamatsu. b. Kobe, Japan, Dec. 10, 1933. e. Pratt Inst.
THEATER: *NY*: Pacific Overtures (Tony nom.), Shimada. *Regional*: Rashomon.
PICTURES: The Ugly Dachshund, The Sand Pebbles (Acad. Award nom.), The Private Navy of Sgt. O'Farrell, The Great Bank Robbery, The Hawaiians, The Island at the Top of the World, Prisoners, The Killer Elite, The Big Brawl, The Bushido Blade, Under the Rainbow, An Eye for an Eye, Conan the Barbarian, The House Where Evil Dwells, Testament, Conan the Destroyer, Armed Response, P.O.W. The Escape, Silent Assassins, The Wash, Tucker: The Man and His Dream, An Unremarkable Life, Taking Care of Business, Pacific Heights, The Perfect Weapon, Sidekicks, Robocop 3, Rising Sun, Cultivating Charlie, A Dangerous Place, Highlander III: The Sorcerer.
TELEVISION: *Series*: Hawaiian Heat. *Movies*: The Challenge, If Tomorrow Comes, The Streets of San Francisco (pilot), Judge Dee and the Monastery Murders, Farewell to Manzanar, When Hell Was in Session, The Last Ninja, Girls of the White Orchid. *Guest:* McHale's Navy, Ensign O'Toole, 77 Sunset Strip, I Spy, F Troop, Hawaii Five-O.

MALDEN, KARL
Actor. r.n. Mladen Sekulovich. b. Gary, IN, March 22, 1914. e. Art Inst. of Chicago 1933-36; Goodman Theatre Sch. Elected pres., Acad. of Motion Picture Arts & Sciences, 1989.
THEATER: *B'way*: Golden Boy, Key Largo, Flight to West, Missouri Legend, Uncle Harry, Counterattack, Truckline Cafe, All My Sons, Streetcar Named Desire, Desperate Hours, Desire Under the Elms, The Egghead.
PICTURES: They Knew What They Wanted (debut, 1940), Winged Victory, 13 Rue Madeleine, Boomerang!, Kiss of Death, The Gunfighter, Where the Sidewalk Ends, Halls of Montezuma, A Streetcar Named Desire (Acad. Award, best supporting actor, 1951), The Sellout, Diplomatic Courier, Operation Secret, Ruby Gentry, I Confess, Take the High Ground, Phantom of the Rue Morgue, On the Waterfront (Acad. Award nom.), Baby Doll, Bombers B-52, Time Limit (dir. only), Fear Strikes Out, The Hanging Tree, One Eyed Jacks, Pollyanna, The Great Impostor, Parrish, All Fall Down, Birdman of Alcatraz, Gypsy, How the West Was Won, Come Fly With Me, Cheyenne Autumn, Dead Ringer, The Cincinnati Kid, Nevada Smith, Murderer's Row, Hotel, Blue, The Adventures of Bullwhip Griffin, Billion Dollar Brain, Hot Millions, Patton, Cat O'Nine Tails, Wild Rovers, Summertime Killer, Beyond the Poseidon Adventure, Meteor, The Sting II, Twilight Time, Billy Galvin, Nuts.
TELEVISION: *Series*: Streets of San Francisco, Skag. *Movies*: Captains Courageous, Word of Honor, With Intent to Kill, Alice in Wonderland, Fatal Vision (Emmy Award, 1985), My Father My Son, The Hijacking of the Achille Lauro, Call Me Anna, Absolute Strangers, Back to the Streets of San Francisco.

MALICK, TERRENCE
Wrtier, Director. b. Bartlesville, OK, November 30, 1943. e. Harvard University. Former Rhodes Scholar.
PICTURES: *Writer*: Deadhead Miles, Pocket Money, The Gravy Train. *Writer, Director*: Days of Heaven, Badlands (also prod.), The Thin Red Line (Acad. Award nom for dir., s.p. adapt.), The Moviegoe(also prod.). *Producer*: Endurance.
TELEVISION: *Actor*: Golden Fiddles, The Beast.

MALIN, AMIR JACOB
Producer, Executive. b. Tel-Aviv, Israel, March 22, 1954. e. Brandeis U., 1972-76, Boston U. School of Law, 1976-79. Staff atty., WGBH-TV, Boston, 1979-81; president and co-CEO, Cinecom Entertainment Grp., Inc., 1982-88; co-president, October Films, Inc., where he oversaw some of the industry's most important films and championed its most important filmmakers; 1989-97; president & CEO, Millennium Pictures, a joint venture with Nu-Image, Inc., Phoenician Films, and October Films; CEO, Artisan Entertainment, 1997-present.
PICTURES: *Executive producer*: Swimming to Cambodia, Matewan, Miles From Home, Scenes from the Class Struggle in Beverly Hills, The Handmaid's Tale, Tune in Tomorrow.

MALKOVICH, JOHN
Actor. b. Christopher, IL, Dec. 9, 1953. e. Illinois State U. Founding member Steppenwolf Ensemble in Chicago with group of college friends, 1976. Starred in Say Goodnight Gracie and True West (Obie Award).Stage work includes Death of Salesman, Burn This, States of Shock. *Dir.:* Balm in Gilead, Arms and the Man, The Caretaker, Libra (also writer).
PICTURES: Places in the Heart (Acad. Award nom.), The Killing Fields, Eleni, Making Mr. Right, The Glass Menagerie, Empire of the Sun, Miles From Home, Dangerous Liaisons, The Accidental Tourist (co-exec. prod. only), The Sheltering Sky, Queens Logic, The Object of Beauty, Shadows and Fog, Of Mice and Men, Jennifer Eight, Alive, In the Line of Fire (Acad. Award nom.), The Convent, Beyond the Clouds, Mary Reilly, Mulholland Falls, Portrait of a Lady, Con Air, Rounders, The Man in the Iron Mask, Time Regained, Ladies Room, Being John Malkovich, The Messenger: The Story of Joan of Arc, RKO 281, Burned to Light.
TELEVISION: *Special*: Rocket to the Moon. *Movies*: True West, Word of Honor, American Dream, Death of a Salesman (Emmy Award, 1986), Heart of Darkness.

MALMUTH, BRUCE
Director, Actor. b. Brooklyn, NY, Feb. 4, 1937. e. City Coll. of New York, Brooklyn Coll. Grad. studies in film, Columbia U. and U. of Southern California. Acted in and dir. college productions. Moved to California and obtained job as page at NBC. In Army assigned to special services as dir.; reassigned to New York. Upon release began 10-year Clio-winning career as dir. of TV commercials. Debut as dir. of features with Nighthawks, 1981. Founder, Los Angeles Aspiring Actors and Directors Workshop. Theatre incl.: Two Guys Second Wind (writer, dir., prod.), Thanksgiving Cries (writer, dir.).
PICTURES: *Director*: Nighthawks, The Man Who Wasn't There, Where Are the Children? (also actor), Hard to Kill, Pentathalon (also actor). *Actor*: The Karate Kid (also Part II), For Keeps?, Happy New Year, Lean on Me.
TELEVISION: Baseballs or Switchblades? (prod., writer, dir., Emmy Award), A Boy's Dream, Twilight Zone, Beauty and the Beast, Heartbreak Winner.

MALONE, DOROTHY
Actress. b. Chicago, IL, Jan. 30, 1925. e. Southern Methodist U., USC, AADA. Started as RKO starlet, 1943. Stage work incl. Little Me, Practice to Deceive.
PICTURES: The Big Sleep, Night and Day, One Sunday Afternoon, Two Guys From Texas, The Nevadan, The Bushwackers, Jack Slade, The Killer That Stalked New York, Scared Stiff, Torpedo Alley, The Lone Gun, Pushover, Security Risk, Private Hell 36, The Fast and the Furious, Young at Heart, Battle Cry, Sincerely Yours, Artists and Models, At Gunpoint, Five Guns West, Tall Man Riding, Pillars of the Sky, Tension at Table Rock, Written on the Wind (Acad. Award, best supporting actress, 1956), Man of a Thousand Faces, Quantez, The Tarnished Angels, Tip on a Dead Jockey, Too Much Toon Soon, Warlock, The Last Voyage, The Last Sunset, Beach Party, Fate is the Hunter (unbilled), Abduction, Golden Rendezvous, Good Luck Miss Wyckoff, Winter Kills, The Day Time Ended, The Being, Basic Instinct, Beverly Hills.
TELEVISION: *Series*: Peyton Place. *Guest*: Dick Powell Theatre, Loretta Young Show (twice hosted), Philip Morris Playhouse, Dr. Kildare, Bob Hope Show, Jack Benny Show, The Untouchables, Phyllis Diller Show, Ken Murray's Blackouts, Death Valley Days. *Movies*: The Pigeon, Little Ladies of the Night, Murder in Peyton Place, Katie: Portrait of a Centerfold, Condominium, Peyton Place: The Next Generation. *Mini-Series*: Rich Man Poor Man. *Specials*: Gertrude Stein Story, The Family That Prays Together.

MALONE, JOHN C.
Executive. b. Milford, CT, Mar. 7, 1941. e. Yale U. Pres. & CEO of Telecommunications Inc., 1973-present. With National Cable Television Association as: dir., 1974-77; treasurer, 1977-78; dir., 1980-94. Dir. of TCI; on bd. of dirs. for Turner Bordacasting, Cable Television Laboratories Inc. BET, Discovery.

MAMET, DAVID
Writer, Director. b. Chicago, IL, Nov. 30, 1947. m. actress Rebecca Pidgeon. e. Goddard Coll. Artist-in-residence, Goddard Coll. 1971-73. Artistic dir. St. Nicholas Theatre Co., Chicago, 1973-75. Co-founder Dinglefest Theatre; assoc. artistic dir., Goodman Theatre, Chicago. Appeared as actor in film Black Widow. *Novel:* The Village (1994).
THEATER: Lakefront, The Woods, American Buffalo, Sexual Perversity in Chicago, Duck Variations, Edmond, A Life in the Theatre, The Water Engine, Prairie du Chien, Glengarry Glen Ross (Pulitzer Prize, Tony Award, 1984), Speed-the-Plow, Sketches of War (benefit for homeless Vietnam Veterans), Oleanna, An Interview (Death Defying Acts), The Cryptogram.
PICTURES: *Writer*: The Postman Always Rings Twice, The Verdict, The Untouchables, House of Games (also dir.), Things Change (also dir.), We're No Angels, Homicide (also dir.), Hoffa, Vanya on 42nd Street (adaptation), Oleanna (also dir.), The Spanish Prisoner (also dir.), The Edge, Wag the Dog, Ronin, The Winslow Boy (also dir.), State and Maine, The Heist, Lakeboat (writer only), Whistle (writer only), Hannibal (writer only).
TELEVISION: Lip Service (exec. prod.), Hill Street Blues, A Life in the Theatre, Texan, Lansky (also exec. prod.), Catastrophe.

MANASSE, GEORGE
Producer. b. Florence, Italy, Jan. 1, 1938. e. U. of North Carolina.
PICTURES: *Prod.*: Who Killed Mary What's 'er Name?, Squirm, Blue Sunshine, He Knows You're Alone. Prod. Mgr.: Greetings, Joe, Fury on Wheels, Slow Dancing in the Big City, Tribute, Porky's II: The Next Day, Neighbors, Death Wish III, Torch Song Trilogy, Indecent Proposal, Coneheads, Lassie, Die Hard With a Vengeance, Eraser.
TELEVISION: *Line Prod.: Series*: American Playwright's Theatre (Arts & Ent.) The Saint in Manhattan (pilot), *Movie*: The Killing Floor, Vengeance: The Story of Tony Cimo. *Prod. Mgr.: Series*: St. Elsewhere, Annie McGuire. *Movies*: Sanctuary of Fear, Mr. Griffith and Me, Peking Encounter, When the Circus Came to Town, Murder, Inc. Muggable Mary, Running Out, Dropout Father, He's Hired, She's Fired, Intimate Strangers, Drop Out Mother, Vengeance: The Story of Tony Cimo, The Saint in Manhattan, The Diamond Trap, The Prize Pulitzer (also suprv. prod.), Orpheus Descending (also suprv. prod.), John and Yoko, Marilyn and Me, The Woman Who Sinned.

MANCIA, ADRIENNE
Curator, Dept. of Film, Museum of Modern Art. b. New York, NY. e. U. of Wisconsin. B.A.; Columbia U., M.A. Worked in film distribution industry in New York prior to joining Dept. of Film & Video, Museum of Modern Art, 1964; responsible for film exhibition since 1965. 1977, appointed curator. Restructured Museums' Auditorium Exhibition Prog., creating a balance between classic cinema and contemporary work. Initiated innovative programs such as Cineprobe and New Documentaries (formerly What's Happening?) Served on numerous int'l film juries. Co-founder New Directors/New Films. Chevalier de l'Ordre des Arts et des Lettres (France, 1985). Ufficiale dell Ordine al Merito della Repubblica Italiana, 1988.

MANCUSO, FRANK G.
Executive. b. Buffalo, NY, July 25, 1933. e. State U. of New York. Film buyer and operations supvr. for Basil Enterprises, theatre circuit, 1958-62. Joined Paramount as booker in Buffalo branch, 1962. Named sls. repr. for branch in 1964 and branch mgr. in 1967. 1970 appt. v.p./gen. sls. mgr., Paramount Pictures Canada, Ltd., becoming pres. in 1972. 1976 relocated with Paramount in U.S. as western div. mgr. in LA. 1977, appt. gen. sls. mgr. of NY, office; two months later promoted to v.p. domestic distribution; 1979, named exec. v.p., distrib. & mktg. 1983 made pres. of entire Paramount Motion Picture Group. 1984, appointed chmn. and CEO, Paramount Pictures; resigned 1991. Appointed chmn. and CEO, MGM. Resigned from post, April 1999 but will remain on MGM's board. Named Motion Picture Pioneers Man of the Year, 1987. Member of Board: AMPAS, M.P. Assoc. of America, Will Rogers Memorial Fund, Variety Clubs Intl., Sundance Institute, Amer. Film Institute, Museum of Broadcasting, Motion Picture Pioneers. Appointed Chmn. & CEO of MGM, 1993. 1998 Women in film Mentor Award. 1998 Ellis Island Medal of Honor Award.

MANCUSO, JR., FRANK
Producer. b. Buffalo, NY, Oct. 9, 1958. Son of Frank G. Mancuso. e. Upsala Coll. Began with industry at age 14, booking short subjects in Canadian theatres. Worked in gross receipts dept. in Paramount corporate offices in New York and later with paralegal div. Initial prod. work as location asst. for Urban Cowboy in Houston, TX. Served as assoc. prod. of Friday the 13th Part II and prod. of Friday the 13th Part III in 3-D.
PICTURES: Off the Wall, The Man Who Wasn't There, April Fool's Day, Friday the 13th, Part IV: The Final Chapter; Friday the 13th—A New Beginning (exec. prod.), Friday the 13th, Part VII (exec. prod.); Back to the Beach; Permanent Record, Internal Affairs, He Said/She Said, Species, Fled, Hoodlum, Toby's Story, Species II, Ronin.
TELEVISION: Friday the 13th: The Series (exec. prod.), The Escape.

MANDEL, BABALOO
Writer. r.n. Marc Mandel. b. 1949. Started as comedy writer for Joan Rivers, among others. First teamed with Lowell Ganz on script for 1982 film Night Shift.
PICTURES: Night Shift, Splash (Acad. Award nom.; also actor), Spies Like Us, Gung Ho, Vibes, Parenthood, City Slickers, A League of Their Own, Mr. Saturday Night, Greedy, City Slickers II: The Legend of Curly's Gold, Forget Paris, Multiplicity, Father's Day, The Secret LIfe of Walter Mitty, Edtv, Where the Heart Is.
TELEVISION: *Series co-writer*: Laverne and Shirley, Busting Loose, Take Five (also co-creator). *Series co-exec. prod.*: Gung Ho, Knight and Daye, Parenthood.

MANDEL, LORING
Writer. b. Chicago, IL, May 5, 1928. e. U. of Wisconsin, B.S. 1949. Long career writing scripts for TV, dating back to 1955 when penned Shakedown Cruise. Governor, Natl. Acad. of TV Arts & Sciences 1964-68; Pres. Writers Guild of America East 1975-77; Natl. Chmn. 1977-79.
PICTURES: Countdown, Promises in the Dark, The Little Drummer Girl.
TELEVISION: Do Not Go Gentle Into That Good Night (Emmy, 1967), Breaking Up, Project Immortality (Sylvania Award, 1959), A House His Own, Trial of Chaplain Jensen, The Raider.

MANDEL, ROBERT
Director. e. Columbia Univ.
PICTURES: Night at O'Rears (also prod.), Independence Day, F/X, Touch and Go, Big Shots, School Ties, The Substitute.
TELEVISION: *Movies:* Hard Time on Planet Earth, The X Files (pilot), Kansas. Series: Nash Bridges, The Practice.

MANDELL, ABE
Executive. b. Oct. 4, 1922. e. U. of Cincinnati. Entered broadcasting as actor on Cincinnati radio station prior to W.W.II. Served U.S. Army in Southwest Pacific, 1942-45. Formed indep. motion picture distribution co. in the Far East. Company, also operated and owned motion picture theaters throughout the Phillipines and Indonesia, 1946-56; network-regional sales exec., Ziv Television, 1956-58; dir. foreign operations, Independent Television Corporation, 1958; v.p.-foreign oper., 1960; v.p.-sales and adm., 1961; exec. v.p., 1962; pres. 1965. 1976 corporate name changed to ITC Entertainment, Inc. President to 1983 of ITC Ent.; with Robert Mandell heads New Frontier Prods.

MANDOKI, LUIS
Director. b. Mexico City, Mexico. e. San Francisco Art Institute, London Intl. Film School, London College's School of Film. Dir. short film Silent Music which won Intl. Amateur Film Fest. Award at 1976 Cannes Film Fest. Back in Mexico dir. shorts and documentaries for the Instituto Nacional Indignista Concaine, Centro de Produccionde Cortometraje. Won Ariel
PICTURES: Motel (debut, 1982), Gaby--A True Story, White Palace, Born Yesterday, When a Man Loves a Woman, Message in a Bottle.

MANES, FRITZ
Producer. b. Oakland, CA, April 22, 1936. e. U.C., Berkeley, B.A. UCLA, 1956. Armed Service: 1951-54. U.S. Marines, Korea, Purple Heart. TV ad. exec. and stuntman before becoming exec. prod. on films for Clint Eastwood. Has formed own production co., Sundancer Prods. Membership, DGA, SAG.
PICTURES: *in various capacities*: The Outlaw Josey Wales, The Enforcer. *Assoc. prod.*: The Gauntlet, Every Which Way But Loose, Escape From Alcatraz, Bronco Billy. *Prod.*: Any Which Way You Can (Acad. of Country Music Tex Ritter award), Firefox (exec. prod.), Honky Tonk Man (exec. prod.), Tightrope (prod.), Sudden Impact (exec. prod.), City Heat (prod.), Pale Rider (exec. prod.), Ratboy (exec. prod.), Heartbreak Ridge (exec. prod., prod. mgr.), James Dean.

MANHEIM, CAMRYN
Actress. b. 1961.
PICTURES: The Bonfire of the Vanities, The Road to Wellville, David Searching, Jeffrey, Eraser, Romy and Michele's High School Reunion, The Tic Code, Mercury Rising, Fool's Gold, Happiness, Wide Awake, David Searching, Way of the Gun.
TELEVISION: *Movies*: Deadley Whispers, Jackie's Back. *Series*: The Practice (Emmy Award, 1998).

MANKIEWICZ, DON M.
Writer. b. Berlin, Germany, Jan. 20, 1922. p. Herman J. Mankiewicz. e. Columbia, B.A., 1942; Columbia Law Sch. Served in U.S. Army, 1942-46; reporter, New Yorker magazine, 1946-48; author of novels See How They Run, Trial, It Only Hurts a Minute; magazine articles, short stories. President, Producers Guild of America, 1987; on Board of Directors, Writers Guild of America, 1992.
PICTURES: Trial, I Want to Live, (Acad. Award nom.), The Chapman Report, The Black Bird.
TELEVISION: Studio One, On Trial, One Step Beyond, Playhouse 90, Profiles in Courage. Exec. story consultant: Hart to Hart, Simon & Simon, Crazy Like a Fox, Adderly. Pilots: Ironside, Marcus Welby M.D., Sarge, Lanigan's Rabbi (collab.), Rosetti and Ryan (collab.)

MANKIEWICZ, TOM
Writer, Director. b. Los Angeles, CA, June 1, 1942. e. Yale U.
PICTURES: *Writer*: The Sweet Ride (debut), Diamonds Are Forever, Live and Let Die, The Man with the Golden Gun, Mother Jugs and Speed (also prod.), The Cassandra Crossing, The Eagle Has Landed, Ladyhawke. *Exec. Prod.:* Hot Pursuit. *Creative consultant:* Superman, Superman II. *Director*: Dragnet (also s.p.), Delirious.
TELEVISION: *Pilot*: Hart to Hart (writer, dir.). *Movie*: Taking the Heat (dir.), `Till Death Do Us Hart. *Episode*: Tales of the Crypt (dir.)

MANN, ABBY
Writer. b. Philadelphia, PA, 1927. e. NYU. First gained fame on TV writing for Robert Montgomery Theatre, Playhouse 90, Studio One, Alcoa, Goodyear Theatre. Acad. Award for film adaptation of own teleplay Judgment at Nuremberg into theatrical film.
PICTURES: Judgment at Nuremberg, A Child Is Waiting, The Condemned of Altona, Ship of Fools (Acad. Award nom.), The Detective, Report to the Commissioner.
TELEVISION: *Series*: Kojak (creator), Skag, Medical Story. *Movies*: The Marcus-Nelson Murders (Emmy Award, 1973; also exec. prod.), Medical Story (also exec. prod.), The Atlanta Child Murders, King (Emmy nom.), Murderers Among Us: The Simon Wiesenthal Story (Emmy Award, 1989; co-writer, co-exec. prod.), Teamster Boss: The Jackie Presser Story (also co-exec. prod.), Indictment: The McMartin Trial (also co-exec. prod.; Emmy Award, 1995, Golden Globe Award).

MANN, DELBERT
Director, Producer. b. Lawrence, KS, Jan. 30, 1920. e. Vanderbilt U., Yale U. U.S. Air Force, 1942-45. Stage mgr., summer stock, dir. Columbia, S.C. Town Theatre, 1947-49. Asst. dir., NBC-TV, 1949; dir., NBC-TV, 1949-55. Past pres., Directors Guild of America.
THEATER: A Quiet Place, Speaking of Murder, Zelda, The Glass Menagerie, The Memoirs of Abraham Lincoln; *opera*: Wuthering Heights (NY City Center).
PICTURES: Marty (Acad. Award, 1955), The Bachelor Party, Desire Under the Elms, Separate Tables, Middle of the Night, The Dark at the Top of the Stairs, The Outsider, Lover Come Back, That Touch of Mink, A Gathering of Eagles, Dear Heart, Quick Before It Melts (also prod.), Mister Buddwing (also prod.), Fitzwilly, The Pink Jungle, Kidnapped, Birch Interval, Night Crossing.
TELEVISION: Philco-Goodyear TV Playhouse, Producer's Showcase, Omnibus, Playwrights '56, Playhouse 90, Ford Star Jubilee, Lights Out, Mary Kay and Johnny, The Little Show, Masterpiece Theatre, Ford Startime. *Movies/Specials:* Heidi, David Copperfield, No Place to Run, She Waits (also prod.), Jane Eyre, The Man Without a Country, A Girl Named Sooner, Francis Gary Powers: The True Story of the U-2 Spy Incident, Tell Me My Name, Breaking Up, Home to Stay, Love's Dark Ride, Thou Shalt Not Commit Adultery, All Quiet on the Western Front, Torn Between Two Lovers, To Find My Son, All the Way Home, The Member of the Wedding, The Gift of Love, Bronte, Love Leads the Way, A Death in California, The Last Days of Patton, The Ted Kennedy, Jr. Story, April Morning (also co-prod.), Ironclads, Against Her Will: An Incident in Baltimore (also prod.), Incident in a Small Town (also prod.), Lily in Winter.

MANN, MICHAEL
Director, Writer, Producer. b. Chicago, IL, Feb. 5, 1943. e. U. of Wisconsin, London Film Sch. Directed shorts, commercials and documentaries in England. Returned to U.S. in 1972. Wrote for prime-time TV (episodes of Starsky and Hutch, Police Story, created Vegas).
PICTURES: *Exec. Prod.*: Band of the Hand. *Director-Writer*: Thief (also exec. prod.), The Keep, Manhunter, The Last of the Mohicans (also co-prod.), Heat, The Insider (also prod.).
TELEVISION: The Jericho Mile (writer, dir.; DGA Award for dir., Emmy Award for writing, 1980), Miami Vice (exec. prod.), Crime Story (exec. prod.), L.A. Takedown (dir., writer, exec. prod.). *Mini-Series*: Drug Wars: The Camarena Story (exec. prod.; Emmy Award, 1990), Drug Wars: The Cocaine Cartel (exec. prod.).

MANNE, S. ANTHONY
Executive. b. New York, NY, July 19, 1940. e. Wharton School, Univ. of Pennsylvania, B.S. economics. Joined Columbia Pictures, 1963; intl. dept., 1964; asst. mgr., Brazil, 1968; mgr., Brazil, 1969-72. Joined JAD Films, 1976. V.p. United Artists, Latin American supervisor, 1980. V.p. Columbia Pictures Intl., continental mgr., 1981; sr. v.p., sales manager, 1984; exec. v.p., Tri-Star Intl, 1987; exec. v.p., Columbia Tri-Star Film Dist. Intl., 1988-.

MANNING, MICHELLE
Executive. Began production career at Zoetrope Studios as prod. supervisor, then VP Production, Orion Pictures. Sr. VP Production, Viacom, Inc., 1991; promoted to Exec. VP, 1993. Pres. production, Paramount Motion Pictures, 1997.
PICTURES: Blue City (dir.), Another 48 Hours (musical dir.).
TELEVISION: Miami Vice (dir.), Friday the 13th (dir.).

MANOFF, DINAH
Actress. b. New York, NY, Jan. 25, 1958. e. CalArts. Daughter of actress-dir. Lee Grant and late writer Arnold Manoff. Prof. debut in PBS prod., The Great Cherub Knitwear Strike. Guest starred on Welcome Back Kotter.
THEATER: I Ought to Be in Pictures (Tony & Theatre World Awards, 1980), Gifted Children, Leader of the Pack, Alfred and Victoria: A Life (L.A. Theatre Center), Kingdom of Earth (TheatreWest).
PICTURES: Grease (debut, 1978), Ordinary People, I Ought to Be in Pictures, Child's Play, Staying Together, Bloodhounds of Broadway, Welcome Home Roxy Carmichael.
TELEVISION: *Series*: Soap, Empty Nest. *Movies*: Raid on Entebee, Night Terror, The Possessed, For Ladies Only, A Matter of Sex, The Seduction of Gina, Flight No. 90: Disaster on the Potomac, Classified Love, Crossing the Mob, Backfire, Babies, Maid for Each Other (also co-exec. prod., co-story). *Mini-Series*: Celebrity.

MANSON, ARTHUR
Executive. b. Brooklyn, NY, Feb. 21, 1928. e. City Coll. of New York, grad. Inst. Film Technique, 1945. Editor, American Traveler, U.S. Army, 1946. Advance agent, co. mgr., Henry V, U.S., 1948-50; producer's publ. rep., Stanley Kramer Distributing Corp., Samuel Goldwyn Productions, 1951-52, dir. of adv. and publ., MGM Pictures of Canada, Ltd., 1952-53; publ. and adv. rep., Cinerama widescreen process, 1953-58; dir. worldwide ad-pub Cinerama 1958-60; adv. mgr., Columbia Pictures, 1961-62; nat'l dir. of adv., publ., Dino De Laurentiis, 1962-64; exec. asst. to v.p. adv. & pub., 20th Century-Fox, 1964-67; v.p., adv. & pub. Cinerama. Inc., and Cinerama Releasing Corp.; 1967-74; exec. v.p., sales & marketing, BCP, service of Cox Broadcasting Corp., 1974-75; v.p. worldwide marketing Warner Bros., 1976. 1977 formed own company, CineManson Mkt. & Dist. Corp. and is pres. Chmn. and founder NY events committee, AMPAS.

MANTEGNA, JOE
Actor. b. Chicago, IL, Nov. 13, 1947. e. Morton Jr. Coll., Goodman Sch. of Drama, 1967-69. Member: The Organic Theatre Company, Chicago (The Wonderful Ice Cream Suit, Cops, and 2 European tours with ensemble). Later member of Goodman Theater where he began long creative assoc. with playwright-dir. David Mamet (A Life in the Theatre, The Disappearance of the Jews). In national co. of Hair, Godspell, Lenny. B'way debut: Working. Narrated documentaries Crack U.S.A. and Death on the Job.

THEATER: Bleacher Bums (also conceived and co-author), Leonardo (L.A., co-author), Glengarry Glen Ross (Tony Award), Speed-the-Plow.
PICTURES: Who Stole My Wheels? (Towing), Second Thoughts, Compromising Positions, The Money Pit, Off Beat, Three Amigos, Critical Condition, House of Games, Weeds, Suspect, Things Change (Venice Film Fest. Award, 1988), Wait Until Spring Bandini, Alice, The Godfather Part III, Queens Logic, Homicide, Bugsy, Body of Evidence, Family Prayers, Searching for Bobby Fisher, Baby's Day Out, Airheads, For Better or Worse, Forget Paris, Up Close and Personal, Eye for an Eye, Thinner, Albino Alligator, Personal Unknowns, For Hire, Underworld, The Wonderful Ice Cream Suit, Jerry & Tom, Conundrum, Celebrity, Body And Soul, Airspeed, The Runner.
TELEVISION: *Series*: Comedy Zone. *Guest*: Soap, Bosom Buddies, Archie Bunker's Place, Magnum P.I., Open All Night, Fallen Angels, The Simpsons (voice). *Special*: Bleacher Bums (Emmy Award). *Movies*: Elvis, Comrades of Summer, The Water Engine, State of Emergency, Above Suspicion, A Call to Remember, Face Down, Merry Christmas George Bailey, The Rat Pack, Spenser: Small Vices. *Mini-series:* The Last Don, The Last Don II.

MANULIS, MARTIN
Producer, Director. b. New York, NY, May 30, 1915. e. Columbia Col., B.A. 1935. Lt. USN, 1941-45. Head of prod. John C. Wilson, 1941-49; mgr. dir., Westport Country Playhouse, 1945-50; dir. B'way plays; staff prod. & dir. CBS-TV, 1951-58; head prod. 20th-Fox Television. Now pres., Martin Manulis Prods. Ltd. 1987, artistic dir., Ahmanson Theatre, L.A.
THEATER: *B'way/and on tour*: Private Lives, Made in Heaven, The Philadelphia Story, Pride's Crossing, Laura, The Men We Marry, The Hasty Heart, The Show Off.
PICTURES: *Producer*: Days of Wine and Roses, Dear Heart, Luv, Duffy, The Out-of-Towners.
TELEVISION: Suspense, Studio One, Climax, Best of Broadway, Playhouse 90. *Mini-Series*: Chiefs, Space, The Day Christ Died, Grass Roots.

MARA, ADELE
Actress. r.n. Adelaida Delgado; b. Dearborn, MI, April 28, 1923. m. writer-prod. Roy Huggins. Singer, dancer with Xavier Cugat.
PICTURES: Navy Blues (feature debut, 1941), Shut My Big Mouth, Blondie Goes to College, Alias Boston Blackie, You Were Never Lovelier, Lucky Legs, Vengeance of the West, Reveille With Beverly, Riders of the Northwest Mounted, The Magnificent Rogue, Passkey to Danger, Traffic in Crime, Exposed, The Trespasser, Blackmail, Campus Honeymoon, Twilight on the Rio Grande, Robin Hood of Texas, Nighttime in Nevada, The Gallant Legion, Sands of Iwo Jima, Wake of the Red Witch, Rock Island Trail, California Passage, The Avengers, The Sea Hornet, Count The Hours, The Black Whip, Back from Eternity, Curse of the Faceless Man, The Big Circus.
TELEVISION: *Series*: Cool Million. *Mini-Series*: Wheels.

MARBUT, ROBERT GORDON
Broadcast Executive. b. Athens, GA, April 11, 1935. Bachelor Industrial Engineering, Georgia Tech, 1957. M.B.A., Harvard, 1963. Copley Newspapers, 1963-91, named pres. & CEO 1971. Founder, chmn. & CEO Argyle communications, 1991.

MARCHAND, NANCY
Actress. b. Buffalo, NY, June 19, 1928. m. actor-dir. Paul Sparer. e. Carnegie Tech. Stage debut The Late George Apley (1946).
THEATER: The Taming of the Shrew (B'way debut, 1951), The Balcony (Obie Award, 1960), Morning's at Seven (Drama Desk & Outer Critics Circle Awards), Sister Mary Ignatius Explains It All to You, Taken in Marriage, The Plough and the Stars, Awake and Sing, The Cocktail Hour (Obie Award, 1990), The End of the Day, Black Comedy/White Liars. Was an original mem of APA-Phoenix Theater.
PICTURES: The Bachelor Party (debut, 1957), Ladybug Ladybug, Me Natalie, Tell Me That You Love Me Junie Moon, The Hospital, The Bostonians, From the Hip, The Naked Gun: From the Files of Police Squad, Jefferson in Paris, Sabrina, Dear God.
TELEVISION: *Specials*: Little Women, Marty, Kiss Kiss Dahlings, many others. *Series*: Beacon Hill, Adams Chronicles, Love of Life, Search for Tomorrow, Lou Grant (4 Emmy Awards: 1978, 1980, 1981, 1982), The Sopranos. *Movies*: Some Kind of Miracle, Willa, Once Upon a Family, Killjoy, The Golden Moment—An Olympic Love Story, Sparkling Cyanide. *Mini-Series*: North and South Book II.

MARCOVICCI, ANDREA
Actress, Singer. b. New York, NY, Nov. 18, 1948. e. Bennett Col. Studied acting with Herbert Berghof. Acted on NY stage in The Wedding of Iphigenia, The Ambassadors, Nefertiti, Hamlet, Any Given Day. Frequent performer in night clubs.
PICTURES: The Front (debut, 1976), The Concorde: Airport 1979, The Hand, Spacehunter: Adventures in the Forbidden Zone, Kings and Desperate Men, The Stuff, Someone to Love, White Dragon, Jack the Bear.
TELEVISION: *Series*: Love Is a Many-Splendored Thing, Berrenger's, Trapper John M.D. *Movies:* Cry Rape!, Smile Jenny You're Dead, Some Kind of Miracle, A Vacation in Hell, Packin' It In, Spraggue, Velvet, The Canterville Ghost, The Water Engine.

MARCUS, BEN
Executive. b. Poland, Aug. 10, 1911. Emigrated 1914. e. U. Minnesota. Opened first theatre 1935, acq'd. restaurants and hotels, formed Marcus Corp. at which he is pres. and COO. Holdings include Budgetel hotel chain, KFC restaurants, and 46 theatres.

MARCUS, JEFFREY A.
Executive. Began cable TV career selling cable door-to-door in college. Founded Marcus Communiations, Inc., in 1982 which merged in 1988 with Western Tele-Communications, Inc. to form WestMarc Communications, Inc. at which he served as Chairman and CEO. Created Marcus Cable Co. in 1990 by merging cable systems in Wisconsin, Texas, Delaware and Maryland and is currently Chairman and CEO of this continuously expanding company.

MARCUS, MICHAEL E.
Executive. b. Pittsburgh, PA, June 5, 1945. e. Penn State, 1963-67. Moved to LA where he started in industry in mailroom of General Artists Corp. Promoted to agent when co. merged with Creative Management Assocs. 1972 joined Bart/Levy Agency; 1980, became full partner and co-owner of Kohner/Levy/Marcus Agency. 1981, became sr. agent at Creative Artists Agency. 1993, named pres. & COO of MGM Pictures.

MARENSTEIN, HAROLD
Executive b. New York, NY, Nov. 30, 1916. e. City Coll. of New York, 1937. Shipping, picture checking service, Warner Bros., 1935-45; booking, Loew's Inc., 1945-48; booking, contracts, Selznick Rel. Org., 1948-51; contracts, Paramount, 1951-52; asst. sls. gr., International Rel. Org., 1952; asst. sls. mgr., Janus Films, 1961-64; sls. exec., Rizzoli Films, 1965; 1967, nat'l. sales dir., Continental Dist.; gen. sales mgr., Cinemation Industries, 1968; v.p.-sales, dir., Cinemation Industries, 1971; 1976, gen. sls. mgr., General National Films; 1980, gen. sls. mgr., Lima Productions. Now retired.

MARGOLIN, STUART
Actor, Director, Writer. b. Davenport, IA, Jan. 31, 1940. Wrote play Sad Choices which was produced Off-B'way when he was only 20.
PICTURES: The Gamblers, Kelly's Heroes, Limbo, Death Wish, The Big Bus, Futureworld, Days of Heaven, S.O.B., Class, Running Hot, A Fine Mess, Paramedics (dir. only), Iron Eagle II, Bye Bye Blues, Guilty By Suspicion, The Lay of the Land, Hi-Line.
TELEVISION: *Series*: Occasional Wife, Love American Style, Nichols, The Rockford Files (Emmy Awards, 1979, 1980), Bret Maverick, Mr. Smith. *Guest*: Hey Landlord, He & She, The Monkees, M*A*S*H, Gunsmoke, The Mary Tyler Moore Show (also dir.), Rhoda, Magnum P.I., Hill Street Blues. *Movies*: The Intruders, The Ballad of Andy Crocker (writer, associate prod. only), A Summer Without Boys (voice), The Rockford Files (pilot), The California Kid, This is the West That Was, Lanigan's Rabbi, Perilous Voyage, A Killer in the Family, Three of a Kind, To Grandmother's House We Go, How the West Was Fun (dir. only), The Rockford Files: I Still Love L.A, The Rockford Files: A Blessing in Disguise. *Director*: Suddenly Love, A Shining Season, The Long Summer of George Adams, Double Double Toil and Trouble, Salt Water Moose (Dir's. Guild of America Award, 1997).

MARGULIES, JULIANNA
Actor. b. Spring Valley, NY, June 8, 1966. e. Sarah Lawrence College, BA.
PICTURES: Out of Justice, Paradise Road, Traveller, A Price Below Rubies, The Newton Boys, Dinosaur.
TELEVISION: *Series*: ER (Emmy Award, 1995). *Guest*: The Larry Sanders Show, Homicide: Life on the Street, Murder She Wrote, Law & Order.

MARGULIES, STAN
Producer. b. New York, NY, Dec. 14, 1920. e. De Witt Clinton H.S., NYU, B.S., June, 1940. Army Air Force, May, 1942; p.r., Air Force and the Infantry, wrote service magazines, newspapers including Yank; spec. feature writer & asst. Sunday editor, Salt Lake City Tribune; publicist, RKO Studios, Hollywood, March, 1947; continued publicity work at CBS-Radio, 20th Century-Fox, Walt Disney Productions. Bryna Films, 1955; became vice-pres., 1958; also served exec. prod., TV series, Tales of the Vikings; prod. asst., Spartacus.
PICTURES: 40 Pounds of Trouble, Those Magnificent Men in Their Flying Machines, Don't Just Stand There, The Pink Jungle, If It's Tuesday This Must Be Belgium, I Love My Wife, Willy Wonka and the Chocolate Factory, One Is a Lonely Number, Visions of Eight.
TELEVISION: *Movies*: The 500 Pound Jerk, She Lives, The Morning After, Unwed Father, Men of the Dragon, I Will Fight No More Forever, Roots (Emmy Award, 1977), Roots: The Next Generations (Emmy Award, 1979), Moviola, Agatha Christie's Murder Is Easy, The Thorn Birds, Agatha Christie's A Caribbean Mystery, A Killer in the Family, Sparkling Cyanide, The Mystic Warrior, A Bunny's Tale, Out on a Limb, Broken Angel, Crossing to Freedom, Separate But Equal (Emmy Award, 1991).

MARILL, ALVIN H.
Writer. b. Brockton, MA, Jan. 10, 1934. e. Boston U., 1955. Dir. music programming, writer/prod., WNAC, Boston 1961-65; dir. music prog., WRFM, NY 1966-67; publicity writer, RCA Records 1967-72; sr. writer/editor, RCA Direct Marketing 1972-80; partner, TLK Direct Marketing 1977-80; mgr., A & R Administration, RCA Direct Marketing 1980-83; exec. editor, CBS TV (1984-88); editor, Carol Publ. Group (1988-94); v.p., Sandal Enterprises (1994-present). Television editor, Films in Review 1973-84. Writer/researcher: The Great Singers (record/tape collections). Jury member: 1983 Locarno Film Fest. Television Movie Hall of Fame.
AUTHOR: Samuel Goldwyn Presents, Robert Mitchum on the Screen, The Films of Anthony Quinn, The Films of Sidney Poitier, Katharine Hepburn: A Pictorial Study, Boris Karloff—A Pictorial Biography, Errol Flynn—A Pictorial Biography, The Complete Films of Edward G. Robinson, More Theatre: Stage to Screen to Television, Movies Made for Television 1964-96, The Films of Tyrone Power; Editor: Moe Howard & The 3 Stooges, The Films of Tommy Lee Jones, The Ultimate John Wayne Trivia Book. Assoc. editor: Leonard Maltin's Movie & Video Guide.

MARIN, CHEECH (RICHARD)
Actor, Writer. b. Los Angeles, CA, July 13, 1946. e. California State U, B.S. Teamed with Tommy Chong in improvisational group, City Works (Vancouver). Comedy recordings include Sleeping Beauty, Cheech and Chong Big Bama, Los Cochinos, The Wedding Album (Grammy Award), Get Out of My Room.
PICTURES: Up in Smoke (also co-s.p.), Cheech and Chong's Next Movie (also co-s.p.), Cheech and Chong's Nice Dreams (also co-s.p.), Things Are Tough All Over (also co-s.p.), It Came from Hollywood, Still Smokin' (also co-s.p.), Yellowbeard, Cheech and Chong's The Corsican Brothers (also co-s.p.), After Hours, Echo Park, Born in East L.A. (also s.p., dir.), Fatal Beauty, Oliver & Company (voice), Troop Beverly Hills (cameo), Ghostbusters II (cameo), Rude Awakening, Far Out Man, The Shrimp on the Barbie, FernGully... The Last Rainforest (voice), A Million to Juan, The Lion King (voice), Desperado, From Dusk Till Dawn, The Great White Hype, Tin Cup, Paulie, Picking up the Pieces, Luminarias.
TELEVISION: *Series*: The Golden Palace, Nash Bridges. *Movie*: The Cisco Kid. *Specials*: Get Out of My Room (also dir., songs), Charlie Barnett—Terms of Enrollment.

MARK, LAURENCE M.
Producer, Executive. b. New York, NY. e. Wesleyan U., B.A.; NYU, M.A. Started career as trainee and publicist for United Artists; also asst. to prod. on Lenny, Smile. Joined Paramount Pictures as mktg./prod. liaison dir. and then exec. dir., pub. for m.p. division in NY. Named v.p., prod./mktg. at Paramount Studio; 1980, v.p., west coast mktg.; 1982 promoted to post as v.p., prod. 1984 (projects incl. Trading Places, Terms of Endearment, Falling in Love, Lady Jane); joined 20th Century-Fox as exec. v.p., prod. (projects incl. The Fly, Broadcast News); 1986, established Laurence Mark Productions at Fox; 1989 moved headquarters to Walt Disney Studios.
THEATER: Brooklyn Laundry (L.A.), Big (N.Y.).
PICTURES: *Producer/Exec. prod.*: Black Widow, Working Girl , My Stepmother is an Alien, Cookie, Mr. Destiny, True Colors , One Good Cop, The Adventures of Huck Finn, Gunmen, Sister Act 2: Back in the Habit, Cutthroat Island, Tom & Huck, Jerry Maguire, Romy & Michele's High School Reunion, Deep Rising, As Good As It Gets, The Object of My Affection, Simon Birch.
TELEVISION: *Exec. prod.*: Sweet Bird of Youth, Oliver Twist.

MARKHAM, MONTE
Actor. b. Manatee, FL, June 21, 1938. e. U. of Georgia. Military service in Coast Guard after which joined resident theatre co. at Stephens College, MO, where he also taught acting. Joined Actor's Workshop Theatre, San Francisco, for three years. Made TV debut in Mission: Impossible episode. June, 1992 formed Perpetual Motion Films with Adam Friedman.
THEATER: *B'way*: Irene (Theatre World Award), Same Time Next Year.
PICTURES: Hour of the Gun, Guns of the Magnificent Seven, One Is a Lonely Number, Midway, Airport '77, Ginger in the Morning, Off the Wall, Jake Speed, Hot Pursuit, Defense Play (also dir.), Neon City (also dir.), At First Sight.
TELEVISION: *Series*: The Second Hundred Years, Mr. Deeds Goes to Town, The New Perry Mason, Dallas, Rituals, Baywatch (also dir. episodes), Melrose Place, Campus Cops. *Movies*: Death Takes a Holiday, The Astronaut, Visions, Hustling, Ellery Queen, Relentless, Drop-Out Father, Hotline, Baywatch: Panic at Malibu Pier. *Host-narrator-prod.-dir.*: Air Combat, Combat at Sea, Master of War, Epic Biographies, The Great Ships.

MARKLE, PETER
Director. b. Danville, PA, Sept. 24, 1946.
PICTURES: The Personals (also s.p., photog.), Hot Dog ... The Movie, Youngblood (also co-story, s.p.), Bat-21, Wagons East!, The Last Days of Frankie the Fly, A Night at the Roxbury.
TELEVISION: *Movies*: Desperate, Nightbreaker, Breaking Point, El Diablo, Through the Eyes of a Killer, Jake Lassiter: Justice on the Bayou, White Dwarf, Mob Justice. *Series*: Millenium.

MARKOWITZ, ROBERT
Director. b. Irvington, NJ, Feb. 7, 1935. e. Boston Univ. Mostly on TV before theatrical debut with Voices, 1979.
TELEVISION: *Movies*: Children of the Night, Phantom of the Opera, The Deadliest Season, The Storyteller, Kojak: The Belarus File, My Mother's Secret Life, Pray TV, A Long Way Home, Alex: The Life of a Child, Adam: His Song Continues, The Wall, A Cry for Help: The Tracey Thurman Story, Too Young to Die, A Dangerous Life, Decoration Day, Love Lies and Murder, Afterburn, Overexposed, Murder in the Heartland, Because Mommy Works, The Tuskegee Airmen. *Special*: Twilight Zone: Rod Serling's Lost Classics.

MARKS, ALFRED
O.B.E. Actor-Comedian. b. London, 1921. TV, own series, Alfred Marks Time with wife, comedienne Paddie O'Neil.
PICTURES: Desert Mice, There Was a Crooked Man, Weekend with Lulu, The Frightened City, She'll Have to Go, Scream and Scream Again, Our Miss Fred, Valentino, Sleeps Six.
TELEVISION: Blanding's Castle, Hobson's Choice, Paris 1900, The Memorandum.

MARKS, ARTHUR
Producer, Director, Writer, Film Executive. b. Los Angeles, CA, Aug. 2, 1927. At 19 began work at MGM Studios as production messenger. Became asst. dir. in 1950, youngest dir. member of Directors Guild of Amer., 1957. President and board member of Arthur Prod., Inc.
PICTURES: Togetherness (prod., dir., s.p.), Class of '74 (dir., s.p.), Bonnie's Kids (dir., s.p.), Roommates (dir., s.p.), Detroit 9000 (prod., dir.), The Centerfold Girls (prod., dir.), A Woman For All Men (dir.), Wonder Woman (exec. prod.), The Candy Snatchers (exec. prod.), Bucktown (dir.), Friday Foster (prod., dir.), J.D.'s Revenge (prod., dir.), Monkey Hustle (prod., dir.). Writer: Empress of the China Seas, Gold Stars, Mean Intentions, Hot Times, Starfire, There's A Killer in Philly.
TELEVISION: *Series*: Perry Mason series (1961-66; prod., also dir. of over 100 episodes); writer-dir. of numerous TV shows including: I Spy, Mannix, Starsky & Hutch, Dukes of Hazzard, Young Daniel Boone, My Friend Tony.

MARKS, RICHARD E.
Executive. e. UCLA; UCLA Sch. of Law. 1978-82, v.p., legal & business affairs for Ziegler/Diskant Literary Agency. Joined Paramount Pictures 1984 as sr. atty. for Network TV Div., as project atty. for Family Ties, Cheers, etc. 1985, named sr. atty. for M.P. Group for The Golden Child, Beverly Hills Cop II, etc.; 1987 joined Weintraub Ent. Group as v.p. business affairs; m.p. div. 1990; counsel for Disney projects such as The Rocketeer, Beauty and the Beast. 1991, joined Media Home Entertainment as sr. v.p. in charge of all business and legal affairs. 1994, joined the Kushner-Locke Company as sr. v.p., business affairs for feature division; currently exec. v.p., gen. counselor.

MARS, KENNETH
Actor. b. Chicago, IL, 1936.
PICTURES: The Producers, Butch Cassidy and the Sundance Kid, Desperate Characters, What's Up Doc?, The Parallax View, Young Frankenstein, Night Moves, The Apple Dumpling Gang Rides Again, Full Moon High, Yellowbeard, Protocol, Prince Jack, Beer, Fletch, Radio Days, For Keeps?, Illegally Yours, Rented Lips, Police Academy 6: City Under Siege, The Little Mermaid (voice), Shadows and Fog, We're Back (voice), The Land Before Time II: The Great Valley Adventure (voice), Thumbelina (voice), Land Before Time III, Rough Magic, Citizen Ruth.
TELEVISION: *Series*: He & She, The Don Knotts Show, Sha Na Na, The Carol Burnett Show (1979). *Guest:* Facts of Life, Murder She Wrote, The Twilight Zone, Garfield & Friends, Civil Wars, Tom, Star Trek Deep Space Nine, The Drew Carrey Show and many others. *Movies*: Second Chance, Guess Who's Sleeping in My Bed?, Someone I Touched, The New Original Wonder Woman, Before and After, The Rules of Marriage, Get Smart Again.

MARSH, JEAN
Actress, Writer. b. London, England, July 1, 1934. NY stage debut in Much Ado About Nothing, 1959. As a child appeared in films: Tales of Hoffman; as principal dancer in Where's Charley. Co-creator, co-author and starred as Rose, in Upstairs, Downstairs.
THEATER: *B'way*: Travesties, The Importance of Being Earnest, Too True to Be Good, My Fat Friend, Whose Life Is It Anyway?, Blithe Spirit.
PICTURES: Cleopatra, Unearthly Stranger, The Limbo Line, Frenzy, Dark Places, The Eagle Has Landed, The Changeling, Return to Oz, Willow.
TELEVISION: Upstairs Downstairs (Emmy Award, 1975), Nine to Five, The Grover Monster, A State Dinner with Queen Elizabeth II, Mad About the Boy: Noel Coward—A Celebration, Habeas Corpus, Uncle Vanya, Twelfth Night, Pygmalion, On the Rocks Theatre, The Corsican Brothers, Master of the Game, Danny, the Champion of the World, Act of Will, A Connecticut Yankee in King Arthur's Court.

MARSHALL, ALAN
Producer. b. London, England, Aug. 12, 1938. Co-founder Alan Parker Film Company, 1970. Formerly film editor. Received Michael Balcon Award, British Acad., Outstanding Contribution to Cinema, 1985.
PICTURES: Bugsy Malone, Midnight Express, Fame, Shoot the Moon, Pink Floyd: The Wall, Another Country (Cannes Film Fest. Award, 1984), Birdy (Special Jury Award, Cannes Film Fest., 1985), Angel Heart, Homeboy, Jacob's Ladder, Basic Instinct, Cliffhanger, Showgirls, Starship Troopers, The Hollow Man.
TELEVISION: No Hard Feelings, Our Cissy, Footsteps.

MARSHALL, FRANK
Producer, Director. b. 1954. Raised in Newport Beach, CA. Worked on first feature film in 1967 while still a student at UCLA. Protege of Peter Bogdanovich, working on his production crew and as asst. on Targets, location manager on The Last Picture Show, What's Up Doc?, assoc. prod. on Paper Moon, Daisy Miller, Nickelodeon, etc. Line prod. on Orson Welles' The Other Side of the Wind (unreleased) and Martin Scorsese's The Last Waltz. Worked with Walter Hill on The Driver (assoc. prod.) and The Warriors (exec. prod.). Began collaboration with Steven Spielberg as prod. for Raiders of the Lost Ark. 1992, with wife and partner Kathleen Kennedy formed The Kennedy/Marshall Company.
PICTURES: Raiders of the Lost Ark (prod.), Poltergeist (prod.), E.T.: The Extra-Terrestrial (prod. supvr.). *Exec. Producer*: Twilight Zone—The Movie, Indiana Jones and the Temple of Doom, Fandango, Gremlins, The Goonies, Back to the Future (also 2nd unit dir.), The Color Purple (prod.), Young Sherlock Holmes, An American Tail, Innerspace, The Money Pit (prod.), Empire of the Sun (prod.), Who Framed Roger Rabbit (prod., 2nd unit dir.), The Land Before Time, Indiana Jones and the Last Crusade, Dad, Back to the Future Part II, Always (prod.), Joe Versus the Volcano, Back to the Future Part III, Gremlins II, Arachnophobia (also dir.), Cape Fear, An American Tail: Fievel Goes West, Hook (co-prod.), Noises Off (prod.), Alive (also dir.), Swing Kids, A Far Off Place, We're Back, Milk Money, Congo (also dir.), The Indian in the Cupboard, The Thief of Always, Snow Falling on Cedars.
TELEVISION: Amazing Stories (series exec. prod.), Roger Rabbit and the Secrets of Toontown (exec. prod.), Alive: The Miracle of the Andes (exec. prod.).

MARSHALL, GARRY
Producer, Director, Writer, Actor. r.n. Garry Marscharelli. b. New York, NY, Nov. 13, 1934. Sister is dir.-actress Penny Marshall. e. Northwestern U. Copy boy and reporter for NY Daily News while writing comedy material for Phil Foster, Joey Bishop. Was drummer in his own jazz band and successful stand-up comedian and playwright. Turned Neil Simon's play The Odd Couple into long running TV series (1970). Partner with Jerry Belson many years. *Playwright:* The Roast (with Belson, 1980), Wrong Turn at Lungfish (with Lowell Ganz, 1992; also dir., actor). *Autobiography:* Wake Me When It's Funny (1995).
PICTURES: *Writer-Producer*: How Sweet It Is, The Grasshopper. *Director:* Young Doctors in Love (also exec. prod.), The Flamingo Kid (also co-s.p.), Nothing in Common, Overboard, Beaches, Pretty Woman, Frankie and Johnny (also co-prod.), Exit to Eden, Dear God (also cameo), Runaway Bride (also cameo), The Other Sister (also story). *Actor:* Psych-Out, Mary Jane, The Escape Artist, Lost in America, Jumpin' Jack Flash, Soapdish, A League of Their Own, Hocus Pocus, With Friends Like These, This Space Between Us, Can't Be Heaven, Never Been Kissed.
TELEVISION: *Series Writer*: Jack Paar Show, Joey Bishop Show, Bill Dana Show, Danny Thomas Show, Lucy Show, Dick Van Dyke Show, I Spy, Sheriff Who??, Love, American Style. *Series creator/exec. prod./writer*: Hey Landlord! (also dir.), The Odd Couple, Barefoot in the Park, Me and the Chimp, The Little People, Happy Days, Laverne & Shirley, Angie. *Series exec. prod./writer*: Blansky's Beauties (also dir.), Who's Watching the Kids?, Mork and Mindy (also dir.), Joanie Loves Chachi. *Series exec. prod.*: The New Odd Couple, Nothing in Common. *Actor: Series* A League of Their Own, Murphy Brown. *Movie*: Evil Roy Slade (also co-prod., co-writer), The Twilight of the Golds, CHiPs '99. *Special*: The Last Shot.

MARSHALL, PENNY
Actress, Director. b. New York, NY, Oct. 15, 1942. Father: industrial filmmaker and Laverne and Shirley prod., Tony Marscharelli. Brother is prod.-dir. Garry Marshall. Daughter is actress Tracy Reiner. Dropped out of U. of New Mexico to teach dancing. Acted in summer stock and competed on The Original Amateur Hour before going to Hollywood to make TV debut in The Danny Thomas Hour (1967-68).
PICTURES: *Actress*: How Sweet It Is, The Savage Seven, The Grasshopper, 1941, Movers and Shakers, The Hard Way, Hocus Pocus, Odd Couple: Together Again, Get Shorty. *Director*: Jumpin' Jack Flash (debut, 1986), Big, Awakenings, A League of Their Own (also exec. prod.), Renaissance Man (also exec. prod.), The Preacher's Wife. *Prod.*: Calendar Girl (exec.), Getting Away with Murder, With Friends Like These, Saving Grace, Live from Baghdad.
TELEVISION: *Actress: Series*: The Bob Newhart Show, The Odd Couple, Friends and Lovers, Laverne and Shirley. *Guest*: Danny Thomas Hour, The Super, Happy Days, Comedy Zone, Chico and the Man. *Movies*: The Feminist and the Fuzz, Evil Roy Slade, The Couple Takes a Wife, The Crooked Hearts, Love Thy Neighbor, Let's Switch, More Than Friends, Challenge of a Lifetime, The Odd Couple: Together Again. *Specials*: Lily for President, The Laverne and Shirley Reunion. *Series Director*: Laverne and Shirley, Working Stiffs, Tracey Ullman Show, A League of Their Own (also prod.).

MARSHALL, PETER
Actor, TV Show Host. r.n. Pierre La Cock. b. Clarksburg, WV, March 30. Sister is actress Joanne Dru. Began career as NBC page in N.Y. Teamed with the late Tommy Noonan in comedy act for nightclubs, guesting on Ed Sullivan Show and other variety shows. In 1950, made Las Vegas stage debut and since has been headliner there and in Reno and Lake Tahoe. New York stage, in B'way musical Skyscraper. On London stage in H.M.S. Pinafore, Bye Bye Birdie. In La Cage aux Folles (national company and B'way), 42nd St. (Atlantic City), Rumors (natl. co.).
PICTURES: The Rookie, Swingin' Along (Double Trouble), Ensign Pulver, The Cavern, Americathon, Annie.
TELEVISION: *Host*: Two of the Most (local N.Y. show), The Hollywood Squares, NBC Action Playhouse, The Peter Marshall Variety Show, Mrs. America Pageant, Mrs. World.

MARSHALL, MERYL
Executive. b. Los Angeles, CA, Oct. 16, 1949. e. UCLA, BA sociology, 1971. JD Loyola Marymount U., 1974. Deputy pub. defender, LA County, 1975-77. Partner, Markman & Markman, 1978-79. NBC: Sr. Atty., 1979-80. Dir. programs/contracts/bus. affairs, 1980; asst. gen'l counsel, 1980-82; VP, compliance/practices, 1982-87. VP prog. affairs, Group W Prods., 1987-92. Founder, Two Oceans Ent. Grp., 1992. Pres., Acad. of TV Arts and Sciences, 1997-.

MARTEL, GENE
Producer, Director. b. New York, NY, June 19, 1906. e. City Coll. of New York , U. of Alabama, Sorbonne, Paris. Newspaperman, New York and Birmingham, AL; dancer, actor, choreographer, dir. Broadway; prod. dir., many documentaries; films for State Dept., others; dir. for Paramount Pictures. Joined Princess Pictures 1952 to make films in Europe; formed own co., Martel Productions Inc., 1956.
PICTURES: Check-mate, Double-Barrelled Miracle, The Lie, Double Profile, Sergeant and the Spy, Black Forest, Eight Witnesses, Fire One, Phantom Caravan, Doorway to Suspicion, Diplomatic Passport, Immediate Disaster.

MARTIN, ANDREA
Actress. b. Portland, ME, Jan. 15, 1947.
THEATRE: *NY*: My Favorite Year (Tony Award & Theatre World Award), The Merry Wives of Windsor.
PICTURES: Cannibal Girls, Soup for One, Club Paradise, Rude Awakening, Worth Winning, Too Much Sun, Stepping Out, All I Want for Christmas, Ted and Venus,. Bogus, Anastasia, Wag the Dog, The Rugrats Movie (voice), Believe.
TELEVISION: *Series*: Second City TV, SCTV Network 90 (2 Emmy Awards for writing), The Martin Short Show, Life and Stuff, Damon. *Special*: In Search of Dr. Seuss. *Movie:* Harrison Bergeron.

MARTIN, DEWEY
Actor. b. Katy, TX, Dec. 8, 1923. e. U. of Georgia. U.S. Navy, WWII. In stock before film debut in 1949.
PICTURES: Knock on Any Door, Kansas Raiders, The Thing, The Big Sky, Tennessee Champ, Prisoner of War, Men of the Fighting Lady, Land of the Pharaohs, Desperate Hours, The Proud and Profane, 10,000 Bedrooms, Battle Ground, The Longest Day, Savage Sam, Seven Alone.
TELEVISION: G.E. Theatre, U.S. Steel, Playhouse 90, Playwrights 56, Daniel Boone, Doc Holliday, Wheeler and Murdoch, Outer Limits, Twilight Zone.

MARTIN, EDWIN DENNIS
Executive. b. Columbus, GA, Jan. 30, 1920. e. U. of Georgia, B.S., 1940. Past pres., Martin Theatre Cos.; past pres., TOA, International, past pres., Variety. Retired.

MARTIN, GARY
Executive. b. Santa Monica, CA, Aug, 14, 1944. e. CSU Northridge, 1962-65. V.P. of production, Columbia Pictures, 1984-86; exec. v.p., production, 1986-88. Pres. of production admin., Columbia Pictures and TriStar Pictures 1988-95, Columbia TriStar Motion Pictures, 1995-. Member, AMPAS., D.G.A. 1994, named pres. of prod. admn. for Columbia/TriStar.

MARTIN, JUDSON W.
Executive. Began career with Pricewaterhouse Coopers in Calgary, Alberta, Canada, 1979. Twenty years in various mgmt roles with affiliates of EdperBrascan Corp., including president & CEO, Trilon Securities Corp., v.p., corporate finance & treasurer, Trizec Hahn; senior exec. v.p., CEO, and director, MDC Corp. Currently director and non-exec. chairman, Board of Intl. Properties Group, Ltd.; director, TGS Properties, Ltd.. exec. v.p. & CFO, Alliance Atlantis Communications, Inc.

MARTIN, MILLICENT
Actress, Singer. b. Romford, England, June 8, 1934. Toured U.S. in The Boy Friend, 1954-57.
THEATER: Expresso Bongo, The Crooked Mile, Our Man Crichton, Tonight at 8:30, The Beggar's Opera, Puss 'n Boots, Aladdin, Peter Pan, The Card, Absurd Person Singular, Aladdin, Side by Side by Sondheim, King of Hearts, Move Over Mrs. Markham, Noises Off, One Into Two, 42nd Street (N.Y. & L.A.), The Cemetery Club, Shirley Valentine, The Boyfriend, Noel, Follies, The Rivals, The Rise and Fall of Little Voice.
TELEVISION: *Series*: The Picadilly Palace, From a Bird's Eye View, Mainly Millicent, Millie, Dowtown. Also: Harry Moorings, Kiss Me Kate, London Palladium Color Show, Tom Jones, Englebert Humperdinck show, That Was the Week That Was, LA Law, Max Headroom, Newhart, Murphy Brown, Coach.
PICTURES: Libel, The Horsemasters (tv in U.S.), The Girl on the Boat, Nothing But the Best, Those Magnificent Men in Their Flying Machines, Alfie, Stop the World I Want To Get Off, Invasion Quartet.

MARTIN, PAMELA SUE
Actress. b. Westport, CT, Jan. 15, 1953. Did modelling and TV commercials before entering films.
PICTURES: To Find a Man, The Poseidon Adventure, Buster and Billie, Our Time, The Lady in Red, Torchlight (also assoc. prod. & s.p.), Flicks, A Cry in the Wild.
TELEVISION: *Series*: Nancy Drew Mysteries, Hardy Boys Mysteries, Dynasty, The Star Games (host). *Movies*: The Girls of Huntington House, The Gun and the Pulpit, Human Feelings, Bay Coven.

MARTIN, STEVE
Actor, Writer. b. Waco, TX, Aug. 14, 1945. e. Long Beach Col., UCLA. Raised in Southern California. Worked at Disneyland, teaching himself juggling, magic and the banjo. Became writer for various TV comedy shows, incl. Smothers Brothers Comedy Hour (Emmy Award for writing, 1968-69), Glen Campbell Show, Sonny & Cher. Co-writer for special Van Dyke and Company. Wrote and starred in Acad. Award nominated short The Absent-Minded Waiter. *Author:* Cruel Shoes (1980). *Albums:* Let's Get Small (Grammy Award, 1977), A Wild and Crazy Guy (Grammy Award, 1978), Comedy Is Not Pretty, The Steve Martin Brothers. Gold Record for single King Tut.
THEATER: *Actor*: Waiting for Godot (Off-B'way debut, 1988). *Author*: Picasso at the Lapin Agile (regional, 1993), WASP (Off-B'way).
PICTURES: Sgt. Pepper's Lonely Hearts Club Band (debut, 1978), The Kids Are Alright, The Muppet Movie, The Jerk (also co-s.p.), Pennies From Heaven, Dead Men Don't Wear Plaid (also co-s.p.), The Man With Two Brains (also co-s.p.), The Lonely Guy, All of Me (NY Film Critics & Natl. Board of Review Awards, 1984), Movers and Shakers, Three Amigos! (also co-s.p., exec. prod.), Little Shop of Horrors, Roxanne (also s.p., exec. prod.; Natl. Society of Film Critics & L.A. Film Critics Awards for actor, WGA Award for adapt. s.p., 1987), Planes Trains & Automobiles, Dirty Rotten Scoundrels, Parenthood, My Blue Heaven, L.A. Story (also s.p., co-exec. prod.), Father of the Bride, Grand Canyon, Housesitter, Leap of Faith, A Simple Twist of Fate (also s.p., exec. prod.), Mixed Nuts, Father of the Bride 2, Sgt. Bilko, The Spanish Prisoner, The Prince of Egypt (voice), Joe Gould's Secret, The Out-of-Towners, Bowfinger (also s.p.).
TELEVISION: *Series*: Andy Williams Presents Ray Stevens, The Ken Berry "WOW" Show, Half the George Kirby Comedy Hour, The Sonny and Cher Comedy Hour, The Smothers Brothers Show (1975), The Johnny Cash Show. *Guest*: The Tonight Show, Cher, The Carol Burnett Show, The Simpsons (voice), The Muppet Show, Steve Allen Comedy Hour. *Specials*: HBO On Location: Steve Martin, Steve Martin—A Wild and Crazy Guy, Comedy Is Not Pretty, All Commercials: A Steve Martin Special, Steve Martin's Best Show Ever, The Winds of Whoopie, Texas 150--A Celebration, The Smothers Brothers Comedy Hour 20th Reunion, Learned Pigs and Fireproof Women. *Producer*: Domestic Life (series). *Pilot*: Leo & Liz in Beverly Hills (writer, creator, co-prod., dir.). *Movies*: The Jerk Too (exec. prod. only), And the Band Played On.

MARTIN, TONY
Singer, Musician, Actor. r.n. Alvin Morris. b. Oakland, CA, Dec. 25, 1913. e. Oakland H.S., St. Mary's Coll. m. actress-dancer Cyd Charisse. Sang, played saxophone & clarinet in high school band, engaged by nearby theatres for vaudeville; with Five Red Peppers, jazz group at 14 yrs.; two yrs. later with band, Palace Hotel, San Francisco; radio debut Walter Winchell program, 1932; joined Tom Gerund's band, World's Fair Chicago, 1933; played night clubs. First starring radio show, Tune Up Time (singer & emcee); on Burns and Allen program; own show for Texaco, Carnation Contented Hour. Recordings: Begin the Beguine, Intermezzo, The Last Time I Saw Paris, I'll See You in My Dreams, Domino, September Song, For Every Man There's a Woman.
PICTURES: Pigskin Parade (debut, 1936), Banjo on My Knee, Sing Baby Sing, Follow the Fleet, Back to Nature, The Holy Terror, Sing and Be Happy, You Can't Have Everything, Life Begins in College, Ali Baba Goes to Town, Sally Irene and Mary, Kentucky Moonshine, Thanks for Everything, Up the River, Winner Take All, Music in My Heart, Ziegfeld Girl, The Big Store, Till the Clouds Roll By, Casbah, Two Tickets to Broadway, Here Come the Girls, Easy to Love, Deep in My Heart, Hit the Deck, Quincannon—Frontier Scout, Let's Be Happy, Dear Mr. Wonderful.

MASLANSKY, PAUL
Producer. b. New York, NY, Nov. 23, 1933. e. Washington and Lee U., 1954. Moved to Europe performing as jazz musician in Paris, 1959-60. Entered film business with documentary, Letter from Paris. Asst. to prods. Charles Shneer and Irving Allen in England, Italy and Yugoslavia, 1961-62. In charge of physical prod. in Europe for UA, 1965-67.
PICTURES: Castle of the Living Dead, Revenge of the Blood Beast, Sudden Terror (Eye Witness), Raw Meat, Deathline, Sister of Satan, Big Truck, Poor Claire, Deathline, Sugar Hill (also dir.), Race With the Devil, Hard Times, The Blue Bird, Circle of Iron, Damnation Alley (co-prod.), When You Comin' Back Red Ryder (co-prod.), Hot Stuff, The Villain, Scavenger Hunt, The Salamander, Ruckus, Love Child, Police Academy, Police Academy 2: Their First Assignment, Return to Oz, Police Academy 3: Back in Training, Police Academy 4: Citizens on Patrol, Police Academy 5: Assignment Miami Beach, For Better or Worse (exec. prod.), Police Academy 6: City Under Siege, Ski Patrol (exec. prod.), Honeymoon Academy (exec. prod.). The Russia House, Cop and a Half, Police Academy: Mission to Moscow, Fluke.
TELEVISION: *Movie*: The Gun and the Pulpit. *Mini-Series*: King.

MASON, JACKIE
Comedian, Actor. b. Sheboygan, WI June 9, 1934. e. City College. Was a rabbi before becoming stand-up comedian. Records include The World According to Me! Has lectureship in his name at Oxford Univ. in England.
THEATER: Enter Solly Gold (1965), A Teaspoon Every Four Hours (Amer. National Theatre & Academy Theatre), Sex-a-Poppin (revue, prod. only), The World According to Me! (one-man show, special Tony Award, 1987), Jackie Mason: Brand New, Politically Incorrect.
PICTURES: Operation Delilah (debut, 1966), The Stoolie (also prod.), The Jerk, History of the World Part I, Caddyshack II.
TELEVISION: *Guest*: Steve Allen, Ed Sullivan, Jack Paar, Garry Moore, Perry Como and Merv Griffin Shows. Johnny Carson, Arsenio Hall, Evening at the Improv, Late Night with David Letterman. *Series*: Chicken Soup, Jackie Mason (synd.). *Specials*: Jack Paar is Alive and Well!, The World According to Me! (ACE Award), Jackie Mason on Broadway (Emmy Award for Writing).

MASON, JOHN DUDLEY
Executive. b. Ashland, KY, Oct 29, 1949. e. Amherst Coll., B.A., cum laude, 1971; Claremont Graduate Sch. and University Center, M.A., 1973; Amos Tuck Sch. of Business Administration, Dartmouth Coll., M.B.A., 1978. Program officer, National Endowment for the Humanities, 1972-76; analyst (1978-79), asst. mgr. (1979-80), mgr. (1980) strategic planning, Consolidated Rail Corp.; Consultant, Frito-Lay, Division, PepsiCo (1980-82); mgr, corporate planning, Dun & Bradstreet Corp. (1982-86); finance dir., anti-piracy (1986-90), v.p. finance, anti-piracy (1990-92), Motion Picture Association of America, Inc. Chmn., New Century Artists' Mgmt., 1990-98. Chmn., Finance Comm. and mem., bd. of dir. Association de Gestion Int'l. Collective des Oeuvres Audiovisuelles (AGICOA) 1987-88. Dir., Instituto Venezolano de Representacion Cinematografica (INVERECI), Caracas, Venezuela (1988-92). Dir.: Foundation for the Protection of Film & Video Works (FVWP), Taipei, Taiwan (1987-92). Dir. sec. Korean Federation Against Copyright Theft, 1990-92; Dir., Japan & Intl. M.P. Copyright Assn., Tokyo, 1990-92; Trustee and Treasurer, Design Industries Foundation for AIDS, 1990-94. Mng. dir., B.L. Nickerson & Associates, 1997-present.

MASON, KENNETH M.
Executive. b. Rochester, NY; Sept. 21, 1917. e. Washington and Jefferson Coll. (BA, 1938); U. of Rochester, graduate work; Dr. of Laws (H), Washington & Jefferson Coll., 1989. Began career with Eastman Kodak Co. in Kodak Park cine processing dept. in 1935; transferred following year to film dev. dept., Kodak Research Lab. Later joined film planning dept., remaining there until entering U.S. Navy in 1943. Returned to Kodak in 1946 as staff engineer in Kodak Office motion picture film dept. 1950 appt. mgr. of Midwest Division, of M.P. Film Dept.; became gen. mgr., Midwest Division, m.p. products sales dept. in 1963; named sls. mgr. of NYC region in 1965; appt. regional sls. mgr., Pacific Southern Region, Hollywood, in 1970; 1974 appt. mgr., product programs and research, Motion Picture and Audiovisual Markets Division, Kodak Office; 1974 named gen. mgr. of that division. Elected asst. v.p. of co., 1974, then v.p., 1978. Retired 1982. Former chmn., Inter-Society Committee for the Enhancement of Theatrical Presentation. Member, Trustee emeritus, Board of Trustees of Washington and Jefferson Coll. (and former chmn); past pres. of Society of Motion Picture & Television Engineers and honorary member; honorary fellow of British Kinematograph Sound & Television Society; mem. of University Film & Video Assn., Motion Picture Academy, American Society of Cinematographers. Board of dir.: Univ. Film & Video Foundation.

MASON, MARSHA
Actress. b. St. Louis. April 3, 1942. e. Webster Coll. Came to N.Y. to continue dramatic studies and embark on theatre career. Member of American Conservatory Theatre, San Francisco.

THEATER: The Deer Park, Cactus Flower, The Indian Wants the Bronx, Happy Birthday Wanda June, King Richard III, Cactus Flower, Private Lives, You Can't Take It With You, Cyrano de Bergerac, A Doll's House, The Merchant of Venice, The Crucible, Twelfth Night, The Good Doctor, Old Times, The Big Love, Lake No Bottom. Escape from Happiness, Amazing Grace, Night of the Iguana. *Director*: Juno's Swans.
PICTURES: Hot Rod Hullabaloo (debut, 1966), Blume in Love, Cinderella Liberty (Acad. Award nom.), Audrey Rose, The Goodbye Girl (Acad. Award nom.), The Cheap Detective, Promises in the Dark, Murder by Death, Max Dugan Returns, Chapter Two (Acad. Award nom.), Only When I Laugh (Acad. Award nom.), Max Dugan Returns, Heartbreak Ridge, Stella, Drop Dead Fred, I Love Trouble, Nick of Time, 2 Days in the Valley.
TELEVISION: *Series*: Love of Life, Sibs, Frazier. *Specials*: Brewsie and Willie, The Good Doctor, Cyrano de Bergerac. Movies: Lois Gibbs and the Love Canal, Surviving, Trapped in Silence, The Image, Dinner at Eight, Broken Trust. *Dir.*: Little Miss Perfect.

MASSEN, OSA
Actress. b. Denmark, Copenhagen. Jan. 13, 1916.
PICTURES: Honeymoon in Bali, Honeymoon for Three, A Woman's Face, Accent on Love, You'll Never Get Rich, The Devil Pays Off, Iceland, Jack London, Cry of the Werewolf, Tokyo Rose, Strange Journey, Night Unto Night, Deadline at Dawn, Gentleman Misbehaves, Rocketship XM, Outcasts of the City.

MASSEY, ANNA
Actress. b. Sussex, England, Aug. 11, 1937. Daughter of late actor Raymond Massey. Brother is actor Daniel Massey. On London stage in The Reluctant Debutante (debut, 1958), The Prime of Jean Brodie, Slag, The Importance of Being Earnest, Spoiled, Doctor's Delimma, School for Scandal, With National Theatre, 1989.
PICTURES: Gideon of Scotland Yard, Peeping Tom, Bunny Lake Is Missing, DeSade, The Looking Glass War, David Copperfield (TV in U.S.), Frenzy, A Doll's House, Vault of Horror, A Little Romance, Sweet William, Another Country, The Chain, Five Days One Summer, Foreign Body, Mountains of the Moon, La Couleur du Vent, The Tall Guy, Killing Dad, Impromptu, Haunted.
TELEVISION: Remember the Germans, Wicked Woman, The Corn Is Green, Sakharov, Hotel Du Lac (BAFTA Award), A Hazard of Hearts, Around the World in 80 Days, Tears in the Rain, The Man from the Pru.

MASTERS, BEN
Actor. b. Corvallis, OR, May 6, 1947. e. Univ. of Oregon.
THEATER: The Cherry Orchard, Waltz of the Toreadors, Plenty, Captain Brassbound's Conversion, The Boys in the Band, Eden Court, What the Butler Saw, The White Whore and the Bit Player, Key Exchange.
PICTURES: Mandingo, All That Jazz, Key Exchange, Dream Lover, Making Mr. Right.
TELEVISION: *Series*: Heartbeat. *Guest*: Barnaby Jones, Kojack. *Movies*: One of Our Own, The Shadow Box, The Neighborhood, Illusions, The Deliberate Stranger, Street of Dreams, Cruel Doubt, Running Mates, A Twist of the Knife, A Time to Heal, Lady Killer. *Mini-Series*: Loose Change, Celebrity, Noble House.

MASTERSON, MARY STUART
Actress. b. Los Angeles, CA, June 28, 1966. Daughter of writer-dir.-actor Peter Masterson and actress Carlin Glynn. e. Goddard Col. Made film debut at age 8 in The Stepford Wives (1975), which featured her father. Spent summer at Stage Door Manor in Catskills; two summers at Sundance Inst. Studied acting with Gary Swanson. Member of the Actor's Studio. Off-off B'way debut in Been Taken. Off-B'way debut in Lily Dale followed by The Lucky Spot (Manhattan Theatre Club). Regional: Moonlight and Valentines, Three Sisters.
PICTURES: The Stepford Wives (debut, 1975), Heaven Help Us, At Close Range, My Little Girl, Some Kind of Wonderful, Gardens of Stone, Mr. North, Chances Are, Immediate Family (Natl. Board of Review Award, 1989), Funny About Love, Fried Green Tomatoes, Mad at the Moon, Married to It, Benny & Joon, Bad Girls, Radioland Murders, Heaven's Prisoners, Bed of Roses, Dogtown, On the Second Day of Christmas, The Postman, The Florentine, Digging to China, The Book of Stars.
TELEVISION: *Movie*: Love Lives On, Lily Dale. *Guest*: Amazing Stories (Go to the Head of the Class).

MASTERSON, PETER
Actor, Writer, Director. r.n. Carlos Bee Masterson, Jr. b. Houston, TX, June 1, 1934. m. actress Carlin Glynn. Daughter is actress Mary Stuart Masterson. e. Rice U., Houston, BA. 1957. NY stage debut, Call Me By My Rightful Name, 1961.
THEATER: Marathon '33, Blues for Mr. Charlie, The Trial of Lee Harvey Oswald, The Great White Hope, That Championship Season, The Poison Tree, The Best Little Whorehouse in Texas (co-author, dir.), The Last of the Knucklemen (dir.).
PICTURES: *Actor*: Ambush Bay (debut, 1965), Counterpoint, In the Heat of the Night, Tomorrow, The Exorcist, Man on a Swing, The Stepford Wives, Gardens of Stone. *Writer*: The Best Little Whore House in Texas. *Director*: The Trip to Bountiful, Full Moon in Blue Water, Blood Red, Night Game, Convicts, The Only Thrill.
TELEVISION: Camera Three, Pueblo; The Quinns; A Question of Guilt.

MASTORAKIS, NICO
Writer, Director, Producer. b. Athens, Greece, 1941. Writer of novels and screenplays, including Fire Below Zero, and Keepers of the Secret (co-author). Pres. Omega Entertainment Ltd. since 1978.
PICTURES: *Writer/dir./prod.*: The Time Traveller, Blind Date, Sky High, The Zero Boys, The Wind, Terminal Exposure, Nightmare at Noon, Glitch, Ninja Academy, Hired to Kill, In the Cool of the Night, At Random. Prod.: The Greek Tycoon, Red Tide, Grandmother's House, Darkroom, Bloodstone (prod., co-s.p.).

MASTRANTONIO, MARY ELIZABETH
Actress. b. Oak Park, IL, Nov. 17, 1958. e. U. of Illinois 1976-78 where she trained for opera. m. dir. Pat O'Connor. Worked as singer & dancer for summer at Opryland Theme Park in Nashville. Came to NY as understudy and vacation replacement as Maria in West Side Story revival.
THEATER: *NY*: Copperfield (1981), Oh Brother, Amadeus, Sunday in the Park With George (Playwright's Horizons), The Human Comedy, Henry V, The Marriage of Figaro, Measure for Measure, The Knife, Twelfth Night.
PICTURES: Scarface (debut, 1983), The Color of Money (Acad. Award nom.), Slamdance, The January Man, The Abyss, Fools of Fortune, Class Action, Robin Hood: Prince of Thieves, White Sands, Consenting Adults, A Day to Remember, Three Wishes, Two Bits, My Life So Far, Limbo, The Perfect Storm.
TELEVISION: *Mini-Series*: Mussolini: The Untold Story, Witness Protection. *Special*: Uncle Vanya (BBC).

MASUR, RICHARD
Actor. b. New York, NY, Nov. 20, 1948. Directed Oscar-nominated short, Love Struck, 1987. Pres., Screen Actors Guild, 1995.
THEATRE: *B'way*: The Changing Room.
PICTURES: Whiffs (debut, 1975), Bittersweet Love, Semi-Tough, Who'll Stop the Rain, Hanover Street, Scavenger Hunt, Heaven's Gate, I'm Dancing as Fast as I Can, The Thing, Timerider, Risky Business, Under Fire, Nightmares, The Mean Season, My Science Project, Head Office, Heartburn, The Believers, Walker, Rent-a-Cop, Shoot to Kill, License to Drive, Far from Home, Flashback, Going Under, My Girl, Encino Man, The Man Without a Face, Six Degrees of Separation, My Girl 2, Forget Paris, Multiplicity, Fire Down Below.
TELEVISION: *Series*: Hot L Baltimore, One Day at a Time, Empire. *Mini-Series*: East of Eden. *Movies*: Having Babies, Betrayal, Mr. Horn, Walking Through the Fire, Fallen Angel, Money on the Side, An Invasion of Privacy, The Demon Murder Case, Adam, John Steinbeck's The Winter of Our Discontent, Flight #90: Disaster on the Potomac, The Burning Bed, Obsessed With a Married Woman, Wild Horses, Embassy, Adam: His Song Continues, Roses Are for the Rich, Cast the First Stone, When the Bough Breaks, Settle the Score, Always Remember I Love You, Stephen King's IT, The Story Lady, And the Band Played On, Search for Grace, My Brother's Keeper, The Face on the Milk Carton, Hiroshima, It Was Him or Us, Undue Influence. *Director*: Torn Between Two Fathers (After School Special, DGA nom.).

MATARAZZO, HEATHER
Actress. b. Nov. 10, 1982.
PICTURES: Welcome to the Dollhouse, Arresting Gena, The Devil's Advocate, The Deli, Hurricane Streets, 54, The Hairy Bird, Getting to Know You, Cherry, Blue Moon, Scream 3, Company Man, The Princess Diaries.
TELEVISION: *Movies:* Our Guys: Outrage at Glen Ridge. *Series*: The Adventures of Pete & Pete, Roseanne, Now & Again. *Guest*: Townies, Roseanne, ER.

MATHESON, TIM
Actor. b. Los Angeles, CA, Dec. 31, 1947. e. California State U. Debut on TV at age 12 in Window on Main Street. At 19, contract player for Universal. 1985, turned to direction: St. Elsewhere episode and music videos. Set up production co. at Burbank Studios 1985; acted off-B'way in True West. With partner Daniel Grodnick bought National Lampoon from founder Matty Simons, becoming exec. officer and chmn. 1989; resigned in 1991.
PICTURES: Divorce American Style (debut, 1967), Yours Mine and Ours, How to Commit Marriage, Magnum Force, Almost Summer, National Lampoon's Animal House, Dreamer, The Apple Dumpling Gang Rides Again, 1941, House of God, A Little Sex, To Be or Not To Be, Up the Creek, Impulse, Fletch, Speed Zone, Drop Dead Fred, Solar Crisis, Black Sheep, A Very Brady Sequel, A Very Unlucky Leprechaun, She's All That.
TELEVISION: *Movies*: Owen Marshall: Counselor-at-Law, Lock Stock and Barrel, Hitched, Remember When, The Last Day, The Runaway Barge, The Quest, Mary White, Listen to Your Heart, Obsessed with a Married Woman, Blind Justice, Warm Hearts Cold Feet, Bay Coven, The Littlest Victims, Little White Lies, Buried Alive, Joshua's Heart, Stephen King's Sometimes They Come Back, The Woman Who Sinned, Quicksand: No Escape, Relentless: Mind of a Killer, Trial & Error, Dying to Love You, A Kiss to Die For, Robin Cook's Harmful Intent, Target of Suspicion, Breach of Conduct (dir., co-exec. prod. only), While Justice Sleeps, Fast Company, An Unfinished Affair,

Buried Alive 2, Sleeping with the Devil, Forever Love, Catch Me If You Can, Fishing with John. *Series:* Window on Main Street, Jonny Quest (voice), The Virginian, Bonanza, The Quest, Tucker's Witch, Just in Time (also co-exec. prod.), Charlie Hoover, The Legend of Calamity Jane (voice), The West Wing. *Pilot*: Nikki & Alexander. *Special*: Bus Stop.

MATHIS, SAMANTHA
Actress. b. New York, NY, 1971. Mother is actress Bibi Besch; grandmother was actress Gusti Huber. Began acting as teen landing role in tv pilot Aaron's Way at age 16.
PICTURES: The Bulldance (debut, 1988 in Yugoslav film), Pump Up the Volume, This Is My Life, FernGully ... The Last Rainforest (voice), Super Mario Bros., The Music of Chance, The Thing Called Love, Little Women, Jack and Sarah, How to Make an American Quilt, The American President, Broken Arrow, Waiting for Woody, Sweet Jane, Freak City, American Psycho.
TELEVISION: *Series*: Knightwatch, Harsh Realm. *Movies*: Cold Sassy Tree, To My Daughter, 83 Hours 'Til Dawn.

MATLIN, MARLEE
Actress. b. Morton Grove, IL, Aug. 24, 1965. e. John Hersey H.S., Chicago, public school with special education program for deaf; William Rainey Harper Coll., majoring in criminal justice. Performed at Children's Theatre of the Deaf in Des Plaines at age 8, playing many leading roles. As adult appeared in only one stage show. Theatrical film debut in Children of a Lesser God. Production company, Solo One Productions.
PICTURES: Children of a Lesser God (debut, 1986; Acad. Award, Golden Globe), Walker, The Player, The Linguini Incident, Hear No Evil, It's My Party, Snitch, Two Shades of Blue.
TELEVISION: *Series*: Reasonable Doubts, The Outer Limits, Picket Fences. *Movies*: Bridge to Silence, Against Her Will: The Carrie Buck Story, Dead Silence. *Specials*: Face the Hate, Meaning of Life, Free to Laugh, Creative Spirit, The Big Help, People In Motion (host). *Guest*: Sesame Street, Adventures in Wonderland, Picket Fences (Emmy Award nom.), Seinfeld (Emmy Award nom.).

MATTHAU, CHARLES
Director. b. New York, NY, Dec. 10, 1964. Son of actor Walter Matthau. e. U. of Southern California Film School. While at USC wrote and dir. The Duck Film, a silent comedy short (Golden Seal Award, London Amateur Film Fest. and C.I.N.E. Eagle Award.) Also dir. short, I Was a Teenage Fundraiser. President, The Matthau Company, organized 1990.
PICTURES: Doin' Time on Planet Earth. (nom. Saturn Award, best dir., Acad. of Science Fiction.), The Grass Harp (dir., prod.; Acad. of Family Films award, best dir., 1996)
TELEVISION: *Movie*: Mrs. Lambert Remembers Love (dir., prod.; Golden Eagle, Golden Medal & Houston Fest. Grand & Angel Awards, 1993).

MATTHAU, WALTER
Actor. b. New York, NY, Oct. 1, 1920. Served in Air Force WWII. Studied journalism at Columbia U. and acting at New Sch. for Social Research's dramatic workshop, 1946, then acted in summer stock.
THEATER: *B'way*: Anne of the Thousand Days (debut, 1948), Will Success Spoil Rock Hunter?, Once More With Feeling, Once There Was a Russian, A Shot in the Dark (Tony Award, 1962), The Odd Couple (Tony Award, 1965). LA: Juno and the Paycock.
PICTURES: The Kentuckian (debut, 1955), The Indian Fighter, Bigger Than Life, A Face in the Crowd, Slaughter on Tenth Avenue, King Creole, The Voice in the Mirror, Ride a Crooked Trial, Onionhead, Strangers When We Meet, The Gangster Story (also dir.), Lonely Are the Brave, Who's Got the Action?, Island of Love, Charade, Ensign Pulver, Fail Safe, Goodbye Charlie, Mirage, The Fortune Cookie (Acad. Award, best supporting actor, 1966), A Guide for the Married Man, The Odd Couple, The Secret Life of an American Wife, Candy, Cactus Flower, Hello Dolly!, A New Leaf, Plaza Suite, Kotch (Acad. Award nom.), Pete n' Tillie, Charley Varrick, The Laughing Policeman, Earthquake, The Taking of Pelham One Two Three, The Front Page, The Sunshine Boys (Acad. Award nom.), The Bad News Bears, Casey's Shadow, House Calls, California Suite, Little Miss Marker (also exec. prod.), Hopscotch, First Monday in October, Buddy Buddy, I Ought to Be in Pictures, The Survivors, Movers and Shakers, Pirates, The Couch Trip, Il Piccolo Diavolo (The Little Devil), JFK, Dennis the Menace, Grumpy Old Men, I.Q., The Grass Harp, I'm Not Rappaport, Grumpier Old Men, Out to Sea, The Odd Couple II, The Marriage Fool.
TELEVISION: Many appearances 1952-65 on Philco-Goodyear Playhouse, Studio One, Playhouse 90, Kraft Theatre, Awake and Sing, Insight. *Series*: Tallahassee 7000 (1961). *Movies*: The Incident, Mrs. Lambert Remembers Love, Against Her Will: An Incident in Baltimore, Incident in a Small Town. *Special*: The Stingiest Man in Town (voice).
(d. July 1, 2000)

MAURA, CARMEN
Actress. b. Madrid, Spain, Sept. 15, 1945. e. Madrid's Catholic Inst. Daughter of ophthalmologist; faced family disapproval and custody battle when she became an actress. After working as cabaret entertainer, translator, and occasional voiceover dubber, met aspiring dir. Pedro Almodovar when they were cast in stage prod. of Sartre's Dirty Hands and starred in several of his films. Hosted weekly Spanish tv talk show Esta Noche.
PICTURES: El Hombre Oculto (debut, 1970), El Love Feroz, The Petition, Paper Tigers, Que Hace una Chica Como tu en un Sitio Como Este?, Pepi Luci Bom ... And Other Girls on the Heap (1980), El Cid Cabreador, Dark Habits, What Have I Done to Deserve This?, Extramuros, Se Infiel y No Mires Con Quien, Matador, Law of Desire, Women on the Verge of a Nervous Breakdown, Baton Rouge, How to Be a Woman and Not Die Trying, Ay Carmela!, Chatarra, Between Heaven and Earth, The Anonymous Queen, Shadows in a Conflict, Louis the Child King, How to Be Miserable and Enjoy It, The Flowers of My Secret, Una Pareja de Tres, El Palomo cojo, Happiness Is in the Field, Tortilla y cinema, Alliance cherche doigt, Elles.

MAUREY, NICOLE
Actress. b. France, Dec. 20, 1926. Studied dancing; French films include Blondine, Pamela, Le Cavalier Noir, Journal D'Un Cure De Campagne, Les Compagnes de la Nuit; many television and stage appearances in France; U.S. film debut in Little Boy Lost (1953).
PICTURES: Little Boy Lost, The Secret of the Incas, The Bold and the Brave, The Weapon, The Constant Husband, The Scapegoat, Me and the Colonel, The Jayhawkers, House of the Seven Hawks, High Time, Day of the Triffids, Why Bother to Knock?, The Very Edge.
TELEVISION: *U.S.* and *U.K.*: Tomorrow We Will Love, Casablanca, The Billion Franc Mystery, Champion House, I Thought They Died Years Ago.

MAXWELL, LOIS
Actress. r.n. Lois Hooker. b. Canada, 1927. Started in U.S. films in late 1940's before working in Italy then Britain. Has done numerous Canadian films for tv.
PICTURES: That Hagen Girl, The Decision of Christopher Blake, The Big Punch, The Dark Past, Kazan, Domani e troppa Tardi (Tomorrow Is Too Late), La Grande Speranza (The Great Hope), Aida, Passport to Treason, Satellite in the Sky, Time Without Pity, Lolita, Dr. No, Come Fly With Me, The Haunting, From Russia With Love, Goldfinger, Thunderball, Operation Kid Brother, You Only Live Twice, On Her Majesty's Secret Service, Adventure in Rainbow Country, The Adventurers, Diamonds Are Forever, Live and Let Die, The Man With the Golden Gun, The Spy Who Loved Me, Moonraker, Mr. Patman, For Your Eyes Only, Octopussy, A View to a Kill, Martha Ruth and Eddie.

MAXWELL, RONALD F.
Director, Writer, Producer. b. Jan. 5, 1947. e. NYU Coll. of Arts & Sciences; NYU Sch. of the Arts, Inst. of Film & Television Graduate Sch., M.F.A., 1970. Prod., dir,. for PBS Theater-in-America (1974-78).
PICTURES: *Director*: The Guest, Little Darlings, The Night the Lights Went Out in Georgia, Kidco, Gettysburg (also co-s.p.), Joan of Arc: The Virgin Warrior.
TELEVISION: *Director*: Sea Marks (also prod.), Verna: USO Girl (also prod.), Parent Trap II.

MAY, ELAINE
Actress, Director, Writer. b. Philadelphia, PA, April 21, 1932. Daughter is actress Jeannie Berlin. Father was prod.-dir. Jack Berlin whose travelling theater she acted with from age 6 to 10. Repertory theatre in Chicago, 1954; comedy team with Mike Nichols starting in 1955. Appeared with improvisational theater group, The Compass, Chicago. Co-starred in An Evening with Mike Nichols and Elaine May.
THEATRE: *Playwright*: A Matter of Position, Not Enough Rope, Hot Line, Better Point of Valour, Mr. Gogol & Mr. Preen, Hotline (Death Defying Acts).
PICTURES: Luv (actress), Enter Laughing (actress), A New Leaf (actress, dir., s.p.), Such Good Friends (s.p. as Esther Dale), The Heartbreak Kid (dir.), Mikey and Nicky (dir., s.p.), Heaven Can Wait (co-s.p.), California Suite (actress), Ishtar (dir., s.p.), In the Spirit (actress), The Birdcage (s.p.), Primary Colors (Acad, Award nom. for s.p. adapt.), Small Times Crooks.
TELEVISION: *Series regular*: Keep Talking (1958-59). *Guest*: Jack Paar, Omnibus, Dinah Shore Show, Perry Como, Laugh Lines.

MAY, JODHI
Actress. b. 1975.
PICTURES: A World Apart, Isabelle Eberhardt, Eminent Domain, The Last of the Mohicans, Sister My Sister, Second Best, The Scarlet Letter (voice), The Woodlanders, The Gambler.
TELEVISION: Max and Helen. *Mini-series*: Signs and Wonders.

MAYER, GERALD
Producer, Director. b. Montreal, Canada, 1919. Father was Jerry G. Mayer, mgr. MGM studio. e. Stanford U., journalism; corresp. for San Francisco Examiner; pres. Sigma Delta Chi, prof. journalism soc. Navy lieut., amphibious forces, WWII. Entered m.p. ind. in prod. dept. MGM studios; first dir. assignment Dial 1119 (1950).
PICTURES: Dial 1119, Inside Straight, The Sellout, Holiday for Sinners, Bright Road (Christopher Award for direction), The Marauders, African Drumbeat, The Man Inside (Canadian).

TELEVISION: Canadian Broadcasting Corp. (prod./dir., TV drama), prod. The Swiss Family Robinson (British-Canadian-West German TV series). Dir. for U.S. TV: One Last Ride (mini-series), Airwolf, Night Heat, Lou Grant, Eight Is Enough, Quincy, Logan's Run, Mannix, Mission Impossible, Police Surgeon, Cimarron Strip, Peyton Place, Judd for the Defense, Bonanza, The Fugitive, Chrysler Thea., Ben Casey, Slattery's People, Profiles in Courage, The Defenders, Gunsmoke.

MAYER, MICHAEL F.
Attorney, Executive. b. White Plains, NY, Sept. 8, 1917. e. Harvard Coll., B.S., 1939; Yale Law Sch., L.L.B., 1942. Armed Forces 1942-46, Air Medal (1945). V.P., Kingsley International Pictures Corp., 1954-62. Exec. dir. and gen. counsel, Independent Film Importers and Distributors of America Inc. (IFIDA), 1959-67. Special Counsel, French Society of Authors, Composers and Publishers, 1961-72; British Performing Rights Society, 1962-67. Author: Foreign Films on American Screens (1966), Divorce and Annulment (1967), What You Should Know About Libel and Slander (1968), Rights of Privacy (1972), The Film Industries (1973, revised ed. pub. in 1978). Teacher of courses on Business Problems in Film, New School (1971-82). Secty. of Film Society of Lincoln Center, Inc. (1972-88).

MAYER, ROGER LAURANCE
Executive. b. New York, NY, April 21, 1926. e. Yale U., B.A. 1948; Yale Law Sch., L.L.B. and J.D. 1951. In 1952 was practicing attorney; joined Columbia Pictures that year as atty. and named general studio exec., 1957. Left in 1961 to join MGM Studio as asst. gen. mgr. With MGM as follows: v.p., operations, 1964; v.p., administration, 1975-84. Also exec. v.p., MGM Laboratories, 1974-83. Named pres., MGM Laboratories and sr. v.p., studio admin.; MGM Entertainment Co. 1983-86; joined Turner Entertainment Co. as pres. and COO, 1986-present. Member of Los Angeles County Bar Assn., Calif. Bar Assn., Los Angeles Copyright Society, bd of govs., Acad. of Motion Picture Arts & Sciences. Trustee, chmn. Motion Picture & TV Fund. Chmn National Film Preservation Foundation.

MAYO, VIRGINIA
Actress. r.n. Virginia Jones. b. St. Louis, MO, Nov. 30, 1920. e. St. Louis dramatic school. With Billy Rose's Diamond Horseshoe; then N.Y. stage, Banjo Eyes.
PICTURES: Jack London (debut, 1943), Up in Arms, The Princess and the Pirate, Wonder Man, The Kid from Brooklyn, The Best Years of Our Lives, The Secret Life of Walter Mitty, Out of the Blue, A Song Is Born, Smart Girls Don't Talk, The Girl from Jones Beach, Flaxy Martin, Colorado Territory, Always Leave Them Laughing, White Heat, Red Light, Backfire, The Flame and the Arrow, West Point Story, Along the Great Divide, Captain Horatio Hornblower, Painting the Clouds with Sunshine, Starlift, She's Working Her Way Through College, Iron Mistress, She's Back on Broadway, South Sea Woman, Devil's Canyon, King Richard and the Crusaders, The Silver Chalice, Pearl of the South Pacific, Great Day in the Morning, The Proud Ones, Congo Crossing, The Big Land, The Story of Mankind, The Tall Stranger, Fort Dobbs, Westbound, Jet Over the Atlantic, Young Fury, Fort Utah, Castle of Evil, Won Ton Ton the Dog Who Saved Hollywood, French Quarter, Evil Spirits, Seven Days Ashore.

MAYRON, MELANIE
Actress, Director. b. Philadelphia, PA, Oct. 20, 1952. e. American Academy of Dramatic Arts, 1972. Debut Godspell (tour), NY stage debut: The Goodbye People, 1979. Gethsemane Springs, (Mark Taper Forum, 1976), Crossing Delancey, (1986, Jewish Rep. Theatre, NY). With Catlin Adams, co-prod., co-wrote short, Little Shiny Shoes.
PICTURES: *Actress:* Harry and Tonto (debut, 1974), Gable and Lombard, Car Wash, The Great Smokey Roadblock, You Light Up My Life, Girl Friends (Locarno Film Fest. Award) Heartbeeps, Missing, The Boss' Wife, Sticky Fingers (also co-s.p., co-prod), Checking Out, My Blue Heaven. *Director:* The Babysitters Club.
TELEVISION: *Series*: thirtysomething (Emmy Award, 1989). *Movies*: Playing For Time, Will There Really Be a Morning?, Hustling, The Best Little Girl in the World, Wallenberg: A Hero's Story, Ordeal in the Arctic, Other Women's Children. *Guest*: Rhoda. Specials: Lily Tomlin: Sold Out, Cinder Ella: A Modern Fairy Tale, Wanted: The Perfect Guy, Mad About You, Toothless, Something So Right. *Director*: Tribeca: Stepping Back (also writer), thirtysomething, Sirens, Moon Over Miami, Winnetka Road, Freaky Friday, Nash Bridges, New York Undercover, Arliss, The Larry Sanders Show.

MAYSLES, ALBERT
Director, Cinematographer. b. Boston, MA, Nov. 1926. e. Syracuse (B.A.), Boston U, M.A. Taught psychology there for 3 years. With late brother David (1932-87) pioneer in direct cinema documentary filmmaking, using a hand-held synchronous sound camera, no narration, to capture the drama of daily life, without need to invent stories. Entered filmmaking photographing Primary with D.A. Pennebaker, Richard Leacock and Robert Drew, 1960. Formed Maysles Films, Inc. 1962, making non-fiction feature films, commercials and corp. films.
PICTURES: Showman (1962), Salesman, What's Happening! The Beatles in the U.S.A., Meet Marlon Brando, Gimme Shelter, Christo's Valley Curtain, Grey Gardens, Running Fence, Vladimir Horowitz: The Last Romantic, Ozawa, Islands, Horowitz Plays Mozart, Fellow Passengers, Christo in Paris, Soldiers of Music: Rostropovitch Returns to Russia, Baroque Duet, Umbrellas.
TELEVISION: Vladimir Horowitz: The Last Romantic (Emmy Award, 1987), Soldiers of Music: Rostopovich Returns to Russia (Emmy Award, 1991), Sports Illustrated: The Making of the Swimsuit Issue (co-dir.), Abortion: Desperate Choices (Emmy Award, 1992, Cable Ace Award), Letting Go: A Hospice Journey (Emmy Award, 1996), A Concept of Wills: The Making of the Getty Art Center.

MAZURSKY, PAUL
Producer, Director, Writer, Actor. b. Brooklyn, NY, April 25, 1930. e. Brooklyn Coll. Started acting in 1951 Off-B'way (Hello Out There, The Seagull, Major Barbara, Death of a Salesman, He Who Gets Slapped), TV and films. Was nightclub comic 1954-1960 and directed plays. Began association with Larry Tucker by producing, directing, writing and performing in Second City, semi-improvisational revue. For four years they wrote the Danny Kaye TV show and created and wrote the Monkees series. First theatrical film I Love You Alice B. Toklas, 1968, which he wrote and exec. produced with Tucker. Exec. prod. of film Taking Care of Business.
PICTURES: *Dir.-Writer*: Bob and Carol and Ted and Alice, *Dir.-Prod.-Writer-Actor*: Alex in Wonderland, Blume in Love, Harry and Tonto, Next Stop Greenwich Village (dir., prod., s.p. only), An Unmarried Woman, Willie and Phil, Tempest, Moscow on the Hudson, Down and Out in Beverly Hills, Moon Over Parador, Enemies: a Love Story, Scenes From a Mall, The Pickle, Faithful. *Actor:* Fear and Desire, Blackboard Jungle, Deathwatch, A Star Is Born, A Man a Woman and a Bank, History of the World Part 1, Into the Night, Punchline, Scenes From the Class Struggle in Beverly Hills, Man Trouble, Carlito's Way, Love Affair, Miami Rhapsody, Faithful, 2 Days in the Valley, Touch.
TELEVISION: *Movies*: Weapons of Mass Distruction.

MAZZELLO, JOSEPH
Actor. b. Rhineback, NY, Sept. 21, 1983. Made acting debut at age 5 in tv movie Unspeakable Acts.
PICTURES: Presumed Innocent (debut, 1990), Radio Flyer, Jurassic Park, Shadowlands, The River Wild, The Cure, Three Wishes, The Lost World: Jurassic Park, Star Kid, Simon Birch.
TELEVISION: *Movies*: Unspeakable Acts, Desperate Choices: To Save My Child, A Father for Charlie.

McBRIDE, JIM
Director, Writer. b. New York, NY, Sept. 16, 1941. e. NYU. m. costume designer Tracy Tynan. Began in underground film scene in New York. First film: David Holzman's Diary, 1967, which won grand prize at Mannheim and Pesaro Film Festivals, and was named to the Library of Congress' list of important American films designated for preservation in 1991. Appeared as actor in film Last Embrace.
PICTURES: *Director*: David Holzman's Diary (also prod.), My Girlfriend's Wedding (also actor, s.p.), Glen and Randa (also s.p.), Hot Times (also s.p., actor), Breathless (also co-s.p.), The Big Easy, Great Balls of Fire (also co-s.p.), Uncovered (also co-s.p.).
TELEVISION: *Series*: The Wonder Years (3 episodes), Twilight Zone (The Once and Future King, 1986). *Movies*: Blood Ties, The Wrong Man, The Informant, Pronto, Dead by Midnight. *Special*: Fallen Angels (Fearless), Dead Before Midnight.

McCALL, JOAN
Writer, Actress. b. Grahn, KY. e. Berea Coll. Staff writer for Days of Our Lives, Another World, As the World Turns, under the pen name Joan Pommer; also Search for Tomorrow, Capitol, Santa Barbara, Divorce Court. Starred on B'way in Barefoot in the Park, The Star Spangled Girl, A Race of Hairy Men, and road companies of Barefoot in the Park, Any Wednesday, Star Spangled Girl, and Don't Drink the Water, Los Angeles co. of Jimmy Shine.
PICTURES: Grizzly, Act of Vengeance, The Devil Times Five. Screenwriter: Predator, Between Two Worlds, Timelapse, Heart Like a Wheel.

McCALLUM, DAVID
Actor. b. Glasgow, Scotland, Sept. 19, 1933. Early career in rep. theatres and dir. plays for Army. Entered industry in 1953.
PICTURES: The Secret Place (debut, 1957), Hell Drivers, Robbery Under Arms, Violent Playground, A Night to Remember, The Long and the Short and the Tall, Carolina, Jungle Street, Billy Budd, Freud, The Great Escape, The Greatest Story Ever Told, To Trap a Spy, The Spy With My Face, Around the World Under the Sea, One Spy Too Many, Three Bites of the Apple, Sol Madrid, Mosquito Squadron, The Kingfisher Caper, Dogs, King Solomon's Treasure, The Watcher in the Woods, Terminal Choice, The Wind, The Haunting of Morella, Hear My Song, Dirty Weekend, Healer.

TELEVISION: *Series*: The Man From U.N.C.L.E., Colditz (BBC, 1972-74), The Invisible Man, Sapphire and Steel (BBC), Trainer (BBC). *Guest*: Hitchcock, Murder She Wrote. *Movies*: Teacher Teacher, Hauser's Memory, Frankenstein: The True Story, Behind Enemy Lines, Freedom Fighters, She Waits, The Man Who Lived at the Ritz, The Return of Sam McCloud, Mother Love (BBC), Shattered Image.

McCAMBRIDGE, MERCEDES
Actress. b. Joliet, IL, March 17, 1918. e. Mundelein Coll., Chicago, B.A. Did some radio work while in college; opposite Orson Welles two seasons, on Ford Theatre, other air shows; New York stage in: Hope for the Best, (1945); Place of Our Own, Twilight Bar, Woman Bites Dog, The Young and Fair, Lost in Yonkers. Starred on own radio show, 1952. Autobiography: The Two of Us.
PICTURES: All the King's Men (debut, 1949; Acad. Award, best supporting actress), Lightning Strikes Twice, Inside Straight, The Scarf, Johnny Guitar, Giant, A Farewell to Arms, Touch of Evil (cameo), Suddenly Last Summer, Cimarron, Angel Baby, 99 Women, Like a Crow on a June Bug, The Exorcist (voice), Thieves, The Concorde—Airport '79, Echoes.
TELEVISION: *Series*: One Man's Family, Wire Service; also numerous guest appearances. *Movies*: Killer By Night, Two For the Money, The Girls of Huntington House, The President's Plane Is Missing, Who Is the Black Dahlia?, The Sacketts.

McCARTHY, ANDREW
Actor. b. Westfield, NJ, Nov. 29, 1962. Raised in Bernardsville, NJ. e. NYU. While at college won role in film Class. Studied acting at Circle-in-the-Square.
THEATER: *B'way*: The Boys of Winter. *Off B'way*: Bodies Rest and Motion, Life Under Water, Neptune's Hips, Mariens Kammer.
PICTURES: Class (debut, 1983), Heaven Help Us, St. Elmo's Fire, Pretty in Pink, Mannequin, Waiting for the Moon, Less Than Zero, Kansas, Fresh Horses, Weekend at Bernie's, Quiet Days in Clichy, Dr. M, Year of the Gun, Only You, Weekend at Bernie's 2, The Joy Luck Club, Getting In, Night of the Running Man, Mrs. Parker & the Vicious Circle, Dream Man, Dead Funny, Mulholland Falls, Things I Never Told You, Stag, I Woke Up Early the Day I Died, Bela Donna A Breed Apart, New World Disorder, Jump, A Twist of Faith.
TELEVISION: *Movie:* The Courtyard. *Specials*: Dear Lola, Common Pursuit. *Guest*: Amazing Stories (Grandpa's Ghost), Tales From the Crypt (Loved to Death), A Father for Brittany.

McCARTHY, KEVIN
Actor. b. Seattle, WA, Feb. 15, 1914. Sister was late author Mary McCarthy. e. U. of Minnesota. Acted in sch. plays, stock; B'way debut in Abe Lincoln in Illinois. Served in U.S. Army.
THEATER: *B'way*: Flight to West, Winged Victory, Truckline Cafe, Joan of Lorraine, The Survivors, Death of a Salesman (London), Anna Christie, The Deep Blue Sea, Red Roses For Me, A Warm Body, Something About a Soldier, Love's Labour's Lost, Advise and Consent, The Day The Money Stopped, Two For the Seesaw, Cactus Flower, Alone Together, The Three Sisters, Happy Birthday Wanda June.
PICTURES: Death of a Salesman (debut, 1951; Acad. Award nom.), Drive a Crooked Road, The Gambler From Natchez, Stranger on Horseback, Annapolis Story, Nightmare, Invasion of the Body Snatchers, The Misfits, 40 Pounds of Trouble, A Gathering of Eagles, The Prize, The Best Man, An Affair of the Skin, Mirage, A Big Hand for the Little Lady, Three Sisters, Hotel, The Hell With Heroes, If He Hollers Let Him Go, Revenge in El Paso, Ace High, Kansas City Bomber, Alien Thunder, Order to Kill, Buffalo Bill and the Indians, Piranha, Invasion of the Body Snatchers (1978, cameo), Hero at Large, Those Lips Those Eyes, The Howling, My Tutor, Twilight Zone—The Movie, Hostage, Innerspace, UHF, Fast Food, Dark Tower, Love or Money, The Sleeping Car, Eve of Destruction, Final Approach, The Distinguished Gentleman, Matinee, Greedy, Just Cause, Steal Big Steal Little, The Sister in Law.
TELEVISION: Active on TV since 1949. *Movies*: U.M.C., A Great American Tragedy, Exo-Man, Mary Jane Harper Cried Last Night, Flamingo Road, Portrait of an Escort, Rosie: The Story of Rosemary Clooney, Making of a Male Model, Invitation to Hell, Deadly Intentions, The Midnight Hour, A Masterpiece of Murder, Poor Little Rich Girl: The Barbara Hutton Story, The Long Journey Home, Once Upon a Texas Train, In the Heat of the Night, Channel 99, The Rose and the Jackal, Dead on the Money, Duplicates, The Sister-in-Law, Liz: The Elizabeth Taylor Story, Marlon Brando: The Wild One, The Second World War, Elvis Meets Nixon. *Mini-series:* Passion and Paradise. *Series*: The Colbys, The Survivors, Flamingo Road, Amanda's, Second Start. *Guest*: Dynasty. *Pilot*: Second Stage.

McCARTNEY PAUL
Singer, Musician. r.n. James Paul McCartney. b. Liverpool, England, June 18, 1942. Formerly with The Beatles, Wings.
PICTURES: *Performer:* A Hard Day's Night, (debut, 1964; also songs) Help! (also songs), Yellow Submarine (cameo; also songs), Let It Be (also songs; Acad. Award for best original song score, 1970), Rockshow (concert film), Give My Regards to Broad Street (also s.p., songs), Eat the Rich (cameo), Get Back (concert film) *Songs for films:* Live and Let Die (title song; Acad. Award nom.), Oh Heavenly Dog, Spies Like Us. *Scores:* The Family Way, Beyond the Limit.

TELEVISION: *Specials:* James Paul McCartney, Sgt. Pepper: It Was 20 Years Ago Today, Put It There, Paul McCartney Live in the New World, The Beatles Anthology.

McCLANAHAN, RUE
Actress. b. Healdton, OK, Feb. 21. e. U. of Tulsa (B.A. cum laude). Member: Actors Studio, NYC.
THEATER: *On B'way* in Sticks and Bones, Jimmy Shine, California Suite. *Off-B'way*: Who's Happy Now? (Obie Award, 1970), After Play. Vienna: Lettice and Lovage. London: Harvey.
PICTURES: Five Minutes to Love, Hollywood After Dark, How to Succeed With Girls, They Might Be Giants, The People Next Door, The Pursuit of Happiness, Modern Love, This World Then The Fireworks, Dear God, Starship Troopers, Out to Sea.
TELEVISION: *Series*: Maude, Mama's Family, The Golden Girls (Emmy Award, 1987), The Golden Palace, Apple Pie, Balckbird Hall. *Movies:* Having Babies III, Sgt. Matlovich Vs. the U.S. Air Force, Rainbow, Topper, The Great American Traffic Jam, Word of Honor, The Day the Bubble Burst, The Little Match Girl, Liberace, Take My Daughters Please, Let Me Hear You Whisper, To the Heroes, After the Shock, Children of the Bride, To My Daughter, The Dreamer of Oz, Baby of the Bride, Mother of the Bride (also co-exec. prod.), A Burning Passion: The Margaret Mitchell Story, Innocent Victims, A Christmas Love. *Specials*: The Wickedest Witch, The Man in the Brown Suit, Nunsense 2: The Sequel. *Mini-Series*: Message From Nam.

McCLORY, SEÁN
Actor. b. Dublin, Ireland, March 8, 1924. e. Jesuit Coll., Nat'l U. at Galway (medical sch.). With Gaelic Theatre, Galway; Abbey Theatre, Dublin. Brought to U.S. in 1946 under contract to RKO Pictures, then Warners, then Batjac (John Wayne's co.). Prod. and dir. numerous plays, member of the Directors Guild of America and author of drama, Moment of Truth; Pax: The Benedictions in China. Editor: The Jester: The Masques Club 50th Anniv. Mng. Editor: A.N.T.A. News (2 yrs). For past 4 years starred in 40 ninety-minute radio dramas for California Artists Radio Theatre and written some 90 min. shows for National Public Radio. Recipient, Irish American Partnership Special CA Achievement Award, 1998.
THEATER: Shining Hour, Juno and the Paycock, Anna Christie, Escape to Autumn, King of Friday's Men, Lady's Not for Burning, Billy Budd, Dial M for Murder, The Winslow Boy, Shadow of a Gunman (Dramalogue Award), Saint Joan, The Importance of Being Earnest, many others.
PICTURES: Roughshod, Beyond Glory, The Daughter of Rosie O'Grady, Anne of the Indies, Storm Warning, Lorna Doone, What Price Glory?, The Quiet Man, Rogue's March, Plunder of the Sun, Island in the Sky, Them, Ring of Fear, Man in the Attic, The Long Grey Lane, Diane, I Cover the Underworld, The King's Thief, Moonfleet, Guns of Fort Petticoat, Valley of the Dragons, Cheyenne Autumn, Follow Me Boys, The Gnome-Mobile, Bandolero, Day of the Wolves, Roller Boogie, In Search of Historic Jesus, My Chauffeur, The Dead.
TELEVISION: *Series*: The Californians (also dir. episodes), Kate McShane, Bring 'Em Back Alive, General Hospital. *Mini-Series*: The Captains and the Kings, Once an Eagle. *Movies:* Kate McShane (pilot), The New Daughters of Joshua Cabe, Young Harry Houdini. *Guest*: Matinee Theatre, Climax, Lost in Space, My Three Sons, Suspense, The Untouchables, Hitchcock, Thriller, Beverly Hillbillies, Bonanza, Gunsmoke, Mannix, Little House on the Prairie, Perry Mason, S.W.A.T., Fish, Columbo, How the West Was Won, Fantasy Island, Battlestar Galactica, Trapper John M.D., Blue Knight, Falcon Crest, Simon and Simon, Murder She Wrote.

McCLUGGAGE, KERRY
Executive. b. 1955. e. USC, Harvard U. 1978, programming asst. at Universal; 1979, dir. of current srs. programming; 1980, became v.p., Universal TV. 1982, sr. v.p. creative affairs. Served as v.p. of production, Universal Pictures and supv. prod. on series Miami Vice. 1987-991, pres. of Universal Television. 1991, joined Paramount as pres. of the Television Group. 1992, named chmn. of the Television Group of Paramount Pictures.

McCLURE, MARC
Actor. b. San Mateo, CA, March 31, 1957.
PICTURES: Freaky Friday, Coming Home, I Wanna Hold Your Hand, Superman, Superman II, Superman III, Supergirl, Back to the Future, Superman IV: The Quest for Peace, Amazon Women on the Moon, Perfect Match, Chances Are, After Midnight, Back to the Future Part III, Grim Prairie Tales, The Vagrant, Apollo 13, Sleepstalker.
TELEVISION: *Series*: California Fever. *Movies*: James at 15, Little White Lies. *Guest*: The Commish.

McCLURG, EDIE
Actress. b. Kansas City, MO, July 23, 1951. e. Syracuse Univ. Newswriter and documentary prod. for National Public Radio affiliate, KCUR-FM. Joined the Pitschel Players in LA in 1975; then became member of the Groundlings Improv Comedy Revue.
PICTURES: Carrie (debut, 1976), Cheech and Chong's Next Movie, Oh God Book II, Secret of NIMH (voice), Pandemonium, Cracking Up, Eating Raoul, Mr. Mom, The Corsican Brothers, Ferris Bueller's Day Off, Back to School, The Longshot, Planes Trains and Automobiles, She's Having a Baby, Elvira: Mistress of the Dark, The Little Mermaid (voice), Curly Sue, A River Runs Through It, Stepmonster, Airborne, Natural Born Killers,

Under the Hula Moon, Carpool, Circuit Breaker, Casper: A Spirited Beginning, Flubber, Meeting Daddy, A Bug's Life (voice), Holy Man, The Rugrats Movie (voice), Can't Stop Dancing, The Manor.
TELEVISION: *Series*: Tony Orlando and Dawn, The Kallikaks, The Big Show, Harper Valley PTA, No Soap Radio, Madame's Place, Small Wonder, Toegther We Stand, Valerie (The Hogan Family), Drexell's Class, Life with Louie, Martin Mull's White Politics in America. *Specials*: Cinderella (Faerie Tale Theatre), The Pee-wee Herman Show, Martin Mull's History of White People in America, Once Upon a Brothers Grimm, The Chevy Chase Show, A Home Run for Love. *Guest*: WKRP in Cincinnati, The Richard Pryor Show, The Jeffersons, Trapper John M.D., Alice, Diff'rent Strokes, The Incredible Hulk, Madame's Place, Picket Fences. *Movies*: Bill on His Own, Crash Course, Dance 'til Dawn, Menu for Murder, Columbo: Ashes to Ashes, Murder She Purred. *Voice Characterizations*: The Snorks, The 13 Ghosts of Scooby Doo, The New Jetsons, Casper, Problem Child, Bobby's World of Monsters.

MCCONAUGHEY, MATTHEW
Actor. b. Uvalde, Texas, November 4, 1969
PICTURES: Dazed and Confused, My Boyfriend's Back, Angels in the Outfield, The Return of the Texas Chainsaw Massacre, Boys on the Side, Scorpion Spring, Submission, Glory Daze, Larger Than Life, A Time to Kill, Lone Star, Amistad, Contact, Making Sandwiches, The Newton Boys, South Beach, Last Flight of the Raven (prod. only), Johnny Diamond, Edtv, U-571, Last Flight of the Raven, The Wedding Planner, Reign of Fire, Dexterity.

McCORMICK, PAT
Writer, Actor. b. July 17, 1934. Served as comedy writer for such performers as Jonathan Winters, Phyllis Diller.
PICTURES: *Actor*: Buffalo Bill and the Indians, Smokey and the Bandit, A Wedding, Hot Stuff, Scavenger Hunt, Smokey and the Bandit 2, History of the World Part 1, Under the Rainbow (also co-s.p.), Smokey and the Bandit 3, Bombs Away, Rented Lips, Scrooged, Beverly Hills Vamp.
TELEVISION: *Series* (as writer): Jack Paar Show, Tonight Show, etc. *Series* (as actor): The Don Rickles Show, The New Bill Cosby Show, Gun Shy. *Movies* (as actor): Mr. Horn, Rooster, The Jerk Too.

McCOWEN, ALEC
Actor. b. Tunbridge Wells, England, May 26, 1925. e. Royal Acad. of Dramatic Art. On stage in London in Hadrian the Seventh, among others. On B'way in Antony and Cleopatra, After the Rain, The Philanthropist, The Misanthrope, Equus, Someone Who'll Watch Over Me, etc.
PICTURES: The Cruel Sea, The Divided Heart, The Deep Blue Sea, The Good Companions, The Third Key (The Long Arm), Time Without Pity, Town on Trial, The Doctor's Dilemma, A Night to Remember, The One That Got Away, Silent Enemy, The Loneliness of the Long Distance Runner, In the Cool of the Day, The Devil's Own, The Hawaiians, Frenzy, Travels with My Aunt, Stevie, Hanover Street, Never Say Never Again, The Assam Garden, Personal Services, Cry Freedom, Henry V, The Age of Innocence.

McCRANE, PAUL
Actor. b. Philadelphia, PA, Jan. 19, 1961. Stage debut at age 16 in NY Shakespeare Fest. prod. of Landscape of the Body.
THEATER: *NY:* Dispatches, Runaway, Split, The House of Blue Leaves, The Palace of Amateurs, Hooters, The Hostage, Curse of an Aching Heart
PICTURES: Rocky II (debut, 1979), Fame (also songwriter), The Hotel New Hampshire, Purple Hearts, Robocop, The Blob, The Shawshank Redemption.
TELEVISION: *Series:* Cop Rock, Under Suspicion. *Movies*: Baby Comes Home, We're Fighting Back, Money—Power—Murder, With Murder in Mind, The Portrait, Strapped, Zelda. *Mini-series*: North & South II.

McDERMOTT, DYLAN
Actor. b. Connecticut, Oct. 26, 1961. Raised in New York City. e. Fordham U., studied acting at Neighborhood Playhouse with Sanford Meisner.
THEATER: The Seagull, Golden Boy, The Glass Menagerie, Biloxi Blues (B'way), Floating Rhoda and the Glue Man.
PICTURES: Hamburger Hill, The Blue Iguana, Twister, Steel Magnolias, Where Sleeping Dogs Lie, Hardware, In the Line of Fire, The Cowboy Way, Miracle on 34th Street, Destiny Turns on the Radio, Home for the Holidays, `Til There Was You, Three to Tango.
TELEVISION: *Movies*: The Neon Empire, Into the Badlands, The Fear Inside. *Series*: The Practice

McDONNELL, MARY
Actress. b. Wilkes Bare, PA.
THEATER: *NY*: Buried Child, Savage in Limbo, All Night Long, Black Angel, A Weekend Near Madison, Three Ways Home, Still Life, The Heidi Chronicles, Summer and Smoke. *Regional:* National Athems, A Doll's House, A Midsummer Night's Dream, The Three Sisters.
PICTURES: Matewan, Tiger Warsaw, Dances With Wolves (Acad. Award nom., Golden Globe Award), Grand Canyon, Sneakers, Passion Fish (Acad. Award nom.), Blue Chips, Mariette in Ecstasy, Independence Day, You Can Thank Me Later, Spanish Fly (voice), Mumford.
TELEVISION: *Series*: E/R, High Society, Ryan Caulfield. *Movies:* Money on the Side, Courage, The American Clock, 12 Angry Men, Replacing Dad, Evidence of Blood, Behind the Mask. *Special*: O Pioneers!

McDORMAND, FRANCES
Actress. b. Illinois, 1958. m. dir. Joel Coen. Daughter of a Disciples of Christ preacher, traveled Bible Belt with family settling in PA at 8. e. Yale Drama School. Regional theater includes Twelfth Night, Mrs. Warren's Profession, The Three Sisters, All My Sons. Two seasons with O'Neill Playwrights Conference.
THEATER: Awake and Sing, Painting Churches, On the Verge, A Streetcar Named Desire (Tony nom.), The Sisters Rosensweig, The Swan.
PICTURES: Blood Simple, Raising Arizona, Mississippi Burning (Acad. Award nom.), Chattahoochee, Dark Man, Miller's Crossing (unbilled), Hidden Agenda, The Butcher's Wife, Passed Away, Short Cuts, Beyond Rangoon, Fargo (Acad. Award, 1996; Chicago Film Critics Award; Screen Actors Guild Award; Ind't Spirit Award), Lone Star, Primal Fear, Palookaville, Paradise Road, Johnny Skidmarks, Madeline, Talk of Angels, Wonder Boys.
TELEVISION: *Series*: Leg Work. *Guest*: Twilight Zone, Spenser: For Hire, Hill St. Blues. *Movies*: Crazy in Love, The Good Old Boys.

McDOWELL, MALCOLM
Actor. b. Leeds, England, June 13, 1943. Was spearholder for the Royal Shakespeare Co. in season of 1965-66 when turned to TV and then to films. *NY stage:* Look Back in Anger (also on video), In Celebration, Another Time. *LA stage:* Hunting Cockroaches.
PICTURES: Poor Cow (debut, 1967), If..., Figures in a Landscape, The Raging Moon (Long Ago Tomorrow), A Clockwork Orange, O Lucky Man!, Royal Flash, Voyage of the Damned, Aces High, The Passage, Time After Time, Caligula, Cat People, Britannia Hospital, Blue Thunder, Cross Creek, Get Crazy, Sunset, Buy and Cell, The Caller, Class of 1999, Disturbed, In the Eye of the Snake, Moon 44, The Maestro, Schweitzer, Assassin of the Tsar, The Player, Happily Ever After (voice), Chain of Desire, East Wind, Night Train to Venice, Bopha!, Milk Money, Star Trek: Generations, Tank Girl, Kids of the Round Table, Where Truth Lies, Hugo Pool, Mr. Magoo, The Gardener, The First 9 1/2 Weeks, Beings, Y2K, Southern Cross, My Life So Far.
TELEVISION: *Series:* Pearl, Fantasy Island. *Guest*: Faerie Tale Theatre (Little Red Riding Hood), Tales from the Crypt (Reluctant Vampire). *Movies*: Arthur the King, Gulag, Monte Carlo, Seasons of the Heart, The Man Who Wouldn't Die.

McELWAINE, GUY
Executive. b. Culver City, CA, June 29, 1936. Started career in pub. dept. of MGM, 1955; 1959, joined m.p. div. of Rogers and Cowen; 1964, formed own public relations firm; then joined CMA. Left to become sr. exec. v.p. in chg. worldwide m.p. production, Warner Bros., 1975. 1977 became sr. exec. v.p. in chg. worldwide m.p. activities and pres. of intl. film mktg. at Intl. Creative Management (ICM), formerly CMA. 1981, named pres. and CEO, Rastar Films. Left in 1982 to become pres., Columbia Pictures; given additional title of CEO, 1983. 1985 named chmn. and on board of Columbia Pictures Industries. Resigned, 1986. Joined Weintraub Entertainment Group as exec. v.p. and chmn., m.p. div. 1987-89; returned to ICM, 1989 as vice chmn.

McEVEETY, BERNARD
Director. Father was pioneer as unit mgr. at New York's Edison Studios; Brothers dir. Vincent and writer Joseph. Began career in 1953 at Paramount where he was asst. dir. for 6 yrs. Dir. debut on TV series, The Rebel.
PICTURES: Ride Beyond Vengeance, Brotherhood of Satan, Napoleon and Samantha, One Little Indian, The Bears and I.
TELEVISION: Numerous episodes of Bonanza, Gunsmoke, Combat and Cimarron Strip (also prod.), Centennial, Roughnecks, The Machans.

McEVEETY, VINCENT
Director. Brother is dir. Bernard McEveety. Joined Hal Roach Studios in 1954 as second asst. dir. Then to Republic for The Last Command. First Disney assignments: Davy Crockett shows and Mickey Mouse Club. Moved to Desilu as first asst. dir. on The Untouchables; made assoc. prod. with option to direct. Did segments of many series, including 34 Gunsmoke episodes.
PICTURES: Firecreek (debut, 1968), $1,000,000 Duck, The Biscuit Eater, Charley and the Angel, Superdad, The Strongest Man in the World, Gus, Treasure of Matecumbe, Herbie Goes to Monte Carlo, The Apple Dumpling Gang Rides Again, Herbie Goes Bananas, Amy.
TELEVISION: Blood Sport, Wonder Woman, High Flying Spy, Ask Max, Gunsmoke: Return to Dodge, Murder She Wrote, Simon and Simon (26 episodes), Columbo: Rest in Peace Mrs. Columbo.

McGAVIN, DARREN
Actor. b. Spokane, WA, May 7, 1922. e. Coll. of the Pacific. Studied acting at Neighborhood Playhouse, Actors Studio. Landed bit roles in films starting in 1945.
THEATER: Death of a Salesman, My Three Angels, The Rainmaker, The Lovers, The King and I, Dinner at Eight (revival), Captain Brassbound's Conversion (LA), The Night Hank Williams Died, Greetings.
PICTURES: A Song to Remember (debut, 1945), Kiss and Tell, Counter-Attack, She Wouldn't Say Yes, Fear, Queen for a Day, Summertime, The Man With the Golden Arm, The Court Martial of Billy Mitchell, Beau James, The Delicate Delinquent, The Case Against Brooklyn, Bullet for a Badman, The Great Sioux Massacre, Ride the High Wind, Mission Mars, Mrs. Polifax—Spy, Happy Mother's Day... Love George (dir. only), No Deposit No Return, Airport '77, Hot Lead and Cold Feet, Zero to Sixty, Hangar 18, Firebird 2015 A.D., A Christmas Story, The Natural, Turk 182, Raw Deal, From the Hip, Dead Heat, Blood and Concrete: A Love Story, Billy Madison, Still Waters Burn, Small Time.
TELEVISION: *Series*: Crime Photographer, Mike Hammer, Riverboat, The Outsider, Kolchak: The Night Stalker, Small & Frye. *Movies*: The Outsider (pilot), The Challenge, The Challengers, Berlin Affair, Tribes, Banyon, The Death of Me Yet, Night Stalker, Something Evil, The Rookies, Say Goodbye Maggie Cole, The Night Strangler, The Six Million Dollar Man (pilot), Brink's: The Great Robbery, Law and Order, The Users, Love for Rent, Waikiki, Return of Marcus Welby M.D., My Wicked Wicked Ways, Inherit the Wind, The Diamond Trap, By Dawn's Early Light, The American Clock, Danielle Steel's A Perfect Stranger, Derby. *Specials*: Unclaimed Fortunes (host), Clara (ACE Award), Mastergate, Miracles and Ohter Wonders (host), The Secret Discovery of Noah's Ark (host). *Mini-Series*: Ike, The Martian Chronicles, Around the World in 80 Days. *Guest*: Goodyear TV Playhouse, Alfred Hitchcock Presents, Route 66, U.S. Steel Hour, The Defenders, Love American Style, The Name of the Game, Owen Marshall, Police Story, The Love Boat, Murphy Brown (Emmy Award, 1990), The X Files.

McGILLIS, KELLY
Actress. b. Newport Beach, CA, July 9, 1957. Studied acting at Pacific Conservatory of Performing Arts in Santa Maria, CA; Juilliard. While at latter, won role in film Reuben Reuben.
THEATER: *D.C. Stage*: The Merchant of Venice, Twelfth Night, Measure for Measure, Much Ado About Nothing. *NY Stage*: Hedda Gabler.
PICTURES: Reuben Reuben (debut, 1983), Witness, Top Gun, Once We Were Dreamers, Made in Heaven, The House on Carroll Street, The Accused, Winter People, Cat Chaser, Before and After Death, The Babe, North, Painted Angels, Morgan's Ferry, At First Sight.
TELEVISION: *Movies*: Sweet Revenge, Private Sessions, Grand Isle (also prod.), Bonds of Love, In the Best of Families: Marriage Pride & Madness, We the Jury, The Third Twin, Perfect Prey, Storm Chasers: Revenge of the Twister. *Special*: Out of Ireland (narrator).

McGINLEY, JOHN C.
Actor. b. New York, NY, Aug. 3, 1959. e. NYU (M.F.A.), 1984.
THEATRE: *NY*: Danny and the Deep Blue Sea, The Ballad of Soapy Smith, Jesse and the Games, Requiem for a Heavyweight, Love as We Know It, Talk Radio, Florida Crackers, Breast Men.
PICTURES: Sweet Liberty, Platoon, Wall Street, Shakedown, Talk Radio, Lost Angels, Fat Man and Little Boy, Born on the Fourth of July, Point Break, Highlander 2: The Quickening, Article 99, Little Noises, A Midnight Clear, Fathers and Sons, Hear No Evil, Watch It (also co-prod.), Car 54 Where Are You?, On Deadly Ground, Surviving the Game, Suffrin' Bastards (also co-s.p.), Wagons East!, Born to Be Wild, Captive (co-prod. only), Seven, Nixon, Johns, The Rock, Nothing to Lose, A.W.O.L, Three to Tango.
TELEVISION: *Movies*: Clinton & Nadine, Cruel Doubt, The Last Outlaw, The Return of Hunter, Intensity, The Pentagon Wars, Target Earth. *Guest*: Frasier.

McGOOHAN, PATRICK
Actor, Director. b. New York, March 19, 1928. Early career in repertory in Britain. London stage 1954 in Serious Charge; 1955, Orson Welles' Moby Dick. On B'way in Pack of Lies (1987).
PICTURES: The Dam Busters (debut, 1954), I Am a Camera, The Dark Avenger, Passage Home, Zarak, High Tide at Noon, Hell Drivers, The Gypsy and the Gentleman, Nor the Moon by Night, Two Living One Dead, All Night Long, Life for Ruth (Walk in the Shadow), The Quare Fellow, The Three Lives of Thomasina, Dr. Syn: Alias the Scarecrow (U.S. tv as: The Scarecrow of Romney Marsh), Ice Station Zebra, The Moonshine War, Mary—Queen of Scots, Catch My Soul (dir. only), Un Genio due Campari e un Pollo, Porgi d'altra Guancia, Silver Streak, Brass Target, Escape From Alcatraz, Scanners, Kings and Desperate Men, Finding Katie, Baby: Secret of the Lost Legend, Braveheart, The Phantom, A Time to Kill.
TELEVISION: *Series*: Danger Man (also dir. episodes), Secret Agent, The Prisoner (also creator, prod.), Rafferty. *Movies/ Specials*: The Hard Way, Jamaica Inn, Of Pure Blood, The Man in the Iron Mask, Three Sovereigns for Sarah. *Guest*: Columbo (Emmy Awards: 1975, 1990; also dir. episodes).

McGOVERN, ELIZABETH
Actress. b. Evanston, IL, July 18, 1961. Family moved to Southern California when she was 10. Acted in high school in North Hollywood; performance in prod. of The Skin of Our Teeth won her agency represenation. Studied at American Conservatory Theatre, San Francisco and Juilliard Sch. of Dramatic Art. Open audition for Ordinary People resulted in her film debut. Appeared in IMAX film Wings of Courage.
THEATER: *NY*: To Be Young Gifted and Black (1981, debut), My Sister in This House (Theatre World, Obie Awards), Painting Churches, The Hitch-Hiker, A Map of the World, Aunt Dan and Lemon (L.A.), Two Gentlemen of Verona, A Midsummer Night's Dream (NY Shakespeare Fest.), Love Letters, Twelfth Night (Boston), Major Barbara (Alaska), Ring Aroung the Moon (D.C.), Maids of Honor, The Three Sisters, As You Like It.
PICTURES: Ordinary People (debut, 1980), Ragtime (Acad. Award nom.), Lovesick, Racing with the Moon, Once Upon a Time in America, Native Son, The Bedroom Window, She's Having a Baby, Johnny Handsome, The Handmaid's Tale, A Shock to the System, Tune in Tomorrow, King of the Hill, Me and Veronica, The Favor.
TELEVISION: *Series*: If Not for You. *Movies*: Women and Men: Stories of Seduction (The Man in the Brooks Brothers Shirt), Broken Trust. *Specials*: Ashenden, Tales From Hollywood, The Changeling (BBC).

McGRATH, JUDY
Executive. e. Cedar Crest Coll. President, MTV. Began at MTV as on-air promotions writer. Created Unplugged, MTV Books, MTV Online.

McGRATH, THOMAS J.
Producer, Attorney, Writer, Lecturer. b. New York, NY, Oct. 8, 1932. e. Washington Square Coll. of NYU, B.A., 1956; NYU Sch. of Law, LL.B., 1960. Served in Korea with U.S. Army, 1953-54. Has practiced law in N.Y. from 1960 to date. Became indep. prod. with Deadly Hero in 1976; Author, Carryover Basis Under The 1976 Tax Reform Act, published in 1977. Cobntributing author, Estate and Gift Tax After ERTA, 1982. Lecturer and writer: American Law Institute 1976-81; Practicing Law Institute, 1976-97. Dir., New York Philharmonic; Oloffson Corp.; Fast Food Development Corp. Pres.: American Austrian Foundation; Tanzania Wildlife Fund.

McGREGOR, CHARLES
Executive. b. Jersey City, NJ, April 1, 1927. e. NYU. 1958-69, co-founder, pres. and CEO, Banner Films, Inc. (World Wide TV Distribution); 1955-58, salesman and div. mgr., Flamingo Films (domestic TV Dist.); Professional mgr. ABC Music Publishing. 1951-53: Prod. and partner Telco Prods. and GM Productions (prods. of network and local shows). 1969-77: exec. v.p. in chg. of worldwide dist., WB-TV; 1977-89, pres. WB-TV Distribution; 1989, named exec. v.p., corp. projects, WB.

McGREGOR, EWAN
Actor. b. Crieff, Scotland, March 31, 1971. Formed Natural Nylon, prodn. co., with Johnny Lee Miller & Jude Law.
PICTURES: Being Human, Shallow Grave, Blue Juice, The Pillow Book, Trainspotting, Emma, Brassed Off, The Serpent's Kiss, Nightwatch, A Life Less Ordinary, Velvet Goldmine, Little Voice, Desserts, Nightwatch, Rogue Trader, Nora, Star Wars: Episode I-The Phantom Menace, Eye of the Beholder, Moulin Rouge, Nora, Killing Priscella, Anno Domini, Star Wars: Episode II.
TELEVISION: *Movies*: Lipstick on Your Collar. *Mini-series*: Scarlet & Black, Karaoke. *Guest*: Tales from the Crypt, ER.

McGUIRE, DOROTHY
Actress. b. Omaha, NE, June 14, 1919. e. Ladywood convent, Indianapolis; Pine Manor, Wellesley, MA. Acting debut as teenager at Omaha Community Playhouse. Following summer stock and radio work, made B'way debut in 1938 as Martha Scott's understudy in Our Town. Came to Hollywood to repeat stage role in film version of Claudia.
THEATER: Our Town, My Dear Children, Swinging the Dream, Claudia, Legend of Lovers, Winesberg Ohio, Night of the Iguana (1976), Cause Celebre, Another Part of the Forest, I Never Sang for My Father.
PICTURES: Claudia (debut, 1943), A Tree Grows in Brooklyn, The Enchanted Cottage, The Spiral Staircase, Claudia and David, Till the End of Time, Gentleman's Agreement (Acad. Award nom.), Mother Didn't Tell Me, Mister 880, Callaway Went Thataway, I Want You, Invitation, Make Haste to Live, Three Coins in the Fountain, Trial, Friendly Persuasion, Old Yeller, The Remarkable Mr. Pennypacker, This Earth Is Mine, A Summer Place, The Dark at the Top of the Stairs, Swiss Family Robinson, Susan Slade, Summer Magic, The Greatest Story Ever Told, Flight of the Doves, Jonathan Livingston Seagull (voice).

TELEVISION: *Series*: Little Women. *Movies*: She Waits, The Runaways, Little Women, The Incredible Journey of Dr. Meg Laurel, Ghost Dancing, Amos, Between the Darkness and the Dawn, Caroline? *Mini-Series*: Rich Man Poor Man. *Specials*: The Philadelphia Story, To Each His Own, Another Part of the Forest, I Never Sang for My Father. *Guest*: The Love Boat, The Young & the Restless, Highway to Heaven, Fantasy Island, St. Elsewhere.

McHATTIE, STEPHEN
Actor. b. Antigonish, Nova Scotia, Canada, Feb. 3, e. Acadia U. Trained for stage at American Acad. of Dramatic Arts.
THEATER: *NY*: The American Dream (debut, 1968), Pictures in the Hallway, Twelfth Night, Mourning Becomes Electra, The Iceman Cometh, Alive and Well in Argentina, The Winter Dancers, Casualties, The Three Sisters, The Misanthrope, Heartbreak House, Mensch Meier, Haven, Search and Destroy.
PICTURES: Von Richthofen and Brown (debut, 1970), The People Next Door, The Ultimate Warrior, Moving Violation, Tomorrow Never Comes, Death Valley, Best Revenge, Belizaire the Cajun, Salvation!, Call Me, Sticky Fingers, Caribe, Bloodhounds on Broadway, Erik, The Dark, Geronimo: An American Legend, Beverly Hills Cop III, Art Deco Detective.
TELEVISION: *Series*: Highcliffe Manor, Mariah, Scene of the Crime. *Mini-series*: Centennial. *Movies*: Search for the Gods, James Dean, Look What's Happened to Rosemary's Baby, Mary and Joseph: A Story of Faith, Roughnecks, Terror on Track 9, Jonathan Stone: Threat of Innocence, Deadlocked: Escape From Zone 14, Convict Cowboy.

McKEAN, MICHAEL
Actor, Writer. b. NYC, Oct. 17, 1947. e. NYU. Featured on L.A. radio show, The Credibility Gap.
THEATRE: Accomplice (Theatre World Award).
PICTURES: 1941, Used Cars, Young Doctors in Love, This is Spinal Tap (also co-s.p., co-wrote songs), D.A.R.Y.L., Clue, Jumpin' Jack Flash, Light of Day, Planes Trains and Automobiles, Short Circuit 2, Earth Girls Are Easy, The Big Picture (also co-s.p.), Hider in the House, Flashback, Book of Love, True Identity, Memoirs of an Invisible Man, Man Trouble, Coneheads, Airheads, Radioland Murders, Across the Moon, The Brady Bunch Movie, Edie and Pen, Jack, No Strings Attached, That Darn Cat, Nothing to Lose, With Friends Like These, Still Breathing, The Pass, Archibald the Rainbow Painter, Final Justice, Small Soldiers (voice), Teaching Mrs. Tingle, Kill the Man, True Crime.
TELEVISION: *Series*: Laverne & Shirley, Grand, Sessions, Saturday Night Live, Dream On, Road Rovers, Secret Service Guy, Totally Ridiculous (host). *Movies*: More Than Friends, Classified Love, Murder in High Places, MacShayne: The Final Roll of the Dice. *Specials*: Spinal Tap Reunion, The Laverne and Shirley Reunion. *Guest:* The X Files, The Simpsons (voice).

McKEE, GINA
Actress. b. 1964.
PICTURES: The Lair of the White Worm, The Rachel Papers, The Misadventures of Mr. Wilt, Naked, Element of Doubt, Croupier, Wonderland, Notting Hill, The Loss of Sexual Innocence.
TELEVISION: *Movies:* Treasure Seekers, Mothertime, Beyond Fear, Our Friends in the North, The Passion. *Series:* An Actor's Life for Me, The Lenny Henry Show, Brass Eye. *Guest:* Drop the Dead Donkey.

McKELLEN, SIR IAN
Actor. b. Burnley, England, May 25, 1939. e. Cambridge. C.B.E. 1979, Knighted 1991.
THEATRE: *London*: A Scent of Flowers (debut, 1964), Trelawny of the Wells, A Lily in Little India, The Man of Destiny, Black Comedy, Dr. Faustus, Henceforward, Bent, Uncle Vanya, Hamlet, Macbeth, Romeo & Juliet, Richard III. B'way: The Promise, Amadeus (Tony Award, 1981), Ian McKellen Acting Shakespeare, Wild Honey (also London), Richard III (Brooklyn), A Knight Out. Assoc. Dir. Nat'l Theatre. Prof. of Contemporary Theatre, Oxford Univ., 1991.
PICTURES: Alfred the Great, Thank You All Very Much, A Touch of Love, Priest of Love, The Keep, Plenty, Zina, Scandal, Last Action Hero, The Ballad of Little Jo, Six Degrees of Separation, The Shadow, Jack & Sarah, Restoration, Thin Ice, Richard III (also co-s.p.), Apt Pupil, Gods and Monsters (Acad, Award nom.), X-Men, The Lord of the Rings: The Fellowship of the Ring, Cirque du Soleil: Journey of Man (voice), The Lord of the Rings: The Two Towers, The Lord of the Rings, The Return of the King.
TELEVISION: Hamlet, David Copperfield, The Scarlet Pimpernel, Hedda Gabler, Ian McKellen Acting Shakespeare, Every Good Boy Deserves Favor, Loving Walter, Windmills of the Gods, Macbeth, Othello, Countdown to War, And the Band Played On, Mister Shaw's Missing Millions, Tales of the City, Cold Comfort Farm, Rasputin (Golden Globe Award, 1997), Great Composers (voice).

McKEON, DOUG
Actor. b. Pompton Plains, NJ, June 10, 1966.
THEATRE: Dandelion Wine, Truckload, Brighton Beach Memoirs, Death of a Buick, The Big Day.
PICTURES: Uncle Joe Shannon, On Golden Pond, Night Crossing, Mischief, Turnaround, Where the Red Fern Grows Part 2, The Empty Mirror.
TELEVISION: *Series*: Edge of Night, Big Shamus Little Shamus, Little Niagra. *Mini-Series*: Centennial, At Mother's Request, From the Earth to the Moon. *Movies*: Tell Me My Name, Daddy I Don't Like It Like This, The Comeback Kid, An Innocent Love, Desperate Lives, Silent Eye, Heart of a Champion: The Ray Mancini Story, Breaking Home Ties, Without Consent, Sub Down.

McKEON, NANCY
Actress. b. Westbury, NY, April 4, 1966.
PICTURE: Where the Day Takes You.
TELEVISION: *Series:* Stone, The Facts of Life, Can't Hurry Love. *Movies:* A Question of Love, The Facts of Life Goes to Paris, High School U.S.A., This Child Is Mine, Poison Ivy, Firefighter (also co-exec. prod.), The Facts of Life Down Under, Strange Voices (also co-exec. prod.), A Cry for Help: The Tracey Thurman Story, A Mother's Gift, Style and Substance, Just Right. *Specials:* Schoolboy Father, Scruffy (voice), Please Don't Hit Me Mom, Candid Kids (co-host).

McKERN, LEO
Actor. r.n. Reginald McKern. b. Sydney, New South Wales, Australia, March 16, 1920.
THEATER: She Stoops to Conquer, Hamlet, Merry Wives of Windsor, Cat on a Hot Tin Roof, A Man for All Seasons, Boswell for the Defence, Hobson's Choice.
PICTURES: Murder in the Cathedral, All For Mary, X the Unknown, Time Without Pity, A Tale of Two Cities, The Mouse That Roared, Yesterday's Enemy, Scent of Mystery, Jazz Boat, Mr. Topaze, The Day the Earth Caught Fire, Lisa, Doctor in Distress, A Jolly Bad Fellow, King and Country, Agent 8 3/4, Help!, The Amorous Adventures of Moll Flanders, A Man for All Seasons, Assignment K, Decline and Fall of a Bird Watcher, The Shoes of the Fisherman, Ryan's Daughter, Massacre in Rome, The Adventure of Sherlock Holmes' Smarter Brother, The Omen, Candleshoe, Damien: Omen II, The Last Tasmanian, The Blue Lagoon, The French Lieutenant's Woman, Ladyhawke, The Chain, Traveling North (Australian Film Award), Dave and Dad on Our Selection.
TELEVISION: King Lear, Murder with Mirrors, House on Garibaldi Street, Reilly: Ace of Spies, Rumpole of the Bailey, The Master Builder, The Last Romantics, A Foreign Field, Good King Wenceslas.

McLAGLEN, ANDREW V.
Director. b. London, England, July 28, 1920. Son of late actor Victor McLaglen. e. U. of Virginia, 1939-40. Asst. m.p. dir., 1944-54.
PICTURES: Gun the Man Down (debut, 1956), Man in the Vault, The Abductors, Freckles, The Little Shepherd of Kingdom Come, McLintock!, Shenandoah, The Rare Breed, The Way West, Monkeys Go Home!, The Ballad of Josie, The Devil's Brigade, Bandolero, Hellfighters, The Undefeated, Chisum, Fool's Parade (also prod.), Something Big (also prod.), One More Train to Rob, Cahill: U.S. Marshal, Mitchell, The Last Hard Men, The Wild Geese, Breakthrough (Sergeant Steiner), ffolkes (North Sea Hijack), The Sea Wolves, Sahara, Return to the River Kwai, Eye of the Widow.
TELEVISION: *Series*: Gunsmoke, Have Gun—Will Travel, Perry Mason, Rawhide, The Lineup, The Lieutenant. *Movies*: Log of the Black Pearl, Stowaway to the Moon, Banjo Hackett: Roamin' Free, Murder at the World Series, Louis L'Amour's The Shadow Riders, Travis McGee, The Dirty Dozen: The Next Mission. *Mini-Series*: The Blue and the Gray, On Wings of Eagles.

MCLEAN, SEATON
Executive. b. Florida, raised in Montreal, Quebec, Canada. Founding partner, Atlantis Films, Ltd., 1978. Writer and editor of several award-winning films. producer/co-producer, Boys and Girls, Lost in the Barrens, Ray Bradbury Theater, Traders. Co-exec. producer, Marlowe, Petticoat Wars. Formerly in charge of Television Production for Alliance Atlantis. Currently president motion picture production, Alliance Atlantis Motion Picture Production.

McLERIE, ALLYN ANN
Actress. b. Grand Mere, Quebec, Canada, Dec. 1, 1926. e. Prof. childrens school. m. actor-singer George Gaynes. e. high school, N.Y. Dancer since 15 in many B'way shows.
THEATER: One Touch of Venus, On the Town, Finian's Rainbow, Where's Charley?, Miss Liberty, Time Limit, South Pacific, Night of the Iguana, Julius Caesar, West Side Story, My Fair Lady, The Beast in Me, To Dorothy a Son.
PICTURES: Words and Music (debut 1948), Where's Charley?, Desert Song, Calamity Jane, Phantom of the Rue Morgue, Battle Cry, They Shoot Horses Don't They?, Monte Walsh, The Cowboys, Jeremiah Johnson, The Magnificent Seven Ride, The Way We Were, Cinderella Liberty, All the President's Men.
TELEVISION: *Series*: Tony Randall Show, Punky Brewster, Days and Nights of Molly Dodd. *Mini-Series*: The Thorn Birds, Beulah Land. *Specials*: Oldest Living Graduate, The Entertainer, Return Engagement, Shadow of a Gunman. *Guest*: WKRP in Cincinnati, Barney Miller, St. Elsewhere, Hart to Hart, Love Boat, Dynasty.

McMAHON, ED
Performer. b. Detroit, MI, March 6, 1923. e. Boston Coll.; Catholic U. of America, B.A., 1949. U.S. Marines, 1942-53. First job on TV was as the clown on Big Top, 1950-51. First joined Johnny Carson as his sidekick on daytime quiz show Who Do You Trust? in 1958.
THEATRE: stock; *B'way*: Impossible Years.
PICTURES: The Incident, Slaughter's Big Rip-Off, Fun with Dick and Jane, The Last Remake of Beau Geste (cameo), Butterfly, Full Moon High, Love Affair.
TELEVISION: *Series*: Big Top, Who Do You Trust?, The Tonight Show (1962-92), Missing Links (emcee), Snap Judgment (emcee), The Kraft Music Hall (host, 1968), Concentration (emcee), NBC Adventure Theatre (host), Whodunnit? (emcee), Star Search (host), TV's Bloopers and Practical Jokes (host). Movies: Star Marker, The Great American Traffic Jam (Gridlock), The Kid From Left Field. *Specials*: Macy's Thanksgiving Day Parade (host), Jerry Lewis Labor Day Telethon (co-host).

McMAHON, JOHN J.
Executive. b. Chicago, IL, 1932. e. Northwestern U. Served with U.S. Army in Korea, beginning career on WGN-TV, Chicago; associated with ZIV-United Artists TV Productions during 1950s; joined ABC in 1958; v.p. & gen. mgr., WXYTZ-TV, Detroit, then KABC-TV, Los Angeles, 1968; v.p., ABC, 1968-72; joined NBC in 1972 as v.p., programs, west coast, NBC-TV; president, Hollywood Radio & Television Society; board member, Permanent Charities Committee. 1980, named pres. of Carson Prods. (Johnny Carson's prod. co.).
TELEVISION: John & Yoko: A Love Story, If It's Tuesday It Still Must Be Belgium (exec. prod.), My Father My Son (exec. prod.), Passions, Brother of the Wind.

McMARTIN, JOHN
Actor. Warsaw, IN, e. Columbia U. Off-B'way debut: Little Mary Sunshine (1959: Theatre World Award).
THEATER: The Conquering Hero, Blood Sweat and Stanley Poole, Children from Their Games, A Rainy Day in Newark, Pleasures and Palaces (Detroit), Sweet Charity (Tony nom.), Follies, The Great God Brown (Drama Desk Award), Sondheim: A Musical Tribute, Forget-Me-Not-Lane (Mark Taper Forum), The Visit, Chemin de Fer, The Rules of the Game, A Little Family Business, Passion (Mark Taper), Solomon's Child, Julius Caesar, A Little Night Music (Ahmanson), Love for Love, Happy New Year, Don Juan (Drama Desk Award, Tony nom.), Artist Descending a Staircase, Henry IV (Kennedy Ctr.), Custer (Kennedy Ctr.), Money & Friends (L.A.), Show Boat (Tony nom.), High Society.
PICTURES: A Thousand Clowns, What's So Bad About Feeling Good?, Sweet Charity, All The President's Men, Thieves, Brubaker, Blow Out, Pennies From Heaven, Dream Lover, Legal Eagles, Native Son, Who's That Girl, A Shock to the System.
TELEVISION: *Series*: Falcon Crest, Beauty and the Beast. *Guest*: Cheers, Mary Tyler Moore Show, Murder She Wrote, Magnum P.I., The Golden Girls, Empty Nest, Law and Order, others. American Playhouse *Specials*: Edith Wharton Story, Rules of the Game, The Greatest Man in the World, Private Contentment, The Fatal Weakness, Concealed Enemies. *Movies*: Ritual of Evil, Fear on Trial, The Defection of Simas Kudirka, The Last Ninja, Murrow, Day One, Roots: The Gift, Citizen Cohn.

McMILLAN, RAY
Special Effects.
PICTURES: Rude, Iron Eagle IV, Getting Away with Murder, That Old Feeling, Trial and Error, Mimic, The Edge, Urban Legend, eXistenZ, Detroit Rock City, Rated X, Lakeboat, Frequency, X-Men, Bait, Knockaround Guys, Steal This Move.
TELEVISION:Maniac Mansion, Due South, Flight for Justice: The Nancy Conn Story, The Abduction, Keeping the Promise, Walking on Air, A Slight Case of Murder, Possessed.

McNAMARA, WILLIAM
Actor. b. Dallas, TX, March 31, 1965. e. Columbia U. Joined Act I theatre group at Williamstown Theatre Festival, 1986; studied acting at Lee Strasberg Institute.
PICTURES: The Beat (debut, 1988), Stealing Home, Dream a Little Dream, Stella, Texasville, Terror at the Opera, Aspen Extreme, Surviving the Game, Chasers, Storybook, Girl in the Cadillac, Copycat, Dead Girl, The Brylcreem Boys, Sweet Jane, Something to Believe In, Stag, The Deli, Knockout, Implicated.
TELEVISION: *Series*: Island Son. *Specials*: Soldier Boys (Afterschool Special), Secret of the Sahara, The Edge (Indian Poker), It's Only Rock 'n' Roll (Afterschool Special). *Movies:* Wildflower (ACE Award nom.), Doing Time on Maple Drive, Honor Thy Mother, Sworn to Vengeance, Radio Inside, Liz: The Elizabeth Taylor Story, Natural Enemy. *Pilot*: The Wyatts.

McNAUGHTON, JOHN
Director. b. Chicago, IL, Jan. 13, 1950.
PICTURES: Henry: Portrait of a Serial Killer, The Borrower, Sex Drugs Rock & Roll, Mad Dog and Glory, Girls in Prison, Normal Life, Veeck as a Wreck, Condo Painting, Wild Things.
TELEVISION: *Movies:* Lansky.

McNEELY, JOEL
Composer.
PICTURES: The Pick-Up Artist (add'l. music score), Iron Will (orchestration), You Talkin' to Me?, Samantha, Police Story III: Supercop, Squanto: A Warrior's Tale, Iron Will, Terminal Velocity, Radioland Murders, Gold Diggers: The Secret of Bear Mountain, Flipper, Virus, Vegas Vacation, Wild America, Air Force One (add'l.), The Avengers, Zack and Reba, Soldier, Virus.
TELEVISION: *Movies*: Parent Trap III, Parent Trap Hawaiian Honemoon, Frankenstein: The College Years, Buffalo Soldiers. *Series*: Tiny Toon Adventures, The Young Indiana Jones Chronicles, Buddy Faro.

McNICHOL, KRISTY
Actress. b. Los Angeles, CA, Sept. 11, 1962. Brother is actor Jimmy McNichol. Made debut at age of 7 performing in commercials. Given regular role in Apple's Way; began appearing on such series as Love American Style and The Bionic Woman. Attracted attention of Spelling-Goldberg Productions, who cast her as Buddy Lawrence in Family series, 1976-80.
PICTURES: The End (debut, 1978), Little Darlings, The Night the Lights Went Out in Georgia, Only When I Laugh, White Dog, The Pirate Movie, Just the Way You Are, Dream Lover, You Can't Hurry Love, Two Moon Junction, The Forgotten One.
TELEVISION: *Series*: Apple's Way, Family (2 Emmy Awards: 1977, 1979), Empty Nest. *Movies*: The Love Boat II, Like Mom Like Me, Summer of My German Soldier, My Old Man, Blinded by the Light, Love Mary, Women of Valor, Children of the Bride, Baby of the Bride, Mother of the Bride (also co-exec. prod.).

McRANEY, GERALD
Actor. b. Collins, MS, Aug. 19, 1948. m. actress Delta Burke. e. U. of Mississippi. Left school to become surveyor in oil fields after which joined acting company in New Orleans. Studied acting with Jeff Corey; landed guest role on TV series, Night Gallery.
PICTURES: Night of Bloody Horror, Keep Off My Grass, The Neverending Story, American Justice.
TELEVISION: *Series*: Simon & Simon, Major Dad (also exec. prod.), Home of the Brave, Promised Land. *Guest:* The Incredible Hulk, The Rockford Files, The Dukes of Hazzard, Eight Is Enough, How the West Was Won, Hawaii Five-O, Barnaby Jones, Gunsmoke, Designing Women. *Movies*: Roots II, The Jordan Chance, Women in White, Trial of Chaplain Jenson, The Law, The Haunting Passion, A Hobo's Christmas, Where the Hell's That Gold?!!?, The People Across the Lake, Dark of the Moon, Murder By Moonlight, Blind Vengeance, Vestige of Honor, Love and Curses... And All That Jazz (also dir., co-exec. prod.), Fatal Friendship, Scattered Dreams: The Kathryn Messenger Story, Armed and Innocent, Motorcycle Gang, Deadly Vows, Someone She Knows, Not Our Son, Simon & Simon: In Trouble Again, The Stranger Beside Me, Nothing Lasts Forever. *Special:* Fast Forward.

McSHANE, IAN
Actor. b. Blackburn, England, Sept. 29, 1942. e. RADA.
THEATRE: *England*: The House of Fred Ginger, The Easter Man, The Glass Menagerie, Rashomon, Next Time I'll Sing to You, Loot, The Big Knife, The Admirable Crichton. *NY*: The Promise. *LA*: Inadmissible Evidence, Betrayal, As You Like It.
PICTURES: The Wild and the Willing (debut, 1962), The Pleasure Girls, Gypsy Girl (Sky West and Crooked), If It's Tuesday This Must Be Belgium, The Battle of Britain, Freelance, Pussycat Pussycat I Love You, The Devil's Widow (Tam-Lin), Villain, Sitting Target, The Left Hand of Gemini, The Last of Sheila, Ransom, Journey Into Fear, The Fifth Musketeer, Yesterday's Hero, Cheaper to Keep Her, Exposed, Torchlight, Ordeal By Innocence, Too Scared to Scream.
TELEVISION: Wuthering Heights, The Pirate, Disraeli, The Letter, Marco Polo, Bare Essence, Grace Kelly, Evergreen, A.D., The Murders in the Rue Morgue, Grand Larceny, War and Remembrance, Chain Letter (pilot), The Great Escape II: the Untold Story, The Young Charlie Chaplin, Lovejoy, Sauce For Goose, Dick Francis Mysteries (Blood Sport), Perry Mason: The Case of the Desperate Deception, Columbo: Rest in Peace Mrs. Columbo, White Goods, Soul Survivors (prod.), Madson (prod.), Lovejoy (prod., dir.).

McTEER, JANET
Actress. b. New Castle, England, May 8, 1961. Tony Award Winner in 1991 as Best Actress in a revival of Ibsen's "A Doll's House."
PICTURES: Half Moon Street, Hawks, I Dreamt I Woke Up, Prince, Wuthering Heights, Carrington, Saint-Ex, Velvet Goldmine (voice), Tumbleweeds, Waking the Dead, Songcatcher, The King is Alive.
TELEVISION: *Movies:* Precious Bane, Portrait of a Marriage, Yellowbacks, A Masculine Ending, Don't Leave Me This Way, The Black Velvet Gown. *Series:* The Governor.

McTIERNAN, JOHN
Director. b. Albany, NY, Jan. 8, 1951. e. Juilliard (acting), SUNY/Old Westbury (filmmaking). m. prod. Donna Dubrow. First effort was film The Demon's Daughter, unreleased to date. Appeared in film Death of a Soldier.

PICTURES: Nomads (also s.p.), Predator, Die Hard, The Hunt for Red October, Medicine Man, Last Action Hero (also co-prod.), Die Hard With a Vengeance, The Thomas Crown Affair, The 13th Warrior.

MEADOWS, JAYNE
Actress. b. Wu Chang, China, Sept. 27, 1924. m. performer Steve Allen. Sister of deceased actress Audrey Meadows. Parents were Episcopal missionaries. Came to U.S. in 1931. Studied acting with Stella Adler, Lee Strasberg, David Craig. Made B'way debut in 1941 in Spring Again.
THEATRE: *NY*: Once in a Lifetime (revival), The Gazebo, Spring Again, Another Love Story, Kiss Them for Me, Many Happy Returns, Odds on Mrs. Oakley. *Regional*: Lost in Yonkers, Love Letters, Cinderella, The Fourposter, Tonight at 8:30, Powerful Women in History (1 woman show).
PICTURES: Undercurrent (debut, 1946), Dark Delusion, Lady in the Lake, Luck of the Irish, Song of the Thin Man, David and Bathsheba, Enchantment, Norman Is That You?, The Fat Man, College Confidential, Da Capo (Finland), City Slickers (voice), City Slickers II: The Legend of Curly's Gold (voice), The Player, Casino.
TELEVISION: *Series*: Meeting of Minds, St. Elsewhere, Medical Center, I've Got a Secret, High Society, It's Not Easy, The Steve Allen Show, Art Linkletter Show, Steve Allen Comedy Hour, Steve Allen's Laugh Back. *Movies*: Alice in Wonderland, Alice Through the Looking Glass, Ten Speed and Brownshoe, Masterpiece of Murder, The Ratings Game, Miss All-American Beauty, The James Dean Story, Sex and the Married Woman, The Gossip Columnist, Parent Trap Hawaiian Honeymoon, Now You See It Now You Don't. *Guest*: Your Show of Shows, The Hollywood Palace, The Red Skelton Show, The Love Boat, Fantasy Island, The Paper Chase, Here's Lucy, Uncle Buck, Sisters, The Nanny, Murder She Wrote.

MEANEY, COLM
Actor. b. Ireland. Started acting as a teen, appearing at Gate Theatre in Dublin in play, The Hostage. Studied at Abbey Theatre then joined London's 7-84 Theatre Co., Half Moon Theatre Co., Belt and Braces touring co. On NY stage in Breaking the Code. Also acted with Great Lakes Fest. in Cleveland, OH, in Nicholas Nickelby.
PICTURES: The Dead, Dick Tracy, Die Hard 2, Come See the Paradise, The Commitments, The Last of the Mohicans, Under Siege, Far and Away, Into the West, The Snapper (Golden Globe nom.), The Road to Wellville, The Englishman Who Went Up a Hill But Came Down a Mountain, The Van, The Last of the High Kings, Con Air, This is My Father, Snitch, October 22, Claire Dolan, Four Days, Chapter Zero, Mystery Alaska, Star Trek 3D.
TELEVISION: *Series*: Star Trek: The Next Generation, Deep Space Nine. *Movies/Mini-Series:* Scarlett, Vig, Leprechauns.

MEANEY, DONALD V.
Executive. b. Newark, NJ. e. Rutgers U. Sch. of Journalism. Worked as reporter for Plainfield (NJ) Courier-News, Newark Evening News. Became news dir. of radio station WCTC in New Brunswick, NJ; later for WNJR, Newark. Joined NBC in 1952 as news writer; two years later became nat'l TV news editor. Promoted to mgr., national news, 1960 and mrg., special news programs, 1961. Appt. dir. of news programs 1962 and gen. mgr., NBC News, 1965; v.p., news programming, NBC, 1967; v.p. news, Washington, 1974; mng. dir., affiliate & intl. liaison, 1979; sr. mng. editor, intl. liaison, 1984; retired from NBC, 1985. Now on faculty of American U. Sch. of Communications.

MEARA, ANNE
Actress, Writer. b. Brooklyn, NY Sept. 20, 1929. m. actor-writer Jerry Stiller. Son is actor-dir. Ben Stiller; daughter is actress Amy Stiller. e. Herbert Berghof Studio, 1953-54. Apprenticed in summer stock on Long Island and Woodstock NY, 1950-53. Acted with NY Shakespeare Fest. 1957 and 1988 (Romeo and Juliet). With husband joined St. Louis improv. theater The Compass, 1959 and Chicago's Medium Rare. They formed comedy act in 1962 appearing (34 times) on The Ed Sullivan Show and making the nightclub and comedy club circuit incl. The Village Gate, The Blue Angel, The Establishment. Formed own prod. company, writing, prod. and recording award-winning radio and TV commercials. With husband co-hosted video, So You Want to Be an Actor?
THEATER: A Month in the Country, Maedchen in Uniform, Ulysses in Nightown, The House of Blue Leaves, Spookhouse, Bosoms and Neglect, Eastern Standard, Anna Christie (Tony nom.), After-Play (also author, Outer Critics Circle Award, 1996).
PICTURES: The Out-of-Towners, Lovers and Other Strangers, Nasty Habits, The Boys From Brazil, Fame, The Perils of P.K., The Longshot, My Little Girl, Awakenings, Highway to Hell, Reality Bites, Heavyweights, Kiss of Death, An Open Window, The Daytrippers, Brass Ring, Fish in the Bathtub.
TELEVISION: Guest on numerous TV game and talk shows and variety shows. *Series*: The Greatest Gift (1954 soap opera), The Paul Lynde Show, The Corner Bar, Take Five with Stiller and Meara (1977-78; synd.), Kate McShane, Rhoda, Archie Bunker's Place, ALF, All My Children. *Movies*: Kate McShane (pilot), The Other Woman (co-writer), Jitters. *Specials*: The Sunset Gang, Avenue Z Afternoon.

MECHANIC, WILLIAM M.
Executive. V.p. & Head of Programming, Select TV Programming, Inc., 1978-82. v.p., pay TV & post-theatrical markets, Paramount; senior creative exec., Paramount Pictures; senior v.p. & v.p., pay TV sales, Walt Disney Co., 1984; president, Intl. Distribution & Worldwide Video, Walt Disney Studios, where he set up Buena Vista Intl;. president & COO, Twentieth Century Fox, 1993; president & COO, Fox Filmed Entertainment, 1994-96. Currently chairman & CEO, Fox Filmed Entertainment, where he oversees all operations including worldwide feature film production, marketing, and distribution, and all worldwide operations for Fox Video, Fox Interactive, Licensing & Merchandising, and Fox Music.

MEDAK, PETER
Director. b. Budapest, Hungary, Dec. 23, 1940. Appeared in film Beverly Hills Cop III.
THEATRE: Miss Julie. *Operas*: Salome, La Voix Humaine, Rigoletto.
PICTURES: Negatives, A Day in the Death of Joe Egg, The Ruling Class, Ghost in the Noonday Sun, The Odd Job, The Changeling, Zorro the Gay Blade, The Men's Club, The Krays, Let Him Have It, Romeo Is Bleeding, Pontiac Moon, Species 2.
TELEVISION: Third Girl from the Left, The Babysitter, The Dark Secret of Black Bayou, Mistress of Paradise, Cry for the Stranger, Faerie Tale Theatre, Twilight Zone, Nabokov, Crime Story, Mount Royal, La Voix Humaine, Tales From the Crypt, Homicide, The Kindred, Falls Road, Homicide, The Hunchback of Notre Dame.

MEDAVOY, MIKE
Executive. b. Shanghai, China, Jan. 21, 1941. e. UCLA, grad. 1963 with honors in history. Lived in China until 1947 when family moved to Chile. Came to U.S. in 1957. Started working in mail room at Universal Studios and became a casting dir., then went to work for Bill Robinson as an agent trainee. Two years later joined GAC and CMA where he was a v.p. in the m. p. dept. 1971 joined IFA as v.p. in charge of m. p. dept. Represented American and foreign creative talents, incl. Jane Fonda, Donald Sutherland, Michelangelo Antonioni, Jean-Louis Trintignant, Karel Reisz, Steven Spielberg, Robert Aldrich, George Cukor, John Milius, Terry Malick, Raquel Welch, Gene Wilder and Jeanne Moreau. While at IFA was involved in packaging The Sting, Young Frankenstein, Jaws and others, before joining United Artists Corp. in 1974, as sr. v.p. in chg. of West Coast prod. While at UA, was responsible for One Flew Over the Cuckoo's Nest, Annie Hall and Rocky among others. 1978 named exec. v.p., Orion Pictures Co. where he was responsible for Platoon, Amadeus, Dances With Wolves and Silence of the Lambs. (In 1982 Orion team took over Filmways, Inc.). 1990, apptd. chmn. Tri-Star Pictures, & mem. Columbia Pictures Bd. of Dir. Resigned in 1994. Became chmn. and CEO of Phoenix Pictures in 1995. Co-chmn., St. Petersburg Film Festival, 1994. Chmn. of the Jury, Tokyo Film Festival, 1994. Member of Filmex bd.; bd. of trustees, UCLA Foundation; chmn. advisory bd., College for Intl. Strategic Affairs at UCLA; steering comm. of Royce 270, UCLA; visiting comm., Boston Museum of Fine Arts; advisory bd., Tel Aviv U.; bd., Museum of Science & Industry; Co-Chmn.: Olympic Sports Federation, Music Center Unified Fund Campaign; founding bd. of governors, Sundance Inst. Recipient: Motion Picture Pioneer Award, 1993; Cannes Film Festival Award, 1998; UCLA Alumni Award for Excellence.

MEDOFF, MARK
Writer. e. U. of Miami, Stanford U. Honorary doctor of humane letters, Gallaudet Univ. Prof. & dramatist in residence, New Mexico St. Univ. Novel: Dreams of Long Lasting.
THEATER: When You Comin' Back Red Ryder? (Obie Award), Children of a Lesser God (Tony Award), The Wager, Kringle's Window.
PICTURES: Good Guys Wear Black, Children of a Lesser God (Acad. Award nom.), Clara's Heart, City of Joy, Homage (also prod.), Santa Fe, Mighty Joe Young.
TELEVISION: *Movie*: Apology, The Twilight of the Golds..

MEDWIN, MICHAEL
Actor, Writer, Producer. b. London, England, 1923. e. Institut Fischer, Switzerland. Stage debut 1940; m.p. acting debut in Root of All Evil, 1946. Acted with National Theatre 1977-78.
THEATRE: Spring and Port Wine, Joe Egg, Forget-me-not Lane, Chez Nous, Alpha Beta, Another Country, Crystal Clear, Interpreters, Orpheus, Noises Off.
PICTURES: *Actor*: My Sister and I, Mrs. Christopher, Gay One, Children of Chance, Operation Diamond, Black Memory, Just William's Luck, Ideal Husband, Picadilly Incident, Night Beat, Courtney's of Curzon Street, Call of the Blood, Anna Karenina, William Comes to Town, Woman Hater, Look Before You Love, Forbidden, For Them That Trespass, Queen of Spades, Trottie True, Boys in Brown, Trio, Long Dark Hall, Curtain Up, Street Corner, I Only Asked, Carry on Nurse, Wind Cannot Read, Heart of a Man, Crooks Anonymous, It's All Happening, Night Must Fall, I've Gotta Horse, 24 Hours To Kill, Scrooge, The Jigsaw Man. *Prod.*: Charlie Bubbles, If..., Spring and Port Wine, O Lucky Man! Gumshoe, Law and Disorder, Memoirs of a Survivor, Diamond's Edge.
TELEVISION: Granada's Army Game, Shoestring, The Love of Mike, Three Live Wires.

MEIER, JIM
Executive. b. Newport Beach, CA, Aug. 9, 1971. Pres., Meier Entertainment Group, Vancouver, BC, 1994-98. Dir., British Columbia Motion Picture Assoc., 1996-98. Member, Academy of Canadian Cinema and Television. Pres., CEO and Chairman, Meier Worldwide Intermedia, Inc., 1996-.

MELCHIOR, IB
Director, Writer. b. Copenhagen, Denmark, Sept. 17, 1917. Son of late singer Lauritz Melchior. e. Coll., Stenhus, Denmark, 1936; U. of Copenhagen, 1937. Actor. stage mgr., English Players, 1937-38; co-dir. 1938; actor in 21 stage prod. in Europe and U.S. on radio; set designer; stage man. dept., Radio City Music Hall, 1941-42; U.S. Military Intelligence, 1942-45; writer, dir., m.p. shorts for TV, 1947-48; TV actor, 1949-50; assoc. dir., CBS-TV, 1950; assoc. prod., G-L Enterprises, 1952-53; dir., Perry Como Show, 1951-54; dir. March of Medicine, 1955-56. Documentary writ. & dir., received Top Award by Nat'l. Comm. for Films for Safety, 1960. Golden Scroll Award, Acad. of Science Fiction, Best Writing, 1976; Hamlet Award, Shakespeare Society of America, excellence in playwriting, Hour of Vengeance, 1982.
AUTHOR: Order of Battle, Sleeper Agent, The Haigerloch Project, The Watchdogs of Abaddon, The Marcus Device, The Tombstone Cipher, Eva, V-3, Code Name: Grand Guignol, Steps & Stairways, Quest, Order of Battle: Hitler's Werewolves, Case by Case.
PICTURES: *Writer:* When Hell Broke Loose, Live Fast—Die Young, The Angry Red Planet (also dir.), The Case of Patty Smith (assoc. prod.), Reptilicus, Journey to the Seventh Planet, Robinson Crusoe on Mars, The Time Travellers (also dir.), Ambush Bay, Planet of the Vampires, Death Race 2000.

MELNICK, DANIEL
Executive. b. New York, NY, April 21, 1934. e. NYU. 1952-54, prod. The Children's Theatre at Circle in the Sq., NY. In 1954 was (youngest) staff prod. for CBS-TV; then exec. prod., East Side West Side and N.Y.P.D. Joined ABC-TV as v.p. in chg. of programming. Partner in Talent Associates. Joined MGM as v.p. in chg. of prod.; in 1974 named sr. v.p. & worldwide head of prod.; 1977 in charge of worldwide production, Columbia Pictures; named pres., 1978. Resigned to form independent production co., IndieProd. Company.
PICTURES: *Prod.*: Straw Dogs, That's Entertainment (exec. prod.), That's Entertainment Part 2, All That Jazz (exec. prod.), Altered States (exec. prod.), First Family, Making Love, Unfaithfully Yours (exec. prod.), Footloose (exec. prod.), Quicksilver, Roxanne, Punchline, Mountains of the Moon, Total Recall, Air America, L.A. Story.
TELEVISION: *Specials*: Death of a Salesman (prod.; Emmy Award, 1967), The Ages of Man (prod.; Emmy Award, 1966). *Exec. prod.*: East Side/West Side, N.Y.P.D., Get Smart, Chain Letter (pilot, exec. prod.). *Movie*: Get Smart Again! (exec. prod.).

MELNIKER, BENJAMIN
Producer, Attorney. b. Bayonne, NJ. e. Brooklyn Coll., LL.B., Fordham Law Sch. Loew's Theatres usher; private law practice. Employed by Legal Department MGM; v.p. & gen. counsel, 1954-69; exec. v.p., 1968-70; resigned from MGM, 1971; also member MGM bd. of dirs. and mem. MGM exec. com. Pres., & CEO of Jerry Lewis Cinemas, 1972. Prod. & exec. prod. motion pictures and television movies and series, 1974 to present. Adjunct assoc. prof., NY Law Sch., 1976-77. Former m.p. chmn. Anti-Defamation League, B'nai Brith. Mem. Amer., NY State bar assns., Bar Assn. of City NY, AMPAS.
PICTURES: Winter Kills. *Exec. prod.*: Mitchell, Shoot, Batman, Batman Returns, Batman Forever, Batman & Robin. *Producer*: Swamp Thing. The Return of the Swamp Thing, Batman: Mask of the Phantasm.
TELEVISION: *Exec. prod.*:Three Sovereigns for Sarah, Television's Greatest Bits, Where On Earth Is Carmen Sandiego (Emmy Award), Little Orphan Annie's Very Animated Christmas , Swamp Thing, Harmful Intent, Fish Police, Dinosaucers.

MELVIN, MURRAY
Actor. b. London, England, 1932. On stage with Theatre Workshop.
PICTURES: The Criminal (debut, 1960), A Taste of Honey, HMS Defiant (Damn the Defiant), Sparrows Can't Sing, The Ceremony, Alfie, Kaleidoscope, Smashing Time, The Fixer, Start the Revolution Without Me, A Day in the Death of Joe Egg, The Devils, The Boy Friend, Ghost in the Noonday Sun, Barry Lyndon, The Bawdy Adventures of Tom Jones, Joseph Andrews, Comrades, Testimony, Little Dorrit, The Krays, Let Him Have It, Princess Caraboo.
TELEVISION: Little World of Don Camilllo, The Soldiers Tale, A Christmas Carol, This Office Life, Bulman, William Tell, Stuff of Madness, Sunday Pursuit, The Memorandum, The Stone of Montezuma, Surprises, England My England, The Village.

MENDES, SAM
Director. England, UK, August 1, 1965. Runs the Donmar Warehouse in London.
THEATER: The Rise and Fall of Little Voice, The Blue Room, Cabaret, Cat on a Hit Tin Roof.
PICTURES: American Beauty (Academy Award), Road to Perdition.

MENGES, CHRIS
Cinematographer, Director. b. Kington, England, Sept. 15, 1940.
PICTURES: *Cinematographer*: Kes, Gumshoe, The Empire Strikes Back (second unit), Local Hero, Comfort and Joy, The Killing Fields (Acad. Award, 1984), Marie, The Mission (Acad. Award, 1986), Singing the Blues in Red, Shy People, High Season, Michael Collins (LA Film Critics Award, 1997). *Director*: A World Apart, Crisscross, Second Best.
TELEVISION: World in Action, Opium Warlords, Opium Trail, East 103rd Street.

MENKEN, ALAN
Composer. b. New York, NY, July 22, 1949. Raised in New Rochelle, NY. e. NYU. Began composing and performing at Lehman Engel Musical Theatre Workshop at BMI, where he met future partner, lyricist Howard Ashman. With Ashman made Off-B'way debut in 1979 with score of God Bless You Mr. Rosewater. Wrote music for workshop Battle of the Giants, and music and lyrics for Manhattan Theatre Club Prod. of Real Life Funnies. With Ashman wrote 1982 Off-B'way hit Little Shop of Horrors. Other theatre credits include: The Apprenticeship of Duddy Kravitz, Diamonds, Personals, Let Freedom Sing, Weird Romance, Beauty and the Beast, A Christmas Carol. Grammy Awards: The Little Mermaid (2), Beauty and the Beast (3), Aladdin (4), Pocahontas (1).
PICTURES: Little Shop of Horrors (Acad. Award nom. for song Mean Green Mother From Outer Space), The Little Mermaid (2 Acad. Awards: best song, Under the Sea, and music score, 1989), Rocky V (song), Beauty and the Beast (2 Acad. Awards: best song, title song, and music score, 1991), Newsies, Aladdin (2 Acad. Awards: for song, A Whole New World, and music score, 1992), Home Alone 2: Lost in New York (song), Life With Mikey, Pocahontas (Acad. Awards for Best Score & Best Original Song), The Hunchback of Notre Dame, Hercules.
TELEVISION: *Special*: Lincoln. *Movie:* Polly (song).

MENZEL, JIRI
Actor, Director. b. Prague, Czechoslovakia, February 23, 1938.
PICTURES: *Actor:* Defendant, Kdyby tisic klarinetu, Everday Courage, Closely Watched Trains, Return of the Prodigal Son, Soukroma vichrie, Hotel pro ciznice, Dita Saxova, Capricious Summer, The Cremator, Sechse kommen durch die ganze Welt, 30 panen a Pythagoras, The Apple Game, The Blue Planet, Magicians of the Silverscreen, Miniden szerdain, Koportos, Upir z Feratu, Szivzur, Buldoci a tresme, Srdecny pozdrav ze zemekoule, Fandy, O Fandy, Albert, Utekajme, uzide, Hard Bodies, Tender Barbarians, Larks on a String, The Elementary School, Long Conversation with a Bird, Everything I Like, The Little Apocalypse, Joint Venture, Vengeance is Mine, Jak si zaslouzi-at princeznu, Truck Stop, Every Sunday, Hannah's Ragtime. *Director;* Domy z panleu, Umrel nam pan Forester, Crime at the Girls School, Pearls of the Deep, Koncert 65, Closely Watched Trains, Capricious Summer, Zlocin v santanu, Promeny krajiny, Who Looks for Gold?, Seclusion Near A Forest, Magicians of the Silverscreen, Short Cut, Krasosmutneni, The Snowdrop Festival, My Sweet Little Village, Die Schokladenschnuffler, Prague, The End of Old Times, Larks on a String, The Beggar's Opera, Life and Extraordinary Adventures of Private Ivan Chonkin.

MERCHANT, ISMAIL
Producer, Director. b. Bombay, India, Dec. 25, 1936. e. St. Xavier's Coll., Bombay; NYU, M.A. business admin. Formed Merchant Ivory Prods., 1961 with James Ivory. First film, The Creation of Women (theatrical short, 1961, nom. for Acad. Award). Published 3 cookbooks: Ismail Merchant's Indian Cuisine, Ismail Merchant's Passionate Meals, Ismail Merchant's Florence. Other books: Hullabaloo in Old Jeypore: The Making of The Deceivers (1989), The Proprietor: The Screenplay and Story Behind the Film.
PICTURES: *Producer*: The Householder, Shakespeare Wallah, The Guru, Bombay Talkie, Savages, Autobiography of a Princess, The Wild Party, Roseland, Hullabaloo Over Georgie and Bonnie's Pictures, The Europeans, Jane Austen in Manhattan, Quartet, Heat and Dust, The Bostonians, A Room With a View, Maurice, My Little Girl (exec. prod.), The Deceivers, Slaves of New York, The Perfect Murder (exec. prod.), Mr. and Mrs. Bridge, Ballad of the Sad Cafe, Howards End (BAFTA Award), The Remains of the Day, In Custody (dir. debut), Jefferson in Paris (also cameo), Feast of July (exec. prod.), The Proprietor (dir.).
TELEVISION: *Director*: Mahatma and the Mad Boy, Courtesans of Bombay.

MEREDITH, ANNE
Writer, Producer.
TELEVISION: Losing Chase, Bastard Out of Carolina (writer only, Writers' Guild Award, 1998).

MERHIGE, E. ELIAS
Director. b. Brooklyn, NY 1964. r.n. Edmund Elias Merhige.
PICTURES: Begotten (also prod.,s.p.,photog.), Shadow of the Vampire.

MERRICK, DAVID
Producer. r.n. David Margulois. b. St. Louis, Nov. 27, 1911. e. Washington U.; St. Louis U. L.L.B.
THEATER: *B'way*: Fanny, The Matchmaker, Look Back in Anger, The Entertainer, Jamaica, The World of Suzie Wong, La Plume de Ma Tante, Epitaph for George Dillon, Destry Rides Again, Gypsy, Take Me Along, Irma La Douce, A Taste of Honey, Becket (Tony Award, 1961), Do Re Mi, Carnival, Sunday in New York, Ross, Subways Are For Sleeping, I Can Get It for You Wholesale, Stop the World—I Want to Get Off, Tchin Tchin, Oliver!, Luther (Tony Award, 1964), 110 in the Shade, Arturo Ui, One Flew Over the Cuckoo's Nest, The Milk Train Does't Stop Here Anymore, Hello Dolly! (Tony Award, 1964), Oh What a Lovely War, Pickwick, The Roar of the Greasepaint—The Smell of the Crowd, Inadmissible Evidence, Cactus Flower, Marat/Sade (Tony Award, 1966), Philadelphia Here I Come, Don't Drink the Water, I Do! I Do!, How Now Dow Jones, The Happy Time, Rosencrantz and Guildenstern Are Dead (Tony Award, 1968), 40 Carats, Promises Promises, Play It Again Sam, Child's Play, Four on a Garden, A Midsummer Night's Dream, The Philanthropist, Vivat Vivat Regina, Moonchildren, Sugar, Out Cry, Mack and Mabel, The Misanthrope, A Patriot for Me, Travesties, Very Good Eddie, Private Lives, 42nd Street (Tony Award, 1981), I Won't Dance, Loot, Oh Kay!, State Fair.
PICTURES: Child's Play (debut, 1972), The Great Gatsby, Semi-Tough, Rough Cut.

MERRILL, DINA
Actress. r.n. Nedenia Hutton. b. New York, NY, Dec. 29, 1928. Fashion model, 1944-46. A co-owner and vice-chmn., RKO Pictures, m.p. and TV prod. co.
THEATER: *Regional*: My Sister Eileen, Major Barbara, Misalliance, Othello, Twelfth Night, Loved, Surprise. Off-B'way: Importance of Being Earnest, Smile of the Cardboard Man, Suddenly Last Summer. *B'way*: Angel Street, Are You Now or Have You Ever Been?, On Your Toes.
PICTURES: The Desk Set (debut, 1957), A Nice Little Bank That Should Be Robbed, Don't Give Up the Ship, Operation Petticoat, The Sundowners, Butterfield 8, Twenty Plus Two, The Young Savages, The Courtship of Eddie's Father, I'll Take Sweden, Running Wild, The Meal, The Greatest, A Wedding, Just Tell Me What You Want, Twisted, Caddyshack II, True Colors, The Player, Open Season, The Point of Betrayal, Milk & Money.
TELEVISION: *Debut:* Kate Smith Show 1956. *Guest*: Four Star Theatre, Playwrights '56, Climax!, Playhouse 90, Westinghouse Presents, The Investigators, Checkmate, The Rogues, Bob Hope Presents, To Tell the Truth, The Doctors, The Name of the Game, Hotel, Hawaii Five-O, Murder She Wrote, Something Wilder, The Nanny, Rosanne. *Series*: Hot Pursuit. *Mini-Series*: Roots: The Next Generations. *Movies*: The Sunshine Patriot, Seven in Darkness, The Lonely Profession, Mr. & Mrs. Bo Jo Jones, Family Flight, The Letters, Kingston: The Power Play, The Tenth Month, Repeat Performance, Turn Back the Clock, Fear, Brass Ring, Anne to the Infinite, Not in My Family, Something Borrowed Something Blue.

MERSON, MARC
Producer. b. New York, NY, Sept. 9, 1931. e. Swarthmore Coll. Entered Navy in 1953; assigned as publicist to Admiral's Staff of Sixth Fleet Command in the Mediterranean. Upon discharge joined trade paper Show Business as feature editor. Joined CBS-TV as asst. to casting dir.. Left after 3 yrs. to work for Ely Landau as casting dir., packager and sometime prod. of The Play of the Week on TV. Returned to CBS for 3-yr. stint doing specials and live programs. Left to organize Brownstone Productions as indep. prod. Partner with Alan Alda in Helix Productions to package and produce TV shows.
PICTURES: The Heart Is a Lonely Hunter, People Soup (short), Leadbelly, Doc Hollywood (exec. prod.).
TELEVISION: *Series*: Kaz, We'll Get By, Off the Rack, Jessica Novak, Waverly Wonders, Stage 67, Androcles and the Lion, Dummler and Son (pilot), The David Frost Revue (synd. series), We'll Get By. *Movie*: Rules of Marriage (spr. prod.).

MESTRES, RICARDO A. III
Executive. b. New York, NY, Jan. 23, 1958. e. Harvard U., A.B. 1980. Gained filmmaking experience during summers as prod. asst. on TV features. Joined Paramount Pictures as creative exec. 1981. Promoted to exec. dir. of production in 1982 and to v.p., prod. in 1984. Named v.p. of prod., Walt Disney Pictures, 1985. Promoted to sr. v.p., prod.,1986-88. Named pres. production, Touchstone Pictures, 1988-89. In 1989, became pres., Hollywood Pictures. Resigned, 1994. Co-founder Great Oaks Entertainment with John Hughes, 1995-1997. Principal Ricardo Mestres Productions. Disney Studios, 1997-present. Member, AMPAS.
PICTURES: *Prod.:* Jack, 101 Dalmatians, Flubber, Home Alone III, The Visitors

METCALF, LAURIE
Actress. b. Edwardsville, IL, June 16, 1955. e. Illinois St. Univ. One of the original members of the Steppenwolf Theatre Company. On B'way in My Thing of Love.
THEATRE: Chicago: True West, Fifth of July. NY: Balm in Gilead (Obie & Theatre World Awards). LA: Wrong Turn at Lungfish.
PICTURES: Desperately Seeking Susan (debut, 1985), Making Mr. Right, Candy Mountain, Stars and Bars, Miles From Home, Uncle Buck, Internal Affairs, Pacific Heights, JFK, Mistress, A Dangerous Woman, Blink, Leaving Las Vegas, Dear God, U Turn, Scream 2, Chicago Cab, Bulworth, Runaway Bride, Toy Story 2 (voice).
TELEVISION: *Series*: Roseanne (3 Emmy Awards: 1992-4), Norm. *Movie*: The Execution of Raymond Graham, Balloon Farm, Always Outnumbered, The Long Island Incident.

METZLER, JIM
Actor. b. Oneonta, NY, June 23, 1951. e. Dartmouth Coll.
PICTURES: Four Friends, Tex, River's Edge, Hot to Trot, Sundown: The Vampire in Retreat, 976-EVIL, Old Gringo, Circuitry Man, Delusion, One False Move, Waxwork II: Lost in Time, A Weekend with Barbara und Ingrid, Gypsy Eyes, C.I.A. Trackdown, Plughead Rewired: Circuitry Man II, Children of the Corn III: Urban Harvest, Cadillac Ranch, A Gun A Car A Blonde, L.A. Confidential, St Patrick's Day, Under the Influence, Phantom Town, Warm Texas Rain.
TELEVISION: *Series*: Cutter to Houston, The Best Times. *Mini-Series*: North and South, North and South Book II, On Wings of Eagles. *Movies*: Do You Remember Love, Princess Daisy, Christmas Star, The Alamo: 13 Days to Glory, The Little Match Girl, Murder By Night, Crash: The Mystery of Flight 1501, Love Kills, French Silk, Don't Look Back, Apollo II, Little Girls in Pretty Boxes, A Wing and a Prayer.

MEYER, BARRY M.
Executive. b. New York, NY, Nov. 28, 1943. e. B.A., U. of Rochester, J.D., Case Western Reserve U. School of Law. Began in legal & business affairs, ABC Television Network, 1968; director, Business Affairs, 1971; v.p., Business Affairs, 1972, Warner Bros. Television; exec. v.p., Television Division, Warner Bros., 1978; exec. v.p., Warner Bros., Inc., 1984, in charge of all television operations. Became CEO, Warner Bros., Inc., 1994. Named chairman & CEO, Warner Bros., 1999. Currently member and former Governor, Academy of Television Arts & Sciences; member and past board member, Hollywood Radio & Television Society; member, Academy of Motion Picture Arts & Sciences; member, Board of Councilors, USC School of Cinema-Television; member of the board, Museum of Radio & Television; member, Board of Directors, City National Corp. and City National Bank; involved in various charitable and community service activities.

MEYER, BRECKIN
Actor. b. Minneapolis, MN, May 7, 1974.
PICTURES: Freddy's Dead: The Final Nightmare, Payback, Clueless, The Craft, Escape from L.A., Prefontaine, Touch, Dancer Texas Pop. 81, Can't Hardly Wait, 54, Go.
TELEVISION: *Movies:* Camp Cucamonga, Betrayed: A Story of Three Women. *Series:* The Jackie Thomas Show, The Home Court. *Guest:* The Wonder Years, Clueless, Party of Five.

MEYER, NICHOLAS
Director, Writer. b. New York, NY, Dec. 24, 1945. e. U. of Iowa. Was unit publicist for Love Story, 1969. Story ed. Warner Bros. 1970-71.
AUTHOR: The Love Story Story, The Seven Percent Solution, Target Practice, The West End Horror, Black Orchid, Confession of a Homing Pigeon, The Canary Trainer.
PICTURES: The Seven Percent Solution (s.p.), Time After Time (s.p., dir.), Star Trek II: The Wrath of Khan (dir.), Volunteers (dir.), The Deceivers (dir.), Company Business (dir., s.p.) Star Trek VI: The Undiscovered Country (dir., co-s.p.), Sommersby (co-s.p.), Voices, The Informant.
TELEVISION: *Movies*: Judge Dee (writer), The Night That Panicked America (writer), The Day After (dir.).

MEYER, RON
Executive. b. 1945. Served in US Marine Corps. 1985, co-founded, with Mike Ovitz, Creative Artists talent agency, eventually serving as pres. 1995, appointed pres. & COO of MCA.

MEYER, RUSS
Producer, Director. b. Oakland, CA, March 21, 1922. In 1942 joined Army Signal Corps, learned m.p. photography and shot combat newsreels. Worked as photographer for Playboy Magazine. Pres., RM Films Intl. Inc. 3 vol. autobiography: A Clean Breast: The Life and Loves of Russ Meyer.
PICTURES: The Immoral Mr. Teas, Eve and the Handyman, Erotica, Wild Gals of the Naked West, Heavenly Bodies, Lorna, Motor Psycho, Fanny Hill, Mudhoney, Mondo Topless, Faster Pussycat Kill Kill, Finders Keepers Lovers Weepers, Goodmorning and Goodbye, Common Law Cabin, Vixen, Cherry Harry & Raquel, Beyond the Valley of the Dolls, The Seven Minutes, Black Snake, Supervixens, Up, Beneath the Valley of the Ultra Vixens, Amazon Women on the Moon (actor), Pandora Peaks, Europe In the Raw!, Melissa Mounds.

MEYERS, NANCY
Writer, Producer. b. Philadelphia, PA. e. American U., D.C. Began as story editor for Ray Stark. First teamed with Charles Shyer to write screenplay for Private Benjamin.

PICTURES: *Writer/Producer*: Private Benjamin (Acad. Award nom., Writers Guild Annual Award), Irreconcilable Differences, Baby Boom, Father of the Bride, I Love Trouble, Father of the Bride II.

MEYERS, ROBERT
Executive. b. Mount Vernon, NY, Oct. 3, 1934. e. NYU. Entered m.p. industry as exec. trainee in domestic div. of Columbia Pictures, 1956; sales and adv. 1956-60; transferred to sales dept. Columbia Pictures Int'l, NY: posts there included supervisor of int'l roadshows and exec. assistant. to continental mgr. Joined National General Pictures as v.p.-foreign sales, 1969. Created JAD Films International Inc. in Feb. 1974 for independent selling and packaging of films around the world. September, 1977, joined Lorimar Productions Inc. as sr. v.p. of Lorimar Distribution Intl. Became pres. in 1978. Joined Filmways Pictures in 1980, named pres. & COO. Pres. of American Film Mktg. Assn.; 1982, formed new co., R.M. Films International. Rejoined Lorimar 1985. as pres., Lorimar Motion Pictures, int'l distribution. 1988-92, pres., Orion Pictures Int'l. 1993-94, pres., Odyssey Entertainment. In 1995, joined Village Roadshow International as pres.

MEYRINK, MICHELLE
Actress.
PICTURES: Valley Girl, The Outsiders, Revenge of the Nerds, Joy of Sex, Real Genius, One Magic Christmas, Nice Girls Don't Explode, Permanent Record.
TELEVISION: *Guest:* Family Ties.

MICHAELS, HELENE
Executive. Began career in television at Triad Artists. V.p., series development, New World Television, 1988. after serving in a number of key roles, including exec. v.p. of programming and v.p. of primetime series. Was named exec. v.p., Columbia TriStar Television (CTT), 1996-99. Currently president, network production, CTT.

MICHAELS, JOEL B.
Producer. b. Buffalo, NY, Oct. 24, 1938. Studied acting with Stella Adler. Many co-prods. with Garth Drabinsky, Cineplex Corp. Pres. of Cineplex Odeon, 1986-90.
PICTURES: The Peace Killers, Your Three Minutes Are Up (prod. spvr.), Student Teachers (prod. spvr.), The Prisoners (assoc. prod.), Lepke (assoc. prod.), The Four Deuces (asso. prod.), Bittersweet Love, The Silent Partner, The Changeling, Tribute, The Amateur, Losin' It (exec. prod.), The Philadelphia Experiment, Black Moon Rising, Universal Soldier, Three of Hearts (exec. prod.), Stargate, Cutthroat Island (co-prod.), Last of the Dogmen, Lolita.

MICHAELS, LORNE
Writer, Producer. b. Toronto, Canada, Nov. 17, 1944. e. U. of Toronto, 1966. CEO, Broadway Video, since 1979. Named B'caster of the Year by the International Radio and TV Society, 1992.
THEATER: Gilda Radner Live From New York (prod., dir.).
PICTURES: *Producer*: Gilda Live (also co-s.p.), Nothing Lasts Forever, Three Amigos (also co-s.p.), Wayne's World, Coneheads, Wayne's World 2, Lassie, Tommy Boy, Stuart Saves His Family, Black Sheep.
TELEVISION: *Series*: Rowan and Martin's Laugh-In (writer, 1968-69), Saturday Night Live (creator, prod., writer: 1975-80, 4 Emmy Awards; 1985-), The New Show (prod.), The Kids in the Hall (series co-prod.), Late Night With Conan O'Brien (exec. prod.). *Specials*: Lily Tomlin Specials (writer, prod.: 1972-75, 2 Emmy Awards), Perry Como (writer, prod., 1974), Flip Wilson (writer, prod.), Beach Boys (writer, prod.), The Paul Simon Special (writer, prod., Emmy Award, 1978), The Rutles: All You Need Is Cash (writer, prod.), Steve Martin's Best Show Ever (prod.), Simon and Garfunkel: The Concert in the Park (exec. prod.), The Coneheads (exec. prod.), 1988 Emmy Awards (prod.), Coca-Cola Presents Live: The Hard Rock, On Location: Kids in the Hall (exec. prod.), The Rolling Stones: Steel Wheels Concert (exec. prod.), Paul Simon: Born at the Right Time in Central Park (exec. prod.).

MICHAELS, RICHARD
Director. b. Brooklyn, NY, Feb. 15, 1936. e. Cornell U. Script supervisor 1955-64 and associate prod. before starting directing career in 1968 with Bewitched (54 episodes; also assoc. prod.).
PICTURES: How Come Nobody's On Our Side?, Blue Skies Again.
TELEVISION: *Series*: Love American Style, The Odd Couple, Delvecchio, Ellery Queen, Room 222. *Movies*: Once an Eagle (mini-series), Charlie Cobb, Having Babies II, Leave Yesterday Behind, My Husband Is Missing, ... And Your Name Is Jonah (winner, Christopher Award), Once Upon a Family, The Plutonium Incident, Scared Straight, Another Story (Scott Newman Drug Abuse Prevention Award), Homeward Bound (Banff Intl. TV Fest. Special Jury Award & Christopher Award), Berlin Tunnel 21, The Children Nobody Wanted, One Cooks, The Other Doesn't, Jessie (pilot), Silence of the Heart, Heart of a Champion: The Ray Mancini Story, Rockabye, Kay O'Brien (pilot), Leg Work (pilot), Red River (movie), Indiscreet, Love and Betrayal, Her Wicked Ways, Leona Helmsley: The Queen of Mean, Triumph of the Heart: The Ricky Bell Story, Backfield in Motion, Miss America: Behind the Crown, Father and Scout. *Mini-series*: Sadat, I'll Take Manhattan.

MICHEL, WERNER
Executive. e. U. of Berlin, U. of Paris, Ph.D., Sorbonne, 1931. Radio writer, dir., co-author two Broadway revues, 1938, 1940. Broadcast dir., Voice of America, 1942-46. Prod. & dir., CBS, 1946-48; asst. prog. dir., CBS, 1948-50. Prod. Ford TV Theatre, 1950-52 Prod. DuMont TV network, 1952-55. Dir. Electronicam TV-Film Prod., 1955-56. Prod. of Edge of Night, Procter and Gamble, 1956-57. V.P. & dir., TV-radio dept., Reach, McClinton Advertising, Inc., 1957-62. Consultant, TV Programming & Comm'l-Prod., N.W. Ayer & Son Inc. V.P. & dir., TV dept., SSCB Advertising, 1963. Program exec. at ABC-TV Hollywood, 1975. Sr. v.p. of creative affairs, MGM-TV, 1977. Exec. v.p., Wrather Entertainment Intl., 1979. Returned to MGM-TV as sr. v.p., creative affairs, 1980-82. COO, Guber-Peters TV, 1982-84. Sr. v.p., corporate TV dept., Kenyon & Eckhart, & NY, 1984-86. Currently sr. v.p., sr. partner of TV dept., Bozell, Inc. NY.

MICHELL, KEITH
Actor. b. Adelaide, Australia, Dec. 1, 1926. Early career as art teacher, radio actor; toured Australia with Stratford Shakespearean Co. 1952-53; Stratford Memorial Theatre 1954-55, Old Vic Theatre 1956-57. Served as artistic dir., Chichester Festival Theatre, touring Australia.
THEATER: Irma la Douce, Art of Seduction, The First 400 Years, Robert & Elizabeth, Kain, The King's Mare, Man of La Mancha, Abelard & Heloise, Hamlet, Crucifer of Blood, On the Twentieth Century, Pete McGynty, Captain Beaky Christmas Show, On the Rocks, The Tempest, Amadeus, La Cage aux Folles, Portraits, The Bacarat Scandal, Henry VIII, Aspects of Love, Scrooge, Brazilian Blue, Caesar & Cleopatra.
PICTURES: True as a Turtle, Dangerous Exile, Gypsy and the Gentleman, The Hellfire Club, All Night Long, Seven Seas to Calais, Prudence and the Pill, House of Cards, Henry VIII and his Six Wives, Moments, The Deceivers.
TELEVISION: *U.K.*: Pygmalion, Act of Violence, Mayerling Affair, Wuthering Heights, The Bergonzi Hand, Ring Round The Moon, Spread of the Eagle, The Shifting Heart, Loyalties, Julius Caesar, Antony and Cleopatra, Kain, The Ideal Husband, The Six Wives of Henry VIII (series), Dear Love, Captain Beaky & His Band, Captain Beaky, Volume 2, The Gondoliers, The Pirates of Penzance, Ruddigore. *U.S.*: Story of the Marlboroughs, Jacob and Joseph, Story of David, The Tenth Month, The Day Christ Died, The Miracle, Murder She Wrote. *Australia: Series*: My Brother Tom, Captain James Cook.

MIDLER, BETTE
Actress, Singer. b. Honolulu, HI, Dec. 1, 1945. e. U. of Hawaii. Studied acting at Berghof Studios. Appeared on B'way in Fiddler on the Roof, Salvation; also in Tommy with Seattle Opera Co., 1971. Gained fame as singer-comic in nightclubs and cabarets. Has toured extensively with own stage shows: The Divine Miss M, Clams on the Half-Shell, Divine Madness, Art of Bust, Experience the Divine. Grammy Awards: The Divine Miss M, The Rose, Blueberry Pie (from In Harmony), Wind Beneath My Wings. *Author*: A View From a Broad, The Saga of Baby Divine. Special Tony Award, 1973.
PICTURES: Hawaii (debut, 1966), The Rose (Acad. Award nom.; 2 Golden Globe Awards), Divine Madness, Jinxed, Down and Out in Beverly Hills, Ruthless People, Outrageous Fortune, Big Business, Oliver & Company (voice), Beaches (also co-prod.), Stella, Scenes from a Mall, For the Boys (Acad. Award nom., Golden Globe Award; also co-prod.), Hocus Pocus, Get Shorty, First Wives Club, That Old Feeling, Isn't She Great, Get Bruce, Drowning Mona.
TELEVISION: *Series*: Bette. *Specials*: The Fabulous Bette Midler Show, Ol' Red Hair is Back (Emmy Award, 1978; also co-writer), Art or Bust (also prod., co-writer), Bette Midler's Mondo Beyondo (also creator, co-writer), Mud Will Be Flung Tonight, Bette Midler in Concert: Diva Las Vegas. *Movies*: Gypsy, Jackie's Back!. *Guest*: Cher, The Tonight Show (Emmy Award, 1992).
RECORDINGS: The Divine Miss M, Bette Midler, Songs for the New Depression, Live at Last, The Rose, Thighs and Whispers, Divine Madness, No Frills, Mud Will Be Flung Tonight, Beaches, Some People's Lives, For the Boys, Experience the Divine, Bette of Roses.

MIGDEN, CHESTER L.
Executive. b. New York, NY, May 21, 1921; e. City Coll. of New York, B.A., 1941, Columbia U., J.D., 1947. Member New York Bar. Attorney for National Labor Relations Board 1947-51. Exec of Screen Actors Guild 1952-81. Nat'l exec. dir., 1973-81. Exec. dir., Assn. of Talent Agents, 1982-94. Arbitrator, consultant 1994-present.

MIKELL, GEORGE
Actor. b. Lithuania. In Australia 1950-56 acting with Old Vic Co. Ent. films 1955. TV 1957. To England 1957.
THEATER: Five Finger Exercise, Altona, The Millionairess, Love from a Stranger, Portrait of a Queen, Farewell, Judas, Flare Path.
PICTURES: The Guns of Navarone, The Password Is Courage, The Great Escape, Deadline for Diamonds, Where The Spies Are, The Spy Who Came in From the Cold, I Predoni Del Sahara (Italy), Sabina (Israel), The Double Man, Attack on the Iron Coast, Zeppelin, Young Winston, Scorpio, The Tamarind Seed, Sweeney Two, The Sea Wolves, Victory, Emerald, Kommissar Zufall (Germany).

TELEVISION: Counsel at Law, Six Eyes on a Stranger, The Mask of a Clown, Green Grows the Grass, Opportunity Taken, OSS Series, Espinage, The Danger Man, Strange Report, The Survivors, The Adventurer, Colditz, The Hanged Man, Quiller, Martin Hartwell, Flambards, Sweeney, The Secret Army, Sherlock Holmes, When the Boat Comes In, Brack Report, Bergerac, The Brief, Glass Babies (Australia), Hannay, Night of the Fox (mini-series), Secrets (Australia), Stark (Australia).

MILCH, DAVID
Producer, Consultant.
TELEVISION: *Movies*: Capital News. *Mini-series*: Murder One: Diary of a Serial Killer. *Series*: Capital News, NYPD Blue (Emmy Award, 1997), Murder One, Total Security, Brooklyn South.

MILCHAN, ARNON
Producer. b. Israel, Dec. 6, 1944. Began producing and financing films in Israel. Also prod. of stage plays including: Ipi Tombi, It's So Nice to be Civilized, and Amadeus in Paris starring Roman Polanski. Appeared in film Can She Bake a Cherry Pie?
PICTURES: Black Joy, The Medusa Touch, Dizengoff 99, The King of Comedy, Once Upon a Time in America (also actor), Brazil, Stripper (exec. prod.), Legend, Man on Fire, Who's Harry Crumb?, The War of the Roses, Big Man on Campus, Pretty Woman, Q & A, Guilty by Suspicion, JFK (exec. prod.), The Mambo Kings, Memoirs of an Invisible Man (exec. prod.), The Power of One, Under Siege, Sommersby, Falling Down (exec. prod.), Made in America, Free Willy (exec. prod.), That Night, Striking Distance, George Balanchine's The Nutcracker (exec. prod.), Six Degrees of Separation, Heaven and Earth, The Client, The New Age, Second Best, Boys on the Side, Copycat (co-prod.), Under Siege 2: Dark Territory, Free Willy 2: The Adventure Home, Heat, Bogus, Tin Cup (exec. prod.), A Time to Kill, The Mirror Has Two Faces, Murder at 1600, L.A. Confidential, Fight Club.
TELEVISION: *Mini-Series:* Masada. *Series:* John Grisham's The Client (exec. prod.), Michael Hayes.

MILES, CHRISTOPHER
Director. b. London, England, April 19, 1939. e. I.D.H.E.C., 1962. Sister is actress Sarah Miles. Studied film in Paris at the Institut des Hautes Etudes Cinematographiques.
PICTURES: The Six-Sided Triangle, Up Jumped a Swagman, The Virgin and the Gypsy, Time for Loving, The Maids (also co-s.p.), That Lucky Touch, Alternative 3 (also co-s.p.), Priest of Love (also prod.), The Marathon (also co-s.p.), Aphrodisias (also co-s.p.), Some Stones of No Value (also co-s.p.), Love In The Ancient World (also s.p.).

MILES, SARAH
Actress. b. Ingatestone, England, Dec. 31, 1941. e. RADA. Was married to late writer Robert Bolt. Brother is actor Christopher Miles. Appeared in short film Six-Sided Triangle.
THEATER: Dazzling, World War 2 1/2, Kelly's Eye, Vivat! Vivat Regina!
PICTURES: Term of Trial (debut, 1962), The Servant, The Ceremony, Those Magnificent Men in Their Flying Machines, I Was Happy Here, Blow-Up, Ryan's Daughter (Acad. Award nom.), Lady Caroline Lamb, The Man Who Loved Cat Dancing, The Hireling, Bride to Be, The Sailor Who Fell From Grace With the Sea, The Big Sleep, Priest of Love, Venom, Ordeal by Innocence, Steaming, Hope and Glory, White Mischief, The Silent Touch.
TELEVISION: Loving Walter (Walter and June), James Michener's Dynasty, Great Expectations, Harem, Queenie, A Ghost in Monte Carlo, Dandelion Dead, Ring Round the Moon, The Rehearsal.

MILES, SYLVIA
Actress. b. New York, NY, Sept. 9, 1934. Attended Pratt Inst., NYC. e. Washington Irving H.S., Actors Studio, Dramatic Workshop of the New School.
THEATER: Rosebloom, The Iceman Cometh, The Balcony, The Riot Act, Vieux Carre, Before Breakfast, The Night of the Iguana, Tea with Mommy and Jack, Ruthless.
PICTURES: Murder Inc. (debut, 1960), Parrish, Pie in the Sky, Violent Midnight, Terror in the City, Midnight Cowboy (Acad. Award nom.), The Last Movie, Who Killed Mary Whats'ername?, Heat, 92 in the Shade, Farewell My Lovely (Acad. Award nom.), The Great Scout and Cathouse Thursday, The Sentinel, Shalimar, Zero to Sixty, The Funhouse, Evil Under the Sun, No Big Deal, Critical Condition, Sleeping Beauty, Wall Street, Crossing Delancey, Spike of Bensonhurst, She-Devil, Denise Calls Up.
TELEVISION: *Series*: All My Children. *Guest*: Miami Vice, The Equalizer, Tonight Show, etc.

MILES, VERA
Actress. r.n. Vera Ralston. b. Boise City, OK, Aug. 23, 1929. e. public schools, Pratt and Wichita, KS.
PICTURES: Two Tickets to Broadway (debut, 1951), For Men Only, Rose Bowl Story, Charge at Feather River, So Big, Pride of the Blue Grass, Tarzan's Hidden Jungle, Wichita, The Searchers, 23 Paces to Baker Street, Autumn Leaves, Wrong Man, Beau James, Web of Evidence, FBI Story, Touch of Larceny, Five Branded Women, Psycho, Back Street, The Man Who Shot Liberty Valance, A Tiger Walks, Those Calloways, Follow Me Boys!, The Spirit Is Willing, Gentle Giant, Sergeant Ryker, Kona Coast, It Takes All Kinds, Hellfighters, Mission Batangas, The Wild Country, Molly and Lawless John, One Little Indian, The Castaway Cowboy, Twilight's Last Gleaming, Thoroughbred, Run for the Roses, Brainwaves, Psycho II, The Initiation, Into the Night.
TELEVISION: *Movies*: The Hanged Man, In Search of America, Cannon (pilot), Owen Marshall: Counselor at Law (pilot), A Howling in the Woods, Jigsaw, A Great American Tragedy, Baffled!, Runaway!, Live Again Die Again, Underground Man, The Strange and Deadly Occurence, NcNaughton's Daughter, Judge Horton and the Scottsboro Boys, Smash-up on Interstate 5, Fire!, And I Alone Survived, Roughnecks, Our Family Business, Rona Jaffe's Mazes and Monsters, Travis McGee, Helen Keller: The Miracle Continues, The Hijacking of the Achille Lauro. *Guest*: Climax, Pepsi Cola Playhouse, Schlitz Playhouse, Ford Theatre.

MILGRAM, HANK
Theatre Executive. b. Philadelphia, PA, April 20, 1926. e. U. of PA, Wharton Sch. Exec. v.p., Milgram Theatres. Variety Club Board member, past president and chairman of the board of Variety Club of Philadelphia; past Variety Club Intl. v.p.; President's council. Served for 12 yrs. as bd. member, Hahneman Univ. until 1993.

MILIUS, JOHN
Writer, Director. b. St. Louis, MO. April 11, 1944. e. Los Angeles City Coll., U. of Southern California (cinema course). While at latter, won National Student Film Festival Award. Started career as ass't. to Lawrence Gordon at AIP. Began writing screenplays, then became dir. with Dillinger (1973). Appeared in documentary Hearts of Darkness.
PICTURES: The Devil's Eight (co-s.p.), Evel Knievel (co-s.p.), The Life and Times of Judge Roy Bean (s.p.), Jeremiah Johnson (co-s.p.), Deadhead Miles (actor), Dillinger (dir. debut, 1973; also s.p.), Magnum Force (co-s.p.), The Wind and the Lion (dir., s.p.), Big Wednesday (dir., co-s.p., actor), Hardcore (exec. prod.), Apocalypse Now (s.p.), 1941 (exec. prod., co-story), Used Cars (co-exec. prod.), Conan the Barbarian (dir., co-s.p.), Uncommon Valor (co-prod.), Red Dawn (dir., co-s.p.), Extreme Prejudice (story), Farewell to the King (dir., s.p.), Flight of the Intruder (dir., co-s.p), Geronimo: An American Legend (co-s.p., story), Clear and Present Danger (co-s.p.), Rough Riders, Mexico.

MILKIS, EDWARD
Producer. b. Los Angeles, CA, July 16, 1931. e. U. of Southern California. Began career as asst. editor, ABC-TV, 1952; Disney, 1954; MGM, 1957; editor, MGM, 1960-65; assoc. prod., Star Trek, 1966-69; exec. in chg. post-prod., Paramount, 1969-72; formed Miller-Milkis Prods., 1972; Miller-Milkis-Boyett, 1979. Now heads Edward K. Milkis Prods.
PICTURES: Silver Streak, Foul Play, The Best Little Whorehouse in Texas.
TELEVISION: Petrocelli, Bosom Buddies (exec. prod.), Happy Days, Laverne and Shirley, Feel the Heat.

MILLAR, STUART
Producer, Director. b. New York, NY, 1929. e. Stanford U.; Sorbonne, Paris. Ent. industry working for Motion Picture Branch, State Dept., Germany. documentaries, Army Signal Corps, Long Island, Germany; journalist, International News Service, San Francisco; assoc. prod.-dir., The Desperate Hours; assoc. prod.-dir., Friendly Persuasion.
PICTURES: *Producer*: The Young Stranger, Stage Struck, Birdman of Alcatraz, I Could Go On Singing, The Young Doctors, Stolen Hours, The Best Man, Paper Lion, Little Big Man, When The Legends Die (also dir.), Rooster Cogburn (dir. only), Shoot the Moon (co-exec. prod.).
TELEVISION: *Producer*: Isabel's Choice, Vital Signs (also dir.), Killer Instinct, Dream Breaker (also dir.), Lady in a Corner.

MILLER, ANN
Actress. r.n. Lucille Ann Collier. b. Houston, TX, April 12, 1923. e. Albert Sidney Johnson H.S., Houston; Lawler Prof. Sch., Hollywood. Studied dance as child; played West Coast vaudeville theatres. Autobiography: Miller's High Life (1974), Tapping Into the Force.
THEATER: George White's Scandals, Mame, Sugar Babies.
PICTURES: Anne of Green Gables (debut, 1934), The Good Fairy, Devil on Horseback, New Faces of 1937, Life of the Party, Stage Door, Radio City Revels, Having Wonderful Time, Room Service, You Can't Take It with You, Tarnished Angel, Too Many Girls, Hit Parade of 1941, Melody Ranch, Time Out for Rhythm, Go West Young Lady, True to the Army, Priorities on Parade, Reveille with Beverly, What's Buzzin' Cousin?, Jam Session, Hey Rookie, Carolina Blues, Eadie Was a Lady, Eve Knew Her Apples, Thrill of Brazil, Easter Parade, The Kissing Bandit, On the Town, Watch the Birdie, Texas Carnival, Two Tickets to Broadway, Lovely To Look At, Small Town Girl, Kiss Me Kate, Deep in My Heart, Hit the Deck, The Opposite Sex, The Great American Pastime, Won Ton Ton the Dog Who Saved Hollywood, That's Entertainment III.
TELEVISION: *Specials*: Dames at Sea, Disney-MGM Special. *Guest*: Love American Style, The Love Boat.

MILLER, ARTHUR
Writer. b. New York, NY, Oct. 17, 1915. e. U. of Michigan. Plays include All My Sons, Death of a Salesman (Pulitzer Prize, 1949), The Crucible (Tony Award), A View from the Bridge, After the Fall, Incident at Vichy, The Price, Up From Paradise, Situation Normal, The American Clock, I Can't Remember Anything, Some Kind of Love Story, Clara, Broken Glass. Novel: Focus. Novella: Homely Girl. *Autobiography*: Time-bends (1987).
PICTURES: Film versions of plays: All My Sons, Death of a Salesman, The Crucible, A View From the Bridge. Original s.p.: The Misfits, Everybody Wins, The Crucible.
TELEVISION: Death of a Salesman (Emmy Award, 1967), Fame, After The Fall, Playing for Time (Emmy Award, 1981).

MILLER, BARRY
Actor. b. Los Angeles, CA, Feb. 6, 1958. New York stage debut, My Mother My Father and Me, 1980.
THEATER: Forty Deuce, The Tempest, Biloxi Blues (Tony, Theatre World, Outer Critics Circle and Drama Desk Awards, 1985), Crazy He Calls Me.
PICTURES: Lepke (debut, 1975), Saturday Night Fever, Voices, Fame, The Chosen, The Journey of Natty Gann, Peggy Sue Got Married, The Sicilian, The Last Temptation of Christ, Love at Large, The Pickle, Love Affair.
TELEVISION: *Specials*: The Roommate, Conspiracy: The Trial of the Chicago Eight. *Series*: Joe and Sons, Szysznyk, Equal Justice, The Practice (3 episodes). *Guest*: The Bill Cosby Show. *Movies*: Brock's Last Case, Having Babies, The Death of Richie.

MILLER, CHERYL
Actress. b. Sherman Oaks, CA, Feb. 4, 1942. e. UCLA, Los Angeles Conservatory of Music.
PICTURES: Casanova Brown, Marriage is a Private Affair, Unconquered, Cheaper by the Dozen, Fourteen Hours, Mr. 880, Executive Suite, The Next Voice You Hear, The Matchmaker, Blue Denim, North by Northwest, The Parent Trap, The Monkey's Uncle, Clarence the Cross-Eyed Lion, The Initiation, Doctor Death, Mr. Too Little.
TELEVISION: *Series*: Daktari, Bright Promise. *Guest*: Perry Mason, Bachelor Father, Flipper, Donna Reed, Leave It to Beaver, Farmer's Daughter, Wonderful World of Color, Moutain Man, Dobie Gillis, Bright Promise, Love American Style, Emergency, Cade's County. *Movie*: Gemini Man.

MILLER, DENNIS
Comedian, Actor. b. Pittsburgh, PA, Nov. 3, 1953. e. Point Park Coll., (journalism degree). Began as stand-up comic in local clubs, then moved to NY appearing at Catch a Rising Star and the Comic Strip. Back in Pittsburgh wrote essays for PM Magazine and hosted Saturday-morning series for teens, Punchline. Recording: The Off-White Album.
PICTURES: Madhouse, Disclosure, The Net, Tales From the Crypt: Bordello of Blood, Murder at 1600.
TELEVISION: *Series*: Saturday Night Live (1985-91), The Dennis Miller Show (talk), Dennis Miller Live (also writer; Emmy Award for writing, 1996), Monday Night Football. *Specials* (also exec. prod./writer): Mr. Miller Goes to Washington, Dennis Miller: Black and White, They Shoot HBO Specials Don't They?, MTV Video Awards (host, 1996), Dennis Miller: Citizen Arcane (also exec. prod./writer; Emmy Award, 1996, Writers' Guild Award, 1998).

MILLER, DICK (RICHARD)
Actor, Writer. b. New York, NY, Dec. 25, 1928. e. City Coll. of New York, Columbia U. Grad. NYU. Theater Sch. of Dramatic Arts. Commercial artist, psychologist (Bellevue Mental Hygiene Clinic, Queens General Hosp. Psychiatric dept.) Served in U.S. Navy, WWII. Boxing champ, U.S. Navy. Semi-pro football. Broadway stage, radio disc jockey, The Dick Miller Show, WMCA, WOR-TV. Over 500 live shows. Did first live night talk show with Bobby Sherwood, Midnight Snack, CBS, 1950. Wrote, produced and directed radio and TV shows in NY in early 1950s. Wrote screenplays; T.N.T. Jackson, Which Way to the Front, Four Rode Out and others. Has appeared on many major TV series and was a regular on Fame (3 years) and The Flash.
PICTURES: Has appeared in over 150 features, including: Apache Woman, Oklahoma Woman, It Conquered the World, The Undead, Not of This Earth, The Gunslinger, War of the Satellites, Naked Paradise, Rock All Night, Sorority Girl, Carnival Rock, A Bucket of Blood, Little Shop of Horrors, Atlas, Capture That Capsule, Premature Burial, X—The Man With the X Ray Eyes, The Terror, Beach Ball, Ski Party, Wild Wild Winter, Wild Angels, Hell's Angels on Wheels, The Trip, St. Valentine's Day Masacre, A Time for Killing, The Dirty Dozen, Targets, The Legend of Lilah Clare, Wild Racers, Target Harry, Which Way to the Front (also co-s.p.), Night Call Nurses, The Grissom Gang, Ulzana's Raid, Executive Action, The Slams, Student Nurses, Big Bad Mama, Truck Turner, Capone, T.N.T. Jackson, The Fortune, White Line Fever, Crazy Mama, Moving Violation, Hustle, Cannonball, Vigilante Force, New York New York, Mr. Billion, Hollywood Boulevard, Grand Theft Auto, I Wanna Hold Your Hand, Piranha, Corvette Summer, Rock 'n' Roll High School, Lady in Red, Dr. Heckle and Mr. Hype, The Happy Hooker Goes Hollywood, Used Cars, The Howling, Heartbeeps, White Dog, Get Crazy, Lies, Heart Like a Wheel, All the Right Moves, Twilight Zone: The Movie, National Lampoon Goes to the Movies, Space Raiders, Swing Shift, Gremlins, The Terminator, Explorers, After Hours, Night of the Creeps, Project X, Armed Response, Chopping Mall, Amazon Women on the Moon, Innerspace, Angel III, The 'Burbs, Under the Boardwalk, Far From Home, Mob Boss, Gremlins 2: The New Batch, Unlawful Entry, Amityville 1992: It's About Time, Motorama, Matinee, Batman: Mask of the Phantasm (voice), Mona Must Die, Number One Fan, Tales From the Crypt Presents Demon Knight, Second Civil War, Small Soldiers.

MILLER, (DR.) GEORGE
Director, Producer. b. Chinchilla, Queensland, Australia, 1945. Practiced medicine in Sydney; quit to work on films with Byron Kennedy, who became longtime partner until his death in 1983. Early work: Violence in the Cinema Part One (short: dir., s.p.), Frieze—An Underground Film (doc.: editor only), Devil in Evening Dress (doc.: dir., s.p.). First worldwide success with Mad Max.
PICTURES: Mad Max (dir., s.p.), Chain Reaction (assoc. prod.), The Road Warrior (dir., co-s.p.), Twilight Zone—The Movie (dir. segment), Mad Max Beyond Thunderdome (co-dir., prod., co-s.p.), The Witches of Eastwick (dir.), The Year My Voice Broke (exec. prod.), Dead Calm (exec. prod.), Flirting (exec. prod.), Lorenzo's Oil (dir., co-s.p., co-prod.), Babe (co-s.p.), 40000 Years of Dreaming (also s.p.), Babe: Pig in the City (also s.p.).
TELEVISION: The Dismissal (mini-series; exec. prod., co-writer & dir. of first episode). Prod.: Bodyline, The Cowra Breakout. Exec. Prod.: Vietnam (mini-series), Dirtwater Dynasty, Sports Crazy.

MILLER, GEORGE
Director. b. Australia.
PICTURES: In Search of Anna (asst. dir.), The Man from Snowy River, The Aviator, The Never Ending Story II, Over the Hill, Frozen Assets, Gross Misconduct, Andre, Zeus and Roxanne.
TELEVISION: Cash and Company, Against the Wind, The Last Outlaw, All the Rivers Run.

MILLER, JAMES R.
Executive. Began m.p. industry career in 1971 in legal dept. of United Artists (N.Y.). Left to go with Paramount Pictures in legal dept.; then moved to Columbia in 1977 as sr. counsel; later assoc. gen. counsel. In 1979, named Warner Bros. v.p., studio business affairs; 1984, v.p. in chg. world-wide business affairs; 1987, sr. v.p.; 1989, exec. v.p. business and acquisition.

MILLER, JASON
Writer, Actor. b. Scranton, PA, April 22, 1939. Entered regional playwriting contest during high school in Scranton, PA and since has moved back and forth between acting and writing. Wrote Nobody Hears a Broken Dream, That Championship Season (NY Drama Critics & Tony Awards, Pulitzer Prize, 1973). Acted on stage in Juno and the Paycock, Long Day's Journey Into Night.
PICTURES: *Actor*: The Exorcist (Acad. Award nom.), The Nickel Ride, The Ninth Configuration (Twinkle Twinkle Killer Kane), Monsignor, Toy Soldiers, Light of Day, The Exorcist III, Rudy. *Director-Writer*: That Championship Season, Small Kill, Rudy, Murdered Innocence, Mommy.
TELEVISION: *Movies*: A Home of Our Own, F. Scott Fitzgerald in Hollywood, Vampire, The Henderson Monster, Marilyn: The Untold Story, The Best Little Girl in the World, Deadly Care, A Mother's Courage: The Mary Thomas Story. *Mini-Series*: The Dain Curse.

MILLER, JP
Writer. b. San Antonio, TX, Dec. 18, 1919. e. Rice U., 1937-41; Yale Drama Sch., 1946-47. U.S. Navy, Lieut., 1941-46; pub. poetry, short stories. Author of novels The Race for Home, Liv, The Skook.
THEATER: Days of Wine and Roses, The People Next Door, Privacy.
PICTURES: The Rabbit Trap, (story, s.p.) Days of Wine and Roses (story, s.p.) The Young Savages (co-author, s.p.) Behold a Pale Horse (s.p.) The People Next Door (story, s.p.).
TELEVISION: Philco TV Playhouse: Hide and Seek, Old Tasslefoot, The Rabbit Trap, The Pardon-me Boy; Playhouse 90, Days of Wine and Roses, CBS Playhouse, The People Next Door (Emmy Award, 1969), The Unwanted, The Lindbergh Kidnapping Case, Helter Skelter, Gauguin the Savage, I Know My First Name is Steven (story, co-s.p.).

MILLER, MAX B.
Executive. b. Los Angeles, Feb. 23, 1937. Father, Max Otto Miller, prod. silent features and shorts. Great grandfather was Brigham Young. e. Los Angeles Valley Coll., UCLA, Sherwood Oaks Coll. Writer of articles on cinema for American Cinematographer and other publications. Owns and manages Fotos Intl., entertainment photo agency with offices in 46 countries. Recipient of Golden Globe Award in 1976 for Youthquake, documentary feature. Also dir. of Films International (prod., Shoot Los Angeles) and pres. of MBM Prod., Inc. Active member of Hollywood Foreign Press Assn. (from 1974-82 bd member; twice chmn.), Independent Feature Project, Acad. of TV Arts & Sciences, L.A. Int'l, Film Exhibition, Soc. of M.P. & TV Engineers, Film Forum, Amer. Cinemateque.

MILLER, PENELOPE ANN
Actress. b. Los Angeles, CA, Jan. 13, 1964. Daughter of actor-filmmaker Mark Miller and journalist-yoga instructor Bea Ammidown. e. studied acting with Herbert Berghof.
THEATER: *NY*: The People From Work (1984), Biloxi Blues (B'way and LA), Moonchildren, Our Town (Tony nom.), On the Waterfront.
PICTURES: Adventures in Babysitting (1987, debut), Biloxi Blues, Big Top Pee-Wee, Miles From Home, Dead-Bang, Downtown, The Freshman, Awakenings, Kindergarten Cop, Other People's Money, Year of the Comet, The Gun in Betty Lou's Handbag, Chaplin, Carlito's Way, The Shadow, The Relic, Rhapsody in Bloom, Little City, The Break Up, Outside Ozona, Killing Moon, Chapter Zero, All the Fine Lines, Loving Lulu.
TELEVISION: *Series*: The Guiding Light, As the World Turns, The Popcorn Kid, The Closer. *Guest*: Tales From the Darkside, Miami Vice, St. Elsewhere, Family Ties, The Facts of Life. *Specials:* Tales From the Hollywood Hills: The Closed Set, Our Town. *Movie*: Witchhunt, The Last Don, The Hired Heart, Merry Christmas George Bailey, Ruby Bridges, Rocky Marciano.

MILLER, ROBERT ELLIS
Director. b. New York, NY, July 18, 1932. e. Harvard U. Worked on Broadway and TV before feature film debut with Any Wednesday (1966).
PICTURES: Any Wednesday (debut, 1966), Sweet November, The Heart Is a Lonely Hunter, The Buttercup Chain, The Big Truck, The Girl from Petrovka, The Baltimore Bullet, Reuben Reuben, Brenda Starr, Hawks, Bed and Breakfast.
TELEVISION: The Voice of Charlie Pont, The Other Lover, Madame X, Just an Old Sweet Song, Her Life as a Man, Ishi: Last of His Tribe, Intimate Strangers, Killer Rules, Point Man (pilot), A Walton Wedding.

MILLS, DONNA
Actress. b. Chicago, IL, Dec. 11, 1945. e. U. of Illinois. Left school to pursue career in theatre, beginning as dancer with stage companies around Chicago and touring. In NY became regular on soap opera, The Secret Storm. On B'way in Don't Drink the Water.
PICTURES: The Incident (debut, 1968), Play Misty for Me.
TELEVISION: *Series*: Love Is a Many Splendored Thing, The Good Life, Knots Landing. *Guest*: Lancer, Dan August. *Movies/Mini-Series*: Haunts of the Very Rich, Rolling Man, Night of Terror, The Bait, Live Again Die Again, Who is the Black Dahlia?, Beyond the Bermuda Triangle, Look What's Happened to Rosemary's Baby, Smash-Up on Interstate 5, Fire!, Curse of the Black Widow, The Hunted Lady, Superdome, Doctors' Private Lives, Hanging by a Thread, Waikiki, Bare Essence, He's Not Your Son, Woman on the Run, Outback Bound, The Lady Forgets, Intimate Encounters (also exec. prod.), The World's Oldest Living Bridesmaid (also exec. prod.), Runaway Father (also co-exec. prod.), False Arrest, In My Daughter's Name (also co-exec. prod.), The President's Child, Barbara Taylor Bradford's Remember, My Name Is Kate (also exec. prod.), Dangerous Intentions, Element of Truth (exec. prod.), Stepford Husbands.

MILLS, HAYLEY
Actress. b. London, England, April 18, 1946. Father is actor John Mills. Sister is actress Juliet Mills. e. Elmhurst Boarding Sch., Surrey, and Institute Alpine Vidamanette, Switz. Made m.p. debut in Tiger Bay 1959 with father; then signed Disney contract 1960. Received special Academy Award for her role in Pollyana.
THEATER: The Wild Duck, Peter Pan, Trelawney of the Wells, The Three Sisters, A Touch of Spring, The Importance of Being Earnest, Rebecca, The Summer Party, Hush & Hide, My Fat Friend, Tally's Folly, Dial M for Murder, The Secretary Bird, Toys in the Attic, The Kidnap Game, The King and I (Australian tour), Fallen Angels (U.K., Australia, New Zealand), Dead and Guilty.
PICTURES: Tiger Bay (debut, 1959), Pollyanna, The Parent Trap, Whistle Down the Wind, In Search of the Castaways, Summer Magic, The Chalk Garden, The Moonspinners, That Darn Cat, The Truth About Spring, Sky West and Crooked (Gypsy Girl), The Trouble With Angels, The Family Way, A Matter of Innocence (Pretty Polly), Twisted Nerve, Take a Girl Like You, Mr. Forbush and the Penguins (Cry of the Penguins), Endless Night, Deadly Strangers, Silhouettes, What Changed Charley Farthing, The Kingfisher Caper, Appointment with Death, After Midnight, A Troll in Central Park (voice).
TELEVISION: The Flame Trees of Thika (mini-series), Parent Trap (Parts II, III, IV, V), Amazing Stories, Illusion of Life, Good Morning Miss Bliss (series), Murder She Wrote, Back Home (series), Tales of the Unexpected, Deadly Strangers, Only a Scream Away, Walk of Life.

MILLS, SIR JOHN
Actor, Producer. b. Suffolk, England, February 22, 1908, m. Mary Hayley Bell. Father of actresses Hayley and Juliet Mills. Worked as clerk before becoming actor. One of top ten money-making Brit. stars in Motion Picture Herald-Fame Poll, 1945, 1947, 1949-50, 1954, 1956-58. Knighted, 1977. Recipient special award 1988, British Academy of Film and Television Arts. Autobiography: Up in the Clouds Gentlemen Please (1981).
THEATER: *London*: Good Companions, Great Expectations, Separate Tables, Goodbye Mr. Chips, Little Lies (also Toronto), The Petition, Pygmalion (NY), An Evening With John Mills.
PICTURES: The Midshipmaid (debut, 1932), Britannia of Billingsgate, The Ghost Camera, The River Wolves, A Political Party, The Lash, Those Were the Days, Blind Justice, Doctor's Orders, Regal Cavalcade, Born for Glory, Car of Dreams, Charing Cross Road, First Offence, Nine Days a Queen, OHMS, The Green Cockatoo, Goodbye Mr. Chipes, Old Bill and Son, Cottage to Let, The Black Sheep of Whitehall, The Big Blockade, The Young Mr. Pitt, In Which We Serve, We Dive at Dawn, This Happy Breed, Waterloo Road, The Way to the Stars, Great Expectations, So Well Remembered, The October Man, Scott of the Antarctic, The History of Mr. Polly, The Rocking Horse Winner (also prod.), Morning Departure, Mr. Denning Drives North, The Gentle Gunman, The Long Memory, Hobson's Choice, The End of the Affair, The Colditz Story, Above Us the Waves, Escapade, It's Great to Be Young, War and Peace, Around the World in 80 Days, Baby and the Battleship, Town on Trial, Vicious Circle, I Was Monty's Double, Dunkirk, Ice Cold in Alex, Summer of the 17th Doll, Tiger Bay, Tunes of Glory, The Singer Not the Song, Swiss Family Robinson, Flame in the Streets, Tiara Tahiti, The Valiant, The Chalk Garden, The Truth About Spring, Operation Crossbow,
King Rat, The Wrong Box, Sky West and Crooked (dir., prod. only), The Family Way, Africa—Texas Style, Chuka, Emma Hamilton, La Morte non ha Sesso, Oh! What a Lovely War, Run Wild Run Free, Ryan's Daughter (Acad. Award, best supporting actor, 1970), A Black Veil for Lisa, Adam's Woman, Dulcima, Oklahoma Crude, Young Winston, Lady Caroline Lamb, The Human Factor, Trial By Combat, The Devil's Advocate, The Big Sleep, Zulu Dawn, The 39 Steps, Gandhi, Sahara, Who's That Girl, When the Wind Blows (voice), Deadly Advice.
TELEVISION: Masks of Death, Murder with Mirrors, Woman of Substance, Hold the Dream, Edge of the Wind, When the Wind Blows, Around the World in 80 Days, The Lady and the Highwayman, The True Story of Spit MacPhee, A Tale of Two Cities, Ending Up, Frankenstein, The Big Freeze.

MILLS, JULIET
Actress. b. London, England, Nov. 21, 1941. m. actor Maxwell Caulfield. Father is actor John Mills. Mother is writer Mary Hayley Bell. Sister is actress Hayley Mills. Made stage debut at 14 in Alice Through the Looking Glass. Also toured with Fallen Angels with sister; 1995, The Cherry Orchard, in Canada. Also in 1995, The Molière Comedies and Time of My Life; in 1996, It Could Be Any One of Us..
PICTURES: So Well Remembered, The History of Mr. Polly, No My Darling Daughter, Twice Round the Daffodils, Nurse on Wheels, Carry on Jack, The Rare Breed, Oh! What a Lovely War, Avanti!, Beyond the Door, The Man With the Green Cross, Primevals.
TELEVISION: *Series*: Nanny and the Professor. *Movies*: Wings of Fire, The Challengers, Letters from Three Lovers, Alexander: The Other Side of Dawn, The Cracker Factory, Barnaby and Me (Australia), Columbo: No Time to Die, A Stranger in the Mirror. *Mini-Series*: QB VII (Emmy Award, 1975), Once an Eagle. *Guest*: Hotel, Dynasty, The Love Boat. *Special*: She Stoops to Conquer.

MILNER, MARTIN
Actor. b. Detroit, MI, Dec. 28, 1927. e. USC. Army 1952-54, directed 20 training films.
PICTURES: Life With Father (debut, 1947), Sands of Iwo Jima, The Halls of Montezuma, Our Very Own, Operation Pacific, I Want You, The Captive City, Battle Zone, Mr. Roberts, Pete Kelly's Blues, On the Threshold of Space, Gunfight at the O.K. Corral, Sweet Smell of Success, Marjorie Morningstar, Too Much Too Soon, Compulsion, 13 Ghosts, Valley of the Dolls.
TELEVISION: *Series*: The Stu Erwin Show, The Life of Riley, Route 66, Adam-12, Swiss Family Robinson. *Movies*: Emergency!, Runaway!, Hurricane, Swiss Family Robinson (pilot), Flood, SST—Death Flight, Black Beauty, Little Mo, Crisis in Mid-Air, The Seekers, The Ordeal of Bill Carney, Nashville Beat. *Mini-Series*: The Last Convertible.

MIMIEUX, YVETTE
Actress. b. Los Angeles, CA, Jan. 8, 1942. e. Vine Street Sch., Le Conte Jr. H.S., Los Angeles, Los Ninos Heroes de Chapultepec, Mexico City, Hollywood H.S., CA. Appeared with a theatrical group, Theatre Events; Concerts: Persephone, Oakland Orchestra, 1965, N.Y. Philharmonic, Lincoln Center, L.A. Philharmonic, Hollywood Bowl.
THEATER: I Am a Camera (1963), The Owl and the Pussycat.
PICTURES: Platinum High School (debut, 1960), The Time Machine, Where the Boys Are, The Four Horsemen of the Apocalypse, Light in the Piazza, The Wonderful World of the Brothers Grimm, Diamond Head, Toys in the Attic, Joy in the Morning, The Reward, Monkeys Go Home, The Caper of the Golden Bulls, Dark of the Sun, The Picasso Summer, Three in the Attic, The Delta Factor, Skyjacked, The Neptune Factor, Journey Into Fear, Jackson County Jail, The Black Hole, Mystique, Lady Boss.
TELEVISION: *Series*: The Most Deadly Game, Berrenger's. *Movies*: Death Takes A Holiday, Black Noon, Hit Lady (also writer), The Legend of Valentino, Snowbeast, Ransom for Alice, Devil Dog: The Hound of Hell, Outside Chance, Disaster on the Coastliner, Forbidden Love, Night Partners, Obsessive Love (also co-prod., co-writer), Perry Mason: The Case of the Desperate Deception.

MINER, STEVE
Director. b. Chicago, IL, June 18, 1951. e. Dean Junior Col. Began career as prod. asst. on Last House on the Left (1970). Launched a NY-based editorial service, and dir., prod., edited sport, educational and indust. films.
PICTURES: Here Come the Tigers! (co-prod.), Manny's Orphans (co-prod., s.p.), Friday the 13th (assoc. prod.). *Director*: Friday the 13th Part 2 (also prod.), Friday the 13th Part 3, Soul Man, House, Warlock (also prod.), Wild Hearts Can't Be Broken, Forever Young, My Father the Hero, Big Bully, Halloween H20: Twenty Years Later, Lake Placid.
TELEVISION: *Series*: The Wonder Years (sprv. prod., dir., DGA Award for pilot), Chicago Hope, The Practice, Dawson's Creek (also prod.). *Pilots*: B-Men, Elvis, Laurie Hill, Against the Grain.

MINGHELLA, ANTHONY
Director, Writer. b. Ryde, Isle of Wight, UK, Jan. 6, 1954.
PICTURES: Truly Madly Deeply, Mr Wonderful (writer only), The English Patient (Acad. award., Golden Globe nom.), The Talented Mr. Ripley, Cold Mountain.
TELEVISION: *Writer*: Jim Henson's The Storyteller, Living With Dinosaurs.

MINNELLI, LIZA
Actress, Singer. b. Los Angeles, CA, March 12, 1946. p. actress-singer Judy Garland & dir. Vincente Minnelli. e. attended sch. in CA, Switzerland, and the Sorbonne. Left to tour as lead in The Diary of Anne Frank, The Fantastiks, Carnival and The Pajama Game. In concert with mother, London Palladium 1964. In concert Carnegie Hall, 1979, 1987, 1993. Film debut as child in mother's film In the Good Old Summertime (1949). Recordings incl. Liza with a Z, The Singer, Live at the Winter Garden, Tropical Nights, Live at Carnegie Hall, Liza Minnelli at Carnegie Hall, Results, Live at Radio City Music Hall, The Day After That.
THEATER: Best Foot Forward (off-B'way debut, 1963, Theatre World Award), Flora The Red Menace (Tony Award, 1965), Liza at the Winter Garden (special Tony Award, 1974), Chicago, The Act (Tony Award, 1978), Are You Now or Have You Ever Been?, The Rink (Tony nom.).
PICTURES: In the Good Old Summertime, Journey Back to Oz (voice; 1964, released in U.S. in 1974), Charlie Bubbles, The Sterile Cuckoo (Acad. Award nom.), Tell Me That You Love Me Junie Moon, Cabaret (Acad. Award; also British Acad. & Golden Globe Awards, 1972), That's Entertainment!, Lucky Lady, Silent Movie, A Matter of Time, New York New York, Arthur, The Muppets Take Manhattan, That's Dancing!, Rent-a-Cop, Arthur 2 on the Rocks, Stepping Out.
TELEVISION: *Specials*: Judy and Liza at the London Palladium, The Dangerous Christmas of Red Riding Hood, Liza, Liza with a Z (Emmy Award, 1972). Goldie and Liza Together, Baryshnikov on Broadway, Liza in London, Faerie Tale Theater (Princess and the Pea), A Triple Play: Sam Found Out, Frank Sammy and Liza: The Ultimate Event, Liza Minnelli Live From Radio City Music Hall. *Movies*: A Time to Live (Golden Globe Award), Parallel Lives, The West Side Waltz.

MIOU-MIOU
Actress r.n. Sylvette Herry. b. Paris, France, Feb. 22, 1950. First job as apprentice in upholstery workshop. In 1968, helped to create Montparnasse cafe-theatre, Cafe de la Gare, with comedian Coluche. Returned to stage in Marguerite Duras' La Musica, 1985.
PICTURES: La Cavale (debut, 1971), Themroc, Quelques Messieurs Trop Tranquilles, Elle Court, Elle Court La Banlieue, Les Granges Brulees, The Mad Adventures of Rabbi Jacob, Going Places, Un Genie Deux Associes une Cloche, D'Amour et D'Eau Fraiche, Victory March, F... comme Fairbanks, On Aura Tout Vu, Jonah Who Will Be 25 in the Year 2000, Dites-lui Que Je l'aime, Les Routes du Sud, Le Grand Embouteillage, Memoirs of a French Whore, Au Revoir...a Lundi, La Femme Flic (Lady Cop), Est-ce Bien Raisonnable?, La Geule du Loup, Josepha, Guy De Maupassant, Coup de Foudre, Canicule, Le Vol du Sphinx, Blanche et Marie, Menage, The Revolving Doors, La Lectrice, Milou in May, La Totale, Le Bal des Casse-Pieds, Tango, Montparnasse-Pondichery, Germinal.

MIRISCH, DAVID
Executive. b. Gettysburg, PA, July 24, 1935. e. Ripon Coll. United Artists Corp., 1960-63. Former exec. with Braverman-Mirisch, adv. public rel. firm. Pres. of David Mirisch Ent., intl prom. firm. Also member of Mirisch Film Co, which has produced Hawaii, West Side Story, Fiddler on the Roof, The Great Escape, The Pink Panther, Some Like it Hot, In the Heat of the Night and The Magnificent Seven.

MIRISCH, MARVIN E.
Executive. b. New York, NY, March 19, 1918. e. CCNY, B.A., 1940. Print dept., contract dept., asst. booker, NY exch.; head booker, Grand National Pictures, Inc., 1936-40; officer, gen. mgr. vending concession operation 800 theatres, Midwest, Theatres Candy Co., Inc., Milwaukee, Wisc., 1941-52; exec., corporate officer in chg., indep. prod. negotiations, other mgmt. functions, Allied Artists Pictures, Inc., 1953-57; chmn. of bd., CEO in chg. of all business affairs, admin. & financing, distr. liaison, The Mirisch Company, Inc., 1957 to present. Member of Board of Governors and former v.p., AMPAS. Member Motion Pictures Pioneers.
PICTURES: *Exec. prod.*: Dracula, Romantic Comedy.

MIRISCH, WALTER
Producer. b. New York, NY, Nov. 8, 1921. e. U. of Wisconsin, B.A., 1942; Harvard Grad. Sch. of Business Admin., 1943. In m.p. indust. with Skouras Theatres Corp., 1938-40; Oriental Theatre Corp., 1940-42. 1945 with Monogram/Allied Artists; apptd. exec. prod. Allied Artists, 1951 (spv. such films as The Big Combo, The Phoenix City Story, Invasion of the Body Snatchers, Friendly Persuasion, Love in the Afternoon); established The Mirisch Company, supervising such films as Some Like It Hot, The Horse Soldiers, The Apartment, West Side Story, Irma La Douce, The Great Escape, The Pink Panther, A Shot in the Dark, The Fortune Cookie, The Russians Are Coming the Russians Are Coming,
Fiddler on the Roof; 1960-61 Pres. of Screen Prod. Guild; 1962, mem. bd. dir., MPAA; bd. Gvnrs., AMPAS, 1964, 1972; 1967, pres., Center Thea. Group of L.A.; named pres. and exec. head of prod., The Mirisch Corporation, 1969; pres., Permanent Charities Committee 1962-63; pres., AMPAS, 1973-77. Recipient: Irving Thalberg Award 1978, Jean Hersholt Humanitarian Award 1984, Honorary Doctor of Humanities, Univ. of WI 1989, UCLA Medal 1989.
PICTURES: *Producer or Exec. Producer*: Fall Guy, I Wouldn't Be in Your Shoes, Bomba on Panther Island, Bomba the Jungle Boy, Bomba and the Hidden City, County Fair, The Lost Volcano, Cavalry Scout, Elephant Stampede, Flight to Mars, The Lion Hunters, Rodeo, African Treasure, Wild Stallion, The Rose Bowl Story, Flat Top, Bomba and the Jungle Girl, Hiawatha, Safari Drums, The Maze, The Golden Idol, Killer Leopard, The Warriors, Annapolis Story, Lord of the Jungle, Wichita, The First Texan, The Oklahoman, The Tall Stranger, Fort Massacre, Man of the West, Cast a Long Shadow, Gunfight at Dodge City, The Man in the Net, The Magnificent Seven, By Love Possessed, Two for the Seesaw, Toys in the Attic, In the Heat of the Night (Acad. Award for Best Picture, 1967), Sinful Davey, Some Kind of a Nut, Halls of Anger, The Hawaiians, They Call Me Mister Tibbs, The Organization, Scorpio, Mr. Majestyk, Midway, Gray Lady Down, Same Time Next Year, The Prisoner of Zenda, Dracula, Romantic Comedy.
TELEVISION: *Movies* (exec. prod.): Desperado, Return of Desperado, Desperado: Avalanche at Devil's Ridge, Desperado: The Outlaw Wars, Desperado: Badlands Justice, Troubleshooters: Trapped Beneath the Earth, Lily In Winter, A Case for Life.

MIRREN, HELEN
Actress. b. London, England, 1946.
THEATER: Troilus and Cressida, 2 Gentlemen of Verona, Hamlet, Miss Julie, Macbeth, Teeth 'n' Smiles, The Seagull, Bed Before Yesterday, Henry VI, Measure for Measure, The Duchess of Malfi, Faith Healer, Antony and Cleopatra, Roaring Girl, Extremities, Madame Bovary, Two Way Mirror, Sex Please We're Italian!, Woman in Mind (LA), A Month in the Country (also B'way).
PICTURES: A Midsummer's Night Dream (debut, 1968), Age of Consent, Savage Messiah, O Lucky Man!, Hamlet, Caligula, Hussy, The Fiendish Plot of Dr. Fu Manchu, Excalibur, The Long Good Friday, Cal, 2010, White Nights, Heavenly Pursuits, The Mosquito Coast, Pascali's Island, When the Whales Came, The Cook The Thief His Wife and Her Lover, The Comfort of Strangers, Where Angels Fear to Tread, Dr. Bethune, The Gift, The Hawk, Prince of Jutland, The Madness of King George (Acad. Award nom.; Cannes Film Fest. Award), Losing Chase, (Golden Globe Award, 1997), Some Mother's Son, Critical Care, The Prince of Egypt (voice), Teaching Mrs. Tingle Prime Suspect, The Passion of Ayn Rand.
TELEVISION: Miss Julie, The Applecart, The Little Minister, The Changeling, Blue Remembered Hills, As You Like It, A Midsummer Night's Dream, Mrs. Reinhart, After the Party, Cymbeline, Coming Through, Cause Celebre, Red King White Knight, Prime Suspect (BAFTA Award), Prime Suspect 2, Prime Suspect 3 (Emmy Award, 1996), Prime Suspect 5: Errors of Judgment, Painted Lady.

MISCHER, DON
Producer, Director. b. San Antonio, TX, March 5, 1941. e. U. of TX, B.A. 1963, M.A. 1965. Pres., Don Mischer Productions. Founded Don Mischer Productions, 1978. Recipient of 12 Emmy Awards, 9 Directors Guild Awards, 3 NAACP Image Awards, Peabody Award.
TELEVISION: *Producer*: Opening and closing ceremonies of the 1996 Centennial Olympics Games (Emmy Award, 1997), Michael Jackson's Super Bowl XXVII Halftime Show, The Kennedy Center Honors (Emmy Awards, 1981, 1987, 1994, 1996), Tony Awards (3 yrs; Emmy Awards, 1987, 1989), Carnegie Hall 100th Anniversary, Gregory Hines Tap Dance in America, Opening of EuroDisney, The Muppets Celebrate Jim Henson, AFI Salutes to Billy Wilder and Gene Kelly, Irving Berlin's 100th Birthday (Emmy Award, 1988), Baryshnikov by Tharp, Motown 25: Yesterday Today Forever (Emmy Award, 1983), Motown Returns to the Apollo (Emmy Award, 1985), Grand Reopening of Carnegie Hall, specials with Goldie Hawn, Liza Minnelli, Bob Hope, Robin Williams, Pointer Sisters. Also: The Great American Dream Machine, Donohue and Kids: Project Peacock (Emmy Award, 1981), The Presidential Inaugural, 6 Barbara Walters Specials, Ain't Misbehavin', It's Garry Shandling's Show.

MOCIUK, YAR W.
Executive. b. Ukraine, Jan. 26, 1927. e. CCNY; World U.; Peoples U. of Americas, Puerto Rico. Expert in field of m.p. care and repair; holds U.S. patent for method and apparatus for treating m.p. film. Has also been film prod. and dir.. Founder and pres. of CM Films Service, Inc. until 1973. Now chmn. of bd. and pres. of Filmtreat International Corp. Member: M.P. & TV Engineers; Univ. Film Assn. Pres., Ukrainian Cinema Assn. of America.

MODINE, MATTHEW
Actor. b. Loma Linda, CA, March 22, 1959. Raised in Utah. Studied acting with Stella Adler. Stage work incl. Our Town, Tea and Sympathy, The Brick and the Rose.
PICTURES: Baby It's You (debut, 1983), Private School, Streamers, The Hotel New Hampshire, Mrs. Soffel, Birdy, Vision Quest, Full Metal Jacket, Orphans, Married to the Mob, La Partita, Gross Anatomy, Pacific Heights, Memphis Belle, Wind, Equinox, Short Cuts, The Browning Version, Bye Bye Love, Fluke, Cutthroat Island., The Real Blonde, The Blackout, The Maker, If...Dog...Rabbit, Notting Hill (cameo), Any Given Sunday, Very Mean Men, Bamboozled, In the Shadows.
TELEVISION: *Movies*: And the Band Played On, Jacob, What the Deaf Man Heard, Flowers for Algernon. *Specials*: Amy and the Angel, Eugene O'Neill: Journey Into Greatness. *Series*: Texas (daytime serial).

MOFFAT, DONALD
Actor. b. Plymouth, England, Dec. 26, 1930. Studied acting Royal Academy of Dramatic Art, 1952-54. London stage debut Macbeth, 1954. With Old Vic before Broadway debut in Under Milkwood, 1957. Worked with APA-Phoenix Theatre Co. and as actor and dir. of numerous B'way and regional productions.
THEATER: The Bald Soprano, Jack, Ivanov, Much Ado About Nothing, The Tumbler, Duel of Angels, A Passage to India, The Affair, The Taming of the Shrew, The Caretaker, Man and Superman, War and Peace, You Can't Take It With You, Right You Are... If You Think You Are, School for Scandal, The Wild Duck, The Cherry Orchard, Cock-a-Doodle Dandy, Hamlet, Chemin de Fer, Father's Day, Forget-Me-Not-Lane, Terra Nova, The Kitchen, Waiting for Godot, Painting Churches, Play Memory, Passion Play, The Iceman Cometh, Uncommon Ground, Love Letters, As You Like It, The Heiress.
PICTURES: Pursuit of the Graf Spee (The Battle of the River Plate; debut, 1957), Rachel Rachel, The Trial of the Catonsville Nine, R.P.M., The Great Northfield Minnesota Raid, Showdown, The Terminal Man, Earthquake, Land of No Return, Promises in the Dark, Health, On the Nickel, Popeye, The Thing, The Right Stuff, Alamo Bay, The Best of Times, Monster in the Closet, The Unbearable Lightness of Being, Far North, Music Box, The Bonfire of the Vanities, Class Action, Regarding Henry, Housesitter, Clear and Present Danger, Trapped in Paradise.
TELEVISION: *Series*: The New Land, Logan's Run. *Guest*: Camera Three (1958), You Can't Have Everything (U.S. Steel Hour), Murder, She Wrote, Dallas. *Specials*: Forget-Me-Not Lane, Tartuffe, Waiting for Godot. *Movies*: Devil and Miss Sarah, Call of the Wild, Eleanor and Franklin: The White House Years, Exo-Man, Mary White, Sergeant Matlovich vs. the U.S. Air Force, The Word, The Gift of Love, Strangers: The Story of a Mother and Daughter, Ebony Ivory and Jade, Mrs. R's Daughter, The Long Days of Summer, Jacqueline Bouvier Kennedy, Who Will Love My Children?, Through Naked Eyes, License to Kill, Cross of Fire, A Son's Promise, Kaleidoscope, The Great Pretender, Babe Ruth, Columbo: No Time to Die, Teamster Boss: The Jackie Presser Story, Majority Rule, Love Cheat and Steal, Is There Life Out There? *Mini-Series*: Tales of the City.

MOGER, STANLEY H.
Executive. b. Boston, MA, Nov. 13, 1936. e. Colby Coll., Waterville, ME, B.A., 1958. Announcer/TV personality/WVDA and WORL (Boston) 1953-54; WGHM (Skowhegan) 1955-56; WTWO-TV (Bangor) 1955; WMHB (Waterville) 1956-57; WTVL (Waterville) 1957-58; unit pub. dir., Jaguar Prods., 1958-59; US Army reserve, 1958-64, with calls to active duty in 1958-59, 1961-62. Account exec., NBC Films/California National Productions, Chicago 1959-60; asst. sales mgr., Midwest, RCA/NBC Medical Radio System, 1960; acct. exec. Hollingbery Co., Chicago, 1960-63; and NY 1963-66; acct. exec., Storer TV Sales, 1966-69; co-founded SFM, 1969. 1978, named pres., SFM Entertainment which was responsible for the revival of Walt Disney's Mickey Mouse Club, The Adventures of Rin-Tin-Tin; Mobil Showcase Network, SFM Holiday Network. Pres.: SFM Entertainment, Inc. Exec. prod.: Television-Annual, 1978-79: Your New Day with Vidal Sassoon, The Origins Game, Believe You Can and You Can, Walt Disney Presents Sport Goofy (series), The World of Tomorrow, March of Time ... on the March (England), Sports Pros and Cons, Unclaimed Fortunes, Sea World Summer Night Magic, America's Dance Honors, Allen & Rossi's 25th Anniversary Special, Paris '89 Celebration, U.S. Sports Academy Awards, K-Nite Color Radio, Into the Night With Brad Garrett (ABC-TV), Family Film Awards (CBS), Sea World/Busch Gardens Annual Specials (CBS and Nickelodeon), Everybody Rides the Carousel (Lifetime), Gift of the Magi (Lifetime), Zoobilee Zoo (PBS), Pillar of Fire (History Channel), AFI Life Achievement Awards (CBS, ABC, NBC, Fox), AFI's 100 Years...100 Movies (CBS & TNT), The Journey Inside (Sci-Fi), Open Book (A&E), Indomitable Teddy Roosevelt (ABC), Ray Harryhausen Chronicles (AMC), Crusade in Europe (History/A&E), Visions of Light (PBS/Encore), Alice Through the Looking Glass (Disney), Witness to the Execution (HBO/Cinemax.)

MOKAE, ZAKES
Actor. b. Johanesburg, South Africa, Aug. 5, 1935. e. RADA. Came to US in 1969. Has appeared in many plays written by Athol Fugard incl. Master Harold...and the Boys, Blood Knot.
PICTURES: The Comedians, The Island, Roar, Cry Freedom, The Serpent and the Rainbow, A Dry White Season, Gross Anatomy, Dad, A Rage in Harlem, The Doctor, Body Parts, Dust Devil, Outbreak, Waterworld, Vampire in Brooklyn, Krippendorf's Tribe.
TELEVISION: *Special*: Master Harold... and the Boys. *Movies*: One in a Million: The Ron LeFlore Story, Parker Kane, Percy & Thunder, Slaughter of the Innocents, Rise & Walk: The Dennis Byrd Story.

MOL, GRETCHEN
Actress. b. Deep River, CT, November 8, 1973. e. William Esper Studio.
PICTURES: The Funeral, Girl 6, Donnie Brasco, The Last Time I Committed Suicide, The Deli, Rounders, The 13th Floor, Music From Another Room, Bleach, Too Tired to Die, Celebrity, Sweet and Lowdown, Forever Mine, Just Looking, Attraction, Get Carter.
TELEVISION: *Movie*: Calm at Sunset Calm at Dawn, Subway Stories, Tales from the Underground. *Mini-series*: Dead Man's Walk, The Magnificent Ambersons.

MOLEN, GERALD R.
Producer. Unit prod. mngr. on The Postman Always Rings Twice, Tootsie, Let's Spend the Night Together, A Soldier's Story, The Color Purple. Assoc. prod. on Batteries Not Included. Co-prod. on Rain Man. Joined Amblin Entertainment to oversee prod. of feature film projects.
PICTURES: *Exec. Producer*: Bright Lights Big City, Days of Thunder, A Far Off Place, The Flintstones, The Little Rascals, Little Giants, Casper, Twister, The Trigger Effect. *Producer*: Hook, Jurassic Park, Schindler's List (Acad. Award for Best Picture, 1993), The Lost World.

MOLINA, ALFRED
Actor. b. London, England, May 24, 1953. e. Guildhall Sch. of Music and Drama. Began acting with the National Youth Theatre. Worked as stand-up comic for street theatre group. Joined Royal Shakespeare Co., 1977.
THEATER: Frozen Assets, The Steve Biko Inquest, Dingo, Bandits, Taming of the Shrew, Happy End, Serious Money, Speed-the-Plow, Accidental Death of an Anarchist (Plays and Players' Most Promising New Actor Award), The Night of the Iguana, Molly Sweeney (off-B'way).
PICTURES: Raiders of the Lost Ark (debut, 1981), Meantime, Number One, Ladyhawke, Eleni, Water, Letter to Brezhnev, Prick Up Your Ears, Manifesto, Not Without My Daughter, Enchanted April, American Friends, The Trial, When Pigs Fly, Cabin Boy, White Fang 2: Myth of the White Wolf, Maverick, Hideaway, The Perez Family, The Steal, Species, Before and After, Dead Man, Scorpion Spring, Anna Karenina, Boogie Nights, The Man Who Knew Too Little, The Treat, The Imposters, The Odd Couple II, Dudley Do-Right, Texas Rangers, Magnolia.
TELEVISION: The Losers, Anyone for Dennis, Joni Jones, Cats' Eyes, Blat, Casualty, Virtuoso, Apocolyptic Butterflies, The Accountant, Drowning in the Shallow End, El C.I.D., Ashenden, Hancock, A Polish Practice, Year in Provence, Requiem Apache, Nervous Energy, Ladies Man (series).

MOLL, RICHARD
Actor. b. Pasadena, CA, Jan. 13, 1943.
PICTURES: Caveman, The Sword and the Sorcerer, Metalstorm: The Destruction of Jared-Syn, The Dungeonmaster, House, Wicked Stepmother, Think Big, Driving Me Crazy, National Lampoon's Loaded Weapon 1, Sidekicks, The Flintstones, Storybook, Galaxis, The Glass Cage, The Secret Agent Club, The Perils of Being Walter Wood, Jingle All the Way,.Ghost Central Station
TELEVISION: *Series*: Night Court. *Movies*: The Jericho Mile, The Archer: Fugitive from the Empire, Combat High, Dream Date, Class Cruise, Summertime Switch, The Ransom of Red Chief. *Specials*: Reach for the Sun, The Last Halloween, Words Up! *Guest*: Remington Steele, Facts of Life, Sledge Hammer, My Two Dads, Highlander, Weird Science, Married...With Children.

MONASH, PAUL
Producer, Writer. b. New York, NY, June 14, 1917. e. U. of WI, Columbia U. Was in U.S. Army Signal Corps and Merchant Marine; newspaper reporter, high school teacher, and civilian employee of U.S. gov't. in Europe. Wrote two novels: How Brave We Live, The Ambassadors. Entered industry writing TV scripts for Playhouse 90, Studio One, Theatre Guild of the Air, Climax, etc. Authored two-part teleplay which launched The Untouchables. 1958 won Emmy award for The Lonely Wizard (Schlitz Playhouse of Stars), dramatization of life of German-born electrical inventor Charles Steinmetz. Made m.p. debut as exec. prod. of Butch Cassidy and the Sundance Kid, 1969.

PICTURES: *Exec. Prod.*: Butch Cassidy and the Sundance Kid. *Producer*: Slaughterhouse-Five, The Friends of Eddie Coyle (also s.p.), The Front Page, Carrie, Big Trouble in Little China.
TELEVISION: *Series*: Peyton Place (exec. prod.). *Movies* (exec. prod.): The Trial of Chaplain Jensen, The Day the Loving Stopped, Child Bride of Short Creek, Killer Rules (writer), Stalin (writer), Kingfish: A Story of Huey P. Long (writer).

MONICELLI, MARIO
Director. b. Rome, Italy, May 15, 1915. Ent. m.p. industry in production; later co-authored, collab., comedies.
PICTURES: The Tailor's Maid (also s.p.), Big Deal on Madonna Street (also s.p.), The Great War, The Passionate Thief, Boccaccio '70 (dir. segment; cut for U.S. release), The Organizer (also s.p.), Casanova '70 (also s.p.), Girl With a Pistol, The Queens, Lady Liberty (Mortadella), Romanzo Popolare (also s.p.), My Friends, Caro Michele, Signore e Signori Buonanotte (also s.p.), The New Monsters, Hurricane Rosy, Sono Fotogencio, Lovers and Liars (also s.p.), Il Marchese del Grillo (also s.p.), Amici Miei Atto (All My Friends 2; also s.p.), Bertoldo Bertoldino e Cacasenna (also s.p.), The Two Lives of Mattia Pascal (also s.p.), Let's Hope It's a Girl (also s.p.), The Rogues (also co-s.p.), The Obscure Illness (also s.p.), Looking for Paradise.

MONKHOUSE, BOB
Comedian, Writer. b. Beckenham, Kent, England, June 1, 1928. e. Dulwich Coll. Debut 1948 while serving in RAF, own radio comedy series 1949-83 (winters), own TV series, BBC 1952-56, ITV 1956-83, BBC 1983-90, ITV 1990-. Major cabaret attraction. Voted Comedian of the Year, 1987. After-Dinner Speaker of the Year, 1989.
THEATER: The Boys from Syracuse, Come Blow Your Horn; The Gulls, several West End revues.
PICTURES: Carry On Sergeant, Weekend with Lulu, Dentist in the Chair, She'll Have to Go, The Bliss of Mrs. Blossom
TELEVISION: *Series*: What's My Line?; Who Do You Trust?, Mad Movies, Quick on the Draw, Bob Monkhouse Comedy Hour, The Golden Shot, Celebrity Squares, I'm Bob He's Dickie!, Family Fortunes, Bob Monkhouse Tonight (1983-86), Bob's Full House (1984-90), Bob Says Opportunity Knocks (1987-89), $64,000 Question (1990-ongoing).

MONKS, JOHN, JR.
Writer, Actor, Producer, Director. b. Brooklyn, NY, June 25, 1910. e. Virginia Military Inst., A.B. Actor, stock, B'way, radio, m.p. U.S. Marines, 1942; commissioned Major, 1945. Co-author of Brother Rat. Wrote book A Ribbon and a Star.
PICTURES: *Writer*: Brother Rat, Brother Rat and a Baby, Strike Up the Band, The House on 92nd Street, 13 Rue Madeleine, Wild Harvest, Dial 1119, The West Point Story, People Against O'Hara, Where's Charley, So This Is Love, Knock on Any Door, No Man Is an Island.
TELEVISION: Climax (The Gioconda Smile, A Box of Chocolates), 20th Century-Fox Hour (Miracle on 34th St.), Gen. Electric Theatre: (Emily), CBS Special: High Tor, SWAT. *Creator serial*: Paradise Bay.

MONTAGNE, EDWARD J.
Producer, Director. b. Brooklyn, NY, May 20, 1912. e. Loyola U., Univ. of Notre Dame. RKO Pathe, 1942; U.S. Army, 1942-46; prod. many cos. after army. Exec. prod. of film-CBS-N.Y. Prod. & head of programming, Wm. Esty Adv. Co., 1950; Program consultant, William Esty Co.; v.p. Universal TV prod. & dir.
PICTURES: Tattooed Stranger, The Man with My Face, McHale's Navy, McHale's Navy Joins the Air Force, P.J., The Reluctant Astronaut, Angel in My Pocket.
TELEVISION: Man Against Crime, Cavalier Theatre, The Vaughn Monroe Show, The Hunter, I Spy, McHale's Navy, Phil Silvers Show. TV *Movies*: Ellery Queen: A Very Missing Person, Short Walk to Daylight, Hurricane, Terror on the 40th Floor, Francis Gary Powers, Million Dollar Ripoff, Crash of Flight 401, High Noon—Part 2.

MONTALBAN, RICARDO
Actor. b. Mexico City, Mex., Nov. 25, 1920. Appeared in Mexican pictures 1941-45. On B'way in Her Cardboard Lover with Tallulah Bankhead. Later in Jamaica, The King and I, Don Juan in Hell. Autobiography: Reflections: A Life in Two Worlds (1980).
PICTURES: Fiesta (U.S. debut, 1947), On an Island With You, The Kissing Bandit, Neptune's Daughter, Battleground, Border Incident, Mystery Street, Right Cross, Two Weeks with Love, Across the Wide Missouri, Mark of the Renegade, My Man and I, Sombrero, Latin Lovers, The Saracen Blade, The Courtesans of Babylon (Queen of Babylon), Sombra Verde, A Life in the Balance, Untouched, The Son of the Sheik, Three for Jamie Dawn, Sayonara, Let No Man Write My Epitaph, The Black Buccaneer, Hemingway's Adventures of a Young Man, The Reluctant Saint, Love Is a Ball, Cheyenne Autumn, The Money Trap, Madame X, The Singing Nun, Sol Madrid, Blue, Sweet Charity, The Deserter, Escape From the Planet of the Apes, Conquest of the Planet of the Apes, The Train Robbers, Joe Panther, Won Ton Ton the Dog Who Saved Hollywood, Star Trek II: The Wrath of Khan, Cannonball Run II, The Naked Gun: From the Files of Police Squad.
TELEVISION: *Series*: Fantasy Island, The Colbys, Heaven Help Us. *Guest*: How the West Was Won Part II (Emmy Award, 1978). *Movies*: The Longest Hundred Miles, The Pigeon, Black Water Gold, The Aquarians, Sarge: The Badge or the Cross, Face of Fear, Desperate Mission, Fireball Foreward, Wonder Woman, The Mark of Zorro, McNaughton's Daughter, Fantasy Island (pilot), Captains Courageous, Return to Fantasy Island.

MONTENEGRO, FERNANDA
Actress. r.n. Arlette Pinheiro Monteiro Torres. b. Rio de Janeiro, Brazil, 1929.
PICTURES: Tudo Bem, A Hora da Estrela, O Que E Isso, Companheiro, Central Station (Acad. Award nom.).
TELEVISION: *Movies:* O Auto da Compadecida. *Series:* Baila Comigo, Brilhante, Guerra dos Sexos, Cambalacho, O Dono do Mundo, Renascer, Zaza.

MONTGOMERY, GEORGE
Actor. r.n. George Montgomery Letz. b. Brady, MT, Aug. 29, 1916. e. U. of MT. Armed Services, WWII. Was champion heavyweight boxer. Debuted in films as extra, stuntman, then bit player billed as George Letz.
PICTURES: Singing Vagabond (debut, 1935), Springtime in the Rockies, The Lone Ranger, Rough Riders' Round-up, Frontier Pony Express, Man of Conquest, Star Dust, Jennie, Cisco Kid and the Lady, Charter Pilot, Hi-Yo Silver, Young People, The Riders of the Purple Sage, Cadet Girl, Accent on Love, The Cowboy and the Blonde, The Last of the Duanes, Ten Gentlemen from West Point, Roxie Hart, Orchestra Wives, China Girl, Coney Island, Bomber's Moon, Three Little Girls in Blue, The Brasher Doubloon, Lulu Belle, The Girl from Manhattan, Belle Starr's Daughter, Dakota Lil, Davy Crockett Indian Scout, The Iroquois Trail, The Texas Rangers, Cripple Creek, Jack McCall Desperado, Gun Belt, Fort Ti, The Pathfinder, The Battle of Rogue River, Seminole Uprising, Robber's Roost, Masterson of Kansas, Huk!, Canyon River, Street of Sinners, Pawnee, Gun Duel in Durango, Black Patch, Last of the Badmen, Toughest Gun in Tombstone, Badman's Country, Man from God's Country, King of the Wild Stallions, Watusi, The Steel Claw (also dir., s.p., prod.), Samar (also dir., s.p., prod.), Guerillas in Pink Lace (also dir., s.p., prod.), Satan's Harvest (also dir.), Proscrito del rio Colorado, Battle of the Bulge, Hell of Borneo (also dir., s.p., prod.), Hallucination Generation, Hostile Guns, The Daredevil, Wild Wind.
TELEVISION: *Series*: Cimarron City.

MOODY, RON
Actor. r.n. Ronald Moodnick. b. London, England, Jan. 8, 1924. e. London Sch. of Economics. *Novels:* The Devil You Don't, Very Very Slightly Imperfect, Off The Cuff, The Amazon Box.
THEATER: *London:* Intimacy at Eight (debut, 1952), For Adults Only, Candide, Oliver! (also NY revival: Theatre World Award), Joey Joey (Bristol; also writer, composer, lyricist), Peter Pan, Hamlet, The Clandestine Marriage, The Showman (also writer), Sherlock Holmes—The Musical. *Author:* Saturnalia, Move Along Sideways.
PICTURES: Davy (debut, 1958), Follow a Star, Make Mine Mink, Five Golden Hours, The Mouse on the Moon, A Pair of Briefs, Summer Holiday, Ladies Who Do, Murder Most Foul, San Ferry Ann, The Sandwich Man, Oliver! (Acad. Award nom.), The Twelve Chairs, Flight of the Doves, Dogpound Shuffle, Dominique, Unidentified Flying Oddball, Wrong Is Right, Where Is Parsifal?, A Kid in King Arthur's Court.
TELEVISION: *Series:* Nobody's Perfect, Tales of the Gold Monkey. *Mini-Series:* The Word. *Movies:* David Copperfield (theatrical in U.K.), Dial M for Murder (U.S.), The Caucasian Chalk Circle, Hideaway. *Specials:* Portrait of Petulia, Bing Crosby's Merrie Olde Christmas, Winter's Tale, Othello, Other Side of London, Baden Powell, Lights Camera Action, Last of the Summer Wine.

MOONJEAN, HANK
Producer, Director. Began as asst. dir. at MGM. Later producer.
PICTURES: *Assoc. Prod.*: The Great Gatsby, WUSA, The Secret Life of An American Wife, Child's Play, Welcome to Hard Times, The Singing Nun. *Exec. Prod.*: The Fortune, The End. *Producer*: Hooper, Smokey and the Bandit II, The Incredible Shrinking Woman, Paternity, Sharky's Machine, Stroker Ace, Stealing Home, Dangerous Liaisons.

MOORE, CONSTANCE
Actress. b. Sioux City, IA, Jan. 18, 1922. Sang on radio: Lockheed program, Jurgen's Show. Screen debut 1938. TV shows, nightclubs. N.Y. Stage: The Boys from Syracuse, By Jupiter, Annie Get Your Gun, Bells Are Ringing, Affairs of State.
PICTURES: Prison Break, A Letter of Introduction, You Can't Cheat an Honest Man, I Wanted Wings, Take a Letter Darling, Show Business, Atlantic City, Delightfully Dangerous, Earl Carroll Vanities, In Old Sacramento, Hit Parade of 1947, Spree.

MOORE, DAN
Costumer Designer.
PICTURES: Southern Comfort, Rocky III, Brewster's Millions, Blue City, Crossroads, Punchline, Red Heat, She's Out of Control, Johnny Handsome, Another 48 Hrs., Necessary Roughness, Trespass, Geronimo: An American Legend, Wild Bill, This World Then the Fireworks, Last Man Standing, Broken Arrow.

TELEVISION: *Movies*: Twisted Desire, The Cherokee Kid, The Second Civil War, 12 Angry Men. *Series*: The Magnificent Seven (Emmy Award, 1998).

MOORE, DEMI
Actress. r.n. Demetria Guynes. b. Roswell, NM, Nov. 11, 1962. Began modeling at age 16. *Off-B'way debut*: The Early Girl, 1987 (Theatre World Award).
PICTURES: Choices (debut, 1981), Parasite, Young Doctors in Love, Blame It on Rio, No Small Affair, St. Elmo's Fire, About Last Night, One Crazy Summer, Wisdom, The Seventh Sign, We're No Angels, Ghost, Nothing But Trouble, Mortal Thoughts (also co-prod.), The Butcher's Wife, A Few Good Men, Indecent Proposal, A Century of Cinema, Disclosure, The Scarlett Letter, Now and Then (also co-prod.), The Juror, The Hunchback of Notre Dame (voice), Striptease, Destination Anywhere, G.I. Jane (also prod.), Austin Powers: International Man of Mystery (prod. only), Deconstructing Harry, Passion of Mind, Airframe.
TELEVISION: *Series*: General Hospital. *Guest*: Kaz, Vega$, Moonlighting, Tales from the Crypt (Dead Right). *Specials*: Bedrooms, The New Homeowner's Guide to Happiness. *Movies*: If These Walls Could Talk.

MOORE, DICKIE
Actor. b. Los Angeles, CA, Sept. 12, 1925. m. actress Jane Powell. Began picture career when only 11 months old, playing John Barrymore as a baby in The Beloved Rogue. Appeared in numerous radio, television and stage prods. in NY and L.A. and over 100 films; appeared in several Our Gang shorts. Co-author and star, RKO short subject, The Boy and the Eagle (Acad. Award nom.). Author: Opportunities in Acting, Twinkle Twinkle Little Star (But Don't Have Sex or Take the Car), 1984. Now public relations executive.
PICTURES: Passion Flower, The Squaw Man, Manhattan Parade, Million Dollar Legs, Blonde Venus, So Big, Gabriel Over the White House, Oliver Twist, Cradle Song, This Side of Heaven, Upper World, Little Men, Peter Ibbetson, So Red the Rose, The Story of Louis Pasteur, The Life of Emile Zola, The Arkansas Traveler, The Under-Pup, The Blue Bird, A Dispatch From Reuters, Sergeant York, Adventures of Martin Eden, Miss Annie Rooney, Heaven Can Wait, The Happy Land, The Eve of St. Mark, Youth Runs Wild, Out of the Past, Killer Shark, 16 Fathoms Deep, Eight Iron Men, The Member of the Wedding.

MOORE, DUDLEY
Actor, Writer, Musician. b. Dagenham, Essex, England, April 19, 1935. e. Oxford, graduating in 1958. Toured British Isles with jazz group before joining Peter Cook, Jonathan Miller and Alan Bennett in creating hit revue, Beyond the Fringe, in U.K. and N.Y. Appeared later with Peter Cook on B'way in Good Evening. Composed film scores: Inadmissible Evidence, Staircase.
PICTURES: The Wrong Box (debut, 1966), Bedazzled (also composer), 30 is a Dangerous Age Cynthia (also co-s.p., composer), Monte Carlo or Bust (Those Daring Young Men in Their Jaunty Jalopies), The Bed Sitting Room, Alice's Adventures in Wonderland, The Hound of the Baskervilles, Foul Play, "10", Wholly Moses, Arthur (Acad. Award nom.), Six Weeks, Lovesick, Romantic Comedy, Unfaithfully Yours, Best Defense, Micki and Maude, Santa Claus, Like Father Like Son, Arthur 2 On the Rocks (also exec. prod.), The Adventures of Milo and Otis (narrator), Crazy People, Blame It on the Bellboy, The Pickle, A Weekend in the Country.
TELEVISION: *Series*: Dudley, Daddy's Girls. *Movie*: Parallel Lives.

MOORE, ELLIS
Consultant. b. New York, NY, May 12, 1924. e. Washington and Lee U., 1941-43. Newspaperman in AK, TN, 1946-52. Joined NBC 1952; mgr. of bus. pub., 1953; dir., press dept., 1954; dir., press & publicity, 1959; vice-pres., 1961; pub. rel. dept., Standard Oil Co. (N.J.), 1963-66; v.p. press relations, ABC-TV Network, 1966-68; v.p. public relations ABC-TV Network, 1968-70; v.p. public relations, ABC, 1970, v.p. public relations, ABC, Inc., 1972; v.p. corporate relations, ABC, Inc., 1979; v.p., public affairs, ABC, Inc., 1982-85. P.R. consultant, 1985. Retired, 1992.

MOORE, JULIANNE
Actress. b. 1961. e. Boston Univ. Sch. for the Arts.
THEATRE: *Off-B'way*: Serious Money, Ice Cream/Hot Fudge, The Road to Nirvana, Hamlet, The Father.
PICTURES: Tales From the Darkside (debut, 1990), The Hand That Rocks the Cradle, Body of Evidence, Benny & Joon, The Fugitive, Short Cuts, Vanya on 42nd Street, Roommates, Safe, Nine Months, Assassins, Surviving Picasso, The Lost World: Jurassic Park, The Myth of Fingerprints, Boogie Nights (LA Film Crits. Award, Best Supporting Actress, 1997), The Big Lebowski, Psycho, A Map of the World, Cookie's Fortune, An Ideal Husband, The End of the Affair, Magnolia, The Ladies Man, Hannibal, Evolution.
TELEVISION: *Series*: As the World Turns (Emmy Award). *Movies*: I'll Take Manhattan, Money Power Murder, The Last to Go, Cast a Deadly Spell.

MOORE, MARY TYLER
Actress. b. Brooklyn. NY, Dec. 29, 1936. Began as professional dancer and got first break as teenager in commercials (notably the elf in Hotpoint appliance ads); then small roles in series Bachelor Father, Steve Canyon, and finally as the switchboard oper. in series Richard Diamond Private Detective (though only her legs were seen). Chairman of Bd., MTM Enterprises, Inc, which she founded with then-husband Grant Tinker.
THEATER: *B'way*: Breakfast at Tiffany's (debut), Whose Life Is It Anyway? (special Tony Award, 1980), Sweet Sue.
PICTURES: X-15, Thoroughly Modern Millie, Don't Just Stand There, What's So Bad About Feeling Good?, Change of Habit, Ordinary People (Acad. Award nom.), Six Weeks, Just Between Friends, Flirting With Disaster, Reno Fins Her Mom, Keys to Tulsa.
TELEVISION: *Series*: Richard Diamond—Private Detective, The Dick Van Dyke Show (2 Emmy Awards: 1964, 1966), The Mary Tyler Moore Show (1970-77; 4 Emmy Awards: 1973, 1974 (2), 1976), Mary (1978), The Mary Tyler Moore Hour (1979), Mary (1985-86), Annie McGuire, New York News, Mary & Rhoda. *Guest*: Bachelor Father, Steve Canyon, 77 Sunset Strip, Hawaiian Eye, Love American Style, Rhoda. *Movies*: Run a Crooked Mile, First You Cry, Heartsounds, Finnegan Begin Again, Gore Vidal's Lincoln, The Last Best Year, Thanksgiving Day, Stolen Babies (Emmy Award, 1993), Forbidden Memories, Payback, Three Cats from Miami and Other Pet Practicioners (host). *Specials*: Dick Van Dyke and the Other Woman, How to Survive the 70's, How to Raise a Drugfree Child.

MOORE, MICHAEL
Director, Writer. b. Davison, MI, 1954. e. Univ. of MI. Was editor of The Michigan Voice and Mother Jones magazine, commentator on radio show All Things Considered, before gaining fame with first film Roger & Me. Established Center for Alternative Media to support indept. filmmakers.
PICTURES: *Dir./Prod./Writer/Actor:* Roger & Me (debut, 1989), Canadian Bacon, The Big One.
TELEVISION: *Series*: *Dir., Exec. Prod., Writer, Host:* TV Nation, The Awful Truth. *Special*: Pets and Meat: The Return to Flint.

MOORE, ROGER
Actor. b. London, England, Oct. 14, 1927. e. art school, London; Royal Acad. of Dramatic Art. Had bit parts in British films Vacation From Marriage, Caesar and Cleopatra, Piccadilly Incident, Gay Lady. Appointed Special Ambassador for UNICEF, 1991.
THEATER: Mr. Roberts, I Capture the Castle, Little Hut, others. *B'way*: A Pin to See the Peepshow.
PICTURES: The Last Time I Saw Paris, Interrupted Melody, The King's Thief, Diane, The Miracle, Gold of the Seven Saints, The Sins of Rachel Cade, Rape of the Sabines, Crossplot, The Man Who Haunted Himself, Live and Let Die, Gold, The Man With the Golden Gun, That Lucky Touch, Street People, Shout at the Devil, The Spy Who Loved Me, The Wild Geese, Escape To Athena, Moonraker, ffolkes, The Sea Wolves, Sunday Lovers, For Your Eyes Only, The Cannonball Run, Octopussy, The Curse of the Pink Panther, The Naked Face, A View to a Kill, The Magic Snowman (voice), Fire Ice and Dynamite, Bed and Breakfast, Bullseye!, The Quest.
TELEVISION: *Series*: The Alaskans, Maverick, The Saint, The Persuaders. *Movies*: Sherlock Holmes in New York, The Man Who Wouldn't Die (also co-exec. prod.).

MOORE, TERRY
Actress. r.n. Helen Koford. b. Los Angeles, CA, Jan. 7, 1929. Mother was Luella Bickmore, actress. Photographer's model as a child; acted on radio; with Pasadena Playhouse 1940. Voted Star of Tomorrow: 1958. Author: The Beauty and the Billionaire (1984). Formed Moore/Rivers Productions, 1988 with partner-manager Jerry Rivers. Has also acted as Helen Koford, Judy Ford, and Jan Ford.
PICTURES: Maryland (debut as Helen Koford, 1940), The Howards of Virginia, On the Sunny Side (billed as Judy Ford), A-Haunting We Will Go, My Gal Sal, True to Life, Date With Destiny, Gaslight, Since You Went Away, Son of Lassie, Sweet and Low Down, Shadowed, Summer Holiday, Devil on Wheels, The Return of October (1st billing as Terry Moore), Mighty Joe Young, The Great Ruppert, He's a Cockeyed Wonder, Gambling House, The Barefoot Mailman, Two of a Kind, Sunny Side of the Street, Come Back Little Sheba (Acad. Award nom.), Man on a Tightrope, Beneath the 12-Mile Reef, King of the Khyber Rifles, Daddy Long Legs, Shack Out on 101, Postmark for Danger (Portrait of Alison), Between Heaven and Hell, Peyton Place, Bernardine, A Private's Affair, Cast a Long Shadow, Why Must I Die?, Platinum High School, City of Fear, Black Spurs, Town Tamer, Waco, A Man Called Dagger, Daredevil, Death Dimension, Double Exposure, Hellhole, W.A.R., Beverly Hills Brats (also co-prod., co-story), Mighty Joe Young.
TELEVISION: *Series*: Empire. *Movies*: Quarantined, Smash-Up on Interstate 5, Jake Spanner: Private Eye, Marilyn and Me.

MOORE, THOMAS W.
Executive. e. U. of Missouri. Naval aviator, USNR, 1940-45. Adv. dept., The Star, Meridian, MS; v.p., adv. mgr., Forest Lawn Memorial Park; account exec., CBS-TV Film Sales, Los Angeles; gen. sales mgr., CBS-TV Film Sales, 1956; v.p. in chg. programming & talent, 1958; pres., ABC-TV Network, 1962; chmn. bd., Ticketron, 1968; pres., Tomorrow Entertainment, Inc. 1971; chmn., 1981.

MORALES, ESAI
Actor. b. Brooklyn, NY, 1963. e. NY's High School for the Performing Arts. NY stage debut at age 17 in NY Shakespeare Fest. prod. of The Tempest, 1981.
THEATRE: Short Eyes, Tamer of Horses, El Mermano, Salome.
PICTURES: Forty Deuce (debut, 1982), Bad Boys, L.A. Bad, Rainy Day Friends, La Bamba, The Principal, Bloodhounds of Broadway, Naked Tango, Amazon, Freejack, In the Army Now, Rapa Nui, My Family/Mi Familia, Scorpion Spring.
TELEVISION: *Mini-Series*: On Wings of Eagles. *Movies*: The Burning Season, Deadlocked: Escape From Zone 14. *Special*: The Great Love Experiment. *Guest*: The Equalizer, Miami Vice.

MORANIS, RICK
Actor, Writer. b. Toronto, Canada, April 18, 1954. Began career as part-time radio engineer while still in high school. Hosted own comedy show on radio then performed in Toronto cabarets and nightclubs and on TV. Joined satirical TV series SCTV during its 3rd season on CBC, for which he won Emmy for writing when broadcast in U.S. Created characters of the McKenzie Brothers with Dave Thomas and won Grammy nom. for McKenzie Brothers album. With Thomas co-wrote, co-directed and starred in film debut Strange Brew, 1983. Supplied voice for cartoon series Rick Moranis in Gravedale High.
PICTURES: Strange Brew (debut, 1983; also co-dir., co-s.p.), Streets of Fire, Ghostbusters, The Wild Life, Brewster's Millions, Head Office, Club Paradise, Little Shop of Horrors, Spaceballs, Ghostbusters II, Honey I Shrunk the Kids, Parenthood, My Blue Heaven, L.A. Story, Honey I Blew Up the Kid, Splitting Heirs, The Flintstones, Little Giants, Big Bully.

MOREAU, JEANNE
Actress. b. Paris, France, Jan. 23, 1928. e. Nat'l Conservatory of Dramatic Art. Stage debut with Comedie Francaise, acting there until 1952 when she joined the Theatre Nationale Populaire. Directorial debut: La Lumiere (film), 1976. Recipient of 1995 BAFTA Film Craft Fellowship Award.
THEATER: A Month in the Country, La Machine Infernale, Pygmalion, Cat on a Hot Tin Roof.
PICTURES: The She-Wolves, Elevator to the Scaffold, The Lovers, Le Dialogue Des Carmelites, Les Liaisons Dangereuses, Moderato Cantabile, La Notte, Jules and Jim, A Woman Is a Woman, Eva, The Trial, Bay of Angels, The Victors, Le Feu Follet, Diary of a Chambermaid, The Yellow Rolls-Royce, The Train, Mata Hari, Viva Maria, Mademoiselle, Chimes at Midnight, Sailor From Gibraltar, The Bride Wore Black, The Immortal Story, Great Catherine, Monte Walsh, Alex in Wonderland, The Little Theatre of Jean Renoir, Louise, The Last Tycoon, French Provincial, La Lumiere (also dir., s.p.), Mr. Klein, The Adolescent (dir., s.p. only), Plein Sud, Querelle, The Trout, Le Miracule, La Femme Nikita, The Suspended Step of the Stork, La Femme Farde, Until the End of the World, Alberto Express, The Lover (voice), Map of the Human Heart, Anna Karamazova, The Summer House, See You Tomorrow, My Name Is Victor, The Old Lady Who Walks in the Sea, Beyond the Clouds, I Love You I Love You Not, The Proprietor.
TELEVISION: A Foreign Field (BBC).

MORENO, RITA
Actress. r.n. Rosa Dolores Alvario. b. Humacao, Puerto Rico, Dec. 11, 1931. Spanish dancer since childhood; night club entertainer. Has won all 4 major show business awards: Oscar, Tony, 2 Emmys and Grammy (for Best Recording for Children: The Electric Company, 1972).
THEATER: Skydrift (debut, 1945), The Sign in Sidney Brustein's Window, Gantry, Last of the Red Hot Lovers, The National Health (Long Wharf, CT), The Ritz (Tony Award, 1975), Wally's Cafe, The Odd Couple (female version), Sunset Boulevard (London).
PICTURES: So Young So Bad (debut, 1950, as Rosita Moreno), Pagan Love Song, The Toast of New Orleans, Singin' in the Rain, The Ring, Cattle Town, Ma and Pa Kettle on Vacation, Latin Lovers, Fort Vengeance, Jivaro, El Alamein, Yellow Tomahawk, Garden of Evil, Untamed, Seven Cities of Gold, Lieutenant Wore Skirts, The King and I, The Vagabond King, The Deerslayer, This Rebel Breed, Summer and Smoke, West Side Story (Acad. Award, best supporting actress, 1961), Cry of Battle, The Night of the Following Day, Marlowe, Popi, Carnal Knowledge, The Ritz, The Boss' Son, Happy Birthday Gemini, The Four Seasons, Life in the Food Chain, The Italian Movie, Blackout, I Like It Like That, Angus, Slums of Beverly Hills, Carlo's Wake.
TELEVISION: *Series*: The Electric Company, Nine to Five, B.L. Styker, Top of the Heap, The Cosby Mysteries, Oz. *Movies*: Evita Peron, Anatomy of a Seduction, Portrait of a Showgirl, The Spree, Resurrection, The Rockford Files: It It Bleeds...It Leads. *Guest*: The Muppet Show (Emmy Award, 1977), The Rockford Files (Emmy Award, 1978). *Special*: Tales From the Hollywood Hills: The Golden Land.

MORGAN, ANDRE
Producer. b. Morocco, 1952. e. U. of Kansas. Golden Harvest Films prod., 1972-84. Exec. v.p., Golden Communications 1976-84. Formed Ruddy-Morgan Organization with Albert S. Ruddy, 1984.
PICTURES: Enter the Dragon, The Amsterdam Kill, The Boys in Company C, Cannonball Run II, High Road to China, Lassiter, Farewell to the King, Speed Zone, Impulse, Ladybugs, Bad Girls, The Scout, Heaven's Prisoners.
TELEVISION: *Series*: Walker Texas Ranger. *Movies*: Miracle in the Wilderness, Staying Afloat.

MORGAN, DEBBI
Actress. b. Dunn, NC, Sept. 20, 1956.
PICTURES: Cry Uncle! (debut, 1971), Mandingo, Monkey Hustle, Dirty Mary, Eve's Bayou (Chicago Crits. Award, Best Supporting Actress, 1997), Asunder.
TELEVISION: *Movies*: Love's Savage Fury, The Jesse Owens Story, Guilty of Innocence: The Lenell Geter Story, Perry Mason: The Case of the Fatal Framing. *Mini-series*: Roots: The Next Generations. *Series*: General Hospital, Behind the Screen, All My Children, Generations, Loving, The City, Port Charles.

MORGAN, HARRY
Actor. r.n. Harry Bratsburg. b. Detroit, MI, April 10, 1915. e. U. of Chicago. Previously acted as Henry Morgan.
THEATER: Gentle People, My Heart's in the Highlands, Thunder Rock, Night Music, Night Before Christmas.
PICTURES: To the Shores of Tripoli (debut, 1942), The Loves of Edgar Allen Poe, Crash Dive, Orchestra Wives, The Ox-Bow Incident, Happy Land, Wing and a Prayer, A Bell for Adano, Dragonwyck, From This Day Forward, The Gangster, All My Sons, The Big Clock, Moonrise, Yellow Sky, Madame Bovary, The Saxon Charm, Dark City, Appointment with Danger, The Highwayman, When I Grow Up, The Well, The Blue Veil, Bend of the River, Scandal Sheet, My Six Convicts, Boots Malone, High Noon, What Price Glory, Stop You're Killing Me, Arena, Torch Song, Thunder Bay, The Glenn Miller Story, About Mrs. Leslie, Forty-Niners, The Far Country, Not as a Stranger, Backlash, Strategic Air Command, The Teahouse of the August Moon, Inherit the Wind, The Mountain Road, How the West Was Won, John Goldfarb Please Come Home, What Did You Do in the War Daddy?, Frankie and Johnny, The Flim Flam Man, Support Your Local Sheriff, Viva Max!, The Barefoot Executive, Support Your Local Gunfighter, Scandalous John, Snowball Express, Charlie and the Angel, The Apple Dumpling Gang, The Greatest, The Shootist, The Cat From Outer Space, The Apple Dumpling Gang Rides Again, Dragnet.
TELEVISION: *Series*: December Bride, Pete and Gladys, The Richard Boone Show, Kentucky Jones, Dragnet, The D.A., Hec Ramsey, M*A*S*H (Emmy Award, 1980), After M*A*S*H, Blacke's Magic, You Can't Take It With You. *Movies*: Dragnet (pilot), But I Don't Want to Get Married!, The Feminist and the Fuzz, Ellery Queen: Don't Look Behind You, Hec Ramsey (pilot), Sidekicks, The Last Day (narrator), Exo-Man, The Magnificent Magnet of Santa Mesa, Maneaters Are Loose!, Murder at the Mardi Gras, The Bastard, Kate Bliss and the Ticker Tape Kid, The Wild Wild West Revisited, Better Late Than Never, Roughnecks, Scout's Honor, More Wild Wild West, Rivkin: Bounty Hunter, Agatha Christie's Sparkling Cyanide, The Incident, Against Her Will: An Incident in Baltimore, Incident in a Small Town. *Mini-Series*: Backstairs at the White House, Roots: The Next Generations.

MORGAN, MICHELE
Actress. r.n. Simone Roussel. b. Paris, France, Feb. 29, 1920. e. Dieppe, dramatic school, Paris. Won starring role at 17 opposite Charles Boyer in Gribouille (The Lady in Question). Made several pictures abroad; to U.S. 1941. Recent theatre includes Les Monstres Sacres. *Autobiography*: With Those Eyes (1977).
PICTURES: Gribouille, Port of Sahadows, Joan of Paris (U.S. debut, 1942), The Heart of a Nation, Two Tickets to London, Higher and Higher, Passage to Marseilles, The Chase, La Symphonie Pastorale, The Fallen Idol, Fabiola, Souvenir, The Naked Heart (Maria Chapdelaine), The Moment of Truth, Daughters of Destiny, The Proud and the Beautiful, Napoleon, Grand Maneuver, Marguerite de la Nuit, Marie Antoinette, There's Always a Price Tag, The Mirror Has Two Faces, Maxime, Love on the Riviera, Three Faces of Sin, Crime Does Not Pay, Landru (Bluebeard), Web of Fear, Lost Command, Benjamin, Cat and Mouse, Robert et Robert, A Man and a Woman: 20 Years Later, Everybody's Fine.

MORIARTY, CATHY
Actress. b. Bronx, NY, Nov. 29, 1960. Raised in Yonkers, NY.
PICTURES: Raging Bull (debut, 1980; Acad. Award nom.), Neighbors, White of the Eye, Burndown, Kindergarten Cop, Soapdish, The Mambo Kings, The Gun in Betty Lou's Handbag, Matinee, Another Stakeout, Me and the Kid, Pontiac Moon, Forget Paris, Casper, Foxfire, Opposite Corners, Cop Land, Hugo Pool, P.U.N.K.S., Digging to China, New Waterford Girl, But I'm A Cheerleader, Gloria, Crazy in Alabama.
TELEVISION: *Series*: Bless This House. *Movie*: Another Midnight Run. *Guest*: Tales from the Crypt (ACE Award).

MORIARTY, MICHAEL
Actor. b. Detroit, MI, April 5, 1941. e. Dartmouth. Studied at London Acad. of Music and Dramatic Arts. Appeared with New York Shakespeare Festival, Charles Street Playhouse (Boston), Alley Theatre (Houston) and Tyrone Guthrie Theatre (Minneapolis). B'way debut in The Trial of the Catonsville Nine.

THEATER: Find Your Way Home (Tony & Theatre World Awards, 1974), Richard III, Long Day's Journey Into Night, Henry V, GR Point, Whose Life Is It Anyway (Kennedy Center), The Ballad of Dexter Creed, Uncle Vanya, The Caine Mutiny Court-Martial, My Fair Lady.
PICTURES: Glory Boy (debut, 1971), Hickey and Boggs, Bang the Drum Slowly, The Last Detail, Shoot It Black Shoot It Blue, Report to the Commissioner, Who'll Stop the Rain, Q, Blood Link, Odd Birds, Pale Rider, The Stuff, Troll, The Hanoi Hilton, It's Alive III: Island of the Alive, Return to Salem's Lot, Dark Tower, Full Fathom Five, The Secret of the Ice Cave, Courage Under Fire.
TELEVISION: *Series*: Law and Order. *Movies*: A Summer Without Boys, The Glass Menagerie (Emmy Award, 1974), The Deadliest Season, The Winds of Kitty Hawk, Too Far to Go (also distributed theatrically), Windmills of the Gods, Frank Nitti: The Enforcer, Tailspin: Behind the Korean Airline Tragedy, Born Too Soon, Children of the Dust. *Mini-Series*: Holocaust (Emmy Award, 1978). *Guest*: The Equalizer.

MORITA, NORIYUKI "PAT"
Actor. b. Isleton, CA, June 28, 1932. Began show business career as comedian in nightclubs for such stars as Ella Fitzgerald, Johnny Mathis, Diana Ross and the Supremes, Glen Campbell, etc. Worked in saloons, coffee houses, and dinner theatres before becoming headliner in Las Vegas showrooms, Playboy Clubs, Carnegie Hall, etc. Guest on most TV talk, variety shows and series: M*A*S*H, Love Boat, Magnum, P.I. etc.
PICTURES: Thoroughly Modern Millie, Every Little Crook and Nanny, Cancel My Reservation, Where Does It Hurt?, Midway, When Time Ran Out, Full Moon High, Savannah Smiles, Jimmy the Kid, The Karate Kid (Acad. Award nom.), Night Patrol, Slapstick of Another Kind, The Karate Kid Part II, Captive Hearts, Collision Course, The Karate Kid Part III, Do Or Die, Lena's Holiday, Honeymoon in Vegas, Miracle Beach, Even Cowgirls Get the Blues, The Next Karate Kid, American Ninja 5, Singapore Sling: Road to Mandalay, The Misery Brothers, Captured Alive, Timemaster, Reggie's Prayer, Earth Minus Zero, Bloodsport 3, Bloodsport 2, Spy Hard, Beyond Barbed Wire, Seth, Mulan (voice), I'll Remember April.
TELEVISION: *Series*: The Queen and I, Sanford and Son, Happy Days, Mr. T and Tina, Blansky's Beauties, Ohara, The Karate Kid (voice for animated series), The Mystery Files of Shelby Woo, Adventures with Kanga Roddy. *Movies*: Evil Roy Slade, A Very Missing Person, Brock's Last Case, Punch and Jody, Farewell to Manzanar, Human Feelings, For the Love of It, The Vegas Strip Wars, Amos, Babes in Toyland, Hiroshima: Out of the Ashes, Greyhounds, Hart to Hart: Secrets of the Hart.

MORITZ, MILTON I
Executive. b. Pittsburgh, PA, April 27, 1933. e. Woodbury Coll., grad. 1955. Owned, operated theatres in L.A., 1953-55; U.S. Navy 1955-57; American International Pictures asst. gen. sls. mgr., 1957; nat'l. dir. of adv. and publ. 1958; v.p. and bd. mem. of American International Pictures, 1967; pres. of Variety Club of So. Cal, Tent 25, 1975-76; 1975, named sr. v.p.; in 1980, formed own co., The Milton I. Moritz Co., Inc., Inc., mktg. & dist. consultant. 1987-94, joined Pacific Theatres as v.p. in chg. of adv., p.r. & promotions. 1995, reactived the Milton I. Moritz Co., Inc.

MORRICONE, ENNIO
Composer, Arranger. b. Rome, Italy, Nov. 10, 1928. Studied with Goffredo Petrassi at the Acad. of Santa Cecilia in Rome. Began career composing chamber music and symphonies as well as music for radio, TV and theater. Wrote for popular performers including Gianni Morandi. Early film scores for light comedies. Gained recognition for assoc. with Italian westerns of Sergio Leone (under name of Dan Davio).
PICTURES: Il Federal (1961, debut), A Fistful of Dollars, The Good the Bad and the Ugly, El Greco, Fists in the Pocket, Battle of Algiers, Matcheless, Theorem, Once Upon a Time in the West, Investigation of a Citizen, Fraulein Doktor, Burn, The Bird with the Crystal Plumage, Cat O'Nine Tails, The Red Tent, Four Flies in Grey Velvet, The Decameron, The Black Belly of the Tarantula, Bluebeard, The Serpent, Blood in the Streets, Eye of the Cat, The Human Factor, Murder on the Bridge, Sunday Woman, The Inheritance, Partner, Orca, Exorcist II: The Heretic, 1900, Days of Heaven, La Cage aux Folles, Bloodline, Stay as You Are, The Humanoid, The Meadow, A Time to Die, Travels With Anita (Lovers and Liars), When You Comin' Back Red Ryder?, Almost Human, La Cage aux Folles II, The Island, Tragedy of a Ridiculous Man, Windows, Butterfly, So Fine, White Dog, Copkiller, Nana, The Thing, Treasure of the Four Crowns, Sahara, Once Upon a Time in America, Thieves After Dark, The Cage, La Cage aux Folles III, The Forester's Sons, The Red Sonja, Repentier, The Mission, The Venetian Woman, The Untouchables, Quartiere, Rampage, Frantic, A Time of Destiny, Casualties of War, Cinema Paradiso, State of Grace, Hamlet, Bugsy, City of Joy, The Bachelor, In the Line of Fire, Wolf, Love Affair, Disclosure, Lolita, U Turn, Phantom of the Opera, Bulworth, The Legend of 1900, Canone Inverso.
TELEVISION: *U.S.*: Marco Polo, Moses—The Lawgiver, Scarlet and the Black, C.A.T. Squad, The Endless Game, Octopus 4, Abraham.

MORRIS, ERROL
Director, Writer. b. Hewlett, NY, 1948. e. Univ. of WI, Univ. of CA/Berkeley.
PICTURES: Gates of Heaven, Vernon Florida, The Thin Blue Line, The Dark Wind, A Brief History of Time, Fast Cheap & Out Of Control, Stairway to Heaven, Mr. Death: The Rise and Fall of Fred A Leuchter Jr..

MORRIS, GARRETT
Actor. b. New Orleans, LA, Feb. 1, 1937. e. Dillard Univ., Julliard Sch. of Music, Manhattan Sch. of Music. Was singer and arranger for Harry Belafonte Folk Singers and B'way actor before achieving fame as original cast member of Saturday Night Live.
THEATER: Porgy and Bess, I'm Solomon, Show Boat, Hallelujah Baby!, The Basic Training of Pavlo Hummel, Finian's Rainbow, The Great White Hope, Ain't Supposed to Die a Natural Death, The Unvarnished Truth.
PICTURES: Where's Poppa? (debut, 1970), The Anderson Tapes, Cooley High, Car Wash, How to Beat the High Cost of Living, The Census Taker, The Stuff, Critical Condition, The Underachievers, Dance to Win, Motorama, Children of the Night, Almost Blue, Coneheads, Black Rose of Harlem, Black Scorpion II: Aftershock, Santa with Muscles.
TELEVISION: *Series*: Roll Out, Saturday Night Live (1975-80), It's Your Move, Hunter, Martin, Cleghorne!, The Jamie Foxx Show. *Movies*: The Invisible Woman, Earth Angel, Maid for Each Other, Black Scorpion. *Guest*: Scarecrow and Mrs. King, Love Boat, Married With Children, Murder She Wrote, The Jeffersons.

MORRIS, HOWARD
Actor, Director, Writer. b. New York, NY, Sept. 4, 1919. e. NYU. U.S. Army, 4 yrs.
THEATER: Hamlet, Call Me Mister, John Loves Mary, Gentlemen Prefer Blondes, Finian's Rainbow.
PICTURES: *Director*: Who's Minding the Mint?, With Six You Get Egg Roll, Don't Drink the Water, Goin' Cocoanuts. *Actor*: Boys' Night Out, 40 Pounds of Trouble, The Nutty Professor, Fluffy, Way... Way Out, High Anxiety, History of the World Part 1, Splash, Transylvania Twist, Life Stinks.
TELEVISION: *Series*: Your Show of Shows (also writer), Caesar's Hour. *Movies*: The Munster's Revenge, Portrait of a Showgirl, Return to Mayberry. *Voices*: Jetsons, Flintstones, Mr. Magoo. *Producer*: The Corner Bar. *Director*: Dick Van Dyke Show, Get Smart, Andy Griffith Show (also frequent guest); also many commericals.

MORRIS, JOHN
Composer, Conductor, Arranger. b. Elizabeth, NJ. e. Juilliard Sch. Music 1946-48, U. of Washington. 1947, New Sch. Social Research 1946-49. Member: ASCAP, Acad. of M.P. Arts & Sciences, American Federation of Musicians.
THEATER: *Composer*. *B'way:* My Mother My Father and Me, A Doll's House, Camino Real, A Time For Singing (musical), Take One Step, Young Andy Jackson, 15 Shakespeare plays for NY Shakespeare Fest. & Amer. Shakespeare Fest, Stratford CT. Musical supervisor, conductor, dance music arranger: Mack and Mabel, Much Ado About Nothing, Bells Are Ringing, Bye Bye Birdie and 23 other B'way musicals. *Off-B'way*: Hair.
PICTURES: The Producers, The Twelve Chairs, Blazing Saddles (Acad. Award nom.), Bank Shot, Young Frankenstein, The Adventure of Sherlock Holmes' Smarter Brother, Silent Movie, The Last Remake of Beau Geste, The World's Greatest Lover, High Anxiety, The In-Laws, In God We Trust, The Elephant Man (Acad. Award nom.), History of the World Part 1, Table for Five, Yellowbeard, To Be or Not to Be, The Woman in Red, Johnny Dangerously, The Doctor and the Devils, Clue, Haunted Honeymoon, Dirty Dancing, Spaceballs, Ironweed, The Wash, Second Sight, Stella, Life Stinks.
TELEVISION: *Composer*: Fresno, Katherine Anne Porter, Ghost Dancing, The Firm, The Mating Season, Splendor in the Grass, The Electric Grandmother, The Scarlet Letter, Georgia O'Keeffe, The Adams Chronicles, The Franken Project, The Tap Dance Kid (Emmy Award, 1986), Make Believe Marriage, The Desperate Hours, The Skirts of Happy Chance, Infancy and Childhood, The Fig Tree, The Little Match Girl, Favorite Son, The Last Best Year, The Last to Go, The Sunset Gang, Our Sons, When Lions Roared, Scarlett. Themes: ABC After School Special, Making Things Grow, The French Chef, Coach. Musical sprv., conductor, arranger Specials: Anne Bancroft Special (Emmy Award), S'Wonderful S'Marvelous S'Gershwin (Emmy Award), Hallmark Christmas specials.
RECORDINGS: Wildcat, All-American, Bells Are Ringing, First Impressions, Bye Bye Birdie, Kwamina, Baker Street, Rodgers and Hart, George Gershwin Vols. 1 & 2, Jerome Kern, Lyrics of Ira Gershwin, Cole Porter, others.

MORRIS, OSWALD
Cinematographer. b. London, England, Nov. 22, 1915. Left school at 16 to work for two years as camera dept. helper at studios. Was lensman for cameraman Ronald Neame who gave Morris first job as cameraman; in 1949, when Neame directed The Golden Salamander, he made Morris dir. of photography.

PICTURES: The Golden Salamander, The Card, The Man Who Never Was, Moulin Rouge, Beat the Devil, Moby Dick, Heaven Knows Mr. Allison, A Farewell to Arms, The Roots of Heaven, The Key, The Guns of Navarone, Lolita, Term of Trial, Of Human Bondage, The Pumpkin Eater (BFA Award, 1964), Mister Moses, The Hill (BFA Award, 1965), The Spy Who Came in from the Cold, Life at the Top, Stop the World- -I Want to Get Off, The Taming of the Shrew, Reflections in a Golden Eye, Oliver!, Gooodbye Mr. Chips, Scrooge, Fiddler on the Roof (Acad. Award, 1971), Sleuth, Lady Caroline Lamb, The Mackintosh Man, The Odessa File, The Man Who Would Be King, The Seven Per Cent Solution, Equus, The Wiz, Just Tell Me What You Want, The Great Muppet Caper, The Dark Crystal.
TELEVISION: Dracula (1974).

MORRISSEY, PAUL
Writer, Director, Photographer. b. New York, NY, 1938. e. Fordham U. 2nd lt. in Army. A writer, cameraman and dir. in indt. film prod. prior to becoming Andy Warhol's mgr. in all areas except painting. Discovered and managed The Velvet Underground and Nico. Founded Interview magazine. Story, casting, dir. & photog. for Warhol Productions' Chelsea Girls, Four Stars, Bike Boy, I A Man, Lonesome Cowboys, Blue Movie, and San Diego Surf.
PICTURES: *writer/photog./edit./dir.*: Flesh, Trash, Heat, L'Amour, Women in Revolt. *writer/dir.*: Flesh For Frankenstein, Blood for Dracula, The Hound of the Baskervilles, Madame Wang's, Forty Deuce, Mixed Blood, Beethoven's Nephew, Spike of Bensonhurst.

MORROW, ROB
Actor. b. New Rochelle, NY, Sept. 21, 1962.
THEATRE: *NY*: The Substance of Fire, Aven'U Boys, The Chosen, Scandal (workshop), Soulful Scream of a Chosen Son, The Boys of Winter, Slam, Third Secret.
PICTURES: Private Resort, Quiz Show, The Last Dance, Mother, Magic, Labor Pains.
TELEVISION: Movies: The Day Lincoln Was Shot, Only Love. *Series*: Tattinger's, Northern Exposure, Nearly Yours. *Guest*: Spenser: For Hire, Everything's Relative, Fame.

MORSE, DAVID
Actor. b. Beverly, MA, Oct. 11, 1953.
THEATRE: *B'way*: On the Waterfront.
PICTURES: Inside Moves, Desperate Hours, The Indian Runner, The Good Son, The Getaway, The Crossing Guard, Twelve Monkeys, The Rock, Contact, The Legend of Pig Eye, A.W.O.L., The Negotiator, The Green Mile.
TELEVISION: *Series*: St. Elsewhere, Big Wave Dave's, Friday the 13th (dir. only). *Movies*: Shattered Vows, When Dreams Come True, Prototype, Downpayment on Murder, Six Against the Rock, Winnie, Brotherhood of the Rose, Cross of Fire, A Cry in the Wild: The Taking of Peggy Ann, Dead Ahead: The Exxon Valdez Disaster, Miracle on Interstate 880, Tecumseh: The Last Warrior. *Mini-Series*: Stephen King's The Langoliers. *Guest*: Nurse. *Special*: A Place at the Table.

MORSE, ROBERT
Actor. b. Newton, MA, May 18, 1931. Served U.S. Navy. Studied with American Theatre Wing, New York. Following radio work, appeared on B'way stage in The Matchmaker, 1956.
THEATER: *B'way*: The Matchmaker, Say Darling (Theatre World Award), Take Me Along, How to Succeed in Business Without Really Trying (Tony Award, 1962), Sugar, So Long 174th Street, Tru (Tony Award, 1990).
PICTURES: The Proud and the Profane (debut, 1956), The Matchmaker, The Cardinal, Honeymoon Hotel, Quick Before It Melts, The Loved One, Oh Dad Poor Dad Mama's Hung You in the Closet and I'm Feeling So Sad, How to Succeed in Business Without Really Trying, A Guide for the Married Man, Where Were You When the Lights Went Out?, The Boatniks, Hunk, The Emperor's New Clothes.
TELEVISION: *Series*: The Secret Storm (1954), That's Life, All My Children, Pound Puppies (voice). *Specials*: The Stingiest Man in Town (voice), Kennedy Center Tonight—Broadway to Washington, Tru (Emmy Award, 1993). *Movie*: The Calendar Girl Murders, Here Come the Munsters. *Mini-Series*: Wild Palms. *Guest*: Masquerade, Alfred Hitchcock Presents, Naked City, Love American Style, Twilight Zone, Murder She Wrote.

MORTENSEN, VIGGO
Actor. b. Oct. 20, 1958, Manhattan, NY.
PICTURES: Witness, Salvation!, Prison, Fresh Horses, Tripwire, Leatherface: Texas Chainsaw Massacre III, Young Guns II, The Reflecting Skin, The Indian Runner, The Young Americans, Ruby Cairo, Ewangelia wedlug Harry'ego, Carlito's Way, Boiling Point, Floundering, Desert Lunch, The Crew, American Yakuza, The Passion of Darkly Noon, Gimlet, Crimson Tide, The Prophecy, Albino Alligator, The Portrait of a Lady, Daylight, La Pistola de mi hermano, G. I. Jane, Blouse Man, A Perfect Murder, Psycho, A Walk on the Moon, 28 Days, Original Sin.
TELEVISION: *Movie*: Vanishing Point. *Mini-series*: George Washington.

MORTON, ARTHUR
Composer, Arranger. b. Duluth, MN, Aug. 8, 1908. e. U. of MN.
PICTURES: Night Life of the Gods, Princess O'Hara, Riding on Air, Fit for a King, Turnabout, Walking Hills, The Nevadan, Rogues of Sherwood Forest, Father is a Bachelor, Never Trust a Gambler, Harlem Globetrotters, Big Heat, Pushover, He Laughed Last. Orchesrtal Arrangements: Laura, From Here to Eternity, Jolson Story, Salome, Born Yesterday, The Long Gray Line, Man from Laramine, My Sister Eileen, Picnic, Strangers When We Meet, That Touch of Mink, Diamond Head, Toys in the Attic, Von Ryan's Express, In Harm's Way, What a Way to Go, The New Interns, Our Man Flint, Planet of the Apes, Patton, Tora Tora Tora, Papillon, Chinatown, Logan's Run, The Omen, MacArthur, The Boys from Brazil, Magic, Superman, Alien, Star Trek: The Motion Picture, Poltergeist, First Blood, Gremlins, Rambo: First Blood Part II, Hoosiers, The 'Burbs, Star Trek V: The Final Frontier, Total Recall, Medicine Man, Gladiator, Mr. Baseball, Forever Young, The Vanishing, Rudy, Angie, The Shadow, The River Wild.
TELEVISION: Black Saddle, Laramie, Bus Stop, Follow the Sun, My Three Sons, Peyton Place, Medical Center, Daniel Boone, Lancers, National Geographic, Say Goodbye, How to Stay Alive, Hooray For Hollywood, The Waltons, Apple's Way, Masada, Medical Story.
(d. April 15, 2000)

MORTON, JOE
Actor. b. New York, NY, Oct. 18, 1947. e. Hofstra U.
THEATRE: *NY*: Hair, Raisin (Theatre World Award), Oh Brother, Honky Tonk Nights, A Midsummer Night's Dream, King John, Cheapside, Electra, A Winter's Tale, Oedipus Rex, Julius Caesar, The Tempest. Dir.: Heliotrope Bouquet.
PICTURES: ...And Justice for All, The Brother From Another Planet, Trouble in Mind, Zelly and Me, The Good Mother, Tap, Terminator 2: Judgment Day, City of Hope, Of Mice and Men, Forever Young, The Inkwell, Speed, The Walking Dead, Lone Star, Executive Decision, Lone Star, The Pest, Speed 2: Cruise Control, Trouble on the Corner, Blues Brothers 2000, Apt Pupil, When It Clicks, The Astronaut's Wife, What Lies Beneath, Bounce.
TELEVISION: *Series*: Grady, Equal Justice, Tribeca (also dir.), Under One Roof, New York News, Prince Street, Mercy Point. *Movies*: The Challenger, Terrorist on Trial: The United States vs. Salim Ajami, Howard Beach: Making a Case for Murder, Death Penalty, Legacy of Lies, In the Shadow of Evil, Y2K, Mutiny, Ali: An American Hero. *Special*: The File of Jill Hatch. *Guest*: A Different World, Hawk, Homicide: Life on the Street.

MOSK, RICHARD M.
Executive. b. Los Angeles, CA, May 18, 1939. e. Stanford U, Harvard Law School. Admitted to California Bar, 1964. Principal in firm of Sanders Barnet Goldman Simons & Mosk, a prof. corp. Named chmn. of the movie industry's voluntary rating system, the Classification & Rating Administration, June 1994; co-chmn, 1997-. Judge, Iran-U.S. Claims Tribunal.

MOSLEY, ROGER E.
Actor. b. Los Angeles, CA. Planned career in broadcasting but turned to acting, first appearing in small roles on TV in: Night Gallery, Baretta, Kojak, Cannon, Switch.
PICTURES: The New Centurions (debut, 1972), Hit Man, Terminal Island, Stay Hungry, Leadbelly, The Greatest, Semi-Tough, Steel, Heart Condition, Unlawful Entry.
TELEVISION: *Series*: Magnum P.I., You Take the Kids. *Guest*: Baretta, Kojak, Cannon, Switch. *Movies*: Cruise Into Terror, I Know Why the Caged Bird Sings, The Jericho Mile, Attica. *Mini-Series*: Roots: The Next Generations.

MOSS, CARRIE-ANNE
Actress. b. Vancouver, Canada, Aug. 21, 1970.
PICTURES: Flashfire, The Soft Kill, Terrified, Sabotage, Secret Life of Algernon, Lethal Tender, New Blood, The Matrix.
TELEVISION: *Series:* Dark Justice, Matrix, Models Inc., F/X: The Series. *Guest:* Street Justice, Nightmare Cafe, Forever Knight, Silk Stalkings, Baywatch, Nowhere Man, Due South.

MOSS, IRWIN
Executive. e. Syracuse U., Harvard Law Sch. Member NY State Bar. Began industry career as dir. of package negotiations for CBS-TV; 1970-80, exec. v.p. & natl. head of business affairs for I.C.M.; 1978-80, sr. v.p., NBC Entertainment; 1980, pres., Marble Arch TV. 1982, joined Paramount Pictures as sr. v.p. for motion picture div. 1984, exec. v.p., L. Taffner Ltd.

MOSTEL, JOSH
Actor, Director. b. New York, NY, Dec. 21, 1946. Father was late actor Zero Mostel. m. prod. Peggy Rajski. e. Brandeis U., B.A. 1970. Part of The Proposition, a Boston improvisational comedy group. Stage debut, The Homecoming (Provincetown Playhouse, MA).
THEATER: *Actor*: Unlikely Heroes, The Proposition, An American Millionaire, A Texas Trilogy, Gemini, Men in the Kitchen, The Dog Play, The Boys Next Door, A Perfect Diamond, Threepenny Opera, My Favorite Year, The Flowering Peach. *Director*: Ferocious Kisses, Love As We Know It, Misconceptions, Red Diaper Baby.

PICTURES: Going Home (debut, 1971), The King of Marvin Gardens, Jesus Christ Superstar, Harry and Tonto, Deadly Hero, Fighting Back, Sophie's Choice, Star 80, Almost You, The Brother from Another Planet, Windy City, Compromising Positions, The Money Pit, Stoogemania, Radio Days, Matewan, Wall Street, Heavy Petting, Animal Behavior, City Slickers, Naked Tango, Little Man Tate, City of Hope, Searching for Bobby Fischer, The Chase, City Slickers II: The Legend of Curly's Gold, Billy Madison, The Basketball Diaries, The Maddening, Big Daddy.
TELEVISION: *Series*: Delta House, At Ease, Murphy's Law. *Mini-Series*: Seventh Avenue. *Special*: The Boy Who Loved Trolls (PBS). *Co-writer*: Media Probes: The Language Show.

MOUND, FRED
Executive. b. St. Louis, MO, April 10, 1932. e. St. Louis U., Quincy Coll. 1946-52, assoc. with father, Charles Mound, at Park Theatre in Valley Park, Mo.; 1952-53, Universal Pictures (St. Louis); 1953, booker, UA, St. Louis; 1955 promoted to salesman in Kansas City; 1957, salesman, St. Louis; 1962, Indianapolis branch mgr. 1967 named UA regional mgr., Dallas and in 1970 became S.W. div. mgr; 1976-77, asst. gen. sls. mgr. for Southern, N.W. and S.W. div. operating out of Dallas. 1977 appt. v.p., asst. gen. sls. mgr. of UA; 1978, appt. v.p. gen sls. mgr. for AFD Pictures in Los Angeles; 1981, v.p. asst. gen. sls. mgr. for Universal; 1984, sr. v.p., gen. sls. mgr., Universal Pictures Distribution; named exec. v.p. 1988. Foundation of Motion Picture Pioneers v.p., 1989. Appointed pres. Universal distrib., 1990.

MOUNT, THOM
Executive. b. Durham, NC, May 26, 1948. e. Bard Coll.; CA Institute of the Arts, MFA. Started career with Roger Corman and as asst. to prod., Danny Selznick at MGM. Moved to Universal under prod. exec. Ned Tanen. At 26, named pres. and head of prod. at Universal. During 8-year tenure, was responsible for dev. and prod. of more than 140 films (including Smokey and the Bandit, Animal House, others).
THEATER: Open Admissions (co-prod.), Death and the Maiden.
PICTURES: Pirates (exec. prod.), My Man Adam, Can't Buy Me Love, Frantic, Bull Durham (co-prod.), Stealing Home, Tequila Sunrise, Roger Corman's Frankenstein Unbound, The Indian Runner (exec. prod.), Death and the Maiden, Natural Born Killers, Night Falls on Manhattan (prod.).
TELEVISION: Son of the Morning Star, Open Admissions.

MOYERS, BILL
TV Correspondent. b. Hugo, OK, June 5, 1934. e. U. of Texas; Southwestern Baptist Theological Sem. Aide to Lyndon B. Johnson; assoc. dir., Peace Corps, 1961-62, and deputy dir., 1963. Spec. asst. to Pres. Johnson, 1963-65 and press secty., 1965-67. Editor and chief corr., CBS Reports. Bill Moyers Journal on PBS. Established Public Affairs TV, Inc., 1986.

MUDD, ROGER
Newscaster. b. Washington, DC, Feb. 9, 1928. e. Washington & Lee U., U. of North Carolina. Reporter for Richmond News-Leader, 1953; news. dir., WRNL, 1954; WTOP, Washington, 1956; joined CBS News 1961 as Congressional correspondent (2 Emmy Awards). 1977, Natl. Aff. corr.; 1978, corr., CBS Reports; 1980-87: NBC News as chief Washington corr., chief political corr., co-anchor; 1987 joined The MacNeil/Lehrer News Hour as special correspondent; essayist, and chief congressional correspondent. 1992 became contributing correspondent.

MUELLER-STAHL, ARMIN
Actor. b. Tilsit, East Prussia, Dec. 17, 1930. Moved to West Germany in 1980. e. Berlin Conservatory. Studied violin before turning to acting. Author: Verordneter Sonntag (Lost Sunday), Drehtage, Nuterwegs Nach Hause (On the Way Home).
PICTURES: Naked Among the Wolves, The Third, Jacob the Liar, The Flight, Lite Trap, Lola, Wings of Night, Veronika Voss, A Cop's Sunday, A Love in Germany, Thousand Eyes, Trauma, Colonel Redl, L'Homme blesse, God Doesn't Believe in Us Anymore, Angry Harvest, The Blind Director, Following the Fuhrer, Momo, The Jungle Mission, Lethal Obsession, Midnight Cop, Music Box, Das Spinnenetz, Just for Kicks, Avalon, Bronstein's Children, Kafka, The Power of One, Night on Earth, Utz, The House of the Spirits, Holy Matrimony, The Last Good Time, A Pyromaniac's Love Story, Taxandria, Shine, Theodore Rex, The Peacemaker, The Game, The Commissioner, The X Files: Fight the Future, Jakob the Liar, The Thirteenth Floor.
TELEVISION: *Mini-Series*: Amerika, Jesus.

MUHL, EDWARD E.
Executive, Producer. b. Richmond, IN, Feb. 17, 1907. Gen. mgr., Universal 1948-53; v.p., studio in charge of prod. 1953-68. Consultant, Alcor Prods., Ft. Smith, AR, 1985-90. Co-author, consultant, s.p., Soldier: Other Side of Glory, 1991-92.

MUIR, E. ROGER
Producer. b. Canada, Dec. 16, 1918. e. U. of Minnesota. Partner Minn. Advertising Services Co.; Photographer, Great Northern Railway; motion picture prod. Army Signal corps; NBC TV prod., Howdy Doody; exec. prod., Concentration. Now pres. Nicholson-Muir Prods, TV program packager, U.S. Spin-Off, Pay Cards, Canada Pay Cards, Headline Hunters, Definition, Celebrity Dominoes; co-creator Newlywed Game, exec. prod. I Am Joe's Heart, I Am Joe's Lung, I Am Joe's Spine, I Am Joe's Stomach, The New Howdy Doody Show, Supermates, Second Honeymoon, Groaner, Generation Jury, Shopping Game, Guess What, I Am Joe's Kidney, I Am Joe's Liver, It's Howdy Doody Time: A 40 Year Celebration. Retired 1993.

MULDAUR, DIANA
Actress. b. New York, NY, Aug. 19, 1943. e. Sweet Briar Coll. Began on New York stage then turned to films and TV, appearing on numerous major network shows.
PICTURES: The Swimmer (debut, 1968), Number One, The Lawyer, One More Train to Rob, The Other, McQ, Chosen Survivors, Beyond Reason.
TELEVISION: *Series*: The Secret Storm, The Survivors, McCloud, Born Free, The Tony Randall Show, Hizzoner, Fitz and Bones, A Year in the Life, L.A. Law, Star Trek: The Next Generation. *Movies*: McCloud: Who Killed Miss U.S.A.?, Call to Danger, Ordeal, Planet Earth, Charlie's Angels (pilot), Pine Canyon is Burning, Deadly Triangle, Black Beauty, To Kill a Cop, Maneaters Are Loose!, The Word, The Miracle Worker, The Return of Frank Cannon, Terror at Alcatraz, The Return of Sam McCloud.

MULGREW, KATE
Actress. b. Dubuque, IA, April 29, 1955. e. NYU. Stage work includes stints with American Shakespeare Festival, NY Shakespeare Festival, Seattle Rep. Theatre, Mark Taper Forum (LA). B'way: Black Comedy.
PICTURES: Lovespell, A Stranger Is Watching, Remo Williams: The Adventure Begins, Throw Momma from the Train, Camp Nowhere, Round Numbers, Lovespell.
TELEVISION: *Series*: Ryan's Hope (1975-77), Kate Columbo (Kate Loves a Mystery), Heartbeat, Man of the People, Star Trek: Voyager. *Movies*: The Word, Jennifer: A Woman's Story, A Time for Miracles, The Manions of America, Roses Are for the Rich, Roots: The Gift, Danielle Steel's Daddy, Fatal Friendship, For Love and Glory.

MULHERN, MATT
Actor. b. Philadelphia, PA, July 21, 1960. e. Rutgers Univ.
THEATRE: *NY*: Biloxi Blues, Wasted, The Night Hank Williams Died.
PICTURES: One Crazy Summer, Extreme Prejudice, Biloxi Blues, Junior, Infinity, The Sunchaser, Walking the Waterline.
TELEVISION: *Series*: Major Dad. *Movie*: Gunsmoke: To the Last Man, Terror in the Night, A Burning Passion: The Margaret Mitchell Story.

MULHOLLAND, ROBERT E.
Executive. b. 1933. e. Northwestern U. Joined NBC News as newswriter in Chicago in 1962. 1964 made midwestern field prod. for Huntley-Brinkley Report. 1964 moved to London as European prod. for NBC News; 1965, named Washington prod. of Huntley-Brinkley Report. Transferred to L.A. in 1967 to be dir. of news, west coast. Named exec. prod. of NBC Nightly News. 1973 appt. v.p., NBC news.; 1974 exec. v.p. of NBC News. 1977 appt. pres. of NBC Television Network; also elected to board of directors; 1981, pres. & CEO. Resigned, 1984. Dir. Television Info. Office, NYC 1985-87. Prof. Northwestern U. 1988-.

MULL, MARTIN
Actor. b. Chicago, IL, Aug. 18, 1943. e. Rhode Island Sch. of Design. Started as humorist, making recordings for Warner Bros., Capricorn, ABC Records.
PICTURES: FM (debut, 1978), My Bodyguard, Serial, Take This Job and Shove It, Flicks, Mr. Mom, Bad Manners, Clue, O.C. and Stiggs, Home Is Where the Hart Is, Rented Lips (also s.p., exec. prod.), Cutting Class, Ski Patrol, Far Out Man, Think Big, Ted and Venus, The Player, Miracle Beach, Mrs. Doubtfire, Mr. Write, Edie and Pen.
TELEVISION: *Series*: Mary Hartman Mary Hartman, Fernwood 2-Night, America 2-Night, Domestic Life, His and Hers, Roseanne, The Jackie Thomas Show, Family Dog (voice). *Specials*: The History of White People in America (also prod.), Candid Camera Christmas Special (1987), Portrait of a White Marriage, The Whole Shebang. *Movies*: Sunset Limousine, California Girls, The Day My Parents Ran Away, How the West Was Fun.

MULLAN, PETER
Actor.
PICTURES: The Big Man, Shallow Grave, Ruffian Hearts, Good Day for the Bad Guys, Braveheart, Trainspotting, Fairy Tale: A True Story, My Name Is Joe (Cannes Film Fest. Award, Best Actor, 1998).
TELEVISION: *Movies*: Bogwoman, Nightlife.

MULLER, ROBBY
Cinematographer. b. Netherlands, April 4, 1940. e. Dutch Film Acad. Asst. cameraman in Holland before moving to Germany where he shot 9 films for Wim Wenders.

PICTURES: Alabama: 2000 Light Years, Summer in the City, Jonathan, Carlos, The Goalkeeper's Fear of the Penalty Kick, The Scarlet Letter, Die Reise Nach Wien, Kings of the Road, Alice in the Cities, Perahim Die Zweite Chance, Wrong Move, The American Friend, Mysteries, The Glass Cell, Opname, Saint Jack, Honeysuckle Rose, A Cop's Sunday, They All Laughed, Body Rock, Repo Man, Paris Texas, To Live and Die in L.A., The Longshot, Down By Law, Tricheurs, The Believers, Barfly, Il Piccolo Diavolo (The Little Devil), Mystery Train, Korczak, Until the End of the World, When Pigs Fly, The Ditvoorst Domains (actor only), Mad Dog and Glory, Breaking the Waves (NY Society of Film Critics Award and Natl Society of Film Critics Awards, 1997), Dead Man (NY Society of Film Critics Awards, 1997), Last Call, Beyond the Clouds, The Tango Lesson, Shattered Image, Ghost Dog: The Way of the Samurai, Buena Vista Social Club.

MULLIGAN, RICHARD
Actor. b. New York, NY Nov. 13, 1932
THEATER: Nobody Loves an Albatross, All the Way Home, Never Too Late, Mating Dance, Hogan's Goat, Thieves, etc.
PICTURES: Love With the Proper Stranger (debut, 1963), One Potato Two Potato, The Group, The undefeated, Little Big Man, Irish Whiskey Rebeliion, From the Mixed-Up Files of Mrs. Basil E. Frankweiler, The Big Bus, Scavenger Hunt, S.O.B., Trail of the Pink Panther, Meatballs Part II, Teachers, Micki and Maude, Doin' Time, The Heavenly Kid, A Fine Mess, Quicksilver, Oliver & Company (voice).
TELEVISION: *Movies:* Having Babies III, Malibu, Jealousy, Poler Alice, Gore Vidal's Lincoln, Guess Who's Coming for Christmas? *Series:* The Hero, Diana, Soap (Emmy Award, 1980), Reggie, Empty Nest (Emmy Award 1989, Golden Globe), London Suite, Dog's Best Friend.

MULLIGAN, ROBERT
Director. b. Bronx, NY. Aug. 23, 1925. e. Fordham U. Served in Navy during WWII. After working as copyboy for NY Times joined CBS in mailroom. Eventually became TV dir. before moving into features.
PICTURES: Fear Strikes Out (debut, 1957), The Rat Race, The Great Imposter, Come September, The Spiral Road, To Kill a Mockingbird, Love With the Proper Stranger, Baby the Rain Must Fall, Inside Daisy Clover, Up the Down Staircase, The Stalking Moon, The Pursuit of Happiness, Summer of '42, The Other, The Nickel Ride, Bloodbrothers, Same Time Next Year, Kiss Me Goodbye, Clara's Heart, The Man in the Moon.
TELEVISION: The Moon and the Sixpence (Emmy Award, 1960), Billy Budd, Ah Wilderness, A Tale of Two Cities, The Bridge of San Luis Rey, Playhouse 90, Philco-Goodyear, Suspense, Studio One, Hallmark Hall of Fame.

MULRONEY, DERMOT
Actor. b. Alexandria, VA, Oct. 31, 1963. e. Northwestern Univ.
PICTURES: Sunset, Young Guns, Survival Quest, Staying Together, Longtime Companion, Career Opportunities, Bright Angel, Where the Day Takes You, Samantha, Point of No Return, The Thing Called Love, Silent Tongue, Bad Girls, Angels in the Outfield, There Goes My Baby, Living in Oblivion, Copycat, How to Make an American Quilt, Kansas City, Trigger Effect, My Best Friend's Wedding, Where the Money Is, Trixie, Goodbye Lover.
TELEVISION: *Movies*: Sin of Innocence, Daddy, Unconquered, Long Gone, The Heart of Justice, Family Pictures, The Last Outlaw. *Special:* Toma: The Drug Knot.

MUMY, BILL
Actor. r.n. Charles William Mumy Jr. b. El Centro, CA, Feb. 1, 1954. Began acting as Billy Mumy at age 6. Played with band America in 1970's, also with bands Bill Mumy & The Igloos, and The Jenerators. Has made 8 albums with Barnes & Barnes. With actor Miguel Ferrer, wrote comic books Comet Man and Trip to the Acid Dog. Has also written stories for Star Trek, The Hulk, and Spiderman comic books, and Lost in Space comic published by Innovation. Wrote music for Disney's Adventures in Wonderland series (Emmy nom.)
PICTURES: Tammy Tell Me True, Palm Springs Weekend, A Ticklish Affair, A Child is Waiting, Dear Brigitte, Rascal, Bless the Beasts and Children, Papillon, Twilight Zone—The Movie, Hard to Hold, Captain America, Double Trouble, Three Wishes, The Fantasy Worlds of Irwin Allen.
TELEVISION: *Series*: Lost in Space, Sunshine. *Movies*: Sunshine, The Rockford Files (pilot), Sunshine Christmas. *Guest*: The Twilight Zone, Alfred Hitchcock Presents, Bewitched, The Virginian, I Dream of Jeannie, The Adventures of Ozzie and Harriet, Ben Casey, The Red Skelton Show, Lancer, Here Come the Brides, Riverboat, Have Gun Will Travel, Matlock, Me and Mom, The Flash, Superboy, Babylon 5. *Pilots*: The Two of Us, Archie, Space Family Robinson. *Host*: Inside Space (SciFi Channel).

MURDOCH, RUPERT
Executive. b. Australia, March 11, 1931. Son of Sir Keith Murdoch, head of The Melbourne Herald and leading figure in Australian journalism. e. Oxford U., England. Spent two years on Fleet St. before returning home to take over family paper, The Adelaide News. Acquired more Australian papers and in 1969, expanded to Britain, buying The News of the World. Moved to U.S. in 1973, buying San Antonio Express and News. Conglomerate in 1985 included New York Post, New York Magazine, The Star, The Times of London, The Boston Herald, The Chicago Sun-Times along with TV stations, book publishing companies, airline, oil and gas companies, etc. 1985, made deal to buy 20th Century-Fox Film Corp. from owner Martin Davis. Sold the NY Post, 1988 to conform with FCC regulations. Purchased Triangle Publications 1988 (including TV Guide).

MUREN, DENNIS E.
Visual Effects Creator and Director. b. Glendale, CA, Nov. 1, 1946. AA Pasadena CC, 1966. Studied at UCLA. Freelance special effects 1968-75. Cameraman Cascade 1975-76. Dir. of photography, visual effects Industrial Light Magic 1976-80. AMPAS Scientific/Technical Award, 1981. Member ASC, AMPAS.
PICTURES: Star Wars, Close Encounters of the Third Kind, The Empire Strikes Back (Acad. Award), Dragonslayer, E.T.: the Extraterrestrial (Acad. Award), Return of the Jedi (Acad. Award, BAFTA Award), Indiana Jones and the Temple of Doom (Acad. Award, BAFTA award), Young Sherlock Holmes, Captain Eo (short feature), Innerspace (Acad. Award), Empire of the Sun, Willow, Ghostbusters II, The Abyss (Acad. Award), Terminator 2 (Acad. Award, BAFTA award), Jurassic Park (Acad. Award, BAFTA award), Casper, The Lost World: Jurassic Park.
TELEVISION: Battlestar Galactica, Caravan of Courage (Emmy award).

MURPHY, BEN
Actor. b. Jonesboro, AR, March 6, 1942. e. U. of Illinois. Degree in drama from Pasadena Playhouse. Acted in campus productions and toured in summer stock. Film debut with small role in The Graduate, 1967.
PICTURES: Yours Mine and Ours, The Thousand Plane Raid, Sidecar Racers, Time Walker.
TELEVISION: *Movies*: The Letters, Wild Bill Hickock, Bridger, Heat Wave, Runaway, This Is the West That Was, Gemini Man, Hospital Fire, The Cradle Will Fall, Stark: Mirror Image. *Series*: The Name of the Game, Alias Smith and Jones, Griff, Gemini Man, The Chisholms, Lottery!, Berrenger's, The Dirty Dozen. *Mini-Series*: The Winds of War.

MURPHY, BRITTANY
Actress. b. Nov. 10, 1977.
PICTURES: Family Prayers, Clueless, Drive, Freeway, The Prophecy II, Phoenix, Falling Sky, Bongwater, Trixie, Piece of My Heart, Drop Dead Gorgeous, Cherry Falls, Girl Interrupted.
TELEVISION: *Movies:* David and Lisa, Devil's Arithmetic. *Series:* Drexell's Class, Almost Home, Sister Sister, King of the Hill (voice). *Guest:* Murphy Brown, Blossom, Frasier, Party of Five, SeaQuest DSV, Boy Meet World, Clueless, Nash Bridges.

MURPHY, EDDIE
Actor. b. Brooklyn, NY, April 3, 1961. e. Roosevelt High Sch. Wrote and performed own comedy routines at youth centers and local bars at age 15. Worked on comedy club circuit; at 19 joined TV's Saturday Night Live as writer and performer. Recordings: Eddie Murphy, Eddie Murphy: Comedian, How Could It Be?, Love's Alright. Voted Top-Money Making Star of 1988 on Quigley Poll, NATO/ShoWest Star of the Decade, for 1980's.
PICTURES: 48 HRS. (debut, 1982), Trading Places, Best Defense, Beverly Hills Cop, The Golden Child, Beverly Hills Cop II, Eddie Murphy Raw (also s.p., exec. prod.), Coming to America (also story), Harlem Nights (also dir., s.p, exec. prod.), Another 48 HRS., Boomerang (also story), The Distinguished Gentleman, Beverly Hills Cop III, Vampire in Brooklyn (also co-prod.), The Nutty Professor (also co-exec. prod.; Nat'l Society of Film Critics Award, 1997), Metro, Mulan (voice), Doctor Dolittle, Holy Man, Life, Bowfinger, The Nutty Professor II.
TELEVISION: *Series:* Saturday Night Live (1981-84), The PJs. *Pilots (exec. prod.):* What's Alan Watching? (also cameo), Coming to America. *Movie (exec. prod.):* The Kid Who Loved Christmas.

MURPHY, MICHAEL
Actor. b. Los Angeles, CA, May 5, 1938. e. U. of Arizona. m. actress Wendy Crewson. Taught English and Drama in L.A. city school system, 1962-64. N.Y. stage debut as dir. of Rat's Nest, 1978.
PICTURES: Double Trouble (debut, 1967), Countdown, The Legend of Lylah Clare, The Arrangement, That Cold Day in the Park, M*A*S*H, Count Yorga: Vampire, Brewster McCloud, McCabe and Mrs. Miller, What's Up Doc?, The Thief Who Came to Dinner, Phase IV, Nashville, The Front, An Unmarried Woman, The Great Bank Hoax, The Class of Miss MacMichael, Manhattan, The Year of Living Dangerously, Strange Behavior, Cloak and Dagger, Salvador, Mesmerized, Shocker, Folks!, Batman Returns, Clean Slate, Bad Company, Kansas City.
TELEVISION: *Series*: Two Marriages, Hard Copy. *Guest:* Saints and Sinners, Ben Casey, Dr. Kildare, Bonanza, Combat. *Movies*: The Autobiography of Miss Jane Pittman, The Caine Mutiny Court-Martial, Tailspin: Behind the Korean Airlines Tragedy. *Specials*: John Cheever's Oh Youth and Beauty, Tanner '88.

MURPHY, THOMAS S.
Executive. e. Cornell Univ (B.S.M.E.), Harvard U. Grad. Sch. of Bus. Admin. (M.B.A.). Joined Capital Cities at its inception in 1954. Named a dir. in 1957, then pres. in 1964. Chmn. & CEO of Capital Cities, 1966-90. Company named Capital Cities/ABC Inc. in 1986 after acquistion of American Broadcasting Companies Inc. 1990-94, chmn. of bd. Resumed position of chmn. & CEO in Feb., 1994.

MURRAY, BARBARA
Actress. b. London, England, Sept. 27, 1929. Stage debut in Variety, 1946.
PICTURES: Badger's Green (debut, 1948), Passport to Pimlico, Don't Ever Leave Me, Boys in Brown, Poets Pub, Tony Draws a Horse, Dark Man, Frightened Man, Mystery Junction, Another Man's Poison, Hot Ice, Street Corner (Both Sides of the Law), Meet Mr. Lucifer, Doctor at Large, Campbell's Kingdom, A Cry from the Streets, Girls in Arms, A Dandy in Aspic, Tales From the Crypt.
TELEVISION: *Series*: The Power Game, The Bretts.

MURRAY, BILL
Actor. b. Wilmette, IL, Sept. 21, 1950. e. attended Regis Coll. Was pre-med student; left to join brother, Brian Doyle-Murray, in Second City the Chicago improvisational troupe. Appeared with brother on radio in National Lampoon Radio Hour, and in off-B'way revue, National Lampoon Show. Also on radio provided voice of Johnny Storm the Human Torch on Marvel Comics' Fantastic Four. Hired by ABC for Saturday Night Live with Howard Cosell; then by NBC for Saturday Night Live, 1977.
PICTURES: Jungle Burger (debut, 1975), Meatballs, Mr. Mike's Mondo Video, Where the Buffalo Roam, Loose Shoes, Caddyshack, Stripes, Tootsie, Ghostbusters, The Razor's Edge (also co-s.p.), Nothing Lasts Forever, Little Shop of Horrors, Scrooged, Ghostbusters II, Quick Change (also co-dir., co-prod.), What About Bob?, Groundhog Day, Mad Dog and Glory, Ed Wood, Space Jam, Larger Than Life, Kingpin, The Man Who Knew Too Little, With Friends Like These, Veeck As in Wreck, Rushmore, Wild Things, The Cradle Will Rock, Hamlet, Scout's Honor, Company Man, Charlie's Angels, Veeck as In Wreck, Osmosis Jones, Ocean's Eleven, Speaking of Sex.
TELEVISION: *Series*: Saturday Night Live (1977-80; also writer; Emmy Award for writing 1977). Pilot: The TV TV Show. *Movie*: All You Need Is Cash. *Specials*: It's Not Easy Being Me—The Rodney Dangerfield Show, Steve Martin's Best Show Ever, Second City—25 Years in Revue.

MURRAY, DON
Actor, Director, Writer. b. Hollywood, CA, July 31, 1929. e. AADA. Mother was a Ziegfeld Girl, father was dance dir. for Fox Studio.
THEATER: *B'way*: Insect Comedy, The Rose Tattoo, The Skin of Our Teeth, The Hot Corner, Smith (musical), The Norman Conquests, Same Time Next Year. *National tours*: California Suite, Chicago.
PICTURES: Bus Stop (debut, 1956; Acad. Award nom.), The Bachelor Party, A Hatful of Rain, From Hell to Texas, These Thousand Hills, Shake Hands With the Devil, One Foot in Hell, The Hoodlum Priest (also co-prod., co-s.p. as Don Deer), Advise and Consent, Escape From East Berlin, One Man's Way, Baby the Rain Must Fall, Kid Rodelo, The Plainsman, Sweet Love Bitter, The Viking Queen, Childish Things (Confession of Tom Harris; also prod., co-s.p.), The Cross and the Switchblade (dir., co-s.p. only), Happy Birthday Wanda June, Conquest of the Planet of the Apes, Cotter, Call Me by My Rightful Name (also prod., co-s.p.), Deadly Hero, Damien (dir., s.p. only), Endless Love, I Am the Cheese, Radioactive Dreams, Peggy Sue Got Married, Scorpion, Made in Heaven, Ghosts Can't Do It.
TELEVISION: *Series*: Made in America (panelist), The Outcasts, Knots Landing, Brand New Life, Sons and Daughters. *Movies*: The Borgia Stick, Daughter of the Mind, The Intruders, The Girl on the Late Late Show, The Sex Symbol, A Girl Named Sooner, Rainbow, Crisis in Mid-Air, If Things Were Different, The Boy Who Drank to Much, Fugitive Family, Return of the Rebels, Thursday's Child, Quarterback Princess, License to Kill, A Touch of Scandal, Something in Common, Stillwatch, The Stepford Children, Mistress, Brand New Life. *Specials*: For I Have Loved Strangers (also writer), Hasty Heart, Billy Budd, Winterset, Alas Babylon, Justin Morgan Had a Horse, My Dad Isn't Crazy Is He?, Montana Crossroads (Emmy nom.)

MURRAY, JAN
Comedian, Actor. b. Bronx, NY, Oct. 4, 1917. Started as comedian, nightclub performer, continuing on radio, tv.
THEATER: A Funny Thing Happened on the Way to the Forum, Guys and Dolls, Silk Stockings, Bye Bye Birdie, A Thousand Clowns, Come Blow Your Horn, The Odd Couple, Make a Million, Don't Drink the Water, Critic's Choice, You Know I Can't Hear You When the Water Is Running.
PICTURES: Who Killed Teddy Bear? (debut, 1965), Tarzan and the Great River, The Busy Body, A Man Called Dagger, Which Way to the Front?, History of the World Part I, Fear City.
TELEVISION: *Series (emcee/host)*: Songs for Sale, Go Lucky, Sing It Again, Blind Date, Dollar a Second (also creator, prod.), Jan Murray Time, Treasure Hunt (also creator, prod.), Charge Account (also creator, prod.), Chain Letter. *Guest*: Zane Grey Theatre, Dr., Kildare, Burke's Law, The Lucy Show, Love American Style, Mannix, Ellery Queen, Hardcastle and McCormick. *Movies*: Roll Freddy Roll, Banjo Hackett: Roamin' Free, The Dream Merchants.

MUSANTE, TONY
Actor. b. Bridgeport, CT, June 30. e. Oberlin Coll. B.A. Directed local theatre, then appeared off-Broadway, in regional theater, and on Dupont Show of the Month (Ride With Terror).
THEATER: *B'way*: The Lady From Dubuque, P.S. Your Cat Is Dead, 27 Wagons Full of Cotton, Memory of Two Mondays. *Off-B'way*: Grand Magic, Cassatt, A Gun Play, Benito Cereno, L'Histoire du Soldat, Match-Play, The Zoo Story, The Pinter Plays (The Collection), Kiss Mama, The Balcony, Snow Orchid, The Flip Side, Frankie and Johnny in the Claire de Lune. *Regional*: The Big Knife, A Streetcar Named Desire, The Taming of the Shrew, Widows, The Archbishop's Ceiling, Dancing in the Endzone, Two Brothers, Souvenir, APA Shakespeare Rep., Wait Until Dark, Anthony Rose, Mount Allegro, Double Play, Falling Man, Breaking Legs, Love Letters, The Sisters, Italian Funerals and Other Festive Occasions.
PICTURES: Once a Thief, The Incident, The Detective, The Mercenary, The Bird with the Crystal Plumage, The Grissom Gang, The Last Run, Anonymous Venetian, Collector's Item, The Repenter, The Pisciotta Case, Goodbye and Amen, Break Up, Nocturne, The Pope of Greenwich Village, One Night at Dinner, Appointment in Trieste, Devil's Hill, The Deep End of the Ocean.
TELEVISION: *Series*: Toma, Oz. *Guest*: Chrysler Theatre, Alfred Hitchcock Hour, N.Y.P.D., The Fugitive, Trials of O'Brien, Police Story, Medical Story, Thomas Gottschallk's Late Night TV, Loving, Acapulco H.E.A.T., Nothing Sacred. *Movies*: Rearview Mirror, The Court Martial of Lt. William Calley, Desperate Miles, The Quality of Mercy, Nowhere to Hide, My Husband is Missing, The Story of Esther, High Ice, Last Waltz on a Tightrope, Weekend (Amer. Playhouse), Nutcracker: Money Madness & Murder, Breaking Up Is Hard To Do, The Baron, The Seventh Scroll, Deep Family Secrets.

MYERS, JULIAN F.
Public Relations Executive. b. Detroit, MI, Feb. 22, 1918. e. Wayne U., 1935-37, USC, 1937-39. Distribution, Loew's Detroit, 1941-42; asst. story editor, idea man, Columbia, 1942-46; publicist, 20th Century-Fox, 1948-62; public relations, Julian F. Myers, Inc., 1962; pres., Myers Studios, Inc., 1966; pres., New Horizons Broadcasting Corp., 1968-69; sr. publicist American Intl. Pictures, 1970-80. Pres., Hollywood Press Club; former member Variety Club; Academy of Motion Pictures Arts & Sciences; Board of Governors Film Industry Workshops, Inc. 1977, 1979, western v.p., Publicists Guild; Recipient of Publicists Guild's Robert Yeager Award. First male member Hollywood Women's Press Club. Co-founder HANDS (Hollywood Answering Needs of Disaster Survivors). Member, M.P. Pioneers. Winner, 1980 Publicists Guild Les Mason Award. Instructor in publicity, UCLA, 1979-present, and at Loyola Marymount U, 1991-present. Filmways Pictures, pub. dept., 1980-81. Exec. v.p., worldwide m.p. and TV pub./mktg., Hanson & Schwam Public Relations 1981-91. Author of Myersystem and Myerscope guides. Member: USC Cinema & TV Alumni Assn., West Coast P.R. Will Rogers Inst., Acad. TV Arts Sciences; p.r. coord. comm., Academy of Motion Picture Arts & Sciences. Bd. of dirs., Show Biz Expo. Publicist, Prods. Guild of America. Pres. Julian Myers Public Relations, nominated MoPic Showmanship of the Year, Publicists Guild of America, 1993. Columnist, Drama-Logue Magazine. Special Award of Merit, Publicists Guild of America, 1998. Member, Women in Film.

MYERS, MIKE
Actor. b. Scarborough, Ontario, Canada, May 25, 1963.
PICTURES: Elvis Stories, Wayne's World (also s.p.), So I Married an Axe Murderer(also s.p.), Wayne's World 2 (also s.p.), Austin Powers: International Man of Mystery (also s.p., prod.), 54, Austin Powers: The Spy Who Shagged Me (also s.p., prod.), Mystery Alaska, Sprockets (also s.p.).
TELEVISION: *Series:* Mullarky & Myers, Saturday Night Live. *Guest:* King of Kensington, The Littlest Hobo.

MYERS, PETER S.
Executive. b. Toronto, Ont., Canada, May 13, 1923. e. U. of Toronto. Toronto branch mgr., 20th Century-Fox, 1948; mng. dir., Canada, 1951; gen. sales mgr. in charge of domestic distrib., 1968; sr. v.p., 20th-Fox Ent.; pres., 20th-Fox Classics, 1983; pres., Hemdale Releasing Corp., 1986; pres. & CEO, Four Seasons Ent., 1989.

MYERS, STANLEY
Composer. b. London, England, 1939.
PICTURES: Kaleidoscope (debut, 1966), Ulysses, No Way to Treat a Lady, Michael Kohlhaas, Otley, Two Gentlemen Sharing, Take a Girl Like You, Tropic of Cancer, The Walking Stick, Long Ago Tomorrow, A Severed Head, Tam Lin, King Queen Knave, Sitting Target, Summer Lightning, X Y & Zee, The Blockhouse, The Apprenticeship of Duddy Kravitz, Caravan to Vaccares, Little Malcolm, The Wilby Conspiracy, Coup de Grace, The Greek Tycoon, The Deer Hunter, The Class of Miss MacMichael, A Portrait of the Artist as a Young Man, The Secret Policeman's Other Ball, Yesterday's Hero, Watcher in the Woods, Absolution, The Incubus, Lady Chatterly's Lover, Eureka, Moonlighting, Blind Date, Beyond the Limit, The Next One, Success is the Best Revenge, The Chain, Dreamchild, Insignificance, The Lightship, The Wind, Castaway, My Beautiful Laundrette, Prick Up Your Ears, Wish You Were Here, The Second Victory, Taffin, Track 29, Stars and Bars, Trading Hearts, Sammy and Rosie Get Laid, Scenes From the Class Struggle in Beverly Hills, Torrents of Spring.

TELEVISION: *Series* (U.K.): Widows (parts 1 & 2), Nancy Astor, Diana. *Series* (U.S.): The Martian Chronicles, Florence Nightingale. *Movies*: Strong Medicine, Smart Money, Baja Oklahoma, Monte Carlo.

MYERSON, BERNARD
Executive. b. New York, NY, March 25, 1918. Entered m.p. ind. with Fabian Theatres, 1938-63; last position as exec. v.p.; joined Loew's Theatres as v.p., 1963; exec. v.p. and board member, Loew's Corp.; pres. Loew's Theatres, 1971. Chmn. & pres., Loews Theatre Management Corp., 1985, presently retired. Member of Executive Committee Greater N.Y. Chapter, National Foundation of March of Dimes; Honorary chmn., bd. mem., & former pres., Will Rogers Memorial Fund; exec. comm., bd., National Assn. Theatre Owners; bd. member & former pres., Motion Picture Pioneers; treas. Variety Intl.; member bd. of dirs., Burke Rehabilitation Center; member, N.Y.S. Governor's Council on M.P. & T.V. Development; vice-chmn., adv. bd. of Tisch Sch. of Arts, NYU.

N

NABORS, JIM
Actor. b. Sylacauga, AL, June 12, 1932. Discovered performing in an L.A. nightclub in early 1960's by Andy Griffith, who asked him to appear on his series. Developed a second career as a singer. Between 1966-72 had 12 albums on best selling charts.
PICTURES: The Best Little Whorehouse in Texas, Stroker Ace, Cannonball Run II.
TELEVISION: *Series*: The Andy Griffith Show, Gomer Pyle USMC, The Jim Nabors Hour, The Lost Saucer, The Jim Nabors Show (synd. talk show). *Movie*: Return to Mayberry.

NADER, GEORGE
Actor. b. Pasadena, CA, Oct. 19, 1921. e. Occidental Coll., B.A.; Pasadena Playhouse, B.T.A. Served in U.S. Navy. Wrote novel: Chrome (Putnam).
PICTURES: Monsoon (debut, 1953), Memory of Love, Robot Monster, Rustlers on Horseback, Overland Telegraph, Carnival Story, Miss Robin Crusoe, Sins of Jezebel, Phone Call from a Stranger, Four Guns to the Border, Six Bridges to Cross, Lady Godiva, The Second Greatest Sex, Away All Boats, Appointment With a Shadow, Congo Crossing, The Unguarded Moment, Four Girls in Town, Man Afraid, The Female Animal, Flood Tide, Joe Butterfly, Nowhere to Go, The Secret Mark of D'Artagnan, The Great Space Adventure, Zigzag, The Human Duplicators, House of a Thousand Dolls, The Million Eyes of Sumuru, Alarm on 83rd Street, Murder at Midnight, Count-Down for Manhattan, Dynamite in Green Silk, The Check and an Icy Smile, Murder Club from Brooklyn, Death in Red Jaguar, End Station of the Damned, Beyond Atlantis.
TELEVISION: *Series*: Ellery Queen, Man and the Challenge, Shannon. *Guest*: Letter to Loretta, Fireside Theatre, Chevron Theatre, Alfred Hitchcock, Andy Griffith Show, etc. *Movie*: Nakia.

NAIFY, ROBERT
Executive. b. Sacramento, CA. e. Attended Stanford U. Worked for United California Theatres starting in 1946 in various capacities including: theatre manager, purchasing agent, film buyer, general manager and president. 1963 became exec. v.p. United Artists Communications; 1971 became pres. & CEO until 1987. Currently president, Todd-AO Corporation.

NAIR, MIRA
Director, Producer. b. Bhubaneshwar, India, October 15, 1957. e. Irish Catholic Missionary School in India, Delhi U., Harvard U. A course in documentary filmmaking at Harvard led to directing 4 non-fiction films including India Cabaret (1985) and Children of Desired Sex.
PICTURES: *Director-Producer*: Salaam Bombay! (Cannes Film Fest. Camera d'Or/Prix du Publique; Acad. Award nom.), Mississippi Masala (also s.p.), The Perez Family, Kama Sutra: A Tale of Love.

NALLE, BILLY
Theatre Concert Organist, Composer. b. Fort Myers, FL, Apr. 24, 1921. Postgrad, Juilliard Sch. Over 5,000 major telecasts from NY; now artist emeritus, Wichita Theatre Organization, Inc. RCA, Telarc, Reader's Digest & WTO Records Artist. Now residing in Fort Myers, FL.

NAMATH, JOE
Actor. b. Beaver Falls, PA, May 31, 1943. e. U. of Alabama. Former professional football star.
PICTURES: Norwood (debut, 1970), C.C. & Company, The Last Rebel, Avalanche Express, Chattanooga Choo Choo, Going Under.
TELEVISION: *Series*: The Waverly Wonders. *Host*: Monday Night Football (1985). *Movie*: Marriage Is Alive and Well. *Guest*: Here's Lucy, The Brady Bunch, The Love Boat, Kate and Allie.

NARIZZANO, SILVIO
Producer, Director. b. Montreal, Canada, Feb. 8, 1927. e. U. of Bishop's, Lennoxville, Quebec, B.A. Was active as actor-director in Canadian theatre before going to England for TV and theatrical film work.
PICTURES: *Director*: Under Ten Flags (co-dir.), Die! Die! My Darling!, Georgy Girl, Blue, Loot, Redneck (also prod.), The Sky Is Falling, Why Shoot the Teacher?, The Class of Miss MacMichael, Choices, Double Play. *Producer*: Negatives, Fade-In.
TELEVISION: The Babysitter, Poet Game, The Little Farm, Come Back Little Sheba, Staying On, Young Shoulders, The Body in the Library. *Series*: Miss Marple.

NASH, N. RICHARD
Writer. b. Philadelphia, PA, June 8, 1913.
AUTHOR: Cry Macho, East Wind, Rain, The Last Magic, Aphrodite's Cave, Radiance, Behold the Man, The Wildwood.
THEATER: *B'way*: Second Best Bed, The Young and Fair, See the Jaguar, The Rainmaker, Girls of Summer, Handful of Fire, Wildcat, 110 in the Shade, Fire, The Happy Time, Echoes, Wildfire, The Torch, Magic, The Bluebird of Happiness, The Loss of D-Natural, Breaking the Tie, Come As You Are, Everybody Smile, Life Anonymous, The Green Clown.
PICTURES: Nora Prentiss, Welcome Stranger, The Vicious Years, The Rainmaker, Dear Wife, Porgy and Bess, Sainted Sisters, Dragonfly.
TELEVISION: Many TV plays for Television Playhouse, U.S. Steel, General Electric.

NATHANSON, MICHAEL
Executive. Began his career at NBC Sports, NY. In 1977 moved to LA and worked as prod. asst. on The Deep, Sinbad the Eye of the Tiger. 1980-85, v.p., prod., MGM, United Artists, Warner Bros. 1987, exec. v.p., prod., Columbia Pictures; 1989-94, pres. of Worldwide Prod. at Columbia Pictures; projects included: Awakenings, The Prince of Tides, Boyz N the Hood, A River Runs Through It, A League of Their Own, In the Line of Fire, Groundhog Day, Bram Stoker's Dracula, and others. 1994-97, chmn, & CEO, Regency Productions; produced: A Time to Kill, Tin Cup, Natural Born Killers, Heat, Copy Cat. 1997-, pres. & CEO, MGM Pictures; produced: Species 2, Dirty Work.

NAUGHTON, DAVID
Actor, Singer. b. Hartford, CT, Feb. 13, 1951. Brother is actor James Naughton. e. U. of Pennsylvania, B.A. Studied at London Acad. of Music and Dramatic Arts. Numerous TV commercials, including music for Dr. Pepper. On B'way in Hamlet, Da, Poor Little Lambs.
PICTURES: Midnight Madness (debut, 1980), An American Werewolf in London, Separate Ways, Hot Dog... The Movie, Not for Publication, The Boy in Blue, Separate Vacations, Kidnapped, Quite By Chance, Beanstalk, The Sleeping Car, Overexposed, Wild Cactus, Desert Steel, Amityville: A New Generation, Beanstalk, Ice Cream Man, Urban Safari.
TELEVISION: *Series*: Makin' It, At Ease, My Sister Sam, Temporary Insanity, The Belles of Bleeker St., Those Two. *Movies*: I Desire, Getting Physical, Goddess of Love. *Guest*: Twilight Zone, Murder She Wrote, Touched By An Angel, Seinfeld, Cybil, Melrose Place.

NAUGHTON, JAMES
Actor. b. Middletown, CT, Dec. 6, 1945. Father of actors Greg Naughton and Keira Naughton. e. Brown U., A.B., 1967; Yale U., M.F.A., drama, 1970.
THEATER: *NY*: I Love My Wife (B'way debut, 1977), Long Day's Journey Into Night (Theatre World, Drama Desk and New York Critics Circle Awards, 1971), Whose Life Is It Anyway?, Losing Time, Drinks Before Dinner, City of Angels (Tony & Drama Desk Awards, 1990), Four Baboons Adoring the Sun. Regional: Who's Afraid of Virginia Woolf? (Long Wharf), The Glass Menagerie (Long Wharf), Hamlet (Long Wharf), Julius Caesar (Amer. Shakespeare Festival), 8 seasons at Williamstown Theatre Festival, Chicago (B'way, 1996-97).
PICTURES: The Paper Chase (debut, 1973), Second Wind, A Stranger is Watching, Cat's Eye, The Glass Menagerie, The Good Mother, First Kid.
TELEVISION: *Special*: Look Homeward Angel (1972). *Series*: Faraday and Company, Planet of the Apes, Making the Grade, Trauma Center, Raising Miranda, The Cosby Mysteries. *Movies*: F. Scott Fitzgerald and the Last of the Belles, The Last 36 Hours of Dr. Durant, The Bunker, My Body My Child, Parole, The Last of the Great Survivors, Between Darkness and the Dawn, Sin of Innocence, Traveling Man, Antigone, The Cosby Mysteries (pilot), The Birds II: Land's End, Cagney & Lacey: The Return, Cagney & Lacey: Together Again, Raising Caines.

NEAL, PATRICIA
Actress. b. Packard, KY, Jan. 20, 1926. e. Northwestern U. Worker as doctor's asst., cashier, hostess, model, jewelry store clerk prior to prof. career as actress. In summer stock before B'way debut in The Voice of the Turtle, 1946. Autobiography: As I Am (with Richard DeNeut, 1988).
THEATER: *NY*: The Voice of the Turtle, Another Part of the Forest (Tony, Donaldson & Drama Critic Awards), The Children's Hour, Roomful of Roses, The Miracle Worker. *England*: Suddenly Last Summer.

PICTURES: John Loves Mary (debut 1949), The Fountainhead, It's a Great Feeling, The Hasty Heart, Bright Leaf, Three Secrets, The Breaking Point, Raton Pass, Operation Pacific, The Day the Earth Stood Still, Weekend With Father, Diplomatic Courier, Washington Story, Something for the Birds, Stranger From Venus (Immediate Disaster), Your Woman, A Face in the Crowd, Breakfast at Tiffany's, Hud (Academy Award, BFA Award, 1963), Psyche '59, In Harm's Way (BFA Award, 1965), The Subject Was Roses (Acad. Award nom.), The Night Digger, Baxter, Happy Mother's Day Love George, "B" Must Die, The Passage, Ghost Story, An Unremarkable Life.
TELEVISION: *Movies*: The Homecoming, Things in Their Season, Eric, Tail Gunner Joe, A Love Affair: The Eleanor and Lou Gehrig Story, The Bastard, All Quiet on the Western Front, Shattered Vows, Love Leads the Way, Caroline?, A Mother's Right: The Elizabeth Morgan Story, Heidi. Guest: Little House on the Prairie, Murder She Wrote. *BBC*: Days & Nights of Beebee Finstermaker, The Country Girl, Clash By Night, The Royal Family.

NEAME, RONALD
C.B.E. Cinematographer, Producer, Director. b. Hendon, Eng. April 23, 1911. e. U. Coll. Sch., London. p. Elwin Neame, London photog., & Ivy Close, m.p. actress. Entered m.p. ind. 1928; asst. cameraman on first full-length Brit. sound film, Blackmail, dir. by Alfred Hitchcock, 1929; became chief cameraman & lighting expert, 1934; in 1945 joint assoc. prod., Noel Coward Prods.
PICTURES: *Cinematographer*: Girls Will Be Boys (co-cine.), Happy (co-cine.), Elizabeth of England, Honours Easy (co-cine.), Invitation to the Waltz (co-cine.), Joy Ride, Music Hath Charms, The Crimes of Stephen Hawke, The Improper Dutchess, A Star Fell From Heaven, Against the Tide, Brief Ecstasy, Feather Your Nest, Keep Fit, Weekend Millionaire, Gaunt Stranger, The Phantom Strikes, The Crime of Peter Frame, Dangerous Secrets, I See Ice (co-cine.), Penny Paradise, Who Goes Next? Cheers Boys Cheer, Sweeney Todd: The Demon Barber of Fleet Street, Let's Be Famous, Trouble Brewing, The Ware Case, It's In the Air (co-cine.), Let George Do It, Return to Yesterday, Saloon Bar, Four Just Men, Major Barbara, A Yank in the R.A.F. (Brit. flying sequence), One of Our Aircraft is Missing, In Which We Serve, This Happy Breed, Blithe Spirit, Brief Encounter, Great Expectations (also co-s.p.), Oliver Twist (also co-s.p.), A Young Man's Fancy, Passionate Friends. *Director*: Take My Life, Golden Salamander (also co-s.p.), The Card (The Promoter; also prod.), Man With a Million (The Million Pound Note), The Man Who Never Was, The Seventh Sin, Windom's Way, The Horse's Mouth, Tunes of Glory, Escape from Zahrain, I Could Go on Singing, The Chalk Garden, Mister Moses, Gambit, A Man Could Get Killed (co-dir.), Prudence and the Pill (co-dir.), The Prime of Miss Jean Brodie, Scrooge, The Poseidon Adventure, The Odessa File, Meteor, Hopscotch, First Monday in October, Foreign Body, The Magic Balloon.

NEEDHAM, HAL
Director, Writer. b. Memphis, TN, March 6, 1931. e. Student public schools. Served with Paratroopers, U.S. Army 1951-54. Founder Stunts Unlimited, Los Angeles, 1970; stuntman Stunts Unlimited, 1956-65; dir. and stunt coordinator second unit, 1965-75. Chmn. of bd., Camera Platforms International, Inc. 1985. Owner Budweiser Rocket Car (fastest car in the world). Member Screen Actors Guild, AFTRA, Writers Guild of America, Directors Guild of America.
PICTURES: *Dir.*: Smokey and the Bandit (debut, 1977; also co-story), Hooper, The Villain, Smokey and the Bandit II, The Cannonball Run, Megaforce (also co-s.p.), Stroker Ace (also co-s.p.), Cannonball Run II (also co-s.p.), RAD, Body Slam.
TELEVISION: *Series*: Hal Needham's Wild World of Stunts (synd. series; also writer, star). *Movie*: Death Car on the Freeway. *Pilot*: Stunts Unlimited (pilot). *Episode*: B.L. Stryker.

NEESON, LIAM
Actor. b. Ballymena, Northern Ireland, June 7, 1952. m. actress Natasha Richardson. Former amateur boxer. Was driving a fork lift truck for a brewery when he joined the Lyric Player's Theatre in Belfast. Made prof. debut in The Risen (1976) and stayed with rep. co. 2 years. Moved to Dublin as freelance actor before joining the Abbey Theatre.
THEATER: The Informer (Dublin Theatre Fest.), Translations (National Theatre, London). NY theatre debut 1992 in Anna Christie (Theatre World Award).
PICTURES: Excalibur (debut, 1981), Krull, The Bounty, Lamb, The Innocent, The Mission, Duet For One, A Prayer for the Dying, Suspect, Satisfaction, The Dead Pool, The Good Mother, High Spirits, Next of Kin, Dark Man, Crossing the Line (The Big Man), Shining Through, Under Suspicion, Husbands and Wives, Leap of Faith, Ethan Frome, Deception, Schindler's List (Acad. Award nom.), Nell, Rob Roy, Before and After, Michael Collins, A Leap of Faith (voice), Alaska: Spirit of the Wild (voice), Ambrose Chapel, Everest (narrator), Les Miserables, The Haunting, Star Wars: Episode I-The Phantom Menace.
TELEVISION: Merlin and the Sword, Across the Water (BBC), Ellis Island, A Woman of Substance, Sweet As You Are, The Great War.

NEILL, SAM
Actor. r.n. Nigel Neill. b. Northern Ireland, Sept. 14, 1947. Raised in New Zealand. e. U. of Canterbury. In repertory before joining N.Z. National Film Unit, acting and directing documentaries and shorts. 1992, awarded the O.B.E. for his services to acting. Co-directed, co-wrote and appeared in New Zealand documentary Cinema of Unease: A Personal Journey by Sam Neill.
PICTURES: Sleeping Dogs (debut, 1977), The Journalist, My Brilliant Career, Just Out of Reach, Attack Force Z, The Final Conflict, Possession, Enigma, Le Sang des Autres, Robbery Under Arms, Plenty, For Love Alone, The Good Wife, A Cry in the Dark (Australian Film Inst. Award), Dead Calm, The French Revolution, The Hunt for Red October, Until the End of the World, Hostage, Memoirs of an Invisible Man, Death in Brunswick, Jurassic Park, The Piano, Sirens, Rudyard Kipling's The Jungle Book, In the Mouth of Madness, Country Life, Restoration, Victory, Event Horizon, The Revengers' Comedies, The Horse Whisperer, My Mother Frank, Molokai: The Story of Father Damien, Bicentennial Man, The Magic Pudding (voice).
TELEVISION: The Sullivans, Young Ramsay, Lucinda Brayford, The Country Girls. *Mini-Series*: Kane and Abel, Reilly Ace of Spies, Amerika, Merlin. *Movies*: From a Far Country: Pope John Paul II, Ivanhoe, The Blood of Others, Arthur Hailey's Strong Medicine, Leap of Faith, Fever, One Against the Wind, The Sinking of the Rainbow Warrior, Family Pictures. *Guest*: The Simpsons (voice).

NELLIGAN, KATE
Actress. r.n. Patricia Colleen Nelligan. b. London, Ontario, Canada, March 16, 1951.
THEATER: Barefoot in the Park, A Streetcar Named Desire, Playboy of the Western World, Private Lives, Plenty, Serious Money, Spoils of War, Bad Habits.
PICTURES: The Romantic Englishwoman (debut, 1975), Dracula, Mr. Patman, Eye of the Needle, Without a Trace, The Mystery of Henry Moore, Eleni, Frankie and Johnny (BAFTA Award), The Prince of Tides (Acad. Award nom.), Shadows and Fog, Fatal Instinct, Wolf, Margaret's Museum, How to Make an American Quilt, Up Close and Personal, U.S. Marshals, Stolen Moments.
TELEVISION: *Movies/Specials*: The Onedin Line, The Lady of the Camelias, Therese Raquin, Count of Monte Cristo, Victims, Kojak: The Price of Justice, Love and Hate: The Story of Colin and Joann Thatcher, Three Hotels, Terror Strikes the Class Reunion, Diamond Fleece, Liar Liar, Shattered Trust: The Shari Karney Story, Spoils of War, Million Dollar Babies, Captive Heart: The James Mink Story.

NELSON, BARRY
Actor. r.n. Robert Neilson. b. Oakland, CA, Apr. 16, 1920. e. U. of California. London stage in No Time for Sergeants, 1957.
THEATER: *B'way*: Light Up the Sky, The Rat Race, The Moon Is Blue, Mary Mary, Cactus Flower, Everything in the Garden, Seascape, The Norman Conquests, The Act, 42nd Street.
PICTURES: Shadow of the Thin Man, Johnny Eager, Dr. Kildare's Victory, Rio Rita, Eyes in the Night, Bataan, The Human Comedy, A Guy Named Joe, Winged Victory, The Beginning or the End, Undercover Maisie, The Man With My Face, The First Traveling Saleslady, Mary Mary, Airport, Pete 'n' Tillie, The Shining, Island Claws.
TELEVISION: *Series*: The Hunter, My Favorite Husband. *Mini-Series*: Washington: Behind Closed Doors. *Movies*: The Borgia Stick, Seven in Darkness, Climb an Angry Mountain. *Guest*: Suspense, Alfred Hitchcock Presents, Longstreet, Taxi, Magnum P.I., Murder She Wrote.

NELSON, CRAIG T.
Actor. b. Spokane, WA, April 4, 1946. Began career as writer/performer on Lohman and Barkley Show in Los Angeles. Teamed with Barry Levinson as a comedy writer. Wrote for Tim Conway Show, Alan King TV special; guest appearances on talk shows and Mary Tyler Moore Show. Produced series of 52 half-hour films on American artists, American Still. Returned to L.A. in 1978 and acting career.
PICTURES: And Justice for All (debut, 1979), Where the Buffalo Roam, Private Benjamin, Stir Crazy, The Formula, Poltergeist, Man Woman and Child, All the Right Moves, The Osterman Weekend, Silkwood, The Killing Fields, Poltergeist II, Red Riding Hood, Action Jackson, Rachel River, Me and Him, Troop Beverly Hills, Turner & Hooch, I'm Not Rappaport, Ghosts of Mississippi.
TELEVISION: *Series*: Call to Glory, Coach (Emmy Award, 1992). *Guest*: Wonder Woman, Charlie's Angels, How the West Was Won. *Movies*: Diary of a Teenage Hitchhiker, Rage, Promise of Love, Inmates: A Love Story, Chicago Story, Paper Dolls, Alex: The Life of a Child, The Ted Kennedy Jr. Story, Murderers Among Us: The Simon Wiesenthal Story, Extreme Close-Up, The Josephine Baker Story, The Switch, The Fire Next Time, Ride With the Wind (also co-writer), Probable Cause, Take Me Home Again. *Mini-Series*: Drug Wars: The Camarena Story.

NELSON, DAVID
Actor. b. New York, NY, Oct. 24, 1936. e. Hollywood H.S., U. of Southern California. Son of Ozzie Nelson and Harriet Hilliard Nelson; brother of late Rick Nelson.

PICTURES: Here Comes the Nelsons, Peyton Place, The Remarkable Mr. Pennypacker, Day of the Outlaw, The Big Circus, "30," The Big Show, No Drums No Bugles, Cry-Baby. *Director*: A Rare Breed, The Last Plane Out.
TELEVISION: *Series*: The Adventures of Ozzie and Harriet (also dir. episodes). *Movies*: Smash-Up on Interstate 5, High School U.S.A. *Guest*: Hondo, The Love Boat. *Dir.*: Easy To Be Free (special), OK Crackerby (series).

NELSON, JUDD
Actor. b. Portland, ME, Nov. 28, 1959. e. Haverford/Bryn Mawr Coll. Studied acting at Stella Adler Conservatory. NY theatre includes Carnal Knowledge.
PICTURES: Making the Grade (debut, 1984), Fandango, The Breakfast Club, St. Elmo's Fire, Blue City, Transformers (voice), From the Hip, Relentless, Far Out Man, New Jack City, The Dark Backward, Primary Motive, Entangled, Conflict of Interest, Caroline at Midnight, Hail Caesar, Every Breath (also s.p.), Flinch, Circumstances Unknown, Blackwater Trail, Steel, Endsville.
TELEVISION: *Series*: Suddenly Susan. *Guest*: Moonlighting. *Movies*: Billionaire Boys Club, Hiroshima: Out of the Ashes, Conflict of Interest, Blindfold: Acts of Obsession, Cabin by the Lake, Mr. Rock 'n' Roll.

NELSON, LORI
Actress. r.n. Dixie Kay Nelson. b. Santa Fe, NM, Aug. 15, 1933. e. Canoga Park H.S. Started as child actress, photographer's model before film debut in 1952.
THEATER: The Pleasure of His Company, Who Was That Lady I Saw You With, Affairs of Mildred Wilde, Sweet Bird of Youth, Picnic, 'Night Mother.
PICTURES: Ma and Pa Kettle at the Fair (debut, 1952), Bend of the River, Francis Goes to West Point, All I Desire, All-American, Walking My Baby Back Home, Tumbleweed, Underwater, Destry, Revenge of the Creature, I Died a Thousand Times, Sincerely Yours, Mohawk, Day the World Ended, Pardners, Hot Rod Girl, Ma and Pa Kettle at Waikiki, Gambling Man, Untamed Youth.
TELEVISION: *Series*: How to Marry a Millionaire. *Guest:* Wagon Train, Laramie, Family Affair, The Texan, Wanted Dead or Alive, Sam Spade, G.E. Theatre, Riverboat, Sugarfoot, The Young and the Restless, Climax, The Millionaire, Wells Fargo, etc. *Special*: The Pied Piper of Hamelin.

NELSON, TRACY
Actress, Singer, Dancer. b. Santa Monica, CA, Oct., 1963. e. Bard Coll. Daughter of late singer-actor Rick Nelson. Sister of singers Matthew & Gunnar Nelson. Studied acting in England.
THEATER: Grease (Nat'l touring co. & B'way).
PICTURES: Yours Mine and Outs (debut, 1968), Maria's Lovers, Down and Out in Beverly Hills, Chapters.
TELEVISION: *Series*: Square Pegs, Glitter, Father Dowling Mysteries, A League of Their Own, Melrose Place, The Man from Snowy River. *Movies*: Katie's Secret, Tonight's the Night, If It's Tuesday It Still Must Be Belgium, Fatal Confessions, For Hope, In the Shadow of Evil, Pleasures, Highway Heartbreaker, Ray Alexander: Murder in Mind, Ray Alexander: A Taste for Justice, No Child of Mine. *Guest*: The Adventures of Ozzie and Harriet, Hotel, Family Ties, The Love Boat.

NELSON, WILLIE
Composer, Singer, Actor. b. Abbott, TX, April 30, 1933. Worked as salesman, announcer, host of country music shows on local Texas stations; bass player with Ray Price's band. Started writing songs in the 60's; performing in the 70's.
PICTURES: The Electric Horseman (debut, 1979), Honeysuckle Rose, Thief, Barbarosa, Hell's Angels Forever, Songwriter, Red-Headed Stranger (also prod.), Walking After Midnight, Gone Fishin', Anthem, Wag the Dog, Half Baked, Dill Scallion (cameo), Austin Powers: The Spy Who Shagged Me (cameo).
TELEVISION: *Movies*: The Last Days of Frank and Jesse James, Stagecoach, Coming Out of the Ice, Baja Oklahoma, Once Upon a Texas Train, Where the Hell's That Gold?!!?, Pair of Aces, Another Pair of Aces, Wild Texas Wind, Big Dreams & Broken Hearts: The Dottie West Story, Outlaw Justice. *Special*: Willie Nelson—Texas Style (also prod.).

NEMEC, CORIN
Actor. r.n. Joseph Charles Nemec IV. b. Little Rock, AR, Nov. 5, 1971. Began acting in commercials at age 13.
PICTURES: Tucker: The Man and His Dream, Solar Crisis, Drop Zone, Operation Dumbo Drop, The War at Home, Mojave Moon, Quality Time, The First to Go, Goodbye America, Legacy, Foreign Correspondents.
TELEVISION: *Series*: Parker Lewis Can't Lose. *Movies*: I Know My First Name is Steven (Emmy nom.), For the Very First Time, My Son Johnny, The Lifeforce Experiment, Summer of Fear, Blade Squad, Silencing Mary. *Mini-Series*: The Stand. *Pilot*: What's Alan Watching? *Guest*: Webster, Sidekicks.

NERO, FRANCO
Actor. r.n. Franceso Spartanero. b. Parma, Italy, Nov. 23, 1942. e. Univ. La Bocconi, Milan. m. Vanessa Redgrave.
PICTURES: Celestina (Made at Your Service; debut, 1964), The Deadly Diaphanoids, I Knew Her Well, Wild Wild Planet, The Third Eyes, The Bible, The Tramplers, Django, The Avenger, Hired Killer, The Brute and the Beast, Mafia, Camelot, L'uomo l'Orgoglio la Vendetta, Island of Crime, The Mercenary, The Day of the Owl, A Quiet Place in the Country, The Battle of Neretva, Detective Belli, Sardinia: Ramsom, Companeros, Tristana, The Virgin and the Gypsy, Drop Out!, Confessions of a Police Commissioner, Killer From Yuma, Redneck, The Monk, The Vacation, Pope Joan, Deaf Smith and Johnny Ears, The Fifth Day of Peace, The Aquarian, High Crime, Blood Brothers, Cry Onion, The Anonymous Avenger, Challenge to White Fang, Death Drive, Violent Breed, Submission, The Last Days of Mussolini, Force Ten From Navarone, The Man With Bogart's Face, The Visitor, Shark Hunter, Blue-Eyed Bandit, Danzig Roses, Day of the Cobra, The Falcon, The Salamander, Sahara Cross, Enter the Ninja, Mexico in Flames, Querelle, Wagner, Sweet Country, The Girl, Garibaldi the General, Race to Danger, Marathon, Django Strikes Again, Top Line, Silent Night, Young Toscanini, The Betrothed, The Magistrate, Heart of Victory, The Repenter, The Forester's Sons, Die Hard 2, Brothers and Sisters, Crimson Down, Oro, Deep Blue, The Lucona Affair, Babylon Complot, A Breath of Life, Jonathan of the Bears, Conflict of Interest, The Dragon's Ring, Talk of Angels, The Innocent Sleep, The King and Me.
TELEVISION: *Mini-series*: The Last Days of Pompeii, Desideria, The Return of Sandokan, Bella Mafia, Painted Lady. *Movies*: The Legend of Valentino, 21 Hours at Munich, The Pirate, Young Catherine, David, The Versace Murder, Das Babylon Komplott, Il Deserto di fuoco.

NESMITH, MICHAEL
Musician, Producer. r.n. Robert Michael Nesmith. b. Houston, TX, Dec. 30, 1942. Original member of The Monkees, later became producer of videos and films. Chmn. & CEO Pacific Arts Publishing video company. Won Grammy award for music video Elephant Parts. Exec. prod. & performer in video Dr. Duck's Super Secret All-Purpose Sauce.
PICTURES: *Actor*: Head, Burglar (cameo), Heart and Soul. *Exec. Prod.*: Timerider (also co-s.p.), Repo Man, Square Dance, Tapeheads.
TELEVISION: *Series*: The Monkees, Michael Nesmith in Television Parts (also prod.). *Special*: 33-1/3 Revolutions Per Monkee.

NETTER, DOUGLAS
Executive, Producer. b. Seattle, WA. 1955-57, gen. mgr. Todd A.O.; 1958-60, Sam Goldwyn Productions; 1961-67, formed own co. representing producers; 1968-69, Jalem Productions; 1969-75, exec. v.p. MGM. Films: Mr. Ricco (prod.), The Wild Geese (co-prod.).
TELEVISION: Louis L'Amour's The Sacketts (prod.), The Buffalo Soldiers (exec. prod.), Wild Times (prod.), Roughnecks (exec. prod.), Cherokee Trail (exec. prod.), Five Mile Creek (exec. prod.; Australian based TV series for Disney Channel), Captain Power and the Soldiers of the Future (exec. prod.), Stealth F22 (exec. prod.), Babylon 5 (exec. prod.).

NETTLETON, LOIS
Actress. b. Oak Park, IL, 1931. e. Studied at Goodman Theatre, Chicago and Actors Studio. Replaced Kim Hunter in Darkness at Noon on B'way. Emmy Award: Performer Best Daytime Drama Spec., The American Woman: Portraits in Courage (1977). Also Emmy: Religious Program, Insight (1983).
THEATER: Cat on a Hot Tin Roof, Silent Night, Lonely Night, God and Kate Murphy, The Wayward Stork, The Rainmaker, A Streetcar Named Desire.
PICTURES: A Face in the Crowd (debut, 1957), Period of Adjustment, Come Fly with Me, Mail Order Bride, Valley of Mystery, Bamboo Saucer, The Good Guys and the Bad Guys, Dirty Dingus Magee, The Sidelong Glances of a Pigeon Kicker, The Honkers, The Man in the Glass Booth, Echoes of a Summer, Deadly Blessing, Butterfly, Soggy Bottom U.S.A., The Best Little Whorehouse in Texas.
TELEVISION: *Series*: Accidental Family, You Can't Take It With You. *Guest*: Medical Center, Barnaby Jones, Alfred Hitchcock, All That Glitters, In the Heat of the Night. *Movies*: Any Second Now, Weekend of Terror, The Forgotten Man, Terror in the Sky, Women in Chains, Fear on Trial, Tourist, Brass, Manhunt for Claude Dallas. *Mini-Series*: Washington: Behind Closed Doors, Centennial. *Specials*: Rendezvous, Meet Me in St. Louis, Traveler's Rest.

NEUFELD, MACE
Producer. b. New York, NY, July 13, 1928. e. Yale Col. Started as professional photographer, before becoming prod. asst. at Dumont Television Network. Wrote musical material for performers incl. Sammy Davis Jr., Dorothy Loudon, Ritz Brothers, etc., and theme for Heckle and Jeckle animated series. In 1951, formed independent TV prod. and personal mgmt. co. For TV produced programs for Dick Van Dyke, Elaine May and Mike Nichols. Formed independent production co. with Nichols and Buck Henry. In 1980, created Neufeld-Davis Prods. with Marvin Davis. Formed Neufeld/Rehme Prods. with Robert G. Rehme in 1989; Mace Neufeld Prods., 1997. On B'way, prod. Flying Karamazov Brothers show. Voted Producer of the Year by NATO/ShoWest, 1992.

PICTURES: The Omen, Damien: Omen II, The Frisco Kid, The Funhouse, The Aviator, Transylvania 6-5000, No Way Out, The Hunt for Red October, Flight of the Intruder, Necessary Roughness, Patriot Games, Gettysburg, Beverly Hills Cop III, Clear and Present Danger, The Saint, The General's Daughter, Lost in Space.
TELEVISION: *Movies/Miniseries*: East of Eden, Angel on My Shoulder, American Dream, Cagney and Lacey (pilot), A Death in California, White Hot. *Specials*: The Magic Planet, The Flying Karamazov Brothers, Blind Faith, A Woman Undone, Escape—Human Cargo.

NEUWIRTH, BEBE
Actress. b. Newark, NJ, Dec. 31, 1958. e. Juilliard. Started as chorus dancer.
THEATER: *NY*: Little Me, Dancin', Upstairs at O'Neal, The Road to Hollywood, Sweet Charity (Tony Award, 1986), Showing Off, Damn Yankees. *Tour*: A Chorus Line. Regional: Just So, Kicks (also choreog.), Chicago. *London*: Kiss of the Spider Woman.
PICTURES: Say Anything... (debut, 1989), Green Card, Bugsy, Paint Job, Malice, Jumanji, All Dogs Go to Heaven (voice), The Associate, The Faculty, Celebrity, An All Dogs Christmas Carol (voice), Summer of Sam, Getting to Know You.
TELEVISION: *Series*: Cheers (2 Emmy Awards), All Dogs Go to Heaven: The Series (voice). *Movies*: Without Her Consent, Unspeakable Acts, Dash and Lilly. *Mini-Series*: Wild Palms. *Guest*: Frasier.

NEWELL, MIKE
Director. b. St. Albans, England, March 28, 1942. e. Cambridge U. Took directorial training course at Granada Television.
PICTURES: The Awakening (debut, 1980), Bad Blood, Dance With a Stranger, The Good Father, Amazing Grace and Chuck, Common Ground, Enchanted April, Into the West, Four Weddings and a Funeral, An Awfully Big Adventure, Donnie Brasco, Photographing Fairies (exec. prod.), Pushing Tin, Best Laid Plan (exec. prod.).
TELEVISION: Baa Baa Black Sheep, Silver Wedding, Jill and Jack, Ready When You Are Mr. McGill, Lost Your Tongue, Mr. & Mrs. Bureaucrat, Just Your Luck, The Man in the Iron Mask, The Gift of Friendship, Destiny, Tales Out of School, Birth of a Nation, Blood Feud.

NEWHART, BOB
Actor, Comedian. b. Chicago, IL, Sept. 5, 1929. e. Loyola U. In Army 2 yrs., then law school; left to become copywriter and accountant. Acted with theatrical stock co. in Oak Park; hired for TV man-in-street show in Chicago. Recorded hit comedy album for Warner Bros., The Button-Down Mind of Bob Newhart (Grammy Award, 1960), followed by two more successful albums. Did series of nightclub engagements and then acquired own TV variety series in 1961. Grand Marshall: Tournament of Roses Parde, 1991. Inducted into TV Hall of Fame, 1993.
PICTURES: Hell Is for Heroes (debut, 1962), Hot Millions, Catch-22, On a Clear Day You Can See Forever, Cold Turkey, The Rescuers (voice), Little Miss Marker, First Family, The Rescuers Down Under (voice), In & Out.
TELEVISION: *Series*: The Bob Newhart Show (1961-62, variety), The Entertainers, The Bob Newhart Show (1972-78, sitcom), Newhart, Bob, George & Leo. *Movies*: Thursday's Game, Marathon, The Entertainers.

NEWLAND, JOHN
Actor, Director. b. Cincinnati, OH, Nov. 23, 1917. Began as a singer-dancer in vaudeville and on B'way; many TV appearances, especially as host of One Step Beyond. Actor, dir., Robert Montgomery Show, My Lover, My Son. Turned to full-time dir. and prod. in the 1960's.
PICTURES: T-Men, Nora Prentiss, Gentleman's Agreement, Let's Live a Little, Homicide for Three, The Challenge, 13 Lead Soldiers, Bulldog Drummond, That Night!, The Violators, The Spy With My Face, Hush-a-Bye Murder, Purgatory, My Lover My Son.
TELEVISION: *Movies*: The Gold Diggers, Crawlspace, The Deadly Hunt (also prod.), The Legend of Hillbilly John, Don't Be Afraid of the Dark, A Sensitive Passionate Man, Overboard, The Suicide's Wife, The Five of Me (exec. prod.), The Execution (exec. prod.), Arch of Triumph (prod.), Timestalkers (prod.), Too Good to Be True (prod.). *Series*: One Man's Family, Alfred Hitchcock Presents, Bachelor Father, Naked City, Robert Montgomery Presents, Alcoa Presents: One Step Beyond (host), Daniel Boone, Star Trek, Route 66, Dr. Kildare, Man from U.N.C.L.E., The Young Lawyers, Police Woman, Harry O, Executive Suite, The Next Step Beyond (host, prod.), Fantasy Island. *Guest*: Philco TV Playhouse, Eye Witness, Schlitz Playhouse of Stars, Loretta Young Show, Thriller.
(d. Jan. 10, 2000)

NEWLEY, ANTHONY
Actor, Writer, Composer, Singer. b. Hackney, Eng., Sept. 24, 1931. Recipient of Male Singer of the Year Award, Las Vegas, 1972; Elected to Songwriters Hall of Fame, 1989. Gold records for composing Goldfinger, Candy Man, What Kind of Fool Am I?
THEATER: *West End stage*: Cranks (also dir., writer), Stop The World—I Want to Get Off (also composer with Leslie Bricusse, dir., writer; also NY), The Roar of the Greasepaint—The Smell of the Crowd (also composer with Bricusse, writer, dir.; also NY), The Good Old Bad Old Days (also composer with Bricusse, writer, dir.), Royalty Follies (also dir., writer), The World's Not Entirely to Blame, It's a Funny Old World We Live In. *Regional*: Chaplin, Once Upon a Song. *British tour:* Scrooge (1992-96).
PICTURES: Adventures of Dusty Bates (debut, 1946), Little Ballerina, The Guinea Pig, Vice Versa, Oliver Twist, Vote for Huggett, Don't Ever Leave Me, A Boy a Girl and a Bike, Golden Salamander, Madeleine, Highly Dangerous, Those People Next Door, Top of the Form, The Weak and the Wicked, Up to His Neck, Blue Peter, The Cockleshell Heroes, Battle of the River Plate, Above Us the Waves, Port Afrique, The Last Man to Hang, Fire Down Below, How to Murder a Rich Uncle, Good Companions, X the Unknown, High Flight, No Time to Die (Tank Force), The Man Inside, The Bandit of Zhobe, The Lady Is a Square, Idle on Parade, Killers of Kilimanjaro, Let's Get Married, Jazz Boat, In the Nick, The Small World of Sammy Lee, Play It Cool, Stop the World I Want to Get Off (songs only), Doctor Dolittle, Sweet November, Can Hieronymus Merkin Ever Forget Mercy Humppe and Find True Happiness? (also dir., s.p., songs), Willie Wonka and the Chocolate Factory (songs only), Summertree (dir. only), Mr. Quilp (also music), It Seemed Like a Good Idea at the Time, The Garbage Pail Kids Movie.
TELEVISION: *Specials*: Sunday Night Palladium, Saturday Spectaculars, Anthony Newley Special (London). *Guest*: The Johnny Darling Show, Limited Partners, Fame, Magnum P.I., Alfred Hitchcock Theatre, Murder She Wrote, Simon & Simon. *Movies*: Malibu, Alice in Wonderland, Blade in Hong Kong, Stagecoach, Coins in a Fountain, Polly Comin' Home, Boris and Natasha, Anna Lee: Dupe. *Series* (BBC): Sammy, The Strange World of Gurney Slade, The Anthony Newley Show (1972).

NEWMAN, ALFRED S.
Executive. b. Brooklyn, NY, Nov. 16. e. NYU. Public relations work for Equitable Life Insurance, Trans World Airlines prior to joining Columbia Pictures in 1968 as writer in publicity dept.; named New York publicity mgr., 1970; national publicity mgr., 1972; joined MGM as East adv.-pub. dir., 1972; named director of adv., pub. and promotion, 1974; named v.p., worldwide adv., pub., promo., 1978; v.p., pub.-promo., MGM/UA, 1981. With 20th Century-Fox as v.p. adv.-pub.-promo. for TV & corporate, 1984-85; joined Rogers & Cowan as sr. v.p. & head of film and corporate entertainment dept., 1985; named exec. v.p., 1987; Oct. 1988 named pres. and CEO. Sterling Entertainment Co. and exec. v.p. worldwide marketing of parent co. MCEG; formed Newman & Associates, 1989; joined Hill and Knowl Entertainment as founding mng. dir., 1990. Re-opened Newman and Assocs., 1991. Joined Imax Corp. as Sr V.P. & Head of Worldwide Communications, 1996. Formed Newman & Company, 1998.

NEWMAN, BARRY
Actor. b. Boston, MA, Nov. 7, 1938. e. Brandeis U.
PICTURES: Pretty Boy Floyd (debut, 1960), The Moving Finger, The Lawyer, Vanishing Point, The Salzburg Connection, Fear is the Key, City on Fire, Amy.
TELEVISION: *Series*: Petrocelli, Nightingales. *Movies*: Night Games, Sex and the Married Woman, King Crab, Fantasies, Having It All, Second Sight: A Love Story, Fatal Vision, My Two Loves, The Mirror Crack'd (BBC).

NEWMAN, DAVID
Composer. b. Los Angeles, CA, Mar. 11, 1954. e. USC (masters degree). Son of late composer Alfred Newman. Cousin of composer Randy Newman. Music director at Robert Redford's Sundance Institute.
PICTURES: Critters, Vendetta, The Kindred, My Demon Lover, Malone, Dragnet, Throw Momma from the Train, Pass the Ammo, Bill & Ted's Excellent Adventure, Disorganized Crime, The Brave Little Toaster, Heathers, Little Monsters, Gross Anatomy, The War of the Roses, Madhouse, Fire Birds, The Freshman, DuckTales: The Movie, Mr. Destiny, Meet the Applegates, The Marrying Man, Talent for the Game, Don't Tell Mom the Babysitter's Dead, Bill & Ted's Bogus Journey, Rover Dangerfield, Paradise, Other People's Money, The Runestone, The Mighty Ducks, Hoffa, The Sandlot, Coneheads, The Air Up There, My Father the Hero, The Flintstones, The Cowboy Way, Tommy Boy, Operation Dumbo Drop, The Phantom, Mathilda, The Nutty Professor, Out to Sea.

NEWMAN, DAVID
Writer. b. New York, NY, Feb. 4, 1937. e. U. of Michigan, M.S., 1959. Was writer-editor at Esquire Magazine where he met Robert Benton, an art director, and formed writing partnership. All early credits co-written with Benton; later ones with Leslie Newman and others.
THEATER: It's a Bird... It's a Plane... It's Superman (libretto), Oh! Calcutta (one sketch).
PICTURES: Bonnie and Clyde, There Was a Crooked Man, What's Up Doc?, Bad Company, Superman, Superman II, Jinxed, Still of the Night (co-story), Superman III, Sheena, Santa Claus, Moonwalker.

NEWMAN, EDWIN
News Correspondent. b. New York, NY, Jan. 25, 1919. Joined NBC News in 1952, based in N.Y. since 1961. Reports news on NBC-TV and often assigned to anchor instant specials. Has been substitute host on Today, appeared on Meet the Press and has reported NBC News documentaries. Series host: Edwin Newman Reporting, The Nation's Future, What's Happening to America, Comment, Speaking Freely, Television (PBS series).

NEWMAN, JOSEPH M.
Producer, Director, Writer. b. Logan, UT, Aug. 7, 1909. Started as office boy MGM, 1925; jobs in production dept. to 1931; asst. to George Hill, Ernst Lubitsch, etc., 1931-37; asstd. in organization of MGM British studios 1937; dir. short subjects 1938; dir. Crime Does Not Pay series 1938-42; Major in U.S. Army Signal Corps 1942-46; dir. 32 Army Pictorial Service Pictures. TV work includes Alfred Hitchcock Presents, Twilight Zone. Member of AMPAS, SDG Masons.
PICTURES: Northwest Rangers, Abandoned, Jungle Patrol, Great Dan Pitch, 711 Ocean Drive, Lucky Nick Cain, The Guy Who Came Back, Love Nest, Red Skies of Montana, Outcasts of Poker Flat, Pony Soldier, Dangerous Crossing, Human Jungle, Kiss of Fire, This Island Earth, Flight to Hong Kong, Fort Massacre, The Big Circus, Tarzan the Ape Man, King of the Roaring Twenties, Twenty Plus Two, The George Raft Story, Thunder of Drums.

NEWMAN, LARAINE
Actress. b. Los Angeles, CA, Mar. 2, 1952. Founding member of comedy troupe the Groundlings.
THEATER: *B'way*: Fifth of July.
PICTURES: Tunnelvision (debut, 1976), American Hot Wax, Wholly Moses!, Stardust Memories (cameo), Perfect, Sesame Street Presents Follow That Bird (voice), Invaders from Mars, Problem Child 2, Witchboard II, Coneheads, The Flintstones, Jingle All the Way.
TELEVISION: *Series*: Manhattan Transfer, Saturday Night Live, Bone Chillers. *Guest*: George Burns Comedy Week, St. Elsewhere, Laverne & Shirley, Alfred Hitchcock Presents, Amazing Stories, Faerie Tale Theatre (The Little Mermaid), Twilight Zone, Dream On, Likely Suspects, Friends, Chicago Hope, Third Rock From the Sun. *Specials*: Steve Martin's Best Show Ever, The Lily Tomlin Special, Bob Ray Jane Laraine & Gilda. *Movies*: Her Life as a Man, This Wife for Hire. *Voice*: Pinky and the Brain, Sylvester & Tweetie, The Tick, Rapunzel, Superman, Wonder Woman.

NEWMAN, NANETTE
Actress, Writer. b. Northampton, Eng., 1934. m. prod.-dir.-writer Bryan Forbes. Ent. films in 1946 and TV in 1951.
AUTHOR: God Bless Love, That Dog, Reflections, The Root Children, Amy Rainbow, Pigalev, Archie, Christmas Cookbook, Summer Cookbook, Small Beginnings, Bad Baby, Entertaining with Nanette Newman and Her Daughters, Charlie the Noisy Caterpillar, Sharing, The Pig Who Never Was, ABC, 123, Cooking for Friends, Spider the Horrible Cat, There's a Bear in the Bath, Karmic Mothers, There's a Bear in the Classroom, The Importance of Being Ernest, The Earwig, Take 3 Cooks.
PICTURES: The Personal Affair, The League of Gentlemen, The Rebel, Twice Around the Daffodils, The L-Shaped Room, The Wrong Arm of the Law, Of Human Bondage, Seance on a Wet Afternoon, The Wrong Box, The Whisperers, Deadfall, The Madwoman of Chaillot, Captain Nemo and the Underwater City, The Raging Moon, The Stepford Wives, It's a 2'2" Above the Ground World, Man at the Top, International Velvet, Restless Natives, The Mystery of Edwin Drood.
TELEVISION: The Glorious Days, The Wedding Veil, Broken Honeymoon, At Home, Trial by Candlelight, Diary of Samuel Pepys, Faces in the Dark, Balzac (BBC), Fun Food Factory, TV series, Stay with Me Till Morning, Let There Be Love (series), West Country Tales, Jessie, Late Expectations (series), Ideal Cooks (presenter), The Endless Game.

NEWMAN, PAUL
Actor, Director, Producer. b. Cleveland, OH, Jan. 26, 1925. m. actress Joanne Woodward. e. Kenyon Coll., Yale Sch. of Drama, The Actors Studio. Formed First Artists Prod. Co., Ltd. 1969 with Sidney Poitier, Steve McQueen and Barbra Streisand. Appeared in documentaries: King: A Filmed Record... Memphis to Montgomery, Hello Actors Studio. Recipient of special Academy Award, 1986; Jean Hersholt Humanitarian Award, 1994.
THEATER: *B'way*: Picnic, The Desperate Hours, Sweet Bird of Youth, Baby Want a Kiss.
PICTURES: The Silver Chalice (debut, 1954), The Rack, Somebody Up There Likes Me, The Helen Morgan Story, Until They Sail, The Long Hot Summer, The Left-Handed Gun, Cat on a Hot Tin Roof, Rally 'Round the Flag Boys!, The Young Philadelphians, From the Terrace, Exodus, The Hustler, Paris Blues, Sweet Bird of Youth, Hemingway's Adventures of a Young Man, Hud, A New Kind of Love, The Prize, What a Way to Go!, The Outrage, Harper, Lady L, Torn Curtain, Hombre, Cool Hand Luke, The Secret War of Harry Frigg, Rachel Rachel (dir. prod. only), Winning, Butch Cassidy and the Sundance Kid, WUSA (also prod.), Sometimes a Great Notion (also dir.), Pocket Money, The Life and Times of Judge Roy Bean, The Effect of Gamma Rays on Man-in-the-Moon Marigolds (dir., prod. only), The Mackintosh Man, The Sting, The Towering Inferno, The Drowning Pool, Buffalo Bill and the Indians or Sitting Bull's History Lesson, Silent Movie, Slap Shot, Quintet, When Time Ran Out..., Fort Apache the Bronx, Absence of Malice, The Verdict, Harry and Son (also dir., co-s.p., co-prod.), The Color of Money (Academy Award, 1986), The Glass Menagerie (dir. only), Fat Man & Little Boy, Blaze, Mr. and Mrs. Bridge, The Hudsucker Proxy, Nobody's Fool, Twilight, Where the Money Is, Message in a Bottle.
TELEVISION: *Guest* (on 1950's anthology series): The Web (Bell of Damon, One for the Road), Goodyear TV Playhouse (Guilty is the Stranger), Danger (Knife in the Dark), Appointment With Adventure (Five in Judgment), Philco TV Playhouse (Death of Billy the Kid), Producers Showcase (Our Town), Kaiser Aluminum Hour (The Army Game, Rag Jungle), U.S. Steel Hour (Bang the Drum Slowly), Playhouse 90 (The 80-Yard Run). *Movie* (dir. only): The Shadow Box.

NEWMAN, RANDY
Composer, Singer. b. Los Angeles, CA, Nov. 28, 1943. Nephew of musicians Lionel and Alfred Newman. Studied music at UCLA. Debut album: Randy Newman Creates Something New Under the Sun. Songs include Short People, I Think It's Gonna Rain Today, I Love L.A. Was music director on film Performance. Began writing songs and scores for films in 1971 with The Pursuit of Happiness. Composed opera, Faust.
PICTURES: Pursuit of Happiness, Cold Turkey, Ragtime, The Natural, Three Amigos (also co-wrote s.p.), Parenthood, Avalon, Awakenings, The Paper, Maverick, James and the Giant Peach, The Quest, Michael, Cat's Don't Dance, Pleasantville (Acad. Award nom.), A Bug's Life (Acad. Award nom.), Toy Story 2.

NEWMAR, JULIE
Actress. r.n. Julie Newmeyer. b. Hollywood, CA, Aug. 16, 1933. e. UCLA. Studied acting with Lee Strasberg at the Actor's Studio. Holds patent for special panty hose design. Appeared in George Michael video Too Funky.
THEATER: *NY*: Silk Stockings, Li'l Abner, The Marriage-Go-Round (Tony Award, 1959). Other: In the Boom Boom Room (L.A.), Damn Yankees, Irma La Douce, Guys and Dolls, Dames at Sea, Stop the World, The Women.
PICTURES: Just for You (debut, 1952), Seven Brides for Seven Brothers, The Rookie, Li'l Abner, The Marriage-Go-Round, For Love or Money, McKenna's Gold, The Maltese Bippy, Hysterical, Streetwalkin', Body Beat, Nudity Required, Ghosts Can't Do It, Oblivion, To Wong Foo—Thanks for Everything—Julie Newmar.
TELEVISION: *Series*: My Living Doll, Batman (frequent guest; as Catwoman). *Movies*: McCloud: Who Killed Miss U.S.A.?, The Feminist and the Fuzz, A Very Missing Person, Terraces. *Guest*: Omnibus, Route 66, Jonathan Winters Show, Beverly Hillbillies, The Monkees, Love American Style, Love Boat, Half Nelson, Fantasy Island, Hart to Hart, Buck Rogers.

NEWTON-JOHN, OLIVIA
Actress, Singer. b. Cambridge, Eng. Sept. 26, 1948. m. actor Matt Lattanzi. Brought up in Melbourne, Australia, where won first talent contest at 15, winning trip to England. Stayed there 2 yrs. performing as part of duo with Australian girl singer Pat Carroll (Farrar) in cabarets and on TV. Started recording; several hit records. Became a regular guest on TV series, It's Cliff Richard. Gained world-wide prominence as singer, winning several Grammys and other music awards. 1983 opened Koala Blue, U.S. Clothing Stores featuring Australian style clothes and goods.
PICTURES: Tomorrow (debut, 1970), Grease, Xanadu, Two of a Kind.
TELEVISION: *Specials*: Olivia Newton-John: Let's Get Physical, Standing Room Only: Olivia Newton-John, Olivia Newton-John in Australia, Christmas in Washington. *Movies*: A Mom for Christmas, A Christmas Romance.

NEY, RICHARD
Actor, Writer, Producer, Financier. b. New York, NY, Nov. 12, 1917. e. Columbia U., B.A., 1940. Acted in RCA TV demonstration, New York World's Fair; on stage in Life with Father. Was Naval Officer in WWII. Financial advisor consultant, Richard Ney and Associates; financial advisor, lecturer; author, The Wall Street Jungle, The Wall Street Gang, Making it in the Market.
PICTURES: Mrs. Miniver, The War Against Mrs. Hadley, The Late George Apley, Ivy, Joan of Arc, The Fan, Secret of St. Ives, Lovable Cheat, Babes in Bagdad, Miss Italia, Sergeant and The Spy, Midnight Lace, The Premature Burial.

NICHOLAS, DENISE
Actress, Writer. b. Detroit, MI, July 12, 1946. e. USC.
THEATER: Performances with the Free Southern Theatre, The Negro Ensemble Company, Crossroads Theatre Co., New Federal Theatre, Los Angeles Theatre Company, Media Forum.
PICTURES: Ghost Dad, Capricorn One, A Piece of the Action, Let's Do It Again, Blacula, The Soul of Nigger Charley, Marvin and Tige.

TELEVISION: *Series*: Room 222, Baby I'm Back, In the Heat of the Night (also wrote 6 episodes). *Movies*: incl. The Sophisticated Gents, On Thin Ice, Mother's Day, Ring of Passion, In the Heat of the Night. *Guest*: The Cosby Show, A Different World, Benson, Magnum P.I., The Paper Chase, Police Story, Living Single, many others.
AUTHOR: Buses (one act play), Augustine, Myrtle, Marty and Me (short story, Essence Magazine), various published articles and poetry.

NICHOLS, MIKE
Director, Producer, Performer. r.n. Michael Igor Peschkowsky. b. Berlin, Germany, Nov. 6, 1931. m. news correspondent Diane Sawyer. e. U. of Chicago. Member of Compass Players; later teamed with Elaine May in night clubs.
THEATER: *Director*: Barefoot in the Park (Tony Award), The Knack, Luv (Tony Award), The Odd Couple, The Apple Tree, The Little Foxes, Plaza Suite (Tony Award), Uncle Vanya, The Prisoner of 2nd Avenue (Tony Award), Streamers, Comedians, The Gin Game, Drinks Before Dinner, Annie (prod. only; Tony Award), The Real Thing (2 Tony Awards), Hurlyburly, Social Security, Waiting for Godot, Elliot Loves, Death and the Maiden.
PICTURES: *Director*: Who's Afraid of Virginia Woolf? (debut, 1966), The Graduate (Academy Award, 1967), Catch-22, Carnal Knowledge, The Day of the Dolphin, The Fortune, Gilda Live, Silkwood (also co-prod.), The Longshot (exec. prod. only), Heartburn, Biloxi Blues, Working Girl, Postcards From the Edge, Regarding Henry, The Remains of the Day (co-prod. only), Wolf, The Birdcage, Primary Colors, What Planet Are You From? (also prod.).
TELEVISION: *Specials*: B'way, An Evening with Mike Nichols and Elaine May. *Exec. prod.*: Family, The Thorns.

NICHOLS, NICHELLE
Actress. b. Robbins, IL, 1936. Started singing and dancing with Duke Ellington and his band at age 16. Was appointee to the bd. of dirs. of the National Space Institute in the 1970's; recruited women and minority astronauts for Space Shuttle Program. Received NASA's distinguished Public Service Award. Member of the bd. of govs. of the National Space Society. One of the original founders of KWANZA Foundation. Awarded star on Hollywood Walk of Fame (1992). *Autobiography*: Beyond (1994). Novels: Saturn's Child (1995), Saturna's Quest (1996).
THEATER: Horowitz and Mrs. Washington, Reflections (one woman show). Nominated for Sarah Siddons Award for performances in Kicks and Company, The Blacks.
PICTURES: Porgy and Bess, Mr. Buddwing, Made in Paris, Truck Turner, Star Trek: The Motion Picture, Star Trek II: The Wrath of Khan, Star Trek III: The Search for Spock, Star Trek IV: The Voyage Home, The Supernaturals, Star Trek V: The Final Frontier, Star Trek VI: The Undiscovered Country, Trekkies.
TELEVISION: *Series*: Star Trek. *Guest*: The Lieutenant, Tarzan. *Special*: Antony and Cleopatra.

NICHOLSON, JACK
Actor, Producer, Director, Writer. b. Neptune, NJ, April 22, 1937. Began career in cartoon department of MGM. Made acting debut in Hollywood stage production of Tea and Sympathy. Made directing debut with Drive, He Said (1971). Has received 10 Academy Award nominations for acting. Recipient of American Film Institute's Life Achievement Award, 1994.
PICTURES: Cry Baby Killer (debut, 1958), Too Soon to Love, Little Shop of Horrors, Studs Lonigan, The Wild Ride, The Broken Land, The Raven, The Terror, Thunder Island (co-s.p. only), Back Door to Hell, Flight to Fury (also s.p.), Ensign Pulver, Ride in the Whirlwind (also co-prod., s.p.), The Shooting (also co-prod.), The St. Valentine's Day Massacre, Rebel Rousers, Hell's Angels on Wheels, The Trip (s.p. only), Head (also co-prod., co-s.p.), Psych-Out, Easy Rider, On a Clear Day You Can See Forever, Five Easy Pieces, Carnal Knowledge, Drive He Said (dir., co-prod., co-s.p. only), A Safe Place, The King of Marvin Gardens, The Last Detail, Chinatown, Tommy, The Passenger, The Fortune, One Flew Over the Cuckoo's Nest (Academy Award, 1975), The Missouri Breaks, The Last Tycoon, Goin' South (also dir.), The Shining, The Postman Always Rings Twice, Reds, The Border, Terms of Endearment (Academy Award, best supporting actor, 1983), Prizzi's Honor, Heartburn, The Witches of Eastwick, Broadcast News, Ironweed, Batman, The Two Jakes (also dir.), Man Trouble, A Few Good Men, Hoffa, Wolf, The Crossing Guard, Mars Attacks!, The Evening Star, As Good As It Gets (Acad. Award, Golden Globe Award, Best Actor, 1997), Playmate Pajama Party, The Pledge.
TELEVISION: *Guest*: Tales of Wells Fargo, Cheyenne, Hawaiian Eye, Dr. Kildare, Andy Griffith Show, Guns of Will Sonnett.

NICHOLSON, WILLIAM
Writer. b. England, 1948. e. Cambridge U. Was graduate trainee at BBC, becoming prod./dir./writer of over 40 documentaries.
THEATER: Shadowlands, Map of the Heart.
PICTURES: Sarafina!, Shadowlands (Acad. Award nom.), Nell, First Knight, Firelight (also dir.), Gray Owl.
TELEVISION: *Exec. Prod.*: Everyman, Global Report, Lovelaw. *Writer*: Martin Luther, New World, Life Story, The Vision, Shadowlands, Sweet as You Are, The Race for the Double Helix, The March, A Private Matter, Crime of the Century.

NICKSAY, DAVID
Executive, Producer. e. Mass., Hampshire Coll. Entered industry through Directors Guild of America's training program, apprenticing on Rich Man Poor Man and rising to second asst. dir. on Oh, God. Producer of many TV projects and theatrical films with Edgar Scherick prod. co. In 1986, joined Paramount Pictures as v.p., prod., for M.P. Group. Assoc. prod., prod. mgr.: I'm Dancing as Fast as I Can. Became sr. v.p., prod. Paramount, M.P. Group, 1987; resigned 1989 to become pres. and head of prod. at Morgan Creek Prods. Mem. of bd.
PICTURES: The One & Only, When I am King, Mrs. Soffel, Lucas, Young Guns II, Pacific Heights, Robin Hood:Prince of Thieves, Freejak, White Sands, Big Top Pee-Wee, Summer School, Coming to America, The Untouchables, Scrooged, Star Trek V: The Final Frontier, Major League, We're No Angels, Harlem Nights, The Two Jakes, Stay Tuned, Addams Family Values, Up Close and Personal, Flubber, The Negotiator.
TELEVISION: Call to Glory (pilot), Little Gloria Happy at Last.

NICOL, ALEX
Actor, Director. b. Ossining, NY, Jan. 20, 1919. e. Fagin Sch. of Dramatic Arts, Actor's Studio. U.S. Cavalry.
THEATER: Forward the Heart, Sundown Beach, Hamlet, Richard II, South Pacific, Mr. Roberts, Cat on a Hot Tin Roof.
PICTURES: The Sleeping City, Tomahawk, Target Unknown, Air Cadet, Raging Tide, Meet Danny Wilson, Red Ball Express, Because of You, Redhead From Wyoming, Lone Hand, Law and Order, Champ for a Day, Black Glove, Heat Wave, About Mrs. Leslie, Dawn at Socorro, Strategic Air Command, Man from Laramie, Great Day in the Morning, The Gilded Cage, Sincerely Yours, Five Branded Women, Via Margutta, Under 10 Flags, Gunfighters at Casa Grande, The Screaming Skull (dir.), Then There Were Three (dir.), The Brutal Land, Bloody Mama, Homer, Point of Terror (dir.), The Night God Screamed, A-P-E.

NIELSEN, LESLIE
Actor. b. Regina, Sask., Canada, Feb. 11, 1926. e. Victoria H.S., Edmonton. Disc jockey, announcer for Canadian radio station; studied at Lorne Greene's Acad. of Radio Arts, Toronto and at Neighborhood Playhouse; N.Y. radio actor summer stock. Toured country in one-man show, Darrow, 1979. *Author:* The Naked Truth (1993), Leslie Nielsen's Stupid Little Golf Book (1995).
PICTURES: Ransom (debut, 1956), Forbidden Planet, The Vagabond King, The Opposite Sex, Hot Summer Night, Tammy and the Bachelor, The Sheepman, Night Train To Paris, Harlow, Dark Intruder, Beau Geste, The Plainsman, Gunfight in Abilene, The Reluctant Astronaut, Rosie!, Counterpoint, Dayton's Devils, How to Commit Marriage, Change of Mind, Four Rode Out, The Resurrection of Zachary Wheeler, The Poseidon Adventure, And Millions Will Die, Day of the Animals, Viva Knievel!, The Amsterdam Kill, City on Fire, Airplane!, Prom Night, The Creature Wasn't Nice, Wrong Is Right, Creepshow, The Patriot, Soul Man, Nightstick, Nuts, Home Is Where the Hart Is, The Naked Gun: From the Files of Police Squad!, Dangerous Curves, Repossessed, The Naked Gun 2 1/2: The Smell of Fear, All I Want for Christmas, Surf Ninjas, Naked Gun 33 1/3: The Final Insult, Dracula: Dead and Loving It, Spy Hard (also co-exec. prod.), Family Plan, Mr. Magoo, Wrongfully Accused, Camouflage, Titanic Too: It Missed the Iceberg.
TELEVISION: *Series*: The New Breed, Peyton Place, The Protectors, Bracken's World, The Explorers (host), Police Squad, Shaping Up. *Guest*: Studio One, Kraft, Philco Playhouse, Robert Montgomery Presents, Pulitzer Prize Playhouse, Suspense, Danger, Justice, Man Behind the Badge, Ben Casey, Walt Disney (Swamp Fox), Wild Wild West, The Virginian, The Loner. *Special*: Death of a Salesman. *Movies*: See How They Run, Shadow Over Elveron, Hawaii Five-O (pilot), Companions in Nightmare, Trial Run, Deadlock, Night Slaves, The Aquarians, Hauser's Memory, Incident in San Francisco, They Call It Murder, Snatched, The Letters, The Return of Charlie Chan, Can Ellen Be Saved?, Brink's: The Great Robbery, Little Mo, Institute for Revenge, OHMS, The Night the Bridge Fell Down, Cave-In!, Reckless Disregard, Blade in Hong Kong, Fatal Confession: A Father Dowling Mystery, Chance of a Lifetime, Safety Patrol. *Mini-Series*: Backstairs at the White House.

NIMOY, LEONARD
Actor, Director. b. Boston, MA, Mar. 26, 1931. e. Boston Col. Joined Pasadena Playhouse. Along with active career in films, TV and stage, has been writer and photographer. Author of three books on photography and poetry, as well as autobiography, I Am Not Spock. Has also been speaker on college lecture circuit. Created comic book Primortals.
THEATER: Full Circle, Equus, Sherlock Holmes, Vincent (also dir., writer; one-man show), Love Letters.

PICTURES: Queen for a Day, Rhubarb, Francis Goes to West Point, Them!, Satan's Satellite's (edited from serial Zombies of the Stratosphere), The Brain Eaters, The Balcony, Catlow, Invasion of the Body Snatchers, Star Trek—The Motion Picture, Star Trek II: The Wrath of Khan, Star Trek III: The Search for Spock (also dir.), Transformers: The Movie (voice), Star Trek IV: The Voyage Home (also. dir., co-story), Three Men and a Baby (dir. only), The Good Mother (dir. only), Star Trek V: The Final Frontier, Funny About Love (dir. only), Star Trek VI: The Undiscovered Country (also exec. prod., co-story), Holy Matrimony (dir. only), The Pagemaster (voice), Jellies & Other Ocean Drifters (voice), Carpati: 50 Miles, 50 Years (voice), A Life Apart: Hasidism in America (voice), Sinbad: Beyond the Veil of Mists, Trekkies.
TELEVISION: *Series*: Star Trek, Mission: Impossible, In Search Of... (host), Outer Limits. *Movies*: Assault on the Wayne, Baffled, The Alpha Caper, The Missing Are Deadly, The Sun Also Rises, A Woman Called Golda, Never Forget (also co-prod.), Bonanza: Under Attack, David, Alien Voices, Brave New World. *Mini-Series*: Marco Polo. *Guest*: Bonanza, Twilight Zone, Perry Mason, Laramie, Wagon Train, Man From U.N.C.L.E., The Virginian, Get Smart, Night Gallery, Columbo, T.J. Hooker, Star Trek: The Next Generation, The Simpsons (voice). *Special*: Seapower: A Global Journey (narrator). *Episode Dir.:* Deadly Games.

NIVEN, DAVID, JR.
Executive. b. London, England, Dec. 15, 1942. e. Univ. of Grenoble; London Sch. of Economics. Joined William Morris Agency in Beverly Hills in 1963. Transferred same yr. to New York; over next five yrs. worked for agency's European offices in Rome, Madrid and London. 1968-72, Columbia Pictures' U.K. office as v.p. of production; 1972-76, mng. dir. and v.p. of Paramount Pictures in U.K. 1976 became indep. prod. West Coast corresp. & interviewer for Inside Edition. Appeared as actor in films Lisa, Cool Surface, and on tv series, America's Most Wanted. 1993, became chmn. of R.A.D.D. (Recording-Artists Against Drunk Driving)
PICTURES: *Producer*: The Eagle Has Landed, Escape to Athena, Monsignor, Better Late Than Never, Kidco, That's Dancing!, Pyscho Cop II, Girl With the Hungry Eyes, Cool Surface (also actor), Blue Flame.
TELEVISION: The Night They Saved Christmas (exec. prod., s.p.), Cary Grant: A Celebration, Minnelli on Minnelli, The Wonderful Wizard of Oz. Panelist: To Tell the Truth (1991-92).

NIX, WILLIAM PATTERSON
Executive. b. Philadelphia, PA, April 10, 1948. e. Georgetown U., A.B., 1970; Antioch, M.A., 1971; Hofstra U. Sch. of Law, J.D., 1976; NYU Sch. of Law, LL.M., 1979. Member, Baker & Botts, LLP New York, NY. Formerly, V.P. Bus. Affairs, NBA Properties Inc., NY, ent. & media firm. Prior to that, was sr. v.p. of both the MPAA and Motion Picture Export Assoc. of America. Chmn. of MPAA committee on copyright and literary property matters, and COO of film industry's intellectual property protection division (1976-91). Lifetime voting member, AMPAS.

NIXON, AGNES
Writer, Producer. b. Nashville, TN, Dec. 10, 1927. e. Northwestern Sch. of Speech, Catholic U. Landed 1st job writing radio serial dialogue (Woman in White, 1948-51), three days after graduating from college. Became a freelance writer for TV dramatic series. Guest writer, New York Times 1968-72, and TV Guide. Trustee, Television Conference Inst., 1979-82. Received National Acad. of Television Arts & Sciences' Trustee Award, 1981; Junior Diabetic Assn. Super Achiever Award, 1982; Communicator Award for American Women in Radio and Television, 1984. Gold Plate Award, American Acad. Achievement, 1993; inducted into TV Hall of Fame, 1993. Popular Culture Lifetime Achievement Award, 1995; Public Service Award, Johns Hopkins Hospital, 1995. Humanitarian Award, National Osteoporosis Foundation, 1996. Member, Int'l Radio & TV Society; Nat'l Acad. of TV Arts & Sciences; bd. of Harvard Foundation; The Friars Club.
TELEVISION: *Series writer*: Studio One, Philco Playhouse, Robert Montgomery Presents, Somerset Maugham Theatre, Armstrong Circle Theatre, Hallmark Hall of Fame, My True Story, Cameo Theatre, Search For Tomorrow, As The World Turns, Guiding Light, Another World. *Series creator-producer*: One Life to Live, All My Children, Loving. *Mini-Series*: The Manions of America.

NIXON, CYNTHIA
Actress. b. New York, NY, April 9, 1966. e. Barnard Coll. Started stage career at age 14.
THEATER: *B'way*: The Philadelphia Story (Theatre World Award), Hurlyburly, The Real Thing, The Heidi Chronicles, Angels in America: Millenium Aproaches/Perestroika, Indiscretions. *Off-B'way*: Moonchildren, Romeo and Juliet, The Balcony Scene, Servy N Bernice 4-Ever, On the Bum, The Illusion, The Scarlet Letter.
PICTURES: Little Darlings (debut, 1980), Tattoo, Prince of the City, I Am the Cheese, Amadeus, The Manhattan Project, Let It Ride, Addams Family Values, The Pelican Brief, Baby's Day Out, Marvin's Room, The Out-of-Towners.
TELEVISION: *Movies*: The Murder of Mary Phagan, The Love She Sought, Love Lies and Murder, Face of a Stranger. *Specials:* The Fifth of July, Kiss Kiss Dahlings, Tanner '88. *Series:* Sex and the City. *Guest*: The Equalizer, Gideon Oliver, Murder She Wrote.

NOIRET, PHILIPPE
Actor. b. Lille, France, Oct. 1, 1930. e. Centre Dramatique de l'Ouest. Company member of Theatre National Populaire 1951-63; nightclub entertainer before film debut in Agnes Varda's short, La Pointe Court. B'way debut Lorenzaccio (1958).
PICTURES: Gigi (debut, 1948), Olivia, Agence Matrimoniale, La Pointe Courte, Ravissante, Zazie dans le Metro, The Billionaire, Crime Does Not Pay, Therese Desqueyroux, Cyrano and D'Artagnan, None But the Lonely Spy, Death Where Is Thy Victory?, Monsieur, Les Copains, Lady L, La Vie de Chateau, Tender Scoundrel, The Night of the Generals, Woman Times Seven, The Assassination Bureau, Mr. Freedom, Justine, Topaz, Clerambard, Give Her the Moon, A Room in Paris, Murphy's War, A Time for Loving, Five-Leaf Clover, The Assassination, Sweet Deception, Poil de Carotte, The French Conspiracy, The Serpent, The Day of the Jackel, La Grande Bouffe, Let Joy Reign Supreme, The Old Gun, The Judge and the Assassin, A Woman at Her Window, Purple Taxi, Dear Inspector, Due Pezzi di Pane,
Who Is Killing the Great Chefs of Europe?, Death Watch, Street of the Crane's Foot, A Week's Vacation, Heads or Tails, Three Brothers, Kill Birgitt Haas, Coup de Torchon, L'Etoile du Nord, Amici, Miei, Atto 2, L'Africain, A Friend of Vincents, Le Grand Carnival, Fort Saganne, Les Ripoux, Souvenirs, Next Summer, The Gold-Rimmed Glasses, No Downing Allowed, My New Partner, 'Round Midnight, Let's Hope It's a Girl, The 4th Power, The Thrill of Genius, The Secret Wife, Twist Again in Moscow, Masks, The Family Chouans!, IL Frullo del Passero, Young Toscanini, The Return of the Musketeers, Moments of Love, Cinema Paradiso, Life and Nothing But, Palermo Connection, My New Partner 2, Uranus, I Don't Kiss, The Two of Us, Especially on Sunday, The Postman, Grosse Fatigue, D'Artagnan's Daughter, The King of Paris, Marianna Ucria, Le Grand ducs, Fantome avec Chauffeur, Soleil, Les Palmes de M. Schutz, On Guard.

NOLTE, NICK
Actor. b. Omaha, NB, Feb. 8, 1941. Attended 5 colleges in 4 yrs. on football scholarships, including Pasadena City Coll. and Phoenix City Coll. Joined Actors Inner Circle at Phoenix and appeared in Orpheus Descending, After the Fall, Requiem For a Nun. Did stock in Colorado. In 1968, joined Old Log Theatre in MN and after 3 yrs. left for New York, appearing at Cafe La Mama. Went to L.A. and did plays The Last Pad and Picnic, as well as several guest spots on TV series before big break in mini-series, Rich Man Poor Man as Tom Jordache.
PICTURES: Return to Macon County (debut, 1975), The Deep, Who'll Stop the Rain, North Dallas Forty, Heart Beat, Cannery Row, 48 HRS., Under Fire, Teachers, Grace Quigley, Down and Out in Beverly Hills, Extreme Prejudice, Weeds, Three Fugitives, New York Stories (Life Lessons), Farewell to the King, Everybody Wins, Q&A, Another 48 HRS, Cape Fear, The Prince of Tides (Golden Globe Award, Acad. Award nom.), The Player, Lorenzo's Oil, I'll Do Anything, Blue Chips, I Love Trouble, Jefferson in Paris, Mulholland Falls, Nightwatch, Mother Night, Afterglow, Affliction (Acad. Award nom.), U-Turn, Thin Red Line, Breakfast of Champions.
TELEVISION: *Mini-Series*: Rich Man Poor Man. *Movies:* Winter Kill (pilot), The California Kid, Death Sentence, The Runaway Barge. *Guest*: Medical Center, Streets of San Francisco, The Rookies.

NOONAN, TOM
Actor, Writer. b. Greenwich, CT, Apr. 12, 1951. e. Yale.
THEATER: Buried Child (Off-B'way debut, 1978), Invitational Farmyard, The Breakers, Five of Us, Spookhouse, What Happened Was (also writer), Wifey (also writer).
PICTURES: Heaven's Gate, Wolfen, Eddie Macon's Run, Easy Money, The Man With One Red Shoe, F/X, Manhunter, The Monster Squad, Mystery Train, Robocop 2, Last Action Hero, What Happened Was (also dir., s.p.), The Wife (also composer, s.p., & dir.), Heat, Phoenix, The Astronaut's Wife.
TELEVISION: *Mini-series*: Monsters, North & South II. *Movies*: Rage, Red Wind (s.p.), The 10 Million Dollar Getaway, Heaven & Hell: North & South Book III. *Guest*: X-Files.

NORMAN, BARRY
Writer/presenter. b. London. Early career as show business editor London Daily Mail; humorous columnist for The Guardian. Entered TV as writer, presenter FILM 1972-81 and 1983-93. 1982, presenter Omnibus. Writer/host: The Hollywood Greats and Talking Pictures. Radio work incl.: Going Places, The News Quiz, Breakaway, The Chip Shop.
AUTHOR: The Hollywood Greats, Movie Greats, Film Greats, Talking Pictures, 100 Best Films of the Century. Novels: A Series of Defeats, Have a Nice Day, Sticky Wicket, The Bird Dog Tapes.
PICTURES: Blues for the Avatar (dir.).

NORRIS, CHUCK
Actor. r.n. Carlos Ray Norris. b. Ryan, OK, Mar. 10, 1940. World middle weight karate champion 1968-74. Owner of LA karate schools which led to film career.

PICTURES: The Wrecking Crew (debut, 1969), Slaughter in San Francisco, Return of the Dragon, The Student Teachers, Breaker! Breaker!, Good Guys Wear Black, Game of Death, A Force of One, The Octagon, An Eye for an Eye, Silent Rage, Forced Vengeance, Lone Wolf McQuade, Missing in Action, Missing in Action 2, Code of Silence, Invasion U.S.A. (also co-s.p.), Delta Force, Firewalker, Braddock: Missing in Action III (also co-s.p.), Hero and the Terror, Delta Force II, The Hitman, Sidekicks (also co-exec. prod.), Hellbound, Top Dog, Forest Warrior.
TELEVISION: *Series*: Chuck Norris's Karate Kommandos (animated series, voice), Walker: Texas Ranger (also co-exec. prod.). Movie: Logan's War: Bound by Honor. *Special*: The Ultimate Stuntman: A Tribute to Dar Robinson (host), Wind in the Wire.

NORTH, SHEREE
Actress. r.n. Dawn Bethel. b. Los Angeles, CA, Jan. 17, 1933. e. Hollywood H.S. Amateur dancer with USO at 11; prof. debut at 13; many TV appearances
THEATER: *B'way*: Hazel Flagg (Drama Desk Award, Critics' Award), I Can Get It For You Wholesale. *Other*: Madwoman of Chaillot, ... And to My Daughter, Stepping Out, California Dogfight, 6 Rms. Riv Vue, Turnstyle, Thursday Is a Good Night, Dutchman, Private Lives, Irma La Douce, Bye Bye Birdie, Your Own Thing, Can-Can, Two for the Seesaw, Breaking Up the Act, etc. Also directed and produced several productions.
PICTURES: Excuse My Dust, Here Come the Girls, Living It Up, How to Be Very Very Popular, The Lieutenant Wore Skirts, The Best Things in Life Are Free, Way to the Gold, No Down Payment, In Love and War, Mardi Gras, Destination Inner Space, Madigan, The Gypsy Moths, The Trouble With Girls, Lawman, The Organization, Charley Varick, The Outfit, Breakout, The Shootist, Telefon, Rabbit Test, Telefon, Cold Dog Soup, Defenseless.
TELEVISION: *Series*: Big Eddie, I'm a Big Girl Now, Bay City Blues. *Guest*: Hawaii 5-0, Kojak, Family, Archie Bunker's Place, Murder She Wrote, Golden Girls, Matlock, Seinfeld, Hunter, Magnum P.I., many others. *Movies*: Then Came Bronson (pilot), Vanished, Rolling Man, Trouble Comes to Town, Snatched, Maneater, Key West, Winter Kill, A Shadow in the Streets, Most Wanted, The Night They Took Miss Beautiful, A Real American Hero, Amateur Night at the Dixie Bar and Grill, Women in White, Portrait of a Stripper, Marilyn: The Untold Story, Legs, Scorned and Swindled, Jake Spanner—Private Eye, Dead on the Money.

NORTON, EDWARD
Actor. b. Boston, MA, Aug. 18, 1969. e. Yale University. Board member of Edward Albee's Signature Company. Works as a board member of the Enterprise Foundation in New York.
PICTURES: Everyone Says I Love You, Primal Fear, The People vs. Larry Flynt, Rounders, Out of the Past (voice), American History X (Acad. Award nom), Fight Club, Keeping the Faith (also dir. and prod.), The Score, Frida Kahlo.
TELEVISION:*Specials:* A Salute to Dustin Hoffman, AFI's 100 Years...100 Stars.

NOSSECK, NOEL
Director, Producer. b. Los Angeles, CA, Dec. 10, 1943. Began as editor with David Wolper Prods; made documentaries; turned to features.
PICTURES: *Director*: Best Friends (also prod.), Youngblood, Dreamer, King of the Mountain.
TELEVISION: *Movies*: Return of the Rebels, The First Time, Night Partners, Summer Fantasies, Different Affair, Stark, A Mirror Image, Roman Holiday, Full Exposure: The Sex Tapes Scandal, Follow Your Heart, Opposites Attract, A Mother's Justice, Without a Kiss Goodbye, Born Too Soon, French Silk, Sister in Law, Down Out and Dangerous. *Pilots*: Aaron's Way, Half 'n Half, Fair Game, Heaven Help Us.

NOURI, MICHAEL
Actor. b. Washington, DC, Dec. 9, 1945. e. Avon Old Farms, Rollins Coll., Emerson Coll. Studied for theatre with Larry Moss and Lee Strasberg. New York stage debut in Forty Carats, 1969.
THEATER: Forty Carats, Victor/Victoria.
PICTURES: Goodbye Columbus (debut, 1969), Flashdance, Gobots (voice), The Imagemaker, The Hidden, Chamelleon, Fatal Sky, Total Exposure, Black Ice, Fortunes of War, To the Limit.
TELEVISION: *Series*: Beacon Hill, Search for Tomorrow, The Curse of Dracula, The Gangster Chronicles, Bay City Blues, Downtown, Love and War. *Movies*: Contract on Cherry Street, Fun and Games, Secrets of a Mother and Daughter, Spraggue, Between Two Women, Rage of Angels: The Story Continues, Quiet Victory: the Charlie Wedemeyer Story, Shattered Dreams, Danielle Steel's Changes, In the Arms of a Killer, Psychic, Exclusive, The Sands of Time, The Hidden 2, Eyes of Terror, Between Love and Honor. *Mini-Series*: The Last Convertible.

NOVAK, KIM
Actress. r.n. Marilyn Novak. b. Chicago, IL, Feb, 13, 1933. e. Wright Junior Coll., Los Angeles City Coll. Started as model, named World's Favorite Actress, Brussels World's Fair.
PICTURES: The French Line (debut, 1954), Pushover, Phffft!, Five Against the House, Son of Sinbad, Picnic, The Man with the Golden Arm, The Eddy Duchin Story, Jeanne Eagles, Pal Joey, Vertigo, Bell Book and Candle, Middle of the Night, Pepe, Strangers When We Meet, The Notorious Landlady, Boys' Night Out, Of Human Bondage, Kiss Me Stupid, The Amorous Adventures of Moll Flanders, The Legend of Lylah Clare, The Great Bank Robbery, Tales That Witness Madness, The White Buffalo, The Mirror Crack'd, Just a Gigolo, The Children, Liebestraum.
TELEVISION: *Series*: Falcon Crest. *Guest*: Alfred Hitchcock Presents (1985). *Movies*: Third Girl From the Left, Satan's Triangle, Malibu.

NOVELLO, DON
Writer, Comedian, Actor. b. Ashtabula, OH, Jan. 1, 1943. e. U. of Dayton, B.A., 1964. Best known as Father Guido Sarducci on Saturday Night Live. Was advertising copy writer before writing and performing on The Smothers Brothers Comedy Hour (1975). Writer for Van Dyke and Company, and writer-performer on Saturday Night Live 1978-80. Producer: SCTV Comedy Network (1982) and performer-writer on B'way in Gilda Radner—Live From New York (1979), as well as filmed version (Gilda Live!). Recordings: Live at St. Douglas Convent, Breakfast in Heaven. Author: The Lazlo Letters: The Amazing Real-Life Actual Correspondence of Lazlo Toth, American!, The Blade, Citizen Lazlo.
PICTURES: Gilda Live!, Head Office, Tucker: The Man and His Dream, New York Stories (Life Without Zoe), The Godfather Part III, Casper (cameo), One Night Stand, Jack.
TELEVISION: *Cable specials*: Fr. Guido Sarducci Goes to College, The Vatican Inquirer—The Pope Tour.

NOYCE, PHILLIP
Director. b. Griffith, New South Wales, Australia, April 29, 1950. Began making films at school and university. Made first short film at age 15, Better to Reign in Hell. In 1980, became part-time mgr., Sydney Filmmaker's Co-operative and in 1973 was selected for Australian Nat'l Film School in Sydney, for year-long training prog. which resulted in shorts, Good Afternoon, Caravan Park, Castor and Pollux, God Knows Why But It Works, and 60-minute film Backroads.
PICTURES: Backroads (also prod., s.p.), Newsfront (also s.p.; Australian Acad. Awards for best dir. & s.p., 1978), Heatwave (also co-s.p.), Echoes of Paradise, Dead Calm, Blind Fury, Patriot Games, Sliver (also cameo), Clear and Present Danger, The Saint, The Bone Collector, Blast Off (also s.p.), The Repair Shop, Rabbit Proof Fence, The Quiet American.
TELEVISION: *Mini-Series*: Dismissal, Cowra Breakout. *Episodes*: The Hitchhiker, Nightmare Cafe.

NOZOE, YUKI
Executive. Began career with Sony Pictures Entertainment (SPE) in 1972. Director, senior v.p. & gen. mgr. , Sony Electronics Consumer Video Co., 1986; exec. v.p. & senior v.p. of mktg., Consumer Products Group, Sony Electronics, Inc., 1993-96, where he was instrumental in developing and standardizing DVD format; co-president, Digital Entertainment, SPE, 1999.

NUNN, BILL
Actor. b. Pittsburgh, PA. Teamed with friend Al Cooper as member of comedy team Nunn and Cooper in nightclubs, 1980-83. On stage with various theatrical companies including the Alliance, the Academy, Theatrical Oufit, Just Us Theatre.
THEATER: T-Bone and Weasel, Split Second, Home, A Lesson From Aloes, A Soldier's Play, Macbeth, The River Niger, Fences.
PICTURES: School Daze, Do the Right Thing, Def by Temptation, Cadillac Man, Mo' Better Blues, New Jack City, Regarding Henry, Sister Act, National Lampoon's Loaded Weapon 1, The Last Seduction, Canadian Bacon, Things to Do in Denver When You're Dead, Candyman 2, Money Train, Mr. & Mrs. Loving, BulletProof, Extreme Measures, Kiss the Girls, Mad City, He Got Game.
TELEVISION: *Movies:* The Littlest Victims, The Affair, Carriers, Quicksilver Highway, Ellen Foster, Always Outnumbered. *Specials:* Native Strangers, Dangerous Heart, War Stories, A Yankee in King Arthur's Court. *Guest:* Fallen Angels.

NYKVIST, SVEN
Cinematographer. b. Moheda, Sweden, Dec. 3, 1922. e. Stockholm Photog. Sch. Asst. cameraman 1941-44. Became internationally known by photographing most of Ingmar Bergman's pictures. Recipient of American Society of Cinematographers Life Achievement Award, 1996.
PICTURES: Sawdust and Tinsel, The Virgin Spring, Winter Light, Karin Mansdotter, The Silence, Loving Couples, Persona, Hour of the Wolf, Cries and Whispers (Academy Award, 1973), The Dove, Black Moon, Scenes from a Marriage, The Magic Flute, Face to Face, One Day in the Life of Ivan Denisovich, The Tenant, The Serpents' Egg, Pretty Baby, Autumn Sonata, King of the Gypsies, Hurricane, Starting Over, Willie and Phil, From the Life of the Marionettes, The Postman Always Rings Twice, Cannery Row, Fanny and Alexander (Academy Award, 1983), Swann in Love,

The Tragedy of Carmen, After the Rehearsal, Agnes of God, Dream Lover, The Sacrifice, The Unbearable Lightness of Being, Katinka, Another Woman, New York Stories (Oedipus Wrecks), Crimes and Misdemeanors, The Ox (dir., co-s.p. only), Chaplin, Sleepless in Seattle, What's Eating Gilbert Grape, With Honors, Kirsten Lavrandatter, Only You, Mixed Nuts, Something to Talk About, Celebrity, Curtain Call.
TELEVISION: *Movie:* Nobody's Child, Private Confessions.

O

O'BRIAN, HUGH
Actor. r.n. Hugh C. Krampe. b. Rochester, NY, Apr. 19, 1925. Raised in Chicago. e. Kemper Military Sch., U. of Cincinnati, UCLA. U.S. Marine Corps, where at age 18 he served as youngest drill instructor in Marine Corps history. Actor in stock cos. before film career. Founder, chmn. development: Hugh O'Brian Youth Foundation, 1958; Nat'l Chmn., Cystic Fibrosis Research Foundation 1969-74; Co-founder and pres. Thalians 1955-58; Founder Hugh O'Brian Annual Acting Awards at UCLA, 1962.
THEATER: *B'way*: Destry Rides Again, First Love, Guys and Dolls, Cactus Flower, The Decision. Regional: The Music Man, Rainmaker, Plaza Suite, On 20th Century, Stalag 17, Thousand Clowns, etc.
PICTURES: Young Lovers (debut, 1949), Never Fear, Rocketship X-M, The Return of Jesse James, Vengeance Valley, Fighting Coast Guard, Little Big Horn, On the Loose, The Cimarron Kid, Red Ball Express, The Battle at Apache Pass, Sally and Saint Anne, Son of Ali Baba, The Raiders, The Lawless Breed, Meet Me at the Fair, Seminole, Man from the Alamo, Back to God's Country, The Stand at Apache River, Saskatchewan, Fireman Save My Child, Drums Across the River, Broken Lance, There's No Business Like Show Business, White Feather, The Twinkle in God's Eye, Brass Legend, The Fiend Who Walked the West, Alias Jesse James, Come Fly with Me, Love Has Many Faces, In Harm's Way, Ten Little Indians, Ambush Bay, Africa--Texas Style!, Killer Force, The Shootist, Game of Death, Doin' Time on Planet Earth, Twins.
TELEVISION: *Series*: The Life and Legend of Wyatt Earp, Search. *Specials*: Dial M for Murder, A Punt a Pass and a Prayer, Going Home, Engagement Ring, Invitation to a Gunfighter, Reunion, Chain of Command, It's a Man's World, Wyatt Earp: Return to Tombstone. *Movies*: Wild Women, Harpy, Probe (Search), Murder on Flight 502, Benny & Barney: Las Vegas Undercover, Fantasy Island, Murder at the World Series, Cruise Into Terror, The Seekers, Gunsmoke: The Last Apache, The Gambler Returns: Luck of the Draw.

O'BRIEN, CONAN
Performer, Writer. b. Brookline, MA, Apr. 18, 1963. e. Harvard. Served two years as pres. of Harvard Lampoon before landing work as tv writer for The Simpsons, Saturday Night Live (Emmy Award, 1989). Prod. of pilot Lookwell. *Series:* Not Necessarily the News, NBC's Late Night With Conan O'Brien (Emmy nom., 1996).

O'BRIEN, MARGARET
Actress. r.n. Angela Maxine O'Brien. Los Angeles, CA, Jan. 15, 1938. Screen debut at 3 in Babes on Broadway (1941). Awarded special Academy Award as best child actress, 1944. Voted one of ten best money-making stars in Motion Picture Herald-Fame Poll 1945-46.
PICTURES: Babes on Broadway (debut, 1941), Journey for Margaret, Dr. Gillespie's Criminal Case, Lost Angel, Thousands Cheer, Madame Curie, Jane Eyre, The Canterville Ghost, Meet Me in St. Louis, Music for Millions, Our Vines Have Tender Grapes, Bad Bascomb, Three Wise Fools, Unfinished Dance, Tenth Avenue Angel, The Big City, The Secret Garden, Little Women, Her First Romance, Two Persons Eyes (Jap.), Agente S3S Operazione Uranio (It.), Glory, Heller in Pink Tights, Anabelle Lee, Diabolic Wedding, Amy, Sunset After Dark.
TELEVISION: *Movies*: Death in Space, Split Second to an Epitaph, Testimony of Two Men. *Guest*: Robert Montgomery Presents, Lux Video Theatre, Playhouse 90, Wagon Train, Studio One, U.S. Steel Hour, Dr. Kildare, Love American Style, Marcus Welby M.D.

O'BRIEN, VIRGINIA
Actress. b. Los Angeles, CA, Apr. 18, 1919. e. North Hollywood h.s. Singer, comedienne with a distinctive dead-pan delivery. On stage in Meet the People. 1990, performed at London Palladium.
PICTURES: Hullabaloo (debut, 1940), The Big Store, Lady Be Good, Ringside Maisie, Ship Ahoy, Panama Hattie, DuBarry Was a Lady, As Thousands Cheer, Meet the People, Two Girls and a Sailor, The Harvey Girls, Ziegfeld Follies, Till Clouds Roll By, The Showoff, Merton of the Movies, Francis in the Navy, Gus.

OBST, LYNDA
Producer. b. New York, NY, Apr. 14, 1950. e. Pomona Col., Columbia Univ. Former editor for New York Times Magazine, 1976-79; then exec. at Polygram Pictures, 1979-81; Geffen Films, 1981-83, co-prod. at Paramount, 1983-85; prod. for Walt Disney, 1986, before moving over to Columbia. Co-Author: Dirty Dreams (with Carol Wolper).
PICTURES: Flashdance (assoc. prod.). *Producer*: Adventures in Babysitting, Heartbreak Hotel, The Fisher King, This Is My Life, Bad Girls, One Fine Day, Hope Floats, The Siege, The Wishbones. *Exec. Prod.*: Sleepless in Seattle.
TELEVISION: The '60s (exec. prod.)
AUTHOR: Hello, He Lied and Other Truths From the Hollywood Trenches.

OCHS, MILLARD L.
Executive. e. U. of Akron. Beginning in July 1946, worked as an usher, projectionist and concession manager and later as cinema manager for his father Lee A. Ochs, while in college. After graduation, became city mng'r. for RKO Stanley Warner Theatre, Cincinnati, OH; followed by district mng'r. for AMC, covering SW territoris of AR and S. CA. 1985, while with AMC, transferred to England and began developing the multiplex concept at Milton Keynes; over next three years, AMC opened eight locations in England, then sold their interest to Univ./Paramount Studio Joint Venture of United Cinema Int'l.; stayed on with UCI until June 1993. Joined WB Int'l. Theatres as exec. v.p.; July 1994, promoted to pres. and began working with Ira Stiegler, v.p., architecture & planning, to introduce the Looney Tune Themed lobby. Awards: Exhibitor of the Year, Cinema Expo in Amsterdam, June 1996; co-recipient, Exhibitor of the Year, ShoWest, March 1998.

O'CONNELL, JACK
Producer, Director, Writer. b. Boston, MA. e. Princeton U., Harvard Business Sch. After being a creative group head in all media and doing 500 tv commercials entered feature films working with Fellini on La Dolce Vita, then asst. dir. to Antonioni on L'Avventura.
PICTURES: *Writer/Prod./Dir.:* Greenwich Village Story, Revolution, Christa (aka Swedish Flygirls), Up the Girls Means Three Cheers for Them All, The Hippie Revolution.

O'CONNOR, CARROLL
Actor. b. New York, NY, Aug. 2, 1924. e. University Coll., Dublin; U. of Montana. Three years with Dublin's Gate Theatre, then N.Y.
THEATER: *NY*: Ulysses in Nighttown, Playboy of the Western World, The Big Knife, Brothers (also dir.), Home Front. Author: Ladies of Hanover Tower.
PICTURES: A Fever in the Blood (debut, 1961), Parrish, By Love Possessed, Lad: A Dog, Belle Sommers, Lonely Are the Brave, Cleopatra, In Harm's Way, What Did You Do in the War Daddy?, Hawaii, Not With My Wife You Don't, Warning Shot, Point Blank, Waterhole No. 3, The Devil's Brigade, For Love of Ivy, Death of a Gunfighter, Marlowe, Kelly's Heroes, Doctors' Wives, Law and Disorder.
TELEVISION: *Series*: All in the Family (4 Emmy Awards: 1972, 1977, 1978, 1979; later retitled Archie Bunker's Place), In the Heat of the Night (Emmy Award, 1989). *Guest*: U.S. Steel Hour, Armstrong Circle Theatre, Kraft Theatre, The Untouchables, Dr. Kildare, East Side/West Side, Gunsmoke, Wild Wild West, Party of Five, Mad About You. *Special*: Of Thee I Sing. *Movies*: Fear No Evil, The Last Hurrah (also writer), Brass, Convicted, The Father Clements Story, In the Heat of the Night: A Matter of Justice (also co-exec. prod.), In the Heat of the Night: Who Was Geli Bendl? (also co-exec. prod.), In the Heat of the Night: By Duty Bound (also co-exec. prod.), In the Heat of the Night: Grow Old With Me (also co-exec. prod.).

O'CONNOR, DONALD
Actor. b. Chicago, IL, Aug. 28, 1925. In vaudeville with family and Sons o' Fun (Syracuse, N.Y.) before screen debut 1938 in Sing You Sinners; return to vaudeville 1940-41, then resumed screen career with What's Cookin'?, 1942. Entered armed services, 1943. Voted Star of Tomorrow, 1943; best TV performer by M.P. Daily poll, 1953.
PICTURES: Sing You Sinners (debut, 1938), Sons of the Legion, Men With Wings, Tom Sawyer—Private Detective, Unmarried, Death of a Champion, Million Dollar Legs, Night Work, On Your Toes, Beau Geste, Private Buckaroo, Give Out Sisters, Get Hep to Love, When Johnny Comes Marching Home, Strictly in the Groove, It Comes Up Love, Mr. Big, Top Man, Chip Off the Old Block, Patrick the Great, Follow the Boys, The Merry Monahans, Bowery to Broadway, This Is the Life, Something in the Wind, Are You With It?, Feudin' Fussin' and a-Fightin', Yes Sir That's My Baby, Francis, Curtain Call at Cactus Creek, The Milkman, Double Crossbones, Francis Goes to the Races, Singin' in the Rain, Francis Goes to West Point, I Love Melvin, Call Me Madam, Francis Covers the Big Town, Walking My Baby Back Home, Francis Joins the WACS, There's No Business Like Show Business, Francis in the Navy, Anything Goes, The Buster Keaton Story, Cry for Happy, The Wonders of Aladdin, That Funny Feeling, That's Entertainment, Ragtime, Pandemonium, A Time to Remember, Toys, Out to Sea.

TELEVISION: *Series*: The Colgate Comedy Hour (host: 1951-54; Emmy Award, 1954), The Donald O'Connor Texaco Show (1954-55), The Donald O'Connor Show (synd., 1968). *Movies*: Alice in Wonderland, Bandit and the Silver Angel. *Guest*: Dinah Shore, Hollywood Palace, Carol Burnett, Julie Andrews, Ellery Queen, The Love Boat, Highway to Heaven, Tales From the Crypt. *Specials*: The Red Mill, Hollywood Melody, Olympus 7-0000.

O'CONNOR, GLYNNIS
Actress. b. New York, NY, Nov. 19, 1955. Daughter of ABC News prod. Daniel O'Connor and actress Lenka Peterson. e. State U., NY at Purchase. Stage includes Domestic Issues (Circle Rep., NY, 1983), The Taming of the Shrew (Great Lakes Shakespeare Fest.), The Seagull (Mirror Rep.).
PICTURES: Jeremy (debut, 1973), Baby Blue Marine, Ode to Billy Joe, Kid Vengeance, California Dreaming, Those Lips Those Eyes, Night Crossing, Melanie, Johnny Dangerously.
TELEVISION: *Series*: Sons and Daughters. *Mini-series*: Black Beauty. *Movies*: The Chisholms, Someone I Touched, All Together Now, The Boy in the Plastic Bubble, Little Mo, My Kidnapper, My Love, The Fighter, Love Leads the Way, Why Me?, Sins of the Father, The Deliberate Stranger, To Heal a Nation, Death in Small Doses, Past the Bleachers.

O'CONNOR, KEVIN J.
Actor. b. 1964. e. DePaul Univ.'s Goodman Sch. of Drama. On stage in Colorado Catechism (NY), El Salvador (Chicago).
PICTURES: One More Saturday Night, Peggy Sue Got Married, Candy Mountain, The Moderns, Signs of Life, Steel Magnolias, Love at Large, F/X 2, Hero, Equinox, No Escape, Color of Night, Virtuosity, Lord of Illusions, Canadian Bacon, Hit Me, Amistad, Gods & Monsters, Chicago Cab, Deep Rising, If...Dog...Rabbit, Chill Factor, The Mummy.
TELEVISION: *Movie:* The Caine Mutiny Court Martial, The Love Bug. *Special:* Tanner 88. *Guest:* Birdland. *Guest*: Law & Order, Birdland.

O'CONNOR, PAT
Director. b. Ardmore, Ireland, 1943. After working in London at odd jobs (putting corks in wine bottles, paving roads), came to U.S. e. UCLA, B.A. Studied film and TV at Ryerson Institute in Toronto. 1970, trainee prod., dir. with Radio Telefis Eireann. 1970-78 prod. and dir. over 45 TV features and current affairs documentaries. (The Four Roads, The Shankhill, Kiltyclogher, One of Ourselves, Night in Ginitia). A Ballroom of Romance won BAFTA Award (1981).
PICTURES: Cal (debut, 1984), A Month in the Country, Stars and Bars, The January Man, Fools of Fortune, Circle of Friends, Sacred Hearts, Inventing the Abbotts.
TELEVISION: *Movie*: Zelda.

O'DONNELL, CHRIS
Actor. b. Winetka, IL, 1970. e. Boston College.
PICTURES: Men Don't Leave (debut, 1990), Fried Green Tomatoes, School Ties, Scent of a Woman, The Three Musketeers, Blue Sky, Circle of Friends, Mad Love, Batman Forever, The Chamber, In Love and War, Batman & Robin, Cookie's Fortune, The Bachelor (also exec. prod.), Vertical Limit.

O'DONNELL, ROSIE
Actress. b. Commack, NY, 1961. e. Dickinson Col., Boston Univ. Stand-up comic first gaining attention on series Star Search.
THEATER: Grease! (B'way debut, 1994).
PICTURES: A League of Their Own, Sleepless in Seattle, Another Stakeout, Car 54 Where Are You?, I'll Do Anything, The Flintstones, Exit to Eden, Now and Then, Beautiful Girls, Harriet the Spy, A Very Brady Sequel (cameo), Wide Awake, Tarzan (voice), Get Bruce.
TELEVISION: *Series:* Gimme a Break, Stand-Up Spotlight (host, exec. prod.), Stand by Your Man, The Rosie O'Donnell Show (host; Emmy, 1997-98). *Movies/Specials:* Elmopalooza!, The Twilight of the Golds, Jackie's Back!.

O'HARA, CATHERINE
Actress, Writer, Director. b. Toronto, Canada, Mar. 4, 1954. Professional debut in 1974 with Toronto's Second City. Co-founder of SCTV in 1976 (Emmy and Canadian Nellie Awards for writing).
PICTURES: Nothing Personal, Rock & Rule (voice), After Hours, Heartburn, Beetlejuice, Dick Tracy, Betsy's Wedding, Home Alone, Little Vegas, There Goes the Neighborhood, Home Alone 2: Lost in New York, The Nightmare Before Christmas (voice), The Paper, Wyatt Earp, A Simple Twist of Fate, Tall Tale, Last of the High Kings, Pippi Longstocking, Home Fries, The Life Before This.
TELEVISION: *Series*: SCTV, Steve Allen Comedy Hour, SCTV Network 90. *Movie:* Hope. *Guest*: Trying Times, Dream On (also dir.), The Simpsons (voice).

O'HARA, GERRY
Director, Writer. b. Boston-Lincs, England 1924. e. St. Mary's Catholic Sch., Boston. Junior Reporter Boston Guardian. Entered industry in 1942 with documentaries and propaganda subjects.
PICTURES: *Director*: That Kind of Girl (debut, 1963), Game for Three Lovers, Pleasure Girls (also s.p.), Maroc 7, Love in Amsterdam, All the Right Noises (also s.p.), Leopard in the Snow, The Bitch, Fanny Hill, The Mummy Lives (also co-s.p.). *Writer*: Ten Little Indians, Havoc in Chase County, Phantom of the Opera, De Sade's Nightmare, Sherlock Holmes and the Affair in Transylvania, Catherine the Great.
TELEVISION: The Avengers, Man in a Suitcase, Journey into the Unknown, The Professionals (story editor, writer), Special Squad (story consultant), Cats Eyes (exec. story editor), Operation Julie (writer; mini-series), Sherlock Holmes & The Leading Lady, Sherlock Holmes & The Incident at Victoria Falls (co-writer).

O'HARA, MAUREEN
Actress. r.n. Maureen FitzSimons. b. Dublin, Ireland. Aug. 17, 1921. Abbey Sch. of Acting. Won numerous prizes for elocution. Under contract to Erich Pommer-Charles Laughton. Co-starred, Abbey & Repertory Theatre.
PICTURES: Kicking the Moon Around (debut, 1938), My Irish Molly, Jamaica Inn, The Hunchback of Notre Dame, A Bill of Divorcement, Dance Girl Dance, They Met in Argentina, How Green Was My Valley, To the Shores of Tripoli, Ten Gentlemen From West Point, The Black Swan, The Immortal Sergeant, This Land Is Mine, The Fallen Sparrow, Buffalo Bill, The Spanish Main, Sentimental Journey, Do You Love Me?, Miracle on 34th Street, Sinbad the Sailor, The Homestretch, The Foxes of Harrow, Sitting Pretty, Woman's Secret, Forbidden Street, Father Was a Fullback, Bagdad, Comanche Territory, Tripoli, Rio Grande, At Sword's Point, Flame of Araby, The Quiet Man, Kangaroo, Against All Flags, The Redhead From Wyoming, War Arrow, Fire Over Africa, The Magnificent Matador, Lady Godiva, Long Gray Line, Lisbon, Everything But the Truth, Wings of Eagles, Our Man in Havana, The Parent Trap, The Deadly Companions, Mr. Hobbs Takes a Vacation, McLintock!, Spencer's Mountain, The Battle of the Villa Fiorita, The Rare Breed, How Do I Love Thee?, Big Jake, Only the Lonely.
TELEVISION: *Movie*: The Red Pony, The Christmas Box. *Specials*: Mrs. Miniver, Scarlet Pimpernel, Spellbound, High Button Shoes, Who's Afraid of Mother Goose.

O'HERLIHY, DAN
Actor. b. Wexford, Ireland, May 1, 1919. e. National U. of Ireland (Bachelor of Architecture). Actor with Abbey Theatre, Dublin Gate, Longford Prod.; announcer on Radio Eireann; on Broadway in The Ivy Green.
PICTURES: Odd Man Out (debut, 1946), Kidnapped, Larceny, Macbeth, Iroquois Trail, The Blue Veil, The Desert Fox, The Highwayman, Soldiers Three, At Swords Point, Invasion U.S.A., Operation Secret, Actors and Sin, Sword of Venus, The Adventures of Robinson Crusoe (Acad. Award nom.), The Black Shield of Falworth, Bengal Brigade, The Purple Mask, The Virgin Queen, City After Midnight, Home Before Dark, Imitation of Life, The Young Land, Night Fighters, One Foot in Hell, The Cabinet of Caligari, Fail-Safe, The Big Cube, 100 Rifles, Waterloo, The Carey Treatment, The Tamarind Seed, MacArthur, Halloween III: The Season of the Witch, The Last Starfighter, The Whoopee Boys, Robocop, The Dead, Robocop 2.
TELEVISION: *Series*: The Travels of Jamie McPheeters, The Long Hot Summer, Hunter's Moon, Whiz Kids, Man Called Sloane, Twin Peaks. *Mini-series*: QB VII, Jennie: Lady Randolph Churchill, Nancy Astor. *Movies*: The People, Deadly Game, Woman on the Run, Good Against Evil, Love Cheat and Steal. *Guest*: The Equalizer, L.A. Law, Murder She Wrote, Ray Bradbury Theatre, Father Dowling. BBC: Colditz, The Secret Servant, Artemis, The Last Day, Jennie, Nancy Astor, The Rat Pack.

OHLMEYER, DONALD W., JR.
Executive, Producer, Director. b. New Orleans, LA, Feb. 3, 1945. e. U. of Notre Dame, B.A. (Communications), 1967. Producer and director at both ABC and NBC. Formed Ohlmeyer Communications Company, 1982 (diversified prod. and dist. of entertainment and sports prog.). Assoc. dir., ABC Sports, NY 1967-70; director, ABC Sports, 1971-72 (dir. 1972 Olympic Games); prod.: ABC Sports, NY 1972-77 (prod. and dir. 1976 Winter and Summer Olympics; prod. ABC's Monday Night Football, 1972-76); exec. prod.: NBC Sports, NY 1977-82 (exec. prod., 1980 Olympics, The World Series, The Super Bowl). Special Bulletin (exec. prod.), John Denver's Christmas in Aspen (exec. prod.). Chmn. and CEO, Ohlmeyer Communications Co., LA, 1982-present. 1993, named pres. NBC West Coast. Resigned from post 1999. Recipient of 14 Emmy Awards, Humanitas Prize, Award for Excellence, National Film Board. Member, Directors Guild of America.
TELEVISION: *Specials*: Heroes of Desert Storm (dir.), Disney's Christmas on Ice (dir.), Crimes of the Century (prod.). *Series*: Lifestories (dir./exec. prod.), Fast Copy (prod.). *Movies*: Cold Sassy Tree (exec. prod.), Crazy in Love (exec. prod.), Right to Die.

OKAWARA, TAKAO
Director.
PICTURES: Psychic Girl Reiko, Godzilla and Mothra: The Battle for Earth, Godzilla vs. Mechagodzilla II, Orochi the Eight-Headed Dragon, Godzilla vs. Destroyah, Abduction, Godzilla 2000.

O'KEEFE, MICHAEL
Actor. b. Larchmont, NY, April 24, 1955. e. NYU, AADA. m. singer Bonnie Raitt. Co-founder, Colonnades Theatre Lab, NY.
THEATER: *B'way*: Mass Appeal (Theatre World Award), Fifth of July. *Off-B'way*: Killdere (NYSF), Moliere in Spite of Himself, Christmas on Mars, Short Eyes. *Regional*: Streamers, A Few Good Men (tour).
PICTURES: Gray Lady Down (debut, 1978), The Great Santini (Acad. Award nom.), Caddyshack, Split Image, Nate and Hayes, Finders Keepers, The Slugger's Wife, Ironweed, Out of the Rain, Me and Veronica, Nina Takes a Lover, Three Lovers, Edie and Pen, Ghosts of Mississippi.
TELEVISION: *Series*: Against the Law, Roseanne. *Movies*: The Lindbergh Kidnapping Case, Friendly Persuasion, Panache, The Dark Secret of Harvest Home, A Rumor of War, Unholy Matrimony, Bridge to Silence, Disaster at Silo 7, Too Young to Die?, In the Best Interest of the Child, Fear, Incident at Deception Ridge, The People Next Door.

OLDKNOW, WILIAM H.
Executive. b. Atlanta, GA, Sept. 3, 1924. e. U.S.C. Served in USNR from 1943-46. Pres., Sero Development Co., (formerly Sero Amusement Co.) 1947-present (drive-in theatres, shopping centers, and commercial real-estate). Sole proprietor, Starlight Drive-in Theatre, Atlanta, GA. Chmn. and pres., De Anza Land & Leisure Corp.

OLDMAN, GARY
Actor. r.n. Leonard Gary Oldman. b. New Cross, South London, England, March 21, 1958. Won scholarship to Rose Bruford Drama College (B.A. Theatre Arts) after studying with Greenwich Young People's Theatre. Acted with Theatre Royal, York and joined touring theatre co. Then in 1980 appeared with Glasgow Citizens Theatre in Massacre at Paris, Chinchilla, Desperado Corner, A Waste of Time (also touring Europe and South America). Received Evening Standard Film Award for Best Newcomer for Sid and Nancy, 1986.
THEATER: *London*: Minnesota Moon, Summit Conference, Rat in the Skull, Women Beware Women, The War Plays, Real Dreams, The Desert Air, Serious Money (Royal Shakespeare Co.), The Pope's Wedding (Time Out's Fringe Award, best newcomer 1985-86; British Theatre Assc. Drama Mag. Award, Best Actor 1985).
PICTURES: Sid and Nancy (debut, 1986), Prick Up Your Ears, Track 29, We Think the World of You, Criminal Law, Chattahoochee, State of Grace, Rosencrantz and Guildenstern Are Dead, Exile, Before and After Death, JFK, Bram Stoker's Dracula, True Romance, Romeo Is Bleeding, The Professional, Immortal Beloved, Murder in the First, Dead Presidents, The Scarlet Letter, Basquiat, Air Force One, Nil by Mouth (s.p., dir., prod. only, BAFTA Award, Outstanding Brit. Film, Best Orig. Screenplay, 1997), Lost in Space, Quest for Camelot (voice), The Contender, Anasazi Moon, Hannibal, Interstate 60.
TELEVISION: Remembrance, Meantime, Honest Decent and True, Rat in the Skull, The Firm, Heading Home, Fallen Angels, Jesus (mini-series).

OLIN, KEN
Actor, Director. b. Chicago, IL, July 30, 1954. e. Univ. of PA. m. actress Patricia Wettig. Studied acting with Warren Robertson and Stella Adler. Made Off-B'way deput in Taxi Tales, 1978.
PICTURES: Ghost Story, Queen's Logic, White Fang 2: Myth of the White Wolf (dir.), 'Til There Was You.
TELEVISION: *Series*: The Bay City Blues, Hill Street Blues, Falcon Crest, thirtysomething (also dir.). *Movies* (actor): Women at West Point, Flight 90: Disaster on the Potomac, There Must Be a Pony, Tonight's the Night, Cop Killer, A Stoning in Fulham County, Goodnight Sweet Wife: A Murder in Boston, Telling Secrets, Nothing But the Truth. *Movies (director)*: The Broken Cord, Doing Time on Maple Drive, In Pursuit of Honor. *Guest*: Murder She Wrote, Hotel, The Hitchhiker.

OLIN, LENA
Actress. b. Stockholm, Sweden, 1955. Member of the Royal Dramatic Theatre in Stockholm. Daughter of actor-director Stig Olin. m. director Lasse Hallstrom.
THEATER: *NY*: Miss Julie.
PICTURES: The Adventures of Picasso, Karleken, Fanny and Alexander, Grasanklingar, After the Rehearsal, A Matter of Life and Death, Friends, The Unbearable Lightness of Being, S/Y Joy (Gladjen), Enemies a Love Story (Acad. Award nom.), Havana, Mr. Jones, Romeo Is Bleeding, The Night and the Moment, Night Falls on Manhattan, Polish Wedding, Hamilton, Mystery Men, The Ninth Gate.

OLMI, ERMANNO
Director, Writer, Producer, Editor. b. Bergamo, Italy, July 24, 1931. e. Accademia d'Arte Drammatica, Milan. Worked as a clerk for an electric company Edisonvolta 1949-52, until 1952 when he began directing theatrical and cinematic activities sponsored by co. 1952-61, directed or supervised over 40 short 16mm and 35mm documentary films. 1959 first feature film, semi-doc. Time Stood Still. With other friends and Tullio Kezich formed prod. co., 22 December S.P.A., 1961. 1982, Helped found Hypothesis Cinema, a sch. for aspiring dirs.
PICTURES: *Director/Writer*: Time Stood Still (debut, 1959), The Sound of Trumpets, The Fiances (also prod.), And There Came a Man (A Man Named John), One Fine Day (also edit.), The Tree of the Wood Clogs (Cannes Film Fest. Award, 1978; also photog., edit.), Camminacammina (also photog., edit., design), Milano '83 (also photog., edit.), Long Live the Lady (also co-photog., edit.), Legend of the Holy Drinker (also edit.), Il Segreto Del Bosco Vecchio. Documenatries: Artigiani Veneti, Lungo Il Fiume, The Secret of the Old Woods.
TELEVISION: The Scavengers (also photog.), During the Summer (also photog., edit.), The Circumstance (also photog., edit.), Genesis: The Creation & the Flood.

OLMOS, EDWARD JAMES
Actor. b. East Los Angeles, CA, February 24, 1947. e. East Los Angeles City Coll., CA State U. m. actress Lorraine Bracco. Started as rock singer with group Eddie James and the Pacific Ocean. By the early 1970s acted in small roles on Kojak and Hawaii Five-O. 1978 starred in Luis Valdez's musical drama Zoot Suit at Mark Taper Forum (L.A. Drama Critics Circle Award, 1978), later on B'way (Theatre World Award, Tony nom.), and in film version. Formed YOY Productions with director Robert Young. Numerous awards for humanitarian work.
PICTURES: Aloha Bobby and Rose (debut, 1975), Alambrista!, Virus, Wolfen, Zoot Suit, Blade Runner, The Ballad of Gregorio Cortez (also assoc. prod., composer and musical adaptor), Saving Grace, Stand and Deliver (Acad. Award nom.; also co-prod.), Triumph of the Spirit, Talent for the Game, American Me (also dir., co-prod.), A Million to Juan, Mirage, My Family/Mi Familia, Roosters, Caught, Selena, The Wonderful Ice Cream Suit.
TELEVISION: *Movies*: Evening in Byzantium, 300 Miles for Stephanie, Menendez: A Killing in Beverly Hills, The Burning Season, The Taking of Pelham One Two Three, Bonanno: A Godfather's Story. *Specials*: Sequin, Y.E.S. Inc, The Story of Fathers & Sons. *Series*: Miami Vice (Golden Globe & Emmy Awards, 1985; also dir. episodes). *Mini-series*: Mario Puzo's The Fortunate Pilgrim.

O'LOUGHLIN, GERALD STUART
Actor. b. New York, NY, Dec. 23, 1921. e. Lafayette Col., U. of Rochester, Neighborhood Playhouse. U.S. Marine, WWII.
THEATER: *B'way*: Streetcar (ANTA series), Shadow of a Gunman, Dark at the Top of the Stairs, A Touch of the Poet, Cook for Mr. General, One Flew Over the Cuckoo's Nest, Calculated Risk, Lovers and Other Strangers. *Off-B'way:* Who'll Save the Plowboy (Obie Award), Harry Noon and Night, Machinal.
PICTURES: Lovers and Lollipops, Cop Hater, A Hatful of Rain, Ensign Pulver, A Fine Madness, In Cold Blood, Ice Station Zebra, Desperate Characters, The Organization, The Valachi Papers, Twilight's Last Gleaming, Frances, Crimes of Passion, City Heat, Quicksilver. Audio narration, The Secret Kingdom.
TELEVISION: *Movies*: The D.A.: Murder One, Murder at the World Series, Something for Joey, A Love Affair: The Eleanor and Lou Gehrig Story, Crash of Flight 401, Detour to Terror, Pleasure Palace, A Matter of Life and Death, Under Siege, Perry Mason: The Case of the Notorious Nun, Child's Cry, In the Arms of a Killer, The Crime of the Century. *Mini-Series*: Wheels, Roots: The Next Generations, Blind Ambition, Women in White, The Blue and the Gray. *Series*: The Storefront Lawyers (Men at Law), The Rookies, Automan, Our House. *Guest*: Alcoa Premiere, Philco-Goodyear, Suspense, The Defenders, Ben Casey, Dr. Kildare, 12 O'Clock High, Going My Way, Naked City, Gunsmoke, Green Hornet, Mission Impossible, Mannix, Judd For The Defense, Hawaii 5-0, Cannon, Room 222, Charlie's Angels, M*A*S*H, Trapper John M.D., Fame, T.J. Hooker, Murder She Wrote, Highway to Heaven, Dirty Dancing, Equal Justice, ER.

OLSON, DALE C.
Executive. b. Fargo, ND, Feb. 20, 1934. e. Portland State Coll., OR. Owner, Dale C. Olson & Associates; formerly sn. v.p. & pres., m.p. div., Rogers & Cowan public relations. Journalist on Oregonian newspaper, West Coast editor, Boxoffice Magazine, 1958-60; critic and reporter, Daily Variety, 1960-66; dir. of publ., Mirisch Corp., 1966-68; Rogers & Cowan, 1968-85. Past pres., Hollywood Press Club, awarded Bob Yaeger and Les Mason award by Publicists Guild; v.p. Diamond Circle, City of Hope; delegate for U.S. to Manila International Film Festival. Chmn. public rltns. coordin. committee & member nat'l bd. of trustees, A.M.P.A.S., 1989-91. Chmn. Western Council, Actors Fund of America, 1991. On Nat'l Bd. of Trustees, 1992-present.

OLSON, JAMES
Actor. b. Evanston, IL, Oct. 8, 1930. e. Northwestern U.
THEATER: *NY*: The Young and the Beautiful, Romulus, The Chinese Prime Minister, J.B., Slapstick Tragedy, Three Sisters, Sin of Pat Muldoon, Winter's Tale, Of Love Remembered, Twelve Dreams.
PICTURES: The Sharkfighters, The Strange One, Rachel Rachel, Moon Zero Two, The Andromeda Strain, The Groundstar Conspiracy, The Mafu Cage, Ragtime, Amityville II: The Possession, Commando, Rachel River.
TELEVISION: *Movies*: Paper Man, Incident on a Dark Street, Manhunter, A Tree Grows in Brooklyn, The Sex Symbol, The Family Nobody Wanted, Someone I Touched, Man on the Outside, Strange New World, Law and Order, The Spell, Moviola: The Silent Years, Cave-In!, The Parade. *Specials*: Missiles of October, Vince Lombardi Story, Court-Martial of Geoge Armstrong Custer.

OLSON, NANCY
Actress. b. Milwaukee, WI, July 14, 1929. e. U. of Wisconsin, UCLA. No prof. experience prior to films.
PICTURES: Canadian Pacific (debut, 1949), Sunset Boulevard (Acad. Award nom.), Union Station, Mr. Music, Submarine Command, Force of Arms, Big Jim McLain, So Big, The Boy From Oklahoma, Battle Cry, Pollyanna, The Absent-Minded Professor, Son of Flubber, Smith!, Snowball Express, Airport 1975, Making Love.
TELEVISION: *Series*: Kingston: Confidential, Paper Dolls. *Special*: High Tor.

OLYPHANT, TIMOTHY
Actor. b. Hawaii, May 20, 1968.
PICTURES: The First Wives Club, A Life Less Ordinary, Scream 2, 1999, No Vacancy, Go.
TELEVISION: *Movies:* When Trumphets Fade. *Guest:* High Incident, Mr. & Mrs. Smith, Sex and the City.

O'NEAL, RON
Actor. b. Utica, NY, Sept. 1, 1937. e. Ohio State U. Spent 9 yrs. at Karamu House in Cleveland (inter-racial theatre) from 1957 to 1966, acting in 40 plays. 1967-68 spent in N.Y. teaching acting in Harlem. Appeared in all-black revue 1968, The Best of Broadway, then in summer stock. Acted off-B'way in American Pastorale and The Mummer's Play. 1970 joined the Public Theatre. Break came with No Place To Be Somebody, which won him the Obie, Clarence Derwent, Drama Desk and Theatre World Awards.
THEATER: Tiny Alice, The Dream of Monkey Mountain.
PICTURES: Move (debut, 1970), The Organization, Super Fly, Super Fly TNT (also dir., co-story), The Master Gunfighter, Brothers, A Force of One, When a Stranger Calls, The Final Countdown, St. Helens, Red Dawn, Mercenary Fighters, Hero and the Terror, Up Against the Wall (also dir.), Death House.
TELEVISION: *Series*: Bring 'em Back Alive, The Equalizer. *Mini-Series*: North and South. *Movies*: Freedom Road, Brave New World, Guyana Tragedy: The Story of Jim Jones, Sophisticated Gents, Playing with Fire, North Beach and Rawhide, As Summers Die.

O'NEAL, RYAN
Actor. r.n. Patrick Ryan O'Neal. b. Los Angeles, CA, April 20, 1941. Parents, screenwriter-novelist, Charles O'Neal, and actress Patricia Callaghan. Daughter is actress Tatum O'Neal; son is actor Griffin O'Neal. Boxer, L.A. Golden Gloves, 1956-57. Began career as stand-in, stunt man, then actor in Tales of the Vikings series, in Germany, 1959; freelanced in Hollywood.
PICTURES: The Big Bounce (debut, 1969), The Games, Love Story (Acad. Award nom.), Wild Rovers, What's Up Doc?, Paper Moon, The Thief Who Came to Dinner, Barry Lyndon, Nickelodeon, A Bridge Too Far, The Driver, Oliver's Story, The Main Event, So Fine, Green Ice, Partners, Irreconcilable Differences, Fever Pitch, Tough Guys Don't Dance, Chances Are, Faithful, Hacks, An Alan Smithee Film: Burn Hollywood Burn, Zero Effect, Coming Soon.
TELEVISION: *Series*: Empire, Peyton Place, Good Sports. *Movies*: Love Hate Love, Small Sacrifices, The Man Upstairs. *Special*: Liza Minnelli: A Triple Play. *Guest*: Dobie Gillis, Bachelor Father, Leave It to Beaver, My Three Sons, Perry Mason, The Larry Sanders Show. *Pilot*: 1775.

O'NEAL, TATUM
Actress. b. Los Angeles, CA, Nov. 5, 1963. p. actors Ryan O'Neal and Joanna Moore. NY stage debut 1992 in A Terrible Beauty, followed by Adroscoggin Fugue.
PICTURES: Paper Moon (debut, 1973; Academy Award, best supporting actress), The Bad News Bears, Nickelodeon, International Velvet, Little Darlings, Circle of Two, Certain Fury, Little Noises, Basquiat.
TELEVISION: *Movie*: Woman on the Run: The Lawrencia Bembenek Story. *Special*: 15 and Getting Straight. *Guest*: Cher, Faerie Tale Theatre (Goldilocks and the Three Bears).

O'NEILL, ED
Actor. b. Youngstown, OH, Apr. 12, 1946. e. Ohio Univ., Youngstown State. Taught social studies in Youngstown prior to becoming an actor. Made NY stage debut Off-Off-B'way in Requiem for a Heavyweight at SoHo Rep. Theatre. B'way debut in Knockout.
PICTURES: Deliverance, Cruising, The Dogs of War, Disorganized Crime, K-9, The Adventures of Ford Fairlane, Sibling Rivalry, Dutch, Wayne's World, Wayne's World 2, Blue Chips, Little Giants, Prefontaine, The Spanish Prisoner, The Bone Collector.
TELEVISION: *Series*: Married... With Children. *Pilot*: Farrell for the People. *Movies*: When Your Lover Leaves, The Day the Women Got Even, Popeye Doyle, A Winner Never Quits, Right to Die, Police School, The Whereabouts of Jenny, W.E.I.R.D. World, The Tenth Kingdom.

O'NEILL, JENNIFER
Actress. b. Rio de Janeiro, Brazil, Feb. 20, 1949. e. Dalton Sch. Model before entering films. Spokeswoman: CoverGirl cosmetics. Pres., Point of View Productions and Management.
PICTURES: Rio Lobo, Summer of '42, Such Good Friends, The Carey Treatment, Glass Houses, Lady Ice, The Reincarnation of Peter Proud, Whiffs, Caravans, The Psychic, The Innocent, A Force of One, Cloud Dancer, Steel, Scanners, Committed, I Love N.Y., Love is Like That, Invasion of Privacy, The Gentle People, Discretion Assured, The Corporate Ladder.
TELEVISION: *Series*: Bare Essence, Cover Up. *Movies*: Love's Savage Fury, The Other Victim, An Invasion of Privacy, Chase, Perry Mason: The Case of the Shooting Star, The Red Spider, Glory Days, Full Exposure: The Sex Tapes Scandal, Personals, Perfect Family, The Cover Girl Murders, Frame-up, Jonathan Stone: Threat of Innocence, Silver Strand. *Mini-Series*: A.D.

ONTKEAN, MICHAEL
Actor. b. Vancouver, British Columbia, Canada, Jan. 24, 1946. e. U. of New Hampshire. Son of Leonard and Muriel Cooper Ontkean, actors. Acting debut at 4 with father's rep. theater. Child actor with Stratford Shakespeare Fest., CBC and Natl Film Bd. Attended coll. 4 years on hockey scholarship. Has performed with Public Theatre, NY, Willamstown Theatre Fest., Mark Taper Lab, The Kitchen, Soho.
PICTURES: The Peace Killers (debut, 1971), Pick Up on 101, Necromancy, Hot Summer Week, Slap Shot, Voices, Willie and Phil, Making Love, Just the Way You Are, The Allnighter, Maid to Order, Clara's Heart, Street Justice, Cold Front, Bye Bye Blues, Postcards From the Edge, Bayou Boy, The Toy Factory, Summer, Access All Areas, Le Sang des Autres, Cutting Loose, Square Deal, Rapture.
TELEVISION: *Series*: The Rookies, Twin Peaks. *Movies*: The Rookies (pilot), The Blood of Others, Kids Don't Tell, The Right of the People, Twin Peaks (pilot), Defense of a Married Man, In a Child's Name, Legacy of Lies, Whose Child Is This? The War for Baby Jessica, Vendetta 2: The New Mafia, Danielle Steel's Family Album, The Man Next Door, Man From the South.

OPHULS, MARCEL
Director, Writer. r.n. Hans Marcel Oppenheimer. b. Frankfurt-am-Main, Germany, Nov. 1, 1927. Son of German director Max Ophuls. e. Occidental Coll., U. of California, Berkeley, Sorbonne (philosophy). Family moved to France, 1932, then to Hollywood, 1941. Military service with Occupation forces in Japan, 1946; performed with theater unit, Tokyo. 1951 began working in French film industry as asst. dir., using name Marcel Wall. Asst. dir. on Moulin Rouge, Act of Love, Marianne de ma Jeunesse, Lola Montes. 1956-59, radio and TV story ed., West Germany. Later worked for French TV as reporter and dir. news mag. features. Dir. & wrote short film Henri Matisse. 1968 doc. dir. for German TV. 1975-78 staff prod. CBS News, then ABC News. MacArthur Fellowship 1991. Member of AMPAS.
PICTURES: *Director/Writer*: Love at 20 (dir. segment), Banana Peel, Fire at Will, Munich or Peace in Our Time, The Sorrow and the Pity (also prod.; Natl. Soc. of Film Critics, NY Film Critics & Prix de Dinard Awards, 1970), The Harvest at Mai Lai, A Sense of Loss, The Memory of Justice, Hotel Terminus--The Life and Times of Klaus Barbie (also prod.; Academy Award, Berlin Peace Prize, Cannes Jury Prize, 1988), The Troubles We've Seen (also prod., Intl. Film Critics Prize, 1994).
TELEVISION: America Revisited, Two Whole Days, November Days.

OPOTOWSKY, STAN
Executive. b. New Orleans, LA, Apr. 13, 1923. e. Tulane U. Served in U.S. Marine Corps as combat corr. and later joined United Press, working in New Orleans, Denver, and New York. Published own weekly newspaper in Mississippi before returning to N.Y. to join New York Post as mgr. editor and traveling natl. corr. Is also cinematographer and film editor. Joined ABC News as TV assignment editor; named asst. assignment mgr. 1974 named dir. of operations for ABC News TV Documentaries. 1975 named dir. of TV News Coverage, ABC News.
TELEVISION: *Author*: The Big Picture, The Longs of Louisiana, The Kennedy Government, Men Behind Bars.

O'QUINN, TERRY
Actor. b. Michigan.
THEATER: *B'way*: Foxfire, Curse of an Aching Heart. *Off-B'way:* Richard III, Groves of Academy, Total Abandon. *Regional*: Streamers, Measure for Measure, The Front Page.
PICTURES: Heaven's Gate, Without a Trace, All the Right Moves, Places in the Heart, Mrs. Soffel, Mischief, Silver Bullet, SpaceCamp, The Stepfather, Black Widow, Young Guns, Pin, Stepfather 2, Blind Fury, The Rocketeer, Prisoners of the Sun, Company Business, The Cutting Edge, Amityville: A New Generation, Tombstone, Lipstick Camera.
TELEVISION: *Movies*: FDR: The Final Year, Prisoner Without a Name Cell Without a Number, Right to Kill, Unfinished Business, An Early Frost, Stranger on My Land, Women of Valor, When the Time Comes, Perry Mason: The Case of the Desperate Deception, Son of the Morning Star, The Last to Go, Deliver Them From Evil: The Taking of Alta View, Trial: The Price of Passion, Sexual Advances, Wild Card, The Good Fight, Born Too Soon, Visions of Murder, Heart of a Child, Don't Talk to Strangers, Justice in a Small Town, A Friend to Die For, Ray Alexander: A Menu for Murder.

ORBACH, JERRY
Actor. b. Bronx, NY, Oct. 20, 1935. e. U. of Illinois, Northwestern U. Trained for stage with Herbert Berghof and Lee Strasberg. N.Y. stage debut in Threepenny Opera, 1955.
THEATER: The Fantasticks (original cast, 1960), Carnival, The Cradle Will Rock, Guys and Dolls, Scuba Duba, Promises Promises (Tony Award, 1969), 6 Rms Riv Vu, Chicago, 42nd Street.
PICTURES: Cop Hater, Mad Dog Coll, John Goldfarb Please Come Home, The Gang That Couldn't Shoot Straight, A Fan's Notes, Foreplay (The President's Woman), The Sentinel, Underground Aces, Prince of the City, Brewster's Millions, F/X, The Imagemaker, Dirty Dancing, Someone to Watch Over Me, Crimes and Misdemeanors, Last Exit to Brooklyn, I Love N.Y., A Gnome Named Norm, California Casanova, Dead Women in Lingerie, Out for Justice, Toy Soldiers (cameo), Delusion, Delirious, Beauty and the Beast (voice), Straight Talk, Universal Soldier, Mr. Saturday Night, The Cemetery Club.
TELEVISION: *Series*: The Law and Harry McGraw, Law and Order. *Guest*: Shari Lewis Show, Jack Paar, Bob Hope Presents, Love American Style, Murder She Wrote, Kojak, Golden Girls, Hunter. *Movies*: An Invasion of Privacy, Out on a Limb, Love Among Thieves, In Defense of a Married Man, Broadway Bound, Quiet Killer. *Mini-Series*: Dream West.

ORMOND, JULIA
Actress. b. England, 1965. Studied acting at Webber Douglas Acad., London.
THEATER: The Rehearsal, Wuthering Heights, Arms and the Man, The Crucible, Faith Hope and Charity (London Drama Critics Award, 1989).
PICTURES: The Baby of Macon, Nostradamus, Legends of the Fall, First Knight, Captives, Sabrina, Smilla's Sense of Snow, The Barber of Siberia, The Prime Gig.
TELEVISION: *Mini-Series:* Traffik. *Movies:* Young Catherine, Stalin, Animal Farm (voice), Varian's War.

ORTEGA, KENNY
Director, Choreographer. b. Palo Alto, CA. e. American Conserv. Theatre, Canada Coll. Started acting at age 13. Earned several scholarships to dance academies in San Francisco Bay area. Regional theatre roles in Oliver, Hair, The Last Sweet Days of Isaac, before staging shows for rock band The Tubes. First major tv job choreographing Cher special. Directed/choreographed concerts and/or music videos for such performers as Michael Jackson, Kiss, Elton John, Cher, Rod Stewart, Diana Ross, Madonna, Billy Joel, Oingo Boingo, Miami Sound Machine, Pointer Sisters, Toto. Artistic dir. and choreographer, 1996 Centennial Olympic Games opening and closing ceremonies.
PICTURES: *Director/Choreographer*: Newsies, Hocus Pocus. *Choreographer*: Quest for Camelot, Ferris Bueller's Day Off, To Wong Foo–Thanks for Everything–Julie Newmar, Dirty Dancing, Road House, Shag, The Great Outdoors, Lost Boys, Pretty in Pink, Salsa, God Created Woman, One from the Heart, St. Elmo's Fire, Xanadu, The Rose.
TELEVISION: *Series Director*: Dirty Dancing (also choreog.), Hull Street High, Chicago Hope (also choreog.), Fame L.A., McKenna, Second Noah. *Choreographer*: American Music Awards, Academy Awards, NAACP Awards, 1996 Olympics, Mickey's 60th Birthday, Totally Mine, America Picks the #1 Hit, Nosotros Awards, Good Time Rock 'n' Roll, Jump. *Specials Choreographer*: Olivia Newton-John, Cher, The Pointer Sisters, Neil Diamond, Smokey Robinson, Cheryl Ladd.

O'SHEA, MILO
Actor. b. Dublin, Ireland, June 2, 1926. Member of Dublin Gate Theatre Co., 1944, before screen career.
THEATER: *NY*: Staircase, Dear World, The Comedians, A Touch of the Poet, Waiting For Godot (Brooklyn Acad. of Music), Mass Appeal, My Fair Lady, Corpse!, Meet Me in St. Louis, Remembrance (Off-B'way), Philadelphia Here I Come!, Alive Alive Oh! (alo co-writer), Mrs. Warren's Profession. *London*: Treasure Hunt, Glory Be, Hans Andersen, Corpse, Can-Can.
PICTURES: Carry on Cabby, Never Put It in Writing, Ulysses, Romeo and Juliet, Barbarella, The Adding Machine, The Angel Levine, Paddy, Sacco and Vanzetti, Loot, Theatre of Blood, Digby: The Biggest Dog in the World, It's Not the Size That Counts, Arabian Adventure, The Pilot, The Verdict, The Purple Rose of Cairo, The Dream Team, Opportunity Knocks, Only the Lonely, The Playboys, Rooney, Never Put It In Writing, The Butcher Boy.
TELEVISION: *Series*: Once a Hero, Frasier. *Mini-Series*: QB VII, Ellis Island, The Best of Families. *Movies/Specials*: Two By Forsythe, Peter Lundy and the Medicine Hat Stallion, Portrait of a Rebel: Margaret Sanger, And No One Could Save Her, A Times for Miracles, Broken Vows, Angel in Green, Murder in the Heartland. *Guest*: The Golden Girls, Cheers, Who's the Boss, Beauty and the Beast, St. Elsewhere.

OSHIMA, NAGISA
Director, Writer. b. Kyoto, Japan, March 31, 1932. e. U. of Kyoto (law), 1954. Joined Shochiku Ofuna Studios in 1954 as asst. dir.; 1956 wrote film criticism and became editor-in-chief of film revue Eiga hihyo; 1959 promoted to director. 1962-65 worked exclusively in TV; 1962-64 made documentaries in Korea and Vietnam; 1975 formed Oshima Prods. 1976, his book of Realm of the Senses seized by police. With editor, prosecuted for obscenity, acquitted. Pres. of Directors Guild of Japan, 1980-present.
PICTURES: *Dir./Writer*: A Town of Love and Hope (debut, 1959), Cruel Story of Youth, The Sun's Burial, Night and Fog in Japan, The Catch (dir. only), The Christian Rebel, A Child's First Adventure, I'm Here Bellett, The Pleasures of the Flesh, Violence at Noon (dir. only), Band of Ninja (also co-prod.), Sing a Song of Sex (also co- prod.), Japanese Summer: Double Suicide (also co-prod.), Death By Hanging, Three Resurrected Drunkards, Diary of a Shinjuku Thief, Boy (dir. only), He Died After the War, The Ceremony, Dear Summer Sister, In the Realm of the Senses, Phantom Love, Empire of Passion (also co-prod.), Merry Christmas Mr. Lawrence, Max My Love.

OSMENT, HALEY JOEL
Actor. b. Los Angeles, CA, April 10, 1988.
PICTURES: Forrest Gump, Mixed Nuts, Bogus, For Better or Worse, The Sixth Sense, I'll Remember April, Discover Spot (voice), Pay It Forward, Edwurd Fudwupper Fibbed Big (voice), A.I., The Hunchback of Notre Dame II (voice), Edges of the Lord.
TELEVISION: *Series:* Thunder Alley, The Jeff Foxworthy Show, Murphy Brown. *Movies:* Lies of the Heart: The Story of Laurie Kellog, Beauty and the Beast: The Enchanted Christmas (voice), The Ransom of Red Chief, Cab to Canada. *Guest:* The Larry Sanders Show, Touched By An Angel, The Pretender, Alley McBeal, Walker, Texas Ranger, Chicago Hope.

OSMOND, DONNY
Singer, TV Host. b. Ogden, UT, Dec. 9, 1957. Seventh of 9 children, he was fifth member of family to become professional singer. (Four brothers: Alan, Wayne, Merrill and Jay, were original members of Osmond Bros., who originally sang barbershop quartet.) Made debut at 4 on Andy Williams Show. Has had 12 gold albums. Was co-host with sister of Donny & Marie on TV.
THEATER: Little Johnny Jones, Joseph and the Amazing Technicolor Dreamcoat.
PICTURE: Goin' Coconuts, Mulan (voice).
TELEVISION: *Series*: The Andy Williams Show, Donny and Marie. *Movie*: The Wild Women of Chastity Gulch. *Guest*: The Jerry Lewis Show, Here's Lucy, The Love Boat.

OSMOND, MARIE
Singer, TV Host. b. Ogden, UT, Oct. 13, 1959. Began career at age of 3 on Andy Williams Show. Her first album, Paper Roses went gold. Appeared with brother Donny in feature film Goin' Coconuts.
TELEVISION: *Series*: Donny and Marie, Marie, Ripley's Believe It or Not (co-host), Maybe This Time. *Movies*: Gift of Love, I Married Wyatt Earp, Side By Side.

O'STEEN, SAM
Editor, Director. b. Nov. 6, 1923. Entered m.p. industry 1956 as asst. to editor George Tomassini on The Wrong Man. Became full editor in 1963 on Youngblood Hawke. Directorial debut with TV film A Brand New Life, 1972.
PICTURES: Youngblood Hawke, Kisses for My President, Robin and the 7 Hoods, Marriage on the Rocks, None But the Brave, Who's Afraid of Virginia Woolf?, Cool Hand Luke, The Graduate, Rosemary's Baby, The Sterile Cuckoo (spv. edit.), Catch-22, Carnal Knowledge, Portnoy's Complaint, The Day of the Dolphin, Chinatown, Sparkle (dir.), Straight Time, Hurricane, Amityville II: The Possession, Silkwood, Heartburn, Nadine, Biloxi Blues, Frantic, Working Girl, A Dry White Season (co-edit.), Postcards from the Edge, Regarding Henry, Wolf.
TELEVISION: *Director*: A Brand New Life, I Love You Goodbye, Queen of the Stardust Ballroom (DGA Award), High Risk, Look What's Happened to Rosemary's Baby, The Best Little Girl in the World, Kids Don't Tell.

O'SULLIVAN, KEVIN P.
Executive. b. New York, NY, April 13, 1928. e. Queens Coll., Flushing, NY. Associated with television 40 yrs., initially as a talent; later as businessman. Won first prize in Arthur Godfrey Talent Scouts competition in 1948. 1950-55 professional singer, actor on TV, in theatre, night clubs. 1955-57 on radio-TV promotion staff, Ronson Corp. 1958-61, salesman, Television Programs of America. 1961-67 dir. of program services, Harrington, Righter and Parsons. 1967 joined ABC Films, domestic sales div. as v.p. & gen. sales mgr. 1969 named v.p., gen. mgr. then pres., ABC Films, Inc.; 1970 made pres., ABC Int'l. TV, while retaining position as pres., ABC Films. 1973 became pres., COO, Worldvision Enterprises, Inc., co. formed to succeed ABC Films when FCC stopped networks from TV program dist. Elected chmn. & CEO, Worldvision, 1982. Named pres., Great American Broadcasting Group, 1987. Resigned, 1988. Named pres., Kenmare Prods. Inc., 1988.

O'TOOLE, ANNETTE
Actress. b. Houston, TX, April 1, 1953. e. UCLA.
PICTURES: Smile (debut, 1975), One on One, King of the Gypsies, Foolin' Around, Cat People, 48 HRS, Superman III, Cross My Heart, Love at Large, Andre (voice), Imaginary Crimes.
TELEVISION: *Movies*: The Girl Most Likely To..., The Entertainer, The War Between the Tates, Love For Rent, Stand By Your Man, Copacabana, Arthur Hailey's Strong Medicine, Broken Vows, Stephen King's It, The Dreamer of Oz, White Lies, Kiss of a Killer, Love Matters, A Mother's Revenge, My Brother's Keeper. *Mini-Series*: The Kennedys of Massachusetts. *Specials*: Vanities, Best Legs in the Eighth Grade, Secret World of the Very Young, Unpublished Letters, On Hope.

O'TOOLE, PETER
Actor. b. Connemara, Ireland, Aug. 2, 1932. Studied at Royal Acad. of Dramatic Art. Early career with Bristol Old Vic. Partner with Jules Buck, Keep Films, Ltd. Autobiography: Loitering With Intent (1993).
THEATER: *London*: Major Barbara, Oh My Papa, The Long the Short and the Tall, Baal, Hamlet, Ride a Cock Horse, Macbeth, Man and Superman, Jeffrey Bernard is Unwell, Our Song. 1960, with the Stratford-on-Avon Company (The Taming of the Shrew, Merchant of Venice, etc). *Dublin*: Arms and the Man, Waiting for Godot. *Toronto*: Present Laughter, Uncle Vanya. B'way debut 1987: Pygmalion.
PICTURES: Kidnapped (debut, 1959), The Savage Innocents, The Day They Robbed the Bank of England, Lawrence of Arabia, Becket, Lord Jim, What's New Pussycat?, The Bible, How to Steal a Million, The Night of the Generals, Casino Royale (cameo), Great Catherine, The Lion in Winter, Goodbye Mr. Chips, Brotherly Love (Country Dance), Murphy's War, Under Milk Wood, The Ruling Class, Man of La Mancha, Rosebud, Man Friday, Foxtrot, Caligula, Power Play, Zulu Dawn, The Stunt Man, My Favorite Year, Supergirl, Creator, Club Paradise, The Last Emperor, High Spirits, On a Moonlit Night, Helena, Wings of Fame, The Nutcracker Prince (voice), The Rainbow Thief, Isabelle Eberhardt, King Ralph, Rebecca's Daughters, The Seventh Coin, FairyTale: A True Story, Phantoms, The Manor, Molokai: The Story of Father Damien.
TELEVISION: *Movies*: Rogue Male (BBC), Svengali, Kim, Crossing to Freedom, Civvies, Gulliver's Travels, Coming Home. *Specials*: Present Laughter, Pygmalion, The Dark Angel. *Series*: Strumpet City (BBC), Heavy Weather. *Mini-Series*: Masada, Heaven & Hell: North and South Book III, Joan of Arc.

OTWELL, RONNIE RAY
Theatre Executive. b. Carrollton, GA, Aug. 13, 1929. e. Georgia Inst. of Technology. Entered industry as mgr., Bremen Theatre, GA, 1950; dir. pub., adv., Martin Theatres, Columbus, GA, 1950-63; v.p., dir. Martin Theatres of Ga., Inc., 1963, Martin Theatres of Ala., Inc., 1963; dir. Martin Theatres of Columbus, 1963; sr. v.p., Martin Theatres Companies, 1971.

OVERALL, PARK
Actress. b. Nashville, TN, March 15, 1957. Attended British boarding school, earned teaching degree, before turning to acting.
THEATER: *NY*: Biloxi Blues, Wild Blue, Only You, Loose Ends, Something About Baseball, Marathon '88.
PICTURES: Body Passion, Biloxi Blues, Mississippi Burning, Talk Radio (voice), Lost Angels, Kindergarten Cop, The Vanishing, House of Cards, Undercover Blues.
TELEVISION: *Series*: Empty Nest. *Movies*: Luck of the Draw: The Gambler Returns, Overkill: The Aileen Wuornos Story, Precious Victims, The Good Old Boys. *Pilot*: The Line.

OVITZ, MICHAEL
Talent Agent, Executive. b. Chicago, IL, Dec. 14, 1946. e. UCLA, 1968. Began ent. career as a tour guide at Universal Studios. Started as a trainee at William Morris Agency before becoming agent, 1969-75. Co-founder of Creative Artists Agency, 1975; became chmn. and chief stock holder. 1995 named pres. The Walt Disney Company; resigned from The Walt Disney Company, Jan. 1997. Co-founder of Artists Management Group, 1999.
Member: Bd. of Dir. Gulfstream Aerospace Corp., Bd. of Dir. J. Crew Inc., Bd. of Dir. Livent Inc., Bd. of Dir. of D.A.R.E. America, National Bd. of Advisors for the Children's Scholarship Fund, Bd. of Advisors at the UCLA School of Theater Film and Television. Also serves on the Exec. Advisory Bd. of the Pediatric Aids Foundations.

OWENSBY, EARL
Producer, Actor. b. North Carolina, 1935. Set up his own studio in Shelby, NC. Built new studio in Gaffney, SC, 1985.
PICTURES: Challenge, Dark Sunday, Buckstone County Prison, Frank Challenge—Manhunter, Death Driver, Wolfman, Seabo, Day of Judgment, Living Legend, Lady Grey, Rottweiler, Last Game, Hyperspace, Hit the Road Running, Rutherford County Line.

OXENBERG, CATHERINE
Actress. b. NY, NY, Sept. 21, 1961. Daughter of the exiled Princess Elizabeth of Yugoslavia, raised among intl. jet set with Richard Burton acting as her tutor. Modeled before making TV debut in The Royal Romance of Charles and Diana (1982).
PICTURES: The Lair of the White Worm, The Return of the Musketeers.
TELEVISION: *Series*: Dynasty, Acapulco H.E.A.T. *Movies*: The Royal Romance of Charles and Diana, Roman Holiday, Swimsuit, Trenchcoat in Paradise, Ring of Scorpio, K-9000, Charles & Diana: Unhappily Ever After, Rubdown, Treacherous Beauties.

OZ, FRANK
Puppeteer, Director, Performer. r.n. Frank Oznowicz. b. Hereford, England, May 25, 1944. Gained fame as creator and performer of various characters on Sesame Street and the Muppet Show (Fozzie Bear, Miss Piggy, Animal, Cookie Monster, Grover and Bert). V.P., Jim Henson Prods.
PICTURES: *Performer*: The Muppet Movie, The Blues Brothers, Star Wars: Episode V-The Empire Strikes Back, The Great Muppet Caper (also prod.), An American Werewolf in London, The Dark Crystal (also co-dir.), Star Wars: Episode VI-Return of the Jedi, Trading Places, The Muppets Take Manhattan (also dir., co-s.p.), Spies Like Us, Labyrinth, Innocent Blood, The Muppet Christmas Carol (also exec. prod.), Muppet Treasure Island (voice), Blues Brothers 2000, Star Wars: Episode I-The Phantom Menace (voice), Muppets from Space (voice), The Adventures of Elmo in Grouchland (voice). *Director only*: Little Shop of Horrors, Dirty Rotten Scoundrels, What About Bob?, Housesitter, The Indian in the Cupboard, In & Out, Bowfinger, Ump, The Score.
TELEVISION: *Series*: Sesame Street (3 Emmy Awards), The Muppet Show (Emmy Award, 1978), Saturday Night Live; various variety shows.

P

PAAR, JACK
Actor. b. Canton, OH, May 1, 1918. Radio announcer in Cleveland, Buffalo; served in U.S. Armed Forces, WWII; entertained in Pacific zone with 28th Special Service Div. On radio with own show, then quiz show Take It or Leave It. First host of The Tonight Show; various specials.
AUTHOR: I Kid You Not, My Sabre Is Bent, Three on a Toothbrush, P.S. Jack Paar.
PICTURES: Variety Time (debut, 1948), Easy Living, Walk Softly Stranger, Footlight Varieties, Love Nest, Down Among the Sheltering Palms.
TELEVISION: Series: Up to Paar (emcee, 1952), Bank on the Stars (emcee, 1953), The Jack Paar Show (1954), The Morning Show (1954), The Tonight Show (retitled The Jack Paar Show: 1957-62), The Jack Paar Program (1962-65), ABC Late Night (1973). Specials: Jack Paar Diary, Jack Paar Remembers, Jack Paar Is Alive and Well (also prod.), He Kids You Not.

PACINO, AL
Actor. b. New York, NY, April 25, 1940. e. High Sch. for the Performing Arts, NY; Actors Studio, 1966; HB Studios, NY. Gained attention as stage actor initially at Charles Playhouse, Boston (Why Is a Crooked Letter, The Peace Creeps, Arturo Ui). Served as artistic dir. (with Ellen Burstyn), Actors Studio (1982-84).
THEATER: NY: The Indian Wants the Bronx (Obie Award), Does a Tiger Wear a Necktie? (Tony & Theatre World Awards, 1969), The Local Stigmatic, Camino Real, The Connection, Hello Out There, Tiger at the Gates, The Basic Training of Pavlo Hummel (Tony Award, 1977), Richard III, American Buffalo, Julius Caesar, Chinese Coffee, Salome, Hughie (also dir.).
PICTURES: Me Natalie (debut, 1969), The Panic in Needle Park, The Godfather, Scarecrow, Serpico, The Godfather Part II, Dog Day Afternoon, Bobby Deerfield, ... And Justice for All, Cruising, Author! Author!, Scarface, Revolution, Sea of Love, Dick Tracy, The Godfather Part III, Frankie and Johnny, Glengarry Glen Ross, Scent of a Woman (Acad. Award, 1992), Carlito's Way, A Day to Remember, City Hall, Heat, Two Bits, Looking for Richard (also dir.), Donnie Brasco, The Devil's Advocate, Chinese Coffee (also dir.), The Insider, Any Given Sunday, Chinese Coffee, Simone.

PACULA, JOANNA
Actress. b. Tomszowau, Poland, Jan. 2, 1957. Member of Polish National Theatre School. Model in Poland, France, then U.S. where she moved in early 1980's.
PICTURES: Gorky Park, Not Quite Paradise, Death Before Dishonor, The Kiss, Sweet Lies, Options, Marked for Death, Husbands and Lovers, Tombstone.
TELEVISION: Series: E.A.R.T.H. Force. Movies: Escape From Sobribor, Breaking Point, Not Like Us.

PAGE, ANTHONY
Director. b. Bangalore, India, Sept. 21, 1935. e. Oxford. Stage work includes Inadmissible Evidence, Waiting for Godot, A Patriot for Me, Look Back in Anger, Uncle Vanya, Mrs. Warren's Profession, Alpha Beta, Heartbreak House, Absolute Hell.
PICTURES: Inadmissible Evidence (debut, 1968), Alpha Beta, I Never Promised You a Rose Garden, Absolution, The Lady Vanishes.
TELEVISION: *Specials:* Pueblo, The Missiles of October, The Parachute, Sheppey. Movies: Collision Course, F. Scott Fitzgerald in Hollywood, FDR—The Last Year, The Patricia Neal Story, Bill, Johnny Belinda, Grace Kelly, Bill—On His Own, Murder: By Reason of Insanity, Forbidden, Monte Carlo, Second Serve, Pack of Lies, Scandal in a Small Town, The Nightmare Years, Chernobyl: The Final Warning, Absolute Hell, Guests of the Emperor, Middlemarch.

PAGE, PATTI
Performer, Recording Artist. r.n. Clara Ann Fowler. b. Claremore, OK, Nov. 8, 1927. e. U. of Tulsa. Staff performer, radio stat. KTUL, Tulsa; Top recording star of the 1950's and 60's (The Tennessee Waltz, Cross Over the Bridge, How Much is That Doggie in the Window?, etc.). Appeared on CBS radio show. Author of Once Upon a Dream.
PICTURES: Elmer Gantry (debut, 1960), Dondi, Boys' Night Out.
TELEVISION: *Series host:* Music Hall, Scott Music Hall, The Patti Page Show, The Big Record, The Patti Page Olds Show. *Guest:* Appointment With Adventure, U.S. Steel Hour, Bachelor Father.

PAGET, DEBRA
Actress. r.n. Debrahlee Griffin. b. Denver, CO, Aug. 19, 1933. e. Hollywood Prof. Sch. , also studied drama & dancing privately. Stage debut in Merry Wives of Windsor, 1946; in Jeanne D'Arc little theatre prod.
PICTURES: Cry of the City (debut, 1948), It Happens Every Spring, House of Strangers, Broken Arrow, Fourteen Hours, Bird of Paradise, Anne of the Indies, Belles on Their Toes, Les Miserables, Stars & Stripes Forever, Prince Valiant, Demetrius & the Gladiators, Princess of the Nile, Gambler from Natchez, White Feather, Seven Angry Men, Last Hunt, The Ten Commandments, Love Me Tender, The River's Edge, Omar Khayyam, From the Earth to the Moon, Why Must I Die?, Cleopatra's Daughter, Journey to the Lost City, The Most Dangerous Man Alive, Tales of Terror, The Haunted Palace.
TELEVISION: *Guest*: Steve Allen, Colgate Comedy Hour, Climax, Wagon Train, Rawhide.

PAGETT, NICOLA
Actress. r.n. Nicola Scott. b. Cairo, Egypt, June 15, 1945. e. Royal Acad. of Dramatic Art. Appeared with Citizen's Rep. Theatre, Glasgow.
THEATER: Cornelia (debut, 1964, Worthing, U.K.), A Boston Story (London debut, 1968), A Midsummer Night's Dream, Widowers' Houses, The Misanthrope, A Voyage 'Round My Father, The Ride Across Lake Constance, Ghosts, The Seagull, Hamlet, The Marriage of Figaro, A Family and a Fortune, Gaslight, Yahoo, Old Times (L.A.).
PICTURES: Anne of the Thousand Days, There's a Girl in My Soup, Operation Daybreak, Oliver's Story, Privates on Parade.
TELEVISION: *Series*: Upstairs Downstairs. *Movies*: Frankenstein: The True Story, The Sweeney, Aren't We All, A Woman of Substance (mini-series), Anna Karenina.

PAIGE, JANIS
Actress r.n. Donna Mae Jaden. b. Tacoma, WA, Sept. 16, 1923. Sang with Tacoma Opera Co. Star of Tomorrow, 1947. Album: Let's Fall in Love. Owns and operates Ipanema, Janeiro, Rio-Cali, and Dindi Music Cos.
THEATER: Pajama Game, Remains to Be Seen, Here's Love, Mame, Alone Together.
PICTURES: Hollywood Canteen (debut, 1944), Of Human Bondage, Two Gals and a Guy, The Time the Place and the Girl, Two Guys from Milwaukee, Her Kind of Man, Cheyenne, Love and Learn, Always Together, Wallflower, Winter Meeting, One Sunday Afternoon, Romance on the High Seas, House Across the Street, The Younger Brothers, Mr. Universe, Fugitive Lady, Two Guys and a Gal, Silk Stockings, Please Don't Eat the Daisies, Bachelor in Paradise, The Caretakers, Welcome to Hard Times, Love at the Top, The Dark Road (It.), Follow the Boys (Fr.), Natural Causes.
TELEVISION: *Special*: Roberta (1958 and 1969). *Series*: It's Always Jan, Lanigan's Rabbi, Gun Shy, Baby Makes Five, Trapper John M.D, Capitol, General Hospital, Santa Barbara. *Guest*: Plymouth Playhouse, Alcoa Premiere, Columbo, Banacek, Flamingo Road, St. Elsewhere. *Movies*: The Turning Point of Jim Malloy, Return of Joe Forrester, Lanigan's Rabbi (pilot), Valentine Magic on Love Island, Angel on My Shoulder, The Other Woman, No Man's Land.

PAINE, CHARLES F.
Executive. b. Cushing, TX, Dec. 23, 1920. e. Stephen F. Austin U. Pres. Tercar Theatre Company; pres., NATO of Texas, 1972-73. NATO board member, 1973 to present; Motion Picture Pioneers member; Variety Club of Texas member.

PALANCE, JACK
Actor. r.n. Vladimir Palanuik. b. Lattimer, PA, Feb. 18, 1920. e. U. of North Carolina. Professional fighter; U.S. Air Corps.
THEATER: The Big Two, Temporary Island, The Vigil, A Streetcar Named Desire, Darkness at Head.
PICTURES: Panic in the Streets (debut, 1950), Halls of Montezuma, Sudden Fear (Acad. Award nom.), Shane (Acad. Award nom.), Flight to Tangier, Arrowhead, Second Chance, Man in the Attic, Sign of the Pagan, Silver Chalice, Kiss of Fire, Big Knife, I Died a Thousand Times, Attack!, Lonely Man, House of Numbers, The Man Inside, Ten Seconds to Hell, Battle of Austerliz, Sword of the Conqueror, The Mongols, Barabbas, Warriors Five, Contempt, Once a Thief, The Professionals, Torture Garden, Kill a Dragon, The Mercenary, Deadly Sanctuary, They Came to Rob Las Vegas, The Desperados, Che, Legion of the Damned, A Bullet for Rommel, The McMasters, Monte Walsh, Companeros, The Horsemen, Chato's Land, Oklahoma Crude, Craze, The Four Deuces, The Great Adventure, The Sensuous Nurse, Portrait of a Hitman, One Man Jury, Angel's Brigade, The Shape of Things to Come, Cocaine Cowboys, Hawk the Slayer, Without Warning, Alone in the Dark, Gor, Bagdad Cafe, Young Guns, Outlaw of Gor, Batman, Tango and Cash, City Slickers (Acad. Award, best supporting actor, 1991), Solar Crisis, Cops and Robbersons, City Slickers II: The Legend of Curly's Gold, The Swan Princess (voice), Treasure Island,.
TELEVISION: *Specials*: Requiem for a Heavyweight (Emmy Award, 1957), Dr. Jekyll and Mr. Hyde, Twilight Zone: Rod Serling's Lost Classics: Where the Dead Are. *Movies*: Dracula, The Godchild, The Hatfields and the McCoys, Bronk (pilot), Last Ride of the Dalton Gang, The Ivory Ape, Golden Moment: An Olympic Love Story, Keep the Change, Buffalo Girls, Ebenezer, I'll Be Home for Christmas, Sarah Plan and Tall 3. *Series*: The Greatest Show on Earth, Bronk, Ripley's Believe It or Not (host).

PALCY, EUZHAN
Director. b. Martinique, 1957. e. Earned a degree in French lit., Sorbonne and a film degree from Vaugirard School in Paris. Began career working as TV writer and dir. in Martinique. Also made 2 children's records. In Paris worked as film editor, screenwriter and dir. of shorts. She received grant from French gov. to make 1st feature Sugar Cane Alley which cost $800,000 and won Silver Lion Prize at Venice Film Fest., 1983.
PICTURES: Sugar Cane Alley (also writer), A Dry White Season (also co-s.p.), Simeon (also writer), Aime Cesaire: A Voice for History, Wings Against the Wind (also story).

PALIN, MICHAEL
Actor, Writer. b. Sheffield, Yorkshire, England, May 5, 1943. e. Oxford. Performed there in Pinter's The Birthday Party and in revue Hang Your Head Down and Die (also in West End prod., 1964). At Oxford met Terry Jones, began writing comedy together, incl. TV series The Frost Report. Became member of Monty Python's Flying Circus. On stage with troupe both in London and on B'way.
PICTURES: And Now for Something Completely Different (also co-s.p.), Monty Python and the Holy Grail (also co-s.p.), Jabberwocky, Life of Brian (also co-s.p.), Time Bandits, The Secret Policeman's Other Ball, Monty Python Live at the Hollywood Bowl (also co-s.p.), The Missionary (also co-prod., s.p.), Monty Python's The Meaning of Life (also co-music, co-s.p.), A Private Function, Brazil, A Fish Called Wanda, American Friends (also co-s.p.), Fierce Creatures, The Wind In The Willows (voice).
TELEVISION: Do Not Adjust Your Set, The Frost Report, Monty Python's Flying Circus, Marty Feldman Comedy Machine, How To Irritate People, Pythons in Deutschland, Secrets, Ripping Yarns, Around the World in 80 Days, GBH, Pole to Pole.

PALMER, BETSY
Actress. b. East Chicago, IN, Nov. 1, 1929. e. DePaul U. Studied at Neighborhood Playhouse, HB Studio with Uta Hagen. On Broadway in The Grand Prize, South Pacific, Affair of Honor, Cactus Flower, Roar Like a Dove, Eccentricities of a Nightingale, Same Time Next Year and many regional prods.
PICTURES: Mister Roberts, The Long Gray Line, Queen Bee, The Tin Star, The Last Angry Man, Friday the 13th, Friday the 13th Part 2, Unveiled, The Fear: Halloween Night.

TELEVISION: All major live shows such as Studio One, U.S. Steel Hour, Kraft Theatre. *Series*: Masquerade Party (panelist), What's It For? (panelist), I've Got a Secret (panelist, 11 years), No. 96 (series), Candid Camera (host), The Today Show (host), Wifeline (host). *Guest*: As the World Turns, Murder She Wrote, Out of This World, Charles in Charge, Knots Landing, Newhart, Love Boat. *Movies*: Isabel's Choice, Windmills of the Gods, Goddess of Love, Still Not Quite Human, Columbo: Death Hits the Jackpot.

PALMER, GREGG
Actor. r.n. Palmer Lee. b. San Francisco, CA, Jan. 25, 1927. e. U. of Utah. U.S. Air Force, 1945-46; radio announcer, disc jockey; then to Hollywood.
PICTURES: Cimarron Kid, Battle at Apache Pass, Son of Ali Baba, Red Ball Express, Francis Goes to West Point, Sally and St. Anne, The Raiders, Back at the Front, The Redhead From Wyoming, Column South, Veils of Bagdad, Golden Blade, The All American, Taza Son of Cochise, Magnificent Obsession, Playgirl, To Hell and Back, Creature Walks Among Us, Hilda Crane, Zombies of Mora Tau, Revolt of Fort Laramie, Rebel Set, Commacheros, Quick Gun, Prize, It Happened Every Thursday, Female Animal, Thundering Jets, Forty Pounds of Trouble, Night Hunt, The Undefeated, Chisum, Rio Lobo, Big Jake, Providenza (It.), Ci Risiamo Vero Providenza (It-Sp), Cat Man, The Sad Horse, Most Dangerous Man Alive, Cutter's Trail, The Shootist, The Man With Bogart's Face, Scream.
TELEVISION (has appeared in over 400 TV programs): *Series*: Run Buddy Run. *Guest* appearances incl: Wagon Train, Loretta Young, Wyatt Earp, Have Gun Will Travel, Sea Hunt, Roaring 20's, Mannix, The High Chaparral, Cannon, Baretta, Gunsmoke, etc.). *Movies*: Mongo's Back in Town, Go West Young Girl, Hostage Heart, How the West Was Won, True Grit, Beggarman Thief, The Blue and the Gray (mini-series).

PALMER, PATRICK J.
Producer. b. Los Angeles, CA, Dec. 28, 1936. Began career with 10-year apprenticeship at Mirisch Company, involved in making of West Side Story, Seven Days in May, The Fortune Cookie, etc. 1966, began association with Norman Jewison, serving as assoc. prod. on The Landlord, Fiddler on the Roof, Jesus Christ Superstar, Rollerball. 1972, prod., with Jewison, Billy Two Hats; exec. prod. on The Dogs of War.
PICTURES: *Co-prod.*: And Justice for All, Best Friends, Iceman, A Soldier's Story, Agnes of God, Children of a Lesser God, Moonstruck, Stanley & Iris, Mermaids, Paradise (also writer), Made in America, Don Juan Demarco. *Exec. prod:* Milk Money, Iron Will, Mrs. Winterbourne, The Rage: Carrie 2

PALMINTERI, CHAZZ
Actor, Writer. r.n. Calogero Lorenzo Palminteri. b. Bronx, NY, May 15, 1951. e. Bronx Comm. Coll. NY stage in The Guys in the Truck (B'way), The King's Men, 22 Years, The Flatbush Faithful, A Bronx Tale (which he also wrote).
PICTURES: The Last Dragon (debut, 1985), Oscar, Innocent Blood, There Goes the Neighborhood, A Bronx Tale (also s.p.), Bullets Over Broadway (Acad. Award nom.), The Perez Family, The Usual Suspects, Faithful (also s.p.), Jade, Mulholland Falls, Diabolique, Scar City, A Night at the Roxbury (cameo), Hurlyburly, Excellent Cadavers, Analyze This, Stuart Little (voice), Company Man, Down to Earth, One Eyed King, Lady and the Tramp II, Scamp's Adventure (voice), Just Like Mona.
TELEVISION: *Movie:* The Last Word.

PALTROW, BRUCE
Director, Producer, Writer. b. New York, NY, Nov. 26, 1943. e. Tulane U., B.F.A. m. actress Blythe Danner. Daughter is actress Gwyneth Paltrow. Has also produced stage plays.
PICTURE: A Little Sex (co-prod., dir.), Duets.
TELEVISION: *Movies*: Shirts and Skins (co-prod., writer), Ed McBain's 87th Precinct (dir.). *Series*: The White Shadow (creat. dir.), St. Elsewhere (exec. prod.-dir.), Tattinger's (exec. prod., dir., co-writer), Nick & Hillary (exec. prod.).

PALTROW, GWYNETH
Actress. b. Los Angeles, CA, Sept. 28, 1973. p. actress Blythe Danner, dir.-prod. Bruce Paltrow. Family moved to NY when she was 11.
THEATER: *Williamstown:* Picnic, The Adventures of Huck Finn, Sweet Bye and Bye, The Seagull.
PICTURES: Shout (debut, 1991), Hook, Malice, Flesh and Bone, Mrs. Parker and the Vicious Circle, Jefferson in Paris, Moonlight and Valentino, Seven, The Pallbearer, Sydney, Emma, Hush, Out of the Past, Sliding Doors, Great Expectations, A Perfect Murder, Duets, Shakespeare in Love (Acad. Award for best actress), The Talented Mr. Ripley, The Intern, Duets, Bounce, View from the Top, Shallow Hal, Possession, How to Lose a Guy in 10 Days, The Anniversary Party.
TELEVISION: *Movie*: Cruel Doubt.

PANAMA, CHARLES A. (CHUCK)
Publicist, b. Chicago, IL, Feb. 2, 1925. e. Northwestern U., Beloit Coll., UCLA. Publicist, Los Angeles Jr. Chamber of Commerce; So. Calif. sports ed., Los Angeles bureau, INS; publicist, 20th Century-Fox Studios; adv.-pub. dir., Arcola Pics.; opened L.A. office, John Springer Associates; v.p. Jerry Pam & Assoc.; account exec., Rogers, Cowan & Brenner, Inc.; dir. m.p. div., Jim Mahoney & Assoc.; v.p. Guttman & Pam, Ltd.; asst. pub. dir., Twentieth TV. Owner, pres. Chuck Panama P.R.; winner 1990 Les Mason Award and 1993 Robert Yeager Award, Publicists Guild of America. Docent, Santa Monica (CA) Museum of Flying.

PANAMA, NORMAN
Writer, Producer, Director. b. Chicago, IL, April 21, 1914. Co-authored The Glass Bed (novel), and plays: A Talent for Murder, The Bats of Portobello.
PICTURES: *Co-Writer*: My Favorite Blonde, Happy Go Lucky, Star-Spangled Rhythm, Thank Your Lucky Stars, And the Angels Sing, Duffy's Tavern, Road to Utopia (Acad. Award nom.), Our Hearts Were Growing Up, Monsieur Beaucaire, It Had to Be You, Mr. Blandings Builds His Dream House, Return of October, White Christmas, Li'l Abner, The Facts of Life. *Co-Dir./Co-Writer* (with Melvin Frank): The Reformer and the Redhead, Strictly Dishonorable, Callaway Went Thataway, Above and Beyond, Knock on Wood (Acad. Award nom. for s.p.), The Court Jester. *Dir./Writer*: The Road to Hong Kong, Not With My Wife You Don't, How to Commit Marriage, I Will I Will... for Now.
TELEVISION: *Dir.*: Barnaby and Me, The Stewardesses, Li'l Abner, Mrs. Katz and Katz (pilot), How Come You Never See Dr. Jekyll and Mr. Hyde Together?, Coffee Tea or Me.

PANKIN, STUART
Actor. b. Philadelphia, PA, April 8, 1946. e. Dickinson Coll., Columbia U. Stage debut 1968 in The War of the Roses.
THEATER: *NY*: Timon of Athens, Tale of Cymbeline, Mary Stuart, The Crucible, Twelfth Night, Glorious Age, Wings, Gorky, Joseph and the Amazing Technicolor Dreamcoat, Three Sisters, The Inspector General.
PICTURES: Scavenger Hunt, Hangar 18, The Hollywood Knights, An Eye for an Eye, Earthbound, Irreconcilable Differences, The Dirt Bike Kid, Fatal Attraction, Love at Stake, Second Sight, That's Adequate, Arachnophobia, Mannequin 2 on the Move, The Vagrant, I Love Trouble, The Silence of the Hams, Squanto: A Warrior's Tale, Congo, Striptease, Honey We Shrunk Ourselves.
TELEVISION: *Series*: The San Pedro Beach Bums, No Soap Radio, Not Necessarily the News (ACE Award), Nearly Departed, Dinosaurs (voice). *Movies:* Valentine Magic on Love Island, Father & Scout, Down Out and Dangerous. *Pilots*: Car Wash, Wonderful World of Philip Malley. *Guest*: Night Court, Crazy Like a Fox, Golden Girls, Stingray, Family Ties, It's Garry Shandling's Show, Hooperman, Barney Miller. *Special*: Stuart Pankin (also co-exec. prod., co-writer).

PANTOLIANO, JOE
Actor. b. Jersey City, NJ, Sept. 12, 1954.
THEATER: *NY*: The Kitchen, The Off Season, The Death Star, Visions of Kerouac. *Regional*: One Flew Over the Cuckoo's Nest, Skaters, Brothers, Italian American Reconciliation (Dramalogue Award), Orphans (Dramalogue Award, Drama Critic Circle nomination), Pvt. Wars.
PICTURES: The Idolmaker, Monsignor, Risky Business, Eddie and the Cruisers, The Mean Season, The Goonies, Running Scared, La Bamba, The Squeeze, Amazon Women on the Moon, Empire of the Sun, The In Crowd, Midnight Run, Downtown, The Last of the Finest, Short Time, Zandalee, Used People, Three of Hearts, Goin' to Mexico, The Fugitive, Calendar Girl, Me and the Kid, Teresa's Tattoo, Baby's Day Out, Bad Boys, Congo (cameo), Steal Big Steal Little, Bound, The Immortals, Top of the World, Tinseltown, U.S. Marshals, The Taxman, New Blood, The Life Before This, Black and White, The Matrix.
TELEVISION: *Series*: Free Country, The Fanelli Boys, EZ Streets, Godzilla: The Series (voice), Sugar Hill. *Mini-Series*: Robert F. Kennedy: His Life and Times, From Here to Eternity. *Guest*: Tales from the Crypt (ACE Award nomination), Amazing Stories, L.A. Law, The Hitchhiker. *Movies*: More Than Friends, Alcatraz: The Whole Shocking Story, Nightbreaker, Destination America, El Diablo, One Special Victory, Through the Eyes of a Killer, The Last (also co-assoc. prod.), EZ Streets (pilot), Ed McBain's 87th Precinct: Ice, Natural Enemy.

PAPAS, IRENE
Actress. b. Chiliomodion, Greece, Sept. 3, 1926. Entered dramatic school at 12. At 16 sang and danced in variety shows before debuting in Greek films, 1950. 1958 appeared with Greek Popular Theatre in Athens. Received Salonika Film Fest. Awards for the films Antigone, Electra.
THEATER: The Idiot, Journey's End, The Merchant of Venice, Inherit the Wind, That Summer, That Fall, Iphigenia in Aulis.

PICTURES: Lost Angels (debut, 1950), Dead City, The Unfaithful, Atilla the Hun, Theodora the Slave Empress, Whirlpool, Tribute to a Bad Man, Antigone, The Guns of Navarone, Electra, The Moon-Spinners, Zorba the Greek, We Still Kill the Old Way, The Desperate Ones, The Brotherhood, Anne of the Thousand Days, Z, A Dream of Kings, The Trojan Women, Roma Bene, Bambina, Mohammed: Messenger of God, Iphigenia, Bloodline, Eboli, Lion of the Desert, Erendira, Into the Night, The Assisi Underground, Sweet Country, High Season, Chronicle of a Death Foretold, Island, Drums of Fire, Banquet, Zoe, Up Down and Sideways.
TELEVISION: Moses the Lawgiver.

PAQUIN, ANNA
Actress. b. Winnipeg, Manitoba, Canada, July 24, 1982.
PICTURES: The Piano (Acad. Award, 1994; Golden Globe nom.), Fly Away Home, Jane Eyre, Amistad, Hurlyburly, Begin the Beguine, A Walk on the Moon, Sleepless Beauty, Castle in the Sky (voice), All the Rage, She's All That, X-Men, Almost Famous, Finding Forrester.
TELEVISION: *Movie*: The Member of the Wedding.

PARE, MICHAEL
Actor. b. Brooklyn, NY, Oct. 9, 1959. e. Culinary Inst. of America, Hyde Park, NY. Worked as chef and model before being discovered by ABC talent agent.
PICTURES: Eddie and the Cruisers (debut, 1983), Streets of Fire, The Philadelphia Experiment, Under Cover (Aust.), Space Rage, Instant Justice, The Women's Club, World Gone Wild, Eddie and the Cruisers II: Eddie Lives, Moon 44, Dragon Fight, Concrete War, The Closer, Into the Sun, Midnight Heat, First Light, Point of Impact, Village of the Damned, Bad Moon.
TELEVISION: *Series*: The Greatest American Hero, Houston Knights. *Movie*: Crazy Times.

PARISH, JAMES ROBERT
Film Historian, Biographer. b. Cambridge, MA, April 21, 1944. e. U. of PA (BA, Phi Beta Kappa); U. of PA Law School (LLB). Member of NY Bar. Founder Entertainment Copyright Research Co., Inc. 1968-69, film reporter, Motion Picture Daily, Weekly Variety. 1969-70, entertainment publicist, Harold Rand & Co. (NY). Currently author, contributor to arts sections of major national newspapers and entertainment trade papers, on-air interviewee for cable/TV documentaries, and series editor of show business book series.
AUTHOR: Hollywood's Great Musicals, Prostitution in Hollywood Films, Ghosts & Angels in Hollywood Films, Hollywood Songsters, Prison Pictures From Hollywood, Hollywood Baby Boomers, The Great Detective Pictures, The Great Cop Pictures, The Great Science Fiction Pictures II, Complete Actors TV Credits (1948-88), The Great Combat Pictures, Black Action Pictures From Hollywood, The Great Detective Pictures, The Great Western Pictures II: The Great Gangster Pictures II: The Great Spy Pictures II, Actors TV Credits, The Best of MGM, The Forties Gals, The Great American Movies Book, Hollywood Happiness, The Funsters, Hollywood on Hollywood, The Hollywood Beauties, Elvis!, The Great Science Fiction Pictures, The Child Stars, The Jeannette MacDonald Story, Great Movie Heroes, Liza!, The RKO Gals, Vincent Price Unmasked, The George Raft File, The Emmy Awards, Hollywood Death Book, Gays & Lesbians in Mainstream Cinema, Hollywood Celebrity Death Book (updated), Let's Talk! America's Favorite TV Talk Show Hosts, Today's Black Hollywood, Pirates and Seafaring Swashbucklers, Rosie: Rosie O'Donnell's Story, The Unofficial 'Murder She Wrote' Casebook, Whoopi Goldberg: Her Journey From Poverty to Mega-Stardom.

PARK, NICK
Director, Writer, Animator. b. Preston, Lancashire, England, December 6, 1958. e. Sheffield Hallam Univeristy. Awarded honorary doctor of arts degree by Bath University, UK.
PICTURES: War Story (anim. only), Creature Comforts, Wallace & Gromit: A Grand Day Out, Wallace & Gromit: The Wrong Trousers, Wallace & Gromit: A Close Shave, Wallace & Gromit: The Best of Aardman Animation, Wallace & Gromit: The Aardman Collection 2, Chicken Run (also prod.).

PARKER, ALAN
Director, Writer. b. Islington, London, England, Feb. 14, 1944. Worked way up in advertising industry from mail room to top writer and dir. of nearly 500 TV commercials between 1969-78. Appointed chmn. of British Film Institute, 1997.
PICTURES: Melody (s.p., 1968). *Director/Writer*: No Hard Feelings, Our Cissy, Footsteps, Bugsy Malone (Brit. Acad. Award for best s.p.), Midnight Express (Brit. Acad. Award), Fame, Shoot the Moon, Pink Floyd—The Wall, Birdy, Angel Heart, Mississippi Burning, Come and See the Paradise, The Commitments (also cameo; BAFTA Award for best dir., 1991), The Road to Wellville (also co-prod.), Evita (also prod), Angela's Ashes (also prod.).
TELEVISION: The Evacuees (Brit. Acad. Award).

PARKER, COREY
Actor. b. New York, NY, July 8, 1965. e. NYU.
THEATER: *NY:* Meeting the Winter Bike Rider (Off-B'way debut, 1984), Been Taken, The Bloodletters, The Semi-Formal.
PICTURES: Scream for Help (debut, 1984), Friday the 13th Part V: A New Beginning, Something Special, Nine 1/2 Weeks, Biloxi Blues, How I Got Into College, Big Man on Campus, White Palace, Flesh Suitcase, Mr. & Mrs. Loving, Fool's Paradise, Scream 2.
TELEVISION: *Series:* Eddie Dodd, Flying Blind, Blue Skies, The Love Boat: The Next Wave. *Movies*: Courage, At Mother's Request, Liz: The Elizabeth Taylor Story, A Mother's Prayer, Encino Woman. *Specials*: Don't Touch, Teen Father, The Lost Language of Cranes. *Pilot:* Sons of Gunz. *Guest:* The Bronx Zoo, thirtysomething.

PARKER, ELEANOR
Actress. b. Cedarville, OH, June 26, 1922. In Cleveland play group; in summer stock Martha's Vineyard; at Pasadena Community Playhouse.
PICTURES: They Died With Their Boots On (debut, 1941), Buses Roar, Mysterious Doctor, Mission to Moscow, Between Two Worlds, The Very Thought of You, Crime By Night, Hollywood Canteen, Last Ride, Pride of the Marines, Never Say Goodbye, Of Human Bondage, Escape Me Never, Woman in White, Voice of the Turtle, It's a Great Feeling, Chain Lightning, Caged (Acad. Award nom.), Three Secrets, Valentino, Millionaire for Christy, Detective Story (Acad. Award nom.), Scaramouche, Above and Beyond, Escape from Fort Bravo, Naked Jungle, Valley of the Kings, Many Rivers to Cross, Interrupted Melody (Acad. Award nom.), Man with the Golden Arm, King and Four Queens, Lizzie, Seventh Sin, A Hole in the Head, Home from the Hill, Return to Peyton Place, Madison Avenue, Panic Button, The Sound of Music, The Oscar, An American Dream, Warning Shot, Tiger and the Pussycat, Eye of the Cat, Sunburn.
TELEVISION: *Series*: Bracken's World. *Movies*: Maybe I'll Come Home in the Spring, Vanished, Home for the Holidays, The Great American Beauty Contest, Fantasy Island (pilot), The Bastard, She's Dressed to Kill, Once Upon a Spy, Madame X, Dead on the Money. *Pilot*: Guess Who's Coming to Dinner. *Special*: Hans Brinker. *Guest*: Buick Electra Playhouse, Kraft Suspense Theatre, The Man from U.N.C.L.E., Vega$, Hawaii 5-0, The Love Boat, Hotel, Murder She Wrote.

PARKER, FESS
Actor. b. Fort Worth, TX, Aug. 16, 1924. e. USC. U.S. Navy, 1943-46; national co., Mr. Roberts, 1951.
PICTURES: Untamed Frontier (debut, 1952), No Room for the Groom, Springfield Rifle, Thunder Over the Plains, Island in the Sky, The Kid From Left Field, Take Me to Town, Them!, Battle Cry, Davy Crockett—King of the Wild Frontier (from Disney TV show), Davy Crockett and the River Pirates (from TV show), The Great Locomotive Chase, Westward Ho! the Wagons, Old Yeller, The Light in the Forest, The Hangman, Alias Jesse James (cameo), The Jayhawkers, Hell Is for Heroes, Smoky.
TELEVISION: *Series*: Mr. Smith Goes to Washington, Daniel Boone. *Guest*: Jonathan Winters, Walt Disney presents (Davy Crockett), Playhouse 90 (Turn Left at Mount Everest), Ed Sullivan, Danny Kaye Show, Phyllis Diller, Joey Bishop, Dean Martin, Red Skelton, Glen Campbell, Andy Williams, Vicki Lawrence. *Movie*: Climb an Angry Mountain.

PARKER, JAMESON
Actor. b. Baltimore, MD, Nov. 18, 1947. e. Beloit Coll. Professional stage debut in Washington Theatre Club production, Caligula. Acted with Arena Stage in DC; worked in dinner theatres and summer stock. Moved to N.Y., working in TV commercials and acted in play, Equus (Coconut Grove Playhouse).
PICTURES: The Bell Jar (debut, 1979), A Small Circle of Friends, White Dog, American Justice (also prod.), Jackals, Prince of Darkness, Curse of the Crystal Eye.
TELEVISION: *Series*: Somerset, One Life to Live, Simon and Simon. *Movies*: Women at West Point, Anatomy of a Seduction, The Gathering Part II, The Promise of Love, Callie and Son, A Caribbean Mystery, Who Is Julia?, Spy, She Says She's Innocent, Dead Before Dawn, Simon & Simon: In Trouble Again, Have You Seen My Son?, Dead Man's Island; Something Borrowed, Something Blue.

PARKER, MARY-LOUISE
Actress. b. Ft. Jackson, SC, Aug. 2, 1964. e. Bard Coll. 1990, received Clarence Derwent Award for her work in the theatre.
THEATER: *B'way*: Prelude to a Kiss (Theatre World Award). *Off-B'way*: Hayfever, The Girl in Pink, Babylon Gardens, Throwing Your Voice, Four Dogs and a Bone, Communicating Doors. *Regional*: The Importance of Being Earnest, Up in Saratoga, The Miser, Hay Fever, The Night of the Iguana, The Age of Pie.
PICTURES: Signs of Life (debut, 1989), Longtime Companion, Grand Canyon, Fried Green Tomatoes, Mr. Wonderful, Naked in New York, The Client, Bullets Over Broadway, Boys on the Side, Reckless, The Portrait of a Lady, Murder in Mind, The Maker, Let the Devil Wear Black, Goodbye Lover.
TELEVISION: *Movies*: Too Young the Hero, A Place for Annie, The Simple Life of Noah Dearborn.

PARKER, SARAH JESSICA
Actress. b. Nelsonville, OH, March 25, 1965. Was dancer with Cincinnati Ballet and American Ballet Theatre. Professional debut at age 8 in TV special The Little Match Girl.
THEATER: *NY*: The Innocents, By Strouse, Annie (title role for 2 yrs.), To Gillian on Her 37th Birthday, The Heidi Chronicles, The Substance of Fire, Sylvia, How To Succeed In Business Without Really Trying, Once Upon A Mattress.
PICTURES: Rich Kids (debut, 1979), Somewhere Tomorrow, Footloose, Firstborn, Girls Just Want to Have Fun, Flight of the Navigator, L.A. Story, Honeymoon in Vegas, Hocus Pocus, Striking Distance, Ed Wood, Miami Rhapsody, If Lucy Fell, The Substance of Fire, First Wives Club, Extreme Measures, Mars Attacks!, 'Til There Was You, Isn't She Great, Dudley Do-Right, State and Main, Life Without Dick.
TELEVISION: *Series*: Square Pegs, A Year in the Life, Equal Justice, Sex and the City. *Specials*: The Almost Royal Family, Life Under Water. *Movies*: My Body My Child, Going for the Gold: The Bill Johnson Story, A Year in the Life (pilot), The Room Upstairs, Dadah Is Death, Twist of Fate, The Ryan White Story, In the Best Interest of the Children, The Sunshine Boys.

PARKER, SUZY
Actress. r.n. Cecelia Parker. b. San Antonio, TX, Oct. 28, 1933. m. actor Bradford Dillman. Began career at 17 as fashion model; becoming the highest paid fashion model and cover girl in U.S.; went to Paris under contract to fashion magazine; film debut as model in Funny Face (1957); signed by 20th-Fox prod. chief Buddy Adler for part opposite Cary Grant in Kiss Them for Me.
PICTURES: Funny Face, Kiss Them For Me, Ten North Frederick, The Best of Everything, Circle of Deception, The Interns, Flight From Ashiya, Chamber of Horrors.

PARKES, WALTER F.
Producer, Writer. b. Bakersfield, CA. e. Yale, Stanford Univ. 1978 prod. & dir. documentary The California Reich which was nominated for Acad. Award.
PICTURES: WarGames (s.p.; Acad. Award nom.). *Exec. Prod.*: Volunteers, Project X, True Believer, Awakenings (Acad. Award nom.), Sneakers (also co-s.p.), Little Giants; To Wong Foo,- Thanks for Everything-Julie Newmar; How to Make an American Quilt, Twister, The Trigger Effect, Amistad, Men In Black, The Peacemaker, Deep Impact, Small Soldiers, The Mask of Zorro.
TELEVISION: *Series*: Eddie Dodd (prod., writer). *Pilot*: Birdland (prod., writer).

PARKINS, BARBARA
Actress. b. Vancouver, British Columbia, Canada, May 22, 1942.
PICTURES: Valley of the Dolls, The Kremlin Letter, The Mephisto Waltz, Puppet on a Chain, Asylum, Shout at the Devil, Bear Island, Breakfast in Paris.
TELEVISION: *Series*: Peyton Place, Scene of the Crime. *Mini-Series*: Captains and the Kings. *Movies*: A Taste of Evil, Snatched, Law of the Land, Testimony of Two Men, Young Joe: The Forgotten Kennedy, Ziegfield: The Man and His Women, The Critical List, The Manions of America, Uncommon Valor, To Catch a King, Calendar Girl Murders, Peyton Place: The Next Generation, Jennie: Lady Randolph Churchill. *Guest*: G.E. Theatre, My Three Sons, Dr. Kildare, Gibbsville, Hotel, The Love Boat, Murder She Wrote. *Special*: Jennie.

PARKS, GORDON
Director, Writer, Photographer, Composer, Photojournalist. b. Fort Scott, KS, Nov. 30, 1912. From the age of 15 worked as piano player, bus boy, dining car waiter and prof. basketball player in MN before taking up photography in late 1930's. Awarded 1st Julius Rosenwald Fellowship in photog., 1942. Worked with Roy Stryker at Farm Security Admin., WWII Office of War Info. correspondent. Photo-journalist, Life Mag., 1949-68, editorial dir. (and founder): Essence Magazine 1970-73. Film debut 1961 with doc. Flavio (dir. and writer), followed by Diary of a Harlem Family (doc.; Emmy Award). Winner of numerous awards including NAACP's Spingarn Medal and Kansas Governor's Medal of Honor, Nat'l Medal of Arts, 1988. Recipient of 23 honorary degrees in lit., fine arts, humane letters. Member of NAACP, AMPAS, PEN American Center, AFI, etc.
AUTHOR: The Learning Tree, A Choice of Weapons, A Poet and His Camera, Whispers of Intimate Things, In Love, Born Black, Moments Without Proper Names, Flavio, To Smile in Autumn, Shannon, Voices in the Mirror, Irias In Silence, Glimpses Toward Infinity.
PICTURES: The Learning Tree (Library of Congress Nat'l Film Registry Classics honor, 1989), Shaft, Shaft's Big Score, Super Cops, Leadbelly.
TELEVISION: The Odyssey of Solomon Northup, Moments Without Proper Names, Martin.

PARKS, MICHAEL
Actor. b. Corona, CA, April 4, 1938.
PICTURES: Wild Seed (debut, 1964), Bus Riley's Back in Town, The Bible, The Idol, The Happening, The Last Hard Men, Sidewinder One, ffolkes, Hard Country, Savannah Smiles, Spiker, Club Life, The Return of Josey Wales (also dir.), Spiker, Arizona Heat, Nightmare Beach, Prime Suspect, The Hitman, Storyville, Death Wish 5: The Face of Death, Stranger by Night.
TELEVISION: *Series*: Then Came Bronson, The Colbys, Twin Peaks. *Movies*: Can Ellen Be Saved?, Savage Bees, Chase, Dangerous Affection, Gore Vidal's Billy the Kid, The China Lake Murders, Hart to Hart: Secrets of the Hart.

PARKS, VAN DYKE
Composer, actor. Albums include: Song Cycle, Discover America, Clang of the Yankee Reaper, Jump!, Tokyo Rose, Orange Crate Art (with Brian Wilson).
PICTURES: The Swan, A Gift for Heidi (actor only), Goin' South, Popeye (actor only), Loose Shoes (actor only), Sesame Street Presents Follow That Bird, Club Paradies, The Brave Little Toaster (songs), Vibes (actor only), Casual Sex?, The Two Jakes (actor only), He Said She Said (actor only), Out on a Limb, Wild Bill, Bastard Out of Carolina, Private Parts, Shadrach.
TELEVISION: *Movies*: Mother Goose Rock 'n' Rhyme (actor only), One Christmas, Next Door, The Summer of Ben Tyler, Oliver Twist. *Series*: Bonino (actor only).

PARRETTI, GIANCARLO
Executive. b. Orvieto, Italy, Oct. 23, 1941. Hotelier in Sicily in the late 1970's. Managing dir. of Naples newspaper Diario, until 1981. 1987, purchased Cannon Group, renaming it Pathe Communications. 1990, company acquired MGM/UA, Communications. Resigned 1991.

PARSONS, ESTELLE
Actress. b. Marblehead, MA, Nov. 20, 1927. e. Connecticut Coll. for Women, Bachelor's degree in political science. Attended Boston U. Law Sch. Helped harvest crops in England with the Women's Land Army. Was active in politics; worked for the Committee for the Nation's Health in Wash. and the Republican Finance Committee in Boston. Was elected to public office in Marblehead, Mass. Joined NBC-TV's Today Show as prod. asst.; then writer, feature prod. and commentator. Appeared in two Julius Monk revues, Jerry Herman's Nightcap.
THEATER: Happy Hunting, Whoop Up, Beg Borrow or Steal, Mrs. Dally Has a Lover (Theater World Award), Next Time I'll Sing to You (Obie Award), In the Summer House (Obie Award), Ready When You Are C.B., Malcolm, The Seven Descents of Myrtle, ...And Miss Reardon Drinks a Little, The Norman Conquests, Ladies of the Alamo, Miss Margarida's Way, Pirates of Penzance, The Unguided Missile, Threepenny Opera, Lincoln Center Repertory Theatre, Mahagonny, Forgiving Typhoid Mary, Shimada, The Shadow Box, Twice Removed, Grace & Glorie.
PICTURES: Ladybug Ladybug (debut, 1963), Bonnie and Clyde (Acad. Award, best supporting actress, 1967), Rachel Rachel (Acad. Award nom.), Don't Drink the Water, Watermelon Man, I Walk the Line, I Never Sang for My Father, Two People, For Pete's Sake, Foreplay, Dick Tracy, The Lemon Sisters, Boys on the Side, That Darn Cat, Looking for Richard.
TELEVISION: *Mini-Series*: Backstairs at the White House. *Special*: The Front Page. *Movies*: Terror on the Beach, The Gun and the Pulpit, The UFO Incident, The Gentleman Bandit, Open Admissions, A Private Matter, The American Clock. *Series*: Roseanne. *Guest*: All in the Family.

PARTON, DOLLY
Singer, Composer, Actress. b. Sevierville, TN, Jan. 19, 1946. Gained fame as country music singer, composer and radio and TV personality. Co-partner with Sandy Gallin, Sandollar Prods. *Author*: My Life and Other Unfinished Business (autobiography), Coat of Many Colors.
PICTURES: Nine to Five (debut, 1980; also wrote & sang title song), The Best Little Whorehouse in Texas (also wrote addtl. songs), Rhinestone (also songs), Steel Magnolias, Straight Talk (also songs), The Beverly Hillbillies.
TELEVISION: *Series*: Dolly (1976), Dolly (1987-88). *Guest*: Porter Wagoner Show, Cass Walker Program, Bill Anderson Show, Wilbur Bros. Show. *Specials*: Kenny Dolly & Willie: Something Inside So Strong, A Tennessee Mountain Thanksgiving. *Movies*: A Smoky Mountain Christmas (also songs), Wild Texas Wind (also co-writer, co-prod.), Big Dreams & Broken Hearts: The Dottie West Story.

PASDAR, ADRIAN
Actor. b. Pittsfield, MA, 1965. e. Univ. of Central FL. Studied acting with People's Light and Theatre Co., Lee Strasberg Institute.
THEATER: *Regional*: The Glass Menagerie, Shadow Box, Hotters, Sorry Wrong Number, Cold Foot, Monkey's Paw.
PICTURES: Top Gun (debut, 1986), Streets of Gold, Solarbabies, Near Dark, Made in USA, Cookie, Vital Signs, Torn Apart, Just Like a Woman, The Pompatus of Love, Ties to Rachel, Wounded, A Brother's Kiss.
TELEVISION: *Series*: Profit, Feds. *Movies*: The Lost Capone, A Mother's Gift, Touched by Evil, Love in Antother Town, The Perfect Getaway. *Mini-Series:* House of Frankenstein. *Special*: Big Time.

PASETTA, MARTY
Producer-Director. b. June 16, 1932. e. U. Santa Clara.
TELEVISION: AFI Salutes to Fred Astaire, John Huston, Lillian Gish, Alfred Hitchcock and Jimmy Stewart, Gene Kelly Special, Elvis Aloha From Hawaii, Oscar (17), Emmy (2) and Grammy (8) Award Shows, A Country Christmas (1978-81), The Monte Carlo Show, Texaco Star Theatre-Opening Night, Burnett Discovers Domingo, Disneyland's 30th Anniversary Celebration, 15 Years of Cerebral Palsy Telethons, A Night at the Moulin Rouge, Soap Opera Awards, An All-Star Celebration Honoring Martin Luther King, Disneyland's Summer Vacation Party, Disney's Captain EO Grand Opening, 15th Anniversary of Disney World; Beach Boys... 25 Years Together, Super Night at the Superbowl, 20th Anniversary of Caesars Palace, Paris by Night with George Burns, I Call You Friend Papal Spacebridge '87, Walt Disney World's Celebrity Circus, Las Vegas: An All-Star 75th Anniversary, Julio Iglesias—Sold Out, The Ice Capades with Kirk Cameron, American All-Star Tribute Honoring Elizabeth Taylor.

PASOLINI, UBERTO
Producer.
PICTURES: The Killing Fields, The Frog Prince, The Mission, Meeting Venus, Palookaville, The Full Monty (BAFTA Award, Outstanding Brit. Film, 1997).
TELEVISION: *Movies*: A Dangerous Man: Lawrence After Arabia.

PASSER, IVAN
Director, Writer. b. Prague, Czechoslovakia, July 10, 1933. e. Film Faculty of Acad. of Musical Arts, Prague. 1961, asst. dir. to Milos Forman on Audition which led to scripting for Forman. 1969, moved to U.S., worked in NY as longshoreman while studying Eng. U.S. dir. debut: Born to Win, 1971.
PICTURES: *Writer*: Loves of a Blonde, A Boring Afternoon, Fireman's Ball. *Director*: Intimate Lighting (also s.p.), Born to Win, Law and Disorder, Crime and Passion, The Silver Bears, Cutter and Bone, Creator, Haunted Summer.
TELEVISION: *U.S.*: Faerie Tale Theatre. *Movies*: Fourth Story, Stalin, While Justice Sleeps, Kidnapped.

PASTER, GARY M.
Executive. b. St. Louis, MO, July 4, 1943. e. U. of MO, B.A.; UCLA, USC Graduate Sch. of Business. 1970, joined Burbank Studios as asst. to pres., treas.; 1976 v.p., admin. and chmn. of the exec. comm.; 1977 pres. Member: AMPAS, LA Film Dev. Council, Hollywood Radio & T.V. Society, Acad. of Television Arts and Sciences. Advisory bd., Kaufman Astoria Studios, N.Y.

PASTORELLI, ROBERT
Actor. b. New Brunswick, NJ, June 21, 1954.
TELEVISION: I Married a Centerfold, California Girls, Hands of a Stranger, Outrageous Fortune, Beverly Hills Cop II, Memories of Me, Lady Mobster, Dances with Wolves, Painted Heart, Folks!, Fern Gully: The Last Rainforest, Striking Distance, Sister Act 2: Back in the Habit, Robin Cook's Harmful Intent, The Yam Princess, The West Side Waltz, Eraser, Michael, A Simple Wish. *Series*: Murphy Brown, Double Rush, Cracker. *Guest*: Tucker's Witch, Hill Street Blues, MacGyver, Batman.

PATINKIN, MANDY
Actor. r.n. Mandel Patinkin. b. Chicago, IL, Nov. 30, 1952. e. U. of Kansas, Juilliard Sch. (Drama Div.; 1972-74). m. actress Kathryn Grody. In regional theatre before coming to New York where played with Shakespeare Festival Public Theater (Trelawny of the Wells, Hamlet, Rebel Women). Recordings: Mandy Patinkin, Dress Casual, Experiment.
THEATER: Savages, The Shadow Box (B'way debut), Evita (Tony Award, 1980), Henry IV, Part I (Central Park), Sunday in the Park With George (Tony nom.), The Knife, Follies in Concert, A Winter's Tale, Mandy Patinkin: Dress Casual (solo concert), The Secret Garden, Falsettos.
PICTURES: The Big Fix (debut, 1978), Last Embrace, French Postcards, Night of the Juggler, Ragtime, Daniel, Yentl, Maxie, The Princess Bride, The House on Carroll Street, Alien Nation, Dick Tracy, True Colors, Impromptu, The Doctor, The Music of Chance, Life With Mikey (cameo), Squanto: A Warrior's Tale, Men with Guns, Lulu on the Bridge, The Adventures of Elmo in Grouchland.
TELEVISION: *Series*: Chicago Hope (Emmy Award, 1995). *Guest*: That Thing on ABC, That 2nd Thing on ABC, Taxi, Sparrow, Streets of Gold, Midnight Special. *Movie*: Charleston, Broken Glass, The Hunchback, Strange Justice.

PATRIC, JASON
Actor. Jason Patric Miller Jr .b. Queens, NY, June 17, 1966. Son of playwright-actor Jason Miller. Grandson of performer Jackie Gleason. Began professional career with Vermont's Champlain Shakespeare Festival.
THEATER: *NY*: Beirut. *LA*: Out of Gas on Lovers' Leap.
PICTURES: Solarbabies (debut, 1986), The Lost Boys, The Beast, Denial, After Dark My Sweet, Roger Corman's Frankenstein Unbound, Rush, Geronimo: An American Legend, The Journey of August King, Sleepers, Speed 2: Cruise Control, Incognito, Your Friends & Neighbors (also prod.), 3 Days of Rain.
TELEVISION: *Movie*: Tough Love. *Special*: Teach 109.

PATRICK, Sr., C.L.
Theatre Executive. b. Honaker, VA, Dec. 6, 1918. Former pres. of Fuqua Industries which owned Martin Theatres and Gulf States Theatres. Prior to this was pres. and chairman of Martin Theatres. Presently chairman of board Carmike Cinemas, Inc.; v.p. Variety International; dir., Will Rogers Institute; Motion Picture Pioneer of 1976; Recipient of: Sherrill Corwin Award, 1984; Salah Hassanein Humanitarian Award, ShowEast '88; Show South's Exhibitor of the Decade Award, 1990.

PATRICK, MICHAEL W.
Executive. b. Columbus, GA, May 17, 1950. e. Columbus Coll., B.S., 1972. Pres., CEO, Carmike Cinemas. 1989. *Board of dir.:* Columbus Bank and Trust Co. *Member:* exec. comm., Will Rogers Institute; Variety Int'l; Motion Picture Pioneers. *Bd. of Trustees:* Columbus State University Foundation Inc.

PATRICK, ROBERT
Actor. b. Marietta, GA. 1959.
PICTURES: Eye of the Eagle, Equalizer 2000, Killer Instinct, Hollywood Boulevard II, Future Hunters, Die Hard 2, Terminator 2: Judgment Day, Double Dragon, Body Shot, Fire in the Sky, Zero Tolerance, Hong Kong 97, The Cool Surface, Last Gasp, Decoy, Asylum, Striptease, The Only Thrill, Hacks, Rosewood, Cop Land, Ravager (prod. only), Very Bad Things, Winter, Counter Force, A Breed Apart, From Dusk Till Dawn 2: Texas Blood Money, The Faculty, Ambushed, Texas Funeral, Shogun Cop, All the Pretty Horses.
TELEVISION: *Movies*: Resident Alien, Body Language. *Series*: Real Adventures of Jonny Quest. *Guest*: The Outer Limits. The X- Files.

PATTON, WILL
Actor. b. Charleston, SC, June 14, 1954. e. NC School of the Arts, 1975.
THEATER: *NY*: Tourists and Refugees #2 (La Mama E.T.C., Obie Award), Fool For Love (Obie Award), Goose and Tomtom (Public Theatre), A Lie of the Mind.
PICTURES: King Blank, Silkwood, Variety, Desperately Seeking Susan, After Hours, Chinese Boxes, Belizaire the Cajun, No Way Out, Stars and Bars, Wildfire, Signs of Life, Everybody Wins, A Shock to the System, The Rapture, Cold Heaven, In the Soup, The Paint Job, Romeo Is Bleeding, Natural Causes, Midnight Edition, Tollbooth, The Client, The Puppet Masters, Copycat, Johns, Inventing the Abbotts, The Postman, O.K. Garage, I Woke Up Early the Day I Died, Breakfast of Champions, Armageddon.
TELEVISION: *Movies*: Kent State, Dillinger, A Gathering of Old Men, The Deadly Desire, In the Deep Woods, A Child Lost Forever, Taking the Heat, Judicial Consent. *Series*: Ryan's Hope, Search For Tomorrow.

PAULEY, JANE
TV Host, Journalist. b. Indianapolis, IN, Oct. 31, 1950. m. Doonesbury creator Garry Trudeau. e. Indiana U. Involved in Indiana state politics before joining WISH-TV, Indianapolis, as reporter. Co-anchored midday news reports and anchored weekend news reports. Co-anchor of nightly news at WMAQ-TV, NBC station in Chicago. Joined Today Show in October, 1976, as featured regular, prior to which had made guest appearances on that program; co-host until 1990. Began own series Real Life With Jane Pauley in 1991.

PAVAN, MARISA
Actress, r.n. Marisa Pierangeli. b. Cagliari, Sardinia, Italy, June 19, 1932. e. Torquato Tasso Coll. Twin sister of late actress Pier Angeli. Came to U.S. 1950.
PICTURES: What Price Glory? (debut, 1952), Down Three Dark Streets, Drum Beat, The Rose Tattoo (Acad. Award nom.), Diane, The Man in the Gray Flannel Suit, The Midnight Story, John Paul Jones, Solomon and Sheba, A Slightly Pregnant Man.

PAVLIK, JOHN M.
Executive. b. Melrose, IA, Dec. 3, 1939. e. U. of Minnesota, B.A., 1963. Reporter, Racine (WI) Journal-Times, San Bernardino (CA) Sun-Telegram, 1963-66; writer, News Bureau, Pacific Telephone, Los Angeles, 1966-68; asst. dir. of publ. rltns., Association of Motion Picture and Television Producers, 1968-72; dir. of PR, 1972-78; v.p., 1978-79; special consultant, California Motion Picture Council, 1974-79; member, exec. council, Los Angeles Film Dev. Committee, v.p., 1977-78; exec. admin., Academy of Motion Picture Arts and Sciences, 1979-82; member, bd. of dir., Permanent Charities Comm. of the Entertainment Industries, 1979-84; member, bd. of dir., Hollywood Chamber of Commerce, 1979-85; exec. dir., M.P. & TV Fund, 1982-88; consultant, 1988-89; member, advisory board, Assn. of Film Commissioners Int'l, 1988-91; dir. of endowment dev., Academy Foundation, 1989-92; dir. of communications, AAMPA, 1992-present.

PAXSON, LOWELL W.
Executive. b. Rochester, NY. e. Syracuse U. As teenager worked in radio in Rochester and became announcer while in college. Purchased first broadcast entity, WACK radio in Newark NY, 1954. Began selling merchandise on a Florida AM station in 1977. Conceived and founded Home Shopping Network, 1982. Est. Silver King Communications, 1986. Sold interest in HSN and Silver King in 1990 and bought WCRJ radio in Florida, start of Paxson Communications Corp. Sold radio interests in 1997 and acquired The Travel Channel, which has since been sold to Discovery Communications, Inc. Launched PAX TV, the seventh US TV network, in 1998. CEO and Chairman, Paxson Communications Corp.

PAXTON, BILL
Actor. b. Fort Worth, TX, May 17, 1955. e. NYU. First professional job as set dresser for film Big Bad Mamma. Studied acting in NYC with Stella Adler. Dir. short films Fish Heads, Scoop (also s.p.)
PICTURES: Stripes, The Lords of Discipline, Mortuary, Streets of Fire, Impulse, The Terminator, Weird Science, Commando, Aliens, Near Dark, Pass the Ammo, Slipstream, Next of Kin, Back to Back, Brain Dead, The Last of the Finest, Navy SEALS, Predator 2, The Dark Backward, One False Move, The Vagrant, Trespass, Indian Summer, Boxing Helena, Future Shock, Monolith, Tombstone, True Lies, Apollo 13, The Last Supper, Twister, The Evening Star, Titanic, Traveller, A Simple Plan, Mighty Joe Young, U-571, Vertical Limit, Mexicali (also prod.), Frailty (dir. only).
TELEVISION: *Mini-Series*: Fresno. *Movies*: Deadly Lessons, The Atlanta Child Murders, An Early Frost, Frank and Jesse, A Bright Shining Lie. *Guest*: Miami Vice.

PAY, WILLIAM
UK Manager Quigley Publishing Co., Inc. b. London, England. Joined London office Quigley Publications. Served in RAF, 1941-46; rejoined Quigley; dir. Burnup Service Ltd., 1951; London news ed., Quigley Pub., 1955; dir., Quigley Pub. Ltd., 1961; appt. mgr. dir., 1963; mgr. dir., Burnup Company. Appt. Sec. British Kinematograph Sound & TV Society. Conference Co-ordinator biennial Intern. Film & TV Technology Conferences in U.K., 1975-87. Retired from Quigley Publishing Co., Inc. 1998.

PAYMER, DAVID
Actor. b. Long Island, NY, Aug. 30, 1954. e. Univ. of Mich. First professional job with natl. company of Grease, which he later appeared in on B'way. Has also taught acting at UCLA and the Film Actor's Workshop, performed stand-up comedy and served as staff writer on The New Leave It to Beaver Show.
PICTURES: The In-Laws (debut, 1979), Airplane II: The Sequel, Best Defense, Irreconcilable Differences, Perfect, Howard the Duck, No Way Out, Crazy People, City Slickers, Mr. Saturday Night (Acad. Award nom.), Searching for Bobby Fischer, Heart and Souls, City Slickers II: The Legend of Curly's Gold, Quiz Show, City Hall, The American President, Unforgettable, Nixon, Get Shorty, The Sixth Man, Amistad, The Long Way Home (voice), Gang Related, Mighty Joe Young, Mumford, Payback, Outside Ozona.
TELEVISION: *Series*: The Commish. *Guest*: Cagney & Lacy, The Paper Chase, Taxi, Cheers, L.A. Law, Hill Street Blues, Moonlighting, Murphy Brown. *Movies*: Grace Kelly, Pleasure, Cagney & Lacey: The Return, Cagney & Lacey: Together Again, Crime of the Century. *Special*: In Search of Dr. Seuss.

PAYNE, ALEXANDER
Director, Writer. b. Omaha, Nebraska, 1961.
PICTURES: The Passion of Martin (dir. only), Inside Out, Citizen Ruth, Election, Jurassic Park III (s.p. only), Sideways (dir. only), About Schmidt.

PAYNTER, ROBERT
Cinematographer. b. London, England, March 12, 1928. e. Mercer Sch. First job in industry at 15 years as camera trainee with Government Film Dept.
PICTURES: Hannibal Brooks (debut, 1969), The Games, Lawman, The Nightcomers, Chato's Land, The Mechanic, Scorpio, The Big Sleep, Superman, Firepower, The Final Conflict, Superman II, An American Werewolf in London, Superman III, Trading Places, The Muppets Take Manhattan, Into the Night, National Lampoon's European Vacation, Spies Like Us, Little Shop of Horrors, When the Whales Came, Strike It Rich, Get Back.

PAYS, AMANDA
Actress. b. Berkshire, England, June 6, 1959. m. actor Corbin Bernsen. Began as a model. Studied French, art and pottery at Hammersmith Polytechnic. Acting debut: Cold Room (HBO).
PICTURES: Oxford Blues, The Kindred, Off Limits, Leviathan, Exposure, Solitaire for Two.
TELEVISION: *Series*: Max Headroom, The Flash. *Mini-Series*: A.D. *Movies*: 13 at Dinner, The Pretenders, Parker Kane, Dead on the Money, The Thorn Birds: The Lost Years.

PAYSON, MARTIN D.
Executive. b. Brooklyn, NY, Jan. 4, 1936. e. Cornell U., NYU Sch. of Law, LLB, 1961. Practiced law privately before joining Warner Communications, Inc. as v.p. 1970. Later named exec. v.p., gen. counsel. 1987, appt. to 3-member office of pres., WCI. Was vice chmn. Time Warner Inc., until Dec. 1992. Retired.

PEAKER, E. J.
Actress, Singer, Dancer. r.n. Edra Jeanne Peaker. b. Tulsa, OK, Feb. 22. e. U. of New Mexico, U. of Vienna, Austria. Stage debut Bye, Bye Birdie
PICTURES: Hello Dolly! (debut, 1969), All American Boy, Private Roads, The Four Deuces, Graduation Day, Fire in the Night, I Can't Lose, Out of This World.
TELEVISION: *Series*: That's Life. *Guest*: The Flying Nun, That Girl, Love American Style, Odd Couple, Police Woman, Rockford Files, Get Christie Love, Houston Knights, Hunter, Quincy, Charlie's Angels, Six Million Dollar Man. *Movies*: Three's a Crowd, Getting Away From It All, Broken Promises (assoc. prod., writer).

PEARCE, CHRISTOPHER
Producer. b. Dursley, Eng, Nov. 19, 1943. Entered industry as gen. mgr. American Zoetrope. From 1982 to 1985 served as exec. in chg. of prod. for Cannon Films Inc. overseeing prod. on 150 films incl. That Championship Season, Runaway Train, Fool For Love and Barfly. 1987 became sr. v.p. and COO Cannon Group. Has since become pres. & CEO Cannon Pictures. TV movie: Coming Out of the Ice.

PEARCE, CRAIG
Actor.
PICTURES: I Can't Get Started, Vicious!, Strictly Ballroom (s.p. only), Mad Bomber in Love, The Seventh Floor, Romeo + Juliet (BAFTA Award, Best Adapted Screenplay, 1997).

PEARCE, RICHARD
Director, Cinematographer. b. San Diego, CA, Jan. 25, 1943. e. Yale U., B.A. degree in Eng. lit., 1965. New School for Social Research, M.A., degree in political economics. Worked with Don Pennebaker and Richard Leacock on documentaries. Photographed Emile de Antonio's America Is Hard to See. In 1970 went to Chile where he dir., photographed and edited Campamento, an award-winning documentary.
PICTURES: As photographer (Acad. Award winning documentaries): Woodstock, Marjoe, Interviews With My Lai Veterans, Hearts and Minds. *Director*: Heartland (debut, 1979), Threshold, Country, No Mercy, The Long Walk Home, Leap of Faith, A Family Thing.
TELEVISION: The Gardener's Son, Siege, No Other Love, Sessions, Dead Man Out, The Final Days.

PECK, GREGORY
Actor, Producer. r.n. Eldred Gregory Peck. b. La Jolla, CA, April 5, 1916. e. U. of California; Neighborhood Playhouse Sch. of Dramatics. Father of actors Tony and Cecilia Peck. On dramatic stage (The Doctor's Dilemma, The Male Animal, Once in a Lifetime, The Play's the Thing, You Can't Take It With You, The Morning Star, The Willow and I, Sons and Soldiers, etc.). Voted one of ten best Money-Making Stars Motion Picture Herald-Fame Poll, 1947, 1952. Co-prod. and starred in Big Country, for his company, Anthony Productions; prod. the Trial of the Catonsville Nine, The Dove (St. George Productions). Pres., Acad. M.P. Arts and Sciences, 1967-70. Founding mem., bd. mem. and chmn. American Film Inst. Recipient, Jean Hersholt Humanitarian Award, 1986. AFI Life Achievement Award, 1989. Voice of Florenz Ziegfeld in 1991 B'way musical The Will Rogers Follies.
PICTURES: Days of Glory (debut, 1944), The Keys of the Kingdom, The Valley of Decision, Spellbound, The Yearling, Duel in the Sun, The Macomber Affair, Gentleman's Agreement, The Paradine Case, Yellow Sky, The Great Sinner, Twelve O'Clock High, The Gunfighter, Only the Valiant, David and Bathsheba, Captain Horatio Hornblower, The World in His Arms, The Snows of Kilimanjaro, Roman Holiday, Night People, Man With a Million, The Purple Plain, The Man in the Gray Flannel Suit, Moby Dick, Designing Woman, The Bravados, The Big Country (also co-prod.), Pork Chop Hill (also prod.), Beloved Infidel, On the Beach, Guns of Navarone, To Kill a Mockingbird (Acad. Award, 1962), Cape Fear (also prod.), How the West Was Won, Captain Newman M.D., Behold a Pale Horse (also prod.), John F. Kennedy: Years of Lightning—Day of Drums (narrator), Mirage, Arabesque, MacKenna's Gold, Stalking Moon, The Chairman, Marooned, I Walk the Line, Shootout, Billy Two Hats, The Omen, MacArthur (also prod.), The Boys from Brazil (also prod.), The Sea Wolves (also prod.), Amazing Grace and Chuck, Old Gringo, Other People's Money, Cape Fear (1991).
TELEVISION: *Mini-series*: The Blue and the Gray. *Movies*: The Scarlet and the Black (also prod.), The Portrait. *Special*: We the People 200: The Constitutional Gala, The First 50 Years.

PEDAS, JIM
Executive. b. Youngstown, OH. e. Thiel College. Opened Circle Theatre in Washington, D.C. in 1957 with brother Ted. 1984 formed Circle Releasing, serving as Secretary/ Treasurer; Circle Films, serving as v.p. See Ted Pedas entry for releases.

PEDAS, TED
Executive. b. Farrell, PA, May 6, 1931. e. B.S.B.A, Youngstown St. Univ. M.B.A., Wharton Sch. of Business at Univ. of PA. J.D., Geo. Washington Univ. 1957, with brother Jim, opened Circle Theatre in Washington D.C. one of the first repertory houses. Circle/Showcase group of m.p. theatres expanded to over 80 quality screens before being sold in 1988. 1973-78, served on board of Cinema 5 in NY. 1984. Pres. NATO D.C.; National Film Preservation Board, Joseph Wharton Award 1988. Circle Releasing formed to distribute films with Ted serving as president. Releases include Blood Simple, The Navigator and the Killer. Circle Films has produced: Raising Arizona, Miller's Crossing, Barton Fink, Caught, Whatever.

PEERCE, LARRY
Director. b. Bronx, NY. Father was late singer Jan Peerce.
PICTURES: One Potato Two Potato, The Big T.N.T. Show, The Incident, Goodbye Columbus, The Sporting Club, A Separate Peace, Ash Wednesday, The Other Side of the Mountain, Two Minute Warning, The Other Side of the Mountain—Part II, The Bell Jar (also exec. prod.), Why Would I Lie?, Love Child, Hard to Hold, Wired.
TELEVISION: *Movies*: A Stranger Who Looks Like Me, Love Lives On, I Take These Men, The Fifth Missile, Prison for Children, Queenie, Elvis and Me, The Neon Empire, The Court-Martial of Jackie Robinson, Child of Rage, Poisoned by Love: The Kern County Murders, Heaven & Hell: North and South Book III, A Burning Passion: The Margaret Mitchell Story, In Pursuit of Honor (co-exec. prod. only), An Element of Truth, The Abduction, Love-Struck.

PEÑA, ELIZABETH
Actress. b. N.J., Sept. 23, 1961 of Cuban parents. Moved to New York in 1969 where she attended NY High School for Performing Arts. Off-B'way in Blood Wedding, Antigone, Romeo & Juliet, Act One & Only, Italian American Reconciliation, and many others.
PICTURES: El Super, Times Square, They All Laughed, Fat Chance, Crossover Dreams, Down and Out in Beverly Hills, La Bamba, Batteries Not Included, Vibes, Blue Steel, Jacob's Ladder, The Waterdance, Across the Moon, Free Willy 2: The Adventure Home, Dead Funny, Lone Star (Ind't Spirit Award, 1997), Strangeland, The Pass, Rush Hour, Strangeland, Seven Girlfriends.
TELEVISION: *Series*: Tough Cookies, I Married Dora, Shannon's Deal. *Movies*: Fugitive Among Us, Roommates, It Came From Outer Space, Contagious, The Second Civil War, Border Line. *Miniseries*: Drug War, The Camarena Story, The Invaders, Aldrich Ames: America Betrayed.

PENDLETON, AUSTIN
Actor. b. Warren, OH, March 27, 1940. e. Yale Univ. Started acting with Williamstown Theatre Festival. Teaches acting at the Herbert Berghof Studio. Named artistic dir. of NY's Circle Rep. Theatre, 1995.
THEATER: *Actor*: Oh Dad Poor Dad Mama's Hung You in the Closet and I'm Feeling So Sad, Fiddler on the Roof, The Little Foxes, The Last Sweet Days of Isaac (NY Drama Critics & Outer Critics Circle Awards), Educating Rita, Doubles, The Sorrows of Frederick, Grand Hotel, Hamlet, Sophistry. *Director*: The Runner Stumbles, Say Goodnight Gracie, John Gabriel Borkman, The Little Foxes. *Author*: Booth, Uncle Bob.
PICTURES: Skidoo (debut, 1968), Catch-22, What's Up Doc?, Every Little Crook and Nanny, The Thief Who Came to Dinner, The Front Page, The Great Smokey Roadblock (The Last of the Cowboys), The Muppet Movie, Starting Over, Simon, First Family, My Man Adam, Off Beat, Short Circuit, Hello Again, Mr. & Mrs. Bridge, The Ballad of the Sad Cafe, True Identity, My Cousin Vinny, Charlie's Ear, Rain Without Thunder, My Boyfriend's Back, Searching for Bobby Fischer, Mr. Nanny, Greedy, Guarding Tess, Dangerous Minds, Two Much, Home for the Holidays, Sgt. Bilko, Trial and Error.
TELEVISION: *Movie*: Don't Drink the Water. *Guest*: Miami Vice, The Equalizer.

PENN, ARTHUR
Director. b. Philadelphia, PA, Sept. 27, 1922. e. Black Mountain Coll., Asheville, NC; U. of Perugia, U. of Florence in Italy. Began as TV dir. in 1953, twice winner of Sylvania Award. Appeared in 1994 film Naked in New York.
THEATER: Two for the Seesaw, Miracle Worker (Tony Award, 1960), Toys in the Attic, All the Way Home, Golden Boy, Wait Until Dark, Sly Fox, Monday After the Miracle, Hunting Cockroaches.
PICTURES: The Left-Handed Gun (debut, 1958), The Miracle Worker (Acad. Award nom.), Mickey One (also prod.), The Chase, Bonnie and Clyde (Acad. Award nom.), Alice's Restaurant (Acad. Award nom.; also co-s.p.), Little Big Man, Visions of Eight (dir. segment: The Highest), Night Moves, The Missouri Breaks, Four Friends (also co-prod.), Target, Dead of Winter, Penn and Teller Get Killed (also prod.), Inside.
TELEVISION: *Movie*: The Portrait.

PENN, CHRISTOPHER
Actor. b. Malibu, CA. Son of dir. Leo Penn and actress Eileen Ryan. Brother of actor Sean Penn and musician Michael Penn. Studied acting with Peggy Feury.
PICTURES: Rumble Fish (debut, 1983), All the Right Moves, Footloose, The Wild Life, Pale Rider, At Close Range, Made in USA, Return From the River Kwai, Best of the Best, Mobsters, Leather Jackets, Reservoir Dogs, Best of the Best 2, The Pickle, The Music of Chance, True Romance, Short Cuts, Josh and S.A.M., Beethoven's 2nd, Imaginary Crimes, Fist of the Northstar, Under the Hula Moon, To Wong Foo–Thanks for Everything–Julie Newmar, Sacred Cargo, Mulholland Falls, The Boys Club, The Funeral, Papertrail, Deceiver, One Tough Cop, Rush Hour, The Florentine, Cement.
TELEVISION: *Guest*: Magnun P.I., The Young Riders, North Beach, Rawhide, Chicago Hope.

PENN, ROBIN WRIGHT
Actress. b. Dallas, TX, 1966. m. actor Sean Penn. Was model at age 14 before making acting debut on tv series The Yellow Rose.
PICTURES: Hollywood Vice Squad (debut, 1986), The Princess Bride, Denial, State of Grace, The Playboys, Toys, Forrest Gump, The Crossing Guard, Moll Flanders, Loved, She's So Lovely, Message In a Bottle, Hurlyburly, How to Kill Your Neighbor's Dog.
TELEVISION: *Series*: Santa Barbara. *Pilot*: Home.

PENN, SEAN
Actor, Director, Writer. b. Burbank, CA, Aug. 17, 1960. Son of actor-dir. Leo Penn and actress Eileen Ryan. Brother of actor Christopher Penn and musician Michael Penn. m. actress Robin Wright. e. Santa Monica H.S. Served as apprentice for two years at Group Repertory Theatre, L.A. Acted in: Terrible Jim Fitch, Earthworms, The Girl on the Via Flaminia. First prof. appearance as guest star on TV's Barnaby Jones. On B'way in Heartland, Slab Boys. Also in Hurlyburly (Westwood Playhouse, LA), Goose & Tom Tom (Lincoln Center Theater). Directed, The Kindness of Women (Santa Monica Pink Theater); exec. prod., Remembrance (Santa Monica Playhouse),
PICTURES: *Actor*: Taps (debut, 1981), Fast Times at Ridgemont High, Bad Boys, Crackers, Racing with the Moon, Falcon and the Snowman, At Close Range, Shanghai Surprise, Colors, Judgment in Berlin, Casualties of War, We're No Angels, State of Grace, Carlito's Way, Dead Man Walking, She's So Lovely (also exec. prod.; Cannes Film Festival Award, 1997), Loved (also prod.), U-Turn (also prod.), The Game, Hurlyburly, The Thin Red Line, Sweet and Lowdown, Being John Malkovich (cameo), The Weight of Water, Beaver Trilogy. *Dir./Writer*: The Indian Runner, The Crossing Guard (also co-prod.), The Pledge.
TELEVISION: *Movie*: The Killing of Randy Webster. *Guest*: Barnaby Jones. *Special*: Dear America (reader).

PENNEBAKER, D.A.
Director. r.n. Donn Alan Pennebaker. b. Evanston, IL, July 15, 1925. e. Yale U. Studied engineering, set up own electronics firm. Worked in advertising, before writing and directing documentaries, as well as experimental films. 1958 joined Richard Leacock, Willard Van Dyke and Shirley Clarke in equipment-sharing film co-op, Filmakers. 1960 joined Robert Drew operating out of Time Life with Leacock, Albert Maysles and others. Set up Leacock Pennebaker with Leacock and made several films that were blown up from 16mm to 35mm and released in theatres. Currently works with co-dir. and wife Chris Hegedus and son Frazer Pennebaker, continuing to film unscripted dramas of real events in cinema verite style. Dir. music videos for Suzanne Vega, Victoria Williams, Branford Marsalis, Randy Newman.
PICTURES: Daybreak Express (1956), Opening in Moscow, Primary, David, Jane, Crisis, The Chair, On the Pole, Mr. Pearson, Don't Look Back, Monterey Pop, Beyond the Law, One P.M., Sweet Toronto, Maidstone, Ziggy Stardust and the Spiders From Mars, On the Pole, Town Bloody Hall, The Energy War, Dance Black America, Rockaby, Delorean, Happy Come Home, Depeche Mode: 101, The Music Tells You, The War Room, Keine Zeit, Moon Over Broadway, Woodstock Diary (also ed.).
TELEVISION: Searching for Jimi Hendrix (also d.p., ed).

PEPLOE, MARK
Writer. b. Kenya. Sister is writer Clare Peploe. Raised in England and Italy. e. Magdalen Col., Oxford. Became researcher for documentary dept. of the BBC; then worked as research, writer and dir. for series Creative Persons.
PICTURES: The Pied Piper, The Passenger, The Babysitter, High Season, The Last Emperor (Acad. Award, 1987), The Sheltering Sky, Afraid of the Dark (also dir.), Little Buddha, Victory.

PERAKOS, SPERIE P.
Executive. b. New Britain, CT, Nov. 12, 1920. e. Cheshire Acad., Yale U., Harvard Law Sch. Student mgr., Stanley-Warner Theatres, 1939-40; Perakos Theatres 1940 to present; Capt., U.S.A. Intelligence with 35 inf. division. Fellow, Pierson Coll., Yale, 1946-present; Yale Alumni Bd., 1949 to present; Yale Alumni Film Bd. 1952 to 1980; member Alumni Council for Yale Drama Sch.;

Past pres. Yale Club of New Britain, Conn.; dir. of Films & Filmings Seminars, Pierson Coll., Yale; prod. Antigone, 1964; pres. Norma Film Prod., Inc., 1962 to present. Past pres. and chmn. Yale's Peabody Museum Associates. Pres., Perakos Theatres, Conn. Theatre Associates, Inc. Past Pres., Connecticut Association of Theatre Owners, Secretary, ShowEast. *Member:* Exec. Board of Natl' Assn. of Theatre Owners, C.A.R.A.

PERENCHIO, ANDREW J.
Executive. b. Fresno, CA, Dec. 20, 1930. e. U. of California. Vice pres., Music Corp. of America, 1958-62; General Artists Corp., 1962-64; pres., owner, Chartwell Artists, Ltd., theatrical agency, Los Angeles, 1964; pres. & CEO, Tandem Productions, Inc., and TAT Communications Co., 1973-83, then became principal with Norman Lear in Embassy Communications. Held post of pres. & CEO of Embassy Pictures.

PEREIRA, VANESSA
Casting Director.
PICTURES: Jude, Hamlet, Welcome to Sarajevo, Under the Skin, Spice World, My Son the Fanatic, Resurrection Man, I Want You, Dark City, What Rats Won't Do, Appetite, Elizabeth, Hilary and Jackie, Alegria, The Lost Son, Heart.
TELEVISION: Flowers of the Forest, The Hunger.

PEREZ, ROSIE
Actress. b. Brooklyn, 1964. Attended sch. in L.A. where she became a dancer on Soul Train; then choreographer for music videos and stage shows for such performers as Bobby Brown, The Boys, Diana Ross, LL Cool J, etc. Acting debut in Do the Right Thing.
PICTURES: Do the Right Thing (also choreog.; debut, 1989), White Men Can't Jump, Night on Earth, Untamed Heart, Fearless (Acad. Award nom.), It Could Happen to You, Somebody to Love, A Brother's Kiss, Perdita Durango, The 24 Hour Woman (also co-prod.).
TELEVISION: *Movie*: Criminal Justice, Subway Stories: Tales from the Underground (also exec. prod.). *Series*: In Living Color (choreographer). *Specials*: Rosie Perez Presents Society's Ride (exec. prod.), In a New Light: Sex Unplugged (co-host).

PERKINS, ELIZABETH
Actress. b. Forest Hills, Queens, NY, Nov. 18, 1960. Grew up in Vermont. After high school moved to Chicago to study at Goodman School of Drama. Two months after moving to NY in 1984, landed a role in the national touring co. of Brighton Beach Memoirs, later performing part on Broadway. Acted with Playwright's Horizon, NY Ensemble Theater, Shakespeare in the Park and Steppenwolf Theatre Co. Appeared in short film Teach 109.
PICTURES: About Last Night... (debut, 1986), From the Hip, Big, Sweet Hearts Dance, Love at Large, Avalon, Enid Is Sleeping, He Said She Said, The Doctor, Indian Summer, The Flintstones, Miracle on 34th Street, Moonlight and Valentino, Lesser Prophets, I'm Losing You, Crazy in Alabama.
TELEVISION: *Movie*: For Their Own Good, Cloned. *Mini-series*: The Rescuers: Two Women.

PERKINS, MILLIE
Actress. b. Passaic, NJ, May 12, 1938. Was model when chosen by dir. George Stevens for starring role in The Diary of Anne Frank.
PICTURES: The Diary of Anne Frank (debut, 1959), Wild in the Country, Dulcinea, Ensign Pulver, Ride in the Whirlwind, The Shooting, Wild in the Streets, Cockfighter, Lady Cocoa, The Witch Who Came From the Sea, Table for Five, At Close Range, Jake Speed, Slam Dance, Wall Street, Necronomicon, Two Moon Junction, The Pistol, Bodily Harm, The Chamber.
TELEVISION: *Series*: Knots Landing, Elvis. *Guest*: U.S. Steel Hour, Breaking Point, Murder She Wrote, Our House, Jessie, Hart to Hart, Glitter, Wagon Train, thirtysomething, Touched By An Angel. *Movies*: A.D., The Thanksgiving Promise, Penalty Phase, Anatomy of an Illness, Shattered Vows, License to Kill, Strange Voices, Broken Angel, Best Intentions, The Other Love, Haunting Passion, A Gun in the House, Model Mother, Macbeth (cable tv), Call Me Anna, 72 Hours, Murder of Innocence, The Writing on the Wall, God, The Universe and Hot Fudge Sundaes, The Bounty Hunter: Miles To Go Before I Sleep, The Summer of Ben Tyler, Harvest of Fire.

PERKINS, ROWLAND
Executive. Vice-President, Creative Services, William Morris Agency, 1952–75. Founding President, Creative Artists Agency, 1975–95. Established The Rowland Perkins Company (a.k.a. Double Eagle Entertainment) in 1994 to develop and produce feature, network and cable films; television series and specials; Broadway shows.

PERLMAN, RHEA
Actress. b. Brooklyn, NY, March 31, 1948. e. Hunter Coll. m. actor-dir. Danny DeVito. Co-founder Colonnades Theatre Lab., NY and New Street prod. co with Danny DeVito.
PICTURES: Love Child, My Little Pony (voice), Enid is Sleeping (Over Her Dead Body), Ted & Venus, Class Act, There Goes the Neighborhood, Canadian Bacon, Sunset Park, Matilda.
TELEVISION: *Series*: Cheers (4 Emmy Awards: 1984, 1985, 1986, 1989), Pearl (co-exec. prod.). *Movies*: I Want to Keep My Baby!, Stalk the Wild Child, Having Babies II, Intimate Strangers, Mary Jane Harper Cried Last Night, Like Normal People, Drop-out Father, The Ratings Game, Dangerous Affection, A Family Again, To Grandmother's House We Go, A Place to Be Loved, Spoils of War, In the Doghouse, Houdini, H.E. Double Hockey Sticks. *Specials*: Funny You Don't Look 200, Two Daddies (voice), The Last Halloween.

PERLMAN, RON
Actor. b. New York, NY, April 13, 1950. While in high school, part of comedy team that played clubs. e. City U. of NY, U. of Minnesota, M.F.A. Joined Classic Stage Company, NY, for 2 years.
THEATER: *NY*: The Architect and the Emperor of Assyria (also toured Europe), American Heroes, The Resistible Rise of Arturo Ui, Tiebele and Her Demon, La Tragedie de Carmen, A Few Good Men.
PICTURES: Quest for Fire, The Ice Pirates, The Name of the Rose, Sleepwalkers, The Adventures of Huck Finn, Double Exposure, Romeo Is Bleeding, Crime and Punishment, Cronos, Fluke, The City of Lost Children, The Last Summer, The Island of Dr. Moreau.
TELEVISION: *Series*: Beauty and the Beast. *Movies*: A Stoning in Fulham County, Blind Man's Bluff, Original Sins.

PERLMUTTER, DAVID M.
Producer. b. Toronto, Canada, 1934. e. U. of Toronto. Pres., Quadrant Films Ltd.
PICTURES: The Neptune Factor, Sunday in the Country, It Seemed Like a Good Idea at the Time, Love at First Sight, Find the Lady, Blood and Guts, The Third Walker, Two Solitudes, Fast Company, Double Negative, Nothing Personal, Misdeal, Love.

PERMUT, DAVID A.
Producer. b. New York, NY, March 23, 1954. In 1974, became pres., Diversified Artists Intl.; 1975, pres., Theatre Television Corp.; 1979, formed Permut Presentations, Inc., of which is pres. Production deals with Columbia Pictures (1979), Lorimar Productions (1981), Universal (1985), United Artists (1986), and New Line Cinema (1991).
PICTURES: Give 'Em Hell Harry, Fighting Back (exec. prod.), Blind Date, Richard Pryor—Live in Concert (exec. prod.), Dragnet, The Marrying Man, 29th Street, Captain Ron, Consenting Adults, The Temp, Three of Hearts, Surviving the Game, Trapped in Paradise, Eddie, Face/Off, Chippendales.
TELEVISION: Mistress (sprv. prod.), Love Leads the Way (exec. prod.), Triumph of the Heart: The Ricky Bell Story (prod.), Breaking the Silence (prod.).

PERREAU, GIGI
Actress. r.n. Ghislaine Perreau. b. Los Angeles, CA, Feb. 6, 1941. e. Immaculate Heart H.S. & College. Many stage and TV guest appearances. Now teaching and directing. Among first 50 stars to be honored with star on Hollywood Walk of Fame.
PICTURES: Madame Currie (debut, 1943), Abigail, Dear Heart, Dark Waters, San Diego I Love You, Two Girls and a Sailor, The Master Race, The Seventh Cross, Mr. Skeffington, Yoland and the Thief, Voice of the Whistler, God Is My Co-Pilot, To Each His Own, Alias Mr. Twilight, High Barbaree, Song of Love, Green Dolphin Street, Family Honeymoon, Enchantment, Sainted Sisters, Roseanna McCoy, Song of Surrender, My Foolish Heart, Shadow on the Wall, For Heaven's Sake, Never a Dull Moment, Reunion in Reno, The Lady Pays Off, Weekend with Father, Has Anybody Seen My Gal, Bonzo Goes to College, There's Always Tomorrow, The Man in the Gray Flannel Suit, Dance With Me Henry, Wild Heritage, The Cool and the Crazy, Girls' Town, Tammy Tell Me True, Look in Any Window, Journey to the Center of Time, Hell on Wheels, The Sleepless.
TELEVISION: *Series*: The Betty Hutton Show, Follow the Sun. *Guest*: Alfred Hitchcock Presents, Perry Mason, The Rifleman, The Brady Bunch.

PERRINE, VALERIE
Actress. b. Galveston, TX, Sept. 3 1943. e. U. of Arizona. Was showgirl in Las Vegas before discovered by agent Robert Walker who got her contract with Universal Pictures.
PICTURES: Slaughterhouse 5 (debut, 1972), The Last American Hero, Lenny (NY Film Critics & Cannes Film Fest. Awards; Acad. Award nom.), W. C. Fields & Me, Mr. Billion, Superman, The Magician of Lublin, The Electric Horseman, Can't Stop the Music, Superman II, Agency, The Border, Water, Maid to Order, Reflections in a Dark Sky, Bright Angel, Boiling Point, Girl in the Cadillac, The Break, My Girlfriend's Boyfirend, Curtain Call, 54.
TELEVISION: *Movies*: The Couple Takes a Wife, Ziegfeld: The Man and His Women, Marian Rose White, Malibu, When Your Lover Leaves, Sweet Bird of Youth, Un Casa a Roma, The Burning Shore. Series: Leo and Liz in Beverly Hills. *Special*: Steambath.

PERRY, LUKE
Actor. r.n. Coy Luther Perry III. b. Mansfield, OH, Oct. 11, 1966. To LA then NY as teen to become actor, landing role on daytime serial Loving.
PICTURES: Terminal Bliss (debut, 1992), Scorchers, Buffy the Vampire Slayer, At Home With the Webbers (cameo), 8 Seconds, From the Edge, Christmas Vacation, Normal Life, American Strays, Lifebreath, The Fifth Element, Last Breath, Indiscreet, The Florentine.
TELEVISION: *Movies*: Riot, Storm. *Series*: Loving, Another World, Beverly Hills 90210. *Guest:* The Simpsons (voice), Spin City.

PERRY, MATTHEW
Actor. b. Williamstown, MA, Aug. 19, 1969.
PICTURES: A Night in the Life of Jimmy Reardon, She's Out of Control, Getting In, Fools Rush In, Almost Heroes, Three to Tango, The Whole Nine Yards, The Kid, Servicing Sarah.
TELEVISION: *Movies:* Dance 'til Dawn, Call Me Anna, Deadly Relations, Parallel Lives. *Series:* Second Chance, Sydney, Home Free, Friends. *Guest:* Silver Spoons, The Tracey Ullman Show, Just the Ten of Us, Highway to Heaven, Growing Pains, Empty Nest, Who's the Boss, Beverly Hills 90210, Dream On, Caroline in the City.

PERRY, SIMON
Producer, Writer. b. Farnham, England, Aug. 5, 1943. e. Cambridge Univ., 1965. Ent. ind. 1974. Early career in stage and television production. Prod. mini-budget feature Knots; prod. dir. Eclipse. Served on bureau staff of Variety. Ran the National Film Development Fund for two years. 1982 set up Umbrella Films to produce Another Time Another Place, Loose Connections, Nineteen Eighty Four, Hotel Du Paradis, Nanou, White Mischief, The Playboys, Innocent Lies. Chief exec. of British Screen Finance since 1991.

PERSKY, LESTER
Executive. b. New York, NY, July 6, 1927. e. Brooklyn Coll. Officer in U.S. Merchant Marine, 1946-48. Founder and pres. of own adv. agency, 1951-1964. Theatrical stage prod., 1966-69. 1973, creative dir. and co-owner Persky Bright Org. (owner-financier of numerous motion pictures for private investment group). Films: Last Detail, Golden Voyage of Sinbad, For Pete's Sake, California Split, The Man Who Would Be King, The Front, Shampoo, Hard Times, Taxi Driver, Missouri Breaks, Funny Lady, Gator, Bound for Glory, Sinbad and the Eye of the Tiger. Lester Persky Productions, Inc.
PICTURES: *Producer*: Fortune and Men's Eyes, Equus, Hair, Yanks.
TELEVISION: *Mini-Series*: Poor Little Rich Girl (Golden Globe Award, 1987), A Woman Named Jackie (Emmy Award, 1992), Liz: The Elizabeth Taylor Story.

PERSOFF, NEHEMIAH
Actor. b. Jerusalem, Israel, Aug. 2, 1919. e. Hebrew Technical Inst., 1934-37. Electrician, 1937-39; signal maint., N.Y. subway, 1939-41. Studied acting with Stella Adler and the Actors Studio. L.A. Critics Award 1971 for Sholem-Sholem Alecheim, and The Dybbuk. Has had exhibitions of his watercolor paintings in California, Florida; on permanent exhibit in Cambria, Ca.
THEATER: Sundown Beach, Galileo, Richard III, King Lear, Peter Pan, Peer Gynt, Tiger At the Gates, Colombe, Flahooly, Montserrat, Only in America. Tour: Fiddler on the Roof, Man of La Mancha, Oliver, Death of a Salesman (Stratford, Ont.), Peter Pan, I'm Not Rappaport, Sholem Aleichem (Drama Log & Bay Area Critics Circle Awards).
PICTURES: On the Waterfront, The Wild Party, The Harder They Fall, The Wrong Man, Men in War, This Angry Age, The Badlanders, Never Steal Anything Small, Al Capone, Some Like It Hot, Green Mansions, The Big Show, The Comancheros, The Hook, A Global Affair, Fate Is the Hunter, The Greatest Story Ever Told, The Power, The Money Jungle, Panic in the City, Mafia, The People Next Door, Mrs. Pollifax—Spy, Red Sky at Morning, Psychic Killer, Voyage of the Damned, In Search of Historic Jesus, Yentl, An American Tail (voice), The Last Temptation of Christ, Twins, Day of the Outlaw, The Dispossessed, An American Tail: Fievel Goes West (voice), An American Tail III (voice).
TELEVISION: *Guest*: Playhouse 90, Philco-Goodyear Show, Kraft, For Whom the Bells Tolls (Sylvania Award, 1958), Producers Showcase, Danger, You Are There, Untouchables, Route 66, Naked City, Wagon Train, Rawhide, Gunsmoke, Thriller, Hitchcock, Bus Stop, Mission Impossible, Henderson Monster, Rebels, Twilight Zone, Five Fingers, Mr. Lucky, The Wild Wild West, I Spy, Hawaii 5-0, Columbo, Barney Miller, L.A. Law, Star Trek, Law and Order, Reasonable Doubts. *Movies*: Sadat, Adderly, The French Atlantic Affair, Sex Symbol, Stranger Within.

PESCI, JOE
Actor. b. Newark, NJ, Feb. 9, 1943. Raised in Belleville, NJ. First show business job as child on TV's Star Time Kids. Worked as mason's laborer, restaurant owner, prior to becoming actor.
PICTURES: Death Collector, Raging Bull, I'm Dancing as Fast as I Can, Dear Mr. Wonderful (Ruby's Dream), Easy Money, Eureka, Once Upon a Time in America, Man on Fire, Moonwalker, Lethal Weapon 2, Betsy's Wedding, Goodfellas (Acad. Award, best supporting actor, 1990), Home Alone, The Super, JFK, My Cousin Vinny, Tuti Dentro, Lethal Weapon 3, The Public Eye, Home Alone 2: Lost in New York, A Bronx Tale, Jimmy Hollywood, With Honors, Casino, 8 Heads in a Duffel Bag, Gone Fishing, Lethal Weapon 4.
TELEVISION: *Series*: Half Nelson. *Movies*: Half Nelson (pilot), Backtrack. *Guest*: Tales From the Crypt (Split Personality).

PETERS, BERNADETTE
Actress. r.n. Bernadette Lazzara. b. New York, NY, Feb. 28, 1948. e. Quintano Sch. for Young Professionals, NY. Professional debut at age 5 on TV's Horn & Hardart Children's Hour, followed by Juvenile Jury and Name That Tune. Stage debut with N.Y. City Center production of The Most Happy Fella (1959).
THEATER: Gypsy (1961), This is Goggle, Riverwind, The Penny Friend, Curley McDimple, Johnny No-Trump, George M! (Theatre World Award), Dames at Sea (Drama Desk Award), La Strada, W.C. & Me, On the Town (1971 revival), Tartuffe, Mack and Mabel, Sally and Marsha, Sunday in the Park With George, Song and Dance (Tony, Drama Desk & Drama League Awards), Into the Woods, The Goodbye Girl.
PICTURES: Ace Eli and Rodger of the Skies (debut, 1973), The Longest Yard, W.C. Fields & Me, Vigilante Force, Silent Movie, The Jerk, Tulips, Pennies from Heaven, Heartbeeps, Annie, Slaves of New York, Pink Cadillac, Alice, Impromptu.
TELEVISION: *Series*: All's Fair. *Mini-Series*: The Martian Chronicles. *Specials*: George M, They Said It with Music, Party at Annapolis, Rich Thin and Beautiful (host), Faerie Tale Theatre, The Last Mile. *Pilot*: The Owl and the Pussycat. *Movies*: The Islander, David, Fall from Grace, The Last Best Year.

PETERS, BROCK
Actor. r.n. Brock Fisher. b. Harlem, NY, July 2, 1927. e. CCNY, U. of Chicago. Had numerous featured roles on and off B'way. in road and stock cos., nightclubs, TV. Toured with DePaur Infantry Chorus as bass soloist, 1947-50. Appeared in short film From These Roots.
THEATER: Porgy and Bess (debut, 1943), Anna Lucasta, My Darlin' Aida, Mister Johnson, King of the Dark Chamber, Othello, Kwamina, The Great White Hope (tour), Lost in the Stars, Driving Miss Daisy (Natl. Co.).
PICTURES: Carmen Jones (debut, 1954), Porgy and Bess, To Kill a Mockingbird, Heavens Above, The L-Shaped Room, The Pawnbroker, Major Dundee, The Incident, P.J., The Daring Game, Ace High, The MacMasters, Black Girl, Soylent Green, Slaughter's Big Rip-off, Lost in the Stars, Million Dollar Dixie Deliverance, Framed, Two-Minute Warning, Star Trek IV: The Voyage Home, Star Trek VI: The Undiscovered Country, Alligator II: The Mutation, The Importance of Being Earnest.
TELEVISION: Arthur Godfrey's Talent Scouts (debut, 1953), *Series*: The Young and the Restless. *Guest*: Eleventh Hour, It Takes a Thief, Mannix, Mod Squad. *Mini-series*: Seventh Avenue, Black Beauty, Roots: The Next Generations. *Movies*: Welcome Home Johnny Bristol, SST: Death Flight, The Incredible Journey of Doctor Meg Laurel, The Adventures of Huckleberry Finn, Agatha Christie's Caribbean Mystery, To Heal a Nation, Broken Angel, The Big One: The Great Los Angeles Earthquake, Highway Heartbreakers, The Secret. *Specials*: Challenge of the Go Bots (voice), Living the Dream: A Tribute to Dr. Martin Luther King. *Co-prod.*: This Far By Faith.

PETERS, JANICE C.
Executive. e. Wayne State U., BS, and Stanford U., masters in mgmt. Began in local/long distance telecom. field. Became pres., CEO, U S WEST NewVector Group, a cellular comm. co., and pres. of wireless ops., U S WEST MediaOne before becoming managing dir. of One 2 One, a cellular comm. co. in the UK in 1996. Currently pres. and CEO of MediaOne, broadband svcs. under MediaOne Group.

PETERS, JON
Producer. b. Van Nuys, CA, 1947. Started hair-styling business; built it into multimillion-dollar firm before turning film producer. Formed Jon Peters Organization. 1980, joined with Peter Guber and Neil Bogart to form The Boardwalk Co. (dissolved 1981). Later Guber-Peters-Barris Company. 1989, became co-chairman of Columbia Pictures. Resigned, 1991.
PICTURES: A Star Is Born, Eyes of Laura Mars, The Main Event, Die Laughing, Caddyshack. *Co-Prod./Co-Exec. Prod. with Peter Guber*: An American Werewolf in London, Missing, Six Weeks, Flashdance, D.C. Cab, Vision Quest, Legend of Billie Jean, Clue, The Color Purple, Head Office, The Clan of the Cave Bear, Youngblood, The Witches of Eastwick, Innerspace, Who's That Girl, Gorillas in the Mist, Caddyshack II, Rain Man, Batman, Tango and Cash, The Bonfire of the Vanities, Batman Returns, This Boy's Life, With Honors, Money Train. *Also: Prod.*: My Fellow Americans (prod.), Rosewood, Wild Wild West.

TELEVISION: *Movies*: Bay Coven (co-exec. prod.), Nightmare at Bitter Creek (exec. prod.).

PETERSEN, PAUL
Actor. b. Glendale, CA, Sept. 23, 1945. e. Valley Coll. Original Disney Mouseketeer (TV). Recorded hit songs She Can't Find Her Keys, and My Dad in 1962. In the late 1960's turned to writing beginning with a Marcus Welby script followed by paperback novels in 1970's. Author of book about Disney empire, Walt Mickey and Me (1977), and co-author of It's a Wonderful Life Trivia Book (1992). President and founder of A Minor Consideration, a support foundation for former kid actors with a current membership of 150 movie, tv and sports stars spanning the past 70 years.
PICTURES: Houseboat, This Could Be the Night, The Happiest Millionaire, Journey to Shiloh, A Time for Killing.
TELEVISION: *Series*: The Donna Reed Show. *Guest*: Playhouse 90, Lux Video Theatre, GE Theatre, The Virginian, Ford Theatre, Valentine's Day, Shindig. *Movies*: Something for a Lonely Man, Gidget Grows Up, Scout's Honor.

PETERSEN, WILLIAM
Actor. b. Chicago, IL, 1953. e. Idaho State U. Active in Chicago theatre; helped to found Ix, an ensemble acting group now called the Remains Theatre. Acted in Moby Dick, In the Belly of the Beast, A Streetcar Named Desire, etc. 1986, formed company with prod. Cynthia Chvatal called High Horse Prods.
THEATER: *NY*: Night of the Iguana.
PICTURES: To Live and Die in L.A., Manhunter, Amazing Grace and Chuck, Cousins, Young Guns II, Hard Promises (also co-prod.), Passed Away, Fear.
TELEVISION: *Movies*: Long Gone (HBO), Keep the Change (also co-prod.), Curacao. *Mini-Series*: The Kennedys of Massachusetts, Return to Lonesome Dove, The Beast.

PETERSEN, WOLFGANG
Director, Writer. b. Emden, Germany, March 14, 1941. Career as asst. stage dir. at Ernst Deutsch Theatre in Hamburg before entering 4 year program at the German Film & TV Academy wher he directed for television and later theatrical films.
PICTURES: One of Us Two, Black and White Like Day and Night (also s.p.), The Consequence (also s.p.), Das Boot (The Boat; also s.p.; Acad. Award nom. for dir.), The Neverending Story (also s.p.), Enemy Mine, Shattered (also s.p., co-prod.), In the Line of Fire (also co-exec.prod.), Outbreak (also co-prod.), Air Force One (also prod.), The Perfect Storm (also prod.).
TELEVISION: I Will Kill You Wolf (dir. debut 1970), Tatort (series), Smog (Prix Futura Award, 1975), For Your Love Only (also released theatrically), Scene of the Crime (series).

PETERSON, S. DEAN
Executive. b. Toronto, Canada, December 18, 1923. e. Victoria Coll., U. of Toronto. WWII service RCNVR; 1946 TV newsreel cameraman NBC; founded own prod. co. in 1947; incorporated Dordean Realty Limited to acquire new studios 1959; formed Peterson Productions Limited in 1957 to make TV commercials and sponsored theatrical shorts; formed Studio City Limited in 1965 to produce TV series and features acquiring an additional studio complex and backlot in Kleinberg, Ontario; 1972 formed SDP Communications Ltd. to package M.P. and TV; 1970 incorporated Intermedia Financial Services Limited to provide specialized financing and consultation to companies in M.P. and TV industries. Past-President Canadian Film and Television Production Assn., mbr. Variety Club, Tent 28; Canadian Society of Cinematographers; Directors Guild of America, Directors Guild of Canada, SMPTE.

PETERSON, RICHARD W.
Executive. b. Denver, CO, June 15, 1949. e. Col. Sch. of Broadcasting, Harper Coll. Joined Kennedy Theatres, Chicago, 1966. 1968 went with Great States Theatres (now Cineplex Odeon), Chicago. Was city mgr. of Crocker and Grove Theatres, Elgin, IL. 1973 joined American Automated Theatres, Oklahoma City, as dir. of adv., pub. Promoted to dir. of U.S. theatre operations. Worked for American International Pictures, Dallas, TX. Then moved to Dal Art Film Exchange and B & B Theatres as general mgr.; 1987 took over 7 screens from McLendon and formed own co., Peterson Theatres, Inc, now operating 17 screens.

PETIT, HENRI-DOMINIQUE
Executive. b. Baden-Baden, Germany. e. Ecole Superieure de Physique et Chimie de Paris, Univ. of Paris. Joined Kodak 1975 as asst. mgr. of the Purchasing Division, Kodak Pathe, France. 1980, asst., then mgr. of Kodak Pathe Photofinishing Lab (1981). 1984, became bus. mgr. Business Information Systems and Corporate Accounts, Kodak Pathe. 1987, named bus. mgr. of Photofinishing Systems Division. 1989, appointed gen. mgr. and v.p. Motion Picture and Television Imaging, Europe/Africa/Middle East Region. Dec., 1992, named v.p. and gen. mgr. Motion Picture and Television Imaging.

PETRIE, DANIEL
Director. b. Glace Bay, Nova Scotia, Nov. 26, 1920. e. St. Francis Xavier U., Nova Scotia; Columbia U., MA, 1945; post-grad. Northwestern U. Broadway actor 1945-46. TV dir. from 1950. Son Daniel Petrie Jr. is a screenwriter; son Donald Petrie is a dir.
THEATER: Shadow of My Enemy, Who'll Save the Plowboy?, Mornin' Sun, Monopoly, The Cherry Orchard, Volpone, A Lesson from Aloes.
PICTURES: The Bramble Bush (debut, 1960), A Raisin in the Sun, The Main Attraction, Stolen Hours, The Idol, The Spy With a Cold Nose, The Neptune Factor, Buster and Billie, Lifeguard, The Betsy, Resurrection, Fort Apache The Bronx, Six Pack, The Bay Boy (also s.p.; Genie Award), Square Dance (also prod.), Rocket Gibraltar, Cocoon: The Return, Lassie, The Associate.
TELEVISION: *Movies*: Silent Night Lonely Night, A Howling in the Woods, A Stranger in Town, Moon of the Wolf, Trouble Comes to Town, Mousey, Returning Home, Eleanor and Franklin (Emmy Award, 1976), Sybil, Eleanor and Franklin: The White House Years (Emmy Award, 1977), Harry Truman, Plain Speaking (Emmy nom.), The Dollmaker (Emmy nom.), The Execution of Raymond Graham (Emmy nom.), Half a Lifetime, My Name is Bill W. (also prod.; Emmy nom.), Mark Twain and Me (also prod., Emmy Award), A Town Torn Apart (also prod., Emmy nom.), Kissinger and Nixon, Calm at Sunset.

PETRIE, DONALD
Director. b. New York, NY. Son of dir. Daniel Petrie. Moved to LA as teenager, becoming tv actor. Attended American Film Inst. dir. program, where he made short film The Expert. Was then hired to dir. Mister Magic esisode of Amazing Stories.
PICTURES: Mystic Pizza (debut, 1988), Opportunity Knocks, Grumpy Old Men, The Favor, Richie Rich, The Associate, My Favorite Martian.
TELEVISION: *Series episodes*: MacGyver, The Equalizer, L.A. Law, Players. *Special*: Have You Tried Talking to Patty?

PETROU, DAVID MICHAEL
Writer, Producer, Public Relations Executive. b. Washington, DC, Nov. 3, 1949. e. U. of Maryland, B.A.; Georgetown U., M.A. Publicity assoc., Psychiatric Institutes of America, Washington, DC, 1971; assoc. dir. of publicity & film liaison, Random House, 1974; guest lecturer, screen writing & film production, The American University Consortium, Washington, DC, spring, 1980; Woodrow Wilson Fellowship, 1971. Entered industry in 1975. Joined Salkind Organization in chg. of literary projects. Worked in numerous production capacities on Crossed Swords, Superman, Superman II. 1977, exec. in chg. of literary development, Salkind. Wrote Crossed Swords (1978) and The Making of Superman. Co-authored screenplay, Shoot to Kill. 1978-79, promotional dev. on Time after Time for Warner Bros.; 1980-83, dir., special projects Joseph Kennedy Foundation. 1983-84, sr. edit. for entertainment, Regardie's Magazine; 1984-86, sr. exec., p.r. div., Abramson Associates; 1986-88, sr. v.p., Eisner, Held & Petrou, Inc., p.r. agency; 1988-present, pres. & COO, Eisner Petrou & Associates Inc. Baltimore-Wash., marketing communications agency. 1992, named chmn. of American Film Institute's Second Decade Council. Bd. Member: Choral Arts Society of Washington, University of Maryland Center for the Performing Arts, Foundation for Contemporary Mental Health, Washington Men's Camerata.

PETTET, JOANNA
Actress. b. London, England, Nov. 16, 1944. Raised in Canada. Studied acting at Neighborhood Playhouse in NY.
PICTURES: The Group (debut, 1966), The Night of the Generals, Casino Royale, Robbery, Blue, The Best House in London, Welcome to Arrow Beach, The Evil, An Eye for an Eye, Double Exposure, Sweet Country, Terror in Paradise.
TELEVISION: *Series*: Knots Landing. *Mini-Series*: Captains and the Kings. *Movies*: Footsteps, The Delphi Bureau, The Weekend Nun, Pioneer Woman, A Cry in the Wilderness, The Desperate Miles, The Hancocks, The Dark Side of Innocence, Sex and the Married Woman, Cry of the Innocent, The Return of Frank Cannon.

PETTY, LORI
Actress. b. Chattanooga, TN, 1965. Worked as graphic artist before turning to acting.
PICTURES: Cadillac Man, Point Break, A League of Their Own, Free Willy, Poetic Justice, In the Army Now, Tank Girl, The Glass Shield, Relax...It's Just Sex, Clubland.
TELEVISION: *Series*: The Thorns, Booker, Lush Life, Brimstone.

PEYSER, JOHN
Producer, Director. b. New York, NY, Aug. 10, 1916. e. Colgate U., 1938. In TV ind. since 1939, with Psychological Warfare Div., ETO., W.W.II; pres. Peyser/Vance Productions, Woodland Hills, CA.
PICTURES: The Open Door, Kashmiri Run, Four Rode Out, Massacre Harbor.
TELEVISION: *Director*: Hawaii Five-O, Mannix, Movin On, Swiss Family Robinson, Bronk, Combat, Untouchables, Rat Patrol, Honeymoon with a Stranger.

PFEIFFER, MICHELLE
Actress. b. Santa Ana, CA, April 29, 1957. Sister of actress Deedee Pfeiffer. While attending jr. coll. and working as supermarket checkout clerk, won Miss Orange County beauty contest. Began taking acting classes in L.A. Stage debut in L.A. prod. of A Playground in the Fall. NY Theatre debut 1989 in Twelfth Night (Central Park).
PICTURES: The Hollywood Nights (debut, 1980), Falling in Love Again, Charlie Chan and the Curse of the Dragon Queen, Grease 2, Scarface, Into the Night, Ladyhawke, Sweet Liberty, The Witches of Eastwick, Amazon Women on the Moon, Married to the Mob, Tequila Sunrise, Dangerous Liaisons (Acad. Award nom.), The Fabulous Baker Boys (NY, LA & & Natl. Society of Film Critics Awards; Acad. Award nom.), The Russia House, Frankie and Johnny, Batman Returns, Love Field (Acad. Award nom.), The Age of Innocence, Wolf, Dangerous Minds, Up Close and Personal, To Gillian On Her 37th Birthday, One Fine Day (also exec. prod.), A Thousand Acres, A Midsummer Night's Dream, The Deep End of the Ocean (also prod.), Prince of Egypt (voice), The Story of Us, What Lies Beneath.
TELEVISION: *Series*: Delta House, B.A.D. Cats. *Movies*: The Solitary Man, Callie and Son, Splendor in the Grass, The Children Nobody Wanted. *Specials*: One Too Many, Tales from the Hollywood Hills (Natica Jackson). *Guest*: Fantasy Island, The Simpsons (voice).

PHILLIPPE, RYAN
Actor. r.n. Matthew Ryan Phillippe. b. New Castle, DE, Sept. 10, 1974. m. actress Reese Witherspoon.
PICTURES: Crimson Tide, Invader, White Squall, Nowhere, I Know What You Did Last Summer, Playing by Heart, Homegrown, Little Boy Blue, 54, Cruel Intentions, The Way of the Gun, Anti-Trust, Company Man, Lukas-En mordares biografi.
TELEVISION: *Movies/Specials:* The Secrets of Lake Success, Deadly Invasion: The Killer Bee Nightmare. *Series:* One Life to Live. *Guest:* Matlock, Due South, Chicago Hope, The Outer Limits.

PHILLIPS, JULIA
Producer. b. Brooklyn, NY, April 7, 1944. e. Mt. Holyoke Coll. Production asst. at McCall's Magazine; later became textbook copywriter for Macmillan; story editor, Paramount; creative exec., First Artists Prods., NY. In 1970 with former husband, Michael Phillips and actor Tony Bill formed Bill/Phillips Productions to develop film projects. Author of You'll Never Eat Lunch in This Town Again (Random House, 1991).
PICTURES: Steelyard Blues, The Sting (Acad. Award for Best Picture, 1973), Taxi Driver, The Big Bus, Close Encounters of the Third Kind, The Beat (co-prod.).

PHILLIPS, LESLIE
Actor, Producer. b. London, England, April 20, 1924. Early career as child actor. Ent. m.p. ind. 1935.
PICTURES: A Lassie From Lancashire (debut, 1935), The Citadel, Rhythm Serenade, Train of Events, The Woman With No Name, Pool of London, The Galloping Major, Breaking the Sound Barrier, The Fake, The Limping Man, Time Bomb, The Price of Greed, Value for Money, The Gamma People, As Long as They're Happy, The Big Money, Brothers in Law, The Barretts of Wimpole Street, Just My Luck, Les Girls, The Smallest Show on Earth, High Flight, I Was Monte's Double, The Man Who Liked Funerals, The Angry Hills, Carry on Nurse, Ferdinand of Naples, This Other Eden, Carry on Teacher, Please Turn Over, The Navy Lark, Doctor in Love, Watch Your Stern, No Kidding, Carry on Constable, Inn for Trouble, Raising the Wind, In the Doghouse, Very Important Persons, Crooks Anonymous, The Longest Day, The Fast Lady, Father Came Too, Doctor in Clover, You Must Be Joking, Maroc 7, Some Will Some Won't, Doctor in Trouble, The Magnificent 7 Deadly Sins, Not Now Darling, Don't Just Lie There Say Something!, Spanish Fly, Not Now Comrade, Out of Africa, Empire of the Sun, Scandal, Mountains of the Moon, King Ralph, Carry on Columbus, August, Caught In The Act.
TELEVISION: Our Man at St. Marks, Impasse, The Gong Game, Time and Motion Man, Reluctant Debutante, A Very Fine Line, The Suit, The Culture Vultures (series), Edward Woodward Show, Casanova 74 (series), Redundant—or the Wife's Revenge, You'll Never See Me Again, Mr. Palfrey of Westminister, Monte Carlo, Rumpole, Summers Lease, Chancer, Comic Strip, Who Bombed Birmingham, Life After Life, Thacker, Chancer II, The Oz Trial, Lovejoy, Boon, The Changeling, Bermuda Grace, Royal Celebration, Honey for Tea, House of Windsor, Two Golden Balls, Love on a Branch Line, Vanity Dies Hard, Edgar Wallace (Germany), Canterville Ghost, Woof, The Bill, The Pale Horse.

PHILLIPS, LOU DIAMOND
Actor. r.n. Lou Upchurch. b. Philippines, Feb. 17, 1962. Raised in Corpus Christi, TX. e. U. of Texas, Arlington (BFA. drama). Studied film technique with Adam Roarke, becoming asst. dir./instructor with the Film Actor's Lab, 1983-86. Regional theater includes: A Hatful of Rain, Whose Life Is It Anyway?, P.S. Your Cat Is Dead, The Lady's Not for Burning, Doctor Faustus, Hamlet.
THEATER: *NY*: The King and I (Bdwy. debut, Tony nom.)
PICTURES: Angel Alley, Interface, Trespasses (also co-s.p.), Harley, La Bamba, Stand and Deliver, Young Guns, Dakota (also assoc. prod.), Disorganized Crime, Renegades, The First Power, A Show of Force, Young Guns II, Ambition (also s.p.), The Dark Wind, Shadow of the Wolf, Dangerous Touch (also dir.), Teresa's Tattoo, Sioux City (also dir.), Undertow, Boulevard, Courage Under Fire, Another Day in Paradise (cameo), The Big Hit, Picking Up the Pieces, Brokedown Palace, Bats, Supernova.
TELEVISION: *Movies*: Time Bomb, The Three Kings, Extreme Justice, The Wharf Rat, In a Class of His Own, Hangman. *Specials*: Avenue Z Afternoon, Wind in the Wire. *Guest*: Dallas, Miami Vice.

PHILLIPS, MICHAEL
Producer. b. Brooklyn, NY, June 29, 1943. e. Dartmouth Coll., B.A., 1965. NYU, Law Sch. J.D., 1968. Indep. m.p. prod. 1971.
PICTURES: Steelyard Blues, The Sting (Acad. Award for Best Picture, 1973), Taxi Driver (Golden Palm Award at Cannes), The Big Bus, Close Encounters of the Third Kind, Heartbeeps, Cannery Row, The Flamingo Kid, Don't Tell Mom the Babysitter's Dead, Mom and Dad Save the World, Eyes of an Angel, The Companion, Mimic (exec.).
TELEVISION: *Movie*: Jane's House.

PHILLIPS, MICHELLE
Actress. r.n. Holly Michelle Gilliam. b. Long Beach, CA, June 4, 1944. Daughter is actress-singer Chynna Phillips. Former member of The Mamas and the Papas. Co-wrote hit single California Dreamin'. *Author:* California Dreamin': The Story of The Mamas and The Papas (1986).
PICTURES: Monterey Pop, The Last Movie, Dillinger, Valentino, Sidney Sheldon's Bloodline, The Man With Bogart's Face, Savage Harvest, American Anthem, Let It Ride, Scissors, Army of One, Keep on Running.
TELEVISION: *Series*: Hotel, Knots Landing, Second Chances. *Mini-Series*: Aspen, The French Atlantic Affair. *Movies*: The Death Squad, The California Kid, The Users, Moonlight, Mickey Spillane's Mike Hammer: Murder Me Murder You, Secrets of a Married Man, Stark: Mirror Image, Assault and Matrimony, Trenchcoat in Paradise, Rubdown, Paint Me a Murder, Covenant. *Guest*: Owen Marshall, Matt Houston, The Fall Guy, Murder She Wrote, T.J. Hooker, Hotel, Fantasy Island, Love Boat, Burke's Law, Robin's Hood, Lois & Clark, Herman's Head.

PHILLIPS, SIAN
Actress. b. Bettws, Wales. e. Univ. of Wales. Studied acting at RADA. London stage debut 1957 in title role in Hedda. Has made numerous recordings including Pal Joey, Gigi, A Little Night Music, Remember Mama.
THEATER: Saint Joan, The Three Sisters, Taming of the Shrew, Duchess of Malfi, Lizard on the Rock, Gentle Jack, The Night of the Iguana, Ride a Cock Horse, Man and Superman, The Burglar, The Cardinal of Spain, Alpha Beta, Spinechiller, A Woman of No Importance, You Never Can Tell, Dear Liar, Pal Joey (SWET nom.), Major Barbara, Gigi, Paris Match, Painting Churches, Vanilla, Ghosts (Artist of the Year nom.), Marlene, A Little Night Music (Olivier nom.), Snow Spider, many others. B'way debut 1994 in An Inspector Calls.
PICTURES: Becket, Young Cassidy, Laughter in the Dark, Goodbye Mr. Chips (NY Film Critics & Critics Circle Awards, 1969), Murphy's War, Under Milk Wood, Clash of the Titans, Dune, The Doctor and the Devils, Valmont, The Age of Innocence, A Painful Case, House of America.
TELEVISION: *Mini-Series*: Shoulder to Shoulder, How Green Was My Valley (BAFTA Award), I Claudius (BAFTA & Royal TV Society Awards), Crime and Punishment, Tinker Tailor Soldier Spy, Vanity Fair. *Movies*: Ewoks: The Battle for Endor–Dark River, The Two Mrs. Grenvilles, Out of Time, Dark River. *Specials*: Off to Philadelphia in the Morning, Sean O'Casey, How Many Miles to Babylon?, Lady Windermere's Fan, Language and Landscape, Heartbreak House, Don Juan in Hell, Summer Silence, Shadow of the Noose, Snow Spider, The Quiet Man, The Sex Game, A Mind To Kill, Ivanhoe, Chestnut Soldier (BAFTA nom.).

PHOENIX, JOAQUIN
Actor. b. Puerto Rico, Oct. 28, 1974. Brother of the late River Phoenix.
PICTURES: SpaceCamp, Russkies, Parenthood, To Die For, Inventing the Abbotts, U Turn, Clay Pigeons, 8 MM, The Yards, Gladiator, Quills, Buffalo Soldiers.
TELEVISION: *Movie*: Secret Witness. *Series*: Morningstar/Eveningstar.

PIALAT, MAURICE
Director, Writer. b. Cunlhat, Puy de Dome, France, Aug. 21, 1925. Worked as a painter and sometime actor before turning to film in 1952. Made a number of short films including L'Amour Existe (award winner Venice Film Fest., 1960). Worked in television before feature debut in 1967.

PICTURES: *Dir./Writer*: L'Enfance Nue (Naked Childhood; Prix Jean Vigo Award), We Will Not Grow Old Together, La Gueule Ouverte (also prod.), Passe ton Bac d'Abord (Graduate First), Loulou, A Nos Amours (also actor; Prix Louis Delluc Award), Police, Under Satan's Sun (also actor; Golden Palm Award, Cannes Festival), Van Gogh, Le Garcu, Bastard Brood (actor only), Les Auto-Stoppeuses.
TELEVISION: Janine, Maitre Galip, La Maison des Bois.

PICARDO, ROBERT
Actor. b. Philadelphia, PA, Oct. 27, 1953. e. Yale. Studied acting at Circle in the Square Theater School.
THEATER: *NY:* Sexual Perversity in Chicago, Gemini, Tribute.
PICTURES: The Howling, Star 80, Oh God You Devil, Explorers, Legend, Back to School, Munchies, Innerspace, Amazon Women on the Moon, Jack's Back, Dead Heat, The 'burbs, 976-EVIL, Loverboy, Total Recall, Gremlins II, Samantha, Motorama, Matinee, Wagons East!, The Pagemaster (voice), Menno's Mind, Star Trek: First Contact, Small Soldiers.
TELEVISION: *Series:* China Beach, The Wonder Years, Star Trek: Voyager. *Movies:* The Dream Merchants, The Violation of Sarah McDavid, Lois Gibbs and the Love Canal, Dixie: Changing Habits, The Other Woman, Runaway Daughters, White Mile, Out There, The Second Civil War.

PICCOLI, MICHEL
Actor. r.n. Jacques Piccoli. b. Paris, France, Dec. 27, 1925. Since his film debut in The Sorcerer in 1945 has had impressive career on the French stage and in films working for major French dirs. Renoir, Bunuel, Melville, Resnais, Clouzot, Godard as well as Hitchcock. Until 1957 was mgr. of Theatre Babylone in Paris. Formed prod. co. Films 66. Produced: Themroc (1972); La Faille; Les Enfants Gates.
PICTURES: The Sorcerer, Le Point du Jour, French Can Can, The Witches of Salem, Le Bal des Espiona, Gina, Le Doulos, Contempt, Diary of a Chambermaid, Lady L, La Guerre Est Finie, The Young Girls of Rochefort, Un Homme de Trop, Belle de Jour, La Chamade, Dillinger Is Dead, L'Invasion, The Milky Way, Topaz, The Things of Life, Ten Days' Wonder, The Discreet Charm of the Bourgeoisie, Themroc, Wedding in Blood, La Grande Bouffe, The Last Woman, Leonor, 7 Deaths by Prescription, The Weak Spot, F For Fairbanks, Mado, Todo Modo, Rene the Cane, Spoiled Children, Strauberg Is Here, The Fire's Share, Little Girl in Blue Velvet, The Savage State, The Sugar, The Bit Between the Teeth, La Divorcement, Leap into the Void, The Price for Survival, Atlantic City, The Prodigal Daughter, Beyond the Door, The Eyes The Mouth, Passion, A Room in Town, Will the High Salaried Workers Please Raise Their Hands!!!, The General of the Dead Army, La Passante, The Prize of Peril, Adieu Bonaparte, Dangerous Moves, Danger in the House, Long Live Life!, Success Is the Best Revenge, The Sailor 512, Departure, Return, Mon Beau-Frere a Tue Ma Soeur, The Nonentity, The Prude, Bad Blood, Undiscovered Country, Blanc de Chine, Le Peuple Singe (narrator), The French Revolution, May Fools, La Belle Noiseuse, The Children Thief, Archipelago, Punctured Life, Martha and I, Traveling Companion.

PICERNI, PAUL
Actor. b. New York, NY, Dec. 1, 1922. e. Loyola U., Los Angeles. U.S. Air Force 1943-46; head of drama dept. Mt. St. Mary's Coll., 1949-50.
PICTURES: Saddle Tramp, Breakthrough, Operation Pacific, The Tanks Are Coming, Force of Arms, I Was a Communist for the FBI, Mara Maru, Operation Secret, The Desert Song, She's Back on Broadway, House of Wax, The System, Shanghai Story, To Hell and Back, Bobby Ware Is Missing, Miracle in the Rain, Omar Khayyam, The Brothers Rico, Marjorie Morningstar, The Young Philadelphians, Strangers When We Meet, The Young Marrieds, The Scarface Mob, The Scalphunters, Che!, Airport, Kotch, Beyond the Poseidon Adventure.
TELEVISION: *Series*: The Untouchables. *Guest*: Philco Playhouse, Climax, Lux, Loretta Young Show, Desilu, Kojak, Mannix, Police Story, Lucy Special, Quincy, Alice, Trapper John M.D., Vegas, Fall Guy, Capitol, Hardcastle and McCormick, Matt Houston, Simon and Simon.

PICKER, DAVID V.
Executive. b. New York, NY, May 14, 1931. e. Dartmouth Coll., B.A., 1953. Father Eugene Picker, exec. Loew's Theatres. Ent. industry in 1956 as adv. pub. & exploitation liaison with sls. dept., United Artists Corp.; exec. v.p. U.A. Records; asst. to Max Youngstein, v.p.; v.p. U.A.; first v.p. UA; pres. 1969. Resigned 1973 to form own production co. 1976 joined Paramount Pictures as pres. of m.p. div.; v.p., Lorimar Productions; independent; 1987, pres. & COO, Columbia Pictures. Resigned.
PICTURES: Juggernaut, Lenny, Smile, Royal Flash, Won Ton Ton the Dog Who Saved Hollywood, The One and Only, Oliver's Story, Bloodline (prod.), The Jerk (prod.), Dead Men Don't Wear Plaid (prod.), The Man with Two Brains, Beat Street (prod.), The Appointments of Dennis Jennings (short, prod.), Stella (exec. prod.), Traces of Red, Leap of Faith, Matinee, The Saint of Fort Washington, The Crucible.

PICKMAN, JEROME
Executive. b. New York, NY, Aug. 24, 1916. e. St. John's U.; Brooklyn Law Sch. of St. Lawrence U., LL.B. Reporter N.Y. newspapers; U.S. Army World War II; Ad-pub exec. 20th-Fox, 1945-46; v.p., dir., adv. & pub., later v.p. domestic gen. sls. mgr., Paramount Pictures; sr. sls. exec. Columbia Pictures; pres. Motion Picture Div. of Walter Reade Org.; pres., Levitt-Pickman Film Corp.; sr. v.p., domestic distribution, Lorimar Productions; pres., Pickman Film Corp., Cineworld Enterprises Corp.; pres. Scotti Bros. Pictures Distribution, 1986. Consultant, various entertainment entities, legal and financial individuals and organizations.

PIDGEON, REBECCA
Actress. b. Cambridge, MA, 1963. m. wr.-dir. David Mamet.
PICTURES: The Dawning, She's Been Away, Oleanna (comp. only), The Spanish Prisoner, The Winslow Boy, State and Main, The Heist.
TELEVISION: *Movies:* Uncle Vanya, Homicide (pilot), The Water Engine, Catastrophe.

PIERCE, DAVID HYDE
Actor. b. Albany, NY, April 3, 1959. e. Yale U.
THEATER: *Off-B'way:* Summer, That's It Folks, Donuts, Hamlet, The Moderati, The Cherry Orchard, Zero Positive, Much About Nothing, Elliot Loves. *B'way:* Beyond Therapy, The Heidi Chronicles. *Regional:* work with Long Wharf, Guthrie, Goodman, Doolittle Theatres.
PICTURES: Bright Lights Big City, Crossing Delancey, Rocket Gibraltar, The Fisher King, Little Man Tate, Sleepless in Seattle, Addams Family Values, Wolf, Nixon, The Mating Habits of the Earthbound Human, A Bug's Life (voice), Isn't She Great.
TELEVISION: *Movies:* Jackie's Back!. *Series:* The Powers That Be, Frasier (Emmy Award, 1995, 1997, 1999; Emmy nom., 1996), Hercules (voice). *Guest:* Dream On, Crime Story, Spenser: For Hire, The Outer Limits, The Simpsons (voice).

PIERCE, FREDERICK S.
Executive. b. New York, NY, April 8, 1933. e. Bernard Baruch Sch. of B.A., City Coll. of New York. Served with U.S. Combat Engineers in Korean War. Associated with Benj. Harrow & Son, CAP, before joining ABC in 1956. Served as analyst in TV research dep.; prom. to supvr. of audience measurements, 1957, named mgr. next year. 1961 made dir. of research; 1962 dir. of research, sales dev. Named dir. of sales planning, sales devel. 1962; elec. v.p., 1964 and made nat. dir. of sales for TV. 1968 named v.p., planning; 1970 named asst. to pres.; 1972, named v.p, in chg. ABC TV planning and devel. and asst. to pres. ABC TV, 1973. Named sr. v.p., ABC TV, 1974. Elected pres., ABC Television Division, 1974. Pres. & COO, ABC, Inc., 1983. Formed Frederick Pierce Co. and also Pierce/Silverman Co. with Fred Silverman, 1989.

PIERSON, FRANK
Producer, Director, Writer. b. Chappaqua, NY, May 12, 1925. e. Harvard U. Was correspondent for Time magazine before entering show business as story editor of TV series, Have Gun, Will Travel. Later served as both prod. and dir. for show. Developed a number of properties for Screen Gems before writing theatrical screenplays.
PICTURES: *Writer*: Cat Ballou, The Happening, Cool Hand Luke, The Anderson Tapes, Dog Day Afternoon (Acad. Award, 1975), In Country, Presumed Innocent. *Director-Writer*: The Looking Glass War, A Star Is Born, King of the Gypsies.
TELEVISION: *Series*: Nichols (prod.), Alfred Hitchcock Presents (1985; dir.). *Movies*: The Neon Ceiling (dir.), Haywire (co-writer), Somebody Has to Shoot the Picture (dir.; ACE Award, 1990), Citizen Cohn (dir.), Lakota Woman: Siege at Wounded Knee (dir.), Truman.

PIGOTT-SMITH, TIM
Actor. b. Rugby, England, May 13, 1946. e. U. of Bristol, B.A., Bristol Old Vic Theatre Sch., 1969. Acted with Bristol Old Vic, Royal Shakespeare Co. Artistic Director of Compass Theatre, 1989-93.
THEATER: *Actor*: As You Like It, Major Barbara, Hamlet, School for Scandal, Sherlock Holmes (B'way debut, 1974), Benefactors, Entertaining Strangers, The Winter's Tale, Antony and Cleopatra, Cymbeline, The Tempest, Jane Eyre, The Picture of Dorian Gray, Retreat. *Director*: Company, Royal Hunt of the Sun, Playing the Wife, Hamlet, The Letter, Retreat, Mary Stuart.
PICTURES: Aces High (debut, 1975), Man in a Fog, Sweet William, Richard's Things, Joseph Andrews, Clash of the Titans, Lucky Village, Victory, State of Emergency, The Remains of the Day.
TELEVISION: Dr. Who (debut, 1970). *Mini-series*: Winston Churchill: The Wilderness Years, The Jewel in the Crown. *Movies*: Eustace and Hilda, The Lost Boys, I Remember Nelson, Measure for Measure, Henry IV, Day Christ Died, The Hunchback of Notre Dame, Fame Is the Spur, Glittering Prizes, Dead Man's Folly, The Case of Sherlock Holmes (host), Life Story, Hannah, The True Adventures of Christopher Columbus, The Chief, Bullion Boys, The Shadowy Third, Calcutta Chronicles.

PIKE, CORNELIA M.
Executive. b. Holyoke, MA, 1933. e. Boston U. Sch. of Comm., BS Magna Cum Laude. Asst. Promotion & Publicity Dir. WNAC/WNAC-TV 1954-56, Boston, MA. Women's Dir./On-air personality: WKNE Keene, NH 1957-60; WSMN Nashua, NH 1963-67; WHOB, Nashua, NH 1967-68. Mngr. Trade Winds Interior Design, Boston, MA 1979-81. Sls. Mngr./VP Pike Productions, Inc. 1981 to present. Company produces and markets trailers to exhibitors in U.S., UK, Germany, Australia and New Zealand. Alpha Epsilon Rho, Natl. Bdcstg. Soc. 1st VP, Variety Club of New England. Bd. dirs., Variety Club of New England. Life Patron, Variety Clubs International.

PIKE, JOHN S.
Executive. b. Cleveland, OH, Oct. 26, 1946. e. Univ. of Miami. Joined Paramount Pictures as v.p., video programming; promoted to sr. v.p., video prog. 1984, named sr. v.p., current network programming; 1985, promoted to exec. v.p., Paramount Network TV. Appt. pres., Network TV and Intl. co-production, 1991.

PINCHOT, BRONSON
Actor. b. New York, NY, May 20, 1959. e. Yale U. Grew up in Pasadena. Studied acting at Yale. On NY stage in Poor Little Lambs, Zoya's Apartment.
PICTURES: Risky Business (debut, 1983), Beverly Hills Cop, The Flamingo Kid, Hot Resort, After Hours, Second Sight, Blame It on the Bellboy, True Romance, Beverly Hills Cop III, It's My Party, Courage Under Fire.
TELEVISION: *Series*: Sara, Perfect Strangers, The Trouble With Larry, Meego. *Movie*: Jury Duty—The Comedy. *Mini-Series*: Stephen King's The Langoliers.

PINKETT-SMITH, JADA
Actress. b. Baltimore, MD, Sept. 18, 1971. m. actor Will Smith.
PICTURES: Menace II Society, A Low Down Dirty Shame, Jason's Lyric, The Inkwell, Tales from the Crypt Presents: Demon Knight, The Nutty Professor, Set It Off, Scream 2, Love For Hire (writer only), Return to Paradise, Woo, Welcome to Hollywood, Bamboozled, Kingdom Come.
TELEVISION: *Series*: A Different World. *Movie*: If These Walls Could Talk. *Guest*: 21 Jump Street.

PINSKER, ALLEN
Executive. b. New York, NY, Jan. 23, 1930. e. NYU. Mgr., Hempstead Theatre, 1950. 1954 joined Island Theatre Circuit as booker-buyer; named head buyer 1958. 1968 joined United Artists Eastern Theatres as film buyer; head buyer, 1969, v.p., 1970. Named v.p. United Artists Theatre Circuit, 1972. 1973 named UAET exec. v.p., member bd., 1974. Appt. pres. & COO, UA Communications, Inc., theatre division, 1987. 1987, named pres. and CEO, United Artists Theatre Circuit, Inc. and exec. v.p., United Artists Communications, Inc.; 1988, became member, bd. dir. United Artists Comm. Inc.

PINTER, HAROLD
Writer, Director, Actor. b. London, England, Oct. 10, 1930. Began career as actor then turned to writing and direction.
THEATER: The Dumb Waiter, Slight Ache, The Room, The Birthday Party, The Caretaker, The Homecoming, The Collection, Landscape, Silence, Old Times, No Man's Land, The Hothouse, Betrayal, One for the Road, Mountain Language, Party Time, Moonlight.
PICTURES: *Writer*: The Caretaker (The Guest), The Servant (also actor), The Pumpkin Eater, The Quiller Memorandum, Accident (also actor), The Birthday Party, The Go-Between, The Homecoming, Butley (dir. only), The Last Tycoon, The French Lieutenant's Woman, Betrayal, Turtle Diary (also actor), The Handmaid's Tale, Reunion, The Comfort of Strangers, The Trial.
TELEVISION: A Night Out, Night School, The Lover, Tea Party, The Basement, Langrishe Go Down, Heat of the Day.

PISANO, A. ROBERT
Executive. e. San Jose St. Univ., Boalt Hall School of Law at Univ. of CA, Berkeley. Was partner at law firm of O'Melveny & Myers prior to entering m.p. industry. 1985-91, exec. v.p. of Paramount Pictures serving as gen. counsel, member of office of chmn.; 1993, named exec. v.p. of MGM responsible for all business and legal affairs, home video and pay tv. In 1997, became Vice Chairman, with overall responsibility for business operations of MGM.

PISCOPO, JOE
Actor, Comedian. b. Passaic, NJ, June 17, 1951. Stage appearances in regional and dinner theaters in South and Northeast. Worked as stand-up comic at the Improvisation and the Comic Strip clubs, NY 1976-80. Author: The Piscopo Tapes. Television debut as regular on Saturday Night Live, 1980.
PICTURES: American Tickler or the Winner of 10 Academy Awards (1976), King Kong, Johnny Dangerously, Wise Guys, Dead Heat, Sidekicks, Huck and the King of Hearts, Two Bits & Pepper, Captain Nuke and the Bomber Boys, Open Season.
TELEVISION: *Series*: Saturday Night Live (1980-84). *Guest*: Comic Relief. *Special*: The Joe Piscopo Special (HBO). *Movie*: Huck and the King of Hearts.

PISIER, MARIE-FRANCE
Actress. b. Dalat, Indochina, May 10, 1944. Began appearing in French films at age 17. Returned to school at Univ. of Paris for degrees in law and political science; continued to work in films.
PICTURES: Qui ose nous Accuser? (debut, 1961), Love at Twenty (Truffaut episode), La Mort d'un Tueur, Les Yeux cernes, Trans-Europe Express, Stolen Kisses, Celine and Julie Go Boating, French Provincial, Cousin Cousine, Serail, Barocco, The Other Side of Midnight, Love on the Run, Les Apprentis Sourciers, The Bronte Sisters, French Postcards, La Banquiere, Chanel Solitaire, Der Zauberberg (The Magic Mountain), Miss Right, Hot Touch, The Prize of Peril, The Silent Ocean, L'Ami de Vincent, Les Nanas, Parking, Blue Note, Why is My Mother in My Bed?
TELEVISION: *U.S.*: French Atlantic Affair, Scruples.

PITT, BRAD
Actor. r.n. William Bradley Pitt. b. Shawnee, OK, Dec. 18, 1963. m. actress Jennifer Anniston. Raised in Springfield, MO. Studied journalism at Univ. of MO at Columbia. Moved to L.A. to attend art school, instead studied acting with Roy London. Appeared in short film Contact.
PICTURES: Cutting Class (debut, 1989), Happy Together, Across the Tracks, Thelma & Louise, Cool World, Johnny Suede, A River Runs Through It, Kalifornia, True Romance, The Favor, Interview With the Vampire. Legends of the Fall, Se7en, Twelve Monkeys (Golden Globe, 1996), Sleepers, The Devil's Own, Seven Years In Tibet, Meet Joe Black, Fight Club, Being John Malkovich (cameo), Snatch, The Mexican, Ocean's Eleven, To the White Sea.
TELEVISION: *Series*: Another World, Glory Days. *Movies*: A Stoning in Fulham County, Too Young to Die, The Image. *Guest*: Dallas, Growing Pains, Head of the Class, Tales From the Crypt.

PIVEN, JEREMY
Actor. b. New York, NY. Raised in Chicago where parents ran Piven Theater Workshop. e. Drake Univ. Studied acting at Eugene O'Neill Theater Center, Natl. Theater of Great Britain, NYU. Eventually joined Chicago's Second City comedy troupe. Co-founded Chicago's New Criminals Theatre Company, 1988.
THEATER: Fear & Loathing in Las Vegas, Peacekeeper, Methusalen, Knuckle, Macbeth.
PICTURES: Lucas, One Crazy Summer, Say Anything..., White Palace, The Grifters, Pay Dirt, The Player, Bob Roberts, Singles, Judgment Night, Twenty Bucks, Car 54 Where Are You?, Twogether, PCU, Miami Rhapsody, Dr. Jekyll and Ms. Hyde, Heat, Grosse Pointe Blank, Very Bad Things, Music From Another Room, Phoenix, The Crew, Red Letters, The Family Man, Serendipity, Highway.
TELEVISION: *Series:* Carol and Company, The Larry Sanders Show, Pride and Joy, Ellen, Cupid. *Pilots:* Heads Will Roll, Ready or Not. *Movie*: Don King: Only in America. *Guest:* The Drew Carey Show, Chicago Hope, Seinfeld.

PLACE, MARY KAY
Actress, Writer. b. Tulsa, OK, Sept. 23, 1947. e. U. of Tulsa. Worked in production jobs and as Tim Conway's asst. for his TV show also as sect. for Norman Lear on Maude before starting to write for TV series (Mary Tyler Moore Show, Phyllis, Maude, M*A*S*H, etc.).
PICTURES: Bound For Glory (debut, 1976), New York New York, More American Graffiti, Starting Over, Private Benjamin, Modern Problems, Waltz Across Texas, The Big Chill, Smooth Talk, A New Life, Bright Angel, Captain Ron, Samantha, Teresa's Tattoo, Manny and Lo, Precious, Citizen Ruth.
TELEVISION: *Series*: Mary Hartman Mary Hartman (Emmy Award, 1977). *Guest*: All in the Family, Mary Tyler Moore Show, Fernwood 2-Night, Tonight Show, Saturday Night Live (host), thirtysomething. *Movies*: The Girl Who Spelled Freedom, Act of Love, For Love or Money, Out on the Edge, Just My Imagination, Telling Secrets, In the Line of Duty: The Pride of Vengeance. *Specials*: John Denver Special, Martin Mull's History of White People in America I & II, Portrait of a White Marriage, The Gift, Tales of the City, Leslie's Folly.

PLATT, OLIVER
Actor. b. 1962. Raised in Asia, Africa and Washington DC. e. Tufts Univ.
THEATER: *Off-B'way*: The Tempest, Moon Over Miami, Sparks in the Park, Urban Blight, Ubu, Elliot Loves.
PICTURES: Married to the Mob (debut, 1988), Working Girl, Crusoe, Flatliners, Postcards From the Edge, Beethoven, Diggstown, The Temp, Indecent Proposal, Benny & Joon, The Three Musketeers, Tall Tale, Funny Bones, Executive Decision, A Time to Kill, Dangerous Beauty, Bulworth, Simon Birch, Lake Placid, Three to Tango, Bicentennial Man, Gun Shy, Ready to Rumble.
TELEVISION: *Movie*: The Infiltrator, Cinderelmo. *Series:* Deadline.

PLESHETTE, SUZANNE
Actress. b. New York, NY. e. H.S. for the Performing Arts, Finch Coll., Syracuse U. Broadway debut, Compulsion.

THEATER: The Cold Wind and the Warm, The Golden Fleecing, The Miracle Worker, Compulsion, Two for the Seesaw, Special Occasions.
PICTURES: The Geisha Boy (debut, 1958), Rome Adventure, 40 Pounds of Trouble, The Birds, Wall of Noise, A Distant Trumpet, Fate Is the Hunter, Youngblood Hawke, A Rage to Live, The Ugly Dachshund, Nevada Smith, Mister Buddwing, The Adventures of Bullwhip Griffin, Blackbeard's Ghost, The Power, If It's Tuesday This Must Be Belgium, Suppose They Gave a War and Nobody Came, Target Harry, Support Your Local Gunfighter, The Shaggy D.A., Hot Stuff, Oh God! Book II, Lion King II.
TELEVISION: *Series*: The Bob Newhart Show, Suzanne Pleshette Is Maggie Briggs, Bridges to Cross, Nightingales, The Boys Are Back, The Single Guy. *Movies*: Wings of Fire, Along Came a Spider, Hunters Are for Killing, River of Gold, In Broad Daylight, Law and Order, Richie Brockelman: Missing 24 Hours, Kate Bliss and the Ticker Tape Kid, Flesh and Blood, For Love or Money, Fantasies, If Things Were Different, Help Wanted—Male, Dixie Changing Habits, Starmaker, One Cooks, The Other Doesn't, Legend of Valentino, Kojak The Belarus File, A Stranger Waits, Alone in the Neon Jungle, Leona Helmsley: The Queen of Mean, Battling for Baby, A Twist of the Knife. *Special*: Where Are They Now.

PLESKOW, ERIC
Executive. b., Vienna, Austria, April 24, 1924. Served as film officer, U.S. War dept., 1946-48; entered industry in 1948 as asst. gen. mgr., Motion Picture Export Association, Germany; 1950-51, continental rep. for Sol Lesser Prods.; joined United Artists in 1951 as Far East Sales Mgr.; named mgr., S. Africa, 1952; mgr., Germany, 1953-58; exec. asst. to continental mgr., 1958-59; asst. continental mgr., 1959-60; continental mgr., 1960-62; v.p. in charge of foreign distrib., 1962; exec. v.p. & CEO, Jan., 1973; pres. & CEO, Oct. , 1973. Resigned in 1978 to become pres. and CEO of Orion Pictures Co.; 1982, became pres. & CEO, Orion Pictures Corp; appointed chmn. of bd. 1991. Resigned 1992. Partner, Pleskow/Spikings Partnership, Beverly Hills, 1992-present. Prod., Beyond Rangoon.

PLIMPTON, MARTHA
Actress. b. New York, NY, Nov. 16, 1970. Daughter of actors Shelley Plimpton and Keith Carradine. Acting debut in film workshop of Elizabeth Swados's musical Runaways. At 11 gained recognition as model in Richard Avedon's commercials for Calvin Klein jeans. Also on stage in The Hagadah, Pericles, The Heidi Chronicles, Robbers, subUrbia, The Great Unwashed.
PICTURES: Rollover (debut 1981, in bit role), The River Rat, The Goonies, The Mosquito Coast, Shy People, Stars and Bars, Running on Empty, Another Woman, Parenthood, Stanley and Iris, Silence Like Glass, Samantha, Inside Monkey Zetterland, Josh and S.A.M., My Life's in Turnaround, Mrs. Parker and the Vicious Circle, The Beans of Egypt Maine, Last Summer in the Hamptons, Beautiful Girls, I Shot Andy Warhol, I'm Not Rappaport, Eye of God, Pecker, Music From Another Room, 200 Cigarettes.
TELEVISION: *Movies*: Daybreak, Chantilly Lace, The Defenders: Choice of Evils, The Defenders: Taking the First. *Guest:* Family Ties.

PLOWRIGHT, JOAN
C.B.E. Actress. b. Scunthrope, Brigg, Lincolnshire, England, Oct. 28, 1929. m. late actor, Lord Laurence Olivier. Trained for stage at Laban Art of Movement Studio, 1949-50; Old Vic Theatre Sch. 1950-52; with Michel St. Denis, Glen Byam Shaw and George Devine. London stage debut The Duenna, 1954. Broadway debut The Entertainer, 1958. Won Tony Award in 1961 for A Taste of Honey. With Bristol Old Vic Rep., Royal Court, National Theatre in numerous classics and contemporary plays.
RECENT THEATER: Saturday Sunday Monday, The Seagull, The Bed Before Yesterday, Filumena, Enjoy, Who's Afraid of Virginia Woolf?, Cavell, The Cherry Orchard, The Way of the World, Mrs. Warren's Profession, Time and the Conways, If We Are Women.
PICTURES: Moby Dick (debut, 1956), Time Without Pity, The Entertainer, Uncle Vanya, Three Sisters, Equus, Brimstone and Treacle, Britannia Hospital, Wagner (tv in U.S.), Revolution, The Dressmaker, Drowning By Numbers, I Love You to Death, Avalon, Enchanted April (Acad. Award nom.), Last Action Hero, Dennis the Menace, A Pin for the Butterfly, The Summer House, Widow's Peak, A Pyromaniac's Love Story, Hotel Sorrento, The Scarlett Letter, Jane Eyre, Mr. Wrong, Surviving Picasso, 101 Dalmatians, The Assistant, Dance with Me, Tom's Midnight Garden, Tea with Mussolini.
TELEVISION: Odd Man In, Secret Agent, School for Scandal, The Diary of Anne Frank, Twelfth Night, Merchant of Venice, Daphne Laureola, Saturday Sunday Monday, The Divider, Conquest of the South Pole, A Nightingale Sang, House of Bernarda Alba, Stalin, On Promised Land, A Place for Annie, The Return of the Native, This Could Be the Last Time, Encore! Encore!. *Pilot*: Driving Miss Daisy (U.S.).

PLUMMER, AMANDA
Actress. b. New York, NY, March 23, 1957. e. Middlebury Coll. Daughter of actors Christopher Plummer and Tammy Grimes.
THEATER: Artichokes, A Month in the Country, A Taste of Honey (Theatre World Award), Agnes of God (Tony Award, 1982), The Glass Menagerie, A Lie of the Mind, Life Under Water, You Never Can Tell, Pygmalion, The Milk Train Doesn't Stop Here Anymore.
PICTURES: Cattle Annie and Little Britches (debut, 1981), The World According to Garp, Daniel, The Hotel New Hampshire, Static, The Courtship, Made in Heaven, Prisoners of Inertia, Joe Versus the Volcano, California Casanova, The Fisher King, Freejack, So I Married an Axe Murderer, Needful Things, Nostradamus, Pulp Fiction, Pax, Butterfly Kiss, The Propechy, Drunks, Freeway, A Simple Wish, American Perfekt, You Can Thank Me Later, L.A. Without a Map, Elizabeth Jane, 8 1/2 Women, Great Sex.
TELEVISION: *Movies*: The Dollmaker, The Unforgivable Secret, Riders to the Sea, Miss Rose White (Emmy Award, 1992), The Sands of Time, Last Light, Whose Child Is This? The War for Baby Jessica. *Guest*: Outer Limits (Emmy Award, 1996). *Specials*: Gryphon, The Courtship. *Pilot*: True Blue.

PLUMMER, CHRISTOPHER
Actor. b. Toronto, Canada, Dec. 13, 1927. Daughter is actress Amanda Plummer. Stage & radio career began in Canada (French & English).
THEATER: toured U.S. in The Constant Wife; B'way debut in The Starcross Story, 1953. *B'way*: The Dark is Light Enough, Home Is the Hero, J.B., The Lark, The Good Doctor, Cyrano (Tony Award, 1974), Othello (Tony nom.), Macbeth, No Man's Land. *London*: leading actor, Royal Shakespeare Theatre, 1961-62, Becket (Evening Standard Award), Natl. Theatre, 1969-70. *Canada*: leading actor, Stratford Festival (6 yrs.).
PICTURES: Stage Struck (debut, 1958), Wind Across the Everglades, The Fall of the Roman Empire, The Sound of Music, Inside Daisy Clover, The Night of the Generals, Triple Cross, Oedipus the King, The High Commissioner (Nobody Runs Forever), The Battle of Britain, The Royal Hunt of the Sun, Lock Up Your Daughters, Waterloo, The Pyx, The Return of the Pink Panther, Conduct Unbecoming, The Man Who Would Be King, The Spiral Staircase, Aces High, Assassination at Sarajevo (The Day That Shook the World), The Assignment, The Disappearance, International Velvet, Murder by Decree, The Silent Partner, Hanover Street, Starcrash, RIEL, Highpoint, Somewhere in Time, Eyewitness, Being Different (narrator), The Amateur, Dreamscape, Ordeal by Innocence, Lily in Love, The Boy in Blue, The Boss' Wife, An American Tail (voice), Dragnet, Souvenir, Light Years (voice), Nosferatu in Venice, I Love N.Y., Shadow Dancing, Mindfield, Kingsgate, Red-Blooded American Girl, Where the Heart Is, Don't Tell Mom the Babysitter's Dead, Star Trek VI: The Undiscovered Country, Firehead, Rock-a-Doodle (voice), Money, Liar's Edge, Impolite, Malcolm X, Wolf, Dolores Claiborne, Twelve Monkeys, Skeletons, Babes in Toyland, Hidden Agenda, The Clown at Midnight, Blackheart, All the Fine Lines, The Insider, The Dinosaur Hunter, Dracula 2000, Star Trek: Klingon Academy, Lucky Break, Full Disclosure.
TELEVISION: *Series*: Counterstrike. *Movies/Specials*: Hamlet at Elsinore (Emmy nom.), Don Juan in Hell (BBC), Little Moon of Alban, Prince and the Pauper, Jesus of Nazareth, Steiglitz and O'Keefe, Oedipus Rex, Omnibus, After the Fall, The Moneychangers (Emmy Award, 1977), Desperate Voyage, The Shadow Box, When the Circus Came to Town, Dial M for Murder, Little Gloria—Happy at Last, The Scarlet and the Black, The Thorn Birds, The Velveteen Rabbit, Crossings, A Hazard of Hearts, A Ghost in Monte Carlo, Young Catherine, Danielle Steel's Secrets, Stranger in the Mirror, Liar's Edge, Madeline (narrator; Emmy Award, 1994), Harrison Bergeron, We the Jury, The Conspiracy of Fear, The Arrow, Winchell, Celebrate the Century (narrator), Nuremberg.

PODELL, ALBERT N.
Attorney. b. New York, NY, Feb. 25, 1937. e. Cornell U., U. of Chicago, NYU Sch. of Law. Non-fiction ed., Playboy magazine, 1959-60; dir. of photog. and m.p. reviewer Argosy magazine, 1961-64; Author: Who Needs a Road? (Bobbs-Merrill, 1967; republished, Wolfenden, 1999), mng. ed., The Players Magazine, 1965-66; acct. exec. on 20th Century-Fox at Diener, Hauser, Greenthal, 1966-68; natl. advt. mgr., Cinema Center Films, 1969; acct. supervisor and creative dir. on Columbia Pictures at Charles Schlaifer, 1969-72; creator & dir. of Annual Motion Picture Advertising Awards sponsored by Cinema Lodge, B'nai B'rith. Attorney specializing in litigation, matrimonial law, rep. of performers and producers (1976-present). Pres., 1990-95 Jean Cocteau Rep. Th. Chmn. of Trustees; 1980-90, Assn. for Development of Dramatic Arts. Pres., Far Above Films. *Dir. & Writer:* A Class Above, The Class on the Cutting Edge, Lift the Chorus, This Is Christmas.

PODHORZER, MUNIO
Executive. b. Berlin, Germany, Sept. 18, 1911. e. Jahn-Realgymnasium, U. of Berlin Medical Sch. U.S. Army, 1943-47; pres. United Film Enterprises, Inc.; formerly secy.-treas. 86th St. Casino Theatre, N.Y.; former v.p. Atlantic Pictures Corp.; former pres. Casino Films, Inc.; former pres. Film Development Corp.; former rep. Export-Union of the German Film Ind.; former U.S. rep. Franco-London Film, Paris; former pres., Venus Productions Corp.; former U.S. rep. Atlas Int'l Film GmbH, Munich; former U.S. rep. Bavaria Atelier Gesellschaft U.S.; past rep. Israfilm Ltd., Tel-Aviv; past rep. Tigon British Film Prod., London; past rep. Elias Querejeta, P.C., Madrid; past rep. Equiluz Films, Madrid; past rep. Airport Cine, Haiti; Les Films Du Capricorne, Paris; Schongerfilm, German; Profilmes, Spain; Ligno, Spain; Films D'Alma, France; Intra Films, Italy. Member: Variety Club, Cinema Lodge, B'nai B'rith, Past Board of Governors IFIDA; past pres. CID Agents Assoc. Former gen. foreign sales mgr., theatrical division of National Telefilm Associates; past rep. Barcino Films, S.A. Spain; Eagle Films Ltd., UK; Les Films Jacques Leitienne, France; Nero Film Classics, USA; Schongerfilm, Germany; Profilmes, S.A. Spain; VIP Ltd., Israel. Presently representing Atlas Film & AV, Germany; KFM Films, Inc. U.S.A.; Compagnie France Film, Canada; Cia. Iberoamerican de TV, S.A. Spain; Israel. Co-chmn., entertainment div., United Jewish Appeal, Federation of Jewish Philanthropies, 1981-83.

PODHORZER, NATHAN
Executive. b. Brody, Poland, Nov. 27, 1919. e. City Coll. of New York, Rutgers U., U. of Southern California. U.S. Army, 1942-46; documentary film prod., Israel, 1946-57; CEO, United Film Enterprises, Inc. U.S. purchasing agent: Atlas Air, Atlas Film & Medien (Germany), Co. France Film (Canada).

POE, STEPHEN
Executive. Began career as lawyer with Rutan & Tucker; 1976, joined 20th Century-Fox as prod. counsel; later v.p., business affairs. Turned to producing in 1982, first in association with Frank Mancuso Jr. Productions. 1986, acted as consultant and indep. prod. counsel for United Artists Pictures. 1987, joined CBS/Fox Video as sr. v.p. of acquisitions and programming.

POITIER, SIDNEY
Actor, Director. b. Miami, FL, Feb. 20, 1927. Raised in the Bahamas. m. actress Joanna Shimkus. e. Miami, FL. On stage with Amer. Negro Theatre in Days of Our Youth. Appeared in Army Signal Corps documentary From Whence Cometh My Help. Formed First Artists Prod. Co. Ltd., 1969, with Paul Newman and Barbra Streisand. *Autobiography*: This Life (1980). Recipient 1992 AFI Life Achievement Award.
THEATER: Strivers Road, You Can't Take It With You, Anna Lucasta (B'way debut, 1948), Lysistrata, Freight, A Raisin in the Sun.
PICTURES: No Way Out (debut 1950), Cry the Beloved Country, Red Ball Express, Go Man Go, Blackboard Jungle, Goodbye My Lady, Edge of the City, Something of Value, Band of Angels, Mark of the Hawk, The Defiant Ones, Virgin Island, Porgy and Bess, All the Young Men, A Raisin in the Sun, Paris Blues, Pressure Point, Lilies of the Field (Acad. Award, 1963), The Long Ships, The Greatest Story Ever Told, The Bedford Incident, The Slender Thread, A Patch of Blue, Duel at Diablo, To Sir With Love, In the Heat of the Night, Guess Who's Coming to Dinner, For Love of Ivy, The Lost Man, They Call Me Mister Tibbs, Brother John, The Organization, Buck and the Preacher (also dir.), A Warm December (also dir.), Uptown Saturday Night (also dir.), The Wilby Conspiracy, Let's Do It Again (also dir.), A Piece of the Action (also dir.), Stir Crazy (dir. only), Hanky Panky (dir. only), Fast Forward (dir. only), Shoot To Kill, Little Nikita, Ghost Dad (dir. only), Sneakers, The Jackal.
TELEVISION: *Movies*: Separate But Equal, Children of the Dust, To Sir With Love II, Mandela and de Klerk, Free of Eden, The Simple Life of Noah dearborn, The Last Bricklayer in America. *Guest*: Philco TV Playhouse, ABC Stage '67.

POLANSKI, ROMAN
Director, Writer. b. Paris, France, Aug. 18, 1933. m. actress Emmanuelle Seigner. Lived in Poland from age of three. Early career, art school in Cracow; Polish Natl. Film Acad., Lodz 1954-59. Radio Actor 1945-47; on stage 1947-53; asst. dir., Kamera film prod. group 1959-61. Co-founder Cadre Films, 1964. Wrote, dir. and acted in short films: Two Men and a Wardrobe, When Angels Fall, The Fat and the Lean, Mammals. On stage as actor in Amadeus (and dir., Warsaw & Paris), Metamorphosis (Paris, 1988). *Autobiography*: Roman (1984).
PICTURES: *Dir./Writer*: Knife in the Water (feature debut, 1962), Repulsion, Cul-de-Sac, The Fearless Vampire Killers or: Pardon Me But Your Teeth Are in My Neck (also actor), Rosemary's Baby, A Day at the Beach (s.p. only), Weekend of a Champion (prod. only), Macbeth (also prod.), What? (a.k.a. Che?; also actor), Chinatown (dir. & actor only), The Tenant (also actor), Tess, Pirates, Frantic, Bitter Moon, Death and the Maiden, The Ninth Gate. *Actor only:* The Generation, The Magic Christian, Andy Warhol's Dracula, Back in the U.S.S.R., A Pure Formality, Grosse Fatigue.

POLEDOURIS, BASIL
Composer. b. Kansas City, MO, Aug. 21, 1945. e. Long Beach St. Univ., USC. While at USC composed music for short films by John Milius and Randal Kleiser. Became first American Film Institute intern.
PICTURES: Big Wednesday, Tintorera, Dolphin, The Blue Lagoon, Conan the Barbarian, Summer Lovers, House of God, Conan the Destroyer, Making the Grade, Red Dawn, Protocol, Flesh and Blood, Iron Eagle, Robocop, No Man's Land, Cherry 2000, Spellbinder, Split Decisions, Farewell to the King, Wired, The Hunt for Red October, Quigley Down Under, Flight of the Intruder, White Fang, Return to the Blue Lagoon, Harley Davidson & the Marlboro Man, Wind, Hot Shots Part Deux, Free Willy, Robocop 3, On Deadly Ground, Serial Mom, Lassie, The Jungle Book, Under Siege 2: Dark Territory, Free Willy 2: The Adventure Home, It's My Party, Celtic Pride, Breakdown, Starship Troopers, Les Miserables.
TELEVISION: *Mini-Series*: Amerika, Lonesome Dove (Emmy Award, 1989). *Movies*: Congratulations It's a Boy, A Whale for the Killing, Fire on the Mountain, Amazons, Single Women Single Bars, Prison for Children, Misfits of Science, Island Sons, Intrigue, L.A. Takedown, Nasty Boys, Ned Blessing, Lone Justice, Danielle Steel's Zoya.

POLL, MARTIN H.
Producer. b. New York, NY, Nov. 24, 1926. e. Wharton Sch., U. of Pennsylvania. Pres. Gold Medal Studios (1956-61).
PICTURES: A Face in the Crowd, Middle of the Night, The Goddess, Butterfield 8, Love Is a Ball, Sylvia, The Lion in Winter, The Appointment, The Magic Garden of Stanley Sweetheart, The Man Who Loved Cat Dancing, Night Watch, Love and Death (exec. prod.); The Man Who Would Be King, The Sailor Who Fell From Grace with the Sea, Somebody Killed Her Husband, Nighthawks, Gimme an F, Haunted Summer, My Heroes Have Always Been Cowboys.
TELEVISION: *Series*: Car 54 Where Are You? *Movies*: Arthur the King, Stunt Seven. *Mini-Series*: A Town Called Alice, The Dain Curse, Diana: Her True Story.

POLLACK, SYDNEY
Director, Producer. b. South Bend, IN, July 1, 1934. m. Claire Griswold. e. Neighborhood Playhouse. Assistant to Sanford Meisner at Neighborhood Playhouse. Appeared as actor on B'way in A Stone for Danny Fisher, The Dark is Light Enough. Dir. debut in 1960. Dir. play at UCLA, P.S. 193. Prepared the American version of The Leopard.
PICTURES: *Director*: The Slender Thread (debut, 1965), This Property Is Condemned, The Scalphunters, Castle Keep, They Shoot Horses Don't They? (also prod.), Jeremiah Johnson, The Way We Were (also prod.), The Yakuza (also prod.), Three Days of the Condor, Bobby Deerfield (also prod.), The Electric Horseman, Asence of Malice (also prod.), Tootsie (also prod., actor), Out of Africa (also prod.; Acad. Awards for Best Picture & dir., 1985), Havana (also prod.), The Firm, Sabrina (also prod.), Random Hearts. *Producer:* Songwriter, Bright Lights Big City, The Fabulous Baker Boys, Presumed Innocent, Random Hearts (also prod.). *Exec. Producer:* Honeysuckle Rose, White Palace, King Ralph, Dead Again, Leaving Normal, Searching for Bobby Fischer, Flesh and Bone, Sense and Sensibility, The Talented Mr. Ripley. *Actor:* War Hunt, The Player, Death Becomes Her, Husbands and Wives, A Civil Action, Eyes Wide Shut, Random Hearts, The Talented Mr. Ripley, Up at the Villa.
TELEVISION: *As actor*: Playhouse 90 (several segments), Shotgun Slade. *Dir.*: Ben Casey (15 episodes), The Game (Bob Hope-Chrysler Theatre; Emmy Award), Two is the Number. *Co-prod.* (movie): A Private Matter. *Exec. prod.* (series): Fallen Angels.

POLLAK, KEVIN
Actor. b. San Francisco, CA, Oct. 30, 1958. Started doing stand-up comedy in the San Francisco Bay area, then continued in L.A. clubs.
PICTURES: Million Dollar Mystery (debut, 1987), Willow, Avalon, L.A. Story, Another You, Ricochet, A Few Good Men, The Opposite Sex and How to Live With Them, Indian Summer, Wayne's World 2, Grumpy Old Men, Reality Bites, Clean Slate, Miami Rhapsody, The Usual Suspects, Canadian Bacon, Casino, Nowhere Man, Chameleon, House Arrest, Grumpier Old Men, That Thing You Do!, National Lampoon's The Don's Analyst, Truth or Consequences N.M., Buffalo 66, Outside Ozona, Steal This Movie, The Sex Monster, She's All That, Deterrence, The Whole Nine Yards, Deal of a Lifetime, The Wedding Planner.
TELEVISION: *Series*: Coming of Age, Morton and Hayes, Work with Me. *Specials*: One Night Stand (also prod., writer), Stop With the Kicking (also prod., writer), The Seven Deadly Sins (also writer, dir.). *Movie*: Ruby Bridges. *Mini-series*: From the Earth to the Moon.

POLLAN, TRACY
Actress. b. New York, NY, June 22, 1960. m. actor Michael J. Fox.
THEATER: *B'way*: Jake's Women.
PICTURES: Promised Land, Bright Lights Big City, A Stranger Among Us.

TELEVISION: *Series*: Family Ties, Anna Says (also exec. prod.). *Movies*: For Lovers Only, Sessions, Trackdown: Finding the Goodbar Killer, A Good Sport, Dying to Love You, Children of the Dark. *Guest*: Law and Order.

POLLARD, MICHAEL J.
Actor. r.n. Michael J. Pollack. b. Passaic, NJ, May 30, 1939. e. Montclair Academy, Actors Studio.
THEATER: Comes a Day, Loss of Roses, Enter Laughing, Bye Bye Birdie, Leda Had a Little Swan, Our Town.
PICTURES: Adventures of a Young Man (debut, 1962), The Stripper, Summer Magic, The Russians Are Coming the Russians Are Coming, The Wild Angels, Caprice, Enter Laughing, Bonnie and Clyde (Acad. Award nom.), Jigsaw, Hannibal Brooks, Little Fauss and Big Halsy, The Legend of Frenchie King, Dirty Little Billy, Between the Lines, Melvin and Howard, Heated Vengeance, America, The Patriot, The American Way, Roxanne, Scrooged, Fast Food, Season of Fear, Next of Kin, Tango and Cash, Night Visitor, Sleepaway Camp 3, Why Me?, Dick Tracy, I Come in Peace, Joey Takes a Cab, The Art of Dying, Another You, Enid Is Sleeping (Over Her Dead Body), Split Second, The Arrival, Heartstopper, Arizona Dream, Motorama, Skeeter.
TELEVISION: *Series*: Leo and Liz in Beverly Hills. *Guest*: Alfred Hitchcock Presents (Anniversary Gift), Going My Way, Route 66, Here's Lucy, Mr. Novak, Honey West, I Spy, Lost in Space, Dobie Gillis, Get Christie Love, Star Trek, Simon & Simon, The Fall Guy, Gunsmoke, Guns of Paradise, The Young Riders, Nasty Boys. *Movies*: The Smugglers, Stuck With Each Other, Working Trash.

POLLEXFEN, JACK
Producer, Director, Writer. b. San Diego, CA, June 10, 1918. e. Los Angeles City Coll. Newspaperman, magazine writer, playwright: prod. for RKO, United Artists, Columbia, Allied Artists.
PICTURES: Son of Sinbad, At Swords Point, Secret of Convict Lake, Desert Hawk, Lady in the Iron Mask, Dragon's Gold, Problem Girls, Captive Women, Captain Kidd and the Slave Girl, Neanderthal Man, Captain John Smith and Pocahontas, Return to Treasure Island, Sword of Venus, Daughter of Dr. Jekyll, Monstrosity, Son of Dr. Jekyll, Mr. Big, Man from Planet X, Indestructible Man, Port Sinister, Treasure of Monte Cristo, Bulldog Drummond, Grey City.

POLLEY, SARAH
Actress. b. Canada, Jan. 8, 1979. Daughter of late actress and casting director Diane Polley.
PICTURES: One Magic Christmas, The Big Town, The Adventures of Baron Munchausen, Babar: The Movie (voice), Exotica, Joe's So Mean to Josephine, The Sweet Hereafter, The Planet of Junior Brown, The Hanging Garden, Last Night, Guinevere, Go, eXistenZ, The Life Before This, The Weight of Water, Love Come Down, The Law of Enclosures, The Claim, Monster.
TELEVISION: *Movies:* Lantern Hill, Johann's Gift to Christmas, White Lies. *Series:* Ramona, Road to Avonlea. *Guest:* Friday the 13th.

POLLOCK, DALE
Producer. b. Cleveland, OH, May 18, 1950. e. Brandeis U., B.A. anthropology, San Jose State, M.S., mass communication. Began journalistic career in Santa Cruz in early '70s, serving as reporter and film critic for Daily Variety, 1977-80. Joined Los Angeles Times as film writer, winning paper's Award for Sustained Excellence in 1984. 1985 left to take post with The Geffen Film Co. as executive in chg. creative development. Joined A&M Films as v.p. in chg. prod., 1986. Became pres., 1989. Author: Skywalking (about George Lucas).
PICTURES: The Beast (exec. prod.), The Mighty Quinn (exec. prod.). *Producer*: House of Cards, Worth Winning, Blaze, Crooked Hearts, A Midnight Clear, A Home of Our Own, S.F.W., Mrs. Winterbourne, Set It Off, Meet the Deedles (also s.p.), Bats.

POLLOCK, THOMAS
Executive. b. 1943. In 1971, after 3 years as business mgr. for American Film Institute's film marketing wing, formed law firm Pollock Bloom, and Dekom with young filmmakers such as George Lucas and Matthew Robbins as clients. Served as chmn. Filmex, 1973-81. 1986, named chmn. MCA's Universal motion picture group., then vice chmn., MCA, Inc.

POLONSKY, ABRAHAM
Writer, Director. b. New York, NY, Dec. 5, 1910. e. CCNY, B.A.; Columbia Law Sch. Taught at City Coll. 1932 until war. Blacklisted from 1951-66.
AUTHOR: The Enemy Sea, The Discoverers, The World Above, The Season of Fear, Zenia's Way.
PICTURES: *Writer*: Golden Earrings, Body and Soul (also story), Force of Evil (also dir.), I Can Get It for You Wholesale, Odds Against Tomorrow, Madigan, Tell Them Willie Boy is Here (also dir.), Romance of a Horse Thief, Avalanche Express, Monsignor.
(d. Oct. 26, 1999)

PONTECORVO, GILLO
Director. b. Pisa, Italy, Nov. 19, 1919. Younger brother of Prof. Bruno Pontecorvo, Harwell scientist who defected in 1950. Former photo-journalist. Worked as asst. dir., directed documentary shorts before feature debut in 1957.
PICTURES: Die Windrose (Giovanna episode), La Grande Strada Azzurra (The Long Blue Road; also co-s.p.), Kapo (also co-s.p.), The Battle of Algiers (also story; Acad. Award noms. as dir. & writer), Queimada! (Burn; also co-story), Ogro (The Tunnel; also co-s.p.).

PONTI, CARLO
Producer. b. Milan, Italy, Dec. 11, 1913. m. actress Sophia Loren. e. U. of Milan, 1934. Prod. first picture in Milan, Little Old World; prod. Lux Film Rome; prod. first of a series of famous Toto pictures, Toto Househunting.
PICTURES: A Dog's Life, The Knight Has Arrived, Musolino, The Outlaw, Romanticism, Sensuality, The White Slave, Europe 1951, Toto in Color, The Three Corsairs, The Gold of Naples, Ulysses, The Woman of the River, An American of Rome, Attila, La Strada, War and Peace, The Last Lover, The Black Orchid, That Kind of Woman, A Breath of Scandal, Heller in Pink Tights, Two Women, Boccaccio '70, Bluebeard, The Condemned of Altona, Marriage Italian Style, Casanova '70, Operation Crossbow, Doctor Zhivago, Lady L, Blow Up, More Than a Miracle, The Girl and the General, Sunflower, The Best House in London, Zabriskie Point, The Priest's Wife, Lady Liberty, White Sister, What?, Andy Warhol's Frankenstein, The Passenger, The Cassandra Crossing, A Special Day, Saturday Sunday Monday.
TELEVISION: Mario Puzo's The Fortunate Pilgrim (exec. prod.).

POP, IGGY
Musician, Actor. r.n. James Osterberg. b. MI, April 21, 1947. Has recorded 16 albums with band the Stooges and solo.
PICTURES: *Actor*: Cry Baby, Hardware (voice only), Dead Man, The Crow: City of Angels, Private Parts (cameo), The Rugrats Movie (voice). *Songs*: Rock 'N' Rule. *Score*: The Brave, Repo Man.

POPE, DICK
Cinematographer.
PICTURES: The Girl in the Picture, Coming Up Roses, The Fruit Machine, The Reflecting Skin, Life is Sweet, Dark City, Naked, The Air Up There, An Awfully Big Adventure, Nothing Personal, Secrets and Lies, Career Girls, Swept from the Sea, The Debt Collector, Topsy-Turvey, The Way of the Gun.
TELEVISION: *Series:* Porterhouse Blue, Forever Green. *Movies:* A Sense of History, Fool's Gold: The Story of the Brink's-Mat Robbery, The Blackheath Poisonings, Pleasure, The Great Kandinsky.

PORTMAN, NATALIE
Actress. b. Jerusalem, Israel, June 9, 1981. e. Stagedoor Manor Performing Arts. B'way debut in The Diary of Anne Frank, 1997.
PICTURES: The Professional, Heat, Everyone Says I Love You, Beautiful Girls, Mars Attacks!, South Beach, Prince of Egypt (voice), The Little Black Book, Anywhere But Here, Star Wars: Episode I-The Phantom Menace, Where the Heart Is, Better Living Through Circuitry, Star Wars: Episode II.

PORTMAN, RACHEL
Composer. b. Haslemere, England, Dec. 11, 1960.
PICTURES: Privileged, First Love, Last Day of Summer, Sharma and Beyond, 90 Degrees South, High Hopes, Oranges Are Not the Only Fruit, Life Is Sweet, Antonia and Jane, Where Angels Fear to Tread, Used People, Rebecca's Daughters, The Joy Luck Club, Great Moments in Aviation, Friends, Ethan Frome, Benny & Joon, War of the Buttons, Only You, Sirens, The Road to Wellville, To Wong Foo—Thanks for Everything! Julie Newmar, A Pyromaniac's Love Story, Smoke, The Adventures of Pinocchio, Emma (Acad. Award, 1996), Palookaville, Marvin's Room, Home Fries, Beauty and the Beast: The Enchanted Christmas, Addicted to Love, Mulan, Beloved, The Other Sister, Ratcatcher, Cider House Rules, The Leggend of Bagger Vance.
TELEVISION: *Movies*: Reflections, Four Days in July, Good as Gold, The Short and Curlies, 1914 All Out, Sometime in August, Loving Hazel, Young Charlie Chaplin, The Woman in Black, Precious Bane, Monster Maker, Living with Dinosaurs, The Widowmaker, Shoot to Kill, Flea Bites, The Cloning of Joanna May. *Mini-series*: A Little Princess, Jim Henson's The Storyteller, Jim Henson's The Storyteller: Greek Myths.

POSEY, PARKER
Actress. b. Laurel, MS, Nov. 8, 1968. e. NC School of the Arts; SUNY Purchase.
PICTURES: Joey Breaker, Dazed and Confused, Coneheads, Mixed Nuts, Dead Connection, Amateur, Sleep with Me, Frisk, Drunks, Party Girl, Kicking and Screaming, The Doom Generation, Flirt, Waiting for Guffman, The Daytrippers, Basquiat, Henry Fool, Dinner at Fred's, SubUrbia, Clockwatchers, The House of Yes, The Misadventures of Margaret, Cross Country, You've Got Mail, Dinner at Fred's, Scream 3, Best in Show, Josie and the Pussycats, The Anniversary Party.

TELEVISION: *Series*: As The World Turns. *Mini-series*: Tales of the City, More Tales of the City.

POST, TED
Producer, Director. b. Brooklyn, NY, March 31, 1918. Dir. many stage plays; dir. CBS-TV Repertoire Thea.; Prod.-dir., NBC-TV Coney Island of the Mind. Directed Everyone Can Make Music.
PICTURES: The Peacemaker (debut, 1956), The Legend of Tom Dooley, Hang 'em High, Beneath The Planet of the Apes, The Baby, The Harrad Experiment, Magnum Force, Whiffs, Good Guys Wear Black, Go Tell the Spartans, Nightkill, The Human Shield.
TELEVISION: *Series*: Studio One, Ford Theatre, Playhouse of Stars, Alcoa Theatre, Gunsmoke, Rawhide, Twilight Zone, Wagon Train, Combat, Peyton Place, Alcoa, Defenders, Route 66, Baretta, Columbo. *Movies*: Night Slaves, Dr. Cook's Garden, Yuma, Five Desperate Women, Do Not Fold Spindle or Mutilate, The Bravos, Sandcastles, Girls in the Office, Diary of a Hitchhiker, Stagecoach. *Pilots*: Cagney & Lacey, Beyond Westworld, Steve Canyon, Perry Mason. *Mini-series*: Rich Man, Poor Man II (episode 3).

POSTER, STEVEN
Cinematographer. A.S.C. b. Chicago, IL, March 1, 1944. e. L.A. Art Center Coll. Started as commercial cinematographer before moving into feature films. 2nd unit work includes: Close Encounters of the Third Kind, Blade Runner. 2nd v.p., American Society of Cinematographers.
PICTURES: Blood Beach, Dead and Buried, Spring Break, Strange Brew, Testament, The New Kids, The Heavenly Kid, Blue City, The Boy Who Could Fly, Aloha Summer, Someone to Watch Over Me, Big Top Pee-wee, Next of Kin, Opportunity Knocks, Rocky V, Life Stinks, The Cemetery Club, Once You Meet a Stranger, A Midwife's Tale, Boy's Life 2, Rocket Man.
TELEVISION: *Movies*: The Grass is Always Greener, The Night Rider, The Beggarman Thief, Coward of the County, Mysterious Two, The Cradle Will Fall, I'll Take Manhattan, Class of '65, Courage, Shanghai La Plaza, Roswell, The Color of Justice.

POSTLETHWAITE, PETE
Actor. b. Lancashire, England. Feb. 16, 1946.
THEATER: *RSC:* Every Man and His Humour, A Midsummer Night's Dream, MacBeth, King Lear, The Taming of the Shrew.
PICTURES: The Duellists, A Private Function, Distant Voices Still Lives, The Dressmaker, To Kill a Priest, Hamlet, Alien^3, The Last of the Mohicans, Waterland, In the Name of the Father (Acad. Award nom.), Anchoress, The Usual Suspects, James and the Giant Peach (voice), Dragonheart, When Saturday Comes, William Shakespeare's Romeo + Juliet, Brassed Off, Bandyta, Amistad, The Serpent's Kiss, The Lost World: Jurrasic Park, Among Giants, The Divine Ryans.
TELEVISION: The Muscle Market, A Child From the South, Treasure Island (theatrical in U.K.), Martin Chuzzlewit, Lost for Words, Alic in Wonderland, Butterfly Collectors (mini-series), Animal Farm (voice).

POSTON, TOM
Actor. b. Columbus, OH, Oct. 17, 1927. Made B'way debut 1947 in Cyrano de Bergerac.
PICTURES: City That Never Sleeps (debut, 1953), Zotz!, The Old Dark House, Soldier in the Rain, Cold Turkey, The Happy Hooker, Rabbit Test, Up the Academy, Carbon Copy, Krippendorf's Tribe.
TELEVISION: *Movies*: The Girl The Gold Watch and Everything, Save the Dog!, A Quiet Little Neighborhood A Perfect Little Murder. *Series*: The Steve Allen Show (Emmy Award, 1959), Pantomime Quiz, To Tell the Truth, On the Rocks, We've Got Each Other, Mork and Mindy, Newhart, Grace Under Fire. *Guest*: Goodyear Playhouse, Phil Silvers Show, Password, The Defenders, Fame, The Love Boat, Dream On, The Simpsons (voice).

POTTS, ANNIE
Actress. b. Nashville, TN, Oct. 28, 1952. e. Stephens Coll., MO, BFA. Amateur stage debut at 12 in Heidi. Then in summer stock; on road in Charley's Aunt, 1976. Serves on auxilliary bd. of MADD (Mothers Against Drunk Driving). Ambassador for Women for the Amer. Arthritis Fdn.
PICTURES: Corvette Summer (debut, 1978), King of the Gypsies, Heartaches, Ghostbusters, Crimes of Passion, Pretty in Pink, Jumpin' Jack Flash, Pass the Ammo, Who's Harry Crumb?, Ghostbusters II, Texasville, Breaking the Rules, Toy Story (voice), Toy Story 2 (voice).
TELEVISION: *Movies*: Black Market Baby, Flatbed Annie and Sweetie Pie, Cowboy, It Came Upon the Midnight Clear, Why Me?, Her Deadly Rival. *Series*: Goodtime Girls, Designing Women, Love & War, Dangerous Minds, Over the Top, Any Day Now. *Guest*: Remington Steele, Magnum P.I., Twilight Zone.

POUND, LESLIE
Executive. b. London, England, Nov. 3, 1926. Entered industry in 1943 as reporter on British trade paper, The Cinema. Now, Screen International. Following military service in India and Singapore returned to work for that publication until 1952 when joined Paramount pub. office in London on the The Greatest Show on Earth. Named dir. of adv./pub. in U.K. for Paramount. 1958, retained Paramount position when Cinema Int'l Corp. was formed. 1977, joined Lew Grade in ITC Entertainment as worldwide dir. of pub./adv. 1977, int'l pub. chief for Embassy Pictures in Los Angeles. 1982, named Paramount Pictures v.p., int'l mktg. for motion picture div., N.Y. 1983. Relocated to L.A. with mktg. div. as sr. v.p. Returned to London, 1993 as sr. v.p. International markets for Paramount Pictures.

POWELL, JANE
Actress, Singer. r.n. Suzanne Burce. b. Portland, OR, April 1, 1929. m. pub. relations exec. Dick Moore. Had own radio program over KOIN, Portland; singer on nat'l networks; Star of Tomorrow, 1948. Autobiography: The Girl Next Door ... and How She Grew (1988). Video: Jane Powell's Fight Back With Fitness.
THEATER: Irene (B'way, 1974). After-Play (off-B'way, 1996). Toured nationally with South Pacific, Peter Pan, My Fair Lady, The Unsinkable Molly Brown, I Do I Do, Same Time Next Year, Chapter Two.
PICTURES: Song of the Open Road (debut, 1944), Delightfully Dangerous, Holiday in Mexico, Three Daring Daughters, A Date With Judy, Luxury Liner, Nancy Goes to Rio, Two Weeks With Love, Royal Wedding, Rich Young and Pretty, Small Town Girl, Three Sailors and a Girl, Seven Brides for Seven Brothers, Athena, Deep in My Heart, Hit the Deck, The Girl Most Likely, The Female Animal, Enchanted Island.
TELEVISION: *Specials*: Ruggles of Red Gap, Give My Regards to Broadway, Meet Me in St. Louis, Jane Powell Show. *Series*: Alcoa Theatre, Loving, As the World Turns. *Guest*: The Love Boat, Growing Pains, Murder She Wrote, others. *Movies*: The Letters, Mayday at 40,000 Feet, The Making of Seven Brides for Seven Brothers. *Host*: The Movie Musicals.

POWELL, MICHAEL
Executive. b. Birmingham, AL, March 23, 1963. e. College of William and Mary, AB, government, 1985. Georgetown U. Law Center, JD, 1993. US Army officer, 1985-88. Policy adviser to Sec'y of Defense, Defense Dept., 1988-90. Law clerk for Harry Edwards, chief judge, US Court of Appeals, 1993-94. Associate, O'Melveny & Myers, 1994-96. Chief of staff, Justice Dept. antitrust div., 1996-97. Commissioner of the FCC, 1997.

POWELL, ROBERT
Actor. b. Salford, England, June 1, 1944. e. Manchester U. Stage work includes Tovarich.
PICTURES: Robbery (debut, 1967), Far From the Madding Crowd, Joanna, The Italian Job, Walk a Crooked Path, Secrets, Running Scared, Asylum, The Asphyx, Mahler, Tommy, Oltre il Bene e il Male, Cocktails for Three, The Thirty-Nine Steps, The Dilessi Affair, Harlequin, Jane Austin in Manhattan, The Survivor, Imperative (Venice Film Fest. Award), The Jigsaw Man, What Waits Below, D'Annunio and I Down There in the Jungle, Romeo-Juliet (voice), The Sign of Command, Once on Chunuk Bar.
TELEVISION: *Series*: Doomwatch, Hannay, The First Circle. *Mini-Series*: Jesus of Nazareth. *Movies/Specials*: Shelley, Jude the Obscure, Mrs. Warren's Profession, Mr. Rolls & Mr. Royce, Looking for Clancy, The Four Feathers, The Hunchback of Notre Dame, Pygmalion, Frankenstein, Shaka Zulu, Merlin of the Crystal Cave, The Golden Years.

POWERS, MALA
Actress. r.n. Mary Ellen Powers. b. San Francisco, CA, Dec. 20, 1931. p. George and Dell Powers, latter, dramatic coach. e. Studied acting with Michael Chekhov. e. UCLA. Pasadena Playhouse in For Keeps, 1946, followed by Distant Isle; Actor's Lab, Hollywood; did considerable radio, theatre and tv work. Writer, narrator Children's Story, and Dial A Story (1979). *Author:* Follow the Star (1980), Follow the Year (1984). Teaches Michael Chekhov technique of acting.
PICTURES: Tough as They Come (debut, 1942), Outrage, Edge of Doom, Cyrano de Bergerac, Rose of Cimarron, City Beneath the Sea, City That Never Sleeps, Geraldine, The Yellow Mountain, Rage at Dawn, Bengazi, Tammy and the Bachelor, The Storm Rider, Death in Small Doses, The Colossus of New York, Sierra Baron, The Unknown Terror, Man on the Prowl, Flight of the Lost Balloon, Rogue's Gallery, Doomsday, Daddy's Gone-A-Hunting, Six Tickets to Hell.
TELEVISION: *Series*: Hazel, The Man and the City. *Guest*: Daniel Boone.

POWERS, C. F. (MIKE) JR.
Executive. b. San Francisco, CA, March 6, 1923. e. Park Coll., MO, Columbia U., N.Y., graduated U. of Oregon. Entered film business with P.R.C. in Portland, OR, 1947. Became Eagle Lion branch mgr. in Portland, 1950, and then United Artists. Moved to Seattle, WA as branch mgr. of 20th Century Fox, 1960. Was then western division mgr. for 20th Century Fox until 1967, then western division mgr. for Cinerama until 1973. Became exec. v.p., head film buyer for Robert L. Lippert Theatres, Transcontinental Theatres and Affiliated Theatres until 1978. Western div. mgr. Orion Pictures, 1982-4. Mike Powers Ent. (a buying and booking combine and indept. film distrib.). 1984-86 Western district mgr. Embassy Pictures. Became western division mgr. for Filmways Pictures. Past president of Catholic Entertainment Guild of

Northern Calif.; past pres. of Variety Club Tent 32, San Francisco. Currently m.p. consultant to U.S. Federal Govt.

POWERS, STEFANIE
Actress. r.n. Stefania Federkiewicz. b. Hollywood, CA, Nov. 2, 1942. After graduation from Hollywood High signed by Columbia Studios.
PICTURES: Tammy Tell Me True (debut, 1962), Experiment in Terror, The Young Sinner, The Interns, If a Man Answers, McClintock!, Palm Springs Weekend, The New Interns, Love Has Many Faces, Die Die My Darling, Stagecoach, Warning Shot, The Boatniks, Crescendo, The Magnificent 7 Ride, Herbie Rides Again, Gone With the West, It Seemed Like a Good Idea at the Time, Escape to Athena, Invisible Stranger.
TELEVISION: *Series*: The Girl From U.N.C.L.E., Feather and Father Gang, Hart to Hart. *Mini-series*: Washington: Behind Closed Doors, Hollywood Wives. *Movies*: Five Desperate Women, Paper Man, Sweet Sweet Rachel, Hardcase, No Place to Run, Shootout in a One-Dog Town, Skyway to Death, Sky Heist, Return to Earth, Family Secrets (also prod.), A Death in Canaan, Nowhere to Run, Mistral's Daughter, Deceptions, At Mother's Request, Beryl Markham: A Shadow on the Sun (also co-prod.), She Was Marked for Murder, Love and Betrayal, When Will I Be Loved?, The Burden of Proof, Survive the Night, Hart to Hart Returns (also co-prod.), Hart to Hart: Home is Where the Hart Is, Hart to Hart: Crimes of the Hart (also co-prod.), Hart to Hart: Old Friends Never Die, The Good Ride, Good King Wenceslas, Hart to Hart: Secrets of the Hart, Hart to Hart: Til Death Do Us Hart.

PREISNER, ZBIGNIEW
Composer. b. Bielsko-Biala, Poland, May 20, 1955.
PICTURES: The Weather Forecast, No End, By Touch, Ucieczka, The Lullabye, Kocham Kino, To Kill a Priest, A Short Film About Killing, A Short Film About Love, The Last Schoolbell, Europa, Europa, The Double Life of Veronique, Eminent Domain, At Play in the Fields of the Lord, Dismissed from Life, Olivier, Olivier, Damage, The Secret Garden, Blue, White, Red, The Line of the Horizon, To Have and to Hold, Desire in Motion, Elisa, Feast of July, Kryszstof Kieslowski: I'm So-So, De Aegypto, Bridges, Fairy Tale: A True Story, The Island on Bird Street, Foolish Heart, Liv, The Last September, Dreaming of Joseph Lees, Aberdeen.
TELEVISION: *Mini-series:* The Decalogue, Radetzky March.

PRENTISS, PAULA
Actress. r.n. Paula Ragusa. b. San Antonio, TX, March 4, 1939. m. actor-dir. Richard Benjamin. e. Northwestern U., Bachelor degree in drama, 1959. On stage in As You Like It, Arf!, The Norman Conquests, Love Letters, Secrets, Demons (Amer. Rep. Theatre, Cambridge, MA), Angel's Share (Tiffany Theater, L.A.).
PICTURES: Where the Boys Are (debut, 1960), The Honeymoon Machine, Bachelor in Paradise, The Horizontal Lieutenant, Follow the Boys, Man's Favorite Sport?, The World of Henry Orient, Looking for Love, In Harm's Way, What's New Pussycat?, Catch-22, Move, Born to Win, Last of the Red Hot Lovers, Crazy Joe, The Parallax View, The Stepford Wives, The Black Marble, Saturday the 14th, Buddy Buddy, Mrs. Winterbourne.
TELEVISION: *Series*: He & She, Burke's Law. *Movies*: The Couple Takes a Wife, Having Babies II, No Room to Run (Australian), Friendships Secrets and Lies, Top of the Hill, Packin' It In, M.A.D.D.: Mothers Against Drunk Drivers.

PRESLE, MICHELINE
Actress. r.n. Micheline Chassagne. b. Paris, France, Aug. 22, 1922. e. Raymond Rouleau Dram. Sch. m.p. debut in Je Chante; on stage in Colinette. Am. Stram Gram, Spectacle des Allies; to U.S., 1945; Flea in Her Ear, Magic Circus, Who's Afraid of Virginia Woolf? (tour), Gigi, Nuit de Valognes, Boomerang, Adriana Mont, etc.
PICTURES: Jeunes Filles en Detresse, L'Histoire de Rire, La Nuit Fantastique, Felicie Nanteuil, Seul Amour, Faibalas, Boule de Suif, Jeux Sont Faix, Diable au Corps, Under My Skin, Some Kind of News, An American Guerilla in the Philippines, Adventures of Captain Fabian, Sins of Pompeii, House of Ricordi, Archipelago of Love, Thieves After Dark, Le Chien, At the Top of the Stairs, Le Jour de Rois. Fine Weather, But Storms Due Towards Evening, Confidences, Alouette, Je te plumerai, I Want to Go Home.
TELEVISION: The Blood of Others.

PRESLEY, PRISCILLA
Actress. b. Brooklyn, NY, May 24, 1945. Raised in Connecticut. e. Wiesbaden, West Germany where met and married Elvis Presley (1967-73). Studied acting with Milton Katselas, dance at Steven Peck Theatre Art School and karate at Chuck Norris Karate School. Formed a business, Bis and Beau, marketing exclusive dress designs. Became TV spokesperson for beauty products.
PICTURES: The Naked Gun: From the Files of Police Squad! (debut, 1988), The Adventures of Ford Fairlane, The Naked Gun 2 1/2: The Smell of Fear, Naked Gun 33 1/3: The Final Insult.
TELEVISION: *Series*: Those Amazing Animals (host, 1980-81), Dallas. *Movies*: Love is Forever, Elvis and Me (prod. only).

PRESSMAN, EDWARD R.
Producer. b. New York, NY. e. Fieldston Sch.; grad., Stanford U.; studied at London Sch. of Economics. Began career with film short, Girl, in collaboration with dir. Paul Williams in London. They formed Pressman-Williams Enterprises.
PICTURES: *Prod. or Exec. prod.*: Out of It, The Revolutionary, Dealing: or the Berkeley to Boston Forty Brick, Lost Bag Blues, Sisters, Badlands, Phantom of the Paradise, Despair, Paradise Alley, Old Boyfriends, Heartbeat, The Hand, Conan the Barbarian, Das Boot, The Pirates of Penzance, Crimewave, Plenty, Half Moon Street, True Stories, Good Morning Babylon, Masters of the Universe, Walker, Wall Street, Cherry 2000, Paris By Night, Talk Radio, Martians Go Home, Blue Steel, Reversal of Fortune, To Sleep with Anger, Waiting for the Light, Homicide, Year of the Gun, Iron Maze (co-exec. prod.), Storyville, Bad Lieutenant, Hoffa, Dream Lover, The Crow, Street Fighter, Judge Dredd, City Hall, The Island of Dr. Moreau, The Crow: City of Angels, The Winter Guest, Two Girls and a Guy, The Blackout, The Crow: World of Gods and Monsters, American Psycho, The Crow: Salvation.

PRESSMAN, LAWRENCE
Actor. b. Cynthiana, KY, July 10, 1939. e. Kentucky Northwestern U. On B'way in Man in the Glass Booth, Play It Again, Sam.
PICTURES: The Man in the Glass Booth, The Crazy World of Julius Vrooder, Hellstrom Chronicle, Shaft, Making It, Walk Proud, Nine to Five, Some Kind of Hero, The Hanoi Hilton, The Waterdance, The Maker, Trial & Error, Mighty Joe Young, My Giant.
TELEVISION: *Series*: Mulligan's Stew, Doogie Howser M.D., Law and Order, N.Y.P.D. Blue, The Late Shift. *Movies*: Cannon, The Snoop Sisters, The Marcus-Nelson Murder, Winter Kill, The First 36 Hours of Dr. Durant, Rich Man, Poor Man, Man from Atlantis, The Trial of Lee Harvey Oswald, The Gathering, Like Mom, Like Me, Blind Ambition, Little Girl Lost, Breaking Point, White Hot: The Mysterious Murder of Thelma Todd.

PRESSMAN, MICHAEL
Director, Producer. b. New York, NY, July 1, 1950. e. California Inst. of Arts. From show business family; was actor in college.
PICTURES: *Director*: The Great Texas Dynamite Chase, The Bad News Bears Breaking Training, Boulevard Nights, Those Lips Those Eyes (also prod.), Some Kind of Hero, Doctor Detroit, Teenage Mutant Ninja Turtles II: The Secret of the Ooze, To Gillian On Her 37th Birthday.
TELEVISION: *Movies*: Like Mom, Like Me, The Imposter, The Christmas Gift, Final Jeopardy, Private Sessions, Haunted by Her Past, To Heal a Nation, Shootdown, The Revenge of Al Capone, Incident at Dark River, Man Against the Mob (also co-prod.), Joshua's Heart, Quicksand: No Escape. *Series*: The Practice.

PRESTON, KELLY
Actress. b. Honolulu, HI, Oct. 13, 1962. e. UCLA, USC. m. actor John Travolta.
PICTURES: Metalstorm: The Destruction of Jared-Syn (debut, 1983), Christine, Mischief, Secret Admirer, SpaceCamp, 52 Pick-Up, Amazon Women on the Moon, A Tiger's Tale, Love at Stake, Spellbinder, Twins, The Experts, Run, Only You, Love Is a Gun, Cheyenne Warrior, Waiting to Exhale, From Dusk Till Dawn, Citizen Ruth, Addicted to Love, Jerry Maguire, Nothing to Lose, Jack Frost, Holy Man, For Love of the Game, Bar Hopping, Standing Room Only.
TELEVISION: *Series*: For Love and Honor, Capitol. *Movies*: The Perfect Bride, The American Clock, Mrs. Munck. *Guest*: Quincy, Blue Thunder, Riptide.

PREVIN, ANDRE
Composer, Conductor. b. Berlin, Germany, April 6, 1929. Composed and conducted over 50 m.p. scores. Music dir., Pittsburgh Symphony Orchestra, & conductor emeritus of London Symphony Orchestra. Music dir., Royal Philharmonic Orch., 1985-89. Guest conductor of most major symphony orchestras in U.S. and Europe. Music dir., Pittsburgh Symphony 1972-81. Conductor, London Symphony, 1968-78. Conductor Emeritus London Symphony, 1992-present. Received Knighthood of British Empire in 1996.
PICTURES: Three Little Words, Cause for Alarm, It's Always Fair Weather, Bad Day at Black Rock, Invitation to the Dance, Catered Affair, Designing Woman, Silk Stockings, Gigi (Acad. Award, 1958), Porgy and Bess (Acad. Award, 1959), The Subterraneans, Bells Are Ringing, Pepe, Elmer Gantry, The Four Horsemen of the Apocalypse, One Two Three, Two for the Seesaw, Long Day's Journey Into Night, Irma LaDouce (Acad. Award, 1963), My Fair Lady (Acad. Award, 1964), Goodbye Charlie, Inside Daisy Clover, The Fortune Cookie, Thoroughly Modern Millie, Valley of the Dolls, Paint Your Wagon, The Music Lovers, Jesus Christ Superstar, Rollerball, One Trick Pony.

PRICE, FRANK
Executive. b. Decatur, IL, May 17, 1930. e. Michigan State U. following naval service. Joined CBS in N.Y. in 1951 as story editor and writer. Moved to Hollywood in 1953, serving as story editor first at Columbia and then NBC (Matinee Theatre). In 1958 joined Universal as an assoc. prod. and writer. In 1961 named exec. prod. of The Virginian TV series. Appt. exec. prod. of Ironside; later did It Takes a Thief and several World Premiere movies. 1964 named v.p. of Universal TV; 1971, sr. v.p.; 1974, pres. Also v.p., MCA, Inc. 1978 left to join Columbia as pres. of new company unit, Columbia Pictures Productions. In 1979 named chmn. & CEO of Columbia Pictures. In 1983 joined Universal: named chmn., motion picture group, pres. of Universal Pictures, and v.p. of MCA. In 1987 formed Price Entertainment Inc. as chmn. & CEO to produce movies and create TV shows for dist. through Columbia Pictures Entertainment. 1990, integrated Price Entertainment Inc., into Columbia and was named chairman. Resigned, 1991. Prod. tv movie, The Tuskegee Airmen; prod. film, Zeus and Roxanne, 1997.

PRICE, RICHARD
Writer. b. Bronx, NY, Oct. 12, 1949. e. Cornell U., Columbia U.
AUTHOR: The Wanderers, Bloodbrothers, Ladies' Man, The Breaks, Clockers.
PICTURES: *Cameos:* The Wanderers, The Paper. *Writer:* The Color of Money (Acad. Award nom.; also cameo), Streets of Gold, New York Stories (Life Lessons; also cameo), Sea of Love, Night and the City (also cameo), Mad Dog and Glory (also exec. prod., cameo), Ethan Frome (exec. prod. only), Kiss of Death (also co-prod., cameo), Clockers (also co-prod.), Ransom (also cameo), Money Train.

PRIES, RALPH W.
Executive. b. Atlanta, GA, August 31, 1919. Graduated Georgia Inst. of Technology. V.P., MEDIQ, Inc.; pres. MEDIQ/PRN Life Support Services, Inc.; past pres., Odgen Food Service Corp.; exec. comm. and bd., Firstrust Savings Bank and chmn. of audit comm.; Boards of St. Christopher's Hospital for Children, Moss Rehabilitation Hospital, United Hospital Corp., Philadelphia Heart Instit. Former intl pres., Variety Clubs Intl.; previously on bd. of Hahnemann U. and Hosp., chmn. of bd. Likoff Cardiovascular Instit., pres. Main Line Reform Temple, Wynnewood, PA.

PRIESTLEY, JASON
Actor. b. Vancouver, Canada, Aug. 28, 1969. First screen appearance was as baby in 1969 film That Cold Day in the Park, in which his mother had bit part. Child actor in many Canadian TV commercials. First major U.S. acting job in 1986 TV movie Nobody's Child. Moved to L.A. in 1987. Theatre includes The Addict, The Breakfast Club.
TELEVISION: *Series*: Sister Kate, Beverly Hills 90210 (also co-prod., dir.). *Movies*: Stacie (Canada), Nobody's Child, Teen Angel & Teen Angel Returns (Disney TV), Vanishing Point, Kiss Tomorrow Goodbye. *Guest*: Danger Bay (Canada), MacGyver, 21 Jump Street, Adventures of Beans Baxter, Quantum Leap, Parker Lewis Can't Lose.
PICTURES: The Boy Who Could Fly, Nowhere to Run, Watchers, Calendar Girl, Tombstone, Coldblooded, Love and Death on Long Island, Hacks, Standing on Fishes, Dill Scallion, Barenaked in America (also dir., prod.), Eye of the Beholder.

PRIMUS, BARRY
Actor. b. New York, NY, Feb. 16, 1938. e. Bennington Coll., City Coll. of NY.
THEATER: The King and the Duke, The Nervous Set, Henry IV, Parts I and II, Creating the World, Teibele and the Demon, Lincoln Center Rep. (The Changling, After the Fall).
PICTURES: The Brotherhood, Puzzle of a Downfall Child, Been Down So Long It Looks Like Up to Me, Von Richtofen and Brown, Boxcar Bertha, The Gravy Train, New York New York, Avalanche, Autopsy, The Rose, Heartland, Night Games, Absence of Malice, The River, Down and Out in Beverly Hills, Jake Speed, SpaceCamp, Talking Walls, The Stranger, Big Business, Cannibal Women in the Avocado Jungle of Death, Torn Apart, Guilty by Suspicion, Mistress (dir., s.p. only), Night and the City.
TELEVISION: *Series*: Cagney and Lacey. *Mini-Series*: Washington Behind Closed Doors. *Movies*: Big Rose, Roger & Harry: The Mitera Target, Portrait of a Showgirl, Paper Dolls, I Want to Live, Heart of Steel, Brotherly Love, The Women of Spring Break. *Guest*: Law and Order.

PRINCE
Singer, Actor. r.n. Prince Rogers Nelson. b. Minneapolis, MN, June 7, 1958. Rock star and recording artist.
PICTURES: Purple Rain (also wrote songs; Acad. Award for best orig. song score, 1984), Under the Cherry Moon (also dir., s.p., songs), Sign O' the Times (also dir., songs), Batman (songs only), Graffiti Bridge (also dir., s.p., songs).

PRINCE, HAROLD
Director. b. New York, NY, Jan. 30, 1928. e. U. of Pennsylvania. Worked as stage mgr. for George Abbott on three shows, later co-produced, produced and/or directed the following: The Pajama Game (Tony Award), Damn Yankees (Tony Award), New Girl In Town, West Side Story, A Swim in the Sea, Fiorello! (Tony Award, Pulitzer Prize), Tenderloin, A Call on Kurpin, Take Her She's Mine, A Funny Thing Happened on the Way to the Forum (Tony Award), She Loves Me, The Matchmaker (revival), Fiddler on the Roof, Poor Bitos, Baker Street, Flora, The Red Menace, Superman, Cabaret (Tony Award), Zorba, Company, Follies, The Great God Brown, The Visit, Love for Love (the last three all revivals), A Little Night Music (Tony Award), Candide (Tony Award), Pacific Overtures, Side by Side by Sondheim, Some of My Best Friends, On the Twentieth Century, Evita (also London), Sweeney Todd (Tony Award 1979; also London), Merrily We Roll Along, A Doll's Life, Play Memory, End of the World, Diamonds, Grind, Roza, Cabaret (revival), Phantom of the Opera (Tony Award, 1988; also London), Grandchild of Kings (dir. & adapt.), Kiss of the Spider Woman (Tony Award, 1993), Show Boat (Tony Award, 1995); and also directed the operas Ashmadei, Silverlake, Sweeney Todd, Candide and Don Giovanni for N.Y. City Opera, Girl of Golden West for Chicago Lyric Opera Co. and San Francisco Opera; Willie Stark for Houston Grand Opera; Madama Butterfly for Chicago Lyric Opera and Turandot for Vienna State Opera and Faust for Metropolitan Opera.
AUTHOR: Contradictions: Notes on Twenty-Six Years in the Theatre (1974).
PICTURES: *Co-producer*: The Pajama Game, Damn Yankees. *Director*: Something for Everyone, A Little Night Music.

PRINCIPAL, VICTORIA
Actress. b. Fukuoka, Japan, Jan 3, 1950. Father was in U.S. air force. Went to New York to become model; studied acting privately with Jean Scott at Royal Acad. of Dramatic Art in London before moving to Hollywood. Worked as talent agent in the mid-1970's.
PICTURES: The Life and Times of Judge Roy Bean (debut, 1972), The Naked Ape, Earthquake, I Will I Will... for Now, Vigilante Force.
TELEVISION: *Series*: Dallas. *Guest*: Fantasy Island (pilot), Love Story, Love American Style, Greatest Heroes of the Bible. *Movies*: The Night They Stole Miss Beautiful, The Pleasure Palace, Last Hours Before Morning, Not Just Another Affair, Mistress, Naked Lie (also exec. prod.), Blind Witness (also exec. prod.), Sparks: The Price of Passion (also exec. prod.), Don't Touch My Daughter (also exec. prod.), The Burden of Proof, Seduction: Three Tales From the Inner Sanctum (also co-exec. prod.), Midnight's Child (exec. prod. only), Beyond Obsession, River of Rage: The Taking of Maggie Keene, Dancing in the Dark, The Abduction.

PRINE, ANDREW
Actor. b. Jennings, FL, Feb. 14, 1936. e. U. of Miami. m. actress Heather Lowe. Mem. Actors Studio. On stage in Look Homeward, Angel, A Distant Bell, Mrs. Patterson, Borak. Ahmanson Theatre, LA: Long Day's Journey into Night, The Caine Mutiny. South Coast Rep.: Goodbye Freddy.
PICTURES: The Miracle Worker, Advance to the Rear, Texas Across the River, Bandolero!, The Devil's Brigade, This Savage Land, Generation, Chisum, Riding Tall, Simon: King of the Witches, Barn of the Naked Dead (Terror Circus), One Little Indian, The Centerfold Girls, Grizzly, The Town That Dreaded Sundown, Winds of Autumn, High Flying Lowe, The Evil, Amityville II: The Possession, Playing with Fire, Eliminators, Chill Factor, The Big One, Life on the Edge, Double Exposure, Gettysburg, Inferno, Dark Dancer, Gathering Evidence, Without Evidence.
TELEVISION: *Series*: The Wide Country, The Road West, W.E.B., Dallas, Room for Two, Weird Science. *Movies*: And the Children Shall Lead, Roughing It, Callie & Son, The Deputies, Another Part of the Forest, Night Slaves, Split Second to an Epitaph, Along Came a Spider, Night Slaves, Wonder Woman, Law of the Land, Tail Gunner Joe, Last of the Mohicans, A Small Killing, Mind over Murder, M-Station Hawaii, Christmas Miracle in Caulfield, Young Abe Lincoln, U.S.A., Donner Pass: The Road to Survival, Mission of the Shark, Scattered Dreams: The Kathryn Messenger Story, The Avenging Angel. *Mini-Series*: V: The Final Battle.

PRINZE, JR., FREDDIE
Actor. b. Los Angeles, CA, March 8, 1976. Son of late actor Freddie Prinze.
PICTURES: To Gillian on Her 37th Birthday, The House of Yes, I Know What You Did Last Summer, Sparkler, I Still Know What You Did Last Summer, Down to You, She's All That, Wing Commander, Head Over Heels, Boys and Girls, Summer Catch.
TELEVISION: *Movies:* Detention: The Siege at Johnson High, Vig. *Guest:* Family Matters.

PROCHNOW, JURGEN
Actor. b. Berlin, Germany, June 10, 1941. Studied acting at the Folkwang-Schule. In provinical theatre before making tv debut on the series Harbour at the Rhine River, 1970.

PICTURES: Zoff (debut, 1971), Zartlichkeit der Wolfe, The Lost Honor of Katharina Blum, The Consequence, Einer von uns beiden, Das Boot (The Boat; Berlin Film Fest. Award), The Keep, Dune, Der Bulle und das Madchen, Killing Cars, Terminus, Beverly Hills Cop II, Devil's Paradise, The Seventh Sign, A Dry White Season, The Fourth War, The Man Inside, Twin Peaks: Fire Walk With Me, Body of Evidence, In the Mouth of Madness, Judge Dredd, The Replacement Killers, The Fall, Chinadream, The Last Stop, Wing Commander.
TELEVISION: Forbidden, Murder by Reason of Insanity, Danielle Steel's Jewels, The Lucona Affair, Love Is Forever, Robin Hood, The Fire Next Time, Esther, Heaven's Fire.

PROSKY, ROBERT
Actor. b. Philadelphia, PA, Dec. 13, 1930. Won TV amateur talent search contest, leading to scholarship with American Theatre Wing. 23-year veteran with Washington's Arena stage. Taught acting and appeared in over 150 plays
THEATER: Death of a Salesman, Galileo, The Caucasian Chalk Circle, You Can't Take it With You, Our Town, The Price (Helen Hayes Award). *B'way*: Moonchildren, A View from the Bridge, Pale Horse Pale Rider, Arms and the Man, Glengarry Glen Ross (Tony nom.), A Walk in the Woods (Tony nom.). Off-B'way: Camping With Henry and Tom. Tours incl.: Our Town, Inherit the Wind, A Walk in the Woods (Soviet Union), After the Fall (Hong Kong).
PICTURES: Thief, Hanky Panky, Monsignor, The Lords of Discipline, Christine, The Keep, The Natural, Outrageous Fortune, Big Shots, Broadcast News, The Great Outdoors, Things Change, Loose Cannons, Gremlins II: The New Batch, Funny About Love, Green Card, Life in the Food Chain (Age Isn't Everything), Far and Away, Hoffa, Last Action Hero, Rudy, Mrs. Doubtfire, Miracle on 34th Street, The Scarlet Letter, Dead Man Walking, Mad City, Dudley Do-Right.
TELEVISION: *Series*: Hill Street Blues, Lifestories (host), Veronica's Closet. *Movies*: World War III, The Ordeal of Bill Carny, Lou Grant, The Adams Chronicles, Old Dogs, Into Thin Air, The Murder of Mary Phagan, Home Fires Burning, From the Dead of Night, Heist, Dangerous Pursuit, Johnny Ryan, Against the Mob, A Green Journey, The Love She Sought, Double Edge, Life on the High Wire, Teamster Boss: The Jackie Presser Story, The Lake, Swing Vote. *Guest*: Coach, Frasier, The Practice.

PROVINE, DOROTHY
Actress. b. Deadwood, SD, Jan. 20, 1937. e. U. of Washington. Retired from films in 1969.
PICTURES: The Bonnie Parker Story (debut, 1958), Live Fast Die Young, Riot in Juvenile Prison, The 30 Foot Bride of Candy Rock, Wall of Noise, It's a Mad Mad Mad Mad World, Good Neighbor Sam, The Great Race, That Darn Cat, One Spy Too Many, Kiss the Girls and Make Them Die, Who's Minding the Mint?, Never a Dull Moment.
TELEVISION: *Series*: The Alaskans, The Roaring 20's. *Movie*: The Sound of Anger.

PRYCE, JONATHAN
Actor. b. North Wales, June 1, 1947. e. Royal Acad. of Dramatic Art. Actor and artistic dir. of Liverpool Everyman Theatre Co.
THEATER: *London*: Comedians, Taming of the Shrew, Antony and Cleopatra, Tally's Folly, Hamlet (Olivier Award), The Caretaker, Macbeth, The Seagull, Uncle Vanya, Miss Saigon (Olivier & Variety Club Awards), Oliver! *NY*: Comedians (Tony & Theatre World Awards, 1977), Accidental Death of an Anarchist, Miss Saigon (Tony & Drama Desk Awards, 1991).
PICTURES: Voyage of the Damned (debut, 1976), Breaking Glass, Loophole, The Ploughman's Lunch, Something Wicked This Way Comes, The Doctor and the Devils, Brazil, Haunted Honeymoon, Jumpin' Jack Flash, Man on Fire, Consuming Passions, The Adventures of Baron Munchausen, The Rachel Papers, Freddie as F.R.O. 7 (voice), Glengarry Glen Ross, The Age of Innocence, A Business Affair, Great Moments in Aviation, A Troll in Central Park (voice), Deadly Advice, Shopping, Carrington (Cannes Film Fest. Award, 1995), Evita, Tomorrow Never Dies, Ronin, Stigmata, The Testimony of Taliesin Jones, Very Annie Mary, The Suicide Club.
TELEVISION: Comedians, Playthings, Partisans, For Tea on Sunday, Timon of Athens, Praying Mantis, Murder Is Easy, Daft as a Brush, Martin Luther Heretic, The Caretaker, Glad Day, The Man From the Pru, Roger Doesn't Live Here Anymore, Selling Hitler, Whose Line is It Anyway?, Mr. Wroes Virgins, Barbarians at the Gate, Thicker Than Water, David, The Union Game: A Rugby History.

PRYOR, RICHARD
Actor. b. Peoria, IL, Dec. 1, 1940. At age 7 played drums with professionals. Made NY debut as standup comic in 1963, leading to appearances on TV (Johnny Carson, Merv Griffin, Ed Sullivan). Co-wrote TV scripts for Lily Tomlin (Emmy Award, 1974) and Flip Wilson. Won Grammy Awards for albums That Nigger's Crazy, Is It Something I Said?, Bicentennial Nigger. *Autobiography*: Pryor Convictions and Other Life Sentences (1995).
PICTURES: The Busy Body (debut, 1967), The Green Berets, Wild in the Streets, The Phynx, You've Got to Walk It Like You Talk It Or You'll Lose That Beat, Dynamite Chicken, Lady Sings the Blues, Hit!, Wattstax, The Mack, Some Call It Loving, Blazing Saddles (co-s.p. only), Uptown Saturday Night, Adios Amigo, The Bingo Long Traveling All-Stars and Motor Kings, Car Wash, Silver Streak, Greased Lightning, Which Way Is Up?, Blue Collar, The Wiz, California Suite, Richard Pryor—Live in Concert (also prod., s.p.), The Muppet Movie, Richard Pryor Is Back Live in Concert (also s.p.), Wholly Moses, In God We Trust, Stir Crazy, Bustin' Loose (also co-prod., co-s.p.), Richard Pryor Live on the Sunset Strip (also prod., s.p.), Some Kind of Hero, The Toy, Superman III, Richard Pryor Here and Now (also dir., s.p.), Brewster's Millions, Jo Jo Dancer Your Life Is Calling (also dir., prod., s.p.), Critical Condition, Moving, See No Evil Hear No Evil, Harlem Nights, Another You, A Century of Cinema, Mad Dog Time, Lost Highway.
TELEVISION: *Series*: The Richard Pryor Show (1977), Pryor's Place. *Guest*: Wild Wild West, The Partridge Family, The Mod Squad, Chicago Hope. *Movies*: The Young Lawyers, Carter's Army.

PRYOR, THOMAS M.
Journalist. b. New York, NY, May 22, 1912. Joined NY Times, 1929; m.p. dept. 1931 as reporter, editor, asst. film critic; Hollywood bureau chief, corres., NY Times, 1951-59; editor, Daily Variety, 1959-88; 1988-90. Consultant to Variety & Daily Variety. 1990, retired.

PTAK, JOHN
Agent. b. San Diego, CA. Graduated UCLA film department, 1968. Theatre mgr. and booker for Walter Reade Organization and Laemmle Theatres, 1966-1969. Admin. exec. at American Film Institute's Center for Advanced Studies, 1969-1971. International Famous Agency (ICM), 1971-1975, William Morris Agency, 1976-91, Creative Artists Agency, 1991-. Represents motion picture and television talent. Co-chmn., Center for Film & Video Preservation at AFI. Member, National film Preservation Board. Bd. of dir., National Film Preservation Foundation, Motion Picture & Television Fund Foundation.

PULLMAN, BILL
Actor. b. Hornell, NY, Dec. 17, 1953. e. SUNY at Oneonta, Univ. of Mass. at Amherst.
THEATER: *NY*: Dramathon '84, Curse of the Starving Class. *LA*: All My Sons, Barabbas, Nanawatai, Demon Wine, Control Freaks.
PICTURES: Ruthless People (debut, 1986), Spaceballs, The Serpent and the Rainbow, Rocket Gibraltar, The Accidental Tourist, Cold Feet, Brain Dead, Sibling Rivalry, Bright Angel, Going Under, Newsies, A League of Their Own, Singles, Nervous Ticks, Sommersby, Sleepless in Seattle, Malice, Mr. Jones, The Favor, Wyatt Earp, While You Were Sleeping, Casper, Mr. Wrong, Independence Day, The End of Violence, Lost Highway, Zero Effect, The Virginian (also dir.), A Man is Mostly Water, The Guilty, Lake Placid, Brokedown Palace, Titan A.E. (voice).
TELEVISION: *Movies*: Home Fires Burning, Crazy in Love, The Last Seduction (also released theatrically), Merry Christmas George Bailey.

PURCELL, PATRICK B.
Executive. b. Dublin, Ireland, March 16, 1943. e. Fordham U., M.B.A., 1973. In pub. & acct., England, 1969-69; acct., Associated Hosp. Service, N.Y., 1968-70; joined Paramount Pictures, 1970; v.p., fin., 1980-83; exec. v.p. chief fin. & admin. officer 1983-.

PURI, OM
Actor.
PICTURES: Ghashiram Kotwal, The Strange Fate of Arvind Desai, Sparsh, A Folk Tale, Cry of the Wounded, Gandhi, The Ascent, Market Place, Who Pays the Piper, Half Truth, The Wave, Party, The Crossing, The Festival of Fire, Spices, New Delhi Times, Genesis, Sam & Me, Narasimha, The Inner Voice, City of Dreams, City of Joy, In Custody, The Burning Season, Ankuram, The Kite, Wold, Target, Kartavya, Brothers in Trouble, The Ghost and the Darkness, Maachis, Ghatak, Droh Kaal, Mrityu Dand, Gupt, My Son the Fanatic, Such a Long Journey, China Gate, Chachi 420, East is East, Hey Ram, Zandagi Zindabad, Kunuwara, The Zookeeper.
TELEVISION: Deliverance, The Jewel in the Crown.

PURL, LINDA
Actress. b. Greenwich, CT, Sept. 2, 1955. Moved to Japan at age 2. Appeared in Japanese theatre, TV. e. Toho Geino Academy. Back to US in 1971.
THEATER: The Baby Dance (New Haven, NYC), Hedda Gabler, The Real Thing (Mark Taper), The Merchant of Venice (Old Globe Theatre), Romeo & Juliet, Doll's House, Hallelujah Hallelujah (NYC), Three Penny Opera, Nora, All the Way Home, The Road to Mecca, Long Wharf, Beyond Therapy.

PICTURES: Jory, Crazy Mama, W.C. Fields & Me, Leo and Loree, The High Country, Visiting Hours, Viper, Natural Causes. TELEVISION: *Series*: The Secret Storm, Beacon Hill, Happy Days, Matlock, Under Cover, Young Pioneers, Robin's Hoods. *Movies*: Eleanor and Franklin, Little Ladies of the Night, Testimony of Two Men, A Last Cry for Help, Women at West Point, Like Normal People, The Flame is Love, The Night the City Screamed, The Adventures of Nellie Bly, The Last Days of Pompeii, The Manions of America, Addicted to His Love, Spies Lies and Naked Thighs, Before the Storm, Spy Games, Danielle Steel's Secrets, Body Language, Accidental Meeting, Incident at Deception Ridge, Absolute Truth.

PUTTNAM, LORD DAVID
CBE: Hon. LL.D Bristol 1983; Hon. D. Litt, Leicester 1986. Hon. Litt. D., Leeds 1992. Knighted, 1995. Producer. b. London, England 1941. e. Michenden Sch. In advertising before joining VPS/Goodtimes Prod. Co. Dir. of Britain's National Film Finance Corp. (1980-85); Also served on Cinema Films Council and governing council of the British Acad. of Film & Television Arts. Officier dans L'Ordre des Arts et des Lettres, 1986. Chmn. National Film and Television Sch., 1988. Past Pres., Council for the Protection of Rural England; Fellow, Royal Soc. of Arts; Fellow, Royal Geographical Soc., Hon. Fellow, The Chartered Society of Designers. appt. Chmn. & CEO, Columbia Pictures. Resigned 1987. Received Eastman 2nd Century Award, 1988. 1988 formed a joint venture for his Enigma Productions Ltd. with Warner Bros., Fujisankei Comm. Gp. of Japan, British Satellite Broadcasting & Country Nat West to prod. 4 films. Appt. chmn. ITEL intl. TV dist. agency, 1989. Dir., Anglia Television Group and Survival Anglia. V.P., BAFTA. Founding pres., Atelier du Cinema Europeen. Member, European Commission's 'Think Tank' for audio-visual policy.
PICTURES: Melody, The Pied Piper, That'll Be The Day, Stardust, Mahler, Bugsy Malone, The Duellists, Midnight Express, Foxes, Chariots of Fire (Acad. Award for Best Picture, 1981), Local Hero, Cal, The Killing Fields, The Mission, Defence of the Realm, Memphis Belle, Meeting Venus, Being Human, War of the Buttons, Le Confessional. Co-produced documentaries: Swastika, James Dean—The First American Teenager, Double-Headed Eagle, Brother Can You Spare a Dime?
TELEVISION: P'Tang Yang Kipperbang, Experience Preferred, Secrets, Those Glory Glory Days, Sharma and Beyond, Winter Flight, Josephine Baker, Without Warning: The James Brady Story, A Dangerous Man: Lawrence After Arabia, The Burning Season.

Q

QUAID, DENNIS
Actor. b. Houston, TX Apr. 9, 1954. Brother is actor Randy Quaid. m. actress Meg Ryan. e. U. of Houston. Appeared in Houston stage productions before leaving for Hollywood. On N.Y. stage with his brother in True West, 1984. Performer with rock band The Electrics; wrote songs for films The Night the Lights Went Out in Georgia, Tough Enough, The Big Easy. Formed Summers/Quaid Productions with producer Cathleen Summers, 1989.
PICTURES: Crazy Mama (debut, 1975), I Never Promised You a Rose Garden, September 30, 1955, Our Winning Season, Seniors, G.O.R.P., Breaking Away, The Long Riders, All Night Long, Caveman, The Night the Lights Went Out in Georgia, Tough Enough, Jaws 3-D, The Right Stuff, Dreamscape, Enemy Mine, The Big Easy, Innerspace, Suspect, D.O.A., Everybody's All-American, Great Balls of Fire, Postcards From the Edge, Come See the Paradise, Wilder Napalm, Undercover Blues, Flesh & Bone, Wyatt Earp, Hideaway (co-prod. only), Something to Talk About, Dragonheart, Gang Related, Switchback, Playing by Heart, The Parent Trap, Savior, Any Given Sunday.
TELEVISION: *Movies*: Are You in the House Alone?, Amateur Night at the Dixie Bar and Grill, Bill, Johnny Belinda, Bill: On His Own, Everything That Rises (also dir., exec. prod.).

QUAID, RANDY
Actor. b. Houston, TX, Oct. 1, 1950. Brother is actor Dennis Quaid. Discovered by Peter Bogdanovich while still jr. at Drama Dept. at U. of Houston and cast in his Targets and The Last Picture Show, 1971. Off-B'way debut: True West (1983).
PICTURES: Targets (debut, 1968), The Last Picture Show, What's Up Doc?, Paper Moon, Lolly-Madonna XXX, The Last Detail (Acad. Award nom.), The Apprenticeship of Duddy Kravitz, Breakout, The Missouri Breaks, Bound for Glory, The Choirboys, Midnight Express, Three Warriors, Foxes, The Long Riders, Heartbeeps, National Lampoon's Vacation, The Wild Life, The Slugger's Wife, Fool for Love, The Wraith, Sweet Country, No Man's Land, Moving, Caddyshack II, Parents, Bloodhounds of Broadway, Out Cold, National Lampoon's Christmas Vacation, Martians Go Home!, Days of Thunder, Quick Change, Cold Dog Soup, Texasville, Freaked, The Paper, Major League 2, Bye Bye Love, The Last Dance, Independence Day, Kingpin, Vegas Vacation, P.U.N.K.S., Bug Buster, Hard Rain, The Adventures of Rocky and Bullwinkle.

TELEVISION: *Movies*: Getting Away From It All, The Great Niagara, The Last Ride of the Dalton Gang, To Race the Wind, Guyana Tragedy: The Story of Jim Jones, Of Mice and Men, Inside the Third Reich, Cowboy, A Streetcar Named Desire, LBJ: The Early Years, Dead Solid Perfect, Evil in Clear River, Frankenstein, Roommates, Next Door, Ed McBain's 87th Precinct, Purgatory West of the Pecos, Mail to the Chief, Leprechauns. *Series*: Saturday Night Live (1985-86), Davis Rules, Gun. *Special*: Dear America (reader).

QUIGLEY, MARTIN, JR.
Educator, Writer. b. Chicago, IL, Nov. 24, 1917. e. A.B. Georgetown U.; M.A., Ed. D., Columbia U. M.P. Herald, Oct. 1939; spcl. ed. rep., M.P. Herald & M.P. Daily, May, 1941. U.S. Office of Coordination of Info., 1942; U.S. Office of Strategic Svc's., Special Intelligence Div., Eire & Italy, 1943-45. Assoc. ed., Quigley Pub., Oct. 1945; ed. M.P. Herald, July, 1949; also edit. dir. of all Quigley Pub., 1956; pres. Quigley Pub. Co., 1964. Editor: New Screen Techniques, 1953; m.p. tech. section, Encyclopaedia Brit., 1956. Co-author: Catholic Action in Practice, 1963; Films in America, 1929-69, 1970. Pres., QWS, Inc., ed. cons., 1975-81. Adjunct prof. of higher ed., Baruch College Univ. City of N.Y. 1977-89; Teachers College, Columbia Univ., 1990. Village of Larchmont, N.Y., trustee, 1977-79; mayor, 1980-84. Bd. of trustees, American Bible Society, 1984-; Religious Ed. Ass'n., treasurer, 1975-80 & chairperson, 1981-84; Laymen's Nat'l. Bible Ass'n., chmn. ed. com., 1983-93; Will Rogers Institute, chmn. Health ed. com., 1980-97; dir., William J. Donovan Memorial Foundation, 1995-. Publisher of The International Motion Picture Almanac and International Television & Video Almanac.
AUTHOR: Great Gaels, 1944; Roman Notes, 1946; Magic Shadows—The Story of the Origin of Motion Pictures, 1948; Gov't. Relations of Five Universities, 1975; Peace Without Hiroshima, 1991; First Century of Film, 1995; A U.S. Spy In Ireland, 1999.

QUIGLEY, WILLIAM J.
Executive. b. New York, NY, July 6, 1951. e. Wesleyan U., B.A., 1973; Columbia U., M.S., 1983. From 1973 to 1974 was advt. circulation mgr. for Quigley Publishing Co. Taught school in Kenya in 1974; returned to U.S. to join Grey Advt. as media planner. 1975 joined Walter Reade Organization as asst. film buyer; promoted to head film buyer in 1977. Named v.p., 1982. In 1986 joined Vestron, Inc. as sr. v.p. to establish Vestron Pictures. Named pres., Vestron Pictures, 1987-89. In 1990 joined Fair Lanes Entertainment, Inc. as v.p. mktg. 1993, joined United Artists Theatre as sr. v.p., marketing & new business. 1997, pres. Entertainment Express; partner, Spellbound Pictures. 1999, Exec. V.P. Mann Theatres, 1998-99. CEO of ECinemaHub, resigned 2000.
PICTURES: *Exec. prod.*: Steel Dawn, The Dead, Salome's Last Dance, The Unholy, Waxwork, Burning Secret, The Lair of the White Worm, Paint It Black, The Rainbow, Twister.

QUINLAN, KATHLEEN
Actress. b. Pasadena, CA, Nov. 19, 1954. Played small role in film, One Is a Lonely Number, while in high school.
THEATER: Taken in Marriage (NY Public Theatre; Theatre World Award), Uncommon Women and Others, Accent on Youth (Long Wharf, CT), Les Liaisons Dangereuses.
PICTURES: One Is a Lonely Number (debut, 1972), American Graffiti, Lifeguard, Airport '77, I Never Promised You a Rose Garden, The Promise, The Runner Stumbles, Sunday Lovers, Hanky Panky, Independence Day, Twilight Zone—The Movie, The Last Winter, Warning Sign, Wild Thing, Man Outside, Sunset, Clara's Heart, The Doors, Trial by Jury, Apollo 13, Zeus and Roxanne, Breakdown, Event Horizon, Lawn Dogs, A Civil Action, My Giant.
TELEVISION: *Movies*: Can Ellen Be Saved?, Lucas Tanner (pilot), Where Have All the People Gone?, The Missing Are Deadly, The Abduction of St. Anne, Turning Point of Jim Malloy, Little Ladies of the Night, She's in the Army Now, When She Says No, Blackout, Children of the Night, Dreams Lost Dreams Found, Trapped, The Operation, Strays, An American Story, Stolen Babies, Last Light, Perfect Alibi, Too Rich: The Secret Life of Doris Duke. *Series:* Family Law.

QUINN, AIDAN
Actor. b. Chicago, IL, March 8, 1959. Raised in Rockwell, IL, also spent time in Ireland as a boy and following high sch. graduation. Returned to Chicago at 19, worked as tar roofer before debuting on Chicago stage in The Man in 605, followed by Scheherazade, The Irish Hebrew Lesson, Hamlet.
THEATER: Fool for Love (off-B'way debut), A Lie of the Mind, A Streetcar Named Desire (Theatre World Award).
PICTURES: Reckless (debut, 1984), Desperately Seeking Susan, The Mission, Stakeout, Crusoe, The Handmaid's Tale, The Lemon Sisters, Avalon, At Play in the Fields of the Lord, The Playboys, Benny & Joon, Blink, Mary Shelley's Frankenstein, Legends of the Fall, The Stars Fell on Henrietta, Haunted, Looking for Richard, Michael Collins, Commandments, The Assignment, This is My Father (also exec. prod.), Practical Magic, Songcatcher, Music of the Heart, In Dreams, Wings Against the Wind, Songcatcher, The Messiah XXI.

TELEVISION: *Special*: All My Sons. *Movies*: An Early Frost, Perfect Witness, Lies of the Twins, A Private Matter, Forbidden Territory: Stanley's Search for Livingstone, Two of Us, The Passenger List, Night Visions.

QUINN, ANTHONY
Actor. r.n. Anthony Quinones. b. Chihuahua, Mexico, Apr. 21, 1915. Came to U.S. as child. Brief stage work before bit roles in films. Autobiographies: The Original Sin (1972), One Man Tango (1995).
THEATER: *B'way*: A Streetcar Named Desire, Beckett, Zorba.
PICTURES: Parole (debut, 1936), Daughter of Shanghai, Last Train From Madrid, Partners in Crime, The Plainsman, Swing High Swing Low, Waikiki Wedding, The Buccaneer (1938), Bulldog Drummond in Africa, Dangerous to Know, Hunted Men, King of Alcatraz, Tip-Off Girls, Island of Lost Men, King of Chinatown, Television Spy, Union Pacific, City for Conquest, Emergency Squad, Ghost Breakers, Parole Fixer, Road to Singapore, Blood and Sand, Bullets for O'Hara, Knockout, Manpower, The Perfect Snob, Texas Rangers Ride Again, They Died With Their Boots On, Thieves Fall Out, The Black Swan, Larceny Inc., Road to Morocco, Guadalcanal Diary, The Ox-Bow Incident, Buffalo Bill, Irish Eyes Are Smiling, Roger Touhy Gangster, Ladies of Washington, China Sky, Back to Bataan, Where Do We Go From Here?, California, Imperfect Lady, Sinbad the Sailor, Black Gold, Tycoon, The Brave Bulls, Mask of the Avenger, Viva Zapata! (Academy Award for Best Supporting Actor, 1952), The Brigand, The World in His Arms, Against All Flags, Ride Vaquero, City Beneath the Sea, Seminole, Blowing Wild, East of Sumatra, Long Wait, Magnificent Matador, Ulysses, Naked Street, Seven Cities of Gold, La Strada, Attila the Hun, Lust for Life (Academy Award for Best Supporting Actor, 1956), Wild Party, Man from Del Rio, The Hunchback of Notre Dame, Ride Back, The River's Edge, Wild is the Wind, The Buccaneer (1958; dir. only), Hot Spell, Black Orchid, Last Train From Gun Hill, Warlock, Portrait in Black, Heller in Pink Tights, Savage Innocents, The Guns of Navarone, Barabbas, Requiem for a Heavyweight, Lawrence of Arabia, Behold a Pale Horse, The Visit, Zorba the Greek (also assoc. prod.), High Wind in Jamaica, Marco the Magnificent, Lost Command, The 25th Hour, The Happening, Guns for San Sebastian, The Rover, The Magus, Shoes of the Fisherman, The Secret of Santa Vittoria, A Dream of Kings, A Walk in the Spring Rain, R.P.M., Flap, Across 110th Street (also exec. prod.), Deaf Smith and Johnny Ears, The Don Is Dead, The Destructors, The Inheritance, The Con Artists, Mohammad: Messenger of God, The Greek Tycoon, Caravans, The Passage, Lion of the Desert, High Risk, The Salamander, A Man of Passion, Stradivarius, Revenge, Ghosts Can't Do It, A Star for Two, Only the Lonely, Jungle Fever, Mobsters, Last Action Hero, Somebody to Love, A Walk in the Clouds, Il Sindaco Di Rione Sanita, The Seven Servants.
TELEVISION: Much dramatic work in the early 1950s. *Series*: The City, American Playwrights Theater (host). *Movies*: Jesus of Nazareth, Treasure Island (Italian TV), Onassis: The Richest Man in the World, The Old Man and the Sea, This Can't Be Love, Hercules and the Amazon Women, Hercules and the Lost Kingdom, Hercules and the Circle of Fire, Gotti.

R

RABE, DAVID WILLIAM
Writer. b. Dubuque, IA, March 10, 1940. m. actress Jill Clayburgh. e. Loras Coll.
THEATER: The Basic Training of Pavlo Hummel (Obie Award, 1971), Sticks and Bones (Tony Award, 1971), The Orphan, In the Boom Boom Room, Streamers, Hurlyburly, Those the River Keeps.
PICTURES: I'm Dancing As Fast As I Can (also exec. prod.), Streamers, Casualties of War, State of Grace, The Firm, Hurly-burly.
TELEVISION: *Special*: Sticks and Bones.

RABINOVITZ, JASON
Executive. b. Boston, MA, e. Harvard Coll., B.A. where elected to Phi Beta Kappa. Following WWII service as military intelligence captain with paratroops, took M.B.A. at Harvard Business Sch., 1948. Started in industry in 1949 as asst. to secty.-treas., United Paramount Theatres. Asst. controller, ABC, 1953; adm. v.p., ABC-TV, 1956; joined MGM as asst. treas., 1957; named MGM-TV gen. mgr., dir. of business & financial affairs, 1958; treas. & CFO, MGM, Inc., 1963; financial v.p. & CFO, 1967. 1971, named exec. v.p. & dir. Encyclopedia Britannica Education Corp.; sr. v.p., American Film Theatre, 1974-75. Rejoined MGM as v.p./exec. asst. to the pres., 1976. Elected v.p. finance, 1979; promoted to sr. v.p., finance & corporate admin., MGM Film Co. & UA Communications, Inc. Resigned, 1984. Now film & TV consultant and indep. prod. Dir., Pacific Rim Entertainment, 1993-95.

RADFORD, MICHAEL
Director, Writer. b. New Dehli, India, Feb. 24, 1946. e. Oxford U. Worked briefly as a teacher before beginning work as documentary filmmaker.
PICTURES: *Director & Writer*: Another TIme Another Place, Nineteen Eight-Four (1984), White Mischief, Il Postino (Academy Award nom., Directors Guild Award nom.), The Swedish Cavalier. *Director:* Delta of Venus, The Elixir, Tania, B. Monkey.
TELEVISION: *Series:* Homicide: Life on the Street.

RADIN, PAUL
Producer. b. New York, NY, Sept. 15, 1913. e. NYU. After college went in adv. Became v.p. in chg. of m.p. div. of Buchanan & Co. During WWII posted in Middle East as film chief for Office of War Information for that area. On return to U.S. assigned by Buchanan to ad campaign for Howard Hughes' The Outlaw. Turned to talent mgr., joining the Sam Jaffe Agency. Then joined Ashley-Famous Agency. Became exec. prod. for Yul Brynner's indep. prod. co. based in Switzerland, with whom made such films as The Journey, Once More with Feeling, Surprise Package.
PICTURES: Born Free, Living Free, Phase IV, The Blue Bird, The Ghost and the Darkness.
TELEVISION: The Incredible Journey of Dr. Meg Laurel, The Ordeal of Dr. Mudd, Crime of Innocence. *Series*: Born Free, The Wizard.

RADNITZ, ROBERT B.
Producer. b. Great Neck, NY, Aug. 9, 1924. e. U. of VA. Taught 2 years at U. of VA, then became reader for Harold Clurman; wrote several RKO This Is America scripts, then to Broadway where co-prod. The Frogs of Spring; prod. The Young and the Beautiful; to Hollywood working at United Artists, then as story consultant to Buddy Adler, head of prod., 20th Century-Fox, 1957-58. V.P., Producer Guild of America, 1982, 1984, 1985; bd. member, Producers Branch, AMPAS, last 4 yrs. First producer with retrospective at Museum of Modern Art, and first producer honored by joint resolution of both houses of Congress for his work, 1973. Pres. Robert B. Radnitz Productions, Ltd.
PICTURES: *Producer*: A Dog of Flanders (debut, 1960; first U.S. film to win Golden Lion Award at Venice Film Fest.), Misty, Island of the Blue Dolphins, And Now Miguel, My Side of the Mountain, The Little Ark, Sounder (Acad. Award nom.), Where the Lilies Bloom, Birch Interval, Sounder 2, A Hero Ain't Nothin' But a Sandwich, Cross Creek.
TELEVISION: Mary White (Emmy & Christopher Awards), Never Forget (ACE Award nom.).

RAFELSON, BOB
Producer, Director, Writer. b. New York, NY, Feb. 21, 1933. e. Dartmouth, B.A. (philosophy). Left NY in teens to ride in rodeos in AZ. Worked on cruise ship, then played drums and bass with jazz combos in Acapulco. 1953 won Frost Natl. Playwriting competition. Dir. his award-winning play at Hanover Experimental Theatre, N.H. After Army Service did program promotion for a radio station, was advisor for Shochiku Films, Japan, then hired by David Susskind to read scripts for Talent Assocs. Writer-assoc.
prod., DuPont Show of the Month and Play of the Week (also script sprv.). Joined Screen Gems in California, developing program ideas for Jackie Cooper, then head of TV prod. arm of Columbia. Later formed BBS Productions with Burt Schneider and Steve Blauner. Appeared as actor in 1985 film Always.
PICTURES: *Co-Prod.* only: Easy Rider, The Last Picture Show, Drive He Said. *Director*: Head (debut, 1968; also co-prod., co-s.p.), Five Easy Pieces (also co-prod., co-story; Acad. Award noms. for picture & writing), The King of Marvin Gardens (also prod., co-s.p), Stay Hungry (also co-prod., co-s.p.), The Postman Always Rings Twice (also co-prod.), Black Widow, Mountains of the Moon (also co-s.p.), Man Trouble, Blood and Wine, Wet (also s.p.), Tales of Erotica, Always (actor only), Leaving Las Vegas.
TELEVISION: *Series*: The Monkees (1966-68, creator, writer, dir.; Emmy Award, 1967), Adapted 34 prods., Play of the Week. *Dir. music video*: All Night Long, with Lionel Ritchie.

RAFFERTY, FRANCES
Actress. b. Sioux City, IA, June 26, 1922. e. U. of California, premed student UCLA. TV series, December Bride, Pete and Gladys.
PICTURES: Seven Sweethearts, Private Miss Jones, Girl Crazy, War Against Mrs. Hadley, Thousands Cheer, Dragon Seed, Honest Thief, Mrs. Parkington, Barbary Coast Gent, Hidden Eye, Abbott and Costello in Hollywood, Adventures of Don Coyote, Money Madness, Lady at Midnight, Old Fashioned Girl, Rodeo, Shanghai Story, Wings of Chance.

RAFFIN, DEBORAH
Actress. b. Los Angeles, CA, March 13, 1953. m. producer Michael Viner. Mother is actress Trudy Marshall. e. Valley Coll. Was active fashion model before turning to acting when discovered by Ted Witzer. Author: Sharing Christmas (Vols. I & II). Debut in 40 Carats (1973). Publisher Dove Books On Tape. Head of Dove Films, prod. co.

PICTURES: 40 Carats (debut, 1973), The Dove, Once Is Not Enough, God Told Me To, Assault on Paradise, The Sentinel, Touched by Love, Dance of the Dwarfs, Death Wish 3, Claudia, Scanners II, Wilde, Family Blessings.
TELEVISION: *Series*: Foul Play. *Movies*: A Nightmare in Badham County, Ski Lift to Death, How to Pick Up Girls, Willa, Mind Over Murder, Haywire, For the Love of It, Killing at Hell's Gate, For Lovers Only, Running Out, Sparkling Cyanide, Threesome, The Sands of Time, Morning Glory (also co-s.p.), A Perry Mason Mystery: The Case of the Grimacing Governor, Home Song, Unwed Father. *Mini-Series*: The Last Convertible, James Clavell's Noble House, Windmills of the Gods (also co-prod.). *Guest*: B.L. Stryker.

RAGLAND, ROBERT O.
Composer. b. Chicago, IL, July 3, 1931. e. Northwestern U., American Conservatory of Music, Vienna Acad. of Music. Professional pianist at Chicago nightclubs. In U.S. Navy; on discharge joined Dorsey Bros. Orchestra as arranger. On sls. staff at NBC-TV, Chicago. 1970, moved to Hollywood to become composer for movies; has scored 67 feature films plus many TV movies and series segments. Has also written some 45 original songs.
PICTURES: The Touch of Melissa, The Yin and Yang of Mr. Go, The Thing with Two Heads, Project: Kill, Abby, Seven Alone, The Eyes of Dr. Chaney, Return to Macon County, The Daring Dobermans, Shark's Treasure, Grizzly, Pony Express Rider, Mansion of the Doomed, Mountain Family Robinson, Only Once in a Lifetime, Jaguar Lives, The Glove, Lovely But Deadly, "Q", The Day of the Assassin, A Time To Die, The Winged Serpent, Trial by Terror, The Guardian, Ten to Midnight, Dirty Rebel, Hysterical, Brainwaves, Where's Willie?, The Supernaturals, Nightstick, Pretty Kill, Deep Space, Messenger of Death, The Fifth Monkey, No Place to Hide, The Buffalo Soldiers, The Raffle, Morty, Crime and Punishment, The Fear, Evil Obsession, Warhead, Top of the World, Plato's Run, Motel Blue.
TELEVISION: Photoplay's Stars of Tomorrow, Wonder Woman, Barnaby Jones, Streets of San Francisco, High Ice, The Girl on the Edge of Town, The Guardian.

RAILSBACK, STEVE
Actor. b. Dallas, TX, 1948. Studied with Lee Strasberg. On stage in Orpheus Descending, This Property Is Condemned, Cherry Orchard, Skin of Our Teeth, etc.
PICTURES: The Visitors, Cockfighter, Angela, The Stunt Man, Deadly Games, Turkey Shoot, The Golden Seal, Torchlight, Lifeforce, Armed and Dangerous, Blue Monkey, The Wind, Distortions, Deadly Intent, Alligator II: The Mutation, After-Shock, Private Wars, Forever, Calendar Girl, Nukie, Save Me.
TELEVISION: *Movies*: Helter Skelter, Good Cops Bad Cops, The Forgotten, Spearfield's Daughter, Sunstroke, Bonds of Love, Separated by Murder. *Mini-Series*: From Here to Eternity.

RAIMI, SAM
Director, Writer, Producer, Actor. b. Royal Oak, MI, Oct. 23, 1959. e. Michigan St. Univ. Formed Renaissance Pictures, Inc.
PICTURES: *Dir./Writer*: The Evil Dead, Crimewave, Evil Dead II, Darkman, Army of Darkness, The Quick and the Dead (dir. only), A Simple Plan, For Love of the Game, Doomsday Man, Spider Man. *Co-Producer*: Hard Target, Timecop, Darkman III (exec. prod). *Actor*: Spies Like Us, Thou Shalt Not Kill... Except, Maniac Cop, Miller's Crossing, Innocent Blood, Indian Summer, Intruder, The Hudsucker Proxy (also co-writer), The Flintstones, Galaxis.
TELEVISION: *Movies*: Journey to the Center of the Earth (actor), Mantis (prod., writer), Body Bags (actor), The Stand (actor). *Series:* American Gothic (exec. prod.), Xena: Warrior Princess (exec. prod.), Hercules: The Legendary Journeys (exec. prod.), Spy Game (exec. prod.), Hercules and Xena-The Animated Movie:The Battle for Mount Olympus, Young Hercules, Jack of All Trades, Cleopatra 2525. *Mini-Series:* The Shining (actor).

RAJSKI, PEGGY
Producer. b. Stevens Point, WI. e. Univ. of Wisconsin. m. actor Josh Mostel. Began film career as prod. manager on John Sayles film Lianna, before becoming producer. Prod. of Bruce Springsteen music videos, incld. Glory Days which won American Video Award. Received 1994 Academy Award for short film Trevor.
PICTURES: The Brother From Another Planet, Matewan, Eight Men Out, The Grifters, Little Man Tate, Used People, Home for the Holidays, Boy's Life 2.

RAKSIN, DAVID
Composer. b. Philadelphia, PA, Aug. 4, 1912. e. U. of Pennsylvania, studied music with Isadore Freed and Arnold Schoenberg. Composer for films, ballet, dramatic and musical comedy, stage, radio and TV, symphony orchestra and chamber ensembles. Arranger of music of Chaplin film, Modern Times; pres. Composers and Lyricists Guild of America, 1962-70; animated films include Madeline and The Unicorn in the Garden (UPA). Professor of Music and Urban Semester, U. of Southern California. Coolidge Commission from the Library of Congress: Oedipus Memneitai (Oedipus Remembers) for bass/baritone, part chorus and chamber orchestra premiered there under dir. of composer, Oct. 1986. Pres., Society for the Preservation of Film Music, 1992. Recipient of ASCAP Golden Score Award for Career Achievement, 1992. Elected to ASCAP bd. of dirs., 1995.
PICTURES: Laura, Secret Life of Walter Mitty, Smoky, Force of Evil, Across the Wide Missouri, Carrie, Bad and the Beautiful, Apache, Suddenly, Big Combo, Jubal, Hilda Crane, Separate Tables, Al Capone, Night Tide, Too-Late Blues, Best of the Bolshoi (music for visual interludes), Two Weeks in Another Town, The Redeemer, Invitation to a Gunfighter, Sylvia, A Big Hand for the Little Lady, Will Penny, Glass Houses, What's the Matter With Helen?
TELEVISION: *Series*: Five Fingers, Life With Father, Father of the Bride, Ben Casey, Breaking Point. *Specials*: Journey, Tender is the Night, Prayer of the Ages, Report from America, The Olympics (CBC), The Day After, Lady in a Corner.

RALPH, SHERYL LEE
Actress. b. Waterbury, CT, Dec. 30, 1956. e. Rutgers U. Studied with Negro Ensemble Company in NYC.
THEATER: *NY*: Reggae, Dreamgirls. *LA*: Identical Twins From Baltimore.
PICTURES: A Piece of the Action (debut, 1977), Oliver and Company (voice), The Mighty Quinn, Skin Deep, To Sleep With Anger, Mistress, The Distinguished Gentleman, Sister Act 2: Back in the Habit, The Flintstones, White Man's Burden, Bogus, Deterrence, Unconditional Love, Lost in the Pershing Point Hotel.
TELEVISION: *Series*: Code Name: Foxfire, Search for Tomorrow, It's a Living, Designing Women, George. *Movies*: The Neighborhood, Sister Margaret and the Saturday Night Ladies, Luck of the Draw: The Gambler Returns, No Child of Mine. *Specials*: Happy Birthday Hollywood, Voices That Care, Story of a People: The Black Road to Hollywood (host).

RAMIS, HAROLD
Writer, Director, Actor, Producer. b. Chicago, IL, Nov. 21, 1944. e. Washington U., St. Louis. Assoc. ed. Playboy Mag. 1968-70; writer, actor, Second City, Chicago 1970-73; National Lampoon Radio Show, 1974-75. Recipient of Chicago Film Critics "Commitment to Chicago" Award, 1997.
PICTURES: National Lampoon's Animal House (co-s.p.), Meatballs (co-s.p.), Caddyshack (co-s.p., dir.), Stripes (co-s.p., actor), Heavy Metal (voice), National Lampoon's Vacation (dir.), Ghostbusters (co-s.p., actor), Back to School (co-s.p., exec. prod.), Club Paradise (co-s.p., dir.), Armed and Dangerous (exec. prod., co-s.p.), Baby Boom (actor), Caddyshack II (co-s.p.), Stealing Home (actor), Ghostbusters II (co-s.p., actor), Rover Dangerfield (co-story), Groundhog Day (dir., co-s.p., co-prod., actor), Airheads (actor), Love Affair (actor), Stuart Saves His Family (dir.), Multiplicity (dir., co-prod.), As Good As It Gets (actor), Run for Your Wife (dir., prod.), Analyze This (dir.), High Fidelity (actor), American Storytellers (actor), Bedazzled (dir).
TELEVISION: *Series*: SCTV (head writer, performer, 1976-78), Rodney Dangerfield Show (head writer, prod.). *Special*: Will Rogers—Look Back and Laugh (exec. prod.).

RAMPLING, CHARLOTTE
Actress. b. Sturmer, England, Feb. 5, 1946. e. Jeanne D'Arc Academie pour Jeune Filles, Versailles; St. Hilda's, Bushey, England.
PICTURES: The Knack... and How to Get It (debut, 1965), Rotten to the Core, Georgy Girl, The Long Duel, Sequestro di Persona, The Damned, Target: Harry, Three, The Ski Bum, Corky, Addio Fratello Crrudele, Asylum, The Night Porter, Giordano Bruno, Zardoz, Caravan to Vaccares, La Chair de L'orchidee, Farewell My Lovely, Foxtrot, Yuppi-Du, Orca, Purple Taxi, Stardust Memories, The Verdict, Viva La Vie, Tristesse et Beaute, On ne Meurt que deux Fois, Angel Heart, Mascara, D.O.A., Max My Love, Rebus, Paris By Night, Helmut Newton: Frames from the Edge (doc.), Hammers Over the Anvil, Time is Money, Invasion of Privacy, Asphalt Tango.
TELEVISION: *BBC Series*: The Six Wives of Henry VIII, The Superlative Seven, The Avengers. *Movies*: Sherlock Holmes in New York, Mystery of Cader Iscom, The Fantasists, What's in it for Henry, Zinotchka, Infidelities, La Femme Abandonnee, Radetzky March, Murder In Mind, Samson Le Maqnifique, La Dernière Fête.

RAND, HAROLD
Executive. b. New York, NY, Aug. 25, 1928. e. Long Island U., B.S., 1948-50; CCNY, 1945-46. U.S. Army 1946-48; ent. m.p. ind. 1950, pub. dept. 20th-Fox; variety of posts incl. writer, trade press, newspaper contacts; joined Walt Disney's Buena Vista pub. mgr., 1957; pub. mgr. Paramount Pictures, 1959; formed own pub. rel. firm, 1961; dir. of pub. Embassy Picture Corp. 1962; dir. of world pub. 20th Century Fox 1962; resigned 1963; dir. of adv. & pub., Landau Co., 1963; dir. world pub., Embassy Pictures, 1964; est. Harold Rand & Co., Inc., 1966, pres. of p.r. & mktg. firm. Appt. mktg., dir., Kaufman Astoria Studios, 1984; elected v.p., 1985.

RANDALL, TONY
Actor. r.n. Leonard Rosenberg. b. Tulsa, OK, Feb. 26, 1920. e. Northwestern U. Prof. N.Y. debut as actor in Circle of Chalk; U.S. Army 1942-46; radio actor on many shows. Founder/Artistic Director of National Actors Theatre in NYC, 1991.
THEATER: Candida, The Corn is Green, Antony & Cleopatra, Caesar & Cleopatra, Inherit the Wind, Oh Men! Oh Women!, Oh Captain, The Sea Gull, The Master Builder, M. Butterfly, A Little Hotel on the Side, Three Men on a Horse, The Government Inspector, The Odd Couple (tour).
PICTURES: Oh Men! Oh Women! (debut, 1957), Will Success Spoil Rock Hunter?, No Down Payment, The Mating Game, Pillow Talk, The Adventures of Huckleberry Finn, Let's Make Love, Lover Come Back, Boys' Night Out, Island of Love, The Brass Bottle, 7 Faces of Dr. Lao, Send Me No Flowers, Fluffy, The Alphabet Murders, Bang Bang You're Dead, Hello Down There, Everything You Always Wanted to Know About Sex* But Were Afraid to Ask, Scavenger Hunt, Foolin' Around, The King of Comedy, My Little Pony (voice), It Had to Be You, That's Adequate, Gremlins 2: The New Batch (voice), Fatal Instinct.
TELEVISION: *Series*: One Man's Family, Mr. Peepers, The Odd Couple (Emmy Award, 1975), The Tony Randall Show, Love Sidney. *Guest*: TV Playhouse, Max Liebman Spectaculars, Sid Caesar, Dinah Shore, Playhouse 90, Walt Disney World Celebrity Circus. *Movies*: Kate Bliss and the Ticker Tape Kid, Sidney Shorr: A Girl's Best Friend, Off Sides, Hitler's SS: Portrait in Evil, Sunday Drive, Save the Dog!, The Odd Couple: Together Again.

RANSOHOFF, MARTIN
Executive. b. New Orleans, LA, 1927. e. Colgate U., 1949. Adv., Young & Rubicam, 1948-49; slsmn, writer, dir., Caravel Films, 1951; formed own co., Filmways, 1952; industrial films, commercials; formed Filmways TV Prods., Filmways, Inc., Filmways of Calif.; bd. chmn. Filmways, Inc. Resigned from Filmways in 1972 and formed Martin Ransohoff Prods., Inc, independent m. p. and tv prod. co.
PICTURES: Boys' Night Out, The Wheeler Dealers, The Americanization of Emily, The Loved One, The Sandpiper, The Cincinnati Kid, The Fearless Vampire Killers, Don't Make Waves, Ice Station Zebra, Castle Keep, Hamlet (exec. prod.), Catch-22, The Moonshine War, King Lear, See No Evil, 10 Rillington Place, Fuzz, Save The Tiger, The White Dawn, Silver Streak (exec. prod.), Nightwing, The Wanderers, The Mountain Men, A Change of Seasons, American Pop, Hanky Panky, Class, Jagged Edge, The Big Town, Switching Channels, Physical Evidence, Welcome Home, Guilty as Sin, Turbulence (prod.).
TELEVISION: *Series*: Mister Ed, The Beverly Hillbillies, Petticoat Junction, Green Acres, The Addams Family.

RAPAPORT, MICHAEL
Actor. b. New York, NY, 1970. Started as stand-up comic appearing at Improv in LA before becoming actor.
PICTURES: Zebrahead, Point of No Return, Poetic Justice, Money for Nothing, True Romance, The Scout, Higher Learning, The Basketball Diaries, Kiss of Death, Mighty Aphrodite, The Pallbearer, A Brother's Kiss, Metro, Cop Land, Men, Palmetto, Kiss Toledo Goodbye, Deep Blue Sea, Navy Diver.
TELEVISION: Subway Stories: Tales from the Underground. *Guest:* Friends, ER, NYPD Blue.

RAPHAEL, FREDERIC
Writer. b. Chicago, IL, Aug. 14, 1931. e. Charterhouse, St. John's Coll., Cambridge.
AUTHOR: The Earlsdon Way, The Limits of Love, A Wild Surmise, The Graduate Wife, The Trouble With England, Lindmann, Orchestra and Beginners, Like Men Betrayed, Who Were You With Last Night?, April June and November, Richard's Things, California Time, The Glittering Prizes, Sleeps Six & Other Stories, Oxbridge Blues & Other Stories, Heaven & Earth, Think of England and other stories, After the War, A Double Life, The Latin Lover and other stories, Old Scores. Biographies: Somerset Maugham and His World, Byron. Translations: (with Kenneth McLeish), Poems of Catullus The Oresteia. Essays: Cracks in the Ice, Of Gods and Men, La Putain du roi, Eyes Wide Shut.
THEATER: From the Greek (1979), An Early Life.
PICTURES: Nothing But the Best, Darling (Academy Award, 1965), Two for the Road, Far from the Madding Crowd, A Severed Head, Daisy Miller, Richard's Things, Women and Men: Stories of Seduction, Women and Men 2: In Love There Are No Rules.
TELEVISION: The Glittering Prizes (Royal TV Society Writer Award 1976), Rogue Male, School Play, Something's Wrong, Best of Friends, Richard's Things, Oxbridge Blues (ACE Award, best writer), After the War, Byrow, The Man in the Brooks Brothers Shirt (also dir.; ACE Award best picture).

RAPHEL, DAVID
Executive. b. Boulogne-Seine, France, Jan. 9, 1925. e. university in France. Entered m.p. ind. as asst. to sales mgr. in France, 20th-Fox, 1950-51; asst. mgr. in Italy, 1951-54; mgr. in Holland, 1954-57; asst. to European mgr. in Paris, 1957-59; European mgr. for TV activities in Paris, 1959-61; Continental mgr. in Paris, 1961-64, transferred to NY as v.p. in chg. of intl. sales, 1964; named pres., 20th Century-Fox International, 1973. 1975, also appointed sr. v.p., worldwide marketing, feature film division, for 20th-Fox, (L.A.). 1976, joined ICM, appointed dir. general of ICM (Europe) headquartered in Paris. 1979 elected pres. ICM (L.A.) 1980, formed Cambridge Film Group Ltd.

RAPPER, IRVING
Director. b. London, Eng., Jan. 16, 1904. Stage prod. London: Five Star Final, Grand Hotel. NY: The Animal Kingdom, The Firebird, The Late Christopher Bean.
PICTURES: Shining Victory (debut, 1941), One Foot in Heaven, The Gay Sisters, Now Voyager, The Adventures of Mark Twain, Rhapsody in Blue, The Corn Is Green, Deception, The Voice of the Turtle, Anna Lucasta, The Glass Menagerie, Another Man's Poison, Forever Female, Bad for Each Other, The Brave One, Strange Intruder, Marjorie Morningstar, The Miracle, Joseph and His Brethren, Pontius Pilate, The Christine Jorgensen Story, Born Again, Justus.

RAPPOPORT, GERALD J.
Executive, Film Producer. b. New York, NY, Aug. 25, 1925. e. NYU. U.S. Marine Corps. Pres., Major Artists Representatives Corp., 1954-58; dir. of Coast Sound Services, Hollywood; 1959-61, pres., International Film Exchange Ltd.; 1960-91, CEO of IFEX Int'l; 1991-94, pres. CIFEX Corporation, 1995-present.

RASHAD, PHYLICIA
Actress-singer. b. Houston, TX, June 19, 1948. m. sportscaster Ahmad Rashad. Sister of Debbie Allen. e. Howard U., B.F.A., magna cum laude, 1970. NY School of Ballet. Acted under maiden name of Phylicia Ayers-Allen. Recording, Josephine Superstar (1979). Conceived (with Michael Peters) and appeared in revue Phylicia Rashad & Co. in 1989 in Las Vegas.
THEATER: Ain't Supposed to Die a Natural Death, The Duplex, The Cherry Orchard, The Wiz, Weep Not For Me, Zooman and the Sign, In an Upstate Motel, Zora, Dreamgirls, Sons and Fathers of Sons, Puppetplay, A Raisin in the Sun, Into the Woods, Jelly's Last Jam.
PICTURE: Once Upon A Time...When We Were Colored.
TELEVISION: *Series*: One Life to Live, The Cosby Show (People's Choice Award, NAACP Image Award, Emmy nom.), Cosby. *Movies*: Uncle Tom's Cabin, False Witness, Polly, Polly—Comin' Home!, Jailbirds, David's Mother, The Possession of Michael D. *Specials*: Nell Carter—Never Too Old to Dream, Superstars and Their Moms, Our Kids and the Best of Everything, The Debbie Allen Special, Hallelujah.

RATHER, DAN
News Correspondent, Anchor. b. Wharton, TX, Oct. 31, 1931. e. Sam Houston State Teachers Coll., BA journalism, 1953. Instructor there for 1 year. Graduate e.: U. of Houston Law School, S. Texas School of Law. Worked for UPI and Houston Chronicle. Radio: KSAM, Huntsville, KTRH, Houston. Joined CBS News in 1962 as chief of southwest bureau in Dallas. Transferred to overseas burs. (including chief of London Bureau 1965-66), then Vietnam before returning as White House corr. 1966. White House Correspondent, 1964-74.
Covered top news events, from Democratic and Republican national conventions to President Nixon's trip to Europe (1970) and to Peking and Moscow (1972). Anchored CBS Reports, 1974-75. Presently co-editor of 60 minutes (since 1975) and anchors Dan Rather Reporting on CBS Radio Network (since 1977). Anchor for 48 Hours, 1988. Winner of numerous awards, including 5 Emmys. Anchorman on CBS-TV Evening News, 1981-. Books: The Palace Guard (1974); The Camera Never Blinks (1977); I Remember (1991); The Camera Never Blinks Twice (1994); Mark Sullivan's Our Times (editor, 1995).

RAUCHER, HERMAN
Writer. b. Apr. 13, 1928. e. NYU. Author of novels Watermelon Man, Summer of '42 and Ode to Billy Joe, adapted to films by him. Other novels inc. A Glimpse of Tiger, There Should Have Been Castles, Maynard's House.
PICTURES: Sweet November, Can Hieronymous Merkin Ever Forget Mercy Humppe and Find True Happiness?, Watermelon Man, Summer of '42, Class of '44, Ode to Billy Joe, The Other Side of Midnight.
TELEVISION: Studio One, Alcoa Hour, Goodyear Playhouse, Matinee Theatre, Remember When? (movie).

RAVETCH, IRVING
Writer, Producer. b. Newark, NJ, Nov. 14, 1920. e. UCLA. m. Harriet Frank, with whom he often collaborated.
PICTURES: *Writer*: Living in a Big Way, The Outriders, Vengeance Valley, Ten Wanted Men, The Long Hot Summer, The Sound and the Fury, Home from the Hill, The Dark at the Top of the Stairs, Hud (also co-prod.), Hombre (also co-prod.), The Reivers (also prod.), House of Cards (as James P. Bonner), The Cowboys, Conrack, Norma Rae, Murphy's Romance, Stanley and Iris.

RAYBURN, GENE
Performer, b. Christopher, IL, Dec. 22, 1917. e. Knox Coll., Galesburg, IL. NBC guide; with many radio stations in Baltimore, Philadelphia, NY; US Army Air Force, 1942-45; Rayburn and Finch Show, WNEW, NY, 1945-52; Gene Rayburn Show, NBC radio; TV shows: Many appearances as host-humorist on game shows, variety shows, drama shows. Also acted in summer stock; AFTRA, past pres. NY local; trustee on H&R Board for over 25 years.
THEATER: *B'way*: Bye Bye Birdie, Come Blow Your Horn.
TELEVISION: *Series*: The Name's the Same, Tonight (second banana), Make the Connection, The Steve Allen Show, The Steve Lawrence-Eydie Gorme Show (announcer), The Match Games, Dough Re Mi, The Sky's the Limit, Choose Up Sides, Tic Tac Dough, Play Your Hunch, Snap Judgment, Amateur's Guide to Love, Break the Bank. *Guest*: The Love Boat, Fantasy Island.
(d. Nov. 15, 1999)

RAYMOND, PAULA
Actress. r.n. Paula Ramona Wright, b. San Francisco, CA., Nov. 23, 1925. e. San Francisco Jr. Coll. 1942. Started career in little theatre groups, concerts, recitals, San Francisco; leading stage roles in Ah! Wilderness, Peter Pan, etc.; also sang lead coloratura rules in Madame Butterfly, Aidia, Rigoletto, Faust, etc.; ballerina with S.F. Opera Ballet; classical pianist; model, Meade-Maddick Photographers.
PICTURES: Racing Luck, Rusty Leads the Way, Blondie's Secret, East Side West Side, Challenge of the Range, Adam's Rib, Devil's Doorway, Sons of New Mexico, Duchess of Idaho, Crisis, Grounds For Marriage, Inside Straight, The Tall Target, Texas Carnival, The Sellout, Bandits of Corsica, City That Never Sleeps, The Beast from 20,000 Fathoms, The Human Jungle, King Richard & the Crusaders, The Gun That Won the West, Hand of Death, The Flight That Disappeared, The Spy With My Face, Blood of Dracula's Castle, Five Bloody Graves, Mind Twister.
TELEVISION: *Guest*: Perry Mason, 77 Sunset Strip, Wyatt Earp, Man from U.N.C.L.E., Maverick, The Untouchables, Bachelor Father, Bat Masterson, Temple Houston, Peter Gunn.

RAYNOR, LYNN S.
Producer, Production Executive. b. Chicago, IL, Feb. 11, 1940. Produced West Coast premiere of The Balcony by Genet, The Crawling Arnold Review by Feiffer. Joined Television Enterprises, 1965; Commonwealth United, 1968 as business affairs exec. later prod. spvr. 1972 opened London branch of the Vidtronics Co. 1974, formed Paragon Entertainment & RAH Records. 1980-95, prod. of TV Movies and Mini-Series. Prod. & editor of 12 minute tv vignettes, A Hall of Fame Story.
PICTURE: Freejack.
TELEVISION: *Special*: Waiting for Godot. *Movies*: Marilyn: The Untold Story, The Execution, A Winner Never Quits, On Wings of Eagles, Stranger in My Bed, Hands of a Stranger, The High Price of Passion, The Kennedys of Massachusetts, Common Ground, Face of Love, The Rape of Doctor Willis, Quiet Killer, Love Honor & Obey: The Last Mafia Marriage, Tony & Nancy: The Inside Story, Tecumseh: The Last Warrior, It Was Him Or Us, The Lover Letter, Glory & Honor. *Series*: Camp Wilderness. *Mini-Series:* True Women. *Pilot*: Murphy's Law.

REA, STEPHEN
Actor. b. Belfast, Northern Ireland, Oct. 31, 1948. e. Queens Univ. (BA in English Lit.). Started acting at Abbey Theatre in Dublin. Formed the Field Day Theatre Co. in 1980 in Londonderry, acting in or directing most of their productions. Also acted with Royal Natl. Theatre.
THEATER: Playboy of the Western World, Comedians, High Society, Endgame, Freedom of the City, Someone Who'll Watch Over Me (also B'way; Theatre World Award, Tony nom.).
PICTURES: Danny Boy (Angel), Loose Connections, The Company of Wolves, The Doctor and the Devils, The House, Life Is Sweet, The Crying Game (Acad. Award nom.), Bad Behavior, Angie, Princess Caraboo, Ready to Wear (Pret-a-Porter), Between the Devil and the Deep Blue Sea, Interview With A Vampire, All Men Are Mortal, ,Trojan Eddie, Michael Collins, A Further Gesture, Last of the High Kings, Hacks, Fever Pitch, Double Top, This Is My Father, Still Crazy, The Butcher Boy, Blue Vision, The Life Before This, Guinevere, In Dreams, The End of the Affair, Catch the Sun, D'Artagnan.
TELEVISION: Shadow of a Gunman, Fugitive, I Didn't Know You Cared, Professional Foul, The Seagull, Out of Town Boys, Calbe Williams, Joyce in June, The House, Four Days in July, Shergar, Scout, Lost Belongings, The Big Gamble, Not With a Bang, Saint Oscar, Hedda Gabler, Citizen X, Crime of the Century.

REAGAN, RONALD
Actor, Politician. b. Tampico, IL, Feb. 6, 1911. e. high school, Eureka Coll. m. former actress Nancy Davis. Wrote weekly sports column for a Des Moines, IA newspaper; broadcast sporting events. Signed as actor by Warner Bros. in 1937. In WWII 1942-45, capt., USAAF. Actor until 1966. Served as Governor, California, 1967-74. Businessman and rancher. Elected President of the United States, 1980. Re-elected, 1984. Autobiography: Where's the Rest of Me? (1965).
PICTURES: Love Is On the Air (debut, 1937), Hollywood Hotel, Sergeant Murphy, Swing Your Lady, Brother Rat, Going Places, Accidents Will Happen, Cowboy from Brooklyn, Boy Meets Girl, Girls on Probation, Dark Victory, Naughty but Nice, Hell's Kitchen, Code of the Secret Service, Smashing the Money Ring, Angels Wash Their Faces, Brother Rat and a Baby, Murder in the Air, Tugboat Annie Sails Again, Knute Rockne—All American, Santa Fe Trail, Angel From Texas, Nine Lives Are Not Enough, The Bad Man, International Squadron, Million Dollar Baby, Kings Row, Juke Girl, Desperate Journey, This Is the Army, Stallion Road, That Hagen Girl, The Voice of the Turtle, Night Unto Night, John Loves Mary, The Girl From Jones Beach, It's a Great Feeling (cameo), The Hasty Heart, Louisa, Storm Warning, The Last Outpost, Bedtime for Bonzo, Hong Kong, She's Working Her Way Through College, The Winning Team, Tropic Zone, Law & Order, Prisoner of War, Cattle Queen of Montana, Tennessee's Partner, Hellcats of the Navy, The Young Doctors (narrator), The Killers.
TELEVISION: *Series*: The Orchid Award (emcee), General Electric Theater (host, frequent star), Death Valley Days (host). *Guest*: Ford Theatre, Schlitz Playhouse of Stars, Lux Video Theatre, Startime.

REARDON, BARRY
Executive. b. Hartford, CT, Mar. 8, 1931. e. Holy Cross Col., Trinity Col. Began industry career with Paramount Pictures; named v.p.; left to join General Cinema Theatres Corp. as sr. v.p. Now with Warner Bros. as pres. of domestic distribution co.

REASON, REX
Actor. b. Berlin, Germany, Nov. 30, 1928. e. Hoover H.S., Glendale, CA. Worked at various jobs; studied dramatics at Pasadena Playhouse.
PICTURES: Storm Over Tibet, Salome, Mission Over Korea, Taza Son of Cochise, This Island Earth, Smoke Signal, Lady Godiva, Kiss of Fire, Creature Walks Among Us, Raw Edge, The Rawhide Trail, Under Fire, Thundering Jets, The Sad Horse, Yankee Pasha, Band of Angels, Miracle of the Hills.
TELEVISION: *Series*: Man Without a Gun, Roaring Twenties.

REDDY, HELEN
Singer. b. Melbourne, Australia, Oct. 25, 1942. Parents were producer-writer-actor Max Reddy and actress Stella Lamond. e. in Australia. Began career at age four as singer and appeared in hundreds of stage and radio roles with parents by age of 15. Came to New York in 1966, played nightclubs, appeared on TV. First single hit record: I Don't Know How To Love Him (Capitol). Grammy Award, 1973, as best female singer of year for I Am Woman. Most Played Artist by the music operators of America: American Music Award 1974; Los Angeles Times Woman of the Year (1975); No. 1 Female Vocalist in 1975 and 1976; Record World, Cash Box and Billboard. Heads prod. co. Helen Reddy, Inc.
THEATER: *B'way*: Blood Brothers.
PICTURES: Airport 1975 (debut), Pete's Dragon.
TELEVISION: *Series*: The Helen Reddy Show (Summer, 1973), Permanent host of Midnight Special. *Appearances*: David Frost Show, Flip Wilson Show, Mike Douglas Show, Tonight Show, Mac Davis Show, Merv Griffin Show (guest host), Sesame Street, Live in Australia (host, 1988); Muppet Show, Home for Easter.

REDFORD, ROBERT
Actor, Director, Producer. r.n. Charles Robert Redford Jr.. b. Santa Monica, CA, Aug. 18, 1937. Attended U. of Colorado; left to travel in Europe, 1957. Attended Pratt Inst. and American Acad. of Dramatic Arts. Founded Sundance Film Institute, Park City, Utah, workshop for young filmmakers.
THEATER: *B'way*: Tall Story (walk on), The Highest Tree, Sunday in New York (Theatre World Award), Barefoot in the Park.
PICTURES: *Actor*: War Hunt (debut, 1962), Situation Hopeless But Not Serious, Inside Daisy Clover, The Chase, This Property Is Condemned, Barefoot in the Park, Downhill Racer (also exec. prod.), Butch Cassidy and the Sundance Kid, Tell Them Willie Boy is Here, Little Fauss and Big Halsy, The Hot Rock, The Candidate (also co-exec. prod.), Jeremiah Johnson, The Way We Were, The Sting (Acad. Award nom.), The Great Gatsby, The Great Waldo Pepper, Three Days of the Condor, All The President's Men (also exec. prod.), A Bridge Too Far, The Electric Horseman, Brubaker, The Natural, Out of Africa, Legal Eagles, Havana, Sneakers, Indecent Proposal, Up Close and Personal, Anthem. *Exec. Producer*: Promised Land, Some Girls, Yosemite: The Fate of Heaven (also narrator), The Dark Wind, Incident at Oglala (also narrator), Strawberry & Chocolate (presenter), She's the One, Slums of Beverly Hills, A Civil Action, No Looking Back. *Director*: Ordinary People (Acad. Award, 1980), The Milagro Beanfield War (also co-prod.), A River Runs Through It (also prod., narrator), Quiz Show (also prod.; NY Film Critics Award for Best Picture; Acad. Award noms. for picture & dir.), The Horse Whisperer (also actor, prod.), The Legend of Bagger Vance (also prod.).

TELEVISION: *Actor: Guest*: Maverick, Playhouse 90, Play of the Week (The Iceman Cometh), Alfred Hitchcock Presents, Route 66, Twilight Zone, Dr. Kildare, The Untouchables, The Virginian, The Defenders. *Exec. Prod.:* Grand Avenue.

REDGRAVE, CORIN
Actor. b. London, England, July 16, 1939. e. Cambridge. p. late Sir Michael Redgrave and Rachel Kempson. Brother of Vanessa and Lynn Redgrave.
THEATER: On stage with England Stage Co.: A Midsummer Night's Dream, Chips with Everything. RSC: Lady Windermere's Fan, Julius Caesar, Comedy of Errors, Antony and Cleopatra. Young Vic: Rosmersholm.
PICTURES: A Man for All Seasons, The Deadly Affair, Charge of the Light Brigade, The Magus, Oh What a Lovely War, When Eight Bells Toll, Serail, Excalibur, Eureka, Between Wars, The Fool, In the Name of the Father, Four Weddings and a Funeral, Persuasion.
TELEVISION: I Berlioz, Measure for Measure, Persuasion, Henry IV, Circle of Deceit.

REDGRAVE, LYNN
Actress. b. London, England, Mar. 8, 1943. Sister of Vanessa and Corin Redgrave. p. late Sir Michael Redgrave and Rachel Kempson. m. dir.-actor-manager John Clark. Ent. m.p. and TV industries, 1962.
THEATER: *NY*: Black Comedy (B'way debut), My Fat Friend (1974), Mrs. Warren's Profession, Knock Knock, Misalliance, St. Joan, Twelfth Night (Amer. Shakespeare Fest), Sister Mary Ignatius Explains It All For You, Aren't We All?, Sweet Sue, A Little Hotel on the Side, The Master Builder, Shakespeare for My Father (also writer). *LA*: Les Liaisons Dangereuses.
PICTURES: Tom Jones (debut, 1963), Girl With Green Eyes, Georgy Girl (Acad. Award nom.), The Deadly Affair, Smashing Time, The Virgin Soldiers, Last of the Mobile Hot-Shots, Los Guerilleros, Viva la Muerta—Tua!, Every Little Crook and Nanny, Everything You Always Wanted to Know About Sex* But Were Afraid to Ask, The National Health, The Happy Hooker, The Big Bus, Sunday Lovers, Morgan Stewart's Coming Home, Midnight, Getting It Right, Shine, Strike, Gods and Monsters (Acad. Award nom.), Touched.
TELEVISION: *BBC*: Pretty Polly, Ain't Afraid to Dance, The End of the Tunnel, I Am Osango, What's Wrong with Humpty Dumpty, Egg On the Face of the Tiger, Blank Pages, A Midsummer Night's Dream, Pygmalion, William, Vienna 1900, Daft as a Brush, Not For Women Only, Calling the Shots. *United States: Co-host*: A.M. America. *Movies*: Turn of the Screw, Sooner or Later, Beggarman Thief, Gauguin the Savage, Seduction of Miss Leona, Rehearsal for Murder, The Bad Seed, My Two Loves, Jury Duty: The Comedy, What Ever Happened to Baby Jane?, Toothless, Indefensible: The Truth About Edward Brannigan, White Lies, Different. *Mini-Series*: Centennial. *Series*: House Calls, Teachers Only, Chicken Soup, Rude Awakening. *Guest*: The Muppet Show, Walking on Air, Candid Camera Christmas Special, Woman Alone, Tales From the Hollywood Hills: The Old Reliable, Death of a Son.

REDGRAVE, VANESSA
O.B.E. Actress. b. London, England, Jan. 30, 1937. p. Sir Michael Redgrave and Rachel Kempson. Sister of Lynn and Corin Redgrave. Mother of actresses Joely and Natasha Richardson. Early career with Royal Shakespeare Company. Appeared in documentary Tonight Let's All Make Love in London. Autobiography, 1994.
THEATER: Daniel Deronda, Cato Street, The Threepenny Opera, Twelfth Night, As You Like It, The Taming of the Shrew, Cymbeline, The Sea Gull, The Prime of Miss Jean Brodie, Antony & Cleopatra, Design for Living, Macbeth, Lady from the Sea, The Aspern Papers, Ghosts, Anthony and Cleopatra, Tomorrow Was War, A Touch of the Poet, Orpheus Descending, Madhouse in Goa, The Three Sisters, When She Danced, Maybe, Heartbreak House, Vita & Virginia.
PICTURES: Behind the Mask (debut, 1958), Morgan!: A Suitable Case for Treatment (Acad. Award nom.), A Man for All Seasons, Blow-Up, The Sailor From Gibraltar, Red and Blue, Camelot, The Charge of the Light Brigade, Isadora (Acad. Award nom.), Oh! What a Lovely War, The Sea Gull, A Quiet Place in the Country, Drop Out, The Trojan Women, La Vacanza, The Devils, Mary—Queen of Scots (Acad. Award nom.), Murder on the Orient Express, Out of Season, The Seven Percent Solution, Julia (Acad. Award, best supporting actress, 1977), Agatha, Yanks, Bear Island, The Bostonians (Acad. Award nom.), Steaming, Wetherby, Prick Up Your Ears, Consuming Passions, Comrades, The Ballad of the Sad Cafe, Romeo-Juliet (voice), Howards End (Acad. Award nom.), Breath of Life, Sparrow, The House of the Spirits, Crime and Punishment, Mother's Boys, Great Moments in Aviation, Little Odessa, A Month by the Lake, Mrs. Dalloway, Deep Impact, Lulu on the Bridge, A Rumor of Angels, Mirka, Girl Interrupted, The Cradle Will Rock.
TELEVISION: *Movies/Specials*: A Farewell to Arms, Katherine Mansfield, Playing for Time (Emmy Award, 1981), My Body My Child, Wagner (theatrical in Europe), Three Sovereigns for Sarah, Peter the Great, Second Serve, A Man For All Seasons, Orpheus Descending, Young Catherine, What Ever Happened to Baby Jane?, They, Down Came a Blackbird, Bella Mafia, If These Walls Could Talk 2. *Guest*: Faerie Tale Theatre (Snow White and the 7 Dwarfs).

REDSTONE, EDWARD S.
Exhibitor. b. Boston, MA, May 8, 1928. e. Colgate U., B.A., 1949; Harvard Grad. Sch. of Bus. Admin., M.B.A., 1952. v.p., treas., Northeast Drive-In Theatre Corp.; v.p., Theatre Owners of New England, 1962; chmn., advis. coms., mem. bd. dirs., TOA; gen. conven. chmn., joint convention TOA & NAC, 1962; pres. National Assn. of Concessionaires, 1963; chief barker. Variety Club of New England, 1963; pres., Theatre Owners of New England; gen. chmn., 35th annual reg. convention.

REDSTONE, SUMNER M.
Executive, Attorney; b. Boston, MA, May 27, 1923. e. Harvard, B.A., 1944, LLB., 1947. Served to 1st Lt. AUS, 1943-45. Admitted to MA Bar 1947; U.S. Ct. Appeals 1st Circuit 1948, 8th Circuit 1950, 9th Circuit 1948; D.C. 1951; U.S. Supreme Ct. 1952; law sec. U.S. Ct. Appeals for 9th Circuit 1947-48; instr. U. San Francisco Law Sch. and Labor Management Sch., 1947; special asst. to U.S. Atty. General, 1948-51; partner firm Ford Bergson Adams Borkland & Redstone, Washington, D.C. 1951-54; exec. v.p. Northeast Drive-In Theatre Corp., 1954-68; pres. Northeast Theatre Corp.; chmn. bd., pres. & CEO, National Amusements, Inc.; chmn. bd., Viacom Int'l, Inc., 1987; asst. pres. Theatre Owners of America, 1960-63; pres. 1964-65; bd. chmn, National Assoc. of Theatre Owners, 1965-66. Member: Presidential Advisory Committee John F. Kennedy Center for the Performing Arts; chmn. Jimmy Fund, Boston 1960; chmn., met. div. Combined Jewish Philanthropies 1963; sponsor Boston Museum of Science; Trustee Children's Cancer Research Foundation; Art Lending Library; bd. of dirs. of TV Acad. of Arts and Sciences Fund; bd. dirs. Boston Arts Festival; v.p., exec. committee Will Rogers Memorial Fund; bd. overseers Dana Farber Cancer Institute; corp. New England Medical Center; Motion Picture Pioneers; bd. mem. John F. Kennedy Library Foundation; 1984-85; 1985-86 State Crusade Chairman American Cancer Society; Board of Overseers Boston Museum of Fine Arts; Professor, Boston U. Law Sch. 1982-83, 1985-86; Boston Latin School's Graduate of the Year, 1989; Acquired Viacom in 1987 which purchased Paramount Communications in 1993. Member of exec. committe of the National Assoc. of Theatre Owners. Member, exec. bd., Combined Jewish Philanthropies. Judge on Kennedy Library Foundation. Founding trustee, American Cancer Society. Visiting professor, Brandeis University; lecturer, Harvard Law School.
AWARDS: (Entertainment related) include: Communicator of the Year B'nai B'rith Communications, Cinema Lodge 1980; Man of the Year, Entertainment Industries div.; UJA-Federation, NY, 1988; Variety of New England Humanitarian Award, 1989; Motion Picture Pioneers Pioneer of the Year, 1991; Golden Plate Award American Acad. Achievement 32nd Annual Salute to Excellence Program; 1994, Man of the Year Award from MIP-COM, the Int'l Film and Programme Market for TV Video Cable and Satellite; 1995, Variety Club International Humanitarian Award; Hall of Fame Award, Broadcast & Cable Magazine, 1995; Honoree 7th Annual Fundraiser, Montefiore Medical Center; Expeditioner's Award, New York City Outward Bound Center, 1996; Patron of the Arts Award, Songwriter's Hall of Fame, 1996; Vision 21 Award and Doctor of Humane Letter, New York Institute of Technology, 1996; Trustees Award, The National Academy of Television Arts and Sciences, 1997; Gold Medal Award, International Radio and Television Society, 1998.

REED, PAMELA
Actress. b. Tacoma, WA, Apr. 2, 1953. Ran day-care center and worked with Head Start children before studying drama at U. of Washington. Worked on Trans-Alaska pipeline. Off-Broadway showcases.
THEATER: Curse of the Starving Class (Off-B'way debut, 1978), All's Well That Ends Well (Central Park), Getting Out (Drama Desk Award), Aunt Dan and Lemon, Fools, The November People (Broadway debut), Sorrows of Stephen, Mrs. Warren's Profession, Getting Through the Night, Best Little Whorehouse in Texas, Fen, Standing on My Knees, Elektra.
PICTURES: The Long Riders (debut, 1980), Melvin and Howard, Eyewitness, Young Doctors in Love, The Right Stuff, The Goodbye People, The Best of Times, Clan of the Cave Bear, Rachel River, Chattahoochee, Cadillac Man, Kindergarten Cop, Passed Away, Bob Roberts, Junior, Santa Fe, Bean.
TELEVISION: *Series*: The Andros Targets (TV debut, 1977), Grand, Family Album, The Home Court. *Movies*: Inmates—A Love Story, I Want To Live, Heart of Steel, Scandal Sheet, Caroline?, Woman With a Past, Born Too Soon, Deadly Whispers, The Man Next Door, Critical Choices, Carriers. *Special*: Tanner '88. *Mini-Series*: Hemingway. *Guest*: L.A. Law, The Simpsons (voice).

REES, ROGER
Actor. b. Aberystwyth, Wales, May 5, 1944. e. Camberwell Sch. of Art, Slade Sch. of Fine Art. Stage debut Hindle Wakes (Wimbledon, U.K., 1964). With Royal Shakespeare Co. from 1967. Starred in the title role The Adventures of Nicholas Nickleby (London and NY, Tony Award), also on stage in Hapgood (London, L.A.), Indiscretions (NY). Off-B'way in The End of the Day. Assoc. dir. Bristol Old Vic Theatre Co., 1986-present. Playwright with Eric Elice of Double Double and Elephant Manse.
PICTURES: Star 80 (debut, 1983), Keine Storung Bitte, Mountains of the Moon, If Looks Could Kill, Stop! Or My Mom Will Shoot, Robin Hood: Men in Tights, Sudden Manhattan.
TELEVISION: *Movies*: A Christmas Carol (released theatrically in Europe), Place of Peace, Under Western Eyes, Bouquet of Barbed Wire, Saigon: The Year of the Cat, Imaginary Friends, The Adventures of Nicolas Nickleby, The Comedy of Errors, Macbeth, The Voysey Inheritance, The Ebony Tower, The Finding, The Return of Sam McCloud, Charles & Diana: Unhappily Ever After, The Tower, The Possession of Michael D. *Series*: Cheers, Singles, M.A.N.T.I.S.

REESE, DELLA
Actress, Singer. r.n. Deloreese Patricia Early. b. Detroit, MI, July 6, 1932. e. Wayne St. Univ. As teen toured with Mahalia Jackson. Began recording in 1950's. Hit songs include Don't You Know.
PICTURES: Let's Rock!, Psychic Killer, Harlem Nights, The Distinguished Gentleman, A Thin Line Between Love and Hate.
TELEVISION: *Series*: The Della Reese Show, Chico and the Man, It Takes Two, Charlie & Company, The Royal Family, Touched by an Angel. *Guest*: The Ed Sullivan Show, Sanford and Son, The Rookies, McCloud, Welcome Back Kotter, The Love Boat, Night Court, The A-Team. *Movies*: The Voyage of the Yes, Twice in a Lifetime, The Return of Joe Forrester, Nightmare in Badham County. *Mini-Series*: Roots: The Next Generations.

REEVE, CHRISTOPHER
Actor. b. New York, NY, Sept. 25, 1952. e. Cornell U., B.A.; graduate work at Juilliard. Stage debut at McCarter Theatre in Princeton at age 9. B'way debut with Katharine Hepburn in A Matter of Gravity.
THEATER: *NY*: A Matter of Gravity, My Life, Fifth of July, The Marriage of Figaro, A Winter's Tale, Love Letters. *LA*: Summer and Smoke. *Williamstown*: The Front Page, Mesmer, Richard Corey, Royal Family, The Seagull, The Greeks, Holiday, Camino Real, John Brown's Body, Death Takes a Holiday, The Guardsman. *Regional*: The Irregular Verb to Love, Beggar's Opera, Troilus and Cressida, The Love Cure. *London debut*: The Aspern Papers.
PICTURES: Gray Lady Down (debut, 1978), Superman, Somewhere in Time, Superman II, Deathtrap, Monsignor, Superman III, The Bostonians, The Aviator, Street Smart, Superman IV: The Quest for Peace (also co-story), Switching Channels, Noises Off, Morning Glory, The Remains of the Day, Above Suspicion, Speechless, Village of the Damned, A Step Toward Tomorrow.
TELEVISION: *Series*: Love of Life. *Mini-Series*: Kidnapped. *Movies*: Anna Karenina, The Great Escape II: The Untold Story, The Rose and the Jackal, Bump in the Night, Death Dreams, Mortal Sins, Nightmare in the Daylight, The Sea Wolf, Black Fox, Black Fox: The Price of Peace, Black Fox: Good Men and Bad, Rear Window (also exec. prod.). *Specials*: Faerie Tale Theatre (Sleeping Beauty), The Last Ferry Home, Earth and the American Dream, Without Pity: A Film About Abilities. *Guest*: Tales From the Crypt, Frasier.

REEVES, KEANU
Actor. b. Beirut, Lebanon, Sept. 2, 1964. Lived in Australia and NY before family settled in Toronto. e. Toronto's High School for the Performing Arts, then continued training at Second City Workshop. Made Coca-Cola commercial at 16. At 18 studied at Hedgerow Theatre in PA for summer. Professional debut on Hanging In, CBC local Toronto TV show. Toronto stage debut in Wolf Boy; later on stage in Romeo and Juliet, Hamlet.
PICTURES: Youngblood (debut, 1986), River's Edge, The Night Before, Permanent Record, The Prince of Pennsylvania, Dangerous Liaisons, Bill and Ted's Excellent Adventure, Parenthood, I Love You to Death, Tune in Tomorrow, Point Break, Bill and Ted's Bogus Journey, My Own Private Idaho, Bram Stoker's Dracula, Much Ado About Nothing, Freaked (cameo), Even Cowgirls Get the Blues, Little Buddha, Speed, Johnny Mnemonic, A Walk in the Clouds, Chain Reaction, Feeling Minnesota, The Last Time I Committed Suicide, The Devil's Advocate, Me and Will (cameo), The Matrix, The Replacements, The Watcher, The Gift, Sweet November, Hardball, The Matrix 2, The Matrix 3.
TELEVISION: *Movies*: Act of Vengeance, Under the Influence, Brotherhood of Justice, Babes In Toyland. *Specials*: I Wish I Were Eighteen Again, Life Under Water. *Guest*: The Tracey Ullman Show, Action.

REEVES, STEVE
Actor. b. Glasgow, MT, Jan. 21, 1926. Delivered newspapers before winning body building titles Mr. Pacific, Mr. America, Mr. World, Mr. Universe. On stage in Kismet, The Vamp, Wish You Were Here.
PICTURES: Athena (debut, 1954), The Hidden Face, Jail Bait, Hercules, Hercules Unchained, Goliath and the Barbarians, The White Warrior, The Giant of Marathon, Morgan the Pirate, Thief of Baghdad, The Last Days of Pompeii, Duel of the Titans, The Trojan Horse, The Avenger, The Slave, The Shortest Day, Sandokan the Great, A Long Ride From Hell.
(d. May 1, 2000)

REGNIER, NATACHA
Actress. b. in Belgium.
PICTURES: The Motorcycle Girl, Le nid tombe de l'oiseau, Dis-moi oiu..., Cecile mon enfant, Encore, La Mouette, The Dreamlife of Angels (Cannes Film Fest. Award, Best Actress, 1998).

REHME, ROBERT G.
Executive. b. Cincinnati, OH, May 5, 1935. e. U. of Cincinnati. 1953, mgr., RKO Theatres, Inc., Cincinnati; 1961, adv. mgr., Cincinnati Theatre Co.; 1966, dir. of field adv., United Artists Pictures; 1969, named dir. of pub. and field adv./promotion, Paramount Pictures; 1972, pres., BR Theatres and v.p., April Fools Films, gen. mgr. Tri-State Theatre Service; 1976, v.p. & gen. sls. mgr., New World Pictures; 1978, joined Avco Embassy Pictures as sr. v.p. & COO, then named exec. v.p.; 1979, named pres., Avco Embassy Pictures, Inc.; 1981, joined Universal Pictures as pres. of distrib. & marketing; 1982, named pres. of Universal Pictures; 1983, joined New World Pictures as co-chmn. & CEO; elected pres., Academy Foundation, 1988; pres. Foundation of Motion Picture Pioneers, 1989; 1st v.p., AMPAS; 1989, partner, Neufeld/Rehme prods. at Paramount; 1992, pres. of Academy of Motion Picture Arts & Sciences.
PICTURES: Flight of the Intruder, Necessary Roughness, Patriot Games, Gettysburg, Beverly Hills Cop III, Clear and Present Danger, Woman Undone, Blind Faith, Lost in Space, Black Dog, Joan of Arc: The Virgin Warrior, The General's Daughter.
TELEVISION: *Movies:* Gridock, For the Children: The Irvine Fertility Scandal, Escape, Human Cargo. *Series:* Lightning Force.

REID, TIM
Actor. b. Norfolk, VA, Dec. 19, 1944. m. actress Daphne Maxwell. Started as half of comedy team of Tim and Tom in 1969, before becoming solo stand-up comedian. Published photo/poetry collection As I Feel It, 1982.
PICTURES: Dead Bang, The Fourth War, Out of Sync (also prod.). *Prod/dir.* Once Upon A Time...When We Were Colored.
TELEVISION: *Series*: Easy Does It... Starring Frankie Avalon, The Marilyn McCoo and Billy Davis Jr. Show, The Richard Pryor Show, WKRP in Cincinnati, Teachers Only, Simon and Simon, Frank's Place (also co-exec. prod.), Snoops (also co-exec. prod.), Sister Sister, Save Our Streets, Lincs (also exec. prod.). *Guest*: That's My Mama, Rhoda, What's Happening, Matlock. *Movies*: Perry Mason: The Case of the Silenced Singer, Stephen King's It, Race to Freedom: The Underground Railroad (also co-exec. prod.), Simon & Simon: In Trouble Again. *Special:* Mastergate.

REILLY, CHARLES NELSON
Actor, Director. b. New York, NY, Jan. 13. 1931. e. U. of CT. On Broadway mostly in comedy roles before turning to TV and films. Recently directed stage plays.
THEATER: *As actor*: Bye Bye Birdie (debut), How to Succeed in Business Without Really Trying (Tony Award, 1962), Hello Dolly!, Skyscraper, God's Favorite. Acted in 22 off-B'way plays. Founded musical comedy dept. HB Studios. Conceived and dir.: The Belle of Amherst, Paul Robeson, The Nerd (dir.). *Resident dir.*: Burt Reynolds' Jupiter Theatre.
PICTURES: A Face in the Crowd, Two Tickets to Paris, The Tiger Makes Out, Cannonball Run II, Body Slam, All Dogs Go to Heaven (voice), Rock-a-Doodle (voice), A Troll in Central Park (voice).
TELEVISION: *Series*: The Steve Lawrence Show, The Ghost and Mrs. Muir, Dean Martin Presents The Golddiggers, Liddsville, Arnie, It Pays to Be Ignorant (1973-74), Match Game P.M., Sweethearts (game show host). *Guest*: Tonight Show (guest host), Dean Martin Show. *Movies*: Call Her Mom, The Three Kings, Bandit, Bandit Goes Country. *Special*: Wind in the Wire.

REINAUER, RICHARD
Executive. b. Chicago, IL, April 28, 1926. e. U. of Illinois, grad. 1952. Prod., dir., freelance, 1952-59; bus. mgr., asst. prod., Showcase Theatre Evanston, 1952; prod., dir., NBC, Chicago, 1953-55; film dir., Kling Studios, 1956; broadcast supervisor. Foote Cone & Belding, 1956-59; dir., radio, TV & m.p., American Medical Assoc., 1959-64; pres., Communications Counselors, 1963-64; exec. dir., TV Arts & Sciences Foundation, 1964; pres., Acad. of TV Arts & Sciences, Chicago Chapter, 1970-72; assoc. prod. & asst. dir. Wild Kingdom & asst. to pres., Don Meier Prods., 1965-1988. Member: Illinois Nature Preserve Commission. Lifetime member: Acad. of TV Arts & Sciences, Pres. Pinewood Prods. Film Co. Communications consultant and advisor.

REINER, CARL
Actor, Director, Writer, Producer. b. New York, NY, March 20, 1922. Son is actor-director-writer Rob Reiner. Comedian on B'way: Call Me Mr., Inside U.S.A., Alive and Kicking. *Author* (novels): Enter Laughing, All Kinds of Love, Continue Laughing. *Playwright:* Something Different.
PICTURES: *Actor only*: Happy Anniversary, Gidget Goes Hawaiian, It's a Mad Mad Mad Mad World, The Russians Are Coming! The Russians Are Coming!, Don't Worry We'll Think of a Title, A Guide for the Married Man, Generation, The End, The Spirit of '76. *Writer-Actor*: The Gazebo, The Thrill of It All (also co-prod.), The Art of Love. *Director*: Enter Laughing (also co-s.p.), The Comic (also s.p., actor), Where's Poppa?, Oh God! (also actor), The One and Only, The Jerk (also actor), Dead Men Don't Wear Plaid (also co-s.p., actor), The Man With Two Brains (also co-s.p.), All of Me, Summer Rental, Summer School (also actor), Bert Rigby You're a Fool (also s.p.), Sibling Rivalry, Fatal Instinct (also actor), That Old Feeling.
TELEVISION: *Series*: The Fashion Story, The Fifty-Fourth Street Revue, Eddie Condon's Floor Show, Your Show of Shows (also writer), Droodles (panelist), Caesar's Hour (also writer; 2 Emmy Awards for supporting actor, 1956, 1957), Sid Caesar Invites You, Keep Talking, Dinah Shore Chevy Show (writer), Take a Good Look (panelist), The Dick Van Dyke Show (also creator-prod.-dir.-writer; 5 Emmy Awards: writing: 1962, 1963, 1964, producing: 1965, 1966), Art Linkletter Show, The Celebrity Game (host), The New Dick Van Dyke Show (creator-prod.-writer), Good Heavens (also exec. prod.), Sunday Best (host). *Movies*: Medical Story, Skokie. *Guest*: Comedy Spot, Judy Garland Show, Burke's Law, That Girl, Night Gallery, Faerie Tale Theatre (Pinocchio), It's Garry Shandling's Show, Mad About You (Emmy Award, 1995). *Special*: The Sid Caesar-Imogene Coca-Carl Reiner-Howard Morris Special (Emmy Award for writing, 1967).
RECORDINGS: Carl Reiner and Mel Brooks, The 2000 Year Old Man, The 2001 Year Old Man, The 2013 Year Old Man, Continue Laughing, A Connecticut Yankee in King Arthur's Court, Miracle on 34th Street, Jack and the Beanstalk, Aesop's Fables, The Prince and the Pauper.

REINER, ROB
Actor, Director, Writer. b. New York, NY, March 6, 1947. Father is actor-writer-director-producer Carl Reiner. Worked as actor with regional theatres and improvisational comedy troupes. Wrote for the Smothers Brothers Comedy Hour. Breakthrough as actor came in 1971 when signed by Norman Lear for All in the Family. Directorial debut with This Is Spinal Tap, 1984. Co-founder of Castle Rock Entertainment.
PICTURES: *Actor*: Enter Laughing, Halls of Anger, Where's Poppa?, Summertree, Fire Sale, Throw Momma From the Train, Postcards From the Edge, The Spirit of '76, Sleepless in Seattle, Bullets Over Broadway, Mixed Nuts, Bye Bye Love, Mad Dog Time, For Better or Worse, The First Wives Club, Primary Colors, Edtv, The Muse (cameo). *Director/Prod.:* This is Spinal Tap (also actor, co-s.p., co-prod.), The Sure Thing (dir. only), Stand by Me (dir. only), The Princess Bride (dir. only), When Harry Met Sally..., Misery, A Few Good Men (Acad. Award nom. for best picture; DGA nom.), North, The American President, Ghosts of Mississippi, The Story of Us (also actor).
TELEVISION: *Series*: All in the Family (2 Emmy Awards: 1974, 1978), Free Country (also co-writer), Morton & Hayes (also co-creator, co-exec. prod.). *Movies*: Thursday's Game, More Than Friends (also co-writer, co-exec. prod.), Million Dollar Infield (also co-prod., co-writer). *Guest*: Gomer Pyle, Batman, Beverly Hillbillies, Room 222, Partridge Family, Odd Couple, It's Garry Shandling's Show. *Special*: But... Seriously (exec. prod.).

REINHOLD, JUDGE
Actor. r.n. Edward Ernest Reinhold Jr. b. Wilmington, DE, May 21, 1957. e. Mary Washington Coll., North Carolina Sch. of Arts. Acted in regional theatres including Burt Reynolds dinner theater in FL before signed to TV contract at Paramount.
PICTURES: Running Scared (debut, 1979), Stripes, Pandemonium, Fast Times at Ridgemont High, Lords of Discipline, Roadhouse 66, Gremlins, Beverly Hills Cop, Head Office, Off Beat, Ruthless People, Beverly Hills Cop II, Vice Versa, Rosalie Goes Shopping, Daddy's Dyin', Enid is Sleeping, Zandalee, Near Misses, Baby on Board, Bank Robber, Beverly Hills Cop III, The Santa Clause, Crackerjack 2, Last Lives, Family Plan, Homegrown, Redemption High, My Brother the Pig, Beethoven's 3rd.
TELEVISION: *Series*: Secret Service Guy. *Movies*: Survival of Dana, A Matter of Sex, Promised a Miracle, Black Magic, Four Eyes and Six-Guns, Dad the Angel and Me, As Good as Dead, The Wharf Rat, The Right to Remain Silent, Runaway Car, Netforce. *Guest*: Seinfeld. *Specials*: A Step Too Slow, The Willmar Eight, The Parallax Garden.

REISENBACH, SANFORD E.
Executive. e. NYU. Associated with Grey Advertising for 20 years; exec. v.p. and pres./founder of Grey's Leisure & Entertainment division in N.Y. In August, 1979, joined Warner Bros. as exec. v.p. of worldwide adv. & pub.; named pres. worldwide adv. & pub., 1985. Appt. corporate exec. of marketing and planning, Warner Bros., 1989.

REISER, PAUL
Actor. b. New York, NY, Mar. 30, 1957. e. SUNY/Binghamton. Started performing as a stand-up comic in such clubs as Catch a Rising Star, the Improv, and the Comic Strip. Author: Couplehood (1994).
PICTURES: Diner (debut, 1982), Beverly Hills Cop, Aliens, Beverly Hills Cop II, Cross My Heart, Crazy People, The Marrying Man, Mr. Write, Bye Bye Love, Get Bruce (cameo), the Story of Us, One Night at McCool's, Purpo$e.
TELEVISION: *Series*: My Two Dads, Mad About You. *Special*: Paul Reiser—Out on a Whim. *Movies*: Sunset Limousine, The Tower. *Pilots*: Diner, Just Married.

REISNER, ALLEN
Director. b. New York, NY.
PICTURES: The Day They Gave the Babies Away, St. Louis Blues, All Mine to Give.
TELEVISION: *Movies/Specials*: Captain and the Kings, Mary Jane Harper Cried Last Night, Your Money or Your Wife, To Die in Paris, The Clift, Skag, They're Playing Our Song, The Gentleman From Seventh Avenue, Escape of Pierre Mendes-France, Deliverance of Sister Cecelia, The Sound of Silence. *Series*: Murder She Wrote, Twilight Zone, Hardcastle & McCormick, Airwolf, The Mississippi, Hawaii Five-O, Blacke's Magic, Law and Harry McGraw, Playhouse 90, Studio One, Climax, United States Steel Hour, Suspense, Danger.

REISS, JEFFREY C.
Executive. b. Brooklyn, NY, April 14, 1942. e. Washington U., St. Louis, B.A., 1963. Consultant at NYU and Manhattanville Coll. and instructor at Brooklyn Coll. before entering industry. Agent in literary dept. for General Artists Corp., 1966. Supervised development in NY of Tandem Prods. for Norman Lear, 1968. Produced off-B'way plays 1968-70. Dir. of program acquistion devel. for Cartridge TV, Inc. (mfg. of first home video cassette players-recorders), 1970-73. Joined ABC Entertainment as director of network feature films, 1973-75. Founder and pres., Showtime Pay TV Network, 1976-80. Co-founder, pres. & CEO, Cable Health Network, 1981-83. 1983, named vice chmn. & CEO, Lifetime Cable Network following Cable Health Network merger with Daytime. Chmn. of the board, pres. & CEO, Reiss Media Enterprises, Inc. 1984. Founder & chmn. of board, Request Television (pay-per-view svc.), 1985.

REISS, STUART A.
Set Decorator. b. Chicago, IL, July 15, 1921. e. L.A. High Sch., 1939. Property man, 20th-Fox, 1939-42; U.S. Army Air Corps, 1942-45; joined 20th-Fox as set decorator in 1945. Worked on over 30 tv shows and over 100 motion pictures, receiving 6 Academy Award noms. and 2 Oscars.
PICTURES: Titanic, How to Marry a Millionaire, Hell and High Water, There's No Business Like Show Business, Soldier of Fortune, The Seven Year Itch, Man in the Grey Flannel Suit, Teen Age Rebel, The Diary of Anne Frank (Academy Award, 1959), What a Way to Go, Fantastic Voyage (Academy Award, 1966), Doctor Doolittle, Oh God!, The Swarm, Beyond the Poseidon Adventure, Carbon Copy, All the Marbles, The Man Who Loved Women, Micki and Maude, A Fine Mess.

REITMAN, IVAN
Director, Producer. b. Komarmo, Czechoslovakia, Oct. 26, 1946. Moved to Canada at age 4. e. McMaster U. Attended National Film Board's Summer Institute directing three short films including Orientation (1968) which received theatrical distribution. Produced Canadian TV show in 1970s with Dan Aykroyd as announcer.
THEATER: *Prod.:* The National Lampoon Show, The Magic Show, Merlin (also dir.).
PICTURES: *Dir./Prod.*: Foxy Lady (debut, 1971; also edit., music), Cannibal Girls, Meatballs (dir. only), Stripes, Ghostbusters, Legal Eagles (also co-story), Twins, Ghostbusters II, Kindergarten Cop, Dave, Junior, Father's Day, Six Days Seven Nights, Evolution. *Prod. only:* Columbus of Sex, They Came From Within (Shivers), Death Weekend, Rabid (co-exec. prod.), Blackout, National Lampoon's Animal House, Heavy Metal, Spacehunter: Adventures in the Forbidden Zone (exec. prod.), Big Shots (exec. prod.), Casual Sex? (exec. prod.), Feds (exec. prod.), Stop! Or My Mom Will Shoot, Beethoven (exec. prod.), Beethoven's 2nd (exec. prod.), Space Jam, Commandments (exec. prod.), Private Parts, Road Trip (exec.), Killing Me Softly, Evolution.
TELEVISION: *Series*: Delta House.

RELPH, MICHAEL
Producer, Director, Writer, Designer. 1942, became art dir. Ealing Studios then assoc. prod. to Michael Balcon on The Captive Heart, Frieda, Kind Hearts and Coronets, Saraband (also designed: Oscar nom.). 1948 appt. producer and formed prod/dir. partnership Basil Dearden (until 1972). 1971-76, Governor, Brit. Film Institute. Chairman BFI Prod. Board. Chairman Film Prod. Assoc. of G.B.; member Films Council.

PICTURES: For Ealing: The Blue Lamp (BFA Award, 1950), I Believe in You, The Gentle Gunman, The Square Ring, The Rainbow Jacket, Out of the Clouds, The Ship That Died of Shame, Davy, The Smallest Show on Earth (for Brit. Lion), Violent Playground (for Rank), Rockets Galore (Island Fling), Sapphire (BFA Award, 1959). 1960 Founder Dir. Allied Film Makers: Prod. The League of Gentlemen, Man in the Moon (co-s.p.), Victim, Life For Ruth (Walk in the Shadow). *Also produced*: Secret Partner, All Night Long, The Mind Benders, A Place To Go (s.p.), Woman of Straw (co-s.p.), Masquerade (co-s.p.), The Assassination Bureau (prod., s.p., designer), The Man Who Haunted Himself (prod., co-s.p.). 1978, exec. in chg. prod., Kendon Films, Ltd. Exec. prod., Scum, 1982. Co-prod., An Unsuitable Job for a Woman. 1984, exec. prod.: Treasure Houses of Britain; TV series, prod., Heavenly Pursuits, 1985-86; Gospel According to Vic (U.S.). Prod. Consultant: Torrents of Spring.

RELPH, SIMON
Producer. b. London, Eng., April 13, 1940. Entered industry 1961.
PICTURES: Reds (exec. prod.), The Return of the Soldier, Privates on Parade, The Ploughman's Lunch, Secret Places, Laughterhouse (exec. prod.), Wetherby, Comrades, Enchanted April (exec. prod.), Damage (coprod.), The Secret Rapture, Camilla, Look Me In The Eye, Blue Juice, The Slab Boys, The Land Girls.

RELYEA, ROBERT E.
Producer, Executive. b. Santa Monica, CA, May 3, 1930. e. UCLA, B.S., 1952. In Army 1953-55. Entered industry in 1955; asst. dir. on The Magnificent Seven and West Side Story; assoc. prod. and 2nd unit dir. on The Great Escape; partnered with Steve McQueen as exec. prod. on Bullitt and The Reivers. 1979-82, exec. v.p. with Melvin Simon Prods. Served as exec. v.p. in chg. world wide prod., Keith Barish Prods. 1983-85. Served as sr. v.p. prod., Lorimar Prods. 1985-90. Named sr. v.p. features prod. management, Paramount Pictures Motion Picture Gp., 1989.
PICTURES: *Exec. Prod.*: Bullitt, The Reivers, Day of the Dolphin. *Prod.*: Love at First Bite, My Bodyguard, Porky's, Blame It On Rio (assoc. prod.), Last Action Hero (co-prod). *Actor:* Seven.

REMAR, JAMES
Actor. b. Boston, MA, Dec. 31, 1953. Studied acting at NY's Neighborhood Playhouse and with Stella Adler. Appeared on NY stage in Yo-Yo, Early Dark, Bent, California Dog Fight.
PICTURES: On the Yard (debut, 1979), The Warriors, Cruising, The Long Riders, Windwalker, Partners, 48 HRS, The Cotton Club, The Clan of the Cave Bear, Band of the Hand, Quiet Cool, Rent-a-Cop, The Dream Team, Drugstore Cowboy, Tales from the Darkside, Silence Like Glass, White Fang, Fatal Instinct, Blink, Renaissance Man, Miracle on 34th Street, Boys on the Side, Session Man (Academy Award, Best Action Short, 1991), Across the Moon, Judge Dredd (cameo), The Quest, The Phantom, Robo-Warriors, Tale From The Darkside: The Movie, Wlld Bill, Exquisite Tenderness, The Phantom, Born Bad, Mortal Kombat: Annihilation, Psycho, Rites of Passage.
TELEVISION: *Movies*: The Mystic Warrior, Desperado, Deadlock, Brotherhood of the Gun, Fatal Charm, Indecency, Night Vision, Inferno. *Guest*: Hill Street Blues, Miami Vice, The Equalizer, The Hitchhiker, Tales From The Crypt, Total Security.

REMBUSCH, MICHAEL J.
Executive. b. Indianapolis, IN, April 8, 1950. e. Ball State U. Son of Trueman T. Rembusch. Began working for father's circuit, Syndicate Theatres, Inc., in 1967. From 1970-80, managed various theatres in circuit. 1980-85, v.p., operations. 1985-90, acquired Heaston circuit (Indianapolis). Became pres., Syndicate Theatres, Inc. 1987-90, chmn, Indiana Film Commission. 1992 to present, pres., Theatre Owners of Indiana.

REMBUSCH, TRUEMAN T.
Exhibitor. b. Shelbyville, IN, July 27, 1909. f. Frank J. Rembusch, pioneer exhibitor. Inventor & manufacturer Glass Mirror Screen. e. U. of Notre Dame Sch. of Commerce, 1928. m. Mary Agnes Finneran. Ent. m.p. ind., 1928, servicing sound equip., father's circuit; became mgr., 1932; elect. bd. of dir., Allied Theatre Owners of Ind., 1936-45, pres. 1945-51, 1952-53; dir. chmn. Allied TV Committee, 1945-50; pres. Allied States Assn., 1950-51; 1952, named by Allied as one of triumvirate heading COMPO; 1953, named by Gov. of Indiana as dir. State Fair Board; elected chmn. Joint Com. on Toll TV, 1954; currently pres. Syndicate Theatres, Inc., Franklin, Ind; member, Notre Dame Club of Indianapolis (Man of Yr., 1950); BPOE, 4th Degree K of C, Meridian Hills Country Club, Marco Island Country Club. American Radio Relay League (amateur & commerce, licenses); OX5 Aviation Pioneers; awarded patent, recording 7 counting device, 1951; dir. Theatre Owners of Indiana; dir. to NATO; dir. NATO member ad hoc comm; 1972 chair., NATO Statistical Committee; 1976, NITE Award service to Independent Exhibition.

RENO, JEAN
Actor. r.n. Juan Moreno b. Casablanca, Morocco July 30, 1948. To France in early 1970's to serve in French military. Began acting in Paris with theatre workshop, then established his own travelling acting company.
PICTURES: Claire de Femme, Le Dernier Combat, Subway, Signes Exterieurs de Richesse, Notre Histoire, I Love You, The Big Blue, La Femme Nikita, L'homme au Masque d'Or, L'Operation Corned Beef, Loulou Graffiti, The Professional (Leon), French Kiss, The Visitors (also s.p.), Beyond the Clouds, Mission Impossible, Le Jaguar, Witch Way Love, Roseanna's Grave, Ronin, Le Couloirs du Temps, Godzilla, Tripwire, Les Rivieres pourpres, The Visitors, Rollerball.

RESNAIS, ALAIN
Director. b. Cannes, France, June 3, 1922. Began career as asst. dir. to Nicole Vedres on compilation of film for Paris 1900. During '50s worked as asst. editor and editor; experimented with making his own 16mm films. Directed or co-dir. several short films: Van Gogh, Gauguin, Guernica, The Statues Also Die, Night and Fog, etc.
PICTURES: Hiroshima Mon Amour (feature debut, 1959), Last Year at Marienbad, Muriel, La Guerre Est Finie (The War Is Over), Je t'Aime Je t'Aime (also co-s.p.), Stavisky, Providence, Mon Oncle d'Amerique, Life Is a Bed of Roses, L'Amour a Mort (Love Unto Death), Melo (also s.p.), I Want to Go Home, Smoking/No Smoking, Same Old Song.

RESNICK, JOEL H.
Executive. b. New York, NY, April 28, 1936. e. U. of PA, B.A., 1958; NY Law Sch. 1961, admitted to NY State Bar. 1962 received Masters of Law degree in taxation; 1961-66 served as associate with NY law firm, Phillips Nizer Benjamin Krim & Ballon; Was in-house counsel to United Artists Corp. 1967, joined UA as spec. asst. to the sr. v.p. & gen. mgr.; 1970, moved to American Multi-Cinema, Inc., Kansas City, as asst. to pres.; 1972, named v.p. in chg. dev.; 1976, promoted to v.p. in chg. film development; 1977, named exec. v.p.; 1983, elected exec. v.p. & dir., AMC Entertainment; 1984, appt. to office of pres. as chmn. & CEO, film mktg.; 1986, resigned to join Orion Pictures Distribution Corp. as pres.; has served as co-chmn. NATO trade practices comm. since 1979. 1982 elected pres., NATO; 1984, became chmn. NATO bd.; 1989, v.p. Foundation of Motion Picture Pioneers; 1990, resigned from Orion; pres., GKC Theatres, Springfield, IL, 1991-92; Cinemark Theatres, Intl. Dev., 1994-.

REUBENS, PAUL
Actor, Writer. r.n. Paul Rubenfeld. b. Peekskill, NY, Aug. 27, 1952. Raised in Sarasota, FL. e. Boston U., California Inst. of the Arts (1976). Also acted as Pee-Wee Herman. Pee-wee character made debut, 1978 at Groundlings, improvisational theater, Los Angeles followed by The Pee-wee Herman Show, a live show which gave 5 months of sold-out performances at the L.A. rock club, Roxy, and was later taped for HBO special. Guest appearances on Late Night With David Letterman, The Gong Show, 227, Tonight Show, Mork & Mindy, Joan Rivers' The Late Show, and The Dating Game.
PICTURES: Midnight Madness, The Blues Brothers, Cheech & Chong's Next Movie, Cheech and Chong's Nice Dreams, Pandemonium, Meatballs Part II, Pee-wee's Big Adventure (also co-s.p.), Flight of the Navigator (voice), Back to the Beach, Big Top Pee-wee (also co-s.p., co-prod.), Batman Returns, Buffy the Vampire Slayer, Tim Burton's The Nightmare Before Christmas (voice), Dunston Checks In, Matilda, Buddy, Doctor Doolittle (voice), Mystery Men, Great Sex.
TELEVISION: *Series*: Pee-wee's Playhouse (also creator, co-dir., co-writer, exec. prod.; 12 Emmy Awards). *Specials*: Pinocchio (Faerie Tale Theatre), Pee-wee Herman Show, Pee-wee's Playhouse Christmas Special (also exec. prod., co-dir. co-writer). *Guest*: Murphy Brown.

REVELL, GRAEME
Composer.
PICTURES: Spontaneous Combustion, Dead Calm, Till There Was You, Child's Play 2, Love Crimes, Until the End of the Crime, Traces of Red, Deadly, The People Under the Stairs, The Hand That Rocks the Cradle, Hear No Evil, Ghost in the Machine, The Crush, Body of Evidence, Boxing Helena, Hard Target, Street Fighter, S.F.W., No Escape, The Crow, Killer: A Journal of Murder, The Basketball Diaries, Tank Girl, Mighty Morphin Power Rangers: The Movie, The Tie That Binds, Strange Days, From Dusk Till Dawn, Race the Sun, The Craft, Fled, The Crow: City of Angels, Chinese Box, The Saint, Spawn, Suicide Kings, Lulu on the Bridge, The Big Hit, The Negotiator, Phoenix, Strike, Bride of Chucky, The Siege, Idle Hands, Three to Tango, Gossip, Bats.

REVILL, CLIVE
Actor. r.n. Clive Selsby. b. Wellington, New Zealand, Apr. 18, 1930. e. Rongotal Coll., Victoria U.
THEATER: Irma La Douce, The Mikado, Oliver, Marat/Sade, Jew of Malta, Sherry, Chichester Season, The Incomparable Max, Sherlock Holmes, Lolita, Pirates of Penzance, Mystery of Edwin Drood, My Fair Lady, Bandido.

PICTURES: Reach for the Sky, The Headless Ghost, Bunny Lake Is Missing, Once Upon a Tractor, Modesty Blaise, A Fine Madness, Kaleidoscope, The Double Man, Fathom, Italian Secret Service, Nobody Runs Forever, Shoes of the Fisherman, Assassination Bureau, The Private Life of Sherlock Holmes, The Buttercup Chain, A Severed Head, Boulevard de Rhum, Avanti!, Escape to the Sun, Ghost in the Noonday Sun, The Legend of Hell House, The Little Prince, The Black Windmill, One of Our Dinosaurs Is Missing, Galileo, Matilda, Zorro the Gay Blade, Transformers (voice), Rumpelstiltskin, The Emperor's New Clothes, Mack the Knife, CHUD II: Bud the Chud, Frog Prince, Let Him Have It, Robin Hood: Men in Tights, Crime and Punishment, Arabian Knight (voice), The Wacky Adventures of Dr. Boris and Nurse Shirley, Dracula—Dead and Loving It!, Possums.
TELEVISION: Chicken Soup with Barley, Volpone, Bam Pow Zapp, Candida, Platonov, A Bit of Vision, Mill Hill, The Piano Player, Hopcroft in Europe, A Sprig of Broome, Ben Franklin in Paris, Pinocchio, The Great Houdini, Show Business Hall of Fame, Feather and Father, Winner Take All, The New Avengers, Licking Hitler, Columbo, Centennial, A Man Called Sloane, Nobody's Perfect, Marya, Moviola, Diary of Anne Frank, Mikado, The Sorcerer, Wizards & Warriors, George Washington, Murder She Wrote, Faerie Tale Theatre, Twilight Zone, Newhart, Hunter, Star Trek, The Sea Wolf, Babylon 5, Fortune Hunter, The Preston Episodes (series), Murphy Brown.

REYNOLDS, BURT
Actor, Director. b. Waycross, GA, Feb. 11, 1936. Former Florida State U. football star; TV and film stunt performer. Won fame as actor on TV in series Riverboat. Founded the Burt Reynolds Dinner Theater in Jupiter, FL, 1979. *Autobiography*: My Life (1994).
THEATER: Mister Roberts (NY City Center), Look We've Come Through (B'way debut, 1956), The Rainmaker.
PICTURES: Angel Baby (debut, 1961), Armored Command, Operation CIA, Navajo Joe, Fade In, Impasse, Shark, Sam Whiskey, 100 Rifles, Skullduggery, Fuzz, Deliverance, Everything You Always Wanted To Know About Sex, Shamus, White Lightning, The Man Who Loved Cat Dancing, The Longest Yard, W.W. & The Dixie Dancekings, At Long Last Love, Hustle, Lucky Lady, Gator (also dir.), Silent Movie, Nickelodeon, Smokey and the Bandit, Semi-Tough, The End (also dir.), Hooper, Starting Over,
Rough Cut, Smokey and the Bandit II, Cannonball Run, Paternity, Sharky's Machine (also dir.), The Best Little Whorehouse in Texas, Best Friends, Stroker Ace, Smokey and the Bandit III (cameo), The Man Who Loved Women, Cannonball Run II, City Heat, Stick (also dir.), Uphill All the Way (cameo), Heat, Malone, Rent-a-Cop, Switching Channels, Physical Evidence, Breaking In, All Dogs Go to Heaven (voice), Modern Love, The Player (cameo), Cop and a Half, The Maddening, Devil Inside, Meet Wally Sparks, Striptease, Mad Dog Time, Citizen Ruth, Boogie Nights (Golden Globe Award, Chicago Film Crits. Award, LA Film Crits. Award, NY Film Circle Crits. Award, Best Supporting Actor, 1997), Raven, Bean, Crazy Six, Pups, The Last Producer (also dir.), The Hunter's Moon, Mystery Alaska, The Crew, The Last Producer, The Hollywood Sign, Driven, Big City Blues.
TELEVISION: *Series*: Riverboat, Gunsmoke, Hawk, Dan August, Out of This World (voice), B.L. Stryker (also co-exec. prod.), Evening Shade (Emmy Award, 1991). *Movies*: Hunters Are for Killing, Run Simon Run, The Man Upstairs (co-exec. prod. only), The Man From Left Field (also dir.), Universal Soldier II: Brothers in Arms, Universal Soldier III: Unfinished Business, Hard Time (also dir.), Hard Time: Hostage Hotel, Hard Time: Hide and Seek, Hard Time: The Premonition. *Host*: The Story of Hollywood. *Special*: Wind in the Wire. *Dir.*: Alfred Hitchcock Presents (1985).

REYNOLDS, DEBBIE
Actress. r.n. Mary Frances Reynolds. b. El Paso, TX, April 1, 1932. Daughter is actress Carrie Fisher. e. Burbank & John Burroughs H.S., Burbank, CA. With Burbank Youth Symphony during h.s.; beauty contest winner (Miss Burbank) 1948; signed by Warner Bros.; on stage in Personal Appearances, Blis-Hayden Theater. Voted Star of Tomorrow, 1952. *Autobiography*: Debbie: My Life (1988).
THEATER: *B'way*: Irene, Woman of the Year.
PICTURES: June Bride (debut, 1948), The Daughter of Rosie O'Grady, Three Little Words, Two Weeks With Love, Mr. Imperium, Singin' in the Rain, Skirts Ahoy, I Love Melvin, Give a Girl a Break, The Affairs of Dobie Gillis, Susan Slept Here, Athena, Hit the Deck, The Tender Trap, The Catered Affair, Bundle of Joy, Tammy and the Bachelor, This Happy Feeling, The Mating Game, Say One for Me, It Started with a Kiss, The Gazebo, The Rat Race, Pepe (cameo), The Pleasure of His Company, The Second Time Around, How the West Was Won, My Six Loves, Mary Mary, Goodbye Charlie, The Unsinkable Molly Brown (Acad. Award nom.), The Singing Nun, Divorce American Style, How Sweet It Is, What's the Matter with Helen?, Charlotte's Web (voice), That's Entertainment!, The Bodyguard (cameo), Heaven and Earth, That's Entertainment III, Mother, In & Out, Wedding Bell Blues, Fear and Loathing in Las Vegas (voice), Keepers of the Frame.
TELEVISION: *Series*: The Debbie Reynolds Show, Aloha Paradise. *Movies*: Sadie and Son, Perry Mason: The Case of the Musical Murders, Battling for Baby, Halloweentown, The Christmas Wish, Virtual Mom. *Special*: Jack Paar Is Alive and Well.

REYNOLDS, GENE
Actor, Executive, Producer. b. Cleveland, OH, April 4, 1925. Acted from 1936-55. Currently pres. Director's Guild of America, Inc.
PICTURES: *Actor:* Thank You, Jeeves; Sins of Man, Thunder Trail, In Old Chicago, The Californian, Of Human Hearts, Love Finds Andy Hardy, The Crowd Roars, Boys Town, The Spirit of Culver, The Flying Irishman, Bad Little Angel, They Shall Have Music, Santa Fe Trail, The Mortal Storm, Gallant Sons, The Blue Bird; Edison, the Man; Andy Hardy's Private Secretary, Adventure in Washington, The Penalty, The Tuttles of Tahiti, Junior G-men of the Air, Eagle Squadron, Jungle Patrol, The Big Cat, Slattery's Hurricane, 99 River Street, The Country Girl, The Bridges at Toko-Ri, Down Three Dark Streets.
TELEVISION: *Director: Series:* Wanted: Dead or Alive, My Three Sons, Hogan's Heroes, F Troop, The Ghost and Mrs. Muir, M*A*S*H (also exec. prod.), Lou Grant (also exec. prod), Christy, Touched by and Angel. *Movies:* In Defense of Kids, Doing Life (also exec. prod.), The Whereabouts of Jenny (also prod.).

REYNOLDS, KEVIN
Director, Writer. b. 1950. e. Texas Marine Acad., Trinity Univ., Baylor Univ. (law degree), USC film school. Student film Proof led to offer to do expanded feature version subsequently retitled Fandango.
PICTURES: Red Dawn (co-s.p.). *Director:* Fandango (dir. debut, 1985; also s.p.), The Beast, Robin Hood: Prince of Thieves, Rapa Nui (also s.p.), Waterworld, 187.

REYNOLDS, NORMAN
Production Designer, Art Director.
PICTURES: *Production Designer:* The Empire Strikes Back, Raiders of the Lost Ark, Return of the Jedi, Return to Oz, Young Sherlock Holmes, Empire of the Sun, Mountains of the Moon, Avalon, Alien 3, Alive, Clean Slate, Mission: Impossible, Sphere, Bicentennial Man. *Art Director:* The Old Curiosity Shop, Lucky Lady, The Incredible Sarah, Star Wars, Superman.

REYNOLDS, SHELDON
Writer, Producer, Director. b. Philadelphia, PA, 1923. e. NYU. Radio-TV writer; programs include My Silent Partner, Robert Q. Lewis Show, We the People, Danger, Adventures of Sherlock Holmes (prod., dir., writer), Dick and the Duchess (prod., dir., writer), Foreign Intrigue (dir., prod., writer). TV Special: Sophia Loren's Rome (dir., writer). Movies: Foreign Intrigue (dir., prod., s.p.), Assignment to Kill (dir., s.p.).

REYNOLDS, STUART
Producer. b. Chicago, IL, March 22, 1907. e. Chicago law schools. Adv. exec., Lord and Thomas, BBDO. General Mills; sales exec. Don Lee-Mutual; formed Stuart Reynolds Prod., TV films. Now motion picture & TV program consultant.
TELEVISION: General Electric Theatre, Cavalcade of America, Your Jeweler's Showcase, Wild Bill Hickok. Producer and world-wide distributor of educational/training films; Eye of the Beholder.

REZNOR, TRENT
Composer. r.n. Michael Trent Reznor. b. Mercer, PA, May 17, 1965. Head of Nothing Records, a division of Interscope Records. Fronts industrial-rock band Nine Inch Nails. Composed music and sounds for id Software's computergame QUAKE.
PICTURES: Light of Day (actor), Seven, Natural Born Killers, Lost Highway, Closure.

RHAMES, VING
Actor. e. Juilliard Sch. of Drama.
THEATER: *B'way:* The Boys of Winter. *Off-B'way:* Map of the World, Short Eyes, Richard III, Ascension Day. *Europe:* Ajax.
PICTURES: Native Son, Patty Hearst, Casualties of War, Jacob's Ladder, The Long Walk Home, Flight of the Intruder, Homicide, The People Under the Stairs, Stop! Or My Mom Will Shoot, Bound by Honor, Dave, The Saint of Fort Washington, Pulp Fiction, Drop Squad, Kiss of Death, Mission: Impossible, Striptease, Rosewood, Con Air, Dangerous Ground, The Split, Out of Sight, Mission: Impossible 2, Duets, Bringing Out the Dead, Entrapment, Final Fantasy (voice), Night Train.
TELEVISION: *Series:* Another World, Men, ER, American Tragedy. *Movies:* Go Tell It on the Mountain, Rising Son, When You Remember Me, Iran: Days of Crisis, Terror on Track 9, Ed McBain's 87th Precinct: Lightning, Deadly Whispers, Don King: Only in America (Golden Globe Award, 1998), Holiday Heart. *Guest:* Miami Vice, Spenser: For Hire, Tour of Duty, Crime Story.

RHODES, CYNTHIA
Actress, Dancer. b. Nashville, TN, Nov. 21, 1956. m. singer Richard Marx. Appeared on many TV specials, inc. Opryland USA, Music Hall America.
PICTURES: Xanadu, One From the Heart, Flashdance, Staying Alive, Runaway, Dirty Dancing, Curse of the Crystal Eye.

RHYS-DAVIES, JOHN
Actor. b. Salisbury, England, 1944. Grew up in Wales and East Africa. Began acting at Truro School in Cornwall at 15. e. U. of East Angelia where he founded school's dramatic society. Worked as teacher before studying at Royal Academy of Dramatic Art, 1969. Appeared in 23 Shakespearean plays.
PICTURES: The Black Windmill, Sphinx, Raiders of the Lost Ark, Victor/Victoria, Sahara, Sword of the Valiant, Best Revenge, King Solomon's Mines, In the Shadow of Kilimanjaro, Firewalker, The Living Daylights, Waxwork, Rising Storm, Indiana Jones and the Last Crusade, Young Toscanini, Journey of Honor, Unnameable II, The Seventh Coin, The Great White Hype.
TELEVISION: *Mini-series*: Shogun, James Clavell's Noble House, Riley, Ace of Spies, I, Claudius, War and Remembrance. *Movies*: The Little Match Girl, Sadat, Kim, The Naked Civil Servant, The Trial of the Incredible Hulk, Goddess of Love, The Gifted One, Great Expectations, Desperado, Secret Weapon, Before the Storm, Spy Games, Perry Mason: The Case of the Fatal Framing. *Series*: Under Cover, The Untouchables, Archaeology, Sliders.

RIBISI, GIOVANNI
Actor. b. Los Angeles, CA, March 31, 1976.
PICTURES: The Outpost, That Thing You Do!, The Grave, First Love Last Rites, Lost Highway, SubUrbia, The Postman, Scotch and Milk, Phoenix, Men, Saving Private Ryan, The Virgin Suicides (voice), The Mod Squad, The Other Sister, The Boiler Room, Gone in 60 Seconds, The Gift, Tell Me, Heaven.
TELEVISION: *Movies:* Promised a Mircle, Blossom, The Positively True Adventures of the Alleged Texas Cheerleader-Murdering Mom, Alptraum im Airport. *Series:* My Two Dads, The Wonder Years, Davis Rules, Family Album. *Guest:* Highway to Heaven, Married...with Children, The Commish, Walker Texas Ranger, Ellen, NYPD Blue, Marker, The X Files, Chicago Hope, Friends.

RICCI, CHRISTINA
Actress. b. Santa Monica, CA, February 12, 1980. Raised in Long Island, NY, and Montclair, NJ. Started prof. acting career in commercials.
PICTURES: Mermaids (debut, 1990), The Hard Way, The Addams Family, The Cemetery Club, Addams Family Values, Casper, Gold Diggers: The Secret of Bear Mountain, Now and Then, Last of the High Kings, The Ice Storm, That Darn Cat, Souvenir, I Woke Up Early the Day I Died, Buffalo 66, 200 Cigarettes, The Opposite of Sex, Fear and Loathing in Las Vegas, Pecker, Desert Blue, Small Soldiers (voice), No Vacancy, Sleepy Hollow, Bless the Child, The Man Who Cried, Prozac Nation, All Over the Guy.

RICH, JOHN
Producer, Director. b. Rockaway Beach, NY, e. U. of Michigan, B.A., Phi Beta Kappa, 1948; M.A. 1949; Sesquicentennial Award, 1967; bd. of dir., Screen Dir. Guild of America, 1954-1960; v.p. 1958-1960, Founder-Trustee, Producers-Directors Pension Plan, chmn. of bd. 1965, 1968, 1970; treasurer, Directors Guild of America, 1966-67; v.p. 1967-72. Awards: Directors Guild Award, Most Outstanding Directorial Achievement, 1971. Christopher award: Henry Fonda as Clarence Darrow, 1975. NAACP Image Award, 1974; 2 Golden Globe Awards: All in the Family, 1972-73. DGA Robert B. Aldrich Award for 1992.
PICTURES: *Director*: Wives and Lovers, The New Interns, Roustabout, Boeing-Boeing, Easy Come Easy Go.
TELEVISION: *Director*: Academy Awards, The Dick Van Dyke Show, All in the Family (also prod.), Mr. Sunshine, Dear John, MacGyver, The Good Life.

RICH, LEE
Producer, Executive. b. Cleveland, OH, Dec. 10, 1926. e. Ohio U. Adv. exec.; resigned as sr. v.p., Benton & Bowles, to become producer for Mirisch-Rich TV, 1965 (Rat Patrol, Hey Landlord). Resigned 1967 to join Leo Burnett Agency. Left to form Lorimar Productions in 1969 and served as pres. until 1986 when left to join MGM/UA Communications as chmn. & CEO. Resigned 1988; signed 3-year deal with Warner Bros. setting up Lee Rich Prods. there. Twice named Television Showman of the Year by Publishers' Guild of America.
PICTURES: *Producer*: The Sporting Club, Just Cause, The Amazing Panda Adventure, Big Bully. *Executive Producer*: The Man, The Choirboys, Who Is Killing the Great Chefs of Europe?, The Big Red One, Hard to Kill, Innocent Blood, Passenger 57, Just Cause, The Amazine Panda Adventure, Big Bully, Desperate Measures, Gloria.
TELEVISION: *Exec. Prod.: Series:* The Waltons (Emmy Award, 1973), Dallas, Knots Landing, Against the Grain. *Mini-series*: The Blue Knight, Helter Skelter, Studs Lonigan. *Movies*: Do Not Fold Spindle or Mutilate, The Homecoming: A Christmas Story, The Crooked Hearts, Pursuit, The Girls of Huntington House, Dying Room Only, Don't Be Afraid of the Dark, A Dream for Christmas, The Stranger Within, Bad Ronald, The Runaway Barge, Runaways, Returning Home, Eric, Conspiracy of Terror, Widow, Green Eyes, Killer on Board, Desperate Women, Long Journey Back, Mary and Joseph: A Story of Faith, Mr. Horn, Some Kind of Miracle, Young Love, First Love, A Man Called Intrepid, Flamingo Road, Marriage Is Alive and Well, A Perfect Match, Reward, Skag, Killjoy, A Matter of Life and Death, Our Family Business, Mother's Day on Walton's Mountain, This is Kate Bennett, Two of a Kind, A Wedding on Walton's Mountain, A Day of Thanks on Walton's Mountain, Secret of Midland Heights, Face of Fear, Killer Rules.

RICHARD, SIR CLIFF
O.B.E. Singer, Actor. r.n. Harry Webb. b. India, Oct. 14, 1940. Ent. show business 1958 in TV series Oh Boy. Other TV includes Sunday Night at the London Palladium, several Cliff Richard Shows; top British Singer, 1960-71. Voted top box-office star of Great Britain, 1962-63, 1963-64. Twice rep. U.K. in Eurovision Song Contest. Innumerable platinum, gold and silver discs. 1989 became first UK artist to release 100 singles; voted top male vocalist of the 80's by UK Indept. TV viewers. Has made numerous videos. Knighted, 1995.
THEATER: Aladdin, Five Finger Exercise, The Potting Shed, Time.
PICTURES: Serious Charge (debut, 1959), Expresso Bongo, The Young Ones, Summer Holiday, Wonderful Life, Finder's Keepers, Two a Penny, Take Me High.

RICHARDS, BEAH
Actress. b. Vicksburg, MS. e. Dillard U. On B'way in The Miracle Worker, A Raisin in the Sun, The Amen Corner (Theatre World Award).
PICTURES: Take a Giant Step, The Miracle Worker, Gone Are the Days, In the Heat of the Night, Hurry Sundown, Guess Who's Coming to Dinner, The Great White Hope, Mahogany, Homer and Eddie, Drugstore Cowboy.
TELEVISION: *Series*: The Bill Cosby Show (1970), Sanford and Son, Frank's Place (Emmy Award, 1988), Hearts Afire. *Movies*: Footsteps, Outrage, A Dream for Christmas, Just an Old Sweet Song, Ring of Passion, Roots II—The Next Generation, A Christmas Without Snow, One Special Victory, Out of Darkness.

RICHARDS, DENISE
Actress. b. Downers Grove, IL, Feb. 17, 1972.
PICTURES: Loaded Weapon I, Tammy and the T-Rex, Lookin' Italian, Nowhere, Starship Troopers, Wild Things, Drop Dead Gorgeous, The World is Not Enough, Valentine, The Third Wheel, Good Advice.
TELEVISION: *Movies:* 919 Fifth Avenue, In the Blink of an Eye. *Series:* Melrose Place. *Guest:* Life Goes On, Saved by the Bell, Married...with Children, Beverly Hills 90210, Seinfeld, Bodies of Evidence, Lois & Clark: The New Adventures of Superman.

RICHARDS, DICK
Director, Producer, Writer. b. New York, NY, July 9, 1934. In U.S. Army as photo-journalist; work appeared in Life, Look, Time, Esquire, etc. Won over 100 int'l. awards, for commercials and photographic art work.
PICTURES: *Director*: The Culpepper Cattle Co. (also story), Rafferty and the Gold Dust Twins, Farewell My Lovely, March or Die (also co- prod., co-story), Death Valley, Tootsie (co-prod. only), Man Woman and Child, Heat.

RICHARDS, MICHAEL
Actor. b. Culver City, July 14, 1950. e. California Inst. of Arts. Work as stand-up comedian led to appearances on tv including regular stint on series Fridays. Acted on stage with San Diego Rep. Co.
THEATER: *LA:* The American Clock, Wild Oats.
PICTURES: Young Doctors in Love, Transylvania 6-5000, Whoops Apocalypse, UHF, Problem Child, Coneheads, So I Married an Axe Murderer, Airheads, Unstrung Heroes, Trial and Error.
TELEVISION: *Series*: Fridays, Marblehead Manor, Seinfeld (3 Emmy Awards: 1993, 1994, 1997), The Michael Richards Show.

RICHARDSON, JOELY
Actress. b. London, Eng., January 9, 1965. Daughter of actress Vanessa Redgrave and director Tony Richardson, sister of actress Natasha Richardson. e. Lycee, St. Paul's Girl's School, London; Pinellas Park H.S. (Florida), The Thacher Sch. (Ojai, CA), Royal Acad. of Dramatic Art. London stage: Steel Magnolias, Beauty and the Beast (Old Vic); also at Liverpool Playhouse, RSC.
PICTURES: Wetherby (debut, 1985 with mother), Drowning By Numbers, About That Strange Girl, King Ralph, Shining Through, Rebecca's Daughters, I'll Do Anything, Sister My Sister, Hollow Reed, Lochness, 101 Dalmations, Event Horizon, Wrestling with Alligators, Under Heaven, Patriot.

TELEVISION: Body Contact, Behaving Badly, Available Light, Heading Home, Lady Chatterly, The Tribe, Echo.

RICHARDSON, MIRANDA
Actress. b. Southport, England, 1958. Studied acting at the drama program at Bristol's Old Vic Theatre School. Began acting on stage, 1979. Appeared in Moving, at the Queen's Theatre and continued in All My Sons, Who's Afraid of Virginia Woolf?, The Life of Einstein in provincial theatres. Also A Lie of the Mind (London), The Changeling, Mountain Language.
PICTURES: Dance With a Stranger (debut, 1985), The Innocent, Empire of the Sun, Eat the Rich, Twisted Obsession, The Bachelor, Enchanted April, The Crying Game, Damage (BAFTA Award; Acad. Award nom.), Tom and Viv, Century, The Night and the Moment, Kansas City, The Evening Star, The Apostle, The Designated Mourner, St. Ives, Jacob Two Two Meets the Hooded Fang, The Big Brass Ring, The King and I (voice), Sleepy Hollow, Chicken Run (voice), Get Carter, Constance & Carlotta, The Man Who Killed Don Quixote.
TELEVISION: The Hard Word, Sorrel and Son, A Woman of Substance, After Pilkington, Underworld, Death of the Heart, The Black Adder (series), Die Kinder (mini-series), Sweet as You Are (Royal TV Society Award), Fatherland (Golden Globe Award), A Dance to the Music of Time (mini-series), The Scold's Bridle, Merlin, Ted & Ralph, The Miracle Maker (voice), Alice in Wonderland, Absolutely Fabuolous, Snow White.

RICHARDSON, NATASHA
Actress. b. London, England, May 11, 1963. m. actor Liam Neeson. Daughter of actress Vanessa Redgrave and director Tony Richardson; sister is actress Joely Richardson. e. Central Sch. of Speech and Drama. Appeared at the Leeds Playhouse in On the Razzle, Top Girls, Charley's Aunt. Performed A Midsummer Night's Dream and Hamlet with the Young Vic. 1985 starred with mother in The Seagull (London), also starred in the musical High Society. Won London Theatre Critics Most Promising Newcomer award, 1986. NY stage debut 1992 in Anna Christie.
PICTURES: Every Picture Tells a Story (debut, 1984). Gothic, A Month in the Country, Patty Hearst, Fat Man and Little Boy, The Handmaid's Tale, The Comfort of Strangers, The Favor the Watch and the Very Big Fish, Widow's Peak, Nell, The Parent Trap.
TELEVISION: Ellis Island (mini-series), In a Secret State, The Copper Beeches (epis. of Sherlock Holmes), Ghosts, Past Midnight, Suddenly Last Summer, Hostages, Zelda, Tales From the Crypt (guest).

RICHARDSON, PATRICIA
Actress. b. Bethesda, MD, Feb. 23, 1951. e. Southern Methodist Univ.
THEATER: *NY:* Gypsy, Loose Ends, The Wake of Jamie Foster, The Collected Works of Billy the Kid, The Frequency, Vanities, The Miss Firecracker Contest, The Coroner's Plot, Fables for Friends. *Regional:* The Killing of Sister George, King Lear, The Philadelphia Story, Fifth of July, About Face.
PICTURES: Gas, C.H.U.D., You Better Watch Out, Lost Angels, In Country, Ulee's Gold.
TELEVISION: *Series:* Double Trouble, Eisenhower and Lutz, FM, Home Improvement, Storytime (PBS). *Movies:* Hands of a Stranger, Parent Trap III, Sophie and the Moonhanger, Undue Influence. *Guest:* Love Sidney, Kate and Allie, The Cosby Show, Quantum Leap.

RICHMAN, PETER MARK
Actor. b. Philadelphia, PA, April 16, 1927. e. Philadelphia Coll. of Pharmacy & Science with Bachelor of Science Degree in Pharmacy. Previously acted as Mark Richman. Member of Actors Studio since 1954.
THEATER: *B'way*: End as a Man, Masquerade, A Hatful of Rain. *Off B'way*: The Dybbuk, The Zoo Story, 4 Faces (also author). *Regional*: Blithe Spirit, The Night of the Iguana, 12 Angry Men, Babes in Toyland, Funny Girl, The Best Man, Equus, The Rainmaker, 4 Faces.
PICTURES: Friendly Persuasion, The Strange One, The Black Orchid, Dark Intruder, Agent for H.A.R.M., For Singles Only, Friday 13th Part VIII—Jason Takes Manahattan, The Naked Gun 2 1/2: The Smell of Fear, Judgment Day (Manila).
TELEVISION: *Series*: Longstreet, Dynasty, Cain's Hundred, My Secret Summer (Berlin). *Movies*: House on Greenapple Road, Yuma, Mallory: Circumstantial Evidence, The Islander, The Psi Factor, Dempsey, Blind Ambition, City Killer, Bonanza: The Next Generation. *Guest:* Three's Company, Murder She Wrote, Star Trek: The Next Generation, Matlock, Beverly Hills 90210, Nothing Sacred and over 500 guest roles.

RICHMOND, TED
Producer. b. Norfolk, VA, June 10, 1912. e. MIT. Entered m.p. ind. as publicity dir., RKO Theatres; later mgr. Albany dist.; publ. dir. Fabian circuit, NY, Paramount upper NY state theats.; Grand Nat'l Pictures. Author Grand Nat'l series Trigger Pal, Six Gun Rhythm. Formed T. H. Richmond Prods., Inc., 1941. Formed Copa Prod. with Tyrone Power, 1954. Formed Ted Richmond Prod. Inc. for MGM release, 1959. Reactivated Copa Prod. Ltd., England, 1960.
PICTURES: Hit the Hay, The Milkman, Kansas Raiders, Shakedown, Smuggler's Island, Strange Door, Cimarron Kid, Bronco Buster, Has Anybody Seen My Gal, No Room for the Groom, Weekend with Father, The Mississippi Gambler, Desert Legion, Column South, Bonzo Goes to College, Forbidden, Walking My Baby Back Home, Francis Joins the Wacs, Bengal Brigade, Count Three and Pray, Nightfall, Abandon Ship, Solomon and Sheba, Charlemagne, Bachelor in Paradise, Advance to the Rear, Pancho Villa, Return of the 7, Red Sun, Papillon (exec. prod.), The Fifth Musketeer.

RICHTER, W. D.
Writer, Director. b. New Britain, CT, Dec. 7, 1945. e. Dartmouth Coll, B.A.; U. of Southern California Film Sch., grad. study.
PICTURES: *Writer*: Slither, Peeper, Nickelodeon, Invasion of the Body Snatchers, Dracula, Brubaker, All Night Long, Big Trouble in Little China, Needful Things, Home for the Holidays. *Prod.-Dir.*: Adventures of Buckaroo Banzai Across the Eighth Dimension, Late for Dinner.

RICKERT, JOHN F.
Executive. b. Kansas City, MO, Oct. 29, 1924. e. USC. Joined Universal Pictures in 1951; left in 1957 to start independent productions. 1960-68 handled indep. roadshow distribution (4-walling). 1969 formed Cineworld Corporation, natl. dist. co., of which he is pres. 1975-76 did tax shelter financing for 13 films. Currently involved in distribution, production packaging and intl. co-production as pres. of Coproducers Corp.

RICKLES, DON
Actor, Comedian. b. New York, NY, May 8, 1926. e. AADA.
PICTURES: Run Silent Run Deep, Rabbit Trap, The Rat Race, X: The Man With the X-Ray Eyes, Muscle Beach Party, Bikini Beach, Beach Blanket Bingo, Enter Laughing, The Money Jungle, Where It's At, Kelly's Heroes, Keaton's Cop, Innocent Blood, Casino, Toy Story (voice), Little Redux Riding Hood (voice), Dennis the Menace 2, Quest for Camelot (voice), Dirty Work, Toy Story 2 (voice).
TELEVISION: *Series*: The Don Rickles Show (1968), The Don Rickles Show (1972), C.P.O. Sharkey, Foul-Ups Bleeps and Blunders, Daddy Dearest. *Movie*: For the Love of It. *Guest*: The Big Show, F Troop, Laugh-In, Kraft Music Hall, Dean Martin's Celebrity Roasts, Tales From the Crypt.

RICKMAN, ALAN
Actor. b. London, England. Began as graphic designer before studying acting at RADA. Joined the Royal Shakespeare Co. where he starred in Les Liaisons Dangereuses; received Tony Award nomination for 1987 NY production.
THEATER: Commitments, The Last Elephant, The Grass Widow, Lucky Chance, The Seagull, As You Like It, Troilus and Cressida, Tango At the End of Winter, Hamlet.
PICTURES: Die Hard (debut, 1988), The January Man, Quigley Down Under, Closet Land, Truly Madly Deeply, Robin Hood: Prince of Thieves (BAFTA Award, 1991), Close My Eyes, Bob Roberts, Mesmer, An Awfully Big Adventure, Sense and Sensibility, Michael Collins, The Winter Guest (also dir.), Judas Kiss, Dogma, Dark Harbor.
TELEVISION: *Series*: The Barchester Chronicles (BBC). *Specials*: Romeo and Juliet. *Guest*: Fallen Angels (Murder Obliquely). *Movie*: Rasputin (Emmy, 1996, 1997; Golden Globe, Screen Actors Guild Awards 1996), Revolutionary Witness, Spirit of Man.

RIEGERT, PETER
Actor. b. New York, NY, Apr. 11, 1947. e. U. of Buffalo, B.A. Brief stints as 8th grade English teacher, social worker, and aide de camp to politician Bella Abzug 1970, before turned actor, off-off B'way. Appeared with improvisational comedy group War Babies. Film debut in short, A Director Talks About His Film.
THEATER: Dance with Me (B'way debut), Minnie's Boys (as Chico Marx), Sexual Perversity in Chicago, Isn't it Romantic?, La Brea Tarpits, A Rosen By Any Other Name, The Nerd, Mountain Language/The Birthday Party, The Road to Nirvana.
PICTURES: National Lampoon's Animal House, Americathon, Head Over Heels, National Lampoon Goes to the Movies, Local Hero, City Girl, A Man in Love, Le Grand Carnaval, The Stranger, Crossing Delancey, That's Adequate, The Passport, A Shock to the System, The Object of Beauty, Beyond the Ocean, Oscar, The Runestone, Passed Away, Utz, The Mask, White Man's Burden, Coldblooded, Pie in the Sky.
TELEVISION: *Specials*: Concealed Enemies, The Hit List, W. Eugene Smith: Photography Made Difficult. *Mini-Series*: Ellis Island. *Movies*: News at Eleven, Barbarians at the Gate, Gypsy, The Infiltrator, Element of Truth. *Series*: The Middle Ages.

RIFKIN, MONROE M.
Executive. e. New York U., BA Finance. Began career with Amer. TV and Communications Corp. as CEO, 1968-82, and Chairman, 1974-82. Bd. member, Nat'l. Cable TV Assoc., 1968-84, and as Chairman, 1983-84. Founder, dir. and Chairman of Rifkin & Associates.

RIFKIN, RON
Actor. b. New York, NY, Oct. 31, 1939. e. NYU.
THEATER: *B'way:* Come Blow Your Horn, The Goodbye People, The Tenth Man. *Off-B'way:* Rosebloom, The Art of Dining, Temple, The Substance of Fire.
PICTURES: The Devil's 8 (debut, 1969), Flareup, Silent Running, The Sunshine Boys, The Big Fix, The Sting II, Husbands and Wives, Manhattan Murder Mystery, Wolf, Last Summer in the Hamptons, The Substance of Fire, I'm Not Rappaport, L.A. Confidential, The Negotiator.
TELEVISION: *Series:* Adam's Rib, When Things Were Rotten, Husbands Wives & Lovers, One Day at a Time, Falcon Crest, Leaving L.A. *Mini-Series:* The Winds of War. *Movie*: Norma Jean & Marilyn

RIGG, DIANA
C.B.E. (1987). Actress. b. Doncaster, England, July 20, 1938. With the Royal Shakespeare Co. at Aldwych Theatre, 1962-64. Recent London stage: Follies, Medea (also B'way).
PICTURES: A Midsummer's Night Dream (debut, 1968), The Assassination Bureau, On Her Majesty's Secret Service, Julius Caesar, The Hospital, Theatre of Blood, A Little Night Music, The Great Muppet Caper, Evil Under the Sun, Snow White, A Good Man in Africa.
TELEVISION: *Series*: The Avengers, Diana, Mystery (host). *Movies*: In This House of Brede, Witness for the Prosecution, A Hazard of Hearts, Mother Love, Mrs. 'arris Goes to Paris, Running Delilah, Genghis Cohn, Danielle Steel's Zoya, The Haunting of Helen Walker. *Specials*: King Lear, Bleak House, Rebecca (Emmy, 1997).

RINGWALD, MOLLY
Actress. b. Sacramento, CA, Feb. 16, 1968. Daughter of jazz musician Bob Ringwald; began performing at age 4 with his Great Pacific Jazz Band and at 6 recorded album, Molly Sings. Professional debut at 5 in stage play, The Glass Harp. Appeared in bit on TV's New Mickey Mouse Club, a West Coast stage production of Annie and in TV series, The Facts of Life, *Off-B'way debut*: Lily Dale (Theatre World Award, 1986).
PICTURES: Tempest (debut, 1982), P.K. and the Kid, Spacehunter: Adventures in the Forbidden Zone, Sixteen Candles, The Breakfast Club, Pretty in Pink, The Pick-Up Artist, For Keeps?, King Lear, Fresh Horses, Strike It Rich, Betsy's Wedding, Face the Music, Seven Sundays, Malicious, Baja, Bastard Brood, Office Killer, Requiem for Murder, Teaching Mrs. Tingle.
TELEVISION: *Series*: The Facts of Life, Townies. *Movies*: Packin' It In, Surviving, Women and Men: Stories of Seduction (Dust Before Fireworks), Something to Live For: The Alison Gertz Story, Since You've Been Gone. *Mini-Series*: The Stand.

RISHER, SARA
Executive. Chair of production, New Line Productions, Inc.
PICTURES: *Co-prod./assoc. prod.*: Polyester, A Nightmare on Elm Street, Quiet Cool, Critters. A Nightmare on Elm Street 3: Dream Warriors, My Demon Lover. *Exec. prod.*: A Nightmare on Elm Street 4: The Dream Master, A Nightmare on Elm Street 5: The Dream Child, Book of Love, Pump Up the Volume, Wide Sargasso Sea, Surf Ninjas, Blink, A Nightmare on Elm Street 7 (also actress), In Love & War, Last Man Standing, The Deep Blue.

RISSIEN, EDWARD L.
Executive. b. Des Moines, IA. e. Grinnell Coll., Stanford U., B.A., 1949. Army Air Force, WWII. B'way stage, mgr., 1950-53; v.p., Mark Stevens. Prods., 1954-56; prod., v.p., Four Star, 1958-60; prog. exec., ABC-TV, 1960-62; v.p., Bing Crosby Prods., 1963-66; v.p., Filmways TV Prods.; assoc. prod., Columbia, 1968-69; indept. prod., 1970; prod., WB, 1971; exec. v.p., Playboy Prods., 1972-80; consultant & indept. prod., 1981-82; sr. consultant, cable, Playboy Prods., 1982-85; pres., Playboy Programs, 1985-88; bd. of dirs.: Heritage Entertainment, Inc. 1985-88; indept. prod., 1989-present. Theatre producer in London: The School of Night.
PICTURES: Snow Job (prod.), Castle Keep (prod. exec.), The Crazy World of Julius Vrooder (prod.), Saint Jack (exec. prod.).
TELEVISION: *Movies* (exec. prod.): Minstrel Man, A Whale for the Killing, The Death of Ocean View Park, Big Bob Johnson, The Great Niagara, Third Girl from the Left, A Summer Without Boys.

RISSNER, DANTON
Executive. b. Brooklyn, NY, March 27, 1940. e. Florida So. Col. Began as agent with Ashley Famous (later Intl. Famous), 1967-69. 1969 joined Warner Bros. as v.p., chg. European prod.; 1970, moved to United Artists as v.p., chg. European prod.; 1973, named v.p. in chg. East Coast & European prod. for UA; 1975- 78, v.p. in chg. of world-wide prod.; 1981, exec. v.p., 20th Century-Fox.; 1984, joined UA as sr. v.p., motion pictures.
PICTURES: *Prod.*: Up the Academy, A Summer Story.
TELEVISION: Backfire (prod.).

RITCHIE, MICHAEL
Director. b. Waukesha, WI, Nov. 28, 1938. e. Harvard U. where he directed first production of Arthur Kopit's play, Oh Dad Poor Dad Mama's Hung You in the Closet and I'm Feeling So Sad. Professional career began as ass't. to Robert Saudek on Ford Foundation's Omnibus TV series. Later became assoc. prod. and then dir. on Saudek's Profiles in Courage series; dir. assignments on tv series. Appeared as actor in film Innocent Blood.
PICTURES: Downhill Racer (debut, 1969), Prime Cut, The Candidate, Smile (also prod., lyricist), The Bad News Bears, Semi-Tough, An Almost Perfect Affair (also co-s.p.), The Island, Divine Madness (also prod.), The Survivors, Fletch, Wildcats, The Golden Child, The Couch Trip, Fletch Lives, Diggstown, Cops and Robbersons, The Scout, The Fantasticks, A Simple Wish.
TELEVISION: *Series*: Profiles in Courage (also prod.), The Man from U.N.C.L.E., Run for Your Life, Dr. Kildare, The Big Valley, Felony Squad, The Outsider (pilot), The Sound of Anger. *Movie*: The Positively True Adventures of the Alleged Texas Cheerleader-Murdering Mom, Comfort Texas.

RITTER, JOHN
Actor. b. Burbank, CA, Sept. 17, 1948. Father was late Tex Ritter, country-western star. Attended Hollywood H.S. Began acting at USC in 1968. Appeared with college cast at Edinburgh Festival; later with Eva Marie Saint in Desire Under the Elms.
PICTURES: The Barefoot Executive (debut, 1971), Scandalous John, The Other, The Stone Killer, Nickelodeon, Americathon, Hero at Large, Wholly Moses, They All Laughed, Real Men, Skin Deep, Problem Child, Problem Child II, Noises Off, Stay Tuned, North, Slingblade. Montana, I Woke Up Early the Day I Died, A Gun A Car A Blonde, Bride of Chucky, Shadow of Doubt, TripFall, Lost in the Pershing Point Hotel.
TELEVISION: *Movies*: The Night That Panicked America, Leave Yesterday Behind, The Comeback Kid, Pray TV, In Love With an Older Woman, Sunset Limousine, Love Thy Neighbor, Letting Go, Unnatural Causes, A Smoky Mountain Christmas, The Last Fling, Prison for Children, Tricks of the Trade, My Brother's Wife, Stephen King's It, The Dreamer of Oz, The Summer My Father Grew Up, Danielle Steel's Heartbeat, The Only Way Out, Gramps, The Colony, Unforgivable, Chance of a Lifetime, Dead Husbands, Holy Joe, It Came From the Sky. *Series*: The Waltons, Three's Company (Emmy Award, 1984), Three's a Crowd, Hooper-man, Have Faith (exec. prod.), Anything But Love (exec. prod., also guest), Fish Police (voice), Hearts Afire, Buffy the Vampire (guest).

RIVERA, CHITA
Actress, Dancer. r.n. Concita del Rivero. b. Washington, DC, Jan. 23, 1933. Trained for stage at American School of Ballet.
THEATER: Call Me Madam (1952), Guys and Dolls, Can-Can, Shoestring Revue, Seventh Heaven, Mr. Wonderful, Shinbone Alley, West Side Story, Bye Bye Birdie, Bajour, Sondheim: A Musical Tribute, Chicago, Hey Look Me Over, Merlin, The Rink (Tony Award, 1984), Jerry's Girls, Kiss of the Spider Woman (Tony Award, 1993).
PICTURE: Sweet Charity (1969).
TELEVISION: *Series*: The New Dick Van Dyke Show. *Specials*: Kennedy Center Tonight—Broadway to Washington!, Pippin, Toller Cranston's Strawberry Ice, TV Academy Hall of Fame, 1985. *Movies*: The Marcus-Nelson Murders, Mayflower Madam.

RIVERA, GERALDO
Journalist. b. New York, NY, July 4, 1943. e. U. of Arizona, Brooklyn Law Sch., 1969, Columbia Sch. of Journalism. Started legal career 1st as lawyer with Harlem Assertion of Rights Community Action for Legal Services 1968-70. Switched to journalism, joined WABC-TV, New York, 1970. Made several TV documentaries on such subjects as institutions for retarded, drug addiction, migrant workers, etc. Chmn.: One-to-One Foundation, Maravilla Foundation. Winner 3 national and 4 local Emmys, George Peabody Award, 2 Robert F. Kennedy Awards. Appeared in film The Bonfire of the Vanities.
TELEVISION: *Series*: Good Morning America (contributor), Good Night America, 20/20, The Geraldo Rivera Show, Now It Can Be Told, Rivera Live. *Specials*: The Mystery of Al Capone's Vault, American Vice: The Doping of a Nation, Innocence Lost: The Erosion of American Childhood, Sons of Scarface: The New Mafia, Murder: Live From Death Row, Devil Worship: Exposing Satan's Underground. *Movie*: Perry Mason: The Case of the Reckless Romeo.

RIVERS, JOAN
Actress, Writer, Director. r.n. Joan Molinsky. b. New York, NY, June 8, 1933. e. Barnard Coll. (Phi Beta Kappa). Formerly fashion coordinator for Bond clothing stores. Performed comedy act in nightclubs, then with Second City 1961-62; TV debut: Johnny Carson Show, 1965; nat'l syndicated columnist, Chicago Tribune 1973-76; Hadassah Woman of the Year, 1983; Jimmy Award for Best Comedian 1981; Chair., National Cystic Fibrosis Foundation. 1978 created TV series Husbands Wives and Lovers.

AUTHOR: Having a Baby Can Be a Scream (1974), Can We Talk? (1983), The Life and Hard Times of Heidi Abramowitz (1984), Enter Talking (1986), Still Talking (1990).
THEATER: *B'way*: Fun City (also co-writer), Broadway Bound, Sally Marr... and Her Escorts (also co-writer).
PICTURES: The Swimmer, Rabbit Test (also dir., s.p.), The Muppets Take Manhattan, Spaceballs (voice), Serial Mom.
TELEVISION: *Series*: The Tonight Show (regular substitute guest host: 1983-86), The Late Show (host), The New Hollywood Squares, The Joan Rivers Show (morning talk show). *Movies*: How to Murder a Millionaire, Tears and Laughter: The Joan and Melissa Rivers Story.

ROBARDS, JASON
Actor. b. Chicago, IL, July 26, 1922. Served in Navy during WWII. Studied acting at Acad. of Dramatic Arts. Began with Children's World Theatre (1947), then stock radio parts, asst. stage mgr. and actor in Stalag 17, The Chase, D'Oyly Carte Opera Co., Stratford Ontario Shakespeare Fest. American Gothic, Circle in the Square.
THEATER: The Iceman Cometh (Obie Award, 1956), Long Day's Journey into Night (Theatre World Award), The Disenchanted (Tony Award, 1959), Toys in the Attic, Big Fish Little Fish, A Thousand Clowns, After the Fall, But for Whom Charlie, Hughie, The Devils, We Bombed in New Haven, The Country Girl, A Moon for the Misbegotten, Long Day's Journey Into Night (Brooklyn Acad. of Music, 1975; B'way, 1988), A Touch of the Poet, O'Neill and Carlotta, You Can't Take It With You, Ah Wilderness, A Month of Sundays, Established Price (Long Wharf), Love Letters, Park Your Car in Harvard Yard, No Man's Land.
PICTURES: The Journey (debut, 1959), By Love Possessed, Tender Is the Night, Long Day's Journey Into Night, Act One, A Thousand Clowns, A Big Hand for the Little Lady, Any Wednesday, Divorce American Style, The St. Valentine's Day Massacre, Hour of the Gun, The Night They Raided Minsky's, (Loves of) Isadora, Once Upon a Time in the West, Operation Snafu, The Ballad of Cable Hogue, Tora! Tora! Tora!, Fools, Julius Caesar, Johnny Got His Gun, Murders in the Rue Morgue, The War Between Men and Women, Pat Garrett and Billy the Kid, A Boy and His Dog, Mr. Sycamore, All the President's Men (Academy Award, best supporting actor, 1976), Julia (Academy Award, best supporting actor, 1977), Comes a Horseman, Hurricane, Raise the Titanic!, Caboblanco, Melvin and Howard, Legend of the Lone Ranger, Burden of Dreams, Max Dugan Returns, Something Wicked This Way Comes, Square Dance, Bright Lights Big City, The Good Mother, Dream a Little Dream, Parenthood, Quick Change, Reunion, Storyville, The Adventures of Huck Finn, The Trial, Philadelphia, The Paper, Little Big League, Crimson Tide, A Thousand Acres, Heartwood, Enemy of the State (cameo), Beloved, The Real Macaw, Magnolia.
TELEVISION: *Specials*: Abe Lincoln in Illinois, The Iceman Cometh, A Doll's House, Noon Wine, Belle of 14th Street, The House Without a Christmas Tree, For Whom the Bell Tolls, You Can't Take It With You, Hughie. *Mini-Series*: Washington: Behind Closed Doors, The Irish in America: Long Journey Home. *Movies*: A Christmas to Remember, Haywire, F.D.R.: The Last Year, The Atlanta Child Murders, The Day After, Sakharov, Johnny Bull, The Long Hot Summer, Laguna Heat, Norman Rockwell's Breaking Home Ties, Inherit the Wind (Emmy Award, 1988), The Christmas Wife, The Perfect Tribute, Chernobyl: The Final Warning, An Inconvenient Woman, Black Rainbow, Mark Twain & Me, Heidi, The Enemy Within, My Antonia. *Guest*: Studio One, Philco Playhouse, Hallmark.

ROBARDS, SAM
Actor. b. New York, NY, December 16. m. actress Suzy Amis. Son of actors Jason Robards and Lauren Bacall. e. National Theater Institute and studied with Uta Hagen at H.B. Studios.
THEATER: *Off-B'way*: Album, Flux, Taking Steps, Moonchildren. Kennedy Center: Idiot's Delight and regional theater.
PICTURES: Tempest, Not Quite Paradise, Fandango, Bright Lights Big City, Bird, Casualties of War, The Ballad of Little Jo, Mrs. Parker and the Vicious Circle, Donor Unknown, Beautiful Girls, Dinner and Driving.
TELEVISION: *Series*: Movin' Right Along (PBS), TV 101, Get a Life!, Maximum Bob. *Movies*: Jacobo Timerman: Prisoner Without a Name Cell Without a Number, Into Thin Air, Pancho Barnes, The Man Who Captured Eichmann.

ROBBINS, MATTHEW
Writer, Director. e. U.S.C. Sch. of Cinema. Wrote early scripts in collaboration with Hal Barwood, Robbins branching out into directing with Corvette Summer in 1978.
PICTURES: *Writer*: The Sugarland Express, The Bingo Long Traveling All-Stars and Motor Kings, Corvette Summer (also dir.), Dragonslayer (also dir.), Warning Sign, Batteries Not Included (also dir.), Bingo (dir. only), Mimic (also story).

ROBBINS, RICHARD
Composer. b. Boston, MA, Dec. 4, 1940. Bachelor of Music and Graduate Studies at New England Conservatory of Music. Received Frank Huntington Beebe Fellowship to Austria where he studied musicology, chamber music. Later became dir. of Mannes College of Music Preparatory School, N.Y. Has worked closely with James Ivory and Ismail Merchant. Also dir. doc. films Sweet Sounds, Street Musicians of Bombay. Awards: Best Score, Venice Film Festival for Maurice; Best Score, BFI Anthony Asquith Award for A Room With a View. Acad. Award nom. for Howards End and The Remains of the Day.
PICTURES: The Europeans (supr. score), Jane Austen in Manhattan, Quartet, Heat and Dust, The Bostonians, A Room with a View, Maurice, Sweet Lorraine, My Little Girl, Slaves of New York, Mr. & Mrs. Bridge, The Ballad of the Sad Cafe, Howards End, The Remains of the Day, Jefferson in Paris, Surviving Picasso, The Proprietor.
TELEVISION: Love and Other Sorrows, In The Gloaming.

ROBBINS, TIM
Actor, Director. b. West Covina, CA, Oct. 16, 1958. Son of Greenwich Village folksinger, worked as actor while in high school. e. NYU. Transferred to UCLA theatre program appearing in guest roles on tv. 1981, co-founder and artistic dir., The Actors Gang, in L.A.; dir. them in and co-authored Alagazam: After the Dog Wars, Violence: The Misadventures of Spike Spangle—Farmer, Carnage: A Comedy (also prod. in NY).
PICTURES: Toy Soldiers (debut, 1984), No Small Affair, Fraternity Vacation, The Sure Thing, Top Gun, Howard the Duck, Five Corners, Bull Durham, Tapeheads, Miss Firecracker, Twister (cameo), Erik the Viking, Cadillac Man, Jacob's Ladder, Jungle Fever, The Player (Cannes Film Fest. Award, 1992), Bob Roberts (also dir., s.p., co-wrote songs), Short Cuts, The Hudsucker Proxy, The Shawshank Redemption, Ready to Wear (Pret-a-Porter), I.Q., Dead Man Walking (dir.), Nothing to Lose, Arlington Road, The Cradle Will Rock (dir.), Mission to Mars, High Fidelity, Anti-Trust, Human Nature.
TELEVISION: *Movies*: Quarterback Princess, Malice in Wonderland. *Guest*: Hardcastle and McCormick, St. Elsewhere, Hill Street Blues.

ROBERTS, BRIAN L.
Executive. b. Philadelphia, PA. e. Wharton School at U. of Penn. Joined Comcast Corp. a major cable TV and cell. tele. network operating co., in 1982. Several mgt. positions, incl. exec. VP of ops., before becoming president in 1990. He also serves as a director of Comcast.

ROBERTS, CURTIS
Producer. b. Dover, England. e. Cambridge U. Child actor. England, Germany; numerous pictures for Rank Org.; prod. England, on Broadway in Gertie, Island Visit; co-prod. on Broadway, Horses in Midstream, Golden Apple, Tonight or Never; tour and NY The Journey. Recipient: Lawrence J. Quirk Photoplay Award 1990. Now pres., CGC Films, Munich.
AUTHOR: The History of Summer Theatre, The History of Vaudeville, Other Side of the Coin, History of Music (Popular) 1900-70, The History of English Music Halls, Latta, Then There Were Some, I Live to Love, Gabor the Merrier, I Live to Love II.
THEATER: *Tours*: Blithe Spirit, Showboat, Kiss Me Kate, Generation, The Camel Bell, Farewell Party, Twentieth Century, Great Sebastians, Goodbye Charlie, Time of the Cuckoo, Under Papa's Picture, Everybody's Gal, Divorce Me Darling, Gingerbread Lady, September Song, Same Time Next Year, Funny Girl, Pal Joey, South Pacific, It Girl, Fanny, Breaking Up the Act, Good, Good Friends, Together, I Remember Mama, Applause Too.
PICTURES: An Actress in Love, La Die, Hypocrite, Jet Over the Atlantic, The Vixen, Farewell Party, Polly's Return, Rain Before Seven, Halloween, Malaga, My Dear Children, Norma, The Lion's Consort, Whispers, Golden Idol, London Belongs To Me, The Ann Moriss Story.
TELEVISION: Rendezvous, Deadly Species, Top Secret, The Ilona Massey Show, When In Rome, Ethan Frome, Black Chiffon, Illusion in Java (mini-series), Diamonds Don't Burn (mini-series), *BBC Specials*: My Family Right Or Wrong, The Psychopathic Dog.

ROBERTS, ERIC
Actor. b. Biloxi, MS, April 18, 1956. Father founded Actors and Writers Workshop in Atlanta, 1963. Sister is actress Julia Roberts. Began appearing in stage prods. at age 5. Studied at American Acad. of Dramatic Arts. Stage debut in Rebel Women.
THEATER: Mass Appeal, The Glass Menagerie (Hartford Stage Co.), A Streetcar Named Desire (Princeton's McCarter Theater), Alms for the Middle Class (Long Wharf), Burn This (B'way debut; Theatre World Award).
PICTURES: King of the Gypsies (debut, 1978), Raggedy Man, Star 80, The Pope of Greenwich Village, The Coca Cola Kid, Runaway Train (Acad. Award nom., Golden Globe nom.), Nobody's Fool, Rude Awakening, Blood Red, Best of the Best, The Ambulance, Lonely Hearts, Final Analysis, Best of the Best 2, By the Sword, Freefall, Babyfever, Love Is a Gun, The Specialist, Nature of the Beast, The Grave, Heaven's Prisoners, It's My Party, From the Edge, The Immortals, Power 98, The Cable Guy, American Strays, TNT, The Shadow Men, Making Sandwiches, Most Wanted, Two Shades of Blue, The Prophecy II, La Cucaracha.

TELEVISION: *Series*: Another World, C-16: FBI. *Specials*: Miss Lonelyhearts, Dear America: Letters Home from Vietnam (reader). *Movies*: Pauls' Case, Slow Burn, To Heal a Nation, The Lost Capone, Descending Angel, Vendetta: Secrets of a Mafia Bride, Fugitive Among Us, Love Honor & Obey: The Last Mafia Marriage, Voyage, Love Cheat and Steal, Saved by the Light, The Odyssey, Dr. Who, Dark Angel, In Cold Blood, Purgatory West of the Pecos.

ROBERTS, JULIA
Actress. b. Smyrna, GA, Oct. 28, 1967. Brother is actor Eric Roberts. Parents ran theater workshop in Atlanta. Moved to NY to study acting; modeled for the Click Agency before making prof. debut in brother's film Blood Red. voted Hasty Pudding Woman of the Year, 1997. People's Choice Award, 1991, 1992, 1994, 1998, 2000 and ShoWest Awards, 1991 and 1998. Number one on Quigley's Top Ten MoneyMaking Stars of 1999.
PICTURES: Blood Red (debut, 1986), Firehouse, Satisfaction, Mystic Pizza, Steel Magnolias (Acad. Award nom., Golden Globe award), Pretty Woman (Acad. Award nom., BAFTA nom., Golden Globe award), Flatliners, Sleeping With the Enemy, Dying Young, Hook, The Player, The Pelican Brief, I Love Trouble, Ready to Wear (Pret-a-Porter), Something to Talk About, Mary Reilly, Michael Collins, Everyone Says I Love You, My Best Friend's Wedding (Golden Globe nom.), Conspiracy Theory, Notting Hill (Golden Globe nom.), Runaway Bride, Stepmom (also exec. prod.), Erin Brockovich, The Mexican, Ocean's Eleven.
TELEVISION: *Movie*: Baja Oklahoma. *Guest*: Crime Story, Miami Vice, Inside the Actors Atudio, Friends, Murphy Brown, Sesame Street, Law & Order (Emmy nom.). *Specials*: In the Wild, AFI's 100 Years...100 Stars.

ROBERTS, PERNELL
Actor. b. Waycross, GA, May 18, 1930. e. U. of Maryland. Left college to begin working with summer stock companies, joining Arena Stage in Washington, DC in 1950. 1952 began appearing off-B'way (where he won a Drama Desk Award for Macbeth, 1957); made B'way debut in 1958 in Tonight in Samarkand.
PICTURES: Desire Under the Elms (debut, 1958), The Sheepman, Ride Lonesome, The Errand Boy (cameo), Four Rode Out, The Magic of Lassie.
TELEVISION: *Series*: Bonanza, Trapper John M.D., FBI: The Untold Stories (host). *Movies*: The Silent Gun, San Francisco International, The Bravos, Adventures of Nick Carter, Assignment: Munich, Dead Man on the Run, The Deadly Tower, The Lives of Jenny Dolan, Charlie Cobb: Nice Night for a Hanging, The Immigrants, The Night Rider, Hot Rod, High Noon Part II: The Return of Will Kane, Incident at Crestridge, Desperado, Perry Mason: The Case of the Sudden Death Payoff, Perry Mason: The Case of the All-Star Assassin, Donor. *Mini-Series*: Captains and the Kings, Centennial, Around the World in 80 Days.

ROBERTS, RALPH J.
Executive. b. Philadelphia, PA. e. Wharton School at U. of Penn. Served 4-year tour of duty in US Navy. Began career in 1950's as acct. exec., Aitken Kynett Advertising Agency. VP, Muzak Corp. Exec. VP, dir. of advertising and later pres. and CEO of Pioneer Industries, a men's accessory co. Pres. and Chairman, Comcast Corp., a cable TV and cell. tele. network operating co. Chairman only since 1989.

ROBERTS, TONY
Actor. b. New York, NY, Oct. 22, 1939. e. Northwestern U.
THEATER: *B'way*: How Now Dow Jones, Don't Drink the Water, Play It Again Sam, Promises Promises, Barefoot in the Park, Absurd Person Singular, Sugar, Murder at the Howard Johnson's, They're Playing Our Song, Doubles, Arsenic and Old Lace, Jerome Robbins' Broadway, The Seagull, The Sisters Rosensweig, Victor/Victoria. *Off-B'way*: The Cradle Will Rock, The Good Parts, Four Dogs and a Bone. NY City Opera: Brigadoon, South Pacific. *Dir*: One of the All-Time Greats (Off-B'way).
PICTURES: Million Dollar Duck, Star Spangled Girl, Play It Again Sam, Serpico, The Taking of Pelham One Two Three, Lovers Like Us, Annie Hall, Just Tell Me What You Want, Stardust Memories, A Midsummer Night's Sex Comedy, Amityville 3-D, Key Exchange, Hannah and Her Sisters, Radio Days, 18 Again, Popcorn, Switch.
TELEVISION: *Series*: Rosetti and Ryan, The Four Seasons, The Lucie Arnaz Show, The Thorns. *Movies*: The Lindbergh Kidnapping Case, Girls in the Office, If Things Were Different, Seize the Day, Messiah on Mott Street, A Question of Honor, A Different Affair, Our Sons, Not in My Family, The American Clock, A Perry Mason Mystery: The Case of the Jealous Jokester. *Guest*: The Defenders, Phyllis, Storefront Lawyers, MacMillan, Trapper John M.D., Love American Style, Love Boat, Hotel.

ROBERTSON, CLIFF
Actor, Writer, Director. b. La Jolla, CA, Sept. 9, 1925.
THEATER: Mr. Roberts, Late Love, The Lady and the Tiger, Ghosts of 87 (one-man show). *B'way*: The Wisteria Tree, Orpheus Descending (Theatre World Award), Love Letters.
PICTURES: *Actor:* Picnic (debut, 1955), Autumn Leaves, The Girl Most Likely, The Naked and the Dead, Gidget, Battle of the Coral Sea, As the Sea Rages, All in a Night's Work, Underworld USA, The Big Show, The Interns, My Six Loves, PT 109, Sunday in New York, The Best Man, 633 Squadron, Love Has Many Faces, Masquerade, Up From the Beach, The Honey Pot, The Devil's Brigade (also s.p.), Charly (Academy Award, 1968), Too Late the Hero, J.W. Coop (also dir., s.p.), The Great Northfield Minnesota Raid, Ace Eli and Rodger of the Skies, Man on a Swing, Out of Season, Three Days of the Condor, Shoot, Obsession, Dominique, Fraternity Row (narrator), Class, Brainstorm, Star 80, Shaker Run, Malone, Wild Hearts Can't Be Broken, Wind, Renaissance Man, Dazzle, The Sunset Boys, Escape From L.A.
TELEVISION: *Series*: Falcon Crest. *Guest*: Philco-Goodyear, Studio One, Robert Montgomery Presents, The Game (Emmy Award, 1966), Batman. *Movies*: Man Without a Country, My Father's House, Washington: Behind Closed Doors, Dreams of Gold, Key to Rebecca, Henry Ford—The Man and the Machine, Dead Reckoning, Dazzle, The Last Best Days, Assignment Berlin. *Special*: Days of Wine and Roses (Playhouse 90). Also spokesman for AT&T.

ROBERTSON, DALE
Actor, Producer. r.n. Dayle Robertson. b. Harrah, OK, July 14, 1923. e. Oklahoma Military Coll. Prof. prizefighter; U.S. Army, 1942-45. Film debut as bit player. Voted Star of Tomorrow, M.P. Herald Fame Poll, 1951.
PICTURES: The Boy With Green Hair (debut, 1948), Flamingo Road, Fighting Man of the Plains, Caribou Trail, Two Flags West, Call Me Mister, Take Care of My Little Girl, Golden Girl, Lydia Bailey, Return of the Texan, The Outcasts of Poker Flat, O. Henry's Full House, The Farmer Takes a Wife, Devil's Canyon, The Silver Whip, City of Bad Men, The Gambler from Natchez, Sitting Bull, Son of Sinbad, Day of Fury, Dakota Incident, Hell Canyon Outlaws, Fast and Sexy, Law of the Lawless, Blood on the Arrow, Coast of Skeletons, The One-Eyed Soldier.
TELEVISION: *Series*: Tales of Wells Fargo, The Iron Horse, Death Valley Days, Dynasty, Dallas, J.J. Starbuck. *Movies*: Scalplock, Melvin Purvis: G-Man, Kansas City Massacre, Last Ride of the Dalton Gang. *Guest*: The Love Boat, Matt Houston, Murder She Wrote.

ROBERTSON, KATHLEEN
Actress. b. Hamilton, Canada, July 8, 1973.
PICTURES: Blown Away, Lapse of Memory, Nowhere, Dog Park, Splendor, Runaway Bride (cameo), Psycho Beach Party.
TELEVISION: *Movies:* Liar's Edge, Quiet Killer, Survive the Night. *Series:* Maniac Mansion, Beverly Hills 90210. *Guest:* My Secret Identity, ENG, Burke's Law.

ROBERTSON, TIMOTHY B.
Executive. e. Univ of VA, Gordon-Conwell Thelogical Seminary, Columbia Univ. Manager of WXNE-TV in Boston, 1980-82; supervisor of Christian Broadcasting Network's tv facility; 1982-90, in charge of Middle East Television after purchase by CBN. Became President & CEO of International Family Entertainment Inc., holdings include The Family Channel, Fit TV, United Family Communications.

ROBINSON, BRUCE
Actor, Director, Writer. b. Kent, England, 1946. e. Central School of Speech and Drama. As actor appeared in 12 films but began writing novels and screenplays long before he gave up acting in 1975.
PICTURES: *Actor*: Romeo and Juliet (debut), The Story of Adele H. (last film as actor). *Writer*: The Killing Fields (Acad. Award nom.), Fat Man and Little Boy. *Director-Writer*: Withnail and I, How to Get Ahead in Advertising, Jennifer Eight, Return to Paradise, In Dreams.

ROBINSON, JAMES G.
Executive, Producer. e. Univ. of Maryland. Was prof. photographer and business entrepreneur prior to entering m.p. industry as co-prod. of The Stone Boy, and exec. prod. of Where the River Runs Black, Streets of Gold. Founded Morgan Creek Prods. in 1988, Morgan Creek Intl. in 1989, Morgan Creek Music Group in 1990, Morgan Creek Theatres and Morgan Creek International Theatres in 1992. Chairman and CEO of Morgan Creek.
PICTURES: *Exec. Prod. for Morgan Creek*: Young Guns, Skin Deep, Renegades, Enemies a Love Story, Nightbreed, Coupe de Ville, Young Guns II, The Exorcist III, Pacific Heights, Robin Hood: Prince of Thieves, Freejack, White Sands, The Last of the Mohicans, True Romance. *Prod. for Morgan Creek:* Stay Tuned, The Crush, Ace Ventura: Pet Detective, Major League II, Chasers, Trial by Jury, Silent Fall, Imaginary Crimes, A Walk in the Clouds, Big Bully, Ace Ventura: When Nature Calls, Two If By Sea, Diabolique, Bad Moon, Wild America, Incognito, Major League: Back to the Minors.

ROBINSON, PHIL ALDEN
Director, Writer. b. Long Beach, NY, Mar. 1, 1950. e. Union Coll., Schenectady. Write and directed training films for Air Force, before writing two episodes for series Trapper John M.D.
PICTURES: Rhinestone (co-s.p.), All of Me (s.p., assoc. prod.). *Dir./Writer*: In the Mood, Field of Dreams, Sneakers.
TELEVISION: *Series*: Trapper John M.D. (writer), The George Burns Comedy Week (dir.)

ROCCO, ALEX
Actor. b. Cambridge, MA, Feb. 29, 1936.
PICTURES: Motor Psycho, St. Valentine's Day Massacre, Blood Mania, The Godfather, Slither, Detroit 9000, Friends of Eddie Coyle, The Outside Man, Stanley, Freebie and the Bean, Three the Hard Way, Rafferty and the Gold Dust Twins, Hearts of the West, Fire Sale, House Calls, Rabbit Test, Voices, Herbie Goes Bananas, The Stunt Man, Nobody's Perfekt, The Entity, Cannonball Run II, Stick, Gotcha!, P.K. and the Kid, Return to Horror High, Dream a Little Dream, Wired, The Pope Must Die, That Thing You Do!, Just-Write, Dead of Night, A Bug's Life (voice), Dudley Do-Right, Goodbye Lover.
TELEVISION: Over 400 television shows incl: *Series*: Three for the Road, The Famous Teddy Z (Emmy Award, 1990), Sibs, The George Carlin Show. *Movies*: Hustling, The Blue Knight, A Question of Guilt, The Grass is Always Greener Over the Septic Tank, Badge of the Assassin, Rock 'n' Roll Mom, The First Time, A Quiet Little Neighborhood A Perfect Little Murder, An Inconvenient Woman, Boris & Natasha, Love Honor & Obey: The Last Mafia Marriage, Robin Cook's Harmful Intent. *Mini-Series*: 79 Park Avenue. *Guest:* The Simpsons (voice).

ROCK, CHRIS
Actor, Comedian. b. Brooklyn, NY, Feb. 7, 1966.
PICTURES: Beverly Hills Cop II, I'm Gonna Git You Sucka, New Jack City, Boomerang, CB4 (also writer, co-prod.), The Immortals, Panther, Sgt. Bilko, Beverly Hills Ninja, Doctor Dolittle (voice), Lethal Weapon 4, Dogma, Nurse Betty, Spin Doctor, Bamboozled, Osmosis Jones, Down to Earth, View Askew 5, Pootie Tang.
TELEVISION: *Specials:* Chris Rock: Bigger & Blacker (also exec. prod.), Jackie's Back!, Whatever Happened to Michael Ray?. *Series*: Saturday Night Live, In Living Color, The Chris Rock Show. *Guest*: Miami Vice, The Fresh Prince of Bel-Air, Homicide: Life on the Street, King of the Hill (voice).

RODAT, ROBERT
Writer. b. 1953.
PICTURES: Tall Tale: The Unbelievable Adventures of Pecos Bill, Fly Away Home, Saving Private Ryan (Acad. Award nom.), Patriot.
TELEVISION: The Comrades of Summer, The Ripper, 36 Hours to Die.

RODDAM, FRANC
Director. b. Stockton, England, Apr. 29, 1946. Studied at London Film Sch. Spent two years as adv. copywriter/prod. with Ogilvy, Benson, Mather before joining BBC as documentary filmmaker. Founder of Union Pictures 1991.
PICTURES: Quadrophenia (also co-s.p.), The Lords of Discipline, Rain Forest (s.p. only), The Bride, Aria (sequence), War Party (also co-exec. prod.), K2.
TELEVISION: *Director*: The Family, Mini, Dummy. *Creator*: Aufwiedersehen Pet, Making Out, Masterchief, Harry.

RODRIGUEZ, ROBERT
Director, Writer, Producer, Editor. e. Univ. of TX. While in college created comic strip Los Hooligans. Made many short films including Bedhead which won several festival awards.
PICTURES: *Director/Writer:* El Mariachi (feature debut, 1993; also co-prod., story, photog., editor, sound), Desperado (also prod., editor), Four Rooms (segment), From Dusk Till Dawn (dir.), The Facult, Spy Kids.
TELEVISION: *Movie (dir./writer):* Roadracers.

ROEG, NICOLAS
Director, Cameraman. b. London, England. Aug. 15, 1928. m. actress Theresa Russell. Entered film industry through cutting rooms of MGM's British Studios, dubbing French films into English. Moved into prod. as clapper boy and part of photographer Freddie Young's crew at Marylebone Studios London, 1947. Next became camera operator (Trials of Oscar Wilde, The Sundowners). Had first experience as cameraman on TV series (Police Dog and Ghost Squad). Debut as director on Performance, co-directed with Donald Cammell. First solo dir. film, Walkabout.
PICTURES: *Cameraman*: The Miniver Story, The Trial of Oscar Wilde, The Sundowners, Lawrence of Arabia, Jazz Boat, Information Received, The Great Van Robbery. *Dir. of Photography*: The Caretaker, Dr. Crippen, Nothing But the Best, Masque of the Red Death, A Funny Thing Happened on the Way to the Forum, Fahrenheit 451, Far from the Madding Crowd, The Girl-Getters, Petulia. *Director-Cameraman*: Performance (co.-dir.), Walkabout. *Director*: Don't Look Now, The Man Who Fell To Earth, Bad Timing, Eureka, Insignificance, Castaway, Aria (sequence, also co-s.p.), Track 29, The Witches, Without You I'm Nothing (exec. prod. only), Cold Heaven.
TELEVISION: *Movies*: Sweet Bird of Youth, Heart of Darkness.

ROËVES, MAURICE
Actor, Director, Writer. b. Sunderland, England, Mar. 19, 1937. Ent. industry, 1964. Played Macduff to Alec Guinness's Macbeth, London stage. Early films: Ulysses, Oh! What a Lovely War, Young Winston, The Eagle Has Landed, Who Dares Wins. Dir. many stage plays.
THEATER: The Killing of Michael Malloy.
PICTURES: Hidden Agenda, Last of the Mohicans, Judge Dredd.
TELEVISION: In *USA* and *UK* incl.: Scobie (series), The Gambler, Allergy, Magnum P.I., Remington Steele, Escape to Victoria, Inside the Third Reich, Journal of Bridgitte Hitler, Tutti Frutti, Unreported Incident, Bookie, North & South Part II, 919 Fifth Ave., Moses (mini-series), Hillborough, David.

ROGERS, FRED
Television Host, Producer. b. Latrobe, PA, March 20, 1928. e. Rollins Coll., B.A., music composition, 1951; Pittsburgh Theol. Seminary, M. Div. 1962. 1951 served as asst. prod. of NBC-TV's The Voice of Firestone and NBC-TV Opera Theatre. Later promoted to network floor dir., supervising Your Lucky Strike Hit Parade, Kate Smith Hour, etc. 1953, joined WQED-TV in Pittsburgh, educational TV station, to handle programming. 1954 started Children's Corner series, writing, producing and performing; it ran 7 years. 1963 was ordained minister of Presbyterian Church, dedicated to working with children and families through media. Same year introduced Mister Rogers on Canadian Broadcasting Corp. of 15-min. daily program. Ran for one year—was similar in content to present half-hour program, Mister Rogers' Neighborhood. 1964 programs were incorporated into larger, half-hour format on ABC affiliate in Pittsburgh. 1966, 100 programs acquired by Eastern Educational Network, broadcast in Pittsburgh, and seen for first time in other cities (and on some cable services) with underwriting by Sears & Roebuck Foundation. Mister Rogers' Neighborhood in its present format began on Feb. 19, 1968 on NET (now PBS). Program now carried over 300 PBS stations. Author of numerous fiction books for children and non-fiction books for adults; and albums and videos released by Family Communication. Also prod. 20 part PBS series Old Friends New Friends, interview/documentary format for adults, 1978-9. Produced Fred Rogers' Heroes (adult special for PBS). Recipient of 2 Emmy Awards, 2 Peabody Awards and over 25 honorary degrees from colleges and universities.

ROGERS, IVAN
Actor. b. Indianapolis, IN, Sept. 20, 1954. e. Ball State Univ. on a music scholarship.
PICTURES: Tigershark (co-s.p. only), One Way Out (also prod., s.p.), Two Wrongs Make a Right (also s.p., prod.), Slow Burn, Ballbuster (also co-prod.), The Runner, Karate Commando: Jungle Wolf 3, Striking Point, Caged Women II (also co-prod., s.p., dir.), Laserhawk, Forgive Me Father (also prod., s.p., dir.).

ROGERS, KENNY
Singer, Actor, Songwriter. b. Crockett, TX, Aug. 21, 1938. Country and western singer. Member Bobby Doyle Trio, Christy Minstrels, 1966-67; The First Edition 1967-76. On screen in Six Pack (1982).
TELEVISION: *Series*: McShane (NBC Friday Night Mystery). *Movies*: The Dream Makers, Kenny Rogers as The Gambler, Coward of the County, Kenny Rogers as the Gambler: The Adventure Continues, Wild Horses; Kenny Rogers as The Gambler Part III: The Legend Continues, Christmas in America, The Gambler Returns: Luck of the Draw, Real West, Rio Diablo, MacShayne: The Final Roll of the Dice, Gambler IV: Playing for Keeps, Big Dreams & Broken Hearts: The Dottie West Story. *Specials*: Kenny, Dolly & Willie: Something Inside So Strong, and numerous others. *Guest*: Dr. Quinn, Medicine Woman.

ROGERS, LAWRENCE H., II
Executive, b. Trenton, NJ, Sept. 6, 1921. e. Princeton U. 1942, U.S. Army, 1942-1946; with WSAZ, Huntington, WV, as radio & tv, v.p. & gen. mgr., 1949-55; WSAZ, Inc., pres., 1955-59; Taft Broadcasting Co., v.p., 1959-63; Taft Broadcasting Co., pres., 1963-76; cert., Harvard Business Sch., 1963; vice chmn., Hanna-Barbera Prods., LA, and Cinemobile Systems, Hollywood. Director Cincinnati Financial Corporation, 1963-94. Chmn., Cincinnati Branch, Federal Reserve Bank of Cleveland, 1974-80. Pres., Omega communications, 1979-84; Director: Cine Artists International, Hollywood; Theater Development Fund, NY. Director of Cardinal Group of Mutual Funds, 1970-present. Author: Business of Broadcasting, 1964; Orlando Shoot-Out, 1990.

ROGERS, MIMI
Actress. b. Coral Gables, FL, Jan. 27, 1959.
PICTURES: Blue Skies Again (debut, 1983), Gung Ho, Street Smart, Someone to Watch Over Me, The Mighty Quinn, Hider in the House, Desperate Hours, The Doors, The Rapture, The Palermo Connection, The Player, White Sands, Dark Horse, Monkey Trouble, Far From Home: The Adventures of Yellow Dog, Bulletproof Heart, Reflections in the Dark, The Mirror Has Two Faces, Lost In Space, Austin Powers International Man of Mystery, Seven Girlfriends.

TELEVISION: *Series*: The Rousters, Paper Dolls. *Episodes*: Magnum, P.I., Hart to Hart, Quincy, M.E., Hill Street Blues, Tales From the Crypt, The X Files. *Movies*: Divorce Wars, Hear No Evil, You Ruined My Life, Fourth Story, Deadlock, Ladykiller, Bloodlines: Murder in the Family, A Kiss to Die For, Weapons of Mass Distraction, Full Body Massage, Tricks, The Devil's Arithmetic.

ROGERS, PETER
Executive. b. Rochester, Eng., Feb. 20, 1916. e. Kings Sch., Rochester. Journalist and in theatre and BBC; joined G. W. H. Productions 1941 as script writer; with Gainsborough Studios; asst. scenario ed. to Muriel Box; assoc. prod.; personal asst. to Sydney Box 1949.
PICTURES: Dear Murderer, Holiday Camp, When the Bough Breaks, Here Come the Huggetts, Huggetts Abroad, Vote for Huggett, It's Not Cricket, Marry Me, Don't Ever Leave Me, Appointment with Venus, The Clouded Yellow, The Dog and the Diamonds, Up to His Neck, You Know What Sailors Are, Cash on Delivery, To Dorothy A Son, Gay Dog, Circus Friends, Passionate Stranger, After the Ball, Time Lock, My Friend Charles, Chain of Events, Carry on Sergeant, Flying Scott, Cat Girl, Solitary Child, Carry On Teacher, Carry On Nurse, Carry On Constable, Please Turn Over, Watch Your Stern, The Tommy Steele Story, The Duke Wore Jeans, No Kidding, Carry On Regardless, Raising the Wind, Twice Around the Daffodils, Carry on Cruising, The Iron Maiden, Nurse on Wheels, Carry on Cabby, This Is My Street, Carry On Jack, Carry on Spying, Carry on Cleo, The Big Job, Carry on Cowboy, Carry on Screaming, Don't Lose Your Head, Follow that Camel, Carry on Doctor, Carry on Up the Khyber, Carry on Camping, Carry on Assault, Carry on Henry, Quest, Revenge, Carry on At Your Convenience, All Coppers Are..., Carry on Matron, Carry on Abroad, Bless This House, Carry on Girls, Carry on Dick, Carry on Behind, Carry on England, The Best of Carry On, Carry on Emmanuelle, Carry on Columbus.
TELEVISION: Ivanhoe (series), Carry on Laughing, Carry on Laughing, What a Carry On, Laugh With the Carry On's.

ROGERS, THOMAS C.
Executive. e. Columbia Law School, Wesleyan Univ. 1981-86, sr. counsel, U.S. House of Representatives Subcommittee on Telecommunications, Consumer Protection and Finance; Joined NBC in 1987 as v.p., policy and planning and business development. 1988 became pres. of NBC Cable and Business Development. 1992, also named exec. v.p. of NBC.

ROGERS, WAYNE
Actor. b. Birmingham, AL, April 7, 1933. e. Princeton U. After graduation entered the army for three yrs.; studied at Sanford's Meisner's Neighborhood Playhouse and with Martha Graham. Currently gen. partner of Balanced Value Fund, an investment firm; founder, mem on advisory bd., of Plaza Bank of Commerce. Chmn., Easter Seals. Member: Executive Committee of the Arthritis Foundation; Juvenile Diabetes Foundation; Trustees of the Webb School; Kenan Institute of Private Enterprise. Affiliate, School of Business Adm. of the U of NC. Spokeperson, J.B. Oxford & Co.
PICTURES: Odds Against Tomorrow (debut, 1959), The Glory Guys, Chamber of Horrors, Cool Hand Luke, WUSA, Pocket Money, Once in Paris, The Gig, The Killing Time, Ghosts of Mississippi.
TELEVISION: *Series*: Edge of Night, Stagecoach West, M*A*S*H, City of the Angels, House Calls, High Risk (host). *Movies*: Lamp Unto My Feet, Attack on Terror: The FBI Versus the Ku Klux Klan, Making Babies II, It Happened One Christmas, The Top of the Hill, Chiefs, He's Fired She's Hired, The Lady from Yesterday, American Harvest, Drop-Out Mother, One Terrific Guy, Bluegrass, Passion and Paradise, Miracle Landing, The Goodbye Bird. Guest: The Fugitive, The Invaders, Gunsmoke, The F.B.I., Gomer Pyle. *Mini-Series*: Chiefs. *Exec. prod.*: Perfect Witness, Age-Old Friends, The Charlie Rose Special, AMC Hollywood Report (also host), Money Plays.

ROHRBECK, JOHN H.
Executive. e. Univ. of WA. 1967, account exec. for NBC Spot Sales in San Francisco, then NY. 1969-78, with KNBC-TV in mngmt. and sales, became station manager in 1976. 1978-84, v.p. & gen. mngr. WRC-TV in Washington DC. Became pres. & gen. mngr. of KNBC-TV in 1984. Named pres. of NBC Television Stations, 1991. Also in charge of network's daytime programming 1992-95.

ROHMER, ERIC
Director. Writer. r.n. Jean Maurice Scherer. b. Nancy, France, April 4, 1920. Professor of literature. Film critic for La Gazette du Cinema and its successor Cahiers du Cinema which he edited, 1957-63. With Claude Chabrol wrote book on Alfred Hitchcock as a Catholic moralist, 1957. 1959 directorial debut, Le Signe du Lion. 1962 began a series of 6 Moral Tales; from 1980 with The Aviator's Wife began another series of 7 films called Comedies and Proverbs. Staged Catherine de Heilbronn in Nanterre, 1979.
PICTURES: *Short films*: Presentation ou Charlotte et Son Steack (1961), La Boulangere de Monceau, Veronique et Son Cancre, Nadja a Paris, Place de L'etoile, Une Etudiante d'aujourd'hui, Fermiere a Montfaucon. *Feature films* (dir. & s.p.): Le Signe du Lion (The Sign of Leo; debut, 1959), La Carriere de Suzanne, Six in Paris (episode), La Collectionneuse, My Night at Maude's, Claire's Knee, Chloe in the Afternoon, The Marquise of O, Perceval, The Aviator's Wife, Le Beau Mariage, Pauline at the Beach, Full Moon in Paris, Summer, Boyfriends and Girlfriends, Four Adventures of Reinette and Mirabelle (also prod.), A Tale of Springtime, A Tale of Winter, The Tree, The Mayor and the Mediatheque, Citizen Langlois (actor), Rendezvous in Paris, A Summer's Tale; An Autumn Tale.
TELEVISION: Carl Dreyer, Le Celluloid et le Marbre, Ville Nouvelle, Catherine de Heilbronn. Between 1964-69 directed series of documentaries for French TV: Les Cabinets et Physique du XVIII siecle, Les Metamorphoses du Paysage Industriel, Don Quichotte, Edgar Poe, Pascal, Louis Lumiere.

ROIZMAN, OWEN
Cinematographer. b. Brooklyn, NY, Sept. 22, 1936. e. Gettysburg Col.
PICTURES: The French Connection, The Gang That Couldn't Shoot Straight, Play It Again Sam, The Heartbreak Kid, The Exorcist, The Taking of Pelham 1-2-3, The Stepford Wives, Independence, Three Days of the Condor, The Return of the Man Called Horse, Network, Straight Time, Sgt. Pepper's Lonely Hearts Club Band, The Electric Horseman, The Black Marble, True Confessions, Absence of Malice, Taps, Tootsie, Vision Quest, I Love You to Death, Havana, The Addams Family, Grand Canyon, Wyatt Earp, French Kiss.

ROLLINS, JACK
Producer. b. 1914. Co-founder of talent management firm Rollins, Joffe, Mora and Brezner Inc. handling careers of Woody Allen, Nichols and May, Robin Williams, Robert Klein, David Letterman, Dick Cavett, Billy Crystal.
PICTURES: *Co-prod./exec. prod.* with Charles Joffe: Take the Money and Run, Bananas, Everything You Always Wanted to Know About Sex, Sleeper, Love and Death, The Front, Annie Hall (Acad. Award for Best Picture, 1977), Interiors, Manhattan, Stardust Memories, Zelig, Broadway Danny Rose (also actor), The Purple Rose of Cairo, Hannah and Her Sisters, Radio Days, September, Another Woman, New York Stories (Oedipus Wrecks), Crimes and Misdemeanors, Alice, Shadows and Fog, Husbands and Wives, Manhattan Murder Mystery, Bullets Over Broadway, Mighty Aphrodite, Everyone Says I Love You, Deconstructing Harry, Celebrity, Sweet and Lowdown.
TELEVISION: *Prod./exec. prod.*: The Dick Cavett Show, Late Night With David Letterman.

ROMAN, LAWRENCE
Writer. b. Jersey City, NJ, May 30, 1921. e. UCLA, 1943.
THEATER: *Author*: Under the Yum Yum Tree, P.S. I Love You, Alone Together, Buying Out, Crystal, Crystal Chandelier (prod. in Stockbridge, Mass), Coulda Woulda Shoulda (premiered in Berlin, Germany), Moving Mountains (premiered in Berlin as Grapes and Raisins).
PICTURES: Drums Across the River, Vice Squad, Naked Alibi, One Desire, Man from Bitter Ridge, Kiss Before Dying, Slaughter on Tenth Avenue, Under the Yum Yum Tree, The Swinger, Paper Lion, Red Sun, A Warm December, McQ.
TELEVISION: *Movies*: Anatomy of an Illness, Badge of the Assassin, Three Wishes for Jamie, Final Verdict, The Ernest Green Story (Peabody Award).

ROMERO, GEORGE A.
Director, Writer, Editor. b. New York, NY, 1940. e. Carnegie-Mellon Univ.
PICTURES: *Dir./Writer/Cameraman*: Night of the Living Dead (debut, 1968), There's Always Vanilla, The Crazies, Jack's Wife (also edit.). *Director-Writer*: Martin (also edit., actor), Dawn of the Dead (dir. only), Knightriders, Creepshow (dir., co-edit. only), Day of the Dead (also edit.), Monkey Shines, Night of the Living Dead (s.p., co-exec. prod. only), Two Evil Eyes, The Dark Half (also exec. prod.), Bruiser.
TELEVISION: Tales from the Dark Side (exec. prod., writer).

RONA, JEFF
Composer. b. March 3, 1957.
PICTURES: *Composer*: Lipstick Camera, White Squall, Do Me a Favor. *Additional Music*: Toys, The Net, Assassins, The Fan, Black Cat Run.
TELEVISION: *Movies*: Toys, Death in Small Doses. *Series*: Homicide: Life on the Street, Chicago Hope, Profiler, High Incident, Gun, Teen Angel, Sleepwalkers.

ROOKER, MICHAEL
Actor. b. Jasper, AL, 1955. e. Goodman School of Drama. Studied Japanese martial art of Aikido prior to establishing himself in Chicago theatre, where he appeared in Union Boys, The Crack Walker and Moon Children.

PICTURES: Streets of Fire (debut, 1984), Light of Day, Rent-a-Cop, Eight Men Out, Mississippi Burning, Sea of Love, Music Box, Henry: Portrait of a Serial Killer, Days of Thunder, JFK, The Dark Half, Cliffhanger, Tombstone, The Hard Truth, Mallrats, The Trigger Effect, Rosewood, Liar, The Replacement Killers, Renegade Force, Brown's Requiem, The Bone Collector, A Table for One.
TELEVISION: *Movies*: Afterburn, Johnny & Clyde.

ROONEY, ANDREW A
Writer, Producer. b. Albany, NY, Jan. 14, 1919. e. Colgate U. Started career as writer at MGM 1946-7, then for Arthur Godfrey, Garry Moore; wrote and produced documentaries, including Black History: Lost Stolen or Strayed (Emmy Award, 1969), An Essay on War, An Essay on Bridges, In Praise of New York City, Mr. Rooney Goes to Washington, etc. Commentator, 60 Minutes (CBS), 1978-present. Newspaper columnist for Tribune Syndicate, 1979-present.
AUTHOR: Air Gunner, The Story of the Stars and Stripes, Conqueror's Peace, A Few Minutes With Andy Rooney, And More Any Rooney, Pieces of My Mind, Sweet and Sour, The Fortunes of War, Not That You Asked, Word for Word, My War.

ROONEY, MICKEY
Actor. r.n. Joe Yule, Jr. b. Brooklyn, NY, Sept. 23, 1920. Son of Joe Yule & Nell Carter, vaudeville performers. U.S. Army, WWII. In vaudeville as child with parents and others before m.p. debut and after; from age of 5 to 12 (1926-33) created screen version of Fontaine Fox newspaper comic character Mickey McGuire in series of short subjects (also billed as Mickey McGuire). Adopted name of Mickey Rooney, returned to vaudeville, then resumed screen career in features. Special Academy Award 1940 for Andy Hardy characterization; voted among first ten Money-Making Stars in M.P. Herald-Fame Poll: 1938-43. Autobiographies: i.e. (1965), Life is Too Short (1991). Novel: The Search for Sonny Skies (1994). Received honorary Academy Award, 1983.
THEATER: *B'way*: Sugar Babies, The Will Rogers Follies. *Regional*: W.C., Lend Me a Tenor.
PICTURES: Orchids and Ermine (feature debut, 1927), Emma, The Beast of the City, Sin's Pay Day, High Speed, Officer Thirteen, Fast Companions, My Pal the King, The Big Cage, The Life of Jimmy Dolan, The Big Chance, Broadway to Hollywood, The World Changes, The Chief, Beloved, I Like It That Way, Love Birds, Half a Sinner, The Lost Jungle, Manhattan Melodrama, Upperworld, Hide-Out, Chained, Blind Date, Death on the Diamond, The County Chairman, Reckless, The Healer, A Midsummer Night's Dream, Ah Wilderness, Riff-Raff, Little Lord Fauntleroy, The Devil is a Sissy, Down the Stretch, Captains Courageous, Slave Ship, A Family Affair, Hoosier Schoolboy, Live Love and Learn, Thoroughbreds Don't Cry, You're Only Young Once, Love is a Headache, Judge Hardy's Children, Hold That Kiss, Lord Jeff, Love Finds Andy Hardy, Boys Town, Stablemates, Out West With the Hardys, The Adventures of Huckleberry Finn, The Hardys Ride High,
Andy Hardy Gets Spring Fever, Babes in Arms (Acad. Award nom.), Judge Hardy and Son, Young Tom Edison, Andy Hardy Meets Debutante, Strike Up the Band, Andy Hardy's Private Secretary, Men of Boy's Town, Life Begins for Andy Hardy, Babes on Broadway, The Courtship of Andy Hardy, A Yank at Eton, Andy Hardy's Double Life, The Human Comedy (Acad. Award nom.), Girl Crazy, Thousands Cheer, Andy Hardy's Blonde Trouble, National Velvet, Love Laughs at Andy Hardy, Killer McCoy, Summer Holiday, Words and Music, The Big Wheel, Quicksand, He's a Cockeyed Wonder, The Fireball, My Outlaw Brother, The Strip, Sound Off, All Ashore, Off Limits, A Slight Case of Larceny, Drive a Crooked Road, The Atomic Kid (also prod.), The Bridges at Toko-Ri, The Twinkle in God's Eye, Francis in the Haunted House, The Bold and the Brave (Acad. Award nom.), Magnificent Roughnecks, Operation Mad Ball, Baby Face Nelson, Andy Hardy Comes Home, A Nice Little Bank That Should Be Robbed, The Last Mile, The Big Operator, Platinum High School, The Private Lives of Adam and Eve (also co-dir.), Breakfast at Tiffany's, King of the Roaring Twenties, Requiem for a Heavyweight, Everything's Ducky, It's a Mad Mad Mad Mad World, Secret Invasion, 24 Hours to Kill, The Devil in Love, Ambush Bay, How to Stuff a Wild Bikini, The Extraordinary Seaman, Skidoo, The Comic, 80 Steps to Jonah, The Cockeyed Cowboys of Calico County, Hollywood Blue, B.J. Lang Presents (The Manipulator), Richard, Pulp, The Godmothers (also s.p., music), Ace of Hearts, Thunder County, That's Entertainment, Journey Back to Oz (voice), From Hong Kong With Love, Rachel's Man, Find the Lady, The Domino Principle, Pete's Dragon, The Magic of Lassie, The Black Stallion (Acad. Award nom.), Arabian Adventure, The Fox and the Hound (voice), The Emperor of Peru, The Black Stallion Returns, The Care Bears Movie (voice), Lightning the White Stallion, Erik the Viking, My Heroes Have Always Been Cowboys, Sweet Justice, The Legend of Wolf Mountain, Little Nemo (voice), Silent Night Deadly Night 5: The Toymaker, The Milky Life, Revenge of the Red Baron, That's Entertainment III, Animals.

TELEVISION: *Series*: Hey Mickey, One of the Boys, The Black Stallion. *Many specials including*: Playhouse 90, Pinocchio, Eddie, Somebody's Waiting, The Dick Powell Theater. *Movies*: Evil Roy Slade, My Kidnapper My Love, Leave 'Em Laughing, Bill (Emmy Award, 1982), Senior Trip, Bill: On His Own, It Came Upon the Midnight Clear, Bluegrass, Home for Christmas, The Gambler Returns: Luck of the Draw. *Many guest appearances including*: The Golden Girls, The Judy Garland Show, Naked City, Wagon Train, Twilight Zone, The Lucy Show, Hollywood Squares, Night Gallery, The Love Boat.

ROONEY, PAT E.
Producer. e. Santa Monica College, Marquette U., Denver U., UCLA. Was Captain in U.S. Army. Entertainer Far East Command Forces, Korean War. In 1960, joined CBS Films, producing TV series and pilot films. 1962 formed Pat Rooney Prods. with Del E. Webb and Jerry Buss. Has worked as independent producer for MGM, Paramount, Universal, 20th Century Fox, Warber Bros, Goldwyn. 1993 partnered with John Veitch (former pres. of Columbia Pictures).
PICTURES: Dime With A Halo, Danger Pass, Caged, Law of the Lawless, Requiem for a Gunfighter, Bounty Killer, Young Once, Hell's Angels, Fools, Christmas Couple, Black Eye, Deadman's Curve, Deadly Attack, Secret Ceremony, Kings Row, Devil Planes, Gentlemen of the Night, Kapo Women, Lillies of the Field, Light Fingers, Poison Ivy, Nylon Noose, A Love Story, Gattling Gun.

ROOS, FRED
Producer. b. Santa Monica, CA, May 22, 1934. e. UCLA, B.A. Directed documentary films for Armed Forces Radio and Television Network. Worked briefly as agent for MCA and story editor for Robert Lippert Productions. Worked as casting dir. in 1960s and served as casting dir. on The Godfather, beginning longtime association with filmmakers Francis Coppola and George Lucas.
PICTURES: The Conversation, The Godfather Part II, Apocalypse Now, The Black Stallion, The Escape Artist (exec. prod.), The Black Stallion Returns, Hammett, One From the Heart, The Outsiders, Rumble Fish, The Cotton Club, One Magic Christmas, Seven Minutes in Heaven, Peggy Sue Got Married (special consultant), Barfly, Gardens of Stone (co-exec. prod.), Tucker: The Man and His Dream, New York Stories (Life Without Zoe), Wait Until Spring Bandini, The Godfather Part III, Hearts of Darkness: A Filmmaker's Apocalypse (exec. prod.), The Secret Garden, Radioland Murders, Jack (spec. consultant), The Rainmaker (exec. consultant).
TELEVISION: *Series*: The Outsiders (exec. prod.). *Movie*: Montana.

ROSE, ALEX
Producer. r.n. Alexandra Rose. b. Jan. 20, 1946. e. U. of WI, BS. Started in m.p. distribution with Medford Films. Later became asst. sls. mgr. for New World Pictures.
PICTURES: *Co-prod.*: Drive-In, I Wanna Hold Your Hand, Big Wednesday, Norma Rae, Nothing in Common (solo prod.), Overboard (co-prod.), Quigley Down Under, Frankie and Johnny.
TELEVISION: Nothing in Common (co-exec. prod. with Garry Marshall), *Pilots*: Norma Rae, Just Us Kids.

ROSE, CHARLIE
Talk Show Host. b. Henderson, NC, Jan. 5, 1942. e. Duke Univ. (history, law). Was exec. prod. for Bill Moyers' Journal, 1975.
TELEVISION: *Series (host/anchor):* A.M. Chicago, The Charlie Rose Show (NBC, 1979, 1981), CBS News Nightwatch, E.D.J. Entertainment Daily Journal (Personalities), Charlie Rose (synd; also exec. prod., editor). *Specials:* Public Debate With Charlie Rose, In Concert at the United Nations (host).

ROSE, REGINALD
Writer, b. New York, NY, Dec. 10, 1920. e. City Coll. of New York. Worked as clerk, publicist, Warner Bros.; adv. acct. exec., copy chief; U.S. Air Force, WWII; first TV play, Bus to Nowhere, 1951; since then numerous TV plays, Studio One, Playhouse 90. Creator of The Defenders, other programs.
PICTURES: Crime in the Streets, 12 Angry Men, Dino, Man of the West, The Man in the Net, Baxter, Somebody Killed Her Husband, The Wild Geese, The Sea Wolves, Whose Life Is It Anyway?, Wild Geese II, The Final Option.
TELEVISION: Dear Friends, Thunder on Sycamore Street, Tragedy in a Temporary Town, My Two Loves, The Rules of Marriage, Studs Lonigan, Escape from Sobibor.

ROSE, STEPHEN
Executive. Entered m.p. industry in 1964 with Columbia Pictures; named adv. dir. 1970 joined Cinema V Distributing, Inc. as dir. of adv.; left in 1971 to take post at Cinemation Industries, where was named v.p. and bd. member. 1975 joined Paramount Pictures as dir. of adv.; promoted to v.p./adv. 1979 formed Barrich Prods. with Gordon Weaver. 1982, rejoined Paramount as v.p., mktg; 1983, named v.p. of mktg. for Paramount; sr. v.p., mktg., 1983. Resigned in 1984 to form Barrich Marketing with Gordon Weaver.

ROSEANNE
Actress. b. Salt Lake City, UT, Nov. 3, 1952. Started performing in bars; prod. showcase for women performers, Take Back the Mike at U. of Boulder. 1983 won Denver Laff-Off. Moved to Los Angeles where performed at The Comedy Store, and showcased on TV special Funny and The Tonight Show. Has previously performed under the names Roseanne Barr, Roseanne Arnold. *Autobiographies:* My Life as a Woman (1989), My Lives (1994).
PICTURES: She-Devil (debut, 1989), Look Who's Talking Too (voice), Freddy's Dead, Even Cowgirls Get the Blues, Blue in the Face, Meet Wally Sparks, Get Bruce.
TELEVISION: *Series*: Roseanne (also co-exec. prod.; Peabody & Golden Globe Awards for Best Series; Emmy Award for Best Actress, 1993), The Jackie Thomas Show (co-exec. prod, guest), Tom (co-exec. prod.), The Roseanne Show (also exec. prod.). *Specials*: Fast Copy, Rodney Dangerfield—It's Not Easy Bein' Me, Live From Minneapolis: Roseanne, Roseanne Arnold: Live From Trump Castle. *Movies*: Backfield in Motion, The Woman Who Loved Elvis (also co-exec. prod.), I Am Your Child.

ROSEN, ROBERT L.
Producer. b. Palm Springs, CA, Jan. 7, 1937. e. U. of Southern Calif.
PICTURES: *Exec. prod.:* French Connection II, Black Sunday, Prophecy, Going Ape, The Challenge, Courage (also dir.), Porky's Revenge, World Gone Wild, Dead-Bang (exec. prod.), Year of the Gun, Spy Hard, Mr. Magoo, Wrongfully Accused. *Exec. in chg. of prod.:* Little Big Man, Le Mans, The Reivers, Rio Lobo, Big Jake, Scrooge, Fourth War (Line Producer).
TELEVISION: Gilligan's Island, Hawaii Five-O, Have Gun Will Travel.

ROSENBERG, FRANK P.
Producer, Writer. b. New York, NY, Nov. 22, 1913. e. Columbia U., NYU. Joined Columbia 1929; writer m.p. novelizations & radio dramatizations; 1933, conceived and wrote script for first-ever ship-to-shore CBS network broadcast for Lady for a Day; exploit, mgr., 1941; apptd. national dir. adv., publicity, exploitation, Columbia Pictures, 1944. Pub. dir. M.P. Victory Loan, 1945; dir. pub. Columbia Pictures Studios, Hollywood, 1946. Resigned 1947 to enter production.
PICTURES: Man-Eater of Kumaon, Where the Sidewalk Ends, The Secret of Convict Lake, Return of the Texan, The Farmer Takes a Wife, King of the Khyber Rifles, Illegal, Miracle in the Rain, The Girl He Left Behind, One-Eyed Jacks, Critic's Choice, Madigan, The Steagle, The Reincarnation of Peter Proud, Gray Lady Down.
TELEVISION: Exec. prod. and prod. for Schlitz Playhouse programs during 1957-58; prod., The Troubleshooters; exec. prod., Arrest and Trial, 1963-64; exec. prod. Kraft Suspense Theatre, 1964-65; v.p. MCA Universal 1964-69; co-exec. prod., CBS tv movie Family of Strangers, 1993.

ROSENBERG, GRANT E.
Executive. b. San Francisco, CA, 1952. e. Univ. of Cal. at Davis. Started career in research dept., NBC; 1977, joined Paramount in research and later in development; 1984, v.p., dramatic dev.; then sr. v.p., dev., for TV group, Paramount. 1985, named sr. v.p., network TV for Walt Disney Pictures; 1988, named pres., Lee Rich Productions, TV div., and exec. prod. of Molloy TV series. 1990, writer, prod., Paramount TV. Series: MacGyver (writer), Star Trek: The Next Generation (writer), Time Trax (exec. prod., creator), Lois & Clark (writer, prod.). Writer, prod. for Warner Bros. TV.

ROSENBERG, RICHARD K.
Executive, Attorney. b. Paterson, NJ, Apr. 4, 1942. e. Indiana Univ. Corporation & intl. entertainment attorney for major corps. and celebrities. Formed RKR Entertainment Group in 1977 with subsidiaries RKR Releasing, RKR Artists and RKR Productions. Subsequently consolidated into RKR Pictures Inc. Author: Negotiating Motion Picture Contracts. Films include Alice Sweet Alice (Holy Terror), Hell's Angels Forever, Mother Lode, Best Revenge, The Wild Duck, Primary Motive, Fatal Past, Dutchman's Creek. V.p., Cinetel Films, 1991-93. Exec. v.p. and bd. mem., Jones Entertainment Group Ltd., 1995.

ROSENBERG, RICK
Producer. b. Los Angeles, CA. e. Los Angeles City Coll., UCLA. Started career in mail room of Columbia Pictures, then asst. to prod. Jerry Bresler on Major Dundee and Love Has Many Faces. Asst. to Col. v.p., Arthur Kramer. Was assoc. prod. on The Reivers and in 1970 prod. first feature, Adam at Six A.M., with Bob Christiansen, with whom co-prod. all credits listed below.
PICTURES: Adam at Six A.M., Hide in Plain Sight.
TELEVISION: Suddenly Single, The Glass House, A Brand New Life, The Man Who Could Talk to Kids, The Autobiography of Miss Jane Pittman, I Love You... Goodbye, Queen of the Stardust Ballroom, Born Innocent, A Death in Canaan, Strangers, Robert Kennedy and His Times, Kids Don't Tell, As Summers Die, Gore Vidal's Lincoln, Red Earth White Earth, Heist, A House of Secrets and Lies, The Last Hit, Heart of Darkness, Tad, Kingfish: A Story of Huey P. Long, Redwood Curtain.

ROSENBERG, STUART
Director, Producer. b. New York, NY, Aug. 11, 1927. e. NYU.
PICTURES: Murder, Inc. (co-dir.; debut, 1960), Question 7, Cool Hand Luke, The April Fools, Move (also co-exec. prod.), WUSA (also co-exec. prod.), Pocket Money, The Laughing Policeman (also prod.), The Drowning Pool, Voyage of the Damned, The Amityville Horror, Love and Bullets, Brubaker, The Pope of Greenwich Village, Let's Get Harry (under pseudonym Allan Smithee), My Heroes Have Always Been Cowboys.
TELEVISION: Numerous episodes of such series as The Untouchables, Naked City, The Defenders (Emmy Award, 1963), Espionage, Chrysler Theatre, Twilight Zone, Alfred Hitchcock Theater.

ROSENFELT, FRANK E.
Executive. b. Peabody, MA, Nov. 15, 1921. e. Cornell U., B.S.; Cornell Law Sch., L.L.B. Served as atty. for RKO Radio Pictures, before joining MGM in 1955 as member of legal dept. Appt. secty. in 1966. Named v.p., gen. counsel in 1969 and pres. in 1973. 1974-81, CEO, bd. chmn. & CEO, MGM; now vice chmn., MGM/UA Communications Co. Member: Bd. of Governors, Academy of M.P. Arts & Sciences for 9 years. Retired from MGM/UA in Aug. 1990, now consultant to MGM-Pathe Commun. Co.

ROSENFELT, SCOTT
Producer, Director. b. Easton, PA, Dec. 20, 1955. e. NYU.
PICTURES: *Producer:* Teen Wolf, Extremities, Russkies, Mystic Pizza, Big Man on Campus (co-prod.), Home Alone, Family Prayers (dir.), Smoke Signals, Getting to Know You (exec.), The Book of Stars.
TELEVISION: *Movie*: T-Bone N Weasel.

ROSENFIELD, JR., JONAS
Executive. b. Dallas, TX, June 29, 1915. e. U. of Miami, A.B. In U.S. Navy, WWII. Warner Bros. advertising copy dept., 1936-40; adv. mgr. Walt Disney, 1941; a founder & pres. N.Y. Screen Publicists Guild; adv. mngr. & dir., 20th Cent.-Fox, 1941-1950; v.p. Italian Films Export, 1950-55; v.p. in chg. adv. pub. expl. Columbia Pictures, 1955-63; v.p. worldwide adv., publ. and promotion, 20th Century-Fox, 1963-77; film mktg. consultant, 1977-78; lecturer in mktg., USC, 1978-79; v.p. in chg. of worldwide mktg., Melvin Simon Prods., 1979-1981; Filmways Pictures as exec. v.p., worldwide adv./pub., promo. 1982; lecturer adjunct, USC Sch. of Cinema & TV, 1982-84; pres. AFMA, 1983 to 1999.
(d. May 31, 2000)

ROSENMAN, HOWARD
Producer. b. Brooklyn, NY, Feb. 1, 1945. e. Brooklyn Col. Asst. to Sir Michael Benthall on B'way show; prod., Benton & Bowles Agency; ABC-TV; RSO Prods. Co-pres., Sandollar Prods.; currently pres. Brillstein-Grey Motion Pictures.
PICTURES: Sparkle, The Main Event, Resurrection, Lost Angels, Gross Anatomy, True Identity, Father of the Bride, Shining Through, Straight Talk, A Stranger Among Us, Buffy the Vampire Slayer, The Celluloid Closet.
TELEVISION: *Movies*: Isn't It Shocking? Altogether Now, Death Scream, Virginia Hill, Killer Bees. *Specials*: Common Threads: Stories from the Quilt (co-exec. prod.), Tidy Endings.

ROSENMAN, LEONARD
Composer. b. New York, NY, Sept. 7, 1924.
PICTURES: East of Eden, Cobweb, Rebel Without a Cause, Edge of the City, The Savage Eye, The Chapman Report, Fantastic Voyage, Hellfighters, Beneath the Planet of the Apes, Barry Lyndon (Academy Award, 1975), Birch Interval, Race With the Devil, Bound For Glory (Academy Award, 1976), A Man Called Horse, The Car, September 30, 1955, The Enemy of the People, The Lord of the Rings, Promises in the Dark, Prophecy, Hide in Plain Sight, The Jazz Singer, Making Love, Miss Lonely Hearts, Cross Creek, Heart of the Stag, Star Trek IV: The Voyage Home, Robocop 2, Ambition, The Color of Evening, Mrs. Munck, Levitation.
TELEVISION: *Movies/Mini-Series*: Sybil (Emmy Award), Friendly Fire (Emmy Award), City in Fear, Murder in Texas, Vanished, The Wall, Miss Lonelyhearts, Celebrity, The Return of Marcus Welby MD, Heartsounds, First Steps, Promised a Miracle, Keeper of the City, The Face on the Milk Carton.

ROSENSTEIN, GERTRUDE
Director. b. New York, NY. e. Barnard Coll., B.A., Neighborhood Playhouse. Exec. asst. to George Balanchine & Lincoln Kirstein, N.Y.C. Ballet. Assoc. with Gian Carlo Menotti, Festival of Two Worlds, Spoleto, Italy. Assoc. dir., NBC Opera Theatre, Emmy Awards, Kennedy Memorial Mass. TV staff dir., NBC. Now free-lance director, news programs, election coverages, music and dance programs, commercials. Governor, NY Television Academy. Member, Emmy Awards Committee.

ROSENTHAL, BUD
Executive. b. Brooklyn, NY, Mar. 21, 1934. e. Brooklyn Coll., B.A., 1954, NYU. US Army, 1954-56; college correspondent, NY Times. Entered m.p. ind. as assoc. editor, Independent Film Journal, 1957-59. Publicist, Columbia Pictures, 1959-61.Natl. publ mgr.,

Columbia Pictures, 1962-67. Publ. dir. for Anderson Tapes, Such Good Friends, The Blue Bird; Story edit. and casting dir., Otto Preminger's Sigma Productions, 1972-75. Assoc. prod., Broadway play, Full Circle. Warner Bros. worldwide mtg. coordinator, Superman, Superman II, Superman III, Batman, Space Jam. Project coordinator, Time Warner Earth Day Special, Warner Bros. Studio Rededication, Celebration of Tradition. International mktg. consultant, 1976-present.
PICTURES: Something for Everyone (asst. prod.), Rosebud (assoc. prod.). *Int'l mktg. co-ord. on films*: Ghostbusters, Labyrinth, Tune in Tomorrow, Boyz 'N the Hood, Addams Family, Bugsy, Batman Returns, A Few Good Men, Last Action Hero, Jumanji, Star Trek: Insurrection, The Rugrats Movie.

ROSENTHAL, JANE
Executive. b. Denver, CO. e. NYU. 1976-84, dir. of film for TV at CBS; 1984-87, v.p. prod. Disney; 1987-88, v.p. of TV & Mini-Series, Warners TV; 1988-93, co-founder, Tribeca Prods., Tribeca Film Center; 1993-present, pres. of Tribeca Prods.; 1992-93, exec. prod. of series Tribeca. Producer of films Thunderheart, Faithful, Night and the City, Bronx Tale, Marvin's Room, Wag the Dog, Analyze This, Entropy, Flawless, Rocky and Bullwinkle.

ROSENTHAL, RICK
Director. b. New York, NY, June 15, 1949. e. Harvard, B.A. cum laude, 1971. Launched career as filmmaker-in-residence with New Hampshire TV Network. Moved to Los Angeles to study at American Film Institute where filmed Moonface, 1973.
PICTURES: Halloween II (debut, 1981), Bad Boys, American Dreamer, Russkies, Distant Thunder.
TELEVISION: *Movies*: Fire on the Mountain, Code of Vengeance, Secrets of Midland Heights, Nasty Boys, Devlin, Birds II, The Land's End. *Series*: Life Goes On, Witches of Eastwick, The Practice, Feds, Early Edition, Dellaventura.

ROSENZWEIG, BARNEY
Producer. b. Los Angeles, CA, Dec. 23, 1937. e. USC, 1959. m. actress Sharon Gless.
PICTURES: Morituri (assoc. prod.), Do Not Disturb (assoc. prod.), Caprice (assoc. prod.), Who Fears the Devil (prod.).
TELEVISION: *Prod.*: Daniel Boone (series), Men of the Dragon, One of My Wives Is Missing, Charlie's Angels (series), Angel on My Shoulder, American Dream (pilot), John Steinbeck's East of Eden (mini-series; Golden Globe Award). *Exec. prod.*: Modesty Blasie (pilot), This Girl for Hire (movie), Cagney and Lacey (series; 2 Emmy Awards: 1985, 1986), The Trials of Rosie O'Neill (series), Christy (movie, series), Cagney & Lacey: The Return (movie), Cagney & Lacey: Together Again (movie), Cagney & Lacey: The View Through the Glass Ceiling (movie), Cagney & Lacey: True Convictions (movie).

ROSS, DIANA
Singer, Actress. b. Detroit, MI, Mar. 26, 1944. Formed musical group at age 14 with two friends, Mary Wilson and Florence Ballard. In 1960 they auditioned for Berry Gordy, head of Motown Record Corp. and were hired to sing backgrounds on records for Motown acts. After completing high school, the trio was named the Supremes and went on tour with Motor Town Revue. Over period of 10 yrs. Supremes had 15 consecutive hit records and once had five consecutive records in the number one spot on charts. In 1969 Diana Ross went on her own, appearing on TV and in nightclubs. Memoirs: Secrets of a Sparrow (1993).
PICTURES: Lady Sings the Blues (debut as actress, 1972; Acad. Award nom.), Mahogany, The Wiz.
TELEVISION: *Movie*: Out of Darkness (also co-exec. prod.). *Specials*: Diana! (also exec. prod. & writer), Motown 25: Yesterday Today Forever, Motown Returns to the Apollo, Diana's World Tour.

ROSS, HERBERT
Director. b. New York, NY, May 13, 1927. m. Lee Radziwill. e. studied dance with Doris Humphrey, Helene Platova, Caird Leslie. Trained for stage with Herbert Berghof, 1946-50. As B'way dancer in Laffing Room Only, Beggars Holiday, Bloomer Girl, Look Ma I'm Dancing, Inside U.S.A., and with the American Ballet Theatre. Resident choreographer 1958-59 ABT for Caprichos, Concerto in D, The Maids, Tristan, Thief Who Loved a Ghost. Ent. m.p. ind. as choreographer for Carmen Jones, The Young Ones, Summer Holiday (also dir. musical sequences), Inside Daisy Clover, Dr. Doolittle, Funny Girl (also dir. musical numbers). Exec. prod. on film Soapdish.
THEATER/OPERA: *B'way Choreographer-Director*: A Tree Grows in Brooklyn, The Gay Life, I Can Get It For You Wholesale, Tovarich, Anyone Can Whistle, Do I Hear a Waltz, On a Clear Day You Can See Forever, The Apple Tree, Finian's Rainbow, Wonderful Town. *Dir.*: Chapter Two, I Ought To Be in Pictures, Follies in Concert, Anyone Can Whistle (fundraiser for GMHC; Grammy nom.), La Bohème (L.A. & Dallas).
PICTURES: Goodbye Mr. Chips (debut, 1969), The Owl and the Pussycat, T.R. Baskin, Play It Again Sam, The Last of Sheila (also prod.), Funny Lady, The Sunshine Boys, The Seven Percent Solution (also prod.), The Turning Point (also prod.), The Goodbye Girl, California Suite, Nijinsky (also prod.), Pennies from Heaven (also prod.), I Ought to Be in Pictures (also prod.), Max Dugan Returns (also prod.), Footloose, Protocol (also prod.), The Secret of My Success (also prod.), Dancers (also prod.), Steel Magnolias, My Blue Heaven (also prod.), True Colors (also prod.), Undercover Blues (also exec. prod.), Boys on the Side (also prod.).
TELEVISION: *Choreographer: Series*: Milton Berle Show (1952-57), Martha Raye Show, Bell Telephone Hour (also prod., dir.). *Specials*: Wonderful Town (also dir.), Meet Me in St. Louis, Jerome Kern Special, Bea Lillie and Cyril Ritchard Show (dir.), The Fantastiks, The Fred Astaire Special (1968, dir.).

ROSS, KATHARINE
Actress. b. Los Angeles, CA, Jan. 29, 1943. m. actor Sam Elliott. e. Santa Rosa Coll. Joined the San Francisco Workshop, appeared in The Devil's Disciple, The Balcony. TV debut, 1962 in Sam Benedict segment.
PICTURES: Shenandoah (debut, 1965), Mister Buddwing, The Singing Nun, Games, The Graduate (Golden Globe Award, Acad. Award nom.), Hellfighters, Butch Cassidy and the Sundance Kid, Tell Them Willie Boy is Here, Fools, Get to Know Your Rabbit, They Only Kill Their Masters, The Stepford Wives, Voyage of the Damned, The Betsy, The Swarm, The Legacy, The Final Countdown, Wrong Is Right, Daddy's Deadly Darling, The Red-Headed Stranger.
TELEVISION: *Movies*: The Longest Hundred Miles, Wanted: The Sundance Woman, Murder by Natural Causes, Rodeo Girl, Murder in Texas, Marian Rose White, Shadow Riders, Travis McGee, Secrets of a Mother and Daughter, Conagher (also co-script). *Guest*: Ben Casey, The Bob Hope-Chrysler Theatre, The Virginian, Wagon Train, Kraft Mystery Theatre, The Lieutenant, The Road West. *Series*: The Colbys.

ROSS, KENNETH
Writer. b. London, Sept. 16, 1941. Entered m.p. industry 1970.
THEATER: The Raft, Under The Skin, Mr. Kilt & The Great I Am.
PICTURES: Brother Sun Sister Moon, Slag, The Reckless Years (also orig. story), Abelard & Heloise, The Day of the Jackal (So. Cal. M.P. Council Award; nom. for Writers' Guild, SFTA, and Golden Globes), The Devil's Lieutenant, The Odessa File (nom. for Writers' Guild Award), Quest (also orig. story), Black Sunday (Edgar Allen Poe Award, Mystery Writers of America, 1977), The Fourth War, Epiphany (also orig. story).
TELEVISION: The Roundelay, The Messenger.

ROSSELLINI, ISABELLA
Actress. b. Rome, Italy, June 18, 1952. Daughter of actress Ingrid Bergman and director Roberto Rossellini. Came to America in 1972. Worked as translator for Italian News Bureau. Taught Italian at New Sch. for Social Research. Worked 3 years on second unit assignments for journalist Gianni Mina and as NY corresp. for Ital. TV series, The Other Sunday. Model for Vogue, Harper's Bazaar, Italian Elle, Lancome Cosmetics.
PICTURES: A Matter of Time (debut 1976; with her mother), The Meadow, Il Pap'Occhio, White Nights, Blue Velvet, Tough Guys Don't Dance, Siesta, Red Riding Hood, Zelly and Me, Cousins, Les Dames Galantes, The Siege of Venice, Wild at Heart, Death Becomes Her, The Pickle, Fearless, Wyatt Earp, Immortal Beloved, The Innocent, Big Night, Left Luggage, The Imposters.
TELEVISION: *Movies*: The Last Elephant, Lies of the Twins, The Crime of the Century, The Odyssey, Merlin. *Guest*: The Tracey Ullman Show, Tales From the Crypt (You Murderer), Friends, The Simpsons (voice). *Specials*: The Gift, Fallen Angels (The Frightening Frammis).

ROSSO, LEWIS, T.
Executive. b. Hoboken, NJ, Feb. 3, 1909. Ent. m.p. ind. 1930; prod. & mgt. for Consolidated Film Ind., 1930-44; Republic producer, 1944-50; prod. mgr., 1950-55; asst. sec'y & asst. treas., 1959; exec. asst. to exec. prod. mgr., 20th Century-Fox Films, 1960; plant mgr., Samuel Goldwyn Studios, 1961-71; exec. admin. asst. plant mgr., The Burbank Studios, 1972-88.

ROSSOVICH, RICK
Actor. b. Palo Alto, CA, August 28, 1957. e. Calif. St. Univ. Sacramento (art history). Studied acting with coach Vincent Chase.
PICTURES: The Lords of Discipline (debut, 1983), Losin' It, Streets of Fire, The Terminator, Fast Forward, Warning Sign, Top Gun, Let's Get Harry, The Morning After, Roxanne, Paint It Black, The Witching Hour, Spellbinder, Navy SEALS, Cognac, Tropical Heat, New Crime City, Cover Me, Black Scorpion II, Truth or Consequences N.M., Telling You, Cross Country.
TELEVISION: *Series*: MacGruder and Loud, Sons and Daughters, ER. *Guest*: Tales from the Crypt (The Switch), Pacific Blue. *Special*: 14 Going On 30. *Movies*: Deadly Lessons, The Gambler Returns: Luck of the Draw, Black Scorpion, Fatally Yours, Legend of the Lost Tomb.

ROTH, BOBBY
Director, Writer, Producer.
PICTURES: The Boss' Son, Circle of Power, Independence Day, Heartbreakers, The Man Inside, Amanda.
TELEVISION: *Episodes*: Miami Vice, The Insiders, Crime Story. *Movies*: Tonight's the Night, The Man Who Fell to Earth, Dead Solid Perfect (dir., co-s.p.), Baja Oklahoma (dir., co-s.p.), The Man Inside, Rainbow Drive, Keeper of the City, The Switch, Judgement Day: The John List Story, Ride With the Wind, Nowhere to Hide, Love Can Build a Bridge, In the Line of Duty: Kidnapped, Tell Me No Secrets, Inheritance, The Devil's Child.

ROTH, JOE
Executive, Producer, Director. b. New York, NY, 1948. Began career working as prod. assistant on commercials and feature films in San Francisco. Also ran the lights for improv group Pitchel Players. Moved with them to Los Angeles, and prod. their shows incl. the $250,000 film Tunnelvision. 1987, co-founder of independent film prod. co. Morgan Creek Productions. 1989, left to become chmn. of newly-formed Fox Film Corp., the theatrical film unit of 20th Century Fox Film Corp. Also named head of News Corp. unit. Resigned from Fox, 1993. Pres. & founder, Caravan Pictures, 1993. 1994, became chmn. Walt Disney Motion Pictures Group.
PICTURES: *Producer*: Tunnelvision, Cracking Up, Americathon, Our Winning Season, The Final Terror, The Stone Boy, Where the River Runs Black, Bachelor Party, Off Beat, Streets of Gold (also dir. debut), Tall Tale, Angels in the Outfield. *Exec. prod.*: Revenge of the Nerds II: Nerds in Paradise (also dir.), Young Guns, Dead Ringers, Skin Deep, Major League, Renegades, Enemies a Love Story, Pacific Heights, The Three Musketeers, Angie, I Love Trouble, Angels in the Outfield, A Low Down Dirty Shame, Houseguest, Tall Tale, While You Were Sleeping, Before and After. *Dir.*: Coupe de Ville.

ROTH, PETER
Executive. b. Larchmont, NY. e. U. of Pennsylvania, graduated cum laude, Tufts U., 1972. Began career in television at ABC Television Network as manager, then director, Children's Programs, 1976; moving to director, Current Programs, 1979; became v.p., Current Primetime Series, 1981-86; president, Stephen J. Cannell Prods., 1986-92, president of production, Twentieth Network Television (currently 20th Century Fox Television), 1992; president, Twentieth Network Television, 1993; president, 20th Century Fox Television, 1994.Currently president, Warner Bros. Television.

ROTH, RICHARD A.
Producer. b. Beverly Hills, CA, 1943. e. Stanford U. Law Sch. Worked for L.A. law firm before beginning film career as lawyer and literary agent for Ziegler-Ross Agency. In 1970 left to develop s.p. Summer of '42 with Herman Raucher.
PICTURES: Summer of '42, Our Time, The Adventures of Sherlock Holmes' Smarter Brother, Julia, Outland, In Country, Havana.

ROTH, TIM
Actor. b. London, England, 1961. Started acting with various fringe theatre groups such as Glasgow Citizen's Theatre, The Oval House, and the Royal Court. Also on London stage in Metamorphosis.
PICTURES: The Hit, A World Apart, The Cook the Thief His Wife and Her Lover, Vincent & Theo, Rosencrantz and Guildenstern Are Dead, Jumpin at the Boneyard, Reservoir Dogs, Backsliding, Bodies Rest and Motion, Pulp Fiction, Rob Roy (BAFTA Award, 1995), Little Odessa, Captives, Hoodlum, Four Rooms, Everyone Say I Love You, Liar, Animals, No Way Home, Gridlock'd, The Legend of 1900, The Million Dollar Hotel, Vatel, Lucky Numbers, Invincible, Planet of the Apes, D'Artagnan.
TELEVISION: *Specials/Movies* (BBC): Meantime, Made in Britain, Metamorphosis, Knuckle, Yellow Backs, King of the Ghetto, The Common Pursuit, Murder in the Heartland (U.S.), Heart of Darkness.

ROTHMAN, THOMAS E.
Executive. b. Baltimore, MD, Nov. 21, 1954. m. actress Jessica Harper. e. Brown U., B.A. 1976; Columbia Law Sch., J.D. 1980. Worked as law clerk with Second Circuit Court of Appeals 1981-82 before becoming partner at entertainment law firm, Frankfurt Garbus Klein & Selz 1982-87; exec. v.p. of production, Columbia Pictures; president of worldwide production, Samuel Goldwyn Co.; founder and president, Fox Searchlight Pictures; president of production, Twentieth Century Fox, 1995. Currently president, Twentieth Century Fox Film Group; member, Board of Directors, Sundance Institute; recipient, Arthur B. Krim Award, Columbia U.
PICTURES: *Co-prod.*: Down By Law, Candy Mountain. *Exec. Prod.*: The Program.

ROTUNNO, GIUSEPPE
Cinematographer. b. Rome, Italy, March 19, 1923. Gained fame as leading cinematographer of Italian films working with Federico Fellini. Later worked in Hollywood.
PICTURES: Tosca, Monte Carlo Story, White Nights, The Naked Maja, On the Beach, Fast and Sexy, The Angel Wore Red, Five Branded Women, Rocco and His Brothers, Boccaccio '70, The Leopard, The Organizer, Juliet of the Spirits, The Bible, Anizo, Candy, Spirits of the Dead, Fellini Satyricon, The Secret of Santa Vittoria, Carnal Knowledge, Fellini's Roma, Man of La Mancha, Amarcord, Love and Anarchy, Fellini's Casanova, All Screwed Up, End of the World in Our Usual Bed in a Night Full of Rain, Orchestra Rehearsal, All That Jazz, City of Women, Popeye, Rollover, Five Days One Summer, And the Ship Sails On, American Dreamer, Desire, Nothing Left to Do But Cry, The Red Sonja, Hotel Colonial, Julia and Julia, Rent-a-Cop, Rebus, Haunted Summer, The Adventures of Baron Munchausen, Regarding Henry, Once Upon a Crime, Wolf, The Night the Moment, Sabrina, La Sindrome di Stendhal.
TELEVISION: The Scarlet and the Black.

ROUNDTREE, RICHARD
Actor. b. New Rochelle, NY, July 9, 1942. e. Southern Illinos U. Former model, Ebony Magazine Fashion Fair; joined workshop of Negro Ensemble Company, appeared in Kongi's Harvest, Man Better Man, Mau Mau Room; played lead role in Philadelphia road company of The Great White Hope before film debut.
PICTURES: What Do You Say to a Naked Lady? (debut, 1970), Shaft, Embassy, Charley One-Eye, Shaft's Big Score, Embassy, Shaft in Africa, Earthquake, Diamonds, Man Friday, Portrait of a Hitman, Escape to Athena, Game for Vultures, An Eye for an Eye, Inchon, Q, One Down Two to Go, The Big Score, Young Warriors, Killpoint, City Heat, Opposing Force, Jocks, Maniac Cop, Homer and Eddie, Angel III: The Final Chapter, The Party Line, Getting Even, American Cops, The Banker, Night Visitor, Crack House, Bad Jim, Lost Memories, Body of Influence, Deadly Rivals, Amityville: A New Generation, Gypsy Angels, Mind Twister, Seven, Once Upon A Time...When We Were Colored, Theodore Rex, Original Gangstas, George of the Jungle, Steel.
TELEVISION: *Series*: Shaft, Outlaws, Cop Files (host), 413 Hope St. *Movies*: Firehouse, The Fifth Missile, Christmas in Connecticut, Bonanza: The Return, Shadows of Desire, Bonanza: Under Attack. *Mini-Series*: Roots, A.D.

ROURKE, MICKEY
Actor. b. Schenectady, NY, Sept. 1956. Moved to Miami as a boy. Fought as an amateur boxer 4 years in Miami. Studied acting with Sandra Seacat while working as a nightclub bouncer, a sidewalk pretzel vendor and other odd jobs. Moved to LA, 1978. Debut: TV movie City in Fear (1978).
PICTURES: 1941 (debut, 1979), Fade to Black, Heaven's Gate, Body Heat, Diner (Natl. Society of Film Critics Award, 1982), Rumblefish, Eureka, The Pope of Greenwich Village, Year of the Dragon, 9-1/2 Weeks, Angel Heart, A Prayer for the Dying, Barfly, Homeboy (also wrote orig. story), Francesco, Johnny Handsome, Wild Orchid, Desperate Hours, Harley Davidson and the Marlboro Man, White Sands, F.T.W., Fall Time, Double Team, Another 9-1/2 Weeks, The Rainmaker, Buffalo 66.
TELEVISION: *Movies*: City in Fear, Rape and Marriage: The Rideout Case, Act of Love, The Last Outlaw.

ROUSSELOT, PHILIPPE
Cinematographer. b. Meurthe-et-Moselle, France, 1945. e. Vaugirard Film Sch., Paris. Worked as camera assistant to Nestor Almendros on My Night at Maud's, Claire's Knee, Love in the Afternoon.
PICTURES: The Guinea Pig Couple, Adom ou le sang d'Abel, Paradiso, Pauline et l'ordinateur, Peppermint Soda, For Clemence, Cocktail Molotov, La Provinciale, A Girl From Lorraine, Diva (Cesar, Natl. Society of Film Critics, and Moscow Awards), The Jaws of the Wolf, The Moon in the Gutter, Thieves After Dark, The Emerald Forest, Therese (Cesar Award), Hope and Glory, Dangerous Liaisons, The Bear, We're No Angels, Too Beautiful for You, Henry and June, A River Runs Through It (Academy Award, 1992), Sommersby, Interview With the Vampire, Queen Margot, Mary Reilly, The People vs. Larry Flynt, Instinct, Random Hearts.

ROWE, ROY
Exhibitor. b. Burgaw, May 29, 1905. e. U. of NC. Eng. instructor, private bus. coll., 1926-29; Publix Sch. for Mgrs., NY, 1930-31; mgr. theatres, Spartanburg, SC; Greensboro & Raleigh, NC; Warner Theatre, Pittsburgh, PA, 1931-34; city mgr. for Warner Theatres, Washington, PA, 1934-35; opened own theatres in NC 1935; member NC Senate, 1937, 1941, 1945, 1949, 1957, 1965; 1935-75, House of Rep., 1943; Major, Civil Air Patrol, WWII; pres. Carolina Aero Club, 1943-44; chmn. NC Aeronautics Comm., 1941-49; dir. Theatre Owners No. & So. Carolina 1943-45; pres., Theatre Owners of SC & NC 1944-45; pres., Assn. of Governing Boards of State Univs., 1964; Rowe Insurance Agency, 1967-69; Mem. Exec. Bd., U. of NC Trustees, 1969. Principal Clerk, NC Senate 1969-75. Owner-operator Rowe Amusement Co., Burgaw, NC. Retired.

ROWLANDS, GENA
Actress. r.n. Virginia Cathryn Rowlands. b. Cambria, WI, June 19, 1934. e. U. of Wisconsin. Son is actor Nicholas Cassavetes. Came to New York to attend American Acad. of Dramatic Arts, where she met and married John Cassavetes. Made B'way debut as understudy and then succeeded to role of The Girl in The Seven Year Itch. Launched as star with part in The Middle of the Night, which she played 18 mos.
PICTURES: The High Cost of Loving (debut, 1958), Lonely Are the Brave, The Spiral Road, A Child Is Waiting, Tony Rome, Faces, Machine Gun McCain, Minnie and Moskowitz, A Woman Under the Influence (Acad. Award nom.), Two Minute Warning, The Brink's Job, Opening Night, Gloria (Acad. Award nom.), Tempest, Love Streams, Light of Day, Another Woman, Once Around, Ted and Venus, Night on Earth, The Neon Bible, Something to Talk About, Unhook The Stars, She's So Lovely, Playing by Heart, The Mighty, Paulie, Hope Floats, The Weekend.
TELEVISION: *Movies*: A Question of Love, Strangers: The Story of a Mother & Daughter, Thursday's Child, An Early Frost, The Betty Ford Story (Emmy Award, 1987), Montana, Face of a Stranger (Emmy Award, 1992), Crazy in Love, Silent Cries, Parallel Lives, Best Friends for Life, Grace and Glorie. *Guest*: The Philco TV Playhouse, Studio One, Alfred Hitchcock Presents, Dr. Kildare, Bonanza, The Kraft Mystery Theatre, Columbo. *Series*: Top Secret USA, 87th Precinct, Peyton Place.

ROWLEY, JOHN H.
Executive. b. San Angelo, TX, Oct. 6, 1917. e. U. of TX, 1935-39. Past pres., NATO of Texas; past Int'l Chief barker, Variety Clubs Int'l; past pres., TOA. Currently exec. dir. NATO of TX.

RUBEN, JOSEPH
Director. b. Briarcliff, NY, 1951. e. U. of Michigan, majoring in theater and film; Brandeis U., B.A. Interest in film began in high sch. Bought a Super-8 camera and filmed his first movie, a teenage love story. First feature, The Sister-in-Law, a low budget feature which he wrote and dir. in 1975.
PICTURES: *Dir./Writer*: The Sister-in-Law (also prod.), The Pom-Pom Girls (also prod.), Joy Ride, Our Winning Season. *Dir.*: G.O.R.P., Dreamscape (also co-s.p.), The Stepfather, True Believer, Sleeping With the Enemy, The Good Son, Money Train, Return to Paradise.
TELEVISION: Breaking Away (pilot), Eddie Dodd.

RUBIN, STANLEY
Producer, Writer. b. New York, NY, Oct. 8, 1917; ed. UCLA, 1933-37. Phi Beta Kappa. Writer for radio, magazines, pictures, 1937-41; U.S. Army Air Force, 1942-45; writer, prod., owner, Your Show Time, Story Theatre TV series; winner of 1st Emmy awarded to filmed series: The Necklace, 1949. Producer, RKO, 20th-Fox, U.I., MGM, Paramount, Rastar.
PICTURES: The Narrow Margin, My Pal Gus, Destination Gobi, River of No Return, Destry, Francis in the Navy, Behind the High Wall, Rawhide Years, The Girl Most Likely, Promise Her Anything, The President's Analyst, Revenge, White Hunter Black Heart (co-prod.).
TELEVISION: G.E. Theatre, Ghost and Mrs. Muir, Bracken's World, The Man and the City, Executive Suite. *Movies*: Babe (co-prod.; Golden Globe Award), And Your Name is Jonah, Don't Look Back: The Story of Satchel Page (Image Award), Escape From Iran: The Canadian Caper (exec. prod.).

RUBINEK, SAUL
Actor. b. Fohrenwold, Germany, July 2, 1948. Family moved to Canada when he was a baby. Acting debut at age 8 with local theatre groups. Founding member of the Toronto Free Stage Theatre.
PICTURES: Nothing Personal, Highpoint, Agency, Death Ship, Ticket to Heaven, Soup for One, Young Doctors in Love, By Design, Against All Odds, Martin's Day, Sweet Liberty, Taking Care, Wall Street, Obsessed, The Outside Chance of Maximillian Glick, The Bonfire of the Vanities, Man Trouble, Unforgiven, The Quarrel, True Romance, Undercover Blues, Death Wish V, Getting Even With Dad, I Love Trouble, Open Season, Nixon, Past Perfect, Bad Manners, Dick.
TELEVISION: Concealed Enemies, The Terry Fox Story, Clown White, Interrogation in Budapest, Woman on the Run, And the Band Played On, The Android Affair, Color of Justice, John Woo's Blackjack, 36 Hours to Die.

RUBINSTEIN, JOHN
Actor, Composer, Director. b. Los Angeles, CA, December 8, 1946. Son of concert pianist Arthur Rubinstein and dancer-writer Aniela Rubinstein. e. UCLA.
THEATER: Pippin (NY debut, 1972; Theatre World Award), Picture (Mark Taper, LA), Children of a Lesser God (Tony Award, Drama Desk, L.A. Drama Critics Awards, 1980), Fools, The Caine Mutiny Court-Martial, M. Butterfly, Kiss of the Spider Woman, Love Letters, Hurlyburly, Getting Away With Murder, Camelot, Ragtime, On A Clear Day You Can See Forever, Counsellor-at-Law (also dir; Drama-Logue, Ovation, L.A. Drama Critics Awards, 1995), Into the Woods (also dir.), Merrily We Roll Along, Streamers, The Tempest, Candida, Arms and the Man, Three Hotels, Broken Glass, Sight Unseen. *Director*: The Rover, Les Liaisons Dangereuses, Phantasie, Nightingale, The Old Boy, She Loves Me.
PICTURES: Journey to Shiloh (debut, 1968), The Trouble With Girls, Getting Straight, The Wild Pack, Zachariah, The Car, The Boys From Brazil, In Search of Historic Jesus, Daniel, Someone to Watch Over Me, Another Stakeout, Mercy, Kid Cop.
TELEVISION: *Series*: Family, Crazy Like a Fox. *Guest*: The Virginian, Ironside, Dragnet, Room 222, The Psychiatrist, The Mary Tyler Moore Show, Cannon, The Mod Squad, Nichols, Hawaii Five-O, Barnaby Jones, Policewoman, Barbary Coast, The Rookies, The Streets of San Francisco, Harry O, Vegas, The Class of '65, Movin' On, Stop the Presses, Wonder Woman, Lou Grant, Fantasy Island, The Quest, Quincy, Trapper John M.D., The Love Boat, Father Dowling, The Paper Chase, Murder She Wrote, Against the Grain, Frasier, Jake and the Fatman, Hotel, Matlock, Highway to Heaven, NYPD Blue, Lois and Clark, Party of Five, Diagnosis Murder, Star Trek: Voyager, Early Edition, E.R., Robocop. *Special*: Triple Play—Sam Found Out. *Movies*: The Marriage Proposal, God Bless the Children, A Howling in the Woods, Something Evil, All Together Now, The Gift of the Magi, Roots: The Next Generations, Just Make Me an Offer, The French Atlantic Affair, Corey: For the People, Happily Ever After, Moviola, Skokie, The Mr. and Ms. Mysteries, Killjoy, Freedom to Speak, Someone's Killing the High Fashion Models; I Take These Men, M.A.D.D.: Mothers Against Drunk Driving, Liberace, Voices Within: The Lives of Truddi Chase, In My Daughter's Name, The American Clock, Perry Mason, Norma and Marilyn, Sleepwalker. *Director*: A Matter of Conscience, Summer Stories: The Mall, High Tide.
SCORES: *Films:* Paddy, Jeremiah Johnson, The Candidate, Kid Blue, The Killer Inside Me. *Television:* All Together Now, Emily, Emily, Stalk the Wild Child, Champions: A Love Story, To Race the Wind, The Ordeal of Patty Hearst, Amber Waves, Johnny Belinda, Secrets of a Mother and Daughter, Choices of the Heart, The Dollmaker, Family (Emmy nom.), The Fitzpatricks, The Mackenzies of Paradise Cove, The New Land, For Heaven's Sake, The Lazarus Syndrome, The City Killer, China Beach, A Walton Wedding.

RUBINSTEIN, RICHARD P.
Producer, Executive. b. New York, NY, June 15, 1947. e. American U. B.S. 1969, Columbia U. MBA 1971. Pres. & CEO, New Amsterdam Entertainment, Inc.
PICTURES: Martin, Dawn Of The Dead, Knightriders, Creepshow, Day Of The Dead, Creepshow 2, Pet Sematary, Tales From the Darkside: The Movie, Stephen King's The Night Flier.
TELEVISION: *Exec. Prod.: Series*: Tales From the Darkside, Monsters, Stephen King's Golden Years. *Mini-Series*: Stephen King's The Stand. *Movies*: The Vernon Johns Story, Precious Victims.

RUDDY, ALBERT S.
Producer. b. Montreal, Canada, March 28, 1934. e. U. of Southern California, B.S. in design, Sch. of Architecture, 1956. Exec. prod. of 1991 TV movie Miracle in the Wilderness.
PICTURES: The Wild Seed, Little Fauss & Big Halsey, Making It, The Godfather, The Longest Yard, Coonskin, Matilda, The Cannonball Run, Megaforce, Lassiter, Cannonball Run II, Farewell to the King, Paramedics, Speed Zone, Impulse, Ladybugs, Bad Girls, The Scout, Heaven's Prisoners.
TELEVISION: *Series*: Walker—Texas Ranger. *Movies*: Miracle in the Wilderness, Staying Afloat.

RUDIE, EVELYN
Actress, Singer, Songwriter. r.n. Evelyn Rudie Bernauer, b. Hollywood, Calif. March 28. e. Hollywood H.S., UCLA. At 19, after childstar career in TV and films, stage debut at Gallery Theatre in Hollywood as songwriter, musical dir., choreographer and star performer: Ostrogoths and King of the Schnorrers. Currently producer, artistic dir., Santa Monica Playhouse; founder of own repertoire co. Received Emmy Nomination for first TV leading role, Eloise, Playhouse 90, 1956. Filmdom's Famous Fives critics award, 1958. Star on Hollywood's Walk of Fame.
PICTURES: Daddy Long Legs (debut, 1955). The Wings of Eagles, Gift of Love, Bye Bye Birdie.
TELEVISION: Hostess with the Mostess, Playhouse 90, Dinah Shore, Red Skelton Show, George Gobel Show, Omnibus, Matinee Theatre, Hitchcock Presents, Gale Storm Show, Jack Paar, Wagon Train, G.E. Theatre, 77 Sunset Strip.

RUDIN, SCOTT
Executive. b. New York, NY, July 14, 1958. Began career as prod. asst. on B'way for producers Kermit Bloomgarden, Robert Whitehead; then casting director. 1984, became producer for 20th Century Fox; named exec. v.p. prod.; 1986, appt. pres. prod., 20th-Fox. Resigned 1987 becoming independent producer.
PICTURES: *Prod.*: I'm Dancing as Fast as I Can, Reckless, Mrs. Soffel, Flatliners (exec. prod.), Pacific Heights, Regarding Henry, Little Man Tate, The Addams Family, White Sands, Sister Act, Jennifer Eight, Life With Mikey, The Firm, Searching for Bobby Fisher, Addams Family Values, Sister Act 2: Back in the Habit, Nobody's Fool, I.Q., Clueless, Sabrina, Up Close and Personal, Marvin's Room, In & Out.
TELEVISION: Little Gloria... Happy at Last (exec. prod.).

RUDNER, RITA
Actress, Writer. b. Miami, FL, 1956. m. producer Martin Bergman. Was stage dancer then stand-up comic. Author: Naked Beneath My Clothes, Rita Rudner's Guide to Men.
THEATER: Annie (B'way), Promises Promises, Follies, Mack and Mabel.
PICTURES: The Wrong Guys (debut, 1988), Gleaming the Cube, That's Adequate, Peter's Friends (also co-s.p.), A Weekend in the Country (also s.p.).
TELEVISION: *Series*: George Schlatter's Funny People (co-host). *Specials*: Women of the Night, One Night Stand: Rita Rudner, Rita Rudner: Born to Be Mild, The Rita Rudner Comedy Specials (also writer), Comic Relief, Rita Rudner: Married Without Children.

RUDOLPH, ALAN
Director, Writer. b. Los Angeles, CA, Dec. 18, 1943. Son of Oscar Rudolph, TV director of '50s and '60s. Made his screen debut in his father's The Rocket Man (1954). Began in industry doing odd jobs in Hollywood studios. 1969 accepted for Directors Guild assistant director's training program. Worked with Robert Altman as asst. dir. on California Split, The Long Goodbye and Nashville and co-writer on Buffalo Bill and the Indians.
PICTURES: *Director*: Welcome to L.A. (debut, 1977; also s.p.), Remember My Name (also s.p.), Roadie (also story), Endangered Species (also co-s.p.), Return Engagement, Songwriter, Choose Me (also s.p.), Trouble in Mind (also s.p.), Made in Heaven, The Moderns (also co-s.p.), Love at Large (also s.p.), Mortal Thoughts, The Player (actor only), Equinox (also s.p.), Mrs. Parker and the Vicious Circle (also co-s.p.), Afterglow, Trixie (also s.p.), Breakfast of Champions (also s.p.), Investigating Sex.

RUEHL, MERCEDES
Actress. b. Queens, NY, 1950. Raised in Silver Spring, MD. e. College of New Rochelle, B.A. English lit. Worked for years in regional theater, mostly in classics.
THEATER: *B'way*: I'm Not Rappaport, Lost in Yonkers (Tony Award, 1991), The Shadow Box, The Rose Tattoo. *Off-B'way*: American Notes, The Marriage of Bette and Boo (Obie Award), Coming of Age in Soho, Other People's Money.
PICTURES: The Warriors (debut, 1979), Four Friends, Heartburn, Radio Days, 84 Charing Cross Road, The Secret of My Success, Leader of the Band, Big, Married to the Mob, Slaves of New York, Crazy People, Another You, The Fisher King (Acad. Award, best supporting actress, 1991), Lost in Yonkers, Last Action Hero, Roseanna's Grave, Spooky House, Out of the Cold, The Minus Man.
TELEVISION: *Movie*: Indictment: The McMartin Trial, Gia, Subway Stories: Tales from the Underground. *Pilot*: Late Bloomer. *Guest*: Our Family Honor, Frasier. *Special*: On Hope.

RUGOLO, PETE
Composer, Arranger. b. Sicily, Italy, Dec. 25, 1915. To U.S., 1919. e. San Francisco State Coll., Mills Coll., Oakland. Armed Forces, 1942-46; pianist, arr. for many orch. including Stan Kenton. Conductor and arrang. for Nat King Cole, Peggy Lee, Harry Belafonte, many others. Received 3 Emmy Awards.
PICTURES: The Strip, Skirts Ahoy, Glory Alley, Latin Lovers, Easy to Love, Jack the Ripper, Foxtrot, Buddy Buddy, Chu Chu and the Philly Flash.
TELEVISION: Richard Diamond, The Thin Man, Thriller, The Fugitive, Run for Your Life, The Bold Ones, Leave It to Beaver, more than 25 movies.

RUIZ-ANCHIA, JUAN
Cinematographer. b. Bilbao, Spain, 1949. e. Escuela Official de Cinematografica, 1972. Worked on such Spanish prods. as 19/19, Cornica del Alba, Odd and Even, Soldier of Metal. Moved to L.A. Granted 2 yr. fellowship at American Film Inst. from which he graduated in 1981. First U.S. prod. was Reborn, 1982.
PICTURES: The Stone Boy, That Was Then This Is Now, Maria's Lovers, At Close Range, Where the River Runs Black, House of Games, Surrender, The Seventh Sign, Things Change, Lost Angels, The Last of the Finest, Dying Young, Naked Tango, Liebstraum, Glengarry Glen Ross, A Far Off Place, Mr. Jones, The Jungle Book, Two Bits, The Adventures of Pinocchio, Lorca.

RULE, JANICE
Actress. b. Cincinnati, OH, Aug. 15, 1931. e. Wheaton & Glenbard H.S., Glen Ellyn, IL. Received Phd in Clinical & Research Psychoanalysis, 1983. Dancer 4 yrs. in Chicago & New York nightclubs; stage experience in It's Great To Be Alive, as understudy of Bambi Lynn.
THEATER: Miss Liberty, Picnic (B'way debut, 1953), The Happiest Girl in the World.
PICTURES: Goodbye My Fancy (debut, 1951), Starlift, Holiday for Sinners, Rogue's March, A Woman's Devotion, Gun for a Coward, Bell Book and Candle, The Subterraneans, Invitation to a Gunfighter, The Chase, Alvarez Kelly, Welcome to Hard Times, The Swimmer, The Ambushers, Doctors' Wives, Gumshoe, Kid Blue, 3 Women, Missing, Rainy Day Friends, American Flyers.
TELEVISION: *Movies*: Shadow on the Land, Trial Run, The Devil and Miss Sarah, The Word.

RUSH, BARBARA
Actress. b. Denver, CO, Jan. 4, 1927. e. U. of CA. First stage appearance at age of ten, Loberto Theatre, Santa Barbara, CA, in fantasy, Golden Ball; won acting award in college for characterization of Birdie (The Little Foxes); scholarship, Pasadena Playhouse Theatre Arts Coll.
THEATER: A Woman of Independent Means, 40 Carats, Same Time Next Year, Steel Magnolias, The Golden Age.
PICTURES: Molly (debut, 1950), The First Legion, Quebec, When Worlds Collide, Flaming Feather, Prince of Pirates, It Came From Outer Space, Taza—Son of Cochise, The Magnificent Obsession, The Black Shield of Falworth, Captain Lightfoot, Kiss of Fire, World in My Corner, Bigger Than Life, Flight to Hong Kong, Oh Men! Oh Women!, No Down Payment, The Young Lions, Harry Black and the Tiger, The Young Philadelphians, The Bramble Bush, Strangers When We Meet, Come Blow Your Horn, Robin and the 7 Hoods, Hombre, The Man, Superdad, Can't Stop the Music, Summer Lovers.
TELEVISION: *Series*: Saints and Sinners, Peyton Place, The New Dick Van Dyke Show, Flamingo Road, 7th Heaven. *Movies*: Suddenly Single, Cutter, Eyes of Charles Sand, Moon of the Wolf, Crime Club, The Last Day, Death on the Freeway, The Seekers, Flamingo Road (pilot), The Night the Bridge Fell Down.

RUSH, GEOFFREY
Actor. b. Toowomba, Queensland, Australia, 1951.
PICTURES: Hoodwink, Starstruck, Twelfth Night, Dad and Dave: On Our Selection, Call Me Sal, Shine (Acad. Award, 1996; Golden Globe), Children of the Revolution, Les Miserables, A Little Bit of Soul, Oscar and Lucinda, Shakespeare in Love (Acad. Award nom.), Elizabeth, Mystery Men, The House on Haunted Hill, Quills, The Magic Pudding (voice).

RUSH, HERMAN
Executive. b. Philadelphia, PA, June 20, 1929. e. Temple U., Sales mgr., Official Films Inc., 1952-57. Headed Flamingo Telefilms, Inc. 1957-60; 1960-71, pres., tv div. of Creative Mgt. Assoc.; pres., Herman Rush Assoc. Inc., 1971-77; 1977-78 chmn. bd., Rush-Flaherty Agency, Inc.; 1970 headed Marble Arch TV; 1980 named pres., Columbia TV; 1984, pres. of newly formed Columbia Pictures TV Group; 1986, chmn. of newly formed Coca-Cola Telecommunications, Inc.; 1988, chmn., Rush Entertainment Group; 1989, became creative consultant for CBN Producers Group; 1992, Katz/Rush Ent., partner; co-founder, dir. of Transactional Media, Informercial and Transactional Program Production Co.; 1993-94 exec. prod., Willard Scott's New Original Amateur Hour; 1994-95, exec. prod. Susan Powter Show; exec. prod. of The Montel Williams Show.

RUSH, RICHARD
Director, Producer, Writer. b. New York, NY, 1930.
PICTURES: *Director*: Too Soon To Love (also prod., s.p.), Of Love and Desire (also prod., s.p.), A Man Called Dagger, Fickle Finger of Fate, Thunder Alley, Hell's Angels on Wheels, Psych-Out (also s.p.), Savage Seven, Getting Straight (also prod.), Freebie and the Bean (also prod.), The Stunt Man (also prod., s.p.; Acad. Award nom. for best dir., s.p.), Air America (co-s.p.), Color of Night.

RUSSELL, CHUCK
Director. Asst. dir., and line prod. on many low-budget films for Roger Corman and Sunn Classics, including Death Race 2000.
PICTURES: Dreamscape (co-s.p., line prod.), Back to School (prod.), Nightmare on Elm Street III (dir., co-s.p.), The Blob (dir., co-s.p.), The Mask, Eraser.

RUSSELL, DAVID O.
Director, Writer. b. New York, NY, August 20, 1958
PICTURES: Spanking the Monkey (also exec. prod.), Flirting with Disaster, Three Kings.

RUSSELL, JANE
Actress. r.n. Ernestine Jane Russell. b. Bemidji, MN, June 21, 1921. e. Max Reinhardt's Theatrical Workshop & Mme. Ouspenskaya. Photographer's model.
PICTURES: The Outlaw (debut, 1943), Young Widow, The Paleface, His Kind of Woman, Double Dynamite, Macao, Son of Paleface, Montana Belle, Las Vegas Story, Road to Bali (cameo), Gentlemen Prefer Blondes, The French Line, Underwater, Gentlemen Marry Brunettes, Foxfire, Tall Men, Hot Blood, The Revolt of Mamie Stover, The Fuzzy Pink Nightgown, Fate Is the Hunter, Waco, Johnny Reno, Born Losers, Darker Than Amber.
TELEVISION: *Series*: Yellow Rose.

RUSSELL, KEN
Director, Producer, Writer. b. Southampton, England, July 3, 1927. e. Walthamstow Art Sch. Early career as dancer, actor, stills photographer, TV documentary film-maker. Ent. TV ind. 1959. Made 33 documentaries for BBC-TV. Also made numerous pop videos.

PICTURES: French Dressing, Billion Dollar Brain, Women in Love, The Music Lovers (also prod.), The Devils (also prod., s.p.), The Boy Friend (also prod., s.p.), Savage Messiah (also prod.), Mahler (also s.p.), Tommy (also prod., s.p.), Lisztomania (also s.p.), Valentino, Altered States, Crimes of Passion, Gothic, Aria (sequence), Salome's Last Dance (also s.p., actor), The Lair of the White Worm (also prod., s.p.), The Rainbow (also prod., co-s.p.), The Russia House (actor only), Whore (also s.p.), Mindbender.
TELEVISION: The Secret Life of Sir Arnold Box, Lady Chatterly's Lover, Portrait of a Soviet Composer, Elgar, A House in Bayswater, Always on Sunday, The Debussy Film, Isadora Duncan, Dantes Inferno, Song of Summer—Delius, Dance of the Seven Veils. HBO: Dust Before Fireworks, Prisoner of Honor.

RUSSELL, KERI
Actress. b. Fountain Valley, CA, March 23, 1976.
PICTURES: Honey I Blew Up the Kid, Eight Days a Week, The Curve, Mad About Mambo.
TELEVISION: *Movies:* The Babysitter's Seduction, The Lottery, When Innocence Is Lost. *Series:* The Mickey Mouse Club, Emerald Cove, Daddy's Girls, Malibu Shores, Roar, Felicity. *Guest:* Boy Meets World, Married...with Children, 7th Heaven.

RUSSELL, KURT
Actor. b. Springfield, MA, March 17, 1951. Son of former baseball player-turned-actor Bing Russell (deputy sheriff on Bonanza). At 12 got lead in tv series The Travels of Jamie McPheeters (1963-64). Starred as child in many Disney shows and films. Professional baseball player 1971-73. Host, Kurt Russell Celebrity Shoot Out, 4-day hunting tournament.
PICTURES: It Happened at the World's Fair (debut, 1963), Follow Me Boys, The One and Only Genuine Original Family Band, The Horse in the Grey Flannel Suit, The Computer Wore Tennis Shoes, The Barefoot Executive, Fools' Parade, Now You See Him Now You Don't, Charley and the Angel, Superdad, The Strongest Man in the World, Used Cars, Escape from New York, The Fox and The Hound (voice), The Thing, Silkwood, Swing Shift, The Mean Season, The Best of Times, Big Trouble in Little China, Overboard, Tequila Sunrise, Winter People, Tango and Cash, Backdraft, Unlawful Entry, Captain Ron, Tombstone, StarGate, Executive Decision, Escape From L.A., Breakdown, Soldier, 3000 Miles to Graceland.
TELEVISION: *Series*: The Travels of Jamie McPheeters, The New Land, The Quest. *Movies*: Search for the Gods, The Deadly Tower, The Quest (pilot), Christmas Miracle in Caulfield U.S.A., Elvis, Amber Waves. *Guest*: The Fugitive, Daniel Boone, Gilligan's Island, Lost in Space, The F.B.I., Love American Style, Gunsmoke, Hawaii Five-O.

RUSSELL, THERESA
Actress. r.n. Theresa Paup. b. San Diego, CA, Mar. 20, 1957. m. dir.-cinematographer Nicolas Roeg. e. Burbank H.S. Began modeling career at 12. Studied at Actors' Studio in Hollywood.
PICTURES: The Last Tycoon (debut, 1976), Straight Time, Bad Timing/A Sensual Obsession, Eureka, The Razor's Edge, Insignificance, Black Widow, Aria, Track 29, Physical Evidence, Impulse, Whore, Kafka, Cold Heaven, The Grotesque, Trade Off,The Spy Within, EroticTales II, Wild Things, Running Woman.
TELEVISION: *Mini-Series*: Blind Ambition. *Movie*: Thicker Than Water, Flight of the Dove, The Trade Off, The Proposition, Woman's Guide to Adultery, Hotel Paradise, When You Meet a Stranger, Public Enemy.

RUSSO, JAMES
Actor. b. New York, NY, Apr. 23, 1953. e. NYU, where he wrote and starred in prize-winning short film Candy Store.
THEATER: *NY:* Welcome to Andromeda, Deathwatch, Marat/Sade, Extremities (Theatre World Award).
PICTURES: A Strange Is Watching (debut, 1982), Fast Times at Ridgemont High, Vortex, Exposed, Once Upon a Time in America, Beverly Hills Cop, The Cotton Club, Extremities, China Girl, The Blue Iguana, Freeway, We're No Angels, State of Grace, A Kiss Before Dying, My Own Private Idaho, Cold Heaven, Dangerous Game, Bad Girls, Donnie Brasco, The Postman, Felons, Detour, Sonic Impact, Jimmy Zip, The Ninth Gate.
TELEVISION: *Movie:* The Secretary.

RUSSO, RENE
Actress. b. California, 1955. Raised in Burbank. Worked as top fashion model for Eileen Ford Agency prior to acting.
PICTURES: Major League (debut, 1989), Mr. Destiny, One Good Cop, Freejack, Lethal Weapon 3, In the Line of Fire, Outbreak, Get Shorty, Tin Cup, Ransom, Buddy, Lethal Weapon 4, The Thomas Crown Affair, The Adventures of Rocky and Bullwinkle.
TELEVISION: *Series:* Sable.

RUTHERFORD, ANN
Actress. b. Toronto, Canada, Nov. 2, 1920. Trained by mother (cousin of Richard Mansfield); with parents in stock as child; later on Los Angeles radio programs. Screen debut, 1935.
PICTURES: Waterfront Lady (debut, 1935), Judge Hardy's Children, Of Human Hearts, A Christmas Carol, You're Only Young Once, Dramatic School, Love Finds Andy Hardy, Out West With the Hardys, The Hardys Ride High, Four Girls in White, Dancing Co-Ed, Andy Hardy Gets Spring Fever, Gone With the Wind, These Glamour Girls, Judge Hardy and Son, Wyoming, Pride and Prejudice, The Ghost Comes Home, Andy Hardy Meets Debutante, Washington Melodrama, Life Begins for Andy Hardy, Badlands of Dakota, Andy Hardy's Private Secretary, Whistling in the Dark, Orchestra Wives, The Courtship of Andy Hardy, Whistling in Dixie, Andy Hardy's Double Life, This Time for Keeps, Happy Land, Whistling in Brooklyn, Bermuda Mystery, Two O'Clock Courage, Bedside Manner, The Madonna's Secret, Murder in the Music Hall, Inside Job, The Secret Life of Walter Mitty, Operation Haylift, Adventures of Don Juan, They Only Kill Their Masters, Won Ton Ton the Dog Who Saved Hollywood.

RYAN, ARTHUR N.
Executive. Joined Paramount in N.Y. in 1967 as asst. treas; later made dir. of admin. and business affairs, exec. asst. to Robert Evans and asst. scty. 1970 appt. v.p.-prod. adm. 1975 named sr. v.p. handling all prod. operations for Paramount's m.p. and TV divisions; 1976, asst. to the chmn. & CEO; chmn. & pres. Magicam, Inc.; chmn. Fortune General Corp.; chmn. Paramount Communications; co-chmn. of scholarship comm. of AMPAS; trustee of Univ. Film Study Center in Boston; joined Technicolor in 1976 as pres., COO & dir.; vice chmn., 1983-85; chmn. & CEO, 1985-; chmn. Technicolor Audio-Visual Systems International, Inc.; dir. Technicolor S.P.A.; dir. Technicolor, Film Intl.; and chmn. of exec. committee, Technicolor Graphics Services, Inc.; dir., Technicolor, Inc.; chmn., Technicolor Fotografica, S.A.; chmn. Technicolor Film Intl. Service Company, Inc.; dir. & deputy chmn. Technicolor Ltd.; chmn. & dir., The Vidtronics Company, Inc.; chmn. & CEO, Compact Video, Inc., 1984-; dir, Four Star Int'l., 1983-; dir., MacAndrews & Forbes, Inc. 1985-; Permanent charities committee of the Ent. Industry; Hollywood Canteen Foundations. Vice-chmn. & dir., Calif. Inst. of Arts. Trustee: Motion Picture & Television Fund. 1985 named chmn., Technicolor.

RYAN, JOHN
Actor. b. New York, NY, July 30, 1936. e. City Coll. of NY.
THEATER: *NY*: Duet for Three, Sgt. Musgrave's Dance, Yerma, Nobody Hears a Broken Drum, The Love Suicide at Schofield Barracks, The Silent Partner, Twelve Angry Men, Medea.
PICTURES: The Tiger Makes Out (debut, 1967), A Lovely Way to Die, What's So Bad About Feeling Good?, Five Easy Pieces, The King of Marvin Gardens, The Legend of Nigger Charley, Cops and Robbers, Dillinger, Shamus, It's Alive, The Missouri Breaks, Futureworld, It Lives Again, The Last Flight of Noah's Ark, On the Nickel, The Postman Always Rings Twice, The Escape Artist, Breathless, The Right Stuff, The Cotton Club, Runaway Train, Avenging Force, Death Wish 4: The Crackdown, Delta Force II, Fatal Beauty, Three O'Clock High, Rent-a-Cop, Paramedics, City of Shadows, Best of the Best, White Sands, Hoffa, Star Time, Young Goodman Brown, Batman: Mask of the Phantasm (voice), Tall Tale, Bound.
TELEVISION: *Series*: Archer. *Guest*: M*A*S*H, Kojak, Starsky & Hutch, Matt Helm, Matt Houston, Miami Vice. *Movies*: Target Risk, Death Scream, Kill Me If You Can, A Killing Affair, Houston: The Legend of Texas, Blood River, Shooting Stars.

RYAN, MEG
Actress. b. Fairfield, CT, November 19, 1961. r.n. Margaret Mary Emily Anne Hyra. b. Bethel, CT, Nov. 19, 1961. e. NYU. Supported herself, while studying journalism at NYU, by making commercials. Auditioned for and won first prof. role as Candice Bergen's daughter in film Rich and Famous.
PICTURES: Rich and Famous (debut, 1981), Amityville 3-D, Top Gun, Armed and Dangerous, Innerspace, Promised Land, D.O.A., The Presidio, When Harry Met Sally, Joe Versus the Volcano, The Doors, Prelude to a Kiss, Sleepless in Seattle, Flesh & Bone, When a Man Loves a Woman, I.Q., French Kiss, Restoration, Courage Under Fire, Addicted to Love, Anastasia (voice), Hurlyburly, City of Angels, You've Got Mail, Hanging Up, Proof of Life.
TELEVISION: *Series*: One of the Boys, As the World Turns (1982-84), Wild Side (Disney TV).

RYAN, MITCHELL
Actor. b. Louisville, KY, Jan. 11, 1928. Entered acting following service in Navy during Korean War. Was New York stage actor working off-B'way for Ted Mann and Joseph Papp; on B'way in Wait Until Dark. Member of Arena Stage group in Washington.
PICTURES: Monte Walsh, The Hunting Party, My Old Man's Place, High Plains Drifter, The Friends of Eddie Coyle, ElectraGlide in Blue, Magnum Force, Labyrinth, Winter People.
TELEVISION: *Series*: Chase, Executive Suite, Having Babies, The Chisholms, Dark Shadows, High Performance, King Crossings. *Movies*: Angel City, The Five of Me, Death of a Centerfold—The Dorothy Stratten Story, Uncommon Valor, Medea, Kenny Rogers as the Gambler—The Adventure Continues, Robert Kennedy & His Times, Fatal Vision, Favorite Son, The Ryan White Story, Margaret Bourke-White.

RYDELL, MARK
Director, Producer, Actor. b. New York, NY March 23, 1934. e. Juilliard Sch. of Music. Studied acting with Sanford Meisner of NY Neighborhood Playhouse. Became member of Actors Studio. Was leading actor for six years on daytime CBS serial, As The World Turns. Made Broadway debut in Seagulls over Sorrento and film debut in Crime in the Streets. Went to Hollywood as TV director (Ben Casey, I Spy, Gunsmoke, etc.). Partner with Sydney Pollack in Sanford Prods., film, TV prod. co. Formed own production co., Concourse Productions.
PICTURES: *Director*: The Fox (debut, 1968), The Reivers, The Cowboys (also prod.), Cinderella Liberty (also prod.), Harry and Walter Go To New York, The Rose, On Golden Pond, The River, Man in the Moon (prod. only), For the Boys (also exec. prod.), Intersection (also co-prod.), Crime of the Century. *Actor:* Crime in the Streets, The Long Goodbye, Punchline, Havana.

RYDER, WINONA
Actress. r.n. Winona Horowitz. b. Winona, MN, Oct. 29, 1971. Grew up in San Francisco. At 7, moved with family to Northern CA commune. At 13 discovered by talent scout during a performance at San Francisco's American Conservatory theatre, where she was studying, and given screen test.
PICTURES: Lucas (debut, 1986), Square Dance, Beetlejuice, 1969, Heathers, Great Balls of Fire, Welcome Home Roxy Carmichael, Edward Scissorhands, Mermaids, Night on Earth, Bram Stoker's Dracula, The Age of Innocence (Golden Globe Award; Acad. Award nom.), Reality Bites, The House of the Spirits, Little Women (Acad. Award nom.), How to Make an American Quilt, Boys, Looking for Richard, The Crucible, Alien: Resurrection, Just to Be Together, Celebrity, Lost Souls, Girl Interrupted (also exec. prod.), Autumn in New York, Simone, Just to Be Together.

RYDSTROM, GARY
Sound.
PICTURES: Indiana Jones and the Temple of Doom, Cocoon, Luxo Jr., Red's Dream, Spaceballs, Tin Toy, Cocoon: The Return, Willow, Colors, Knickknack, Ghostbusters II, Always, Romero, The Hot Spot, Rush, Luxo Jr. in 'Surprise' and 'Light & Heavy,' Backdraft, Terminator 2: Judgment Day, F/X2, A River Runs Through It, Single White Female, Mrs. Doubtfire, Meteor Man, Jurassic Park, Quiz Show, Baby's Day Out, Casper, Strange Days, Toy Story, Jumanji, James and the Giant Peach, Mission: Impossible, Sleepers, Titanic (Acad. Award, Best Sound, 1997), Hercules, The Lost World: Jurassic Park, A Bug's Life, The Horse Whisperer, Saving Private Ryan, Reach the Rock, Rules of Engagement, The Haunting, Star Wars: Episode I-The Phantom Menace.

S

SACKHEIM, WILLIAM B.
Producer, Writer. b. Gloversville, NY, Oct. 31, 1921. e. UCLA.
PICTURES: The Art of Love, The In-Laws (co-prod.), The Competition, First Blood (co-s.p.), The Survivors (prod.), No Small Affair (prod.), The Hard Way (prod.), Pacific Heights (prod.), White Sands (prod.).
TELEVISION: The Law (Emmy Award, Peabody Award, 1975), Gideon Oliver (series, exec. prod.), Almost Grown (exec. prod.), The Antagonists (exec. prod.), The Human Factor (exec. prod.), The Harness (prod.), The Neon Ceiling (prod.), The Senator.

SACKS, SAMUEL
Attorney, Agent. b. New York, NY, March 29, 1908. e. CCNY, St. John's Law Sch., LL.B., 1930. Admitted Calif. Bar, 1943; priv. law practice, NY 1931-42; attorney, William Morris Agency, Inc., 1942; head of west coast TV business affairs, 1948-75; bd. of dir., Alliance of Television Film Producers, 1956-60; LA Copyright Society Treasurer, Beverly Hills Bar Assn., LA Bar Assn., American Bar Assn.; Academy of TV Arts & Sciences; Hollywood Radio & TV Society; counsel, entertainment field, Simon & Sheridan, 1975-89, Los Angeles Citizens' Olympic Committee; arbitrator for Screen Actors Guild, Assn. of Talent Agents and American Arbitration Assn.; bd. of dirs., Friars Club, 1991-95; Counsel for the Caucus for Producers, Writers & Directors, 1975-95.

SADLER, WILLIAM
Actor. b. Buffalo, NY, April 13, 1950. e. SUNY, Cornell U. Made stage debut in title role in Hamlet for Colorado Shakespeare Fest. Also acted with La Jolla Playhouse, Yale Rep.
THEATER: *NY:* Ivanov (Off-B'way debut, 1975), Limbo Tales (Obie Award), Chinese Viewing Pavilion, Lennon, Necessary Ends, Hannah, Biloxi Blues (B'way debut, 1985; Clarence Derwent & Dramalogue Awards). *Regional:* Journey's End, A Mad World My Masters, Romeo and Juliet, Night Must Fall, etc.
PICTURES: Hanky Panky, Off Beat, Project X, K-9, Hard to Kill, Die Hard 2, The Hot Spot, Bill & Ted's Bogus Journey, Rush, Trespass, Freaked, The Shawshank Redemption, Tales From the Crypt Presents Demon Knight, Solo, Skippy, Rocket Man, Ambushed, Disturbing Behavior, Reach the Rock, The Green Mile.
TELEVISION: *Series:* Private Eye, Roswell. *Movies:* The Great Walendas, Charlie and the Great Balloon Race, Face of Fear, The Last to Go, Bermuda Grace. *Guest:* Hooperman, Roseanne, Dear John, Gideon Oliver, The Equalizer, In the Heat of the Night, Tales From the Crypt, Murphy Brown.

SAFER, MORLEY
News Correspondent. b. Toronto, Ont., 1931. e. U. of Western Ontario. Started as corresp. and prod. with Canadian Broadcasting Corp. Joined CBS News London Bureau 1964, chief of Saigon Bureau, 1965. Chief of CBS London bureau 1967-70. Joined 60 Minutes as co-editor in Dec., 1970.

SAFFLE, M. W. "BUD"
Executive. b. Spokane, WA, June 29, 1923. e. U. of Washington. In service 1943-46. Started in m.p. business as booker, 1948. Entire career with Saffle Theatre Service as buyer-booker; named pres. in 1970. Also pres. of Grays Harbor Theatres, Inc., operating theatres in Aberdeen, WA. Also operates drive-in in Centralia, WA. On bd. of NATO of WA for 15 yrs; pres. of same for 2 terms and secty.-treas. 6 yrs. Elected to National NATO bd. in 1972. Founder of Variety Tent 46, serving as chief barker three times.

SAGAL, KATEY
Actress. b. Los Angeles, CA, Nov. 18, 1953.
PICTURES: Maid to Order, The Good Mother.
TELEVISION: *Movies:* The Failing of Raymond, Mother Goose Rock 'n' Rhyme, She Says She's Innocent, Trail of Tears, Mr. Headmistress, Chance of a Lifetime, God's New Plan. *Series:* Mary, Married...with Children, Futurama (voice). *Guest:* Tales from the Crypt, Duckman (voice), That '70s Show (voice).

SAGANSKY, JEFF
Executive. b. 1953. Joined CBS 1976 in bdcst. finance; 1977, NBC, assoc. in pgm. development.; 1977, mgr. film pgms.; 1978, dir. dramatic dev.; 1978, v.p., dev. David Gerber Co.; 1981, returned to NBC as series dev. v.p.; 1983, sr. v.p. series programming; 1985, joined Tri-Star Pictures as pres. of production; 1989 promoted to president of Tri-Star, later that year joined CBS as entertainment division president. Resigned, 1994.

SAGEBRECHT, MARIANNE
Actress. b. Starnberg, Germany, Aug. 27, 1945. In 1977 conceived revue Opera Curiosa.
PICTURES: Die Schaukel (debut, 1983), Sugarbaby, Crazy Boys, Bagdad Cafe, Moon Over Parador, The War of the Roses, Rosalie Goes Shopping, Martha and I, The Milky Life, Dust Devil, Mr. Bluesman, Il Piccolo lord, Erotique, Mona Must Die, All Men Are Mortal, Lorenz Im Land Der Lugner, The Ogre, Soleil, Johnny, Left Luggage, Asterix et Obelix.
TELEVISION: *Movies*: Herr Kischott, Eine Mutter Kampft un Ihren Sohn, My Lord, Und Plotzlich War Alles Anders, Frau Nach Mab Eine.

SAGET, BOB
Actor. b. Philadelphia, PA, May 17, 1956. Started as stand-up comedian.
PICTURE: Critical Condition.
TELEVISION: *Series*: Full House, America's Funniest Home Videos (host). *Movie*: Father and Scout (also co-exec. prod.).

SAINT, EVA MARIE
Actress. b. Newark, NJ, July 4, 1924. e. Bowling Green State U., Ohio, Actors Studio. Radio, tv actress; on Broadway in Trip to Bountiful before film debut.
THEATER: Trip to Bountiful, The Rainmaker, Desire Under the Elms, The Lincoln Mask, Summer and Smoke, Candida, Winesburg Ohio, First Monday in October, Duet for One, The Country Girl, Death of a Salesman, Love Letters, The Fatal Weakness, On The Divide.
PICTURES: On the Waterfront (debut, 1954; Acad. Award, best supporting actress), That Certain Feeling, Raintree County, Hatful of Rain, North by Northwest, Exodus, All Fall Down, 36 Hours, The Sandpiper, The Russians Are Coming! The Russians Are Coming!, Grand Prix, The Stalking Moon, Loving, Cancel My Reservation, Nothing in Common, Mariette in Ecstasy.
TELEVISION: *Movies*: Carol for Another Christmas, The Macahans, A Christmas to Remember, When Hell Was in Session, Fatal Weakness, Curse of King Tut's Tomb, Best Little Girl in the World, Splendor in the Grass, Malibu, Jane Doe, Love Leads the Way, Fatal Vision, The Last Days of Patton, A Year in the Life, Norman Rockwell's Breaking Ties, I'll Be Home for Christmas, Voyage of Terror: The Achille Lauro Affair, People Like Us (Emmy Award, 1991), Danielle Steel's Palomino, Kiss of a Killer, My Antonia, After Jimmy, Titanic. *Series*: Campus Hoopla, One Man's Family, Moonlighting. *Special*: Our Town, First Woman President, Primary Colors: The Story of Corita.

SAINT JAMES, SUSAN
Actress. r.n. Susan Miller. b. Los Angeles, CA, Aug. 14, 1946. e. Connecticut Coll. for Women. Was model for 2 years; then signed to contract by Universal Pictures.

PICTURES: P.J., Where Angels Go... Trouble Follows, What's So Bad About Feeling Good?, Jigsaw, Outlaw Blues, Love at First Bite, How to Beat the High Cost of Living, Carbon Copy, Don't Cry It's Only Thunder.
TELEVISION: *Series*: The Name of the Game (Emmy Award, 1969), McMillan & Wife, Kate and Allie. *Movies*: Fame Is the Name of the Game, Alias Smith and Jones, Once Upon a Dead Man, Magic Carpet, Scott Free, Night Cries, Desperate Women, The Girls in the Office, Sex and the Single Parent, S.O.S. Titanic, The Kid from Nowhere, I Take These Men. *Special*: A Very Special Christmas Party.

SAJAK, PAT
TV Host. b. Chicago, IL, Oct. 26, 1946. e. Columbia Coll., Chicago. Broadcasting career began as newscaster for Chicago radio station. 1968 drafted into Army, where served 4 years as disc jockey for Armed Forces Radio in Saigon, Vietnam. Moved to Nashville, where continued radio career while also working as weatherman and host of public affairs prog. for local TV station. 1977 moved to LA to become nightly weatherman on KNBC. Took over as host of daytime edition of Wheel of Fortune and later the syndicated nighttime edition (4 Emmy nom.; Emmy, 1997). 1989, The Pat Sajak Show.
PICTURE: Airplane II: The Sequel.
TELEVISION: *Host*: The Thanksgiving Day Parade, The Rose Parade.

SAKS, GENE
Director, Actor. b. New York, NY, Nov. 8, 1921. e. Cornell U. Attended dramatic workshop, New School for Social Research. Active in off-Broadway in 1948-49, forming cooperative theatre group at Cherry Lane Theatre. Joined Actor's Studio, followed by touring and stock. Also appeared in live TV dramas (Philco Playhouse, Producer's Showcase). Directed many Broadway plays before turning to film direction with Barefoot in the Park (1967) President of SSDC.
THEATER: *B'way: Director*: Enter Laughing, Nobody Loves an Albatross, Generation, Half a Sixpence, Mame, A Mother's Kisses, Sheep on the Runway, How the Other Half Loves, Same Time Next Year, California Suite, I Love My Wife (Tony Award), Brighton Beach Memoirs (Tony Award), Biloxi Blues (Tony Award), The Odd Couple (1985), Broadway Bound, Rumors, Lost in Yonkers, Jake's Women. *Actor:* Middle of the Night, Howie, The Tenth Man, A Shot in the Dark, A Thousand Clowns.
PICTURES: *Director*: Barefoot in the Park, The Odd Couple, Cactus Flower, Last of the Red Hot Lovers, Mame, Brighton Beach Memoirs, Tchin-Tchin, A Fine Romance. *Actor:* A Thousand Clowns, Prisoner of Second Avenue, The One and Only, Lovesick, The Goodbye People, Nobody's Fool, I.Q., Deconstructing Harry.
TELEVISION: *Movie*: Bye Bye Birdie. *Guest*: Law & Order.

SALANT, RICHARD S.
Executive. b. New York, NY, April 14, 1914. e. Harvard Coll. A.B., 1931-35; Harvard Law Sch., 1935-38. Atty. Gen.'s Com. on Admin. Procedure, 1939-41; Office of Solicitor Gen., U.S. Dept. of Justice, 1941-43; U.S. Naval Res., 1943-46; assoc., Roseman, Goldmark, Colin & Kave, 1946-48; then partner, 1948-51; pres. CBS news div., 1961-64; v.p. special asst. to pres. CBS, Inc., 1951-61, 1964-66; pres., CBS news div., 1966; mem. bd. of dir., CBS, Inc. 1964-69; vice chmn., NBC bd., 1979-81; sr. adviser, 1981-83; pres. CEO, National News Council, 1983-84. Retired.

SALDANA, THERESA
Actress. b. Brooklyn, NY, Aug. 20, 1954. Following attack by stalker founded advocacy group Victims for Victims. *Author*: Beyond Survival, 1986.
PICTURES: Nunzio, I Wanna Hold Your Hand, Defiance, Raging Bull, Double Revenge, Angel Town.
TELEVISION: *Series*: The Commish, All My Children. *Movies*: Sophia Loren: Her Own Story, Victims for Victims: The Theresa Saldana Story, Confessions of a Crime, The Highwayman, Shameful Secrets, She Woke Up Pregnant.

SALEM, KARIO
Actor, Writer.
PICTURES: Underground Aces, Triumph of the Spirit, 1492: Conquest of Paradise, Killing Zoe, Savage.
TELEVISION: *Movies*: Under the Influence, The Red Spider, Shooter, Liberace, Kojak: Ariana, Jericho Fever, Without Warning, Mr. Stitch, Divas (writer), Don King: Only in America (writer, Emmy Award, 1998), The Rat Pack (writer). *Mini-series*: Centennial. *Series*: Heart of the City,

SALES, SOUPY
Comedian. r.n. Milton Hines. b. Franklinton, NC, Jan. 8, 1926. Was radio DJ before debuting with his own children show in Detroit, 1953. Program was picked up by ABC in 1955. Continued to perform on radio over the years.
PICTURES: Birds Do It, And God Spoke.
TELEVISION: *Series*: Soupy Sales (1955), Lunch With Soupy Sales, The Soupy Sales Show (1962), The Soupy Sales Show (1965-67), What's My Line (panelist), The Soupy Sales Show (1978-79), Sha Na Na. *Guest*: The Rebel, The Real McCoys, Route 66, The Beverly Hillbillies, Love American Style, The Love Boat, Wings.

SALHANY, LUCIE
Executive. e. Kent State U., Kent, OH. Began career 1967 WKBF-TV, Cleveland, OH. Prog. mgr., WLVI-TV, Boston, 1975. VP, TV and cable prog., Taft Broadcasting Co., 1979-85. Pres. & CEO, Paramount Domestic TV, 1985. Chairman, 20th TV, 1991. Chairman, Fox Broadcasting Co., 1993. Pres., UPN, 1995.

SALKIND, ILYA
Producer. b. Mexico City, 1947. e. U. of London. Father is producer, Alexander Salkind. First film job as production runner on The Life of Cervantes for father.
PICTURES: The Three Musketeers, The Four Musketeers, Superman, Superman II (exec. prod.), Supergirl (exec. prod.), Superman III (exec. prod.), Christopher Columbus: The Discovery.
TELEVISION: Superboy (exec. prod.).

SALKOW, SIDNEY
Director, Writer. b. New York, NY, June 16, 1911. e. City Coll. of New York, B.A.; Harvard Law Sch. Master of Fine Arts, USC. Stage dir. & prod. asst. number N.Y. dram. prods. (Dir. Bloodstream, Black Tower, etc.) and mgr. summer theatre. From 1933 variously dialogue dir., assoc. dir., writer & dir. numerous pictures Paramount, Universal, Republic, Columbia, etc.; dir. number of pictures in Lone Wolf series (for Columbia), Tillie the Toiler, Flight Lieutenant, etc. In armed service, WWII. Head of film dept., CSUN, emeritus prof. Headed prod. for FF Prod. in Rome, 1967-71.
PICTURES: Murder With Pictures (prod. only), Rhythm on the Range (prod. only), Girl Overboard, Four Days' Wonder, Exclusive (prod. only), That's My Story, Behind the Mike, Storm Over Bengal, The Night Hawk, Prison Nurse (prod. only), Come On Leathernecks! (prod. only), The Zero Hour, Woman Doctor, Street of Missing Men, She Married a Cop, Flight at Midnight, Fighting Thoroughbreds, The Lone Wolf Strikes, The Lone Wolf Meets a Lady, Girl from God's Country, Street of Missing Women, Tillie the Toiler, The Lone Wolf Takes a Chance (also prod.), The Lone Wolf Keeps a Date (also prod.), Time Out for Rhythm, Flight Lieutenant, The Adventures of Martin Eden, City Without Men, Faithful in My Fashion, Millie's Daughter, Bulldog Drummond at Bay, Sword of the Avenger (also prod.), Fugitive Lady, The Admiral Was a Lady (prod. only), Shadow of the Eagle, Golden Hawk, Scarlet Angel, Prince of Pirates, Jack McCall Desperado, Raiders of the 7 Seas (also prod.), The Pathfinder, Sitting Bull, Robbers' Roost, Las Vegas Shakedown, Toughest Man Alive, Gun Brothers, Duel in Durango, Chicago Confidential, Iron Sheriff, The Big Night, Twice-Told Tales, The Last Man on Earth, The Quick Gun, Blood on the Arrow, Great Sioux Massacre, The Murder Game, Martin Eden.
TELEVISION: *Creator/prod./dir.*: This Is Alice (for Desilu), Lassie, Fury, Wells Fargo, The Addams Family.

SALOMON, MIKAEL
Cinematographer, Director. b. Copenhagen, Feb. 24, 1945.
PICTURES: *Europe*: The Dreamers, Z.P.G., Three From Haparanda, The Five, Me and My Kid Brothers, The Owlfarm Brothers, Five on the Run, Magic in Town, 24 Hours With Ilse, Why?, Bedside Freeway, My Sister's Children Goes Astray, Around the World, Tumult, Welcome to the Club, Violets Are Blue, Tintomare, Tell It Like It Is Boys, Cop, Elvis Elvis, Hearts Are Trump, The Marksman, The Flying Devils, Peter von Scholten, The Baron, Once a Cop..., Early Spring, The Wolf at the Door. U.S.: Zelly and Me, Torch Song Trilogy, Stealing Heaven, The Abyss (Acad. Award nom.), Always, Arachnophobia, Backdraft, Far and Away, A Far Off Place (dir. only), Congo (2nd unit dir.), Judge Dredd (trailer dir.), Hard Rain (dir. only).
TELEVISION: *Movie*: The Man Who Broke 1,000 Chains (ACE Award). *Series*: Space Rangers (dir.). Also commercials for Mitsubishi, Nescafe, Converse, Mazda, etc.

SALZBURG, JOSEPH S.
Producer, Editor. b. New York, NY, July 27, 1917. Film librarian, then rose to v.p. in chg. of prod., Pictorial Films, 1935-42; civilian chief film ed. U.S. Army Signal Corps Photo Center, 1942-44; U.S. Army Air Forces, 1944-46; prod. mgr., Pictorial Films, 1946-50; prod. mgr. Associated Artists Prod., then M.P. for TV, 1950-51; org. m.p. prod. & edit. service for theatrical, non-theatrical & TV films 1951-56; prod. mgr., dir. of films oper., official Films. 1956-59; prod. sup. tech. dir. Lynn Romero Prod. features and TV; assoc. prod. Lynn Romero Prod. TV series, Counterthrust 1959-60; v.p., sec'y, B.L. Coleman Assoc., Inc. & Newspix, Inc. 1961; pres. National Production Assoc., Inc. 1960-1962, chief of production, UPI Newsfilm, 1963-66. Prod./account exec. Fred A. Niles Comm. Center, 1966. Appt. v.p., F.A. Niles Communications Centers Inc., N.Y., 1969. 1979 appointed in addition exec. producer & gen. mgr., F. A. Niles Comm., N.Y. studio. 1989, elected mem. bd. dir., Florida Motion Pictures & Television Assn., Palm Beach area chap.; 1989 professor m.p. & TV prod. course at Palm Beach Comm. Coll.: Breaking into TV and Movie Making in South Florida.

SAMMS, EMMA
Actress. b. London, England, Aug. 28, 1960. Former fashion model. Has worked as commercial photographer for such magazines as Ritz, Metro, and Architectural Digest. Co-founder of charitable org. the Starlight Foundation.
PICTURES: Arabian Adventure (debut, 1979), The Shrimp on the Barbie, Delirious.
TELEVISION: *Series*: General Hospital, Dynasty, The Colbys. *Movies*: Goliath Awaits, Agatha Christie's Murder in Three Acts, The Lady and the Highwayman, A Connecticut Yankee in King Arthur's Court, Bejeweled, Shadow of a Stranger, Robin Cook's Harmful Intent, Treacherous Beauties. *Guest*: Hotel, The New Mike Hammer, Murder She Wrote, Newhart, My Two Dads.

SAMPSON, LEONARD E.
Exhibitor. b. New York, NY, Oct. 9, 1918. e. City Coll. of New York, B.B.A., 1939. Entered m.p. industry as stagehand helper and usher, Skouras Park Plaza, Bronx 1932-36; asst. mgr. Gramercy Park, 1937-38; mgr., 5th Avenue Playhouse, 1939-41; mgr., Ascot Bronx, 1941-42. In Army 1942-46. Entered into partnership with cousin Robert C. Spodick in Lincoln, a New Haven art house. Org. Nutmeg Theatres in 1952 in assn. with Norman Bialek, operating 6 art and conventional theatres in Conn., mainly in Westport and Norwalk. Sold Nutmeg in 1968 to Robert Smerling (became Loews Theatres, now Sony Theatres). Built Groton, CT, Cinemas I & II in 1970 and Norwich, CT, Cinema I & II, 1976 and acquired Village Cinemas I, II & III, Mystic, in association with Spodick and William Rosen. Operated as Gemini Theatres. Acquired Westerly Cinema I, II & III, 1982. Sold Gemini Theatre Circuit to Hoyts Theatres, 1987. Retained partnership with Spodick in New Haven's York Sq., until 1996 when he became an inactive partner due to illness.

SAMUELSON, DAVID W.
F.R.P.S., F.B.K.S., B.S.C.: Executive. b. London, England, July 6, 1924. Son of early producer G.B. Samuelson. Joined ind. 1941 with British Movietone News. Later film cameraman, 1947. Left Movietone 1960 to join family company, Samuelson Film Service Ltd. Dir., Samuelson Group Plc, 1958-84. Past president British Kinematograph Sound & TV Soc., Past Chmn, British Board of Film Classification, London Intl. Film Sch. Author: Hands On Manual for Cinematographer, Motion Picture Camera and Lighting Equipment, Motion Picture Camera Techniques, Motion Picture Camera Data, Samuelson Manual of Cinematography, Panaflex User's Manual and Cinematographers Computer Program. Currently consultant on technology film making, author, lecturer. Won Acad. Award for Engineering, 1980 and Acad. Award for Tech. Achievement, 1987.

SAMUELSON, PETER GEORGE WYLIE
Producer. b. London, England, October 16, 1951. e. Cambridge U., M.A., English literature. Early career as interpreter, production assistant, then prod. mgr. 1975, Return of the Pink Panther. 1979-85, exec. v.p., Interscope Comm., Inc. 1982-present, Intl. Pres., Starlight Foundation. 1986-present, pres., Film Associates, Inc. 1985-90 chmn., Samuelson Group, Inc. 1990-present, partner, Samuelson Prods. of L.A. and London.
PICTURES: Speed Merchants, High Velocity, One by One, Return of the Pink Panther, Santa Fe, A Man a Woman and a Bank, Revenge of the Nerds, Turk 182, Tom and Viv, Playmaker, Dog's Best Friend, Wilde.

SAMUELSON, SIR SYDNEY
C.B.E., B.S.C., Hon. F.B.K.S., Executive. b. London, England, Dec. 7, 1925. e. Irene Avenue Council Sch., Lancing, Sussex. Early career as cinema projectionist, 1939-42; Gaumont British News, 1942-43; Royal Air Force, 1943-47; asst. cameraman, cameraman, director/cameraman until 1960; founded Samuelson Film Service, 1954; Trustee and chmn. board of management, British Acad. of Film and Television Arts (chmn. of Council 1973-76). Member (Pres. 1983-86; Trustee: 1982-89) Cinema and Television Benevolent Fund. Member of Executive, Cinema & Television Veterans (pres. 1980-81); assoc. member, American Society of Cinematographers. Hon. Tech. Adviser, Royal Naval Film Corp. Hon. member, Guild of British Camera Technicians, 1986 (now BECTU); Member, British Society of Cinematographers (governor, 1969-79; 1st vice pres., 1976-77), Hon. Mem. for Life, Assn. of Cinema & Television Technicians, 1990. Appointed first British Film Commissioner by U.K. government, 1991. Recipient of two British Academy Awards: Michael Balcon (1985), Fellowship (1993). Received knighthood for services to British Film Industry, 1995. Lifetime Honorary Fellowship, British Kinematograph, Sound & Television Society, 1995.

SANDA, DOMINIQUE
Actress. r.n. Dominique Varaigne. b. Paris, France, March 11, 1951. e. Saint Vincent de Paul, Paris. Was a popular model for women's magazines when cast by Robert Bresson as the tragic heroine in his Dostoyevsky adaptation Un Femme Douce (1968).
THEATER: Madame Klein, Les Liaisons Dangereuses, Un Mari Ideal, Carte Blanche de Dominique Sanda.
PICTURES: Un Femme Douce, First Love, The Conformist, The Garden of the Finzi-Continis, La Notte Dei Fiori, Sans Mobile Apparent, Impossible Object, Steppenwolf, Conversation Piece, 1900, L'Heritage, Le Berceau de Cristal, Damnation Alley, Au Dela du Bien et du Mal, Beyond Good and Evil, The Song of Roland, Utopia, The Navire Night, Travels on the Sly, Caboblanco, A Room in Town, Dust of the Empire, The Way to Bresson, The Sailor 512, Corps et Biens, Les Mendiants, On a Moonlit Night, Warrior and Prisoners, Je Ne Vous Derangerai Plus, Moi La Pire De Toutes, Le Voyage, Emile Rosen, Henri Le Vert.
TELEVISION: The Sealed Train, La Naissance Du Jour, Il Decimo Clandestino, Voglia Di Vivere, Achille Lauro, Warburg, Comme Par Hazard, Non Siamo Soli, Albert Savarus, Der Lange Weg des Lukas B, The Lucona Affair, Nobody's Children, Brennendes Herz, Joseph.

SANDERS, JAY O.
Actor. b. Austin, TX, April 16, 1953. e. SUNY/Purchase. First professional theatre experience with NY Shakespeare-in-the Park prods. of Henry V and Measure for Measure. Appeared in Abel's Sister for England's Royal Court Theatre.
THEATER: *NY*: Loose Ends, The Caine Mutiny Court-Martial, Buried Child, In Trousers, Geniuses, The Incredibly Famous Willy Powers, Heaven on Earth, Girls Girls Girls, King John, Saint Joan, Three Birds Alighting on a Field.
PICTURES: Starting Over (debut, 1979), Hanky Panky, Eddie Macon's Run, Cross Creek, Tucker: The Man and His Dream, The Prince of Pennsylvania, Glory, Just Like in the Movies, Mr. Destiny, V.I. Warshawski, Defenseless, Meeting Venus, JFK, Angels in the Outfield, Kiss of Death, Down Came a Blackbird, The Big Green, Three Wishes, Kiss the Girls, Daylight, The Matchmaker, For Richer or Poorer, Wrestling With Alligators, The Odd Couple II, Tumbleweeds, Music of the Heart, Endsville, The Confession.
TELEVISION: *Series*: Aftermash, Crime Story, Lonesome Dove. *Movies*: The Day Christ Died, Living Proof: The Hank Williams Jr. Story, A Doctor's Story, Cold Sassy Tree, Hostages, State of Emergency, Nobody's Children, Rio Shannon, The Prosecutors, Earthly Possessions, The Jack Bull. *Special:* The Revolt of Mother. *Guest*: Roseanne, The Young Riders, Spenser: For Hire, A Man Called Hawk, Kate and Allie, Miami Vice, Northern Exposure, NY Undercover, The Outer Limits, Nothing Sacred.

SANDERS, TERRY BARRETT
Producer, Director, Writer. b. New York, NY, Dec. 20, 1931. e. UCLA, 1951; Co-prod., photographed, A Time Out of War, 1954. Academy Award best two-reel subject, and won first prize Venice Film Festival, etc.; co-wrote The Day Lincoln Was Shot, CBS-TV; s.p. The Naked and the Dead; prod. Crime and Punishment—USA., prod., co-dir. War Hunt; prod. and dir. Portrait of Zubin Mehta for U.S.I.A. Assoc. dean, Film Sch., California Inst. of the Arts. Prod.-Dir.: Four Stones for Kanemitsu (Acad. Award nom.). Prod.-Dir.-Writer: Rose Kennedy: A Life to Remember (Acad. Award nom.) Professor, UCLA. Pres., American Film Foundation.
PICTURES: Maya Lin: A Strong Clear Vision (prod., Acad. Award), Never Give Up: The 20th Century Odyssey of Herbert Zipper (prod., dir., Acad. Award nom.).
TELEVISION: *Prod./dir.*: Hollywood and the Stars, The Legend of Marilyn Monroe, National Geographic Society specials, The Kids from Fame, Film Bios Kennedy Center Honors, Slow Fires, Lillian Gish: The Actor's Life for Me (Emmy Award).

SANDLER, ADAM
Actor, Writer, Comedian. b. Manchester, NH, Sept. 9, 1966.
PICTURES: Going Overboard, Shakes the Clown, Coneheads, Mixed Nuts, Airheads, Billy Madison (also s.p.), Happy Gilmore (also s.p.), Bulletproof, The Wedding Singer (also comp. 2 songs), Dirty Work, The Waterboy (also s.p., exec. prod.), Big Daddy (also s.p., exec. prod.), Little Nicky (also s.p.).
TELEVISION: *Series:* Remote Control, Saturday Night Live. *Guest:* The Cosby Show, The Marshall Chronicles, The Larry Sanders Show.

SANDRICH, JAY
Director. b. Los Angeles, CA, Feb. 24, 1932. e. UCLA.
TELEVISION: *Special:* The Lily Tomlin Show (DGA Award, 1975). *Movies:* The Crooked Hearts, What Are Best Friends For?, For Richer For Poorer. *Series:* The Mary Tyler Moore Show (Emmy Awards: 1971, 1973), Soap, Phyllis (pilot), Tony Randall Show (pilot), Bob Newhart Show (pilot), Benson (pilot), Golden Girls (pilot; DGA Award, 1985), Empty Nest (pilot), The Cosby Show (Emmy Awards: 1985, 1986; DGA Award 1985).
PICTURE: Seems Like Old Times, Neil Simon's London Suite.

SANDS, JULIAN
Actor. b. Yorkshire, England, 1958. e. Central School of Speech and Drama, London 1979. Formed small theater co. that played in schools and youth clubs. Professional debut in Derek Jarman's short, Broken English and one-line part in Privates on Parade. Then opposite Anthony Hopkins in British TV series A Married Man (1981).

PICTURES: Privates on Parade (debut, 1982), Oxford Blues, The Killing Fields, After Darkness, The Doctor and the Devils, A Room with a View, Gothic, Siesta, Vibes, Wherever You Are, Manika: The Girl Who Lived Twice, Arachnophobia, Warlock, Night Sun, Impromptu, Naked Lunch, Wicked, Husbands and Lovers, Tale of a Vampire, Boxing Helena, Warlock: The Armageddon, Black Water, The Browning Version, Leaving Las Vegas, Never Ever, One Night Stand, Long Time Since, Phantom of the Opera, The Loss of Sexual Innocence, Autumn Heart, The Million Dollar Hotel, Mercy, Love Me.
TELEVISION: *Series*: A Married Man. *Movies*: Romance on the Orient Express, Harem, The Room, Murder By Moonlight, Grand Isle, Crazy in Love, Witch Hunt, The Great Elephant Escape, The Tomorrow Man, End of Summer.

SANDS, RICK
Executive. Began career as v.p. of distribution, Columbia Pictures, 1978; exec. v.p. & CFO, Miramax Films, 1990; exec. v.p. & CFO, Hallmark/RHI Entertainment, 1993; president, Miramax Intl., 1995. Currently chairman, Worldwide Distribution, Miramax, (since1997), where he is responsible for worldwide theatrical, home video, television, co-productions and acquisitions; member, Board of Directors, AFMA, AMPAS, BAFTA, and IFP; awarded Distributor of the Year, Cinema Expo Intl., 2000.

SANDS, TOMMY
Singer. b. Chicago, IL, Aug. 27, 1937. e. Schools there and Houston, TX, Greenwood, LA. Father, Benny Sands, concert pianist. Started career as guitar player, singer when 5, at KWKH station, Shreveport. One of pioneers of rock music. First manager was Col. Tom Parker. Acting debut: Kraft TV show The Singin' Idol; recording contract won him million record sales of Teen Age Crush.
PICTURES: Sing Boy Sing, Mardi Gras, Love in a Goldfish Bowl, Babes in Toyland, The Longest Day, Ensign Pulver, None But the Brave, The Violent Ones.

SANFORD, ISABEL
Actress. b. New York, NY, Aug. 29, 1929. e. Textile H.S., Evander Childs H.S. Began acting in elementary school and continued through high school. Joined American Negro Theatre in the 1930's (then The Star Players) which disbanded in W.W.II. Later associated with YWCA project and off-B'way plays. B'way debut in The Amen Corner.
PICTURES: Guess Who's Coming to Dinner, The Young Runaways, Pendulum, The Comic, Stand Up and Be Counted, The New Centurions, Love at First Bite, South Beach, Original Gangstas.
TELEVISION: *Series*: All in the Family, The Jeffersons (Emmy Award, 1981). *Movie*: The Great Man's Whiskers. *Guest*: Fresh Prince of Bel Air, Roseanne, Hangin' With Mr. Cooper, Living Single, In the House, Fresh Prince of Bel Air, Lois & Clark, Cybill.

SAN GIACOMO, LAURA
Actress. b. New Jersey, 1962. e. Carnegie Melon Univ. m. actor Cameron Dye. Appeared Off-B'way in North Shore Fish, Beirut, The Love Talker, Italian American Reconciliation, Wrong Turn at Lungfish, Three Sisters.
PICTURES: Sex Lies and Videotape (debut, 1989), Pretty Woman, Vital Signs, Quigley Down Under, Once Around, Under Suspicion, Where the Day Takes You, Nina Takes a Lover, Stuart Saves His Family, Suicide Kings, Eat Your Heart Out, The Apocalypse, With Friends Like These, Mom's on the Roof.
TELEVISION: *Series*: Just Shoot Me. *Movie*: For Their Own Good, The Right to Remain Silent. *Mini-Series*: Stephen King's The Stand. *Guest*: The Equalizer, Crime Story.

SANSOM, LESTER A.
Producer. b. Salt Lake City, UT, April 24, 1910. e. U. of Utah. Radio singer under name of Jack Allen, 1930; ent. m.p. ind. in editorial dept., Fox Film Corp., 1931; served in U.S. Navy as head of film library, Washington, DC, 1942-45; head of edit. dept. & post-prod., Allied Artists, from 1953; assoc. prod. Skabenga; prod., co-writer, Battle Flame; assoc. prod. Hell to Eternity, exec. prod. The Thin Red Line, prod. Crack in the World; prod. Bikini Paradise, Battle of the Bulge, Custer of the West, Co-prod., Krakatoa—East of Java; exec. prod. 12+1.

SAPERSTEIN, DAVID
Writer, Director. b. Brooklyn, NY. e. Bronx H.S. of Science, CCNY, Film Institute, Chemical Engineering. 1960-80 wrote, prod. and dir. documentary films, TV commercials. Also wrote lyrics and managed rhythm and blues and rock 'n roll groups. Assoc. Professor NYU Graduate Film & TV, Manhattan Marymount College. Has directed various music videos.Wrote libretto and lyrics for Blue Planet Blue, Clowns and Cocoon: The Musical.
AUTHOR: Cocoon, Metamorphosis, Red Devil, Funerama, Fatal Reunion, Dark Again.
PICTURES: Cocoon (story), Killing Affair (dir., s.p.), Personal Choice (dir., s.p.), Fatal Reunion (s.p.), Queen of America (s.p.), Torch, Sara Deri, Hearts & Diamonds, Vets, Do Not Disturb, Point of Honor, Snatched, Jack in the Box, Schoolhouse, Roberto: The Roberto Clemente Story, Roamers, Joshua's Golden Band, Beyond the Stars (dir., s.p.), Bab's Labs (s.p.), Fighting Back (s.p.), Silyan (s.p.).
TELEVISION: The Vintage Years (pilot), Dance of the Athletes (dir., writer), Rodeo—A Matter of Style (dir., writer), Mama Sings, The Corky Project, OB/GYN (pilot), Reppies (prod.).

SARA, MIA
Actress. b. Brooklyn, NY, 1968. Started doing TV commercials; landed role in soap opera, All My Children.
PICTURES: Legend (debut, 1986), Ferris Bueller's Day Off, The Long Lost Friend, Apprentice to Murder, A Row of Crows, Imagination, Any Man's Death, Shadows in the Storm, A Stranger Among Us, By the Sword, Timecop, The Pompatus of Love, The Maddening, Undertow, Bullet to Beijing, Black Day Blue Night.
TELEVISION: *Movies*: Queenie, Till We Meet Again, Daughter of Darkness, Blindsided, Call of the Wild, The Set Up. *Special*: Big Time. *Guest*: Alfred Hitchcock Presents. *Mini-series*: 20,000 Leagues Under the Sea.

SARAFIAN, RICHARD C.
Director. b. New York, NY. April 28, 1935. Studied medicine and law before entering film industry with director Robert Altman making industrial documentaries.
PICTURES: Andy (debut, 1965), Run Wild Run Free, Ballad of a Badman, Fragment of Fear, Man in the Wilderness, Vanishing Point, Lolly Madonna XXX, The Man Who Loved Cat Dancing, The Next Man (also prod.), Sunburn, The Bear, Songwriter (actor only), Street Justice (also actor), Crisis 2050, Truk Lagoon.
TELEVISION: Gunsmoke, Bonanza, Guns of Will Sonnet, I Spy Wild, Wild West; Maverick, Twilight Zone, Gangster Chronicles. *Movies*: Shadow on the Land, Disaster on the Coastline, Splendor in the Grass, A Killing Affair, Liberty, Golden Moment—An Olympic Love Story. *As Actor*: Foley Square, Long Time Gone, Miami Hustle.

SARANDON, CHRIS
Actor. b. Beckley, WV, July 24, 1942. e. U. of West Virginia. Mem. Catholic U.'s National Players touring U.S. in Shakespeare and Moliere. Acted with Washington, D.C. improvisational theater co. and Long Wharf. B'way debut, The Rothschilds.
THEATER: Two Gentlemen of Verona, Censored Scenes from King Kong, Marco Polo Sings a Solo, The Devil's Disciple, The Soldier's Tale, The Woods, Nick & Nora.
PICTURES: Dog Day Afternoon (debut, 1975; Acad. Award nom.), Lipstick, The Sentinel, Cuba, The Osterman Weekend, Protocol, Fright Night, Collision Course, The Princess Bride, Child's Play, Slaves of New York, Forced March, Whispers, The Resurrected, Dark Tide, The Nightmare Before Christmas (voice), Just Cause, Tales From the Crypt: Bordello of Blood, Edie and Pen, Road Ends, Little Men, American Perfekt, Great Sex.
TELEVISION: *Series*: The Guiding Light. *Movies*: Thursday's Game, You Can't Go Home Again, The Day Christ Died, A Tale of Two Cities, This Child Is Mine, Broken Promises, Liberty, Mayflower Madam, Tailspin: Behind the Korean Airliner Tragedy, The Stranger Within, A Murderous Affair: The Carolyn Warmus Story, David's Mother, When the Dark Man Calls, No Greater Love.

SARANDON, SUSAN
Actress. r.n. Susan Abigail Tomaling. b. New York, NY, Oct. 4, 1946. e. Catholic U. Raised in Metuchen, New Jersey. Returned to New York to pursue acting, first signing with Ford Model Agency.
THEATER: *NY*: An Evening with Richard Nixon and..., A Coupla White Chicks Sitting Around Talking, Extremities.
PICTURES: Joe (debut, 1970), Lady Liberty, Lovin' Molly, The Front Page, The Great Waldo Pepper, The Rocky Horror Picture Show, Dragonfly (One Summer Love), Checkered Flag or Crash, The Last of the Cowboys (The Great Smokey Roadblock; also co-prod.), The Other Side of Midnight, Pretty Baby, King of the Gypsies, Something Short of Paradise, Loving Couples, Atlantic City (Acad. Award nom.), Tempest, The Hunger, The Buddy System, Compromising Positions, The Witches of Eastwick, Bull Durham, Sweet Hearts Dance, The January Man, A Dry White Season, Through the Wire (narrator), White Palace, Thelma & Louise (Acad. Award nom.), The Player, Light Sleeper, Bob Roberts, Lorenzo's Oil (Acad. Award nom.), The Client (Acad. Award nom.), Little Women, Safe Passage, The Celluloid Closet, Dead Man Walking (Acad. Award), James and the Giant Peach (voice), 187, Illuminata, Twilight, Stepmom (also exec. prod.), Joe Gould's Secret, The Cradle Will Rock, Anywhere But Here, Our Friend, Martin (voice), Rugrats in Paris: The Movie (voice), Like Cats & Dogs, Baby's in Black.
TELEVISION: *Series*: Search For Tomorrow. *Guest*: Calucci's Dept, Owen Marshall: Counsellor at Law, The Simpsons (voice). *Specials:* Rimers of Eldritch, June Moon, Who Am I This Time?, One Woman One Vote (narrator). *Mini-Series*: A.D. *Movies*: F. Scott Fitzgerald & the Last of the Belles, Mussolini: Decline and Fall of Il Duce, Women of Valor, Father Roy: Inside the School of Assassins, Earthly Possessions.

SARDI, JAN
Writer.
PICTURES: Moving Out, Street Hero, Ground Zero, Breakaway, Secrets, Shine.

TELEVISION: Mission Impossible, Phoenix, The Feds, The Man From Snowy River, Halifax f.p.

SARGENT ALVIN
Writer. b. Philadelphia, PA, April 12, 1927. Began career as writer for TV, then turned to theatrical films.
PICTURES: Gambit (co-s.p.), The Stalking Moon, The Sterile Cuckoo, I Walk the Line, The Effect of Gamma Rays on Man-in-the-Moon Marigolds, Paper Moon (Acad. Award nom.), Love and Pain (and the Whole Damn Thing), Julia (Acad. Award, 1977), Bobby Deerfield, Straight Time (co-s.p.), Ordinary People (Acad. Award, 1980), Nuts (co-s.p.), Dominick and Eugene (co-s.p.), White Palace (co-s.p.), What About Bob? (co-story), Other People's Money, Hero (co-story), Bogus, Anywhere But Here.
TELEVISION: *Movies*: Footsteps, The Impatient Heart. *Series*: The Naked City, Route 66, Ben Casey, Alfred Hitchcock Presents, The Nurses, Mr. Novak, Empire.

SARGENT, HERB
Executive. Pres., Writer Guild of America East, Inc. Prod. radio program, NPR's Backfire; s.p., Bye Bye Branerman; writer, prod. for many comedy shows.

SARGENT, JOSEPH
Director. r.n. Giuseppe Danielle Sargente. b. Jersey City, NJ, July 25, 1925. e. studied theatre, New Sch. for Social Research 1946-49.
PICTURES: One Spy Too Many, The Hell With Heroes, Colossus: The Forbin Project, White Lightning, The Taking of Pelham One Two Three, MacArthur, Goldengirl, Coast to Coast, Nightmares, Jaws—The Revenge (also prod.).
TELEVISION: *Special*: The Spy in the Green Hat. *Mini-series*: The Manions of America, James Mitchener's Space. *Movies*: The Sunshine Patriot, The Immortal (pilot), The Man, Tribes, The Marcus-Nelson Murders (Emmy Award, 1973), Maybe I'll Come Home in the Spring (also prod.), The Man Who Died Twice, The Night That Panicked America, Sunshine (also prod.), Friendly Persuasion, Amber Waves, Hustling, Freedom, Tomorrow's Child, Memorial Day, Terrible Joe Moran, Choices of the Heart (also prod.), Space, Love Is Never Silent (Emmy Award, 1986), Passion Flower, Of Pure Blood, There Must Be a Pony, The Karen Carpenter Story, Day One, The Incident, Caroline? (Emmy Award, 1990), The Last Elephant, Never Forget, Miss Rose White (Emmy Award, 1992), Somebody's Daughter (also prod.), Skylark (also prod.), Abraham, World War II: When Lions Roared, My Antonia.

SARLUI, ED
Executive. b. Amsterdam, The Netherlands, Nov. 10, 1925. Owner, Peruvian Films, S.A.; pres., Radio Films of Peru, S.A.; pres. Bryant Films Educatoriana, S.A.; partner, United Producers de Colombia Ltd.; pres. Royal Film N.V.; pres., United Producers de Centroamerica, S.A.; pres. United Producers de Mexico, S.A.; pres., United Producers Int'l, Inc., Continental Motion Pictures, Inc. 1988, formed Cinema Corp. of America with Moshe Diamant and Elliott Kastner. Co-chmn. Epic Prods. Inc.
PICTURES: *Exec. prod.*: Full Moon in Blue Water, High Spirits, Teen Witch, Courage Mountain, Night Game.

SARNOFF, THOMAS W.
Executive. b. New York, NY, Feb. 23, 1927. e. Phillips Acad., Andover, MA, 1939-43, Princeton U., 1943-45, Stanford U. grad. 1948, B.S. in E.E.; Grad Sch. of Bus. Admin. 1948-49. Sgt., U.S. Army Signal Corps, 1945-46; prod. & sales, ABC-TV, Hollywood, 1949-50; prod. dept. MGM, 1951-52; asst. to dir. of finance and oper., NBC, 1952-54; dir. of prod. and bus. affairs, 1954-57; v.p., prod. and bus. affairs, 1957-60; v.p. adm. west coast, 1960-62; v.p. west coast, 1962; exec. v.p. 1965-77; bd. of dir., NBC prods 1961-77; bd of dir. Hope Enterprises 1960-75; dir. NABCAT, Inc. 1967-75; dir. Valley County Cable TV, Inc. 1969-75; Pres. NBC Entertainment Corp. 1972-77; pres. Sarnoff International Enterprises, Inc. 1977-81; pres., Sarnoff Entertainment Corp., 1981-; pres., Venturetainment Corp. 1986-93; past pres. Research Foundation at St. Joseph Hospital of Burbank; past pres. Permanent Charities of the Entertainment Ind.; past ch. bd. of trustees, National Acad. of TV Arts and Sciences. Pres. Acad. of TV Arts & Sciences Foundation 1990-99. Chairman and C.E.O. Acad. of TV Arts & Sciences Foundation, 1999-. Bd. of Dir. Multimedia Games Inc., 1998-

SARRAZIN, MICHAEL
Actor. r.n. Jacques Michel Andre Sarrazin. b. Quebec, Canada, May 22, 1940. Began acting at 17 on CBC TV; signed by Universal, 1965.
PICTURES: Gunfight in Abilene (debut, 1967), The Flim-Flam Man, The Sweet Ride, Journey to Shiloh, A Man Called Gannon, Eye of the Cat, In Search of Gregory, They Shoot Horses Don't They?, The Pursuit of Happiness, Sometimes a Great Notion, Believe in Me, The Groundstar Conspiracy, Harry in Your Pocket, For Pete's Sake, The Reincarnation of Peter Proud, The Loves and Times of Scaramouche, The Gumball Rally, Caravans, Double Negative, The Seduction, Fighting Back, Joshua Then and Now, Captive Hearts, Mascara, Keeping Track, Malarek, Lena's Holiday, Bullet to Beijing.

TELEVISION: *Movies*: The Doomsday Flight, Frankenstein: The True Story, Beulah Land, Passion and Paradise. *Guest*: Chrysler Theatre, The Virginian, World Premiere.

SAUNDERS, DAVID
Executive. Pres., Triumph Films, Inc.
PICTURES: *Exec. prod.*: Hellraiser, High Spirits, Bat *21 (co-prod.), Wild Orchid, Wild Orchid II: Two Shades of Blue, The Assignment, Masterminds, In God's Hands, Baby Geniuses.
TELEVISION: *Series*: Red Shoe Diaries. *Movies*: Red Shoe Diaries, Red Shoes Diaries 3: Another Woman's Lipstick.

SAUNDERS, WILLIAM
Executive. b. London, England, Jan. 4, 1923. e. left Upton House Central Sch. at 16. Served in British Eighth Army, 1941-47. Entered industry in 1947 as salesman with 20th Century Fox Film Co. in London; sales mgr., Anglo-Amalgamated Film Co., London, 1951-61; with Motion Picture Producers Assoc. of Amer. as sales dir. in Lagos, Nigeria, dist. Amer. feature films to West African countries, 1962-64; joined 20th Century Fox TV Intl., Paris as v.p. European TV sales, 1964-83; 20th Century TV Intl., Los Angeles as sr. v.p., 1983; named exec. v.p. 1987 and pres., 1988. Retired.

SAURA, CARLOS
Director. b. Huesca, Spain, January 4, 1932. e. educated as engineer. Worked as professional photographer from 1949. Studied at Instituto de Investigaciones y Experiencias Cinematograficos, Madrid, 1952-57 where he then taught from 1957-64 until being dismissed for political reasons. 1957-58 dir. shorts La tarde del domingo and Cuenca.
PICTURES: *Director &/or Writer*: Los Golfos (The Urchins), Lament for a Bandit, La Caza (The Hunt), Peppermint Frappe, Stress es Tres Tres, La Madriguera (The Honeycomb), The Garden of Delights, Anna and the Wolves, Cousin Angelica (Cannes Fest. jury prize, 1974), Cria! (Cannes Fest. jury prize, 1976), Elisa Vide Mia, Los ojos Vendados (Blindfold), Mama Turns 100, Hurry Hurry (Golden Bear, Berlin Fest., 1981), Blood Wedding, Dulces Horas (Sweet Hours), Antonieta, Carmen, Los Zancos (The Stilts), El Amor Brujo (Love the Magician), El Dorado, The Dark Night, Ay Carmela!, Sevillanas, Outrage, Flamenco, Taxi, Tango, Pajarico, Esa luz!.

SAVAGE, DAVID
Executive Producer, Advertising Executive, b. New York, NY, March 17, 1929. e. Rochester Inst. of Technology. In research development & testing div., Eastman Kodak Co., 2 yrs.; adv. mgr. asst. nat'l sales mgr., Official Films; org., film dept. mgr. WCBS-TV; dir. of film procurement, CBS; mgr. of film procurement, NBC; mgr. planning, merchandising, Recorded Tape Dept., RCA Records; promo. mgr., special products mktg. RCA Records Div.; program and marketing chmn. RCA SelectaVision group; v.p., operations, Wunderman, Rilotto, & Kline, 1970; pres., Response Industries, Inc., (direct response adv. agency), 1973 which became affiliate of McCann Erickson, and was sr. v.p. of McCann Erickson Pres., Mattel Direct Marketing, 1982; v.p. and man. dir., Foote Cene Belding, subsid. Knipp-Taylor USA, 1985.

SAVAGE, FRED
Actor. b. Highland Park, IL, July 9, 1976. e. Stanford Univ. While in kindergarten auditioned for commercial at local community center. Didn't get the job but called back by same dir. for two more tests. Chosen for Pac-Man vitamin ad which led to 27 on-camera TV commercials and 36 voice-over radio spots.
PICTURES: The Boy Who Could Fly, The Princess Bride, Vice Versa, Little Monsters, The Wizard.
TELEVISION: *Series*: Morningstar/Eveningstar, The Wonder Years, Working. *Movies*: Convicted: A Mother's Story, Run Till You Fall, When You Remember Me, Christmas on Division Street, No One Would Tell. *Special*: Runaway Ralph. *Guest*: The Twilight Zone, Seinfeld, The Outer Limits.

SAVAGE, JOHN
Actor. r.n. John Youngs. b. Old Bethpage, Long Island, NY, Aug. 25, 1949. Studied at American Acad. of Dramatic Arts. In Manhattan organized Children's Theatre Group which performed in public housing. Won Drama Desk Award for performance in One Flew Over the Cuckoo's Nest (Chicago & LA).
THEATER: Fiddler on the Roof, Ari, Siamese Connections, The Hostage, American Buffalo, Of Mice and Men.
PICTURES: Bad Company (debut, 1972), Steelyard Blues, The Killing Kind, The Sister in Law (also composed score), The Deer Hunter, Hair, The Onion Field, Inside Moves, Cattle Annie and Little Britches, The Amateur, Brady's Escape, Maria's Lovers, Salvador, Beauty and the Beast, Hotel Colonial, Soldier's Revenge, The Beat, Caribe, Do the Right Thing, Point of View, Any Man's Death, The Godfather Part III, Hunting, Primary Motive, My Forgotten Man, C.I.A. II: Target Alexa, Red Scorpion 2, Killing Obsession, Carnosaur 2, From the Edge, The Dangerous, Centurion Force, The Crossing Guard, White Squall, Where Truth Lies, American Strays, Little Boy Blue, The Mouse, Club Vampire, Burning Down the House, Amnesia, Hostile Intent, The Virginian, Summer of Sam, Frontline, Message in a Bottle.

TELEVISION: *Series*: Gibbsville. *Movies*: All the Kind Strangers, Eric (also wrote and performed songs), The Turning Point of Jim Malloy, Coming Out of the Ice, The Tender Age (The Little Sister), Silent Witness, The Nairobi Affair, Desperate, The Burning Shore, Daybreak, Shattered Image, Tom Clancy's Op Center, Before Women Had Wings, The Jack Bull. *Special:* Date Rape (Afterschool Special). *Guest*: Tales From the Crypt, Birdland, X Files, Walker Texas Ranger, The Outer Limits.

SAVOCA, NANCY
Director. e. NYU film sch. m. prod.-writer Richard Guay. While in school directed and wrote short films Renata and Bad Timing. Received Haig P. Manoogian Award for filmmaking at 1984 NYU Student Film Festival. Made feature debut with True Love which won Grand Jury Prize at 1989 United States Film Festival.
PICTURES: True Love (also co-s.p.), Dogfight, Household Saints (also co-s.p.), 24-Hour Woman.

SAWYER, DIANE
News Correspondent, Anchor. b. Glasgow, KY, Dec. 22, 1945. m. director Mike Nichols. e. Wellesley Coll. Studied law before deciding on career in TV. Former Junior Miss winner and weather reporter on a Louisville TV station before arriving in Washington, 1970. Worked for Nixon Administration in press office from 1970-74; assisted Nixon in writing memoirs, 1975-78. Joined CBS News as reporter in Washington bureau in 1978; named correspondent in 1980. Served as CBS State Dept. correspondent 1980-81. Joined Charles Kuralt as co-anchor of the weekday editions of CBS Morning News in 1981; 1984-89 correspondent on 60 Minutes; 1989, signed by ABC News as co-anchor of Primetime Live news prog. with Sam Donaldson. 1994, co-anchor of Turning Point.

SAXON, JOHN
Actor. r.n. Carmine Orrico. b. Brooklyn, NY, Aug. 5, 1936.
PICTURES: Running Wild (debut, 1955), The Unguarded Moment, Rock Pretty Baby, Summer Love, The Reluctant Debutante, This Happy Feeling, The Restless Years, The Big Fisherman, Cry Tough, Portrait in Black, The Unforgiven, The Plunderers, Posse from Hell, Mr. Hobbs Takes a Vacation, War Hunt, Evil Eye, The Cardinal, The Ravagers, The Cavern, The Appaloosa, Queen of Blood, Night Caller From Outer Space, For Singles Only, Death of a Gunfighter, Company of Killers, Joe Kidd, Enter The Dragon, Black Christmas, Mitchell, The Swiss Conspiracy, Strange Shadows in an Empty Room, Moonshine County Express, Shalimar, The Bees, The Glove, The Electric Horseman, Battle Beyond the Stars, Beyond Evil, Blood Beach, Cannibal in the Streets, Wrong Is Right, The Big Score, Nightmare on Elm Street, Prisioners of the Lost Universe, Fever Pitch, Nightmare on Elm Street 3: Dream Warriors, Criminal Act, Death House (also dir.), My Mom's a Werewolf, Aftershock, Blood Salvage, Hellmaster, Crossing the Line, Maximum Force, No Escape No Return, Jonathan of the Bears, Killing Obsession, Beverly Hills Cop III, Wes Craven's New Nightmare.
TELEVISION: *Series*: The Bold Ones (The New Doctors), Falcon Crest. *Movies*: The Doomsday Flight, Winchester 73, Istanbul Express, The Intruders, Snatched, Linda, Can Ellen Be Saved?, Planet Earth, Crossfire, Strange New World, Raid on Entebbe, The Immigrants, Golden Gate, Rooster, Prisoners of the Lost Universe, Payoff, Blackmail, Genghis Khan, Liz: The Elizabeth Taylor Story.

SAYLES, JOHN
Writer, Director, Editor, Actor. b. Schnectady, NY, Sept. 28, 1950. e. Williams Coll., B.S. psychology, 1972. Wrote two novels: Pride of the Bimbos, 1975 and Union Dues, 1978; also The Anarchist's Convention, collection of short stories and, Thinking in Pictures: The Making of the Movie Matewan (1987). Wrote and directed plays off-B'way (New Hope for the Dead, Turnbuckle). Directed Bruce Springsteen music videos (Born in the U.S.A., I'm on Fire, Glory Days). Recipient of MacArthur Foundation Grant for genius.
PICTURES: Piranha (s.p., co-story, actor), Lady in Red (s.p.), Battle Beyond the Stars (story, s.p.), Return of the Secaucus Seven, Alligator (s.p., story), The Howling (co-s.p., actor), The Challenge (co-s.p.), Lianna, Baby It's You (dir., s.p.), The Brother from Another Planet, Enormous Changes at the Last Minute (co-s.p.), The Clan of the Cave Bear (s.p.), Hard Choices (actor), Something Wild (actor), Wild Thing (s.p.), Matewan (dir., s.p., actor), Eight Men Out (dir., s.p., actor), Breaking In (s.p.), Little Vegas (actor), City of Hope, Straight Talk (actor), Malcolm X (actor), Passion Fish (dir., s.p., edit.), Matinee (actor), My Life's in Turnaround (actor), The Secret of Roan Inish (dir., s.p., edit.), Lone Star (dir., s.p.), Men With Guns (dir., s.p., edit.), Mimic, Limbo (dir., s.p., ed.).
TELEVISION: *Movies*: A Perfect Match, Unnatural Causes (actor, writer), Shannon's Deal (writer, creative consult.). *Special*: Mountain View (Alive From Off Center).

SCACCHI, GRETA
Actress. b. Milan, Italy, Feb. 18, 1960. e. England and Australia. Acted in Bristol Old Vic Theatre in England.
PICTURES: Das Zweiter Gesicht, Heat and Dust, The Coca Cola Kid, Burke & Wills, Defence of the Realm, A Man in Love, Good Morning Babylon, White Mischief, Paura e Amore (Fear and Love), Woman in the Moon, Presumed Innocent, Fires Within, Shattered, The Player, Turtle Beach, Desire, The Browning Version, Jefferson in Paris, Country Life, Cosi (cameo), Emma, The Serpent's Kiss, The Red Violin, Love and Rage, Tom's Midnight Garden, Ladies Room, Cotton Mary, The Manor.
TELEVISION: *Mini-Series*: Waterfront (Australia), The Odyssey. *Movies*: Ebony Tower, Dr. Fischer of Geneva, Camille, Rasputin (Emmy Award, 1996), Macbeth.

SCARWID, DIANA
Actress. b. Savannah, GA. e. St. Vincent's Acad., American Acad. of Dramatic Arts, Pace U., 1975. Member of National Shakespeare Conservatory (Woodstock, NY) and worked in regional theatres before moving to Hollywood 1976.
PICTURES: Pretty Baby (debut, 1978), Honeysuckle Rose, Inside Moves (Acad. Award nom.), Mommie Dearest, Rumble Fish, Strange Invaders, Silkwood, The Ladies Club, Psycho III, Extremities, Heat, Brenda Starr, Gold Diggers: The Secret of Bear Mountain, The Cure, The Neon Bible, Bastard Out of Carolina.
TELEVISION: *Mini-Series*: Studs Lonigan. *Movies*: In the Glitter Palace, The Possessed, Forever, Battered, Guyana Tragedy: The Story of Jim Jones, Desperate Lives, Thou Shalt Not Kill, A Bunny's Tale, After the Promise, Night of the Hunter, Simple Justice, Labor of Love: The Arlette Schweitzer Story, JFK: Reckless Youth, Truman. *Series*: The Outer Limits.

SCHAEFER, CARL
Media Consultant, Publicist, b. Cleveland, OH, Sept. 2, 1908. e. UCLA. Contr. to mag., including Vanity Fair, Hollywood Citizen-News, 1931-35; Warner Bros., 1935.; Huesped de Honor, Mexico, 1943; OSS WWII, 1944-45; Int'l Comt. AMPS, chmn. 1966-67; Italian Order of Merit, 1957; Chevalier de l'ordre de la Couronne, Belgium, 1963. Pres., Foreign Trade Assn. of Southern Calif., 1954; chmn. of bd., 1955; British-American C. of C., Dir., 1962; Chevalier French Legion d'Honneur, 1955; Comm. Hollywood Museum; dir., intl. relations, Warner Bros. Seven Arts Int'l Corp., 1960; formed own firm, Carl Schaefer Enterprises, 1971. Dir. pub. rel., British-American Chamber of Commerce, 1971; dir. pub. rel. for Iota Intl. Pictures, 1971; dir. pub. rel. Lyric Films Intl., 1971; bureau chief (Hollywood) Movie/TV Marketing, 1971; man. dir., Intl. Festival Advisory Council, 1971; dir. pub. rel. & adv. Francis Lederer Enterprises Inc. (American National Acad. of Performing Arts, and Canoga Mission Gallery) 1974; West Coast rep. Angelika Films of N.Y. 1974, Hwd. rep Korwitz/Geiger Products. 1975-; Hwd. corresp. Movie News, S'pore, & Femina, Hong Kong, 1974-; member Westn. Publications Assn. 1975-; field rep. Birch Records 1975; Hollywood rep Antena Magazine, Buenos Aires; dir. pub. rel., Style Magazine. Coordinator Hollywood Reporter Annual Key Art Awards; coordinator Hollywood Reporter Annual Marketing Concept Awards; exec. comm. & historian ShoWest; Mem: National Panel of Consumer Arbitrators, 1985; Hollywood Corr., Gold Coast Times of Australia, 1986-87. Winner 1990 Key Art Award. Member: AMPAS, awarded certif. of Appreciation, 1962; charter member, Publicists Guild of America; pres. Pacific Intercollegiate Press Assn., while UCLA Daily Bruin Editor, 1930-31. Poetry anthologies, 1995-96, National Library of Poetry.

SCHAFFEL, ROBERT
Producer. b. Washington, DC, March 2, 1944. Partner with Jon Voight in Voight-Schaffel Prods. Now heads Robert Schaffel Prods.
PICTURES: Gordon's War, Sunnyside, Lookin' to Get Out, Table for Five, American Anthem, Distant Thunder, Jacknife, Diggstown, Pontiac Moon.

SCHAPIRO, KEN
Executive. e. B.A., UC Berkeley, graduate, Harvard Law School. Joined Morgan Creek films, 1990, where he was responsible for business & legal affairs on the production of all films; executive v.p., Morgan Creek Prods. & Morgan Creek Intl.; executive v.p., Artisan Entertainment, 1998. Currently COO, Artisan.

SCHATZBERG, JERRY
Director. b. New York, NY, June 26, 1927. e. U. of Miami, 1947-48. Early career in photography as asst. to Bill Helburn 1954-56. Freelance still photographer and TV commercials dir. 1956-69. Contrib. photographs to several mags. incl. Life.
PICTURES: Puzzle of a Downfall Child (debut, 1970), The Panic in Needle Park, Scarecrow, Sweet Revenge (also prod.), The Seduction of Joe Tynan, Honeysuckle Rose, Misunderstood, No Small Affair, Street Smart, Reunion.
TELEVISION: *Movie*: Clinton and Nadine.

SCHEIDER, ROY
Actor. b. Orange, NJ, Nov. 10, 1932. e. Franklin and Marshall Coll. where he twice won the Theresa Helburn Acting Award. First professional acting in 1961 NY Shakespeare Festival prod. of Romeo and Juliet. Became member of Lincoln Center Repertory Co. and acted with Boston Arts Festival, American Shakespeare Festival, Arena Stage (Wash., DC) and American Repertory Co. Appeared in documentary In Our Hands.

THEATER: Richard III, Stephen D, Sergeant Musgrave's Dance, The Alchemist, Betrayal.
PICTURES: Curse of the Living Corpse (debut, 1964), Paper Lion, Star!, Stiletto, Loving, Puzzle of a Downfall Child, Klute, The French Connection (Acad. Award nom.), The Outside Man, The French Conspiracy, The Seven Ups, Sheila Levine is Dead and Living in New York, Jaws, Marathon Man, Sorcerer, Jaws 2, Last Embrace, All That Jazz (Acad. Award nom.), Still of the Night, Blue Thunder, 2010, Mishima (narrator), The Men's Club, 52 Pickup, Cohen and Tate, Listen to Me, Night Game, The Fourth War, The Russia House, Naked Lunch, Romeo Is Bleeding, The Rage, Plato's Run, The Peacekeeper, The Myth of Fingerprints, Executive Target, The Definite Maybe, The Rainmaker, The White Raven, Better Living, Silver Wolf, Falling Through.
TELEVISION: *Movies*: Assignment Munich, Jacobo Timerman: Prisoner Without a Name Cell Without a Number, Tiger Town, Somebody Has to Shoot the Picture, Wild Justice, Money Plays, RKO 281. *Series*: seaQuest DSV. *Guest*: Hallmark Hall of Fame, Studio One, N.Y.P.D. *Special*: Portrait of the Soviet Union (host).

SCHEINMAN, ANDREW
Producer. b. 1948. e. Univ. of VA, law degree. Professional tennis player before entering film business as producer of three Charlton Heston films. Became one of 5 founding partners of Castle Rock Entertainment.
PICTURES: *Prod/Exec. Prod.*: The Mountain Man, The Awakening, Modern Romance, Mother Lode, The Sure Thing, Stand By Me, The Princess Bride, When Harry Met Sally..., Misery, A Few Good Men, North (also co-s.p.), Ghosts of Mississippi, Extreme Measures. *Director*: Little Big League.
TELEVISION: *Series*: Seinfeld (exec. prod.)

SCHELL, MARIA
Actress. b. Vienna, Austria, Jan. 5, 1926. Brother is actor Maximilian Schell. Made debut as teenager in Swiss film, Steinbruch (Quarry). Subsequently appeared in many British and American films.
PICTURES: Quarry (debut, 1941), Angel with the Trumpet, The Affairs of Dr. Holl, The Magic Box, Angelika, So Little Time, The Heart of the Matter, Der Traumende Mund (Dreaming Lips), The Last Bridge (Cannes Film Fest. Award, 1954), Angelika, The Rats, Napoleon, Gervaise (Venice Film Fest. Award, 1956), Liebe (Love), Rose Bernd, Le Notti Bianche (White Nights), Une Vie (End of Desire), The Brothers Karamazov, The Hanging Tree, Der Schinderhanners (Duel in the Forest), As the Sea Rages, Cimarron, The Mark, Only a Woman, La Assassin connait la Musique, Rendevzous in Trieste, Who Has Seen the Wind?, 99 Women, Devil By the Tail, Night of the Blood Monster, Lust in the Sun, The Odessa File, Voyage of the Damned, Folies Bourgeoises (The Twist), Superman, Just a Gigolo, 1919.
TELEVISION: *U.S.*: Heidi, Christmas Lilies of the Field, Inside the Third Reich, Martian Chronicles, Samson and Delilah.

SCHELL, MAXIMILIAN
Actor, Director. b. Vienna, Dec. 8, 1930. Sister is actress Maria Schell. e. Switzerland. Stage debut 1952. B'way debut in Interlock.
PICTURES: Children Mother and the General (debut, 1955), The Young Lions (U.S. debut, 1958), Judgment at Nuremberg (Acad. Award, 1961), Five Finger Exercise, The Reluctant Saint, The Condemned of Altona, Topkapi, Return from the Ashes, The Deadly Affair, Counterpoint, The Desperate Ones, The Castle (also prod.), Krakatoa—East of Java, Simon Bolivar, First Love (also dir., co-s.p., co-prod.), Trotta (co-s.p.), Pope Joan, Paulina 1880, The Pedestrian (also dir., prod., s.p.), The Odessa File, The Man in the Glass Booth, End of the Game (also dir., co-prod., co-s.p.), St. Ives, The Day That Shook the World, A Bridge Too Far, Cross of Iron, Julia, Players, Avalanche Express, Together?, The Black Hole, Tales From the Vienna Woods (also prod., s.p.), The Chosen, Les Iles, Morgen in Alabama, Marlene (dir., s.p., interviewer), The Rose Garden, The Freshman, Labyrinth, A Far Off Place, Little Odessa.
TELEVISION: Judgment at Nuremberg (Playhouse 90), The Fifth Column, The Diary of Anne Frank, Turn The Key Deftly, Phantom of the Opera, Heidi, The Assisi Underground, Peter the Great (mini-series), Young Catherine, Stalin, Miss Rose White, Candles in the Dark (also dir.).

SCHEPISI, FRED
Producer, Director, Writer. b. Melbourne, Australia, Dec. 26, 1939. e. Assumption Col., Marist Bros. Juniorate, Marcellin Col. Assessed student films at Melbourne's Swinburne Inst. of Tech.; worked on gov. sponsored experimental Film Fund; made TV commercials. Founded The Film House prod. co. Dir. short film The Party.
PICTURES: *Director*: Libido (co-dir.), Barbarosa, Iceman, Plenty, Roxanne, A Cry in the Dark (also co-s.p.; Australian Film Inst. Award for best dir. & s.p.), Fierce Creatures. *Dir./Prod.*: The Devil's Playground (also s.p.), The Chant of Jimmie Blacksmith (also s.p.), The Russia House, Mr. Baseball, Six Degrees of Separation, I.Q., Fierce Creatures. *Producer*: That Eye the Sky (exec.)

SCHERICK, EDGAR J
Executive, Producer. b. New York, NY, Oct. 16, 1924. e. Harvard U.; elected to Phi Beta Kappa. Asst. dir. of radio and TV; assoc. media dir. and dir. of sports special events, Dancer-Fitzgerald-Sample ad agency, NY during 1950s. Introduced Wide World of Sports on TV through his co., Sports Programs, Inc. Was v.p. in chg. of network programming at ABC-TV. Pres. of Palomar Pictures Int'l. Now independent producer.
PICTURES: For Love of Ivy, The Birthday Party, Take the Money and Run, They Shoot Horses Don't They?, The Killing of Sister George, Ring of Bright Water, Jenny, Sleuth, The Heartbreak Kid, Law and Disorder, The Stepford Wives, I Never Promised You a Rose Garden, The Taking of Pelham One Two Three, American Success Company, I'm Dancing As Fast As I Can, Shoot the Moon, White Dog, He Makes Me Feel Like Dancin' (Acad. Award, 1983), Reckless, Mrs. Soffel.
TELEVISION: The Man Who Wanted to Live Forever, The Silence, Circle of Children, Raid on Entebbe, Panic in Echo Park, Zuma Beach, An American Christmas Carol, The Seduction of Miss Leona, Revenge of the Stepford Wives, Hitler's SS, The High Price of Passion, The Stepford Children, Unholy Matrimony, Little Gloria... Happy at Last, On Wings of Eagles, Hands of a Stranger, Home Fires, He Makes Me Feel Like Dancin' (Emmy Award, 1983), Stranger on My Land (exec. prod.), And the Band Played On, The Kennedys of Massachusetts, Satin's Touch (exec. prod.), Phantom of the Opera, The Secret Life of Ian Fleming, Tyson.

SCHIAVELLI, VINCENT
Actor. b. Brooklyn, NY. e. NYU. On Stage in Hunting Cockroaches, Alphabetical Order, Angel City.
AUTHOR: Papa Andrea's Sicilian Table, Bruculinu America.
PICTURES: Taking Off, The Great Gatsby, For Pete's Sake, One Flew Over the Cuckoo' Nest, The Happy Hooker, Next Stop Greenwich Village, An Unmarried Woman, The Frisco Kid, Butch and Sundance: The Early Days, Seed of Innocence, The Return, American Pop (voice), Chu Chu and the Philly Flash, Night Shift, Fast Times at Ridgemont High, Kidco, The Adventures of Buckaroo Banzai Across the 8th Dimension, Amadeus, Better Off Dead, Valmont, Homer and Eddie, Cold Feet, Ghost, Waiting for the Light, Playroom, Penny Ante, Mister Frost, Ted and Venus, Another You, Miracle Beach, Batman Returns, Lurking Fear, Cultivating Charlie, Lod of Illusions, A Little Princess, Ninjas Knuckle Up, Two Much, The People vs. Larry Flynt, Back to Back, The Beautician and the Beast, Tomorrow Never Dies, Milo, The Prince and the Surfer, Coyote Moon.
TELEVISION: *Series*: The Corner Bar, Taxi, Fast Times. *Movies*: Rescue from Gilligan's Island, White Mama, Escape, The Ratings Game, Bride of Boogedy, Escape to Witch Mountain, The Whipping Boy. *Guest*: Moonlighting, Shell Game, Star Trek: The Next Generation, Batman: The Animated Series (voice), Knots Landing, Eerie Indiana, The X Files, Buffy the Vampire Slayer.

SCHIFRIN, LALO
Composer, b. Buenos Aires, Argentina, June 21, 1932. Father was conductor of Teatro Colon in B.A. for 30 years. Schifrin studied with Juan Carlos Paz in Arg. and later Paris Cons. Returned to homeland and wrote for stage, modern dance, TV. Became interested in jazz and joined Dizzie Gillespie's band in 1962 as pianist and composer. Settled in L.A. Pres. Young Musicians Fed. Music; dir. and conductor, Paris Philharmonic 1987.
PICTURES: El Jefe, Rhino!, Joy House/Les Felins, Once A Thief, Gone With the Wave, Dark Intruder, The Cincinnati Kid, Way...Way Out!, The Liquidator, I Deal in Danger, Blindfold, Who's Minding the Mint?, The Venetian Affair, Sullivan's Empire, The President's Analyst, Murderer's Row, Cool Hand Luke (Acad. Award nom.), Sol Madrid, Hell in the Pacific, The Fox (Acad. Award nom.), Coogan's Bluff, Bullitt, The Bortherhood/The Heroin Gang, The Eye of the Cat, Che!, W.U.S.A., Pussycat Pussycat I love You, Kelly's Heroes, Imago, I Love My Wife, THX-1138, Pretty Maids All in a Row, Mrs. Pollifax–Spy, The Hellstrom Chronicle, Dirty Harry, The Christian Licorice Store, The Beguiled, The Wrath of God, Rage, Prime Cut, Joe Kidd, The Neptune Factor,
Magnum Force, Hit!, Harry in Your Pocket, Enter the Dragon, Charlie Varrick, Man On a Swing, Golden Needles, The Master Gunfighter, The Four Musketeers, Voyage of the Damned (Acad. Award nom.), St. Ives, Special Delivery, The Sky Riders, Return From Witch Mountain, Telefon, Rollercoaster, The Eagle Has Landed, The Day of the Animals, Nunzio, The Manitou, The Cat From Outer Space, Love and Bullets, Escape to Athena, Boulevard Nights, The Concorde: Airport '79, The Amityville Horror, When Time Ran Out, Serial, The Nude Bomb, The Competition (Acad. Award nom.), Brubaker, The Big Brawl, The Seduction, La Pelle, Loophole, Caveman, Buddy Buddy, Las Viernes de la Etertnidad, Fast-Walking, The Class of 1984, A Stranger Is Watching, Amytiville II–The Possession, Airplane II–The Sequel, Sudden Impact, The Sting II, The Osterman Weekend, Dr. Detroit, Tank, The New Kids, The Mean Season, The Ladies Club, Black Moon Rising, The Fourth Protocol, The Silence at Bethany, Little Sweetheart, The Dead Pool,

Berlin Blues, Return to the River Kwai, Fridays to Eternity, Naked Tango, FX 2, The Beverly Hillbilles, Rice Beans & Ketchuo, Scoprion Spring, Mission: Impossible, Tango, Something to Believe In, Money Talks.
TELEVISION: *Theme, Episode, Movie & Miniseries scores*: Mission Impossible, Mannix, Medical Center, T.H.E. Cat, Planet of the Apes, Starsky and Hutch, Bronk, Braddock, The Blue Light, Dr. Kildare, 90 Bristol Court, The Young Lawyers, The Black Cloak, The Cliff Dwellers, Ben Casey, I.F.M., Johnny Comes Home, Delancy Street, Foster and Laurie, Egan, How I Spent My Summer Vacation, The World of Jacques Cousteau, Three for Danger, Brenda Starr, Good Against Evil, The Chicago Story, The Victims, Starflight One, Princess Diasy, Sprague, House Detective, Command 5, Glitter, A.D., Hollywood Wives, Terror at London Bridge, Private Sessions, The Equalizer, Beverly Hills Madam, Out on a Limb, Hunter, The Doomsday Flight, Jericho, The Highest Fall of All, Maryk, The Nativity, Quest, Petrocelli, The President's Mistress, Pay the Piper, The Rise and Fall of the Third Reich, The Hidden World of Insects, The Way-Out Men, Sullivan Country, The Aquarians, Shipwreck, Sam Sheppard, Sixth Sense, Memo From Purgatory, Kraft Suspense Theatre, The Virginians, Wagon Train, Private Eye, Shakedown on the Sunset Strip, Earthstar Voyager, Neon Empire, Little White Lies, Face to Face, Original Sins, Berlin Blues, El Quixote, A Woman Named Jackie, Danger Theater.

SCHILLER, FRED
Playwright, Screen & TV Writer. b. Vienna, Austria, Jan. 6, 1924. e. Columbia Univ. (B.A.). Awarded: New York Literary Prize for McCall magazine story Ten Men and a Prayer. Member of Dramatists' Guild and Writer's Guild of America. Formerly chief corresp. European Newspaper Feature Services. Honored by the U. of Wyoming and the American Heritage Center for literary achievements with a special Fred Schiller Collection for their library. Awarded the Honor Silver Cross by Austrian Govt., for literary achievements and for furthering cultural relations between Austria and U.S. Screen plays for pictures by MGM, Columbia, RKO, Republic, Harry Sokal Productions.
THEATER: Come On Up (U.S. key citiies , London), Anything Can Happen (London), Demandez Vicky (Paris), Finder Please Return (L.A., San Francisco, Madrid, Vienna), Finder Bitte Melden (Berlin, Baden-Baden, Vienna), The Love Trap.
TELEVISION: Wrote some 53 TV plays incl. The Inca of Perusalem, Demandez Vicky! for Paris and Finder Bitte Melden! for Austria.

SCHILLER, LAWRENCE J.
Producer, Director. b. New York, NY, Dec. 28, 1936. Photojournalist with Life Magazine & Saturday Evening Post, 1958-70; collaborated on numerous books including three by Norman Mailer: The Executioner's Song, Marilyn, and The Faith of Graffiti; also Muhammad Ali (with Wilfrid Sheed), Minamata (with Eugene Smith).
PICTURES: The Man Who Skied Down Everest (editorial concept & direction), Butch Cassidy & the Sundance Kid (conceived and executed special still montages & titles); The American Dreamer (prod., dir.).
TELEVISION: *Prod.:* Hey I'm Alive (also dir.), The Trial of Lee Harvey Oswald, The Winds of Kitty Hawk, Marilyn, The Untold Story, An Act of Love, Child Bride of Short Creek, The Executioner's Song (also dir.), Peter the Great, Margaret Bourke-White (also dir.).

SCHINE, G. DAVID
Executive. b. Gloversville, NY, Sept. 11, 1927. e. Harvard U., Pres., gen. mgr. Schine Hotels 1950-63. Film exhibitor until 1966 in New York, Ohio, Kentucky, Maryland, Delaware, and West Virginia. Exec. prod. of French Connection, 1971. Writer, prod., dir. of That's Action!, 1977. Chief Exec. officer of Schine Productions (production) and Epic Productions (distribution), Visual Sciences, Inc., High Resolution Sciences, Inc., and Studio Television Services, Inc.

SCHLAIFER, CHARLES
Executive. b. Omaha, NB, July 1, 1909. Reporter Daily News, World-Herald (Omaha). 1930 appt. adv. mngr. Paramount theatres, then Publix theatres in Omaha; then mngr. of Tri-State circuit, NE, Iowa; 1936-42 mng. dir. UA Theatres, San Francisco; advisor, nat'l adv., United Artists prods.; 1942 appt. adv. mgr. 20th Cent.-Fox; 1944, named asst. dir. adv., publicity, & exploitation; 1945-49, v.p. & dir. of advertising, pub., exploitation and radio; 1949, resigned to establish own adv. agency becoming pres., Charles Schlaifer & Co., Inc.; chmn. advertising advisory council, MPAA; revised m.p. adv. code; permanent chmn. first MPAA public relations committee.

SCHLATTER, GEORGE
Producer, Director, Writer. b. Birmingham, AL, Dec. 31, 1932. m. former actress Jolene Brand. e. Pepperdine U. on football scholarship. First industry job was MCA agent in band and act dept. Then gen. mgr. and show producer Ciro's nightclub (where he met Dick Martin and Dan Rowan). Produced shows at Frontier Hotel and Silver Slipper, Las Vegas. Sang 2 seasons St. Louis Municipal Opera Co.
TELEVISION: *Created*: Laugh-In, Real People (3 Emmys, 27 nominations). *Specials with*: Goldie Hawn, Robin Williams, Shirley MacLaine, Doris Day, John Denver, Frank Sinatra, Jackie Gleason, Danny Thomas, Bob Hope, Milton Berle, Danny Kaye, George Burns, Dinah Shore, Lucille Ball, Goldie & Liza Together, Salute to Lady Liberty, Las Vegas 75th Anniversary, Speak Up America, Real Kids, Best of Times, Look At Us, Shape of Things, Magic or Miracle, Grammy Awards (first 5 years: also writer), series with Dinah Shore, Judy Garland, Bill Cosby, Steve Lawrence; also ABC American Comedy Awards (3 years), George Schlatter's Comedy Club, George Schlatter's Funny People, Beverly Hills 75th Anniversary, Humor and the Presidency, Frank Liza & Sammy... The Ultimate Event, Comedy Hall of Fame, She TV (series), Sinatra's 75th Birthday, The Best Is Yet to Come, Muhammad Ali's 50th Birthday, Welcome Home America, Laugh-In 25th Anniversary Reunion.

SCHLESINGER, JOHN
Director, Producer. b. London, England, Feb. 16, 1926. e. Oxford U., BBC dir. 1958-60: Wrote and dir. Terminus for British Transport Films (Golden Lion, best doc., Venice); The Class. Some episodes The Valiant Years series. Appeared as actor in films: Sailor of the King (1953), Pursuit of the Graf Spee, Brothers in Law, The Divided Heart, The Last Man to Hang, Fifty Years of Action (DGA doc.). Assoc. dir., National Theatre, London 1973-89. Recipient of 1995 BAFTA Fellowship.
THEATER: No Why (RSC), Timon of Athens (RSC), Days in the Trees (RSC), I and Albert, Heartbreak House (NT), Julius Caesar (NT), True West (NT).
PICTURES: A Kind of Loving (Berlin Golden Bear Award, 1961), Billy Liar, Darling (NY Film Critics Award), Far From the Madding Crowd, Midnight Cowboy (Acad. Award, 1969), Sunday Bloody Sunday, Visions of Eight (sequence), The Day of the Locust, Marathon Man, Yanks, Honky Tonk Freeway, The Falcon and the Snowman (also co-prod.), The Believers (also co-prod.), Madame Sousatzka (also co-s.p.), Pacific Heights (also cameo), The Innocent, Eye for an Eye, Cold Comfort Farm, The Next Best Thing.
TELEVISION: Separate Tables, An Englishman Abroad (BAFTA Award), The Lost Language of Cranes (actor only), A Question of Attribution (BAFTA Award), The Tale of Sweeney Todd.
OPERA: Les Contes d'Hoffmann (Royal Opera House 1981; SWET award), Der Rosenkavalier, Un Ballo in Maschera (Salzburg Fest., 1989).

SCHLONDORFF, VOLKER
Director. b. Wiesbaden, Germany, March 31, 1939. m. dir.-actress Margarethe von Trotta. Studied in France, acquiring degree in political science in Paris. Studied at French Intl. Film Sch. (IDHEC) before becoming asst. to Jean-Pierre Melville, Alain Resnais, and Louis Malle.
PICTURES: Young Torless (debut, 1966; also s.p.), A Degree of Murder (also s.p.), Michael Kohlhass, Baal, The Sudden Fortune of the Poor People of Kombach, Die Moral der Ruth Halbfass, A Free Woman, The Lost Honor of Katharina Blum (also s.p.), Coup de Grace, The Tin Drum (also s.p.), Valeska Gert (also s.p.), Circle of Deceit, Swann in Love (also s.p.), The Handmaid's Tale, Voyager (also co-s.p.).
TELEVISION: Death of a Salesman, A Gathering of Old Men.

SCHLOSSBERG, JULIAN
Producer, Distributor, Director, Radio TV Host. b. New York, NY, Jan. 26, 1942. e. N.Y. Joined ABC-TV network 1964 as asst. acct. rep.; named act. rep. 1965; 1966, joined Walter Reade Organization as asst. v.p. chg. of TV; 1969, moved to WRO Theatre Div.; 1970, joined faculty of School of Visual Arts; 1971 named v.p. of WRO Theatres; 1976, joined Paramount Pictures as v.p. in charge of feature film acquisition. Since 1978 pres. & owner of Castle Hill Productions; 1974, prod. & moderated An Evening with Joseph E. Levine at Town Hall, N.Y.; 1974-1980, host of radio show Movie Talk on WMCA (N.Y.), WMEX (Boston), WICE (Providence); 1982-83 host of syndicated TV show, Julian Schlossbergs' Movie Talk; producers' rep. for Elia Kazan, Dustin Hoffman, Elaine May, George C. Scott. Responsible for restored version of Orson Welles' Othello, re-released in 1992.
THEATER: It Had To Be You, An Evening with Nichols and May, Rainbow Room N.Y., Mr. Gogol and Mr. Preen, Damn Yankees, Vita & Virginia, Death Defying Acts, Moscow Stations, Below the Belt, Cakewalk.
PICTURES: Going Hollywood: The War Years, Hollywood Uncensored, Hollywood Ghost Stories, No Nukes, Going Hollywood: The 30's, 10 From Your Show of Shows, In the Spirit, Bad Girls, Widow's Peak.
TELEVISION: Steve Allen's Golden Age of Comedy; All the Best, Steve Allen, Sex & Justice: The Anita Hill/Clarence Thomas Hearings, Slapstick Too, Elia Kazan: A Director's Journey (Emmy nom.), Nichols & May: Take Two.

SCHLOSSER, HERBERT S.
Executive. b. Atlantic City, NJ, April 21, 1926. e. Princeton U., Yale Law Sch. Joined law firm of Phillips, Nizer, Benjamin, Krim & Ballon, 1954; attorney, California National Productions

subsidiary of National Broadcasting Company) 1957; v.p. & gen. mgr., 1960; joined NBC-TV as director, talent & program admin., 1961; v.p., talent & program admin., 1962; v.p. programs, west coast, 1966-72; exec. v.p., NBC-TV, 1972; pres., 1973; pres. & COO, 1974-76; pres. & CEO, 1977-78; exec. v.p. RCA, 1978-85; sr. advisor, broadcasting & entertainment, Schroder Wertheim & Co., 1986.

SCHMIDT, WOLF
Producer, Distributor. b. Freiburg/Br., Germany, June 30, 1937. Came to U.S. 1962 as freelance journalist. Started producing in 1969, distributing independently since 1972. Now pres. Big Bearing Licensing Corp.
PICTURES: *Prod./Exec. Prod.:* Ski Fever, Stamping Ground, Young Hannah, Things Fall Apart, The Passover Plot, Run for the Roses, Ghost Fever, Defense Play, Riding the Edge, The Fourth War, Neon City, Extreme Justice, Silent Hunter.

SCHMOELLER, DAVID
Writer, Director. b. Louisville, KY, Dec. 8, 1947. e. Universidad de Las Americas, 1967-69, studied film and theater under Luis Bunuel and Alejandro Jodorowsky; U. of TX, B.A., M.A., 1969-74. Wrote and directed 7 short films while studying at college; won 27 intl. awards. In Hollywood spent 6 months working as intern to Peter Hyams on film, Capricorn One. Now heads own co., The Schmoeller Corp.
AUTHOR: The Seduction.
PICTURES: Tourist Trap (debut as dir.), The Seduction (dir., s.p.), Crawlspace (dir., s.p.). *Writer:* The Day Time Ended, The Peeper, Last Chance Romance, Thrill Palace, Warriors of the Wind (Eng. adaptation), Ghost Town (story). *Director:* Catacombs, Puppet Master, The Arrival, Netherworld, Catch the Wind (also s.p.).
TELEVISION: James at 15 (writer), Kid Flicks (cable; writer, prod.), Silk Stalkings (dir.), Renegades (dir.).

SCHNEER, CHARLES H.
Producer, b. Norfolk, VA, May 5, 1920. e. Columbia Coll. pres., Morningside Prods. Inc. & Pictures Corp.; 1956. Founded Andor Films 1974. Chmn, Acad. of MP Arts & Sciences, London Screening Committee.
PICTURES: *Prod.*: The 3 Worlds of Gulliver, The 7th Voyage of Sinbad, I Aim at the Stars, Face of a Fugitive, Good Day for a Hanging, Battle of the Coral Sea, Tarawa Beachhead, Mysterious Island, Jason and the Argonauts, First Men In The Moon, Half A Sixpence, Land Raiders, Valley of Gwangi, The Executioner, The Golden Voyage of Sinbad, Sinbad & The Eye of the Tiger, Clash of the Titans.

SCHNEIDER, DICK
Producer, Director. b. Cazadero, CA, March 7. e. Univ. of the Pacific, Stockton, CA. US Navy, WWII. Has received 9 Emmy Awards.
TELEVISION: Dough Re Mi, Wide Wide World, Colgate Comedy Hour, Beatrice Lillie, Jackie Gleason, Henry Morgan Show, Kate Smith Show, Big Story, Treasury Men in Action, Doorway to Danger, Today Show, Home, Tonight Show, General Mills Circus, Princess Margaret's Wedding, Paris Summit Conference, Eleanor Roosevelt Specials, Something Special 61, At This Very Moment, Inauguration, Gemini, Papal Mass for all networks at Yankee Stadium, Orange Bowl, Jr. Miss Pageant, College Queen (Emmy Award), New Communication, Big Sur, Dream House, Who What or Where, Stars and Stripes, Post Parade, Salute to Sir Lew, NBC Star Salute, Rose Parade, UCP Telethons, Macy's Parade, People's Choice, Jeopardy, Photo Finish.

SCHNEIDER, JOHN
Actor. b. Mount Kisco, NY, April 8, 1954. Active in drama club in high school in Atlanta. Worked as fashion model and played guitar singing own compositions in various Atlanta clubs. Active in local community theatre. Summer stock in New Hampshire. B'way debut 1991 in Grand Hotel.
PICTURES: Smokey and the Bandit, Million Dollar Dixie Deliverance, Eddie Macon's Run, The Curse, Cocaine Wars, Speed Zone, Ministry of Vengeance.
TELEVISION: *Series*: Dukes of Hazzard, Grand Slam, Second Chances, Heaven Help Us. *Specials*: John Schneider—Back Home, Wild Jack. *Movies*: Dream House, Happy Endings, Stagecoach, Christmas Comes to Willow Creek, Outback Bound, Gus Brown and Midnight Brewster, Highway Heartbreaker, Desperate Journey: The Allison Wilcox Story, Texas.

SCHNEIDER, PETER
Executive. e. B.A., theatre, Purdue U., 1971. Theatrical director, The WPA, Playwrights Horizon, and Circle Repetory Theater, New York; producer & managing director, Chicago's St. Nicholas Theater; general mgr., Apollo Theater Productions; director, 1984 Olympic Arts Festival; president (1985) and supervisor of the development and production of all Disney animated motion pictures; president, Walt Disney Studios; supervised the release of Disney's most successful release to date, The Lion King. Currently chairman, The Walt Disney Studios.

SCHNEIER, FREDERICK
Executive. b. New York, NY, May 31, 1927; e. NYU, 1951, bus. admin.; NYU Grad. Sch., M.B.A., 1953. Dir. sls. planning, Mutual Broadcasting System, 1947-53; media research dir., RKO Teleradio, 1953-55; RKO Teleradio Advisory Comm., 1955-56; exec. staff RKO Teleradio & dir., marketing services, 1956-58; exec. vice-pres., Showcorporation, 1958-71; v.p. TV programming, RKO General, 1972-1973; v.p., Hemdale Leisure Corp., 1973-79; Viacom Enterprises v.p., feature films, 1979; sr. v.p., program acquisitions & motion pictures, 1980-83; sr. v.p., acquisitions, Showtime/The Movie Channel, 1983-85; sr. v.p. program acquisitions, program enterprises, 1985-87; exec. v.p., programming; 1987-89; pres. & CEO, Viacom Pictures Inc., 1989-92; pres. & CEO, FSA Film Enterprises.

SCHOEFFLING, MICHAEL
Actor. b. Philadelphia, PA. e. Temple Univ.
PICTURES: Sixteen Candles (debut, 1984), Vision Quest, Sylvester, Bellizaire the Cajun, Let's Get Harry, Slaves of New York, Longtime Companion, Mermaids, Wild Hearts Can't Be Broken.

SCHOENFELD, LESTER
Executive. b. Brooklyn, NY, Dec. 6, 1916. e. CCNY, 1934-38. Asst. mgr., Randforce Amusement, 1936-38; mgr., Rugoff & Becker circuit, 1938-47; mgr., Golden & Ambassador Theatres, 1948; print & sales dept., Film Classics, 1948-50; chg. of theatrical, non-theatrical & TV dist., Brit. Info. Serv.; est. Lester A. Schoenfeld Films, 1958; Schoenfeld Films Distributing Corp., 1960.

SCHOONMAKER, THELMA
Editor. b. January 3, 1940.
PICTURES: Finnegan's Wake, Who's That Knocking at My Door?, Woodstock, Street Scenes, Taxi Driver, Rock Show, Raging Bull, The King of Comedy, After Hours, The Color of Money, Bad, The Last Temptation of Christ, New York Stories, Made in Milan, Goodfellas, Cape Fear, The Age of Innocence, Casino, Grace of My Heart, Kundun, Bringing out the Dead, The Gangs of New York.

SCHORR, DANIEL
Radio, Television News Correspondent. b. New York, NY, Aug. 31, 1916. e. City Coll. of New York. Started with various news services and newspapers. Joined CBS in 1953 as Washington correspondent; 1955, reopened CBS bureau in Moscow; 1958-60, roving assignment; 1960-1966, chief German Bureau; 1966-76, Washington Bureau; 1979, Public Radio and TV; 1980, sr. Washington correspondent for Cable News Network; 1985, sr. news analyst, National Public Radio.

SCHRADER, PAUL
Writer, Director. b. Grand Rapids, MI, July 22, 1946. m. actress Mary Beth Hurt. e. Calvin Coll. (theology & philosophy); Columbia U., UCLA, M.A., cinema. Served as film critic for L.A. Free Press and Cinema 1970-72. Former professor at Columbia U.
PICTURES: *Writer &/or Director*: The Yakuza (co-s.p.), Taxi Driver, Rolling Thunder, Obsession, Blue Collar (co-s.p., dir). Hardcore, Old Boyfriends (co-s.p., exec. prod.), American Gigolo, Raging Bull (co-s.p.), Cat People, Mishima (co-s.p.), The Mosquito Coast, Light of Day, The Last Temptation of Christ, Patty Hearst, The Comfort of Strangers, Light Sleeper, City Hall (co-s.p.), Touch, Affliction, Bringing out the Dead (s.p.), Forever Mine (dir., s.p.), Dino (s.p.).
TELEVISION: *Movie*: Witch Hunt (dir.), The Hollywood Fashion Machine (act. only).

SCHREIBER, LIEV
Actor. b. San Francisco, CA, October 4, 1967. e. Yale School of Drama. Attended London's Royal Academy of Art and Hampshire College, Amherst, Mass.
PICTURES: Mixed Nuts, Denise Calls Up, Mad Love, Party Girl, Big Night, Walking and Talking, Ransom, Scream, The Daytrippers, Baggage, Scream 2, His and Hers, Phantoms, Sphere, Twilight, Desert Blue (voice), A Walk on the Moon, Jakob the Liar, The Hurricane, Spring Forward, Hamlet, Scream 3, Dial 9 For Love.
TELEVISION: Janek: The Silent Betrayal, Buffalo Girls, The Sunshine Boys, Since You've Been Gone, Babe Ruth (voice), RKO 281.

SCHRODER, RICK
Actor. b. Staten Island, NY, April 13, 1970. Started modelling while only four months; did many TV commercials before theatrical film debut in The Champ, at age eight.
PICTURES: The Champ, The Last Flight of Noah's Ark, The Earthling, Apt Pupil, Across the Tracks, There Goes My Baby, Crimson Tide.
TELEVISION: *Series*: Silver Spoons, NYPD Blue. *Movies*: Little Lord Fauntleroy, Something So Right, Two Kinds of Love, A Reason to Live, Too Young the Hero, Terror on Highway 91, Out on the Edge, A Son's Promise, The Stranger Within, Blood River, My Son Johnny, Miles From Nowhere, Call of the Wild, To My Daughter with Love, Texas, Heart Full of Rain, Ebenezer, Too Close To Home, Detention: The Siege at Johnson High. *Mini-Series*: Lonesome Dove, Return to Lonesome Dove.

SCHROEDER, BARBET
Producer, Director. b. Teheran, Iran, Aug. 26, 1941. Critic for Cahiers du Cinema and L'Air de Paris, 1958-63. 1963: asst. to Jean-Luc Godard on Les Carabiniers. 1964: formed own prod. co. Les Films du Losange. As actor only: Paris vu par, La Boulangere de Monceau Roberte, Celline and Julie Go Boating, Beverly Hills Cop III, La Reine Margot, Mars Attacks!
PICTURES: *Producer*: La Boulangere de Monceau (26 mins.), La Carriere de Suzanne (52 mins.), Mediterrannee, Paris Vu Par, La Collectionneuse, Tu Imagines Robinson, My Night at Maud's, Claire's Knee, Chloe in the Afternoon, Out One (co-prod.), The Mother and the Whore (co-prod.), Celine and Julie Go Boating, Flocons D'Or, The Marquise of O, Roulette Chinoise (co-prod.), The American Friend (co-prod.), Le Passe-Montagne, The Rites of Death, Perceval Le Gallois, Le Navire Night, Le Pont du Nord, Mauvaise Conduite, Une Sale Historie. *Director & Producer*: More (1969), Sing-Sing (doc.), La Vallee, General Idi Amin Dada (doc.), Maitresse, Koko a Talking Gorilla (doc.), Charles Bukowski Tapes (doc.), Tricheurs, Barfly, Reversal of Fortune, Single White Female, Kiss of Death, Before and After, Desperate Measures.

SCHUCK, JOHN
Actor. b. Boston, MA, Feb. 4, 1940. e. Denison (BA). Cabaret act: An Evening With John Schuck.
THEATER: *B'way*: Annie. *Off-B'way*: The Streets of NY, The Shrike. London: The Caine Mutiny. Regional incl. Long Day's Journey Into Night, As You Like It.
PICTURES: M*A*S*H, The Moonshine War, Brewster McCloud, McCabe and Mrs. Miller, Hammersmith Is Out, Blade, Thieves Like Us, Butch and Sundance: The Early Days, Just You and Me Kid, Earthbound, Finders Keepers, Star Trek VI: The Voyage Home, Outrageous Fortune, The New Adventures of Pippi Longstocking, My Mom's a Werewolf, Second Sight, Dick Tracy, Star Trek IV: The Undiscovered Country, Holy Matrimony, Pontiac Moon, Tales From the Crypt Presents Demon Knight.
TELEVISION: *Series*: McMillan and Wife, Holmes and Yoyo, Turnabout, The New Odd Couple, The Munsters Today. Mini-Series: Roots. *Movies*: Once Upon a Dead Man, Hunter, Till Death Us Do Part. *Guest*: Murder She Wrote, Time Trax, Deep Space Nine.

SCHULBERG, BUDD WILSON
Writer. b. New York, NY, March 27, 1914. son of B. P. Schulberg, prod. e. Dartmouth Coll. Publicist, Paramount Pictures, 1931; writer for screen from 1932. Armed services WWII. Syndicated newspaper columnist: The Schulberg Report.
AUTHOR: *Novels*: What Makes Sammy Run?, The Disenchanted, The Harder They Fall, On the Waterfront, Some Faces in the Crowd, Everything That Moves, Sanctuary V, Love Action Laughter and Other Sad Tales. *Non-fiction books:* Writers in America, Moving Pictures: Memories of a Hollywood Prince, Swan Watch, Loser and Still Champion: Muhammad Ali, Sparring With Hemingway and Other Legends of the Fight Game. *Short stories*: Some Faces In the Crowd, Love, Action, Laughter and Other Sad Tales
THEATER: The Disenchanted (with Harvey Breit, 1958), What Makes Sammy Run? (book for musical), On the Waterfront (with Stan Silverman).
PICTURES: A Star is Born (additional dial.), Nothing Sacred (add. dial.), Little Orphan Annie (co-s.p.), Winter Carnival (co-s.p. with F. Scott Fitzgerald), Weekend for Three (orig. and co-s.p.), City Without Men (co-story), Government Girl (adapt.). Original s.p.: On the Waterfront (Acad. Award, & Writers Guild Award, 1954), A Face in The Crowd, Wind Across the Everglades, Joe Louis: For All Time (doc., Cine Golden Eagle Award, 1985).
TELEVISION: *Teleplays*: What Makes Sammy Run?, Paso Doble, The Pharmacist's Mate, Memory In White, The Legend That Walks Like A Man, A Question of Honor, A Table at Ciro's.

SCHULMAN, JOHN A.
Executive. b. Washington, D.C., June 13, 1946. e. Yale U., 1968; law degree from Boalt Hall, U. of California, Berkeley, 1972. Founding partner in Beverly Hills law firm, Weissmann, Wolff, Bergman, Coleman & Schulman in 1981 after nine years with firm of Kaplan, Livingston, Goodwin, Berkowitz & Selvin. Joined Warner Bros. 1984 as v.p. & gen. counsel; 1989 sr. v.p. and gen. counsel; 1991, exec. v.p. and gen. counsel.

SCHULMAN, TOM
Writer. e. Vanderbilt U, BA.
PICTURES: Dead Poets Society (Acad. Award, 1989), What About Bob?, Honey I Shrunk the Kids, Second Sight, Medicine Man, Indecent Proposal (exec. prod.)

SCHULTZ, DWIGHT
Actor. b. Baltimore, MD, Nov. 24, 1947. e. Townson St. Univ. Acted with Williamstown Theatre Fest. prior to NY stage work, incl. The Crucifer of Blood, The Water Engine, Night and Day.
PICTURES: The Fan, Alone in the Dark, Fat Man and Little Boy, The Long Walk Home, The Temp.
TELEVISION: *Series*: The A-Team, Star Trek: The Next Generation. *Movies*: Child of Rage, When Your Lover Leaves, Perry Mason: The Case of the Sinister Spirit, Perry Mason: The Case of the Musical Murder, A Woman With a Past, The Last Wish, A Killer Among Us, Victim of Love: The Shannon Mohr Story, Menendez: A Killing in Beverly Hills.

SCHULTZ, MICHAEL
Director, Producer. b. Milwaukee, WI, Nov. 10, 1938. e. U. of Wisconsin, Marquette U.
THEATER: The Song of the Lusitainian Bogey, Kongi's Harvest, Does a Tiger Wear a Necktie?, Operation Sidewinder, What the Winesellers Buy, The Cherry Orchard, Mulebone, Dream on Monkey Mountain.
PICTURES: *Director*: Together for Days, Honeybaby Honeybaby, Cooley High, Car Wash, Greased Lightning, Which Way Is Up?, Sgt. Pepper's Lonely Hearts Club Band, Scavenger Hunt, Carbon Copy, The Last Dragon, Krush Groove (also prod.), Disorderlies (also co-prod.), Livin' Large.
TELEVISION: *Specials*: To Be Young Gifted and Black, Ceremonies in Dark Old Men, For Us the Living, Fade Out: The Erosion of Black Images in the Media (documentary), Hollywood Follies, Travels With Father. *Series*: The Young Indiana Jones Chronicles, Picket Fences, Chicago Hope, Sisters. *Pilot*: Shock Treatment. *Movies*: Benny's Place, The Jerk Too, Timestalkers, Rock 'n' Roll Mom, Tarzan in Manhattan, Jury Duty, Dayo.

SCHUMACHER, JOEL
Director, Writer. b. New York, NY, Aug. 29, 1939. Worked as design and display artist for Henri Bendel dept. store NY while attending Parson's Sch. of Design. As fashion designer opened own boutique, Paraphernalia. Joined Revlon as designer of clothing and packaging before entering m.p. indus. as costume designer on Play It As It Lays, Sleeper, The Last of Sheila, Blume in Love, Prisoner of 2nd Avenue, Interiors.
PICTURES: *Writer*: Car Wash, Sparkle, The Wiz. *Director*: The Incredible Shrinking Woman (debut, 1981), D.C. Cab (also s.p.), St. Elmo's Fire (also s.p.), The Lost Boys, Cousins, Flatliners, Dying Young, Falling Down, The Client, Batman Forever, A Time to Kill, Batman & Robin, Tigerland, 8mm (also prod.), Flawless (also s.p., prod.), Tigerland, Phone Booth, Dare, The Church of the Dead Girls.
TELEVISION: *Director: Movies*: The Virginia Hill Story (also writer), Amateur Night at the Dixie Bar & Grill (also writer). *Music video*: Devil Inside for rock group INXS (dir.). *Series*: 2000 Malibu Drive. *Exec. Prod.*: Slow Burn.

SCHUMACHER, MARTHA
Producer. a.k.a Martha De Laurentiis. m. Dino De Laurentiis, producer.
PICTURES: Firestarter (assoc. prod.), Silver Bullet, Cat's Eye, King Kong Lives, Raw Deal, Maximum Overdrive, The Bedroom Window, Desperate Hours (exec. prod.). *As Martha De Laurentiis*: Once Upon a Crime (exec. prod.), Temptation (exec. prod.), Slave of Dreams, Unforgettable, Breakdown, U-571

SCHUMACHER, THOMAS
Producer, Executive. e. UCLA. Began as production asst., Taper Mainstage, Taper Too, and the literary cabaret, Mark Taper Forum. Producer, three original productions for the Improvisational Theater Project. Olympic Arts Festival staff, 1984; asst. gen. mgr., Los Angeles Ballet; co-founder and assoc. dir., 1987 Los Angeles Festival of Arts. Responsible for the American premiere of Canada's Cirque du Soleil. Producer: The Rescuers Down Under (1990), Walt Disney Feature Animation, 1988; exec. producer, The Lion King, 1994; exec. v.p., Disney Feature Animation and Theatrical Productions, 1994-98. Currently president of Walt Disney Feature Animation, Walt Disney Television Animation, and Buena Vista Theatrical Group. Serves on the Education Council, the Presentations Committee of the Performing Arts Center of Los Angeles County, and the board of directors of the Rachel Rosenthal Co.

SCHWAB, SHELLY
Executive. Station mgr., WAGA-TV, Atlanta; various sls. & mgr. posts with CBS. Joined MCA, 1978, becoming exec. v.p., MCA-TV. 1986, appt. pres., MCA TV Enterprises, 1989 appt. pres. MCA TV.

SCHWARTZ, BERNARD
Producer. Brought to Hollywood by the late Howard Hughes to watch his film interests; Schwartz teamed with atty. Greg Bautzer to package movie deals for clients. Re-cut number of Buster Keaton's silent movies into documentary anthologies (The Golden Age of Comedy, When Comedy Was King.). Subsequently made TV series, One Step Beyond, followed by The Wackiest Ship in the Army, Miss Teen International specials, etc. Named pres. Joseph M. Schenck Enterprises, for which he made Journey to the Center of the Earth, Eye of the Cat, A Cold Wind in August, I Passed for White, The Shattered Room, Trackdown. Presently partnered with Alan Silverman.
PICTURES: Coal Miner's Daughter (prod.), Road Games (exec. prod.) Psycho II (exec. prod.), St. Elmo's Fire (co-exec. prod.).
TELEVISION: Elvis and Me (co-exec. prod.).

SCHWARTZ, SHERWOOD
Producer. Also composed themes for television shows Gilligan's Island and The Brady Bunch.
PICTURES: The Brady Bunch Movie, A Very Brady Sequel.
TELEVISION: *Movies:* Rescue from Gilligan's Island (exec., s.p.), The Invisible Woman (exec., s.p.), The Harlem Globetrotters on Gilligan's Island (s.p. only), The Brady Girls Get Married (s.p. only). *Series:* Gilligan's Island (also creator), It's About Time, The Brady Bunch (exec.), The brady Kids (exec. consult. only), Dusty's Trail, Big John Little John (exec., also creator), The Brady Bunch Hour, Harper Valley P.T.A., The Bradys (creator only).

SCHWARY, RONALD L.
Producer. b. Oregon, May 23, 1944. e. U. of Southern California. Started as movie extra before becoming asst. dir.; served as assoc. prod. on The Electric Horseman.
PICTURES: Ordinary People (Acad. Award for Best Picture, 1980), Absence of Malice, Tootsie, A Soldier's Story, Batteries Not Included, Havana, Scent of a Woman, Cops and Robbersons, Sabrina, The Mirror Has Two Faces (co-exec. prod.).
TELEVISION: Tour of Duty.

SCHWARZENEGGER, ARNOLD
Actor. b. Graz, Austria, July 30, 1947. m. NBC reporter Maria Shriver. e. U. Wisconsin, B.A. Bodybuilding Titles: Junior Mr. Europe (at age 18), Mr. Universe (3 time winner), Mr. Olympia (7 times), Mr. Europe, Mr. World. Special Olympics weightlifting Coach (1989), Prison Weightlifting Rehabilitation Prog. Awards: Sportsman of the Year (1977, Assn. Physical Fitness Ctrs.), Golden Globe (best newcomer, 1977), ShoWest '85 Intl. Star., ShoWest Career Achievement Award, NATO Male Star of Yr. (1987).
AUTHOR: Arnold: The Education of a Bodybuilder, Arnold's Bodyshaping for Women, Arnold's Bodybuilding for Men, The Encyclopedia of Modern Bodybuilding, Arnold's Fitness for Kids (3 Vols.).
PICTURES: Hercules in New York (debut, 1970; billed as Arnold Strong), The Long Goodbye, Stay Hungry, Pumping Iron, The Villain, Scavenger Hunt, Conan the Barbarian, Conan the Destroyer, The Terminator, Red Sonja, Commando, Raw Deal, Predator, The Running Man, Red Heat, Twins, Total Recall, Kindergarten Cop, Terminator 2: Judgment Day, Beretta's Island (cameo), Dave (cameo), Last Action Hero (also exec. prod.), True Lies, Junior, Eraser, Jingle All the.Way, Batman and Robin, End of Days, The 6th Day, Collateral Damage, Terminator 3.
TELEVISION: *Movie*: The Jayne Mansfield Story. *Special*: A Very Special Christmas Party (host). *Guest*: Streets of San Francisco. *Director*: Tales from the Crypt (The Switch), Christmas in Connecticut (movie).

SCHWIMMER, DAVID
Actor. b. Queens, NY, Nov. 12, 1966.
PICTURES: Flight of the Intruder, Crossing the Bridge, Twenty Bucks, Wolf, The Pallbearer, Apt Pupil, Kissing a Fool (also exec. prod.), Six Days Seven Nights, Love & Sex, Picking up the Pieces.
TELEVISION: *Movies:* Breast Men, Since You've Been Gone (also dir.). *Series:* The Wonder Years, Monty, Friends, Band of Brothers. *Guest:* L.A. Law, NYPD Blue, Blossom, The Single Guy, ER.

SCHYGULLA, HANNA
Actress. b. Kattowitz, Germany, Dec. 25, 1943. Worked with Rainer Werner Fassbinder in Munich's Action Theater; a founder of the ``anti-theatre" group. Made film debut in 1968 short Der Brautigam die Komodiantin und der Zuhalter (The Bridegroom, the Comedienne and the Pimp).
PICTURES: Love Is Colder Than Death (feature debut, 1969), Gods of the Plague, Beware of a Holy Whore, The Merchant of Four Seasons, The Bitter Tears of Petra Von Kant, House by the Sea, Jail Bait, Effi Briest, The Marriage of Maria Braun, Berlin Alexanderplatz, Lili Marleen, The Night of Varennes, Passion, A Labor of Love, A Love in Germany, The Delta Force, The Future Is a Woman, Forever Lulu, Miss Arizona, The Summer of Ms. Forbes, Dead Again.
TELEVISION: *U.S.*: Rio das Mortes, Peter the Great, Barnum, Casanova.

SCIORRA, ANNABELLA
Actress. b. New York, NY, 1964. As teen studied acting at HB Studio; then AADA. Founded The Brass Ring Theatre Co. Won role of Sophia Loren's daughter in mini-series Fortunate Pilgrim.
THEATER: Orpheus Descending, Bus Stop, Three Sisters, Snow Angel, Cries and Shouts, Trip Back Down, Love and Junk, Stay With Me, Those the River Keeps.
PICTURES: True Love (debut, 1989), Internal Affairs, Cadillac Man, Reversal of Fortune, The Hard Way, Jungle Fever, The Hand That Rocks the Cradle, Whispers in the Dark, The Night We Never Met, Mr. Wonderful, Romeo is Bleeding, The Cure, The Addiction, The Innocent Sleep, The Funeral, Cop Land, What Dreams May Come, New Rose Hotel, Little City.
TELEVISION: *Mini-Series*: The Fortunate Pilgrim. *Movie*: Prison Stories: Women on the Inside.

SCOFIELD, PAUL
Actor. b. Hurstpierpoint, England, Jan. 21, 1922.
THEATER: Adventure Story, Ring Round the Moon, Richard II, The Way of the World, Venice Preserved, Time Remembered, Hamlet, Power and the Glory, Family Reunion, Espresso Bongo, A Man For All Seasons (also B'way: Tony Award, 1962), Coriolanus, Don Armando, King Lear, Timon, Troilus, Pericles, Henry V, MacBeth, Staircase, Hotel In Amsterdam, Uncle Vanya, The Captain of Kopernik, Rules of the Game, Savages, The Tempest, Volpone, Madras House, The Family, Amadeus, Othello, Don Quixote, A Midsummer Night's Dream, I'm Not Rappaport, Heartbreak Housem, John Gabriel Borkman.
PICTURES: That Lady (debut, 1955), Carve Her Name With Pride, The Train, A Man for All Seasons (Acad. Award, 1966), Tell Me Lies, King Lear, Bartleby, Scorpio, A Delicate Balance, 1919, When the Whales Came, Henry V, Hamlet, Utz, Quiz Show, London (narrator), The Crucible (BAFTA Award, 1997), Robinson in Space (narrator).
TELEVISION: *Movies*: Anna Karenina, The Attic: The Hiding of Anne Frank, The Disabled Century, Animal Farm (voice). *Specials*: The Male of the Species (Emmy Award, 1969), The Ambassadors, The Potting Shed, Martin Chuzzlewit, Little Riders.

SCOGGINS, TRACY
Actress. b. Galveston, TX, Nov. 13, 1959. Studied acting at H.B. Studies, Wynn Handman Studios. Appeared on stage in L.A. in The Sicilian Bachelor.
PICTURES: Some Kind of Hero, Toy Soldier, In Dangerous Company, The Gumshoe Kid, Watchers II, Time Bomb, Silhouette, Ultimate Desires, Alien Intruder, Demonic Toys, Dead On.
TELEVISION: *Series*: Renegades, Hawaiian Heat, The Colbys, Lois & Clark: The New Adventures of Superman. *Movies*: Twirl, Jury Duty, Dan Turner: Hollywood Detective, Jake Lassiter: Justice on the Bayou. *Pilots*: The Naturals, High Life, Unauthorized Biographies. *Guest*: Hotel, Crazy Like a Fox, Dallas, Magnum P.I., The Fall Guy, Mike Hammer, The Heights.

SCOLA, ETTORE
Director, Writer. b. Trevico, Italy, May 10, 1931. e. U. of Rome. Began career in 1947 as journalist; 1950, wrote for radio shows. Then made first film as script writer 1954; debut as director-writer, 1964. Has written 50 other scripts for other directors.
PICTURES: *Dir/Writer*: Let's Talk about Women (debut, 1964), La Congiuntura, Thrilling (segment: Il Vittimista), The Devil in Love, Will Your Heroes Find Their Friends Who Disappeared so Mysteriously in Africa?, Inspector Pepe, The Pizza Triangle, Rocco Papaleo, The Greatest Evening of My Life, We All Loved Each Other So Much, Down and Dirty, Signore e Signori Buonanotte (segment), A Special Day, Viva Italia! (segment), The Terrace, Passion d'Amore, La Nuit de Varennes, Le Bal, Macaroni, The Family, Splendor, What Time is It?, Le Capitain Fracassa, Mario Maria and Mario, Romanzo di un Giovane Povero

SCOLARI, PETER
Actor. b. New Rochelle, NY, Sept. 12, 1954.
PICTURES: The Rosebud Beach Hotel, Corporate Affairs, Ticks, Camp Nowhere, That Thing You Do!.
TELEVISION: *Series*: Goodtime Girls, Bosom Buddies, Baby Makes Five, Newhart, Family Album, Dweebs, Honey I Shrunk the Kids: The TV Show. *Movies*: Carpool, Amazon, Fatal Confession, The Ryan White Story, Stop the World I Want to Get Off, From the Earth to the Moon. *Guest*: Remington Steele, The Love Boat, Family Ties, The New Mike Hammer, Trying Times, Fallen Angels.

SCORSESE, MARTIN
Writer, Director, Editor, Actor. b. New York, NY, Nov. 17, 1942. Began career while film arts student at NYU, doing shorts What's A Nice Girl Like You Doing in a Place Like This? (dir., s.p.), It's Not Just You Murray and The Big Shave. Other short films: Street Scenes, Italianamerican, American Boy, Mirror Mirror, Somewhere Down the Crazy River. *Dir.* 2 commercials for Armani. Currently campaigning for the preservation and restoration of historic films. Recipient of the American Film Institute Life Achievement Award, ,1997.
THEATER: The Act.
PICTURES: *Editor*: Woodstock, Medicine Ball Caravan, Unholy Rollers, Elvis on Tour. *Producer*: The Grifters, Mad Dog and Glory, Naked in New York (exec. prod.), Clockers. *Actor*: Cannonball, 'Round Midnight, Akira Kurosawa's Dreams, Guilty by Suspicion, Quiz Show, Search and Destroy (also co-exec. prod.). *Director*: Who's That Knocking at My Door? (also s.p., assoc. prod., actor), Boxcar Bertha (also actor), Mean Streets (also co-s.p., actor), Alice Doesn't Live Here Anymore, Taxi Driver (also actor), New York New York, The Last Waltz (also cameo), Raging Bull, The King of Comedy (also actor), After Hours (also cameo), The Color of Money, The Last Temptation of Christ, New York Stories (Life Lessons; also cameo), GoodFellas (also co-s.p.), Cape Fear, The Age of Innocence (also co-s.p., cameo), Casino (also co-s.p.), Kundun, Bringing Out the Dead, The Gangs of New York, Dino.

TELEVISION: *Series episode*: Amazing Stories (dir.). *Specials*: A Personal Journey With Martin Scorsese Through American Movies (dir. writer), Il Dolce Cinema.

SCOTT, CAMPBELL
Actor. b. New York, NY, July 19, 1962. e. Lawrence Univ. Son of George C. Scott and Colleen Dewhurst. Studied with Geraldine Page and Stella Adler.
THEATER: *NY*: The Last Outpost, The Real Thing, Copperhead, The Queen and the Rebels, Hay Fever, A Man For All Seasons, Long Day's Journey Into Night, Measure for Measure, Pericles, On the Bum. *Regional*: Romeo and Juliet, Our Town, Gilette, School for Wives, Hamlet.
PICTURES: Five Corners (debut, 1988), From Hollywood to Deadwood, Longtime Companion, The Sheltering Sky, Dying Young, Dead Again, Singles, Mrs. Parker and the Vicious Circle, The Innocent, The Daytrippers, Big Night (also co-dir., prod.), The Spanish Prisoner, The Imposters, Hi-Life, Top of the Food Chain, Lush.
TELEVISION: *Mini-Series*: The Kennedys of Massachusetts, LIBERTY! The American Revolution. *Guest*: Family Ties, L.A. Law. *Movie*: The Perfect Tribute, The Love Letter, The Tale of Sweeney Todd.

SCOTT, DEBORAH LYNN
Costume Designer.
PICTURES: The Private Eyes, Don't Answer the Phone!, E.T. the Extra-Terrestrial, Never Cty Wolf, Back to the Future, Armed and Dangerous, Blue City, About Last Night..., Who's That Girl?, Life Is Sweet, Coupe de Ville, Hear My Song, Defending Your Life, Eve of Destruction, Blame It on the Bellboy, Hoffa, Jack the Bear, Sliver, Legends of the Fall, Sister My Sister, Persuasion, Funny Bones, Jack and Sarah, The Indian in the Cupboard, Othello, Heat, Looking for Richard, To Gillian on Her 37th Birthday, Titanic (Acad. Award, 1997), Wild Wild West.
TELEVISION: *Movies*: Dancing Queen.

SCOTT, MARTHA
Actress. b. Jamesport, MO, September 22, 1914. e. U. of Michigan. In little theatres over U.S.; summer stock NY; on radio with Orson Welles; Broadway debut Our Town (1938), film debut in film adaptation of same. Became theater producer in 1968 with Henry Fonda and Alfred De Liagre at Kennedy Center and on B'way (Time of Your Life, First Monday in October).
THEATER: Our Town, Soldier's Wife, The Voice of the Turtle, The Number, The Male Animal, The Remarkable Mr. Pennypacker, Forty-Second Cousin, The Crucible.
PICTURES: Our Town (debut, 1940; Acad. Award nom.), The Howards of Virginia, Cheers for Miss Bishop, They Dare Not Love, One Foot in Heaven, In Old Oklahoma (The War of the Wildcats), Hi Diddle Diddle, So Well Remembered, Strange Bargain, When I Grow Up, The Desperate Hours, The Ten Commandments, Eighteen and Anxious, Sayonara, Ben-Hur, Charlotte's Web (voice), Airport 1975, The Turning Point, Doin' Time on Planet Earth.
TELEVISION: *Movies*: The Devil's Daughter, Thursday's Game, The Abduction of Saint Anne, Medical Story, Charleston, Father Figure, Summer Girl, Adam, Adam: His Song Continues, Love and Betrayal, Daughter of the Streets. *Mini-Series*: The Word, Beulah Land. *Guest*: Murder She Wrote, Hotel, A Girl's Life (pilot).

SCOTT, RIDLEY
Director, Producer. b. South Shields, Northumberland, England, Nov. 30, 1937. Brother is director Tony Scott. e. Royal College of Art, London. Joined newly formed Film Sch. First film: Boy on Bicycle (short). Won design scholarship in NY. Returned to London and joined BBC as set designer (Z-Cars, The Informer series). Directed almost 3,000 commercials in 18 years. Formed Percy Main Prods. Also mng. dir. of Ridley Scott Assocs.Exec.
PICTURES: *Director*: The Duellists (debut, 1978), Alien, Blade Runner, Legend, Someone to Watch Over Me (also exec. prod.), Black Rain, Thelma & Louise (also prod.), 1492: Conquest of Paradise (also prod.), White Squall (also exec. prod.), G.I. Jane (also prod.), G.I. Jane, Gladiator, Hannibal. *Prod:* Monkey Trouble, The Browning Version, Clay Pigeons.

SCOTT, TONY
Director. b. Newcastle, England, July 21, 1944. Began career in TV commercials, being partnered with his brother Ridley in prod. co. Winner of numerous Clios, Gold & Silver Lions, and other awards. Entered m.p. industry 1972, directing half-hr. film, One of the Missing, for British Film Inst. and Loving Memory, 1-hr. feature for Albert Finney.
PICTURES: The Hunger (debut, 1983), Top Gun, Beverly Hills Cop II, Revenge, Days of Thunder, The Last Boy Scout, True Romance, Crimson Tide, The Fan, Clay Pigeons (exec. prod. only), Enemy of the State.
TELEVISION: *Series Dir.:* The Hunger.

SCOTT-THOMAS, KRISTIN
Actress. b. Redruth, Cornwall, England, May 24, 1960. Lived in France since 18. e. Central School of Speech and Drama, London; Ecole Nationale des Arts et Technique de Theatre, Paris. Stage debut in La Lune Declinante Sur 4 Ou 5 Personnes Qui Danse. Other theater work in Paris.
PICTURES: Djomel et Juliette, L'Agent Troube, La Meridienne, Under the Cherry Moon, A Handful of Dust, Force Majeure, Bille en tete, Autobus/In the Eyes of the World, The Governor's Party, The Bachelor, Bitter Moon, Somebody to Love, Four Weddings and a Funeral, An Unforgettable Summer, Mayday, The Confessional, Angels and Insects, Les Milles, Richard III, The Pompatus of Love, Portraits Chinois, Mission: Impossible, Microcosmos: Le Peuple de L'Herbe, The English Patient, Amour et Confusions, The Revengers' Comedies, The Horse Whisperer, Up at the Villa, Random Hearts.
TELEVISION: L'Ami D'Enfance de Maigret, Blockhaus, Chameleon/La Tricheuse (Aust.), Sentimental Journey (Germany), The Tenth Man, The Endless Game, Framed, The Secret Life of Ian Fleming, Titmuss Regained, Look at it This Way, Weep No More My Lady, Body & Soul, La Belle Epoque, Gulliver's Travels.

SCULLY, JOE
Talent Executive, Casting Director, Producer, Writer. b. Kearny, NJ, March 1, 1926. e. Goodman Memorial Theatre of the Art Inst. of Chicago, 1946. m. Penelope Gillette. Acted until 1951. CBS-TV, NY. Casting Dir., Danger, You Are There, Omnibus, The Web, 1951-56. Wrote The Little Woman for CBS Danger Anthology Series, 1954. 1956-60, CBS-TV, Associate Prod., Studio One, Dupont Show of the Month, Playhouse 90; 1962-64, Writer for CBS Repertoire Workshop anthology series; 1963-64, CBS Stations div. KNXT, prod., Repertoire Workshop; 1965-70 casting dir., 20th Century-Fox Films; 1970-74, indept. casting dir.; 1974-75 Universal TV, casting dir. Member, AMPAS since 1975; NBC-TV Manager, Casting & Talent; 1978, re-established Joe Scully Casting, indept. service to the industry. Founding member, CSA, 1982; 1983, casting dir., Walt Disney Pictures. 1991 published story in Emmy Magazine: Have You Ever... You Know? Conducted AMPAS Seminar, 'The Casting Process in Motion Pictures.'
PICTURES: Hello Dolly, In Like Flint, Valley of the Dolls, Planet of the Apes, The Flim-Flam Man, Sounder, Lady Sings the Blues, Play It as It Lays, The Stone Killer, Parallax View, Lifeguard, Man in the Glass Booth, Middle Age Crazy, Death Wish II, Frankenweenie (short), North of Chiang Mai, Chained in Paradiso (video).
TELEVISION: *Series*: Peyton Place, Bonanza, Room 222, Nichols, Snoop Sisters, Columbo, Switch, McMillan & Wife, Tales of the Unexpected, Gone Are the Days (Disney Channel). *Pilots*: Julia, The Ghost and Mrs. Muir, The Bill Cosby Show. *Movies*: Thief, Missiles of October, Gone Are the Days, Earth II. Australian: Flair (mini-series), Ebb Tide (movie).

SEAGAL, STEVEN
Actor, Director, Producer, Writer. b. Lansing, MI, April 10, 1952. Became skilled at martial arts at an early age, studying Aikido. Lived in Japan for 15 yrs. where he opened a martial arts academy. Opened similar academy upon his return to U.S. in Los Angeles. Was martial arts choreographer/coordinator on film The Challenge.
PICTURES: Above the Law (debut, 1988; also co-prod., co-story), Hard to Kill, Marked for Death (also co-prod.), Out for Justice (also co-prod.), Under Siege (also co-prod.), On Deadly Ground (also dir., co-prod.). Under Siege 2: Dark Territory (also co- prod.), Executive Decision, The Glimmer Man, Fire Down Below (also prod.), My Giant (cameo), The Patriot (also prod.).

SEAGROVE, JENNY
Actress. b. Kuala Lumpur, Malaysia. e. Bristol Old Vic. Theatre Sch. Stage debut 1979. Early TV: The Brack Report, The Woman in White, Diana. Recent stage: Jane Eyre, King Lear, Present Laughter, The Miracle Worker, Dead Guilty.
PICTURES: Moonlighting, Local Hero, Nate and Hayes, Appointment With Death, A Chorus of Disapproval, The Guardian, Bullseye!, Miss Beatty's Children.
TELEVISION: A Woman of Substance, Hold The Dream, In Like Flynn, Killer, Lucy Walker, Magic Moments, Some Other Spring, The Betrothed, Deadly Game, The Sign of Four, The Incident at Victoria Falls, A Shocking Accident.

SEALE, JOHN
Cinematographer. b. Warwick, Australia, 1943. Camera operator on several films before becoming director of photography.
PICTURES: Deathcheaters, Fatty Finn, The Survivor, Doctors & Nurses, Fighting Back, Ginger Meggs, Goodbye Paradise, Careful He Might Hear You, BMX Bandits, Silver City, Witness, The Empty Beach, The Mosquito Coast, The Hitcher, Children of a Lesser God, Stakeout, Gorillas in the Mist, Rain Man, Dead Poets Society, Till There Was You (dir. only), The Doctor, Lorenzo's Oil, The Firm, The Paper, Beyond Rangoon, The American President, Ghosts of Mississippi, The English Patient, City of Angels, The Talented Mr. Ripley, Cold Mountain, At First Sight, The Perfect Storm.
TELEVISION: *Movies:* Top Kid.

SECOMBE, SIR HARRY
C.B.E.: Singer, Comedian, Actor. b. Swansea, Wales, Sept. 8, 1921. Awarded, C.B.E., 1963. Awarded Knight Bachelor, 1991. AUTHOR: Twice Brightly, Goon for Lunch, Katy and the Nurgla, Welsh Fargo, Goon Abroad, The Harry Secombe Diet Book, Harry Secombe's Highway, The Highway Companion. Autobiography: Arias and Raspberries.
THEATER: *London*: Pickwick (also NY), The Four Musketeers, The Plumber's Progress, Pickwick (revival: Chichester Fest., Sadlers Wells Theatre, natl. tour, 1993-95).
PICTURES: Hocus Pocus (debut, 1948), Helter Skelter, London Entertains, Penny Points to Paradise, Forces' Sweetheart, Down Among the Z Men, Svengali, Davy, Jet Storm, Oliver!, The Bed Sitting Room, Song of Norway, Rhubarb, Doctor in Trouble, The Magnificent Seven Deadly Sins, Sunstruck.
TELEVISION: Numerous appearances, incl. own *series*: Secombe and Friends, The Harry Secombe Show, Secombe with Music. Also special version, Pickwick. Presenter of Tyne Tees TV's Highway 1983-93; Presenter of BBC-TV Songs of Praise, 1995-96.

SEDGWICK, KYRA
Actress. b. New York, NY, Aug. 19, 1965. e. USC. m. actor Kevin Bacon.
THEATER: *NY*: Time Was, Dakota's Belly Wyoming, Ah Wilderness (Theatre World Award), Maids of Honor. *LA*: Oleanna.
PICTURES: War and Love, Tai-Pan, Kansas, Born on the Fourth of July, Mr. & Mrs. Bridge, Pyrates, Singles, Heart & Souls, Murder in the First, Something to Talk About, The Low Life, Losing Chase, Phenomenon, Montana (also assoc. prod.), Critical Care, Labor Pains.
TELEVISION: *Movies*: The Man Who Broke 1000 Chains, Women & Men II (In Love There Are No Rules), Miss Rose White, Family Pictures, The Wide Net, Twelfth Night, Lemon Sky. *Series*: Another World. *Guest*: Amazing Stories. *Specials*: Cinder Ella: A Modern Fairy Tale.

SEGAL, GEORGE
Actor. b. New York, NY, Feb. 13, 1934. e. Columbia U., B.A., 1955. Worked as janitor, ticket-taker, soft-drink salesman, usher and under-study at NY's Circle in the Square theatre. Acting debut: Downtown Theatre's revival of Don Juan. Formed a nightclub singing act with Patricia Scott. Record album of rag-time songs and banjo music: The Yama Yama Man. *Dir. debut*: Bucks County Playhouse prod. Scuba Duba.
THEATER: The Iceman Cometh (1956 revival), Antony and Cleopatra N.Y. Shakespeare Festival, Leave It to Jane, The Premise (satiric improv revue), Gideon, Rattle of a Simple Man, The Knack, Requiem for a Heavyweight, The Fourth Wall.
PICTURES: The Young Doctors (debut, 1961), The Longest Day, Act One, The New Interns, Invitation to a Gunfighter, Ship of Fools, King Rat, Lost Command, Who's Afraid of Virginia Woolf? (Acad. Award nom.), The Quiller Memorandum, The St. Valentine's Day Massacre, Bye Bye Braverman, No Way to Treat a Lady, The Southern Star, The Bridge at Remagen, The Girl Who Couldn't Say No, Loving, The Owl and the Pussycat, Where's Poppa?, Born to Win, The Hot Rock, A Touch of Class, Blume in Love, The Terminal Man, California Split, Russian Roulette, The Black Bird, The Duchess and the Dirtwater Fox, Fun with Dick and Jane, Rollercoaster, Who Is Killing the Great Chefs of Europe?, Lost and Found, The Last Married Couple in America, Carbon Copy, Killing 'em Softly, Stick, All's Fair, Look Who's Talking, The Clearing, For the Boys, Look Who's Talking Now, Army of One, Direct Hit, Deep Down, Flirting With Disaster, The Cable Guy, The Feminine Touch, The Mirror Has Two Faces.
TELEVISION: *Series*: Take Five, Murphy's Law, High Tide, Just Shoot Me. *Specials*: Death of a Salesman, Of Mice and Men, The Desperate Hours. *Guest*: The Nurses, Naked City, Alfred Hitchcock Presents. *Movies*: Trackdown: Finding the Goodbar Killer, The Cold Room, The Zany Adventures of Robin Hood, Not My Kid, Many Happy Returns, Endless Game, Taking the Heat, Following Her Heart, Houdini.

SEGAL, MAURICE
Publicist. b. New York, NY, July 22, 1921. e. CCNY, 1937-41. Entered m.p. ind., adv. dept., 20th Fox, 1941-42; U.S. Army 1942-46; feature writer, publ. dept., 20th Fox, 1946; asst. to dir., adv., publ., Century Circuit, 1947; press book dept., Paramount, 1949; trade press rep. 1950; trade press rep. RKO Radio, 1952; resigned to join Richard Condon-Kay Norton, publicists, 1953; adv., pub. dept., U-I. 1954; asst. pub. mgr., United Artists 1957; Hollywood publ. coordinator, 1958; exec. in chg. of M.P. press dept., Universal City Studios, 1966; West Coast adv.-publ. dir., National Gen. Pictures, 1971; pres., Maurice E. Segal Co., 1974; dir., West Coast operations, Charles Schlaifer & Co., 1976; v.p., Max Youngstein Enterprises, 1979; exec. v.p., Taft Intl. Pictures, 1980; pres. Maurice E. Segal Co., 1982; pres. The Segal Company, 1987.

SEIDELMAN, ARTHUR ALLAN
Director, Producer, Writer. b. New York, NY, October 11. e. Whittier Coll., B.A.; UCLA, M.A. Former staff member, Repertory Theatre of Lincoln Center and Phoenix Theatre, NY.
THEATER: *Dir.: LA*: The Sisters, Gypsy Princess, The Beautiful People, Five Finger Exercise, The Purification, etc. *Dir.: NY*: Awakening of Spring, Hamp, Ceremony of Innocence, The Justice Box, Billy, Vieux Carre, The World of My America, Awake and Sing, The Four Seasons, Inherit the Wind, The Most Happy Fella, as well as numerous regional prods. and national tours.
PICTURES: Hercules in New York, Children of Rage (dir., s.p.), Echoes, The Caller, Rescue Me.
TELEVISION: *Director*: Family, Magnum, P.I., Murder She Wrote, Hill Street Blues, Trapper John M.D., Paper Chase, Knots Landing, Bay City Blues, Capitol News, WIOU, L.A. Law, FBI: The Untold Stories, Sweet Justice, Heaven Help Us, Amazing Grace. *Movies*: Which Mother is Mine? A Special Gift, Schoolboy Father, A Matter of Time, I Think I'm Having a Baby, Sin of Innocence, Kate's Secret, Ceremony of Innocence, Poker Alice, The People Across the Lake, Addicted to His Love, Kate's Secret, A Friendship in Vienna, A Place at the Table, An Enemy Among Us, Glory Years, Strange Voices, A Taste of Honey, Look Away, False Witness, The Kid Who Loved Christmas, Body Language, Trapped in Space, Dying to Remember, Wing and a Prayer, Harvest of Fire, I Love Liberty, The Summer of Ben Tyler, Deep Family Secrets.

SEIDELMAN, SUSAN
Director. b. near Philadelphia, PA, Dec.11, 1952. e. Drexel Univ. B.A. Worked at a UHF television station in Phila., NYU film school M.F.A. Debut: 28-min. student film And You Act Like One Too. Then dir. Deficit (short, funded by AFI), and Yours Truly, Andrea G. Stern.
PICTURES: Smithereens (dir., prod., co-s.p.; 1st Amer. indep. feature accepted into competition at Cannes Film Fest., 1982), Desperately Seeking Susan, Making Mr. Right, Cookie (also exec. prod.), She-Devil, The Dutch Master (short, Acad. Award nom.), Tales of Erotica, A Cooler Climate.
TELEVISION: Sex and the City, Confessions of a Suburban Girl (BBC; also writer, actress), The Barefoot Executive.

SEINFELD, JERRY
Comedian, Actor. b. Brooklyn, NY, April 29, 1954. e. Queens Col. Stand-up comic; guested on such shows as The Tonight Show, Late Night With David Letterman. Received American Comedy Award for funniest male comedy stand-up, 1988. Author: Seinlanguage (1993).
TELEVISION: *Series*: Benson, Seinfeld (also co-creator, writer). *Pilot*: The Seinfeld Chronicles. *Specials*: Jerry Seinfeld—Stand-Up Confidental (also writer), Abott and Costello Meet Jerry Seinfeld (host).

SELBY, DAVID
Actor. b. Morganstown, WV. Feb. 5, 1941. e. West Virginia U. Acted in outdoor dramas in home state and did regional theatre elsewhere. Was asst. instructor in lit. at Southern Illinois U.
PICTURES: Night of Dark Shadows, Up the Sandbox, Super Cops, Rich Kids, Raise the Titanic, Rich and Famous, Dying Young, Intersection, Headless Body in Topless Bar.
TELEVISION: *Series*: Dark Shadows, Flamingo Road, Falcon Crest. *Mini-Series*: Washington: Behind Closed Doors. *Movies*: Telethon, The Night Rider, Love for Rent, Doctor Franken, King of the Olympics: The Lives and Loves of Avery Brundage, Grave Secrets: The Legacy of Hilltop Drive, Lady Boss. *Guest*: Kojak, Doogie Howser M.D.

SELF, WILLIAM
Producer. b. Dayton, OH, June 21, 1921. e. U. of Chicago, 1943. Prod.-dir., Schlitz Playhouse of Stars, 1952-56; prod., The Frank Sinatra Show, 1957; exec. prod., CBS-TV, The Twilight Zone, Hotel De Paree; 1960-61 exec. prod., 20th Century-Fox TV: Hong Kong, Adventures in Paradise, Bus Stop, Follow The Sun, Margie; v.p. in chg. of prod., 20th Century-Fox TV, 1962; exec. v.p., 1964; pres., Fox TV 1969; v.p. 20th Century Fox Film Corp., 1969; pres. of William Self Productions, Inc., partner, Frankovich/Self Productions; 1975; v.p., programs, Hollywood CBS TV Network, 1976; 1977, v.p. motion pictures for tv and miniseries, CBS TV; 1982, pres., CBS Theatrical Films; 1985, pres., William Self Prods. in association with CBS Prods; 1990, pres. Self Productions, Inc.
TELEVISION: *Movies* (exec. prod.): The Tenth Man (also prod.), Sarah Plain & Tall, Skylark.

SELIG, ROBERT WILLIAM
Exhibitor. b. Cripple Creek, CO, Feb., 1910. e. U. of Denver, 1932, B.A.; doctorate, 1959. 1932 joined advertising sales div., 20th Century Fox, Denver. Founding mem. Theatre Owners of Amer. and NATO. Consultant, Pacific Theatres. Lifetime Trustee, U. of Denver. Member Kappa Sigma, Omicron Delta Kappa, Beta Gamma Sigma; Nat'l Methodist Church Foundation; Past Pres., Theatre Association of California and CEO NATO of CA; board of directors L.A. Chamber of Commerce; founder NATO/ShoWest Conventions. Received NATO Sherrill C. Corwin Award, 1989.

SELLECCA, CONNIE
Actress. b. Bronx, NY, May 25, 1955. m. anchor-host John Tesh.
TELEVISION: *Series*: Flying High, Beyond Westworld, The Greatest American Hero, Hotel, P.S. I Luv U, Second Chances. *Movies*: The Bermuda Depths (debut, 1978), Flying High (pilot), Captain America II, She's Dressed to Kill, The Last Fling, International Airport, Downpayment on Murder, Brotherhood of the Rose, Turn Back the Clock, Miracle Landing, People Like Us, A House of Secrets and Lies (also co-exec. prod.), Passport to Murder, She Led Two Lives, A Dangerous Affair. *Specials*: The Celebrity Football Classic, Celebrity Challenge of the Sexes, Circus of the Stars.

SELLECK, TOM
Actor. b. Detroit, MI, Jan. 29, 1945. e. U. of Southern California. Grew up in Southern California, appearing in several commercials before being signed to 20th Century Fox. First acting job was on tv series Lancer.
PICTURES: Myra Breckenridge (debut, 1970), Midway, The Washington Affair, Coma, High Road to China, Lassiter, Runaway, Three Men and a Baby, Her Alibi, An Innocent Man, Quigley Down Under, Three Men and a Little Lady, Folks!, Christopher Columbus: The Discovery, Mr. Baseball, In & Out, The Love Letter.
TELEVISION: *Series*: Magnum P.I. (Emmy Award, 1984; also Golden Globe & People's Choice Awards), The Closer. *Movies*: Most Wanted, Superdome, Returning Home, The Sacketts, The Concrete Cowboys, Divorce Wars, Louis L'Amour's The Shadow Riders, Broken Trust, Ruby Jean and Joe, Last Stand at Saber River, Memoir of the 1997 Cowboy, Hall of Fame Heritage Award. *Exec. prod.*: Magnum P.I., B.L. Stryker (series), Revealing Evidence, The Silver Fox. *Guest*: The Young and the Restless, The Rockford Files, Friends.

SELTZER, DAVID
Writer, Director. b. Highland Park, IL, 1940. m. flutist Eugenia Zukerman. e. Northwestern U. School for Film and Television. Moved to NY where worked on TV game show I've Got a Secret. Made short My Trip to New York. 1966 moved to LA to write for David Wolper's Incredible World of Animals. Then dir. and prod. Wolper documentaries. Worked as ghostwriter on film Willy Wonka and the Chocolate Factory.
PICTURES: *Writer*: The Hellstrom Chronicle, One Is a Lonely Number, The Omen, Damien: The Omen Part II, The Other Side of the Mountain, Six Weeks, Table for Five, Lucas (also dir.), Punchline (also dir.), Bird on a Wire, Shining Through (also dir., co-exec. prod.).
TELEVISION: National Geographic Specials (prod., dir., writer), William Holden in Unconquered Worlds (prod., dir., writer), The Underworld World of Jacques Cousteau. Movies (writer): The Story of Eric, Green Eyes, My Father's House, Larry.

SELTZER, WALTER
Executive. b. Philadelphia, PA, Nov. 7, 1914. e. U. of PA. Publicity Asst. for Warner Bros. Theatres, Philadelphia; Fox West Coast Theatres; with MGM 1936-39; Warner Bros., 1939-40; Columbia, 1940-41. Enlisted U.S. Marine Corp., 1941-44. Publ. dir., Hal Wallis, 1945-54; v.p. in chg. adv & pub., Hecht-Lancaster Orgn., 1954-56; assoc. prod., The Boss; partner, Glass-Seltzer, pub. rel. firm; v.p. & exec. prod, Pennebaker Production; 1982, v.p., M.P. & TV Fund; Pres., WSP Inc. Bd. of trustees of Motion Picture and TV Fund.
PICTURES: One-Eyed Jacks, Shake Hands With the Devil, Paris Blues, The Naked Edge, Man in the Middle, Wild Seed, War Lord, Beau Geste, Will Penny, Number One, Darker Than Amber, The Omega Man, Skyjacked, Soylent Green, The Cay, The Last Hard Men.

SEMEL, TERRY
Executive. b. New York, NY, Feb. 24, 1943. e. Long Island Univ., B.S. Accounting 1964. Warner Bros. sales trainee 1966. Branch mgr., Cleveland, Los Angeles. V.P. Domestic sls. mgr. for CBS, 1971-73. Buena Vista as v.p., gen. sls. mgr., 1973-5. 1975 went to Warner Bros. as pres. domestic sls. 1978 named exec. v.p. and COO WB Inc. Named pres., Warner Bros. & COO, 1980. Named Pioneer of the Year by Foundation of Motion Picture Pioneers, 1990.

SEMLER, DEAN
Cinematographer. b. Australia. Served as 2nd unit dir. and cameraman on the mini-series Lonesome Dove, Son of the Morningstar.
PICTURES: The Earthling, The Coca Cola Kid, The Road Warrior, Hoodwink, Kitty and the Bagman, Razorback, Mad Max Beyond Thunderdome, The Coca-Cola Kid, Going Sane, The Lighthorsemen, Cocktail, Young Guns, Farewell to the King, K-9, Dead Calm, Impulse, Young Guns II, Dances With Wolves (Acad. Award, 1990), City Slickers, The Power of One, Super Mario Bros., Last Action Hero, The Three Musketeers, The Cowboy Way, Waterworld, Gone Fishin', Firestorm, The Bone Collector, The Nutty Professor II, The Patriot (dir.).

SEMPLE, LORENZO, JR.
Writer.
THEATER: The Golden Fleecing.
PICTURES: Fathom, Pretty Poison, Daddy's Gone A-Hunting (co-s.p.), The Sporting Club, The Marriage of a Young Stockbroker, Papillon (co-s.p.), Super Cops, The Parallax View (co-s.p.), The Drowning Pool (co-s.p.), Three Days of the Condor (co-s.p.), King Kong, Hurricane (and exec. prod.), Flash Gordon, Never Say Never Again, Sheena (co-s.p.), Never Too Young to Die.
TELEVISION: *Series*: Batman (1966). *Movie*: Rearview Mirror.

SENA, DOMINIC
Director. b. Niles, Ohio, April 26, 1949.
PICTURES: Rhythm Nation 1814, Kalifornia, Gone in Sixty Seconds, Swordfish.

SENDREY, ALBERT
Music Composer, Arranger, Conductor. b. Chicago, IL, Dec. 26, 1921. e. Trinity Coll. Music, London, USC, Paris, & Leipzig Conservatories. Composer, arr., orch. for many plays, films and TV. On stage was pianist/conductor for Lauritz Melchior, Kathryn Grayson, Ray Bolger, Danny Kaye, Tony Martin, Buddy Ebsen. Numerous B'way productions, including Mary Martin's Peter Pan, Ginger Rogers' Pink Jungle and Yul Brynner's Penelope.
PICTURES: *Orchestrations*: The Yearling, Three Musketeers, Father's Little Dividend, Duchess of Idaho, Royal Wedding, Easy to Love, Great Caruso, An American in Paris, Brigadoon, Guys and Dolls, Meet Me in Las Vegas, High Society, Raintree County, Ride the High Country, Hallelujah Trail, The Hook, The Comancheros, Nevada Smith, The Oscar, Thoroughly Modern Millie, Hello Down There, Private Navy of Sgt. O'Farrell, Bad Day at Black Rock (with Andre Previn), Undercurrent, Sea of Grass (with H. Stothart).
TELEVISION: *Comp. music*: Laramie, Wagon Train, Ben Casey, Wolper Documentaries, Americans Abroad, J. F. Kennedy Anthology, Young Man from Boston, High Chaparral, The Monroes, Ken Murray's Hollywood.

SERNA, ASSUMPTA
Actress. b. Barcelona, Spain, Sept. 16, 1957. Abandoned plans to be a lawyer, making stage debut 1978 with anti- Franco theatre company.
PICTURES: Sweet Hours (debut, 1980), The Hunting Ground, Crime of Cuenca, Revolt of the Birds, Circle of Passions, Tin Soldier, Secret Garden, Extramuros, The Old Music, Lola, Matador, Ballad of Dogs, Lucky Ravi, La Brute, La Nuite de L'Ocean, What Belongs to Caesar, Neon Man, Wild Orchid, I the Worst of All, Rossini Rossini, Adelaide, Chain of Desire, Cracked Nut, Fencing Master, Green Henry, Nostradamus, Shortcut to Paradise, Belle al Bar, The Shooter, Como un Relampago, The Craft, Stolen Moments.
TELEVISION: Valentina, First Brigade, Falcon Crest, Fur Elise, Drug Wars, Revolver, Sharpe, Day of Reckoning, Les Derniers Jours de la Victime.

SEWELL, RUFUS
Actor. b. Twickenham, England, Oct. 29, 1967. e. London's Central School of Speech and Drama.
THEATER: *London*: (stage debut) Making It Better, Arcadia. *B'way*: (debut) Translations.
PICTURES: Twenty-One, Dirty Weekend, A Man of No Importance, Victory, Cold Comfort Farm, Carrington, Hamlet, The Woodlanders, Illuminata, Dark City, Dangerous Beauty, Martha Meet Frank Daniel and Laurence.
TELEVISION: *Movie*: The Last Romantics. *Mini-series*: Middlemarch.

SEYMOUR, JANE
Actress. r.n. Joyce Frankenberg. b. Hillingdon, England, Feb. 15, 1951. Dancer with London Festival Ballet at 13. On B'way in Amadeus (1980). British Repetory including Canterbury, Harrogate, Sussex, Windsor.
PICTURES: Oh! What a Lovely, The Only Way, Young Winston, Live and Let Die, Sinbad and the Eye of the Tiger, Battlestar Galactica, Oh Heavenly Dog, Somewhere in Time, Lassiter, Head Office, The Tunnel, The French Revolution, Keys to Freedom.
TELEVISION: *Series*: The Onedine Line, Dr. Quinn: Medicine Woman (Golden Globe, 1996). *Movies/Mini-Series*: Here Come the Double Deckers, Frankenstein: The True Story, Captains and the Kings, Benny and Barney: Las Vegas Undercover, Seventh Avenue, Killer on Board, Our Mutual Friend, The Four Feathers, The Awakening Land, Love's Dark Ride, The Hanged Man, Dallas Cowboys Cheerleaders, The Story of David, McCloud, East of Eden, The Scarlet Pimpernal, Phantom of the Opera, The Haunting Passion, Dark Mirror, The Sun Also Rises, Obsessed with a Married Woman, Jamaica Inn, Crossings, War and Remembrance, The Woman He Loved, Onassis: The Richest Man in the World (Emmy Award, 1988), Jack the Ripper, Angel of Death, I Remember You, Memories of Midnight, Are You Lonesome Tonight?, Matters of the Heart, Sunstroke (also exec. prod.), Heidi, Praying Mantis (also co-exec. prod.), A Passion for Justice: The Hazel Brannon Smith Story (also co-exec. prod.), The Absolute Truth. *Host*: The Heart of Healing.

SHABER, DAVID
Writer. b. Cleveland, OH. e. Western Reserve U., Yale U., Taught at Allegheny Coll. and Smith Coll. in speech and drama dept. Prof. of screenwriting Columbia Univ. Film School. Contributor to Cosmopolitan, Life, Esquire; had several short stories in O'Henry prize collections. Also wrote dramas (Shake Hands with the Clown, The Youngest Shall Ask, Bunker Reveries, etc.). First screenplay was Such Good Friends for Otto Preminger.
PICTURES: The Last Embrace, The Warriors, Those Lips, Those Eyes, Night Hawks, Rollover, The Hunt for Red October (uncredited), Flight of the Intruder, Lion's Share.

SHAFER, MARTIN
Producer, Executive. b. 1954. e. UCLA, 1975. J.D., Southwestern U. Law School, 1978.president of production, Embassy Pictures, 1985; exec. v.p., Twentieth Century Fox Film Corp. Motion Picture Division, 1986; co-founder, Castle Rock Entertainment, 1987. Currently president, Castle Rock Pictures, where his is responsible for the development, production, and distribution of all movies.
PICTURES: The Awakening, Mother Lode, Modern Romance; co-producer, The Mountain Men (Columbia Pictures)

SHAGAN, STEVE
Writer. b. New York, NY. Oct. 25, 1927. Apprenticed in little theatres, film lab chores, stagehand jobs. Wrote, produced and directed film short, One Every Second; moved to Hollywood in 1959. Was IATSE technician, working as grip, stagehand, electrician to support film writing. Also did freelance advertising and publicity; produced Tarzan TV show. In 1968 began writing and producing two-hour films for TV.
AUTHOR: Save the Tiger, City of Angels, The Formula, The Circle, The Discovery, Vendetta, Pillars of Fire, A Cast of Thousands.
PICTURES: *Writer*: Save the Tiger (also prod.; Acad. Award nom., WGA Award, 1973), W.W. and the Dixie Dancekings (exec. prod.), Hustle, Voyage of the Damned (co.-s.p.; Acad. Award nom.), Nightwing (co-s.p.), The Formula (also prod.), The Sicilian, Primal Fear (co-s.p.).
TELEVISION: *Writer-producer*: River of Mystery, Spanish Portrait, Sole Survivor, A Step Out of Line, House on Garibaldi Street (exec. prod.), John Gotti.

SHAIMAN, MARC
Composer, Arranger. b. Newark, NJ, Oct. 22, 1959. Began career at 16 as vocal arranger for Bette Midler; became her Musical Director and Co-producer as well as writing special material for The Divine Miss M! Wrote music for Saturday Night Live; co-wrote musical material for Billy Crystal for the Academy Awards (Emmy Award for "Oscar Medleys"). Prod. and arranger for several Harry Connick, Jr. albums. Received Grammy noms. for "When Harry Met Sally" and "We Are In Love". Appeared on stage in Harlem Nocturne.
PICTURES: Divine Madness (music dir., arranger), The Cotton Club (music sprv., arranger), Broadcast News (cameo), Big Business (music sprv., arranger), Beaches (arranger), When Harry Met Sally... (music spvr.), Misery (music), Scenes From a Mall (music, adapt., cameo), City Slickers (music), Hot Shots (cameo), For the Boys (music sprv., arranger, co-composer), The Addams Family (music, cameo, co-wrote song "Mamuschka"), Sister Act (music, adapt.), Mr. Saturday Night (music, cameo), A Few Good Men (music), Life With Mikey (music spvr.), Sleepless in Seattle (musical spvr., co-wrote song "With a Wink and a Smile"; Acad. Award nom.), Hocus Pocus (music prod.), Heart and Souls (music, cameo), For Love or Money (co-composer), Addams Family Values (music), Sister Act 2: Back in the Habit (music, adaptations), That's Entertainment III (music spvr.), City Slickers II: The Legend of Curly's Gold (music), North (music, cameo), The American President (Acad. Award nom.), Speechless, Stuart Saves His Family, Forget Paris, The First Wives Club (Acad. Award nom.), Ghosts of Mississippi, Mother, George of the Jungle, In & Out, Patch Adams, My Giant, Simon Birch, The Out-of-Towners, South Park: Bigger Longer and Uncut, The Story of Us.
TELEVISION: From the Earth to the Moon (part eleven), Jackie's Back!.

SHALIT, GENE
Critic. b. New York, NY, 1932. e. U. of Illinois. Started as freelance writer; joined NBC Radio Network, working on Monitor, 1968. Has been book and film critic, sports and general columnist. Since 1973 has been featured regular on NBC Today Show. Edits newsletter Shalit's Sampler.

SHANDLING, GARRY
Actor, Comedian, Writer, Producer. b. Chicago, IL, Nov. 29, 1949. e. Univ. of AZ. Moved to LA where he became writer for such sitcoms as Sandford & Son, Welcome Back Kotter, Three's Company. Became stand-up comedian in nightclubs which led to appearances on The Tonight Show.
PICTURES: The Night We Never Met (debut, 1993), Love Affair, Mixed Nuts, Hurlyburly, Doctor Dolittle (voice).
TELEVISION: *Series*: It's Garry Shandling's Show (also exec. prod., writer; ACE Awards for Best Series & Actor), The Larry Sanders Show (also co-exec. prod., co-creator, co-writer, Emmy Award, 1998). *Specials*: Garry Shandling—Alone in Las Vegas (also writer, prod.), It's Garry Shandling's Show—25th Anniversary Special (also exec. prod., writer), Grammy Awards (host), Garry Shandling: Stand-Up (also writer). Guest: Tonight Show (also frequent guest host), Dr Katz: Professional Therapist (voice).

SHANLEY, JOHN PATRICK
Writer, Director. b. New York, NY, 1950. e. NYU. Cameo appearance in 1988 film Crossing Delancey. Dir. and wrote short I am Angry.
THEATER: *Writer*: Rockaway, Welcome to the Moon, Danny and the Deep Blue Sea, Savage in Limbo, Dreamer Examines His Pillow. *Writer-Dir.*: Italian-American Reconciliation, Beggars in the House of Plenty, Four Dogs and a Bone.
PICTURES: *Writer*: Moonstruck (Acad. Award & Writers Guild Award, 1987), Five Corners (also assoc. prod.), The January Man, Joe Versus the Volcano (also dir.), Alive, We're Back!, Congo.

SHAPIRO, ROBERT W.
Producer. b. Brooklyn, NY, March 1, 1938. e. USC. Joined William Morris Agency, Inc., 1958; dir. and head of motion picture dept., William Morris Agency (UK) Ltd., 1969; mng. dir., 1970; 1974 v.p., head int'l. m.p. dept.; 1977 joined Warner Bros. as exec. v.p. in chg. of worldwide production; 1981, named WB pres., theatrical production div. Resigned 1983 to produce films.
PICTURES: Pee-Wee's Big Adventure, Empire of the Sun (exec. prod.), Arthur 2 On the Rocks, There Goes My Baby, Black Beauty, Dr. Jekyll and Ms. Hyde, An Alan Smithee Film: Burn Hollywood Burn (actor only), Somewhere in the City (actor only).
TELEVISION: *Movie*: The Summer My Father Grew Up, Do You Know the Muffin Man.

SHARE, MICHAEL
Executive. Began career with Paramount Pictures 1974 as booker in Indianapolis; 1975-76 appt. salesman; 1976-77 sls. mgr. in Philadelphia; 1977, Cincinnati branch mgr.; 1980, Chicago branch mgr.; 1985, promoted to v.p., eastern div., Paramount.

SHARIF, OMAR
Actor. r.n. Michel Shahoub. b. Alexandria, Egypt, April 10, 1932. e. Victoria Coll., Cairo.; pres. of College Dramatic Society. Starred in 21 Egyptian (billed as Omar el Cherif or Omar Cherif) and two French films prior to English-language debut in Lawrence of Arabia. Left Egypt 1964. Champion contract bridge player. 1983 made rare stage appearance in The Sleeping Prince (Chichester, then West End).
PICTURES: The Blazing Sun (debut, 1954), Our Happy Days, La Chatelane du Liban, Goha, The Mameluks, Lawrence of Arabia (Acad. Award nom.), The Fall of the Roman Empire, Behold a Pale Horse, Marco the Magnificent, Genghis Khan, The Yellow Rolls-Royce, Doctor Zhivago, The Poppy Is Also a Flower, The Night of the Generals, More Than a Miracle, Funny Girl, Mackenna's Gold, The Appointment, Mayerling, Che!, The Last Valley, The Horsemen, The Burglars, The Right to Love (Brainwashed), The Tamarind Seed, The Mysterious Island of Captain Nemo, Juggernaut, Funny Lady, Crime and Passion, The Pink Panther Strikes Again (cameo), Ashanti, Bloodline, The Baltimore Bullet, Oh Heavenly Dog, Green Ice, Chanel Solitaire, Top Secret!, The Possessed, Paradise Calling, The Blue Pyramids, Keys to Freedom, Novice, Mountains of the Moon, Michelangelo and Me, Drums of Fire, Le Guignol, The Puppet, The Rainbow Thief, Journey of Love, Mother, 588 Rue Paradis.
TELEVISION: S*H*E, Pleasure Palace, The Far Pavilions, Peter the Great, Harem, Anastasia, Grand Larceny, Omar Sharif Returns to Egypt, The Mysteries of the Pyramids Live (host), Memories of Midnight, Mrs. 'arris Goes to Paris, Lie Down with Lions.

SHARP, ALAN
Writer. b. Glasgow, Scotland.
PICTURES: The Hired Hand, Ulzana's Raid, Billy Two Hats, Night Moves, The Osterman Weekend, Little Treasure (also dir.), Freeway, Cat Chaser (co-s.p.).
TELEVISION: Coming Out of the Ice.

SHATNER, WILLIAM
Actor. b. Montreal, Quebec, March 22, 1931. e. McGill U. Toured Canada in various stock, repertory companies before U.S. tv debut in 1956. *Author*: TekWar, TekLords, TekLab, Tek Vengeance, TekSecret, Believe, Star Trek Memories (co-author with Chris Kreski), Star Trek Movie Memories (co-author with Kreski), The Return, Man O'War.
THEATER: *NY*: Tamburlaine the Great, The World of Susie Wong (Theatre World Award), A Shot in the Dark, L'Idiote.
PICTURES: The Brothers Karamazov (debut, 1958), Judgment at Nuremberg, The Explosive Generation, The Intruder, The Outrage, Incubus, White Comanche, Impulse, Big Bad Mama, The Devil's Rain, Kingdom of the Spiders, Land of No Return,

Star Trek—The Motion Picture, The Kidnapping of the President, Visiting Hours, Star Trek II: The Wrath of Khan, Airplane II: The Sequel, Star Trek III: The Search for Spock, Star Trek IV: The Voyage Home, Star Trek V: The Final Frontier (also dir., orig. story), Bill & Ted's Bogus Journey (cameo), Star Trek VI: The Undiscovered Country, National Lampoon's Loaded Weapon 1, Star Trek: Generations, Trekkies, Land of the Free.
TELEVISION: *Series*: For the People, Star Trek, Barbary Coast, T.J. Hooker, Rescue 911 (host), TekWar: The Series (also dir., co-exec. prod.), Hercules (voice). *Movies*: Sole Survivor, Vanished, Owen Marshall: Counselor at Law (pilot), The People, The Hound of the Baskervilles, Incident on a Dark Street, Go Ask Alice, The Horror at 37000 Feet, Pioneer Woman, Indict and Convict, Pray for the Wildcats, Barbary Coast (pilot), Perilous Voyage, The Bastard, Little Women, Crash, Disaster on the Coastliner, The Baby Sitter, Secrets of a Married Man, North Beach and Rawhide, Broken Angel, Family of Strangers, Columbo: Butterfly in Shades of Grey, TekWar (also dir., co-exec. prod.), TekLab, TekWar: TekJustice, Janek: The Silent Betrayal, Prisoner of Zenda Inc., Dead Man's Island. *Special*: The Andersonville Trial, TekPower, TekMoney, Ashes of Money, Trinity and Beyond. *Mini-Series*: Testimony of Two Men.

SHAVELSON, MELVILLE
Writer, Director. b. Brooklyn, NY, April 1, 1917. e. Cornell U., 1937, A.B. Radio writer: We The People, Bicycle Party, 1937, Bob Hope Show, 1938-43, then screen writer; apptd. prod., Warner Bros, 1951. Conceived for TV: Make Room for Daddy, My World and Welcome To It. Author: book, How To Make a Jewish Movie, Lualda, The Great Houdinis, The Eleventh Commandment, Ike, Don't Shoot It's Only Me. Pres., Writers Guild of America, West, 1969-71, 1979-81, 1985-87; Pres., Writers Guild Foundation 1978-96.
PICTURES: *Writer*: The Princess and the Pirate, Wonder Man, The Kid From Brooklyn, Sorrowful Jones, It's a Great Feeling, The Daughter of Rosie O'Grady, Always Leave Them Laughing, Where There's Life, On Moonlight Bay, Double Dynamite, I'll See You in My Dreams, Room for One More, April in Paris, Trouble Along the Way, Living It Up. *Director-Writer*: The Seven Little Foys (dir. debut, 1955), Beau James, Houseboat, It Started in Naples, The Five Pennies, On the Double, The Pigeon That Took Rome (also prod.), A New Kind of Love (also prod.), Cast a Giant Shadow (also prod.), Yours Mine and Ours, The War Between Men and Women, Mixed Company.
TELEVISION: *Movies*: The Legend of Valentino, The Great Houdinis, Ike, The Other Woman, Deceptions. *Specials:* Academy Awards, 1988, 1990 (writer).

SHAVER, HELEN
Actress. b. St. Thomas, Ontario, Canada, Feb. 24, 1951. e. Banff Sch. of Fine Arts, Alberta. Worked on stage and screen in Canada before coming to Los Angeles 1978.
THEATER: Tamara, Are You Lookin'? Ghost on Fire, A Doll's House, The Master Builder, The Hostage, Jake's Women (B'way debut; Theatre World Award).
PICTURES: Christina, Shoot, Starship Invasions, Outrageous!, High-Ballin', The Amityville Horror, In Praise of Older Women, Who Has Seen the Wind, Gas, Harry Tracy, The Osterman Weekend, Best Defense, Desert Hearts, The Color of Money, The Believers, The Land Before Time (voice), Walking After Midnight, Innocent Victim (Tree of Hands), Zebrahead, That Night, Dr. Bethune, Morning Glory, Change of Heart, Open Season, Born to Be Wild.
TELEVISION: *Series*: United States, Jessica Novak, WIOU. *Movies*: Lovey: Circle of Children II, Between Two Brothers, Many Happy Returns, The Park is Mine, Countdown To Looking Glass, No Blame, B.L. Stryker: The Dancer's Touch, Pair of Aces, Columbo: Rest in Peace Mrs. Columbo, Survive the Night, Poisoned By Love: The Kern County Murders, Trial & Error, The Forget-Me-Not Murders, Ride With the Wind, Without Consent, Janek: A Silent Betrayal. *Guest*: Ray Bradbury Theatre, Amazing Stories.

SHAW, MICHAEL M. (JOHN)
Executive. b. Ashland, KY, Jan. 10, 1945. e. Eastern KY Univ., Univ. of KY, Univ of MS. 1968-69, asst. booker, 20th Century Fox, Denver; 1969, head booker, Fox; 1970, salesman, Paramount Pictures, S.F.; 1970-71, head booker, sales Paramount L.A.; 1971-73, booker, Commonwealth Theatres; 1973, booker, McLendon theatres, Dallas; 1973-78, div. mngr. Mulberry Square Prods., Dallas; 1978-79, branch mngr. Filmways Pictures, Dallas; 1980-82, owner, Sequoyah Cinema Svc., Denver; 1983-87, head film buyer, Presidio Theatres, Austin; 1987-88, head film buyer, Santikos Theatres, San Antonio; 1988-present, pres./CEO, Film Booking Office Corp., Movieline Int'l, Dallas. Member: Motion Picture Pioneers, Variety Club.

SHAW, STAN
Actor. b. Chicago, IL, July 14, 1952. On stage received NAACP Image Award for West Coast premiere of Home, 1982.
PICTURES: The Bingo Long Travelling All-Stars and Motor Kings, Rocky, The Boys in Company C, The Great Santini, Tough Enough, Runaway, The Monster Squad, Harlem Nights, Fried Green Tomatoes, Body of Evidence, Rising Sun, Houseugest, Cutthroat Island, Daylight, Snake Eyes.
TELEVISION: *Series*: The Mississippi. *Mini-Series*: Roots: The Next Generations. *Movies*: Call to Glory, Maximum Security, The Gladiator, The Billionaire Boys Club, The Three Kings, The Court-Martial of Jackie Robinson, Lifepod. *Guest*: Starsky and Hutch, Wiseguy, Murder She Wrote, Hill Street Blues, Matlock.

SHAWN, WALLACE
Playwright, Actor. b. New York, NY, Nov. 12, 1943. Son of former New Yorker editor William Shawn. e. Harvard; Oxford U. Taught English in India on a Fulbright scholarship 1965-66. English, Latin and drama teacher, NY 1968-70.
THEATER: *Writer*: Our Late Night (1975, Obie Award), The Mandrake (translation, also actor), A Thought in Three Parts, Marie and Bruce, The Hotel Play, Aunt Dan and Lemon (also actor), The Fever (Obie Award, 1991; also actor). *Opera*: The Music Teacher (with Allen Shawn). *Actor*: The Master and Margarita, Chinchilla, Wifey.
PICTURES: Manhattan (debut, 1979), Starting Over, All That Jazz, Strong Medicine, Simon, Atlantic City, My Dinner With Andre (also co-s.p.), A Little Sex, Lovesick, The First Time, Deal of the Century, Strange Invaders, Saigon—Year of the Cat, Crackers, The Hotel New Hampshire, The Bostonians, Micki and Maude, Heaven Help Us, Head Office, The Bedroom Window, Radio Days, Prick Up Your Ears, Nice Girls Don't Explode, The Princess Bride, The Moderns, She's Out of Control, Scenes From the Class Struggle in Beverly Hills, We're No Angels, Shadows and Fog, Mom and Dad Save the World, Nickel and Dime, The Cemetery Club, Un-Becoming Age, The Meteor Man, Vanya on 42nd Street, Mrs. Parker and the Vicious Circle, A Goofy Movie (voice), Clueless, Canadian Bacon, Toy Story (voice), The Wife, House Arrest, All Dogs Go to Heaven II (voice), Just Write, National Lampoon's Vegas Vacation, Critical Care, My Favorite Martian, Toy Story 2 (voice).
TELEVISION: *Series:* Clueless, The Lionharts.

SHAYE, ROBERT
Executive. b. Detroit, MI, March 4, 1939. e. U. of Michigan, B.B.A.; Columbia U. Law. At 15 wrote, prod. dir. training film for father's supermarket staff. Later won first prize in Society of Cinematologists' Rosenthal Competition (best m.p. by American dir. under 25). Wrote, prod., dir., edited short films, trailers and TV commercials, including award-winning shorts, Image and On Fighting Witches (prod., dir.). Founded New Line Cinema 1967. Chmn. & CEO, New Line Cinema.
PICTURES: *Prod./exec. prod.*: Stunts, XTRO, Alone in the Dark, The First Time, Polyester, Critters, Quiet Cool, My Demon Lover, A Nightmare on Elm Street (also parts 2,3,4,5,6), The Hidden, Stranded, Critters 2, Hairspray, Heart Condition, Book of Love (dir.), Wes Craven's New Nightmare (also actor).
TELEVISION: Freddy's Nightmare: the Series (exec. prod.).

SHEA, JOHN
Actor. b. Conway, NH, April 14, 1949. Raised in MA. e. Bates Coll., ME, B.A. 1970; Yale Drama School, M.F.A. 1973. Worked as asst. dir. Chelsea Theater; taught part-time at Pratt Inst.
THEATER: Yentl (debut 1975, Off-B'way and B'way; Theatre World Award), Sorrows of Stephen, Long Day's Journey Into Night (Joseph Jefferson Award nom.), The Master and Margarita, Romeo and Juliet (Circle in the Sq.), American Days (Drama Desk Award), The Dining Room, End of the World (B'way), The Normal Heart (London, 1987), Animal Kingdom, Rosmersholm (La Mama), Impossible Spy (China's Golden Panda Award).
PICTURES: Hussy, Missing, Windy City (Best Actor Montreal Film Festival), A New Life, Unsettled Land, Honeymoon, Stealing Home, Freejack, Honey I Blew Up the Kid, A Weekend in the Country, Brass Ring (also dir., co-writer).
TELEVISION: *Series*: WIOU, Lois and Clark. *Movies*: The Nativity, Family Reunion, Coast to Coast (BBC), Hitler's S.S.: Portrait in Evil, A Case of Deadly Force, The Impossible Spy, Magic Moments, Baby M (Emmy Award), Do You Know the Muffin Man, Small Sacrifices, Notorious, Ladykiller, Justice in a Small Town, See Jane Run, Forgotten Sins, The Dining Room. *Mini-Series*: The Last Convertible, Kennedy, The Apocalypse Watch. *Special*: Leslie's Folly.

SHEAFF, DONALD J.
Executive. b. Oct. 23, 1925. e. U.of California at L.A., 1948; Pierce Coll., 1957. Served 4 yrs. during W.W.II in Navy Air Corps in South Pacific. 1946, joined Technicolor Motion Picture Div. in supervisory capacity; 1957, lab. supervisor, Lookout Mountain Air Force Station, handling Top Secret film for Air Force and Atomic Energy Commission; est. and org. the installation of Vandenberg Air Force Base Lab. facilities, which Technicolor designed; 1961 joined Panacolor Corp.; 1963, joined Pacific Title and Art Studio in charge of color control for special effects and titles; returned to Technicolor Corp. app't. Plant Mgr. of TV div., 1966; v.p. & gen. mngr. of the TV div., 1973; appt v.p. & gen. mgr., Motion Picture Division, 1976; mgr., special visual effects, Universal City Studios. Member: SMPTE, Nat'l Academy of Television Arts & Sciences. Has conducted scientific seminars for SMPTE.

SHEARER, HARRY
Writer, Actor. b. Los Angeles, CA, Dec. 23, 1943. e. UCLA (pol. science); grad. work in urban gov., Harvard. At 7 appeared on The Jack Benny Show. Worked as freelance journalist for Newsweek, L.A. Times and publ. articles in New West, L.A. Magazine and Film Comment. Also taught h.s. Eng. and social studies and worked in CA State Legislature in Sacramento. Founding mem. The Credibility Gap, co-wrote, co-prod. and performed on comedy group's albums (A Great Gift Idea, The Bronze Age of Radio). Co-wrote, co-prod. Albert Brooks' album A Star is Bought. Performed with group Spinal Tap. Host of Le Show, L.A. radio prog. Writer-cast mem. Saturday Night Live (1979-80 & 1984-85).
THEATER: Accomplice (Pasadena Playhouse).
PICTURES: *Actor*: Abbott and Costello Go to Mars (debut, as child, 1953), Cracking Up, Real Life (also co-s.p.), Animalympics (voice), The Fish That Saved Pittsburgh, Serial, One-Trick Pony, The Right Stuff, This is Spinal Tap (also co-s.p.), Plain Clothes, My Stepmother is an Alien (voice), Oscar, Pure Luck, Blood & Concrete, The Fisher King, A League of Their Own, Wayne's World 2, I'll Do Anything, Speechless, My Best Friend's Wedding, Godzilla, Encounters in the Third Dimension (voice), Almost Heroes, The Truman Show, Small Soldiers (voice), Dick, Edtv.
TELEVISION: *Series*: Fernwood 2-Night (creative consultant), The Simpsons (voice), Harry Shearer's News Quiz. *Specials*: Likely Stories, It's Just TV, Paul Shaffer: Viva Shaf Vegas, Comedy Hour, Portrait of a White Marriage (also dir.), The Magic of Live, Spinal Tap Reunion (also co-writer).

SHEEDY, ALLY
Actress. r.n. Alexandra Sheedy. b. New York, NY, June 13, 1962. e. USC. m. actor David Lansbury. Daughter of literary agent Charlotte Sheedy. As child performed with American Ballet Theatre. At age 12 wrote children's book, She Was Nice to Mice; later wrote pieces for NY Times, Village Voice, Ms. Published book of poetry: Yesterday I Saw the Sun. Began acting in TV commercials at 15. Chicago Theatre in Wrong Turn at Lungfish; NY stage debut in Advice from a Caterpillar.
PICTURES: Bad Boys (debut, 1983), WarGames, Oxford Blues, The Breakfast Club, St. Elmo's Fire, Twice in a Lifetime, Blue City, Short Circuit, Maid to Order, Heart of Dixie, Betsy's Wedding, Only the Lonely, Home Alone 2: Lost in New York (cameo), Tattletale, The Pickle, Man's Best Friend, One Night Stand, High Art, Sugar Town, Autmn Heart.
TELEVISION: *Movies*: The Best Little Girl in the World, The Violation of Sarah McDavid, The Day the Loving Stopped, Splendor in the Grass, Deadly Lessons, We Are the Children, Fear, The Lost Capone, Lethal Exposure, Chantilly Lace, Ultimate Betrayal, Parallel Lives, The Haunting of Seacliff Inn, The Tin Soldier, The Fury Within, Our Guys: Outrage at Glen Ridge. *Guest*: Hill Street Blues, St. Elsewhere.

SHEEN, CHARLIE
Actor. r.n. Carlos Irwin Estevez. b. Los Angeles, Sept. 3, 1965. Father is actor Martin Sheen. Brother of actors Emilio, Ramon and Renee Estevez. Made debut as extra in TV movie, The Execution of Private Slovik (starring father) and as extra in Apocalypse Now (also starring father).
PICTURES: Grizzly II—The Predator, Red Dawn, The Boys Next Door, Lucas, Ferris Bueller's Day Off, The Wraith, Platoon, Wisdom, Three for the Road, No Man's Land, Wall Street, Never on Tuesday, Young Guns, Eight Men Out, Major League, Beverly Hills Brats, Courage Mountain, Navy Seals, Men at Work, The Rookie, Cadence, Hot Shots!, National Lampoon's Loaded Weapon 1 (cameo), Hot Shots Part Deux!, DeadFall, The Three Musketeers, The Chase (also co-exec. prod.), Major League 2, Beyond the Law, Terminal Velocity, The Shadow Conspiracy, All Dogs Go to Heaven II (voice), The Arrival, Money Talks, Postmortem, No Code of Conduct, Free Money, Being John Malkovich (cameo), Five Aces, Rated X, Famous, Good Advice, The Colored Star.
TELEVISION: *Movies*: Silence of the Heart, Backtrack. *Series:* Sugar Hill, Spin City.

SHEEN, MARTIN
Actor. r.n. Ramon Estevez. b. Dayton, OH, Aug. 3, 1940. Father of actors Emilio Estevez, Charlie Sheen, Ramon Estevez and Renee Estevez. Wrote play (as Ramon G. Estevez) Down the Morning Line (prod. Public Theatre, 1969). Emmy Award as dir., exec. prod. Babies Having Babies (1986).
THEATER: The Connection (debut, 1959 with the Living Theater), Women of Trachis, Many Loves, In the Jungle of Cities, Never Live Over a Pretzel Factory, The Subject Was Roses, The Wicked Crooks, Hamlet, Romeo and Juliet, Hello Goodbye, The Happiness Cage, Death of a Salesman (with George C. Scott), Julius Caesar, The Crucible.
PICTURES: The Incident (debut, 1967), The Subject Was Roses, Catch-22, No Drums No Bugles, Rage, Pickup on 101, Badlands, The Legend of Earl Durrand, The Cassandra Crossing, The Little Girl Who Lives Down the Lane, Apocalypse Now, Eagle's Wing, The Final Countdown, Loophole, Gandhi, That Championship Season, Enigma, Man Woman and Child, The Dead Zone, Firestarter, The Believers, Siesta, Wall Street, Walking After Midnight, Da (also co-exec. prod.), Judgment in Berlin (also exec. prod.), Beverly Hills Brats, Cold Front, Beyond the Stars, The Maid, Cadence (also dir.), JFK (narrator), Hear No Evil, Hot Shots Part Deux (cameo), Gettysburg, Trigger Fast, Hits!, Fortunes of War, Sacred Cargo, The Break, Dillinger & Capone, Captain Nuke and the Bomber Boys, Ghost Brigade, The Cradle Will Rock, Dead Presidents, Dorothy Day, Gospa, The American President, The War At Home, Spawn, Taylor's Campaign, Stranger in the Kingdom, Snitch, Shadrach (voice), No Code of Conduct, Gunfighter, Free Money, Texas Funeral, Ninth Street, Lucky Town, Lost & Found, O, The Papp Project.
TELEVISION: *Series*: As the World Turns, The West Wing. *Movies*: Then Came Bronson, Mongo's Back in Town, Welcome Home Johnny Bristol, That Certain Summer, Letters for Three Lovers, Pursuit, Catholics, Message to My Daughter, The Execution of Private Slovik, The California Kid, The Missiles of October, The Story of Pretty Boy Floyd, Sweet Hostage, The Guardian, The Last Survivors, Blind Ambition, The Long Road Home (Emmy Award, 1981), In the Custody of Strangers, Choices of the Heart, The Atlanta Child Murders, Consenting Adult, Shattered Spirits, News at Eleven, Out of the Darkness, Samaritan, Conspiracy: The Trial of the Chicago 8, No Means No (exec. prod. only), Nightbreaker (also exec. prod.), Guilty Until Proven Innocent, The Water Engine (voice), The Last P.O.W.?: The Bobby Garwood Story, A Matter of Justice, One of Her Own, Roswell, Voyage of Terror, Babylon 5: The River of Souls, Storm, The Time Shifters. *Mini-Series*: Kennedy, Queen, Medusa's Child. *Guest*: Tales From the Crypt, Murphy Brown (Emmy Award, 1994), The Simpsons (voice). *Narrator*: Eyewitness (PBS).

SHEFFER, CRAIG
Actor. b. York, PA, 1960. e. East Stroudsberg Univ., PA. Started career in tv commercials; in soap opera, One Life to Live. On NY stage in Fresh Horses, G.R. Point, Torch Song Trilogy (B'way & Off-B'way). Starred in IMAX film Wings of Courage.
PICTURES: That Was Then This Is Now (debut, 1985), Fire with Fire, Some Kind of Wonderful, Voyage of the Rock Aliens, Split Decisions, Nightbreed, Instant Karma (also exec. prod.), Blue Desert, Eye of the Storm, A River Runs Through It, Fire in the Sky, The Program, Sleep With Me, Roadflower, The Grave, Head Above Water, Flypaper, Double Take, Bliss, Executive Power, The Fall, Rhapsody in Bloom, Shadow of Doubt, Net Worth.
TELEVISION: *Series*: The Hamptons. *Movies*: Babycakes, In Pursuit of Honor, The Desperate Trail, Miss Evers' Boys, Merry Christmas George Bailey.

SHEFFIELD, JOHN
Actor. b. Pasadena, CA, April 11, 1931. e. UCLA. Stage debut at 7 in On Borrowed Time. Created screen role of Tarzan's son in Tarzan Finds a Son, followed by 7 other entries in Tarzan series, and role of Bomba in Bomba series.
PICTURES: Babes in Arms, Tarzan Finds a Son, Lucky Cisco Kid, Little Orvie, Knute Rockne—All-American, Million Dollar Baby, Tarzan's Secret Treasure, Tarzan's New York Adventure, Tarzan Triumphs, Tarzan's Desert Mystery, Tarzan and the Amazons, Tarzan and the Leopard Woman, Tarzan and the Huntress, Roughly Speaking, Bomba the Jungle Boy, Bomba on Panther Island, Lost Volcano, Bomba and the Hidden City, The Lion Huntress, Bomba and the Elephant Stampede, African Treasure, Bomba and the Jungle Girl, Safari Drums, The Golden Idol, Killer Leopard, Lord of the Jungle.
TELEVISION: *Series*: Bantu the Zebra Boy.

SHEINBERG, SIDNEY JAY
Executive. b. Corpus Christi, TX, Jan. 14, 1935. e. Columbia Coll., A.B. 1955; LL.B., 1958. Admitted to Calif. bar, 1958; assoc. in law U. of California Sch. of Law, Los Angeles, 1958-59; joined MCA, Inc, 1959; pres., TV div., 1971-74; exec. v.p., parent co., 1969-73. Named MCA pres. & chief oper. off., 1973. Resigned from position 1995 to form company The Bubble Factory to produce films for MCA. 1997, prod. films: The Pest, A Simple Wish.

SHELDON, DAVID
Producer, Director, Writer. b. New York, NY. e. Yale U. Sch. of Drama, M.F.A.; Principia Coll., B.A.; Actors Studio, directors unit. 1972-74 was exec. at American Int'l Pictures supervising development and production of 18 films include: Futureworld, Walking Tall, Dillinger, Sisters, Macon County Line, Reincarnation of Peter Proud, Slaughter, Dr. Phibes. *Prod./Dir.*, The Gateway Playhouse in NY where dir. over 50 plays and musicals. Started the Sheldon/Post Company in 1991 with Ira Post. *Exec. prod./writer* of Secret of a Small Town.
PICTURES: *Prod./Dir.*: Grizzly Adams and The Legend of Dark Mountain. *Producer*: Just Before Dawn, Abby, Day of the Animals, The Manitou. *Director*: Lovely But Deadly. *Writer*: The Predator. *Prod./Writer*: Grizzly, Sheba Baby, The Evil, Project: Kill.

SHELDON, JAMES
Director. r.n. James Schleifer. b. New York, NY. Nov. 12. e. U. of NC. Page boy, NBC; announcer-writer-dir., NBC Internat'l Div.; staff dir., ABC radio; staff prod. dir., Young & Rubicam; free lance prod. dir. of many programs live tape and film, N.Y. and Hollywood.

TELEVISION: *Series* (prod./ dir.): Mr. Peepers, Armstrong Circle Theatre, Robert Montgomery Presents, Schlitz Playhouse, West Point, Zane Grey Theatre, The Millionaire, Desilu Playhouse, Perry Mason, Twilight Zone, Route 66, Naked City, The Virginian, Alfred Hitchcock Presents, Fugitive, Espionage, Defenders, Nurses, Bing Crosby Show, Family Affair, Wonderful World of Disney, Man From UNCLE, Felony Squad, That Girl, Ironside, My World and Welcome To It, To Rome With Love, Owen Marshall, Room 222, Apple's Way, Love American Style, McMillan and Wife, Sanford and Son, Ellery Queen, Rich Man, Poor Man II, Family, MASH, Switch, Loveboat, Sheriff Lobo, Knots Landing, The Waltons, 240-Robert, Nurse, Dukes of Hazard, Todays F.B.I., McLain's Law, 7 Brides for 7 Brothers, Lottery, Partners in Crime, Jessie, Santa Barbara, Half Nelson, Stir Crazy, The Equalizer, Sledge Hammer, Cagney & Lacey. *Movies*: Gidget Grows Up, With This Ring, The Gossip Columnist.

SHELDON, SIDNEY
Writer, Director, Producer, Novelist. b. Chicago, IL, Feb. 11, 1917. e. Northwestern U.
AUTHOR: The Naked Face, The Other Side of Midnight, A Stranger in the Mirror, Bloodline, Rage of Angels, Master of the Game, If Tomorrow Comes, Windmills of the Gods, The Sands of Time, Memories of Midnight, The Doomsday Conspiracy, The Stars Shine Down, Nothing Lasts Forever, Morning Noon & Night, The Best Laid Plans, Tell Me Your Dreams.
THEATER: Redhead (Tony Award, 1959). Alice in Arms, Jackpot, Dream With Music, Merry Widow (revision), Roman Candle.
PICTURES: *Writer*: The Bachelor and the Bobbysoxer (Acad. Award, 1947), Easter Parade, Annie Get Your Gun, Three Guys Named Mike, Dream Wife (also dir.), Remains to Be Seen, You're Never Too Young, Pardners, The Buster Keaton Story (also prod., dir.), The Birds and the Bees, Gambling Daughters, Dangerous Lady, Bill Rose's Jumbo. *Novels made into films:* The Naked Face, The Other Side of Midnight, Bloodline.
TELEVISION: *Series*: Patty Duke Show (creator), I Dream of Jeannie (creator, prod.), Nancy (creator, prod.), Hart to Hart (creator). *Novels made into Mini-Series/Movies*: Rage of Angels, Master of the Game, Windmills of the Gods, If Tomorrow Comes, Memories of Midnight, The Sands of Time, Stranger in the Mirror, Nothing Lasts Forever.

SHELLEY, CAROLE
Actress. b. London, England, Aug. 16, 1939. e. Arts Educational Sch., RADA.
THEATER: *NY:* The Odd Couple (debut, 1965), The Astrakhan Coat, Loot, Sweet Potato, Little Murders, Hay Fever, Absurd Person Singular (Tony nom.), The Norman Conquests, The Elephant Man (Tony Award, 1979), Twelve Dreams (Obie Award), The Misanthrope, Noises Off, Stepping Out (Tony nom.), What the Butler Saw, The Miser, Maggie and Misha, The Destiny of Me, Later Life, London Suite, Show Boat. *London:* Simon and Laura (debut, 1955), New Cranks, Boeing-Boeing, Mary Mary, Lettice and Lovage. Also appearances with Shaw Festival, Stratford Fest., Amer. Shakespeare Fest., etc.
PICTURES: Give Us this Day (debut, 1949), Cure for Love, It's Great to Be Young, Carry on Regardless, Carry on Cabby, The Odd Couple, The Boston Strangler, The Aristocats (voice), Robin Hood (voice), The Super, Little Noises, Quiz Show, The Road to Wellville, Hercules (voice), Jungle2Jungle.
TELEVISION: *Series:* The Odd Couple. *Specials:* Coconut Downs, Gabby, A Salute to Noel Coward. *Movie:* Devlin. *Guest:* Brian Rix, Dickie Henderson Show, The Avengers.

SHELTON, RON
Writer, Director, Producer. b. Whittier, CA, Sept. 15, 1945. e. Westmont Coll., Santa Barbara, CA, 1967; U of Arizona, Tucson, AZ, 1974. For 5 years played second base for Baltimore Orioles farm team. Cleaned bars and dressed mannequins to support his art: painting and sculpture. A script he wrote, A Player to Be Named Later (which he later filmed himself as Bull Durham), attracted attention of dir. Roger Spottiswoode who directed his first two scripts.
PICTURES: The Pursuit of D. B. Cooper (assoc. prod.), Open Season (exec. prod.). Writer: Under Fire (also 2nd unit dir.), The Best of Times (also 2nd unit dir.), Bull Durham (also dir.), Blaze (also dir.), White Men Can't Jump (also dir.), Blue Chips (also co-exec. prod.), Cobb (also dir.), The Great White Hype (co-s.p.), Tin Cup (also prod., s.p.).

SHENSON, WALTER
Producer. b. San Francisco, CA. e. Stanford U., Calif.; Ent. m.p. ind. 1941; studio exec., writing, prod., prom. shorts, trailers, Columbia; sup. publ., expl., London, Columbia European production, 1955.
PICTURES: *Prod.*: The Mouse That Roared, A Matter of Who, The Mouse on the Moon, A Hard Day's Night, Help!, 30 Is a Dangerous Age Cynthia, Don't Raise the Bridge Lower the River, A Talent for Loving, Welcome to the Club (also dir.), The Chicken Chronicles, Reuben Reuben, Echo Park, Ruby Jean and Joe.
(d. October 17, 2000)

SHEPARD, SAM
Writer, Actor. r.n. Samuel Shepard Rogers. b. Fort Sheridan, IL, Nov. 5, 1943. Raised in California, Montana and South Dakota. Worked as stable hand, sheep shearer, orange picker in CA, a car wrecker in MA and musician with rock group Holy Modal Rounders. Lived near San Francisco, where, in addition to writing, ran a drama workshop at the U. of California at Davis. Recipient of Brandeis U. Creative Arts Citation, 1976, and American Acad. of Arts and Letters Award, 1975.
THEATER: *Playwright*: Icarus' Mother, Red Cross (triple bill—Obie Award, 1966), La Turista (Obie Award, 1967), Forensic and the Navigators, Melodrama Play, Tooth of Crime (Obie Award, 1973), Back Dog Beast Bait, Operation Sidewinder, 4-H Club, The Unseen Hand, Mad Dog Blues, Shaved Splits, Rock Garden, Curse of the Starving Class (Obie Award, 1978), Buried Child (Obie Award & Pulitzer Prize, 1979), True West, Fool For Love, A Lie of the Mind, Simpatico.
PICTURES: *Actor*: Renaldo and Clara (debut, 1978), Days of Heaven, Resurrection, Raggedy Man, Frances, The Right Stuff (Acad. Award nom.), Country, Fool for Love, Crimes of the Heart, Baby Boom, Steel Magnolias, Bright Angel, Defenseless, Voyager, Thunderheart, The Pelican Brief, Safe Passage, The Only Thrill. *Writer*: Me and My Brother (co-s.p.), Zabriskie Point (co-s.p.), Oh Calcutta! (contributor), Renaldo and Clara (co-s.p.), Paris Texas, Fool for Love, Far North (also dir.), Silent Tongue (also dir.), Snow Falling on Cedars, Hamlet, Curtain Call.
TELEVISION: *Special*: Fourteen Hundred Thousand Blue Bitch (BBC). *Movie*: The Good Old Boys, Purgatory, Dash and Lilly.

SHEPHERD, CYBILL
Actress, Singer. b. Memphis, TN, Feb. 18, 1950. e. Hunter Coll., NYU, USC. Was fashion model (won Model of the Year title, 1968) before acting debut in 1971. Debut record album, Cybill Does It... To Cole Porter, 1974, followed by Stan Getz: Mad About the Boy, Vanilla, Somewhere Down the Road.
PICTURES: The Last Picture Show (debut, 1971), The Heartbreak Kid, Daisy Miller, At Long Last Love, Taxi Driver, Special Delivery, Silver Bears, The Lady Vanishes, The Return, Chances Are, Texasville, Alice, Once Upon a Crime, Married to It, The Muse (cameo).
TELEVISION: *Series*: The Yellow Rose, Moonlighting, Cybill (also co-exec. prod.; Golden Globe, 1996). *Movies*: A Guide for the Married Woman, Secrets of a Married Man, Seduced, The Long Hot Summer, Which Way Home, Memphis (also co-writer, co-exec. prod.), Stormy Weathers, Telling Secrets, There Was a Little Boy, Baby Brokers, For the Love of My Daughter, While Justice Sleeps, The Last Word, Journey of the Heart.

SHEPHERD, RICHARD
Producer. b. Kansas City, MO, June 4, 1927. e. Stanford U. In U.S. Naval Reserve, 1944-45. Entered entertainment field as exec. with MCA, 1948, functioning in radio, TV, and m.p. fields until 1956, with time out for U.S. Army, 1950-52. 1956 became head of talent for Columbia Pictures. 1962 joined CMA talent agency on its founding, becoming exec. v.p. in chg. of m.p. div.; 1972-74, exec. v.p. for prod. Warner Bros.; 1974 became indept. prod.; 1976 named MGM sr. vp. & worldwide head of theatrical prod. 1985 to present, partner in The Artists Agency.
PICTURES: Twelve Angry Men, The Hanging Tree, The Fugitive Kind, Breakfast at Tiffany's, Alex and the Gypsy, Robin and Marian, Volunteers, The Hunger.

SHER, LOUIS K.
Executive. b. Columbus, OH, Feb. 25, 1914. e. Ohio State U., 1933. Exec., Stone's Grills Co., 1934-37; owned & operated, Sher Vending Co., 1937-43. U.S. Army, 1943-46. V.p., Sons Bars & Grills, 1947-54; org. & pres. Art Theatre Guild, 1954; opened art theatres for first time in many cities, org. opera film series, film classic series and similar motion picture activities in many cities; org., Film Festival at Antioch Coll., 1960; pioneer in fighting obscenity laws in Ohio; operates 4 theatres in midwest and western states. Co-producer of the musical broadway production Shenandoah and American Dance Machine. Produced film, Deathmask.

SHERAK, THOMAS
Executive. e. B.A., marketing, New York City Community College. Began film career in distribution, Paramount Pictures, 1970; v.p. & head film buyer, General Cinema; president, domestic dist. & mktg, Twentieth Century Fox, 1983-84 & 1986-90; senior exec. v.p., Twentieth Century Fox. Currently chairman, 20th Domestic Film Group (since 1997); senior exec. v.p., Fox Filmed Entertainment, 1994-present. Board member, National Multiple Sclerosis Society, the Weizmann Institute, Fulfillment Fund of Southern Calif., and Southern Calif. Variety; member, Endowment Campaign Committee for the Academy Found.; chairman, Found. for Motion Picture Pioneers.

SHERIDAN, JAMEY
Actor. b. Pasadena, CA, July 12, 1951. e. UC Santa Barbara.
THEATER: *Off-B'way:* Just a Little Bit Less Than Normal, The Arbor, One Wedding Two Rooms Three Friends. *B'way:* The Man Who Came to Dinner, Hamlet, Biloxi Blues, All My Sons, Long Day's Journey Into Night, Ah Wilderness, The Shadow Box. *Regional*: Major Barbara, Loose Ends, Deathtrap, Homesteaders.

PICTURES: Jumpin' Jack Flash (debut, 1986), The House on Carroll Street, Distant Thunder, Stanley & Iris, Quick Change, Talent for the Game, All I Want for Christmas, A Stranger Among Us, Whispers in the Dark, White Squall.
TELEVISION: *Series*: Shannon's Deal, Chicago Hope. *Movies*: One Police Plaza, Shannon's Deal (pilot), A Mother's Courage: The Mary Thomas Story, Murder in High Places, My Breast, Spring Awakening, Killer Rules. *Mini-Series*: The Stand. *Guest*: The Doctors, Another World, St. Elsewhere, Spenser: For Hire, Picket Fences, The Equalizer.

SHERIDAN, JIM
Director, Writer. b. Dublin, Ireland, 1949. e. Univ Col. in Dublin, NYU Inst. of Films & TV. Started as director-writer at Lyric Theatre in Belfast and Abbey Theatre in Dublin; also at Project Arts Theatre (1976-80), NY Irish Arts Center (1982-87) as artistic director. Founded Children's Theatre Company in Dublin.
PICTURES: *Dir.-Writer*: My Left Foot, The Field, Into the West (s.p. only), In the Name of the Father, Some Mother's Son (also prod.), The Boxer (also prod.).
THEATER: *Writer*: Mobile Homes, Spike in the First World War (Edinburgh Festival Fringe Award for best play, 1983).

SHERIDAN, NICOLLETTE
Actress. b. Worthing, Sussex, England, Nov. 21, 1963. Moved to LA in 1973. Became model in NYC before turning to acting.
PICTURES: The Sure Thing (debut, 1985), Noises Off, Spy Hard, Beverly Hills Ninja, Raw Nerve.
TELEVISION: *Series*: Paper Dolls, Knots Landing. *Movies*: Dark Mansions, Agatha Christie's Dead Man's Folly, Jackie Collins' Lucky/Chances, Deceptions, A Time to Heal, Shadows of Desire, Robin Cook's Virus, Murder in My Mind, Knots Landing: Back to the Cul-de-Sac, Dead Husbands.

SHERMAN, RICHARD M.
Composer, Lyricist, Screenwriter. b. New York, NY, June 12, 1928. e. Bard Coll., B.A., 1949. Info. & Educ. Br., U.S. Army, 1953-55. Songwriter, composer, Walt Disney Prods 1960-71, then freelance. With partner-brother Robert has won, 9 Acad. Award nom., 2 Grammys, 17 gold and platinum albums, 1st Prize, Moscow Film Fest. (for Tom Sawyer) and a star on Hollywood Walk of Fame. Have written over 500 pub. and recorded songs. Also wrote score for B'way musical Over Here (1974) and songs for Disney Theme Parks.
SONGS: Things I Might Have Been, Tall Paul, Christmas in New Orleans, Mad Passionate Love, Midnight Oil, The Ugly Bug Ball, You're Sixteen, That Darn Cat, The Wonderful Thing About Tiggers, It's a Small World, A Spoonful of Sugar, Supercalifragilistic, Feed the Birds, Let's Go Fly a Kite, Age of Not Believing, When You're Loved, Pineapple Princess, Let's Get Together, Maggie's Theme, Chim Chim Cheree (Acad. Award, 1964), Chitty Chitty Bang Bang, Hushabye Mountain, Winnie the Pooh, Fortuosity, Slipper and the Rose Waltz, many others. Comedy Album: Smash Flops.
PICTURES: Nightmare, The Cruel Tower, The Absent Minded Professor, The Parent Trap, Big Red, In Search of the Castaways, Moon Pilot, Bon Voyage, Legend of Lobo, Summer Magic, Miracle of the White Stallions, The Sword in the Stone, The Misadventures of Merlin Jones, Mary Poppins (2 Acad. Awards for song & score, 1964), Those Calloways, The Monkey's Uncle, That Darn Cat, Follow Me Boys!, Winnie the Pooh, Monkeys Go Home!, Chitty Chitty Bang Bang, The Gnome-Mobile, The Jungle Book, The Happiest Millionaire, The One and Only Genuine Original Family Band, The Aristocats, Bedknobs & Broomsticks, Snoopy Come Home, Charlotte's Web, Beverly Hills Cop III, The Mighty Kong. Songs & S.P.: Tom Sawyer, The Slipper and the Rose, The Magic of Lassie, Huckleberry Finn, Little Nemo: Adventures in Slumberland.
TELEVISION: Wonderful World of Color, Bell Telephone Hour, Welcome to Pooh Corner, The Enchanted Musical Playhouse, The Timberwood Tales, Goldilocks, Harry Anderson's Sideshow.

SHERMAN, ROBERT B.
Composer, Lyricist, Screenwriter. b. New York, NY, Dec. 19, 1925. e. Bard Coll., B.A., 1949. U.S. Army, WWII, 1943-45 (purple heart). Songwriter, 1952-60; pres., Music World Corp., 1958; songwriter, composer, Walt Disney, 1971, then freelance. Hon. Phd., Lincoln Col, 1990. With partner-brother Richard Sherman, has won, 9 Acad. Award nom., 2 Grammys, 17 gold and platinum albums, 1st Prize, Moscow Film Fest. (for Tom Sawyer) and a star on Hollywood Walk of Fame. Have written over 500 pub. and recorded songs. Also wrote score for B'way musical Over Here (1974) and songs for Disney Theme Parks. (see Richard M. Sherman for co-writing credits.)

SHERMAN, SAMUEL M.
Producer, Director, Writer. b. New York, NY. e. CCNY, B.A. Entered m.p. ind. as writer, cameraman, film ed., neg. & sound cutter; nat'l mag. ed., Westerns Magazine 1959; pres., Signature Films; prod., dir., TV pilot, The Three Mesquiteers, 1960; prod., Pulse Pounding Perils, 1961; helped create, ed., dir., Screen Thrills Illustrated; exec. prod., Screen Thrills; v.p., Golden Age Films, 1962; prod., Joe Franklin's Silent Screen, 1963; NY rep., Victor Adamson Prods.; NY rep., Tal prods., Hlywd.; adv. & pub. Hemisphere Pictures; prod., writer, Chaplin's Art of Comedy, The Strongman; prod., Hollywood's Greatest Stuntman; story adapt., Fiend With the Electronic Brain; tech. consul., Hal Roach Studios, Music from the Land; 1968, NY rep. East West Pict. of Hollywood. 1968, N.Y. rep., Al Adamson Prods. of Hollywood; Ed.-in-chief, bk., The Strongman; pres., Independent-International Pictures Corp. (and tv div.); pres., Producers Commercial Productions, Inc. Chmn. of Creditors' Committee, Allied Artists Television Corp.; pres., Technovision Inc.; pres., Super Video, Inc.
PICTURES: *Assoc. prod.*: Horror of the Blood Monsters, Blood of Ghastly Horror. *Prod., s.p.*: Brain of Blood. *Prod. supervisor*: Dracula vs. Frankenstein. *Exec. prod.*: Angels, Wild Women, The Naughty Stewardesses (prod., s.p.), Girls For Rent, The Dynamite Brothers, Blazing Stewardesses (prod., s.p.), Cinderella 2000, Team-Mates (also story), Raiders of the Living Dead (dir., s.p.).

SHERMAN, VINCENT
Director. b. Vienna, GA, July 16, 1906. e. Oglethorpe U. B.A. Writer, actor, dialogue dir., then prod. dir.
PICTURES: The Return of Doctor X (debut, 1939), Saturday's Children, The Man Who Talked Too Much, Underground, Flight from Destiny, The Hard Way, All Through the Night, Old Acquaintance, In Our Time, Mr. Skeffington, Pillow to Post, Janie Gets Married, Nora Prentiss, The Unfaithful, Adventures of Don Juan, The Hasty Heart, The Damned Don't Cry, Harriet Craig, Goodbye My Fancy, Lone Star, Affair in Trinidad, Difendo il mio Amore, The Garment Jungle, The Naked Earth, The Young Philadelphians, Ice Palace, A Fever in the Blood, The Second Time Around, Cervantes.
TELEVISION: 35 episodes of Medical Center, Westside Medical, Baretta, Waltons, Doctors Hospital, Trapper John, Movies: The Last Hurrah, Women at West Point, The Yeagers (pilot), Bogey, The Dream Merchants, Trouble in High Timber Country, High Hopes—The Capra Years.

SHERRIN, NED
Producer, Director, Writer. b. Low Ham, Somerset, England, Feb. 18, 1931. Early career writing plays and musical plays. Prod., dir., ATV Birmingham, 1955-57; prod., Midlands Affairs, Paper Talk, etc. Joined BBC-TV 1957 and produced many TV talk programs. Novels: (with Caryl Brahms) Cindy-Ella or I Gotta Shoe (also prod. as stage play), Rappell 1910, Benbow Was His Name.
AUTHOR: *Autobiography*: A Small Thing Like a Earthquake. *Anthology*: Cutting Edge Theatrical Anecdotes. 1995, edit. of Oxford Dictionary of Humorous Quotations. *Novel*: Scratch an Actor. *Diaries*: Serrin's Year: 1995.
PICTURES: *Prod.*: The Virgin Soldiers (with Leslie Gilliat), Every Home Should Have One, Up Pompeii, Girl Stroke Boy (co-author with Caryl Brahms), Up the Chastity Belt, Rentadick, The Garnet Saga, Up the Front, The National Health, The Cobblers of Umbridge (dir. with Ian Wilson). *Actor*: Orlando.
TELEVISION: *England: Prod.*: Ask Me Another, Henry Hall Show, Laugh Line, Parasol. *Assoc. prod.*: Tonight series, Little Beggars. *Prod., creator*: That Was The Week That Was. *Prod., dir.*: Benbow Was His Name (co-author), Take a Sapphire (co-author), The Long Garden Party, The Long Cocktail Party. ABC of Britain revue, Not So Much a Programme—More a Way of Life. Appearances inc.: Your Witness, Quiz of The Week, Terra Firma, Who Said That, The Rather Reassuring Programme, Song by Song, Loose Ends Radio 4.

SHERWOOD, MADELEINE
Actress. b. Montreal, Canada, Nov. 13, 1922. e. Yale Drama Sch. Trained with Montreal Rep. and Actors Studio. Has dir. prods. at Actors Studio and regional theaters, as well as 2 AFI films Goodnight Sweet Prince and Sunday.
THEATER: The Crucible, Sweet Bird of Youth, Cat on a Hot Tin Roof, Invitation to a March, The Garden of Sweets, Camelot, Hey You, Light Man!, Brecht on Brecht, Night of the Iguana, Arturo Ui, Do I Hear a Waltz?, Inadmissible Evidence, All Over, Older People, Getting Out, The Suicide, Eclipse, Miss Edwina.
PICTURES: Baby Doll, Cat on a Hot Tin Roof, Parrish, Sweet Bird of Youth, The 91st Day, Hurry Sundown, Pendulum, Wicked Wicked, The Changeling, Resurrection, Teachers, An Unremarkable Life, Silence Like Glass.
TELEVISION: *Series*: The Flying Nun. *Mini-Series*: Rich Man Poor Man. *Movies*: The Manhunter, Nobody's Child, Palace Guard; many guest appearances.

SHIELDS, BROOKE
Actress. r.n. Christa Brooke Camille Shields. b. New York, NY, May 31, 1965. e. Princeton U. Honors in French Lit. Discovered at age 11 months by photographer Francesco Scavullo to pose in Ivory Soap ads.
THEATER: *Off-B'way*: The Eden Cinema; *B'way debut* 1994 in Grease! (Theatre World Award).
PICTURES: Alice Sweet Alice (debut 1977), Pretty Baby, King of the Gypsies, Tilt, Wanda Nevada, Just You and Me Kid, The Blue Lagoon, Endless Love, Sahara, The Muppets Take Manhattan (cameo), Speed Zone (cameo), Back Street Dreams, Brenda Starr, An American Love (It.), The Seventh Floor, Freeway, The Misadventures of Margaret, Black and White, The Weekend.

TELEVISION: *Movies*: The Prince of Central Park, Wet Gold, The Diamond Trap, I Can Make You Love Me: The Stalking of Laura Black; Nothing Lasts Forever; numerous specials. *Guest*: Friends, The Simpsons (voice). *Series*: Suddenly Susan.

SHIELDS, WILLIAM A.
Executive. b. New York, NY, 1946. e. El Camino Coll., California State Coll. at LA. Entered the motion picture industry in 1966 with Pacific Theatres, then MGM sales dept., L.A. and Denver, 1970; New World Pictures, 1972; 20th Century-Fox, Washington, 1973; NY district manager, 20th Century-Fox, 1973-75; joined Mann Theatres Corp. of California as head booker in 1975; gen. sls. mgr., Far West Films, 1977-79; joined Avco Embassy as Western div. mgr., promoted to asst. gen. sls. mgr., 1980; promoted to v.p.-gen. sls. mgr., 1981; 1983 joined New World Pictures as exec. v.p., worldwide mktg. & acquisitions; promoted to pres., worldwide sls. & mktg., 1985; 1987, pres. CEO, New World Intl.; 1989, joined Trans Atlantic Pictures as pres., CEO when company purchased assets of New World's feature film division. Sold ownership in Trans Atlantic and formed G.E.L. Prod. & Distrib., 1992. Exec. prod. Au Pair (1991); exec. in charge of prod. Death Ring (1992). Exec. prod. of Uninvited. Past chmn, American Film Mktg. Assn. (1987-91). Presently chmn. American Film Export Assn.

SHIFF, RICHARD
Executive. b. New York, NY, March 3, 1942. e. Queens College, B.A., M.A., Brooklyn Col., P.D. Joined Warner Bros. as sales analyst, 1977. 1979 named dist. coordinator; 1980, asst. dir. sls. admin. 1982, promoted to post, dir. sls. admin. 1987, v.p., theatrical sls. operations.

SHIRE, DAVID
Composer. b. Buffalo, NY, July 3, 1937. m. actress Didi Conn. e. Yale U., 1959, B.A. Composer of theater scores: The Sap of Life, Urban Blight, Starting Here Starting Now, Baby, Closer Than Ever, Big. Emmy noms. Raid on Entebbe, The Defection of Simas Kudirka, Do You Remember Love? and The Kennedys of Massachusetts. Grammy Awards for Saturday Night Fever.
PICTURES: One More Train to Rob, Summertree, Drive, He Said; Skin Game, To Find a Man, Showdown, Two People, Steelyard Blues (adapt.), Class of '44, The Conversation, The Taking of Pelham 1-2-3, The Fortune, Farewell My Lovely, The Hindenberg, All the President's Men, The Big Bus, Harry and Walter Go to New York, Saturday Night Fever (adapt. & add. music), Straight Time, The Promise (Acad. Award nom.), Old Boyfriends, Norma Rae (Acad. Award for best song, It Goes Like It Goes, 1979), Only When I Laugh, The Night the Lights Went Out in Georgia, Paternity, The World According to Garp, Max Dugan Returns, Oh God You Devil, 2010, Fast Break, Return to Oz, Short Circuit, 'night Mother, Vice Versa, Monkey Shines, Bed and Breakfast, One Night Stand.
TELEVISION: *Series themes*: Sarge, McCloud, The Practice, Sirota's Court, Joe & Sons, Lucas Tanner, Alice, Tales of the Unexpected, Brewster Place, Room for Two. *Movies*: Priest Killer, McCloud, Harpy, Three Faces of Love, Killer Bees, Tell Me Where It Hurts, The Defection of Simus Kudirka, Three for the Road, Amelia Earhart, Something for Joey, Raid on Entebbe, The Storyteller, Promise, Mayflower Madam, Echoes in the Darkness, Jesse, God Bless the Child, Common Ground, The Clinic, Convicted, The Women of Brewster Place, I Know My First Name is Steven, The Kennedys of Massachusetts (mini-series), The Great Los Angeles Earthquake, The Boys, Sarah: Plain and Tall, Always Remember I Love You, Paris Trout, Four Eyes, Broadway Bound, Bed of Lies, Last Wish, Alison, Habitation of Dragons, Lily in Winter, Reunion, Serving in Silence, My Brother's Keeper, My Antonia, The Heidi Chronicles, The Man Who Wouldn't Die, Tecumseh: The Last Warrior, Almost Golden: The Jessica Savitch Story, many others.

SHIRE, TALIA
Actress. r.n. Talia Coppola. b. New York, NY, April 25, 1946. Raised on road by her father, arranger-conductor Carmine Coppola, who toured with Broadway musicals. After 2 yrs. at Yale Sch. of Drama she moved to L.A. where appeared in many theatrical productions. Brother is dir. Francis Ford Coppola. Started in films as Talia Coppola.
PICTURES: The Wild Racers, The Dunwich Horror, Gas-s-s-s, The Christian Licorice Store, The Outside Man, The Godfather, The Godfather Part II (Acad. Award nom.), Rocky (Acad. Award nom.), Old Boyfriends, Prophecy, Rocky II, Windows, Rocky III, Rocky IV, RAD, Lionheart (co-prod.), New York Stories (Life Without Zoe), Rocky V, The Godfather III, Bed and Breakfast, Cold Heaven, DeadFall, One Night Stand (dir. only), She's So Lovely, Lured Innocence.
TELEVISION: *Mini-Series*: Rich Man Poor Man. *Movies*: Foster and Laurie, Kill Me If You Can, Daddy I Don't Like It Like This, For Richer For Poorer, Chantilly Lace, Born Into Exile. *Special*: Please God I'm Only 17.

SHIVAS, MARK
Producer. e. Oxford.
PICTURES: *Producer*: Richard's Things, Moonlighting, A Private Function, The Witches. *Exec. Prod.*: Bad Blood, Truly Madly Deeply, Enchanted April, The Grass Arena, Memento Mori, The Snapper, Priest, An Awfully Big Adventure, Jude, The Van, Small Faces.
TELEVISION: Presenter of Cinema. *Producer*: The Six Wives of Henry VIII, Casanova, The Edwardians, The Evacuees, The Glittering Prizes, Abide With Me, Rogue Male, 84 Charing Cross Road, The Three Hostages, She Fell Among Thieves, Professional Foul, Telford's Change, On Giant's Shoulders, The Price, What If it's Raining?, The Storytellers. *Exec. prod.*: Regeneration.

SHORE, HOWARD
Composer, Musician. b. Oct., 18, 1994, Toronto, Ontario, Canada. Began as musical director for Saturday Night Live, 1975.
PICTURES: I Miss You Hugs and Kisses, The Brood, Scanners, Gilda Live (actor), Videodrome, The Fly, Nothing Lasts Forever, After Hours, Fire with Fire, The Fly, Heaven, Belizaire the Cajun, Nadine, Moving, Big, Dead Ringers, Signs of Life, She-Devil, The Local Stigmatic, An Innocent Man, The Lemon Sisters, Made in Milan, Postcards From the Edge (musical numbers sprv.), The Silence of the Lambs, A Kiss Before Dying, Naked Lunch, Prelude to a Kiss, Single White Female, Sliver, Guilty as Sin, M. Butterfly, Mrs. Doubtfire, Philadelphia, Ed Wood, The Truth About Cats & Dogs, Striptease, Looking for Richard, Crash, That Thing You Do!, The Game, Cop Land, eXistenZ, Chinese Coffee, Fight Club, Dogma, Gloria, Analyze This.
TELEVISION: Saturday Night Live, Coca-Cola Presents Live: The Hard Rock, Late Night with Conan O'Brien.

SHORE, PAULY
Actor. b. Los Angeles, CA, 1968. Son of comedian Sammy Shore and nightclub owner Mitzi Shore. Worked as stand-up comedian at mother's club, The Comedy Store.
PICTURES: For Keeps? (debut, 1988), 18 Again!, Lost Angels, Phantom of the Mall, Wedding Band, Encino Man, Class Act, Son-in-Law, In the Army Now, Jury Duty, Bio-Dome.
TELEVISION: *Series*: Totally Pauly, Totally Different Pauly, Paul. *Special*: Pauly Does Dallas. *Movie*: Home By Midnight, The Curse of Inferno, Casper Meets Wendy. *Guest*: 21 Jump Street, Married... with Children, King of the Hill (voice).

SHORT, MARTIN
Actor, Comedian, Writer. b. Toronto, Can., March 26, 1950. e. McMaster U. Trained as social worker but instead performed on stage in Godspell as well as in revues and cabarets in Toronto, 1973-78, including a stint as a member of the Toronto unit of the Second City comedy troupe, 1977-78. Created such characters as Ed Grimley, Jackie Rogers Jr. B'way debut 1993 in The Goodbye Girl (Theatre World Award; Tony nom.).
PICTURES: Lost and Found, The Outsider, Three Amigos!, Innerspace, Cross My Heart, Three Fugitives, The Big Picture, Pure Luck, Father of the Bride, Captain Ron, Clifford, The Pebble and the Penguin (voice), Father of the Bride Part 2, An Indian in the City, Mars Attacks!, Jungle 2 Jungle, A Simple Wish, Mumford, Akbar's Adventure Tours, Prince of Egypt (voice).
TELEVISION: *Series*: The Associates, I'm a Big Girl Now, SCTV Network (Emmy Award for writing, 1983), Saturday Night Live (1985- 86), The Completely Mental Misadventures of Ed Grimley (cartoon series), The Martin Short Show (also exec. prod., writer). *Specials*: All's Well That Ends Well, Really Weird Tales, Martin Short's Concert for the North Americas (SHO), Martin Short Goes Hollywood (HBO), The Show Formerly Known as the Martin Short Show (also exec. prod., co-writer). *Movies*: The Family Man, Sunset Limousine, Money for Nothing (BBC), Alice in Wonderland. *Mini-Series:* Merlin.

SHORT, THOMAS C.
Executive. International Pres., International Alliance of Theatrical Stage Employees, Moving Picture Technicians, Artists and Allied Crafts of the United States and Canada AFL-CIO, CLC.

SHOWALTER, MAX
Actor, Composer. r.n. Casey Adams. b. Caldwell, KS, June 2, 1917. e. Caldwell H.S.; Pasadena Playhouse. Composed background music for films: Vicki, Return of Jack Slade, B'way Harrigan 'n Hart (composer), Touch of the Child (lyricist-composer). Recordings incl. The Brementown Musicians, The Gold Dog (as narrator, composer, pianist and singer). On bd. of trustees: Eugene O'Neill Theatre Center, Natl. Theatre of the Deaf, Ivorytown Playhouse, Shoreline Alliance for the Arts. Gov's Bd.: Commission for the Arts.
THEATER: *B'way*: Knights of Song, Very Warm for May, My Sister Eileen, Showboat, John Loves Mary, Make Mine Manhattan, Lend an Ear, Hello Dolly!, The Grass Harp.
PICTURES: Always Leave Them Laughing (debut, 1949), With a Song in My Heart, What Price Glory?, My Wife's Best Friend, Niagara, Destination Gobi, Dangerous Crossing, Vicki, Night People, Naked Alibi, The Indestructible Man, The Return of Jack Slade, Never Say Goodbye, Bus Stop, Dragoon Wells Massacre, Down Three Dark Streets, Designing Woman, Female Animal, The Monster That Challenged the World, Voice In the Mirror, The Naked and the Dead, It Happened to Jane, Elmer Gantry, Return to Peyton Place, Summer and Smoke, The Music Man, Bon Voyage, My Six Loves, Move Over Darling, Sex and the Single Girl, Fate Is the Hunter, How to Murder Your Wife, Lord Love a Duck, A Talent for Loving, The Moonshine War, The Anderson Tapes, "10", Racing with the Moon, Sixteen Candles.
(d. July 30, 2000)

SHUE, ELISABETH
Actress. b. South Orange, NJ, Oct. 6, 1963. e. Harvard. Brother is actor Andrew Shue.
PICTURES: The Karate Kid (debut, 1984), Adventures in Babysitting, Link, Cocktail, Back to the Future Part II, Back to the Future Part III, The Marrying Man, Soapdish, Twenty Bucks, The Underneath, Leaving Las Vegas (Chicago Film Critics Award; Nat'l Film Critics Award; LA Film Critics Award), Trigger Effect, The Saint, Radio Inside, Palmetto, Deconstructing Harry, Cousine Bette (LA Film Critics Award), Molly, The Hollow Man.
TELEVISION: *Series*: Call to Glory. *Movies*: Charles and Diana, Double Switch, Hale the Hero, Blind Justice.

SHULER-DONNER, LAUREN
Producer. b. Cleveland, OH. B.S. in film & bdcstg., Boston U. m. dir.-prod. Richard Donner. Began filmmaking career as ed. of educational films then camera-woman in TV prod., assoc. prod., story editor, creative affairs exec.; TV movie: Amateur Night at the Dixie Bar and Grill (prod.). Assoc. prod. on film Thank God It's Friday. Cameo in film Maverick.
PICTURES: Mr. Mom, Ladyhawke, St. Elmo's Fire, Pretty in Pink, Three Fugitives, The Favor, Radio Flyer, Dave, Free Willy, Free Willy 2: The Adventure Home, Assassins, Volcano, Free Willy 3, Bulworth, You've Got Mail, Any Given Sunday, X-Men.

SHULL, RICHARD B.
Actor. b. Evanston, IL, Feb. 24, 1929. e. State U. of Iowa. B.A. drama, 1950., Kemper Mil. Sch. AA Humanities, 1986. U.S. Army, 1953. Armed Forces Korea Network. 1953-56, exec. asst. prod. Gordon W. Pollock Prods.; 1954-56 stage mgr. Hyde Park Playhouse; other prod. jobs and freelance stage mgr. and dir. 1950-70. NY stage debut in Wake Up Darling (1956), also in Minnie's Boys, Goodtime Charley (Tony nom.; Drama Desk nom.), The Marriage of Bette and Boo (Obie Award), One of the All-Time Greats, Ain't Broadway Grand, Victor Victoria.
PICTURES: The Anderson Tapes (debut, 1971), B.S. I Love You, Such Good Friends, Hail to the Chief, Slither, Sssss, Cockfighter, The Fortune, The Black Bird, Hearts of the West, The Big Bus, The Pack, Dreamer, Wholly Moses, Heartbeeps, Spring Break, Lovesick, Unfaithfully Yours, Splash, Garbo Talks, Tune in Tomorrow, Housesitter, For Love or Money, Trapped in Paradise, Cafe Society, Private Parts.
TELEVISION: *Series*: Diana, Holmes & Yoyo. *Guest*: Your Hit Parade (1950), Rockford Files, Good Times, Love American Style, Hart to Hart, Lou Grant. *Movies*: Ziegfeld: A Man and His Women, Studs Lonigan, Will There Really Be a Morning? The Boy Who Loved Trolls, Keeping the Faith, Seize the Day.
(d. Oct. 30, 1999)

SHURPIN, SOL
Executive. b. New York, NY, Feb. 22, 1914. e. Pace Inst., 1936. Law stenog., 1932-33; Joe Hornstein, Inc., 1933-41; National Theatre Supply, 1941-48; purchased interest in Raytone Screen Corp., became v.p., 1948; pres., Raytone, 1952; pres., Technikote Corp., which succeeded Raytone Screen, 1956-present; sole owner, Technikote Corp., 1962.

SHUTT, BUFFY
Executive. e. Sarah Lawrence Col. Joined Paramount 1973 as sect. with N.Y. pub. staff; 1975, natl. mag. contact. 1978, named dir. of pub.; later exec. dir. of pub. Promoted 1980 to v.p., pub. & promo. Resigned to join Time-Life Films as v.p. east coast prod; returned to Paramount in 1981 as sr. v.p. & asst. to pres. of Motion Picture Group. 1983, appointed pres. of mktg. 1986, resigned. Formed Shutt-Jones Communications, 1987, marketing consultancy with Kathy Jones. 1989, pres. of marketing, Columbia Pictures & TriStar Pictures. 1991, pres. of marketing, TriStar Pictures. 1994, pres. of marketing, Universal Pictures.

SHYER, CHARLES
Director, Writer. b. Los Angeles, CA. e. UCLA. Was asst. dir. and prod. mgr. before becoming head writer for tv series The Odd Couple. First teamed with Nancy Meyers on Private Benjamin.
PICTURES: *Writer*: Smokey and the Bandit, House Calls, Goin' South, Private Benjamin (Acad. Award nom.; also prod.), The Parent Trap (also prod.). *Director-Writer*: Irreconcilable Differences, Baby Boom, Father of the Bride, I Love Trouble, Father of the Bride Part II.

SHYAMALAN, M. NIGHT
Writer, Director. b. Pondicherry, Tamil-Nadu province, India, August 6, 1970.
PICTURES: Praying With Anger, Wide Awake, The Sixth Sense, Stuart Little (s.p. only), Unbreakable.

SIDARIS, ANDY
Producer, Director, Writer. b. Chicago, IL, Feb. 20, 1932. e. Southern Methodist U., B.A., radio-TV. Began television career in 1950 in Dallas, TX as a director at station WFAA-TV; now pres., The Sidaris Company. Won 8 Emmy Awards.
PICTURES: *Dir.*: Stacey, The Racing Scene, M*A*S*H (football sequences), Seven (also prod.). *Dir.-Writer*: Malibu Express (also prod.), Hard Ticket to Hawaii, Picasso Trigger, Savage Beach, Guns, Do or Die, Hard Hunted, Fit to Kill, Day of the Warrior, Return to Savage Beach. *Exec. Prod.*: Enemy Gold, The Dallas Connection.
TELEVISION: *Dir.*: The Racers/Mario Andretti/Joe Leonard/Al Unser, ABC's Championship Auto Racing, ABC's NCAA Game of the Week, 1968 Summer Olympics: 1968 (Mexico City), 1972 (Munich), 1976 (Montreal), 1984 (L.A.), Winter Olympics: 1964 (Innsbruck), 1968 (Grenoble), 1976 (Innsbruck), 1980 (Lake Placid), 1988 (Calgary), Wide World of Sports, The Racers/Craig and Lee Breedlove, The Burt Reynolds Late Show, Kojak episode, Nancy Drew episodes.

SIDNEY, GEORGE
Director, Producer. b. New York, NY, Oct. 4, 1916. Son of L. K. Sidney, veteran showman and v.p. MGM, and Hazel Mooney, actress. From 1932 at MGM as test, second unit and short subjects dir. Won Academy Awards for shorts: Quicker 'n' a Wink (Pete Smith speciality), Of Pups and Puzzles (Passing Parade). In 1941 made feature dir. debut, MGM. Pres., Director's Guild of America, 16 yrs; spec. presidential assignment to Atomic Energy Commission and U.S. Air Force; 1961-66, pres., Hanna-Barbera Productions; Doctorate of Science Hanneman Medical University and Hospital. Member ASCAP. Pres., Directors, Inc., since 1969; v.p., Directors Foundation; v.p., D.W. Griffith Foundation; life mem., ACTT (England) and DGA. Directed U.N. special, Who Has Seen the Wind? Awarded Gold Medal for service to D.G.A. 1959, Doctorate from Collegio Barcelona 1989, Life Membership in D.G.A.
PICTURES: Free and Easy (debut, 1941), Pacific Rendezvous, Pilot No. 5, Thousands Cheer, Bathing Beauty, Anchors Aweigh, The Harvey Girls, Holiday in Mexico, Cass Timberlane, The Three Musketeers, The Red Danube, Key to the City, Annie Get Your Gun, Show Boat, Scaramouche, Young Bess, Kiss Me Kate, Jupiter's Darling, The Eddy Duchin Story, Jeanne Eagels (also prod.), Pal Joey, Who Was That Lady? (also prod.), Pepe (also prod.), Bye Bye Birdie, A Ticklish Affair, Viva Las Vegas (also co-prod.), The Swinger (also prod.), Half a Sixpence (also co-prod.).

SIEMASZKO, CASEY
Actor. r.n. Kazimierz Siemaszko. b. Chicago, IL, March 17, 1961. e. Goodman Theatre School of Drama, Chicago.
PICTURES: Class (debut, 1983), Secret Admirer, Back to the Future, Stand By Me, Gardens of Stone, Three O'Clock High, Biloxi Blues, Young Guns, Breaking In, Back to the Future Part II, Of Mice and Men, Teresa's Tattoo, My Life's in Turnaround, Milk Money, The Phantom, Bliss, The Taxman, Limbo.
TELEVISION: *Movie*: Miracle of the Heart: A Boys Town Story, The Chase, Children Remember the Holocaust, Black Scorpion, Rose Hill, Mistrial. *Mini-series*: Storm of the Century.

SIGHVATSSON, SIGURJON (JONI)
Producer. b. Reykjavik, Iceland, June 15, 1952. e. Iceland Community Col, Univ. of Iceland. Came to U.S. in 1978. Also attended USC. Was film and music video prod. for Blue-Ice Prods. Founder and chairperson with Steve Golin of Propaganda Films.
PICTURE: *Assoc. Prod*: Hard Rock Zombies, American Drive-In. *Producer:* Private Investigations, The Blue Iguana, Kill Me Again, Fear Anxiety and Depression, Daddy's Dyin'... Who's Got the Will?, Wild at Heart, Truth or Dare, Ruby, A Stranger Among Us, Candyman, Kalifornia, Red Rock West, S.F.W., Lord of Illusions, Canadian Bacon, The Kids in the Hall: Brain Candy, Basquiat, A Thousand Acres. *Exec. Prod.:* 'Til There Was You , The Real Blonde, Polish Wedding, Phoenix, Homegrown, 200 Cigarettes, Arlington Road.
TELEVISION: *Movie*: Memphis. *Specials*: Rock the Vote, Education First, Tales of the City. *Series*: Twin Peaks.

SIKKING, JAMES B.
Actor. b. Los Angeles, CA, March 5, 1934. e. UCLA, B.A. Theatre includes Waltz of the Toreadors, Plaza Suite, Damn Yankees, The Big Knife.
PICTURES: The Magnificent Seven, Von Ryan's Express, Chandler, The New Centurions, The Electric Horseman, Capricorn One, Ordinary People, Outland, The Star Chamber, Up the Creek, Star Trek III—The Search for Spock, Morons from Outer Space, Soul Man, Narrow Margin, Final Approach.
TELEVISION: *Series*: General Hospital, Turnabout, Hill Street Blues. Doogie Howser, M.D., Brooklyn South. *Movies*: The Jesse Owens Story, First Steps, Bay Coven, Brotherhood of the Rose, Too Good to be True, Desperado: Badlands Justice, Doing Time on Maple Drive, Jake Lassiter: Justice on the Bayou, In Pursuit of Honor, Tyson. *Mini-Series*: Around the World in 80 Days. *Specials*: Tales from the Hollywood Hills (Golden Land), Ollie Hopnoodle's Haven of Bliss.

SILVA, HENRY
Actor. b. Brooklyn, NY, 1928. Studied acting with Group Theatre, Actors Studio.
PICTURES: Viva Zapata!, Crowded Paradise, A Hatful of Rain, The Law and Jake Wade, The Bravados, Green Mansions, Cinderfella, Ocean's Eleven, Sergeants 3, The Manchurian Candidate, A Gathering of Eagles, Johnny Cool, The Secret Invasion, Hail Mafia, The Return of Mr. Moto, The Reward, The Hills Ran Red, The Plainsman, Matchless, Never a Dull Moment, The Animals, Man and Boy, The Italian Connection,

The Kidnap of Mary Lou, Shoot, Thirst, Buck Rogers in the 25th Century, Love and Bullets, Virus, Alligator, Sharky's Machine, Wrong Is Right, Megaforce, Cannonball Run II, Lust in the Dust, Code of Silence, Alan Quartermain and the Lost City of Gold, Amazon Women on the Moon, Above the Law, Bulletproof, Dick Tracy, Fists of Steel, Trained to Kill, Possessed by the Night, The Silence of the Hams, The Prince, Mad Dog Time, The End of Violence, Unconditional Love, Ghost Dog: The Way of the Samurai.
TELEVISION: *Movies*: Black Noon, Drive Hard Drive Fast, Contract on Cherry Street, Happy. *Series*: Buck Rogers in the 25th Century.

SILVER, CASEY
Executive. Chmn., Universal Pictures, Inc. Began career in motion picture industry as a screenwriter. Was asst. to dir. Adrian Lyne on Flashdance. Became dir. of devt. and prod. for Simpson-Bruckheimer Prods. V.P., prod., TriStar Pictures. Sr. v.p., prod., TriStar. Joined Universal Pictures as exec. v.p., prod., 1987. Became pres. of prod. in January, 1989; pres., Universal Pictures, June, 1994. Appointed chmn., Universal Pictures, November,. 1995. Responsible for leadership of prod., mktg., dist., and home video.

SILVER, JOAN MICKLIN
Writer, Director. b. Omaha, NB, May 24, 1935. m. producer Raphael Silver. Daughter is dir. Marisa Silver. e. Sarah Lawrence Coll. Began career as writer for educational films. Original s.p., Limbo, purchased by Universal Pictures. In 1972 Learning Corp. of Am. commissioned her to write and direct a 30-min. film, The Immigrant Experience. Also wrote and directed two children's films for same co; dir. & wrote short film Bernice Bobs Her Hair. First feature was Hester Street, which she wrote and directed.
THEATER: *Director*: Album, Maybe I'm Doing It Wrong, A ... My Name is Alice, A ... My Name is Still Alice (co-conceived & co-dir. with Julianne Boyd).
PICTURES: *Director*: Hester Street (also s.p.), Between the Lines, On the Yard (prod.), Head Over Heels (also s.p.; retitled Chilly Scenes of Winter), Crossing Delancey, Loverboy, Big Girls Don't Cry... They Get Even, A Fish In the Bathtub.
TELEVISION: Finnegan Begin Again (dir.), The Nightingale: Faerie Tale Theatre (writer), Parole Board (Prison Stories: Women on the Inside), A Private Matter (dir.), In the Presence of Mine Enemies.

SILVER, JOEL
Producer. b. South Orange, NJ, July 14, 1952. e. NYU. Made first film, a short called Ten Pin Alley; moved to Los Angeles with job as asst. to Lawrence Gordon. Named pres., Lawrence Gordon Prods.; developed with Gordon and produced and marketed Hooper, The End, The Driver, The Warriors (also assoc. prod.). At Universal Pictures as prod. v.p.; supervising Smokey and the Bandit II. Honored 1990 as NATO/Showest's Producer of the Year. Appeared in 1988 film Who Framed Roger Rabbit.
PICTURES: Xanadu (co-prod.), Jekyll & Hyde ... Together Again (exec. prod.), 48 HRS., Streets of Fire, Brewster's Millions, Weird Science, Commando, Jumpin' Jack Flash, Lethal Weapon, Predator, Action Jackson, Die Hard, Road House, Lethal Weapon 2, The Adventures of Ford Fairlane, Die Hard 2, Predator 2, Hudson Hawk, Ricochet, The Last Boy Scout, Lethal Weapon 3, Demoliton Man, The Hudsucker Proxy, Richie Rich, Tales From the Crypt Presents Demon Knight (co-exec. prod.), Fair Game, Assassins, Executive Decision, Conspiracy Theory, Father's Day, Conspiracy Theory, The Matrix, Lethal Weapon 4, Romeo Must Die, The House on Haunted Hill, Made Men, Wonder Woman, Dungeon & Dragons.
TELEVISION: Tales from the Crypt (exec. prod. & prod.; also dir. episode), Two Fisted Tales, Parker Can, W.E.I.R.D. World (co-exec. prod.), The Strip (exec. prod), Action (exec. prod.).

SILVER, LEON J.
Executive. b. Boston, MA, March 25, 1918. e. USC, 1935-39. Independent prod. of short subjects, 1939; story analyst, Paramount, 1940, film writer, U.S. Army Pictorial Service, 1941-45; freelance writer, 1946; film writer. prod., U.S. Public Health Service, 1946-51; asst. chief, foreign film prod., U.S. Dept. of State, 1951-54; acting chief, domestic film prod., U.S. Information Agency, 1955; division chief, Worldwide Documentary Film & Television Product, U.S. Information Agency, 1968; 1978-79, sr. advisor IV, film production. Coordinator of TV & film, all Fed Govt. Agencies Private Industry under Exec. Office, pres. of U.S. 1980. Resigned, 1980. Now TV network writer-producer-novelist.

SILVER, MARISA
Director. b. New York, NY, April 23, 1960. Daughter of director Joan Micklin Silver and prod.-dir. Raphael Silver. e. Harvard U. where she directed short Dexter T. and edited doc. Light Coming Through: a Portrait of Maud Morgan.
PICTURES: Old Enough, Permanent Record, Vital Signs, He Said/She Said (co-dir.), Indecency.
TELEVISION: *Co-dir.*: A Community of Praise (an episode of PBS series Middletown, 1982).

SILVER, RAPHAEL D.
Producer. b. Cleveland, OH, 1930. e. Harvard Coll. and Harvard Graduate Sch. of Business Adm. Is pres. of Middex Devel. Corp. 1973 formed Midwest Film Productions to produce Hester Street, written and directed by Joan Micklin Silver. Also distributed film independently. Also produced Between the Lines. Exec. prod. of Crossing Delancey. Directed On the Yard, A Walk on the Moon; writer/prod. A Fish in the Bathtub. Currently pres. Silverfilm Prods. Inc.

SILVER, RON
Actor, Director. b. New York, NY, July 2, 1946. e. U. of Buffalo, St. John's U., Taiwan, M.A. Trained for stage at Herbert Berghof Studios and Actors Studio. N.Y. stage debut in Kasper and Public Insult, 1971. Elected pres. of Actors Equity Assn., 1991.
THEATER: El Grande de Coca Cola, Lotta, More Than You Deserve, Angel City (Mark Taper, LA), Hurlyburly, Social Security, Hunting Cockroaches, Speed-the-Plow (Tony & Drama Desk Award), Gorilla (Chicago, Jefferson Award nom.; N.YU. & L.A., Dramalogue Award), Friends, And, Broken Glass.
PICTURES: Tunnelvision, Welcome to L.A., Semi-Tough, Silent Rage, Best Friends, The Entity, Lovesick, Silkwood, Garbo Talks, Oh God! You Devil, Goodbye People, Eat and Run, Enemies A Love Story, Blue Steel, Reversal of Fortune, Mr. Saturday Night, Married to It, Timecop, Danger Zone, Deadly Takeover, Girl 6, The Arrival, Rhapsody in Bloom, Black & White.
TELEVISION: *Series*: Mac Davis Show, Rhoda, Dear Detective, The Stockard Channing Show, Baker's Dozen, Chicago Hope. *Movies*: The Return of the World's Greatest Detective, Murder at the Mardi Gras, Betrayal, Word of Honor, Billionaire Boys Club, Fellow Traveler, Forgotten Prisoners: The Amnesty Files, Live Wire, Blindside, Lifepod (also dir.), Almost Golden: The Jessica Savitch Story, Billionaire Boys Club (Emmy nom.), Shadow zone, The Undead, Express, The Beneficiary, In the Company of Spies. *Mini-Series*: A Zoman of Independent Means. *Guest*: Trying Times, Hill Street Blues. *Special*: Loyalty and Betrayal: The Story of the American Mob (narrator).

SILVERMAN, FRED
Producer. b. New York, NY, Sept., 1937. e. Syracuse U., Ohio State U., master's in TV and theatre arts. Joined WGN-TV, indep. sta. in Chicago. Came to NY for exec. post at WPIX-TV, where stayed only six weeks. CBS-TV hired him as dir. of daytime programs. Named v.p., programs 1970. 1975 left CBS to become pres., ABC Entertainment. 1978, named pres. and CEO of NBC. Now Pres., The Fred Silverman Company, Los Angeles.
TELEVISION: *Prod./exec. prod.: Series:* Perry Mason Movies, Matlock, In the Heat of the Night, Jake and the Fatman, Father Dowling Mysteries, Diagnosis Murder, Bonechillers, Bedtime Stories. *Movies*: Gramps, My Very Best Friend, Journey to Mars.

SILVERMAN, JONATHAN
Actor. b. Los Angeles, CA, Aug. 5, 1966. e. USC, NYU.
THEATER: *NY*: Brighton Beach Memoirs, Biloxi Blues, Broadway Bound. *LA*: The Illusion (Dramalogue Award), Pay or Play (Dramalogue Award), Sticks and Stones (Dramalogue Award).
PICTURES: Brighton Beach Memoirs (debut, 1986), Caddyshack II, Stealing Home, Weekend at Bernie's, Class Action, Breaking the Rules, Life in the Food Chain, Little Sister, Weekend at Bernie's II, Little Big League, Teresa's Tattoo, French Exit, At First Sight, Denial, 12 Bucks, The Odd Couple II, Just a Little Harmless Sex, Freak City, Kat and Allison.
TELEVISION: *Series*: Gimme a Break, The Single Guy. *Movies*: Challenge of a Lifetime, Traveling Man, For Richer For Poorer, Broadway Bound, 12:01, Sketch Artist II: Hands That See, London Suite, The Inspectors.

SILVERSTEIN, ELLIOT
Director. b. Boston, MA, Aug. 3, 1937. e. Boston Coll., Yale U. Started career on television.
PICTURES: Cat Ballou, The Happening, A Man Called Horse, Deadly Honeymoon, The Car (also co-prod.), Flashfire.
TELEVISION: *Pilot*: Belle Sommers (debut, 1962). *Movies*: Betrayed by Innocence, Night of Courage, Fight for Life, Rich Men Single Women. *Series*: Tales From the Crypt.

SILVERSTONE, ALICIA
Actress. b. California, 1977. Made stage debut at Met Theater in Los Angeles in Carol's Eve. Starred in three Aerosmith videos including Cryin'. Formed own production co., First Kiss Prods.
PICTURES: The Crush (debut, 1993), The Babysitter, True Crime, Le Nouveau Monde, Hideaway, Clueless, Excess Baggage (also prod.), Batman & Robin, Love's Labour's Lost, Blast from the Past.
TELEVISION: *Movies*: Torch Song, Shattered Dreams, The Cool and the Crazy. *Guest*: The Wonder Years.

SILVESTRI, ALAN
Composer.
PICTURES: The Doberman Gang, The Amazing Dobermans, The Fifth Floor, Romancing the Stone, Summer Rental, Fandango, Cat's Eye, Back to the Future, No Mercy, Flight of the Navigator, American Anthem, The Delta Force, The Clan of the Cave Bear, Overboard, Critical Condition, Predator, Outrageous Fortune, My Stepmother Is an Alien, Mac and Me, Who Framed Roger Rabbit, She's Out of Control, The Abyss, Back to the Future Part II, Downtown, Back to the Future Part III, Young Guns II, Predator 2, Father of the Bride, Dutch, Back to the Future... The Ride, Soapdish, Shattered (also orchestration), Ricochet, FernGully: The Last Rainforest, Stop! Or My Mom Will Shoot, The Bodyguard, Sidekicks, Death Becomes Her, Judgment Night, In Search of the Obelisk, Grumpy Old Men, Super Mario Bros., Cop & 1/2, Richie Rich, Clean Slate, Forrest Gump (Acad. Award nom., Golden Globe nom.), Blown Away, The Quick and the Dead, The Perez Family, Judge Dredd, Father of the Bride Part II, Grumpier Old Men, Sgt. Bilko, Eraser, The Long Kiss Goodnight, Fools Rush In, Volcano, Contact, Mouse Hunt, The Odd Couple II, Holy Man, Practical Magic, Stuart Little, Hanging Up.
TELEVISION: Starsky and Hutch, CHiPs, Airwolf, Tales From the Crypt.

SIMMONS, ANTHONY
Director, Writer. b. London, England. e. Grad. from the LSE with LL.B. Practiced briefly as a barrister before entering the industry as writer/director of documentaries, then commercials and feature films. Awards: Grand Prix (shorts), Venice, Grand Prix, Locarno; 2 Int. Emmys, Intl. Awards for commercials. Publications: The Optimists of Nine Elms, A Little Space for Issie Brown.
PICTURES: Sunday By the Sea, Bow Bells, Time Without Pity (co- prod.), Four in the Morning, The Optimists, Black Joy, Little Sweetheart, Poison Candy.
TELEVISION: On Giant's Shoulders, Supergran and the Magic Ray, Harry Carpenter Never Said It Was Like This, Life After Death, Day After the Fair, Inspector Morse, Van de Valk, Inspector Frost, The Good Guys, 99-1.

SIMMONS, JEAN
Actress. b. London, England, Jan. 31, 1929. e. Aida Foster Sch., London. Screen debut 1944 at age 14. Voted one of top ten British money-making stars in M.P. Herald-Fame Poll, 1950-51. London stage: A Little Night Music. Awards: Cannes Film Festival Homage 1988, Italian Outstanding Film Achievement Award 1989, French Govt. Commandeur de L'Ordre des Arts des Lettres. 1990.
PICTURES: Give Us the Moon (debut, 1944), Mr. Emmanuel, Meet Sexton Blake, Kiss the Bride Goodbye, Sports Day, Caesar and Cleopatra, Way to the Stars, Great Expectations, Hungry Hill, Black Narcissus, Uncle Silas, The Women In the Hall, Hamlet (Acad. Award nom.), Blue Lagoon, Adam and Evelyne, Trio, So Long at the Fair, Cage of Gold, The Clouded Yellow, Androcles and the Lion (U.S. film debut, 1953), Angel Face, Young Bess, Affair with a Stranger, The Actress, The Robe, She Couldn't Say No, A Bullet Is Waiting, The Egyptian, Desiree, Footsteps in the Fog, Guys and Dolls, Hilda Crane, This Could Be the Night, Until They Sail, The Big Country, Home Before Dark, This Earth Is Mine, Elmer Gantry, Spartacus, The Grass Is Greener, All the Way Home, Life at the Top, Mister Buddwing, Rough Night in Jericho, Divorce American Style, The Happy Ending (Acad. Award nom.), Say Hello to Yesterday, Mr. Sycamore, Dominique, Going Undercover, The Dawning, How to Make an American Quilt.
TELEVISION: *Movies & Specials:* Heidi, Beggarman Thief, The Easter Promise, The Home Front, Golden Gate, Jacqueline Susann's Valley of the Dolls 1981, A Small Killing, Inherit the Wind, Great Expectations, Sensibility and Sense, The Laker Girls, Perry Mason: The Case of Lost Love, People Like Us, December Flower. *Mini-Series*: The Dain Curse, The Thorn Birds (Emmy Award, 1983), North and South Book II. *Series*: Dark Shadows (1991).

SIMMONS, MATTY
Producer. b. Oct. 3. As bd. chmn., National Lampoon, Inc. produced National Lampoon Radio Hour, National Lampoon Lemmings, National Lampoon Show. Resigned from National Lampoon Inc. 1989. Now heads Matty Simmons Productions.
PICTURES: National Lampoon's Animal House, National Lampoon's Vacation, National Lampoon Goes to the Movies, National Lampoon's Class Reunion, National Lampoon's European Vacation, National Lampoon's Christmas Vacation (exec. prod.), National Lampoon's Vegas Vacation (exec. prod.).
TELEVISION: National Lampoon's Disco Beavers, National Lampoon's Class of '86 (exec. prod.), Delta House.

SIMON, MELVIN
Executive. b. New York, NY, Oct. 21, 1926. e. City Coll.of New York, B.B.A., 1949; graduate work at Indiana U. Law Sch. Owner and operator, in partnership with two brothers, of over 110 shopping centers in U.S. 1978 formed Melvin Simon Productions, privately owned corp., to finance films. Dissolved Co. in 1983.
PICTURES: *Exec. Prod.*: Dominique, Love at First Bite, When a Stranger Calls, The Runner Stumbles, Scavenger Hunt, Cloud Dancer, The Stunt Man, My Bodyguard, Zorro the Gay Blade, Chu Chu and the Philly Flash, Porky's, Porky's II—The Next Day, Uforia, Wolf Lake, Porky's Revenge.

SIMON, NEIL
Playwright, Screenwriter, Producer. r.n. Marvin Neil Simon. b. Bronx, NY, July 4, 1927. e. NYU. U.S. Army Air Force, 1945-46. Wrote comedy for radio with brother, Danny, (Robert Q. Lewis Show and for Goodman Ace), also TV scripts for Sid Caesar, Red Buttons, Jackie Gleason, Phil Silvers, Garry Moore, Tallulah Bankhead Show. With Danny contributed to B'way revues Catch a Star (1955), and New Faces of 1956.
THEATER: *Playwright*: Come Blow Your Horn, Little Me, Barefoot in the Park, The Odd Couple (Tony Award, 1965), Sweet Charity, The Star Spangled Girl, Plaza Suite, Promises Promises, Last of the Red Hot Lovers, The Gingerbread Lady, The Prisoner of Second Avenue, The Sunshine Boys, The Good Doctor, God's Favorite, California Suite, Chapter Two, They're Playing Our Song, I Ought to Be in Pictures, Fools, Little Me (revised version), Brighton Beach Memoirs, Biloxi Blues (Tony Award, 1985), The Odd Couple (female version), Broadway Bound, Rumors, Lost in Yonkers (Pulitzer Prize, Tony Award, 1991), Jake's Women, The Goodbye Girl (musical), Laughter on the 23rd Floor, London Suite (Off-B'way), The Out-of-Towners, The Odd Couple II.
PICTURES: After the Fox, Barefoot in the Park (also assoc. prod.), The Odd Couple, The Out-of-Towners, Plaza Suite, Last of the Red Hot Lovers, The Heartbreak Kid, The Prisoner of Second Avenue, The Sunshine Boys, Murder by Death, The Goodbye Girl, The Cheap Detective, California Suite, Chapter Two, Seems Like Old Times, Only When I Laugh (also co-prod.), I Ought to Be in Pictures (also co-prod.), Max Dugan Returns (also co-prod.), The Lonely Guy (adaptation), The Slugger's Wife, Brighton Beach Memoirs, Biloxi Blues (also co-prod.), The Marrying Man, Lost in Yonkers, The Odd Couple II, The Out-of-Towners (1999).
TELEVISION: *Specials*: The Trouble With People, Plaza Suite. *Movie*: Broadway Bound, Jake's Women, London Suite.

SIMON, PAUL
Singer, Composer, Actor. b. Newark, NJ, Oct. 13, 1941. e. Queens Coll., BA; postgrad. Brooklyn Law Sch. Teamed with Art Garfunkel in 1964, writing and performing own songs; they parted in 1970. Reunited for concert in New York, 1982, which was televised on HBO. Songs: With Garfunkel incl.: Mrs. Robinson (Grammy Award), The Boxer, Bridge Over Troubled Water (Grammy Award).
ALBUMS: with Garfunkel: Wednesday Morning 3 a.m., Sounds of Silence, Parsley, Sage, Rosemary and Thyme, The Graduate (Grammy Award), Bookends, Bridge Over Troubled Water (Grammy Award), Simon & Garfunkel's Greatest Hits, Concert in the Park. *Solo*: Paul Simon, There Goes Rhymin' Simon, Live Rhymin', Still Crazy After All These Years (Grammy Award), Greatest Hits, One Trick Pony, Hearts and Bones, Graceland (Grammy Award), Negotiations and Love Songs, The Rhythm of the Saints, Paul Simon's Concert in the Park.
PICTURES: The Graduate (songs), Annie Hall (actor), One Trick Pony (s.p., actor, composer)
TELEVISION: *Specials*: The Fred Astaire Show, The Paul Simon Special (Emmy Award), Home Box Office Presents Paul Simon, Graceland: The African Concert, Mother Goose Rock 'n' Rhyme, Paul Simon's Concert in the Park. *Guest*: Sesame Street.

SIMON, SIMONE
Actress. b. April 23, 1911, Marseilles, France. Played in many films in Europe, among them Les Beaux Jours, La Bete Humaine, and Lac aux Dames. On stage in Toi C'est Moi, and others.
PICTURES: Girl's Domitory (U.S. debut, 1936), Ladies in Love, Seventh Heaven, All That Money Can Buy, Cat People, Tahiti Honey, Johnny Doesn't Live Here Any More, The Curse of the Cat People, Mademoiselle Fifi, Petrus, Temptation Harbor, La Ronde, Olivia (Pit of Loneliness), Le Plaisir (House of Pleasure), Double Destin, The Extra Day, La Femme en Bleu.

SIMPSON, GARRY
Producer, Director, Executive. b. Camden, MI, Feb. 16, 1914. e. Stanford U. Major shows with NBC-TV: Jimmy Durante Show, Armstrong Circle Theatre, Campbell Soundstage, Comedy Hour, Ford Festival, Chevrolet Tele-Theater, Ed Wynn Show, The World of Mr. Sweeney, Philco TV Playhouse, Wide Wide World, Ballet Theatre. Dir. of programming, Vermont State PBS Network and writer-prod. of documentary films. Awards: Peabody, NY Film & TV Fest., Chicago Film Fest., & 3 Emmys.

SIMPSON, O.J.
Actor. r.n. Orenthal James Simpson. b. San Francisco, CA, July 9, 1947. e. U. of Southern California. Was star collegiate and professional football player and winner of Heisman Trophy. Began sportscasting in 1969.
PICTURES: The Klansman (debut, 1974), The Towering Inferno, Killer Force, The Cassandra Crossing, Capricorn One, Firepower, Hambone & Hillie, The Naked Gun: From the Files of Police Squad, The Naked Gun 2 1/2: The Smell of Fear, Naked Gun 33 1/3: The Final Insult.

TELEVISION: *Mini-Series*: Roots. *Movies*: A Killing Affair, Goldie and the Boxer (also exec. prod.), Detour to Terror (also exec. prod.), Goldie and the Boxer Go to Hollywood (also exec. prod.), Cocaine and Blue Eyes (also exec. prod.), Student Exchange. Prod.: High Five (pilot), Superbowl Saturday Night (host & co-prod.). *Series*: First and Ten (HBO), NFL Live (co-host).

SIMS, JOAN
Actress. b. Laindon, England, May 9, 1930. e. Trained at RADA. Early career in repertory and West End Theatre.
PICTURES: Dry Rot, Off the Record, No Time for Tears, Just My Luck, The Naked Truth, The Captain's Table, Passport to Shame, Emergency Ward 10, Most of the Carry On' films, Doctor in Love, Watch Your Stern, Twice Round the Daffodils, The Iron Maiden, Nurse on Wheels, Doctor in Clover, Doctor in Trouble, The Garnett Saga, Not Now Darling, Don't Just Lie There Say Something, Love Among the Ruins, One of Our Dinosaurs Is Missing, Till Death Us Do Part, The Way of the World, Deceptions, The Fool, My Good Friend, As Time Goes By, The Canterville Ghost.
TELEVISION: Over 100 shows incl. Stanley Baxter Show, Dick Emery Show, Carry on Shows, Love Among the Ruins, Born and Bred, Worzel Gummidge, Ladykillers, Crown Court, Cockles, Fairly Secret Army, Tickle on the Tum, Miss Marple: A Murder Is Announced, Hay Fever, In Loving Memory, Drummonds, Farrington of the F.O., Dr. Who, On the Up (3 series), Boys From the Bush, Simon & the Witch, Children's TV, Boys From the Bush, Tender Loving Care, Canterville Ghost, My Good Friend, Smokescreen, As Time Goes By, Just William, Henrietta Wainthrop Investigates.

SINBAD
Actor. r.n. David Adkins. b. Benton Harbor, MI, Nov. 10, 1956. e. Univ. of Denver. Served in Air Force before becoming stand-up comic. Career was subsquently launched by appearances on tv series Star Search.
PICTURES: Necessary Roughness (debut, 1991), Coneheads, The Meteor Man, Houseguest, First Kid (also co-exec. prod.), Jingle All the Way, Homeward Bound II: Lost in San Francisco, First Kid, Jingle All the Way, Good Burger.
TELEVISION: *Series*: The Redd Foxx Show, A Different World, It's Showtime at the Apollo (host), The Sinbad Show (also exec. prod.). *Specials*: Sinbad: Brain Damaged, Afros and Bellbottoms, Take No Prisoners, Sinbad and Friends All the Way Live... Almost (also writer), Aliens for Breakfast. *Guest*: The Cosby Show.

SINDEN, DONALD
Actor. b. Plymouth, England, Oct. 9, 1923. Stage debut 1942 in fit-up shows; London stage includes There's a Girl in My Soup, The Relapse, Not Now Darling, King Lear, Othello, Present Laughter, Uncle Vanya, The School for Scandal, Two Into One, The Scarlet Pimpernel, Oscar Wilde, Major Barbara, Out of Order, Venus Observed, She Stoops to Conquer, Hamlet, That Good Night. B'way: London Assurance, Habeas Corpus. TV debut 1948.
PICTURES: Portrait From Life (The Girl in the Painting; debut, 1948), The Cruel Sea, Mogambo, A Day to Remember, You Know What Sailors Are, Doctor in the House, The Beachcomber, Mad About Men, An Alligator Named Daisy, Black Tent, Eyewitness, Tiger in the Smoke, Doctor at Large, Rockets Galore (Mad Little Island), The Captain's Table, Operation Bullshine, Your Money or Your Wife, The Siege of Sydney Street, Twice Around the Daffodils, Mix Me a Person, Decline and Fall, Villain, Rentadick, The Island at the Top of the World, That Lucky Touch, The Children, The Canterville Ghost.
TELEVISION: Bullet in the Ballet, Road to Rome, Dinner With the Family, Odd Man In, Love from Italy, The Frog, The Glove, The Mystery of Edwin Drood, The Happy Ones, The Comedy of Errors, The Wars of the Roses, The Red House, Blackmail, A Bachelor Gray, Our Man at St. Marks (3 series), The Wind in the Tall Paper Chimney, A Woman Above Reproach, Call My Bluff, Relatively Speaking, Father Dear Father, The 19th Hole, Seven Days in the Life of Andrew Pelham (serial), The Assyrian Rejuvenator, The Organization (serial), The Confederacy of Wives, Tell It to the Chancellor, The Rivals, Two's Company (4 series), All's Well That Ends Well, Never the Twain (11 series), Cuts.

SINGER, LORI
Actress. b. Corpus Christi, TX, Nov. 6, 1962. Brother is actor Marc Singer; father was symphony conductor Jacques Singer. Concert cellist while in teens. Won starring role in TV series Fame (1981).
PICTURES: Footloose (debut, 1984), The Falcon and The Snowman, The Man with One Red Shoe, Trouble in Mind, Summer Heat, Made in U.S.A., Warlock, Equinox, Sunset Grill, Short Cuts (Golden Globe Award), F.T.W.
TELEVISION: *Series*: Fame, VR5. *Movies*: Born Beautiful, Storm and Sorrow, Inspired by Bach. *Special*: Sensibility and Sense.

SINGER, MARC
Actor. b. Vancouver, B.C., Canada, Jan. 29. Brother of actress Lori Singer. Son of symphony conductor Jacques Singer. Trained in summer stock and regional theatre.
PICTURES: Go Tell the Spartans, If You Could See What I Hear, The Beastmaster, Born to Race, A Man Called Sarge, Watchers II, Body Chemistry, Dead Space, In the Cold of the Night, Beastmaster 2, Sweet Justice, The Berlin Conspiracy, Alien Intruder, Beastmaster 3.
TELEVISION: *Series*: The Contender, V, Dallas. *Mini-Series*: 79 Park Avenue, Roots: The Next Generation. *Movies*: Things in Their Season, Journey from Darkness, Something for Joey, Never Con a Killer, Sergeant Matlovich vs. the U.S. Air Force, The Two Worlds of Jennie Logan, For Ladies Only, Paper Dolls, V, Her Life as a Man, V—The Final Battle, Deadly Game, The Sea Wolf.

SINGLETON, JOHN
Director, Writer. b. Los Angeles, CA, Jan. 6, 1968. Entered USC's Filmic Writing Program, where he received a Robert Riskin Writing Award and two Jack Nicholson Writing Awards. With debut feature Boyz N the Hood (1991) he became the first African-American and youngest person ever to be nominated for an Academy Award for Best Director. Appeared in film Beverly Hills Cop III.
PICTURES: *Director-Writer*: Boyz N the Hood (Acad. Award noms. for dir. & s.p.), Poetic Justice (also co-prod.), Higher Learning (also co-prod.), Rosewood, Shaft.

SINGLETON, PENNY
Actress. r.n. Dorothy McNulty. b. Philadelphia, PA, September 15, 1908. e. Columbia U. First Broadway success came as top comedienne in Good News., exec. pres. AGVA.
PICTURES: Outside of Paradise, Swing Your Lady, Men Are Such Fools, Boy Meets Girl, Mr. Chump, Mad Miss Manton, Garden of the Moon, Secrets of an Actress, Hard to Get, 28 films in Blondie series (from Blondie, 1938, to Blondie's Hero, 1950), Rocket Busters, Go West Young Lady, Footlight Glamor, Young Widow, The Best Man, Jetsons: The Movie (voice).
TELEVISION: *Series*: The Jetsons (voice).

SINISE, GARY
Actor, Director. b. 1955. Co-founder and artistic dir. of Chicago's Steppenwolf Theatre Company, 1974.
THEATER: *NY*: Balm in Gilead, True West, The Caretaker, The Grapes of Wrath. Chicago: Of Mice and Men, Getting Out. *Director*: True West (Obie Award), Orphans, Buried Child.
PICTURES: Miles From Home (dir. only), A Midnight Clear, Of Mice and Men (also dir., co-prod.), Jack the Bear, Forrest Gump (Acad. Award nom.), The Quick and the Dead, Apollo 13, Albino Alligator, Ransom., Snake Eyes, Bruno, All the Rage, The Green Mile, Reindeer Games, Mission to Mars, Imposter.
TELEVISION: *Mini-Series*: The Stand. *Movies*: Family Secrets, My Name is Bill W, The Final Days, Truman (Golden Globe Award), George Wallace (Emmy Award, 1998), That Championship Season. *Director*: Crime Story, thirtysomething, China Beach.

SIODMAK, CURT
Director, Writer. b. Dresden, Germany, Aug. 10, 1902. e. U. of Zurich. Engineer, newspaper reporter, writer in Berlin; novelist, including F.P.1 Does Not Answer, adapt. 1932 for Ufa. Originals and screenplays in France and England including France (Le Bal), Transatlantic Tunnel, GB.
PICTURES: *Writer*: Her Jungle Love (co-story), The Invisible Man Returns, Black Friday, The Ape, Aloma of the South Sea (co-story), The Wolf Man, Invisible Agent, Frankenstein Meets the Wolf Man, I Walked With a Zombie, Son of Dracula (co-story), The Mantrap, House of Frankenstein (story), The Climax, Shady Lady, The Beast with Five Fingers, Berlin Express (story), Tarzan's Magic Fountain, Four Days Leave, Bride of the Gorilla (also dir.), The Magnetic Monster (also dir.), Curucu—Beast of the Amazon (also dir.), Love Slaves of the Amazon (also dir., prod.), Riders to the Stars, Creature with the Atom Brain, Earth vs. the Flying Saucers.
(d. Sept. 2, 2000)

SIZEMORE, TOM
Actor. b. Detroit, MI. e. Wayne St. Univ., Temple Univ.Stage incl. The Land of the Astronauts in NYC and D.C.
PICTURES: Lock Up, Rude Awakening, Penn and Teller Get Killed, Born on the Fourth of July, Blue Steel, Flight of the Intruder, Guilty by Suspicion, Harley Davidson and the Marlboro Man, A Matter of Degrees, Passenger 57, Watch It, Heart and Souls, True Romance, Striking Distance, Wyatt Earp, Natural Born Killers, Devil in a Blue Dress, Strange Days, Heat, The Relic, Enemy of the State (cameo), Saving Private Ryan, The Florentine, The Match, Bringing Out the Dead, Play It To The Bone, Red Planet, Pearl Harbor, Ticker, Big Trouble.
TELEVISION: Witness to the Mob, Witness Protection.

SKARSGARD, STELLAN
Actor. b. Gothenburg, Vastergotland, Sweden, June 13, 1951.
PICTURES: Raid in the Summer, The Office Party, Brollopet, Anita, Taboo, Homeward in the Night, The Simple-Minded Murder, P & B, Ake and His World, False as Water, Peter-No-Tail in Americat, The Serpents Way, Jim and the Pirates, Hipp hipp hurra!, Time of the Wolf, Friends, The Unbearable Lightness of Being, S/Y Joy, Code Name Coq Rouge,

The Women on the Roof, The Hunt for Red October, The Perfect Murder, The Ox, The Democratic Terrorist, Wind, The Slingshot, The Last Dance, Jonssonligans storsta kupp, Zero Kelvin, Hundarna i Riga, Harry och Sonja, Breaking the Waves, Insomnia, The Volcano Man, The Kingdom 2, Amistad, Good Will Hunting, Tranceformer - A Portait of Lars von Trier, My Son the Fanatic, The Glass-Blower's Children, Savior, Ronin, Deep Blue Sea, Passion of Mind, Light Keeps Me Company, Signs & Wonders, Timecode, Dancer in the Dark, Aberdeen, Kiss Kiss Bang Bang, The Glass House.

SKASE, CHRISTOPHER
Executive. b. Australia, 1946. Began career as reporter for Fairfax publication, Australian Financial Review. In 1970s set up investment company with about $20,000. Revived Australian TV Seven network in Melbourne and then in U.S. bought Hal Roach Studios and NY based prod.-dist. Robert Halmi which he merged into Qintex Entertainment. Qintex Entertainment produced TV mini-series Lonesome Dove.

SKERRITT, TOM
Actor. b. Detroit, MI, Aug. 25, 1933. e. Wayne State U., UCLA. Model for Guess? jeans ads.
PICTURES: War Hunt (debut, 1962), One Man's Way, Those Calloways, M*A*S*H, Wild Rovers, Fuzz, Harold and Maude, Run Joe Run, Big Bad Mama, Thieves Like Us, The Devil's Rain, La Madonna, The Turning Point, Up in Smoke, Ice Castles, Alien, Savage Harvest, The Silence of the North, A Dangerous Summer (The Burning Man), Fighting Back, The Dead Zone, Top Gun, Opposing Force (Hell Camp), SpaceCamp, Wisdom, Maid to Order, The Big Town, Poltergeist III, Steel Magnolias, Big Man on Campus, Honor Bound, The Rookie, Wild Orchid II: Two Shades of Blue, Poison Ivy, Singles, A River Runs Through It, Knight Moves, Contact, Not Like You, Smoke Signals, The Other Sister.
TELEVISION: *Series*: Ryan's Four, Cheers, Picket Fences (Emmy Award, 1993). *Movies*: The Bird Men, The Last Day, Maneaters Are Loose!, The Calendar Girl Murders, Miles to Go, Parent Trap II, A Touch of Scandal, Poker Alice, Moving Target, Nightmare at Bitter Creek, The Heist, Red King White Knight, The China Lake Murders, Child of the Night, In Sickness and in Health, Getting Up and Going Home, What the Deaf Man Heard, Two for Texas, The Hunt for the Unicorn Killer, Aftershock. *Director*: A Question of Sex (Afterschool Special), Picket Fences (3 episodes), Divided by Hate.

SKLAR, MARTIN A.
Executive. e. UCLA, 1956. editor, the Daily Bruin, 1955. Began as asst. news editor, MAC (Media Agency Clients) Publications, 1956. Worked in publicity & mktg., Disneyland, 1956-61; writer, advertising and publicity, WED Enterprises (now Walt Disney Imagineering - WDI) where he served on a team assigned by Walt Disney to develop special projects for industry. Wrote personal materials for Showman of the World and other publications, television and special films aimed at communicating Walt Disney's visionary concepts. Primary strategist, Imagineering, 1960s-90s; v.p., concepts/planning, 1974; v.p., creative development, 1979; exec. v.p., 1982; president, 1987-96, Walt Disney Imagineering, responsible for the creation and expansion of Disney's theme parks and other creative initiatives. Currently vice chairman and principal creative executive, Walt Disney Imagineering (WDI), which is responsible for all aspects of every theme park project; featured speaker at numerous art design and recreation-related conferences. Elected member & president, Board of Education, Anaheim City School District, 1969 & 1973; former president, Orange Cty. School Board Assoc.; former City Commissioner, Anaheim; founding chairman, Michael L. Roston Creative Writing Awards; recipient, Community Service Award for Anaheim, 1977; Disney Legend Award, 1995; recipient, Lifetime Achievement Award, Themed Entertainment Assoc., 1995; member, Board of the Manned Space Flight Education Found.; president, Ryman-Carroll Found., which fosters the teaching of art and cultural diversity in public education.

SKOLIMOWSKI, JERZY
Director, Writer. b. Lodz, Poland, May 5, 1938. e. Warsaw U., State Superior Film Sch., Lodz, Poland. Scriptwriter for Wajda's Innocent Sorcerers (also actor), Polanski's Knife in the Water and Lomnicki's Poslizg. Author: Somewhere Close to Oneself, Somebody Got Drowned.
PICTURES: *Director-Writer*: Identification Marks—None (also actor, edit., art dir.), Walkover (also actor, edit.), Barrier, The Departure, Hands Up (also actor), Dialogue, The Adventures of Gerard, Deep End, King Queen Knave (dir. only), The Shout, Circle of Deceit (actor only), Moonlighting (also prod., actor), Success Is the Best Revenge, The Lightship, White Nights (actor), Big Shots (actor), Torrents of Spring (also actor), 30 Door Key (also co-s.p., prod.), The Hollow Men (prod.).

SKYE, IONE
Actress. r.n. Ione Skye Leitch. b. London, England, Sept. 4, 1971. Daughter of folksinger Donovan (Leitch) and sister of actor Donovan Leitch. Raised in San Francisco, Connecticut, Los Angeles. Fashion photo of her in magazine led to audition for film River's Edge.
PICTURES: River's Edge (debut, 1987 as Ione Skye Leitch), Stranded, A Night in the Life of Jimmy Reardon, Say Anything..., The Rachel Papers, Mindwalk, Samantha, Guncrazy, Carmilla, Wayne's World, The Color of Evening, Gas Food Lodging, Four Rooms, The Size of Watermelons, One Night Stand, Dream for an Insomniac, Went to Coney Island on a Mission from God...Be Back by Five, Jump, The Good Doctor, Mascara.
TELEVISION: *Series*: Covington Cross. *Movies*: Napoleon and Josephine, Girls in Prison. *Specials*: It's Called the Sugar Plum, Nightmare Classics (Carmilla).

SLATER, CHRISTIAN
Actor. r.n. Christian Michael Leonard Hawkins. b. New York, NY, Aug. 18, 1969. Mother is NY casting dir. Mary Jo Slater; father Los Angeles stage actor Michael Hawkins. Made prof. debut at 9 in The Music Man starring Dick Van Dyke, natl. tour, then on B'way Also on B'way in Macbeth, A Christmas Carol, David Copperfield and Merlin. Off-B'way in Landscape of the Body, Between Daylight and Boonville, Somewhere's Better. Also summer theatre. Directed 1992 L.A. prod. of The Laughter Epidemic.
PICTURES: The Legend of Billie Jean (debut, 1985), Twisted, The Name of the Rose, Tucker: The Man and His Dream, Gleaming the Cube, Heathers, The Wizard, Tales from the Dark Side: The Movie, Beyond the Stars (Personal Choice), Young Guns II, Pump Up the Volume, Robin Hood: Prince of Thieves, Mobsters, Star Trek VI: The Undiscovered Country (cameo), Kuffs, FernGully... The Last Rainforest (voice), Where the Day Takes You, Untamed Heart, True Romance, Jimmy Hollywood, Interview With the Vampire, Murder in the First, Broken Arrow, Austin Powers: International Man of Mystery (cameo), Bed of Roses, Julian Po, Very Bad Things, Hard Rain, Basil, Love Stinks (cameo), The Contender, 3000 Miles to Graceland, Windtalkers, Cletis Tout.
TELEVISION: *Series*: One Life to Live, Ryan's Hope. *Specials*: Sherlock Holmes, Pardon Me for Living, The Haunted Mansion Mystery, Cry Wolf, The Edge (Professional Man). *Movies*: Living Proof: The Hank Williams Jr. Story, Desperate For Love, Merry Christmas George Bailey.

SLATER, HELEN
Actress. b. New York, NY, Dec. 19, 1963. *Off-B'way*: Responsible Parties, Almost Romance.
PICTURES: Supergirl (debut, 1984), The Legend of Billie Jean, Ruthless People, The Secret of My Success, Sticky Fingers, Happy Together, City Slickers, A House in the Hills, Betrayal of the Dove, Lassie, The Steal, The Long Way Home (voice).
TELEVISION: *Series*: Capital News. *Movies*: 12:01, Chantilly Lace, Parallel Lives, Toothless, Best Friend for Life.

SLATZER, ROBERT FRANKLIN
Writer, Director, Producer. b. Marion, OH, April 4, 1927. e. Ohio State U., UCLA, 1947. Radio news commentator sportscaster, wrote radio serials; adv. dir., Brush-Moore Newspapers; feature writer, Scripps-Howard Newspapers; adv. exec., The Columbus Dispatch; syn. columnist, NY Journal-American; wrote guest columns for Dorothy Kilgallen; author of western short stories and novels; wrote, dir., prod. industrial films, docs., sports specials and commercials; 1949-51, writer for Grand National Studios Prods, Monogram Pictures, Republic Studios, Eagle-Lion Films; 1951, publicist, Hope Enterprises; pub. dir., Paramount Pictures; 1952, personal mgr. to Marilyn Monroe, Ken Maynard, James Craig, Gail Russell and other stars; 1953, story editor and assoc. prod., Joe Palooka Productions; 1953-54, staff writer Universal Studios, RKO Radio Pictures, MGM, Columbia and Paramount; 1958, formed Robert F. Slatzer Productions; 1960, exec. in chg. of prod., Jaguar Pictures Corp.; 1963-65, pres., Slatzer Oil & Gas Co.; 1966-67, bd. dir., United Mining & Milling Corp.; 1970-74, exec., Columbia Pictures Corp.; 1974, resumed producing and financing features and television films; 1976, honored as Fellow, Mark Twain Inst.
AUTHOR: *Novels*: Desert Empire, Rose of the Range, Rio, Rawhide Range, The Cowboy and the Heiress, Daphne, Campaign Girl, Scarlet, The Dance Studio Hucksters, Born to be Wild, Single Room Furnished, The West is Still Wild, Gusher, The Young Wildcats. *Biographies*: The Life and Curious Death of Marilyn Monroe, The Life and Legend of Ken Maynard, Who Killed Thelma Todd?, The Duke of Thieves, Bing Crosby—The Hollow Man, Duke: The Life and Times of John Wayne, The Marilyn Files.
PICTURES: White Gold, The Obsessed, Mike and the Heiress, Under Texas Skies, They Came To Kill, Trail of the Mounties, Jungle Goddess, Montana Desperado, Pride of the Blue, Green Grass of Wyoming, The Naked Jungle, Warpaint, Broken Lance, Elephant Walk, South of Death Valley, The Big Gusher, Arctic Flight, The Hellcats, Bigfoot, John Wayne's No Substitute for Victory', Joniko-Eskimo Boy, Operation North Slope, Claws, Don't Go West, Mulefeathers, The Unfinished, Single Room Furnished, Viva Zapata, Inchon.
TELEVISION: The Great Outdoors, Adventures of White Arrow, Let's Go Boating, The Joe Palooka Story, Amos & Andy, I Am the Law, Files of Jeffrey Jones, Fireside Theatre, The Unser Story, Year of Opportunity, The Big Ones, Ken Maynard's West,

Where are They Now?, The Groovy Seven, The Untouchables, The Detectives, Wild Wild West, Wagon Train, Playhouse 90, Highway Patrol, David Frost Special, Today Show, ABC News, 20/20, Inside Edition, The Reporters, Current Affair, The Geraldo Show, Hard Copy, Larry King Show, Marilyn and Me, The Marilyn Files.

SLAVIN, GEORGE
Writer. b. Newark, NJ, March 2, 1916. e. Bucknell U., drama, Yale U. Has written over 300 TV episodes & pilots. WGA TV Award. Collected works at U. Wyoming. Received Stanford U, Maxwell Anderson Playwriting Award.
PICTURES: Intrigue, Woman on Pier 13, The Nevadan, Mystery Submarine, Peggy, Red Mountain, City of Bad Men, Weekend with Father, Thunder Bay, Rocket Man, Smoke Signal, Uranium Boom, Desert Sands, The Halliday Brand, Son of Robin Hood, Big House USA, Fighting Stallions.

SLOAN, JOHN R.
Producer. e. Merchiston Castle Sch., Edinburgh, 1932-39; asst. dir. and prod. man. Warners, London, Hollywood; 1939-46, Army.
PICTURES: Sea Devils, The End of the Affair, Port Afrique, Abandon Ship, The Safecracker, Beyond this Place, The Killers of Kilimanjaro, Johnny Nobody, The Reluctant Saint, The Running Man, The Last Command, To Sir With Love, Fragment of Fear, Dad's Army, Lord Jim, No Sex Please, We're British, The Odessa File, High-Ballin', Force 10 From Navarone, The Children's Story.

SLOCOMBE, DOUGLAS
Cinematographer. b. England, Feb. 10, 1913. Former journalist. Filmed the invasion of Poland and Holland. Under contract to Ealing Studios 17 years.
PICTURES: Dead of Night, The Captive Heart, Hue and Cry, The Loves of Joanna Godden, It Always Rains on Sunday, Saraband for Dead Lovers, Kind Hearts and Coronets, Cage of Gold, The Lavender Hill Mob, Mandy, The Man in the White Suit, The Titfield Thunderbolt, Man in the Sky, Ludwig II, Lease on Life, The Smallest Show on Earth, Tread Softly, Stranger, Circus of Horrors, The Young Ones, The Mark, The L-Shaped Room, Freud, The Servant (BAFTA Award), Guns at Batashi, A High Wind in Jamaica, The Blue Max, Promise Her Anything, The Vampire Killers, Fathom, Robbery, Boom, The Lion in Winter, The Italian Job, The Music Lovers, Murphy's War, The Buttercup Chain, Travels With My Aunt (Acad. Award nom.), Jesus Christ Superstar, The Great Gatsby, Rollerball, Hedda, The Sailor Who Fell From Grace With the Sea, Nasty Habits, Julia (Acad. Award nom.), Close Encounters of the Third Kind (co-photog.), Caravans, Lost and Found, The Lady Vanishes, Nijinsky, Raiders of the Lost Ark (Acad. Award nom.), The Pirates of Penzance, Never Say Never Again, Indiana Jones and the Temple of Doom, Water, Lady Jane, Indiana Jones and the Last Crusade.
TELEVISION: Movie: Love Among the Ruins.

SLUIZER, GEORGE
Director. b. Paris, France, June 25, 1932.
PICTURES: De lage landen, Jolio en het mes, Twice a Woman, Red Desert Penetentiary, Spoorloos, Utz, The Vanishing, Dying to Go Home, Crimetime, The Commissioner, The Stone Raft.

SMART, JEAN
Actress. b. Seattle, WA, Sept. 13, 1951. e. Univ. of WA. Member of Oregon Shakespeare Fest, 1975-77; also with Hartford Stage Co., Pittsburgh Public Theatre Co., Intiman Theatre Co.
THEATER: *Regional*: Equus, Much Ado About Nothing, A Moon for the Misbegotten, Terra Nova, Cat's Play, Saint Joan, A History of the American Film, Last Summer at Bluefish Cove (LA Drama Critics Circle, Dramalogue & LA Drama Desk Awards), Mrs. California, Strange Snow. *NY*: Last Summer at Bluefish Cove, Piaf (B'way debut, 1981).
PICTURES: Flashpoint (debut, 1984), Protocol, Fire With Fire, Project X, Mistress, Homeward Bound: The Incredible Journey, The Brady Bunch Movie, Edie & Pen, The Odd Couple II.
TELEVISION: *Series*: Reggie, Teachers Only, Designing Women, High Society, Hey Arnold, Style and Substance. *Movies*: Single Bars Single Women, A Fight for Jenny, A Seduction in Travis County, A Stranger in Town (also co-prod.), The Yarn Princess, The Yearling, A Stranger in Town, Undue Influence. *Specials*: Piaf, Maximum Security, Royal Match, A Palce at the Table.

SMITH, CHARLES MARTIN
Actor, Director. b. Los Angeles, CA, Oct. 30, 1953. e. California State U. Father is animation artist Frank Smith.
PICTURES: The Culpepper Cattle Company (debut, 1972), Fuzz, The Spikes Gang, American Graffiti, Pat Garrett and Billy the Kid, Rafferty and the Gold Dust Twins, No Deposit No Return, The Hazing, The Buddy Holly Story, More American Graffiti, Herbie Goes Bananas, Never Cry Wolf (also co-wrote narration), Starman, Trick or Treat (also dir.), The Untouchables, The Experts, The Hot Spot, Deep Cover, Fifty-Fifty (also dir.), I Love Trouble, Perfect Alibi, Speechless, He Ain't Heavy, The Final Cut, Wedding Bell Blues, Deep Impact.
TELEVISION: *Series*: Speed Buggy (voice). *Guest*: The Brady Bunch, Monte Nash, Baretta, Streets of San Francisco, Petrocelli, The Rookies, Grizzly Adams, Twilight Zone, Ray Bradbury Theatre, Outer Limits, L.A. Law, Picket Fences, Northern Exposure, Tales From the Crypt. *Movies*: Go Ask Alice, Law of the Land, Cotton Candy, Boris and Natasha (also dir.), And the Band Played On, Roswell, Brother's Destiny, dead Silence, Blackout Effect. *Special*: Partners. *Mini-Series*: Streets of Laredo, The Beast, P.T. Barnum.

SMITH, DAVID R.
Archivist. b. Pasadena, CA, Oct. 13, 1940. e. Pasadena City Coll., A.A., 1960; U. of California, Berkeley, B.A. 1962, MLS 1963. Writer of numerous historical articles. Worked as librarian at Library of Congress, 1963-65 and as reference librarian, UCLA 1965-70 before becoming archivist for The Walt Disney Co. 1970-present. Exec. dir., The Manuscript Society, 1980-; member, Society of CA Archivists, Fellow of the Manuscript Society, 1993. Received service award, ASIFA, and award of distinction, Manuscript Soc, 1983. *Co-Author:* The Ultimate Disney Trivia Book (1992, 1994, 1997), Disney: The First 100 Years (1999). *Author:* Disney A to Z: The Official Encyclopedia (1996, 1998).

SMITH, HOWARD K.
News commentator. b. Ferriday, LA, May 12, 1914. e. Tulane U., 1936; Heidelberg U., Germany; Oxford U., Rhodes scholarship. United Press, London, 1939; United Press Bureau, Copenhagen; United Press, Berlin, 1940; joined CBS News, Berlin corr., 1941. Reported on occupied Europe from Switzerland to 1944; covered Nuremberg trials, 1946; ret. to U.S., moderator, commentator or reporter, CBS Reports, Face the Nation, Eyewitness to History, The Great Challenge, numerous news specials (Emmy Award, 1960 for The Population Explosion). Sunday night news analysis. CBS News Washington corr., 1957; chief corr. & mgr., Washington Bureau, 1961; joined, ABC News, Jan. 1962. News and comment, ABC news. Anchorman and commentator, ABC Evening News. Author: Last Train from Berlin, 1942, The State of Europe, 1949. Washington, D.C.—The Story of Our Nation's Capital, 1967, Events Leading Up to My Death —The Life of a 10th Century Reporter, 1996.

SMITH, HY
Executive. b. New York, NY, June 3, 1934. e. Baruch Sch., CCNY, B.B.A. Joined Paramount Pictures 1967, foreign ad.-pub coordinator; 1969, joined United Artists as foreign ad.-pub mgr.; named intl. ad.-pub dir., 1970; named v.p., intl. adv.-pub. 1976; v.p. worldwide adv., publ. & promo., 1978; 1981, named first v.p., adv./pub./promo; 1982, joined Rastar Films as v.p., intl. project director for Annie; 1983, joined United Intl. Pictures as sr. v.p., adv/pub, based in London. 1984, named sr. v.p., mktg. 1995, promoted to exec. v.p., mktg.

SMITH, JACLYN
Actress. b. Houston, TX, Oct. 26, 1947. Started acting while in high school and studied drama and psychology at Trinity U. in San Antonio. Appeared in many commercials as model.
PICTURES: The Adventurers, Bootleggers, Nightkill, Deja Vu.
TELEVISION: *Series*: Charlie's Angels, Christine Cromwell. *Guest*: McCloud, Get Christy Love, The Rookies. *Movies*: Probe (Switch), Charlie's Angels (pilot), Escape From Bogen County, The Users, Jacqueline Bouvier Kennedy, Rage of Angels, The Night They Saved Christmas, Sentimental Journey, Florence Nightingale, Rage of Angels: The Story Continues, Windmills of the Gods, The Bourne Identity, Settle the Score, Danielle Steel's Kaleidoscope, Lies Before Kisses, The Rape of Dr. Willis, In the Arms of a Killer, Nightmare in the Daylight, Love Can Be Murder, Cries Unheard: The Donna Yalich Story, Danielle Steel's Family Album.

SMITH, JOSEPH P.
Executive. b. Brooklyn, NY, March 28, 1921. e. Columbia U. Started career Wall Street; joined RKO Radio Pictures, served in sales and managerial posts; exec. v.p., Lippert Productions, Hollywood; v.p., Telepictures, Inc.; formed and pres., Cinema-Vue Corp.; pres., Pathe Pictures, Inc., Pathe News, Inc.

SMITH, KEVIN
Director, **Writer**. b. Red Bank, NJ, Aug. 2, 1970. also co-authored comic book series featuring Jay and Silent Bob characters.
PICTURES: Clerks (debut, 1994. also actor, editor, prod.), Mallrats (also actor), Drawing Flies (prod. only), Chasing Amy (also actor, editor), Good Will Hunting (co-exec. prod. only), Vulgar (exec. prod., actor only), Dogma (also actor, editor), Coyote Ugly (s.p. only), View Askew 5.

SMITH, KURTWOOD
Actor. b. New Lisbon, WI, July 3, 1943. e. B.A. San Jose (1966), M.F.A. Stanford (1969). Starred in Oscar-nom short 12:01 P.M.
THEATER: Plymouth Rock, The Price, Faces by Chekhov, Familiar Faces, Enemy of the People, The Debutante Ball (all in Calif.), The Lucky Spot (Williamston), Signature (Poughkeepsie), Hamlet, Taming of the Shrew, and over 20 other Shakespeare productions in CA.

PICTURES: Roadie (debut, 1980), Zoot Suit, Going Berserk, Staying Alive, Flashpoint, Robocop, Rambo III, True Believer, Dead Poets Society, Heart of Dixie, Quick Change, Oscar, Company Business, Star Trek VI: The Undiscovered Country, Shadows and Fog, The Crush, Heart and Souls, Fortress, Boxing Helena, Under Siege 2: Dark Territory, Last of the Dogmen, To Die For, Broken Arrow, A Time to Kill, Citizen Ruth, Precious, Shelter, Prefontaine, Deep Impact.
TELEVISION: *Series*: The Renegades, The New Adventures of Beans Baxter, Big Wave Dave's, That '70s Show. *Movies*: Murder in Texas, Missing Pieces, The Midnight Hour, International Airport, Deadly Messages, The Christmas Gift, Doorways, While Justice Sleeps, A Bright Shining Lie. *Mini-Series*: North and South Book II, The Nightmare Years (Ace Award nom.). *Guest*: Stir Crazy, Stingray, Newhart, 21 Jump Street, It's Garry Shandling's Show, The Famous Teddy Z, Picket Fences.

SMITH, LANE
Actor. b. Memphis, TN, April 29.
THEATER: *NY*: Visions of Kerouac, Brechtesgarten, Glengarry Glen Ross (Drama Desk Award).
PICTURES: Network, Honeysuckle Rose, Prince of the City, Frances, Purple Hearts, Red Dawn, Places in the Heart, Weeds, Prison, Race for Glory, Air America, My Cousin Vinny, The Mighty Ducks, The Distinguished Gentleman, Son-in-Law, The Scout, Lost & Found.
TELEVISION: *Series*: V, Kay O'Brien, Good Sports, Good and Evil. *Mini-Series*: Chiefs, From the Earth to the Moon. *Movies*: A Death in Canaan, Crash, The Solitary Man, Disaster on the Coastliner, City in Fear, Gideon's Trumpet, A Rumor of War, The Georgia Peaches, Mark I Love You, Dark Night of the Scarecrow, Prime Suspect, Thou Shalt Not Kill, Special Bulletin, Something About Amelia, Dress Gray, The Final Days, False Arrest, Duplicates, Alien Nation: The Udara Legacy. Specials: Displaced Person, Member of the Wedding.

SMITH, DAME MAGGIE
D.B.E. C.B.E. Actress. b. Ilford, England, Dec. 28, 1934. Early career Oxford Playhouse. With the Old Vic 1959-60. Also with Stratford Ontario Shakespeare Fest. 1975-78, & 1980. Received C.B.E. 1970; D.B.E., 1990.
THEATER: Twelfth Night (debut, 1952), Cakes and Ale, New Faces of 1956 (NY debut, as comedienne), Share My Lettuce, The Stepmother, What Every Woman Knows, Rhinoceros, The Rehearsal, The Private Ear, The Public Eye, Mary Mary, The Recruiting Officer, Othello, The Master Builder, Hay Fever, Much Ado About Nothing, Black Comedy, Miss Julie, Trelawney of the Wells, The Beaux Stratagem, The Three Sisters, Hedda Gabler, Design for Living (L.A.), Private Lives (London & NY), Slap, Peter Pan, As You Like It, Macbeth, Night and Day (London & NY), Virginia, Way of the World, Lettice and Lovage (London & NY, Tony Award), The Importance of Being Earnest, Three Tall Women.
PICTURES: Nowhere to Go (debut, 1958), Go to Blazes, The V.I.P.s, The Pumpkin Eater, Young Cassidy, Othello, The Honey Pot, Hot Millions, The Prime of Miss Jean Brodie (Acad. Award, BAFTA Award, 1969), Oh! What a Lovely War, Travels With My Aunt, Love and Pain and the Whole Damn Thing, Murder by Death, Death on the Nile, California Suite (Acad. Award, best supporting actress, 1978), Clash of the Titans, Quartet, Evil Under the Sun, The Missionary, Better Late Than Never, A Private Function (BAFTA Award, 1985), Lily in Love, A Room with a View, The Lonely Passion of Judith Hearne, Romeo-Juliet (voice), Hook, Sister Act, The Secret Garden, Sister Act 2: Back in the Habit, Richard III, Washington Square.
TELEVISION: Much Ado About Nothing, Man and Superman, On Approval, Home and Beauty, Mrs. Silly, Bed Among the Lentils, Memento Mori, Suddenly Last Summer.

SMITH, ROGER
Actor, Producer. b. South Gate, CA, Dec. 18, 1932. m. actress-performer Ann Margret. e. U. of Arizona. Started career at age 7, one of the Meglin Kiddies, appearing at the Mayan Theater, Wilshire, Ebell. Sings, composes, American folk songs. Producer: Ann-Margret cabaret and theater shows.
PICTURES: No Time to Be Young, Crash Landing, Operation Madball, Man of a Thousand Faces, Never Steal Anything Small, Auntie Mame, Rogues Gallery.
TELEVISION: The Horace Heidt Show, Ted Mack Original Amateur Hour, 77 Sunset Strip (series), writer, ABC-TV. *Co-prod.*: Homestead.

SMITH, WILL
Actor, Singer. b. Philadelphia, PA, Sept. 25, 1968. Teamed with musician Jeff Townes as rap duo D.J. Jazzy Jeff & the Fresh Prince. Albums: Rock the House, He's the DJ I'm the Rapper, And in This Corner, Homebase. Recipient of 2 Grammy Awards.
PICTURES: Where the Day Takes You (debut, 1992), Made in America, Six Degress of Separation, Bad Boys, Independence Day, Men in Black, Enemy of the State, Wild Wild West, The Legend of Bagger Vance, Men in Black 2.
TELEVISION: *Series*: Fresh Prince of Bel Air (also co-exec. prod.).

SMITH, WILLIAM
Actor. b. Columbia, MO, March 24, 1932. e. Syracuse, U., BA; UCLA, MA.
PICTURES: Darker Than Amber, C.C. and Company, The Losers, Run, Angel, Run, Blood and Guts, Seven, Fast Company, No Knife, Twilight's Last Gleaming, The Frisco Kid, Any Which Way You Can, Rumble Fish, Red Dawn, Eye of the Tiger, Commando Squad, Moon in Scorpio, Hell Comes to Frogtown, Maniac Cop, Red Nights, Nam, B.O.R.N., Action U.S.A., Deadly Breed, Evil Altar, Jungle Assault, L.A. Vice, Slow Burn, Terror in Beverly Hills, Hell on the Battleground, Forgotten Heroes, Instant Karma, Empire of Ash, Emperor of the Bronx, Rock n' Roll Cops, Broken Vessels.
TELEVISION: *Mini-Series*: Rich Man Poor Man. *Series*: Laredo, Rich Man Poor Man: Book II. *Series*: Laredo, Rich Man Poor Man: Book II, Hawaii 5-0, Wildside. *Movies*: The Over-the-Hill Gang, Crowhaven Farm, The Rockford Files (pilot), The Sex Symbol, Death Among Friends, Manhunter, The Rebels, Wild Times, The Jerk Too.

SMITROVICH, BILL
Actor. b. Bridgeport, CT, May 16, 1947. e. Univ. of Bridgeport, Smith Col. Studied acting at Actors and Directors Lab.
THEATER: *B'way*: The American Clock. *Off-B'way*: Never Say Die, Frankie and Johnny in the Claire de Lune, Seks. Regional: Requeim for a Heavyweight, Food from Trash, Of Mice and Men, The Love Suicide at Schofield Barracks.
PICTURES: A Little Sex, Without a Trace, Splash, Maria's Lovers, Key Exchange, Silver Bullet, Band of the Hand, Manhunter, A Killing Affair, Her Alibi, Renegades, Crazy People, Bodily Harm, The Phantom, The Trigger Effect, Independence Day, Air Force One, Around the Fire, Kiss Toledo Goodbye.
TELEVISION: *Series*: Crime Story, Life Goes On. *Guest*: Miami Vice, Millenium, L.A. Medical. *Movies*: Born Beautiful, Muggable Mary, Gregory K, Labor of Love: The Arlette Schweitzer Story, Children of the Dark, Texas Justice, Mr. Murder, Futuresport, The '60s.

SMITS, JIMMY
Actor. b. New York, NY, July 9, 1955. e. Brooklyn Coll., B.A.; Cornell U., M.F.A. Worked as community organizer before acting with NY Shakespeare Fest. Public Theater.
THEATER: Hamlet (NY Shakespeare Fest., 1983), Little Victories, Buck, The Ballad of Soapy Smith, Death and the Maiden.
PICTURES: Running Scared (debut, 1986), The Believers, Old Gringo, Vital Signs, Fires Within, Switch, Gross Misconduct, My Family/Mi Familia, Marshal Law, Murder in Mind, Lesser Prophets, The Million Dollar Hotel, Bless the Child, Price of Glory.
TELEVISION: *Series*: L.A. Law (Emmy Award, 1990), NYPD Blue (Golden Globe, 1996). *Pilot*: Miami Vice. *Movies*: Rockabye, The Highwayman, Dangerous Affection, Glitz, The Broken Cord, The Tommyknockers, The Cisco Kid, Solomon and Sheba, The Last Word. *Specials*: The Other Side of the Border (narrator), Happily Ever After Fairy Tales: Cinderella, Hispanic Americans: The New Frontier (host), The Story of the Western.

SMOTHERS BROTHERS
Comedians, Singers.
SMOTHERS, DICK: b. New York, NY, Nov. 20, 1939. e. San Jose State College. Films: The Silver Bears (debut, 1978), Casino.
SMOTHERS, TOM: b. New York, NY, Feb. 2, 1937. e. San Jose State College. In films Get to Know Your Rabbit, The Silver Bears, There Goes the Bride, Serial, Pandemonium.
Began career as coffeehouse folk singers with a bit of comic banter mixed in. After success at some of hipper West Coast clubs, appeared on Jack Paar's Tonight Show, The Jack Benny Show and as regulars on Steve Allen's show, 1961. 1962-65 had a series of popular albums. After starring in a situation comedy show, they hosted their own variety program. On B'way in musical I Love My Wife. Both appeared in film Speed Zone.
TELEVISION: *Series*: The Steve Allen Show (1961), The Smothers Brothers Show (1965-66), The Smothers Brothers Comedy Hour (1967-69), The Smothers Brothers Show (1970), The Smothers Brothers Show (1975), Fitz and Bones, The Smothers Brothers Comedy Hour. *Specials*: The Smothers Brothers Reunion.

SNELL, PETER R. E.
Producer. b. Nov. 17, 1941. Entered industry 1967. Appt. head of prod. and man. dir. British Lion 1973. Joined Robert Stigwood group 1975. Returned to indep. prod., 1978; Hennessy. Appt. chief exec., Britannic Film & Television Ltd. 1985, purchased British Lion Film Prods., Ltd. from Thorn/EMI 1986-87. 1988: chmn. and chief executive British Lion.
PICTURES: *Prod.*: Winters Tale, Some May Live, A Month in the Country, Carnaby 68, Subterfuge, Julius Caesar, Goodbye Gemini, Antony and Cleopatra, The Wicker Man, Hennessy, Bear Island, Mother Lode, Lady Jane, Turtle Diary, A Prayer for the Dying.

TELEVISION: *Exec. Prod.*: A Man For All Seasons, Tears in the Rain, Treasure Island, The Crucifer of Blood. *Prod.*: Death Train, Nightwatch.

SNIDER, STACEY
Executive. Co-President of production, Universal Pictures.

SNIPES, WESLEY
Actor. b. Bronx, NY, July 31, 1962. e. SUNY/Purchase. Performed with puppet theatre group called Struttin Street Stuff before landing NY stage work. Appeared in Michael Jackson video Bad.
THEATER: *B'way*: The Boys of Winter, Death and the King's Horsemen, Execution of Justice.
PICTURES: Wildcats (debut, 1986), Streets of Gold, Critical Condition, Major League, Mo' Better Blues, King of New York, New Jack City, Jungle Fever, White Men Can't Jump, The Waterdance, Passenger 57, Boiling Point, Rising Sun, Demolition Man, Sugar Hill, Drop Zone, To Wong Foo—Thanks for Everything—Julie Newmar, Money Train, Waiting to Exhale, The Fan, Murder at 1600, Down in the Delta, Blade (also prod.), U.S. Marshals, One Night Stand, The Art of War, Blade 2.
TELEVISION: *Series*: H.E.L.P. *Special*: Vietnam War Stories (ACE Award, 1989). *Guest*: Miami Vice. *Movies:* Futuresport.

SNODGRESS, CARRIE
Actress. b. Chicago, IL, Oct 27, 1945. e. Northern Illinois U. and M.A. degree from the Goodman Theatre. Plays include All Way Home, Oh What a Lovely War, Caesar and Cleopatra and Tartuffe (Sarah Siddons Award, 1966), The Price, Vanities, The Curse of the Starving Class.
PICTURES: Rabbit Run (debut, 1970), Diary of a Mad Housewife (Acad. Award nom.), The Fury, The Attic, Homework, Trick or Treats, A Night in Heaven, Pale Rider, Rainy Day Friends, Murphy's Law, Blueberry Hill, The Chill Factor, Nowhere to Run, Across the Tracks, The Ballad of Little Jo, 8 Seconds, Blue Sky, White Man's Burden.
TELEVISION: *Movies*: The Whole World Is Watching, Silent Night Lonely Night, The Impatient Heart, Love's Dark Ride, Fast Friends, The Solitary Man, Nadia, The Rose and the Jackal, Woman With a Past, Rise & Walk: The Dennis Byrd Story. *Guest*: The Outsider, The Virginian, Judd for the Defense, Medical Center, Marcus Welby, M.D.

SNOW, MARK
Composer. b. Brooklyn, NY, 1946. e. Juilliard School of Music, 1968. As co-founder and member of New York Rock 'n' Roll Ensemble, appeared with the Boston Pops, at Carnegie Hall concerts and on the college circuit in the 1960s and 1970s.
PICTURES: Skateboard, Something Short of Paradise, High Risk, Jake Speed, Born to Be Wild, The X-Files: Fight the Future, Disturbing Behavior, Crazy in Alabama.
TELEVISION: *Series*: The Rookies, Starsky and Hutch, The Gemini Man, Family, The San Pedro Beach Bums, The Love Boat, The Next Step Beyond, Vega$, Hart to Hart, When the Whistle Blows, Dynasty, Falcon Crest, Strike Force, Cagney and Lacey, T.J. Hooker, The Family Tree, Lottery!, Double Trouble, Crazy Like a Fox, Hometown, The X-Files, Millenium, La Femme Nikita, Harsh Realm. *Mini-series*: Blood and Orchids, Night Sins. *Movies*: The Boy in the Plastic Bubble, Overboard, The Return of the Mod Squad, Angel City, Games Mother Never Taught You, John Steinbeck's Winter of Our Discontent, Packin' It In, I Married a Centerfold, Something About Amelia, Challenge of a Lifetime, California Girls, I Dream of Jeannie: Fifteen Years Later, Not My Kid, The Lady From Yesterday, Beverly Hills Cowgirl Blues, Acceptable Risks, News at Eleven, The Girl Who Spelled Freedom (Emmy nom.), Murder By the Book, A Hobo's Christmas, The Father Clements Story, Still Crazy Like a Fox, Cracked Up, Roman Holiday, Pals, Murder Ordained, Louis L'Amour's Down the Long Hills, The Saint, The Return of Ben Casey, Bluegrass, Alone in the Neon Jungle, Those She Left Behind, Stuck With Each Other, Settle the Score, Archie: To Riverdale and Back Again, Child of the Night, Dead Reckoning, Follow Your Heart, The Girl Who Came Between Them, The Little Kidnappers, Miracle Landing, When He's Not a Stranger, Opposites Attract, Crash: The Mystery of Flight 1501, In the Line of Duty, The Marla Hanson Story, A Woman Scorned: The Betty Broderick Story, Highway Heartbreaker, Deliver Them From Evil: The Taking of Alta View, An American Story, Telling Secrets, The Man With 3 Wives, Born Too Soon, In the Line of Duty: Ambush in Waco, Precious Victims, Scattered Dreams: The Kathryn Messenger Story, In the Line of Duty: The Price of Heaven, Murder Between Friends, Moment of Truth: Cradle of Conspiracy, Substitute Wife, Down Out and Dangerous, Cloned, The Day Lincoln Was Shot, Le Dernier Combat, Mr. Murder, A Memory in My Heart *Specials*: Day-to-Day Affairs, Vietnam War Story.

SNYDER, BRUCE M.
Executive. b. New York, NY, July 1, 1946. e. Queens Coll. Began entertainment career with Paramount Pictures as a booker in San Francisco, 1968-69. Paramount sales, NY 1969-76. Became eastern div. mgr., 20th century Fox, 1976-80. New York sales mgr., American Cinema Releasing, 1980-82. Eastern div. mgr., Embassy Pictures, 1982-83. Eastern div. mgr., TriStar Pictures, 1984-85. General sales mgr., 20th Century Fox, 1985-89. Pres., domestic distribution, 20th Century Fox, 1989-present.

SNYDER, TOM
Newscaster, Host. b. Milwaukee, WI, May 12, 1936. e. Marquette U. First job in news dept. of WRIT, Milwaukee. Subsequently with WSAV-TV, Savannah; WAII-TV, Atlanta; KTLA-TV, Los Angeles; and KYW-TV, Philadelphia, before moving to KNBC in L.A. in 1970 as anchorman for weeknight newscast. Named host of NBC-TV's Tomorrow program in 1973 (Emmy Award), moved to NY in 1974, as anchorman of one-hour segment of NewsCenter 4. 1975, inaugurated the NBC News Update, one-minute weeknight prime time news spot. Host for Tomorrow talk show, Tom Snyder Show (ABC Radio), The Late Late Show With Tom Snyder.

SOADY, WILLIAM C.
Executive. b. Toronto, Canada, Oct. 7, 1943. Career with Universal Pictures started in 1970 when named Toronto branch mgr.; promoted to v.p. & gen. sls. mgr. of Universal Film (Canada) in 1971. Promoted to v.p. & gen. sls. mgr., Universal Pictures, 1981, in NY relocating to L.A. later that year. 1983 named pres. of Universal Pictures Distribution, new domestic dist. div. of Universal; resigned, 1988. Named exec. v.p. distrib., Tri-Star Pictures, 1988; pres. of distrib., 1992. Named pres. & CEO of Showscan Entertainment Inc. in 1994. Became pres. of distrib. for Polygram Films in 1997.

SOAMES, RICHARD
Executive. b. London, England, June 6, 1936. Joined Film Finances Ltd. 1972; Appt. director Film Finances Ltd., 1977: Appt. man. dir. 1979. Appt. pres. Film Finances Canada Ltd. 1982: Appt. pres., Film Finances Inc. Also formed Doric Prods, Inc.
PICTURES: The Boss's Wife, The Principal, Honey I Shrunk the Kids, Tap.

SOBIESKI, LEELEE
Actress. r.n. Liliane Rudabet Gloria Elsveta Sobieski. b. New York, NY, June 10, 1982.
PICTURES: Jungle 2 Jungle, A Soldier's Daughter Never Cries, Deep Impact, Never Been Kissed, Eyes Wide Shut, Here on Earth, Squelch, My First Mister, The Glass House.
TELEVISION: *Movies:* Reunion, A Horse for Danny, Joan of Arc. *Series:* Charlie Grace. *Guest:* F/X: The Series, NewsRadio.

SODERBERGH, STEVEN
Director, Writer, Editor. b. Atlanta, GA, Jan. 14, 1963. First major professional job was directing concert film for rock group Yes for Grammy-nominated video, 1986.
PICTURES: *Director-Editor*: Sex Lies and Videotape (debut, 1989; also s.p.; Cannes Fest. Palme d'Or Award; Acad. Award nom. for s.p.), Kafka, King of the Hill (also s.p.), The Underneath (also s.p.), Schizopolis (also actor), Gray's Anatomy, Out of Sight, The Limey, Erin Brockovich, Traffic, Ocean's Eleven. *Producer*: Suture (exec. prod.), The Day Trippers, Pleasantville.
TELEVISION: *Series*: Fallen Angels (The Quiet Room).

SOKOLOW, DIANE
Executive. b. New York, NY. e. Temple U. m. Mel Sokolow. 1975, v.p., East Coast operations, for Lorimar; with Warner Bros. 1977-81; served as v.p. of East Coast production. Left to form The Sokolow Co. with husband, Mel, to produce films. 1982, returned to WB as v.p., East Coast prod. 1984, joined Motown Prods. as exec. v.p.; producer, MGM-UA 1986-87. Currently S.V.P., East Coast Production, Phoenix Pictures.
PICTURE: My Son's Brother (co-prod.).
TELEVISION: *Exec. Prod.*: Miles from Nowhere, Trial: The Price of Passion, Lady Against the Odds, Fallen Champ, Silent Cries.

SOLO, ROBERT H.
Producer. b. Waterbury, CT, Dec. 4, 1932. e. U. of Connecticut, BA. Early career as agent with Ashley-Famous; later production as exec. asst. to Jack Warner and Walter MacEwen at Warner Bros. 1971, named WB v.p., foreign production 1974, named exec. v.p., prod. at Burbank Studio. Now indep. prod.
PICTURES: Scrooge, The Devils (co-prod.), Invasion of the Body Snatchers, The Awakening, I the Jury, Bad Boys, Colors, Above the Law (exec. prod.), Winter People, Blue Sky, Car 54 Where Are You?, Body Snatchers.

SOLONDZ, TODD
Director, Producer, Writer. b. Newark, NJ, October 15, 1959. e. NYU Film Sch. After first feature film release, left filmmaking to teach English as a Second Language. Returned with Welcome to the Dollhouse.
PICTURES: Feelings (NYU short), Babysitter (NYU short), Schatt's Last Shot (NYU short), Fear Anxiety and Depression, Married to the Mob (actor only), Welcome to the Dollhouse (Jury Prize, Sundance Film Fest.), Happiness. *Actor*: As Good as It Gets.
TELEVISION: How I Became a Leading Artistic Figure in New York City's East Village Cultural Landscape (short for Saturday Night Live).

SOLT, ANDREW W.
Producer, Writer, Director. b. London, England, December 13, 1947. e. UCLA.

PICTURES: Imagine: John Lennon, This is Elvis, It Came From Hollywood.
TELEVISION: Honeymooners' Reunion, The Muppets... A Celebration of 30 Years, Cousteau's Mississippi, Happy Birthday Donald Duck, America Censored, Remembering Marilyn, Great Moments in Disney Animation, ET & Friends, Disney's DTV, Heroes of Rock 'n Roll, Bob Hope's Christmas Tours, Disney Goes To The Oscars, Cousteau: Oasis In Space (series), Cousteau: Odyssey, Best of the Ed Sullivan Show (4 specials), The History of Rock 'n' Roll, Sesame Street's 25th Birthday Special, Grammy's Greatest Moments, TV Guide's 40th Anniversary Special, 25x5: The Continuing Adventures of the Rolling Stones, Andy Griffith Show Reunion, Cousteau: Search for Atlantis I&II, All My Children 25th Anniversary Special, Hunt for Amazing Treasure, Great Moments in Disney Animation.

SOMERS, SUZANNE
Actress. r.n. Suzanne Mahoney. b. San Bruno, CA, Oct. 16, 1946. e. Lone Mountain Sch., San Francisco Coll. for Women. Pursued modeling career; worked as regular on Mantrap, syndicated talk show. Did summer stock and theatrical films. *Author*: Touch Me Again, Keeping Secrets, Some People Live More Than Others, Wednesday's Children: Adult Survivors of Abuse Speak Out.
PICTURES: Bullitt (debut, 1968), Daddy's Gone A-Hunting, Fools, American Graffiti, Magnum Force, Yesterday's Hero, Nothing Personal, Serial Mom.
TELEVISION: *Series*: Three's Company, She's the Sheriff, Step by Step, The Suzanne Somers Show (talk). *Guest*: One Day at a Time, Lotsa Luck, The Rockford Files, Starsky & Hutch, The Rich Little Show, Battle of the Network Stars, Love Boat. *Movies*: Sky Heist, It Happened at Lakewood Manor (Ants), Happily Ever After, Zuma Beach, Rich Men Single Women, Keeping Secrets (also exec. prod.), Exclusive (also co-exec. prod), Seduced by Evil. *Mini-Series*: Hollywood Wives. *Specials*: Us Against the World, Suzanne, Suzanne Somers Presents: Showtime's Triple Crown of Comedy, Disney's Totally Minnie.

SOMMER, ELKE
Actress. r.n. Elke Schletz. b. Berlin, Germany, Nov. 5, 1940. Entered films in Germany, 1958.
PICTURES: Das Totenschiff (debut, 1958), Lampenfieber, The Day It Rained, Heaven and Cupid, Love the Italian Way, Why Bother to Knock? (English-language debut, 1961), Daniela by Night, Violent Ecstasy, Auf Wiedersehen, Cafe Oriental, Bahia de Palma, The Victors, Island of Desire, The Prize, Frontier Hellcat, Le Bambole (The Dolls), A Shot in the Dark, The Art of Love, The Money Trap, The Corrupt Ones, The Oscar, Boy Did I Get a Wrong Number, The Venetian Affair, Deadlier Than the Male, The Wicked Dreams of Paula Schultz, The Invincible Six, They Came to Rob Las Vegas, The Wrecking Crew, Baron Blood, Zeppelin, Percy, It's Not the Size That Counts (Percy's Progress), Ten Little Indians, The Swiss Conspiracy, Carry on Behind, House of Exorcism (Lisa and the Devil), Das Netz, The Astral Factor (Invisible Strangler), Thoroughbreds, I Miss You—Hugs and Kisses, The Prisoner of Zenda, A Nightingale Sang in Berkeley Square, The Double McGuffin, Exit Sunset Blvd., The Man in Pyjamas, Lily in Love, Death Stone, Himmelsheim, Neat and Tidy, Severed Ties.
TELEVISION: *Movies*: Probe, Stunt Seven, The Top of the Hill, Inside the Third Reich, Jenny's War, Anastasia: The Mystery of Anya. *Mini-Series*: Peter the Great.

SOMMER, JOSEF
Actor. b. Greifswald, Germany, June 26, 1934. Raised in North Carolina. e. Carnegie-Mellon U. Studied at American Shakespeare Festival in Stratford, CT, 1962-64. US Army, 1958-60. NY stage debut in Othello, 1970.
PICTURES: Dirty Harry (debut, 1971), Man on a Swing, The Front, Close Encounters of the Third Kind, Oliver's Story, Hide in Plain Sight, Absence of Malice, Reds, Rollover, Hanky Panky, Still of the Night, Sophie's Choice (narrator), Independence Day, Silkwood, Iceman, Witness, D.A.R.Y.L., Target, The Rosary Murders, Chances Are, Dracula's Widow, Forced March, Bloodhounds of Broadway, Shadows and Fog, The Mighty Ducks, Malice, Cultivating Charlie, Nobody's Fool, Strange Days, Moonlight & Valentino, The Chamber, The Proposition.
TELEVISION: *Series*: Hothouse, Under Cover. *Specials*: Morning Becomes Electra, The Scarlet Letter, Saigon. *Movies*: Too Far to Go, Doctor Franken, The Henderson Monster, Sparkling Cyanide, The Betty Ford Story, A Special Friendship, Bridge to Silence, The Bionic Showdown: The Six Million Dollar Man and the Bionic Woman, Money Power Murder, Spy Games, An American Story, Citizen Cohn, Hostages, The Enemy Within, Don't Drink the Water, The Minutes, Kansas, Letter to My Killer, Hidden in America, Mistrial, The Widenet. *Mini-Series*: The Kennedys of Massachusetts, A Woman Named Jackie.

SONDHEIM, STEPHEN
Composer, Lyricist. b. New York, NY, March 22, 1930. e. Williams Coll. Writer for Topper TV series, 1953. Wrote incidental music for The Girls of Summer (1956), Invitation to a March (1961), Twigs (1971). Winner of 6 Grammy Awards: Cast Albums 1970, 1973, 1979, 1984, 1988 and song of the year 1975. Named Visiting Prof. of Contemporary Theater, Oxford U. 1990.
THEATER: *Lyrics only:* West Side Story, Gypsy, Do I Hear a Waltz? *Music and lyrics*: A Funny Thing Happened on the Way to the Forum, Anyone Can Whistle, Company (Tony Award, 1971), Follies (Tony Award, 1972), A Little Night Music (Tony Award, 1973), The Frogs, Candide (new lyrics for revival), Pacific Overtures, Sweeney Todd, (Tony Award, 1979), Merrily We Roll Along, Sunday in the Park with George (Pulitzer Prize, 1985), Into the Woods (Tony Award, 1988), Assassins, Passion (Tony Award, 1994). Theater anthologies of his songs: Side By Side By Sondheim; Marry Me a Little, You're Gonna Love Tomorrow, Putting It Together. *Play:* Getting Away With Murder.
PICTURES: West Side Story (lyrics), Gypsy (lyrics), A Funny Thing Happened on the Way to the Forum (music, lyrics), The Last of Sheila (s.p.), Stavisky (score), A Little Night Music (music, lyrics), Reds (score), Dick Tracy (music, lyrics; Acad. Award for best song: Sooner or Later, 1990).
TELEVISION: *Special*: Evening Primrose (music, lyrics; ABC Stage '67).

SONNENFELD, BARRY
Director, Cinematographer. b. 1953. Received Emmy Award for photography on series Out of Step.
PICTURES: *Cinematographer:* Blood Simple (debut, 1984), Compromising Positions, Raising Arizona, Three O'Clock High, Throw Momma From the Train, Big, When Harry Met Sally..., Miller's Crossing, Misery. *Director:* The Addams Family (debut, 1991), For Love or Money (also co-prod.), Addams Family Values (also cameo), Get Shorty (also exec. prod.), Men in Black., Wild Wild West.
TELEVISION: *Movies*: Doubletake, Welcome Home Bobby, Classified Love.

SORVINO, MIRA
Actress. b. Tenafly, NJ, 1968. Father is actor Paul Sorvino. e. Harvard U., A.B., 1990.
PICTURES: Amongst Friends (also assoc. prod.), Quiz Show, Parallel Lives, Barcelona, Tarantella, Sweet Nothing, Mighty Aphrodite (Acad. Award, Golden Globe), The Dutch Master (short), The Second Greatest Story Ever Told (short), Blue in the Face, Tales of Erotica, New York Cop, Beautiful Girls, Romy and Michele's High School Reunion, Mimic, The Replacement Killers, Too Tired to Die, Lulu on the Bridge, Free Money, At First Sight, Summer of Sam, Joan of Arc: The Virgin Warrior, The Triumph of Love, The Grey Zone.
TELEVISION: *Movies*: Norma Jean and Marilyn, Jake's Women. *Series*: Swans Crossing. *Mini-series*: The Buccaneers.

SORVINO, PAUL
Actor. b. New York, NY, 1939. Daughter is actress Mira Sorvino.
THEATER: Bajour, An American Millionaire, The Mating Dance, King Lear, That Championship Season, Marlon Brando Sat Right Here.
PICTURES: Where's Poppa? (debut, 1970), The Panic in Needle Park, Made for Each Other, A Touch of Class, The Day of the Dolphin, The Gambler, Shoot It Black Shoot It Blue, I Will I Will... For Now, Oh God, Bloodbrothers, Slow Dancing in the Big City, The Brink's Job, Lost and Found, Cruising, Reds, I The Jury, That Championship Season, Off the Wall, Very Close Quarters, Turk 182, The Stuff, A Fine Mess, Vasectomy, Dick Tracy, GoodFellas, The Rocketeer, Life in the Food Chain (Age Isn't Everything), The Firm, Nixon, Romeo + Juliet, Money Talks, American Perfekt, Most Wanted, Bulworth, Knock Off, Harlem Aria, Goodnight Joseph Parker, Dead Broke.
TELEVISION: *Series*: We'll Get By, Bert D'Angelo: Superstar, The Oldest Rookie, Law and Order. *Mini-Series*: Seventh Avenue, Chiefs. *Movies*: Tell Me Where It Hurts, It Couldn't Happen to a Nicer Guy, Dummy, A Question of Honor, My Mother's Secret Life, With Intent to Kill, Surviving, Don't Touch My Daughter, The Case of the Wicked Wives, Parallel Lives, Without Consent, Joe Torre: Curveballs Along the Way, Houdini. *Guest*: Moonlighting, Murder She Wrote. *Special*: The Last Mile.

SOTHERN, ANN
Actress. r.n. Harriet Lake. b. Valley City, ND, Jan. 22, 1909. e. Washington U. p. Annette Yde-Lake, opera singer. In m.p. since 1927. Star of 10 Maisie movies in series from 1939-47. Has recently become noted painter.
PICTURES: Broadway Nights (debut in bit part, 1927), Hearts in Exile, The Show of Shows, Hold Everything, Whoopee, Doughboys, Broadway Through a Keyhole, Let's Fall in Love, Melody in Spring, The Party's Over, The Hellcat, Blind Date, Kid Millions, Folies Bergere, Eight Bells, Hooray for Love, The Girl Friend, Grand Exit, You May Be Next, Hell Ship Morgan, Don't Gamble With Love, My American Wife, Walking on Air, The Smartest Girl in Town, Dangerous Number, Fifty Roads to Town, There Goes My Girl, Super Sleuth, Danger: Love at Work, There Goes the Groom, She's Got Everything, Trade Winds, Hotel For Women, Maisie (and subsequent series of 9 other films), Fast and Furious, Joe and Ethel Turp Call on the President, Brother Orchid, Dulcy, Lady Be Good, Panama Hattie, Cry Havoc, Thousands Cheer, Three Hearts for Julia, April Showers, Words and Music, The Judge Steps Out, A Letter to Three Wives, Shadow on the Wall, Nancy Goes to Rio, The Blue Gardenia, Lady in a Cage, The Best Man, Sylvia,

Chubasco, The Killing Kind, Golden Needles, Crazy Mama, The Manitou, The Little Dragons, The Whales of August (Acad. Award. nom).
TELEVISION: *Series*: Private Secretary, The Ann Sothern Show, My Mother The Car (voice of the car). *Movies*: The Outsider, Congratulations It's a Boy, A Death of Innocence, The Weekend Nun, The Great Man's Whiskers, A Letter to Three Wives. *Mini-Series*: Captains and the Kings.

SOUL, DAVID
Actor. r.n. David Solberg. b. Chicago, IL, Aug. 28, 1943.
PICTURES: Johnny Got His Gun, Magnum Force, Dog Pound Shuffle, The Hanoi Hilton, Appointment with Death, Pentathalon.
TELEVISION: *Series*: Here Come the Brides, Owen Marshall-Counselor at Law, Starsky and Hutch, Casablanca, Yellow Rose, Unsub. *Movies*: The Disappearance of Flight 412, Starsky and Hutch (pilot), Little Ladies of the Night, Salem's Lot, Swan Song (also co-prod.), Rage, Homeward Bound, The Manions of America, World War III, Through Naked Eyes, The Fifth Missile, Harry's Hong Kong, In the Line of Duty: The FBI Murders, Prime Target, So Proudly We Hail, Bride in Black, A Cry in the Wild, The Taking of Peggy Ann, Perry Mason: The Case of the Fatal Framing, Grave Secrets: The Legacy of Hilltop Drive.

SPACEK, SISSY
Actress. r.n. Mary Elizabeth Spacek. b. Quitman, TX, Dec. 25, 1949. m. director Jack Fisk. Cousin of actor Rip Torn. Attended acting classes in New York under Lee Strasberg. Had bit role in Andy Warhol's Trash. Worked as set decorator on films Death Game, Phantom of the Paradise.
PICTURES: Prime Cut (debut, 1972), Ginger in the Morning, Badlands, Carrie, Welcome to L.A., 3 Women, Heart Beat, Coal Miner's Daughter (Acad. Award, 1980), Raggedy Man, Missing, The Man With Two Brains (voice), The River, Marie, Violets Are Blue, 'night Mother, Crimes of the Heart, The Long Walk Home, JFK, Hard Promises, Trading Mom, The Grass Harp, Affliction, Blast from the Past.
TELEVISION: *Movies*: The Girls of Huntington House, The Migrants, Katherine, A Private Matter, The Good Old Boys, If These Walls Could Talk. *Special*: Verna: USO Girl. *Guest*: The Rookies, The Waltons.

SPACEY, KEVIN
Actor. r.n. Kevin Spacey Fowler. b. South Orange, NJ, July 26, 1959. Raised in southern CA. e. L.A. Valley Coll., appearing in stage productions as well as stand-up comedy clubs, before attending Juilliard Sch. of Drama. Has appeared in numerous regional and repertory productions including Kennedy Center (The Seagull), Williamstown Theatre Fest. and Seattle Rep. Theatre, and with New York Shakespeare Fest.
THEATER: Henry IV Part I, The Robbers, Barbarians, Ghosts, Hurlyburly, Long Day's Journey into Night, National Anthems, Lost in Yonkers (Tony Award, 1991), Playland.
PICTURES: Heartburn (debut, 1986), Rocket Gibraltar, Working Girl, See No Evil Hear No Evil, Dad, A Show of Force, Henry and June, Glengarry Glen Ross, Consenting Adults, Iron Will, The Ref, Outbreak, Swimming With Sharks (also co-prod.), The Usual Suspects (Acad. Award, Chicago Film Critics Award), Seven, Albino Alligator (dir.), A Time to Kill, Looking for Richard, L.A. Confidential, Midnight in the Garden of Good and Evil, Hurly-burly, The Negotiator, A Bug's Life (voice), The Negotiator, Ordinary Decent Criminal, American Beauty, Pay It Forward, The Shipping News.
TELEVISION: *Specials*: Long Day's Journey into Night, Darrow, Steve McQueen: The King of Cool, Hitchcock: Shadow of a Genius. *Movies*: The Murder of Mary Phagan, Fall from Grace, When You Remember Me, Doomsday Gun. *Series*: Wiseguy, Tribeca. *Guest*: L.A. Law.

SPADE, DAVID
Actor. b. Birmingham, MI. Raised in Scottsdale, AZ. Performed stand-up comedy in clubs and colleges which led to debut on Saturday Night Live in 1990.
PICTURES: Light Sleeper (debut, 1982), Coneheads, Reality Bites, P.C.U., Tommy Boy, Black Sheep, 8 Heads in a Duffel Bag, Senseless, The Rugrats Movie (voice), Lost & Found (also s.p.), Loser, Little Nicky, The Emperor's New Groove, Joe Dirt.
TELEVISION: *Series*: Saturday Night Live, Just Shoot Me.

SPADER, JAMES
Actor. b. Boston, MA, Feb. 7, 1960. e. Phillips Academy. Studied acting at Michael Chekhov Studio.
PICTURES: Endless Love (debut, 1981), The New Kids, Tuff Turf, Pretty in Pink, Mannequin, Baby Boom, Less Than Zero, Wall Street, Jack's Back, The Rachel Papers, Sex Lies and Videotape (Cannes Fest. Award, 1989), Bad Influence, White Palace, True Colors, Storyville, Bob Roberts, The Music of Chance, Dream Lover, Wolf, Stargate, 2 Days in the Valley, Crash, Critical Care, Curtain Call, Supernova.
TELEVISION: *Series*: The Family Tree. *Movies*: Cocaine: One Man's Seduction, A Killer in the Family, Starcrossed, Family Secrets, Keys to Tulsa.

SPANO, VINCENT
Actor. b. New York, NY, Oct. 18, 1962. While attending Stuyvesant H.S. made stage debut at 14 in The Shadow Box (Long Wharf and B'way).
THEATER: The Shadow Box, Balm in Gilead.
PICTURES: Over the Edge (debut, 1979), The Double McGuffin, The Black Stallion Returns, Baby It's You, Rumblefish, Alphabet City, Maria's Lovers, Creator, Good Morning Babylon, And God Created Woman, 1753: Venetian Red, High Frequency (Aquarium), Oscar, City of Hope, Alive, Indian Summer, The Ascent, The Tie That Binds, A Brooklyn State of Mind, The Unknown Cyclist.
TELEVISION: *Series*: Search for Tomorrow. *Movies*: The Gentleman Bandit, Senior Trip, Blood Ties, Afterburn.

SPEARS, JR., HAROLD T.
Executive. b. Atlanta, GA, June 21, 1929. e. U. of Georgia, 1951. With Floyd Theatres, Lakeland, FL, since 1953; now pres. Pres., Sun South Theatres, Inc., 1996.

SPECKTOR, FREDERICK
Executive. b. Los Angeles, CA, April 24, 1933. e. USC, UCLA. M.P. agent, Ashley Famous Agency, 1962-64; Artists Agency Corp., 1964-68; exec. M.P. dept., William Morris Agency, 1968-78; exec. Creative Artists Agency, 1978-present. Trustees Council, Education First, bd. of dirs., Amer. Jewish Committee. Bd. of dirs. for the ACLU and Center for Gun-Violence Prevention.

SPEEDMAN, SCOTT
Actor. b. London, England, Sept. 1, 1975.
PICTURES: Ursa Major, Kitchen Party, Duets.
TELEVISION: *Movies:* Net Worth, A Brother's Promise: The Dan Jansen Story, Giant Mine, Rescuers Stories of Courage: Two Couples, Dead Silence, What Happened to Bobby Earl?, Every 9 Seconds. *Series:* Nancy Drew, Felicity. *Guest:* Kung Fu: The Legend Continues, Goosebumps.

SPELLING, AARON
Executive. b. Dallas, TX, April 22, 1928. e. SMU. Daughter is actress Tori Spelling. Was actor/writer before becoming producer at Four Star in 1957. Won Harvard Award for Best Original One-act Play. Producer of series and tv movies: 1967, formed Thomas/Spelling Productions; 1969, formed his own co., Aaron Spelling Productions; 1972, partnered with Leonard Goldberg. Chairman/CEO Spelling TV, Inc. Produced so far over 111 movies for television. Winston Churchill Medal of Wisdom, 1988. Special People's Choice Award, 1992.
PICTURES: *Exec Prod.:* Mr. Mom, Surrender, Three O'Clock High, Cross My Heart, Satisfaction (co-prod.), Loose Cannons, Soapdish, The Mod Squad.
TELEVISION: *Exec. Prod./Prod.: Series*: The Mod Squad, The Rookies, Charlie's Angels, Fantasy Island, Starsky and Hutch, Hart to Hart, T.J. Hooker, Family, The Love Boat, Vega$, Dynasty, Matt Houston, Hotel, The Colbys, Life with Lucy, Nightingales, HeartBeat, Beverly Hills 90210, The Heights, Melrose Place, The Round Table, Winnetka Road, 7th Heaven, Sunset Beach, Pacific Palisades, The Love Boat: The Next Wave, Buddy Faro, Charmed, Safe Harbor. *Movies:* The Over-the-Hill Gang, Wake When the War Is Over, The Monk, The Pigeon, The Ballad of Andy Crocker, Say Goodbye Maggie Cole, Rolling Man, Shooting Stars, Dark Mirror, Making of a Male Model, The Three Kings, Nightingales, Day One (Emmy Award, 1989), Rich Men Single Women, The Love Boat: The Valentine Voyage, Jailbirds, Back to the Streets of San Francisco, Grass Roots, Terror on Track 9, A Stranger in the Mirror, And the Band Played On (Emmy Award, 1994), Jane's House, Green Dolphin Beat, Satan's School for Girls.

SPELLING, TORI
Actress. r.n. Victoria Davey Spelling. b. Los Angeles, CA, May 16, 1973. Father is prod. Aaron Spelling.
PICTURES: Troop Beverly Hills, The House of Yes, Scream 2, Perpetrators of the Crime, Trick.
TELEVISION: *Movies:* Shooting Stars, Beverly Hills 90210 (pilot), A Friend to Die For, Awake to Murder, Mother May I Sleep with Danger, Deadly Pursuits, Co-ed Call Girl. *Series:* Saved by the Bell, Beverly Hills 90210. *Guest:* Vega$, Fantasy Island, The Love Boat, T.J. Hooker, Hotel, Blossom, Parker Lewis Can't Lose, Burke's Law, Melrose Place, Malibu Shores.

SPENGLER, PIERRE
Producer. b. Paris, France, 1947. Went on stage at 15; returned to language studies at Alliance Franccaise. Entered film industry as production runner and office boy. Teamed for first time with friend Ilya Salkind on The Light at the Edge of the World, produced by Alexander Salkind.
PICTURES: Bluebeard, The Three Musketeers, The Four Musketeers, Crossed Swords, Superman, Superman II, Superman III, Santa Claus: The Movie, The Return of the Musketeers (tv in U.S.).

SPHEERIS, PENELOPE
Director. b. New Orleans, LA, 1945. e. UCLA. Film Sch., MFA.
PICTURES: Real Life (prod. only). *Director*: The Decline of Western Civilization (also prod., s.p.), Suburbia (also s.p.), The Boys Next Door, Summer Camp Nightmare (s.p. only), Hollywood Vice Squad, Dudes, The Decline of Western Civilization-Part II: The Metal Years, Wedding Band (actress only), Wayne's World, The Beverly Hillbillies, The Little Rascals, Black Sheep, The Decline of Western Civilization Part III: Gutterpunks, Senseless.
TELEVISION: Saturday Night Live (prod. only), Danger Theatre (co-creator, dir., co-writer). *Movie*: Prison Stories: Women on the Inside (New Chicks), Applewood 911 (dir.).

SPIEGEL, LARRY
Producer, Writer, Director. b. Brooklyn, NY. e. Ohio U. With CBS-TV; Benton & Bowles; Wells, Rich, Green; BBDO. Now heads Appledown Films, Inc.
PICTURES: Hail (s.p.), Book of Numbers (s.p.), Death Game (prod.), Stunts (prod.), Spree (dir., s.p.), Phobia (prod.), Remo Williams: The Adventure Begins (prod.), Dove Against Death (prod.), The Sunchaser (prod.).
TELEVISION: *ABC Afterschool Specials*, Bear That Slept Through Christmas (writer), Never Fool With A Gypsy Ikon (writer), Planet of The Apes (animated; writer), Jan Stephenson Golf Video (prod.), Remo Williams (pilot ABC; prod.).

SPIELBERG, STEVEN
Director, Producer. b. Cincinnati, OH, Dec. 18, 1947. e. California State Coll. m. actress Kate Capshaw. Made home movies as child; completed first film with story and actors at 12 yrs. old in Phoenix. At 13 won film contest for 40-min. war movie, Escape to Nowhere. At 16 made 140-min. film, Firelight. At California State Coll. made five films. First professional work, Amblin', 20 min. short which led to signing contract with Universal Pictures at age 20. Formed own co. Amblin Entertainment, headquartered at Universal Studios. Received Irving G. Thalberg Memorial Award, 1987; American Film Institute Life Achievement Award, 1995. Parterned with David Geffen and Jeffrey Katzenberg formed film company DreamWorks, 1995.
PICTURES: *Director*: The Sugarland Express (debut, 1974; also story), Jaws, Close Encounters of The Third Kind (also s.p.; Acad. Award nom. for dir.), 1941, Raiders of the Lost Ark (Acad. Award nom.), E.T. The Extra-Terrestrial (also co-prod.; Acad. Award noms. for dir. & picture), Twilight Zone—The Movie (sequence dir.; also exec. prod.), Indiana Jones and the Temple of Doom, The Color Purple (also co-prod.; Acad. Award nom. for picture), Empire of the Sun (also co-prod.), Indiana Jones and the Last Crusade, Always (also co-prod.), Hook, Jurassic Park, Schindler's List (also co-prod.; Acad. Awards for Best Director & Picture, 1993; DGA, Golden Globe & Natl. Society of Film Critics Awards for director; NY Film Critics, LA Film Critics, Natl. Board of Review. Natl. Society of Film Critics & Golden Globe Awards for picture), The Lost World: Jurassic Park, Amistad (also prod.), Saving Private Ryan (also prod.; Acad. Award for Best Director), The Unfinished Journey, A.I., Minority Report. *Co-exec. prod.*: I Wanna Hold Your Hand, Used Cars, Continental Divide (exec. prod.), Poltergeist (co-prod., co-s.p.), Gremlins (also cameo), The Goonies (also story), Back to the Future, Young Sherlock Holmes, The Money Pit, An American Tail, Innerspace, Batteries Not Included, Who Framed Roger Rabbit, The Land Before Time, Dad, Back to the Future Part II, Joe Versus the Volcano, Back to the Future Part III, Gremlins 2: The New Batch, Arachnophobia, Cape Fear, An American Tail: Fievel Goes West (co-prod.), We're Back!: A Dinosaur's Story, The Flintstones, The Little Rascals, Casper (co-prod.), The Bridges of Madison County (co-prod.), Men in Black, Deep Impact (also cameo), The Last Days, The Mask of Zorro, Gladiator. *Actor only:* The Blues Brothers, Listen Up: The Lives of Quincy Jones.
TELEVISION: *Series episodes* (dir.): Columbo, Owen Marshall: Counsellor-at-Law, The Pyschiatrist, Toonsylvania. *Movies* (dir.): Night Gallery (episode dir.), Duel, Something Evil, Savage. *Exec. prod.*: Amazing Stories (series; also dir. of 2 episodes), Tiny Toon Adventures (series; Emmy Award, 1991), Class of '61 (movie), Family Dog (series), seaQuest DSV (series), Pinky and the Brain (series), Band of Brothers (mini-series).

SPIKINGS, BARRY
Executive. b. Boston, England, Nov. 23, 1939. Ent. m.p. ind. 1973. Joint man. dir. British Lion Films Ltd., 1975. Appt. jnt. man. dir. EMI Films Ltd., 1977. 1979, appt. chmn. & chief exec., EMI Film & Theatre Corp.; chmn. & chief exec, EMI Films, Ltd., chmn. EMI Cinemas, Ltd.; chmn., Elstree Studios, Ltd.; chmn. EMI-TV Programs, Inc., 1980; appt. chmn. chief exec., EMI Films Group, 1982; 1985 Barry Spikings Productions Inc. (U.S.A.); 1985 became director Galactic Films Inc. (with Lord Anthony Rufus Issacs); 1986, acquired Embassy Home Entertainment from Coca Cola Co., renamed Nelson Entertainment Inc., appointed pres. and COO. 1992, Pleskow/Spikings Partnership, film prod. and distrib. partnership with Eric Pleskow.
PICTURES: *Prod.*: Conduct Unbecoming, The Man Who Fell to Earth, The Deer Hunter, Texasville, Beyond Rangoon. *Exec. prod.*: Convoy.

SPINELLA, STEPHEN
Actor.
THEATER: Angels in America: Millenium Approaches (Tony award), Angels in America: Perestroika (Tony award).
PICTURES: Tarantella, Virtuosity, Faithful, The Unknown Cyclist, Love! Valour! Compassion!, The Jackal, Ravenous, Out of the Past (voice), Great Expectations, David Searching.

SPINER, BRENT
Actor. b. Houston, TX. Recorded album Ol' Yellow Eyes Is Back.
THEATER: *NY:* The Seagull, The Three Musketeers, Sunday in the Park With George, Big River.
PICTURES: Stardust Memories, The Miss Firecracker Contest, Corrina Corrina, Star Trek: Generations, Independence Day, Phenomenon, Star Trek: First Contact, Out to Sea, Trekkies, Star Trek: Insurrection, South Park: Bigger Longer and Uncut (voice), Geppetto.
TELEVISION: *Series:* Star Trek: The Next Generation. Movie: Introducing Dorothy Dandridge

SPINETTI, VICTOR
Actor. b. South Wales, Sept. 2, 1933. e. Monmouth School. Entered industry in 1955. Appeared on Broadway in Oh! What a Lovely War winning 1965 Tony and Theatre World Awards.
THEATER: *London*: Expresso Bongo, Candide, Make Me an Offer, Oh What a Lovely War (also B'way), The Odd Couple, Cat Among the Pigeons.
PICTURES: A Hard Day's Night, The Wild Affair, Help!, The Taming of the Shrew, The Biggest Bundle of Them All, Can Hieronymous Merkin Ever Forget Mercy Humppe and Find True Happiness?, Under Milk Wood, The Little Prince, The Return of the Pink Panther, Under the Cherry Moon, The Krays, The Princess and the Goblin (voice).
TELEVISION: The Magical Mystery Tour, Vincent Van Gogh, Paradise Club, The Attic.

SPINOTTI, DANTE
Cinematographer. b. Tolmezzo, Italy, Aug. 22, 1943.
PICTURES: La Disubbidienza, Cinderella '80, Hearts and Armour, Sogno di una notte di meza estate, Softly Softly, Cosi parlo Bellavista, The Berlin Affair, The Dark Side of Love, Manhunter, Crimes of the Heart, Choke Canyon, From the Hip, The Legend of the Holy Drinker (actor), Illegally Yours, Fair Game, Beaches, Torrents of Spring, A Violent Life, The Comfort of Strangers, True Colors, Hudson Hawk, Frankie and Johnny, The Last of the Mohicans, The Secret of the Old Woods, The End Is Known, Blink, Nell, The Quick and the Dead, The Star Maker, Heat, The Mirror Has Two Faces, L.A. Confidential (LA Film Crits. Award, Best Cinematography, 1997), Goodbye Lover, Man of the People.
TELEVISION: Basileus Quartet.

SPIRA, STEVEN S.
Executive. b. New York, NY, March 25, 1955. e. City Coll. of New York; Benjamin Cardozo Sch. of Law. Associated 10 years with N.Y. law firm, Monasch Chazen & Stream. 1984, joined 20th Century Fox as sr. counsel; 1985, to Warner Bros. Now exec. v.p., theatrical business affairs, Warner Bros.

SPODICK, ROBERT C.
Exhibitor. b. New York, NY, Dec. 3, 1919. e. CCNY, 1940; ent. NYC m.p. ind. as errand boy Skouras Park Plaza, Bronx 1932-33; reel boy, asst. mgr., Loew's Theatres; mgr., Little Carnegie and other art theatres; exploitation man, United Artists.
Acquired Lincoln, New Haven art house in 1945 in partnership with cousin Leonard E. Sampson; developed Nutmeg Theatre circuit, which was sold in 1968 to Robert Smerling. Beginning in 1970, built Groton, CT., Cinemas I and II; Norwich Cinemas I and II, Mystic Village Cinemas I, II and III, and Westerley Triple Cinemas in RI as Gemini Cinema Circuit in partnership with Sampson and William Rosen. Gemini sold to Interstate Theatres, 1986. With Sampson presently operates York Square I & II and The New Lincoln in New Haven. Pres., Allied of CT, 1962-64; Pres. NATO of Conn. 1968-73. Past Chmn. Exec. Comm., CT Ass'n of Theatre Owners, and still active member of Board of Directors in 1997.

SPOTTISWOODE, ROGER
Director. b. England. Film editor of TV commercials and documentaries before turning to direction.
PICTURES: *Editor*: Straw Dogs, The Getaway, Pat Garrett and Billy the Kid, Hard Times, The Gambler; Who'll Stop the Rain? (assoc. prod.), Baby: Secret of the Lost Legend (exec. prod.). *Director:* Terror Train (debut, 1980), The Pursuit of D.B. Cooper, Under Fire, The Best of Times, Shoot to Kill, Turner & Hooch, Air America, Stop Or My Mom Will Shoot.
TELEVISION: *Movies*: The Renegades, The Last Innocent Man, Third Degree Burn, And the Band Played On, Hiroshima. *Special*: Time Flies When You're Alive.

SPRADLIN, G.D.
Actor. b. Daylight Township, Garvin County, OK, Aug. 31, 1920. e. Univ. of Oklahoma-doctor of Juris Prudence (1948). Started career as lawyer, became Independent Oil Producer. Active in local politics before turning to acting. Joined Oklahoma Repertory Theatre in 1964.
PICTURES: Will Penny (debut, 1968), Number One, Zabriskie Point, Monte Walsh, Tora! Tora! Tora!, The Hunting Party, The Godfather Part II, MacArthur, One on One, North Dallas Forty, Apocalypse Now, The Formula, Wrong Is Right, The Lords of Discipline, Tank, The War of the Roses, Clifford, Ed Wood, Canadian Bacon, Nick of Time, The Long Kiss Goodnight, Dick.
TELEVISION: *Series*: Rich Man Poor Man Book II. *Mini-Series*: Space, Dream West, Nutcracker: Money Madness and Murder, Robert Kennedy and His Times, War and Remembrance. *Movies*: Dial Hot Line, Sam Hill: Who Killed the Mysterious Mr. Foster?, Oregon Trail, Maneaters Are Loose!, And I Alone Survived, Jayne Mansfield Story, Resting Place, Shoot First: A Cop's Vengeance, Telling Secrets, Riders of the Purple Sage.

SPRINGER, PAUL D.
Executive. e. Brooklyn Law Sch. Served as assoc. for NY law firm, Johnson & Tannebaum. Later with legal dept. of Columbia Pics. 1970, joined Paramount Pictures N.Y. legal dept. 1970; promoted to v.p. Theatrical Distrib. Counsel, 1979; promoted to sr. v.p., chief resident counsel, 1987; promoted to sr. v.p., asst. general counsel responsible for all legal functions for Paramount's distribution and marketing depts. Mem., NY and California Bars.

SPRINGFIELD, RICK
Actor, Singer, Songwriter. b. Sydney, Australia, Aug. 23, 1949.
PICTURES: Battlestar Galactica, Hard to Hold (act., addl. music).
TELEVISION: *Series*: General Hospital, Human Target, High Tide. *Specials*: An Evening at the Improv, Countdown '81. *Movies*: Nick Knight, Dead Reckoning, In the Shadows Someone's Watching.

SQUIRES, BUDDY
Cinematographer.
PICTURES: Brooklyn Bridge (also prod.), Huey Long, The Statue of Liberty (Acad. Award nom.), The Donner Party, High Lonesome: The Story of Bluegrass Music, Out of the Past, Frank Lloyd Wright.
TELEVISION: *Mini-series*: The Civil War, Baseball, The West, Lewis & Clark, The Irish in America: Long Journey Home.

STACK, ROBERT
Actor. b. Los Angeles, CA, Jan. 13, 1919. e. U. of Southern California. In U.S. Armed Forces (Navy), W.W.II. Studied acting at Henry Duffy School of Theatre 6 mo. then signed a contract with Universal. National skeet champion at age 16. Autobiography: Straight Shooting (1980).
PICTURES: First Love (debut, 1939), When the Daltons Rode, The Mortal Storm, A Little Bit of Heaven, Nice Girl?, Badlands of Dakota, To Be or Not To Be, Eagle Squadron, Men of Texas, Fighter Squadron, A Date With Judy, Miss Tatlock's Millions, Mr. Music, The Bullfighter and the Lady, My Outlaw Brother, Bwana Devil, War Paint, Conquest of Cochise, Sabre Jet, The Iron Glove, The High and the Mighty, House of Bamboo, Good Morning Miss Dove, Great Day in the Morning, Written on the Wind (Acad. Award nom.), The Gift of Love, The Tarnished Angels, John Paul Jones, The Last Voyage, The Caretakers, Is Paris Burning?, The Corrupt Ones, Action Man, Story of a Woman, A Second Wind, 1941, Airplane!, Uncommon Valor, Big Trouble, Transformers (voice), Plain Clothes, Caddyshack II, Dangerous Curves, Joe Versus the Volcano, Beavis and Butt-Head Do America (voice), BASEketball (cameo), Totally Irresponsible, Top Speed (cameo), Mumford (cameo).
TELEVISION: *Series*: The Untouchables (Emmy Award, 1960), The Name of the Game, Most Wanted, Strike Force, Unsolved Mysteries (host), Final Appeal (host), Hercules (voice). *Guest*: Playhouse 90 (Panic Button). *Movies*: The Strange and Deadly Occurance, Adventures of the Queen, Murder on Flight 502, Most Wanted (pilot), Undercover With the KKK (narrator), Midas Valley, Perry Mason: The Case of the Sinister Spirit, The Return of Eliot Ness. *Mini-Series*: George Washington, Hollywood Wives.

STAHL, AL
Executive. b. July 3, 1916. Syndicated newspaper cartoonist; asst. animator, Max Fleischer, gag ed. Terrytoons; U.S. Signal Corps; opened own studios, 1946; prod. first animated TV cartoon show; pres., Animated Prod., prod. live and animated commercials; member of bd. NTFC. Developed and built first animation camera and stand, 1950. Designed and produced opening animation for The Honeymooners, The Electric Company, Saturday Night Live. Produced over 5,000 tv spots. Prod. 50 min. documentary War and Pieces for U.S. Army Commandy of War in the Gulf, 1991.

STAHL, NICK
Actor. b. Dallas, TX, 1980. Started acting at age 4.
PICTURES: The Man Without a Face, Safe Passage, Tall Tale, Eye of God, The Thin Red Line, Disturbing Behavior.
TELEVISION: *Movies*: Stranger at My Door, Woman With a Past, Incident in a Small Town, My Son Is Innocent, Seasons of Love.

STALLONE, SYLVESTER
Actor, Writer, Director. b. New York, NY, July 6, 1946. After high school taught at American Coll. of Switzerland instructing children of career diplomats, young royalty, etc. Returned to U.S. in 1967 and studied drama at U. of Miami, 1969. Came to New York to seek acting career, taking part-time jobs, including usher for Walter Reade Theatres. Then turned to writing, selling several TV scripts.
PICTURES: *Actor:* Party at Kitty and Studs (debut, 1970), Bananas, Rebel (A Man Called Rainbo), The Lords of Flatbush (also co-s.p.), The Prisoner of 2nd Avenue, Capone, Death Race 2000, Farewell My Lovely, Cannonball, Rocky (also s.p.; Acad. Award noms. for actor & s.p.), F.I.S.T. (also co-s.p.), Paradise Alley (also s.p., dir.), Rocky II (also s.p., dir.), Nighthawks, Victory, Rocky III (also s.p., dir.), First Blood (also co-s.p.), Staying Alive (cameo; also dir., prod., co-s.p.), Rhinestone (also co-s.p.), Rambo: First Blood Part II (also co-s.p.), Rocky IV (also dir., s.p.), Cobra (also s.p.), Over the Top (also co-s.p.), Rambo III (also co-s.p.), Lock Up, Tango and Cash, Rocky V (also s.p.), Oscar, Stop Or My Mom Will Shoot, Cliffhanger (also co-s.p.), Demolition Man, The Specialist, Judge Dredd, Assassins, Daylight, Cop Land, Antz (voice), Get Carter, Eye See You, Driven.
TELEVISION: *Guest*: Kojak, Police Story, Dream On.

STAMOS, JOHN
Actor. b. Cypress, CA, Aug. 19, 1963. m. model Rebecca Romijn Stamos. Landed role of Blackie Parrish on daytime serial General Hospital in 1982. Has toured with his own band John Stamos and the Bad Boyz.
THEATER: *B'way*: How to Succeed in Business Without Really Trying.
PICTURES: Never Too Young to Die, Born to Ride, Private Parts.
TELEVISION: *Series*: General Hospital, Dreams, You Again?, Full House. *Movies*: Daughter of the Streets, Captive, The Disappearance of Christina, Fatal Vows: The Alexandra O'Hara Story, A Match Made in Heaven.

STAMP, TERENCE
Actor. b. London, England, July 23, 1938. Stage experience including Alfie on Broadway. Recent stage: Dracula, The Lady from the Sea, Airborne Symphony. *Autobiography:* Coming Attractions (1988).
PICTURES: Billy Budd (debut 1962; Acad. Award nom.), Term of Trial, The Collector (Cannes Film Fest. Award, 1965), Modesty Blaise, Far from the Madding Crowd, Poor Cow, Blue, Teorema, Spirits of the Dead, The Mind of Mr. Soames, A Season in Hell, Hu-Man, The Divine Nymph, Strip-Tease, Superman, Meetings with Remarkable Men, Together?, Superman II, Monster Island, Death in the Vatican, The Hit, The Company of Wolves, Link, Legal Eagles, The Sicilian, Wall Street, Young Guns, Alien Nation, Stranger in the House (also dir., co-s.p.), Genuine Risk, Beltenebros, The Real McCoy, The Adventures of Priscilla--Queen of the Desert, Mindbender, Limited Edition, Bliss, Kiss the Sky, Love Walked In, The Limey, Bowfinger, Star Wars: Episode I-The Phantom Menace.
TELEVISION: *Movie*: The Thief of Bagdad.

STANFILL, DENNIS C.
Executive. b. Centerville, TN, April 1, 1927. e. Lawrenceburg H.S.; U.S. Naval Acad., B.S., 1949; Oxford U. (Rhodes Scholar), M.A., 1953; U. of S. Carolina, L.H.D. (hon.). Corp. finance specialist, Lehman Bros 1959-65; v.p. finance, Times Mirror Company, Los Angeles, 1965-69; exec. v.p. finance, 20th C.-Fox Film Corp., 1969-71, pres., 1971, chmn. bd./CEO, 1971-81; pres., Stanfill, Bowen & Co., venture capital firm, 1981-90; chmn. bd./CEO, AME, Inc., 1990-92; co-chmn. bd./co-CEO, MGM, 1992-93. Sr. advisor to Credit Lyonnais, 1993-95. Private Investments, 1995-.

STANG, ARNOLD
Performer, b. Chelsea, MA, Sept. 28, 1927. Radio, 1935-50; on B'way, in five plays and in m.p. and short subjects; guest appearances on TV shows. Much voice-over cartoon work. Starred in 36 shorts.
TELEVISION: *Series*: School House, Henry Morgan Show, Doc Corkle, Top Cat (voice), Broadside. *Guest*: Captain Video, Milton Berle, Danny Thomas, Perry Como, Ed Sullivan, Red Skelton, Frank Sinatra, Wagon Train, Jack Benny, Johnny Carson, December Bride, Playhouse 90, Batman, Bonanza, Bob Hope, Danny Kaye, Jackie Gleason, Emergency, Feeling Good, Chico & the Man, Super Jaws & Catfish, Busting Loose, Flying High, Robert Klein Specials, Tales from the Dark Side, True Blue, Cosby Show.
PICTURES: Seven Days Leave, My Sister Eileen, Let's Go Steady, They Got Me Covered, So This is New York, Double for Della, Return of Marco Polo, Spirit of '76, The Man with the Golden Arm, Dondi, The Wonderful World of the Brothers Grimm, It's a Mad Mad Mad Mad World, Pinocchio in Outer Space (voice), Alakazam the Great (voice), Hello Down There,

Skidoo, The Aristocats (voice), Raggedy Ann & Andy (voice), Gang That Couldn't Shoot Straight, That's Life, Hercules in New York, Ghost Dad, Dennis the Menace, At The Cottonwood.

STANLEY, KIM
Actress. r.n. Patricia Reid. b. Tularosa, NM, Feb. 11, 1925. e. U. of NM. Began stage acting in college and later in stock. Worked as model in NY while training with Elia Kazan and Lee Strasberg at Actors Studio. In late 1960s and 1970s taught drama, Coll. of Santa Fe, NM.
THEATER: The Dog, Beneath the Skin (NY debut, 1948), Him, Yes Is For a Very Young Man, Montserrat, The House of Bernarda Alba, The Chase, Picnic (NY Drama Critics Award, 1953), The Traveling Lady, The Great Dreamer, Bus Stop, A Clearing in the Woods, A Touch of the Poet, A Far Country, Natural Affection, The Three Sisters.
PICTURES: The Goddess (debut, 1958), Seance on a Wet Afternoon (Acad. Award nom.), The Three Sisters, Frances (Acad. Award nom.), The Right Stuff.
TELEVISION: *Specials*: Clash by Night, The Travelling Lady, Cat on a Hot Tin Roof (Emmy Award, 1985). *Movie*: U.M.C. *Guest*: Ben Casey (A Cardinal Act of Mercy; Emmy Award, 1963).

STANTON, HARRY DEAN
Actor. b. West Irvine, KY, July 14, 1926. Acting debut at Pasadena Playhouse. Billed in early film appearances as Dean Stanton.
PICTURES: Revolt at Fort Laramie (debut, 1957), Tomahawk Trail, The Proud Rebel, Pork Chop Hill, The Adventures of Huckleberry Finn, A Dog's Best Friend, Hero's Island, The Man From the Diner's Club, Ride in the Whirlwind, The Hostage, A Time for Killing, Rebel Rousers, Cool Hand Luke, Day of the Evil Gun, The Miniskirt Mob, Kelly's Heroes, Cisco Pike, Two-Lane Blacktop, Face to the Wind (Cry for Me Billy), Pat Garrett and Billy the Kid, Dillinger, Where the Lilies Bloom, Cockfighter, Zandy's Bride, The Godfather Part II, Rafferty and the Gold Dust Twins, Rancho Deluxe, Farewell My Lovely, 92 in the Shade, Win Place or Steal, The Missouri Breaks, Straight Time, Renaldo and Clara, Alien, The Rose, Wise Blood, Death Watch, The Black Marble, Private Benjamin, Escape From New York, One From the Heart, Young Doctors in Love, Christine, Repo Man, Red Dawn, The Bear, Paris Texas, The Care Bears Movie (voice), One Magic Christmas, Fool for Love, UFOria, Pretty in Pink, Slamdance, Stars and Bars, Mr. North, The Last Temptation of Christ, Dream a Little Dream, Twister, The Fourth War, Stranger in the House, Wild at Heart, Man Trouble, Twin Peaks: Fire Walk With Me, Blue Tiger, Never Talk to Strangers, Down Periscope, She's So Lovely, Fire Down Below, The Mighty, Fear and Loathing in Las Vegas, The Straight Story, The Green Mile.
TELEVISION: *Movies*: Flatbed Annie & Sweetpie: Lady Truckers, I Want to Live, Payoff, Hostages, Against the Wall. *Special*: Hotel Room (Tricks).

STAPLETON, JEAN
Actress. r.n. Jeanne Murray. b. New York, NY. e. Wadleigh H.S. Summer stock in NH, ME, MA, and PA. Broadway debut in In the Summer House (1954). Chair, Advisory bd., Women's Research and Education Inst. (Wash., D.C.); bd.: Eleanor Roosevelt Val-kill, Hyde Park; trustee: Actors Fund of America.
THEATER: Harvey, Damn Yankees, Bells Are Ringing, Juno, Rhinoceros, Funny Girl, Arsenic and Old Lace (B'way and tour), Mountain Language/The Birthday Party (Obie Award), The Learned Ladies, Bon Appetit, The Roads to Home, Night Seasons, Morning's at Seven, You Can't Take It With You, The Show-Off, The Mystery of Edwin Drood (natl. tour). and extensive regional work at the Totem Pole Playhouse, Fayetteville, PA, Pocono Playhouse, Mountain Home Pa; Peterborough Playhouse, N.H. and others. Operatic debut with Baltimore Opera Co. in Candide, then The Italian Lesson and Bon Appetit. Cinderella, NY City Opera. Starred in San Jose Civic Light Opera Co.'s Sweeney Todd. Off B'way in The Entertainer. The Matchmaker, A.C.T. San Francisco.
PICTURES: Damn Yankees (debut, 1958), Bells Are Ringing, Something Wild, Up the Down Staircase, Cold Turkey, Klute, The Buddy System, Michael.
TELEVISION: *Series*: All in the Family (3 Emmy Awards: 1971, 1972, 1978), Bagdad Cafe, Mrs. Piggle-Wiggle. *Movies*: Tail Gunner Joe, Aunt Mary, Angel Dusted, Isabel's Choice, Eleanor: First Lady of the World (Emmy nom.), A Matter of Sex, Dead Man's Folly, Fire in the Dark, The Habitation of Dragons, Ghost Mom, Lily Dale. *Specials*: You Can't Take It With You, Grown-Ups (ACE nom.), Jack and the Beanstalk and Cinderella (Faerie Tale Theatre), Something's Afoot, Let Me Hear You Whisper, Mother Goose Rock 'n' Rhyme, Parallax Garden.

STAPLETON, MAUREEN
Actress. b. Troy, NY, June 21, 1925. e. Siena Col. Worked as a model and waitress while studying acting with Herbert Berghof in NY. Became member of Actors Studio. Broadway debut, 1946, in The Playboy of the Western World. *Autobiography:* A Hell of a Life (1995).
THEATER: *NY*: Antony and Cleopatra, Detective Story, The Bird Cage, The Rose Tattoo (Tony Award, 1951), The Emperor's Clothes, The Crucible, Richard III, The Seagull, 27 Wagons Full of Cotton, Orpheus Descending, The Cold Wind and the Warm, Toys in the Attic, The Glass Menagerie (1965 & 1975), Plaza Suite, Norman Is That You?, The Gingerbread Lady (Tony Award, 1971), The Country Girl, The Secret Affairs of Mildred Wild, The Gin Game, The Little Foxes. *LA*: Juno and the Paycock.
PICTURES: Lonelyhearts (debut, 1958; Acad. Award nom.), The Fugitive Kind, A View From the Bridge, Bye Bye Birdie, Airport (Acad. Award nom.), Plaza Suite, Interiors (Acad. Award nom.), Lost and Found, The Runner Stumbles, The Fan, On the Right Track, Reds (Acad. Award, best supporting actress, 1981), Johnny Dangerously, The Cosmic Eye (voice), Cocoon, The Money Pit, Heartburn, Sweet Lorraine, Made in Heaven, Nuts, Doin' Time on Planet Earth (cameo), Cocoon: The Return, Passed Away, Trading Mom, The Last Good Time.
TELEVISION: *Series*: What Happened? (panelist, 1952), The Thorns. *Specials*: For Whom the Bell Tolls, Among the Paths to Eden (Emmy Award, 1968).*Movies*: Tell Me Where It Hurts, Queen of the Stardust Ballroom, Cat on a Hot Tin Roof, The Gathering, Letters From Frank, The Gathering Part II, The Electric Grandmother, Little Gloria--Happy at Last, Family Secrets, Sentimental Journey, Private Sessions, Liberace: Behind the Music, Last Wish, Miss Rose White.

STARGER, MARTIN
Producer, Executive. b. New York, NY, May 8, 1932. e. CCNY. Served in U.S. Army Signal Corp., where prod. training films. Joined BBDO, starting in TV prod. dept.; later made v.p. & assoc. dir. of TV. Joined ABC in 1966, as v.p. of programs, ABC-TV, East Coast. 1968, promoted to v.p. and natl prog. dir; 1969 named v.p. in chg. progr.; named pres., ABC Entertainment, 1972; 1975 formed & became pres. of Marstar Productions Inc., M.P. & TV prod. co.; 1978 formed Marble Arch Productions, of which he was pres. Formed Rule/Starger Co. with Elton Rule, 1988.
PICTURES: *Exec. prod./Producer*: Nashville, The Domino Principle, Movie/Movie, The Muppet Movie, Raise the Titanic, Saturn 3, The Great Muppet Caper, Hard Country, The Legend of the Lone Ranger, On Golden Pond, Sophie's Choice, Barbarosa, Mask.
TELEVISION: Friendly Fire (Emmy Award, 1979), Escape from Sobibor, Consenting Adult, Earth Star Voyager, Marcus Welby M.D., A Holiday Affair, The Return of Marcus Welby M.D., The Elephant Man, All Quiet on the Western Front.

STARK, RAY
Producer. e. Rutgers U. Began career after WWII as agent handling Red Ryder radio scripts, and later literary works for such writers as Costain, Marquand and Hecht. Publicity writer, Warner Bros. Joined Famous Artists Agency, where he represented such personalities as Marilyn Monroe, Kirk Douglas and Richard Burton; in 1957, resigned exec. position to form Seven Arts Prods. with Eliot Hyman, serving as exec. v.p. and head of production until 1966, when he left to take on personal production projects. Founded Rastar Prods. and Ray Stark Prods. Received Irving Thalberg Award from Acad. of M.P. Arts and Sciences 1980. TV production: Barbarians at the Gate (Emmy Award).
PICTURES: The World of Susie Wong, The Night of the Iguana, This Property Is Condemned, Oh Dad Poor Dad Mama's Hung You in the Closet and I'm Feeling So Sad, Reflections in a Golden Eye, Funny Girl, The Owl and the Pussycat, Fat City, The Way We Were, Summer Wishes Winter Dreams, For Pete's Sake, Funny Lady, The Sunshine Boys, Robin and Marian, Murder by Death, The Goodbye Girl, Casey's Shadow, The Cheap Detective, California Suite, The Electric Horseman, Chapter Two, Seems Like Old Times, Annie, The Slugger's Wife, Nothing in Common, Brighton Beach Memoirs, Biloxi Blues, Steel Magnolias, Revenge, Lost in Yonkers, Harriet the Spy, To Gillian on Her 37th Birthday, Random Hearts.

STARR, MIKE
Actor. b. Queens, NY. e. Hofstra Univ. Theatre debut with Manhattan Punchline.
THEATER: NY: Requiem for a Heavyweight, The Guys in the Truck, Map of the World, Vesper's Ever.
PICTURES: Bushido Blade, Cruising, The Natural, The Last Dragon, Cat's Eye, The Money Pit, Violets Are Blue, Off-Beat, Collision Course, Five Corners, Funny Farm, Lean on Me, Blue Steel, Uncle Buck, Last Exit to Brooklyn, Miller's Crossing, GoodFellas, Billy Bathgate, Freejack, The Bodyguard, Mac, Mad Dog and Glory, Son of the Pink Panther, Cabin Boy, On Deadly Ground, The Hudsucker Proxy, Blown Away, Baby's Day Out, Trial by Jury, Ed Wood, Radioland Murders, Dumb & Dumber, A Pyromaniac's Love Story, Clockers, Two If By Sea, James & the Giant Peach, Blood & Wine, Hoodlum, The Deli, Frogs for Snakes, The Adventures of Ragtime, Summer of Sam, Gloria.

TELEVISION: *Series:* Hardball. *Mini-series*: The Last Don. *Movies:* The Frank Nitti Story, Hot Paint, Stone Pillow, Path to Paradise, Murder in a Small Town. *Guest:* Kojak, Hawk, The Equalizer, Crime Story, Spenser: For Hire.

STARR, RINGO
O.B.E. Singer, Musician, Songwriter, Actor. r.n. Richard Starkey. b. Liverpool, England, July 7, 1940. m. actress Barbara Bach. Former member of The Beatles.
PICTURES: A Hard Day's Night (debut, 1964), Help!, Yellow Submarine (cameo), Candy, The Magic Christian, Let It Be, 200 Motels, Blindman, The Concert for Bangladesh, Lisztomania, The Last Waltz, Sextette, The Kids Are Alright, Caveman, Give My Regards to Broad Street, Water (cameo), Walking After Midnight.
TELEVISION: *Movies*: Princess Daisy, Alice in Wonderland. *Series*: Shining Time Station

STEADMAN, ALISON
Actress. b. Liverpool, England, Aug. 26, 1946. m. director Mike Leigh. Studied acting with East 15 Acting School.
THEATER: The Prime of Miss Jean Brodie, Hamlet, Wholesome Glory, The Pope's Wedding, The Anchor, The King, Abigail's Party, Joking Apart, Unlce Vanya, The Rise and Fall of Little Voice, Othello, The Plotters of Cabbage Patch Corner.
PICTURES: Kipperbang (debut, 1982), Champions, Number One, A Private Function, Clockwise, Stormy Monday, The Misadventures of Mr. Wilt, Shirley Valentine, Life Is Sweet, Blame It on the Bellboy.
TELEVISION: Virtuoso, The Singing Detective, The Finding, Hard Labour, Nuts in May, Throught the Night, Pasmore.

STEELE, BARBARA
Actress. b. Trenton Wirrall, England, Dec. 29, 1937. Studied to be painter prior to joining rep. cos. in 1957.
PICTURES: Bachelor of Hearts (debut, 1958), Sapphire, Your Money or Your Wife, Black Sunday, The Pit and the Pendulum, Revenge of the Mercenaries, The Horrible Dr. Hitchcock, 8 1/2, Danse Macabre (Castle of Blood), The Ghost, The Hours of Love, White Voices, Nightmare Castle, The Maniacs, Terror Creatures From the Grave, The She Beast, Young Torless, Crimson Cult, They Came From Within, Caged Heat, I Never Promised You a Rose Garden, Piranha, Pretty Baby, The Silent Scream.

STEELE, TOMMY
Performer. r.n. Tommy Hicks. b. London, Dec. 17, 1936. Early career Merchant Navy. 1956 first gained fame as successful pop singer. First TV and film appearances, 1957. Composed and sang title song for The Shiralee.
THEATER: Half a Sixpence, Hans Andersen, Singin' in the Rain, Some Like It Hot.
PICTURES: Kill Me Tomorrow (debut, 1957), The Tommy Steele Story (Rock Around the World), The Duke Wore Jeans, Tommy the Toreador, Light Up the Sky, It's All Happening (The Dream Maker), The Happiest Millionaire, Half a Sixpence, Finian's Rainbow, Where's Jack?
TELEVISION: Tommy Steele Spectaculars, Richard Whittington Esquire (Rediffusion), Ed Sullivan Show, Gene Kelly in NY NY, Perry Como Show, Twelfth Night, The Tommy Steele Hour, Tommy Steele in Search of Charlie Chaplin, Tommy Steele and a Show, Quincy's Quest.

STEENBURGEN, MARY
Actress. b. Newport, AR, Feb. 8, 1953. Graduated from Neighborhood Playhouse. Received honorary doctorate degrees from Univ. of Ark. at Little Rock and Hendrix Col. in Conway, AR. On B'way stage 1993 in Candida.
PICTURES: Goin' South (debut, 1978), Time After Time, Melvin and Howard (Acad. Award, best supporting actress, 1980), Ragtime, A Midsummer Night's Sex Comedy, Cross Creek, Romantic Comedy, One Magic Christmas, Dead of Winter, End of the Line (also exec. prod.), The Whales of August, Miss Firecracker, Parenthood, Back to the Future Part III, The Long Walk Home (narrator), The Butcher's Wife, What's Eating Gilbert Grape, Philadelphia, Clifford, It Runs in the Family (My Summer Story), Pontiac Moon, My Family/Mi Familia, Powder, The Grass Harp, Nixon.
TELEVISION: *Series*: Ink (also co-exec. prod.), Back to the Future (voice). *Mini-Series*: Tender Is the Night. *Specials*: Faerie Tale Theatre (Little Red Riding Hood), The Gift. *Movie*: The Attic: The Hiding of Anne Frank, Gulliver's Travels, About Sarah.

STEIGER, ROD
Actor. b. Westhampton, NY, April 14, 1925. e. Westside H.S., Newark, NJ. Served in U.S. Navy, then employed in Civil Service; studied acting at N.Y. Theatre Wing Dramatic Workshop Actors' Studio; numerous TV plays; on Broadway in ANTA prod. of Night Music.
PICTURES: Teresa (debut, 1951), On the Waterfront, The Big Knife, Oklahoma!, The Court Martial of Billy Mitchell, Jubal, The Harder They Fall, Back From Eternity, Run of the Arrow, The Unholy Wife, Across the Bridge, Cry Terror, Al Capone, Seven Thieves, The Mark, World in My Pocket, 13 West Street, Convicts 4, The Longest Day, Hands Over the City, Time of Indifference, The Pawnbroker, The Loved One, Dr. Zhivago, And There Came a Man (A Man Called John), In the Heat of the Night (Acad. Award, 1967), The Girl and the General, No Way to Treat a Lady, The Sergeant, The Illustrated Man, Three Into Two Won't Go, Waterloo, Happy Birthday Wanda June, Duck You Sucker! (A Fistful of Dynamite), The Heroes, Lolly Madonna XXX, Lucky Luciano, Mussolini: Dead or Alive (The Last Days of Mussolini), Hennessey, Dirty Hands, W.C. Fields and Me, Wolf Lake, F.I.S.T., Breakthrough (Sgt. Steiner), The Amityville Horror, Love and Bullets, Klondike Fever, The Lucky Star, Lion of the Desert, Cattle Annie and Little Britches, The Chosen, The Magic Mountain, Portrait of a Hitman (Jim Buck), The Naked Face, The Kindred, Catch the Heat, American Gothic, The January Man, Men of Respect, The Ballad of the Sad Cafe, Midnight Murders, Guilty as Charged, That Summer of White Roses, The Player, The Neighbor, The Last Tattoo, Black Water, The Specialist, Mars Attacks!, Animals.
TELEVISION: Many appearances in 1950s live TV including Marty. *Movies*: Jesus of Nazareth, Cook & Perry: The Race to the Pole, Sword of Gideon, Desperado: Avalanche at Devil's Ridge, Passion and Paradise, In the Line of Duty: Manhunt in the Dakotas, Sinatra, Tom Clancy's Op Center, Choices of the Heart: The Margaret Sanger Story, In Pursuit of Honor, Columbo: Strange Bedfellows. *Mini-Series*: Hollywood Wives. *Special*: Tales of the City. Guest: The Simpsons (voice).

STEINBERG, DAVID
Actor, Writer, Director. b. Winnipeg, Canada, Aug. 9, 1942. e. U. of Chicago; Hebrew Theological Coll. Member Second City troupe; comedian at comedy clubs: Mr. Kelly's Hungry i, Bitter End. Starred in London and B'way stage prods. B'way includes Little Murders, Carry Me Back to Morningside Heights.
PICTURES: *Actor*: The Lost Man, The End, Something Short of Paradise, The Best of the Big Laff Off, The Tommy Chong Roast. *Director*: Paternity, Going Berserk (also co.-s.p.), Cats Don't Dance (exec. prod. only), The Wrong Guy, Kids in the Hall: Brain Candy (exec. prod. only) .
TELEVISION: *Series*: Music Scene (writer, co-host), Tonight Show (guest host), David Steinberg Show, Good Grief (exec. prod.). *Special*: Second City: 25 Years in Revue. *Director*: Newhart, The Popcorn Kid, Golden Girls, One Big Family, Faerie Tale Theatre, Richard Belzer Special, Baby on Board, Annie McGuire, Seinfeld, Mad About You, Evening Shade, Designing Women, Friends, Good Grief, and many commercials.

STEINBERG, HERB
Executive. b. New York, NY, July 3, 1921. e. City Coll. of New York, 1937-41. Capt. U.S. Army, 1942-46; pub. PRC, 1946, Eagle Lion, 1946-49, Paramount 1949; pub. mgr. 1951; expl. mgr., 1954; studio adv. & pub. dir., 1958; exec. chg. of spec. proj., press dept., Universal City Studio, 1963; v.p., Universal Studio Tours, 1971; 1974 v.p., MCA Recreation Services. Appt. to California Tourism Commission, Calif. Tourism Hall of Fame, 1984; consultant, MCA, Inc., 1987; bd. trustees, Motion Picture & TV Fund, 1987; bd. of trustees Hollywood Canteen Foundation, 1988; Communications dir. Alliance of Motion Picture & Television Producers.
(d. May 8, 2000)

STEINMAN, MONTE
Executive. b. New York, NY, May 18, 1955. e. Wharton Sch. of Univ. of PA. Joined Paramount Pictures 1980 as sr. financial analyst. Series of promotions followed, culminating in appt. as dir. of financial planning of Gulf & Western's Entertainment and Communications Group, 1984. 1985, named exec. dir., financial planning. 1990, joined Viacom Intl., as mgr. financial planning. 1993, dir. financial planning, MTV Networks. 1994, v.p. finance at MTV Networks.

STEMBLER, JOHN H.
Executive. b. Miami, FL, Feb. 18, 1913. e. U. of FL Law Sch., 1937. Asst. U.S. att., South. dist. of FL, 1941; U.S. Air Force, 1941-45; pres. Georgia Theatre Co., 1957; named chmn., 1983; NATO member exec. comm. and past pres.; Major Gen. USAF (Ret); past bd. chmn., National Bank of Georgia.

STEMBLER, WILLIAM J.
Executive. b. Atlanta, GA, Nov. 29, 1946. e. Westminster Sch., 1964; U. of FL, 1968; U. of GA Law Sch., 1971. 1st. lt. U.S. Army, 1971; capt., U.S. Army Reserve; resigned 1976. Enforcement atty., SEC, Atlanta office, 1972-73; joined Georgia Theatre Co., 1973; pres. 1983-86; joined United Artists Communications, Inc., 1986, as v.p.; Incorporated Value Cinemas 1988 and Georgia Theatre Co. II in 1991 as its chmn. & pres. Bd. of dir., & vice chmn., NATO; member, NATO OF GA & past-pres., 1983-85; Rotary Club of Atlanta, pres. 1991-92.

STERLING, JAN
Actress. r.n. Jane Sterling Adriance. b. New Yor, NY, April 3, 1923. e. private tutors; Fay Compton Sch. of Dramatic Art, London. N.Y. stage debut: Bachelor Born.
THEATER: Panama Hattie, Present Laughter, John Loves Mary, Two Blind Mice, Front Page, Over 21, Born Yesterday, The November People.
PICTURES: Johnny Belinda (debut, 1948), Appointment with Danger, Mystery Street, Caged, Union Station, The Skipper Surprised His Wife, The Big Carnival (Ace in the Hole), The Mating Season, Rhubarb, Flesh and Fury, Sky Full of Moon, Pony Express, The Vanquished, Split Second, Alaska Seas, The High and the Mighty (Acad. Award nom.), Return From the Sea, Human Jungle, Women's Prison, Female on the Beach, Man with the Gun, 1984, The Harder They Fall, Slaughter on Tenth Avenue, Kathy O', The Female Animal, High School Confidential, Love in a Goldfish Bowl, The Incident, The Angry Breed, The Minx, First Monday in October.
TELEVISION: *Series*: You're in the Picture (panelist, 1961), Made in America, The Guiding Light (1969-70). *Mini-Series*: Backstairs at the White House. *Movies*: Having Babies, Dangerous Company, My Kidnapper My Love.

STERLING, ROBERT
Actor. r.n. William Sterling Hart. b. Newcastle, PA, Nov. 13, 1917. e. U. of Pittsburgh. m. Anne Jeffreys, actress. Daughter is actress Tisha Sterling. Fountain pen salesman, day laborer, clerk, industrial branch credit mgr., clothing salesman on West Coast; served as pilot-instructor U.S. Army Corps. 3 yrs.
PICTURES: The Amazing Mr. Williams (debut, 1939), Blondie Brings Up Baby, Blondie Meets the Boss, Only Angels Have Wings, Manhattan Heartbeat, Yesterday's Heroes, Gay Caballero, Penalty, I'll Wait for You, Get-Away, Ringside Maisie, Two-Faced Woman, Dr. Kildare's Victory, Johnny Eager, This Time for Keeps, Somewhere I'll Find You, Secret Heart, Roughshod, Bunco Squad, Sundowners, Show Boat, Column South, Voyage to the Bottom of the Sea, Return to Peyton Place, A Global Affair.
TELEVISION: *Series*: Topper, Love That Jill, Ichabod and Me. *Movies*: Letters from Three Lovers, Beggarman, Thief.

STERN, DANIEL
Actor, Director. b. Bethesda, MD, Aug. 28, 1957. e. H.B. Studios. Appeared in 1984 short film Frankenweenie.
PICTURES: Breaking Away (debut, 1979), Starting Over, A Small Circle of Friends, Stardust Memories, It's My Turn, One-Trick Pony, Honky Tonk Freeway, I'm Dancing As Fast As I Can, Diner, Blue Thunder, Get Crazy, C.H.U.D., Key Exchange, The Boss' Wife, Hannah and Her Sisters, Born in East L.A., D.O.A., The Milagro Beanfield War, Leviathan, Little Monsters, Friends Lovers and Lunatics, Coupe de Ville, My Blue Heaven, Home Alone, City Slickers, Home Alone 2: Lost in New York, Rookie of the Year (also dir.), City Slickers II: The Legend of Curly's Gold, Bushwhacked (also exec. prod.), Celtic Pride, Very Bad Things.
TELEVISION: *Movies*: Samson and Delilah, Weekend War, The Court-Martial of Jackie Robinson, Big Guns Talk: The Story of the Western. *Series*: Hometown, The Wonder Years (narrator; also episode dir.), Dilbert (voice). *Guest:* The Simpsons (voice).

STERN, EDDIE
Film buyer. b. New York, NY, Jan. 13, 1917. e. Columbia Sch. of Journalism. Head film buyer and booker, specializing in art theatres, for Rugoff and Becker, NY; Captain, USAF; joined Wometco Ent. in 1952 as asst. to film buyer; v.p. motion picture theatre film buying and booking, Wometco Enterprises, Inc. Retired from Wometco 1985. 1985-96, film buying and booking, Theatres of Nassau, Ltd. Retired in 1996.

STERN, EZRA E.
Attorney. b. New York, NY, March 22, 1908. e. Southwestern U. 1930, LL.B. pres., Wilshire Bar Assn. Former legal counsel for So. Calif. Theatre Owners Assn. Member: Calif. State Bar; member, Int'l Variety Clubs; former chief barker, Variety Club So. Calif. Tent 25; pres., Variety Int'l Boys' Club; board of dir., Los Angeles Metropolitan Recreation & Youth Services Council; bd. of trustees, Welfare Planning Council, Los Angeles Region; former mem. Los Angeles Area Council, Boys' Club of America; pres., Variety International Boys' Club 1976-77 and 1979-80. Member bd., Will Rogers Inst., M.P. Pioneers. 1984, honored by Variety Boys and Girls Club as founder of youth recreational facility.

STERN, STEWART
Writer. b. New York, NY, March 22, 1922. e. Ethical Culture Sch., 1927-40; U. of Iowa, 1940-43. Rifle Squad Leader, S/Sgt. 106th Inf. Div., 1943-45; actor, asst. stage mgr., The French Touch, B'way, 1945-46; dialogue dir. Eagle-Lion Studios, 1946-48. 1948 to date: screenwriter.
TELEVISION: Crip, And Crown Thy Good, Thunder of Silence, Heart of Darkness, A Christmas to Remember, Sybil (Emmy Award, 1977).
PICTURES: Teresa, Rebel Without a Cause, The Rack, The James Dean Story, The Outsider, The Ugly American, Rachel Rachel, The Last Movie, Summer Wishes Winter Dreams.

STERNHAGEN, FRANCES
Actress. b. Washington, DC, Jan. 13, 1930. e. Vassar Coll., drama dept.; Perry-Mansfield School of Theatre. Studied with Sanford Meisner at Neighborhood Playhouse, NY. Was teacher at Milton Acad. in MA. Acted with Arena Stage, Washington, DC, 1953-54.
THEATER: Thieves Carnival (off-B'way debut, 1955), The Skin of Our Teeth, The Carefree Tree, The Admirable Bashville, Ulysses in Night Town, Viva Madison Avenue!, Red Eye of Love, Misalliance, Great Day in the Morning, The Right Honorable Gentleman, The Displaced Person, The Cocktail Party, Cock-a-Doodle Dandy, Playboy of the Western World, The Sign in Sidney Brustein's Window, Enemies, The Good Doctor (Tony Award, 1974), Equus, Angel, On Golden Pond, The Father, Grownups, Summer, You Can't Take It With You, Home Front, Driving Miss Daisy, Remembrance, A Perfect Ganesh, The Heiress (Tony Award, 1995), Long Day's Journey Into Night.
PICTURES: Up the Down Staircase (debut, 1967), The Tiger Makes Out, The Hospital, Two People, Fedora, Starting Over, Outland, Independence Day, Romantic Comedy, Bright Lights Big City, See You in the Morning, Communion, Sibling Rivalry, Misery, Doc Hollywood, Raising Cain, Curtain Call, Landfall.
TELEVISION: *Series*: Love of Life, Doctors, Golden Years, Under One Roof, The Road Home. *Movies*: Who'll Save Our Children?, Mother and Daughter: The Loving War, Prototype, Follow Your Heart, She Woke Up, Labor of Love: The Arlette Schweitzer Story, Reunion. *Guest*: Cheers, Tales From the Crypt, Outer Limits, The Con, To Live Again.

STEUER, ROBERT B.
Executive. b. New Orleans, LA, Nov. 18, 1937. e. U. of Illinois, & 1955-57; Tulane U., 1957-59, B.B.A. Booker-Southern D.I. circuit, New Orleans, 1959; assoc., prod., Poor White Trash; 1960; v.p. Cinema Dist. America, 1961; co-prod., Flesh Eaters, Common Law Wife, Flack Black Pussy Cat; partner, gen. mgr., radio station WTVF, Mobile, 1963; dir. special projects, American Intl. Pictures, 1967; so. div. sls. mgr., AIP, 1971; v.p. asst. gen. sls. mgr., AIP, 1974; partner, United Producers Organization, producing Screamers, 1977; v.p., sls., Ely Landau Org., 1979; v.p., gen. sls. mgr., Film Ventures Intl., 1981; exec. v.p. world-wide mktg., 1983; pres., FVI, 1986-89. 1987, exec. v.p. world-wide mktg. Film Ventures Intl; 1987-88 exec. prod. Operation: Take No Prisoners, Most Dangerous Women Alive, Tunnels, Criminal Act, Au Pair; 1989 sales consultant, 20th Century Fox. 1990-93 Prod. rep: When the Whales Came, China Cry, Twogether, Sweet and Short, Taxi to Soweto, Bound and Gagged: A Love Story, Skin Art, Yankee Zulu. 1994-97 formed Robert B. Steuer and Assoc. distribution and sales consult. to ent. industry. U.S. Rep 1997-98 Marche International du Film (Cannes Film Market). 1998-present, partner in Encore Int'l. Group LTD, a comp. of diversified experienced marketing and public relations specialists.

STEVENS, ANDREW
Actor, Director, Writer, Producer. b. Memphis, TN, June 10, 1955. Mother is actress Stella Stevens. e. Antioch U., L.A., B.A. (psychology). L.A. stage includes Journey's End, Mass Appeal, Leader of the Pack, Billy Budd (also prod.), P.S. Your Cat is Dead, Bouncers (L.A. Drama Circle Critics Award). Pres., CEO Royal Oaks Entertainment Intl. Film Distributors.
PICTURES: *Actor*: Shampoo, Day of the Animals, Massacre at Central High, Las Vegas Lady, Vigilante Force, The Boys in Company C, The Fury, Death Hunt, The Seduction, Ten to Midnight, Scared Stiff, Tusks, Fine Gold, Deadly Innocents, Down the Drain, Eyewitness to Murder, The Ranch, The Terror Within, Blood Chase, Counterforce, The Terror Within II (also dir., s.p.), Red Blooded American Girl, Night Eyes (also s.p., prod.), Munchie, Double Threat, Night Eyes II (also s.p., prod.), Deadly Rivals, Night Eyes III (also s.p., dir.), Body Chemistry III (also prod.), Scorned (also dir.), Illicit Dreams (also dir.), Victim of Desire (prod. only), The Skateboard Kid 2 (also dir.), Body Chemistry 4 (prod. only), Hard Bounty (prod. only), Grid Runners (dir. only), Munchie Strikes Back. Producers: Victim of Desire, Body Chemistry 4, Starhunter, Cyber Zone, Masseuse, Virtual Desire, Alone in the Woods, Invisible Mom, Innocence Betrayed, Illicit Dreams 2, Over the Wire, Terminal Rush, Flash Frame (also dir.)
TELEVISION: *Series*: Oregon Trail, Code Red, Emerald Point N.A.S., Dallas. *Mini-Series*: Hollywood Wives, Once an Eagle. *Movies*: Beggarman Thief, The Rebels, The Bastard, The Last Survivors, The Oregon Trail, Secrets, Topper (also prod.), Women at Westpoint, Code Red, Miracle on Ice, Journey's End, Forbidden Love, Murder in Malibu (Columbo). *Special*: Werewolf of Woodstock. *Guest*: Adam-12, Apple's Way, The Quest, Police Story, Shazam, Hotel, Westside Medical, Murder She Wrote, Love Boat. *Director*: Swamp Thing (3 episodes), Silk Stalkings (2 episodes), General Hospital (3 eps), Walker—Texas Ranger, Marker.

STEVENS, CONNIE
Actress. r.n. Concetta Ann Ingolia. b. Brooklyn, NY, August 8, 1938. e. Sacred Heart Acad., Hollywood Professional Sch. Began career as winner of several talent contests in Hollywood; prof. debut, Hollywood Repertory Theatre's prod. Finian's Rainbow; B'way in Star Spangled Girl (Theatre World Award); recordings include: Kookie Kookie Lend Me Your Comb, 16 Reasons, What Did You Wanna Make Me Cry For, From Me to You, They're Jealous of Me, A Girl Never Knows.
PICTURES: Eighteen and Anxious (debut, 1957), Young and Dangerous, Dragstrip Riot, Rock-a-Bye Baby, The Party Crashers, Parrish, Susan Slade, Palm Springs Weekend, Two on a Guillotine, Never Too Late, Way ... Way Out, The Grissom Gang, The Last Generation, Scorchy, Sgt. Pepper's Lonely Hearts Club Band (cameo), Grease 2, Back to the Beach, Tapeheads, Love Is All There Is.
TELEVISION: *Movies*: Mister Jerico, Call Her Mom, Playmates, Every Man Needs One, The Sex Symbol, Love's Savage Fury, Scruples, Bring Me the Head of Dobie Gillis, Race with Destiny: The James Dean Story. *Series*: Hawaiian Eye, Wendy and Me, Kraft Music Halls Presents The Des O'Connor Show, Starting from Scratch.

STEVENS, CRAIG
Actor. r.n. Gail Shikles. b. Liberty, MO, July 8, 1918. Was married to late actress Alexis Smith. e. U. of Kansas. Played in coll. dramatics.
THEATER: Here's Love, King of Hearts, Plain and Fancy, Critics Choice, Mary Mary, Cactus Flower (natl. co.), My Fair Lady.PICTURES: Affectionately Yours (debut, 1941), Law of the Tropics, Dive Bomber, Steel Against the Sky, Secret Enemies, Spy Ship, The Hidden Hand, Hollywood Canteen, Since You Went Away, The Doughgirls, God Is My Co-Pilot, Roughly Speaking, Too Young to Know, Humoresque, The Man I Love, That Way With Women, Love and Learn, Night Unto Night, The Lady Takes a Sailor, Where the Sidewalk Ends, Blues Busters, The Lady From Texas, Drums in the Deep South, Phone Call from a Stranger, Murder Without Tears, Abbott and Costello Meet Dr. Jekyll Mr. Hyde, The French Line, Duel on the Mississippi, The Deadly Mantis, Buchanan Rides Alone, Gunn, S.O.B., La Truite (The Trout).
TELEVISION: *Guest*: Lux Video Theatre, Four Star Playhouse, Loretta Young Show, Schlitz Playhouse, Dinah Shore, Ernie Ford Shows, Chevy Show, Summer on Ice, The Millionaire, The Bold Ones. *Series:* Peter Gunn (1958-61), Man of the World (ATV England), Mr. Broadway, The Invisible Man, Dallas. *Movies*: The Killer Bees; The Cabot Connection, The Home Front, Supercarrier, Marcus Welby, M.D.-A Holiday Affair. *Mini-Series*: Rich Man Poor Man.
(d. May 10, 2000)

STEVENS, FISHER
Actor. b. Chicago, IL, Nov. 27, 1963. e. NYU. Artistic Director of Naked Angels Theatre Co. in NYC.
THEATER: *NY*: Torch Song Trilogy (Off-B'way & B'way), Brighton Beach Memoirs, A Perfect Ganesh, Carousel.
PICTURES: The Burning, Baby It's You, The Brother From Another Planet, The Flamingo Kid, My Science Project, Short Circuit, The Boss's Wife, Short Circuit 2, Point of View, Reversal of Fortune, The Marrying Man, Mystery Date, Bob Roberts, Hero, When the Party's Over, Super Mario Bros., Nina Takes a Lover, Only You, Hackers, Cold Fever, Four Days in September.
TELEVISION: *Series*: Key West, Early Edition. *Guest*: Columbo. *Special*: It's Called the Sugar Plum, The Right to Remain Silent.

STEVENS, GAIL
Casting Director.
PICTURES: High Season, The Rachel Papers, Antonia and Jane, Captives, Paprazzo, Trainspotting, Beautiful Thing, The Slab Boys, Swept From the Sea, The Woodlanders, Still Crazy, Bedrooms & Hallways, Mansfield Park, Hold Back the Night, Saving Grace, The Beach, Late Night Shopping.
TELEVISION: A Murder of Quality, Oliver's Travels, Deadly Voyage, Truth or Dare, Painted Lady, Touching Lady, Butterfly Collectors, Great Expectations, All the Kings Men.

STEVENS, JR., GEORGE
Director, Writer, Producer. b. Los Angeles, CA, April 3, 1932. Son of late director George Stevens. e. Occidental Coll., 1949-53, B.A. 1st Lieut. U.S. Air Force; TV dir., Alfred Hitchcock Presents, Peter Gunn, 1957-61; prod. asst. Giant Productions, 1953-54; prod. asst. Mark VII, Ltd., 1956-57; dir. M.P. Service, U.S. Information Agency 1962-67; chmn., U.S. deleg. to Film Festivals at Cannes (1962, 1964), Venice (1962, 1963), Moscow (1963); Founding director, American Film Institute, 1967-79; co-chmn., American Film Institute, 1979 to present.
PICTURES: The Diary of Anne Frank (assoc. prod.), The Greatest Story Ever Told (assoc. prod.), John F. Kennedy: Years of Lightning Day of Drums (prod.), America at the Movies (prod.), George Stevens: A Filmmaker's Journey (dir., s.p., prod.; 1988 WGA Award for TV broadcast).
TELEVISION: *Specials*: American Film Institute's Salutes (exec. prod./writer, 1973-; received 1975 Emmy Award as exec. prod. of The American Film Institue Salute to James Cagney), The Stars Salute America's Greatest Movies (exec. prod.), The Kennedy Center Honors (prod./writer, 1978-; Emmy Awards: 1984, 1986, 1989, 1996), America Entertains Vice Premier Deng (prod./writer), Christmas in Washington, (exec. prod./writer, 1982-), *Movies:* The Murder of Mary Phagan (co-writer, prod., 1988; Emmy Award for prod.; also Christopher & Peabody Awards), Separate But Equal (dir., writer, co-exec. prod.; Emmy Award for exec. prod.; also Christopher Award, Ohio State Award, Paul Selvin Award by the Writers Guild of America), George Stevens: D-Day to Berlin, The Kennedy Center Honors (co. prod., co-writer; Emmy Award, 1996).

STEVENS, STELLA
Actress, Director. r.n. Estelle Eggleston. b. Yazoo City, MS, Oct. 1, 1938. Mother of actor Andrew Stevens. e. Attended Memphis State U. Modeled in Memphis when she was discovered by talent scouts. Was briefly a term contract actress at 20th Century-Fox, later under exclusive contract to Paramount, then Columbia. *Director*: The American Heroine (feature length doc.), The Ranch (feature comedy). Creator/owner of Sexy Fragrances.
PICTURES: Say One For Me (debut, 1959), The Blue Angel, Li'l Abner, Man Trap, Girls! Girls! Girls!, Too Late Blues, The Nutty Professor, The Courtship of Eddie's Father, Advance to the Rear, Synanon, The Secret of My Success, The Silencers, Rage, Where Angels Go Trouble Follows, How to Save a Marriage and Ruin Your Life, Sol Madrid, The Mad Room, The Ballad of Cable Hogue, A Town Called Hell, Slaughter, Stand Up & Be Counted, The Poseidon Adventure, Arnold, Cleopatra Jones and the Casino of Gold, Las Vegas Lady, Nickelodeon, The Manitou, Wacko, Chained Heat, The Longshot, Monster in the Closet, Down the Drain, Last Call, The Terror Within II, Eye of the Stranger, The Guest, Exiled in America, The Nutty Nut, Hard Drive, Molly & Gina, Body Chemistry 3: Point of Seduction, Illicit Dreams, The Granny.
TELEVISION: *Series*: Ben Casey, Flamingo Road, Santa Barbara. *Guest*: Bob Hope Bing Crosby Special, Frontier Circus, Johnny Ringo, Alfred Hitchcock, Love Boat, Highway to Heaven, Murder She Wrote, Martin Mull's White America, A Table at Ciros, In the Heat of the Night, Hotel, Night Court, Newhart, Dangerous Curves, The Commish, Burke's Law. *Movies*: In Broad Daylight, In Cold Blood, Climb an Angry Mountain, Linda, The Day The Earth Moved, Honky Tonk, New Original Wonder Woman (pilot), Kiss Me Kill Me, Wanted: The Sundance Woman, Charlie Cobb (pilot), The Night They Took Miss Beautiful, Murder in Peyton Place, The Jordan Chance, Cruise into Terror, New Love Boat (pilot), Friendship Secrets and Lies, Hart to Hart (pilot), The French Atlantic Affair, The Pendragon Affair (Eddie Capra Mystery pilot), Make Me an Offer, Children of Divorce, Twirl, Amazons, Women of San Quentin, No Man's Land, A Masterpiece of Murder, Fatal Confessions (Father Dowling pilot), Man Against The Mob, Jake Spanner: Private Eye. *Special:* Attack of the 5'2" Woman, The Christmas List, Reunion in Hazzard.

STEVENSON, CYNTHIA
Actress. b. Oakland, CA, Aug. 2, 1963. Raised in Washington, Vancouver.
THEATER: Ladies Room.
PICTURES: The Player, The Gun in Betty Lou's Handbag, Watch It, Forget Paris, Home for the Holidays, Live Nude Girls, Happiness, Air Bud: Golden Receiver.
TELEVISION: *Series*: My Talk Show, Bob, Hope and Gloria, Oh Baby. *Movie*: Double Your Pleasure, From the Earth to the Moon. *Guest*: Empty Nest, Cheers, Dream On.

STEVENSON, JULIET
Actress. b. England, Oct. 30, 1956. e. RADA.
THEATER: Other Worlds, Measure for Measure, Breaking the Silence, Troilus and Cressida, As You Like It, Les Liaisons Dangereuses, Yerma, Hedda Gabler, On the Verge, Burn This, Death and the Maiden, Scenes From an Execution (LA), The Duchess of Malfi.
PICTURES: Drowning by Numbers (debut, 1988), Ladder of Swords, Truly Madly Deeply, The Trial, The Secret Rapture, Emma.
TELEVISION: The Mallens (TV debut), Maybury, Bazaar and Rummage, Life Story, Stanley, Out of Love, Antigone, Oedipus at Colonus, Living With Dinosaurs, Amy, The March, A Doll's House, The Politician's Wife.

STEVENSON, PARKER
Actor. b. Philadelphia, PA, June 4, 1952. e. Princeton U. m. actress Kirstie Alley. Began professional acting career by starring in film, A Separate Peace, while high school senior, having attracted attention through work on TV commercials.
PICTURES: A Separate Peace (debut, 1972), Our Time, Lifeguard, Stroker Ace, Stitches, Official Denial.

TELEVISION: *Series:* Hardy Boys Mysteries, Falcon Crest, Probe, Baywatch, Melrose Place. *Guest*: The Streets of San Francisco, Gunsmoke. *Mini-Series*: North & South Book II, All the Rivers Run. *Movies*: This House Possessed, Shooting Stars, That Secret Sunday, Baywatch: Panic at Malibu Pier, The Cover Girl and the Cop, Are You Lonesome Tonight?, Nighttide, Shadow of a Stranger, Official Denial, Not of This Earth.

STEWART, DOUGLAS DAY
Writer, Director.
PICTURES: *Writer*: The Blue Lagoon, An Officer and a Gentleman, The Scarlet Letter. *Director-Writer*: Thief of Hearts, Listen to Me, The Visionary (dir. only).
TELEVISION: *Writer*: Boy in the Plastic Bubble, The Man Who Could Talk to Kids, Murder or Mercy, Silver Strand.

STEWART, JAMES L.
Executive. e. U. of Southern California, B.A. in cinema-TV and M.B.A. in finance. Worked for two years in sales for CBS Radio Network-West Coast. Spent four years with MGM in promotion and marketing. With Walt Disney Prods. for 12 years, functioning in marketing, management and administrative activities; named v.p.-corp. relations & admin. asst. to pres. 1978 joined in formation of Aurora Pictures, as exec. v.p., secty., & COO.
PICTURES: *Exec. prod.*: Why Would I Lie?, The Secret of NIMH, Eddie and the Cruisers, Heart Like a Wheel, East of the Sun, West of the Moon, Maxie.

STEWART, MARILYN
Marketing & Public Relations Executive. b. New York, NY. e. Hunter Coll. Entered ind. as scty. then asst. to MGM dir. of adv. Left to become prom.-pub. dir. for Verve/Folkways Records; duties also included ar and talent scouting. In 1966 joined 20th-Fox as radio/tv pub. coordinator. In 1969 went to Para. Pictures as mag. pub. coordinator; 1970 named worldwide dir. of pub. for Para., including creation of overall mkt. concepts, becoming 1st woman to be appt. to that position at major co. Campaigns included Love Story and The Godfather. 1972 opened own consulting office specializing in m.p. marketing and p.r. Headquarters in NY; repr. in L.A. Has represented The Lords of Flatbush, Bang the Drum Slowly, The Kids Are Alright, Autumn Sonata, The Tin Drum, A Cry in the Dark, The Russia House, Filmex, Michael Moriarty, Arthur Hiller, John Shea, Fred Schepisi, Volker Schlondorff, Hemdale Pictures, Lucasfilm.

STEWART, PATRICK
Actor. b. Mirfield, England, July 13, 1940. Trained at Bristol Old Vic Theatre School. Made professional stage debut 1959 in Treasure Island with Lincoln Rep. Co. at the Theatre Royal in Lincoln.
THEATER: *NY*: A Midsummer Night's Dream, A Christmas Carol, The Tempest. Numerous London theatre credits incl.: The Investigation, Henry V, The Caretaker, Body and Soul, Who's Afraid of Virginia Woolf?, Yonadab. Associate artist with Royal Shakespeare Co. since 1967; many appearances with them incl. Antony and Cleopatra for which he received the Olivier Award for Best Supporting Actor in 1979.
PICTURES: Hennessey, Hedda, Excalibur, The Plague Dogs (voice), Races, Dune, Lifeforce, Code Name: Emerald, Wild Geese II, The Doctor and the Devils, Lady Jane, L.A. Story, Robin Hood: Men in Tights, Gunmen, Star Trek: Generations, The Pagemaster (voice), Liberation (narrator), Jeffrey, Star Trek: First Contact, Conspiracy Theory, Masterminds, The Prince of Egypt (voice), Dad Savage, Star Trek: Insurrection, Safe House, X-Men.
TELEVISION: *Series*: Eleventh Hour (BBC), Maybury (BBC), Star Trek: The Next Generation (U.S.). *Mini-Series*: I Claudius, Smiley's People. *Movies*: Little Lord Fauntleroy, Pope John Paul II, Death Train, Moby Dick, Animal Farm (voice). *Special*: In Search of Dr. Seuss. *BBC Specials*: Oedipus Rex, Miss Julie, Hamlet, The Devil's Disciple, Fall of Eagles, The Artist's Story, Love Girl and the Innocent, Conrad, A Walk With Destiny, Alfred the Great, The Madness, When the Actors Come, Tolstoy: A Question of Faith, The Anatomist, The Mozart Inquest. *Guest:* The Simpsons (voice).

STIERS, DAVID OGDEN
Actor. b. Peoria, IL, Oct. 31, 1942. Guest conductor: 50 American orchestras incl. Chicago, San Diego, Dallas, Utah, and Chamber Orchestra of Baltimore. Resident conductor of Yaquina Chamber Orchestra in Oregon.
THEATER: *NY*: The Magic Show, Ulysses in Nighttown, The Three Sisters, Beggar's Opera, Measure for Measure.
PICTURES: Drive He Said, THX 1138, Oh God!, The Cheap Detective, Magic, Harry's War, The Man With One Red Shoe, Better Off Dead, Creator, Another Woman, The Accidental Tourist, Doc Hollywood, Beauty and the Beast (voice), Shadows and Fog, Iron Will, Bad Company, Pocahontas (voice), Steal Big Steal Little, Mighty Aphrodite, Meet Wally Sparks, The Hunchback of Notre Dame (voice), Jungle 2 Jungle, Krippendorf's Tribe, Toy Story 2 (voice).
TELEVISION: *Series*: Doc, M*A*S*H, Two Guys and a Girl. *Movies*: Charlie's Angels (pilot), A Circle of Children, A Love Affair: The Eleanor and Lou Gehrig Story, Sgt. Matlovich Vs. the U.S. Air Force, Breaking Up is Hard to Do, Damien: The Leper Priest, The Day the Bubble Burst, Anatomy of an Illness, The First Olympics: Athens 1896, The Bad Seed, 5 Perry Mason Movies (Shooting Star, Lost Love, Sinister Spirit, Avenging Ace, Lady in the Lake), Mrs. Delafield Wants to Marry, The Alamo: 13 Days to Glory, The Kissing Place, Final Notice, The Final Days, How to Murder a Millionaire, Wife Mother Murderer, The Last of His Tribe, Without a Kiss Goodbye. *Specials:* The Oldest Living Graduate, The Innocents Abroad, Mastergate. *Mini-Series*: North and South (also Book II), MacArthur, Reagan.

STILES, JULIA
Actress. b. New York, NY, March 28, 1981.
PICTURES: I Love You I Love You Not, The Devil's Own, Wicked, Wide Awake, Hamlet, 10 Things I Hate About You, O.
TELEVISION: *Movies:* Before Women Had Wings, The '60s. *Guest:* Ghostwriter, Promised Land, Chicago Hope.

STILES, RYAN
Actor. b. April 22, 1959.
PICTURES: Hot Shots!, Hot Shots! Part Deux.
TELEVISION: *Series:* Whose Line Is It Anyway?, The Drew Carey Show, Whose Line Is It Anyway? (USA, also exec. prod.). *Guest:* Parker Lewis Can't Lose, The John Larroquette Show, Mad About You, Weird Science, Murphy Brown.

STILLER, BEN
Actor, Director. b. New York, NY, November 30, 1966. Son of performers Jerry Stiller and Anne Meara. e. UCLA. Made short film parody of The Color of Money, called The Hustler of Money which landed him work on Saturday Night Live. Acting debut in 1985 B'way revival of The House of Blue Leaves.
PICTURES: Hot Pursuit, Empire of the Sun, Fresh Horses, Next of Kin, That's Adequate, Stella, Highway to Hell, Reality Bites (also dir.), Heavyweights, Get Shorty, Flirting With Disaster, The Cable Guy (also dir.), If Lucy Fell, Permanent Midnight, Zero Effect, There's Something About Mary, Your Friends & Neighbors, Mystery Men, Black and White, The Suburbans (also prod.), Meet the Parents, Zoolander (also dir.), Nobody Knows Anything, What Makes Sammy Run (dir only).
TELEVISION: *Series*: Saturday Night Live (also writer), The Ben Stiller Show (also creator, dir., writer; Emmy Award as writer). *Specials*: House of Blue Leaves, Colin Quinn Back in Brooklyn (dir., writer). *Movie*: Working Trash. *Guest:* Frasier, Friends, Duckman, NewsRadio, The Larry Sanders Show, Mr. Show.

STILLER, JERRY
Actor. b. New York, NY, June 8, 1929. m. actress Anne Meara. Son is actor Ben Stiller, daughter is acress Amy Stiller. With partner Meara gained recognition as comedy team in nightclubs, theatres and on tv, most notably The Ed Sullivan Show. Video with Meara, So You Want to Be An Actor?
THEATER: *B'way*: The Ritz, Passione, Hurlyburly, Three Men on a Horse, What's Wrong With This Picture?, The Three Sisters.
PICTURES: The Taking of Pelham One Two Three, Airport 1975, The Ritz, Nasty Habits, Those Lips Those Eyes, Hot Pursuit, Nadine, Hairspray, That's Adequate, Little Vegas, Highway to Hell, The Pickle, Heavyweights, The Fish in the Bathtub, Stag, The Deli, The Suburbans.
TELEVISION: *Movies*: Madame X, The Other Woman, Seize the Day, Subway Stories: Tales from the Underground. *Series:* The Paul Lynde Show, Joe and Sons, Take Five With Stiller and Meara (synd), Tattingers, Seinfeld, The King of Queens. *Guest*: L.A. Law, In the Heat of the Night, Homicide, Murder She Wrote, Touched By an Angel.

STING
Musician, Actor. r.n. Gordon Matthew Sumner. b. Newcastle-Upon-Tyne, England, Oct. 2, 1951. e. Warwick U. A schoolteacher before helping form rock group, The Police as songwriter, singer and bass player. B'way debut, Threepenny Opera, 1989.
PICTURES: Quadrophenia, Radio On, The Great Rock 'n' Roll Swindle, The Secret Policeman's Other Ball, Brimstone and Treacle, Urgh! A Music War, Dune, The Bride, Plenty, Bring on the Night, Julia and Julia, Stormy Monday, The Adventures of Baron Munchausen, Resident Alien, The Music Tells You, The Grotesque, Lock Stock and Two Smoking Barrels.

ST. JOHN, JILL
Actress. r.n. Jill Oppenheim. b. Los Angeles, CA, Aug. 19, 1940. m. actor Robert Wagner. On radio series One Man's family. Television debut, A Christmas Carol, 1948.
PICTURES: Summer Love, The Remarkable Mr. Pennypacker, Holiday for Lovers, The Lost World, The Roman Spring of Mrs. Stone, Tender Is the Night, Come Blow Your Horn, Who's Minding the Store?, Who's Been Sleeping in My Bed?, Honeymoon Hotel, The Liquidator, The Oscar, Banning, Tony Rome, Eight on the Lam, The King's Pirate, Diamonds Are Forever, Sitting Target, The Concrete Jungle, The Act, The Player.

TELEVISION: *Series*: Emerald Point. *Movies*: Fame Is the Name of the Game, How I Spent My Summer Vacation, The Spy Killer, Foreign Exchange, Brenda Starr, Telethon, Hart to Hart (pilot), Rooster. *Guest*: Dupont Theatre, Fireside Theatre, Batman, The Love Boat. *Mini-Series*: Around the World in 80 Days.

STOCKWELL, DEAN
Actor. r.n. Robert Dean Stockwell. b. Hollywood, CA, March 5, 1935. p. Harry and Betty Veronica Stockwell. Brother is actor Guy Stockwell. e. Long Island public schools and Martin Milmore, Boston. On stage in Theatre Guild prod. Innocent Voyage. Appeared on radio in Death Valley Days and Dr. Christian. Named in 1949 M.P. Herald-Fame Stars of Tomorrow poll; 1976 retired to Santa Monica as a licensed real estate broker but soon returned to acting.
PICTURES: Anchors Aweigh (debut, 1945), The Valley of Decision, Abbott and Costello in Hollywood, The Green Years, Home Sweet Homicide, The Mighty McGurk, The Arnelo Affair, The Romance of Rosy Ridge, Song of the Thin Man, Gentleman's Agreement, Deep Waters, The Boy With Green Hair, Down to the Sea in Ships, The Secret Garden, The Happy Years, Kim, Stars in My Crown, Kim, Cattle Drive, Gun for a Coward, The Careless Years, Compulsion, Sons and Lovers, Long Day's Journey Into Night, Rapture, Psych-Out, The Dunwich Horror, The Last Movie, The Loners, The Werewolf of Washington, Win Place or Steal (The Big Payoff), Won Ton Ton The Dog Who Saved Hollywood, Stick Fighter (South Pacific Connection), Tracks, She Came to the Valley, Alsino and the Condor, Sandino, Human Highway (also co-dir., s.p.), Wrong Is Right, To Kill a Stranger, Paris Texas, Dune, The Legend of Billie Jean, To Live and Die in L.A., Blue Velvet, Gardens of Stone, Beverly Hills Cop II, Banzai Runner, The Blue Iguana, Tucker: The Man and His Dream, Married to the Mob (Acad. Award nom.), Palais Royale, Limit Up, Buying Time, Time Guardian, The Player, Chasers, Mr. Wrong, Air Force One, McHale's Navy, The Rainmaker, Water Damage, Rites of Passage.
TELEVISION: *Series*: Quantum Leap, It's True, The Tony Danza Show. *Guest*: Miami Vice, Hart to Hart, Simon and Simon, The A-Team, Wagon Train, Twilight Zone, Playhouse 90, Bonanza, Hallmark Hall of Fame, Hunter, Police Story, Greatest Show on Earth. *Movies*: Paper Man, The Failing of Raymond, The Adventures of Nick Carter, The Return of Joe Forrester, Three for the Road, A Killing Affair, Born to Be Sold, Sweet Smell of Death (U.K.), The Gambler III: The Legend Continues, Son of the Morning Star, Backtrack, Shame, Fatal Memories, Bonanza: The Return, In the Line of Duty: The Price of Vengeance, Justice in a Small Town, The Innocent, Madonna: Innocence Lost, Deadline for Murder: From the Files of Edna Buchanan, Stephen King's The Langoliers. *Pilot:* Caught in the Act.

STODDARD, BRANDON
Executive. b. Brideport, CT, March 31, 1937. e. Yale U., BS Amer. Studies, 1958. Columbia Law Sch. Was program ass't. at Batton, Barton, Durstine and Osborn before joining Grey Advertising, 1962, where was successively prog. ops. supvr., dir. daytime prog., VP TV/radio prog. Joined ABC in 1970; named v.p. daytime programs for ABC Entertainment, 1972; v.p. children's programs, 1973. Named v.p., motion pictures for TV, 1974; 1976 named v.p., dramatic progs. and m.p. for TV; 1979, named pres., ABC Motion Pictures; 1985 appt. pres., ABC Entertainment. Resigned 1989 to head ABC Prods. unit to create and prod. series and movies for ABC and other networks. Resigned that position, 1995.

STOLNITZ, ART
Executive. b. Rochester, NY, March 13, 1928. e. U. of Tennessee, LL.B., 1952. U.S. Navy Air Force. Legal dept., William Morris Agency, 1953, dir. business affairs, ZIV, 1959; dir. new program development, ZIV-United Artists, 1960; literary agent, MCA, 1961; dir. business affairs, Selmur Productions, Selmur Pictures, 1963; v.p. ABC Pictures, 1969; v.p. Metromedia Producers Corporation, 1970, executive v.p. Metromedia Producers Corporation; 1975 exec. v.p. and prod. Charles Fries Prods. 1976, prod. Edgar J. Scherick Productions; 1976-77 prod., Grizzly Adams (TV); 1977; v.p. business affairs, Warner Bros.-TV; 1980, sr. v.p., business affairs; 1990, exec. v.p. business & financial affairs, Lorimar; 1993, exec. v.p. business and financial affairs, Warner Bros. TV.

STOLOFF, VICTOR
Producer, Writer, Director, Editor. b. March 17, 1913. e. French Law U. Ac. Fines Arts. Prod. dir. writer of award winning documentaries (Warner Bros. release); Prod. dir. writer first U.S. film made in Italy, When in Rome; contract writer, dir. to Sidney Buchman, Columbia.
PICTURES: *Writer*: Volcano, The Sinner, Shark Reef, Journey Around the World. Of Love and Desire (also prod.), Intimacy (also prod., dir.), The Washington Affair (prod., dir.), The 300 Year Weekend (also dir.).
TELEVISION: Ford Theatre, Lloyd Bridges series, National Velvet, High Adventure with Lowell Thomas, *Prod.:* Hawaii Five-O. *Created* Woman of Russia (dir., writer), Audience (exec. prod., dir.).

STOLTZ, ERIC
Actor. b. Los Angeles, CA, 1961. Moved to American Samoa at age 3; family returned to California when he was 8. Spent 2 years at U. of Southern California in theatre arts; left to study with Stella Adler and later William Traylor and Peggy Feury.
THEATRE: *Off-B'way*: The Widow Claire, The American Plan, Down the Road, The Importance of Being Earnest. *B'way*: Our Town (B'way debut; Theatre World Award, Tony nom. & Drama Desk nom., 1988), Two Shakespearean Actors, Three Sisters. *Regional*: Tobacco Road, You're a Good Man Charlie Brown, Working (all with an American Rep. Co. in Scotland), Arms and the Man, Glass Menagerie (Williamstown Theater Festival).
PICTURES: Fast Times at Ridgemont High (debut, 1982), Surf II, Running Hot, The Wild Life, The New Kids, Mask, Code Name: Emerald, Some Kind of Wonderful, Lionheart, Sister Sister, Haunted Summer, Manifesto, The Fly II, Say Anything... (cameo), Memphis Belle, The Waterdance, Singles (cameo), Bodies Rest & Motion (also co-prod.), Naked in New York, Killing Zoe, Sleep With Me (also prod.), Pulp Fiction, Little Women, Rob Roy, Fluke, The Prophecy, Kicking and Screaming, Grace of My Heart, 2 Days in the Valley, Inside, Anaconda, Mr. Jealousy (also prod.), The Passion of Ayn Rand, Hi-Life, A Murder of Crows, The House of Mirth, Jesus & Hutch, It's A Shame About Ray, Things Behind the Sun, Harvard Man.
TELEVISION: *Movies*: The Grass Is Always Greener Over the Septic Tank, The Seekers, The Violation of Sarah McDavid, Paper Dolls, Thursday's Child, A Killer in the Family, Money, The Heart of Justice, Foreign Affairs, Roommates, Keys to Tulsa, Our Guys: Outrage at Glen Ridge, The Lot, Annus Horribilis. *Specials*: Things Are Looking Up, Sensibility and Sense, Our Town. *Guest*: Mad About You, Homicide. *Series*: Chicago Hope.

STONE, ANDREW L.
Director, Producer, Writer. b. Oakland, CA, July 16, 1902. e. U. of CA. Ent. ind. 1918 at Universal San Francisco exch.; later author, prod., dir. series of pictures for Paramount; prod., dir. for Sono-Art; 1932-36 org. and oper. Race Night company. Formed Andrew Stone Prods., 1943. Co-prod. with wife Virginia beginning in 1958.
PICTURES: *Dir.:* Dreary House (debut, 1928; also prod.), Hell's Headquarters, The Girl Said No (also prod., story), Stolen Heaven (also prod., story), Say It in French (also prod.), The Great Victor Herbert (also prod., co-story), There's Magic in Music (also prod., co-story), Stormy Weather, Hi Diddle Diddle (also prod.), Sensations of 1945 (also prod., co-s.p.), Bedside Manner (also prod.), The Bachelor's Daughters (also prod., s.p.), Fun on a Weekend (also prod., s.p.), Highway 301 (also s.p.), Confidence Girl (also prod., story, s.p.), The Steel Trap (also story, s.p.), Blueprint for Murder (also story, s.p.), The Night Holds Terror (also prod., story), Julie (also s.p.). *Dir./Co-Prod./Writer:* Cry Terror, The Decks Ran Red, The Last Voyage, Ring of Fire, The Password Is Courage, Never Put It in Writing, The Secret of My Success, Song of Norway, The Great Waltz.

STONE, AUBREY
Executive. b. Charlotte, NC, Jan. 14, 1964. e. U. of NC-Chapel Hill. Joined Consolidated Theatres Inc. in 1987. Helped to found a new motion picture exhibition company, Consolidated Theatres/The Stone Group, 1990. V.P., Consolidated Theatres/The Stone Group, 1990-95. Assumed role of v.p./general mgr. in 1996. Bd. of dir., NATO of NC & SC, 1991-present; pres., NATO of NC & SC, 1995-96. Bd of dir., National NATO, 1995-present; chmn., Programs & Services Committee, National NATO, present.

STONE, BURTON
Executive. b. Feb. 16, 1928; e. Florida Southern Coll. Was film ed., Hollywood Film Co. 1953-61; serv. mgr., sales mgr. and gen. mgr., Consolidated Film Inds., 1953-61; nat'l sales mgr., Movielab, 1961-63; pres., Allservice Film Laboratories, 1963-64; v.p. Technicolor, Inc., 1964-70. Pres., Precision Film Labs., 1965-76. Pres., Deluxe Laboratories, Inc., a wholly-owned subsidiary of 20th Century Fox, 1976-91. 1991, pres. Deluxe color, a sub of the Rank Org. Member: Board of directors, Will Rogers Foundation and Motion Picture Pioneers; member Acad. of Motion Picture Arts & Sciences, American Society of Cinematographers; awarded fellowship in Society of Motion Picture & Television Engineers; past pres., Association of Cinema & Video Laboratories; awarded fellowship in British Kinematograph, Sound & Television Society.

STONE, DEE WALLACE
Actress. r.n. Deanna Bowers. b. Kansas City, MO, Dec. 14, 1948. m. actor Christopher Stone. e. U. of Kansas, theater and education. Taught high school English. Came to NY to audition for Hal Prince and spent 2 years working in commercials and industrial shows. First break in Police Story episode.

PICTURES: The Stepford Wives (debut, 1975), The Hills Have Eyes, 10, The Howling, E.T:. The Extra-Terrestrial, Jimmy the Kid, Cujo, Critters, Secret Admirer, Club Life, Shadow Play, The White Dragon, Alligator II: The Mutation, Popcorn, Rescue Me, The Frighteners.
TELEVISION: *Series*: Together We Stand, Lassie, High Sierra Search and Rescue. *Movies*: The Sky's No Limit, Young Love First Love, The Secret War of Jackie's Girls, Child Bride of Short Creek, The Five of Me, A Whale for the Killing, Skeezer, Wait Til Your Mother Gets Home, Happy, I Take These Men, Hostage Flight, Sin of Innocence, Addicted to His Love, Stranger on My Land, Terror in the Sky, The Christmas Visitor, I'm Dangerous Tonight, Prophet of Evil: The Ervil LeBaron Story, Witness to the Execution, Search and Rescue, Moment of Truth: Cradle of Conspiracy, Huck and the King of Hearts. *Guest*: CHiPs.

STONE, MARIANNE
Actress. b. London, England. Studied Royal Acad. of Dramatic Art, West End debut in The Kingmaker, 1946.
PICTURES: Brighton Rock, Seven Days to Noon, The Clouded Yellow, Wrong Arm of the Law, Heavens Above, Stolen Hours, Nothing But the Best, Curse of the Mummy's Tomb, Hysteria, The Beauty Jungle, A Hard Day's Night, Rattle of a Simple Man, Echo of Diana, Act of Murder, Catch Us If You Can, You Must Be Joking, The Countess from Hong Kong, The Wrong Box, To Sir With Love, The Bliss of Mrs. Blossom, Here We Go Round the Mulberry Bush, Carry on Doctor, The Twisted Nerve, The Best House in London, Oh! What a Lovely War; The Raging Moon, There's a Girl in My Soup, All the Right Noises, Assault, Carry On at Your Convenience, All Coppers Are..., Carry on Girls, Penny Gold, The Vault of Horror, Percy's Progress, Confessions of a Window Cleaner, Carry on Dick, That Lucky Touch, Sarah, Carry on Behind, Confessions From a Holiday Camp, The Chiffy Kids, What's Up Superdoc?; The Class of Miss McMichael, The Human Factor, Dangerous Davies, Funny Money, Terry on the Fence, Carry on Laughing, The Wicked Lady, Deja Vu.
TELEVISION: Maigret, Bootsie and Snudge, Jimmy Edwards Show, Wayne and Schuster Show, Roy Hudd Show, Harry Worth Show, Steptoe and Son, Informer, Love Story, Father Dear Father, Bless This House, The Man Outside, Crown Court, Public Eye, Miss Nightingale, She, Little Lord Fauntleroy, The Secret Army (2 series), Shillingbury Tale, The Bright Side (series), Tickets for the Titanic (series), The Balance of Nature, Always, Hammer House of Mystery & Suspense, The Nineteenth Hole, In Possession.

STONE, OLIVER
Director, Writer. b. New York, NY, Sept. 15, 1946. e. Yale U., NYU, B.F.A., 1971. Teacher in Cholon, Vietnam 1965-66. U.S. Infantry specialist 4th Class. 1967-68 in Vietnam (Purple Heart, Bronze Star with Oak Leaf Cluster honors).
PICTURES: Sugar Cookies (assoc. prod.), Seizure (dir., s.p., co-editor, 1974), Midnight Express (s.p.; Acad. Award, 1978), The Hand (dir., s.p., cameo), Conan the Barbarian (co-s.p.), Scarface (s.p.), Year of the Dragon (co-s.p.), Salvador (dir., co-s.p., co-prod.), 8 Million Ways to Die (co-s.p.), Platoon (dir., s.p., cameo; Acad. Award & DGA Award for Best Director, 1986), Wall Street (dir., co-s.p., cameo), Talk Radio (dir., co-s.p.), Born on the Fourth of July (dir., co-s.p., cameo; Acad. Award & DGA Award for Best Director, 1989), Blue Steel (co-prod.), Reversal of Fortune (co-prod.), The Doors (dir., co-s.p., cameo), Iron Maze (co-exec. prod.), JFK (dir., co-prod., co-s.p.), South Central (co-exec. prod.), Zebrahead (co-exec. prod.), Dave (actor), The Joy Luck Club (co-exec. prod.), Heaven and Earth (dir., co-prod., s.p.), Natural Born Killers (dir., co-prod., co-s.p.), The New Age (exec. prod.), Nixon (dir., co-s.p., co-prod.; Chicago Film Critics Award), Killer: A Journal of Murder (co-exec. prod.), The People vs. Larry Flynt (prod.), Evita, U-Turn, Savior (prod.), Scud: The Disposable Assassin (prod.), Any Given Sunday (dir., prod.), Chains (exec. prod.), The Art of War (prod.), The Corrupter (prod.), Beyond Borders.
TELEVISION: *Mini-Series*: Wild Palms (co-exec. prod.). *Movie:* Indictment: The McMartin Trial (co-exec. prod.), Frank Capra's American Dream.

STONE, PETER
Writer. b. Los Angeles, CA, Feb. 27, 1930. Son of film prod. John Stone and screenwriter Hilda Hess Stone. e. Bard Col., B.A. 1951; Yale U, M.F.A., 1953. Won Mystery Writers of America Award for Charade, Christopher Award for 1776.
THEATER: Kean, Skyscraper, 1776 (Tony and NY Drama Critics Circle Awards, 1969), Two By Two, Sugar, Full Circle, Woman of the Year (Tony Award, 1981), My One and Only, Will Rogers Follies (Tony, Grammy and NY Drama Critics Circle Awards, 1991), Titanic.
PICTURES: Charade, Father Goose (Acad. Award, 1964), Mirage, Arabesque, The Secret War of Harry Frigg, Jigsaw, Sweet Charity, Skin Game, The Taking of Pelham One Two Three, 1776, The Silver Bears, Who Is Killing the Great Chefs of Europe?, Why Would I Lie?, Grand Larceny, Just Cause.
TELEVISION: *Movies*: Studio One, Brenner, Witness, Asphalt Jungle, The Defenders (Emmy Award, 1962). Androcles and the Lion, Baby on Board, The Taking of Pelham One Two Three. *Series*: Adam's Rib, Ivan the Terrible.

STONE, SHARON
Actress. b. Meadville, PA, March 10, 1958. e. Edinboro St. Univ. Started as model, appearing in several TV commercials.
PICTURES: Stardust Memories (debut, 1980), Deadly Blessing, Bolero, Irreconcilable Differences, King Soloman's Mines, Allan Quartermain and the Lost City of Gold, Cold Steel, Police Academy 4: Citizens on Patrol, Action Jackson, Above the Law, Blood and Sand, Beyond the Stars (Personal Choice), Total Recall, He Said/She Said, Scissors, Year of the Gun, Basic Instinct, Diary of a Hit Man, Where Sleeping Dogs Lie, Sliver, Last Action Hero (cameo), Intersection, The Specialist, The Quick and the Dead (also co- prod.), Casino (Golden Globe Award), The Last Dance, Diabolique, The Mighty, Sphere, Gloria, Antz (voice), Simpatico, Picking up the Pieces, Gloria, The Muse.
TELEVISION: *Series*: Bay City Blues. *Mini-Series*: War and Remembrance. *Movies*: Not Just Another Affair, The Calendar Girl Murders, The Vegas Strip Wars, Tears in the Rain, If These Walls Could Talk 2. *Pilots*: Mr. & Mrs. Ryan, Badlands 2005. *Guest*: T.J. Hooker, Magnu P.I., Roseanne, Big Guns Talk: The Story of the Western.

STOPPARD, TOM
Writer, Director. r.n. Tomas Straussler. b. Zlin, Czechoslovakia, July 3, 1937. Playwright whose works include Rosencrantz and Guildenstern Are Dead, Jumpers, Travesties, The Real Thing, Hapgood, Arcadia.
PICTURES: *Writer:* The Romantic Englishwoman, Despair, The Human Factor, Squaring the Circle, Brazil, Empire of the Sun, The Russia House, Rosencrantz and Guildenstern Are Dead (also dir.), Billy Bathgate, Fifteen Minute Hamlet, Shakespeare in Love (Acad. Award for orig. s.p.), Enigma, Vatel, Sleepy Hollow.
TELEVISION: *Movies*: Three Men in a Boat, The Dog It Was That Died, Poodle Springs.

STORARO, VITTORIO
Cinematographer. b. Rome, Italy, June 24, 1940. Trained at Rome's Centro Sperimentale Cinematografia and began filming short films. His work as Bernardo Bertolucci's regular cinematographer won him an international reputation and award-winning work in Europe and America, including 3 Academy Awards.
PICTURES: Giovinezza Giovinezza (Youthful Youthful), The Gallery Murders, The Conformist, The Spider's Stratagem, The Fifth Cord, Malice, 'Tis Pity She's a Whore, Last Tango in Paris, Giordano Bruno, Footprints, The Driver's Seat, 1900, Submission, Agatha, Apocalypse Now (Acad. Award, 1979), La Luna, Reds (Acad. Award, 1981), One From the Heart, Wagner, Ladyhawke, Captain Eo, Ishtar, The Last Emperor (Acad. Award, 1987), Tucker: The Man and His Dream, New York Stories (Life Without Zoe), Dick Tracy, The Sheltering Sky, Tosca, Little Buddha, Roma! Imago Urbis, Flamenco, Taxi, Tango (Canne Film Fest. Award, Tech. Prize, 1998), Bulworth.

STOREY, FREDERICK
Executive. b. Columbus, GA, Nov. 12, 1909. e. Georgia Tech. Adv. staff Atlanta Journal, 1933-38; adv. staff C. P. Clark Adv. Agcy., 1938; partner 1940; U.S. Navy, 1941-46; staff Georgia Theatre Co., 1946; v.p. 1947-52. Founded Storey Theatres Inc., Atlanta, GA; 1952, now bd. chmn. emeritus (formerly pres.) of Georgia State Theatres; dir. numerous theatre cos.; v.p. dir., Motion Picture Theatre Owners of Georgia, Dist. Alumnus award, Georgia Tech, 1979.

STORKE, WILLIAM F.
Producer. b. Rochester, NY, Aug. 12, 1927. e. UCLA, B.A. 1948. In Navy, WWII. First position with NBC Hollywood guest relations staff, 1948. Moved to continuity acceptance dept. as comm. editor. Prom. to asst. mgr, comm. spvr. before joining NBC West Coast sales dept., 1953. Transferred to N.Y. as prog. acct. exec., 1955; named administrator, participating prog. sales, 1957. Named dir., participating program sales, 1959. Named dir., program adm., NBC-TV, 1964; then elected v.p., program adm.; 1967 named v.p., programs, East Coast; 1968, appt. v.p., special programs, NBC-TV Network; 1979, pres., Claridge Group, Ltd.; exec. v.p. Entertainment Partners, Inc., N.Y., 1982-. Pres., Storke Enterprises Inc. 1988-.
TELEVISION: *Producer*: Oliver Twist, To Catch A King, A Christmas Carol, The Last Days of Patton, A Special Friendship, The Ted Kennedy Jr. Story, Buck James (series, exec. prod.), Old Man and the Sea, Hands of a Murderer (Sherlock Holmes).

STORM, GALE
Actress. r.n. Josephine Cottle. b. Bloomington, TX, April 5, 1922. Won Gateway to Hollywood talent contest while still in high school, in 1939. Also launched successful recording career. *Autobiography*: I Ain't Down Yet (1981).

PICTURES: Tom Brown's Schooldays (debut, 1939), Smart Alecks, Foreign Agent, Nearly Eighteen, Where Are Your Children?, Revenge of the Zombies, The Right to Live, Sunbonnet Sue, Swing Parade of 1946, It Happened on Fifth Avenue, The Dude Goes West, Stampede, The Kid From Texas, Abandoned, Between Midnight and Dawn, Underworld Story, Curtain Call at Cactus Creek, Al Jennings of Oklahoma, Texas Rangers, Woman of the North Country.
TELEVISION: *Series*: My Little Margie, The Gale Storm Show.

STOSSEL, JOHN
News Correspondent. b. 1947. e. Princeton U. Started as producer-reporter with KGW-TV in Portland, OR. Joined WCBS-TV in New York as investigative reporter and consumer editor, winning 15 local Emmy Awards. 1981 joined ABC-TV, appearing on Good Morning America and 20/20 as consumer editor. Also provides twice-weekly consumer reports on ABC Radio Information Network. Author: Shopping Smart (1982).

STOWE, MADELEINE
Actress. b. Los Angeles, CA, Aug. 18, 1958. e. USC. m. actor Brian Benben. Began acting at the Solari Theatre in Beverly Hills where she appeared in The Tenth Man.
PICTURES: Stakeout (debut, 1987), Tropical Snow, Worth Winning, Revenge, The Two Jakes, Closet Land, China Moon, Unlawful Entry, The Last of the Mohicans, Another Stakeout, Short Cuts, Blink, Bad Girls, Twelve Monkeys, The Proposition, Imposter, The General's Daughter.
TELEVISION: *Series*: The Gangster Chronicles. *Movies*: The Nativity, The Deerslayer, Amazons, Blood and Orchids. *Mini-Series*: Beulah Land.

STRAIGHT, BEATRICE
Actress. b. Old Westbury, NY, Aug. 2, 1914. Trained in classics; won Tony award early in career for best actress in Arthur Miller's The Crucible.
THEATER: *NY*: King Lear, Twelfth Night, The Possessed, Land of Fame, Eastward in Eden, The Heiress (B'way & on tour), The Crucible (Tony Award), Phedra, Everything in the Garden, Ghosts, All My Sons. *Regional*: A Streetcar Named Desire, The Lion in Winter, Old Times.
PICTURES: Phone Call from a Stranger (debut, 1952), Patterns, The Nun's Story, Garden Party, Network (Acad. Award, best supporting actress, 1976), The Promise, Bloodline, The Formula, Endless Love, Poltergeist, Two of a Kind, Power.
TELEVISION: *Series*: Beacon Hill, King's Crossing, Jack and Mike. *Mini-Series*: The Dain Curse, Robert Kennedy and His Times. *Specials*: The Borrowers, Faerie Tale Theatre (The Princess and the Pea). *Movies*: Killer on Board, Under Siege, Run Till You Fall, Chiller, People Like Us.

STRATHAIRN, DAVID
Actor. b. San Francisco, CA, 1949. e. Williams Col.
THEATER: Einstein and the Polar Bear, Blue Plate Special, Fen, I'm Not Rappaport, Salonika, A Lie of the Mind, The Birthday Party, Danton's Death, Mountain Language, L'Atelier, A Moon for the Misbegotten, Temptation.
PICTURES: Return of the Secaucus 7, Lovesick, Silkwood, Iceman, The Brother from Another Planet, When Nature Calls, Enormous Changes at the Last Minute, At Close Range, Matewan, Stars and Bars, Dominick and Eugene, Call Me, Eight Men Out, The Feud, Memphis Belle, City of Hope, Big Girls Don't Cry... They Get Even, A League of Their Own, Bob Roberts, Sneakers, Passion Fish, Lost in Yonkers, The Firm, A Dangerous Woman, The River Wild, Losing Isaiah, Dolores Claiborne, Mother Night, Home for the Holidays, Song of Hiawatha, L.A. Confidential, The Climb, With Friends Like These, Meschugge, A Good Baby, Simon Birch, Bad Manners, A Midsummer Night's Dream, A Map of the World, Limbo.
TELEVISION: *Series*: The Days and Nights of Molly Dodd. *Movies*: Day One, Son of the Morning Star, Heat Wave, Judgment, Without Warning: The James Brady Story, O Pioneers!, The American Clock, Beyond the Call, In the Gloaming, Evidence of Blood. *Guest*: Miami Vice, The Equalizer.

STRAUSS, PETER
Actor. b. Croton-on-Hudson, NY., Feb. 20, 1947. e. Northwestern U. Spotted at N.U. by talent agent and sent to Hollywood. On stage at Mark Taper Theatre in Dance Next Door, The Dirty Man.
PICTURES: Hail Hero! (debut, 1969), Soldier Blue, The Trial of the Catonsville Nine, The Last Tycoon, Spacehunter: Adventures in the Forbidden Zone, Nick of Time.
TELEVISION: *Series*: Moloney. *Movies*: The Man Without a Country, Attack on Terror: The FBI Versus the Ku Klux Klan, Young Joe: The Forgotten Kennedy, The Jericho Mile (Emmy Award, 1979), Angel on My Shoulder, Heart of Steel, Under Siege, A Whale for the Killing, Penalty Phase, Proud Men, Brotherhood of the Rose, Peter Gunn, 83 Hours Till Dawn, Flight of Black Angel, Fugitive Among Us, Trial: The Price of Passion, Men Don't Tell, Thicker Than Blood: The Larry McLinden Story, The Yearling, Reunion, Texas Justice. *Mini-Series*: Rich Man Poor Man, Masada, Kane & Abel, Tender Is The Night.

STRAUSS, PETER E.
Executive. b. Oct. 7, 1940. e. Oberlin Coll., London Sch. of Economics, Columbia U. Sch. of Law, L.L.B., 1965. Vice pres., University Dormitory Dev. Co., 1965-68; v.p., Allart Cinema 16, 1968-69; v.p. prod., Allied Artists Pictures Corp., 1970; 1978-80, exec. v.p. Rastar Films; left to become independent as pres., Panache Prods., 1980-86. 1987, pres. & CEO of The Movie Group.
PICTURE: *Producer*: Best of the Best, Cadence, By the Sword, Best of the Best II, Best of the Best III.

STREEP, MERYL
Actress. r.n. Mary Louise Streep. b. Summit, NJ, June 22, 1949. e. Vassar. Acted for a season with traveling theater co. in VT. Awarded scholarship to Yale Drama School, 1972. NY stage debut: Trelawny of the Wells (1975) with New York Shakespeare Fest. Appeared in 1984 documentary In Our Hands.
THEATER: *Off-B'way*: 27 Wagons Full of Cotton (Theatre World Award), A Memory of Two Mondays, Secret Service, Henry V, (NY Shakespeare Fest.), Measure for Measure (NYSF), The Cherry Orchard, Happy End (B'way debut, 1977), The Taming of the Shrew (NYSF), Taken in Marriage, Alice in Concert, Isn't It Romantic?
PICTURES: Julia (debut, 1977), The Deer Hunter, Manhattan, The Seduction of Joe Tynan, Kramer vs. Kramer (Acad. Award, best supporting actress, 1979), The French Lieutenant's Woman, Still of the Night, Sophie's Choice (Acad. Award, 1982), Silkwood, Falling in Love, Plenty, Out of Africa, Heartburn, Ironweed, A Cry in the Dark, She-Devil, Postcards From the Edge, Defending Your Life, Death Becomes Her, The House of the Spirits, The River Wild, The Bridges of Madison County, Before and After, Marvin's Room, One True Thing (Acad. Award nom.), Antz (voice), Dancing at Lughnasa, Music of the Heart, Clint Eastwood: Out of the Shadows, The Papp Project.
TELEVISION: *Mini-Series*: Holocaust (Emmy Award, 1978). *Movies*: The Deadliest Season. *Specials* (PBS): Secret Service, Uncommon Women and Others, Age 7 in America (host), First Do No Harm. *Guest:* The Simpsons (voice).

STREISAND, BARBRA
Singer, Actress, Director, Producer. b. New York, NY, April 24, 1942. e. Erasmus H.S., Brooklyn. Son is actor Jason Gould. Appeared as singer in NY night clubs. NY stage debut: Another Evening with Harry Stoones (1961), followed by Pins and Needles. On Broadway in I Can Get It For You Wholesale, Funny Girl. Performed song Prisoner for 1978 film Eyes of Laura Mars. Appeared in 1990 documentary Listen Up.
PICTURES: Funny Girl (debut; Acad. Award, 1968), Hello Dolly!, On a Clear Day You Can See Forever, The Owl and the Pussycat, What's Up Doc?, Up the Sandbox, The Way We Were (Acad. Award nom.), For Pete's Sake, Funny Lady, A Star Is Born (also co-composer, exec. prod.; Acad. Award for best song: Evergreen, 1976), The Main Event (also co-prod.), All Night Long, Yentl (also dir., prod., co- s.p.), Nuts (also prod., co-composer), The Prince of Tides (also dir., co-prod.; Acad. Award nom. for picture), The Mirror Has Two Faces (also dir.).
TELEVISION: *Specials*: My Name Is Barbra (Emmy Award, 1965), Color Me Barbra, The Belle of 14th Street, A Happening in Central Park, Barbra Streisand... And Other Musical Instruments, Putting It Together, One Voice, Barbra Streisand: The Concert (also co-prod.; 2 Emmy Awards, 1995). *Movie:* Serving in Silence: The Margarethe Cammermeyer Story (co-exec. prod. only). *Guest*: Ed Sullivan, Merv Griffin, Judy Garland Show.

STRICK, WESLEY
Writer. b. New York, NY, Feb. 11, 1954. e. UC at Berkeley, 1975. Was rock critic for magazines Rolling Stone, Cream, Circus.
PICTURES: True Believer, Arachnophobia, Cape Fear, Final Analysis, Batman Returns, Wolf, The Tie That Binds (dir.), The Saint, Return to Paradise.
TELEVISION: *Series*: Eddie Dodd (pilot).

STRICKLAND, GAIL
Actress. b. Birmingham, AL, May 18. e. Florida St. Univ. NY Theatre includes Status Quo Vadis, I Won't Dance.
PICTURES: The Drowning Pool, Bittersweet Love, Bound for Glory, One on One, Who'll Stop the Rain, Norma Rae, Lies, Oxford Blues, Protocol, The Man in the Moon, Three of Hearts, When a Man Loves a Woman, How to Make an American Quilt, The American President.
TELEVISION: *Series*: The Insiders, What a Country, Heartbeat. *Movies*: Ellery Queen, My Father's House, The Dark Side of Innocence, The Gathering, A Love Affair: The Eleanor and Lou Gehrig Story, The President's Mistress, Ski Lift to Death, Letters from Frank, King Crab, Rape and Marriage: The Rideout Case, A Matter of Life and Death, My Body My Child, Eleanor: First Lady of the World, Life of the Party: The Story of Beatrice, Starlight: The Plane That Couldn't Land, The Burden of Proof, Silent Cries, Spies, Barbara Taylor Bradford's Remember, A Mother's Prayer.

STRICKLYN, RAY
Actor. b. Houston, TX, October 8, 1928. e. U. of Houston. Official U.S. representative at Edinburgh Int'l Festival (1988); and Israel Intl. Festival (1989).
THEATER: The Climate of Eden (B'way debut; Theatre World Award). Tour: Stalag 17. Off-B'way: The Grass Harp, Confessions of a Nightingale (also LA, tour; LA Drama Critics, LA Weekly, Dramalogue, Oscar Wilde Awards). LA: Vieux Carre, Compulsion, The Caretaker, Naomi Court, Bus Stop.
PICTURES: The Proud and the Profane, Crime in the Streets, Somebody Up There Likes Me, The Catered Affair, The Last Wagon, Return of Dracula, 10 North Frederick, The Remarkable Mr. Pennypacker, The Big Fisherman, Young Jesse James, The Plunderers, The Lost World, Track of Thunder, Arizona Raiders, Dogpound Shuffle.
TELEVISION: *Movies*: Jealousy, Danielle Steel's Secrets, Hart to Hart Returns.

STRINGER, HOWARD
Executive. b. Cardiff, Wales. Feb. 19, 1942. e. Oxford U., B.A., M.A., modern history/international relations. Received Army Commendation Medal for meritorious achievement for service in Vietnam (1965-67). Joined CBS, 1965, at WCBS-TV, NY, rising from assoc. prod., prod. to exec. prod. of documentary broadcasts. Served as prod., dir. and writer of CBS Reports: The Palestinians (Overseas Press Club of America, Writers Guild Awards, 1974); The Rockefellers (Emmy Award, 1973). Won 9 Emmy Awards as exec. prod., prod., writer or dir: CBS Reports: The Boston Goes to China; CBS Reports: The Defense of the United States; CBS Evening News with Dan Rather: The Beirut Bombing; The Countdown Against Cancer; The Black Family. Exec. prod., CBS Reports; exec. prod., CBS Evening News with Dan Rather, 1981-84. Appointed exec. vice pres., CBS News Division, 1984; pres., CBS News, 1986; pres., CBS/Broadcast Group, 1988. Chmn. & CEO, Tele-TV 1995. Pres., Sony Corporation of America.

STRITCH, ELAINE
Actress. b. Detroit, MI, Feb. 2, 1926. e. studied acting with Erwin Piscator at the New Sch. for Social Research. Major career on stage. B'way debut 1946 in Loco.
THEATER: *NY*: Made in Heaven, Angel in the Wings, Call Me Madam, Pal Joey, On Your Toes, Bus Stop, Goldilocks, Sail Away, Who's Afraid of Virginia Woolf?, Wonderful Town, Company, Show Boat, A Delicate Balance (Tony Award nom.). *London:* Gingerbread Lady, Small Craft Warnings, Company.
PICTURES: The Scarlet Hour (debut, 1955), Three Violent People, A Farewell to Arms, The Perfect Furlough, Who Killed Teddy Bear?, Sidelong Glances of a Pigeon Kicker, The Spiral Staircase, Providence, September, Cocoon: The Return, Cadillac Man, Out to Sea.
TELEVISION: *Series*: Growing Paynes (1948), Pantomine Quiz (regular, 1953-55, 1958), My Sister Eileen, The Trials of O'Brien, Two's Company (London), Nobody's Perfect (London; also adapt.) The Ellen Burstyn Show. *Specials*: Company: the Making of the Album, Kennedy Center Tonight, Follies in Concert, Sensibility and Sense. Movies: The Secret Life of Archie's Wife, An Inconvenient Woman, Chance of a Lifetime. *Guest*: Law & Order (Emmy Award, 1993).

STROCK, HERBERT L.
Producer, Writer, Director, Film editor. b. Boston, MA, Jan. 13, 1918. e. USC, A.B., M.A. in cinema. Prof. of cinema, USC, 1941. Started career, publicity leg man, Jimmy Fidler, Hollywood columnist; editorial dept., MGM, 1941-47; pres., IMPPRO, Inc., 1955-59; assoc. prod.-supv. film ed., U.A.; director: AIP, Warner Bros. independent, Phoenix Films. Pres., Herbert L. Strock Prods. Lecturer at American Film Institute.
PICTURES: Storm Over Tibet, Magnetic Monster, Riders to the Stars, The Glass Wall. *Director*: Gog, Battle Taxi, Donovan's Brain, Rider on a Dead Horse, Devil's Messenger, Brother on the Run, One Hour of Hell, Witches Brew, Blood of Dracula, I Was a Teenage Frankenstein, The Crawling Hand; Soul Brothers Die Hard, Monstroids. *Writer-film editor*, Hurray for Betty Boop (cartoon). *Sound Effects editor* on Katy Caterpillar (cartoon feature). Editor: Night Screams, Detour. *Post-prod. spvr.*: King Kung Fu, Sidewalk Motel. *Co-director*: Deadly Presence. *Editor*: Snooze You Lose, Gramma's Gold, Distance, Fish Outta Water. *Prod/edit.:* The Visitors, Statistically Speaking.
TELEVISION: Highway Patrol, Harbor Command, Men of Annapolis, I Led Three Lives, The Veil, Dragnet, 77 Sunset Strip, Maverick, Cheyenne, Bronco, Sugarfoot, Colt 45, Science Fiction Thea., Seahunt, Corliss Archer, Bonanza, Hallmark Hall of Fame, The Small Miracle, Hans Brinker, The Inventing of America (specials); What Will We Say to a Hungry World (telethon), They Search for Survival (special), Flipper (series). *Documentaries*: Atlantis, Legends, UFO Journals, UFO Syndrome, Legend of the Lochness Monster, China-Mao to Now, El-Papa—Journey to Tibet. *Editor*: Peace Corps' Partnership in Health. *L.A. Dept. of Water & Power:* Water You Can Trust. Olympic Comm. Your Olympic Legacy—AAF.

STROLLER, LOUIS A.
Producer. b. Brooklyn, NY, April 3, 1942. e. Nicholas Coll. of Business Admin., BBA, 1963. Entered film business in 1963 doing a variety of jobs in local NY studios, and TV commercials. Unit manager on The Producers. Moved to L.A. in 1970s. First asst. dir. Charley, Take the Money and Run, Lovers and Other Strangers, They Might Be Giants, Man on a Swing, 92 in the Shade. Prod. mgr.: Mortadella, Sisters, Sweet Revenge, The Eyes of Laura Mars, Telefon. *Assoc. prod.*: Badlands, Carrie, The Seduction of Joe Tynan.
PICTURES: *Exec. prod. or prod.*: Simon, The Four Seasons, Venom, Eddie Macon's Run, Scarface, Sweet Liberty, Real Men, A New Life, Sea of Love, Betsy's Wedding, Back in the U.S.S.R., The Real McCoy, Carlito's Way, The Shadow, The Rock, Nothing to Lose.
TELEVISION: Half a Lifetime (exec. prod.; nom. 4 ACE Awards), Blue Ice.

STRONG, JOHN
Producer, Director, Writer, Actor. b. New York, NY, Dec. 3. e. U. of Miami, Cornell U., B.S., architectural engineering. Began acting in small role in film Duel in the Sun; on B'way in Annie Get Your Gun and understudy for James Dean in Immoralist. Appeared in many radio and TV serials, regular on Captain Video and the Video Ranger, later under contract as actor to Universal and Warner Bros. Member, Writers Guild America West, Directors Guild of America, Producers Guild of America, Dramatists Guild. Pres., Cinevent Corp.
PICTURES: Perilous Journey (exec. prod., s.p.), Eddie & the Cruisers (sprv. prod.), Heart Like a Wheel (sprv. prod.), For Your Eyes Only (s.p.), The Earthling (prod.), The Mountain Men (actor, prod.), Savage Streets (prod.), Steel Justice (prod.), Knights of the City (prod.), Garbage Pail Kids (sprv. prod.), Cop (sprv. prod.), Wild Thing (sprv. prod.), Summer Heat (sprv. prod.), Teen Wolf II (sprv. prod.), Atlantic Entertainment (sprv. prod.), Show of Force (prod., s.p.), Prime Directive (prod., s.p.), Sinapore Sling (prod., s.p.), Willie Sutton Story (prod.), Bandit Queen (prod.), Fatal Charm (exec. prod.), Colors of Love (prod.), Black Ice (dir., s.p.).
TELEVISION: The John Strong Show (host, exec. prod.), The Nurse (special, writer), McCloud (prod., writer), The Thrill of the Fall (prod.), Search (prod., writer, 2nd unit dir.), Outer Limits (exec. chg. prod.), Name of the Game (exec. chg. prod.), I Spy (writer), Love American Style (writer), All in the Family (writer), Changes (prod., dir., writer), Charlie's Angels (writer), Hawaii Five O' (writer).

STROUD, DON
Actor. b. Honolulu, Hawaii, Sept. 1, 1943. e. Kaimuki h.s. Was surfing champion, ranked 4th in the world.
PICTURES: Games, Madigan, Journey to Shiloh, What's So Bad About Feeling Good?, Coogan's Bluff, Bloody Mama, Explosion, Angel Unchained, Tick Tick Tick, Von Richtofen and Brown, Joe Kidd, Slaughter's Big Rip-Off, Scalawag, Murph the Surf, The Killer Inside Me, The House by the Lake, The Choirboys, The Buddy Holly Story, The Amityville Horror, The Night the Lights Went Out in Georgia, Search and Destroy, Sweet Sixteen, Armed and Dangerous, Licence to Kill, Down the Drain, The Divine Enforcer, King of the Kickboxers, Cartel, Mob Boss, Street Wars, Frogtown, Deady Avenger, Danger Sign, Carnosaur II, Of Unknown Origin, Sudden Death, Dillinger and Capone, Twisted Justice, Two to Tango, Ghost Ship, Precious Find, Wild America, Perdita Durango.
TELEVISION: *Series*: Kate Loves a Mystery, Mike Hammer, The New Gidget, Dragnet. *Pilot*: Barefoot in Paradise. *Movies*: Split Second to an Epitaph, Something for a Lonely Man, DA: Conspiracy to Kill, Deadly Dream, Daughters of Joshua Cabe, Rolling Man, The Elevator, Return of Joe Forrester, High Risk, Katie: Portrait of a Centerfold, Out on a Limb, I Want to Live, Manhunters, Murder Me Murder You, The Alien Within, Sawbones, Barefoot in Paradise. *Special:* Hatful of Rain. *Guest*: Murder She Wrote, Quantum Leap, The FBI, Gunsmoke, Baywatch, Starsky and Hutch, The Mod Squad, Marcus Welby, Babylon 5, Walker: Texas Ranger, Nash-Bridges.

STRUTHERS, SALLY
Actress. b. Portland, OR, July 28, 1948. First tv appearance was as dancer on a Herb Alpert special. Appeared on Broadway stage in Wally's Cafe.
PICTURES: The Phynx, Five Easy Pieces, The Getaway.
TELEVISION: *Series*: The Summer Smothers (1970), The Tim Conway Comedy Hour, All in the Family (Emmy Awards: 1972, 1979), Pebbles and Bamm-Bamm (voice), Flintstones Comedy Hour (voice), Gloria, 9 to 5, Dinosaurs (voice). *Movies*: The Great Houdinis, Aloha Means Goodbye, Hey I'm Alive, Intimate Strangers, My Husband is Missing, And Your Name is Jonah, A Gun in the House, A Deadly Silence, In the Best Interests of the Children.

STUBBS, IMOGEN
Actress. b. Newcastle-upon-Tyne, England, Feb. 2, 1961. Brought up in West London on sailing barge on the Thames. Grandmother was playwright Esther McCracken. e. Exeter Coll. First class degree at Oxford U. in English. Joined Oxford U. Dramatic Society appearing in revues and at Edinburgh Festival in play called Poison. Trained for stage at Royal Acad. of Dramatic Art. Prof. stage debut in Cabaret and The Boyfriend, in Ipswich. Acted with Royal Shakespeare Co. in The Two Noble Kinsmen, The Rover (promising newcomer critics award), Richard II, Othello, Heartbreak House, St. Joan, Uncle Vanya.
PICTURES: Privileged, A Summer Story, Nanou, Erik the Viking, True Colors, A Pin for the Butterfly, Sandra C'est la Vie, Jack & Sarah, Sense and Sensibility, Twelfth Night.
TELEVISION: The Browning Version, Deadline, The Rainbow, Fellow Traveller, After the Dance, Relatively Speaking, Othello, Anna Lee, Mother Time.

STULBERG, GORDON
Executive. b. Toronto, Canada, Dec. 17, 1927. e. U. of Toronto, B.A., Cornell Law Sch., LL.B. Was assoc. & member, Pacht, Ross, Warne & Bernhard; ent. m.p. ind. as exec. asst. to v.p., Columbia Pictures Corp., 1956-60; v.p. & chief studio admin. off., 1960-67; pres. of Cinema Center Films, a division of CBS 1967-71; pres. 20th Century-Fox, 1971-75; 1980, named president & COO, PolyGram Pictures. Member of NY, Calif. bars, Chairman, American Interactive Media (Polygram subsidiary).

SUGAR, LARRY
Executive. b. Phoenix, AZ, May 26, 1945. m. Bonnie Sugar. e. Cheshire Acad., 1962; CSUN, B.A., 1967; U. of Southern Calif., J.D., 1971. Writer and co-author, Calif. Primary Reading Program, 1967-68. Joined Warner Bros. as dir., legal and corp. affairs, 1971-74; 20th Century Fox legal staff, 1974-77; co-owner with Bonnie Sugar, Serendipity Prods., 1977-81; named president, international., Lorimar Prods. 1981-84; executive v.p., distribution, CBS 1984-85; exec. v.p. worldwide distribution, Weintraub Entertainment Group 1987-89; formed Sugar Entertainment, chairman., 1989-1991; president, international, Republic Pictures, Inc. 1991-93; pres. Larry Sugar Entertainment, 1993-.
PICTURES: *Exec. prod.*: Slapstick, Steel Dawn, Options, Damned River, Fatal Sky, Graveyard Shift, Shattered, Dark Horse, Family Prayers, The Plague, Boxing Helena. *Prod.*: With Deadly Intent, Annie O, Robin of Locksley, Ronnie & ulie.
TELEVISION: *Movies*: The Prisoner of Zenda Inc., The Halfback of Notre Dame, Dead Man's Gun.

SUGARMAN, BURT
Producer. b. Beverly Hills, CA, Jan. 4. e. U. of Southern California. Chmn. & CEO, GIANT GROUP, LTD., diversified co. traded on NYSE.
PICTURES: Kiss Me Goodbye, Extremities, Children of a Lesser God, Crimes of the Heart.
TELEVISION: Midnight Special, Switched on Symphony, The Mancini Generation, Johnny Mann's Stand Up and Cheer.

SULLIVAN, REV. PATRICK J.
S.J., S.T.D.: Provost, Graduate Center at Tarrytown, Fordham U. b. New York, NY, March 25, 1920. e. Regis H.S.: Georgetown U., A.B., 1943; Woodstock Coll., M.A., 1944; Fordham U., 1945-47; S.T.L. Weston Coll., 1947-51; S.T.D. Gregorian U. (Rome), 1952-54. Prof. of Theology, Woodstock Coll., 1954-57; Consultor, Pontifical Commission for Social Communications, 1968-82; Exec. Dir., U.S. Catholic Conference, Film & Broadcasting Office, 1965-80; Fordham Univ. Graduate School of Business, Assoc. Dean 1982-83, Dean 1983-85.

SUMMERS, GARY
Sound.
PICTURES: Star Wars: Episode IV-A New Hope, Star Wars: Episode V-The Empire Strikes Back, Raiders of the Lost Ark, Star Wars: Episode VI-Return of the Jedi, Indiana Jones and the Temple of Doom, Cocoon, Captain Eo, Howard the Duck, Spaceballs, Always, Indiana Jones and the Last Crusade, Defenseless, The Cross the Rubicon, Rush, The Five Heartbeats, Terminator 2: Judgment Day, F/X2, The Addams Family, House of Cards, Jurassic Park, Miracle on 34th Street, Casper, Toy Story, Special Effects: Anything Can Happen, Titanic (Acad. Award, Best Sound, 1997), The Lost World: Jurassic Park, Stepmom, A Bug's Life, Saving Private Ryan.
TELEVISION: *Series*: Fame L.A.

SUNSHINE, ROBERT HOWARD
Publisher. b. Brooklyn, NY, Jan. 17, 1946. e. U. of RI; Brooklyn Law Sch., 1971. Admitted to NY State Bar, 1971. President of Pubsun Corp., owner of Film Journal International (formerly Film Journal). Publisher of Film Journal International. Exec. dir., International Theatre Equipment Association, 1979-present; sec. and exec. dir. Foundation of the Motion Picture Pioneers, 1975-present; exec. dir., Natl. Assoc. of Theatre Owners of NY State, 1985-present; Producer of Variety Telethon, 1985-present; coordinator and producer, Show East Convention; coordinator and prod., Cinema Expo Intl., Amsterdam, Holland; coordinator and producer, CineAsia, Singapore.

SURTEES, BRUCE
Cinematographer. b. Carmel, CA, Aug. 3, 1944. Son of cinematographer Robert L. Surtees.
PICTURES: The Beguiled, Play Misty for Me, Dirty Harry, The Great Northfield Minnesota Raid, Conquest of the Planet of the Apes, Joe Kidd, The Outfit, High Plains Drifter, Blume in Love, Lenny (Acad. Award nom.), Night Moves, Leadbelly, The Outlaw Josey Wales, The Shootist, Three Warriors, Sparkle, Big Wednesday, Movie Movie (segment: Baxter's Beauties of 1933), Dreamer, Escape from Alcatraz, Ladies and Gentlemen the Fabulous Stains, White Dog, Firefox, Inchon, Honkytonk Man, Bad Boys, Risky Business, Sudden Impact, Tightrope, Beverly Hills Cop, Pale Rider, Psycho III, Out of Bounds, Ratboy, Back to the Beach, License to Drive, Men Don't Leave, Run, The Super, The Crush, That Night. Corrina Corrina, The Stars Fell on Henrietta, The Substitute, Isn't It Romantic, Just A Little Harmless Sex.
TELEVISION: Murder in a Small Town, That Championship Season, Dash and Lilly.

SUSCHITZKY, PETER
Cinematographer. Spent long time in Latin America as documentatory cinematographer. Later made commercials in France, England and U.S. First feature was It Happened Here, 1962.
PICTURES: Over 30 features including: A Midsummer Night's Dream, Charlie Bubbles, Leo the Last, Privilege, That'll Be the Day, Lisztomania, The Rocky Horror Picture Show, All Creatures Great and Small (TV in U.S.), Valentino, The Empire Strikes Back, Krull, Falling in Love, In Extremis, Dead Ringers, Where the Heart Is, Naked Lunch, The Public Eye, The Vanishing, M. Butterfly, Immortal Beloved, Crash, Mars Attacks, The Man in the Iron Mask, eXistenZ.

SUTHERLAND, DONALD
Actor. b. St. John, New Brunswick, Canada, July 17, 1935. Son is actor Kiefer Sutherland. e. U. of Toronto, B.A., 1956. At 14 became a radio announcer and disc jockey. Worked in a mine in Finland. Theatre includes: The Male Animal (debut), The Tempest (Hart House Theatre, U. of Toronto), Two years at London Acad. of Music and Dramatic Art. Spent a year and a half with the Perth Repertory Theatre in Scotland, then repertory at Nottingham, Chesterfield, Bromley and Sheffield.
THEATER: August for the People (London debut), On a Clear Day You Can See Canterbury, The Shewing Up of Blanco Posnet, The Spoon River Anthology, Lolita (B'way debut, 1981).
PICTURES: Castle of the Living Dead (debut, 1964), The World Ten Times Over, Dr. Terror's House of Horrors, Die Die My Darling (Fanatic), The Bedford Incident, Promise Her Anything, The Dirty Dozen, Billion Dollar Brain, Sebastian, Oedipus the King, Interlude, Joanna, The Split, M*A*S*H, Start the Revolution Without Me, Act of the Heart, Kelly's Heroes, Alex in Wonderland, Little Murders, Klute, Johnny Got His Gun, F.T.A. (also co-prod., co-dir., co-s.p.), Steelyard Blues (also exec. prod.), Lady Ice, Alien Thunder (Dan Candy's Law), Don't Look Now, S*P*Y*S, The Day of the Locust, End of the Game (cameo), Fellini's Casanova, The Eagle Has Landed, 1900, The Disappearance, The Kentucky Fried Movie, National Lampoon's Animal House, Invasion of the Body Snatchers, The Great Train Robbery, Murder by Decree, Bear Island, A Man a Woman and a Bank, Nothing Personal, Ordinary People, Blood Relatives, Gas, Eye of the Needle, Threshold, Max Dugan Returns, Crackers, Ordeal by Innocence, Heaven Help Us, Revolution, Wolf at the Door, The Rosary Murders, The Trouble With Spies, Apprentice to Murder, Lost Angels, Lock Up, A Dry White Season, Eminent Domain, Backdraft, Buster's Bedroom, JFK, Scream of Stone, Buffy the Vampire Slayer, Shadow of the Wolf, Benefit of the Doubt, Dr. Bethune (Bethune: The Making of a Hero), Younger and Younger, Six Degrees of Separation, Robert A. Heinlein's The Puppet Masters, Disclosure, Outbreak, Hollow Point, The Shadow Conspiracy, A Time to Kill, The Assignment, Free Money, Fallen, Without Limits, Virus, Toscano, Instinct.
TELEVISION: *Specials*: (British) Marching to the Sea, The Death of Bessie Smith, Hamlet at Elsinore, Gideon's Way, The Champions, Bethune (Canada), Give Me Your Answer True, The Prize (narrator), People of the Forest: The Chimps of Gombe (narrator). *Guest*: The Saint, The Avengers. *Movies*: The Sunshine Patriot, The Winter of Our Discontent, Quicksand: No Escape, The Railway Station Man, The Lifeforce Experiment, Oldest Living Confederate Widow Tells All, Citizen X (Emmy Award, 1995; Golden Globe Award 1995), Natural Enemy. *Series*: Great Books (narrator).

SUTHERLAND, KIEFER
Actor. r.n. William Frederick Dempsey George Sutherland. b. London, England, CA, Dec. 18, 1966. Son of actor Donald Sutherland and actress Shirley Douglas. Moved to Los Angeles at age 4, then to Toronto at 8. Debut with L.A. Odyssey Theater at age 9 in Throne of Straw. Worked in local Toronto theater workshops before landing starring role in The Bay Boy (1984) for which he won Canadian Genie Award.

PICTURES: Max Dugan Returns (debut, 1983), The Bay Boy, At Close Range, Stand By Me, Crazy Moon, The Lost Boys, The Killing Time, Promised Land, Bright Lights Big City, Young Guns, 1969, Renegades, Flashback, Chicago Joe and the Showgirl, Flatliners, Young Guns II, The Nutcracker Prince (voice), Article 99, Twin Peaks: Fire Walk With Me, A Few Good Men, The Vanishing, The Three Musketeers, The Cowboy Way, Teresa's Tattoo, Eye for an Eye, Freeway, A Time To Kill, Truth or Consequences—N.M. (also dir.), Dark City, The Break Up, Woman Wanted, Picking up the Pieces.
TELEVISION: *Movies*: Trapped in Silence, Brotherhood of Justice, Last Light (also dir.), Dark Reflection (co-exec. prod. only). *Guest*: Amazing Stories (The Mission).

SUTTON, JAMES T.
Executive. b. California, Sept. 13. e. Columbia U. Film inspector, U.S. government; overseas m.p. service, WW II; co-owner, gen. mgr., Hal Davis Studios; hd. TV commercial div., Allan Sandler Films; Academy Art Pictures; pres., chmn. of bd., exec. prod., Royal Russian Studios, Inc., western hemisphere div.; pres. exec. prod. Gold Lion Prods., Inc.; pres. exec. prod. James T. Sutton-John L. Carpenter Prods.; pres., exec. dir., Airax Corp.; pres. of Skyax (div. of Airax).

SUVARI, MENA
Actress. b. Newport, RI, February 9, 1979. e. Providence High School, Burbank. m. cinematographer Robert Brinkmann.
PICTURES: Nowhere, Kiss the Girls, Slums of Beverly Hills, Snide and Prejudice, The Rage: Carrie 2, American Pie, American Beauty, American Virgin, Loser, Sugar & Spice, D'Artagnan.
TELEVISION: *Movies:* Atomic Train. *Guest:* Boy Meets World, High Incident, Minor Adjustments, ER, Chicago Hope, 413 Hope St.

SUZMAN, JANET
Actress. b. Johannesburg, South Africa, Feb. 9, 1939. e. Kingsmead Coll., U. of Witwaterstrand. Trained at L.A.M.D.A. London stage debut in The Comedy of Errors. *Recent theater*: Another Time, Hippolytos, The Sisters Rosensweig. *Director*: Othello for Market Theatre and Channel 4 (TV), Death of a Salesman, A Dream of People, The Deep Blue Sea.
PICTURES: Nicholas and Alexandra (Acad. Award nom.), A Day in the Death of Joe Egg, The Black Windmill, Nijinsky, Priest of Love, The Draughtsman's Contract, And the Ship Sails On, A Dry White Season, Nuns on the Run, Leon the Pig Farmer.
TELEVISION: *Specials/Movies*: The Three Sisters, Hedda Gabler, The House on Garibaldi Street, The Zany Adventures of Robin Hood, Miss Nightingale, Macbeth, The Miser, Revolutionary Witness, Saint Joan, Twelfth Night, Master Class on Shakespearean Comedy, Inspector Morse, The Ruth Rendell Mysteries. *Series:* Mountbatten—Last Viceroy of India, The Singing Detective, Clayhanger.

SVENSON, BO
Actor. b. Goteborg, Sweden, Feb. 13, 1941. e. UCLA, 1970-74. U.S. Marine Corps 1959-65.
PICTURES: Maurie (debut, 1973), The Great Waldo Pepper, Part 2: Walking Tall, Breaking Point, Special Delivery, Portrait of a Hitman, Final Chapter: Walking Tall, Our Man in Mecca, The Inglorious Bastard, North Dallas Forty, Virus, Night Warning, Thunder Warrior, Deadly Impact, Wizards of the Lost Kingdom, The Manhunt, The Delta Force, Choke Canyon, Heartbreak Ridge, War Bus 2, Silent Hero, Thunder Warrior II, White Phantom, Deep Space, Justice Done, The Train, Soda Cracker, Curse II: The Bite, Captain Henkel, Running Combat, Steel Frontier, Private Obsession, Speed 2: Cruise Control.
TELEVISION: *Series*: Here Come the Brides, Walking Tall. *Movies*: The Bravos, Frankenstein, You'll Never See Me Again, Hitched, Target Risk, Snowbeast, Gold of the Amazon Women, Jealousy, Dirty Dozen: The Deadly Mission, 3 Days to Kill, Heartless.

SWAIM, BOB
Director, Writer. b. Evanston, IL, Nov. 2, 1943. e. Calif. State U, B.A.; L'Ecole Nationale de la Cinematographie, Paris, BTS 1969. American director who has often worked in France. Began career making shorts: Le Journal de M Bonnafous, Self Portrait of a Pornographer, Vive les Jacques. Received Cesar award French Acad. M.P., 1982; Chevalier des Arts et des Lettres 1985.
PICTURES: La Nuit de Saint-Germain-des-Pres (1977), La Balance, Spies Like Us, (actor), Half Moon Street, Masquerade, Atlantide, Da Costa, Parfum de Meurte, Femme de Passions, The Climb.
TELEVISION: Series: Rainbow Drive (actor), Frauen in Angst (s.p.), Target of Suspicion (actor, dir., cam.).

SWANK, HILARY
Actress. Bellingham, Washington, July 30, 1974. m. actor Chad Lowe. Won the Best Actress Oscar in 2000.
PICTURES: Buffy the Vampire Slayer, The Next Karate Kid, Sometimes They Come Back...Again, Kounterfeit, Quiet Days in Hollywood, Heartwood, Boys Don't Cry, The Gift, The Affair of the Necklace.
TELEVISION: *Series:* Camp Wilder, Beverly Hills 90210, Leaving L.A. *Movies:* Cries Unheard: The Donna Yaklich Story, Terror in the Family, Dying to Belong, The Sleepwalker Killing. *Guest:* Growing Pains.

SWANSON, DENNIS
Executive. e. Univ. of IL. B.A. in journalism, 1961, M.S. in communications/political science, 1966. 1966-67, news prod. & assignment mngr. for WGN radio & tv in Chicago; 1968-70, assign. edit. & field prod. for NBC news at WMAQ TV in Chicago; 1971-74, sportscaster and prod. WMAQ; worked for TVN in Chicago and served as company's NY dir. of news division; 1976, became exec. prod. of KABC-TV in LA; 1981, appointed station mngr. KABC-TV; 1983, v.p. & gen. mngr. WLS-TV, Chicago; 1985, named pres. of ABC Owned TV Stations; 1986, became pres. of ABC Sports; 1990, pres., ABC Daytime and ABC Children's Programming.

SWANSON, KRISTY
Actress. b. Mission Viejo, CA, Dec. 12, 1969. Signed with modeling agency at age 9, appearing in over 30 commercials. Acting debut at 13 on Disney series Dreamfinders.
PICTURES: Pretty in Pink, Ferris Bueller's Day Off, Deadly Friend, Flowers in the Attic, Diving In, Mannequin Two on the Move, Hot Shots, Highway to Hell, Buffy the Vampire Slayer, The Program, The Chase, Getting In (Student Body), Higher Learning, The Phantom, Marshal Law, Lover Girl, 8 Heads in a Duffel Bag, Tinseltown, Supreme Sanction, Past Imperfect, Meeting Daddy, Big Daddy.
TELEVISION: *Series*: Dreamfinders, Knots Landing, Nightingales, Early Edition. *Movies*: Miracle of the Heart: A Boys Town Story, Not Quite Human, Bad to the Bone, Supreme Sanction.

SWAYZE, PATRICK
Actor, Dancer. b. Houston, TX. Aug. 18, 1952. e. San Jacinto Col. m. actress-dancer Lisa Niemi. Son of choreographer Patsy Swayze (Urban Cowboy). Brother is actor Don Swayze. Began as dancer appearing in Disney on Parade on tour as Prince Charming. Songwriter and singer with 6 bands. Studied dance at Harkness and Joffrey Ballet Schs. On B'way as dancer in Goodtime Charley, Grease. Co-author of play Without a Word.
PICTURES: Skatetown USA (debut, 1979), The Outsiders, Uncommon Valor, Red Dawn, Grandview USA (also choreographer), Youngblood, Dirty Dancing (also co-wrote and sang She's Like the Wind), Steel Dawn, Tiger Warsaw, Road House, Next of Kin, Ghost, Point Break, City of Joy, Father Hood, Tall Tale, To Wong Foo—Thanks for Everything—Julie Newmar, Three Wishes, Black Dog, Letters from a Killer.
TELEVISION: *Mini-Series*: North and South: Books I and II. *Movies*: The Comeback Kid, Return of the Rebels, The Renegades (pilot), Off Sides. *Series*: Renegades. *Guest*: M*A*S*H, Amazing Stories.

SWEENEY, ANNE
Executive. e. B.A., College of New Rochelle, and Ed. M., Harvard U. President, Disney Channel and exec. v.p., Disney/ABC Cable Networks, 1996-98. Under her leadership, Disney channel has more than quadrupled its subscriber base to over 62 million homes. Oversaw the launch of Toon Disney, the all-animation cable channel and SoapNet, the 24-hr. soap opera network. Currently president of Disney/ABC Cable Networks, where she is responsible for nonsports cable programming for The Walt Disney Co. and its ABC subsidiary. Oversees the operation of Disney Channel, Toon Disney, and SoapNet, as well as ABC's interests in Lifetime, A&E Television Network, The History Channel, and E! Entertainment Television. Also oversees the creation and management of ABC's Saturday morning children's programming schedule and is in charge of developing future television programming for cable and other platforms. Currently a board member of the National Assoc. of Television Program Executives (NATPE) and the Walter Kaitz Foundation, and honorary chair of Cable Positive. Founding member, Women in Cable, who awarded her Executive of the Year in 1994, Woman of the Year in 1997, and the 1998 Advocate Leader Award from the So. Calif. chapter. Received prestigious STAR Award from American Women in Radio and Television in 1995 and was inducted into the American Adverstising Federation's Advertising Hall of Achievement in 1996. Named to the board of directors, Special Olympics, 2000.

SWEENEY, D. B.
Actor. r.n. Daniel Bernard Sweeney. b. Shoreham, NY, 1961. e. NYU, 1984 B.F.A.
THEATER: *NY*: The Caine Mutiny Court-Martial (B'way), The Seagull: The Hamptons: 1990, Distant Fires (L.A.), among others.
PICTURES: Power (debut, 1986), Fire With Fire, Gardens of Stone, No Man's Land, Eight Men Out, Memphis Belle, Blue Desert, Sons, Leather Jackets, Heaven Is a Playground, The Cutting Edge, A Day in October, Hear No Evil, Fire in the Sky,

Roommates, Three Wishes (cameo), Spawn, Goosed, The Book of Stars, The Weekend.
TELEVISION: *Series*: Strange Luck, C-16: FBI, Harsh Realm. *Mini-Series*: Lonesome Dove. *Movies*: Out of the Darkness, Miss Rose White, Introducing Dorothy Dandridge.

SWERLING, JO, JR.
Executive, Producer. b. Los Angeles, CA, June 18, 1931. e. UCLA, 1948-51; California Maritime Acad., 1951-54. Son of writer Jo Swerling. Active duty US Navy 1954-56. Joined Revue Prods./Universal Television, 1957-81, as prod. coordinator, assoc. prod., prod., assoc. exec. prod., exec. prod., writer, director, actor; currently sr. v.p. and supervising prod., The Cannell Studios.
TELEVISION: *Series*: Kraft Suspense Theater (prod.), Run for Your Life (prod., writer, Emmy, nom.), The Rockford Files (prod., writer), Cool Million (prod.), Alias Smith & Jones (assoc. exec. prod.), Baretta (prod., Emmy nom.), City of Angels (exec. prod.), Toma (exec. prod.), Jigsaw (prod.), The Bold Ones (prod., writer), Lawyers (prod., writer). Mini-series: Captains and the Kings (prod., Emmy nom.), Aspen (prod.), The Last Convertible (exec. prod., dir.). Movies (prod.): This Is the West That Was, The Whole World Is Watching, The Invasion of Johnson County, The Outsider, Do You Take This Stranger, Burn the Town Down, The Three-Thousand Mile Chase, How to Steal an Airplane. Supervising prod., Stephen J. Cannell Productions: The Greatest American Hero, Quest, The A-Team, Hardcastle & McCormick, Riptide, The Last Precinct, Hunter, Stingray, Wiseguy, 21 Jump Street, J.J. Starbuck, Sonny Spoon, The Rousters, Unsub, Booker, Top of the Hill, Broken Badges, Dead End Brattigan, The Hat Squad, Traps, Profit.

SWIFT, LELA
Director.
TELEVISION: Studio One, Suspense, The Web, Justice, DuPont Show of the Week, Purex Specials For Women (Emmy Award) Dark Shadows, Norman Corwin Presents, ABC Late Night 90 min. Specials, ABC Daytime 90 min. Play Break, Ryan's Hope (Emmy Awards: 1977, 1979, 1980; Montior Awards: 1985, 1989), The Rope (A & E).

SWINK, ROBERT E.
Film Editor. b. Rocky Ford, CO, June 3, 1918. Joined editorial dept., RKO Radio, 1936; appt. film ed., 1941. U.S. Army Signal Corps, 1944-45; supv. editor, Fox studio. Edited numerous productions.
PICTURES: Detective Story, Carrie, Roman Holiday, Desperate Hours, Friendly Persuasion, The Big Country, The Diary of Anne Frank, The Young Doctors, The Children's Hour, The Best Man, The Collector, How to Steal a Million, The Flim Flam Man, Funny Girl, The Liberation of L.B. Jones, The Cowboys, Skyjacked, Lady Ice, Papillion, Three the Hard Way, Rooster Cogburn, Midway, Islands in the Stream, Gray Lady Down, The Boys From Brazil, The In-Laws, Going in Style, Sphinx, Welcome Home.
(d. Aug 15, 2000)

SWIT, LORETTA
Actress. b. Passaic, NJ, Nov. 4, 1939. Stage debut in Any Wednesday. Toured in Mame for year. Arrived in Hollywood in 1971 and began TV career.
THEATER: Same Time Next Year, The Mystery of Edwin Drood (B'way), Shirley Valentine (Sarah Siddons Award).
PICTURES: Stand Up and Be Counted (debut, 1972), Freebie and the Bean, Race with the Devil, S.O.B., Beer, Whoops Apocalypse, Lords of Tanglewood.
TELEVISION: *Series*: M*A*S*H (Emmy Awards, 1980, 1982; also Genii, Silver Satellite & People's Choice Awards), Those Incredible Animals (host). *Guest*: Perry Como Show, Mac Davis, Dolly Parton, Bobby Vinton. *Movies*: Hostage Heart, Shirts/Skins, The Last Day, Coffeeville, Valentine, Mirror Mirror, Friendships Secrets and Lies, Cagney & Lacey, Games Mother Never Taught You, Friendships Secrets & Lies, First Affair, The Execution, Dreams of Gold: The Mel Fisher Story, Hell Hath No Fury, A Killer Among Friends. Specials: 14 Going on 30, Best Christmas Pageant Ever, Texaco Salute to Broadway, It's a Bird It's a Plane It's Superman, Miracle at Moreaux, My Dad Can't Be Crazy Can He?, A Matter of Principal.

SWOPE, HERBERT BAYARD, JR.
Director, Producer, Commentator. b. New York, NY. e. Horace Mann Sch., Princeton U. U.S. Navy, 1941-46; joined CBS-TV as remote unit dir., 1946 directing many firsts in sportscasting; winner, Variety Show Management Award for sports coverage & citation by Amer. TV Society, 1948; joined NBC as dir., 1949; prod. dir., 1951; winner, 1952 Sylvania TV Award Outstanding Achievement in Dir. Technique; became exec. prod., NBC-TV in charge of Wide Wide World; film prod., 20th Century-Fox; 1960-62, exec. prod. 20th-Fox TV; 1970-72 exec. at N.Y. Off-Track Betting Corp. 1973-74; v.p., Walter Reade Organization, Inc.; 1975-76 producer-host, This Was TV, Growth of a Giant; 1976 to present commentator-interviewer, Swope's Scope, (radio—WSBR-AM)); Critic's Views (TV: WTVJ, Ch. 5); Column: Now and Then (Palm Beach Pictorial).
THEATER: *Dir./Co-Prod.*: Step on a Crack, Fragile Fox, Fair Game for Lovers.
PICTURES: *Producer*: Hilda Crane, Three Brave Men, True Story of Jesse James, The Bravados, The Fiend Who Walked the West.
TELEVISION: *Prod/Dir.*: Lights Out, The Clock, The Black Robe, Robert Montgomery Presents, Arsenic and Old Lace, Climax, Many Loves of Dobie Gillis, Five Fingers.

SYKES, ERIC
O.B.E.: Writer, Comedian, Actor. b. Oldham, England, May 4, 1923. Early career as actor; 1948 wrote first three series, BBC's Educating Archie TV comedy series for Frankie Howerd, Max Bygraves, Harry Secombe. BBC panel show member. Sykes Versus TV, The Frankie Howerd Series. Longterm contract with ATV 1956. Own BBC series 1958-78, Sykes and A... Specials: Silent Movies for TV, The Plank (also dir. & s.p.), If You Go Down Into the Woods Today, Rhubarb, It's Your Move, Mr. H Is Late, 19th Hole, The Big Freeze.
THEATER: Big Bad Mouse (tour: 1966-9 in America, Rhodesia, Australia, Canada), One Man Show (1982), Time and Time Again, Run for Your Wife, Two Into One, The 19th Hole.
PICTURES: Watch Your Stern, Very Important Person, Invasion Quartet, Village of Daughters, Kill or Cure, Heavens Above, The Bargee, One Way Pendulum, Those Magnificent Men in Their Flying Machines, Rotten to the Core, The Liquidator, The Spy With The Cold Nose, Shalako, Monte Carlo or Bust, Theatre of Blood, Boys in Blue, Gabrielle and the Doodleman, Absolute Beginners, Splitting Heirs.

SYLBERT, ANTHEA
Executive. b. New York, NY, Oct. 6, 1939. e. Barnard Coll., B.A.; Parsons Sch. of Design, M.A. Early career in costume design with range of B'way (The Real Thing), off-B'way and m.p. credits (Rosemary's Baby, John & Mary, Carnal Knowledge, A New Leaf, The Heartbreak Kid, The Cowboys, Bad Company, Shampoo, The Fortune, The Last Tycoon, F.I.S.T.). Two Acad. award. nominations for costume designs for Julia and Chinatown. Joined Warner Bros. in 1977, as v.p., special projects, acting as liaison between creative execs., prod. dept., and creative talent producing films for company. 1978, named v.p., prod. (projects included One Trick Pony, Personal Best.). 1980 appointed v.p. prod., for United Artists, working on Jinxed, Still of the Night, Yentl, etc. 1982 became indept. prod. in partnership with Goldie Hawn (Hawn/Sylbert Movie Co.) producing Swing Shift, Protocol, Wildcats, Overboard, My Blue Heaven, Deceived, Crisscross, Something to Talk About. *TV Movie:* Truman, Hope.

SYMES, JOHN
Executive. e. Univ. of CA at Berkeley. Started at Paramount in tech. opts. dept. of Paramount's domestic tv distrib. div., then became mngr. of videotape opts., dir. of opts. Became sr. v.p. current programs for Paramount Network tv, then exec. v.p. crative affairs for same. Jan. 1994, became pres. of MGM Worldwide TV.

SYMS, SYLVIA
Actress. b. London, June 1, 1934. e. Convent and Grammar Sch.
PICTURES: My Teenage Daughter (debut, 1956), No Time For Tears, The Birthday Present, Woman in a Dressing Gown, Ice Cold in Alex (Desert Attack), The Moonraker, Bachelor of Hearts, No Trees in the Street, Ferry to Hong Kong, Expresso Bongo, Conspiracy of Hearts, The Virgins of Rome, The World of Suzie Wong, Flame in the Streets, Victim, The Quare Fellow, The Punch and Judy Man, The World Ten Times Over, East of Sudan, Operation Crossbow, The Big Job, Hostile Witness, Danger Route, Run Wild Run Free, The Desperados, Asylum, The Tamarind Seed, Give Us Tomorrow, There Goes the Bride, Absolute Beginners, A Chorus of Disapproval, Shirley Valentine, Shining Through, Dirty Weekend, Staggered, The House of Angelo, Food of Love.
TELEVISION: Something to Declare, Bat Out of Hell, Department in Terror, Friends and Romans, Strange Report, Half-hour Story, The Root of All Evil, The Bridesmaid, Clutterbuck, Movie Quiz, My Good Woman, Looks Familiar, Love and Marriage, The Truth About Verity, I'm Bob, He's Dickie, Blankety Blank, The Story of Nancy Astor, Give Us a Clue, Sykes, Crown Court, A Murder Is Announced, Murder at Lynch Cross, Rockcliffes Follies, Dr. Who, Countdown, Ruth Rendell Mystery, May to December, Intimate Contact, Thatcher: The Final Days, Natural Lies, Mulberry, Peak Practice, Half the Picture, Master of the Moor, Original Sin. *Series*: The Human Jungle, The Saint, The Baron, *Mini-series*: The Glass Virgin.

SZABO, ISTVAN
Director. b. Budapest, Hungary, Feb. 18, 1938. e. Academy of Theatre and Film Art, Budapest, 1961. Debut Koncert (short, diploma film) 1961. Short films: Variations on a Theme, You, Piety, Why I Love It, City Map. Appeared in film Tusztortenet (Stand Off).

PICTURES: Age of Illusions (feature debut, 1964), Father, A Film About Love, 25 Fireman's Street, Premiere, Tales of Budapest, The Hungarians, Confidence (Silver Bear Award, Berlin Fest.), The Green Bird, Mephisto (Hungarian Film Critics Award; Acad. Award, Best Foreign Film, 1982), Bali, Colonel Redl, Hanussen (also co-s.p.), Opera Europa, Meeting Venus, Dear Emma—Sweet Bobe, Offenbach Titkai.

SZWARC, JEANNOT
Director. b. Paris, France, Nov. 21, 1939.
PICTURES: Extreme Close-Up, Bug, Jaws II, Somewhere in Time, Enigma, Supergirl, Santa Claus, Honor Bound.
TELEVISION: *Series*: Ironside, To Catch a Thief, Kojak, Columbo, Night Gallery, Crime Club, True Life Stories, Twilight Zone (1986). *Movies*: Night of Terror, The Weekend Nun, The Devil's Daughter, You'll Never See Me Again, The Small Miracle, Lisa: Bright and Dark, A Summer Without Boys, Crime Club, Code Name: Diamond Head, Murders in the Rue Morgue, The Rockford Files: A Blessing in Disguise.

T

MR. T
Actor. r.n. Lawrence Tero. b. Chicago, IL, May 21, 1953. Professional bodyguard when hired by Stallone in 1980 for Rocky.
PICTURES: Penitentiary II, Rocky III, D.C. Cab, Freaked, The Magic of the Golden Bear: Goldy III.
TELEVISION: *Series*: The A Team, T & T. *Movie*: The Toughest Man in the World. *Guest*: Silver Spoons.

TAFFNER DONALD L.
Executive. b. New York, NY. e. St. Johns U. William Morris Agency, 1950-59; Paramount Pictures. 1959-63; D. L. Taffner Ltd., 1963-present.
TELEVISION: *Prod.*: Three's Company, Too Close For Comfort.

TAGAWA, CARY-HIROYUKI
Actor.
PICTURES: Armed Response, The Last Emperor, Spellbinder, Twins, The Last Warrior, License to Kill, Showdown in Little Tokyo, The Perfect Weapon, Kickboxer 2: The Road Back, Raven: Return of the Black Dragons, American Me, Nemesis, Rising Sun, Natural Causes, The Dangerous, Soldier Boyz, Picture Pride, Mortal Kombat, White Tiger, Provocateur, Danger Zone, The Phantom, Top of the World, American Dragons, Vampires.
TELEVISION: *Movies:* Star Trek: The Next Generation - Encounter at Farpoint, L.A. Takedown, Murder in Paradise, Vestige of Honor, Not of This World, Mission of the Shark: The Saga of the U.S.S Indianapolis, Raven: Return of the Black Dragons, Day of Reckoning. *Series*: Nash Bridges.

TAKEI, GEORGE
Actor. b. Los Angeles, CA, April 20, 1937. e. UCLA. Professional debut in Playhouse 90 production while training at Desilu Workshop in Hollywood. Gained fame as Sulu in Star Trek TV series. *Author*: Mirror Friend Mirror Foe (novel), To the Stars (autobiography; 1994).
PICTURES: Ice Palace, A Majority of One, Hell to Eternity, PT 109, Red Line 7000, An American Dream, Walk Don't Run, The Green Berets, Star Trek: The Motion Picture, Star Trek II: The Wrath of Khan, Star Trek III: The Search for Spock, Star Trek IV: The Voyage Home, Star Trek V: The Final Frontier, Return From the River Kwai, Prisoners of the Sun, Star Trek VI: The Undiscovered Country, Live by the Fist, Oblivion, Chongbal, Oblivion 2: Backlash, Star Trek: Starfleet Academy, Mulan (voice), Bug Buster, Trekkies.
TELEVISION: *Series:* Star Trek, Hercules (voice). *Movies*: Kissinger and Nixon, Space Cases, Star Trek Voyager. *Guest*: Perry Mason, Alcoa Premiere, Mr. Novak, The Wackiest Ship in the Army, I Spy, Magnum PI, Trapper John M.D., Miami Vice, Murder She Wrote, McGyver, Hawaiian Eye, Californian, Hawaii Five-O, My Three Sons, John Forsythe Show, Death Valley Days, Theatre in America, Game Night, Kung Fu: The Legend Continues, The Simpsons (voice).

TAMBLYN, RUSS
Actor b. Los Angeles, CA, Dec. 30, 1934. e. No. Hollywood H.S. West Coast radio shows; on stage with little theater group; song-and-dance act in Los Angeles clubs, veterans hospitals.
PICTURES: The Boy with Green Hair, Reign of Terror, Samson and Delilah, Gun Crazy, Kid from Cleveland, The Vicious Years, Captain Carey U.S.A., Father of the Bride, As Young As You Feel, Father's Little Dividend, Cave of Outlaws, Winning Team, Retreat Hell, Take the High Ground, Seven Brides for Seven Brothers, Deep in My Heart, Many Rivers to Cross, Hit the Deck, Last Hunt, Fastest Gun Alive, The Young Guns, Don't Go Near the Water, Peyton Place (Acad. Award nom.), High School Confidential, Tom Thumb, Cimarron, West Side Story, Wonderful World of the Brothers Grimm, How the West Was Won, Follow the Boys, The Haunting, Long Ships, Son of a Gunfighter, War of the Gargantuas, Scream Free, Dracula Vs. Frankenstein, Satan's Sadists, The Female Bunch, The Last Movie, Win Place or Steal, Murder Gang, Human Highway, Aftershock, Commando Squad, Cyclone, Necromancer, B.O.R.N., Phantom Empire, Bloodscream, Wizards of the Demon Sword, Desert Steel, Cabin Boy, Attack of the 60 Ft. Centerfold, Johnny Mysto: The Boy Wizard, Little Miss Magic, Invisible Dad, Ghost Dog.
TELEVISION: *Series*: Twin Peaks. *Guest*: The Walter Winchell Show, ABC's Wide World of Entertainment, The Ed Sullivan Show, Gunsmoke, Name of the Game, Tarzan, Rags to Riches, Channing, Iron Horse, Perry Como Show, Love American Style, Grizzly Adams, Fame, Running Mates, Greatest Show on Earth, Burke's Law, Cade's County, The Quest, Quantum Leap, Babylon 5, Invisible Mom, Nash Bridges. *Specials*: The Making of Seven Brides for Seven Brothers.

TAMBOR, JEFFREY
Actor. b. San Francisco, CA, July 8, 1944. e. San Francisco St. (BA), Wayne St. (MA). Acted with Seattle Rep., Actors Theatre of Louisville, Loeb Drama Ctr. (Harvard), Milwaukee Rep. Theatre, Acad. Festival Theatre (Chicago), Old Globe Theatre in San Diego, South Coast Rep. Theatre. B'way in Measure for Measure, Sly Fox.
PICTURES: And Justice for All, Saturday the 14th, Mr. Mom, The Man Who Wasn't There, No Small Affair, Three O'Clock High, Lisa, City Slickers, Life Stinks, Pastime, Article 99, Brenda Starr, Crossing the Bridge, At Home with the Webbers, Face Dancer, Under Pressure, A House in the Hills, Radioland Murders, Heavyweights, Big Bully, Learning Curves, Bad with Numbers, Big Bully, Meet Joe Black, Teaching Mrs. Tingle, Doctor Dolittle, There's Something About Mary, Girl Interrupted, The Freshman, Muppets From Space, Pollock, How the Grinch Stole Christmas, Never Again
TELEVISION: *Series*: The Ropers, Hill Street Blues, 9 to 5, Mr. Sunshine, Max Headroom, Studio 5-B, American Dreamer, The Larry Sanders Show, Me and George, The Lionhearts, Everything's Relative, Sammy (voice). *Movies*: Alcatraz: The Whole Shocking Story, A Gun in the House, The Star Maker, Take Your Best Shot, Cocaine: One Man's Seduction, Sadat, The Awakening of Candra, The Three Wishes of Billy Grier, The Burden of Proof, Honey Let's Kill the Neighbors, Another Midnight Run, The Man Who Captured Eichmann, Weapons of Mass Destruction, The Lot. *Mini-Series*: Robert Kennedy & His Times, The Lot. *Guest*: Three's Company, M*A*S*H, Barney Miller, Tales From the Crypt, The Golden Globe, Empty Nest, Doogie Howser M.D., Equal Justice, Murder She Wrote.

TANEN, NED
Executive. b. Los Angeles, CA, 1931. e. UCLA, law degree. Joined MCA, Inc. 1954; appt. v.p. in 1968. Brought Uni Records, since absorbed by MCA Records, to best-seller status with such artists as Neil Diamond, Elton John, Olivia Newton-John. First became active in theatrical film prod. in 1972. 1975 began overseeing feature prod. for Universal. 1976 named pres. of Universal Theatrical Motion Pictures, established as div. of Universal City Studios. Left in 1982 to become independent producer. 1985, joined Paramount Pictures as pres. of Motion Picture Group. Resigned 1988 to continue as sr. advisor at Paramount. Producer: Guarding Tess, Cops and Robbersons.

TANKERSLEY, ROBERT K.
Executive. b. Decatur, IL, July 31, 1927. In U.S. Navy, 1945-46; Marine Corps, 1949-55. With Natl. Theatre Supply as salesman in Denver 13 yrs. 1959-87, pres. Western Service & Supply, Denver, theatre equip. co.; 1987-present, mgr., Tankersley Enterprises theatre equip. Also was CEO of Theatre Operators, Inc., Bozeman, Mont. Member: Theatre Equipment Assn. (past pres.), National NATO Presidents Advisory Council; Rocky Mt. Motion Picture Assn. (past pres.), SMPTE, Motion Picture Pioneers, past chief barker, Variety Club Tent #37. Colorado, Wyoming NATO (past pres.) chmn.-elect Exhibitors West.

TAPLIN, JONATHAN
Producer. b. Cleveland, OH, July 18, 1947. e. Princeton U.
PICTURES: Mean Streets, The Last Waltz, Carny (exec. prod.), Grandview U.S.A. (co-exec. prod.), Under Fire, Baby, My Science Project, Until the End of the World, K2, To Die For (exec. prod.), Rough Magic (exec. prod.).
TELEVISION: Shelly Duvall's Faerie Tale Theatre (6 episodes), 1968: The 25th Anniversary, The Native Americans, The Prize, *Mini-series*: Cadillac Desert (exec. prod.).

TAPS, JONIE
Producer. Executive. Columbia Studio. Member of Friars Club, Hillcrest Country Club.

PICTURES: *Produced*: When You're Smiling, Sunny Side of Street, Sound Off, Rainbow Round My Shoulder, All Ashore, Cruisin' Down the River, Drive a Crooked Road, The Eddy Duchin Story, Three for the Show, Bring Your Smile Along, He Laughed Last, Shadow on the Window.

TARADASH, DANIEL
Writer, Director. b. Louisville, KY, Jan. 29, 1913. e. Harvard Coll., B.A., 1933; Harvard Law Sch., LL.B., 1936. Passed NY Bar, 1937; won nationwide playwriting contest, 1938; U.S. Army WWII. Pres. Screen Writers Branch, WGA, 1955-56; v.p., Writers Guild of America, West 1956-59; mem. Writers Guild Council, 1954-65; mem., bd. of govnrs. Motion Picture Acad. Arts & Sciences, 1964-74, 1990-93; v.p. 1968-70 and pres. 1970-73. Trustee, Producers-Writers Guild Pension plan 1960-73. chmn., 1965. Mem. Bd. of Trustees of American Film Institute 1967-69. WGA's Valentine Davies Award, 1971. Pres., Academy M.P. Arts & Sciences, 1970-73, mem. bd. trustees, Entertainment Hall of Fame Foundation. Mem., Public Media General Programs panel for the National Foundation for the Arts, 1975-85, 1992; Pres. Writers Guild of America, West, 1977-79. Natl. chmn., Writers Guild of America, 1979-81. WGA's Morgan Cox Award, 1988. WGA's Edmund H. North Founders Award 1991. Festival to present Taradash Screenwriting Award 1992-; USC retrospective and tribute, 1992. Writer of TV special Bogie. Recipient of the Writers Guild of America West Laurel Award, 1996.
PICTURES: Golden Boy, A Little Bit of Heaven, Knock on Any Door, Rancho Notorious, Don't Bother to Knock, From Here to Eternity (Academy Award 1953), Desiree, Storm Center (also dir., co-story), Picnic, Bell Book and Candle, The Saboteur Code Name—Morituri, Hawaii, Castle Keep, Doctors' Wives, The Other Side of Midnight.

TARANTINO, QUENTIN
Writer, Director, Actor, Producer. b. Knoxville, TN, March 27, 1963. Graduate of Sundance Institute Director's Workshop and Lab. With producer Lawrence Bender, formed production co. A Band Apart.
PICTURES: Past Midnight (assoc. prod., co-s.p.), Reservoir Dogs (dir., s.p., actor), True Romance (s.p.), Killing Zoe (co-exec. prod.), Natural Born Killers (story), Sleep With Me (actor), Pulp Fiction (dir., s.p., co-story, actor; Cannes Film Fest. Award for Best Film; LA Film Critics, NY Film Critics, Natl. Soc. of Film Critics, Chicago Film Critics & Independent Spirit Awards for dir. & s.p.; Academy Award & Golden Globe for s.p.; Natl. Bd. of Review Award for dir., 1994), Destiny Turns on the Radio (actor), Somebody to Love (actor), Desperado (actor), Four Rooms (co-s.p., co-exec. prod., actor), From Dusk Till Dawn (s.p., actor, co-exec. prod.), Girl 6 (actor), Curdled (exec. prod.), God Said, Ha (actor); Full Tilt Boogie (actor), Jackie Brown, Forever Hollywood (actor), Little Nicky (actor), From Dusk Till Dawn 2:Texas Blood Money (exec. prod), From Dusk Till Dawn 3: The Hangman's Daughter (exec. prod.).
TELEVISION: *Guest*: The Golden Girls, All-American Girl. *Dir*: ER (1 episode).

TARNOFF, JOHN B.
Producer. b. New York, NY, Mar. 3, 1952. e. UCLA, motion pictures & TV, 1973-74; Amherst Coll., B.A., 1969-73. Named field exec. with Taylor-Laughlin Distribution (company arm of Billy Jack Enterprises) 1974; left in 1975 to be literary agent with Bart/Levy, Inc.; later with Michael Levy & Associates, Paul Kohner/Michael Levy Agency; Headed TV dept., Kohner/Levy, 1979. Joined MGM as production exec., 1979; v.p., development, 1979-80; sr. v.p. production & devel., 1981-82; exec. v.p., Kings Road Prods., 1983-84; v.p., prod., Orion Pictures Corp., 1985; exec. prod., Out of Bounds, Columbia Pictures, 1986; v.p., prod., De Laurentiis Entertainment Group, 1987. Head of production, DeLaurentiis Entertainment, Australia, 1987-88. Exec. v.p. production, Village Roadshow Pictures, 1988-. Exec. prod.: The Delinquents, Blood Oath. 1990-93, personal mngr., Addis-Wechsler & Assoc. 1994, New Line Cinema/Overseas Film Group; prod., Nature of the Beast. 1995, founder, Newspeak Media Inc. 1996, founder, Personality Factory, Inc. 1998, exec. prod. Big Brother, cd-rom adventure based on Orwell's 1984; writer/designer, WarGames, cd-rom.

TARSES, JAMIE
Executive. b. Pittsburgh, PA. e. Williams Coll. Prior to joining NBC, worked as a casting director for Lorimar Productions. Joined NBC in Sept. 1987 as Mgr., Creative Affairs for NBC Productions. In Dec. 1987, named Mgr., Current Comedy Programs, NBC Entertainment and was NBC's Program Exec. for such series as Cheers, Amen, 227 and A Different World. In 1988, named Mgr., Comedy Development. In Feb. 1989, promoted to Director, Comedy Development, NBC Entertainment. Was directly involved in the development of Friends, NewsRadio, Caroline in the City, Mad About You, Frasier and several other NBC programs. In Aug. 1994, was named to supervise one of NBC's two programming teams before being promoted in 1995 to S.V.P., Primetime Series. In June of 1996, joined ABC Entertainment as President. Resigned, July 1999.

TARSES, JAY
Producer, Writer, Actor. b. Baltimore, MD, July 3, 1939. e. Williams Coll., Ithaca Coll., BFA theatre. Daughter is executive Jamie Tarses. Wrote and acted with little-theater co. in Pittsburgh, drove a truck in NY for Allen Funt's Candid Camera and worked in advertising and promotion for Armstrong Cork Co. in Lancaster, PA where he met Tom Patchett. Formed Patchett and Tarses, stand-up comedy team played coffee-house circuit in the late 1960s. Later twosome became TV writing team and joined writing staff of Carol Burnett Show winning Emmy in 1972.
PICTURES: *Co-s.p. with Patchett*: Up the Academy, The Great Muppet Caper, The Muppets Take Manhattan.
TELEVISION: *Series*: *Actor*: Make Your Own Kind of Music, Open All Night, The Duck Factory, The Days and Nights of Molly Dodd. *Specials*: *With Tom Patchett*: The Bob Newhart Show (exec. prod., writer), The Tony Randall Show (creator, exec. prod., writer), We've Got Each Other (creator, exec. prod., writer), Mary (prod.), Open All Night (creator, prod., writer), Buffalo Bill (creator, exec. prod., writer). *Solo*: The Days and Nights of Molly Dodd (creator, prod., writer), The "Slap" Maxwell Story (creator, prod., writer), Smoldering Lust (creator, prod., writer), Public Morals (co-creator, exec. prod., writer). *Pilots*: The Chopped Liver Brothers (exec. prod., writer), The Faculty (exec. prod., dir., writer), Baltimore (creator, prod., writer), Harvey Berger: Salesman (co-creator, prod., writer), Jackass Junior High (creator, prod., writer).

TAVERNIER, BERTRAND
Director, Writer. b. Lyon, France, April 25, 1941. After 2 yrs. of law study, quit to become film critic for Cahiers du Cinema and Cinema 60. Asst. to dir. Jean-Pierre Melville on Leon Morin Priest (1961), also worked as film publicist. Wrote film scripts and a book on the Western and a history of American cinema. Partner for 6 yrs. with Pierre Rissient in film promotion company, during which time he studied all aspects of film-making. 1963: directed episode of Les Baisers. Pres., Lumiere Inst., Lyon. Book: 50 Years of American Cinema, Qu'est ce Qu'on Attend?, Amis Americains.
PICTURES: *Director-Co-writer*: The Clockmaker (L'Horloger de Saint-Paul), Let Joy Reign Supreme (Que La Fête Commence), The Judge and the Assassin (Le Judge et l'Assassin), Spoiled Children (also co-prod.), Deathwatch. *Dir./Co-Writer/Prod.*: A Week's Vacation, Clean Slate (Coup de Torchon; 11 César nom., Oscar nom.), Mississippi Blues (co-dir. with Robert Parrish), A Sunday in the Country (Un Dimanche a la Campagne; Best Direction Cannes, New york Critics Prize), 'Round Midnight, Beatrice (dir. co-prod. only), Life and Nothing But, Daddy Nostalgia, The Undeclared War (co-dir. with Patrick Rutman), L627, La Fille de D'Artagnan, L'Appat, Capitaine Conan, Ca Commence Aujourd'hui.
TELEVISION: Phillippe Soupault, October Country (co-dir. with Robert Parrish), Lyon, le regard interieur, La Lettre, The Other Side of the Tracks.

TAVIANI, PAOLO and VITTORIO
Directors, Writers. b. San Miniato, Pisa, Italy, (Paolo: Nov. 8, 1931; Vittorio: Sept. 20, 1929); e. Univ. of Pisa (Paolo: liberal arts; Vittorio: law). The two brothers always work in collaboration from script preparation through shooting and editing. 1950: With Valentino Orsini ran cine-club at Pisa. 1954: In collab. with Caesare Zavattini directed short about Nazi massacre at San Miniato. 1954-59: with Orsini made series of short documentaries (Curatorne e Montanara; Carlo Pisacane; Ville della Brianza; Lavatori della pietra; Pitori in cita; I Pazzi della domenica; Moravia, Cabunara). Worked as assistant to Rosellini, Luciano Emmer and Raymond Pellegrini. 1960: collaborated on an episode of Italy Is Not a Poor Country.
PICTURES (all by both): A Man for Burning (debut, 1962; co-dir. with Valentino Orsini), Matrimonial Outlaws (co-dir. with Orsini), The Subversives, Under the Sign of Scorpio, Saint Michael Had a Rooster, Allonsanfan, Padre Padrone (Cannes Film Fest.: Grand Prix & Critics International Prize, 1977), The Meadow, The Night of the Shooting Stars (1981, Best Director Award, Natl. Society of Film Critics; Special Jury Prize, Cannes), Kaos, Good Morning Babylon, The Sun Also Shines at Night, Fiorile, The Elective Affinities (Le Affinata elettive), You Laugh (Tu ridu).

TAVOULARIS, DEAN
Production Designer. b. Lowell, MA.
PICTURES: Candy, Zabriskie Point, Little Big Man, The Godfather, The Godfather: Part II, The Conversation, Farewell, My Lovely, The Brink's Job, Apocalypse Now, One From the Heart, The Escape Artist, Hammett, The Outsiders, Rumble Fish, Peggy Sue Got Married, Gardens of Stone, Tucker: The Man and His Dream, New York Stories, The Godfather: Part III, Final Analysis, Rising Sun, I Love Trouble, Jack, Bulworth, The Parent Trap, The Ninth Gate, Angel Eyes, C.Q.

TAYLOR, DELORES
Actress, Writer, Producer. b. Winner, SD, Sept. 27, 1939. e. U. of South Dakota, studying commercial art. m. Tom Laughlin. First TV experience was heading art dept. at RCA wholesale center in Milwaukee. Established first Montessori School in U.S. in Santa Monica for several yrs., with husband. Made feature film debut as actress in Billy Jack in 1971. Wrote s.p. with husband for that and sequels, The Trial of Billy Jack, Billy Jack Goes to Washington, under pseudonym Teresa Christina.
PICTURES: *Exec. Prod., Writer:* Proper Time, Young Sinners, Born Losers, The Master Gunfighter. *Exec. Prod., Writer, Actress*: Billy Jack, Trial of Billy Jack, Billy Jack Goes to Washington, Return of Billy Jack.

TAYLOR, ELIZABETH
Actress. b. London, Eng., Feb. 27, 1932. e. Bryon House, London. When 3 years old danced before Princess Elizabeth, Margaret Rose. Came to U.S. at outbreak of WWII. *Author*: World Enough and Time (with Richard Burton; 1964), Elizabeth Taylor (1965), Elizabeth Takes Off (1988). Initiated Ben Gurion U.—Elizabeth Taylor Fund for Children of the Negev, 1982. Co-founded American Foundation for AIDS Research, 1985. Named Comdr. Arts & Letters (France) 1985, Legion of Honor, 1987. Established the Elizabeth Taylor AIDS Foundation in 1991. Developed various perfume products: Elizabeth Taylor's Passion, Passion Body Riches, Passion for Men, White Diamonds, Diamonds and Emeralds, Diamonds and Sapphires, Diamond and Rubies; 1993 launched Elizabeth Taylor Fashion Jewelry Collection. Recipient of AFI Life Achievement Award (1993), Jean Hersholt Humanitarian Award (1993).
THEATER: *B'way*: The Little Foxes (also London), Private Lives.
PICTURES: There's One Born Every Minute (debut, 1942), Lassie Come Home, Jane Eyre, White Cliffs of Dover, National Velvet, Courage of Lassie, Life with Father, Cynthia, A Date With Judy, Julia Misbehaves, Little Women, Conspirator, The Big Hangover, Father of the Bride, Father's Little Dividend, A Place in the Sun, Callaway Went Thataway (cameo), Love Is Better Than Ever, Ivanhoe, The Girl Who Had Everything, Rhapsody, Elephant Walk, Beau Brummel, The Last Time I Saw Paris, Giant, Raintree County, Cat on a Hot Tin Roof, Suddenly Last Summer, Scent of Mystery (cameo), Butterfield 8 (Academy Award, 1960), Cleopatra, The V.I.P.s, The Sandpiper, Who's Afraid of Virginia Woolf? (Academy Award, 1966), The Taming of the Shrew, Doctor Faustus, Reflections in a Golden Eye, The Comedians, Boom!, Secret Ceremony, The Only Game in Town, X Y and Zee (Zee and Company), Under Milk Wood, Hammersmith Is Out, Night Watch, Ash Wednesday, That's Entertainment!, The Driver's Seat, The Blue Bird, A Little Night Music, Winter Kills (cameo), The Mirror Crack'd, Genocide (narrator), Young Toscanini, The Flintstones, The Visit.
TELEVISION: *Movies*: Divorce His/Divorce Hers, Victory at Entebbe, Return Engagement, Between Friends, Malice in Wonderland, There Must Be a Pony, Poker Alice, Sweet Bird of Youth. *Mini-Series*: North and South. *Guest*: Here's Lucy (1970 with Richard Burton), General Hospital (1981), All My Children (1983), Hotel, The Simpsons (voice). *Specials*: Elizabeth Taylor in London, America's All-Star Salute to Elizabeth Taylor.

TAYLOR, JULIET
Casting Director. e. Smith College, Massachussetts.
PICTURES: The Exorcist, The Stepford Wives, Love and Death, Taxi Driver, Next Stop, Greenwich Village, Network, The Front, Close Encounters of the Third Kind, Annie Hall, Julia, Between the Lines, Cindy, Pretty Baby, An Unmarried Woman, Manhattan, Stardust Memories, Willie and Phil, Arthur, Shoot the Moon, A Midsummer Night's Sex Comedy, Tempest, Still of the Night, Zelig, Terms of Endearment, Broadway Danny Rose, The Killing Fields, Falling in Love, Birdy, The Purple Rose of Cairo, Alamo Bay, The Mission, Heartburn, Hannah and Her Sisters, September, Radio Days, Big, Another Woman, Working Girl, Mississippi Burning, Dangerous Liasons, New York Stories, Crimes and Misdemeanors, The Grifters, The Sheltering Sky, Postcards from The Edge, Alice, Harley Davidson and the Marlboro Man, Regarding Henry, Shadows and Fog, This is My Life, Husbands and Wives, Hero, Sleepless in Seattle, Schindler's List, Bullets Over Broadway, Mixed Nuts, Wolf, The Road To Welville, Angie, Mighty Aphrodite, Mary Reilly, The Birdcage, Everyone Says I Love You, Deconstructing Harry, Primary Colors, Celebrity, Meet Joe Black, Sweet and Lowdown, Angela's Ashes, Small Time Crooks, The Curse of the Jade Scorpion.

TAYLOR, LILI
Actress. b. Chicago, 1967.
THEATER: *NY*: What Did He See, Aven U Boys. *Regional*: Mud, The Love Talker, Fun. *Director*: Collateral Damage.
PICTURES: Mystic Pizza (debut, 1988), Say Anything, Born on the Fourth of July, Bright Angel, Dogfight, Watch It, Household Saints, Short Cuts, Rudy, Arizona Dream, Mrs. Parker and the Vicious Circle, Ready to Wear (Pret-a-Porter), The Addiction, Cold Fever, Four Rooms, Things I Never Told You, I Shot Andy Warhol, Girl's Town, Ransom, Pecker, Kicked in the Head, O.K. Garage, The Imposters, A Slipping Down Forward, Janis, The Haunting, High Fidelity, Julie Johnson, Gaudi Afternoon.
TELEVISION: *Movies*: Subway Stories: Tales from the Underground. *Guest:* Mad About You, The X Files.

TAYLOR, MESHACH
Actor. b. Boston, MA, Apr. 11. e. Florida A & M Univ. Hosted Chicago TV show Black Life.
THEATER: Streamers, Sizwe Banzi is Dead, The Island, Native Son, Wonderful Ice Cream Suit, Bloody Bess, Sirens of Titan, Night Feast, Huckleberry Finn, Cops.
PICTURES: Damien: Omen II, The Howling, The Beast Within, Explorers, Warning Sign, One More Saturday Night, From the Hip, Mannequin, The Allnighter, House of Games, Welcome to Oblivion, Mannequin 2 on the Move, Class Act.
TELEVISION: *Series*: Buffalo Bill, Designing Women, Dave's World. *Guest*: Lou Grant, Barney Miller, Melba, Golden Girls, M*A*S*H, The White Shadow, What's Happening Now, ALF. *Movies*: An Innocent Man, How to Murder a Millionaire, Double Double Toil and Trouble, Virtual Seduction. *Specials*: Huckleberry Finn, The Rec Room.

TAYLOR, RENEE
Actress, Writer. b. New York, NY, March 19, 1935. Wife of actor Joseph Bologna, with whom she collaborates in writing. Their B'way plays include Lovers and Other Strangers, It Had to Be You. *Stage actress*: One of the All-Time Greats.
PICTURES: *Actress*: The Errand Boy, The Detective, The Producers, A New Leaf, Lovers and Other Strangers (also s.p.), Made for Each Other (also s.p.), Last of the Red Hot Lovers, Lovesick, It Had to Be You (also co-dir., co-s.p.), That's Adequate, White Palace, End of Innocence, Delirious, All I Want for Christmas, Forever.
TELEVISION: *Writer*: Acts of Love... and Other Comedies (Emmy Award, 1973), Paradise, Calucci's Department, The American Dream Machine, Bedrooms (Writers Guild Award, 1984), etc. Actress: *Series regular*: The Jack Paar Show, Mary Hartman Mary Hartman, Daddy Dearest, The Nanny. *Movie*: Woman of the Year (also co-writer).

TAYLOR, ROD
Actor. b. Sydney, Australia, Jan. 11, 1930. e. East Sydney Fine Arts Coll. Started out as artist then turned to acting on stage. Formed own company, Rodler, Inc., for TV-film production.
PICTURES: The Sturt Expedition (debut, 1951), King of the Coral Sea, Long John Silver, Top Gun, The Virgin Queen, Hell on Frisco Bay, World Without End, The Rack, Giant, The Catered Affair, Raintree County, Step Down to Terror, Separate Tables, Ask Any Girl, The Time Machine, Seven Seas to Calais, 101 Dalmatians (voice), The Birds, A Gathering of Eagles, The V.I.P.s, Sunday in New York, Fate is the Hunter, 36 Hours, Young Cassidy, Do Not Disturb, The Glass Bottom Boat, The Liquidator, Hotel, Chuka (also prod.), Dark of the Sun, High Commissioner (Nobody Runs Forever), The Hell with Heroes, Zabriskie Point, Darker Than Amber, The Man Who Had Power Over Women, The Heroes, The Train Robbers, Trader Horn, The Deadly Trackers, Hell River, Blondy, Picture Show Man, A Time To Die, On the Run, Close Enemy, Open Season, Point of Betrayal, Welcome to Woop-Woop.
TELEVISION: *Movies*: Powerkeg, Family Flight, The Oregon Trail, Cry of the Innocent, Jacqueline Bouvier Kennedy, Charles and Diana: A Royal Love Story, Outlaws, Danielle Steel's Palomino, Grass Roots. *Series*: Hong Kong, Bearcats, Masquerade, The Oregon Trail, Outlaws, Falcon Crest.

TAYLOR, RONNIE
Director of Photography. b. London, England, 1924. Ent. m.p. ind. 1941 at Gainsborough Studios
PICTURES: Tommy, The Silent Flute, Circle of Iron, Savage Harvest, Gandhi, High Road to China, The Hound of the Baskervilles, The Champions, Master of the Game (UK shoot), A Chorus Line, Foreign Body, Cry Freedom, Opera (Italy), The Experts, Sea of Love, Popcorn, The Rainbow Thief, Jewels, Age of Treason, The Steal, The Good King.

TAYLOR, JOHN RUSSELL
Writer, Critic. b. Dover, England, June 19, 1935. e. Cambridge U., B.A., 1956. Editor: Times Educational Supplement, London, 1959-60; film critic, The Times, London, 1962-73; art critic, 1978-; editor, Films and Filming, 1983-; prof., division of Cinema, USC, 1972-78. Member: London Film and TV Press Guild, London Critics Circle, NY Society of Cinematologists.
BOOKS: Joseph L. Mankiewicz: An Index, The Angry Theatre, Anatomy of a Television Play, Cinema Eye Cinema Ear, Shakespeare: A Celebration (cont.), New English Dramatists 8 (ed. & intr.), The Hollywood Musical, The Second Wave: Hollywood Dramatists for the 70s, Masterworks of the British Cinema, *Directors and Directions*: Peter Shaffer, Hitch, Cukor's Hollywood, Impressionism, Strangers in Paradise, Ingrid Bergman, Alec Guinness: A Celebration, Vivien Leigh, Hollywood 1940s, Portraits of the British Cinema.

TAYLOR-YOUNG, LEIGH
Actress. b. Washington, DC, Jan. 25, 1945. e. Northwestern U. B'way debut 1966 in Three Bags Full. Additional stage: The Beckett Plays (Off-B'way, LA), Knives, Sleeping Dogs.
PICTURES: I Love You Alice B. Toklas (debut, 1968), The Games, The Big Bounce, The Adventurers, The Buttercup Chain, The Horsemen, The Gang That Couldn't Shoot Straight, Soylent Green, Can't Stop the Music, Looker, Secret Admirer, Jagged Edge, Honeymoon Academy, Accidents.
TELEVISION: *Series*: Peyton Place, The Devlin Connection, The Hamptons, Dallas, Picket Fences (Emmy Award, 1994). *Movies*: Marathon, Napoleon and Josephine: A Love Story, Perry Mason: The Case of the Sinister Spirit, Who Gets the Friends, Bonnie and McCloud, Moment of Truth: Murder or Memory? *Guest*: Civil Wars, The Young Riders, Alfred Hitchcock Presents, Spenser for Hire, Evening Shade. *Pilots*: Ghostwriter, Houston Knights.

TEAGUE, LEWIS
Director. b. 1941. e. NYU. Editor and/or 2nd unit dir. on such films as Cockfighter, Crazy Mama, Death Race 2000, Avalanche, Fast Charlie: The Moonbeam Rider, The Big Red One.
PICTURES: Dirty O'Neil (co-dir.), Lady in Red (also editor), Alligator, Fighting Back, Cujo, Cat's Eye, The Jewel of the Nile, Collision Course, Navy SEALS, Fortune Hunter.
TELEVISION: *Series episodes*: Alfred Hitchcock Presents, Daredevils, Shannon's Deal. *Movies*: T Bone N Weasel, Tom Clancy's Op Center, Time Traxx, Saved by the Light, Profiler, Justice League of America, The Reunion: Dukes of Hazzard.

TECHINE, ANDRE
Director, Writer. b. Valence d'Agen, Tarn-et- Garonne, France, March 13, 1943.
PICTURES: Paulina s'en va (dir. only), French Provincial, Barocco, The Bronte Sisters, Hotel des Ameriques, La Matiouette, Rendez-vous, Scene of the Crime, The Innocents, Mauvaise Fille (s.p. only), I Don't Kiss, My Favorite Season, The Wild Reeds, The Child of the Night, Transatlantique (s.p. only), Alice and Martin, Terminus des anges.

TELLER, IRA
Executive, b. New York, NY, July 3, 1940. e. City Coll. of New York, & 1957-61; NYU Graduate Sch. of Arts, 1961-62. Publicist, Pressbook Dept., 20th Century Fox., 1961-62; asst. to adv. mgr., Embassy Pictures Corp., 1962-63; asst. adv. mgr., Columbia Pictures Corp., 1963; adv. mgr., Columbia Pictures Corp., 1964, 1964-65; asst. to chmn. of bd., Diener, Hauser, Greenthal Agy., 1966; adv. mgr., 20th Century-Fox, 1966-67; 1967, adv. dir. 20th Cent.-Fox.; dir. of adv., Nat'l General Pictures Corp., 1969; eastern dir., adv.-pub., 1972; national dir., adv-pub., 1973; Bryanston Distributors, Inc. v.p. adv.-pub., 1974; Cine Artists Pictures Corp. v.p. adv-pub., 1975; Lorimar Productions, v.p., adv.-marketing, 1976-77; 1977-present, pres. Ira Teller and Company, Inc.; This Is It Productions, prod. Instructor, UCLA Extension.

TEMPLE, JULIEN
Director. b. London, England, Nov. 26, 1953. e. Cambridge, London's National Film School. Dir. many rock videos.
PICTURES: The Great Rock 'n' Roll Swindle (debut, 1979), The Secret Policeman's Other Ball, Undercover (also s.p.), Running Out of Luck (also s.p.), Absolute Beginners, Aria (segment: Rigoletto), Earth Girls Are Easy, Rolling Stones: At the Max (creative consultant), Bullet, Catching Fire.

TEMPLE (BLACK), SHIRLEY
Actress, Diplomat. b. Santa Monica, CA, April 23, 1928. In 1932 screen debut, Red Haired Alibi. In 1933 To the Last Man; then leading figure in series of Educational shorts called Baby Burlesque and Frolics of Youth, until breakthrough role in Stand Up and Cheer, 1934, which resulted in career as child and teen star. Voted one of ten best Money-Making Stars in Motion Picture Herald-Fame Poll, 1934-39. As an adult, turned her attention to government and international issues. Republican candidate for U.S. House of Representatives, 1967. Rep. to 24th General Assembly of U.N. (1969-70). Special asst. to chmn., President's Council on the Environment (1970-72). U.S. Ambassador to Ghana (1974-76). Chief of Protocol, White House (1976-77); member of U.S. delegation on African Refugee problems, Geneva, 1981; 1987 made 1st honorary U.S. Foreign Service Rep. for State Dept.; 1989, appt. Ambassador to Czechoslovakia. *Autobiography*: Child Star (1988).
PICTURES: The Red-Haired Alibi (feature debut, 1932), To the Last Man, Out All Night, Mandalay, Carolina, Stand Up and Cheer, Baby Take a Bow, Now and Forever, Bright Eyes, Now I'll Tell, Change of Heart, Little Miss Marker, The Little Colonel, Our Little Girl, Curly Top, The Littlest Rebel, Captain January, Poor Little Rich Girl, Dimples, Stowaway, Wee Willie Winkle, Heidi, Rebecca of Sunnybrook Farm, Little Miss Broadway, Just Around the Corner, Little Princess, Susannah of the Mounties, The Blue Bird, Young People, Kathleen, Miss Annie Rooney. Since You Went Away, I'll Be Seeing You, Kiss and Tell, That Hagen Girl, Honeymoon, Bachelor and the Bobby-Soxer, Fort Apache, Mr. Belvedere Goes to College, Adventure in Baltimore, Story of Seabiscuit, Kiss for Corliss.
TELEVISION: *Series*: Shirley Temple's Storybook (host, performer).

TENNANT, VICTORIA
Actress. b. London, England, Sept. 30, 1953. e. Central Sch. of Speech & Drama. Daughter of ballerina Irina Baronova and talent agent Cecil Tennant.
THEATER: Love Letters (Steppenwolf), Getting Married (NY), Taming of the Shrew (NY).
PICTURES: The Ragman's Daughter, Strangers Kiss, All of Me, The Holocraft Covenant, Best Seller, Flowers in the Attic, Fool's Mate, The Handmaid's Tale, L.A. Story, Whispers, The Plague.
TELEVISION: *Mini-Series*: Voice of the Heart, Winds of War, Chiefs, War and Remembrance, Act of Will, The Man from Snowy River. *Movies*: Maigret, Dempsey, Under Siege.

TETZLAFF, TED
Director. b. Los Angeles, CA, June 3, 1903. Joined camera dept. Fox Studios, became first cameraman; dir., 1940; served in U.S. Air Corps as a Major, WWII.
PICTURES: *Cameraman*: Enchanted Cottage, Notorious. *Dir.*: World Premiere, Riffraff, Fighting Father Dunne, Window, Johnny Allegro, Dangerous Profession, Gambling House, White Tower, Under the Gun, Treasure of Lost Canyon, Terror on a Train, Son of Sinbad, Seven Wonders of the World, The Young Land.

TEWKESBURY, JOAN
Writer, Director. b. Redlands, CA, April 8, 1936. e. USC. Student American Sch. Dance 1947-54. Was ostrich and understudy in Mary Martin's Peter Pan. Directed and choreographed Theatre prods. in L.A., London, Edinburgh Festival, Scotland. Taught dance and theory, American Sch. of Dance 1959-64; taught in theatre arts depts. of two universities: USC, Immaculate Heart. Became script supvr. for Robert Altman on McCabe & Mrs. Miller. *Off-B'way*: Cowboy Jack Street (writer, dir.). Teacher in film dept. UCLA. Sundance advisor, 1992-93: directors lab-writers lab. American Musical Theatre Festival in Philadelphia. Chippy (dir.), Jammed (Edinburgh Festival; writer, dir.). Dance Card (Oregon Ballter Theatre; writer, dir., choreo.)
PICTURES: Thieves Like Us (co.-s.p.), Nashville, (s.p.), Old Boyfriends (dir.), Hampstead Center (doc. of Anna Freud, writer, dir.), A Night in Heaven (s.p.), The Player (actress).
TELEVISION: *Series*: *Director*: Alfred Hitchcock Presents (also writer), Elysian Fields (pilot; also writer, exec. prod.), Almost Grown, Shannon's Deal (also writer), Nothing Sacred. *Movies*: *Director/Writer*: The Acorn People, The Tenth Month, Cold Sassy Tree, Sudie and Simpson, Wild Texas Wind, The Stranger, On Promised Land, Scattering Dad.

THALHIMER, JR., MORTON G.
Former Theatre Executive. b. Richmond, VA, June 27, 1924. e. Dartmouth Coll., 1948, B.A.; U. of Virginia, 1959. Naval aviator in WWII. Joined Century Theatres as trainee 1948; Jamestown Amusement, 1949-50. Past pres. Neighborhood Theatre, Inc. 1967-86. Charter member of Theatre Owners of America; past member and v.p. of NATO, served on finance comm. and Trade Practice comm. bd. member and past president of NATO of VA, 1973-75. Mem. Variety Club Int'l., Tent 11; patron life member, Variety Club of Israel, Tent 51.

THAXTER, PHYLLIS
Actress. b. Portland, ME, Nov. 20, 1919. e. St. Genevieve Sch., Montreal. Daughter is actress Skye Aubrey.
PICTURES: Thirty Seconds Over Tokyo (debut, 1944), Bewitched, Weekend at the Waldorf, Sea of Grass, Living in a Big Way, Tenth Avenue Angel, Sign of the Ram, Blood on the Moon, Act of Violence, No Man of Her Own, The Breaking Point, Fort Worth, Jim Thorpe_All American, Come Fill the Cup, She's Working Her Way Through College, Springfield Rifle, Operation Secret, Women's Prison, Man Afraid, The World of Henry Orient, Superman.
TELEVISION: *Movies*: Incident in San Francisco, The Longest Night, Three Sovereigns for Sarah. *Mini-Series*: Once an Eagle. *Guest*: Wagon Train, Alfred Hitchcock, Twilight Zone, Purex Specials For Women, Playhouse 90, The Fugitive, The Defenders, Murder She Wrote.

THEODORAKIS, MIKIS
Composer. b. Greece, 1925.
PICTURES: Eva, Night Ambush, Shadow of the Cat, Phaedra, Five Miles to Midnight, Zorba the Greek, The Day the Fish Came Out, The Trojan Women, State of Siege, Serpico, Iphigenia.

THEWLIS, DAVID
Actor. b. Blackpool, England, 1962. e. Guildhall School of Music and Drama, The Barbicon, London. First prof. job in breakfast food commercial.
PICTURES: Little Dorrit, Resurrected, Life Is Sweet, Afraid of the Dark, Damage, The Trial, Naked (Cannes Film Fest., NY Film Critics & Natl. Soc. of Film Critics Awards, 1993), Black Beauty, Restoration,Total Eclipse, Dragonheart, James and the Giant Peach (voice), The Island of Dr. Moreau, Seven Years in Tibet, American Perfekt, Divorcing Jack, The Big Lebowski, Besieged, Whatever Happened to Harold Smith?, Gangster No. 1, Great Sex.
TELEVISION: Only Fools and Horses, The Singing Detective, Filipino Dreamgirls, Prime Suspect, Dandelion Dead, Love Story, The Miracle Maker (voice). *Mini-series*: Dinotopia.

THIGPEN, LYNNE
Actress, Singer. b. Joliet, IL, Dec. 22, 1948.
THEATER: *NY*: Godspell, The Magic Show, But Never Jam Today, Tintypes, And I Ain't Finished Yet, Full Hookup, Balm in Gilead, A Month of Sundays, Fences, Boesman & Lena, An American Daughter (B'way).
PICTURES: Godspell (debut, 1973), The Warriors, Tootsie, Streets of Fire, Sweet Liberty, Hello Again, Running on Empty, Lean on Me, Impulse, Article 99, Bob Roberts, The Paper, Naked in New York, Blankman, Just Cause, Random Hearts.
TELEVISION: *Series*: Love Sidney, The News is the News, FM, All My Children, Where in the World is Carmen Sandiego?, Where in Time is Carmen Sandiego?, Bear in the Big Blue House (voice) *Pilot*: Pottsville. *Guest*: The Equalizer, Gimme a Break, L.A. Law, Days and Nights of Molly Dodd, Roseanne, Frank's Place, The Cosby Show, Dear John, thirtysomething, Preston Episodes, Law & Order, King of the Hill (voice). *Movies*: Fear Stalk, Separate But Equal, A Mother's Instinct, Boys Next Door, Cagney & Lacey. *Pilot*: For the People, Those Two, A Mother Instinct, The Boys Next Door, Chance of a Lifetime.

THINNES, ROY
Actor. b. Chicago, IL, April 6, 1938. Made tv debut as teen on DuPont Theatre, 1957.
PICTURES: Journey to the Far Side of the Sun, Charlie One-Eye, Airport 75, The Hindenburg, Rush Week.
TELEVISION: *Series*: General Hospital (1963-65), The Long Hot Summer, The Invaders, The Psychiatrist, From Here to Eternity, One Life to Live, Falcon Crest, Dark Shadows, The X Files. *Movies*: The Other Man, The Psychiatrist: God Bless the Children, Black Noon, The Horror at 37000 Feet, The Norliss Tales, Satan's School for Girls, Death Race, The Manhunter, Secrets, Code Name: Diamond Head, Sizzle, The Return of the Mod Squad, Freedom, Dark Holiday, Blue Bayou, The Hand in the Glove, An Inconvenient Woman, Lady Against the Odds, Stormy Weathers, The Indians. *Mini-Series*: From Here to Eternity, Scruples.

THOMAS, BETTY
Director, Actress. b. St. Louis, MO, July 27, 1949. e. Ohio U, Chicago Art Inst., Roosevelt U. Former member of Chicago's Second City improv group.
PICTURES: *Actress*: Tunnelvision, Chesty Anderson—U.S. Navy, Loose Shoes, Used Cars, Homework, Troop Beverly Hills, Jackson County Jail. *Director*: Only You, The Brady Bunch Movie, Private Parts, Doctor Dolittle, 28 Days, Surviving Christmas, The Dreyfus Affair: A Love Story. *Prod.*: Can't Hardly Wait.
TELEVISION: *Series*: Hill Street Blues (Emmy Award, 1985). *Movies*: Outside Chance, Nashville Grab, When Your Lover Leaves, Prison for Children. Director (series): Doogie Howser M.D., Dream On (Emmy Award, 1993), Hooperman, Mancusco FBI, Arresting Behavior, Couples. *Movie*: My Breast. *Specials*: The Late Shift (Dir's Guild of America Award, 1997).

THOMAS, DAVE
Actor, Writer, Director. b. St. Catherines, Ontario, Canada, May 20, 1949. e. McMaster Univ.
PICTURES: Stripes (debut, 1981), Strange Brew (also co-dir., co-s.p.), My Man Adam, Sesame Street Presents Follow That Bird, Love at Stake, Nightflyers, Moving, The Experts (dir. only), Cold Sweat, Coneheads.
TELEVISION: *Series (actor/writer):* Second City TV, SCTV Network The New Show, The Dave Thomas Comedy Show (also exec. prod., dir.), Maniac Mansion, Grace Under Fire (actor only). *Movies:* Home to Stay, Just Me and You, The Canadian Conspiracy, Boris and Natasha, Ghost Mom (writer). *Pilot:* From Cleveland. *Specials:* Twilight Theatre, Martin Short Concert for the North, Dave Thomas: The Incredible Time Travels of Henry Osgood (also dir., exec. prod., writer), Andrea Martin: Together Again, Inside America's Totally Unsolved Lifestyles (also exec. prod., writer).

THOMAS, HARRY E.
Exhibitor. b. Monroe, LA, May 22, 1920. e. Louisiana State U., 1938-41. Psychological Branch of Army Air Force, 1942-46. Past pres., secy., and treas. of NATO of MS. Dir. of Design & Const. & Sec. Gulf State Theatres Inc. Retired 1978.

THOMAS, HENRY
Actor. b. San Antonio, TX, Sept. 8, 1971. Made film debut at the age of 9 in Raggedy Man, 1981. On stage in Artichoke, The Guardsman.
PICTURES: Raggedy Man (debut, 1981), E.T.: The Extra-Terrestrial, Misunderstood, Cloak and Dagger, The Quest, Murder One, Valmont, Fire in the Sky, Legends of the Fall, Bombshell, Suicide Kings, Niagara Niagara, Hijacking Hollywood, A Good Baby, Fever.
TELEVISION: *Movies*: Psycho IV: The Beginning, A Taste for Killing, Curse of the Starving Class, Indictment: The McMartin Trial, Riders of the Purple Sage, Moby Dick, Happy Face Murders. *Special*: The Steeler and the Pittsburgh Kid.

THOMAS, JAY
Actor. b. New Orleans, LA, July 12, 1948. Started as stand-up comedian before pursuing acting career in NY. Appeared on NY stage with Playwrights Horizons and Off-B'way in Isn't It Romantic? Also morning disc jockey on L.A. radio station KPWR-FM.
PICTURES: C.H.U.D., The Gig, Straight Talk, Mr. Holland's Opus, A Smile Like Yours, Dirty Laundry, A Smile Like Yours, The Adventures of Ragtime, Last Chance.
TELEVISION: *Movies*: Miracle Landing, A Husband A Wife A Lover, Deserts Edge, Killing Mr. Griffin, My Date with the President's Daughter. *Series*: Mork & Mindy, Cheers, Married People, Love & War, Katie Joplin. *Guest*: Murphy Brown (Emmy Award, 1991).

THOMAS, JEREMY
Producer. b. London, Eng., July 26, 1949. e. Millfield School. Son of dir. Ralph Thomas (Doctor comedies) and nephew of dir. Gerald Thomas (Carry On... comedies). Entered industry 1969. Worked as film edit. on Brother Can You Spare a Dime, 1974. Received Evening Standard Special Award for Outstanding Contribution to Cinema in 1990, BAFTA's Michael Balcon Award in 1991. Appointed chmn. of British Film Institute, 1992.
PICTURES: Mad Dog Morgan, The Shout, The Great Rock 'n' Roll Swindle, Bad Timing: A Sensual Obsession, Eureka, Merry Christmas Mr. Lawrence, The Hit, Insignificance, The Last Emperor (Academy Award, 1987), Everybody Wins, The Sheltering Sky, Let Him Have It (exec. prod.), Naked Lunch, Little Buddha, Stealing Beauty, Blood and Wine, The Brave, All the Little Animals (dir.).

THOMAS, LEO J.
Executive. b. Grand Rapids, MN. e. Univ. of MI, Univ. of IL. Started as research chemist in 1961 at Color Photog. Division of the Kodak Research Labs. 1967-70, head of Color Physics and Engingeering Lab; 1970-72, asst. head of Color Photog. Division; 1972-74, tech. asst. to dir. of the Research Labs; 1974, appointed sec. of Technical Affairs Committe. 1977, named dir. of Research Laboratories; later that year became v.p. of the company; 1978 elected sr. v.p. 1984, appointed gen. mgr. Life Sciences. 1988, v.p. Sterling Drug; 1989, gen. mgr. of Health Group; 1989, v.p. of Health Group; 1991, pres. of Imaging Group; 1994, exec. v.p. Eastman Kodak Company.

THOMAS, MARLO
Actress. b. Detroit, MI, Nov. 21, 1938. Daughter of late Danny Thomas. m. Phil Donahue. Brother is TV producer Tony Thomas. e. U. of Southern California. Started career with small TV roles, summer stock. Appeared in London stage prod. of Barefoot in the Park. Most Promising Newcomer Awards from both Fame and Photoplay for series That Girl. Conceived book, record and TV special Free to Be You and Me (Emmy Award, 1974).
THEATER: *NY*: Thieves, Social Security, The Shadow Box.Regional: Six Degrees of Separation.
PICTURES: Jenny, Thieves, In the Spirit, The Real Blonde, Starfucker.
TELEVISION: *Series*: The Joey Bishop Show, That Girl. *Specials*: Acts of Love and Other Comedies, Free To Be You and Me (also prod.; Emmy Award, 1974), The Body Human: Facts for Girls (Emmy Award, 1981), Love Sex... and Marriage (also exec. prod.), Free to Be a Family (host, exec. prod.; Emmy Award, 1989). *Movies*: It Happened One Christmas (also co-prod.), The Lost Honor of Kathryn Beck (also exec. prod.), Consenting Adult, Nobody's Child (Emmy Award, 1986), Leap of Faith (co-exec. prod. only), Held Hostage: The Sis and Jerry Levin Story, Ultimate Betrayal, Reunion (also co-exec. prod.). *Guest*: Dobie Gillis, Zane Grey Theatre, Thriller.

THOMAS, PHILIP MICHAEL
Actor. b. Columbus, OH, May 26, 1949. e. Oakwood Coll.
PICTURES: Black Fist, Sparkle, Death Drug, The Wizard of Speed and Time.
TELEVISION: *Series*: Miami Vice. *Movies*: Toma, The Beasts Are on the Streets, This Man Stands Alone, Valentine, A Fight for Jenny, False Witness. *Special*: Disney's Totally Minnie, The Debbie Allen Special.

THOMAS, RALPH
Director. b. Hull, Yorkshire, England, Aug. 10, 1915. e. Tellisford Coll., Clifton and University Coll., London. Journalist in early career, entered m.p. ind. 1932 as film ed.; service with 9th Lancers, 1939-45; then film director.
PICTURES: Helter Skelter, Once Upon a Dream, Traveller's Joy, The Clouded Yellow, Appointment With Venus (Island Rescue), The Assassin (The Venetian Bird), A Day to Remember, Doctor in the House, Mad about Men, Above Us the Waves, Doctor at Sea, The Iron Petticoat, Checkpoint, Doctor at Large, Campbell's Kingdom, A Tale of Two Cities, The Wind Cannot Read, The 39 Steps, Upstairs and Downstairs, Conspiracy of Hearts, Doctor in Love, No Love for Johnnie, No My Darling Daughter, A Pair of Briefs, The Wild and the Willing, Doctor in Distress, Hot Enough for June (Agent 8 3/4), The High Bright Sun (McGuire Go Home!), Doctor in Clover, Deadlier Than the Male, Nobody Runs Forever (The High Commissioner), Some Girls Do, Doctor in Trouble, Percy, Quest for Love, The Love Ban, Percy's Progress (It's Not the Size That Counts), A Nightingale Sang in Berkeley Square, Pop Pirates.

THOMAS, RICHARD
Actor. b. New York, NY, June 13, 1951. e. Columbia U. Made TV debut at age 7 on Hallmark Hall of Fame The Christmas Tree. That same year appeard on Brodawy in Sunrise at Campobello.
THEATER: Sunrise at Campobello, Everything in the Garden, Fifth of July, The Front Page, Love Letters, Square One, The Lisbon Traviata, Danton's Death, Richard II, Richard III.
PICTURES: Winning (debut, 1969), Last Summer, Red Sky at Morning, The Todd Killings, You'll Like My Mother, September 30, 1955; Battle Beyond the Stars.
TELEVISION: *Series*: One Two Three Go, As the World Turns, The Waltons (Emmy Award, 1973). *Guest*: Great Ghost Tales, Bonanza, Love American Style, Medical Center, Marcus Welby M.D., The F.B.I., Tales From the Crypt (Mute Witness to Murder), The Outer Limits. *Movies*: Homecoming, The Red Badge of Courage, The Silence, Getting Married, No Other Love, All Quiet on the Western Front, To Find My Son, Berlin Tunnel 21, Johnny Belinda, Living Proof: The Hank Williams Jr. Story, Hobson's Choice, The Master of Ballantrae, Final Jeopardy, Glory Glory, Go To the Light, Common Ground, Stephen King's IT, Mission of the Shark, Yes Virginia There Is a Santa Claus, Crash Landing: The Rescue of Flight 232, I Can Make You Love Me: The Stalking of Laura Black, Precious Victims, Linda, A Walton Thanksgiving Reunion, Death in Small Doses, A Walton Wedding, Down Out and Dangerous. *Specials:* A Doll's House, Give Us Barabbas, HMS Pinafore, Barefoot in the Park, Fifth of July, Andre's Mother.

THOMAS, ROBERT G.
Producer, Director. b. Glen Ridge, NJ, July 21, 1943. e. U. of Bridgeport, Fairleigh Dickinson U. Prod. educational radio programs, 1962, WPKN-FM. Asst. stage mgr. Meadowbrook Dinner Theatre, 1963; 1964, began career as TV cameraman for NY stations. Worked both full-time and freelance for major TV and video tape studios. 1968, started Bob Thomas Productions, producing business/sales films and TV commercials. Has 8 awards from natl. film festivals; nominated for 5 Emmys for TV series called The Jersey Side he produced for WOR-TV. Inventor of Futurevision 2000 multi-imaging video system for conventions and exhibits and museums (American Museum of Natural History: Hall of Human Biology to be shown over 15 years). Inventor and pres. of Video Mail Marketing Inc., low cost, light weight paper board video cassettes for the direct mail video marketing industry. *Shorts:* Valley Forge with Bob Hope, New Jersey—200 Years, Road-Eo '77.
TELEVISION: The Jersey Side (talk/entertainment), Jersey People (weekly talk/entertainment prog.), Movies '89 (synd. film preview series).

THOMAS, ROBERT J. (BOB)
Columnist, Associated Press, Hollywood. b. San Diego, CA, Jan. 26, 1922. p. George H. Thomas, publicist. e. UCLA. Joined Associated Press staff, Los Angeles, 1943; corr. Fresno, 1944; Hollywood since 1944. Writer mag. articles; appearances, radio; orig. story Big Mike.
AUTHOR: The Art of Animation, King Cohn, Thalberg, Selznick, Winchell—Secret Boss of California, The Heart of Hollywood, Howard—The Amazing Mr. Hughes, Weekend '33, Marlon—Portrait of the Rebel as an Artist, Walt Disney—An American Original, Bud and Lou—The Abbott and Costello Story, The Road to Hollywood (with Bob Hope), The One and Only Bing, Joan Crawford, Golden Boy: The Secret Life of William Holden, Astaire: The Man the Dancer, I Got Rhythm— The Ethel Merman Story, Liberace, Clown Prince of Hollywood (Jack L. Warner), Disney's Art of Animation.

THOMOPOULOS, ANTHONY D.
Executive. b. Mt. Vernon, NY, Feb. 7, 1938. e. Georgetown U. Began career in broadcasting at NBC, 1959, starting as mailroom clerk and moving to radio division in prod. & admin. Shortly named to post in int'l division sales, involved with programming for stations and in dev. TV systems for other nations. Joined Four Star Entertainment Corp. as dir. of foreign sales, 1964; named v.p., 1965; exec. v.p., 1969; 1970 joined RCA SelectaVision Div. as dir. of programming; 1971 joined Tomorrow Entertainment as v.p.; 1973 joined ABC as v.p., prime-time programs in N.Y.; 1974, named v.p., prime-time TV creative operations, ABC Entertainment; 1975 named v.p. of special programs, ABC Entertainment; 1976 made v.p., ABC-TV, assisting pres. Frederick S. Pierce in supervising all activities of the division; 1978 named pres. of ABC Entertainment; 1983 promoted to pres., ABC Broadcast Group in chg. all TV & radio operations; 1986-88, pres. & COO, United Artists Corp.; independent prod. with Columbia, 1989. Formed Thomopoulos Productions in 1989. Pres., Amblin Television, 1991-95. Responsible for the original placement of ER in addition to several other series on network television.

THOMPSON, CAROLINE
Writer. b. Washington, DC, Apr. 23, 1956. e. Amherst Col., Harvard. Started as free-lance journalist. Wrote novel First Born, which led to screenwriting.
PICTURES: Edward Scissorhands (also assoc. prod.), The Addams Family, Homeward Bound: The Incredible Journey, The Secret Garden (also assoc. prod.), The Nightmare Before Christmas, Black Beauty (also dir.), Buddy (also dir.).

THOMPSON, EMMA
Actress. b. London, England, Apr. 15, 1959. e. Cambridge Univ. Daughter of actors Eric Thompson and Phyllida Law. Acted with the Footlights at the Edinburgh Fringe. At Cambridge co-wrote, co-produced, co-directed and co-starred in school's first all-female revue Woman's Hour, as well as solo show Short Vehicle.
THEATER: *London*: Me and My Girl, Look Back in Anger. Renaissance Theatre Company (World Tour): A Midsummer Night's Dream, King Lear.
PICTURES: Henry V, The Tall Guy, Impromptu, Dead Again, Howards End (Academy Award, BAFTA, NY Film Critics, LA Film Critics, Golden Globe, Nat'l Society of Film Critics & Nat'l Board of Review Awards for Best Actress of 1992), Peter's Friends, Much Ado About Nothing, The Remains of the Day (Acad. Award nom.), In the Name of the Father (Academy Award nom.), My Father the Hero, Junior, Carrington, Sense and Sensibility (also s.p.; BAFTA Award, 1995; Academy Award for s.p.,1996; Writers Guild Award, 1996; Golden Globe Award, 1996), The Winter Guest, Judas Kiss, Primary Colors, Maybe Baby.
TELEVISION: *Series*: Thompson (also writer). *Mini-Series*: Tutti Frutti, Fortunes of War (BAFTA Best Actress award). *Specials*: The Emma Thompson Special, The Winslow Boy, Look Back in Anger, Knuckle, The Blue Boy, Hospital. *Guest*: Cheers, Ellen. *Movies*: Wit.

THOMPSON, FRED (DALTON)
Actor. b. Sheffield, AL, Aug. 19, 1942. Raised in TN. e. Memphis St. U, Vanderbilt U, studying law. Was Federal prosecutor before going to DC to serve as minority counsel on the Senate Select Committe on Presidential Campaign Activies, which involved investigation of the Watergate scandal. Hired to serve as consultant on film Marie, then was asked to play himself in the movie, resulting in acting career. 1994 elected to U.S. senate as Republican representative from Tennessee. *Author*: At That Point in Time (1975).
PICTURES: Marie (debut, 1985), No Way Out, Feds, Fat Man and Little Boy, The Hunt for Red October, Days of Thunder, Die Hard 2, Flight of the Intruder, Class Action, Necessary Roughness, Curly Sue, Cape Fear, Thunderheart, White Sands, Aces: Iron Eagle III, Born Yesterday, In the Line of Fire, Baby's Day Out.
TELEVISION: *Movies*: Bed of Lies, Keep the Change, Stay the Night, Day-O, Barbarians at the Gate.

THOMPSON, J. LEE
Director, Writer, Producer. b. Bristol, England, 1914. On Brit. stage as actor with Nottingham Rep. Co.; *Playwright*: Murder Without Crime, Cousin Simon, Curious Dr. Robson (collab.) Thousands of Summers, Human Touch. To films, 1934 as actor, then writer, before turning to directing.

PICTURES: *Writer*: The Middle Watch, For Them That Trespass. *Director*: Murder Without Crime (dir. debut, 1950; also story, s.p.), The Yellow Balloon (also s.p.), The Weak and the Wicked (also co-s.p.), For Better or Worse (also s.p.), As Long as They're Happy, An Alligator Named Daisy, Yield to the Night, The Good Companions (also co-prod.), Woman in the Dressing Gown (also co-prod.), Ice Cold in Alex (Desert Attack), No Trees in the Street (also co-exec. prod.), Northwest Frontier (Flame Over India), Tiger Bay, I Aim at the Stars, The Guns of Navarone, Cape Fear, Taras Bulba, Kings of the Sun, What a Way to Go!, John Goldfarb Please Come Home (also co-exec. prod.), Return From the Ashes (also prod.), Eye of the Devil, Mackenna's Gold, Before Winter Comes, The Chairman, Country Dance (Brotherly Love), Conquest of the Planet of the Apes, Battle for the Planet of the Apes, Huckleberry Finn, The Reincarnation of Peter Proud, St. Ives, The White Buffalo, The Greek Tycoon, The Passage, Caboblanco, Happy Birthday to Me, 10 to Midnight, The Evil That Men Do, The Ambassador, King Solomon's Mines, Murphy's Law, Firewalker, Death Wish IV: The Crackdown, Messenger of Death, Kinjite.
TELEVISION: A Great American Tragedy, The Blue Knight, Widow.

THOMPSON, JACK
Actor. r.n. John Payne. b. Sydney, Australia, Aug. 31, 1940. e. Queensland U. Joined drama workshop at school; first part was in TV soap opera as continuing character. 1988, appt. to bd. of Australian Film Finance Corp. Formed Pan Film Enterprises.
PICTURES: The Savage Wild, Outback (Wake in Fright), Libido, Petersen, A Sunday Too Far Away, Caddie, Scobie Malone, Mad Dog Morgan, The Chant of Jimmie Blacksmith, The Journalist, Breaker Morant, The Earthling, The Club, The Man From Snowy River, Bad Blood, Merry Christmas Mr. Lawrence, Flesh + Blood, Burke & Willis, Ground Zero, Waterfront, Turtle Beach, Wind, A Far Off Place, Deception, The Sum of Us, The Last Dance, Excess Baggage, Midnight in the Garden of Good and Evil.
TELEVISION: The Last Frontier, A Woman Called Golda, Waterfront, The Letter, Beryl Markham: A Shadow on the Sun, Paradise, Last Frontier, Wreck of the Stinson, A Woman of Independent Means, Thornbirds: The Missing Years.

THOMPSON, LEA
Actress. b. Rochester, MN, May 31, 1961. m. director Howard Deutch. Danced professionally since age of 14; won scholarship to Pennsylvania Ballet Co., American Ballet Theatre, San Francisco Ballet. Gave up that career for acting, appearing in several commercials for Burger King. *L.A. stage*: Bus Stop, The Illusion.
PICTURES: Jaws 3-D (debut, 1983), All the Right Moves, Red Dawn, The Wild Life, Back to the Future, SpaceCamp, Howard the Duck, Some Kind of Wonderful, Casual Sex?, Going Undercover, The Wizard of Loneliness, Back to the Future Part II, Back to the Future Part III, Article 99, Dennis the Menace, The Beverly Hillbillies, The Little Rascals, The Unknown Cyclist, Right to Remain Silent, A Will of Their Own.
TELEVISION: *Series*: Caroline in the City. *Movies*: Nightbreaker, Montana, Stolen Babies, The Substitute Wife, The Unspoken Truth. *Guest*: Tales From the Crypt.

THOMPSON, PATRICIA
Publisher, Editor. b. Portsmouth, UK, June 28, 1927. Co-found. Ontario Film Institute and Theatre, Ontario Science Center, 1969; co-ordinator, 1970-72. Co-ordinator, Stratford International Film Festival. Exec. dir., Canadian Film Awards (Genie Awards), 1977-78. Edit., Canadian Film Digest Yearbook, 1977-85. Short Film programmer for Cineplex cinemas. Columnist and contributor, Cinema Canada, 1983-89. Contributor, Kinema (Jour. for Film and Audiovisual Media), 1996-. Pub., edit., Film Canada Yearbook. Can. edit., Intl. M.P. Almanac and Intl. TV & Video Almanac, Quigley Pub. Awarded Queen's Silver Jubilee Medal, for svc's. to arts/film in Can., 1977.
(d. July, 1999)

THOMPSON, SADA
Actress. b. Des Moines, IA, Sept. 27, 1929. e. Carnegie Inst. of Technology, Pittsburgh. First N.Y. stage appearance in Under Milk Wood. B'way incl. The Effect of Gamma Rays (Obie, Drama Desk, Variety Poll), Twigs (Tony Award, 1972), Saturday, Sunday, Monday. Recent theater: Real Estate, Any Given Day.
PICTURES: Pursuit of Happiness, Desperate Characters.
TELEVISION: *Specials*: Sandburg's Lincoln, Our Town, The Skin of Our Teeth, Andre's Mother, Painting Churches. *Movies*: The Entertainer, Princess Daisy, My Two Loves, Fatal Confession: A Father Dowling Mystery, Home Fires Burning, Fear Stalk, Indictment: The McMartin Trial. *Series*: Family (Emmy Award, 1978). *Mini-Series*: Queen.

THORNTON, BILLY BOB
Actor, Director, Writer. b. Hot Springs, AR, Aug. 5, 1955. m. actress Angelina Jolie.
PICTURES: *Actor*: Hubter's Blood, South of Reno, Babes Ahoy, One False Move (also s.p.), For the Boys, Trouble Bound, Chopper Chicks in Zombietown, Tombstone, Some Folks Call It a Sling Blade (also s.p., dir.), Bound by Honor, On Deadly Ground, Floundering, Stars Fell on Henrietta, Dead Man, The Winner, Sling Blade (also dir., s.p.; Acad. Award, for best adapt. s.p., 1996; Chicago Film Critics Award for best actor; Ind't Spirit Awards), U-Turn, A Thousand Miles, Primary Colors, Homegrown, The Apostle, A Gun A Car A Blonde, Armageddon, A Simple Plan (Acad. Award nom.), Pushing Tin, Franky Goes to Hollywood, The Last Real Cowboys, Wakin' Up in Reno, Daddy and Them (also s.p.), The Barber Project, Bandits. *Writer*: A Family Thing, The Shipping News.
TELEVISION: *Movies*: The 1,000 Chains (actor), Don't Look Back (actor., writer). *Series*: The Outsiders (actor), Hearts Afire (actor). *Guest*: Matlock, Ellen.

THULIN, INGRID
Actress, Director. b. Solleftea, Sweden, Jan. 27, 1929. m. Harry Schein. Made acting debut at 18 at the Municipal Theatre in Norrkoping. Studied at Stockholm's Royal Dramatic Theatre. Worked with Malmo and Stockholm repertory. Appeared on Swedish stage in nearly 50 plays including Gigi, Peer Gynt, Two for the Seesaw, Twelfth Night, Miss Julie. Has directed plays and films in Stockholm. N.Y. stage debut, 1967: Of Love Remembered. Author: Somebody I Knew (1993).
PICTURES: Where the Wind Blows, Love Will Conqueror, Jack of Hearts, Foreign Intrigue, Wild Strawberries, Brink of Life (Cannes Film Fest. Award), The Magician, The Judge, The Four Horsemen of the Apocalypse, Winter Light, The Silence, Games of Desire, Return From the Ashes, La Guerre est Finie, Night Games, Adelaide, Hour of the Wolf, I a Virgin, The Ritual, The Damned, Cries and Whispers, A Handful of Love, La Cage, Moses, Madame Kitty, The Cassandra Crossing, Broken Sky, At the Rehearsal, Control, House of Smiles, Rabbit Face.

THURMAN, UMA
Actress. b. Boston, MA, Apr. 29, 1970. m. Named after a Hindu deity. Raised in Woodstock, NY and Amherst, MA where father taught Asian studies. Father's work took family to India where they lived three years. e. Professional Children's School, NY. Worked as model while still in high school.
PICTURES: Kiss Daddy Good Night (debut, 1988), Johnny Be Good, Dangerous Liaisons, The Adventures of Baron Munchausen, Where the Heart Is, Henry and June, Final Analysis, Jennifer Eight, Mad Dog and Glory, Even Cowgirls Get the Blues, Pulp Fiction (Acad. Award nom.), A Month by the Lake, The Truth About Cats and Dogs, Beautiful Girls, Batman and Robin, Gattaca, Les Miserables, The Avengers, Sweet and Lowdown, Vatel, The Golden Bowl.
TELEVISION: *Movie*: Robin Hood.

THURSTON, BARRY
Executive. b. Hackensack, NJ. e. B.S., economics, Lehigh U. Began career as broadcaster, director and producer for network telecasts, Sports Network; program mgr., Kaiser Broadcasting, and station mgr., WKBD, 1965-1970; dir. of programming, v.p., programming, Field Communications (formerly Kaiser Broadcasting); v.p., domestic synd., Embassy Communications, 1983-85; senior v.p., domestic synd., and president, Embassy Comm., 1985-86; president of syndication, Columbia/Embassy Television, 1986-87; president of syndication, Columbia Pictures Entertainment and Columbia Pictures Television, 1987-92; president, Columbia Pictures Television Distribution (now Columbia TriStar Television Distribution - CTTD), 1992-present. Responsible for ushering CTTD into new areas of first-run syndication and first-run production for cable, and formed Columbia TriStar Advertiser Sales, 1993. Served on the board for NATPE and Combined Broadcasting and was a member of INTV's planning committee. Currently on the board of directors, TVB.

THURSTON, DONALD A.
Executive. b. Gloucester, MA, April 2, 1930. Began career in broadcasting in 1949. Former Chmn., National Assoc. of Broadcasters. Past Pres., Massachusetts Broadcasters Assoc. Former Commissioner of Massachusetts Cable TV Commission. Former Chmn. of Broadcast Capital Fund, Inc. a venture capital co. that assists minorities in the acquisition of broadcast properties. Pres. Berkshire Broadcasting Co. Inc. Director and Former Chmn., Broadcast Music, Inc. Received Honorary Doctor of Humanities from North Adams State College (1977), Doctor of Humane Letters, Emerson college (1995). Recipient of the Distinguished Service Award of the National Association of Broadcasters.

TICOTIN, RACHEL
Actress. b. Bronx, NY, Nov. 1, 1958. Began career as dancer with the Ballet Hispanico of New York, before becoming a production assist. on such films as The Wanderers, Dressed to Kill and Raging Bull.

PICTURES: King of the Gypsies, Fort Apache: The Bronx, Critical Condition, Total Recall, One Good Cop, FX2, Falling Down, Natural Born Killers, Don Juan DeMarco, Steal Big Steal Little, Turbulence, Con-Air, The Day October Died.
TELEVISION: *Series*: For Love and Honor, Ohara, Crime and Punishment. *Movies*: Love Mary, Rockabye, When the Bough Breaks, Spies Lies and Naked Thighs, Prison Stories: Women on the Inside, Keep the Change, From the Files of Joseph Wambaugh: A Jury of One, Thicker Than Blood: The Larry McLinden Story, Deconstructing Sarah, The Wharf Rat, First Time Felon.

TIERNEY, LAWRENCE
Actor. b. Brooklyn, NY, Mar. 15, 1919. Brother of actor Scott Brady. e. Manhattan Coll. Track athlete (natl. championship Cross Country Team, N.Y. Athletic Club). Stage actor before screen debut 1943.
PICTURES: The Ghost Ship (debut, 1943), Government Girl, Gildersleeve on Broadway, The Falcon Out West, Youth Runs Wild, Back to Bataan, Dillinger, Mama Loves Papa, Those Endearing Young Charms, Badman's Territory, Step By Step, San Quentin, The Devil Thumbs a Ride, Born to Kill, Bodyguard, Kill or Be Killed, Shakedown, The Hoodlum, The Bushwhackers, Best of the Bad Men, The Greatest Show on Earth, The Steel Cage, Female Jungle, Singing in the Dark, A Child Is Waiting, Custer of the West, Such Good Friends, Abduction, Andy Warhol's Bad, The Kirlian Witness, Never Pick Up a Stranger, Gloria, Arthur, Rosemary's Killer, Midnight, Prizzi's Honor, Stephen King's Silver Bullet, Murphy's Law, Tough Guys Don't Dance, The Offspring, The Horror Show, Wizards of the Demon Sword, Why Me?, City of Hope, The Runestone, Reservoir Dogs, A Kiss Goodnight, Junior, Fatal Passion, Ben Johnson: Third Cowboy on the Right, 2 Days in the Valley, American Hero, Southie, Armageddon.
TELEVISION: *Movies*: Terrible Joe Moran, Dillinger. *Guest*: Hill Street Blues, Star Trek: The Next Generation, Tales From the Dark Side, Hunter, The Simpsons (voice).

TIERNEY, MAURA
Actress. b. Boston, MA, Feb. 3, 1965.
PICTURES: Dead Women in Lingerie, The Linguini Incident, White Sands, The Temp, Fly by Night, Primal Fear, Mercy, Liar Liar, Primary Colors, Oxygen (also exec. prod.), Forces of Nature, Instinct.
TELEVISION: *Movies:* Student Exchange, Crossing the Mob, Flying Blind, Out of Darkness. *Series:* The Van Dyke Show, 704 Hauser, NewsRadio. *Guest:* Booker, Law & Order.

TIFFIN, PAMELA
Actress. r.n. Pamela Wonso. b. Oklahoma City, OK, Oct. 13, 1942. e. Hunter Coll., Columbia U., Loyola U, Rome Center. Studied acting with Stella Adler and Harold Clurman. Started modeling as a teenager.
THEATER: Dinner at Eight (Theatre World Award), Uncle Vanya.
PICTURES: Summer and Smoke (debut, 1961), One Two Three, State Fair, Come Fly with Me, For Those Who Think Young, The Lively Set, The Pleasure Seekers, Kiss the Other Sheik, The Hallelujah Trail, Harper, Paranoia, Viva Max!, The Godson, Giornata Nera per l'Ariete, Deaf Smith and Johnny Ears, Puntto e a Capo, Evil Fingers.

TIGHE, KEVIN
Actor. b. Los Angeles, CA, Aug. 13, 1944. e. Cal. State, B.A. in psychology; USC M.F.A. in performing arts. Served in U.S. Army, 1967-69. Received N.E.A. Director's Fellowship, Seattle Rep. Theatre, 1988-89.
PICTURES: The Graduate (debut, 1967), Matewan, Eight Men Out, K-9, Lost Angels, Road House, Another 48 HRS, Bright Angel, City of Hope, Newsies, School Ties, A Man in Uniform (Genie Award), Geronimo: An American Legend, What's Eating Gilbert Grape, Scorpion Spring, Jade, Race the Sun, The Wentonicawa Flash, Mumford.
TELEVISION: *Series*: Emergency, Murder One. *Guest*: Tales From the Crypt (Cutting Cards). *Movies*: Better Off Dead, Betrayal of Trust, The Avenging Angel, Winchell.

TILLY, JENNIFER
Actress. b. Harbour City, CA, 1962. Sister is actress Meg Tilly.
THEATER: One Shoe Off (Off-B'way debut, 1993; Theatre World Award).
PICTURES: No Small Affair, Moving Violations, Inside Out, He's My Girl, Johnny Be Good, Rented Lips, High Spirits, Far From Home, Let It Ride, The Fabulous Baker Boys, Made in America, The Getaway, Bullets Over Broadway (Acad. Award nom.), Man With a Gun, Embrace of the Vampire, House Arrest, The Pompatus of Love, Bound, Bird of Prey, Edie and Pen, American Strays, Liar Liar, Bride of Chucky, Relax...It's Just Sex, The Wrong Guy, Hoods, Music From Another Room, Goosed, The Muse (cameo).
TELEVISION: *Series*: Shaping Up. *Movie*: Heads, Bella Mafia. *Guest:* Hill Street Blues.

TILLY, MEG
Actress. b. Long Beach, CA, Feb. 14, 1960. m. Producer John Calley. Sister is actress Jennifer Tilly. Began acting and dancing in community theatrical prods. while in high school. To New York at 16; appeared on TV in Hill Street Blues. *Author*: Singing Songs (1994).
PICTURES: Fame (debut, 1980), Tex, Psycho II, One Dark Night, The Big Chill, Impulse, Agnes of God (Acad. Award nom.), Off Beat, Masquerade, The Girl in a Swing, Valmont, The Two Jakes, Leaving Normal, Body Snatchers, Sleep with Me.
TELEVISION: *Series*: Winnetka Road. *Specials*: The Trouble With Grandpa, Camilla (Nightmare Classics). *Movies*: In the Best Interest of the Child, Trick of the Eye. *Guest*: Fallen Angels (Dead-End for Delia).

TINKER, GRANT A.
Executive. b. Stamford, CT., Jan. 11, 1926. e. Dartmouth Coll., 1947. Joined NBC radio prog. dept. 1949. In 1954 with McCann-Erickson ad agency, TV dept. In 1958, Benton & Bowles Ad Agency, TV dept.; 1961-66 with NBC, v.p., programs, West Coast; v.p. in chg. of programming, NY, 1966-67; joined Universal Television as v.p., 1968-69; 20th-Fox, v.p., 1969-70. Became pres. MTM Enterprises, Inc. 1970. Named NBC bd. chmn. & CEO, 1981-86. Received ATAS Governor's Award in 1987. Formed indep. prod. co. G.T.G. Entertainment, 1988.

TINKER, MARK
Director, Producer.
TELEVISION: *Movies*: Private Eye, Capital News, N.Y.P.D. Mounted, Babe Ruth, Bonanza: Under Attack. *Series*: L.A. Law, NYPD Blue, Chicago Hope, ER, Brooklyn South (prod., Emmy Award, 1998).

TISCH, LAURENCE A.
Executive. b. Brooklyn, NY, March 5, 1923. e. NYU, 1941; U. of Pennsylvania Wharton Sch., 1942; Harvard Law Sch., 1946. Pres. Tisch Hotels, Inc., 1950-59; pres. Americana Hotel, Inc., Miami Beach, 1956-59; Chmn. of bd. and co-chief executive officer of Loews Corp since 1960. Also chmn. of bd. of CNA Financial Corp since 1947. President and chief executive officer and chmn. of board, CBS since 1986.

TISCH, PRESTON ROBERT
Executive. b. Brooklyn, NY, April 29, 1926. e. Bucknell U., Lewisberg, PA, 1943-44; U. of Michigan, B.A., 1948. Pres. Loew's Corporation. Postmaster General of the U.S. 1986-1988. March, 1988 returned to Loews Corp. as president and co-chief executive. Elected member of bd. CBS Inc. 1988, 1994, position changed to co-chmn. & co-CEO of Loews Corp.

TISCH, STEVE
Producer. b. Lakewood, NJ, 1949. e. Tufts U. Son of Preston Tisch. Worked during school breaks for John Avildsen and Fred Weintraub. Signed upon graduation as exec. asst. to Peter Guber, then prod. head at Columbia Pics. Entered producer ranks with Outlaw Blues, 1977, collaborating with Jon Avnet with whom formed Tisch/Avnet Prods. Alliance with Phoenix Entertainment 1988.
PICTURES: Outlaw Blues, Almost Summer, Coast to Coast, Risky Business, Deal of the Century, Soul Man, Big Business, Hot to Trot, Heart of Dixie, Heart Condition, Bad Influence, Forrest Gump (Academy Award for Best Picture, 1994), Corrina Corrina. *Exec. Prod.:* The Long Kiss Goodnight, Dear God, Wild America, American History X, The Postman, Nico the Unicorn, Lock Stock and Two Smoking Barrels, Wayward Son, Looking for an Echo, Snatch.
TELEVISION: Homeward Bound, No Other Love, Prime Suspect, Something So Right, Calendar Girl Murders, The Burning Bed (exec. prod.), Call to Glory (series), Triple Cross, Silence of the Heart, In Love and War (sole prod.), Evil in Clear River, Dirty Dancing (series), Out on the Edge (exec. prod.), Judgment (exec. prod.), Lies of the Heart, The Vidiots (pilot), Victim of Love, Keep the Change, Afterburn (exec. prod.), Freshman Dorm (pilot & series), The People Next Door, Mission Extreme (series).

TOBACK, JAMES
Writer, Producer, Director. b. New York, NY, Nov. 23, 1944. e. Harvard U. Taught literature at City Coll. of New York; contributed articles and criticism to Harper's, Esquire, Commentary, etc. Wrote book Jim, on actor-athlete Jim Brown (1971). First screenplay, The Gambler, filmed in 1974.
PICTURES: *Writer*: The Gambler, Fingers (also dir.), Love and Money (also dir., prod.), Exposed (also dir., prod.), The Pick-Up Artist (also dir.), The Big Bang (also dir., actor), Alice (actor), Bugsy (also actor).

TOBOLOWSKY, STEPHEN
Actor. b. Dallas, TX, May 30, 1951. e. Southern Methodist Univ.
THEATER: *Actor*: Whose Life Is It Anyway?, Crimes of the Heart, Godspell, Three Sisters, The Glass Menagerie, Barabass, The Wake of Jamey Foster, The Wild Duck, No Scratch, The Miss Firecracker Contest, The Importance of Being Earnest, Purlie, Whispers in the Wind. *Director*: The Miss Firecracker Contest, The Lucky Spot, The Bridgehead (Dramalogue Award), The Secret Rapture (Dramalogue Award), Our Town, The Debutante Ball.
PICTURES: Swing Shift, True Stories (co-s.p.), Nobody's Fool, Spaceballs, Mississippi Burning, Checking Out, Two Idiots in Hollywood (dir. & s.p.), Great Balls of Fire!, In Country, Breaking In, Bird on a Wire, Funny About Love, Welcome Home Roxy Carmichael, The Grifters, Thelma & Louise, Memoirs of an Invisible Man, Basic Instinct, Roadside Prophets, Single White Female, Where the Day Takes You, Sneakers, Hero, Groundhog Day, The Pickle, Calendar Girl, Josh and S.A.M., My Father the Hero, Radioland Murders, Murder in the First, Dr. Jekyll and Ms. Hyde, Power 98, The Glimmer Man, The Curse of the Inferno, The Curse of Inferno, The Brave Little Toaster Goes to Mars, Boys Life II, Mr. Magoo, An Alan Smithee Film: Burn Hollywood Burn, The Operator, Black Dog, One Man's Hero, The Insider, Bossa Nova, Alien Fury: Countdown to Invasion, THe Prime Gig, Memento, Urban Chaos Theory, Sleep Easy Hutch Rimes, Freddy Got Fingered, Par 6.
TELEVISION: *Movies*: Last Flight Out, Marla Hanson Story, Perry Mason: The Case of the Maligned Mobster, Tagget, Deadlock, Deadly Medicine, When Love Kills: The Seduction of John Hearn, Night Visitors. *Series*: Against the Grain, Blue Skies, A Whole New Ballgame, Dweebs. *Guest*: Crazy Like a Fox, Designing Women, L.A. Law, Days and Nights of Molly Dodd, Seinfeld, Picket Fences, Chicago Hope, Hearts of the West, Baby Talk, Knots Landing, Falcon Crest.

TODD, BEVERLY
Actress, Director, Producer. b. Chicago, IL, July 11.
THEATER: *NY*: Carry Me Back to Morningside Heights, Black Visions. *Producer*: A Tribute to Ella Fitzgerald. *Director*: I Need a Man, Sneaky.
PICTURES: The Lost Man, They Call Me Mister Tibbs!, Brother John, Vice Squad, Homework, The Ladies Club, Happy Hour, Baby Boom, Moving, Clara's Heart, Lean on Me, The Surgeon.
TELEVISION: *Series*: Love of Life, Having Babies, The Redd Foxx Show. *Mini-Series*: Roots. *Movies*: Deadlock, The Ghost of Flight 401, Having Babies II, The Jericho Mile, Don't Look Back, A Touch of Scandal, A Different Affair. *Guest*: Magnum P.I., The Robert Guillaume Show, Falcon Crest, Quincy M.E., Hill Street Blues, Family, Benson, Lou Grant, A Different World, Good News, Sparks. *Special*: A Laugh a Tear: The Story of Black Humor in America (prod.), Don't Hit Me Mom (Afterschool Special), The Class of '61.

TODD, RICHARD
O.B.E. Actor. b. Dublin, Ireland, June 11, 1919. e. Shrewsbury. In repertory, 1937; founder-member, Dundee Repertory Theatre, 1939; distinguished war service, 1939-46; Dundee Repertory, 1946-48; screen debut, 1948; For Them That Trespass, 1948. 1970 Founder-Director Triumph Theatre Productions. Published autobiography, 1986, Volume II, 1989. Awarded O.B.E., 1993.
THEATER: An Ideal Husband, Dear Octopus. Co-founder, Triumph Theatre Prods., Ltd. plays since 1970: Roar Like a Dove, Grass Is Greener, The Marquise (U.S.). Sleuth (England and Australia). Murder by Numbers, The Hollow Crown (with RSC), Equus. On Approval, Quadrille, This Happy Breed, The Business of Murder (London), Intent to Kill, The Woman in Black, Beyond Reasonable Doubt, Sweet Revenge, Brideshead Revisted.
PICTURES: For Them That Trespass (debut, 1948), The Hasty Heart, Interrupted Journey, Stage Fright, Portrait of Clare, Lightning Strikes Twice (U.S.), Flesh and Blood, Story of Robin Hood, 24 Hours of a Woman's Life, The Venetian Bird, Sword and the Rose, Rob Roy, Les Secrets d'Alcove (Fr.), A Man Called Peter (U.S.), The Virgin Queen (U.S.), Dam Busters, D-Day the Sixth of June (U.S.), Marie Antoinette (Fr.), Yangtse Incident, Saint Joan, Chase a Crooked Shadow, The Naked Earth, Intent to Kill, Danger Within, Never Let Go, The Long the Short and the Tall, Don't Bother to Knock (also exec. prod.), The Hellions, The Longest Day, Crime Does Not Pay (Fr.), The Boys, The Very Edge, Death Drums Along the River, Battle of the Villa Fiorita, Operation Crossbow, Coast of Skeletons, The Love-Ins, Subterfuge, Dorian Gray, Asylum, The Sky is Falling, Number One of the Secret Service, The Big Sleep, House of the Long Shadows, Incident at Victoria Fall.s .
TELEVISION: Wuthering Heights, Carrington V.C., The Brighton Mesmerists, Beautiful Lies, The Boy Dominic, Murder She Wrote, Virtual Murder., Murder One, Marlene Dietrich: Shadows and Light.

TOKOFSKY, JERRY H.
Executive. b. New York, NY, Apr. 14, 1936. e. NYU, B.S., journalism, 1956; New York Law, 1959. Entered William Morris Agency while at NYU 1953, working in night club dept. to live TV. Moved to Beverly Hills office, 1959. Entered m.p. div. WMA, 1960. Joined Columbia Pictures, as Prod. V.P., 1963-70. Joined Paramount Pictures 1970 as prod. v.p. To MGM as prod. v.p., 1971. Producer & Exec. V.P., Zupnik Enterprises, Inc. until 1992.
PICTURES: *Producer*: Where's Poppa, Born to Win, Paternity, Dreamscape, Fear City, Wildfire, Glengarry Glen Ross.

TOLAN, PETER
Producer, Writer.
PICTURES: Alice (actor), My Fellow Americans, Analyze This.
TELEVISION: *Series*: Murphy Brown (Emmy Award, 1992), The Larry Sanders Show (Emmy Award, 1998), Style and Substance.

TOLKAN, JAMES
Actor. b. Calumet, MI, June 20, 1931. e. Univ. of Iowa. Trained with Stella Adler.
THEATER: *NY*: Abe Lincoln in Illinois, Once in a Lifetime, Three Sisters, The Cannibals, Mary Stuart, The Silent Partner, 42 Seconds from Broadway, Full Circle, Macbeth, Dream of a Blacklisted Actor, Jungle of Cities, Wings.
PICTURES: Stiletto, They Might Be Giants, The Friends of Eddie Coyle, Serpico, Love and Death, The Amityville Horror, Wolfen, Prince of the City, Author! Author!, Hanky Panky, Nightmares (voice), WarGames, Iceman, The River, Turk 182!, Flanagan, Back to the Future, Off Beat, Top Gun, Armed and Dangerous, Masters of the Universe, Made in Heaven, Viper, Split Decisions, True Blood, Second Sight, Back to the Future Part II, Family Business, Opportunity Knocks, Back to the Future Part III, Dick Tracy, Hangfire, Problem Child 2, Driving Me Crazy, Boiling Point, Love in Ambush.
TELEVISION: *Series*: Mary, The Hat Squad, Cobra. *Movies*: Little Spies, Leap of Faith, Weekend War, The Case of the Hillside Stranglers, Sketch Artist, Beyond Betrayal, Sketch Artist II: Hands That See. *Guest*: Remington Steele, Miami Vice, The Equalizer, Tales From the Crypt.

TOLKIN, MICHAEL
Writer, Director, Producer. b. New York, NY, Oct. 17, 1950. e. Middlebury Col, VT. Started as writer for LA Times, Village Voice, before becoming story editor on tv series Delta House. Novels: The Player (1988), Among the Dead (1992).
PICTURES: *Writer*: Gleaming the Cube, The Rapture (also dir.), The Player (also co-prod., actor; WGA Award, Acad. Award nom.), Deep Cover (also story), The New Age (also dir.), Deep Impact, 20 Billion.
TELEVISION: *Movie*: The Burning Season (co-writer).

TOLL, JOHN
Cinematographer.
PICTURES: *Cam. Op.:* Tom Horn, Norma Rae, Zorro: The Gay Blade, Scarface, The Falcon and the Snowman, Peggy Sue Got Married, Black Widow, Tequila Sunrise, The Milagro Beanfield War, Blaze, Always. *Cinematographer:* Wind, Legends of the Fall, Braveheart, Jack, The Rainmaker, The Thin Red Line (Acad. Award nom.), Simpatico.
TELEVISION: The Boy Who Drank Too Much (cam. op.), The Kid, The Young Riders, Good Night Sweet Wife: A Murder in Boston.

TOMEI, MARISA
Actress. b. Brooklyn, NY, Dec. 4, 1964. e. Boston U.
THEATER: Beiruit (L.A.). *NY*: Daughters (Theatre World Award), The Comedy of Errors, What the Butler Saw, Slavs!
PICTURES: The Flamingo Kid (debut, 1984), Playing for Keeps, Oscar, Zandalee, My Cousin Vinny (Academy Award, best supporting actress, 1992), Chaplin, Untamed Heart, Equinox, The Paper, Only You, The Perez Family, Four Rooms, A Brother's Kiss, Unhook the Stars, Welcome to Sarajevo, The Women, The Slums of Beverly Hills, Only Love.
TELEVISION: *Series*: As the World Turns, A Different World. *Guest:* Seinfeld. *Movie*: Parker Kane, Since You've Been Gone.

TOMLIN, LILY
Actress. r.n. Mary Jean Tomlin. b. Detroit, MI, Sept. 1, 1939. e. Wayne State U. (studied pre-med). Studied mime with Paul Curtis. Started inventing characters for comedy sketches in college, used them in cafe and night club dates in Detroit. 1965 went to NY performing skits on coffee-house circuit, landed job on The Garry Moore Show. Moved to L.A. where she appeared on The Music Scene. 1969, first appeared on Laugh-In TV series, gaining national attention with such characters as telephone operator Ernestine and child Edith Ann.
RECORDS: This Is a Recording (Grammy Award, 1971), Modern Scream, And That's the Truth, Lily Tomlin On Stage.

THEATER: Appearing Nitely (special Tony Award, 1977), The Search for Signs of Intelligent Life in the Universe (1985, on B'way and on tour; Tony Award).
PICTURES: Nashville (debut, 1975; NY Film Critics Award; Acad Award nom.), The Late Show, Moment by Moment, Nine to Five, The Incredible Shrinking Woman, All of Me, Big Business, The Search for Signs of Intelligent Life in the Universe, Shadows and Fog, The Player, Short Cuts, The Beverly Hillbillies, Blue in the Face, Getting Away With Murder, The Celluloid Closet (narrator), Flirting With Disaster, Krippendorf's Tribe, Get Bruce (cameo), Tea with Mussolini.
TELEVISION: *Series*: The Music Scene (host, 1969), Rowan and Martin's Laugh-In (1969-73), Magic School Bus (voice for animated series; Emmy Award), Murphy Brown. *Specials*: Lily (Emmy Award as writer, 1974), Lily Tomlin (Emmy Award as writer, 1976), The Paul Simon Special (Emmy Award as writer, 1978), Lily: Sold Out! (also exec. prod.; Emmy Award as exec. prod., 1981), The Muppets Go to the Movies, Lily for President?, Live—and in Person, Funny You Don't Look 200, Free to Be... a Family, Edith Ann: A Few Pieces of the Puzzle (voice, exec. prod.), Edith Ann: Homeless Go Home (voice, exec. prod.), Edith Ann's Christmas: Just Say Noel (voice, exec. prod; Peabody Award). *Movie*: And the Band Played On. *Guest:* Homicide, The X Files, Frasier.

TOPOL
Actor. r.n. Chaim Topol. b. Tel-Aviv, Israel, Sept. 9, 1935.
THEATER: Fiddler on the Roof (London, 1967, 1994-95 also U.K. tour; NY 1989: Tony nom.; Canada & Japan tour) Chicester Fest. Theatre: Caucasian Chalk Circle, Romanov and Juliet, Othello, View From the Bridge.
PICTURES: Sallah, Cast a Giant Shadow, Before Winter Comes, A Talent for Loving, Fiddler on the Roof (Acad. Award nom.), Follow Me, Galileo, Flash Gordon, For Your Eyes Only, Ervinka, A Dime Novel.
TELEVISION: *Movies*: House on Garibaldi Street, Queenie. *Mini-Series*: The Winds of War, War and Remembrance. *Series* (BBC): It's Topol, Topol's Israel.

TORME, MEL
Singer, Actor. b. Chicago, IL, Sept. 13, 1925. Singing debut at age of 4; won radio audition 1933; on radio; composed song Lament to Love; with Chico Marx's orchestra as drummer, arranger & vocalist 1942; served in U.S. Army, WWII; org. vocal group Meltones; many recordings; night club and concert appearances. *Author*: The Other Side of the Rainbow: With Judy Garland on the Dawn Patrol (1970), It Wasn't All Velvet (1988), My Singing Teachers: Reflections on Singing Popular Music (1994).
PICTURES: Higher and Higher (debut, 1943), Pardon My Rhythm, Let's Go Steady, Janie Gets Married, Junior Miss, Night and Day, Good News, Words and Music, Duchess of Idaho, The Big Operator, Girls Town, Walk Like a Dragon, The Patsy, A Man Called Adam, The Land of No Return (Snowman), Daffy Duck's Quackbusters (voice), The Naked Gun 2 1/2: The Smell of Fear.
TELEVISION: Series: TV's Top Tunes, The Judy Garland Show (musical advisor, frequent guest), It Was a Very Good Year (host). Movie: Pray TV. *Guest*: Night Court.
(d. June 5, 1999)

TORN, RIP
Actor. r.n. Elmore Torn, Jr. b. Temple, TX, Feb. 6, 1931. e. Texas A & M U., U. of TX. Served in army. Signed as understudy for lead in Cat on a Hot Tin Roof on Broadway.
THEATER: Orpheus Descending, Sweet Bird of Youth (Theatre World Award), Daughter of Silence, Macbeth, Desire Under the Elms, Strange Interlude, Blues For Mr. Charlie, The Kitchen, The Deer Park (Obie Award), The Beard, The Cuban Thing, Dream of a Blacklisted Actor, The Dance of Death, Anna Christie.
PICTURES: Baby Doll (debut, 1956), A Face in the Crowd, Time Limit, Pork Chop Hill, King of Kings, Hero's Island, Sweet Bird of Youth, Critic's Choice, The Cincinnati Kid, One Spy Too Many, You're a Big Boy Now, Beach Red, Sol Madrid, Beyond the Law, Coming Apart, Tropic of Cancer, Maidstone, Slaughter, Payday, Crazy Joe, Birch Interval, The Man Who Fell to Earth, Nasty Habits, The Private Files of J. Edgar Hoover, Coma, The Seduction of Joe Tynan, Heartland, One Trick Pony, First Family, A Stranger is Watching, The Beastmaster, Jinxed, Airplane II: The Sequel, Cross Creek (Acad. Award nom.), Misunderstood, Songwriter, Flashpoint, City Heat, Summer Rental, Beer, Extreme Prejudice, Nadine, The Telephone (also dir.), Cold Feet, Hit List, Blind Curve, The Hunt for Red October, Defending Your Life, Silence Like Glass, Beautiful Dreamers, Hard Promises, Robocop 3, Dolly Dearest, Where the Rivers Flow North, Canadian Bacon, How to Make an American Quilt, Down Periscope, Hercules (voice), Trial and Error, Men in Black, The Mouse, Senseless, Wonder Boys.
TELEVISION: *Series*: The Larry Sanders Show (Emmy Awatd, 1996), Hercules (voice), Ghost Stories (voice). *Movies*: The President's Plane Is Missing, Attack on Terror: The FBI vs. the Ku Klux Klan, Betrayal, Steel Cowboy, A Shining Season, Sophia Loren—Her Own Story, Rape and Marriage—The Rideout Case, Laguna Heat, When She Says No, The Execution, The Atlanta Child Murders, Manhunt for Claude Dallas, J. Edgar Hoover, The King of Love, April Morning, Sweet Bird of Youth, Pair of Aces, By Dawn's Early Light, Another Pair of Aces, My Son Johnny, Death Hits the Jackpot, T Bone N Weasel, A Mother's Right: The Elizabeth Morgan Story, Dead Ahead: The Exxon Valdez Disaster, She Stood Alone: The Tailhook Scandal, Letter to My Killer, Balloon Farm, Seasons of Love. *Mini-Series*: Blind Ambition, The Blue and the Gray, Heaven & Hell: North and South Book III, Heart of a Child.

TORNATORE, GIUSEPPE
Director. b. Bagheria, Sicily, Italy, 1956. Made directorial debut at age 16 with short film Il Carretto. 1978- 85, served as pres. of the CLTC filmmaking cooperative.
PICTURES: The Professor (debut, 1986), Cinema Paradiso, Everybody's Fine, The Blue Dog (segment), Especially on Sunday (segment), A Pure Formality, The Star Maker (L'uomo delle stelle), 1900 (La Leggenda del pianista sull'oceano), Malena.
TELEVISION: Portrait of a Thief, Metting With Francesco Rosi, Sicilian Writers and Films, Il Diario di Guttuso, Ethnic Minorities in Sicily (Salerno Film Fest. Prize), A Hundred Days in Palermo (also writer, 2nd unit dir.).

TOTTER, AUDREY
Actress. b. Joliet, IL, Dec. 20, 1918. In many stage plays. On radio 1939-44.
THEATER: Copperhead, Stage Door, Late Christopher Bean, My Sister Eileen.
PICTURES: Main Street After Dark (debut, 1944), Her Highness and the Bellboy, Dangerous Partners, The Sailor Takes a Wife, Adventure, The Hidden Eye, The Secret Heart, The Postman Always Rings Twice, Cockeyed Miracle, Lady in the Lake, Beginning or the End, Unsuspected, High Wall, The Saxon Charm, Alias Nick Beal, Any Number Can Play, Tension, The Set-Up, Under the Gun, The Blue Veil, Sellout, F.B.I. Girl, Assignment-Paris, My Pal Gus, Woman They Almost Lynched, Cruisin' Down the River, Man in the Dark, Mission Over Korea, Champ for a Day, Massacre Canyon, Women's Prison, A Bullet for Joey, Vanishing American, Ghost Diver, Jet Attack, Man or Gun, The Carpetbaggers, Harlow, Chubasco, The Apple Dumpling Gang Rides Again.
TELEVISION: *Series*: Cimarron City, Our Man Higgins, Medical Center (1972-76). *Movies*: The Outsider, U.M.C., The Nativity, The Great Cash Giveaway, City Killer. Guest: Murder, She Wrote.

TOWERS, CONSTANCE
Actress. b. Whitefish, MT, May 20, 1934. m. John Gavin, actor and former U.S. Ambassador to Mexico. e. Juilliard Sch. of Music. Stage work on Broadway and tour. In Concert with John Raitt, 1998.
THEATER: *B'way*: Ari, Anya, Engagement Baby, The King and I (1977-79 opp. Yul Brynner), Showboat. *Regional*: Steel Magnolias, Follies, Sound of Music, I Do I Do, Mame, 110 In the Shade, Carousel, Oklahoma, Dumas & Son, Guys & Dolls, Oh Coward.
PICTURES: Bring Your Smile Along, Horse Soldiers, Sergeant Rutledge, Fate Is the Hunter, Shock Corridor, Naked Kiss, Sylvester, Fast Forward, Nutty Nut, The Next Karate Kid, The Relic, A Perfect Murder.
TELEVISION: *Series*: Love Is a Many Splendored Thing, VTV, Capitol, 2000 Malibu Road, General Hospital. *Mini-Series*: On Wings of Eagles, Sands of Time. *Guest*: Home Show, The Loner, Murder, She Wrote, Hour Mag, MacGyver, Designing Women, Midnight Caller, Matlock, Baywatch, Prince of Bel Air, Thunder in Paradise, L.A. Law, Civil Wars, Frasier, Robin's Nest, Caroline In the City, The Young & the Restless.

TOWERS, HARRY ALAN
Executive, Producer. b. London, England, 1920.
PICTURES: Sanders of the River (also s.p.), Code Seven Victim Five (also s.p.), City of Fear, Mozambique, Coast of Skeletons, Sandy the Seal, 24 Hours to Kill, The Face of Fu Manchu, Ten Little Indians, Marrakesh, Circus of Fear, The Brides of Fu Manchu, Sumuru, Five Golden Dragons, The Vengeance of Fu Manchu, Jules Verne's Rocket to the Moon, House of a Thousand Dolls, The Face of Eve, Blood of Fu Manchu, 99 Women, Girl From Rio, Marquis de Sade's Justine, Castle of Fu Manchu, Venus in Furs, Philosophy in the Boudoir, Eugenie, Dorian Gray, Count Dracula, The Bloody Judge. Black Beauty, Night Hair Child, The Call of the Wild, Treasure Island, White Fang, Death in Persepolis, Ten Little Indians, End of Innocence, Black Cobra, Black Velvet—White Silk, Night of The High Tide, King Solomon's Treasure, Shape of Things to Come,

Klondike Fever, Fanny Hill, Frank and I, Black Venus, Christmas, Black Arrow, Pompeii, Love Circles, Lightning—The White Stallion, Gor, Outlaw of Gor, Dragonard, Skeleton Coast, Master of Dragonard Hill, Nam, Fire With Fire, Jekyll and Hyde, River of Death, Cobra Strike, The Howling IV: The Original Nightmare, Skeleton Coast, Edge of Sanity, Ten Little Indians, Platoon Leader, Captive Rage, American Ninja III: Blood Hunt, The Fall of the House of Usher, Edgar Allan Poe's Buried Alive, Phantom of the Opera, Oddball Hall, Terror of Manhattan, The Lost World, Return to the Lost World, Black Museum, Golden Years of Sherlock Holmes, The Mangler, Midnight in St. Petersburg, Bullet to Beijing (The Return of Harry Palmer), Cry the Beloved Country, China Bill, She, Stanley & Livingstone, The Zodiak Conspiracy, The House of Usher, Edge of Sanity, Ten Little Indians, River of Death, Outlaw of Gor, American Ninja 3: Blood Hunt, Masque of Red Death, Buried Alive, Incident at Victoria Falls, The Hitman, Delta Force 3: The Killing Game, Tobe Hooper's Night Terrors, The Mummy Lives, The Mangler, Cry the Beloved Country, Midnight in St. Petersburg, Bullet to Beijing, Treasure Island, City of Fear, Queen's Messenger, High Explosive.

TOWNE, ROBERT
Writer, Director, Producer. b. Los Angeles, CA, 1936. Raised in San Pedro. Was member of Warren Beatty's production staff on Bonnie and Clyde and contributed to that screenplay. Also uncredited, wrote Pacino-Brando garden scene in The Godfather; script doctor on Marathon Man, The Missouri Breaks and others.
PICTURES: *Writer*: The Last Woman on Earth (as Edward Wain), The Tomb of Ligeia, Villa Rides, The Last Detail, Chinatown (Academy Award, 1974), Shampoo (co-s.p.), The Yazuka (co-s.p.), Personal Best (also dir., prod.), Greystoke: The Legend of Tarzan (s.p., uncredited), Tequila Sunrise (also dir.), Days of Thunder, The Two Jakes, The Firm (co-s.p.), Love Affair (co-s.p.), Mission: Impossible (co-s.p.), Without Limits.

TOWNSEND, ROBERT
Actor, Producer, Director, Writer. b. Chicago, IL, Feb. 6, 1957. e.Illinois State U., Hunter Coll. Veteran of Experimental Black Actors Guild and Second City. TV commercials; stand-up comedy at NY Improvisation; taped Evening at the Improv.
PICTURES: *Actor*: Cooley High (debut, 1974), Willie and Phil, Streets of Fire, A Soldier's Story, American Flyers, Odd Jobs, Ratboy, Hollywood Shuffle (also prod., dir., co-s.p.), Eddie Murphy Raw (dir. only), The Mighty Quinn, That's Adequate, The Five Heartbeats (also dir., exec. prod., co-s.p.), The Meteor Man (also dir., s.p., co-prod.), B.A.P.S. (dir. only).
TELEVISION: *Series*: Another Page (PBS series), Townsend Television, The Parent 'Hood (also co-creator, exec. prod.). *Specials*: Robert Townsend and His Partners in Crime, Take No Prisoners: Robert Townsend and His Partners in Crime II (HBO). *Movies*: Women at West Point, Senior Trip!, In Love With an Older Woman.

TRAMBUKIS, WILLIAM J.
Executive. b. Providence, R.I., July 26, 1926. e. Mt. Pleasant Bus. Col. Began career as usher with Loew's in Providence, RI, 1941. Served 1943-46 with Navy Seabees. Recipient of Quigley Awards. Managed/supervised Loew's Theatres in several New England cities, Harrisburg, PA, Syracuse, Rochester, Buffalo, NY, Washington, DC, Richmond, Norfolk, VA, Toronto, Canada, Atlanta, GA. Appt. Loew's NorthEastern Division mgr. 1964, Loew's gen. mgr. 1975: v.p. in 1976; sr. v.p., 1985. Retired, 1987.

TRAVANTI, DANIEL J.
Actor. b. Kenosha, WI, March 7, 1940. e. U. of Wisconsin (B.A.), Loyola Marymount Univ. (M.A.), Yale Sch. of Drama. Woodrow Wilson fellow, 1961. Formerly acted as Dan Travanty. On stage in Twigs, Othello, I Never Sang for My Father, Only Kidding, The Taming of the Shrew, Les Liaisons Dangereuses, A Touch of the Poet, Antony & Cleopatra, A Touch of the Poet.
PICTURES: St. Ives, Midnight Crossing, Millenium, Megaville, Weep No More My Lady, Just Cause, Siao Yu, Who Killed Teddy Bear.
TELEVISION: *Series*: General Hospital, Hill Street Blues (Emmy Awards, 1981, 1982; Golden Globe Award, 1981), Missing Persons, Poltergeist: The Legacy. *Movies*: The Love War, Adam, Aurora, Murrow, Adam: His Song Continues, I Never Sang for My Father, Fellow Traveler, Howard Beach: Making the Case for Murder, Tagget, Eyes of a Witness, The Christmas Stallion, In the Shadows Someone's Watching, My Name is Kate, Wasp Woman, A Case of Libel, To Sir With Love II.

TRAVIS, NANCY
Actress. b. New York, NY, Sept. 21, 1961. Raised in Baltimore, MD, and Farmingham, MA. e. NYU. Attended Circle-in-the-Square Theatre school. Acted with NY Amer. Jewish Theatre before landing role in touring prod. of Brighton Beach Memoirs.3
THEATER: *NY*: It's Hard to Be a Jew, The Signal Season of Dummy Hoy, I'm Not Rappaport (B'way). Tour: Brighton Beach Memoirs. *La Jolla Playhouse*: My Children My Africa, Three Sisters.
PICTURES: Three Men and a Baby (debut, 1987), Married to the Mob, Eight Men Out, Internal Affairs, Loose Cannons, Air America, Three Men and a Little Lady, Passed Away, Chaplin, The Vanishing, So I Married an Axe Murderer, Greedy, Destiny Turns on the Radio, Fluke, Bogus.
TELEVISION: *Series*: Almost Perfect, Work with Me. *Movies*: Malice in Wonderland, Harem, I'll Be Home for Christmas, Body Language, My Last Love (prod.). *Special*: High School Narc (ABC Afterschool Special).

TRAVOLTA, JOHN
Actor. b. Englewood, NJ, Feb. 18, 1954. m. actress Kelly Preston. First stage role in Who Will Save the Plowboy? Did off-B'way prod. of Rain; then on Broadway in Grease (also on tour for 10 months), Over Here (with the Andrew Sisters). Author of Staying Fit, 1984.
PICTURES: The Devil's Rain (debut, 1975), Carrie, Saturday Night Fever (Acad. Award nom.), Grease, Moment by Moment, Urban Cowboy, Blow Out, Staying Alive, Two of a Kind, Perfect, The Experts, Look Who's Talking, Look Who's Talking Too, Shout, Eyes of an Angel, Look Who's Talking Now, Pulp Fiction (Acad. Award nom.), White Man's Burden, Get Shorty (Golden Globe winner), Broken Arrow, Phenomenon, Michael, Face/Off, She's So Lovely (also exec. prod.), Mad City, The Thin Red Line, A Civil Action, Primary Colors, The General's Daughter, Our Friend, Martin (voice), Forever Hollywood, Battlefield Earth (also prod.), Lucky Numbers, Swordfish, Domestic Disturbance.
TELEVISION: *Series*: Welcome Back Kotter. *Movies*: The Boy in the Plastic Bubble, Chains of Gold, Boris & Natasha (cameo). *Special*: The Dumb Waiter. *Guest*: Emergency, Owen Marshall--Counselor at Law, The Rookies, Medical Center.

TREMAYNE, LES
Actor. b. London, England, Apr. 16, 1913. e. Northwestern U., Chicago Art Inst., Columbia U., UCLA. First professional appearance in British mp., 1916, with mother; stock, little theatres, vaudeville, 1925-40; entered radio field, 1930. Blue ribbon award for best perf. of the month for A Man Called Peter; dir. Hollywood Rep. Theatre, 1957; pres. Hollywood Actors' Council, 1951-58; chmn. Actors Div. workshop com. Acad. TV Arts & Sciences; Mem.: The Workshop Comm. of the Hollywood M.P. & TV Museum Comm. One of 17 founding members, Pacific Pioneer Broadcasters; Life member, Actor's Fund; charter/founding mem. AFTRA, Chicago local. (delegate to most conventions since 1938). mem. Local, L.A, and Natl. AFTRA bds.
THEATER: Woman in My House, Errand of Mercy, You Are There, One Man's Family, Heartbeat Theatre, The First Nighter (lead 7 yrs.); on Broadway in Heads or Tails, Detective Story.
PICTURES: The Racket, Blue Veil, Francis Goes to West Point, It Grows on Trees, I Love Melvin, Under the Red Sea, Dream Wife, War of the Worlds, Susan Slept Here, Lieutenant Wore Skirts, Unguarded Moment, Everything But the Truth, Monolith Monsters, Perfect Furlough, North by Northwest, Say One for Me, The Gallant Hours, The Angry Red Planet, The Story of Ruth, The Fortune Cookie, Daffy Duck's Movie: Fantastic Island (voice), Starchaser (voice), Rainbow Brite and the Star Stealer.
TELEVISION: Lux Video Theatre, 20th Century-Fox Hour, Navy Log, One Man's Family, Meet Mille, The Millionaire, The Whistler, Truth or Consequences, NBC Matinee, The Girl, O'Henry series, Rin Tin Tin, Bachelor Father, The Texan, Adventures of Ellery Queen, Court of Last Resort, Rifleman, State Trooper, Rescue 8, June Allyson-Dupont Show, Wagon Train, M Squad, Hitchcock Presents, Mr. Ed., Perry Mason.

TREUT, MONIKA
Director, Writer, Editor.
PICTURES: Seduction: The Cruel Woman, Virgin Machine, My Father is Coming, Female Misbehavior, Erotique ("Taboo Parlor" segment), Danish Girls Show Everything (dir. only), Didn't Do It for Love, Gendernauts (dir. only).

TREVOR, CLAIRE
Actress. b. New York, NY, Mar. 8, 1910. e. American Acad. of Dramatic Arts; Columbia U. On Broadway in Party's Over, Whistling in the Dark, Big Two. On radio in Big Town for 4 yrs.
PICTURES: Life in the Raw, The Last Trail, Mad Game, Jimmy and Sally, Hold That Girl, Baby Take a Bow, Elinore Norton, Wild Gold, Dante's Inferno, Spring Tonic, Navy Wife, Black Sleep, Human Cargo, My Marriage, The Song and Dance Man, To Mary—With Love, 15 Maiden Lane, Career Woman, Star for a Night, One Mile From Heaven, Time Out for Romance, Second Honeymoon, Big Town Girl, Dead End (Acad. Award nom.), King of Gamblers, The Amazing Dr. Clitterhouse, Walking Down Broadway, Valley of the Giants, Two of a Kind, I Stole a Million, Stagecoach, Allegheny Uprising, Dark Command, Texas, Honky Tonk, Street of Chance,

The Adventures of Martin Eden, Crossroads, Woman of the Town, The Desperadoes, Good Luck Mr. Yates, Murder My Sweet, Johnny Angel, Crack-Up, The Bachelor's Daughters, Born to Kill, Raw Deal, The Babe Ruth Story, The Velvet Touch, Key Largo (Academy Award, best supporting actress, 1948), The Lucky Stiff, Borderline, Best of the Bad Men, Hard Fast and Beautiful, Hoodlum Empire, My Man and I, Stop You're Killing Me, The Stranger Wore a Gun, The High and the Mighty (Acad. Award nom.), Man Without a Star, Lucy Gallant, The Mountain, Marjorie Morningstar, Two Weeks in Another Town, The Stripper, How to Murder Your Wife, The Capetown Affair, Kiss Me Goodbye.
TELEVISION: *Specials/Movies*: If You Knew Elizabeth, Dodsworth (Emmy Award, 1957), No Sad Songs for Me, Ladies in Retirement, Breaking Home Ties. *Guest*: Alfred Hitchcock Presents, The Untouchables, Love Boat, Murder She Wrote.
(d. April 8, 2000)

TREXLER, CHARLES B.
Exhibitor. b. Wadesboro, NC, Feb. 8, 1916. 1937-48 was practicing CPA except for 2 yrs. in U.S. Army in WWII. Joined Stewart & Everett Theatres in 1948 as controller. 1953 named gen. mgr.; 1954, exec. v.p., treas.; 1962 named pres.; 1983, named bd. chmn.; former bd. chmn., NATO of North and South Carolina; v.p. & bd. mem., National NATO.

TRIKONIS, GUS
Director. b. New York, NY. Started career in chorus of West Side Story on B'way. Turned to directing, making low-budget weekenders (films shot in 12 days only on weekends).
PICTURES: *Actor*: West Side Story, Pajama Party, The Unsinkable Molly Brown, The Sand Pebbles, The Hell Cats, St. Valentine's Day Massacre, *Director*: Five the Hard Way, The Swinging Mermaids, Supercock (also actor), The Student Body, Nashville Girl, Moonshine County Express, The Evil, Touched by Love, Take This Job and Shove It.
TELEVISION: *Movies*: The Darker Side of Terror, She's Dressed To Kill, Flamingo Road (pilot), Elvis and the Beauty Queen, Twirl, Miss All-American Beauty, Dempsey, First Affair, Dempsey, Dance of the Dwarfs, Midas Valley, Malice in Wonderland, Love on the Run, Open Admissions, Unknown Subject, The Great Pretender, Insel der Furcht. *Mini-Series*: The Last Convertible (co-dir.). *Episode*: Twilight Zone (1985). *Series*: Burke's Law, Hercules: The Legendary Journeys, Baywatch Nights, The Sentinel.

TRINTIGNANT, JEAN-LOUIS
Actor. b. Piolenc, France, Dec. 11, 1930. m. Nadine Marquand, director. Theatre debut: 1951, To Each According to His Hunger. Then Mary Stuart, Macbeth (at the Comedie de Saint-Etienne). 1955 screen debut.
PICTURES: Si Tous Les Gars du Monde, La Loi des Rues, And God Created Woman, Club de Femmes, Les Liaisons Dangereuses, L'Estate Violente, Austerlitz, La Millieme Fenetre, Pleins Feux sur L'Assasin, Coeur Battant, L'Atlantide, The Game of Truth, Horace 62, Les Sept Peches Capitaux (7 Capital Sins), Le Combat dans L'Ile, The Easy Life, Il Successo, Nutty Naughty Chateau, Les Pas Perdus, La Bonne Occase, Mata-Hari, Meurtre a L'Italienne, La Longue Marche, Un Jour a Paris, Is Paris Burning?, The Sleeping Car Murders, A Man and a Woman, Enigma, Safari Diamants, Trans-Europ-Express, Mon Amour, Mon Amour, Un Homme a Abattre, La Morte Ha Fatto L'Uovo, Les Biches, Grand Silence, Z, Ma Nuit Chez Maud (My Night at Maud's), The Conformist, The Crook, Without Apparent Motive, The Outside Man, The French Conspiracy, Simon the Swiss, Agression, Les Violons du Bal, The Sunday Woman, Under Fire, La Nuit de Varennes, Long Live Life!, Next Summer, Departure, Return, The Man With the Silver Eyes, Femme Je Personne, Confidentially Yours, A Man and a Woman: 20 Years Later, La Vallee Fantome; Rendezvous, Bunker Palace Hotel, Three Colors: Red, The City of Lost Children, Fiesta, Un homme est tombe dans la rue, L'Insoumise, Les Bidochon, C'est jamais loin, Self-Made Hero, Tykho Moon, Those Who Love Me Can Take the Train.

TRIPP, STEVEN L.
Executive. b. Worthington, MN, Sept. 29, 1958. e. St. Cloud State U. Managed local hometown theatres from 1978-82, then promoted to operation mgr., Tentelino Enterprises Circuit. Became general mgr. after Tentelino was purchased by Lakes & Rivers Cinemas in 1989. 1994-present, general mgr. and film buyer. Formed Midwest Theatres Corp. dba Cinemagic Theatres in 1996. Currently serving as Pres. & COO.

TRIPPLEHORN, JEANNE
Actress. b. Tulsa, OK, 1964. e. Julliard Sch. of Drama. On stage at NY's Public Theatre in The Big Funk, 'Tis Pity She's a Whore.
PICTURES: Basic Instinct (debut, 1992), The Night We Never Met, The Firm, Waterworld, Reality Bites (cameo), Office Killer, 'Til There Was You, Very Bad Things, Snitch, Sliding Doors, Steal This Movie, Mickey Blue Eyes.
TELEVISION: *Movie*: The Perfect Tribute, Old Man. *Guest:* The Ben Stiller Show.

TRUMBULL, DOUGLAS
Director, Cinematographer. b. Los Angeles, CA, Apr. 8, 1942. Inventor Showscan Film process. Produced and directed Universal Studios attraction Back to the Future: The Ride; Luxor Las Vegas attractions. Director: Showscan short films New Magic, Let's Go, Big Ball, Leonardo's Dream, Night of the Dreams, Chevy Collector. Former Vice Chmn., The Imax Corp. Currently Pres. & CEO, Entertainment Design Workshop.
PICTURES: *Cinematographer*: 2001: A Space Odyssey, Silent Running (also dir.), The Andromeda Strain, Close Encounters of the Third Kind, Star Trek: The Motion Picture, Blade Runner, Brainstorm (also dir., prod.).

TSAI, MING-LIANG
Director, Writer. b. Kuching, Malaysia, Oct. 27, 1957.
PICTURES: Rebels of the Neon God, Vive L'Amour (Golden Horse Award, 1994), The River, Last Dance (dir. only), Dong.

TUBB, BARRY
Actor. b. Snyder, TX, 1963. Former rodeo star. Studied acting at Amer. Conservatory Theatre in SF.
THEATER: Sweet Sue (B'way), The Authentic Life of Billy the Kid.
PICTURES: Mask, The Legend of Billie Jean, Top Gun, Valentino Returns, Warm Summer Rain, Guilty By Suspicion.
TELEVISION: *Series*: Bay City Blues. *Guest*: Hill Street Blues. *Movies*: Consenting Adult, The Billionaire Boys Club, Without Her Consent. *Mini-Series*: Lonesome Dove, Return to Lonesome Dove.

TUCCI, STANLEY
Actor. b. Peekskill, NY. e. SUNY.
THEATER: *B'way:* The Misanthrope, Brighton Beach Memoirs, The Iceman Cometh. Moon Over Miami, Scapin, Dalliance, Balm in Gilead.
PICTURES: Who's That Girl, Monkey Shines, Slaves of New York, Fear Anxiety and Depression, The Feud, Quick Change, Men of Respect, Billy Bathgate, Beethoven, Prelude to a Kiss, The Public Eye, In the Soup, Undercover Blues, The Pelican Brief, It Should Happen to You, Mrs. Parker and the Vicious Circle, Kiss of Death, A Modern Affair, The Daytrippers, Big Night (also co-dir; Ind't Spirit Awards, 1997.), Life During Wartime, The Eighteenth Angel, Deconstructing Harry, A Life Less Ordinary, Montana, The Imposters (also prod., dir., s.p.), A Midsummer Night's Dream, Joe Gould's Secret (also prod., dir.), In Too Deep.
TELEVISION: *Series:* The Street, Wiseguy, Murder One. *Guest:* Miami Vice, The Equalizer, thirtysomething, Equal Justice. *Movies:* Winchell.

TUCKER, MELVILLE
Executive. b. New York, NY, Mar. 4, 1916. e. Princeton U. Asst. purchasing agent Consolidated Laboratories, N.Y., 1934-36; sound effects & picture ed., Republic Productions, Inc. 1936-8; then asst. production mgr. & first asst. dir., 1938-42; served in U.S. Army 1942-46; asst. prod. Republic 1946; assoc. producer, 1947-52; prod., Universal 1952-54; prod. exec. v.p., Universal, 1955-70; production exec. U-I, 1954-71; became prod.Verdon Prods., 1971.
PICTURES: *Prod.*: The Missourians, Thunder in God's Country, Rodeo King and the Senorita, Utah Wagon Train, Drums Across the River, Black Shield of Falworth, A Warm December, Uptown Saturday Night, Let's Do It Again, A Piece of the Action. *Exec. prod.*: Stir Crazy, Hanky Panky, Fast Forward.

TUCKER, MICHAEL
Actor. b. Baltimore, MD, Feb. 6, 1944. m. actress Jill Eikenberry. e. Carnegie Tech. Drama Sch. Worked in regional theater (Long Wharf, Washington's Arena Stage, Milwaukee Rep.) and with the NY Shakespeare Festival in Trelawney of the Wells, Comedy of Errors, Measure for Measure, The Merry Wives of Windsor. Also prod. revival of El Grande de Coca Cola (1986).
THEATER: Moonchildren, Modigliani, The Goodbye People, The Rivals, Mother Courage, Waiting for Godot, Oh What a Lovely War, I'm Not Rappaport (American Place Theatre).
PICTURES: A Night Full of Rain (debut, 1977), An Unmarried Woman, Eyes of Laura Mars, Diner, The Goodbye People, The Purple Rose of Cairo, Radio Days, Tin Men, Checking Out, For Love or Money, D2: The Mighty Ducks.
TELEVISION: *Series*: L.A. Law. *Movies:* Concealed Enemies, Vampire, Assault and Matrimony, Day One, Spy, Too Young to Die?, Casey's Gift: For Love of a Child, The Secret Life of Archie's Wife, In the Nick of Time, A Town Torn Apart. *Specials*: Love Sex... and Marriage, A Family Again, On Hope. *Guest*: Hill Street Blues.

TUCKERMAN, DAVID R.
Executive. b. Perth Amboy, NJ, Nov. 9, 1949. e. Monmouth Coll., F.L.U. 1967-70; B.S.B.A. Entered industry with A.I.T. Theatres, 1967; gen. mgr., Music Makers Theatres, 1973; v.p., Leigh Group, MMT, head film buyer, 1976; sr. v.p., MMT, 1980; Loews Film Buyer, 1986; Loews (now Sony) v.p. film, 1993. U.A., Head Film Buyer, Southeat region, 1998. New Line Cinema, Exec. V.P. and Gen. Sales Mgr., 1999. *Member:* SMPTE, Variety Int., MPBC, AFI, Motion Picture Pioneers.

TUGGLE, RICHARD
Director, Writer. b. Coral Gables, FL, Aug. 8, 1948. e. U. Virginia, B.A. 1970. Wrote screenplays before directorial debut with Tightrope, 1984.
PICTURES: Escape from Alcatraz (s.p.), Tightrope (dir., s.p.), Out of Bounds (dir.).

TUNE, TOMMY
Actor, Director, Choreographer, Dancer. b. Wichita Falls, TX, Feb. 28, 1939. e. Univ of Texas at Austin. Began professional career dancing in chorus of B'way shows (Baker Street, A Joyful Noise, How Now Dow Jones, etc.). Recipient of 9 Tony Awards.
THEATER: *Performer:* Seesaw, My One and Only, Bye Bye Birdie (tour), Tommy Tune Tonite! (B'way & tour). *Director and/or choreographer*: The Club, Cloud 9, The Best Little Whorehouse in Texas, Nine, A Day in Hollywood/A Night in the Ukraine, Stepping Out, My One and Only, Grand Hotel, The Will Rogers Follies.
PICTURES: Hello Dolly!, The Boy Friend.
TELEVISION: *Series*: Dean Martin Presents the Goldiggers, The Bold and the Beautiful, also numerous specials, Tony Award Shows.

TURMAN, LAWRENCE
Producer. b. Los Angeles, CA, Nov. 28, 1926. e. UCLA. In textile business 5 years, then joined Kurt Frings Agency; left in 1960 to form Millar-Turman Prods.
PICTURES: *Prod.*: The Young Doctors, I Could Go on Singing, The Best Man. Formed own prod. co., Lawrence Turman, Inc., to make The Flim-Flam Man, The Graduate, Pretty Poison (exec. prod.), The Great White Hope, The Marriage of a Young Stockbroker (also dir.), The Nickel Ride (exec. prod.), The Drowning Pool, First Love, Heroes, Walk Proud, Tribute, Caveman, The Thing, Second Thoughts (also dir.), Mass Appeal, The Mean Season, Short Circuit, Running Scared, Short Circuit 2, Full Moon in Blue Water, Gleaming the Cube, The Getaway, The River Wild, The Getaway, Booty Call (exec. prod.), American History X (exec. prod.).
TELEVISION: *Co-prod. with David Foster*. The Gift of Love, News at Eleven, Between Two Brothers. *Prod.*: The Morning After, She Lives, Unwed Father. *Co-exec. prod.*: Jesse.

TURNER, JANINE
Actress. r.n. Janine Gauntt. b. Lincoln, NE, Dec. 6, 1962. Raised in Texas. Studied dance, joined Forth Worth Ballet. Started modeling at age 15 in NYC, enrolled in Professional Children's School. First major acting job was on series Dallas. On stage in Full Moon and High Tide in the Ladies Room.
PICTURES: Young Doctors in Love, Knights of the City, Tai-Pan, Monkey Shines, Steel Magnolias, The Ambulance, Cliffhanger, The Curse of the Inferno, Leave It to Beaver.
TELEVISION: *Movies*: Stolen Women Captured Hearts, Circle of Deceit. *Series*: Behind the Screen, General Hospital (1982-83), Another World (1986-87), Northern Exposure. *Guest*: The Love Boat, The A-Team, Mike Hammer.

TURNER, KATHLEEN
Actress. b. Springfield, MO, June 19, 1954. e. U. of Maryland, SMSU.
THEATER: *B'way*: Gemini, Cat on a Hot Tin Roof (Theatre World Award), Indiscretions. *Regional*: Camille (Long Wharf), A Midsummer Night's Dream (DC), Toyer (DC).
PICTURES: Body Heat (debut, 1981), The Man With Two Brains, Romancing the Stone, Crimes of Passion, A Breed Apart, Prizzi's Honor, The Jewel of the Nile, Peggy Sue Got Married (Acad. Award nom.), Julia and Julia, Switching Channels, Who Framed Roger Rabbit (voice), The Accidental Tourist, The War of the Roses, V.I. Warshawski, House of Cards, Undercover Blues, Serial Mom, Naked in New York, Moonlight & Valentino, A Simple Wish, Legalese, Baby Geniuses, The Virgin Suicides.
TELEVISION: *Series*: The Doctors. *Movies*: Friends at Last, Love in the Ancient World. *Special*: Dear America: Letters Home From Vietnam (reader). *Director*: Leslie's Folly.

TURNER, TED
Executive. r.n. Robert Edward Turner. b. Cincinnati, OH., Nov. 19, 1938. e. Brown U. m. actress Jane Fonda. Began career in Savannah in family's outdoor adv. business, selling space on billboards. Inherited co. in 1963 and in 1970 entered broadcasting with purchase of a failing TV station in Atlanta which he turned into WTBS, a "superstation" which in 1994 reached 95% of U.S. homes equipped with cable. 1980, established CNN a 24-hr. cable news service. Purchased MGM film library. Co-owner of two professional sports teams in Atlanta: Braves (baseball) and Hawks (basketball). Started Headline News, 1982; CNN International 1985; Turner Network Television 1988; Sportsouth, 1990; Cartoon Network in 1992; acquired Castle Rock Entertainment, 1993; merger with New LIne Cinema, 1994; started Turner Classic Movies, 1994; CNNfn Financial Network, 1995.

TURNER, TINA
Singer, Actress. r.n. Annie Mae Bullock. b. Nutbush, TN, Nov. 26, 1939. Previously married to Ike Turner and appeared with him on road in Ike and Tina Turner Revue. Many hit records. *Autobiography*: I Tina.
PICTURES: Gimme Shelter, Taking Off, Soul to Soul, Tommy, Sound of the City, Mad Max Beyond Thunderdome, What's Love Got to Do With It (vocals), Last Action Hero.
TELEVISION: *Special*: Tina—Live From Rio.

TURTURRO, JOHN
Actor. b. Brooklyn, NY, Feb. 28, 1957. e. SUNY/New Paltz; Yale Drama School, 1983. m. actress Katherine Borowitz. Worked in regional theater and off-B'way.
THEATER: Danny and the Deep Blue Sea (Obie & Theatre World Awards, 1985), Men Without Dates, Tooth of the Crime, La Puta Viva, Chaos and Hard Times, The Bald Soprano, Of Mice and Men, The Resistible Rise of Arturo Ui, Death of a Salesman (B'way debut, 1984).
PICTURES: Raging Bull (debut, 1980), Exterminator II, The Flamingo Kid, Desperately Seeking Susan, To Live and Die in L.A., Hannah and Her Sisters, Gung Ho, Off Beat, The Color of Money, The Sicilian, Five Corners, Do the Right Thing, Mo' Better Blues, State of Grace, Miller's Crossing, Men of Respect, Jungle Fever, Barton Fink (Cannes Film Fest. Award), Brain Donors, Mac (also dir., co-s.p.), Fearless, Being Human, Quiz Show, Search and Destroy, Clockers, Unstrung Heroes, Grace of My Hear, Box of Moonlight, Girl 6, The Search for One-eye Johnny, Lesser Prophets, Animals, O.K. Garage, Illuminata, The Big Lebowski, He Got Game, Rounders, The Cradle Will Rock, Summer of Sam, Company Man, O Brother, Where Art Thou?, Two Thousand and None, The Man Who Cried, The Luzhin Defence.
TELEVISION: *Mini-Series*: The Fortunate Pilgrim. *Movie:* Backtrack.

TUSHINGHAM, RITA
Actress. b. Liverpool, England, March 14, 1942. Student at Liverpool Playhouse.
THEATER: The Giveaway, Lorna and Ted, Mistress of Novices, The Undiscovered Country, Mysteries.
PICTURES: A Taste of Honey (debut, 1961; BFA Award), The Leather Boys, A Place to Go, Girl With Green Eyes, The Knack... and How to Get It, Doctor Zhivago, The Trap, Smashing Time, Diamonds for Breakfast, The Guru, The Bed Sitting Room, Straight on Till Morning, The Case of Laura C., Where Do You Go From Here?, Situation, Instant Coffee, The Human Factor, Rachel's Man, The Slum Boy, The Black Journal, Bread Butter and Jam, Mysteries, Felix Krull, Spaghetti Thing, Dream to Believe, Flying, Seeing Red, The Housekeeper, Resurrected, Dante and Beatrice in Liverpool, Hard Days Hard Nights, Paper Marriage, Desert Lunch, An Awfully Big Adventure, The Boy From Mercury, Under the Sun, Swing.
TELEVISION: *U.S.*: Green Eyes, Bread, Sunday Pursuit, Gutt Ein Journalist, Hamburg Poison.

TUTIN, DOROTHY
Actress. b. London, Eng., Apr. 8, 1930. e. St. Catherine's Sch. Bramley, Guildford (Surrey). Stage debut in The Thistle & the Rose, 1949.
THEATER: Much Ado About Nothing, The Living Room, I Am a Camera, The Lark, Wild Duck, Juliet, Ophelia, Viola, Portia, Cressida, Rosalind, The Devils, Once More With Feeling, The Cherry Orchard, Victoria Regina-Portrait of a Queen, Old Times, Peter Pan, What Every Woman Knows, Month in the Country, Macbeth, Antony and Cleopatra, Undiscovered Country, Reflections, After the Lions, Ballerina, A Kind of Alaska, Are You Sitting Comfortably?, Chalk Garden, Brighton Beach Memoirs, Thursday's Ladies, The Browning Version, A Little Night Music, Henry VIII, Party Time, The Seagull, Getting Married.
PICTURES: The Importance of Being Earnest, The Beggar's Opera, A Tale of Two Cities, Cromwell, Savage Messiah, The Shooting Party, The Great Kandinsky.

TELEVISION: Living Room, Victoria Regina, Invitation to a Voyage, Antigone, Colombe, Carrington V.C., The Hollow Crown, Scent of Fear, From Chekhov With Love, The Queen and the Welshman, Flotsam and Jetsam, Mother & Son, South Riding, Willow Cabins, Ghosts, Sister Dora, The Double Dealer, The Combination, La Ronde, Tales of the Unexpected, 10 Downing Street, Life After Death, King Lear, Murder with Mirrors, Great Moments in Aviation, Dancing Queen, Landscape, The Father, The Demon Lover, Robin Hood, All Creatures Great and Small, A Kind of Alaska, The Bill, Lease of Death, Anglo-Saxon Attitudes, The Great Kandinsky, Indian Summer. *Mini-series*: The Six Wives of Henry VIII, Vienna 1900, Body and Soul, Scarlett, Jake's Progress.

TWAINE, MICHAEL
Actor, Director. b. New York, NY, Nov. 1, 1939. e. Ohio State U. Served U.S. Army. While studying with Lee Strasberg, worked as private detective, school teacher. Made stage debut City Center, 1956, in Mr. Roberts. Became village coffee house and club comedian 1968 to 1972.
PICTURES: Marriage Italian Style (voice), American Soap, Blood Bath, F.I.S.T., Cheap Shots, Platoon (voice), Billy Bathgate (voice).
TELEVISION: The Silent Drum, Starsky & Hutch, Wonder Woman, Streets of San Francisco, Soap, Lou Grant, Diff'rent Strokes, Nurse, Stalk the Wild Child, The Courage and the Passion, Eischied, America's Most Wanted, Beyond the Universe.

TWIGGY
Actress. r.n. Leslie Hornby. b. London, England, Sept. 19, 1949. m. actor Leigh Lawson. At 17 regarded as world's leading high fashion model. Made m.p. debut in The Boy Friend, 1971. Starred in many London West End Shows, including Cinderella and Captain Beaky Presents. 1983: on Broadway in musical, My One and Only.
PICTURES: The Boyfriend (debut, 1971), W, There Goes the Bride, The Blues Brothers, The Doctor and the Devils, Club Paradise, Madame Sousatzka, Istanbul.
TELEVISION: *Series*: Twiggy, Twiggy and Friends, Juke Box (U.S.), Princesses (U.S.). *Specials*: Pygmalion, Sun Child, Young Charlie Chaplin. *Movies*: The Diamond Trap, Body Bags.

TYKWER, TOM
Director, **Writer**, **Composer**. b. Wuppertal, Germany, 1965.
PICTURES: Deadly Maria (also prod.), Winter Sleeper, Life Is All You Get (s.p. only), Run Lola Run.

TYLER, LIV
Actress. b. July, 1977. Daughter of fashion model Bebe Buell and musician Steven Tyler. Began as a model at age 14.
PICTURES: Silent Fall (debut), Empire Records, Heavy, Stealing Beauty, That Thing You Do!, Inventing the Abbotts, U-Turn, Plunkett & MacLeane, Eugene Onegin, Armageddon, The Little Black Book, Cookie's Fortune, Franky Goes to Hollywood, Dr.T and the Women, One Night at McCool's, The Lord of the Rings: The Fellowship of the Ring, The Lord of the Rings: The Two Towers, The Lord of the Rings: The Return of the Kings.

TYRRELL, SUSAN
Actress. b. San Francisco, CA, 1946. Made first prof. appearance with Art Carney in summer theatre tour prod. of Time Out for Ginger. Worked in off-B'way prods. and as waitress in coffee house before attracting attention in Lincoln Center Repertory Co. prods. of A Cry of Players, The Time of Your Life, Camino Real.
THEATER: The Knack, Futz, Father's Day, A Coupla White Chicks Sitting Around Talking, The Rotten Life.
PICTURES: Shoot Out (debut, 1971), The Steagle, Been Down So Long It Looks Like Up to Me, Shoot Out, Fat City (Acad. Award nom.), Catch My Soul, Zandy's Bride, The Killer Inside Me, Islands in the Stream, Andy Warhol's Bad, I Never Promised You a Rose Garden, Another Man Another Chance, September 30, 1955, Racquet, Loose Shoes, Forbidden Zone, Subway Riders, Night Warning, Fast-Walking, Liar's Moon, Tales of Ordinary Madness, Fire and Ice (voice), Angel, The Killers, Avenging Angel, Flesh and Blood, The Chipmunk Adventure (voice), The Offspring, Big Top Pee-Wee, Tapeheads, The Underachievers, Far From Home, Cry-Baby, Motorama, Powder.
TELEVISION: *Series*: Open All Night. *Movies*: Lady of the House, Midnight Lace, Jealousy, Thompson's Last Run, Poker Alice, The Christmas Star, Windmills of the Gods. *Mini-Series*: If Tomorrow Comes.

TYSON, CICELY
Actress. b. New York, NY, Dec. 19, 1933. e. NYU. Studied at Actor's Studio. Former secretary and model. Co-founder, Dance Theatre of Harlem.
THEATER: The Blacks, Moon on a Rainbow Shawl, Tiger Tiger Burning Bright, The Corn Is Green.
PICTURES: A Man Called Adam (debut, 1966), The Comedians, The Heart Is a Lonely Hunter, Sounder (Acad. Award nom.), The Blue Bird, The River Niger, A Hero Ain't Nothin' But a Sandwich, The Concorde—Airport '79, Bustin' Loose, Fried Green Tomatoes, The Grass Harp, Hoodlum.
TELEVISION: *Series*: East Side West Side, The Guiding Light, Sweet Justice. *Movies*: Marriage: Year One, The Autobiography of Miss Jane Pittman (Emmy Award, 1974), Just An Old Sweet Song, Wilma, A Woman Called Moses, The Marva Collins Story, Benny's Place, Playing with Fire, Acceptable Risks, Samaritan: The Mitch Snyder Story, The Women of Brewster Place, Heat Wave, The Kid Who Loved Christmas, Duplicates, When No One Would Listen, House of Secrets, Oldest Living Confederate Widow Tells All (Emmy Award, 1994), Mama Flora's Family, Road to Galveston, Bridge of Time, Riot, The Price of Heaven, Ms. Scrooge, Always Outnumbered, A Lesson Before Dying. *Guest*: B.L. Stryker. *Special*: Without Borders (host). *Mini-Series*: Roots, Aftershock. *Pilot*: Clippers.

U

UGGAMS, LESLIE
Singer. b. New York, NY, May 25, 1943. e. Professional Children's Sch., grad., 1960. Juilliard Sch. of Music. Beg. singing career age 5. TV debut as Ethel Waters' niece on Beulah. Also on Johnny Olsen's TV kids at age 7, Your Show of Shows as singer, 1953; Recording artist for Columbia Records, Atlantic, Motown Wrote The Leslie Uggams Beauty Book (1962).
THEATER: Hallelujah Baby (Tony & Theatre World Awards, 1968), Her First Roman, Blues in the Night, Jerry's Girls, Anything Goes (natl. co. & Bdwy), Stringbean (Dallas), Into the Woods (Long Beach, CA).
PICTURES: Two Weeks in Another Town, Poor Pretty Eddie, Black Girl, Heartbreak Motel, Skyjacked, Sugar Hill.
TELEVISION: *Series*: Sing Along With Mitch, The Leslie Uggams Show (1969), Fantasy (Emmy Award, 1984). *Guest*: Beulah (1949), Kids and Company, Milton Berle Show, Name That Tune, Jack Paar Show, Garry Moore. *Mini-Series*: Roots, Backstairs at the White House. *Movie*: Sizzle. *Specials*: The Book of Lists (co-host). Fantasy (Emmy Award, 1983, host), I Love Men, 'S Wonderful, 'S Marvelous, 'S Gershwin, Sinatra and Friends, Placido Domingo Steppin' Out With the Ladies, Jerry Herman Tribute, Rooms for Improvement.
RADIO: Peter Lind Hayes-Mary Healy Show, Milton Berle, Arthur Godfrey, Star Time.

ULANO, MARK
Sound.
PICTURES: Think Me Nothing, Hospital Massacre, Time Walker, Cujo, Lovelines, Once Bitten, Sweet Hearts Dance, Desperado, Rough Magic, The Winner, From Dusk Till Dawn, Titanic (Acad. Award, Best Sound Mixing, 1997), The Pest, Austin Powers: International Man of Mystery, Jackie Brown, The Patriot, Molly, Making Sandwiches, 68, Stuart Little.
TELEVISION: *Movies*: High School U.S.A., The Parade, The Cartier Affair, A Time to Triumph, Shattered Spirits, Lena: My 100 Children, Dance 'Til Dawn, Shadow of a Doubt, Empty Cradle, If These Walls Could Talk 2 *Series*: The Trials of Rosie O'Neill, Significant Others, Time of Your Life. *Mini-series*: Drug Wars: The Camarena Story.

ULLMAN, TRACEY
Actress, Comedian, Singer. b. Hackbridge, England, Dec. 29, 1959. m. British TV prod. Allan McKeown. e. won a performance sch. scholarship at 12. Attended the Italia Conti School for 4 years. Soon after appeared on British TV and onstage in Grease and The Rocky Horror Picture Show. Also performed in improvisational play Four in a Million (1981) at the Royal Court Theatre, London (London Theatre Critics Award). Recorded gold-selling album You Broke My Heart in Seventeen Places. Appeared in music video They Don't Know. U.S. TV debut, The Tracey Ullman Show (debuted April, 1987).
THEATRE: *NY*: The Taming of the Shrew, The Big Love.
PICTURES: Give My Regards to Broad Street, Plenty, Jumpin' Jack Flash, I Love You to Death, Happily Ever After (voice), Robin Hood: Men in Tights, Household Saints, Bullets Over Broadway, Ready to Wear (Pret-a-Porter).
TELEVISION: *Series*: Three of a Kind (BBC), The Tracey Ullman Show (Emmy Awards, 1989, 1990),. *Specials*: The Best of the Tracey Ullman Show (Emmy Award, 1990), Tracey Ullman—A Class Act. *Guest*: Love & War (Emmy Award, 1993), Tracey Ullman: Takes on New York (Emmy Award, 1994) Tracey Takes On... (Emmy, Cable Ace Awards, 1997), Ally McBeal (recurring).

ULLMANN, LIV
Actress. b. Tokyo, Japan, of Norwegian parents, Dec. 16, 1939. Accompanied parents to Canada when WWII began and later returned to Norway. Was catapulted to fame in a succession of Swedish films directed by Ingmar Bergman. *Author*: Changing, Choices. Ambassador for UNICEF since 1980. Youngest person to date to receive the Order of St. Olav from the King of Norway. Recipient of 11 honorary doctorates.
THEATER: *U.S.*: A Doll's House, Anna Christie, I Remember Mama (musical), Ghosts, Old Times.
PICTURES: Fjols til Fjells (debut, 1957), The Wayward Girl, Tonny, Kort ar Sommaren, De Kalte Ham Skarven, Persona, Hour of the Wolf, Shame, The Passion of Anna, The Night Visitor, Cold Sweat, The Emigrants, Pope Joan, Cries and Whispers, Lost Horizon, Forty Carats, The New Land, Scenes From a Marriage, Zandy's Bride, The Abdication, Leonor, Face to Face, Couleur Chair, A Bridge Too Far, The Serpent's Egg, Autumn Sonata, Players (cameo), Richard's Things, The Wild Duck, Bay Boy, Dangerous Moves, Let's Hope It's a Girl, Gaby—A True Story. Moscow Adieu (Donatello Award, 1987), A Time of Indifference, La Amiga, The Rose Garden, Mindwalk, The Ox, The Long Shadow, Sophie (dir., co-s.p. only), Kristin Lavrandsdatter (dir., s.p. only).
TELEVISION: Lady From the Sea, Jacobo Timerman: Prisoner Without a Name Cell Without a Number.

ULRICH, SKEET
Actor. r.n. Bryan Ray Ulrich. b. NC, Jan. 20, 1970.
PICTURES: Albino Alligator, Last Dance, The Craft, Boys, Scream, Touch, As Good As It Gets, The Newton Boys, A Soldier's Sweetheart, Takedown, Ride with the Devil, Chill Factor, Kevin of the North, Anasazi Moon.

UNDERWOOD, BLAIR
Actor. b. Tacoma, WA, Aug. 25, 1964. e. Carnegie-Mellon Univ. NY stage: Measure for Measure.
PICTURES: Krush Groove, Posse, Just Cause, Set It Off, The Eighth Day, Gattaca, Deep Impact, Asunder, The Wishing Tree, Rules of Engagement.
TELEVISION: *Series*: One Life to Live, Downtown, L.A. Law, High Incident. *Movies*: The Cover Girl and the Cop, Heat Wave, Murder in Mississippi, Father & Son: Dangerous Relations (also assoc. prod.), Soul of the Game, Mistrial, Mama Flora's Family. *Guest*: Scarecrow and Mrs. King, The Cosby Show, Knight Rider, 21 Jump Street.

UNDERWOOD, RON
Director. b. Glendale, CA, Nov. 6, 1953. e. USC, AFI.
PICTURES: Tremors (also co-story), City Slickers, Heart and Souls, Speechless, Mighty Joe Young.
TELEVISION: The Mouse and the Motorcycle (Peabody Award), Runaway Ralph (Emmy nom.).

UNGER, ANTHONY B.
Executive, Producer. b. New York, NY, Oct. 19, 1940. e. Duke U., USC. Prod. ass't Third Man, TV series, 1961. v.p. Unger Productions, Inc., 1964; v.p. Landau-Unger Co., Inc., 1965; v.p. Commonwealth United Entertainment in London, 1968; pres., Unger Prods. Inc., 1978-present.
PICTURES: The Desperate Ones. The Madwoman of Chaillot. The Battle of Neretva, The Magic Christian, Julius Caesar, The Devil's Widow, Don't Look Now, Force Ten From Navarone, The Unseen, Silent Rage, The Dark Side of Hollywood (doc., prod.).

UNGER, STEPHEN A.
Executive. b. New York, NY, May 31, 1946. e. NYU, Grad. Film and Television Instit. Started as independent prod. and dist. of theatrical and TV films. 1978, joined Universal Pictures Intl. Sales as foreign sls. mgr.; named v.p. Universal Theatrical Motion Pictures in 1979, responsible for licensing theatrical or TV features not handled by U.I.P. in territories outside U.S. & Canada and worldwide acquisitions; 1980 joined CBS Theatrical Films as intl. v.p., sls.; 1982-88, pres., Unger Intl. Distributors, Inc.; 1988 joined Korn/Ferry Intl. as exec. v.p., worldwide entertainment div. Promoted to mng. dir., 1989-91. Joined Spencer Stuart Exec. Search Consultants as mng. dir., Worldwide Ent. Div. 1991. Elected Partner, 1994-98. Joined Heidrick & Struggles in 1998 as Managaing Partner Media, Entertainment, and Interactive Content. Elected to Bd. of Dirs. in 1999.

URBANSKI, DOUGLAS
Producer.
PICTURES: Nil By Mouth (BAFTA Award, Outstanding Brit. Film, 1997).

URICH, ROBERT
Actor. b. Toronto, OH, Dec. 19, 1946. e. Florida State U., B.A., radio and TV communications; Michigan State U., M.A. Communications Mgmt. Appeared in university plays. Was sales account executive at WGN Radio, Chicago, before turning to stage acting (Ivanhoe Theatre, Chicago).
PICTURES: Magnum Force, Endangered Species, The Ice Pirates, Turk 182.
TELEVISION: *Series*: Bob & Carol & Ted & Alice, S.W.A.T., Soap, Tabitha, Vega$, Gavilan, Spenser For Hire, American Dreamer, Crossroads, National Geographic Explorers (host), It Had to Be You, Lazarus Man, Boatworks, The Love Boat: The Next Wave, Invasion: America (voice), Boatworks (host). *Guest*: The FBI, Gunsmoke, Kung Fu, Marcus Welby MD, The Love Boat. *Movies*: Killdozer, Vega$ (pilot), Leave Yesterday Behind, When She Was Bad, Fighting Back, Killing at Hell's Gate, Take Your Best Shot, Princess Daisy, Invitation to Hell, His Mistress, Scandal Sheet, Young Again, April Morning, The Comeback, She Knows Too Much, Murder By Night, Night Walk, Blind Faith, Spooner, A Quiet Little Neighborhood A Perfect Little Murder, Stranger at My Door, And Then She Was Gone, Survive the Savage Sea, Blind Man's Bluff (also co-prod.), Double Edge, Revolver, Deadly Relations, Spenser: Ceremony (also co-exec. prod.), Spenser: Pale Kings and Princes (also co-exec. prod.), Danielle Steel's A Perfect Stranger, Spenser: The Judas Goat, A Horse for Danny, She Stood Alone: The Tailhook Scandal, Captains Courageous, Final Descent, Final Run, Miracle on the 17th Green. *Mini-Series*: Mistral's Daughter, Amerika, Lonesome Dove.

URMAN, MARK
Executive. b. New York, NY, Nov. 24, 1952. e. Union Coll., 1973; NYU, cinema, 1973-74. m. story analyst Deborah Davis. 1973, apprentice publicist, Universal Pictures; 1973-82, United Artists intl. dept. as assoc. publicist, sr. publicist and ultimately asst. to v.p. worldwide ad-pub.; 1982-84, dir., publicity and marketing, Triumph Films (Columbia/Gaumont); 1985-86, exec. dir. East Coast pub., Columbia Pictures; 1986-89, v.p. East Coast pub., Columbia Pictures. Joined Dennis Davidson Associates as v.p., 1989; promoted to sr. v.p., 1991. Member: Motion Picture Academy.

USLAN, MICHAEL E.
Producer, Writer. b. Bayonne, NJ, June 2, 1951. e. Indiana U., A.B., M.S., J.D. Wrote 12 books, including Dick Clark's 1st 25 Years of Rock 'n' Roll; 1976-80 atty. with United Artists; writer of syndicated comic strip Terry and the Pirates; produced with Benjamin Melniker.
PICTURES: Swamp Thing (prod.), The Return of Swamp Thing (prod.), Batman (exec. prod.), Batman Returns (exec. prod.), Batman: The Animated Movie (prod.), Batman Forever (exec. prod), Batman & Robin (exec. prod.), Batman Beyond: Return of the Joker 2000 (direct-to-video).
TELEVISION: Three Sovereigns for Sarah (exec. prod.), Dinosaucers (exec. prod., creator, writer), Swamp Thing (exec. prod. for both live-action and animated series), Fish Police (exec. prod.), South Korea cultural segments NBC Summer Olympics 1988 (exec. prod.), Television's Greatest Bits (prod., creator, writer), 1st National Trivia Quiz (prod., writer), Where On Earth Is Carmen Sandiego? (animated, exec. prod.; Emmy Award), Robin Cook's Harmful Intent (exec. prod.), Little Orphan Annie's Very Animated Christmas (exec. prod., writer); remakes of The Kiss, The Sneeze, The Great Train Robbery, The Barbershop, Streetcar Chivalry, Smashing a Jersey Mosquito (prod., dir.), Doomsday.

USTINOV, SIR PETER
Actor, Writer, Director. b. London, Eng., Apr. 16, 1921. e. Westminster Sch. In Brit. Army, W.W.II. On Brit. stage from 1937. Screen debut 1941 in Brit. picture Mein Kampf, My Crimes. Awards: 3 Emmy Awards (Specials: Life of Samuel Johnson, Barefoot in Athens, A Storm in Summer); Grammy Award for Peter and the Wolf; NY Critics Award and Donaldson Award for best foreign play (The Love of Four Colonels); British Critics Award (Romanoff and Juliet). Chancellor, Durham Univ., 1992. Received Britannia Award from BAFTA, 1992; Critics Circle Award, 1993; German Cultural Award, 1994; German Bambi, 1994; Rudolph Valentino Award, 1995.
THEATER: Romanoff and Juliet, N.Y., London; and 17 other plays. Dir., acted, Photo Finish; wrote, Life In My Hands, The Unknown Soldier and His Wife, Half Way Up The Tree, King Lear, Beethoven's Tenth, An Evening With Peter Ustinov.
PICTURES: *Actor*: The Goose Steps Out, One of Our Aircraft Is Missing, The Way Ahead (co-s.p.), School for Secrets (wrote, dir. & co-prod. only), Vice Versa (dir., s.p. only), Private Angelo (also adapt., dir., co-prod.), Odette, Quo Vadis (Acad. Award nom.), The Magic Box, Hotel Sahara, The Egyptian, Beau Brummell, We're No Angels, Lola Montez, The Spies, The Man Who Wagged His Tail, School for Scoundrels (adapt. only), The Sundowners, Spartacus (Academy Award, best supporting actor, 1960), Romanoff and Juliet (also prod., s.p.), Billy Budd (also prod., dir., s.p.), Topkapi (Academy Award, best supporting actor, 1964), John Goldfarb Please Come Home, Lady L. (also dir., s.p.), The Comedians, Blackbeard's Ghost, Hot Millions, Viva Max. Hammersmith Is Out (also dir.), Robin Hood (voice), One of Our Dinosaurs Is Missing, Logan's Run,

Treasure of Matecumbe, Purple Taxi, The Last Remake of Beau Geste, Doppio Delitto, Death on the Nile, Ashanti, Charlie Chan and the Curse of the Dragon Queen, Grendel Grendel Grendel (voice), The Great Muppet Caper, Evil Under the Sun, Memed My Hawk (also dir., s.p.), Appointment with Death, Lorenzo's Oil, The Phoenix and the Magic Carpet.
RECENT TV: The Well Tempered Bach, 13 at Dinner, Deadman's Folly, Peter Ustinov's Russia, World Challenge, Murder in Three Acts, The Secret Identity of Jack the Ripper (host), Around the World in 80 Days, The Mozart Mystique, Ustinov on the Orient Express, Ustinov Meets Pavarotti, Inside the Vatican, The Old Curiosity Shop, Haydn Gala, An Evening With Sir Peter Ustinov, Paths of the Gods.

V

VACCARO, BRENDA
Actress. b. Brooklyn, NY, Nov. 18, 1939. e. Thomas Jefferson H.S., Dallas; studied two yrs. at Neighborhood Playhouse in N.Y. Was waitress and model before landing first B'way role in Everybody Loves Opal. Toured in Tunnel of Love and returned to N.Y. for role in The Affair.
THEATER: Everybody Loves Opal (Theatre World Award), Tunnel of Love (tour), The Affair, Children From Their Games, Cactus Flower (Tony Award, 1965), The Natural Look, How Now Dow Jones (Tony nom.), The Goodbye People (Tony nom.), Father's Day, The Odd Couple, Jake's Women.
PICTURES: Where It's At (debut, 1969), Midnight Cowboy, I Love My Wife, Summertree, Going Home, Once Is Not Enough (Acad. Award nom., Golden Globe Award), Airport '77, House by the Lake (Death Weekend), Capricorn One, Fast Charlie the Moonbeam Rider, The First Deadly Sin, Zorro the Gay Blade, Supergirl, Water, Cookie, Heart of Midnight, Masque of the Red Death, Ten Little Indians, Lethal Games, Love Affair, The Mirror Has Two Faces.
TELEVISION: *Series*: Sara, Dear Detective, Paper Dolls. *Guest*: The F.B.I., The Name of the Game, The Helen Reddy Show, The Shape of Things (Emmy Award, 1974), The Golden Girls, Columbo, Murder She Wrote, Flesh & Blood, Golden Girls (Emmy nom.), Civil Wars, Red Shoe Diaries, Spawn, Friends, Johnny Bravo (voice). *Movies*: Travis Logan D.A., What's a Nice Girl Like You...?, Honor Thy Father, Sunshine, The Big Ripoff, Guyana Tragedy, The Pride of Jesse Hallam, The Star Maker, A Long Way Home, Deceptions, Julius and Ethel Rosenberg, Stolen: One Husband, Red Shoes Diaries, Following Her Heart, When Husbands Cheat.

VADIM, ROGER
Director, Writer. r.n. Roger Vadim Plemiannikow. b. Paris, Jan. 26, 1928. m. actress Marie-Christine Barrault. Appeared in films Rich and Famous, Into the Night.
PICTURES: Futures Vedettes (s.p.). *Writer-Director*: And God Created Woman, No Sun in Venice, The Night Heaven Fell, Les Liaisons Dangereuses, Blood and Roses, Please Not Now!, Seven Capital Sins (Pride segment), Love on a Pillow, Vice and Virtue (also prod.), Nutty Naughty Chateau, La Ronde (Circle of Love), The Game is Over (also prod.), Spirits of the Dead (Metzengerstein segment), Barbarella, Pretty Maids All in a Row, Helle, Ms. Don Juan, Night Games, Hot Touch, Surprise Party, Come Back, And God Created Woman (1988), Safari.
TELEVISION: Beauty and the Beast (Faerie Tale Theatre), The Hitchhiker (series), Amour Fou (Mad Love), La Nouvelle tribu (mini-series), Mon Pere avait raison (My Father Was Right), Un coup de baguette magique.
(d. February 11, 2000)

VAJNA, ANDREW
Executive. b. Budapest, Hungary, Aug. 1, 1944. e. UCLA. Launched career with purchase of m.p. theaters in Far East. Founded Panasia Film Ltd. in Hong Kong. Exhibitor and dist. of feature films since 1970. Formed Carolco Service, Inc. (foreign sls. org.), with Mario Kassar 1976. Founder and Pres., American Film Mkt. Assn., 1982. Resigned from Carolco, 1989; formed independent production co., Cinergi Prods., 1989.
PICTURES: *Exec. Prod.*: The Deadly China Doll, The Silent Partner, The Changeling, Victory, The Amateur, First Blood, Superstition, Rambo: First Blood Part II, Angel Heart, Extreme Prejudice, Rambo III, Red Heat, Iron Eagle II, Deepstar Six, Johnny Handsome, Music Box, Mountains of the Moon, Total Recall, Air America, Narrow Margin, Jacob's Ladder, Medicine Man, Tombstone, Renaissance Man, Color of Night, Die Hard With a Vengeance, Judge Dredd, The Scarlet Letter, The Shadow Conspiracy, Nixon, Evita, Alan Smithee Film: Burn Hollywood Burn, Out of Order, The 13th Warrior, Eyes of the Holocaust, Basic Instinct 2, Terminator 3.

VALENTI, JACK J.
Executive. b. Sept. 5, 1921. e. U. of Houston, B.A., 1946; Harvard U., M.B.A., bus. admin., 1948. Air force pilot in European theatre, W.W.II; adv. and pub. rel. exec. in Houston; special asst. and advisor to Pres. Lyndon B. Johnson, 1963-66, elected pres., Motion Picture Association of America, MPEA and AMPTP, since June, 1966. Named Motion Picture Pioneer of the Year, 1988.

VALENTINE, DEAN
Executive. b. Romania, 1954. e. U. of Chicago, English major, honors grad. Began career in journalism at *Time*, *Life* and *The Saturday Review*. Dir., comedy programming, NBC. 1988, joined Walt Disney Television as dir., of TV dev't; 1990, sr. v.p.; appt'd. pres. of WD Television and WD Television Animation. 1997, appointed COO, United Paramount Networks, then chairman & CEO, UPN.

VALENTINE, KAREN
Actress. b. Sebastopol, CA, May 25, 1947.
PICTURES: Forever Young Forever Free, Hot Lead and Cold Feet, The North Avenue Irregulars.
TELEVISION: *Series*: Room 222 (Emmy Award, 1970), Karen, Our Time (host). *Guest*: My Friend Tony, Hollywood Squares, Laugh-In, The Bold Ones, Sonny and Cher, Mike Hammer, Murder, She Wrote. *Movies*: Gidget Grows Up, The Daughters of Joshua Cabe, Coffee Tea or Me?, The Girl Who Came Gift-Wrapped, The Love Boat (pilot), Having Babies, Murder at the World Series, Return to Fantasy Island, Go West Young Girl, Muggable Mary: Street Cop, Money on the Side, Skeezer, Illusions, Jane Doe, Children in the Crossfire, He's Fired She's Hired, A Fighting Choice, Perfect People. *Special*: The Emancipation of Lizzie Stern (Afterschool Special).

VALLI, ALIDA
Actress. r.n. Alida von Altenburger. b. Pola, Italy, May 31, 1921. e. M.P. Acad., Rome (dramatics); m. Oscar de Mejo, pianist-composer. In Italian m.p.; won Venice Film Festival Award in Piccolo Mondo Antico (Little Old World); to U.S. in 1947, billed simply as Valli.
PICTURES: Vita Ricomincia, Giovanna; The Paradine Case, The Miracle of the Bells, The Third Man, Walk Softly Stranger, The White Tower, Lovers of Toledo, We the Women, Senso, The Stranger's Hand, The Outcry, The Night Heaven Fell, This Angry Age (The Sea Wall), The Horror Chamber of Dr. Faustus, The Long Absence, The Happy Thieves, The Castilian, Ophelia, Oedipus Rex, The Spider's Stratagem, Tender Dracula, La Jeu de Solitaire, The Cassandra Crossing, Suspiria, 1900, The Tempter, Luna, Inferno, Le Jupon Rouge, A Notre Regrettable Epoux, A Month by the Lake.

VALLONE, RAF
Actor. b. Turin, Italy, Feb. 17, 1916. e. U. of Turin. Former newspaper writer. Directed operas Norma, La Traviata, Adrianna in NY, San Francisco and Houston.
PICTURES: Bitter Rice (debut, 1949), Vendetta, Under the Olive Tree, Anna, Path of Hope, White Line, Rome 11 O'Clock, Strange Deception, Anita Garibaldi, Daughters of Destiny, Teresa Raquin, Riviera, The Secret Invasion. Two Women, El Cid, Phaedra, A View From the Bridge, The Cardinal, Harlow, Nevada Smith, Kiss the Girls and Make Them Die, The Desperate Ones, The Secret Invasion, The Italian Job, The Kremlin Letter, Cannon for Cordoba, A Gunfight, Summertime Killer, Rosebud, The Human Factor, That Lucky Touch, The Other Side of Midnight, The Devil's Advocate, The Greek Tycoon, An Almost Perfect Affair, A Time to Die, Lion of the Desert, The Godfather Part III.
TELEVISION: Fame (Hallmark Hall of Fame), Honor Thy Father, Catholics, The Scarlet and the Black, Christopher Columbus, Goya.

VAN ARK, JOAN
Actress. b. New York, NY. m. NBC news reporter John Marshall. e. Yale U of Drama. Began career in touring co., then on Broadway and in London in Barefoot in the Park. Also appeared on B'way with the APA-Phoenix Rep. Co. in the 1970s. As a runner has competed in 12 marathons, incl. Boston Marathon. On TV also created voices for animated series Spiderwoman, Thundarr and Dingbat, Dumb and Dumber, Santo Bugito and the Creeps and special Cyrano de Bergerac. Estee Lauder spokesperson.
THEATER: School for Wives (Tony Award nom.; Theatre World Award), The Rules of the Game (Theatre World Award). L.A.: Cyrano de Bergerac, Ring Around the Moon, Chemin de Fer, As You Like It (L.A. Drama Critics Award). Williamstown Theatre Fest.: Night of the Iguana, The Legend of Oedipus, Little Night Music. *Off-B'way & L.A.*: Love Letters, Three Tall Women.
PICTURES: Frogs, Dedication Day (dir. only).

TELEVISION: *Series*: Temperatures Rising, We've Got Each Other, Dallas, Knots Landing. *Guest*: The F.B.I., The Girl with Something Extra, Quark, Dallas, Quincy, Rockford Files, Rhoda. *Co-host*: Miss USA and Miss Universe Pageants, Battle of the Network Stars, Macy's Thanksgiving Parade, Tournament of Roses Parade. *Movies*: The Judge and Jake Wyler, Big Rose, Testimony of Two Men, Shell Game, The Last Dinosaur, Red Flag—The Ultimate Game, Glitter, Shakedown on the Sunset Strip, My First Love, Always Remember I Love You, The Grand Central Murders, Tainted Blood, In the Shadows Someone's Watching (also co-exec. prod.), Moment of Truth: A Mother's Deception, When the Dark Man Calls, Loyal Opposition: Terror in the White House. *Special*: Boys Will Be Boys (also dir.). *Mini-series*: Knots Landing: Back to the Cul-de-Sac.

VANCE, COURTNEY B.
Actor. b. Detroit, MI, Mar. 12, 1960. e. Harvard (B.A.), Yale Drama Sch. (M.A.).
THEATER: *B'way:* Fences (Theatre World & Clarence Derwent Awards; Tony nom.), Six Degrees of Separation (Tony nom.). *Off-B'way:* My Children My Africa (Obie Award), Romeo and Juliet, Temptation. *Regional:* A Lesson From Aloes, Rosencrantz and Guildenstern Are Dead, Hamlet, Butterfly, Jazz Wives Jazz Lives, Geronimo Jones.
PICTURES: Hamburger Hill, The Hunt for Red October, The Adventures of Huck Finn, Holy Matrimony, Panther, Dangerous Moves, The Last Supper, The Preacher's Wife, Blind Faith, Ambushed, Love and Action in Chicago (also co-prod.), Cookie's Fortune, Space Cowboys, The Acting Class, Eye See You.
TELEVISION: *Movies:* Percy and Thunder, Race to Freedom, Tuskegee Airmen, The Affair, Black Tuesday, 12 Angry Men, Naked City: Justice with a Bullet, Naked City: A Killer Christmas, Parting the Waters. *Series*: Boston Public.

VAN DAMME, JEAN-CLAUDE
Actor. r.n. Jean-Claude Van Varenberg. b. Brussels, Belgium, Apr. 1, 1961. Former European karate champion, began studying martial arts at 11 yrs. old. Won the European Professional Karate Association's middleweight championship. As teen established the California Gym in Brussels; also worked as a model before coming to U.S. in 1981. Resumed career teaching martial arts before landing first film role.
PICTURES: No Retreat No Surrender, Bloodsport, Black Eagle, Cyborg, Kickboxer (also co-story), Death Warrant, Lionheart (also co-s.p., story), Double Impact (also co-prod., co-s.p., co-story, fight choreog.), Universal Soldier, Nowhere to Run, Last Action Hero (cameo), Hard Target, Timecop, Street Fighter, Sudden Death, The Quest (also dir. & story), Maximum Risk, Double Team, Legionnaire (also s.p., prod.), Knock Off, Inferno, Universal Soldier: The Return (also prod.).

VAN DER BEEK, JAMES
Actor. b. Cheshire, CT, March 8, 1977
PICTURES: Angus, I Love You I Love You Not, Castle in the Sky (voice), Varsity Blues.
TELEVISION: *Series:* As the World Turns, Dawson's Creek. *Guest:* Clarissa Explains It All.

VAN DEVERE, TRISH
Actress. b. Englewood Cliffs, NJ, March 9, 1945. e. Ohio Wesleyan U. m. late actor George C. Scott. *On B'way* in Sly Fox, Tricks of the Trade.
PICTURES: The Landlord (debut, 1970), Where's Poppa?, The Last Run, One Is a Lonely Number, Harry in Your Pocket, The Day of the Dolphin, The Savage Is Loose, Movie Movie, The Changeling, The Hearse, Uphill All the Way, Hollywood Vice Squad, Messenger of Death.
TELEVISION: *Movies*: Stalk the Wild Child, Beauty and the Beast, Sharon: Portrait of a Mistress, Mayflower—The Pilgrim's Adventure, All God's Children, Haunted, Curacao.

VAN DOREN, MAMIE
Actress. r.n. Joan Lucille Olander. b. Rowena, SD, Feb. 6, 1933. e. Los Angeles H.S. Secy. law firm, L.A.; prof. debut as singer with Ted Fio Rita orch.; debuted in films as Joan Olander.
PICTURES: His Kind of Woman (debut, 1951), Forbidden, The All-American, Yankee Pasha, Francis Joins the WACs, Ain't Misbehavin', The Second Greatest Sex, Running Wild, Star in the Dust, Untamed Youth, The Girl in Black Stockings, Teacher's Pet, Guns Girls and Gangsters, High School Confidential, The Beat Generation, The Big Operator, Born Reckless, Girls' Town, The Private Lives of Adam and Eve, Sex Kittens Go to College, College Confidential, Vice Raid, The Sheriff Was a Lady, The Candidate, Three Nuts in Search of a Bolt, The Navy vs. the Night Monsters, Las Vegas Hillbillies, You've Got to Be Smart, Voyage to the Planet of the Prehistoric Women, The Arizona Kid, Boarding School (Free Ride).

VAN DYK, NICOLAS
Executive. e. B.A., political science (Phi Beta Kappa), UCLA, M.B.A., Harvard Business School. Served as consultant, LEK Partnership, where he worked on strategies for clients in the media & entertainment industries; manager, The Walt Disney Co., where he was responsible for technology-related acquisitions and strategies for business units such as ABC, ESPN, Disney Regional Entertainment, and Disney Interactive, as well as the acquisition of Dream Quest Images. Became v.p. of strategic planning, Artisan Entertainment, 1997, helping to acquire LIVE Entertainment. Currently executive v.p. & CSO, Artisan, and president, Artisan Digital Media. Oversees company-wide business development, strategic planning, mergers & acquisitions, and corporate finance, as well as all strategic and operational aspects of Artisan's Internet initiatives, including the management of iArtisan, LLC, an Internet investment vehicle.

VAN DYKE, DICK
Actor. b. West Plains, MO, Dec., 13, 1925. Brother is actor Jerry Van Dyke. Son is actor Barry Van Dyke. Served in USAF, WWII. After discharge from service, opened advertising agency in Danville, IL. Teamed with friend in nightclub act called Eric and Van, The Merry Mutes, and for 4 yrs. toured country doing a routine in which they pantomimed and lip-synched to records. 1953 hosted local TV show in Atlanta, then New Orleans. 1955 to NY as host of CBS Morning show.
THEATER: *NY*: The Girls Against the Boys (Theatre World Award), Bye Bye Birdie (Tony Award, 1961), The Music Man (revival).
PICTURES: Bye Bye Birdie (debut, 1963), What a Way to Go!, Mary Poppins, The Art of Love, Lt. Robin Crusoe USN, Divorce American Style, Fitzwilly, Chitty Chitty Bang Bang, Some Kind of a Nut, The Comic, Cold Turkey, The Runner Stumbles, Dick Tracy.
TELEVISION: *Series*: The Morning Show (host), CBS Cartoon Theatre (host), The Chevy Showroom, Pantomime Quiz, Laugh Line (emcee), The Dick Van Dyke Show (3 Emmy Awards: 1964, 1965, 1966), The New Dick Van Dyke Show, Van Dyke and Company (Emmy Award, 1977), The Carol Burnett Show, The Van Dyke Show, Diagnosis Murder. *Guest*: Jake and the Fat Man, Highway to Heaven, Matlock. *Movies*: The Morning After, Wrong Way Kid, Drop-Out Father, Found Money, The Country Girl, Ghost of a Chance, Keys to the Kingdom, Daughters of Privilege, The House on Sycamore Street, A Twist of the Knife. *Pilot*: Harry's Battles. *Specials*: The Dick Van Dyke Special, Dick Van Dyke and the Other Woman, Julie and Dick in Covent Garden, The Confessions of Dick Van Dyke, CBS Library: The Wrong Way Kid (Emmy Award, 1984), Breakfast With Les and Bess, The Town Santa Forgot (narrator), The People's Choice Awards (host).

VAN DYKE, JERRY
Actor. b. Danville, IL, July 27, 1931. Brother is actor Dick Van Dyke. Served in U.S. Air Force before becoming standup comic, banjo player in nightclubs. Guested on The Dick Van Dyke Show, playing Van Dyke's brother.
PICTURES: The Courtship of Eddie's Father (debut, 1963), McLintock!, Palm Springs Weekend, Love and Kisses, Angel in My Pocket, W.A.R.: Women Against Rape, Run If You Can, Annabelle's Wish.
TELEVISION: *Series*: Picture This, The Judy Garland Show, My Mother the Car, Accidental Family, Headmaster, 13 Queens Boulevard, Coach, You Wish, Teen Angel. *Mini-Series*: Fresno. *Movie*: To Grandmother's House We Go. *Pilots*: My Boy Googie, You're Only Young Twice, Merry Christmas, George Bailey.

VANGELIS
Composer, Conductor. r.n. Vangelis Papathanassiou. b. Greece, March 23, 1943. Began composing as child, performing own compositions at 6. Left Greece for Paris by late 1960s. Composed and recorded his symphonic poem Faire que Ton Reve Soit Plus Long que la Nuit, and album Terra. Collaborated with filmmaker Frederic Rossif for whom composed La Cantique des Creatures. Moved to London then to Greece in 1989. Formed band Formynx in Greece; then Aphrodite's Child in Paris.
PICTURES: Chariots of Fire (Academy Award, 1981), Antarctica, Missing, Blade Runner, The Year of Living Dangerously, The Bounty, Wonders of Life, Wild and Beautiful, Nosferatu in Venice, Francesco, 1492: Conquest of Paradise, Bitter Moon, Cavafy.

VANOCUR, SANDER
News Commentator. b. Cleveland, OH, Jan. 8, 1928. e. Northwestern U. Began career as journalist on London staff of Manchester Guardian 1954-5; City staff, NY Times 1956-57. Joined NBC in 1957, hosting First Tuesday series. Resigned in 1971 to be correspondent of the National Public Affairs Center for PBS. TV Critic for Washington Post, 1975-7. In 1977 joined ABC News as v.p., special reporting units 1977-80. Chief overview corr. ABC news, 1980-81; sr. corr. 1981-present. Anchor: Business World.

VAN PALLANDT, NINA
Actress. b. Copenhagen, Denmark, July 15, 1932. e. USC. Returned to Denmark where she was married to Baron Frederik Van Pallandt with whom she appeared as folk singer throughout Europe, as well as making 3 films with him; went on world tour together before divorcing. Has appeared in New York as singer.
PICTURES: The Long Goodbye, Assault on Agathon, A Wedding, Quintet, American Gigolo, Cloud Dancer, Cutter and Bone, Asi Como Habian Sido, The Sword and the Sorcerer, Jungle Warriors, Time Out, O.C. and Stiggs.
TELEVISION: *Movie*: Guilty or Innocent: The Sam Shepherd Murder Case.

VAN PATTEN, DICK
Actor. b. New York, NY, Dec. 9, 1928. Sister is actress Joyce Van Patten. Father of actors James and Vincent Van Patten. Began career as child actor with B'way debut at 7 yrs., playing son of Melvyn Douglas in Tapestry in Gray.
THEATER: The Lady Who Came to Stay, O Mistress Mine, On Borrowed Time, Ah, Wilderness, Watch on the Rhine, The Skin of Our Teeth, Kiss and Tell, Mister Roberts, Thieves.
PICTURES: Reg'lar Fellers (debut, 1941), Psychomania, Charly, Zachariah, Making It, Joe Kidd, Soylent Green, Dirty Little Billy, Westworld, Superdad, The Strongest Man in the World, Gus, Treasure of Matecumbe, The Shaggy D.A., Freaky Friday, High Anxiety, Spaceballs, The New Adventures of Pippi Longstocking, Robin Hood: Men in Tights, A Dangerous Place, Demolition High, Love Is All There Is, The Price of Air.
TELEVISION: *Series*: Mama, The Partners, The New Dick Van Dyke Show, When Things Were Rotten, Eight Is Enough, WIOU. *Guest*: Arnie, The Rookies, Cannon, Banyon, The Little People, The Streets of San Francisco, Hotel, Growing Pains, Love Boat, Murder She Wrote. *Specials*: Jay Leno's Family Comedy Hour, A Mouse A Mystery and Me, 14 Going On 30. Movies: Hec Ramsey (pilot), The Crooked Hearts, The Love Boat (pilot), With This Ring, Diary of a Hitchhiker, Eight Is Enough Reunion, Going to the Chapel, An Eight Is Enough Wedding, Jake Spanner—Private Eye, The Odd Couple: Together Again, The Gift of Love, Eight is Enough: The E! True Hollywood Story.

VAN PATTEN, JOYCE
Actress. b. New York, NY, March 9, 1935. Brother is actor Dick Van Patten. Mother of actress Talia Balsam.
THEATER: *NY*: Spoon River Anthology, Same Time Next Year, The Supporting Cast, The Seagull, I Ought to Be in Pictures, Brighton Beach Memoirs, Murder at the Howard Johnson's, Rumors, Jake's Women.
PICTURES: Reg'lar Fellers (debut, 1941), Fourteen Hours, The Goddess, I Love You Alice B. Toklas, Making It, Something Big, Thumb Tripping, The Manchu Eagle Murder Caper Mystery, Mame, The Bad News Bears, Mikey and Nicky, The Falcon and the Snowman, St. Elmo's Fire, Billy Galvin, Blind Date, Trust Me, Monkey Shines, Show and Tell.
TELEVISION: *Series*: The Danny Kaye Show, The Good Guys, The Don Rickles Show, Mary Tyler Moore Hour, Unhappily Ever After. *Guest*: Brooklyn Bridge. *Movies*: But I Don't Want to Get Married!, Winter Kill, The Stranger Within, Let's Switch, Winner Take All, To Kill a Cop, Murder at the Mardi Gras, The Comedy Company, Eleanor: First Lady of the World, Another Woman's Child, The Demon Murder Case, In Defense of Kids, Malice in Wonderland, Under the Influence, The Haunted, Maid for Each Other, Breathing Lessons, The Gift of Love, Grandpa's Funeral, Jake's Women. *Mini-Series*: The Martian Chronicles. *Special*: Bus Stop.

VAN PEEBLES, MARIO
Actor, Director, Producer, Writer. b. Mexico D.F., Mexico, Jan. 15, 1957. Father is filmmaker Melvin Van Peebles. e. Columbia U., B.A. economics, 1980. Studied acting with Stella Adler 1983. Served as budget analyst for NY Mayor Ed Koch and later worked as a Ford model. Directed music videos for Kid Creole and the Coconuts, Nighttrain (also prod., cameo) and for film Identity Crisis. Appeared as child in father's film Sweet Sweetback's Baadasssss Song. Dir., prod., wrote and starred in short, Juliet. Exec. prod. of soundtracks for Posse and Gunmen.
THEATER: Waltz of the Stork (B'way debut, 1984), Take Me Along, The Legend of Deadwood Dick, Champeen, Friday the 13th.
PICTURES: *Actor:* The Cotton Club, Delivery Boys, Exterminator II, 3:15, Rappin' (also wrote and performed 5 songs), South Bronx Heroes, Heartbreak Ridge (also songs), Last Resort, Jaws: the Revenge, Hot Shot, Identity Crisis (also s.p.), New Jack City (also dir.), Posse (also dir.), Gunmen, Highlander: The Sorcerer, Panther (also dir., prod.), Jaws IV: The Revenge, Solo, Los Locos (also s.p., prod., exec. prod.), Stag, Love Kills (also. dir., prod., s.p.), Crazy Six, Raw Nerve, Judgement Day, Blowback.
TELEVISION: *Series*: Sonny Spoon, Rude Awakening. *Guest*: L.A. Law, One Life to Live, The Cosby Show, The Pat Sajack Show (guest host), In Living Color, Living Single, Outer Limits: Bodies of Evidence. *Movies*: The Cable Car Murder, Sophisticated Gents, Children of the Night (Bronze Halo Award), The Facts of Life Down Under, The Child Saver, Blue Bayou, Triumph of the Heart: The Ricky Bell Story, Stompin' at the Savoy, In the Line of Duty: Street War, Crosscurrents: Cable Car Murder, Full Eclipse. Specials: American Masters: A Glory of Ghosts (Emperor Jones, All God's Chillun), Third & Oak: The Pool Hall (CBS play), Strangers: Leave, Gang In Blue, Riot, Gang In Blue (also. co-direct, co-prod.), Valentine's Day, Mama Flora's Family, Killers in the House. *Director*: Sonny Spoon, 21 Jump Street, Top of the Hill, Wise Guy, Malcolm Takes a Shot (DGA nom.), Gabriel's Fire, Missing Persons, Sally Hemming: An America Scandal.

VAN PEEBLES, MELVIN
Producer, Director, Writer, Composer, Editor, Actor. b. Chicago, IL, Aug. 21, 1932. e. Ohio Wesleyan U., 1953. Father of actor Mario Van Peebles. Was portrait painter in Mexico, cable car driver in San Francisco; journalist in Paris and (in 1970s) options trader on Wall Street. Dir. Funky Beat music video.
AUTHOR: *Books*: The Big Heart, A Bear for the FBI, Le Chinois de XIV, La Permission (Story of a Three Day Pass) La Fete a Harlem, The True American, Sweet Sweetback's Baadassss Song, Just an Old Sweet Song, Bold Money, No Identity Crisis (co-author with Mario Van Peebles), Panther.
ALBUMS: *Composer*: Brer Soul, Watermelon Man, Sweet Sweetback's Baadassss Song, As Serious as a Heart Attack, Don't Play Us Cheap, Ain't Suppose to Die a Natural Death, What the #*!% You Mean I Can't Sing, Ghetto Gothic.
THEATER: *B'way* (writer, prod., dir.): Ain't Supposed to Die a Natural Death, Don't Play Us Cheap, Waltz of the Stork (also actor). *Off-B'way*: Champeen, Waltz of the Stork, Kickin the Science.
PICTURES: The Story of a Three-Day Pass (dir., s.p., music), Watermelon Man (dir., music), Sweet Sweetback's Baadassss Song (prod., dir., s.p., edit., music, actor), Don't Play Us Cheap (prod., dir., s.p., edit., music), Greased Lightning (co-s.p.), America (actor), O.C. and Stiggs (actor), Jaws: The Revenge (actor), Identity Crisis (prod., dir., co-edit., actor), True Identity (actor), Boomerang (actor), Posse (actor), Last Action Hero (actor), Terminal Velocity (actor), Fist of the North Star (actor), Panther (s.p., actor, prod., co-edit.).
TELEVISION: *Writer*: Down Home, Just an Old Sweet Song, The Day They Came to Arrest the Book (Emmy Award). *Actor*: Taking Care of Terrific, Sophisticated Gents, Sonny Spoons (series). *Director*: Nipsey Russell at Harrah's, Vroom Vroom Vroom (also writer; German TV).

VAN PRAAG, WILLIAM
Executive, Producer, Director, Writer, Editor, Advertising Consultant. b. New York, NY, Sept. 13, 1924. e. CREI, Columbia U. U.S. Army, 1942. Paramount, 1945; Brandt Bros. Prods., 1946; NBC, 1947; v.p. Television Features, 1948; devlpd. vidicon system in m.p. prod., 1949; Started, pres., Van Praag Prod. Inc. 1951; formed Ernst-Van Praag, Inc. 1971, a communications and marketing counseling firm (NY, Brussels, Tokyo); pres., International Film, TV and A-V Producers Assn, 1969; creator of Van-O-Vision. Winner of commercial, short subject and feature theatrical awards. Author of Color Your Picture, Primer of Creative Editing, and Van Praag's Magic Eye. Past pres., Film Producer's Assn, mem. DGA, SAG, 771 IATSE, National Academy of TV Arts and Sciences, International Radio and TV Executive Society and Soc. of MP and TV Engineers.

VAN SANT, GUS
Director, Writer. b. Louisville, KY, 1952. Raised in Darien, CT, then moved to Oregon at age 17. e. Rhode Island Sch. of Design, where he studied painting. Went to L.A. in 1976, becoming prod. asst. to dir. Ken Shapiro. Made first low-budget film, Alice in Hollywood, which was never released. Later made commercials for NY ad agency before returning to filmmaking.
PICTURES: Mala Noche, Drugstore Cowboy (Natl. Soc. of Film Critics Awards for best dir. & s.p.; NY Film Critics & L.A. Film Critics Award for s.p.), My Own Private Idaho, Even Cowgirls Get the Blues, To Die For, Ballad of the Skeletons, Good Will Hunting, Psycho, Finding Forrester.

VARNEY, JIM
Actor. b. Lexington, KY, June 15, 1949. Studied acting at the Barter Theatre. Performed as stand-up comedian in NY and LA. Appeared in dinner theatre productions of Death of a Salesman, Camelot, Guys and Dolls, etc. During 1970's starred as Sgt. Glory in long running series of TV commercials. Became famous with character of Ernest P. Worrell in TV commercials beginning in 1980.

PICTURES: Ernest Goes to Camp, Ernest Saves Christmas, Fast Food, Ernest Goes to Jail, Ernest Scared Stupid, Wilder Napalm, The Beverly Hillbillies, Ernest Rides Again, Ernest Goes to School, Toy Story (voice), The Expert, Snowboard Academy, 3 Ninjas, Ernest Goes to Africa, 100 Proof, Ernest in the Army, 3 Ninjas: High Noon at Mega Mountain, Treehouse Hostage, Existo, Ernest the Pirate, Toy Story 2 (voice).
TELEVISION: *Series*: The Johnny Cash Show (1976), Operation Petticoat, Pink Lady, Tom T.'s Pop Goes the Country, The Rousters, Hey Vern It's Ernest (Emmy Award, 1989). *Guest*: Fernwood 2-Night, Alice, America 2-Nite, Roseanne, The Simpsons (voice). *Pilot*: Operation Petticoat.
(d. February 10, 2000)

VAUGHN, ROBERT
Actor. b. New York, NY, Nov. 22, 1932. e. L.A. State coll., B.S. and M.A. Theatre Arts 1956; USC, Ph.D. Communications, 1970. Gained fame as Napoleon Solo in The Man From U.N.C.L.E. TV series. *Author*: Only Victims, 1972.
PICTURES: The Ten Commandments (debut, 1956), Hell's Crossroads, No Time to Be Young, Teenage Caveman, Unwed Mother, Good Day for a Hanging, The Young Philadelphians (Acad. Award nom.), The Magnificent Seven, The Big Show, The Caretakers, To Trap a Spy, The Spy With My Face, One Spy Too Many, The Glass Bottom Boat (cameo), The Venetian Affair, How to Steal the World, Bullitt, The Bridge at Remagen, If It's Tuesday This Must Be Belgium (cameo), The Mind of Mr. Soames, Julius Caesar, The Statue, Clay Pigeon, The Towering Inferno, The Babysitter, Lucifer Complex, Demon Seed (voice), Starship Invasions, Brass Target, Good Luck Miss Wycoff, Hangar 18, Sweet Dirty Tony, Battle Beyond the Stars, Virus, S.O.B., Superman III, Black Moon Rising, The Delta Force, Rampage, Nightstick, Hour of the Assassin, Skeleton Coast, River of Death, Captive Rage, Nobody's Perfect, Fair Trade, Edgar Allan Poe's Buried Alive, That's Adequate, Blind Vision, C.H.U.D. II: Bud the Chud, Transylvania Twist, Going Under, Twilight Blue, Joe's Apartment, Vulcan, The Sender, Motel Blue, Milk and Money, Anak ng Bulkan, An American Affair, McCinsey's Island, BASEketball.
TELEVISION: *Series*: The Lieutenant, The Man From U.N.C.L.E., The Protectors, Emerald Point N.A.S., The A-Team, Danger Theatre, As the World Turns. Mini-Series: Captains and the Kings, Washington: Behind Closed Doors (Emmy Award, 1978), Centennial, Backstairs at the White House, The Blue and the Gray, Evergreen. *Movies*: The Woman Hunter, Kiss Me Kill Me, The Islander, The Rebels, Mirror Mirror, Doctor Franken, The Gossip Columnist, City in Fear, Fantasies, The Day the Bubble Burst, A Question of Honor, Inside the Third Reich, Intimate Agony, The Return of the Man From U.N.C.L.E., International Airport, Murrow, Prince of Bel Air, Desperado, Perry Mason: The Case of the Defiant Daughter, Dark Avenger, Dancing in the Dark. BBC: One of Our Spies is Missing, The Spy in the Green Hat, The Karate Killers, Virtual Obsession.

VAUGHN, VINCE
Actor. b. Minneapolis, MN, March 28, 1970.
PICTURES: For the Boys (uncredited), Rudy, At Risk, Swingers, Just Your Luck, The Locusts, The Lost World: Jurassic Park, Return to Paradise, Clay Pigeons, A Cool Dry Place, The Cell, Psycho, South of Heaven, West of Hell, The Prime Gig, Zoolander, Made (also prod.), Domestic Disturbance.
TELEVISION: *Guest*: Doogie Howser M.D., China Beach, 21 Jump Street.

VEL JOHNSON, REGINALD
Actor. b. Queens, NY, Aug. 16, 1952. e. Long Island Inst. of Music and Arts, NYU.
THEATER: *NY*: But Never Jam Today, Inacent Black, World of Ben Caldwell, Staggerlee.
PICTURES: Wolfen (debut, 1981), Ghostbusters, The Cotton Club, Remo Williams, Armed and Dangerous, Crocodile Dundee, Die Hard, Turner & Hooch, Die Hard 2, Posse, Ground Zero.
TELEVISION: *Series*: Perfect Strangers, Family Matters. *Movies*: Quiet Victory: The Charlie Wedemeyer Story, The Bride in Black, Jury Duty: The Comedy, Grass Roots, One of Her Own, Deadly Pursuits.

VENORA, DIANE
Actress. b. Hartford, CT, 1952. e. Juilliard Sch. (BFA degree). Member of Juilliard's Acting Company, Circle Repertory Co. and the Ensemble Studio Theatre.
THEATER: A Midsummer Night's Dream, Hamlet (New York Shakespeare Festival), Uncle Vanya (at La Mama), Messiah (Manhattan Theatre Club), Penguin Toquet, Tomorrow's Monday (Circle Rep), Largo Desolato, School for Scandal, The Seagull, A Man for All Seasons (Roundabout Theatre Co.), Peer Gynt (Williamstown Fest.), The Winter's Tale, Hamlet (NYSF).
PICTURES: All That Jazz, Wolfen, Terminal Choice, The Cotton Club, F/X, Ironweed, Bird (NY Film Critics Award, 1988; Golden Globe nom.), Heat, Three Wishes, Surviving Picasso, The Subsitute, Romeo and Juliet, The Jackal, Young Girl and the Monsoon, Looking for an Echo, The Joyriders, The Insider, Hamlet, True Crime, The 13th Warrior.
TELEVISION: *Mini-Series*: A.D. *Movie*: Cook and Peary: The Race to the Pole. *Specials*: Getting There, Rehearsing Hamlet, Hamlet. *Guest*: Law and Order. *Series*: Thunder Alley, Chicago Hope.

VERDON, GWEN
Actress, Dancer, Choreographer. b. Culver City, CA, Jan. 13, 1925. Married to late dir.-choreographer Bob Fosse. Studied dancing with her mother, E. Belcher, Carmelita Marrachi, and Jack Cole.
THEATER: Bonanza Bound!, Magdalena (asst. choreographer to Jack Cole), Alive and Kicking, Can-Can (Donaldson & Tony Awards, 1954), Damn Yankees (Tony Award, 1956), New Girl in Town (Tony Award, 1958), Redhead (Tony Award, 1959), Sweet Charity, Children! Children!, Milliken's Breakfast Show, Damn Yankees (revival Westbury), Chicago, Dancin' (asst. choreographer, prod. sprv. road co.), Sing Happy (tribute to Kander and Ebb), Parade of Stars Playing the Palace (Actors' Fund benefit), Night of 100 Stars II (1985).
PICTURES: On the Riviera (debut, 1951), David and Bathsheba, The Mississippi Gambler, Meet Me After the Show, The Merry Widow, The I Don't Care Girl, Farmer Takes a Wife, Damn Yankees, The Cotton Club, Cocoon, Nadine, Cocoon: The Return, Alice, Marvin's Room.
TELEVISION: *Movies*: Legs, The Jerk Too, Oldest Living Confederate Widow Tells All, Best Friends for Life. *Special*: Steam Heat. *Guest*: M*A*S*H, Fame, All My Children, Magnum P.I., The Equalizer, All is Forgiven, Dear John, Dream On, Homicide, many others.

VEREEN, BEN
Singer, Dancer, Actor. b. Miami, FL, Oct. 10, 1946. e. High School of Performing Arts.
THEATER: *NY*: Hair, Sweet Charity, Jesus Christ Superstar (Theatre World Award), Pippin (Tony Award, 1973), Grind.
PICTURES: Sweet Charity, Gasss, Funny Lady, All That Jazz, The Zoo Gang, Buy and Cell, Friend to Friend, Once Upon a Forest (voice).
TELEVISION: *Movies*: Louis Armstrong—Chicago Style, The Jesse Owens Story, Lost in London, Intruders. *Mini-Series*: Roots, Ellis Island, A.D.. *Series*: Ben Vereen... Comin' at Ya, Ten Speed and Brown Shoe, Webster, Zoobilee Zoo, You Write the Songs (host), J.J. Starbuck, Silk Stalkings. *Specials*: Ben Vereen—His Roots, Uptown— A Tribute to the Apollo Theatre.

VERHOEVEN, PAUL
Director. b. Amsterdam, The Netherlands, July 18, 1938. e. U. of Leiden, Ph.D., (mathematics and physics) where he began making films.
PICTURES: Business Is Business, Turkish Delight, Keetje Tippel (Cathy Tippel), Soldier of Orange, Spetters, The Fourth Man, Flesh + Blood, Robocop, Total Recall, Basic Instinct, Showgirls, Starship Troopers, Hollow Man.

VERNON, ANNE
Actress. r.n. Edith Antoinette Alexandrine Vignaud. b. Paris, Jan. 7, 1924. e. Ecole des Beaux Arts, Paris. Worked for French designer; screen debut in French films; toured with French theatre group; first starring role, Le Mannequin Assassine 1948. Wrote French cookbooks. Was subject of 1980 French TV film detailing her paintings, Les Peintres Enchanteurs.
PICTURES: Edouar et Caroline, Terror on a Train, Ainsi Finit La Nuit, A Warning to Wantons, Patto Col Diavolo, A Tale of Five Cities, Shakedown, Song of Paris, The Umbrellas of Cherbourg, General Della Rovere, La Rue L'Estrapade, Love Lottery, Therese and Isabelle.

VERNON, JOHN
Actor. r.n. Adolphus Raymondus Vernon Agopowicz. b. Montreal, Canada, Feb. 24, 1932. e. Banff Sch. of Fine Arts, Royal Acad. of Dramatic Art. Worked on London stage and radio. First film work as voice of Big Brother in 1984 (1956). Daughter is actress Kate Vernon.
PICTURES: 1984 (voice; debut, 1956), Nobody Waved Goodbye, Point Blank, Justine, Topaz, Tell Them Willie Boy is Here, One More Train to Rob, Dirty Harry, Fear Is the Key, Charley Varrick, W (I Want Her Dead), The Black Windmill, Brannigan, Sweet Movie, The Outlaw Josey Wales, Angela, A Special Day, The Uncanny, Golden Rendevzous, National Lampoon's Animal House, It Rained All Night the Day I Left, Crunch, Fantastica, Herbie Goes Bananas, Heavy Metal (voice), Airplane II: The Sequel, Chained Heat, Curtains,

Savage Streets, Jungle Warriors, Fraternity Vacation, Doin' Time, Double Exposure (Terminal Exposure), Ernest Goes to Camp, Blue Monkey, Nightstick, Border Heat, Deadly Stranger, Dixie Lanes, Killer Klowns From Outer Space, Bail-Out, I'm Gonna Git You Sucka, Office Party, War Bus Commando, Mob Story, The Naked Truth.
TELEVISION: *Series*: Tugboat Annie (Canadian TV), Wojeck (Canadian TV), Delta House, Hail to the Chief. *Movies*: Trial Run, Escape, Cool Million, Hunter, The Questor Tapes, Mousey, The Virginia Hill Story, The Imposter, Swiss Family Robinson, The Barbary Coast, Matt Helm, Mary Jane Harper Cried Last Night, The Sacketts, The Blood of Others, Two Men (Can.), The Woman Who Sinned, The Fire Next Time, The Forget-Me-Not Murders. *Mini-Series*: The Blue and the Gray, Louisiana (Fr.). *Pilots*: B-Men, War of the Worlds. *Guest*: Tarzan, Kung Fu, Faerie Tale Theatre (Little Red Riding Hood), The Greatest American Hero, Fall Guy, Alfred Hitchcock Presents, Knight Rider, Tales From the Crypt.

VERONA, STEPHEN
Director, Producer, Writer. b. Illinois, Sept. 11, 1940. e. Sch. of Visual Arts. Directed and wrote some 300 commercials (over 50 award-winners) before turning to feature films in 1972, which he wrote as well. Also dir. award-winning short subjects (featuring Barbra Streisand, The Beatles, Simon and Garfunkle and The Lovin' Spoonful). Also prod., dir. of Angela Lansbury's Positive Moves video. Is an artist whose works have been exhibited at numerous CA and NY galleries. Dir. Acad. Award nom. short subject, The Rehearsal, 1971.
PICTURES: *Director*: The Lords of Flatbush (prod., co-dir., co-s.p.), Pipe Dreams (also prod., s.p.), Boardwalk (also co-s.p.), Talking Walls (also s.p.).
TELEVISION: Class of 1966 (prod. designer, ani. dir.), Diff'rent Strokes, The Music People, Sesame Street, Take a Giant Step, Double Exposure, Flatbush Avenue (pilot, prod., co-s.p.).

VETTER, RICHARD
Executive. b. San Diego, CA, Feb. 24, 1928. e. Pepperdine Coll., B.A., 1950; San Diego State Coll., M.A., 1953; UCLA, Ph.D., 1959. U.S. Navy: aerial phot., 1946-48, reserve instr., San Diego County Schools, 1951-54; asst. prof., audio-vis. commun., U.C.L.A., 1960-63. Inventor, co-dev., Dimension 150 Widescreen Process. 1957-63: formed D-150 Inc., 1963; exec. v.p. mem.: SMPTE, Technical & Scientific Awards Committee, AMPAS.

VIANE, CHUCK
Executive. e. B.S., marketing, De Paul U. Began as film buyer, v.p. & head buyer, General Cinema Theater Corp., 1973-85; v.p. & asst. gen. sales mgr., Buena Vista Pictures, 1986; senior v.p. & gen. sales mgr., Buena Vista Pictures, 1995. Currently president, Buena Vista Pictures Distribution (since 1999), overseeing sales and distribution operations throughout U.S. and Canada for all motion pictures released by Walt Disney, Touchstone, and Hollywood Pictures. His tenure with Buena Vista has seen the company break numerous industry records and finish as the industry leader for six of the last ten years, surpassing the $1 billion mark at the box office for five of the past six years.

VICTOR, JAMES
Actor. r.n. Lincoln Rafael Peralta Diaz. b. Santiago, Dominican Republic, July 27, 1939. e. Haaren H.S., N.Y. Studied at Actors Studio West. Member of Academy of Mo. Pic. Arts & Sciences, Actors Branch. Recipient of Cleo Award, 1975, for Mug Shot; Golden Eagle Award, 1981, for consistent outstanding performances in motion pictures.
THEATER: Bullfight, Ceremony for an Assassinated Blackman, Latina (Drama-Logue Critics Award, 1980), The Man in the Glass Booth, The M.C. (Drama-Logue Critics, and Cesar best actor awards, 1985), I Gave You a Calendar (Drama-Logue Critics Award, 1983), I Don't Have To Show You No Stinking Badges (Drama-Logue Critics Award, 1986), The Rooster and the Egg, One Hour Without Television, The Red Devil Battery Sign.
PICTURES: Fuzz, Rolling Thunder, Boulevard Nights, Defiance, Losin' It, Borderline; Stand and Deliver, Gunfighter's Moon.
TELEVISION: *Series*: Viva Valdez, Condo, I Married Dora, Angelica Mi Vida, The New Zorro, Murder She Wrote. Many appearances on specials. *Movies*: Robert Kennedy and His Times, Twin Detectives, Remington Steel, The Streets of L.A., I Desire, Second Serve, Grand Slam, Falcon Crest. *Mini-Series*: Streets of Laredo.

VIGODA, ABE
Actor. b. New York, NYU, Feb. 24, 1921.
PICTURES: The Godfather, The Don Is Dead, Newman's Law, The Cheap Detective, Vasectomy - A Delicate Matter, Plain Clothes, Look Who's Talking, Prancer, Joe vs. the Volcano, Sugar Hill, Jury Duty, Good Burger.
TELEVISION: *Series*: Dark Shadow, Barney Miller, Fish, One Life to Live. *Movies*: The Devil's Daughter, Tomaa, Having Babies, How to Pick Up Girls, Death Car on the Freeway. *Guest*: Mannix, Kojak, The Rookies, B.J. and the Bear, B.K. Stryker.

VINCENT, JR., FRANCIS T
Executive. b. Waterbury, CT, May 29, 1938. e. Williams Coll. B.A., 1960; Yale Law Sch. LL.B., 1963. Bar, CT 1963; NY, 1964; D.C. 1969. 1969-78, partner in law firm of Caplin & Drysdale, specializing in corporate banking and securities matters; 1978, assoc. dir. of, Division of Corporation Finance of Securities & Exchange Commission; exec. v.p. of the Coca-Cola Company and pres. & CEO of its entertainment business sector. Also chmn. & CEO of Columbia Pictures Industries, Inc.; appt. pres. CEO, 1978; mem. bd. of dir. of The Coca-Cola Bottling Co. of NY. 1987-88; rejoined law firm of Caplin & Drysdale, Washington, D.C., 1988. Trustee of Williams Coll. & The Hotchkiss Sch.

VINCENT, JAN-MICHAEL
Actor. b. Denver, CO, July 15, 1945. e. Ventura City (CA) Coll. as art major. Joined National Guard. Discovered by agent Dick Clayton. Hired by Robert Conrad to appear in his film, Los Bandidos. Signed to 6-mo. contract by Universal, for which made U.S. debut in Journey to Shiloh. Then did pilot TV movie for 20th-Fox based on Hardy Boys series of book. Originally called self Michael Vincent; changed after The Undefeated.
PICTURES: Los Bandidos (debut, 1967), Journey to Shiloh, The Undefeated, Going Home, The Mechanic, The World's Greatest Athlete, Buster and Billie, Bite the Bullet, White Line Fever, Baby Blue Marine, Vigilante Force, Shadow of the Hawk, Damnation Alley, Big Wednesday, Hooper, Defiance, Hard Country, The Return, The Last Plane Out, Born in East L.A., Enemy Territory, Hit List, Deadly Embrace, Demonstone, Hangfire, Raw Nerve, Alienator, Haunting Fear, Gold of the Samurai, The Divine Enforcer, Beyond the Call of Duty, Sins of Desire, Hidden Obsession, Xtro II, Deadly Avenger, Midnight Witness, Ice Cream Man, Abducted II: The Reunion, Red Line, Orbit, Codename: Silencer, Buffalo '66, White Boy, The Thundering 8th, Escape to Grizzly Mountain.
TELEVISION: *Series*: Dangerous Island (Banana Splits Hour), The Survivors, Airwolf. *Movies*: Tribes, The Catcher, Sandcastles, Deliver Us From Evil, Six Against the Rock, Tarzan in Manhattan. *Mini-Series*: The Winds of War. *Guest*: Lassie, Bonanza.

VINCENT, KATHARINE
Actress. r.n. Ella Vincenti. b. St. Louis, MO, May 28, 1918.
THEATER: *B'way*: Love or Bust, Could She Tell?, Banners of 1939, Czarina Smith.
PICTURES: Peptipa's Waltz, Error in Her Ways, Stars and Stripes on Tour, Skin Deep, The Hungry, Voodoo Village, Welcome to Genoa, Unknown Betrayal, The Hooker, Study by M. Atget.
TELEVISION: The Untouchables, Moses the Lawgiver, Dolce Far Niente (mini-series, Roma).

VINER, MICHAEL
Producer, Writer. b. 1945. m. actress Deborah Raffin. e. Harvard U., Georgetown U. Served as aide to Robert Kennedy; was legman for political columnist Jack Anderson. Settled in Hollywood, where worked for prod. Aaron Rosenberg, first as prod. asst. on three Frank Sinatra films; then asst. prod. on Joaquin Murietta. In music industry was record producer, manager, executive, eventually heading own division, at MGM. Debut as writer-producer in 1976 with TV special, Special of the Stars. Theatrical film debut as prod.-co-writer of Touched by Love, 1980. Television: Windmills of the Gods (exec. prod.). *Exec. Prod.*: Rainbow Drive; *Prod.*: Memories of Midnight. *President*: Dove Audio.

VIOLANTE, JOSEPH
Executive, Dailies Advisor. b. Brooklyn, NY. Vice President, Technicolor, New York.
PICTURES: Dawn of the Dead, The Protector, The Unotuchables, The Last Temptation of Christ, Zelly and Me, Signs of Life, Night Game, Reversal of Fortune, The Lemon Sisters, Jacob's Ladder, The Ballad of the Sad Cafe, Consenting Adults, Mad Dog and Glory, A Bronx Tale, Life With Mikey, Serial Mom, Only You, Radio Inside, Die Hard With A Vengeance, Clockers, Twelve Monkeys, Beautiful Girls, Girl 6, Kama Sutra: A Tale of Love, When We Were Kings, A Brother's Kiss, The Blackout, Julian Po, The Spanish Prisoner, Two Girls and a Guy, Nigh Flier, Great Expectations, The Last Days of Disco, Rounders, Simply Irresistable, Summer of Sam, Wirey Spindell, Flawless.

VITALE, RUTH
Executive. e. Tufts U., B.A.; Boston U., M.S. Prior to motion picture career, worked in advertising and media. Senior v.p., Vestron Pictures then s.v.p. of feature production at United Artists and management at Constantin Film Development before joining New Line. Joined New Line as exec. v.p. of worldwide acquisitions. Currently pres., Fine Line Features, a wholly owned division of New Line Cinema.

VITTI, MONICA
Actress. r.n. Maria Luisa Ceciarelli. b. Rome, Italy, Nov. 3, 1933. Started acting in plays as teen, studying at Rome's Natl. Acad. of Dramatic Arts.
PICTURES: Ridere Ridere Ridere (debut, 1955), Smart Girls, L'Avventura, La Notte, L'Eclipse, Dragees du Poivre (Sweet and Sour), Three Fables of Love, The Nutty Naughty Chateau, Alta Infidelitata (High Infidelity), The Red Desert, Le Bambole (The Dolls), Il Disco Volante, Le Fate (The Queens), Modesty Blaise, The Chastity Belt (On My Way to the Crusades I Met a Girl Who...), Girl with a Pistol, La Femme Ecarlate, The Pizza Triangle, The Pacifist, Teresa la Ladra, Tosca, The Phantom of Liberty, Midnight Pleasures, My Loves, Duck in Orange Sauce, An Almost Perfect Affair, The Mystery of Oberwald, Tigers in Lipstick, The Flirt (also s.p.), When Veronica Calls, Secret Scandal (also dir., co- s.p.).

VOIGHT, JON
Actor. b. Yonkers, NY. Dec. 29, 1938. e. Archbishop Stepinac H.S., White Plains, NY; Catholic U. of Amer., D.C. (B.F.A.) 1960; studied acting at the Neighborhood Playhouse and in private classes with Stanford Meisner, four yrs.
THEATER: *B'way*: The Sound of Music (debut, 1959), That Summer That Fall (Theatre World Award), The Seagull. *Off-B'way*: A View From the Bridge (1964 revival). *Regional*: Romeo & Juliet, A Streetcar Named Desire, Hamlet.
PICTURES: Hour of the Gun (debut, 1967), Fearless Frank, Midnight Cowboy, Out of It, Catch-22, The Revolutionary, Deliverance, All-American Boy, Conrack, The Odessa File, End of the Game, Coming Home (Acad. Award, 1978), The Champ, Lookin' To Get Out (also co-s.p., prod.), Table for Five (also prod.), Runaway Train, Desert Bloom, Eternity, Heat, Rosewood, U-Turn, Mission Impossible, Anaconda, The Rainmaker, Enemy of the State, The General, A Dog of Flanders, Varsity Blues.
TELEVISION: *Movies*: Chernobyl: The Final Warning, The Last of His Tribe, The Tin Soldier (also dir.), Convict Cowboy, The Fixer. *Mini-Series*: Return to Lonesome Dove, Noah. *Special*: The Dwarf (Public Broadcast Lab). *Guest*: Gunsmoke, Naked City, The Defenders, Coronet Blue, NYPD.

VON SYDOW, MAX
Actor. b. Lund, Sweden, April 10, 1929. Theatrical debut in a Cathedral Sch. of Lund prod. of The Nobel Prize. Served in the Swedish Quartermaster Corps two yrs. Studied at Royal Dramatic Theatre Sch. in Stockholm. Tour in municipal theatres. Has appeared on stage in Stockholm, London (The Tempest, 1988), Paris and Helsinki in Faust, The Legend and The Misanthrope. 1954 won Sweden's Royal Foundation Cultural Award. Appeared on B'way in Duet for One.
PICTURES: Bara en Mor (Only a Mother; debut, 1949), Miss Julie, Ingen Mans Kvinna, Ratten att Alska, The Seventh Seal, Prasten i Uddarbo, Wild Strawberries, Brink of Life, Spion 503, The Magician, The Virgin Spring, Brollopsdagen, Through a Glass Darkly, Nils Holgerssons Underbara Resa, Alskarinnen, Winter Light, 4x4, The Greatest Story Ever Told (English-language debut, 1965), The Reward, Hawaii, The Quiller Memorandum, Hour of the Wolf, Here Is Your Life, Svarta Palmkronor, Shame, Made in Sweden, The Kremlin Letter, The Passion of Anna, The Night Visitor, The Touch, The Emigrants, Appelbriget, Embassy, The New Land, The Exorcist, Steppenwolf, Egg! Egg!, Illustrious Corpses, Three Days of the Condor, The Ultimate Warrior, Foxtrot (The Other Side of Paradise), Cuore di Cane, Voyage of the Damned, Les Desert des Tartares, Exorcist II: The Heretic, March or Die, Brass Target, Gran Bolitto, Hurricane, Deathwatch, Venetian Lies, Flash Gordon, Victory, She Dances Alone (voice), Conan the Barbarian, Flight of the Eagle, Strange Brew, Never Say Never Again, Target Eagle, Dreamscape, Dune, Code Name: Emerald, Hannah and Her Sisters, Duet for One, The Second Victory, Wolf at the Door, Pelle the Conqueror (Acad. Award nom.), Katinka (dir.), Cellini: A Violent Life, Awakenings, A Kiss Before Dying, Until the End of the World, Zentropa (narrator), The Bachelor, The Best Intentions, The Ox, Father, Grandfather's Journey, Needful Things, The Silent Touch, Time Is Money, The Atlantic (narrator), Judge Dredd, Needful Things, Jerusalem, Hamsun, What Dreams May Come, Snow Falling on Cedars.
TELEVISION: *Movies/Mini-Series*: Samson and Delilah, Christopher Columbus, Kojak: The Belarus File, Brotherhood of the Rose, Hiroshima: Out of the Ashes, Red King White Knight, Radetzky March, Citizen X, A Que Punto E La Notte, Uncle Vanya, Confessions, Hostile Waters, Fantasma Per Caso, Salomone, La Principessa E Il Povero.

VON TRIER, LARS
Director, Writer, Editor, Actor. r.n. Lars Trier. b. Copenhagen, Denmark, April 30, 1956. e. Danish Film Institute. Attracted international attention with Forbrydelsens Element (The Element of Crime). Is working on a film project taking a 3 minute shot every year from different locations all over Europe for a period of 33 years; begun in 1991, the premiere is expected in the year 2024.
PICTURES: *Director*: Orchidegartneren (1976), Menthe la bienheureuse, Den Sidste detalje, Befrielsesbilleder (also s.p.), The Element of Crime (also actor, s.p.), Epidemic (also actor, s.p., edit.), Medea (also s.p.), Un Monde de Difference (actor only), Zentropa (a.k.a. Europa; also actor, s.p.), The Kingdom (orig. for Danish TV; also s.p.), Breaking the Waves (also s.p.; Grand Jury Prize, Cannes, 1996), The Kingdom 2 (orig. for Danish TV; also s.p.), The Idiots (also s.p.), Dancer in The Dark (also s.p.).

VON TROTTA, MARGARETHE
Director, Writer. b. Berlin, Germany, Feb. 21, 1942. e. Studied German and Latin literature in Munich and Paris. Studied acting in Munich and began career as actress. 1970 began collaborating on Schlondorff's films as well as acting in them.
PICTURES: *Actress*: Hands Up!, Madchen zwischen Nacht und Morgen, Schrage Vogel, Brandstifter, Gotter der Pest, Baal, Drucker, Der Amerikanische Soldat, Gods of the Plague, Why Does Herr R. Run Amok?, The Sudden Wealth of the Poor People of Kombach (also co-s.p.), Beware the Holy Whore, Die Moral der Ruth Halbfass, Free Woman (also co-s.p.), Desaster, Ubernachtung in Tirol, Die Atlantikschwimmer, Bierkampf, Coup de Grace (also co-s.p.). *Dir./ Co-s.p.*: The Lost Honor of Katharina Blum (co-dir., co-s.p., with Schlondorff), The Second Awakening of Christa Klages, Sisters or the Balance of Happiness, Circle of Deceit, Marianne and Julianne, Friends & Husbands, Unerreichbare Nahe, Rosa Luxemburg, Felix, Paura e Amore (Three Sisters), The African Woman, The Long Silence, The Promise.

VON ZERNECK, FRANK
Producer. b. New York, NY, Nov. 3, 1940. e. Hofstra Coll., 1962. Has produced plays in New York, Los Angeles and on national tour. Partner, von Zerneck/Sertner Films. Devised Portrait film genre for TV movies: Portrait of a Stripper, Portrait of a Mistress, Portrait of a Centerfold, etc. Past chmn. of California Theatre Council; former officer of League of Resident theatres; member of League of New York Theatres & Producers; Producers Guild of America; chmn's council, the Caucus for Producers, Writers and Directors; Board of Directors, Allied Communications, Inc. Museum of Radio & Television in NYC, Hollywood Television & Radio Society, Acad. of TV Arts & Sciences, Natl. Acad. of Cable Programming. Received American Film Institute Charles Fries Producer of the Year Award.
PICTURE: God's Lonely Man, Living In Oblivion.
TELEVISION: 21 Hours at Munich, Dress Gray, Miracle on Ice, Combat High, Queenie, In the Custody of Strangers, The First Time, Baby Sister, Policewoman Centerfold, Obsessive Love, Invitation to Hell, Romance on the Orient Express, Hostage Flight. *Exec. prod.*: The Proud Men, Man Against the Mob, To Heal a Nation, Lady Mobster, Maybe Baby, Full Exposure: the Sex Tapes Scandal, Gore Vidal's Billy the Kid, Too Young to Die, The Great Los Angeles Earthquake, The Court-Martial of Jackie Robinson, White Hot: The Mysterious Murder of Thelma Todd, Survive the Savage Sea, Opposites Attract, Menu for Murder, Battling for Baby, Woman With a Past, Jackie Collins' Lady Boss, Danger Island, The Broken Chain, Beyond Suspicion, French Silk, The Corpse Had a Familiar Face, Robin Cook's Mortal Fear, Take Me Home Again, The Other Woman, Seduced and Betrayed, Robin Cook's Virus, The West Side Waltz, Crazy Horse, Robin Cook's Terminal, She Said No, Terror In the Family, My Son Is Innocent, Tornado!, Border Music, No One Would Tell, Robin Cook's Invasion, Nightscream, Mother Knows Best, Dying To Belong, Still Holding on: The Legend of Cadillac Jack, Two Came Back, Murder Live!, Holiday in Your Heart, Virtual Obsession, Don't Look Down, Too Rich: The Secret Life of Doris Duke, Fatal Error, Serial Predators.

W

WADLEIGH, MICHAEL
Director. b. Akron, OH, Sept. 24, 1941. e. Ohio State U., B.S., B.A., M.A., Columbia Medical Sch.
PICTURES: Woodstock (dir.), Wolfen (dir., co-s.p.), Out of Order, The Village at the End of the Universe (dir., s.p.).

WAGGONER, LYLE
Actor. b. Kansas City, KS, April 13, 1935. e. Washington U., St. Louis. Was salesman before becoming actor with road co. prod. of Li'l Abner. Formed own sales-promo co. to finance trip to CA for acting career in 1965. Did commercials, then signed by 20th-Fox for new-talent school.
PICTURES: Love Me Deadly, Journey to the Center of Time, Catalina Caper, Surf II, Murder Weapon, Dead Women in Lingerie, Gypsy Angels.
TELEVISION: *Series*: The Carol Burnett Show, The Jimmie Rodgers Show, It's Your Bet (host), Wonder Woman. *Movies*: Letters from Three Lovers, The New Original Wonder Woman, The Love Boat II, The Gossip Columnist, Gridlock.

WAGNER, JANE
Writer, Director, Producer. b. Morristown, TN, Feb. 26, 1935. e. attended Sch. of Visual Arts, NY. Worked as designer for Kimberly Clark, created Teach Me Read Me sheets for Fieldcrest.
THEATER: *B'way*: Appearing Nitely (dir., co-writer), The Search for Signs of Intelligent Life in the Universe (dir., writer; NY Drama Desk Award & Special NY Drama Critics Award), both starring Lily Tomlin.
PICTURES: Moment by Moment (s.p., dir.), The Incredible Shrinking Woman (s.p., exec. prod.), The Search for Signs of Intelligent Life in the Universe (s.p., exec. prod.).
TELEVISION: *Specials*: *Exec. prod./writer*: J.T. (Peabody Award), Lily (prod., co-writer; Emmy & WGA Awards, 1974), Lily Tomlin (also prod.; Emmy Award for writing, 1976), People (also prod.), Lily—Sold Out (co-writer; Emmy Award for producing, 1981), Lily for President? (co-writer), The Edith Ann Show , Edith Ann: A Few Pieces of the Puzzle, Edith Ann: Homeless Go Home, Edith Ann's Christmas: Just Say Noel (Peabody Award).

WAGNER, LINDSAY
Actress. b. Los Angeles, CA, June 22, 1949. Appeared in school plays in Portland, OR; studied singing and worked professionally with rock group. In 1968 went to L.A. Signed to Universal contract in 1971.
PICTURES: Two People, The Paper Chase, Second Wind, Nighthawks, High Risk, Martin's Day, Ricochet, Frog and Wombat, The Fourth Horseman.
TELEVISION: *Series*: The Bionic Woman (Emmy Award, 1977), Jessie, Peaceable Kingdom. *Guest*: The F.B.I., Owen Marshall: Counselor at Law, Night Gallery, The Bold Ones, Marcus Welby M.D., The Six Million Dollar Man. *Movies*: The Rockford Files (pilot), The Incredible Journey of Dr. Meg Laurel, The Two Worlds of Jennie Logan, Callie and Son, Memories Never Die, I Want to Live, Princess Daisy, Two Kinds of Love, Passions, This Child Is Mine, Child's Cry, Convicted, Young Again, Stranger in My Bed, The Return of the Six Million Dollar Man and the Bionic Woman, Student Exchange, Evil in Clear River, The Taking of Flight 847, Nightmare at Bitter Creek, From the Dead of Night, The Bionic Showdown: The Six-Million Dollar Man and the Bionic Woman, Shattered Dreams, Babies, Fire in the Dark, She Woke Up, Treacherous Crossing, To Be the Best, A Message From Holly, Nurses on the Line: The Crash of Flight 7, Danielle Steel's Once in a Lifetime, Bionic Ever After?, Fighting for My Daughter, Their, Second Chance, Contagious, Sins of Silence, A Mother's Instinct.

WAGNER, RAYMOND JAMES
Producer. b. College Point, NY, Nov. 3, 1925. e. Middlebury Coll., Williams Coll. Joined Young & Rubicam, Inc., as radio-TV commercial head in Hollywood, 1950-59. Head of pilot devt., Universal Studios, 1960-65. V.P. of prod. (features) for MGM, 1972-79. Presently indt. prod.
PICTURES: *Prod.*: Petulia, Loving (exec. prod.), Code of Silence, Rent-a-Cop, Hero and the Terror, Turner and Hooch, Run, Fifty Fifty.

WAGNER, ROBERT
Actor. b. Detroit, MI, Feb. 10, 1930. e. Saint Monica's H.S. m. actress Jill St. John. Signed to contract with 20th Century-Fox, 1950.
PICTURES: The Happy Years (debut, 1950), The Halls of Montezuma, The Frogmen, Let's Make It Legal, With a Song in My Heart, What Price Glory?, Stars and Stripes Forever, The Silver Whip, Titanic, Beneath the 12-Mile Reef, Prince Valiant, Broken Lance, White Feather, A Kiss Before Dying, The Mountain, Between Heaven and Hell, The True Story of Jesse James, Stopover Tokyo, The Hunters, In Love and War, Say One for Me, All the Fine Young Cannibals, Sail a Crooked Ship, The Longest Day, The War Lover, The Condemned of Altona, The Pink Panther, Harper, Banning, The Biggest Bundle of Them All, Don't Just Stand There, Winning, The Towering Inferno, Midway, The Concorde—Airport '79, Trail of the Pink Panther, Curse of the Pink Panther, I Am the Cheese, Delirious, The Player, Dragon: The Bruce Lee Story, Austin Powers: International Man of Mystery, Wild Things, Something to Believe In, No Vacancy, The Kidnapping of Chris Burden, Austin Powers: The Spy Who Shagged Me, Crazy in Alabama.
TELEVISION: *Series*: It Takes A Thief, Colditz (UK), Switch, Hart to Hart, Lime Street. *Movies*: How I Spent My Summer Vacation, City Beneath the Sea, The Cable Car Murder, Killer by Night, Madame Sin (also exec. prod.), Streets of San Francisco (pilot), The Affair, The Abduction of St. Anne, Switch (pilot), Death at Love House, Cat on a Hot Tin Roof, The Critical List, Hart to Hart (pilot), To Catch a King, There Must Be a Pony, Love Among Thieves, Windmills of the Gods, Indiscreet, This Gun for Hire, False Arrest, Daniel Steel's Jewels, Deep Trouble, Hart to Hart Returns (also co-exec. prod.), Hart to Hart: Home is Where the Hart Is, Hart to Hart: Crimes of the Hart, Hart to Hart: Old Friends Never Die, Parallel Lives, Hart to Hart: Secrets of the Heart, Fatal Error. *Mini-Series*: Pearl, Around the World in 80 Days, Heaven & Hell: North and South Book III.

WAHL, KEN
Actor, Producer. b. Chicago, IL, Feb. 14, 1957. No acting experience when cast in The Wanderers in 1978.
PICTURES: The Wanderers (debut, 1979), Fort Apache The Bronx, Race to the Yankee Zephyr, Jinxed, The Soldier, Purple Hearts, The Omega Syndrome, The Taking of Beverly Hills (also co-exec. prod.), The Favor, Back in the U.S.A.
TELEVISION: *Movies*: The Dirty Dozen: The Next Mission, The Gladiator, Search for Grace, Wise Guy. *Series*: Double Dare, Wiseguy.

WAITE, RALPH
Actor. b. White Plains, NY, June 22, 1929. e. Bucknell U.; Yale U. Social worker, publicity dir., assistant editor and minister before turning to acting. Founder of the Los Angeles Actors Theatre.
THEATER: *B'way*: Hogan's Goat, The Watering Place, Trial of Lee Harvey Oswald. *Off-B'way*: The Destiny of Me, The Young Man From Atlanta. *Regional*: Hometown Heroes.
PICTURES: Cool Hand Luke, A Lovely Way to Die, Last Summer, Five Easy Pieces, Lawman, The Grissom Gang, The Sporting Club, The Pursuit of Happiness, Chato's Land, The Magnificent Seven Ride, Trouble Man, Kid Blue, The Stone Killer, On the Nickel (also dir., prod., s.p.), Crash and Burn, The Bodyguard, Cliffhanger, Sioux City, Homeward Bound II: Lost in San Francisco.
TELEVISION: *Series*: The Waltons, The Mississippi. *Movies*: The Secret Life of John Chapman, The Borgia Stick, Red Alert, Ohms, Angel City, The Gentleman Bandit, A Wedding on Waltons Mountain, Mother's Day on Waltons Mountain, A Day for Thanks on Waltons Mountain, A Good Sport, Crime of Innocence, Red Earth White Earth, A Walton Thanksgiving Reunion, Sin and Redemption, A Season of Hope, A Walton Wedding. *Mini-Series*: Roots.

WAITE, RIC
Cinematographer. b. Sheboygan, WI, July 10, 1933. e. Univ. of CO. Photographed more than 40 movies-of-the-week for TV, 1979-83.
PICTURES: The Other Side of the Mountain (debut, 1975), Defiance, On the Nickel, The Long Riders, The Border, Tex, 48 Hrs., Class, Uncommon Valor, Footloose, Red Dawn, Volunteers, Summer Rental, Brewster's Millions, Cobra, Adventures in Babysitting, The Great Outdoors, Marked for Death, Out for Justice, Rapid Fire, On Deadly Ground, Last Stand at Saber River, Truth or Consequences—N.M.
TELEVISION: Nakia, The November Plan, Captains and the Kings (Emmy Award, 1977), Tail Gunner Joe (Emmy nom.), Huey P. Long (Emmy nom.), The Initiation of Sarah, And Baby Makes Six, Revenge of the Stepford Wives, Baby Comes Home, Dempsey, Police Story: Burnout, Scam, Last Light, Andersonville, Money Plays, Hope, Andersonville (Emmy nom.), Last Stand at Saber River.

WAITS, TOM
Singer, Composer, Actor. b. Pomona, CA, Dec. 7, 1949. Recorded numerous albums and received Acad. Award nom. for his song score of One from the Heart. Composed songs for On the Nickel, Streetwise, Paradise Alley, Wolfen, American Heart, Dead Man Walking, Night on Earth (score). Featured songs in Smoke and Things to Do in Denver When You're Dead.

Has starred in Chicago's Steppenwolf Theatre Co.'s Frank's Wild Years (also co-wrote, wrote the music) and Los Angeles Theatre Co.'s Demon Wine. Wrote songs and music for opera The Black Rider (1990). Co-wrote songs and music for opera Alice by Robert Wilson. Received Grammy Award for album, Bone Machine, 1992.
PICTURES: *As actor*: Paradise Alley, Poetry in Motion, The Outsiders, Rumble Fish, The Cotton Club, Down by Law (also music), Ironweed, Candy Mountain, Big Time (also co-s.p.), Cold Feet, Bearskin, Night On Earth (music only), The Two Jakes, Queens Logic, The Fisher King, At Play in the Fields of the Lord, Bram Stoker's Dracula, Short Cuts.

WAJDA, ANDRZEJ
Director, Writer. b. Suwalki, Poland, March 6, 1926. e. Fine Arts Academy, Krakow, Poland, 1945-48; High School of Cinematography, Lodz, Poland, 1950-52. 1940-43, worked as asst. in restoration of church paintings. 1942, joined Polish gov. in exile's A.K. (Home Army Resistance) against German occupation. 1950-52, directed shorts (While You Sleep; The Bad Boy, The Pottery of Ilzecka) as part of film school degree; 1954, asst. dir. to Aleksander Ford on 5 Boys from Barska Street. 1981, concentrated on theatrical projects in Poland and film prods. with non-Polish studios. 1983, gov. dissolved his Studio X film prod. group. 1984, gov. demanded Wajda's resignation as head of filmmakers' assoc. in order to continue org.'s existence. 1989, appt. artistic dir. of Teatr Powszechny, official Warsaw theater. Also leader of the Cultural Comm. of the Citizen's Committee. 1989, elected senator. Short films: While You Sleep, The Bad Boy, The Pottery of Ilza, I Go to the Sun. Received Honorary Academy Award, 1998.
PICTURES: *Dir.-Writer*: A Generation (debut, 1957), Kanal, Ashes and Diamonds, Lotna, Innocent Sorcerers, Samson, Siberian Lady Macbeth (Fury Is a Woman), Love at 20 (Warsaw Poland episode), Ashes, Gates to Paradise, Everything for Sale, Hunting Flies, Landscape After the Battle, The Wedding, Promised Land, Shadow Line, Man of Marble, Without Anesthetic, The Girls From Wilko, The Orchestra Conductor, Man of Iron (Golden Palm Award, Cannes, 1981), Danton, A Love in Germany, Chronicle of Love Affairs, The Possessed, Korczak, The Ring with a Crowned Eagle, Nastasja, Holy Week, Miss Nobody, Pan Nikt, Pan Tadeusz.
TELEVISION: Roly-Poly, The Birch Wood, Pilate and the Others, The Dead Class, November Night, Crime and Punishment.

WALD, MALVIN
Writer, Producer. b. New York, NY, Aug. 8, 1917. e. Brooklyn Coll., B.A., J.D. Woodland U. Coll. of Law; grad. work Columbia U., NYU, USC. Newspaper reporter, editor, publicist, social worker, radio actor. Screenplays and original stories for Columbia, 20th-Fox, UA, MGM, WB. U.S. Air Force tech. sgt., wrote 30 doc. films for film unit. Exec. prod., 20th Century Fox tv doc. unit, 1963-64. Writer-prod. U.S.I.A., 1964-65. Writer-prod., Ivan Tors Films, 1965-69. Prof., USC Sch. of Cinema, TV, 1956-96. Bd. of dir., Writer's Guild of America; 1983-85, Trustee, Writers Guild Foundation. Edit. bd. WGA Journal, 1996; editorial bd., Creative Screenwriting, 1996. Acad. of Motion Picture Arts and Sciences, co-author of book, Three Major Screenplays. Contributor to books, American Screenwriters, The Search for Reality, Close-Ups, Henry Miller: A Book of Tributes, Tales From the Casting Couch. Published s.p., Naked City. Consultant, Natl. Endowment for Humanities and Corp. for Public Broadcasting. Visiting professor, Southern Illinois Univ., Univ of PA. Pre-selection judge, Focus writing awards. Media & prod. consultant, Apache Mountain Spirit (PBS). Playwright, ANTA-West, Actors Alley, Rep. Theatre. Co-author, L.A. Press Club 40th Anniversary Show, 1987. Mag. articles published in Film Comment, Journal of Popular Film & TV, Journal of Writers Guild of America, American Heritage, Creative Screenwriting, Directors Guild Magazine, Hollywood: Then and Now, Writers Digest, Producers Guild Magazine, 1991-. Shorts: An Answer, Employees Only (Acad. Award nom.), Boy Who Owned a Melephant (Venice Children's Film Fest. gold medal), Unarmed in Africa, The Policeman, James Weldon Johnson, Me an Alcoholic?, Problem Solving, Managerial Control, UFO—Fact or Fiction? Was admitted to Producers Guild Hall of Fame, 1996.
PICTURES: The Naked City (Acad. Award nom., best story), Behind Locked Doors, The Dark Past, Ten Gentlemen from West Point, The Powers Girl, Two in a Taxi, Undercover Man, Outrage, On the Loose, Battle Taxi, Man on Fire, Al Capone, Venus in Furs, In Search of Historic Jesus, Legend of Sleepy Hollow, Mysteries From Beyond Earth.
TELEVISION: Many credits including Playhouse 90, Marilyn Monroe, Hollywood: The Golden Years, The Rafer Johnson Story, D-Day, Project: Man in Space, Tales of Hans Christian Andersen, John F. Kennedy, Biography of A Rookie, Alcoa-Goodyear Hour, Climax, Shirley Temple Storybook, Life of Riley, Peter Gunn, Perry Mason, Dobie Gillis, Combat, Moonport (U.S.I.A.; prod., writer), Daktari, (assoc. prod.) Primus, California Tomorrow (prod.), Mod Squad, Untamed World, Around the World of Mike Todd, The Billie Jean King Show, Life and Times of Grizzly Adams, Mark Twain's America, Greatest Heroes of the Bible, Littlest Hobo, Rich Little's You Asked For It, Hugh Hefner's Bunny Memories, Hollywood Commandoes, Visiting with Huell Howser.

WALKEN, CHRISTOPHER
Actor. r.n. Ronald Walkenb. Astoria, NY, Mar. 31, 1943. Began career in off-B'way play J.B. billed as Ronnie Walken. Appeared in Madonna video Bad Girl.
THEATER: *NY*: Best Foot Forward (Clarence Derwent Award), Kid Champion (Obie Award), High Spirits (B'way debut, 1964), The Lion in Winter (Clarence Derwent Award). The Rose Tattoo (Theatre World Award), Hurlyburly (B'way), Him (also author). NY Shakespeare Festival: Coriolanus, Othello.
PICTURES: The Anderson Tapes (debut, 1971), The Happiness Cage, Next Stop Greenwich Village, The Sentinel, Annie Hall, Roseland, The Deer Hunter (Academy Award, best supporting actor, 1978), Last Embrace, Heaven's Gate, The Dogs of War, Shoot the Sun Down, Pennies from Heaven, Brainstorm, The Dead Zone, A View to a Kill, At Close Range, Deadline, The Milagro Beanfield War, Biloxi Blues, Puss in Boots, Homeboy, Communion, King of New York, The Comfort of Strangers, McBain, All-American Murder, Batman Returns, Mistress, Le Grand Pardon, Day of Atonement, True Romance, Wayne's World 2, A Business Affair, Pulp Fiction, Search and Destroy, The Prophecy, The Addiction, Wild Side, Things to Do in Denver When You're Dead, Nick of Time, The Funeral, Last Man Standing, Touch, Excess Baggage, Suicide Kings, Mouse Hunt, Trance, The Prophecy II, New Rose Hotel, Illuminata, Antz (voice), Vendetta, The Prophecy III: The Ascent, The Opportunists, Kiss Toledo Goodbye, Blast from the Past, Sleepy Hollow, Inside Job, Joe Dirt, The Papp Project, The Affair of the Necklace.
TELEVISION: *Movies*: Sarah: Plain and Tall, Skylark, Scam, Sarah: Plain and Tall 3. *Special*: Who Am I This Time?

WALKER, E. CARDON
Executive. b. Rexburg, ID, Jan. 9, 1916. e. UCLA, B.A. 1938. Four years officer, U.S. Navy. Started with Walt Disney Productions, camera, story, unit dir. short subjects, budget control, 1938; headed adv. & pub., 1950; v.p. in chg. of adv. & sales, 1956; member bd. of dir. & exec. comm., 1960; v.p., mkt., 1965; exec. v.p. operations, 1967; exec. v.p. and COO, 1968; pres., 1971; pres. and CEO, 1976; named bd. chmn. & CEO, 1980; chmn. of exec. committee, 1983-84. Remains a bd. member.

WALKER, KATHRYN
Actress. b. Philadelphia, PA, Jan. 9. e. Wells Coll., Harvard. m. singer-songwriter James Taylor. Studied acting at London Acad. of Music and Dramatic Art on Fulbright Fellowship. Stage roles include part in Private Lives with Elizabeth Taylor and Richard Burton, and Wild Honey with Ian McKellen.
PICTURES: Slap Shot, Rich Kids, Neighbors, D.A.R.Y.L., Dangerous Game, Emma and Elvis.
TELEVISION: *Series*: Beacon Hill. *Movies*: The Winds of Kitty Hawk, Too Far to Go, FDR: The Last Year, A Whale for the Killing, Family Reunion, Special Bulletin, The Murder of Mary Phagan. *Mini-Series*: The Adams Chronicles (Emmy Award, 1976).

WALKER, SHIRLEY
Composer.
PICTURES: *Composer*: The End of August, Touched, Violated, Ghoulies, The Dungeonmaster, Batman (mus. conductor only), Immediate Family (mus. conductor only), Strike It Rich, Chicago Joe and the Showgirl, Nightbreed, Days of Thunder, Born to Ride, Memoirs of an Invisible Man, A League of Their Own (mus. conductor only), Batman: Mask of the Phantasm, It Came from Outer Space II, John Carpenter's Escape from L.A., Turbulence (also mus. conductor). *Orchestration*: The Accused, Black Rain, Arachnophobia, Defending Your Life, The Butcher's Wife, Backdraft (also mus. conductor), Johnny Mnemonic (also mus. conductor),
TELEVISION: *Movie*: The Flash, Majority Rule, Rasputin, (mus. conductor), The Garbage Picking Field Goal Kicking Philadelphia Phenomenon. *Series*: The Flash, Batman: The Animated Series, Space: Above and Beyond, Superman, Spawn. *Mini-series*: Asteroid.

WALLACE, MIKE
TV Commentator, Interviewer. b. Brookline, MA, May 9, 1918. e. U. of Michigan, 1939. Night Beat, WABD, N.Y., 1956; The Mike Wallace Interview, ABC, 1956-58; newspaper col., Mike Wallace Asks, N.Y. Post, 1957-58; News Beat, WNTA-TV, 1959-61; The Mike Wallace Interview, WNTA-TV, 1959-61; Biography, 1962; correspondent, CBS News, 1963, CBS Radio; Personal Closeup, Mike Wallace at Large; Co-editor, 60 Minutes (Emmy Awards, 1971, 1972, 1973), CBS News, Host, 20th Century, 1994.

WALLACH, ELI
Actor. b. Brooklyn, NY, Dec. 7, 1915. e. U. of TX. m. actress Anne Jackson. Capt. in Medical Admin. Corps during WWII. After college acting, appeared in summer stock. Charter member of the Actors Studio.
THEATER: Skydrift (B'way debut, 1945), Antony & Cleopatra, The Rose Tattoo (Tony Award, 1951), Mademoiselle Colombe, Camino Real, The Teahouse of August Moon (also London), Major Barbara, Rhinoceros, Luv, Twice Around the Park, Cafe Crown, The Price, In Persons (Off-B'way), The Flowering Peach, Visiting Mr. Green.
PICTURES: Baby Doll (debut, 1956; BFA Award), The Line Up, The Magnificent Seven, Seven Thieves, The Misfits, Hemingway's Adventures of A Young Man, How the West Was Won, The Victors, Act One, The Moonspinners, Kisses for My President, Lord Jim, Genghis Khan, How to Steal a Million, The Good the Bad and the Ugly, The Tiger Makes Out, How to Save a Marriage and Ruin Your Life, MacKenna's Gold, A Lovely Way to Die, Ace High, The Brain, Zigzag, The People Next Door, The Angle Levine, The Adventures of Gerard, Romance of a Horse Thief, Cinderella Liberty, Crazy Joe, Stateline Motel, Don't Turn the Other Cheek, The Sentinel, Nasty Habits, The Deep, The Domino Principle, Girlfriends, Movie Movie, Circle of Iron, Firepower, Winter Kills, The Hunter, The Salamander, Sam's Son, Tough Guys, Nuts, Funny, The Two Jakes, The Godfather Part III, Article 99, Mistress, Night and the City, Two Much, The Associate, Keeping the Faith.
TELEVISION: *Series*: Our Family Honor. *Guest*: Studio One, Philco Playhouse, Playhouse 90, The Poppy Is Also a Flower (Emmy Award, 1967), Law & Order. *Movies*: Cold Night's Death, Indict and Convict, Seventh Avenue, The Pirate, Fugitive Family, Pride of Jesse Halam, Skokie, The Wall, Anatomy of an Illness, Murder: By Reason of Insanity, Something in Common, Executioner's Song, Christopher Columbus, Embassy, The Impossible Spy, Vendetta: Secrets of a Mafia Bride, Legacy of Lies, Teamster Boss: The Jackie Presser Story, Vendetta 2: The New Mafia.

WALLACH, GEORGE
Producer, Writer, Director. b. New York, NY, Sept. 25, 1918. e. SUNY-Westbury. Actor in theater & radio 1936-45. U.S. Navy 1942-45. Supvr. radio-TV Div. of American Theatrical Wing, 1946-48. Dir., WNEW, 1946-48. Prod./dir., Wendy Barrie Show, 1948-49. Prod.-dir. for WNBC-WNBT, 1950; dir., news, spec. events WNBT-WNBC, 1951-52; prod. mgr., NBC Film Div. 1953-56, appt. TV officer, U.S.I.A., 1957. Film-TV officer American Embassy, Bonn, 1961; Film-TV officer American Embassy, Tehran, 1965-66. MoPix Prod. Officer, JUSPAO, American Embassy, Saigon, 1966. Prod., dir.,writer, Greece Today, 1967-68. Exec. prod.,dir., George Wallach Productions, spec. doc., travel, and industrial films. Chmn., Film-TV Dept., N.Y. Institute of Photography, 1968-75. Prof. film-TV-radio, Brooklyn Coll., 1975-80. Dir., special projects, DGA 1978-88. Presently: intl. rep. for Denver Film Festival; U.S. Contact for Moscow Film Festival; U.S. prod. for A Native of Beijing in NY, a series of 20 1 hr. programs for Beijing TV.
PICTURES: It Happened in Havana, Bwana Devil.
TELEVISION: *NBC producer*: Inner Sanctum, The Falcon, His Honor Homer Bell, Watch the World. *Dir.*: Wanted.

WALLMAN, KATHLEEN
Attorney. e. Catholic U. of America, BA; Georgetown U, MS, JD. Clerked for various judges on the U.S. Court of Appeals, District of Columbia & Federal Circuits, 1984-86. Became assoc., Arnold & Porter, 1987-92; partner, 1992-94. In 1994, became Deputy Chief, FCC Cable Services Bureau. Chief, FCC Common Carrier Bureau, 1994-95. Deputy Counsel to the President, 1995-97. Deputy Asst. to the Pres. for Economic Policy/Chief of Staff, National Economic Council, 1997.

WALSH, DYLAN
Actor. Raised in Africa, Indonesia, India, Washington D.C. e. Univ. of VA. On D.C. stage with Arena Stage and Studio Theatre, Heritage Rep. Co. Appearing in A Midsummer Night's Dream, Curse of the Starving Class, Romeo & Juliet, Death of a Salesman.
PICTURES: Where the Heart Is, Betsy's Wedding, Arctic Blue, Nobody's Fool, Congo, Eden, Changing Habits, Men.
TELEVISION: *Series:* Gabriel's Fire, Brooklyn South. *Guest*: Kate and Allie. *Movies:* Telling Secrets, Radio Inside.

WALSH, M. EMMET
Actor. r.n. Michael Emmet Walsh. b. Ogdensburg, NY, Mar. 22, 1935. e. Clarkson Col. (B.B.A., 1958), American Academy of Dramatic Arts (1959-61).
THEATER: *B'way*: Does the Tiger Wear a Necktie?, That Championship Season. *Off-B'way*: Shepherds of the Shelf, The Old Glory, The Outside Man, Death of the Well Loved Boy, Three From Column 'A', Are You Now or Have You Ever Been, Marathon '93. Extensive summer stock and regional theatre.
PICTURES: End of the Road, Midnight Cowboy, Alice's Restaurant, Stiletto, Loving, They Might Be Giants, The Traveling Executioner, Little Big Man, Escape from the Planet of the Apes, Get to Know Your Rabbit, The Gambler, The Prisoner of 2nd Avenue, What's Up Doc?, Kid Blue, The Fish That Saved Pittsburgh, Serpico, Mikey and Nicky, Cold Turkey, At Long Last Love, Nickelodeon, Bound for Glory, Airport '77, Slap Shot, Straight Time, The Jerk, Raise the Titanic, Brubaker, Ordinary People, Reds, Back Roads, Fast-Walking, The Escape Artist, Cannery Row, Blade Runner, Silkwood, Blood Simple, Scandalous, (Raw) Courage, Grandview USA, The Pope of Greenwich Village, Back to School, Critters, Missing in Action, Fletch, Wildcats, The Best of Times, Raising Arizona, Harry and the Hendersons, The Milagro Beanfield War, No Man's Land, Sunset, War Party, Clean and Sober, Catch Me If You Can, Thunderground, Sundown: The Vampire in Retreat, Chattahoochee, Red Scorpion, The Mighty Quinn, Narrow Margin, Killer Image, The Naked Truth, White Sands, Equinox, Wilder Napalm, The Music of Chance, Bitter Harvest, Cops and Robbersons, Relative Fear, The Glass Shield, Probable Cause, Dead Badge, Camp Nowhere, Panther, Free Willy 2: The Adventure Home, Criminal Hearts, Portraits of a Killer, Albino Alligator, The Killing Jar, A Time to Kill, Romeo & Juliet, Retroactive, Carrot Top–Chairman of the Board, My Best Friend's Wedding, Legal Tender, Twilight, Me and Will, Iron Giant, Jack of Hearts, Eyeball Eddie, Wild Wild West, Random Hearts (cameo).
TELEVISION: *Series*: The Sandy Duncan Show, Dear Detective, Unsub. *Movies*: Sarah T.—Portrait of a Teenage Alcoholic, Crime Club, Invasion of Johnson County, Red Alert, Superdome, A Question of Guilt, No Other Love, The Gift, Skag, City in Fear, High Noon Part II, Hellinger's Law, Night Partners, The Deliberate Stranger, Resting Place, Broken Vows, Hero in the Family, The Abduction of Kari Swenson, Murder Ordained, Brotherhood of the Rose, Love and Lies, Fourth Story, Wild Card, Four Eyes and Six-Guns, From the Mixed-Up Files of Mrs. Basil E. Frankweiler, The Lottery, Dogs, Monster. *Mini-Series*: The French-Atlantic Affair, East of Eden. *Guest*: Julia, Amy Prentiss, The Jimmy Stewart Show, Bonanza, All in the Family, Rockford Files, Baretta, The Waltons, Nichols, Starsky & Hutch, Amazing Stories, Twilight Zone, The Flash, Jackie Thomas Show, Tales From the Crypt, Home Improvement, The Outer Limits, The X Files. *Pilot*: Silver Fox.

WALSTON, RAY
Actor. b. New Orleans, LA, Nov. 2, 1918. Stage debut in Houston, 1936. To NY where he appeared on stage in South Pacific, The Front Page, Me and Juliet, Damn Yankees (Tony Award, 1956).
PICTURES: Kiss Them For Me (debut, 1957), South Pacific, Damn Yankees, Say One for Me, Tall Story, The Apartment, Portrait in Black, Convicts Four, Wives and Lovers, Who's Minding the Store?, Kiss Me Stupid, Caprice, Paint Your Wagon, The Sting, Silver Streak, The Happy Hooker Goes to Washington, Popeye, Galaxy of Terror, Fast Times at Ridgemont High, O'Hara's Wife, Private School, Johnny Dangerously, RAD, From the Hip, O.C. and Stiggs, A Man of Passion, Blood Relations, Saturday the 14th Strikes Back, Paramedics, Ski Patrol, Blood Salvage, Popcorn, The Player, Of Mice and Men, House Arrest, Early Bird Special, My Favorite Martian.
TELEVISION: *Series*: My Favorite Martian, Stop Susan Williams (Cliffhangers), Silver Spoons, Fast Times, Picket Fences (Emmy Awards, 1995 & 1996). *Guest*: You Are There, Producers Showcase, There Shall Be No Night, Studio One, Playhouse 90, Oh Madeline, Crash Course, Parker Lewis Can't Lose. *Movies*: Institute for Revenge, The Kid With the Broken Halo, The Fall of the House of Usher, This Girl for Hire, The Jerk Too, Amos, Red River, I Know My First Name Is Steven, One Special Victory, Tricks, The Westing Game, Addams Family Reunion, Swing Vote. *Mini-Series*: Stephen King's The Stand.

WALTER, JESSICA
Actress. b. Brooklyn, NY, Jan. 31, 1944. m. actor Ron Leibman. e. H.S. of the Performing Arts. Studied at Bucks County Playhouse and Neighborhood Playhouse. Many TV performances plus lead in series, For the People. Broadway debut in Advise and Consent, 1961. Also, Photo Finish (Clarence Derwent Award), Night Life, A Severed Head, Rumors.
PICTURES: Lilith (debut, 1964), The Group, Grand Prix, Bye Bye Braverman, Number One, Play Misty for Me, Goldengirl, Going Ape, Spring Fever, The Flamingo Kid, Tapeheads, Ghost in the Machine, PCU, Dark Goddess, Slums of Beverly Hills.
TELEVISION: *Series*: For the People, Love of Life, Amy Prentiss (Emmy Award, 1975), Bare Essence, Aaron's Way, Dinosaurs (voice), The Round Table, One Life to Live, Oh Baby. *Movies*: The Immortal (pilot), Three's a Crowd, They Call It Murder, Women in Chains, Home for the Holidays, Hurricane, Having Babies, Victory at Entebbe, Black Market Baby, Wild and Wooly, Dr. Strange, Secrets of Three Hungry Wives,

Vampire, She's Dressed to Kill, Miracle on Ice, Scruples, Thursday's Child, The Return of Marcus Welby M.D., The Execution, Killer in the Mirror, Leave of Absence, Mother Knows Best, Doomsday Rock. *Mini-Series*: Wheels. *Guest:* Just Shoot Me.

WALTER, TRACEY
Actor. b. Jersey City, NJ, Nov. 25.
PICTURES: Goin' South, Blue Collar, Hardcore, The Hunter, The Hand, Raggedy Man, Honkytonk Man, Timerider, Rumble Fish, Conan the Destroyer, Repo Man, At Close Range, Something Wild, Malone, Mortuary Academy, Married to the Mob, Under the Boardwalk, Out of the Dark, Batman, Homer and Eddie, Young Guns II, The Two Jakes, Pacific Heights, The Silence of the Lambs, City Slickers, Delusion, Amos and Andrew, Philadelphia, Mona Must Die, Destiny Turns on the Radio, Wild America, Road to Ruin, Dorothy Day, Junior, Amanda, Larger Than Life, Matilda, Desperate Measures, Playing God, Kiss the Girls, Beloved, Mighty Joe Young.
TELEVISION: *Series*: Best of the West, On the Air, Nash Bridges. *Movies*: Ride With the Wind, In the Line of Duty: Kidnapped, Buffalo Girls, Bill On His Own, Mad Bull, Out of this World, Tell Me No Secrets, The Devil's Child.

WALTERS, BARBARA
Broadcast Journalist. b. Boston, MA, Sept. 25, 1931. e. Sarah Lawrence Coll. Daughter of Latin Quarter nightclub impressario Lou Walters. Began working in TV after graduation. Joined The Today Show in 1961 as writer-researcher, making occasional on-camera appearances. In 1963, became full-time on camera. In April, 1974, named permanent co-host. Also hosted own synd. prog., Not for Women Only. In 1976, joined ABC-TV Evening News, (host, 1976-78), correspondent World News Tonight (1978); corresp. 20/20 (1979-present). Host of The Barbara Walters Specials (1979-present). Author: How to Talk with Practically Anybody About Practically Anything (1970). Recipient of numerous awards including Emmy, Media, Peabody. Named one of women most admired by American People in 1982 & -84 Gallup Polls. Inducted into the Television Academy Hall of Fame, 1990. 1994, co-anchor of Turning Point.

WALTERS, JULIE
Actress. b. Birmingham, England, Feb. 22, 1950. Trained for 2 years to be a nurse before studying drama at Manchester Polytechnic, followed by year at Granada's Stables Theatre. Joined Everyman Theatre, Liverpool. Also toured Dockland pubs with songs, dance and imitations.
THEATER: Breezeblock Park, Funny Perculiar, The Glad Hand, Good Fun, Educating Rita, Jumpers, Fool for Love, When I Was a Girl I Used to Scream and Shout, Frankie and Johnnie in the Claire de Lune, Macbeth, Having a Ball, The Rose Tattoo, Jumpers, Fool for Love, When I Was a Girl I Used to Scream and Shout, Frankie and Johnny.
PICTURES: Educating Rita (debut, 1983; Acad. Award nom.), She'll Be Wearing Pink Pyjamas, Car Trouble, Personal Services, Prick Up Your Ears, Buster, Mack the Knife, Killing Dad, Stepping Out, Wide Eyed and Legless, The Summer House, The Wedding Gift, Just Like a Woman, Sister My Sister.
TELEVISION: Unfair Exchanges, Talent, Nearly a Happy Ending, Family Man, Happy Since I Met You, The Secret Diary of Adrian Mole (series), Wood and Walters (series), Say Something Happened, Intensive Care, The Boys from the Black Stuff, Talking Heads, Victoria Wood As Seen on TV (series & special), The Birthday Party, Her Big Chance, Nearly a Happy Ending, Julie Walters & Friends (special), GBH (series), The All-Day Breakfast Show (special).

WALTERS, MELORA
Actress.
PICTURES: Dead Poets Society, Underground, Beethoven, Twenty Bucks, Ed Wood, Cabin Boy, America's Deadliest Home Video, All Tied Up, Eraser, American Strays, Hard Eight, Boogie Nights, Los Locos, Magnolia, Desert Saints, Speaking of Sex.
TELEVISION: *Movies:* How to Murder a Millionaire, Telling Secrets, Dead Man's Revenge, Midnight Run for Your Life. *Series:* Roseanne, L.A. Doctors. *Guest:* NYPD Blue, Seinfeld, The Wonder Years, Murphy Brown, Walker, Texas Ranger, Bakersfield, P.D., The Marshal, Picket Fences, Dream On, Nash Bridges.

WANG, WAYNE
Director. b. Hong Kong, 1949. e. came to U.S. to study photography at College of Arts and Crafts, Oakland, CA. m. actress Cora Miao. With a Master's Degree in film and television, returned to Hong Kong. Worked on TV comedy series. First dir. work, as asst. dir. for Chinese sequences of Golden Needle. First film was A Man, A Woman and a Killer. Won grant from AFI and National Endowment for the Arts, used to finance Chan is Missing (1982) which cost $22,000.
PICTURES: Chan is Missing (also s.p., editor, prod.), Dim Sum: A Little Bit of Heart (also prod., story), Slam Dance, Eat a Bowl of Tea, Life is Cheap... But Toilet Paper is Expensive (also exec. prod., story), The Joy Luck Club, Smoke, Blue in the Face (also co-s.p.), Chinese Box (also prod., s.p.), Anywhere But Here, Center of the World.

WARBECK, STEPHEN
Composer.
PICTURES: Sister My Sister, Skallagrigg, O Mary This London, Nervous Energy, Brothers in Trouble, Different for Girls, Element of Doubt, Mrs. Brown, My Son the Fanatic, Shakespeare in Love, Heart, Mystery Men, Fanny and Elvis, Billy Elliot, Quills, Captain Corelli's Mandolin.
TELEVISION: *Movies:* Prime Suspect, Femme Fatale, The Mother, The Changeling, Bambino mio, Prime Suspect 4: The Lost Child, Prime Suspect 4: inner Circles, Devil's Advocate, Truth or Dare, Bright Hair, The Student Prince, A Christmas Carol. *Mini-series:* Prime Suspect 2, Prime Suspect 3, Prime Suspect 5: Errors of Judgement.

WARD, DAVID S.
Writer, Director. b. Providence, RI, Oct. 24, 1947. Raised in Cleveland. e. Pomona Col. (BA), UCLA (MFA).
PICTURES: *Writer*: Steelyard Blues, The Sting (Academy Award, 1973), Cannery Row (also dir.), The Milagro Beanfield War (co-s.p.), Major League (also dir.), King Ralph (also dir.), Sleepless in Seattle (co-s.p.; Acad. Award nom.), The Mask of Zorro. *Director*: Major League II (also s.p., prod.), Down Periscope, The Program (also s.p.), The Best Man (also s.p.).

WARD, FRED
Actor. b. San Diego, CA, 1943. Raised in Louisiana and Texas. Studied at Herbert Berghof Studio. Moved to Rome to work in experimental theatre. Returned to U.S. to appear on San Fransico stage with Sam Shepard's Magic Theatre in Inacoma and Angel City. Additional stage work in The Glass Menagerie, One Flew Over the Cuckoo's Nest, Domino Courts, Simpatico.
PICTURES: Escape From Alcatraz (debut, 1979), Tilt, Carny, Southern Comfort, Timerider, The Right Stuff, Silkwood, Uncommon Valor, Swing Shift, Uforia, Secret Admirer, Remo Williams: The Adventure Begins, Off Limits, Big Business, The Prince of Pennsylvania, Tremors, Miami Blues (also co-exec. prod.), Henry and June, Thunderheart, The Player, Bob Roberts, The Dark Wind, Equinox, Short Cuts, Naked Gun 33 1/3: The Final Insult, Two Small Bodies, The Blue Villa, Chain Reaction, Best Men, Dangerous Beauty, Circus, All the Fine Lines.
TELEVISION: *Movies*: Belle Starr, Noon Wine, Florida Straits, Cast a Deadly Spell, Backtrack, Four Eyes and Six-Guns, ...First Do No Harm, Invasion: Earth. *Special*: Noon Wine (Amer. Playhouse).

WARD, RACHEL
Actress. b. London, 1957. m. actor Bryan Brown. Top fashion and TV commercial model before becoming actress. Studied acting with Stella Adler and Robert Modica. On stage in Sydney in A Doll's House, Hopping to Byzantium.
PICTURES: Night School (debut, 1981), The Final Terror, Sharky's Machine, Dead Men Don't Wear Plaid, Against All Odds, The Good Wife, Hotel Colonial, How to Get Ahead in Advertising, After Dark My Sweet, Christopher Columbus: The Discovery, Wide Sargasso Sea, The Ascent.
TELEVISION: *Mini-Series*: The Thorn Birds, Shadow of the Cobra (U.K.). *Movies*: Christmas Lillies of the Field, Fortress, And the Sea Will Tell, Black Magic, Double Jeopardy, My Stepson My Lover, Seasons of Love. *Series:* In the Name of Love.

WARD, SELA
Actress. b. Meridian, MS, July 11, 1956.
PICTURES: The Man Who Loved Women, Rustler's Rhapsody, Nothing in Common, Steel Justice, Hello Again, The Fugitive, My Fellow Americans, The Reef, 54, Runaway Bride.
TELEVISION: *Series:* Emerald Point N.A.S., Sisters (Emmy Award, 1994), Once and Again. *Movies:* Almost Golden: The Jessica Savitch Story (Cable Ace Award, 1996), The Haunting of Sarah Hardy, Bridesmaids, Killer Rules, Double Jeopardy, Rescuers: Two Women, Passion's Way.

WARD, SIMON
Actor. b. London, England, Oct. 19, 1941. Ent. ind. 1964.
PICTURES: If... (debut, 1969), Frankenstein Must Be Destroyed, I Start Counting, Quest for Love, Young Winston, Hitler—The Last Ten Days, The Three Musketeers, The Four Musketeers, Deadly Strangers. Aces High, Children of Rage, Battle Flag, The Chosen, Dominique, Zulu Dawn, La Sabina, The Monster Club, L'Etincelle, Supergirl, Leave All Fair, Double X, Wuthering Heights.

TELEVISION: Spoiled, Chips with Everything, The Corsican Brothers, All Creatures Great and Small, Dracula, Valley Forge, The Last Giraffe (Raising Daisy Rothschild), Around the World in 80 Days.

WARD, VINCENT
Director, Writer. b. New Zealand, 1956. e. Ilam Sch. of Art. At 21 dir. & co-wrote short film A State of Siege (Hugo Award, Chicago Film Fest.)
PICTURES: In Spring One Plants Alone (Silver Hugo, Chicago Film Fest.), Vigil (Grand Prix Awards, Madrid & Prades Film Fests), The Navigator (Australian Film Awards for Best Picture & Director), Alien^3 (story only), Map of the Human Heart, Leaving Las Vegas (actor only), The Shot (actor only), One Night Stand (actor only), What Dreams May Come.

WARDEN, JACK
Actor. r.n. Jack Warden Lebzelter. b. Newark, NJ, Sept. 18, 1920. Started with Margo Jones theatre in Dallas (rep. co.).
THEATER: *B'way*: Golden Boy, Sing Me No Lullaby, Very Special Baby, Cages (Obie Award), A View from the Bridge, The Man in the Glass Booth, The Body Beautiful. *Repertory*: Twelfth Night, She Stoops to Conquer, The Importance of Being Earnest, Summer and Smoke, The Taming of the Shrew, etc.
PICTURES: You're in the Navy Now (U.S.S. Teakettle; debut, 1951), The Frogmen, The Man With My Face, Red Ball Express, From Here to Eternity, Edge of the City, 12 Angry Men, The Bachelor Party, Darby's Rangers, Run Silent Run Deep, The Sound and the Fury, That Kind of Woman, Wake Men When It's Over, Escape From Zahrain, Donovan's Reef, The Thin Red Line, Blindfold, Bye Bye Braverman, The Sporting Club, Summertree, Who Is Harry Kellerman?, Welcome to the Club, Billy Two Hats, The Man Who Loved Cat Dancing, The Apprenticeship of Duddy Kravitz, Shampoo (Acad. Award nom.), All the President's Men, The White Buffalo, Heaven Can Wait (Acad. Award nom.), Death on the Nile, The Champ, Dreamer, Beyond the Poseidon Adventure, And Justice for All, Being There, Used Cars, The Great Muppet Caper, Chu Chu and the Philly Flash, Carbon Copy, So Fine, The Verdict, Crackers, The Aviator, September, The Presidio, Everybody Wins, Problem Child, Problem Child 2, Passed Away, Night and the City, Toys, Guilty As Sin, Bullets Over Broadway, While You Were Sleeping, Things to Do in Denver When You're Dead, Mighty Aphrodite, Ed, The Island of Bird Street, Chairman of the Board, Bulworth, Dirty Work, A Dog of Flanders.
TELEVISION: *Series*: Mr. Peepers, Norby, The Asphalt Jungle, The Wackiest Ship in the Army, N.Y.P.D., Jigsaw John, The Bad News Bears, Crazy Like a Fox. *Guest*: Philco Goodyear Producer's Showcase, Kraft, Norm. *Movies*: The Face of Fear, Brian's Song (Emmy Award, 1972), What's a Nice Girl Like You...?, Man on a String, Lt. Schuster's Wife, Remember When, The Godchild, Journey From Darkness, They Only Come Out at Night, Raid on Entebbe, Topper, A Private Battle, Hobson's Choice, Helen Keller: The Miracle Continues, Hoover vs. The Kennedys, The Three Kings, Dead Solid Perfect, Judgment, Problem Child 3: Junior in Love. *Mini-Series*: Robert Kennedy and His Times, A.D.

WARNER, DAVID
Actor. b. Manchester, England, July 29, 1941. e. Royal Acad. of Dramatic Art. Made London stage debut in Tony Richardson's version of A Midsummer Night's Dream (1962). Four seasons with Royal Shakespeare Co. Theater includes Afore Night Comes, The Tempest, The Wars of the Roses, The Government Inspector, Twelfth Night, I Claudius.
PICTURES: Tom Jones (debut, 1963), Morgan!, The Deadly Affair, A King's Story (voice), Work Is a Four Letter Word, A Midsummer's Night Dream, The Bofors Gun, The Fixer, The Seagull, Michael Kolhaus, The Ballad of Cable Hogue, Perfect Friday, Straw Dogs, A Doll's House, From Beyond the Grave, Little Malcolm (and His Struggle Against the Eunuch), Mr. Quilp, The Omen, Providence, The Disappearance, Cross of Iron, Silver Bears, Nightwing, The Concorde—Airport '79, Time After Time, The 39 Steps, The Island, The French Lieutenant's Woman, Time Bandits, Tron, The Man With Two Brains, The Company of Wolves, Hansel and Gretel, My Best Friend Is a Vampire, Waxworks, Mr. North, Silent Night, Office Party, Hanna's War, Pulse Pounders, Keys to Freedom, Star Trek V: The Final Frontier, S.P.O.O.K.S., Tripwire, Mortal Passions, Teenage Mutant Ninja Turtles II: The Secret of the Ooze, Star Trek VI: The Undiscovered Country, Blue Tornado, Drive, Unnameable II, Dark at Noon, In the Mouth of Madness.
TELEVISION: *Movies*: S.O.S. Titantic, Desperado, A Christmas Carol, Hitler's SS—Portrait in Evil, Perry Mason: The Case of the Poisoned Pen, The Secret Life of Ian Fleming, Cast a Deadly Spell, The House on Sycamore Street, Perry Mason: The Case of the Skin-Deep Scandal, John Carpenter Presents Body Bags, Danielle Steel's Zoya. *Mini-Series*: Holocaust, Masada (Emmy Award, 1981), Marco Polo, Wild Palms. *Specials*: Love's Labour's Lost, Uncle Vanya.

WARNER, JULIE
Actress. b. New York, NY. e. Brown Univ., B.A. in Theatre Arts.
PICTURES: Doc Hollywood (debut, 1991), Mr. Saturday Night, Indian Summer, The Puppet Masters, Tommy Boy, White Lies, Wedding Bell Blues.
TELEVISION: *Series*: Pride and Joy. *Guest*: Star Trek: The Next Generation, 21 Jump Street, The Outsiders.

WARNER, MALCOLM-JAMAL
Actor. b. Jersey City, NJ, Aug. 18, 1970. Raised in Los Angeles.
THEATER: Three Ways Home (off-B'way debut, 1988).
PICTURE: Drop Zone (debut, 1994), Restaurant.
TELEVISION: *Series*: The Cosby Show (also dir. episode), Here and Now, Magic School Bus (voice), Malcolm & Eddie. *Movies*: The Father Clements Story, Mother's Day, Tyson. *Special*: Kids Killing Kids (host).

WARREN, GENE
Executive. b. Denver, CO, Aug. 12, 1916. Pres. of Excelsior Prods., prod. co. specializing in special effects and animation. Has headed 2 other cos. of similar nature over past 20 years, functioning at various times as prod., dir., studio prod. head and writer. Prod., dir., of following shorts: The Tool Box, Suzy Snowflake, Santa and the Three Dwarfs, Land of the Midnight Sun and these documentaries/training films: Mariner I, Mariner III, Apollo, U.S. Navy titles. Special effects on theatrical features incl: Black Sunday, tom thumb, The Time Machine (Academy Award, 1960), The Wonderful World of the Brothers Grimm, 7 Faces of Dr. Lao, The Power, Legend of Hillybilly John. TV series include: The Man from Atlantis, Land of the Lost, Star Trek, Outer Limits, Twilight Zone, Mission Impossible. *TV Movie*: Satan's School for Girls.

WARREN, JENNIFER
Actress, Producer. b. New York, NY, Aug. 12, 1941. e. U. of Wisconsin, Madison, B.A. Graduate work at Wesleyan U. Studied acting with Uta Hagen at HB Studios. As part of AFI Women's Directing Workshop, directed Point of Departure, short film which received Cine Golden Eagle and Aspen Film Festival Awards. Formed Tiger Rose Productions, indep. film-TV prod. co., 1988. Exec. prod., You Don't Have to Die (Acad. Award, doc. short, 1989). Dir., The Beans of Egypt Maine, 1994. Recipient of 2 Spirit Awards.
THEATER: Scuba Duba (off-B'way debut, 1967), 6 RMS RIV VU (Theatre World Award), Harvey, P.S., Your Cat Is Dead, B'way: Saint Joan, Volpone, Henry V (Guthrie Theatre).
PICTURES: Night Moves (debut, 1975), Slapshot, Another Man Another Chance, Ice Castles, Fatal Beauty.
TELEVISION: *Series*: Paper Dolls. *Pilots*: Double Dare, Knights of the Kitchen Table. *Guest*: Kojak. *Movies*: Banjo Hackett: Roamin' Free, Shark Kill, First You Cry, Steel Cowboy, Champions: A Love Story, Angel City, The Choice, The Intruder Within, Freedom, Paper Dolls (pilot), Confessions of a Married Man, Amazons, Full Exposure: The Sex Tape Scandal. *Mini-Series*: Celebrity.

WARREN, LESLEY ANN
Actress. b. New York, NY, Aug. 16, 1946. Studied acting under Lee Strasberg. Big break came in Rodgers and Hammerstein's 1964 tv prod. of Cinderella, where she was seen by Disney scout. Broadway debut in 110 in the Shade (1963, Theatre World Award), followed by Drat! The Cat! Appeared in Aerosmith video Janie's Got a Gun.
PICTURES: The Happiest Millionaire (debut, 1967), The One and Only Genuine Original Family Band, Pickup on 101, Harry and Walter Go to New York, Victor/Victoria (Acad. Award nom.), A Night in Heaven, Songwriter (Golden Globe nom.), Choose Me, Race to the Yankee Zephyr, Clue, Burglar, Cop, Worth Winning, Life Stinks, Pure Country, Color of Night, Bird of Prey, The First Man, Going All the Way, Love Kills, Twin Falls Idaho, Trixie, Teaching Mrs. Tingle, Spoken in Silence, The Limey, All of It.
TELEVISION: *Series*: Mission: Impossible. *Mini-Series*: 79 Park Avenue (Golden Globe Winner), Pearl, Evergreen, Family of Spies, Joseph. *Movies*: Seven in Darkness, Love Hate Love, Assignment Munich, The Daughters of Joshua Cabe, The Letters, The Legend of Valentino, Betrayal, Portrait of a Stripper, Beulah Land, Portrait of a Showgirl, A Fight for Jenny, Apology, Baja Oklahoma (Ace Award nom.), A Seduction in Travis County, In Sickness and in Health, Willing to Kill: The Texas Cheerleader Story, A Mother's Revenge, Family of Spies (Emmy nom.), Murderous Intent, 27 Wagons Full of Cotton, Natural Enemy. *Specials*: The Saga of Sonora, It's a Bird It's a Plane It's Superman, A Special Eddie Rabbit, The Dancing Princess, 27 Wagons Full of Cotton (Ace Award nom.), Willie Nelson: Big Six-O.

WARRICK, RUTH
Actress. b. St. Joseph, MO, June 29, 1916. Started as radio singer. Autobiography: The Confessions of Phoebe Tyler (1980).

PICTURES: Citizen Kane (debut, 1941), Obliging Young Lady, The Corsican Brothers, Journey Into Fear, Forever and a Day, Perilous Holiday, The Iron Major, Secret Command, Mr. Winkle Goes to War, Guest in the House, China Sky, Song of the South, Driftwood, Daisy Kenyon, Arch of Triumph, The Great Dan Patch, Make Believe Ballroom, Three Husbands, Let's Dance, One Too Many, Roogie's Bump, Ride Beyond Vengeance, The Great Bank Robbery, Deathmask, The Returning, The Battle Over Citizen Kane.
TELEVISION: *Movie*: Peyton Place—The Next Generation. *Series*: Peyton Place, All My Children. *Guest*: Studio One, Robert Montgomery Presents, Lux Star Playhouse. *Special*: Sometimes I Don't Love My Mother.

WARZEL, PETER C.
Executive. b. Buffalo, NY, May 31, 1952. e. Univ. of Rochester, Canisius Col. Joined Tele-Communications Inc., 1982, also serving as v.p. of industrial relations at Community Tele-Communications Inc., a TCI subsidiary. 1988, became sr. v.p. of United Artists Entertainment Co.; 1990, promoted to pres. & CEO of United Artists Theatre Circuit. 1992, was party to management buy-out of UATC as pres. & COO.

WASCO, DAVID
Production Designer.
PICTURES: Goldy: The Last of the Golden Bears, Smooth Talk, Student Confidential, Stacking, Rachel River, The Wash, Twister, In A Shallow Grave, Reservoir Dogs, Where the River Flows North, Killing Zoe, Pulp Fiction, Oleanna, Bottle Rocket, Touch, She's So Lovely, Jackie Brown, Rushmore, Bounce, The Heist.
TELEVISION: Traveling Man, A Life in the Theater.

WASHBURN, DERIC
Writer. b. Buffalo, NY. e.Harvard U., English lit. Has written number of plays, including The Love Nest and Ginger Anne.
PICTURES: Silent Running (co-s.p.), The Deer Hunter (co-s.p.), The Border, Extreme Prejudice.

WASHINGTON, DENZEL
Actor. b. Mt. Vernon, NY, Dec. 28, 1954. e. Fordham U., B.A., journalism. Studied acting with American Conservatory Theatre, San Francisco.
THEATER: When the Chickens Come Home to Roost (Audelco Award), Coriolanus, Spell #7, The Mighty Gents, Ceremonies in Dark Old Men, A Soldier's Play, Checkmates, Richard III.
PICTURES: Carbon Copy (debut, 1981), A Soldier's Story, Power, Cry Freedom (Acad. Award nom.), The Mighty Quinn, For Queen and Country, Glory (Academy Award, best supporting actor, 1989; Golden Globe Award), Heart Condition, Mo' Better Blues, Ricochet, Mississippi Masala, Malcolm X (NY Film Critics Award; Acad. Award nom.), Much Ado About Nothing, Philadelphia, The Pelican Brief, Crimson Tide, Virtuosity, Devil in a Blue Dress, Courage Under Fire, The Preacher's Wife, Fallen, He Got Game, The Siege, The Hurricane, The Bone Collector.
TELEVISION: *Movies*: Wilma, Flesh and Blood, License to Kill, The George McKenna Story. *Series*: St. Elsewhere.

WASSERMAN, DALE
Writer, Producer. b. Rhinelander, WI, Nov. 2, 1917. *Stage:* lighting designer, dir., prod.; dir. for. attractions, S. Hurok; began writing, 1954. Founding member & trustee of O'Neill Theatre Centre; artistic dir. Midwest Playwrights Laboratory; member, Acad. M.P. Arts & Sciences; awards include Emmy, Tony, Critics Circle (Broadway), Outer Circle; Writers Guild.
PICTURES: Cleopatra, The Vikings, The Sea and the Shadow, Quick Before It Melts, Mister Buddwing, A Walk with Love and Death, Man of La Mancha.
TELEVISION: The Fog, The Citadel, The Power and the Glory, Engineer of Death, The Lincoln Murder Case, I Don Quixote, Elisha and the Long Knives, and others.PLAYS: Livin' the Life, 998, One Flew Over the Cuckoo's Nest, The Pencil of God, Man of La Mancha, Play With Fire, Shakespeare and the Indians, Mountain High, Western Star, Green.

WASSERMAN, LEW
Executive. b. Cleveland, OH, March 15, 1913. Natl. dir. advertising and pub., Music Corporation of Amer. 1936-38; v.p. 1938-39; v.p. motion picture div. 1940; chmn. of the bd., CEO, MCA, Inc., Universal City, CA. Named chmn. emeritus of MCA in 1995. Received Jean Hersholt Humanitarian Award, 1973; awarded Presidential Medal of Freedom, 1995.

WASSON, CRAIG
Actor. b. Ontario, OR, March 15, 1954. Also musician/songwriter.
THEATER: Godspell, All God's Chillun Got Wings, Death of a Salesman (also wrote incidental music), Jock, Children of Eden, M. Butterfly, Skin of Our Teeth, The Sisters (Pasadena Playhouse). Wrote incidental music for prod. of The Glass Menagerie and Death of a Salesman.
PICTURES: Rollercoaster, The Boys in Company C (also wrote and performed song Here I Am), Go Tell the Spartans, The Outsider, Carny, Schizoid, Ghost Story, Four Friends, Second Thoughts (also wrote and performed music), Body Double, The Men's Club, A Nightmare on Elm Street 3, The Trackers, Midnight Fear (co-s.p.), Malcolm X, Bum Rap (also wrote and performed music), Velocity Trap, The Debt, Father, The Image Maker, The Outfitters.
TELEVISION: *Series*: Phyllis (also wrote and performed orig. songs), Skag, One Life to Live, The Tomorrow Man. *Guest*: M*A*S*H, Baa Baa Black Sheep, Rockford Files, Hart to Hart, L.A. Law, Kung Fu: The Legend Continues, Dr. Quinn Medicine Woman, Murder She Wrote, Walker Texas Ranger, Deep Space Nine, Dangerous minds, Profiler, The Practice, Touched By an Angel. *Movies*: The Silence, Mrs. R's Daughter, Skag, Thornwell, Why Me?, Strapped, Trapped in Space, The Calvin Mire Story, The Becky Bell Story, Sister in Law, Harvest of Fire, Deep Family Secrets, Seed. *Specials*: A More Perfect Union, Innocents Abroad.

WATANABE, GEDDE
Actor. b. Ogden, UT, June 26. Trained for stage at American Conservatory Theatre, San Francisco. Appeared with N.Y. Shakespeare Fest. Shakespeare in the Park series and with Pan Asian Repertory Theatre, N.Y.
THEATER: Pacific Overtures (debut, as Tree Boy, B'way and on tour, 1976), Bullet Headed Birds, Poor Little Lambs, Dispatches, Music Lesson, Good Person.
PICTURES: Sixteen Candles (debut, 1984), Gremlins, Volunteers, Gung Ho, Vamp, UHF, Boys on the Side, That Thing You Do!, Nick and Jane, Booty Call, Mulan (voice), Guinevere, EDtv.
TELEVISION: *Series*: Gung Ho, ER. *Movie*: Miss America: Behind the Crown. *Guest:* The Simpsons (voice).

WATERHOUSE, KEITH
Writer. b. Leeds, England, Feb. 6, 1929. Early career as journalist, novelist. Author: There is a Happy Land, Billy Liar, Jubb, The Bucket Shop. Ent. m.p. ind. 1960.
PICTURES: *Writer* (with Willis Hall): Whistle Down the Wind, A Kind of Loving, Billy Liar, Man in the Middle, Pretty Polly, Lock Up Your Daughters, The Valiant, West Eleven.
TELEVISION: *Series*: Inside George Webley, Queenie's Castle, Budgie, Billy Liar, There is a Happy Land, Charters and Caldicott.

WATERS, JOHN
Director, Writer. b. Baltimore, MD, April 22, 1946. First short film Hag in a Black Leather Jacket (1964) shot in Baltimore, as are most of his films. Other shorts include Roman Candles, Eat Your Makeup. Feature debut, Mondo Trasho. Appeared as actor in films Something Wild, Homer and Eddie. On tv in Homicide: Life on the Streets.
PICTURES: *Director/Writer/Prod.*: Mondo Trasho (also photo., edit.), Multiple Maniacs (also ed., sound), Pink Flamingos (also photo., edit.), Female Trouble (also photo.), Desperate Living, Polyester, Hairspray (also co-prod., actor), Cry-Baby, Serial Mom, Pecker, Cecil B. Demented. *Actor:* Divine Trash, Anthem.
TELEVISION: *Guest*: The Simpsons (voice).

WATERSTON, SAM
Actor. b. Cambridge, MA, Nov. 15, 1940. e. Yale U. Spent jr. year at Sorbonne in Paris as part of the Amer. Actors' Workshop run by American dir. John Berry. Broadway debut in Oh Dad Poor Dad ... (1963). Film debut, The Plastic Dome of Norma Jean (made 1965; unreleased). TV debut Pound (Camera Three). Has worked in New York Shakespeare Festival prods. since As You Like It (1963).
THEATER: *N.Y.* Shakespeare Festival: As You Like It, Ergo, Henry IV (Part I & II), Cymbeline, Hamlet, Much Ado About Nothing, The Tempest. *Off-B'way*: The Knack, La Turista, Waiting for Godot, The Three Sisters. *B'way*: The Paisley Convertible, Halfway Up the Tree, Indian, Hay Fever, The Trial of Cantonsville Nine, A Meeting by the River, Much Ado About Nothing (Drama Desk and Obie Awards), A Doll's House, Lunch Hour, Benefactors, A Walk in the Woods, Abe Lincoln in Illinois.
PICTURES: Fitzwilly, Three, Generation, Cover Me Babe, Mahoney's Estate, Who Killed Mary What's 'er Name?, Savages, The Great Gatsby, Journey Into Fear, Rancho Deluxe, Sweet Revenge, Capricorn One, Interiors, Eagle's Wing, Sweet William, Hopscotch, Heaven's Gate, The Killing Fields, Warning Sign, Hannah and Her Sisters, Just Between Friends, A Certain Desire, The Devil's Paradise, September, Welcome Home, Crimes and Misdemeanors, The Man in the Moon, Mindwalk, A Captive in the Land, Serial Mom, The Journey of August King (also co-prod.), The Proprietor, The Shadow Conspiracy.

TELEVISION: *Specials*: Pound, Robert Lowell, The Good Lieutenant, Much Ado About Nothing, Oppenheimer, A Walk in the Woods. *Movies*: The Glass Menagerie, Reflections of Murder, Friendly Fire, Games Mother Never Taught You, In Defense of Kids, Dempsey, Finnegan Begin Again, Love Lives On, The Fifth Missile, The Room Upstairs, Terrorist on Trial: The United States vs. Salim Ajami, Gore Vidal's Lincoln, Lantern Hill, The Shell Seekers, Assault at West Point: The Court-Martial of Johnson Whittaker, David's Mother, The Enemy Within, Miracle at Midnight, Exiled: A Law & Order Movie. *Mini-Series*: The Nightmare Years, The Civil War (voice), Thomas Jefferson, Lewis & Clark. *Series*: Q.E.D., I'll Fly Away, Law & Order. *Guest*: Amazing Stories.

WATKIN, DAVID
Director of Photography. b. Margate, England, March 23, 1925. Entered British documentary ind. in Jan., 1948. With British Transport Films as asst. cameraman, 1950 -55; as cameraman, 1955 -61. Feature film debut The Knack beginning long creative relationship with director Richard Lester.
PICTURES: The Knack... and How to Get It (debut, 1965), Help!, Marat/Sade, How I Won the War, The Charge of the Light Brigade, The Bed-Sitting Room, Catch-22, The Devils, The Boyfriend, The Homecoming, A Delicate Balance, The Three Musketeers, The Four Musketeers, Mahogany, To the Devil a Daughter, Robin and Marian, Joseph Andrews, Hanover Street, Cuba, That Summer, Endless Love, Chariots of Fire, Yentl, The Hotel New Hampshire, Return to Oz, White Nights, Out of Africa (Academy Award, 1985), Moonstruck, Sky Bandits, Masquerade, The Good Mother, Last Rites, Journey to the Center of the Earth, Memphis Belle, Hamlet, The Object of Beauty, Used People, This Boy's Life, Bopha!, Milk Money, Jane Eyre, Bogus, Night Falls on Manhattan, Obsession, Critical Care, Gloria, Tea with Mussolini.

WATROS, CYNTHIA
Actress. b. Sept. 2, 1968.
PICTURES: Cafe Society, His and Hers.
TELEVISION: *Series*: Guiding Light (Emmy Award, 1998), Another World. *Guest*: Spin City.

WATSON, BARRY
Actor. r.n. Michael Barret Watson. b. Traverse City, MI, April 23, 1974.
PICTURES: Teaching Mrs. Tingle.
TELEVISION: *Movies:* Fatal Deception: Mrs. Lee Harvey Oswald, Attack of the 50 Ft. Woman, Co-ed Call Girl. *Series:* 7th Heaven. *Guest:* Malibu Shores.

WATSON, EMILY
Actress. b. London, England, 1966.
PICTURES: Breaking the Waves (Acad. Award nom., 1997; Golden Globe nom.; NY Society of Film Critics Award; Nat'l Society of Film Critics Award;), Mill on the Floss, Metroland, The Boxer, Hilary and Jackie (Acad. Award nom.), Trixie, The Cradle Will Rock, Angela's Ashes.

WAX, MORTON DENNIS
Public Relations Executive. b. New York, NY, March 13, 1932. e. Brooklyn Coll., 1952. President of Morton Dennis Wax & Assoc., Inc., p.r. and marketing firm servicing int'l creative marketplace, established 1956. Recent PR & Marketing for foreign films: Hungarian Fairy Tale, December Bride, Eden Valley. Contrib. writer to Box Office Magazine, Film Journal. Recent articles: Creativity (Advertising Age), Rolling Stone's Marketing Through Music, Words & Music, Campaign Magazine, Songwriters Guild of America National Edition. As sect. of VPA, conceptualized int'l Monitor Award, an annual event, currently under auspices of ITS. Public relations counsel to London Int'l Advertising Awards. Member of The Public Relations Society of America, Nat'l Academy of TV Arts & Sciences, Nat'l Acadrmy of Recording Arts & Sciences, Publishers Publicity Association. Morton Dennis Wax & Assocs. in NY was awarded the first EPM Entertainment Marketing Cause Event Award for creating, developing and promoting a nat'l fund raising campaign to combat homelessness, called Brother Can You Spare a Dime Day.

WAYANS, DAMON
Actor, Writer, Producer. b. New York, NY, Sept. 4, 1960. Brother is comedian-actor Keenen Ivory Wayans. Started as stand up comedian.
PICTURES: Beverly Hills Cop (debut, 1984), Hollywood Shuffle, Roxanne, Colors, Punchline, I'm Gonna Git You Sucka, Earth Girls Are Easy, Look Who's Talking Too (voice), The Last Boy Scout, Mo' Money (also s.p., co-exec. prod.), Last Action Hero (cameo), Blankman (also co-s.p., exec. prod.), Major Payne (also co-s.p., co-exec. prod.), The Great White Hype, Bulletproof.
TELEVISION: *Series*: Saturday Night Live (1985-6), In Living Color (also writer), 413 Hope St., (also prod.), Damon. *Special*: The Last Stand? (HBO).

WAYANS, KEENEN IVORY
Actor, Director, Writer. b. NYC, June 8, 1958. e. Tuskegee Inst. Began as stand-up comic at The Improv in NYC and L.A. Brother is comedian-actor Damon Wayans.
PICTURES: Star 80 (debut, 1983), Hollywood Shuffle (also co-s.p.), Eddie Murphy Raw (co-prod., co-s.p. only), I'm Gonna Git You Sucka, The Five Heartbeats (co-s.p. only), A Low Down Dirty Shame, The Glimmer Man, America's Most Wanted, Scart Movie, Scary Movie 2.
TELEVISION: *Series*: For Love and Honor, In Living Color (also exec. prod. & writer; Emmy Award 1990), Keenen Ivory Wayans Show (also exec. prod., writer). *Guest*: Benson, Cheers, CHiPS, A Different World. *Special*: Partners in Crime (also co-writer).

WAYLAND, LEN
Actor. b. California, Dec. 28. e. Junior Coll., Modesto, CA. Wrote, prod. weekly radio series 1939-41, KPAS, KTRB, Calif. Service, radar navigator, 1941-45; theatre, Tobacco Road, 1946; 1973, formed Len Wayland Prods. for prod. of theatrical pictures and TV series. 1976-77: *prod./dir.*: Don't Let It Bother You. 1978, *prod., dir.*, You're not there yet, for own co.
THEATER: A Streetcar Named Desire (B'way, tour), Heaven Can Wait, My Name Is Legion, Love of Four Colonels, Stalag 17, A Man For All Seasons.
TELEVISION: A Time to Live (serial), First Love, Armstrong Circle Theatre, Justice, Sgt. Bilko, Kraft Theatre; Dr. Weaver, From These Roots. Profiles in Courage, Dr. Kildare, Gunsmoke, Slattery's People, Ben Casey, A Noise in the World, Love Is a Many Splendored Thing; Dragnet, Outsider; Ironside, Name of the Game, The Bold Ones, Daniel Boone, The Virginian, Project U.F.O., Sam (series), The Blue and the Gray, Hunter, A-Team, Dallas, Amy on the Lips, Generations (serial).

WAYNE, JOEL
Executive. Began career with Grey Advertising; in 17 years won many awards (60 Clios, 25 N.Y. Art Director Club Awards, etc.). Was exec. v.p. & creative dir. of agency when left in 1979 to join Warner Bros. as v.p., creative adv. 1987, named sr. v.p., worldwide creative adv., then exec. v.p. worldwide creative adv. & publicity.

WAYNE, MICHAEL A.
Executive. r.n. Michael A. Morrison. b. Los Angeles, CA, Nov. 23, 1934. Father was late actor John Wayne. e. Loyola H.S.; Loyola U., B.B.A. Asst. dir., various companies, 1955-56; asst. dir., Revue Prods., 1956-57; pres. Batjac Prods, and Romina Prods., 1961.
PICTURES: *Asst. to producer*: China Doll, Escort West, The Alamo (asst. to prod.). *Prod.*: McLintock!, Cast Giant Shadow (co- prod.), The Green Berets, Chisum (exec. prod.), Big Jake, The Train Robbers, Cahill: U.S. Marshal, McQ (exec. prod.), Brannigan (exec. prod.).

WAYNE, PATRICK
Actor. b. Los Angeles, July 15, 1939. e. Loyola U, 1961, BS in biology. Father was late actor John Wayne. Made film debut at age 11 in Rio Grande with father.
PICTURES: The Long Gray Line, Mister Roberts, The Searchers, The Alamo, The Comancheros, McClintock, Donovan's Reef, Cheyenne Autumn, Shenandoah, An Eye for an Eye, The Green Berets, The Deserter, Big Jake, The Gatling Gun, Beyond Atlantis, The Bears and I, Mustang Country, Sinbad and the Eye of the Tiger, The People Time Forgot, Rustler's Rhapsody, Young Guns, Blind Vengeance, Deep Cover.
TELEVISION: *Series*: The Rounders, Shirley. *Movies*: Sole Survivor, Yesterday's Child, Flight to Holocaust, The Last Hurrah, Three on a Date. *Guest*: Frank's Place.

WEATHERS, CARL
Actor. b. New Orleans, LA, Jan. 14, 1948. e. San Diego State U.
PICTURES: Bucktown (debut, 1975), Friday Foster, Rocky, Close Encounters of the Third Kind, Semi-Tough, Force Ten From Navarone, Rocky II, Death Hunt, Rocky III, Rocky IV, Predator, Action Jackson, Hurricane Smith, Happy Gilmore.
TELEVISION: *Series*: Fortune Dane, Tour of Duty, Street Justice, In the Heat of the Night. *Movies*: The Hostage Heart, The Bermuda Depths, Breaker, Dangerous Passion, In the Heat of the Night: A Matter of Justice, In the Heat of the Night: Who Was Geli Bendl?, In the Heat of the Night: By Duty Bound, Tom Clancy's Op Center, In the Heat of the Night: Grow Old With Me, The Defiant Ones, Shadow Warriors, Shadow Warriors II. *Director*: Silk Stalkings (7 episodes), Renegade (1 episode).

WEAVER, DENNIS
Actor, Director. b. Joplin, MO, June 4, 1925. e. U. of Oklahoma, B.A., fine arts, 1948.

PICTURES: Horizons West (debut, 1952), The Raiders, The Redhead From Wyoming, The Lawless Breed, Mississippi Gambler, Law and Order, It Happens Every Thursday, Column South, The Man From the Alamo, The Golden Blade, The Nebraskan, War Arrow, Dangerous Mission, Dragnet, Ten Wanted Men, The Bridges at Toko-Ri, Seven Angry Men, Chief Crazy Horse, Storm Fear, Touch of Evil, The Gallant Hours, Duel at Diablo, Way... Way Out, Gentle Giant, Mission Batangas, A Man Called Sledge, What's the Matter With Helen?, Walking After Midnight, Two Bits & Pepper, Escape From Wildcat Canyon, The Virginian.
TELEVISION: *Series*: Gunsmoke (Emmy Award, 1959), Kentucky Jones, Gentle Ben, McCloud, Stone, Emerald Point NAS, Buck James, Lonesome Dove: The Outlaw Years. *Movies*: McCloud: Who Killed Miss USA?, The Forgotten Man, Duel, Rolling Man, Female Artillery, The Great Man's Whiskers, Terror on the Beach, Intimate Strangers, The Islander, Ishi: The Last of His Tribe, The Ordeal of Patty Hearst, Stone (pilot), Amber Waves, The Ordeal of Dr. Mudd, The Day the Loving Stopped, Don't Go to Sleep, Cocaine: One Man's Seduction, Bluffing It, Disaster at Silo 7, The Return of Sam McCloud (also co-exec. prod.), Greyhounds, Seduction in a Small Town. *Mini-Series*: Centennial, Pearl. *Special*: Mastergate.

WEAVER, FRITZ
Actor. b. Pittsburgh, PA, Jan. 19, 1926. e. U. of Chicago.
THEATER: The Chalk Garden (Theatre World Award), Miss Lonelyhearts, All American, A Shot in the Dark, Baker Street, Child's Play (Tony, 1970), The Price, The Crucible, The Professional, etc.
PICTURES: Fail Safe (debut, 1964), The Guns of August (narrator), The Maltese Bippy, A Walk in the Spring Rain, Company of Killers, The Day of the Dolphin, Marathon Man, Demon Seed, Black Sunday, The Big Fix, Jaws of Satan, Creepshow, Power.
TELEVISION: *Movies*: The Borgia Stick, Berlin Affair, Heat of Anger, The Snoop Sisters, Hunter, The Legend of Lizzie Borden, Captains Courageous, The Hearst and Davies Affair, A Death in California, My Name is Bill W, Ironclads, Citizen Cohn, Blind Spot. *Mini-Series*: Holocaust, The Martian Chronicles, Dream West, I'll Take Manhattan.

WEAVER, SIGOURNEY
Actress. r.n. Susan Weaver. b. New York, NY, Oct. 8, 1949. e. Stanford U., Yale U. Daughter of Sylvester (Pat) Weaver, former NBC pres. Mother, actress Elizabeth Inglis (one-time contract player for Warner Bros.). After college formed working partnership with fellow student Christopher Durang for off-B'way improv. productions. First professional appearance on stage in 1974 in The Constant Wife with Ingrid Bergman. Formed Goat Cay Prods.
THEATER: *Off-Off-B'way*: The Nature and Purpose of the Universe. *Off-B'way*: Titanic/Das Lusitania Songspiel (also co-writer), Gemini, Marco Polo Sings a Solo, New Jerusalem, The Merchant of Venice, Beyond Therapy. *B'way*: Hurlyburly.
PICTURES: Madman (Israeli; debut, 1976), Annie Hall, Alien, Eyewitness, The Year of Living Dangerously, Deal of the Century, Ghostbusters, One Woman or Two, Aliens (Acad. Award nom.), Half Moon Street, Gorillas in the Mist (Acad. Award nom.), Working Girl (Acad. Award nom.), Ghostbusters II, Alien 3 (also co-prod.), 1492: Conquest of Paradise, Dave, Death and the Maiden, Jeffrey, Copycat, The Ice Storm (BAFTA Award, Best Supporting Actress, 1997), Alien: Resurrection (also co-prod.), Snow White, A Map of the World, Get Bruce, Galaxy Quest, Company Man.
TELEVISION: *Series*: The Best of Families (PBS), Somerset. *Special*: The Sorrows of Gin.

WEAVER, SYLVESTER L., JR.
Executive. b. Los Angeles, CA, Dec. 21, 1908. e. Dartmouth Coll. Daughter is actress Sigourney Weaver. CBS, Don Lee Network, 1932-35; Young & Rubicam adv. agency, 1935-38; adv. mgr., American Tobacco Co., 1938-47; v.p. Young & Rubicam, 1947-49; joined NBC as v.p., chg. TV, 1949; appt'd v.p. chg. NBC Radio & TV networks, 1952; vice-chmn. bd., NBC, 1953; pres., NBC, 1953; bd. chmn., 1955; as head of NBC during TV's formative years, Weaver is credited as the father of TV talk/service program, founding both Tonight and Today shows, also innovated the rotating multi-star anthology series, the Wide Wide World series and concept of TV "special;" Own firm, 430 Park Avenue., N.Y., 1956; chmn. of bd. McCann-Erickson Corp. (Intl.), 1959; pres., Subscription TV, Inc. Comm. Consultant in Los Angeles, CA and President, Weaver Productions, Inc. On magazine series Television: Inside and Out (1981-82). Author: The Best Seat in the House (1994). Awards: Emmy Trustees' and Governor's Award (1967) and Governor's Award (1983), TV Hall of Fame (1984), NAB Hall of Fame (1986), Dartmouth Lifetime Achievement Award, 1993.

WEBB, CHLOE
Actress. b. New York, NY. e. Boston Conservatory of Music and Drama. On stage with Boston Shakespeare Co., Goodman Theatre in Chicago and Mark Taper Forum, L.A., improv. groups Imagination Theatre Co., Paul Sills Theatre.
THEATER: Forbidden Broadway (Off-B'way and L.A.), Addiction, Family Album, The Model Apartment (LA Critics Circle & Dramalogue Awards), House of Blue Leaves (Dramlogue Award), School Talk, A Midsummer Night's Dream.
PICTURES: Sid and Nancy (debut, 1986; Natl. Society of Film Critics Award), Twins, Heart Condition, The Belly of an Architect, Queens Logic, A Dangerous Woman, Love Affair, She's So Lovely, The Newton Boys, Practical Magic.
TELEVISION: *Series*: Thicke of the Night. *Special*: Who Am I This Time? *Movies*: Lucky Day, Silent Cries. *Mini-Series*: Tales of the City. *Guest*: Remington Steele, China Beach (pilot).

WEBER, STEVEN
Actor. e. Purchase Col. Acted with Mirror Rep. Co. Off-B'way.
THEATER: *NY:* Paradise Lost, The Real Thing (B'way debut, 1985), Something About Baseball. *Regional:* Made in Bangkok, Come Back Little Sheba, Naked at the Coast, Death of a Salesman.
PICTURES: The Flamingo Kid, Flanagan, Hamburger Hill, Les Anges, Single White Female, The Temp, Jeffrey, Dracula: Dead and Loving It, I Woke Up Early the Day I Died, The Breakup, Sour Grapes, At First Sight.
TELEVISION: *Series:* Wings. *Mini-Series:* The Kennedys of Massachusetts, The Shining. *Movies:* In the Company of Darkness, In the Line of Duty: The Undercover Murders, Deception: A Mother's Secret, Betrayed by Love. *Special:* Pudd'nhead Wilson.

WEDGEWORTH, ANN
Actress. b. Abilene, TX, Jan. 21, 1935. e. U. of Texas. On stage in Thieves, Blues for Mr. Charlie, Chapter Two (Tony Award, 1978).
PICTURES: Andy, Bang the Drum Slowly, Scarecrow, The Catamount Killing, Law and Disorder, Dragonfly (One Summer Love), Birch Interval, Thieves, Handle With Care, No Small Affair, Sweet Dreams, The Men's Club, Made in Heaven, A Tiger's Tale, Far North, Miss Firecracker, Steel Magnolias, Green Card, Hard Promises, Love and a .45, The Whole Wide World.
TELEVISION: *Series*: The Edge of Night, Another World, Somerset, Three's Company, Filthy Rich, Evening Shade. *Movies*: The War Between the Tates, Bogie, Elvis and the Beauty Queen, Killjoy, Right to Kill?, A Stranger Waits, Cooperstown, A Burning Passion: The Margaret Mitchell Story, Fight for Justice: The Nancy Conn Story. *Pilot*: Harlan & Merleen.

WEILER, GERALD E.
Producer. b. Mannheim, Germany, May 8, 1928. e. Harvard, 1946-48; Columbia, B.S., 1949-51; New York U. Grad. Sch., 1951-53. Writer, WHN, N.Y. writer, sports ed., news ed., Telenews Prod., Inc., 1948-52; asst. to prod., Richard de Rochemont, Vavin, Inc., 1952; U.S. Army, 1953-55; v.p., Vavin Inc. 1955-73; President, Weiler Communications Inc. 1973. Winner, NY "Lotto" Lottery, 1988; retired 1989.

WEILL, CLAUDIA
Director. b. New York, NY 1947. e. Radcliffe, B.A., 1969. Teacher of acting, Cornish Institute, 1983; guest lecturer on film directing, NYU and Columbia U. Winner of Donatello Award, best director, 1979; Mademoiselle Woman of the Year, 1974; AFI Independent Filmmakers Grant, 1973. Worked as prod. asst. on doc., Revolution.
THEATER: An Evening for Merlin Finch (debut, 1975, Williamstown), Stillife, Found a Peanut, The Longest Walk.
PICTURES: *Doc. shorts*: This Is the Home of Mrs. Levant Grahame, Roaches' Serenade, Joyce at 34. *Director*: The Other Half of the Sky—A China Memoir (also photog., edit.), Girlfriends (also prod., story), It's My Turn.
TELEVISION: *Series*: The 51st State, Sesame Street, Joyce at 34, The Great Love Experiment, thirtysomething, My So-Called Life, Chicago Hope. *Movie*: A Child Lost Forever, Critical Choices.

WEINBLATT, MIKE
Executive. b. Perth Amboy, NJ, June 10, 1929. e. Syracuse U. Served in Army as counter-intelligence agent, mostly in Japan, 1952-53. Joined NBC in 1957; has headed two major TV network functions—talent/program admin. & sls.; joined network business affairs dept. in 1958 as mgr., business affairs, facilities operations; rose to post of director, pricing & financial services before moving to sales in 1962, as mgr., participating program sales; named v.p., eastern sales, NBC-TV, 1968; named v.p., talent & program admin., 1968; promoted to v.p. sales, 1973; 1975 named sr. v.p., sales; later became exec. v.p.; appointed exec. v.p. & gen. mgr. of NBC TV network, 1977; appointed Pres., NBC Entertainment, 1978; 1980, joined Showtime/Movie Channel as pres. & COO; 1984, pres., Multi Media Entertainment; 1990, chmn. Weinblatt Communications Co. Inc. 1991, mng. dir. Interequity Capital Corp.

WEINGROD, HERSCHEL
Writer, Producer. b. Milwaukee, WI, Oct. 30, 1947. e. U. of Wisconsin, 1965-69; London Film Sch., 1969-71.
PICTURES: *Co-writer* with Timothy Harris: Cheaper to Keep Her, Trading Places (BAFTA nom.), Brewster's Millions, My Stepmother Is An Alien, Paint It Black, Twins, Kindergarten Cop, Pure Luck, Falling Down (prod. only), Space Jam (co-s.p.).
TELEVISION: Street of Dreams (exec. prod.).

WEINSTEIN, BOB
Executive. With brother Harvey founded distribution company Miramax Films in 1979. Company branched into feature production in 1989 with film Scandal. Serves as Miramax co-chairman.
PICTURES: Light Years (Bob: prod., Harvey: dir. of U.S. version). *Co-Executive Producers*: Scandal, The Lemon Sisters, Hardware, A Rage in Harlem, The Miracle, Crossing the Line, The Night We Never Met, Benefit of the Doubt, True Romance, Into the West, Mother's Boys, Pulp Fiction, Ready to Wear (Pret-a-Porter), The Englishman Who Went Up a Hill But Came Down a Mountain, Smoke, The Crossing Guard, The Journey of August King, Last of the High Kings, Addicted to Love, Air Bud, Cop Land, The English Patient, Scream , Wishful Thinking, The Wings of the Dove, She's So Lovely, Mimic, Good Will Hunting, Scream 2, Jackie Brown, Velvet Goldmine, Shakespeare in Love (Acad. Award for Best Picture), Rounders, The Prophecy II, A Price Above Rubies, Playing by Heart, The Mighty, Little Voice, Heaven, Halloween H20: Twenty Years Later, The Faculty, B. Monkey, Phantoms, Senseless, Ride, Wide Awake, Nightwatch, 54, Talk of Angels, The Yards, Teaching Mrs. Tingle, Outside Providence, My Life So Far, Music of the Heart, Masfield Park, Holy Smoke, Guinevere, The Cider House Rules, Allied Forces, She's All That, In Too Deep, Scream If You Know What I Did Last Halloween, Reindeer Games, The Yards, Boys and Girls, Scary Movie, Highlander: Endgame, Backstage, Chocolat, The Lord of the Rings: The Fellowship of the Ring, Scary Movie II.
TELEVISION: *Series:* Wasteland, Clerks: The Animated Series.

WEINSTEIN, HARVEY
Executive. With brother Bob founded distribution company Miramax Films in 1979. Company branched into feature production in 1989 with film Scandal. Serves as Miramax co-chairman. (For list of films see Bob Weinstein).

WEINSTEIN, PAULA
Producer. b. Nov. 19, 1945. e. Columbia U. Daughter of late prod. Hannah Weinstein. Raised in Europe. Partnered with Gareth Wigan in WW Productions at Warner Brothers. Started as theatrical agent with William Morris and ICM. With Warner Brothers, 1976-78 as production v.p.; left to go to 20th Century-Fox in same capacity; named Fox sr. v.p., worldwide prod; 1980, appointed v.p., prod., the Ladd Company; 1981, joined United Artists as pres., m.p. div.; 1983, began own prod. company at Columbia Pictures, also serving as a consultant for Columbia; 1987, joined MGM as exec. consultant; With late husband Mark Rosenberg formed Spring Creek Prods.
PICTURES: *Prod.*: A Dry White Season, The Fabulous Baker Boys, Fearless, Flesh and Bone, With Honors, Something to Talk About, The Incredible Mr. Limpet, Analyze This, Liberty Heights, The Perfect Storm, An Everlasting Piece, Possession, Bandits.
TELEVISION: *Movies*: The Rose and the Jackal, Citizen Cohn, Truman (Emmy Award, 1996), The Cherokee Kid, First-time Felon, Cloned.

WEINTRAUB, FRED
Executive, Producer. b. Bronx, NY, April 27, 1928. e. U. of PA, Wharton Sch. of Bus. Owner of The Bitter End Coffeehouse to 1971. Personal management, Campus Coffee House Entertain-ment Circuit; TV Production Hootenanny, Popendipity; syndicated TV show host: From The Bitter End; motion picture prod.; v.p., creative services, Warner Bros. 1969; exec. in chg. Woodstock; prod. motion pictures, Weintraub-Heller Productions, 1974; then Fred Weintraub Productions, which became Weintraub/Kuhn Prods. in 1990.
PICTURES: Enter the Dragon, Rage, Black Belt Jones, Truck Turner, Golden Needles, Animal Stars, Hot Potato, The Ultimate Warrior, Dirty Knights Work, Those Cuckoo Crazy Animals, Crash, Outlaw Blues, The Pack, The Promise, Tom Horn, Battle Creek Brawl, Force Five, High Road to China, Out of Control, Gymkata, Princess Academy, Born to Ride.
TELEVISION: My Father My Son (prod.), Triplecross. Produced: Trouble Bound, Dead Wrong, JFK Assassination (doc.), The Bruce Lee Story (doc.), The New Adventures of Robin Hood.

WEINTRAUB, JERRY
Producer. b. New York, NY, Sept. 26, 1937. m. former singer Jayne Morgan. Sole owner and chmn. of Management Three, representing entertainment personalities, including John Denver, John Davidson, Frank Sinatra, Neil Diamond, etc. Also involved with Intercontinental Broadcasting Systems, Inc. (cable programming) and Jerry Weintraub/Armand Hammer Prods. (production co.). 1985, named United Artists Corp. chmn. Resigned, 1986. 1987: formed Weintraub Entertainment Group.
PICTURES: Nashville, Oh God!, Cruising, All Night Long, Diner, The Karate Kid, The Karate Kid Part II, The Karate Kid Part III, Pure Country, The Firm (actor), The Next Karate Kid, The Specialist, National Lampoon's Vegas Vacation, The Avengers, Soldier.

WEINTRAUB, SY
Executive. b. New York, NY, 1923. e. U. of Missouri, B.A., journalism, 1947; graduate of American Theater Wing. Started career in 1949 forming with associates a TV syndication co., Flamingo Films, Inc., which merged with Associated Artists to form Motion Pictures for Television, Inc., largest syndicator at that time. Originated Superman and Grand Ol' Opry series for TV. 1958, bought Sol Lesser Prods., owners of film rights for Tarzan, and began producing and distributing Tarzan films through Banner Productions, Inc. Also formerly chmn. of Panavision, Inc.; bd. mem. and pres. of National General TV Corp., and pres. of KMGM-TV in Minneapolis. In 1978, named chmn. of Columbia Pictures Industries' new Film Entertainment Group, also joining office of the chief executive of CPI.
(d. April 4, 2000)

WEIR, PETER
Director, Writer. b. Sydney, Australia, Aug. 21, 1944. e. attended Scots Coll. and Sydney U. Briefly worked selling real estate, traveled to England 1965. Entered Australian TV industry as stagehand 1967 while prod. amateur revues. *Dir. shorts*: Count Vim's Last Exercise, The Life and Times of Reverend Buck Shotte, Homeside, Incredible Floridas, What Ever Happened to Green Valley? 1967-73.
PICTURES: *Director*: Three to Go (debut, 1970; segment: Michael), The Cars That Ate Paris (also s.p., co-story; a.k.a. The Cars That Eat People), Picnic at Hanging Rock, The Last Wave (also s.p.), The Plumber (also s.p.; tv in Australia). Gallipoli (also story), The Year of Living Dangerously (also co-s.p.), Witness (Academy Award nom.), The Mosquito Coast, Dead Poets Society (Academy Award nom.), Green Card (also prod., s.p.; Academy Award nom.), Fearless, The Truman Show (Acad. Award nom. for dir.).

WEIS, DON
Director, Writer, Producer. b. Milwaukee, WI, May 13, 1922. e. USC. Started as dialogue dir. on such films as Body and Soul, The Red Pony, Champion, Home of the Brave, The Men.
PICTURES: Bannerline (debut, 1951), It's a Big Country (segment), Just This Once, You for Me, I Love Melvin, Remains to Be Seen, A Slight Case of Larceny, Half a Hero, The Affairs of Dobie Gillis, The Adventures of Haji Baba, Ride the High Iron, The Gene Krupa Story, Critic's Choice, Looking for Love, Pajama Party, Billie (also prod.), The King's Pirate, Did You Hear the One About the Traveling Saleslady?, Zero to Sixty.
TELEVISION: Dear Phoebe, The Longest Hundred Miles, It Takes a Thief, Ironside, M*A*S*H., Happy Days, Planet of the Apes, Bronk, Petrocelli, The Magician, Mannix, Night Stalker, Barbary Coast, Courtship of Eddie's Father, Starsky & Hutch, Hawaii Five-O, Chips, Charlie's Angels, Love Boat, Fantasy Island, Remington Steele, Hill St. Blues, Murphy's Law.
(d. July 25, 2000)

WEISS, STEVEN ALAN
Executive. b. Glendale, CA, Oct. 19, 1944. e. Los Angeles City Coll., A.A., 1964; USC, M.S., 1966; Northwestern U., B.S., 1967; LaSalle Extension U., J.D., 1970. U.S. Navy-San Diego, Great Lakes, Vallejo & Treasure Island, 1966-67; shipyard liaison officer, Pearl Harbor Naval Shipyard, U.S. Navy, 1967-70; gen. mgr., Adrian Weiss Prods., 1970-74; organized Weiss Global Enterprises with Adrian Weiss 1974 for production, acquisition & distribution of films. Purchased with Tom J. Corradine and Adrian Weiss from the Benedict E. Bogeaus Estate nine features, 1974. Sec./Treas. of Film Investment Corp. & Weiss Global Enterprises which own, control or have dist. rights to over 300 features, many TV series, documentaries, etc. CFO/COO Flo-Fowes, a full service telecommunications corp., 1992-present. Member of the Nat'l Assn. of TV Program Executive Int'l, National Cable TV Assn., AFI.

WEISSMAN, MURRAY
Executive. b. New York, NY, Dec. 23. e. USC. Asst. dir. of press info., CBS, 1960-66; mgr., TV press dept., Universal Studio, 1966-68; executive in charge of m.p. press dept., Universal Studios & asst. secy., Universal Pictures, 1968-76; marketing exec., Columbia Pictures, 1976-77; vice pres. of advertising & publicity, Lorimar Productions, 1977; vice pres., ICPR Public Relations Company, 1978-81; now principal, Weissman/Delson Comm.

WEISWASSER, STEPHEN A.
Executive. e. Wayne St. Univ., John Hopkins Univ., Harvard Law School. Partner at Wilmer Cutler & Pickering law firm until he joined Capital Cities/ABC in 1986 as sr. v.p. Aug. 1993 became pres. of Capital Cities/ABC Multimedia Group until Oct. 1995. Nov. 1995, became pres. & CEO of Americast.

WEITZNER, DAVID
Executive. b. New York, NY, Nov. 13, 1938. e. Michigan State U. Entered industry in 1960 as member Columbia Pictures adv. dep't; later with Donahue and Coe as ass't exec. and Loew's Theatres adv. dep't; later with Embassy Pictures, adv. mgr.; dir. of adv. and exploitation for Palomar Pictures Corp.; v.p. in charge of adv., pub., and exploitation for ABC Pictures Corp.; v.p., entertainment/leisure div., Grey Advertising; v.p., worldwide adv., 20th Century Fox; exec. v.p. adv./pub./promo., Universal Pictures; exec. v.p., mktg. & dist., Embassy Pictures; 1985, joined 20th Century-Fox Films as pres. of mktg. 1987, pres., mktg., Weintraub Entertainment Group; 1988 joined MCA/Universal as pres. worldwide marketing, MCA Recreation Services.

WELCH, RAQUEL
Actress. r.n. Raquel Tejada. b. Chicago, IL, Sept. 5, 1940. e. La Jolla H.S. Theatre arts scholarship San Diego State Coll. Worked as model before landing bit parts in films. Broadway debut, Woman of the Year, 1981.
PICTURES: A House Is Not a Home (debut, 1964), Roustabout, Do Not Disturb, A Swingin' Summer, Fantastic Voyage, Shoot Loud Louder... I Don't Understand, One Million Years B.C., Fathom, The Oldest Profession, Bedazzled, The Biggest Bundle of Them All, Le Fate (The Queens), Bandolero, Lady in Cement, 100 Rifles, Flare Up, The Magic Christian, Myra Breckinridge, Restless, Hannie Caulder, Kansas City Bomber, Fuzz, Bluebeard, The Last of Sheila, The Three Musketeers, The Four Musketeers, The Wild Party, Mother Jugs and Speed, Crossed Swords, L'Animal, Naked Gun 33 1/3: The Final Insult.
TELEVISION: *Specials*: Really Raquel, Raquel. *Movies*: The Legend of Walks Far Woman, Right to Die, Scandal in a Small Town, Trouble in Paradise, Tainted Blood, Judith Krantz's Torch Song, Hollyrock-a-Bye Baby (voice). *Guest*: Cher, The Muppet Show.

WELD, TUESDAY
Actress. r.n. Susan Weld. b. New York, NY, Aug. 27, 1943. m. violinist Pinchas Zuckerman. e. Hollywood Professional Sch. Began modeling at 4 yrs.
PICTURES: Rock Rock Rock (debut, 1956), Rally 'Round the Flag Boys! The Five Pennies, Because They're Young, High Time, Sex Kittens Go to College, The Private Lives of Adam and Eve, Return to Peyton Place, Wild in the Country, Bachelor Flat, Soldier in the Rain, I'll Take Sweden, The Cincinnati Kid, Lord Love a Duck, Pretty Poison, I Walk the Line, A Safe Place, Play It As It Lays, Looking for Mr. Goodbar (Acad. Award nom.), Who'll Stop the Rain, Serial, Thief, Author! Author!, Once Upon a Time in America, Heartbreak Hotel, Falling Down.
TELEVISION: *Series*: The Many Loves of Dobie Gillis (1959-60). *Movies*: Reflections of Murder, F. Scott Fitzgerald in Hollywood, A Question of Guilt, Mother and Daughter: The Loving War, Madame X, The Winter of Our Discontent, Scorned and Swindled, Something in Common, Circle of Violence. *Special*: The Rainmaker.

WELLER, PETER
Actor. b. Stevens Point, WI, June 24, 1947. Acting since 10 years old. e. North Texas State U. Studied at American Acad. of Dramatic Arts with Uta Hagen. Member, Actor's Studio.
THEATER: Sticks and Bones (moved up from understudy, B'way debut), Full Circle, Summer Brave, Macbeth, The Wool-Gatherer, Rebel Women, Streamers, The Woods, Serenading Louie, Daddy Wolf.
PICTURES: Butch and Sundance: The Early Years (debut, 1979), Just Tell Me What You Want, Shoot the Moon, Of Unknown Origin, The Adventures of Buckaroo Banzai Across the 8th Dimension, Firstborn, Robocop, Shakedown, A Killing Affair, Leviathan, The Tunnel, Robocop 2, Cat Chaser, Naked Lunch, Fifty Fifty, Sunset Grill, The New Age, Screamers, Mighty Aphrodite, Beyond the Clouds, Top of the World, Enemy of My Enemy, Diplomatic Siege, Falling Through.
TELEVISION: *Movies*: The Man Without a Country, The Silence, Kentucky Woman, Two Kinds of Love, Apology, Women & Men: Stories of Seduction (Dust Before Fireworks), Rainbow Drive, The Substitute Wife, The Road to Ruin, Decoy, Michael Hayes (dir.), Gold Coast (dir.). *Guest*: Lou Grant, Exit 10. *Special*: Partners (also dir., co-writer).

WENDERS, WIM
Director, Writer. b. Dusseldorf, Germany, August 14, 1945. Studied film 1967-70 at Filmhochschule in Munich. Worked as film critic 1968-70 for Filmkritik and Die Suddeutsche Zeitung. 1967 made first short films (Schauplatze) and three others before first feature, Summer in the City.
PICTURES: *Director-Writer*: Summer in the City (debut, 1970; also prod., actor), The Scarlet Letter, The Goalie's Anxiety at the Penalty Kick, Alice in the Cities, Wrong Move (dir. only), Kings of the Road (also prod.), The American Friend, Lightning Over Water (also actor), Chambre 66 (dir., actor), Hammett (dir. only), The State of Things, Paris Texas (dir. only), I Played It for You (dir., actor only), Tokyo-Ga (also edit.), Wings of Desire (also prod.), Notebooks on Cities and Clothes (also photog.), Until the End of the World, Faraway So Close! (also prod.), Lisbon Story, Beyond the Clouds (co-dir. & co-s.p. with Michelangelo Antonioni), The End of Violence (also prod.), City of Angels (s.p. only), The Million Dollar Hotel (also prod.), Buena Vista Social Club, Vill Passiert. *Actor:* Long Shot, King Kong's Faust, Helsinki Napoli All Night Long, Motion and Emotion.

WENDKOS, PAUL
Director. b. Philadelphia, PA, Sept. 20, 1926. e. Temple U., Columbia, the New School.
PICTURES: The Burglar, Tarawa Beachhead, Gidget, Face of a Fugitive, Battle of the Coral Sea, Because They're Young, Angel Baby, Gidget Goes to Rome, Miles to Terror, Guns of the Magnificent Seven, Cannon for Cordova, The Mephisto Waltz, Special Delivery.
TELEVISION: Hawaii 5-0 (pilot), Fear No Evil, The Brotherhood of the Bell, Travis Logan D.A., A Tattered Web, A Little Game, A Death of Innocence, The Delphi Bureau, Haunts of the Very Rich, Footsteps, The Strangers in 7-A, Honor Thy Father, Terror on the Beach, The Underground Man, The Legend of Lizzie Borden, Death Among Friends, The Death of Ritchie, Secrets, Good Against Evil, Harold Robbins' 79 Park Avenue, A Woman Called Moses, The Ordeal of Patty Hearst, Act of Violence, Ordeal of Doctor Mudd, A Cry for Love, The Five of Me, Golden Gate, Farrell for the People, Cocaine: One Man's Seduction, Intimate Agony, The Awakening of Candra, Celebrity, Scorned and Swindled, The Execution, The Bad Seed, Picking Up the Pieces, Rage of Angels: The Story Continues, Sister Margaret and the Saturday Night Ladies, Six Against the Rock, Right to Die, The Taking of Flight 847: The Uli Derickson Story, The Great Escape II: The Untold Story (co-dir.), From the Dead of Night, Cross of Fire, Blind Faith, Good Cops Bad Cops, The Chase, White Hot: The Murder of Thelma Todd, Guilty Until Proven Innocent, The Trail, Bloodlines.

WENDT, GEORGE
Actor. b. Chicago, IL, Oct. 17, 1948. e. Rockhurst Col. Joined Second City's acting troupe in 1973. Appeared in NBC pilot Nothing but Comedy.
PICTURES: My Bodyguard, Somewhere in Time, Airplane II: The Sequel, Jekyll & Hyde Together Again, The Woman in Red, Dreamscape, Thief of Hearts, No Small Affair, Fletch, House, Gung Ho, Plain Clothes, Guilty by Suspicion, Forever Young, The Little Rascals, Man of the House, Spice World, Anarchy TV, Space Truckers, The Lovemaster, Rupert's Land, The Pooch and the Pauper, Outside Providence.
TELEVISION: *Series*: Making the Grade, Cheers, The George Wendt Show, The Naked Truth. *Guest*: Alice, Soap, Taxi, Hart to Hart, Seinfeld, The Simpsons (voice). *Movies*: Oblomov (BBC), The Ratings Game, Hostage for a Day, Shame II: The Secret, Bye Bye Birdie, Alien Avengers, Alien Avengers II, The Price of Heaven, Alice in Wonderland.

WERNER, PETER
Producer, Director. b. New York, NY, Jan. 17, 1947. e. Dartmouth Coll., AFI. Received Academy Award for short subject, In the Region of Ice, 1976.
PICTURES: Don't Cry It's Only Thunder, No Man's Land.
TELEVISION: *Movies*: *Director*: Battered, William Faulkner's Barn Burning, Sins of the Father, Aunt Mary, No Man's Land, Women in Song, No Man's Land, LBJ: The Early Years. Men (exec. prod., dir.; Emmy nom.), The Image (Ace Award), Hiroshima: Out of the Ashes (D.G.A. nom.), The Good Policeman, Doorways, Middle Ages (co-exec. prod.), Substitute Wife, The Four Diamonds, The Unspoken Truth, Inflammable, Almost Golden: The Jessica Savitch Story (D.G.A. nom.), For the Love of Zachary, On the Edge of Innocence, House of Frankenstein, Parallels. *Series*: Moonlighting (Emmy & D.G.A. nom.), Outlaws (pilot), The Wonder Years, D.E.A. (pilot), Ned Blessing (pilot), Nash Bridges (pilot).

WERTHEIMER, THOMAS
Executive. b. 1938. e. Princeton U., B.A. 1960; Columbia U., LLB, 1963. V.p. business affairs subs. ABC 1964-72; joined MCA Inc, 1972; v.p. Universal TV dir.; corp. v.p. 1974 -83; exec. v.p. 1983-; chmn., MCA Television and Home Entertainment Groups. Consultant, 1996-present

WERTMULLER, LINA
Director, Writer. b. Rome, Italy, Aug. 14, 1928. m. sculptor-set designer Enrico Job. e. Acad. of Theatre, Rome, 1951. Began working in theatre in 1951; Prod.-dir. avant-garde plays in Italy 1951-52; member puppet troupe 1952-62; actress, stage mgr., set designer, publicity writer, for theater, radio & TV, 1952-62. Began film career as asst. to Fellini on 8 1/2 in 1962. Following year wrote and directed first film, The Lizards. Had big TV success with series called Gian Burasca and then returned to theatre for a time. 1988, named Special Commissioner of Centro Sperimentale di Cinematografia. Was the first woman to be nominated for an Academy Award for Best Director (Seven Beauties, 1976).
PICTURES: *Director-Writer*: The Lizards (dir. debut, 1963), Let's Talk About Men, The Seduction of Mimi (Cannes Film Fest Award, 1972), Love and Anarchy, All Screwed Up, Swept Away... By an Unusual Destiny in the Blue Sea of August, Seven Beauties (Acad. Award noms. for dir. & s.p., 1976), The End of the World in Our Usual Bed in a Night Full of Rain, Blood Feud, A Joke of Destiny (Lying in Wait Around the Corner Like a Bandit), A Complex Plot About Women, Sotto Sotto (Softly Softly), Summer Night With Greek Profile Almond Eyes and a Scent of Basil, The Tenth One in Hiding, On a Moonlit Night, Saturday Sunday Monday, Ciao Professore!
TELEVISION: Rita the Mosquito, Il Decimo Clandestino (Cannes Fest. Award).

WEST, ADAM
Actor. r.n. William West Anderson. b. Walla Walla, WA, Sept. 19, 1929. e. Whitman Col. (B.A.), Stanford Univ. Created classic Batman role. Appeared in interactive short film Ride for Your Life, and CD-ROM The Golden Nugget.
PICTURES: The Young Philadelphians, Geronimo, Soldier in the Rain, Tammy and the Doctor, Robinson Crusoe on Mars, The Outlaws Is Coming!, Mara of the Wilderness, Batman, The Girl Who Knew Too Much, Marriage of a Young Stockbroker, The Specialist, Hell River, Hooper, The Happy Hooker Goes to Hollywood, Blonde Ambition, One Dark Night, Young Lady Chatterly, Hell Raiders, Zombie Nightmare, Doin' Time on Planet Earth, Mad About You, John Travis: Solar Survivor, Maxim Xul, Night of the Kickfighter, The New Age, Not This Part of the World, Bigger Than Watermelon, An American Vampire Story.
TELEVISION: *Series*: The Detectives, Batman, The Last Precinct, Danger Theatre, The Clinic. *Movies*: The Eyes of Charles Sands, For the Love of It, I Take These Men, Nevada Smith, Poor Devil, The Last Precinct. *Guest*: Hawaiian Eye, 77 Sunset Strip, Bonanza, The Outer Limits, Petticoat Junction, Bewitched, The Big Valley, Love American Style, Night Gallery, Mannix, Alice, Murder She Wrote, Hope and Gloria, Lois and Clark, Burke's Law, The Simpsons (voice), The Critic (voice), Batman (animated series; voice), Politically Incorrect, Weird Science, Rugrats (voice), Animaniacs (voice), Murphy Brown, Pauly Shore Show, Wayans Brothers, MTV's Singled Out. *Pilots*: Lookwell, 1775, Reel Life, Doc Holliday, Burnett, Johnny Cinderella, Alexander the Great.

WEST, TIMOTHY
Actor. b. Yorkshire, England, Oct. 20, 1934. m. actress Prunella Scales. e. John Lyon Sch. Harow. Ent. ind. 1960. Began acting 1956 after two years as recording engineer. Worked in regional repertory, London's West End and for Royal Shakespeare Company. Dec., 1979 appointed artistic controller of Old Vic. Has directed extensively in the theatre.
PICTURES: Twisted Nerve, The Looking Glass War, Nicholas and Alexandra, The Day of the Jackal, Hedda, Joseph Andrews, The Devil's Advocate, Agatha, The Thirty Nine Steps, Rough Cut, Cry Freedom, Consuming Passions.
TELEVISION: Edward VII, Hard Times, Crime and Punishment, Henry VIII, Churchill and the Generals, Brass, The Monocled Mutineer, The Good Doctor Bodkin Adams, What the Butler Saw, Harry's Kingdom, The Train, When We Are Married, Breakthrough at Reykjavik, Strife, A Shadow on the Sun, The Contractor, Blore, m.p., Survival of the Fittest, Oliver Twist, Why Lockerbie, Framed, Smokescreen, Eleven Men Against Eleven, Cuts, The Place of the Dead.

WESTON, JAY
Producer. b. New York, NY, March 9, 1929. e. New York U. Operated own pub. agency before moving into film prod. In 1965 launched Weston Production; sold orig. s.p., The War Horses, to Embassy Pictures; acquired and marketed other properties. Became prod. story exec. for Palomar-ABC Pictures in 1967.
THEATER: Does a Tiger Wear a Necktie? (co-prod.).
PICTURES: For Love of Ivy (co-prod.), Lady Sings the Blues (co-prod.), W.C. Fields and Me, Chu Chu and the Philly Flash, Night of the Juggler, Buddy Buddy, Side Out.
TELEVISION: Laguna Heat (exec. prod.).

WETTIG, PATRICIA
Actress. b. Cincinnati, OH, Dec. 4, 1951. m. actor Ken Olin. e. Temple Univ. Studied at Neighborhood Playhouse. Began acting career with NY's Circle Repertory Company appearing in The Wool Gatherer, The Diviners and A Tale Told. Other theatre work includes The Dining Room, Talking With (LA), Threads, Innocent Thoughts, My Mother Said I Never Should.
PICTURES: Guilty by Suspicion, City Slickers, Veronica & Me, City Slickers II: The Legend of Curly's Gold.
TELEVISION: *Series*: St. Elsewhere, thirtysomething (2 Emmy Awards), Courthouse. *Movies*: Silent Motive, Taking Back My Life: The Nancy Ziegenmeyer Story, Parallel Lives, Nothing But the Truth, Kansas. *Mini-Series*: Stephen King's The Langoliers.

WEXLER, HASKELL
Cinematographer, Director. b. Chicago, IL June 2, 1922. Photographed educational and industrial films before features. Documentaries as cinematographer include: The Living City, The Savage Eye, T. for Tumbleweed, Stakeout on Dope Street, Brazil—A Report on Torture, Interviews With Mai Lai Veterans, Interview—Chile's President Allende, Introduction to the Enemy. Elected by AMPAS to Bd. of Governors, Cinematographers Branch. 1991, elected by AMPAS to bd. of govs., Cinematographers Branch; 1993, received lifetime achievement award from American Society of Cinematographers.
PICTURES: *Cinematographer:* Studs Lonigan, Five Bold Women, The Hoodlum Priest, Angel Baby, A Face in the Rain, America America, The Best Man, The Bus (also dir., prod.), The Loved One (also co-prod.), Who's Afraid of Virginia Woolf? (Academy Award, 1966), In the Heat of the Night, The Thomas Crown Affair, Medium Cool (also dir., co-prod., s.p.), Trial of Catonsville Nine, American Graffiti, One Flew Over the Cuckoo's Nest, Bound for Glory (Academy Award, 1976), Coming Home, Days of Heaven (addit. photog.), No Nukes (also co-dir.), Second Hand Hearts, Richard Pryor: Live on the Sunset Strip, Lookin' to Get Out, The Man Who Loved Women, Matewan (Oscar nom.), Colors, Latino (dir., writer only), Three Fugitives, Blaze (Oscar nom.), Through the Wire, Other People's Money, Rolling Stones at the MAX, The Babe, The Secret of Roan Inish, Canadian Bacon, The Sixth Sun: Mayan Uprising in Chiapas, Mulholland Falls, The Rich Man's Wife, IMAX: Mexico, Stakeout on Dope Street, Limbo.
TELEVISION: Steve McQueen: The King of Cool.

WHALEY, FRANK
Actor. b. Syracuse, NY, July 20, 1963. e. SUNY, Albany. With his brother formed rock band the Niagaras. Member of Malaparte Theatre Co. in NY.
THEATER: *NY*: Tigers Wild (debut, 1986), Face Divided, The Indian Wants the Bronx, The Years, Good Evening, Hesh, The Great Unwashed.
PICTURES: Ironweed (debut, 1987), Field of Dreams, Little Monsters, Born on the Fourth of July, The Freshman, Cold Dog Soup, The Doors, Career Opportunities, JFK, Back in the U.S.S.R., A Midnight Clear, Hoffa, Swing Kids, Pulp Fiction, I.Q., Swimming With Sharks, Homage, Cafe Society, Broken Arrow, Retroactive, Glam, When Trumpets Fade, Went to Coney Island on a Mission from God...Be Back By Five, The Wall, Curtain Call, Pursuit of Happiness.
TELEVISION: *Specials*: Soldier Boys, Seasonal Differences. *Movies*: Unconquered, Flying Blind, Fatal Deception: Mrs. Lee Harvey Oswald, To Dance With the White Dog, The Desperate Trail, Dead Man's Gun, Shake, Rattle, and Roll: An American Love Story, When Trumpets Fade. *Pilot:* Flipside. *Guest*: Spenser: For Hire, The Equalizer.

WHALLEY-KILMER, JOANNE
Actress. b. Manchester, England, Aug. 25, 1964. Began stage career while in teens including season of Edward Bond plays at Royal Court Theatre (Olivier Award nom.) and The Three Sisters, The Lulu Plays. *NY*: What the Butler Saw (Theatre World Award).
PICTURES: Dance with a Stranger, No Surrender, The Good Father, Willow, To Kill a Priest, Scandal, Kill Me Again, Navy SEALS, Crossing the Line, Shattered, Storyville, Mother's Boys, The Secret Rapture, Trial by Jury, A Good Man in Africa, The Man Who Knew Too Little, Texas Funeral, Run the Wild Fields, The Guilty.
TELEVISION: The Singing Detective, A Quiet Life, Edge of Darkness, A Christmas Carol, Save Your Kisses, Will You Love Me Tomorrow, Scarlett.

WHEATON, WIL
Actor. r.n. Richard William Wheaton III. b. Burbank, CA, July 29, 1972. Began acting in commercials at age 7. Graduated L.A. Professional H.S., June, 1990.

PICTURES: The Secret of NIMH (voice), The Buddy System, Hambone and Hillie, The Last Starfighter, Stand by Me, The Curse, Toy Soldiers, December, The Liars' Club, Pie in the Sky, Trekkies, Tales of Glamour and Excess, Flubber, Fag Hag, The Girls' Room, Foreign Correspondents.
TELEVISION: *Series*: Star Trek: The Next Generation. *Pilots*: Long Time Gone, 13 Thirteenth Avenue, The Man Who Fell to Earth. *Movies*: A Long Way Home (debut, 1981), The Defiant Ones, Young Harry Houdini, The Last Prostitute, The Day Lincoln Was Shot. *Specials*: The Shooting, My Dad Can't Be Crazy Can He?, Lifestories (A Deadly Secret). *Guest*: St. Elsewhere, Family Ties, Tales From the Crypt, Outer Limits.

WHEDON, JOSS
Writer. b. June 23, 1964. e. Wesleyan University.
PICTURES: Buffy the Vampire Slayer, Speed, Waterworld, Toy Story, Twister, Alien Resurrection, Titan A.E.
TELEVISION: Roseanne, Angel (dir. and prod. only), Buffy the Vampire Slayer (also prod. and dir.), Boy Meets World (prod. and dir. only).

WHITAKER, FOREST
Actor, Director. b. Longview, TX, July 15, 1961. Raised in Los Angeles. e. Pomona Col., studying music; USC, studying opera and drama. Prof. debut in prod. of The Beggar's Opera. Directed Whitney Houston's "Exhale (Shoop Shoop)" video.
THEATER: Swan, Romeo and Juliet, Hamlet, Ring Around the Moon, Craig's Wife, Whose Life Is It Anyway?, The Greeks (all at Drama Studio London); School Talk (LA), Patchwork Shakespeare (CA Youth Theatre), The Beggar's Opera, Jesus Christ Superstar. *Dir.*: Look Back in Anger, Drums Across the Realm.
PICTURES: Tag: The Assassination Game (debut, 1982), Fast Times at Ridgemont High, Vision Quest, The Color of Money, Platoon, Stakeout, Good Morning Vietnam, Bloodsport, Bird (Cannes Film Fest. Award, 1988), Johnny Handsome, Downtown, Rage in Harlem (also co-prod.), Article 99, Diary of a Hit Man, Consenting Adults, The Crying Game, Bank Robber, Body Snatchers, Blown Away, Jason's Lyric, Ready to Wear (Pret-a-Porter), Smoke, Species, Phenomenon, The Split, Ghost Dog: The Way of the Samurai, Four Dogs Playing Poker, Light It Up, Battlefield Earth, Clint Eastwood: Out of the Shadows, American Storytellers, The Panic Room, Green Dragon, The Fourth Angel. *Dir.*: Waiting to Exhale, Hope Floats.
TELEVISION: *Movies*: Hands of a Stranger, Criminal Justice, Last Light, Strapped (dir. only), Lush Life, The Enemy Within, Rebound: The Legend of Earl 'The Goat' Manigault, Witness Protection. *Guest*: Amazing Stories, Hill Street Blues, Cagney and Lacey, Trapper John M.D., The Fall Guy, Different Strokes. *Mini-Series*: North and South Parts I & II, Feast of All Saints.

WHITE, BETTY
Actress. b. Oak Park, IL, Jan. 17, 1924. Graduated from Beverly Hills H.S. Performed on radio beginning in early 1940's on such shows as Blondie, The Great Gildersleeve, This Is Your FBI. Became local L.A. tv personality in early 1950's prior to starring in her first series to be seen nationwide, Life With Elizabeth, in 1953. Was married to late tv host Allen Ludden. Inducted into Academy of Television Arts & Sciences Hall of Fame, 1994. Recipient of Comedy Lifetime Achievement Award.
AUTHOR: Betty White's Pet Love (1983), Betty White In Person (1987), The Leading Lady: Dinah's Story (1991), Here We Go Again: My Life in Television (1995).
PICTURES: Advise and Consent, The Flood.
TELEVISION: *Series*: Life With Elizabeth, Make the Connection (panelist), Date With the Angels, The Betty White Show (1958), The Jack Paar Show, The Pet Set, The Mary Tyler Moore Show (2 Emmy Awards: 1975, 1976), Match Game P.M. (panelist), Liar's Club (panelist), The Betty White Show (1977-78), Just Men (host; Emmy Award, 1983), Mama's Family, The Golden Girls (Emmy Award, 1986), The Golden Palace, Bob, Maybe This Time. *Movies*: Vanished, With This Ring, The Best Place to Be, Before and After, The Gossip Columnist, Chance of a Lifetime. *Host*: Macy's Thanksgiving Parade for 10 yrs, Tournament of Roses Parade (20 yrs.). *Guest*: The Millionaire, U.S. Steel Hour, Petticoat Junction, The Odd Couple, Sonny and Cher, The Love Boat, Hotel, Matlock, The John Laroquette Show (Emmy Award, 1996), Suddenly Susan.

WHITE, ROY B.
Executive, Exhibitor. b. Cincinnati, OH, July 30, 1926. e. U. of Cincinnati. U.S. Air Force during WWII; sales department of 20th Century-Fox, 1949-52; began in exhibition, 1952; past pres., Mid-States Theatres; chmn. R. M. White Management, Inc.; past president, National Association of Theatre Owners, past Chairman of the Board, NATO, Board of Trustees—American Film Inst.; bd.of dirs. NATO of Ohio, Motion Picture Pioneers Foundation; Will Rogers Hospital, Nat'l. Endowment for Arts.

WHITELAW, BILLIE
C.B.E., D.Litt.: Actress. b. Coventry, England, June 6, 1932. Acted on radio and television since childhood. Winner of the TV Actress of the Year and 1972, Guild Award, Best Actress, 1960. British Acad. Award 1969; U.S. National Society of Film Critics Award best supp. actress, 1968. Evening News, Best Film Actress, 1977; best actress Sony Radio Radio Award 1987, 1989. 1988 Evening Standard Award for Best Actress.
THEATER: England Our England (revue), Progress to the Park, A Touch of the Poet, Othello; 3 yrs. with Natl. Theatre of Great Britain; Trelawney of the Wells, After Haggerty, Not I, Alphabetical Order, Footfalls, Molly, The Greeks, Happy Days, Passion Play, Rockaby (also in N.Y. and Adelaide Festival), Tales from Hollywood, Who's Afraid of Virginia Woolf?
PICTURES: The Fake (debut, 1953), Companions in Crime, The Sleeping Tiger, Room in the House, Small Hotel, Miracle in Soho, Gideon of Scotland Yard, Carve Her Name With Pride, Bobbikins, Mania, Hell Is a City, Make Mine Mink, No Love for Johnnie, Mr. Topaze (I Like Money), Payroll, The Devil's Agent, The Comedy Man, Charlies Bubbles, The Adding Machine, Twisted Nerve, Start the Revolution Without Me, Leo the Last, Eagle in a Cage, Gumshoe, Frenzy, Night Watch, The Omen, Leopard in the Snow, The Water Babies, An Unsuitable Job for a Woman, The Dark Crystal (voice), Tangier, Slayground, Shadey, The Chain, Murder Elite, Maurice, The Dressmaker, Joyriders, The Krays, Freddie as F.R.O.7 (voice), Deadly Advice.
TELEVISION: Over 100 leading roles including: No Trains to Lime Street, Lady of the Camelias, Resurrection, Beyond the Horizon, Anna Christie, You and Me, A World of Time, Dr. Jekyll and Mr. Hyde, Poet Game, Sextet (8 plays for BBC), Wessex Tales, The Fifty Pound Note, Supernatural (2 plays), Four plays by Samuel Beckett, Eustace and Hilda, The Oresteia of Aeschylus, The Haunted Man, Private Schultz, Jamaica Inn, Happy Days, Camille, Imaginary Friends, The Secret Garden, The Picnic, A Tale of Two Cities, The Fifteen Streets, Three Beckett plays, Lorna Doone, Duel of Love, A Murder of Quality, The Cloning of Joanna May, The Entertainer, Firm Friends, Skallagrigg.

WHITEMORE, HUGH
Writer. b. England, 1936. Studied acting at Royal Acad. of Dramatic Art. Has since written for television, film, theatre.
THEATER: Stevie, Pack of Lies, Breaking the Code, The Best of Friends, It's Ralph.
PICTURES: All Neat in Black Stockings, All Creatures Great and Small, Stevie, The Return of the Soldier, 84 Charing Cross Road, Utz, Jane Eyre.
TELEVISION: Cider With Rosie (Writers' Guild Award 1971), Elizabeth R (Emmy Award, 1971), Country Matters (Writers' Guild Award, 1972), Dummy (RAT—Prix Italia, 1979), Rebecca, All For Love, A Dedicated Man, Down at the Hydro, A Bit of Singing and Dancing, Concealed Enemies (Emmy & Neil Simon Awards, 1984), Pack of Lies, The Final Days, The Best of Friends, The Turn of the Screw.

WHITMAN, STUART
Actor. b. San Francisco, CA., Feb. 1, 1928. Army Corp. of Engineers (1945-1948), at Fort Lewis, WA; while in army, competed as light heavyweight boxer. Studied drama under G.I. Bill at Ben Bard Drama Sch. and L.A. City Coll. Performed in Heaven Can Wait and became member of Michael Chekhov Stage Society and Arthur Kennedy Group. Entered films in early 1950's. TV debut on 26 episodes of Highway Patrol.
PICTURES: When Worlds Collide, The Day The Earth Stood Still, Rhapsody, Seven Men From Now, War Drums, Johnny Trouble, Darby's Rangers, Ten North Frederick, The Decks Ran Red, China Doll, The Sound and the Fury, These Thousand Hills, Hound Dog Man, The Story of Ruth, Murder Inc., Francis of Assisi, The Fiercest Heart, The Mark (Acad. Award nom.), The Comancheros, Convicts 4, The Longest Day, The Day and the Hour (Fr./It.), Shock Treatment, Rio Conchos, Those Magnificent Men In Their Flying Machines, Sands of the Kalahari, Signpost to Murder, An American Dream, The Invincible Six, The Last Escape, Captain Apache (US/Sp.), Night Of The Lepus, Welcome To Arrow Beach (Tender Flesh), Crazy Mama, Call Him Mr. Shatter, Assault on Paradise (Maniac/Ransom), Mean Johnny Barrows, Las Vegas Lady, Eaten Alive!, Tony Saitta/Tough Tony (It.), Strange Shadows In An Empty Room, Ruby, The White Buffalo; Delta Fox, Thoroughbred (Run for the Roses), Oil (It. as Red Adair), La Murjer de la Tierra Caliente (Sp./It.); Guyana: Cult of the Damned, Cuba Crossing, Jamaican Gold, The Monster Club, Demonoid, Butterfly, Treasure of The Amazon, John Travis: Solar Survivor, Deadly Reactor, Moving Target, Mob Boss, Private Wars, Trail by Jury, Improper Conduct, Land of Milk and Honey.

TELEVISION: *Series*: Cimarron Strip, Shaunessy (pilot). *Guest*: The Crowd Pleaser (Alcoa-Goodyear), Highway Patrol, Dr. Christian, Hangman's Noose (Zane Grey), Walker Texas Ranger, Adventures of Brisco County Jr., Time Trax, Courthouse. *Mini-Series*: The Last Convertible, Hemingway. *Movies*: The Man Who Wanted to Live Forever, City Beneath the Sea, Revenge, The Woman Hunter, The Man Who Died Twice, Cat Creature, Go West Young Girl, The Pirate, Women in White, The Seekers, Condominium, Stillwatch, Once Upon a Texas Train, Wounded Heart.

WHITMORE, JAMES
Actor. r.n. James Allen Whitmore, Jr. b. White Plains, NY, Oct. 1, 1921. e. Yale U. In Yale Drama Sch. players; co-founder Yale radio station, 1942; U.S. Marine Corps, W.W.II; in USO, in American Wing Theatre school, in stock. Broadway debut in Command Decision, 1947.
THEATER: Give 'em Hell Harry, Will Rogers USA, Almost an Eagle.
PICTURES: The Undercover Man (debut, 1949), Battleground (Acad. Award nom.), The Asphalt Jungle, The Next Voice You Hear, Mrs. O'Malley and Mr. Malone, The Outriders, Please Believe Me, Across the Wide Missouri, It's a Big Country, Because You're Mine, Above and Beyond, The Girl Who Had Everything, All the Brothers Were Valiant, Kiss Me Kate, The Command, Them!, Battle Cry, The McConnell Story, The Last Frontier (Savage Wilderness), Oklahoma!, Crime in the Streets, The Eddie Duchin Story, The Deep Six, Face of Fire, Who Was That Lady?, Black Like Me, Chuka, Waterhole No. 3, Nobody's Perfect, Planet of the Apes, Madigan, The Split, Guns of the Magnificent Seven, Tora! Tora! Tora!, Chato's Land, The Harrad Experiment, Where the Red Fern Grows, Give 'em Hell Harry (Acad. Award nom.), The Serpent's Egg, Bully, The First Deadly Sin, The Adventures of Mark Twain (voice), Nuts, Old Explorers, The Shawshank Redemption, The Relic, Old Hats.
TELEVISION: *Series*: The Law and Mr. Jones, My Friend Tony, Temperature's Rising. *Movies*: The Challenge, If Tomorrow Comes, I Will Fight No More Forever, Rage, Mark I Love You, Glory! Glory!, Sky High, Swing Vote. *Mini-Series*: The Word, Celebrity, Favorite Son. *Special*: All My Sons.

WHITTON, MARGARET
Actress. b. Baltimore, MD, Nov. 30, 1950. Raised in Haddonfield, NJ. Has written articles for Village Voice, The National.
THEATER: *NY*: Nourish the Beast (Off-B'way debut, 1973), Another Language, The Art of Dining, Chinchilla, Othello, One Tiger to a Hill, Henry IV Part 1, Don Juan, Steaming, Aunt Dan and Lemon, Ice Cream/Hot Fudge. *Regional*: Hamlet, Camille, Time and the Conways, The House of Blue Leaves.
PICTURES: National Lampoon Goes to the Movies (debut, 1981), Love Child, The Best of Times, 9-1/2 Weeks, The Secret of My Success, Ironweed, Major League, Little Monsters, Big Girl Don't Cry... They Get Even, The Man Without a Face, Major League 2, Trial by Jury.
TELEVISION: *Series*: Search for Tomorrow, Hometown, A Fine Romance, Good and Evil. *Special*: Motherlove. *Movies*: The Summer My Father Grew Up, Menendez: A Killing in Beverly Hills.

WIDMARK, RICHARD
Actor. b. Sunrise, MN, Dec. 26, 1914. e. Lake Forest U. Was drama instructor, 1936, before going to NY where he acted on many radio dramas, then stage.
PICTURES: Kiss of Death (debut, 1947), Road House, Street With No Name, Yellow Sky, Down to the Sea in Ships, Slattery's Hurricane, Night and the City, Panic in the Streets, No Way Out, Halls of Montezuma, The Frogmen, Red Skies of Montana, Don't Bother to Knock, O. Henry's Full House, My Pal Gus, Destination Gobi, Pickup on South Street, Take the High Ground, Garden of Evil, Hell & High Water, Broken Lance, Prize of Gold, The Cobweb, Backlash, Run for the Sun, The Last Wagon, Saint Joan, Time Limit, The Law and Jake Wade, The Tunnel of Love, The Trap, Warlock, The Alamo, The Secret Ways, Two Rode Together, Judgment at Nuremberg, How the West Was Won, Flight from Ashiya, The Long Ships, Cheyenne Autumn, The Bedford Incident, Alvarez Kelly, The Way West, Madigan, Death of a Gunfighter, A Talent for Loving, The Moonshine War, When The Legends Die, Murder on the Orient Express, The Sell Out, To the Devil a Daughter, Twilight's Last Gleaming, The Domino Principle, Rollercoaster, Coma, The Swarm, Dinero Maldito, Bear Island, National Lampoon Goes to the Movies, Hanky Panky, Who Dares Wins, The Final Option, Against All Odds, True Colors.
TELEVISION: *Series*: Madigan. *Movies*: Vanished, Brock's Last Case, The Last Day, Mr. Horn, All God's Children, A Whale for the Killing, Blackout, A Gathering of Old Men, Once Upon a Texas Train, Cold Sassy Tree. *Special*: Benjamin Franklin.

WIESEN, BERNARD
Producer, Director, Writer, Executive. b. New York, NY. e. City Coll. of New York, B.A.; Pasadena Playhouse Coll. of Theatre, Master of Theatre Arts; Dramatic Workshop of New School.
THEATER: First Monday in October (B'way, co. prod).
PICTURES: *Producer-Director*: Fear No More. *Asst. Dir.*: The King and I, The Left Hand of God, The Rains of Ranchipur, To Catch a Thief, The Trouble with Harry.
TELEVISION: *Director*: How to Marry a Millionaire, Valentine's Day. *Assoc. Producer*: Valentine's Day, Three on an Island, Cap'n Ahab, Sally and Sam. *Assoc. Prod.*: Daniel Boone. *Producer/Director*: Julia, *Co-Producer-Director*: The Jimmy Stewart Show. *Prod. Exec.*: Executive Suite (pilot). *Exec.* Paramount TV, director of current programming. *Writer*: Love 4 Love, The Grand Turk.

WIEST, DIANNE
Actress. b. Kansas City, MO, March 28, 1948. e. U. of Maryland. Studied ballet but abandoned it for theatre. Did regional theatre work (Yale Repertory, Arena Stage), performed with NY Shakespeare Festival, toured with American Shakespeare Co.
THEATER: *Regional*: Arena Stage (DC): Heartbreak House, Our Town, The Dybbuk, Inherit the Wind. *Yale Rep.*: Hedda Gabler, A Doll's House. *NY*: Ashes (NY debut, 1977, at Public Theatre), Agamemnon, Leave It to Beaver Is Dead, The Art of Dining (Obie & Theatre World Awards), Bonjour La Bonjour, Frankenstein (B'way), Three Sisters, Othello, Beyond Therapy, Other Places, Serenading Louie (Obie Award), After the Fall, Not About Heroes (dir.; also at Williamstown Fest.), Hunting Cockroaches, Square One, In the Summer House, Blue Light, The Shawl (Off B'way), One Flea Spare (NY Public Theatre).
PICTURES: It's My Turn (debut, 1980), I'm Dancing as Fast as I Can, Independence Day, Footloose, Falling in Love, The Purple Rose of Cairo, Hannah and Her Sisters (Acad. Award, supporting actress, 1986), Radio Days, The Lost Boys, September, Bright Lights Big City, Parenthood (Acad. Award nom.), Cookie, Edward Scissorhands, Little Man Tate, Cops and Robbersons, The Scout, Bullets Over Broadway (Academy Award, best supporting actress, 1994; also Golden Globe, NY Film Critics, LA Film Critics, Natl. Bd. of Review Awards), Drunks, The Birdcage, The Associate, Practical Magic, The Horse Whisperer, Portofino.
TELEVISION: *Specials*: Zalman or the Madness of God, Out of Our Father's House. *Movies*: The Wall, The Face of Rage. *Guest*: Avonlea (Emmy Award, 1997). *Series*: Law and Order.

WIGAN, GARETH
Executive. b. London, England. e. Oxford U.. Began career in the industry as theatrical agent and film producer. v.p. of production, Twentieth Century Fox, 1975-79; partner & producer, The Ladd Co. (Warner Communications), 1979-83; producer, American Flyers, produced by his own company with Paula Weinstein under Warner Bros;, 1983-87; consultant, exec. of production, exec. v.p., Columbia Pictures, 1987-97. Currently co-vice chairman, Columbia TriStar Motion Picture Group.

WILBY, JAMES
Actor. b. Rangoon, Burma, Feb. 20, 1958. Lived a nomadic childhood moving from Burma to Ceylon, then Jamaica and finally England. e. Durham U. Trained at Royal Acad. of Dramatic Art where he played Shakespearean roles and landed a part in Oxford Film Foundation's Privileged (1982). West End stage debut Another Country. Also acted in regional theater. 1988: The Common Pursuit.
PICTURES: Privileged (debut, 1982), Dreamchild, Maurice, A Handful of Dust, A Summer Story, Immaculate Conception, Howards End, The Chess Game, Une Partie d'Echec, Regeneration: Tom's Midnight Garden.
TELEVISION: Dutch Girls, A Tale of Two Cities, Mother Love, Tell Me That You Love Me, Adam Bede, Lady Chatterly, You Me and It, Crocodile Shoes, Treasure Seekers, Original Sin, Witness Against Hitler, The Woman in White.

WILDE, ARTHUR L.
Publicist. b. San Francisco, CA, May 27. S.F. Daily News; Matson Lines; pub. dept., Warner Bros., 1936; photo editor at Columbia Pictures, RKO Pictures, Universal Pictures; dir. exploitation, CBS; pub. dir., Hal Wallis Prod.; pub. dept., Paramount; pub., Hecht-Hill-Lancaster; v.p., Arthur Jacobs, public rel.; Blowitz-Maskell Publicity Agency; pub. dir., C. V. Whitney Pictures; gen. v.p., 1958; owner, pub.-ad. agency, The Arthur L. Wilde Co., 1961-65; freelance publicist, 1965-66; pub. rel. consultant, Marineland of Florida 1965; unit publicity dir., United Artists, National General, Paramount, 1966-69; freelance publicity, 1971; unit publicist, MGM, Paramount, United Artists, 1972-74; staff position; Features Publicity at Paramount Pictures, 1973. Freelance unit publicist again in 1976 at Universal, Paramount and Lorimar Productions. 1978-79, Columbia Pictures & Universal Studios; 1980, Marble Arch. Prods. & Northstar Intl. Pictures; 1981, studio pub. mgr. 20th Century-Fox; recently staff unit publicist for 20th-Fox; 1984-89; currently freelance unit publicist for feature films.

WILDER, BILLY
Director, Writer, Producer. r.n. Samuel Wilder. b. Austria, June 22, 1906. Newspaperman in Vienna and Berlin; then author of screen story People on Sunday (debut, 1929) followed by 10 other German films. including Emil and the Detectives (s.p.). Co-dir. French film Mauvaise Graine with Alexander Esway (also story), marking debut as director, 1933. To Hollywood 1934. Head of Film Section, Psych. Warfare Div., U.S. Army, 1945, American Zone, Germany. Recipient: American Film Institute Life Achievement Award, 1987; Irving Thalberg Memorial Award, 1988.
PICTURES: *U.S.: Co-Writer*: Adorable (co-story), Music in the Air, Lottery Lover, Champagne Waltz (co-story), Bluebeard's Eighth Wife, Midnight, Ninotchka, What a Life, Rhythm on the River (co-story), Arise My Love, Ball of Fire, Hold Back the Dawn. *Director/Co-Writer*: The Major and the Minor (U.S. dir. debut, 1942), Five Graves to Cairo, Double Indemnity, The Lost Weekend (Academy Awards for Best Director and Adapted Screenplay, 1945), The Emperor Waltz, A Foreign Affair, Sunset Boulevard (Academy Award for Best Original Story & Screenplay, 1950). *Director-Co-Writer-Producer*: Ace in the Hole (The Big Carnival), Stalag 17, Sabrina, The Seven Year Itch (dir. & co-s.p. only), The Spirit of St. Louis, Love in the Afternoon, Witness for the Prosecution (dir. & co-s.p. only), Some Like It Hot, The Apartment (Academy Awards for Best Picture, Director and Original Story & Screenplay, 1960), One Two Three, Irma La Douce, Kiss Me Stupid, The Fortune Cookie, The Private Life of Sherlock Holmes, Avanti!, The Front Page (dir. & co-s.p. only), Fedora, Buddy Buddy (dir. & co-s.p. only).

WILDER, GENE
Actor, Director, Writer. r.n. Jerry Silberman. b. Milwaukee, WI, June 11, 1935. e. U. of Iowa. Joined Bristol Old Vic company in England, became champion fencer; in NY, worked as chauffeur, fencing instructor, etc. before NY off-B'way debut in Roots. Co-founder of Gilda's Club, a cancer support center in Manhattan.
THEATER: *B'way*: The Complacent Lover, Mother Courage, Luv, One Flew Over the Cuckoo's Nest.
PICTURES: Bonnie and Clyde (debut, 1967), The Producers (Acad. Award nom.), Start the Revolution Without Me, Quackser Fortune Has a Cousin in the Bronx, Willy Wonka and the Chocolate Factory, Everything You Always Wanted to Know About Sex* But Were Afraid to Ask, Rhinoceros, Blazing Saddles, The Little Prince, Young Frankenstein (also co-s.p.), The Adventure of Sherlock Holmes' Smarter Brother (also dir., s.p.), Silver Streak, The World's Greatest Lover (also dir., s.p., prod.), The Frisco Kid, Stir Crazy, Sunday Lovers (also dir. & s.p.; episode: Skippy), Hanky Panky, The Woman in Red (also dir., s.p.), Haunted Honeymoon (also dir., s.p., prod.), See No Evil Hear No Evil (also co-s.p.), Funny About Love, Another You, Stuart Little (voice).
TELEVISION: *Series*: Something Wilder. *Specials*: The Man Who Refused to Die, Death of a Salesman (1966), The Scarecrow, Acts of Love—And Other Comedies, Annie and the Hoods, The Trouble With People, Marlo Thomas Special. *Movie*: Thursday's Game, Murder in a Small Town, Alice in Wonderland, The Lady in Question, Murder in A Small Town.

WILKINSON, TOM
Actor.
PICTURES: A Pocketful of Rye, Wetherby, Sylvia, Sharma and Beyond, Paper Mask, In the Name of the Father, Priest, All Things Bright and Beautiful, Business Affair, Sense and Sensibility, The Ghost and the Darkness, Wilde, Smilla's Sense of Snow, The Full Monty (BAFTA Award, Best Supporting Actor, 1997), Oscar and Lucinda, The Governess, Rush Hour, Shakespeare in Love, Molokai: The Story of Father Damien, Ride with the Devil, Patriot.
TELEVISION: *Movies*: Sakharov, Shake Hands Forever, The Woman He Loved, The Attic: The Hiding of Anne Frank, First and Last, Prime Suspect, Resnick: Lonely Hearts, Eskimo Day, Crossing the Floor, Cold Enough for Snow. *Mini-series*: Spyship, Martin Chuzzlewit.

WILLENBORG, GREGORY H.
Producer. b. Miami, FL, Feb. 18, 1959. e. Geroge Washington U., B.B.A. 1981; UCLA M.B.A. Marketing & Strategic Planning 1983. During grad. school, worked at the political fundraising firm of Lynn, Bryan & Associates. In 1983, he formed Willenborg & Associates, a consulting grp. specializing in marketing and fundraising. Raised 25 million for the Bob Hope Cultural Center in Palm Desert, CA.
TELEVISION: America's Hope Awards (creator), America's Dance Awards (creator), America's Hope Award Honoring Bob Hope, America's All-Star Tribute to Elizabeth Taylor, Ray Charles: 50 Years in Music, An All-Star Tribute to Oprah Winfrey, Jerry Herman's Broadway at the Hollywood Bowl.

WILLIAMS, ANDY
Singer, Performer. b. Wall Lake, IA, Dec. 3, 1927. Sang as teen with brothers, performing on radio in Des Moines, Chicago, and Los Angeles. William Brothers were back up singers on Bing Crosby's hit recording of Swinging on a Star. Andy dubbed singing voice of Lauren Bacall in To Have and Have Not. Went solo after group disbanded in early 1950's.
PICTURES: Something to Sing About, I'd Rather Be Rich.
TELEVISION: *Series:* The College Bowl, Tonight (with Steve Allen; 1954-57), The Andy Williams and June Valli Show, The Chevy Showroom, The Andy Williams Show (1958), The Andy Williams Show (1962-67, 1969-71), The Andy Williams Show (synd.: 1976-77). *Specials:* Love Andy, Kaleidoscope Company, Magic Lantern Show Company, The NBC Kids Search for Santa, The NBC Kids Easter in Rome, many Christmas specials.

WILLIAMS, BERT
Executive, Actor. b. Newark, NJ, April 12, 1922. e. USC. Navy, 1942-45. Summer Stock, 1940-41; world's prof. diving champion, 1945-48; star diver, Larry Crosby, Buster Crabbe, Johnny Weismuller, Dutch Smith Shows, 1945-48; writer, asst. prod., Martin Mooney Prods., PRC, Goldwyn Studios; pres., Bert Prods., Bert Williams Motion Picture Producers and Distributors, Inc. Member, MP Academy of Fine Arts & TV Academy of Arts & Science. Masters Outdoor & Indoor National Diving, 1985-87, 89, 90. 1989 World Masters Diving Champion; 1990 & 1994 World Games Diving Champion.
THEATER: Cat on a Hot Tin Roof, Hamlet, Run From The Hunter, Sugar and Spice, Hope Is a Thing Called Feathers, 69 Below, Tribute.
PICTURES: *Actor*: Fort Apache, Rio Grande, American Bandito, Angel Baby; The Nest of the Cuckoo Birds (also prod., dir.), Around the World Under the Sea, Deathwatch 28 (s.p.), Gambit, No Secret, This Must Be the Last Day of Summer, Twenty Eight Watched (dir.), Adventure To Treasure Reef (prod., dir.), Knife Fighters (s.p.). Black Freedom; A Crime of Sex, The Masters (prod., dir.), Crazy Joe, Serpico, Lady Ice, The Klansman, Report to the Commissioner, Tracks, All the President's Men, From Noon Till Three, While Buffalo, Shark Bait (s.p.), The Big Bus, Wanda Nevada, Cuba Crossing, Sunnyside, Cuba, The Last Resort, The All Night Treasure Hunt. Tom Horn, Kill Castro, Midnight Madness, The All-American Hustler, 10 to Midnight, Police Academy 2, One More Werewolf Picture, Silent Scream, Murphy's Law, Cobra, Assassinations, Penitentiary III, Messenger of Death, Death Under the Rock, Innocent Blood, Public Access, Tropic of Desire, Duel at Pueblo Solo, Project Eliminators, No Secret, The Usual Suspects.
TELEVISION: Flipper, Sea Hunt, Final Judgment, Project Eliminator, Speargun, Gentle Ben, The Law (pilot) and Police Story (actor), Get Christy Love, General Hospital, Columbo, Brenner for the People, Mayday 40,000 Feet, Jigsaw John (Blue Knight episode), Police Woman, Chips, Mobil One, Street Killing, East of Eden, Rose for Emily, Brett Maverick, Today's F.B.I., The Judge, Fifth St. Gym (also prod., dir., s.p.; pilot), Helter Skelter, The Green Eyed Bear, The Amazing Howard Hughes, Mike Douglas Show, Johnny Carson Show, Tales from the Dark Side, The Last Car, This Is the Life, Deadly Intentions, Divorce Court, Man Who Broke 1000 Chains, Nightmare Classics (Eye of the Panther), Man from Atlantis, Land's End.

WILLIAMS, BILLY DEE
Actor. b. New York, NY, April 6, 1937. e. National Acad. of Fine Arts and Design. Studied acting with Paul Mann and Sidney Poitier at actor's workshop in Harlem. Was child actor in the Firebrand of Florence with Lotte Lenya; Broadway adult debut in The Cool World in 1961.
THEATER: A Taste of Honey, Hallelujah Baby, I Have a Dream, Fences.
PICTURES: The Last Angry Man (debut, 1959), The Out-of-Towners, The Final Comedown, Lady Sings the Blues, Hit!, The Take, Mahogany, The Bingo Long Travelling All-Stars and Motor Kings, Scott Joplin, Star Wars: Episode V-The Empire Strikes Back, Nighthawks, Star Wars: Episode VI-Return of the Jedi, Marvin and Tige, Fear City, Number One with a Bullet, Deadly Illusion, Batman, The Pit and the Pendulum, Driving Me Crazy, Giant Steps, Alien Intruder, Steel Sharks, The Prince, Moving Target, Mask of Death, Woo, The Contract, Fear Runs Silent, The Visit, The Ladies Man, The Last Place on Earth, Good Neighbor.
TELEVISION: *Series*: The Guiding Light, Double Dare. *Mini-Series*: Chiefs. *Movies*: Carter's Army, Brian's Song, The Glass House, Christmas Lilies of the Field, Children of Divorce, The Hostage Tower, The Imposter, Courage, Oceans of Fire, The Right of the People, Dangerous Passion, The Jacksons: An American Dream, Marked for Murder, Percy & Thunder, Heaven & Hell: North and South Book III, Falling for You. *Guest*: The F.B.I., The Interns, Mission Impossible, Mod Squad, Dynasty, In Living Color.

WILLIAMS, CARA
Actress. r.n. Bernice Kamiat. b. Brooklyn, NY, June 29, 1925. e. Hollywood Professional Sch. Ent. ind., 20th Century Fox, child actress.
PICTURES: The Happy Land (debut, 1943), Something for the Boys, In the Meantime Darling, Boomerang!, Don Juan Quilligan, Sitting Pretty, The Saxon Charm, Knock on Any Door, The Girl Next Door, Monte Carlo Baby, The Great Diamond Robbery, Meet Me in Las Vegas, The Helen Morgan Story, Never Steal Anything Small, The Defiant Ones (Acad. Award nom.), The Man from the Diners' Club, Doctors' Wives, The White Buffalo.
TELEVISION: *Series*: Pete and Gladys, The Cara Williams Show, Rhoda. *Guest*: Alfred Hitchcock Presents, Desilu Playhouse, The Jackie Gleason Show, Henry Fonda Special.

WILLIAMS, CARL W.
Executive. b. Decatur, IL, March 9, 1927. e. Illinois State Normal U., B.S., 1949; UCLA, M.A., 1950. dir. adv. photo., Clark Equipment Co., 1951-54; film dir., WKAR-TV, E. Lansing, MI, 1954-56; Prod., dir., Capital Films, E. Lansing, MI, 1957; dir., A-V Laboratory, U.C.L.A., 1957-63; co-dev. Dimension 150 Widescreen process, 1957; formed D-150 Inc., 1963; Filbert Co., 1970, v.p., 1977; v.p., Cinema Equipment Sales of Calif., Inc., 1986; pres. 1992. Member: AMPAS, SMPTE, AFI.

WILLIAMS, CINDY
Actress. b. Van Nuys, CA., Aug. 22, 1947. e. Los Angeles City Coll. Appeared in high school and college plays; first prof. role in Roger Corman's film Gas-s-s-s. Made TV debut in Room 222 and had recurring role.
PICTURES: Gas-s-s-s (debut, 1970), Beware! the Blob, Drive He Said, The Christian Licorice Store, Travels With My Aunt, American Graffiti, The Conversation, Mr. Ricco, The First Nudie Musical, More American Graffiti, UFOria, Rude Awakening, Big Man on Campus, Bingo!, Father of the Bride II (co-prod. only), Meet Wally Sparks.
TELEVISION: *Series*: The Funny Side, Laverne and Shirley, Normal Life, Getting By. *Guest*: Barefoot in the Park, My World and Welcome to It, Love American Style, Nanny and the Professor, Getting Together, Lois and Clark. *Movies*: The Migrants, Helped Wanted: Kids, Save the Dog, Tricks of the Trade, The Leftovers, Perry Mason: The Case of the Poisoned Pen, Menu for Murder (Murder at the PTA Luncheon), Earth Angel, Escape From Terror: The Teresa Stamper Story, The Stepford Husbands. *Special*: The Laverne and Shirley Reunion. *Pilot*: Steel Magnolias, The Neighbors.

WILLIAMS, CLARENCE, III
Actor. b. New York, NY, Aug. 21, 1939. B'way stage: Slow Dance on the Killing Ground (Tony nom.; Theatre World Award), The Great Indoors, Night and Day.
PICTURES: Rituals, The End, Judgment, Road to Galveston, Purple Rain, 52 Pick-Up, Tough Guys Don't Dance, I'm Gonna Git You Sucka, My Heroes Have Always Been Cowboys, Deep Cover, Dead Fall, Sugar Hill, Tales From the Hood, The Immortals, Ritual, The Brave, Sprung, Hoodlum, Starfucker, Frogs for Snakes, Half Baked, The Legend of 1900, Life, The Day October Died, The General's Daughter.
TELEVISION: *Series*: The Mod Squad. *Guest*: The Nasty Boys, Crazy Love, Miami Vice, Twin Peaks, Uptown Undercover, Cosby Mysteries. *Movies*: The Return of the Mod Squad, Against the Wall, Encino Woman, Rebound: The Legend of Earl 'The Goat' Manigault, George Wallace, The Love Bug.

WILLIAMS, ELMO
Film Editor, Director, Producer. b. Oklahoma City, OK, Apr. 30, 1913. Film editor 1933-39, with British & Dominion Studio, England. Since then with RKO-Radio as film editor for numerous major productions; mgr., dir., 20th Century Fox Prod. Ltd. v.p., worldwide production, 20th Century-Fox Film 1971. President Ibex Films. Exec. v.p., Gaylord Prods., 1979; promoted to pres., worldwide prods.
PICTURES: High Noon (edit; Academy Award, 1952), Tall Texan (dir., edit.), The Cowboy (prod., dir., edit.), 20,000 Leagues Under the Sea (edit.), Apache Kid (dir.), The Vikings (2nd unit dir., film ed.), The Big Gamble (2nd Unit dir.), The Longest Day (assoc. prod.), Zorba the Greek (exec. prod.), Those Magnificent Men in Their Flying Machines (exec. prod.), The Blue Max (exec. prod.), Tora! Tora! Tora! (prod.), Sidewinder One (edit.), Caravans (edit.), Man Woman and Child (prod.).
TELEVISION: Tales of the Vikings (co-prod., dir.).

WILLIAMS, ESTHER
Actress, Swimmer. b. Los Angeles, CA, Aug. 8, 1923. e. USC. Swimmer at San Francisco World's Fair Aquacade; professional model. Signed to movie contract by MGM. Voted one of Top Ten Money-Making Stars in M.P. Herald-Fame poll, 1950.
PICTURES: Andy Hardy's Double Life (debut, 1942), A Guy Named Joe, Bathing Beauty, Thrill of a Romance, Ziegfeld Follies, The Hoodlum Saint, Easy to Wed, Fiesta, This Time for Keeps, On an Island With You, Take Me Out to the Ball Game, Neptune's Daughter, Pagan Love Song, Duchess of Idaho, Texas Carnival, Callaway Went Thataway (cameo), Skirts Ahoy!, Million Dollar Mermaid, Dangerous When Wet, Easy to Love, Jupiter's Darling, The Unguarded Moment, Raw Wind in Eden, The Big Show, The Magic Fountain, That's Entertainment III.
TELEVISION: *Specials*: Esther Williams in Cypress Gardens, Live From New York, Esther Williams Aqua Spectacular.

WILLIAMS, JO BETH
Actress. b. Houston, TX, Dec. 6, 1948. m. director John Pasquin. e. Brown U. One of Glamour Magazine's top 10 college girls, 1969-70. Acted with rep. companies in Rhode Island, Philadelphia, Boston, Washington, DC, etc. Spent over two years in New York-based daytime serials, Somerset and The Guiding Light.
THEATER: Ladyhouse Blues (1979), A Coupla White Chicks Sitting Around Talking, Gardenia.
PICTURES: Kramer vs. Kramer (debut, 1979), Stir Crazy, The Dogs of War, Poltergeist, Endangered Species, The Big Chill, American Dreamer, Teachers, Desert Bloom, Poltergeist II, Memories of Me, Welcome Home, Switch, Dutch, Stop Or My Mom Will Shoot, Me Myself & I, Wyatt Earp, Jungle 2 Jungle, Little City, It Came From the Sky.
TELEVISION: *Movies*: Fun and Games, The Big Black Pill, Feasting with Panthers, Jabberwocky, The Day After, Adam, Kids Don't Tell, Adam: His Song Continues, Murder Ordained, Baby M, My Name is Bill W, Child of the Night, Bump in the Night (co-exec. prod. only), Victim of Love, Jonathan: The Boy Nobody Wanted, Sex Love and Cold Hard Cash, Chantilly Lace, Final Appeal, Parallel Lives, Voices From Within, A Season of Hope. *Series*: Fish Police (voice), John Grisham's The Client.

WILLIAMS, JOHN
Composer. b. New York, NY, Feb. 8, 1932. e. UCLA, Juilliard Sch. Worked as session musician in '50s; began career as film composer in late '50s. Considerable experience as musical director and conductor as well as composer. Since 1977 conductor of Boston Pops.
PICTURES: I Passed for White, Because They're Young, The Secret Ways, Bachelor Flat, Diamond Head, Gidget Goes to Rome, The Killers, None But the Brave, John Goldfarb Please Come Home, The Rare Breed, How to Steal a Million, The Plainsman, Not with My Wife You Don't, Penelope, A Guide for the Married Man, Fitzwilly, Valley of the Dolls, Daddy's Gone A-Hunting, Goodbye Mr. Chips (music supvr. & dir.), The Reivers, Fiddler on the Roof (musc. dir.; Acad. Award, 1971). The Cowboys, Images, Pete 'n' Tillie, The Poseidon Adventure, Tom Sawyer (musc. supvr.), The Long Goodbye, The Man Who Loved Cat Dancing, The Paper Chase, Cinderella Liberty, Conrack, The Sugarland Express, Earthquake, The Towering Inferno, The Eiger Sanction, Jaws (Acad. Award, 1975), Family Plot, The Missouri Breaks, Midway, Black Sunday, Star Wars: Episode IV-A New Hope (Acad. Award, 1977), Raggedy Ann & Andy, Close Encounters of the Third Kind, The Fury, Jaws II, Superman, Meteor, Quintet, Dracula, 1941, Star Wars: Episode V-The Empire Strikes Back, Raiders of the Lost Ark, Heartbeeps, E.T.: The Extra-Terrestrial (Acad. Award, 1982), Yes Giorgio, Monsignor, Star Wars: Episode VI-Return of the Jedi, Indiana Jones and the Temple of Doom, The River, SpaceCamp, The Witches of Eastwick, Empire of the Sun, The Accidental Tourist, Indiana Jones and the Last Crusade, Born on the Fourth of July, Always, Stanley & Iris, Presumed Innocent, Home Alone, Hook, JFK, Far and Away, Home Alone 2: Lost in New York, Jurassic Park, Schindler's List (Acad. Award, 1993), Sabrina., The Lost World: Jurassic Park, Seven Years In Tibet, Amistad, Rosewood, Stepmom, Saving Private Ryan, Angela's Ashes, Star Wars: Episode I-The Phantom Menace, Memoirs of a Geisha, Star Wars: Episode II, Minority Report, Star Wars: Episode III, Harry Potter and the Sorcerer's Stone, A.I., The Patriot.
TELEVISION: Once Upon a Savage Night, Jane Eyre (Emmy Award), Sergeant Ryker, Heidi (Emmy Award), The Ewok Adventure. *Series themes*: Checkmate, Alcoa Premiere, Wide Country, Lost in Space, The Time Tunnel, NBC News Theme, Amazing Stories.

WILLIAMS, KENNETH S.
Executive. b. Tulsa, OK, Dec. 31, 1955. e. Harvard Coll., B.A. 1978; Columbia U., M.S. 1985. Began as team leader of Chase Manhattan's motion picture lending group 1978-81. Joined Sony Pictures Entertainment in Jan. 1982 as director of corporate finance, was promoted to assistant treas. Oct. 1982. He became treas. in Feb. 1984 and named assistant v.p. in Nov. 1984. Served as v.p. & treas. of both Columbia Pictures Industries, Inc. and the Entertainment Business Sector of the Coca-Cola Co. (Sony Pictures previous parent co.), 1986-87.

1987-90, corporate v.p. & treas. of Sony Pictures Entertainment and was then promoted to senior v.p., Corporate Operations. Was named executive v.p. of Sony Pictures Entertainment in Aug. 1995. Named pres. of Digital Division of Sony Pictures in Jan. 1997.

WILLIAMS, MICHELLE
Actress. b. Kalispell, MT, Sept. 9, 1980.
PICTURES: Lassie, Species, Timemaster, A Thousand Acres, Halloween H20: Twenty Years Later, Dick, But I'm a Cheerleader.
TELEVISION: *Movies:* Killing Mr. Griffin, Kangaroo Palace, If These Walls Could Talk 2. *Series:* Dawson's Creek. *Guest:* Home Improvement.

WILLIAMS, PAUL
Actor, Composer. b. Omaha, NE, Sept. 19, 1940. Began career at studios as set painter and stunt parachutist. Bit and character parts in commercials followed. Became song writer, collaborating briefly with Biff Rose and later with Roger Nichols, with whom wrote several best-sellers, including We've Only Just Begun, Rainy Days and Mondays, Just an Old-Fashioned Love Song.
PICTURES: *Actor*: The Loved One (debut, 1965), The Chase, Watermelon Man, Battle for the Planet of the Apes, Phantom of the Paradise (also songs), Smokey and the Bandit, The Cheap Detective, The Muppet Movie (also songs), Stone Cold Dead, Smokey and the Bandit II, Smokey and the Bandit 3, Zombie High, The Chill Factor, The Doors, Solar Crisis (voice), A Million to Juan, Headless Body in Topless Bar. *Songs for Films*: Cinderella Liberty, Bugsy Malone (also vocals), Lifeguard, A Star Is Born (co-composer; Academy Award for best song: Evergreen, 1976), One on One, The End, Agatha, Ishtar, The Muppet Christmas Carol, Headless Body in Topless Bar.
TELEVISION: *Series*: Sugar Time! (songs, music spvr.). *Movies (actor):* Flight to Holocaust, The Wild Wild West Revisted, Rooster, The Night They Saved Christmas, People Like Us, Hart to Hart Returns.

WILLIAMS, PAUL
Director. b. New York, NY, Nov. 12, 1943. e. Harvard (Phi Beta Kappa, 1965). First gained attention as director of film short, Girl, which won Golden Eagle award, made in collaboration with producer Edward R. Pressman, with whom he formed Pressman-Williams Enterprises which prod. Badlands, Phantom of the Paradise, etc. Now with Fulcrum Productions. In Rose Against the Odds, tv movie.
PICTURES: Out of It (also s.p.), The Revolutionary, Dealing: or the Berkeley-to-Boston Forty-Brick Lost-Bag-Blues (also s.p.), Nunzio, Miss Right (also story), The November Men (also actor), Mirage (also actor), Men (prod.).

WILLIAMS, RICHARD
Producer, Painter, Film Animator. b. March, 1933, Toronto, Canada. Entered industry in 1955. Founded Richard Williams Animation Ltd. in 1962, having entered films by producing The Little Island (1st Prize, Venice Film Festival) in 1955. His company produces TV commercials for England, America, France and Germany, entertainment shorts and animated films. Designed animated feature titles/sequences for What's New Pussycat?, A Funny Thing Happened On The Way To The Forum, Casino Royale, The Charge of the Light Brigade, A Christmas Carol (Academy Award for best animated short, 1972), Who Framed Roger Rabbit (dir. of animation), Arabian Knight (dir., prod., co-s.p.). Awards: at Festivals at Venice, Edinburgh, Mannheim, Montreal, Trieste, Melbourne, West Germany, New York, Locarno, Vancouver, Philadelphia, Zagreb, Hollywood, Cork, Los Angeles. 1989, Academy Award, BAFTA Award, AMPAS Award, special effects, also Special Achievement Awards for work over 30 years, esp. Roger Rabbit by both BAFTA and AMPAS.

WILLIAMS, ROBIN
Actor, Comedian. b. Chicago, IL, July 21, 1951. e. Claremont Men's Coll. (CA), Coll. of Marin (CA), studying acting at latter. Continued studies at Juilliard with John Houseman in New York augmenting income as a street mime. As San Francisco club performer appeared at Holy City Zoo, Intersection, The Great American Music Hall and The Boardinghouse. In Los Angeles performed as stand-up comedian at The Comedy Store, Improvisation, and The Ice House. First TV appearance on 1977 Richard Pryor series followed by The Great American Laugh Off. Guest on Happy Days as extraterrestrial Mork from Ork, led to own series.
PICTURES: Can I Do It...Til I Need Glasses? (debut, 1977), Popeye, The World According to Garp, The Survivors, Moscow on the Hudson, The Best of Times, Club Paradise, Good Morning Vietnam (Acad. Award nom.), The Adventures of Baron Munchausen, Dead Poets Society (Acad. Award nom.), Cadillac Man, Awakenings, Dead Again, The Fisher King (Acad. Award nom.), Hook, Shakes the Clown, FernGully... The Last Rainforest (voice), Aladdin (voice), Toys, Mrs. Doubtfire (also co-prod.), Being Human, Nine Months, To Wong Foo—Thanks for Everything—Julie Newmar, Jumanji, Birdcage, Jack, Hamlet, Good Will Hunting (Acad. Award, Best Supporting Actor, 1997), Flubber, What Dreams May Come, Patch Adams, Jakob the Liar, Get Bruce, Bicentennial Man, A.I. (voice).
TELEVISION: *Series*: The Richard Pryor Show (1977), Laugh-In (1977-78 revival; later aired as series in 1979), Mork and Mindy, Shakespeare: The Animated Tales (host). *Guest*: America Tonight, Ninety Minutes Live, The Alan Hamel Show. *Specials*: An Evening With Robin Williams, E.T. & Friends, Faerie Tale Theatre (The Frog Prince), Carol Carl Whoopi and Robin (Emmy Award, 1987), Free To Be... a Family, Dear America: Letters Home from Vietnam (reader), ABC Presents a Royal Gala (Emmy Award, 1988), In Search of Dr. Seuss. *Movie*: Seize the Day.

WILLIAMS, ROGER
Pianist, Concert, Film, TV Personality. b. Omaha, NE, Oct. 1, 1924. e. Drake U., Idaho State Coll. Hon. Ph.D. Midland and Wagner Colls. Served U.S. Navy WWII. Appeared as guest artist in number of films. Public debut on TV's Arthur Godfrey Talent Scouts and Chance of a Lifetime. Other TV appearances include Ed Sullivan, Hollywood Palace, Kraft Summer Series, Celanese Special. Recorded 75 Albums, Kapp (now MCA) Records, with sales over 15 million albums.

WILLIAMS, TREAT
Actor. r.n. Richard Williams. b. Rowayton, CT, Dec. 1, 1952. e. Franklin and Marshall Coll. Landed role on B'way in musical, Over Here! also played leading role in Grease on B'way.
THEATER: Over Here, Bus Stop (Equity Library Theatre), Once in a Lifetime, The Pirates of Penzance, Some Men Need Help, Oh Hell, Oleanna.
PICTURES: Deadly Hero (debut, 1976), The Ritz, The Eagle Has Landed, Hair, 1941, Why Would I Lie?, Prince of the City, The Pursuit of D. B. Cooper, Once Upon a Time in America, Flashpoint, Smooth Talk, The Men's Club, Dead Heat, Sweet Lies, Heart of Dixie, Night of the Sharks, Russicum, Beyond the Ocean, Where the Rivers Flow North, Hand Gun, Things to Do in Denver When You're Dead, Mulholland Falls, The Phantom, The Devil's Own, Deep Rising, The Deep End of the Ocean.
TELEVISION: *Movies*: Dempsey, A Streetcar Named Desire, J. Edgar Hoover, Echoes in the Darkness, Third Degree Burn, Max and Helen, Final Verdict, Till Death Us Do Part, The Water Engine, Deadly Matrimony, Bonds of Love (also co-exec. prod), Parallel Lives, In the Shadow of Evil, Escape: Human Cargo, The Substitute 2: School's Out. *Mini-Series*: Drug Wars: The Camarena Story. *Specials*: The Little Mermaid (Faerie Tale Theatre), Some Men Need Help, Texan (also dir.), Edgar Allan Poe: Terror of the Soul. *Series*: Eddie Dodd, Good Advice. *Guest*: Tales From the Crypt.

WILLIAMS-JONES, MICHAEL
Executive. b. England, June 3, 1947. Joined United Artists as trainee, 1967; territorial mgr., South Africa, 1969; territorial mgr., Brazil, 1971; territorial mgr., England, 1976; appt. v.p., continental European mgr., 1978; sr. v.p. foreign mgr., 1979; 1982 joined United Intl. Pictures as sr. v.p. intl. sls., based in London. 1984, named pres. UIP motion picture group; 1986, named pres. & CEO. In Dec. 96, retired from UIP to create own production co., Merlin Angelsey U.K. Ltd.

WILLIAMSON, FRED
Actor, Director, Producer, Writer. b. Gary, IN, March 5, 1937. e. Northwestern U. Spent 10 yrs. playing pro football before turning to acting.
PICTURES: M*A*S*H (debut, 1970), Tell Me That You Love Me Junie Moon, Fist of Fear Touch of Death, Taxi Killer (prod.), The Legend of Nigger Charlie, Hammer, That Man Bolt, The Soul of Nigger Charlie, Hell Up in Harlem, Black Caesar, Three Tough Guys, Three Days to a Kill (also dir., s.p.), Justice Done (also dir.), Soda Cracker (also dir., prod.), Three the Hard Way, Crazy Joe, Black Eye, `Boss Nigger, Death Journey (also dir., prod.), Bucktown, The Black Bounty Killer (also prod.), Adios Amigo (also dir., prod., s.p.), Take a Hard Ride, Mean Johnny Barrows (also dir., prod.), Joshua, No Way Back (also dir., prod., s.p.), Quel Maledetto Treno Blindato, Mr. Mean (also dir., prod.), Hell's Heroes, Blind Rage, Express to Terror, Fist of Fear Touch of Death, Vigilante, Warriors of the Wasteland, One Down Two to Go (also dir., prod.), The Last Fight (also dir., s.p.), Warriors of the Year 2072, The Big Score (also dir.), 1990: The Bronx Warriors, Warrior of the Lost World, White Fire, Deadly Impact, Foxtrap (also dir., prod.), Delta Force Commando, The Black Cobra, Deadly Intent, Taxi Killer (prod. only), The Kill Reflex (also dir.), Detective Malone, Steele's Law (also dir.), Critical Action (also dir.), Delta Force Commando II: Priority Red One, South Beach (also dir., prod.), Silent Hunter (also dir.), From Dusk Till Dawn, Original Gangstas (also prod.), Full Tilt Boogie.

TELEVISION: *Series*: Julia, Monday Night Football, Half Nelson, Fast Track. *Guest*: Police Story, The Rookies, Lou Grant. *Movies*: Deadlock, 3 Days to a Kill. *Mini-series*: Wheels

WILLIAMSON, KEVIN
Writer. b. New Bern, NC, March 14, 1965.
PICTURES: Scream, I Know What You Did Last Summer, Scream 2 (also exec. prod., actor), Halloween H20: Twenty Years Later (also co-exec. prod.), The Faculty, Teaching Mrs. Tingle (also dir.), Scream 3 (also prod.), Her Leading Man (also prod & dir.), Cursed (also prod.).
TELEVISION: *Series:* Dawson's Creek (exec. prod., creator), Wasteland (exec. prod.)

WILLIAMSON, NICOL
Actor. b. Hamilton, Scotland, Sept. 14, 1938. Has played many classical roles with Royal Shakespeare Co., including Macbeth, Malvolio, and Coriolanus. Starred on Broadway in Inadmissible Evidence, Rex (musical debut), Macbeth, I Hate Hamlet. *London*: Jack.
PICTURES: Inadmissible Evidence (debut, 1968), The Bofors Gun, Laughter in the Dark, The Reckoning, Hamlet, The Jerusalem File, The Monk, The Wilby Conspiracy, Robin and Marian, The Seven Percent Solution, The Goodbye Girl (cameo), The Cheap Detective, The Human Factor, Excalibur, Venom, I'm Dancing as Fast as I Can, Return to Oz, Black Widow, The Exorcist III, Apt Pupil, The Advocate.
TELEVISION: *Movies*: Sakharov, Passion Flower. *Mini-Series*: Lord Mountbatten, The Word, Christopher Columbus. *Specials*: Of Mice and Men, Macbeth, I Know What I Meant.

WILLIAMSON, PATRICK
Executive. b. England, Oct. 1929. Joined Columbia Pictures London office 1944—career spanned advertising & publicity responsibilities until 1967 when appt. managing dir. Columbia Great Britain; also mng. dir. on formation of Columbia-Warner; promoted to exec. position in Columbia's home office, NY, 1973, and pres. of intl. optns. 1974; v.p., Coca-Cola Export Corp., 1983; exec. v.p. Columbia Pictures Industries, 1985; director, CPI, 1985; exec. v.p., Coca-Cola Entertainment Business Sector, 1987; promoted to special asst. to pres. & CEO of Coca-Cola Entertainment Business Sector, 1987; served on boards of Tri-Star Pictures, RCA/Columbia Home Video, RCA/ Columbia Int'l. Video; 1987, named pres. Triumph Releasing Corp., a unit of Columbia Pictures Entertainment; Consultant to Sony Pictures Entertainment, 1989. 1994, dir. & co-founder, Sports Alliance Intl. TV.

WILLIS, BRUCE
Actor. r.n. Walter Bruce Willis. b. Germany, March 19, 1955. Moved to New Jersey when he was 2. After graduating high school, worked at DuPont plant in neighboring town. First entertainment work was as harmonica player in band called Loose Goose. Formed Night Owl Promotions and attended Montclair State Coll. NJ, where he acted in Cat on a Hot Tin Roof. *NY stage debut*: Heaven and Earth. Member of Barbara Contardi's First Amendment Comedy Theatre; supplemented acting work by doing Levi's 501 jeans commercials and as bartender in NY nightclub, Kamikaze. Appeared as extra in film The First Deadly Sin. Star on the Hollywood Walk of Fame, 1998.
THEATER: Fool for Love.
PICTURES: Blind Date, Sunset, Die Hard, In Country, Look Who's Talking (voice), That's Adequate, Die Hard 2, Look Who's Talking Too (voice), The Bonfire of the Vanities, Mortal Thoughts, Hudson Hawk (also co-story), Billy Bathgate, The Last Boy Scout, The Player, Death Becomes Her, National Lampoon's Loaded Weapon 1 (cameo), Striking Distance, North, Color of Night, Pulp Fiction, Nobody's Fool, Die Hard With a Vengeance, Twelve Monkeys, Last Man Standing, Mercury Rising, Armageddon, The Siege, The Sixth Sense, Breakfast of Champions, The Story of Us, The Kid, The Whole Nine Yards, Unbreakable, Hart's War, Bandits.
TELEVISION: *Series*: Moonlighting (Emmy Award, Golden Globe Award, 1987). *Guest*: Hart to Hart, Miami Vice, Twilight Zone, Friends (Emmy Award, 2000). *Special*: Bruce Willis: The Return of Bruno (also writer, prod.).

WILLIS, GORDON
Cinematographer. Acted two summers in stock at Gloucester, MA, where also did stage settings and scenery. Photographer in Air Force; then cameraman, making documentaries. In TV did commercials and documentaries.
PICTURES: End of the Road, Loving, The Landlord, The People Next Door, Little Murders, Klute, The Godfather, Bad Company, Up the Sandbox, The Paper Chase, The Parallax View, The Godfather Part II, The Drowning Pool, All the President's Men, Annie Hall, Interiors, September 30, 1955, Comes a Horseman, Manhattan, Stardust Memories, Pennies from Heaven, A Midsummer Night's Sex Comedy, Zelig, Broadway Danny Rose, The Purple Rose of Cairo, Perfect, The Money Pit, The Pick-Up Artist, Bright Lights Big City, Presumed Innocent, The Godfather Part III, Malice, The Devil's Own. *Director*: Windows (1980; debut).
TELEVISION: *Movie*: The Lost Honor of Kathryn Beck.

WILSON, ELIZABETH
Actress. b. Grand Rapids, MI, April 4, 1921.
THEATER: *B'way*: Picnic (debut, 1953), The Desk Set, The Tunnel of Love, Little Murders, Big Fish Little Fish, Sheep on the Runway, Sticks and Bones (Tony Award, 1972), Uncle Vanya, Morning's at Seven, Ah! Wilderness, The Importance of Being Earnest, You Can't Take It With You, A Delicate Balance. *Off-B'way*: Sheep on the Runway, Token in Marriage (Drama Desk Award), Three Penny Opera, Salonika, Ante Room, Eh?, All's Well That Ends Well. Tour: The Cocktail Hour.
PICTURES: Picnic (debut, 1955), Patterns, The Goddess, The Tunnel of Love, Happy Anniversary, A Child is Waiting, The Birds, The Tiger Makes Out, The Graduate, Jenny, Catch-22, Little Murders, Day of the Dolphin, Man on a Swing, The Happy Hooker, The Prisoner of Second Avenue, Nine to Five, The Incredible Shrinking Woman, Grace Quigley, Where Are the Children?, The Believers, Regarding Henry, The Addams Family, Quiz Show, Nobody's Fool.
TELEVISION: *Series*: East Side West Side, Doc, Morningstar/ Eveningstar, Delta. *Movies*: Miles to Go Before I Sleep, Once Upon a Family, Million Dollar Infield, Sanctuary of Fear, Morning's at Seven, Nutcracker: Money Madness and Murder (Emmy nom.), Conspiracy of Love, Skylark, In the Best of Families: Marriage Pride & Madness, Bitter Blood, In the Best Families, Spring Awakening, Journey to Mars. *Mini-Series*: Queen, Scarlett, Promised Land, Delaventure. *Specials*: Patterns, Happy Endings, You Can't Take It With You. *Guest*: U.S. Steel Hour, Maude, All in the Family, Love Sidney, Murder She Wrote, The Boys Next Door.

WILSON, HUGH
Producer, Director, Writer. b. Miami, FL, Aug. 21, 1943. e. Univ. of FL., 1965. Gained fame for creating, writing, producing and directing TV series, WKRP in Cincinnati, Frank's Place and The Famous Teddy Z. Feature film dir. debut with Police Academy (1984).
PICTURES: *Director &/or Writer*: Stroker Ace, Rough Riders, Police Academy, Rustler's Rhapsody, Burglar, Guarding Tess (also voice), Down Periscope (co-s.p.), Blast From the Past, The First Wives Club.

WILSON, LUKE
Actor. b. Dallas, TX, 1971. Brother is actor-writer Owen Wilson. Debuted in short film Bottle Rocket, which was later expanded to a feature.
PICTURES: Bottle Rocket, Telling Lies in America, Best Men, Scream 2, Rushmore, Home Fries, Dog Park, Bongwater, My Dog Skip, Kill the Man, Committed, Blue Streak, Preston tylk, Charlie's Angels, Soul Survivors, The Third Wheel, Legally Blonde.
TELEVISION: *Guest:* The X Files.

WILSON, OWEN
Actor. Brother is actor Luke Wilson. Debuted in short film Bottle rocket, which he co-wrote and later expanded to feature.
PICTURES: Bottle Rocket (also co-s.p.), The Cable Guy, Anaconda, As Good As It Gets (assoc. prod. only), Rushmore (also co-s.p., exec. prod.), Permanent Midnight, Armageddon, The Minus Man, The Haunting, Breakfast of Champions, Shangai Noon, Kingdom of the Sun (voice), Meet the Parents, Zoolander, Behind Enemy Lines.

WILSON, ROYCE
Executive. b. Rison, AR, Feb. 19, 1957. e. U. of Arkansas, BS/BA, 1980. Sales mgr., Viacom: 1980-83. Sales mgr., KATV Little Rock, 1983-84. VP (southwest), Paramount TV, 1984-87. East. reg. mgr., 1987-90. SVP, syndication, Columbia TriStar Domestic TV, 1990-94. Founder, MaXaM, 1994-96. Pres., Eyemark Entertainment, CBS Entertainment Division, CBS, Inc., 1996-.

WILSON, SCOTT
Actor. b. Atlanta, GA, 1942. Was college athlete on basketball scholarship when injured and had to leave school. Moved to L.A. and enrolled in local acting class.
PICTURES: In the Heat of the Night (debut, 1967), In Cold Blood, The Gypsy Moths, Castle Keep, The Grissom Gang, The New Centurions, Lolly Madonna XXX, The Great Gatsby, Twinkle Twinkle Killer Kane (The Ninth Configuration), The Right Stuff, The Aviator, On the Line, A Year of the Quiet Sun, Blue City, Malone, Johnny Handsome, The Exorcist III, Young Guns II, Femme Fatale, Pure Luck, Flesh and Bone, Geronimo: An American Legend, Tall Tale, Judge Dredd, The Grass Harp, Dead Man Walking, Shiloh, G.I. Jane, Our God's Brother, Clay Pigeons, Pride.

TELEVISION: *Movies*: Jesse, Elvis and the Colonel, Soul Survivors, California Quartet, Tracker.

WINCER, SIMON
Director. b. Australia. Directed over 200 hours of dramatic programs for Australian TV, including Cash and Company, Tandarra, Ryan, Against the Wind, The Sullivans, etc. Exec. prod. of The Man from Snowy River, then the top-grossing theatrical film in Australia.
PICTURES: Snapshot (The Day After Halloween), Harlequin, Phar Lap, D.A.R.Y.L., The Lighthorsemen (also co.-prod.), Quigley Down Under, Harley Davidson and the Marlboro Man, Free Willy, Lightning Jack (also co-prod.), Operation Dumbo Drop, The Phantom, Flash.
TELEVISION: *Movies*: The Last Frontier, Bluegrass, Lonesome Dove (Emmy Award, 1989), The Girl Who Spelled Freedom. *Series*: Homicide (prod.) Matlock Police, The Box, Cash & Company, Young Ramsey, The Young Indiana Jones Chronicles, Escape: Human Cargo. *Mini-series*: Against the Wind.

WINCHELL, PAUL
Actor, Ventriloquist. b. New York, NY, Dec. 21, 1922. e. Sch. of Industrial Arts. At 13 won first prize Major Bowes Radio Amateur Hour; signed by Ted Weems; created dummies Jerry Mahoney and Knucklehead Smiff. On radio as host of his own show in 1940's. In the news in 1975 as inventor of an artificial heart.
PICTURES: Stop! Look! and Laugh! (actor), Winnie the Pooh and the Blustery Day (short; voice), The Aristocats (voice), Which Way to the Front? (actor), Winnie the Pooh and Tigger Too (short; voice), The Fox and the Hound (voice).
TELEVISION: *Series*: The Bigelow Show, The Paul Winchell-Jerry Mahoney Spiedel Show (also prod., writer), Jerry Mahoney's Club House (also writer), What's My Name?, Circus Time (ringmaster), Toyland Express (also prod.), The Paul Winchell Show (1957-60), Banana Splits Adventure Hour (voice), Runaround. *Voices for series:* The Wacky Races, Cartoonsville, Dastardly and Mutley, Help It's the Hair Bear Bunch, Goober and the Ghost Chaser, The Oddball Couple, Clue Club, The C.B. Bears, Wheelie and the Chopper, Heathcliff and Marmaduke Show, The Smurfs, Winnie the Pooh Hour, various Dr. Seuss specials, Smurf specials. *Movie*: The Treasure Chest. *Guest*: Pat Boone Show, Polly Bergen Show, The Lineup, Candid Camera, The Beverly Hillbillies, 77 Sunset Strip, Donna Reed Show, Perry Mason, Dick Van Dyke Show, Lucy Show, Love American Style, Brady Bunch, many others.

WINCOTT, MICHAEL
Actor. b. Canada, Jan. 6, 1959. Studied acting at Juilliard. NY stage incl. Talk Radio, States of Shock.
PICTURES: Wild Horse Hank (debut, 1979), Circle of Two, Ticket to Heaven, Curtains, The Sicilian, Talk Radio, Suffering Bastards, Bloodhounds of Broaway, Born on the Fourth of July, The Doors, Robin Hood: Prince of Thieves, 1492: Conquest of Paradise, The Three Musketeers, Romeo Is Bleeding, The Crow, Panther, Strange Days, Dead Man, Basquiat, Alien: Resurrection, Metro, Gunshy.
TELEVISION: *Movies*: Tragedy of Flight 103: The Inside Story. *Guest*: Miami Vice, Crime Story, The Equalizer. *Special*: High School Narc.

WINDOM, WILLIAM
Actor. b. New York, NY, Sept. 28, 1923.
PICTURES: To Kill a Mockingbird (debut, 1962), Cattle King, For Love or Money, One Man's Way, The Americanization of Emily, Hour of the Gun, The Detective, The Gypsy Moths, The Angry Breed, Brewster McCloud, Fool's Parade, Escape From the Planet of the Apes, The Mephisto Waltz, The Man, Now You See Him Now You Don't, Echoes of a Summer, Mean Dog Blues, Separate Ways, Last Plane Out, Grandview U.S.A., Prince Jack, Space Rage, Funland, Pinocchio and the Emperor of the Night (voice), Planes Trains and Automobiles, She's Having a Baby, Sommersby, Miracle on 34th Street.
TELEVISION: *Series*: The Farmer's Daughter, My World and Welcome to It (Emmy Award, 1970), The Girl With Something Extra, Brothers and Sisters, Murder She Wrote, Parenthood. *Movies*: Prescription: Murder, U.M.C., The House on Greenapple Road, Assault on the Wayne, Escape, A Taste of Evil, Marriage: Year One, The Homecoming, Second Chance, A Great American Tragedy, Pursuit, The Girls of Huntington House, The Day the Earth Moved, The Abduction of St. Anne, Journey from Darkness, Guilty or Innocent: The Sam Sheppard Murder Case, Bridger, Richie Brockelman: Missing 24 Hours, Hunters of the Reef, Portrait of a Rebel: Margaret Sanger, Leave 'Em Laughing, Side Show, Desperate Lives, The Rules of Marriage, Why Me?, Off Sides, Velvet, Surviving, There Must Be a Pony, Dennis the Menace, Chance of a Lifetime, Attack of the 50 Ft. Woman. *Mini-Series*: Once an Eagle, Seventh Avenue, Blind Ambition. *Guest*: Robert Montgomery Presents, Ben Casey, Lucy Show, The FBI, Gunsmoke, Partridge Family, That Girl, The Rookies, Streets of San Francisco, Barney Miller, Kojak, Police Woman, Love Boat, St. Elsewhere, Newhart, Night Gallery, Twilight Zone, Star Trek.

WINDSOR, MARIE
Actress. r.n. Emily Marie Bertelsen. b. Marysvale, UT, Dec. 11, 1919. Winner of beauty contests, including Queen of Covered Wagon Days. Worked as telephone girl, dancing teacher. Trained for acting by Maria Ouspenskaya. Won Look Mag. Award, best supporting actress, 1957.
PICTURES: All-American Co-Ed (debut, 1941), Song of the Thin Man, Unfinished Dance, On an Island With You, Three Musketeers, Kissing Bandit, Force of Evil, Oupost in Morocco, Fighting Kentuckian, Beautiful Blonde From Bashful Bend, Frenchie, Dakota Lil, Little Big Horn, Two Dollar Bettor, Hurricane Island, The Narrow Margin, Japanese War Bride, The Jungle, The Sniper, The Tall Texan, The City That Never Sleeps, The Eddie Cantor Story, Trouble Along the Way, Cat Women of the Moon, Hell's Half Acre, The Bounty Hunter, No Man's Woman, Abbott & Costello Meet the Mummy, Swamp Women, Two Gun Lady, The Killing, The Unholy Wife, The Story of Mankind, Girl in Black Stockings, Parson and the Outlaw, Island Woman, Paradise Alley, The Day Mars Invaded Earth, Critics Choice, Mail Order Bride, Bedtime Story, Chamber of Horrors, Support Your Local Gunfighter, The Good Guys and the Bad Guys, One More Train To Rob, Cahill U.S. Marshall, The Outfit, Hearts of the West, Freaky Friday, Lovely But Deadly.
TELEVISION: *Series*: Supercarrier. *Movies*: Wild Women, Manhunter, Salem's Lot, J.O.E. and the Colonel.

WINFIELD, PAUL
Actor. b. Los Angeles, CA, May 22, 1940. e. attended U. of Portland 1957-59, Stanford U., L.A. City Coll, and UCLA. Inducted in Black Filmmakers Hall of Fame.
THEATER: Regional work at Dallas Theatre Center (A Lesson From Aloes), Goodman Theatre (Enemy of the People), Stanford Repertory Theatre and Inner City Cultural Center, L.A.; At Lincoln Center in The Latent Heterosexual, and Richard III. B'way: Checkmates, Othello, Merry Wives of Windsor.
PICTURES: The Lost Man (debut, 1969), R.P.M., Brother John, Sounder (Acad. Award nom.), Trouble Man, Gordon's War, Conrack, Huckleberry Finn, Hustle, Twilight's Last Gleaming, The Greatest, Damnation Alley, A Hero Ain't Nothin' But a Sandwich, High Velocity, Carbon Copy, Star Trek II—The Wrath of Khan, White Dog, On the Run, Mike's Murder, The Terminator, Blue City, Death Before Dishonor, Big Shots, The Serpent and the Rainbow, Presumed Innocent, Cliffhanger, Dennis the Menace, Original Gangstas, Mars Attacks!, Strategic Command, Relax...It's Just Sex, Assignment Berlin, Knockout.
TELEVISION: *Series*: Julia, The Charmings, Wiseguy, 227, Built to Last, Teen Angel. *Movies*: The Horror at 37,000 Feet, It's Good to Be Alive (The Fight), Green Eyes, Angel City, Key Tortuga, The Sophisticated Gents, Dreams Don't Die, Sister Sister, For Us the Living, Go Tell It on the Mountain, Under Siege, The Roy Campanella Story, Guilty of Innocence, Women of Brewster Place, Roots: The Gift, Back to Hannibal, Breathing Lessons, Tyson, Strange Justice. *Mini-Series*: King, Backstairs at the White House, The Blue and the Gray, Roots: The Next Generations, Queen, Scarlett.

WINFREY, OPRAH
TV Talk Show Hostess, Actress, Producer. b. Kosciusko, MS, Jan. 29, 1954. e. Tennessee State U. Started as radio reporter then TV news reporter-anchor in Nashville. Moved to Baltimore in same capacity, later co-hosting successful morning talk show. Left for Chicago to host own show AM Chicago which became top-rated in only a month; expanded to national syndication in 1986. Formed own production co., Harpo Productions, Inc. in 1986 which assumed ownership and prod. of The Oprah Winfrey Show in 1988. Named Broadcaster of the Year by Intl. Radio and TV Soc., 1988. Purchased Chicago movie and TV production facility, 1988; renamed Harpo Studios. National Daytime Emmy Award, 1987, Outstanding Talk/Service Program Host. Was given Emmy Lifetime Achievement Award in 1998, and then permanently withdrew her name from annual award consideration. Received Honorary National Book Award, 1999. Launched magazine "O" in 2000.
PICTURES: The Color Purple (debut, 1985; Acad. Award nom.), Native Son, Throw Momma From the Train (cameo), Listen Up: The Lives of Quincy Jones, Beloved.
TELEVISION: *Movies*: The Women of Brewster Place (actress, co-exec. prod.), Overexposed (co-prod. only), There Are No Children Here, Lincoln (voice), Before Women Had Wings, About Us: The Dignity of Children. *Series*: The Oprah Winfrey Show (many Emmy Awards), Brewster Place (also exec. prod.). *Special*: Pee-wee's Playhouse Christmas Special. *Mini-series*: The Wedding.

WINGER, DEBRA
Actress. b. Cleveland, OH, May 16, 1955. e. California State U. Began career on TV series Wonder Woman.
PICTURES: Slumber Party '57 (debut, 1977), Thank God It's Friday, French Postcards, Urban Cowboy, Cannery Row, An Officer and a Gentleman (Acad. Award nom.), Terms of Endearment (Acad. Award nom.), Mike's Murder, Legal Eagles, Black Widow, Made in Heaven, Betrayed, Everybody Wins, The Sheltering Sky, Leap of Faith, Wilder Napalm, A Dangerous Woman, Shadowlands (Acad. Award nom.), Forget Paris., Rumi: Poet of the Heart, Big Bad Love.
TELEVISION: *Movie*: Special Olympics. *Guest*: Wonder Woman, James at 16. *Specials*: The Wizard of Oz in Concert: Dreams Come True, In the Wild: Pandas.

WINITSKY, ALEX
Producer. b. New York, NY, Dec. 27, 1924. e. NYU, BS, LLB, JD. In partnership as attorneys in L.A. for 20 years with Arlene Sellers before they turned to financing and later production of films.
PICTURES: *Co-prod. with Sellers*: End of the Game, The White Dawn, The Seven-Per-Cent Solution, Cross of Iron, Silver Bears, The Lady Vanishes, Cuba, Blue Skies Again, Irreconcilable Differences, Scandalous, Swing Shift, Bad Medicine, Stanley & Iris, Circle of Friends.
TELEVISION: Ford—The Man and the Machine.

WINKLER, HENRY
Actor, Producer, Director. b. New York, NY, Oct. 30, 1945. e. Emerson Coll., Yale Sch. of Drama, MA. Appeared with Yale Repertory Co.; returned to N.Y. to work in radio. Did 30 TV commercials before starring in The Great American Dream Machine and Masquerade on TV. Formed Fairdinkum Productions with Ann Daniel.
PICTURES: *Actor*: Crazy Joe (debut, 1974), The Lords of Flatbush, Heroes, The One and Only, Night Shift, Scream, The Waterboy, P.U.N.K.S, Dill Scallion, Ugly Naked People, Down To You. *Exec. Prod*: The Sure Thing, Sightings 6 Years, Dead Man's Gun. *Director*: Memories of Me, Cop and a Half.
TELEVISION: *Series* (actor): Happy Days, Monty. *Series (prod.)*: Ryans Four (co-prod.), Mr. Sunshine (co-exec. prod.), McGyver, A Life Apart. *Guest*: The Mary Tyler Moore Show, The Bob Newhart Show, The Paul Sand Show, Rhoda, Laverne & Shirley, The Larry Sanders Show. *Specials*: Henry Winkler Meets William Shakespeare, America Salutes Richard Rodgers, A Family Again (exec. prod.), Two Daddies (voice, exec. prod.). *Movies*: Katherine, An American Christmas Carol, Absolute Strangers, The Only Way Out, Truman Capote's One Christmas, A Child Is Missing. *Director*: A Smoky Mountain Christmas (movie), All the Kids Do It (also actor, exec. prod.; Emmy Award as exec. prod., 1985). *Exec. prod.*: Who Are the DeBolts and Where Did They Get 19 Kids?, Scandal Sheet, When Your Lover Leaves, Starflight, Second Start, Morning Glory (pilot), MacGyver: Lost Treasure of Atlantis, MacGyver: Trail to Doomsday.

WINKLER, IRWIN
Producer, Director. b. New York, NY, May 28, 1934. e. NYU.
PICTURES: *Producer*: Double Trouble, Blue, The Split, They Shoot Horses Don't They?, The Strawberry Statement, Leo the Last, Believe in Me, The Gang That Couldn't Shoot Straight, The Mechanic, The New Centurions, Up the Sandbox, Busting, S*P*Y*S, The Gambler, Breakout, Peeper, Rocky (Academy Award for Best Picture, 1976), Nickelodeon, New York New York, Valentino, Comes a Horseman, Uncle Joe Shannon, Rocky II, Raging Bull, True Confessions, Rocky III, Author! Author!, The Right Stuff, Rocky IV, Revolution, 'Round Midnight, Betrayed, Music Box, GoodFellas, Rocky V, The Juror. *Director*: Guilty by Suspicion (also s.p.), Night and the City, The Net (also co-s.p., co-prod.), At First Sight (also s.p., prod.,), The Shipping News.
TELEVISION: *Series:* The Net (exec. prod.).

WINNER, MICHAEL
Producer, Director, Writer. b. London, England, Oct. 30, 1935. e. Cambridge U. Ent. m.p. ind. as columnist, dir., Drummer Films. *Presenter*: Michael Winner's True Crimes. *Actor*: For the Greater Good, Decadence, Calliope, Kenny Everett Show, The Full Wax, Birds of a Feather.
PICTURES: *Writer*: Man With A Gun. *Dir.-Writer*: Haunted England (also prod.), Shoot to Kill, Swiss Holiday, Climb Up the Wall, Out of the Shadow, Some Like It Cool, Girls Girls Girls, It's Magic, Behave Yourself, The Cool Mikado, You Must Be Joking, West 11 (dir. only). *Dir./Prod.*: The System (The Girl-Getters), I'll Never Forget What's 'is Name, The Jokers, Hannibal Brooks (also s.p.), The Games, Lawman, The Nightcomers, Chato's Land, The Mechanic (dir. only), Scorpio (also s.p.), The Stone Killer, Death Wish, Won Ton Ton the Dog Who Saved Hollywood, The Sentinel (also s.p.), The Big Sleep (also s.p.), Firepower (also s.p.), Death Wish II, The Wicked Lady (also s.p.), Scream for Help, Death Wish III (dir. only), Appointment With Death (also s.p.), A Chorus of Disapproval (also s.p.), Bullseye (also s.p.), Dirty Weekend (also s.p.), Parting Shots (also s.p., ed.).
TELEVISION: *Series*: White Hunter, Dick and the Duchess.

WINNINGHAM, MARE
Actress. r.n. Mary Megan Winningham. b. Phoenix, AZ, May 16, 1959. TV debut at age 16 as a singer on The Gong Show. Debut solo album What Might Be released in 1992.
PICTURES: One-Trick Pony, Threshold, St. Elmo's Fire, Nobody's Fool, Made in Heaven, Shy People, Miracle Mile, Turner and Hooch, Hard Promises, Teresa's Tattoo, Wyatt Earp, The War, Georgia (Indep. Spirit Award, Best Supporting Actress, 1996), The Deliverance of Elaine, Bad Day on the Block.
TELEVISION: *Mini-Series*: The Thorn Birds, Studs Lonigan. *Movies*: Special Olympics, The Death of Ocean View Park, Amber Waves (Emmy Award, 1980), Off the Minnesota Strip, The Women's Room, Freedom, A Few Days in Weasel Creek, Missing Children: A Mother's Story, Helen Keller: The Miracle Continues, Single Bars Single Women, Love Is Never Silent, Who is Julia, A Winner Never Quits, Eye on the Sparrow, God Bless the Child, Love and Lies, Crossing to Freedom, Fatal Exposure, She Stood Alone, Those Secrets, Intruders, Better Off Dead, Betrayed by Love, Letter to My Killer, The Boys Next Door, George Wallace (Emmy Award, 1998), Little Girl Fly Away, Everything That Rises.

WINSLET, KATE
Actress. b. Reading, England, Oct. 5, 1975. Began studying drama at age 11.
THEATER: *U.K. Regional*: Adrian Mole, Peter Pan, What the Butler Saw, A Game of Soldiers.
PICTURES: Heavenly Creatures, Sense and Sensibility (BAFTA, Screen Actors Guild Awards, Academy Award nom. 1996), A Kid In King Arthur's Court, Jude, Hamlet, Titanic, Hideous Kinky, Plunge, Holy Smoke, Faeries (voice), Quills, Therese Raquin, Enigma, Christmas Carol: The Movie (voice).
TELEVISION: *Series*: Casualty, Dark Season, Get Back.

WINSTON, STAN
Makeup and Special Effects Artist. b. 1946. e. UofVA. Started in business in 1970 as apprentice to Robert Schiffer at makeup dept. of Walt Disney Studios. Established Stan Winston Studio in Van Nuys, CA.
PICTURES: W.C. Fields and Me, The Wiz, Dead and Buried, Heart Beeps, The Thing, The Entity, Something Wicked This Way Comes, The Terminator, Starman, Invaders From Mars, Aliens (Academy Award for Visual Effects, 1986), Predator, The Monster Squad, Alien Nation, Pumpkinhead (dir. debut), Leviathan, Predator 2, Edward Scissorhands, Terminator 2: Judgment Day (2 Academy Awards: Visual Effects and Makeup, 1991), A Gnome Named Gnorm (dir.), Batman Returns, Jurassic Park (Academy Award for Visual Effects, 1993), Interview With the Vampire, Tank Girl, Congo, Ghosts (dir.), The Ghost and the Darkness, The Relic, The Lost World: Jurassic Park, Mouse Hunt, Paulie, Small Soldiers, End of Days, Inspector Gadget, Galaxy Quest, Instinct, Lake Placid.
TELEVISION: *Movies*: Gargoyles (Emmy Award for Makeup, 1972), The Autobiography of Miss Jane Pittman (Emmy Award for Makeup, 1974), Roots, Creature. *Specials*: Masquerade, Pinocchio, An Evening With Diana Ross.

WINTER, ALEX
Actor. b. London, England, July 17, 1965. e. NYU. At age 4 began studying dance. Played opposite Vincent Price in St. Louis Opera production of Oliver! Co-founder of Stern-Winter Prods. Produced videos for Red Hot Chili Peppers, Human Radio, Ice Cube, etc. Co-directed TV special Hard Rock Cafe Presents: Save the Planet.
THEATER: *B'way*: The King and I (1977 revival), Peter Pan (1979 revival). *Off-B'way*: Close of Play.
PICTURES: Death Wish III, The Lost Boys, Haunted Summer, Bill & Ted's Excellent Adventure, Rosalie Goes Shopping, Bill & Ted's Bogus Journey, Freaked (also co-dir., co-s.p., co-prod.), Fever (dir., s.p.).
TELEVISION: *Movie*: Gaugin the Savage. *Series*: Idiot Box (also co-creator, co-dir., co-writer).

WINTERS, DAVID
Choreographer, Actor, Director. b. London, April 5, 1939. Acted in both Broadway and m.p. version of West Side Story (as A-rab). Directed and acted in number of TV shows. Pres., A.I.P. Distribution, A.I.P. Productions and A.I.P. Home Video, 1989, formed Pyramid Distributors.
PICTURES: *Choreographer*: Viva Las Vegas, Billie, Send Me No Flowers, Bus Riley's Back In Town, Tickle Me, Pajama Party, Girl Happy, The Swinger, Made in Paris, Easy Come, Easy Go, The Island of Doctor Moreau, Roller Boogie, A Star is Born, Blame It on the Night. *Director*: Welcome to My Nightmare, Racquet, The Last Horror Show, The Last Horror Film (also prod., s.p., act.),

Thrashin', Rage to Kill, The Mission... Kill, Space Mutiny (also prod.), Code Name Vengeance. *Producer*: Young Lady Chatterley, Future Force, Raw Nerve, Operation Warzone, Raw Justice, Good Cop Bad Cop, The Dangerous, Codename: Silencer. *Actor*: Rock Rock Rock, West Side Story, The Crazy-Quilt.
TELEVISION: *Choreographer: Series*: Hullabaloo, Shindig, Donny and Marie Osmond, The Big Show, and Steve Allen Show. *Specials starring:* Joey Heatherton, Nancy Sinatra, Diana Ross, Raquel Welch, Ann Margret, Lucille Ball. *Movies*: Firehead, Raw Nerve, Center of the Web, Double Vision.

WINTERS, DEBORAH
Actress. b. Los Angeles, CA. e. Professional Children's Sch., New York; began studying acting at Stella Adler's with Pearl Pearson. at age 13 and Lee Strasberg at 16. Acting debut at age 5 in TV commercials. Casting dir.: Aloha Summer (asst.), Breakdancers From Mars (assoc. prod., casting dir.), Into the Spider's Web, The Hidden Jungle, Haunted, Broken Spur, Behind the Mask (also assoc. prod.).
PICTURES: Me Natalie, Hail Hero!, The People Next Door, Kotch, Class of '44, Blue Sunshine, The Lamp, The Outing.
TELEVISION: *Special*: Six Characters in Search of an Author. *Guest*: Matt Houston, Medical Center. *Movies*: Lottery, Gemini Man. Tarantulas: The Deadly Cargo, Little Girl Lost, Space City. *Mini-Series*: The Winds of War.

WINTERS, JONATHAN
Actor. b. Dayton, OH, Nov. 11, 1925. e. Kenyon Coll.; Dayton Art Inst., B.F.A. Disc jockey, Dayton and Columbus stations; night club comedian performing at Blue Angel and Ruban Bleu (NY), Black Orchid (Chicago), Flamingo, Sands, Riviera (Las Vegas), then on B'way in John Murray Anderson's Almanac. Author: Mouse Breath, Conformity and Other Social Ills, Winters Tales, Hang Ups (book on his paintings). Recorded 7 comedy albums. Won Grammy Award for "Crank Calls" comedy album, 1996.
PICTURES: Alakazam the Great! (voice), It's a Mad Mad Mad Mad World, The Loved One, The Russians Are Coming the Russians Are Coming, Penelope, Oh Dad Poor Dad Mama's Hung You in the Closet and I'm Feeling So Sad, Eight on the Lam, Viva Max, The Fish That Saved Pittsburgh, The Longshot, Say Yes, Moon Over Parador, The Flintstones, The Shadow, Arabian Knight (voice).
TELEVISION: *Series*: And Here's the Show, NBC Comedy Hour, The Jonathan Winters Show (1956-57), Masquerade Party (panelist), The Andy Williams Show, The Jonathan Winters Show (1967-69), Hot Dog, The Wacky World of Jonathan Winters, Mork and Mindy, Hee Haw, The Smurfs (voice of Papa Smurf), The Completely Mental Misadventures of Ed Grimley (voices), Davis Rules (Emmy Award, 1991), Fish Police (voice). *Guest*: Steve Allen Show, Garry Moore Show, Jack Paar, Omnibus, Twlight Zone, Bob Hope specials, Tonight Show, Hollywood Squares. *Specials*: The Jonathan Winters Special, The Jonathan Winters Show (1964, 1965), Jonathan Winters Presents 200 Years of American Humor, 'Tis the Season to Be Smurfy (voice). *Movies*: Now You See It—Now You Don't, More Wild Wild West.

WINTERS, SHELLEY
Actress. r.n. Shirley Schrift. b. St. Louis, MO, Aug. 18, 1922. e. Wayne U. Clerked in 5 & 10 cent store; in vaudeville, chorus girl in night clubs; NY stage (Conquest, Night Before Christmas, Meet the People, Rosalinda, A Hatful of Rain, Girls of Summer, Minnie's Boys, One Night Stand of a Noisy Passenger. (Off-B'way).
AUTHOR: Shelley Also Known as Shirley (1981), Shelley II: The Middle of My Century (1989).
PICTURES: What a Woman! (debut, 1943), Nine Girls, Sailor's Holiday, Knickerbocker Holiday, Cover Girl, A Double Life, Cry of the City, Larceny, Take One False Step, Johnny Stool Pigeon, The Great Gatsby, South Sea Sinner, Winchester '73, Frenchie, A Place in the Sun, He Ran All the Way, Behave Yourself, The Raging Tide, Phone Call From a Stranger, Meet Danny Wilson, Untamed Frontier, My Man and I, Tennessee Champ, Executive Suite, Saskatchewan, Playgirl, To Dorothy a Son (Cash on Delivery), Mambo, Night of the Hunter, I Am a Camera, Big Knife, Treasure of Pancho Villa, I Died a Thousand Times, The Diary of Anne Frank (Academy Award, best supporting actress, 1959), Odds Against Tomorrow, Let No Man Write My Epitaph, Young Savages, Lolita, Chapman Report, The Balcony, Wives and Lovers, Time of Indifference, A House Is Not a Home, A Patch of Blue (Academy Award, best supporting actress, 1965), The Greatest Story Ever Told, Harper, Alfie, Enter Laughing, The Scalphunters, Wild in the Streets, Buona Sera Mrs. Campbell, The Mad Room, How Do I Love Thee?, Bloody Mama, Flap, What's the Matter with Helen?, Who Slew Auntie Roo?, The Poseidon Adventure, Cleopatra Jones, Something to Hide, Blume in Love, Diamonds, Journey Into Fear, That Lucky Touch, Next Stop Greenwich Village, The Tenant, Tentacles, Pete's Dragon, King of the Gypsies, The Magician of Lublin, The Visitors, City on Fire, S.O.B., Over the Brooklyn Bridge, Ellie, Witchfire (also assoc. prod.), Deja Vu, Very Close Quarters, The Delta Force, The Order of Things, Purple People Eater, An Unremarkable Life, Touch of a Stranger, Stepping Out, Weep No More My Lady, The Pickle, The Silence of the Hams, Heavy, Jury Duty, Portrait of a Lady.
TELEVISION: *Special*: Bob Hope Chrysler Theatre: Two Is the Number (Emmy Award, 1964). *Movies*: Revenge, A Death of Innocence, The Adventures of Nick Carter, The Devil's Daughter, Big Rose, The Sex Symbol, The Initiation of Sarah, Elvis, Alice in Wonderland, Mrs. Munck. *Mini-Series*: The French Atlantic Affair.

WINTMAN, MELVIN R.
Theatre Executive, b. Chelsea, MA. e. U. of Massachusetts, Northeastern U., J.D. Major, infantry, AUS, W.W.II. Attorney. Now consultant & dir., General Cinema Corp.; formerly exec. v.p., GCC and pres., GCC Theatres, Inc., Boston. Dir. Will Rogers Memorial Fund. Former pres. Theatre Owners of New England (1969-70); past dir. NATO (1969-70); treas., Nat'l Assoc. of Concessionaires (1960).

WISDOM, NORMAN
O.B.E. Actor, Singer, Comedian. b. London, England, Feb. 4, 1915. Awarded Order of the British Empire (O.B.E.), 1995. Many London West End stage shows including royal command performances. N.Y. B'way shows include Walking Happy and Not Now Darling.
PICTURES: A Date With a Dream (debut, 1948), Meet Mr. Lucifer, Trouble in Store, One Good Turn, As Long as They're Happy, Man of the Moment, Up in the World, Just My Luck, The Square Peg, Follow a Star, There Was a Crooked Man, The Bulldog Breed, The Girl on the Boat, On the Beat, A Stitch in Time, The Early Bird, Press for Time, The Sandwich Man, The Night They Raided Minsky's, What's Good for the Goose, Double X.
TELEVISION: Androcles and the Lion.

WISE, ROBERT
Director, Producer. b. Winchester, IN, Sept. 10, 1914. e. Franklin Coll., Franklin, IN. Ent. m.p. ind. in cutting dept. RKO, 1933; sound cutter, asst. edit.; film edit., 1938; edited Citizen Kane, Magnificent Ambersons; 1944, became dir.; to 20th Century-Fox, 1949; ass'n. Mirisch Co. independent prod. 1959; assn. MGM independent prod., 1962; assn. 20th Century Fox Independent Prod. 1963. Partner, Filmakers Group, The Tripar Group. Amer. Film Inst. Life Achievement Award, 1998.
PICTURES: Curse of the Cat People (debut as co-dir., 1944), Mademoiselle Fifi, The Body Snatcher, A Game of Death, Criminal Court, Born to Kill, Mystery in Mexico, Blood on the Moon, The Set-Up, Three Secrets, Two Flags West, The House on Telegraph Hill, The Day the Earth Stood Still, The Captive City, Something for the Birds, Destination Gobi, The Desert Rats, So Big, Executive Suite, Helen of Troy, Tribute to a Bad Man, Somebody Up There Likes Me, Until They Sail, This Could Be the Night, Run Silent Run Deep, I Want to Live!, Odds Against Tomorrow (also prod.), West Side Story (co-dir., prod.; Acad. Awards for Best Picture & Director, 1961), Two For the Seesaw, The Haunting (also prod), The Sound of Music (also prod.; Acad. Awards for Best Picture & Director, 1965), The Sand Pebbles (also prod.), Star! (also prod.), The Andromeda Strain (also prod.), Two People (also prod.), The Hindenburg (also prod.), Audrey Rose, Star Trek: The Motion Picture, Wisdom (exec. prod. only), Rooftops.

WISEMAN, FREDERICK
Documentary Filmmaker, Producer, Director & Editor. b. Boston, MA, Jan. 1, 1930. e. Williams College, B.A., 1951; Yale Law Sch., L.L.B., 1954. Member: MA Bar. Private law practice, Paris, 1956-57. Lecturer-in-Law, Boston U. Law Sch., 1959-61; Russell Sage Fndn. Fellowship, Harvard U., 1961-62; research assoc., Brandeis U., dept. of sociology, 1962-66; visiting lecturer at numerous universities. Author: Psychiatry and Law: Use and Abuse of Psychiatry in a Murder Case (American Journal of Psychiatry, Oct. 1961). Co-author: Implementation (section of report of President's Comm. on Law Enforcement and Administration of Justice). Fellow, Amer. Acad. of Arts & Sciences, 1991; John D. and Catherine T. MacArthur Foundation Fellowship, 1982-87; John Simon Guggenheim Memorial Foundation Fellowship, 1980-81. Films are distributed through his Zipporah Films, located in Cambridge, MA. Awards include 3 Emmys, Peabody Award, Intl. Documentary Assn. Career Achievement Award, 3 Columbia Dupont Awards for Excellence in Broadcast Journalism, among others.
PICTURES: Titicut Follies, High School, Law and Order, Hospital, Basic Training, Essene, Juvenile Court, Primate, Welfare, Meat, Canal Zone, Sinai Field Mission, Manoeuvre, Model, Seraphita's Diary, The Store, Racetrack, Deaf, Blind, Multi-Handicapped, Adjustment and Work, Missile, Near Death, Central Park, Aspen, Zoo, High School II, Ballet, La Comedie Francaise, Public Housing.

WISEMAN, JOSEPH
Actor. b. Montreal, Canada, May 15, 1918.
THEATER: King Lear, Golden Boy, The Diary of Anne Frank, Uncle Vanya, The Last Analysis, Enemies, Detective Story, Three Sisters, Tenth Man, Incident at Vickey, Marco Williams, Unfinished Stories, many others.
PICTURES: Detective Story (debut, 1951), Viva Zapata, Les Miserables, Champ for a Day, The Silver Chalice, The Prodigal, Three Brave Men, The Garment Jungle, The Unforgiven, Happy Thieves, Dr. No, Bye Bye Braverman, The Counterfeit Killer, The Night They Raided Minsky's, Stiletto, Lawman, The Valachi Papers, The Apprenticeship of Duddy Kravitz, Journey Into Fear, The Betsy, Buck Rogers in the 25th Century, Jaguar Lives.
TELEVISION: *Mini-Series*: QB VII, Masada, Rage of Angels. *Movies*: Pursuit, Murder at the World Series, Seize the Day, Lady Mobster, Ghost Writer. *Series*: Crime Story.

WITHERS, GOOGIE
Actress. b. Karachi, India, Mar. 12, 1917. Trained as a dancer under Italia Conti, Helena Lehmiski & Buddy Bradley; stage debut Victoria Palace in Windmill Man, 1929. Best Actress Award, Deep Blue Sea, 1954. Began screen career at 18. TV also. Theatrical tours Australia, Sun Award, Best Actress, 1974. Awarded officer of the Order of Australia (A.O.) 1980. U.S. ACE Cable award, best actress for Time After Time, 1988.
THEATER: *Britain*: Winter Journey, Deep Blue Sea, Hamlet, Much Ado About Nothing. *Australia*: Plaza Suite, Relatively Speaking, Beckman Place, Woman in a Dressing Gown, The Constant Wife, First Four Hundred Years, Roar Like a Dove, The Cherry Orchard, An Ideal Husband. *London*: Getting Married, Exit the King. *New York*: The Complaisant Lover. Chichester Festival Theatre and Haymarket, London, in The Circle, The Kingfisher, Importance of Being Earnest, The Cherry Orchard, Dandy Dick, The Kingfisher (Australia and Middle East), Time and the Conways (Chichester), School for Scandal (London), Stardust (UK tour). 1986: The Chalk Garden, Hay Fever, Ring Round the Moon, The Cocktail Hour (UK, Australian tour), High Spirits (Aus. tour), On Golden Pond (UK tour).
PICTURES: Haunted Honeymoon, Jeannie, One of Our Aircraft Is Missing, On Approval, Dead of Night, It Always Rains on Sunday, Miranda, Traveler's Joy, Night and the City, White Corridors, Lady Godiva Rides Again, Derby Day, Devil on Horseback, Safe Harbor, Nickel Queen, Country Life, Shine.
TELEVISION: *Series*: Within These Walls, Time After Time, *Movies*: Hotel Du Lac, Northanger Abbey, Ending Up.

WITHERS, JANE
Actress. b. Atlanta, GA, April 12, 1927. By 1934 attracted attention as child player on screen, after radio appearance in Los Angeles and experimental pictures parts, in 1934 in Fox production Bright Eyes, Ginger; thereafter to 1942 featured or starred in numerous 20th-Fox prod. Voted Money-Making Star M.P. Herald-Fame Poll, 1937, 1938. Starred as Josephine the Plumber in Comet tv commercials. TV Movie: All Together Now.
PICTURES: Handle With Care (debut, 1932), Bright Eyes, Ginger, This Is the Life, The Farmer Takes a Wife, Paddy O'Day, Pepper, Gentle Julia, Little Miss Nobody, Can This Be Dixie?, Wild and Woolly, The Holy Terror, Checkers, Angel's Holiday, Forty-Five Fathers, Always in Trouble, Rascals, Keep Smiling, Arizona Wildcat, Pack Up Your Troubles, Chicken Family Wagon, Boy Friend, Shooting High, High School, Youth Will Be Served, The Girl From Avenue A, Golden Hoofs, A Very Young Lady, Her First Beau, Small Town Deb, Young America, The Mad Martindales, Johnny Doughboy, The North Star, My Best Gal, Faces in the Fog, The Affairs of Geraldine, Danger Street, Giant, The Right Approach, Captain Newman M.D., The Hunchback of Notre Dame (voice), The Hunchback of Notre Dame II (voice).

WITHERSPOON, REESE
Actress. r.n. Laura Jean Reese Witherspoon. b. Nashville, TN, March 22, 1976. m. actor Ryan Phillippe.
PICTURES: The Man in the Moon, Jack the Bear, A Far Off Place, S.F.W., Fear, Freeway, Pleasantville, Overnight Delivery, Twilight, Cruel Intentions, Election, Best Laid Plans, American Psycho, Little Nicky, The Trumpet of the Swan, Slow Motion, Legally Blonde.
TELEVISION: *Movies:* Wildflower, Desperate Choices: To Save My Child, Return to Lonesome Dove.

WITT, PAUL JUNGER
Producer. b. New York, NY, Mar. 20, 1941. e. Univ. of VA. Was assoc. prod., prod. and dir. for Screen Gems, starting in 1965; prod. for Spelling-Goldberg Prods., 1972; Prod.-exec. prod. for Danny Thomas Prods., 1973. With Tony Thomas became co-founder, exec. prod. of Witt/Thomas Prods., 1975.
PICTURES: Firstborn, Dead Poets Society, Final Analysis, Mixed Nuts, Three Kings.
TELEVISION: *Series*: Here Come the Brides, The Partridge Family, The Rookies, Soap, Benson, It's a Living, I'm a Big Girl Now, It Takes Two, Condo, Hail to the Chief, The Golden Girls (Emmy Awards: 1986, 1987), Beauty and the Beast, Empty Nest, Blossom, Good and Evil, Herman's Head, Nurses, Woops, Golden Palace, The John Larroquette Show, Brotherly Love, Minor Adjustments, Common Law, Pearl, Local Heroes, The Secret Lives of Men, Everything's Relative. *Movies*: Brian's Song (Emmy Award: 1972), No Place to Run, Home for the Holidays, A Cold Night's Death, The Letters, Blood Sport, Remember When, The Gun and the Pulpit, Satan's Triangle, Griffin and Phoenix, High Risk, Trouble in High Timber Country, Radiant City.

WOLF, DICK
Producer, Writer. b. New York, NY, Dec. 20, 1946. e. Univ. of PA. Started in advertising winning three Clio Awards for excellence.
PICTURES: *Prod./Writer:* Skateboard, Gas, No Man's Land, Masquerade (exec. prod., writer, actor), School Ties (story only).
TELEVISION: *Series (exec. prod.):* Miami Vice (also writer), Gideon Oliver (also writer), Christine Cromwell (also creator), Nasty Boys (also creator, writer), H.E.L.P. (also creator, writer), Law and Order (also creator, writer), Mann and Machine (also writer), The Human Factor, Crime and Punishment (also creator), South Beach (also creator), New York Undercover (also creator), The Wright Verdicts (also creator), FEDS (creator), Players (prod.), Law & Order: Special Victims Unit, Deadline.

WOLF, EMANUEL L.
Executive b. Brooklyn, NY, Mar. 27, 1927. e. Syracuse U., B.A., 1950; Maxwell Sch., Syracuse U., M.A. 1952; Maxwell Scholar in Public Admin.-Economics; Chi Eta Sigma (Econ. Hon.). 1952-55. Management consultant, exec. office of Secretary of Navy & Dept. of Interior, Wash, DC, 1956; pres. E.L. Wolf Assocs., Washington, DC, 1961-65; Kalvex, Inc., treas: 1962, dir.: 1963, pres./chmn. of bd.: 1966; dir. Allied Artists Pictures Corp., 1965; chmn. of bd. Vitabath, Inc., Lexington Instruments, Pharmaceutical Savings Plan, Inc. (also pres.) Syracuse U.; corp. advisory bd., American Committee for the Weizmann Institute of Science (Bd. of Directors); pres. & chmn. of bd., Allied Artists Pictures Corp: 1976: pres., bd. chmn. & CEO, Allied Artists Industries Inc., created by Merger of Allied Artists Pictures Corp., Kalvex Inc. and PSP, Inc. 1985, formed indep. prod. co., Emanuel L. Wolf Prods.; 1986-90, pres. & chmn. of bd., Today Home Entertainment. 1991-present. Emanuel L. Wolf Prods., Inc. Chmn., Allied Artists Entertainment Group. Member, AMPAS.

WOLF, THOMAS HOWARD
TV News Exec. b. New York, NY, April 22, 1916. e. Princeton U., B.A., magna cum laude, 1937. Time & Life Mag. 1937-39; 1937-39 NEA (Scripps-Howard) 1940-46; European mgr., NEA, 1942-46. War correspondent, (ETO, MTO) NBC radio correspondent, Paris, 1944-45; co-owner, pres., Information Prod., Inc. founded 1951; co-owner, chmn. Butterfield & Wolf, Inc. founded 1955; prod. CBS series Tomorrow, 1960; exec. prod., CBS daily live Calendar Show, 1961-62; sr. prod., ABC News Report, 1963; exec. prod., ABC Scope, 1964-66. v.p. dir. of TV Documentaries, 1966; v.p., dir. of TV Public Affairs, 1974; dir. TV Cultural Affairs, 1976. Pres., Wolf Communications, Inc., 1981-; consultant Smithsonian Institution, 1981-88.
TELEVISION: ABC News Reports, ABC Scope, Now, Issues and Answers, Directions, Make a Wish, Animals Animals Animals.

WOLFSON, RICHARD
Executive. b. New York, NY, Jan. 7, 1923. e. Harvard Coll., Yale Law Sch., 1945-47, law clerk to Justice Wiley Rutledge, U.S. Supreme Court. Law instructor at NYU Law Sch.; 1952, joined Wometco Ent. as counsel and asst. to pres.; named v.p. and dir. in 1959 and sr. v.p. in 1962; named exec. v.p. and general counsel in 1973; named chmn., exec. comm., 1976; retired from Wometco 1982.

WOLPER, DAVID L.
Producer. b. New York, NY, Jan. 11, 1928. m. Gloria Diane Hill. e. Drake U., U. of Southern California. Treas., Flamingo Films, 1948; merged with Associated Artist to form M.P. for TV, Inc., acting as v.p. in chg. of West Coast oper., 1950; v.p. reactivated Flamingo Films, 1954; also pres. Harris-Wolper Pictures, Inc.; pres. Wolper Prod. 1958; pres. Dawn Prod.; v.p. bd. dir. Metromedia, 1965; pres. Wolper Pictures Ltd. 1967; ch. of bd. Wolper Prod., Inc., 1967; pres. Wolper Pictures, 1968; pres. Wolper Productions, 1970; pres. & chmn. of bd. of dir. The Wolper Organization, Inc., 1971; consultant to Warner Bros. & Warner Communications. Pres., David L. Wolper Prods., Inc. 1977. Received Jean Hersholt Humanitarian Award, 1985; Intl. Documentary Assn. Career Achievement Award, 1988. Also received French Natl. Legion of Honor Medal, Lifetime Achievement Award from Producers Guild, Charles de Gaulle Centennial Medal. Shows have won 52 Emmys, 5 Peabody Awards and 7 Golden Globes.

PICTURES: Four Days in November, If It's Tuesday This Must Be Belgium, One Is a Lonely Number, The Hellstrom Chronicle, Willy Wonka and the Chocolate Factory, I Love My Wife, Visions of Eight, Birds Do it Bees Do It, This Is Elvis, The Man Who Saw Tomorrow, Imagine: John Lennon, Murder in the First, Surviving Picasso, L.A. Confidential.
TELEVISION: *Specials*: The Race For Space, The Making of the President (1960, 1964, 1968), National Geographic Society Specials (1965-68, 1971-75), The Rise and Fall of the Third Reich, The Undersea World of Jacques Cousteau (1967-68), George Plimpton specials (1970-72), American Heritage specials (1973-74), Primal Man specials (1973-75), Judgment specials (1974), Smithsonian Specials, Sandburg's Lincoln, The Man Who Saw Tomorrow, Opening & Closing Ceremonies: Olympic Games 1984, Liberty Weekend 1986, A Celebration of Tradition for Warner Bros, Here's Looking at You Warner Bros., Golf—The Greatest Game. *Series*: Story of..., Biography, Hollywood and the Stars, Men in Crisis, The March of Time (1965-66), Appointment With Destiny, Get Christie Love, Chico and the Man, Welcome Back Kotter, Casablanca, Golf: Heroes of the Game. *Movies*: Say Goodbye, The 500 Pound Jerk, I Will Fight No More Forever, Victory at Entebbe, Agatha Christie's Murder Is Easy, What Price Victory, Roots: The Gift, When You Remember Me, The Betty Ford Story, Dillinger, The Plot to Kill Hitler, Murder in Mississippi, Bed of Lies, The Flood: Who Will Save Our Children?, Fatal Deception: Mrs. Lee Harvey Oswald, Without Warning, Prince For a Day. *Mini-Series*: Roots (Emmy Award, 1977), Roots: The Next Generations, (Emmy Award, 1979), Moviola (This Year's Blonde, The Scarlett O'Hara War, The Silent Lovers), The Thorn Birds, North & South, North & South Book II: Love & War, North & South Book III: Heaven & Hell, Napoleon & Josephine: A Love Story, Queen, The Thorn Birds: The Missing Years.

WONG, VICTOR
Actor. b. San Francisco, CA. e. UC Berkeley, poli. sci. & journalism; U of Chicago; San Francisco Art Institute. Was reporter in San Francisco's Chinatown, 1968-75, before working on stage at Joseph Papp's Public Theatre.
PICTURES: Dim Sum: A Little Bit of Heart, Year of the Dragon, Big Trouble in Little China, Shanghai Surprise, The Golden Child, Bloodsport, Prince of Darkness, The Last Emperor, Eat a Bowl of Tea, Tremors, Life Is Cheap... But Toilet Paper Is Expensive, 3 Ninjas, The Joy Luck Club, The Ice Runner, 3 Ninjas Kick Back, 3 Ninjas Knuckle Up, The Stars Fell on Henrietta, Jade, Seven Years in Tibet, 3 Ninjas: High Noon at Mega Mountain.
TELEVISION: *Series*: Search for Tomorrow. *Movies/Specials*: Night Song, Fortune Cookie, Paper Angel, Mild Bunch, Search, China Nights.

WOO, JOHN
Director. r.n. Yusen Wu. b. Guangzhou, China, 1948. e. Matteo Ricci Col, Hong Kong. Started making experimental 16 mm films in 1967. Joined film industry in 1969 as prod. asst. for Cathay Film Co., then asst. dir. 1971 joined Shaw Brothers working as asst. dir. to Zhang Che.
PICTURES: The Young Dragons (debut, 1973), The Dragon Tamers, Countdown in Kung Fu, Princess Chang Ping, From Riches to Rags, Money Crazy, Follow the Star, Last Hurrah for Chivalry, To Hell With the Devil, Laughing Times, Plain Jane to the Rescue, Sunset Warriors (Heroes Shed No Tears), The Time You Need a Friend, Run Tiger Run, A Better Tomorrow, A Better Tomorrow II, Just Heroes, The Killer, Bullet in the Head, Once a Thief, Hard Boiled, Hard Target (U.S. debut, 1993), Cinema of Vengeance (act. only), Broken Arrow, Face/Off, The Big Hit (exec. prod. only), The Replacement Killers (exec. prod. only), King's Ransom, Mission: Impossible 2, The Devil's Pale Moonlit Kiss (prod. only), Windtalkers (also prod.), King's Ransom, Bulletproof Monk (prod. only).
TELEVISION: *Movie*: John Woo's Once a Thief (prod.), Black Jack (also prod.).

WOOD, ELIJAH
Actor. b. Cedar Rapids, IA, Jan. 28, 1981. Started in commercial modeling. Landed first acting job in Paula Abdul video Forever Your Girl.
PICTURES: Back to the Future Part II (debut, 1989), Internal Affairs, Avalon, Paradise, Radio Flyer, Forever Young, The Adventures of Huck Finn, The Good Son, North, The War, Flipper, The Ice Storm, The Faculty, Deep Impact, The Bumblebee Flies Away, Black and White, The Adventures of Tom Thumb and Thumbelina (voice), The Lord of the Rings: The Fellowship of the Ring, The Lord of the Rings: The Two Towers,The Lord of the Rings: The Return of the King.
TELEVISION: *Movies*: Child of the Night, Day-O, Oliver Twist.

WOODARD, ALFRE
Actress. b. Tulsa, OK, Nov. 8, 1953. e. Boston U., B.A. Soon after graduation landed role in Washington, D.C. Arena Stage theater in Horatio, and Saved.
THEATER: A Christmas Carol, Bugs Guns, Leander Stillwell, For Colored Girls Who Have Considered Suicide/When the Rainbow Is Enuf, A Map of the World, A Winter's Tale, Two By South.
PICTURES: Remember My Name, Health, Cross Creek (Acad. Award nom.), Extremities, Scrooged, Miss Firecracker, Grand Canyon, The Gun in Betty Lou's Handbag, Passion Fish, Rich in Love, Heart and Souls, Blue Chips, Crooklyn, How to Make an American Quilt, Primal Fear, Star Trek: First Contact, Follow Me Home, Mumford, Down in the Delta, Dinosaur, Brown Sugar.
TELEVISION: *Series*: Tucker's Witch, Sara, St. Elsewhere. *Guest*: Palmerstown USA, What Really Happened to the Class of '65?, Hill Street Blues (Emmy Award, 1984), L.A. Law (Emmy Award, 1987). *Mini-series*: Cadillac Desert. *Movies*: Freedom Road, Sophisticated Gents, Go Tell It on the Mountain, Sweet Revenge, Unnatural Causes, The Killing Floor, Mandela, A Mother's Courage: The Mary Thomas Story, Blue Bayou, Race to Freedom: The Underground Railroad, The Piano Lesson, Member of the Wedding, Miss Evers' Boys (Golden Globe Award, 1998). *Specials*: For Colored Girls Who Haved Considered Suicide/When the Rainbow Is Enuf, Trial of the Moke, Words by Heart, Aliens for Breakfast.

WOODS, JAMES
Actor. b. Vernal UT, Apr. 18, 1947. e. Massachusetts Inst. of Technology (appeared in 36 plays at MIT, Harvard and Theatre Co. of Boston). Left college to pursue acting career in New York.
THEATER: Borstal Boy (B'way debut, 1970), followed by Conduct Unbecoming (off-B'way, Obie Award), Saved, Trial of the Catonsville Nine, Moonchildren (Theatre World Award), Green Julia (off-B'way), Finishing Touches.
PICTURES: The Visitors (debut, 1971), Hickey and Boggs, The Way We Were, The Gambler, Distance, Night Moves, Alex and the Gypsy, The Choirboys, The Onion Field, The Black Marble, Eyewitness, Fast-Walking, Split Image, Videodrome, Against All Odds, Once Upon a Time in America, Cat's Eye, Joshua Then and Now, Salvador (Acad. Award nom.; Indept. Film Project Spirit Award, 1986), Best Seller, Cop (also co-prod.), The Boost, True Believer, Immediate Family, The Hard Way, Straight Talk, Diggstown, Chaplin, The Getaway, The Specialist, For Better or Worse, Casino, Nixon, Killer: A Journal of Murder, Ghosts of Mississippi, Hercules (voice), Contact, Another Day in Paradise, John Carpenter's Vampires, The Virgin Suicides, True Crime, Any Given Sunday, The General's Daughter, Race to Space, Play it to the Bone, Final Fantasy (voice), John Q.
TELEVISION: *Movies*: Footsteps, A Great American Tragedy, Foster and Laurie, F. Scott Fitzgerald in Hollywood, The Disappearance of Aimee, Raid on Entebbe, Billion Dollar Bubble, The Gift of Love, The Incredible Journey of Dr. Meg Laurel, And Your Name Is Jonah, Badge of the Assassin, Promise (Emmy & Golden Globe Awards, 1987), In Love and War, My Name is Bill W. (Emmy Award, 1989), Women & Men: Stories of Seduction (Hills Like White Elephants), The Boys, Citizen Cohn, Jane's House, Next Door, Curse of the Starving Class, Indictment: The McMartin Trial, The Summer of Ben Tyler, Dirty Pictures, Hercules: Zero to Hero (voice). *Specials*: All the Way Home, Crimes of Passion (host), Wildfire (host), Mobs and Mobsters (host), Fallen Angels, A Salute to Martin Scorcese, America's Endangered Species: Don't Say Goodbye (narrator), World's Deadliest Earthquakes. *Mini-series*: Holocaust. *Guest*: Kojak, Rockford Files, Streets of San Francisco, The Rookies, Police Story, Dream On, The Simpsons (voice).

WOODWARD, EDWARD
O.B.E.: Actor, Singer. b. Croydon, England, June 1, 1930. e. Royal Acad. of Dramatic Art. As singer has recorded 11 LPs. 2 Gold Discs. Television Actor of the Year, 1969-70; also Sun Award, Best Actor, 1970-72. Has received 15 national & international awards.
THEATER: With Royal Shakespeare Company, 1958-59; Cyrano, 20 West End plays and musicals, including The Art of Living, The Little Doctor, A Rattle of a Simple Man (West End/B'way), The High Bid, The Male of the Species, High Spirits (B'way musical), The Best Laid Plans, On Approval, The Wolf, Richard III, The Assassin.
PICTURES: Where There's a Will (debut, 1955), Becket, File on the Golden Goose, Incense for the Damned, Young Winston, Sitting Target, Hunted, Wicker Man, Callan, Stand Up Virgin Soldiers, Breaker Morant, The Appointment, The Final Option (Who Dares Wins), Champions, King David, Mister Johnson, Deadly Advice.
TELEVISION: *Series*: Callan, Nice Work, The Equalizer (4 Emmy noms., Golden Globe Award), Over My Dead Body, In Suspicious Cirumstances. *Movies/Specials*: Sword of Honour, Bassplayer and Blonde (mini-series), Saturday, Sunday, Monday, Rod of Iron, The Trial of Lady Chatterly, Wet Job–Callan Special, Churchill: The Wilderness Years,

Blunt Instrument, Killer Contract, Arthur the King, Uncle Tom's Cabin, A Christmas Carol, Codename: Kyril, Hunted, The Man in the Brown Suit, Hands of a Murderer, World War II, Suspicious Circumstances, The Shamrock Conspiracy, Common as Muck, Harrison, Gulliver's Travels.

WOODWARD, JOANNE
Actress. b. Thomasville, GA, Feb. 27, 1930. m. Paul Newman. e. Louisiana State U. Studied at Neighborhood Playhouse Dramatic Sch. and the Actors Studio. Appeared in many TV dramatic shows.
THEATER: Picnic, The Lovers, Baby Want a Kiss, Candida, The Glass Menagerie (Williamstown, The Long Wharf), Golden Boy (dir., the Blue Light Theatre Company).
PICTURES: Count Three and Pray (debut, 1955), A Kiss Before Dying, Three Faces of Eve (Academy Award, 1957), No Down Payment, The Long Hot Summer, Rally 'Round the Flag Boys, The Sound and the Fury, The Fugitive Kind, From the Terrace, Paris Blues, The Stripper, A New Kind of Love, Signpost to Murder, A Big Hand for the Little Lady, A Fine Madness, Rachel Rachel (Acad. Award nom.), Winning, WUSA, They Might Be Giants, The Effect of Gamma Rays on Man-in-the-Moon Marigolds, Summer Wishes Winter Dreams (Acad. Award nom.), The Drowning Pool, The End, Harry and Son, The Glass Menagerie, Mr. and Mrs. Bridge (Acad. Award nom.), The Age of Innocence (narrator), Philadelphia, Even If A Hundred Ogres (voice), Remembering the Kindertransports.
TELEVISION: *Specials*: Broadway's Dreamers: The Legacy of The Group Theater (host, co-prod.; Emmy Award, 1990), Family Thanksgiving Special (dir. only). *Movies*: Sybil, Come Back Little Sheba, See How She Runs (Emmy Award, 1978), A Christmas to Remember, The Streets of L.A., The Shadow Box, Crisis at Central High, Passions, Do You Remember Love? (Emmy Award, 1985), Foreign Affairs, Blind Spot (also co-prod.), Breathing Lessons, James Dean: A Portrait.

WOOLDRIDGE, SUSAN
Actress. b. London, England. e. Central Sch. of Speech & Drama/Ecole/Jacques LeCoq. Paris. Ent. ind. 1971.
THEATER: Macbeth, School for Scandal, Merchant of Venice, The Cherry Orchard, Look Back in Anger, 'night Mother, Map of the Heart.
PICTURES: The Shout, Butley, Loyalties, Hope and Glory, How to Get Ahead in Advertising, Bye Bye Blues, Twenty-One, Afraid of the Dark, Just Like a Woman, The Hummingbird Tree.
TELEVISION: The Naked Civil Servant, John McNab, The Racing Game, The Jewel in the Crown, The Last Place on Earth, Hay Fever, Time and the Conways, Dead Man's Folly, The Devil's Disciple, The Dark Room, Pastoralcare, The Small Assassin, A Fine Romance, Ticket to Ride, Changing Step, Pied Piper, Crimestrike, Broke, Miss Pym's Day Out, An Unwanted Woman, The Humming Bird Tree, Inspector Alleyn Mysteries, Tracey Ullman Show, Bad Company, Under the Hammer, All Quiet on the Preston Front, Wycliffe, The Writing Game. *Guest*: The Ray Bradbury Theatre.

WOPAT, TOM
Actor. b. Lodi, WI, Sept. 9, 1951. e. U. of Wisconsin. Left school to travel for two years with rock group as lead singer and guitarist. Spent two summers at Barn Theater in MI. Came to New York; *Off-B'way* in A Bistro Car on the CNR. *On B'way* in I Love My Wife, City of Angels, Guys and Dolls.
TELEVISION: *Series*: The Dukes of Hazzard, Blue Skies, A Peaceable Kingdom, Cybill, Prime Time Country (host). *Movies*: Christmas Comes to Willow Creek, Burning Rage, Just My Imagination, Contagious, The Dukes of Hazzard: Reunion!, Meteorites.

WORKMAN, CHUCK
Director, Writer, Producer. b. Philadelphia, PA. June 5. e. Rutgers U., B.A.; Cornell U. Pres., International Documentary Assoc. 1987-88; Member: Directors Guild of America, National Board. Lecturer, U. of Southern California. Pres. Calliope Films, Inc. Winner Clio Award, 1969, 1970. Acad. Award, 1987; ShowEast Achievement Award, 1996; Cable Ace Award, 1996.
THEATER: Bruno's Ghost (1981, writer, dir.), Diplomacy (writer, dir.), The Man Who Wore White Shoes (writer), Bloomers (writer).
PICTURES: Monday's Child (1967, editor), Traitors of San Angel (editor), The Money (dir., s.p.), Protocol (dir., media sequences), Stoogemania (dir., co-s.p.), Precious Images (Acad. Award, Best Live Action Short, 1986; Gold Hugo Award, Cannes Film Fest., N.Y. Film Fest.), Words (Best Short, Houston Fest., N.Y. Film Fest., 1988), Pieces of Silver, Superstar (dir.-prod.), The First 100 Years (dir., prod.).
DOCUMENTARIES: The Making of the Deep (prod., dir., writer), The Director and the Image (CINE Golden Eagle Award, 1980), The Game, The Best Show in Town (CINE Golden Eagle), And the Winner Is..., The Keeper of the Light.

WORONOV, MARY
Actress. b. Brooklyn, NY, Dec. 8, 1946. e. Cornell. On NY stage in In the Boom Boom Room (Theatre World Award).
PICTURES: The Chelsea Girls, Kemek: It's Controlling Your Mind, Sugar Cookies, Seizure, Cover Girl Models, Death Race 2000, Cannonball, Jackson County Jail, Hollywood Boulevard, Bad Georgia Road, Mr. Billion, The One and Only, The Lady in Red, Rock 'n' Roll High School, National Lampoon Goes to the Movies, Angel of H.E.A.T., Heartbeeps, Eating Raoul, Get Crazy, Night of the Comet, Hellhole, My Man Adam, Nomads, Movie House Massacre, Chopping Mall, Terrorvision, Black Widow, Scenes From the Class Struggle in Beverly Hills, Let It Ride, Mortuary Academy, Dick Tracy, Watchers II, Warlock, Club Fed, Where Sleeping Dogs Lie, Motorama, Good Girls Don't, Hell-Rollers, Grief.
TELEVISION: *Movies*: In the Glitter Palace, Challenge of a Lifetime, Acting on Impulse.

WORTH, IRENE
Actress. r.n. Hattie Abrams. b. Nebraska, June 23, 1916. e. UCLA. Formerly a teacher. B'way debut in The Two Mrs. Carrolls, after which went to London where made her home. Appeared with Old Vic and Royal Shakespeare Co.; returned to U.S. to appear on B'way in the Cocktail Party.
THEATER: Hotel Paradiso, Mary Stuart, The Potting Shed, Toys in the Attic, Tiny Alice (Tony Award, 1965), Sweet Bird of Youth (Tony Award, 1976), Cherry Orchard, Old Times Happy Days, Coriolanus (NY Shakespeare Fest), Lost in Yonkers (Tony Award, 1991).
PICTURES: One Night With You, Secret People, Orders to Kill (British Acad. Award, best actress), The Scapegoat, Seven Seas to Calais, King Lear, Nicholas and Alexander, Rich Kids, Eyewitness, Deathtrap, Fast Forward, Lost in Yonkers, Onegin, Just the Ticket.
TELEVISION: The Lady from the Sea, The Duchess of Malfi, The Way of the World, Prince Orestes, Forbidden, The Big Knife, The Shell Seekers. *Guest*: Remember WENN.

WOWCHUK, HARRY N.
Actor, Writer, Photographer, Producer, Executive. b. Philadelphia, PA. Oct. 16, 1948. e. Santa Monica City Coll., UCLA, theater arts, 1970. Started film career as actor, stunt-driver-photographer. T.V. and commercial credits include: TV Guide, Seal Test, Camel Cigarettes, Miller High Life, American Motors, Camera V, AW Rootbeer. Former exec. v.p. International Cinema, in chg. of prod. and distribution; V.P. J. Newport Film Productions; pres., United West Productions.
PICTURES: The Lost Dutchman, Las Vegas Lady, This Is a Hijack, Tidal Wave, Tunnel Vision, Incredible 2-Headed Transplant, Jud, Bad Charleston Charlie, Some Call It Loving, Summer School Teachers, Five Minutes of Freedom, Pushing Up Daisies, Money-Marbles-Chalk, The Models, Love Swedish Style, Up-Down-Up, Sunday's Child, Soul Brothers, Freedom Riders, Perilous Journey, Claws of Death, Georgia Peaches.

WOWCHUK, NICHOLAS
Executive, Producer, Writer, Editor, Financier. b. Philadelphia, PA. e. St. Basil's Coll., UCLA. Founder-publisher: All-American Athlete Magazine, Sports and Health Digest, The Spectator. Former sports writer: Phila. Evening Public Ledger; Phila. Daily Record; Phila. Inquirer. Founder & bd. chmn.: Mutual Realty Investment Co.; Mutual Mortgage Co., Beverly Hills, CA. President: Mutual General Films, Bev. Hills, CA; Abbey Theatrical Films, NY; Mutual Film Distribution Co.; Mutual Recording & Broadcasting Enterprises.
PICTURES: *Exec. Prod.*: Perilous Journey, The Incredible 2-Headed Transplant, Pushing Up Daisies, Money-Marbles-Chalk, Five Minutes of Freedom, The Campaign, Claws of Death. *Prod.*: Scorpion's Web, Pursuit, Brave Men, Sea of Despair, Cossacks in Battle, The Straight White Line, Tilt, Rooster, To Live... You Gotta Win.

WRAY, FAY
Actress. b. Alberta, Canada, Sept. 15, 1907. On stage in Pilgrimage Play, Hollywood, 1923; m.p. debut in Gasoline Love; thereafter in many m.p. for Paramount to 1930; then in films for various Hollywood and Brit. prod. Autobiography: On the Other Hand (1989).
PICTURES: Streets of Sin, The Wedding March, The Four Feathers, The Texan, Dirigible, Doctor X, The Most Dangerous Game, The Vampire Bat, The Mystery of the Wax Museum, King Kong, The Bowery, Madame Spy, The Affairs of Cellini, The Clairvoyant, They Met in a Taxi, Murder in Greenwich Village, The Jury's Secret, Smashing the Spy Ring, Navy Secrets, Wildcat Bus, Adam Had Four Sons, Melody for Three, Not a Ladies' Man, Small Town Girl, Treasure of the Golden Condor, Queen Bee, The Cobweb, Hell on Frisco Bay, Crime of Passion, Rock Pretty Baby, Tammy and the Bachelor, Summer Love, Dragstrip Riot, Frank Capra's American Dream.
TELEVISION: *Series*: Pride of the Family. *Movie*: Gideon's Trumpet.

WRIGHT, AMY
Actress. b. Chicago, IL, Apr. 15, 1950. e. Beloit Col. Studied acting with Uta Hagen; 1976, joined Rip Torn's Sanctuary Theatre. B'way in Fifth of July, Noises Off, Mrs. Klein.
PICTURES: Not a Pretty Picture, Girlfriends, The Deer Hunter, Breaking Away, The Amityville Horror, Heartland, Wise Blood, Stardust Memories, Inside Moves, Off Beat, The Telephone, Crossing Delancey, The Accidental Tourist, Miss Firecracker, Daddy's Dyin', Deceived, Love Hurts, Hard Promises, Josh and S.A.M., Tom and Huck.
TELEVISION: *Movies*: Trapped in Silence, Settle the Score, To Dance With the White Dog. *Special*: Largo Desolato. *Pilot*: A Fine Romance.

WRIGHT, ROBERT C.
Executive. b. Hempstead, NY, April 23, 1943. e. Coll. Holy Cross, B.A. history, 1965; U. of Virginia, LLB 1968. Mem. NY, VA, MA, NJ Bar. 1969, joined General Electric; lawyer in plastics div. Later moved into product & sls. management in plastics div. 1980, moved to Cox Cable as pres. Returned to GE 1983 heading small appliances div.; moved to GE Financial Services & GE Credit Corp. as pres., which posts he held when named head of NBC following purchase of NBC's parent RCA by GE. Pres. and CEO, National Broadcasting Co. (NBC), 1986-. Humanitarian Award from Foundation Fighting Blindness, 1995.

WRIGHT, TERESA
Actress. b. New York, NY, Oct. 27, 1918. e. Columbia H.S., Maplewood, NJ, 1938.
THEATER: *Tours*: Mary Mary, Tchin-Tchin, The Effect of Gamma Rays on Man-in-the-Moon Marigolds, Noel Coward in Two Keys, The Master Builder. *Regional*: Long Day's Journey into Night, You Can't Take It With You, All The Way Home, Wings. *NY*: Life with Father, Dark at the Top of the Stairs, I Never Sang for My Father, Death of a Salesman, Ah Wilderness!, Morning's at Seven (also London), On Borrowed Time.
PICTURES: The Little Foxes (debut, 1941), Pride of the Yankees, Mrs. Miniver (Academy Award, best supporting actress, 1942), Shadow of a Doubt, Casanova Brown, The Best Years of Our Lives, The Trouble With Women, Pursued, Imperfect Lady, Enchantment, The Capture, The Men, Something to Live For, California Conquest, Steel Trap, Count the Hours, The Actress, Track of the Cat, The Search for Bridey Murphy, Escapade in Japan, The Restless Years, Hail Hero, The Happy Ending, Roseland, Somewhere in Time, The Good Mother, The Red Coat, The Rainmaker.
TELEVISION: *Specials*: The Margaret Bourke-White Story, The Miracle Worker, The Golden Honeymoon, The Fig Tree, A Century of Women. *Movies*: Crawlspace, The Elevator, Flood, Bill—On His Own, Perry Mason: The Case of the Desperate Deception, Lethal Innocence, Diamonds on the Silver Screen. *Mini-series*: A Century of Women. *Guest*: The U.S. Steel Hour, Climax, The Alcoa Hour, Playhouse 90, Picket Fences.

WUHL, ROBERT
Actor, Writer. b. Union, NJ, Oct. 9, 1951. e. Univ. of Houston. Worked as stand-up comedian and joke writer. Was story editor on series Police Squad! Appeared in 1988 Academy Award winning short Ray's Male Heterosexual Dance Hall.
PICTURES: The Hollywood Knights (debut, 1980), Flashdance, Good Morning Vietnam, Bull Durham, Batman, Blaze, Wedding Band, Mistress, A Kiss Goodnight, Blue Chips, Cobb, Dr. Jekyll and Ms. Hyde, Open Season (also dir., s.p.), Good Burger.
TELEVISION: *Series*: Arliss. *Pilots*: Rockhopper, Sniff. *Guest*: Tales from the Crypt, Moonlighting, L.A. Law, Falcon Crest. *Specials*: The Big Bang (also dir.), Comic Relief IV, The Earth Day Special, The Real Deal. *Movie*: Percy & Thunder, The Last Don, The Last Don II. *Writer*: Police Squad, Sledge Hammer, Grammy Awards (1987-89), Academy Awards (Emmy Award, 1991).

WYATT, JANE
Actress. b. Campgaw, NJ, Aug. 12, 1910. e. Miss Chapin's Sch., Barnard Coll. m. Edgar B. Ward. Joined Apprentice Sch., Berkshire Playhouse, Stockbridge, Mass. Understudied in Tradewinds and The Vinegar Tree. Appeared in Give Me Yesterday and the Tadpole. In 1933 succeeded Margaret Sullavan in Dinner at Eight.
THEATER: The Autumn Garden (NY), The Bishop Misbehaves, Conquest, Eveningsong, The Mad Hopes, Hope for the Best, The Joyous Season For Services Rendered, Driving Miss Daisy, Love Letters.
PICTURES: One More River (debut, 1934), Great Expectations, We're Only Human, The Luckiest Girl in the World, Lost Horizon, The Girl From God's Country, Kisses for Breakfast, Hurricane Smith, Weekend for Three, Army Surgeon, The Navy Comes Through, The Kansan, Buckskin Frontier, None But the Lonely Heart, Strange Conquest, The Bachelor's Daughters, Boomerang!, Gentleman's Agreement, Pitfall, No Minor Vices, Bad Boy, Canadian Pacific, Task Force, House By the River, Our Very Own, My Blue Heaven, The Man Who Cheated Himself, Criminal Lawyer, Interlude, Two Little Bears, Never Too Late, Treasure of Matecumbe, Star Trek IV: The Voyage Home.
TELEVISION: *Series*: Father Knows Best (1954-59; 3 Emmy Awards: 1957, 1958, 1959), Confidential For Women. *Guest*: Bob Hope Chrysler Theater, The Virginian, Wagon Train, U.S. Steel Hour, Bell Telephone Hour, My Father My Mother, Barefoot in the Park, The Ghost and Mrs. Muir, Here Come the Brides, Love American Style, Fantasy Island, Love Boat. *Movies*: Katherine, Tom Sawyer, Father Knows Best Reunion, A Love Affair, Amelia Earhart, Superdome, The Nativity, The Millionaire, Missing Children—A Mother's Story, Legacy of the Hollywood Blacklist, Amityville: The Evil Escapes, Neighbors, Ladies of the Corridor, Star Trek, Frank Capra's American Dream.

WYMAN, THOMAS H.
Executive. b. 1931. Joined CBS, Inc. in 1980 as pres. & chief exec. Then chmn until 1986. William H. Donaldson Faculty Fellow at Yale School of Mgmt., 1987. Prior career as chief exec. of Green Giant Co.; became v. chmn. to 1988, of Pillsbury Co. when it acquired Green Giant in 1979. Chairman of Bd., Amherst College. Trustee, Ford Foundation.

WYNN, TRACY KEENAN
Writer. b. Hollywood, CA, Feb. 28, 1945. e. UCLA Theatre Arts Dept., BA in film/TV division, 1967. Fourth generation in show business: son of actor Keenan Wynn, grandson of Ed Wynn, great-grandson of Frank Keenan, Irish Shakespearean actor who made B'way debut in 1880.
PICTURES: The Longest Yard, The Drowning Pool (co-s.p.), The Deep (co. s.p.).
TELEVISION: *Movies*: The Glass House, Tribes (also assoc. prod.: Emmy & WGA Awards, 1971), The Autobiography of Miss Jane Pittman (Emmy Award & WGA Awards, 1974), Hit Lady (dir. only), Quest, Bloody Friday (also co-prod.), Capone in Jail, Carolina Skeletons.

Y

YABLANS, FRANK
Executive. b. Brooklyn, NY, Aug. 27, 1935. Entered m.p. ind. as Warner Bros. booker, 1957. Warner Bros. salesman in N.Y., Boston, Milwaukee, Chicago, 1957-59. Milwaukee br. mgr. Buena Vista, 1959-66. Midwest sales mgr., Sigma III, 1966. Eastern sales mgr., 1967, sales v.p. 1968. V.P. general sales mgr., Paramount Pic. Corp., 1969; v.p.-dist., 1970; sr. v.p.-mkt., 1970; exec. v.p., 1971; named pres. 1971. 1975, became an indep. prod. for his company, Frank Yablans Presentations Inc. 1983, MGM/UA Entertainment Co. as bd. chmn. & CEO. Held titles of bd. chmn. & CEO with both MGM and UA Corp when resigned, 1985. Same year teamed with PSO Delphi to form Northstar Entertainment Co.; 1986, non-exclusive deal with Empire Entertainment; 1988, non-exclusive 3-year deal with Columbia Pictures; 1989, pres. Epic Prods., pres., CEO Nova Intl. Films Inc.
PICTURES: *Producer*: Silver Streak (exec. prod.), The Other Side of Midnight, The Fury, North Dallas Forty (also co-s.p.), Mommie Dearest (also co-s.p.), Monsignor (co.-prod), Star Chamber, Kidco, Buy and Cell, Lisa, Congo (exec. prod.).

YABLANS, IRWIN
Executive. b. Brooklyn, NY, July 25, 1934. Began career in industry at WB in 1956 after two-yr. stint with U.S. Army in Germany. Held m.p. sales posts in Washington, DC, Albany, Detroit, Milwaukee and Portland. In 1962 joined Paramount as L.A. mgr.; in 1964 made western sales mgr. In 1972 entered production as assoc. prod. on Howard W. Koch's Badge 373. Pres. of Compass Int'l. Pictures. Exec. v.p., low budget films, Lorimar Productions. Resigned June, 1984. In 1985 named chmn., Orion Pictures Distributing Corp. 1988: named chmn. and CEO of newly formed Epic Pictures.
PICTURES: The Education of Sonny Carson. *Exec. prod.*: Halloween, Roller Boogie (also story), Fade To Black (also story), Seduction (prod.), Halloween II, Halloween III: Season of the Witch, Parasite, Tank, Hell Night, Prison Arena, Why Me?, Men at Work.

YATES, PETER
Producer, Director. b. Ewshoot, England, July 24, 1929. e. Royal Acad. of Dramatic Art. Entered m.p. ind. as studio mgr. and dubbing asst. with De Lane Lea. Asst. dir.: The Entertainer, The Guns of Navarone, A Taste of Honey, The Roman Spring of Mrs. Stone. Stage dir.: The American Dream, The Death of Bessie Smith, Passing Game, Interpreters. Received Acad. Award noms. for Best Director/Picture (Producer): Breaking Away, The Dresser.

PICTURES: Summer Holiday, One Way Pendulum, Robbery (also co-s.p.), Bullitt, John and Mary, Murphy's War, The Hot Rock, The Friends of Eddie Coyle, For Pete's Sake, Mother Jugs and Speed (also prod.), The Deep, Breaking Away (also prod.), Eyewitness (also prod.), Krull, The Dresser (also prod.), Eleni, Suspect, The House on Carroll Street (also prod.), An Innocent Man, Year of the Comet (also co-prod.), Needful Things (exec. prod. only), Roommates, The Run of the Country (also co-prod.).
TELEVISION: *Series*: Danger Man (Secret Agent), The Saint.

YELLEN, LINDA
Producer, Director, Writer. b. New York, NY, July 13. e. Barnard Coll., B.A.; Columbia U., M.F.A., Ph.D. Lecturer Barnard Coll., Yale U.; asst. professor, City U. of N.Y. Member: exec. council, DGA.
THEATER: Chantilly Lace (dir., prod., writer), Parallel Lives (dir., prod. writer).
PICTURES: The End of Summer (dir., prod., s.p.), Looking Up (prod., dir.), Prospera, Come Out Come Out, Everybody Wins (prod.).
TELEVISION: *Movies*: Mayflower: The Pilgrims' Adventure (prod.), Playing for Time (exec. prod.; Emmy, Peabody & Christopher Awards, 1980), Hardhat and Legs (prod.), The Royal Romance of Charles and Diana (exec. prod., co-writer), Prisoner Without a Name Cell Without a Number (prod., dir., co-writer; Peabody & WGA Awards), Liberace: Behind the Music (exec. prod.), Sweet Bird of Youth (exec. prod.), Rebound (dir., co-writer).

YEOH, MICHELLE
Actress. r.n. Yeoh Chu-Kheng. b. Ipoh, Malaysia, August 6, 1962. Has acted under the name Michelle Khan.
PICTURES: In the Line of Duty, Magnificent Warriors, The Heroic Trio, Police Story 3: Supercop, Butterfly Sword, Heroic Trio 2: Executioners, Seven Maidens, Tai-Chi, Wing Chun, The Stunt Woman, The Soong Sisters, Tomorrow Never Dies, Moonlight Express, Crouching Tiger, Hidden Dragon.

YORDAN, PHILIP
Writer. b. Chicago, IL, April 1, 1914. e. U. of Illinois, B.A., Kent Coll. of Law, LL.D. Was attorney, then author, prod., playwright (Anna Lucasta). Began screen writing 1942 with collab. s.p. Syncopation.
PICTURES: Syncopation, The Unknown Guest, Johnny Doesn't Live Here Anymore, When Strangers Marry, Dillinger, Whistle Stop, Suspense, The Chase, Reign of Terror, Bad Men of Tombstone, Anna Lucasta, House of Strangers, Edge of Doom, Drums in the Deep South, Detective Story, Mutiny, Mara Maru, Man Crazy, Houdini, Blowing Wild, The Naked Jungle, Broken Lance, Johnny Guitar, Joe MacBeth, Conquest of Space, The Big Combo, Man from Laramie, The Last Frontier, The Harder They Fall, No Down Payment, Gun Glory, Four Boys and a Gun, Men in War, The Fiend Who Walked the West, The Bravados, God's Little Acre, Day of the Outlaw, The Bramble Bush, Studs Lonigan, King of Kings, El Cid, The Day of the Triffids, 55 Days at Peking, Fall of the Roman Empire, Circus World, Battle of the Bulge, Royal Hunt of the Sun, Captain Apache, Bad Man's River, Night Train to Terror, Fort Saganne, Bloody Wednesday, Cry Wilderness, The Unholy.

YORK, MICHAEL
Actor. r.n. Michael York-Johnson. b. Fulmer, England, March 27, 1942. Early career with Oxford U. Dramatic Society and National Youth Theatre; later Dundee Repertory, National Theatre. Chmn., California Youth Theatre. 1992 *Autobiography*: Accidentally on Purpose (Simon & Schuster).
THEATER: Any Just Cause, Hamlet, Ring Round the Moon (Los Angeles), Cyrano de Bergerac, Ira Gershwin At 100. *B'way*: Outcry, Bent, The Little Prince and the Aviator, Whisper in the Mind, The Crucible, Someone Who'll Watch Over Me, Nora.
PICTURES: The Taming of the Shrew, Accident, Red and Blue, Smashing Time, Romeo and Juliet, The Strange Affair, The Guru, Alfred the Great, Justine, Something for Everyone, Zeppelin, La Poudre D'Escampette, Cabaret, England Made Me, Lost Horizon, The Three Musketeers, Murder on the Orient Express, The Four Musketeers, Conduct Unbecoming, Logan's Run, Seven Nights in Japan, The Last Remake of Beau Geste, The Island of Dr. Moreau, Fedora, The Riddle of the Sands (also assoc. prod.), Final Assignment, The White Lions, The Weather in the Streets, Success Is the Best Revenge, Dawn, Lethal Obsession (Der Joker), The Return of the Musketeers, Phantom of Death, The Secret of the Sahara, Midnight Cop, The Wanderer, The Long Shadow, Wide Sargasso Sea, Rochade, Discretion Assured, The Shadow of a Kiss, Gospa, Goodbye America, Austin Powers: International Man of Mystery, Dark Planet, The Treat, Perfect Little Angels, Wrongfully Accused, 54, Austin Powers: The Spy Who Shagged Me, The Omega Code, The Haunting of Hell House, Puss in Boots, Borstal Boy.
TELEVISION: *Specials*: The Forsyte Saga, Rebel in the Grave, Jesus of Nazareth, True Patriot, Much Ado About Nothing. *Series*: Knots Landing. *Guest*: Seaquest, The Naked Truth, Babylon 5, Sliders. *Movies*: Great Expectations, A Man Called Intrepid, The Phantom of the Opera, The Master of Ballantrae, Space, For Those I Loved, The Far Country, Dark Mansions, Sword of Gideon, Four Minute Mile, The Lady and the Highwayman, The Heat of the Day, Till We Meet Again, Night of the Fox, A Duel of Love, The Road to Avonlea, Charles Dickens' David Copperfield (voice), Fall from Grace, Tek War: Tek Lab, September, A Young Connecticut Yankee in King Arthur's Court, Not of This Earth, The Out of Towner, Danielle Steel's The Ring, True Women, The Ripper, A Knight in Camelot. *Host*: The Hunt for Stolen War Treasure, The Magic Paint Brush, Gardens of the World.

YORK, SUSANNAH
Actress. b. London, England, Jan. 9, 1941. Ent. tv 1959; m.p. 1960. Author: In Search of Unicorns, Lark's Castle.
THEATER: A Cheap Bunch of Flowers, Wings of the Dove, Singular Life of Albert Nobbs, Man and Superman, Mrs. Warren's Profession, Peter Pan, The Maids, Private Lives, The Importance of Being Earnest, Hedda Gabler (N.Y.), Agnes of God, The Human Voice, Penthesilea, Fatal Attraction, The Apple Cart, Private Treason, Lyric for a Tango, The Glass Menagerie, A Streetcar Named Desire, September Tide. Produced The Big One, a variety show for peace, 1984.
PICTURES: Tunes of Glory (debut, 1960), There Was a Crooked Man, Greengage Summer (Loss of Innocence), Freud, Tom Jones, The Seventh Dawn, Sands of the Kalahari, Kaleidoscope, A Man for All Seasons, Sebastian, Duffy, The Killing of Sister George, Oh What a Lovely War, The Battle of Britain, Lock Up Your Daughters, They Shoot Horses Don't They? (Acad. Award nom.), Brotherly Love (Country Dance), Zee & Co. (X Y & Zee), Happy Birthday Wanda June, Images, The Maids, Gold, Conduct Unbecoming, That Lucky Touch, Sky Riders, The Silent Partner, Superman, The Shout, Falling in Love Again, The Awakening, Superman II, Loophole, Yellowbeard, Land of Faraway, Superman IV (voice), Prettykill, Bluebeard Bluebeard, A Summer Story, American Roulette, Diamond's Edge, Melancholia, En Hanfull Tio, Fate, Pretty Princess.
TELEVISION: *Movies*: The Crucible, The Rebel and the Soldier, The First Gentleman, The Richest Man in the World, Slaughter of St. Teresa's Day, Kiss On A Grass Green Pillow, Fallen Angels, Prince Regent, Second Chance, Betjeman's Briton, We'll Meet Again, Jane Eyre, A Christmas Carol, Star Quality, Macho, Return Journey, After the War, The Man From the Pru, The Haunting of the New, Devices and Desires, Boon, Little Women, Illusions. *Series*: Trainer.

YORKIN, BUD
Producer, Director. r.n. Alan Yorkin. b. Washington, PA, Feb. 22, 1926. e. Carnegie Tech., Columbia U. U.S. Navy, 1942-45. Began career in tv in NBC's engineering dept. Moved into prod., first as stage mgr., then assoc. dir. of Colgate Comedy Hour (Martin and Lewis) and dir. of Dinah Shore Show. Formed Tandem Productions with Norman Lear; 1974 formed own production co.
PICTURES: Come Blow Your Horn (dir., co-prod., adapt.), Never Too Late (dir), Divorce American Style (dir.), The Night They Raided Minsky's (exec. prod.), Inspector Clouseau (dir.), Start the Revolution Without Me (prod., dir.), Cold Turkey (exec. prod.), Thief Who Came to Dinner (prod., dir.), Deal of the Century (prod.), Twice in a Lifetime (prod., dir.), Arthur 2 on the Rocks (dir.), Love Hurts (prod., dir.), For the Boys (actor), Intersection (co-prod.).
TELEVISION: *Series dir*: Songs at Twilight, Martin & Lewis Show, Abbott and Costello Show, Spike Jones Show, Tony Martin Show (also prod., writer), George Gobel Show, The Ford Show Starring Tennesse Ernie Ford (also prod.). *Specials (dir.)*: An Evening with Fred Astaire (Emmy Award, 1959), Another Evening with Fred Astaire, The Jack Benny Hour Specials (Emmy Award, 1960), Henry Fonda and the Family, We Love You Madly with Duke Ellington, TV Guide Awards Show, Bobby Darin and Friends, Danny Kaye Special, Where It's At with Dick Cavett, Many Sides of Don Rickles, Robert Young and the Family, owner. *Series co-prod.*: All In The Family, Sanford and Son, Maude, Good Times, What's Happening!, Carter Country, Diff'rent Strokes, Archie Bunker's Place.

YOUNG, ALAN
Actor. r.n. Angus Young. b. North Shield, Northumberland, England, Nov. 19, 1919. First acted as monologist for 13 years in Canada; radio comedian 10 yrs. in Canada and U.S. Served in Canadian Navy as sub-lt. 1942-44. Wrote, dir. and acted in comedy broadcasts.
AUTHOR: Mister Ed and Me.
PICTURES: Margie (debut, 1946), Chicken Every Sunday, Mr. Belvedere Goes to College, Aaron Slick from Punkin Crick, Androcles and the Lion, Gentlemen Marry Brunettes, Tom Thumb, The Time Machine, Baker's Hawk, The Cat from Outer Space, The Great Mouse Detective (voice), Duck Tales: The Movie (voice), Beverly Hills Cop III.

TELEVISION: *Series*: The Alan Young Show (Emmy Award, 1950), Saturday Night Revue, Mr. Ed, Coming of Age. *Movies:* Earth Angel, Hart to Hart: Home is Where the Hart Is.

YOUNG, BURT
Actor, Writer. b. New York, NY, April 30, 1940. Worked at variety of jobs (boxer, trucker, etc.) before turning to acting and joining Actor's Studio. Appeared in off-B'way plays which led to Hollywood career. On B'way in Cuba and His Teddy Bear.
PICTURES: The Gang that Couldn't Shoot Straight, Carnival of Blood, Across 110th Street, Cinderella Liberty, Chinatown, The Gambler, Murph the Surf, You Can't Steal Love, The Killer Elite, Rocky (Acad. Award nom.), Harry & Walter Go to New York, Twilight's Last Gleaming, The Choirboys, Uncle Joe Shannon (s.p. only), Convoy, Uncle Joe Shannon (also s.p.), Rocky II, Blood Beach, ...All the Marbles, Rocky III, Lookin' To Get Out, Amityville II: The Possession, Over the Brooklyn Bridge, Once Upon a Time in America, The Pope of Greenwich Village, Rocky IV, Back to School, Bandini, Going Overboard, Blood Red, Beverly Hills Brats, Last Exit to Brooklyn, Medium Rare, Betsy's Wedding, Wait Until Spring Bandini, Diving In, Backstreet Dreams, Rocky V, Bright Angel, Red American, Club Fed, Excessive Force, North Star, Red Blooded American Girl II, The Undertaker's Wedding, She's So Lovely, Kicked in the Head, Heaven Before I Die, Firehouse, The Deli, The Mouse, Mickey Blue-Eyes, Loser Love, The Florentine.
TELEVISION: *Series*: Roomies. *Guest*: M*A*S*H, The Rockford Files, Miami Vice, The Equalizer, Alfred Hitchcock Presents, Tales From the Crypt, Miami Vice, The Equilizer, Law & Order, Walker Texas Ranger, The Outer Limits, Law & Order. *Movies*: The Great Niagara, Hustling, Serpico: The Deadly Game, Woman of the Year, Daddy I Don't Like It Like This (also s.p.), Murder Can Hurt You, A Summer to Remember, Vendetta: Secrets of a Mafia Bride, Double Deception, Vendetta 2: The New Mafia, Before Women Had Wings, Greener Fields. *Mini-series*: The Maharaja's Daughter, Crocodile Shoes, The Last Don.

YOUNG, CHRIS
Actor. b. Chambersburg, PA, April 28, 1971. Stage debut in college production of Pippin, followed by On Golden Pond.
PICTURES: The Great Outdoors (debut, 1988), Book of Love, December, The Runestone, Warlock: The Armageddon, PCU, Deep Down, Falling Sky, The Brave Little Toaster Goes to Mars (voice).
TELEVISION: *Series*: Max Headroom, Falcon Crest, Live-In, Married People. *Pilot*: Jake's Journey. *Movies*: Dance 'Til Dawn, Breaking the Silence, MacShayne: The Final Roll of the Dice, Runaway Daughters, Killing Mr. Griffin. *Special*: Square One. *Guest*: Crime & Punishment.

YOUNG, KAREN
Actress. b. Pequonnock, NJ, Sept. 29, 1958. Trained at Image Theatre/Studio in NYC.
THEATER: A Lie of the Mind, 3 Acts of Recognition, Five of Us, Mud People.
PICTURES: Deep in the Heart (debut, 1983), Almost You, Birdy, 9-1/2 Weeks, Heat, Jaws the Revenge, Torch Song Trilogy, Criminal Law, Night Game, The Boy Who Cried Bitch, Hoffa, The Wife, Daylight, Pants on Fire, Pleasant View Avenue.
TELEVISION: *Movies*: The Execution of Raymond Graham, The 10 Million Dollar Getaway, The Summer My Father Grew Up, Drug Wars: The Cocaine Cartel, On the Edge of Innocence. *Guest*: The Equilizer.

YOUNG, LORETTA
Actress. r.n. Gretchen Young. b. Salt Lake City, UT, Jan. 6, 1913. e. Ramona Convent, Alhambra, CA, Immaculate Heart Coll. Hollywood. Family moved to Hollywood when she was 3 yrs. old; began acting as child. After small part in Naughty But Nice, lead in Laugh Clown, Laugh. Played in almost 100 films. *Autobiography*: The Things I Had to Learn (1962).
PICTURES: Laugh Clown Laugh (debut, 1928), Loose Ankles, The Squall, Kismet, I Like Your Nerve, The Devil to Pay, Platinum Blonde, The Hatchet Man, Big Business Girl, Life Beings, Zoo in Budapest, Life of Jimmy Dolan, Midnight Mary, Heroes for Sale, The Devil's in Love, She Had to Say Yes, A Man's Castle, The House of Rothschild, Bulldog Drummond Strikes Back, Born to Be Bad, Caravan, The White Parade, Clive of India, Call of the Wild, Shanghai, The Crusades, The Unguarded Hour, Private Number, Ramona, Ladies in Love, Love is News, Cafe Metropolis, Wife Doctor and Nurse, Second Honeymoon, Four Men and a Prayer, Suez, Kentucky, Three Blind Mice, Wife Husband and Friend, The Story of Alexander Graham Bell, Eternally Yours, The Doctor Takes a Wife, He Stayed for Breakfast, Lady from Cheyenne, The Men in Her Life, Bedtime Story, A Night to Remember, China, Ladies Courageous, And Now Tomorrow, Along Came Jones, The Stranger, The Perfect Marriage, The Farmer's Daughter (Acad. Award, 1947), The Bishop's Wife, Rachel and the Stranger, The Accused, Mother Is a Freshman, Come to the Stable, Key to the City, Cause for Alarm, Half Angel, Paula, Because of You, It Happens Every Thursday.
TELEVISION: *Series*: The Loretta Young Show (1953-61; 3 Emmy Awards: 1954, 1956, 1959), The New Loretta Young Show (1962-63). *Movies*: Christmas Eve, Lady in a Corner.
(d. August 12, 2000)

YOUNG, ROBERT M.
Director. b. New York, NY, Nov. 22, 1924. e. Harvard.
PICTURES: Nothing But a Man (prod., co-s.p.), The Plot Against Harry (co-prod., photog.), Short Eyes, Rich Kids, One-Trick Pony, The Ballad of Gregorio Cortez (also s.p. adapt.), Alambrista! (also s.p., photog.), Extremities, Saving Grace, Dominick and Eugene, Triumph of the Spirit, Talent for the Game, American Me (co-prod. only), Children of Fate (exec. dir. & exec. prod. only), Roosters, Caught.
TELEVISION: *Specials*: Sit-In, Angola—Journey to a War (Peabody Award), The Inferno (Cortile Cascino; also prod., writer, edit.), Anatomy of a Hospital, The Eskimo: Fight for Life (Emmy Award, 1971). *Movie*: Solomon and Sheba.

YOUNG, SEAN
Actress. r.n. Mary Sean Young. b. Louisville, KY, Nov. 20, 1959. e. Interlochen Arts Acad., MI, studied dance, voice, flute and writing. After graduating, moved to N.Y., worked as receptionist, model for 6 months and signed with ICM. Shortly after signing with ICM debuted in Jane Austen in Manhattan. On L.A. Stage in Stardust.
PICTURES: Jane Austen in Manhattan (debut, 1980), Stripes, Blade Runner, Young Doctors in Love, Dune, Baby: The Secret of the Lost Legend, No Way Out, Wall Street, The Boost, Cousins, Fire Birds, A Kiss Before Dying, Love Crimes, Once Upon a Crime, Hold Me Thrill Me Kiss Me, Forever,Fatal Instinct, Ace Ventura: Pet Detective, Even Cowgirls Get the Blues, Mirage, Dr. Jekyll and Ms. Hyde, The Proprietor, Motel Blue, Exception to the Rule, The Invader, Men, Out of Control, Special Delivery, Poor White Trash, The Amati Girls, Sugar & Spice.
TELEVISION: *Special*: Under the Biltmore Clock. *Mini-Series*: Tender Is the Night. *Movies*: Blood and Orchids, The Sketch Artist, Blue Ice, Witness to the Execution, Model by Day, Evil Has a Face, Everything to Gain, The Cowboy and the Movie Star, Secret Cutting.

YU, JESSICA
Director. b. 1966. e. Yale University.
PICTURES: Sour Death Balls, Breathing Lessons: The Life and Work of Mark O'Brien (also edit., prod., s.p.), Better Late, The Living Museum (also edit.).

YULIN, HARRIS
Actor. b. Los Angeles, Nov. 5, 1937. On B'way in Watch on the Rhine, A Lesson from Aloes, etc. Founder of the Los Angeles Classic Theatre.
THEATER: Numerous productions including: The Little Foxes, Who's Afraid of Virginia Woolf?, Becket, The Entertainer, Uncle Vanya, Tempest, Timon of Athens, The Seagull, A Midsummer Night's Dream, Hamlet, Julius Caesar, Tartuffe, Henry V, The Visit (B'way), Arms and the Man, It's a Mad Mad World, Arts and Leisure, Diary of Anne Frank, The Visit. *Director*: Baba Goya, The Front Page, The Guardsman, Sheba, The Man Who Came to Dinner, Guns of Carrar, Cuba Si, Candida, Don Juan in Hell, Jitta's Atonement, As You Like It, The Rehearsal, After the Fall, Winterplay, Last Meeting of the Knights of the White Magnolia.
PICTURES: End of the Road, Doc, The Midnight Man, Night Moves, Steel, Scarface, The Believers, Fatal Beauty, Candy Mountain, Bad Dreams, Judgement in Berlin, Another Woman, Ghostbusters II, Narrow Margin, Final Analysis, There Goes the Neighborhood, Clear and Present Danger, Stuart Saves His Family, The Baby-sitters Club, Looking for Richard, Multiplicity, Loch Ness, Bean.
TELEVISION: *Specials/Movies*: The Thirteenth Day—The Story of Esther, When Every Day Was the Fourth of July, Missiles of October, Conspiracy: Trial of the Chicago Seven, Last Ride of the Dalton Gang, Robert Kennedy and His Times, Tailspin: Behind the Korean Airlines Tragedy, Face of a Stranger, The Last Hit, Incident at Vichy, How the West Was Won, Truman. *Series*: WIOU, Frasier.

YUN-FAT, CHOW
Actor. b. May 18, 1955, Nam Nga Island, Hong Kong.
PICTURES: Massage Girls, Heroic Cops, Miss O, See-Bar, Patrol Horse, Woo Yuet's Story, Blood Money, Shanghai Beach, Shanghai Beach 2, The Head Hunter, Flower City, Love in a Fallen City, The Occupant, Waiting for Daybreak, Woman, Witch from Nepal, The Story of Rose, The Phantom Bride, The Seventh Curse, A Better Tomorrow, A Hearty Response, 100 Ways to Murder Your Wife, You Will I Will, Dream Lovers, Lunatic's True Story, Love Unto Waste, The Missed Date, Blacklist, A Better Tomorrow II, Heroic Hero, Scared Stiff, City on Fire, An Autumn's Tale, Dragon and Tiger Fight, Drifter Love, Prison Turbulence, The Romancing Star, Goodbye My Friend, Legend of Yu Ta Fu,

City War, Tiger Goes on the Beat, The Greatest Lover, Diary of a Big Man, Fractured Follies, The Eighth Happiness, All About Ah-Long, A Better Tomorrow III, Brotherhood, The Inside Story, The Fun The Luck and the Tycoon, God of Gamblers, The Killer, Wild Search, Once a Thief, Black Vengeance, Prison on Fire II, Full Contact, Now You See Love Now You Don't, Hard-Boiled, All for the Winner, Treasure Hunt, God of Gamblers Returns, The Peach Hotel, The Replacement Killers, The Corruptor, Anna and the King, Crouching Tiger, Hidden Dragon, King's Ransom, Bulletproof Mask.
TELEVISION: *Movies*: The Reincarnation.

Z

ZAENTZ, SAUL
Producer. b. Passaic, NJ. Irving R. Thalberg Award, 1997.
PICTURES: One Flew Over the Cuckoo's Nest (Acad. Award: Best Picture, 1975), Three Warriors, The Lord of the Rings, Amadeus (Acad. Award: Best Picture, 1984), The Mosquito Coast (exec. prod.), The Unbearable Lightness of Being, At Play in the Fields of the Lord, The English Patient (Acad. Award: Best Picture, 1996).

ZAHN, STEVE
Actor. b. Marshall, MN, 1968.
PICTURES: Rain Without Thunder, Reality Bites, Crimson Tide, That Thing You Do!, Race the Sun, SubUrbia, The Object of My Affection, Out of Sight, Safe Men, You've Got Mail, Hamlet, Freaks Talk About Sex, Forces of Nature, Happy Texas, Stuart Little (voice), Hamlet, Chain of Fools, Squelch, Saving Silverman, Riding in Cars with Boys.
TELEVISION: *Movies:* Subway Stories: Tales from the Underground, From the Earth to the Moon. *Guest:* Friends.

ZAILLIAN, STEVEN
Writer. Director. b. 1951.
PICTURES: The Falcon and the Snowman, Awakenings, Jack the Bear, Searching for Bobby Fischer (also dir.), Schindler's List (Acad. Award, 1993; WGA & Golden Globe Awards), Clear and Present Danger (co-s.p.), Mission: Impossible (co-s.p.), Amistad, A Civil Action.

ZANE, BILLY
Actor. b. Chicago, IL, 1966. Sister is actress Lisa Zane. Studied acting at American School in Switzerland. To Hollywood in 1984 landing small role in Back to the Future. On stage in American Music (NY), The Boys in the Backroom (Actors' Gang, Chicago).
PICTURES: Back to the Future (debut, 1985), Critters, Dead Calm, Back to the Future Part II, Megaville, Memphis Belle, Blood & Concrete: A Love Story, Millions, Femme Fatale, Sniper, Posse, Orlando, Flashfire, Tombstone, The Silence of the Hams, Cyborg Agent, Only You, Tales From the Crypt Presents Demon Knight, Reflections in the Dark, Danger Zone, The Phantom, Titanic, This World—Then the Fireworks, Head Above Water, Susan's Plan, I Woke Up Early the Day I Died, Taxman, Morgan's Ferry, Claim, The Believer.
TELEVISION: *Series*: Twin Peaks, Sole Survivor. *Movie*: Brotherhood of Justice, The Case of the Hillside Stranglers, Lake Consequence, Running Delilah, The Set Up, Cleopatra, Howard Hughes: His Women and His Movies, Hendrix.

ZANE, DEBRA
Casting Director.
PICTURES: Days of Thunder, Cadillace Man, Delirious, The Addams Family ,My Cousin Vinny, Whitesands, Hoffa, Joshua Tree, Addams Family Values, Mr. Wonderful, Ghost in the Machine, The War, The Firm, Disclosure, The Last Supper, Get Shorty, The Truth About Cats & Dogs, Men In Black, Washington Square, Wag the Dog, Red Meat, A Cool, Dry Place, Home Fries, Pleasantville, The Limey, American Beauty, Liberty Heights, Stuart Little, Galaxy Quest, The Legend of Bagger Vance, Traffic.
TELEVISION: *Movies:* The Nightman, The Last Seduction, David and Lisa. *Series:* Maximum Bob.

ZANUCK, LILI FINI
Producer, Director. b. Leominster, MA, April 2, 1954. e. Northern VA Community Coll. Worked for Carnation Co. in LA prior to entering film business. Joined Zanuck/Brown Company in 1978 working in development and various phases of production; 1984-present, prod. Made directorial debut in 1991 with Rush. Named Producer of the Year (1985) by NATO, along with Richard D. Zanuck and David Brown; Producer of the Year (1989) by Producers Guild of America, with Zanuck.
PICTURES: Cocoon, Cocoon: The Return, Driving Miss Daisy (Academy Award, Golden Globe & Natl. Board of Review Awards for Best Picture 1989), Rush (dir.), Rich in Love, Clean Slate, Wild Bill, Mulholland Falls, The Double, True Crime.
TELEVISION: *Movies*: Rush, Into Thin Air. *Mini-series*: From the Earth to the Moon.

ZANUCK, RICHARD DARRYL
Executive, b. Los Angeles, CA, Dec 13, 1934. e. Stanford U. 1952-56. Father was exec. Darryl Zanuck. Story dept., 20th Century Fox, 1954; NY pub. dept., 1955; asst. to prod.: Island in the Sun, The Sun Also Rises, The Longest Day; v.p. Darryl F. Zanuck Prods. 1958; first credit as prod. Compulsion (1959); president's prod. rep., 20th Century Fox Studio, 1963; v.p. charge prod., 20th Fox; pres., 20th Fox TV exec. v.p. chge. prod.; 1968 Chmn. of Bd., Television div., 20th Century Fox, 1969 Pres., 20th Century Fox Film Corp. Joined Warner Bros., 1971, as sr. exec. v.p.; resigned 1972 to form Zanuck-Brown Production Company, Universal Pictures. Joined 20th Century-Fox, 1980-83. To Warner Bros., 1983. To MGM Entertainment, 1986. 1988, dissolved 16-year partnership with David Brown. Formed The Zanuck Company, 1989. Recipient: Irving Thalberg Award (1991).
PICTURES: Compulsion, The Chapman Report, Sssssss, The Sting (Acad. Award for Best Picture, 1973), The Sugarland Express, Willie Dynamite, The Black Windmill, The Girl from Petrovka, The Eiger Sanction, Jaws, MacArthur, Jaws 2, The Island, Neighbors, The Verdict, Cocoon, Target, Cocoon: The Return, Driving Miss Daisy (Acad. Award for Best Picture, 1989), Rush, Rich in Love, Clean Slate, Wild Bill, Mulholland Falls.

ZEFFIRELLI, FRANCO
Director, Writer. b. Florence, Italy, Feb. 12, 1923. e. Florence Univ. Was stage director before entering film industry. Set designer 1949 -52 for Visconti plays (A Streetcar Named Desire, The Three Sisters). Worked as asst. dir. on La Terra Trema, Bellissima, Senso. Director of operas.
PICTURES: *Dir./Writer*: The Taming of the Shrew (also co-prod.), Romeo and Juliet (also exec. prod.), Brother Sun Sister Moon, The Champ (dir. only), Endless Love (dir. only), La Traviata (also prod. design), Othello, Young Toscanini (also story), Hamlet, Jane Eyre, Tea with Mussolini (also story).
TELEVISION: *Mini-Series*: Jesus of Nazareth.

ZELLWEGER, RENEE
Actress. b. Katy, TX, 1969. e. Univ. of Texas, Radio-Television-Film major, 1991.
PICTURES: A Taste for Killing, My Boyfriend's Back, Murder in the Heartland, Shake-Rattle and Rock!, The Return of the Texas Chainsaw Massacre, The Low Life, 8 Seconds, Reality Bites, Love and a .45, Empire Records, Jerry Maguire, The Whole Wide World, A Price Below Rubies, Liar, One True Thing, Nurse Betty, Me, Myself, and Irene, Bridget Jones' Diary.

ZELNICK, STRAUSS
Executive. b. Boston, MA, June 26, 1957. e. Wesleyan U. B.A., 1979 (Summa Cum Laude); Harvard Grad. School of Business Administration, M.B.A., 1983; Harvard Law School, J.D., 1983 (Cum Laude). 1983-86, VP Int'l. TV for Columbia Pictures. 1988-89, pres. & COO, Vestron, Inc.; 1989-93, pres. & COO, 20th Century Fox. CEO, Crystal Dynamics. Currently pres. & CEO of BMG Entertainment North America. Bd. member BMG Entertainment and Recording Industry Association of America.

ZEMECKIS, ROBERT
Director, Writer. b. Chicago, IL, May, 1951. e. U. of Film Awards sponsored by M.P. Academy of Arts & Sciences, plus 15 intl. honors. m. actress Mary Ellen Trainor. Has film editing background, having worked as cutter on TV commercials in Illinois. Also cut films at NBC News, Chicago, as summer job. After schooling went to Universal to observe on set of TV series, McCloud. Wrote script for that series in collab. with Bob Gale. Turned to feature films, directing I Wanna Hold Your Hand and co-writing s.p. with Gale.
PICTURES: *Director*: I Wanna Hold Your Hand (also co-s.p.), Used Cars (also co-s.p.), Romancing the Stone, Back to the Future (also co-s.p.), Who Framed Roger Rabbit, Back to the Future II (also story), Back to the Future III (also story), Death Becomes Her (also co-prod.), Forrest Gump (Acad. Award, Golden Globe & DGA Awards, 1994), Contact (also prod.), What Lies Beneath (also prod.), Cast Away (also prod.), Macabre (also prod.), 13 Ghosts (prod. only), Revelation (prod. only), Clink, Inc. (prod. only). *Co-Writer*: 1941, Trespass. *Exec. Prod.*: The Public Eye, Tales From the Crypt Presents Demon Knight, The Frighteners, Tales From the Crypt Presents Bordello of Blood.
TELEVISION: Amazing Stories, Tales From the Crypt (exec. prod.; also dir., All Through the House, You Murderer).

ZERBE, ANTHONY
Actor. b. Long Beach, CA, May 20, 1936. Studied at Stella Adler Theatre Studio.
THEATER: *NY*: Solomon's Child, The Little Foxes.
PICTURES: Cool Hand Luke, Will Penny, The Liberation of L.B. Jones, The Molly Maguires, The Call Me Mister Tibbs, Cotton Comes to Harlem, The Omega Man, The Life and Times of Judge Roy Bean, The Strange Vengeance of Rosalie, The Laughing Policeman, Papillon, The Parallax View, Farewell My Lovely, Rooster Cogburn, The Turning Point, Who'll Stop the Rain, The First Deadly Sin, The Dead Zone, Off Beat, Opposing Force, Private Investigation, Steel Dawn, Listen to Me, See No Evil Hear No Evil, Licence to Kill, Touch, Star Trek: Insurrection, True Crime.
TELEVISION: *Series*: Harry-O (Emmy Award, 1976), The Young Riders. *Movies*: The Priest Killer, The Hound of the Baskervilles, Snatched, She Lives, The Healers, In the Glitter Palace, KISS Meets the Phantom of the Park, Child of Glass, Attica, The Seduction of Miss Leona, Rascals and Robbers: The Secret Adventures of Tom Sawyer and Huck Finn, A Question of Honor, The Return of the Man from U.N.C.L.E., One Police Plaza, Independence, Baja Oklahoma, Onassis: The Richest Man in the World, Columbo: Columbo Goes to the Guillotine, To Save a Child, Treasure Island: The Adventure Begins, On Seventh Avenue. *Mini-Series*: Once an Eagle, Centennial, The Chisholms, George Washington, A.D., North and South II, Dream West, Asteroid.

ZETA-JONES, CATHERINE
Actress. b. Swansea, Wales, Sept. 25, 1969.
PICTURES: Les 1001 Nuits, Out of the Blue, Christopher Columbus: The Discovery, Splitting Heirs, Blue Juice, The Phantom, The Mask of Zorro, The Haunting, Entrapment, High Fidelity, Traffic.
TELEVISION: *Movies:* The Cinder Path, The Return of the Native, Catherine the Great, Titanic. *Series:* Darling Buds of May. *Guest:* The Young Indiana Jones Chronicles.

ZIDE, LARRY M.
Executive. b. Flushing, NY, Oct. 16, 1954. 3rd generation in mp. industry. Started 1972 with American Intl. Pictures in sls. & adv.; 1973, named branch sls. mgr., Memphis. 1975, joined Dimension Pictures as print controller; 1978, formed Zica Films Co. serving m.p. industry; 1985, Zica merged with Filmtreat Intl. Corp; named pres., newly formed Filmtreat West Corp.

ZIDE, MICHAEL (MICKEY)
Executive. b. Detroit, MI, May 31, 1932. Joined m.p. ind. with American Intl. Pictures as print controller; 1962, promoted to asst. gen. sls. mgr. Named v.p., special projects, 1970; 1972, joined Academy Pictures as v.p. of prod. Later went with Zica Film Co.; 1985, named exec. v.p., Filmtreat West Corp.

ZIEFF, HOWARD
Director. b. Chicago, IL. e. Art Center School in Los Angeles. Started as artist and photographer, working as newsreel photographer for L.A. TV station. Went to N.Y. to do still photography; became top photo artist in advertising. Turned to film direction with Slither.
PICTURES: Slither (debut, 1973), Hearts of the West, House Calls, The Main Event, Private Benjamin, Unfaithfully Yours, The Dream Team, My Girl, My Girl 2.

ZIMBALIST, JR., EFREM
Actor. b. New York, NY, Nov. 30, 1923. e. Fay Sch., Southboro, MA; St. Paul's, Concord, NH; Yale. Son of violinist Efrem Zimbalist and soprano Alma Gluck. Daughter is actress Stephanie Zimbalist. Studied drama, Neighborhood Playhouse. N.Y. Stage debut, The Rugged Path. Shows with American Repertory Theatre; Henry VIII, Androcles and the Lion, What Every Woman Knows, Yellow Jack, Hedda Gabler, Fallen Angels. Co-prod., The Medium, The Telephone, The Consul. Gave up acting after death of his wife and served as asst. to father, Curtis Inst. of Music for 4 years. Returned to acting, stock co., Hammonton, NJ, 1954.
PICTURES: House of Strangers (debut, 1949), Bombers B-52, Band of Angels, The Deep Six, Violent Road, Girl on the Run, Too Much Too Soon, Home Before Dark, The Crowded Sky, A Fever in the Blood, By Love Possessed, The Chapman Report, The Reward, Harlow, Wait Until Dark, Airport 1975, Elmira, Hot Shots!, Batman: Mask of the Phantasm (voice).
TELEVISION: *Series*: Concerning Miss Marlowe (daytime serial), 77 Sunset Strip, The FBI, Hotel, Spiderman the Series. *Guest*: Philco, Goodyear Playhouse, U.S. Steel Hour. *Movies*: Who Is the Black Dahlia?, A Family Upside Down, Terror Out of the Sky, The Best Place to Be, The Gathering Part II, Baby Sister, Shooting Stars. *Host*: You Are the Jury, The Tempest. *Mini-Series*: Scruples.

ZIMBALIST, STEPHANIE
Actress. b. New York, NY, Oct. 8. Father is actor Efrem Zimbalist Jr.; grandparents: violinist Efrem Zimbalist and soprano Alma Gluck; aunt: novelist Marcia Davenport.
THEATER: *LA*: Festival, The Tempest, American Mosaic, Love Letters, The Baby Dance, The Crimson Thread, AdWars, Sylvia. Williamstown Theatre Festival: Barbarians, Summer and Smoke, Threepenny Opera. *Tours*: My One and Only, Carousel. *Regional*: The Philadelphia Story, The Cherry Orchard, The Baby Dance.
PICTURES: The Magic of Lassie, The Awakening.
TELEVISION: *Series*: Remington Steele. *Mini-Series*: Centennial. *Movies*: Yesterday's Child, In the Matter of Karen Ann Quinlan, The Gathering, The Long Journey Back, Forever, The Triangle Factory Fire Scandal, The Best Place to Be, The Baby Sitter, The Golden Moment—An Olympic Love Story, Elvis and the Beauty Queen, Tomorrow's Child, Love on the Run, A Letter to Three Wives, Celebration Family, The Man in the Brown Suit, Caroline?, Personals, The Killing Mind, The Story Lady, Some Kind of Love, Breaking the Silence, Sexual Advances, Jericho Fever, Incident in a Small Town, Voices From Within, The Great Elephant Escape, Whose Daughter Is She? Stop the World—I Want to Get Off, Dead Ahead, Prison of Secrets.

ZIMMER, HANS
Composer. b. Germany. Member of the Buggles, producing hit song Video Killed the Radio Star. Pioneered use of digital synthesizers with computer technology and traditional orchestras.
PICTURES: Burning Secret, A World Apart, Rain Man, Paperhouse, Wonderland, Black Rain, Driving Miss Daisy, Bird on a Wire, Days of Thunder, Pacific Heights, Green Card, Thelma & Louise, Backdraft, Radio Flyer, The Power of One, K-2, A League of Their Own, Toys, Younger and Younger, True Romance, Cool Runnings, I'll Do Anything, The House of the Spirits, Renaissance Man, The Lion King (Acad. Award, Golden Globe, 1994), Drop Zone, Crimson Tide, Nine Months, Something to Talk About, Beyond Rangoon, Muppet Treasure Island, Broken Arrow, The Preacher's Wife, Smilla's Sense of Snow, The Peacemaker, As Good As It Gets, The Thin Red Line, The Prince of Egypt, The Last Days, Gladiator, Chill Factor, The Road to El Dorado, Mission Impossible II, The Pledge, Hannibal, Pearl Harbor.
TELEVISION: Two Deaths, El Candidato.

ZINNEMANN, TIM
Producer. b. Los Angeles, CA. e. Columbia U. Son of dir. Fred Zinnemann. Entered m.p. ind. as film editor; then asst. dir. on 20 films. Production mgr. for 5 projects; assoc. prod. on The Cowboys and Smile. Prod., Straight Time for Warners with Stanley Beck.
PICTURES: A Small Circle of Friends, The Long Riders, Tex, Impulse, Fandango, Crossroads, The Running Man, Pet Sematary (exec. prod.), Streetfighter, The Island of Dr. Moreau.
TELEVISION: The Jericho Mile, Lies of the Twins.

ZISKIN, LAURA
Producer. e. USC Cinema School. Worked as game show writer, development exec. before joining Jon Peters' prod. co. where she worked on A Star is Born, Eyes of Laura Mars (assoc. prod.). Formed Fogwood Films with Sally Field. Became pres. of company Fox 2000 Pictures.
PICTURES: Murphy's Romance, No Way Out, D.O.A., The Rescue, Everybody's All American, Pretty Woman (exec. prod.), What About Bob?, The Doctor, Hero (also co-story), To Die For, Courage Under Fire, As Good As It Gets.

ZSIGMOND, VILMOS
Cinematographer. b. Szeged, Hungary, June 16, 1930. e. National Film Sch. Began career photographing Hungarian Revolution of 1956. Later escaped from Hungary with friend Laszlo Kovacs, also a cinematographer. Winner of Academy Award and British Academy Award for cinematography, also several int'l and domestic awards as dir. of TV commercials.
PICTURES: The Time Travelers (1964), The Sadist, The Name of the Game Is Kill, Futz, Picasso Summer, The Monitors, Red Sky at Morning, McCabe and Mrs. Miller, The Hired Hand, The Ski Bum, Images, Deliverance, Scarecrow, The Long Goodbye, Cinderella Liberty, The Sugarland Express, The Girl From Petrovka, Sweet Revenge, Death Riders, Obsession, Close Encounters of the Third Kind (Academy Award, 1977), The Last Waltz, The Deer Hunter (BAFTA Award; Acad. Award nom.), Winter Kills, The Rose, Heaven's Gate, Blow Out, The Border, Jinxed, Table for Five, No Small Affair, The River (Acad. Award nom.), Real Genius, The Witches of Eastwick, Fat Man and Little Boy, The Two Jakes, Journey to Spirit Island, The Bonfire of the Vanities, The Long Shadow (dir.), Sliver, Intersection, Maverick (also actor), The Crossing Guard, Assassins, The Ghost and the Darkness (A.S.C. Award nom.), Playing by Heart.
TELEVISION: Flesh and Blood, Stalin (Emmy Award, ACE Award, ASC Award).

ZORADI, MARK
Executive. e. B.A. economics and sociology, Westmont College, 1976. M.B.A., Marketing & Finance, UCLA Graduate School of Management, 1980. Mktg. mgr., Walt Disney Home Video. Participated in Home Video and Disney Channel start-ups in the early 1980s, and growth of Buena Vista Pictures Distribution in the mid 1980s; mktg. dir., The Disney Channel, 1983-85; dir. of sales, establishing national adverstising sales division generating $100 million in first-yr. sales, Buena Vista Pictures Distribution, 1985-87; senior v.p. & gen. mgr., Buena Vista Television, 1987-92; president, Buena Vista Intl., 1992-99. Currently president, Buena Vista Intl. (BVI) and Buena Vista Home Entertainment (BVHE) Intl. Named to head BVI & BVHE Intl. Distribution groups, combining groups to generate over $1.5 billion in revenue. Currently member, Los Angeles chapter of Young Presidents Org. and board of trustees, Westmont College.

ZUCKER, DAVID
Producer, Director, Writer. b. Milwaukee, WI, Oct. 16, 1947. e. U. of Wisconsin, majoring in film. With brother, Jerry, and friend Jim Abrahams founded the Kentucky Fried Theatre in Madison in 1971 (moved theater to L.A. 1972); later wrote script for film of that name released in 1977.
PICTURES: The Kentucky Fried Movie (co-s.p., actor), Airplane! (co-s.p., co-dir., actor), Top Secret (co-dir., co-s.p., co-exec. prod.), Ruthless People (co-dir.), The Naked Gun: From the Files of Police Squad! (exec. prod., dir., co-s.p.), The Naked Gun 2 1/2: The Smell of Fear (dir., exec. prod., co-s.p., actor), Brain Donors (co-exec. prod.), The Naked Gun 33 1/3: The Final Insult (prod., co-s.p., actor), A Walk in the Clouds (co-prod.), High School High (prod., s.p.), BASEketball, For Goodness Sake, Santa Claus Conquers the Martians (prod. only), Phone Booth (prod. only).
TELEVISION: Police Squad (series), Our Planet Tonight (special).

ZUCKER, JERRY
Producer, Director. Writer. b. Milwaukee, WI, March 11, 1950. e. U. of Wisconsin. With brother, David, and friend Jim Abrahams founded the Kentucky Fried Theatre in Madison in 1970 and wrote script for film of that name released in 1977.
PICTURES: The Kentucky Fried Movie (co-s.p., actor), Airplane! (co-dir., co-s.p.), Top Secret (co-dir., co-s.p.), Ruthless People (co-dir.), The Naked Gun (exec. prod., co-s.p.), Ghost (dir.), The Naked Gun 2-1/2 (exec. co-prod.), Brain Donors (co-exec. prod.), My Life (co-prod.), Naked Gun 33-1/3 (co-exec. prod.), First Knight (dir., co-prod.), A Walk in the Clouds (co-prod.), First Knight, My Best Friend's Wedding, Toddlers, Imagining Nathan, Unconditional Love (prod.), Rat Race (prod.).
TELEVISION: *Series*: Police Squad! (co-exec. prod., dir.; co-wrote first episode).

ZUNIGA, DAPHNE
Actress. b. Berkeley, CA, October 28, 1962. e. UCLA.
PICTURES: Pranks (debut, 1982), The Dorm That Dripped Blood, The Initiation, Vision Quest, The Sure Thing, Modern Girls, Spaceballs, Last Rites, The Fly II, Gross Anatomy, Staying Together, Eight Hundred Leagues Down the Amazon, Cityscrapes: Los Angeles, Charlie's Ghost Story, Stand-ins, Naked in the Cold Sun, Enermies of Laughter, Artificial Lies.
TELEVISION: *Movies*: Quarterback Princess, Stone Pillow, Prey of the Chameleon, Degree of Guilt, Pandora's Clock, Loss of Faith. *Series*: Melrose Place, Stories from My Childhood. *Guest*: Family Ties, Nightmare Classics (Eye of the Panther).

ZWICK, EDWARD
Writer, Producer, Director. b. Chicago, IL, Oct. 8, 1952. e. Harvard U., B.A., 1974; AFI Advanced Film Studies, M.F.A., 1976. Editor and feature writer, The New Republic and Rolling Stone, 1972-74. Author: Literature and Liberalism (1975). Formed Bedford Falls Production Co. with Marshall Herskovitz.
PICTURES: *Director*: About Last Night... (debut, 1986), Glory (Golden Globe nom.), Leaving Normal, Legends of the Fall (also co-prod., Golden Globe nom.), Courage Under Fire, Against All Enemies, The Siege (also prod.). *Prod.:* Shakespeare in Love (Acad. Award for Best Picture, BAFTA award), Dangerous Beauty, Executive Search, Traffic.
TELEVISION: *Series*: Family (writer, then story editor, dir., prod., Humanitas Prize Award, 1980), thirtysomething (co-exec. prod.; Emmy Award, 1988), Dream Street (exec. prod.), My So-Called Life (also ep. dir.), Relativity, Once and Again (exec.prod). *Movies (dir.)*: Paper Dolls, Having It All, Extreme Close-Up (also co-exec. prod., co-story), Relativity (pilot).

ZWICK, JOEL
Director. b. Brooklyn, NY, Jan. 11, 1942. e. Brooklyn Coll., M.A.
THEATER: Dance with Me, Cold Storage, Esther, Cafe La Mama.
PICTURES: *Producer*: Can't Be Heaven. TELEVISION: *Series*: Laverne and Shirley, Mork and Mindy, It's a Living, America 2100, Goodtime Girls, Hot W.A.C.S. (also exec. prod.), Little Darlings, Joanie Loves Chachi, The New Odd Couple (also supv. prod.), Webster, Brothers (supv. prod.), Perfect Strangers (also pilot), Full House (also pilot), Getting By (also prod.), Kirk, Meego, The Wayans Brothers, The Parent 'Hood, The Love Boat: The Next Wave. *Pilots*: Angie, Bosom Buddies, Struck by Lightning, Family Matters, Adventures in Babysitting, Morning Glory, Star of the Family, Up to No Good, Going Places, Hangin' With Mr. Cooper, Life Happens, On Our Own, Making Out, Nowhere Fast. *Movies*: Adventures in Babysitting.

OBITUARIES

(OCT. 1, 1999 - SEPT. 30, 2000)

Edward Anhalt . . . . . Sept. 3, 2000
Ian Bannen . . . . . Nov. 3, 1999
Paul Bartel . . . . . May 13, 2000
Hugh Benson . . . . . Oct. 28, 1999
John Berry . . . . . Nov. 29, 1999
Bill Colleran . . . . . June 1, 2000
George Duning . . . . . Feb. 27, 2000
Douglas Fairbanks Jr. . . . . . May 7, 2000
William Fairchild . . . . . May 9, 2000
William Fineshriber . . . . . Nov. 6, 1999
Vittorio Gassman . . . . . June 29, 2000
John Gielgud . . . . . May 21, 2000
James Goldstone . . . . . Nov. 5, 1999
Ernie Grossman . . . . . July 25, 2000
Alec Guinness . . . . . Aug. 5, 2000
Madeline Kahn . . . . . Dec. 3, 1999
Hedy Lamarr . . . . . Jan. 19, 2000
David Levy . . . . . Jan. 25, 2000
Nancy Marchand . . . . . June 18, 2000
Walter Matthau . . . . . July 1, 2000
David Merrick . . . . . April 25, 2000
Arthur Morton . . . . . April 15, 2000
John Newland . . . . . Jan 10, 2000
Abraham Polonsky . . . . . Oct. 26, 1999
Gene Rayburn . . . . . Nov. 29, 1999
Steve Reeves . . . . . May 1, 2000
Jonas Rosenfield . . . . . May 31, 2000
Max Showalter . . . . . July 30, 2000
Richard Shull . . . . . Oct. 13, 1999
Curt Siodmak . . . . . Sept. 2, 2000
Herb Steinberg . . . . . May 8, 2000
Craig Stevens . . . . . May 10, 2000
Robert E. Swink . . . . . Aug. 15, 2000
Claire Trevor . . . . . April 8, 2000
Roger Vadim . . . . . Feb. 11, 2000
Jim Varney . . . . . Feb. 10, 2000
Sy Weintraub . . . . . April 4, 2000
Don Weis . . . . . July 25, 2000
Loretta Young . . . . . Aug. 12, 2000

Motion Pictures

U.S. Releases, 1999-2000 459

Foreign Releases, 1999-2000 485

U.S. & Foreign Releases, 1990-1999 530

Film Festivals 630

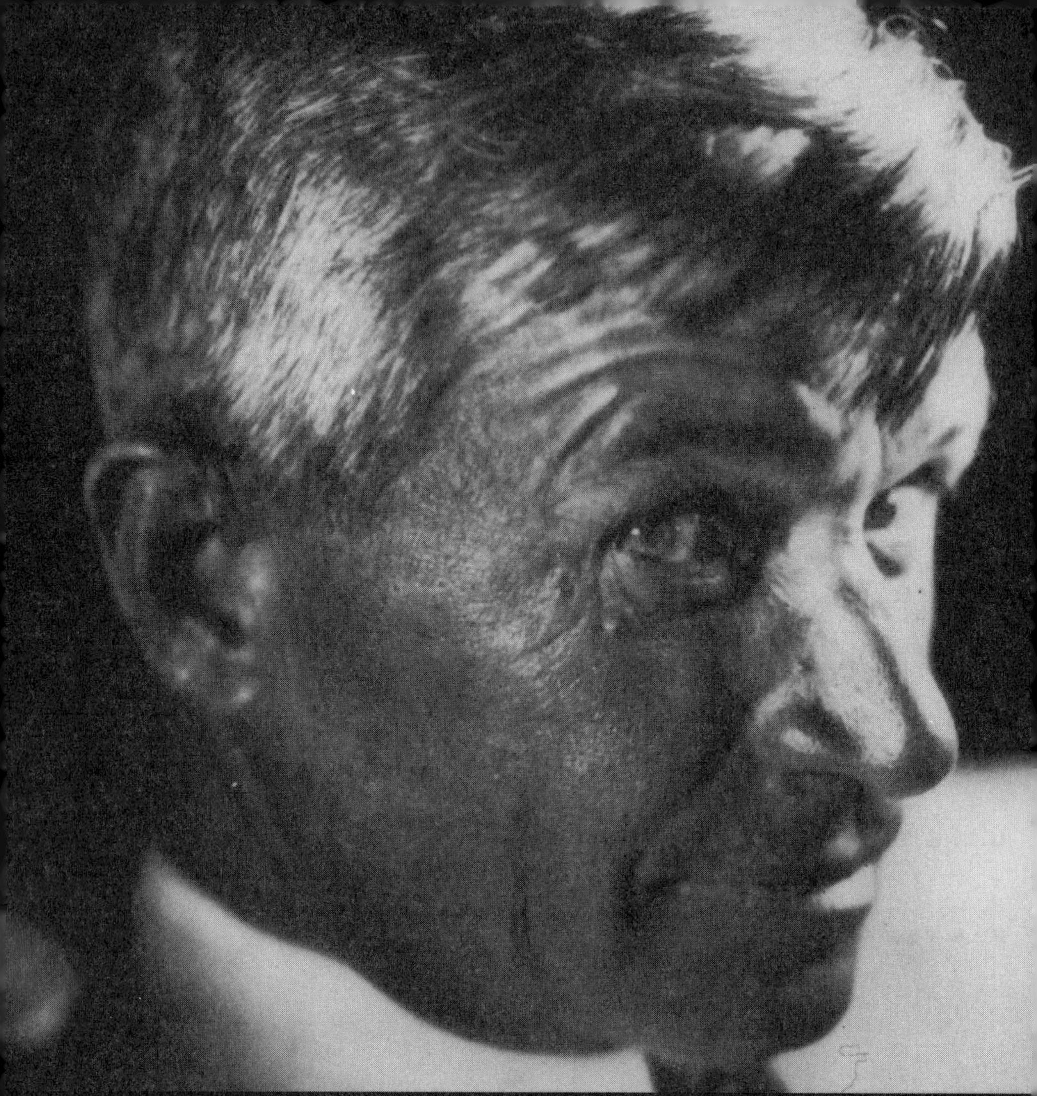

U.S. Motion Picture Releases

(October 1, 1999—September 30, 2000)

This list includes motion pictures from major studios and independents. Many release dates are review or festival release dates.

ABCD
A Laxmi Pictures presentation, in association with the Business. (International sales: the Business, N.Y./Laxmi, N.J.) Producers: Tejal Desai, Brian Wray, Krutin Patel. Executive producer: Madhur Jaffrey. Director: Krutin Patel. Screenplay: Patel, James Ambrose; story: Patel. Camera: Milton Kam. Editor: Ravi Subramaniam. Music: Deirdre Broderick. In color. Release date: Nov. 13, 1999. Running time: 106 Min.
Cast: Madhur Jaffrey, Faran Tahir, Sheetal Sheth, Aasif Andvi, David Ari, Jennifer Dorr White, Adriane Forlana Erdos, Rex Young.

ABILENE
A Clear Stream Pictures production. Producer: Tom Gamble. Executive producer: Ian Jessel. Director/Screenplay: Joe Camp III. Camera: Rob Sweeney. Editor: Olof Kallstrom. Music: Charles Engstrom. In color, Panavision widescreen. Release date: Sept. 19, 1999. Running time: 102 Min.
Cast: Ernest Borgnine, Kim Hunter, James Morrison, Wendell Pierce, Park Overall, Adrian Richard, Alan North, Zouanne Leroy, Mary Jo Catlett, Rance Howard.

THE ADVENTURES OF ELMO IN GROUCHLAND
A Sony Pictures Entertainment release of a Columbia Pictures presentation of a Jim Henson Pictures presentation of a Children's Televison Workshop production. Producers: Alex Rockwell, Marjorie Kalins. Executive producers: Brian Henson, Stephanie Allain, Martin G. Baker. Co-producers: Kevin Clash, Thomas M. Bourne. Director: Gary Halvorson. Screenplay: Mitchell Kriegman, Joseph Mazzarino. Camera: Alan Caso. Editor: Alan Baumgarten. Music: John Debney. In Deluxe color. Release date: Sept. 25, 1999. MPAA Rating: G. Running time: 73 Min.
Voices: Kevin Clash, Fran Brill, Stephanie, D'Abruzzo, Dave Goelz, Joseph Mazzarino, Jerry Nelson, Martin P. Robinson, David Rudman, Caroll Spinney, Steve Whitmire.

THE ADVENTURES OF ROCKY AND BULLWINKLE
A Universal release presented in association with Capella/KC Medien of a Tribeca production. Producers: Jane Rosenthal, Robert De Niro. Executive producers: Tiffany Ward, David Nicksay. Co-producer: Brad Epstein. Director: Des McAnuff. Screenplay: Kenneth Lonergan, based on characters developed by Jay Ward. Camera: Thomas Ackerman. Editor: Dennis Virkler. Music: Mark Mothersbaugh. In Deluxe color. Release date: June 27, 2000. MPAA Rating: PG. Running time: 88 Min.
Cast: Rene Russo, Jason Alexander, Piper Perabo, Randy Quaid, Robert De Niro, Janeane Garofalo, Jonathan Winters, John Goodman, Kenan Thompson.
Voices: June Foray, Keith Scott.

ALL THE RAGE
A Mutual Film Co./Scanbox Entertainment/Newmarket Film Co. presentation of a Screenland Pictures production. (International sales: Mutual Film Co., Los Angeles.) Producers: James D. Stern, Peter Gilbert, Ash R. Shah, Anne McCarthy, Mary Vernieu. Executive producers: Will Tyrer, Chris Ball, Gary Levinsohn, Mark Gordon. Co-executive producers: Adam Del Deo, Todd King. Director: James D. Stern. Screenplay: Keith Reddin, based on his play. Camera: Alex Nepomniaschy. Editor: Tony Lombardo. Music: Mark Mothersbaugh. In FotoKem color. Release date: Sept. 13, 1999. Running time: 97 Min.
Cast: Joan Allen, Andre Braugher, Josh Brolin, Jeff Daniels, Robert Forster, Anna Paquin, Giovanni Ribisi, David Schwimmer, Gary Sinise, Bokeem Woodbine.

ALMOST FAMOUS
A DreamWorks Pictures release of a Vinyl Films production. Producers: Cameron Crowe, Ian Bryce. Co-producer: Lisa Stewart. Director/Screenplay: Cameron Crowe. Camera: John Toll. Editors: Joe Hutshing, Saar Klein. Music score: Nancy Wilson. Release date: Aug.18, 2000. MPAA Rating: R. Running time: 122 Min.
Cast: Billy Crudup, Frances McDormand, Kate Hudson, Jason Lee, Patrick Fugit, Anna Paquin, Fairuza Balk, Noah Taylor, Zooey Deschanel, John Fedevich, Bijou Phillips, Philip Seymour Hoffman, Eion Bailey, Terry Chen.

ALWAYS A BRIDESMAID
A Nina Davenport production, in co-production with Cinemax and Channel Four. (International sales: Sunshine AmalgaMedia, N.Y.) Producer/Director/Screenplay/Editor: Nina Davenport. Camera: Davenport. Music: Sheldon Mirowitz. In digital video color. Release date: Mar. 29, 2000. Running time: 101 Min. Documentary.

AMARGOSA
A Triple Play Pictures presentation. Producers: Sidney Sherman, Kenneth A. Carlson. Executive producer: Traci Robinson. Director/Screenplay: Todd Robinson. Camera: Curt Apduhan. Editor: Clarinda Wong. Music: Randy Miller. In FotoKem color. Release date: Mar. 29, 2000. Running time: 92 Min. Documentary.
With: Marta Becket, Tom Willet, Ray Bradbury, Paul Lyday.
Narrator: Mary McDonnell.

AMERICAN BABYLON
A Court TV release of an RS production in association with Court TV. Producers: David Heilbroner, Robert Stone. Executive producer: Anthony Horn. Director: Robert Stone. Camera: Stone. Editor: Kate Davis. Music: Joel Harrison. In color, 16mm. Release date: May 30, 2000. Running time: 86 Min. Documentary.
With: Jeff Fauntleroy, Lonell Jones.

AMERICAN GYPSY: A STRANGER IN EVERYBODY'S LAND
A Little Dust Production. Producer: Jasmine Dellal. Producer: Jasmine Dellas. Director: Jasmine Dellal. Camera: Michele Zaccheo, Dellal. Editors: Joseph De Francesco, Dellal. Music: John Filcich. In color, video-to-16mm. Release date: Apr. 29, 2000. Running time: 80 Min. Documentary.

AMERICANOS: LATINO LIFE IN THE UNITED STATES
An Olmos Prods./BAK Prods. production in association with the Reflections Joint Venture. Producers: Nick Athas, Edward James Olmos. Executive producers: Lea Ybarra, Manuel Monterrey. Directors: Susan Todd, Andrew Young. Camera: Young. Editors: Harvey Greenstein, Young. In color. Release date: Jan. 22, 2000. Running time: 81 Min. Documentary.

AMERICAN PSYCHO
A Lions Gate release of a Lions Gate Films/Edward R. Pressman Film Corp. production. Producers: Edward R. Pressman, Chris Hanley, Christian Halsey Solomon. Executive producers: Michael Paseornek, Jeff Sackman, Joe Drake. Co-producers: Ernie Barbaresh, Clifford Streit, Joseph Drake. Director: Mary Harron. Screenplay: Harron, Guinevere Turner, based on the novel by Bret Easton Ellis. Camera: Andrzej Sekula. Editor: Andrew Marcus. In color, Panavision widescreen. Release date: Jan. 21, 2000. MPAA Rating: NC-17. Running time: 97 Min.
Cast: Christian Bale, Willem Dafoe, Jared Leto, Reese Witherspoon, Samantha Mathis, Chloe Sevigny, Justin Theroux, Josh Lucas, Matt Ross, Bill Sage, Cara Seymour.

THE AMERICAN TAPESTRY
A Showtime presentation of an El Norte production. Producers: Gregory Nava, Barbara Martinez-Jitner. Executive producer: Sandra M. Itkoff. Co-producer: Lesli Klainberg. Director: Gregory Nava. Mexican sequence director: Barbara Martinez-Jitner. Camera: Martinez-Jitner, Stephen Constentino, Kirk Gardner, Frances Kenny. Editor: Sandy Guthrie. Music: John Adams. In color, digital video. Release date: Feb. 26, 2000. Running time: 96 Min. Documentary.

ANGELA'S ASHES
A Paramount release (in U.S.) of a Paramount Pictures and Universal Pictures Intl. presentation of a David Brown/Scott Rudin/Dirty Hands production. Producers: Rudin, Brown, Alan Parker. Executive producers: Adam Schroeder, Eric Steel. Director: Alan Parker. Screenplay: Laura Jones, Parker, based on the book by Frank McCourt. Camera: Michael Seresin. Editor: Gerry Hambling. Music: John Williams. In Technicolor. Release date: Nov. 22, 1999. MPAA Rating: R. Running time: 145 Min.
Cast: Emily Watson, Robert Carlyle, Joe Breen, Ciaran Owens, Michael Legge, Ronnie Masterson, Pauline McLynn, Liam Carney, Eanna Macliam, Andrew Bennett.

ANGELS!
A Diet Angels production. Producers: T.J. Di Reda, Jessica Caggiano. Executive producers: Rico Martinez, Ruben Zambrano, Caggiano, John Stapleton. Director: Rico Martinez. Screenplay: John Stapleton, Martinzez. Camera: Richard Avalon. Editors: Jett Sally, Jim Makiej. Music: Nazario Alonzo, Craig Sherrad. In color, video. Release date: July 8, 2000. Running time: 86 Min.
Cast: Ruben Zambrano, John Stapleton, Raja, Monty Freeman, Christian Campbell, Yvette Saunders.

ANIMAL FACTORY
A Franchise Pictures presentation of a Phoenician Entertainment/Industry Entertainment/Arts Production Corp. production. Producers: Julie Yorn, Elie Samaha, Steve Buscemi, Andrew Stevens. Executive producers: Alan Cohen, Barry Cohen, Edward Bunker, Danny Trejo. Co-producers: Tracee Stanley, Edward Bunker, Danny Trejo. Director: Steve Buscemi. Screenplay: Edward Bunker, based on his novel. Camera: Phil Parmet. Editor: Kate Williams. Music: John Lurie. In color. Release date: Jan. 24, 2000. Running time: 90 Min.
Cast: Willem Dafoe, Edward Furlong, Seymour Cassel, Mickey Rourke, Steve Buscemi, Tom Arnold, John Heard, Danny Trejo, Jake La Botz, Mark Boone, Edward Bunker.

ANIMAL FARM
A Hallmark Entertainment production for TNT. (International sales: Lakeshore Intl., Los Angeles.) Producer: Greg Smith. Executive producer: Robert Halmi Sr. Co-producer (Ireland): Morgan O'Sullivan. Director: John Stephenson. Screenplay: Alan Janes, Martyn Burke, based on the novel by George Orwell. Camera: Mike Brewster. Editor: Colin Green. Music: Richard Harvey. In color. Release date: Sept. 19, 1999. Running time: 89 Min.
Voices: Pete Postlethwaite, Kelsey Grammer, Ian Holm, Julia Louis-Dreyfus, Julia Ormond, Paul Scofield, Patrick Stewart, Peter Ustinov.

ANNA AND THE KING
A 20th Century Fox release of a Fox 2000 Pictures presentation of a Lawrence Bender production. Producers: Lawrence Bender, Ed Elbert. Executive producer: Terence Chang. Co-producers: Jon Jashni, G. Mac Brown, Wink Mordaunt, Julie Kirkham. Director: Andy Tennant. Screenplay: Steve Meerson, Peter Krikes, based upon the diaries of Anna Leonowens. Camera: Caleb Deschanel. Editor: Roger Bondelli. Music: Geroge Fenton. In Technicolor, Panavision widescreen. Release date: Nov. 27, 1999. MPAA Rating: PG-13. Running time: 147 Min.
Cast: Jodie Foster, Chow Yun-Fat, Bai Ling, Tom Felton, Syed Alwi, Randall Duk Kim, Lim Kay Siu, Melissa Campbell, Deanna Yusoff.

ANY GIVEN SUNDAY
A Warner Bros. release of an Ixtlan/The Donners' Co. production. Producers: Lauren Shuler, Donner, Clayton Townsend, Dan Halsted. Executive producers: Richard Donner, Oliver Stone. Co-producers: Eric Hamburg, Jonathan Krauss, Richard Rutowski. Director: Oliver Stone. Screenplay: John Logan, Stone,; screen story by Daniel Pyne, Logan. Camera: Salvatore Totino. Editors: Tom Nordberg, Keith Salmon, Stuart Waks, Stuart Levy. Music score: Robbie Robertson, Paul Kelly, Richard Horowitz. In Technicolor, Panavision widescreen. Release date: Dec. 9, 1999. MPAA Rating: R. Running time: 162 Min.
Cast: Al Pacino, Cameron Diaz, Dennis Quaid, James Woods, Jamie Foxx, LL Cool J, Matthew Modine, Jim Brown, Charlton Heston, Ann-Margret.

ARTISTS IN EXILE: A STORY OF MODERN DANCE IN SAN FRANCISCO
A Rapt Prods. presentation. Producer/Director/Editor: Austin Forbord, Shelley Trott. Camera: Forbord. Editing consultant: Dave Cerf. Original music: Albert Mathias. In color and B&W. Release date: Sept. 18, 2000. Running time: 85 Min. Documentary.
With: Anna Halprin, Terry Sendgraff, Tumbleweed, Mangrove, Margaret Jenkins, Brenda Way, K.T. Nelson, ODC/San Francisco, the Wallflower Collective, Drissy Keefer, Dance Brigade, Joe Goode Performance Group, Sara Shelton Mann.

THE ART OF WAR
A Warner Bros. release of a Morgan Creek Prods., Franchise Pictures and Amen Ra Films presentation of a Filmline Intl. production. Producer: Nicolas Clermont. Executive producers: Elie Samaha, Dan Halsted, Wesley Snipes. Co-producer: Richard Lalonde. Director: Christian Duguay. Screenplay: Wayne Beach, Simon Davis Barry, based on a story by Beach. Camera: Pierre Gill. Editor: Michel Arcand. Music: Normand Corbeil. In Deluxe color, widescreen. Release date: Aug. 16, 2000. MPAA Rating: R. Running time: 117 Min.
Cast: Wesley Snipes, Anne Archer, Maury Chaykin, Cary-Hiroyuki Tagawa, Donald Sutherland, Michael Biehn, Marie Matiko, Liliana Kmorowska, James Hong.

ASTORIA
A Marevan Pictures presentation in association with Astoria Partners. Producer: Athena Efter, Jamie Dakoyannis. Executive producers: Paul S. Mezey. Co-producers: Elsa Tsartsidou, David Marcellino. Director/Screenplay: Nick Efteriades. Camera: Elia Lyssy. Editor: Stuart Emanuel. Music: Nikos Papazoglou. In Duart color. Release date: Mar. 10, 2000. Running time: 103 Min.
Cast: Paige Turco, Rick Stear, Ed Setrakain, Joseph D'Onofrio, Geraldine Librandi, Steven J. Christofer, Yianni Sfinias, Gregory Sims, Stelio Savante, Chelsea Altman.

ASUNDER
An Obsidian Prods./World Intl. Network production. (International sales: New Millennium Studios, Petersburg, VA.) Producers: Tim Reid, Martin Jones. Co-executive producers: Daphne Maxwell Reid, Blair Underwood. Director: Tim Reid. Screenplay: Eric Lee Bowers. Camera: Johnny Simmons. Editor: John Lafferty. Music: Lionel Cole. In color. Release date: Oct. 10, 1999. Running time: 102 Min.
Cast: Blair Underwood, Michael Beach, Debbi Morgan, Marva Hicks, Desiree Marie Velez, Ira Hawkins, Alene Dawson, Wendy Moore.

THE ATROCITY EXHIBITION
A the Business (New York) production. Producers: Robert Jason, Alexander Lasky, Jonathan Weiss, Robert Kravitz. Co-producers: Bud Gardner, Adam Ernst, Catherine Ernst. Director: Jonathan Weiss. Screenplay: Weiss, Michael Kirby, based on the novel by J.G. Ballard. Camera: Bud Gardner. Editors: Chad Sipkin. Ravi Subramanian, Jed Parker. Music: J.G. Thitlwell. In B&W and color. Release date: June 5, 2000. Running time: 102 Min.
Cast: Victor Slezak, Anna Juvander, Michael Kirby, Mariko Takai, Rob Brink, Diane Grotke, Caroline McGee, Robert Morgan, Tom Constantine, Jeremy Graham.

ATTACK OF THE BAT MONSTERS
An Attack Prods. presentation. Producers: Mark Spacek, Kelly Greene. Executive producers: Greene, Alexis Bakaysa, James Jongebloed. Director/Screenplay/Editor: Kelly Greene. Camera: Tom Hennig. Music: Tim Bushong. In color and B&W, Super 16mm. Release date: June 24, 2000. Running time: 92 Min.
Cast: Michael Dalmon, Fred Ballard, Casie Waller, Ryan Wickerham, Douglas Taylor, Robert Graham, Bill Wise, Rob Bassetti.

ATTRACTION
A Trimark Pictures release of a Krauss-DeGrazier/Capital Arts production. Producers: Mike Elliot, Jon Krauss. Executive producers: Mark Amin, Robin Schorr. Co-producer: Steven Pearl. Director/Screenplay: Russell DeGrazier. Camera: Mike Price. Editor: Glen Garland. Music: Graeme Revell. In CFI color. Release date: Sept. 11, 2000. MPAA Rating: R. Running time: 94 Min.
Cast: Samantha Mathis, Gretchen Mol, Tom Everett Scott, Matthew Settle.

AUGGIE ROSE
A Franchise Pictures presentation in association with Persistent Pictures. (International sales: Franchise Pictures, L.A.) Producers: Dan Stone, Matthew Rhodes, Andrew Stevens, Elie Samaha. Executive producers: Jeremiah Samuels, Mark McGarry. Co-producers: Tracee Stanley, Rick Pacano. Director/Screenplay: Matthew Tabak. Camera: Adam Kimmel. Editor: Brian Berdan. Music: Don Harper, Mark Mancina. In FotoKem color. Release date: May 14, 2000. Running time: 108 Min.
Cast: Jeff Goldblum, Anne Heche, Nancy Travis, Timothy Olyphant, Richard T. Jones, Kim Coates, Joe Santos, Page Moss.

THE AUTEUR THEORY
A Theoretical Films production. Producer: Holly Sorenson. Director/Screenplay: Evan Oppenheimer. Camera: Ruurd M. Fenenga Jr. Editors: Todd Busch, John Axelrad. Music: Joshua Kramon. In FotoKem color. Release date: Nov. 9, 1999. Running time: 77 Min.
Cast: Alan Cox, Natasha Lyonne, Angeline Ball, Rachel True, Armin Shimerman, Ian McNeice, Jeremy Sisto, Garrett Wang, Dana Lee.

AUTUMN IN NEW YORK
An MGM release and presentation, in association with Lakeshore Entertainment of a Gary Lucchesi/Amy Robinson production. Producers: Amy Robinson, Gary Lucchesi, Tom Rosenberg. Executive producers: Ted Tannenbaum, Ron Bozman. Co-producer: Andre Lamal. Director: Joan Chen. Screenplay: Allison Burnett. Camera: Changwei Gu. Editor: Ruby Yang. Music: Gabriel Yared. In Deluxe color. Release date: Aug. 11, 2000. MPAA Rating: PG-13. Running time: 103 Min.
Cast: Richard Gere, Winona Ryder, Anthony LaPaglia, Elaine Stritch, Vera Farmiga, Sherry Stringfield, Jill Hennessy.

THE BACHELOR
A New Line Cinema release of a Lloyd Segan Co. production in association with George Street Pictures. Producers: Segan, Bing Howenstein. Executive producers: Michael De Luca, Chris O'Donnell, Donna Langley. Co-producers: Leon Dudevoir, Sephen Hollocker. Director: Gary Sinyor. Screenplay: Steve Cohen, based on the play "Seven Chances" by Roi Copper Megrue and the screenplay by Clyde Bruckman, Jean Havez, Joseph Mitchell for the film starring and directed by Buster Keaton. Camera: Simon Archer. Editor: Robert Reitano. Music: David A. Hughes, John Murphy. In FotoKem color. Release date: Nov. 1, 1999. MPAA Rating: PG-13. Running time: 101 Min.
Cast: Chris O'Donnell, Renee Zellweger, Hal Holbrook, James Cromwell, Artie Lange, Edward Asner, Marley Shelton.

BACKROADS
An Offline Entertainment Group production. Producers: Shirley Cheechoo, Phyllis Ellis, Christine K. Walker. Executive producers: Henri Kessler, Ezra Swerdlow, David Peipers, Steve Gottlieb. Director/Screenplay: Shirley Cheechoo. Camera: Jonathan Brown. Editor: Lee Percy. In color. Release date: Jan. 26, 2000. Running time: 82 Min.
Cast: Renae Morriseau, Sheila Tousey, Shirley Cheechoo, Greta Cheechoo, Max Martini.

BACKSTAGE
A Dimension Films presentation in association with Roc-a-Fella Records and the Island Def Jam Music Group. Producer: Damon Dash. Executive producers: Bob Weinstein, Harvey Weinstein, Cary Granat, Lyor Cohen. Co-producers: Keri Weisblum, Cha-Ka Pilgrim, Martne Capalbo, Jesse Berdinka, Peter Scherwin. Director: Chris Fiore. Camera: Elena "EZ" Sorre, Mark Peterson, Lenny Santiago. Editors: Chris Fiore, Richard Calderon. In color, video. Release date: Sept. 1, 2000. MPAA Rating: R. Running time: 86 Min. Documentary.
With: Jay-Z, DMX, Method Man, Redman, Beanie Sigel, Memphis Bleek, DJ Clue, Amil, Ja Rule.

BAD CITY BLUES

A Bad City Pictures presentation of a Michael Stevens production. (International sales: Bad City Pictures, Studio City, Calif.) Producers: Stevens, Tim Willocks. Executive producer: Tom Scott. Director: Michael Stevens. Screenplay: Tim Willocks, based on his novel. Camera: Zoran Popovic. Editor: John Ganem. Music: Mick Taylor, Max Middleton. In Technicolor. Release date: Oct. 26, 1999. Running time: 116 Min.

Cast: Michael Massee, Michael McGrady, Judith Hoag, Jim Metzler, Simon Billig, Earl Holliman, Dennis Hopper, Ruth Livier, Scott MacDonald, Virginia Capers, Bob Clendenin, Armando Duran.

BAIT

A Warner Bros. release of a Castle Rock Entertainment presentation. Producer: Sean Ryerson. Executive producers: Tony Gilroy, Jaime Rucker King. Co-producer: Joseph Boccia. Director: Antoine Fuqua. Screenplay: Andrew Scheinman, Adam Scheinman, Tony Gilroy. Camera: Tobias Schleisser. Editor: Alan Edward Bell. Music: Mark Mancina. In Technicolor, Panavision widescreen. Release date: Aug. 29, 2000. MPAA Rating: R. Running time: 119 Min.

Cast: Jamie Foxx, David Morse, Doug Hutchison, Robert Pastorelli, Kimberly Elise, David Paymer, Mike Epps, Jamie Kennedy, Nestor Serrano, Kirk Acevedo.

THE BALLAD OF RAMBLIN' JACK

A Plantain Films presentation in association with Crawford Communications. Producers: Aiyana Elliott, Paul Mezey, Dan Partland. Executive producers: Hunter Gray, Tyler Brodie, Jesse Crawford. Co-producer: Dick Dahl. Director: Aiyana Elliott. Screenplay: Elliott, Dick Dahl. Camera: Elliott. Editors: David Baum. Susan Littenberg. In color. Release date: Jan. 26, 2000. Running time: 112 Min. Documentary.

BARTOK THE MAGNIFICENT

A 20th Century Fox Home Entertainment release of a Gary Goldman production. Producers/Directors: Don Bluth, Goldman. Executive producer: Lori Foster. Screenplay: Jay Lacopo. Director of animation: Len Simon. In color. Release date: Nov. 22, 1999. MPAA Rating: G. Running time: 67 Min. Animated.

Voices: Hank Azaria, Kelsey Grammer, Andrea Martin, Catherine O'Hara, Tim Curry, Jennifer Tilly.

BATS

A Destination Films release. Producers: Brad Jenkel, Louise Rosner. Executive producers: Steve Stabler, Brent Baum, John Logan, Dale Pollock. Director: Louis Morneau. Screenplay: John Logan. Camera: George Mooradian. Editor: Glenn Garland. Music: Graeme Revell. In Technicolor. Release date: Oct. 18, 1999. MPAA Rating: PG-13. Running time: 91 Min.

Cast: Lou Diamond Phillips, Dina Meyer, Bob Gunton, Leon, Carlos Jacott, David Shawn McConnell, Marcia Dangerfield, Oscar Rowland.

BATTLEFIELD EARTH

A Warner Bros. release of a Morgan Creek and Franchise Pictures presentation of a Franchise Pictures, Jonathan D. Krane and JTP Films production. Producers: Elie Samaha, Jonathan D. Krane, John Travolta. Executive producers: Andrew Stevens, Ashok Amritraj, Don Carmody. Co-producers: Tracee Stanley, James Holt. Director: Roger Christian. Screenplay: Corey Mandell, JD Shapiro, based on the novel by L. Ron Hubbard. Camera: Giles Nuttgens. Editor: Robin Russell. Music: Elia Cmiral. In color, widescreen. Release date: May 10, 2000. MPAA Rating: PG-13. Running time: 117 Min.

Cast: John Travolta, Barry Pepper, Forest Whitaker, Kim Coates, Richard Tyson, Sabine Karsenti, Michael Byrne, Sean Hewitt, Michel Perron, Shaun Austin-Olsen, Christian Tessler, Marie-Josee Croze.

THE BEACH

A 20th Century Fox release of a Figment Film. Producer: Andrew Macdonald. Co-producer: Callum McDougall. Director: Danny Boyle. Screenplay: John Hodge, based on the novel by Alex Garland. Camera: Darius Khondji. Editor: Masahiro Hirakubo. Music: Angelo Badalamenti. In Technicolor, widescreen. Release date: Feb. 2, 2000. MPAA Rating: R. Running time: 120 Min.

Cast: Leonardo DiCaprio, Tilda Swinton, Virginie Ledoyen, Guillaume Canet, Paterson Joseph, Robert Carlyle, Peter Youngblood Hills, Jerry Swindall, Lars Arentz Hansen.

BEAT

A Millennium Pictures presentation of a Pfilmco/Donald Zuckerman/Pendragon Film production, in association with Walking Pictures, Martien Holding and Background Prods. Producers: Zuckerman, Andrew Pfeffer, Alain Silver. Executive producers: Avi Lerner, Willi Baer, Danny Dimbort, Trevor Short. Co-executive producers: Michael Beugg, Antonio Zavala, Victor Zavala. Co-producers: Wendy Cassileth, Heidi Levitt. Director/Screenplay: Gary Walkow. Camera: Ciro Cabello. Editors: Steve Vance, Peter B. Ellis. Music: Ernest Troost. In color. Release date: Jan. 29, 2000. Running time: 89 Min.

Cast: Courtney Love, Norman Reedus, Ronn Livingston, Kiefer Sutherland, Daniel Martinez, Kyle Secor, Sam Trammell, Lisa Sheridan, Rene Rubio, Georgiana Sirbu, Tommy Perna.

BEAUTIFUL

A Destination Films presentation, in association with Flashpoint and Prosperity Pictures, of a 2 Drivers/Fogwood Films production. Producers: John Bertolli, B.J. Rack. Executive producers: Dick Vane, Kate Driver, Wendy Japhet, Barry London, Brent Baum, Steve Stabler, Marty Fink, David Forrest, Beau Rogers. Co-producers: Mark Morgan, Jon Bernstein, Jade Ramsey. Director: Sally Field. Screenplay: Jon Bernstein. Camera: Robert Yeoman. Editor: Debra Neil-Fischer. Music: Mohn Frizzell. In color. Release date: Sept. 10, 2000. Running time: 112 Min.

Cast: Minnie Driver, Joey Lauren Adams, Hallie Kate Eisenberg, Kathleen Turner, Leslie Stefanson, Bridgette Wilson, Kathleen Robertson.

BEFORE NIGHT FALLS

A Fine Line Features release (in U.S.) of a Grandview Pictures/El Mar Pictures production. Producer: Jon Kilik. Director: Julian Schnabel. Screenplay: Cunningham O'Keefe, Lazaro Gomez Carriles, Schnabel, based on the book by Reinaldo Arenas. Camera: Xavier Perez Grobet, Guillermo Rosas. Editor: Michael Berenbaum. Music: Carter Burwell. Additional music: Lou Reed, Laurie Anderson. In Technicolor. Release date: Sept. 3, 2000. Running time: 132 Min.

Cast: Javier Bardem, Olivier Martinez, Andrea Di Stefano, Johnny Depp, Sean Penn, Michael Wincott, Najwa Nimri, Hector Babenco, Olatz Lopez Garmendia, Vito Maria Schnabel, Jerzy Skolimowski.

BEL AIR

A PlasterCity Prods. production in association with Morgan Digital Studios. Producer: Alain Silver. Executive producers: Nicolas Cage, Christopher Coppola, Marc Coppola. Co-producers: Jack Oliver, Mark Ean, Jonas Hudson. Director: Chris Coppola. Screenplay: Nicholas Johnson. Camera: Richard Cantu. Eitors: Travis Spangler, Dan Perrett, Nate Bashor. Music: Jim Fox. In color, digital. Release date: Mar. 5, 2000. Running time: 110 Min.

Cast: Marc Coppola, Barbara Bain, Jennifer Rubin, Esteban Powell, Lou Rawls, Charles Fleischer, Ernie Mirich, Brad Wyman, Noah Blake.

BENJAMIN SMOKE

A Cowboy Booking Intl. release (in U.S., Canada) of a C-Hundred Film Corp./Cowboy Booking Intl. presentation of a Gravity Hill Films/Pumpernickel production. (International sales: Cowboy Booking Intl., New York.) Producers: Jem Cohen, Peter Sillen. Executive producer: Noah Cowan. Director/Screenplay: Jem Cohen, Peter Sillen. Camera: Cohen, Sillen, Sarah Cawley. Editors: Nancy Roach, Cohen, Sillen. Music: Smoke. In color and B&W. Release date: Feb. 17, 2000. Running time: 73 Min. Documentary.

With: Benjamin, Tim Campion, Brian Halloran, Coleman Lewis, Bill Taft, Todd Butler, Will Fratesi.

BEST IN SHOW

A Warner Bros. release of a Castle Rock Entertainment production. Producer: Karen Murphy. Executive producer: Gordon Mark. Director: Christopher Guest. Screenplay: Guest, Eugene Levy. Camera: Robert Schaefer. Editor: Robert Leighton. Music: Jeffery CJ Vanston. In Technicolor. Release date: Sept. 7, 2000. Running time: 90 Min.

Cast: Bob Balaban, Jennifer Coolidge, Christopher Guest, John Michael Higgins, Michael Hitchcock, Eugene Levy, Jane Lynch, Michael McKean, Catherine O'Hara, Parker Posey, Fred Willard, Patrick Cranshaw, Don Lake.

BEYOND THE MAT

A Universal release of an Imagine Entertainment production. Producers: Brian Grazer, Ron Howard, Michael Rosenberg, Barry Bloom, Barry W. Blaustein. Co-producer: Debra Marie Simon. Director/Screenplay: Barry W. Blaustein. Camera: Michael Grady. Editor: Jeff Werner. Music: Nathan Barr. In Foto-Kem color. Release date: Oct. 15, 1999. MPAA Rating: R. Running time: 102 Min. Documentary.

With: Terry Funk, Mick Foley, Jake Roberts, Vince McMahon, Roland Alexander, Collette Foley, Dewey Foley, Noelle Foley, Brandy Smith, Paul Heyman, Tony Jones, Mike Modest, Darren Drozdov.

BICENTENNIAL MAN

A Buena Vista Pictures release of a Touchstone Pictures and Columbia Pictures presentation of a 1492 Pictures production in association with Laurence Mark Prods. and Radiant Prods. Producers: Wolfgang Petersen, Gail Katz, Neal Miller, Laurence Mark, Chris Columbus, Mark Radcliffe, Michael Barnathan. Executive producer: Dan Kolsrud. Director: Chris Columbus. Screenplay: Nicholas Kazan, based on the short story by Isaac Asimov and the novel "The Positronic Man" by Asimov and Robert Silverberg. Camera: Phil Meheux. Editor: Neil Travis. Music: James Horner. In Technicolor. Release date: Dec. 8, 1999. MPAA Rating: PG. Running time: 131 Min.

Cast: Robin Williams, Sam Neill, Embeth Davidtz, Oliver Platt, Wendy Crewson, Hallie Kate Eisenberg, Stephen Root, Lynne Thigpen, Bradley Whitford, Kiersten Warren, John Michael Higgins.

BIG EDEN

A Chaiken Films production. Producer: Jennifer Chaiken. Co-producer: John D. Vaughan. Director/Screenplay: Thomas Bezucha. Camera: Rob Sweeney. Editor: Andrew London. Music: Joseph Conlan. In FotoKem color. Release date: Apr. 18, 2000. Running time: 119 Min.

Cast: Arye Gross, Eric Schweig, Tim DeKay, Louise Fletcher, George Coe, Nan Martin, O'Neal Compton, Corinne Bohrer, Veanne Cox.

BIG MOMMA'S HOUSE

A 20th Century Fox release of a Fox and Regency Enterprises presentation of a David T. Friendly/Runteldat Entertainment production in association with Taurus Film. Producers: Friendly, Michael Green. Executive producers: Martin Lawrence, Jeffrey Kwatinetz, Rodney Liber, Arnon Milchan. Co-producers: Peaches Davis, David W. Higgins, Aaron Ray. Director: Raja Gosnell. Screenplay: Darryl Quarles, Don Rhymer, story by Quarles. Camera: Michael D. O'Shea. Editors: Bruce Green, Kent Beyda. Music: Richard Gibbs. In Deluxe color. Release date: May 20, 2000. MPAA Rating: PG-13. Running time: 98 Min.
Cast: Martin Lawrence, Nia Long, Paul Giamatti, Terrence Howard, Anthony Anderson, Ella Mitchell, Jascha Washington, Carl Wright.

THE BIG SPLIT

A Kramer/Tornell production in association with Crossroads Films. Producers: Stacy Kramer, Lisa Tornell. Director/Screenplay: Martin Hynes. Camera: Dino Parks. Editor: David Birdsell. Music: Tom Hynes. In color. Release date: Oct. 23, 1999. Running time: 90 Min.
Cast: Martin Hynes, Judy Greer, Darryl McCane, Rachel True, Maggie Baird, Casey Lee, Lindsay Price.

BITTERSWEET MOTEL

An Image Entertainment release in association with Aviva Entertainment and Little Villa Features of a Stanger Than Fiction presentation of a Bittersweet Films production. Producer: Todd Phillips. Executive producer: Joshua Plank. Director: Todd Phillips. Camera: Elia Lyssy. Editor: Alan Oxman. In color. Release date: Aug. 18, 2000. Running time: 82 Min. Documentary.

BLACK EYED DOG

An Aisling Works presentation. Producers: Paul Barnett, Mikel O'Riordan. Director/Screenplay: Richard O'Connell. Camera: Brian Tramontana. Editor: Megan B. Agosto. Music: Patrick Francis. In color. Release date: Sept. 7, 1999. Running time: 89 Min.
Cast: Paul Barnett, Dermot Carroll, Lorcan Keating, Clive Worsley, Kevin Kearns, Suzanne Nece, Bernadette McCarthy, Pamela Wylie.

BLACK TAR HEROIN: THE DARK END OF THE STREET

A Home Box Office presentation of a Farallon, Films production in association with Imagineer Co. and Tapestry Intl. Producer: Sheila Nevins. Co-producers: Takayuki Kamikura, Nancy Walzog. Director/Editor: Steven Okazaki. Camera: Okazaki; additional camera: Balke McHugh, Michael Chin, Justin Schein. Music: Will Bernard, Ovarian Trolley. In color, video-to-16mm. Release date: Nov. 8, 1999. Running time: 74 Min. Documentary.

BLESSED ART THOU

A Yucca Street Prods. presentation. Producer: William Haney. Executive producer: Edward R. Pressman. Director/Screenplay: Tim Disney, based on a story by Rachel Ingalls. Camera: Claudio Rocha. Editor: Nancy Richardson. Music: Steven Taylor. In FotoKem color. Release date: Jan. 26, 2000. Running time: 92 Min.
Cast: Bernard Hill, Paul Guilfoyle, Daniel von Bargen, Naveen Andrews, Joe Spano, M.E. Hackett, Michael Cudlizt, David Thornton, Brent Hinkley, Kenneth Tigar, Randy Oglesby, Lupe Ontiveros.

BLESS THE CHILD

A Paramount Pictures release of a Paramount Pictures and Icon Prods. presentation of a Mace Neufeld production. Producer: Mace Neufeld. Executive producers: Robert Rehme, Lis Kern, Bruce Davey. Co-producer: Stratton Leopold. Director: Chuck Russell. Screenplay: Tom Rickman, Clifford Green, Ellen Green, based on the novel by Cathy Cash Spellman. Camera: Peter Menzies. Editor: Alan Heim. Music: Christopher Young. In Deluxe color, Panavision widescreen. Release date: Aug. 9, 2000. MPAA Rating: R. Running time: 107 Min.
Cast: Kim Basinger, Jimmy Smits, Holliston Coleman, Rufus Sewell, Angela Bettis, Christina Ricci, Michael Gaston, Ian Holm.

BLOSSOMS OF FIRE

An Intrepidas Production. Producer: Maureen Gosling. Co-producers: Ellen Osborne, Toni Hanna, Maria Therese Garcia de la Noceda. Director: Maureen Gosling, Ellen Osborne. Camera: Xavier Perez Grobet. Editor: Gosling. Music: Gosling. In color, 16mm. Release date: Apr. 25, 2000. Running time: 74 Min. Documentary.

BLUE MOON

A Paradise Pictures presentation of a Blue Moon production. Producers: Ronnie Shapiro, Sylvia Caminer. Executive producer: Norman Chanes. Director/Screenplay: John Gallagher, story by Stephen Carducci. Camera: Craig DiBona. Editors: Craing McKay, Naomi Geraghty. Music: Stephen Endelman. In Technicolor. Release date: Jan. 20, 2000. Running time: 89 Min.
Cast: Ben Gazzara, Rita Moreno, Alanna Ubach, Brian Vincent, Shawn Elliot, David Thornton, Burt Young, Vincent Pastore, Heather Matarazzo.

BOILER ROOM

A New Line Cinema release of a Team Todd production. Producers: Suzanne Todd, Jennifer Todd. Executive producers: Claire Rudnick Polstein, Richard Brener. Co-producer: E. Bennett Walsh. Director/Screenplay: Ben Younger. Camera: Enrique Chediak. Editor: Chris Peppe. Music: the Angel. In Deluxe color. Release date: Jan. 30, 2000. MPAA Rating: R. Running time: 120 Min.
Cast: Giovanni Ribisi, Vin Diesel, Nia Long, Nicky Katt, Scott Caan, Ron Rifkin, Jamie Kennedy, Taylor Nichols, Bill Nichols, Tom Everett Scott, Ben Affleck.

BORICUA'S BOND

A USA Films release of an October Films/Rogue Picutres presentation in association with Mindz in Action. Producers: Greg Scheinman, Robyn Karp, Val Lik. Executive producers: Alan Novich, Pharmboys Partners. Co-producer: Akivah Bloom. Co-executive producers: Abraham Meisner, Mitchell Levinton, Marco Sorisio. Director/Screenplay: Val Lik. Camera: Brendan Flynt. Editor: Doug Abel. In DuArt color, Cinemascope widescreen. Release date: June 22, 2000. MPAA Rating: R. Running time: 95 Min.
Cast: Frankie Negron, Val Lik, Ramses Ignacio, Jorge Gautier, Jesglar Cabral, Geovanny Pineda, Erica Torres, Kaleena Justiniano.

BORN TO LOSE: THE LAST ROCK 'N' ROLL MOVIE

A KW Filmworks production. (International sales: KW Filmworks, New York.) Producers: Lech Kowalski, Bette Wanderman. Executive producer: Catherine Bourdeau. Director: Lech Kowalski. Camera: Marc Brady, Eric Bulder; archival footage: Bob Gruen. Editor: Kowalski. Music: Johnny Thunders, various. In B&W and color, Beta. Release date: Sept. 14, 1999. Running time: 125 Min. Music Documentary.
With: Dee Dee Ramone, Johnny Thunders, Willy DeVille, John Spacely, Stiv Bators, Cheetah Chrome, Wayne Kramer, Sylvain Sylvain, Chris Spedding, Walter Lure.

BOUNCE

A Dendrobium Films production. (International sales: Dendrobium Films, N.Y.) Producers: Adam Watstein, story by Walter Velasquez, Anthony Young. Camera: Peter Olsen. Editor: Ron Kalish. Music: Lord Finesse. In color. Release date: Oct. 14, 1999. Running time: 108 Min.
Cast: Walter Velasquez, Jamal Mackey, L. Vee Anduze, Anthony Young, Pamela Johnson.

BOUNCE: BEHIND THE VELVET ROPE

A Stick Figures production. Producers: Steven Cantor, Daniel Laikind. Director/Screenplay: Steven Cantor. Camera: Paul Dokuchitz. Editors: Pax Wasserman, Iain Kennedy. Music: Samantha Maloney. In DuArt color. Release date: Apr. 15, 2000. Running time: 72 Min. Documentary.
With: Lenny "The Guv'nor" McLean, Terence "The Black Prince" Buckley, Mike and Frank DeMaio, Jordan Maldonado, Alan Crosley, Homer "Omar" Cook.

BOYS AND GIRLS

A Miramax release of a Dimension Films presentation of a Punch 21 production. Producers: Jay Cohen, Lee Gottsegen, Murray Schisgal. Executive producers: Bob Weinstein, Harvey Weinstein, Jeremy Kramer, Jill Sobel Messick. Co-producer: Sue Baden-Powell. Director: Robert Iscove. Screenplay: the Drews. Camera: Ralf Bode. Editor: Casey O. Rohrs. Music: Stewart Copeland. In Deluxe color. Release date: June 14, 2000. MPAA Rating: PG-13. Running time: 94 Min.
Cast: Freddie Prinze Jr., Claire Forlani, Jason Biggs, Amanda Detmer, Heather Donahue, Alyson Hannigan, Raquel Beaudine.

BRINGING OUT THE DEAD

A Paramount release of a Paramount and Touchstone Pictures presentation of a Scott Rudin-Cappa/De Fina production. Producers: Rudin, Barbara De Fina. Executive producers: Adam Schroeder, Bruce S. Pustin. Co-producers: Joseph Reidy, Eric Steel. Director: Martin Scorcese. Screenplay: Paul Schrader, based on the novel by Joe Connelly. Camera: Robert Richardson. Editor: Thelma Schoonmaker. Music: Elmer Bernstein. In Deluxe color, Panavision widescreen. Release date: Oct. 13, 1999. MPAA Rating: R. Running time: 120 Min.
Cast: Nicolas Cage, Patricia Arquette, John Goodman, Ving Rhames, Tom Sizemore, Marc Anthony, Mary Beth Hurt, Cliff Curtis.

BRING IT ON

A Universal release of a Universal Pictures and Beacon Pictures presentation. Producer: Marc Abraham, Thomas A. Bliss, John Ketcham. Executive producers: Armyan Bernstein, Max Wong, Caitlin Scanlon, Paddy Cullen. Co-producers: Patricia Wolff, Jessica Bendinger. Director: Peyton Reed. Screenplay: Jessica Bendinger. Camera: Shawn Maurer. Editor: Larry Bock. Music: Christophe Beck. In FotoKem color. Release date: Aug. 15, 2000. MPAA Rating: PG-13. Running time: 98 Min.
Cast: Kirsten Dunst, Eliza Dushku, Jesse Bradfor, Gabrielle Union, Glare Kramer, Nicole Bilderback, Tsianina Joelson, Rini Bell.

BROKE EVEN

A Broke Even Prods. presentation. Producers: Marc Rizzo, Pamela Russell. Executive producer: Rizzo. Director: David Feldman. Screenplay: Feldman, Carl V. Dupre. Camera: Peter Hawkins. Editor: Livio Sanchez. Music: John Trivers, Elizabeth Myers. In CFI color. Release date: Apr. 3, 2000. Running time: 94 Min.
Cast: Kevin Corrigan, Elizabeth Berridge, Mick Cunningham, Michael Lowry, Michael Kenneth Williams, Mary Diveny, Austen Pendleton.

BRUNO

A J & M Entertainment presentation. Producer: David Kirkpatrick. Executive producers: Jim Lotfi, Doug Mankoff, Jonathan King, Julia Palau, Ivan Gulas. Co-producers: Joe Burns, Robert Leveen, Andrew J. Sacks, David Ciminello. Director: Shirley MacLaine. Screenplay: David Ciminello. Camera: Jan Kiesser. Editor: Bonnie Koehler. Music: Chris Boardman. In Deluxe color. Release date: Apr. 16, 2000. Running time: 108 Min.
Cast: Alex D. Linz, Shirley MacLaine, Gary Sinise, Kathy Bates, Stacey Halprin, Kiami Davael, Joey Lauren Adams, Jennifer Tilly.

BUDDY BOY

An Independent Pictures production. Producers: Cary Woods, Gina Mingacci. Executive producer: Elliot Lewis Rosenblatt. Director/ Screenplay: Mark Hanlon. Camera: Hubert Taczanowski. Editor: Hughes Winborne. Music: Michael Brook. In FotoKem color. Release date: Sept. 3, 1999. Running time: 107 Min.
Cast: Aiden Gillen, Emmanuelle Seigner, Susan Tyrrell, Mark Boone Junior, Harry Groener, Hector Elias, Jon Huertas, Richard Assad.

BURNING MAN: THE BURNING SENSATION

Producer: Alex Nohe, Alan Roberts. Co-producer: Travis Harrod. Director: Alex Nohe. Camera: Nohe, Pilar Otero, David Smith, Chris Stong, Ted Trost. Editors. James Frisa, Nohe. Assoc. editor: Mark Oguschewitz. In color. Release date: Mar. 11, 2000. Running time: 73 Min. Documentary.

BUS RIDERS UNION

Producer/Director: Haskell Wexler. Co-director/Editor: Johanna Demetrakas. Camera: Wexler. Music: Greg Landau. Additional camera: Joan Churchill, Scott Miller, Demetrakas, Bill Bryn Russell. In color, video-to-film. Release date: Mar. 29, 2000. Running time: 86 Min. Documentary.

BUT I WAS A GIRL: THE STORY OF FREIDA BELINFANTE

A First Run/Icarus Films release. A Frame Media and HPS production. Producer: Bernard Neuhaus. Director: Toni Boumans. Camera: Maarten Kramer. Editors: Tenn Pfeil, Berenike Rozgonui. In color. Release date: Apr. 25, 2000. Running time: 69 Min. Documentary.
Narrator: Kenneth Kuhn.

CECIL B. DEMENTED

An Artisan Entertainment release of an Artisan Entertainment presentation, in association with Le Studio Canal Plus, of a Polar Entertainment production. (International sales: Studio Canal Plus, Paris.) Producers: John Fielder, Joe Caracciolo Jr., Mark Tarlov. Executive producers: Anthony DeLorenzo, Fred Bernstein. Director/Screenplay: John Waters. Camera: Robert Stevens. Editor: Jeffrey Wolf. Music: Zoe Poledouris, Basil Poledouris. In color. Release date: May 17, 2000. MPAA Rating: R. Running time: 88 Min.
Cast: Melanie Griffith, Stephen Dorff, Alicia Witt, Larry Giliard Jr., Maggie Gyllenhall, Eric M. Barry, Zenzele Uzoma, Erika Lynn Rupli, Harriet Dodge, Adrian Grenier, Jack Noseworthy, Ricki Lake.

THE CELL

A New Line release and presentation of a Caro-McLeod/Radical Media production. Producers: Julio Caro, Eric McLeod. Executive producers: Donna Langley, Carolyn Manetti. Co-producers: Mark Protosevich, Stephen J. Ross. Director: Tarsem. Screenplay: Mark Protosevich. Camera: Paul Laufer. Editors: Paul Rubell, Robert Duffy. Music: Howard Shore. In Deluxe color, widescreen. Release date: Aug. 9, 2000. MPAA Rating: R. Running time: 107 Min.
Cast: Jennifer Lopez, Vince Vaughn, Vincent D'Onofrio, Jake Weber, Dylan Baker, Marianne Jean-Baptiste, James Gammon, Tara Subkoff.

CENTER STAGE

A Sony Pictures Entertainment release of a Columbia Pictures presentation of a Laurence Mark production. Producer: Mark. Co-producer: Caroline Baron. Director: Nicholas Hytner. Screenplay: Carol Heikkinen. Camera: Geoffrey Simpson. Editor: Tariq Anwar. MusicL Geroge Fenton. In Deluxe color, Panavision widescreen. Release date: May 1, 2000. MPAA Rating: PG-13. Running time: 114 Min.
Cast: Amanda Schull, Zoe Saldana, Susan May, Peter Gallagher, Donna Murphy, Debra Monk, Ethan Stiefel, Sascha Radetsky, Julie Kent, Ilia Kulik, Eion Bailey, Shakiem Evans.

CHARMING BILLY

A Beech Hill Films presentation of a SledgeHammer MFA Films/ Mohawk Films production. Producer: Alexa L. Fogel, Joseph Infantolino, Doug Huebner, Tom Rondinella. Co-producer: Greg Jennings. Director/Screenplay: William R. Pace, story by Pace, Huebner, Rondinella. Camera: William Newell. Editors: Tom Rondinella, James P. Mann. Music: David Barkley. In Astro color. Release date: Oct. 28, 1999. Running time: 79 Min.
Cast: Michael Hayden, Sally Murphy, Tony Mockus, Chelcie Ross, Bernadette O'Malley, Adam Tanguay, Oksana Fedunyszyn.

CHASING SLEEP

A TVA Intl. presentation of a Glaski Prods. and Forensic Films production in association with Le Studio Canal+. (International sales: Le Studio Canal Plus, Paris.) Producer: Oliver Glaas, Thomas Bidegain. Executive producers: Robin O'Hara, Scott Macaulay. Director/ Screenplay: Michael Walker. Camera: Jim Denault. Editor: David Leonard. In color. Release date: Sept. 8, 2000. Running time: 104 Min.
Cast: Jeff Daniels, Emily Bergl, Gil Bellows, Zach Grenier, Julian McMahon, Ben Shenkman, Molly Price.

CHINESE COFFEE

A 20th Century Fox release of a Fox Searchlight presentation from Chal Prods. in association with the Shooting Gallery. Producer: Michael Hadge, Larry Meistrich, Robert Salerno. Executive producer: Anne D'Amato. Co-producer: Jim Bulleit. Director: Al Pacino. Screenplay: Ira Lewis, based on his play. Camera: Frank Prinzi. Editor: Michael Berenbaum. Music: Elmer Bernstein. In Technicolor. Release date: Sept. 2, 2000. Running time: 99 Min.
Cast: Al Pacino, Jerry Orbach, Susan Floyd, Ellen McElduff.

CHUCK & BUCK

An Artisan Entertainment release of a Blow Up Pictures presentation of a Flan de Coco production. Producer: Matthew Greenfield. Executive producers: Jason Kliot, Joana Vicente. Co-producers: Scott M. Cort, Beth Colt. Co-executive producers: Thomas Brown, Charles J. Rusbasan, Judith Zarin, Michael Escott. Director: Miguel Arteta. Screenplay: Mike White. Camera: Chuy Chavez. Editor: Jeff Betancourt. Music: Joey Waronker, Tony Maxwell; theme song: Gwendolyn Stafford. In color, digital-to-35mm. Release date: Jan. 29, 2000. Running time: 99 Min.
Cast: Mike White, Chris Weitz, Lupe Ontiveros, Beth Colt, Paul Weitz, Maya Rudolph, Mary Wigmore, Paul Sand, Gino Buccola.

CIRQUE DU SOLEIL: JOURNEY OF MAN

A Sony Pictures Classics release of a Cirque du Soleil/Motion International production. Producer: Andre Picard, Peter Wagg. Co-producers: Antoine Compin, Charis Horton. Executive producer: Mitchell Cannold. Director: Keith Melton, story by Peter Wagg, Steve Roberts. Camera: Reed Smoot. Editor: Harry B. Miller III. Music: Benoit Jutras. In color, 70mm 3-D. Release date: Jan. 9, 2000. Running time: 38 Min.
Cast: Ian McKellan, Nicky Dewhurst, Brian Dewhurst, Anait Karagyezyan, Mikhail Matorin, Chris Van Wagenen, Kenny Raskin, Cully Smoller, Yves Decoste, Marie-Laure Mesnage.

CITIZEN JAMES

A Doug E. Doug World Inc. presentation of a Doug E. Doug Moving Picture Co. Film. Producers: Doug E. Doug, Anna Southall, Charlynne Hopson. Director: Doug E. Doug. Screenplay: Doug, Guy Margo. Camera: Andre Banks. Editor: Nzingah Clarke. In B&W. Release date: Mar. 31, 2000. Running time: 74 Min.
Cast: Doug E. Doug, Kayinde Harris, Tyrone Jefferson, Albert Shiver Jr.

THE CLEAN AND NARROW

A Del Mar production, presented in association with Sneak Preview Entertainment. Producers: Edward Lopatin, Kermit Christman. Executive producer: Del Tenney. Director: William Katt. Screenplay: Kermit Christman, Katt. Camera: M. David Mullen. Editors: Eric Albertson, Sean Albertson. Music: Jimmy Webb. In FotoKem color. Release date: Jan. 21, 2000. Running time: 82 Min.
Cast: Jack Noseworthy, Laura Keighton, Wings Hauser, Paul Francis, Wes Culwell, William Katt, Sondra Locke.

COMING TO LIGHT: EDWARD S. CURTIS AND THE NORTH AMERICAN INDIANS

A co-production of Anne Makepeace Prods. and Thirteen/WNET for American Masters. Producer: Makepeace. Executive producer (for American Masters): Susan Lacy. Director/Screenplay: Anne Makepeace. Camera: Uta Briesewitz, Jennifer Lane, Emiko Omori. Editor: Jennifer Chinlund. Music: Todd Boekelheide. In B&W and color. Release date: Jan. 28, 2000. Running time: 85 Min. Documentary.
Narrator: Sheila Tousey.

COMMITTED

A Miramax release and presentation of a Dean Silvers/Marlen Hecht production. Producers: Silvers, Hecht. Executive producers: Bob Weinstein, Harvey Weinstein, Jonathan Gordon, Amy Slotnick. Co-producer: Guy J. Louthan. Director/Screenplay: Lisa Krueger. Camera: Tom Krueger. Editor: Colleen Sharp. Music: Calexico. In color. Release date: Jan. 22, 2000. Running time: 98 Min.
Cast: Heather Graham, Casey Affleck, Luke Wilson, Goran Visnjic, Patricia Velasquez, Alfonso Arau, Mark Ruffalo, Kim Dickens, Clea Duvall.

COMPANY MAN

A Paramount Classics (in U.S.)/UFD (in France) release of an Intermedia Films presentation, in association with Foundry Film Partners and UGC Ph. Producers: John Penotti, James W. Skotchdopole, Rick Leed, Guy East. Co-executive producers: Nigel Sinclair, Matt Williams, Susan Cartsonis, Jon Ein, Robert Greenhut. Director/Screenplay: Douglas McGrath, Peter Askin. Camera: Russell Boyd. Editor: Camilla Toniolo. Music: David Nessim Lawrence. In color. Release date: May 7, 2000. Running time: 86 Min.
Cast: Douglas McGrath, Sigourney Weaver, John Turturro, Anthony LaPaglia, Ryan Phillippe, Denis Leary, Woody Allen, Alan Cumming.

COMPENSATION

A Wimmin With a Mission Prods. production. Producers: Zeinabu Irene Davis, Marc Arthur Chery. Director: Davis. Screenplay:Chery. Camera: Pierre H.L. Desir Jr. Editors: Dana Briscoe, Davis. Music: Reginald B. Robinson, Atiba Y. Jali. In B&W. Release time: Jan. 28, 2000. Running time: 91 Min.
Cast: John Earl Jelks, Michelle A. Banks, Christopher Smith.

THE CONTENDER

A DreamWorks Pictures release of a Cinerenta/Cinecontender presentation of a Battleground production, in association with the SE8 Group. Producers: Marc Frydman, Douglas Urbanski, Willi Baer, James Spies. Executive producers: Rainer Bienger, Gary Oldman, Maurice Leblond, Co-producers: Scott Shiffman, Steve Loglisci. Director/Screenplay: Rod Lurie. Camera: Denis Maloney. Editor: Michael Jablow. Music: Larry Groupe. In color. Release date: Aug. 31, 2000. Running time: 126 Min. In color. Release date: Aug. 31, 2000. Running time: 126 Min.
Cast: Joan Allen, Gary Oldman, Jeff Bridges, Sam Elliott, Christian Slater, William Petersen, Philip Baker Hall, Saul Rubinek.

THE CONVENT

An Alpine Pictures production. Producer: Jed Nolan. Executive producers: Roland Carroll, Ryan Carroll, Elliot Metz. Co-producer: Chaton Anderson. Director: Mike Mendez. Screenplay: Chaton Anderson. Camera: Jason Lowe. Editor: John Rosenberg. Music: Joseph Bishara. In color. Release date: Jan. 22, 2000. Running time: 84 Min.
Cast: Adrienne Barbeau, Joanna Canton, Megahn Perry, Dax Miller, Richard Trapp, Coolio, David Gunn, Jim Golden, Liam Kyle Sullivan.

A CONVERSATION WITH GREGORY PECK

A Turner Classic Movies presentation of an On Tour Prods. production in association with Cabin Creek Films. Producers: Barbara Kopple, Cecilia Peck, Linda Saffire. Director: Barbara Kopple. Camera: Don Lenzer, Tom Hurwitz, Sandy Sissel. Editor: Bob Eisenhardt. Music: Art Labrola. In color. Release date: Oct. 14, 1999. Running time: 97 Min. Documentary.

COWBOYS AND ANGELS

A Smokin' Dawgs release. Producers: Greggory B. Peck, Kathryn Arnold. Director/Screenplay: Gregory C. Haynes. Camera: Kramer Morgenthau. Editor: Rocco DeVilliers. Music: Steve Edwards, main theme by Frank Fitzpatrick. In color. Release date: Apr. 15, 2000. Running time: 113 Min.
Cast: Adam Trese, Mia Kirshner, Radha Mitchell, Hamilton Von Watts, Carmen Llywellyn, Steve Lisk, Duane Stephens, Alissa Rice.

COYOTE UGLY

A Buena Vista Pictures release of a Touchstone Pictures and Jerry Bruckheimer Films presentation. Producers: Jerry Bruckheimer, Chad Oman. Executive producers: Mike Stenson, Scott Gardenhour. Director: David McNally. Screenplay: Gina Wendkos. Camera: Amir Mokri. Editor: William Goldenberg. Music: Trevor Horn. In Technicolor, Panavision widescreen. Release date: July 31, 2000. MPAA Rating: PG-13. Running time: 100 Min.
Cast: Piper Perabo, Adam Garcia, Maria Bello, John Goodman, Melanie Lynskey, Izabella Miko, Bridget Moynahan, Tyra Banks.

CREMASTER 2

A Glacier Field release of a Glacier Field production. Producers: Barbara Gladstone, Mathew Barney. Director/Screenplay: Barney. Camera: Peter Strietmann. Music: Jonathan Bepler. In digital HDTV-to-35mm. Release date: Oct. 16,1999. Running time: 79 Min.
Cast: Norman Mailer, Mathew Barney, Lauren Pine, Scot Ewalt, Patty Griffin, Michael Thompson, Dave Lombardo, Bruce Steele, Steve Tucker, Cat Kubic, Sam Jalhej.

THE CREW

A Buena Vista release of a Touchstone Pictures presentation of a George Litto Pictures production in association with Sonnenfeld/Josephson Worldwide Entertainment. Producers: Barry Sonnenfeld, Barry Josephson. Executive producers: George Litto, Michael S. Glick. Co-producer: Zane Weiner. Director: Michael Dinner. Screenplay: Barry Fanaro. Camera: Juan Ruiz-Anchia. Editor: Nicholas C. Smith. Music: Steve Bartek. In Technicolor. Release date: Aug. 22, 2000. MPAA Rating: PG-13. Running time: 87 Min.
Cast: Richard Dreyfuss, Burt Reynolds, Dan Hedaya, Seymour Cassel, Carrie-Anne Moss, Jennifer Tilly, Lainie Kazan, Miguel Sandoval, Jeremy Piven, Casey Siemaszko, Matt Borlenghi.

CRIME + PUNISHMENT IN SUBURBIA

An MGM release of a United Artists Films presentation of a Killer Films production. Producers: Pamela Koffler, Larry Gross, Christine Vachon. Co-producer: Dara L. Weintraub. Director: Rob Schmidt. Screenplay: Larry Gross. Camera: Bobby Bukowski. Editor: Gabriel Wrye. Music: Michael Brook. In CFI color. Release date: Jan. 24, 2000. Running time: 100 Min.
Cast: Monica Keena, Vincent Kartheiser, Ellen Barkin, Jeffrey Wright, James DeBello, Michael Ironside, Christian Payne, Conchata Ferrell, Marshall Teague, Nicki Aycox, Brad Greenquist, Lucinda Jenney.

THE CROW: SALVATION

An SND release (in France) of an IMF presentation of a Pacific Film/Ed Pressman/IMF/Jeff Most Prods. production. Producers: Edward R. Pressman, Jeff Most, Alessandro Camon. Executive producers: Bob Weinstein, Harvey Weinstein, Chris Sievernich, Moritz Borman. Co-producer: Russ Markowitz. Director: Bharat Nalluri. Screenplay: Chip Johannessen, based on the comic book by James O'Barr. Camera: Carolyn Chen. Editor: Howard E. Smith. Music: Marco Beltrami. In color. Release date: June 14, 2000. Running time: 102 Min.
Cast: Kirsten Dunst, Eric Mabius, Jodi Lyn O'Keefe, William Atherton, Fred Ward, Debbie Fan, Grant Shaud, David Stevens, Dale Midkiff, Bill Mondy, Walton Goggins, Tim DeKay.

DANCING IN SEPTEMBER

A Weecan Films presentation in association with StarRise Entertainment. Producers: Reuben Cannon, Don Kurt, Reggie Rock Bythewood. Co-producers: Ligiah Villalobos, Tammy Garnes. Director/Screenplay: Reggie Rock Bythewood. Camera: Bill Dill. Editor: Kevin Krasny. Music: K.C. Saney, Kurt Farquhar, Kwame, Mark Sparks. In Deluxe color. Release date: Feb. 24, 2000. Running time: 107 Min.
Cast: Isaiah Washington, Nicole Ari Parker, Vicellous Reon Shannon, Jay Underwood, Marcia Cross, Jenifer Lewis, James Avery, Michael Cavanaugh, Malinda Williams.

DARK DAYS

A Picture Farm production. Producer: Marc Singer. Executive producers: Paolo Seganti, Randall Mesdon, Morton Swinsky, Gordon Paul. Co-producer: Ben Freedman. Director: Marc Singer. Camera: Singer. Editor: Melissa Neidich. Music: DJ Shadow. In B&W. Release date: Jan. 27, 2000. Running time: 81 Min. Documentary.

DAUGHTER OF SUICIDE

An HBO presentation of Daughter One Prods. production. Producer: Dempsey Rice. Executive producer: Sheila Nevins. Director: Dempsey Rice. Camera: Jim Denault. Editor: Dena Seidel. Music: John Califra. In color and B&W. Release date: June 24, 2000. Running time: 71 Min. Documentary.

DESI'S LOOKING FOR A NEW GIRL

A Mary Guzman production. Producers: Fontana Butterfield, Mary Guzman. Director/Screenplay: Mary Guzman. Camera: Sophie Constantinou. Editor: Lidia Szajko. Music: Alfred O. Guzman Jr. In color, 16mm. Release date: June 16, 2000. Running time: 68 Min.
Cast: Desi del Valle, Yesenia Aguirre, Sandra Carola, Rosa Medina, Michelle T. Cordero, Richard A. Bracho, Alisa Rodriguez, Janelle Jacoo, Marga Gomez.

DETENTION

An Andersonfilm production. Producers: Robert Castaldo, K.C. Irick. Director/Screenplay: Andy Anderson. Camera: Gary Watson. Editor: Castaldo. Music: Johnny Reno. In color. Release date: Dec. 27, 1999. Running time: 130 Min.
Cast: John Davies, Marsha Dietlein, Susana Gibb, Meason Wiley, Rebecca Sanabria, Brandy Little, Jonathan Brent, Kirk Kelley Kahn, Forrest Denbow, Gail Cronauer.

DEUCE BIGALOW: MALE GIGOLO

A Buena Vista Pictures release of a Touchstone Pictures presentation of a Happy Madison production in association with Out of the Blue ... Entertainment. Producers: Sid Ganis, Barry Bernardi. Executive producers: Adam Sandler, Jack Giarraputo. Co-producers: Alex Siskin, Harris Goldberg. Director: Mike Mitchell. Screenplay: Harris Goldberg, Rob Schneider. Camera: Peter Lyons Collister. Editors: George Bowers, Lawrence Jordan. Music: Teddy Castellucci. In Technicolor. Release date: Dec. 6, 1999. Running time: 88 Min.
Cast: Rob Schneider, William Forsythe, Eddie Griffin, Arija Bareikis, Oded Fehr, Gail O'Grady, Richard Riehle, Jacqueline Obradors, Big Boy, Amy Poehler, Dina Platias, Torsten Voges.

DIAL H FOR HITCHCOCK

A Universal Television Enterprises release of a Universal Television Enterprises/Encore Media Group presentation of a Rocket Science Laboratories production. Producer: Nicole Lucas. Executive producers: Jean-Michel Michenaud. Chris Cowan. Co-producer: Arnold Glassman. Director/Screenplay: Ted Haimes. Camera: Michael Barry, Brain Dowley, Brian Duggan, Sam Painter, Mark Petersson, Sam Sewell, Mark Zavad. Editor: Arnold Glassman. Music: Taylor M. Uhler. In color and B&W. Release date: Oct. 13, 1999. Running time: 101 Min. Documentary.
With: Jonathan Demme, Joseph Stefano, John Michael Hayes, Janet Leigh, Brian De Palma, Curtis Hanson, Pat Hitchcock O'Connell, Norman Lloyd, Herb Steinberg, Peter Bogdanovich. Narrator: Kevin Spacey.

DINOSAUR

A Buena Vista release of a Walt Disney Pictures presentation. Producer: Pam Marsden. Co-producer: Baker Bloodworth. Director: Ralph Zondag, Eric Leighton. Screenplay: John Harrison, Robert Nelson Jacobs, based on an original screenplay by Walon Green, story by Thom Enriquez, Harrison, Jacobs, Zonday. Camera: Steven Douglas Smith, Dave Hardberger. Editor: H. Lee Peterson. Music: James Newton Howard. In Hollywood Film and Video color. Release date: May 5, 2000. MPAA Rating: PG. Running time: 82 Min.
Voices: D.B. Sweeney, Alfre Woodard, Ossie Davis, Max Casella, Hayden Panettiere, Samuel E. Wright, Julianne Margulies, Peter Siragusa, Joan Plowright, Della Reese.

DISNEY'S THE KID

A Buena Vista release of a Walt Disney Pictures presentation of a Junction Entertainment production. Producers: Jon Turteltaub, Christina Steinberg, Hunt Lowry. Executive producers: Arnold Rifkin, David Willis. Co-producers: Bill Johnson, William M. Elvin. Director: Jon Turteltaub. Screenplay: Audrey Wells. Camera: Peter Menzies Jr. Editors: Peter Honess, David Rennie. Music: Marc Shaiman. In Technicolor. Release date: June 28, 2000. MPAA Rating: PG. Running time: 104 Min.
Cast: Bruce Willis, Spencer Breslin, Emily Mortimer, Lily Tomlin, Chi McBride, Jean Smart, Dana Ivey, Daniel von Bargen, Stanley Anderson, Susan Dalian.

DOG STORY

A Dog Story Films presentation of a Shovel Guy Movie production. Producers: Adam Golomb, Christopher Hatton, Jian Hong Kuo. Director: Jian Hong Kuo. Screenplay: Adam Golomb. Camera: Patrick Neary. Editor: Christopher L. Walter. Music: Jonathan Price. In FotoKem color. Release date: June 20, 2000. Running time: 80 Min.
Cast: Adam Golomb, Maria Cina, Lyle Schwarz, Kevin Cahill, ALice Lentz, Paul Wadleigh, James Servais, Emmett.

THE DOGWALKER

A Rita Films production in association with Soundelux Entertainment Group and Bouquet Multimedia. Producer: Vera Anderson. Executive producers: Lon Bender, Wylie Stateman, Stanton Kaye, Terry Myers. Co-producers: Roderick Spencer, Stacy Leah Winkler. Director/Screenplay: Paul Duran. Camera: Dean Lent. Editor: Julie Rogers. Music: Joey Altruda. In color. Release date: Jan. 16, 2000. Running time: 105 Min.
Cast: Will Stewart, Stepfanie Kramer, Tony Todd, John Randolph, Allan Rich, Stacey Williams, Carol Gustafson, Nicki Aycox.

DOUBLE PARKED

A Fierce Films presentation of a 44th Street Films production. (International sales: Fierce Films, New York.) Producers: Stephen Kinsella, Matthew Myers. Executive producer, Mark Montgomery. Director: Stephen Kinsella. Screenplay: Kinsella, Paul Solberg, from a story by Kinsella. Camera: Jim Denault. Editor: Seth E. Anderson. Music: Craig Hazen, David Wolfert. In Duart color. Release date: Mar. 11, 2000. Running time: 98 Min.
Cast: Callie Thorne, William Sage, Noah Fleis, Rufus Read, P.J. Brown, Michelle Hurd, Eileen Galindo, Anthony De Sando.

DOWNTOWN

A New York Beat Films production. (International sales: Celluloid Dreams, Paris.) Producer: Michael Zilkha. Co-producer: Glenn O'Brien. Director: Edo Bertoglio. Screenplay: Glenn O'Brien. Camera: John McNulty. Editor: Pamela French. Music: Gray, John Lurie, DNA, Tuxedo Moon.
Cast: Jean Michel Basquiat, Anna Schroeder, Giorgio Giomelsky, Marshall Chess, Danny Rosen, Daniela Morera, Lisa Rosen, Steve Mass, Saul Williams.

DOWN TO YOU

A Miramax release of an Open City Film production. Producers: Jason Kliot, Joana Vicente. Executive producers: Bob Weinstein, Harvey Weinstein, Jeremy Kramer, Bobby Cohen. Co-producer: Trish Hoffmann. Director/Screenplay: Kris Isacsson. Camera: Robert Yeoman. Editor: Stephen A. Rotter. Music: Edmund Choi. In color. Release date: Jan 21, 2000. MPAA Rating: PG-13. Running time: 92 Min.
Cast: Freddie Prinze Jr., Julia Stiles, Selma Blair, Shawn Hatosy, Zak Orth, Ashton Kutcher, Rosario Dawson, Henry Winkler, Lucie Arnaz.

DREAMERS

An American Anvil presentation of a Dark Lantern Pictures production. Producer: Artie Glackin. Executive producers: Peiti Feng, Yang-Wen Lu, Carl L. Fredericks, Henry Zhao. Co-producer: Craig Hall. Director/Screenplay: Ann Lu. Camera: Neil L. Fredericks. Editor: Andrea Zondler. Music: Bob Mithoff. In FotoKem color. Release date: June 13, 2000. Running time: 93 Min.
Cast: Jeremy Jordan, Mark Ballou, Courtney Gains, Paul Bartel, Brian Krause, Portia Dawson, Ruth de Sosa.

DRIVE ME CRAZY

A 20th Century Fox release of an Amy Robinson production. Producer: Robinson. Co-producer: Nancy Paloian-Breznikar. Director: John Schultz. Screenplay: Rob Thomas, based on the novel "How I Created My Perfect Prom Date" by Todd Strasser. Camera: Kees Van Oostrum. Editor: John Pace. Music: Greg Kendall. In Deluxe color. Release date: Sept. 23, 1999. MPAA Rating: PG-13. Running time: 91 Min.
Cast: Melissa Joan Hart, Adrian Grenier, Susan May Pratt, Kris Park, Mark Webber, Ali Larter, Stephen Collins, Gabriel Carpenter, Mark Metcalf, William Converse-Roberts.

DROP BACK TEN

An E Films production. Producer: Stacy Cochran. Supervising producer: Molly Bradford. Co-producer: Todd Thaler. Director/Screenplay: Stacy Cochran. Camera: Spencer Newman. Editor: Nancy I. Novak. Music: Pat Irwin. In color. Release date: Jan. 22, 2000. Running time: 88 Min.
Cast: James LeGros, Amber Valletta, Desmond Harrington, Josh Lucas, Jodie Markell, Laila Robins, Penny Balfour, Ilana Levine, Kelly De Martino, Eddie Kaye Thomas Courtney Jines, Tate Donovan.

DROPPING OUT

A Flemington Pictures and Bad Clams production. Producers: Steve Kalafer, Neil Machlis, Michelle Imperato-Stabile. Executive producer: Daniel M. Stillman. Director: Mark Osborne. Screenplay: Kent Osborne. Camera: Brian Capener. Editor: Kris Cole. Music: Jack Pendarvis. In color. Release date: Mar. 11, 2000. Running time: 109 Min.
Cast: Kent Osborne, David Koechner, Vince Vieluf, Adam Arkin, John Stamos, Jennifer Elise Cox, Dylan Haggerty.

DROWNING MONA

A Destination Films release of a Neverland Films/Jersey Shore production. Producers: Al Corley, Bart Rosenblatt, Eugene Musso. Executive producers: Danny DeVito, Michael Shamberg, Stacey Sher, Jonathan Weisgal. Director: Nick Gomez. Screenplay: Peter Steinfeld. Camera: Bruce Douglas Johnson. Editor: Richard Pearson. Music: Michael Tavera. In FotoKem color. Release date: Feb. 23, 2000. MPAA Rating: PG-13. Running time: 95 Min.
Cast: Danny DeVito, Bette Midler, Neve Campbell, Jamie Lee Curtis, Casey Affleck, William Fichtner, Marcus Thomas, Peter Dobson, Kathleen Wilhoite, Tracey Walter, Paul Ben-Victor, Paul Schulze, Mark Pellegrino.

DROWNING ON DRY LAND

A Cineville presentation, in association with Unapix Entertainment. (International sales: Cineville Intl., Santa Monica, CA.) Producers: Ruth Charney, Susan Shapiro. Co-producer: Allison Emilio. Director: Carl-Jan Colpaert. Screenplay: Sheila Nayar, Julie Jacobs, story by Jacobs. Camera: Dean Lent. Editor: Gail Yasunaga. Music: Richard Horowitz. In FotoKem color. Release date: Oct. 9, 1999. Running time: 88 Min.
Cast: Barbara Hershey, Naveen Andrews, Carol Lynley, John Joe, Steven Polk.

DR. T & THE WOMEN

An Artisan Entertainment release of a Sandcastle 5 production. Producers: Robet Altman, James McLindon. Executive producer: Cindy Cowan. Co-producers: Tommy Thompson, David Levy. Director: Robert Altman. Screenplay: Anne Rapp. Camera: Jan Kiesser. Editor: Geraldine Peroni. Music: Lyle Lovett. In Deluxe color, Panavision widescreen. Release date: Aug. 29, 2000. MPAA Rating: R. Running time: 121 Min.
Cast: Richard Gere, Helen Hunt, Farrah Fawcett, Laura Dern, Shelley Long, Tara Reid, Kate Hudson, Liv Tyler, Robert Hays.

DUETS

A Buena Vista release of a Hollywood Pictures presentation in association with Seven Arts Pictures and Beacon Pictures of a Kevin Jones production. Producers: Jones, Bruce Paltrow, John Byrum. Executive producers: Lee R. Mayes, Neil Canton. Tony Ludwig, Alan Riche. Director: Bruce Paltrow. Screenplay: John Byrum. Camera: Paul Sarossy. Editor: Jerry Greenberg. Music: David Newman. Release date: Sept. 9, 2000. MPAA Rating: R. Running time: 112 Min.
Cast: Maria Bello, Andre Braugher, Paul Giamatti, Huey Lewis, Gwyneth Paltrow, Scott Speedman, Marian Seldes, Kiersten Warren, Angie Phillips, Angie Dickinson.

EAST OF A

A Span Prods. presentation. (International sales: Menemsah Entertainment.) Producer: Michele Carnes Ellis. Director: Amy Goldstein. Screenplay: Patrick Breen, Scott Kraft, Nadine van der Velde. Camera: Ernest Holzman. Editor: Dawn Hogatt. Music: John McCarthy. In Deluxe color, Panavision widescreen. Release date: Mar. 3, 2000. Running time; 86 Min.
Cast: Patrick Breen, Nadine van der Velde, David Alan Grier, Glen Chin, Adam Arkin, Mary McCormack, Melanie Mayron, Camryn Manheim.

EASTSIDE

A Hollywood Independents release of a Candlelight Films presentation of a Kingsize Entertainment production. Producers: Mark Roberts, Ravi Chopra. Executive producer: H.K. Chopra. Director: Lorena David. Screenplay: Eric P. Sherman, based on a story by Ravi Chopra. Camera: Lisa Wiegand. Editor: Ned Kerwin. Music: Armando Avila. In color. Release date: June 14, 2000. Running time: 94 Min.
Cast: Mario Lopez, Elizabeith Bogush, Mark D. Espinoza, Efrain Figueroa, Maurice Compte, Richard Lynch.

EBAN AND CHARLEY

A Monqui Films/Harcamone Films production. Producer: Chris Monlux. Director/Screenplay: James Bolton. Camera: Judy Irola. Editor: Elizabeth Edwards. Music: Stephen Merritt. In color, video. Release date: June 12, 2000. Running time: 86 Min.
Cast: Brent Fellows, Giovanni Andrade, Ellie Nicholson, Drew Zeller, Pam Munter, Ron Upton, Nolan V. Chard.

EL VALLEY CENTRO

A James Benning production. Producer/Director/Editor: James Benning. Camera: Benning. In 16mm. Release date: Jan. 23, 2000. Running time: 90 Min. Documentary.

END OF DAYS

A Universal release of a Universal and Beacon Pictures presentation. Producers: Armyan Berstein, Bill Borden. Executive producers: Marc Abraham, Thomas A. Bliss. Co-producers: Paul Deason, Andrew W. Marlowe. Director: Peter Hyams. Screenplay: Andrew W. Marlowe. Camera: Hyams. Editor: Steve Kemper. Music: John Debney. In Deluxe color, Panavision widescreen. Release date: Nov. 18, 1999. MPAA Rating: R. Running time: 120 Min.
Cast: Arnold Schwarzenegger, Gabriel Byrne, Kevin Pollack, Robin Tunney, C.C.H. Pounder, Rod Steiger, Derrick O'Connor.

THE END OF THE ROAD

A Slow Loris Films presentation of a Joint Prods. production. Producers: Brent Meeske, Michael Dong, Douglas Hosdale. Director: Brent Meeske. Camera: Meeske, Douglas Hosdale. Editor: Meeske. Music: Merl Saunders, Jerry Garcia. In color, video. Release date: Aug. 1, 2000. Running time: 97 Min. Documentary.
With: Bob Weir, Phil Lesh, Mickey Hart, Bill Kruetzmann, Marl Saunders, Wavy Gravy, Babatunde Olatunji.

ERIN BROCKOVICH

A Universal release (in U.S.) of a Universal and Columbia Pictures presentation of a Jersey Films production. Producers: Danny DeVito, Michael Shamberg, Stacey Sher. Executive producers: John Hardy, Carla Santos Shamberg. Co-producer: Gail Lyon. Director: Steven Soderbergh. Screenplay: Susannah Grant. Camera: Ed Lachman. Editor: Anne V. Coates. Music: Thomas Newman. In CFI color. Release date: Feb. 29, 2000. MPAA Rating: R. Running time: 131 Min.
Cast: Julia Roberts, Albert Finney, Aaron Eckhart, Cherry Jones, Marg Helgenberger, Veanne Cox, Conchata Ferrell, Peter Coyote.

EVERYTHING PUT TOGETHER

A Furst Films production. Producer: Sean Furst. Executive producer: Adam Forgash. Co-producer: Jill Silversthorne. Director: Marc Forster. Screenplay: Adam Forgash, Catherine Lloyd Burns, Forster. Camera: Roberto Schaefer. Editor: Matt Chesse. In color, digital. Release date: Jan. 24, 2000. Running time: 85 Min.
Cast: Radha Mitchell, Megan Mullally, Justin Louis, Catherine Lloyd Burns, Alan Ruck, Michele Hicks, Matt Malloy.

EVERYTHING'S JAKE

A Blackjack Entertainment presentation of a Christopher Fetchko production in association with Boz Prods. Producers: Christopher Fetchkoi, Matthew Miele, Andrew Charas, Chris D'Annibale. Executive producer: Bo Zenga. Co-producer: Ernie Hudson. Director: Matthew Miele. Screenplay: Christopher Fetchko, Miele. Camera: Anthony Jannelli. Editor: Noelle Webb. In color. Release date: Mar. 5, 2000. Running time: 92 Min.
Cast: Ernie Hudson, Graeme Malcolm, Debbie Allen, Lou Myers, Robin Givens, Willis Burks II, Stephen Furst, Lou Rawls.

THE EYES OF TAMMY FAYE

A Lions Gate release of a World of Wonder production in association with Cinemax. Producer/Director: Fenton Bailey, Randy Barbain. Camera: Sandra Chandler. Editor: Paul Wiesepape. Music producer: Jim Harry. In color. Release date: Jan. 25, 2000. Running time: 79 Min. Documentary.
Narrator: RuPaul Charles.

FAG HAG

A Troma Team release of a Lloyd Kaufman and Michael Herz presentation. (International sales: Troma, New York.) Producers: Damion Dietz, George Orff. Director/Screenplay: Damion Dietz. Camera: Pedro Castro. Editor: Vince Fillipone. Music: Dietz. In color. Release date: May 19, 2000. Running time: 73 Min.
Cast: Damion Dietz, Stephanie Orff, Saadia Billman, Wil Wheaton.

FALLEN ARCHES

A Saraghine Film Co. presentation in association with Pemdola Prods. Producers: Libby Osborn, Ron Cosentino. Co-producer: Victor Cosentino. Director/Screenplay/Editor: Ron Cosentino. Camera: Darko Suvak. Music: Rick Giovinazzo. In color. Release date: Jan. 15, 2000. Running time: 69 Min.
Cast: Carmine D. Giovinazzo, Justin Louis, Karen Black, Peter Onorati, Richard Portnow.

FAMILY TREE

An Independent Artists release of a WarnerVision Films presentation in association with Curb Entertainment of a Curb Entertainment production. Producers: Mike Curb, Carole Curb Nemoy. Co-producer: Jordan Leibert. Director: Duane Clark. Screenplay: Paul Canterna. Camera: John Peters. Editor: Matthew Booth. Music: Mike Curb, Randy Miller. In FotoKem color. Release date: Apr. 18, 2000. MPAA Rating: G. Running time: 90 Min.
Cast: Robert Forster, Naomi Judd, Cliff Robertson, Andy Laurence, Matthew Laurence.

FAMOUS

A Stella Maris Films and Dolly Hall production of a GreeneStreet Films presentation in association with Sidney Kimmel Entertainment/ Longfellow Pictures. Producers: Mira Sorvino, Dolly Hall. Executive producers: Kimmel, John Penotti, Fisher Stevens, Bradley Yonover, Andrew S. Karsch. Co-producer: Celeste Peterka. Director: Griffin Dunne. Screenplay: Nat De Wolf, Laura Kirk. Camera: William Rexer II. Editor: Nancy Baker. Music: Evan Lurie. In Duart color. Release date: May 14, 2000. Running time: 90 Min.
Cast: Laura Kirk, Nat De Wolf, Daniel London, Griffin Dunne, L.M. Kit Carson, Buck Henry, Sandra Bullock, Carrie Fisher, Linda Blair, Spike Lee, Penelope Ann Miller, Charles Sheen, Mira Sorvino.

THE FANTASTICKS

A United Artists Films release and presentation. Producers: Michael Ritchie, Linne Radmin. Executive producer: Art Schaefer. Director: Michael Ritchie. Screenplay: Tom Jones, Harvey Schmidt, based on their play. Camera: Fred Murphy. Editor: William Scharf. Additional editor: Melissa Kent. Music: Harvey Schmidt, arranged & adapted by Jonathan Tunick; lyrics: Tom Jones. In Deluxe color, Panavision widescreen. Release date: Sept. 12, 2000. MPAA Rating: PG. Running time: 86 Min.
Cast: Joel Grey, Barnard Hughes, Jean Louisa Kelly, Joe McIntyre, Jonathon Morris, Brad Sullivan, Teller.

FASHIONABLY L.A.

A Glam Slam Prods. production. Producers: Ania Sikorska, Patricia Hanten. Executive producer: Adriana AJ Cohen. Director/Screenplay: Tamara Olson. Camera: Steve Yedlin. Editors: Ray Daniels, Daniel Candib, Arthur Klein, William Grayburn. Music: Mark Kilian. In color and B&W. Relase date: Nov. 6, 1999. Running time: 96 Min.
Cast: Tamara Olson, Darienne Arnold, Holly Laningham, Miranda Gibson, Jenya Lano.

FIGHTER

A Next Wave Films production. Producers: Amir Bar-Lev, Jonathan Crosby, Alex Mamlet. Executive producer: Peter Broderick. Director/ Screenplay/Editor: Amir Bar-Lev. Camera: Gary Griffin. In color. Release date: Apr. 14, 2000. Running time: 91 Min. Documentary.
With: Jan Wiener, Arnost Lustig.

A FIGHT TO THE FINISH: STORIES OF POLIO

A Mandel/Herring production, in association with the Texas Scottish Rite Hospital for Children. Producer: Tony Herring, Ken Madden. Executive producer: J.C. Montgomery. Director: Ken Mandel. Screenplay: Ralph Meyers. Camera: Mandel. Editors: Mandel, Meyers. Music: John Bryant, Frank Hames, Tony Herring. In color, video. Release date: June 10, 2000. Running time: 90 Min. Documentary.

FINAL DESTINATION

A New Line Cinema release of a Waren Zide/Craig Perry production. Producers: Warren Zide, Craig Perry, Glen Morgan. Executive producers: Brian Witten, Richard Brenner. Co-producer: Art Schaefer. Director: James Wong. Screenplay: Glen Morga, Wong, Jeffrey Reddick. Camera: Robert McLachlan. Editor: James Coblentz. Music: Shirley Walker. In Deluxe color. Release date: Mar. 15, 2000. MPAA Rating: R. Running time: 97 Min.
Cast: Devon Sawa, Ali Larter, Kerr Smith, Kristen Cloke, Daniel Roebuck, Chad E. Donella, Roger Guenveur Smith, Seann William Scott, Tony Todd, Amanda Detmer.

FIRST, LAST AND DEPOSIT

A Hecht Co. production. Producer: Duffy Hecht. Director: Peter Hyoguchi. Screenplay: Hyoguchi, from a story by Duffy. Camera: Hyoguchi. Editor: Julius Braunschweig. Music: Christopher James Thomas. In color, digital-to-35mm. Release date: Apr. 16, 2000. Running time: 90 Min.
Cast: Jessica White, Sara Wilcox, Don Margolin, Alanna Learned, Alison Coutts-Jordan, Glen Phillips, Jason Hallows.

FIRST PERSON PLURAL

An Independent Television Service presentation in association with National Asian American Telecommunications Assn. Producer: Deann Borshay Liem. Executive producer: Vivian Kleiman. Director: Deann Borshay Liem. Screenplay: Liem, Vivien Hillgrove. Camera: Michael Chin. Editor: Hillgove. Music: Mark Adler. In color. Release date: Jan. 21, 2000. Running time: 59 Min. Documentary.

FLAWLESS

An MGM release of a Tribeca production. Producers: Joel Schumacher, Jane Rosenthal. Executive producer: Neil Machlis. Co-producers: Caroline Baron, Amy Sayre. Director/Screenplay: Joel Schumacher. Camera: Declan Quinn, Editor: Mark Stevens. Music: Bruce Roberts. In Deluxe color. Release date: Nov.11, 1999. MPAA Rating: R. Running time: 112 Min.
Cast: Robert De Niro, Philip Seymour Hoffman, Barry Miller, Chris Bauer, Skipp Sudduth, Wilson Jermaine Heredia, Bashom Benjamin, Scott Allen Cooper, Rory Cochrane, Daphne Rubin-Vega, Wande De Jesus.

THE FLINTSTONES IN VIVA ROCK VEGAS

A Universal release of a Hanna-Barbera/Ambline Entertainment production. Producer: Bruce Cohen. Executive producers: William Hanna, Joseph Barbera, Dennis E. Jones. Co-producer: Bart Brown. Director: Brain Levant. Screenplay: Deborah Kaplan, Harry Elfont, Jim Cash, Jack Epps Jr., based on the animated television series by Hanna-Barbera Prods. Camera: Jamie Anderson. Editor: Kent Beyda. Music: David Newman. In Deluxe color. Release date: Apr., 2000. MPAA Rating: PG. Running time: 90 Min.
Cast: Mark Addy, Stephen Baldwin, Kristen Johnston, Jane Krakowski, Thomas Gibson, Joan Collins, Alan Cumming, Harvey Korman, Alex Meneses.

A FORCE MORE POWERFUL

A Santa Monica Pictures presentation of a Peter Ackerman-York Zimmerman production. Producers: Steve York, Peter Ackerman. Executive producers: Dalton Delan, Jack DuVall. Director/Screenplay: Steve York. Camera: Giulio Biccari, Peter Rearce, Dilip Varma. Rostrum camera: Berle Cherney. Editors: Joseph Wiedenmayer, Anny Lowery Meza. Music: John D. Keltonic. In color. Release date: Nov. 10, 1999. Running time: 110 Min. Documentary.
With: Prod. Devavrat Pathak, Alyque Padamsee, Rev. James Lawson, John Lewis, Diane Nash, Mkhuseli Jack, Prof. Janet Cherry, Tango Lamani. Narrator: Ben Kingsley.

FOREVER HOLLYWOOD

A Kodak presentation of an American Cinematheque production in association with Esplanade Prods. Producer: Sasha Alpert. Executive producer: Barbara Zicka Smith. Director/Screenplay: Todd McCarthy. Co-director: Arnold Glassman. Camera: Nancy Schreiber; additional camera: Paul Ryan. Editor: Glassman. In Deluxe color and B&W. Release date: Dec. 3, 1999. Running time: 57 Min. Documentary.
With: Warren Beatty, Annette Bening, Jeff Bridges, Andre de Toth, Michael Douglas, Clint Eastwood, Mel Gibson, Salma Hayek, Charlton Heston, Samuel L. Jackson, Angela Lansbury, Jack Lemmon, Shirley MacLaine, Edward Norton.

FOREVER LULU

A Millenium Films presentation, in association with Cinerenta, of a Green Moon Prods./Abra Edelman production. Producers: Diane Sillan Isaacs, Abra Edelman, Boaz Davidson, John Thompson. Executive producers: Willi Baer, Avi Lerner, Danny Dimbort, Trevor Short. Co-producer: Tani Cohen. Director/Screenplay: John Kaye. Camera: Dion Beebe. Editor: Alain Jakubowicz. Music: Serge Colbert. In color. Release date: July 7, 2000. Running time: 99 Min.
Cast: Melanie Griffith, Patrick Swayze, Penelope Ann Miller, Joseph Gordon-Levin, Richard Schiff, Annie Corley, Lee Garlington.

FOUR DOGS PLAYING POKER

A Half Moon Entertainment production, in association with New Moon Prods. Producers: Steve Hoffman, Matt Salinger. Executive producers: William Sherak, Jason Shuman. Director: Paul Rachman. Screenplay: Thomas Durham, William Quist. Camera: Claudio Rocha. Editor: Conrad Gonzales. Music: Bryan Tyler, Scott Hackwith. In color. Release date: June 6, 2000. Running time: 98 Min.
Cast: Olivia Williams, Balthazar Getty, Stacy Edwards, Daniel London, Tim Curry, Forest Whitaker, George Lazenby, Stephen Phillip Jones.

FREAK WEATHER

A Sparring Partners I presentation of an HKM Films/Blurco production. (International sales: Freak Films, Los Angeles.) Producers: Andrea Sperling, Alexis Magnagni-Seely. Executive producer: James Delliquanti. Director/Screenplay: Mary Kuryla, based on her short story. Camera: Arturo Smith. Editors: Joe D'Augustine, Gail Yasunaga. Music: Joe Gore, Ralph Carney. Release date: Sept. 17, 1999. Running time: 84 Min.
Cast: Jacqueline McKenzie, Aida Turturro, John Carroll Lynch, Jacob Chase, Jerry Adler, Robert Wisdom, Justin Pierce, John Heard, Mink.

FREESTYLE

An Organic Films release. Producers: Kevin Fitzgerald, Youree Henley, Charles Raggio. Executive producer: Tiare White. Co-producers: Casey Bridges, Brian Bellamy, Tisha Harris, Peter Giblin. Director: Kevin Fitzgerald. Camera: Todd Hickey, Daniel Kozman, Brian Bellamy. Editors: S. Leo Chaing, Isaac Solotaroff, Lee Edwards, Rachel Raimist. In color, 16mm and digital video. Release date: Apr. 14, 2000. Running time: 63 Min.
Cast: Mos Def, the Last Poets, Freestyle Fellowship, Pharoahe Monch, Medusa, Divine Styler, Supernatural, Cut Chemist.

FREQUENCY

A New Line Cinema release. Producers: Hawk Koch, Gregory Hoblit, Bill Carraro, Toby Emmerich. Executive producers: Robert Shaye, Richard Saperstein. Co-executive producer: Janis Chaskin. Director: Gregory Hoblit. Screenplay: Toby Emmerich. Camera: Alar Kivilo. Editor: David Rosenbloom. Music: Michael Kamen. In Deluxe color, widescreen. Release date: Apr. 11, 2000. MPAA Rating: PG-13. Running time: 117 Min.
Cast: Dennis Quaid, Jim Caviezel, Andre Braugher, Elizabeth Mitchell, Noah Emmerich, Shawn Doyle, Jordan Bridges, Melissa Errico.

FRESHMEN

A Stoddard Temple production. Producer/Director/Screenplay: Tom Huang. Camera: Brian Harding. Editors: Huang, Monina Verano. In color, 16mm. Release date: Feb. 21, 2000. Running time: 121 Min.
Cast: N.D. Brown, Tom Huang, Kurt Kohler, Margaret Scarborough, Wendy Speake, Mary Chen, Richard Guiton, Jake White, Sonya Leslie, Partick Gorman.

FRIENDLY PERSUASION: IRANIAN CINEMA AFTER THE REVOLUTION

A Jam-Hi Prods. presentation. Producer/Director/Screenplay: Jamsheed Akrami. Camera: Dan Nocera, Shahram Asadi, Albert Xavier, Akrami. Editors: Akrami, Dah Nan Kou. Music: Ahmad Pejman. In color, video. Release date: Aug. 30, 2000. Running time: 113 Min. Documentary.
With: Abbas Kiarosami, Mohsen Makhmalbaf, Dariush Mehrjui, Bahram Bayzai, Masoud Kimiai, Rakhshan Bani Etemad, Ebraheem Hatami Kia, Majid Majidi, Jafar Panahi, Tahmineh Milani.

GALAPAGOS

An Imax Film Distribution release of an Imax and Smithsonian Institution presentation in association with the National Science Foundation of a Mandalay Media Arts production, sponsored by America Online. Producers: Al Giddings, David Clark. Executive producers: Laurence O'Reilly, Andrew Gellis, Peter Guber, Barry Clark. Director: Al Giddings, David Clark. Screenplay: David Clark, Barry Clark. Camera: Giddings, Andrew Kitzanuk, Reed Smoot. Editor: James Lahti. Music: Mark Isham. In Dolby Digital/DTS/SDDS. Release date: Nov. 9, 1999. Running time: 40 Min. Documentary.

GALAXY QUEST

A DreamWorks Pictures release of a Mark Johnson production. Producers: Johnson, Charles Newirth. Co-producers: Suzann Ellis, Sona Gourgouris. Director: Dean Parisot. Screenplay: David Howard, Robert Gordon. Camera: Jerzy Zielinski. Editor: Don Zimmerman. Music: David Newman. In Technicolor, Panavision widescreen. Release date: Dec. 17, 1999. MPAA Rating: PG. Running time: 104 Min.
Cast: Tim Allen, Sigourney Weaver, Alan Rickman, Tony Shalhoub, Sam Rockwell, Daryl Mitchell, Enrico Colantoni, Robin Sachs.

GEORGE WALLACE: SETTIN' THE WOODS ON FIRE

A Big House production in association with Midnight Films for the American Experience. Producers: Daniel McCabe, Paul Steckler. Screenplay: Steve Fayer, McCabe, Steckler, based on Dan Carter's "The Politics of Rage: George Wallace, the Origins of the New Conservatism and the Transformation of American Politics." Camera: John Hazard. Editor: McCabe. Music: Mason Daring, Duke Levine. In color. Release date: Jan. 29, 2000. Running time: 160 Min. Documentary.
Narrator: Randy Quaid.

GEORGE WASHINGTON

A Youandwhatarmy Filmed Challenges production in association with Blue Moon Film Prods. and Down Home Entertainment. Producers: David Gordon Green, Sacha Mueller, Lisa Muskat. Executive producer: Sam Froelich. Co-producers: Erin Aldridge, R. Craig Zobel. Director/Screenplay: David Gordon Green. Camera: Tim Orr. Editors: Steven Gonzales, Zene Baker. Music: Michael Linnen, David Wingo. In color, widescreen. Release date: Feb. 11, 2000. Running time: 89 Min.
Cast: Candace Evanofski, Donald Holden, Curtis Cotton III, Eddie Rouse, Paul Schneider, Damian Jewan Lee, Rachel Handy, Jonathan Davidson, Janet Taylor.

GET YOUR STUFF

A reVision Films presentation in association with Wey-Man Prods. and Peoples Prods. Producers: Max Mitchell, Jasper Cole, Carl Peoples. Director/Screenplay: Max Mitchell, based on his play. Camera: Jeff Orsa. Editor: Christopher Koefoed. In color, video. Release date: June 17, 2000. Running time: 93 Min.
Cast: Cameron Watson, Anthony Meindl, Elaine Hendrix, Patience Cleveland, Grady Hutt, Blyan Barbosa, Kimberly Scott, Kelly Packard, David Faustino, Jim J. Bullock, Denis Simpson.

GIRLFIGHT

A Screen Gems release of an Independent Film Channel and Green/Renzi production. Producers: Sarah Green, Martha Griffin, Maggie Renzi. Executive producers: John Sayles, Jonathan Sehring, Caroline Kaplan. Director/Screenplay: Karyn Kusama. Camera: Patrick Cady. Editor: Plummy Tucker. Music: Theodore Shapiro. In color. Release date: Jan 22, 2000. Running time: 113 Min.
Cast: Michelle Rodriguez, Jaime Tirelli, Paul Calderon, Santiago Douglas, Ray Santiago, Elisa Bocanegra, Shannon Walker Williams, Iris Little-Thomas, John Sayles.

GIRL, INTERRUPTED

A Sony Pictures Entertainment release of a Columbia Pictures presentation of a Red Wagon production. Producers: Douglas Wick, Cathy Konrad. Executive producers: Carol Brodie, Winona Ryder. Co-producer: Georgia Kacandes. Director: James Mangold. Screenplay: Mangold, Lisa Loomer, Anna Hamilton Phelan, based on the book by Susanna Kaysen. Camera: Jack Green. Editor: Kevin Tent. Music: Mychael Danna. In Deluxe color. Release date: Dec. 1, 1999. MPAA Rating: R. Running time: 127 Min.
Cast: Winona Ryder, Angelina Jolie, Clea Duvall, Brittany Murphy, Elisabeth Moss, Jared Leto, Jeffrey Tambor, Vanessa Redgrave, Whoopi Goldberg, Mary Kay Place.

THE GIRL NEXT DOOR

An Indican Pictures release of a Cafe Sisters production in association with Berns Brothers Prods. Producers: Christine Fugate, Adam Berns, Eren McGinnis. Executive producer: Michael Berns. Co-executive producers: Chris Korbin, Craig Steel. Director: Christine Fugate. Camera: Fugate, Neal Brown. Editors: Fugate, Kate Amend. Music: Denis M. Harrigan. In color. Release date: Apr. 3, 2000. Running time: 83 Min. Documentary.

THE GIRLS' ROOM

Producers: Carol Ann Shine, Barclay DeVeau, Irene Turner. Co-producer: Michael Hirshenson. Director: Irene Turner. Screenplay: Amanda L. Beall. Camera: Cort Fey. Editors: Jeff Betancourt, Robert C. Winn. Music: Alan Ari Lazar. In color. Release date: Mar. 3, 2000. Running time: 101 Min.
Cast: Soleil Moon Frye, Wil Wheaton, Cat Taber, Gary Wolf, Michelle Brookhurst, Crystall Carmen, Malinda Williams.

GLADIATOR

A DreamWorks release (in U.S.)/Universal release (foregin) of a DreamWorks Pictures/Universal Pictures presentation of a Douglas Wick production in association with Scott Free Prods. Produced by Wick, David Franzoni, Branko Lustig. Executive producers: Walter F. Parks, Laurie MacDonald. Director: Ridley Scott. Screenplay: David Franzoni, John Logan, William Nicholson, story by Franzoni. Camera: John Mathieson. Editor: Pietro Scalia. Music: Hans Zimmer, Lisa Gerrard. In Technicolor, Panavision widescreen. Release date: Apr. 19, 2000. MPAA Rating: R. Running time: 154 Min.
Cast: Russell Crowe, Joaquin Phoenix, Connie Nielsen, Oliver Reed, Derek Jacobi, Djimon Hounsou, Richard Harris, David Schofield, John Shrapnel, Tomas Arana, Ralf Moeller, Spencer Treat Clark, David Hemmings.

THE GLASS JAR

A Sterling Pacific Films presentation of a McAboy/Wadsworth production. Producers: Any Sydorick, Scott Hohnbaum. Executive producers: Scott McAboy, Tom Standish, Gil Wadsworth. Director/Screenplay: Gil Wadsworth. Camera: Jacques Haitkin. Editor: Chris Worland. Music: Louis Durra. In FotoKem color. Release date: Sept. 12, 1999. Running time: 92 Min.
Cast: Anthony Crivello, John Kasir, C. Thomas Howell.

GODASS

A Hell's Bells production. Producers: Lori Cheatle, Mindy Pfeffer, Rob Hall, Esther Bell. Executive producer: Pfeffer. Director/Screenplay: Esther Bell. Camera: Milton Kam. Editor: Rob Hall. In color, video. Release date: June 21, 2000. Running time: 73 Min.
Cast: Nika Feldman, Preston Miller, Arik Roper, Julianne Nicholson, George Crowley, Fred Schneider, David Ilku, Tina Holmes, Lola Labelle.

GOD'S ARMY

A Zion Films presentation. Producer: Richard Dutcher. Director/Screenplay: Richard Dutcher. Camera: Ken Glassing. Editor: Michael Chaskes. Music: Miriam Cutler. In color. Release date: May 7, 2000. MPAA Rating: PG. Running time: 117 Min.
Cast: Richard Dutcher, Matthew Brown, DeSean Terry, Michael Buster, Luis Robledo.

GONE IN SIXTY SECONDS

A Buena Vista release of a Touchstone Pictures and Jerry Bruckheimer Films presentation. Producers: Bruckheimer, Mike Stenson. Executive producers: Jonathan Hensleigh, Chad Oman, Barry Waldman, Denice Shakarian Halicki, Robert Stone, Webster Stone. Director: Dominic Sena. Screenplay: Scott Rosenberg, based on the 1974 motion picture written and directed by H.B. Halicki. Camera: Paul Cameron. Editors: Tom Muldoon, Chris Lebenzon. Music: Trevor Rabin. In Technicolor, Panavision widescreen. Release date: June 6, 2000. MPAA Rating: PG-13. Running time: 117 Min.
Cast: Nicolas Cage, Angelina Jolie, Giovanni Ribisi, Delroy Lindo, Will Patton, Christopher Eccleston, Chi McBride, Robert Duvall, Scott Caan, Timothy Olyphant, William Lee Scott.

GOOD HOUSEKEEPING

A Modernica production. Producer: Mark Mathis. Executive producer: Jay Novak. Director/Screenplay: Frank Novak. Camera: Alex Vendler. Editor: Fritz Feick. In FotoKem color, 16mm. Release date: Feb. 17, 2000. Running time: 90 Min.
Cast: Bob Mills, Petra Westen, Tacey Adams, Zia, Andrew Eichner, Maeve Kerrigan, Scooter Stephan, Al Schuermann, Jerry O'Connor, Doug Duane, Borma Barbour.

GOOD KURDS, BAD KURDS: NO FRIENDS BUT THE MOUNTAINS

An Access production. Producer/Director/Screenplay: Kevin McKiernan. Camera: Haskell Wexler, McKiernan. Editor: Thomas G. Miller. Music: Bronwen Jones. In color. Release date: Feb. 24, 2000. Running time: 79 Min. Documentary.

GOSSIP

A Warner Bros. release presentation in association with Village Roadshow Pictures and NPV Entertainment, of an Outlaw production. Producers: Jeffrey Silver, Bobby Newmyer. Executive producers: Joel Schumacher, Bruce Berman. Co-producer: John M. Eckert. Director: Davis Guggenheim. Screenplay: Gregory Poirier, Theresa Rebeck, story by Poirier. Camera: Andrezej Bartkowiak. Editor: Jay Cassidy. Music: Graeme Revell. In Deluxe color, Panavision widescreen. Release date: Apr. 18, 2000. MPAA Rating: R. Running time: 91 Min.
Cast: James Marsden, Lena Headey, Norman Reedus, Kate Hudson, Joshua Jackson, Marisa Coughlan, Edward James Olmos, Sharon Lawrence, Eric Bogosian.

THE GREEN MILE

A Warner Bros. release of a Castle Rock Entertainment presentation of a Darkwoods production. Producers: David Valdes, Frank Darabont. Director/Screenplay: Frank Darabont, based on the novel by Stephen King. Camera: David Tattersall. Editor: Richard Francis-Bruce. Music: Thomas Newman. In Technicolor. Release date: Nov. 20, 1999. MPAA Rating: R. Running time: 187 Min.
Cast: Tom Hanks, David Morse, Bonnie Hunt, Michael Clarke Duncan, James Cromwell, Michael Jeter, Graham Greene, Doug Hutchinson, Sam Rockwell, Barry Pepper, Jeffrey DeMunn, Patricia Clarkson, Harry Dean Stanton.

GROOVE

A Sony Pictures Classics release of a 415.com presentation. Producers: Danielle Renfrew, Greg Harrison. Executive producers: Jeff Southard, Michael Bayne. Director/Screenplay: Greg Harrison. Camera: Matthew Irving. Editor: Harrison. In color. Release date: Jan. 22, 2000. Running time: 83 Min.
Cast: Lola Glaudini, Hamish Linklater, Denny Kirkwood, MacKenzie Firgens, Rachel True, Steve Van Wormer, Nick Offerman, Ari Gold, DJ Dmitri.

GUN SHY

A Buena Vista release of a Hollywood Pictures presentation of a Fortis Films production. Producer: Sandra Bullock. Co-producer: Marc S. Fischer. Director/Screenplay: Eric Blakeney. Camera: Tom Richmond. Editor: Pamela Martin. Music: Rolfe Kent. In Technicolor. Release date: Feb. 2, 2000. MPAA Rating: R. Running time: 102 Min.
Cast: Liam Neeson, Oliver Platt, Sandra Bullock, Jose Zuniga, Richard Schiff, Andy Lauer, Mitch Pileggi, Paul Ben-Victor, Mary McCormack, Frank Vincent, Gregg Daniel.

GYPSY BOYS

An Another B.S. Production production. Producer: Brian Shepp. Co-producer: Jason Blumenfeld. Director/Screenplay: Brian Shepp. Co-producer: Jason Blumenfeld. Director/Screenplay: Brian Shepp. Camera: Gary Rohan. Editor: Rick Lobo. Music: Rich McCracken. In color, 16mm-to-35mm. Release date: Dec. 14, 1999. Running time: 103 Min.
Cast: Adam Gavzer, Robert Hampton, Tom McCann, Jud Parker, Alberto Rosas, Zeke Wheeler, Andrew Abelson, Matt Boucher.

HAMLET

A Miramax presentation of a Double A Films production. Producers: Andrew Fierberg, Amy Hobby. Executive producers: Jason Blum, John Sloss. Director: Michael Almereyda. Screenplay: Almereyda, based on the play by William Shakespeare. Camera: John De Borman. Editor: Kristina Boden. Music; Carter Burwell. In color and B&W. Release date: Jan. 24, 2000. Running time: 111 Min.
Cast: Ethan Hawke, Kyle MacLachlan, Sam Shepard, Diane Verona, Bill Murray, Liev Schreiber, Julia Stiles, Karl Geary, Paula Malcomson, Steve Zahn, Dechen Thurman.

HANGING UP

A Sony Pictures Entertainment release of a Columbia Pictures presentation of a Nora Ephron and Laurence Mark production. Producers: Mark, Ephron. Executive producers: Delia Ephron, Bill Robinson. Co-producer: Diana Pockorny. Director: Diane Keaton. Screenplay: Delia Ephron, Nora Ephron, based on the book by Delia Ephron. Camera: Howard Atherton. Editor: Julie Monroe. Music: David Hirschfelder. In Deluxe color. Release date: Feb. 9, 2000. MPAA Rating: PG-13. Running time: 93 Min.
Cast: Meg Ryan, Diane Keaton, Lisa Kudrow, Walter Matthau, Adam Arkin, Duke Moosekian, Ann Bortolotti, Cloris Leachman, Maree Cheatham, Myndy Crist, Jesse James.

HAPPY ACCIDENTS

An Independent Film Channel presentation of an Accidental Production. Producer: Susan A. Stover. Executive producers: Jonathan Sehring, Caroline Kaplan, John Sloss. Director/Screenplay: Brad Anderson. Camera: Terry Stacy. Editor: Anderson. Music: Evan Lurie. In Technicolor. Release date: Jan.25, 2000. Running time: 110 Min.
Cast: Marisa Tomei, Vincent D'Onofrio, Nadia Dajani, Tovah Feldshuh, Holland Taylor, Richard Portnow, Sean Gullette, Cara Buono, Liana Pai, Tamara Jenkins, Jose Zuniga, Anthony Michael Hall.

HELD UP

A Trimark Pictures release of a Minds Eye Pictures presentation of a Neil H. Moritz/Trimark Pictures production. Producers: Neal H. Moritz, Jonathon Komack Martin, Stokely Chaffin. Executive producers: Mark Amin, Devin Dewalt. Co-producers: Jay Heit, Jaime Rucker King. Director: Steve Rash. Screenplay: Jeff Eastin, story by Eastin, Erik Fleming. Camera: David A. Makin. Editor: Jonathan Chibnall. Music: Robert Folk. In FotoKem color. Release date: May 10, 2000. MPAA Rating: PG-13. Running time: 89 Min.
Cast: Jamie Foxx, Nia Long, Barry Corbin, Eduardo Yanez, John Cullum, Jake Busey, Michael Shamus Wiles, Sarah Paulson.

HELLHOUNDS ON MY TRAIL: THE AFTERLIFE OF ROBERT JOHNSON

A Non Fiction Films and Mug-Shot Prods. production. Producers: Robert Mugge, Jeff Sanders. Executive producers: Julie R. Goldman, Michael Olivieri. Director/Editor: Robert Mugge. Camera: Lawrence McConkey. Music recording/mixing: Big Mo. In color and B&W. Release date: Oct. 11, 1999. Running time: 95 Min. Music Documentary.
With: Bob Weir, Rob Wasserman, Keb' Mo', Robert Lockwood Jr., Joe Louis Walker, Billy Branch, Sonny Landreth, Chris Whitley.

HENRY HILL

A Henry Hill LLC production. Producer/Director/Screenplay: David G. Kantar. Camera: Luke Eder. Editors: Susan Littenberg, Brian Kates. Music: Dave Eggar. In color. Release date: Oct. 13, 1999. Running time: 81 Min.
Cast: Moira Kelly, Jamie Harrold, Susan Blommaert, Eden Riegel, John Griesemer, Michael Kimbal.

HERE ON EARTH

A 20th Century Fox release of a Fox 200 presentation of a David T. Friendly production. Producer: Friendly. Executive producer: Jeffrey Downer. Co-producer: David W. Higgins. Director: Mark Piznarski. Screenplay: Michael Seitzman. Camera: Michael D. O'Shea. Editor: Robert Frazen. Music: Andrea Morricone. In Deluxe color, panavision, widescreen. Release date: Mar. 15, 2000. MPAA Rating: PG-13. Running time: 96 Min.
Cast: Chris Klein, Leelee Sobieski, Josh Hartnett, Michael Rooker, Annie Corley, Bruce Greenwood, Annette O'Toole, Elaine Hendrix.

THE HIDING PLACE

An Unleashed Picture presentation. Producer: Tom Koranda. Director: Douglas Green. Screenplay: Mitch Giannunzio, based on his play: "A Smaller Place." Camera: John Leuba. Editor: Robert Gordon. Music: Kevin Klingler. In FotoKem color. Release date: June 18, 2000. Running time: 97 Min.
Cast: Kim Hunter, Timothy Bottoms, Kim Greist, Katie Hagan.

HIGH FIDELITY

A Buena Vista release of a Touchstone Pictures presentation of a Working Title Films production in association with Dogstar Films/New Crime Prods. Producers: Tim Bevan, Rudd Simmons. Executive producers: Mike Newell, Alan Greenspan, Lisa Chasin. Co-producers: D.V. DeVincentis, Steve Pink, John Cusack. Director: Stephen Frears. Screenplay: D.V. DeVincentis, Steve Pink, John Cusack, Scott Rosenberg, based on the novel by Nick Hornby. Camera: Seamus McGarvey. Editor: Mick Audsley. Music: Howard Shore. In Technicolor. Release date: Mar. 16, 2000. MPAA Rating: R. Running time: 113 Min.
Cast: John Cusack, Iben Hjejle, Todd Louiso, Jack Black, Lisa Bonet, Catherine Zeta-Jones, Tim Robbins, Chris Rehmann, Ben Carr., Lili Taylor, Joelle Carter, Natasha Gregson Wagner, Sara Gilbert.

HIGHLANDER: ENDGAME

A Miramax release of a Dimension Films presentation of a Davis/Panzer production. Producers: Peter Davis, William Panzer. Executive producers: Bob Weinstein, Harvey Weinstein, Cary Granat. Co-executive producers: H. Daniel Gross, Beth Anne Calabro. Co-producer: Patrick Peach. Director: Douglas Aarniokoski. Screenplay: Joel Soisson, story by Eric Bernt, Gillian Horvath, William Panzer, based on characters created by Gregory Widen. Camera: Doug Milsome. Editors: Christopher Blunden, Michael N. Nue, Robert Feretti, Tracy Granger, Rod Dean, Donald J. Paonessa. Associate editor: Asim Main. Music: Stephen Graziano. In Deluxe color, widescreen. Release date: Aug. 30, 2000. MPAA Rating: R. Running time: 88 Min.
Cast: Christopher Lambert, Bruce Payne, Lisa Barbuscia, Donnie Yen, Jim Byrnes, Peter Wingfield, Damon Dash, Beatie Edney, Sheila Gish.

HISTORY LESSONS

A Barbara Hammer production. Producer/Director/Camera/Editor: Barbara Hammer. Additional camera: Carolyn McCartney, Ann T. Rossetti. Music: Eve Beglarian, Lisa Ben, Mikael Karlsson, Gretchen Phillips, Jean Paul Keenon. In B&W and color. Release date: June 21, 2000. Running time: 65 Min. Documentary.
With: Ann Maguire, Kaja Aman, Antonio Caputo, Denise Coles, Elvis Herselvis, Cambrea Ezell, Dred, Coco Feliciano, Mo Fisher.

HOLLOW MAN

A Sony Pictures Entertainment release of a Columbia Pictures presentation of a Douglas Wick production. Producers: Douglas Wick, Alan Marshall. Executive producer: Marion Rosenburg. Co-producer: Stacy Lumbrezer. Director: Paul Verhoeven. Screenplay: Andrew W. Marlowe, story by Gary Scott Thompson, Marlowe. Camera: Jost Vacano. Editor: Mark Goldblatt. Music: Jerry Goldsmith. In Deluxe color. Release date: July 28, 2000. MPAA Rating: R. Running time: 114 Min.
Cast: Kevin Bacon, Elisabeth Shue, Josh Brolin, Greg Grunberg, Mary Jo Randle, Steve Altes, Kim Dickens.

HONEST

A Pathe Distribution release (in France) of a Seven Dials film in association with Pathe Entertainment Ltd. (International sales: Pandor.) Producers: Eileen Gregory, Michael Peyser. Executive producer: Keith Northrop. Director: David A. Stewart. Screenplay: Stewart, Dick Clement, Ian La Fresnais, Karen Street. Camera: David Johnson. Editor: David Martin. Music: David A. Stewart. In color. Release date: May 13, 2000. Running time: 109 Min.
Cast: Peter Facinelli, Nicole Appleton, Melanie Blatt, James Cosmo, Jonathan Cake, Corin Redgrave, Rick Warren, Annette Badland, Paul Rider, Sean Gilder, Matt Bardock.

A HOUSE DIVIDED

A Showtime and Paramount Network Television presentation of an Avnet/Kerner Co. production in association with Atkinson Way. Producers: Beth Colt, Sam Waterston. Executive producers: Jordan Kerner, Jon Avnet. Co-executive producer: Phyllis Rossheim-Pierce. Director: John Kent Harrison. Screenplay: Paris Qualles, based on the book "Woman of Color, Daughter of Privilege: Amanda Dickson" by Kent Anderson Leslie. Camera: Kees Van Oostrum. Editors: Henk van Eeghen. Music: Lawrence Shragge. In color. Release date: Jan. 17, 2000. Running time: 101 Min.
Cast: Jennifer Beals, Lisa Gay Hamilton, Sam Waterston, Tim Daly, Ron White.

HOUSE ON HAUNTED HILL

A Warner Bros. release of a Dark Castle Entertainment production. Producers: Robert Zemeckis, Joel Silver, Gilbert Adler. Executive producers: Dan Cracchiolo, Steve Richards. Co-producer: Terry Castle. Director: William Malone. Screenplay: Dick Beebe, based on a story by Robb White. Camera: Rick Bota. Editor: Anthony Adler. Music: Don Davis. In Technicolor, Panavision widescreen. Release date: Oct. 29, 1999. MPAA Rating: R. Running time: 96 Min.
Cast: Geoffrey Rush, Famke Janssen, Taye Diggs, Peter Gallagher, Chris Kattan, Ali Larter, Bridgette Wilson, Max Perlich, Lisa Loeb.

HOW TO KILL YOUR NEIGHBOR'S DOG

A Millennium Films presentation, in association with Cinerenta, of a South Fork Pictures production in association with Lonsdale Pictures. (International sales: Nu Image, Los Angeles.) Producers: Michael Nozik, Nancy M. Ruff, Brad Weston. Executive producer: Robert Redford. Co-executive producers: Willi Baer, Avi Lerner, Danny Dimbort, Trevor Short, John Thompson. Co-producers: Tani Cohen, Amanda Nelligan. Director/Screenplay: Michael Kalesniko. Camera: Hubert Taczanowski. Editor: Pamela Martin. Music: David Robbins. In FotoKem color. Release date: May 17, 2000. Running time: 107 Min.
Cast: Kenneth Branagh, Robin Wright Penn, Jared Harris, Johnathon Schaech, Peter Riegert, Lynn Redgrave, Suzi Hofrichter.

THE HUNGRY BACHELOR'S CLUB

A Mama's Boys Prods. release of a Taggart Transcontinental and Managed Passion Films presentation of a Mama's Boys production . Producers: Dan Gifford, Amy Sommer Gifford. Executive producer: Kimberly Becker. Co-producer: Robert Lynn New. Director: Gregory Ruzzin. Screenplay: Fred Dresch, Ron Ratliff, based on the novel by Lynn Scott Myers. Camera: Robert Smith. Supervising editors: Stephen Myers, Andrew Frank. Music: Larry Brown. In FotoKem color. Release date: Nov. 13, 1999. Running time: 93 Min.
Cast: Candice Azzara, Michael Des Barres, Jorja Fox, Katherine Kendall, Suzanne Mara, Peter Murnik, Bill Nunn, Paul Provenza.

THE HURRICANE

A Universal release of a Beacon Pictures presentation of an Azoff Films/Rudy Langlais production. Producers: Armyan Bernstein, John Ketcham, Norman Jewison. Executive producers: Irving Azoff, Tom Rosenberg, Rudy Langlais, Thomas A. Bliss, Marc Abraham, William Teitler. Co-producers: Suzann Ellis, Michael Jewison, Jon Jashni. Director: Norman Jewison. Screenplay: Armyan Berstein, Dan Gordon, based on the books, "The Sixteenth Round" by Rubin "Hurricane" Carter and "Lazarus and the Hurricane" by Sam Chaiton and Terry Swinton. Camera: Roger Deakins. Editor: Stephen Rivkin. Music: Christopher Young. In Deluxe color. Release date: Nov. 29, 1999. MPAA Rating: R. Running time: 125 Min.
Cast: Denzel Washington, Vicellous Reon Shannon, Deborah Kara Unger, Liev Schreiber, John Hannah, Dan Hedaya.

IDITAROD...A FAR DISTANT PLACE

A Mineral King Prods. production. Producer/Director: Alice Dungan Bouvrie. Screenplay: Bouvrie, Julia Dixon Eddy. Camera: Tom Curran. Editor: Dixon Eddy. Music: Jeanine Cowen. Release date: June 9, 2000. Running time: 88 Min. Documentary.

I DREAMED OF AFRICA

A Sony Pictures Entertainment release of a Columbia Pictures presentation of a Jaffilms production. Producers: Stanley R. Jaffe, Allyn Stewart. Co-producer: John D. Schofield. Director: Hugh Hudson. Screenplay: Paula Milne, Susan Shilliday, based on the book by Kuki Gallmann. Camera: Bernard Lutic. Editor: Scott Thomas. Music: Maurice Jarre. In Technicolor, widescreen. Release date: Apr. 18, 2000. MPAA Rating: PG-13. Running time: 114 Min.
Cast: Kim Basinger, Vincent Perez, Liam Aiken, Garrett Strommen, Eva Marie Saint, Daniel Craig, Lance Reddick.

I'LL REMEMBER APRIL

A Flashpoint presentation of a Regent Entertainment production. Producers: Paul Colichman, Mark Harris. Executive producers: Stephen P. Jarchow, Beau Rogers, David Forrest. Co-producer: Sam Irvin. Director: Bob Clark. Screenplay: Mark Sanderson. Camera: Stephan Katz. Editor: Stan Cole. Music: Paul J. Zaza. In CFI color. Release date: Jan. 17, 2000. Running time: 90 Min.
Cast: Trevor Morgan, Pam Dawber, Mark Harmon, Pat Morita, Haley Joel Osment, Yuji Okumoto.

I'LL TAKE YOU THERE

A Jim Stark presentation in association with Hollywood Partners. (International sales: Jim Stark, Film 49 Inc., New York.) Producer: Stark. Executive producer: Sandra Schulberg. Director/Screenplay: Adrienne Shelly. Camera: Vanja Cernjul. Editor: Duncan Pettigrew. Music: Andrew Hollander. In Duart color. Release date: Sept. 3, 1999. Running time: 93 Min.
Cast: Ally Sheedy, Reg Rogers, Lara Harris, John Pyper-Ferguson.

IMAGINE: SURFING AS SADHANA

A Gaia Co-op presentation in association with Koko Prods. Producer: Marshall K. Hattori. Executive producers: Al Merrick, Terry Merrick, Roger Nance, Kelly Brown. Director/Screenplay/Editor: Marshall K. Hattori. Camera/On-line editor/Sound: Peter Trow. In video-to-16mm. Release date: Apr. 11, 2000. Running time: 75 Min. Documentary.

I'M THE ONE THAT I WANT

A Cho Taussig Prods. presentation. Producer: Lorene Machado. Executive producers: Margaret Cho, Karen Taussig. Director: Lionel Coleman. Writer: Cho. Camera: Coleman. Editor: Robyn T. Migel. Music: Joan Jett & the Blackhearts. In color. Release date: June 23, 2000. Running time: 94 Min.
With: Margaret Cho.

THE IN CROWD

A Warner Bros. release of a Morgan Creek production. Producer: James G. Robinson. Executive producers: Jonathan A. Zimbert, Michael Rachmil. Director: Mary Lambert. Screenplay: Mark Gibson, Philip Halprin. Camera: Tom Priestley. Editor: Pasquale Buba. Music: Jeff Rona. In color. Release date: July 19, 2000. MPAA Rating: PG-13. Running time: 104 Min.
Cast: Lori Heuring, Susan Ward, Daniel Hugh Kelly, Matthew Settle, Nathan Bexton, Laurie Fortier, Kim Murphy, Ethan Erickson.

THE INDEPENDENT

A United Lotus group production. Producer: Mike Wilkins. Executive producer: Jerry Weintraub. Co-executive producer: Lesa Lakin Richardson. Co-producer: Jack Ziga. Director: Stephen Kessler. Screenplay: Mike Wilkins, Kessler. Camera: Amir Hamed. Editor: Chris Franklin. Music: Ben Vaughn. Music: Ben Vaughn. In Technicolor. Release date; Mar. 12, 2000. Running time: 93 Min.
Cast: Jerry Stiller, Janeane Garofalo, Max Perlich, Ginger Lynn Allen, Billy Burke, Andy Dick, Fred Dryer, Ethan Embry, Jonathan Katz, John Lydon, Anne Meara, Ben Stiller.

THE INSIDER

A Buena Vista release of a Touchstone Pictures presentation of a Mann/Roth production of a Forward Pass picture. Producers: Michael Mann, Pieter Jan Brugge. Co-producers: Michael Waxman. Director: Michael Mann. Screenplay: Eric Roth, Mann, based on the Vanity Fair article "The Man Who Knew Too Much" by Marie Brenner. Camera: Dante Spinotti. Editors: William Goldenberg, Paul Rubell, David Rosenbloom. Music: Lisa Gerrard, Pieter Bourke. In Technicolor, Panavision widescreen. Release date: Sept. 22, 1999. MPAA Rating: R. Running time: 157 Min.
Cast: Al Pacino, Russell Crowe, Christopher Plummer, Dianne Venora, Philip Baker Hall, Lindsay Crouse, Debi Mazar, Stephen Tobolowsky.

INSTRUMENT: TEN YEARS WITH THE BAND FUGAZI

A LAL/Gravity Hill presentation. Producer: Jem Cohen, Fugazi. Co-producer, Good Machine. Director: Jem Cohen, Fugazi. Camera: Cohen. Editors: Cohen, Fugazi, David Frankel. In video, Super 8, 16mm-to-video, color and B&W. Release date: Oct. 19, 1999. Running time: 115 Min. Documentary.
With: Fugazi (Ian MacKaye, Guy Picciotto, Joe Lally, Brendan Canty).

INTERN

A Moonstone Entertainment and Given Films production. Producers: Galt Neiderhoffer, Daniela Etchie Stroh, Soto-Taplin. Executive producer: Randy Simon. Co-producers: Karen Jaroneski, Alex Orlovsky. Director: Michael Lange. Screenplay: Caroline Doyle, Jill Kopelman. Camera: Rodney Charters. Editor: Anita Brandt-Burgoyne. Music: Jimmy Harry. In color. Release date: Jan. 23, 2000. Running time: 90 Min.
Cast: Dominique Swain, Ben Pullen, Peggy Lipton, Joan Rivers, Kathy Griffin.

IN THE WEEDS

A Glatzer production. Producer: Peter Glatzer. Director/Screenplay: Michael Rauch. Camera: Horacio Marquinez. Editor: Susan Graef. Music: Douglas J. Cuomo. In color. Release date: June 11, 2000. Running time: 91 Min.
Cast: Joshua Leonard, Molly Ringwald, Ellen Pompeo, Michael Buchman Silver, Sam Harris, J.P. Pitoc, Bonnie Root, Kirk Acevedo, Peter Riegert, Caroleen Feeney, Eric Bogosian.

INTO THE ARMS OF STRANGERS: STORIES OF THE KINDERTRANSPORT

A Warner Bros. release of a Sabine Films production, in cooperation with the U.S. Holocaust Memorial Museum. Producer: Deborah Oppenheimer. Director/Screenplay: Mark Jonathan Harris. Camera: Don Lenzer. Editor: Kate Amend. Music: Lee Holdridge. In B&W and color. Release date: Aug. 30, 2000. Running time: 122 Min. Documentary.
Narrator: Judi Dench.

AN INVITED GUEST

A Picture Me Rollin Prods. production. (International sales: Picture Me Rollin, Columbus, OH.) Producers: Larry Spud Raymond, Harold Folsome, William Hightower, Keith Hightower. Executive producer: Kevin D. Hightower. Director/Screenplay: Timothy Wayne Folsome. Camera: Wayne Sells. Editor: Edward Abrams. Music: Stanley Clarke. In color. Release date: Oct. 9, 1999. Running time: 116 Min.
Cast: Mekfi Phifer, Mel Jackson, Mari Morrow, Malinda Williams, Wayna Morris, Kim Fields.

ISN'T SHE GREAT

A Universal release of a Mutual Film Co. presentation of a Lobell/Bergman production. Producer: Mike Lobell. Executive producers: Ted Kurdyla, Gary Levinsohn, Mark Gordon. Director: Andrew Bergman. Screenplay: Paul Rudnick, based on an article by Michael Korda. Camera: Karl Walter Lindelaub. Editor: Barry Malkin. Music: Burt Bacharach. In Deluxe color. Release date: Jan. 12, 2000. MPAA Rating: R. Running time: 93 Min.
Cast: Bette Midler, Nathan Lane, Stockard Channing, David Hyde Pierce, John Cleese, John Larroquette. Amanda Peet.

IVANSXTC. (TO LIVE AND DIE IN HOLLYWOOD)

A Rhino Films presentation of an Enos/Rose production in association with Alternative Investments of Michigan. (International sales: the Sales Co., London.) Producer: Lisa Enos. Executive producers: Steven Nemeth, Kenneth Enos, Cat Villiers, Lisa Henson. Co-producers: Heidi Jo Markel, Galina Tuchinsky. Director: Bernard Rose. Screenplay: Rose, Lisa Enos, based on "The Death of Ivan Illyich" by Leo Tolstoy. Camera: Rose, Ron Forsythe. Editor: Rose. Release date: Sept. 13, 2000. Running time: 94 Min.
Cast: Danny Huston, Peter Weller, Lisa Enos, Joanne Duckman, Angela Featherstone, Caroleen Feeney, Valeria Golino'.

JACKS OR BETTER

A Trips to Win production. Producer: Hilton H. Smith. Executive producer: Ken Meyer. Director/Screenplay: Robert Sidney Mellette. Camera: David M. Russell. Editor: Neil L. Felder. Music: Ross Levinson. In FotoKem color. Release date: June 25, 2000. Running time: 76 Min.
Cast: Jack Wallace, Nathan Anderson, Matt Landers, Vincent Guastaferro, Meshach Taylor, Garthering Marbet.

JERKS

An Allied Entertainment Group presentation of a Cinema Arts Magic production. Producer/Director/Screenplay: Ted Grouya. Camera: John Skotchdopole. Editor: Andrea Zondler. Music: Kareen Roustom, Ted J. Grouya. In color. Release date: Jan. 21, 2000. Running time: 89 Min.
Cast: Emmanuel Xuereb, Francis Fallon, Patrick Sheehan.

JOE GOULD'S SECRET

A USA Films release of an October Films presentation of a First Cold Press/Charles Weinstock production. Producers: Weinstock, Elizabeth W. Alexander, Stanley Tucci. Executive producers: Michael Lieber, Chisann Verges. Director: Stanley Tucci. Screenplay: Howard A. Rodman, based on "Professor Seagull" and "Joe Gould's Secret" by Joseph Mitchell. Camera: Maryse Alberti. Editor: Suzy Elmiger. Music: Evan Lurie. In Duart color. Release date: Jan. 21, 2000. MPAA Rating: R. Running time: 104 Min.
Cast: Ian Hom, Stanley Tucci, Patricia Clarkson, Hope Davis, Steve Martin, Susan Sarandon, Patrick Tovatt, Celia Weston.

JOURNEY TO A HATE-FREE MILLENNIUM

A New Light Media production. Producers: Brent Scarpo, Martin Bedogne. Director/Screenplay: Martin Bedgone, Brent Scarpo. Camera: Lowel Pierce. Editor: Davis Coombe. In color. Release date: Apr. 15, 2000. Running time: 80 Min. Documentary.

JUNK

A Piecemeal Films/Fallen Cinema presentation. Producer: Chris Hoover. Director/Screenplay, Editor: Roddy Bogawa. Camera: Ben Speth. Music: Ward Shelley. In color, 16mm. Release date: Feb. 21, 2000. Running time: 85 Min.
Cast: William Schefferine, Tara Milutis, Tommy Bigelow, Lazar Stojanovic, Michael Joo, Gloria Park, Victor Bloom.

JUST LOOKING

A Jean Doumanian production. Producer: Doumanian. Co-producer: Mike Jackman. Director: Jason Alexander. Screenplay: Marshall Karp. Camera: Fred Schuler. Editor: Norman Hollyn. In color. Release date: Oct. 22, 1999. Running time: 97 Min.
Cast: Ryan Merriman, Joseph Franquinha, Peter Onorati, Gretchen Mol, Amy Braverman, Ilana Levine, Richard V. Licata, Patti LuPone, John Bolger, Robert Weil, Alex Sobol.

JUST MELVIN

A James Ronald Whitney/Production 920 production. Producer/Director/Screenplay: James Ronald Whitney. Executive producer: Richard Reichgut. Camera: John Taggart. Editors: Connie Walsh, Whitney. Music: Whitney, Brent Argovitz. In color. Release date: Jan. 27, 2000. Running time: 96 Min. Documentary.

JUST ONE TIME

An Alliance Atlantis presentation of a Danger Filmworks production. Producers: Jasmine Kosovic, Lane Janger, Exile Ramirez, Jeff Roth. Executive producers: Marcus Hu, Charlotte Mickie, David R. Ginsburgh. (International sales: Alliance Atlantis Pictures Intl., Santa Monica.) Director: Lane Janger. Screenplay: Janger, Jennifer Vandever, Based on Janger's original story. Camera; Michael St. Hilaire. Editor: Mitch Stanley. Music: Edward Bilous. In color. Release date: Sept. 14, 1999. Running time: 124 Min.
Cast: Lane Janger, Joelle Carter, Guillermo Diaz, David Lee Russek, Jennifer Esposito.

KEEPING THE FAITH

A Buena Vista Pictures release of a Touchstone Pictures/Spyglass Entertainment production. Producers: Howard Koch, Edward Norton, Stuart Blumberg. Executive producers: Gary Barber, Roger Birnbaum Jonathan Glickman. Director: Edward Norton. Screenplay: Stuart Blumberg. Camera: Anastas Michos. Editor: Malcolm Campbell. Music: Elmer Bernstein. In Technicolor. Release date: Mar. 29, 2000. MPAA Rating: PG-13. Running time: 127 Min.
Cast: Ben Stiller, Edward Norton, Jenna Elfman, Anne Bancroft, Eli Wallach, Ron Rifkin, Milos Forman, Holland Taylor, Lis Edelstein, Rena Sofer, Ken Leung, Brian George.

KEEP THE RIVER ON YOUR RIGHT: A MODERN CANNIBAL TALE

A Next Wave Films production. Producers: David Shapiro, Laurie Gwen Shapiro. Camera: Jonathan Kovel. Editor: Tula Goenka. Music: Steve Bernstein. In color. Release date: Apr. 15, 2000. Running time: 90 Min. Documentary.
With: Tobias Schneebaum, Norman Mailer, Charlie Rose, Mike Douglas.

KILL BY INCHES

A CineBlast! production. Producer: Gill Holland. Executive producers: Michael Morley, Raymond Demarco. Directors/Screenplay: Diane Doniol-Valcroze, Arthur Flam. Camera: Richard Rutkowski. Editors: Elizabeth Gazzara, Ethan Spigland. Music: Geir Jenssen. In color. Release date: Sept. 14, 1999. Running time: 85 Min.
Cast: Emmanuel Salinger, Myriam Cyr, Marcus Powell, Christopher Zach.

KING OF THE JUNGLE

A Bombo Sports & Entertainment presentation of a Forensic Films/Media Ventures production. Producers: Bob Potter, Scott Macaulay, Robin O'Hara. Executive producers: John Leguizamo, Jay Rifkin, Hans Zimmer. Director/Screenplay: Seth Zvi Rosenfeld. Camera: Fortunato Procopio. Editor: Katherine Sanford. Music: Harry Gregson-Williams. In DuArt color. Release date: Apr. 14, 2000. Running time: 86 Min.
Cast: John Leguizamo, Rosie Perez, Julie Carmen, Cliff Gorman, Michael Rapaport, Marisa Tomei, Justin Pierce, Annabella Sciorra.

KNOCKOUT

A Renegade Pictures release of a Ceo Films presentation of a DMG Entertainment production. Producers: Simone Sheffield, Lorenzo Doumani. Director: Doumani. Screenplay: Mark Stevens, Doumani, story by Doumani. Camera: Hisham Abed. Editor: Dayle Mustain. Music: Sidney James. In Deluxe color. Release date: Jan. 31, 2000. MPAA Rating: PG-13. Running time: 99 Min.
Cast: Sophia-Adella Hernandez, Eduardo Yanez, Tony Plana, Paul Winfield, William McNamara, Maria Conchita Alonso, Gina La Piana, Fredia Gibbs, Erick Vazquez.

LAKEBOAT

An Oregon Trail Films presentation, in association with One Vibe Entertainment of a Lakeboat production. Producer: Joe Mantegna, Tony Mamet, Morris Ruskin. Executive producers: Eric. R. Epperson, Alan James. Co-producers: Ande Hecht Endewardt, Stacia Sekuler Miehe, Vicky Pike. Director: Joe Mantegna. Screenplay: David Mamet, based on his stage play. Camera: Paul Sarossy. Editor: Christopher Cibelli. Music: Bob Mamet. In FotoKem color. Release date: Apr. 13, 2000. Running time: 98 Min.

Cast: Charles Durning, Peter Falk, Robert Forster, J.J. Johnson, Denis Leary, Jack Wallace, George Wendt, Tony Mamet, Roberta Angelica, Saul Rubinek.

THE LAST MAN

An ID Films production. Producer: Tamara Hernandez, Harry Ralston, Jessica Rains. Executive producer: Roger Avery. Director/Screenplay: Harry Ralston. Camera: Michael Grady. Editor: Tony Miller. Music: Woody Jackson, Ivan Knight. In color, 35mm-to-video. Release date: Oct. 24, 1999. Running time: 95 Min.

Cast: David Arnott, Jeri Ryan, Dan Montgomery.

LEFT OVERS

A Troma Team release of a Deadbeat Prods. presentation iin association with Andre's World Inc. and Montego Films. Producers: Patric Z, Margo Romero. Executive producers: Lionel Luna, Dave Parker. Co-producers: Travis Daking, Bill Hamilton. Director/Screenplay: Jason Phillips. Camera: Cory Christiansen. Editor: Bob Stone. Music: Brian Schey. In color. Release date: Apr. 27, 2000. Running time: 101 Min.

Cast: Mark Fite, Jason Oliver, Todd Stanton, Timothy DiPri, Cyndy Preston, Jason Cross, Christina Karras, Miranda Viscoli, Jack Moore, David Dickerson, Marine Palmier-Gonzalez.

LEGACY

A Nomadic Pictures production. Producer: Todd S. Lending. Executive producer: Sheila Nevins. Co-producer: Daniel Alpert. Director/Screenplay: Lending. Camera: Slawomir Grunberg, Max Miler, Therese Sherman, Sid Lubitsch, Don Winter, Keith Walker, Randell Blakely, Phil Cantor. Editor: Alpert. Music: Sheldon Mirowitz. In color. Release date: Jan. 27, 2000. Running time: 90 Min. Documentary.

L5: FIRST CITY IN SPACE

An Imax production. Producer: Toni Myers. Co-producer: GraemeFerguson. Executive producer: Jonathan Barker. Supervising director: Toni Myers. Screenplay: Myers. Live-action director: Allan Kroeker. Camera: Andrew Kitzanuk. Editor: Myers. Music: Micky Erbe, Meribeith Solomon. In color, 15/70mm 3-D. Release date: Nov. 16, 1999. MPAA
Rating: G. Running time: 40 Min.

Cast: Colin Fox, Rachel Walker, Denis Akiyama, Genevieve Langlois, Martha Henry.

LIAR'S POKER

A North Branch release of a Savino Brothers production. Producers: Billy Savino, Carlos H. Sanchez, Jeff Santo. Executive producer: Billy Savino. Co-executive producers: Johnny Savino, Patrick Savino, Paul Savino. Director/Screenplay: Santo. Camera: Giles M.I. Dunning. Editor: Kathryn Himoff. Music: Peter Himmelman. In color. Release date: Oct. 26, 1999. Rating: R. Running time: 93 Min.

Cast: Richard Tyson, Caesar Luisi, Jimmy Blondell, Flea, Neith Andrina, Pamela Gidley, Amelia Heinle, Colin Partrick Lynch.

LIBERTY HEIGHTS

A Warner Bros. release of a Baltimore/Spring Creek Pictures production. Producers: Barry Levinson, Paula Weinstein. Executive producer: Patrick McCormick. Director/Screenplay: Barry Levinson. Camera: Chris Doyle. Editor: Stu Linder. Music: Andrea Morricone. In Technicolor. Release date: Nov. 3, 1999. MPAA Rating: R. Running time: 127 Min.

Cast: Adrien Brody, Ben Foster, Orlando Jones, Bebe Neuwirth, Joe Mantegna, Rebekah Johnson, David Krumholtz, Richard Kline, Vincent, Guastaferro, Justin Chambers, Carolyn Murphy.

LIGHT IT UP

A 20th Century Fox release of a Fox 2000 Pictures presentation of an Edmonds Entertainment production. Producer: Tracey E. Edmonds. Executive producer: Kenneth "Babyface" Edmonds. Co-producers: Bridget D. Davis, Helena Echegoyen. Co-executive producer: David Starke. Director/Screenplay: Craig Bolotin. Camera: Elliot Davis. Editor: Wendy Greene Bricmont. Music: Harry Gregson-WIlliams. In Astro color. Release date: Nov. 2, 1999. MPAA Rating: R. Running time: 99 Min.

Cast: Usher Raymond, Forest Whitaker, Rosario Dawson, Robert Richard, Judd Nelson, Fredro Starr, Sara Gilbert, Clifton Collins Jr., Glynn Turman, Vic Polizos, Vanessa L. Williams.

THE LITTLE MERMAID II: RETURN TO THE SEA

A Walt Disney Home Video release of a Walt Disney Television Animation production. Producers: David Lovegren, Leslie Hough. Director: Jim Kammerud. Co-director: Brian Smith. Screenplay: Elizabeth Andersen, Temple Mathews. Art director: Fred Cline. Music: Danny Troop; songs: Michael and Patty Silversher. In color. Release date: Sept. 19, 2000. MPAA Rating: G. Running time: 75 Min. Animated.

Voices: Jodi Benson, Samuel E. Wright, Tara Charendoff, Pat Carroll, Buddy Hackett, Kenneth Mars, Max Casella, Stephen Furst, Rob Paulsen.

LIVE NUDE GIRLS, UNITE!

A Query? production. Producers: John Montoya, Julia Query. Executive producer: Gini Reticker. Co-producers: Sarah Kennedy, Avilla Peterson. Director: Query, Vicky Funari. Camera: Query, John Montoya, Sarah Kennedy, Funari. Editors: Funari, Heidi Rahlmann Plumb. Music: Allison Hennesy, Kali and Alex Kort, Blaise Smith, Dale Everingham. In color, video-to-16mm. Release date: Apr. 26, 2000. Running time: 70 Min. Documentary.

LOOKING FOR AN ECHO

A Steve Tisch/Paul Kurta production. Producers: Kurta, Martin Davidson. Executive producer: Tisch. Co-producers: Mary Jo Slater, Anthony Esposito. Director: Martin Davidson. Screenplay: Jeffrey Goldenberg, Robert Held, Davidson. Camera: Charles Minsky. Editor: Jerrold Lludwig. Music producer and supervisor: Kenny Vance. In color. Release date: Oct. 12, 1999. Running time: 97 Min.

Cast: Armand Assante, Diane Venora, Joe Grifasi, Tom Mason, Tony Denison, Johnny Williams, Edoardo Ballerini, Christy Romano.

LONG NIGHT'S JOURNEY INTO DAY

A Reid/ Hoffman production. Producer: Frances Reid. Co-producer: Johnny Symons. Directors: Frances Reid, Deborah Hoffmann. Camera: Reid, Ezra Jwili. Editors: Hoffmann, Kim Roberts. Music: Lebo M. In color. Release date: Jan. 29, 2000. Running time: 90 Min. Documentary.

With: Desmond Tutu, Glenda Wildschut, Mary Burton, Pumla Gobodo-Madikizela, Jann Turner, Tony Weaver.

LOSER

A Sony Pictures Entertainment release of a Columbia Pictures presentation. Producers: Amy Heckerling, Twink Caplan. Executive producer: John M. Eckert. Director/Screenplay: Amy Heckerling. Camera: Rob Hahn. Editor: Debra Chiate. Music: David Kitay. In Deluxe color. Release date: July 18, 2000. MPAA Rating: PG-13. Running time: 95 Min.

Cast: Jason Biggs, Mena Suvari, Zak Orth, Tom Sadoski, Jimmi Simpson, Greg Kinnear, Dan Aykroyd, Twink Caplan, Bobby Slayton, Robert Miano, Mollee Israel, Colleen Camp, Andy Dick.

LOST IN THE PERSHING POINT HOTEL

A Pierrepont Prods. and Pershing Point Prods. presentation. Producers: Julia Jay Pierrepont II, Erin Chandler. Co-producers: Grant Gilmore, Elizabeth Carney. Director: Julia Jay Pierrepoint II. Screenplay: Leslie Jordan, based on his play. Camera: Sacha Sarchielli. Editor: Ila von Hasperg. Music: Dan Gilboy. In color. Release date: May 31, 2000. Running time: 102 Min.

Cast: Leslie Jordan, Erin Chandler, Mark Pellegrino, Carlos Gomez, Luke Eberl, John Ritter, Marilu Henner, Michelle Phillips.

LOUIS PRIMA: THE WILDEST!

A Blue Sea Prods./Historic Films production. Producer: Joe Lauro. Executive producers: Don McGlynn, Celia Zaentz. Director: Don McGlynn. Camera, sound: Steve Wacks, Randy Drummond, Alex Vlasco. Editors: Christian Moltke-Leth, McGlynn. In color and B&W. Release date: Oct. 13, 1999. Running time: 82 Min. Documentary.

LOVE AND ACTION IN CHICAGO

A Flashpoint presentation with Gold/Basulto Entertainment in association with Prosperity Pictures. (International sales: Artist View Entertainment, North Hollywood.) Producers: Richard Mann, Danny Gold, Dave Basulto, Leszek Burzynski, B.J. Rack. Executive producers: David Forrest, Beau Rogers. Co-producers: Courtney B. Vance, Greg Bernstein, Betsy Chasse. Director/Screenplay: Swayne Johnson-Cochran. Camera: Phil Parmet. Editors: J. Kathleen Gibson, Carol Oblath. Music: Russ Landau. In Deluxe color. Release date: Sept. 15, 1999. Running time: 91 Min.

Cast: Courtney B. Vance, Regina King, Jason Alexander, Kathleen Turner, Edward Asner, Robert Breuler, Michael Gilio.

LOVE AND BASKETBALL

A New Line release of a 40 Acres and a Mule Filmworks production. Producers: Spike Lee, Sam Kitt. Executive producers: Andrew Z. Davis, Jay Stern, Cynthia Guidry. Director/Screenplay: Gina Prince-Bythewood. Camera: Reynaldo Villalobos. Editor: Terilyn Shropshire. Music: Terence Blanchard. In Deluxe color. Release date: Jan. 26, 2000. MPAA Rating: R. Running time: 124 Min.

Cast: Sanaa Lathan, Omar Epps, Alfre Woodard, Dennis Haysbert, Debbie Morgan, Harry J. Lennix, Kyla Pratt, Glenndon Chatman.

LOVE & SEX

A Behaviour Worldwide presentation of a Bogart/Wyman production. Producers: Timothy Scott Bogart, Martin J. Barab, Brad Wyman. Executive producer: Mark Damon. Director/Screenplay: Valerie Breiman. Camera: Adam Kane. Editor: Martin Applebaum. In FotoKem color. Release date: Jan. 24, 2000. Running time: 80 Min.

Cast: Famke Janssen, Jon Favreau, Noah Emmerich, Ann Magnuson, Cheri Oteri, Josh Hopkins, Robert Knepper, Vincent Ventresca.

LOVING JEZEBEL

A Starz! presentation, in association with BET Movies, of a David Lancaster Prod. production. (International sales: BET Movies, Englewood, CO.) Producer: David Lancaster. Director/Screenplay: Kwyn Bader. Camera: Horacio Marquinez. Editor: Tom McArdle. Music: Tony Prendatt, Wendy Melvoin, Lisa Coleman. In color. Release date: Oct. 8, 1999. Running time: 86 Min.

Cast: Hill Harper, Nicole Ari Parker, Laurel Holloman, Sandrine Holt, David Moscow, Andre Blake, John Doman, Elisa Donovan, Phylicia Rashad.

LUCKYTOWN

A Plus Entertainment presentation of a Mediapix production. Producer: Paul Nicholas. Executive producers: Adam Goldworm, John Rogers. Director: Paul Nicholas. Screenplay: Brendon Beseth. Camera: Denis Maloney. Editor: Roberto Silvi. Music: Greg Edmonson. In Fotokem color. Release date: Aug. 4, 2000. Running time: 101 Min.
Cast: Kirsten Dunst, Vincent Kartheiser, James Caan, Luis Guzman, Robert Miano, Jennifer Gareis.

LUSH

An i5 Picture. Producers: David Siegel, Scott McGehee, Patrick Dollard. Executive producers: Robert Nathan, Eileen Jones. Co-producer: Alicia Allain. Director/Screenplay: Mark Gibson. Camera: Caroline Champetier. Editor: Sarah Flack. Music: Barrett Martin. In CFI color. Release date: Jan. 24, 2000. Running time: 94 Min.
Cast: Campbell Scott, Jared Harris, Laurel Holloman, Laura Linney, Nick Offerman, Kimo Wills, James R. Hall Jr., Don Hood, Joe Chrest, David Sellars, Michael Cahill.

MAD ABOUT MAMBO

A USA Films release of a Gramercy Pictures presentation, in association with Phoenix Pictures, of a First City production in association with Plurabelle Films. Producer: David P. Kelly. Executive producers: Gabriel Byrne, Martin Bruce-Clayton. Director/Screenplay: John Forte. Camera: Ashley Rowe. Editor: David Martin. Music: Richard Hartley. In Technicolor. Release date: Aug. 1, 2000. MPAA Rating: PG-13. Running time: 92 Min.
Cast: William Ash, Keri Russell, Brian Cox, Theo Fraser Steele, Rosaleen Linehan, Maclean Stewart, Tim Loane, Julian Littman, Russell Smith, Joe Rea, Aingeal Grehan, Jim Norton, Daniel Caltagirone.

THE MAGIC OF MARCIANO

A Lumiere Films Intl. presentation of a Lila Cazes production. Producer: Lila Cazes. Executive producers: Claude Leger, Luciano Lisi, Wendy Cary, Mickey Cottrell. (International sales: Lumiere Intl., L.A.) Director/Screenplay: Tony Barbieri. Camera: Matthew Irving. Editor: Jeffery Stephens. Music: Harry Gregson-Williams. In FotoKem color. Release date: Apr. 15, 2000. Running time: 101 Min.
Cast: Nastassja Kinski, Robert Forster, Cody Morga, Jason Cairns.

MAGNOLIA

A New Line release of a Joanne Sellar/Ghoulardi Film production. Producer: Joanne Sellar. Executive producers: Michael De Luca, Lynn Harris. Co-producer: Daniel Lupi. Director/Screenplay: Paul Thomas Anderson. Camera: Robert Elswit. Editor: Dylan Tichenor. Music: John Brion, songs by Aimee Mann. In Deluxe color, Panavision widescreen. Release date: Nov. 30, 1999. MPAA Rating: R. Running time: 188 Min.
Cast: Jason Robards, Julianne Moore, Tom Cruise, Philip Seymour Hoffman, John C. Reilly, Melora Walters, Jeremy Blackman, Michael Bowen, William H. Macy, Philip Baker Hall, Melinda Dillon.

MAN ON THE MOON

A Universal release of a Universal Pictures and Mutual Film Co. presentation of a Jersey Films/Cinehaus production. Producers: Danny DeVito, Michael Shamberg, Stacey Sher. Executive producers: George Shapiro, Howard West, Michael Hausman. Co-executive producer: Bob Zmuda. Director: Milos Forman. Screenplay: Scott Alexander, Larry Karaszewski. Camera: Anastas Michos. Editors: Christopher Tellefsen, Lynzee Klingman. Music: R.E.M. In Deluxe color, Panavision widescreen. Release date: Nov. 5, 1999. MPAA Rating: R. Running time: 118 Min.
Cast: Jim Carrey, Danny DeVito, Courtney Love, Paul Giamatti, Vincent Schiavelli, Peter Bonerz, Jerry Lawler, Gerry Becker, Leslie Lyles.

MARINE LIFE

An Odeon Films/Alliance Atlantis production. (International sales: Alliance Atlantis Pictures International, Santa Monica.) Producers: Jeanne Stromberg, Arvi Liimatainen. Executive producers: Harold Tichenor, John Delmage. Director: Anne Wheeler. Screenplay: Lori Lansens, Rob Forsyth, based on the book by Linda Svendsen. Camera: David Pelletier. Editor: Alison Grace. Music: George Blondheim. In color. Release date: Sept. 15, 2000. Running time: 95 Min.
Cast: Cybill Shepherd, Peter Outerbridge, Alexandra Purvis, Gabrielle Miller, Michael Hogan.

MARRIAGE PREP

A Lighted Pathway production. Producer: Donahue Tuitt. Executive producer: Rosalind Keith. Director/Screenplay: Donahue Tuitt. Camera: Armand Gazarian. Editor: Yousef Shehadeh. Music: Ann Moore. In color. Release date: Feb. 27, 2000. Running time: 102 Min.
Cast: Donahue Tuitt, Temple Parker, Skip Mullen, Darlene Rene, Thomas lazare, Sonya Leslie, Joel Kindrick, Roe Williams, Baron Jay, Alicia Mallory.

MARYAM

A Streetlight Films production. Producer: Shauna Lyon. Executive producer: Cyrus Serry. Co-producers: Jonathan Shoemaker, Derrick Tseng. Director/Screenplay: Ramin Serry. Camera: Harlan Bosmajian. Music: Ahrin Mishan. In Duart color. Release date: Apr. 3, 2000. Running time: 90 Min.
Cast: Mariam Parris, David Ackert, Shaun Toub, Shohreh Aghdashloo, Maziyar Jobrani, Victor Jory.

MAU MAU SEX SEX

A 7th Planet production. Producer: Ted Bonnitt. Executive producer: Keith Robinson. Co-producer: Eddie Muller. Director: Ted Bonnitt. Camera: Bonnitt. Editors: Bonnitt, Christopher Rowland, Eddie Muller. Music: Eddie Baytos & the Nervis Brothers. In color, Digi-Beta digital video. Release date: Apr. 5, 2000. Running time: 78 Min. Documentary.
With: David Friedman, Dan Sonney, Frank Henenlotter, Mike Vraney, Carol Friedman, Margaret Sonney.

ME & ISAAC NEWTON

A Paul G. Allen presentation of a Clear Blue Sky Prods. production. (International sales: Myriad Pictures, Santa Monica.) Producers: Jody Patton, Eileen Gregor. Director: Michael Apted. Camera: Maryse Alberti. Editor: Susanne Szabo Rostock. Music: Patrick Seymour. In color. Release date: Sept. 16, 1999. Running time: 105 Min. Documentary.
With: Gertrude Elion, Ashok Gadgil, Michio Kaku, Maja Mataric, Steven Pinker, Karol Likora, Patricia C. Wright.

MEET THE PARENTS

A Universal (in U.S.) /DreamWorks release (foreign) of a Universal Pictures and DreamWorks Pictures presentation. Producers: Nancy Tenenbaum, Jane Rosenthal, Robert De Niro, Jay Roach. Co-producers: Amy Sayres, Shauna Weinberg. Director: Roach. Screenplay: Jim Herzfeld, John Hamburg, story by Greg Glienna, Mary Ruth Clarke. Camera: Peter James. Editor: Jon Poll. Music: Randy Newman. In Deluxe color. Release date: Sept. 18, 2000. MPAA Rating: PG-13. Running time: 108 Min.
Cast: Robert De Niro, Ben Stiller, Blythe Danner, Teri Polo, James Rebhorn, Jon Abrahams, Phyllis George, Kali Rocha, Tom McCarthy, Nicole DeHuff, Owen Wilson.

MEMENTO

A Newmarket (in U.S.)/UGC Ph release (in France) of a Newmarket presentation, in association with Summit Entertainment, of a Team Todd production. Producers: Suzanne Todd, Jennifer Todd. Executive producer: Aaron Ryder. Co-producer: Elaine Dysinger. Director/Screenplay: Christopher Nolan, based on a short story by Jonathan Nolan. Camera: Wally Pfister. Editor: Dody Dorn. Music: David Julyan. Release date: Sept. 7, 2000. Running time: 116 Min.
Cast: Guy Pearce, Carrie-Anne Moss, Joe Pantoliano, Mark Boone Jr., Stephen Tobolowsky, Harriet Sansom Harris, Callum Keith Rennie, Russ Fega, Kimberly Campbell, Larry Holden.

ME, MYSELF & IRENE

A 20th Century Fox release of a Conundrum Entertainment production. Producers: Bradley Thomas, Bobby Farrelly, Peter Farrelly. Executive producers: Charles B. Wessler, Tom Schulman. Co-producers: Marc S. Fischer, James B. Rogers, Mark Charpentier. Directors: Bobby Farrelly, Peter Farrelly. Screenplay: Peter Farrelly, Mike Cerrone, Bobby Farrelly. Camera: Mark Irwin. Editor: Christopher Greenbury. Music: Peter Yorn, Lee Scott. In Duart color. Release date: June 14, 2000. MPAA Rating: R. Running time: 117 Min.
Cast: Jim Carrey, Renee Zellweger, Chris Cooper, Robert Forster, Richard Jenkins, Rob Moran, Traylor Howard, Daniel Greene, Zen Gesner, Tony Cox, Anthony Anderson, Mongo Brownlee.

MEN OF HONOR

A 20th Century Fox release of a Fox 2000 Pictures presentation of State Street Pictures production. Producers: Robert Teitel, Bill Badalato. Executive producers: Bill Cosby, Stanley Robertson. Director: George Tillman Jr. Screenplay: Scott Marshall Smith, based on the life of Carl Brashear. Camera: Anthony B. Richmond. Editor: John Carter. Music: Mark Isham. In Deluxe color, Joe Dunton & Co. widescreen. Release date: Sept. 14, 2000. MPAA Rating: PG-13. Running time: 129 Min.
Cast: Robert De Niro, Cuba Gooding Jr., Charlize Theron, Aunjanue Ellis, Hal Holbrook, David Keith, Michael Rapaport, Powers Boothe, Joshua Leonard, David Conrad, Glynn Turman, Holt McCallany, Lonette McKee, Carl Lumbly.

MERCY

A Franchise Pictures presentation of a Jazz Pictures production. Producers: Amedeo Ursini, Elie Samaha, Andrew Stevens. Executive producers: Damian Lee, Ashok Armitraj. Co-executive producer: Paul Wynn. Director/Screenplay: Damian Harris, based on the novel by David L. Lindsey. Camera: Manuel Teran. Editor: Stephan Fanfara. In color. Release date: Feb. 23, 2000. Running time: 117 Min.
Cast: Ellen Barkin, Wendy Crewson, Peta Wilson, Karen Young, Julian Sands, Stephen Baldwin, Marshell Bell, Beau Starr, Bill MacDonald, Steward Bick, Ellen-Ray Hennessey.

METAL

A 21st Century Pictures Group presentation in association with Ubuntu Filmworks. Producer: Adryenn Ashley. Executive producer: Christopher E. Brown. Co-producer: Christina Funk. Director/Screenplay/Editor: Christopher E. Brown. Camera: Andy Lilien. Music supervisors: Sundan Moore, Helen Sanderson. In B&W, 16mm. Release date: Sept. 15, 1999. Running time: 88 Min.
Cast: Wedrell James, Venieta Porter, Khafre James, R. Tyrone Fields, Thea-Marie Perkins, Andre C. Andre, Earl "Robbie" Robertson, Alyce James.

MEXICO
A Sol Films production. Producer/Director: Lorena M. Parlee. Screenplay: Carlos Blanco Aguinaga, Parlee. Camera: David Douglas, Haskell Wexler, Alex Phillips. Editors: Miroslav Janek, Robert Lower, Tonichka Janek. Music: Daniel Valdez. In color, Imax. Release date: Feb. 27, 2000. Running time: 43 Min. Documentary.
Narrators: Martin Sheen, Enrique Rocha.

MICHAEL JORDAN TO THE MAX
A Giant Screen Sports release of an mvp.com presentation of a Giant Screen Sports-James D. Stern Prods.-NBA Entertainment production. Producers: Don Kempf, Steve Kempf, James D. Stern. Executive producers: David Falk, Curtis Polk Adam Silver Gregg Winik. Directors: James D. Stern, Don Kempf. Narration written by Jonathan Hock. Camera: James Neihouse, John Bailey. Editor: Hock. Music: John Debney. In CFI color. Release date: May 2, 2000. Running time: 46 Min. Documentary.
With: Michael Jordan, Phil Jackson, Doug Collins, Bob Greene, Bob Costas, Dean Smith, Deloris Jordan, Fred Lynch, Walter Iosss Jr., Bill Murray, Laurence Fishburne.

MISSION: IMPOSSIBLE 2
A Paramount Pictures release of a Cruise/Wagner production. Producers: Tom Cruise, Paula Wagner. Executive producers: Terence Change, Paul Hitchcock. Director: John Woo. Screenplay: Robert Towne, story by Ronald D. Moore, Brannon Braga, based on the television series created by Bruce Geller. Camera: Jeffrey L. Kimball. Editors: Christian Wagner, Steven Kemper. Music: Hans Zimmer, original theme by Lalo Schifrin. In Deluxe color, Panavision widescreen. Release date: May 22, 2000. MPAA Rating: PG-13. Running time: 123 Min.
Cast: Tom Cruise, Dougray Scott, Thandie Newton, Ving Rhames, Richard Roxburgh, John Polson, Brendan Gleeson, Rade Sherbedgia, Anthony Hopkins.

MISSION TO MARS
A Buena Vista release of a Touchstone Pictures presentation of a Jacobson Co. production. Producer: Tom Jacobson. Executive producer: Sam Mercer. Co-producers: David Goyer, Justis Greene, Jim Wedda. Director: Brian De Palma. Screenplay: Jim Thomas, John Thomas, Graham Yost, story by Lowell Cannon, Thomas & Thomas. Camera: Stephen H. Burum. Editor: Paul Hirsch. Music: Ennio Morricone. In Technicolor, Panavision widescreen. Release date: Mar. 6, 2000. MPAA Rating: PG. Running time: 112 Min.
Cast: Gary Sinise, Tim Robbins, Don Cheadle, Connie Nielsen, Jerry O'Connell, Kim Delaney, Elise Neal, Peter Outerbridge, Jill Teed, Kavan Smith.

MR. DEATH: THE RISE AND FALL OF FRED A. LEUCHTER JR.
A Lions Gate Films release of an Independent Film Channel presentation, in association with Channel 4, of a Fourth Floor/Scout production. (International sales: Sloss Special Projects, New York.) Producers: Michael Williams, David Collins, Dorothy Aufiero. Executive producers: Jonathan Sehring, Caroline Kaplan, John Sloss. Director: Errol Morris. Camera: Peter Donohue. Editor: Karen Schmeer. Music: Caleb Sampson. In Technicolor. Release date: Sept. 14, 1999. Running time: 90 Min. Documentary.

MOLLY
An MGM release of a Cockamamie/Absolute Entertainment production. Producer: WIlliam J. Macdonald. Executive producer: Amy Heckerling. Co-producer: Frank Bodo. Director: John Duigan. Screenplay: Dick Christie. Camera: Gabriel Beristain. Editor: Humphrey Dixon. Music: Trevor Jones. In Deluxe color. Release date: Oct. 14, 1999. MPAA Rating: PG-13. Running time: 89 Min.
Cast: Elisabeth Shue, Aaron Eckhart, Jill Hennessy, Thomas Jane, D.W. Moffett, Elizabeith Mitchell, Robert Harper, Elaine Hendrix, Michael Paul Chan, Lucy Liu.

MY DOG SKIP
A Warner Bros. release of an Alcon Entertainment presentation of a Mark Johnson/John Lee Hancock production. Producers: Broderick Johnson, Andrew A. Kosove, Mark Johnson, Hancock. Executive producers: Marty P. Ewing, Jay Russell. Director: Jay Russell. Screenplay: Gail Gilchriest, based on the book by Willie Morris. Camera: James L. Carter. Editors: Harvey Rosenstock, Gary Winter. Music: William Ross. In Deluxe color. Release date: Jan. 6, 2000. MPAA Rating: PG. Running time: 95 Min.
Cast: Frankie Muniz, Diane Lane, Like Wilson, Kevin Bacon, Caitlin Wachs, Bradley Coryell, Daylan Honeycutt, Cody Linley, Peter Crombie, Clint Howard, Harry Connick Jr.

THE NEXT BEST THING
A Paramount release of a Paramount/Lakeshore Entertainment presentation of a Lakeshore Entertainment production. Producer: Tom Rosenberg, Leslie Dixon, Linne Radmin. Executive producers: Gary Lucchesi, Ted Tannebaum, Lewis Manilow. Co-producers: Marcus Viscidi, Richard S. Wright. Director: John Schlesinger. Screenplay: Thomas Ropelewski. Camera: Elliot Davis. Editor: Peter Honess. Music: Gabriel Yared. In Deluxe color. Release date: Feb. 29, 2000. MPAA Rating: PG-13. Running time: 108 Min.
Cast: Rupert Everett, Madonna, Benjamin Bratt, Michael Vartan, Josef Sommer, Lynn Redgrave, Malcolm Stumpf, Neil Patrick Harris, Illeana Douglas, Mark Valley, Suzanne Krull, Stacy Edwards.

NEXT FRIDAY
A New Line Cinema release of a Cubevision production. Producer: Ice Cube. Executive producers: Michael Gruber, Claire Rudnick Polstein. Co-executive producer: Matt Moore. Co-producers: Douglas Curtis, Matt Alvarez. Director: Steve Carr. Screenplay: Ice Cube, based on characters created by Ice Cube and DJ Pooh. Camera: Christopher J. Baffia. Editor: Elena Maganini. Music: Terence Blanchard. In FotoKem color. Release date: Jan 7, 2000. MPAA Rating: R. Running time: 93 Min.
Cast: Ice Cube, Mike Epps, Justin Pierce, John Witherspoon. Don "DC" Curry, Jacob Vargas, Lobo Sebastian, Rolando Molina, Lisa Rodriguez, Tommy "Tiny" Lister Jr., Kym E. Whitley, Amy Hill, Tamala Jones, Robin Allen.

THE NIGHT LARRY KRAMER KISSED ME
A FilmNext release in association with John Tilley of a FilmNext/Montrose Pictures production. Producers: Michael Kaplan, Kirkland Tibbels. Co-producer: Gill Holland. Director: Tim Kirkman. Screenplay: David Drake, based on his play. Camera: James Carman. Editor: Caitlin Dixon. Music: Steve Sandberg. In Fuji color. Release date: July 12, 2000. Running time: 81 Min.
Cast: David Drake

NIGHT WALTZ: THE MUSIC OF PAUL BOWLES
An Owsley Browne Presents (San Francisco) production, with support from Telefilm Canada. Producer: Owsley Browne III. Co-producer: Robin Burke. Director/Screenplay: Owsley Browne III. Camera: David Golia, Gene Salvitore, Rudy Brukhardt, Nataniel Dorsky. Editor: Dorsky. Music: Paul Bowles. In color and B&W, 16-to-35mm blowup. Release date: Oct. 7, 1999. Running time: 76 Min. Documentary.
With: Paul Bowles, Allen Ginsberg, William S. Burroughs.

NORIEGA: GOD'S FAVORITE
A Showtime and Regency Enterprises presentation of a Nancy Hardin/Industry Entertainment production. (International sales: 20th Century Fox Intl.) Producer: Nancy Hardin. Executive producers: Arnon Milchan, Nick Wechsler, Roger Spottiswoode. Co-producers: Lawrence Wright, Tom Todoroff. Director: Roger Spottiswoode. Screenplay: Lawrence Wright. Camera: Pierre Mignot. Editor: Mark Conte. In Deluxe color. Release date: Mar. 4, 2000. Running time: 120 Min.
Cast: Bob Hoskins, Jeffrey Demunn, Rosa Blasi, Luis Avalos, Denise Blasor, Nestor Carbonell, Tony Plana, John Verea, Richard Masur, David Marshall Grant, Michael Sorich, Jorge Luis Abreu, Edward Edwards.

NORMA JEAN, JACK, AND ME
A New Path Pictures production in association with Maurice Singer. Producer: David De Vos. Executive producer: Singer. Co-producer: Paul Seydor. Director: Cyrus Nowrasteh. Screenplay: Nowrasteh, James Trivers, based on a short story by Trivers. Camera: Nils Erickson. Editor: Paul Seydor. Music: Trivers, Elizabeth Myers. In color. Release date: Mar. 3, 2000. Running time: 95 Min.
Cast: Sally Kirkland, Michael Murphy, Kai Lennox, Dan Mandehr, David De Vos.

NURSE BETTY
A USA Films release of a Gramercy Pictures presentation, in association with Pacifica Film Distribution, of a Propaganda Films/ab'-strakt pictures/IMF production. Producers: Gail Mutrux, Steve Golin. Executive producers: Philip Steuer, Stephen Pevner, Moritz Borman, Chris Sievernich. Director: Neil LaBute. Screenplay: John C. Richards, James Flamberg, based on a story by Richards. Camera: Jean Yves Escoffier. Editors: Joel Plotch, Steven Weisberg. Music: Rolfe Kent. In Technicolor, widescreen. Release date: May 11, 2000. MPAA Rating: R. Running time: 108 Min.
Cast: Renee Zellweger, Morgan Freeman, Chris Rock, Greg Kinnear, Aaron Eckhart, Tia Texada, Crispin Glover, Pruitt Taylor Vince, Allison Janney, Kathleen Wilhoite, Harriet Sanson Harris, Laird Macintosh.

NUTTY PROFESSOR II: THE KLUMPS
A Universal Pictures release of an Imagine Entertainment presentation of a Brian Grazer production. Producer: Brian Grazer. Executive producers: Jerry Lewis, Eddie Murphy, Karen Kehela, Tom Shadyac, James D. Brubaker. Co-producers: James Whitaker, Michael Ewing. Director: Peter Segal. Screenplay: Barry W. Balustein, David Sheffield, Paul Weitz, from a story by Steve Oederkerk, Blaustein, Sheffield, based on characters created by Jerry Lewis, Bill Richmond. Camera: Dean Semler. Editor: William Kerr. Music: David Newman. In Deluxe color. Release date: July 25, 2000. MPAA Rating: PG-13. Running time: 106 Min.
Cast: Eddie Murphy, Janet Jackson, Larry Miller, John Ales, Richard Gant, Anna Maria Horsford, Melinda McGraw, Jamal Mixon.

NUYORICAN DREAM
A Big Mouth Prods. presentation in association with John Leguizamo and Jellybean Benitez. Producers: Laurie Collyer, Julia Pimsleur, Katy Chevigny. Executive producers: Leguizamo, Benitez. Director: Laurie Collyer. Camera: Auroroa M. Aguero, Victoria Garza, Jaime Reyes. Editor: Allan Title. In color. Release date: Jan. 26, 2000. Running time: 97 Min. Documentary.

O BROTHER, WHERE ART THOU?

A Buena Vista (in U.S.)/Universal (foreign) release of a Universal and Touchstone Pictures presentation, in association with StudioCanal, of a Working Title production. Producer: Ethan Coen. Executive producers: Tim Bevan, Eric Fellner. Co-producer: John Cameron. Director: Joel Coen. Screenplay: Ethan and Joel Coen, based on "The Odyssey" by Homer. Camera: Otto Nemenz, Roger Deakins. Editors: Roderick Jaynes, Tricia Cooke. Music: T Bone Burnett. In Deluxe color, widescreen. Release date: May 13, 2000. MPAA Rating: PG-13. Running time: 106 Min.
Cast: George Clooney, John Turturro, Tim Blake Nelson, Charles Durning, John Goodman, Michael Badalucco, Holly Hunter.

OF CIVIL WRONGS & RIGHTS: THE FRED KOREMATSU STORY

A Pushtan Prods. (San Francisco) production. Producers: Dorka Keehn, Shirley Nakoa. Director/Screenplay: Eric Paul Fournier. Camera: Peter McCandless. Editors: Jean Kawahara, Fournier. Music: Bond Bergland, Michael Becker. In color, video. Release date: June 7, 2000. Running time: 60 Min. Documentary.
With: Fred Korematsu, Rosa Parks, Bill Clinton.

THE OMEGA CODE

A Providence Entertainment release of a TBN Films presentation of a Gener8xion Entertainment production. Producers: Matthew Crouch, Rob Marcarelli, Lawrence Mortorff. Executive producer: Paul Crouch. Co-producer: Gary M. Bettman. Director: Rob Marcarelli. Screenplay: Stephan Blinn, Hollis Barton. Camera: Carlos Gonzalez. Editor: Peter Zinner. Music: Harry Manfredini. In FotoKem color. Release date: Oct. 15, 1999. MPAA Rating: PG-13. Running time: 99 Min.
Cast: Casper Van Dien. Michael York, Catherine Oxenberg, Michael Ironside, Jan Triska, Gregory Wagrowski, Devon Odessa.

ONE DAY IN SEPTEMBER

An HBO presentation of a Passion Pictures/Arthur Cohn production. Producers: Cohn, John Battsek. Executive producer: Lilliam Birnbaum. Director: Kevin McDonald. Camera: Alwin Kuchler, Neve Cunningham. Special still photographer: Raymond Depardon. Editor: Justine Wright. Music: Alex Heffes. Release date: Sept. 1, 2000. Running time: 92 Min. Documentary.
Narrator: Michael Douglas.

101 RENT BOYS

A Cinemax presentation of a World of Wonder production. Producers: Randy Barbato, Fenton Bailey. Executive producers: Harry Knapp, John Hoffman. Director: Randy Barbato, Fenton Bailey. Camera: Sandra Chandler, Scott Franse, Thairin Smothers. Editor: William Grayburn. In color, video-to-35mm. Release date: June 7, 2000. Running time: 78 Min. Documentary.

ON TIPTOE: THE MUSIC OF LADYSMITH BLACK MAMBAZO

A Noma Films presentation of an On Tip Toe Prods. (Los Angeles) production. Producers: Lelai Diemoz, Eric Simonson. Co-producer: Corinne Marrinan. Director/Screenplay: Eric Simonson. Camera: Jan Maliszewski. Editors: Tina Imahara, Simonson. Music: Ladysmith Black Mambazo. In color, video. Release date: June 9, 2000. Running time: 58 Min. Documentary.
With: Ladysmith Black Mambazo, Paul Simon, Patrick Bhutelezi.

THE OPERA LOVER

A Gifthorse picture. Producer: Ed Amaya, Tom Bastounes. Co-producers: Lisa Spencer, Tiny Moy. Directors: Ron Lazzeretti, Venturino Liberatore. Screenplay: Lazzeretti, story by Lazzeretti, Tom Bastounes. Camera: Gary Katz. Editor: Brian Clark. In color. Release date: Oct. 23, 1999. Running time: 93 Min.
Cast: Tom Bastounes, Monica Zaffarano, Dean Bastounes, Nick Bastounes, Coren Caldwell, Tom White, Robert Altman.

THE OPERATOR

A Black Wolf Prods. presentation. Producer: Jon Dichter. Co-producers: Doug Bruce, Betty Buckley. Executive producer: Jay Barnet. Director/Screenplay: Jon Dichter. Camera: Bert Guthrie. Editors: Michael Coleman, Darren Kloomok. Music: Victor Zupanc. In FotoKem color. Release date: Mar. 4, 2000. Running time: 102 Min.
Cast: Michael Laurence, Christa Miller, Brion James.

THE OPPORTUNISTS

A Eureka Films production in association with Clinica Estetico and Kalkaska Films. Producers: John Lyons, Tim Perell. Executive producers: Peter Saraf, Jonathan Demme, Edward Saxon. Co-producers: Martin Fink, Richard E. Johnson. Director/Screenplay: Myles O'Connell. Camera: Teodoro Maniaci. Editor: Andy Keir. Music: Kurt Hoffman. In color. Release date: Jan. 27, 2000. Running time: 89 Min.
Cast: Christopher Walken, Peter McDonald, Cyndi Lauper, Donal Logue, Vera Farmiga, Jose Zuniga, Anne Pitoniak, Tom Noonan.

ORDINARY MADNESS

A Legendary Prods. presentation of an Anello/Keane production. Producers: Dean Anello, Paula Keane, Erica Spano. Executive producer: James. J. Smythe. Director/Screenplay: Bernardo Gigliotti. Camera: Keith Holland. Editor: J. Carlos Negrete. Music: Tom Keane. In color, digital. Release date: Feb. 25, 2000. Running time: 94 Min.
Cast: Ron Carlson, Denise Gentile, Mariah O'Brien, Gary D. Mosher, Robert Musgrave, Alan Gelfant, Mark Boone Jr., Steve Richard Harris, Pat Cocran, David Batiste, Aimee Graham.

ORIGINAL DINER GUYS

A Baltimore/Spring Creek Prods. production. Producer/Director: Barry Levinson. Camera: Wayne Ewing, Erich Roland, Bob Dorsey, Josh Dorsey, Josh Spring, Boots Shelton, Blackford Vincent Shelton III. Editors: Neil Kirk, Wayne Ewing. In color, video-to-35mm. Release date: Oct. 9, 1999. Running time: 75 Min. Documentary.

THE ORIGINAL KIINGS OF COMEDY

An MTV Films and Latham Entertainment presentation of a 40 Acres and a Mule Filmworks production. Producers: Walter Latham, David Gale, Spike Lee. Executive producer: Van Toffler. Co-producer: Butch Robinson. Director: Spike Lee. Camera: Malik Sayeed. Editor: Barry Alexander Brown. In color, video. Release date: Aug. 10, 2000. MPAA Rating: R. Running time: 115 Min. Documentary.
With: Steve Harvey, D.L. Hughley, Cedric the Entertainer, Bernie Mac.

THE ORIGIN OF MAN

A Mysterious Offshore Holdings production. (International sales: MOH, San Diego, Calif.) Producer/Director/Screenplay: Stuart Hynson Culpepper. Camera: Zachary Erin Malone. Editor: Culpepper. Music: Bruce Odland. In FotoKem color. Release date: June 30, 2000. Running time: 78 Min.
Cast: Gabe Anderson, Phil Beaumont, Lou Seitchik, Stuart Hynson Culpepper, Kitty Culpepper, Nakissa Eternad.

OTHER VOICES

A Unapix Entertainment presentation of a Charny/Strong production, in association with Redwood Comminications and Phantom Limbs Plays & Pictures. Producers: Ruth Charny, Shelly Strong. Executive producer: Robert Baruc. Co-producer: Alicia Reilly-Larson. Director/Screenplay: Dan McCormack. Camera: Dan Gillham. Editor: Fred Wardell; supervising editor: Martin Hunter. Music: William T. Stromberg. In FotoKem color. Release date: Jan. 23, 2000. Running time: 104 Min.
Cast: Mary McCormack, David Aaron Baker, Campbell Scott, Rob Morrow, Stockard Channing, Peter Gallagher, Ricky Aiello.

OUR SONG

An Independent Fllm Channel presentation, in association with Beech Hill Films and Journeyman Pictures, of a C-Hundred Film Corp. production. Producers: Jim McKay, Paul Mezey, Diana E. Williams. Executive producers: Caroline Kaplan, Jonathan Sehring, Michael Stipe. Co-producers: Alexa L. Fogel, Joseph Infantolino. Director/Screenplay: Jim McKay. Camera: Jim Denault. Editor: Alex Hall. In color, 16mm. Release date: Jan.21, 2000. Running time: 95 Min.
Cast: Kerry Washington, Anna Simpson, Melissa Martinez, Marlene Forte, Ray Anthony Thomas, Rosalyn Coleman, Carmen Lopez.

OUTTAKES

Producers: Katherine Brooks, Karen Klopfenstein. Executive producer: Michael Eisenberg. Director/Screenplay: Katherine Brooks, Karen Klopfenstein. Camera: Jennifer Lane. Editors: Brooks, Scott-E. In color. Release date: Jan. 14, 2000. Running time: 69 Min.
Cast: Katherine Brooks, Karen Klopfenstein, Sean Carlos Larkin.

PANIC

A Bac Films release (in France) of a Vault/Mad Chance production. (International sales: Summit Entertainment, L.A.) Producers: Andrew Lazar, Lori Miller, Matt Cooper. Executive producer: David Cooper. Co-producer: Jody Hedien. Director/Screenplay: Henry Bromell. Camera: Jeffrey Jur. Editors: Lynzee Klingman, Cindy Mollo. Music: Brian Tyler. Release date: Sept. 8, 2000. MPAA Rating: R. Running time: 88 Min.
Cast: William H. Macy, John Ritter, Neve Campbell, Donald Sutherland, Tracey Ullman, Barbara Bain, David Dorfman.

PARAGRAPH 175

A Telling Pictures production. Producers: Rob Epstein, Jeffrey Friedman, Michael Ehrenzweig, Janet Cole. Co-producer: Howard Rosenman. Director: Rob Epstein, Jeffrey Friedman. Screenplay: Sharon Wood. Camera: Bernd Meiners. Editor: Dawn Logsdon. Music: Tibor Szemzo. In color and B&W. Release date: Jan. 22, 2000. Running time: 76 Min. Documentary.
Narrator: Rupert Everett.

PASSION OF MIND

A Paramount Classic release of a Lakeshore Entertainment and Paramount Classic presentation, in association with Ron Bass Prods. Producers: Carole Scotta, Tom Rosenberg, Ron Bass. Executive producers: Gary Lucchesi, William Kepper, Ted Tannenbaum, Sigrion Sighvatsson. Co-producer: Andre Lamal. Director: Alain Berliiner. Screenplay: Ron Bass, David Field. Camera: Eduardo Serra. Editor: Anne V. Coates. Music: Randy Edelman. In Deluxe color. Release date: Apr. 30, 2000. MPAA Rating: PG-13. Running time: 105 Min.
Cast: Demi Moore, Stellan Skarsgard, William Fichtner, Sinead Cusack, Peter Riegert, Joss Ackland, Eloise Eonnet, Chaya Cuenot.

PATRIOT

A Sony Pictures Entertainment release of a Columbia Pictures presentation of a Mutual Film Co./Centropolis Entertainment production. Producers: Dean Devlin, Mark Gordon, Gary Levinsohn. Executive producers: William Fay, Ute Emmerich, Roland Emmerich. Co-producer: Peter Winther. Director: Roland Emmerich. Screenplay: Robert Rodat. Camera: Caleb Deschanel. Editor: David Brenner. Music: John Williams. In Technicolor. Release date: June 9, 2000. MPAA Rating: R. Running time: 164 Min.
Cast: Mel Gibson, Heath Ledger, Joely Richardson, Jason Isaacs, Chris Cooper, Tcheky Karyo, Rene Auberjonois, Lisa Brenner.

PEDESTRIAN

A Pedestrian Prods. production. Producer: Dave Werner. Executive producer: Krikor Satamian. Director/Screenplay: Jason Kartalian. Camera: Ted J. Jacobs. Editors: Jacobs, Kartalian. Music: Jim Lang. In FotoKem color. Release date: June 29, 2000. Running time: 97 Min.
Cast: Jeffrey Stubblefield, Melissa Marie Lewis, Joe Seely, Krikor Satamian, Jerry Corley, Buck Kartalian, Jack Sanderson, Kevin E. West, Peter Onorati, Louis Guss, Izumi Maki, Avery Schreiber.

THE PERFECT STORM

A Warner Bros. release of a Baltimore Spring Creek Pictures production in association with Radiant Prods. Producers: Paula Weinstein, Wolfgang Petersen, Gail Katz. Executive producers: Barry Levinson, Duncan Henderson. Director: Wolfgang Petersen. Screenplay: Bill Wittliff, based on the book by Sebastian Junger. Camera: John Seale. Editor: Richard Francis-Bruce. Music: James Horner. In Technicolor, Panavision widescreen. Release date: June 21, 2000. MPAA Rating: PG-13. Running time: 129 Min.
Cast: George Clooney, Mark Wahlberg, John C. Reilly, Diane Lane, William Fichtner, John Hawkes, Allen Payne, Mary Elizabeth Mastrantonio, Karen Allen, Cherry Jones, Bob Gunton.

PERSONALS

A The Personals Co. production. (International sales: Personals, L.A.) Producers: J. Boyce Harman Jr., Gerrit Van Der Meer. Executive producers: Harman, Van Der Meer, Jody Milano. Director/Screenplay: Mike Sargent. Camera: Giselle Chamma. Editor: Jack Haigis. Music: Bread & Butter. In color. Release date: Oct. 16, 1999. Running time: 92 Min.
Cast: Malik Yoba, Stacey Dash, Monteria Ivey, Rhoda Ross Kendrick, Sheryl Lee Ralph, Jim Gaffigan, Rosalyn Coleman, Delilah Cotto, Angela Bullock, Joe Susannah Lee, Dreena DeNiro.

THE PHOTOGRAPHER

A Photographer Co. presentation. Producers: Peter O. Almond, Chris Moore, Jeremy Stein. Co-producer: Per Melita. Director/Screenplay: Jeremy Stein. Camera: Vanja Cernjul. Editor: Sylvia Waliga. Music: Andrew Hollander. In Duart color. Release date: Apr. 15, 2000. Running time: 90 Min.
Cast: Reg Rogers, Rob Campbell, Chris Bauer, Kristen Wilson, Maggie Gyllenhaal, Tom Noonan, Mary Alice, Tina Holmes, Anthony Michael Hall, John Heard, Marisa Berenson.

PIGEONHOLED

An Eclipse Pictures production. Producer: Tripp Swanhaus. Executive producers: Carder Stout, William McCutcheon, Joe McSpadden. Director: Michael Swanhaus. Screenplay: Michael and Tripp Swanhaus, Luke McMullen. Camera: Kramer Morgenthau. Editor: Stephanie Sterner. Music: Joseph Arther. In color. Release date: Oct. 28, 1999. Running time: 79 Min.
Cast: Justin Pierce, Allison Folland, Galaxy Craze, Tom Lock, Andrea Ciannavei, Jon Abrahams, Chris Noth, Rosanna Arquette.

PINK PUMPKINS AT DAWN

Producer: Per Jorgen Ostby. Director/Screenplay: Rick Onorato. Camera: Alex Wakeford. Editor: Andrew Bullas. Music: Kim Halliday. Release date: Jan. 19, 2000. Running time: 88 Min.
Cast: Chris Gunn, Dominique Debroux, Robert Brown, John Stonehill, Rick Onorato, Jeb Eastman, Glory Gallo.

PITCH BLACK

A USA Films release of a Gramercy Pictures presentation of an Interscope Communication production. Producer: Tom Engelman. Executive producers: Ted Field Scott Kroopf, Anthony Winley. Director: David Twohy. Screenplay: Jim Wheat, Ken Wheat, Twohy, based on a story by Jim and Ken Wheat. Camera: David Eggby. Editor: Rick Shaine. Music: Graeme Revell. In Atlab QLD color. Release date: Jan. 8, 2000. MPAA Rating: R. Running time: 108 Min.
Cast: Radha Mitchell, Vin Diesel, Cole Hauser, Lewis Fitz-Gerald, Claudia Black, Rhiana Griffith, John Moore, Simon Burke.

THE POET AND THE CON

A Poet Prods. presentation. Producer/Director/Screenplay/Editor: Eric Trules. Camera: Arnie Sirlan. Music: Ron Sures. In B&W and color. Release date: Sept. 13, 1999. Running time: 78 Min. Documentary.

POLES APART

A Lead Dog Prods. presentation. Producer/Director: Greg Stiever. Screenplay: Chris Jones. Camera: Bill Strohm, Mike Laumann, John Wahatton. Editors: Stiever, Kathleen Laughlin. Music: Paul Hartwig. Video. Release date: July 8, 2000. Running time: 86 Min. Documentary.
With Ann Bancroft, Sunniva Sorby, Anne Dal Vera, Sue Giller. Narrator: Louise Woehrle.

POLLOCK

A Sony Pictures Classics release of a Brant-Allen production in association with Zeke Films, Ed Harris, Fred Berner Films. (International sales: Alliance Atlantis Communications, Toronto.) Producer: Fred Berner, Ed Harris, Jon Kilik. Executive producers: Peter M. Brant, Joseph Allen. Co-producer: Cecilia Kate Roque. Director: Ed Harris. Screenplay: Barbara Turner, Susan J. Emshwiller, based on the book "Jackson Pollock: An American Saga," by Steven Naifeh, Gregory White Smith. Camera: Lisa Rinzler. Editor: Kathryn Himoff. Music: Jeff Beal. In color. Release date: Sept. 6, 2000. Running time: 122 Min.
Cast: Ed Harris, Marcia Gay Harden, Amy Madigan, Jennifer Connelly, Jeffrey Tambor, Bud Cort, John Heard, Val Kilmer.

POOR WHITE TRASH

A Kingsize Entertainment presentation. Producers: Mark Roberts, Lorena David. Executive producer: Michael Lawrence. Co-producer: Justin Conley. Director/Screenplay: Michael Addis. Camera: Peter Kowalski. Editor: Tom McArdle. Music: Tree Adams. In FotoKem color. Release date: June 18, 2000. Running time: 85 Min.
Cast: Sean Young, William Devane, Jason London, Tony Denman, Jacob Tierney, Jamie Pressly, M. Emmet Walsh, Tim Kazurinsky.

POST CONCUSSION

A Daniel D. Yoon (Toronto) production. Co-producer: Destry Miller. Director/Screenplay/Editor: Daniel Yoon, from a story by Jean Yoon. Camera: Yoon. Music: Eric Macris. In color, 16mm. Release date: Oct. 9, 1999. Running time: 80 Min.
Cast: Daniel Yoon, Jennifer Welch, Michael Hohmeyer, Niloufar Talebi, C.B. Yoon, Kristy Bright, Felecia Faulkner, Dr. Lester Luz.

PRESTON TYLK

A Next Generation (Burbank) production, in association with Cutting Edge Entertainment. Producers: James Frey, Dan Glasser, Roni Eguia. Executive producers: Brian Sullivan, Kevin Morris. Co-producers: Marty Cohen, Lisa Hope. Director/Screenplay: Jon Bokenkamp. Camera: Joey Forsyte. Editor: Ann Truelove. Music: Kurt Kuenne. In color. Release date: June 6, 2000. Running time: 93 Min.
Cast: Luke Wilson, Norman Reedus, Dennis Farina, Mili Avital, Vincent kartheiser, T.J. Thyne, Larry Boothby.

PRICE OF GLORY

A New Line Cinema release of an Esparza-Katz production in association with Arthur E. Friedman Prods. Producers: Moctesuma Esparza, Robert Katz, Arthur Friedman. Executive producers: Carolyn Manetti, Stephanie Striegel, Loretha Jones. Co-executive producers: Morris Ruskin, Laurie Wagman. Director: Carlos Avila. Screenplay: Phil Berger. Camera: Affonso Beato. Editor/Music supervisor: Margaret Guerra Rogers. In Deluxe color. Release date: Mar. 7, 2000. MPAA Rating PG-13. Running time: 118 Min.
Cast: Jimmy Smits, Jon Seda, Clifton Collins Jr., Maria del Mar, Sal Lopez, Louis Mandylor, Danielle Camastra, Ernesto Hernandez, Paul Rodriguez, Ron Perlman.

PRIDE AND PERIL

A Paradiddle Pictures production. Producer: Tony Mortillaro. Executive producers: Tony L. Della Ripa, Mortillaro. Director/Screenplay: Tony Mortillaro. Camera: F. Smith Martin. Editor: David Dill. Music: Pro Music. In color, high-definition video. Release date: Apr. 29, 2000. Running time: 98 Min.
Cast: Bernie Sparago, Catherine McGoohan, Brian Whitman, Tony Mortillaro, James O'Leary, Heather McClurg, Sparkle, Sofia Milos.

THE PRIME GIG

A Fine Line release of an Independent Pictures production. Producers: Cary Woods, Gina Mingacci, Elliot Lewis Rosenblatt. Co-producer: William Wheeler. Director: Gregory Mosher. Screenplay: William Wheeler. Camera: John A. Alonzo. Editor: James Kwei. Music: David Robbins. In CFI color. Release date: Sept.1, 2000. Running time: 96 Min.
Cast: Vince Vaughn, Julia Ormond, Ed Harris, Rory Cochrane, Wallace Shawn, George Wendt, Stephen Tobolowsky, Jeannetta Arnette, Shishir Kurup, Harper Roisman, Romany Malco Jr., Brian George, Amber Benson.

PSYCHO BEACH PARTY

A Strand/New Oz and Red Horse Films presentation. Producers: Virginia Biddle, Jon Gerrans, Marcus Hu, Victor Smyris. Executive producer: John Hall. Director: Robert Lee King. Screenplay: Charles Busch, based on his play. Camera: Arturo Smith. Editor: Suzanne Hines. Music: Ben Vaughn. In color. Release date: Jan. 23, 2000. Running time: 95 Min.
Cast: Lauren Ambrose, Thomas Gibson, Nicholas Brendon, Kimberly Davies, Matt Keeslar, Charles Busch, Beth Broderick, Danni Wheeler, Nick Cornish, Andrew Levitas, Amy Adams.

PUNKS

An E2 Filmworks presentation of a Tall Skinny Black Boy production. Producers: Patrik-Ian Polk, Tracy E. Edmonds, Michael McQuarn. Executive producer: Kenneth "Babyface" Edmonds. Co-producer: Robi Reed-Humes, Doran Reed. In color. Release date: Jan. 27, 2000. Running time: 104 Min.
Cast: Seth Gilliam, Dwight Ewell, Rockmond Dunbar, Jazzmun, Renoly Santiago, Loretta Devine, Vanessa Williams, Devon O'Dessa.

QUANTUM PROJECT

A SightSound.com and Metafilmics production. Producers: Stephen Simon, Barnet Bain. Executive producer: Scott Sander. Director: Eugenio Zanetti. Screenplay: David Aaron Cohen. Camera: Robert Primes. Editor: Jay Nelson. Music: Emilio Kauderer. In color. Release date: May 4, 2000. Running time: 32 Min.
Cast: Stephen Dorff, Fay Masterson, John Cleese, Russell Brown, Wendy Worthington.

QUEEN: THE MAKING OF AN AMERICAN BEAUTY

An Anima Prods. presentation. Producer/Director: Mimi Riley. Camera: David Smith. Editor: Mayin Lo. Music: Jimmy Rip. In color, video. Release date: July 9, 2000. Running time: 91 Min. Documentary.
With: Angela McCulley, Tara Watson, Joe Wilmouth, Jack Newsom, Mike Graham.

QUILLS

A 20th Century Fox release of a Fox Searchlight Pictures presentation of an Industry Entertainment/A Walrus & Associates Production in association with Hollywood Partners. Producers: Julia Chasman, Nick Wechsler, Peter Kaufman. Executive producers: Des McAnuff, Sandra Schulberg, Rudulf Wiesmeier. Co-producer: Mark Huffam. Director: Philip Kaufman. Screenplay: Doug Wright, based on his play. Camera: Rogier Stoffers. Editor: Peter Boyle. Music: Stephen Warbeck. In Deluxe color. Release date: Sept. 2, 2000. MPAA Rating: R. Running time: 123 Min.

Cast: Geoffrey Rush, Kate Winslet, Joaquin Phoenix, Michael Caine, Billie Whitelaw, Patrick Malahide, Amelia Warner, Jane Menelaus.

RANDOM HEARTS

A Sony Pictures Entertainment release of a Columbia Pictures presentation of a Rastar/Mirage Enterprises production. Producers: Sydney Pollack, Marykay Powell. Executive producers: Ronald L. Schwary, Warren Adler. Director: Sydney Pollack. Screenplay: Kurt Luedtke, adaptation by Darryl Ponicsan, based on the novel by Warren Adler. Camera: Philippe Rousselot. Editor: William Steinkamp. Music: Dave Grusin. In Deluxe color. Release date: Sept. 23, 1999. MPAA Rating: R. Running time: 133 Min.

Cast: Harrison Ford, Kristin Scott Thomas, Charles S. Dutton, Bonnie Hunt, Dennis Haysbert, Sydney Pollack, Richard Jenkins, Paul Guilfoyle, Susanna Thompson, Peter Coyote.

RATED X

A Showtime presentation of a District production. Producers: Dick Berg, Allan Marcil. Co-producer: Lisa Niedenthal. Director: Emilio Estevez. Screenplay: Norman snider, Anne Meredith, David Hollander, based on the book "X-Rated: The Mitchell Brothers, a True Story of Sex, Money and Death" by David McCumber. Camera: Paul Arossy. Editor: Craig Bassett. Music: Tyler Bates. In Deluxe color. Release date: Jan. 25, 2000. Running time: 115 Min.

Cast: Charlie Sheen, Emilio Estevez, Rafer Weigel. Tracy Hutson, Megan Ward, Terry O'Quinn, Danielle Brett, Peter Bogdanovich.

RATS

A Zoo Prods. presentation. Producer: Tracy M. Cones. Executive producer: James M. Felter. Director/Screenplay: James M. Felter. Camera: Felter. Editors: Felter, Tracy M. Cones. Music: Tom Barrick. In color. Release date: Sept. 17, 1999. Running time: 74 Min. Documentary.

READY TO RUMBLE

A Warner Bros. release, presented in association with Bel-Air Entertainment, of an Outlaw production in association with Tollin/Robbins Prods. Producer: Bobby Newmyer, Jeffrey Silver. Executive producers: Steven Reuther, Mike Tollin. Co-producers: Herbert W. Gains, Scott Strauss, John Gatins. Director: Brian Robbins. Screenplay: Steven Brill, based on World Championship Wrestling characters. Camera: Clark Mathis. Editors: Ned Bastille, Cindy Mollo. Music: George S. Clinton. In Technicolor. Release date: Apr. 4, 2000. MPAA Rating: PG-13. Running time: 107 Min.

Cast: David Arquette, Oliver Platt, Scott Caan, Bill Goldberg, Rose McGowan, Richard Lineback, Joe Pantoliano, Martin Landau.

REBELS WITH A CAUSE

A Shire Films (Los Gatos, Calif.) production. Producer/Director/Screenplay/Editor: Helen Garvey. Camera: Emiko Omori. Associate producer: Robert Pardun. Release date: June 3, 2000. Running time: 110 Min. Documentary.

With: Tom Hayden, Cathy Wilkerson, Todd Gitlin, Carl Ogelsby, Junius Williams, Juan Gonzales, Robert Pardun, Elizabeth Stanley.

RED DIRT

A Sweet Tea production. Producer: Cyril Bijaoui. Director/Screenplay: Tag Purvis. Camera: Theodore Cohen. Editor: Nikko Tsiotsias. Music: Nathan Barr. In Duart color. Release date: Apr. 17, 2000. Running time: 107 Min.

Cast: Karen Black, Dan Montgomery, Aleksa Palladino, Walton Goggins.

RED INK

A Krescent Films production. Producer: Cyndi Johnson. Executive producer: Stephen Allen. Director: Jerry A. Henry. Screenplay: Stephen Allen. Camera: John Snavely. Editor: Snavely. Music: Mark Brown. In color. Release date: Feb. 27, 2000. Running time: 103 Min.

Cast: Davi Jay, Clarence Whitmore, Diego Villareal Garcia, Errol Wilks, Deborah Flowers, David Parker, Lew Temple, David Hickox.

RED RAIN

A Lola Films production. Producer/Director: Laura Plotkin. Camera: Caitlin Manning. Editor: Gabriel Rhodes. Music: E.J. Sharpe, John Birdsong. In color, video. Release date: June 20, 2000. Running time: 60 Min. Documentary.

REINDEER GAMES

A Dimension Films release of a Marty Katz production. Producers: Katz, Bob Weinstein, Chris Moore. Executive producers: Harvey Weinstein, Cary Granat, Andrew Rona. Co-producers: B. Casey Grant, Mark Indig. Director: John Frankenheimer. Screenplay: Ehren Kruger. Camera: Alan Caso. Editors: Tony Gibbs, Michael Kahn. Music: Alan Silverstri. In Deluxe color, Panavision widescreen. Release date: Feb. 18, 2000. MPAA Rating: R. Running time: 104 Min.

Cast: Ben Affleck, Gary Sinise, Charlize Theron, Dennis Farina, James Frain, Donal Logue, Danny Trejo, Isaac Hayes.

RENDEZVOUS IN SAMARKAND

A Samarkand Pictures production. Producer: Tim Bridwell. Supervising producer: Lee Beckett. Director/Screenplay: Tim Bridwell. Camera: Jan Maliszewski. Editor: George Chiochios. Music: Hassan Hakmoun. In color. Release date: Oct. 13, 1999. Running time: 100 Min.

Cast: John Littlefield, Marie Ravel, Tsuyu Shimizu, Miho Mikaido, Lyes Salem.

THE REPLACEMENTS

A Warner Bros. release of a Bel Air Entertainment presentation of a Dylan Sellers production. Producer: Dylan Sellers. Executive producers: Erwin Stoff, Jeffrey Chernov, Steven Reuther. Director: Howard Deutch. Screenplay: Vince McKewin. Camera: Tak Fujimoto. Editors: Bud Smith, Seth Flaum. Music: John Debney. In Technicolor. Release date: July 29, 2000. MPAA Rating: PG-13. Running time: 118 Min.

Cast: Keanu Reeves, Gene Hackman, Orlando Jones, Jon Favreau, Brooke Langton, Rhys Ifans, Jack Warden, Faizon Love.

REQUIEM FOR A DREAM

An Artisan Entertainment release of an Artisan Entertainment and Thousand Words presentation. Producers: Eric Watson, Palmer West. Executive producers: Nick Wechsler, Beau Flynn, Stefan Simchowitz. Co-producers: Randy Simon, Jonah Smith, Scott Vogel, Scott Franklin. Co-executive producer: Ben Barenholtz. Director: Darren Aronofsky. Screenplay: Hubert Selby Jr., Aronofsky, based on the novel by Selby. Camera: Matthew Libatique. Editor: Jay Rabinowitz. Music: Clint Mansell. In Deluxe color. Release date: May 14, 2000. Running time: 102 Min.

Cast: Ellen Burstyn, Jared Leto, Jennifer Connelly, Marlon Wayans, Christopher McDonald, Louise Lasser, Keith David, Sean Gullette.

RETURN TO ME

An MGM release of a JLT production. Producer: Jennie Lew Tugend. Executive producers: C.O. Erickson, Melanie Greene. Director: Bonnie Hunt. Screenplay: Hunt, Don Lake, based on a story by Hunt, Lake, Andrew Stern, Samantha Goodman. Camera: Laszlo Kovacs. Editor: Garth Craven. Music: Nicholas Pike. In Deluxe color. Release date: Mar. 16, 2000. MPAA Rating: PG. Running time: 113 Min.

Cast: David Duchovny, Minnie Driver, Carroll O'Connor, Robert Loggia, Bonnie Hunt, David Alan Grier, Joely Richardson.

THE REUNION

A Good Medicine release of an Asylum Pictures presentation of an Esquire films production. Producers: Leticia Gomez, Paul Corvino, Dallas Hartnett. Executive producers: Joseph S. DiMarco, Sean P. Casey. Co-producers: Glenn Conte, Richard Lefkowitz, David Michaels, Jonathan Fisher. Director: Larry Eudene. Screenplay: Paul Corvino. Camera: Patrick Capone. Editors: Robert Fitzgerald, Glenn Conte. Music: Kristen Vogelsand. In color and B&W. Release date: Jan. 17, 2000. Running time: 84 Min.

Cast: Tim Devlin, Elizabeth P. McKay, Patrick Ferraro, Leila Sbatini, Jack Mulcahy, Mimi Langeland, Kristopher Medina, Edouard DeSoto.

RITUAL

A Gotham Entertainment in association with Raslan Co. of America presentation. Producers: Beth Hubbard, Michael Hubbard. Executive producer: Nick Raslan. Co-producers: David Raynr, Thomas D. Adelman. Director/Screenplay: Stanley Bennett Clay. Camera: M. David Mullen. Editors: Nicholas Elipoulos, Michael Schultz. Music: Curt Sobel, Lumelle Humes. In FotoKem color. Release date: July 13, 2000. Running time: 78 Min.

Cast: Clarence Williams III, Denise Nicholas, Shawn Michael Howard, Angelle Brooks, Gerrie Ellis.

RIVERS OF BABYLON

A Marian Urban/Alef Film & Media Group/Ceska Televize/Ateliery Zlin/Pokium/TV Markiza presentation. Producer: Marian Urban. Director: Vlado Balco. Screenplay: Peter Pistanek, Marian Urban, based on the novel by Pistanek. Camera: Martin Strba. Editor: Dusan Milko. Music: Jaroslav Filip. In color. Release date: Sept. 16, 1999. Running time: 102 Min.

Cast: Andrej Hryc, Ady Hajdu, Diana Morova, Barbara Kodetova.

ROAD DOGS

Producer: Dan Halperin. Director/Screenplay: Detdrich McClure. Camera: David Morrison. Editor: David Lindblum. In color. Release date: Feb. 28, 2000. Running time: 90 Min.

Cast: Glenn Plummer, Chris Spencer, J. Lamont Pope.

ROADS AND BRIDGES

Producers: Marc H. Glick, Abraham Lim. Executive producers: Robert Altman, Glick, Lim. Director/Screenplay/Editor: Abraham Lim. Camera: Robert Learner, Diego Quemada, Dennis Maloney. Music: Bradford Athey, Adam Gorgoni. In color. Release date: Apr. 16, 2000. Running time: 100 Min.

Cast: Gregory Sullivan, Abraham Lim, Matt Malloy, Soon-Tek Oh, Jim Akman, Emmet Brennan, Joe Michaelski.

THE ROAD TO EL DORADO

A DreamWorks Pictures release. Producers: Bonne Radford, Brooke Breton. Executive producer: Jeffrey Katzenberg. Co-executive producer: Bill Damaschke. Director: Eric "Bibo" Bergeron, Don Paul. Screenplay: Ted Elliott, Terry Rossio. Supervising editors: John Carnochan, Dan Molina. Editor: Vicki Hiatt. Music: Elton John. Lyrics: Time Rice. Score: Hans Zimmer, John Powell. In Technicolor. Release date: Mar. 28, 2000. MPAA Rating: PG. Running time: 89 Min. Animated.

Voices: Kevin Kline, Kenneth Branagh, Rosie Perez, Armand Assante, Edward James Olmos, Elton John.

ROAD TRIP

A DreamWorks Pictures production in association with the Montecito Picture Co. Producers: Daniel Goldberg, Joe Medjuck. Executive producers: Ivan Reitman, Tom Pollock. Director: Todd Phillips. Screenplay: Phillips, Scot Armstrong. Camera: Mark Irwin. Editor: Sheldon Kahn. Music: Mike Simpson. In Technicolor. Release date: Apr., 19, 2000. MPAA Rating: R. Running time: 91 Min.

Cast: Breckin Meyer, Seann William Scott, Amy Smart, Paulo Costanzo, D.J. Qualls, Rachel Blanchard, Anthony Rapp, Fred Ward.

ROBERT LOUIS STEVENSON'S THE SUICIDE CLUB

A New Concorde production. Producer: Roger Corman. Co-producers: Rachel Samuels, John Brady. Director: Rachel Samuels. Screenplay: Lev. L. Spiro, based on the story by Robert Louis Stevenson. Camera: Chris Manley. Editor: Bernadette Kelly. Music: Adrian Johnston. In FotoKem color. Release date: Jan. 21, 2000. Running time: 89 Min.

Cast: David Morrissey, Jonathan Pryce, Catherine Siggins, Paul Bettany, Neil Stuke.

ROCK OPERA

A Crashcam Cineproductions presentation. Producer: Barna Kantor. Executive producers: Bob Ray, Nicole Ray. Co-executive producers: Kantor, Tamas Kovacs, Kurtis D. Machler, Victor Soares. Director/Screenplay/Editor: Bob Ray. Camera: Jackson W. Saunders. Music: Kurtis D. Machler. In color video. Release date: Jan. 11, 2000. Running time: 90 Min.

Cast: Jerry Don Clark, Ted Jarrell, Chad Holt, Paul Wright, Luis Olmeda, Rob Gasper, Mike Guihan, Bob Ray.

ROMEO MUST DIE

A Warner Bros. release of a Silver Pictures production. Producers: Joel Silver, Jim Van Wyck. Executive producer: Dan Cracchiolo. Co-producer: Warren Carr. Director: Andrzej Bartkowiak. Screenplay: Eric Bernt, John Jarrell, story by Mitchell Kapner. Camera: Glen MacPherson, Editor: Derek G. Brechin. Music: Stanley Clarke, Timbaland. In Technicolor, Panavision widescreen. Release date: Mar. 14, 2000. MPAA Rating: R. Running time: 115 Min.

Cast: Jet Li, Aaliyah, Isaiah Washington, Russell Wong, DMX.

ROW YOUR BOAT

A Gullane Pictures presentation of a 49th Parallel Prods./Preferred Films/Water Street Pictures production. (International sales: Catalyst Distribution, Toronto.) Producers: Chip Duncan, Claudia Vianello, Hervey Kahn. Executive produers: Charles Reiner, Lindsay Marx, Jennifer Dewis. Co-executive producer: Charles Falzon. Co-producer: Karen Montgomery. Director/Screenplay: Sollace Mitchell. Camera: Zoltan David, Michael Barrow. Editor: Alex Albanese. Music: Mader. In Duart color. Release date: Apr. 4, 2000. Running time: 89 Min.

Cast: Jon Bon Jovi, Bai Ling, William Forsythe, Jill Hennessy, Peter Kwong, John Ventimiglia.

RULES OF ENGAGEMENT

A Paramount release presented in association with Seven Arts Pictures of a Richard D. Zanuck/Scott Rudin production. Producers: Zanuck, Rudin. Executive producers: Adam Schroeder, James Webb. Co-producer: Arne Schmidt. Director: William Friedkin. Screenplay: Stephen Gaghan, story by James Webb. Camera: Nicola Percorini, William Fraker. Editor: Augie Hess. Music: Mark Isham. In CFI color. Release date: Mar. 30, 2000. MPAA Rating: R. Running time: 128 Min.

Cast: Tommy Lee Jones, Samuel L. Jackson, Guy Pearce, Bruce Greenwood, Blair Underwood, Philip Baker Hall, Anne Archer, Ben Kingsley, Mark Feuerstein, Dale Dye.

RUM AND COKE

A Rum and Coke presentation of an Escobedo/Gherardi production. Producer: Charles Gherardi. Co-producer: Dick Fisher. Director/Screenplay/Editor: Maria Escobedo. Camera: Dick Fisher. Music: John Escobedo. In color. Release date: Feb. 25, 2000. Running time: 97 Min.

Cast: Diana Marquis, Juan Carlos Hernandez, Christopher Marazzo, Kevin A. King, Jacqueline Torres, Rosa Nino, Susana Crisan.

A RUMOR OF ANGELS

A CineTel Films production. (International sales: A Rumor of Angels, Inc., L.A.) Producers: Lisa Hansen, Paul Hertzberg, Peter O'Fallon. Executive producer: John Hamilton. Co-producers: John Paul Pettinato, Meg Liberman. Director: Peter O'Fallon. Screenplay: James Eric, Jamie Horton, O'Fallon, based on "Thy Son Liveth, Messages From a Soldier to His Mother" by Grace Duffie Boylan. Camera: Roy H. Wagner. Editor: Louise Rubacky. Music: Tim Simone. In color. Release date: Sept. 10, 2000. Running time: 106 Min.

Cast: Vanessa Redgrave, Ray Liotta, Catherine McCormack, Trevor Morgan, Ron Livingston, George Coe.

RUNNING FREE

A Sony Pictures Entertainment release of a Columbia Pictures presentation of a Reperage production. Producer: Jean-Jacques Annaud. Executive producers: Alisa Tager, Lloyd Phillips. Director: Sergei Bodrov. Screenplay: Jeanne Rosenberg, story by Jean-Jacques Annaud. Camera: Dan Laustsen. Editor: Ray Lovejoy. Music: Nicola Piovani. In Deluxe color, widescreen. Release date: May 15, 2000. MPAA Rating: G. Running time: 81 Min.

Cast: Chase Moore, Jan Decleir, Maria Geelbooi, Lukas Haas, Arie Cerveen.

RUNNING ON THE SUN: THE BADWATER 135

A Mel Stuart presentation in association with Galaxy Entertainment, with the participation of Qualcomm. Producers: Stuart, Leland Hammerschmitt. Executive producers: Richard Houghton, Kirk Friedman. Co-producer: Chris Wiser. Director: Mel Stuart. Camera: John Malvino, Kevin O'Brien, David West. Editor: Greg Byers. Music: Michel Colombier. In color. Release date: Aug. 4, 2000. Running time: 98 Min. Documentary.

THE ST. FRANCISVILLE EXPERIMENT

A Trimark Pictures release. Producers: Dana Scanlan, Paul Salamoff. Camera: Tim Baldini. Editors: Tom Vater, Jeff Bradley. Video. Release date: Apr. 15, 2000. Running time: 79 Min.

Cast: Tim Baldini, Madison Charap, Ryan Larson, Paul Palmer.

SCARY MOVIE

A Dimension Pictures release of a Wayans Bros. Entertainment production in association with Gold-Miller and Brad Grey Pictures. Producer: Eric L. Gold, Lee R. Mayes. Executive producers: Brad Grey, Peter Safran, Bo Zenga, Bob Weinstein, Harvey Weinstein, Cary Granat, Peter Schwerin. Co-producer: Lisa Suzanne Blum. Director: Keenen Ivory Wayans. Screenplay: Shawn Wayans, Marlon Wayans, Buddy Johnson, Phil Beauman, Jason Friedberg, Aaron Seltzer. Camera: Francis Kenny. Editor: Mark Helfrich. Music: David Kitay. In Deluxe color. Release date: June 27, 2000. MPAA Rating: R. Running time: 88 Min.

Cast: Shawn Wayans, Marlon Wayans, Cheri Oteri, Shannon Elizabeth, Anna Faris, Jon Abrahams, Lochlyn Munro.

SCOTTSBORO: AN AMERICAN TRAGEDY

A Social Media Prods. production in association with the American Experience. Producer/Director: Barak Goodman, Daniel Anker. Screenplay: Goodman. Camera: Buddy Squires. Editor: Jean Tsien. Music: Ed Bilous. In color. Release date: Jan. 28, 2000. Running time: 90 Min. Documentary.

Narrator: Andre Braugher.

SCREAM 3

A Dimension Films release of a Konrad Pictures production in association with Craven/Maddalena Films. Producers: Cathy Konrad, Kevin Williamson, Marianne Maddalena. Executive producers: Bob Weinstein, Harvey Weinstein, Cary Granat, Andrew Rona. Co-executive producer: Stuart M. Besser. Co-producers: Dan Arredondo, Dixie J. Capp, Julie Plec. Director: Wes Craven. Screenplay: Ehren Kruger, based on characters created by Kevin Williamson. Camera: Peter Deming. Editor: Patrick Lussier. Music: Marco Beltrami. In FotoKem color. Release date: Feb. 2, 2000. MPAA Rating: R. Running time: 116 Min.

Cast: David Arquette, Neve Campbell, Courteney Cox Arquette, Patrick Dempsey, Scott Foley, Lance Henriksen, Matt Keeslar, Jenny McCarthy, Emily Mortimer, Parker Posey.

SCREWED

A Universal Pictures release of a Robert Simonds/Brad Grey production. Producer: Robert Simonds. Executive producers: Brad Grey, Ray Reo. Co-producers: Fitch Cady, Julia Dray. Directors/Screenplay: Scott Alexander, Larry Karaszewski. Camera: Robert Brinkman. Editor: Michael Jablow. In Deluxe color. Release date: May 12, 2000. MPAA Rating: PG-13. Running time: 81 Min.

Cast: Norm Macdonald, Dave Chappelle, Elaine Stritch, Danny DeVito, Daniel Benzali, Sherman Hemsley, Sarah Silverman.

SEED

A Working Pictures production. Producers: Bobby Sheehan, Sara Feldmann Sheehan, Alex Albanese. Director: Bobby Sheehan. Editor: Alex Albanese. Music: Joel Goodman. In color. Release date: Apr. 14, 2000. Running time: 75 Min.

Cast: John Michael Bolger, Chuck Negron.

SEVEN GIRLFRIENDS

A White Dwarf Prods./J. Todd Harris/Barry Opper production. Producers: Paul Lazarus, Harris, Opper. Executive producer: Steven Lazarus. Co-producer: George Conda. Director: Paul Lazarus. Screenplay: Stephen Gregg, based on a story by Lazarus, Gregg. Camera: Don E. FauntLeRoy. Editor: Ed Marx. Music: Christopher Tyng. In color. Release date: Feb. 21, 2000. Running time: 99 Min.

Cast: Tim Daly, Olivia D'Abo, Jami Gertz, Melora Hardin, Laura Leighton, Elizabeth Pena, Mimi Rogers, Katy Selverstone.

75 DEGREES IN JULY

A Stockyard Films presentation. Producers: Hyatt Bass, Jeanne O'Brien. Director/Screenplay: Hyatt Bass. Camera: Michael Barrett. Editor: Thom Zimny. Original music: Steven Edwards. In color. Release date: Aug. 26, 2000. Running time: 86 Min.

Cast: Shirley Knight, William Moses, Karen Sillas, Heidi Swedberg, Harris Yulin.

SHADOW HOURS

A Newmark Films presentation in association with 5150 Prods. Producers: Peter McAlevey, Isaac H. Eaton. Executive producer: Michael Thomas Shannon. Co-producers: Balthazar Getty, Shon Greenblatt. Co-executive producer: Andrea Mia. Director/Screenplay: Isaac H. Eaton. Camera: Frank Byers. Editors: Annamaria Szanto, Clayton Halsey, Bill Yarhaus. Music: Brian Tyler. In CFI color. Release date: Jan. 23,2000. Running time: 92 Min.

Cast: Balthazar Getty, Peter Weller, Rebecca Gayheart, Peter Greene, Michael Dorn, Richard Moll, Johnny Whitworth, Corin Nemec.

SHAFT

A Paramount Pictures release of a Scott Rudin/New Deal production. Producers: Scott Rudin, John Singleton. Executive producers: Adam Schroeder, Paul Hall, Steve Nicolaides. Co-producer: Eric Steel. Directors: John Singleton, Shane Salerno, story by Singleton, Salerno, based on the novel by Ernest Tidyman. Camera; Donald E. Thorin. Editors; John Bloom, Antonia Van Drimmelen. Music: David Arnold, Isaac Hayes. In Deluxe color, Panavision widescreen. Release date: July 7, 2000. MPAA Rating: R. Running time: 98 Min.
Cast: Samuel L. Jackson, Vanessa Williams, Jeffrey Wright, Christian Bale, Busta Rhymes, Dan Hedaya, Toni Collette, Richard Roundtree, Ruben Santiago-Hudson, Josef Sommer.

SHANGHAI NOON

A Buena Vista release of a Touchstone Pictures and Spyglass Entertainment presentation of a Birnbaum/Barber production in association with Jackie Chan Films. Producers: Roger Birnbaum, Gary Barber, Jonathan Glickman. Executive producers: Jackie Chan, Willie Chan, Solon So. Co-producers: Ned Dowd, Jules Daly. Director: Tom Dey. Screenplay: Alfred Gough, Miles Millar. Camera: Dan Mindel. Editor: Richard Chew. In Technicolor, widescreen. Release date: May 16, 2000. MPAA Rating: PG-13. Running time: 110 Min.
Cast: Jackie Chan, Owen Wilson, Lucy Liu, Brandon Merrill, Roger Yuan, Xander Berkeley, Rong Guang Ye, Chi Ya Hi, Eric Chi Cheng Chen, Walton Goggins, P. Adrien Dorval, Rafael Baez, Stacy Grant.

SHOW ME THE ALIENS!

A No More Rice and Beans Productions presentation. (International sales: No More Rice and Beans, New York.) Producers: Steve Hermanos, Devin Crowley. Co-producer: Philip Farha. Executive producer: Jon Miles. Director/Screenplay: Devin Crowley, based on a story by Crowley, Steve Hermanos, Kirk Davis. Additional writing: Hermanos, Davis. Camera: John Kovel. Editor: Nelson Ryland. In color. Release date: May 16, 2000. Running time: 79 Min.
Cast: Devin Crowley, Aaron Rudelson, Kim Reinle, Denny Siegel, Misty Greer, Lorrel Manning, Andy Smart, Richard Pohlers.

SIEGFRIED & ROY: THE MAGIC BOX

An Imax Ltd. release of an L-Squared Entertainment production in association with Lexington Road Prods. and Foundry Film Partners. Producer: Michael Lewis. Executive producers: Lou Gonda, Jon Ein, Robert Greenhut, Bernie Yuman. Co-producer: Jini Dayaneni. Director: Brett Leonard. Screenplay: Lyn Vaus, Leonard. Camera: Sean MacLeod Phillips. Editor: Jonathan P. Shaw. Music: Alan Silverstri. In color, Imax 3-D. Release date: Oct. 13, 1999. Running time: 50 Min.
Cast: Siegfried Fischbacher, Roy Uwe, Ludwig Horn, John Summers, Andrew Dunlap, Dillon McEwin, Cameron Alexander.
Narrator: Anthony Hopkins.

A SIGN FROM GOD

An Over a Rope production. Producers: Greg Watkins, Caveh Zahedi. Executive producer: Richard Clark. Director/Screenplay: Greg Watkins. Camera: Jennifer Jew. Editor: Caveh Zahedi. Music: Jonathan Richman, Tommy Larkins. In color. Release date: Mar. 9, 2000. Running time: 71 Min.
Cast: Laura Macias, Caveh Zahedi, Celia Gamburg, Francesca Schneider, Henry Rosenthal, Moe Ghassemi.

THE SIMIAN LINE

An S.L. production in association with Da Wa movies. Producers: Linda Yellen, Robert Renfield. Executive producers: Montel Williams, Daniel Bennett, Michael Escott. Co-producer: Jordan Walker-Pearlman. Camera: David Bridges. Editor: Bob Jorissen. Music: Patrick Seymour. In color. Release date: Jan. 15, 2000. Running time: 106 min.
Cast: Lynn Redgrave, Jamey Sheridan, Cindy Crawford, Samantha Mathis, Dylan Bruno, Monica Keena, Harry Connick Jr., Tyne Daly, William Hurt, Jeremy Zelig, Eric Stoltz.

THE SINISTER SAGA OF MAKING "THE STUNT MAN"

A Bart Pierce and Richard Rush production for the Film Organization. Producers: Pierce, Rush. Director/Screenplay: Richard Rush. Camera: Bruce Schermer. Editor: Bart Pierce. Video. Release date: Feb. 21, 2000. Running time: 112 Min. Documentary.
With: Peter O'Toole, Steve Railsback, Barbara Hershey, Chuck Bail, Sharon Farrell, Mario Tosi, Nelson Tyler.
Narrator: Richard Rush

SIX DAYS IN ROSWELL

A Benevolent Authority production in association with Neo Art and Logic. Producer: Roger Nygard. Executive producers: Hiroshi Sano, Aki Komine. Joel Soisson, Michael Leachy, W.K. Border. Director: Tomothy B. Johnson. Camera: David Doyle, Adam Olson. Editor: Rogher Nygard. Music: Walter Werzowa, Jimmie Wood, J.J. Holiday, Billy Sullivan. In color. Release date: Oct. 14, 1999. Running time: 80 Min. Documentary
With: Richard Kronfeld, Dennis Balthaser, Bob Barnes, Deon Crosby, Stanton T. Friedman, Peter Gersten, Budd Hopkins, Debra L. Lindemann, Donald R. Schmitt, Yvonne Smith, Whitley Streiber. .

SKIPPED PARTS

A Trimark presentation of a Skipped Parts production. Producers: Shelby Stone, Alison Dickey, Sharon Oreck. Executive producers: Mark Amin, Tamra Davis, Mike Elliot, Co-producers: Jennifer Jason Leigh, Gordon McLennan, Robin Schorr, Peter Marshall. Director: Tamra Davis. Screenplay: Tim Sandlin, based on his novel. Camera: Claudio Rocha. Editor: Luis Colina. Music: Stewart Copeland. In color. Release date: June 6, 2000. Running time: 93 Min.
Cast: Jennifer Jason Leigh, Bug Hall, Mischa Barton, Peggy Lipton, Brad Renfro, Michael Greyeyes, Alison Pill, Angela Featherstone, Drew Barrymore, R. Lee Ermey, Gerald Lenton-Young.

THE SKULLS

A Universal release of a Universal Pictures production in association with Original Film/Newmarket Capital Group. Producers: Neal H. Moritz, John Pogue. Executive producers: William Tyrer, Chris J. Ball, Bruce Mellon. Co-producer: Fred Caruso. Director: Rob Cohen. Screenplay: John Pogue. Camera: Shane Hurlbut. Editor: Peter Amundson. Music: Randy Edelman. In Deluxe color. Release date: Mar. 29, 2000. MPAA Rating: PG-13. Running time: 106 Min.
Cast: Joshua Jackson, Paul Walker, Hill Harper, Leslie Bibb, Christopher McDonald, Steve Harris, Craig T. Nelson.

SLEEPY HOLLOW

A Paramount release of a Paramount and Mandalay Pictures presentation of a Scott Rudin/American Zoetrope production. Producers: Rudin, Adam Schroeder. Executive producers: Francis Ford Coppola, Larry Franco. Co-producer: Kevin Yagher. Director: Tim Burton. Screenplay: Andrew Kevin Walker, Screen story by Kevin Yagher, Walker, based on the story "The Legend of Sleepy Hollow" by Washington Irving. Camrera: Emmanuel Lubezki. Editor: Chris Lebenzon. Music: Danny Elfman. In Deluxe color. Release date: Nov. 1, 1999. MPAA Rating: R. Running time: 105 Min.
Cast: Johnny Depp, Christina Ricci, Miranda Richardson, Michael Gambon, Casper Van Dien, Jeffrey Jones, Christopher Lee, Richard Griffiths, Ian McDiarmid, Michael Gough, Christopher Walken.

SMALL TIME CROOKS

A DreamWorks release of a Sweetland Films presentation of a Jean Doumanian production. Producer: Doumanian. Executive producer: J.E. Beaucaire. Co-producer: Helen Robin. Co-executive producers: Jack Rollins, Charles H. Joffe, Letty Aronson. Director/Screenplay: Woody Allen. Camera: Zhao Fei. Editor: Alisa Lepselter. In Duart color. Release date: May 3, 2000. MPAA Rating: PG. Running time: 94 Min.
Cast: Woody Allen, Tracey Ullman, Tony Darrow, Hugh Grant, George Grizzard, Jon Lovitz, Elaine May, Michael Rapaport, Elaine Stritch.

SMOKE AND MIRRORS: A HISTORY OF DENIAL

A Rosenzweig Co. production, in association with the American Lung Assn. Producers: Torrie Rosenzweig, Elise Pearlstein. Executive producer: Bonnie Rosenzweig. Director: Torrie Rosenzweig. Screenplay: Rosenzweig, Elise Pearlstein. Camera: Shana Hagan, John Hessler, Paul Young, David Zapatka. Editor: Brad Byers. Music: Murielle Hamilton. In color. 16mm. Release date: Jan. 11, 2000. Running time: 74 Min. Documentary.
Narrator: Sharon Gless.

THE SMOKERS

An Intl. Prod. Co. production. Producer: Nicholas Loeb. Executive producers: Quincy Jones, Michael Niemtzow, Ted Roesgen. Director/Screenplay: Christina Peters. Camera: J.B. Lechtinger. Editor: Elias Chalhub. Music: Lawrence Gingold. In color. Release date: Mar. 5, 2000. Running time: 97 Min.
Cast: Dominque Swain, Busy Phillipps, Keri Lynn Pratt, Nicholas Loeb, Oliver Hudson, Thora Birch.

SNOW DAY

A Paramount release of a Nickelodeon Movies presentation. Producers: Albie Hecht, Julia Pistor. Executive producer: Raymond Wagner. Co-producers: Grace Gilroy, Will McRobb, Chris Viscardi. Director: Chris Koch. Screenplay: Will McRobb, Chris Viscardi. Camera: Robbie Greenberg. Editor: David Finfer. Music: Steve Bartek. In Deluxe color. Release date: Feb. 3, 2000. MPAA Rating: PG. Running time: 89 Min.
Cast: Chris Elliott, Mark Webber, Jean Smart, Schuyler Fisk, Iggy Pop, Pam Grier, Chevy Chase, John Schneider, Zena Grey.

SNOW DAYS

A Girl and Boy Prods. presentation of a Marcus Bros. production. Producer: Kipp Marcus. Executive producers: Donny Epstein, Yeeshai Gross. Director: Adam Marcus. Screenplay: Kipp Marcus. Camera: Ben Weinstein. Editor: Joe Klotz. Music: Sean McCourt. In Duart color. Release date: Oct. 24, 1999. Running time: 90 Min.
Cast: Kipp Marcus, Alice Dylan, Bernadette Peters, Henry Simmons, Miriam Shor, Judith Malina, Larry Pine, Debra Sullivan.

SOFT TOILET SEATS

A Phaedra Cinema release of a Shirley Craig production. Producer: Shirley Craig. Executive producer: Dave Stauffacher. Director/Screenplay: Tina Valinsky. Camera: Stephen Timberlake. Editors: Lynel Moore Cioffi, Nancy Rosenblum, John Refoua, Robbie Adler. Music: Louis Durra, Jeffrey R. Gund. In FotoKem color. Release date: Mar. 1, 2000. MPAA Rating: R. Running time: 112 Min.
Cast: David Alex Rosen, Alexa Jago, Sammi Davis, Jonathan Aube, Michael Greene.

SOLID ONES

An Artists' Colony production in association with S&J Entertainment. Producers: Lloyd A. Silverman, Brent Florence. Director/Screenplay: Brent Florence. Camera: Matthew Davis. Editor: Sam Bauer. Music: Todd Hannigan. In color, digital. Release date: Mar. 5, 2000. Running time: 95 Min.

Cast: Brent Florence, Josh Holland, Tracy Zahoryin, Christian Leffler, Michael Trucco, Tava Smiley, Kenny Luper, June Allyson.

SONGCATCHER

A Rigas Entertainment presentation, in association with the Independent Film Project, of an ErgoArts production. Producers: Ellen Rigas Venetis, Richard Miller. Executive producers: Jonathan Sehring, Caroline Kaplan. Co-producers: Jennifer Roth, Wendy Sax. Director/Screenplay: Maggie Greenwald. Camera: Enrique Chediak. Editor: Keith Reamer. Music: David Mansfield. In color. Release date: Jan. 25, 2000. Running time: 112 Min.

Cast: Janet McTeer, Aidan Quinn, Pat Carroll, Jane Adams, Gregory Cook, Iris DeMent, Stephanie Roth Haberle, David Patrick Kelly, E. Katherine Kerr, Taj Mahal, Emmy Rossum, Muse Watson.

SORDID LIVES

A Del Shores production, in association with Daly/Harris & Davis Classics. Producers: Sharyn Lane, Victoria Alonso, Max CiVon. Director/Screenplay: Del Shores, based on his play. Camera: Max CiVon. Editor: Ed Max. Music: Geroge S. Clinton. In color, digital beta. Release date: June 5, 2000. Running time: 111 Min.

Cast: Bonnie Bedelia, Delta Burke, Beth Grant, Ann Walker, Leslie Jordan, Rosemary Alexander, Beau Bridges, Kirk Giger, Olivia Newton-John, Sarah Huntley, Newell Alexander, Earl H. Bullock.

SOUND AND FURY

An Aronson Film Associates production in association with Public Policy productions, Thirteen/WNET, Channel 4. Producer: Roger Weisberg. Director: Josh Aronson. Camera: Brian Danitz, Kenny Gronningsater, Mead Hunt, Gordy Waterman, Brett Wiley. Editor: Ann Collins. Music: Mark Suozzo. In color. Release date: Jan. 27, 2000. Running time: 77 Min. Documentary.

SPACE COWBOYS

A Warner Bros. release presented in association with Village Roadshow Pictures/Clipsal Films of a Malpaso and Mad Chance production. Producers: Clint Eastwood, Andrew Lazar. Executive producer: Tom Rooker. Director: Clint Eastwood. Screenplay: Ken Kaufman, Howard Klausner. Camera: Jack N. Green. Editor: Joel Cox. Music: Lennie Niehaus. In Technicolor, Panavision widescreen. Release date: July 25, 2000. MPAA Rating: PG-13. Running time: 129 Min.

Cast: Clint Eastwood, Tommy Lee Jones, Donald Sutherland, James Garmer, James Cromwell, Marcia Gay Harden, William Devane, Loren Dean, Courtney B. Vance, Barbara Babcock, Rade Sherbedgia.

THE SPECIALS

A Regent Entertainment release and presentation of a Mindfire Entertainment production in association with Brillstein/Grey Entertainment. Producers: Dan Bates, Mark A. Altman, Rick Mischel. Executive producers: Mark Gottwald, Ellie Gottwald. Co-executive producer: Peter Safran. Co-producers: James Gunn, Sean Gunn, Jamie Kennedy, Craig Mazin. Director: Craig Mazin. Screenplay: James Gunn. Camera: Eliot Rockett. Editor: Stephen Garrett. In FotoKem color. Release date: Sept. 18, 2000. MPAA Rating: R. Running time: 82 Min.

Cast: Rob Lowe, Jamie Kennedy, Thomas Haden Church, Paget Brewster, Kelly Coffield, Judy Greer, James Gunn, Sean Gunn, Jordan Ladd, Mike Schwartz, Jim Zulevic, John Doe.

SPECTRES OF THE SPECTRUM

An Other City (San Francisco) production. Producer/Director/Screenplay: Craig Baldwin. Camera: Bill Daniel, others. Editor: Daniel. Music: John Watermann, Korla Pandit. In color, 16 mm. Release date: Sept. 25, 1999. Running time: 94 Min. Docu-Drama.

With: Sean Kilcoyne, Caroline Koebel, Beth Liseck.

SPENT

A Regent Entertainment release of a Trademark Entertainment presentation of a THF Pictures production. Producers: Rana Joy Glickman, Jordan Summers, Gil Cates Jr. Executive producers: Joe Cates, Jordan Zevon. Co-producer: Deborah Henderson. Director/Screenplay: Gil Cates Jr. Camera: Robert D. Tomer. Editor: Jonathan Cates. Music: Stan Ridgway. In FotoKem color. Release date: July 17, 2000. Running time: 91 Min.

Cast: Jason London, Charlie Spradling, Phill Lewis, Erin Beaux, James Parks, Richmond Arquette, Barbara Barrie, Gil Cates, Sr., Rain Phoenix, Margaret Cho.

SPRING FORWARD

An Independent Film Channel Prods. presentation of a C-Hundred Film Corp./cineBLAST! production. (International sales: Sloss Special Projects/IFC Films, New York.) Producer: Jim McKay, Gill Holland, Tom Gilroy, Paul Mezey. Executive producers: Jonathan Sehring, Caroline Kaplan, William Gilroy, Michael Stipe. Director/Screenplay: Tom Gilroy. Camera: Terry Stacey. Editor: James Lyons. Music: Hahn Rowe. In color. Release date: Jan. 23, 2000. Running time: 111 Min.

Cast: Ned Beatty, Liev Schreiber, Campbell Scott, Peri Gilpin, Bill Raymond, Catherine Kellner, Hallee Hirsh.

STANLEY'S GIG

A Left Hook Films and Lampedusa Films presentation. Producers: Justin Hogan, Todd Traina. Executive producers: Justin Lazard, Panos Nicolaou. Co-producer: Cameron McIntyre. Co-executive producer: Cathryn Jaymes. Director: Marc Lazard. Screenplay: Lazard, Gadi Dechter. Camera: John Rhode. Editor: Alan Roberts. Music: Frank Fitzpatrick. In FotoKem color. Release date: June 20, 2000. Running time: 92 Min.

Cast: William Sanderson, Marla Gibbs, Faye Dunaway, Steven Tobolowsky, Paul Benjamin, Kevin Jackson, Ian Whitcomb.

STATE AND MAIN

A Fine Line Features release and presentation, in association with Filmtown Entertainment, of a Green/Renzi production in association with El Dorado Pictures. (International sales: Filmtown Entertainment, Los Angeles.) Producer: Sarah Green. Executive producers: Jon Cornick, Alec Baldwin. Co-producers: Mark Ordesky, Rachel Horowitz, Alan Mruvka, Joseph Nittolo. Director/Screenplay: David Mamet. Camera: Oliver Stapleton. Editor: Barbara Tulliver. Music: Theodore Shapiro. In color. Release date: Aug. 26, 2000. Running time: 106 Min.

Cast: Alec Baldwin, Charles Durning, Philip Seymour Hoffman, Patti LuPone, William H. Macy, Sarah Jessica Parker, David Paymer, Rebecca Pidgeon, Julia Stiles, Ricky Jay, Jim Frangione.

STEAL THIS MOVIE

A Lions Gate Films release of a Lakeshore Intl. presentation of a Greenlight production in association with Ardent Films. Producers: Robert Greenwald, Jacobus Rose. Executive producers: Jon Avnet, Vincent D'Onofrio, Ken Christmas. Co-producers: Elizabeth Selzer Lang, Bradley H. Gordon. Director: Robert Greenwald. Screenplay: Bruce Graham. Camera: Denis Lenoir. Editor: Kimberly Ray. Music: Mader. In Deluxe color. Release date: Mar. 4, 2000. Running time: 111 Min.

Cast: Vincent D'Onofrio, Janeane Garofalo, Jeanne Tripplehorn, Kevin Pollak, Donal Logue, Kevin Corrigan, Alan Van Sprang, Troy Garity, Ingrid Veninger.

THE STERLING CHASE

A Weinberg Entertainment and Indyssey Entertainment presentation in association with Redwood Communications. Producers: Tanya Fenmore, Katrina S. Pavlos, Cynthia Perez-Brown. Executive producers: Ronald E. Weinberg, Vanessa Wingate. Co-producer: Robert Trehy. Co-executive producers: Milena Rimassa, Lucas E. Devenn. Director/Screenplay: Tanya Fenmore, story by Fenmore, Jeremy Dauber. Camera: David Bridges. Editors: David Codron, Edward R. Abroms. Music: Mark Adler. In color. Release date: Sept. 17, 1999. Running time: 92 Min.

Cast: Andrea Ferrell, John Livingston, Irene Ng, Jack Noseworthy, Devon Odessa, Sean Patrick Thomas, Nicholle Tom, Alanna Ubach.

STING OF CHANCE

A New Path Cinema presentation. Producer/Director/Screenplay/Editor: Babak Sarrafan. Camera: Jim Orr. Music: Sarrafan. In color, 16mm. Release date: Feb. 24, 2000. Running time: 107 Min.

Cast: Mohammad Ali Golabaz, Behzad Maghadam, Mohsen Rastegar-panah, Ramsin Eivaspour-adeh, Scott D. Apel, Steve Schultz, Michael Stange.

A STORM IN SUMMER

A Showtime Original Pictures for All Ages presentation in association with Hallmark Prods. of a Renee Valente production. Producer: Valente. Executive producers: Valente, Robert Halmi Jr. Director: Robert Wise. Screenplay: Rod Serling. Camera: Bert Dunk. Editor: Jack Hofstra. Music: Cynthia Millar. In color. Release date: Jan. 18, 2000. Running time: 94 Min.

Cast: Peter Falk, Aaron Meeks, Natassja Kinski, Andrew McCarthy, Ruby Dee.

STRAIGHTMAN

A Benzfilm Group production. Producers: Ben Redgrave, Ben Berkowitz. Co-producers: Victoria Kallay, Michael Palmerio. Director: Ben Berkowitz. Screenplay: Ben Redgrave, Berkowitz. Camera: Jerome Biron. Editor: Michael Palmeria. Music: Joaquin De La Puente, Berkowtiz. In color, 16mm. Release date: Apr. 4, 2000. Running time: 98 Min.

Cast: Ben Redgrave, Ben Berkowitz, Rachel Tomlinson, Butch Jerinic, Joaquin De La Puente, Victoria Kallay, Scott Holme.

STRAIGHT RIGHT

Producers: Marcel Pagulayan, Chris Donahue, Brent Smith. Director: P. David Ebersole. Screenplay: Brent Smith, Ebersole. Camera: Mark Putnam. Editor: Poppy Das. Music: Peter Golub. In Deluxe color. Release date: Apr. 15, 2000. Running time: 82 Min.

Cast: Brent Smith, Lynn Evans, Zeke Rippy, Mary Woronov, Bob Romanus, Mickey Cottrell.

STRIPPERS

A Hollywood Independents release and presentation in association with A.J. Prods. Producers: Jorge Ameer, Janine Gosselin, Marianne Marx, John Greenlaw, Rochelle Jefferson. Executive producers: Ameer, Greenlaw. Director/Screenplay: Jorge Ameer. Camera: Aaron Kirsch, Gary Tachell. Editor: Rollin Olson. Music: Paul McCarty. In Deluxe color. Release date: Sept. 13, 2000. Running time: 71 Min.

Cast: Tony Tucci, John Greenlaw, Kerrie Clark, Jeff Seal, JD Roberto, Linda Graybel, Kirsten Holly Smith, Jane Grogan.

STUART LITTLE

A Sony Pictures Entertainment release of a Columbia Pictures presentation of a Douglas Wick and Franklin/Waterman production. Producer: Douglas Wick. Executive producers: Jeff Franklin, Steve Waterman, Jason Clark. Director: Rob Minkoff. Screenplay: M. Night Shyamlan, Greg Brooker, based on the book by E.B. White. Camera: Guillermo Navarro, Editor: Tom Finan. Music: Alan Silvestri. In Deluxe color. Release date: Nov. 21, 1999. MPAA Rating: PG. Running time: 92 Min.

Cast: Geena Davis, Hugh Laurie, Jonathan Lipnicki, Brian Doyle-Murray, Estelle Getty, Julia Sweeney, Dabney Coleman.

Voices: Michael J. Fox, Nathan Lane, Chazz Palminteri, Steve Zahn, Jim Doughan, David Alan Grier, Bruno Kirby, Jennifer Tilly.

SUCKERS

A Neo Motion Pictures presentation of a Neo Art and Logic production. Producer: W.K. Border. Executive producers: Joel Soisson, Michael Leahy, Michael Peyser. Co-producers: Jane Gordon, Aki Komine. Director/Editor: Roger Nygard. Screenplay: Nygard, Joe Yannetty. Camera: Nathan Hope. Music: Walter Werzowa, Jimmie Wood, J.J. Holiday, Billy Sullivan. In color. Release date: Oct. 13, 1999. Running time: 86 Min.

Cast: Daniel Benzali, Louis Mandylor, Lori Loughlin, David A. Brooks, William Shockley, Michael D. Roberts, Wayne Duvall, Eli Danker, BT.

A SUDDEN LOSS OF GRAVITY

A Bangor Films production. Producers: Jim Dwyer, Todd Verow. Director: Verow. Screenplay: Verow, Jim Dwyer. Camera: Verow. Editors: Verow, Dwyer. Music: Colin Owens, DJ Rake. In color, digital video-to16mm. Release date: Feb. 18, 2000. Running time: 84 Min.

Cast: Devery Doleman, Jim Dwyer, Aaron Falls, Brenda Velez, Philly, Erma Verow, Leanne Whitney, Craig Bowden, Rebecca Denise, Jesse Manson, Eric Sapp.

SUGIHARA: CONSPIRACY OF KINDNESS

A Seventh Art release of a Dentsu Inc. in association with David Rubinson and Creative Production Group presentation. Producer: Diane Estelle Vicari. Executive producers: Shozo Katsuta, Norio Hayashi, Alan Ett, David Rubinson. Director: Robert Kirk. Camera: Paul Dougherty. Editor: Matt Stevenson. Music: Bill Conti. In video color. Release date: Aug. 6, 2000. Running time: 103 Min. Documentary.

With: Hiroki Sugihara, Benjamin Fishoff, Rabbi Moses Zupnik, Susan Bluman.

Narrator: Neil Ross.

SUNSET STRIP

A 20th Century Fox release of a Fox 2000 Pictures presentation of a Linson Films production. Producer: Art Linson, John Linson. Executive producer: James Dodson. Director: Adam Collis. Screenplay: Randall Jahnson, Russell Degrazier, story by Jahnson. Camera: Ron Fortunato. Editors: Bruce Cannon, Angus Wall. Music: Stewart Copeland. In Deluxe color. Release date: Aug. 8, 2000. MPAA Rating: R. Running time: 90 Min.

Cast: Simon Baker, Anna Friel, Nick Stahl, Rory Cochrane, Adam Goldberg, Tommy J. Flanagan, Jared Leto, Stephanie Romanov, John Randolph, Sebastian Robertson.

SUPER CHIEF

An Io Pictures production. Producer/Director/Screenplay: Nick Kurzon. Camera: Kurzon. Editor: David Allen. Music: Joel Goodman. In color, digital video. Release date: Oct. 28, 1999. Running time: 72 Min. Documentary.

With: Darrell "Chip" Wadena, Eugene "Bugger" McArthur, Lowell Bellanger, Erma Vizenor, Doyle Turner.

SUPERNOVA

An MGM release of a Screenland Pictures/Hammerhead production. Producers: Ash R. Shah, Daniel Chuba, Jamie Dixon. Executive producer: Ralph S. Singleton. Director: Thomas Lee. Screenplay: David Campbell Wilson, story by William Malone. Camera: Lloyd Ahern II. Editors: Michael Schweitzer, Melissa Kent. Music: David Williams. In Deluxe color. Release date: Jan. 14, 2000. MPAA Rating: PG-13. Running time: 90 Min.

Cast: James Spader, Angela Bassett, Robert Forster, Lou Diamond Phillips, Peter Facinelli, Robin Tunney, Wilson Cruz.

SURFING FOR LIFE

A David L. Brown production in association with Seniority Inc. Producers: Brown, Roy Earnest. Director/Screenplay: David L. Brown. Camera: Brown, David Collier, Stephen Lighthill. Editors: Brown, Shirley Thompson. Music: Tom Disher; additional music: Sons of Hawai'i, Gabby Pahinui. In color. Release date: Mar. 29, 2000. Running time: 68 Min. Documentary.

Narrator: Beau Bridges.

SWIMMING

An Oceanside Pictures production. Producers: Robert J. Siegel, Linda Moran. Executive producer: Reginald Shelbourne. Co-producers: Ciro Silva, Grace Woodard, Lisa Bazadona. Director: Robert J. Siegel. Screenplay: Lia Bazadona, Siegel, Grace Woodard. Camera: John Leuba. Editor: Frank Reynolds. Music: Mark Wike. In color. Release date: Feb. 2, 2000. Running time: 93 Min.

Cast: Laruen Ambrose, Jennifer Dundas Lowe, Joelle Carter, Jamie Harrold, James Villemaire, Josh Pais, Sharon Scruggs, Joshua Harto.

THE TALENTED MR. RIPLEY

A Paramount release of a Paramount Pictures and Miramax Films presentation of a Mirage Enterprises/Timnick Films production. Producers: William Horberg, Tom Sternberg. Executive producer: Sydney Pollack. Co-producer: Paul Zaentz. Director/Screenplay: Anthony Minghella, based on the novel by Patricia Highsmith. Camera: John Seale. Editor: Walter Murch. Music: Gabriel Yared. In Deluxe color. Release date: Dec. 9, 1999. MPAA Rating: R. Running time: 139 Min.

Cast: Matt Damon, Gwyneth Paltrow, Jude Law, Cate Blanchett, Philip Seymour Hoffman, Jack Davenport, James Rebhorn, Sergio Rubini, Philip Baker Hall, Celia Weston, Rosario Fiorello, Stefania Rocca.

THE TAO OF STEVE

A Good Machine production in association with Thunderhead Prods. Producer: Anthony Bregman. Executive producer: Ted Hope. Co-producer: Alton Walpole. Director: Jenniphr Goodman. Screenplay: Duncan North, with Greer Goodman, Jenniphr Goodman. Camera: Teodoro Maniaci. Editor: Sarah Gartner. Music: Joe Delia. In Technicolor. Release date: Jan. 26, 2000. Running time: 88 Min.

Cast: Donal Logue, Greer Goodman, Kimo Wills, Ayelet Kaznelson, David Aaron Baker, Nina Jaroslaw.

THE TARGET SHOOTS FIRST

Producer/Director/Screenplay: Christopher Wilcha. Camera: Wilcha. Editors: Bil Yoelin, Wilcha. Music: Sasha Frere Jones, Adam S. Goldman. In Hi-8 video. Release date: Feb. 20, 2000. Running time: 71 Min. Documentary.

TEMPS

A Five Sisters Productions presentation. Producers: Maria, Gabrielle, Ursula, Jennifer and Charity Burton. Director: Maria Burton. Screenplay: Gabrielle Burton. Camera: Edward Slattery. Editors: Marc Laub, Bret Marnell, Maja Vrivlo. Music: Mark Northam, Jim Latham. In Duart color. Release date: Nov. 6, 1999. Running time: 93 Min.

Cast: Gabrielle C. Burton, Robert Perberton, Ursula Burton, Tim Bohn, Katrina Stevens, Seymour Cassel, Maria Burton, Kim Mansfield, Guy Strauss, Ariel Martinez.

A TEXAS FUNERAL

A Dragon Pictures production. (International sales: J&M Entertainment, L.A.) Producer: Damian Jones, Graham Broadbent. Director/Screenplay: William Blake Herron. Camera: Mike Bonvillain. Editor: Paul Trejo. Music: James Legg. In Deluxe color, widescreen. Release date: Mar. 30, 2000. Running time: 102 Min.

Cast: Robert Patrick, Joanne Whalley, Isaiah Washington, Quinton Jones, Jane Adams, Chris Noth, Olivia D'Abo, Martin Sheen.

THICKER THAN WATER

A Palm Pictures release of a Marsmedia production of a Hoo-Bangin'/Priority Film. Producer: Darryl Taja, Andrew Shack. Executive producer, Mack 10. Co-producers: David "Wavy" Green, Taj Lewis. Co-executive producer: Stavros Merjos. Director: Ernest Nyle Brown. Camera: Robert Benavides. Editor: Danny Rafic. Music: QDIII. In color, video-to-35mm. Release date: Oct. 21, 1999. MPAA Rating: R. Running time: 91 Min.

Cast: Mack 10, Fat Joe, Ice Cube, MC Eiht, CJ Mac, Big Pun, K-Mack, Tom'ya Bowden, Kidada Jones, Buddy Lewis, Drayzie Bone, Flesh 'N' Bone, B-Real, Bad Azz, WC.

THINGS YOU CAN TELL JUST BY LOOKING AT HER

An MGM release from United Artists of a Jon Avnet and Franchise Pictures presentation. Producers: Avnet, Lisa Lindstrom, Marsha Oglesby. Executive producers: Elie Samaha, Andrew Stevens. Director/Screenplay: Rodrigo Garcia. Camera: Emmanuel Lubezki. Editor: Amy E. Duddleston. Music: Edward Shearmur. In Deluxe color. Release date: Jan. 13, 2000. MPAA Rating: PG-13. Running time: 106 Min.

Cast: Glenn Close, Cameron Diaz, Calista Flockhart, Kathy Baker, Amy Brenneman, Valeria Golino, Holly Hunter, Matt Craven, Gregory Hines, Miguel Sandoval.

30 DAYS

An Arielle Tepper/Araca Group presentation of an Araca Group/Arielle Tepper production. (International sales: Araca Group, New York.) Producers: Matthew Rego, Michael Rego, Arielle Tepper. Director/Screenplay: Aaron Harnick. Camera: David Tumblety. Editor: Sean J. Campbell. Music: Andrew Sherman, Stephen J. Walsh. In color. Release date: Sept. 12, 1999. Running time: 87 Min.

Cast: Ben Shenkman, Arija Bareikis, Alexander Chaplin, Bradley White, Thomas McCarthy, Catherine Kellner, Jerry Adler, Barbara Barrie, Arden Myrin, Mark Feuerstein.

THOMAS AND THE MAGIC RAILROAD

An Icon (in U.K.)/Destination Films (In U.S.) release of a Destination Films/Gullane Pictures production, in association with the Isle of Man FIlm Commission. (International sales: Kathy Morgan Intl., Los Angeles.) Producers: Britt Allcroft, Phil Fehrle. Executive producers: Charles Falzon, Nancy Chapelle, Barry London, Brent Baum, John Bertilli. Co-producer: Mark Jacobson. Director/Screenplay: Britt Allcroft. Camera: Paul Ryan. Editor: Ron Wisman. Music: Hummie Mann. In Deluxe color. Release date: July 14, 2000. Running time: 86 Min.

Cast: Peter Fonda, Mara Wilson, Alec Baldwin, Didi Conn, Michael E. Rodgers, Cody McMains.

3 STRIKES

An MGM release of an Absolute Entertainment/Motion Picture Corp. of America production in association with Lithium Entertainment Group. Producer: Marcus Morton. Executive producers: Julio Caro, Benny Medina, Brad Krevoy. Co-producer: Jeremiah Samuels. Director/Screenplay: D.J. Pooh. Camera: John W. Simmons. Editor: John Carter. In FotoKem color. Release date: Mar. 1, 2000. MPAA Rating: R. Running time: 82 Min.

Cast: Brian Hooks, N'Bushe Wright, Faizon Love, E40, Starletta DuPois, George Wallace, David Alan Grier, Dean Norris.

THREE TO TANGO

A Warner Bros. release, presented in association with Village Roadshow Pictures and Village-Hoyts Film Partnership, of an Outlaw production. Producers: Bobby Newmyer, Jeffrey Silver, Bettina Sofia Viviano. Executive producers: Lawrence B. Abramson, Bruce Berman. Co-producers, John M. Eckert, Keri Selig. Director: Damon Santostefano. Screenplay: Rodney Vaccaro, Aline Brosh McKenna. Camera: Walt Lloyd. Editor: Stephen Semel. Music: Graeme Revell. In Technicolor. Release date: Oct. 9, 1999. MPAA Rating: PG-13. Running time: 98 Min.

Cast: Matthew Perry, Neve Campbell, Dylan McDermott, Oliver Platt, Cylk Cozart, John C. McGinley, Bob Balaban, Deborah Rush.

TIGERLAND

A 20th Century Fox release of a Regency Enterprise presentation of a Haft Entertainment/New Regency production. Producers: Arnon Milchan, Steven Haft, Beau Flynn. Executive producer: Ted Kurdyla. Director: Joel Schumacher. Screenplay: Ross Klavan, Michael McGruther. Camera: Matthew Libatique. Editor: Mark Stevens. Music: Nathan Larsen. In Deluxe color. Release date: Sept.12, 2000. Running time: 109 Min.

Cast: Colin Farrell, Matthew Davis, Clifton Collins Jr., Thomas Guiry, Shea Whigham, Russell Richardson Cole Hauser.

THE TIGGER MOVIE

A Buena Vista Pictures release of a Walt Disney Pictures presentation, produced by Walt Disney Television Animation, with animation production by Walt Disney Animation (Japan). Producer: Cheryl Abood. Director/Screenplay: Jun Falkenstein, story by Eddie Guzelian, based on characters by A.A. Milne. Supervising film editor: Robert Fisher Jr., songs by Richard M. Sherman, Robert B. Sherman, score by Harry Gregson-Williams. In Technicolor. Release date: Feb. 6, 2000. MPAA Rating: G. Running time: 77 Min. Animated.

Voices: Jim Cummings, Nikita Hopkins, Ken Sansom, John Fiedler, Peter Cullen, Andre Stojka, Kath Soucie, Tom Attenborough, John Hurt.

TIMECODE

A Screen Gems release of a Red Mullet production. Producers: Mike Figgis, Annie Steward. Co-producers: Dustin Bernard, Gary Scott Marcus. Director: Mike Figgis, story by Figgis. Camera: Patrick Alexander Stewart. Music: Figgis, Anthony Marinelli. In color, HDD video-to-35mm. Release date: Apr., 18, 2000 . MPAA Rating: R. Running time: 97 Min.

Cast: Xander Berkeley, Golden Brooks, Saffron Burrows, Viveka Davis, Richard Edson, Aimee Graham, Salma Hayek, Glenne Headly, Andrew Heckler, Holly Hunter, Danny Huston.

TITAN A.E.

A 20th Century Fox release of a 20th Century Fox Animation presentation of a Gary Goldman production in association with David Kirschner Prods. Producers: Kirschner, Don Bluth, Gary Goldman. Executive producer, Paul Gertz. Directors: Don Bluth, Gary Goldman. Screenplay: Ben Edlund, John August, Joss Whedon, story by Hans Bauer, Randall McCormick. Animation director: Len Simon. Digital technology director: Mark Weathers. Editors: Fiona Trayler, Bob Bender. Music: Graeme Revell. In Technicolor, Technicolor, CinemaScope widescreen. Release date: June 1, 2000. MPAA Rating: PG. Running time: 95 Min. Animated.

Voices: Matt Damon, Drew Barrymore, Bill Pullman, John Leguizamo, Nathan Lane, Janeane Garofalo, Ron Perlman, Alex D. Linz, Tone-Loc.

TOTALLY IRRESPONSIBLE

A Killer Bud Films/Prosperity Pictures production. Producers: Ellen Erwin, Richard Mann. Executive producers: David Forrest, Beau Rogers. Co-producer: Betsy Chasse. Director: Karl Hirsch. Screenplay: Hank Nelken, Greg DePaul. Camera: David Lewis. Editor: Carol Oblath. Music: Russ Landau. In color. Release date: Feb. 5, 2000. Running time: 95 Min.

Cast: Corin Nemec, David Faustino, Caroline Keenan, Danielle Harris, Robert Stack, Maurice Chasse, Bunny Summers, Patrick Cupo.

TOY STORY 2

A Buena Vista Pictures release of a Walt Disney Pictures presentation of a Pixar Animation Studios film. Producers: Helene Plotkin, Karen Robert Jackson. Executive producer: Sarah McArthur. Director: John Lasseter. Co-directors: Lee Unkrich, Ash Brannon. Screenplay: Andrew Stanton, Rita Hsiao, Doug Chamberlin, Chris Webb, original story by Lesseter, Peter Docter, Brannon, Stanton. Camera: Sharon Calahan. Editors: Edie Bleiman, David Ian Salter, Unkrich. Music: Randy Newman. In Monaco Labs color. Release date: Nov. 6, 1999. Running time: MPAA Rating: G. 92 Min. Animated.

Voices: Tom Hanks, Tim Allen, Kelsey Grammer, Don Rickles, Jim Varney, Wallace Shawn, John Ratzenberger, Annie Potts.

TRADE OFF

A Wright Angle Media (Seattle) production. Producer: Thomas Lee Wright. Co-producers: Shaya Mercer, Tammy Strange. Director: Shaya Mercer. Camera: Chris Towey; additional camera: Mercer, Mark Brian Smith, Robert Bennett. (DC) editor: Charlese Stobbs. Music: Spearhead, Laura Love. In color, digital beta. Release date: June 8, 2000. Running time: 95 Min. Documentary.

With: Mike Dolan, Michael Moore, Jello Biafra, Jerry Mander, Vandana Shiva, Charlene Barshefsky, Bill Clinton, Tom Hayden, Michael Franti.

TRASH

A Dancing Babies Entertainment presentation of a Todd Feldman production. Producers: Scott Tiano, Sean Entin, Todd Feldman. Executive producer: Gary J. Miller. Co-producer: Shawn Albertbum. Director/Screenplay: Mark Anthony Galluzzo. Camera: Thom Stukas. Editor: Adam P. Scott. Music: Michael Muhlfriedel. In FotoKem color. Release date: Sept. 14, 1999. Running time: 95 Min.

Cast: Jeremy Sisto, Eric Michael Cole, Jaime Pressly, Grace Zabriskie, Jonathan Bank, Charles Venturi, Marisa Ryan.

A TRIAL IN PRAGUE

A Pick production, in association with Space Films. Producers: Zuzana Justman, Jiri Jezek, Zuzana Cervenkova, David Charap. (International sales: Pick Prods., New York.) Director/Screenplay: Justman. Camera: Miro Gabor, Marek Jicha. Editor: Charap. Music: Peter Fish. In color and B&W. Release date: Aug. 27, 2000. Running time: 84 Min. Documentary.

TRIFLING WITH FATE

A Separate Star production. Producers: Michael Bergmann, Lexi Robertson, Sarah Winkler. Director/Screenplay: Michael Bergmann. Camera: Michael Bergmann. Editors: Michael Bergmann, Ardythe Ashley. Music: Doug Scofield. In color, video. Release date: June 26, 2000. Running time: 95 Min.

Cast: Teri Lamm, Ryan Dunn, Bridget Moynahan, Vivienne Benesch, Rob Gerlach, Holter Graham, Robin Dorian, Michael Hayward-Jones.

TRIXIE

A Sony Pictures Classics release. Producer: Robert Altman. Executive producer: James McLindon. Co-producer: Joseph Patrick Finn. Director/Screenplay: Alan Rudolph, based on a story by Rudolf, John Binder. Camera: Jan Kiesser. Editor: Michael Ruscio. Music: Mark Isham, Roger Neill. In Deluxe color, widescreen. Release date: Jan. 25, 2000. MPAA Rating: R. Running time: 117 Min.

Cast: Emily Watson, Dermot Mulroney, Nick Nolte, Nathan Lane, Brittany Murphy, Lesley Ann Warren, Will Patton, Stephen Lang.

TROIS

A Rainforest Prods. release in association with TRF Prods. Producer: William Packer. Executive producers: Gabe Group, Eric and Aaron Goowin, Madison Gray. Co-producer: Gregory Anderson. Director/Screenplay: Rob Hardy, based on a story by Willpower. Camera: Charles Mills. Editor: Griff Thomas. Music: Steven Gutheinz. In FotoKem color. Release date: July 15, 2000. Running time: 93 Min.

Cast: Gary Dourdan, Kenya Moore, Gretchen Palmer, Soloman K. Smith, Thom Byrd, Chrystale Wilson, Bryce Wilson.

TURN IT UP

A New Line Cinema release. Producers: Guy Oseary, Happy Walters. Executive producers: Gary Ventimiglia, Lennox Parris, Lester Parris. Co-producers: E. Bennett Walsh, Pras Michel. Director/Screenplay: Robert Adetuyi, based on a story by Ray "Cory" Daniels, Chris Hudson, Kelly Hilaire. Camera: Hubert Taczanowski. Editor: Jeff Freeman. Music: Frank Fitzpatrick. In Deluxe color. Release date: Aug. 30, 2000. MPAA Rating: R. Running time: 86 Min.

Cast: Pras, Ja Rule, Vondie Curtis-Hall, Tamala Jones, Jason Statham, Eugene Clark, John Ralston, Chris Messina.

28 DAYS

A Sony Pictures Entertainment release of a Columbia Pictures presentation of a Columbia Pictures presentation of a Tall Trees production. Producer: Jenno Topping. Co-producer: Celia Costas. Director: Betty Thomas. Screenplay: Susannah Grant. Camera: Declan Quinn. Editor: Peter Teschner. Music: Richard Gibbs. In Deluxe color. Release date: Apr. 3, 2000. MPAA Rating: PG-13. Running time: 103 Min.

Cast: Sandra Bullock, Viggo Mortensen, Dominic West, Diane Ladd, Elizabeth Perkins, Steve Buscemi, Alan Tudyk, Michael O'Malley, Azura Skye, Reni Santoni, Marianne Jean-Baptiste.

TWILIGHT: LOS ANGELES

An Anna Deavere Smith presentation in association with Offline. Entertainment Group. Producer: Smith, Ezra Swerdlow. Executive producer: Cherie Fortis. Co-producer: Daphne Pinkerson. Director: Marc Levin. Screenplay: Anna Deavere Smith, based on her play: "Twilight: Los Angeles, 1992." Camera: Maryse Alberti, Joan Churchill. Editor: Bob Eisenhardt. Original music: Camara Kambon. In color, digital video. Release date: Jan. 22, 2000. Running time: 76 Min.

TWO FAMILY HOUSE

A Lions Gate release of a Filbert Steps production. Producers: Anne Harrison, Alan Klingenstein. Executive producers: Jim Kohlberg, Adam Brightman. Director/Screenplay: Raymond De Felitta. Camera: Michael Mayers. Editor: David Leonard. In color. Release date: Jan. 22, 2000. Running time: 107 Min.

Cast: Michael Rispoli, Kelly Macdonald, Katherine Narducci, Kevin Conway, Matt Servitto, Michele Santopietro, Louis Guss.

TWO NINAS
A King Brook Entertainment presentation in association with Castlerea Films and Accidental Pictures. Producers: Greg Scheinmen, Denis Doyle. Executive producers: Seth Kanegis, Adam Sender. Director/Screenplay: Neil Turitz. Camera: Joaquin Baca-Asay. Editor: Jumbulingam Chandrasekhar. Music: Joseph Saba. In Duart color. Release date: Sept. 15, 1999. Running time: 88 Min.
Cast: Cara Buono, Amanda Peet, Bray Poor, Linda Larkin, Ron Livingston, Jill Hennessy.

U-571
A Universal release of a Universal Pictures and Studio Canal Plus presentation in association with Dino De Laurentiis. Producers: Dino De Laurentiis, Martha De Laurentiis. Executive producer: Hal Lieberman. Director: Jonathan Mostow. Screenplay: Mostow, Sam Montgomery, David Ayer, story by Mostow. Camera: Oliver Wood. Editor: Wayne Wahrman. Music: Richard Marvin. In Deluxe color, Joe Dunton Cameras widescreen. Release date: Apr. 12, 2000. MPAA Rating: PG-13. Running time: 116 Min.
Cast: Matthew McConaughey, Bill Paxton, Harvey Keitel, Jon Bon Jovi, Jake Weber, David Keith, T.C. Carson, Jack Noseworth.

UNBOWED
A Filmanthropic presentation. Producers: Nanci Rossov, Lisa Karadijian. Co-producer: Clive Endersby. Director: Nanci Russov. Screenplay: Mildred Inez Lewis. Camera: Tom Feldman. Editor: Taatshing Hui. Music: Elizabeth Sellers. In color. Release date: Nov. 19, 1999. Running time: 122 Min.
Cast: Tembi Locke, Jay Tavare, Edward Albert, Orson Bean, Ron Glass, Hattie Winston, Michelle Thomas, Mark Abbott, Fran Bennett.

UNDER HELLGATE BRIDGE
A Fortune Films presentation in association with Cavu Pictures, of an El-Train production. Producers: Michael Sergio. Isil Bagdadi. Executive producer: John M. Fortune III. Co-executive producers: Vivian Jang, Heinz Kluetmeier, David Anthony. Director/Screenplay: Michael Sergio. Camera: Leland Krane. Editor: Stan Warnow. Music: Stephan Moccio. In color. Release date: Aug. 28, 1999. Running time: 87 Min.
Cast: Michael Rodrick, Jonathan LaPaglia, Frank Vincent, Jordan Bayne, Brian Vincent, Dominic Chianese, Vincent Pastore.

URBANIA
A Shear/Golden/Harris production. Producers: Jon Shear, Stephanie Golden, J. Todd Harris. Co-producers: Meta Puttkammer, Douglas Hunter. Director: Jon Shear. Screenplay: Shear, Daniel Reitz, based on the play "Urban Folk Tales" by Reitz. Camera: Shane Kelly. Editors: Randolph K. Bricker, Ed Marx. Music: Marc Anthony Thompson. Release date: Jan. 24, 2000. Runnning time: 107 Min.
Cast: Dan Futterman, Alan Cumming, Matt Keeslar, Josh Hamilton, Lothaire Bluteau, Bill Sage, Barbara Sukowa, Paige Turco, Meagan Dodds, Gabriel Olds, Samuel Ball.

URBAN LEGENDS: FINAL CUT
A Sony Pictures Entertainment release of a Columbia Pictures and Phoenix Pictures presentation of a Neal H. Moritz/Gina Matthews production. Producers: Neal H. Moritz, Gina Matthews, Richard Luke Rothschild. Executive producers: Nicholas Osborne, Brad Luff. Co-producer: Michael McDonnell. Director: John Ottman. Screenplay: Paul Harris Boardman, Scott Derrickson, based on characters created by Silvio Horta. Camera: Brian Pearson. Editor: Ottman, Rob Kobrin. Music: Ottman. In Deluxe color, Panavision widescreen. Release date: Sept. 18, 2000. MPAA Rating: R. Running time: 98 Min.
Cast: Jennifer Morrison, Matthew Davis, Hart Bochner, Loretta Devine, Joseph Lawrence, Anson Mount, Eva Mendez.

VERY MEAN MEN
A Giants Entertainment presentation of a Baio/White production. Producers: David Dadon, Steven Baio, Neil P. White. Executive producers: Lydia Dadon, Anthony Cataldo. Director: Tony Vitale. Screenplay: Paul T. Murray. Camera: Alex Vendler. Editor: Gregory Hobson. Music: Ennio Di Berardo. In color. Release date: June 10, 2000. Running time: 93 Min.
Cast: Mathew Modine, Martin Landau, Ben Gazzara, Scott Baio, Burt Young, Paul Ben-Victor, Billy Drago, Charles Durning, Louise Fletcher, Jack McGee, Patrick Renna, Idalis DeLeon.

VIA DOLOROSA
A Booth Theater production in association with Lincoln Center Theater, Royal Court Theater, Brandman Prods. Producer: Iris Merlis. Executive producers: Simon Curtis, Michael Brandman. Director: John Bailey. Stage director: Stephen Daldry. Camera: Bailey. Editor: Raul Davalos. Music: Christopher Klatman. In color, digital video. Release date: Jan 22, 2000. Running time: 90 Min.
Cast: David Hare.

THE VISIT
A DaWa Movies presentation of a Jordan Walker-Pearlman production. Producer: Walker-Pearlman. Executive producers: Susanne Columbia, Anastasia King, Vicky Pike, Morris Ruskin, Kosmond Russell. Director/Screenplay: Jordan Walker-Pearlman, based on the play by Kosmond Russell. Camera: John Ndiaga Demps. Editors: Alison Learned, Walker-Pearlman. Music: Michael Bearden, Stefan Dickerson, Ramsey Lewis, Wallace Roney, Stanley A. Smith. In Deluxe color. Release date: June 18, 2000. Running time: 123 Min.
Cast: Hill Harper, Obba Babatunde, Rae Dawn Chong, Billy Dee WIlliams, Marla Gibbs, Phylicia Rashad, Talia Shire, David Clennon.

A VOICE FROM HEAVEN
A Crossmedia Communications production. Producers: Alessandro Sforza, Giuseppe Asaro, Shafiq Saddiqui. Co-producers: Vikas Bushan, Ian Fletcher. Director/Screenplay: Giuseppe Asaro. Camera: Asaro. Editors: Asaro, Tom Acito. Music: Ustad Nusrat Fateh Ali Khan, Rahat Nusrat Fateh Ali Khan. Farrukh Ali Khan. In color, digital video. Release date: Oct. 28, 1999. Running time: 80 Min. Documentary.
With: Ustad Nusrat Fateh Ali Khan, Rahat Nusrat Fateh Ali Khan, Farrukh Ali Khan, Dildar Hussein, Rick Rubin, Michael Brook, Talvin Singh, Bally Sagoo, Iqbal Nagibi, Imran Khan, Lubana Saeed.

VULGAR
A Lions Gate release of a View Askew Production. (International sales: Sloss Special Projects, N.Y.) Producer: Monica Hampton. Executive producers: Kevin Smith, Scott Mosier. Director/Screenplay: Bryan Johnson. Camera: David Klein. Editors: Scott Mosier, Johnson. Music: Ryan Shore. In color, 16mm. Release date: Sept. 13, 2000. Running time: 91 Min.
Cast: Scott O'Halloran, Bryan Johnson, Ralph Lamblase, Scott Mosier, Brian Quinn, Scott Schiaffo, Kevin Smith, Ethan Suplee.

A WAKE IN PROVIDENCE
A Mister P. Prods. presentation in association with Gladiator Pictures. Producers: William Redner, Vincent Pagano, Rosario Roveto Jr., Patrick Coppola. Executive producer: Michael Williams. Director: Rosario Roveto Jr. Screenplay: Billy Van Zandt, Jane Milmore, Vincent Pagano, Mike Pagano. Camera: Mark Kohl. Editor: Gareth O'Neil. Music: Ed Alton. In FotoKem color. Release date: Sept. 7, 1999. Running time: 94 Min.
Cast: Vincent Pagano, Victoria Rowell, Mike Pagano, Adrienne Barbeau, Micole Mercurio, Lisa Raggio, Dan Lauria, Kaye Kingston, Louis Guss, Sam Coppola, John Capodice, Mark DeCarlo.

WAKING THE DEAD
A USA Films release presented in association with Gramercy Pictures and Polygram Filmed Entertainment, of an Egg Pictures production. Producers: Keith Gordon, Stuart Kleinman, Linda Reisman. Executive producer: Jodie Foster. Co-producer: Irene Litinsky. Director: Keith Gordon. Screenplay: Robert Dillon, based on the novel by Scott Spencer. Camera: Tom Richmond. Editor: Jeff Wishengrad. Music: tomandandy. In color. Release date: Jan. 24, 2000. Running time: 105 Min.
Cast: Billy Crudup, Jennifer Connelly, Molly Parker, Janet McTeer, Paul Hipp, Sandra Oh, Hal Holbrook, Laurence Dane.

WALKING ACROSS EGYPT
A Mitchum Entertainment production. (International sales: Keystone Entertainment.) Producers: Madeline Bell, Heath McLaughlin, Bettina Tendler O'Mara, Paul Tamasy, Executive producers: Stan Tendler, Lance Tendler. Director: Arthur Allan Seidelman. Screenplay: Paul Tamasy, based on the novel by Clyde Edgerton. Camera: Amelia Vincent. Editors: Jonathan Shaw, Bert Glatstein. Music: Marco Beltrami. In Deluxe color. Release date: Feb. 1, 2000. Running time: 110 Min.
Cast: Ellen Burstyn, Jonathan Taylor Thomas, Mark Hamill, Judge Reinhold, Gail O'Grady, Gwen Verdon, Edward Herrmann, Harve Presnell, Pat Corley, James Colman III, Patrick David.

WALTER ROSENBLUM: IN SEARCH OF PITT STREET
A Daedalus Prods. presentation. Producers: Nina Rosenblum, Sonya Starr. Co-producer: Daniel V. Allentuck. Director: Rosenblum. Camera: Dejan Georgevich; additional camera: Nancy Schreiber, Nina Rosenblum. Editors: Steven Olswang. Satoko Sugiyama. In color and B&W. Release date: Oct. 11, 1999. Running time: 60 Min. Documentary.

THE WATCHER
A Universal Pictures release in association with Interlight of a Lewitt/Eberts-Choi/Niami production. Producer: Christopher Eberts, Elliot Lewitt, Jeff Rice, Nile Niami. Executive producers: Patrick Choi, Paul Pompian. Director: Joe Charbanic. Screenplay: David Elliott, Clay Ayers, from a story by Darcy Meyers, Elliott. Camera: Michael Chapman. Editor: Richard Nord. Music: Marco Beltrami. In Deluxe color. Release date: Sept. 5, 2000. MPAA Rating: R. Running time: 96 Min.
Cast: James Spader, Marisa Tomei, Keanu Reeves, Ernie Hudson, Chris Ellis, Robert Cicchini, Yvonne Niami, Jennifer McShane.

THE WAY OF THE GUN
An Artisan Entertainment release. Producer: Kenneth Kokin. Executive producer: Russ Markowitz. Director/Screenplay: Christopher McQuarrie. Camera: Dick Pope. Editor: Stephen Semel. Music: Joe Kraemer. In Deluxe color. Release date: Aug. 31, 2000. Running time: 118 Min.
Cast: Ryan Phillippe, Benicio Del Toro, James Caan, Juliette Lewis, Taye Diggs, Nicky Katt, Dylan Kussman, Scott Wilson, Kristin Lehman.

WAYWARD SON
An Avenue Pictures production, in association with Maccabee Prods. (International sales: Arthur Kananack & Associates, Santa Monica.) Producer: Cary Brokaw. Executive producers: Michael Hammer, Steve Tisch. Co-executive producers: Rachel Frazin, Harmon M. Kaslow. Co-producer: Tom Luse. Director/Screenplay: Randall Harris. Camera: David Hennings. Editor: Louise Rubacky. Music: James Newton Howard, Steve Porcaro. In color, widescreen. Release date: Sept. 15, 1999. Running time: 97 Min.
Cast: Harry Connick Jr., Peter Postlethwaite, Patricia Clarkson, Vinessa Shaw, Michael Gaston.

THE WEIGHT OF WATER

A Lions Gate release of a StudioCanal presentation of a Manifest Film Co./Palomar Pictures/Miracle Pictures production. Producers: Janet Yang, Sigurjon Sighvatsson, A. Kitman Ho. Executive producers: Lisa Henson, Steven-Charles Jaffe. Co-producers: Sean Wimmer, Chris Zimmer. Director: Kathryn Bigelow. Screenplay: Alice Arlen, Christopher Kyle, based on the novel by Anita Shreve. Camera: Adrian Biddle. Editor: Howard E. Smith. Music: David Hirschfelder. Release date: Sept. 8, 2000. Running time: 113 Min.
Cast: Catherine McCormack, Sarah Polley, Sean Penn, Josh Lucas, Elizabeth Hurley, Ciaran Hinds, Ulrich Thomsen.

WE MET ON THE VINEYARD

A Can You Spot Me a Twenty Pictures film. Producers: Forrest Murray, Andy Buckley, Nancy Banks. Director: Ian McCrudden. Screenplay: Forrest Murray, Andy Buckley, Nancy Banks. Camera: Tony Cucchiari. Editor: McCrudden. Score: Dr. John. In color. Release date: Oct. 23, 1999. Running time: 88 Min.
Cast: Julianna Margulies, Ivan Sergi, Kevin Tighe, Dixie Carter, Clayton Rohner, Kathleen York, Alanna Ubach, C.C.H. Pounder.

THE WETONKAWA FLASH

A Goner Prods. production. Producer/Director: Boyd Hale, Wendy Hopkins. Screenplay: Hale. Camera: Michael Spicer. Editor: A.Z. Novak. Music: Bob Derkach. In color. Release date: Nov. 6, 1999. Running time: 90 Min.
Cast: Mark Boone Jr. Kevin Tighe, Toby Huss, Neil Giutoli, Algie Kirkland, Brian Shoop, Craig Walter, Betty Haynes.

WHATEVER IT TAKES

A Sony Pictures Entertainment release of a Columbia Pictures presentation of a Paul Schiff production. Producer: Schiff. Executive producers: Bill Brown, Vicki Dee Rock. Co-producers: Matt Berenson, Mark Schwahn. Director: David Raynr. Screenplay: Mark Schwahn. Camera: Tim Suhrstedt. Editor: Ronald Roose. Music: Edward Shearmur. In CFI color. Release date: Mar. 22, 2000. MPAA Rating: PG-13. Running time: 94 Min.
Cast: Shane West, Marla Sokoloff, Jodi Lyn O'Keefe, James Franco, Aaron Paul, Richard Schiff, Julia Sweeney, Manu Intiraymi.

WHAT HAPPENED TO TULLY

A Tell Tale Films production. Producers: Annie Sundberg, Hilary Birmingham. Director: Hilary Birmingham. Screenplay: Birmingham, Matt Drake, based on the short story by Tom McNeal. Camera: John Foster. Editor: Affonso Goncalves. Music: Marcelo Zarvos. In color. Release date: Apr. 14, 2000. Running time: 102 Min.
Cast: Anson Mount, Julianne Nicholson, Glenn Fitzgerald, Catherine Kellner, Bob Burrus, Natalie Canerday, John Diehl.

WHAT I LIKE ABOUT YOU

A Misery Loves Company Inc. presentation, in association with Hockeyrado Prods., of a Tony Hewett production. Producer: Hewett. Co-producers: Merle Bertrand, Jimmy Jongebloed. Director: Jeff Stolhand. Screenplay: Marie Black, Scott Van Doviak. Camera: William Ambrico. Editors: Merle Bertrand, Stolhand. Music: Mark David, William Tabanou. In color, 16mm. Release date: Mar. 11, 2000. Running time: 90 Min.
Cast: Marie Black, Ryan Wickerham, Cameron Johnson, Ben Pascoe, Scott Von Doviak, Tim Curry.

WHAT LIES BENEATH

A DreamWorks Pictures release of a DreamWorks and Twentieth Century Fox presentation of an Imagemover production. Producers: Steve Starkey, Robert Zemeckis, Jack Rapke. Executive producers: Joan Bradshaw, Mark Johnson. Director: Robert Zemeckis. Screenplay: Clark Gregg, based on a story by Sarah Kernochan, Gregg. Camera: Don Burgess. Editor: Aethur Schmidt. Music: Alan Silvestri. In Technicolor, Panavision widescreen. Release date: July 7, 2000. MPAA PG-13. Running time: 126 Min.
Cast: Harrison Ford, Michelle Pfeiffer, Diana Scarwid, Miranda Otto, James Remar, Joe Morton, Amber Valletta, Victoria Birdwell.

WHAT PLANET ARE YOU FROM?

A Sony Pictures Entertainment release of a Columbia Pictures presentation of a Brad Grey/Bernie Brillstein production. Producers: Mike Nichols, Garry Shandling, Neil Machlis. Executive producers: Grey, Brillstein. Co-producer: Michele Imperato-Stabile. Director: Mike Nichols. Screenplay: Garry Shandling, Michael Leeson, Ed Solomon, Peter Toland, story by Shandling, Leeson. Camera: Michael Ballhaus. Editor: Richard Marks. Music: Carter Burwell. In Deluxe color. Release date: Feb. 17, 2000. MPAA Rating: R. Running time: 104 Min.
Cast: Garry Shandling, Annette Bening, Greg Kinnear, Ben Kingsley, Linda Fiorentino, John Goodman, Richard Jenkins, Caroline Aaron, Judy Greer, Nora Dunn, Ann Cusack, Camryn Manheim.

WHERE THE HEART IS

A 20th Century Fox release of a Wind Dancer production. Producers: Susan Cartsonis, David McFadzean, Patricia Whitcher, Matt Williams. Executive producers: Carmen Finestra, Rick Leed. Co-producers: Gerrit Folsom, Dianne Minter Lewis. Director: Matt Williams. Screenplay: Lowell Ganz, Babaloo Mandel, based on the novel by Billie Letts. Camera: Richard Greatrex. Editor: Ian Crafford. Music: Mason Daring. In Deluxe color. Release date: Apr. 6, 2000. MPAA Rating: PG-13. Running time: 120 Min.
Cast: Natalie Portman, Ashley Judd, Stockard Channing, Joan Cusack, James Frain, Dylan Bruno, Keith David, Sally Field.

WHERE THE MONEY IS

A USA Films release of a Gramercy Pictures presentation, in association with Intermedia Films and Pacific Film Distribution, of a Scott Free/IMF production. Producers: Ridley Scott, Charles Weinstock, Chris Zarpas, Christopher Dorr. Executive producers: Tony Scott, Guy East, Nigel Sinclair, Chris Sievernick, Moritz Borman. Co-producer: Beau E.L. Marks. Director: Marek Kanievska. Screenplay: E. Max Frye, Topper Lilien, Carroll Cartwright, based on a story by Frye. Camera: Thomas Burstyn. Editors: Sam Craven, Garth Craven, Dan Lebental. Music: Mark Isham. In Deluxe color. Release date: Apr. 7, 2000. MPAA Rating: PG-13. Runing time: 90 Min.
Cast: Paul Newman, Linda Fiorentino, Dermot Mulroney, Susan Barnes, Anne Pioniak, Bruce MacVittie, Irma St. Paul, Michel Perron.

WHIPPED

An Emotion Motion Pictures production. Producers/Directors: Iana Porter, Sasha Waters. Camera: Porter, Peter Hawkins, Nina Davenport, Tom Hurwitz. Editor: Nancy Roach. Music: Jason Glassner. In color, 16mm. Release date: Feb. 24, 2000. Running time: 63 Min. Documentary.

WHIPPED

A Destination Films release of a Hi-Rez Films production. Producer: Peter M. Cohen. Executive producers: Anthony Armetta, Taylor MacCrae, Barry London, Brent Baum, Brad Jenkel. Co-producers: Zorie Barber, Andrew R. Shakman. Director/Screenplay: Peter M. Cohen. Camera: Peter B. Kowalski. Editor: Tom McArdle. Music: Michael Montes. in Technicolor. Release date: Aug. 30, 2000. MPAA Rating: R. Running time: 82 Min.
Cast: Armanda Peet, Brian Van Holt, Judah Domke, Zorie Barber, Jonathan Abrahams, Callie Thorne.

THE WHOLE NINE YARDS

A Warner Bros. release of a Morgan Creek Prods. and Franchsie Pictures presentation of a Rational Packaging Films production, in association with Lansdown Films. Producers: David Willis, Allan Kaufman. Executive producers: Elie Samaha, Andrew Stevens. Co-producers: Don Carmody, James Holt, Tracee Stanley. Director: Jonathan Lynn. Screenplay: Mitchell Kapner. Camera: David Franco. Editor: Tom Lewis. Music. Randy Edelman. In Deluxe color. Release date: Feb. 8, 2000. MPAA Rating: PG-13. Running time: 101 Min.
Cast: Bruce Willis, Matthew Perry Rosanna Arquette, Michael Clarke Duncan, Natasha Henstridge, Amanda Peet, Kevin Pollak.

WILDFLOWERS

A Fried Film Group presentation of a Filmsmith production. Producers: Zachary Matz, Thomas Garvin, Timothy Bird. Executive producers: Christine Vachon, Daryl Hannah. Director/Screenplay: Melissa Painter. Camera: Paul Ryan. Editor: Brent White. Music: Sam Bisbee. In CFI color. Release date: Mar. 4, 2000. Running time: 98 Min.
Cast: Clea DuVall, Daryl Hannah, Tomas Arana, Eric Roberts.

WIREY SPINDELL

A WinStar Cinema release of a Five Minutes Before the Miracle production. Producers: Terence Michael, Lloyd Segan, Dolly Hall, Eric Schaeffer. Executive producers: Bruce Greenfield, Van Greenfield. Director/Screenplay: Eric Schaeffer. Camera: Kramer Morgenthau. Editor: Mitch Stanley. Music: Amanda Kravat, Peter Millrose. In Technicolor. Release date: Sept. 8, 1999. Running time: 101 Min.
Cast: Eric Schaeffer, Eric Mabius, Devon Matthews, Zane Adlum, Callie Thorne, Samantha Buck, John Doman.

THE WOMAN CHASER

A Definitive Films production in association with Tarmac Films. Producer: Soly Haim. Executive producer: Joe McSpadden. Co-producer: Fuller French. Director/Screenplay: Robinson Devor, based on the novel by Charles Williford. Camera: Kramer Morgenthau. Editor: Mark Winitsky. Music: Daniele Luppi. In B&W. Release date: Oct. 4, 1999. Running time: 96 Min.
Cast: Patrick Warburton, Eugene Roche, Ron Morgan, Emily Newman, Paul Malevitz, Lynette Bennett, Joe Durrenberger, Marilyn Rising, Pat Crowder.

WOMAN ON TOP

A Fox Searchlight (in U.S.)/UFD (in France) release of a 20th Century Fox Intl./Fox Searchlight Pictures production. Producer: Alan Poul. Co-producer: Nancy Paloian-Breznikar. Director: Fina Torres. Screenplay: Vera Blasi. Camera: Thierry Arbogast. Editor: Leslie Jones. Music: Luis Bacalov. In color, widescreen. Release date: Apr. 28, 2000. Running time: 83 Min.
Cast: Penelope Cruz, Murilo Benicio, Harold Perrineau Jr., Mark Feuerstein, John De Lancie.

WONDER BOYS

A Paramount release of a Paramount and Mutual Film Co. presentation of a Scott Rudin/Curtis Hanson production, produced in association with BBC, Maruben/Toho-Towa and Tele Munchen, in association with MFF Feature Film Productions. Producers: Rudin, Hanson. Executive producers: Adam Schroeder, Ned Dowd. Director: Curtis Hanson. Screenplay: Steve Kloves, based on the novel by Michael Chabon. Camera: Dante Spinotti. Editor: Dede Allen. Music: Christopher Young. In Deluxe color, Panavision widescreen. Release date: Feb. 10, 2000. MPAA Rating: R. Running time: 112 Min.
Cast: Michael Douglas, Tobey Maguire, Frances McDormand, Robert Downey Jr., Katie Holmes, Richard Thomas, Rip Torn, Philip Bosco, Jane Adams, Richard Knox, Michael Cavaias.

THE WORLD IS NOT ENOUGH

An MGM release of an Albert R. Broccoli's Eon Prods. Ltd. presentation. Producer: Michael G. Wilson, Barbara Broccoli. Director: Michael Apted. Screenplay: Neal Purvis, Robert Wade, Bruce Feirstein, story by Purvis, Wade. Camera: Adrian Biddle. Editor: Jim Clark. Music: David Arnold. In Deluxe color, Panavision widescreen. Release date: Nov. 10, 1999. MPAA Rating: PG-13. Running time: 125 Min.
Cast: Pierce Brosnan, Sophie Marceau, Robert Carlyle, Denise Richards, Robbie Coltrane, Judi Dench, Desmond Llewelyn, John Clelese, Maria Grazia Cucinotta, Samantha Bond.

THE WORLDS OF MEI LANFANG

A Blue Moon Prods. presentation of a Lotus Film production. (International sales: Blue Moon, N.Y.) Producer: Lisa Muskat, Shi Jian. Director: Mei-juin Chen. Screenplay: Bronwyn Barkan, Ross Blaufarb, Chen. Camera: Christian Iseli, David Shao. Editor: Chen. Music: Jean-Pierre Bedoyan. In part color, video. Release date: Mar. 14, 2000. Running time: 58 Min. Documentary.
With: Alan Chow, Lu Wenchin, Mei Shaowu, Wen Ruhua, Song Xiaochuan, Gold Star.
Narrators: Syou-ling Fu, Daxing Chang.

X-MEN

A 20th Century Fox release presented in associated with Marvel Entertainment Group of the Donners' Co./Bad Hat Harry production. Producers: Lauren Shuler-Donner, Ralph Winter. Executive producers: Avi Arad, Stan Lee, Richard Donner, Tom DeSanto. Co-producers: Joel Simon, William S. Todman Jr. Director: Bryan Singer. Screenplay: David Hayter, story by Tom DeSanto, Singer, based on the Marvel Comics series by Stan Lee. Camera: Newton Thomas Sigel. Editors: Steven Rosenblum, Devin Stitt, John Wright. Music: Michael Kamen. In Deluxe color, Panavision widescreen. Release date: July 11, 2000. MPAA Rating: PG-13. Running time: 104 Min.
Cast: Hugh Jackman, Patrick Stewart, Ian McKellan, Famke Janssen, James Marsden, Halle Berry, Anna Paquin, Tyler Mane, Ray Park, Rebecca Romijn-Stamos, Bruce Davison, Matthew Sharp.

THE YARDS

A Miramax release of a Paul Webster/Industry Entertainment production. Producers: Nick Wecksler, Paul Webster, Kerry Orent. Executive producers: Bob Weinstein, Harvey Weinstein, Jonathan Gordon. Co-producers: Matt Reeves, Christopher Goode. Director: James Gray. Screenplay: Gray, Matt Reeves. Camera: Harris Savides. Editor: Jeffrey Ford. Music: Howard Shore. In Deluxe color, Panavision widescreen. Release date: May 19, 2000. MPAA Rating: R. Running time: 115 Min.
Cast: Mark Wahlberg, Joaquin Phoenix, Charlize Theron, James Caan, Ellen Burstyn, Faye Dunaway, Chad Aaron, Andrew Davoli, Steve Lawrence, Tony Musante, Victor Argo, Tomas Milian, Robert Montano, Victor Arnold.

YOU CAN COUNT ON ME

A Shooting Gallery release of a Hart Sharp Entertainment/Shooting Gallery production. Producers: John Hart, Jeff Sharp, Larry Meistrich, Barbara De Fina. Executive producers: Martin Scorsese, Steve Carlis, Don Carter, Morton Swinsky. Director/Screenplay: Kenneth Lonergan. Camera: Stephen Dazmierski. Editor: Anne McCabe. Music: Lesley Barber. In color. Release date: Jan 28, 2000. Running time: 109 Min.
Cast: Laura Linney, Mark Ruffalo, Rory Culkin, Matthew Broderick, Jon Tenney, V. Smith-Cameron, Kenneth Lonergan.

THE YOUNG AND THE DEAD

A Tail Slate Pictures production. Producer: Ellin Baumel. Executive producer: Sheila Nevins. Co-producer: Julia King. Director: Shari Springer Berman, Robert Pulcini. Camera: Michael Barrow, Sandra Chandler. Editor: Robert Pulcini. Music: Mark Suozzo. In color. Release date: Sept. 7, 2000. Running time: 93 Min. Documentary.

THE YOUNG GIRL AND THE MONSOON

A Monsoon production. Producer: James Ryan. Executive producers: Richard Mehrlich, Beverly Mehrlich. Director/Screenplay: James Ryan. Camera: Ben Wolf. Editor: John David Allen. Music: David Carbonara. In Technicolor. Release date: Mar. 31, 2000. Running time: 90 Min.
Cast: Terry Kinney, Ellen Muth, Mili Avital, Diane Venora, Tom Guinee.

FOREIGN FEATURE FILMS

(OCTOBER 1, 1999—SEPTEMBER 30, 2000)

Many of the following films have been released in a limited fashion at film festivals or other similar venues but have not yet been nationally distributed.

ABERDEEN

A Norsk Film production in association with Freeway Films. (International sales: Trust Film Sales, Hvidovre, Denmark.) Producers: Tom Remlov, Petter J. Borgli. Co-producers: Kastro Khatib, John McGrath. Director: Hans Petter Moland. Screenplay: Moland, Kristin Amundsen. Camera: Philip Ogaard. Editor: Sophie Hesselberg. Music: Zbigniew Preisner. In color. Release date: July 5, 2000. Running time: 113 Min. NORWEGIAN-BRITISH.

Cast: Stellan Skarsgard, Lena Headey, Ian Hart, Charlotte Rampling.

ABOUT ADAM

A Miramax HAL Films and BBC Films presentation of a Venus production in association with Bord Scannian NA Herireann and the Irish Film Board. Producers: Anna Devlin, Marina Hughes. Executive producers: Harvey Weinstein, David M. Thompson, David Aukin, Trea Leventhal, Rod Stoneman. Director/Screenplay: Gerard Stembridge. Camera: Bruno De Keyser. Editor: Mary Finlay. Music: Adrian Johnston. In color. Release date: Jan. 28, 2000. Running time: 105 Min. BRITISH-IRISH.

Cast: Stuart Townsend, Kate Hudson, Frances O'Connor, Charlotte Bradley, Rosaleen Linehan, Tommy Tiernan, Alan Maher.

ABOUT JULY

A Rice Film Intl. (Taipei) production. Producer: Liu Xiao-Shu. Executive producer: Lim Min-Uan. Director/Screenplay: Wei Te-Sheng. Camera: Chin Ding-Chang, Liu San-lang. Editor: Chen Pau-Wen. Music: Luo Ji-Yi. In color, 16mm. Release date: Oct. 10, 1999. Running time: 72 Min. TAIWANESE.

Cast: Wan En-Yong, Si-ma San-San, Dong Wai-Xiu, Zeng Mian, Zhang Long.

ACROSS A GOLD PRAIRIE

A Prime Pictures Prod. production, in association with Filmmakers Inc. (International sales: Pony Canyon, Tokyo.) Producers: Osamu Kubota, Masataka Izumi. Director: Isshin Inudo. Screenplay: Sakichi Sato, Inudo, based on the manga by Yumiko Oshima. Camera: Taku Murakami. Editor: Inudo. Music: Elephant Love. In color. Release date: Feb. 13, 2000. Running time: 96 Min. JAPANESE.

Cast: Yusuke Iseya, Chizuru Ikewaki, Masatoshi Matsuo, Miako Tadano, Takeshi Kato.

(AN ACT OF...) SABOTAGE

A Big Head production in association with ZDF. Producer: Claudia Trunnier. Director/Screenplay: Christopher Anderson. Camera: Cyrus Amini, Anderson. Editor: Anton Herbert. In color, 16mm. Release date: Nov. 9, 1999. Running time: 80 Min. U.S.-GERMAN.

Cast: Bettina Hurzner, Rehane Abrahams, Ross Campbell, Kevin Evensen, Peter Van Lenger.

ACTORS

A Bac Films release of a Les Films Alain Sarde/Planete A/TF1 Films Prod./Le Studio Canal Plus production. (International sales: Le Studio Canal Plus, Paris.) Producer: Alain Sarde. Executive producer: Christine Gozlan. Director/Screenplay: Bertrand Blier. Camera: Francois Catonne. Editors: Claudine Merlin, Philippe Heissler. Music: Martial Solal. In color, widescreen. Release date: Apr. 5, 2000. Running time: 99 Min. FRENCH.

Cast: Pierre Arditi, Josiane Balasko, Jean-Paul Belmondo, Francois Berleand, Dominique Blanc, Bertrand Blier, Gerard Depardieu.

ADULT BEHAVIOR: IT'S ALL IN THE MIND

A Svensk Filmindustri release (in Sweden) of a Svensk Filmindustri production, in association with SVT Drama, FLAB and FLX Comedy. (International sales: Svensk Filmindustri, Stockholm.) Producers: Waldemar Bergendahl, Jan Blomgren. Director: Fredrik Lindstrom, Felix Herngren. Screenplay: Lindstrom, based on an idea by Lindstrom, Herngren. Camera: Goran Hallberg. Editor: Hanne Persson. Music: Bo Kasper's Orchestra. In color. Release date: Sept. 20, 1999. Running time: 97 Min. SWEDISH.

Cast: Felix Herngren, Karin Bjurstrom, Cecilia Ljung, Mikael Persbrandt, Kalla Bie, Magnus Harenstam, Fredrik Lindstrom.

THE ADVENTURES OF GOD

A CQ3 Films/Estudios Darwin production, in association with XL Films. (International sales: Orgon Films, Buenos Aires.) Producers: Victor Catania, Alejandro Galindo, Eliseo Subiela. Director/Screenplay: Eliseo Subiela. Camera: Daniel Rodriguez Maseda. Editor: Laura Bua. Music: Osvaldo Montes. In color and B&W, digital video. Release date: Sept. 1, 2000. Running time: 85 Min. ARGENTINE.

Cast: Pasta Dioguardi, Flor Sabatella, Daniel Freire, Lorenzo Quinteros, Maria Concepcion Cesar, Jose Maria Gutierrez, Walter Balsarini, Enrique Blugerman.

ADWA: AN AFRICAN VICTORY

A Negod Gwad Prods. production, in association with ZDF/Arte. (International sales: Mypheduh Films, Washington.) Producer: Haile Gerima. Director/Screenplay: Haile Gerima. Camera: Agustin Cubano. Editor: Gerima. In color. Release date: Sept. 5, 1999. Running time: 96 Min. Documentary. ETHIOPIAN-U.S.-ITALIAN.

AFTER THE FALL

An Umbrella Films production. Producer: Frauke Sandig. Executive producers: Barbara Frankenstein, Jurgen Tomm, Peter Bruggner. Director/Screenplay: Frauke Sandig, Eric Black. Camera: Black. Editor: Inge Schneider. In color, video-to-35mm. Release date: Apr. 22, 2000. Running time: 88 Min. Documentary. GERMAN-U.S.

AGATHA

An Alpha Plus/Studio Virtual production. (International sales: Alpha, Prague.) Director/Screenplay: Dan Krames. Camera: Radek Chmel. Editors: Petr Svoboda, Petr Stanek. Music: Karol Szymanowski. In B&W and color. Release date: Dec. 22, 1999. Running time: 79 Min. CZECH.

Cast: Eva Salzmannova, David Prachar, Jiri Ornest, Michal Dosedla, Michaela Dolinova, Alice Dvorakova, Radka Fidlerova.

AGUJETAS, CANTAOR

An Ideale Audience/Imalyre-Group France Telecom production in association with La Sept ARTE and TVE. Producer: Pierre-Olivier Bardet. Director: Dominique Abel. Camera: Jean-Yves Escoffier, Christophe Michelet. Editor: Christine Benoit. In B&W and color, Super 16mm. Release date: Apr. 30, 2000. Running time: 58 Min. Documentary. FRENCH.

ALI AZOUA

A Playtime presentation in co-production with Remstar, in association with Alexis Films and Ali'N Prods. Producers: Nabil Ayouch, Martine Lambrechts. Director: Nabil Ayouch. Screenplay: Ayouch, Nathalie Saugeon. Camera: Vincent Mathias, Renaat Lambeets. Editor: Jean-Robert Thomann. Music: Krishna Levy, Keith Jarrett, Lili Boniche, Reinette L'Orannaise. In color, widescreen. Release date: Aug. 29, 2000. Running time: 95 Min. FRENCH-MOROCCAN-BELGIAN.

Cast: Maunim Kbab, Mustapha Hansali, Hicham Moussane, Abdelhak Zhayra, Said Taghmaoui.

ALIEN ADVENTURE

An nWave Pictures release and presentation in association with Iwerks Entertainment and Movida/Trix. Producers: Charlotte Huggins, Caroline Van Iseghem. Executive producer: Ben Stassen. Co-producer: Kim Nelson-Frey. Director/Screenplay: Ben Stassen. Camera: Stassen. Editors: James Manke, Edwin Escalante, Todd Portugal. Music: Louis Vyncke, Lele & the Puzzlers. In CFI color, Imax 3-D. Release date: Aug. 22, 2000. Running time: 36 Min. BELGIAN-U.S.

Voices: Phil "Bouli" Lanners, Pierre "Lele" Lebecque.

Narrator: John Boyle.

ALL MY LOVED ONES

An In Film Praha presentation, supported by Eurimages. Producers: Rudolf Biermann, Jiri Bartoska, Lyn Clinton. Executive producer: Veronika Marczuk-Pazura. Co-producers: Olaf Lubaszenko, Cestmir Kopecky, Cezary Pazura, Martin Sulik. Director: Matej Minac. Screenplay: Jiri Hubac. Camera: Dodo Simoncic. Editor: Patrik Pass. Music: Janusz Stoklosa. In Filmmove color. Release date: Jan. 19, 2000. Running time: 92 Min. SLOVAK-CZECH-POLISH-GERMAN.

Cast: Josef Abrham, Jiri Bartoska, Branislav Holicek, Libuse Safrankova, Ondrej Vetchy, Rupert Graves, Marian Labuda.

ALL THE LOVE THERE IS

A Cecchi Gori Distribuzione release of a Mario & Vittorio Cecchi Gori presentation of a CGG production. Producer: Vittorio Cecchi Gori. Director: Sergio Rubini. Screenplay: Domenico Starnone, Rubini. Camera: Paolo Carnera. Editor: Angelo Nicolini. Music: Michele Fazio. In Cinecitta color. Release date: Mar. 15, 2000. Running time: 95 Min. ITALIAN.

Cast: Damiano Russo, Michele Venitucci, Francesco Cannito, Pierluigi Ferrandini, Marcello Introna, Antonio Lanera, Francesco Lamacchia.

ALL THE MORON'S MEN

A Medusa Film release (in Italy) of a Palomar production, in association with Medusa Film, of a Gialappa's Band film. Producer: Carlo Degli Esposti. Medusa producer: Antonino Antonucci. Director: Paolo Costella. Screenplay: Gialappa's Band, Andrea Salvadore, Enzo Santin, Costella. Camera: Fabrizio Luce. Editor: Esmeralda Calabria. Music: Elio & Le Storie Tese. In Cinecitta color. Release date: Dec. 13, 1999. Running time: 109 Min. ITALIAN.

Cast: Claudia Gerini, Paolo Hendel. Marina Massironi, Giovanni Esposito, Gigio Alberti, Fabio De Luigi, maurizio Crozza, Ugo Dighero.

ALMOST NOTHING
A Morena Filmes/Filmania production (International sales: Morena Filmes, Rio de Janeiro.) Producers: Mariza Leao, Renata Gentil. Director/Screenplay: Sergio Rezende. Camera: Guy Goncalves. Editor: Isabelle Rathery. Music: David Tygel. In color. Release date: Aug. 27, 2000. Running time: 100 Min. BRAZILIAN-MEXICAN.
Cast: Genesio de Barros, Denise Weinberg, Augusto Pompeu, Caio Jungueria, Camilo Bevilacqua, Ana Luisa Rabelo.

AMAZON
A Bac Distribution release of a Les Films Alain Sarde, TF1 Films Prod. (France)/PHF Films (Spain) production. (International sales: Le Studio Canal Plus, Paris.) Producer: Alain Sarde. Executive producer: Christine Gozlan. Director: Philippe de Broca. Screenplay: De Broca, Serge Frydman, story by De Broca. Camera: Jean-Francois Robin. Editor: Henri Lanoe. Music: Alexandre Desplat. In color, widescreen. Release date: June 18, 2000. Running time: 88 Min. FRENCH-SPANISH.
Cast: Jean-Paul Belmondo, Arielle Dombasle, Patrick Bouchitey, Thylda Bares, Andre Penvern, Jackie de la Nuea.

ANATOMY
A Sony Pictures release (in U.S.)/Columbia TriStar release (foreign) of a Deutsche Columbia Pictures Filmproduktion/Claussen & Woebke Filmproduktion production. (International sales: Columbia TriStar, Culver City/Berlin.) Producers: Jakob Claussen, Thomas Woebke, Andrea Willson. Director/Screenplay: Stefan Ruzowitzky. Camera: Peter von Haller. Editor: Ueli Christen. Music: Marius Ruhland. In color, widescreen. Release date: July 29, 2000. Running time: 99 Min. GERMAN.
Cast: Franka Potente, Benno Fuermann, Anna Loos, Holger Speckhahn, Sebastian Blomberg, Traugott Buhre, Rudiger Vogler.

ANDRE THE MAGNIFICENT
A UFD release of a Noe Prods./Andre Prods. production. (International sales: UGC Intl., Paris.) Executive producers: Frederic Dumas, Marc Baschet, Daniela Romano. Directors: Emmanuel Silvestre, Thibault Staib. Screenplay: Isabelle Candelier, Loic Houdre, Gilles Laurent, Patrick Ligardes, Jean-Luc Porraz, Staib, Silvestre, Michel Vuillermoz, based on the play "Andre le magnifique" by Candelier, Denis Podalydes, Houdre, Ligardes, Vuillermoz. Camera: Florent Herry. Editor: Eric Berruchon. Music: Pascal Comelade. In color. Release date: Apr. 10, 2000. Running time: 87 Min. FRENCH.
Cast: Michel Vuillermoz, Patrick Ligardes, Isabelle Candelier, Jean-Luc Porraz, Loic Houdre.

ANGELOS' FILM
A Lumen Film production in association with VPRO Television. Producer: Cesar Messemaker. Director: Peter Forgacs. Camera: Angelos Papanasstassiou, various. Editor: Kati Juhasz. Original music: Tibor Szemzo. In B&W, 16mm-to-BETA. Release date: May 2, 2000. Running time: 60 Min. Documentary. DUTCH.
Voices: Caroline Bodoczky, Peter Forgacs, Johanna Ter Steege, Charlotte Van Dijk, Ad Van Kempen.

ANGELS OF THE UNIVERSE
An Icelandic Film Corp. (Iceland)/Filmhuset (Norway)/Peter Rommel Prods., SDF-Arte, ORB (Germany)/SVT (Sweden)/Zentropa Prods. (Denmark) production. (International sales: Trust Film Sales, Hvidore, Denmark.) Producer: Fridrik Thor Fridriksson. Co-producers: Egil Odegaard, Peter Rommel, Peter Aalbaeck Jensen, Anna Maria Karlsdottir, Gunnar Carlsson. Director: Fridrik Thor Fridriksson. Screenplay: Einar Mar Gudmundsson, from his novel. Camera: Harald Paalgaard. Editors: Sigvaldi Karason,. Skule Eriksen. Music: Hilmar Orn Hilmarsson. In color. Release date: Jan. 28, 2000. Running time: 95 Min. ICELANDIC-NORWEGIAN-GERMAN-SWEDISH-DANISH.
Cast: Ingvar E. Sigurdsson, Baltasar Kormakur, Bjorn Jorundur Fridbjornsson, Jilmir Snaer Gudnason, Margret Helga Johanssdottir.

ANGST
A UIP (Australia) release of an Australian Film Finance Corp. presentation of a Green Light production, in association with the NSW Film and TV Office, Australian Film Commission. (International sales: Beyond Films, Sydney.) Producer: Jonathon Green. Director: Daniel Nettheim. Screenplay: Anthony O'Connor. Camera: Tristan Milani. Editor: Martin Connor. Music: David Thrussell. In Movielab color. Release date: July 22, 2000. Running time: 85 Min. AUSTRALIAN.
Cast: Sam Lewis, Jessica Napier, Justin Smith, Abi Tucker, Luke Lennox, Lara Cox.

ANNE FRANK'S DIARY OF A YOUNG GIRL
A Globe Trotter Network, Animation Production Multimedia Investissement, Associated Studios Global Toon Network (France)/Brookfield BS (U.K.)/Cleeve Studios (Ireland) production, with participation of the Anne Frank Fonds (Switzerland). (International sales: Globe Trotter, Paris.) Producer: Stephane Dykman. Director: Julian Y. Wolff. Screenplay: Daniel Holender, Wolff. Music: Carine Gutlerner. In color. Release date: Oct. 10, 1999. Running time: 88 Min. Animated. FRENCH-BRITISH-IRISH.

ANOTHER PLANET
A Domino Film & Television presentation of a Syncopated Prods. (Toronto) production. Producer/Director/Screenplay: Christene Browne. Camera: Candide Franklyn. Editor: Le Michael Searles. Music: Donald Quan. In color. Release date: Oct. 3, 1999. Running time: 90 Min. CANADIAN.
Cast: Sandy Daley, Kevin White, Marcia Brown, Daniel Levesque, Monique MacDonald, Tiemoko Simaga, Natalie Eta, Mathieu Dutan.

THE ANTO WAR
A Cecchi Gori Distribuzione release of a Cecchi Gori Group production. Producer: Vittorio Cecchi Gori. Executive producer: Alessandro Calosci. Director: Riccardo Milani. Screenplay: Sandro Petraglia, Domenico Starnone, Milani. Camera: Alessandro Pesci. Editor: Marco Spoletini. Music: Piccola Orchestra Avion Travel. In color. Release date: Oct. 10, 1999. Running time: 98 Min. ITALIAN.
Cast: Flavio Pistilli, Paolo Setta, Danilo Mastracci, Federico Di Flauro, Regina Orioli.

ANTS IN THE PANTS
A Constantin release of Constantin Film Produktion production. (International sales: Atlas Intl., Munich.) Producer: Bernd Eichinger. Co-producer: Martin Moszkowicz. Director: Marc Rothemund. Screenplay: Granz Henman. Camera: Hans-Guenther Buecking. Editor: Sandy Saffeels. Music: Johnny Klimek, Xaver Naudascher. In color. Release date: July 18, 2000. Running time: 83 Min. GERMAN.
Cast: Tobias Schenke, Axel Stain, Luise Helm, Bjorn Kirschniok, Mina Tander, Nicky Kantor, Tom Lass, Christian Schneller, Andrea Sawitzki.

APRIL
A Consortium Film Georgia production (International sales: Pierre Grise Prods., Paris.) Director/Editor: Otar Iosseliani. Screenplay: Iosseliani, Erlon Akhvlediani. Camera: Yuri Fednev. Music: Sulkhan Nassidze. In B&W. Release date: May 15, 2000. Running time: 50 Min. GEORGIAN.
Cast: Tania Tchantouria, Guia Tchirakadze.

THE APRIL CHILDREN
An Inter Nationales release of a Ventura Films presentation of a Zero Film production in association with ZDF. Producer: Thomas Kufus. Executive producers: Aneke Reddering. Director: Yuksel Yavuz. Screenplay: Yavuz, Britta Ohm. Henner Winckler. Camera: Ciro Cappellari. Editor: Arpad Bondy. In color. Release date: Jan 14, 2000. Running time: 85 Min. GERMAN.
Cast: Erdal Yildiz, Inga Busch, Bulent Esrungun, Senem Tepe, Serif Sezer, Cemel Yavuz, Kaan Emre.

AROUND THE PINK HOUSE
A Mille et Une Prods. presentation. Producers: Anne-Cecile Berthomeau, Edouard Mauriat. Executive producer: Djinn House Prods. Co-producer: Les Lateles du Cinema Quebecois, Jean Dansereau. Director/Screenplay: Joana Hadjithomas, Khalil Joreige. Camera: Pierre David. Editor: Tina Baz Le Gall. In color. Release date: Apr. 6, 2000. Running time: 92 Min. FRENCH-CANADIAN-LEBANESE.
Cast: Joseph Bon Nassar, Mireille Safa, Chadi El Zein, Hassan Mrad, Ziad Said, Rabih Mroue, Aline Aoun, Tony Balabane, Hassan Ferat.

THE ART OF DYING
An Aurum release of an Aurum production, in association with TVE, Canal Plus. (International sales: Aurum, Madrid.) Producer: Francisco Ramos. Director: Alvaro Fernandez Armero. Screenplay: Juan Vicente Pozuelo, Francisco Javier Roy. Camera: Javier Salmones. Editor: Ivan Aledo. Music: Bingen Mendizabal. In color. Release date: Mar. 29, 2000. Running time: 103 Min. SPANISH.
Cast: Fele Martinez, Maria Esteve, Gustavo Salmeron, Lucia Jimenez, Adria Collado, Elsa Pataky, Sergio Peris-Mencheta.

ASPHALT
An Alta Films release of a Jose Maria Lara P.C. production, in association with Albares Prods., Sur Films, TVE, Canal Plus, ETB. (International sales: TF1 Intl., Paris.) Producer: Jose Maria Lara. Director: Daniel Calparsoro. Screenplay: Calparsoro, Santiago Tabernero, Frank Palacios. Camera: Josep M. Civit. Editor: Julia Juaniz. Music: Mastreta, Najwajean. In color. Release date: Feb. 5, 2000. Running time: 94 Min. SPANISH.
Cast: Najwa Nimri, Juan Diego Botto, Gustavo Salmeron, Alfredo Villa, Antonia San Juan, Roger Ibanez.

AT MIDNIGHT AND A HALF
A Sudaka Films (Caracas) production, in association with Futuro Films (Lima). Producers: Mariana Rondon, Marite Ugas. Director/Screenplay: Ugas, Rondon. Camera: Micaela Cajahuaringa. Editor: Alberto Gomez. Music: Trina Medina, Ignacio Barreto, Los Rodriguez. In color. Release date: June 5, 2000. Runnning time: 90 Min. VENEZUELAN-PERUVIAN.
Cast: Salvador Del Solar, Maria Fernanda Ferro, Constanza Morales.

ATTACK THE GAS STATION!
A Cinema Service release (in South Korea) of a Fun & Happiness production. (International sales: Mirovision, Seoul.) Producer: Lee Kwan-su. Executive producer: Kim Miheui. Director: Kim Sang-jin. Screenplay: Park Jeong-wu. Camera: Choi Jeong-wu. Editor: Go Im-pyo. In color. Release date: Oct. 21, 1999. Running time: 109 Min. SOUTH KOREAN.
Cast: Lee Seong-jae, Yu Oh-seong, Kang Seong-jin, Yu Ji-tae, Park Yeong-kyu.

AT THE HEIGHT OF SUMMER
A Lazennec presentation of a Studio Canal Plus/Arte France Cinema/Hang Phim Truyen production, with the participation of Canal Plus, ZDF/Arte. (International sales: Studio Canal, Paris.) Producer: Christophe Rossignon. Director/Screenplay: Tran Anh Hung. Camera: Mark Lee. Editor: Mario Battistel. Music: Ton That Tiet. In color. Release date: May 18, 2000. Running time: 112 Min. FRENCH-VIETNAMESE.
Cast: Than Nu Yen Khe, Nguyen Nhu Quynh, Le Khanh, Ngo Quang Hai, CHu Hung, Trn Manh Cuong, Le Tuan Anh, Le Ngoc Dung.

AUDITION

An Omega Project (Tokyo) production. Producers: Akemi Suyama, Satoshi Hukushima. Executive producer: Toyoyuki Yokohama. Director: Takashi Miike. Screenplay: Daisuke Tengan, based on a novel by Ryu Murakami. Camera: Jideo Yamamoto, Editor: Yasushi Shimamura. Music: Koji Endo. In color. Release date: Oct. 6, 1999. Running time: 115 Min. JAPANESE.
Cast: Ryo Ishibashi, Eihi Shiina, Miyuki Matsuda, Renji Ishibashi.

AUGUSTIN, KING OF KUNG-FU

A Pathe Distribution release (in France) of an Alain Sarde Prods., Cine B, Cinea, France 2 (France)/BocaBoca Producciones (Spain) production, with participation of Canal Plus, Sofinergie 5. (International sales: President Film, Paris.) Producers: Philippe Carcassonne, Alain Sarde. Executive producer: Antonio Barzga. Director: Anne Fontaine, Screenplay: Fontaine, Jacques Fieschi, Gilles Taurand, Camera: Christophe Polloc. Editor: Luc Barnier. Music: Ri-Mah, Olivier Lebe. In color, widescreen. Release date: Aug. 29, 1999. Running time: 87 Min. FRENCH-SPANISH.
Cast: Jean-Chretien Sibertin-Blanc, Maggie Cheung, Darry Cowl, Bernard Campan, Paulette Dubost, Pascal Bonitzer, Ming Shan.

AUTUMN

A BIM Distribuzione release (in Italy) of a Dodici Dicembre production in association with RAI Radiotelevisione Italiana, Telepiu. Producer: Giorgio Magliulo. Director/Screenplay: Nina di Majo. Camera: Cesare Accetta. Editor: Giogio Franchini. Music: Giulio di Majo, Davide Mastropaolo, Leandro Sorrentino, Stefano Ulisse. In color. Release date: Aug. 26, 1999. Running time: 95 Min. ITALIAN.
Cast: Giovanni Bruno, Francesca Caracciolo, Marco Mario De Notaris, Nina di Majo, Pietro Alessio di Majo, Angelica di Majo, Sonia Gessner.

AUTUMN BLOSSOMS

A CineQuanon/Nikkatsu production. (International sales: Cine Quanon, Tokyo.) Executive producers: Bong-ou Lee, Masaya Nakamura, Mizue Kunizane. Director/Screenplay: Shunsaku Ikehata. Camera: Masao Tochizawa. Editor: Tomoyo Oshima. Music: Taro Iwashiro. Release date: Sept. 3, 1999. Running time: 120 Min. JAPANESE.
Cast: Ken Ogata, Jijiri Kojima, Yoshi Oida.

AVEC MON MARI

A Muto Kiichi Office production in association with New Cinema Workshop and Cineman Brain. (International sales: Pony Canyon, Tokyo.) Producer: Kiichi Muto. Director/Screenplay/Editor: Kentaro Otani. Camera: Kazuhiro Suzuki. Music: Reinaldo Pineda. In color. Release date: Dec. 21, 1999. Running time: 97 Min. JAPANESE.
Cast: Hirofumi Kobayashi, Yuka Itaya, Kaori Tsuji, Ren Osugi, Kentaro Otani, Mayumi Terashima.

AZZURRO

A C-Films, TSI (Switzerland)/Alhena Films, Machinassou, PCT Cinema & Television (France)/Gam Film, Technovisual (Italy) production. (International sales: C-Films, Zurich.) Executive producer: Edi Hubschmid. Director: Denis Rabaglia. Screenplay: Rabaglia, Luca De Benedettis, Antoine Jaccoud. Camera: Dominique Grosz. Editor: Claudio Di Mauro. Music: Louis Crelier. In color. Release date: Aug. 11, 2000. Running time: 85 Min. SWISS-FRENCH-ITALIAN.
Cast: Paolo Villaggio, Francesca Pipoli, Marie-Christine Barrault, Jean-Luc Bideau, Renato Scarpa, Julien Boisselier.

BACK DOOR

An IdeeFixe production, in association with the Greek Film Centre, Alpha TV, Rosebud SA, Netmed, JBA Productions, Filmex, TNT. (International sales: Greek Film Centre, Athens.) Producers: Fenia Cossovitsa, Amanda Livanou, Hercules Mavroides. Director: Yorgos Tsemberopoulos. Screenplay: Dennis Iliades, Tsemberopoulos. Camera: Platon Andronides. Editor: Takis Yannopoulos. Music: Marios Strofalis. In color. Release date: May 17, 2000. Running time: 104 Min. GREEK.
Cast: Constantinos Papadimitriou, Alexandriani Kikelianou, Haris Sozos, Ierkolis Michailides, Antonis Kafetzopoulos.

BAD COMPANY

A Universal Pictures (France) release (in France) of a Pan-Europeenne Prod., Les Films Alain Sarde, M6 Films presentation, in association with Universal Pictures (France), and with participation of Canal Plus, M6 and Sofygram 3, of a PFP Prods. production. Producers: Philippe Godeau, Alain Sarde. Director: Jean-Pierre Ameris. Screenplay: Alain Layrac, Ameris. Camera: Yves Vandermeeren. Editor: Martine Giordano. Music director: Valerie Lindon. In color. Release date: Oct. 27, 1999. (Original title: Mauvaises frequentations.) Running time: 95 Min. FRENCH.
Cast: Maud Forget, Lou Doillon, Micheline Presle, Ariane Ascaride, Robinson Stevenin, Maxime Mansion, Delphinie Rich.

BAD GIRL TRILOGY

A Central Motion Picture Co. production. Producer: Shun-Ching Chiu. Executive producer:. Itu-Bin Chung. Co-producer: Shi-Feng Wang. Director: Yan-Ting Wen, Jin-Jie Lin, Ying-Yu Chan. Screenplays: Yao-ting Wen, Jing-jie Lin, Ying-yu Chan. Camera: Ming-guo Lin, Wen-chung Sung. Editors: Hsiao-dong Chen, Chen-ching Lei. Music: Jie-ren Cheng, Shen Hu, Huan-fu Yu. In color. Release date: Mar. 1, 2000. Running time: 114 Min. TAIWANESE.
Cast: Rui-Jun Fan, Chi-Yao Chang, Tsan-De Tsai, Jing-Wen Jia, Han-Liang Chung, Pei-Wen Huang, Hsin-Ru Lin, Shi Chang.

BAD GUYS

A Magic Media/Medien & Television Munchen production, in association with HBO, MTV. Producer: Peter Barbalics. Director: Tamas Sas. Screenplay: Laszlo Bernat Czeto, Erika Ozsda, Sas. Camera: Gergely Poharnok. Editor: Klara Major. Music: Pierrot. In color. Release date: Feb. 5, 2000. Running time: 104 Min. HUNGARIAN-GERMAN.
Cast: Viktor Bodo, Zoltan Rajkai, Andras Stohl, Anna Palmai, Andrea Fullajtar, Laszlo Banszky, Gabor Mate.

BAD MONEY

A Red Sky Entertainment release (in Canada) of a Security Film Corp. (Calgary) production, with support from Telefilm Canada and Rogers Telefund Canada. (International sales: Myriad Pictures, Santa Monica.) Producers: James Gottselig, John Hazlett. Director: John Hazlett. Screenplay: Hazlett, Blake Brooker, Michael Gregory. Camera: Alex Vendler. Editor: Michael Dowse. Music: Schaun Tozer. In color. Release date: Sept. 25, 1999. Running time: 95 Min. CANADIAN.
Cast: Graham Greene, Karen Sillas, Stephen Spender, Alison Down, Tamsin Kelsey.

BALKAN BAROQUE

A Regards Prods./Institut National de l'Audiovisuel (France) production, in association with Wega Film (Austria), Scarabee (Netherlands), with support from Arte-WDR (Germany) and ORF (Austria). (International sales: Regards Prods., Paris.) Producer: Chantal Delanoe. Co-producers: Veit Heiduschka, Hetty Naaijkens-Retel Helmrich. Director: Pierre Coulibeuf. Screenplay: Marina Abramovic. Camera: Domonique le Rigoleur. Editor: Thierry Rouden. In color. Release date: Sept. 26, 1999. Running time: 63 Min. Documentary. FRENCH.
With: Marina Abramovic, Ulay, Michel Butor, Sean Kelly.

BANKRUPT

A La Vie est Belle Films Associes production in co-production with Les Films en Hiver, Elison, Horizon Mars, Les Productions de l'Amour Fou. (International sales: Celluloid Dreams, Paris.) Producer: Celine Maugis. Director: Antoine Desrosieres. Screenplay: Philippe Barassat, Desrosieres, Swennola Bothorel. Camera: George Lechaptois. Editor: Nicolas Le Du. Music: Dominique A. In B&W and color. Release date: Feb. 5, 2000. Running time: 75 Min. FRENCH.
Cast: Mathieu Demy, Gwennola Bothorel, Zinedine Soualem, Antoine Chappey, Howard Vernon.

THE BEATING OF THE BUTTERFLY'S WINGS

A Les Films des Tournelles release of a Les Films des Tournelles/Les Films en Hiver production, with participation of Gimages and Canal Plus. Producers: Anne-Dominique Toussaint, Pascal Judelewicz. Executive producer: Franck Landron. Director/Screenplay: Laurent Firode. Camera: Jean-Rene Duveau. Editor: Didier Rantz. Music: Peter Chase. In color. Release date: July 4, 2000. Running time: 97 Min. FRENCH.
Cast: Audrey Tautou, Faudel, Eric Feldman, Eric Savin, Lysiane Meis, Francoise Bertin, Irene Ismailoff, Said Ferrai, Felicite Wouassi.

BEAUTIFUL CREATURES

A UIP (in U.K.)/Universal (in U.S.) release of a DNA Films presentation, in association with United Pictures Intl. and the Arts Council of England, of a Snakeman production. Producers: Alan J. Wands, Simon Donald. Director: Bill Eagles. Screenplay: Simon Donald. Camera: James Welland. Editor: Jon Gregory. Associate editor: Ian Seymour. Music: Murray Gold. In Technicolor. Release date: Aug. 23, 2000. Running time: 86 Min.
Cast:Rachel Weisz, Susan Lynch, Alex North, Iain Glen, Maurice Roeves, Tom Mannion, Robin Laing.

BEAUTIFUL SUMMER

A Kiev Studio production. Director: Boris Barnet. Screenplay: Evgeni Pomeshchikov, N. Daleky. Camera: Aleksei Mishurin. Music: German Zhukovsky. In color. Release date: Aug. 10, 2000. Running time: 87 Min. SOVIET UNION–1950.
Cast: Nikolai Kryuchkov, Nina Arkhipova, Mikhail Kuznetsov, Marina Bebutova, Viktor Dobrovolsky, Konstantin Sorokin.

BELLYFUL

A Euripide Distribution release (in France) of a Havas Image, Les Voleurs d'Ombres Prods. (France)/Harlenkijn Holland, Kro-TV Holland (Netherlands) production, in association with Accolade Pictures, with participation of Canal Plus, CNC. (International sales: Film Distribution, Paris.) Producers: Jean-Pierre Saire. Co-executive producers: Frederic Sichler, Daniel Toscan du Plantier, Melvin Van Peebles. Co-producer: Yves Pasquier. Director/Screenplay: Melvin Van Peebles, based on his novel. Camera: Philippe Pavans de Ceccaty. Editor: Catherine d'Hoir. Music: Van Peebles. In color, digital video-to-35mm. Release date: June 21, 2000. Running time: 107 Min. FRENCH-DUTCH.
Cast: Andrea Ferreol, Jacques Boudet, Meiji U Tum'si, Claude Perron, Franck Delhaye, Herman van Veen.

A BENCH IN THE PARK

An Alta Films release (in Spain) of a Fernando Colomo PC/Alta Films production with participation of Canal Plus. Executive producer: Beatriz de la Gandara. Director/Screenplay: Agusti Vila. Camera: David Omedes. Editor: Miguel Angel Santamaria. Music: Ian Briton. In color. Release date: Sept. 21, 1999. Running time: 81 Min. SPANISH.
Cast: Alex Brendemuhl, Victoria Freire, Monica Lopez, Aitor Merino, Gary Piquer, Francesco Garrido, Vicenta Ndongo, Ingrid Rubior.

BERLIN-CINEMA
A Les Filmes de la Terrasse (Vevey)/La Sept-Arte (Paris) production. (International sales: Les Films de la Terrasse, Vevey, Switzerland.) Director: Samira Gloor Fadel. Texts: Franz Hessel, Ruth-Andreas Friedrich, Ilma Rakusa. Camera: Philippe Bonnier, Patrice Cologne, Fadel, Denis Jutzeler, Jacques Loiseleux, Sophie Maintigneux, Jugues Ryffel. Editors: Camille Bordes Resnais, Isabelle Dedieu, Alexandre Malcotti. Music: Mahmut Demir, Jean-Louis Valero. In B&W and color. Release date: Sept. 14, 1999. Running time: 106 Min. SWISS-FRENCH.
Cast: Wim Wenders, Jean Nouvel, Thomas, Jean-Luc Godard (voice), Rudiger Vogler (voice).

BESAME MUCHO
A Terzp Mondo production. Producers: Mosh Dannon, Shai Goldman, Jospeh Pitchhadze, Dov Steuer. Director/Screenplay: Joseph Pitchhadze. Camera: Shai Goldman. Editor: Dov Steuer. Music: Berry Sakharof. In color. Release date: July 20, 2000. Running time: 114 Min. ISRAELI.
Cast: Ryan Early, Carmel Betto, Eli Danker, Ayala Verete, Ezra Kafri, Moni Moshonov, Michael Sarne.

BESIDE MYSELF
A Pablo Distribuzione release (in Italy) of a Pupkin production. Producers: Gianluca Arcopinto, Rita Zanasi. Director/Screenplay: Gianni Zanasi. Camera: Giulio Pietromarchi. Editor: Rita Rognoni. Music: Giuliano Taviani. In Technicolor. Release date: Nov. 23, 1999. Running time: 75 Min. ITALIAN.
Cast: Paolo Sassanelli, Lorenzo Viaconzi, Marit Nissen, Dino Abbrescia.

BEST
An Optimum Releasing release of an IAC Film/Sky Films/Isle of Man Film Commission production, in association with Smoke & Mirrors Film Prods. and Pembridge Pictures. Producers: Mary McGuckian, Chris Roff, Elvira Bolz. Executive producers: Steve Christian, Guy Collins, Michael Ryan, John Lynch. Director: Mary McGuckian. Screenplay: John Lynch, McGuckian. Camera: Witold Stok. Editor: Kant Pan. Music: Mark Stevens. In Metrocolor B&W, Technicolor. Release date: May 5, 2000. Running time: 106 Min. BRITISH.
Cast: John Lynch, Ian Bannen, Jerome Flynn, Ian Hart, Patsy Kensit, Cal Macaninch, Linus Roache, Adrian Lester, David Hayman, James Ellis, Roger Daltrey, Clive Anderson, Sophie Dahl, Stephen Fry.

BETTER THAN SEX
A Samuel Goldwyn Films (in U.S.)/New Vision (in Australia) release of a New South Wales Film & TV Office/France Television Distribution-Meercat Films/New Vision Films presentation of a Better Than production. (International sales: President Films, Paris.) Producers: Bruna Papandrea, Frank Cox. Executive producer: Marc Bonduel. Director/Screenplay: Jonathan Teplitzky. Camera: Garry Phillips. Editor: Shawn Seet. Music: David Hirschfelder. In Movielab color. Release date: June 8, 2000. Running time: 81 Min. AUSTRALIAN-FRENCH.
Cast: David Wenham, Susie Porter, Catherine McClements, Kris McQuade, Simon Bossell.

BEWARE OF GREEKS BEARING GUNS
A Palace Films (Australia) release of an Australian Film Finance Corp. presentation of a Media World Features (Melbourne)/Mythos Prods. (Athens) co-production, in association with Film Victoria, Mega Channel, the Greek Film Center. (International sales: Trident Releasing, L.A.) Producers: Colin J. South, Dionyssis Samiotis, Anastasios Vasiliou, John Tatoulis. Director: Tatoulis. Screenplay: Tom Galbraith. Camera: Peter Zakharov. Editor: Michael Collins. Music: Mikis Theodorakis. In Cinevex color. Release date: Mar. 30, 2000. Running time: 88 Min. AUSTRALIAN-GREEK.
Cast: Lakis Lazopoulos, Zoe Carides, John Bluthal, Claudia Buttazzoni, Tasso Kavvadia, Noni Ionannidou,. Osvaldo Maione.

BEYOND
A Thura Film, Bech Film, Danish Film Institute, TV2, (Denmark)/Nordic Screen Production, Svenska Filmkompaniet, SVT Drama (Sweden) production. (International sales: Nordisk Film, Copenhagen.) Producers: Peter Bech, Michael Obel. Director: Ake Sandgren. Screenplay: Bent E. Rasmussen, Anders Thomas Jensen. Camera: Dan Laustsen. Editor: Kasper Leick. Music: Randall Meyers. In color. Release date: Aug. 18, 2000. Running time: 91 Min. DANISH-SWEDISH.
Cast: Robert Hansen, Ralf J. Hollander, Otto Brandenburg, Baard Owe, Jesper Asholt, Laura Aagaard, Jytte Abildstrom.

BEYOND FORGIVIN'
A Magna Pictures (Bangkok) production, in association with Five Star Productions. Producers: Sorajak Kasemsuvan, Chochart Toprateep. Executive producer: Charum Eamphungporn. Director/Screenplay: Manop Udomdej. Camera: Sutas Intranupakorn. Editor: Manop Jenjarassakul. Music: Tewan Sapsanayakorn. In color. Release date: Oct. 4, 1999. Running time: 112 Min. THAI.
Cast: Dom Hetrakul, Nuchnart Saichompoo, Juthamas Chantasorn, Chaianant Trisarnsri, Vit Pimkarnchanapong.

BEYOND OUR DREAMS
A UGC Intl. and Les Films du Rivage production in association with MK2 Diffusion and Canal Plus. Producer: Marc Ruscart. Executive producers: Norair Azatian, Enrico Ballarine, Guido Cerasuolo. Director/Screenplay: Hiner Saleem. Camera: Andreas Sinanos. Editor: Monique Prim. Music: Nikos Kipourgos. In color. Release date: Aug. 28, 2000. Running time: 100 Min. FRENCH-ARMENIAN-ITALIAN.
Cast: Olivier Sitruk, Roasanna Vite Mesropian, Ramen Avinian, Edik Bagdassarian, Noris Maloyan, Mariana Dourgarian, Kamal Hamarash.

BEYOND THE OCEAN
A Go East Prods. and Intrinsic Value production in association with Persistence of Vision Films. Producers: Isen Robbins, Unsula Wolschlager. Executive producer: Go East Prods. Director: Tony Pemberton. Screenplay: Pemberton, Alexis Brunner. Camera: Ted Sappington, Phil Robertson. Editor: Svetlana Guralskaya. Music: Christian Fennesz. In color and B&W. Release date: Jan. 22, 2000. Running time: 87 Min. U.S.-RUSSIAN-AUSTRIAN.
Cast: Dasha Volga, Rik Nagel, Donovan Barton, Sage, Tatiana Kuznetsova, Tatiana Kamina.

BHOPAL EXPRESS
A Highlight Films production in association with Kintop Pictures and Alive Entertainment. Producers: Philip Von Alvensleben, Tabrez Noorani, Deepak Nayar. Director: Mahesh Mathai. Screenplay: Piyush Pandey, Prasoon Pandey. Camera: Mathai. Editor: Priya Krishnaswamy. In color. Release date: Mar. 7, 2000. Running time: 92 Min. INDIA.
Cast: Kay Kay, Nethra Raghuraman, Naseeruddin Shah, Zeenat Aman, Vijay Raaz.

THE BIG ANIMAL
A Telewizja Polska production. (International sales: Poltel Enterprises, Warsaw.) Producer: Slawomir Rogowski. Executive producer: Film Srugio Perspektyewa. Director: Jerzy Stuhr. Screenplay: Krzysztof Kieslowski, from a story by Kazimierz Orlos. Camera: Pawel Edelman. Editor: Elzbieta Kurkowska. Music: Abel Korzeniowski. In Kodak color and B&W. Release date: July 8, 2000. Running time: 70 Min. POLISH.
Cast: Anna Dymna, Jerzy Stuhr, Dominika Dednarczyk, Blazej Wojcik, Rubio.

THE BIG BANG
A Cecchi Gori Distribuzione release of a Cecchi Gori Group production. Producer: Vittorio Cecchi Gori. Executive producers: Bruno Altissimi, Claudio Saraceni. Director: Leone Pompucci. Screenplay: Gennaro Nunziante, Paolo Rossi, Pompucci. Camera: Massimo Pau. Editor: Mauro Bonanni. Music: Rossi. In color. Release date: Apr. 7, 2000. Running time: 90 Min. ITALIAN.
Cast: Carlo Buccirosso, Emilio Solfrizzi, Alessandro Di Carlo, Gennaro Nunziante, Francesca Nunzi, Claudio Amendola.

BIGGER THAN TINA
A Palace Films release (in Australia and New Zealand) of a Backyard Prods./Palace Films production, with the assistance of Film Victoria. (International sales: Backyard Prods., Melbourne.) Producer: Grant Hardie. Executive producer: Daniel Scharf. Co-producer: Jenny Loncaric. Director/Screenplay: Neil Foley. Camera: Ben Milward-Bason. Editor: John Leonard. Music: Hugo Cran, Michael Conolon, Henri Crave. In Cinevex color. Release date: Nov. 18, 1999. Running time: 95 Min. AUSTRALIAN.
Cast: Michael Dalley, Sally Lightfoot, Barry Friedlander, Dobe Newton, Phillipa Chapple, Annie Finsterer, Fraser Grey, Greg Francis.

THE BIRTHDAY
A Sonet Film release of a Cimbria Film production, in association with SVT Drama Malmo and Film pa Osterlen. (International sales: BV Intl. Pictures, Avaldsnes, Norway.) Producer: Goran Lindstrom. Executive producers: Lindstrom, Bengt Linne. Director/Screenplay: Richard Hobert. Camera: lars Crepin. Editor: Leif Kristiansson. Music: Bjorn Hallman Hobert. In color. Release date: Jan. 31, 2000. Running time: 114 Min. SWEDISH.
Cast: Camilla Lunden, Goran Stangertz, Lena Endre, Pernilla August, Sven Lindberg, Mona Malm, Sven-Bertil Taube, Jakob Eklund.

BLACK & WHITE IN COLOR
A Czech Television/Arcimboldo production. Producer: Peter Ott. Director/Screenplay: Mira Erdevicki-Charap. Camera: Marek Jicha. Editor: David Charap. Music: Vera Bila and KALE. In color. Release date: Aug. 21, 1999. Running time: 58 Min. Documentary. CZECH.

BLACKBOARDS
A Makhmalbaf Film House (Tehran)/Fabrica Cinema (Rome) production, in association with Raicinema, T-Mark (Japan). (International sales: Wild Bunch/Le Studio Canal Plus, Paris.) Producers: Mohsen Makmalbaf, Marco Muller. Executive producer: Mohamad Ahmadi. Director: Samira Makmalbaf. Screenplay: Mohsen Makmalbaf, Samira Makmalbaf. Camera: Ebrahim Ghafori. Editor: Mohsen Makmalbaf. Music: Mohamed Reza Darvishi. In color. Release date: May 11, 2000. Running time: 84 Min. IRANIAN-ITALIAN.
Cast: Bahman Ghobadi, Said Mohamadi, Behnaz Jafari.

BLACK HOLE
A Cinerock Pictures Co. production. (International sales: Cinerock, Seoul.) Producer: Kweon Yeong-rak. Executive producer: Kim Won-rae. Director/Screenplay: Kim Kuk-hyeong, from the novel by Choe In-ho. Camera: Seok Hyeong-jin. Editor: Kim Hyeon. Music: Kim Kyu-yang. In color. Release date; Oct. 16, 1999. Running time: 92 Min. SOUTH KOREAN.
Cast: Ahn Sung-ki, Kim Min, Sa Hyun-jin, Bang Eun-jin.

THE BLACK HOUSE
An Asmik Ace Entertainment production. (International sales: Asmik Ace, Tokyo.) Producers: Yasushi Tsuge, Kazuko Misawa, Tsutomu Yamamoto. Executive producer: Masato Hara. Senior executive producers: Tsuguhiko Kadokawa, Nobuyoshi Otani. Director: Yoshimitsu Morita. Screenplay: Sumi Omori, based on the novel by Yusuke Kishi. Camera: Nobuyasu Kita. Editor: Shinji Tanaka. Music: Tetsuo Yamazaki. In color. Release date: Feb. 16, 2000. Running time: 117 Min. JAPANESE.
Cast: Shinobu Otake, Masaki Uchino, Masahiko Nishimura, Misato Tanaka.

BLAME IT ON THE KING
An Alta Films release of a Pedro Costa PC/Enrique Cerezo PC production, in association with Canal Plus, TVE. (International sales: Pedro Costa, Madrid.) Producers: Pedro Costa, Enrique Cerezo. Director: Jose Antonio Quiros. Screenplay: Quiros, Alicia Luna, Clara Perez Escriva, Pedro Costa. Camera: Julio Madurga. Editor: Fernando Pardo. Music: Juan Carlos Cuello. In color. Release date: Feb. 7, 2000. Running time: 94 Min. SPANISH.
Cast: Antonio Resines, Adriana Ozores, Jesus Bonilla, Manuel Alexandre, Manuel Manquina, Nicolas Fernandez Luna

BLUE CLEAR ACROSS TO AMERICA
A Noria Films/Little Big Films release (in France) of an Alta Loma Films/Mact Prods./Le Studio Canal Plus/Arte France Cinema production. (International sales: UGC Intl., Paris.) Producers: Didier Boujard, Martine de Clermont-Tonnerre. Director/Screenplay: Sarah Levy. Camera: Jean-Max Bernard. Editor: Jacqueline Mariani. Music: Ramon Pipin. In color. Release date: Dec. 14, 1999. Running time: 96 Min. FRENCH.
Cast: Samuel Jouy, Marion Cotillard, Albert Dupontel, Claude Perron, Zabou Breitman, Feodor Atkine, Franck Gourlat, Edouard Montoute.

BLUE END
An eXtra Film production. Producer: Kaspar Kasics. (International sales: First Hand Films, Zurich.) Director/Screenplay: Kaspar Kasics. Camera: Pierre Mennel. Editor: Kasics. Music: Mich Gerber. In color. Release date: Aug. 10, 2000. Running time: 83 Min. Documentary. SWISS.

BOESMAN & LENA
A Pathe release (in France) of a Pathe Image presentation, in association with Primedia Pictures, with the participation of Canal Plus and La Sept-Arte. Producers: Francois Ivernel, Pierre Rissient. Co-producers: Jeremy Nathan, John Stodel. (International sales: Pathe International, Paris.) Director: John Berry. Adapted by Berry from the play by Athol Fugard. Camera: Alain Choquart. Editors: Claudine Bouche, Jeanne Moutard. Music: Wally Badarou. In color, widescreen. Release date: Apr. 25, 2000. Running time: 86 Min. FRENCH.
Cast: Danny Glover, Angela Bassett, Willie Jonah.

THE BOOKS AND THE NIGHT
A Universidad Nacional General San Martin/Canal Plus Madrid production. (International sales: Tristan Bauer, Manuela Pedraza, Buenos Aires.) Producer: Diego Dubcovsky. Director: Tristan Bauer. Screenplay: Bauer, Carolina Scaglione. Camera: Javier Julia, Alejandro Fernandez Moujan. Editor: Alejandro Brodersohn. Music: Federico Bonasso. In color. Release date: Feb. 17, 2000. Running time: 83 Min. ARGENTINE.
Cast: Walter Santa Ana, Hector Alterio, Lorenzo Quinteros,.

THE BOOK THAT WROTE ITSELF
A Siar a Rachas Miuid Prods. (Rathmines, Ireland) production. Producer/Director/Screenplay: Liam O'Mochain. Camera: Oisin Bourke. Editor: Ray Fallon. Music: Paul Dwyer. In color, 16mm. Release date: Sept. 28, 1999. Running time: 70 Min. IRISH.
Cast: Liam O'Mochain, Antoinette Guiney, Marco Van Belle, Kristen Marken, Carol Myers.

BOONDOCK SAINTS
An Indican Pictures release of a Franchise Pictures presentation of a Brood Syndicate production in association with Fried Films, the Lloyd Segan Co. and Chris Brinker Prods. Producers: Elie Samaha, Lloyd Sega, Robert Fried, Chris Brinker. Executive producers: Andrew Stevens, Ashok Amritraj, David Della Rocco, Don Carmody. Co-producers: Richard Zinman, Mark McGarry. Director/Screenplay: Troy Duffy. Camera: Adam Kane. Editor: Bill Deronde. Music: Jeff Danna. In FotoKem color. Release date: Jan. 15, 2000. MPAA Rating: R. Running time: 108 Min.
Cast: Willem Dafoe, Sean Patrick Flanery, Norman Reedus, David Della Rocco, Billy Connolly, David Ferry, Brian Mahoney, Bob Marley.

BOOTMEN
A 20th Century Fox release of a Fox Searchlight Pictures presentation in association with the Australian Film Finance Corp. of a Bootmen Prods. (Hilary Linstead-Dein Perry) production. Producer: Hilary Linstead. Co-producer: Antonia Barnard. Executive producer: Dein Perry. Director: Dein Perry. Screenplay: Steve Worland, from a story by Worland, Hilary Linstead, Perry. Camera: Steve Mason. Editor: Jane Moran. Music: Cezary Skubiszewski. In Atlab color. Release date: July 12, 2000. MPAA Rating: R. Running time: 92 Min. AUSTRALIAN-U.S.
Cast: Adam Garcia, Sophie Lee, Sam Worthington, William Zappa, Richard Carter, Susie Porter, Anthony Hayes, Christopher Horsey.

BORN OF A STORK
A Mondo Films release of a Princes Film/Canal Plus production. Director: Tony Gatlif. Screenplay: Gatlif, Michel Medieu. Camera: Claude Garnier, Eric Guichard. Editor: Monique Dartonne. Music: Gatlif. Release date: Dec. 12, 1999. Running time: 75 Min. FRENCH.
Cast: Romain Duris, Rona Hartner, Ouassini Embarek.

BORSTAL BOY
A Hell's Kitchen (Ireland)/Dakota Films (U.K.) production, with participation of British Screen, BSkyB and the Irish Film Board, in association with RTE and Full Schilling Investments. Producers: Pat Moylan, Arthur Lappin. Executive producers: Jim Sheridan, Nye Heron. Co-producer: Judy Counihan. Director: Peter Sheridan. Screenplay: Nye Heron, Sheridan, inspired by the book by Brendan Behan. Camera: Ciaran Tanham. Editor: Stephen O'Connell. Music: Stephen McKeon. In Technicolor. Release date: July 4, 2000. Running time: 93 Min. IRISH-BRITISH.
Cast: Shawn Hatosy, Danny Dyer, Michael York, Lee Ingleby, Robin Laing, Eva Birthistle.

BOSSA NOVA
A Sony Pictures Classics (in U.S.)/Columbia TriStar Film Distributors release of an LC Barreto/Filmes do Equador production in association with Globo Filmes. Producers: Lucy and Luiz Carlos Barreto. Executive producer: Bruno Barreto. Director: Bruno Barreto. Screenplay: Alexandre Machado, Fernanda Young, based on the novel "Miss Simpson" by Sergio Sant'Anna. Camera: Pascal Rabaud. Editor: Ray Hubley. Music: Eumir Deodato. In color, widescreen. Release date: Feb. 20, 2000. MPAA Rating: R. Running time: 93 Min. BRAZILIAN.
Cast: Amy Irving, Antonio Fagundes, Alexandre Borges, Debora Bloch, Drica Moraes, Giovanna Antonelli, Rogerio Cardoso.

BOX LUNCH
A Hot Pictures Co. production. (International sales: Hot Entertainment Co., Tokyo.) Producer: Shinsuke Kaji. Executive producer: Shungo Kaji. Director/Screenplay: Shungo Kaji. Camera: Koichi Ishii. Editor: Naoki Kaneko. In B&W. Release date: Feb. 12, 2000. Running time: 108 Min. JAPANESE.
Cast: Saki Shiratori, Shungo Kaji, Chocoball Mukai.

A BOY AND A GIRL ON THE 14TH FLOOR
A Mondo Films release of a Le Poisson Volant/Les Films du Rond-Pont production, with participation of CNC. Producer: Sophie Goupil. Director/Screenplay: Sophie Blondy. Camera: Renaud Chassaing. Editor: Eric Ambruster. Music: Jam'ba. In B&W. Release date: Nov. 13, 1999. Running time: 88 Min. FRENCH.
Cast: Sophie Blondy, Paul Tang, Guillaume Depardieu, Bass Dhem.

BOY'S CHOIR
A Suncent CinemaWorks presentation of a WOWOW/Bandai Visual Co. production. (International sales: Suncent Cinema-Works, Tokyo.) Producer: Takenori Sento. Director: Akira Ogata. Screenplay: Kenji Aoki. Camera: Masami Inomoto. Editor: Shuichi Kakesu. Music: Shinichiro Ikebe. In color. Release date: Feb. 10, 2000. Running time: 130 Min. JAPANESE.
Cast: Atsushi Ito, Sora Toma, Teruyuki Kagawa, Ryoko Takizawa, Ken Mitsuishi, Reita Serizawa, Jun Kunimura, Shigeru Izumiya.

BREAD AND ROSES
A Parallax Pictures, Road Movies Vierte Produktionen and Tornasol/Alta Films production with the participation of British Screen and BSkyB in association with BAC Films, BIM Distribuzione, Cineart and Film Co-operative, Zurich, and in collaboration with Film Four, WDR/Arte/La Sept Cinema, ARD/Degeto Film and Filmstiftung Nordhein-Westfalen. (International sales: The Sales Co., London.) Producer: Rebecca O'Brien. Executive producer: Ulrich Felsberg. Director: Ken Loach. Screenplay: Paul Laverty. Camera: Barry Ackroyd. Editor: Jonathan Morris. Music: George Fenton. In Deluxe color. Release date: May 10, 2000. Running time: 110 Min. BRITISH-GERMAN-SPANISH.
Cast: Pilar Padilla, Adrien Brody, Elpidia Carrillo, Jack McGee, George Lopez, Alonso Chavez, Monica Rivas, Frank Davila.

BREAD AND TULIPS
An Istituto Luce release of a Monogatari presentation of an Istituto Luce, Monogatari, RAI (Italy)/Amka Films, Televisione Svizzera Italiana (Switzerland) production. Producer: Daniele Maggioni. Director: Silvio Soldini. Screenplay: Doriana Leondeff, Soldini. Camera: Luca Bigazzi. Editor: Carlotta Cristiani. Music: Giovanni Venosta. In Cinecitta color. Release date: Feb. 28, 2000. Running time: 114 Min. ITALIAN-SWISS.
Cast: Licia Maglietta, Bruno Ganz, Giuseppe Battiston, Marina Massironi, Antonio Catania, Felice Andreasi, Tatiana Lepore.

BREAD DAY
A Higher Courses for Scriptwriters presentation of a Sergei Dvortsevoy production. (International sales: Jane Balfour Films, London.) Director/Screenplay: Sergei Dvortsevoy. Camera: Alisher Khamidhkodjaev. Editor: Dvortsevoy. In color. Release date: Jan. 20, 2000. Running time: 58 Min. Documentary. RUSSIAN.

BREAKING THE SILENCE
An Asia Union Film & Entertainment presentation of a Zhujiang Film Co./Guangdong Sanjiu Film Co. production. (International sales: The Film Library, Los Angeles.) Producers: Huang Yong, Zhao Xindian. Executive producers: Sun Zhou, Sun Mian. Director: Sun Zhou. Screenplay: Liu Heng, Sun, Shao Xiaoli. Camera: Lu Yue. Editors: Nancy Muqing, Zhai Ru. Music: Zhao Jiping. In color. Release date: Feb. 13, 2000. Running time: 91 Min. CHINESE.
Cast: Gong Li, Gao Xin, Shi Jingming, Guan Yue, Yue Xiuqing, Li Chengru, Lu Liping, Lei Quesheng, Lin Qing, Zhou Yufeng.

BREATHE IN BREATHE OUT
A B Prods./Dune/ZDF Das Kleine Fernsehspiel production in association with TV 10 Angers, Blow Up Pictures. (International sales: Jane Balfour Films, London.) Producers: Beth B, Chantal Bernheim. Executive producers: Beth B, Bernheim, Tom Brown, Jason Kliot, Robert Nador, Chuck Rusbasan, Sharan Sklar, Eve Vercel, Joana Vicente. Director/Screenplay: Beth B. Camera: Nancy Schreiber. Editor: Steve Hamilton. Music: Jim Coleman. In B&W and color. Release date: Jan. 31, 2000. Running time: 75 Min. Documentary. U.S.-GERMAN.

BREATHTAKING
An IAC Film/Sky Pictures/The Television Co./September Films production. (International sales: IAC Film, London.) Producer: Rachel Brown. Director: David Green. Screenplay: Nicky Cowan. Camera: Gavin Finney. Editor: Kant Pan. Music: Rob Lane. In color. Release date: May 16, 2000. Running time: 105 Min. BRITISH.
Cast: Joanne Whalley, Lorraine Pilkington, Jame Foreman, Cal Macaninch, Neil Dudgeon.

THE BRIAN EPSTEIN STORY

An Arena presentation of a BBC Worldwide and A&E production. Producer: Anthony Wall. Executive producers: Debbie Geller, Diana Mansfield. Director: Anthony Wall. Screenplay: Jon Savage. Camera: Luke Cardiff. 8mm photography: Louis Caulfield. Editors: Guy Crossman, Roy Deverall. In color and B&W, video. Release date: June 12, 2000. Running time: 145 Min. Documentary . BRITISH.
With: Paul McCartney, Gerry Marsden, Billy J. Kramer, Peter Brown, Alistair Taylor, Stella Epstein, Simon Napier-Bell, Robert Stigwood.

THE BRIDE OF FIRE

A Third Eye production. (International sales: Iranian Independents, Tehran.) Producer: Ghasem Ghoolipour. Director: Khosro Sinai. Screenplay: Sinai, Hamid Farrokhnezhad. Camera: Ali Loghmani. Editor: Hayedeh Safiyari. Music: Sinai. In color. Release date: May 17, 2000. Running time: 106 Min. IRANIAN.
Cast: Pasal Soremi, Saeed Poursamimi, Mahdi Ahmadi, Salimeh Rangzan, Hamid Forrokhnezhad, Ghazal Saremi.

BRIGHTER THAN THE MOON

A Virgil Widrich Film und Multimediproduktions production. (International sales: Virgil Widrich, Vienna.) Producer/Director: Virgil Widrich. Screenplay: Widrich, Enrico Jakob. Camera: Martin Putz. Editor: Veronika Mossbock. Music: Alexander Zlamal. In color. Release date: Jan. 28, 2000. Running time: 87 Min. AUSTRIAN.
Cast: Christopher Buchholz, Piroska Szekely, Lars Rudolph, Gerhard Liebmann, Werner Prinz, Alexander Ebeert.

BRONX-BARBES

A Hachette Premiere, Film d'Ici, Arte, France 3 Cinema, CNRS Images-Media production. (International sales: President Films, Paris.) Producers: Rene Cleitman, Serge Lalou. Executive producer: Marie-Frederique Lauriot-dit-Prevost. Director: Eliane de Latour. Screenplay: de Latour, Emmanuel Bourdieu. Camera: Stephane Fontaine. Editor: Anne Weil. Music: Philippe Miller. In color, widescreen. Release date: Aug. 9, 2000. Running time: 110 Min. FRENCH.
Cast: Antony Koulehi Diate, Loss Sylla Ousseni, Edwige Dogo, Shang Lee Souleyman Kere, David Cyril Guen.

BROTHER

A Sony Pictures Classics release (in U.S.) of a Recorded Picture Co. (London)/Office Kitano (Tokyo) production in association with Film Four, BAC Films. (International sales: HanWay Films, London.) Producers: Jeremy Thomas, Masuyuki Mori. Co-producers: Takio Yoshida, Ann Carli. Director/Screenplay/Editor: Takeshi Kitano. Camera: Katsumi Yanagjima. Music: Joe Hisaishi. In color. Release date: Aug. 23, 2000. Running time: 112 Min. JAPANESE-BRITISH.
Cast: Beat Takeshi, Claude Maki, Omar Epps, Masaya Kato, Ren Ohsugi, Susumu Terajima, Ryo Ishibashi, James Shigeta.

BROTHERS

A Paradise Films release of a Brothers Films production. Producers: Martin Dunkerton, Joanna Garvin. Executive producer: Julian Dunkerton. Co-producer: Nick Valentine. Director: Martin Dunkerton. Screenplay: Dunkerton, Nick Valentine. Camera: Richard Terry. Editor: John Grover. Music: Julian Stewart Lindsey. In Fujicolor, Technicolor. Release date: June 23, 2000. Running time: 98 Min. BRITISH.
Cast: Justin Brett, Daniel Fredenburgh, Rebecca Cardinale, Daren Jacobs, Leigh Tapper, Fin Wild, Nick Valentine, Stephen Maggid.

BRUISER

A Le Studio Canal Plus presentation of a Ben Barenholtz production, in association with Romero-Grunwald Prods. (International sales: Le Studio Canal Plus, Paris.) Producer: Ben Barenholtz. Executive producer: Allen M. Shore. Co-producers: Peter Grunwald, Martin Walters, Ric Shore. Director/Screenplay: George A. Romero. Camera: Adam Swica. Editor: Miume Jan Eramo. Music: Donald Rubinstein, The Misfits. Release date: Feb. 13, 2000. Running time: 96 Min. U.S.-FRENCH.
Cast: Jason Flemyng, Peter Stormare, Leslie Hope, Nina Garbiras, Andrew Tarbert, Tom Atkins, Jonathan Higgins, Jeff Monahan.

THE BUILDING

A Giai Phong Film Studio presentation of a Giai Phong (Vietnam)/Le Bureau (France) production. (International sales: Le Bureau, Paris.) Producers: Tran Tan Hung, Franck Vager. Director/Screenplay: Viet Linh, based on the short story by Nguyen Ho. Camera: Hai Bao. Editor: Thien Huong. Music: Phu Quang. In color. Release date: Sept. 3, 1999. Running time: 89 Min. VIETNAMESE-FRENCH.
Cast: Mai Thanh, Hong Anh, Don Duong, Minh Trang, Quyen Linh, Kim Xuan, Le Binh, Huu Tien, Chi Cuong, Hoang Anh, Cam Ha, Ngoe.

BULLETS OVER SUMMER

A Brilliant Idea Group production for Mei Ah. (International sales: Mei Ah, Hong Kong.) Producer: Li Kuo-hsing. Executive producer: Joe Ma. Executive in charge of production: Patrick Tong. Director: Wilson Yip. Screenplay: Matt Chow, Yip, Cheing Man. Camera: Lam Wah-chuen. Editor: Cheung Ka-fai. Music: Wai Kai-leung. In color. Release date: Sept. 16, 1999. Running time: 93 Min. HONG KONG.
Cast: Francis Ng, Louis Koo, Michelle Alicia Saram, Stephanie Lin, Helena Law, Lai Yiu-cheung, David Lee, Lo Mong, Joe Lee.

BUNUEL'S PRISONERS

A Pieter van Huystee Film & TV production. (International sales: Public Film Sales & Distribution, Amsterdam.) Director/Screenplay: Ramon Gieling. Camera: Goert Giltay. Editor: Berenike Rozgonyi. Music: Micha Molthoff. In color. Release date: Feb. 4, 2000. Running time: 78 Min. Documentary. DUTCH.

BURIED COUNTRY

A Film Australia production, in association with SBS Independent. (International sales: Film Australia, Sydney.) Producer: Liz Watts. Executive producer: Mark Hamlyn. Director: Andy Nehl. Screenplay: Clinton Walker, Nehl. Camera: Warwick Thornton. Editor: Karen Johnson. In color. Release date: June 12, 2000. Running time: 74 Min. Documentary. AUSTRALIAN.
Narrator: Kev Carmody.

BURLESK KING

A Seiko Films production. Producer: Robbie Tan. Director: Mel Chionglo. Screenplay: Ricardo Lee. Camera: George Tutanes. Editor: Jess Navarro. Music: Nonong Buencamino. In color. Release date: Sept. 12, 1999. Running time: 109 Min. FILIPINO.
Cast: Rodel Velayo, Nini Jacinto, Leondardo Litton, Raymond Bagsting, Elizabeth Oropesa, Joel Lamangan.

THE BUTTERFLY'S TONGUE

A Warner Sogefilms release (in Spain) of a Sogetel/Las Producciones del Escorpion/Grupo Voz production, in association with Canal Plus and TVG. (International sales: Sogepaq, Madrid.) Executive producers: Fernando Bovaira, Jose Luis Cuerda. Director: Jose Luis Cuerda. Screenplay: Rafael Azcona, based on stories by Manuel Rivas. Camera: Javier Salmones. Editor: Nacho Ruiz-Capillas. Music: Alejandro Amenabar. In color. widescreen. Release date: Sept. 23, 1999. Running time: 95 Min. SPANISH.
Cast: Fernando Fernan Gomez, Manuel Lozano, Uxia Blanco, Gonzalo Martin Uriarte, Alexis de Los Santos, Guillermo Toledo.

BYE BYE AFRICA

A Les Productions de la Lanterne presentation. Producer: Claude Gilaizeau. Director/Screenplay: Mahamet-Saleh Haroun. Camera: Stephane Legoux, Haroun. Editor: Sarah Taouss. Music: Alhadj Ahmat dit Pecos, Issa Bongo, Ringo Efoua-Ela. In color. Release date: May 1, 2000. Running time: 86 Min. CHAD-FRENCH.
Cast: Mahamet-Saleh Haroun, Garba Issa, Aicha Yelena, Mahamat-Saleh Abakar.

BY MY SIDE AGAIN

A Warner Sogefilms release (in Spain) of a Sogetel, Elias Querejeta (Spain)/Albares Prods. (France)/Blue Cinematografica (Italy) production, with participation of Esicma, Continental, TVE, Canal Plus, Tele Plus, TVG. (International sales: Sogetel, Madrid.) Producer: Elias Querejeta. Director: Gracia Querejeta, Elias Querejeta. Camera: Alfredo Mayo. Editor: Nacho Ruiz-Capillas. Music: Angel Illarramendi. In color, widescreen. Release date: July 16, 1999. Running time: 97 Min. SPANISH-FRENCH-ITALIAN.
Cast: Mercedes Sampietro, Jorge Perugorria, Julieta Serrano, Marta Belaustegui, Adriana Ozores, Rosa Mariscal, Ramon Barea.

THE CALL OF THE OBOE

An Imagica Producoes presentation of a Rio Filme, Skylight Cinema, Quanta and Ara Films production. Producer: Claudio MacDowell. Director: Claudio MacDowell. Screenplay: MacDowell, Joaquine Assis. Camera: Toca Seabra. Editors: MacDowell, Snir Wine. Music: Wagner Tiso. In CFI color. Release date: Oct. 24, 1999. Running time: 120 Min. BRAZILIAN-PARAGUAYAN.
Cast: Paulo Betti, Leticia Vota, Mario Lozano, Arturo Fleitas, Graciela Canepa, Mirthita Mazo.

CANONE INVERSO–MAKING LOVE

A Cecchi Gori Distribuzione release of a Mario and Vittorio Cecchi Gori presentation of a Cecchi Gori Group Fin.Ma.Vi. production. Producer: Vittorio Cecchi Gori. Executive producer for Pacific Pictures: Mario Cotone. Director: Ricky Tognazzi. Screenplay: Graziano Diana, Simona Izzo, Tognazzi, based on the novel "Canone inverso" by Paolo Maurensig. Camera: Fabio Cianchetti. Editor: Carla Simoncelli. Music: Ennio Morricone. In Cinecitta color, Panalight widescreen. Release date: May 16, 2000. Running time: 107 Min. ITALIAN.
Cast: Hans Matheson, Melanie Thierry, Lee Williams, Gabriel Byrne, Ricky Tognazzi, Peter Vaughn, Nia Roberts, Adriano Pappalardo.

CAPTAIN PANTOJA AND THE SPECIAL SERVICE

An America production, in association with Inca Films and Tornasol Film, in collaboration with Via Digital. (International sales: Cinevista, Miami Beach, FL.) Producers: Jose Enrique Crousillat, Gerardo Herrero. Executive producer: Gustavo Sanchez. Director: Francisco J. Lombardi. Screenplay: Giovanna Pollarolo, Enrique Moncloa, based on the novel by Mario Vargas Llosa. Camera: Teodoro Delgado. Editor: Danielle Fillios. Music: Bingen Mendizabal. In color. Release date: Feb. 16, 2000. Running time: 137 Min. PERUVIAN.
Cast: Salvador Del Solar, Angie Cepeda, Monica Sanchez, Pilar Bardem, Gianfranco Brero, Gustavo Bueno, Carlos Kaniowsky.

THE CAPTAIN'S DAUGHTER

An NTV Profit (Russia)/Roissy Films, Productions Le Pont, Canal Plus (France) production, in association with Globus Film Studio and Orenburg Region Administration. (International sales: Roissy Films/Celluloid Dreams, Paris.) Producers: Igor Tolstunov, Mikhail Zilberman. Executive producer: Vitaly Koshman. Director: Aleksandr Proshkin. Screenplay: Galina Arbuzova, Stanislav Govorukhin, Vladimir Zheleznikov, based on the books "The Captain's Daughter" and "A History of Pugachev" by Aleksandr Pushkin. Camera: Sergei Yurizditsky. Editor: Tatyana Yegorisheva. Music: Vladimir Martynov. In Technicolor. Release date: Feb. 12, 2000. Running time: 129 Min. RUSSIAN-FRENCH.
Cast: Vladimir Mashkov, Karolina Gruszka, Mateusz Damiecki, Sergei Makovetsky, Vladimir Ilyin, Yuri Belyaev, Natalia Yegorova.

CAPTAINS OF APRIL
A JBA Prod. (Paris)/Mutante Filmes (Lisbon) production in association with Alia Filmes (Lisbon) production in association with Alia Film (Rome). Producer: Jacques Bidou. (International sales: Art Box, Paris.) Director: Maria de Medeiros. Screenplay: Medeiros, Eve Deboise. Camera: Michel Abramowicz. Editor: Jacques Witta. Music: Antonio Victorino D'Almeida. In color. Release date: May 12, 2000. Running time: 124 Min. FRENCH-PORTUGUESE.
Cast: Stefano Accorsi, Maria de Medeiros, Joaquim de Almeida, Frederic Pierrot, Fele Martinez.

THE CAPTIVE
A Gemini Films release of a Gemini Films/Arte France Cinema/Paradise Films production with participation of Canal Plus, Centre National de la Cinematographie, Gimages 3. (International sales: Gemini Films, Paris.) Producer: Paulo Branco. Director: Chantal Akerman. Screenplay: Akerman, Eric de Kuyper, inspired by Marcel Proust's "La prisonniere." Camera: Sabine Lancelin. Editor: Claire Atherton. In color. Release date: May 15, 2000. Running time: 118 Min. FRENCH-BELGIAN.
Cast: Stanislas Merhar, Sylvie Testud, Olivia Bonamy, Liliane Rovere, Francoise Bertin, Aurore Clement.

CASCABEL
A Warner Sogefilms release of an Alma Ata production, in association with Galiardo Producciones and Xaloc Producciones, with participation of Canal Plus. (International sales: Warner Sogefilms, Madrid.) Executive producers: Jose Maria Calleja de la Fuente, Manuel Matji. Director: Daniel Cebrian. Screenplay: Cebrian, Manuel Matji. Camera: Pedro del Rey. Editor: Guillermo Represa. Music: Eva Gancedo, Pedro Guerra. In color. Release date: Feb. 11, 2000. Running time: 104 Min. SPANISH.
Cast: Irene Visedo, Pilar Punzano, Antonio Dechent, Chete Lera, Javier Albala, Jose Coronado, Aitor Merino.

A CENTURY'S END
A Mirae Asset Capital Co. presentation of a Taehung Pictures production. (International sales: Cineclick Asia, Seoul.) Producer: Lee Tae-won. Director/Screenplay: Song Neung-han. Camera: Lee Hu-kon. Editor: Park Kok-ji. Music: Shin Hae-chol. In color. Release date: Sept. 3, 2000. Running time: 102 Min. SOUTH KOREAN.
Cast: Kim Kap-su, Lee Jae-un, Cha Seung-won, Lee Ho-jae, Ahn Seok-hwan.

THE CHARCOAL PEOPLE
A Zazen Producoes production. Producer: Jose Padilha. Co-producers: Josane Resende, Marcos Prado. Director: Nigel Noble. Screenplay: Jose Padilha. Camera: Flavio Zangrandi. Editor: Ann Collins. Music: Joao Nabucco. In color. Release date: Jan. 26, 2000. Running time: 70 Min. Documentary. BRAZILIAN.

CHARGE!
A Diaphana Distribution release of an Agat Film & Cie./Diaphana/TF1 Films Prod. production, with participation of Canal Plus. (International sales: Mercure, Paris.) Producers: Gilles Sandoz, Michel Saint-Jean, Robert Guediguian. Director: Robert Guediguian. Screenplay: Jean Louis Milesi, Guediguian. Camera: Bernard Cavalie. Editor: Bernard Sasia. Music: Jacques Menichetti. In color. Release date: Apr. 9, 2000. Running time: 90 Min. FRENCH.
Cast: Ariane Ascaride, Pierre Banderet, Frederique Bonnal, Patrick Bonnel, Jacques Boudet, Christine Brucher, Jean-Pierre Darroussin.

CHICKEN RUN
A DreamWorks release presented in association with Pathe of an Aardman production. Producers: Peter Lord, David Sproxton, Nick Park. Executive producers: Jake Eberts, Jeffrey Katzenberg, Michael Rose. Director: Peter Lord, Nick Park. Screenplay: Karey Kirkpatrick, based on an original story by Lord, Park. Supervising camera: Dave Alex Riddett. Camera: Tristan Oliver, Frank Passingham. Editor: Mark Solomon. Music: John Powell, Harry Gregson-Williams. In Technicolor. Release date: June 7, 2000. MPAA Rating: G. Running time: 85 Min. Animated. U.S.-BRITISH.
Voices: Mel Gibson, Julia Sawalha, Miranda Richardson, Jane Horrocks, Lynn Ferguson, Imelda Staunton, Benjamin Whitrow.

THE CHILD AND THE SOLDIER
Producer: Vahid Nikkhah Azad. (International sales: Farabi Cinema Foundation, Tehran.) Director: Seyyed Reza Mir-Karimi. Screenplay: Mohammad Rezai-Rad. Camera: Hamid Khozoui Abyane. Editor: Nazanin Mofakham. In color. Release date: May 19, 2000. Running time: 92 Min. IRANIAN.
Cast: Mehdi Lotfi, Rouhallah Hosseini, Mehran Rajabi, Bizhan Soltani.

CHILL OUT
A Jost Hering Filmproduktion, in association with ZDF. Producer: Jost Hering. Director/Screenplay: Andreas Struck. Camera: Andreas Doub. Editor: Phillipp Stahl. Music: Erlandas. In color. Release date: Feb. 15, 2000. Running time: 91 Min. GERMAN.
Cast: Sebastian Blomberg, Tatjana Blacher, Barnaby Metschurat.

A CHINESE IN A COMA
A Cecchi Gori Distribuzione release of a Mario & Vittorio Cecchi Gori presentation of a Cecchi Gori Group production. Producer: Vittorio Cecchi Gori. Director: Carlo Verdone. Screenplay: Verdone, Giovanni Veronesi, Pasquale Plastino. Camera: Danilo Desideri. Editor: Antonio Siciliano. Music: Fabio Liberatori. In Cinecitta color. Release date: Feb. 28, 2000. Running time: 103 Min. ITALIAN.
Cast: Carlo Verdone, Beppe Fiorello, Marit Nissen, Anna Safroncik, Zanni Tamma, Giorgia Bongianni.

CHOPPER
A Palace Films (Australia) release of an Australian Film Finance Corp./Mushroom Pictures presentation of a Pariah Films production. (International sales: Beyond Films, Sydney.) Producer: Michele Bennett. Co-producer: Michael Gudinski. Executive producers: Al Clark, Martin Fabinyi. Director/Screenplay: Andrew Dominik. Camera: Geoffrey Hall, Kevin Hayward. Editor: Ken Sallows. Music: Mick Harvey. In Cinevex color. Release date: June 29, 2000. Running time: 94 Min. AUSTRALIAN.
Cast: Eric Bana, Vince Colosimo, Simon Lyndon, Kate Beahan, David Field, Dan Wyllie, Bill Young, Kenny Graham, Gary Waddell.

CHRISTMAS VACATION 2000
A Filmauro release (in Italy) of a Filmauro production. Producer: Aurelio De Laurentiis. Executive producer: Maurizio Amati. Director: Carlo Vanzina. Screenplay: Carlo and Enrico Vanzina. Camera: Gianlorenzo Battaglia. Editor: Luca Montanari. Music: Manuel De Sica. In color. Release date: Jan. 3, 2000. Running time: 110 Min. ITALIAN.
Cast: Christian De Sica, Massimo Boldi, Magan Gale, Nino D'Angelo, Monica Scattini, Enzo Salvi, Carmen Electra, Irene Ferri.

CHRONICALLY UNFEASIBLE
An Agravo Producoes Cinematograficas production. (International sales: Grupo Novo de Cinema & TV) Director: Sergio Bianchi. Screenplay: Gustavo Steinberg, Bianchi. Camera: Marcelo Coutinho, Antoni Penido. Editor: Paulo Sacramento. Music: Tom Jobim, Arrigo Barnabe, Helena Neirelles, Carlos Lyra. In color. Release date: Aug. 10, 2000. Running time: 101 Min. Docudrama. BRAZILIAN.

CHUNHYANG
A Taenung Pictures/Mirae Asset Capital Co. production, in association with CJ Entertainment, Saehan Industries. (International sales: Wild Bunch, Paris.) Producer: Lee Tai Won. Executive producers: Kim Dong Joo, Seok Dong Jun, Park Do Jun. Director: Im Kwon Taek. Screenplay: Kim Myoung Kon, based on the Pansori song by Cho Sang Hyun. Camera: Jung Il Sung. Editor: Park Soon Duk. Music: Kim Jung Gil. In color. Release date: May 16, 2000. Running time: 121 Min. SOUTH KOREAN.
Cast: Yi Hyo Jeong, Cho Seung Woo, Kim Sung Nyu, Lee Jung Hun, Kim Hak Yong, Lee Hae Eun, Cho Sang Hyun, Kim Myung Hwan.

CINEMA VERITE: DEFINING THE MOMENT
A National Film Board (Toronto) production, with support from Telefilm Canada. Producers: Eric Michel, Adam Symansky. Executive producers: Sally Bochner, Doris Girard, Adrienne Bourneville. Associate producer: Kirwan Cox. Director: Peter Wintonick. Writer-interviewer: Kirwan Cox. Camera: Francis Miquet, various. Editors: Marlo Miazga, Wintonick. Music: various. In B&W. Release date: Oct. 10, 1999. Running time: 110 Min. Documentary. CANADIAN.
With: D.A. Pennebaker, Richard Leacock, Wolf Koenig, Al Maysles, Hope Ryden, Richard Ballentine, Jean Rouch, Richard Leiterman.

THE CIRCLE
A Mikado release (in Italy) of a Jafar Panahi Film Productions (Iran)/Mikado/Lumiere & Co. (Italy) co-production. (International sales: Celluloid Dreams, Paris.) Producer: Jafar Panahi. Screenplay: Kambozia Partovi. Camera: Bahram Badakhshani. Editor: Panahi. In color. Release date: Sept. 67, 2000. Running time: 91 Min. IRANIAN-ITALIAN.
Cast: Maryiam Parvin Almani, Nargess Mamizadeh, Fereshteh Sadr Orafai, Monir Arab, Elham Saboktakin, Fatemeh Naghavi.

CIRCUS
A Columbia TriStar (in U.K.)/Sony Pictures Entertainment (in U.S.) release of a Columbia Pictures presentation of a Film Development Corp. production. Producers: Alan Latham, James Gibb. Executive producer: Alberto Ardissone. Director: Rob Walker. Screenplay: David Logan. Camera: Ben Seresin. Editor: Oral Norrie Ottey. Music: Simon Boswell. In Deluxe color. Release date: May 2, 2000. MPAA Rating: R. Running time: 95 Min. BRITISH-U.S.
Cast: John Hannah, Famke Janssen, Peter Stormare, Eddie Izzard, Fred Ward, Brian Conley, Tiny Lister, Amanda Donohoe, Ian Burfield.

THE CIRCUS
A Mosfilm production. Director/Screenplay: Grigori Aleksandrov. Camera: Vladimir Nilsen, Boris Petrov. Music: Isaak Dunayevsky. In B&W. Release date: Aug. 6, 2000. Running time: 94 Min. SOVIET UNION–1936.
Cast: Lyubov Orlova, Evgenia Melnikova, Vladimir Volodin, Sergei Stoliarov, Pavel Massalsky, Aleksandr Komissarov, Solomon Mikhoels.

CIRCUS PALESTINA
A Transfax Film Prods. (Tel Aviv) production. Producers: Einat Bickel, Marek Rozenbaum, Uri Sabag, Chaim Sharir. Director/Screenplay: Eyal Halfon. Camera: Valentin Belanogov. Editor: Tovah Asher. Music: Shlomo Gronich. In color. Release date: Sept. 29, 1999. Running time: 90 Min. ISRAELI.
Cast: Yoram Hatav, Evgenia Dudina, Amos Lavi, Basaam Zuamot.

CITY LOOP
An Australian Film Commission/Pacific Film & TV Commission/SBS Independent presentation, in association with Showtime Australia, NHK, of a Red Movies production. (International sales: Beyond Films, Sydney.) Producer: Bruce Redman. Director: Belinda Chayko. Screenplay: Stephen Davis. Camera: Josef Demian. Editor: Nick Meyers. Music: Kate Crawford, Nicole Skeltys, B(if)tek. In Atlab color. Release date: June 17, 2000. Running time: 78 Min. AUSTRALIAN.
Cast: Sullivan Stapleton, Ryan Johnson, Megan Dorman, Kellie Jones, Brendan Cowell, Hayley McElhinney, Jessica Napier.

CITY OF DREAMS
A Film Australia production, in association with the Australian Broadcasting Corp. (International sales: Film Australia, Sydney.) Producer: Gaby Mason. Executive producers: Mark Hamlyn, Dasha Ross. Director: Belinda Mason. Screenplay: Belinda and Gaby Mason. Camera: Andre Fleuren. Editor: James Manche. Music: Andree Greenwell. In color. Release date: July 23, 2000. Running time: 56 Min. Documentary. AUSTRALIAN.

THE CLANDESTINE MARRIAGE
A Universal Intl. Pictures release (in U.K.) of a Portman Entertainment and BBC Films presentation of a Portman production, with participation of British Screen, the Gunner & Stables Group and Milesian Films. Producers: Steve Clark-Hill, Rod Gunner, Johnathan B. Stables. Executive producers: Alan Howden, Tim Buxton. Co-producer: Andrew Warren. Director: Christopher Miles. Screenplay: Trevor Bentham, based on the play by George Coleman the Elder and David Garrick. Camera: Denis Crossan. Editor: George Akers. Music: Stanislas Syrewicz. In Technicolor. Release date: Dec. 7, 1999. Running time: 90 Min. BRITISH.
Cast: Nigel Hawthorne, Joan Collins, Timothy Spall, Tom Hollander, Paul Nicholls, Natasha Little, Emma Chambers, Cyril Shaps.

CLINT EASTWOOD: OUT OF THE SHADOWS
A Warner Home Video release of a Rhapsody Films/American Masters/BBC production. Producers: Susan Lacy, Anthony Wall. Director: Bruce Ricker. Screenplay: Dave Kehr. Camera: Vic Losick. Editor: Kate Hirson. Music: Lennie Niehaus. Release date: Aug. 29, 2000. Running time: 87 Min. Documentary. U.S.-BRITISH.
With: Clint Eastwood, Martin Scorsese, Gene Hackman, Meryl Streep, Forest Whitaker, Curtis Hanson, Rip Torn, William Goldman.

THE CLOSER YOU GET
A Fox Searchlight release of a Redwave production. Producer: Uberto Pasolini. Co-producers: Polly Leys, Mark Huffam. Director: Aileen Ritchie. Screenplay: William Ivory, story by Herbie Wave. Camera: Robert Alazraki. Editor: Sue Wyatt. Music: Rachel Portman. In Deluxe London color . Release date: Feb. 8, 2000. MPAA Rating: PG-13. Running time: 90 Min. IRISH-BRITISH.
Cast: Ian Hart, Sean McGinley, Niamh Cusack, Ruth McCabe, Ewan Stewart, Pat Shortt, Cathleen Bradley, Sean McDonagh.

CLOUDS OF MAY
An NBC Ajans production. (International sales: Keriman Ulas Ulusoy, Paris.) Producer: Nuri Bilge Ceylan. Executive producer: Sadik Inescu. Director/Screenplay: Nuri Bilge Ceylan. Camera: Ceylan. Editors: Ayan Ergusel, Ceylan. Music: Bach, Mozart. In color. Release date: Feb. 18, 2000. Running time: 135 Min. TURKISH.
Cast: Muzaffer Ozdemir, M. Emin Ceylan, Fatma Ceylan.

CODE UNKNOWN: INCOMPLETE TALES OF SEVERAL JOURNEYS
An MK2 Diffusion release of an MK2 Prods./Les Films Alain Sarde production in association with Arte France Cinema, France 2 Cinema, Bavaria Film, ZDF, Romanian Culture Ministry, Filmex Romania, with participation of Canal Plus. (International sales: MK2 Diffusion, Paris.) Producers: Marin Karmitz, Alain Sarde. Executive producer: Yvon Crenn. Director/Screenplay: Michael Haneke. Camera: Jurgen Jurges. Editors: Andreas Prochaska, Karin Hartusch, Nadine Muse. Music: Giba Goncalves. In color. Release date: May 19, 2000. Running time: 118 Min. FRENCH.
Cast: Juliette Binoche, Thierry Neuvic, Luminita Gheorghiu, Ona Lu Yenke, Helene Diarra, Sepp Bierbichler, Alexandre Hamidi.

COLD LANDS
A Mercure Distribution release of an Agat Films/La Sept Arte production. Producer: Gilles Sandoz. Director: Sebastien Lifshitz. Screenplay: Lifshitz, Stephane Bouquet. Camera: Pascal Poulet. Editor: Yann Deder. In color. Release date: Sept. 3, 1999. Running time: 65 Min. FRENCH.
Cast: Yasmine Belmadi, Bernard Verley, Sebastien Charles, Valerie Donzelli, Eric Savin.

COLOURFUL
An NHK Enterprises 21 production. (International sales: NHK 21, Tokyo.) Producers: Yasuo Takahashi, Kanji Hagiwara. Director: Shun Nakahara. Screenplay: Yoshimitsu Morita, based on the novel by Eto Mori. Camera: Junichi Fujisawa. Editor: Isao Tomita. Music: Shinichiro Ikebe. In color. Release date: Sept. 2, 2000. Running time: 97 Min. JAPANESE.
Cast: Koki Tanaka, Sawako Agawa, Kanako Magara, Asuka Komayu.

COMEDIAN
A Vega Distribution release of a Vega Film production. (International sales: Vega, Zurich.) Producer: Ruth Waldburger. Director: Markus Imboden. Screenplay: Walter Bretscher, Beat Schlatter. Camera: Rainer Klausman. Editor: Bernhard Lehner. In color. Release date: Aug. 10, 2000. Running time: 93 Min. SWISS.
Cast: Beat Schlatter, Patrick Frey, Brigitte Beyeler, Stephanie Glaser.

COMPLICITY
An Entertainment Film Distributors release of a J&M Entertainment/ Entertainment Film Distributors/Carlton Films presentation of a Talisman Films production. (International sales: J&M, London.) Producers: Richard Jackson, Neil Dunn. Executive producers: Julia Palau, Michael Ryan. Co-producers: Andrew Warren, Peter McAleese. Director: Gavin Millar. Screenplay: Bryan Elsley, based on the novel by Iain Banks. Camera: David Odd. Editor: Angus Newton. Music: Colin Towns. Release date: July 28, 2000. Running time: 100 Min. BRITISH.
Cast: Jonny Lee Miller, Brian Cox, Keeley Hawes, Paul Higgins, Jason Hetherington, Bill Paterson, Samuel West, Rachael Stirling.

CONFLICT
A National Film Development Corp. presentation of a Shyam Benegal production. (International sales: NFDC, Bombay.) Producer: Shyam Benegal. Executive producer: Raj Pius. Director: Shyam Benegal. Screenplay: Ashok Mishra. Camera: Rajen Kothari. Editor: Aseem Sinha. Music: Vanraj Bhatia. In color. Release date: Aug. 28, 2000. Running time: 126 Min. INDIAN.
Cast: Rajeshwari Schdev, Rajit Kapur, Ravi Jhankal, Raghubir Yadav, Kishore Kadam, Seem Biswas, Divya Dutta.

CONVICTS
A Mosfilm production. Director: Evgeni Chervyakov. Screenplay: Nikolai Pogodin, based on his play "Aristocrats." Camera: Mikhail Gindin, Boris Petrov. Music: Yuri Shaporin. In B&W. Release date: Aug. 6, 2000. Running time: 90 Min. SOVIET UNION–1936.
Cast: Mihail Astangov, Aleksandr Cheban, Mikhail Yanshin, Boris Dobronravov, Vera Yanukova, Nadezhda Ermakovich.

CORONATION
An Andrea Films production. (International sales: Andrea Films, Santiago.) Producers: Silvio Caiozzi, Guadalupe Bornand. Director/Screenplay: Silvio Caiozzi, from a novel by Jose Donoso. Camera: David Bravo. Editor: Fernando Guariniello. Music: Luis Advis. Release date: Sept. 1, 2000. Running time: 139 Min. CHILEAN.
Cast: Julio Jung, Maria Canepa, Adela Secall, Gabriela Medina, Jaime Vadell, Myriam Palacios, Paulo Meza, Luis Dubo.

COSY DENS
A Czech TV/Pavel Borovan Creative Group production, in association with Total HelpArt and Studio Barrandov. (International sales: Telexport, Prague.) Producer: Pavel Borovan. Executive producer: Ondrej Trojan. Director: Jan Hrebejk. Screenplay: Petr Jarchovsky, based on the novel "Shit Burns" by Petr Sabach. Camera: Jan Malir. Editor: Vladimir Barak. Music: various. In color. Release date: Sept. 25, 1999. Running time: 116 Min. CZECH.
Cast: Michal Beran, Miroslav Donutil, Jiri Kodet, Kristyna Novakova, Simona Stasova, Smilia Vasaryova, Ondrej Brousek, Eva Holubova.

COTTON MARY
A UIP release (in U.K.) of a Merchant Ivory production. Producers: Nayeem Hafizka, Richard Hawley. Executive producer: Paul Bradley. Director: Ismael Merchant. Co-director: Madhur Jaffrey. Screenplay: Alexandra Viets. Camera: Pierre Lhomme. Editor: John David Allen. Music: Richard Robbins. In Technicolor. Release date: Nov. 5, 1999. Running time: 122 Min. BRITISH.
Cast: Greta Scacchi, Madhur Jaffrey, James Wilby, Nina Gupta, Sakina Jaffrey, Prayag Raj, Sarah Badel, Joanna David.

COUNTY KILBURN
An @radical.media presentation of a Watermark Films production, in association with Breakneck Films. (International sales: Watermark, London.) Producer: Nick Heyworth. Executive producer: Magnus Macintyre. Director/Screenplay: Elliot Hegarty. Camera: John Lynch. Editors: Vincenzo De Cecco, Bill Jones. In color, digital video. Release date: Aug. 17, 2000. Running time: 81 Min. BRITISH.
Cast: Ciaran Mcmenamin, Rick Warden, John Bowe, Georgia Mackenzie, Patrick Duggan, Kay D'Arcy, Norman Rodway.

CRANE WORLD
A Cinematografica Sargentina production. Producers: Lita Stantic, Pablo Trapero. Director/Screenplay: Pablo Trapero. Camera: Coby Migliora. Editor: Nicolas Goldbart. Music: Francisco Canaro. In B&W. Release date: Sept. 7, 1999. Running time: 89 Min. ARGENTINE.
Cast: Luis Margani, Adriana Aizemberg, Daniel Valenzuela, Roly Serrano, Federico Esquerro, Graciana Chironi, Alfonso Rementeria.

CRAZY
A Pieter van Huystee Film & TV/VPRO production. (International sales: Fortuna Films, Amsterdam.) Producer: Pieter van Huystee. Director: Heddy Honigmann. Screenplay, research: Honigmann, with cooperation of Ester Gould. Camera: Gregor Meerman. Editor: Mario Steenbergen. In color. Release date: Feb. 5, 2000. Running time: 97 Min. Documentary. DUTCH.

CRAZY
A Constantin release of a Claussen & Woebke Filmproduktion production. Producers: Thomas Woebke, Jakob Claussen. Director: Hans-Christian Schmid. Screenplay: Schmid, Michael Gutmann, based on the novel by Benjamin Lebert. Camera: Sonja Rom. Editor: Hansjoerg Weissbrich. Music: Christoph M. Kaiser. In color. Release date: June 29, 2000. Running time: 89 Min. GERMAN.
Cast: Robert Stadlober, Tom Schilling, Oona-Devi Liebich, Julia Hummer, Can Taylanlar, Christoph Ortmann, Willy Rachow.

CRIME SCENES
A Rezo Films release of a La Chauve-Souris/Le Studio Canal Plus/Telfrance/M6 Films production. (International sales: UGC Intl., Paris.) Producer: Eric Neve. Director: Frederic Schoendoerffer. Screenplay: Schoendoerffer, Yann Brion, Olivier Douyere. Camera: Jean-Pierre Sauvaire. Editor: Dominique Mazzoleni. Music: Bruno Coulais. In color, widescreen. Release date: Mar. 20, 2000. Running time: 101 Min. FRENCH.
Cast: Charles Berling, Andre Dussollier, Eva Darlan, Camille Japy, Elodie Navarre, Hubert Saint Macary, Balnce Ravalec.

THE CRIMINAL OF BARRIO CONCEPCION
A Good Harvest Unlimited production in association with Regal Films. (International sales: Regal Films, Quezon City, Philippines.) Producer: Joey Gosiengfiao. Executive producer: Lily Monteverde. Director/Screenplay: Lav Diaz. Camera: Ariel Reyes. Editor: Randy Brien. Music: Blitz Padua. In color. Release date: Sept. 10, 1999. Running time: 121 Min. FILIPINO.
Cast: Raymond Bagatsing, Anna Capri, Angel Aquino.

CROSS-HARBOUR TUNNEL
A Billy's Outgrowth Workshop production. (International sales: Billy's Outgrowth Workshop, Hong Kong.) Producers: Karen Chu, Ken Wong, Lawrence Wong, Carly Wong. Director: Lawrence Wong. Screenplay: Wong, GC Goo Bi. Camera: Ng Yuet-fung, Ah Wai. Editor: Chan Chi-wai. Music: Anthony Teoh. In color, Super-16. Release date: Jan. 30, 2000. Running time: 93 Min. HONG KONG.
Cast: Syna Lee, Martin Kam, Anthony Teoh, Pauline Yam, GC Goo Bi, Kwan Lung.

THE CROSSING
An Isabella Films (Netherlands)/Tatfilm (Germany)/Zentropa Prods. (Denmark) production in co-production with NPS Television, ZDF, Arte. (International sales: Proctor Film Sales, Amsterdam.) Producers: Els Vandevorst, Wilfried Depeweg. Executive producer: Christine Ruppert. Director/Screenplay: Nora Hoppe. Camera: Walther Vanden Ende. Editor: Vessela Martschewski. Music: Zaher Howaida. In color. Release date: Sept. 20, 1999. Running time: 91 Min. DUTCH-GERMAN-DANISH.
Cast: Behrouz Vossoughi, Johan Leysen, Viviane de Muynck, Mil Seegers, Juan Carlos Tajes, Michel Israel, Amid Chakir.

THE CROSSING
A Siglo production. (International sales: Brussels Ave., Brussels.) Producers: Tetsujiro Yamagami, Koshiro Sho. Director/Screenplay: Yoichi Higashi, based on a story by Tetsujiro Yamagami. Camera: Takahiro Tsutai. In color. Release date: Feb. 17, 2000. Running time: 116 Min. JAPANESE.
Cast: Michitaka Tsutsui, Takahito Hosoyamada, Miho Tsumiki, Yoichiro Aoi, Akemi Omori, Satoki Abe, Tomoko Nakajima, Hiromitsu Suzuki.

CROUCHING TIGER, HIDDEN DRAGON
A Sony Pictures Classics (in U.S.) release of a United China Vision production of a Sony Pictures Classics and Columbia Pictures Film Production Asia presentation in association with Good Machine Intl., and Edko Films, Zoom Hunt production in collaboration with China Film Co-Production Corp. and Asia Union Film & Entertainment Ltd. (International sales: Good Machine Intl., N.Y.) Producers: Bill Kong, Hsu Li Kong, Ang Lee. Executive producers: James Schamus, David Linde. Co-producers: Zheng Quan Gang, Dong Ping. Director: Ang Lee. Screenplay: James Schamus, Wang Hui Ling, Tsai Kuo Jung, based on the novel by Wang Du Lu. Camera: Peter Pau. Editor: Tim Squyres. Music: Tan Dun; cello solos: Yo-Yo Ma. In Technicolor, widescreen. Release date: May 16, 2000. Running time: 120 Min. HONG KONG-TAIWANESE-U.S.
Cast: Chow Yun-fat, Michelle Yeoh, Zhang Ziyi, Chang Chen, Lung Sihung, Cheng Pei-pei, Li Fazeng, Gao Xian, Hai Yan, Wang Deming.

CRYING HEART
A Charles Heung and Imperial Intl. Ltd. presentation of a Sundy Production Co. Ltd. production. Producer: Jing Wong. Director/Screenplay: Jing Wong. Camera: Herman Yau. Editor: Poon Hung Yi. In color. Release date: Aug. 17, 2000. Running time: 102 Min. HONG KONG.
Cast: Deanie Ip, Patrick Tam, Suki Kwan, Sau Leung, Emotion Cheung, Joe Lee, Jimmy Wong Ga Lok.

CUBA FELIZ
A Pyramide Distribution release of an ADR production in co-production with Le Studio Canal Plus, El Movimento Nacional de Video de Cuba, with participation of CNC, Canal Plus. (International sales: Le Studio Canal Plus, Paris.) Producers: Alain Rozanes, Pascal Verroust, Jacques Debs. Director: Karim Dridi. Screenplay: Pascal Letellier, Dridi. Camera: Dridi. Editors: Lise Bealieu. Marie Kiotard. In color. Release date: May 13, 2000. Running time: 96 Min. FRENCH.
Cast: Miguel Del Morales (El Gallo), Pepin Vaillant, Mirta Gonzales, Anibal Avila, Alberto Pablo, Armandito Machado, Candido Fabre.

CUT
A UIP/Beyond Films release (in Australia) of an MBP/Mushroom Pictures/Beyond Films/South Australian Film Corp. production .(International sales: Beyond FIlms, Sydney.) Producers: Martin Fabinyi, Bill Bennett, Jennifer Bennett. Executive producers: Mikael Borglund, Michael Gudinski, Gary Hamilton, Rainer Mockert. Co-producer: Julia Overton. Director: Kimble Rendall. Screenplay: Dave Warner, based on a story by Warner, Mark Lamprell. Camera: David Foreman. Editor: Henry Dangar. Music: Guy Gross. In Atlab color. Release date: Jan. 20, 2000. Running time: 80 Min. AUSTRALIAN.
Cast: Molly Ringwald, Jessica Napier, Sarah Kants, Kylie Minogue, Simon Bossell, Geoff Revell, Frank Roberts, Sam Lewis.

THE CUT RUNS DEEP
An Ilshin Investment Co. presentation of an Albus Films Intl. production. (International sales: Ilshin, Seoul.) Producer: Ha Kang-hwi. Director/Screenplay: John H. Lee. Camera: Walter Gregg. Editors: Ham Seong-weon, Lee. Music: Jeong Weon-yeong, Kang Ki-yeong. In Duart color, widescreen. Release date: Oct. 15, 1999. Running time: 108 Min. SOUTH KOREAN.
Cast: Alexandre Manning, David L. McInnis, Gio Park,.

DAMN YOU! MOSQUITO
A Neuropa Film production, in association with TV2, MMK, ORTT, NKA, MTV, Duna TV. Producer: Andras Ondorai. Director: Miklos Jancso. Screenplay: Jancso, Ferenc Grunwalsky, Gyula Hernadi. Camera: Grunwalsky. Editor: Zsuzsa Csakany. Music: Andras Lovasi, Lagzi Lajcsi. In color. Release date: Feb. 4, 2000. Running time: 83 Min. HUNGARIAN.
Cast: Zoltan Mucsi, Peter Scherer, Emese Vasvari, Miklos B. Szekeley.

DANCER
A Universal Pictures release of a Working Title Films/BBC Films presentation in association with the Arts Council of England of a Tiger Aspect Pictures production in association with WT2. Producers: Greg Brenman, Jon Finn. Executive producers: Natascha Wharton, Charles Brand, Tessa Ross, David M. Thompson. Director: Stephen Daldry. Screenplay: Lee Hall. Camera: Brian Tufano. Editor: John Wilson. Music: Stephen Warbeck. In color. Release date: May 19, 2000. Running time: 111 Min. BRITISH.
Cast: Julie Walters, Jamie Bell, Jamie Driven, Gary Lewis, Jean Heywood, Stuart Wells, Nicola Blackwell.

THE DANCER
An ARP Selection release of a Leeloo Prods./TF1 Prod. production. Producer: Luc Besson. Executive producer: Bernard Grenet. Director: Fred Garson. Screenplay: Jessica Kaplan, Luc Besson, based on an original idea by Besson. Camera: Thierry Arbogast. Editor: Sylvie Landra. Music: Pascal Lafa & Poz. In color, widescreen. Release date: June 12, 2000. Runnning time: 90 Min. FRENCH.
Cast: Mia Frye, Garland Whitt, Rodney Eastman, Josh Lucas, Feodor Atkine, DJ Atomic.

DANCER IN THE DARK
A Fine Line release (in U.S.) of a Zentropa Entertainments (Denmark)/Trust Film Svenska, Film i Vast (Sweden)/Liberator Prods. (France) presentation, in association with France 3 Cinema, Arte France Cinema, Pain Unlimited Filmproduktion. (International sales: Trust Film Sales, Hvidovre, Denmark.) Producer: Vibeke Windelov. Executive producer: Peter Aalbaek Jensen. Co-executive producers: Lars Jonsson, Marianne Slot. Director/Screenplay: Lars Von Trier. Camera: Robby Mueller. Editors: Molly Malene Stensgaard, Francois Gedigier. Music: Bjork, lyrics by Von Trier, Sjon Sigurdsson. In color, widescreen. Release date: May 17, 2000. Running time: 137 Min. DANISH-SWEDISH-FRENCH.
Cast: Bjork, Catherine Deneuve, David Morse, Peter Stormare, Joel Grey, Vincent Paterson, Cara Seymour, Jean-Marc Barr.

THE DARK ROOM
A Parnasse Intl., Blue Films (France)/Delux Prods. (Luxembourg)/ Gam Films (Italy) production, with participation of CNC, Canal Plus. (International sales: Parnasse, Paris.) Producer: Sylvain Bursztejn. Co-producers: Jimmy de Brabant, Raymond Blumenthal. Director: Marie-Christine Questerbert. Screenplay: Questerbert, Daniele Dubroux, inspired by an episode in "The Decameron." Camera: Emmanuel Machuel. Editor: Catherine Quesemand. Music: Solange Boulanger. In color. Release date: May 3, 2000. Running time: 110 Min. FRENCH-LUXEMBOURGOIS-ITALIAN.
Cast: Caroline Ducey, Melvil Poupaud, Mathiew Demy, Sylvie Testud, Jackie Berroyer, Hugues Quester, Edith Scob, Luis Rego.

DAUGHTERS OF THE SUN
A Farabi Cinema Foundation production. (International sales: Farabi Cinema Foundation, Tehran.) Producer: Jahangir Kosari. Director/Screenplay: Maryam Shahriar. Camera: Homayoun Payvar. Editor: Shahrzad Pouya. Music: Hossein Alizadeh. In color. Release date: Aug. 29, 2000. Running time: 105 Min. IRANIAN.
Cast: Altinary Ghelich Taghani, Soghra Karimi, Zahra Mohamadi, Habib Haddad.

DAYBREAK
A Scottish Arts Council Lottery Fund and FilmFour presentation, in association with Starhaus Produktionen, of a Basilisk Communications production, in association with Traumwerk. (International sales: Basilisk, London.) Producers: Jim Hickey, James Mackay. Executive producer (for Starhaus): Rainer Kolmel. Director/Screenplay: Bernard Rudden. Camera: Jean-Jacques Bouhon. Editor: Alan Knight. Music: Matthew Herbert. In Technicolor . Release date: Aug. 20, 2000. Running time: 98 Min. BRITISH.
Cast: Diane Bell, Flash, Gaynor Purvis, Jean-Philippe Ecoffey, Shauna Macdonald, Karl Shields, James Shaw, Dot Allison.

DAYDRIFT
A DayDrift Prods. (Vancouver) production in association with Telefilm Canada. Producers: Ryan Bonder, Margot Dear. Executive producers: D. Barry Lee, James Head. Director/Screenplay: Ryan Bonder. Camera: Brian Johnson. Editor: Ross Weber, Grace Yuen. Music: Marc Bjorknas. In color. Release date: Sept. 25, 1999. Running time: 82 Min. CANADIAN.
Cast: Jed Rees, Enuka Okuma, Jim Thorburn, Jillian Fargey, Megan Leitch, Kurt Max Runte, Christine Anton.

THE DAY I BECAME A WOMAN
A Makhmalbaf Film House production. (International sales: Makhmalbaf Film House.) Producer: Mohsen Makhmalbaf. Director: Marziyeh Mashkini. Screenplay: Mohsen Makhmalbaf, dialogue by Meshkini. Camera: Ebrahim Ghafori, Mohammad Ahmadi. Editor: Maysam Makhmalbaf, Sharhrzad Poya. Music: Ahmad Reza Darvishi. In color. Release date: Sept. 1, 2000. Running time: 78 Min. IRANIAN.
Cast: Fatemeh Cherag Akhar, Shabnam Toloui, Azizeh Sedighi.

THE DAY SILENCE DIED

A Pegaso Producciones presentation in association with Sandkorn Filmproduktion and Red Atb production. (International sales: Media Luna, Cologne.) Producer: Martin Proctor. Executive producers: Ute Gumz, Paolo Agazzi. Director: Paolo Agazzi. Screenplay: Guillermo Aguirre, Agazzi. Camera: Livio Delgado, Guillermo Medrano. Editors: Agazzi, Nelson Rodriguez. Music: Cergio Prudencio. In Technicolor. Release date: Jan. 22, 2000. Running time: 113 Min. BOLIVIAN-GERMAN.

Cast: Dario Grandinetti, Gustavo Angarita, Maria Laura Garcia.

THE DAY THE PONIES COME BACK

A TVA Intl. presentation of a Lazennec Prods. production, in association with River Quest Entertainment. (International sales: Studio Canal, Paris.) Producer: Alain Rocca. Co-producer: Ed Rivero. Director: Jerry Schatzberg. Screenplay: Schatzberg, Robert Cea. Camera: Bruno de Keyser. Editor: Sabine Hoffman. Music: John Hill. In DuArt color. Release date: Aug. 27, 2000. Running time: 101 Min. FRENCH.

Cast: Guillaume Canet, Burt Young, Monica Trombetta, Nick Sandow, Jay Rivera, Tony Lo Bianco, Norman Matlock.

DEAD OR ALIVE

A Daiei Co./Toei Video Co. production. (International sales: Tokuma Intl., Tokyo.) Producers: Katsumi Ono, Makoto Okada, Toshiki Kimura. Executive producers: Mitsuru Kurosawa, Tsutomu Tsuchikawa. Director: Takashi Miike. Screenplay: Ichiro Ryu. Camera: Jideo Yamamoto. Editor: Taiji Shimamura. Music: Kouji Endou. In color. Release date: Jan. 31, 2000. Running time: 104 Min. JAPANESE.

Cast: Riki Takeuchi, Show Aikawa, Renji Ishibashi, Hitoshi Ozawa, Shingo Turumi, Kaoru Sugita, Dankan, Hirotaro Honda.

THE DEATH OF A COMPOSER: ROSA, A HORSE DRAMA

A Kasander Film Co. production in association with NPS-Television, De Nederlandse Opera, NVC Arts. (International sales: NVC Arts, London.) Producer: Kees Kasander. Executive producer: George van Breeman. Director: Peter Greenaway. Libretto, visual concept: Greenaway. Camera, lighting design: Reinier van Brummelen. Editor: Elmer Leupen. Music: Louis Andriessen. In color, video. Release date: Sept. 5, 1999. Running time: 90 Min. DUTCH.

Cast: Lyndon Terracini, Marie Angel, Miranda van Kralingen, Roger Smeets, Christopher Gillett, Phyliss Blanford.

THE DEBT

A Zebra Film/Canal Plus Poland/ITI Cinema production. (International sales: Film Polski, Warsaw.) Producer: Juliusz Machulski. Co-producers: Jacek Maczydlowski, Jacek Bromski. Director: Krzysztof Krauze. Screenplay: Krauze, Jerzy Morawski. Camera: Bartek Prokopowicz. Editor: Krzysztof Szpetmanski. Music: Michal Urbaniak. In color. Release date: Feb. 18, 2000. Running time: 101 Min. POLISH.

Cast: Robert Gonera, Jacek Boruch, Andrzej Chyra, Joanna Szurmiej, Cezary Kosinski, Agnieszka Warchulska, Joanna Kurowska.

DECEIT

An Adriana Chiesa Enterprises presentation of a Film Master Film production. Producers: Sergio Castellani, Carlos Pasini-Hansen. Director: Claudia Florio. Screenplay: David Ambrose. Camera: Luciano Tovoli. Editor: Claudio Cutri. Music: Luis Bacalov. In color. Release date: Sept. 1, 1999. Running time: 98 Min. ITALIAN.

Cast: Jonathan Pryce, Susan Lynch, Claudia Gerini, Enrico Silvestrio, Alessandra Aciai, Brian Prothroe.

DECEMBER 1-31

A ZDF/Mainz presentation of an Abbildungszentrum production. Producer: Peter Ott. Director/Editor: Jan Peters. Camera: Peters. Editor: Peters. Music: Bachler-Sextett, Pit Przygodda. In color. Release date: Aug. 23, 1999. Running time: 97 Min. Documentary. GERMAN.

DEEP INSIDE CLINT STAR

A National Film Board of Canada production. Producer: Silva Basmajian. Executive producer: Louise Lore. Director/Screenplay: Clint Alberta. Camera: Marcos Arriaga. Editor: Katherine Asals. Music: James Cavalluzzo. In color, Beta-SP. Release date: Oct. 10, 1999. Running time: 89 Min. Documentary. CANADIAN.

DEEP IN THE WOODS

A Pathe release of a Fidelite Prods. production, in association with Le Studio Canal Plus and Glozel Diffusion, with participation of Canal Plus, Gimages 3, Studio Images 6, Cofimage 11 and CNC. (International sales: Wild Bunch, Paris.) Producers: Marc Missonnier, Olivier Delbosc. Director: Lionel Delplanque. Screenplay: Annabelle Perrichon, Delplanque. Camera: Denis Rouden. Editor: Pomme Zhed. Music: Jerome Coullet. In color, widescreen. Release date: Aug. 20, 2000. Running time: 86 Min. FRENCH.

Cast: Clotilde Courau, Clement Sibony, Alexia Stresi, VIncent Lecoeur, Maud Buquet, Francois Berleand, Denis Lavant.

DEEPLY

A Vif Filmproduktion (Germany)/Bellwood Stories Prod. (Canada) production, in association with TiMe Filmproduktion and Meg Media Group. (International sales: Myriad Pictures, Santa Monica, Calif.) Producers: Karen Arikian, Carolynne Bell. Executive producer: Wolfgang Tichy. Director/Screenplay: Sheri Elwood. Camera: Sebastian Edschmid. Editor: Jon Gregory. Music: Micki Meuser. In color. Release date: May 15, 2000. Running time: 99 Min. GERMAN-CANADIAN.

Cast: Kirsten Dunst, Lynn Redgrave, Alberta Watson, Julia Brendler, Brent Carver, Peter Donaldson, Tara Rosling, Trent Ford.

DEVILS ON THE DOORSTEP

An Asian Union Film & Entertainment/China Film Co-Production Corp. production, in assoc. with CMC Xiandai Trade Co., Beijing Zhongbo-Times Film Planning, Huayi Brothers Advertising. (International sales: Fortissimo Film Sales, Amsterdam/Hong Kong.) Producer: Jiang Wen. Executive producers, Dong Ping, Zheng Quangang. Director: Jiang Wen. Screenplay: You Fengwei, Shi Jianquan, Shu Ping, Jiang, story by Jiang, Shu, from by the novella "Shengcun" by You Fengwei. Camera: Gu Changwei. Editors: Zhang Yifan, Folmer Weisinger. Music: Cui Jian, Liu Xing, Li Haiying. In B&W and color. Release date: May 12, 2000. Running time: 162 Min. CHINESE.

Cast: Jiang Wen, Jiang Hongbo, Teruyuki Kagawa, Yuan Ding.

THE DINOSAUR HUNTER

A Credo Releasing presentation of an Independent Moving Pictures production. (International sales: Credo Releasing.) Producer: Gail Tilson. Executive producers: James Brooks, Derek Mazur. Director: Rick Stevenson. Screenplay: Edwina Follows, based on the book "My Daniel" by Pam Conrad. Camera: Gerald Packer. Editor: Jackie Dzuba. Music: Jay Semko, Ross Nykiforuk. In color. Release date: Aug. 5, 2000. Running time: 90 Min. CANADIAN.

Cast: Alison Pill, Bill Switzer, Simon McCorkindale, Christopher Plummer, Enuka Okuma.

THE DIPLOMAT

A Film Australia production, in association with Emerald Films and SBS Independent, with assistance from Australian Film Commission, NSW Film & TV Office. (International sales: Film Australia, Sydney.) Producer: Sally Browning. Executive producers: Stefan Moore, Megan McMurchy. Co-producer: Wilson da Silva. Director: Tom Zubrycki. Screenplay: Wilson da Silva, based on an idea by Geoffrey Barter. Camera: Robert Humphreys, Zubrycki, Jo Parker, Joel Petersen. Editor: Ray Thomas. Music: Jan Preston. In color. Release date: June 12, 2000. Running time: 81 Min. Documentary. AUSTRALIAN.

DISPARUS

A Persona Films and Les Films de L'Atalante presentation, in co-production with Les Productions Crittin & Thiebaud and La Television Suisse Romande, with Canal Plus, Le Centre National de la Cinematographe, L'Office Federal de la Culture, La Fondation Gan pour le Cinema, Procirep. Producer: Serge Duveau. Director: Gilles Bourdos. Screenplay: Brigitte Catillon, Bourdos, Michel Spinosa, based on the novel by Jean-Francois Vilar. Camera: Antoine Roch. Editor: Emmanuelle Castro. Music: Eric Le Lann. In color. Release date: Oct. 30, 1999. Running time: 108 Min. FRENCH.

Cast: Gregoire Colin, Anouk Grinberg, Xavier Beauvois, Frederic Pierrot, Matial Di Fonzo Bo, Redjep Mitrovitsa, Michel Duchassoy.

THE DIVER

A Buena Vista Intl. (Sweden) release of a Filmfabriken, Film i Vast (Sweden)/Smile Entertainment (Denmark) production, in association with Nordic Screen Production. (International sales: Filmfabriken, Stockholm.) Producer: Castro Khatib. Director: Erik Gustavson. Screenplay: Gerald Wilson, Gustavson, Kjetil Indregard, based on an original script by Stefan Sauk, Mats Berglund, Anders Lennberg. Camera: Kjell Vassdal. Editor: Wadt Thomse, Music: Randall Meyers. In color. Release date: Jan. 9, 2000. Running time: 97 Min. SWEDISH-DANISH.

Cast: Stefan Sauk, Izabella Scorupco, Bjorn Floberg, Klaus Maria Brandauer, Alexander Skarsgard, Tomas von Bromssen, Keve Kjelm.

DIVIDED WE FALL

A Total HelpArt THA/Czech Television production. (International sales: Czech Television, Prague.) Producers: Ondrej Trojan, Pavel Borovan. Executive producer: Ondre Trojan. Director: Jan Hrebejk. Screenplay: Petr Jarchovsky, based on his novel. Camera: Jan Malir. Editor: Vladimir Barak. Music: Ales Brezina. In color. Release date: Aug. 27, 2000. Running time: 123 Min. CZECH.

Cast: Boleslav Polivka, Csongor Kassai, Jaroslav Dusek, Anna Siskova, Jiri Pecha, Martin Huba, Simona Stasova, Vladimir Marek.

THE DIVINE RYANS

A Red Sky (Canada) presentation of an Imagex Ltd. production, in association with WIC, Vision TV and TMN, with support from Enterprise Newfoundland & Labrador Corp. (International sales: Myriad Pictures, Santa Monica.) Producer: Christopher Zimmer. Co-producers: Robert Petrie, Wolfram Tichy. Director: Stephen Reynolds. Screenplay: Wayne Johnston, based on his novel. Camera: Alwyn Kumst. Editor: Jeff Warren. Music: Denis Carey, Dave Keary, Ray Fian. In color. Release date: Sept. 26, 1999. Running time: 93 Min. CANADIAN.

Cast: Jordan Harvey, Robert Joy, Peter Postlethwaite, Wendel Meldrum, Mary Walsh, Richard Boland, Marguerite McNeil.

DJOMEH

A Behnegar Films (Tehran) and Lumen Films (Paris) co-production. (International sales: Celluloid Dreams, Paris.) Producer: Ahmad Moussazadeh. Co-producer: Mehran Haguigui. Director/Screenplay: Hassan Yektapanah. Camera: Ali Longhmani. Editor: Hassan Yektapanah. In color. Release date: May 19, 2000. Running time: 93 Min. IRANIAN-FRENCH.

Cast: Jalil Nazari, Mahmoud Behraznia Rashid Akbari

DOLCE FAR NIENTE

A Mact Prods., France 2 Cinema (France)/Sintra, K2 (Italy) production, in association with TelePiu and Canal Plus. Producers: Antoine de Clermont-Tonnerre, Rossanna Seregni. (International sales: UGC Intl., Paris.) Director/Screenplay: Nae Caranfil, based on the novel "The Comedy of Terracina" by Frederic Vitoux. Camera: Cristian Comeaga. Editor: Maryline Monthieux. Music: Nicola Piovani. In color. Release date: Jan. 22, 2000. Running time: 105 Min. FRENCH-ITALIAN.

Cast: Francois Cluzet, Giancarlo Giannini, Isabella Ferrari, Margherita Buy, Pierfrancesco Favino, Teresa Saponangelo.

DON'T BREATHE...LOVE IS IN THE AIR
A Filmax release (in Spain) of an Astrolabio Producciones/Sogedasa/Alma Ata Pictures production, with participation of Via Digital. Producers: Alejandro Bellaba, Julio Fernandez, Jose Maria Calleja. Director/Screenplay: Juan Potau. Camera: Jose Luis Lopez Linares. Editor: Ernest Blasi. Music: Paco Musulen, Luis Elices. In color. Release date: Oct. 4, 1999. Running time: 93 Min. SPANISH.
Cast: Oscar Ladoire, Carlos Fuentes, Leonor Watling, Ana Risueno.

DON'T CRY GERMAINE
A Laurenfilm (Spain)/Cooperative Nouveau Cinema (Belgium) release of a Y.C. Aligator production, in association with Stupid Stupid, Oberon Cinematografica, Tchin Tchin Prods., RTBF. (International sales: Art Box, Paris.) Producer: Eric van Beuren. Director: Alain de Halleux. Screenplay: de Halleux, Eric van Beuren, from the novel by Claude Jasmin. Camera: Philippe Guilbert. Editor: Michele Maquet. Music: Carles Cases. In color. Release date: Aug. 31, 2000. Running time: 96 Min. BELGIAN-FRENCH-SPANISH.
Cast: Rosa Renom, Dirk Roofthooft, Cathy Grosjean, Benoit Skalka, Iwana Krzeptowski, Simon de Thomaz.

DORA-HEITA
A Toho release of a Dora-Heita Projects/Nikkatsu Corp./Yomiko Advertising Co./Mainichi Broadcasting System production, in association with Eizo Kyoto Film Co. (International sales: Nikkatsu Corp., Tokyo.) Producer: Yoshinobu Nishioka. Executive producer: Masaya Nakamura. Director: Kon Ichikawa. Screenplay: Ichikawa, Akira Kurosawa, Keisuke Kinoshita, Masaki Kobayashi, based on the novel "Diary of a Town Magistrate" by Shugoro Yamamoto. Camera: Yukio Isohata. Editor: Chizuko Osada. Music: Kensaku Tanikawa. In color. Release date: Feb. 19, 2000. Running time: 110 Min. JAPANESE.
Cast: Koji Yakusho, Yuko Asano, Bunta Sugawara, Ryudo Uzaki, Tsurutaro Kataoka, Saburo Ishikura, Renji Ishibashi, Tsuyoshi Ujiki.

DOUBLE PACK
A Prokino release of a Catapult Film/Prokino Filmproduktion production, in association with Cine Media Film. (International sales: Bavaria Film Intl., Munich.) Producers: Manya Lutz, Monika Raebel. Executive producer: Lutz. Director: Matthia Lehmann. Screenplay: Lehmann, Eckhard Preuss. Camera: Jo Heim. Editor: Edith Eisenstecken, Evi Oberkofler. Music: various bands. In color. Release date: June 28, 2000. Running time: 88 Min. GERMAN.
Cast: Markus Knuefken, Eckhard Preuss, Margret Voelker, Jeanne Tremsal, Jochen Nichel, Edgar Selge, Manfred Zapatka.

DOUBLE TAP
A Golden Harvest release of a GH Pictures China presentation of a Film Unlimited production. Producers: Derek Yee, Tung-Sing. Executive producers: Stephen Lau, David Chan. Director/Screenplay: Law Chi Leung. Camera: Venus Keung. Editor: Leung. Music: Peter Kam. In color. Release date: Aug. 14, 2000. Running time: 89 Min. HONG KONG.
Cast: Lelie Cheung, Alex Fong, Ruby Wong, Monica Chan.

DRAGONLAND
A Schramm Film production in association with ZDF. Producer: Schramm Film Koerner & Weber. Director/Screenplay: Florian Gartner. Camera: Judith Kaufmann, Sabine Ohle, Ute Freund. Editor: Bettina Bohler. In color. Release date: Jan. 19, 2000. Running time: 93 Min. GERMAN.
Cast: Marek Harloff, Peggy Lukac, Julia Richter, Matthias Matz, Inga Busch, Laura Tonke, Hans Peter Hallwachs.

DREAM
A Mosfilm production. Director: Mikhail Romm. Screenplay: Evgeny Gabrilovich, Tomm. Camera: Boris Volchek. Editor: E. Ladyzhenskaya. Music: Genrikh Vars. In B&W. Release date: Aug. 9, 2000. Running time: 100 Min. SOVIET UNION–1943.
Cast: Elena Kusmina, Vladimir Solovyov, V. Scheglov, Faina Ranevskaya, Arkadi Kislyakov, Ada Voytsik.

DREAMS IN THE MIDDLE WORLD
A Productora Grupo Alyaz production. (International sales: Grupo Alyaz, Madrid.) Producer: Maria Elena Sanchez. Director/Screenplay: Carlos Naranjo Estrella. Camera: Jose Garcia Galisteo. Editor: Miguel A. Lopez. Music: Claudio Jacome, Hugo Idrovo. In color. Release date: Sept. 2, 1999. Running time: 92 Min. ECUADORIAN-SPANISH.
Cast: Hector Alterio, Concha Cuetos, Oscar Iadoire, Maria Kosty, Santiago Naranjo, Claudia Gravi, Mirta Miller, Andrea Guardiola.

DREAMTRIPS
A Munkfilms and Kino Gedanken Experiments production. Producer: Kal Ng. Co-producers: Chow Kaung, Paul Lee. Director/Screenplay: Kal Ng. Camera: Gavin Liew, Derek Rogers. Editor: Louis Yang. Music: Gary Sze. In color, widescreen. Release date: Mar. 2, 2000. Running time: 97 Min. HONG KONG-CANADIAN.
Cast: Jennifer Chan, Wayne Kwok, Gary Sze, WanChi Hong, Jamie Lau, Jane Show, Kal Ng, Damon Mason, Paul Fonoroff, Alex Lee.

DR. K
A Free Cinema production. (International sales: Son-E-Son Film Co., Seoul/Berlin.) Producer: Seo U-sik. Executive producer: Kim In-su. Director/Screenplay: Kwak Kyeong-taek. Camera: Park Hi-ju. Editor: Park Kok-ji. Music: Mun Seung-hyeon, Seong Im-suk. In color. Release date: Nov. 5, 1999. Running time: 100 Min. SOUTH KOREAN.
Cast: Ja In-pyo, Kim Hye-su, Kim Ha-neul, Yu In-chon.

THE DUKE
A Keystone Pictures presentation of a Gone Fishing Prods. production. (International sales: Keystone Entertainment, Malibu, CA.) Producer: Ian Fodie. Executive producers: Robert Vince, Michael Strange, Anne Vince. Director: Philip Spink. Screenplay: Craig Detweiler. Camera: Mike Southon. Editor: Kelly Herron. Music: Brahm Wenger. In color. Release date: Oct. 8, 1999. Running time: 88 Min. CANADIAN.
Cast: John Neville, James Doohan, Courtnee Draper, Jeremy Maxwell, Oliver Muirhead, Sophie Heyman, Judy Geeson.

DURIAN DURIAN
A Golden Network, Nice Top Entertainment (Hong Kong)/Films Studio Canal (Paris) production. (International sales: Wild Bunch, Paris) production. (International sales: Wild Bunch, Paris.) Producer: Doris Yang. Executive producers: Vincent Maraval, Alain de la Mata, Jean-Pierre Dionnet, Carrie Wong. Director: Fruit Chan. Screenplay: Fruit Chan, Sheng Zhi Min, Chan Wai Keung. Camera: Iam Wah Chuen. Editor: Tin Sam Fat. Music: Iam Wah Chuen, Chu Hing Cheung. In color. Release date: Sept. 7, 2000. Running time: 111 Min. HONG KONG-FRENCH.
Cast: Qin Hailu, Mak Wai Fan, Biao Xiao Ming, Yung Wai Yiu.

EATING AIR
A UIP (Singapore) release of a YTC Pictures presentation of a Multi-Story Complex production, with participation of a Yellow River Network. (International sales: Multi-Story Complex, Singapore.) Producers: Loraine Frugniet, Mabelyn Ow. Executive producers: Andrew Yap, Jonathan Yap, Awi Lee. Directors/Screenplay: Kelvin Tong, Jasmine Ng. Camera: Lucas Jodogne, Mary Van Kets. Editor: Ng. Music director: Joe Ng. In color: Release date: Jan. 10, 2000. Running time: 108 Min. SINGAPORE.
Cast: Benjamin Heng, Joseph Cheong, Alvina Toh, Ferris Yeo.

EENY MEENY
A Pozitiv and Czech Television production. Producer: Pavel Sodomka. Executive producer: Klara Bukovska. Director/Screenplay: Alice Nellis. Camera: Ramunas Greicius. Editor: Josef Valusiak. Music: Tomas Polak. In color. Release date: Apr. 13, 2000. Running time: 104 Min. CZECH.
Cast: Iva Janzurova, Leos Sucharipa, Theodora Remundova, Eva Holubova, Vladimir Javorsky, Martina Musilova, Jana Janzurova.

ELISKA LOVES IT WILD
A Bonton Film (in Czech Republic) release of an M.D.M. production, in association with S Pro Alfa Film, Czech Television. Director/Screenplay: Otakaro Schmidt. Camera: Martin Strba. Editor: Olina Kaufmonova. Music: Jan Cechticky, Dan Bauer. In color. Release date: July 7, 2000. Running time: 101 Min. CZECH.
Cast: Bolek Polivka, Zuzana Stivinova, Veronika Zilkova, Martin Dejdar, Jiri Labus, Petr Cyvrtnicke, David Vavra, Dan Nekonecny.

ELZE'S LIFE
A Lietuvos Kino Studio/Q&Q Media production. (International sales: Atlas Intl., Munich.) Producer: Robertas Urbonas. Co-producer: Jan Fantl. Director: Algimantas Puipa. Screenplay: Vytautas Zalakevicius, based on the novel by Ernst Wichert. Camera: Viktoras Radzevicius. Editor: Gintautas Smilga. Music: Juozas Sirvinskas. In color. Release date: Feb. 19, 2000. Running time: 139 Min. LITHUANIAN-GERMAN.
Cast: Egle Jaselskyte, Andrius Paulavicius, Kostas Smoriginas, Janina Lapinskaite, Eduardas Pauliukonis, Antanas Surna.

THE ENCHANTED INTERLUDE
An Ocean Films release of a Dacia Films/France 2 Cinema/Persona Films production, with participation of Canal Plus, CNC. (International sales: UGC Intl., Paris.) Producer: Georges Benayoun. Executive producer: Francoise Guglielmi. Director/Screenplay: Michel Spinosa. Camera: Antoine Roch. Editor: Valerie Deseine. In color. Release date: Apr. 17, 2000. Running time: 88 Min. FRENCH.
Cast: Clotilde Courau, Vincent Elbaz, Geraldine Pailhas, Karin Viard, Roschdy Zem, Eric Caravaca, Brigitte Catillon, Michel Spinosa.

THE END OF THE AFFAIR
A Sony Pictures Entertainment release of a Columbia Pictures presentation of a Stephen Woolley production. Producers: Stephen Woolley, Neil Jordan. Co-producer: Kathy Sykes. Director/Screenplay: Neil Jordan, based on the novel by Graham Greene. Camera: Roger Pratt. Editor: Tony Lawson. Music: Michael Nyman. In Technicolor. Release date: Nov. 11, 1999. MPAA Rating: R. Running time: 109 Min. BRITISH.
Cast: Ralph Fiennes, Julianne Moore, Stephen Rea, Ian Hart, Samuel Bould, Jason Isaacs, James Bolam, Deborah Findlay.

ENGINEER KOCHIN'S ERROR
A Mosfilm production. Director: Aleksandr Macheret. Screenplay: Macheret, Yuri Olesha, based on a play by the Tur brothers. Camera: I. Gelein. Editor: M. Kuzmina. In B&W. Release date: Aug. 8, 2000. Running time: 111 Min. SOVIET UNION–1939.
Cast: M. Zharov, S. Nikonov, Lyubov Orlova, N. Dorokhin, B. Petker, Faina Ranevskaya.

ENGLAND!
A Tossell Pictures production, in association with ZDF, Studio Babelsberg Independents and German Film & TV Academey Berlin. (International sales: Bavaria Film Intl., Munich.) Producers: Judy Tossell, Susanne Marian. Director: Achim von Borries. Screenplay: Von Borries, Karin Astrom, Maria von Heland. Camera: Jutta Pohlmann. Editor: Gergana Voigt. Music: Daler Nazarov, Ingo Frenzel. In Fujicolor. Release date: June 20, 2000. Running time: 97 Min. GERMAN.
Cast: Ivan Shvedoff, Merab Ninidze, Anna Geislerova, Chulpan Khamatova, Maxim Kowalewski, Fabian Busch, Dennis Burgazliev.

ENLIGHTENMENT GUARANTEED
A Constantin Film release of a Bernd Eichinger presentation of a Megaherz production. (International sales: Cinepool World Distribution, Munich.) Producer: Franz X. Gernstl. Executive producer: Louis Saul. Director/Screenplay: Doris Dorrie. Camera: Hans Karl Hu. Editors: Inez Regnier, Arne Sinnwell. In color, digital video-to-film.) Release date: Jan. 29, 2000. Running time: 108 Min. GERMAN.
Cast: Uwe Oschsenknecht, Gustav Peter Wohler, Anica Dobra, Ulrike Kriener, Heiner Lauterbach.

ENTER: A FILM ABOUT LOS ANGELES
A True Pictures presentation of a Verismo Film/True Pictures/Veit Bastian production. Producers: Zuli Aladag, Bastian. Director/Editor: Veit Bastian. Camera: Marcus Hampe, Guido Frenzel, Jennifer Lane, Bastian. Music: David Jazay, Gift, Arab Strap. Video. Release date: Feb. 20, 2000. Running time: 50 Min. Documentary. GERMAN.
With: Edwin Vela, Jim South, Bola Akinwole, Stoo Mundel, Mario Paola.

ENVY
An Adelphi Films production. Producer: Michael Cook. Executive producers: Peter Broderick, Julie Money. (International sales: Next Wave Films, Santa Monica.) Director: Julie Money. Screenplay: Jeff Truman, based on the original script "Snowdrop" by Trevor Shearston. Camera: Graeme Wood. Editor: Roberta Horslie. Music: Andy Evans. In color. Release date: Sept. 13, 1999. Running time: 81 Min. AUSTRALIAN.
Cast: Linda Cropper, Jeff Truman, Anna Lise Phillips, Wade Osborne, Scott Major.

THE ESCORT
A Pathe release (in France & U.K.) of a Claude Berri presentation of a Renn Prods., France 3 Cinema (France)/Pathe Prods. (U.K.) production, with participation of Canal Plus and CNC. (International sales: UGC Intl., Paris.) Executive producers: Annabel Karouby, Pierre Grunstain. Co-producer: Timothy Burrill. Director/Screenplay: Michel Blanc, from an idea by Hanif Dureishi. English dialogue: Nick Love. Camera: Barry Ackroyd. Editor: Maryline Monthieux. Music: Barry Adamson. In color. Release date: Oct. 28, 1999. Running time: 106 Min. FRENCH-BRITISH.
Cast: Daniel Auteuil, Stuart Townsend, Liza Walker, Noah Taylor, Frances Barber, Claire Skinner, Beatrice Agenin, Keith Allen.

ESSEX BOYS
A Pathe Distribution release of a Granada Film production. (International sales: Spring Intl. U.K., London.) Producer: Jeff Pope. Executive producer: Pippa Cross. Director: Terry Winsor. Screenplay: Jeff Pope, Winsor. Camera: John Daly. Editor: Edward Mansell. Music: Colin Towns. In Technicolor. Release date, Mar. 30, 2000. Running time: 102 Min. BRITISH.
Cast: Sean Bean, Alex Kingston, Charlie Creed-Miles, Tom Wilkinson, Larry Lamb, Michael McKell, Billy Murray, Amelia Lowdell.

ESTHER KAHN
A Why Not Prods. & Les Films Alain Sarde presentation of a France 2 Cinema/France 3 Cinema/Zephyr Films/Arts Council of England/BSkyB/British Screen production. (International sales: Studio-Canal, Paris.) Producer: Alain Sarde. Director: Arnaud Desplechin. Screenplay: Desplechin, Emmanuel Bourdieu, based on the story by Arthur Symons. Camera: Eric Gautier. Editor: Herve de Luze. Music: Howard Shore. In color. Release date: May 18, 2000. Running time: 163 Min. FRENCH-BRITISH.
Cast: Summer Phoenix, Ian Holm, Fabrice Desplechin, Frances Barber, Laszlo Szabo, Emmanuelle Devos, Akbar Kurtha.

EUREKA
A J Works/Suncent Cinemaworks presentation, in association with Les Films de l'Observatoire, of a Dentsu/Imagica/Suncent Cinemaworks/Tokyo Theaters production. (International sales: Wild Bunch, Paris.) Producer: Takenori Sento. Co-producer: Philippe Avril. Director/Screenplay: Shinji Aoyama. Camera: Masaki Tamra. Editor: Aoyama. Music: Isao Yamada, Aoyama. In B&W and color, widescreen. Release date: May 18, 2000. Running time: 218 Min. JAPANESE.
Cast: Koji Yakusho, Aoi Miyazaki, Masaru Miyazaki, Yohichiroh Saitoh, Ken Mitsuishi, Go Riju, Yutaka Matsuhige, Sansei Shiomi.

EVA'S EYE
A Northern Lights, NRK (Norway)/Nordisk FIlm (Denmark) production. (International sales: Nordisk Film, Copenhagen.) Producer: Axel Helgeland. Director/Screenplay: Berit Nesheim, based on the novel by Karin Fossum. Camera: Erling Thurmann-Andersen. Editor: Inge-Lise Langfeldt. Music: Geir Bohren, Bent Aserud. In color. Release date: Feb.1, 2000. Running time: 90 Min. NORWEGIAN-DANISH.
Cast: Andrine Saether, Bjorn Sundquist, Gisken Armand, Sverre Anker Ousdal, Linda Tomine Coles, Svein Roger Karlsen.

EVERYBODYLOVES-SUNSHINE
A Lion's Gate release of an IAC Holdings Ltd. presentation in association with the Isle of Man Film Commission and BV Films Intl. of a Gothic production. Producer: Joanne Reay. Executive producers: Guy Collins, Heather Playford Denman, Bjorg Veland, Simon Johnson. Director/Screenplay: Andrew Goth. Camera: Julian Morson. Editor: Jeremy Gibbs. Music: Nicky Matthew. In Deluxe color. Release date: Nov. 17, 1999. Running time: 97 Min. BRITISH.
Cast: Goldie, Andrew Goth, David Bowie, Rachel Shelley, Clint Dyer, Sarah Shackleton, David Baker, Paul Hawkyard, Graham Bryan.

EVERYTHING HAPPENS TO ME
An Iris Star production. Producers: Joan Bosch, Pere Domenech. Director: Miguel Garcia Borda. Screenplay: Toni Martin, Borda, based on a story by Martin. Camera: Jordi Torta. Editor: Lluis Freixa. In color. Release date: July 9, 2000. Running time: 108 Min. SPANISH.
Cast: Javier Albala, Lola Duenas, Mariam Alamany, Jordi Collet, Christian Brondo, Miguel Garcia Bordo.

EVERYTHING'S FINE (WE'RE LEAVING)
A Rezo Prods/France 2 Cinema/Rezp Films/Rhone-Alpes Cinema production, with the participation of La Region Rhone-Alpes, Centre National de la Cinematographie, Canal Plus, France 2, Sofica Sofinergie 5, La Procirep. (International sales: Flach Pyramide Intl., Paris.) Producers: Jean-Michel Rey, Philippe Liegeois. Director/Screenplay: Claude Mourieras. Camera: William Lubtchansky. Editor: Monique Dartonne. In color. Release date: May 11, 2000. Running time: 95 Min. FRENCH.
Cast: Michel Piccoli, Miou Miou, Sandrine Kiberlain, Natacha Regnier.

EVIL
A Rosa Filmes/Radiotelevisao Portuguesa (Portugal)/Metropolitan Films (Ireland)/Camelot Pelis (Spain)/Quimera Filmes (Brazil) production. (International sales: Rosa Filmes, Lisbon.) Producer: Amandio Coroado. Director/Screenplay: Alberto Seixas Santos. Camera: Acacio de Almeida. Editor: Catarina Ruivo. Music: Nuno Carvalho, Vasco Pimentael, Victor Puertas. In color. Release date: Sept. 5, 1999. Running time: 87 Min. PORTUGUESE-IRISH-SPANISH-BRAZILIAN.
Cast: Pauline Cadell, Rui Morrisson, Alexandre Pinto, Maria Santo.

THE EXAM (DADDY'S LAST RUN)
A Shochiku release of a Shochik Co./Kadokawa/Human Dream production. (International sales: Shochiku, Tokyo.) Producers: Nobuyoshi Ohtani, Tsuguhiko Kadokawa. Director: Yojiro Takita. Screenplay: Nobuyuki Isshiki. Camera: Naoki Kayano. Music: Toshihiko Sabashi. In color. Release date: Nov. 28, 2000. Running time: 113 Min. JAPANESE.
Cast: Eikichi Yazawa, Yuko Tanaka, Natsumi Ohira.

EYE BALL
A Europafilm release (in Norway) of a Norsk Film (Norway)/Felicia Film (Sweden)/Per Holst Film (Denmark) production. (International sales: BV Intl. Pictures, Avaldsnes, Norway.) Producer: Tom Remlov. Director: Catrine Telle. Screenplay: Beate Grimsrud. Camera: Peter Mokrosinski. Editor: Pal Gengenback. Music: Nils Petter Molvaer, Jan Bang. In color. Release date: Jan. 31, 2000. Running time: 85 Min. NORWEGIAN-SWEDISH-DANISH.
Cast: Laila Goody, Bjornar Teigen, Marit A. Andreassen, Kristin Kajander, Kjersti Holmen, Anne Krigsvoll, Tom Tellefsen.

EYE OF THE BEHOLDER
A Behaviour Worldwide presentation, in association with Village Roadshow and Ambridge Film Partnership, of a Hit & Run/Filmline Intl. production in association with Eye of the Beholder Ltd. (International sales: Behaviour Worldwide, Los Angeles.) Producers: Nicolas Clermont, Tony Smith. Executive producers: Hilary Shor, Mark Damon. Co-producer: Al Clark. Director/Screenplay: Stephan Elliott, based on the novel by Marc Behm. Camera: Guy Dufaux. Editor: Sue Blainey. Music: Marius De Vries. In color. Release date: Sept. 4, 1999. Running time: 107 Min. CANADIAN-BRITISH.
Cast: Ewan McGregor, Ashley Judd, Patrick Bergin, k.d. lang, Jason Priestley, Genevieve Bujold.

FACE
A Tokyo Theatres Co. release of a Shochiku, Eiga Gekijo, Kuho production. (International sales: Shochiku, Tokyo.) Producer: Yukiko Shii. Director: Junji Sakamoto. Screenplay: Sakamoto, Isamu Uno, story by Uno. Camera: Norimichi Kasamatsu. Editor: Toshihide Fukano. Music: Coba. In color. Release date: Sept. 8, 2000. Running time: 124 Min. JAPANESE.
Cast: Naomi Fujiyama, Etsushi Toyokawa, Michio Ookusu, Kankuro Nakamura, Ittoku Kishibe, Hiroyuki Sato, Junn Kinimura, Riho Makise.

FACE TO FACE
A Rofilm/Artis Foundation production. (International sales: Romaniafilm, Bucharest.) Director/Screenplay: Marius Theodor Barna. Camera: Alexandru Solomon. Editor: Melania Oproiu. Music: Petru Margineanu. In color. Release date: Aug. 28, 1999. Running time: 91 Min. ROMANIAN.
Cast: Maia Morgenstern, Serban Ionescu, Serban Pavlu,.

FACING
A Cinemane Film/Carrere/M6 Films production, in association with Canal Plus. (International sales: RF1, Paris.) Producers: Guillaume Godard, Patrick Gouyou Beauchamps, Thierry Peronne, Claude Carrere. Director: Mathias Ledoux. Screenplay: Valerie Guignabodet. Camera: Stephane Leparc. Editor: Jean-Pierre Baiesi. Music: Gekko. In color. Release date: Feb. 12, 2000. Running time: 90 Min. FRENCH.
Cast: Jean-Hugues Anglade, Clotilde Courau, Christine Boisson, Jose Garcia, Jean Benguigui, Emmanuel Salinger, Laurence Fevrier.

FAITHLESS
An SVT Drama production, in collaboration with AB Svensk Filmindustri, NRK, Classic SRL, RAI, ZDF, with the support of the Swedish Film Institute, Nordic Film and TV Fund. (International sales: AB Svensk Filmindustri, Stockholm.) Producer: Kaj Larsen. Executive producer: Maria Curman. Director: Liv Ullmann. Screenplay: Ingmar Bergman. Camera: Jorgen Persson. Editor: Syliva Ingemarsson. In color. Release date: May 13, 2000. Running time: 154 Min. SWEDISH.
Cast: Lena Endre, Erland Josephson, Krister Henriksson, Thomas Hanzon, Michelle Gylemo, Juni Dahr, Philip Zanden.

THE FALSE SERVANT

A Pyramide release of a Dacia Films Pyramide Prods., Les Films du Camelia production, with participation of Canal Plus. (International sales: Flach Pyramide Intl., Paris.) Producer: Geroges Benayoun. Executive producer: Francoise Guglielmi. Director: Benoit Jacquot, from the play by Marivaux. Camera: Romain Winding. Editor: Pascale Chavance. In color. Release date: Apr. 16, 2000. Running time: 88 Min. FRENCH.

Cast: Isabelle Huppert, Sandrine Kiberlain, Pierre Arditi, Mathieu Amalric, Alexandre Soulie, Philippe Vieux.

FAMILY SECRET

A Blinding Light (New York)/Morgane Production (Paris)/La Sept Arte (Paris) production. (International sales: Jane Balfour Films, London; U.S. sales: Magnet Media, New York.) Producers: Pola Rapaport, Edgard Tenembaum. Director/Screenplay/Editor: Pola Rapaport. Camera: Wolfgang Held. Music: Guy Klucevsek, Loren Toolajian. In color and B&W. Release date: Feb. 3, 2000. Running time: 58 Min. Documentary. U.S.-FRENCH.

FANDANGO

A Buena Vista Intl. (Germany) release of a Calypso Filmproduktion production, in association with BVI Film Production (Germany) and Bavaria Film. (International sales: Bavaria Film Intl., Geiselgasteig, Munich.) Producer: Werner Possardt. Executive producer: Viola Jaeger. Co-producers: Wolfgang Braun, Christoph Ott, Michael Weber. Director/Screenplay: Matthias Glasner, based on the idea "Dee Jay's Day" by Hens Bielefeldt von Kunowski. Camera: Sonja Rom. Editor: Markus Goller. Music: Fetisch & Meister. In color, widescreen. Release date: Feb. 12, 2000. Running time: 115 Min. GERMAN.

Cast: Nicolette Krebitz, Moritz Bleibtreu, Richy Mueller, Lars Rudolph, Ill-Young Kim, Volker Spengler, Corinna Harfouch.

FANNY AND ELVIS

A UIP release (in U.K.) of a Scala Prods., the Film Consortium (U.K.)/Ima Films (France) production. (International sales: Capitol Films, London.) Producer: Laurie Borg. Executive producer: Nik Powell. Co-executive producer: Georges Benayoun. Director/Screenplay: Kay Mellor. Camera: John Daly. Editor: Christopher Blunden. Music: Stephen Warbeck. In color. Release date: Oct. 2, 1999. Running time: 110 Min. BRITISH-FRENCH.

Cast: Kerry Fox, Ray Winstone, David Morrissey, Ben Daniels, Jennifer Saunders, Colin Salmon, Gaynor Faye.

FANS

A Filmauro Distribuzione release of a Filmauro production. Producer: Aurelio De Laurentiis. Director: Neri Parenti. Screenplay: Parenti, Marco Martani, Fausto Brizzi, Enrico Vanzina. Camera: Lorenzo Battaglia. Editor: Alberto Gallitti. Music: Bruno Zambrini. In color. Release date: Oct. 13, 1999. Running time: 120 Min. ITALIAN.

Cast: Massimo Boldi, Christian De Sica, Diego Abatantuono, Enzo Iacchetti, Nino D'Angelo, Maurizio Mattioli, Angelo Bernabucci.

FANTOZZI 2000: THE CLONING

A Cecchi Gori Distribuzione release (in Italy) of an Italian Intl. Film/Cecchi Gori Group production. Producers: Fulvio Lucisano, Vittorio Cecchi Gori. Director: Domenico Saverni. Screenplay: Alessandro Bencivenni, Saverni. Camera: Marco Onorato. Editor: Raimondo Crociani. Music: Fabio Frizzi. In color. Release date: Dec. 20, 1999. Running time: 94 Min. ITALIAN.

Cast: Paolo Villaggio, Milena Vukotic, Anna Mazzamauro, Dodi Conti, Paolo Paoloni.

FARA

An ABA Studio/National Production Center of the Republic of Kazakhstan/Russian State Committee of Cinematography production. (International sales: Sovexportfilm, Moscow.) Producer: Boris Airapetian. Director: Abai Karpykov. Screenplay: Leila Akhinzhanova, Boris Airapetian. Camera: Alexei Berkovich. Editors: Tatiana Belousova, Svetlana Mayzova. Music: Boris Beglar. In color. Release date: Feb. 13, 2000. Running time: 89 Min. RUSSIAN-KAZAKHSTANIAN.

Cast: Farkhat Abdraimov, Kristina Orbakaite, Alexander Alexandrov, Dauren Sarsekeev.

THE FAREWELL

A Novoskop Film/WDR/ORB/SWR/Arte/Studio Babelsberg Independents/Arthur Hofer production with support from Filmforfrung Hamburg, Filmboard Berlin, European Script fund and Kulturstiftung der Deutschen Bank. (International sales: Cinepool, Munich.) Producers: Gesche Carstens, Henryk Romanowski, Jan Schutte. Director: Jan Schutte. Screenplay: Klaus Pohl. Camera: Edward Klosinski. Editor: Renate Merck. Music: John Cale. In color. Release date: May 14, 2000. Running time: 93 Min. GERMAN.

Cast: Josef Bierbichler, Monica Bleibtreu, Margit Rogall, Jeanette Hain, Samuel Fintzi, Elfriede Irrall.

FAST FOOD, FAST WOMEN

An Ocean Films (in France) release of a Lumen Films presentation in association with Bim Distribuzione, Pandora Films, Paradis Films, Orly Films. (International sales: Celluloid Dreams, Paris.) Producer: Hengameh Panahi. Co-producer: Avram Ludwig. Director/Screenplay: Amos Kollek. Camera: Jean-Marc Fabre. Editor: Sheri Bylander. Music: David Carbonara. In color. Release date: May 15, 2000. Running time: 95 Min. FRENCH-U.S.

Cast: Anna Thomson, Jamie Harris, Louise Lasser, Robert Modica, Lonette McKee, Victor Argo, Angelica Torn, Austin Pendleton.

FATHER

A Beijing Film Studio presentation of a Beijing Film Studio/Beijing Shanhe Yingshi Yishu production, in association with Beijing Good Dreams. Producer: Han Sanping. Executive producer: Wang Weijing. Executive in charge of production: Peng Xiaolin. Director: Wang Shuo. Executive director: Lao Yun. Screenplay: Wang, Feng Xiaogang, from Wang's 1991 novel, "I'm Your Dad" (Wo shi ni baba). Camera: Yan Xiaoxiong. Editor: Zhou Ying. Music: Shi Wanchun. In color. Release date: Aug. 9, 2000. Running time: 96 Min. CHINESE.

Cast: Feng Xiaogang, Hu Xiaopei, Xu Fan, Qin Yan, Wang Weining, Ye Qing, Yuan Yuan, Chen Huanyuan, Sima Nan.

FATHERLESS

A Japanese Academy of Moving Images production. Producer: Tetsuo Yamatani. Director: Yoshihisa Shigeno. Camera: Takashi Soga. Editor: Taiki Saito. Music: Tomohiro Hosayama. In color. Release date: Aug. 24, 1999. Running time: 44 Min. Documentary. JAPANESE.

FEMALE COMPANY

An Odeon release of an Odeon/Greek Film Center/A-Sky/Mythos/Nikos Perakis production. (International sales: Greek Film Center, Athens.) Producer: Manos Krezias. Director: Nikos Perakis. Screenplay: Katerina Bei, Perakis. Camera: Yorgos Argyroiliopoulos. Editor: Yorgos Mavropsaridis. Music: Nikos Mamangakis. In color. Release date: Feb. 17, 2000. Running time: 107 Min. GREEK.

Cast: Maria Yorgiadou, Smaragda Diamantidou, Sofi Zanninou, Christina Theodoropoulou, Tania Kapasali, Katia Nikolaidou.

FEMININE, SINGULAR

A Paso Doble Film production. Producer: Giuliana Del Punta. Director/Editor: Claudio Del Punta. Screenplay: Doriana Leondeff, Claudio Del Punta. Camera: Patrizio Patrizi. In Augustus color. Release date: Oct. 14, 1999. Running time: 104 Min. ITALIAN.

Cast: Cristina Moglia, Danny Quinn, Valentina Chico, Vincenzo Peluso, Lorenza Indovina.

FEROCIOUS SAINT LORD OF GOBI

A Nyamgavaa Film production. (International sales: Nyamgavaa Film Production Co.) Producer: Ichinhorloo Nyamgavaa. Director: Ichinmorloo Nyamgavaa. Screenplay: B. Dogmid. Music: N. Jantsannorov. In Fujicolor. Release date: Jan. 22, 2000. Running time: 104 Min. MONGOLIAN.

Cast: Dogmid Sosorbaram, O. Baigal. N. Dolgor, L. Jamsranja.

FIDELITY

A Gemini Films release of a Gemini Films/France 3 Cinema co-production with the participation of Canal Plus. (International sales: Gemini Films, Paris.) Producer: Paulo Branco. Director/Screenplay: Andrzej Zulawski, based on the novel "La Princesse de Cleves" by Madame de La Fayette. Camera: Patrick Blossier. Editor: Marie-Sophie Dubus. Music: Andrzej Korzynski. In color. Release date: Apr. 6, 2000. Running time: 166 Min. FRENCH.

Cast: Sophie Marceau, Guillaume Canet, Pascal Greggory, Michel Subor, Magali Noel, Edith Scob, Aurelien Recoing, Marc Francois.

15 AMORE

A Maurice Murphy & Friends release and presentation of an MTXM Movies production. Producers: Brooke Wilson, Maurice Murphy. Executive producers: Maurice Murphy, Margaret Murphy. Director/Screenplay: Maurice Murphy. Camera: John Brock. Editor: Dana Hughes. Music: Carlo Giacco. In Atlab color. Release date: Apr. 16, 2000. Running time: 92 Min. AUSTRALIAN.

Cast: Lisa Hensley, Steve Bastoni, Domenic Galati, Tara Jakszewicz, Gertraud Ingeborg, Rhiana Griffith, Joel Pieterse, Nicholas Bryant.

THE FIFTH SET: AUSTRALIA AND THE DAVIS CUP

A Film Australia production. (International sales: Film Australia, Sydney.) Producers: Cristina Pozzan, Kate Latimer. Director: Sue Thompson. Screenplay: Nick Place, Kate Latimer. Video. Release date: July 29, 2000. Running time: 56 Min. Documentary: AUSTRALIAN.

FILM

A Lucky Red release of a Brosfilm production. Director/Screenplay: Laura Betti. Camera: Marco Sperduti. Editor: Bruno Sarandrea. Music: Tito Schipa, Jr. In Technicolor and B&W. Release date: July 5, 2000. Running time: 94 Min. ITALIAN.

Cast: Laura Morante, Monica Scattini, Maddalena Crippa, Naike Rivelli, Gigio Alberti, Riccardo Onorato, Vanni Corbellini.

FILM...

A Filmplus production, in association with MMK, ORTT, TV2. Producers: Gabor Varga, Zsuzsanna G. Hollosi. Director: Andras Suranyi. Screenplay: Suranyi, Ilona Nagy, Miklos Meszoly. Camera: Istvan Borbas. Editor: Andras Suranyi. Music: Karoly Binder. In color and B&W. Release date: Feb. 4, 2000. Running date: 84 Min. HUNGARIAN.

Cast: Ivan Darvas, Hedi Temessy, Peter Haumann, Juli Basti, Andras Balint, Tamas Vegvari, Lili Monori.

FILM NOIR

A Monkey Town Prods. production. (International sales: Mercure Distribution, Paris.) Producer: Seiichi Ono. Director/Screenplay: Masahiro Kobayashi. Camera: Akira Sakoh. Editor: Naoki Kaneko. In color. Release date: May 17, 2000. Running time: 86 Min. JAPANESE.

Cast: Ryo Ishibashi, Nene Otsuka, Ken Ogata.

FILM 1

A Luna FIlms production, in association with Flanders Film Fund and Canal Plus. (International sales: Luna, Ceroux-Mousty, Belgium.) Producer: Willem Wallyn. Executive producer: Nadja Benallou. Director/Screenplay: Willem Wallyn. Camera: Lou Berghmans. Editor: Neil Skeet. Music: Dirk Jans. In color. Release date: Oct. 9, 1999. Running time: 99 Min. BELGIAN.

Cast: Peter van den Begin, Herbert Flack, Frank Vander Linden, David Steegen, Carl Ridders, Luc Wallyn, Syliva Kristel, Dora van der Groe.

THE FILTH AND THE FURY

A Fine Line Features release of a Film-Four Ltd. presentation in association with the Sex Pistols/Jersey Shore/Nitrate Film Prods. Producers: Anita Camarata, Amanda Temple. Executive producers: Eric Gardner, Jonathan Weisgal. Director: Julien Temple. Editor: Niven Howie. In Deluxe London color. Release date: Jan. 25, 2000. Running time: 108 Min. Documentary. BRITISH-U.S.

With: the Sex Pistols (Paul Cook, Steve Jones, Glen Matlock, Johnny Rotten, Sid Vicious).

FIRST LOVE

An Engine Network, Tokyo Broadcasting System, Bandai Visual Co., Kadokawa Shoten Publishing Co., Dentsu, Dynasty production. (International sales: TBS, Tokyo.) Producers: Shohei Kotaki, Kazuya Hamana, Kazumi Kawashiro. Executive producers: Masahiro Yasuda, Toshiaki Harada, Tadamichi Abe. Co-producers: Nobuyuki Tohya, Yutaka Okawa, Yoshihiro Kato. Director: Tetsuo Shinohara. Screenplay: Masahiko Nagasawa. Camera: Junichi Fujisawa. Music: Joe Hisaishi. In color. Release date: July 12, 2000. Running time: 115 Min. JAPANESE.

Cast: Rena Tanaka, Mieko Harada, Mitsuru Hirate, Hiroyuki Sanada, Masaki Nishina, Makoto Sato.

FIRST OF THE NAME

An Ognon Picture/JMH Prods. production, with the participation of Canal Plus, CNC, Eurimages, Communaute Urbaine de Strasbourg, SCAM. (International sales: FPI, Paris.) Producer: Humbert Balsan. Director: Sabine Franel. Screenplay: Franel, Nicolas Morel. Camera: Jimmy Glasberg. Editors: Anee Weil, Yannick Kergoat. Music: Jean-Pierre Fouquey. In color and B&W. Release date: May 14, 2000. Running time: 117 Min. Documentary. FRENCH-SWISS.

With: Philippe Blachais, Albert Blin, Claude Bloch, Emile-Jacques Franel, Sabine Franel, Antoine Grumbach, Gilles Wolkowitsch.

FIRST LIGHT OF DAWN

A Caviar Produzioni production. (International sales: Intra Films.) Producers: Andrea De Liberato, Antonio Fusco. Director: Lucio Gaudino. Screenplay: Nicola Molino. Camera: Felice de Maria. Editor: Patrizio Marone. Music: Andrea Guerra. In color. Release date: Feb. 17, 2000. Running time: 86 Min. ITALIAN.

Cast: Gianmarco Tognazzi, Francesco Giuffrida, Laura Morante, Roberto Nobile.

FIRST LOVE: THE LITTER ON THE BREEZE

A Block 2 Pictures presentation, in association with Amuse Group, of a Jet Tone production. (International sales: Block 2, Hong Kong.) Producers: Wong Kar-wai, Yokichi Osato, Jacky Pang, Akira Morishita. Executive producer: Chan Ye-cheng. Director: Eric Kot. Screenplay: Ocean Chan, Yip Lim-sum. Camera: Christopher Doyle. Editor: Chan Ki-hop. Music: Carl Wong. In color. Release date: Feb. 13, 2000. Running time: 96 Min. HONG KING-JAPANESE.

Cast: Takeshi Kaneshiro, Karen Mok, Eric Kot, Lee Wai-wai, Vincent Kuk, Lan Sin, Cheung Tik-lung.

THE FISH IN LOVE

A Cecchi Gori Distribuzione release (in Italy) of a Mario & Vittorio Cecchi Gori presentation of a Cecchi Gori Entertainment Europa production. Producer: Vittorio Cecchi Gori. Executive producer: Alessandro Calosci. Director: Leonardo Peraccioni. Screenplay: Periaccioni, Giovanni Veronesi. Camera: Arnaldo Catinari. Editor: Mirco Garrone. Music: Claudio Guidetti. In Cinecitta color. Release date: Dec. 14, 1999. Running time: 92 Min. ITALIAN.

Cast: Leonardo Peraccioni, Yamila Diaz, Paolo Hendel, Patrizia Loreti,

FLAMES OF PARADISE

An Icelandic Film Corp., Leiknar Myndir (Iceland)/Viking Film (Sweden)/Filmhuset (Norway)/Peter Rommel Filmproduktion (Germany) production. (International sales: Trust Film Sales, Hvidore, Denmark.) Producer: Fridrik Thor Fridriksson. Co-producers: Bo Jonsson, Egil Odegaard, Peter Rommel. Director: Hrafn Gunnlaugsson. Screenplay: Bo Honsson, Gunnlaugsson, Thorarinn Eldjarn. Camera: Ari Kristinsson. Editors: Gunnlaugsson, Skule Eriksen. Music: Gunnlaugsson. In color. Release date: Feb. 1, 2000. Running time: 100 Min. ICELANDIC-SWEDISH-NORWEGIAN-GERMAN.

Cast: Hilmir Snaer Gudnason, Sara Gogg Magnusdottir, Hallgrimur H. Helgason, Alexandra Rappaport, Jon Sigurbjornsson.

FLAT TYRE

An HMC Film Prods. production. (International sales: HMC, Taipei.) Producer: Shell Wang. Director/Screenplay: Huang Min-Chuan. Camera: Zeng Bodo. Editors: Huan, Joy Zhou. Music: T.I.P. In color, 16mm. Release date: Oct. 19, 1999. Running time: 73 Min. TAIWANESE.

Cast: Ding Ning, Yang Ming-hsuing, Zeng Bodo.

A FLEETING PASSAGE TO THE ORIENT

An Aichholzer Film production. (International sales: First Hand Films, Zurich.) Producer: Josef Aichholzer. Director/Screenplay: Ruth Beckermann. Camera: Nurith Aviv, Sophie Cadet. Editor: Gertraud Luschitzky. Music: Bruno Pisek, Peter Ponger, Ernst Zettl. In color. Release date: July 8, 2000. Running time: 82 Min. Documentary. AUSTRIAN.

FLY ME TO POLARIS

A Golden Harvest release of a GH Pictures (China)/Deltamac Co./Sil-Metropole Organization presentation of a Jayline production. (International sales: Golden Harvest, Hong Kong.) Producer: Raymond Chow. Executive producer: David Chan. Director: Jingle Ma. Screenplay: Lo Chi-leung, Yeung Sin-ling. Camera: Ma, Chan Kwok-hung. Editor: Kwong Chi-leong. Music: Peter Kam. In color, widescreen. Release date: Nov. 26, 1999. Running time: 94 Min. HONG KONG.

Cast: Richie Ren, Cecilia Cheung, William So, Eric Tsang, Eric Kot, Sheren Tang, Lam San-san.

THE FOOLISH POMEGRANATE TREE

A Budapest Filmstudio/Kvali Film co-production, in association with Grusia Film, BBSA, MMK, NKA, ORTT. Producers: Ferenc Kardos, Laszlo Kantor, Gela Kandelaki. Director/Screenplay: Peter Meszaros. Camera: Gyorgy Beridze. Editor: Cisana Cihiseli. Music: Zurab Nadaresvilli. In B&W. Release date: Feb. 6, 2000. Running time: 91 Min. HUNGARIAN-GEORGIAN.

Cast: Slava Gasparov, Vahtang Komahidze, Magda Anikasvili, Peter Meszaros.

FOREIGN FIELDS

A Balboa 2 production, in association with Exitfilm and Zentropa Prods. (International sales: Scanbox, Denmark.) Producer: Henrik Danstrup. Executive producer: Peter Aalbaeck Jensen. Director: Aage Reis. Screenplay: Reis, Jens Dahl. Camera: Bo Tengberg. Editor: Darek Hodor. Music: Hilmar Orn Hilmarsson. In color. Release date: Feb. 4, 2000. Running time: 93 Min. DANISH.

Cast: Pelle Hvenegaard, Nicolaj Coster-Waldau, John Widerberg, Julia Jager, Steve Nicolson.

FOREIGN SISTER

A Dan Wolman production. Producer/Director/Screenplay: Dan Wolman. Camera: Itamar Hadar. Editor: Shoshi Wolman. Music: Slava Ganelin. In color. Release date: July 19, 2000. Running time: 124 Min. ISRAELI.

Cast: Tamar Yerushalmi, Askala Marcus, Avi Salton, Miriam Nevo, Neli Tagar, Yosi Asafa.

FORGET AMERICA

An Arthaus Filmverleih release of an Avista Film/Brainpool TV/ Kinowelt Filmproduktion production, in association with WDR. (International sales: Cinepool, Munich.) Producers: Alena and Herbert Rimbach. Director: Vanessa Jopp. Screenplay: Maggie Peren, Jopp. Camera: Judith Kaufmann. Editor: Martina Matuschewski. Music: Beckmann.In Fujicolor. Release date: June 28, 2000. Running time: 90 Min. GERMAN.

Cast: Marek Harloff, Franziska Petri, Roman Knizka, Rita Feldmeier, Andreas Schmidt-Schaller, Gerd Lohmeyer, Ursula Doll.

FORGIVE AND FORGET

A Scottish Television production. Executive producer: Philip Hinchcliffe. Director: Aisling Walsh. Screenplay: Mark Burt. Camera: Kevin Rowley. Editor: Chris Buckland. Music: Hal Lindes. In color, video-to-35mm. Release date: June 12, 2000. Running time: 100 Min. BRITISH.

Cast: John Simm, Steven John Shepherd, Laura Fraser, Maurice Roeves, Ger Ryan, Meera Sya.

THE FORGOTTEN ONES

Producer: Giovanni Schettini. Director/Screenplay: Piero Livi. Camera: Gianfranco Transunto. Editor: Carlo Valerio. Music: Claudio Tallino. Release date: Jan. 16, 2000. Running time: 104 Min. ITALIAN.

Cast: Sandro Ghiani, Alex Partexano, Lucio Salis.

FORTUNA (MY SISTER)

A Sheleg production. Producer: Hagai Levi. Executive producer: Osnat Eitan. Director: Timna Rosenheimer. Camera: Itzik Portal. Editor: Naomi Press Aviram. In color. Release date: Aug. 21, 2000. Running time: 59 Min. Documentary. ISRAELI.

42 UP

A First Run Films release (U.S.) of a Granada Television production for the BBC. Producer: Michael Apted. Executive producers: Ruth Pitt, Stephen Lambert. Co-producer: Claire Lewis. Director: Michael Apted. Camera: George Jesse Turner. Editor: Kim Horton. In color and B&W. Release date: Oct. 9, 1999. Running time: 139 Min. Documentary. BRITISH.

THE FOUL KING

A b.o.m. Film Prods. presentation of a b.o.m. production, in association with KM Culture Investement Co. and Cinema Service Co.. (International sales: Mirovision, Seoul.) Producer: Lee Mi-yeon. Executive producer: Oh Jeong-wan. Director/Screenplay: Kim Jee-soon, story by Kim Dae-woo. Camera: Hong kyeong-pyo. Editor: Go Im-pyo. Music: Uh-Uh-Boo. In color. Release date: May 12, 2000. Runnning time: 109 Min. SOUTH KOREAN.

Cast: Song Kang-ho, Jang Jin-yeong, Jang Hang-seon, Park Sang-myeon, Song Yeong-chang, Jeong Ung-in, Lee Ki-yeong.

FOUR DAYS
A Behaviour Distribution release (in Canada) of a Cite-Amerique/Greg Dummett Films production, with the participation of the Canadian Television Fund, Telefilm Canada, Sodec, the Harold Greeberg Fund, TMN-The Movie Network, City-TV, Government of Quebec, Government of Canada, Government of Ontario. (International sales: Behaviour Worldwide, Los Angeles.) Producers: Lorraine Richard, Greg Dummett. Executive producer: Louis Laverdiere. Co-producer: Marie-France Lemay. Director: Curtis Wehrfritz. Screenplay: Pinckney Benedict, based on the novel by John Buell. Camera: Miroslaw Baszak. Editor: Gaetan Huot. Music: Tom Third. In color. Release date: Sept. 14, 1999. Running time: 92 Min. CANADIAN.
Cast: Kevin Zegers, Lolita Davidovich, Colm Meaney, William Forsythe, Anne-Marie Cadieux, Patrick Goyette.

FRAGMENTS OF LIFE
A Zala'men Prods. (Yaounde)/PBC Pictures (Brussels) co-production. (International sales: PBC Pictures, Brussels.) Producer: Patrice Bauduinet. Executive producer: Francois L. Woukoache. Director/Screenplay: Francois L. Woukoache. Camera: Bonaventure Takoukam. Editor: Jean Thome. In color. Release date: Feb. 14, 2000. Running time: 86 Min. CAMEROON-BELGIAN.
Cast: Tshilombo Lubambu, Deneuve Djobong, Jean Bediebe, Helene Beleck, Jerome Bolo, Therese Ngo Ngambi, Lionnelle Cathy Eteta.

THE FRAME
A Super Vision Prod. production, in association with Asmik Ace Entertainment, Kinema Junposha Co., Environment Art Laboratory Co., Forward Group. (International sales: Asmick Ace, Tokyo.) Producer: Takahiro Iwashita. Executive producer: Yoshiyuki Ohira. Director: Satoshi Isaka. Screenplay: Hisashi Nozawa, based on his novel. Camera: Tetsuro Sano. Editor: Junichi Kikuchi. Music: Tsukasa Tawada. In color. Release date: Feb. 15, 2000. Running time: 110 Min. JAPANESE.
Cast: Hitomi Kuroki, Tetsuo Yamashita, Toshio Kakei, Takanori Jinnai, Akira Shirai, Saburo Shinoda, Takeo Nakahara, Kanta Tsutsumi, Kunio Hatoyama, Atsuo Nakamura, Naomi Akimoto, Kumiko Oba.

FRANCE, HERE WE COME!
A Lotus Film production. (International sales: First Hand Films, Zurich.) Producer: Erich Lackner. Director: Michael Glawogger. Screenplay: Glawogger, Johannes Skocek. Camera: Wolfgang Thaler. Editor: Monika Willi. Music: Armin Pokorn. In color. Release date: July 7, 2000. Running time: 82 Min. Documentary. AUSTRIAN.

FRANK SPADONE
A Cine B/Les Films Alain Sarde/Hachette production. (International sales: Art Box, Paris.) Producers: Philippe Carcassonne, Alain Sarde. Executive producer: Brigitte Faure. Director: Richard Bean. Screenplay: Sophie Feldman. Camera: Philippe Leeuw. Editor: Andree Davanture. Music: Olivier Lebe. In color, widescreen. Release date: Sept. 4, 1999. Running time: 89 Min. FRENCH.
Cast: Monica Bellucci, Stanislas Mehrar, Carlo Brandt, Antoine Fayard, Christophe Le Masne, Jean-Claude Lecas.

FREE THE FISH
A Medusa Film release of a Cattleya presentation of a Cattleya/ Cineritmo production. Producers: Riccardo Tozzi, Gioviannella Zannoni. Director: Cristina Comencini. Screenplay: Comencini, Enzo Monteleone, Gennaro Nunziate. Camera: Roberto Forza. Editor: Jacopo Quadri. Music: Alessio Vlad. In Cinecitta color. Release date: Jan. 24, 2000. Running time: 93 Min. ITALIAN.
Cast: Laura Morante, Francesco Paolantoni, Michele Placido, Lunetta Savino, Emilio Solfrizzi, Angelica Ippoliito, Marco Morandi.

THE FRENCHMAN'S SON
A Pathe Distribution release (in France) of a Film Par Film/TF1 Films Prod. production, with participation of TPS Cinema and Cofimage 10. (International sales: TF1 Intl., Paris.) Producer: Jean-Louis Livi. Executive producer: Bernard Marescot. Director/Screenplay: Gerard Lauzier. Camera: Robert Alazraki. Editor: Georges Klotz. Music: Vladimir Cosma. In color. Release date: Jan. 6, 2000. Running time: 110 Min. FRENCH.
Cast: Josiane Balasko, Fanny Ardant, Thierry Fremont, David-Alexandre Parquier, Luca Barbareschi, George Aguilar.

FRIENDS
A Moneypenny Filmproduktion production, in association with DFFB, Geyer-Werke Berlin, Cine Licht, ZDF. (International sales: Bavaria Film Intl., Munich.) Producers: Sigrid Hoerner, Anne Lapin, Martin Walz. Director: Martin Eigler. Screenplay: Soenke Lars Neuwoehner, Eigler. Camera: Michael Mieke. Editor: Dirk Grau. Music: Johannes Kobilke, Moe Jaksch, Tom Reiss. In color. Release date: June 26, 2000. Running time: 106 Min. GERMAN.
Cast: Benno Fuermann, Erdal Yildiz, Christiane Paul, Michael Gwisdek, Irene Kugler, Erhan Emre, Susanne Bormann.

FROZEN HEART: A FILM ABOUT ROALD AMUNDSEN
A Motlys (Oslo) production, in association with NRK, SVT, YLE, Epidem, ORB, Final Cut and Czech TV, with support from the Norwegian Film Institute. Producers: Sigve Endresen, Orjan Karlsen. Director/Screenplay: Stig Andersen, Kenny Sanders. Camera: Hallgrim Odergard. Editor: Jon Endre Mork. Music: Nils Petter Molvaer. In color. Release date: Oct. 10, 1999. Running time: 87 Min. Documentary. NORWEGIAN.
With: Sidsel Endresen, Espen Skjonberg, Terje Stromdal, Bjarte Hjelmeland, Thomas Seltzer.

FUCKIT
A Nora Production Group production in association with RTV Slovenia. Director/Screenplay: Miha Hocevar. Camera: Simon Pintar. Editor: Olga Toni, Hocevar. Music: Mitja Vrhovnik Smrekar. In color. Release date: Apr., 2, 2000. Running time: 90 Min. SLOVENIAN.
Cast: Polona Juh, Matej Druznik, David Furlan, Marko Miladinovic, Jure Sotlar, Gorazo Obersnel, Damijan, Skafar, Peter Hvalica.

FULL BLAST
An Aska Film Distribution release (in Canada) of a Les Films de L'Isle/Transmar Films production. (International sales: Les Films de L'Isle, Montreal.) Producer: Ian Boyd. Director: Rodrigue Jean. Screenplay: Jean, Nathalie Loubeyre, based on the novel "L'Ennemi que je connais" by Martin Pitre. Camera: Stefan Ivanov. Editor: Mathieu Bouchard-Malo. Music: Robert Marcel Lepage. In color. Release date: Sept. 15, 1999. Running time: 95 Min. CANADA.
Cast: David La Haye, Martin Desgagne, Louise Portal, Marie-Jo Therio, Patrice Godin.

FUNNY FELIX
An Arte France Cinema/Pyramide Production presentation of a Les Films Pelleas production, in association with Gimages and Canal Plus. (International sales: Flach Pyramide Intl., Paris.) Producer: Philippe Martin. Directors/Screenplay: Olivier Ducastel, Jacques Martinuea. Camera: Matthieu Poirot-Delpech. Editor: Sabine Mamou. In color, widescreen. Release date: Feb. 12, 2000. Running time: 95 Min. FRENCH.
Cast: Sami Bouajila, Patachou, Ariane Ascaride, Pierre-Loup Rajot, Charly Sergue, Maurice Benichou.

GAEA GIRLS
A Vixen Films production for BBC Bristol. Producers/Directors/ Screenplay: Kim Longinotto, Jano Williams. Camera: Longinotto. Editor: Brian Tagg. In color. Release date: Aug. 20, 2000. Running time: 104 Min. Documentary. BRITISH.
With: Chigusa Nagayo, Meiko Satomura, Saika Takeuchi, Yuka Sugiyama.

GANGSTER
A Josefine Film Produktion production, in association with WDR, Arte. (International sales: Media Luna, Cologne. Producer: Lothar Kurzawa. Director: Volker Einrauch. Screenplay: Lothar Kurzawa. Camera: Stefan Spreer. Editor: Mana Meyer. Music: Rainer J.G. Uhl. In color. Release date: May 14, 2000. Running time: 85 Min. GERMAN.
Cast: Frank Giering, Laura Tonke, Saskia Vester, Dietmar Mues, Andreas Schmidt, Jochen Nickel, Christian Redl, Stefan Kurt.

GANGSTER NO. 1
A FilmFour Distributors release of a FilmFour presentation of a pagoda Film production, in association with Road Movies Filmproduktion, with participation of British Screen, BSkyB, Filmboard Berlin Brandenburg, in association with NFH and Littlebird Prods. (International sales: FilmFour Intl., London.) Producers: Norma Heyman, Jonathan Cavendish. Executive producer: Peter Bowles. Co-producers: Ulrich Felsberg, Nicky Kentish Barnes. Director: Paul McGuigan. Screenplay: Johnny Ferguson, based on the play by Louis Mellis and David Scinto. Camera: Peter Sova. Editor: Andrew Hulme. Music: John Dankworth. In Technicolor. Release date: June 6, 2000. Running time: 103 Min. BRITISH-GERMAN.
Cast: Malcolm McDowell, David Thewlis, Paul Bettany, Saffron Burrows, Kenneth Cranham, Jamie Foreman, Razaaq Adoti.

GEMINI
A Sedic Intl. Inc./Marubeni Corp. production in association with Kaijyu Theater. (International sales: Sedic Intl., Tokyo.) Producer: Futoshi Nishimura. Executive producers: Toshiaki Nakazawa, Yasuhiko Furusato. Director/Screenplay/Editor: Shinya Tsukamoto, based on the novel by Edogawa Rampo. Camera: Tsukamoto. Music: Chu Ishikawa. In color. Release date: Sept. 3, 1999. Running time: 82 Min. JAPANESE.
Cast: Masahiro Motoki, Tyo, Yasutaka Tsutsui, Shiho Fujimura, Akaji Maro, Naoto Takenaka, Renji Ishibashi, Tadanobu Asano.

GEPPETTO
An Eduardo R. Calcagno Producciones production. (International sales: Primer Plano Film Group, Buenos Aires.) Producer: Eduardo Calcagno. Executive producer: Axel Pauls. Director: Eduardo R. Calcagno. Screenplay: Roberto Cossa, Calcagno, based on Cossa's play. Camera: Roberto Mateo, Andres Mazzon. Music: Mariano Nunez West. In color. Release date: Jan 21, 2000. Running time: 94 Min. ARGENTINE.
Cast: Ulises Dumont, Malena Figo, Nicolas Cabre.

GEOGRAPHY OF FEAR
A Blind Spot Pictures, YTV1 (Finland)/Zentropa Prods. (Denmark)/ Wuste Filmproduktion, NDR, Arte (Germany) production. (International sales: Trust Film Sales, Denmark.) Producer: Tero Kaukomaa. Director: Auli Mantila. Screenplay: Mantila, based on the novel by Anja Kauranen. Camera: Heikki Farm. Editor: Kimmo Taavila. Music: Hilmar Orn Hilmarsson. In color. Release date: Feb. 2, 2000. Running time: 110 Min. FINNISH-DANISH-GERMAN.
Cast: Tanjalotta Raikka, Leena Klemola, Pertti Sveholm, Kari Sorvali, Anna-Elina Lyytikainen, Elsa Saisio, Elja Vilpas, Kaarina Hazard.

GERRY HUMPHRYS: THE LOVED ONE
A Sunrise Picture Co. release and production. (International sales: Sunrise Picture Co., Melbourne.) Producer/Director/Editor: Nigel Buesst. Camera: Buesst. In color. Release date: July 22, 2000. Running time: 65 Min. Documentary. AUSTRALIAN.

THE GHOST OF MARSHAL TITO

An Interfilm production in association with HRT. (International sales: Interfilm, Zagreb.) Producers: Ivan Maloca, Ljubo Sikic. Director: Vinko Bresan. Screenplay: Ivo Zalar. In color. Release date: Feb. 10, 2000. Running time: 95 Min. CROATIAN.
Cast: Drazen Kuhn, Linda Begonja, Ilja Ivezic, Ivo Gregurevic, Boris Buzancic.

GIGANTIC

An X Filme Creative Pool production, in association with Norddeutsche Rundfunk (Hamburg) and Arte. (International sales: Bavaria Film Intl., Munich.) Producers: Stefan Arndt, Tom Tykwer. Director/Screenplay: Sebastian Schipper. Camera: Frank Griebe. Editor: Andrew Bird. Music supervisor: Uwe Kirbach. In color. Release date: Oct. 8, 1999. Running time: 77 Min. GERMAN.
Cast: Frank Giering, Florian Lukas, Antoine Monot Jr., Julia Hummer, Jochen Nickel, Albert Kitzl.

THE GIRL IN THE SNEAKERS

An Art Bureau/Milad Film production. Director: Rassul Sadr Ameli. Screenplay: Peyman Qasemkhani, Fereydoun Farhudi. Camera: Dariuch Ayyari. Editor: Mostafa Kherqu-Poush. Music: Iraj Panahi. In color. Release date: June 30, 2000. Running time: 110 Min. IRANIAN.
Cast: Pegah Ahangarani, Majid Hajizadeh, Akram Mohammadi, Abdolreza Akbari, Mahmud Jafari.

A GIRL IS A GIRL

A Shavick Entertainment production, in association with Masculine-Feminine Films and CityTV, with participation of British Columbia Film. (International sales: Luminous X Velocity, Los Angeles.) Producer: Christina Margellos. Executive producer: Christine Haebler. Director: Reginald Harkema. Screenplay: Harkema, Angus Fraser. Camera: Robert Aschmann. Editor: Janel Hassine. Music: Various. In color. Release date: Sept. 13, 1999. Running time: 86 Min. CANADIAN.
Cast: Andrew McIntyre, Paige Morrison, Laurie Baranyay, Aeryn Twidle, Jo-Ann MacDonald, Keir MacPherson, David Pauls.

GIRLS CAN'T SWIM

A Sepia Prod./YMC Prods. production. (International sales: Celluloid Dreams, Paris.) Producer: Philippe Jacquier. Co-producer: Yvon Cremin. Director: Anne-Sophie Birot. Screenplay: Birot, Christophe Honore. Camera: Nathalie Durand. Editor: Pascale Chavance. Music: extract from chamber work by Ernest Chausson. In color. Release date: Sept. 4, 2000. Running time: 102 Min. FRENCH.
Cast: Isild Le Besco, Karen Alyx, Pascale Bussieres, Pascal Elso, Marie Riviere, Yelda Reynaud, Sandrine Blancke, Julien Cottereau.

GLAMOUR

A Magyar Televizio, Focusfilm (Hungary)/Iloona Grundman Filmproduktion, Arts & Future Film Fabrik (Germany)/Cascadefilm (Switzerland) production. (International sales: S-media 2000, Budapest.) Producers: Kornel Sipos, Ilona Grundman, Gerald W. Kruse. Director/Screenplay: Frigyes Godros. Camera: Sandor Kardos. Editor: Maria Rigo. Music: Laszlo Melis. In color. Release date: Feb. 7, 2000. Running time: 117 Min. HUNGARIAN-GERMAN-SWISS.
Cast: Karoly Eperjes, Eszter Onodi, Gyorgy Barko, Antal Cserna, Katinka Cseke, Lajos Szucs, Janos Szirtes, Tamas Jakab.

GLASS MARBLES

A 41T-Mario Krastev production, in association with Boyana Film Co., Bulgarian National Television, National Film Center of Bulgaria. (International sales: Klasfilm, Sofia.) Producer: Mario Krastev. Director/Screenplay: Ivan Cherkelov. Camera: Emil Hristov. Editor: Ognyan Ivanov. Music: Assen Avramov. In color and B&W. Release date: Feb. 17, 2000. Running time: 100 Min. BULGARIAN.
Cast: Ivan Ivanov, Jana Karaivanova, Rumen Traikov, Georgi Cherkelov.

THE GLEANERS AND I

A Canal Plus (in France) release of a Cine Tamaris production, with the participation of the Centre National de la Cinematographie and Procirep. (International sales: Cine Tamaris, Paris.) Producer/Director: Agnes Varda. Camera: Stephane Krausz, Didier Rouget, Didier Doussin, Pascal Sautelet, Varda. Editors: Varda, Laurent Pineau. Music: Joanna Bruzdowicz. In color, video-to-35mm. Release date: May 15, 2000. Running time: 82 Min. Documentary. FRENCH.

GLOOMY SUNDAY

A Universal Pictures Germany release (in Germany) of a Studio Hamburg Produktion, Polygram Filmproduktion, Dom Film (Germany)/Focus Film (Hungary) production, in association with WDR, Premiere, Arte, MTV2. (International sales: Cinepool, Munich.) Producer: Kerstin Ramcke. Executive producers: Martin Rohrbeck, Aron Sipos. Co-producer: Richard Schoeps. Director: Rolf Schuebel. Screenplay: Ruth Thoma, Schuebel, based on the novel "The Song of Gloomy Sunday" by Nick Barkow. Camera: Edward Klosiniski. Editor: Ursula Hoef. Music: Detlef Petersen, Rezso Seress. In color. Release date: Feb. 10, 2000. Running time: 114 Min. GERMAN-HUNGARIAN.
Cast: Joachim Krol, Stefano Dionisi, Ben Becker, Erika Marozsan, Sebastian Koch, Laszlo I. Kish, Wanja Mues, Ulrike Grote.

GLUE SNIFFER

A Unity Films/CNAC/Tango Bravo/Credesca/Filmart P.C. co-production. Producer: Jose R. Novoa. Director: Elia Schneider. Screenplay: Nestor Caballero, Santiago Tabernero, Schneider. Camera: Oscar Perez. Editor: Jose R. Novoa. Music: Francisco Cabrutas. In color. Release date: Jan. 17, 2000. Running time: 109 Min. ARGENTINE.
Cast: Jose G. Rivas, Luis Campos, Alfredo Medina, Adolfo Cubas, Pedro Lander, Laureano Olivarez.

THE GODDESS OF 1967

A Fandango release (in Italy) of an Australian Film Finance Corp. production in association with the New South Wales Film and Television Office. Producers: Peter Sainsbury, Eddie L.C. Fong. Executive producers: Wouter Barendrecht, Helen Loveridge, Miachel J. Werner, Akiko Funatsu. (International sales: Fortissimo, Amsterdam.) Director: Clara Law. Screenplay: Eddie L.C. Fong, Law. Camera: Dion Beebe. Editor: Kate Williams. Music: Jen Anderson. In color. Release date: Sept. 2, 2000. Running time: 118 Min. AUSTRALIAN.
Cast: Rose Byrne, Rikiya Kurokawa, Nicholas Hope, Elise McCredie.

GODZILLA 2000

A Sony Pictures release of a TriStar Pictures presentation of a Toho Pictures production. Producer: Toshihiro Ogawa. Executive producers: Shogo Tomiyama. Director: Takao Okawara. Screenplay: Hiroshi Kashiwabara, Wataru Mimura. Camera: Katsuhiro Kato. Editor: Yoshiyuki Okuhara. Music: Takayuki Hattori. In Deluxe color. Release date: Aug. 14, 2000. MPAA Rating: PG. Running time: 97 Min. JAPANESE.
Cast: Takehiro Murata, Shiro Sano, Hiroshi Abe, Naomi Nishida, Mayu Suzuki, Tsutomu Kitagawa.

THE GOLDEN BOWL

A Miramax release (U.S.) of a Merchant Ivory Prods./TF1 Intl. presentation in association with Miramax Films. (International sales: TF1 Intl., Paris.) Producer: Ismail Merchant. Executive producers: Paul Bradley, Richard Hawley. Director: James Ivory. Screenplay: Ruth Prawer Jhavbala, based on the novel by Henry James. Camera: Tony Pierce Roberts. Editor: John David Allen. Music: Richard Robbins. In Technicolor, Panavision widescreen. Release date: May 14, 2000. Running time: 134 Min. U.S.-FRENCH-BRITISH.
Cast: Uma Thurman, Jeremy Northam, Kate Beckinsale, Nick Nolte, Anjelica Huston, James Fox, Madeleine Potter, Peter Eyre.

GONE WITH THE FISH

A Per Holst Film production in association with the Danish Film Institute, DR-TV, Norsk Film (Norway), Felicia Film (Sweden), TV1000 (Sweden), SVT Drama (Sweden), the Swedish Film Institute, Nordic Film & Television Fund. (International sales: Nordisk Film, Copenhagen.) Producers: Per Holst, Thomas Lydholm. Director: Lotte Svendsen. Screenplay: Svendsen, Elith Nulle Nykjaer. Camera: Anthony Dod Mantle. Editor: Kasper Leich. Music: Jens Brygmann. In color. Release date: Feb. 3, 2000. Running time: 114 Min. DANISH-NORWEGIAN-SWEDISH.
Cast: Henrik Lykkegaard, Sofie Stougaard, Michelle Bjorn Andersen, Helle Dolleris, Thomas Bo Larsen, Isidor Torkar, Preben Harris.

GOODBYE FROM THE HEART

An Alta Films release (in Spain) of an Alma Ata Intl. Pictures, Galiardo Producciones, Gaila, Rafael Azcona production, with participation of Antena 3 TV and Canal Plus. (International sales: Alta Films, Madrid.) Executive producer: Jose Maria Calleja. Director: Jose Luis Garcia Sanchez. Screenplay: Rafael Azcona. Camera: Alfredo Mayo. Editor: Pablo G. del Amo. Music: Carmelo Bernaola. In color. Release date: June 28, 2000. Running time: 89 Min. SPANISH.
Cast: Juan Luis Galiardo. Laura Ramos, Jesus Bonilla, Neus Asensi, Maria Luisa San Jose, Teresa Gimpera, Juan Echanove.

A GOOD LAD

An Alma Ata Studios production. Director: Boris Barnet. Screenplay: Aleksei Kapler, Pyotr Pavlenko. Camera: Sergei Ivanov. Music: Nikita Bogoslovsky, Nikolai Kryukov; lyrics: Natalia Konchalovskaya. In B&W. Release date: Aug. 5, 2000. Running time: 67 Min. SOVIET UNION–1943.
Cast: E. Grigorev, O. Yakunina, Elena Sipavina, Nikolai Bogolyubov, Viktor Dobrovolsky.

GOOD WORK

A La Sept Arte/Pathe Television/S.M. Films production. (International sales: Mercure, Paris.) Producer: Jerome Minet. Director: Claire Denis. Screenplay: Jean-Pol Fargeau, Denis, based on the novella "Billy Budd, Sailor" by Herman Melville. Camera: Agnes Godard. Editor: Nelly Quettier. Music: Eran Tzur. In color. Release date: Sept. 3, 1999. Running time: 90 Min. FRENCH.
Cast: Denis Lavant, Michel Subor, Gregoire Colin, Richard Courcet.

GOSTANZA DA LIBBIANO

An Arsenali Medicei production. (International sales: Arsenali Medicei, Pisa.) Producer: Giovanni Carratori. Director: Paolo Benvenuti. Screenplay: Stefano Bacci, Benvenuti, Mario Cereghino. Camera: Aldo Di Marcantonio. Editor: Cesar Meneghetti. In B&W. Release date: Aug. 5, 2000. Running time: 93 Min. ITALIAN.
Cast: Lucia Poli, Valentino Davanzati, Renzo Cerrato, Paolo Spaziani, Lele Biagri, Nadia Capocchini, Teresa Soldaini.

GRAN PARADISO

A Warner Bros. presentation of a Letterbox Filmproduktion in co-production with Monty Filmgesellschaft and Warner Bros. Filmproduktion, in association with Cinemedia. Producer: Henrik Meyer. Executive producer: Verena Herfurth. Director: Miguel Alexandre. Screenplay: Georg Heinzen. Camera: Peter Indergand. Editor: Inge Behrens. Music: Dominic Roth. In color, widescreen. Release date: Aug. 28, 2000. Running time: 106 Min. GERMAN.
Cast: Ken Duken, Regula Grauwiller, Gregor Torzs, Max Herbrechter, Frank Giering, Erhan Emre, Alexander Horbe, Antje Westermann.

THE GREAT BAGAROZY

A Constantin Film release (in Germany) of a Constantin Film Produktion production. (International sales: BetaFilm, Ismaning, Germany.) Producer: Bernd Eichinger. Co-producer: Martin Moszkowicz. Director/Screenplay: Bernd Eichinger, from the novel by Helmut Krausser. Camera: Gernot Roll. Editor: Alexander Berner. Music: Norbert Schneider. In color, widescreen. Release date: July 1, 1999. Running time: 103 Min. GERMAN.

Cast: Til Schweiger, Corinna Harfouch, Thomas Heinze, Christine Neubauer, Sonja Kerskes, Patricia Lueger, Neza Selbuz.

GREY OWL

A Remstar Distribution release (in Canada) of a Beaver Prods./Allied Filmmakers/Transfilm production. (International sales: Summit Entertainment, Los Angeles.) Producers: Richard Attenborough, Jake Eberts, Claude Leger. Executive producers: Barr Potter, Lenny Yound. Co-producer: Diana Hawkins. Director: Richard Attenborough. Screenplay: William Nicholson. Camera: Roger Pratt. Editor: Lesley Walker. Music: George Fenton. In color, Panavision widescreen. Release date: Sept. 20, 1999. Running time: 117 Min. BRITISH-CANADIAN.

Cast: Pierce Brosnan, Annie Galipeau, Nathaniel Arcand, Vlasta Vrana, David Fox, Charles Powell, Stephanie Cole, Graham Greene.

GRIZZLY FALLS

A Providence Entertainment release of a Behaviour Worldwide/ Norstar Filmed Entertainment presentation, in association with Le Sabre, of a Peter Simpson and Allan Scott production. Producers: Peter R. Simpson, Scott. Executive producers: Mark Damon, Raylan Jensen, Georges Campana. Director: Stewart Raffill. Screenplay: Richard Beattie, story by Stuart Margolin. Camera: Thom Best. Editor: Nick Rotundo. Music: David Reilly, Paul J. Zaza. In Deluxe color Toronto. Release date: Jan. 24, 2000. MPAA Rating: 94 Min. Running time: 94 Min. CANADIAN-BRITISH.

Cast: Daniel Clark, Bryan Brown, Tom Jackson, Oliver Tobias, Richard Harris, Brock Simpson, Chantal Dick, Trevor Lowden, Marnie McPhai.

GUEST HOUSE PARADISO

A Universal Intl. Pictures release (in U.K.) of a Universal Pictures presentation of a Phil McIntyre production. Producer: McIntyre. Executive producers: Helen Parker, Marc Samuelson, Peter Samuelson. Director: Adrian Edmondson. Screenplay: Edmondson, Rik Mayall. Camera: Alan Almond. Editor: Sean Barton. Music: Colin Towns. In Deluxe London color, widescreen. Release date: Dec. 7, 1999. Running time: 86 Min. BRITISH.

Cast: Rik Mayall, Adrian Edmondson, Vincent Cassel, Helene Mahieu.

THE GUILTY

An SND release (in France) of a J&M Entertainment presentation of a J&M Entertainment/Dogwood Pictures production, in association with Muse Entertainment Enterprises. Producers: Lisa Richardson, Thomas Hedman. Executive producers: Julia Palau, William Davies, Michael Prupas, Anthony Waller. Director: Anthony Waller. Screenplay: William Davies, based on the book "The Guilty" by Simon Burke. Camera: Tobias Schliessler. Editor: Alison Grace. Music: Debbie Wiseman. In color. Release date: July 22, 2000. Running time: 107 Min. BRITISH-CANADIAN.

Cast: Bill Pullman, Gabrielle Anwar, Devon Sawa, Angela Featherstone, Joanne Whalley, Ken Tremblett, Jaimz Woolvet.

GUTS

A C.V. Lef production (International sales: C.V. Lef, Amsterdam.) Producers: Marijke Kloosterman, Ron Termaat. Director/Screenplay: Ron Termaat. Camera: Maarten Kramer. Editors: Annette Otto, Hans Van Dongen. Music: Joep Van Deudekom. In color and B&W. Release date: Sept. 11, 1999. Running time: 94 Min. DUTCH.

Cast: Viggo Waas, Alice Reys, Rick Engelkes, Victor Reinier, Eric Van Sauers, Ineke Veenhooven, Cees Geel.

A HANDFUL OF GRASS

A Kinowelt release of an MTM Cineteve/Kinowelt Filmproduktion production, in association with Bavaria Film and WDR, with participation of Milad Film (Iran). (International sales: Bavaria Film Intl., Munich.) Producers: Guenter Rohrbach, Peter Herrmann. Executive producer: Andreas Bareiss. Co-producer: Ulrich Limmer. Director: Roland Suso Richter. Screenplay: Uwe Timm. Camera: Martin Langer. Editor: Eva Schnare. Music: Harald Kloser, Thomas Wanker. In color, widescreen. Release date: June 27, 2000. Running time: 115 Min. GERMAN.

Cast: Oliver Korittke, Arman Inci, Ercan Durmaz, Lisa Martinek.

HANS STADEN

A Lapfilme Do Brasil (Brazil)/Jorge Neves Producoes Audiovisuais (Portugal) production. (International sales: Grupo Novo de Cinema & TV, Rio de Janeiro.) Director/Screenplay: Luiz Alberto Pereira, based on the memoirs of Hans Staden. Camera: Uli Burton. Editor: Veronica Kovensky. In color. Release date: May 12, 2000. Running time: 92 Min. BRAZILIAN-PORTUGUESE.

Cast: Carlos Evelyn, Beto Simas, Ariana Messias, Clauda Liz, Stenio Garcia.

HANS WARNS–MY 20TH CENTURY

A Gordian Maugg production. (International sales: Pegasos Film, Frankfurt.). Producer/Director/Screenplay: Gordian Maugg. Camera: Hans Moser, Andreas Giesecke. Editor: Monika Schindler. Music: Ferdinand Forsch, Heidi Aydt. In B&W and color. Release date: Sept. 11, 1999. Running time: 105 Min. Historical Docudrama. GERMAN.

Cast: Florian Hober, Shenja Lacher, Klaus Kirchner, Fred Angerstein, Julia Jessen, Leonor Quinteros Ochoa, Albert Hetterle.

HANUMAN

A Gaumont Buena Vista Intl. release (in France) and presentation in co-production with Borealies and Visual Eyes. (International sales: Gaumont, Paris.) Producers: Patrice Ledoux, Fred Fougea. Executive producer: Barthelemy Fougea. Co-executive producers: Anne-Marie Ader, K. Kaarthikeyan. Director: Fred Fougea. Screenplay: Fougea, Michel Fessler. Camera: Bernard Luric. Editors: Yann Deder, Frederique Lebel. Music: Laurent Ferlet. In color. Release date: Oct. 11, 1999. Running time: 87 Min. FRENCH-INDIAN.

Cast: Robert Cavanah, Tabu, Nathalie Auffret, Khalid Thiabji, Sydney Kean, Javed Jaffrey, William Doherthy.

HAPPY END

A CJ Entertainment/Kookmin Finance presentation of a Myung Film/Seoul Movies production. (International sales: CJ Entertainment, Seoul.) Producer: Lee Eun. Executive producer: Seok Dong-jun. Director/Screenplay: Jung Ji-woo. Camera: Kim Woo-hyung. Editor: Kim Hyun, Kim Yong-soo. Music: Cho Young-wook, Kim Kyu-yang. In color. Release date: May 11, 2000. Running time: 99 Min. SOUTH KOREAN.

Cast: Choi Min-shik, Chun Do-yeon, Joo Jin-mo, Hwang Mi-sun, Joo Hyun, Huh Yae-in.

HARD-OFF

A Pathe Distribution release (in France) of a Katharine/Renn Prods., France 2 Cinema production, with participation of Canal Plus and CNC. (International sales: President Films, Paris.) Executive producer: Piere Grunstein. Director: Claude Berri, Arlette Langmann. Camera: William Lubtchansky. Editor: Herve de Luze. Music: Bruno Colais. In color. Release date: Oct. 26, 1999. Running time: 92 Min. FRENCH.

Cast: Claude Berri, Fanny Ardant, Claude Brasseur, Alain Chabat, Daniele Lebrun, Brigitte Bemol, Olga Grumberg. Badia Barentin.

THE HAREM OF MADAME OSMANE

An Ocean Films release (in France) of a France 3 Cinema/Astoria Films/Canal Plus (France)/Tornasol Films/PHF Films (Spain)/Zilis Films (Morocco) production. (International sales: Art Box, Paris.) Producer: Didier Haudepin. Executive producer: Mohamed Ulad-Mohand. Co-producers: Gerardo Herrero, Sarah Halioua. Director/Screenplay: Nadir Mokneche. Camera: Helene Louvart. Editor: Stephanie Mahet. In color. Release date: May 16, 2000. Running time: 100 Min. FRENCH-SPANISH-MOROCCAN.

Cast: Carmen Maura, Biyouna, Myriam Amarouchene, Linda Slimani, Thamila Mesbah-Detraz, Nadia Kaci.

HARRY, HE'S HERE TO HELP

A Diaphana Films production. (International sales: Mercure Distribution, Paris.) Producer: Michel Saint-Jean. Director: Dominik Moll. Screenplay: Moll, Gilles Marchand. Camera: Matthieu Poirot-Delpech. Editor: Yannick Kergoat. Music: David Sinclair Whitaker. In color, Panavision widescreen. Release date: May 11, 2000. Running time: 117 Min. FRENCH.

Cast: Laurent Lucas, Sergi Lopez, Mathilde Seigner, Sophie Guillemin, Liliane Rovere, Dominique Rozan, Michel Fau.

HAZY LIFE

A Midnight Child Theater production. (International sales: Planet Studyo Plus One, Osaka.) Producers: Kosuke Mukai, Nobuhiro Yamashita, Hayato Maeda, Ryuto Kondo, Akira Matsumoto. Director: Nobuhiro Yamashita. Screenplay: Kosuke Mukai, Yamashita. Camera: Tyuto Kondo. Editors: Mukai, Yamashita, Maeda, Ryuto Kondo. Music: Akainu. In color, 16mm. Release date: Oct. 4, 1999. Running time: 84 Min. JAPANESE.

Cast: Hiroshi Yamamoto, Teppei Uda, Hiromichi Maeda, Ko Riran, Maki Imaeda.

A HEAD FOR BUSINESS

A Bac Distribution release of an Alain Sarde presentation of a Cine Valse/Le Studio Canal Plus/AFCL production, with participation of Studio Images. (International sales: Studio Canal, Paris.) Producer: Sarde. Executive producer: Christine Gozlan. Director/Screenplay: Guy-Philippe Bertin. Camera: Carlo Nicolas Errera. In color, widescreen. Release date: Aug. 25, 2000. Running time: 89 Min. FRENCH.

Cast: Feodor Atkine, Claire Keim, Albert Delpy, Guy-Philippe Bertin, Patrice Bornand, Dominique Compagnon, Claude Koener.

THE HEART OF THE WARRIOR

An Altafilms release of a Tornasol/Cartel production, in association with Via Digital, TVE. (International sales: Altafilms, Madrid.) Producers: Gerardo Herroro, Jesus Lopez Blanco, Eduardo Campoy. Director/Screenplay: Daniel Monzon. Camera: Carles Gusi. Editor: Ivan Aledo. Music: Roque Banos. In color. Release date: Jan. 25, 2000. Running time: 114 Min. SPANISH.

Cast: Fernando Ramallo, Neus Asensi, Joel Joan, Santiago Segura, Javier Aller, Adria Collado, Jaime Barnatan, Juan Diaz.

THE HEART'S ROOT

A Suma Filmes (Lisbon) Les Films de l'Atlante (Paris) production. Producers: Paulo Rocha, Gerard Vaugeois. Director: Paulo Rocha. Screenplay: Rocha, Jeanne Waltz, Regina Guimaraes, Raquel Freire. Camera: Elso Roque. Editor: Edgar Feldman. Music: Jose Mario Branco. In color. Release date: Aug. 7, 2000. Running time: 120 Min. PORTUGUESE-FRENCH.

Cast: Luis Miguel Cintra, Joana Barcia, Melvil Poupaud, Isabel Ruth.

HEATER
A Marble Island Pictures Corp. (Winnipeg, Manitoba) production, with support from Telefilm Canada, Vision TV and WIC. Producers: Marc Stephenson, Ritchard Findlay. Executive producer: Findlay. Director/Screenplay: Terrance Odette. Camera: Arthur E. Cooper. Editor: David Wharnsby. Music: Neil Clark. In color. Release date: Oct. 7, 1999. Running time: 87 Min. CANADIAN.
Cast: Gary Farmer, Stephen Ouimette, Tina Keeper, Jan Skene..

HEAVY METAL 2000
A Eurozoom (in France)/Columbia TriStar Home VIdeo (in U.S.) release of a Cinegroupe Animation, Lions Gate Films (Canada)/Helkon Media (Germany) production, in association with Das Werk. (International sales: Sceneries Intl., L.A.) Producers: Jacques Pettigrew, Michel Lemire. Executive producers: Pettigrew, Werner Koenig, Philippe Diaz. Directors: Michel Lemire, Michael Coldewey. Screenplay: Robert P. Cabeen, Carl Masek, based on the graphic novel "The Melting Pot" by Kevin Eastman, Simon Bisley, Eric Talbot. Camera: Bruno Philip. Editor: Brigitte Breault. Music: Frederic Talgorn. In color, widescreen. Release date: Apr. 28, 2000. MPAA Rating: R. Running time: 88 Min. Animated. CANADIAN-GERMAN.
Voices: Michael Ironside, Julie Strain Eastman, Billy Idol, Pierre Kohn, Sonja Ball, Brady Moffatt, Rick Jones.

HERE WE ARE WAITING FOR YOU
Producer/Director/Screenplay: Marcelo Masagao. Camera: Marco Tulio Guglielmoni. Editor: Masagao. Music: Wim Mertens. In B&W and color. Release date: Jan. 14, 2000. Running time: 74 Min. Documentary. BRAZILIAN.

HERR ZWILLING AND FRAU ZUCKERMAN
A Vineta Film production. Executive producer: Fritz Hartthaler. Co-producers: MDR, WDR, SFB. Director: Volker Koepp, Barbara Frankenstein. Camera: Thomas Plenert, Lars Lenski, Michael Loewenberg. Editor: Angelika Arnold. In color. Release date: Jan. 16, 2000. Running time: 131 Min. Documentary. GERMAN.

HER WAY
A Sovkino production. Director: Aleksandr Strizhak. Screenplay: D. Posnansky, Maria Smirnova, from the story "Marina" by D. Nikitin. Camera: V. Semyonov. In B&W. Release date: Aug. 4, 2000. Running time: 65 min. SOVIET UNION–1929. Silent.
Cast: Emma Tserarskaya, Aleksandr Zhukov, Karl Gurniak, A. Otradin.

HIDDEN WHISPER
A Central Motion Picture Corp. presentation. (International sales: Taiwan Film Center, Taipei.) Producer: Chiu Shunching. Executive producers: Yeh Chienchao, Lin-hsiang. Co-producers: Wang Shih-feng, Wang Jean-jean. Director/Screenplay: Vivian Chang. Camera: Shen Rei-yuan. Editors: Chen Xiao-dong, Lei Cheng-cheng. Music: Max Nagl. In color. Release date: May 14, 2000. Running time: 96 Min. TAIWANESE.
Cast: Hsiao Shu-shen, Hsia Ching-ting, Huang Pin-hsuan, Leon Dai.

HIGHWAY MELODY
A UIP Intl. release of a Playtime, France 2 Cinema production, with participation of TPS Cinema. (International sales: Artbox, Paris.) Producers: Jean Cottin, Etienne Comar, Antoine Voituriez. Director: Thierry Boscheron. Screenplay: Philippe Donzelot, Philippe Charazenc, Xavier Mathiew, Boscheron, based on an idea by Boscheron. In color. Release date: June 15, 2000. Running time: 84 Min. FRENCH.
Cast: Sacha Bourdo, Aure Atika, Philippe Nahon, Marc Berman.

HIGHWAY SOCIETY
A Mariette Rissenbeek Filmproduktion (Germany)/Marianna Films (Finland) production, in association with NDR. (International sales: Rissenbeek, Hamburg.) Producer: Mariette Rissenbeek. Director: Mika Kaurismaki. Screenplay: Paul Charles Bailly, Kaurismaki. German dialogue: Beate Langmaack. Camera: Timo Salminen. Editor: Inga Behrens. Music: Steamhammer, Mauri Sumen. In color. Release date: Nov. 13, 1999. Running time: 94 Min. GERMAN-FINNISH.
Cast: Kai Wiesinger, Marie Zielcke, Jochen Nickel, Hannes Hellmann, Michaela Rosen, Siegfried Terpoorten, Michael Schoenborn.

HIPPOLYT
A CinemaStar release of a Europa 2000/RTL Klub production. (International sales: Europa 2000, Budapest.) Producer: Barna Kabay. Co-producer: Bence Gyongyossy. Director: Barna Kabay. Associate director: Katalin Petenyi. Screenplay: Gabor Nogradi, Robert Koltai, based on the 1931 film "Hyppolit, the Butler" (Hyppolit, a lakaj), directed by Istvan Szekely, adapted by Karoly Noti and Istvan Zagon from the play "Hyppolit" by Zagon. Camera: Tibor Mathe. Editor: Mari Miklos. Music: Gabor Berkes, Mihaly Eisemann. In color. Release date: Feb. 6, 2000. Running time: 93 Min. HUNGARIAN.
Cast: Karoly Eperjes, Robert Koltai, Judit Pogany, Agi Szirtes.

HISTORY IS MADE AT NIGHT
A J&M Entertainment/Scala presentation of a Scala production, in association with IMA Films, Smile Entertainment and Helkon Media Filmproduktion, with participation of Canal Plus. (International sales: J&M, London.) Producers: Jonathan Karlsen, Kerry Rock. Executive producers: Nik Powell, Stephen Woolley, Georges Benayoun, Werner Koenig. Director: Ilkka Jarvilaturi. Screenplay: Patrick Amos, story by Jean-Pierre Gorin, Amos. Camera: Michel Amathieu. Editor: Alan Strachan. Music: Courtney Pine. In color. Release date: Sept. 11, 1999. Running time: 94. BRITISH.
Cast: Bill Pullman, Irene Jacob, Bruno Kirby, Glenn Plummer, Udo Kier, Andre Oumansky, Feodor Atkine.

HIS WIFE'S DIARY
A Ministry of Cinematography of Russia-Studio Rock production. (International sales: Studio Rock, St. Petersburg.) Producers: Alexander Golutva, Alexey Uchitel. Director: Alexey Uchitel. Screenplay: Dunya Smirnova. Camera: Yuri Klimenko. Editor: Yelena Andreyeva. Music: Leonid Desyatnikov. In Kodak color. Release date: July 10, 2000. Running time: 103 Min. RUSSIAN.
Cast: Andrey Smirnov, Galina Tyunina, Olga Budina, Yevgeny Mironov.

HOLD-UP
An Allegro Film production. (International sales: Allegro, Vienna.) Producer: Helmut Grasser. Director: Florian Flicker. Screenplay: Susanne Freund, Flicker. Camera: Helmut Pirnat. Editor: Monika Willi. Music: Sam Auinger, Hannes Strobl. In color, widescreen. Release date: Aug. 9, 2000. Running time: 84 Min. AUSTRALIAN.
Cast: Roland Dueringer, Joachim Bissmeier, Josef Hader, Birgit Doll, Sonja Romei, Ulrike Beimpold, Klaus Ortner, Klaus Haendl.

HOLY TONGUE
A Medusa Film release of a Rodeo Drive/Medusa Film production in association with Telepiu. (International sales: Adriana Chiesa Enterprises, Rome.) Producers: Marco Poccioni, Marco Valsania. Director: Carlo Mazzacurati. Screenplay: Franco Bernini, Umberto Contarello, Mazzacurati, Marco Pettenello. Camera: Alessandro Perci. Editor: Paolo Cottignola. In Technicolor, widescreen. Release date: Sept. 8, 2000. Running time: 110 Min. ITALIAN.
Cast: Antonio Albanese, Fabrizio Bentivoglio, Toni Bertorelli.

HOME GAME
A Quinte Film production in association with Arte, Goethe Institute. (International sales: Amberlon Pictures, London.) Producer: Mirjam Quinte. Director/Screenplay: Pepe Danquart. Camera: Michael Hammon. Editor: Mona Brauer. Music: Walter W. Cikan, Eddi Siblik. In color. Release date: Feb. 11, 2000. Running time: 95 Min. Documentary. GERMAN.

HOMESICK
A Mover's Entertainment production. (International sales: Slow Learner, Tokyo.) Producers: Tsuyoshi Miyazaki, Hidenobu Mito, Yukari Hatano. Director: Hineki Mito. Screenplay: Takehiko Tamiya, Mito. Camera: Tamiya. Editor: Yoko Nichioka. Music: Tatsuya Murayama. In color. Release date: Feb. 12, 2000. Running time: 60 Min. JAPANESE.
Cast: Kiminobu Okumura, Aki Onobara, Hana Yamanashi, Masato Kondo, Hiroshi Komiyama, Shingo Tsurumi.

HONOUR OF THE HOUSE
An Umbifilm, Pegasus (Iceland)/Gotafilm, Film i Vast (Sweden)/ Nordisk Film Prod. (Denmark) production. (International sales: Nordisk Film, Copenhapgen.) Producer: Halldor Thorgeirsson. Executive producers: Snorri Thorisson, Erik Crone, Christer Nilsson. Director/Screenplay: Gudny Halldorsdottir, from a novel by Halldor Laxness. Camera: Per Kallberg. Editor: Larus Ymir Oskarsson. Music: Hilmar Orn Hilmarsson. In color. Release date: Feb. 5, 2000. Running time: 100 Min. ICELANDIC-SWEDISH-DANISH.
Cast: Ragnhildur Gisladottir, Tinna Gunnlaugsdottir, Egil Olafsson, Rurik Haraldsson, Agneta Ekmanner, Reine Brynolfsson.

HOPELESS
A Kahukura Prods. production, in association with New Zealand Film Commission. (International sales: NZ Film Commission, Wellington.) Producer: Larry Parr. Director: Stephen Hickey. Screenplay: Hickey, Sean Molloy. Camera: Simon Riera. Editors: Andrew Brettell, Jonno Woodford-Robinson. In Atlab color. Release date: May 12, 2000. Running time: 80 Min. NEW ZEALAND.
Cast: Phil Pinner, Mia Taumoepeau, Adam Gardiner, Scott Wills.

HOTARU
A Dentsu, Imagica, Suncent CinemaWorks, Tokyo Theatre presentation of a Suncent CinemaWorks/Tokyo Theatre production, in association with Les Films de l'Observatoire. (International sales: Wild Bunch, Paris.) Producer: Takenori Sento. Co-producer: Philippe Avril. Director/Screenplay: Naomi Kawase. Camera: Masami Inomoto. Editor: Kawase. Music: Kawase, Naomi Matsuoka. In color. Release date: Aug. 7, 2000. Running time: 165 Min. JAPANESE.
Cast: Yuko Nakamura, Tashiya Nagasawa, Miyako Yamaguchi.

HOTEL SPLENDIDE
A FilmFour/TOC Films presentation of a Renegade Films production. (International sales: FilmFour, London.) Producer: Ildiko Kemeny. Executive producers: Robert Buckler, Charles Gassot. Director/ Screenplay: Terence Gross. Camera: Gyula Pados. Editor: Michael Ellis. Music: Mark Tschanz. In color. Release date: Feb. 16, 2000. Running time: 98 Min. BRITISH-FRENCH.
Cast: Toni Collette, Daniel Craig, Stephen Tompkinson, Katrin Cartlidge, Hugh O'Conor, Helen McCrory, Peter Vaughan.

HOUSE!
A Pathe Distribution release of a Live Wire Films presentation, in association with CF1 and the South Wales Film Commission, of a Victor Film Co. production, with participation of British Screen and the Arts Film Council of England. (International sales: Victor Film Co., London.) Producer: Michael Kelk, Executive producers: Adam Sutcliffe, Christopher Figg. Co-producer: David Ball. Director: Julian Kemp. Screenplay: Jason Sutton, based on an original idea by Eric Styles. Camera: Kjell Vassdal. Editor: Jonathan Rudd. Music: Mark Thomas. In Deluxe color. Release date: Jan. 24, 2000. Running time: 91 Min. BRITISH.
Cast: Kelly Macdonald, Freddie Jones, Miriam Margolyes, Jason Hughes, Mossie Smith, Gwenllian Davies, Sue Hopkins.

HOUSE OF MEMORIES
A Suravi production. (International sales: Suravi Prods., Calcutta.) Producer: Rajesh Agarwal. Director/Screenplay: Aparna Sen. Camera: Abhik Mukopadhyay. Editor: Arghyakamal Mitra. Music: Jyotishka Dasgupta. In color and B&W. Release date: July 13, 2000. Running time: 130 Min. INDIAN.
Cast: Soumitra Chatterjee, Aparna Sen, Rituparna Sengupta, Sohini Haldar, Sailee Sengupta, Rajatabha Dutta, Ratna Ghoshal.

THE HOUSE OF MIRTH
A FilmFour Distribution release of a Granada presentation of a Three Rivers production, in association with the Arts Council of England, FilmFour, the Scottish Arts Council, Showtime Network and Glasgow Film Fund, with participation of Diaphana, Progress and Kinowelt. (International sales: Capitol Films, London.) Producer: Olivia Stewart. Executive producers: Bob Last, Pippa Cross. Co-producer: Alan J. Wands. Director/Screenplay: Terence Davies, from the novel by Edith Wharton. Camera: Remi Adefarasin. Editor: Michael Parker. In Deluxe color. Release date: Aug. 5, 2000. Running time: 143 Min. BRITISH.
Cast: Gillian Anderson, Eric Stoltz, Dan Aykroyd, Eleanor Bron, Terry Kinney, Anthony LaPaglia, Elizabeth McGovern.

THE HOUSE OF THE DEAD
A Mezhrabpomfilm (Moscow) production. Director: Vasili Fyodorov. Screenplay: Viktor Shklovsky, Fyodorov, from the novel by Fyodor Dostoyevsky. Camera: Vasili Pronin. Music: Vasili Kryukov. In B&W. Release date: Aug. 5, 2000. Running time: 91 Min. SOVIET UNION–1932.
Cast: Nikolai Khmelyov, Nikolai Podgorny, Nikolai Vitovtov, Nikolai Radin, Vladimir Belokurov, Vasili Kovrigin.

HUMAN RESOURCES
A La Sept Arte/Haut et Court production with participation of Centre National de la Cinematographie, Procirep, BBC Films. (International sales: Celluloid Dreams, Paris.) Producers: Caroline Benjo, Carole Scotta. Executive producer: Barbara Letellier. Director: Laurent Cantet. Screenplay: Cantet, Gilles Marchand. Camera: Matthieu Poirot Delpech, Claire Caroff. Editor: Robin Campillo. In color. Release date: Sept. 22, 1999. Running time: 103 Min. FRENCH.
Cast: Jalil Lespert, Jean-Claude Vallod, Chantal Barre, Veronique de Pandelaere, Michel Begnez, Lucien Longueville, Danielle Melador.

THE HUMILIATED
A Jesper Jargil Film production, in association with the Danish Film Institute, DRTV, Danish Ministry of Education. (International sales: Trust Film Sales, Hvidovre, Denmark.) Producer: Vinca Wiedermann. Director/Screenplay: Jesper Jargil. Camera: Jargil. Editors: Mette Zeruneith, Daniel Dencik. Music: excerpts from Camille Saint-Saens. In Sony VX-1000 Digital Handycam-to-35mm. Release date: Sept. 10, 1999. Running time: 83 Min. Documentary. DANISH.

THE HUNDRED STEPS
An Istituto Luce release of a Titti Film/Rai Cinema production. (International sales: Intra Movies, Rome.) Producer: Fabrizio Mosca. Director: Marco Tullio Girodana. Screenplay: Claudio Fava, Monica Zapelli, Tullio Girodana. Camera: Roberto Forza. Editor: Toberto Missiroli. In color. Release date: Aug. 30, 2000. Running time: 104 Min. ITALIAN.
Cast: Luigi Lo Cascio, Luigi Maria Burruano, Lucia Sardo, Paolo Briguglia, Tony Sperandeo, Pippo Montalbano, Ninni Bruschetta.

HUNTERS IN THE SNOW
A Wega Filmproduktion production. (International sales: Austrian Film Commission, Vienna.) Producer: Veit Heiduschka. Director/ Screenplay: Michael Kreihsl. Camera: Oliver Bokelberg. Editor: Clemens Bohm. In color. Release date: Feb. 13, 2000. Running time: 86 Min. AUSTRIAN.
Cast: Ulrich Tukur, Julia Filiminow, Johannes Silberschneider, Sophia Gorgi, Claudia Martini, Nikolaus Paryla.

HUNTER'S MOON
An MPC & Associados production. (International sales: Grupo Novo de Cinema e TV Distribution & Diffusion, Rio de Janeiro.) Producer: Luciana Boal Marinho. Director: Alberto Graca. Screenplay: Leopoldo Serran, Alberto Graca. Camera: Toca Seabra. Editor: Isabelle Rathery. Music: Armenio Graca. In color, widescreen. Release date: Feb. 13, 2000. Running time: 113 Min. BRAZILIAN.
Cast: Marcello Antony, Barbara Schulz, Paulo Vespucio, Jean-Louis Tribes, Nelson Pereira Dos Santos, Milton Goncalves, Herson Capri.

HURT
An Australian Film Institute release of a Big hArt and the Omni Group presentation, in association with Arts Northwest, Outback Arts, the Trustees of Casino Development Fund, New South Wales Ministry of Arts and Stephen Grant, of an Outsider Film production. (International sales: Australian Film Institute, Melbourne.) Producer: Julie Torrance. Director/Screenplay: Philip Crawford, Matthew Priestley and 250 young Australians. Video. Release date: July 22, 2000. Running time: 50 Min. AUSTRALIAN.

HYPNOSIS
A Toho Co. release of a Toho/TBS production. Producers: Toru Shibata, Toshiyaki Harada. Director: Masayuki Ochiai. Screenplay: Ochiai, Yasushi Fukuda, based on the novel by Keisuke Matsuoka. Camera: Osamu Fujishi. Editor: Kazuo Miyauchi. Music: Kuniyagi Haijima. In color, widescreen. Release date: Dec. 5, 1999. Running time: 109 Min. JAPANESE.
Cast: Goro Inagaki, Miho Kanno, Ken Utsui, Takeshi Sho, Yuki Watanabe, Shigemitsu Ogi, Kenta Satori, Akira Shirai, Ren Osugi.

I COULDN'T CARE LESS
A Columbia TriStar Spain release of an Enrique Cerezo PC/CR Films production, in association with TVE, Canal Plus. (International sales: Enrique Cerezo, Madrid.) Producer: Enrique Cerezo. Director: David Gordon. Screenplay: Gordon, Alvaro Gallegos, Gustavo Fuertes. Camera: Joaquin Manchado. Editor: Gordon, Bela da Costa. Music: Francis Garcia, Carmelo Martinez. In color. Release date: Aug. 3, 2000. Running time: 98 Min. SPANISH.
Cast: Alejandro Cano, Maria Jurado, Alvaro Gallegos, Fernando Cayo.

IF YOU ONLY KNEW
A Moonstone Entertainment release of an Eternity Pictures presentation of a Cinerenta/Cinefirst production in association with Two Sticks Prods. (International sales: Moonstone Entertainment.) Producers: Richard Salvatore, Carmen M. Miller. Executive producers: Willi Baer, Marc Sferrazza. Co-producers: David E. Ornston, Joey Travolta, Gary Goldstein, David Franco. Director: David Snedeker. Screenplay: Gary Goldstein, Snedeker. Camer: Kristian Bernier. Editor: William Bonomo. Music: Bill Myers. In FotoKem color. Release date: Mar. 5, 2000. Running time: 109 Min. U.S.-GERMAN.
Cast: Jonathan Schaech, Alison Eastwood, James LeGros, Gabrielle Anwar, Lainie Kazan.

I KNOW WHO YOU ARE
A Continental Producciones, Tornasol Films (Spain)/Zarlek Producciones (Argentina) production. Producers: Pancho Casal, Gerardo Herrero, Claudio Pustenlik. Executive producer: Carmen de Miguel. Director: Patricia Ferreira. Screenplay: Ines Paris, Daniela Fejerman, Ferrieira, Enrique Jiminez, Manuel Gutierrez Aragon. Camera: Jose Luis Alcaine. Editor: Marcela Saenz. Music: Jose Nieto. In color. Release date: Feb. 15, 2000. Running time: 107 Min. SPANISH-ARGENTINE.
Cast: Miguel Angel Sola, Ana Fernandez, Roberto Enriquez, Ingrid Rubio, Manuel Manquna, Maria Bouzas, Gonzalo Uriarte, Vicky Pena.

I.K.U.
An Uplink production. Producer: Asai Takashi. Director: Shu Lea Cheang. Screenplay: Cheang with XXX, based on a story by Asai Takashi, Cheang. Camera: Kamoto Tesuya. Editor: Shirao Kazuhiro. Music: the Saboten. In color, digital video. Release date: Jan. 29, 2000. Running time: 92 Min. JAPANESE.
Cast: Tokitoh Ayumu, Zachery Nataf, Akechi Denki, Yumeno Maria, Sasaki Yumeka, Ariga Miho, Asou Myu, Tchuchida Etuyo.

I LOVE ANDREA
A Universal Pictures Italy release of a Francescandrea production, in association with TelePiu. Producers: Andrea Girombelli, Massimo Roviglioni, Francesco Nuti. Director: Francesco Nuti. Screenplay: Carla Giulia Casalini, Ugo Chiti, Nuti. Camera: Maurizio Calvesi. Editor: Ugo De Rossi. Music: Giovanni Nuti, Riccardo Galaradini. In Cinecitta color. Release date: Jan. 11, 2000. Running time: 109 Min. ITALIAN.
Cast: Francesco Nuti, Francesca Neri, Agathe de la Fontaine, Marina Giulia Cavalli, Francesca De Rose, Simona Caparrini, Giulia Weber.

IN A SAVAGE LAND
A Motion Intl. release (in Canada) of an Australian Film Finance Corp. and Hollywood Partners production in association with Showtime Australia, Strand/New Oz Prods. and Polygram Filmed Entertainment. (International sales: Beyond Films, Sydney.) Producers: Bill Bennett, Jennifer Bennett. Executive producers: Mikael Borglund, Gary Hamilton, Hans Huttman. Co-producer: Benda Pam. Director: Bill Bennett. Screenplay: Bill Bennett, Jennifer Bennett. Camera: Danny Ruhlman. Editor: Henry Dangar. Music: David Bridie. In color. Release date: Oct. 2, 1999. Running time: 116 Min. AUSTRALIAN.
Cast: Maya Stange, Martin Donovan, Rufus Sewell, Max Cullen.

IN BED WITH SANTA
A Sonet Film release (in Sweden) of a FilmLance Intl. (Sweden)/ Yellow Cottage (Norway)/Kinoproduction (Finland) production, in association with Sandrew Metronome, Sonet Film, TV1000 and the Chimney Pot. (International sales: BV Intl. Pictures, Avaldsnes, Norway.) Producers: Borje Hansson, Lars Blomgren. Co-producers: Aage Aaberge, Claes Olsson. Director: Kjell Sundvall. Screenplay: Monika Rolfner, Eva Callenbo, Harald Hamrell. Camera: John Christian Rosenlund. Editor: Thomas Tang. Music: Geir Bohren, Bent Aserud. In color. Release date: Oct. 27, 1999. Running time: 95 Min. SWEDISH-NORWEGIAN-FINNISH.
Cast: Katarina Ewerlof, Peter Haber, Leif Andree, Jessica Zanden.

IN EFREN'S PARADISE
A Good Harvest Film production. Producer: Lily Yu Monteverde. Director: Maryo J. Delos Reyes. Screenplay: Jun Lana, story by Robert Silverio. Camera: Shayne Clemente. Editor: Robert Vasadre. Music: Archie Castillo. In color. Release date: Apr. 16, 2000. Running time: 110 Min. FILIPINO.
Cast: Anton Bernardo, Allan Paule, Ynez Veneracion, Ana Capri.

INNOCENCE
A Sharmill release (in Australia) of a Strand/New Oz/Showtime Australia presentation, in association with the South Australian Film Corp., of an Illumination Films production, in association with CineTe, with the support of Cinemedia Corp. Producers: Mark Patterson, Paul Cox. Executive producer: William T. Marshall. Director/Screenplay: Paul Cox. Camera: Tony Clark. Editor: Simon Whittington. Music: Paul Grabowsky. In Cinevex color. Release date: Apr. 20, 2000. Running time: 92 Min. AUSTRALIAN.
Cast: Julia Blake, Charles Tingwell, Terry Norris, Robert Menzies, Marta Dusseldorp, Chris Haywood, Norman Kaye.

THE INNOCENT
A Fuji release of a Tezuka Prods. production. Producer: Binbun Furusawa. Executive producer: Takamasa Matsutani. Director/Screenplay: Macoto Tezka, based on the novella by Ango Sakaguchi. Camera: Junichi Fujisawa. Editor: Yoshiyuki Wada. Music: Ichiko Hashimoto. In color. Release date: Sept. 9, 1999. Running time: 146 Min. JAPANESE.
Cast: Tadanobu Asano, Miyako Koda, Reika Hashimoto, Masao Kusakari, Syunji Fujimura, Kyoko Enami, Anji, Yasutaka Tsutsui.

INSEPARABLE
A Rezo Films release (in France) of a Les Films Balenciaga Productions Cercle Bleu/Arte France Cinema/Telfrance/RFK Distribution Intl./CRRAV/RenNCn Prods. production, in association with Canal Plus, Sofica Gimages 2. (International sales: TF1 Intl., Paris.) Producers: Regine Konckier, Jean-Luc Ormieres. Co-producer: Michel Vermoesen. Director/Screenplay: Michel Couvelard. Camera: Antoine Roch. Editor: Frederic Viger. Music: Arthur H. In color. Release date: Dec. 12, 1999. Running time: 90 Min. FRENCH.
Cast: Jean-Pierre Daroussin, Catherine Frot, Fabienne Babe, Herve Pierre, Sami Bouajila, Brigitte Rouan, Marie Mergey, Daniel Isoppo.

IN VANDA'S ROOM
A Contracosta Producoes (Portugal)/Pandora Film (Germany)/Ventura Film (Switzerland) production, in association with ZDF and RTSI. (International sales: Pandora, Frankfurt.) Producers: Francisco Villa-Lobos, Karl Baumgartner, Andres Pfaeffli. Director: Pedro Costa. Camera: Costa. Editor: Dominique Auvray, Patricia Saramago. In color, digital video. Release date: Aug. 8, 2000. Running time: 179 Min. PORTUGUESE-GERMAN-SWISS.
Cast: Vanda Duarte, Zita Duarte, Lena Duarte, Manuel Gomes Miranda, Diogo Pires Miranda, Evangelina Nelas, Miquelina Barros.

INVASION
A Combined Studio (Alma-Ata) production. Director: Abram Room. Co-director: Oleg Zhakov. Screenplay: Boris Chriskov, based on a play by Leonid Leonov. Camera: Sergei Ivanov. Music: Yuri Biryukov. In B&W. Release date: Aug. 9, 2000. Running time: 100 Min. SOVIET UNION–1945.
Cast: V. Gremin, Olga Zhizneva, Oleg Zhakov, Lyudmila Glazova, Zinaida Morskaya, Lyudmila Shabalina, V. Valersky.

IONE, FLY UP TO HEAVEN
A Zine Zero production, with participation of TVE and ETB. (International sales: Zine Zero, Bilbao.) Executive producer: Luis Goya. Director: Joseba Salegi. Screenplay: Salegi, Jose Antonio Vitoria. Camera: Federico Rives. Editor: Antonio P. Reina. Music: Aitor Amezaga. In color. Release date: June 28, 2000. Running time: 99 Min. SPANISH.
Cast: Kike Diaz de Rada, Martxelo Rubio, Anabel Arrainza, Mario Pardo, Klara Badiola, Esther Esparza.

THE ISLAND TALES
A The Island Tales Seisaku/Kwan's Creative Workshop production. (International sales: TF1 Intl., Paris.) Producers: Shinya Kawai, Naoko Tsukeda. Director: Stanley Kwan. Screenplay: Jimmy Ngai. Camera: Pan-leung Kwan. Editors: Maurice Li, Jimmy Ngai. Music: Yat-yiu Yu. In color. Release date: Feb. 11, 2000. Running time: 100 Min. JAPANESE-HONG KONG.
Cast: Takao Osawa, Shu Qi, Michele Reis, Julian Cheung, Kaori Momoi, Elaine Jin, Gordon Liu.

THE INTER-VIEW
A BKA-Kunstsektion presentation. Director/Screenplay: Jessica Hausner. Camera: Martin Gschlacht. Editor: Karin Hartusch. In color. Release date: Aug.21, 1999. Running time: 48 Min. AUSTRIAN.
Cast: Klaus Handl, Milena Oberndorfer, Birgit Doll, Nica Steinbauer, Andreas Azcharsiewicz.

IN THE MOOD FOR LOVE
A USA Films release of a Block 2 Pictures Inc. presentation with participation of Paradis Films of a Jet Tone Films production. (International sales: Fortissimo Film Sales, Amsterdam.) Producer: Wong Kar-wai. Executive producer: Chan Ye-chang. Director/Screenplay: Wong Kar-wai. Camera: Christopher Doyle, Mark Li Ping-bing. Editor: William Chang Sukping. Music: Michael Galasso, Umebayashi Shigeru. In color. Release date: May 20, 2000. Running time: 97 Min. HONG KONG.
Cast: Tony Leung Chiu-wai, Maggie Cheung Man-yuk, Lai Chin.

THE INTRUDER
A GFT Kingsborough Films (Canada)/Steve Walsh Prods. (U.K.) production, in association with Studio Eight Prods. (International sales: CTV Intl., Paris.) Producers: Jamie Brown, Pieter Kroonenburg. Executive producers: Thierry Wase Bailey, Gary Howsam, Steve Walsh. Director: David Bailey. Screenplay: Jamie Brown, based on the novel by Brooke Leimas. Camera: Jean Lepine. Editor: Angelo Corrao. Music: Frank Ilfman. In color. Release date: Oct. 1, 1999. Running time: 94 Min. CANADIAN-BRITISH.
Cast: Charlotte Gainsbourg, Charles Powell, Nastassja Kinski, Molly Parker, John Hannah.

THE INVESTIGATION MUST GO ON
A Transfix Films production. Producer/Director: Marek Rozenbaum. Screenplay: Haim Merin. Camera: Valentin Belonogov. Editor: Anat Lubarsky. Music: Efi Shoshani. In color. Release date: July 15, 2000. Running time: 94 Min. ISRAELI.
Cast: Moshe Ivgi, Aki Avni, Osnat Fishman, David Danino, Assi Levy, Itzik Juli.

I PREFER THE SOUND OF THE SEA
A Mikado release of a BiancaFilm and Mikado presentation of a BiancaFilm, Mikado, RAI (Italy)/Arcapix (France) production, with participation of Canal Plus. Producers: Donatella Botti, Roberto Cicutto, Luigi Musini. Co-producer: Gilles-Marie Tine. Director: Mimmo Calopresti. Screenplay: Calopresti, Francesco Bruni, story by Calopresti, Heidrun Schleef, Bruni. Camera: Luca Bigazzi. Editor: Massimo Fiocchi. Music: Franco Piersanti. In Cinecitta color. Release date: Mar. 20, 2000. Running time: 84 Min. ITALIAN-FRENCH.
Cast: Silvio Orlando, Michele Raso, Fabrizia Sacchi, Mimmo Calopresti, Andrea Occhipinti, Enrica Rosso, Marcello Mazzarella.

THE IRON LADIES
A Fortissimo Film Sales presentation of a Tai Entertainment production. (International sales: Fortissimo Film Sales, Amsterdam.) Producer: Visute Poolvoralaks. Co-producers: Chatchavarin Klainak, Pasert Wiwatabanonpong, Chanajai Tonsaithong. Director: Yongyoot Thongkongtoon. Screenplay: Visuttichai Boonyakarjana, Jira Maligool, Thongkongtoon. Camera: Jira Maligool. Editor: Sunit Assavinikul. Original music: Wild At Heart. In color. Release date: Sept. 12, 2000. Running time: 104 Min. TAIWANESE.
Cast: Jessadaporn Pholdee, Sahapap Virakamin, Ekachai Buranapanit, Giorio Maiocchi, Chaicharn Nimpoonsawas.

THE IRREFUTABLE TRUTH ABOUT DEMONS
A First Sun presentation in association with New Zealand Film Commission of a First Sun production. (International sales: New Zealand Film Commission, Wellington.) Producer: Dave Gibson. Director/Screenplay: Glenn Standring. Camera: Simon Baumfield. Editor: Paul Sutorius. Music: Victoria Kelly, Joost Langveld. In color. Release date: May 18, 2000. Running time: 89 Min. NEW ZEALAND.
Cast: Karl Urban, Katie Wolfe, Sally Stockwell, Jonathon Hendry.

THE ISLE
A CJ Entertainment presentation of a Myung Film production. (International sales: CJ Entertainment, Seoul.) Producer: Lee Eun. Executive producer: Seok Dong-jun. Director/Screenplay: Kim Ki-duk. Camera: Hwang Suh-shik. Editor: Kyung Min-ho. In color. Release date: May 11, 2000. Running time: 89 Min. SOUTH KOREAN.
Cast: Seoh Jung, Kim Yu-seok, Park Sung-hee, Jang Hang-sun, Jo Jae-hyun.

IT TAKES ALL KINDS
A Pathe release of a Telema/Les Films A4/France 2 Cinema production, with participation of Canal Plus. (International sales: Pathe Intl., Paris.) Producers: Christian Berard, Charles Gassot. Executive producer: Jacques Hinstin. Director: Agnes Jaoui. Screenplay: Jaoui, Jean-Pierre Bacri. Camera: Jean-Paul Dumas-Grillet. Editor: Herve de Luze. Music arranger: Jean-Charles Jarrell. In color, widescreen. Release date: Mar. 1, 2000. Running time: 112 Min. FRENCH.
Cast: Jean-Pierre Bacri, Anne Alvaro, Agnes Jaoui, Gerard Lanvin, Alain Chabat, Brigitte Catillon, Christiane Millet, Wladimir Yordanoff.

IT WILL END UP IN TEARS
A Gonen Glaser production. Producer/Director/Camera: Glaser. Editor: Stephanie Abramovich. Release date: July 17, 2000. Running time: 60 Min. Documentary. ISRAELI.

I WANT IT ALL
A UIP release (in France) of a Les Films Alain Sarde/L'Arbre & La Colombe/M6 Films production, with participation of Canal Plus. (International sales: Le Studio Canal Plus, Paris.) Producers: Alain Sarde, Patrick Braoude. Executive producer: Christine Gozlan. Director/Screenplay: Guila Braoude. Camera: Philippe Pavans de Ceccaty. Editor: Yves Deschamps. Music: Jacques Davidovici. In color. Release date: Dec 23, 1999. Running time: 91 Min. FRENCH.
Cast: Elsa Zylberstain, Frederic Diefenthal, Alain Bashung, Elisabeth Vitali, Sonia Vollereaux, Patrick Braoude, Smadi Wolfman.

I WILL SURVIVE
An Aurum release (in Spain) of an Aurum/El Paso Producciones/Peliculas Freneticas production, in association with Via Digital and with participation of Antena 3. Producer: Francisco Ramos. Director: Alfonso Albacete, David Menkes. Screenplay: Albacete, Menkes, Lucia Etxeberria. Camera: Gonzalo Fernandez-Berridi. Editor: Miguel Angel Santamaria. Music: Paco Ortega. In color. Release date: Nov. 22, 1999. Running time: 105 Min. SPANISH.
Cast: Emma Suarez, Juan Diego Botto, Mirtha Ibarra, Rosana Pastor, Manuel Manquina.

I WON'T GO BACK HOME
A Mandragora production. Producer: Albertina Carri. Director/Screenplay: Albertina Carri. Camera: Paula Grandio. Editor: Rosario Suarez. Music: Edgardo Rudnitzky. In B&W. Release date: Apr. 12, 2000. Running time: 74 Min. ARGENTINE.
Cast: Margara Alonso, Manuel Callau, Martin Churba, Analia Couceyro, Fabiana Falcon, Marta Lubos, Ricardo Merkin.

JACKY
An A-Film Distribution release of a Motel Films production in association with VPRO Television. (International sales: Fortissimo Film Sales, Amsterdam.) Producers: Jeroen Beker, Frans van Gestel. Director/Screenplay: Fow Pyng Hu, Brat Ljatifi. Camera: Benito Strangio. Editors: Hu, Ljatifi, Casper Koetsveld. In color. Release date: Feb. 4, 2000. Running time: 77 Min. DUTCH.
Cast: Fow Pyng Hu, Eveline Wu, Gary Guo, Xuan Wei Zhou, Jian Pau Toh.

JADVIGA'S PILLOW

A Mafilm production in association with ORTT and MMK. Producer: Gyorgy Marosi. Director: Krisztina Deak. Screenplay: Deak, Pal Zavada, based on the novel by Zavada. Camera: Gabor Balogh. Editor: Zsuzsa Csakany. Music: Gyorgy Selmeczi. In color. Release date: Feb. 4, 2000. Running time: 134 Min. HUNGARIAN.
Cast: Ildiko Toth, Viktor Bodo, Roman Luknar, Mari Csomos, Eszter Onodi, Bela Fesztbaum, Djoko Rosic, Marian Labuda.

JAIME

A Jani Thiltges/Claude Waringo presentation of a Samsa Film (Luxembourge)/Fado Filmes, SIC (Portugal)/Videofilmes (Brazil) production. (International sales: Artbox, Paris.) Producer: Jani Thiltges. Executive producer: Serge Zeitoun. Director: Antonio-Pedro Vasconcelos. Screenplay: Carlos Saboga, based on an idea by Vasconcelos. Camera: Edgar Moura. Editor: Frederic Fichefet. Music: Alain Jomy, Rui Veloso, Carlos Te. In color. Release date: Sept. 18, 1999. Running time: 108 Min. LUXEMBOURGOIS-PORTUGUESE-BRAZILIAN.
Cast: Saul Fonseca, Fernanda Serrano, Joaquim Leitao, Sandro Silva.

JANANI

A Badarudeen production. (International sales: Thanal, Kerala.) Producer/Director: Thankamaniamma Rajeevnath. Camera: Suresh P. Nair. Editor: Beena. Music: Ousepachan. In color. Release date: Jan. 22, 2000. Running time: 97 Min. INDIAN.
Cast: Latiff, Kavitha, Rosline, Santhakumari, Rukmimi.

JET SET

A Bac Films release (in France) of a Mandarin Films, TF1 Films Prod. (France)/Filmart (Spain) production, with participation of Canal Plus and Bac Films. Producers: Eric and Nicolas Altmayer. Director: Fabien Onteniente. Screenplay: Onteniente, Emmanuel de Brantes, Bruno Solo, Olivier Chavarot. Camera: Franco Di Giacomo. Editor: Nathalie Hubert. Music: Loik Dury & Crew. In color. Release date: June 22, 2000. Running time: 103 Min. FRENCH-SPANISH.
Cast: Samuel Le Bihan, Lambert Wilson, Ornella Muti, Ariadna Gil.

JOHNNIE GREYEYES

A Nepantla Films production in association with Ravenhead Prods. Producers: Jorge Manzano, Phyllis Ellis, Timothy L. Hill. Director: Jorge Manzano. Screenplay: Manzano, Riel Brown, Vince Manitowabi, Gail Maurice. Camera: Marcos Arriaga. Editor: Jacqueline Carmody. Music: Nano Valverde. In color and B&W. Release date: Jan. 29, 2000. Running time: 79 Min. CANADIAN.
Cast: Gail Maurice, Jonathan Fisher, Columpa C. Bobb, Gloria May Eshkibok, Marion Devries, Shirley Cheechoo, Georgina Lightning.

THE JOLLY BOYS' LAST STAND

A Jolly Prods. production. Producer: Craig Woodrow. Executive producers: Tom McCabe, Richard Holmes, Gavin Emerson. Co-producer: Richard Conway. Director/Screenplay: Christopher Payne. Camera: Will Jacob, Robin Cox. Editor: Tullio Brunt. Music: Jeremy Panufnik. In color, Digibeta video. Release date: July 24, 2000. Running time: 87 Min. BRITISH.
Cast: Milo Twomey, Yolande Davis, Andy Serkis, Rebecca Craig.

JONAH AND LILA, TILL TOMORROW

A Filmograph (Geneva)/Cab Prods. (Lausanne)/Gemini Films (Paris) production in co-production with Television Suisse Romande, Westdeutscher Rundfunk Koln. (International sales: Gemini Films, Paris.) Producers: Alain Tanner, Gerard Ruey, Jean-Louis Porchet, Paulo Branco. Director: Tanner. Screenplay: Tanner, Bernard Comment. Camera: Denis Jutzeler. Editor: Monica Goux. Music: Michel Wintsch. In color. Release date: Sept. 24, 1999. Running time: 120 Min. SWISS-FRENCH.
Cast: Jerome Robart, Aissa Maiga, Natalia Dontcheva, Jean-Pierre Gos, Cecile Tanner, Philippe Demarle, Heinz Bennent.

JUBAKU–SPELLBOUND

A Toei release of a Toei/Kadokawa Shoten presentation of an Asmik Ace Entertainment production, in association with Toei Co. (International sales: Kadokawa Shoten Publishing, Tokyo.) Producers: Masato Hara, Sunao Sakagami. Executive producers: Tsuguhiko Kadokawa, Tan Takaiwa, Shigeaki Hazama. Co-executive producers: Yosho Tobaru, Masao Sato, Yoshiaki Sumita. Director: Masato Harada. Screenplay: Ryo Takasugi, Satoshi Suzuki, Mugita Kinoshita, based on a novel by Takasugi. Camera: Yoshitaka Sakamoto. Editor: Akimasa Kawashima. Music: Masahiro Kawasaki. In color. Release date: Feb. 17, 2000. Running time: 115 Min. JAPANESE.
Cast: Koji Yakusho, Tatsuya Nakadai, Jun Fubuki, Kippei Shiina, Mayumi Wakamura, Kenichi Endo, Masako Motai, Hirotaro Honda.

JULY RAIN

A Mosfilm production. Director: Marlen Khutsiev. Screenplay: Khutsiev, Anatoli Grebnev. Camera: German Lavrov. Editor: A. Abramova. Music: Bulat Okudzhava, Yuri Vizbor. In B&W. Release date: Aug. 10, 2000. Running time: 103 Min. SOVIET UNION–1967.
Cast: Evgeniya Uralova, Aleksandr Belyavsky, Yuri Vizbor, Aleksandr Mitta, Alla Pokrovskaya.

THE JUNK FOOD GENERATION

An Urban Entertainment presentation, in association with Otwo 99. (International sales: Pal Entertainments, Tokyo.) Executive producer: Yoshiyuki Honda. Director/Screenplay: Shinobu Sakagami, Hideo Baba. Music: Hideya Nakazaki. In color. Release date: Oct. 7, 1999. Running time: 98 Min. JAPANESE.
Cast: Shinobu Sakagami, Amiko Kanaya, Nathan Ginn, David Adams, Lisa Noelle, Angel Powers, D.C. Warren, Darwin, Takatoshi Takeda.

JUST MESSING ABOUT

A Next Film production. (International sales: Media Luna, Koln.) Producers: Laurence Straub, Pia Frankenberg. Director: Jochen Kuhn. Screenplay: Claudia Messemer, Kuhn. Camera: Jorg Schmidt-Reitwein. Editor: Sabine Jehnert. Music: Christopher Evans Ironside. In color. Release date: Feb. 18, 2000. Running time: 99 Min. GERMAN.
Cast: Maximilian Schell, Edgar Selge, Tonio Arango, Alexandra Maria Lara, Neza Selbuz, Marianne Schubert, Desiree Nick, Horst Krause.

JUST RUN

An Altafilms release (in Spain) of a Cartel, La Fiera Corrupia (Spain)/Fandango (Italy)/Alien Prods. (Denmark) production, with participation of TVE, Via Digital. (International sales: Media Luna, Cologne.) Producers: Eduardo Campoy, Antonio Saura. Director: Saura Medrano. Screenplay: Anton Martin, Nicolas Casariego, Saura, based on a nvoel by Martin Casariego. Camera: Jose Luis Lopez Linare, Teo Delgado. Editor: Jose Salcedo. Music: Carlo Siliotto. In color. Release date: May 3, 2000. Running time: 91 Min. SPANISH-ITALIAN-DANISH.
Cast: Fele Martinez, Silke, Patxi Freytez, Aitor Merino, Alberto Escobar, Santiago Etombayambo, Geraldine Chapline.

KANAK ATTACK

A Concorde Film Classic release of a Becker & Haeberle Filmproduktion production, in association with ZDF/Arte. (International sales: Bavaria Film Intl., Munich.) Producers: Thomas Haeberle, Christian Becker. Director: Lars Becker. Screenplay: Becker, Feridun Zaimoglu, Bernhard Wutka, based on the novel "Scum" (Abschaum) by Zaimoglu. Camera: Hannes Hubach. Editor: Oliver Gieth. Release date: June 27, 2000. Running time: 86 Min. GERMAN.
Cast: Luke Piyes, David Scheller, Tyron Ricketts, Oezlem Cetin, Nadeshda Brennicke, Ercan Durmaz, Murat Yilmaz, Ralph Herforth.

KAPUTT MUNDI

An RAI Trade and Instituto Luce production in association with Sorpasso Film and Cinecitta. Producers: Marco Risi, Maurizio Tedesco. Director: Marco Risi. Screenplay: Niccolo Ammaniti, Risi, based on the novel "L'ultimo capodanno dell'umanita" by Ammaniti. Camera: Maurizio Calvesi. Editor: Franco Fraticelli. Music: Andrea Rocca. In color. Release date: Sept. 30, 1999. Running time: 105 Min. ITALIAN.
Cast: Monica Bellucci, Alessandro Haber, Francesca D'Aloja, Marco Giallini, Ricky Memphis, Giorgio Tirabassi, Natale Tulli, Piero Naroli.

KARAKUM

A EuroArts Intl. production. Producers: Dietrich Voigtlaender, Gulja Chalmamedova, Kurban Tchekirov. Director: Arend Agthe. Screenplay: Agthe, Usman Saparov. Camera: Michael Wiesweg. Editor: Ursula Hof. Music: Matthias Raue, Martin Cyrus. In color. Release date: Oct. 9, 1999. Running time: 100 Min. GERMAN-TURKMENISTANIAN.
Cast: Max Kullman, Murat Orasov, Pjotr Olev, Neidhart Niedel, Alexander Potapov.

KEEP RUNNING

An MK2 Diffusion release (in France) of a Les Films du Bois Sacre/MK2 Prods./Arte France Cinema production. (International sales: MK2 Diffusion, Paris.) Producers: Fabrice Guez, Marin Karmitz. Director: Dante Desarthe. Screenplay: Dante Desarthe, Fabrice Guez, Agnes Desarthe. Camera: Laurent Macheil. Editor: Martine Rousseau. Music: David Lascot, Bratsch. In color. Release date: Dec. 8, 1999. Running time: 84 Min. FRENCH.
Cast: Clemont Sibony, Rona Hartner, Isaac Sharry, Emmanuelle Devos, Gilbert Levy.

KENNEDY AND I

A Pathe release (in France) of an Elizabeth Films/Les Films A4 presentation of a France 2 Cinema/Roissy Films/Prima/Telema production, with participation of Canal Plus, Gimages 2 and Cofimage 10. (International sales: Roissy Film, Paris.) Producers: Edouard Weil, Christian Berard. Executive Producer: Jean-Claude Bourlat. Director: Sam Karmann. Screenplay: Karmann, Jean-Paul Dubois, based on the novel by Dubois. Camera: Guillaume Schiffman. Editor: Philippe Bourgueil. Music: Pierre Adenot. In color. Release date: Jan. 5, 2000. Running time: 84 Min. FRENCH.
Cast: Jean-Pierre Bacri. Nicole Garcia, Patrick Chesnais, Sam Karmann, Francois Chattot, Eleonore Gosset, Lucas Bonnifait.

KESTREL'S EYE

A First Run Films Release of a Picafilms picture. Producer/ Director/Screenplay/Editor: Mikael Kristersson. Camera: Kristersson. In color, 16mm. Release date: Jan. 26, 2000. Running time: 86 min. Documentary. SWEDISH.

KEVIN & PERRY GO LARGE

An Icon release of an Icon Entertainment Intl. presentation of a Tiger Aspect Pictures production, in association with Icon Prods., and Fragile Films. Producers: Peter Bennett-Jones, Jolyon Symonds, Harry Enfield. Executive producers: Bruce Davey, Ralph Kamp, Barnaby Thompson. Co-producer: Paul Tucker. Director: Ed Bye. Screenplay: Harry Enfield, David Cummings. Camera: Alan Almond. Editor: Mark Wybourn. In Deluxe London color. Release date: Apr. 22, 2000.Running time: 82 Min. British.
Cast: Harry Enfield, Kathy Burke, Rhys Ifans, Laura Fraser, James Fleet, Louisa Rix, Tabith Wady, Paul Whitehouse, Natasha Little.

KIN

A Bard Entertainments production, with participation of BSkyB, British Screen and the Arts Council of England, in asociation with N-Net. (International sales: Regent Entertainment Intl., Santa Monica.) Producer: Margaret Matheson. Executive producer: Miles Donnelly. Director/Screenplay: Elaine Proctor. Camera: Amelia Vincent. Editor: Nicholas Gaster. Music: Justin Adams. In Deluxe color, Panavision widescreen. Release date: July 5, 2000. Running time: 89 Min. BRITISH.
Cast: Miranda Otto, Isaiah Washington, Chris Chameleon, Moses Kandjoze, Ndondoro Hevita, Susan Coetzer, Martin Stefanus.

THE KING IS ALIVE

A Newmarket/Good Machine Intl. presentation of a Zentropa Entertainments 5 production, in co-production with the Danish Broadcasting Corp. in collaboration with SVT Drama, supported by the Danish Film Institute, Nordic Film & TV Fund. (International sales: Good Machine, N.Y.) Producers: Patricia Kruijer, Vibeke Windelov. Executive producers: William A. Tyrer, Chris J. Ball, David Linde, Peter Aalbaek Jensen. Director: Kristian Levring. Screenplay: Levring, Anders Thomas Jensen, inspired by Shakespeare's "King Lear." Camera: Jens Schlosser. Editor: Nicholas Wayman-Harris. In color. Release date: May 11, 2000. Running time: 108 Min. DANISH.
Cast: Miles Anderson, Romane Bohringer, David Bradley, David Calder, Bruce Davison, Brion James, Peter Kubheka, Vusi Kunene.

THE KING'S DAUGHTERS

A UIP release of an Archipel 35/Lichtblick FilmProduktion/Entre Chien et Loup/Arte France Cinema/France 2 Cinema/WDR/FMB Films/Accaan/Les Films du camelia/Cineart production in association with Sofinergie 5, Sofygram 3, Cofimage 10, UGC Intl., with participation of Canal Plus, CNC. (International sales: UGC Intl., Paris.) Producer: Denis Freyd. Co-producers: Helga Bahr, Diana Elbaum. Director: Patricia Mazuy, Yves Thomas, based on the novel "La maison d'Esther" by Yves Dangerfield. Camera: Thomas Mauch. Editor: Ludo Troch. Music: John Cale. In color. Release date: May 16, 2000. Running time: 119 Min. FRENCH.
Cast: Isabelle Huppert, Jean-Pierre Kalfon, Simon Reggiani, Jean-Francois Balmer, Anne Marev, Nina Meurisse, Morgane More.

KIPPUR

An MP Prods./Agav Hafakot co-production, in association with Le Studio Canal Plus, Arte France Cinema, R & C Produzioni, Canal Plus, Telad, Eldan, Tele Plus. (International sales: President Films, Paris.) Producers: Amos Gitai, Michel Propper, Laurent Truchot. Co-producers: Tilde Corsi, Gianni Romoli, Michael Tapuach. Director: Amos Gitai. Screenplay: Gitai, Marie-Jose Sanselme. Camera: Renato Berta. Editors: Monica Coleman, Kobi Netanel. Music: Jan Garbarek. In color. Release date: May 17, 2000. Running time: 123 Min. ISRAELI-FRENCH.
Cast: Liron Levo, Tomer Ruso, Uri Ran Klauzner, Yoram Hattab, Juliano Merr, Ran Kauchinsky, Kobi Livne, Liat Glick Levo.

KISS ME SO LONG I CAN'T BREATHE

A Zone production. (International sales: Zone, Tokyo.) Producers: Shoichi Kanayama, Kenichiro Sato, Kim Taegwan. Executive producer: Kanayama. Director/Screenplay: Kim Taegwan. Camera: Satoshi Maeda. Editor: Fukano Toshihide. In color. Release date: Feb. 17, 2000. Running time: 93 Min. JAPANESE.
Cast: Atsuki Kato, Toshiya Nakamatsu, Ikkoh Suzuki.

THE KITE

A GMA Films presentation of a Teamwork Prods. production. Producer: Gil M. Portes. Executive producer: Marco M. Capistrano. Director: Gil M. Portes. Screenplay: Jose Y. Dalisay Jr., Portes. Camera: Louie Quirino. Editor: Tara Illenberger. Music: Joy Marfil. In color. Release date: Sept. 4, 1999. Running time: 85 Min. PHILIPPINE.
Cast: Ricky Davao, Lester Llansang, Jennifer Sevilla, Mark Gil, Sining Blanco, Daryl Reyes, Connie Lauigan-Chua, Nanding Josef.

KM.O

A Universal Pictures Intl. release of a Universal Pictures Spain/Cuarteto PC production, in association with Media Park. (International sales: UPI, Madrid.) Executive producers: Rafael Alvero, Stefan Nicoll, Marc Cases, Pastora Delgado. Director/Screenplay: Juan Luis Iborra, Yolanda Garcia Serrano. Camera: Angel Luis Fernandez. Editor: Jose Salcedo. Music: Joan Bibiloni. In color. Release date: July 7, 2000. Running time: 108 Min. SPANISH.
Cast: Concha Velasco, George Corraface, Silke, Carlos Fuentes, Merce Pons, Alberto San Juan, Elisa Matilla, Armando del Rio.

KNOCKOUT

A Svensk Filmindustri release (in Sweden) of a Giraff Film, Svensk Filmindustri, SVT Filmpool Nord (Sweden)/SF Norge (Norway) production. (International sales: Svensk Filmindustri, Stockholm.) Producer: John O. Olsson. Director: Agneta Fagerstrom-Olsson. Screenplay: Peter Birro, Fagerstrom-Olsson. Camera: John O. Olsson. Editor: Hakan Karlsson. Music: Christer Engberg, Mats Asplen, Ola Gustavsson. In color. Release date; Feb. 4, 2000. Running time: 110 Min. SWEDISH-NORWEGIAN.
Cast: Orjan Landstrom, Reine Brynolfsson, Ludmila Varfolomeyeva, Igor Chernovich, Kirill Ulyanov, Mikhail Wasserbaum, Aleksei Shulin.

THE KNOT

A Studio Nadezha production. Producer: Svetlana Voloshina. Director: Alexander Sokurov. Camera: Alexander Degtiarev, Alexei Fiudorov. Editor: Konstantin Stafeev. In color. Release date: Oct. 19, 1999. Running time: 91 Min. Documentary. RUSSIAN.

KRAMPACK

An Alta Films release (in Spain) of a Messidor Films production. (International sales: Segepaq, Madrid.) Producers: Marta Esteban, Gerardo Herrero. Director: Cesc Gay. Screenplay: Gay, Tomas Aragay, based on the play by Jordi Sanchez. Camera: Andreu Rebes. Editor: Frank Gutierrez. Music: Riqui Sabates, Joan Diaz, Jordi Prats. In color. Release date: May 15, 2000. Running time: 90 Min. SPANISH.
Cast: Fernando Ramallo, Jordi Vilches, Marieta Orozco, Esther Nubiola, Chisco Amado, Ana Gracia, Myriam Mezieres.

L + R

A Fischer Film production. Producer: Markus Fischer. (International sales: First Hand Films, Bulach, Switzerland.) Director/Screenplay: Edgar Honetschlager. Camera: Norbert Artner, Honetschlager, Karl Neubert. Editor: Kurt Hennrich. In color and B&W. Release date: Jan. 28, 2000. Running time: 79 Min. Documentary. AUSTRIAN.
Narrator: Yukika Kudo.

LA BOSTELLA

A Pathe Distribution release of a La Compagnie Panoptique/Les Productions en Cabine/Le Studio Canal Plus production, with participation of Canal Plus and Sylicone. Producers: Jean Labib, Marco Cherqui. Director: Edouard Baer. Screenplay: Fabrice Roger-Lacan, Baer. Screenplay: Fabrice Roger-Lacan, Baer. Camera: Laurent Machuel. Editor: Marco Cave. Music: Julien Baer. In color. Release date: July 17, 2000. Running time: 99 Min. FRENCH.
Cast: Edouard baer, Rosine Favey, Gilles Gaston-Dreyfus, Jean-Michel Lahm, Pierre-Louis Lanier, Philippe Laudenbach, Emmanuelle Lepoutre, Francis Van Litsenborgh, Joseph Malerba.

LA CARBONARA

A Lion Pictures release of a Letizia Cinematografica production, in association with RAI Cinema. Producers: Letizia Colonna Di Stigliano, Massimo Ferrero. Director/Screenplay: Luigi Magni. Camera: Danilo Desideri. Editor: Fernanada Indoni. Music: Nicola Piovani. In color. Release date: Feb. 16, 2000. Running time: 115 Min. ITALIAN.
Cast: Lucrezia Lante Della Rovere, Nino Manfredi, Valerio Mastrandrea, Fabrizio Gifuni, Claudio Amendola.

LADIES ROOM

A Motion Intl. release (in Canada) of a Cine-Roman/Laurem Prods./Transfilm/-Smallrain Ltd. production. Producers: Tony Roman, Rene Malo, Claude Leger, Jonathan Vanger. Director: Gabriella Christiani. Screenplay: Leila Basen, Andree Pelletier, Genevieve Lefebvre, Natalina Di Leandro, Amanda Roberts, based on an original idea by Tony Roman. Camera: Pierre Mignot. Editors: Dominique Fortin, Gabriella Cristiani. Music: Simon Carpentier, Jean-Patrick Capdevielle, Richard Tate, Tony Roman. In color. Release date: Sept. 1, 1999. Running time: 90 Min. CANADIAN-BRITISH.
Cast: John Malkovich, Lorraine Bracco, Greta Scacchi, Veronica Ferres, Molly Parker, Greg Thomey, Nanette Workman, Alan Fawcett.

THE LADY OF HAMRE

A Zentropa Entertainment S3 production, in association with TV2 (Denmark), Scanbox Entertainment. (International sales: Trust Film Sales, Hvidorvre, Denmark.) Producer: Ib Tardini. Director: Katrine Wiedemann. Screenplay: Vince Wiedemann, based on a novel by Morten Krochs. Camera: Morten Soborg. Editor: Mette Zeruneith. In color. Release date: Feb. 16, 2000. Running time: 88 Min. DANISH.
Cast: Bodil Jorgensen, Bjarne Henriksen, Rikke Louise Andersson, Nikolaj Kopernikus, Bodil Lassen, Regitze Estrup, Tommy Kenter.

THE LADY OF THE HOUSE

A J. Radical Entertainment Co. Private production. Producer: Anupam Kher. Director/Screenplay: Rituparno Ghosh. Camera: Vivek Shah. Editor: Arghyakamal Mitra. Music: Debajyoti Mishra. In color. Release date; Feb. 16, 2000. Running time: 148 Min. INDIAN.
Cast: Kiron Kher, Chiranjeet Chakraborty, Sudipta Chakraborty, Surya Chatterjee, Rupa Ganguly, Abhishek Chatterjee.

L'AMOUR L'ARGENT L'AMOUR

A Philip Groening Filmproduktion (Germany)/Balzli & Fahrer Filmproduktion (Switzerland)/Solera & Cie. (France) production, in association with WDR, BR, Arte, SF, DRS, Taunus Film, Bavaria Film, Teleclub. (International sales: Bavaria Film Intl., Munich.) Producers: Philip Groening, Res Balzli, Dieter Fahrer, Francoise Gazio. Co-producers: Uwe Boll, Michael Weber. Director: Philip Groening. Screenplay: Groening, Michael Busch. Camera: Sophie Maintigneux, Max Jonathan Silberstein. Editors: Silberstein, Valdis Oskarsdottir. Music: various. In color, widescreen. Release date: Aug. 8, 2000. Running time: 138 Min. GERMAN-SWISS-FRENCH.
Cast: Sabine Timoteo, Florian Stetter, Michael Schech, Dierk Prawdzik, Marquardt Bohm, Gerhard Fries.

THE LAND OF THE WANDERING SOULS

An INA/La Sept-Arte production. (International sales: INA, Paris.) Producer: Cati Couteau. Director/Screenplay: Rithy Panh. Camera: Prum Mesar. Editors: Marie-Christine Rougerie, Isabelle Roudy. Music: Marc Marder. In color, digital video. Release date: Aug. 19, 2000. Running time: 98 Min. Documentary. FRENCH.

THE LAST DAY

An Urban Inc./Pug Point production. (International sales: Urban, Tokyo.) Producer: Yoshiyuki Honda. Director/Screenplay: Takumi Kimizuka, based on the novel by Motoko Arai. Camera: Yonezo Maeda. Editor: Yoshinori Ohta. Music: Masaharu Sato. In color. Release date: Sept. 5, 1999. Running time: 118 Min. JAPANESE.
Cast: Nae Yuuki, Kazuya Takahashi, Kazuhiko Kanayama, Noriko Nagi, Masahiro Kiyota, Senjyaku Nakamura, Haruko Mabuchi.

THE LAST ENEMY

A Yona Prods. (Tel Aviv) production, with support from the Peres Center for Peace, the Palestinian Center for Regional Studies. Producer: Nitzan Gilady. Director/Screenplay: Nitzan Gilady. Camera: Nimrod Chaman. Editor: Ron Goldman. Music: Idan Sieberstein. In color, video. Release date: Feb. 6, 2000. Running time: 58 Min. Documentary. ISRAELI.

With: Jim Mirrione, Achim Nowak, Achsen Tourkia.

LAST RESORT

A BBC Films/BBC Documentaries production. Producer: Ruth Caleb. Executive producers: David M. Thompson, Alex Holmes. Director: Paul Pawlikowski. Screenplay: Pawlikowski, Rowan Joffe. Camera: Ryszard Lenczewski. Editor: David Charrup. Music: Max de Wardener. In color, digital video. Release date: Aug. 22, 2000. Running time: 73 Min. BRITISH.

Cast: Dina Korzun, Artiom Strelnikov, Paddy Considine, Lindsey Honey, Dave Bean, Perry Benson, Adrian Scarborough.

LAURA CADIEUX...THE SEQUEL

An Alliance Atlantis release (in Canada) of a Cinemaginaire production. (International sales: Alliance Atlantis Motion Pictures, L.A.) Producer: Denise Robert. Director/Screenplay: Denise Filiatrault. Camera: Daniel Jobin. Editor: Yvann Thibaudeau. Music: Francois Dompierre. In color. Release date: Dec. 2, 1999. Running time: 97 Min. CANADIAN.

Cast: Ginette Reno, Pierrette Robitaille, Denise Dubois, Pauline Lapointe, Daniele Lorain, Dominique Michel, Adele Reinhardt.

THE LEGENDS OF RITA

An Arthaus release of a Babelsberg Film Produktion production, in association with Mitteldeutsches Filmkontor and MDR TV. (International sales: Bavaria Film Intl., Geiselgasteig, Munich.) Producers: Friedrich-Carl Wachs, Arthur Hofer, Emmo Lempert. Director: Volker Schlondorff. Screenplay: Wolfgang Kohlhaase, Schlondorff. Camera: Andreas Hoefer. Editor: Peter Przygodda. In color. Release date: Feb. 16, 2000. Running time: 103 Min. GERMAN.

Cast: Bibiana Beglau, Martin Wuttke, Nadja Uhl, Harald Schrott, Alexander Beyer, Jenny Schily, Mario Irrek, Thomas Arnold.

LES DESTINEES SENTIMENTALES

A Pathe Distribution release of an Arena Films presentation of an Arena Films/TF1 Films Prods. (France)/CAB Prods. (Switzerland) production with the participation of Canal Plus, Cofimage 11, Arcade, with support of CNC, Procirep, Office federal de la Culture (Switzerland), in co-production with Television Suisse Romande. (International sales: Pathe Intl., Paris.) Producer: Bruno Pesery. Co-producers: Jean-Louis Porchet, Gerard Ruey. Director: Olivier Assayas. Screenplay: Jacques Fieschi, Assayas, based on the novel by Jacques Chardonne. Camera: Eric Gautier. Editor: Luc Barnier. Music: Guillaume Lekeu. In color, widescreen. Release date: May 17, 2000. Running time: 180 Min. FRENCH-SWISS.

Cast: Emmanuelle Beart, Charles Berling, Isabelle Huppert, Olivier Perrier, Dominique Reymond, Andre Marcon, Alexandra London.

LES SIESTES GRENADINE

A Hassan Daldoul/Luc Dardenne presentation of a Touza Prods. (France)/Touza Films (Tunisia)/Les Films du Fleuve (Belgium) production, with participation of Canal Plus Horizons Tunisia, ERTT, CNC. Producer: Hassan Daldoul. Director: Mahmoud Ben Mahmoud. Screenplay: Maryse Leon Garcia, Mahmoud, Moncef Dhouib. Camera: Gilberto Azevedo. Editors: Karina Pourtaud, Kahena Attia Riveill. In color. Release date: Nov. 22, 1999. Running time: 92 Min. FRENCH-TUNISIAN-BELGIAN.

Cast: Hicham Rostom, Yasmine Bahri, Loubna Azabaal.

LET IT COME DOWN: THE LIFE OF PAUL BOWLES

A Mongrel Media release (in Canada) of a Requisite Prods. production. (International sales: Rhombus Intl., Toronto.) Producers: Nick de Pencier, Jennifer Baichwal. Executive producer: Daniel Iron. Director: Jennifer Baichwal. Camera: Nick de Pencier, Jim Allodi. Editor: David Wharnsby. Music: Paul Bowles. Release date: Oct. 18, 1999. Running time: 71 Min. Documentary. CANADIAN.

LIAM

A BBC Films presentation of a Liam Films/Road Movies (Berlin) production, in association with Mida, Diaphana, Bim, WDR/Arte, ARD/Degeto Film. (International sales: the Sales Co., London.) Producers: Colin McKeown, Martin Tempia. Executive producers: David M. Thompson, Tessa Ross Sally Hibbin. Co-producer: Ulrich Felsberg. Director: Stephen Frears. Screenplay: Jimmy McGovern. Camera: Andrew Dunn. Editor: Kristina Hetherington. Music: John Murphy. In color. Release date: Sept. 4, 2000. Running time: 91 Min. BRITISH-GERMAN.

Cast: Ian Hart, Claire Hackett, Anthony Borrows, David Hart, Megan Burns, Anne Reid, Julia Deakin, Andrew Schofield, Bernadette Shortt.

THE LIBERTINE

A Pathe Distribution release of a TF1 Films Prod., Bel Ombre Films, Mosca Films, Josy Films, Sans Contrefacon Prods. production, with participation of Canal Plus. (International sales: UGC Intl., Paris.) Producer: Gaspard de Chavagnac. Executive producer: Raphael Cohen. Director: Gabriel Aghion. Screenplay: Eric-Emmanuel Schmitt, Aghion, based on the play by Schmitt. Camera: Jean-Marie Dreujou. Editor: Luc Barnier. Music: Bruno Coulais. In color. Release date: Feb. 28, 2000. Running time: 100 Min. FRENCH.

Cast: Vincent Perez, Fanny Ardant, Josiane Balasko, Michel Serrault, Arielle Dombasle, Christian Charmetant, Francoise Lepine.

LIFE AFTER LOVE

An Alliance Atlantis release (in Canada) of a Max Films production, with the participation of the Canadian Television Fund, Telefilm Canada, Quebec Tax Credit, Sodec, Canadian Tax Credit, Reseau TVA. (International sales: Alliance Atlantis Pictures Intl., Los Angeles.) Producers: Roger Frappier, Luc Vandal. Director: Gabriel Pelletier. Screenplay: Ken Scott. Camera: Eric Cayla. Editor: Alain Baril. Music: Benoit Charest. In color. Release date: July 10, 2000. Running time: 104 Min. CANADIAN.

Cast: Michel Cote, Sylivie Leonard, Patrick Huard, Yves Jacques, Norman Helms, Guylaine Tremblay, Denis Mercier, Pierre-Luc Brillant.

THE LIFE AND ASCENSION OF YURAZ BRATCHIK

A Belarusfilm production. Director: Vladimir Bychkov, S. Skvortsov. Screenplay: V. Korotkevich, based on his novel. Camera: A. Zabolotsky. Editor: V. Kolyadenko. Music: O. Karavaychuk. In color. Release date: Aug. 8, 2000. Running time: 81 Min. SOVIET UNION–1968.

Cast: L. Durov, I. Rutberg, L. Krugly, A. Smirnov, R. Kormunin.

LIFE BLOOD

A Mikado/Pablo release of a Sidecar Films & TV production. (International sales: Pablo-Intrafilm, Rome.) Producer: Maurizio Tini. Director: Edouardo Winspeare. Screenplay: Giorgia Cecere, Winspeare. Camera: Paolo Carnera. Editor: Luca Benedetti. Music: Gruppo Zoe. In color. Release date: May 30, 2000. Running time: 95 Min. ITALIAN.

Cast: Pino Zimba, Lamberto Probo, Claudio Giangreco, Alessandro Valenti, Ivan Verardo, Lucia Chiuri, Addolorata Turco, Nico Cirasola.

LIFE HURTS

A Filmcontract production in association with TVP, Agencja Produkcji Filmowej Komitetu Kinematografii. (International sales: Gutek Film, Warsaw.) Producer: Henryk Romanowski. Director: Lech Majewski. Screenplay: Majewski, Maciej Melecki. Camera: Adam Sikora. Editor: Eliot Ems. In B&W. Release date: Jan. 30, 2000. Running time: 95 Min. POLISH.

Cast: Krzysztof Siwczyk, Dominika Ostalowska, Elzbieta Okupska, Andrzej Mastalerz.

THE LIFE OF THE JEWS IN PALESTINE

A Jerusalem Film Archive presentation, in association with the Archives du Film of Centre National de la Cinematographie, Bois d'Arcy, Cinematheque Francaise and Israel Film Archive, of a HaMizrah Society production. Producer/Director: Noah Sokolovsky. Camera: Miron Osip Grossman. In B&W. Release date: July 24, 2000. Running time: 78 Min. Documentary. RUSSSIAN–ARCHIVAL.

LIGHT KEEPS ME COMPANY

A Beluga Film, Sandrew Metronome, Svensk Filmindustri, SVT Drama (Sweden)/Nordisk Film (Denmark) production. (International sales: Swedish Film Institute, Stockholm.) Producers: Gudrun and Carl-Gustaf Nykvist. Co-producers: Klas Olofsson, Lars Blomgren, Gunnar Carlsson. Director: Carl-Gustaf Nykvist. Screenplay: Michael Leszcylowski, Carl-Gustaf Nykvist, Gudrun Nykvist. Camera: Carl-Gustaf Nykvist, Sven Nykvist, Dan Myhrman, Vilmos Zsigmond, Kidd Johnson, Laszlo Kovacs, Gustaf Mandal, Billy WIlliams, Torbjorn Andersson, Michael Green, Bjorn Henriksson, Lennart Adell, Arne Carlsson. Editor: Lass Summanen. Music: Mynta, Gudrun Nykvist, Kasper Lindgren, An Blom, Peter Hennix. In color and B&W. Release date: Feb. 6, 2000. Running time: 78 Min. Documentary. SWEDISH-DANISH.

LIKE A MAGNET

A Mars Films release of a Why Not Prods. production for Le Studio Canal Plus, Eskwad, La Societe 361. Producer: Richard Granpierre. Director/Screenplay: Kamel Saleh, Akhenaton. Camera: Denis Rouden. Editor: Fabrice Salinie. Music: Bruno Coulais, Akhenaton. In color. Release date: June 6, 2000. Running time: 90 Min. FRENCH.

Cast: Kamel Saleh, Houari Djerir, Brahim Aimad, Sofiane Madjid Mammeri, Kamel Ferrat, Titoff, Akhenaton, Malek Brahimi.

A LINGERING FACE

A Beijing Film Studio, China Film Corp., Center for Satellite Broadcasting production. (International sales: the Company of Chinese Film Group, Beijing.) Producers: Han Sanping, Tong Gang. Executive producers: Cao Wei, Tian Yuping. Director: Lu Xuechang. Screenplay: Lu, Li Jixian. Camera: Wang Yu. Editor: Kong Leujin. Music: Nathan McCree. Release date: Aug. 3, 2000. Running time: 94 Min. CHINESE.

Cast: Ma Xiaoqing, Pan Yueming, Li Min, Ge Yaming, He Xi.

LITTLE CHEUNG

A Meteor Independent (Hong Kong)/NHK Japan Broadcasting Corp. production. (International sales: Golden Network, Hong Kong.) Executive producers: Doris Yang, Makoto Ueda. Director/Screenplay: Fruit Chan. Camera: Lam Wah-chuen. Editor: Tin Sam-fat. Music: Lam, Chu Hing-cheung. In color. Release date: Nov. 26, 1999. Running time: 118 Min. HONG KONG-JAPANESE.

Cast: Yiu Yuet-ming, Mak Wai-fan, Mak Yuet-man, Chu Sun-yau.

LITTLE DARLING

A Tadrart Films release of a 3B Prods./Arte France Cinema/Ognon Pictures production, with participation of Canal Plus, GAN Cinema Foundation. (International sales: Celluloid Dreams, Paris.) Producers: Jean Brehat, Rachid Bouchareb. Director: Anne Villaceque. Screenplay: Villaceque, Elisabeth Barriere-Marquet. Camera: Pierre Milon. Editor: Anne Riegel. In color, widescreen. Release date: May 2, 2000. Running time: 108 Min. FRENCH.

Cast: Corinne Debonniere, Jonathan Zaccai, Laurence Fevrier, Patrick Prejean.

THE LITTLE VAMPIRE

A New Line Cinema release (in U.S.)/Icon release (in U.K.) of a Cometstone Pictures presentation of a Comet Film (German)/ Stonewood Communications (Netherlands) production, in association with Avrora Media (Germany) and Propaganda Films. (International sales: New Line Intl., Los Angeles.) Producer: Richard Claus. Executive producers: Alexander Buchman, Anthony Waller, Larry Wilson. Co-producers: Klaus Bauschulte, Carsten Lorenz. Director: Uli Edel. Screenplay: Karey Kirkpatrick, Larry Wilson, based on the "The Little Vampire" novels by Angela Sommer-Bodenburg. Camera: Bernd Heinl. Editor: Peter R. Adam. Music: Nigel Clarke, Michael Csanyi-Wills. In Geyer Werke color. Release date: Aug. 18, 2000. Running time: 97 Min. GERMAN-DUTCH.

Cast: Jonathan Lipnicki, Richard E. Grant, Jim Carter, Alice Krige, Rollo Weeks, John Wood, Pamela Gidley, Tommy Hinkley.

LITTLE VILMA: THE LAST DIARY

A Dialog Studio (Hungary)/EuroArts Entertainment (Germany)/Akson Studio (Poland) production, in association with Canal Plus (Poland). (International sales: S-media 2000, Budapest.) Producers: Csaba Bereczki, Karoly Makk, Bernd Hellthaler, Michal Kwieczinski. Director: Marta Meszaros. Screenplay: Meszaros, Eva Pataki. Camera: Myika Jancso. Editor: Cezary Grzesiuk. Music: various. In color. Release date: Feb. 6, 2000. Running time: 115 Min. HUNGARIAN-GERMAN-POLISH.

Cast: Jan Nowicki, Barbara Hegyi, Kitty Keri, Lukas Nowiczki, Cleo Ladanyi, Lili Monori.

THE LITTLE VOYAGE

A Zsebcselek Csoport production in association with MMK, ORTT, MAFSZ. Producers: Gyorgy Czaban, Mihaly Buzas. Director: Mihaly Buzas. Screenplay: Buzas, Zoltan Korosi, Gyorgy Palos. Camera: Palos. Editor: Mihaly Buzas. Music: Zoltan Vegso. In color. Release date: Feb. 6, 2000. Running time: 95 Min. HUNGARIAN.

Cast: Jozsef Gyabronka, Arnold Farkas, Jozsef Szikra, Imola Gaspar, Nora Cseszarik, Erzsebet Dozsa.

LIVE VIRGIN

A Granite Releasing release (in U.S.) of a Vertigo Prods./M6 Films production with participation of TPS. (International sales: CLT/Ufa Intl., Luxembourg.) Producers: Aissa Djabri, Farid Lahouassa, Manuel Munz. Co-producer: Aladdin Pojhan. Executive producer: Jean-Pierre Marois. Director: Jean-Pierre Marois. Screenplay: Marois, Ira Israel. Camera: Agle Egilsson. Editor: Georges Klotz. Music: Czerkinsky. In color. Release date: June 26. 2000. Running time: 88 Min. FRENCH.

Cast: Bob Hoskins, Robert Loggia, Mena Suvari, Sally Kellerman, Lamont Johnson, Gabriel Mann, Bobbie Phillips, Esai Morales.

LOOKING FOR ALIBRANDI

A Roadshow release of an Australian Film Finance Corp. presentation of a Miall & Kershaw production, in association with Showtime Australia, NSW Film & TV Office, Beyond Films, Sydney. Producer: Robyn Kershaw. Executive producer: Tristram Miall. Director: Kate Woods. Screenplay: Melina Marchetta, based on her novel. Camera: Toby Oliver. Editor: Martin Connor. Music: Alan John. In Atlab color. Release date: Apr. 4, 2000. Running time: 102 Min. AUSTRALIAN.

Cast: Pia Miranda, Greta Scaachi, Anthony LaPaglia, Elena Cotta, Kerry Walker, Kick Gurry, Matthew Newton, Leanne Carlow.

LONERS

A CinemArt release (in Czech Republic) of a Lucky Man Films production, in association with CinemArt, Czech Television, E-Motion Film. (International sales: Lucky Man Films, Prague.) Producer: David Ondricek. Executive producers: Radek Auer, Robert Vicek. Co-producers: Jaroslav Kucera, Iva Prochazkova. Director: David Ondricek. Screenplay: Petr Zelenka, from a story by Olga Dabrowska, Zelenka. Camera: Richard Rericha. Editor: Michal Lansky. Music: Jan P. Muchow. Release date: July 26, 2000. Running time: 104 Min. CZECH.

Cast: Labina Mitevska, Jitka Schneiderova, Sasa Rasilov, Jiri Machacek, Ivan Trojan, Miki Kren, Dana Sedlakova.

THE LONG HOLIDAY

A Public Film release of a Pieter van Huystee Film & TV production. (International sales: Ideale Audience Distribution, Paris.) Producers: Pieter van Huystee, Sylvia Baan. Director/Screenplay: Johan van der Keuken. Camera: van der Keuken. Editor: Menno Boerema. In color. Release date: Feb. 2, 2000. Running time: 140 Min. Documentary. DUTCH.

LONG LIVE US!

A Gemini Films release of a Gemini Films/Felix Films/France 2 Cinema production, with participation of Canal Plus and CNC. (International sales: Gemini, Paris.) Producer: Paulo Branco. Director/Screenplay: Camille de Casabianca. Camera: Renato Berta. Editor: Morgane Spacagna. Music: Alexandre Desplat. In color. Release date: Feb. 18, 2000. Running time: 93 Min. FRENCH.

Cast: Dieudonne, Camille de Casabianca, Michele Bernier, Daniel Prevost, Emmanuelle Devos, Thibault de Montalembert, Pascal Elbe.

LOOK AT ME

A Filmauro Distribuzione release (in Italy) of a Luigi and Aurelio De Laurentiis presentation of a Trio Film production. (International sales: Filmexport Group, Rome.) Producers: Giuseppe Perugia, Alessandro Giachetti. Executive producer: Piero Amati. Director/Screenplay: Davide Ferrario. Camera: Giovanni Cavallini. Editor: Claudio Cormio. Music: Giorgio Canali. In Cinecitta color. Release date: Sept. 7, 1999. Running time: 95 Min. ITALIAN.

Cast: Elisabetta Cavallotti, Stefania Orsola Garello. Flavio Insinna, Gianluca Gobbi, Claudio Spadaro, Anglica Ippolito, Luigi Diberti.

LOST KILLERS

A Home Run Pictures, Rommel Film co-production with backing from MFG Baden-Wurttemberg, BKM, Filmboard Berlin-Brandenberg and support form ZDF/Arte. (International sales: Christa Saredi, Zurich.) Producer: Peter Rommel. Executive producer: Monika Kintner. Director/Screenplay: Dito Tsintsadze. Camera: Benedict Neuenfels. Editor: Stephan Krumbiegel. Music: Dito Tsintsadze & Mirian, Udo Schobel, Adrian Sherwood, Skip McDonald. In color. Release date: May 17, 2000. Running time: 97 Min. GERMAN.

Cast: Nicole Seelig, Misel Maticevic, Lasha Bakradze.

THE LOST LOVER

A Mikado Film release (in Italy) of a Jean Vigo Italis/Mikado Film(Rome)/Steel Pcitures (London) production in association with RAI Television, British Screen, British Sky Broadcasting, TelePiu. (International sales: Studio Canal Plus.) Producer: Elda Ferri. Director: Roberto Faenza. Screenplay: Sandro Petraglia, Faenza, based on a novel by Abraham B. Yehoshua. Camera: Jose Luis Alcaine. Editor: Massimo Fiocchi. Music: Paolo Buonvino. In color, Cinemascope. Release date: Oct. 11, 1999. Running time: 97 Min. ITALIAN-BRITISH.

Cast: Ciaran Hinds, Juliet Aubrey, Stuart Bunce, Phyllida Law, Erick Vazquez, Clara Bryant.

A LOVE

A Pablo release of a Gianluca Arcopinto production in association with RAI Radiotelevisione Italiana. (International sales: Intrafilms, Rome.) Producer: Gianluca Arcopinto. Director: Gianluca Maria Tavarelli. Screenplay: Tavarelli, with collaboration of Leonardo Fasoli. Camera: Pietro Sciortino. Editor: Marco Spoletini. Music: Ezio Bosso. In Augustus color. Release date: Feb. 3, 2000. Running time: 98 Min. ITALIAN.

Cast: Lorenza Indovina, Fabrizio Gifuni, Luciano Federico, Roberta Lena, Riccardo Montanaro, Ezio Sega, Benedetta Francardo.

LOVE AND HATE

A Mezhrabpomfilm (Moscow) production. Director: Albert Gendelstein. Screenplay: Sergei Ermolinsky, Vasili Pronin. Camera: Pronin. Music: Dmitri Shostakovich. In B&W. Release date: Aug. 3, 2000. Running time: 80 Min. SOVIET UNION–1935

Cast: Emma Tsesarskaya, A. Chistyakov, V. Maretskaya, N. Kryuchkov, V. Stanitsyn, M. Kedrov, V. Popova, Boris Barnet.

LOVE & RAGE

A J&M Entertainment presentation of an Isle of Man Film Commission, Nova Films (U.K.)/Irish Film Board, Cathal Black Prods. (Ireland)/Schlemmer Film (Germany) production. (International sales: J&M Entertainment, London.) Producers: Rudolph Wishmann, Cathal Black. Director: Cathal Black. Screenplay: Brian Lynch, based on the novel "The Playboy and the Yellow Lady" by James Carney. Camera: Slawomir Idziak. Editors: Ulrike Leopold, Emer Reynolds. Music: Ralf Wienrich. In color. Release date: Aug. 29, 1999. Running time: 100 Min. BRITISH-IRISH-GERMAN.

Cast: Greta Scacchi, Daniel Craig, Stephen Dillane, Valerie Edmond.

LOVE AT FIRST HICCOUGH

A Regner Grasten Film production in association with TV2/Denmark, Danish Film Institute. (International sales: Nordisk Film, Copenhagen.) Producer: Regner Grasten. Director/Screenplay: Tomas Villum Jensen. Camera: Dirk Bruel. Editor: Thomas Krag. Music: Innocent Blood. In color. Release date: Feb. 14, 2000. Running time: 83 Min. DANISH.

Cast: Sofie Lassen Kahlke, Robert Hansen, Karl Bille, Mira Wanting.

LOVE AT FIRST SIGHT

A Cecchi Gori Distribuzione release (in Italy) of a Mario and Vittorio Cecchi Gori presentation of a Cecchi Gori Entertainment Europa production. Producer: Vittorio Cecchi Gori. Executive producer: Alessandro Calosci. Director/Screenplay: Vincenzo Salemme. Camera: Mauro Marchetti. Editor: Patrizio Marrone. Music: Pino Daniele. In Cinecitta color. Release date: Oct. 21, 1999. Running time: 87 Min. ITALIAN.

Cast: Vincenzo Salemme, Mandala Tayde, Carlo Buccirosso, Naurizio Casagrande, Nando Paone, Biagio Izzo, Tosca D'Aquino.

LOVE, HONOUR AND OBEY

A UIP (U.K.) release of a BBC Films presentation of a Fugitive production. (International sales: The Sales Co., London.) Producers: Dominic Anciano, Ray Burdis. Executive producers: David M. Thompson, Jane Tranter, Jim Beach. Director/Screenplay: Dominic Anciano, Ray Burdis. Camera: John Ward. Editor: Rachel Meyrick. In Deluxe color. Release date: Jan. 27, 2000. Running time: 103 Min. BRITISH.

Cast: Sadie Frost, Ray Winstone, Jonny Lee Miller, Jude Law.

LOVE INVENTORY

A Muse production, in association with Noga Communications and JCS Content. Producer: Yahaly Gat. Director/Screenplay: David Fisher. Camera: Itzik Portal. Editor: Tali Halter SHenkar. Music: Amnon Fisher, Doron Shenkar. In color. Release date: July 18, 2000. Running time: 90 Min. Documentary. ISRAELI.

LOVE ME

A Pyramide release of a Les Films Alain Sarde production. (International sales: Flach Pyramide Intl., Paris.) Producer: Alain Sarde. Executive producer: Nicolas Daguet. Director/Screenplay: Laetitia Masson. Camera: Antoine Heberle. Editor: Ailo Auguste. Music: John Cale. In color. Release date: Feb. 16, 2000. Running time: 107 Min. FRENCH.

Cast: Sandrine Kiberlain, Johnny Hallyday, Jean-Francois Stevenin, Anh Duong, Julie Depardieu, Christine Boisson, Julian Sands.

LOVER'S GRIEF OVER THE YELLOW RIVER
A Shanghai Paradise Film & TV Group production. (International sales: Shanghai Paradise Film & TV Company.) Producer: Yang Yubing. Executive producer: Jiang Ping. Director/Screenplay: Feng Xiaoning. Camera: Feng, Gang Qiang. Editor: Feng Sihai. Music: Li Ge. Release date: Jan. 19, 2000. Running time: 110 Min. CHINESE.
Cast: Ning Jing, Paul Kersey, Wang Xinjun, Tu Men.

LOVE'S A BITCH
An Alta Vista Films presentation of a Zeta Film/Alta Vista Films production. (International sales: Lions Gate Films Intl., L.A.) Producer: Alejandro Gonzalez Inarritu. Executive producers: Martha Sosa Elizondo, Francisco Gonzalez Compean. Director: Alejandro Gonzalez Inarritu. Screenplay: Guillermo Arriaga Jordan. Camera: Rodrigo Prieto. Editors: Gonzalez Inarritu, Luis Carballar, Fernando Perez Unda. Music: Gustavo Santaolatta. In color. Release date: May 14, 2000. Running time: 153 Min. MEXICO.
Cast: Emilio Echevarria, Gael Garcia Bernal, Goya Toledo.

LOVE'S LABOUR'S LOST
A Pathe Pictures (in U.K.)/Miramax (in U.S.) release of an Intermedia Films and Pathe Pictures presentation, in association with the Arts Council of England, Le Studio Canal Plus and Miramax Films, of a Shakespeare Film Co. production. (International sales: Intermedia, London.) Producers: David Barron, Kenneth Branagh. Executive producers: Guy East, Nigel Sinclair, Alexis Lloyd, Harvey Weinstein, Bob Weinstein. Director/Screenplay: Kenneth Branagh, based on the play by William Shakespeare. Camera: Alex Thomson. Editors: Neil Farrell, Dan Farrell. Music: Patrick Doyle. In Technicolor, Panavision widescreen. Release date: Feb. 14, 2000. Running time: 93 Min. BRITISH.
Cast: Alessandro Nivola, Alicia Silverstone, Natascha McElhone, Kenneth Branagh, Carmen Ejogo, Matthew Lillard, Adrian.

LOVE STORY
A Women Making Movies release of a British Broadcasting production. Producer/Director: Catrine Clay. Camera: Ken Morse. Editor: Edward Roberts. Release date: Jan. 23, 2000. Running time: 48 Min. Documentary. BRITISH.
Narrator: Sara Kestleman.

LOVE TORN IN DREAM
A Madragoa Filmes and Gemini Films co-production in association with Canal Plus, Radiotelevisao Portuguesa, Instituto do Cinema, Audiovisual e Multimedia Fundacao Cultursintra, Camera Municipal de Sintra, Quinta Regaleira. Producer: Paulo Branco. Executive producers: Branco, Valentina Merli, Laurent Baudens. Director/Screenplay: Raoul Ruiz. Camera: Acacio de Almeida. Editor: Valeria Sarmiento. Music: Jorge Arriaga. Release date: Aug. 29, 2000. Running time: 126 Min. CHILEAN-PORTUGUESE-FRENCH.
Cast: Melvil Poupaud, Elsa Zylberstein, Lambert Wilson, Christian Vadim, Diogo Doria, Rogerio Samora, Marie-France Pisier.

THE LOW DOWN
A FilmFour and British Screen presentation, in association with Bozie, of an Oil Factory/Sleeper Films production. (International sales: FilmFour, London.) Producers: John Stewart, Sally Llewellyn. Director/Screenplay: Jamie Thraves. Camera: Igor Jadue-Lillo. Editor: Lucia Zucchetti. Music: Nick Currie, Fred Thomas. In Metrocolor. Release date: Aug. 6, 2000. Running time: 96 Min. BRITISH.
Cast: Aidan Gillen, Kate Ashfield, Kean Lennox Kelly, Tobias Menzies, Rupert Proctor, Samantha Powers, Deanna Smiles.

LOW SELF ESTEEM GIRL
A Blue Curtain (Vancouver) production. Producer: Aaron Lake. Director/Screenplay/Editor: Blaine Thurier. Camera: Thurier. Music: Sun City Girls, Destroyer, Superconductor. In color, video. Release date: June 25, 2000. Running time: 96 Min. CANADIAN.
Cast: Corrina Hammond, Rob McBeth, Ted Dave, Cindy Wolfe.

LULU KREUTZ'S PICNIC
A Les Films du Losange release of a JM Compagnie, France 3 Cinema, Rhone Alpes Cinema production, with participation of Canal Plus, CNC, Procirep. (International sales: Films Distribution, Paris.) Producer: Jean-Philippe Reza. Director: Didier Martiny. Screenplay: Yasmina Reza. Camera: Francois Catonne. Editor: Joelle van Effenterre. Music: extracts from Schumann and J.S. Bach. In color. Release date: Feb. 29, 2000. Running time: 100 Min. FRENCH.
Cast: Philippe Noiret, Carole Bouquet, Niels Arestrup, Stephane Audran, Michel Aumont, Judith Magre, Johan Leysen.

LUMUMBA
An Ocean release (in France)/Cinelux (in Benelux) of a JBA Prods (France)/Entre Chien et Loup (Belgium)/Essential Filmproduktion (Germany)/Velvet S.A.(Haiti)/Arte France Cinema (France)/RTBF (Belgium) production. (International sales: Art Box, Paris.) Producer: Jacques Bidou. Director: Raoul Peck. Screenplay: Peck, Pascal Bonitzer. Camera: Bernard Lutic. Editor: Jacques Comets. Music: Jean-Claude Petit. In color. Release date: May 14, 2000. Running time: 115 Min. FRENCH-BELGIAN-GERMAN-HAITIAN.
Cast: Eriq Ebouaney, Alex Descas, Theophile Moussa Sowie.

THE LUNATICS' BALL
A Platinum Glass Studios production. (International sales: New Zealand Film Commission.) Producer: Michael Thorp. Co-producer: Jamie Selkirk. Director/Screenplay: Michael Thorp. Camera: Neil Cervin. Editors: Mike Horton, Paul Sutorius. Music: Peter Scholes. In Atlab color. Release date: Jan. 19, 2000. Running time: 85 Min. NEW ZEALAND.
Cast: Russel Walder, Jane Irwin, Sara Ashworth, Alan De Malmanche, Jamie Martin.

THE LUZHIN DEFENCE
An Entertainment Film Distributors (in U.K.)/Sony Pictures Classics (in U.S.) release of a Renaissance Films presentation, in association with Clear Blue Sky Prods., of a Renaissance Films (U.K.)/ICE3(France) production, in association with Lantia Cinema, Magic Media, France 2 Cinema. (International sales: Renaissance, London.) Producers: Caroline Wood, Stephen Evans, Louis Becker, Philippe Guez. Executive producer: Jody Patton. Co-producers: Leo Pescarolo, Eric Robison. Director: Marleen Gorris. Screenplay: Peter Berry, based on the novel by Vladimir Nabakov. Camera: Bernard Lutic. Editor: Michael Reichwein. Music: Alexandre Desplat. In Technicolor. Release date: Aug. 21, 2000. Running time: 108 Min. BRITISH-FRENCH.
Cast: John Turturro, Emily Watson, Stuart Wilson, Christopher Thompson, Fabio Sartor, Peter Blythe, Orla Brady, Mark Tandy.

MAD COWS
An Entertainment Film Distributors release (in U.K.) of a Capitol Films, Fewmarket Capital Group and Entertainment Distributors presentation of a Flashlight Films production. (International sales: Capitol, London.) Producers: Frank Mannion, Aaron Simpson. Executive producers: Sharon Harel, Jane Barclay, Chris J. Ball, WIlliam Tyrer. Co-producer: Liz Bunton. Director: Sara Sugarman. Screenplay: Sugarman, Sasha Hails, based on the novel by Kathy Lette. Camera: Pierre Aim. Editor: John Jympson. Original music: Mark Thomas. In Technicolor. Release date: Oct. 30, 1999. Running time: 90 Min. BRITISH.
Cast: Anna Friel, Joanna Lumley, Anna Massey, Phyllida Law, Greg Wise, John Standing, Nicholas Woodeson, Prunella Scales.

MAELSTROM
An Alliance Atlantis Pictures Intl. presentation of a Max Films production in association with Telefilm Canada and Sodec. Producers: Roger Frappier, Luc Vandal. Director/Screenplay: Denis Villeneuve. Camera: Andre Turpin. Editor: Richard Comeau. Music: Pierre Desrochers. In color. Release date: Aug. 30, 2000. Running time: 95 Min. CANADIAN-NORWEGIAN.
Cast: Marie-Josee Croze, Jean-Nicholas Verreault, Stephanie Morgenstern, Pierre LeBeau, Marc Gelinas, Klimbo, Bobby Beshro.

MAGIK AND ROSE
A Kahukura Prods. production, in association with New Zealand Film Commission. (International sales: New Zealand Film Commission, Wellington.) Producer: Larry Parr. Director/Screenplay: Vanessa Alexander. Camera: Fred Renata. Editor: Eric de Beus. Music: Victoria Kelly. In color. Release date: May 15, 2000. Running time: 92 Min. NEW ZEALAND.
Cast: Alison Bruce, Nicola Murphy, Oliver Driver, Simon Ferry.

A MAJOR INCONVENIENCE
A SND release of a Les Films de la Boissiere/France 3 Cinema production, with participation of Canal Plus. (International sales: Artbox, Paris.) Producer: Annie Miller. Director by Bernard Stora. Screenplay: Stora, GIlles Taurand. Camera: Gerard de Battista. Editor: Jacques Comets. Music: Bruno Coulais. In color. Release date: Feb. 24, 2000. Running time: 112 Min. FRENCH.
Cast: Jalil Lespert, Mireille Perrier, Chantal Banlier, Clement Sibony.

THE MAKING OF A NEW EMPIRE
Lava Film Distribution & Sales presents a Stichting Jura Film Production, in association with NPS. (International sales: Films Transit, Montreal.) Producers: Ruud Monster, Jan Heijs. Director/Screenplay: Jos de Putter. Camera: Andrzej Adamczak. Editors: Danniel Danniel, Puck Goossen. Music: Vincent van Warmerdam. In color. Release date: Sept. 10, 1999. Running time: 95 min. Documentary. DUTCH.

MALLBOY
A Buena Vista (in Australia) release of an Australian Film Commission/ SBS Independent/Showtime Australia presentation of a Twenty 20 production. (International sales: Beyond Films, Sydney.) Producer: Fiona Eagger. Director/Screenplay: Vincent Giarrusso. Camera: Brendan Lavelle. Editor: Mark Atkin. Music: Giarrusso, Glenn Bennie. Release date: May 16, 2000. Running time: 84 Min. AUSTRALIAN.
Cast: Kane McNay, Nell Feeney, Brett Swain, Brett Tucker.

MALLI
A Children's Film Society, India, production. (International sales: Children's Film Society, Mumbai, India.) Director: Santosh Sivan. Screenplay: Sivan, Ravi Deshpande, based on a story by Sivan; dialogue: C.K. Raja, Chandrashekhar. Camera: Sivan. Editor: Sreekar Prasad. Music: Aslam Mustafa. In color. Release date: Sept. 11, 1999. Running time: 87 Min. INDIAN.
Cast: Swetha, Vanitha, Janakraj, Parameshwaran, Baby Amma, Priya.

MALOU MEETS INGMAR BERGMAN AND ERLAND JOSEPHSON
A TV4 (Sweden) production. (International sales: TV4, Stockholm.) Producers: Katarina Malmer. Host: Malou von Sivers. Editors: Sofia Owenmark, Sebastian Bank, Stefan Brann. Release date: May 13, 2000. Running time: 52 Min. Documentary. SWEDISH.
With: Ingmar Bergman, Erland Josephson, Malou von Sivers.

A MAN CALLED HERO

A Golden Harvest release (in Hong Kong) of a GH Pictures (China)/Centro Digital Pictures/Bob & Partners Co. production, in association with Sil-Metropole Organization, China Film Co-production Corp. and Shanghai Film Studio. (International sales: Golden Harvest, Hong Kong.) Producers: Raymond Chow, John Chu. Executive producers: Barbie Tung, Manfred Wong. Director: Andrew Lau. Screenplay: Manfred Wong, based on the manga by Ma Song-shing. Camera: Lau. Editor: Pang Fat. Music: Chan Kwong-wing. Release date: Nov. 2, 1999. Running time: 118 Min. HONG KONG.

Cast: Ekin Cheng, Shu Qi, Kristy Yang, Nicholas Tse, Yuen Biao, Jerry Lamb, Dion Lam, Anthony Wong, Elvis Tsui, Harold Low, Grace Yip, Francis Ng.

MANHOOD AND OTHER MODERN DILEMMAS

A Blue Dahlia/France 3 Cinema production, with participation of Canal Plus and Studio Images 6. (International sales: Films Distribution, Paris.) Producer: Gerard Jourd'hui. Director/Screenplay: Ronan Girre. Camera: Dominique Colin. Editor: Anna Ruiz. Music: Girre. In color. Release date: June 23, 2000. Running time: 92 Min. FRENCH.

Cast: Bruno Putzulu, Estelle Skornik, Emmanuelle Meyssignac, Sandrine Le Berre, Olga Sekulic, Philippe Nahon, Yse Tran.

MANILA

A Senator release of a Pantera Film, Cobra Film, Senator Film production. (International sales: Bavaria Film Intl., Munich.) Producer: Romuald Karmakar. Co-producers: Renate Seefeldt, Gerd Huber, Hanno Huth. Director: Romuald Karmakar. Screenplay: Bodo Kirchhoff, Karmakar. Camera: Fred Schuler. Editor: Peter Przygodda. Music: various. Release date: Aug. 9, 2000. Running time: 114 Min. GERMAN.

Cast: Juergen Vogel, Michael Degen, Chin-Chin Gutierrez, Ana Capri, Peter Ruehring, Margit Carstensen, Manfred Zapatka, Sky Du Mont.

MAN OF STEEL

A VCKJ release (in Belgium) of a Favourite Films production. (International sales: Brussels Ave., Brussels.) Producers: Dirk Impens, Rudy Verzyck. Director/Screenplay: Vincent Bal. Camera: Glynn Speeckaert. Editor: Ewin Ryckaert. Music: Wim de Wilde. In color. Release date: Oct. 8, 1999. Running time: 82 Min. BELGIAN.

Cast: Ides Meire, Charlotte de Ruyter, Peter Gorissen.

THE MAN WHO CRIED

A Universal Focus release of a Working Title/Adventure Pictures/PIE/Studio Canal Plus production. (International sales: Studio Canal Plus, Paris.) Producer: Christopher Sheppard. Executive producers: Tim Bevan, Eric Fellner, Simona Benzakein. Director/Screenplay: Sally Potter. Camera: Sacha Vierny. Editor: Herve Schneid. Music: Osvaldo Golijov. In color. Release date: Sept. 2, 2000. Running time: 99 Min. BRITISH-FRENCH.

Cast: Christina Ricci, Cate Blanchett, John Turturro, Johnny Depp, Harry Dean Stanton, Claudia Lander-Duke, Oleg Yankovsky.

THE MARCORELLE AFFAIR

A Euripe Prods./Rhone-Alpes Cinema production, with participation of Canal Plus, the Rhone-Alpes Region and CNC. Producer: Vincent Roget. Co-executive producers: Daniel Toscan du Plantier, Frederic Sichler. Director/Screenplay: Serge Le Peron. Camera: Ivan Kozelka. Editor: Janice Jones. Music: Antoine Duhamel. In color. Release date: Apr. 27, 2000. Running time: 96 Min. FRENCH.

Cast: Jean-Pierre Leaud, Irene Jacob, Mathieu Amalric, Philippe Khorsand, Dominique Reymond, Helene Surgere.

MARLENE

A Senator Film release of a Trebitsch Produktion Intl./Perathon Film production, in association with ZDF, RAI, Studio Babelsberg. (International sales: Amberlon Pictures, London.) Producers: Katharina M. Trebitsch, Jutta Lieck-Klenke. Executive producer: Joseph Vilsmaier. Director: Joseph Vilsmaier. Screenplay: Christian Pfannenschmidt, based on factual material from the book "Marlene Dietrich by Her Daughter" by Maria Riva. Camera: Vilsmaier. Editors: Barbara Hennings, Gabi Kroeber. Music: Harald Kloser. In FotoKem color, widescreen. Release date: May 13, 2000. Running time: 132 Min. GERMAN.

Cast: Katja Flint, Herbert Knaup, Heino Ferch, Hans-Werner Meyer, Christiane Paul, Suzanne von Borsody, Armin Rhode.

MARTA AND SURROUNDINGS

An Alta Films release of a Clave Producciones/ALta Films production, in association with EPC, Cherokee Luz, Canal Plus. (International sales: Alta, Madrid.) Producers: Belen Bernuy, Enrique Gonzalez Macho. Director/Screenplay: Nacho Perez de la Paz, Jesus Ruiz. Camera: Alfonso Sanz. Editor: Fernando Pardo. Music: Lucio Godoy. In color. Release date: Jan. 25, 2000. Running time: 108 Min. SPANISH.

Cast: Marta Belaustegui, Tristan Ulloa, Lola Duenas, Roberto Enriquez, Maria Jose Millan, Nieve de Medina, Sergi Calleja.

MARTYR-IN-LOVE, BOOTA SINGH

A Sain Prods. (Mumbai) production. Producer: Manjeet Maan. Executive producer: Anil Pandit. Director: Manoj Punj. Screenplay: Suraj Sanim. Camera: Pramod Mittal. Editor: Omkar Bhakri. Music director: Amar Haldipur. In color, widescreen. Release date: Sept. 29, 1999. Running time: 130 Min. INDIAN.

Cast: Gurdas Mann, Divya Dutta, Aroon Bakshi, Raghubeer Yadav, Yograj Chedda, Darshan Aulakh, Hari Om Jalota, Gurkitan.

MASHENKA

A Mosfilm production. Director: Yuli Raizman. Screenplay: Evgeni Gabrilovich, Sergei Ermolinsky. Camera: Evgeni Andrikanis. Music: B. Volsky. In B&W. Release date: Aug. 6, 2000. Running time: 77 Min. SOVIET UNION–1942.

Cast: Valentina Karavayeva, Mikhail Kuznetsov, D. Pankratova, Vera Altaiskaya, Georgi Svetlanin.

MASK OF DESIRE

A Milo Prods. and NHK (Japan Broadcasting Corp.) production. Producers: Tsering Rhitar Sherpa, Lobsang Tsultrim. Ang Kusang Sherpa, Sampa Lama. Executive producers: Makoto Ueda, Keiko Iino. Director: Twering Rhitar Sherpa. Screenplay: Kesang Tseten, based on a story by Tseten, Sherpa. Camera: Ranjan Palit. Editor: Reena Mohan. Music: Nhyoo Bajacharya. In color. Release date: Apr. 11, 2000. Running time: 105 Min. NEPALESE-JAPANESE.

Cast: Gauri Malla, Mithila Sharma, Ratan Subedi, Nirmal Pyakurel, Rama Thapalia.

MATRONI AND ME

An Alliance Atlantis Releasing release (in Canada) of a Max films production. (International sales: Alliance Atlantis Pictures Intl., Los Angeles.) Producers: Roger Frappier, Luc Vandal. Director: Jean-Philippe Duval. Screenplay: Duval, Alexis Martin, based on the play by Martin. Camera: Andre Turpin. Editor: Alain Baril. Music: Benoit Charest, Maxime Morin. In color. Release date: Oct. 8, 1999. Running time: 102 Min. CANADIAN.

Cast: Alexis Martin, Guylaine Tremblay, Gary Boudreault, Pierre Lebeau, Maude Guerin, Pierre Curzi, Daniel Briere.

MAYBE

A Warner Bros. Transatlantic release (in France) of a Vertigo Prods., PECF, M6 Films production, with participation of TPS Cinema. (International sales: Flach Pyramide Intl., Paris.) Producers: Aissa Djabri, Rarid Lahouassa, Manuel Munz. Director: Cedric Klapisch. Screenplay: Santiago Amigorena, Alexis Galmot, Klapisch. Camera: Philippe Le Sourd. Editor: Francine Sandberg. Music: Loik Dury, Magister Dixit. In color, widescreen. Release date: Nov. 11, 1999. Running time: 109 Min. FRENCH.

Cast: Romain Duris, Jean-Paul Belmondo, Geraldine Pailhas, Vincent Elbaz, Riton Liebman, Julie Depardieu, Emmanuelle Devos.

MAYBE BABY

A Redbus Film Distribution (in U.K.)/USA Films (in U.S.) release of a Pandora/BBC Films presentation of a Phil McIntyre production. (International sales: Pandora, Paris.) Producer: Phil McIntyre. Executive producers: Ernst Goldschmidt, David M. Thompson. Director/Screenplay: Ben Elton, based on his novel "Inconceivable." Camera: Roger Lanser. Editor: Peter Hollywood. Music: Colin Towns. In Deluxe color. Release date: June 2, 2000. Running time: 104 Min. BRITISH-FRENCH.

Cast: Hugh Laurie, Joely Richardson, Adrian Lester, James Purefoy, Tom Hollander, Joanna Lumley, Rowan Atkinson, Dawn French.

THE MECHANISM

A Horizon 2000/Centar Film production. (International sales: Center Film A.D., Belgrade.) Producer: Ivana Mihic. Executive producer: Miodrag Misa Djordjevic. Director: Djordje Milosavljevic. Screenplay: Gordan Mihic. Camera: Zoran Petrovic. Editor: Marko Glusac. Music: Aleksandar Sasa Habic. In color. Release date: Sept. 1, 2000. Running time: 94 Min. YUGOSLAVIAN.

Cast: Ivana Mihic, Nikola Kojo, Andrej Sepetkovski, Gordan Kicic.

MEMENTO MORI

A Cine 2000 production, in association with Cinema Service. (International sales: Mirovision, Seoul.) Producer: Oh Kimin. Executive producer: Lee Chun-yeon. Director/Screenplay: Kim Tae-yong, Min Kyu-dong. Camera: Kim Yun-su. Editor: Kim Sang-beom. Music: Jo Seong-woo. In color. Release date: Feb. 12, 2000. Running time: 94 Min. SOUTH KOREAN.

Cast: Kim Min-seon, Park Ye-jin, Lee Yeong-jin, Kong Hyo-jin.

MEN ON WINGS

A Mosfilm production. Director: Yuli Raisman. Screenplay: Aleksandr Macheret. Camera: Leonid Kosmatov. Music: Nikolai Kryukov. Release date: Aug. 3, 2000. Running time: 80 Min. SOVIET UNION–1935.

Cast: Boris Shchukin, Ivan Koval-Samborsky, Evgenia Melnikova.

MESSENGERS

A Toho Co. release of a Fuji Television Network/Pony Canyon/ Shogakukan production, in association with Premier Intl. (International sales: Pony Canyon, Tokyo.) Director: Yasuo Baba. Screenplay: Masahi Todayama, story, Hoichoi Prods. Camera: Genkichi Hasegawa. Editor: Takuya Taguchi. Music: Yusuke Honma. In color. Release date: Nov. 28, 1999. Running time: 117 Min. JAPANESE.

Cast: Naoko Iijima, Tsuyoshi Kusanagi, Hiroyuki Yabe, Kotomi Kyono, Yuzo Kayama, Tetsuya Bessho, Shigemitsu Ogi, Shinsuke Kyo.

THE MESSENGER: THE STORY OF JOAN OF ARC

A Sony Pictures Entertainment release (in U.S.) of a Columbia Pictures presentation of a Gaumont production. Producer: Patrice Ledoux. Executive producer: Leeloo Prods. Co-producer: Bernard Grenet. Director: Luc Besson. Screenplay: Andrew Birkin, Besson. Camera: Thierry Arbogast. Editor: Sylvie Landra. Music; Eric Serra. In color, Technovision widescreen. Release date: Oct. 15, 1999. MPAA Rating: R. Running time: 148 Min. FRENCH.

Cast: Milla Jovovich, John Malkovich, Faye Dunaway, Dustin Hoffman, Pascal Greggory, Vincent Cassel, Tcheky Karyo, Richard Ridings.

MESSIAH

A Rezo Films release of a Kuiv/France 2 Cinema production, in association with RAI and the Sacem Action Fund, with participation of Canal Plus, Sofica Gimages, the Mission to Celebrate 2000 in France, Procirep. Producer: Michel Rotman. Director/Screenplay: William Klein. Camera: Klein, Paco Wiser. Pascal Marti. Editor: Francoise Arnaud. Music: Handel's "Messiah." In color. Release date: Dec. 7, 1999. Running time: 117 Min. Documentary. FRENCH.
Cast: Daniel Edinger, Sebastian Gutierrez, Nicholas Savalas, Arjun Spinner.

METADE FUMACA

A Media Asia Distribution release of a Media Asia Films presentation of a United Filmmakers Organization production. (International sales: Media Asia, Hong Kong.) Producers: Thomas Chung, WIllie Chan. Executive producers: Claudie Chung, John Chong, Solon So. Director/Screenplay: Riley Ip (Ip Kamhung). Camera: Peter Pau. Editor: Maruice Li. Music: Chiu Tsang-hei, Lau Chotak. In color. Release date: Nov. 28, 2000. Running time: 101 Min. HONG KONG.
Cast: Eric Tsang, Nicholas Tse, Shu Qi, Kelly Chen, Sandra Ng, Anthony Wong, Terence Yin, Stephen Fung, Sam Lee, Eleaine Jin.

ME, YOU, THEM

A Sony Pictures Classics release of a Conspiracao Filmes/Columbia Pictures production. (International sales: Sony Picutres Classics, New York.) Producers: Leonardo M. De Barros, Pedro B. De Hollanda, Andrucha Waddington, Favio R. Tambelinni. Director: Andrucha Waddington. Screenplay: Elena Soarez. Camera: Breno Silveira. Editor: Vicente Kubrusly. Music: Gilberto Gil. In color, widescreen. Release date: May 16, 2000. Running time: 104 Min. BRAZILIAN.
Cast: Regina Case, Lima Duarte, Stenio Garcia, Luis Carlos Vasconcelos, Nilda Spencer.

MILK

A Sky Pictures presentation, in association with Remil & Associates and Cinequanon Pictures Intl., of an Arcane Pictures production. (International sales: Cinequanon, L.A.) Producers: George Duffield, Galt Niederhoffer, Meg Thomson. Executive producers: Paul Trijbits, Miles Donnelly. Director/Screenplay: Bill Brookfield. Camera: Peter Hannan. Editor: Peter Hollywood. Music: Jools Holland. In color. Release date: Oct. 1, 1999. Running time: 94 Min. BRITISH.
Cast: James Fleet, Phyllida Law, Joss Ackland, Clotilde Coureau, Peter Jones, Francesca Annis, Dawn French, Lelley Manville.

THE MILLION DOLLAR HOTEL

An Icon Entertainment Intl. presentation of a Road Movies production in association with Icon Prods., Kintop Pictures. (International sales: Icon Entertainment, London.) Producers: Deepak Nayar, Bono, Nicholas Klein, Bruce Davey, Wim Wenders. Executive producer: Ulrich Felsberg. Director: Wim Wenders. Screenplay: Nicholas Klein, based on an idea by Bono, Klein. Camera: Phedon Papamichael. Editor: Tatiana S. Riegel. Music: Jon Hassell, Bono, Daniel Lanois, Barian Eno. In FotoKem color, Panavision widescreen. Release date: Feb. 9, 2000. Running time: 122 Min. GERMAN-U.S.
Cast: Jeremy Davies, Milla Jovovich, Mel Gibson, Jimmy Smits, Peter Stormare, Amanda Plummer, Gloria Stuart, Tom Bower, Donal Logue.

THE MIRACLE MAKER

An Icon release (in U.K.) of an S4C Films presentation, with participation of British Screen and Icon Entertainment Intl., in association with BBC Wales, of a Cartwn Cymru (U.K.)/Christmas Films (Russia) production. Producer: Naomi Jones. Executive producer: Christopher Grace. Executive co-producer: Elizabeth Babakhina. Director: Stanislav Sokolov, Derek Hayes. Executive director: Hayes. Screenplay: Murray Watts. Camera: Alexander Vikhanski. Editors: William Oswald, John Richards. Music: Anne Dudley. In Technicolor. Animated. BRITISH-RUSSIAN.
Voices: Ralph Fiennes, Michael Bryant, Julie Christie, Rebecca Callard, James Frain, Richard E. Grant, Ian Holm, William Hurt, Anton Lesser, Daniel Massey, Tim McInnerny, Miranda Richardson.

MIRKA

A Mikado release (in Italy) of a Filmart, Bongiorno Prods., David Prods. (Italy)/DD Prods. (France)/Enrique Cerezo PC Prod. (Spain) production, in association with RAI, Canal Plus, Arcapix, Capitol Films. (International sales: Capitol, London.) Producers: Paolo Boccio, Annamaria Gallone. Executive producers: Jean-Pierre Guerin, Veronique Marchat, Jane Barclay, Sharon Harel. Director/Screenplay: Rachid Benhadj. Camera: Vittorio Storaro. Editor: Anna Napoli. Music: Safy Boutella. In color, Technovision Univisium 1:2 widescreen. Release date: Mar. 3, 2000. Running time: 107 Min. ITALIAN-FRENCH-SPANISH.
Cast: Karim Benhadj, Barbora Bobulova, Vanessa Redgrave, Gerard Depardieu, Sergio Rubini, Franco Nero.

THE MISSING

A Roadshow Film Distributors release (in Australia and New Zealand) of a Jim Stark and Lynda House presentation in association with the Australian Film Finance Corp. and Hollywood Partners of an Upside Down Films-Und Film Produktion production, with the support of Film Victoria. (International sales: G2 Films Lts., London.) Producers: Jim Stark, Lynda House. Executive producers: Hans Huttman, Rudolf Wiesmeier, Sandra Schulberg. Director/Screenplay: Manuela Alberti. Camera: Geoffrey Hall. Editor: Ken Sallows. Music: Bruce Smeaton. In Cinevex color. Release date: Oct. 26, 1999. Running time: 91 Min. AUSTRALIAN-GERMAN.
Cast: Fabrizio Bentivoglio, David Ngoombujarra, John Moore, Rebecca Frith, David Franklin, Fiorenzio Fiorentini, Elise McCredie.

THE MISSING BOY

A Talatta Film Production for Swedish National Television. Producer/Director: Tove Torbiornsson. Camera: Calle Nilsson. Editor: Bernhard Winkler. In color, HD video-to-16mm. Release date: Apr. 29, 2000. Running time: 65 Min. Documentary. SWEDISH.

THE MISSION

An Intl. Films Enterprises presentation of a Milkyway Image (Hong Kong) production. Producer: Chiu Fu-sheng. Executive producer: Johnnie To. Co-producer: Christina Lee. Director: Johnnie To. Executive director: Law Wing-cheong. Screenplay: Yau Naihoi, Milkyway Creative Team. Camera: Cheng Siu-keung. Editor: Andy Chan. Music: Ching Chi-wing. In color, widescreen. Release date: Nov. 22, 1999. Running time: 87 Min. HONG KONG.
Cast: Anthony Wong, Francis Ng, Jackie Lui, Roy Cheung, Lam Suet, Simon Yam, Wong Tin-lan, Ko Hung, Elaine Eca Da Silva, Keiji Sato.

MISTER FEDERMANN

A Jost Hering Filmproduktion, in association with ZDF. (International sales: Jost Hering, Berlin.) Producer: Jost Hering. Executive producer: Anya Grunewald. Director: Christian Diedrichs. Screenplay: Friedrich Ani. Camera: Kurt Schmitz. Editor: Catherine Stegrens. Music: Maurus Ronner. In color, 16mm. Release date: Aug. 29, 1999. Running time: 77 Min. GERMAN.
Cast: Christian Redl, Adelheid Arndt, Teresa Harder, Rolf Zacher, Christos Garyfallakis, Manfred Andrae.

THE MISTRESS

A Wild Horse Prods. production. (International sales: Media Asia Distribution, Hong Kong.) Executive producer, Crystal Kwok. Co-producers, Lawrence Lau, Fiona Lee. Director: Crystal Kwok (Kwok Kamyan.) Screenplay: Kwok, Susan Chan. Camera: Gigo Lee. Editor: Cheung Ka-fai. Music: Charles Valade. In color. Release date: May 11, 2000. Running time: 95 Min. HONG KONG.
Cast: Ray Lui, Moses Chan, Vicky Chen, Jacqueline Peng, Anna Yui, Sarah Hughes, Susan Chan, Dong Yee.

MODERN COMFORTS

A Key Light release of a Key Light production, with participation of CNC and Canal Plus. Producer: Jean-Claude Jean. Director/Screenplay: Dominique Choisy. Camera: Isabelle Czajka. Editor: Laure Blancherie. Music: Philippe Le Baraillec. In color. Release date: June 15, 2000. Running time: 96 Min. FRENCH.
Cast: Nathalie Richard, Valerie Mairesse, Jean-Jacques Vanier.

MODERN LIFE

A Gemini Films release of a Gemini Films, Le Studio Canal Plus, Les Films du Camelia (France)/Light Night Prods. (Switzerland), with participation of Canal Plus, CNC, Cofimages 10, Office Federal de la Culture, Television Suisse Romande. (International sales: Gemini FIlms, Paris.) Producer: Paulo Branco. Director: Laurence Ferreira Barbosa. Screenplay: Ferrieia Barbosa, Yvonne Kerouedan, Bruno Guiblet, Cedric Kahn. Camera: Christophe Beaucarne. Editor: Yann Dedet. Music: Faton Cohen. In color. Release date: Mar. 13, 2000. Running time: 123 Min. FRENCH-SWISS.
Cast: Isabelle Huppert, Frederic Pierrot, Lolita Chammah, Juliette Andrea, Jean-Pierre Gos, Robert Kramer, Aurelien Recoing.

MONDAY

A CineRocket and Media Factory presentation of a CineQuanon production, in association with MME. (International sales: CineQuanon, Tokyo.) Producer: Lee Bong-ou. Director/Screenplay: Sabu. Camera: Kazuhiko Sato. Editor: Kumio Onaga. Music: Keiichiro Shibuya. In color. Release date: Feb. 15, 2000. Running time: 101 Min. JAPANESE.
Cast: Shinichi Tsutsumi, Yasuko Matsuyuki, Ren Osugi, Masanobu Ando, Hideki Noda.

MOON FATHER

A Pandora Film (Cologne)/Prisma Film (Vienna) production in association with Thomas Koerfer Film (Zurich), NTV-Profit (Moscow), Les Films de l'Observatoire (Strasbourg), Euro Space (Tokyo), Viss (Dushanbe), Takjik Filmstudio (Dushanbe). (International sales: Christa Saredi, Zurich.) Producers: Heinz Stussak, Karl Baumgartner. Director: Bakhtiar Khudojnazarov. Screenplay: Irakli Kwirikadze, Khudojnazarov. Camera: Martin Gschlasct, Rotislav Pirumov, Dusan Joksimovic, Rali Ralchev. Editors: Kirk von Heflin, Evi Romen. Music: Daler Nasarov. In color. Release date: Sept. 8, 1999. Running time: 106 Min. GERMAN-AUSTRIAN.
Cast: Chulpan Khamatova, Moritz Bleibtreu, Merab Ninidze.

MOONFISH

A Paulo Branco presentation of a Madragoa Filmes/Gemini Films, Paris/Madragoa Filmes, Alcochete, Portugal. Producer: Paulo Branco. Director: Jose Alvaro Morais. Screenplay: Morais, Jeanne Waltz. Camera: Edgar Moura. Editor: Jackie Bastide. Music: Ricardo Del Fra. In color. Release date: Aug. 29, 2000. Running time: 124 Min. PORTUGUESE-FRENCH-SPANISH.
Cast: Beatriz Batarda, Marcello Urgeghe, Ricardo Aibeo, Luis Miguel Cintra, Isabel Ruth, Assuncion Balaguer, Paula Guedes.

MOSCOW

A Studio Telekino production. (International sales: Studio Telekino, Moscow.) Producer: Arsen Gottlieb. Executive producers: Oleg Gutman, Dmitri Sivozhelezov. Director: Alexander Zeldovich. Screenplay: Vladimir Sorokin, Zeldovich. Camera: Alexander Ilkhovsky. Editor: Tatiana Yegoracheva. Music: Leonid Desyatnikov. In color. Release date: Sept. 3, 2000. Running time: 139 Min. RUSSIAN.
Cast: Ingeborga Dapkunaite, Tatiana Drubich, Natalia Koliakanova, Alexander Baluev, Viktor Gvozditsky, Stanislav Pavlov.

MOST PROMISING YOUNG ACTION

A UFD release of an RF2K/Novo Arturo FIlms/Les Films Ariane/TF1 Films Prod. production, with participation of Canal Plus. (International sales: UGC Intl., Paris.) Producers: Olivier Granier, Dominique Farrugia. Executive producer: Antoine Simkine. Director: Gerard Jugnot. Screenplay: Jugnot, Isabelle Mergault. Camera: Pascal Gennesseaux. Editor: Catherine Kelber. Music: Khalil Chahine. In color. Release date: Apr. 13, 2000. Running time: 100 Min. FRENCH.
Cast: Gerard Jugnot, Berenice Bejo, Antoine Dulery, Sabine Haudepin, Mohamed Hicham, Chantal Lauby, Ticky Holgado.

MR. ACCIDENT

A Roadshow (Australia) release of a United Artists Films presentation of a Serious production. (International sales: United Artists Ltd., London.) Producers: Yahoo Serious, Warwick Ross. Co-producer: Lulu Serious, David Roach. Director/Screenplay: Yahoo Serious. Camera: Steve Arnold. Editor: Simon Martin. Music: Nerida Tyson-Chew. In Atlab color. Release date: Aug. 14, 2000. Running time: 88 Min. AUSTRALIAN-U.S.
Cast: Yahoo Serious, Helen Dallimore, David Field, Grant Piro.

MR. RICE'S SECRET

A New City Prods. (Vancouver) production. (International sales: Horizon Entertainment, West Vancouver.) Producer: Colleen Nystedt. Executive producers: Beau Rogers, David Forrest. Director: Nicholas Kendall. Screenplay: J.H. Wyman. Camera: Gregory Middleton. Editor: Ron E. Yoshida. Music: Simon Kendall, Al Rodger. In color. Release date: June 3, 2000. Running time: 113 Min. CANADIAN.
Cast: David Bowie, Bill Switzer, Garwin Sanford, Teryl Rothery, Zachary Lipovsky, Jason Anderson, Tyler Thompson.

MUGGERS

A REP release (in Australia) of an Australian Film Finance Corp. presentation of a Winchester Films-Clock End Films production, in association with Film Victoria, Australian Film Commission. (International sales: Winchester Films, London.) Producers: Nigel Odell, David Redman. Executive producer: John Wolstenholme. Director: Dean Murphy. Screenplay: Robert Taylor. Camera: Roger Lanser. Editor: Peter Carrodus. Music: Doug Brady. In Cinevex color, Panavision widescreen. Release date: Apr. 19, 2000. Running time: 96 Min. AUSTRALIAN-BRITISH.
Cast: Matt Day, Jason Barry, Petra Yared, Marshall Napier.

MY DETOX

A GagStones/Milk & Honey Films/Czech Television/Space Films production. (International sales: Milk & Honey Films, Prague.) Producer: Tomas Krejci. Director: Victor Taus. Screenplay: Boris Hybner. Camera: David Calek. Editor: Alois Fisarek. Music: Oskar Rozsa. In color and B&W. Release date: July 7, 2000. Running time: 92 Min. CZECH.
Cast: Viktor Taus, Mikulas Kren, Vanda Hybnerova, Milan Hlavsa.

MY FATHER'S ANGEL

A Ranfilm production. (International sales: Ranfilm Prods., North Vancouver.) Producers: Mort Ransen, David Bouck. Executive producers: Raymond Massey, Trevor Hodgson. Director: Davor Marjanovic. Screenplay: Frank Borg, based on a story by Borg, Marjanovic. Camera: Bruce Worrall. Editor: Lenka Svab. Music: Schaun Tozer. In color. Release date: Sept. 12, 1999. Running time: 89 Min. CANADA.
Cast: Tony Nardi, Timothy Webber, Tygh Runyan, Brendan Fletcher, Asja Pavlovic, Lynda Boyd, Vanessa King.

MY GENERATION

A Mikado release (in Italy) of a Cabin Creeks Films presentation of a Mikado Films/Polygram Diversified Ventures/Road Movies Filmproduktion/ Schulberg Prods./Solaris co-production. Producer: Barbara Kopple. Directors: Barbara Kopple, Tom Haneke. Screenplay: Kopple. Camera: Tom Hurwitz. Editor: Haneke. In color. Release date: Sept. 6, 2000. Running time: 103 Min. Documentary. U.S.-ITALIAN-GERMAN.

MY KHMER HEART

A Sir Peter Ustinov presentation of an iCandy production. (International sales: iCandy Prods. Artarmon, Australia.) Producer/ Director: Janine Hosking. Camera: Rod Pollard. Editor: David Schmidt. Music: Thomas Newman, Jocelyn Pook, Barringtron Pheloung. In color. Release date: Aug. 6, 2000. Running time: 95 Min. Documentary. AUSTRALIAN.
With: Geraldine Cox, Hun Sen, Prince Norodom Ranariddh, Peter Ustinov.

MY HEART

A Bae Changho Prod. production, in association with Korean Film Commission. (International sales: Mirovision, Seoul.) Producer: Bae Chang-ho. Director: Bae Chang-ho. Screenplay: Bae, Kim Yu-mi. Camera: Song Haeng-ki. Editor: Kim Hyeon. Music: Lee Seong-jae. SOUTH KOREAN.
Cast: Kim Yu-mi, Kim Myeong-kon, Yun Yu-seon, Nam Jeong-hi, Jeong In-ha, Choi Suk-jin.

MY MOTHER FRANK

A UIP/Beyond Films release (in Australia) of an Australian Film Finance Corp. presentation of an Intrepid Films production, in association with Showtime (Australia) and the support of the NSW Film and TV Office, Australian Film Commission, Channel 4 (U.K.). (International sales: Beyond Films, Sydney.) Producers: Phaedon Vass, Susan Vass, John Winter. Director/Screenplay: Mark Lamprell. Camera: Brian Breheny. Editor: Nicholas Beauman. Music: Peter Best. In Atlab color. Release date: Feb. 19, 2000. Running time: 95 Min. AUSTRALIAN.
Cast: Sinead Cusak, Sam Neill, Matthew Newton, Rose Byrne, Sacha Horler, Joan Lord, Melissa Jaffer, Lynette Curran, Celia Ireland.

MYSTERIOUS OBJECT AT NOON

A 9/6 Cinema Factory production in association with the Thai Film Foundation and the Hubert Bals Foundation. Producers: Gridthiya Gaweewong, Mingmongkol Sonakul. (International sales: Firecracker Film Co., Bangkok.) Director/Screenplay/Editor: Apichatpong Weerasethakul. Camera: Prasong Klinborrom. In B&W. Release date: Feb. 2, 2000. Running time: 83 Min. THAI.
Cast: Duangjai Hiransri, Kongkeirt Komsiri, Saisiri Xoomsai.

THE MYSTERY OF PAUL

An Agat Films & Co. production. Producer: Yvon Davis. Director/Screenplay: Abraham Segal, with Frederic Boyer. Camera: Jacques Pamart, Diane Baratier. Editor: Annie Waks. Music: Jacques Remus. In color. Release date: July 6, 2000. Running time: 105 Min. Documentary. FRENCH.
With: Didier Sandre.

MY TREASURE

A Fuerte Apache Producciones/INCAA production. Director: Sergio Bellotti. Screenplay: Daniel Guebel. Camera: Esteban Sapir. Editor: Santiago Ricci. Music: Daniel Lozano, Mario Siperman. In color. Release date: Sept. 19, 1999. Running time: 91 Min. ARGENTINE.
Cast: Gabriel Goity, Edda Bustamente, Victoria Onetto.

NAKED UNDER THE MOON

A Good Harvest production for Regal Entertainment. (International sales: Regal Films, Quezon City, Philippines.) Producer: Lily Monteverde. Director/Screenplay: Lav Diaz. Camera: Louie Quirino. Editor: Randy Brien. Music: Michelle Pritchard. In color. Release date: Feb. 16, 2000. Running time: 118 Min. FILIPINO.
Cast: Klaudia Koronel, Elizabeth Oropesa, Joel Torre, Julio Diaz, Isabel Granada, Ronnie Lazaro, Richard Joson.

THE NAMELESS

A Filmax release (in Spain) of a Joan Ginard PC/Sogedasa production, in association with Via Digital, TVC. (International sales: Filmax, Barcelona.) Producer: Julio Fernandez. Executive producer: Joan Ginard. Director/Screenplay: Jaime Balaguero, based on the novel by Ramsey Campbell. Camera: Xavi Gimenez. Editor: Luis de la Madrid. Music: Carles Casas. In color. Release date: Nov. 13, 1999. Running time: 102 Min. SPANISH.
Cast: Emma Vilarasau, Karra Elejalde, Tristan Ulloa, Pep Tosar.

NANG NAK

A Tai Entertainment (Bangkok) production in association with Buddy Films & Video. Producer: Nonzee Nimbutr. Executive producer: Visute Poolvoralaks. Director: Nonzee Nimbutr. Screenplay: Wisid Sartsanatieng. Camera: Nattawut Kittikhun. Editor: Wunit Ussavinikul. Music: Pakawat Waiwittaya, Chatchai Pongprapapun. In color. Release date: Sept. 24, 1999. Running time: 99 Min. THAI.
Cast: Intira Jaroenpura, Winai Kraibutr, Pramote Suksatit, Pracha Thawongfia, Manit Meekaewjaroen.

NASTY NEIGHBOURS

An Ipso Facto Films production in association with Glenrinnes Film partnership and MPCE. (International sales: First Hand Films, Switzerland.) Producer: Christine Alderson. Executive producers: Adam Page, Nadine Marsh Edwards, Terje Gaustad, Lukas Erni. Director/Screenplay: Debbie Isitt, based on her play. Camera: Simon Reeves, Sam McCurdy, Editor: Nicky Ager. Music: Jocelyn Pook. In color. Release date: Sept. 6, 1999. Running time: 89 Min. BRITISH.
Cast: Ricky Tomlinson, Marion Bailey, Phil Daniels, Rachel Fielding, Hywel Bennett, Nick Whitfield, Debbie Isitt.

NEJISHIKI: WIND-UP TYPE

A Bitters End release (in Japan) of an Ishii Prod. production. (International sales: Bitters End, Tokyo.) Producer/Director/ Screenplay: Teruo Ishii, based on the manga by Yoshiharu Tsuge. Camera: Takahiro Tsunoi. Editor: Nobutake Kamiya. Music: Kenichi Segawa. In color. Release date: June 21, 1999. Running time: 85 Min. JAPANESE.
Cast: Tadanobu Asano, Miki Fujitani, Kazuhiko Kanayama, Tetsuro Tanba, Nijiko Kiyokawa, Yuko Fujimori, Tsugaumi, Mutsumi Fujita.

THE NEWCOMER

A Sky Planning/Hori Pro production in association with the City of Kyoto. Produced by Toshi Shioya, Motoyuki Suzuki, Shigeji Maeda. Executive producers: Fumiko Honma, Kunio Sasaki. Director: Isao Morimoto. Screenplay: Morimoto, adapted from the novel by David Zoppetti. Camera: Peter Borosh. Editors: Morimoto, Kimitsuka Fujkiwara. Music: S.E.N.S. In color. Release date: Sept. 22, 1999. Running time: 122 Min. JAPANESE.
Cast: Edward Atterton, Honami Suzuki, Yoshiko Nakata, Tetsu Watanabe, Sokyu Fujita, Keizo Kanie.

NEW YEAR'S DAY

A Flashpoint presentation of an Alchymie production with the participation of the ECF, Liberator Prods. and Canal Plus. Producers: Stephen Cleary, Simon Channing-Williams. Executive producers: David Forrest, Beau Rogers. Co-executive producers: Cameron McCracken, Pippa Cross. Co-producers: Charles Steel, Marianne Slot, Vibeke Windelev. Director: Suri Krishnamma. Screenplay: Ralph Brown. Editor: Adam Ross. Music: Julian Nott. In color, widescreen. Release date: Jan. 25, 2000. Running time: 101 Min. BRITISH.
Cast: Andrew Lee Potts, Robby Barry, Marianne Jean-Baptiste, Jacqueline Bisset, Anatasia Hille, Michael Kitchen, Ralph Brown.

NIGHTCAP

An MK2 Diffusion release (in France) of an MK2 Prods. (France)/CAB Prods. (Switzerland) production, in association with France 2 Cinema, Television Suisse Romande, YMC Prods., with participation of Canal Plus, Office Federal de la Culture, Suisse Succes Cinema, Teleclub. (International sales: MK2, Paris.) Producer: Marin Karmitz. Executive producer: Jean-Louis Porchet. Director: Claude Chabrol. Sreenplay: Caroline Eliacheff, Chabrol, based on the novel "The Chocolate Cobweb" by Charlotte Armstrong. Camera: Renato Berta. Editor: Monique Fardoulis. Music: Matthieu Chabrol. In color. Release date: Aug. 2, 2000. Running time: 99 Min. FRENCH-SWISS.
Cast: Isabelle Huppert, Jacques Dutronc, Anna Mouglalis, Rodolphe Pauly, Michel Robin, Brigitte Catillon, Mathieu Simonet.

NIGHTFALL

A Mediopolis/Filmes do Tejo production with Westdeutscher Rundfunk. (International sales: Futura Film/Welvertrieb im Filmverlag der Autoren, Munich.) Producer: Alexander Ris. Executive producer: Jorg Rothe. Director/Screenplay: Fred Kelemen. Camera: Kelemen, Editors: Kelemen, Anja Neraal, Nicola Undritz Cope. Music: Rainer Kirchmann. In color. Release date: Sept. 5, 1999. Running time: 144 Min. GERMAN-PORTUGUESE.
Cast: Wolfgang Michael, Verena Jasch, Adolfo Assor, Isa Hochgerner.

A NIGHT ON THE TOWN

A Buena Vista Intl. (Germany) release (in Germany) of a Hager Moss Film production, in association with Seven Pictures. (International sales: BetaFilm, Ismaning, Germany.) Producers: Kirsten Hager, Eric Moss. Director: Soenke Wortmann. Screenplay: Frank Goehre, from his novel. Camera: Tom Faehrmann. Editor: Hans Funck. Music: Peter Wolf. In color, widescreen. Release date: June 30, 1999. Running time: 91 Min. GERMAN.
Cast: Benno Fuermann, Kathleen Gallego Zapata, Armin Rohde, Maruschka Detmers, Axel Milberg, Oliver Stokowski, Florian Lukas.

NIGHT SERVICE STATION

A Filmakademie Baden/Lilion Film/SN Film production. (International sales: Lilion Film, Berlin.) Producer: Tanino Belanca. Director/Screenplay: Samir Nasr. Camera: Stefan Runge. Editor: Raimund Barthelmes. Music: Dieter Schleip. In color. Release date: Feb. 17, 2000. Running time: 92 Min. Documentary. GERMAN.

NIGHT TIME

An Avista Film production in association with Roxy Film, Luggi Waldleitner and ProSieben. Producers: Herbert, Alena Rimbach. Director: Peter Fratzscher. Screenplay: Nils-Morten Osburg. Camera: Thomas Merker. Editor: Barbara Gies. In color. Release date: Mar. 4, 2000. Running time: 96 Min. GERMAN.
Cast: Jan Josef Liefers, Ulrich Muhe, Marie Baumer, Christoph Waltz.

NIGHTWATCHMAN

An Eagle Pictures release of a Digital Film production, in association with RAI, with participation Telepiu. Producer: Galliano Juso. Director: Francesco Calogero. Screenplay: Calogero, Umberto Contarello, story by Vincenzo Pardini. Camera: Giulio Pietromarchi. Editor: Davide Azzigana. Music: Mario Tronco. Pinomarino Band. In Cinecitta color. Release date: Mar. 28, 2000. Running time: 103 Min. ITALIAN.
Cast: Diego Abatantuono, Anna Safroncik, Flavio Insinna, Marco Messeri, Simona Caramelli, Antonio Petrocelli, Ugo Conti.

THE NINE LIVES OF TOMAS KATZ

A Geissendorfer Films/G2 Films presentation of a Strawberry Vale production. (International sales: G2 Films, London.) Producer: Caroline Hewitt. Executive producer: Hans W. Geissendorfer. Director: Ben Hopkins. Screenplay: Hopkins, Thomas Browne, story by Hopkins, Ben Cheek. Camera: Julian Court. Editor: Alan Levy. Music: Dominik Scherrer. In B&W/tinted and Metrocolor. Release date: Aug.17, 2000. Running time: 87 Min. BRITISH-GERMAN.
Cast: Thomas Fisher, Ian McNeice, Tim Barlow, Janet Henfrey.

NOBODY KNOWS ANYBODY

A Warner Sogefilms release (in Spain) of A Sogetel/Maestranza Films/DMBV Films production, in association with Canal Plus (Spain) and with participation of Canal Sur Television. (International sales: Sogetel, madrid.) Executive producers: Gustavo Ferrada, Antonio P. Perez. Director/Screenplay: Mateo Gil, based on the novel by Juan Bonilla. Camera: Javier Salmones. Editor: Nacho Ruiz Capilla. Music: Alejandro Amenabar. In color, Panavision widescreen. Release date: Nov. 29, 1999. Running time: 108 Min. SPANISH-FRENCH.
Cast: Eduardo Noriega, Jordi Molla, Natalia Verbeke, Paz Vega, Pedro Alvarez Osorio.

NO COFFEE, NO TV, NO SEX

A Latke Films presentation in association with La Television Suisse Romande. Producer: Romed Wyder. Director/Screenplay: Romed Wyder. Camera: Stephane Kuthy. Editor: Orsola Valenti. Music: Thierry Clerc, Daniel Schweizer. In color. Release date: Apr. 23, 2000. Running time: 87 Min. SWISS.
Cast: Vincent Coppey, Alexandra Tidemann, Pietro Musillo, Nalini Selvadoray.

A NON-VIOLENT LIFE

An Istituto Luce release (in Italy) of a Film 7 Intl. production, in association with RAI. Producer: Luciano Emmer. Director/Screenplay: David Emmer. Camera: Roberta Allegrini. Editor: Valentina Girodo. Music: Gabriele Ducros. In Cinecitta color. Release date: Nov. 23, 1999. Running time: 84 Min. ITALIAN.
Cast: Yuri Gugliucci, Ninetto Davoli, Jacqueline Lustig, Gianluca Angelini, Gianfranco Mattioli, Adriana Asti.

NO ONE SLEEPS

A Galeria Alaska Prods. production in association with Hamburger Filmforderung, Medien-und Filmgesellschaft Baden-Wurttemberg, Filmstiftung Nordrhein-Westfalen and WDR/Arte. (International sales: Media Luna Intl. Film Sales, Cologne, Germany.) Producer: Jochen Hick. Director/Screenplay: Hick. Camera: Thomas M. Harting, Michael Maely. Editor: Helga Scharf. In color. Release date: Feb. 16, 2000. Running time: 108 Min. GERMAN.
Cast: Tom Wlaschiha, Irit Levi, Jim Thalman, Richard Thalman, Richard Conti, Kalene Parker, Charles Shaw Robinson.

NO PLACE TO GO

A Distant Dreams Filmproduktion production, in association with ZDF and Geyer Werke Berlin. (International sales: Bavaria Film Intl., Munich.) Producers: Kaete Ehrmann, Ulrich Caspar. Director/Screenplay: Oskar Orehler. Camera: Hagen Bogdanski. Editor: Isabel Meier. Music: Martin Todsharow. In B&W. Release date: May 14, 2000. Running time: 110 Min. GERMAN.
Cast: Hannelore Elsner, Vadim Glowna, Jasmin Tabatabai, Lars Rudolph, Michael Gwisdek, Nina Petri, Tonio Arango, Claudia Geisler.

NORA

An Alliance Atlantis release of a Natural Nylon Entertainment/IAC Holdings production, in association with Volta Films, Road Movies Vierte Produktionen, Gam Film, Metropolitan Films. (International sales: IAC, London.) Producers: Bradley Adams, Damon Bryant, Tracey Seaward. Executive producer: Guy Collins. Co-producers: Ewan McGregor, James Flynn, Ulrich Felsberg, Gherardo Pagliei. Director: Pat Murphy. Screenplay: Murphy, Gerard Stembridge, based on the book by Brenda Maddox. Camera: Jean-Francois Robin. Editor: Pia Di Ciaula. Music: Robert Boyle. In color. Release date: Feb. 14, 2000. Running time: 106 Min. BRITISH.
Cast: Ewan McGregor, Susan Lynch, Peter McDonald, Aedin Moloney, Roberto Citran.

NOROC

A Versatile Pictures (Vancouver) production, with support from Telefilm Canada. Producer: Marc Retailleau. Executive producer: Robert French. Director: Marc Retailleau. Screenplay: Retailleau, Robert French. Camera: James Tocher. Editors: Mark Lemon, Sue Kittler. Music: Lache Cercel, Michael Dunn. In color-JVC D-9. Release date: Oct. 10, 1999. Running time: 92 Min. CANADIAN.
Cast: Peter La Croix, Gina Chiarelli, Jay Brazeaau, Babz Chula, Alan Peterson.

NOT WITH A BANG

An Imbarco Per Citera production. Producers: Gianfranco Isernia, Rosa Russo. Director: Mariano Lambeerti. Screenplay: Mariano Lamberti, Roberta Calandra. Camera: Antonio Grambone. Editor: Alessio Doglione. Music: Roberto Sbolci. In color. Release date: Sept. 3, 1999. Running time: 102 Min. ITALIAN.
Cast: Paola Pitagora, Nello Mascia, Mariano D'Amora, Giovanna Giuliani, Carlo Giuliano, Rita Montes, Elena Cannella.

NOWHERE TO HIDE

A Cinema Service presentation of a Taewon Entertainment production, in association with Kookmin Venture Capital, Samboo Finance Entertainment and Fox Video Korea. (International sales: Taewon, Seoul.) Producer: Cheong Tae-weon. Executive producer: Kang Woo-suk. Director/Screenplay: Lee Myeong-se. Camera: Jeong Kwang-seok, Song Haeng-ki. Editor: Go Im-pyo. Music: Jo Seong-woo. In color. Release date: Oct. 19, 1999. Running time: 112 Min. SOUTH KOREAN.
Cast: Ahn Sung-ki, Park Jung-hun, Jang Dong-keon, Choe Ji-woo.

NUMERO BRUNO

A Hoodwink Pictures production, in association with New Zealand on Air, TV One, Telecom. (International sales: Quardle Ardle Films, Wellington.) Producer: Nicola Saker. Director/Screenplay: Steve La Hood. Camera: Warrick Wka Attewell. Editor: Geoff Conway. In color. Release date: July 3, 2000. Running time: 68 Min. Documentary. NEW ZEALAND.

OF WOMEN AND MAGIC

A La Sept Arte/Les Films de la Boissiere/Telecip presentation of a Les Films de la Boissiere/Telecip production, in association with la Sept Arte Fiction Dept. (International sales: UGC Intl., Paris.) Producers: Annie Miller, Jacques Fansten. Co-producer: Pierre Chevalier. Director/Screenplay: Claude Miller, based on chapter three of the novel "The Blindfold" by Siri Hustvedt. Camera; Philippe Welt, Nathan Miller. Editor: Veronique Lange. Music: Christus Vincit. In color, digital video. Release date: Feb. 19, 2000. Running time: 83 Min. FRENCH.
Cast: Anne Brochet, Mathilde Seigner, Annie Noel, Yves Jacques, Eduard Baer, Jacques Mauclair, Edith Scob, Marc Cennelier.

OLD SCHOOL

An Opening Distribution release of a Scarla Films, Tanka Prods., Glorinda Prods. production. Producer: Eric Houdion. Executive producer: Michel Rosenthal. Co-producer: Dominique Blanchard. Director: Kader Ayd, Karim Abbou. Screenplay: Hocine Ossoukine, Ayd, Abbou. Camera: Eric Cadrieu. Editor: Philippe Doria Machado. Music: Joey Starr, DJ Spank. In color. Release date: June 16, 2000. Running time: 91 Min. FRENCH.
Cast: Fabienne Babe, Julien Courbey, Kader Ayd, Hocine Ossoukine, Stephane Soo Mongo.

ONCE UPON ANOTHER TIME
A Cinema Indie Group release (in Spain) of an Atlantico Films production in association with TVG. Producer: Pilar Sueiro. Director/Screenplay: Juan Pinzas. Camera: Gerardo Moschioni, Tote Trenas. Editor: Maria Lara. Music: Juan Sueiro. In color. Release date: June 29, 2000. Running time: 93 Min. SPANISH.
Cast: Monti Castineiras, Pilar Saavedra, Vicente de Souza, Mara Sanchez, Victor Mosquiera, Isabel Vallejo, Marcos Orsi, Paul Naschy.

A ONE AND A TWO...
A 1+2 Seisaku linkai presentation of an Atom Films production for Pony Canyon/Omega Project. (International sales: Capitol Films, London.) Producers: Shinya Kawai, Naoko Tsukeda. Director/Screenplay: Edward Yang. Camera: Yang Wei-han. Editor: Chen Bowen. Music: Peng Kai-li. In color. Release date: May 14, 2000. Running time: 173 Min. TAIWANESE-JAPANESE.
Cast: Wu Nien-jen, Elaine Jin, Issey Ogata, Kelly Lee, Jonathan Chang, Chen Hsi-sheng, Ko Su-yun, Michael Tao, Hsaio Shu-shen.

ONE DAY IN THE LIFE OF ANDREI ARSENEVITCH
An AMIP-La Sept Arte-INA-Arkeion Films production. (International sales: Doc and C, Paris.) Producers: Thierry Garrel, Jean-Jacques Henry, Claude Guisard, Liane Wilmont, Michele Levelle. Executive producers: Elisabeth Gerard, Richard Delmotte. Director/ Screenplay/ Editor: Chris Marker. Camera: Marc-Andre Batigne, Pierre Camus. Music: Edouard Artemiev, J.S. Bach, Henry Purcell, W. Mozart. Release date: Feb. 16, 2000. Running time: 50 Min. Documentary. FRENCH.
Narrator: Marina Vlady (French), Alexandra Stewart (English).

101 REYKJAVIK
A 101 Ltd. (Iceland)/Zentropa Entertainment (Denmark)/Liberator Prods. (France)/Filmhuset (Norway) production, with participation of Icelandic Film Fund. (International sales: Trust FIlm Sales, Hvidovre, Denmark.) Producers: Ingvar Thordarson, Baltasar Kormakur. Director/Screenplay: Baltasar Kormakur, from the novel by Hallgrimur Helgason. Camera: Pter Steuger. Editors: Skule Eriksen, Sigvaldi Karason. Music: Damon Albarn, Einar Orn Benediktsson. In color. Release date: Aug. 4, 2000. Running time: 89 Min. ICELANDIC-DANISH-FRENCH-NORWEGIAN.
Cast: Victoria Abril, Hilmir Snaer Gudnason, Hanna Maria Karlsdottir, Baltasar Kormakur, Olafur Darri Olafsson, Thrudur Vilhjalmdottir.

ONE LIFE STAND
An Elemental Films production. (International sales: Elemental, Glasgow.) Producer: Karen M. Smyth. Executive producer: Owen Thomas. Director/Screenplay/Editor: May Miles Thomas. Camera: Miles Thomas. Music: Bobby Henry. In B&W, Digital video. Release date: Aug. 21, 2000. Running time: 119 Min. BRITISH.
Cast: Maureen Carr, John Kielty, Gary Lewis, Archie Lal, Alyson Orr, Rohanna Law, Ros McCue.

ONE MORE DAY
A Cima Film production. (International sales: Cine Media Intl., Tehran.) Producer: Babak Payami. Executive producer: Alireza Shoja Noori. Director/Screenplay: Babak Payami, based on an idea by Mahmoud Aiden. Camera: Farzad Jodat. Editor: Parviz Shahbazi. In color. Release date: Feb. 14, 2000. Running time: 73 Min. IRANIAN.
Cast: Ali Hosseini, Leila Saadi.

ONE MORE KISS
A Metrodome Films release (in U.K.) of a Mob Films production, in association with JAM Pictures and Freewheel Intl. (International sales: Mob Films, London.) Producers: Vadim Jean, Paul Brooks. Executive producers: Sara Giles, Derek Roy. Co-producers: Hane Walmsley, Michael Braham. Director: Vadim Hean. Screenplay: Suzie Halewood. Camera: Mike Fox. Editor: Joe McNally. Music: John Murphy, David A. Hughes. In Technicolor, Panavision widescreen. Release date: Nov. 8, 1999. Running time: 100 Min. BRITISH.
Cast: Gerry Butler, James Cosmo, Valerie Edmond, Valerie Gogan, Danny Nussbaum, Carl Proctor.

ONE NIGHT
A Yerevan Studios (Armenia) production. Director: Boris Barnet. Screenplay: Fyodr Knorr, from his story and play. Camera: Stepan Gevorkian. In B&W. Release date: Aug. 6, 2000. Running time: 81 Min. SOVIET UNION–1945.
Cast: Irina Radchenko, Boris Andreyev, I. Kuznetsov, B. Leonov, A. Judin, V. Viazemsky, Boris Barnet.

ONE PIECE!
A Pia Film Festival production. (International sales: PFF, Tokyo.) Director/Editor: Shinobu Yaguchi, Takuji Suzuki. Camera: Yaguchi, Suzuki. Music: Yaguchi, Suzuki. In color, video. Release date: Sept. 17, 1999. Running time: 73 Min. JAPANESE.
Cast: Youji Tanaka, Nao Nekota, Satoru Jitsunashi, Masumi Kiuchi, Keiko Shionoya, Miako Tadano, Yoko Chosokabe, Tsurumi Komatsu.

ON THE BEACH BEYOND THE PIER
An Adriana Chiesa Enterprises presentation of a C.E.P. production in association with Radiotelevisione Italiana. Producers: Arturo and Massimiliano La Pegna. Director: Giovanni Fago. Screenplay: Fago, Massimo Felisatti, Luciana Catalani, story by Fago, based on the novel by Mario Tobino. Camera: Marco Pontecorvo. Editor: Giancarlo Cerosimo. Music: Pino Donaggio. In color. Release date: May 2, 2000. Running time: 140 Min. ITALIAN.
Cast: Lorenza Indovina, Stephane Freiss, Andrea Renzi, Laurent Terzieff, Ludovica Modugno, Omero Antonutti, Eros Pagni.

OPERA FANATIC
A Pars Media presentation. Producer: Pars Media. Director: Jan Schmidt-Garre. Camera: Wedigo von Schultzendorff, Heinrich Chini, Julian Hohnsort. Editor: Gaby Null-Neujahr. In color. Release date: Jan. 17, 2000. Running time: 96 Min. Documentary. GERMAN.
Cast: Stefan Zucker, Leyla Gencer, Gigliola Frazzoni, Iris Adami Corradetti, Giulietta Simionato, Magda Olivero, Gina Cigna.

ORATOR
An Uzbekino production. Producer: Yusup Razykov. Director/ Screenplay: Razykov. Camera: Dankar Abdurakhmanov. Editor: Olga Morova. Music: Dimitri Yanov. In color. Release date: June 10, 2000. Running time: 83 Min. UZBEKISTANIAN.
Cast: Bosh Rollarda, Bahodir Odilov, Lola Eltoeva, Jahovir Zukirov, Asal Alijuheva, Nargiza, Rahmonova, Shohsanam Khamrokulova.

ORDINARY DECENT CRIMINAL
An Icon (in U.K.)/Miramax (in U.S.) release of an Icon Entertainment Intl. presentation of a Little Bird production, in association with Tatfilm and Trigger street Prods., with participation of Miramax Films, the Irish Film Board, the Greenlight Fund and Filmstiftung NRW. Producer: Jonathan Cavendish. Executive producers: James Mitchell, Christine Ruppert. Co-producer: Martha O'Neill. Director: Thaddeus O'Sullivan. Screenplay: Gerard Stembridge. Camera: Andrew Dunn. Editor: William Anderson. Music: Damon Albarn. In Technicolor, Panavision widescreen. Release date: Mar. 23, 2000. Running time: 90 Min. IRISH-BRITISH.
Cast: Kevin Spacey, Linda Fiorentino, Peter Mullan, Stephen Dillane, Helen Baxendale, David Hayman, Patrick Malahide, Garard McSorley.

ORIENTATIONS–CHRISTOPHER DOYLE: STIRRED NOT SHAKEN
An Australian Film Finance Corp. presentation of a Pagan Films production, with the support of the NSW Film & TV Office, SBS Independent, Australian Film Commission. (International sales: TVF Intl., London.) Producer: Karena Slaninka. Director: Rick Farquharson. Screenplay: Farquharson, Karena Slaninka. Camera: Catherine Marciniak, Roman Baska. Editor: Emma Hay. In color. Release date: June 17, 2000. Running time: 54 Min. Documentary. AUSTRALIAN.

ORIUNDI
A Laz Audiovisual LTDA production. (International sales: Triad Media Communications, Los Angeles.) Producers: R.A. Gennaro, Virginia W. Moraes. Executive producers: Telmo Maia, Eliane Ferreira. Co-producer: Luiz Carlos Bravo. Director: Ricardo Bravo. Screenplay: Marcos Bernstein. Camera: Toca Seabra. Editors: Isabelle Rathery, Ana Tiexiera. Music: Arrigo Barnabe. In color, widescreen. Release date: Sept. 24, 1999. Running time: 97 Min. BRAZILIAN.
Cast: Anthony Quinn, Leticia Spiller, Paulo Betti, Gabriela Duarte, Marly Bueno, Raquel Rizzo, Paulo Autran, Lorenzo Quinn, Tiago Real.

OSAKA STORY
A Kindai Eiga Kyokai production (International sales: Dentsu Inc., Tokyo.) Producer: Tetsuo Satonaka. Executive producers: Akira Yokozawa, Matsuki Katagiri, Hideaki Furukawa. Director: Jun Ichikawa. Screenplay: Isshin Inudo. Camera: Tatsuhiko Kobayashi, Takahiro Tsutai. Editor: Yukio Watanabe. Music: Tomoyuki Asakawa. In color. Release date: Oct. 18, 1999. Running time: 118 Min. JAPANESE.
Cast: Chizuru Ikewaki, Kenju Sawada, Yuko Tanaka.

OTHER GIRLS
A Rezo Films release of a TS Prods. production. (International sales: Flach Pyramide Intl., Paris.) Producers: Milena Poylo, Gilles Sacuto. Director/Screenplay: Caroline Vignal. Camera: Jeanne Lapoirie. Editor: Annick Raoul. Music: Jean-Stephane Brosse. In color. Release date: Apr. 27, 2000. Running time: 96 Min. FRENCH.
Cast: Julie Leclercq, Benoite Sapim, Caroline Baehr, Jean-Francois Gallotte, Bernard Menez.

OTOMO
A Filmgalerie 451/ZDF Mainz production. Producers: Irene von Alberti, Thomas Lechner. (International sales: MFA-Filmdistribution, Munich.) Director: Frieder Schlaich. Screenplay: Klaus Pohl, Schlaich. Camera: Volker Tittel. Editor: Magdolna Rokob. Music: Freundeskreis. In color. Release date: Jan. 28, 2000. Running time: 85 Min. GERMAN.
Cast: Isaach de Bankole, Eva Mattes, Hanno Friedrich, Barnaby Metschurat, Lara Kugler, Sigrid Burkholder.

OUCH
A Pierre Grise Prods. production, in association with FMB Films, with participation of Canal Plus and CNC. (International sales: Celluloid Dreams, Paris.) Producers: Martine Marignac, Maurice Tinchant. Director/Screenplay: Sophie Fillieres. Camera: Christophe Pollock. Editor: Valerie Loiseleux. Music: Michel Portal. Release date: Aug. 6, 2000. Running time: 106 Min. FRENCH.
Cast: Andre Dussollier, Helene Fillieres, Emmanuelle Devos, Anne Le Ny, Lucienne Hamon, Alain Rimoux, Gisele Casadeus, Lucien Pascal.

OUR LADY OF THE ASSASSINS
A Les Films du Losange/Le Studio Canal Plus/Vertigo Films/Tucan Producciones Cinematograficas Ltda. presentation, with the participation of Canal Plus. (International sales: Le Studio Canal Plus, Paris.) Producers: Jaime Osorio Gomez, Barbet Schroeder, Margaret Menegoz. Director: Barbet Schroeder. Screenplay: Fernando Vallejo, based on his novel. Camera: Rodrigo Lalinde. Editor: Elsa Vasquez. Music: Jorge Arriagada. Release date: Sept. 1, 2000. Running time: 101 Min. FRENCH-COLOMBIAN.
Cast: German Jaramillo, Anderson Ballesteros, Juan David Restrepo, Manuel Busquets.

OUR LOVE
A Hunnia Filmstudio/Gambit production, in association with TV Polska, MMK, RTL Klub, ORTT, MTV. Producers: Sandor Simo, Jan Kidawa-Blonski. Director/Screenplay: Jozsef Pacskovszky. Camera: Francisco Gozon. Editor: Eva Szentandrasi. Music: Mendelssohn, Bach. In color. Release date: Feb. 7, 2000. Running time: 108 Min. HUNGARIAN-POLISH.
Cast: Melinda Major, Lajos Bartok, Erik Desfosses, Jan Kidawa-Blonski.

AN OUTGOING WOMAN
A Mars Films release of a Sunday Morning Prods./Rhone Alpes Cinema/Groupe TSF production, with participation of CNC, Canal Plus, Sofiga and Gimages 2. (International sales: Mercure Distribution, Paris.) Producers: Bertand Gore, Nathalie Mesuret, Emmanuelle de Reynal. Director: Christophe Blanc. Screenplay: Blanc, Roger Bohbot, Eve Deboise. Camera: Pascal Poucet, Pierre Hemon, Marie Deshayes. Editor: Agnes Bruckert. Music: Martin Wheeler. In color. Release date: Feb. 22, 2000. Running time: 116 Min. FRENCH.
Cast: Agnes Jaoui, Serge Riaboukine, Sarah Haxaire, Richard Morgieve.

OVER THE RAINBOW
An Arsenal Filmverleih release (in Germany) of an LE Vision Film & Fernsehproduktion production, in association with Mitteldeutscher Rundfunk. (International sales: LE Vision, Leipzig.) Producers: Simone Baumann, Jan Peter, Yury Winterberg. Director: Jan Peter. Screenplay: Yury Winterberg, Peter. Camera: Soenke Hansen. Editor: Michael Radeck. Music: Jean-Marie Gilles, Nikolai Tomas. In color. Release date: July 2, 1999. Running time: 88 Min. GERMAN.
Cast: Mareike Fell, Annett Renneberg, Mina Tander, Pascal Ulli, Bela B. Felsenheimer, Tobias Kuenzel.

OWLS' CASTLE
A Toho Co. release of an Owls' Castle Project presentation of a Fuji Television/Hyogensha production. (International sales: Pony Canyon, Tokyo.) Producers: Masaru Kakutani, Masaru Koibuchi. Executive producer: Shigeaki Hazama. Director: Masahiro Shinoda. Screenplay: Shinoda, Katsuo Narita, based on a story by Ryotaro Shiba. Camera: Tatsuo Suzuki. Music: Joji Yuasa. In color. Release date: May 13, 2000. Running time: 138 Min. JAPANESE.
Cast: Kiichi Nakai, Mayu Tsuruta, Riona Hazuki, Takaya Kamikawa, Shima Iwashita, Toshiya Nagasawa, Jinpachi Nezu, Gaku Yamamoto.

PANDAEMONIUM
A BBC Films presentation of a Mariner Films production in association with the Arts Council of England and Moonstone Entertainment. Producer: Nick O'Hagan. Executive producers: Mike Phillips, Tracey Scoffield, David M. Thompson. Co-producer: Michael Kustow. Director: Julien Temple. Screenplay: Frank Cottrell Boyce. Camera: John Lynch. Editor: Niven Howie. Music: Dario Marianecelli. Release date: Sept. 11, 2000. Running time: 124 Min. BRITISH.
Cast: Linue Roache, John Hannah, Samantha Morton, Emily Woof, Emma Fielding, Andy Serkis, Samuel West, Michael Harbour.

PANDORA'S BEAUTY
An Alliance Atlantis release (in Canada) of a Cite-Amerique production, with the participation of Sodec, Telefilm Canada, the Canadian Television Fund, Societe Radio-Canada, Super Ecran. (International sales: Cite-Amerique, Montreal.) Producer: Lorraine Richard. Executive producer: Louis Laverdiere. Director: Charles Biname. Screenplay: Biname, Suzanne Jacob. Camera: Pierre Gill. Editor: Michel Arcand. Music: Francois Bruneau, Jean-Marc Pisapia. In color. Release date: Feb. 18, 2000. Running time: 92 Min. CANADIAN.
Cast: Pascale Bussieres, Jean-Francois Casabonne, Maude Guerin, Gary Boudreault, Pascale Montpetit, Annick Bergeron.

PAN TADEUSZ
A Heritage Films (Warsaw)/Les Films du Losange (Paris) co-production, in association with Canal Plus Poland, Le Studio Canal Plus, Vision Film Production, Cinematography Committee (Poland), Film Production Agency (Poland), Apollo Film, Film Art, Max Film, Neptune Film, Odra Film, Silesia Film. (International sales: Le Studio Canal Plus, Paris.) Producers: Lew Rywin, Margaret Menegoz. Executive producers: Michal Szczerbic, Amira Chemakhi. Director: Andrzej Wajda. Screenplay: Wajda, Jan Nowina Zarzycki, Piotr Weresniak, based on the poem by Adam Mickiewicz. Camera: Pawel Edelman. Editor: Wanda Zeman. Music: Wojciech Kilar. In color, Panavision widescreen. Release date: Feb. 17, 2000. Running time: 125 Min. POLISH-FRENCH.
Cast: Boguslaw Linda, Daniel Olbrychski, Andrzej, Seweryn.

PAPER
A DB production. Producer: Shan Dongbing. Director/Screenplay: Ding Jiancheng. Camera: Xu Wei. Editor: Ding Jiancheng. Music: Su Fang. In color and B&W. Release date: Jan. 30, 2000. Running time: 60 Min. CHINESE.
Cast: Chen Ying, Dan Da, Zhou Zhe, Cong Zhijun, Zhou Yunpeng.

A PARADISE UNDER THE STARS
An Icaic/Wanda production, in association with Ibsermedia and Spanish Television. Producers: Camilo Vives, Jose Maria Morales. Executive producers: Evelio Delgado, Puy Oria. Director: Gerardo Chijona. Screenplay: Chijona, Luis Aguero, Senal Paz. Camera: Raul Perez Ureta. Editor: Rori Sainz De Rozas. Music: Jose Maria Vitier. In color. Release date: Jan. 29, 2000. Running time: 90 Min. CUBAN-SPANISH.
Cast: Thais Valdes, Vladimir Cruz, Ampoaro Munoz, Enrique Molina.

PARADISO–SEVEN DAYS WITH SEVEN WOMEN
A Moana-Film production. (International sales: Moana-Film, Berlin.) Producer: Rudolf Thome. Director/Screenplay: Thome. Camera: Reinhold Vorschneider. Editor: Karin Nowarra. Music: Wolfgang Bohmer. In color. Release date: Feb. 14, 2000. Running time: 102 Min. GERMAN.
Cast: Hanns Zischler, Cora Frost, Adriana Altaras, Sabine Bach, Khyana El Bitar, Irm Hermann, Isabel Hindersin, Amelie zur Muhlen.

PARANOID
A Portman Entertainment & Sky Pictures presentation in association with Isle of Man Film Commission of a Paul Trijbits/Gareth Neame production. (International sales: Portman Entertainment, London.) Producer: Paul Trijbits. Executive producers: Gareth Neame, Steve Christian, Miles Donnelly. Co-producer: Jo Human. Director/Screenplay: John Duigan. Camera: Slawomir Idzlak. Editor: Humphrey Dixon. Music: Charlie Mole. In Deluxe color. Release date: May 12, 2000. Running time: 94 Min. BRITISH.
Cast: Jessica Alba, Iain Glen, Jeanne Tripplehorn, Ewen Bremner, Kevin Whately, Oliver Milburn, Amy Phillips, Gary Love, David Fahm.

PARK
A High-Hat Films production. (International sales: High-Hat, Dublin.) Producers/Directors: John Carney, Tom Hall. Screenplay: Carney. Camera: Mark Waldron. Editor: Brenda Morrisey. Music: Carney. In color, video-to 35 mm. Release date: Aug. 31, 1999. Running time: 88 Min. IRISH.
Cast: Des Nealon, Jayne Snow, Claudia Terry, Pat Laffin, Aidan Walshe, Dereck Young, Suzan Harnett.

PASSING DARKNESS
A Kommunenes Filmsentral release of a Barentsfilm production, in association with Norsk Film and BV Film. Producer: Jan-Erik Gammleng. (International sales: BV Intl. Pictures, Avaldsnes, Norway.) Director: Knut Erik Jensen. Screenplay Alf. R. Jacobsen, Jensen, based on Jacobsen's novel "Tango Bacalao." Camera: Svein Krovel. Editor: Trygve Hagen. Music: Olga Petrova. In color. Release date: Jan. 19, 2000. Running time: 95 Min. NORWEGIAN.
Cast: Stig Henrik Hoff, Snorre Tindberg, Gunnel Lindblom, Gorild Mauseth, Nicholas Hope, Dietrich Hollinderbaumer, Lana Paouli.

PASSIONATELY
An Ocean release of a Film par Film/France 3 Cinema production, with participation of TPS Cinema and Cofimage 10. (International sales: TF1 Intl., Paris.) Producer: Jean-Louis Livi. Executive producer: Bernard Marescot. Director: Bruno Nuytten. Screenplay: Nuytten, Tatiana Vialle. Camera: Eric Gautier. Editor: Dominique Auvray. Music: Richard Galliano, Michel Portal. In color. Release date: June 4, 2000. Running time: 99 Min. FRENCH.
Cast: Gerard Lanvin, Charlotte Gainsbourg, Eric Ruf, Liliane Rovere, Tania Da Costa, Berenice Bejo, Catherine Sola, Angelica Chaves.

PASSION BOULEVARD
A ROI Studio production (International sales: Intercinema Art Agency.) Director: Vladimir Khotinenko. Screenplay: Sergei Koltakov. Camera: Vladimir Shevtsik. Editor: Svetlana Tarik. In color. Release date: Feb. 12, 2000. Running time: 107 Min. RUSSIAN.
Cast: Sergei Koltakov, Nina Usatova, Vladimir Ilyin, Sergei Garmash, Sergei Parshin, Elena Starodub.

THE PAST
A World Circle and Czech TV production in cooperation with the Union of the Deaf and Hard of Hearing in the Czech Republic. Producers: Ivo Trajkov, Vladimir Chrenovsky. Director/Screenplay: Ivo Trajkov. Camera: Klaus Fuxjager. Editor: Bara Kastakova. Music: Vladimir Chrenovsky. In color. Release date: Aug. 22, 1999. Running time: 96 Min. CZECH.
Cast: Karel Zima, Klara Melisova, Peter Georgiev.

THE PENITENT'S TREE
A Columbia TriStar Spain release of a Kanzaman production, in association with Via Digital. Producers: Denise O'Dell, Mark Albela. Director/Screenplay: Jose Maria Borell. Camera: Joan Benet. Editor: Guillermo Represa. Music: Roque Banos. In color. Release date: Apr. 14, 2000. Running time: 89 Min. SPANISH.
Cast: Javier Manrique, Elena Anaya, Alfredo Landa, Ildefonso Tamayo.

PEPPERMINT CANDY
A UniKorea/Dream Venture Capital presentation of an East Film (S. Korea)/NHK (Japan) production. (International sales: East Film, Seoul.) Producers: Myeong Kye-nam, Makoto Ueda, Co-producers, Jeon Jae-yeong, Hay Jeon, Keiko Iino. Director/Screenplay: Lee Chang-dong. Camera: Kim Hyeong-gu. Editor: Kim Hyeon. Music: Lee Jai-jin. In color. Release date: Oct. 14, 1999. Running time: 131 Min. SOUTH KOREAN-JAPANESE.
Cast: Seol Kyeong-gu, Mun So-ri, Kim Yeo-jin.

PERFECT BLUE
A Palm Pictures release of a Manga Entertainment presentation of a Rex Entertainment Co. production. Producers: Hiroaki Inoue, Masao Maruyama. Director: Satoshi Kon. Screenplay: Sadyuki Murai, based on the novel by Yoshikazu Takeuchi. Camera: Hisao Shirai. Editor: Harutoshi Ogata. Music: Masahiro Ikumi. In color. Release date: Oct. 19, 1999. Running time: 80 Min. Animated. JAPANESE.

PETTSON AND FINDUS

A Svensk Filmindustri release (in Sweden) of a Happy Life (Sweden)/TMO-ToonLand Film (Germany) production. (International sales: Svensk, Stockholm.) Producer: Ulf Synnerholm. Executive producers: Peter Gustafsson, Peter Volkle. Director: Albert Hanan Kaminski. Screenplay: Torbjorn Jansson, based on the stories by Sven Nordqvist. Music: Lennart Olsson. In color. Release date: Dec. 22, 1999. Running time: 72 Min. Animated. SWEDISH-GERMAN.

PHANTOM

A Rosa Filmes production in association with Radiotelevisao Portuguesa, with support of ICAM, MC. (International sales: Rosa Filmes, Lisbon.) Producer: Amando Coroado. Director: Joao Pedro Rodrigues. Screenplay: Rodrigues, Jose Neves, Paula Rebelo, Alexandre Melo. Camera: Rui Pocas. Editors: Paulo Rebelo, Rodrigues. In color. Release date: Sept. 8, 2000. Running time: 90 Min. PORTUGUESE.
Cast: Ricardo Meneses, Beatriz Torcato, Andre Barbosa.

PHANTOM, THE SUBMARINE

An Ilshin Investment Co. presentation of an Uno Films production. (International sales: Ilshin, Seoul.) Producer: Kim Seon-ah. Executive producer: Kim Seong-bum. Co-producer: Cha Seung-jae. Director: Min Byeong-cheon. Screenplay: Jan Jun-hwan, Bong Jun-hom, Kim Jong-hun. Camera: Hong Kyeong-pyo. Editor: Ko Im-pyo. Music: Lee Dong-jun. In color. Release date: Oct. 16, 1999. Running time: 103 Min. SOUTH KOREAN.
Cast: Choe Min-su, Cheong Wu-seong, Yun Ju-sang.

THE PILGRIMAGE OF STUDENTS PETER AND JACOB

A Cineart/Czech TV/Slovak TV/Kvartfilm/Kratky Film/Margo Films production. (International sales: Filmexport, Prague.) Producers: Viktor Schwarcz, Marian Postihac. Alice Nemanska, Helena Slavikova, Marian Puobis, Francois Margolin. Director: Drahomira Vihanova. Screenplay: Vihanova, Vladimir Vondra. Camera: Juraj Sajmovic. Editor: Josef Valusiak. Music: Emil Viklicky. In Kodak color. Release date: July 8, 2000. Running time: 95 Min. CZECH-SLOVAK-FRENCH.
Cast: Adrian Jastraban, Gustav Reznicek, Zuzana Stivinova.

PIN-PON–THE FILM

A Lions Gate Films release (in Canada) of a Vision 4 production, with the participation of the Canadian Television Fund, Telefilm Canada, Sodec, Quebec government, Canadian government, Super Ecran, Tele-Quebec. (International sales: Sonoma Entertainment, Los Angeles.) Producers: Jacques Bonin, Claude Veillet, Carmen Bourassa. Director: Ghyslaine Cote. Screenplay: Paul Thinel, Paule Marier. Camera: Serge Ladouceur. Editor: Jose Heppell. Music: Gerard Gerard Cyr. In color. Release date: Dec. 6, 1999. Running time: 80 Min. CANADIAN.
Cast: Thomas Graton, Yves Soutiere, Philippe Lambert, Julien Poulin, Anastassia Fomina, Melven Gilbert, Mireille Levesque.

P.I.N.S.

A Cinemedia production in association with Film Victoria, Australian Film Commission, Australian Broadcasting Corp. (International sales: Cinemedia, Melbourne.) Producer: Luke Kilmany. Director: Garth Davis. Camera: Davis, Greig Fraser. Editor: Jane Usher. In color. Release date: July 28, 2000. Running time: 63 Min. Documentary. AUSTRALIAN.

A PLACE NEARBY

A Nordisk Film production, in association with TV2 Denmark, BG Fund, Danish Film Institute. (International sales: Nordisk Film, Copenhagen.) Producer: Tina Dalhoff. Executive producer: Erik Crone. Director/Screenplay: Kaspar Rostrup. Camera: Eric Kress. Editor: Grete Moldrup. Music: Fuzzy. In color. Release date: Feb. 13, 2000. Running time: 100 Min. DANISH.
Cast: Ghita Norby, Frits Helmuth, Henning Moritzen, Thure Lindhardt.

PLACIDO RIZZOTTO

An Istituto Luce release of an Arbash Film production in association with RAI Cinema. (International sales: Arbash Film, Palermo.) Director/Screenplay: Pasquale Scimeca. Camera: Pasquale Mari. Editor: Babak Karimi. Music: Agricantus. In Cinecitta color, widescreen. Release date: Aug. 24, 2000. Running time: 108 Min. ITALIAN.
Cast: Marcello Mazzarelli, Gioia Spaziani, Arturo Todaro,.

PLATFORM

A Hu-Tong Communication (Hong Kong)/T-Mark Inc. (Japan) Artcam Intl. (France) production in collaboration with Office Kitano, Bandai Visual Co. (International sales: Flach Pyramide Intl., Paris.) Producers: Li Kit-ming, Shozo Ichiyama. Executive producer: Masayuki Mori. Co-producers: Joel Farges, Elise Jalladeau. Director/Screenplay: Jia Zhang-ke. Camera: Yu Lik-wai. Editor: Kong Jing-lei. Music: Yoshihiro Hanno. Release date: Sept. 4, 2000. Running time: 195 Min. HONG KONG-JAPANESE-FRENCH.
Cast: Wang Hong-wei, Zhao Tao, Liang Jing-dong, Yang Tian-yi.

POKEMON: THE FIRST MOVIE

A Warner Bros. Family Entertainment release of a Kids WB! presentation of a Pikachu Project '98-Shogakukan Inc. production in association with 4Kids Entertainment. Producers: Norman J. Grossfeld, Choji Yoshikawa, Tomoyuki Igarashi, Takemoto Mori. Executive producers: Alfred R. Kahn, Masakazu Kubo, Takashi Kawaguchi. Director: Kunihiko Yuyama. Director, English adaptation: Michael Haigney. Screenplay: Takeshi Shudo, based on characters created by Satoshi Tajiri. Camera: Hisao Shirai. Editors: Toshio Henmi, Yutaka Ito. Music: Ralph Schuckett, John Loeffler. In Deluxe color. Release date: Nov. 6, 1999. MPAA Rating: G. Running time: 75 Min. Animated. JAPANESE.
Voices: Veronica Taylor, Philip Bartlett, Rachael Lillis, Eric Stuart, Addie Blaustein, Ikue Otani.

POKEMON THE MOVIE 2000: THE POWER OF ONE

A Warner Bros. Family Entertainment release of a Kids WB! presentation of a Pikachu Project '99-Shogakukan Inc. production in association with 4Kids Entertainment. Producers: Norman J. Grossfeld, Choji Yoshikawa, Yukako Matsusako, Takemoto Mori. Executive producers: Masakazu Kubo, Takashi Kawaguchi, Alfred R. Kahn. Director: Kunihiko Yuyama. Director (English adaptation): Michael Haigney. Screenplay: Takeshi Shudo, based on characters created by Satoshi Tajiri. English adaptation: Norman J. Grossfeld, Haigney. Translation: Paul Taylor. Camera: Hisao Shirai. Editor: Jay Film. Music: Ralph Schuckett, John Loeffler. In Deluxe color. Release date: July 18, 2000. MPAA Rating: PG. Running time: 81 Min. Animated. JAPANESE.
Voices: Veronica Taylor, Rachael Lillis, Addie Blaustein, Eric Stuart.

POLICEWOMAN

A Westdeutsche Universum-Film/Westdeutsche Rundfunks production. Producer: Christian Granderath. Executive producer: Norbert Sauer. Director: Andreas Dresen. Screenplay: Laila Stieler, inspired by Annegret Held's book "My Night Shapes" (Meine Nachtgestalten). Camera: Michael Hammon. Editor: Monika Schindler. In color. Release date: June 29, 2000. Running time: 98 Min. GERMAN.
Cast: Gabriela Maria Schmeide, Axel Prahl, Paul Grubba, Yevgeni Sitokhin, Katrin Sass, Horst Krause, Martin Seifert, Klaus Manchen.

PORNOSTAR

A Little More Co. production. (International sales: Little More, Tokyo.) Producers: Masakazu Takei, Miyoshi Kikuchi. Director/Screenplay: Toshiaki Toyoda. Camera: Norimichi Kasamatsu. Editor: Toshihide Fukano. Music: DIP. In color. Release date: Dec 21, 1999. Running time: 98 Min. JAPANESE.
Cast: Koji Chihara, Onimaru, Rin Ozawa, Tetta Sugimoto, Akaji Maro, Reona Hirota.

POP IN REYKJAVIK

A 101 Ltd. production. Producers: Ingbar H. Poroarson, Baltasar Kormakur. Director/Editor: Agust Jakobsson. Camera: Jakobsson, Arni Pall Hansson. In color. Release date: Mar. 1, 2000. Running time: 103 Min. ICELANDIC.
Cast: Bang Gang, Bellatrix, Botnleoja, Curver, DJ Addi, Ensimi, Gus Gus, Hringir, Magga Stirina, Maus, Moa, Pall Oskar & Casino.

PORNO FILM

An E-Motion Film/TV Slovenia production. (International sales: E-Motion Film, Ljubljana, Slovenia.) Producer: Danijel Hocevar. Director/Screenplay: Damjan Kozole. Camera: Ven Jemersic. Editors: Zlatjan Cuckov, Dafne Jemersic. Music: Drago Ivanusa. In color. Release date: July 12, 2000. Running time: 80 Min. SLOVENIAN
Cast: Matjaz Latin, Natalia Danilova, Primoz Petkovsek, Zoran More.

THE PORT OF LAST RESORT

A Pinball Films (Vienna) production, in association with Estrafilm, with the support of Home Box Office. (International sales: Louise Rosen Ltd., Brookline, MA.) Producers: Joan Grossman, Paul Rosdy. Co-producer: Lukas Stepanik. Director/Screenplay/Editor: Joan Grossman, Paul Rosdy. Camera: Wolfgang Lehner, various. Music: John Zorn. In B&W. Release date: Oct. 10, 1999. Running time: 80 Min. Documentary. AUSTRIAN.
With: Fred Fields, Ernest Heppner, Illo Heppner, Siegmar Simon.

PORTUGUESE

A Hunnia Film Studio production. Producers: Sandor Simo, Gyorgy Budai. Director/Screenplay: Andor Lukats, based on the play by Andras Monori, Zoltan Egressy. Camera: Daniel Garas. Editor: Maria Rigo. Music: Andras Monori. In color. Release date: Feb. 6, 2000. Running time: 100 Min. HUNGARIAN.
Cast: Imre Csuja, Reka Pelsoczy, Agi Szirtes, Ferenc Lengyel, Zoltan Varga, Jozsef Kelemen, Zsolt Kovacs, Viktor Nagy, Eszter Onodi.

PRETEND I'M NOT HERE

An Ocean Films (in France)/Cineart (in Belgium) release of a Quo Vadis Cinema/Arte France Cinema (France)/Mikado Films/Bianca Films (Italy) co-production. (International sales: Flach Pyramide Intl.) Producer: Jerome Vidal. Director: Olivier Jahan. Screenplay: Jahan, Michel C. Pouzel. Camera: Gilles Porte. Editor: Nathalie Langlade, Marie-France Cuenot. Music: Milos Corsiny. In color. Release date: May 18, 2000. Running time: 101 Min. FRENCH-ITALIAN.
Cast: Jeremie Renier, Aurore Clement, Johan Leysen, Sami Bouajila, Alexia Stresi, Natalie Richard, Pierre Berriau, Emma De Caunes.

PRETTY DEVILS

A Les Films du Losange release of an Ocelot Prods. presentation of an Ocelot/Fildebroc/Nef production, with participation of Canal Plus. (International sales: Mercure Distribution, Paris.) Producer: Josee Benabent-Loiseau. Co-producers: Michelle de Broca, Manuel Malle. Director/Screenplay: Serge Meynard. Camera: Bruno Privat. Editor: Katya Chelli. Music: Roland Romanelli. In color. Release date: Nov., 25, 1999. Running time: 100 Min. FRENCH.
Cast: Olivia Bonamy, Audrey Tautou, Axelle Ade-Pasdeloup.

THE PRICE

A Cine Citta Intl. presentation of a Sintra production. Producer: Rosanna Seregni. Director: Rolando Stefanelli. Screenplay: Stefanelli, Claudio Lizza. Camera: Vincenzo Marano. Editor: Roberta Penchini. Music: Palo Fresu. In color. Release date: Nov. 18, 1999. Running time: 114 Min. ITALIAN.
Cast: Stefano Dionisi, Chiara Caselli, Alessandro Repossi.

THE PRICE OF MILK

A Lot 47 Films (in U.S.) release of a John Swimmer presentation in association with the New Zealand Film Commission of a John Swimmer production. (International sales: New Zealand Film Commission, Wellington.) Producer: Fiona Copland. Executive producer: Tim Sanders. Director/Screenplay: Harry Sinclair. Camera: Leon Narbey. Editor: Cushla Dillon. In color, Panavision widescreen. Release date: May 18, 2000. Running time: 87 Min. NEW ZEALAND.
Cast: Danielle Cormack, Karl Urban, Willa O'Neill, Michael Lawrence, Rangi Motu.

THE PRINCE'S MANUSCRIPT

A Warners Italia release of a Sciario production. Producers: Giuseppe and Francesco Tornatore. (International sales: Intrafilm, Rome.) Director: Roberto Ando. Screenplay: Ando, Salvatore Marcarelli. Camera: Enrico Lucidi. Editor: Massimo Quaglia. Music: Marco Betta. In Technicolor. Release date: Mar. 29, 2000. Running time: 93 Min. ITALIAN.
Cast: Michel Bouquet, Jeanne Moreau, Paolo Briguglia, Girogio Lupano, Laurent Terzieff, Massimo de Francovich.

THE PRINCESS AND THE WARRIOR

A Sony Pictures Classics release (in U.S.) of an X Filme Creative Pool production. (International sales: Studio Canal, Paris.) Producers: Stefan Arndt, Maria Kopf. Director, Screenplay: Tom Tykwer. Camera: Frank Griebe. Editor: Mathilde Bonnefoy. Music: Tywker, Johnny Klimek, Reinhold Heil. In color, Panavision widescreen. Release date: Sept. 2, 2000. Running time: 135 Min. GERMAN.
Cast: Franka Potente, Benno Furmann, Joachim Krol, Marita Breuer, Jurgen Tarrach, Lars Rudolph, Melchior Beslon, Ludger Pistor

PRIVATE LIES

A Bernd Burgemeister presentation of a TV-60 Filmproduktion Munich production, in association with BR, NDR, WDR, ORF, SF DRS. (International sales: Cinepool, Munich.) Producers: Otto Grokenberger, Dorothy Aufiero, David Collins. Co-producer: Gabriela Sperl. Director: Sherry Hormann. Screenplay: Gabriela Sperl. Camera: Ken Kelsch. Editor: Christel Suckow. Music: Mason Dering. In color. Release date: June 26, 2000. Running time: 107 Min. GERMAN.
Cast: Martina Gedeck, Vyto Ruginis, John Corbett, Marianne Saegerbrecht, Rosemarie Fendel, Margaret Colin.

THE PRIVATE LIFE OF PYOTR VINOGRADOV

A Moskinokombianat (Moscow) production. Director: Aleksandr Macheret. Screenplay: Lev Slavin. Camera: Aleksei Utkin. Music: L. Knipper. In B&W. Release date: Aug. 7, 2000. Running time: 88 Min. SOVIET UNION–1935.
Cast: Boris Livanov, V. Chishevsky, Konstantin Gradopolov, Galina Pashkova, N. Ardi.

THE PROF

A Rezo Films release of an Alter Films/Le Studio Canal Plus/France 2 Cinema production, with participation of Canal Plus. (International sales: Le Studio Canal Plus, Paris.) Producer: Alain Terzian. Director: Alexandre Jardin. Screenplay: Helene Jousse, Alexandre Jardin, based on the novel "Le petit sauvage" by Jardin. Camera: Manuel Teran. Editor: Veronique Parnet. Music: Jean-Claude Petit. In color. Release date: Apr. 25, 2000. Running time: 94 Min. FRENCH.
Cast: Jean-Hughes Anglade, Yvan Attal, Helene de Fougerolles, Odette Laure, Jean-Marie Winling, Thierry Lhermitte.

THE PROTAGONISTS

A Medusa release (in Italy) of a Massimo Vigliar presentation of a Surf Film production in association with Medusa Film, Telepiu. (International sales: Surf Film, Rome.) Producers: Massimo Viglia, Fulvio Colombo. Executive producer: Roberto Manni. Director/Screenplay: Luca Guadagnino. Camera: Paolo Bravi. Editor: Walter Fasano. Music: Andrea Guerra. In color. Release date: Aug. 26, 1999. Running time: 90 Min. ITALIAN.
Cast: Tilda Swinton, Fabrizia Sacchi, Andrew Tiernan, Claudio Gioe, Paolo Briguglia, Michelle Hunziker, Chiara Conti, Laura Betti, Jhelisa.

PUBLIC ENEMY

An Archipel 33/Egoli Film/Kinotar Oy production. Producer: Denis Freyd. Co-producer: Jens Meurer. Director/Screenplay: Jens Meurer. Camera: Torsten Lippstock. Editor: Anne Weil. Music: Nile Rodgers. In color, 16mm. Release date: Sept. 1, 1999. Running time: 88 Min. Documentary. FRENCH-GERMAN.
Cast: Bobby Seale, Jamal Joseph, Kathleen Cleaver, Nile Rodgers.

PURELY BELTER

A Film Four presentation of a Mumbo Jumbo production. (International sales: Film Four Intl., London.) Producer: Elizabeth Karlsen. Executive producer: Stephen Woolley. Director/Screenplay: Mark Herman, based on the novel "The Season Ticket" by Jonathan Tulloch. Camera: Andy Collins. Editor: Michael Ellis. Music: Ian Broudie, Michael Gibbs. In Deluxe color. Release date: May 12, 2000. Running time: 99 Min. BRITISH.
Cast: Chris Beattie, Greg McLane, Charlie Hardwick, Jody Baldwin.

PURE MOMENT OF ROCK 'N' ROLL

A Universal Pictures Intl. release (in France) of an MP Prods./Breguet Prods./Havas Images production with participation of Centre National du Cinema, Canal Plus, Sofinergie V. (International sales: UGC Intl., Paris.) Producers: Michel Propper, Laurent Thiry, Alain Serror. Director: Manuel Boursinhac. Screenplay: Vincent Ravallec, Boursinhac, Louis Stephane Ulysse, Stephane Cabel. Camera: Kevin Jewison. Editor: Helene de Luze. In color. Release date: Sept. 18, 1999. Running time: 108 Min. FRENCH.
Cast: Vincent Elbaz, Nicolas Abraham, Samy Naceri, Laurence Cote.

PURPLE STORM

A Media Asia Distribution release of a Media Asia Films and Jackie Chan presentation of a Media Asia Films production. (International sales: Media Asia, Hong Kong.) Producers: Thomas Chung, Willie Chan. Executive producers: John Chong, Solon So. Director: Teddy Chen. Screenplay: Jo Jo Hui, Clarence Yip, Lam Oi-wah, story by Chen, Chan Wai. Camera: Arthur Wong. Editor: Kong Chi-leung. Music: Peter Kam. In color. Release date: Nov. 23, 1999. Running time: 112 Min. HONG KONG.
Cast: Daniel Wu, Kam Kwok-leung, Emil Chow, Josie Ho, Joan Chen, Theresa Lee, Tam Yiu-man, Huan Jianxin, Michael Tong, Moses Chan.

A QUESTION OF TASTE

A Pyramide release of a CDP/Le Studio Canal Plus/France 3 Cinema/Rhone-Alpes Cinema production, with participation of Canal Plus, CNC. (International sales: FTD, Paris.) Producers: Catherine Dussart, Chantal Perrin. Director: Bernard Rapp. Screenplay: Gilles Taurand, Rapp, based on the novel "Affaires de gout" by Philippe Balland. Camera: Gerard de Battista. Editor: Juliette Welfling. Music: Jean-Philippe Goude. In color. Release date: Apr., 18, 2000. Running time: 91 Min. FRENCH.
Cast: Bernard Giraudeau, Jean-Pierre Lorit, Florence Thomassin, Jean-Pierre Leaud, Artus de Penguern, Charles Berling.

RAGE

A Granite FilmWorks production. (International sales: Granite, London.) Producers: Maria-Elena L'Abbate, Newton I. Aduaka. Director/Screenplay: Newton I. Aduaka. Camera: Carlos Arango. Editor: Marcela Cueo. Music: various. In color. Release date: Sept. 16, 1999. Running time: 120 Min. BRITISH.
Cast: Fraser Ayres, Shaun Parkes, John Pickard, Shango Baku.

RAINBOW TROUT

A Park Chong-won Prod./Trout Prods. production, in association with Cinema Service. (International sales: Mirovision, Seoul.) Producer: Park Chong-won. Executive producer: Park Keon-seop. Director: Park Chong-won. Screenplay: Park, Kim Dae-woo. Camera: Jin Young-hwan. Editor: Lee Kying-ja. Music: Kim Sung-hyun. In color. Release date: Sept. 4, 1999. Running time: 100 Min. SOUTH KOREAN.
Cast: Kan Su-yeon, Hwang In-sung, Sul Kying-gu, Kim Sae-dong.

RANCID ALUMINIUM

An Entertainment Film Distributors release of an EFD presentation of a Fiction Factory production. Producers: Mike Parker, Mark Thomas. Executive producer: Nigel Green. Co-producer: James Hawes. Director: Ed Thomas. Screenplay: James Hawes, based on his novel. Camera: Tony Imi. Editor: Chris Lawrence. Music: John Hardy. In Fujicolor, Deluxe color, widescreen. Release date: Jan. 23, 2000. Running time: 87 Min. BRITISH.
Cast: Joseph Fiennes. Rhys Ifans, Tara Fitzgerald, Sadie Frost, Stephen Berkoff, Keith Allen, Dani Behr, Andrew Howard, Nick Moran.

RAPE ME

A Pan-Europeenne Distribution release of a Toute Premiere Fois presentation of a Philippe Godeau production, with participation of Canal Plus. (International sales: Wild Bunch, Paris.) Producer: Philippe Godeau. Executive producer: Dominique Chiron. Director/Screenplay: Virginie Despentes, Coralie Trinh Thi, based on the novel by Despentes. Camera: Benoit Chamaillard. Editors: Ailo Auguste, Francine Lemaitre. Music: Varou Jan. In color. Release date: June 30, 2000. Running time: 76 Min. FRENCH.
Cast: Raffaela Anderson, Karen Bach.

RAY: LIFE AND WORK OF SATYAJIT RAY

A Satyajit Ray Archive/Orchid Films production with the support of the Ford Foundation. (International sales: Indrapur Cinematografica, Rome.) Producer/Director/Screenplay: Goutam Ghose. Camera: Ghose. Editor: Moloyt Bannerjee. Music: Stayajut Ray, Ghose. Commentary: Ray, Aparna Sen. In B&W and color. Release date: Sept. 9, 1999. Running time: 105 Min. Documentary. INDIAN.

A REAL YOUNG LADY

A Rezo Films release of a CB Films/Artedis presentation with support from the CNC and GNCR. Producer: Pierre-Richard Muller. (Original uncredited producer: Andre Genoves/Les Films de la Boetie.) Director/Screenplay: Catherine Breillat. Camera: Pierre Fattori. Editor: Annie Charrier. Music: Mort Shuman. In color. Release date: June 7, 2000. Running time: 92 Min. FRENCH.
Cast: Charlotte Alexandra, Hiram Keller, Rita Meiden, Bruno Balp.

RED DUST

An Interfilm/Croation Television production. (International sales: Interfilm.) Producer: Ivan Maloca. Executive producer: Sanja Ivancin. Director: Zrinko Ogresta. Screenplay: Ogresta, Goran Tribuson. Camera: Davorin Gecl. Editor: Josip Podvorac. Music: Neven Franges. In color. Release date: Sept. 8, 1999. Running time: 105 Min. CROATIAN.
Cast: Josip Kusan, Marko Matanovic, Ivo Gregurevic.

RELATIVE VALUES

An Alliance Atlantis release of a Midsummer Films production, in association with the Isle of Man Film Commission. (International sales: Overseas Filmgroup, Los Angeles.) Producer: Christopher Millburn. Executive producers: Steven Christian, Chris Harris. Director: Eric Styles. Screenplay: Paul Rattigan, Michael Walker, based on the play by Noel Coward. Camera: Jimmy Dibling. Editor: Caroline Limmer; Associate editor: Ian Seymour. Music: John Jaeger. In color. Release date: June 23, 2000. Running time: 87 Min. BRITISH.
Cast: Julie Andrews, Sophie Thompson, Edward Atterton, Jeanne Tripplehorn, William Baldwin, Colin Firth, Stephen Fry.

REMBRANDT

A Pyramide release (in France) of an Ognon Pictures, France 2 Cinema (France)/Pain Unlimited, Filmstiftung Nordrhein-Westfalen (Germany)/Argus Film Produktie, Trois Television, Cobo Fund (Netherlands) production, with participation of Canal Plus and CNC. (International sales: Flach Pyramide Intl., Paris.) Produced by Humbert Balsan. Co-producers: Vibeke Windelov, Peter van Vogelpoel, Erik Schut. Director: Charles Matton. Screenplay: Sylvie Matton, Charles Matton. Camera: Pierre Dupouey. Editor: Francois Gedigier. Music: Nicolas Matton. In color. Release date: Sept. 1, 1999. Running time: 100 Min. FRENCH-GERMAN-DUTCH.

Cast: Klaus Maria Brandauer, Romane Bohringer, Jean Rochefort, Johanna ter Steege, Jean-Philippe Ecoffey, Carolinie van Houten.

RENT-A-FRIEND

An A Film Distribution release of a Jordaan Film production in association with BNN-TV, Fu Works. (International sales: SND Films, Amsterdam.) Producer: Marc Heijdemann. Co-producer: San Fu Maltha. Director/Screenplay: Eddy Terstall. Camera: Stefan Bijnen. Editor: Eddy Zoutendijk. Music: Van Dik Hout, Jina Sumedi. In color, widescreen. Release date: Feb. 2, 2000. Running time: 84 Min. DUTCH.

Cast: Marc van Uchelen, Rifka Lodeizen, Nadja Hupscher, Huub Stapel, Femke Lakerveld, Natasja Loturco, Ariane Schlute.

RESISTING REMEMBRANCE

A Sunday Morning Prods. production. (International sales: Films Distribution, Paris.) Producer: Nathalie Mesuret. Director: Orso Miret. Screenplay: Miret, Roger Bohbot, Agnes de Sacy. Camera: Olivier Chambon. Editor: Agnes Bruckert. Music: Gorecki. In color. Release date: May 16, 2000. Running time: 121 Min. FRENCH.

Cast: Yann Goven, Olivier Gourmet, Brigitte Catillon, Martine Audrain, Jocelyne Desverchere, Stephane Bierry, Jacques Spiesser.

A RESPECTABLE MAN

A CDI/Buena Vista Intl. Italia release (in Italy) of a Clemi Cinematografica production in association with Mediatrade. Producer: Giovanni Di Clemente. Director: Maurizio Zaccaro. Screenplay: Umberto Contarello, Zaccaro, based on an idea by Silvia Tortora. Camera: Pasquale Rachini. Editor: Anna Napoli. Music: Pino Donaggio. In color, widescreen. Release date: Sept. 9, 1999. Running time: 120 Min. ITALIAN.

Cast: Michele Placido, Stefano Accorsi, Marianegla Melato, Giovanna Mezzogiorno, Leo Gullotta, Giuliano Gemma, Vincenzo Peluso.

RETURN TO ALGIERS

A Bac Films release of an Alexandre Films presentation of an Alexandre Films production, with participation of Canal Plus, Le Studio Canal Plus, Studio Images 6. (International sales: Le Studio Canal Plus, Paris.) Producer: Alexandre Arcady. Executive producer: Robert Benmussa. Director: Arcady. Screenplay: Antoine Lacomblez, Arcady, with the collaboration of Benjamin Stora, adapted from the novel "Grand vacance" by Rene Bonnell. Camera: Robert Alazraki. Editor: Joele van Effenterre. Music: Philippe Sarde. In color, widescreen. Release date: Mar. 17, 2000. Running time: 115 Min. FRENCH.

Cast: Antoine de Caunes, Nozha Khouadra, Samy Naceri, Said Amadis, Mathilda May, Wadeck Stanczak, Pierre Vaneck, Dora Doll.

RETURN TO GO!

An o-Filmproduktion in association with ZDF. Producers: Frank Loprich, Katrin Schlosser. Director/Screenplay: Pierre Sanoussi-Bliss. Camera: Thomas Plenert. Editor: Gudrun Plenert. In color. Release date: Feb. 18, 2000. Running time: 101 Min. GERMAN.

Cast: Pierre Sanoussi-Bliss, Matthias Freihof, Dieter Bach, Bart Klein, Paul Gilling, Ared Hubert.

REVENGE

A Wood Producciones production in association with Sombrero Verde and Arauco Films. Producer: Pepe Torres. Executive producers: Boris Quercia, Andres Wood. Director: Andres Wood. Screenplay: Boris Quercia, Wood. Camera: Miguel Joan Littin. Editor: Guillermo Cifuentes. Music: Alvaro Henriquez. In color. Release date: Sept. 14, 1999. Running time: 119 Min. CHILEAN.

Cast: Tamara Acosta, Willy Semler, Maria Izquierdo, Belgica Castro, Patricia Lopez, Daniel Munoz, Aldo Parodi.

RHYTHM & BLUES

An Equator Films presentation of a Life on Mars production. (International sales: Equator, London.) Producers: Hugh Bygott-Webb, Dominic Denny. Executive producers: David Winters, Patrick Meehan. Director: Stephen Lennhoff. Screenplay: Michael Jones. Camera: Fiona Cunningham Reid. Editor: Patrick McDonnell. Music: Michael Conn. In color. Release date: Sept. 27, 1999. Running time: 95 Min. BRITISH.

Cast: Angus McInnes, Ian Henderson, Paul Blackthorne, Gary Fairhall, Joe Hutton, Richard Ritchie, Phillipe Sartori, Sue Tilling.

THE RIFLEMAN OF THE VOROSHILOV REGIMENT

An NTV-Profit production. Producers: Igor Tolstunov, Sergei Kozlov. Director: Stanislav Govoruchin. Screenplay: Aleksandr Borodjanski, Govoruchin, Yuri Poljakov, based on the novel "A Woman on Wednesdays" by Viktor Pronin. Camera: Genadij Engstrem. Editor: Vera Kruglova. Music: Vladimir Dasckevic. In color. Release date: Feb. 14, 2000. Running time: 98 Min. RUSSIAN.

Cast: Michail Uljanov, Anna Sinjakina, Aleksandr Porochosikov, Irina Rozanova, Aleksei Makarov, Marat Basarov, Ilja Drevnev.

THE ROAD HOME

A Sony Pictures Classics release (in U.S.) of a Columbia Pictures Film Production Asia presentation of a Guangxi Film Studio/Beijing. New Picture Distribution Co. production. Producer: Zhao Yu. Executive producer: Zhang Weiping. Director: Zhang Yimou. Screenplay: Bao Shi, based on his novel "Remembrance." Camera: Hou Yong. Editor: Zhai Ru. Music: San Bao. In color, widescreen. Release date: Feb. 15, 2000. Running time: 89 Min. CHINESE.

Cast: Zhang Ziyi, Sun Honglei, Zheng Hao, Zhao Yuelin, Li Bin, Chang Guifa, Sung Wencheng, Liu Qi, Ji Bo, Zhang Zhongxi.

RODENTS

A Cabeza Hueca Prods. production. Producer: Lisandra I. Rivera. Executive producer: Isabel Davalos. Director/Screenplay: Sebastian Cordero. Camera: Matthew Jensen. Editors: Cordero, Mateo Herrera. Music: Sergio Sacoto Arias. In Deluxe color. Release date: Sept. 6, 1999. Running time: 107 Min. ECUADORIAN.

Cast: Carlos Valencia, Marco Bustos, Irina Lopez, Simon Brauer, Fabricio Lalama, Cristina Davila, Lupe Machado, Alfredo Martinez

ROLLERCOASTER

A Giraffe production, with the participation of the Canadian Television Fund, Telefilm, Canada, the Canadian Broadcasting Corp., TMN-The Movie Network, and British Columbia Film. (International sales: Buzzmedia, Toronto.) Producers: Scott Smith, Connie Dolphin. Director/Screenplay: Scott Smith. Camera: Robert Aschmann. Editor: Allan Lee. Music: Don MacDonald. In color. Release date: Sept. 21, 1999. Running time: 90 Min. CANADIAN.

Cast: Brendan Fletcher, Kett Turton,. Crystal Buble, Brent Glenen, Seam Amsing, David Lovgren.

ROSA AND CORNELIA

A Lantia Cinema & Audiovisivi release of a Gierre-Film Tre production. Producer: Grazia Volpi. Executive producer: Sandro Frezza. Director: Giorgio Treves. Screenplay: Remo Binosi, Francois de Maulde, Treves, based on the play "Expecting" (L'attesa) by Binosi. Camera: Camillo Bazzoni. Editor: Carla Simoncelli. Music: Franco Piersanti. In color. ITALIAN.

Cast: Stefania Rocca, Chiara Muti, Athina Cenci, Massimo Poggio, Daria Nicolidi, Massimo De Rossi.

A RUN FOR MONEY

A Warner Bros. (Turkey) release of an Atlantik Film production. (International sales: Atlantik, Istanbul.) Producer: Omer Atay. Director/Screenplay: Reha Erdem. Camera: Florent Herry, Jean-Louis Vialard. Editor: Nathalie Le Guay. Music: Pressure Drops. In Fujicolor. Release date: June 25, 2000. Running time: 98 Min. TURKISH.

Cast: Taner Birsel, Bennu Yildirimlar, Zuhal Gencer, Engin Alkan, Sermet Yesil, Bulent Yarar, Ali Dusenkalkar, Ara Guler.

RUNNING OUT OF TIME

A China Star Entertainment Group presentation of a Milkyway Image (Hong Kong) production for Win's Entertainment. (International sales: China Star, Hong Kong.) Producer: Charles Heung. Executive producer: Johnnie To. Co-producer: Christina Lee. Executive in charge of production: Tiffany Chen. Director: Johnnie To. Screenplay: Yau Nai-hoi. Laurent Cortiaud, Julien Carbon. Camera: Cheng Siu-keung. Editor: Andy Chan. Music: Raymond Wong. In color. Release date: Nov. 29, 1999. Running time: 93 Min. HONG KONG.

Cast: Andy Lau, Lau Ching-wan, YoYo Mung, Lee Chi-hung, Hui Shiu-hung, Lam Suet, Ruby Wong.

SACHS' DISEASE

A Pathe Distribution (in France) release of an Elefilm/Renn Prods./Katharina/France2 Cinema production, with participation of Canal Plus. (International sales: Films Distribution, Paris.) Producer: Rosalinde Deville. Director: Michel Deville. Screenplay: Rosalinde and Michel Deville, based on the novel by Martin Winckler. Camera: Andre Diot, Laurent Dhainaut. Editor: Andrea Sedlackova. Music: Jean-Fery Rebel, Quentin Daramane. In color, widescreen. Release date: Sept. 15, 1999. Running time: 107 Min. FRENCH.

Cast: Albert Dupontel, Valerie Dreville, Dominique Reymond, Martine Sarcey, Francois Clavier, Lucienne Hamon, Nathalie Boutefeu.

SACRED FLESH

A Gothica presentation of a Salvation Films production, in association with the 400 Co. Producer: Louise Ross. Executive producer: Mark Sloper. Director/Screenplay: Nigel Wingrove. Camera: Chris Herd, James Macdonald. Editors: Chris Shaw, Jake West. Music: Steve Pittis/Band of Pain. In color, video. Release date: Apr. 27, 2000. Running time: 73 Min. BRITISH.

Cast: Sally Tremaine, Moyna Cope, Simon Hill, Kristina Bill, Rachel Taggart, Eileen Daly, Daisy Weston, Moses Rockman, Emily Booth.

SADE

An Ocean Films release of an Alicelio/TF1 Films Prod. production, in association with Cofimage 11 and with participation of Canal Plus. (International sales: TF1 Intl., Paris.) Producer: Patrick Godeau. Executive producer: Francoise Galfre. Director: Benoit Jacquot. Screenplay: Jacques Fieschi, Bernard Minoret, based on the novel "La terreur du boudoir" by Serge Bramly. Camera: Benoit Delhomme. Editor: Luc Barnier. Music: Poulenc. Release date: Aug. 17, 2000. Running time: 97 Min. FRENCH.

Cast: Daniel Auteuil, Marianne Denicourt, Jeanne Balibar, Gregoire Colin, Isild Le Besco, Jean-Pierre Cassel, Jalil Lespert.

SAFE SEX
A Papandreou S.A.-Mega Channel presentation of a Tassos Papandreou production. (International sales: Papandreou, Athens.) Director/Screenplay: Thanassis Papathanassiou, Michalis Reppas. Camera: Kostis Gikas. Editor: Joanna Spiliopoulou. In color. Release date: Feb. 11, 2000. Running time: 100 Min. GREECE.
Cast: Mina Adamaki, Alexandros Antonopoulos, Kostas Grekas, Vaso Wilielmiaki. Haris Grigoropoulos, Mary Kavogianni, Eleni Kastani.

SAINT JEROME
A Rio Filme release of a TB Producoes production. Producer: Julio Bressane. Executive producer: Guilherme Spinelli. Director/ Screenplay: Bressane. Camera: Jose Tadeu Ribeiro. Editor: Virginia Flores. Music: Fabio Tagliaferri. In color. Release date: Sept. 6, 1999. Running time: 75 Min. BRAZILIAN.
Cast: Everaldo Pontes, Hamilton Vaz Pereira, Balduino Lellis, Helena Ignez, Bia Nunes, Silvia Buarque.

SALTWATER
An Irish Film Board/BBC Films presentation of a Treasure Films production. (International sales: The Sales Co., London.) Producer: Robert Walpole. Executive producers: David M. Thompson, Rod Stoneman, Claire Duigan. Director/Screenplay: Conor McPherson. Camera: Oliver Curtis. Editor: Emer Reynolds. Music: the Plague Monkeys. In Technicolor. Release date: Feb. 15, 2000. Running time: 95 Min. IRISH-BRITISH.
Cast: Peter McDonald, Brian Cox, Conor Mullen, Laurence Kinlan, Brendan Gleeson, Eva Birthistle, Valerie Spelman, David O'Rourke.

SALUZZI, COMPOSITION FOR BANDONEON AND THREE BROTHERS
Producer/Director/Screenplay: Daniel Rosenfeld. Camera: Ramiro Civita. Editor: Lorenzo Bombicci, Rosenfeld. In B&W and color. Release date: Apr. 15, 2000. Running time: 68 Min. Documentary. ARGENTINE.

THE SAME LOVE, THE SAME RAIN
A Warner Bros. (Argentina) release of a Jorge Estrada Mora Producciones production. Executive producer: Ricardo Freixa. Director: Juan Jose Campanella. Screenplay: Fernando Castets, Campanella. Camera: Daniel Shulman. Editor: Camilo Antolini. Music: Emilio Kauderer. In color. Release date: Apr. 15, 2000. Running time: 110 Min. ARGENTINE.
Cast: Ricardo Darin, Soledad Villamil, Eduardo Blanco, Ulises Dumont, Graciela Tenebaum.

SAMPLE PEOPLE
A REP release of a South Australian Film Corp. presentation of a Living Motion Pictures production, in association with Scanbox Asia Pacific. (International sales: Scanbox Asia Pacific.) Producers: Emile Sherman, Barton Smith. Executive producer: Jonathan Shteinman. Director: Clinton Smith. Screenplay: Clinton Smith, Peter Buckmaster. Camera: David Foreman. Editor: Frans Vandenburg. Music: Rafael May. In color. Release date: Mar. 30, 2000. Running time: 96 Min. AUSTRALIAN.
Cast: Kylie Minogue, Ben Mendelsohn, Simon Lyndon, David Field, Joel Edgerton, Paula Arundell, Nathan Page, Nathalie Roy.

SANCTIMONY
A Regent Entertainment presentation of a 1st Boll Kino Beteiligungs production. (International sales: Regent, Santa Monica, Calif.) Producers: Uwe Boll, Shawn Williamson, Paul Colichman. Executive producers: Mark R. Harris, Stephen P. Jarchow, James Shavick. Co-producer: Jeffrey Schenck. Director/Screenplay: Uwe Boll. Camera: Mathias Neumann. Editor: David M. Richardson. Music: Uwe Spies, Ken Williams. In color, Panavision widescreen. Release date: May 18, 2000. Running time: 86 Min. GERMAN-U.S.
Cast: Casper Van Dien, Michael Pare, Eric Roberts, Catherine Oxenburg, Jennifer Rubin, Michael Rasmussen, Tanja Reichert.

THE SANDMEN
A Les Films du Losange release of an Agat Films & Co./Les Films Pelleas production, with participation of CNC, Sofica Gimages 2, Gimages Developpement. La Sept/Arte. Producers: Philippe Martin, Gilles Sandoz. Director: Pierre Salvadori. Screenplay: Nicolas Saada, Salvadori. Camera: Gilles Henry. Editor: Isabelle Devinck. Music: Camille Baz Baz. In color. Release date: July 25, 2000. Running time: 103 Min. FRENCH.
Cast: Robert Castel, Mathieu Demy, Serge Riaboukine, Guillaume Depardieu, Marina Golovine, Patrick Lizana, Michele Moretti.

SARA AMERIKA
A Blackwood Connection/Helkon Media Filmproduction production. (International sales: Blackwood, Todtmoos, Germany.) Producer: Roland Suso Richter. Executive producer: Lucas Schoener. Director: Roland Suso Richter. Screenplay: Tobias Stille, Suso Richter. Camera: Martin Langer. Editor: Eva Schnare. Music: Ulrich Reuter. In color, widescreen. Release date: Oct. 11, 1999. Running time: 118 Min. GERMAN.
Cast: Dennenesch Zoude, Thomas Heinze, Gregor Torzs, Oliver Korittke.

SASHA ENTERS LIFE
A Mosfilm production. Director: Mikhail Shveitser. Screenplay: Vladimir Tendryakov. Camera: Aleksei Temerin. Music: Veniamin Basner. Release date: Aug. 7, 2000. Running time:105 Min. SOVIET UNION–1957.
Cast: Viktor Avdyushko, Oleg Tabakov, Nikolai Sergeyev, Ivan Pereverzev.

SATURDAY NIGHT
A Late Saturday Films production in association with the Australian Film Commission. Producer: Charlie Doane. Executive producers: Steve MacDonald, Martin Guinness. Director/Screenplay: James Balian. Camera: MacDonald. Editor: James Manche. Music: Wayne Goodwin. In color. Release date: Mar. 3, 2000. Running time: 88 Min. AUSTRALIAN.
Cast: Alison Whyte, Aaron Pederson.

SAUDATE FOR THE FUTURE
A Laterit Prods. presentation in association with Cobra Films, LX Filmes, AF Cinema & Video, RTBF Liege, Voyage and Mezzo. Producers: Cesar Paes, Marie-Clemence Blanc-Paes. Director: Cesar Paes. Screenplay: Paes, Marie-Clemence Blanc-Paes. Camera: C. Paes. Editor: Agnes Contensou. In color. Release date: Aug. 30, 2000. Running time: 94 Min. Documentary. BRAZILIAN-FRENCH.

SAUSALITO
A Star East presentation of a Bob & Partners Co. production. (International sales: Golden Network, H.K.) Producer: Wong Jing. Executive producer: Jessinta Liu. Director: Andrew Lau. Screenplay: Thirteen Chan (Chan Sup-sam). Camera: Lau. Editor: Danny Pang. Music: Chan Kwong-wing. In color. Release date: May 16, 2000. Running time: 94 Min. HONG KONG.
Cast: Leon Lai, Maggie Cheung, Eric Kot, Richard Ng, Suki Kwan.

SAVAGE HONEYMOON
Producer: Steve Sachs. Director/Screenplay: Mark Beasley. Camera: Leon Narbey. Editor: Margot Francis. Music: the Dean Savage Band. Release date: Jan. 15, 2000. Running time: 90 Min. NEW ZEALAND.
Cast: Nicholas Eadie, Perry Piercy, Elizabeth Hawthorne.

SAVING GRACE
A Fine Line release of a Portman Entertainment presentation, in association with Sky Pictures and Wave Pictures, of a Homerun production. Producer: Mark Crowdy. Executive producers: Cat Villiers, Xavier Marchand. Co-producers: Craig Ferguson, Torsten Leschley. Director: Nigel Cole. Screenplay: Craig Ferguson, Mark Crowdy. Camera: John de Borman. Editor: Alan Strachan. In Deluxe color, widescreen. Release date: Jan. 24, 2000. Running time: 94 Min. BRITISH.
Cast: Brenda Blethyn, Craig Ferguson, Martin Clunes, Tcheky Karyo.

SCARLET DIVA
A Minerva Pictures release of a Dario Argento, Claudio Argento presentation of an Opera Film production in association with Gianluca Curti, Stefano Curti, Adriana Chiesa Di Palma. (International sales: Adriana Chiesa Enterprises, Rome.) Executive producer: Claudio Argento. Director/Screenplay: Asia Argento. Camera: Frederic Fasano. Editor: Anna Napoli. Music: John Hughes. In Cinecetta color. Release date: May 12, 2000. Running time: 89 Min. ITALIAN.
Cast: Asia Argento, Jean Shepherd, Herbert Fritsch, Joe Coleman, Francesca d'Aloja, Vera Gemma, Justinian Kfoury, Daria Nicolodi.

SCARS
An Instituto Nacional de Cine & Artes Audiovisuales production, in association with Juan Carlos Fisner & Asociados. Director/ Screenplay: Patricio Coll, based on the novel by Juan Jose Saer. Camera: Esteban Courtalon. Editor: Jose Maria del Peon. In color. Release date: Apr. 16, 2000. Running time: 115 Min. ARGENTINE.
Cast: Omar Fantini, Raul Kreig, Pablo Di Crocce, Monica Galan.

SCRATCHES IN THE TABLE
An Egmond Film & Television presentation in co-production with VPRO Television. (International sales: MDC Film Distribution & World Sales.) Producer: Hans de Weers. Director: Ineke Houtman. Screenplay: Rob Arends, Maarten Lebens, based on the book by Guus Kuijer. Camera: Sander Snoep. Editor: Leo de Boer. Music: Henny Vrienten. In color. Release date: Jan. 22, 2000. Running time: 84 Min. DUTCH.
Cast: Madelief Vereist, Rijk de Gooijer, Margo Dames, Freek Bom.

THE SEA
A Massa D'Or Prods. production with support from COFUC, TVE, TVC. (International sales: Gemini Films, Paris.) Producer: Luis Ferrando. Executive producer: Isona Passola. Director: Agusti Villaronga. Screenplay: Toni Aloy, Biel Mesquida, Villaronga, based on the novel by Blai Bonet. Camera: Jaume Paracaula. Editor: Raul Roman. Music: Javier Navarrete. In color. Release date: Feb. 15, 2000. Running time: 112 Min. SPANISH.
Cast: Bruno Bergonzini, Roger Casamajor, Antonia Torrens, Angela Molina, Simon Andreu, Juli Mira, Hernan Gonzalez, David Lozano.

SEALED WITH A KISS
A Mei Ah presentation of a Milkyway Image (Hong Kong) production. Producer: Li Kuo-hsing. Executive producer: Johnnie To. Executive in charge of production: Patrick Tong. Director: Derek Chiu. Screenplay: Hui Hong. Camera: Cheung Tung-leung. Editor: Chan Chi-wai. Music: Van Lock, Chris Cho. In color. Release date: Nov. 28, 1999. Running time: 87 Min. HONG KONG.
Cast: Louis Koo, Yo Yo Mung, Raymond Wong, Siu Au.

SEANCE
A Kansai Telecasting Corp./Twins Japan production. (International sales: Twins Japan, Tokyo.) Producers: Takehiko Tanaka, Yasuyuki Uemura. Director: Kiyoshi Kurosawa. Screenplay: Tetsuya Onishi, Kuorsawa, from the novel "Seance on a Wet Afternoon" by Mark McShane. Camera: Takahide Shibanushi. Editor: Junichi Kikuchi. Music: Gary Ashiya. Release date: Aug. 7, 2000. Running time: 95 Min. JAPANESE.
Cast: Koji Yakusho, Jun Fubuki, Tsuyoshi Kusanagi, Ittoku Kishibe.

SEASIDE, DUSK

A Kep-Arnyek (Hungary)/Hazard Filmproduction (Germany) production, in association with MMK, NKA, TV2, ORTT and Duna TV. Producer: Gyorgy Durst. Co-producer: Sandor Simo. Director: Andras Fesos. Screenplay: Fesos, Gabor Nemeth. Camera: Andras Nagy. Editor: Agnes Mogor. Music: Tibor Szemzo. In color. Release date: Feb. 8, 2000. Running time: 96 Min. HUNGARIAN-GERMAN.
Cast: Gyozo Szabo, Andrea Takats, Laszlo Keszeg, Maria Schuster.

THE SEASON OF GUAVAS

A Youth Studio production, in association with Les Films d'Ici, with participation of Ministry of Culture & Tourism (Vietnam) and Vietnam Cinema Office. (International sales: : Les Film d'Ici, Paris.) Producers: Dang Nhat Minh, Nguyen Thyu Vinh. Director/Screenplay: Dan Nhat Minh, based on his novel "The Old Home." Camera: Vu Duc Tung. Editors: Tran Anh Hoa, Nguyen Viet Nga. Music: Dang Huu Phuc. In color. Release date: Aug. 10, 2000. Running time: 104 Min. VIETNAMESE.
Cast: Bui Bai Binh, Nguyen Lan Huong, Pham Thu Thuy, Le Thi Huong Thao, Huong Thao, Hua Do Pham Khac Lam.

THE SEASON OF MEN

An Appolo Distribution release (in Tunisia) of a Les Films du Losange (Paris)/Maghrebfilms Carthage (Tunis) production in association with Arte France Cinema. (International sales: Les Films du Losange.) Producers: Margaret Menegos, Mohamed Tlatli. Executive producers: Dora Boucoucha Fourati, Nathalie Nghet. Director/Screenplay: Moufida Tlatli. Dialogue adaptation: Nouri Bouzid. Camera: Youssef Ben Youssef. Editor: Isabelle Devinck. Music: Anouar Brahem. In color. Release date: May 13, 2000. Running time: 122 Min. TUNISIAN-FRENCH.
Cast: Rabiaa Ben Abdallah, Sabah Bouzouita, Ghalia Ben Ali, Hend Sabri, Ezzedine Gennoun, Mouna Noureddine.

SECOND SKIN

A Lolafilms Distribucion release of a Lolafilms production, with participation of Via Digital, Antena 3 TV. (International sales: Lolafilms, Madrid.) Producer: Andres Vicente Gomez. Director: Gerardo Vera. Screenplay: Angeles Gonzalez-Sinde. Camera: Julio Madurga. Editor: Nick Wentworth. Music: Roque Banos. In color. Release date: Jan. 17, 2000. Running time: 106 Min. SPANISH.
Cast: Javier Bardem, Jordi Molla, Ariadna Gil, Cecilia Roth.

SECRET

A Tokyo Broadcasting System production. (International sales: TBS, Tokyo.) Producer: Yasuhiro Mase. Director: Yojiro Takita. Screenplay: Hiroshi Saito, original story by Keigo Higashino. Camera: Naoki Kayano. Music: Ryudo Uzaki. In color. Release date: Dec. 5, 1999. Running time: 119 Min. JAPANESE.
Cast: Ryoki Hirosue, Kaoru Kobayashi, Kayoko Kishimoto, Ken Kaneko, Yuriko Ishida, Hideaki Ito, Ren Osugi, Hatsuo Yamaya.

THE SECRET

A Les Prods. Bagheera/France 3 Cinema/Diaphana Films production, in association with Canal Plus, Le Centre National de la Cinematographie, La Procirep, Sofica S. (International sales: Mercure Distribution, Paris.) Producer: Francois Marquis. Director: Virginie Wagon. Screenplay: Wagon, Erick Zonca. Camera: Jean-Marc Fabre. Editor: Yannick Kergoat. Music: Mercury Rev, Chuck Berry. In color. Release date: May 17, 2000. Running time: 107 Min. FRENCH.
Cast: Anne Coesens, Michel Bompoil, Tony Todd, Quentin Rossi, Jacqueline Jehanneuf, Aladin Reibel, Valerie Vogt, Frederic Sauzay.

THE SECRET LAUGHTER OF WOMEN

An Optimum Releasing release (in U.K.) of a Paragon Entertainment Corp./HandMade Films presentation, with participation of the European Co-production Fund and BSkyB, in association with the Arts Council of England, of an ELBA Films (U.K.)/Paragon Entertainment (Canada) production. (International sales: Seven Arts Intl., Hollywood.) Producers: O.O. Sagay, Jon Slan. Executive producer: Gareth Jones. Director: Peter Schwabach. Screenplay: O.O. Sagay. Camera: Martin Fuhrer. Editor: Michael Pacek. Music: Yves Laferriere. In Rank Film Labs color, Deluxe Toronto color. Release date: Nov. 8, 1999. Running time: 99 Min. BRITISH-CANADIAN.
Cast: Colin Firth, Nia Long, Fissy Roberts, Caroline Goodall, Dan Lett, Joke Jacobs, Ariyon Bakare, Joy Elias Rilwan, Hakim Kae-Kazim.

SEE YOU

An Istituto Luce release (in Italy) of a Tangram Film/Instituto Luce/RAI Radiotelevisione Italiana productions. (International sales: RAI Trade, Rome.) Producers: Roberto and Matteo Levi. Director/Screenplay: Gianni Zanasi. Camera: Giulio Pietromarchi. Editor: Rita Rognoni. Music: Giuliano Taviani. In Technicolor. Release date: Sept. 7, 1999. Running time: 103 Min. ITALIAN.
Cast: Stefania Rivi, Andrea Corneti, Wilson Saba, Paolo Sassanelli, Mimmo Mancini, Lorenzo Viaconzi, Umberto Franchini.

SELKIE

A UIP (Australia) release of a Bluestone Pictures production, in association with the Australian Film Commission, South Autralian Film Corp., Showtime Australia. Producers: Jane Ballantyne, Rob George. Executive producer: Jill Green. Director: Donald Crombie. Screenplay: Rob George, based on a concept by Kate Fawkes, David Marlow. Camera: David Foreman. Editor: Edward McQueen-Mason. Music: Sean Timms. In Cinevex color. Release date: Mar. 15, 2000. Running time: 86 Min. AUSTRALIAN.
Cast: Shimon Moore, Chelsea Bruland, Bryan Marshall, Celine O'Leary, Mariana Rego, Elspeth Ballantyne, Edmund Pegge.

SENSITIVE NEW-AGE KILLER

A Frisson production. Producers: John Brousek, Mark Savage. Screenplay: Savage, David Richardson. Camera: Richardson. Editors: Robin Brennan, Anthony Ega. Music: Cesary Skubiszewski. In color. Release date: July 21, 2000. Running time: 87 Min. AUSTRALIAN.
Cast: Paul Moder, Kevin Hopkins, Helen Hopkins, Carolyn Bock, Frank Bren.

7 DAYS TO LIVE

A Senator release of an Indigo Filmproduktion presentation of a Becker & Haeberle Filmproduktion production, in association with Senator Film Produktion, RoofTop Entertainment and EIS Prods. (Prague). (International sales: Amberlon Pictures, London.) Producers: Christian Becker, Thomas Haeberle. Co-producer: Don Maug. Director: Sebastian Niemann. Screenplay: Dirk Ahner. Camera: Gerhard Schirlo. Editor: Moune Barius. Music: Egon Riedel. In color, widescreen. Release date: June 25, 2000. Running time: 96 Min. GERMAN.
Cast: Amanda Plummer, Sean Pertwee, Nick Brimble, Gina Bellman, Sean Chapman, Eddie Cooper, Chris Barlow, Amanda Walker.

SEVEN SONGS FROM THE TUNDRA

A Jorn Donner production. (International sales: Jorn Donner Prods., Helsinki.) Producer: Markku Lehmuskallio. Director: Anatasia Lapsui, Markku Lehmuskallio. Screenplay: Anatasia Lapsui. Camera: Johannes Lehmuskallio. Editor: Markku Lehmuskallio. In B&W. Release date: Feb. 10, 2000. Running time: 89 Min. FINNISH.
Cast: Vitalina Hudi, Hatjako Yzangi, Gregory Anaguritsi, Nadeshda Wolodejeva, Nadeshda Horotetto.

A SEVERE YOUNG MAN

A Ukrainfilm (Kiev) production. Director: Abram Room. Screenplay: Yuri Olesha. Camera: Yuri Ekelchik. Music: Gavriil Popov. In B&W. Release date: Aug. 4, 2000. Running time: 98 Min. SOVIET UNION–1936.
Cast: Dmitri Dorliak, Olga Zhizneva, Yuri Yurev, Maksim Straukh, Valentina Polovikova, Irina Volodko.

SEX OUT OF COMPASSION

A Filmax release (in Spain) of a Sogedasa Visual Grup (Spain)/Resonancia Productora (Mexico) production in association with Via Digital. (International sales: Filmax, Barcelona.) Producers: Julio Fernandez, Miguel Torrente. Executive producers: Carlos Fernandez, J.K. Malou, Fina Torrente. Director/Screenplay: Laura Mana. Camera: Henner Hofmann. Editor: Guillermo S. Maldonado. Music: Francesc Gener. In B&W and color. Release date: June 29, 2000. Running time: 109 Min. SPANISH-MEXICAN.
Cast: Elisabeth Margoni, Alex Angulo, Pilar Bardem, Juan Carlos Colombo, Mariola Fuentes, Jose Sancho, Leticia Huijada.

THE SEXUAL LIFE OF THE BELGIANS 4: PLEASURE AND HYSTERIA

A Transatlantic Films/De Smet Films production. (International sales: Brussels Ave, Brussels.) Producer: Jan Bucquoy. Camera: Bucquoy, Nathan Sartiaux. Editor: Severine De Streyker. In color. Release date: Feb. 17, 2000. Running time: 85 Min. BELGIAN.
Cast: Jan Bucquoy, Evelyne Letwe, Marie Bucquoy, Gail Verjasselt.

SEXY BEAST

A FilmFour (in U.K.)/Fox Searchlight Pictures (in U.S.) release of a Recorded Picture Co./FilmFour production, in association with Fox Searchlight and Kanzaman (Madrid). (International sales: FilmFour, London.) Producer: Jeremy Thomas. Co-producer: Denise O'Dell. Director: Jonathan Glazer. Screenplay: Louis Mellis, David Scinto. Camera: Ivan Bird. Editors: John Scott, Sam Sneade. Music: Roque Banos; additional music: Unkle With South. In Deluxe color, widescreen. Release date: Sept. 12, 2000. Running time: 88 Min. BRITISH.
Cast: Ray Winstone, Ben Kingsley, Ian McShane, Amanda Redman, Cavan Kendall, Julianne White, Alvaro Monje, James Fox.

SHACKY CARMINE

An Aurum release (in Spain) of a Fernando Colomo P.C. production, in association with Via Digital. (International sales: Fernando Colomo P.C., Madrid.) Executive producer: Beatriz de la Gandara. Director: Chema de la Pena. Screenplay, de la Pena, Oscar de Julian. Camera: David Omedes. Editor: Antonio Lara. Music: Undrop, Undershakers, Aneurol 50, Dover, Freak XII, others. In color. Release date: Sept. 11, 1999. Running time: 106 Min. SPANISH.
Cast: Fernando Cayo, Andres Gertrudix, Pau Colera, Manolo Caro, Rebeca Jimenez, Nathalie Sesena, Patxi Freytez.

SHADOW MAGIC

A Sony Pictures Classics release of a Schulberg Prods./Road Movies Veirte Produktionen production, in association with Filmstiftung Nordrhein-Westfalen GmbH. Producer: Ann Hu. Executive producers: Charles Xue, Steve Chang, Chiu Shun-Ching, Han Sanping, Ulrich Felsberg, Eitan Hakami, Katia Milani. Co-producers: Sandra Schulberg, Shang Xia, Lee You-Ning, Cheng Zheng. Director: Ann Hu. Screenplay: Huang Dan, Tang Louyi, Kate Raisz, Bob McAndrew, Hu. Camera: Nancy Schreiber. Editors: Keith Reamer, John Gilroy. Music: Zhang Lida. In Technicolor, widescreen. Release date: Jan. 25, 2000. Running time: 112 Min. U.S.-GERMAN.
Cast: Jared Harris, Xia Yu, Liu Peiqi, Lu Liping, Xing Yufei, Wang Jingming, Li Yusheng, Zhang Yukui, Fang Quingzhuo, Li Bin.

THE SHADOW OF THE GIANT

A Cinema e Societa production, in association with Consiglio dei Ministri/Dipartimento dello Spettacolo and ALBA Produzioni (International sales: Adriana Chiesa Enterprises, Rome.) Producer: Manolo Bolognini. Director: Roberto Petrocchi. Screenplay: Petrocchi, Riccardo De Luca, based on the story "The Giant" by Paola Capriolo. Camera: Camillo Bazzoni. Editor: Paolo Benassi. Music: Andrea Morricone. In color. Release date: Feb. 14, 2000. Running time: 97 Min. ITALIAN.

Cast: Margherita Buy, Arnaud Arbessier, Marisa Solinas.

SHADOW OF THE VAMPIRE

A Lions Gate Films release of a Saturn Films presentation of a Long Shot Films production in association with BBC Films and Delux Prods. (International sales: Lions Gate Films Intl., L.A.) Producers: Nicolas Cage, Jeff Levine. Executive producer: Paul Brooks. Co-producers: Jimmy de Brabant, Richard Johnns. Director: E. Elias Merhige. Screenplay: Steven Katz. Camera: Lou Bogue. Editor: Chris Wyatt. Music: Dan Jones. In Deluxe London color, widescreen. Release date: May 16, 2000. Running time: 93 Min. BRITISH-U.S.

Cast: John Malkovich, Willem Dafore, Cary Elwes, John Aden Gillet, Eddie Izzard, Udo Kier, Catherine McCormack, Ronan Vibert.

SHADOWS IN THE DARK

A Vital Films production in association with National Film Development Corp. (India), JBA Prods. (France), Hubert Bals Fund. (International sales: Vital Films, New Delhi). Producer/Director: Pankaj Butalia. Screenplay: Butalia, Nilofer Kaul. Camera: Ranjan Palit. Editor: Sameera Jain. Music: Susmit Sen. In color. Release date: Sept. 6, 1999. Running time: 104 Min. INDIAN-FRENCH.

Cast: Kitu Gidwani, Subrata Dutta, Srivardhan Trivedi, Ikhlaque Khan.

SHADY GROVE

A Bitters End presentation of a Brandish production. (International sales: Bitters End, Tokyo.) Producer: Kumi Sato. Executive producer: Yuji Sadai. Director: Shinji Aoyama. Screenplay: Aoyama, Sato. Camera: Masaki Tamura. Editor: Sansei Miyata. Music: Isao Yamada, Aoyama. In color. Release date: Nov. 22, 1999. Running time: 98 Min. JAPANESE.

Cast: Urara Awata, Arata, Tomohiro Sekiguchi, Wakaba Nakano.

SHIRI

A Samsung Entertainment Group presentation of a Kan Je-gyu Film Co. production. (International sales: Samsung, Seoul.) Producer/Director/Screenplay: Kand Je-gyu (Jacky Kang). Camera: Kim Seong-bok. Editor: Park Gok-ji. Music: Lee Dong-jun. In color. Release date: Oct. 19, 1999. Running time: 120 Min. SOUTH KOREAN.

Cast: Han Seok-kyu, Choe Min-shik, Song Kang-ho, Kim Yu-jin.

SHIT HAPPENS

A Buena Vista Intl. (Sweden) release of an S/S Fladen Film/SVT Drama Malmo production, in association with Canal Plus. (International sales: S/S Fladen, Stockholm.) Producer: Patrick Ryborn. Director/Screenplay: Mans Herngren, Hannes Holm. Camera: Mats Olofsson. Editor: Sofia Lindgren. Music: Magnus Frykberg, Pal Svende. In color. Release date: Jan. 18, 2000. Running time: 114 Min. SWEDISH.

Cast: Josefin Nilsson, Marie Richardson, Cecilia Frode.

SHOOTING STAR

A Little More Co. production. (International sales: Little More Co., Tokyo.) Producers: Masakazu Takei, Miyoshi Kikuchi. Director: Hiromitsu Yamanaka. Screenplay: Hiroshi Hashimoto. Camera: Isao Ishii. Editor: Tomoo Sanjo. Music: Kazuhisa Uchihashi. In color, Super 16. Release date: Jan. 20, 2000. Running time: 96 Min. JAPANESE.

Cast: Ken Ogata, Yosuke Eguchi, Mami Shimizu, Jun Kunimura, Michio Akiyama.

SHOOT THE SUN BY LYRIC: THE FIGHT FOR THE SCREEN QUOTA IN KOREA

A Unikorea/Dream Venture Capital presentation of a Screen Quota Watchers/Seoul Visual Collective production. (International sales: SVC, Seoul.) Director: Cho Jae-hong. Screenplay: Lee Nam-jin. Camera: Mario Lee. In color. Release date: Oct. 16, 1999. Running time: 88 Min. Documentary. SOUTH KOREAN.

With: Myung Kay-nam, Lee Cheon-yeon, Kim Hae-jin, Chung Ji-yeong, Mun Sung-keun, Ahn Sung-ki, Shim Hye-jin, Kim Hae-su.

SIGNS & WONDERS

An MK2 Prods. production in association with Ideefixe Prods., Industry Entertainment, Sunshine Amalgamedia and Goatworks Films. (International sales: MK2 Diffusion.) Producer: Marin Karmitz. Executive producers: Jed Alpert, Nick Wechsler. Director: Joanthan Nossiter. Screenplay: James Lasdun, Mossiter, based on a story by Lasdun. Camera: Yorgos Arvanitis. Editor: Madeleine Gavin. Music: Adrian Utley. In color. Release date: Feb. 11, 2000. Running time: 108 Min. FRENCH.

Cast: Stellan Skarsgard, Charlotte Rampling, Deborah Kara Unger.

THE SILENCE OF THE ANGELS

An Artline Films production, in association with La Sept Arte and Les Productions Sablier. (International sales: Ideale Audience, Paris.) Producer: Olivier Mille. Director: Mille. Screenplay: Mille, Jean-Francois Colosimo. Camera: Pierre Bourgeois, Antoine-Marie Meert. Editor: Jean-Pierre Bloc. In color-beta SP video. Release date: Sept. 30, 1999. Running time: 90 Min. Music documentary. FRENCH-BELGIAN-GREEK.

THE SISTER BROTHERS

A Bac Distribution release of an Ima Films/FAS production, with the participation of Canal Plus. (International sales: UGC Intl., Paris.) Producer: Georges Benayoun. Executive producer: Veronique Rofe. Director: Frederic Jardin. Screenplay: Edouard Baer, Jarkin, Fabrice Roger-Lacan. Camera: Laurent Machuel. Editor: Monica Coleman. Music: Nicolas Errera, Yussef Lateef, Dizzy Gillespie. In color. Release date: June 5, 2000. Running time: 95 Min. FRENCH.

Cast: Jose Garcia, Denis Podalydes, Jackie Berroyer, Edouard Baer.

SIX-PACK

A Pathe Distribution a Les Films Alain Sarde production. (International sales: Le Studio Canal Plus, Paris.) Producer: Alain Sarde. Executive producer: Christine Gozlan. Director/Screenplay: Alain Berberian, based on the novel "Six-Pack" by Jean-Hugues Oppel. Camera: Jean-Francois Robin. Editor: Catherine Renault. Music: Elia Cmiral. In color, widescreen. Release date: Apr. 25, 2000. Running time: 105 Min. FRENCH.

Cast: Richard Anconina, Frederic Diefenthal, Chiara Mastroianni, Bernard Fresson, Jonathan Firth, Francois Berleand.

6IXTYNIN9

A Five Star production. (International sales: Film Factory, Bangkok.) Producer: Pen-ek Ratanaruang. Executive producer: Charoen Aiempeungporn. Director/Screenplay: Pen-ek Ratanaruang. Camera: Chankit Chamnivikaipong. Editor: Patamanadda Yukol. In color. Release date: Jan. 29, 2000. Running time: 111 Min. THAI.

Cast: Lalita Panyopas, Tasanawalai Ongartittichai, Black Phomtaong

SKIN FLICK

A Cazzo Films production in association with Millivres, Suzuki Akihiro/Stance Co. Executive producer: Juergen Anger. Director/Screenplay: Bruce LaBruce. Camera: James Carman. Editors: Manfred Mancini, Joerg Andreas. Music: Gavin Brown, Kilslug, Nip Drivers, Hype. In color and B&W, video. Release date: Feb. 1, 2000. Running time: 67 Min. GERMAN.

Cast: Steve Master, Eden Miller, Tim Vincent, Jens Hammer, Tom International, Ralph Steel, Bastian, Nikki Richardson, Darren James.

SKY HOOK

A Cinema Design production, in cooperation with RTS and co-production with Cine Enterprise. (International sales: Cinema Design, Belgrade.) Producer: Ljubisa Samardzic. Co-producer: Giacomo Billi. Director: Ljubisa Samardzic. Screenplay: Dorde Milosavljevic. Co-writer: Srdan Koljevic. Camera: Radoslav Vladic. Editor: Marko Glusac. Music: Vlatko Stefanovski. In color. Release date: Feb. 10, 2000. Running time: 93 Min. YUGOSLAVIAN-ITALIAN.

Cast: Nebojsa Glogovac, Ana Sofrenovic, Ivan Jevtovic, Katarina Zutic, Nikola Kojo, Sonja Kolacaric, Dragan Bjelogrlic, Irfan Mensur.

THE SKY WILL FALL

An Istituto Luce release of a Silvia d'Amico Bendico presentation of a Parus Film/Viva Cinematografica/Istituto Luce production, in association with RAI. Producers: Carlo M. Cucchi, Vittorio Noia. Directors: Andrea and Antonio Frazzi. Screenplay: Suso Cecchi D'Amico, freely adapted from Lorenza Mazzetti's novel. Camera: Franco Di Giacomo. Editor: Amedeo Salfa. Music: Luis Bacalov. In color. Release date: June 20, 2000. Running time: 94 Min. ITALIAN.

Cast: Isabella Rossellini, Jeroen Krabbe, Barbara Enrichi, Gianna Giachetti, Luciano Virgilio, Elenca Sofonova, Paul Brooke.

SLOW FADE

A RYMD Industries production. (International sales: Golden Network, Hong Kong.) Producer: Daniel Chan. Executive producer: Frederick Lau. Director: Daniel Chan. Screenplay: Kyle Davisson, story by Davisson, Chan. Camera: Chan. Editor: Ray Chim, Chris Chow. Music: Daniel Lan. In color. Release date: Sept. 2, 1999. Running time: 89 Min. HONG KONG.

Cast: Ken Wong, Jimmy Wong, Josie Ho, Roy Cheung.

SMALL TIME OBSESSION

A Guerilla Films release of a Solo Films production, in association with the Seventh Twelfth Collective. Producer: Piotr Szkopiak. Executive producer: David Nicholas Wilkinson. Co-producers: Ian David Diaz, Julian Boote. Director/Screenplay: Piotr Szkopiak. Additional script material: Ian David Diaz. Camera: Neils Reedtz Johansen. Editor: Szkopiak. Music: Martin Bell. In color. Release date: June 9, 2000. Running time: 118 Min. BRITISH.

Cast: Alex King, Juliette Caton, Jason Merrells, Oliver Young.

SMOKING CUBAN STYLE

A Blow-up Film/Kuba Film production. (International sales: Kuba Film, Berlin.) Producer/Director/Screenplay: Stephan Wagner. Camera: Thomas Benesch. Editor: Gunnar Wanne-Eickel. Music: Peter Ponger, Alexander Zlamal. In B&W. Release date: Oct. 14, 1999. Running time: 87 Min. AUSTRIAN-GERMAN.

Cast: Simon Licht, Thomas Morris, Seymour Cassel, Tatjana Alexander, Eva-Maria Straka, Wolfgang S. Zechmayer, Alfons Haider.

SNATCH

A Columbia (in U.K.)/Screen Gems (in U.S.) release of a Columbia Pictures presentation, in association with SKA Films, of a Matthew Vaughn production. Producer: Vaughn. Executive producers: Peter Morton, Steve Tisch, Stephen Marks, Angad Paul, Trudie Styler. Co-producer: Michael Dreyer. Director/Screenplay: Guy Ritchie. Camera: Tim Maurice-Jones. Editors: John Harris, Les Healey. Music: John Murphy. In Deluxe color. Release date: Sept. 19, 2000. Running time: 102 Min. BRITISH-U.S.

Cast: Benicio Del Toro, Dennis Farina, Vinnie Jones, Brad Pitt.

SNOW ON NEW YEAR'S EVE

A Buena Vista Intl. release of a UFA Filmproduktion in association with Westdeutsche Universum-Film, Buena Vista Intl. Film Production, WDR and Arte. Producers: Norbert Sauer, Christian Granderath. Executive producer: Harald Reinhold. Executive co-producers: Heike Hempel, Georg Steinert. Co-producers: Wolfgang Braun, Christoph Ott. Director: Thorsten Schmidt. Screenplay: Stefan Kolditz. Camera: Klaus Eichhammer. Editor: Claudia Wolscht. Music: Ralf Wienrich. In color. Release date: jan. 19, 2000. Running time: 100 Min. GERMAN.
Cast: Jurgen Tarrach, Tamara Simunovic, Hannes Jaenicke, Dieter Landuris, Andre Hennicke, Niels Bruno Schmidt, Nadja Uhl.

SOCCER RULES!

A Seven X Filmverleih presentation of a Novamedia production in association with Hofmann & Voges Filmproduktion and Sven Pictures. (International sales: Beta Film, Ismaning.) Producers: Philip Voges, Mischa Hofmann. Co-producer: Benjamin Bauheimer. Director: Tomy Wigand. Screenplay: Mathias Dinter, Martin Ritzenhoff. Camera: Diethard Prengel. Editor: Christian Nauheimer. Music: Tobias Neumann. In color. Release date: Feb. 15, 2000. Running time: 97 Min. GERMAN.
Cast: Uwe Ochsenknecht, Ralf Richter, Oscar Ortega Sanchez, Walter Gontermann, Michael Sideris, Tana Schanzara.

SOFT HEARTS

A Viva Films release of a Neo Films presentation of a Kaizz Ventures production. Producers: Vicente del Rosario III, Veronique del Roasrio-Corpus. Executive producer: Vic del Rosario Jr. Directors: Joel Lamangan, Eric Quizon. Screenplay: Ricky Lee, Mel Mendoza-Del Rosario. Camera: Romeo Vitug. Editor: Jess Navarro. Music: Dennis Garcia. In color. Release date: Sept. 13, 1999. Running time: 110 Min. PHILIPPINE.
Cast: Lorna Tolentino, Albert Martinez, Eric Quizon, Caridad Sanchez, Jake Roxas, Matthew Mendoza.

SOME VOICES

A FilmFour presentation, with participation of British Screen, of a Dragon Pictures production. (International sales: Film Four Intl., London.) Producers: Damian Jones, Graham Broadbent. Co-producer: Fiona Morham. Director: Simon Cellan Jones. Screenplay: Joe Penhall, based on his play. Camera: David Odd. Editor: Elen Pierce Lewis. Music: Adrian Johnston. In Deluxe color. Release date: May 15, 2000. Running time: 96 Min. BRITISH.
Cast: Daniel Craig, David Morrissey, Kelly Macdonald, Julie Graham.

SOMEWHERE IN THE NIGHT

A CO2 Films and Multimedia Co. presentation of a Roos Film production in association with Fondart, Corfo and J.J. Harting. Producers: Harting, Hector Porras. Director: Martin Rodriguez. Screenplay: Alberto Fufuet. Camera: Alex Miranda, Jorge Avalos. Editor: Juan Andres Condon. Music: Ricardo Santander. In color. Release date: Mar. 3, 2000. Running time: 100 Min. CHILEAN.
Cast: Francisco Lopez, Luciano Cruz-Coke, Faride Kaid, Paula Pizarro, Diego Munoz.

SONGS FROM THE SECOND FLOOR

A Roy Andersson Filmproduktion production, in association with Sveriges Television, Danmarks Radio, Norsk Rikskringkasting, Arte France Cinema, Societe Parisienne de Production, Essential Filmproduktion, Easy Film, ZDF/Arte-La Sept. (International sales: The Coproduction Office, Berlin.) Producer: Lis Alwert. Executive producer: Philippe Bober. Director/Screenplay: Roy Andersson. Camera: Istvan Borbas, Jesper Klevenas. Editor: Roy Andersson. Music: Benny Andersson. In color. Release date: May 19, 2000. Running time: 97 Min. SWEDISH.
Cast: Lars Nordh, Stefan Larsson, Torbjorn Fahlstrom, Sten Andersson, Lucio Vucino, Hanna Eriksson, Peter Roth.

SON OF TWO MOTHERS OR THE COMEDY OF INNOCENCE

A MACT Prods./TF1 Intl./Les Films du Camelia production. (International sales: TF1Intl., Paris.) Producers: Martine and Antoine de Clermont-Tonnerre. Director: Raul Ruiz. Screenplay: Francoise Dumas, Ruiz, based on the novel by Massimo Bontempelli. Camera: Jacques Bouquin. Editor: Mireille Hannon. Music: Jorge Arriagada. In color. Release date: Sept. 1, 2000. Running time: 102 Min. FRENCH.
Cast: Isabelle Huppert, Jeanne Balibar, Charles Berling, Nils Hugon, Edith Scob, Denis Podalydes, Laure de Clermont-Tonnerre.

SOONER OR LATER

An Ocean Films release of a Blue Dahlia Prod./Studiocanal/France 2 Cinema production. Producer: Gerard Jourd'hui. Executive producer: Gaelle Girre. Director/Screenplay: Anne-Marie Etienne. Camera: Alain Choquart. Editor: Isabelle Dedieu. Music: Roddy Julienne. In color. Release date: July 20, 2000. Running time: 106 Min. FRENCH.
Cast: Philippe Torreton, Amira Casar, Laura Del Sol, Anny Duperey, Jacques Webe, Pascal Legitumus.

SORRY BABY

A Forbidden City Film presentation of a Huayi Brothers Advertising/Asian Film Union/Forbidden City Film production. (International sales: Golden Network, Hong Kong.) Producers: Zhang Heping, Wang Zhongjun, Dong Ping. Executive producer: Wang. Director: Feng Xiaogang. Screenplay: Wang Xiaozhu, Bai Tiejun. Camera: Yang Xiaoxiong. Editor: Zhou Ying. In color. Release date: Feb. 28, 2000. Running time: 95 Min. CHINESE.
Cast: Ge You, Wu Chien-lien, Fu Biao, Ming He, Gao Chengsheng, Liang Jianiang, Shi Xiuyun, Shi Yan, Xu Fan.

SORTED

An Advanced Film release (in Germany) of a Jovy Junior Enterprises production. (International sales: Advanced, Oberhaching, Germany.) Producers: Fabrizio Chiesa, Mark Crowdy. Executive producers: Steve Clarke-Hall, Alex Jovy. Director: Alex Jovy. Screenplay: Nick Villiers, based on a screenplay by Christian Spurrier, Malcolm Campbell, story by Jovy. Camera: Mike Southon. Editor: Justin Krish. Music: Guy Farley. In color, widescreen. Release date: June 28, 2000. Running time: 102 Min. BRITISH.
Cast: Matthew Rhys, Sienna Guillory, Tim Curry, Fay Masterson, Jason Donovan, Steven Marcus, Kelly Brook, Sebastian Knapp.

THE SOUTH: ALICE NEVER LIVED HERE

An Akedia Prods. production. (International sales: Akedia Prods., Tel Aviv, Israel.) Producers: David Benchetrit, Senyora Bar David. Director/Screenplay/Editor: Senyora Bar David. Camera: David Benchetrit. Music: various. In color, Beta SP. Release date: Oct. 14, 1999. Running time: 82 Min. Documentary. ISRAELI.

SOUTH SIDE STORY

An Istituto Luce release (in Italy) of a Gam Film production in association with Istituto Luce. (International sales: Adriana Chiesa Enterprises, Rome.) Producers: Gherardo Pagliei, Elisabetta Riga. Director: Roberta Torre. Screenplay: Torre, Franco Maresco, Francesco Suriano. Camera: Daniele Cipri. Editor: Giogio Franchini. Music: Gino Decrescenzo. In color. Release date: Sept. 6, 2000. Running time: 82 Min. ITALIAN.
Cast: Forstine Ehobor, Roberto Rondelli, Eleonora Teriaca, Rosa D'Alba, Giuseppa Vella, Little Tony (Antonio Ciacci), Mario Merola.

SPEAKERS OF TRUTH

An A-Film Distribution release of a Motel Films production in co-production with NPS Television. (International sales: Fortissimo Film Sales, Amsterdam.) Producers: Jeroen Beker, Frans van Gestel. Director/Screenplay: Karim Traidia. Camera: Jacques Laureys. Editor: Chris Teerink. Music: Fons Merkies. In color. Release date: Jan. 29, 2000. Running time: 74 Min. DUTCH.
Cast: Sid Ahmed Agoumi, Jaap Spijkers, Monic Hendrickx, Mireille Perrier.

SPEAKING OF BUNUEL

A Nirvana Films release (in Spain) of a Cero en Conducta, Arte, TVE (Spain)/Amaranta (Mexico) production. (International sales: TVE, Madrid.) Producers: Jose Luis Lopez Linares, Jorge Sanchez Sosa. Directors: Jose Luis Lopez Linares, Javier Rioyo. Screenplay: Agustin Sanchez-Vidal, based on Luis Bunuel's autobiography "My Last Breath." Camera: Linares. Editor: Fidel Collados. Music: Mauricio Berenguer, Mar Gonzalez, Sergio Burmann. In color. Release date: May 5, 2000. Running time: 91 Min. Documentary. SPANISH-MEXICAN.
Cast: Jose Bello, Angela Molina, Francisco Rabal, Pere Portabella, Jose Luis Barros, Michel Piccoli, Serge Silberman, Luis Bunuel.

SPLIT WIDE OPEN

An Adlabs/BMG Crescendo/Tropicfilm production. Producer: Anuradha Parikh. Co-producers: Manmohan Shetty, Suresh Thomas. Director: Dev Benegal. Screenplay: Farrukh Dhondy, based on a story by Benegal, Upamanyu Chatterjee. Camera: Sukumar Jatania. Editor: Renu Saluja. Music: Nitin Sawhney. In Adlabs color, widescreen. Release date: Sept. 7, 1999. Running time: 107 Min. INDIAN.
Cast: Rahul Bose, Laila Rouass, Shivaji Sathem, Ayesha Dharker, Farida Haider Mulla, Shiv Paul, Kiran Nagarkar, Arti Gosavi.

THE SPREADING GROUND

A Tsunami Entertainment presentation in association with Vine Intl. Pictures Ltd., Alpine Pictures and Stonelock Pictures of a Polson Street production. (International sales: Tsunami Entertainment.) Producer: Ken Nakamura. Executive producers: Beni Tadd Atoori, Susan Wichmann. Director: Derek Vanlint. Screenplay: Mark Katsumi Nakamura, story by Mark Burman, Ross Korte. Camera: Vanlint. Editor: Michael Doherty. Music: Mark Shannon, Mark Nakamura, Shark. In color. Release date: Mar. 5, 2000. Running time: 100 Min. CANADIAN.
Cast: Dennis Hopper, Leslie Hope, Frederic Forrest, Tom McCamus, Elizabeth Shepherd, Chuck Shamata, David Dunbar.

SRI

A Marselli Sumarno production. (International sales: Sumarno, Jakarta.) Producers: Kemala Atmojo, Moetaryanto, Marselli Sumarno. Director/Screenplay: Marselli Sumarno. Camera: Hadi Artmono. Editor: Subagio B. Santoso. Music: Rahayu Supanggah. In color. Release date: Oct. 20, 1999. Running time: 103 Min. INDONESIAN.
Cast: Rina Ariyanti, RMT, Ronosuripto, Sardono W. Kusumo.

STAND-BY

A Diaphana release of a Salome presentation of a Salome, Le Studio Canal Plus, Arte France Cinema, Havas Images, Ista Films, Diaphana Distribution production, with participation of Canal Plus and Studio Images 5. Producer: Maurice Bernart. Director/Screenplay: Roch Stephanik. Camera: Tetsuo Nagata. Editors: Dan Facundo, Stephanik. In color, widescreen. Release date: Aug. 2, 2000. Running time: 122 Min. FRENCH.
Cast: Dominique Blance, Roschdy Zem, Patrick Catalifo, Jean-Luc Bideau, Georges Corrafce, Cecile Brune, Gamil Ratib, Remi Martin.

STARDOM
An Alliance Atlantis Communications/Serendipity Point Films/ Cinemaginaire/Cine B production, with the participation of Telefilm Canada, Quebec Film and Television Tax Credit, Canadian Film or Video Production Tax Credit, the Movie Network, Sodec, Super Ecran, Government of Ontario, Canal Plus, Ministere de la Culture et de la Communication, and the Centre National de la Cinematographie. (International sales: Alliance Atlantis Communications, Toronto.) Producers: Denise Robert, Robert Lantos. Co-producer: Philippe Carcassonne. Director: Denys Arcand. Screenplay: Arcand, Jacob Potashnik. Camera: Guy Dufaux. Editor: Isabelle Dedieu. Music: Francois Dompierre. In color and B&W. Release date: May 17, 2000. Running time: 100 Min. CANADIAN-FRENCH.
Cast: Jessica Pare, Dan Aykroyd, Charles Berling, Thomas Gibson, Frank Langella, Robert Lepage, Patrick Huard.

STRANGERS
A Cima Film Intl. (Iran)/Noruz Prods. (U.S.) production. (International sales: Cima Media Intl., Tehran.) Producers: Ali Reza Shoja Noori, Ramin Bahrani. Director/Screenplay: Ramin Bahrani. Camera: Amir Karimi. Editor: Hassan Ayoubi. Music: Peyman Yazdanian. In color. Release date: May 14, 2000. Running time: 80 Min. IRANIAN-U.S.
Cast: Ramin Bahrani, Karim Kashani.

STRONG LANGUAGE
A Simon Rumley production. (International sales: Stranger Than Fiction, London.) Alex Tate. Director/Screenplay: Simon Rumley. Camera: Armando Smit. Editor: Adrian Begone. Music: Martin Phipps. In color. Release date: Jan. 25, 2000. Running time: 77 Min. BRITISH.
Cast: David Groves, Al Nedjari, Paul Tonkinson, Julie Rice, Charlie De'ath, Kelly Marcel, Ricci Harnet, Stuart Laing, Chris Pavlo.

STUFF
A Bruce McDonald presentation of a Bullseye Film production (Toronto). Producer: James Dunnison. Executive producer: Bruce McDonald. Director/Editor: James Dunnison. Screenplay: James Dunnison, Rebecca Dunnison. Camera: William Morrison. Music: Justin Deneau. In color, Beta-sp video. Release date: Oct. 8, 1999. Running time: 87 Min. CANADIAN.
Cast: Max Danger, Sanda Guerard, Maureen Burgoyne, Joe Sather, Winston Spear, Art Bergman, Moe Berg, Russell Oliver.

SUCH IS LIFE...
A Filmania production, with Gardenia Producciones, Fondo para la Produccion Cinematografica de Calidad, Instituto Mexicano de Cinematografia, Wanda Vision (Spain), DMVB (France) and the support of Programa Ibermedia. Producers: Laura Imperiale, Jorge Sanchez, Alvaro Garnica. Executive producer: Walter Navas. Co-producers: Jose Maria Morales, Thierry Forte. Director: Arturo Ripstein. Screenplay: Paz Alicia Garciadiego, inspired by the tragedy "Medea" by Seneca. Camera: Guillermo Granillo. Editor: Carlos Puente. Music: David Mansfield, Leoncio Lara (Bon). In color, video-to-35mm. Release date: Apr. 27, 2000. Running time: 98 Min. MEXICAN-FRENCH-SPANISH.
Cast: Arcelia Ramirez, Luis Felipe Tovar, Patricia Reyes Spindola, Ernesto Yanez, Francesca Guillen, Martha Aura.

A SUMMER TALE
A Sonet Film release (in Sweden) of a Memfis Film, Film i Vast, SVT Drama Gothenburg (Sweden)/Zentropa Entertainments (Denmark) production, with participation of TV1000. (International sales: Trust Film, Stockholm.) Producer: Lars Jonsson. Executive producer: Peter Aalbaeck Jensen. Director: Ulf Malmros. Screenplay: Malmros, Lars Johansson. Camera: Mats Olofsson. Editors: Michal Leszczylowski, Fredrik Abrahamsen. Music: Dan Sundquist, Henrik Medquist. In color. Release date: Feb. 16, 2000. Running time: 91 Min. SWEDISH-DANISH.
Cast: Kjell Bergqvist, Cecilia Nilsson, Brasse Brannstrom, Rebecka Scheja, Anastasios Soulis, Marcus Hasselborg, Gachugu Makini.

SUN ALLEY
A Delphi Filmverleih release of a Boje Buck Produktion production, in association with O-Filmproduktion and SAT 1. (International sales: Boje Buck, Berlin.) Producers: Claus Boje, Detlev Buck. Co-producers: Katrin Schloesser, Doris Kirch. Director: Leander Haussmann. Screenplay: Thomas Brussig, Haussmann, Detlev Buck, Heike Sperling. Camera: Peter J. Krause. Editor: Sandy Saffeels. Music: Stephen Keusch, Paul Lemp. In color. Release date: Feb. 13, 2000. Running time: 87 Min. GERMAN.
Cast: Alexander Scheer, Alexander Beyer, Katharina Thalbach, Teresa Weissbach, Detlev Buck, Henry Huebchen, Ignaz Kirchner.

SUNDAY'S DREAM
An NHK release and production. (International sales: NHK, Tokyo.) Producer: Fusao Mineshima. Director: Yoichiro Takahashi. Screenplay: Ryo Iwamatsu. Camera: Kazuhiko Ishikawa, Takeshi Hori. Editor: Kiyoko Mizushima. Music: Liliy & Yoz. In color. Release date: May 11, 2000. Running time: 89 Min. JAPANESE.
Cast: Kenji Mizuhashi, Yumika Hayashi, Tetsu Watanabe, Liliy, Shinya Tsukamoto.

SUZHOU RIVER
A Coproduction Office presentation of an Essential Film (Berlin)/Dream Factory (Beijing) production. (International sales: Coproduction Office, Berlin.) Producers: Nai An, Philippe Bober. Director/Screenplay: Lou Ye. Camera: Wang Yu. Editor: Karl Riedl. Music: Jorg Lemberg. In color. Release date: Jan. 29, 2000. Running time: 83 Min. CHINESE-GERMAN.
Cast: Zhou Xun, Jia Hongsheng, Yao Anlian, Nai An.

SWAMP!
A Magloo release (in France) of a Magloo production. (International sales: Magloo, Paris.) Producer: Matthieu Gallou. Director/ Screenplay: Eric Bu. Camera: Jose Boulesteix. Editors: Brigitte Gallot, Eric Marie, Pascale Berson. Music: Cyril Bihi. In color. Release date: Sept. 21, 1999. Running time: 80 Min. FRENCH.
Cast: Satya Esquenazi, Michel Toesca, Thierry Buisson, Carole Frank, Isabelle Leprince, Claude Grinberg, Anne Sylvestre, Jean-Paul Farre.

TABOO
A Shochiku Co./BAC Films/Le Studio Canal Plus/Recorded Picture Co. presentation, in association with Kadokawa Shoten Publishing Co., Imagica, BS Asahi, Eisei Gekijo Co. (International sales: Studio Canal, Paris.) Executive producers: Oshima Prods., Eiko Oshima, Shigehiro Nakagawa, Kazuo Shimizu. Director/Screenplay: Nagis Oshima, based on the novellas "Maegami No Sozaburo" and "Sanjogawara Ranjin" from "Shinsengumi Keppuroku" by Ryotaro Shiba. Camera: Toyomichi Kurita. Editor: Tomoyo Oshima. Music: Ryuichi Sakamoto. In color. Release date: May 15, 2000. Running time: 101 Min. JAPANESE-FRENCH-U.S.
Cast: Beat Takeshi, Ryuhei Matsuda, Shinji Takeda, Tadanobu Asano.

TACKLE HAPPY
A Radiant Industries release and production. Producer/Director: Mick Molloy. Camera: Darren Chow, Steve Curry, Richard Molloy. Editor: Wayne Hyett. Music: Gareth Skinner. In color. Release date: June 11, 2000. Running time: 75 Min. Documentary. AUSTRALIAN.
With: Simon Morley, David Friend.

TAIL LIGHTS FADE
A Motion Intl. release (in Canada) of a Cadence Entertainment production, with the participation of the Canadian Television Fund, Telefilm Canada, City-TV, British Columbia Film, Film Incentive B.C., the Canadian Film or Video Production Tax Credit and the Harold Greenberg Fund. (International sales: Motion Intl., Montreal.) Producer: Christine Haebler. Executive producer: Scott Kennedy. Co-producers: Shawn Williamson, Karen Powell. Director: Malcolm Ingram. Screenplay: Matt Gissing. Camera: Brian Pearson. Editor: Reginal Harkema. Music: Neil Weisensel. In color. Release date: Dec. 10, 1999. Running time: 87 Min. CANADIAN.
Cast: Denise Richards, Breckin Meyer, Jake Busey, Tanya Allen, Elizabeth Berkley, Jaimz Woolvett, Lisa Marie, Ben Derrick.

TALE OF THE SIBERIAN LAND
A Mosfilm production. Director: Ivan Pyriev. Screenplay: Evgeni Pomeshchikov, Nikolai Rozhkov. Camera: Valentin Pavlov. Editor: A. Kulganek. Music: Nikolai Kryukov; songs: Evgeni Dolmatovsky. In color. Release date: Aug. 10, 2000. Running time: 114 Min. SOVIET UNION–1948.
Cast: Vladimir Druzhnikov, Marina Ladynina, Boris Andreyev, Vera Vasileva, Sergei Kalinin.

TANKA THE INNKEEPER
A Sovkino production. Director: Boris Svetozarov. Screenplay: K. Minaev, Svetozarov. Camera: V. Popov. In B&W. Release date: Aug. 4, 2000. Running time: 42 Min. SOVIET UNION–1929. Silent.
Cast: Tania Mukhina, K. Yastrebitsky, L. Nenasheva, A. Antonov.

TAXI 2
An ARP release of a Luc Besson presentation of a Leeloo Prods./ARP/TF1 Films Prod./Le Studio Canal Plus production, with participation of Canal Plus. Producers: Luc Besson, Michele Petin, Laurent Petin. Executive producers: Bernard Grenet, Antoine Simkine. Director: Gerard Krawczyk. Screenplay: Luc Besson. Camera: Gerard Sterin. Editor: Thierry Hoss. Music: Al Khemya. In color. widescreen. Release date: Mar. 28, 2000. Running time: 85 Min. FRENCH.
Cast: Samy Naceri, Frederic Diefenthal, Emma Sjoberg, Barnard Farcy, Marion Cotillard.

TEETH
A Cecchi Gori Distribuzione release of a Cecchi Gori Group/Colorado Film production. Producers: Vittorio Cecchi Gori, Maurizio Totti. Executive producer: Totti. Director/Screenplay: Gabriele Salvatores, based on the novel by Domenico Starnone. Camera: Italo Petriccione. Editor: Massimo Fiocchi. Music: Federico De Robertis, Teho Teardo, Eraldo Bernocchi. In color, Panalight widescreen. Release date: Sept. 1, 2000. Running time: 96 Min. ITALIAN.
Cast: Sergio Rubini, Anouk Grinberg, Tom Novembre, Anita Caprioli.

TELL ME SOMETHING
A Koo & C Film Co. production, in association with Cinema Service and Kookmin Venture Captial. (International sales: Mirovision, Seoul.) Producers: Ku Bonhan, Chang Yoon-hyun (Jang Yun-hyeon). Screenplay: Kyong Su-chang, In Eun-ah, Shim Hye-weon, Kim Eun-jeong, Chang. Camera: Kim Seong-bok. Editor: Kim Sang-beom. Music: Jo Yeong-uk, Bang Jun-seok. In color. Release date: Jan. 12, 2000. Running time: 118 Min. SOUTH KOREAN.
Cast: Han Seok-kyu, Shim Eun-ha, Jang Hang-seon, Yeom Jeong-ah, An Seok-hwan, Park Cheol-ho, Yu Jun-sang, Lee Hwan-jun.

TENEBRAE LESSONS
A Les Films de la Croisade presentation, in association with Carre Noir and RTDF Liege, with participation of La Region Haute Normandie and Prestige Television. Producer: Emmauel Giraud. Executive producer: Catherine Hannoun. Director/Screenplay: Vincent Dieutre. Camera: Jean-Marie Boulet, Benoit Chamaillard, Gilles Marchand. Editor: Ariane Doullet. In color. Release date: June 18, 2000. Running time: 77 Min. FRENCH.
Cast: Andrzej Burzynski, Hubert Geiger, Vincent Dieutre, Leo Bersani.

THAI SAHEBA
A Shri Soundarya Arts (Bangalore) production. Producer: Jaimala Ramachandra. Director/Screenplay: Girish Kasaravalli. Camera: H.M. Ramachandra. Editor: M.N. Swamy. Music: Isaac Thomas Kottukapally, Numlam Nischayov. In color. Release date: Sept. 25, 1999. Running time: 150 Min. INDIAN.
Cast: Jaimala Ramachandra, Suresh Heblikar, Shivaram, Harish Raju.

THANKS FOR THE GESTURE
A Mars Film release of a Telema/Studio Canal Plus/France 2 Cinema production, with participation of Canal Plus. (International sales: Le Studio Canal Plus, Paris.) Producer: Charles Gassot. Executive producers: Jacques Hinstin, Alain Steffen. Director/Screenplay: Claude Faraldo. Camera: Yves Lafaye. Editor: Guy Lecorne. Music: Sergio Tomassi. In color. Release date: Dec. 13, 1999. Running time: 96 Min. FRENCH.
Cast: Jacques Hansen, Marie Rousseau, Agathe de la Boulaye, Erick Deshors, Francoise Arnoul, Steve Kalfa, Annie Mercier.

THAT ONE NO ENOUGH
A Cathay Asia release of a Cathay Asia Films presentation of an Oak 3 Films production. (International sales: Cathay Asia, Singapore.) Executive producer: Meileen Choo. Director/Screenplay: Jack Neo, based on an original story by Neo and Mark Lee. Camera: Tung Seikwong. Editor: Martyn See. Music: Li Yi. In Fujicolor. Release date: Dec. 5, 1999. Running time: 111 Min. SINGAPORE.
Cast: Jack Neo, Mark Lee, Henry Thua, Hong Hui-fang, Patricia Mok, John Cheng, Yan Ni, Yoo Ah-min.

THAT'S JUST LIKE YOU
An Agata Films & Cie./La Sept Arte/Le Theatre National de Strasbourg production. (International sales: Agat, Paris.) Producer: Gilles Sandoz. Director: Claire Simon. Screenplay: Jean-Francois Goyet, Simon. Camera: Katell Dijan. Editor: Catherine Zins. Music: Jesus "Chucho" Valdes. In color. Release date: Aug. 4, 2000. Running time: 122 Min. FRENCH.
Cast: Stephanie Pasquet, Sophie Rodrigues, Marie Eleonore Pourtois, Claire Delaporte, Marika Peryronne, Alexandre Zloto, Ismae.

THEHEADISSPINNING
A Kubla Khan/Munbut production. (International sales: Kubla Khan/Munbut, Rome.) Producers: Alessandro Piva, Umberto Massa, Valerio Bariletti. Director: Alessandro Piva. Screenplay: Andrea Piva. Camera: Gianenrico Bianchi. Editors: Thomas Woschitz, Alessandro Piva. Music: Ivan Iusco. In color. Release date: Feb. 11, 2000. Running time: 70 Min. ITALIAN.
Cast: Dino Abbrescia, Mino Barbarese, Mimmo Mancini, Dante Marmone, Paolo Sassanelli, Teodosio Barresi, Nicola Pignataro.

THERE'S ONLY ONE JIMMY GRIMBLE
A Pathe Distribution release of a Pathe Pictures presentation, in association with the Arts Council of England and Le Studio Canal Plus, of a Sarah Raddyclyffe Prods./Impact Films production. Producers: Sarah Radclyffe, Jeremy Bolt, Alison Jackson. Director: John Hay. Screenplay: Simon Mayle, Hay, Rik Carmichael, story by Mayle. Camera: John de Borman. Editor: Oral Norrie Ottey. Music: Simon Boswell, Alex James. In Deluxe color. Release date: July 27, 2000. Running time: 105 Min. BRITISH.
Cast: Robert Carlyle, Ray Winstone, Gina McKee, Lewis McKenzie, Ben Miller, Bobby Power, Samia Ghadie, Hane Lapotaire.

THE THIEF OF SAINT LUBIN
A Mercure Distribution release of an Agat Films/La Sept Arte production. Producer: Gilles Sandoz. Director: Calire Devers, Jean-Louis Benoit. Camera: Helene Louvart. Editors: Marie Castro, Monica Coleman. Music: Beatrice Thiriet. In color. Release date: Sept. 3, 1999. Running time: 81 Min. FRENCH.
Cast: Dominique Blanc, Denis Podalydes, Michele Goddet, Fanny Florido.

THIRD WORLD COP
A Palm Pictures production in association with Hawk's Nest Prods. Producer: Carolyn Pfeiffer Bradshaw. Executive producers: Chris Blackwell, Dan Genetti. Director: Chris Browne. Screenplay: Suzanne Fenn, Browne, Chris Salewicz. Camera: Richard Lannaman. Editor: Suzanne Fenn. Music: Wally Badarou, Sly Dunbar, Robbie Shakespeare. In color. Release date: Sept. 14, 1999. Running time: 98 Min. JAMAICAN.
Cast: Paul Campbell, Mark Danvers, Carl Bradshaw, Audrey Reid, Winston Bell, Lenford Salmon.

30 YEARS
A Gemini Films release of a Gemini Films production, with participation of Canal Plus, CNC, Gimages 3. (International sales: Gemini, Paris.) Producer: Paulo Branco. Director: Laurent Perrin. Screenplay: Perrin, Camille Taboulay. Camera: Olivier Gueneau. Editor: Alice Lary. Music: Jorge Arriagade. In color. Release date: Aug. 1, 2000. Running time: 101 Min. FRENCH.
Cast: Anne Brochet, Laurent Lucas, Gregori Derangere, Nathalie Richard, Arielle Dombasle, Julie Depardieu, Hector Noguera.

THIS IS ME
A Public Film release of a Pieter van Huystee Film & TVVPRO production. (International sales: Pieter van Huystee Film & TV, Amsterdam.) Producer: Pieter van Huystee. Director/Screenplay: Sonia Herman Dolz. Camera: Hans Fels. Editor: Andrez de Jong. Music: Paul M. van Brugge. In color. Release date: Feb. 2000. Running time: 97 Min. Documentary. DUTCH.

THIS IS THE GARDEN
A Lucky Red release and production. Producer: Andrea Occhipinti. Director: Giovanni Davide Maderna. Screenplay: Giovanni Davide Maderna, Carolina Freschi. Camera: Luga Bigazzi. Editor: Jacopo Quadri. Music: Massimo Mariani. In color. Release date: Sept. 4, 1999. Running time: 89 Min. ITALIAN.
Cast: Carolina Fresche, Denis Fasolo, Allesandro Quattro, Emanuela Macchniz, Delia Boccardo, Tiziana Bergamaschi.

THREE BROTHERS
An East Cinema production. Producers: Serik Aprymov, Sano Sinju. Executive producer: Gulmira Aprymova. Director/Screenplay: Serik Aprymov. Camera: Fedor Aranishev. Editor: Dina Bersugurova. In color. Release date: Feb. 3, 2000. Running time: 78 Min. KAZAKHSTANIAN.
Cast: Kasym Zhakibaev, Shakir Vilyoumov, Bulat Mazhagulov, Bahtiyour Kuatbaev.

THE THREE MADELEINES
A Films Equinox release of a Filmo/La Compagnie France Film production, with participation of Harold Greenberg Fund, Canadian Arts Council, Main Film, Telefilm Canada, National Film Office of Canada, Quebec Council of Arts & Letters. (International sales: France Film, Montreal.) Producers: Francois Landrey, Guylaine Dionne, Michael Mosca, Claire Valade, Pierre Rene. Director/Screenplay: Guylaine Dionne. Camera: Nathalie Moliavko-Visotzky. Editor: Aube Foglia. In B&W. Release date: May 5, 2000. Running time: 81 Min. CANADIAN.
Cast: Sylvie Drapeau, France Arbour, Isadora Galwey, Kathleen Fortin, Maxim Gaudette, Isabelle Blais, Monique Joly, Luc Prouix.

THE THREE MEN OF MELITA ZGANJER
A Kvadar production. Producers: Sanja Vejnovic, Irina Damic, Vesna Mort, Josip Barlovic. Director/Screenplay: Snjezana Tribuson. Camera: Goran Mecava. Editor: Marina Barac. In color. Release date: Feb. 25, 2000. Running time: 97 Min.CROATIAN.
Cast: Mirjana Rogina, Goran Navojec, Sanja Vejnovic, Suzana Nikolic, Filip Sovagovic, Ivo Gregurevic, Ljubomir Keredes, Luka Peros, Rene Bitorajac.

THREE SONGS ABOUT LENIN
A Mezhrabpomfilm (Moscow) production. Director/Screenplay/Editor: Dziga Vertov. Camera: D. Uspensky, D. Magidson, B. Monastyrsky. Release date: Aug. 4, 2000. Running time: 57 Min. Documentary. SOVIET UNION–1935.

THREE STORIES
An Ipotesi Cinema in collaboration with RAI. Producer: ICS. Directors: Piergiorgio Gay with Roberto San Pietro. Screenplay: Gay, San Pietro, in collaboration with Giulio Ciarambino. Camera: Alessandro Bolzoni. Editor: Carlotta Cristiani. In color. Release date: Nov. 20, 1999. Running time: 114 Min. ITALIAN.
Cast: Stefano Dionisi, Chiara Caselli, Alessandro Repossi, Barbara Lerici, Vittorio Amandola, Fabrizio Mele, Hidde Maas.

THROUGH THE WINDOW
An A.F. Cinema e Video/Bial Culture & Arts production. (International sales: A.F. Cinema e Vildeo, Sao Paulo.) Producers: Caio Gullane, Fabiano Gullane. Executive producer: Van Fresnot. Director: Tata Amaral. Screenplay: Jean-Claude Bernardet, Fernando Bonassi, Amaral. Camera: Hugo Kovensky. Editor: Ide Lacreta. Music: Livio Tagtenberg, Wilson Sukorski. In color. Release date: Feb. 1, 2000. Running time: 83 Min. BRAZILIAN.
Cast: Laura Cardoso, Fransergio Araujo, Ana Lucia Torre, Leona Cavalli, Joao Acaiabe, Antonio Petrin, Debora Duboc.

TIERRA DEL FUEGO
An Istituto Luce release (in Italy) of a Surf Film (Italy)/Castelao Prods. (Spain)/Buenaventura Films (Chile) production. (International sales: RAI Trade, Rome.) Producers: Massimo Vigliar, Julio Fernandez, Cristina Littin Mena. Executive producers: Littin Menz, Roberto Manni, Miguel Angel. Director: Miguel Littin. Screenplay: Luis Sepulveda, Littin, in association with Tonino Guerra, based on the novel by Francisco Coloane and the diary of Julius Popper. Camera: Giuseppe Lance. Editor: Ernest Blasi. Music: Milladoiro, Angel Parra. In color, widescreen. Release date: May 17, 2000. Running time: 108 Min. ITALIAN-SPANISH-CHILEAN.
Cast: Jorge Perugorria, Ornella Muti, Claudio Santamaria, Nancho Novo, Nelson Villagra, Alvaro Rudolphy, Tamara Acosta.

THE TIGHT KNOT
A Mosfilm production. Director: Mikhail Shveitser. Screenplay: Vladimir Tendryakov. Camera: Aleksei Temerin. Music: Veniamin Basner. Release date: Aug. 7, 2000. Running time: 97 Min. SOVIET UNION–1957.
Cast: Viktor Avdyushko, Oleg Tabakov, Nikolai Sergeyev, Vladimir Emelyanov.

A TIME FOR DRUNKEN HORSES
An MK2 Diffusion release of a B.H. Films production. (International sales: MK2 Diffusion, Paris.) Producer/Director/Screenplay: Bahman Ghobadi. Camera: Saed Nikzat. Editor: Samad Tavazoi. Music: Hossein Alizadeh. In color. Release date: May 14, 2000. Running time: 80 Min. IRANIAN.
Cast: Nezhad Ekhtiar-Dini, Amaneh Ekhtiar-Dini, Madi Ekhtiar-Dini, Ayoub Ahmadi, Jouvin Younessi.

TO AND FRO
An Imcine presentation of a Centro de Capacitacion Cinematografia production. Producers: Angeles Castro Gurria, Hugo Rodriquez. Director: Salvador Aguirre. Screenplay: Aguirre, Alejandro Lubezki. Camera: Geronimo Denti. Editor: Moises Ortiz-Urquidi. Music: Jorge Fratta. In color. Release date: Aug. 27, 2000. Running time: 83 Min. MEXICAN.
Cast: Gerardo Taracena, Ricardo Esquerra, Tiare Scanda.

TOBIA AL CAFFE
An AB Film release of a Factory Produzioni Cinematografiche production. (International sales: Adriana Chiesa Enterprises, Rome.) Producer: Mariella Li Sacchi. Executive producer: Amedeo Letizia. Director: Gianfranco Mingozzi. Screenplay: Marco Lodoli, Silvia Brembilla, Angelo Orlando, Mingozzi, based on the story by Lodoli in the collection "Grande raccordo." Camera: Luigi Verga. Editor: Alfredo Muschietti. Music: Nicola Piovani. In Augustus color. Release date: July 7, 2000. Running time: 99 Min. ITALIAN.
Cast: Roberto Citran, Nicola Russo, Candice Hugo, Federico Galante.

TO DIE (OR NOT)
A Lauren Films release of an Els Films de la Rambla production, in association with Canal Plus, TVE, TVC. (International sales: Els Films de la Rambla, Barcelona.) Producer: Ventura Pons. Director/Screenplay: Ventura Pons, based on a play by Sergi Belbel. Camera: Jesus Escosa. Editor: Pere Abadal. Music: Carles Cases. In B&W and color. Release date: Jan. 31, 2000. Running time: 92 Min. SPANISH.
Cast: Lluis Homar, Carmen Elias, Roger Coma, Marc Martinez, Anna Azcona, Vicky Pena, Carlota Bantula, Amparo Moreno, Mingo Rafols.

TOGETHER
A Sonet Film release (in Sweden) of a Memfis Film presentation of a Memfis Film, Film i Vast, SVT Drama Gothenburg (Sweden)/Zentropa Entertainments (Denmark)/Keyfilms Roma (Italy) production, in association with TV 1000. (International sales: Trust Film Sales, Copenhagen.) Producer: Lars Jonsson. Co-producer: Peter Aalbaeck Jensen. Director/Screenplay: Luka Moodysson. Camera: Ulf Branta. Editors: Michal Leszczylowksi, Fredrik Abrahamsen. In color. Release date: Aug. 18, 2000. Running time: 106 Min. SWEDISH-DANISH-ITALIAN.
Cast: Lisa Lindgren, Mikael Nyqvist, Gustaf Hammarsten.

TOMORROW'S ANOTHER DAY
A Bac Films release of a Cine Valse, Art Light Prods., France 2 Cinema production, in association with Le Studio Canal. (International sales: Studio Canal Plus, Paris.) Producer: Alain Sarde. Executive producer: Nicole Bechet. Director/Screenplay: Jeanne Labrune. Camera: Jean-Claude Thibaut. Editor: Guy Lecorne. Music: Bruno Fontaine. In color. Release date: Aug. 7, 2000. Running time: 90 Min. FRENCH.
Cast: Nathalie Baye, Jeanne Balibar, Jean-Pierre Darroussin, Danielle Darrieux, Isabelle Carre, Didier Bezace, Sophie Guillemin.

TOP OF THE FOOD CHAIN
A Red Sky Entertainment (Canada) release of an Upstart Pictures production, in association with Bedard/Lalonde Amusements and Victor Film Co., with support from the Ontario Film Development Corp. and Space: The Imagination Station. Producer: Susan Berber. Executive producer: Jana Edelbaum. Co-producers: Phil Bedard, Larry Lalonde. Director: John Paizs. Screenplay: Phil Bedard, Larry Lalond. Camera: Bill Wong. Editor: Albert Kish. Music: David Krystal. In color. Release date: Sept. 20, 1999. Running time: 99 Min. CANADIAN.
Cast: Campbell Scott, Fiona Loewi, Tom Everett Scott, Hardee T. Lineham, Bernard Behrens, Nigel Bennett, Elisa Moolecherry.

TOPS & BOTTOMS
A Barking at Moon production, in association with TVOntario, Arte, Showcase Television, Women's Television Network, Knowledge Network, the Canadian Film Board Women's Equity Program. (International sales: Barking at Moon, Toronto.) Producer/Director: Christine Richey. Screenplay: John Kramer. Camera: Micha Dahan, Peter Walker, Richard Stringer. Editor: Jack Morbin. Music: Nicholas Stirling. In B&W and color, 16mm. Release date: Sept. 15, 1999. Running time: 80 Min. Documentary. CANADIAN.

TORO
A Regal Entertainment Corp. presentation of an Available Light production. Producer: Lily Y. Monteverde. Director/Screenplay: Jose Javier Reyes. Camera: Eduardo Jacinto. Editor: Vito Cajili. Music: Jesse Lucas. In color. Release date: Mar. 2, 2000. Running time: 110 Min. FILIPINO.
Cast: Paolo Rivero, Anna Capri, Klaudia Koronel, Hazel Espinosa.

TOSCA: A TALE OF LOVE AND TORTURE
A Film Australia presentation in association with the Australian Broadcasting Corp. (International sales: Film Australia, Sydney.) Producer: Patricia Lovell. Executive producer: Mark Hamlyn. Director: Trevor Graham. Screenplay: Graham, Rosemary Hesp. Camera: John Witteron, Robert Humphries. Editor: Denise Haslem. Music: Giacomo Puccini. In color. Release date: June 17, 2000. Running time: 86 Min. Documentary. AUSTRALIAN.

TOTAL LOSS
A Warner Bros. presentation of a Lemming Film production in association with V-PRO TV and MaJaDe Film/Heino Deckert. Producers: Leontine Petit, Joost de Vries. Director: Dana Nechushtan. Screenplay: Marco van Geffen, from a novel by Karst Woudstra. Camera: Bert Pot. Editor: Peter Alderliesten. Music: Han Otten, Maurits Overdulve. In color. Release date: Aug. 26, 2000. Running time: 94 Min. DUTCH-GERMAN.
Cast: Franky Ribbens, Roef Ragas, Yorick van Wageningen.

TOTAL WESTERN
A UFD release (in France) of a Lazennec/UGC Images production, with participation of Canal Plus, in association with Studio Images 6, Gimages. (International sales: M6, Paris.) Producers: Alain Rocca, Said Ben Said. Director: Eric Rochant. Screenplay: Laurent Chalumeau, Rochant, based on an idea by Rochant. Camera: Vincenzo Marano, Yves Agostini. Editor: Pascales Fenouillet. Music: Marco Prince. In color, widescreen. Release date: July 18, 2000. Running time: 100 Min. FRENCH.
Cast: Samuel Le Bihan, Jean-Pierre Kalfon, Jean-Francois Stevenin, Kahena Saighi, Alexia Stresi, Youssef Diawara, Ouassini Embarek.

TOUCHED
A Red Sky Entertainment release (in Canada) of a Ranfilm production. (International sales: Ranfilm, Vancouver.) Producer: Mort Ransen. Executive producer: Raymond Massey. Co-producers: Diane Patrick O'Connor, Trevor Hodgson. Director: Mort Ransen. Screenplay: Ransen, Joan Hopper. Camera: Georges Dufaux. Editor: Ransen. Music: Michael Conway Baker. In color. Release date: Sept. 12, 1999. Running time: 105 Min. CANADIAN.
Cast: Lyn Redgrave, Tygh Runyan, Annick Obonsawin, Maury Chaykin, Lolita Davidovich, Ian Tracey, Graham Greene, Gary Farmer.

THE TOWN IS QUIET
A Mercure Film (France) release of an Agat Films & Cie-Diaphana production, in association with Canal Plus. Producers: Gilles Sandoz, Michel Saint-John, Robert Guediguian. Executive producer: Bruno Ghariani. Director: Robert Guediguian. Screenplay: Guediguian, Jean-Louis Milesi. Camera: Bernard Cavalie. Editor: Bernard Sasia. In color. Release date: Aug. 30, 2000. Running time: 143 Min. FRENCH.
Cast: Ariane Ascaride, Jean-Pierre Darroussin, Gerard Meylan, Alexandre Ogou, Pierre Banderet, Jacques Boudet, Pascale Roberts, Julie-Marie Parmentier, Christine Brucher.

THE TRAIN GOES EAST
A Mosfilm production. Director: Yuli Raisman. Screenplay: Leonid Malyugin. Camera: Igor Geleyn, Aleksandr Kaltsati. Editor: T. Lihachyova. Music: Tikhon Khrennikov. In color. Release date: Aug. 6, 2000. Running time: 93 Min. SOVIET UNION–1948.
Cast: Lidia Dranovskaya, Leonid Gallis, Maria Yaroskaya, N. Vorobev, K. Sorokin, V. Lyubimov.

TRANSGRESSION
A Massimo Ferrero presentation (International sales: Film Export Group.) Producer: Massimo Ferrero. Executive producer: Pino Gargiulo. Director: Tinto Brass. Screenplay: Brass, Carla Cipriani, Nicolaj Pennestri, Silvia Rossi, Massimiliano Zanin, story by Brass. Camera: Massimo Di Venanzo. Music: Pino Donaggio. In Cinecitta color. Release date: Jan. 23, 2000. Running time: 89 Min. ITALIAN.
Cast: Yuliya Mayarchuk, Jarno Berardi, Francesca Nunzi, Max Parodi.

A TRIP TO THE COUNTRY
A Les Films du Raphia production in association with ZDF, Arte. (International sales: Les Films du Raphia, Chatillon, France.) Producer/Director: Jean-Marie Teno. Camera: Teno, Moussa Diakite. Editor: Christiane Badgley. Music: Ben's Belinga. In color. Release date: Feb. 12, 2000. Running time: 78 Min. Documentary. CAMEROON-FRENCH-GERMAN.

TUBE TALES
A Sky Pictures presentation of a Horsepower Films production. (International sales: Icon Entertainment Intl., London.) Producer: Richard Jobson. Co-producer: Tony Thompson. Directors: Amy Jenkins, Stephen Hopkins, Mehaj Huda, Bob Hoskins, Ewan McGregor, Armando Iannucci, Jude Law, Gaby Dellal, Charles McDougall. Screenplay: Amy Jenkins, Stephen Hopkins, Harsha Patel, Paul Fraser, Mark Greig, Armando Iannucci, Ed Allen, Gaby Dellal, Atalanta Goulandris, Nick Perry. Camera: Sue Gibson, David Johnson, Brain Tufano. Editors: Niven Howie, Liz Green. Title Music: Faze & Zero. In Deluxe color. Release date: Dec. 15, 1999. Running time: 90 Min. BRITISH.
Cast: Kelly Macdonald, Jason Flemyng, Denise Van Outen, Tom Bell, Stephen Da Costa, Dele Johnson, Ray Winstone, Tom Watson.

TURBULENCE
A Skylight Cinema (Brazil)/Icaic (Cuba)/D & D (Portugal) production. Producers: Ruy Guerra, Buza Ferraz, Daniel D'Olivier, Donald Ranvaud, Renato Padovani. (International sales: Serena Skylight Intl., Santa Monica.) Director/Screenplay: Ruy Guerra, based on the novel by Chico Buarque. Camera: Marcelo Durst. Editor: Mair Tavares. Music: Egberto Gismonti. In color. Release date: May 13, 2000. Running time: 96 Min. BRAZILIAN-CUBAN-PORTUGUESE.
Cast: Jorge Perugorria, Bianca Byington, Susana Ribeiro, Leonor Arocha, Xando Graca.

TUVALU
A Veit Helmer-Filmprodukton production in association with Borough Film, with participation of Buena Vista Intl., Filmboard Berlin-Brandenberg, FFA, SWR, Mitteldeutscher Rundfunk. (International sales: Bavaria Film Intl., Germany.) Producer: Veit Helmer. Executive producers: Vladimir Andreev, George Balkanski. Director: Veit Helmer. Screenplay: Michaela Beck, Helmer. Camera: Emil Christov. Editor: Araksi Mouhibian. Music: Jurgen Knieper. In B&W, widescreen. Release date: Sept. 23, 1999. Running time: 101 Min. GERMAN.
Cast: Denis Lavant, Chulpan Hamatova, Philippe Clary, Terrence Gillespie, EJ Callahan, Djoko Rossich, Catalina Murgea.

24 HOURS IN LONDON

A Blue Dolphin Films release of a One World Films production. (International sales: Victor Film Co., London.) Producer: Fergal McGrath. Director/Screenplay: Alexander Finbow. Camera: Chris Plevin. Editor: Ian Farr. Music: Edmund Butt. In Fujicolor. Release date: July 14, 2000. Running time: 86 Min. BRITISH.
Cast: Gary Olsen, Anjela Lauren-Smith, John Benfield, Amita Dhiri, James Oliver, Sara Stockbridge, Richard Graham, James Hicks.

27 MISSING KISSES

A Jens Meuer and Oliver Damian presentation of an Egoli Films production, in co-production with Le Studio Canal Plus, Moco Films/British Screen, Studio Babelsberg Independents, Wave Pictures. (International sales: Wild Bunch, Paris.) Producers: Meuer, Damian. Director: Nana Djordjadze. Screenplay: Iraklij Kvirikadze. Camera: Phedon Papamichael. Editor: Vessela Martschewski. Music: Goran Bregovic. In color. Release date: May 11, 2000. Running time: 98 Min. GERMAN-GEORGIAN.
Cast: Nino Kuchanidze, Eugenij Sidichin, Shalva Iashvili,.

20–VENTI

A Quattrocentoundici/411 production in association with Bongiomo Prods. and David Prods. (International sales: 411 Prods., Milano.) Producers: Luca Mignani, Augusto Pizzamiglio. Director: Marco Pozzi. Screenplay: Possi, Andrea Bempensante. Camera: Alessio Viola. Editor: Piero Biggi. In color. Release date: Feb., 17, 2000. Running time: 91 Min. ITALIAN.
Cast: Cecilia Dazzi, Anita Caprioli, Ivano Narescotti, Rocco Barbaro.

TWO FOR TEA

A Lauren Films presentation of a Produccions Kilimanjaro production. Producer: Carles Benpar. Director/Screenplay: Isabel Gardela. Camera: Nuria Roldos. Editors: Domi Parra, Victor Vidal. Music: Alex Solana. In color. Release date: Aug. 28, 2000. Running time: 93 Min. SPANISH.
Cast: Nuria Prims, Zack Qureshi, Txell Sust, Olalla Moreno, Teresa Gimpera, Moncia Van Campen, Xavier Graset, Carlos Orellana.

TWO LIKE US, NOT THE BEST

An Istituto Luce release of a Metafilm production. Producer: Laura Cafiero. Director/Screenplay: Stefano Grossi. Camera: Marcello Montarsi. Editor: Graziana Quintalti. Music: Francesco De Luca, Alessandro Forti. In color. Release date: Apr. 30, 2000. Running time: 109 Min. ITALIAN.
Cast: Marcello Sambati, Adel Bakri, Stefania Orsola Garello.

2 MINUTES SILENCE, PLEASE

A Public Film Release (in the Netherlands) of a Pieter van Huystee Film &TV/NPS production. (International sales: Fortuna Film, Amsterdam.) Producer: Pieter van Huystee. Director: Heddy Honigmann. Screenplay, research: Honigmann, Hans Dortmans. Camera: Maarten Kramer. Editor: Mario Steenbergen. In color. Release date: Oct. 15, 1999. Running time: 87 Min. Documentary. DUTCH.

2000 AD

A Media Asia (in Hong Kong)/Raintree (in Singapore) release of a Media Asia Films/Raintree Pictures production. Producers: John Chong, Solon So, David Leong. Executive producers: Thomas Chung, Daniel Yu, Willie Chan. Director: Gordon Chan. Screenplay: Stu Zicherman, Chan, story by Chan, Zicherman. Camera: Arthur Wong. Editor: Chan Ki-hop. Music: Shigeru Umebayashi. In color. Release date: May 12, 2000. Running time: 102 Min. HONG KONG-SINGAPORE.
Cast: Aaron Kwok, Daniel Wu, Phyllis Quek, James Lye, Andrew Lin, GiGi Choi, Ray Lui, Francis Ng, Cynthia Koh, Lim Yubeng.

TWO THOUSAND AND NONE

A Galafilm Prods. production, with participation of Canadian Television Fund, CHUM Television, the Movie Network, Super Ecran and Super Channel. (International sales: Pandora, Paris.) Producer: Arnie Gerlbart. Director/Screenplay: Arto Paragamian. Camera: Norayr Kasper. Editor: Alain Baril. Music: Milan Kymlicka. In color. Release date: July 7, 2000. Running time: 93 Min. CANADIAN.
Cast: John Turturro, Oleg Kisseliov, Katherine Borowitz, Julian Richings, Carl Alacchi, Pascale Devigne, Jayne Heitmeyer.

THE UGLIEST WOMAN IN THE WORLD

An Aurum release (in Spain) of an Aurum production, with participation of Canal Plus, in association withTVE. (International sales: Aurum, Madrid.) Producer: Francisco Ramos. Director: Miguel Bardem. Screenplay: Nacho Faerna. Camera: Nestor Calvo. Editor: Ivan Aledo. Music: Juan Bardem. In color. Release date: Nov. 13, 1999. Running time: 108 Min. SPANISH.
Cast: Elia Galera, Roberto Alvarez, Hector Alterio, Javivi, Alberto San Juan.

UNDER SUSPICION

A Revelations Entertainment (U.S.)/-TF1 Intl. (France) production. (International sales: TF1, Paris.) Producers: Lori McCreary, Anne Marie Gillen, Stephen Hopkins. Executive producers: Morgan Freeman, Gene Hackman, Maurice Leblond, Ross Grayson Bell. Director: Stephen Hopkins. Screenplay: Tom Prevost, W. Peter Iliff, based on the film "Garde a vue," written by Claude Miller, Jean Herman, Michel Audiard, based on the book "Brainwash" by John Wainwright. Camera: Peter Levy. Editor: John Smith. Music: BT. In Technicolor. Release date: May 11, 2000. Running time: 110 Min. U.S.-FRENCH.
Cast: Morgan Freeman, Gene Hackman, Thomas Jane, Monica Bellucci, Nydia Caro, Angel Suarez, Pablo Cunqueiro, Isabel Algaze.

UNDERTAKER'S PARADISE

A Buena Vista Intl. (Germany) release of a Claussen & Woebke Filmproduktion production. (International sales: Bavaria Film Intl., Munich.) Producers: Jakob Claussen, Thomas Woebke. Director: M.X. Oberg. Screenplay: Tim Dabringhaus, Oberg. Camera: Martin Kukula. Editors: Barbara Giess, Mona Braeuer. Music: Niki Reiser. In color. Release date: Aug. 1, 2000. Running time: 91 Min. GERMAN.
Cast: Thomas Schmauser, Ben Gazzara, Michael Fitzgerald, Emma Catherwood, Edward Jewesbury, Sally Dexter, Janine Eser.

UNDER THE SAND

A Fidelite Prods. production, in association with Euro Space, Haut & Court, Arte France Cinema. (International sales: Celluloid Dreams, Paris.) Producers: Olivier Delbosc, Marc Missonnier. Director: Francois Ozon. Screenplay: Ozon, Emmanuele Bernheim, Marina De Van, Marcia Romano. Camera: Jeanne Lapoirie, Antoine Heberle. Editor: Laurence Bawedin. Music: Philippe Rombi. In color. Release date: Sept. 9, 2000. Running time: 96 Min. FRENCH.
Cast: Charlotte Rampling, Bruno Cremer, Jacques Nolot, Alexandra Stewart, Pierre Vernier, Andree Tainsy.

UNINVITED

A Franco Nero/Francesco Papa presentation of a Barolo Films (New York)/No Limit Intl. (Rome) production in association with Mediaset. (International sales: Image Design Entertainment, Los Angeles.) Producers: Nero, Papa, Paul Stepehen Mezey. Director/Screenplay: Carlo Gabriel Nero, based on the novel by James Gabriel Berman. Camera: Giancarlo Ferrando. Editor: Paolo Benassi. Music: Carlo Siliotto. In Cinecitta color. Release date: Sept. 19, 1999. Running time: 112 Min. U.S.-ITALIAN.
Cast: Kevin Isola, Adam Hann-Byrd, Stephen Mendillo, Patricia Dunnock, Eli Wallach, Franco Nero, Vanessa Redgrave.

UNKNOWN FRIEND

A Moneypenny Filmproduktion production, in association with ZDF and DFFB. (International sales: Moneypenny, Berlin.) Producers: Sigrid Hoerner, Anne Leppin, Martin Walz. Director/Screenplay: Anne Hoegh Krohn. Camera: Sebastian Edschmid. Editor: Uta Schmidt. Music: Bernd Jestram, Ronald Lippok. In color. Release date: Feb. 19, 2000. Running time: 81 Min. GERMAN.
Cast: Karoline Eichhorn, Inga Busch, Biroll Uenel, Antonio Wannek, Mario Mentrup, Isabel Tuengerthal, Dirk Borchardt.

AN UNUSUAL LOVE

A Beijing Film Studio release (in China) of a Beijing Xinyingjia/Beijing Film Studio production. (International sales: Beijing Film Studio, Beijing.) Producer: Han Sanping. Executive producers: Lu Yao, He Ping. Director: Wu Tianming. Screenplay: Chen Tong. Camera: Zhao Lei. Editor: Zeng Shiwei. Music: Zhang Qianyi. In color. Release date: Aug. 28, 1999. Running time: 98 Min. CHINESE.
Cast: Yuan Li, Liu Yunlong, Zhu Daoxian, Han Fuyi, Gong Peixin, Tian Chengren, Jiang Yaofen, Mei Lin, Wang Yonggui, Song Banggui.

UP AT THE VILLA

A USA Films (in U.S.)/UIP (in U.K.) release of a Universal Pictures/Intermedia Films presentation of a Mirage/Stanley Buchtal production. Producer: Geoff Stier. Executive producers: Sydney Pollack, Arnon Milchan, Stanley Buchthal. Co-executive producers: Guy East, Nigel Sinclair. Co-producer: David Brown. Director: Philip Haas. Screenplay: Belinda Haas, from the novella by W. Somerset Maugham. Camera: Maurizio Calvesi. Editor: Belinda Haas. Music: Pino Donaggio. In Technicolor. Release date: Apr. 21, 2000. Running time: 114 Min. U.S.-BRITISH.
Cast: Kristin Scott Thomas, Sean Penn, Anne Bancroft, James Fox, Jeremy Davies, Derek Jacobi, Massimo Ghini.

UP TO THE ANGELS

A Medusa Film release (in Italy) of a DueA Film production, in association with Medusa Film. (International sales: Adriana Chiesa Enterprises, Rome.) Producers: Antonio Avati, Fiorenzo Senese. Director: Pupi Avati. Screenplay: Pupi Avati, Antonio Avati, based on an idea by Ines Vigetti, Marco Benardini. Camera: Cesare Bastelli. Editor: Amedeo Salfa. Music: Riz Ortolani. In Cinecitta color, Technovision widescreen. Release date: Dec 7, 1999. Running time: 123 Min. ITALIAN.
Cast: Gianni Cavina, Valentina Cervi, Carlo Delle Piane, Libero De Rienzo, Eliana Miglio, Chiara Muti, Paola Saluzzi, Mario Maranzana.

THE VALLEY

An MBC production in association with Suspect Device for Channel 4. Producer: Dan Reed. Executive producer: Geroge Carey. Director: Dan Reed. Camera: Jacek Petrycki. Editor: Stefan Ronowicz. Music: David Hughes, John Murphy. In color, HD video. Release date: Apr. 25, 2000. Running time: 69 Min. Documentary. BRITISH.

VATEL

A Miramax (U.S.)/Gaumont (France) release of a Gaumont-Legende Enterprises (Paris)/Timothy Burrill Prods. (London) co-production, in association with Nomad, RF1 Films, Canal Plus. (International sales: Gaumont Intl., Paris.) Producers: Alain Goldman, Roland Joffe. Co-producer: Timothy Burrill. Director: Roland Joffe. Screenplay: Jeanne Labrune; English adaptation: Tom Stoppard. Camera: Robert Fraisse. Editor: Noelle Boisson. Music: Ennio Morricone. In color, Panavision widescreen. Release date: May 10, 2000. Running time: 117 Min. FRENCH-BRITISH.
Cast: Gerard Depardieu, Uma Thurman, Tim Roth, Julian Glover, Julian Sands, Timothy Spall, Arielle Dombasle, Hywel Bennett.

VICTIM
A Mei Ah release of a Mei Ah Film Prod. Co./ Brilliant Idea Group production. (International sales: Mei Ah, Hong Kong.) Producer: Li Kuohsing. Executive producer: Joe Ma. Executive in charge of production: Patrick Tong. Director: Ringo Lam. Camera: Ross Clarkson. Editor: Andy Chan. Music: Raymond Wong. In color. Release date: Nov. 24, 2000. Running time: 103 Min. HONG KONG.
Cast: Tony Leung Kar-fai, Lau Ching-wan, Amy Kwok, Lai Yiu-cheung, Colling Chou, Emily Kwan, Shiu Hsiu-hong, David Lee, Tony Chiu.

THE VINEYARD
A Buena Vista Intl. presentation of an Aura Producciones Internacionales and Nueva Imagen production. Producers: Nelson Stratta, Fernando Acuna, Esteban Schroeder. Director: Esteban Schroeder. Screenplay: Schroeder, Pablo Vierci. Camera: Ricardo di Angelis. Editor: Daniel Manques. Music: Gabriel Markarian. In color, video-to-35mm. Release date: Aug. 28, 2000. Running time: 87 Min. URUGUAYAN-CHILEAN.
Cast: Danilo Rodriquez, Liliana Garcia, Fernando Kliche, Eduardo Guerrero, Martin Linares, Sara Laroca, Mario Aguerre.

VIOLET
An Alliance Atlantis Viva Film presentation of a Dark Flowers production. Producer: Mary Sexton. Executive producers: Jim Byrd, Charlotte Mickie, Jan Nathanson. Director/Screenplay: Mary Sexton. Camera: Ivan Gekoff. Editor: Trevor Ambrose. Music: Paul Steffler. In color. Release date: Aug. 27, 2000. Running time: 105 Min. CANADIAN.
Cast: Mary Walsh, Peter MacNeill, Andrew Younghusband, Susan Kent, Berni Stapleton, Janis Spence, Raoul Bhaneja, Barry Newhook.

THE VIRGIN
A Nanook Films production. (International sales: Austrian Film Commission.) Producer: Peter Roehsler. Director/Screenplay: Diego Donnhofer. Camera: Peter Roehsler. Editor: Karina Ressler. Music: John Cale. In color. Release date: Feb. 13, 2000. Running time: 92 Min. AUSTRIAN.
Cast: Joey Kern, Kristy Hinchcliffe, Glenn Cruz.

VIRGIN STRIPPED BARE BY HER BACHELORS
A Unikorea/Miracin Korea production (International sales: Mirovision, Seoul.) Producers: Lee Yu-jin. Executive producers: Ahn Byung-ju, Choi In-ki. Director/Screenplay: Hong Sang-soo. Camera: Choi Yeongtaek. Editor: Yim Dong-suk, Oh Won-chul. In B&W. Release date: May 20, 2000. Running time: 127 Min. SOUTH KOREAN.
Cast: Lee Eun-ju, Jeong Bo-seok, Mun Seong-keun.

VIRTUAL VAMPIRE
A Luxus Film production in association with ZDF, das Kleine Fernsehspiel and Burkhardt Althoff. Producer: Michael Busch. Executive producer: Jaqueline Kaassa. Director/Screenplay: Michael Busch. Camera: Marcus Winterbauer. Editor: Ute Schall. Music: Jammin' Onit, the PSI-Project. In color. Release date: Mar. 3, 2000. Running time: 92 Min. GERMAN.
Cast: Inga Busch, Armin Dallpiccola, Rene Hofschneider, Rudiger Kuhlbrodt, Claudia Splitt.

THE VISITANT
A Tercer Milenio/Aries Cinematografica Argentina production. (International sales: Aries, Bueno Aires.) Producer: Hector Olivera. Executive producer: Marcos Olivera. Director: Javier Olivera. Screenplay: Jose Pablo Feinmann, Olivera, story by Axel Nacher, Fernando Schmidt. Camera: Victor Kino Gonzalez. Editor: Marcel Cluzet. Music: Axel Krygier. In Fuji-color. Release date: Sept. 4, 1999. Running time: 91 Min. ARGENTINE.
Cast: Julio Chavez, Valentina Bassi, Mariano Bertolini, Elsa Berenguer, Alejandro Awada, Silvina Bosco, Roly Serrano.

A VISITOR FROM THE LIVING
A New Yorker Films release (in U.S.) of a Les Films Aleph/Cineteve production in association with La Sept Arte. Producer/Director: Claude Lanzmann. Camera: Dominique Chapuis, William Lubtchansky. Editor: Sabine Mamou. In color, 16mm. Release date: Sept. 23, 1999. Running time: 65 Min. Documentary. FRENCH.

VOLAVERUNT
An Aurum release (in Spain) of a Mate Prod./MDA Films/UGC YM/UGC Intl. production with participation of Television Espanola, Via Digital, Canal Plus (France). (International sales: UGC Intl., Paris.) Producers: Mate Cantero, Stephane Sorlat. Executive producer: Cantero. Director: Bigas Luna. Screenplay: Cuca Canals, Luna, based on the novel by Antonio Larreta. Camera: Paco Femenia. Editor: Kenout Peltier. Music: Alberto Garcia Demestre. In color, widescreen. Release date: Sept. 18, 1999. Running time: 115 Min. SPANISH-FRENCH.
Cast: Aitana Sanchez-Gijon, Penelope Cruz, Jordi Molla, Jorge Perugorria, Stefania Sandrelli, Carlos La Rosa, Zoe Berriatua.

VULCAN JUNCTION
An Eran Riklis Prods. production, with the assistance of the Israel Film Fund, NCP-Reshet Television. Producers: Eran Riklis, Mosh Danon. Director: Eran Riklis. Screenplay: Moshe Zonder, Amir Ben-David. Camera: Amnon Zalait. Editor: Naomi Press-Aviram. Music: Haim Romano, Ben-David. In color. Release date: June 5, 2000. Running time: 102 Min. ISRAELI.
Cast: Oren Shabo, Sammy Ori, Yael Hadar, Danny Shteg, Tomer Sharon, Gilli Shoshan, Jack Adalist.

WAIT FOR ME
A Combined Studio (Alma-Ata) production. Directors: Aleksandr Stolper, Boris Ivanov. Screenplay: Konstantin Simonov, based on his poem. Camera: Samuil Rubashkin. Editor: E. Abdirkina. Music: Nikolai Kryukov. In B&W. Release date: Aug. 9, 2000. Running time: 90 Min. SOVIET UNION–1943.
Cast: Boris Blinov, Valentina Serova, Lev Sverdlin, Mikhail Nasvanov, Nina Zorskaya, Elena Tyapkina.

WAITING FOR THE MESSIAH
A Burman-Dubcovsky Cine production. Producers: Diego Dubcovsky, Daniel Burman. Director: Daniel Burman. Screenplay: Burman, Emilio Torres. Camera: Ramiro Civita. Editor: Veronica Chen. Music: Cesar Lerner, Marcelo Moguilevsky. In color. Release date: Apr. 14, 2000. Running time: 97 Min. ARGENTINE.
Cast: Daniel Hendler, Hector Alterio, Enrique Pineyro.

THE WAITING LIST
A Tornasol Films/Icaic/DMVB/Tabasco Films/Producciones Amaranta/ Road Movies Fillm Produktionen production, with the participation of Via Digital and Canal Plus. (International sales: Artbox-Claudia Rae, Paris.) Producers: Gerardo Herrero, Camilo Vives, Thierry Forte. Executive producer: Mariela Besuievsky. Co-producers: Ignacio Cobo, Jorge Sanchez, Ulrich Felsberg. Director: Juan Carlos Tabio. Screenplay: Tabio, with the collaboration of Senel Paz, based on the story by Arturo Arango. Camera: Hans Burmann. Editor: Carmen Frias. Music: Jose Maria Vitier. In color. Release date: May 13, 2000. Running time: 105 Min. SPANISH-CUBAN-FRENCH-MEXICAN.
Cast: Vladimir Cruz, Thaimi Alvarino, Jorge Perugorria.

WALK THE TALK
A 20th Century Fox release (in Australia) of a DreamWorks Pictures/Jan Chapman production, with the assistance of the Pacific Film and TV Commission. (Internnational sales: Good Machine, New York.) Producer: Jan Chapman. Director/Screenplay: Shirley Barrett. Camera: Mandy Walker. Editor: Denise Haratzis. Music: Todd Hunter, Mark O'Connor. In Atlab color. Release date: Aug. 10, 2000. Running time: 111 Min. AUSTRALIAN-U.S.
Cast: Salvatore Coco, Sacha Horler, Nikki Bennett, Carter Edwards, Robert Coleby, Skye Wansey, John Burgess, Jon English.

WAR BOOTY
A Zafra Cine Difusion (Argentina)/Tornasol Films production, in association with TVE and Arte. Producer: David Blaustein. Director: Blaustein. Screenplay: Blaustein, Irene Ickowicz. Camera: Marcelo Iaccarino. Editor: Juan Carlos Macias. Music: Jorge Drexler. In color. Release date: Apr. 11, 2000. Running time: 118 Min. Documentary. ARGENTINE-SPANISH.

WATER DROPS ON BURNING ROCKS
A Fidelite Prods./Les Films Alain Sarde production, in association with Euro Sage. (International sales: Roissy Films-Celluloid Dreams, Paris.) Producer: Marc Missonier. Co-producer: Kenzo Horikoshi. Director/Screenplay: Francois Ozon, based on the play "Tropfen auf heisse Steine" by Rainer Werner Fassbinder. Camera: Jeanne Lapoirie. Editor: Laurence Bawedin. In color. Release date: Feb. 13, 2000. Running time: 85 Min. FRENCH.
Cast: Bernard Giraudeau, Malick Zidi, Ludivine Sagnier.

WEAK AT DENISE
A Peninsula Films production. (International sales: Peninsula, London.) Producer: Julian Nott. Co-producer: Clare Erasmus. Director: Julian Nott. Screenplay: Graham Williams, Nott, based on the novel by Williams. Camera: Marco Windham. Editors: Simon Beeley, Melanie Adams. Music: Nott. In Deluxe color. Release date: Dec. 22, 1999. Running time: 92 Min. BRITISH.
Cast: Bill Thomas, Chrissie Cotterill, Craig Fairbrass, Tilly Blackwood, Claudine Spiteri, Edna Dore, Jean Ainslie.

THE WEDDING
A Pyramide release (in France) of a CDP/Film Studio Mosfilm Service/Arte France Cinema/WDR/Lichtblick Cologne production in association with Cine B. (International sales: Flach Pyramide Intl., Paris.) Producer: Catherine Dussart. Executive producer: Eric Weisberg. Director: Pavel Lounguine. Screenplay: Lounguine, Alexandre Burov. Editor: Sophie Brunet. Music: Vladimir Chekassine. In color. Release date: May 14, 2000. Running time: 114 Min. FRENCH-RUSSIAN-GERMAN.
Cast: Marat Basharov, Maria Mironova, Andrei Panine, Alexandre Semtchev, Vladimir Simonov, Maria Goloubkina, Natalia Koliakanova.

THE WEDDING COW
A Sudwestrundfunk production in association with FSDRS and ARTE. (International sales: Streiffschuss Films AG.) Producer: Susan Schultz. Executive producer: Carl Bergengruen. Director: Tomi Streiff. Screenplay: Ela Thier, Streiff. Camera: Johannes Hollmann. Editor: Roswitha Gnadig. Music: Oliver Kuka, Holger Nesweda. In color. Release date: Mar. 18, 2000. Running time: 87 Min. GERMAN.
Cast: Isabella Parkinson, Oliver Reinhard, Hannah the Cow, Dani Levy, Maria Schrader, Julia Stohl-Palmer.

THE WEDDING TACKLE
A Viking Films release of a Viking Films production. Producer: Nigel Horne. Executive producer: Don Horne. Director: Rami Dvir. Screenplay: Nigel Horne. Camera: Shelley Hirst. Editors: Matthew Tabern, Mike Latham. Music: Charles Hodgkinson. In Deluxe color. Release date: July 19, 2000. Running time: 91 Min. BRITISH.
Cast: Adrian Dunbar, James Purefoy, Tony Slattery, Neil Stuke, Leslie Grantham, Victoria Smurfit, Susan Vidler, Amanda Redman.

THE WEEKEND

A Strand Releasing/Granada presentation of a Lunatics and Lovers/Granada Film production. Producer: Ian Benson. Executive producers: Pippa Cross, Janette Day. Director/Screenplay: Brian Skeet, based on the novel by Peter Cameron. Camera: Ron Fortunato. Editor: Chris Wyatt. Music: Dan Jones, Sarah Class. In color. Release date: June 6, 2000. Running time: 97 Min. U.S.-BRITISH.

Cast: Deborah Kara Unger, Jared Harris, D.B. Sweeney, Gena Rowlands, Brooke Shields, David Conrad, James Duval.

WE ONLY LIVE ONCE

An Objektiv Filmstudio/Magyar Televizio production, in association with MMK, ORTT, NKA. (International sales: Objektiv, Budapest.) Producer: Janos Rozsa. Director: Gyorgy Molnar. Screenplay: Sandor Tar. Camera: Sandor Kardos. Editor: Hajnal Sello. Music: Laszlo Des. In color. Release date: Feb. 5, 2000. Running time: 94 Min. HUNGARIAN.

Cast: Jozsef Szarvas, Juli Basti, Sandor Gaspar, Mari Csomos, Lujza Orosz, Eniko Borcsok, Gaspar Galgoczy, Szabolcs Hajdu, Ilona Nagy.

WERCKMEISTER HARMONIES

A Goess Film (Hungary)/Von Vietinghoff Filmproduktion (Germany)/13 Production (France) production, in association with Magyar Mozgokep Kozalapitvany, ORTT, Magyar Televizio, Nemzeti Kulturalis Alapprogram, ZDF, Arte, Studio Babelsberg, RAI-3, Fondazione Montecinemaverita. (International sales: Von Vietinghoff/Cotta Media, Berlin. Producers: Miklos Szita, Franz Goess. Director: Bela Tarr. Screenplay: Laszlo Krasznahorkai, Tarr, based on the novel, "The Melancholy of Resistance" by Krasznahorkai. Camera: Gabor Medvigy. Editor: Agnes Hranitzky. Music: Mihaly Vig. In B&W. Release date: May 19, 2000. Running time: 145 Min. HUNGARIAN-GERMAN-FRENCH.

Cast: Lars Rudolph, Peter Fitz, Hanna Schygulla, Janos Derzi, Djoko Rossich.

WHATEVER

A Mars Films release (in France) of a Lazennec/Le Studio Canal Plus production, with participation of Canal Plus. (International sales: Le Studio Canal Plus, Paris.) Producer: Adelinie Lecallier. Director: Philippe Harel. Screenplay: Harel, Michel Houellebecq, based on the novel by Houellebecq. Camera: Gilles Henry. Editor: Benedicte Teiger. In color. Release date: Sept. 22, 1999. Running time: 120 Min. FRENCH.

Cast: Philippe Bianco, Phillipe Harel, Jose Garcia, Catherine Mouchet.

WHATEVER HAPPENED TO HAROLD SMITH?

A UIP (in U.K.)/USA Films (in U.S.) release of an Intermedia Films /October Films presentation, in association with the Arts Council of England, of a West Eleven Films production. (International sales: Intermedia, London.) Producers: Ruth Jackson, David Brown. Executive producers: Guy East, Nigel Sinclair. Director: Peter Hewitt. Screenplay: Ben Steiner. Camera: David Tattersall. Editor: Martin Walsh. Music: Rupert Gregson-Williams. In Deluxe color. Release date: Nov. 13, 1999. Running time: 94 Min. BRITISH.

Cast: Tom Courtenay, Stephen Fry, Michael Legge, Laura Fraser, Lulu, David Thewlis, Rosemary Leach, Amanda Root, Matthew Rhys.

WHAT I SAW IN HEBRON

A Noga Communications, Israeli Film Service and Jerusalem Cinematheque production. Producers/Directors/Editors: Dan and Noit Geva. Screenplay/Research: Noit Geva. Camera: Dan Geva, Gabriel Vagnon. In color and B&W. Release date: July 12, 2000. Running time: 73 Min. Documentary. ISRAELI.

WHAT IS LIFE?

A Diaphana release (in France) of a Salome/Diaphana/Frane 3 Cinema production, with the participation of Canal Plus and CNC. Producer: Maurice Bernart. Director/Screenplay: Francois Dupeyron. Camera: Tetsuo Nagata. Editor: Bernard Sasia. Music: Michel Portal, Brian Yamakoshi. In color, widescreen. Release date: Aug. 30, 1999. Running time: 117 Min. FRENCH.

Cast: Eric Caravaca, Jacques Dufilho, Isabelle Renauld, Jean-Pierre Darroussin, Licinio Da Silva, Elie Tazartes, Michelle Goddet.

WHAT'S COOKING?

A Flashpoint presentation of a Jeffrey Taylor's Stagescreen production. Producer: Jeffrey Taylor. Executive producers: Beau Rogers, David Forrest, Abe Glazer. Director: Gurinder Chadha. Screenplay: Chadha, Paul Mayeda Berges. Camera: Jong Lin. Editor: Janice Hampton. Music: Craig Pruess. In FotoKem color. Release date: Jan. 20, 2000. Running time: 109 Min. BRITISH-U.S.

Cast: Alfre Woodard, Dennis Haysbert, Ann Weldon, Mercedes Ruehl, Victor Rivers, Douglas Spain, Lainie Kazan, Kyra Sedgwick.

THE WHEEL OF FIRE

A Fenda Films production. Producer: Manuel Castelao. Director/ Screenplay: Raul Veiga. Camera: Juan Carlos Gomez. Editor: Guillermo Represa. Music: Charles Cases. In color. Release date: Nov. 7, 1999. Running time: 90 Min. SPANISH.

Cast: Rosana Pastor, Sergi Lopez, Chete Lera, Maria Bouzas, Miguel Pernas.

WHEN BRENDAN MET TRUDY

A Collins Avenue/Deadly Films 2 production. (International sales: The Sales Co., London.) Producer: Lynda Myles. Director: Kieron J. Walsh. Screenplay: Roddy Doyle. Camera: Ashley Rowe. Editor: Scott Thomas. Music: Richard Hartley. In color. Release date: Sept. 12, 2000. Running time: 95 Min. BRITISH-IRISH.

Cast: Peter McDonald, Flora Montgomery, Marie Mullen, Pauline McLynn, Don Wycherley.

WHEN GODS MEET

A UIP release (in Spain) of a Blu Cinematografica (Italy)/Esicma (Spain) production, with participation of RAI, Tele Plus, Canal Plus. Producers: Massimo Ferraro, Leo Pescarolo. Director: Antonello De Leo. Screenplay: Franca De Angelis, Francesca Panzarella. Camera: Marco Onorato. Editor: Maurizio Baglivio. Music: Paulo Buonvino. In color. Release date: Apr. 26, 2000. Running time: 98 Min. ITALIAN-SPANISH.

Cast: Pere Ponce, Claudia Gerini, Ana Risueno, Pia Velsi, Paolo Sassanelli.

WHERE A GOOD MAN GOES

An Intl. Films Interi-Rise presentation of a Milkyway Image (H.K.) production. (International sales: Milkyway, H.K.) Producer: Chiu Fu-sheng. Executive producers: Johnnie To, Wai Ka-fai. Director: Johnnie To. Executive director: Patrick Yau. Screenplay: Yau Naihoi, Milkyway Creative Team. Camera: Cheng Siu-keung. Editor: Chan Chi-wai. Music: Cacine Wong. In color, widescreen. Release date: Oct. 19, 1999. Running time: 88 Min. HONG KONG.

Cast: Lau Ching-wan, Ruby Wong, Lai Yiu-hung, Lam Suet, Raymond Wong, Law Wing-cheung, Tsang Siu-yin, Ah Wai, Chiu Wai-hung.

WHERE THE RAINBOW ENDS

A Sonet Film release (in Sweden) of a Cimbria Film/SVT Drama Malmo/Sonet Film/Film pa Osterlen production. (International sales: BV Intl. Pictures, Avaldsnes, Norway.) Producer: Goran Lindstrom. Executive producers: Goran Lindstrom, Bengt Linni. Director/Screenplay: Richard Hobert. Camera: Lars Cripin. Editor: Leif Kristiansson. Music and lyrics: Hobert. In color. Release date: Oct. 7, 1999. Running time: 116 Min. SWEDISH.

Cast: Goan Stangertz, Camilla Lindin, Rolf Lassgard, Pernilla August, Tommy Korberg, Peter Joback, Helen Sjoholm, Sharon Dyall.

WHERE THE SKY MEETS THE LAND

A Cine Dok/EuroArts Entertainment production. (International sales: EuroArts Intl., Stuttgart.) Producer: Frank Hartwig Hendrik Mueller. Co-producer: Bernd Hellthaler. Director/Camera: Mueller. Editor: Stephan Krumbiegel. Music: Nurlan Nischanov. In color. Release date: Sept. 4, 1999. Running time: 85 Min. GERMAN.

Cast: Bubush Alayeva, Rysbek Jumabayev.

WHERE VIOLENCE ENDS LOVE BEGINS

A Produktionsgruppen Wechselmann (Sweden)/WOWam (South Africa) production. (International sales: Wechselmann, Stockholm.) Producer/Director/Screenplay: Maj Wechselmann. Camera: Hans-Ake Lerin. Editor: Kajsa Grandell. In color. Release date: Jan. 30, 2000. Running time: 84 Min. SWEDISH-SOUTH AFRICAN.

Cast: Ossi Carp, Nadine Naidoo, Bill Curry, Rafiq Jajbhay, Sivan Pillay, Olivia Stevens, Peter Taggart-Holland, Alex Patterson.

WHIRLPOOL

An Omega Micott production. Producer: Sumiji Miyake. Executive producers: Mitsuru Kurosawa, Toyoyuki Yokohama. Director: Higunchinsky. Screenplay: Takao Nitta, based on the comic book by Junji Ito. Camera: Gen Kobayashi. Editor: Chiaki Tohyam. Music: Keiichi Suzuki, Tetsuro Kashibuchi. In color. Release date: Apr. 8, 2000. Running time: 90 Min. JAPANESE.

Cast: Eriko Hatsune, Fhi Fan, Hinako Saeki, Shin Eun Kyung, Keiko Takahasi, Ren Osugi.

THE WHITE

A V & R Planning production. (International sales: V & R Planning, Tokyo.) Director: Katsuyuki Hirano. Camera/Editor: Hirano. Music: Yuji Kitano, Yutaka Suzuki. In color, Hi8 video-to-35mm. Release date: Feb. 13, 2000. Running time: 118 Min. Documentary. JAPANESE.

WHOAFRAIDWOLF

An Ombra-Films production in association with BE-Pictures. (International sales: Ombra-Films, Perugia, Italy. Producer/ Director/Screenplay: Clemens Klopfenstein. Camera: Klopfenstein. Editors: Nicola Bellucci, Vadim Jendreyko, Ben Jeger, Gerhard Grumbach. Music: Jeger. In Eastmancolor. Release datea: Feb. 15, 2000. Running time: 85 Min. SWISS-ITALIAN.

Cast: Bruno Ganz, Tina Engel, Mathias Gnadinger, Charlotte Heinimann, Stefan Kurt, Norbert Klassen, Doraine Green.

THE WIDOW OF SAINT-PIERRE

A Pathe Distribution release of an Epithete Films presentation of an Epithete Films/France 2/France 3/Cineimaginaire production. (International sales: Flach Pyramide Intl., Paris.) Producers: Gilles Legrand, Frederic Brillion. Co-producers: Denise Robert, Daniel Louis. Director: Patrice Leconte. Screenplay: Claude Faraldo. Camera: Eduardo Serra. Editor: Joelle Hache. Music: Pascal Esteve. In color, widescreen. Release date: Mar. 2, 2000. Running time: 112 Min. FRENCH.

Cast: Juliette Binoche, Daniel Auteuil, Emir Kusturica, Michel Duchaussoy, Philippe Magnan, Christian Charmetant.

WILD BLUE, NOTES FOR SEVERAL VOICES

A Les Prods. du Sablier/La Sept Arte/Artline Films/Man's Films/ Navigator Films/RTBF production. (International sales: Films Distribution, Paris.) Producer/Director/Screenplay: Thierry Knauff. Camera: Antoine-Marie Meert. Editors: Knauff, Michele Hubinon, Luc Plantier. In B&W. Release date: May 12, 2000. Running time: 68 Min. Documentary. BELGIAN.

With: Joan Leighton, Neela Bhagwat, Charlene Alenga, Dalila Amali, Sanja Vranes, Kaiga Kayiganwa, Mojgan Cahen, Francoise Guiguet.

WILLOW AND WIND

A Cina Media Intl. and NHK production. Producers: Mohammad Mehdi Dadgon, Makoto Ueda. Executive producers: Ali Reza Shoja Noori. Director: Mohammad Ali Talchi. Screenplay: Abbas Kiarostami. Camera: Farhad Saba. Editor: Sohrab Mirsepassi. Music: Mehrdad Jenabi. In color. Release date: Aug. 30, 2000. Running time: 77 Min. IRANIAN-JAPANESE.
Cast: Hadi Alipour, Amir Janfada, Majid Alipour, Mohammad Sharif Ebrahimi.

THE WINTER OF THE FAIRIES

A Nirvana Films release of a Creacion/Amanda Films/Alma Ata Intl. Pictures production, in association with TVE, Canal Plus. (International sales: Alma Ata, Madrid.) Executive producers: Rodolfo Monteiro de Palacio, Jose Maria Calleja de la Fuente. Director: Pedro Telechea. Screenplay: Telechea, Diego Modino. Camera: Angel Luis Fernandez. Editor: Luis Villar. Music: Mario de Benito. In color. Release date: May 15, 2000. Running time: 92 Min. SPANISH.
Cast: Elena Anaya, Eduardo Noriega, Juan Diego, Elvira Minguez, Ana Gracia, Antonio Resines.

WISCONSIN DEATH TRIP

A BBC Arena and Cinemax presentation of a Hands On production. Producers: Maurren A. Ryan, James Marsh. Executive producers: Carol Hirschi, Nancy Abraham, Sheila Nevins, Anthony Wall. Director/Screenplay: James Marsh, based on the book by Michael Lesy. Camera: Eigil Bryld. Editor: Jinx Godfrey. Music: DJ Shadow. In B&W and color, 16mm-to-35mm. Release date: Apr. 4, 2000. Running time: 76 Min. Documentary. U.S.-BRITISH.
Narrator: Ian Holm.
With: Jo Vukelich, Jeffrey Golden, Marilyn White, John Schneider.

A WITCH IN THE FAMILY

A Sonet Film release of a Filmlance Intl. production, in association with Sonet Film, the Chimney Pot, BV Film (Norway), Yellow Cottage (Norway), Bogaeus Manuskript and Harald Hamrell Filmproduktion. (International sales: BV Intl., Norway.) Producers: Lars Blomgren, Borje Hansson. Director: Harald Hamrell. Screenplay: Johan Bogaeus, based on the novel "Maria Bleknos" by Ulf Stark. Camera: Olof Johnson. Editor: Michal Leszczylowski. Music: Adam Norden. In color. Release date: Jan. 13, 2000. Running time: 84 Min. SWEDISH.
Cast: Johan Rheborg, Tintin Anderzon, Margreth Weivers, Karin Bogaeus, Rebecca Scheja, Fredrik Unger, Anna Lindholm.

THE WOGBOY

A 20th Century Fox (Australia) release of an Australian Film Finance Corp./Third Costa presentation of a G.O. Films production, in association with Film Victoria. (International sales: Beyond Films, Sydney.) Producers: John Brousek, Nick Giannopoulos. Executive producer: Roger Rothfield. Director: Aleksi Vellis. Screenplay: Nick Giannopoulos, Chris Anastassiades. Camera: Roger Lanser. Editor: Suresh Ayyar. Music: Cezary Skubiszewski. In Cinevex color. Release date: Feb. 29, 2000. Running time: 92 Min. AUSTRALIAN.
Cast: Nick Giannopolulos, Lucy Bell, Vince Colosimo, Geraldine Turner, Abi Tucker, John Barresi, Tony Nikolakopoulos, Stephen Curry.

WOMAN ON A TIN ROOF

A Good Harvest Films (Quezon City) production. Producer/Director/Screenplay: Mario O'Hara, based on a play by Agapito Joaquin. Camera: Rey De Leon. Editor: Edmondo Jarlego. Music: Blitz Padua. In color. Release date: Oct. 3, 1999. Running time: 110 Min. FILIPINO.
Cast: Nike Magat, Aya Medel, Anita Linda, Frank Rivera, Renzo Cruz, Allen Dizon.

WOMAN SOUP

A Group Power Workshop Co. production. (International sales: Group Power, Taipei.) Producer: Dale Huang. Executive producers: Kuo Mu-shun, Lee Pei-ling. Director/Screenplay: Emily Liu. Camera: Chen Jui-yuan. Editor: Chen Powen. In color. Release date: Jan. 23, 2000. Running time: 96 Min. TAIWANESE.
Cast: May Chin, Tien Hsin, Elsie Yeh, April Wang, Tony Chang, Andrew, Liu Liang-tso, Khan Lee.

WORD ATTACK

A Filmax release of an Iconica/Freedonia Producciones production, in association with Via Digital, TVV. (International sales: Filmax, Barcelona.) Producers: Jose Nolla, Pepe Ferrandiz. Director: Miguel Albaladejo. Screenplay: Albaladejo, Elvira Lindo. Camera: Alfonso Sanz Alduan. Editor: Angel Hernandez Zoido. Music: Lucio Godoy. In color. Release date: Mar. 30, 2000. Running time: 83 Min. SPANISH.
Cast: Antonia San Juan, Sergi Lopez, Antonio Resines, Fedra Lorente, Adriana Ozores, Roberto Alvarez, Felix Alvarez.

WORKERS FOR THE GOOD LORD

A Rezo Films release of a La Sorciere Rouge/Euripide Prods./Arte France Cinema/Rhone Alpes Cinema production, with participation of Canal Plus. (International sales: UGC Intl., Paris.) Producers: Jean-Claude Brisseau, Frederic Sichler, Daniel Toscan du Plantier. Director/Screenplay: Jean-Claude Brisseau. Camera: Romain Winding, Laurent Fleutot. Editor: Maria Luisa Garcia Martinez. Music: Jean Musy. In color. Release date: Apr. 4, 2000. Running time: 106 Min. FRENCH.
Cast: Stanislas Merhar, Raphaele Godin, Emile Abossolo M'Bo, Coralie Revel, Paulette Dubost.

THE WORKERS' SETTLEMENT

A Lenfilm production. Director: Vladimir Vengerov. Screenplay: Vera Panova. Camera: Genrikh Maradzhyan. Music: Isaak Svats. In B&W. Release date: Aug. 7, 2000. Running time: 138 Min. SOVIET UNION–1965.
Cast: Oleg Borisov, Tatyana Doronina, Viktor Avdyushko, Lyudmila Gurchenko, Nikolai Simonov, Lyubov Sokolova.

THE WRESTLERS

A Buddhadeb Dasgupta Prods. production. Producer: Buddhadeb Dasgupta. Executive producer: Dulal Roy. Director/Screenplay: Dasgupta, from a story by Samaresh Rose. Camera: Asim Bose. Editor: Raviranjan Maitra. Music: Biswadeb Dasgupta. In color. Release date: Aug. 30, 2000. Running time: 99 Min. INDIAN.
Cast: Jaya Seal, Tapas Pal, Shankar Chakraborty. R.I. Asad, Tapas Adhikari, Saurav Das, Gautam Warshi, Masud Akhtar, Subrata Dutta.

X

A Manga Entertainment presentation of an X Committee Clamp/Manga Entertainment production in association with Kadokawa Shoten Publishing Co., Bandai Visual Co., Marubeni Corp., Shelty Co., Sega Enterprises, Victor Entertainment, Animation Studio Mad House Co., Movie Co Ltd. Producers: Kazuo Yokoyama, Masanori Maruyama, Kazuhiko Ikeguchi. Executive producer: Tsunehiko Kadokawa. Director: Rintaro. Screenplay: Asami Watanabe, Nanase Ohkawa, Rintaro, based on the original story by Clamp (Satsuki Igarashi, Mokonaapapa, Ohkawa, Mikku Nekoi). Camera: Jin Yamaguchi. Editors: Harutoshi Ogata, Yukiko Itoh, Satoshi Terauchi. Music: Harumitsu Shimizu. In color. Release date: Apr., 6, 2000. MPAA Rating: R. Running time: 98 Min. Animated. JAPANESE.

THE YEAR OF MARIA

An Aurum release of an Asegarce production, in association with TVE, Via Digital, ETB. (International sales: Aurum, Madrid.) Producer: Juanjo Landa. Executive producer: Fernando Garcillan. Director: Fernando Guillen Cuervo, Karra Elejalde. Screenplay: Guillen Cuervo, Elejalde, Jose Antonio Ortega. Camera: Hans Burmann. Editor: Pablo Blanco. Music: Kike Suarez Alba. Release date: Aug. 26, 2000. Running time: 117 Min. SPANISH.
Cast: Karra Elejalde, Fernando Guillen Cuervo, Manuel Manquina.

YELLOW HAIR

A Piksyeon Baengkeu production, with participation of the Korean Motion Picture Promotion Corp. (International sales: Korean Film Commission, Seoul.) Producer: Yeo Han-ku. Director: Kim Yoo-min. Screenplay: Kim, Son Jeong-seob. Camera: Lee Eun-kil. Editor: Kim Sang-beom. Music: Ahn Ji-hong. In color. Release date: Oct. 2, 1999. Running time: 85 Min. SOUTH KOREAN.
Cast: Lee Jai-eun, Kim Ki-yeon, Kim Hyeon-cheol, Kim Hyeok-euk.

YESTERDAY CHILDREN

A Reynafilms production. Producer/Director: Carlos Siguion-Reyna. Screenplay: Bibeth Orteza, based on a story by Adolfo Alix, Jr. Camera: George Tutanes. Editor: Manet A. Dayrit. Music: Ryan Cayabyab. In color. Release date: Mar. 1, 2000. Running time: 89 Min. FILIPINO.
Cast: Ara Mina, Tonton Gutierrez, Patricia Ann Roque, Carlo Aquino, Pen Medina,Ray Ventura, Jennifer Sevilla, Eva Darren.

YOU ONLY LIVE ONCE

A Cecchi Gori Distribuzione release (in Italy) of a Mario and Vittorio Cecchi Gori presentation of a Cecchi Gori Group/Boccia Film production. Executive producer: Gianluca Arcopinto. Directors/Screenplay: Eugenio Cappuccio, Massimo Gaudioso, Fabio Nunziata. Camera: Vincenzo Marinese. Editor: Nunziata. Music: Daniele Sepe. In Technicolor. Release date: Nov. 22, 1999. Running time: 90 Min. ITALIAN.
Cast: Eugenio Cappuccio, Massimo Gaudioso, Fabio Nunziata, Anna Scaglione, Gianluca Arcopinto, Guiseppe Picciotto.

YOYES

A Columbia TriStar Spain release of an CIPI Cinematografica (Spain)/Mact Prods. (France)/Marvel Movies (Italy) production, in association with Via Digital, TVE, ETB. (International sales: Intrafilm, Rome.) Director: Helena Taberna. Screenplay: Taberna, Andres Martorell. Camera: Federico Rivers. Editor: Rori Saiz de Rosas. Music: Angel Illarramendi. In color. Release date: Apr. 9, 2000. Running time: 104 Min. SPANISH-FRENCH-ITALIAN.
Cast: Ana Torrent, Ernesto Alterio, Florence Pernel, Ramon Langa, Inaki Aierra, Isabel Ordaz, Laura Ballesta.

ZERO TOLERANCE

A Sonet Film release (in Sweden) of a Sonet Film production, in association with Film i vast, Sandrew Metronome, TV4 and TV1000. (International sales: Sonet, Stockholm.) Producers: Joakim Hansson, Bjorn Carlstrom. Executive producer: Peter Possne. Director: Anders Nilsson. Screenplay: Nilsson, Joakim Hansson. Camera: Jacob Jorgenson. Editor: Darek Hodor. Music: Bengt Nilsson. In color. Release date: Oct. 20, 1999. Running time: 105 Min. SWEDISH.
Cast: Jakob Eklund, Marie Richardson, Peter Andersson, Jacqueline Ramel, Lennart Hjulstrom, Helene Soderkvist Henriksson.

ZION, AUTO-EMANCIPATION

A Tal Prods./Agav Films production. (International sales: Agav Films, Tel Aviv.) Producer: Paul Rozemberg. Director/Screenplay: Amos Gitai. Camera: Nurith Aviv. Editor: Roy Shmueli. Music: Marcus and Simon Stockhausen. In color. Release date: Sept. 4, 1999. Running time: 110 Min. Documentary. ISRAELI.
Cast: Uri Avneri, Theo Balmer, Efratia Gitai.

FEATURE PICTURES

JANUARY 1, 1990 – SEPTEMBER 30, 1999

In the following listings, the distributor is followed by the release date, country of origin, the director (in parentheses), and cast. For feature films released from 1980–1989, please see the 1996 edition of the Motion Picture Almanac.

A
"A" PRODUCTION COMMITTEE. Feb., 1999. Japanese. (Mori Tatsua). Documentary.

AARON'S MAGIC VILLAGE
AVALANCHE. Sept., 1997. German-French-Israeli. (Albert Hanan Kaminski) Fyvush Finkel, Tommy Michaels, Tovah Feldshuh.

A,B,C... MANHATTAN
ALPHAVILLE FILMS, NYC & OPEN CITY FILMS. May, 1997. (Amir Naderi) Lucy Knight, Erin Norris, Sara Paul, Maisy Hughes.

ABOVE FREEZING
COOLER PICTURES. June, 1998. (Frank Todaro) Mike O'Malley, Jill Tracy, J. K. Simmons, Phyllis Somerville.

ABOVE THE RIM
NEW LINE. March, 1994. (Jeff Pollack) Duane Martin, Leon, Tonya Pinkins.

THE ABSENT ONE
CINEMA LIBRE. June, 1997. Canadian. (Celine Baril) Roland Breard, Bobo Vian.

ABSOLUTE POWER
SONY PICTURES ENTERTAINMENT. February, 1997. (Clint Eastwood) Clint Eastwood, Gene Hackman, Ed Harris, Laura Linney, Judy Davis.

ACCELERATOR
FLASHPOINT. May, 1999. British-Irish. (Vinny Murphy) Stuart Sinclair Blyth, Gavin Kelty, Aisling O'Neill, Mark Dunne, Georgina McKeritt.

THE ACCIDENT
JOSEPH LOVETT PICTURES. June, 1999.(Joseph Lovett). Documentary.

THE ACCOMPANIST
SONY PICTURES CLASSICS. December, 1993. French. (Claude Miller) Richard Bohringer, Elena Safonova.

ACE VENTURA, PET DETECTIVE
WARNER BROS. February, 1994. (Tom Shadyac) Jim Carrey, Courteney Cox, Sean Young.

ACE VENTURA: WHEN NATURE CALLS
WARNER BROS. November, 1995. (Steve Oedekerk) Jim Carrey, Ian McNeice, Simon Callow, Maynard Eziashi.

ACES: IRON EAGLE III
NEW LINE/7 ARTS. June, 1992. (John Glen) Louis Gossett, Jr., Rachel McLish, Horst Buccholz.

THE ACID HOUSE
PICTURE PALACE NORTH/UMBRELLA PRODS. May, 1998. Scottish. (Paul McGuigan) Stephen McCole, Maurice Roeves.

ACLA
INFRAFILMS/SACIS. December, 1993. Italian (Aurelio Grimaldi) Francesco Cusimano, Tony Sperandeo.

THE ACROBATS
MIKADO. April, 1997. Italian-Swiss. (Silvio Soldini) Valeria Golino, Licia Maglietta, Mira Sardoc, Angela Marraffa, Fabrizio Bentivoglio.

ACROPOLE
GREEK FILM CENTER. May, 1996. Greek-Bulgarian-Italian-German. (Pantelis Voulgaris) Lefteris Voyatzis.

ACROSS THE SEA OF TIME
COLUMBIA/SONY. October, 1995. (Stephen Low) Peter Reznik, John McDonough, Avi Hoffman, Victor Steinbach.

ACROSS THE TRACKS
ACADEMY ENT./DESERT PRODS. February, 1991. (Sandy Tung) Rick Schroder, Brad Pitt, Carry Snodgress.

ACT OF CONSCIENCE
TURNING TIDE PRODS. Jan., 1997. (Robbie Leppzer) Documentary.

ACT OF PIRACY
BLOSSOM. March, 1990. (John "Bud" Cardos) Gary Busey, Belinda Bauer, Ray Sharkey.

ADAM'S RIB
OCTOBER FILMS. May, 1992. Russian. (Vyacheslav Krishtofovich) Inna Churikova, Svetlana Ryabova.

THE ADDAMS FAMILY
PARAMOUNT. November, 1991. (Barry Sonnenfeld) Anjelica Huston, Raul Julia, Christopher Lloyd.

ADDAMS FAMILY VALUES
PARAMOUNT. November, 1993. (Barry Sonnenfeld) Anjelica Huston, Raul Julia, Joan Cusack.

ADDICTED TO LOVE
WARNER BROS. May, 1997. (Griffin Dunne), Meg Ryan, Matthew Broderick, Kelly Preston, Tcheky Karyo, Maureen Stapleton.

THE ADDICTION
OCTOBER FILMS. October, 1995. (Abel Ferrara) Lili Taylor, Christopher Walken, Annabelle Sciorra.

THE ADJUSTER
ORION CLASSICS. May, 1992. Canadian. (Atom Egoyan) Elias Koteas, Arsinee Khanjian, Maury Chaykin.

THE ADOPTED SON
KIRGIZFILM/NOE PRODS. Aug., 1998. Kirghizian-French. (Aktan Abdykalykov) Mirlan Abdykalykov, Albina Imasheva.

ADRENALINE DRIVE
ADRENALINE DRIVE COMMITTEE/KINDAI EIGA KYOKAI CO./GAGA COMMUNICATIONS/THERE'S ENTERPRISE/NIPPON SHUPPAN HANBAI. Mar., 1999. Japanese. (Shinobu Yaguchi) Hikari Ishida, Masanobu Ando, Yutaka Matsushige, Kazue Tsunogae.

THE ADVENTURES OF FORD FAIRLANE
20TH CENTURY FOX. July, 1990. (Renny Harlin) Andrew Dice Clay, Wayne Newton, Priscilla Presley.

THE ADVENTURES OF HUCK FINN
BUENA VISTA. April, 1993. (Stephen Sommers) Elijah Wood, Courtney Vance, Jason Robards.

THE ADVENUTRES OF PINNOCHIO
NEW LINE. June, 1996. British-French-German. (Steve Barron) Martin Landau, Jonathan Taylor.

THE ADVENTURES OF PRISCILLA, QUEEN OF THE DESERT
GRAMERCY. August, 1994. Australian. (Stephan Elliott) Terence Stamp, Hugo Weaving, Guy Pearce.

THE ADVENTURES OF SEBASTIAN COLE
PARAMOUNT CLASSICS. Sept. 1998. (Tod Williams) Adrian Grenier, Clark Gregg, Aleska Palladino, Margaret Colin.

THE ADVOCATE
MIRAMAX. August, 1994. British. (Leslie Megahey) Colin Firth, Lysette Anthony, Ian Holm.

AN AFFAIR
NINE FILM. Sept., 1998. South Korean. (E J-Yong) Lee Mi-suk, Lee Jeong-jae.

AFFENGEIL
FIRST RUN FEATURES. July, 1992. German. (Rosa von Praunheim) Lotte Huber, Rosa von Praunheim, Helga Sloop.

AFFLICTION
LARGO ENTERTAINMENT. Aug, 1997. (Paul Schrader) Nick Nolte, Sissy Spacek, James Coburn, Willem Dafoe, Mary Beth Hurt.

AFRAID OF EVERYTHING
FLORIDA PICTURES AND LOCUS STOTUS. Jan., 1999. (David Barker) Nathalie Richard, Sarah Adler, Daniel Aukin.

AFRAID OF THE DARK
FINE LINE. July, 1992. British. (Mark Peploe) James Fox, Fanny Ardant, Ben Keyworth.

AFRO PROMO
JENNI OLSON. Jan., 1997. (Jenni Olson, Karl Bruce Knapper) Documentary.

AFTER DARK, MY SWEET
AVENUE. August, 1990. (James Foley) Jason Patric, Rachel Ward, Bruce Dern.

AFTERGLOW
MOONSTONE ENT. May, 1997. (Alan Rudolph) Julie Christie, Nick Nolte, Lara Flynn Boyle, Jonny Lee Miller.

AFTER LIFE
TV MAN UNION/ENGINE FILM. Sept., 1998. Japanses. (Hirokazu Koreeda) Erika Oda, Susumu Terajia, Takashi Naito, Kei Tani.

AFTER THE END OF THE WORLD
META BM-4/SAXONIA MEDIA. Feb., 1999. Bulgarian-Greek-German. (Ivan Nichev) Katerina Didaskalo, Stefan Danalyov, Zlatil Davidov, Zhana Dakovska, Vasil Michailov.

AFTER THE RAIN
CAPELLA INTL. June, 1999. South African. (Ross Kettle) Raul Bettany, Louise Lombard, Ariyon Bakare, Hakeem Kae-Kazim.

AFTER THE TRUTH
HELKON FILMVERLEIH. July, 1999. German. (Roland Suso Richter) Kai Wiesinger, Goetz George, Karoline Eichhorn, Doris Schade, Peter Roggisch.

AGNES BROWNE
OCTOBER FILMS. May, 1999. (Angelica Huston) Angelica Huston, Marion O'Dwyer, Niall O'Shea, Ciaran Owens.

THE AGE OF INNOCENCE
COLUMBIA. September, 1993. (Martin Scorsese) Daniel Day-Lewis, Michelle Pfeiffer, Winona Ryder.

AH CHUNG
HONG RONG FILM CO. Sept., 1996. Taiwanese. (Chang Tso-chi) Liu Sheng-Chung, Chou Shio-min, Lu Ying, Ho Huang-chi.

AILEEN WURONOS:
THE SELLING OF A SERIAL KILLER
STRAND. February, 1994. (Nick Broomfield) Documentary.

AIMEE & JAGUAR
SENATOR FILM. Feb., 1999. German. (Max Faerberboeck) Maria Schrader, Juliane Koehler, Heike Makatsch, Johanna Wokalek.

AINSI SOIT-IL
LEO & CIE. Aug. 1999. French. (Gerard Blain). Paul Blain, Sylvie Ollivier, Marie Allanioux, Delphine Dalbin, Michel Subor.

AIR AMERICA
TRISTAR. August, 1990. (Roger Spottiswoode) Mel Gibson, Robert Downey, Jr., Nancy Travis.

AIR BUD
BUENA VISTA. July, 1997. (Charles Martin Smith), Michael Jeter, Kevin Zegers, Wendy Makkena, Bill Cobbs, Eric Christmas.

AIR BUD: GOLDEN RECEIVER
MIRAMAX. Aug., 1998. (Richard Martin) Kevin Zegers, Cynthia Stevenson, Gregory Harrison, Nora Dunn, Perry Anzilotti.

AIR FORCE ONE
SONY PICTURES ENTERTAINMENT. July, 1997. (Wolfgang Petersen), Harrison Ford, Gary Oldman, Glenn Close, William H. Macy.

AN AIR SO PURE
BAC FILMS. Aug., 1997. French-Polish-Belgian. (Yves Angelo) Fabrice Luchini, Andre Dussollier, Jacques Boudet, Edith Scob.

THE AIR UP THERE
BUENA VISTA. January, 1994. (Paul M. Glaser) Kevin Bacon, Charles Gitonga Maina, Yolanda Yazquez.

AIRBORNE
WARNER BROS. September, 1993. (Rob Bowman) Shane McDermott, Seth Green, Brittany Powell.

AIRHEADS
20TH CENTURY FOX. August, 1994. (Michael Lehmann) Brendan Fraser, Steve Buscemi.

AKIRA KUROSAWA'S DREAMS
WARNER BROS. August, 1990. Japanese. (Akira Kurosawa) Mitsunori Isaki, Mieko Harada, Martin Scorsese.

AKSUAT
TOO EAST CINEMA. Feb., 1999. Kazakh-Japanese. (Serik Aprymov) Sabit Kurmanbekov, Erschan Aschim, Erbolat Ospankulov, Inessa Radinova, Nurschuman Ichtymbaev.

A LA PLACE DU COEUR
Agat Films. Sept., 1998. French. (Robert Guediguian) Ariane Ascaride, Christine Bruecher, Jean-Pierre Darroussin, Gerard Meylan.

ALADDIN
BUENA VISTA. November, 1992. (John Musker, Ron Clements) Animated.

ALAN & NAOMI
TRITON. January, 1992. (Sterling VanWagenen) Lukas Haas, Vanessa Zaoui, Michael Gross.

ALASKA
COLUMBIA. August, 1996. (Fraser S. Heston) Thora Birch, Vincent Kartheiser, Dirk Benedict, Charlton Heston.

ALBERTO EXPRESS
MK2. October, 1992. French-Italian. (Arthur Joffe) Sergio Castellitto, Nino Manfredi, Marie Trintignant.

ALBINO ALLIGATOR
MIRAMAX. August, 1996. (Kevin Spacey) Matt Dillion, Faye Dunaway, Gary Sinise.

THE ALCHEMIST AND THE VIRGIN
MAGYAR TV-DIALOG STUDIO-EUROFILM STUDIO-TOR FILM STUDIO. Feb., 1999. Hungarian-Polish. (Zoltan Kamondi) Mariusz Bonazewski, Eszter Onodi, Danuta Zaflarska, Norbert Novenyi.

ALCHEMY
SENECA FALLS. October, 1995. (Suzanne Myers) Rya Kihlsetd, Jeff Webster, D.V. de Vincentis.

ALDOUS HUXLEY: THE GRAVITY OF LIGHT
CINEMA ESPERANCA INTL. June, 1997. Canadian. (Oliver Hockenhull) David Odhiambo, Judy Klassen, Documentary.

ALEGRIA
OVERSEAS FILMGROUP. Jan., 1999. Canadian-French-Dutch. (Franco Dragone) Renee Bazinet, Frank Langella, Julie Cox, Heathcote Williams, Clipper Miano.

ALEX
CORALIE. March, 1992. Portuguese. (Teresa Villaverde) Ricardo Colares, Vincent Gallo, Teresa Roby.

ALFRED
SANDREWS. December, 1995. Swedish. (Vilgot Sjoman) Sven Wollter, Rita Russek, Judit Danyi.

ALGIERS-BEIRUT: A SOUVENIR
CINETEVE/DJINN HOUSE PRODS. Aug., 1998. French-Lebanese. (Merzouk Allouache) Fabienne Babe, Georges Corraface, H. Choutri.

ALICE
ORION. December, 1990. (Woody Allen) Mia Farrow, Joe Mantegna, William Hurt, Alec Baldwin.

ALICE AND MARTIN
LES FILMS ALAIN SARDE, FRANCE 2 CINEMA, FRANCE 3 CINEMA)/VERTIGO FILMS. Oct., 1998. French-Spanish. (Andre Techine) Juliette Binoche, Alexis Loret, Carmen Maura, Mathieu Amalric, Pierre Maguelon.

ALIEN^3
20TH CENTURY FOX. May, 1992. (David Fincher) Sigourney Weaver, Charles S. Dutton, Charles Dance.

ALIEN RESURRECTION
20TH CENTURY FOX. Oct., 1997. (Jean-Pierre Jeunet) Sigourney Weaver, Winona Ryder, Ron Perlman, Dominique Pinon.

ALIVE
BUENA VISTA. January, 1993. (Frank Marshall) Ethan Hawke, Josh Hamilton, Vincent Spano.

ALL ABOUT MY MOTHER
WARNER SOGEFILMS/SONY. Apr., 1999. Spanish-French. (Pedro Almodovar) Cecilia Roth, Eloy Azorin, Marisa Paredes, Penelope Cruz, Candela Pena.

ALL DOGS GO TO HEAVEN 2
MGM/UA. March, 1996. (Paul Sabella, Larry Leker) (voices) Charlie Sheen, Sheena Easton, Dom DeLuise.

ALL FOR ONE
QUO VADIS CINEMA. May, 1998. French-Belgian. (Bruno Bontzolakis) Alexandre Carriere, Nicolas Ducron, Florence Masure.

ALL I WANT FOR CHRISTMAS
PARAMOUNT. November, 1991. (Robert Lieberman) Harley Jane Kozak, Ethan Randall, Thora Birch.

ALL IS BRAZIL
TUPANA FILMS. May, 1998. Brazilian. (Rogerio Sganzerla) documentary with Richard Wilson, Robert Wise, Bill Krohn, Edmar Morel.

ALL OF IT
BLOOMFIELD PARTNERS. Sept., 1999.(Jody Podolsky).Alanna Ulbach, Lesley Ann Warren, James Rebhorn.

ALL OF THEM WITCHES
VIDEOCINE. June, 1996. Mexican. (Daniel Gruener) Susana Zabaleta, Alejandro Tommasi, Delia Casanova.

ALL OF US, EFFENDI
GREEK FILM CENTRE. Nov., 1998. Greek. (Leonidas Vardaros) Vassilis Kolovos, Perikles Moustakis, Antonis Vlissidis, Antonis Maibatzis, Yannis Tsikis.

ALL OVER ME
FINE LINE. July, 1996. (Alex Sichel) Alison Folland, Tara Subkoff, Cole Hauser.

ALL THE LITTLE ANIMALS
RECORDED PICTURES CO. May, 1998. British. (Jeremy Thomas) John Hurt, Christian Bale, Daniel Benzali, James Faulkner.

ALL THE RAGE
PINK PLOT. PRODS. June, 1997. (Roland Tec) John-Michael Lander, David Vincent, Jay Corcoran, Peter Bubriski, Paul Outlaw.

ALL THE VERMEERS IN NEW YORK
STRAND. May, 1992. (Jon Jost) Emmanuelle Chaulet, Katherine Bean, Grace Phillips.

ALL THINGS FAIR
COLUMBIA/TRISTAR. October, 1995. Swedish. (Bo Widerberg) Johan Widerberg, Marika Lagerkrantz.

ALL'S FAIR IN LOVE AND WAR
STAR LAND ENTERTAINMENT. August 1996. (Sartaj Khan) Khan, Miki O'Brien, Bill Trillo, William Night.

ALLIGATOR EYES
CASTLE HILL. November, 1990. (John Feldman) Annabelle Larsen, Roger Kabler.

ALMA'S RAINBOW
PARADISE PLUM. June, 1994. (Ayoka Chenzira) Victoria Gabriella Platt, Kim Weston-Moran, Mizan Nunes.

ALMOST AN ANGEL
PARAMOUNT. December, 1990. (John Cornell) Paul Hogan, Elias Koteas, Linda Kozlowski.

ALMOST HEROES
WARNER BROS. May, 1998. (Christopher Guest) Chris Farley, Matthew Perry, Eugene Levy, Kevin Dunn, Bokeen Woodbine.

ALONE
MAESTRANZA FILMS. Feb., 1999. Spanish. (Benito Zambrano) Ana Fernandez, Maria Galiana, Carlos Alvarez-Novoa.

AMAZING WOMEN BY THE SEA
KINOPRODUCTION. Aug., 1998. Finnish. (Claes Olsson). Marika Krook, Asa Karlin, Nicke Lignell, Onni Thulesius.

AMATEUR
SONY PICTURES CLASSICS. April, 1995. (Hal Hartley) Isabelle Huppert, Martin Donovan, Elina Lowensohn.

THE AMAZING PANDA ADVENTURE
WARNER BROS. August 1995. (Christopher Cain) Stephen Lang, Ryan Slater, Yi Ding, Huang Fei.

AMAZON
CABRIOLET. February, 1992. Brazilian-Finnish. (Mika Kaurismaki) Robert Davi, Rae Dawn Chong, Kari Vaananen.

AMBITION
MIRAMAX. May, 1991. (Scott D. Goldstein) Lou Diamond Phillips, Clancy Brown, Cecilia Peck.

AMBUSH
MATILA & ROHR PRODS. Feb., 1999. Finnish. (Olli Saarela) Peter Franzen, Irina Bjorklund, Kari Heiskanen, Taisto Reimaluoto.

AMERICAN BEAUTY
DREAMWORKS PICTURES. Sept., 1999. (Sam Mendes) Kevin Spacey, Annette Bening, Thora Brich, Wes Bentley.

AMERICAN BLUE NOTE
PANORAMA ENT. November, 1990. (Ralph Toporoff) Peter MacNicol, Carl Capotorto.

AMERICAN BUFFALO
SAMUEL GOLDWYN. October, 1996. (Michael Corrente) Dustin Hoffman, Dennis Franz, Sean Nelson.

AMERICAN CUISINE
POLYGRAM. Aug., 1998. French. (Jean-Yves Pitoun) Eddy Mitchell, Irene Jacob, Jason Lee, Thibault de Montalembert, Michel Muller.

AMERICAN CYBORG
CANNON. January, 1994. (Boaz Davidson) Joe Lara, Nicole Hansen, John Ryan.

AMERICAN DREAM
PRESTIGE. March, 1992. (Barbara Kopple) Documentary.

AMERICAN FABULOUS
FIRST RUN FEATURES. October, 1992. (Reno Dakota) Jeffrey Strouth.

AMERICAN FRIENDS
CASTLE HILL. April, 1993. British. (Tristam Powell) Michael Palin, Connie Booth, Trini Alvarado.

AMERICAN HEART
TRITON. May, 1993. (Martin Bell) Jeff Bridges, Edward Furlong, Lucinda Jenney.

AMERICAN HISTORY X
NEW LINE. Oct., 1999. (Tony Kaye) Edward Norton, Edward Furlong, Fairuza Balk, Beverly D'Angelo.

AMERICAN HOLLOW
HBO. Jan., 1999. (Rory Kennedy) Documentary.

AMERICAN JOB
BLUEMARK. January, 1996. (Chris Smith) Randy Russell, Tom Wheeler, Matt Collier, Charlie Smith.

AMERICAN KICKBOXER
CANNON. February, 1991. South African. (Frans Nel) John Barrett, Keith Vitali, Terry Norton.

AN AMERICAN LOVE STORY
AMERICAN PLAYHOUSE AND INDEPENDENT TELEVISION SERVICE. Jan. 1999. (Jennifer Fox) Documentary.

AMERICAN ME
UNIVERSAL. March, 1992. (Edward James Olmos) Edward James Olmos, William Forsythe, Pepe Serna.

AMERICAN MOVIE
SONY. Jan. 1999. (Chris Smith) Documentary.

AMERICAN NINJA 4: THE ANNIHILATION
CANNON. March, 1991. (Cedric Sundstrom) Michael Dudikoff, David Bradley, James Booth.

AMERICAN PERFEKT
NU IMAGE. May, 1997. (Paul Chart) Fairuza Balk, Robert Foster, Amanda Plummer, Paul Sorvino, David Thewlis, Geoffrey Lewis.

AMERICAN PIE
UNIVERSAL June, 1999. (Paul Weitz) Jason Biggs, Shannon Elizabeth, Alyson Hannigan, Chris Klein, Natasha Lyonne.

AMERICAN PIMP
UNDERWORLD ENTERTAINMENT Jan., 1999. (Allen and Albert Hughes) Rosebudd, Schauntte, Bradley, C-Nolte, Ken Ivy.

THE AMERICAN PRESIDENT
COLUMBIA. November, 1995. (Rob Reiner) Michael Douglas, Annette Bening, Martin Sheen, Michael J. Fox, David Paymer.

AMERICAN PURGATORY: 90 DAYS BEHIND THE WIRE OF GUANTANAMO USNB
NINETY MILES. October, 1995. (Rafael Oller) Documentary.

AMERICAN STRAYS
CANNED PICTURES. April, 1996. (Michael Covert) Jennifer Tilly, Eric Roberts, John Savage.

AN AMERICAN SUMMER
CASTLE HILL. June, 1991. (James Slocum) Michael Landes, Brian Austin Green, Amber Susa.

AN AMERICAN TAIL: FIEVEL GOES WEST
UNIVERSAL. November, 1991. (Phil Nibbelink, Simon Wells) Animated.

AM I BEAUTIFUL?
ATLAS INTL. Sept., 1998. German. (Doris Dorrie) Senta Berger, Gottfried John, Otto Sander, Franka Potente, Anica Dobra.

AMISTAD
DREAMWORKS PICTURES. Nov., 1997. (Steven Spielberg) Morgan Freeman, Anthony Hopkins, Matthew McConaughey, Nigel Hawthorne, Djimon Hounsou.

AMONG GIANTS
CAPITOL FILMS. May, 1998. British. (Sam Miller) Pete Postlethwaite, Rachel Griffiths, James Thornton, Lennie James, Andy Serkis.

AMONGST FRIENDS
FINE LINE. July, 1993. (Rob Weiss) Steve Parlavecchio, Joseph Lindsey, Patrick McGraw.

AMOS & ANDREW
COLUMBIA. March, 1993. (E. Max Frye) Nicolas Cage, Samuel L. Jackson, Dabney Coleman, Brad Dourif.

AMY
VILLAGE ROADSHOW. May, 1998. Australian. (Nadia Tass) Alana De Roma, Rachel Griffiths, Ben Mendelsohn, Nick Barker.

AN AMBIGUOUS REPORT ABOUT THE END OF THE WORLD
FALCON. Feb., 1997. Czechoslovakian. (Juraj Jakubisko) Milan Bahul, Deana Horvathova, Klara Issova, Joachim Kemmer.

AN AMERICAN WEREWOLF IN PARIS
BUENA VISTA PICTURES. Oct., 1997. British-Dutch-Luxembourgois. (Anthony Waller) Tom Everett Scott, Julie Delpy, Vince Vieluf.

ANACONDA
SONY PICTURES ENTERTAINMENT. April, 1997. (Luis Llosa), Jennifer Lopez, Ice Cube, Jon Voight, Eric Stoltz, Kari Wuhrer.

ANALYZE THIS
WARNER BROS. Feb., 1999. (Harold Ramis) Robert De Niro, Billy Crystal, Lisa Kudrow, Joe Vierelli, Chazz Palminteri.

ANASTASIA
20TH CENTURY FOX. Nov., 1997. (Don Bluth, Gary Goldman) Meg Ryan, John Cusack, Kelsey Grammer, Christopher Lloyd (voices).

ANCESTORS IN THE AMERICAS: COOLIES, SAILORS, SETTLERS
CENTER FOR EDUCATIONAL TELECOMM. February, 1996. (Loni Ding) Documentary.

ANCHORESS
INT'L FILM CIRCUIT. May, 1994. British. (Chris Newby) Natalie Morse, Eugene Bervoets, Pete Postlethwaite.

... AND GOD SPOKE
LIVE ENT. September, 1994. (Arthur Borman) R.C. Bates, Michael Riley, Stephen Rappaport, Soupy Sales.

AND YOU THOUGHT YOUR PARENTS WERE WEIRD
TRIMARK. November, 1991. (Tony Cookson) Marcia Strassman, Joshua Miller, Edan Gross.

ANDRE
PARAMOUNT. August, 1994. (George Miller) Keith Carradine, Tina Majorino, Chelsea Field.

ANGEL FACE
PABLO TORRE. Feb., 1999. Argentine. (Pablo Torre) Virginia Innocenti, Mario Pasik, Enrique Pinti, Mariano Marini.

ANGEL OF THE NIGHT
WISE GUY PRODS. Feb., 1999. Danish. (Shaky Gonzalez) Maria Karlsen, Mette Louise Holland, Tomas Villum Jensen, Ulrich Thomsen.

ANGEL ON MY SHOULDER
A D.D. PRODS. Feb. 1998. (Donna Deitch), DOCUMENTARY.

ANGELS AND INSECTS
SAMUEL GOLDWYN. November, 1995. (Philip Haas) Mark Rylance, Kristin Scott Thomas, Patsy Kensit.

ANGEL'S DANCE
PROMARK ENTERTAINMENT GROUP Feb., 1999. (David L. Corley) James Belushi, Sheryl Lee, Kyle Chandler, Frank John Hughes.

ANGELS IN THE OUTFIELD
BUENA VISTA. July, 1994. (William Dear) Danny Glover, Joseph Gordon Levitt, Christopher Lloyd.

ANGIE
BUENA VISTA. March, 1994. (Martha Coolidge) Geena Davis, Stephen Rea, James Gandolfini.

ANGUS
NEW LINE. September, 1995. (Patrick Read Johnson) Charlie Talbert, Kathy Bates, George C. Scott.

ANIMA
TANGENT FILMS/OTHER PICTURES. MAY, 1998. (Craig Richardson) George Bartenieff, Jacqueline Bertrand, Bray Poor, Geoffrey Cantor.

ANIMALS (AND THE TOLLKEEPER)
MAGNOLIA MAE FILMS. Jan., 1998. (Michael Di Jiacomo) Tim Roth, Mili Avital, Rod Steiger, Mickey Rooney, John Turturro, Jacques Herlin.

ANNALUISE AND ANTON
BUENA VISTA INTL. Feb., 1999. German. (Caroline Link) Elea Geissler, Max Felder, Juliane Koehler, August Zirner, Meret Becker.

ANNA MAGDALENA
UNITED FILMMAKERS ORGANISATION. Sept., 1998. Hong Kong. (Yee Chung-man) Takeshi Kaneshiro, Aaron Kwok, Kelly Chen, Leslie Cheung, Anita Yuen.

ANNA OZ
STUDIO CANAL PLUS. September, 1996. French-Italian-Swiss. (Eric Rochant) Charlotte Gainsbourg, Gerard Lanvin.

ANNE FRANK REMEMBERED
SONY PICTURES CLASSICS. January, 1996. (Jon Blair) Kenneth Brabagh, Glenn Close, Miep Gies.

THE ANNIHILATION OF FISH
PAUL HELLER Sept., 1999. (Charles Burnett Lynn Redgrave, James Earl Jones, Margot Kidder.

ANOOSH OF THE AIRWAVES
PACIFIC MOTION PICTURE CO. Aug., 1999. (James Westby) Melik Malkasian, Steven Clark Pachosa, Barbara Niven.

ANOTHER DAY IN PARADISE
TRIMARK PICTURES. Sept. 1998. (Larry Clark) James Woods, Melanie Griffith, Vincent Kartheiser, Natasha Gregson Wagner.

ANOTHER 48 HRS.
PARAMOUNT. June, 1990. (Walter Hill) Eddie Murphy, Nick Nolte, Brion James.

ANOTHER MOTHER
STUDIO NIEUWE GRONDEN/KRO TV. Sept., 1996. Dutch. (Paula van der Oest) Janis Reinis, Arys Adamson, Geert de Jong.

ANOTHER NINE & A HALF WEEKS
JONES FILM/SAGA PICTURES. Sept., 1997. (Anne Goursaud) Mickey Rourke, Agatha de la Fontaine, Angie Everhart.

ANOTHER STAKEOUT
BUENA VISTA. July, 1993. (John Badham) Richard Dreyfuss, Emilio Estevez, Rosie O'Donnell.

ANOTHER YOU
TRISTAR. July, 1991. (Maurice Phillips) Gene Wilder, Richard Pryor, Mercedes Ruehl.

ANTHEM
ZEITGEST FILMS. June, 1997. (Shainee Gabel, Kristin Hahn) Robert Redford, Michael Stipe, Studs Terkel, Documentary.

ANTIGONE/RITES FOR THE DEAD
ASA COMMUNICATIONS. November, 1990. (Amy Greenfield) Amy Greenfield, Bertram Ross.

ANTONIA & JANE
MIRAMAX. October, 1991. British. (Beeban Kidron) Imelda Staunton, Saskia Reeves, Iain Cuthbertson.

ANTONIA'S LINE
FIRST LOOK. October, 1995. Dutch. (Marleen Gorris) Willeke Van Amerooy, Els Dottermans, Jan Decleir.

ANTZ
DREAMWORKS. Sept., 1998. (Eric Darnell, Tim Johnson) Woody Allen, Dan Aykroyd, Anne Bancroft, Jane Curtin, Danny Glover.

ANY MAN'S DEATH
INI ENTERTAINMENT. May, 1990. (Tom Clegg) John Savage, William Hickey, Mia Sara.

ANYWHERE BUT HERE
20TH CENTURY FOX. Sept., 1999. (Wayne Wang) Susan Sarandon, Natalie Portman, Eileen Ryan, Ray Baker.

APEX
REPUBLIC. March, 1994. (Phillip J. Roth) Richard Keats, Mitchell Cox, Lisa Ann Russell.

APOCALYPSE BOP
OL' BAIT SHOP PRODS. April, 1996. (Andrew Osborne) Scott Von Doviak, Bryant Marshall, Holly Harris.

APOLLO 13
UNIVERSAL. June, 1995. (Ron Howard) Tom Hanks, Kevin Bacon, Bill Paxton, Ed Harris, Gary Sinise, Kathleen Quinlan.

THE APOSTLE
OCTOBER FILMS. Sept., 1997. (Robert Duvall) Robert Duvall, Farrah Fawcett, Miranda Richardson, Todd Allen, John Beasley.

APPASSIONATA
UNIVERSAL. Sept., 1999. Italian. (Tonino de Bernardi) Anna Bonaiuto, Ines de Medeiros, Iaia Forte, Galatea Ranzi, Isabel Ruth.

THE APPRENTICES
GALA FILM. November, 1995. French. (Pierre Salvadori) Francois Cluzet, Guillaume Depardieu.

APRIL STORY
ASIAN FILM LIBRARY/ROCKWELL EYES. Aug., 998. Japanese. (Noboru Shinoda) Takako Matsu, Seiichi Tanabe, Kaori Fujii, Rumi.

APRILIE
TANDEM DISTRIBUZIONE. March, 1998. Italian. (Nanni Moretti) documentary with Nanni Moretti, Silvio Orlando, Silvia Nono.

APT PUPIL
SONY PICTURES ENTERTAINMENT. Aug, 1998. (Bryan Singer) Ian McKellen, Brad Renfro, Bruce Davison, Elias Koteas, Joe Morton.

ARABIAN KNIGHT
MIRAMAX. August, 1995. (Richard Williams) Animated.

ARACHNOPHOBIA
BUENA VISTA. July, 1990. (Frank Marshall) Jeff Daniels, Harley Jane Kozak, John Goodman.

ARCHANGEL
ZEITGEIST. March, 1991. Canadian. (Guy Maddin) Kyle McCulloch, Kathy Marykuca. B&W.

ARCHIBALD THE RAINBOW PAINTER
EMPTY BOX. Aug., 1998. (Les Landau) Dorian Harewood, Michael McKean, Patti D'Arbanville.

THE ARCHITECTS
INDEPENDENT. October, 1993. German. (Peter Kahane) Kurt Naumann, Rita Feidmeier, Uta Eisold.

THE ARCHITECTURE OF DOOM
FIRST RUN FEATURES. October, 1991. German-Swedish. (Peter Cohen) Documentary.

THE ARENA OF MURDER
AGAV FILMS. Sept., 1996. Israeli. (Amos Gitai) Documentary.

ARGUING THE WORLD
FIRST RUN FEATURES. Dec., 1997. (Joseph Dorman) DOCUMENTARY.

ARIEL
KINO. August, 1990. Finnish. (Aki Kaurismaki) Turo Pajalo, Susanna Haavisto.

ARISTOTLE'S PLOT
JBA PROD. Sept., 1996. Zimbabwean-French-British. (Jean-Pierre Bekolo) Seputla Sobogohi, Albee Lesotho, Ken Gamou.

ARIZONA DREAM
WARNER. September, 1994. (Emir Kusturica) Johnny Depp, Jerry Lewis, Faye Dunaway, Lili Taylor.

ARLETTE
AMLF. April, 1997. French. (Claude Zidi) Josiane Balasko, Christophe Lambert, Ennio Fantastichini, Jean-Marie Bigard.

ARLINGTON ROAD
SONY. Mar. ,1999. (M Bobby Bukowski) Jeff Bridges, Tim Robbins, Joan Cusack, Hope Davis.

ARMAGEDDON
BUENA VISTA. June, 1998. (Michael Bay) Bruce Willis, Billy Bob Thornton, Liv Tyler, Ben Affleck, Will Patton, Peter Stormare.

ARMY OF DARKNESS
UNIVERSAL. February, 1993. (Sam Raimi) Bruce Campbell, Embeth Davidtz, Marcus Gilbert.

ARRESTING GENA
GOOD MACHINE & KARDNA/SWINSKY. Jan., 1997. (Hannah Weyer) Aesha Waks, Summer Phoenix, Sam Rockwell.

THE ARRIVAL
ORION. May, 1996. (David Twohy) Charlie Sheen, Ron Silver, Lindsay Crouse, Teri Polo, Richard Schiff, Tony T. Johnson.

ART DECO DETECTIVE
TRIDENT. September, 1994. (Philippe Mora, Bruce Critchley) John Dennis Johnston, Stephen McHattie, Brion James.

ART FOR TEACHERS OF CHILDREN
ZEITGEIST. August, 1995. (Jennifer Montgomery) Caitlin Grace McDonnell, Duncan Hannah, Coles Burroughs. B&W.

ART MUSEUM BY THE ZOO
CINE 2000. MAY, 1999. South Korean. (Lee Jeong-hyang) Shim Eun-ha, Ahn Sung-ki, Lee Seong-jae, Song Seon-mi.

THE ART OF REMEMBRANCE: SIMON WIESENTHAL
RIVER LIGHTS PICTURES. May, 1996. German. (Johanna Heer, Werner Schmeidel) Documentary.

ARTEMISIA
POLYGRAM. Sept., 1997. French-German-Italian. (Agnes Merlet) Michel Serrault, Valentina Cervi, Miki Manojlovic, Luca Zingaretti.

ARTICLE 99
ORION. March, 1992. (Howard Deutch) Ray Liotta, Kiefer Sutherland, Kathy Baker.

AS GOOD AS IT GETS
SONY PICTURES ENTERTAINMENT. Dec., 1997. (James L. Brooks) Jack Nicholson, Helen Hunt, Greg Kinnear, Cuba Gooding Jr.

ASTERIX & OBELIX VS. CAESAR
AMLF DISTRIBUTION. Jan., 1999. French-German-Italian. (Claude Zidi) Christian Clavier, Gerard Depardieu, Roberto Benigni, Michel Galabru, Claude Pieplu.

AS TIME GOES BY
TOP FOCUS PROD. Nov., 1997. Taiwanese. (Ann Hui, Vincent Chui) documentary with Ann Hui, Margaret Ng, Dominic Tsim, Emily Luk.

ASPEN EXTREME
BUENA VISTA. January, 1993. (Patrick Hasburg) Paul Gross, Peter Berg, Finola Hughes.

ASSASSINS
WARNER BROS. October, 1995. (Richard Donner) Sylvester Stallone, Antonio Banderas, Julianne Moore.

ASSASSIN(S)
MKL LAZENNEC DIFFUSION/STUDIO CANAL PLUS. May, 1997. French. (Mathieu Kassovitz) Michel Serrault, Kassovitz.

THE ASSIGNMENT
TRIUMPH FILMS. Sept., 1997. (Christian Duguay) Aidan Quinn, Donald Sutherland, Ben Kingsley, Claudia Ferri, Celine Bonnier.

THE ASSOCIATE
BUENA VISTA. October, 1996. (Donald Petrie), Whoopi Goldberg, Dianne Wiest, Eli Wallach, Tim Daly, Helen Hanft, George Morfogen.

THE ASTRONAUT'S WIFE
NEW LINE. Aug., 1999. (Rand Ravich) Johnny Depp, Charlize Theron, Joe Morton, Clea DuVal.

AT FIRST SIGHT
METRO-GOLDWYN-MAYER. Jan., 1999. (Irwin Winkler) Val Kilmer, Mira Sorvino, Kelly McGillis, Steven Weber.

AT FULL GALLOP
TOR FILM STUDIO. May, 1996. Polish. (Krzysztof Zanussi) Maja Komorowska, Bartosz Obuchowicz.

ATILANTO FOR PRESIDENT
CINE CO. Sept., 1998. Spanish. (La Cuadrilla) Manuel Manquina, Ramon Barea, Laura Conejero, Fernando Vivanco, Carlos Lucas.

AT PLAY IN THE FIELDS OF THE LORD
UNIVERSAL. December, 1991. (Hector Babenco) Tom Berenger, Kathy Bates, Aidan Quinn, John Lithgow.

AT SATCHEM FARM
ITASCA PICTURES. Sept., 1998. (John Huddles) Rufus Sewell, Nigel Hawthorne, Minnie Driver, Amelia Heinie, Michael E. Rodgers.

AT THE CROSSROADS: JEWS IN EASTERN EUROPE TODAY
ARTHUR CANTOR FILMS. February, 1991. (Oren Rudavsky, Yale Strom) Documentary.

AT THE MAX
BLC GROUP/IMAX CORP. October, 1991. (Julien Temple) The Rolling Stones.

ATILANO FOR PRESIDENT
CINE CO. Sept., 1998. Spanish. (Luis Guridi, Santiago Aguilar) Manuel Manquina, Ramon Barea, Laura Conejero, Fernando Vivanco.

ATLANTIS
MILESTONE. December, 1993. French. (Luc Besson) Documentary.

ATMAN
BAYERISCHE RUDFUNK. Sept., 1997. Finnish-German. (Pirjo Honkasalo) documentary.

AU PETIT MARGUERY
FILMS DU LOSANGE. November, 1995. French. (Laurent Benegui) Stephane Audran, Michel Aumont.

AUGUST
SAMUEL GOLDWYN. April, 1996. (Anthony Hopkins) Hopkins, Kate Burton, Leslie Phillips, Kate Burton.

AUGUST 32ND ON EARTH
MAX FILMS. May, 1998. Canadian. (Denis Villeneuve) Pascale Bussieres, Alexis Martin, Richard S. Hamilton.

AUGUST VACATION (FERIE D'AGOSTO)
CECCHI GORI. April, 1996. Italian. (Paolo Virzi) Silvio Orlando, Sabrina Ferilli, Ennio Fantastichini.

AUSTIN POWERS: INTERNATIONAL MAN OF MYSTERY
NEW LINE. April, 1997. (Jay Roach), Mike Myers, Elizabeth Hurley, Michael York, Mimi Rogers, Robert Wagner, Seth Green.

AUSTIN POWERS: THE SPY WHO SHAGGED ME
NEW LINE. June, 1999. (Jay Roach) Mike Myers, Heather Graham, Michael York, Robert Wagner, Rob Lowe, Seth Green.

THE AUTUMN HEART
FILM CELLAR. Jan., 1999. (Steven Maler) Tyne Daly, Ally Sheedy, Jack Davidson, Davidlee Willson.

AUTUMN IN PARADISE
SONET. December, 1995. Swedish. (Richard Hobert) Mona Malm, Sven Lindberg, Goran Stangertz.

AUTUMN SUN (SOL DE OTONO)
EDUARDO MIGNOGNA & ASSOCIADOS. September, 1996. Argentine. (Eduardo Mignogna) Norma Aleandro, Jorge Luz.

AUTUMN TALE
LES FILMS DU LOSANGE. Aug., 1998. French. (Eric Rohmer) Marie Riviere, Beatrice Romand, Alain Libolt, Didier Sandre, Alexia Portal.

AVALANCHE
PM ENTERTAINMENT GROUP. May, 1999.(Steve Kroschel) Thomas Ian Griffith, Caroleen Feeney, R. Lee Ermey, C. Thomas Howell.

AVALON
TRISTAR. October, 1990. (Barry Levinson) Aidan Quinn, Armin Mueller Stahl, Elijah Wood.

AVE MARIA
LESTES FILMS, IMCINE AND MANGA FILMS. Mexican-Spanish. Nov., 1999. (Eduardo Rossoff) Tere Lopez Tarin, Damian Alcazar, Demian Bichir, Ana Torrent, Juan Diego Botto.

THE AVENGERS
WARNER BROS. Aug., 1998. (Jeremiah Chechick) Ralph Fiennes, Uma Thurman, Sean Connery, Patrick Macnee, Jim Broadbent.

AWAKENINGS
COLUMBIA. December, 1990. (Penny Marshall) Robert De Niro, Robin Williams, Julie Kavner.

AWAY WITH WORDS
TIMEWARP. May, 1999. Japanese. (Christopher Doyle)Cast: Tadano Asano, Kevin Sherlock, Mavis Xu, Christa Hughes, Georgina Dobson.

AWFULLY BIG ADVENTURE, AN
FINE LINE. July, 1995. British. (Mike Newell) Alan Rickman, Hugh Grant, Georgina Cates.

AY, CARMELA!
PRESTIGE. February, 1991. Spanish. (Carlos Saura) Carmen Maura, Andres Pajares, Gabin Diego.

B

BABAR: KING OF THE ELEPHANTS
ALLIANCE ATLANTIS. Mar., 1999. Canadian-French-German. (Raymond Jafelice). Animated.

BABE
UNIVERSAL. August, 1994. (Chris Noonan) James Cromwell, Magda Szubanski.

THE BABE
UNIVERSAL. April, 1992. (Arthur Hiller) John Goodman, Kelly McGillis, Trini Alvarado.

BABEL
IMA FILM/ALLEGRO FILM. Apr., 1999. French-Canadian. (Gerard Pullicino) Mitchell David Rothpan, Maria de Medeiros, Tcheky Karyo, Michel Jonasz.

BAB EL OUED CITY
JANE BALFOUR FILMS. June, 1995. Algerian. (Merzak Allouache) Nadia Kaci, Mohammed Ourdache.

BABE: PIG IN THE CITY
UNIVERSAL. Nov., 1999.(George Miller) Magda Szubanski, James Cromwell, Mary Stein, Mickey Rooney, Julie Godfrey.

BABY GENIUSES
SONY. Mar. 1999. (Bob Clark) Kathleen Turner, Christopher Lloyd, Kim Cattrall, Peter MacNicol.

BABY, IT'S YOU
ITVS. Jan., 1998. (Anne Makepeace), DOCUMENTARY.

BABY'S DAY OUT
20TH CENTURY FOX. July, 1994. (Patrick Read Johnson) Joe Mantegna, Lara Flynn Boyle.

BABY NOBODY
ALTA FILMS. April, 1997. Spanish. (Jose Luis Borau) Rafael Alvarez, Iciar Bollain, Jose Castillo, Pedro Alonso, Adriana Ozores.

BABYFACE
STABLE FILMS. May, 1998. Canadian. (Jack Blum) Lenore Zann, Elisabeth Rosen, Shawn Doyle, James Gallanders, William Dunlop.

BABYFEVER
RAINBOW. April, 1994. (Henry Jaglom) Frances Fisher, Eric Roberts, Victoria Foyt, Matt Salinger.

BABYMOTHER
FILM FOUR DISTRIBUTORS. July, 1998. British. (Julian Henriques) Anjela Lauren Smith, Wil Johnson, Caroline Chikezie, Jocelyn Esien.

THE BABYSITTER
SPELLING. November, 1995. (Guy Ferland) Alicia Silverstone, J.T. Walsh, Lee Garlington, Nicky Katt.

THE BABYSITTER'S CLUB
COLUMBIA. BEACON. August, 1995. (Melanie Mayron) Schuyler Fisk, Bre Blair, Rachael Leigh Cook.

BACK IN THE U.S.S.R.
20TH CENTURY FOX. February, 1992. (Deran Sarafian) Frank Whaley, Natalya Negoda, Roman Polanski.

BACK OF BEYOND
TOURIST FILMS. November, 1995. Australian. (Michael Robertson) Paul Mercurio, Colin Friels.

BACK TO BACK
CONCORDE. January, 1990. (John Kincade) Bill Paxton, Todd Field, Apolonia Kotero.

BACK TO THE FUTURE PART III
UNIVERSAL. May, 1990. (Robert Zemeckis) Michael J. Fox, Christopher Lloyd, Mary Steenburgen.

BACK TO THE PROMISED LAND
BLUE PRODS. April, 1993. Israeli. (Madeleine Ali) Documentary.

BACKBEAT
GRAMERCY. April, 1994. British. (Iain Softley) Stephen Dorff, Sheryl Lee, Ian Hart.

THE BACK COUNTRY
MARS FILMS. May, 1998. French. (Jacques Nolot) Jacques Nolot, Henri Gardey, Mathilde Mone.

BACKDRAFT
UNIVERSAL. May, 1991. (Ron Howard) Kurt Russell, William Baldwin, Robert De Niro.

BACKGROUND NOISE
LUCKY RED DISTRIBUZIONE. April, 1996. Italian. (Claudio Camarca) Francesco Dominedo, Francesco Meoni.

BACKSTREET DREAMS
VIDMARK. September, 1990. (Rupert Hitzig) Jason O'Malley, Brooke Shields, Burt Young.

BAD BEHAVIOUR
OCTOBER FILMS. September, 1993. British. (Les Blair) Stephen Rea, Sinead Cusack, Philip Jackson.

BAD BOYS
COLUMBIA. April, 1995. (Michael Bay) Martin Lawrence, Will Smith, Tea Leoni, Tcheky Karyo.

BAD COMPANY
BUENA VISTA. January, 1995. (Damian Harris) Ellen Barkin, Laurence Fishburne, Frank Langella.

BAD GIRLS
CASTLE HILL. January, 1994. (Amos Kollek) Amos Kollek, Marla Sucharetz, Mari Nelson.

BAD GIRLS
20TH CENTURY FOX. April, 1994. (Jonathan Kaplan) Madeleine Stowe, Andie MacDowell, Mary Stuart Masterson.

BAD INFLUENCE
TRIUMPH. March, 1990. (Curtis Hanson) Rob Lowe, James Spader, Lisa Zane.

BAD LIEUTENANT
ARIES. November, 1992. (Abel Ferrara) Harvey Keitel, Frankie Thorn, Paul Hipp.

BAD MANNERS
DAVIS ENTERTAINMENT CLASSICS. May, 1997. (Jonathan Kaufer) David Strathairn, Bonnie Bedelia, Saul Rubinek, Caroleen Feeney.

BAD MOON
WARNER BROS. November, 1996. (Eric Red), Mariel Hemingway, Michael Pare, Mason Gamble, Primo.

BAD TIMES
UNIVERSIDAD DEL CINE Y ARTES AUDIOVISUALES. Nov., 1998. Argentine. (Nicolas Saad, Mariano De Roas, Salvador Roselli, Rodrigo Moreno) Pablo Vega, Daniel Valenzuela, Nicolas Leivas, Diego Peretti, Virginia Innocenti.

BAIL JUMPER
ANGELIKA. April, 1990. (Christian Faber) Eszter Balint, B.J. Spalding, Tony Askin.

BALKANISATOR
MYTHOS LTD. GREEK FILM CENTER/THELMA FILM/TCHAPPLINE FILM. Feb, 1997. Greek-Swiss-Bulgarian. (Sotiris Goritsas) Gerassimos Skiadaressis, Stelios Mainas, Yiota Festa, Sabine Berg.

THE BALLAD OF LITTLE JO
FINE LINE. August, 1993. (Maggie Greenwalt) Suzy Amis, Ian McKellen, David Chung.

THE BALLAD OF THE SAD CAFE
ANGELIKA. May, 1991. (Simon Callow) Vanessa Redgrave, Keith Carradine, Cork Hubbert.

THE BALLAD OF THE WINDSHIELD WASHERS
MIKADO. Sept,. 1998. Italian. (Peter Del Monte) Olek Mincer, Agara Buzek, Kim Rossi Stuart, Andrzej Grabowski, Grazyna Wolszak.

BALLET
ZIPPORAH. March, 1995. (Frederick Wiseman) Documentary.

BALLISTIC KISS
CRASH MEDIA. Oct., 1998. Hong Kong. (Donnine Yen) Donnie Yen, Annie Wu, Jimmy Wong, Simon Lui, Yu Rongguang.

BALLOT MEASURE 9
ZEITGEIST. June, 1995. (Heather MacDonald) Documentary.

BALTO
UNIVERSAL. December. 1995. (Simon Wells) (voices) Kevin Bacon, Bridget Fonda, Bob Hoskins, Phil Collins.

BANDWAGON
PAMLICO. January, 1996. (John Schultz) Kevin Corrigan, Steve Parlavecchio, Lee Holmes.

BANDIT QUEEN
ARROW. June, 1995. Hindi. (Shekhar Kapur) Seema Biswas, Nirmal Pandey, Manoj Bajpai.

BANG BOOM BANG: A DEAD-CERT THING
SENATOR. June, 1999. German. (Peter Thorwarth) Oliver Korittke, Markus Knuefken, Ralf Richter, Diether Krebs.

BANK ROBBER
I.R.S. December, 1993. (Nick Mead) Patrick Dempsey, Lisa Bonet, Judge Reinhold.

B.A.P.S.
NEW LINE. March, 1997. (Robert Townsend), Halle Berry, Martin Landau, Ian Richardson, Natalie Desselle, Troy Beyer, Luigi Amodeo.

BARAKA
SAMUEL GOLDWYN. September, 1993. (Ron Fricke) Non-narrative images.

BARBARA
PER HOLST FILM/SVENSK FILMINDUSTRI. Feb., 1998. Danish-Swedish-Norwegian. (Nils Malmros) Anneke von der Lippe, Lars Simonsen, Helene Egelund, Trond Hovik, Peter Hesse Overgaard.

THE BARBER OF SIBERIA
MICHEL SEYDOUX. May, 1999. Russian-French-Italian-Czech. (Nikita Mikhalkov) Julia Ormond, Oleg Menshikov, Richard Harris

BAR GIRLS
ORION CLASSICS. April, 1995. (Marita Giovanni) Nancy Allison Wolfe, Liza D'Agostino, Camilla Griggs.

BARB WIRE
GRAMERCY. May, 1996. (David Hogan) Pamela Anderson Lee, Temuera Morrison, Victoria Rowell, Udo Kier.

BARCELONA
FINE LINE. July, 1994. (Whit Stillman) Taylor Nichols, Chris Eigeman, Tushka Bergen.

BARENAKED IN AMERICA
NETTFILMS. Sept., 1999. Canadian. (Jason Priestley) The Barenaked Ladies, Jon Steward, Jason Priestley, Moses Znaimer.

BARJO
MYRIAD PICTURES. July, 1993. French. (Jerome Boivin) Anne Brochet, Richard Bohringer, Hippolyte Girardot.

BARNONE
BURNING GIRAFFE PICTURES. Oct., 1997. Canadian. (Mark Tuit) William MacDonald, Cavan Cunningham, Anthony Dohm, Frank Topol.

BARRACKS
VGTRK/DAR CINEMATOGRAPHIC CO.. Aug., 1999. Russian. (Valeri Ogorodnikov) Irina Senotova, Yulia Svezhakova, Yevgeni Sidikhin, Nina Usatova, Sergei Kachanov.

BARRIO
WARNER SOGEFILMS. Sept., 1998. Spanish. (Fernando Leon de Aranoa) Crispulo Cabezas, Timy, Eloi Yebra, Marieta Orozco.

BARROCO
INT'L FILM CIRCUIT. January, 1991. Spain/Cuba (Paul LeDuc) Francisco Rabal, Angela Molina.

BARNEY'S GREAT ADVENTURE
POLYGRAM FILMS. March, 1998. (Steve Gomer) George Hearn, Shirley Douglas, Trevor Morgan, Kyla Pratt, Diana Rice, David Joyner.

BARTON FINK
20TH CENTURY FOX. August, 1991. (Joel Coen) John Turturro, John Goodman, Michael Lerner.

BASED ON THE NOVEL
DKP AMSTERDAM. Jan. 1999. Dutch. (Eddy Terstall) Dirk Seelenberg, Nadja Hupscher, Femke Lakerveld, Alette Dirkse.

BASEKETBALL
UNIVERSAL PICTURES. July, 1998. (David Zucker), Trey Parker, Matt Stone, Yasmine Bleeth, Jenny McCarthy, Robert Vaughn.

THE BASEMENT AND THE KITCHEN
DRAMA 3/4. June, 1999.(David Frickas) David Frickas, Pam Cook, Mo Gaffney, Ric Barbera.

BASIC INSTINCT
TRISTAR. March, 1992. (Paul Verhoeven) Michael Douglas, Sharon Stone, George Dzundza.

THE BASKET
NORTH BY NORTHWEST ENTERTAINMENT. May, 1999.(Rich Cowan) Peter Coyote, Karen Allen, Robert Karl Burke.

BASKET CASE 2
SHAPIRO GLICKENHAUS. March, 1990. (Frank Henenlotter) Kevin Van Hentenryck, Annie Ross.

BASKET CASE 3: THE PROGENY
SHAPIRO GLICKENHAUS. February, 1992. (Frank Henenlotter) Annie Ross, Kevin Van Hentenryck.

THE BASKETBALL DIARIES
NEW LINE. April, 1995. (Scott Kalvert) Leonardo DiCaprio, Mark Wahlberg, Lorraine Bracco.

BASQUIAT
MIRAMAX. July 1996. (Julian Schnabel) Jeffrey Wright, Michael Wincott, Benicio Del Toro, David Bowie.

BASTARD BROOD (ENFANTS DE SALAUDY)
UFD. April, 1996. French. (Tonie Marshall) Anemone, Nathalie Baye, Molly Ringwald.

BAT OUT OF HELL
AFMD. Sept., 1997. French. (Xavier Durringer) Arnaud Giovaninetti, Gerald Laroche, Claire Keim, Jean Miez, Brigitte Catillon.

BATMAN & ROBIN
WARNER BROS. June, 1997. (Joel Schumacher), Arnold Schwarzenegger, George Clooney, Chris O'Donnell, Uma Thurman, Alicia Silverstone, Michael Gough, Pat Hingle.

BATMAN FOREVER
WARNER BROS. June, 1995. (Joel Schumacher) Val Kilmer, Tommy Lee Jones, Jim Carrey, Nicole Kidman.

BATMAN: MASK OF THE PHANTASM
WARNER BROS. December, 1993. (Eric Radomski, Bruce W. Timm) Animated.

BATMAN RETURNS
WARNER BROS. June, 1992. (Tim Burton) Michael Keaton, Danny DeVito, Michelle Pfeiffer.

BATTLE FOR THE MINDS
BATTLE FOR THE MINDS. Sept., 1996. (Steven Lipscomb) Documentary.

BATTLE OF THE JAVA SEA
HOLLAND FILM PROMOTION. Oct., 1996. Dutch. (Nick Koppen) Documentary.

THE BATTLE OVER CITIZEN KANE
WGBH. January, 1996. (Thomas Lennon and Michael Epstein) Documentary.

BAY OF ALL SAMBAS
ELIO RUMMA. Sept., 1996. Italian. (Gianni Amico) Documentary.

BAYSIDE SHAKEDOWN
TOHO. May, 1999. Japanese. (Katsuyuki Motohiro) Yuji Oda, Toshiro Yanagiba, Eri Fukatsu, Miki Mizuno, Kyoko Koizumi.

THE BEACH AT TROUVILLE
TRANS-FILM/TIME FILMVERLEIH. Feb., 1999. German. (Michael Hofmann) Boris Aljinovic, Antje Westermann, Katja Zinsmeister, Karin Krawczyk, Christoph Zapatka.

BEAN
POLYGRAM. June, 1997. British. (Mel Smith) Rowan Atkinson, Peter MacNicol, Pamela Reed, Harris Yulin, Burt Reynolds, John Mills.

THE BEANS OF EGYPT, MAINE
I.R.S. November, 1994. (Jennifer Warren) Martha Plimpton, Rutger Hauer, Kelly Lynch.

BEASTCOPS
Media Asia Films. May, 1998. Hong Kong. (Gordon Chan) Michael Fitzgerald Wong, Anthony Wong, Kathy Chau, Roy Cheung, Sam Lee.

BEASTMASTER 2: THROUGH THE PORTAL OF TIME
NEW LINE. August, 1991. (Sylvio Tabet) Marc Singer, Kari Wuhrer, Wings Hauser.

BEAT
SHOCHIKU. Sept., 1998. Japanese. (Amon Miyamoto) Claude Maki, Yuki Uchida, Dean Stapleton, Naoto Harata, Judy Motomura.

BEAUMARCHAIS
ALLIANCE. August, 1996. French. (Edourd Molinaro) Fabrice Luchini, Sandrine Kerlain, Michel Serrault.

THE BEAUTICIAN AND THE BEAST
PARAMOUNT. January, 1997. (Ken Kwapis), Fran Drescher, Timothy Dalton, Ian McNeice, Patrick Malahide, Lisa Jakub, Michael Lerner.

BEAUTIFUL GIRLS
MIRAMAX. February, 1996. (Ted Demme) Matt Dillon, Noah Emmerich, Annabeth Gish, Lauren Holly, Uma Thurman.

BEAUTIFUL MYSTERY
NEK. February, 1996; originally released 1983. Japanese. (Genji Nakamura) Tatuya Nagatomo, Kei Shiyuto, Ren Osugi.

A BEAUTIFUL NEW WORLD
IMAR FILM. Feb., 1999. Chinese. (Shi Runjiu) Jiang Wu, Tao Hong, Chen Ning, Ren Xianqi, Wu Pai.

BEAUTIFUL SUNDAY
JJ-PHONE. Sept., 1998. Japanese. (Tetsuya, Nakashima) Masatoshi Nagase, Momoki Bitoh, Kumiko Nakamura, Mamako Yoneyama, Kyoko Endoh.

BEAUTOPIA
FOX LORBER. Jan., 1998. (Katharina Otto) DOCUMENTARY.

BEAUTY
MARGIN FILMS. Feb., 1999. Hong Kong-Chinese. (Manshih Yonfan): Stephen Fung, Daniel Wu, Jason Tsang, Terence Yiin, Shu Qi.

BEAUTY AND THE BEAST
BUENA VISTA. November, 1991. (Gary Trousdale, Kirk Wise) Animated.

BEAVIS AND BUTT-HEAD DO AMERICA
PARAMOUNT. December, 1996. (Mike Judge), Mike Judge, Cloris Leachman, Robert Stack, Eric Bogosian, Richard Linklater (Voices).

BEBE'S KIDS
PARAMOUNT. July, 1992. (Bruce Smith) Animated.

BECAUSE OF THE WAR
NURIT PRICE. March, 1991. Israeli. (Orna Ben Dor Niv) Documentary.

BECOMING COLETTE
CASTLE HILL. November, 1992. German-U.S. (Danny Huston) Mathilda May, Klaus Maria Brandauer.

THE BED
BARRANDOV BIOGRAFIA. May, 1998. Czech. (Oskar Reif) Micheal Przebinda, Stanslava Jachnicka, Jana Hruskova, Martin Stavel.

BED & BREAKFAST
HEMDALE. August, 1992. (Robert Ellis Miller) Roger Moore, Colleen Dewhurst, Talia Shire.

BED OF ROSES
NEW LINE. February, 1996. (Michael Goldenberg) Christian Slater, Mary Stuart Masterson, Pamela Segall.

BEDROOM & COURTROOM
CINEMA SERVICE CO. Sept., 1998. South Korean. (Kang Wu-seok) Ahn Sung-ki, Mun Seong-keun, Hwang Cine, Shim Hye-jin.

BEDROOMS & HALLWAYS
PANDORA CINEMA. May, 1998. British. (Rose Troche) Kevin McKidd, Hugo Weaving, Jennifer Ehle, Simon Callow, Harriet Walter.

BEEFCAKE
EMOTION PICTURE/ALLIANCE INDEPENDENT FILMS/CHANNEL FOUR/ODEON FILMS/MIKADO FILMS/LA SEPT ARTE. JAN., 1999. Canadian. (Thom Fitzgerald) Daniel MacIvor, Josh Peace, Carroll Godsman, Jonathan Torrens, Jack Griffin Mazeika.

THE BEEKEEPER
MK2. May, 1993. Greek. (Theo Angelopoulous) Marcello Mastroianni, Nadia Mourouzi, Serge Reggiani.

BEETHOVEN
UNIVERSAL. April, 1992. (Brian Levant) Charles Grodin, Bonnie Hunt, Dean Jones.

BEETHOVEN'S 2ND
UNIVERSAL. December, 1993. (Rod Daniel) Charles Grodin, Bonnie Hunt, Nicholle Tom.

BEFORE AND AFTER
HOLLYWOOD. February, 1996. (Barbet Schroder) Meryl Sreep, Liam Neeson, Edward Furlong, Julia Weldon.

BEFORE SUNRISE
COLUMBIA. January, 1995. (Richard Linklater) Ethan Hawke, Julie Delpy.

BEFORE SUNSET
CECCHI GORI GROUP. Aug., 1999. Italian. (Stefano Incerti) Said Taghmaoui, Vincenzo Peluso, Ninni Bruschetta, Gigi Savoia.

BEFORE THE RAIN
GRAMERCY. February, 1995. Macedonian-British-French. (Milcho Manchevski) Katrin Cartlidge, Rade Serbedzija.

BEGOTTEN
THEATRE OF MATERIAL. June, 1991. (E. Elias Merhige) Brian Salzberg, Donna Dempsey. B&W.

BEING HUMAN
WARNER BROS. May, 1994. British-U.S. (Bill Forsyth) Robin Williams, John Turturro, Anna Galiena.

BEING JOHN MALKOVICH
USA FILMS/UNIVERSAL. Sept., 1999. British-U.S. (Spike Jonze) John Cusak, Cameron Diaz, Catherine Keener, Mary Kay Place, John Malkovich.

BELIEVE ME
BL PRODUCOES ARTISTICAS/RIOFILME. Feb., 1997. Brazilian. (Bia Lessa).

BELLE EPOQUE
SONY PICTURES CLASSICS. February, 1994. Spanish. (Fernando Trueba) Fernando Fernan Gomez, Jorge Sanz.

BELLINI'S DRIVE
NEVERTHERE PRODS.. Sept., 1998. Canadian. (Jeff Stephenson) Paul Bellini, Shania Twain.

BELLY
ARTISAN. Nov., 1999.(Hype Williams) Nas, DMX, Taral Hicks, Tionne "T-Boz" Watkins, Method Man.

BELLYFRUIT
INDEPENDENT WOMEN ARTISTS. Apr., 1999 (Kerri Lee) Tamara LaSeon Bass, Tonatzin Mondragon, Kelly Vin.

BELOVED
BUENA VISTA. Sept., 1998. (Jonathan Demme) Oprah Winfrey, Danny Glover, Thandie Newton, Kimberly Elise, Beah Richards.

BELOW UTOPIA
CINETEL FILMS. May, 1997. (Kurt Voss) Justin Theroux, Alyssa Milano, Ice-T, Tiny Lister.

BELLEVILLE
RAI CINEMAFICTION. Sept., 1998. Italian.(Marco Turco) Ennio Fantastichini, Isabella Ferrari, Massimo Bellinzoni.

THE BELLY OF AN ARCHITECT
HEMDALE. May, 1990. British (Peter Greenaway) Brian Dennehy, Chloe Webb, Lambert Wilson.

BELLY TALKERS
MIRAMAX. January, 1996. (Sandra Luckow) Documentary.

BELOVED FRIEND
LAUREN FILMS. Jan., 1999. Spanish. (Ventura Pons): Josep Maria Pou, Rosa Maria Sarda, Mario Gas, David Selvas.

BENEFIT OF THE DOUBT
MIRAMAX. July, 1993. (Jonathan Heap) Donald Sutherland, Amy Irving, Graham Greene.

BENJAMIN DOVE
BALDUR FILM. Oct., 1996. Icelandic. (Gisli Snaer Erlingsson) Sturla Sighvatsson, Gunnar Atli Cauthery, Sigfus Sturluson.

BENNY & JOON
MGM. April, 1993. (Jeremiah Hechik) Johnny Depp, Mary Stuart Masterson, Aidan Quinn.

BENT
METROMEDIA. May, 1997. British. (Sean Mathias) Clive Owen, Lothaire Bluteau, Brian Webber, Ian McKellen, Mick Jagger.

BEOWULF
CTV INTL. May, 1999. (Graham Baker) Christopher Lambert, Rhona Mitra, Oliver Cotton, Goetz Otto, Layla Roberts.

BERESINA OR THE LAST DAYS OF SWITZERLAND
T&C FILM)/PANDORA FILM/PRISMA FILM. May, 1999. Swiss-German-Austrian. (Daniel Schmid) Elena Panova, Geraldine Chaplin, Martin Benrath, Ulrich Noethen, Ivan Darvas.

BERKELEY IN THE SIXTIES
P.O.V. THEATRICAL FILMS. September, 1990. (Mark Kitchell) Documentary.

BERLIN JERUSALEM
JANE BALFOUR FILMS. March, 1991. French-Israeli. (Amos Gitai) Lisa Dreuzer, Rivka Neuman.

BESAME MUCHO
EUROSTAR 95. Jan., 1999. Italian. (Maurizio Ponzi) Toni Bertorelli, Giuliana De Sio, Elena Russon, Duccio Giordano, Francesco Stella.

BESEIGED
FINE LINE CINEMA. Sept., 1998. Italian. (Bernardo Bertolucci) Thandie Newton, David Thewlis, Claudio Santamaria.

THE BEST INTENTIONS
SAMUEL GOLDWYN. July, 1992. Swedish. (Bille August) Samuel Froler, Pernilla August, Max von Sydow.

BEST LAID PLANS
20TH CENTURY FOX. June, 1999. (Mike Barker) Alessandro Nivola, Reese WItherspoon, Josh Brolin, Rocky Carroll.

THE BEST MAN
OCTOBER FILMS. Jan., 1998. Italian. (Pupi Avati) Diego Abantantuono, Ines Sastre, Dario Cantarelli, Cinia Mascoli.

THE BEST MAN
UNIVERSAL. Sept., 1999. (Malcolm D. Lee) Taye Diggs, Nia Long, Morris Chestnut, Harold Perrineau, Terrence Howard.

BEST MEN
FILM FOUR DISTRIBUTORS. March, 1998. (Tamra Davis) Dean Cain, Andy Dick, Sean Patrick Flanery, Luke Wilson, Fred Ward.

BEST OF THE BEST 2
20TH CENTURY FOX. March, 1993. (Robert Radler) Eric Roberts, Phillip Ree, Christopher Penn.

BE THERE OR BE SQUARE
BEIJING FORBIDDEN CITY/BEIJING FILM STUDIO. Dec., 1998. Chinese. (Feng Xiaogeng) Ge You, Xu Fan.

BETSY'S WEDDING
BUENA VISTA. June, 1990. (Alan Alda) Alan Alda, Madeline Kahn, Molly Ringwald.

BETTER AND BETTER
BIOGRAPH FILM. Sept., 1996. Swiss. (Alfredo Knuchel) Documentary.

BETTER LIVING
GOLDHEART PICTURES. Nov. 1998. (Max Mayer) Olympia Dukakis, Roy Scheider, Edward Herrmann, Cathrine Corpeny.

BETTER LIVING THROUGH CIRCUITRY
Cleopatra Pictures. Apr. 1999. (Jon Reiss) The Crystal method, Roni Size, DJ Spooky, Electric.

BETTY
MK2. August, 1993. French. (Claude Chabrol) Marie Trintignant, Stephane Audran, Jean-Francois Garreau.

BETWEEN HEAVEN AND EARTH
ARROW. October, 1993. French. (Marion Mansel) Carmen Maura, Jean-Pierre Cassel, Didier Bezace.

BETWEEN THE TEETH
TODO MUNDO. February, 1994. (David Byrne) David Byrne, 10 Car Pile Up.

BETWEEN YOUR LEGS
COLUMBIA TRISTAR. Jan., 1999. Spanish-French. (Manuel Gomez Pereira) Victoria Abril, Javier Bardem, Carmelo Gomez, Juan Diego, Sergio Lopez.

THE BEVERLY HILLBILLIES
20TH CENTURY FOX. October, 1993. (Penelope Spheeris) Jim Varney, Lily Tomlin, Cloris Leachman.

BEVERLY HILLS COP III
PARAMOUNT. May, 1994. (John Landis) Eddie Murphy, Judge Reinhold, Hector Elizondo.

BEWARE OF MY LOVE
REZO FILMS. Aug., 1998. French. (Jeanne Labrune) Nathalie Baye, Daniel Duval, Hubert Saint Macary.

BEYOND BARBED WIRE
TRIBUTE TO FREEDOM. July, 1997. (Steve Rosen) Noriyuki Morita. Documentary.

BEYOND PARADISE
KAMA'AINA FILM PARTNERS. Oct., 1998. (David L. Cunningham) Roy Newton, David Schultz, Lorenzo Callender, Daryl Bonilla.

BEYOND RANGOON
vCOLUMBIA. August, 1995. (John Boorman) Patricia Arquette, Frances McDormand, U Aung Ko.

BEYOND SILENCE
BUENA VISTA INTL. Sept., 1996. German. (Caroline Link) Tatjana Trieb, Sylvie Testud, Howie Seago, Emmanuelle Laborit.

BEYOND THE PALE
CLARKE/ALVINO. July, 1999.George Bazala) Patrick Clarke, Conn Horgan, Beverley Elder, Malachy McCourts.

BHAJI ON THE BEACH
FIRST LOOK. May, 1994. British. (Gurinder Chadha) Kim Vithana, Jimmi Harkishin, Sarita Khajuria.

THE BIBLE AND GUN CLUB
BIG IN VEGAS PICTURES/UMAGUMMA ENTERTAINMENT. Oct., 1996. (Daniel J. Harris) Andy Kallok, Don Yanan, Al Schuermann.

BIG BAD JOHN
MAGNUM ENT. February, 1990. (Burt Kennedy) Jimmy Dean, Jack Elam, Ned Beatty.

THE BIG BANG
TRITON. May, 1990. (James Toback) Emma Astner, Missy Body, Eugene Fodor.

BIG BULLY
WARNER BROS. January, 1996. (Steve Minor) Rich Moranis, Tom Arnold, Julianne Philips, Carol Kane, Don Knotts.

BIG DADDY
SONY. June, 1999. (Dennis Dugan) Adam Sandler, Joey Lauren Adams, Jon Stewart, Cole Sprouse.

THE BIG DIS
OLYMPIA. June, 1990. (Gordon Eriksen, John O'Brien) James Haig, Kevin Haig. B&W.

BIG FEELINGS
FAMA FILM DISTRIBUTION. Aug., 1999. Swiss-Luxembourgeois. (Christof Schertenleib) Anne Weber, Stefan Suske, Manuela Biedermann, Markus Wolff, Delia Mayer.

BIG GIRLS DON'T CRY... THEY GET EVEN
NEW LINE. May, 1992. (Joan Micklin Silver) Hillary Wolf, David Strathairn, Margaret Whitton.

THE BIG GREEN
BUENA VISTA. September, 1995. (Dennis Bishop) Olivia D'Abo, Steve Guttenberg, Jay O. Saunders.

THE BIG HIT
SONY PICTURES ENTERTAINMENT. April, 1998. (Che-Kirk Wong) Mark Wahlberg, Lou Diamond Phillips, Christina Applegate.

THE BIG KAHUNA
LIONS GATE. Sept. 1999. (John Swanbeck) Kevin Spacey, Danny DeVito, Peter Facinelli.

THE BIG LEBOWSKI
GRAMERCY. March, 1998. (Joel Coen) Jeff Bridges, John Goodman, Julianne Moore, Steve Buscemi, Peter Stormare, Flea, Sam Elliott.

THE BIG MAMBO
KINOWELT. Feb., 1998. German. (Michael Gwisdek) Corinna Harfouch, Michael Gwisdek, Juergen Vogel, Uwe Kokisch.

BIG MAN ON CAMPUS
VESTRON. February, 1990. (Jeremy Paul Kagan) Allan Katz, Corey Parker, Cindy Williams.

BIG NIGHT
RYSHER. January, 1996. (Stanley Tucci, Campbell Scott) Minnie Driver, Ianholm, Osabella Rossellini.

THE BIG ONE
MIRAMAX. Sept., 1997. (Michael Moore) Documentary.

THE BIG SQUEEZE
FIRST LOOK PICTURES. June, 1996. (Marcus De Leon) Peter Dobson, Lara Flynn Boyle, Luca Bercovici.

THE BIG TEASE
WARNER BROS. Aug., 1999. (Kevin Allen).Craig Ferguson, Frances Fisher, Chris Langham, Mary McCormack.

BIKER DREAMS
EPICENTER FILMS. Oct., 1997. (Adam Berman) DOCUMENTARY

BIKINI ISLAND
CURB/ESQUIRE. July, 1991. (Anthony Markes) Holly Floria, Alicia Anne.

BILL & TED'S BOGUS JOURNEY
ORION. July, 1991. (Pete Hewitt) Keanu Reeves, Alex Winter, William Sadler.

BILLY BATHGATE
BUENA VISTA. November, 1991. (Robert Benton) Dustin Hoffman, Loren Dean, Nicole Kidman.

BILLY MADISON
UNIVERSAL. February, 1995. (Tamra Davis) Adam Sandler, Darren McGavin, Bridgette Wilson.

BILLY'S HOLLYWOOD SCREEN KISS
REVOLUTIONARY EYE LLC. Jan., 1998. (Tommy O'Haver) Sean P. Hayes, Brad Rowe, Richard Ganoung, Meredith Scott Lynn.

BIMBOLAND
LEGENDE ENTREPRISES/GAUMONT/TF1 FILMS. May, 1999. French. (Ariel Zeitoun) Judith Godreche, Aure Atika, Gerard Depardieu, Sophie Forte, Armelle,.

BINGO
TRISTAR. August, 1991. (Matthew Robbins) Cindy Williams, David Rasche, Robert J. Steinmiller, Jr.

BINGO: THE DOCUMENTARY
JEFFCOAT FILMS. June, 1999. (John Jeffcoat.) Documentary.

BIO DOME
MGM. January, 1996. (Jason Bloom) Pauly Shore, Stephen Baldwin, William Atherton, Joey Adams, Kylie Minogue.

BIRD ON A WIRE
UNIVERSAL. May, 1990. (John Badham) Mel Gibson, Goldie Hawn, David Carradine.

THE BIRD PEOPLE OF CHINA
SEDIC INT'L. April, 1998. Japanese. (Takashi Miike) Masahiro Motoki, Renji Ishibashi, Mako, Wang Li Li.

THE BIRDCAGE
MGM/UA. March, 1996. (Mike Nichols) Robin Williams, Gene Hackman, Nathan Lane, Dianne Wiest, Hank Azaria.

BIRDCAGE INN
BOOGUI CINEMA. Sept. 1998. South Korean. (Kim Ki-deok) Lee Ji-eun, Lee Hye-un.

THE BIRD THAT STOPS IN THE AIR
DONGNYUK FILM. SEPT., 1999. South Korean. (Jeon Soo-il) Sul Kyung-gu, Kim So-hee, Lee Chung-in.

A BIT OF SCARLET
MAYA VISION. Feb., 1997. British. (Andrea Weiss) documentary.

THE BITTER END
JEMPSA ENTERTAINMENT/APOSTLE PICTURES PROD. Jan., 1997. (Juan Jose Campanella) Denis Leary, Aitana Sanchez Gijon.

BITTER MOON
FINE LINE. March, 1994. French-British. (Roman Polanski) Peter Coyote, Emmanuelle Seigner, Hugh Grant.

BITTER SUGAR (AZUCAR AMARGA)
AZUCAR FILMS. February, 1996. (Leon Ichaso) Rene Lavan. Mayte Vilan, Miguel Guttierez.

BLACK & WHITE: A LOVE STORY
A WOMAN UNDER THE INFLUENCE PRODS. February, 1996. (Susanna Lo) Katherine Donahue, Kenny Ranson.

BLACK & WHITE & RED ALL OVER
CABALLEROS. Jan., 1997. (DeMane Davis) Thomas Braxton Jr., Lord Harrison, MyQuan, Damian, Rob Florestal, Naomi Ramsey.

BLACK ANGEL VOL. 2
SHOCHIKU. Feb., 1999. Japanese. (Takashi Ishii) Yuki Amami, Takeshi Yamato, Reiko Kataoka, Yozaburo Ito, Daisuku Iijima.

BLACK BEAUTY
WARNER BROS. July, 1994. (Caroline Thompson) Sean Bean, David Thewlis, Andrew Knott.

BLACK CAT
HEADLINER. October, 1993. Hong Kong. (Stephen Shin) Jade Leung, Simon Yam, Thomas Lam.

BLACK CAT, WHITE CAT
OCTOBER FILMS/GOLDWYN FILMS. Sept., 1998. French-German-Yugoslav. (Emir Kusturica) Bajram Severdzan, Florijan Ajdini.

BLACK CIRCLE BOYS
LYSA HAYLAND. Jan., 1997. (Matthew Carnahan) Scott Bairstow, Eric Mabius, Heath Lourwood, Chad Lindberg, Tara Subkoff.

BLACK DAY BLUE NIGHT
CAPELLA INTERNATIONAL. November, 1995. (J.S. Cardone) Gil Bellows, Michelle Forbes, Mia Sara, J.T. Walsh.

BLACK DIAMOND RUSH
WARREN MILLER ENT. October, 1993. (Kurt Miller, Peter Speek) Documentary.

BLACK DOG
UNIVERSAL. April, 1998. (Kevin Hooks), Patrick Swayze, Meat Loaf, Randy Travis, Gabriel Casseus, Brian Vincent, Brenda Strong.

BLACK IS . . . BLACK AIN'T
TARA. October, 1995 (Marlon Riggs) Angela Davis, Bell Hooks, Barabara Smith, Cornel West.

BLACK LIZARD
CINEVISTA. September, 1991; originally released 1968. Japanese. (Kinji Fukasaku) Akihiro Maruyama, Isao Kimura.

BLACK OUT
PAUSILYPON FILMS/MACT PRODS./ ANIMATOGRAFO PRODUCAO DES FILMES. Nov., 1998. Greek-French-Portuguese. (Menelaos Karamaghiolis) Alkis Kourkoulos, Myrto Alikaki, Cleon Grigoriadis, Hanna Schygulla, Karyofilia Karabeti.

BLACK RAIN
ANGELIKA. February 1990. Japanese. (Shohei Imamura) Yoshiko Tanaka, Kazuo Kitmamura.

BLACK ROBE
SAMUEL GOLDWYN. October, 1991. Canadian-Australian. (Bruce Beresford) Lothaire Bluteau, Aden Young, Sandrine Holt.

BLACK SHEEP
PARAMOUNT. February, 1996. (Penelope Spheeris) Chris Farley, David Spade, Tim Mattheson, Christine Ebersole.

THE BLACKSHEEP AFFAIR
EASTERN FILM CO. Aug., 1998. Hong Kong. (Allun Lam) Zhao Wenzhuo, Shu Qi, Andrew Lin, Ken Wong, Kent Tseng.

BLACK TEARS
RYNIKS FILMS BV. April, 1998. Dutch. (Sonia Herman Dolz) La Vieja Trova Santiaguera.

BLACK TEARS
ALTA FILMS. Nov., 1998. Spanish. (Ricardo Franco) Ariadne Gil, Fele Martinez, Ana Risueno, Elena Anaya, Elvira Minguez.

THE BLACKOUT
MDP WORLDWIDE. May, 1997. (Abel Ferrara) Matthew Modine, Dennis Hopper, Claudia Schiffer, Beatrice Dalle, Sarah Lassez.

BLACKROCK
POLYGRAM FILMED ENTERTAINMENT. Jan., 1997. Australian. (Steve Vidler) Laurence Breuls, Linda Cropper, Simon Lyndon.

BLACKS AND JEWS
SNITOW-KAUFMAN. Jan., 1997. (Alan Snitow) Documentary. B&W/Color.

BLADE
NEW LINE CINEMA. Aug., 1998. (Stephen Norrington) Wesley Snipes, Stephen Dorff, Kris Kristofferson, N'Bushe Wright.

THE BLAIR WITCH PROJECT
ARTISAN. Jan., 1999. (Daniel Myrick, Eduardo Sanchez) Heather Donahue, Michael Williams, Joshua Leonard, Sandra Sanchez.

BLAME IT ON THE BELLBOY
BUENA VISTA. March, 1992. British. (Mark Herman) Dudley Moore, Bryan Brown, Patsy Kensit.

BLANK CHECK
BUENA VISTA. February, 1994. (Rupert Wainwright) Brian Bonsall, Karen Duffy, Miguel Ferrer.

BLANKMAN
COLUMBIA. August, 1994. (Mike Binder) Damon Wayans, David Alan Grier, Robin Givens.

BLAST 'EM
SILENT FICTION FILMS. July, 1992. Canadian. (Joseph Blasioli) Documentary.

BLAST FROM THE PAST
NEW LINE. Feb. 1999. (Hugh Wilson) Brendan Fraser, Alicia Silverstone, Christopher Walken Sissy Spacek.

BLEEDER
SCANBOX ENTERTAINMENT. May, 1999. Danish. (Nicolas Winding) Kim Bodnia, Mads Mikkelsen, Rikke Louise Andersson, Liv Corfixen, Levino Jensen.

BLESSED ARE THOSE WHO THIRST
NORDIC SCREEN PROD. Aug., 1998. Norwegian. (Carl Jorgen Kionig) Kjersti Elvik, Lasse Kolsrud, Anne Ryg, Bjorn Sundquist, Nils Ole Oftebro.

BLESSING
STARR VALLEY. April, 1995. (Paul Zehrer) Melora Griffis, Carlin Glynn, Guy Griffis.

BLIND DATE
SHOOTING STAR FILM DIST. Sept., 1996. Dutch. (Theo Van Gogh) Renee Fokker, Peer Mascini, Roeland Fernhout.

BLINDFOLDED
DADA/FILMI OY. May, 1999. Finnish. (Matti Ijas) Martti Suosalo, Walter Grohn, Mikko Vanhala, Turo Rannema.

BLIND FURY
TRISTAR. March, 1990. (Phillip Noyce) Rutger Hauer, Brandon Call, Terry O'Quinn.

THE BLIND MAN WHO SHOUTED LIGHT
SOLUTIONS PRODUCAO & COMUNICACAO. Feb., 1997. Brazilian. (Joao Batista de Andrade) Tonico Pereira, Roberto Bontempo.

BLINDED
ARABA FILMS. July, 1997. Spanish. (Daniel Calparsoro) Najwa Nimri, Alfredo Villa, Ramon Barea, Javier Nogueiras, Elena Irureta.

BLINDNESS
PARK AVENUE. Aug., 1998. (Anna Chi) Vivian Wu, Joe Lando, Lisa Lu, Chin Han.

BLINK
NEW LINE. January, 1994. (Michael Apted) Madeleine Stowe, Aidan Quinn, Laurie Metcalf.

BLISS
SONY PICTURES ENTERTAINMENT. April, 1997. (Lance Young), Craig Sheffer, Sheryl Lee, Terence Stamp, Casey Siemaszko.

BLOOD & CONCRETE
I.R.S. September, 1991. (Jeffrey Reiner) Billy Zane, Jennifer Beals, Darren McGavin.

BLOOD AND WINE
FOX SEARCHLIGHT. September, 1996. (Bob Rafelson) Jack Nicholson, Stephen Dorff, Jennifer Lopez.

BLOOD, GUTS, BULLETS & OCTANE
LIONS GATE. Jan., 1998. (Joe Carnahan), Dan Leis, Joe Carnahan, Dan Harlan, Ken Rudulph, Hugh McCord, Mark S. Allen.

BLOOD IN THE FACE
FIRST RUN FEATURES. February, 1991. (Anne Bohlen, Kevin Rafferty, James Ridgeway) Documentary.

THE BLOOD OF HEROES
NEW LINE. February, 1990. (David Peoples) Rutger Hauer, Joan Chen.

THE BLOOD ORANGES
TRIMARK PICTURES. Sept., 1997. (Philip Haas), Charles Dance, Colin Lane, Sheryl Lee, Laila Robins, Rachel Bella, Aida Lopez.

BLOOD SALVAGE
PARAGON ARTS. May, 1990. (Tucker Johnston) Danny Nelson, Lori Birdsong, John Saxon.

BLOODFIST II
CONCORDE. October, 1990. (Andy Blumenthal) Don Wilson, Rina

BLOODFIST III: FORCED TO FIGHT
CONCORDE. January, 1992. (Francis Sassone) Don "The Dragon" Wilson, Richard Roundtree, Gregory McKinney.

BLOODY ANGELS
UNITED MEDIA. May, 1999. Norwegian. (Karin Julsrud) Reidar Sorensen, Gaute Skjegstad, Trond Hovik, Laila Goody.
Reyes.

BLOSSI/810551
ICELANDIC FILM CO. May, 1998. Icelandic-Danish. (Julius Kemp) Pall Banine, Thora Dungal, Finnur Johannsson.

BLOSSOM TIME
POSSUMTOWN PICTURES. Jan., 1997. (David Orr) Laurel Holloman, Greg Farnese, Paul Daniel Gavin, Anthony Gavin.

B. LOVE: COLDER THAN DEATH
SCARABEE FILMS. March, 1996. French-Turkish-Swiss. (Canan Gerede) Bennu Gerede, Kadir Inanir.

BLOWBACK
NORTHERN ARTS. August, 1991. (Marc Levin) Bruce McCarty, Jane Hamper, Eddie Figueroa.

BLOWN AWAY
MGM. July, 1994. (Stephen Hopkins) Jeff Bridges, Tommy Lee Jones, Lloyd Bridges.

BLUE
MIRAMAX. December, 1993. Polish-French. (Krzyzstof Kieslowksi) Juliette Binoche, Benoit Regent.

BLUE
ZEITGEIST. April, 1994. British. (Derek Jarman) John Quentin, Nigel Terry, Tilda Swinton.

BLUE CHIPS
PARAMOUNT. February, 1994. (William Friedkin) Nick Nolte, Mary McDonnell, Shaquile O'Neal.

BLUE FISH
TONPU CO., LTD. Feb., 1998. Japanese. (Yosuke Nagagawa) Mari Ouchi, Keigo Heshiki, Yoshino Tamaki.

BLUE IN THE FACE
MIRAMAX. November, 1995. (Wayne Wang, Paul Auster) Harvey Keitel, Victor Argo, Giancarlo Esposito.

THE BLUE KITE
KINO. April, 1994. Dutch-Hong Kong. (Tian Zhuangzhuang) Zhang Wenyo, Chen Xiaoman, Lu Liping.

THE BLUE MONK
ZENTROPA ENTERTAINMENTS/KOLLEKTIV FILM. Feb., 1999. Danish. (Christian Braad Thomsen) Helle Ryslinge, Ole Meyer, Bent Conradi, Claus Nissen, Jarl Forsmann.

BLUE MOON
BLUE MOON FILMS. Nov,. 1998. Taiwanese. (Ko Yi-cheng) Tarcy Su, Leon Dai, David Wang, Chang Han, Teddy Lo.

BLUE MOUNTAIN
BOA FILMPRODUKTION. Jan., 1997. Swiss. (Thomas Tanner) Chandra Gotz, Eva Scheurer, Wolf Hofer, Sabrina Luthi.

BLUE SKY
ORION. September, 1994. (Tony Richardson) Jessica Lange, Tommy Lee Jones, Powers Boothe, Amy Locane.

BLUE STEEL
MGM/UA. March, 1990. (Kathryn Bigelow) Jamie Lee Curtis, Ron Silver, Clancy Brown.

THE BLUE VILLA
NOMAD. September, 1995. Belgian. (Alain Robbe Grillet) Fred Ward, Arielle Dombasle, Charles Tordjman.

BLUES BROTHERS 2000
UNIVERSAL. Feb., 1998. (John Landis) Dan Aykroyd, John Goodman, Joe Morton, J. Evan Bonifant, Nia Peeples, Kathleen Freeman.

B. MONKEY
BUENA VISTA INTL./MIRAMAX. Nov., 1998. British-U.S. (Michael Radford) Asia Argento, Jared Harris, Rupert Everett, Jonathan Rhys Meyers.

BO A BU
HORUS & BASTET. Nov. 1998. Italian-French-Uzbeck. (Ali Khamraev) Arielle Dombasle, Abdrashid Abdrakhmanov, Djavakhir ZaKhirov.

BOATMAN
SINEVIZYON FILM/MARATHON FILMS, HYPERION PRODS./ADELA MEDIA. Apr., 1999. Turkish-Greek-Bulgarian. (Biket Ilhan) Memet Ali Alabora, Katerina Mousatsos, Mustafa Avkran, Elina Phillippa.

BOBBY G. CAN'T SWIM
CINEBLAST!. Mar., 1999. (John-Luke Montias) John-Luke Montias, Susan Mitchell, Vincent Vega, Norman Milton.

BOB ROBERTS
PARAMOUNT. September, 1992. (Tim Robbins) Tim Robbins, Giancarlo Esposito, Ray Wise, Gore Vidal.

BOCAGE, THE TRIUMPH OF LOVE
Cinema do Seculo XXI. Jan., 1998. Brazilian. (Djalma Limongi Batista) Victor Wagner, Francisco Farinelli, Vietia Rocha, Majo de Castro.

BODIES, REST & MOTION
FINE LINE. April, 1993. (Michael Steinberg) Phoebe Cates, Eric Stoltz, Bridget Fonda.

BODY CHEMISTRY
CONCORDE. March, 1990. (Kristine Peterson) Marc Singer, Lisa Pescia, Mary Crosby.

BODY COUNT
POLYGRAM. April, 1998. (Robert Patton-Spruill), David Caruso, Linda Fiorentino, John Leguizamo, Ving Rhames, Donnie Wahlberg.

BODY OF EVIDENCE
MGM. January, 1993. (Uli Edel) Madonna, Willem Dafoe, Joe Mantegna, Anne Archer.

BODY PARTS
PARAMOUNT. August, 1991. (Eric Red) Jeff Fahey, Lindsay Duncan, Brad Dourif.

BODY SNATCHERS
WARNER BROS. January, 1994. (Abel Ferrara) Gabrielle Anwar, Terry Kinney, Meg Tilly, Billy Wirth.

BODY WITHOUT SOUL
MIROFILM. June, 1996. Czech. (Wiktor Grodecki) Documentary.

THE BODYGUARD
WARNER BROS. November, 1992. (Mick Jackson) Kevin Costner, Whitney Houston, Gary Kemp.

BOGUS
WARNER BROS. August, 1996. (Norman Jewison) Whoopi Goldberg, Gerard Depardieu, Haley Joel, Osmet Denis.

BOMBAY BOYS
KISMET TALKIES. Sept., 1998. Indian. (Kaizad Gustad) Naveen Andrews, Rahul Bose,Alexander Giffor, Naseeruddin Shah.

THE BONE COLLECTOR
UNIVERSAL. Aug., 1999. (Phillip Noyce) Denzel Washington, Angelina Jolie, Queen Latifah, Michael Rooker.

BOOGIE NIGHTS
NEW LINE. September, 1997. (Paul Thomas Anderson), Mark Wahlberg, Burt Reynolds, Julianne Moore, John C. Reilly, Heather Graham.

THE BOOK OF LIFE
COLLECTION 2000. May, 1998. French. (Hal Hartley) Martin Donovan, P. J. Harvey, Thomas Jay Ryan, Dave Simonds.

BOOTLEG FILM
MONKEY TOWN PRODS. May, 1999. Japanese. (Masahiro Kobayashi) Akira Emoto, Kippei Shiina, Maika, Wakaba Nakano.

BOOTY CALL
SONY PICTURES ENTERTAINMENT. February, 1997. (Jeff Pollack), Jamie Foxx, Tommy Davidson, Vivica A. Fox, Tamala Jones.

BOTTLE ROCKET
SONY PICTURES. February, 1996. (Wes Anderson) Owen, C. Wilson, Luk Wilson, Robert Musgrave, Andrew Wilson.

THE BONFIRE OF THE VANITIES
WARNER BROS. December, 1990. (Brian DePalma) Tom Hanks, Bruce Willis, Melanie Griffith.

BONGWATER
ALLIANCE INDEPENDENT FILMS. April, 1998. (Richard Sears) Luke Wilson, Alicia Witt, Amy Locane, Andy Dick, Jeremy Sistos.

BOOK OF DAYS
STUTZ CO. February, 1990. (Meredith Monk) Gerd Wameling, Lucas Hoving.

BOOK OF LOVE
NEW LINE. February, 1991. (Robert Shaye) Chris Young, Keith Coogan, John Cameron Mitchell.

BOOMERANG
PARAMOUNT. July, 1992. (Reginald Hudlin) Eddie Murphy, Robin Givens, Halle Berry.

BOPHA!
PARAMOUNT. September, 1993. (Morgan Freeman) Danny Glover, Malcolm McDowell, Alfre Woodard.

BORN TO BE WILD
WARNER BROS. March, 1995. (John Gray) Will Horneff, Helen Shaver, Peter Boyle.

BORN TO RIDE
WARNER BROS. May, 1991. (Graham Baker) John Stamos, John Stockwell, Teri Polo.

BORN YESTERDAY
BUENA VISTA. March, 1993. (Luis Mandoki) Melanie Griffith, John Goodman, Don Johnson.

THE BORROWER
CANNON. August, 1991. (John McNaughton) Tom Towles, Rae Dawn Chong, Antonio Fargas.

BOSNA!
ZEITGEIST. November, 1994. Bosnian-French. (Bernard Henri Levy, Alain Ferrari) Documentary.

BOUND
GRAMERCY. October, 1996. (Larry and Andy Wachowski) Jennifer Tilly, Gina Gershon, Joe Pantoliano.

BOUND & GAGGED: A LOVE STORY
NORTHERN ARTS. October, 1993. (Daniel Appleby) Ginger Lynn Allen, Chris Denton, Elizabeth Saltarrelli.

BOUND BY HONOR (BLOOD IN, BLOOD OUT)
BUENA VISTA. January, 1993. (Taylor Hackford) Damian Chapa, Jesse Borrego, Benjamin Bratt.

BOWFINGER
UNIVERSAL. Aug., 1999. (Frank Oz) Steve Martin, Eddie Murphy, Heather Graham, Christine Baranski.

BOX OF MOONLIGHT
LARGO ENTERTAINMENT. August, 1996. (Tom DiCillo) John Turturro, Sam Rockwell, Catherine Keeler.

THE BOXER
UNIVERSAL. JAN., 1998. (Jim Sheridan) Daniel Day-Lewis, Emily Watson, Brian Cox, Ken Stott, Gerard McSorley, Eleanor Methven.

BOXING HELENA
ORION CLASSICS. September, 1993. (Jennifer Lynch) Julian Sands, Sherilyn Fenn, Bill Paxton.

THE BOY FROM MERCURY
LE STUDIO CANAL PLUS. June, 1996. Irish-French-British. (Martin Duffy) James Hickey, Rita Tushingham.

THE BOY WHO CRIED BITCH
PILGRIMS 3 CORP. October, 1991. (Juan Jose Campanella) Harley Cross, Karen Young, Jesse Bradford.

BOYS
BUENA VISTA. May, 1996. (Stacy Cochran) Winona Ryder, Lukas Haas, Skeet Ulrich, John C. Reilly, Bill Sage.

THE BOYS (LES BOYS)
MELENNY PRODS. Dec., 1997. Canadian. (Louis Saia) Marc Messier, Remy Girard, Patrick Huard, Serge Theriault.

THE BOYS
GLOBE FILMS. Feb., 1998. Australian. (Rowan Woods) David Wenham, Toni Collette, Lynette Corran, John Poison, Anthony Hayes.

THE BOYS II
LIONS GATE. Dec., 1998. Canadian. (Louis Saia) Marc Messier, Remy Girard, Patrick Huard, Serge Theriault, Paul Houde.

THE BOYS CLUB
LE MONDE ENTERTAINMENT. May, 1996. Canadian. (John Fawcett) Chris Penn, Dominic Amprogna, Devon Sawa.

BOYS LIFE
STRAND. September, 1994. (Brian Sloan, Raoul O'Connell, Robert Lee King) Josh Weinstein, Raoul O'Connell.

BOYS LIFE 2
STRAND. March, 1997. (Various directors) Michael Saucedo, Vincent D'Onofrio, Mary Beth Hurt, Brett Barsky.

BOYS DON'T CRY
FOX SEARCHLIGHT. Aug., 1999. (Kimberly Peirce) Hilary Swank, Chloe Sevigny, Peter Sarsgaard, Brendan Sexton III.

THE BOYS OF ST. VINCENT'S
ALLIANCE. June, 1994. Canadian. (John N. Smith) Henry Czerny, John Morina, Sebastian Spence.

BOYS ON THE SIDE
WARNER BROS. February, 1995. (Herbert Ross) Whoopi Goldberg, Mary Louise Parker, Drew Barrymore.

BOYZ N THE HOOD
COLUMBIA. July, 1991. (John Singleton) Cuba Gooding, Jr., Ice Cube, Laurence Fishburne.

THE BRADY BUNCH MOVIE
PARAMOUNT. February, 1995. (Betty Thomas) Shelley Long, Gary Cole, Michael McKean, Christine Taylor.

BRAIN DONORS
PARAMOUNT. April, 1992. (Dennis Dugan) John Turturro, Mel Smith, Bob Nelson.

BRAIN DRAIN
FERNANDO MUSA PRODUCCIONES. Sept., 1998. Argentine. (Fernando Musa) Nicolas Cabre, Luis Quiroz, Roberto Carnaghi, Enrique Liporace.

BRAINSCAN
TRIUMPH. April, 1994. (John Flynn) Edward Furlong, T. Ryder Smith, Frank Langella.

BRAKHAGE
ZEITGEIST. Jan. 1999. (Jim Shedden) Documentary.

BRAM STOKER'S DRACULA
COLUMBIA. November, 1992. (Francis Ford Coppola) Gary Oldman, Winona Ryder, Anthony Hopkins, Keanu Reeves.

THE BRANCHES OF THE TREE
ERATO FILMS. April, 1992. Indian-French. (Satyajit Ray) Ajit Benerjee, Maradan Benerjee, Soumitra Chatterjee.

THE BRANDON TEENA STORY
BLESS BLESS PRODS. Feb., 1998. (Susan Muska, Greta Olafsdottir) DOCUMENTARY.

BRASSED OFF
FILM FOUR DISTRIBUTORS. Oct., 1996. British. (Mark Herman) Pete Postlethwaite, Tara Fitzgerald, Ewan McGregor, Jim Carter.

THE BRAVE
MAJESTIC FILMS & JEREMY THOMAS. May, 1997. (Johnny Depp) Johnny Depp, Marlon Brando, Marshall Bell, Elipida Carillo.

BRAVEHEART
PARAMOUNT. May, 1995. (Mel Gibson) Mel Gibson, Sophie Marceau, Patrick McGoohan, James Cosmo.

THE BREAK
TRIMARK. September, 1995. (Lee H. Katzin) Vince Van Patten, Martin Sheen, Ben Jorgensen.

BREAK EVEN
DEUTSCHEN FILM AND FERNSEHAKADEMIE BERLIN. Sept., 1998. German. (Eoin Moore) Andreas Schmidt, Tamara Simunovic.

BREAKDOWN
PARAMOUNT. April, 1997. (Jonathan Mostow), Kurt Russell, J.T. Walsh, Kathleen Quinlan, M.C. Gainey, Jack Noseworthy, Rex Linn.

BREAKING OUT
SONET FILMS . Feb., 1999. Swedish. (Daniel Lind Lagerlof) Bjorn Kjellman, Peter Haber, Viveca Seldahl, Thomas Hanzon.

BREAKING THE RULES
MIRAMAX. October, 1992. (Neal Israel) Jason Bateman, C. Thomas Howell, Jonathan Silverman.

BREAKING UP
WARNER BROS. June, 1997. (Robert Greenwald), Russell Crowe, Salma Hayek.

A BREATH OF LIFE
SURF FILM. January, 1993. Italian. (Beppe Cino) Franco Nero, Vanessa Redgrave, Lucrezia Lante Della Rovere.

BREATHING ROOM
ARROW RELEASING. Oct., 1996. (Jon Sherman) Susan Floyd, Dan Futterman, David Thornton, Amy Hohn, Rod McLachlan.

BRENDA STARR
TRIUMPH. April, 1992. (Robert Ellis Miller) Brooke Shields, Timothy Dalton, Tony Peck.

BRIDE OF CHUCKY
UNIVERSAL. Oct., 1999. (Ronnie Yu) Jennifer Tilly, Katherine Heigl, Nick Stabile, John Ritter.

BRIDE OF RE-ANIMATOR
50TH ST. FILMS. February, 1991. (Brian Yuzna) Jeffrey Combs, Bruce Abbott, Kathleen Kinmont.

THE BRIDE'S JOURNEY
CECCHI GORI DISTRIBUZIONE. Aug., 1997. Italian. (Sergio Rubini) Sergio Rubini, Giovanna Mezzogiorno, Umberto Orsini.

A BRIDGE BETWEEN TWO SHORES
AMLF. Apr., 1999. French. (Gerard Depardieu, Frederic Auburtin) Carole Bouquet, Gerard Depardieu, Charles Berling, Stanislas Crevillen, Dominique Reymond.

THE BRIDGES OF MADISON COUNTY
WARNER BROS. June, 1995. (Clint Eastwood) Clint Eastwood, Meryl Streep, Annie Corley, Victor Slezak.

A BRIEF HISTORY OF TIME
TRITON. August, 1992. British. (Errol Morris) Stephen Hawking.

BRIGHT ANGEL
HEMDALE. June, 1991. (Michael Fields) Dermot Mulroney, Lili Taylor, Sam Shepard.

BRILLIANT LIES
VILLAGE ROADSHOW. April, 1996. Australian. (Richard Franklin) Gia Carides, Anthony LaPaglia, Zoe Carides.

BROADWAY DAMAGE
VILLAGE ART PICTURES. June, 1997. (Victor Mignatti) Mara Hobel, Michael Shawn Lucas, Hugh Panaro, Aaron Williams, Gary Janetti.

BROKEDOWN PALACE
20TH CENTURY FOX. Aug., 1999. (Jonathan Kaplan) Claire Danes, Kate Beckinsale, Bill Pullman, Jacqueline Kim.

BROKEN ARROW
20TH CENTURY FOX. February, 1996. (John Woo) Christian Slater, John Travolta, Samantha Mathis, Delroy Lindo.

BROKEN BRIDGES
ARAZ GOLDEN GATE. Jan., 1999. Azerbaijani-U.S. (Rafigh Pooya) Peter Reckell, Rebeccah Bush, Behrouz Vossoughi, Fatima Ibragimbekov.

BROKEN ENGLISH
SONY PICTURES CLASSICS. August, 1996. New Zealand. (Gregor Nicholas) Aleksandra Vujcic, Julian Arahanga.

THE BROKEN JOURNEY
FILMHAUS. May, 1995. Indian. (Satyajit Ray) Soumitra Chatterji, Sadhu Meher, Subhalakshmi Munshi.

BROKEN VESSELS
ZIEHL AND ZAL. April, 1998. (Scott Ziehl) Todd Field, Jason London, Roxana Zal, Susan Traylor, James Hong, Patrick Cranshaw.

A BRONX TALE
SAVOY. September, 1993. (Robert De Niro) Robert De Niro, Chazz Palminteri, Lilo Brancato.

A BROOKLYN STATE OF MIND
NORSTAR ENTERTAINMENT. May, 1997. Canadian. (Frank Rainone) Vincent Spano, Maria Grazia Cucinotta, Danny Aiello.

A BROTHER
PERSONA FILMS. May, 1997. French. (Sylvie Verheyde) Jeannick Gravelines, Emma De Caunes, Nils Tavernier, Karole Rocher, Emmanuel Nicolas.

BROTHER
STW FILM CO./ROSKOMKINO. May, 1997. Russian. (Alexei Balabanov) Sergei Bodrov, Viktor Sukhoroukov.

BROTHER MINISTER: THE ASSASSINATION OF MALCOLM X
X-CEPTIONAL PRODS. January, 1995. (Jack Baxter, Jefri Almuhammed) Documentary.

BROTHER OF SLEEP
SONY PICTURES CLASSICS. October, 1996. Austrian. (Joseph Vilsmaier) Andre Eisermann, Dana Vavrova.

BROTHER'S KEEPER
CREATIVE THINKING. September, 1992. (Joe Berlinger, Bruce Sinofsky) Documentary.

A BROTHER'S KISS
FIRST LOOK PICTURES. July, 1997. (Seth Zvi Rosenfeld) Nick Chinlund, Michael Raynor, Cathy Moriarty, Rosie Perez.

THE BROTHERS MCMULLEN
20TH CENTURY FOX. August, 1995. Irish. (Edward Burns) Edward Burns, Mike McGlone, Jack Mulcahy.

THE BROWNING VERSION
PARAMOUNT. October, 1994. (Mike Figgis) Albert Finney, Greta Scacchi, Matthew Modine, Julian Sands.

BROWN'S REQUIEM
J&T PRODS. Nov., 1998. (Jason Freeland) Michael Rooker, Tobin Bell, Selma Blair, Jack Conley, Kevin Corrigan.

BRUNO'S WAITING IN THE CAR
ITALIAN INTL. FILM. April, 1996. Italian. (Duccio Camerini) Nancy Brilli, Antonello Fassari, Leo Gullotta.

BRUTE
BOJE BUCK FILM/DOUEK PRODS. Feb., 1998. Polish. (Maciej Dejczer) Wojciech Brzezinski, John Hurt, Ida Jablonska.

THE BRYLCREEM BOYS
ROUGH MAGIC FILMS. Nov., 1996. British. (Terence Ryan) Bill Campbell, William McNamara, Angus Macfadyen, Gabriel Byrne.

BUCKMINSTER FULLER: THINKING OUT LOUD
SIMON & GOODMAN PICTURE CO. January, 1996. (Karen Goodman, Kirk Simon) Documentary. Color/B&W.

BUDDY
SONY PICTURES ENTERTAINMENT. May, 1997. (Caroline Thompson), Rene Russo, Robbie Coltrane, Alan Cumming, Irma P. Hall.

BUENAS AIRES VICE VERSA
MGI INTL. May, 1996. Argentine-Dutch. (Alejandro Agresti) Vera Fogwill, Fernan Miras, Mirta Busnelli.

BUENA VISTA SOCIAL CLUB
ROAD MOVIES FILMPRODUKTION. Feb., 1999. German-U.S. (Wim Wenders) Ry Cooder, Compay Segundo, Ruben Gonzalez, Ibrahim Ferrer, Eliades Ochoa.

BUFFALO 66
LIONS GATE FILMS/CINEPIX. Jan., 1998. (Vincent Gallo) Vincent Gallo, Christina Ricci, Anjelica Huston, Ben Gazzara, Mickey Rourke, Rosanna Arquette.

BUFFY THE VAMPIRE SLAYER
20TH CENTURY FOX. July, 1992. (Fran Rubel Kazui) Kristy Swanson, Donald Sutherland, Luke Perry.

A BUG'S LIFE
BUENA VISTA. Oct., 1998. (John Lasseter) Animated.

BUGSY
TRISTAR. December, 1991. (Barry Levinson) Warren Beatty, Annette Bening, Harvey Keitel, Ben Kingsley.

BULLET BALLET
KAIJYU THEATER CO. Sept., 1998. Japanese. (Shinya Tsukamoto) Shinya Tsukamoto, Kirina Mano, Tatsuya Nakamura, Takahiro Murase.

BULLET ON A WIRE
PROVISIONAL. Nov., 1998. (Jim Sikora) Jeff Strong, Lara Phillips, David Yow, Paula Killen, Richard Kern.

BULLETPROOF
UNIVERSAL. August, 1996. (Ernest Dickerson) Damon Wayans, Adam Sandler, James Caan, Kristen Wilson.

BULLETPROOF HEART
KEYSTONE. March, 1995. (Mark Malone) Mimi Rogers, Anthony LaPaglia, Peter Boyle.

BULLETS OVER BROADWAY
MIRAMAX. October, 1994. (Woody Allen) John Cusack, Dianne Wiest, Chazz Palminteri, Jennifer Tilly.

BULWORTH
20TH CENTURY FOX. May, 1998. (Warren Beatty) Warren Beatty, Halle Berry, Don Cheadle, Oliver Platt, Paul Sorvino, Jack Warden.

THE BUMBLEBEE FLIES ANYWAY
SHOOTING GALLERY/HAFT ENTERTAINMENT. Sept., 1999. (Martin Duffy) Elijah Wood, Janeane Garofalo, Rachel Leigh Cook, Roger Rees.

BURN, HOLLYWOOD, BURN
BUENA VISTA. Sept., 1997. (Alan Smithee) Ryan O'Neal, Coolio, Chuck D., Richard Jeni, Eric Idle, Leslie Stefanson, Sandra Bernhard.

THE BURNING SNAIL
JOST HERING FILMPRODUKTION. Jan., 1997. German. (Thomas Stiller) Max Haas, Barbara Auer, Sebastian Koch, Tobias Nath.

BURNT BY THE SUN
SONY PICTRUES CLASSICS. April, 1995. Russian-French. (Nikita Mikhalkov) Nikita Mikhalkov, Ingeborga Dapkounaite.

BURNT EDEN
LES PRODS. JEUX D'OMBRES. June, 1997. Canadian. (Eugene Garcia) Romano Orzari, Marisa Malone, Documentary.

BURY ME IN KERN COUNTY
KRANK. Aug., 1998. (Julien Nitzberg), Mary Sheridan, Judson Mills, Mary Lynn Rajskub, Johnny Strong, Thom Rachford, Sandra Tucker.

BUSHWHACKED
20TH CENTURY FOX. August, 1995. (Greg Beeman) Daniel Stern, Jon Polito, Brad Sullivan, Ann Dowd.

A BUSINESS AFFAIR
CASTLE HILL. December, 1995. (Charlotte Brandstrom) Christopher Walken, Carole Bouquet, Jonathan Pryce.

THE BUTCHER BOY
WARNER BROS. July, 1997. (Neil Jordan), Eamonn Owens, Alan Boyle, Stephen Rea, Fiona Shaw, Andrew Fullerton.

THE BUTCHER'S WIFE
PARAMOUNT. October, 1991. (Terry Hughes) Demi Moore, Jeff Daniels, George Dzundza.

BUT I'M A CHEERLEADER
FINE LINE. Sept., 1999. (Jamie Babbit) Natasha Lyonne, Cathy Moriarty, Bud Cort, Mink Stole, Ru Paul Charles.

BUT FOREVER IN MY MIND
MIKADO. Aug., 1999. Italian. (Gabriele Muccino) Silvio Muccino, Giuseppe Sanfelice di Monteforte, Giula Steigerwalt, Giulia Carmignani.

THE BUTTERFLY EFFECT
UIP. January, 1996. Spanish-French. (Fernando Colomo) Maria Barranco, Coque Malla, James Fleet.

BUTTERSCOTCH AND CHOCOLATE
LANG & ASSOCS. October, 1992. (Nate Grant) Rickey Hendon.

BUUD YAM
CINECOM/CAROLINE. May, 1997. Burkina Faso. (Gastin Jean-Marie Kabore) Serge Yanogo, Amssatou Maiga, Severine Oueddouda.

BWANA
AURUM PRODUCCIONES. Sept., 1996. Spanish. (Imanol Uribe) Andres Pajares, Maria Barranco, Emilio Buale.

BY THE DAWN'S EARLY LIGHT
DANISH FILM INSTITUTE WORKSHOP. June, 1996. Danish. (Knud Vesterkov) Documentary.

BY THE SWORD
MOVIE GROUP. May, 1993. (Jeremy Kagan) F. Murray Abraham, Eric Roberts, Mia Sara.

BYE BYE LOVE
20TH CENTURY FOX. March, 1995. (Sam Weisman) Matthew Modine, Paul Reiser, Randy Quaid.

C

CB4
UNIVERSAL. March, 1993. (Tamra Davis) Chris Rock, Allen Payne, Deezer D., Chris Elliott.

CABEZA DE VACA
CONCORDE. May, 1992. Mexican-Spanish. (Nicolas Eshevarria) Juan Diego, Daniel Gimenez Cacho.

CABIN BOY
BUENA VISTA. January, 1994. (Adam Resnick) Chris Elliott, James Gammon, Brian Doyle-Murray.

THE CABLE GUY
SONY PICTURES. June, 1996. (Ben Stiller) Jim Carrey, Matthew Broderick., Leslie Mann, Jack Black, George Segal.

CADENCE
NEW LINE. January, 1991. (Martin Sheen) Charlie Sheen, Martin Sheen, Laurence Fishburne.

CADILLAC MAN
ORION. May, 1990. (Roger Donaldson) Robin Williams, Tim Robbins, Pamela Reed.

CADILLAC RANCH
DAVIS ENTERTAINMENT. January, 1996. (Lisa Gottlieb) Renee Humphrey, Christopher Lloyd.

CAFE AU LAIT
NEW YORKER. August, 1994. French. (Mathieu Kassovitz) Julie Mauduech, Hubert Kounde, Mathieu Kassovitz.

CAGE/CUNNINGHAM
CUNNINGHAM DANCE FOUNDATION. December, 1991. (Elliot Caplan) Documentary.

CALENDAR
ZEITGEIST. March, 1994. Armenian-Canadian-German. (Atom Egoyan) Arsinee Khanjian, Ashot Adamian.

CALENDAR GIRL
COLUMBIA. September, 1993. (John Whitesell) Jason Priestley, Gabriel Olds, Jerry O'Connell.

CAMELEON
S4C. May, 1997. British. (Ceri Sherlock) Aneirin Hughes, Sara McGaughey, Phylip Hughes, Sue Jones-Davies, Daniel Evans.

CAMILLA
MIRAMAX. December, 1994. Canadian-British. (Deepa Mehta) Jessica Tandy, Bridget Fonda, Elias Koteas.

THE CAMP AT THIAROYE
NEW YORKER. September, 1990. French. (Ousmane Sembene, Thierno Faty Sow) Ibrahima Sane, Sijiri Bakaba.

CAMP NOWHERE
BUENA VISTA. August, 1994. (Jonathan Prince) Christopher Lloyd, Jonathan Jackson, Wendy Makkena.

THE CAMP OF FALLEN WOMEN
STUDIO KOBILA. Feb., 1998. Slovakian-German-Czech. (Laco Halama) Juraj Kukura, Dana Dinkova, Stefan Kvietik.

CAMPING COSMOS
BRUSSELS AVE. May, 1996. Belgian. (Jan Bucquoy) Jean-Henri Compere, Fanny Hanciaux, Eve Ferrari.

CAMPUS
CONSTANTIN FILM. Feb., 1998. German. (Soenke Wortmann) Heiner Lauterbach, Axel Milberg, Sibylle Canonica, Barbara Rudnik.

CANADIAN BACON
GRAMERCY. September, 1995. (Michael Moore) Alan Alda, John Candy, Kevin Pollak, Rip Torn.

CANDYMAN
TRISTAR. October, 1992. (Bernard Rose) Virginia Madsen, Tony Todd, Xander Berkeley.

CANDYMAN: FAREWELL TO THE FLESH
GRAMERCY. March, 1995. (Bill Condon) Tony Todd, Kelly Rowan, Timothy Carhart.

CAN'T HARDLY WAIT
SONY PICTURES ENTERTAINMENT. June, 1998. (Deborah Kaplan) Jennifer Love Hewitt, Ethan Embry, Charlie Korsmo, Lauren Ambrose.

CAN'T STOP DANCING
PM ENTERTAINMENT. Jan., 1999. (Stephen Falick, Ben Zook) Ben Zook, Melanie Hutsell, Margaret Cho, Bruce DanielsDouglas, Taylor Negron.

CAPE FEAR
UNIVERSAL. November, 1991. (Martin Scorsese) Robert De Niro, Nick Nolte, Jessica Lange, Juliette Lewis.

CAPTAIN JACK
WINCHESTER FILMS. May, 1998. British. (Robert Young) Bob Hoskins, Peter McDonald, Sadie Frost, Jemma Jones.

CAPTAIN RON
BUENA VISTA. September, 1992. (Thom Eberhardt) Kurt Russell, Martin Short, Mary Kay Place.

CAPTIVE AUDIENCE
CORPORATE SUCKER FILMS. July, 1999. (Mike Gioscia, Kurt St. Thomas) Michael Kevin Walker, Daniel Haas, Mike Gioscia, Kat Corbett.

CAPTIVE IN THE LAND, A
NORKAT. January, 1993. Soviet-U.S. (John Berry) Sam Waterston, Aleksandr Potapov.

CAR 54, WHERE ARE YOU?
ORION. January, 1994. (Bill Fishman) David Johansen, John C. McGinley, Fran Drescher.

CAREER GIRLS
OCTOBER FILMS. May, 1997. British. (Mike Leigh) Katrin Cartlidge, Lynda Steadman, Kate Byers, Mark Benton, Andy Serkis.

CAREER OPPORTUNITIES
UNIVERSAL. March, 1991. (Bryan Gordon) Frank Whaley, Jennifer Connelly, Dermot Mulroney.

CAREFUL
ZEITGEIST. August, 1993. Canadian. (Guy Maddin) Kyle McCulloch, Gosia Dobrowolska, Sarah Neville.

CARESSES
LAUREN FILMS. Feb., 1998. Spanish. (Ventura Pons) David Selvas, Laura Conejero, Julieta Serrano, Montserrat Salvador.

CARLITO'S WAY
UNIVERSAL. November, 1993. (Brian De Palma) Al Pacino, Sean Penn, Penelope Ann Miller.

CARMEN MIRANDA: BANANAS IS MY BUSINESS
INT'L. CINEMA. July, 1995. Brazilian-U.S. (Helena Solberg) Erick Barreto, Leticia Monte.

CARMEN'S REVENGE
MIGMA. Oct., 1996. Swedish. (Suzanne Osten) Emelie Ekenborn, Lena Klingwall, Erik Gustavssoon, Malin Ek, Simon Norrthon.

CARNIVALE
TERRAGLYPH. July, 1999. Irish. (Deane Taylor). Animated.

CARNOSAUR
CONCORDE. May, 1993. (Adam Simon) Diane Ladd, Raphael Sbarge, Jennifer Runyon.

CARO DIARIO
FINE LINE. September, 1994. Italian-French. (Nanni Moretti) Nanni Moretti, Renato Carpentieri, Valerio Magrelli.

CARPOOL
WARNER BROS. August, 1996. (Arthur Hiller) Tom Arnold, David Paymer, Rhea Perlman, Rod Steiger, Kim Coastes.

CARRIED AWAY
FINE LINE. January, 1996. (Bruno Barreto) Dennis Hopper, Amy Irving, Amy Locane, Julie Harris, Gary Busey.

CARRIED AWAY
HYSTERIA FILMS. June, 1998. (Paul Kostick) Christian Ryser, Susan Tate, Matt Riedy.

THE CARRIERS ARE WAITING
K-STAR/RTBF/CAB PRODS. May, 1999. Belgian-French-Swiss. (Benoit Mariage) Benoit Poelvoorde, Morgane Simon, Bouli lanners, Dominiue Baeyens.

CARRINGTON
GRAMERCY. November, 1995. (Christopher Hampton) Emma Thompson, Jonathan Pryce.

CASA HOLLYWOOD
CASA HOLLYWOOD. June, 1996. (Mark Decker) Estuardo Volty, Michael Banks, Lisa Cobano.

CASCADEUR: THE AMBER CHAMBER
CASCADEUR FILMPRODUKTION/PROSIEBEN/FIMA. May, 1998. German. (Hardy Martins) Hardy Martins, Regula Grauwiller.

CASHING IN
PENDULUM. February, 1996. (Anne Rose Dremman) Paul Ruehl, Cassidy Phillips, John Serge, Brian Wankum.

CASINO
UNIVERSAL/SYALIS D.A/LEGENDE. November, 1995. (Martin Scorsese) Robert De Niro, Joe Pesci, Sharon Stone.

CASPER
UNIVERSAL. May, 1995. (Brad Silberling) Christina Ricci, Bill Pullman, Eric Idle, Cathy Moriarty.

CASSANDRA CAT
CESKOSLOVENSKY FILMEXPORT. July, 1990; originally released 1963. Czech. (Vojtech Jasný) Jan Werich.

CASTLE OF CAGLIOSTRO, THE
STREAMLINE. July, 1992. Japanese. (Hayao Miyazaki) Animated.

CATFISH IN BLACK BEAN SAUCE
BLACK HAWK ENTERTAINMENT. Apr., 1999. (Chi Muoi Lo.) Paul Winfield, Mary Alice, Chi Muoi Lo, Lauren Tom.

CATWALK
ARROW. January, 1996. (Robert Leacock, Milton Moses Ginsberg) Christy Turlington. Documentary.

CAT SWALLOWS PARAKEET AND SPEAKS
ILEANA PIETROBRUNO. June, 1997. Canadian. (Ileana Pietrobruno) Tara Frederick, Rebecca Godin, Alex Ferguson, Christine Taylor.

CATS DON'T DANCE
WARNER BROS. March, 1997. (Mark Dindal), Scott Bakula, Jasmine Guy, Natalie Cole, Ashley Peldon, Kathy Najimy, John Rhys-Davies.

CAUGHT
CINEHAUS/DUART/CIRCLE. January, 1996. (Robert M. Young) Edward James Olmos, Maria Conchita Alonso.

CAUGHT IN THE ACT
MIDSUMMER FILMS. May, 1996. British. (Mark Greenstreet) Sara Crowe, Annette Badland, Nadia Sawalha.

CAUGHT UP
LIVE ENTERTAINMENT. Feb., 1998. (Darin Scott) Bokeem Woodbine, Cynda Williams, Joseph Lindsay, Clifton Powell, LL Cool J.

THE CELEBRATION
OCTOBER FILMS. May, 1998. Danish. (Thomas Vinterberg) Ulrich Rhomsen, Henning Moritzen, Thomas Bo Larsen.

CELEBRITY
MIRAMAX. Aug., 1998. (Woody Allen) Hank Azaria, Kenneth Branaugh, Judy Davis, Leonardo DiCaprio, Melanie Griffith, Famke Janssen.

THE CELLULOID CLOSET
SONY PICTURES CLASSICS. March, 1996. (Rob Epstein, Jeffery Friedman) Tony Curtis, Shirley Maclaine Documentary.

CELTIC PRIDE
BUENA VISTA. April, 1996. (Tom deCherchio) Damon Wayans, Daniel Stern, Dan Aykroyd, Gail O'Grady.

CEMETERY CLUB, THE
BUENA VISTA. February, 1993. (Bill Duke) Ellen Burstyn, Olympia Dukakis, Diane Ladd, Danny Aiello.

CEMETARY MAN
OCTOBER FILMS. April, 1996. Italian-French-British. (Michele Soavi) Rupert Everett, Francois Hadji-Lazaro.

CENTER OF THE WEB
A.I.P. STUDIO. May, 1992. (David A. Prior) Robert Davi, Charlene Tilton, Tony Curtis.

CENTRAL STATION
SONY PICTURES CLASSICS. Jan., 1998. Brazilian-French. (Walter Salles) Fernanda Montenegro, Marilia Pera, Vinicius de Oliveira.

C'EST LA VIE
SAMUEL GOLDWYN. November, 1990. French. (Diane Kurys) Nathalie Baye, Richard Berry, Julie Bataille.

A CHA-CHA FOR THE FUGITIVE
FOUNTAIN FILMS CO. Feb., 1997. Taiwanese. (Wang Tsai-sheng) Julien Chen, Lu Hsin-yu, Chen Chieh-yi, Liu Shen-hsin.

CHA CHA CHA
Sogepaq. July, 1998. Spanish. (Antonio del Real) Eduardo Noriega, Ana Alvarez, Maria Adanez, Jorge Sanz.

CHACUN CHERCHE SON CHAT
MALO FILMS. August, 1996. French. (Cedric Klapisch) Jane Bradbury, Romain Duris, Marine Delterme, Camille Japy.

CHAIN OF DESIRE
MAD DOG PICTURES. June, 1993. (Temistocles Lopez) Malcolm McDowell, Linda Fiorentino, Tim Guinee.

CHAIN REACTION
20TH CENTURY FOX. July, 1996. (Andrew Davis) Keanu Reeves, Morgan Freeman, Rachel Weisz, Fred Ward.

CHAIRMAN OF THE BOARD
TRIMARK PICTURES. March, 1998. (Alex Zamm) Carrot Top, Courtney Thorne-Smith, Larry Miller, Raquel Welch, Mystro Clark.

CHALK
TENDERLOIN ACTION GROUP/PACIFIC RIM MEDIA. April, 1996. (Rob Nillson) Kevin Han Yee, Don Bajema.

THE CHAMBER
UNIVERSAL. October, 1996. (James Foley) Chris O'Donnell, Gene Hackman, Faye Dunaway, Robert Prosky.

CHAMELEON STREET
NORTHERN ARTS. April, 1991. (Wendell B. Harris Jr.) Wendell B. Harris Jr., Angela Leslie.

CHANGING HABITS
TEAGARDEN PICTURES INC. Jan., 1997. (Lynn Roth) Moira Kelly, Christopher Lloyd, Dylan Walsh, Shelley Duvall, Bob Gunton.

CHANNELLING BABY
OCEANIA PARKER LTD. May, 1999. New Zealand. (Christine Parker) Danielle Cormack, Kevin Smith, Anber Sainsbury, Joel Tobeck.

CHANTAL AKERMAN BY CHANTAL AKERMAN
AMIP. May, 1997. French. (Chantal Akerman). Documentary.

CHAPLIN
TRISTAR. December, 1992. (Richard Attenborough) Robert Downey Jr., Geraldine Chaplin, Kevin Kline, Diane Lane.

CHARACTER
FIRST FLOOR FEATURES. May, 1997. Dutch. (Mike van Diem) Fedja Van Huet, Jan Decleir, Betty Schuurman, Victor Low.

CHARISMA
NIKKATSU CORP./KING RECORDS CO./TOKYO THEATERS CO. May, 1999. Japanese. (Kiyoshi Kurosawa) Koji Yakusho, Hiroyuki Ikeuchi, Ren Osugi, Yoriko Doguchi, Jun Fubuki.

CHARLES MINGUS: TRIUMPH OF THE UNDERDOG
WINTER MOON PRODS./JAZZ WORKSHOP. Nov., 1997. (Don McGlynn) DOCUMENTARY.

THE CHASE
20TH CENTURY FOX. March, 1994. (Adam Rifkin) Charlie Sheen, Kristy Swanson, Henry Rollins.

CHASERS
WARNER BROS. April, 1994. (Dennis Hopper) Tom Berenger, William McNamara, Erika Eleniak.

CHASING AMY
MIRAMAX. January, 1997. (Kevin Smith), Ben Affleck, Joey Lauren Adams, Jason Lee, Dwight Ewell, Jason Mewes, Kevin Smith.

CHATTAHOOCHEE
HEMDALE. April, 1990. (Mick Jackson) Gary Oldman, Dennis Hopper, Pamela Reed.

CHEAP SHOTS
HEMDALE/SELECT. November, 1991. (Jeff Ureless) Louis Zorich, David Patrick Kelly, Mary Louise Wilson.

CHEATIN' HEARTS
TRIMARK. July, 1993. (Rod McCall) Sally Kirkland, James Brolin, Kris Kristofferson.

CHECKPOINT
ORT-STW FILM CO. Feb., 1999. Russian. (Alexander Rogoshkin) Andrei Krasko, Alexei Buldakov, Zoya Burjak, Roman Romancov.

A CHEF IN LOVE
UGC. May, 1996. French-Georgian. (Nana Djordjadze) Pierre Richard, Micheline Presle.

CHERRY
CYPRESS FILMS. Apr., 1999. (John Glascoe, Joseph Pierson) Shalom Harlow, Jake Weber, Isaach de Bankole, Laurel Holloman.

THE CHERRY ORCHARD
MELANDA FILM PRODS. Sept., 1999. Greek-French-Cypriot. (Michael Cacoyannis) Charlotte Rampling, Alan Bates, Katrin Cartlidge, Owen Teale, Frances de la Tour.

THE CHERRY PICK
NFM/IAF. Sept., 1996. Dutch. (Arno Kranenborg) Finbarr Wilbrink, Anton Starke, Ricky Koole, Lukas Dijkema.

THE CHERRY TREE
OBERON CINEMATOGRAFICA, S.A. Feb., 1999. Spanish. (Marc Recha) Pere Ponce, Diana Palazon, Jordi Dauder, Isabel Rocatti.

CHEYENNE WARRIOR
CONCORDE. July, 1994. (Mark Griffiths) Kelly Preston, Pato Hoffman, Bo Hopkins.

CHICAGO CAB
GFT ENTERTAINMENT. March, 1998. (Mary Cybulski, John Tintori) Paul Dillon, Michael Ironside, Laurie Metcalf, John C. Reilly, Gillian Anderson, John Cusack, Julianne Moore.

CHICAGO JOE AND THE SHOWGIRL
NEW LINE. July, 1990. British. (Bernard Rose) Kiefer Sutherland, Emily Lloyd, Patsy Kensit.

CHI GIRL
TRISHORE ENTERTAINMENT. Jan., 1999. (Heidi Van Lier) Heidi Van Lier, Joe Kraemer, Scott Benjaminson, Phil Smith.

CHILDHOOD'S END
PLAINVIEW PICTURES. August, 1996. (Jeff Lipsky) Cameron Ford, Heather Gottlieb, Sam Trammell.

THE CHILDREN OF CHABANNES
PERENNIAL PICTURES/WETHERELL & ASSOCIATES. June, 1999. (Lisa Gossels) Documentary.

THE CHILDREN OF HEAVEN
MIRAMAX. Aug., 1997. Iranian. (Majid Majidi) Mohammad Amir Naji, Fereshte Sarabandi, Karnal Mirkarimi.

THE CHILDREN OF THE CENTURY
BAC FILMS. Sept. 1999. French. (Diane Kurys)Juliette Binoche, Benoit Magimel, Stefano Dionisi, Robin Renucci.

CHILDREN OF THE CORN II
DIMENSION. January, 1993. (David Price) Terence Knox, Paul Scherrer, Rosalind Allen.

CHILDREN OF THE MARSHLAND
UGC. Apt., 1999. French. (Jean Becker) Jacques Villeret, Jacques Gamblin, Andre Dussollier, Michel Serrault.

CHILD'S PLAY 2
UNIVERSAL. November, 1990. (John Lafia) Alex Vincent, Christine Elise, Jenny Agutter.

CHILL FACTOR
WARNER BROS. Aug., 1999. (Hugh Johnson) Cuba Gooding, Jr., Skeet Ulrich, Peter Firth, David Paymer.

CHILLICOTHE
BLUE YONDER FILMS. Jan., 1999. (Todd Edwards) Todd Edwards, Peter Bedgood, Cory Edwards, Brad Knull.

CHINA CRY
PENLAND CO. November, 1990. (James E. Collier) Julia Nickson-Soul, Russell Wong, James Shigeta.

CHINA MOON
ORION. March, 1994. (John Bailey) Ed Harris, Madeleine Stowe, Charles Dance.

CHINA, MY SORROW
MILESTONE. January, 1993. Chinese. (Dai Sijie) Guo Liang Yi, Tieu Quan Nghieu.

CHINESE BOX
LE STUDIO. Sept., 1997. French-Japanese-U.S. (Wayne Wang) Jeremy Irons, Gong Li, Maggie Chung, Michael Hui, Ruben Blades.

CHINESE DEFENSE
OBJEKTIV FILMSTUDIO-MAGYAR TV-COVI DESIGN FILM. FEB., 1999. Hungarian-Romanian. (Gabor Tompa) Emil Gyorgy, Ivan Dengyei, Victor Rebengiuc, Maia Morgenstern.

CHIN UP!
DIAPHANA. May, 1999. French-Belgain. (Solveig Anspach) Karin Viard, Laurent Lucas, Julien Cottereau, Philippe Duclos.

CHOCOLATE BABIES
OPEN CITY FILMS. July, 1996. (Stephen Winter) Gregg Ferguson, Dudley Findlay, Jr. Jon Lee.

CHOCOLATE FOR BREAKFAST
ASPECT RATIO. Apr., 1999. (Emily Baer) Isabel Gillies, Brooke Hailey, Marin Hinkle, Callie Thorne.

CHOLERA STREET
OZEN FILM. May, 1998. Turkish-Hungarian-French. (Mustafa Altioklar) Okan Bayulgen, Mujde Ar, Savas Dincel, Burak Sergen.

CHOPPER CHICKS IN ZOMBIETOWN
TRIAX. March, 1990. (Dan Hoskins) Jamie Rose, Catherine Carlen.

CHRISTMAS IN AUGUST
ILSHIN INVESTMENT CO. May, 1998. Korean. (Hur Jin-Ho) Suk-Kyu, Shim Eun-Ha, Shin Koo, Oh Ji-Hae, Lee Han-Wi.

CHRISTMAS VACATION
FILMAURO. December, 1995. Italian. (Neri Parenti) Luke Perry, Massimo Baldi, Christian diSica.

CHRISTOPHER COLUMBUS—THE DISCOVERY
WARNER BROS. August, 1992. (John Glen) George Corraface, Marlon Brando, Tom Selleck.

CHUNGKING EXPRESS
MIRAMAX/ROLLING THUNDER. March, 1996. Chinese. (Wong Kar Wei) Brigitte Lin, Tony Leung.

CIAO, PROFESSORE!
MIRAMAX. July, 1994. Italian. (Lina Wertmuller) Paolo Bonacelli, Pier Francesco Borruto, Esterina Carloni.

THE CIDER HOUSE RULES
MIRAMAX. Sept., 1999 (Lasse Hallstrom) Tobey Maguire, Charlize Theron, Delroy Lindo, Paul Rudd, Michael Caine.

CINEMA PARADISO
MIRAMAX. February, 1990. Italian. (Giuseppe Tornatore) Philippe Noiret, Jacques Perrin.

CINEMATOGRAPHY 3: REVENGE OF IRIS
DAIEI. May, 1999. Japanese. (Shusuke Kaneko) Shinobu Nakayama, Ai Mada, Ayako Fujitani, Senri Yamasaki.

CIRCLE OF FRIENDS
SAVOY. March, 1995. Irish. (Pat O'Connor) Minnie Driver, Chris O'Donnell, Geraldine O'Rawe.

CIRCUITRY MAN
SKOURAS. August, 1990. (Steve Lovy) Jim Metzler, Dennis Christopher, Dana Wheeler Nicholson.

THE CITY
NORTH STAR FILMS. Sept., 1998. (David Riker), Fernando Reyes, Marcos Martinez Garcia, Moises Garcia, Anthony Rivera.

CITY HALL
SONY PICTURES. February, 1996. (Harold Becker) Al Pacino, John Cusack, Bridget Fonda, Danny Aiello.

CITY OF ANGELS
WARNER BROS. March, 1998. (Brad Silberling), Nicolas Cage, Meg Ryan, Andre Braugher, Dennis Franz, Colm Feore, Robin Bartlett.

CITY OF GLASS
GOLDEN HARVEST. Dec., 1998. Hong Kong. (Mabel Cheung) Leon Lai, Shu Qi, Nicola Cheung, Daniel Wu, Enson Chan.

CITY OF HOPE
SAMUEL GOLDWYN. October, 1991. (John Sayles) Vincent Spano, Joe Morton, Tony Lo Bianco, Todd Graff.

CITY OF INDUSTRY
ORION. February, 1997. (John Irvin), Harvey Keitel, Stephen Dorff, Famke Janssen, Timothy Hutton, Wade Dominguez.

CITY OF JOY
TRISTAR. April, 1992. British-French. (Roland Joffé) Patrick Swayze, Om Puri, Pauline Collins.

CITY OF LOST CHILDREN
SONY PICTURES CLASSICS. October, 1995. French. (Jean-Pierre Jeunet) Ron Perlman, Daniel Emilfork.

THE CITY OF MARVELS
FILMAX. June, 1999. Spanish-French-Portuguese. (Mario Camus) Olivier Martinez, Emma Suarez, Francois Marthouret, Joaquin Diaz.

CITY OF PEACE
CABIN JOHN. April, 1998. (Susan Koch) DOCUMENTARY.

CITY SLICKERS
COLUMBIA. June, 1991. (Ron Underwood) Billy Crystal, Daniel Stern, Bruno Kirby, Jack Palance.

CITY SLICKERS II: THE LEGEND OF CURLY'S GOLD
COLUMBIA. June, 1994. (Paul Weiland) Billy Crystal, Daniel Stern, Jon Lovitz, Jack Palance.

CITY UNPLUGGED
FILMHAUS. June, 1995. Estonian. (Ilkka Jarvilaturi) Peeter Oja, Ivo Uukkivi, Milena Gulbe

CITY ZERO
IFEX. March, 1991. Soviet. (Karen Shakhnazarov) Leonid Filatov, Oleg Basilashvili.

A CIVIL ACTION
BUENA VISTA. Dec., 1998. (Steven Zaillian) John Travolta Robert Duvall, Tony Shalhoub, William H. Macy, Zeljko Ivanbeck.

CLAIRE OF THE MOON
DEMI MONDE. October, 1992. (Nicole Conn) Trisha Todd, Karen Trumbo, Faith McDevitt.

CLASS ACT
WARNER BROS. June, 1992. (Randall Miller) Christopher "Kid" Reid, Christopher "Play" Martin.

CLASS ACTION
20TH CENTURY FOX. March, 1991. (Michael Apted) Gene Hackman, Mary Elizabeth Mastrantonio, Colin Friels.

CLASS OF 1999
TAURUS ENTERTAINMENT. May, 1990. (Mark L. Lester) Bradley Gregg, Malcolm McDowell, Traci Lind.

CLASS OF NUKE 'EM HIGH PART 2: SUBHUMANOID MELTDOWN
TROMA. April, 1991. (Eric Louzil) Brick Bronsky, Lisa Gaye.

CLASS TRIP
LES FILMS DE LA BOISSIERE. May, 1998. French. (Claude Miller) Clement Van Den Bergh, Lokman Nalcakan, Francoise Roy.

CLAUDINE'S RETURN
JAZZ PICTURES. April, 1998. (Antonio Tibaldi) Christina Applegate, Stefano Dionisi, Matt Clark, Tony Torn, Gabriel Mann, Perry Anzilotti.

CLAY PIGEONS
GRAMERCY PICTURES. Sept., 1998. (David Dobkin) Vince Vaughn, Janeane Garofalo, Joaquin Phoenix, Georgina Cates, Phil Morris.

CLEAN, SHAVEN
STRAND. April, 1995. (Lodge H. Kerrigan) Peter Greene, Jennifer MacDonald, Robert Albert.

CLEAN SLATE
MGM. May, 1994. (Mick Jackson) Dana Carvey, Valeria Golino, James Earl Jones.

CLEOPATRA'S SECOND HUSBAND
CUCOLORIS FILMS. April, 1998. (Jon Reiss) Paul Hipp, Boyd Kestner, Bitty Schram, Rhada Mitchell, Alexis Arquette.

CLEAR AND PRESENT DANGER
PARAMOUNT. August, 1994. (Phillip Noyce) Harrison Ford, Willem Dafoe, Anne Archer.

CLEARCUT
NORTHERN ARTS. August, 1992. Canadian. (Richard Bugajski) Ron Lea, Graham Greene, Michael Hogan.

CLERKS
MIRAMAX. October, 1994. (Kevin Smith) Brian O'Halloran, Jeff Anderson, Marilyn Ghigliotti. B&W

THE CLIENT
WARNER BROS. July, 1994. (Joel Schumacher) Susan Sarandon, Tommy Lee Jones, Brad Renfro.

CLIFFHANGER
TRISTAR. May, 1993. (Renny Harlin) Sylvester Stallone, John Lithgow, Michael Rooker.

CLIFFORD
ORION. April, 1994. (Paul Flaherty) Martin Short, Charles Grodin, Mary Steenburgen.

THE CLIMB
ELLIPSE PROGRAMME/ISAMBARD PRODS. May, 1997. French-New Zealand. (Bob Swaim) John Hurt, Gregory Smith.

CLOCKERS
UNIVERSAL. September, 1995. (Spike Lee) Harvey Keitel, John Turturro, Delroy Lindo, Mekhi Phifer.

CLOCKWATCHERS
GOLDCREST INT'L. Jan., 1997. (Jill Sprecher) Toni Collette, Parker Posey, Lisa Kudrow, Alanna Ubach, Helen Fitzgerald.

CLOSE MY EYES
CASTLE HILL. November, 1991. British. (Stephen Poliakoff) Alan Rickman, Clive Owen, Saskia Reeves.

CLOSE SHAVE
MKL. March, 1996. French. (Etienne Dhaene) Jean-Marc Barr, Anemone, Olivia Bonamy.

CLOSE TO EDEN
MIRAMAX. October, 1992. Russian. (Nikita Mikhalkov) Bayaertu Badema, Vladimir Gostukhin.

CLOSET LAND
UNIVERSAL. March, 1991. (Radha Bharadwaj) Madeleine Stowe, Alan Rickman.

CLOSE TO LOVE
HUNNIA STUDIO/MAFILM AKTIV STUDIO. Feb., 1999. Hungarian. (Andras Salamon) Ferenc Hujber, Tsuyu Shimizu, Nimrod Antal, Janos Gyuriska, Karoly Gesztesi.

THE CLOUD
CINESUR/LES FILMS DU SUD. Sept., 1998. Argentine-French-Italian-German. (Fernando E. Solanas) Eduardo Pavlovsky, Angela Correa, Franklin Caicedo, Carlos Perez, Leonor Manso.

CLOWNHOUSE
TRIUMPH. July, 1990. (Victor Salva) Nathan Forrest Winters, Brian McHugh.

THE CLOWN SMILES
EUROZOOM. June, 1999. French. (Eric Besnard) Ticky Holgado, Vincent Elbaz, Francois Berleand, Bruno Putzulu.

CLUBBED TO DEATH
MADAR PRODS. Feb., 1997. French. (Yolande Zauberman) Elodie Bouchez, Roschdy Zem, Beatrice Dalle, Richard Courcet.

CLUELESS
PARAMOUNT. July, 1995. (Amy Heckerling) Alicia Silverstone, Stacey Dash, Brittany Murphy, Dan Hedaya.

THE COAST IS CLEAR
UFD. Feb., 1998. French. (Stephane Clavier) Francois Cluzet, Philippine Leroy-Beaulieu, Emma de Caunes, Eric Caravaca.

COBB
WARNER BROS. December, 1994. (Ron Shelton) Tommy Lee Jones, Robert Wuhl, Lolita Davidovitch.

THE COCKROACH THAT ATE CINCINNATI
QUEEN WEST PRODS. Sept., 1996. Canadian. (Michael McNamara) Alan Williams, Deborah Drakeford, Oliver Dennis.

COLD AROUND THE HEART
20TH CENTURY FOX. Nov., 1998. (John Ridley) David Caruso, Kelly Lynch, Stacey Dash, Chris Noth, John Spencer, Pruitt Taylor Vince.

COLD COMFORT FARM
GRAMERCY. May, 1996. (John Schlesinger) Kate Beckinsdale, Eileen Atkins, Ian McKellen.

COLD FEVER
ARTISTIC LICENSE FILMS. April, 1996. (Fridrik Thor Fridriksson) Masatoshi Nagase, Lili Taylor, Fisher Stevens.

COLD HEAVEN
HEMDALE. May, 1992. (Nicolas Roeg) Theresa Russell, Mark Harmon, James Russo.

COLD MOON
GAMUONT. April, 1992. French. (Patrick Bouchitey) Jean Francois Stevenin, Patrick Bouchitey, Jean Pierre Bisson.

COLDBLOODED
I.R.S. September, 1995. (M. Wallace Wolodarsky) Jason Priestley, Peter Riegert, Kimberly Williams.

COLIN FITZ
BABY SHARK INC. Jan., 1997. (Robert Bella) John C. McGinley, Matt McGrath, William H. Macy, Andy Fowle, Julianne Phillips.

COLIN NUTLEY'S HOUSE OF ANGELS
SONY PICTURES CLASSICS. August, 1993. Swedish. (Colin Nutley) Helena Bergstrom, Rikard Wolff, Sven Wollter.

COLONEL CHABERT
OCTOBER FILMS. December, 1994. French. (Yves Angelo) Gérard Depardieu, Fanny Ardant, Fabrice Luchini.

COLOR ADJUSTMENT
CALIFORNIA NEWSREEL. January, 1992. (Marlon T. Riggs) Documentary.

COLOR OF A BRISK AND LEAPING DAY
JIM STARK/ANTARCTIC. January, 1996. (Christopher Munch) Peter Alexander, Michael Stipe, Jeri Arredondo.

THE COLOR OF COURAGE
STUDIOS USA PICTURES. Oct., 1998. (Lee Rose) Linda Hamilton, Lynn Whitfield, Bruce Greenwood, Roger Guenveur Smith.

THE COLOR OF GOD
VARAHONAR CO. Feb., 1999. Iranian. (Majid Majidi) Mohsen Ramezani, Hossein Mahjub, Salime Feizi, Elham Sharifi.

THE COLOR OF LIES
MK2 DIFFUSION. Jan., 1999. French. (Claude Chabrol) Sandrine Bonnaire, Jacques Gamblin, Valeria Bruni-Tedeschi, Antoine de Caunes.

COLOR OF NIGHT
BUENA VISTA. August, 1994. (Richard Rush) Bruce Willis, Jane March, Ruben Blades, Andrew Lowery.

COLORS STRAIGHT UP
ECHO PICTURES. April, 1997. (Michele Ohayon) Documentary.

COMANCHE TERRITORY
TORNASOL FILMS, BMG ENT. Feb., 1997. Spanish-German-French-Argentine. (Gerardo Herrero) Imanol Arias, Carmelo Gomez.

COMBINATION PLATTER
ARROW. November, 1993. (Tony Chan) Jeff Lau, Colleen O'Brien, Colin Mitchell, Kenneth Lu.

COMEDIA INFANTIL
TORROMFILM/PROLE FILME/AVENIDA PRODUCOES. Feb., 1998. Swedish-Mozambican-Portuguese. (Solveig Nordlund) Sergio Titos, Joao Manja, Joaquina Odete, Jaime Julio, Avelino Manhica.

COMFORTABLY NUMB
QUARTET. September, 1995. (Henri Barges) Catherine Ussel, Phillipe Spiteri, Marc Duret.

COME SEE THE PARADISE
20TH CENTURY FOX. December, 1990. (Alan Parker) Dennis Quaid, Tamlyn Tomita, Sab Shimono.

COMEDIAN HARMONISTS
MIRAMAX. Feb., 1998. German. (Joseph Vilsmaier) Ben Becker, Heino Ferch, Ulrich Noethen, Heinrich Schafmeister, Max Tidof.

COMEDY'S DIRTIEST DOZEN
ISLAND. October, 1990. (Lenny Wong) Tim Allen.

THE COMET
INSTITUTO MEXICANO DE CINEMATOGRAPHIA/FONDO DE FOMENTO A LA CALIDAD CINEMATOGRAFICA/FONDO SUD . Jan., 1999. Mexican. (Marisa Sistach, Jose Buil) Diego Luna, Ana Claudia Talancon, Carmen Maura, Gabriel Retes.

COMING OUT UNDER FIRE
ZEITGEIST. July, 1994. (Arthur Dong) Brian Thompson, Kathy Shower. Documentary.

COMING SOON
KEY ENTERTAINMENT. May, 1999. (Colette Burson) Tricia Vessey, Gaby Hoffman, Bonnie Root, James Roday, Mia Farrow.

COMMANDMENTS
GRAMERCY. Jan, 1997. (Daniel Taplitz) Aidan Quinn, Courteney Cox, Anthony LaPaglia, Louis Zorich, Pamela Gray, Pat McNamara.

THE COMMISSIONER
METROPOLIS FILMPRODUKTION/NEW ERA VISION/SAGA FILM. Feb., 1998. German-British-Belgian. (George Sluizer) John Hurt, Rosana Pastor, Alice Krige, Armin Mueller-Stahl, Johan Leysen.

THE COMMITMENTS
20TH CENTURY FOX. August, 1991. British. (Alan Parker) Robert Arkins, Johnny Murphy, Andrew Strong, Angeline Ball.

COMPANY BUSINESS
MGM. September, 1991. (Nicholas Meyer) Gene Hackman, Mikhail Baryshnikov, Kurtwood Smith.

COMPLEX WORLD
HEARTBREAK HITS. November, 1990. (James Wolpaw) Stanley Matis, Dan Von Bargen, Dan Welch.

COMRADES, ALMOST A LOVE STORY
GOLDEN HARVEST. Feb., 1997. Hong Kong. (Peter Chan) Leon Lai, aggie Cheung, Kristy Yeung, Eric Tsang, Irene Tsu.

CON AIR
BUENA VISTA. May, 1997. (Simon West), Nicolas Cage, John Cusack, John Malkovich, Steve Buscemi, Ving Rhames, Colm Meaney.

CONCERTO OF LIFE
BEIJING FILM STUDIO. June, 1998. Chinese. (Xia Gang) Wang Luoyong, Da Shichang, Yan Xiaopin, Shi Ke, Wang Bozhao, Zhang Xi.

CONDO PAINTING
USA FILMS. Aug., 1999. (John McNaughton) George Condo, William S. Burroughs, Allen Ginsberg, John Sampas.

CONEHEADS
PARAMOUNT. July, 1993. (Steve Barron) Dan Aykroyd, Jane Curtin, Michael McKean.

THE CONFESSIONS OF AN INNOCENT MAN
CINEXPORT. April, 1996. French. (Jean-Pierre Ameris) Bruno Putzulu, Elisabeth Depardieu, Michele Laroque.

CONGO
PARAMOUNT. June, 1995. (Frank Marshall) Dylan Walsh, Laura Linney, Ernie Hudson, Tim Curry.

CONFESSIONS OF A SEXIST PIG
PIZZA PRODS. March, 1998. (Sandy Tung) Edward Kerr, Traylor Howard, Michael Trucco, Lauren Graham, Anneliza Scott, Sal Viscuso.

THE CONGRESS OF PENGUINS
ARIANE FILM. January, 1995. Swiss. (Hans Ulrich Schlumpf) Documentary.

THE CONJUGAL BED
LEISURE TIME. July, 1994. Romanian. (Mircea Daneliuc) Gheorghe Dinica, Coca Bloos, Valentin Teodosiu.

CONJURE WOMEN
REBEKAH. September, 1995. (Demetria Royals) Documentary.

CONNECTED TO FATE
TAIWAN FILM CENTER. Sept., 1998. Taiwanese. (Wan Jen) Tsai Cheng-nan, Chang Cheng-yu, Chang Fei-chun, Chen Chiou-yen.

CONSENTING ADULTS
BUENA VISTA. October, 1992. (Alan J. Pakula) Kevin Kline, Mary Elizabeth Mastrantonio, Kevin Spacey.

CONSPIRACY THEORY
WARNER BROS. July, 1997. (Richard Donner), Mel Gibson, Julia Roberts, Patrick Stewart, Cylk Cozart.

CONTACT
WARNER BROS. July, 1997. (Robert Zemeckis), Jodie Foster, Matthew McConaughey, James Woods, John Hurt, Tom Skerritt, Angela Bassett.

THE CONTACT
MYUNG FILM CO./KIID. Sept., 1998. South Korean. (Jang Yun-hyeon) Han Seok-kyu, Jeon Do-yeon, Park Yong-su, Chu Sang-mi, Kim Tae-u.

THE CONTINUED ADVENTURES OF REPTILE MAN (AND HIS FAITHFUL SIDEKICK TADPOLE)
CINEMA ARTS. May, 1996. (Stewart Schill) Tony Curtis, Arye Gross, Ally Walker.

CONVERGENCE
WHITE ROCK FILM. Feb., 1999. Canadian. (Gavin Wilding) Christopher Lloyd, Cynthia Preston, Adrian Paul, Blu Mankuma.

THE CONVICTION
INT'L FILM CIRCUIT. May, 1994. Italian-French. (Marco Bellocchio) Vittorio Mezzogiorno, Claire Nebout.

CONVICTS
M.C.E.G. December, 1991. (Peter Masterson) Robert Duvall, Lukas Haas, James Earl Jones.

COOKIE'S FORTUNE
OCTOBER FILMS. Jan., 1999. (Robert Altman) Glenn Close, Julianne Moore, Liv Tyler, Chris O'Donnell, Charles S. Dutton.

THE COOK, THE THIEF, HIS WIFE & HER LOVER
MIRAMAX. April, 1990. British. (Peter Greenaway) Helen Mirren, Michael Gambon, Alan Howard.

COOL AS ICE
UNIVERSAL. October, 1991. (David Kellogg) Vanilla Ice, Kristin Minter, Michael Gross.

A COOL, DRY PLACE
20TH CENTURY FOX. Feb., 1999. (John N. Smith) Vince Vaughn, Joey Lauren Adams, Monica Potter.

COOL RUNNINGS
BUENA VISTA. October, 1993. (Jon Turteltaub) Leon, Doug E. Doug, Rawle D. Lewis, John Candy.

COOL WORLD
PARAMOUNT. July, 1992. (Ralph Bakshi) Kim Basinger, Brad Pitt, Gabriel Byrne.

COP AND A HALF
UNIVERSAL. April, 1993. (Henry Winkler) Burt Reynolds, Norman D. Golden II, Ray Sharkey, Ruby Dee.

COP LAND
MIRAMAX. August, 1997. (James Mangold), Sylvester Stallone, Harvey Keitel, Ray Liotta, Robert De Niro, Peter Berg, Janeane Garofalo,Michael Rapaport, Annabella Sciorra, Noah Emmerich, Cathy Moriarty.

COPS AND ROBBERSONS
TRISTAR. April, 1994. (Michael Ritchie) Chevy Chase, Jack Palance, Dianne Wiest, David Barry Gray.

COPYCAT
WARNER BROS. October, 1995. (Jon Amiel) Sigourney Weaver, Holly Huner, Dermot Mulroney, William McNamara.

THE COQ IS DEAD
OBJEKTIV FILM. June, 1999. German. (Hermine Huntgebruth) Gisela Schneeberger, August Zirner, Renate Kroessner, Nikolaus Paryla.

CORISCO AND DADA
GRUPO NOVO DE CINEMA ETV. May, 1996. Brazilian. (Rosemberg Cariry) Chico Dias, Dira Paes.

THE CORMORANT
BBC/PUBLIC TH. April, 1995. British. (Peter Markham) Ralph Fiennes, Helen Schlesinger, Thomas Williams.

THE CORNDOG MAN
CORNDOG PRODS. Jan., 1999. (Andrew Shea) Noble Willingham, Jim Holmes.

CORPORATE AFFAIRS
CONCORDE. October, 1990. (Terence H. Winkless) Peter Scolari, Mary Crosby, Chris Lemmon.

CORRINA, CORRINA
NEW LINE. August, 1994. (Jessie Nelson) Whoopi Goldberg, Ray Liotta, Tina Majorino.

THE CORRUPTOR
NEW LINE. Mar., 1999. (James Foley) Chow Yun-Fat, Mark Wahlberg, Ric Young, Paul Ben-Victor.

COSI
MIRAMAX. April, 1996. Autralian. (Mark Joffe) Ben Mendelsohn, Barry Otto, Toni Collette, Greta Scacchi.

COSMOS
MALOFILM DISTRIBUTION. Nov., 1996. Canadian. (Various directors) Marie-Helene Montpetit, Sebastien Joannette, David La Haye, Marie-France Lambert, Sarah-Jeanne Salvy, Igor Ovadis.

COST OF LIVING
SCHOFIELD FILMS PRODUCTION. Oct., 1997. (Stan Schofield) Edie Falco, James Villemaire, Andrew Lowery, Bill Sage.

THE COTTONWOOD
FIRSTBORN PICTURES/BLACK SHEEP ENTERTAINMENT. Oct., 1996. (Steven Feder) Pruitt Taylor Vince, Jack Mulcahy, Cyril O'Reilly

COUNTESS, THE
INT'L FILM CIRCUIT. January, 1991. Bulgarian. (Peter Popzlatev) Svetlana Yancheva, Itzhak Fintsi.

COUNTRY LIFE
MIRAMAX. July, 1995. Australian. (Michael Blakemore) Sam Neill, Greta Scacchi, John Hargreaves.

COUPE DE VILLE
UNIVERSAL. March, 1990. (Joe Roth) Patrick Dempsey, Daniel Stern, Alan Arkin.

COUNT ME OUT
ICELANDIC FILM CORP/FILMHUSET/PETER ROMMEL FILM-PRODUKTION/ ZENTROPA. May, 1998. Icelandic-Norwegian-German-Danish. (Ari Kristinsson) Bergthora Aradottir, Freydis Kristofersdottir.

COURAGE MOUNTAIN
TRIUMPH. February, 1990. (Christopher Leitch) Juliette Caton, Leslie Caron, Charlie Sheen.

COURAGE UNDER FIRE
20TH CENTURY FOX. June, 1996. (Edward Zwick) Denzel Washington, Meg Ryan, Lou Diamond Phillips.

THE COURTYARD
Studio Uljana Kim. May, 1999. Lithuanian-French. (Valdas Navasaitas) Donatas Banionis, Richardas Vitkaitas, Albinas Keleris, Tatjana Liutajeva.

THE COUSIN
LES FILMS ALAIN SARDE/TF1 FILMS PROD./DIVALI FILMS & CO./ CINEMATOGRAPHIQUE PRIMA. Dec., 1997. French. (Alain Corneau) Alain Chabat, Patrick Timsit, Samuel Le Bihan, Caroline Proust.

COUSIN BETTE
FOX SEARCHLIGHT. June, 1998. (Des McAnuff) Jessica Lange, Elisabeth Shue, Bob Hoskins, Hugh Laurie, Kelly Macdonald.

COUSIN BOBBY
CINEVISTA. May, 1992. (Jonathan Demme) Documentary.

COVENTRY
CHIMBORAZO PICTURES. Feb., 1998. (J. Trumbull Foster) Ryan Gibson, Felicity Jones, Clint Jordan, Lynn Jordan, Tia Hunnicut.

THE COW
CZECH TV/PUBLIC TH. February, 1995. Czech. (Karyl Kachyna) Radek Holub, Alena Mikulova.

THE COWBOY WAY
UNIVERSAL. June, 1994. (Gregg Champion) Woody Harrelson, Kiefer Sutherland, Dylan McDermott.

COWS (VACAS)
PUBLIC THEATRE. June, 1994. Spanish. (Julio Medem) Manuel Blasco, Emma Suarez, Carmelo Gomez.

THE COW'S ORGASM
ATTIKA SA/HYPERION PROD. Feb., 1997. Greek. (Olga Malea) Irini Balta, Natalia Stylianou, Eleni Gerasimidou, Katerina Didaskalou.

COYOTES
COYOTE MOON. Jan., 1999. (Kevin McCarey) Leo Gannan, Kristen Carmody, Lina Gallegos, Louis Caracas.

CRACK 6-T
BAC FILMS. May, 1997. French. (Jean-Francois Richet) Arco Descat C., Jean-Marie Robert, Malik Zeggou, Moustapha Ziad.

CRACKDOWN
CONCORDE. January, 1991. (Louis Morneau) Cliff De Young, Robert Beltran, Jamie Rose.

CRACKERS
SHARMILL/BEYOND FILMS. Feb., 1998. Australian. (David Swann) Warren Mitchell, Daniel Kellie, Peter Rowsthorn, Susan Lyons.

CRADLE WILL ROCK
BUENA VISTA. May, 1999. (Tim Robbins) Hank Azaria, Ruben Blades, Joan Cusack, John Cusack.

THE CRAFT
COLUMBIA. May, 1996. (Andrew Fleming) Robin Tunney, Fairuza Balk, Neve Campbell, Rachel True, Skeet Ulrich.

CRASHING EDEN
AXIOM FILMS. Mar., 1999. (Dean Alioto) Paul Ghiringhelli, Jodi Verdu, Rick Williams, Alecia Derwin.

CRAZY ENGLISH
XI'AN FILM STUDIO. Aug., 1999. Chinese. (Zhang Yuan). Documentary..

CRAZY IN ALABAMA
SONY. Aug., 1999. (Antonio Banderas) Melanie Griffith, David Morse, Lucas Black, Cathy Moriarty, Meat Loaf Aday.

CRAZY PEOPLE
PARAMOUNT. April, 1990. (Tony Bill) Dudley Moore, Daryl Hannah, Paul Reiser.

THE CRAZY STRANGER
PRINCES FILM. Aug., 1997. French. (Tony Gatlif) Romain Duris, Rona Hartner, Izidor Serban, Florin Moldovan.

THE CREATOR
REZO FILMS. Apr., 1999. French. (Albert Dupontel) Albert Dupontel, Calude Perron, Philippe Uchan, Michel Vuillermoz.

CREATURE
GRAPEVINE FILMS. June, 1999. (Parris Patton) Stacey"Hollywood" Dean, Butch Dean, Dusty Dean, Filberto "Barbarella" Ascencio. Documentary.

CRIME BROKER
A-PIX. September, 1994. Australian. (Ian Barry) Jacqueline Bisset, Masaya Kato.

CRIMETIME
TRIMARK. August, 1996. (George Sluizer) Stephen Baldwin, Pete Postlethwaite, Sadie Frost, Gerladine Chaplin.

CRIMINAL LOVERS
MARS FILMS. July, 1999. French-Japanese. (Francois Ozon). Natacha Regnier, Jeremie Renier, Miki Manojlovic, Salim Kechiouche.

CRIMSON TIDE
BUENA VISTA. May, 1995. (Tony Scott) Denzel Washington, Gene Hackman, George Dzundza.

CRISSCROSS
MGM. May, 1992. (Chris Menges) Goldie Hawn, Arliss Howard, David Arnott, Keith Carradine.

CRITICAL CARE
LIVE ENTERTAINMENT. Oct., 1997. (Sidney Lumet) James Spader, Kyra Sedgwick, Helen Mirren, Margo Martindale, Jeffrey Wright, Wallace Shawn, Anne Bancroft, Albert Brooks.

CRONOS
OCTOBER FILMS. March, 1994. Mexican. (Guillermo Del Toro) Federico Luppi, Ron Perlman, Claudio Brook.

CROOKED HEARTS
MGM. May, 1991. (Michael Bortman) Vincent D'Onofrio, Jennifer Jason Leigh, Peter Berg.

CROOKLYN
UNIVERSAL. May, 1994. (Spike Lee) Alfre Woodard, Delroy Lindo, Zelda Harris.

THE CROSS
AGRESTI FILMS/ORLER. May, 1997. Argentine. (Alejandro Agresti) Norman Briski, Mirta Busnelli, Carlos Roffe, Laura Melillo.

CROSS MY HEART (LA FRACTURE DU MYOCARDE)
MK2. April, 1991. French. (Jacques Fansten) Sylvain Copans, Nicolas Parodi, Cecilia Rouaud.

CROSSCUT
PAVLIC-RAIMONDI. October, 1995. (Paul Raimondi) Costas Mandylor, Megan Gallagher, Casey Sander.

CROSSFIRE
GEE PEE FILMS. Feb., 1998. Indian. (Rituparno Ghosh) Suchitra Mitra, Indrani Haldar, Rituparna Sengupta, Abhishek Chatterjee.

THE CROSSING GUARD
MIRAMAX. November, 1995. (Sean Penn) Jack Nicholson, Angelica Houston, Robin Wright, David Morse.

CROSSING THE BRIDGE
BUENA VISTA. September, 1993. (Mike Binder) Josh Charles, Jason Gedrick, Stephen Baldwin.

CROSSING THE LINE (THE BIG MAN)
MIRAMAX. August, 1991. British. (David Leland) Liam Neeson, Joanne Whalley-Kilmer, Ian Bannen.

CROSSMAHEART
LEXINGTON FILMS. May, 1998. British. (Henry Herbert) Gerard Rooney, Maria Lennon, Desmond Cave, Tim Sloane.

CROUPIER
CHANNEL FOUR FILMS. Feb., 1998. British-German. (Mike Hodges) Clive Owen, Kate Hardie, Alex Kingston, Gina Mckee, Nicholas Ball.

THE CROW
MIRAMAX. May, 1994. (Alex Proyas) Brandon Lee, Ernie Hudson, Michael Wincott.

THE CROW II: CITY OF ANGELS
MIRAMAX/DIMENSION. August, 1996. (Tim Pope) Vincent Perez, Richard Brooks, Mia Kirschner, Iggy Pop.

THE CRUCIBLE
20TH CENTURY FOX. October, 1996. (Nicholas Hytner), Daniel Day-Lewis, Winona Ryder, Paul Scofield, Joan Allen, Bruce Davison.

THE CRUDE OASIS
MIRAMAX. July, 1995. (Alex Graves) Jennifer Taylor, Aaron Shields, Robert Peterson.

CRUEL INTENTIONS
SONY. Feb., 1999. (Roger Kumble) Sarah Michelle Gellar, Ryan Phillippe, Reese Witherspoon, Selma Blair.

THE CRUISE
CHARTER FILMS. April, 1998. DOCUMENTARY.

CRUMB
SONY PICTURES CLASSICS. April, 1995. (Terry Zwigoff) Documentary.

THE CRUSADE OF ANNE BURIDAN
LOLISTAR. December, 1995. (Judith Cahen) Judith Cahen, Joel Luecht.

CRUSH
STRAND. September, 1993. New Zealand. (Alison MacLean) Marcia Gay Harden, Donogh Rees, Caitlin Bossley.

THE CRUSH
WARNER BROS. April, 1993. (Alan Shapiro) Cary Elwes, Alicia Silverstone, Jennifer Rubin.

CRY BABY
UNIVERSAL. April, 1990. (John Waters) Johnny Depp, Amy Locane, Polly Bergen, Ricki Lake.

A CRY IN THE NIGHT
CFP DISTRIB. April, 1996. Canadian. (Jean Beaudry) Pierre Curzi, Felix-Antoine Leroux, Louise Richer.

A CRY IN THE WILD
CONCORDE. June, 1990. (Mark Griffiths) Jared Rushton, Pamela Sue Martin.

CRY, THE BELOVED COUNTRY
MIRAMAX. December, 1995. (Darrell James Roodt) James Earl Jones, Richard Harris, Charles S. Dutton, Vusi Kunene.

THE CRYING GAME
MIRAMAX. November, 1992. British. (Neil Jordan) Stephen Rea, Forest Whitaker, Miranda Richardson.

LA CUCARACHA
FLASHPOINT LTD. May, 1998. (Jack Perez) Eric Roberts, Joaquim De Almeida, Victor Rivers, Jack McManus, Tara Crespo.

THE CUP
PALM PICTURES. May, 1999. Australian. (Khyentse Norbu) Jamyang Lodro, Orgyen Tobgyal, Neten Chokling.

CUP FINAL
FIRST RUN FEATURES. August, 1992. Israeli. (Eran Riklis) Moshe Ivgi, Muhamad Bacri, Suheil Haddad.

CURDLED
MIRAMAX. September, 1996. (Reb Braddock) William Baldwin, Angela Jones, Bruce Ramsay, Barry Corbin.

CURE
DAIEI CO. Feb., 1998. Japanese. (Kiyoshi Kurosawa) Koji Yakusho, Tsuyoshi Ujiki, Anna Nakagawa.

THE CURE
UNIVERSAL. April, 1995. (Peter Horton) Joseph Mazzello, Brad Renfro, Annabella Sciorra.

THE CURE SHOW
I.R.S. October, 1993. (Aubrey Powell, Leroy Bennett) The Cure.

CURFEW
NEW YORKER. December, 1994. Dutch-Palestinian. (Rashid Masharawai) Salim Daw, Na'ila Zayaad, Younis Younis.

CURLY SUE
WARNER BROS. October, 1991. (John Hughes) James Belushi, Alisan Porter, Kelly Lynch.

CUTTHROAT ISLAND
MGM/MARIO KASSAR. December, 1995. (Benny Harlin) Geena Davis, Matthew Modine, Frank Langella.

THE CUTTING EDGE
MGM. March, 1992. (Paul M. Glaser) D.B. Sweeney, Moira Kelly, Roy Dotrice.

CUTTING LOOSE
LEAPFROG. January, 1996. (Susan Todd & Andrew Young) Documentary.

CYRANO DE BERGERAC
ORION CLASSICS. November, 1990. French. (Jean Paul Rappeneau) Gérard Depardieu, Anne Brochet.

D

D2: THE MIGHTY DUCKS
BUENA VISTA. March, 1994. (Sam Weisman) Emilio Estevez, Kathryn Erbe, Michael Tucker, Jan Rubes.

D3: THE MIGHTY DUCKS
BUENA VISTA. September, 1996. (Robert Lieberman) Emilio Estevez, Jeffrey Nording, Joshua Jackson, David Selby.

DAD SAVAGE
POLYGRAM FILMED ENTERTAINMENT. June, 1998. British. (Betsan Morris Evans) Patrick Stewart, Kevin McKidd, Helen McCrory.

DADDY NOSTALGIA
AVENUE. April, 1991. French. (Bertrand Tavernier) Dirk Bogarde, Jane Birkin, Odette Laure.

DADDY'S DYIN'... WHO'S GOT THE WILL?
MGM/UA. May, 1990. (Jack Fisk) Beau Bridges, Beverly D'Angelo, Keith Carradine, Tess Harper.

DADETOWN
KHXT. September 1995. (Russ Hexter) Bill Harrison, David Phelps, Jim Pryor, Jonathan Shafer.

DAGS
COVENTRY-WINFALZ-NEW OZ. Nov., 1998. Australian. (Murray Fahey) Tanya Bulmer, David Callan, Daniel Cordeaux, Sheena Crouch, Penny Cooper.

DANCE ME TO MY SONG
VERTIGO. April, 1998. Australian. (Rolf de Heer.) Heather Rose, Joey Kennedy, John Brumpton, Rena Owen, Phil Macpherson.

DANCE OF DUST
RASANEH-E-AMA. Aug., 1998. Iranian. (Abolfazl Jalili) Mahmood Khosravi, Limua Rahi.

DANCE WITH ME
SONY PICTURES. June, 1998. (Randa Haines) Vanessa Williams, Chayanne, Kris Kristopherson, Joan Plowright, Jane Krakowski.

DANCED
RADIO TELEVISION SERBIA/VIKTORIJA FILM. Feb., 1998. Serbian. (Purisa Djordjevic) Ana Sofrenovic, Ljuba Tadic, Dragan Micanovic.

DANCEMAKER
WALTER SCHEUER. June, 1998. (Matthew Diamond) DOCUMENTARY.

DANCER, TEXAS POP. 81
SONY PICTURES ENTERTAINMENT. March, 1998. (Tim McCanlies) Breckin Meyer, Peter Facinelli, Eddie Mills, Ethan Embry.

DANCES WITH WOLVES
ORION. November, 1990. (Kevin Costner) Kevin Costner, Mary McDonnell, Graham Greene.

DANCING AT LUGHNASA
SONY PICTURES CLASSICS. Sept., 1998. (Pat O'Connor) Meryl Streep, Michael Gambon, Catherine McCormack, Kathy Burke.

DANDY DUST
HANS SCHEIRL. June, 1998. British-Austrian. ((Hans Scheirl) Hans Scheirl, Suzie Krueger, Leonora Rogers-Wright, Tre Temperilli.

D.A.N.G.A.N RUNNER
NIKKATSU CORP. Feb., 1997. Japanese. (Sabu) Tomorowo Taguchi, Diamond Yukai, Shinichi Tsutsumi, Sabu.

DANG BIRELEY'S AND YOUNG GANGSTERS
TAI ENTERTAINMENT. Oct., 1997. Thai. (Nonzee Nimibutr) Jesdaporn Pholdee, Noppachai Muttaweevong, Attaporn Teemakorn.

DANGEROUS BEAUTY
WARNER BROS. Jan., 1998. (Marshall Herskovitz) Catherine McCormack, Rufus Sewell, Jacqueline Bissett, Oliver Platt.

DANGEROUS DOWRY
WARNER BROS. Feb., 1997. German. (Dennis Satin) Katja Riemann, Hannes Jaenicke, Heinz Hoenig, Daniela Lunkewitz.

DANGEROUS GAME
MGM. November, 1993. (Abel Ferrara) Harvey Keitel, Madonna, James Russo.

DANGEROUS GROUND
NEW LINE. February, 1997. (Darrell James Roodt), Ice Cube, Elizabeth Hurley, Ving Rhames, Eric Moyeni.

DANGEROUS MINDS
BUENA VISTA. August, 1995. (John N. Smith) Michelle Pfeiffer, George Dzundza, Courtney B. Vance.

A DANGEROUS WOMAN
GRAMERCY. December, 1993. (Stephen Gyllenhaal) Debra Winger, Barbara Hershey, Gabriel Byrne.

DANTE'S PEAK
UNIVERSAL. January, 1997. (Roger Donaldson), Pierce Brosnan, Linda Hamilton, Charles Hallahan, Grant Heslov, Elizabeth Hoffman.

DANZON
SONY PICTURES CLASSICS. September, 1992. Mexican. (Maria Novaro) Maria Rojo, Carmen Salinas, Blanca Guerra.

DAREDREAMER
LENSMAN CO. February, 1990. (Barry Caillier) Tim Noah, Alyce LaTourelle.

THE DARIEN GAP
NOMAD. January, 1996. (Brad Anderson) Lyn VBaus, Sandi Carroll.

DARK AT NOON
SIDERAL PRODS. August, 1993. French-Argentine. (Raul Ruiz) John Hurt, Didier Bourdon, David Warner.

THE DARK BACKWARD
GREYCAT FILMS. July, 1991. (Adam Rifkin) Judd Nelson, Bill Paxton, Wayne Newton.

DARK CITY
NEW LINE CINEMA. Feb., 1998. (Alex Proyas), Rufus Sewell, Kiefer Sutherland, Jennifer Connelly, William Hurt, Richard O'Brien.

THE DARKEST LIGHT
PATHE DISTRIBUTORS. Aug., 1999. British. (Bille Eltringham) Stephen Dillane, Kerry Fox, Keri Arnold, Kavita Sungha, Jason Walton.

THE DARK HALF
ORION. April, 1993. (George A. Romero) Timothy Hutton, Amy Madigan, Michael Rooker.

DARK HARBOR
HART SHARP ENTERPRISES. June, 1998. (Adam Coleman) Alan Rickman, Polly Walker, Norman Reedus.

DARK HORSE
REPUBLIC. July, 1992. (David Hemmings) Ed Begley Jr., Mimi Rogers, Ari Meyers.

DARK OBSESSION (DIAMOND SKULLS)
CIRCLE. June, 1991. British. (Nick Broomfield) Gabriel Byrne, Amanda Donohoe, Douglas Hodge.

DARKMAN
UNIVERSAL. August, 1990. (Sam Raimi) Liam Neeson, Frances McDormand, Colin Friels.

DARKNESS AND LIGHT
CHANG TSO-CHI FILM STUDIO. May, 1999. Taiwanese. (Chang Tso-chi Lee Kang-i, Tsai Ming-shiou, Shie Bau-huei, He Huang-ji, Lu Ing, Fan Jr-Uei.

DARK SUMMER
CINERENTA & MARIE HOY FILMS. May, 1999. Canadian. (Gregory Marquette) Jean-Hughes Anglade, Connie Nielsen, Mia Kirshner, Robert Culp, Anne Archer.

DAS BOOT
TRIUMPH. April, 1997. German. (Wolfgang Petersen) Jurgen Prochnow, Herbert Gronemeyer. Re-release of 1981 movie.

DATE WINE
MISR INTL. FILMS. Aug., 1998. Egyptian. (Radwan el-Kashef) Sherihan, Abla Kamel, Hamdy Ahmed, Mohamed Nagati.

DATING THE ENEMY
PANDORA FILM. May, 1996. Australian. (Megan Simpson Huberman) Claudia Karvan, Guy Pearce, Matt Day.

DAUGHTERS OF LUCK
STUDIO DOM, TV POLSKI/BUDAPEST FILMSTUDIO-LENGYEI TV/MANFRED DURNIOK PRODS. Feb., 1999. Polish-Hungarian-German. (Marta Meszaros) Olga Drozdowa, Jan Nowicki, Masha Petraniuk, Olaf Lubashenko, Ewa Telega.

DAUGHTERS OF THE DUST
KINO INT'L. January, 1992. (Julie Dash) Cora Lee Day, Alva Rodgers, Adisa Anderson.

DAVE
WARNER BROS. May, 1993. (Ivan Reitman) Kevin Kline, Sigourney Weaver, Frank Langella, Charles Grodin.

DAVIDE'S SUMMER
RAI CINEMAFICTION. Aug., 1998. Italian. (Carlo Mazzacurati) Stefano Campi, Patrizia Piccinini, Tony Bertorelli, Semsudin Mujic.

DAVY JONES' LOCKER
JACOBY. December, 1995. (Joseph Jacoby) Bil Baird's Marionettes.

DAY AFTER DAY
AGAV FILMS/CINEMA FACTORY. Sept., 1998. Israeli-French. (Amos Gitai) Moshe Ivgi, Hanna Maron, Juliano Merr, Dalit Kahan.

DAY AND NIGHT
LES FILMS DU LENDEMAIN. Feb., 1997. French-Canadian-Belgian-Spanish. (Bernard-Henri Levy) Alain Delon, Lauren Bacall.

DAYBREAK
SUEDDEUTSCHER RUNDFUNK/MARAN FILM. May, 1998. German. (Oliver Storz) Stefan Kurt, Karoline Eichhorn, Bruno Ganz.

A DAY IN BLACK AND WHITE
JON GOLD AND DESMOND HALL. Mar., 1999. (Desmond Hall) Harold Perrineau, Anthony DeSando, Francie Swift, Joseph Siravo.

DAYLIGHT
UNIVERSAL. November, 1996. (Rob Cohen), Sylvester Stallone, Amy Brenneman, Viggo Mortensen, Dan Hedaya, Jay O. Sanders.

THE DAY OF BIRTH
NATIONAL FILM DEVELOPMENT CORP. Feb., 1999. Indian. (Suma Josson) Nandita Das, Surekha Sikri.

DAY OF THE FULL MOON
KURIER STUDIOS. SEPT., 1998. Russian. (Karen Shakhnazarov) Vladimir Ilyin, Valeri Premykhov, Valeri Storozhik, Anna Germ.

DAYS OF THUNDER
PARAMOUNT. June, 1990. (Tony Scott) Tom Cruise, Robert Duvall, Nicole Kidman.

THE DAY THE SUN TURNED COLD
KINO. April, 1995. Chinese. (Yim Ho) Siqin Gowa, Tuo Zhong Hua, Ma Jing Wu.

THE DAYTRIPPERS
March, 1996. (Greg Mottola) Hope Davos, Pat McNamara, Anne Meara, Parker Posey, Stanley Tucci, Campbell Scott.

DAZED AND CONFUSED
GRAMERCY. September, 1993. (Richard Linklater) Jason London, Joey Lauren Adams, Anthony Rapp.

DEAD AGAIN
PARAMOUNT. August, 1991. (Kenneth Branagh) Kenneth Branagh, Emma Thompson, Derek Jacobi.

DEAD–ALIVE
TRIMARK. February, 1993. New Zealand. (Peter Jackson) Timothy Balme, Diana Penalver, Elizabeth Moody.

DEAD AVIATORS
ACCENT ENTERTAINMENT/TEMPLE STREET. Apr., 1999. Canadian. (David Wellington) Lothaire Bluteau, Marsha Mason, Michel Monty.

DEAD DOGS
ONE EIGHT FIVE FILMS. May, 1999. (Clay Eide) Joe Reynolds, Jay Underwood, Margot Demeter, John Durbin.

DEAD END
LIONS GATE. Mar., 1999. Canadian. (Richard Ciupka) Luc Picard, Julien Poulin, Michel Goyette, Serge Houde, Lorne Brass.

DEAD FLOWERS
OAK ISLAND. April, 1993. Austrian. (Peter Ily Huemer) Kate Valk, Thierry van Werveke, Tana Schanzara.

DEAD FUNNY
CINEPIX. July, 1995. (John Feldman) Andrew McCarthy, Elizabeth Pena, Paige Turco.

DEAD LEAVES
RED LION TAMARIS. Oct.,1998. (Constantin Werner) Haim Abramski, Elisabeth Gondek.

DEAD LETTER OFFICE
POLYGRAM FILMED ENTERTAINMENT. May, 1998. Australian. (John Ruane) Miranda Otto, George DelHoyo, Nicholas Bell, Syd Brisbane.

DEAD MAN
MIRAMAX. May, 1996. (Jim Jarmusch) Johnny Depp, Gary Farmer, Lance Henriksen, Iggy Pop, Crispin Glover.

DEAD MAN ON CAMPUS
PARAMOUNT PICTURES. Aug., 1998. (Alan Cohn) Tom Everett Scott, Mark-Paul Gosselaar, Poppy Montgomery, Lochlyn Munro.

DEAD MAN WALKING
GRAMERCY. December, 1995. (Tim Robbins) Susan Sarandon, Sean Penn, Robert Prosky.

DEAD MAN'S CURVE
ALAN SIRITZKY/HOPE STREET ENTERTAINMENT. Jan., 1998. (Dan Rosen), Matthew Lillard, Michael Vartan, Randall Batinkoff.

DEAD MEN DON'T DIE
TRANS ATLANTIC. September, 1991. (Malcolm Marmorstein) Elliott Gould, Melissa Anderson, Mabel King.

DEAD PRESIDENTS
BUENA VISTA. October, 1995. (the Hughes Brothers) Larenz Tate, Keith David, Chris Tucker, N'Bushe Wright.

DEAD RINGER
OGDEN AVE. July, 1991. (Allan Nicholls) Meat Loaf, Josh Mostel, MacIntyre Dixon.

DEAD SILENCE
ALLIANCE COMMUNICATIONS. May, 1997. Canadian-U.S. (Daniel Petrie Jr.) James Garner, Marlee Matlin, Lolita Davidovich.

DEAD SPACE
CONCORDE. January, 1991. (Fred Gallo) Marc Singer, Laura Tate.

DEAD WOMEN IN LINGERIE
AFI USA. November, 1991. (Erica Fox) John Romo, Jerry Orbach, Dennis Christopher.

DEADFALL
TRIMARK. October, 1993. (Christopher Coppola) Michael Biehn, Sarah Trigger, Nicolas Cage.

DEADFUL MELODY
FILM CITY DIST. LTD. Jan., 1997. Hong Kong. (Ng Min-keng) Yuen Biao, Brigitte Lin Chin-hsia, Carina Lay Kar-ling, David Lam Wai.

DEADLY CURRENTS
NORMANDIE. October, 1992. Canadian. (Simcha Jacobovici) Documentary.

DEALER
ZDF/TRANS-FILM. Feb. 1999. German. (Thomas Arslan) Tamer Yigit, Idil Uner, Birol Unel, Hussi Kutlucan, Lea Stefane

DEAR CLAUDIA
UNITED INTL. PICTURES. Jan., 1999. Australian. (Chris Cudlipp) Bryan Brown, Aleksandra Vujcic, Rel Hunt, Deborah Mailman, Kim Hillas.

DEAR GOD
PARAMOUNT. October, 1996. (Garry Marshall), Greg Kinnear, Laurie Metcalf, Maris Pitillo, Tim Conway, Hector Elizondo, Jon Seda.

DEATH: A LOVE STORY
HARKEN. Jan., 1999. (Michelle Le Brun). Documentary.

DEATH AND THE COMPASS
TOGETHER BROS. PRODS. Oct., 1996. (Alex Cox) Peter Boyle, Miguel Sandoval, Christopher Eccleston.

DEATH AND THE MAIDEN
FINE LINE. December, 1994. French-British-U.S. (Roman Polanski) Sigourney Weaver, Ben Kingsley, Stuart Wilson.

DEATH BECOMES HER
UNIVERSAL. July, 1992. (Robert Zemeckis) Meryl Streep, Goldie Hawn, Bruce Willis.

DEATH IMPACT
PARAMOUNT.May, 1998. (Mimi Leder) Robert Duvall, Tea Leoni, Elijah Wood, Vanessa Redgrave, Morgan Freeman, James Cromwell.

DEATH IN GRENADA
COLUMBIA TRISTAR. Feb., 1997. Spanish-Puerto Rican. (Marcos Zurinaga) Andy Garcia, Esai Morales, Edward James Olmos.

DEATH IN THERAPY
ARENA FILMS & CAMERA ONE. Nov., 1996. French. (Francis Girod) Daniel Auteuil, Patrick Timsit, Anne Parillaud, Michele Laroque.

DEATH ON A FULL MOON DAY
PRASANNA VITHANAGE PRODS./JAPAN BROADCASTING. Oct., 1998. Sri Lankan-Japanese. (Prasanna Vithanage) Joe Abeywickrama, Nayana Hettiarachchi, Priyanka Samarawerera.

DEATH SENTENCE
EROS INTL. Nov., 1997. Indian. (Prakash Jha) Shabana Asmi, Madhuri Dixit, Om Puri, Ayub Khan.

DEATH WARRANT
MGM/UA. September, 1990. (Deran Sarafian) Jean Claude Van Damme, Robert Guillaume, Cynthia Gibb.

DEATH WISH V: THE FACE OF DEATH
TRIMARK. January, 1994. Canadian. (Allan A. Goldstein) Charles Bronson, Lesley Anne Down, Michael Parks.

THE DEBT COLLECTOR
FILMFOUR DISTRIBUTORS. Feb., 1999. British. (Anthony Neilson) Billy Connolly, Ken Stott, Francesca Annis, Iain Robertson, Annette Crosbie.

DECEIVED
BUENA VISTA. September, 1991. (Damian Harris) Goldie Hawn, John Heard, Ashley Peldon.

DECEMBER
I.R.S. December, 1991. (Gabe Torres) Wil Wheaton, Chris Young, Balthazar Getty, Brian Krause.

DECEMBER BRIDE
WAX/COURIER. September, 1994. Irish. (Thaddeus O'Sullivan) Saskia Reeves, Donal McCann, Ciaran Hinds.

DECEPTION
MIRAMAX. October, 1993. (Graeme Clifford) Liam Neeson, Andie MacDowell, Viggo Mortensen.

THE DECLINE OF WESTERN CIVILIZATION PART III
SPHEERIS FILMS. Jan., 1998. (Penelope Spheeris), DOCUMENTARY.

DECONSTRUCTING HARRY
FINE LINE. August, 1996. (Woody Allen), Caroline Aaron, Woody Allen, Kirstie Alley, Bob Balaban, Richard Benjamin, Eric Bogosian, Billy Crystal, Judy Davis.

DEEP BLUES
AFI USA. November, 1991. (Robert Mugge) Junior Kimbrough, Jessie Mae Hemphill.

DEEP BLUE SEA
WARNER BROS. July, 1999. (Renny Harlin) Thomas Jane, Saffron Burrows, Samuel L. Jackson, Jacqueline McKenzie.

DEEP COVER
NEW LINE. April, 1992. (Bill Duke) Laurence Fishburne, Jeff Goldblum, Victoria Dillard.

THE DEEP END OF THE OCEAN
SONY. Feb., 1999. (Ulu Grosbard) Michelle Pfeiffer, Treat Williams, Whoopi Goldberg, Jonathan Jackson.

DEEP IMPACT
PARAMOUNT PICTURES. May., 1998. (Mimi Leder) Robert Duvall, Tea Leoni, Vanessa Redgrave, Elijah Wood, Morgan Freeman.

DEEP IN THE FOREIGN LAND
BIM DISTRIBUZIONE. April, 1997. Italian-French-Swiss. (Fabio Carpi) Claude Rich, Valeria Cavalli, Gregoire Colin, Renee Faure.

DEEP RISING
BUENA VISTA. Jan., 1998. (Stephen Sommers) Treat Williams, Famke Janssen, Anthony Heald, Kevin J. O'Connor, Wes Studi.

THE DEER'S ROOM
TELEWIZJA POLSKA. Oct., 1998. Polish. (Lech Majewski) Rafal Olbrychski, Elzbieta Mazur, Mieczyslaw Czepulonis, Agnieszka Wroblewska.

DEE SNIDER'S STRANGELAND
RAUCOUS RELEASING. Oct., 1998. (John Pieplow) Dee Snider, Kevin Gage, Brett Harrelson, Elizabeth Pena.

DEF BY TEMPTATION
TROMA. March, 1990. (James Bond III) James Bond III, Cynthia Bond, Kadeem Hardison.

DEF JAM'S HOW TO BE A PLAYER
GRAMERCY. Aug., 1997. (Lionel C. Martin) Bill Bellamy, Natalie Desselle, Lark Voorhies, Mari Morrow, Pierre, Jermaine (Big Hugg) Hopkins, A.J. Johnson, Max Julien, Beverly Johnson.

DEFENDING YOUR LIFE
WARNER BROS. March, 1991. (Albert Brooks) Albert Brooks, Meryl Streep, Rip Torn.

DEFENSELESS
7 ARTS/NEW LINE. August, 1991. (Martin Campbell) Barbara Hershey, Sam Shepard, Mary Beth Hurt.

DEFYING GRAVITY
BOOM PICTURES. June, 1997. (John Keitel) Daniel Chilson, Niklaus Lange, Don Handfield, Linna Carter, Seabass Diamond, Lesley Tesh.

DEJA VU
RAINBOW FILM CO./REVERE ENTERTAINMENT. Oct., 1998. (Henry Jaglom) Stephen Dillane, Victoria Foyt, Vanessa Redgrave.

THE DELI
GOLDEN MONKEY PICTURES. March, 1997. (John Gallagher) Mike Starr, Matt Keeslar, Judith Malina, Brian Vincent, Ice-T.

THE DELICATE ART OF THE RIFLE
CAMBRAI LIBERATION COLLECTIVE. March, 1996. (D.W. Harper) David Grant, Stephen Grany, John Kessel.

DELICATESSEN
MIRAMAX. April, 1992. French. (Jean Pierre Jeunet, Marc Caro) Marie-Laure Dougnac, Jean Claude Dreyfus.

DELIRIOUS
MGM. August, 1991. (Tom Mankiewicz) John Candy, Mariel Hemingway, Dylan Baker, Emma Samms.

DELIVERED
BANNER ENTERTAINMENT. May, 1998. (Guy Ferland) David Strickland, Ron Eldard, Leslie Stefanson, Scott Bairstow, Nicky Katt.

DELIVERED VACANT
ISLET. May, 1993. (Nora Jacobson) Documentary.

DELPHINE 1—YVAN 0
AMLF. June, 1996. French. (Dominique Farrugia) Julie Gayet, Serge Hazanavicius, Dominique Farrugia.

DELTA FORCE 2
MGM/UA. August, 1990. (Aaron Norris) Chuck Norris, Billy Drago, John P. Ryan.

DELUSION
I.R.S. MEDIA. June, 1991. (Carl Colpaert) Jim Metzler, Jennifer Rubin, Kyle Secor.

DEMOLITION HIGH
SUNSET FILMS INTL. May, 1996. (Jim Wynorski) Corey Haim, Alan Thicke, Jeff Kober.

DEMOLITION MAN
WARNER BROS. October, 1993. (Marco Brambilla) Sylvester Stallone, Wesley Snipes, Sandra Bullock.

DEMONSTONE
FRIES. March, 1990. (Andrew Prowse) Jan Michael Vincent, R. Lee Ermey.

DENIAL
KUSHNER-LOCKE/TAPESTRY FILMS. June, 1998. (Adam Rifkin), Jonathan Silverman, Leah Lail, Ryan Alosio, Amy Yasbeck.

DENNIS THE MENACE
WARNER BROS. June, 1993. (Nick Castle) Walter Matthau, Mason Gamble, Joan Plowright.

DESERET
December, 1995. (James Benning) Documentary.

DESERT BLUE
SAMUEL GOLDWYN CO. Sept., 1998. (Morgan J. Freeman) Brendan Sexton III, Kate Hudson, Christina Ricci, John Heard, Lucinda Jenney.

THE DESIGNATED MOURNER
FIRST LOOK PICTURES. Feb., 1997. British. (David Hare) Mike Nichols, Miranda Richardson, David de Keyser.

DESIRE
AMLF March, 1996. French. (Bernard Murrat) Jean-Paul Belmondo, Fanny Arant, Beatrice Dalle.

DESIRE & HELL AT SUNSET MOTEL
TWO MOON RELEASING. April, 1992. (Allen Castle) Sherilyn Fenn, Whip Hubley, David Hewlett.

DESIRE: SEXUALITY IN GERMANY, 1910–1945
MAYAVISION. June, 1990. British. (Stuart Marshall) Documentary.

DESPERADO
COLUMBIA. August, 1995. (Robert Rodriguez) Antonio Banderas, Joaquim de Almeida, Salma Hayek.

DESPERATE ACQUAINTANCES
MEFISTOFILM AS . Feb., 1999. Norwegian. (Svend Wam) Anders Dale, Bjarte Hjelmeland, Bjornar Teigen.

DESPERATE HOURS
MGM. October, 1990. (Michael Cimino) Mickey Rourke, Anthony Hopkins, Mimi Rogers.

DESPERATE REMEDIES
MIRAMAX. May, 1994. New Zealand. (Stewart Main, Peter Wells) Jennifer Ward Lealand, Kevin Smith, Lisa Chappell.

DESTINY
PYRAMIDE. May, 1997. Fremch-Egyptian. (Youssef Chahine) Nour El Cherif, Laila Eloui, Hani Salama, Khaled El Nabaoui.

DESTINY
LES FILMS DU XXEME/LA SEPT CINEMA. May, 1997. French-Guinean. (Mohamed Camara) Aboubacar Toure, Mamady.

THE DESTINY OF MARTY FINE
ONE-TWO PRDS. March, 1996. (Michael Hacker) Alan Gelfant, James LeGros, Catherine Keener.

DESTINY TURNS ON THE RADIO
SAVOY. April, 1995. (Jack Baran) James LeGros, Dylan McDermott, Quentin Tarantino.

DETECTIVE RIKO
KADOKAWA SHOTEN. Sept., 1998. Japanese. (Satoshi Isaka) Ryoko Takizawa, Toshiya Nagasawa.

DETROIT ROCK CITY
NEW LINE. Aug., 1999. (Adam Rifkin) Edward Furlong, Giuseppe Andrews, James De Bello, Sam Huntington.

DEVIL IN A BLUE DRESS
TRISTAR. September, 1995. (Carl Franklin) Denzel Washington, Jennifer Beals, Tom Sizemore.

THE DEVIL, PROBABLY
NEW YORKER. November, 1994. French. (Robert Bresson) Antoine Monnier, Tina Irissari, Henri de Maublanc.

THE DEVIL'S ADVOCATE
WARNER BROS. Oct., 1998. (Taylor Hackford), Keanu Reeves, Al Pacino, Charlize Theron, Jeffrey Jones, Judith Ivey, Connie Neilsen.

DEVIL'S ISLAND
ICELANDIC FILM CORP. Feb.,1997. Icelandic-German-Norwegian-Danish. (Fridrik Thor Fridriksson) Baltasar Kormakur, Gisli Halldorsson, Sigurveig Jonsdottir, Sveinn Geirsson.

THE DEVIL'S OWN
SONY PICTURES ENTERTAINMENT. March, 1997. (Alan J. Pakula), Harrison Ford, Brad Pitt, Margaret Colin, Ruben Blades, Treat Williams.

DHARMA BLUES
ANDREAS THOMOPOULOS/EPT/GREEK TELEVISION ET-1/FASMA/CINEMAGIC/GREEK FILM CENTRE. Nov., 1997. Greek. (Andreas Thomopoulos) Stavros Paravas, Tamilla Koulieva-Karantinaki.

DIABOLIQUE
WARNER BROS. March, 1996. (Jeremiah Chechik.) Sharon Stone, Isabelle Adjani, Chazz Palminteri, Kathy Bates.

DIALOGUES WITH MADWOMEN
LIGHT/SARAF. August, 1994. (Allie Light) Documentary.

DIAMONDS
MIRAMAX. Sept. 1999. U.S. German. (John Asher) Kirk Douglas, Dan Aykroyd, Corbin Allred, Lauren Bacall, Kurt Fuller.

DIAMOND'S EDGE (JUST ASK FOR DIAMOND)
CASTLE HILL. November, 1990. British. (Stephen Bayly) Colin Dale, Dursley McLinden, Susannah York.

DIARY OF A HIT MAN
VISION INT'L. May, 1992. (Roy London) Forest Whitaker, Sherilyn Fenn, Sharon Stone.

DIARY OF A SEDUCER
GEMINI FILMS. December, 1995. French. (Daniele Dubroux) Chiara Mastroianni, Melvil Poupaud.

DIARY OF A YOUNG FOOL (MEMOIRE D'UN JEUNE CON)
MKL. January, 1996. French. (Patrick Aurignac) Christophe Hemon, Friancois Perier, Daniel Russo, Aurignac.

DICE RULES
7 ARTS. May, 1991. (Jay Dubin) Andrew Dice Clay.

DICK
SONY. July, 1999. (Andrew Fleming) Kirsten Dunst, Michelle Williams, Jim Breuer, Will Ferrell, Dave Foley.

DICK TRACY
BUENA VISTA. June, 1990. (Warren Beatty) Warren Beatty, Madonna, Al Pacino, Charlie Korsmo.

DIE HARD 2
20TH CENTURY FOX. July, 1990. (Remy Harlin) Bruce Willis, Bonnie Bedelia, Franco Nero.

DIE HARD WITH A VENGEANCE
20TH CENTURY FOX. May, 1995. (John McTiernan) Bruce Willis, Jeremy Irons, Samuel L. Jackson.

DIFFERENT FOR GIRLS
BBC FILMS. January, 1996. (Richard Spence) Steven Mackintosh, Rupert Graves, Saskia Reeves.

DIGGING TO CHINA
MOONSTONE ENTERTAINMENT. Jan., 1998. (Timothy Hutton) Kevin Bacon, Mary Stuart Masterson, Cathy Moriarty, Evan Rachel Wood.

DIGGSTOWN
MGM. August, 1992. (Michael Ritchie) James Woods, Louis Gossett, Jr., Bruce Dern.

DILL SCALLION
PEDESTRIAN FILMS. Jan., 1999. (Jordan Brady) Billy Burke, Peter Berg, Lauren Graham, Kathy Griffin, David Koechner.

THE DINNER
ACORN. Aug., 1997. (Bernie Casey) Bernie Casey, Wren T. Brown, Doug Johnson, Meg Register, Lew Tate.

THE DINNER
MEDUSA. Nov., 1998. Italian. (Ettore Scola) Fanny Ardent, Vittorio Gassman, Stefania Sandrelli, Lea Gramsdorff.

THE DINNER GAME
GAUMONT BUENA VISTA INTL. April, 1998. French. (Francis Weber) Jacquest Villeret, Thierry Lhermitte, Francis Huster.

DIPLOMATIC IMMUNITY
FRIES ENT. April, 1991. (Peter Maris) Bruce Boxleitner, Billy Drago, Tom Breznahan.

DIRTY
DIRTY/STEPHEN HEGYES. Jan., 1998. Canadian. (Bruce Sweeney) Tom Scholte, Babz Chula, Benjamin Ratner, Nancy Sivak.

DIRTY LAUNDRY
HOLLYWOOD PRODS./ROGUE FEATURES. Nov., 1996. (Robert Sherwin, Michael Normand) Jay Thomas, Tess Harper.

DIRTY LINEN
CDI. Jan. 1999. Italian. (Mario Monicelli) Mechele Placido, Mariangela Melato, Paolo Bonacelli, Alessandro Haber, Marina Confalone.

DIRTY MONEY
NORTHERN ARTS. May, 1995. (James Bruce) Frederick Deane, Timothy Patrick Cavanaugh, Biff Yeager.

DIRTY WORK
MGM. June, 1998. (Bob Saget) Norm MacDonald, Jack Warden, Artie Lange, Traylor Howard, Don Rickles, Chevy Chase.

THE DISAPPEARANCE OF FINBAR
FILM FOUR DISTRIBUTION. Sept., 1996. British-Irish-Swedish. (Sue Clayton) Jonathan Rhys-Myers, Luke Griffin, Fanny Risberg.

THE DISAPPEARANCE OF KEVIN JOHNSON
BEDFORD COMMS. GROUP. July, 1997. British-U.S. (Francis Megahy) Pierce Brosnan, James Coburn, Dudley Moore.

DISCLOSURE
WARNER BROS. December, 1994. (Barry Levinson) Michael Douglas, Demi Moore, Donald Sutherland.

DISH DOGS
FILMWAVE PICTURES. May, 1998. (Robert Kubilos) Sean Astin, Matthew Lillard, Brian Dennehy, Shannon Elizabeth, Maitland Ward.

THE DISTINGUISHED GENTLEMAN
BUENA VISTA. December, 1992. (Jonathan Lynn) Eddie Murphy, Lane Smith, Sheryl Lee Ralph.

DISTURBED
LIVE ENTERTAINMENT. November, 1990. (Charles Winkler) Malcolm McDowell, Geoffrey Lewis, Priscilla Pointer.

DISTURBING BEHAVIOR
MGM. July, 1998. (David Nutter) James Marsden, Katie Holmes, Nick Stahl, Stever Railsback, Bruce Greenwood, William Sadler.

DIVINE
PRODUCCIONES AMARANTA. Mexican-Argentine-Spanish. (Arturo Ripstein) Francisco Rabal, Katy Jurado, Caroline Papaleo.

DIVINE BODY
UNDERWORLD FILMS. April, 1998. Belgian-Benin. (Dominique Loreau) Alphonse Atacolodjou, Szymon Zaleski, Fidele Gbegnon.

DIVINE OBSESSION
PANORAMA ENTERTAINMENT. March, 1990. (Yuri Sivo) Brian Benben, Deborah Farentino.

DIVINE TRASH
STRATOSPHERE. Jan., 1998. (Steve Yeager) DOCUMENTARY.

DIVING IN
SKOURAS. September, 1990. (Strathford Hamilton) Matt Adler, Burt Young, Matt Lattanzi.

DIVINITY GRATIS
Jan., 1997. (Betzy Bromberg) Claire Dishman, Kirby White, Duchess DeSade, Kory Ivy Vence.

DIVORCE IRANIAN STYLE
TWENTIETH CENTRY VIXEN. Aug., 1998. British. (Kim Longinotto, Ziba Mir-Hosseini). Documentary.

DIVORCING JACK
BBC FILMS/WINCHESTER FILMS. May, 1998. British-French. (David Caffrey) David Thewlis, Rachel Griffiths, Robert Lindsay.

DJEMBEFOLA
INTERAMA. September, 1993. French. (Laurent Chevalier) Documentary.

DO OR DIE
MALIBU BAY. June, 1991. (Andy Sidaris) Pat Morita, Erik Estrada, Dona Speir.

DOC HOLLYWOOD
WARNER BROS. August, 1991. (Michael Caton Jones) Michael J. Fox, Julie Warner, Barnard Hughes.

THE DOCTOR
BUENA VISTA. July, 1991. (Randa Haines) William Hurt, Elizabeth Perkins, Christine Lahti.

THE DOG IN THE MANGER
COLUMBIA TRISTAR. Sept., 1996. Spanish. (Pilar Miro) Emma Suarez, Carmelo Gomez, Fernando Conde, Ana Duato.

A DOG OF FLANDERS
WARNER BROS. Aug., 1999. (Kevin Brodie): Jack Warden, Jeremy James Kissner, Jesse James, Jon Voight, Cheryl Ladd.

DOG PARK
LIONS GATE FILMS. Sept., 1998. Canadian. (Bruce McCulloch) Natasha Henstridge, Luke Wilson, Kathleen Robertson, Janeane Garofalo.

DOG RUN
C&P PRODS. April, 1996. (D. Ze'ev Gilad) Brian Marc, Craid DuPlessis, Lisa Ristorucci, Elizabeth Horsburgh.

DOG TAGS
CINEVEST ENTERTAINMENT. February, 1990. (Romano Scavolini) Clive Wood, Baird Stafford.

DOG YEARS
AGIT JACK FILM. March, 1998. (Robert Loomis) R. Michael Caincross, Ted Parks, Veronica Loomis, Shawn Smith, Charlie Rivers.

DOGFIGHT
WARNER BROS. September, 1991. (Nancy Savoca) River Phoenix, Lili Taylor, Richard Panebianco.

DOGTOWN
DONALD ZUCKERMAN PROD. April, 1997. (George Hickenlooper) Trevor St. John, Mary Stuart Masterson, Jon Favreau.

DOING TIME FOR PATSY CLINE
DENDY FILMS. April, 1997. Australian. (Chris Kennedy) Richard Roxburgh, Miranda Otto, Matt Day, Tony Barry.

THE DOLL
PLUS FILMS. May, 1997. Indian (Goutam Ghose) Mithum Chakraborty, Nandana Dev Sen, Pran, Mohan Agashe.

DOLORES CLAIBORNE
COLUMBIA. March, 1995. (Taylor Hackford) Kathy Bates, Jennifer Jason Leigh, Christopher Plummer.

DON
CMI. May, 1998. Iranian. (Abolfazi Jalili) Farhad Bahremand, Bakhtiyar Bahremand, Farzad Helili.

DON JUAN DEMARCO
NEW LINE. April, 1995. (Jeremy Leven) Marlon Brando, Johnny Depp, Faye Dunaway.

DON JUAN, MY LOVE
IFEX. July, 1991. Spanish. (Antonio Mercero) Juan Luis Galiardo, Maria Barranco, Loles Leon.

DONKA: X-RAY OF AN AFRICAN HOSPITAL
LES FILMS DE LA PASSERELLE/ZEAUX PRODS. April, 1997. Belgian-French. (Thierry Michel) Documentary.

DONNIE BRASCO
SONY PICTURES ENTERTAINMENT. February, 1997. (Mike Newell), Al Pacino, Johnny Depp, Michael Madsen, Bruno Kirby, James Russo, Anne Heche, Zeljko Ivanek.

DON'T BE A MENACE TO SOUTH CENTRAL WHILE DRINKING YOUR JUICE IN THE HOOD
MIRAMAX. January, 1996. (Paris Barclay) Shawn Wayans, Marlon Wayans.

DON'T GO BREAKING MY HEART
POLYGRAM. Jan. 1999. British. (Willi Patterson) Anthony Edwards, Jenny Seagrove, Charles Dance, Jane Leeves, Lynda Bellinghaml.

DON'T LET ME DIE ON A SUNDAY
PROGRAM 33. Sept., 1998. French. (Didier Le Pecheur) Elodie Bouchez, Jean-Marc Barr, Martin Petitguyot, Patrick Catalifo, Gerard Loussine.

DON'T LOOK BACK
EURO SPACE/THE FILM SCHOOL OF TOKYO. Aug., 1999. Japanese. (Akihiko Shiota) Yusaki Suzuki, Shingo Mizuno, Yuria Haga, Yuuya Suzuki.

DON'T TELL ANYONE
LOLAFILMS DISTRIBUCION. Sept., 1998. Spanish-Peruvian. (Franscisco J. Lombardi) Santiago Magill, Lucia Jimenez, Christian Meier, Carmen Elias, Hernan Romero, Giovanni Ciccia.

DON'T TELL HER IT'S ME
HEMDALE. September, 1990. (Malcolm Mowbray) Steve Guttenberg, Shelley Long, Jami Gertz.

DON'T TELL MOM THE BABYSITTER'S DEAD
WARNER BROS. June, 1991. (Stephen Herek) Christina Applegate, Joanna Cassidy, Keith Coogan.

THE DOOM GENERATION
TRIMARK November , 1995. (Gregg Araki) Jonathan Scheach, Margaret Cho, Perry Farrell, James Duval.

THE DOORS
TRISTAR. March, 1991. (Oliver Stone) Val Kilmer, Meg Ryan, Frank Whaley, Kyle MacLachlan.

DOUBLE DRAGON
GRAMERCY. November, 1994. (James Yukich) Robert Patrick, Mark Dacascos, Scott Wolf.

DOUBLE EDGE
CASTLE HILL. September, 1992. Israeli-U.S. (Amos Kollek) Faye Dunaway, Amos Kollek, Mohammad Bakri.

DOUBLE HAPPINESS
FINE LINE. July, 1995. Canadian. (Mina Shum) Sandra Oh, Alannah Ong, Stephen Chang.

DOUBLE IMPACT
COLUMBIA. August, 1991. (Sheldon Lettich) Jean Claude Van Damme, Geoffrey Lewis, Alan Scarfe.

DOUBLE JEOPARDY
PARAMOUNT PICTURES. Sept., 1999. (Bruce Beresford) Tommy Lee Jones, Ashley Judd, Bruce Greenwood, Annbeth Gish.

THE DOUBLE LIFE OF VERONIQUE
MIRAMAX. November, 1991. French-Polish. (Krzysztof Kieslowski) Irene Jacob, Halina Gryglaszewska.

DOUBLE TEAM
SONY PICTURES ENTERTAINMENT. March, 1997. (Tsui Hark), Jean-Claude Van Damme, Dennis Rodman, Mickey Rourke.

DOUBLE THREAT
PYRAMID. December, 1992. (David A. Prior) Sally Kirkland, Andrew Stevens, Richard Lynch.

DOUG'S 1ST MOVIE
BUENA VISTA. Mar., 1999. (Maurice Joyce). Animated.

DOWNHILL CITY
LUNA FILM, ZDF, DFFB/TALENT HOUSE, TV 4. June, 1999. Finnish. (Hannu Salonen) Franka Potente, Teemu Aromaa, Andreas Brucher, Michaela Rosen, Sebastian Rudolph.

DOWN IN THE DELTA
MIRAMAX. Sept., 1998. (Maya Angelou) Alfre Woodard, Al Freeman, Jr., Mary Alice, Esther Rolle, Loretta Devine, Wesley Snipes.

DOWN PERSICOPE
20TH CENTURY FOX. March, 1996. (David S. Ward) Kelsey Grammar, Lauren Holly, Rob Schneider, Rip Torn.

DOWNTIME
FILM FOUR DISTRIBUTORS. Oct., 1997. British. (Bharat Nalluri) . Paul McGann, Susan Lynch, Tom Georgeson, David Roper.

DOWNTOWN
20TH CENTURY FOX. January, 1990. (Richard Benjamin) Anthony Edwards, Forest Whitaker, David Clennon.

DOWN WITH DEATH!
LES FILMS DU LOSANGE. MAY, 1999. FRENCH. (Romain Goupil) Romain Goupil, Marianne Denicourt, Anne Alvaro, Christine Murillo.

DR. AKAGI
IMAMURA PRODUCTIONS/TOEI CO. May, 1998. Japanese. (Shohei Imamura) Akira Emoto, Kumiko Aso, Jyuro Kara, Masanori Sera.

DR. BETHUNE
TARA. September, 1993. Canadian. (Phillip Borsos) Donald Sutherland, Helen Mirren, Helen Shaver.

DR. CALIGARI
STEINER. May, 1990. (Stephen Sayadian) Madeleine Reynal, Fox Harris.

DR. DOLITTLE
20TH CENTURY FOX. June, 1998. (Betty Thomas) Eddie Murphy, Ossie Davis, Oliver Platt, Peter Boyle, Richard Schiff, Kristen Wilson.

DREAMING OF JOSEPH LEES
20TH CENTURY FOX/FOX SEARCHLIGHT. July, 1999. British-U.S. (Eric Styles) Samantha Morton, Lee Ross, Rupert Graves, Holly Aird, Miriam Margolyes, Frank Finlay.

DR. GIGGLES
UNIVERSAL. October, 1992. (Manny Coto) Larry Drake, Holly Marie Combs, Cliff De Young.

DR. JEKYLL AND MS. HYDE
SAVOY. August, 1995. (David F. Price) Tim Daly, Sean Young, Lysette Anthony.

DRACULA: DEAD AND LOVING IT
SONY PICTURES. December, 1995. (Mel Brooks) Leslie Nielsen, Peter MacNichol, Steven Weber, Amy Yasbeck.

DRAGON: THE BRUCE LEE STORY
UNIVERSAL. May, 1993. (Rob Cohen) Jason Scott Lee, Lauren Holly, Robert Wagner.

DRAGON TOWN STORY
CHINA STAR ENTERTAINMENT. March, 1998. Hong-Kong-Chinese. (Yang Fengliang) Wu Chien-lien, You Yong, Huang Zhongqiu.

DRAGONHEART
UNIVERSAL. May, 1996. (Rob Cohen) Dennis Quaid, David Thewlis, Pete Postlethwaite, Dina Meyer, Julie Christie.

DRAWING FLIES
VIEW ASKEW/GOOD LOAD PRODS. Oct., 1996. Canadian. (Matt Gissing) Jason Lee, Renee Humphrey, Jason Mewes, Carmen Lee.

DREAM AND MEMORY
C&A PRODS. May, 1994. Chinese. (Ann Hu) Bing Yang, Shao Bing, Li Wei.

DREAM DECEIVERS
FIRST RUN FEATURES. August, 1992. (David Van Taylor) Documentary.

DREAM FOR AN INSOMNIAC
TRITONE PRODS. April, 1996. (Tiffanie DeBartolo) Ione Skye, Jennifer Aniston, Seymour Cassel, Mackenzie Austin.

THE DREAMLIFE OF ANGELS
BAGHEERA/DIAPHANA/FRANCE 3 CINEMA. May, 1998. French. (Erick Zonca) Elodie Bouchez, Natacha Regnier, Gregoire Colin.

DREAM LOVER
GRAMERCY. May, 1994. (Nicholas Kazan) James Spader, Madchen Amick, Bess Armstrong.

THE DREAM MACHINE
INT'L. CREATIVE EXCHANGE. September, 1991. (Lyman Dayton) Corey Haim, Evan Richards, Jeremy Slate.

DREAM WITH THE FISHES
3 RING CIRCUS FILMS. Jan., 1997. (Finn Taylor) David Arquette, Brad Hunt, Kathryn Erbe, Cathy Moriarty.

DREAMING OF RITA
FIRST RUN. April, 1995. Swedish. (Jon Lindstrom) Per Oscarsson, Marika Lagercrantz, Philip Zanden.

DREAMLAND
SILVER SPINE PRODS. Oct.,1996. (Robert Hein) Nitzan Gilady, Brian Schany, Wayquay, Sarah Heyes.

DRESDEN
Jan., 1999. (Ben Speth) Anne Lobst, Erik Kraus, Carol Schneider, Jeff Taylor.

DRIBBLING FATE
DAVID & GOLIAS /INSTITUTO CINEMA CABOVERDIANO/ACT. Feb., 1998. Portuguese-Cape Verdian-French. (Fernando Vendrell) Carlos Germano, Betina Lopes, Paulo Miranda, Daniel MartinhoO.

DRIFTING CLOUDS
CHRISTA SAREDI. May, 1996. Finnish. (Aki Kaurismaki) Kati Outinen, Kari Vaananen, Elina Salo.

A DRIFTING LIFE
CENTRAL MOTION PICTURE CORP. May, 1996. Taiwanese. (Lin Cheng-sheng) Lee Kang-sheng, Vicky Wei, Grace Chen.

DRIFTWOOD
BLUE DOLPHIN FILM & VIDEO. April, 1997. Irish. (Ronan O'Leary) James Spader, Anne Brochet, Barry McGovern, Anna Massey.

DRINKING GAMES
VILLAGE IDIOT PLAYHOUSE PRODS. March, 1996. (Joseph Lawson) Christian Leffler, Dinah Leffert, Geoffrey L. Smith.

DRIVE
MEGAGIANT ENT. July, 1992. (Jeffery Levy) David Warner, Steven Antin, Dedee Pfeiffer.

THE DRIVE
INDUSTRY ENTERTAINMENT. Jan., 1997. Canadian. (Romy Goulem) Daniel Brochu, Fab Fillipo, Alain Goulem, Jayne Paterson.

DRIVEN
PALISADES PICTURES. August, 1996. (Michael Paradies Shoob) Tony Todd, Whip Hubley, Chad Lowe.

DRIVING ME CRAZY
MOTION PICTURE CORP. OF AMER. November, 1991. (Jon Turtletaub) Thomas Gottschalk, Billy Dee Williams.

DRIVING ME CRAZY
FIRST RUN FEATURES. March, 1990. British. (Nick Broomfield) André Heller, Mercedes Ellington.

DROP DEAD FRED
NEW LINE. May, 1991. (Ate De Jong) Phoebe Cates, Rik Mayall, Marsha Mason.

DROP DEAD GORGEOUS
NEW LINE. June, 1999. (Michael Patrick) Kirsten Dunst, Ellen Barkin, Allison Janney, Denise Richards, Kirstie Alley.

DROP DEAD ROCK
SPAZZ-O PRODS. March, 1996. (Adam Dubin) Adam Ant, Deborah Harry, Ian Maynard, Shelly Mars.

DROP SQUAD
GRAMERCY. October, 1994. (D. Clark Johnson) Eriq La Salle, Vondie Curtis Hall, Ving Rhames.

DROP ZONE
PARAMOUNT. December, 1994. (John Badham) Wesley Snipes, Gary Busey, Yancy Butler, Michael Jeter.

DROWNING
SHANGHAI FILM STUDIO. November, 1995. Chinese. (Hu Xueyang) Xueyang, Saren Gaowa, Yang Ming.

DROWNING BY NUMBERS
PRESTIGE. April, 1991. British. (Peter Greenaway) Joan Plowright, Juliette Stevenson, Bernard Hill.

DRY CLEANING
AMLF. Sept., 1997. French-Spanish. (Anne Fontaine) Miou-Miou, Charles Berling, Stanislas Merhar, Mathilde Seigner.

DRYLONGSO
NATION SACK FILMWORK. Oct., 1998. (Cauleen Smith) Toby Smith, April Barnett, Will Power, Channel Schafer, Salim Akil.

DUCK TALES:
THE MOVIE—TREASURE OF THE LOST LAMP
BUENA VISTA. August, 1990. (Bob Hathcock) Animated.

DUDLEY DO-RIGHT
UNIVERSAL PICTURES. Aug., 1999 (High Wilson) Brendan Fraser, Sarah Jessica Parker, Alfred Molina, Eric Idle.

DUMB AND DUMBER
NEW LINE. December, 1994. (Peter Farrelly) Jim Carrey, Jeff Daniels, Lauren Holly.

DUMBARTON BRIDGE
BRIDGE PARTNERS. Mar., 1999. (Charles Koppelman) Tom Wright, Esperanza Catubig, Daphne Ashbrook, Leo Burmester.

DUNE WARRIORS
CONCORDE. January, 1991. (Cirio H. Santiago) David Carradine, Rick Hill, Luke Askew.

DUNSTON CHECKS IN
20TH CENTURY FOX. January, 1996. (Ken Kwapis) Jason Alexander, Faye Dunaway, Eric Lloyd, Rupert Everett.

DUST OF NAPLES
FULVIO LUCISANO. May, 1998. Italian. (Antonio Capuano) Gigio Morra, Antonio Iuorio, Gianni Ferreri, Alan De Luca.

DUTCH
20TH CENTURY FOX. July, 1991. (Peter Faiman) Ed O'Neill, Ethan Randall, JoBeth Williams.

DWM (DIVORCED WHITE MALE)
ARC ANGEL FILMS. July, 1999. (Lou Volpe) Lou Volpe, Lauren Bailey, Lydia De Luccia, Veronica Dipippo.

DYING OF LAUGHTER
LOLAFILMS. Mar., 1999. Spanish. (Alex de la Iglesia) Santiago Segura, El Gran Wyoming, Alex Angulo, Carla Hidalgo, Eduardo Gomez.

DYING YOUNG
20TH CENTURY FOX. June, 1991. (Joel Schumacher) Julia Roberts, Campbell Scott, Vincent D'Onofrio.

E

THE EAR
INT'L. FILM EXCHANGE. March, 1992. Czech. (Karel Kachyna) Radoslav Brzobahaty, Jirina Bohdalova.

EARTH
SOGEPAQ INTL. May, 1996. Spanish. (Julio Medem) Carmelo Gomez, Emma Suarez, Karra Elejalde.

EARTH
BEHAVIOR/MGM. Sept., 1998. Indian-Canadian. (Deepa Mehta) Aamir Khan, Nandita Das, Rahul Khanna, Maia Sethna, Kitu Gidwani.

EAST OF WAR
JOSEF AICHHOLZER FILMPRODUKTION. Feb., 1997. Austrian. (Ruth Beckermann) Documentary.

EAST PALACE, WEST PALACE
QUELQU'UN D'AUTRE PRODS. May, 1997. Chinese-French (Zhang Yuan) Si Han, Hu Jun, Liu Yuxiao, Wang Quan, Ye Jing.

EAST SIDE STORY
ANDA FILMS. Jan., 1997. German. (Dana Ranga) Documentary.

EAST-WEST
UFD DISTRIBUTION. Aug., 1999. French-Russian-Spanish-Bulgarian. (Regis Wargnier) Sandrine Bonnaire, Oleg Menshikov, Catherine Deneuve, Sergei Bodrov, Jr. Ruben Tapiero.

EAT DRINK MAN WOMAN
SAMUEL GOLDWYN. August, 1994. Taiwanese. (Ang Lee) Sihung Lung, Kuei Mei Yang, Chien Lien Wu.

EATING
INT'L RAINBOW. November, 1990. (Henry Jaglom) Nelly Alard, Mary Crosby, Frances Bergen.

ECHOES FROM A SOMBER EMPIRE
NEW YORKER. July, 1992. German-French. (Werner Herzog) Documentary.

ED
UNIVERSAL. March, 1996. (Bill Couturie) Matt LeBlanck, Jayne Brook, Bill Cobbs, Jack Warden.

ED AND HIS DEAD MOTHER
I.R.S. November, 1993. (Jonathan Wacks) Steve Buscemi, Ned Beatty, Miriam Margolyes.

EDDIE
BUENA VISTA. May, 1996. (Steve Rash) Whoopie Goldberg, Frank Langella, Lisa Ann Walter, John Benjamin Hickey.

EDEN
WATER STREET. January, 1996. (Howard Goldberg) Joanna Going, Dylan Walsh, Sean Patrick Flannery.

THE EDEN MYTH
TUESDAY NIGHT MOVIES. Feb, 1999. (Mark Edlitz) Rebecca Boyd, Julia Dyon, Justin Kirk, Zohra Lampert.

THE EDGE
20TH CENTURY FOX. August, 1997. (Lee Tamahori), Anthony Hopkins, Alec Baldwin, Elle Macpherson, Harold Perrineau.

EDGE CITY
CITY STORY PICTURES. April, 1998. (Eugene Martin) Charlie Hofheimer, Heather Gottlieb, Isidra Vega, Ryan Carmony, Todd Berry.

EDGE OF SEVENTEEN
BLUE STREAK FILMS/LUNA PICTURES. June, 1998. (David Moreton) Chris Stafford, Tina Holmes, Andersen Gabrych, Stephanie McVay.

EDIE & PEN
PACIFIC SHORE MEDIA. May, 1996. (Matthew Irmas) Stockard Channing, Jennifer Tilly, Scott Glenn.

ED'S NEXT MOVE
BLUEHAWK. January, 1996. (John Walsh) Matt Ross, Calliope Thorne, Kevin Carroll.

EDTV
UNIVERSAL. Mar., 1999. (Ron Howard) Matthew McConaughey, Jenna Elfman, Woody Harrelson, Sally Kirkland.

THE EDUCATION OF LITTLE TREE
PARAMOUNT. Nov., 1997. (Richard Friedenburg) James Cromwell, Tantoo Cardinal, Joseph Ashton, Graham Greene.

EDWARD SCISSORHANDS
20TH CENTURY FOX. December, 1990. (Tim Burton) Johnny Depp, Dianne Wiest, Winona Ryder.

EDWARD II
FINE LINE. March, 1992. British. (Derek Jarman) Steven Waddington, Kevin Collins, Andrew Tiernan.

ED WOOD
BUENA VISTA. September, 1994. (Tim Burton) Johnny Depp, Martin Landau, Sarah Jessica Parker, Bill Murray.

THE EEL
SHOCHIKU. May, 1997. Japanese. (Shohei Imamura) Koji Yakusho, Misa Shimizu, Fujio Tsuneta, Mitsuko Baisho, Akira Emoto.

THE EFFICIENCY EXPERT
MIRAMAX. November, 1992. Australian. (Mark Joffe) Anthony Hopkins, Ben Mendelsohn, Toni Collette.

8 1/2 WOMEN
WOODLINE PRODUCTIONS LTD./MOVIE MASTERS/DELUX PRODUCTIONS/CONTINENT FILM. May, 1999. British-Dutch-Luxembourgeois-German.(Peter Greenaway) John Standing, Matthew Delamere, Vivian Wu, Shizuka Inoh, Barbara Sarafian.

8 SECONDS
NEW LINE. February, 1994. (John G. Avildsen) Luke Perry, Stephen Baldwin, James Rebhorn.

EIGHTEEN SPRINGS
MANDARIN FILMS. Oct., 1997. Hong Kong. (Ann Hui) Leon Lai, Wu Chien-lien, Anita Mui, Ge You, Wang Lei.

8MM
SONY. Feb., 1999. (Joel Schumacher) Nicolas Cage, Joaquin Phoenix, James Gandolfini, Peter Stormare, Anthony Heald.

EL MARIACHI
COLUMBIA. February, 1993. (Robert Rodriguez) Carlos Gallardo, Consuelo Gomez, Reinol Martinez.

ELECTION
PARAMOUNT. Apr., 1999. (Alexander Payne) Matthew Broderick, Reese Witherspoon, Chris Klein, Jessica Campbell.

ELECTIVE AFFINITIES
SACIS. May, 1996. French-Italian. (Paolo and Vittorio Taviani) Isabelle Huppert, Jean-Hugues Anglade, Fabrizio Bentivoglio.

ELEPHANT JUICE
MIRAMAX. Aug., 1999. British-U.S. (Sam Miller) Emmanuelle Beart, Sean Gallagher, Daniel Lapaine, Daniela Nardini, Mark Strong.

THE ELEPHANT MASTER
CIBY. December, 1995. French-Spanish. (Patrick Grandperret) Erwan Baynaud, Jacques Dutrone.

THE ELEVENTH CHILD
PARIS NEW YORK. Sept., 1998. French-Canadian-Vietnamese. (Dai Sijie) Akihiro Nishida, Tapa Sudana, Nguyen Minh Chau.

THE ELIMINATOR
COUSINS PICTURES. Sept., 1996. Northern Irish. (Enda Hughes) Barry Wallace, Michael Hughes, Mik Duffy.

ELISA... BEFORE THE END OF THE WORLD
TELEVICINE PROD. March, 1997. Mexican. (Juan Antonio de la Riva) Sherlyn Motserrat, Imanol Goenaga, Ruben Rojo Aura.

ELIZABETH
GRAMERCY/POLYGRAM FILMED ENTERTAINMENT. Sept., 1998. British. (Shekhar Kapur) Cate Blanchett, Geoffrey Rush, Christopher Eccleston, Joseph Fiennes, Richard Attenborough, Fanny Ardant.

ELLES
ARTEMIS. Jan., 1998. Luxembourgeois. (Luis Galvao Teles) Miou-Miou, Carmen Maura, Marthe Keller, Marisa Berenson, Guesch Patti.\

ELLIOT FAUMAN, PH.D.
TAURUS ENTERTAINMENT. March, 1990. (Ric Klass) Randy Dreyfuss, Jean Kasem.

ELVIS & MERILIN
ISTITUTO LUCE. May, 1998. Italian. (Armando Manni) Edyta Olszowka, Goran Navojec, Giorgio Faletti, Toni Bertorelli.

ELVIS GRATTON II-MIRACLE IN MEMPHIS
LIONS GATE. July, 1999. Canadian. (Pierre Falardeau) Julien Poulin, Yves Trudel, Barry Blake, Jacques Theriault.

EMINENT DOMAIN
TRIUMPH. April, 1991. Canadian-Israeli-French. (John Irvin) Donald Sutherland, Anne Archer, Paul Freeman.

EMMA
MIRAMAX. June, 1996. British. (Douglas McGrath) Gwyneth Paltrow, Jeremy Northam, Toni Collette.

EMMA AND ELVIS
NORTHERN ARTS. October, 1992. (Julia Reichert) Kathryn Walker, Mark Blum, Jason Duchin.

THE EMPEROR AND THE ASSASIN
SONY. May, 1999. Japanese-Chinese-French. (Chen Kaige) Gong Li, Zhang Fengyi, Li Xuejian, Sun Zhou, Wang Zhiwen.

THE EMPEROR'S SHADOW
OCEAN FILM. May, 1996. Hong Kong-China. (Zhou Xiaowen) Jiang Wen, Ge You, Xu Qing.

EMPIRE RECORDS
WARNER BROS. September, 1995. (Allan Moyle) Anthony LaPaglia, Rory Cochrane, Johnny Whitworth.

EMPTY DAYS
ADR PRODS. Sept., 1999. French. (Marion Vernoux) Valeria Bruni Tedeschi, Patrick Dell'Isola, Sergi Lopez, Florence Thomassin.

ENCHANTED APRIL
MIRAMAX. July, 1992. British. (Mike Newell) Josie Lawrence, Miranda Richardson, Joan Plowright.

THE ENCHANTMENT
HERALD ACE/NIPPON HERALD. May, 1992. Japanese. (Chun'Ichi Nagaskai) Kumiko Akiyoshi, Masao Kusakari.

ENCINO MAN
BUENA VISTA. May, 1992. (Les Mayfield) Sean Astin, Brendan Fraser, Pauly Shore.

ENCORE
PARIS-NEW YORK PRODUCTION. September, 1996. French. (Pascal Bonitzer) Jacky Berroyer, Valeria Bruni-Tedeschi.

ENCOUNTER AT RAVEN'S GATE
HEMDALE. January, 1990. Australian. (Rolf de Heer) Steven Vidler, Celine Griffin.

ENCOUNTER IN THE THIRD DIMENSION
NWAVE. Mar., 1999. (Ben Stassen): Stuart Pankin, Elvira, Harry Shearer, Andrea Thompson.

THE END OF INNOCENCE
SKOURAS. December, 1990. (Dyan Cannon) Dyan Cannon, John Heard, George Coe.

END OF INNOCENCE
MOONSTONE ENTERTAINMENT. May, 1999. (James Rowe) Peter Facinelli, Jay R. Ferguson, Rodney Eastman, Chris Isaak, Amy Irving.

THE END OF OLD TIMES
IFEX. January, 1992. Czech. (Jiri Menzel) Josef Abraham, Marian Labuda, Jaromir Hanzlik.

THE END OF VIOLENCE
CIBY 2000. Aug., 1997. U.S.-French. (Wim Wenders) Bill Pullman, Andie McDowell, Gabriel Byrne, Loren Dean, Traci Lind.

THE ENDLESS SUMMER II
NEW LINE. June, 1994. (Bruce Brown) Documentary.

ENDURANCE
BUENA VISTA. Sept., 1998. (Leslie Woodhead, Bud Greenspan) Haile Gebrselassie, Shawananness Gebrselassie, Yonas Zergaw.

ENEMY OF MY ENEMY
TRIMARK PICTURES. May, 1999. (Gustavo Graef-Marino) Peter Weller, Daryl Hannah, Tom Berenger, Adrian Pintea

ENEMY UNSEEN
TRIAX ENTERTAINMENT. January, 1990. (Elmo DeWitt) Vernon Wells, Angela O'Neil.

THE ENGLISH PATIENT
MIRAMAX. October, 1996. (Anthony Minghella), Ralph Fiennes, Juliette Binoche, Willem Dafoe, Kristin Scott Thomas.

ENGLISHMAN WHO WENT UP A HILL BUT CAME DOWN A MOUNTAIN, THE
MIRAMAX. May, 1995. British. (Christopher Monger) Hugh Grant, Tara Fitzgerald, Colm Meaney.

ENNUI
GEMINI FILMS/IMA FILMS. Sept., 1998. French. (Cedric Kahn) Charles Berling, Sophie Guillemin, Arielle Dombasle.

ENOUGH ALREADY
WOLFEBORO FILMS. May, 1998. (Tom Keenan) Alanna Ubach, David Wheir, Rick Gomez, Brad Beyer, Paul Wagner.

ENTERTAINING ANGELS: THE DOROTHY DAY STORY
PAULIST PICTURES. September, 1996. (Michael Ray Rhodes) Moira Kelly, Martin Sheen, Melinda Dillon.

ENTHUSIASM
CINE XXI/PARAISO PRODUCTION DIFFUSION/CARTEL. May, 1999. Chilean-French-Spanish. (Ricardo Larrain) Maribel Verdu, Carmen Maura, Alvaro Escobar, Alvaro Rudolphi, Gianfranco Lebrini.

ENTRAPMENT
20TH CENTURY FOX. Apr., 1999. (Jon Amiel) Sean Connery, Catherine Zeta-Jones, Ving Rhames, Will Patton, Maury Chaykin.

ENTROPY
TRIBECA FILMS. Apr., 1999. (Phil Joanou) Stephen Dorff, Judith Godreche, Kelly Macdonald, Lauren Holly.

ENTWINED
CORAZON PRODS. June, 1997. (Raquel Cecilia Harrington) Veronica Sanchez, Kim Ostrenko, Marilyn Romero, Iris Delgado.

EPSILON
MIRAMAX. Jan., 1997. Australian-Italian. (Rolf De Heer) Ulli Birve, Syd Brisbane, Alethe McGrath, Chloe Ferguson, Phoebe Ferguson.

EQUINOX
I.R.S. June, 1993. (Alan Rudolph) Matthew Modine, Lara Flynn Boyle, Marisa Tomei.

ERASABLE YOU
DORIAN. Aug., 1998. (Harry Bromley-Davenport) Timothy Busfield, Jennifer Grant, Melora Hardin, M. Emmet Walsh.

ERASER
WARNER BROS. June, 1996. (Charles Russel) Arnold Schwarzenegger, James Caan, Vanessa Williams.

ERMO
ARROW. May, 1995. Chinese. (Zhou Xiaowen) Alia, Liu Peiqi, Ge Zhijun.

ERNEST GOES TO JAIL
BUENA VISTA. April, 1990. (John Cherry) Jim Varney, Gailard Sartain, Bill Byrge.

ERNEST RIDES AGAIN
EMSHELL. November, 1993. (John R. Cherry III) Jim Varney, Ron K. James, Linda Kash.

ERNEST SCARED STUPID
BUENA VISTA. October, 1991. (John Cherry) Jim Varney, Eartha Kitt, Austin Nagler.

EROTIC TALES II
REGINA ZIEGLER. December, 1995. German. (Cinzia TH Torrini, Nicolas Roeg, Janusz Makewski).

EROTIQUE
GROUP 1/ODYSSEY. April, 1995. U.S.-German. (Lizzie Borden, Monika Truet, Clara Law) Kamela Lopez Dawson.

ESCAPE FROM L.A.
PARAMOUNT. August, 1996. (John Carpenter) Kurt Russell, Stacy Keach, Steve Buscemi, Peter Fonda, Cliff Robertson.

ESCORIANDOLI
ADRIANA CHIESA ENT. September, 1996. Italian. (Antonio Rezza) Isabel Ferrari, Valeria Golino, Claudia Gerrini.

THE ESCORT
CASTOR & POLLUX. Sept., 1996. French-Canadian. (Denis Langlois) Robin Aubert, Paul-Antoine Taillefer, Eric Cabana.

ESMERALDA COMES BY NIGHT
FINE LINE. July, 1997. Mexican. (Jaime Humberto Hermosillo) Maria Rojo, Claudio Obregon, Martha Navarro, Antonio Crestain.

ESPECIALLY ON SUNDAY
MIRAMAX. August, 1993. Italian. (Giuseppe Tornatore) Philippe Noiret, Ornella Muti, Bruno Ganz.

ETERNITY
PAUL ENTERTAINMENT. October, 1990. (Steven Paul) Jon Voight, Armand Assante, Eileen Davidson.

ETERNITY AND A DAY
THEO ANGELOPOULOS FILMS, GREEK FILM CENTRE, GREEK TV/ PARADIS FILMS, LA SEPT CINEMA/INTERMEDIAS. May, 1998. Greek-French-Italian. (Theo Angelopoulos) Bruno Ganz, Isabelle Renauld, Achileas Skevis, Despina Bebedeli, Iris Chatziantoniou.

ETHAN FROME
MIRAMAX. March, 1993. (John Madden) Liam Neeson, Patricia Arquette, Joan Allen.

EUROPA, EUROPA
ORION CLASSICS. June, 1991. German-Russian-Polish. (Agnieszka Holland) Marco Hofschneider.

EUROPA EXPRESS
BEST HOLLYWOOD. Feb., 1999. Hungarian. (Csaba Horvath) Andras Stohl, Kata Dobo, Ivan Kamaras, Tibor Szilagyi, Zoltan Ratoti.

EVA PERON
ALEPH PRODUCCIONES S.A./ARGENTINE INSTITUTE FOR CINEMA. Dec., 1996. Argentine. (Juan Carlos Desanzo) Esther Goris, Victor Laplace, Christina Banegas, Pepe Nuvoa, Irma Cordoba.

EVE OF DESTRUCTION
ORION. January, 1991. (Duncan Gibbins) Gregory Hines, Renee Soutendijk, Michael Greene.

EVEN COWGIRLS GET THE BLUES
FINE LINE. May, 1994. (Gus Van Sant) Uma Thurman, Lorraine Bracco, John Hurt, Rain Phoenix.

THE EVENING STAR
PARAMOUNT. December, 1996. (Robert Harling), Shirley MacLaine, Bill Paxton, Juliette Lewis, Miranda Richardson, Ben Johnson, Scott WolfMackenzie Astin, Donald Moffat, China Kantner, Jack Nicholson.

EVENT HORIZON
PARAMOUNT. August, 1997. (Paul Anderson), Laurence Fishburne, Sam Neill, Kathleen Quinlan, Joely Richardson, Jack Noseworthy.

EVER AFTER
20TH CENTURY FOX. July, 1998. (Andy Tennant) Drew Barrymore, Anjelica Huston, Dougray Scott, Patrick Godfrey, Megan Dodds.

EVER CHANGING WATERS
DIGIART. Feb., 1998. Argentine. (Marcos Loayza) Jorge Marrale, Marcos Woinski, Noemi Frenkel, Mariano Bertolini.

EVEREST
MACGILLIVRAY FREEMAN FILMS. March, 1998. (Greg MacGillivray, David Breashears, Stephen Judson) DOCUMENTARY.

EVERYBODY WINS
ORION. January, 1990. (Karel Reisz) Nick Nolte, Debra Winger, Will Patton.

EVERYBODY'S FINE
MIRAMAX. May, 1991. Italian. (Giuseppe Tornatore) Marcello Mastroianni, Michele Morgan, Marino Cenna.

EVERY LITTLE THING
INTERNATIONAL FILM CIRCUIT. Oct., 1997. French. (Nicolas Philibert) documentary.

EVERYONE SAYS I LOVE YOU
MIRAMAX. November, 1996. (Woody Allen), Alan Alda, Woody Allen, Drew Barrymore, Goldie Hawn, Julia Roberts, Tim Roth, Lukas Haas.

EVERYONE'S CHILD
MEDIA FOR DEV'T TRUST. Sept., 1996. Zimbabwean. (Tsitsi Dangarembga) Nomsa Mlambo, Thulani Sandhla, Walter Muparutsa.

EVERY OTHER WEEKEND
MK2. June, 1991. French. (Nicole Garcia) Nathalie Baye, Joachim Serreau, Felicie Pasotti.

EVERY SUNDAY
NEUROPA FILM. Feb., 1997. Hungarian. (Sandor Simo) Eva Kerekes, Denes Ujlaki, Krisztina Biro, Lazlo Gorog, Eva Igo.

EVERYTHING MUST GO
FAVOURITE FILMS/PHANTOM FILMS. Feb., 1997. Belgian. (Jan Verheyen) Stany Crets, Peter van den Begin, Bart De Pauw.

EVERYTHING RELATIVE
BIG SISTERS. January, 1996. (Sharon Pollack) Ellen McLaughlin, Olivia Negron, Stacey Nelkin.

EVERYTHING'S GONNA BE GREAT
FILMA-CASS. Feb., 1999. Turkish-Hungarian. (Omer Vargi) Cem Yilmaz, Mazhar Alanson, Selim Nasit Ozcan, Ceyda Duvenci.

EVERYTHING WILL BE FINE
NDR DONIS J. HEINZE. July, 1998. German. (Angelina Maccarone) Viati Studemann, Chantal de Freitas, Isabella Pavkinson.

EVE'S BAYOU
TRIMARK. August, 1997. (Kasi Lemmons), Jurnee Smollett, Meagan Good, Samuel L. Jackson, Lynn Whitfield, Debbi Morgan.

EVITA
BUENA VISTA. December, 1996. (Alan Parker), Madonna, Antonio Banderas, Jonathan Pryce, Jimmy Nail.

EXCESS BAGGAGE
SONY PICTURES ENTERTAINMENT. August, 1997. (Marco Brambilla), Alicia Silverstone, Benicio Del Toro, Christopher Walken.

EXCESSIVE FORCE
NEW LINE. May, 1993. (Jon Hess) Thomas Ian Griffith, Charlotte Lewis, James Earl Jones.

THE EXECUTION PROTOCOL
FIRST RUN. April, 1993. British. (Stephen Trombley) Documentary.

EXECUTIONERS
RIM FILMS. June, 1995. Hong Kong. (Johnny To, Ching Siu Tung) Michelle Khan, Anita Mui, Maggie Cheung.

EXECUTIVE DECISION
WARNER BROS. March, 1996. (Stuart Baird) Kurt Russell, Halle Berry, John Leguizamo, Steven Seagal, Oliver Platt.

EXILED
GAELIC ARTISTS PRODS. July, 1999. (Bill Muir) Paul Ronan, Ronan Carr, Jenny Conroy, Paul Anthony McGraine.

EXILE SHANGHAI
ULRIKE OTTINGER FILMPRODUKTION. April, 1997. German-Israeli. (Ulrike Ottinger) Documentary.

EXISTENZ
MIRAMAX. Feb., 1999. Canadian-British. (David Cronenberg) Jennifer Jason Leigh, Jude Law, Willem Dafoe, Ian Holm, Callum Keith Rennie.

EXISTO
HOMETOWN PRODS. Apr., 1999. (Coke Sams) Bruce Arnston, Jackie Welch, Jim Varney, Gailard Sartain.

EXIT TO EDEN
SAVOY. October, 1994. (Garry Marshall) Dana Delany, Paul Mercurio, Rosie O'Donnell, Dan Aykroyd.

THE EXORCIST III
20TH CENTURY FOX. August, 1990. (William Peter Blatty) George C. Scott, Brad Dourif, Ed Flanders.

EXOTICA
MIRAMAX. March, 1995. Canadian. (Atom Egoyan) Bruce Greenwood, Mia Kirshner, Don McKellar.

EXPECT THE UNEXPECTED
MILKYWAY IMAGE. Sept., 1998. Hong Kong. (Patrick Yau) Lau Ching-wan, Simon Yam, Ruby Wong, Hui Shiu-hung, Raymond Wong.

EXPOSURE
MIRAMAX. October, 1991. Brazilian. (Walter Salles, Jr.) Peter Coyote, Tcheky Karyo, Amanda Pays.

EXQUISITE TENDERNESS
GUILD FILM. November, 1995. U.S.-German. (Carl Schenkel) Isabel Glasser, James Remar, Sean Haberle.

EXTRAMUROS
FRAMELINE. June, 1991. Spanish. (Miguel Picazo) Carmen Maura, Mercedes Sampietro, Assumpta Serna.

EXTRAORDINARY VISITOR
CINEMA ESPERANCA. Sept., 1998. Canadian. (John W. Doyle) Mary Walsh, Andy Jones, Raoul Bhaneja, Jordan Canning, Rick Boland.

EXTRAS
SAMBOO FINANCE. Sept., 1998. South Korean. (Shin Seung-Soo) Lim Chang-Jeong, Na Han-Il, Park Joon-Hee, Kim Won-Hee.

EXTREME MEASURES
SONY PICTURES. September, 1996. (Michael Apted) Hugh Grant, Gene Hackman, Sarah Jessica Parker, David Morse.

THE EYE
SONET FILM. Aug., 1998. Swedish. (Richard Hobert) Lena Endre, Samuel Froler, Goran Stangertz, Camilla Lundin.

EYE FOR AN EYE
PARAMOUNT. January, 1996. (John Schlesinger) Sally Field, Kiefer Sutherland, Ed Harris, Beverly D'Angelo.

EYE OF GOD
MINNOW PICTURES. Jan., 1997. (Tom Blake Nelson) Martha Plimpton, Kevin Anderson, Hal Holbrook, Nick Stahl.

EYE OF THE STRANGER
SILVER LAKE. September, 1993. (David Heavener) David Heavener, Martin Landau, Sally Kirkland.

EYES OF THE SPIDER
DAIEI CO.. Aug., 1999. Japanese. (Kiyoshi Kurosawa). Sho Aikawa, Dankan, Ren Osugi, Shun Sugata.

EYES WIDE SHUT
WARNER BROS. July, 19919. (Stanley Kubrick) Tom Cruise, Nicole Kidman, Sydney Pollack, Marie Richardson.

F

FACE
UIP. Aug., 1997. British. (Antonia Bird) Robert Carlyle, Ray Winstone, Steven Waddlington, Philip Davis, Damon Albarn, Lena Headey.

FACE/OFF
PARAMOUNT. June, 1997. (John Woo), John Travolta, Nicolas Cage, Joan Allen, Gina Gershon, Dominique Swain, Nick Cassavetes.

THE FACULTY
Dimension Films. Dec., 1998. (Robert Rodriguez) Jordana Brewster, Clea DuVall, Laura Harris, Josh Harnett, Shawn Hatosy.

FAG HAG
POTENKIN. July, 1998. (Damion Dietz) Stephanie Orff, Damion Dietz, Sasha Cardona, Darryl Therise, Wil Wheaton, Jaush Way.

FAIR GAME
WARNER BROS. November, 1995. (Andrew Sipes) William Baldwin, Cindy Crawford, Steven Berkhoff.

FAIRY TALE: A TRUE STORY
PARAMOUNT. September, 1997. (Charles Sturridge), Florence Hoath, Elizabeth Earl, Paul McGann, Peter O'Toole, Harvey Keitel.

FAITHFUL
NEW LINE. February, 1996. (Paul Mazursky) Cher, Chazz Palminteri, Ryan O'Neal, Amber Smith.

FALL
5 MINUTES BEFORE THE MIRACLE. June, 1997. (Eric Schaeffer) Eric Schaeffer, Amanda DeCadenet, Rudolph Martin, Francie Swift.

THE FALL
ALLIANCE. Feb., 1999. British-Canadian-Hungarian. (Andrew Piddington) Craig Sheffer, Helen de Fougerolles, Jurgen Prochnow, Kim Huffman, Sandor Teri..

FALL AND SPRING
ANYTOWN, ANYWHERE PRODS. Oct., 1996. (Steven Sobel) Jason Cottle, Michael Healey, Beth Kitchen.

FALLEN ANGELS' PARADISE
ART. May, 1999. Egyptian. (Oussama Fawzi) Mahmoud Hamida, Lebleba.

FALL OUT
MKL. June, 1996. French. (Jean-Denis Robert) Stanislas Crevillen, Laure Duthilleul, Pierre-Arnaud Crespeau.

FALLEN
WARNER BROS. Jan., 1998. (Gregory Hoblit) Denzel Washington, John Goodman, Donald Sutherland, Embeth Davidtz.

THE FALLING
SODONA ENTERTAINMENT. Oct., 1998. Canadian. (Raul Sanchez Inglis) Christopher Shyer, Nicole Oliver, Rob Lee, John Cassini

FALLING BODIES
JBA. Aug., 1998. French-German-Haitian. (Raoul Peck) Geno Lechner, Jean-Michel Martial, Bob Meyer, Israel Horovitz.

FALLING DOWN
WARNER BROS. February, 1993. (Joel Schumacher) Michael Douglas, Robert Duvall, Barbara Hershey.

FALLING FROM GRACE
COLUMBIA. February, 1992. (John Mellencamp) John Mellencamp, Mariel Hemingway, Kay Lenz.

FALLING INTO THE EVENING
SHOCHIKU CO. Feb., 1998. Japanese. (Naoe Gozu) Tomoyo Harada, Atsuro Watanabe, Miho Kanno, Midori Kiuchi, Ren Osugi.

FALLOUT
SHOWCASE ENTERTAINMENT. August, 1996. (Robert Palumbo) Claire Beckman, Mark Deakins, David Wasson.

FALSE IDENTITY
RKO PICTURES. June, 1990. (James Keach) Stacy Keach, Genevieve Bujold.

FAME WHORE
APATHY PRODS./BLURCO. Oct., 1998. (Jon Moritsugu) Peter Friedrich, Amy Davis, Victor of Aquitaine, Jason Rail.

FAMILY
AZERBAIJAN FILM STUDIO-AZERKINOVIDEO)/IBRUS FILM. Feb., 1999. Azerbaijan-Russian. (Rustam Ibragimbekov) Gasanaga Turabov, Sijavush Kerimi, Svetlana Metkina, Rafiq Aliev, Tachmina Mamedova.

FAMILY NAME
OPELIKA PICTURES. Jan., 1997. (Macky Alston) Documentary.

FAMILY PRAYERS
ARROW. March, 1993. (Scott Rosenfelt) Joe Mantegna, Anne Archer, Paul Reiser.

A FAMILY THING
MGM/UA. March, 1996. (Richard Pearce) Robert Duvall, James Earl Jones, Michael Beach, Irma P. Hall.

FAMINE–33
INDEPENDENT. December, 1993. Ukranian. (Oles Yanchuk) Halyna Sulyma, Georgi Morozuik. B&W.

THE FAMINE WITHIN
DIRECT CINEMA. July, 1991. (Katherine Gilday) Documentary.

THE FAN
SONY PICTURES. August, 1996. (Tony Scot) Robert De Niro, Wesley Snipes, Ellen Barkin, John Leguizamo.

FAR AND AWAY
UNIVERSAL. May, 1992. (Ron Howard) Tom Cruise, Nicole Kidman, Thomas Gibson.

FAREWELL PAVEL
STUDIO NIEUWE GRONDEN. Feb., 1999. Dutch. (Rosemarie Blank) Valery Kuchareschin, Boris Khvoles, Isil Zabludowskij, Vlatka Simac, Maria Pliatskovskaya.

FAREWELL, TERRA FIRMA!
PIERRE GRIS PRODS./CARAC FILM/ALIA FILM/ISTITUTO LUCE . May, 1999. French-Swiss-Italian. (Otar losseliani) Nico Tarielashvili, Lily Lavina, Philippe Bas, Stephanie Hainque, Mirabelle Kirkland.

FAREWELL TRAVELLING PLAYER
LES FILMS DU SUD. Oct., 1998. Moroccan. (Daoud Aoulad-Syad) Abdellah Didane, Med Bastaoui, Hassen Essaklli, Nezha Rahile.

FAR FROM HOME: THE ADVENTURES OF YELLOW DOG
20TH CENTURY FOX. January, 1995. (Phillip Borsos) Jesse Bradford, Bruce Davison, Mimi Rogers.

FAR FROM SIGHT
MADRAGOA FILMES/GEMINI FILMS. Sept., 1998. Portuguese-French. (Joao Mario Grillo) Cano E Castro, Francisco Nascimento, Henrique Viana, Zita Duarte, Ria Blance.

A FAR OFF PLACE
BUENA VISTA. March, 1993. (Mikael Salomon) Reese Witherspoon, Ethan Randall, Sarel Bok.

FAR OUT MAN
NEW LINE. May, 1990. (Tommy Chong) Tommy Chong, C. Thomas Howell, Shelby Chong.

FARAWAY, SO CLOSE!
SONY PICTURES CLASSICS. December, 1993. German. (Wim Wenders) Otto Sander, Nastassja Kinski, Peter Falk.

FARAW! MOTHER OF THE DUNES
FILME DE LA DUNE ROSE/CENTRE NATIONAL DE PRODUCTION. May, 1997. Mali. (Abdoulaye Ascofare) Aminata Ousmane.

A FARE TO REMEMBER
BENT TREE. Mar., 1999. (Jim Yukich) Malcolm Jamal Warner, Challen ates, Stanley Kamel, Tracee Ellis Ross.

FAREWELL MY CONCUBINE
MIRAMAX. October, 1993. Hong Kong. (Chen Kaige) Leslie Cheung, Zhang Fengyi, Gong Li.

FARGO
GRAMERCY. February, 1996. (Ethan Coen) Steve Buscemi, William H. Macy, Peter Stormare, Frances McDormand.

FARINELLI
SONY PICTURES CLASSICS. March, 1995. Belgian. (Gerard Corbiau) Stefano Dionisi, Erico Lo Verso, Jeroen Krabbe.

THE FARM: ANGOLA, USA
GABRIEL FILMS. Jan., 1998. (Jonathan Stack, Liz Garbus) DOCUMENTARY.

FARMER & CHASE
ARROW. October, 1995. (Michael Seltzman) Todd Field, Ben Gazzara, Lara Flynn Boyle, Ron Kaell.

FAST, CHEAP & OUT OF CONTROL
SONY PICTURES CLASSICS. Jan., 1997. (Errol Morris) Documentary.

FAST FOOD
TWIN PICTURES/FAST FOOD FILMS. May, 1998. British. (Stewart Sugg) Douglas Henshall, Emily Woof, Miles Anderson, Gerard Butler.

FAT WORLD
POLYGRAM FILMED ENTERTAINMENT GMBH. Aug., 1998. British. (Jan Schuette) Juergen Vogel, Julia Filiminow, Stefan Dietrich.

FATAL INSTINCT
MGM. October, 1993. (Carl Reiner) Armand Assante, Kate Nelligan, Sherilyn Fenn, Sean Young.

FATHER
NORTHERN ARTS. July, 1992. Australian. (John Power) Max von Sydow, Carol Drinkwater, Julia Blake.

THE FATHER
FARABI CINEMA FOUNDATION. May, 1996. Iranian. (Majid Majidi) Mohammad Kasebi, Parivash Nazarieh.

FATHER DAMIEN
KINEPOLIS FILM DISTRIBUTION. Mar., 1999. Belgian-Dutch. (Paul Cox) David Wenham, Kate Ceberano, Chris Haywood, Derek Jacobi, Alice Krige.

FATHER HOOD
BUENA VISTA. August, 1993. (Darrell James Roodt) Patrick Swayze, Sabrina Lloyd, Brian Bonsall, Halle Berry.

FATHER OF THE BRIDE
BUENA VISTA. December, 1991. (Charles Shyer) Steve Martin, Diane Keaton, Kimberly Williams.

FATHER OF THE BRIDE II
Buena Vista. December, 1995. (Charles Shyer) Steve Martin, Diane Keaton, Martin Short, Kimberly Williams.

FATHERS AND SONS
PACIFIC PICTURES. November, 1992. (Paul Mones) Jeff Goldblum, Rory Cochrane, Rocky Carroll.

FATHER'S DAY
WARNER BROS. April, 1997. (Ivan Reitman), Robin Williams, Billy Crystal, Julia Louis-Dreyfus, Nastassja Kinski, Charlie Hofheimer.

FATHER'S DAY
BUENA VISTA INTL. May, 1997. German. (Sherry Hormann) Herbert Knaup, Corinna Harfouch, Richy Mueller, Dominik Graf.

FAUST
FILM FORUM. October, 1994. French-Czech-British-German. (Jan Svankmajer) Petr Cepek.

THE FAVOR
ORION. April, 1994. (Donald Petrie) Harley Jane Kozak, Elizabeth McGovern, Bill Pullman, Brad Pitt.

THE FAVOR, THE WATCH AND THE VERY BIG FISH
TRIMARK. May, 1992. British. (Ben Lewin) Bob Hoskins, Natasha Richardson, Jeff Goldblum.

FEAR
UNIVERSAL. April, 1996. (James Foley) Mark Wahlberg, Reese Witherspoon, William Petersen, Amy Brenneman.

FEAR & LEARNING AT HOOVER ELEMENTARY
JOSEPHA PRODUCCIONES. Jan., 1997. (Laura Angelica Simon) Documentary.

FEAR AND LOATHING IN LAS VEGAS
UNIVERSAL. May, 1998. (Terry Gilliam) Johnny Depp, Benicio Del Toro, Craig Bierko, Ellen Barkin, Gary Busey, Cameron Diaz, Flea.

FEAR OF A BLACK HAT
SAMUEL GOLDWYN. June, 1994. (Rusty Cundieff) Mark Christopher Lawrence, Larry B. Scott, Rusty Cundieff.

FEARLESS
WARNER BROS. October, 1993. (Peter Wier) Jeff Bridges, Isabella Rossellini, Rosie Perez, Tom Hulce.

FEDERAL HILL
TRIMARK. December, 1994. (Michael Corrente) Nicholas Turturro, Anthony De Sando, Libby Langdon. B&W

FEED
ORIGINAL CINEMA. October, 1992. (Kevin Rafferty, James Ridgeway) Documentary.

FEELING MINNESOTA
FINE LINE. September, 1996. (Steven Baigelman) Keanu Reeves, Vincent D'Onofrio, Cameron Diaz.

FEELING SEXY
NICHE PICTURES. Aug., 1999. Australian. (Davida Allen) Susie Porter, Tamblyn Lord, Amanda Muggleton, John Donatiu.

FELICE...FELICE...
NFM DISTRIBUTIE. Jan., 1998. Dutch. (Peter Delpeut) Johan Leysen, Toshie Ogura, Rina Yasima, Noriko Sasaki, Kumi Nakamura.

FELICIA'S JOURNEY
ARTISAN. May, 1999. British-Canadian. (Atom Egoyan) Bob Hoskins, Elaine Cassidy, Arsinee Khanjian, Peter McDonald, Gerard McSorley.

FEMALE MISBEHAVIOR
FIRST RUN. April, 1993. German. (Monika Truet) Documentary.

FEMALE PERVERSIONS
OCTOBER FILMS. January, 1996. (Susan Streifeld) Tilda Swinton, Amy Madigan, Karen Sillas, Laila Robins.

THE FEMININE TOUCH
MIRACON PICTURES. April, 1996. (Conrad Janis) Paige Turco, Dirk Benedict, Janis, George Segal, Bo Hopkins.

FERDINAND AND CAROLINA
MEDUSA. Mar., 1999. Italian-French. (Lina Wertmuller) Sergio Assisi, Gabriella Pession, Silvana De Santis, Mario Scaccia, Isa Danieli.

FERNGULLY... THE LAST RAINFOREST
20TH CENTURY FOX. April, 1992. (Bill Kroyer) Animated.

THE FERRY
VILNIS KALNAELLIS. May, 1996. Latvian. (Laila Pakalnina) Documentary.

FESTIVAL
TAEHUNG PICTURES. Feb.,1997. South Korean. (Im Kwon-taek) Ahn Sung-kee, Oh Jung-hae, Han Eun-jin, Chung Kyung-soon.

FETISHES
ITEL. June, 1996. British. (Nick Broomfield) Documentary.

THE FEUD
CASTLE HILL. May, 1990. (Bill D'Elia) Rene Auberjonois, Scott Allegrucci, Ron McLarty.

FEVER
SUNLIGHT PICTURES. May, 1999. British. (Alex Winter) Henry Thomas, David O'Hara, Bill Duke, Teri Hatcher, Sandor Tecsy.

A FEW GOOD MEN
COLUMBIA. December, 1992. (Rob Reiner) Tom Cruise, Jack Nicholson, Demi Moore, Kevin Bacon.

FEW OF US
MERCURE. May, 1996. Portuguese-French-German-Lithuanian. (Sharunas Bartas) Katerina Golubeva.

FIBER OPTICS
CONSEJO NACIONAL PARA LA CULTURA Y LAS ARTES/ INSTITUTO MEXICANO DE LA CINEMATOGRAFIA/HUBERT BAL FUND. Feb., 1998. Mexican. (Francisco Athie) Roberto Sosa, Lumi Cavazos.

FICTION
MOVIE MILL. Feb., 1997. Indian. (Malay Bhattacharya) Dhritiman Chatterjee, Debesh Roy Chowdhury, Debashish Goswami.

FIDDLEFEST
FOUR OAKS. October, 1995. (Lana Miller) Documentary.

THE FIELD
AVENUE. December, 1990. Irish. (Jim Sheridan) Richard Harris, Sean Bean, John Hurt.

MR. FIFTEEN BALLS
MEDUSA. Sept., 1998. Italian. (Francesco Nuti) Francesco Nuti, Sabrina Ferilli, Novello Novelli, Antonio Pertrocelli, Giulia Weber.

THE FIFTH ELEMENT
SONY PICTURES. April, 1997. French. (Luc Besson) Bruce Willis, Gary Oldman, Ian Holm, Milla Jovovich, Chris Tucker, Luke Perry.

THE FIFTH MONKEY
COLUMBIA. October, 1990. French-Brazilian-U.S. (Eric Rochat) Ben Kingsley, Silvia De Carvalho.

FIFTY FIFTY
CANNON. February, 1993. (Charles Martin Smith) Peter Weller, Robert Hays, Ramona Rahman.

54
MIRAMAX. Aug., 1998. (Mark Christopher) Ryan Phillippe, Salma Hayek, Neve Campbell, Mike Myers, Sela Ward, Breckin Meyer.

FIGHT CLUB
20TH CENTURY FOX. Sept., 1999. (David Fincher) Brad Pitt, Edward Norton, Helena Bonham Carter, Meat Loaf Aday, Jared Leto.

THE FIGHT IN THE FIELDS
INDEPENDENT TV SERVICE. Jan., 1997. (Ray Telles) Documentary.

FINAL ANALYSIS
WARNER BROS. February, 1992. (Phil Joanou) Richard Gere, Kim Basinger, Eric Roberts, Uma Thurman.

FINAL APPROACH
TRIMARK. December, 1991. (Eric Steven Stahl) James B. Sikking, Hector Elizondo, Madolyn Smith.

FINAL CUT
FUGITIVE FEATURES. Nov., 1998. British. (Dominic Anciano) Ray Winstone, Jude Law, Sadie Frost, Holly Davidson, John Beckett.

FINAL IMPACT
PM ENTERTAINMENT. February, 1992. (Joseph Merhi) Lorenzo Lamas, Kathleen Kinmont, Michael Worth.

FINAL RINSE
POLYVINYL FILM. June, 1999. (Robert Tucker) Terence Goodman, David Cale, Jennifer Regan, Michael Hannon, Frank Gorshin.

FINDING GRACELAND
TCB PRODS. Sept., 1998. (David Winkler) Harvey Keitel, Johnathon Schaech, Bridget Fonda, Gretchen Mol.

FINDING NORTH
REDEEMABLE FEATURES. Jan., 1998. (Tanya Wexler) Wendy Makkena, John Benjamin Hickey, Jonathan Walker.

FINE POWDER
5600 FILM. Feb., 1997. Argentine. (Esteban Sapir) Facundo Luengo, Belen Blanco, Marcela Guerty, Fanny Robman.

A FINE ROMANCE
CASTLE HILL. September, 1992. Italian. (Gene Saks) Julie Andrews, Marcello Mastroianni.

FINISHED
Jan., 1997. (William E. Jones) Documentary.

FINISTERRE (WHERE THE WORLD ENDS)
ALTA FILMS. Oct., 1998. Spanish. (Xavier Villaverde) Nancho Novo, Elena Anaya, Enrique Alcides, Geraldine Chaplin, Chete Lera.

FINZAN
CALIFORNIA NEWSREEL. March, 1992. Malian Bambara. (Cheik Oumar Sissoko) Diarrah Sanogo.

FIONA
AM KO PRODS. Sept., 1998. (Amos Kollek) Anna Thomas, Felicia Maguire, Alyssa Mulhern, Anna Grace, Bill Dawes.

FIORILE
FINE LINE. February, 1994. Italian. (Paolo and Vittorio Taviani) Claudio Bigagli, Galatea Ranzi.

FIRE DOWN BELOW
WARNER BROS. August, 1997. (Felix Enriquez Alcala), Steven Seagal, Marg Helgenberger, Harry Dean Stanton, Stephen Lang.

FIRE-EATER
MARKO ROHR PRODS./AQUAVITE FILM & MEDIA AB, SVT DRAMA. May, 1998. Finnish-Swedish. (Pirjo Honkasalo) Elina Hurme, Tiina Weckstrom, Elena Leeve, Elsa Saisio, Vappu Jurkka.

FIRE IN THE SKY
PARAMOUNT. March, 1993. (Robert Lieberman) D.B. Sweeney, Robert Patrick, James Garner.

FIRE ON THE MOUNTAIN
GAGE & GAGE. January, 1996. (Beth Gage, George Gage) Documentary.

FIREBIRDS
BUENA VISTA. May, 1990. (David Green) Nicolas Cage, Tommy Lee Jones, Sean Young.

FIREHEAD
PYRAMID DISTRIB. January, 1991. (Peter Yuval) Christopher Plummer, Chris Lemmon, Martin Landau.

FIRELIGHT
MIRAMAX. Sept., 1997. (William Nicholson) Sophie Marceau, Stephen Dillane, Kevin Anderson, Joss Ackland, Lia Williams.

FIRES WITHIN
MGM. June, 1991. (Gillian Armstrong) Jimmy Smits, Greta Scacchi, Vincent D'Onofrio.

FIRESTORM
20TH CENTURY FOX. Jan., 1998. (Dean Semler) Howie Long, Scott Glenn, William Forsythe, Suzy Amis, Christianne Hirt.

THE FIRM
PARAMOUNT. June, 1993. (Sydney Pollack) Tom Cruise, Gene Hackman, Jeanne Tripplehorn, Holly Hunter.

FIRST DATE
PETER WANG FILMS. June, 1991. Taiwanese. (Peter Wang) Chang Shi, Li Xing Wen, Shi Jun.

FIRST KID
BUENA VISTA/WALT DISNEY/CARAVAN. August, 1996. (David Mickey) Sinbad, Brock Pierce Robert Guillaume.

FIRST KNIGHT
COLUMBIA. July, 1995. (Jerry Zucker) Sean Connery, Richard Gere, Julia Ormond, Ben Cross.

THE FIRST NIGHT
A GRUPO TELEVISA FILM PRODUCTIONS. March, 1998. Mexican. (Alejandro Gamboa) Osvaldo Benavides, Mariana Avila.

FIRST ON THE ROPE
MC4 DISTRIBUTION. July, 1999. French-Italian-Swiss. (Edouard Niermans, Pierre-Antoine Hiroz) Silvia de Santis, Frederic Gorny, Andrea Ferreol, Giuliano Gemma, Didier Bienaime.

THE FIRST POWER
ORION. April, 1990. (Robert Resnikoff) Lou Diamond Phillips, Tracy Griffith, Jeff Kober.

THE FIRST TIME
MEDUSA FILM . Apr., 1999. Italian. (Massimo Martella) Alessia Fugardi, Valentina Limongelli, Marco Vivio, Costantino Meloni.

THE FIRST WIVES CLUB
PARAMOUNT. September, 1996. (Hugh Wilson) Goldie Hawn, Bette Midler, Diane Keaton, Maggie Smith.

F. IS A BASTARD
FILMCOOPERATIVE. Aug., 1998. Swiss-French. (Marcel Gisler) Frederic Andrau, Vincent Branchet, Urs-Peter Halter, Martin Schenkel.

THE FISHER KING
TRISTAR. September, 1991. (Terry Gilliam) Robin Williams, Jeff Bridges, Mercedes Ruehl, Amanda Plummer.

FISHES IN AUGUST
NHK DRAMA PROGRAMS DIVISION. Sept., 1998. Japanese. (Yoichiro Takahashi) Kenji Mizuhashi, Ayumi Ito, Yoshiki Sekino, Ryuzo Hayashi, Tomoko Mayumi.

FISHING NET, THE (VISIDELA)
E.A.P. FILMS. November, 1995. Sri Lankan. (H.D. Premaratne) Anosha Sonali, Jackson Anthony, W. Jayasiri.

THE FISHING TRIP
RESOUNDING PICTURES. Sept., 1998. Canadian. (Amnon Buchbinder) Jhene Erwin, Melissa Hood, Anna Henry, Jim Kinney, Dian Tabak.

FISHING WITH GHANDI
VIDEOACTIVE RELEASING. Nov., 1998. (Gabe Weisert) John Reichmuth, James Reichmuth, Dan Klein, Gabe Weisert.

FIST OF THE NORTH STAR
STREAMLINE. October, 1991. Japanese. (Toyoo Ashida) Animated.

A FISTFUL OF FINGERS
BLUE DOLPHIN. November, 1995. British. (Edgar Wright) Graham Low, Martin Curtis, Oliver Evans.

A FIT OF RAGE
RAVINA FILMES. Feb., 1999. Brazilian. (Aluizio Abranches) Alexandre Borges, Julia Lemmertz, Linneu Dias.

FIVE DAYS, FIVE NIGHTS
MADRAGOA FILMES. Feb., 1997. Portuguese-French. (Jose Fonseca Costa) Vitor Norte, Paulo Pires, Ana Padrao.

THE FIVE HEARTBEATS
20TH CENTURY FOX. March, 1991. (Robert Townsend) Robert Townsend, Michael Wright, Harry J. Lenix.

THE FIVE SENSES
ALLIANCE ATLANTIS. May, 1999. Canadian (Jeremy Podeswa) Mary-Louise Parker, Philippe Volter, Gabrielle Rose, Daniel MacIvor.

FLAME
BLACK & WHITE FILM CO. May, 1996. Zimbabwean. (Ingrid Sinclair) Marian Kunonga, Ulla Mahaka, Norman Madawo.

FLAMING EARS
WOMEN MAKE MOVIES. January, 1993. Austrian. (Angela Hans Scheirl, Dietmar Schipek, Ursula Puerrer) Susanna Heilmayr, Ursula Puerrer.

FLASHBACK
PARAMOUNT. February, 1990. (Franco Amurri) Dennis Hopper, Kiefer Sutherland, Carol Kane.

FLATLINERS
COLUMBIA. August, 1990. (Joel Schumacher) Kiefer Sutherland, Julia Roberts, Kevin Bacon.

FLEAS BARK TOO, DON'T THEY?
ASA FILM PROD. Feb., 1997. Danish. (Stellan Olsson) Christina Brix Christensen, Niels Hausgaard, Erik Clausen, Leif Sylvester.

FLED
MGM/UA. July, 1996. (Kevin Hooks) Laurence Fishburne, Stephen Baldwin, Salma Hayek, Will Patton.

FLESH AND BONE
PARAMOUNT. November, 1993. (Steve Kloves) Dennis Quaid, Meg Ryan, James Caan.

FLEX
TRIAX. May, 1990 (Pat Domenico) Harry Grant, Lorin Jean Vail.

THE FLIGHT
PURBANCHAL FILMS CO-OPERATIVE SOCIETY PROD. May, 1997. Indian. (Santwana Bardoloi) Trisha Saikia, Tom Alter.

FLIGHT OF THE BEE
Nov., 1998. Tajik.(Jamshed Usmonov, Min Biong Hun) Muhammadjon Shodi, Mastura Ortik, Tahjoymurod Rozik, Fakhriddin Fakhriddin.

FLIGHT OF THE INNOCENT
MGM. October, 1993. Italian. (Carlo Carlei) Manuel Colao, Francesca Neri, Jacques Perrin.

FLIGHT OF THE INTRUDER
PARAMOUNT. January, 1991. (John Milius) Danny Glover, Willem Dafoe, Brad Johnson.

THE FLINTSTONES
UNIVERSAL. May, 1994. (Brian Levant) John Goodman, Rick Moranis, Elizabeth Perkins, Rosie O'Donnell.

FLIPPER
UNIVERSAL. May, 1996. (Alan Shapiro) Elijah Wood, Paul Hogan, Chelsea Field, Isaac Hayes.

FLIPPING
MON FRERE. January, 1996. (Gene Mitchell) David Amos, David Proval, Keith David, Shant Benjamin.

FLIRT
TRUE FICTION. September, 1995. (Hal Hartley) Bill Sage,, Parker Posey, Dwightt Ewell, Elina Lowensohn.

FLIRTING WITH DISASTER
MIRAMAX. March, 1996. (David O. Russell) Patricia Arquette, Tea Leoni, Alan Alda, Ben Stiller, Mary Tyler Moore.

FLOUNDERING
STRAND. November, 1994. (Peter McCarthy) James LeGros, Sy Richardson, Ethan Hawke, John Cusack.

FLOWER OF MY SECRET, THE
SONY PICTURES CLASSICS. April, 1996. Spanish-French. (Pedro Amaldovar) Marisa Paredez, Juan Echanove.

FLOWER SEASON, RAIN SEASON
SHENZHEN FILM CO./SHENZHEN MUNICIPAL PUBLICITY DEPT. Nov., 1998. Chinese. (Qi Jian) Yan Danchen, Yangzi Baiyun, Li Chen, Liu Yin, Cao Peng.

FLOWERS FROM ANOTHER WORLD
IGUANA/ALTA FILMS. May, 1999. Spanish. (Iciar Bollain) Lissete Mejia, Luis Tosar, Marilin Torres, Jose Sancho.

FLOWERS OF SHANGHAI
SHOCHICKU CO. May, 1998. Taiwanese-Japanese. (Hou Hsiao-hsien) Tony Leung Chiu-wai, Michiko Hada, Michele Reis, Carina Liu.

FLUBBER
BUENA VISTA. Nov., 1997. (Les Mayfield) Robin Williams, Marcia Gay Harden, Christopher McDonald, Raymond Barry, Clancy Brown.

FLUKE
MGM/UA. June, 1995. (Carlo Carlei) Matthew Modine, Nancy Travis, Eric Stoltz, Ron Perlman.

FLY AWAY HOME
COLUMBIA. September, 1996. (Carol Ballard) Jeff Daniels, Anna Paquin, Dana Delany, Terry Kinney.

FLY LOW
SION FILM. Jan., 1999. South Korean. (Kim Sion) Kang Tae-Young, Lee jong-Woo, Jung Jae-Wook, Lim Ji-Eun, Lee Ah-Youngg.

FOLKS!
20TH CENTURY FOX. May, 1992. (Ted Kotcheff) Tom Selleck, Don Ameche, Anne Jackson.

FOLLOW ME HOME
NEW MILENNIA. January, 1996. (Peter Bratt) Jesse Borrego, Benjamin Bratt, Clavin Levels, Alfre Woodard.

FOLLOW THE BITCH
PENNANT PRODS. Jan., 1997. (Julian Stone) Ray Porter, David Teitelbaum, Dion Luther, Mike Cudlitz, Thomas Napier, Matt Foyer.

FOLLOW YOUR HEART (VA' DOVE TI PORTA IL CUORE)
FILMAURO. January, 1996. Italian-French-German. (Cristina Comencini) Virna Lisi, Margherita Buy, Galatea Ranzi.

FOOLISH
ARTISAN ENTERTAINMENT. Apr., 1999. (Dave Meyers) Eddie Griffin, Master P, Amy Petersen, Frank Sivero.

FOOLISH HEART
HB FILMS/OSCAR KRAMER S.A./FLACH FILM. May, 1998. Brazilian-Argentine-French. (Hector Babenco) Miguel Angel Sola, Mari Luisa Mendonca, Walter Quiroz, Xuxa Lopes, Norma Aleandro.

FOOLS GOLD
JANGER. Jan., 1999. (Lane Janger) Blair Singer, Billy Gallo, J.E. Freeman, Camryn Manheim.

FOOLS OF FORTUNE
NEW LINE. September, 1990. British. (Pat O'Connor) Mary Elizabeth Mastrantonio, Iain Glen.

FOOLS RUSH IN
SONY PICTURES ENTERTAINMENT. February, 1997. (Andy Tennant), Matthew Perry, Salma Hayek, Jon Tenney, Carlos Gomez.

FOOTBAL STORIES
ROOS NORTESUR PICTURES/KALFKRATES S.A. PROD. Aug., 1997. Chilean. (Andres Wood) Maria Izquierdo, Elsa Poblete.

FOR A LOST SOLDIER
STRAND. May, 1993. Dutch. (Roeland Kerbosch) Maarten Smit, Andrew Kelley, Jeroen Krabbe.

THE FORBIDDEN DANCE
COLUMBIA. March, 1990. (Greydon Clark) Laura Herring, Jeff James, Richard Lynch.

FORBIDDEN ENCOUNTERS
FILMAURO/AURELIA CINEMATOGRAFICA. Sept., 1998. Italian. (Alberto Sordi) Alberto Sordi, Valeria Marini, Franca Faldini.

FORBIDDEN LOVE:
THE UNASHAMED STORIES OF LESBIAN LIVES
WOMEN MAKE MOVIES. August, 1993. Canadian. (Aerlyn Weissman, Lynne Fernie) Documentary.

THE FORBIDDEN QUEST
ZEITGEIST. January, 1994. Dutch. (Peter Delpeut) Joseph O'Conor, Roy Ward.

FORCE OF CIRCUMSTANCE
UPFRONT. June, 1990. (Liza Bear) Borbala Major, Jessica Stutchbury.

FORCES OF NATURE
DREAMWORKS. Mar., 1999. (Bronwen Hughes) Sandra Bullock, Ben Affleck, Maura Tierney, Steve Zahn, Blythe Danner.

A FOREIGN BODY
ZELIE PRODS., LA SEPT CINEMA, FRENCH PROD. May, 1997. French-Canadian. (Claire Simon) Catherine Mendez, Emmanuel Clarke, Lou Castel, Agnes Regolo, Claude Merlin.

FOREIGN MOON
MIRAMAX. Nov., 1996. Hong Kong. (Zhang Zeming) Vicky Chen Hsiao-hsuan, Harrison Liu, Chen Daming, David Tse.

FOREIGN STUDENT
GRAMERCY. July, 1994. French. (Eva Sereny) Marco Hofschneider, Robin Givens, Charles S. Dutton.

FOREVER ACTIVISTS: STORIES FROM THE VETERANS OF THE ABRAHAM LINCOLN BRIGADE
TARA. June, 1991. (Judith Montell) Documentary.

FOREVER FEVER
SHAW ORGANISATION/MIRAMAX. July, 1998. Singaporean. (Glen Goei) Adrian Pang, Medlaine Tan, Anna Belle Francis, Pierre Png.

FOREVER MARY
CINEVISTA. April, 1991. Italian. (Marco Risi) Michele Placido, Alessandro di Sanzo, Claudio Amendola.

FOREVER MINE
J&M ENTERTAINMENT. Sept., 1999. British-U.S. (Paul Schrader) Esquema/Alan, Joseph Fiennes, Ray Liotta, Gretchen Mol, Vincent Laresca.

FOREVER YOUNG
WARNER BROS. December, 1992. (Steve Miner) Mel Gibson, Elijah Wood, Jamie Lee Curtis.

FORGET PARIS
COLUMBIA. May, 1995. (Billy Crystal) Billy Crystal, Debra Winger, Joe Mantegna, Cynthia Stevenson.

FORGOTTEN SILVER
PANDORA FILM. May, 1996. New Zealand. (Peter Jackson) Sam Neill, Leonard Maltin, Harvey Weinstein.

FOR LOVE OF THE GAME
UNIVERSAL. Sept., 1999. (Sam Raimi) Kevin Costner, Kelly Preston, John C. Reilly, Jena Malone, Brian Cox.

FOR LOVE OR MONEY
UNIVERSAL. October, 1993. (Barry Sonnenfeld) Michael J. Fox, Gabrielle Anwar, Anthony Higgins.

FORREST GUMP
PARAMOUNT. July, 1994. (Robert Zemeckis) Tom Hanks, Robin Wright, Gary Sinise, Sally Field.

FOR RICHER OR POORER
UNIVERSAL PICTURES. Dec., 1997. (Bryan Spicer) Tim Allen, Kirstie Alley, Jay O. Sanders, Michael Lerner, Wayne Knight, Larry Miller.

FOR ROSEANNA
FINE LINE. March, 1997. (Paul Weiland) Jean Reno, Mercedes Ruehl, Polly Walker, Mark Frankel, Trevor Peacock, Fay Ripley.

FOR SALE
PYRAMIDE. May, 1998. French. (Laetitia Masson) Sandrine Kiberlain, Sergio Castellitto, Jean-Francoise Stevenin.

FOR SASHA
MK2. June, 1992. French. (Alexandre Arcady) Sophie Marceau, Richard Berry, Fabien Orcier.

FOR THE BOYS
20TH CENTURY FOX. November, 1991. (Mark Rydell) Bette Midler, James Caan, George Segal.

FORTRESS
DIMENSION. September, 1993. Australian-U.S. (Stuart Gordon) Christopher Lambert, Kurtwood Smith.

FOR WANT OF SUN
PIERRE GRISE. June, 1996. French. (Christophe Blanc) Jean-Jacques Benhamou, Sara Haxaire, Christian Baltauss.

FOUR CORNERS
JAMES BENNING. Oct., 1998. (James Benning). Documentary.

FOUR FOR VENICE
BUENA VISTA INTL. May, 1998. German. (Vivian Naefe) Heino Ferch, Aglaia Szyszkowitz, Gedeon Burkhard, Hilde van Nieghem.

4 LITTLE GIRLS
HBO. July, 1997. (Spike Lee) Documentary.

FOUR ROOMS
MIRAMAX. December, 1995. (Allison Anders, Alexandre Rockwell, Robert Rodriguez, Quentin Tarantino) Tim Roth.

4 SEASONS IN ESPIGOULE
REZO FILMS. Mar., 1999. French. (Christian Philibert) The residents of "Espigoule."

FOUR WEDDINGS AND A FUNERAL
GRAMERCY. March, 1994. British. (Mike Newell) Hugh Grant, Andie MacDowell, Simon Callow, David Bower.

14 DAYS TO LIFE
MIL FILM ART & ENTERTAINMENT. May, 1998. German. (Roland Suso Richter) Kai Wiesinger, Michael Mendl, Katharina Meinecke.

1492: CONQUEST OF PARADISE
PARAMOUNT. October, 1992. (Ridley Scott) Gérard Depardieu, Armand Assante, Michael Wincott.

FOURTH WAR, THE
NEW AGE RELEASING. March, 1990. (John Frankenheimer) Roy Scheider, Jurgen Prochnow.

40,000 YEARS OF DREAMING
AUSTRALIAN FILM FINANCE CORP. Nov., 1996. Australian. (George Miller) Documentary.

FOXFIRE
SAMUEL GOLDWYN. July, 1996. (Annette Haywood-Carter) Hedy Burress, Angelina Jolie, Jenny Lewis.

FRAGMENTS * JERUSALEM
RON AND JACQUELINE HAVILIO. Sept., 1998. Israeli. (Ron Havilio) documentary.

FRANCHESCA PAGE
FLORA FILMS. May, 1997. (Kelley Sane) Varla Jean Merman, Rossy de Palma, Franchesca Leon, Mark Dandy, Linda Smith.

FRANCOIS TRUFFAUT: STOLEN PORTRAITS
MYRIAD PICTURES. July, 1994. French. (Serge Toubiana, Michel Pascal) Documentary.

FRANK CAPRA'S AMERICAN DREAM
COLUMBIA TRISTAR TELEVISION. May, 1997. (Kenneth Bowser) Documentary.

FRANK LLOYD WRIGHT
FLORENTINE FILMS. Jan., 1998. (Ken Burns, Lynn Novick) DOCUMENTARY.

FRANKENHOOKER
SHAPIRO GLICKENHAUS. June, 1990. (Frank Henenlotter) James Lorinz, Patty Mullen.

FRANKENSTEIN AND ME
MALOFILM INTL. April, 1996. Canadian. (Robert Tinnell) Jamieson Boulanger, Burt Reynolds, Louise Fletcher.

FRANKIE AND JOHNNY
PARAMOUNT. October, 1991. (Garry Marshall) Al Pacino, Michelle Pfeiffer, Kate Nelligan, Nathan Lane.

FRANKIE STARLIGHT
FINE LINE. September, 1995. (Michael Lindsay-Hogg) Annie Parillaud, Matt Dillon, Gabriel Byrne.

FRANTZ FANON: BLACK SKIN WHITE MASK
NORMAL FILMS. Jan., 1997. British. (Isaac Julien) Documentary.

FRAUDS
LIVE/J&M. September, 1993. Australian. (Stephan Elliott) Phil Collins, Hugo Weaving, Josephine Byrnes.

FREAKED
20TH CENTURY FOX. October, 1993. (Tom Stern, Alex Winter) Alex Winter, Randy Quaid, Megan Ward.

FREAKIN' BEAUTIFUL WORLD
LASSIHELMI FILMI. Feb., 1997. Finnish. (Jarmo Lampela) Joonas Bragge, Arttu Kapulainen, Pihla Penttinen, Ilkka Koivula.

FREAK TALKS ABOUT SEX
NEW SKY COMMUNICATIONS/LATENT IMAGE ENTERTAINMENT . June, 1999. (Paul Todisco): Josh Hamilton, Steve Zahn, Heather McComb, Arabella Field, David Kinney.

FRED
BAC FILMS. Jan., 1997. French. (Pierre Jolivet) Vincent Lindon, Clotilde Courau, Francois Berleand, Stephane Jobert.

FREDDIE AS F.R.O. 7
MIRAMAX. August, 1992. British. (Jon Acevski) Animated.

FREDDY'S DEAD: THE FINAL NIGHTMARE (3–D)
NEW LINE. September, 1991. (Rachel Talalay) Robert Englund, Lisa Zane, Lezlie Deane.

FREE ENTERPRISE
MINDFIRE ENTERTAINMENT. Oct., 1998. (Robert Meyer) Rafer Weigel, Eric McCormack, Audie England, Patrick Van Horn.

THE FREELANCERS
LES FILMS A UN DOLLAR. Sept., 1998. French. (Denis Dercourt) Pierre Lacan, Marc Citti, Philippe Clay, Henri Garcin, Marie-Christine Laurent.

FREE TIBET
SHOOTING GALLERY. Aug., 1998. (Sarah Pirozek) DOCUMENTARY.

FREE WILLY
WARNER BROS. July, 1993. (Simon Wincer) Jason James Richter, Lori Petty, August Schellenberg.

FREE WILLY 2: THE ADVENTURE HOME
WARNER BROS. July, 1995. (Dwight Little) Jason James Richter, August Schellenberg, Michael Madsen.

FREE WILLY 3: THE RESCUE
WARNER BROS. July, 1997. (Sam Pillsbury), Jason James Richter, August Schellenberg, Annie Corley, Vincent Berrym Patrick Kilpatrick.

FREEJACK
WARNER BROS. January, 1992. (Geoff Murphy) Emilio Estevez, Mick Jagger, Rene Russo.

FREEWAY
KUSHNER-LOCKE. January, 1996. (Matthew Bright) Kiefer Sutherland, Brooke Shileds, Reese Witherspoon.

FREEZE–DIE–COME TO LIFE
IFEX. December, 1990. Soviet. (Vitaly Kanevski) Pavel Nazarov, Dinara Drukarova. B&W.

FRENCH DRESSING
DAIEI CO. Feb., 1998. Japanese. (Hisashi Saito) Munehisa Sakurada, Miako Tadano, Hiroshi Abe, Rumi, Shuuhei Minami.

FRENCH EXIT
CINEVILLE. September 1995. (Daphna Kastner) Madchen Amick, Jonathan Silverman, Molly Hagan, Vince Grant.

FRENCH KISS
20TH CENTURY FOX. May, 1995. (Lawrence Kasdan) Meg Ryan, Timothy Hutton, Kevin Kline, Jean Reno.

FRENCH TWIST
MIRAMAX ZOE. January, 1996. French. (Josiane Balasko) Victoria Abril, Balasko, Alain Chabat.

FRESH
MIRAMAX. August, 1994. (Boaz Yakin) Sean Nelson, Giancarlo Esposito, Samuel L. Jackson.

FRESH AIR
R.B. FILMS/AUSTRALIAN FILM COMMISSION/SBS INDEPENDENT/ PREMIUM MOVIE PARTNERSHP. Jan., 1999. Australian.(Neil Mansfield) Nadine Garner, Bridie Carter, Marin Mimica, Tony Barry, Julie Hamilton.

FRESH KILL
STRAND. January, 1996. (Shu Lea Cheang) Sarita Choudhury, Erin McMurtry, Abraham Lim.

THE FRESHMAN
TRISTAR. July, 1990. (Andrew Bergman) Marlon Brando, Matthew Broderick, Penelope Ann Miller.

FRIDAY
NEW LINE. April, 1995. (F. Gary Gray) Ice Cube, Chris Tucker, Nia Long.

FRIED GREEN TOMATOES
UNIVERSAL. December, 1991. (Jon Avnet) Kathy Bates, Mary Stuart Masterson, Jessica Tandy, Mary Louise Parker.

FRIENDLY FIRE
DEZENOVE SOM E IMAGENS. Sept., 1998. Brazilian. (Beto Brant) Leonardo Villar, ZeCarlos Machados, Caca Amaral, Genesio de Barros.

THE FRIEND OF THE DECEASED
COMPAGNIE DES FILMS/COMPAGNIE EST-OUEST. May, 1997. Ukranian-French. (Viatcheslav Krichtofovitch) Alexandre Lazarev.

FRIENDS & LOVERS
LIONS GATE. Apr., 1999. (George Haas) Stephen Baldwin, Danny Nucci, George Newbern, Claudia Schiffer.

THE FRIGHTENERS
UNIVERSAL. July, 1996. (Peter Jackson) Michael J. Fox, Tino Alvarado, Peter Dobson, John Astin, Jeffrey Combs.

FRISK
STRAND. March, 1996. (Todd Verow) Michael Gunther, Craig Chester, Parker Posey, Alexis Arquette.

FROG AND WOMBAT
PIGTAIL PRODS. Oct., 1998. (Laurie Agard) Katie Stuart, Emily Lipoma, Ronny Cox, Lindsay Wagner.

FROGS FOR SNAKES
SHOOTING GALLERY. Feb., 1998. (Amos Poe) Barbara Hershey, Robbie Coltrane, Harry Hamlin, Ian Hart, John Leguizamo, Lisa Marie.

FROM DUSK TILL DAWN
DIMENSION. January, 1996. (Robert Rodriguez) Harvey Keitel, George Clooney, Quentin Tarantino, Juliette Lewis.

FROM HOLLYWOOD TO HANOI
INDEPT. July, 1993. (Tiana Thi Thanh Nga) Documentary.

FROM RUSSIA TO HOLLYWOOD: THE 100-YEAR OSYSSEY OF CHEKHOV AND SHDANOFF
KEEVE PRODS. Aug., 1999. (Frederick Keeve) John Berry, Dorothy Bridges, Lloyd Bridges, Leslie Caron. Documentary.

FROM RUSSIA WITH ROCK
INT'L. FILM CIRCUIT. December, 1990. Soviet. (Marjaana Mykkanen) Documentary.

FROM THE EDGE OF THE CITY (APO TIN AKRI TIS POLIS)
MYTHOS. Nov., 1998. Greek. (Constantinos Giannaris) Stathis Papadopoulos, Dimitris Papadoulidis, Theodora Tzimou, Costas Cotsianidis.

FROM THE HEART
BHARAT SHAH. Feb., 1999. Indian. (Mani Ratnam) Shahrukh Khan, Manisha Koirala, Preity Zinta, Raghuvir Yadav, Zora Sehgal.

FROSH: NINE MONTHS IN A FRESHMAN DORM
HORIZON UNLTD. October, 1994. (Dan Geller) Documentary.

FROZEN ASSETS
RKO. October, 1992. (George Miller) Shelley Long, Corbin Bernsen, Larry Miller.

FUCKING AMAL
SONET FILM. Oct., 1998. Swedish. (Lukas Moodysson) Alexandra Dahlstrom, Rebecca Liljeberg, Erica Carlson, Mathias Rust.

THE FUGITIVE
WARNER BROS. August, 1993. (Andrew Davis) Harrison Ford, Tommy Lee Jones, Jeroen Krabbe.

FULL ALERT
YOUNG FILMMAKERS. Dec., 1997. Hong Kong. (Ringo Lam) Lau Ching-wan, Francis Ng, Blackie Ko, Amanda Lee.

FULL FATHOM FIVE
CONCORDE. August, 1990. (Carl Franklin) Michael Moriarty, Maria Rangel, Diego Bertie.

THE FULL MONTY
20TH CENTURY FOX/FOX SEARCHLIGHT. July, 1997. British-U.S. (Peter Cattaneo) Robert Carlyle, Tom Wilkinson, Mark Addy, Lesley Sharp, Emily Woof, Steve Huison, Paul Barber, Hugo Speer.

FULL MONTYS WANTED
COLUMBIA TRISTAR. July, 1999. Spanish. (Alex Calvo-Sotelo) Antonio Molero, Guillermo Toledo, Sonia Javaga.

FULL MOON
A T&C FILM/PANDORA FILM/ARENA FILMS. Aug., 1998. Swiss. (Fredi M. Murer) Hanspeter Muller, Lilo Bauer, Benedict Freitag.

FULL MOON IN NEW YORK
SHIOBU FILM CO. June, 1990. Chinese. (Stanley Kwan) Sylvia Chang, Maggie Cheung.

FULL SPEED
POLYGRAM FILM. April, 1996. French. (Gael Morel) Elodie Bouchez, Stephane Rideau, Pascal Cervo.

FULL TILT BOOGIE
MIRAMAX. Sept., 1997. (Sarah Kelly), Robert Rodriguez, Quentin Tarantino, George Clooney, Juliette Lewis, Harvey Keitel.

FUN
INDEPT./FILM FORUM. April, 1995. (Rafael Zelinsky) Alicia Witt, Renee Humphrey, William R. Moses.

FUN DOWN THERE
FRAMELINE. June, 1990. (Roger Stigliano) Michael Waite, Nickolas B. Nagourney.

THE FUNERAL
October Films. August, 1996. (Abel Ferrara) Christopher Walken, Chris Penn, Vincent Gallo.

FUNKYTOWN
DRUMMER BOY PICTURES. March, 1998. (Steven Greenberg) DOCUMENTARY.

FUNNY ABOUT LOVE
PARAMOUNT. September, 1990. (Leonard Nimoy) Gene Wilder, Christine Lahti, Mary Stuart Masterson.

FUNNY BONES
BUENA VISTA. March, 1995. (Peter Chelsom) Oliver Platt, Jerry Lewis, Leslie Caron, George Carl.

FUNNY GAMES
WEGA FILM. May, 1997. Austrian. (Michael Hanecke) Susanne Lothar, Ulrich Muhe, Frank Giering, Arno Frisch.

FURIA
ALEXANDRE FILMS/FRANCE 2 CINEMA/LE STUDIO CANAL PLUS. June, 1999. French. (Alexandre Aja) Stanislas Merhar, Marion Cotillard, Wadek Stanczak, Pierre Vaneck, Carlo Brandt.

A FURTHER GESTURE
CASTLE HILL. May, 1997. British-German-Irish-Japanese. (Robert Dornhelm) Stephen Rea, Alfred Molina.

F/X 2
ORION. May, 1991. (Richard Franklin) Bryan Brown, Brian Dennehy, Rachel Ticotin.

G

GALGAMETH
GALAXY INTL. May, 1996. (Sean McNamara) Devin Oatway, Sean McNamara, Stephen Macht.

THE GAME
AQUARIUS RELEASING. April, 1990. (Curtis Brown) Curtis Brown, Richard Lee Ross.

THE GAME
POLYGRAM. September, 1997. (David Fincher), Michael Douglas, Sean Penn, Deborah Kara Unger, James Rebhorn, Peter Donat.

THE GAMEBAG
BUENA VISTA INT'L. Feb., 1997. Italian. (Maurizio Zaccaro) Massimo Ghini, Antonio Catania, Roberto Zibetti.

GAMERA 3: REVENGE OF IRIS
DAIEI. May, 1999. Japanese. (Shusuke Kaneko) Shinobu Nakayama, Ai Maeda, Ayako Fujitani, Senri Yamasaki.

GANGLAND
NEOFILMS. Sept., 1998. Philippine. (Peque Gallaga) Ryan Eigenmann, Jason Salcedo, Junell Hernando, Jesus Simoy, Blakdyak.

GARAGE OLIMPO
CLASSIC PARADIS FILMS NISARGA. May, 1999. Italian-French-Argentine. (Marco Bechis) Antonella Costa, Carlos Echeverria, Dominique Sanda, Chiara Caselli, Enrique Pineyro.

GARBAGE
PBFM/VOIX. September, 1995. (Peter Byck) Derich Wittliff, Byck.

THE GARDEN
INT'L FILM CIRCUIT. January, 1991. U.K. (Derek Jarman) Tilda Swinton, Johnny Mills, Philip MacDonald, Spencer Lee.

THE GARDEN OF REDEMPTION
PARAMOUNT. June, 1997. (Thomas Michael Donnelly), Anthony LaPaglia, Embeth Davidtz, Dan Hedaya, Peter Firth, David Neal.

GARDEN OF SCORPIONS
LEN FILM. March, 1993. Russian. (Oleg Kovalov). Compilation.

THE GARDEN ON EDEN
MEDUSA FILM. Sept., 1998. Italian. (Alessanro D'Alatri) Kim Rossi Stuart, Said Taghmaoui, Boris Terral, Kassandra Voyagis.

GAS FOOD LODGING
I.R.S. July, 1992. (Allision Anders) Brooke Adams, Ione Skye, Fairuza Balk.

GATE II
TRIUMPH. February, 1992. (Tibor Takacs) Louis Tripp, Simon Reynolds, Pamela Segall.

GATTACA
SONY PICTURES ENTERTAINMENT. September, 1997. (Andrew Niccol), Ethan Hawke, Uma Thurman, Jude Law, Gore Vidal, Alan Arkin.

GAY CUBA
CUBA'S FELIX VARELA CENTER. August, 1996. (Sonja de Vries) Documentary.

GENDERNAUTS
HYENA FILMS. Feb., 1999. German. (Monika Treut) Sandy Stone, Jordy Jones, Susan Stryker, Stafford, Texas Tomboy.

GENEALOGIES OF A CRIME
GEMINI FILMS. Feb., 1997. French. (Raoul Ruiz) Catherine Deneuve, Michel Piccoli, Melvil Poupaud, Andrzej Seweryn.

GENESIS
KORA FILMS. May, 1999. French-Mali. (Cheick Oumar) Sotigui Kouyate, Salif Keita, Balla Moussa Keita, Fatoumata Diawara.

GENUINE RISK
I.R.S. RELEASING. December, 1990. (Kurt Voss) Terence Stamp, Peter Berg, Michelle Johnson.

GEORGE B.
TANGO WEST. Jan., 1997. (Eric Lea) David Morse, Nina Siemaszko, Brad Gregg, John Franklin, Grace Zabriskie, Henry V. Brown Jr.

GEORGE BALANCHINE'S THE NUTCRACKER
WARNER BROS. October, 1993. (Emile Ardolino) Darci Kistler, Macaulay Culkin, Jessica Lynn Cohen.

GEORGE OF THE JUNGLE
BUENA VISTA. July, 1997. (Sam Weisman.), Brendan Fraser, Leslie Mann, Thomas Haden Church, Richard Roundtree, John Cleese.

GEORGE'S ISLAND
NEW LINE. October, 1991. Canadian. (Paul Donovan) Ian Bannen, Sheila McCarthy, Nathaniel Moreau.

GEORGIA
MIRAMAX. December, 1995. (Lilli Grosbard) Jennifer Jason Leigh, Mare Winningham.

GEORGICA
A Q-FILM. June, 1998. Estonian. (Sulev Keedus) Evald Aavik, Mait Marekulski, Ulle Toming.

THE GENERAL'S DAUGHTER
PARAMOUNT. June, 1999. (Simon West) John Travolta, Madeleine Stowe, James Cromwell, Timothy Hutton.

GERMANY YEAR 90 NINE ZERO
BRAINSTORM. January, 1995. French-German. (Jean Luc Godard) Eddie Constantine, Hanns Zischler.

GERMINAL
SONY PICTURES CLASSICS. December, 1993. French. (Claude Berri) Gérard Depardieu, Miou-Miou.

GERONIMO: AN AMERICAN LEGEND
COLUMBIA. December, 1993. (Walter Hill) Jason Patric, Wes Studi, Gene Hackman, Matt Damon.

GET BRUCE!
MIRAMAX. Jan., 1999. (Andrew J. Kuehn) Bruce Vilanch, Bette Midler, Billy Crystal, Robin Williams, Whoopi Goldberg.

GET ON THE BUS
SONY PICTURES. October, 1996. (Spike Lee) Richard Belzer, DeAundre Bonds, Andre Braugher, Thomas Jefferson Byrd.

GET REAL
DISTANT HORIZON. Aug., 1998. British. (Simon Shore) Ben Silverstone, Brad Gorton, Charlotte Brittain, Stacy A. Hart.

GET SHORTY
MGM. October, 1995. (Barry Sonnenfeld) John Travolta, Gene Hackman, Danny DeVito, Rene Russo, Delroy Lindo.

GET THEE OUT
FIRST RUN FEATURES. January, 1993. Russian. (Dimitri Astrakhan) Otar Mengvinetukutsey, Elena Anisimova.

THE GETAWAY
UNIVERSAL. February, 1994. (Roger Donaldson) Alec Baldwin, Kim Basinger, Michael Masden, James Woods.

GETTING EVEN WITH DAD
MGM. June, 1994. (Howard Deutch) Macaulay Culkin, Ted Danson, Glenne Headly.

GETTING OFF
CINEBLAST! Sept., 1998. (Julie A. Lynch) Christine Harnos, Brooke Smith, Bill Sage, David Marshall Grant.

GETTING TO KNOW YOU
SHOWDOWCATCHER ENTERTAINMENT-SEARCH PARTY. Jan., 1999. (Lisanne Skyler) Heather Matarazzo, Zach Braff, Michael Weston, Bebe Neuwirth.

GETTYSBURG
NEW LINE. October, 1993. (Ronald E. Maxwell) Tom Berenger, Jeff Daniels, Martin Sheen.

GHOST
PARAMOUNT. July, 1990. (Jerry Zucker) Patrick Swayze, Demi Moore, Whoopi Goldberg.

THE GHOST AND THE DARKNESS
PARAMOUNT. October, 1996. (Stephen Hopkins) Michael Douglas, Val Kilmer, Tom Wilkinson, John Kani, Bernard Hill.

GHOST DAD
UNIVERSAL. June, 1990. (Sidney Poitier) Bill Cosby, Kimberly Russell, Denise Nicholas.

GHOST DOG: THE WAY OF THE SAMURAI
JVC/BAC FILMS/LE STUDIO CANAL PLUS. May, 1999. U.S.-French. (Jim Jarmusch) Forest Whitaker, John Tormey, Cliff Gorman, Henry Silva, Isaach de Bankole.

GHOST IN THE MACHINE
20TH CENTURY FOX. December, 1993. (Rachel Talalay) Karen Allen, Wil Horneff, Chris Mulkey.

GHOST IN THE SHELL
MANGA ENTERTAINMENT LTD. April, 1996. Japanese. (Mamoru Oshii) Animated.

GHOSTS
M.J.J. May, 1997. (Stan Winston) Michael Jackson.

GHOSTS CAN'T DO IT
TRIUMPH. June, 1990. (John Derek) Bo Derek, Anthony Quinn, Don Murray.

GHOSTS OF MISSISSIPPI
SONY PICTURES ENTERTAINMENT. December, 1996. (Rob Reiner), Alec Baldwin, Whoopi Golberg, James Woods, William H. Macy.

GIDEON
BALDWIN/COHEN PRODS. May, 1999. (Claudia Hoover) Christopher Lambert, Shelley Winters, Charlton Heston, Carroll O'Connor, Shirley Jones.

G.I. JANE
BUENA VISTA. July, 1997. (Ridley Scott), Demi Moore, Viggo Mortensen, Anne Bancroft, Jason Beghe, Scott Wilson.

THE GINKO BED
GOLDEN NETWORK, HONG KONG/MORE IN GROUP, SEOUL. May, 1996. South Korean. (Jacky Kang) Han Suk-kyu, Shim Hae-jin, Jin Hee-kyung.

THE GIRAFFE
Jugendfilm. Sept., 1998. German-Austrian. (Dani Levy) Maria Schrader, Dani Levy, David Strathairn, Nicole Heesters, Jeffrey Wright.

GIRL
KUSHNER-LOCKE. May, 1998. (Jonathan Kahn) Dominique Swain, Sean Patrick Flanery, Summer Phoenix, Tara Reid, Selma Blair.

A GIRL CALLED ROSEMARIE
CONSTANTIN FILM. Feb., 1997. German. (Bernd Eichinger) Nina Hoss, Heiner Lauterbach, Mathieu Carriere, Horst Krause.

THE GIRL OF THE SILENCE
FILM-MAKERS. November, 1995. Japanese. (Genjiro Arato) Mami Nakamura, Kaori Momoi.

THE GIRL OF YOUR DREAMS
LOLA FILMS. Nov., 1998. Spanish. (Fernando Trueba): Penelope Cruz, Antonio Resines, Neus Asensi, Jesus Bonilla, Liles Leon.

THE GIRL ON THE BRIDGE
UFD. Mar., 1999. French. (Patrice Leconte) Daniel Auteuil, Vanessa Paradis, Demetre Georgalas, Isabelle Petit-Jacques, Frederic Pfluger.

GIRL 6
FOX SEARHCLIGHT. March 1996. (Spike Lee) Theresa Randle, Spike Lee, Peter Berg, Naomi Campbell.

GIRLS' NIGHT
GRANADA. Jan., 1998. British. (Nick Hurran) Brenda Blethyn, Julie Walters, Kris Kristofferson, James Gaddas, George Costigan.

GIRL'S NIGHT OUT
SAMSUNG PICTURES. Sept., 1998. South Korean. (Im Sang-su) Kang Su-yeon, Jin Heui-kyeong, Kim Yeo-jin.

GIRL'S TOWN
OCTOBER FILMS. January, 1996. (Jim McKay) Lili Taylor, Anna Grace, Bruklin Harris, Aunjanue Ellis.

THE GIRL WITH BRAINS IN HER FEET
ALLIANCE ELECTRIC PICTURES. Aug., 1997. British. (Roberto Bangura) Amanda Mealing, Joanna Ward, Jamie McIntosh.

GIRLFRIEND FROM HELL
AUGUST ENT. April, 1991. (Daniel M. Peterson) Liane Curtis, Dana Ashbrook, Lezlie Deane.

GIRLS LIKE US
INDEPENDENT TELEVISION SERVICE. Jan., 1997. (Jane C. Wagner) Documentary.

THE GIVING
NORTHERN ARTS. November, 1992. (Eames Demetrios) Jeremiah Pollock, Lee Hampton, Flor Hawkins.

GLADIATOR
COLUMBIA. March, 1992. (Rowdy Herrington) James Marshall, Brian Dennehy, Cuba Gooding Jr.

GLADYS
PRODUCTIONS LA FETE. June, 1999. (Vojtech Jasny). Documentary.

THE GLASS SHIELD
MIRAMAX. June, 1995. (Charles Burnett) Michael Boatman, Lori Petty, Ice Cube.

GLENGARRY GLEN ROSS
NEW LINE. September, 1992. (James Foley) Al Pacino, Jack Lemmon, Ed Harris.

GLIMMER MAN
WARNER BROS. October, 1996. (John Gray) Steven Seagal, Keenan Ivory Wayans, Bob Gundton, Brian Cox.

GLORIA
COLUMBIA. Jan., 1999. (Sidney Lumet) Sharon Stone, Jean-Luke Figueroa, Jeremy Northam, Cathy Moriarty, George C. Scot.

GLORIA
ROSA FILMES/CARO-LINE PRODS./CAMELOT PELIS. Feb., 1999. Portuguese-French-Spanish. (Manuela Viegas) Jean-Christophe Bouvet, Raquel Marques, Francisco Relvas, Ricardo Aibeo, Paul So.

GO
SONY. Jan., 1999. (Doug Liman) Desmond Askew, Taye Diggs, William Fichtner, J.E. Freeman.

GOAT ON FIRE & SMILING FISH
MARTINI/JORDAN. Sept., 1999. (Kevin Jordan) Derick Martini, Christa Miller, Steven Martini, Bill Henderson.

THE GODFATHER PART III
PARAMOUNT. December, 1990. (Francis Ford Coppola) Al Pacino, Andy Garcia, Talia Shire, Diane Keaton.

GODMOTHER
GRAMCO FILMS. Aug., 1999. Indian. (Vinay Shukla) Shabana Azmi, Milind Gunaji, Nirmal Pandey. Gonvind Namdev, Raima Sen.

GOD SAID, HA!
AN OH BROTHER. March, 1998. (Julia Sweeney) Julia Sweeney, Quentin Tarantino.

GODS AND MONSTERS
REGENT ENTERTAINMENT. Jan., 1998. (Bill Condon) Ian McKellen, Brendan Fraser, Lynn Redgrave, Lolita Davidovich, Kevin J. O'connor.

GOD'S LONELY MAN
ST. FRANCES OF ASSISI. January, 1996. (Francis Von Zerneck) Michael Wyle, Heather McComb, Justine Bateman.

THE GODS MUST BE CRAZY II
COLUMBIA. April, 1990. Botswana. (Jamie Uys) N!xau, Lena Farugia.

GOD'S WEDDING
MADRAGOA FILMES/GEMINI FILMS. May, 1999. Portuguese-French. (Joao Cesar Monteiro) Joao Cesar Monteiro, Joana Azevedo, Rita Durao, Jose Airosa, Manuela de Freitas.

GODZILLA
SONY. May., 1998. (Roland Emmerich) Matthew Broderick, Jean Reno, Maria Pitillo, Hank Azaria, Kevin Dunn, Michael Lerner.

GO FISH
SAMUEL GOLDWYN. June, 1994. (Rose Troche) Guinevere Turner, V.S. Brodie, T. Wendy McMillan.

GOING ALL THE WAY
GRAMERCY. Jan., 1997. (Mark Pellington) Jeremy Davies, Ben Affleck, Amy Locane, Rachel Weisz, Rose McGowan, John Lordan.

GOING TO KANSAS CITY
MANDART ENTERTAINMENT LTD. Oct., 1998. Canadian-Finnish. (Pekka Mandart). Mikko Nousiainen, Melissa Galianos, Michael Ironside.

GOING TO SCHOOL WITH DAD ON MY BACK
BEIJING FORBIDDEN CITY FILM COMPANY. Aug., 1998. Chinese. (Zhou Youchao) Zhao Qiang, Jiang Hualin, Yukui, Yan Danchen.

GOLD DIGGERS: THE SECRET OF BEAR MOUNTAIN
UNIVERSAL. November, 1995. (Kevin James Dobson) Anna Chlumsky, Christina Ricci, Polly Draper, Brian Kerwin.

GOLD IN THE STREETS
CARLTON/RFD. April, 1997. British-Irish. (Elizabeth Gill) Karl Geary, James Belushi, Ian Hart, Jared Harris, Aidan Gillen.

THE GOLDEN BOAT
STRAND. June, 1991. (Paul Ruiz) Federico Muchnik, Michael Kirby.

GOLDEN BRAID
CABRIOLET. December, 1991. Australian. (Paul Cox) Chris Haywood, Gosia Dobrowolska, Paul Chubb.

GOLDENEYE
UA. November, 1995. (Martin Campbell) Pierce Brosnan, Sean Bean, Izabella Scorupco, Famke Janssen.

GOLDEN GATE
SAMUEL GOLDWYN. January, 1994. (John Madden) Matt Dillon, Joan Chen, Bruno Kirby, Stan Egi.

GONE FISHIN'
BUENA VISTA. May, 1997. (Christopher Cain), Joe Pesci, Danny Glover, Rosanna Arquette, Lynn Whitfield, Willie Nelson, Nick Brimble.

GONE, GONE, FOREVER GONE
GIAI PHONG FILMS. Sept., 1996. Vietnamese-Swiss. (Ho Quang Minh) Phuong Dung, Le Tuan Anh, Hoang Phuc.

GOOD BURGER
PARAMOUNT PICTURES. July, 1997. (Brian Robbins), Kel Mitchell, Kenan Thompson, Sinbad, Abe Vigoda, Shar Jackson.

GOODBYE AMERICA
QUANTUM ENTERTAINMENT & STAR PACIFIC CINEMA. May, 1997. (Thierry Notz) John Haymes Newton, Corin Nemec.

GOODBYE TOMORROW
RH POLITIC PRODS. INTL./EUROFILM STUDIO/ FRP. Apr., 1999. Turkish-Hungarian-French. (Reis Celik).

GOODBYE, 20TH CENTURY!
MIRCO & SLAVCO FIRST PARTISAN. Feb., 1999. Macedonian. (Aleksandar Popovski) Lazar Ristovski, Mikola Ristanovski, Vlado Jovanovski, Sofija Kunovska, Dejan Acimovic.

GOODFELLAS
WARNER BROS. September, 1990. (Martin Scorsese) Robert De Niro, Ray Liotta, Joe Pesci, Paul Sorvino.

A GOOD MAN IN AFRICA
GRAMERCY. September, 1994. (Bruce Beresford) Colin Friels, Sean Connery, John Lithgow.

THE GOOD SON
20TH CENTURY FOX. September, 1993. (Joseph Ruben) Macaulay Culkin, Elijah Wood, Wendy Crewson.

GOOD WILL HUNTING
MIRAMAX. Nov., 1997. (Gus Van Sant) Matt Damon, Robin Williams, Ben Affleck, Minnie Driver, Stellan Skarsgard, Casey Affleck.

THE GOOD WOMAN OF BANGKOK
ROXIE. November, 1991. Australian. (Dennis O'Rourke) Documentary.

A GOOFY MOVIE
BUENA VISTA. April, 1995. (Kevin Lima) Bill Farmer, Jason Marsden, Jim Cummings, Kellie Martin.

GORDY
MIRAMAX. November, 1994. (Mark Lewis) Doug Stone, Michael Roescher, Kristy Young.

GOREVILLE, U.S.A.
LEANING SILO. Aug., 1998. (Seth Henrikson, Dave Sarno, Rob Shields) DOCUMENTARY.

GORGEOUS
GOLDEN HARVEST. July, 199. Hong Kong. (Vincent Kuk) Jackie Chan, Shu Qi, Tony Leung Chiu-wai, Emil Chow, Jen Hsien-chi.

GORILLA BATHES AT NOON
INDEPT./PUBLIC TH. March, 1995. German-Russian. (Dusan Makavejcu) Svetozar Cvetkovic, Anita Manic. B&W/Color.

GOSHOGAOKA
SHARON LOCKHART. Jan., 1998. (Sharon Lockhart) DOCUMENTARY.

THE GOVERNESS
SONY PICTURES CLASSICS. June, 1998. British. (Sandra Goldbacher) Minnie Driver, Tom Wilkinson, Florence Hoath.

GOYA IN BORDEAUX
LOLAFILMS. Sept., 1999. Spanish-Italian. (Carlos Saura) Francisco Rabal, Jose Coronado, Dafne Fernandez.

GRACE OF MY HEART
GRAMMERCY PICTURES. September, 1996. (Allison Anders) Illeana Douglas, Matt Dillon, Eric Stoltz.

GRADUATE OF INSANITY
MINE FILM/MACT PRODS./OBJEKTIV FILMSTUDIO. Apr., 1999. Turkish-French-Hungarian.(Tunic Basaran) Ayda Aksel, Selcuk Yontem, Guler Okten, Meric Basaran, Gokham Mete.

THE GRADUATES
WARNER ITALIA. December, 1995. Italian. (Leonardo Pieraccioni) Rocco Papaleo, Gianmarco Tognazzi.

GRAFFITI BRIDGE
WARNER BROS. November, 1990. (Prince) Prince, Morris Day, Jerome Benton & The Time.

GRAND CANYON
20TH CENTURY FOX. December, 1991. (Lawrence Kasdan) Kevin Kline, Danny Glover, Steve Martin, Mary McDonnell.

THE GRANDFATHER
COLUMBIA TRISTAR. Nov., 1998. Spanish. (Jose Luis Garcia) Fernando Fernan-Gomez, Rafael Alonso, Cayetana Guillen-Cuervo, Agustin Gonzalez.

GRASS
LIONS GATE . Sept., 1999. Canadian. (Ron Mann). Documentary.

THE GRASS HARP
FINE LINE. September, 1996. (Charles Matthau) Sissy Spacek, Walter Matthau, Jack Lemmon, Piper Laurie.

THE GRAVE
KUSHNER-LOCKE. January, 1996. (Jonas Pate) Craig Sheffer, Garbielle Anwar, Josh Charles, Max Perlich.

GRAVEYARD OF DREAMS
TMS INVEST/GEORGIA FILM/COCA BOTTLERS. Feb., 1997. Georgian. (Georgi Chaindrava) Bacho Bachukaschvili.

GRAY'S ANATOMY
INDEPENDENT FILM CHANNEL. September, 1996. (Steven Soderbergh) Spalding Gray.

A GREAT DAY IN HARLEM
CASTLE HILL. February, 1995. (None credited) Documentary.

THE GREAT WHITE HYPE
20TH CENTURY FOX. May, 1996. (Reginald Hudlin) Samuel L. Jackson, Jeff Goldblum, Peter Berg, Jon Lovitz.

GREED
TURNER CLASSIC MOVIES. Sept., 1999. (Rick Schmidlin). Restoration.

GREEDY
UNIVERSAL. March, 1994. (Jonathan Lynn) Michael J. Fox, Kirk Douglas, Nancy Travis.

GREEN CARD
BUENA VISTA. December, 1990. French-Australian. (Peter Weir) Gérard Depardieu, Andie MacDowell, Bebe Neuwirth.

GREEN DESERT
BUENA VISTA INTL. June, 1999. German. (Anno Saul) Tatjana Trieb, Robert Gwisdek, Martina Gedeck, Ulrich Noethen, Heino Ferch.

GREEN PLAID SHIRT
VICIOUS CIRCLE. July, 1996. (Richard Natale) Gregory Phelan, Kevin Spirtas, Richard Israel.

GREGORY'S TWO GIRLS
FILMFOUR. Aug., 1999. British. (Bill Forsyth) John Gordon Sinclair, Carly McKinnon, Maria Doyle Kennedy, Kevin Anderson, Martin Schwab.

GREMLINS 2: THE NEW BATCH
WARNER BROS. June, 1990. (Joe Dante) Zach Galligan, John Glover, Phoebe Cates.

GRETA
CHARLES STEWART MOTT FOUNDATION/ EUROPEAN CULTURAL FOUNDATION/SOROS DOCUMENTARY FUND OF THE OPEN SOCIETY INSTITUTE/INTERNEWS.Aug., 1999. (Haris Pasovic). Documentary.

GRIEF
STRAND. March, 1994. (Richard Glatzer) Craig Chester, Jackie Beat, Alexis Arquette, Illeana Douglas.

THE GRIFTERS
MIRAMAX. December, 1990. (Stephen Frears) John Cusack, Anjelica Huston, Annette Bening.

GRIM PRAIRIE TALES
COE HAN FILMS. August, 1990. (Wayne Coe) Brad Dourif, James Earl Jones, Marc McClure.

GRIND
KODIAK. April, 1996. (Chris Kentis) Adrienne Shelly, Billy Crudup, Paul Schulze, Frank Vincent, Saul Stein.

GRIZZLY ADAMS AND THE LEGEND OF DARK MOUNTAIN
MARK OF THE BEAR PARTNERSHIP. May, 1999. (John Huneck) Tom Tayback, Lindsay Bloom, Jennifer Waldman, Selina Jayne.

GRIZZLY MOUNTAIN
LEGACY. Oct., 1997. (Jeremy Haft) Dan Haggerty, Dylan Haggerty, Nicole Lund, Kim Morgan Greene, Perry Stephens, Robert Patteri.

GROSSE FATIGUE
MIRAMAX. July, 1995. French. (Michel Blanc) Michael Blanc, Carole Bouquet, Phillipe Noiret.

GROSSE POINTE BLANK
BUENA VISTA. March, 1997. (George Armitage), John Cusack, Minnie Driver, Dan Aykroyd, Alan Arkin, Joan Cusack, Jeremy Piven, Hank Azaria.

GROUNDHOG DAY
COLUMBIA. February, 1993. (Harold Ramis) Bill Murray, Andie MacDowell, Chris Elliott.

GRUMPIER OLD MEN
WARNER BROS December, 1995. (Howard Deutch) Jack Lemmon, Walter Matthau, Ann-Margret, Sophia Loren.

GRUMPY OLD MEN
WARNER BROS. December, 1993. (Donald Petrie) Jack Lemmon, Walter Matthau, Ann-Margret.

THE GUARDIAN
UNIVERSAL. April, 1990. (William Friedkin) Jenny Seagrove, Dwier Brown, Carey Lowell.

GUARDING TESS
TRISTAR. March, 1994. (Hugh Wilson) Shirley MacLaine, Nicolas Cage, Austin Pendleton.

GUELWAAR
NEW YORKER. April, 1993. Senegalese-French. (Ousmane Sembene) Omar Seck, Ndiawar Diop, Isseu Niang.

THE GUEST
FILM DAEDALUS. Feb., 1999. Italian. (Alessandro Colizzi) Elodie Treccani, Anita Zagria, Umberto Orsini, Ignazio Oliva, Maddalena Maggi, Lorenzo Lavia. Yoon C. Joyce.

GUESTS
ARCHIMEDE PRODUZIONE. Sept., 1998. Italian. (Matteo Garrone) Julian Sota, Llazar Sota, Corrado Sassi, Pasqualino Mura, Paola Rota.

GUILT FREE
PRODUCCIONES MEXICO. March, 1997. Mexican. (Marcel Sisniega) Martin Altomaro, Francisco Ribera, Masha Kostiurina.

GUILTY AS CHARGED
I.R.S. January, 1992. (Sam Irvin) Rod Steiger, Lauren Hutton, Zelda Rubinstein.

GUILTY AS SIN
BUENA VISTA. June, 1993. (Sidney Lumet) Rebecca De Morany, Don Johnson, Jack Warden, Stephen Lang.

GUILTY BY SUSPICION
WARNER BROS. March, 1991. (Irwin Winkler) Robert De Niro, Annette Bening, George Wendt.

GUINEVERE
MIRAMAX. Jan., 1999.(Audrey Wells) Stephen Rea, Sarah Polley, Jean Smart, Gina Gershon, Paul Dooley.

GUMBY: THE MOVIE
ARROW. December, 1995. (Art Clokey) Animation.

GUMMO
FINE LINE FEATTURES. Aug., 1997. (Harmony Korine), Jacob Reynolds, Nick Sutton, Jacob Sewell, Chloe Sevigny, Max Perlich.

THE GUMSHOE KID
SKOURAS. February, 1990. (Joe Manduke) Jay Underwood, Tracy Scoggins.

A GUN, A CAR, A BLONDE
SHOWCASE ENTERTAINMENT/VISTA DEL MAR PRODS. May, 1997. (Stefani Ames) Jim Metzler, Kay Lenz, Billy Bob Thornton.

A GUN FOR JENNIFER
CONSPIRACY FILMS. August, 1996. (Todd Morris) Deborah Twiss, Benja Kay, Freida Hoops, Rene Alberta.

THE GUN IN BETTY LOU'S HANDBAG
BUENA VISTA. August, 1992. (Allan Moyle) Penelope Ann Miller, Eric Thal, Alfre Woodard.

GUNMEN
DIMENSION. February, 1994. (Mario Van Peebles) Mario Van Peebles, Christopher Lambert, Patrick Stewart.

GUNS
MALIBU BAY FILMS. November, 1990. (Andy Sidaris) Erik Estrada, Dona Spier, Roberta Vasquez.

GUNS AND ROSES
FALCO FILM. Feb., 1999. Italian. (Carla Apuzzo) Anna Ammirati, Duccio Giordano, Luigi Petrucci, Cristina Donadio, Lello Serao.

GUNS ON THE CLACKAMAS: A DOCUMENTARY
October, 1995. (Bill Plympton) Keith Scales, Michael Thomas Parks, Danny Bruno, William Tate.

GUNSHY
PERISCOPE PICTURE. March, 1998. (Jeff Celentano) William Petersen, Michael Wincott, Diane Lane, Kevin Gage, Michael Byrne.

GURU IN SEVEN
RATPACK FILMS. April, 1998. British. (Shani Grewal) Nitin Chandra Ganatra, Saeed Jaffrey, Jacqueline Pearce, Antony Zaki.

GUY
POLYGRAM FILM INTERNATIONAL. September, 1996. (Michael Lindsay-Hogg) Vincent D'Onofrio, Hope Davis.

GYPSY SOUL
ALTAFILMS. January, 1996. Spanish. (Chuz Gutierrez) Amara Carmona, Pedro Alonso, Peret, Rafael Alvarez. Loles Leon.

H

H–2 WORKER
FIRST RUN FEATURES. November, 1990. (Stephanie Black) Documentary.

HABIT
GLASS EYE PIX. April, 1996. (Larry Fessenden) Fessenden, Meredith Snaider, Aaron Beall, Patricia Coleman.

HACKERS
MGM/UA. September, 1995. (Iain Softley) Johnny Lee Miller, Angelina Jolie, Fisher Stevens, Lorraine Bracco.

HACKS
MATT SALINGER AND MIKE SAYLES. Oct., 1997. (Gary Rosen) Stephen Rea, Illeana Douglas, John Ritter, David Foley, Richard Kind.

HAIR SHIRT
LUNATIC PRODS. Sept., 1998. (Dean Paras) Dean Paras, Katie Wright, Neve Campbell, Kimberly Huie, Stefan Brogren.

THE HAIRDRESSER'S HUSBAND
TRITON. June, 1992. French. (Patrice Leconte) Jean Rochefort, Anna Galiena, Roland Bertin.

HALF A CHANCE
UFD. March, 1998. French. (Patrice Leconte) Jean-Paul Belmondo, Alain Delon, Vanessa Paradis, Eric Defosse, Alexandre Iakovlev.

HALF JAPANESE: THE BAND WHO WOULD BE KING
INDEPENDENT. October, 1993. (Jeff Feuerzeig) Half Japanese.

HALF SPIRIT: VOICE OF THE SPIDER
QUARTET. September, 1995. French. (Henri Barges) Catherine Ussel, Phillipe Spiteri, Marc Duret.

HALLELUJAH! RON ATHEY: A STORY OF DELIVERANCE
AUBIN PICTURES. Feb., 1998. (Catherine Saalfield) DOCUMENTARY.

HALLOWEEN: H2O
DIMENSION FILMS. July, 1998. (Steve Miner) Jamie Lee Curtis, Adam Arkin, Josh Hartnett, Michelle Williams, Adam Hann-Byrd.

HALLOWEEN: THE CURSE OF MICHAEL MYERS
DIMENSION. September, 1995. (Joe Chappelle) Donald Pleasence, Mitch Ryan, Mariann Hagen.

HAMLET
WARNER BROS. December, 1990. British. (Franco Zeffirelli) Mel Gibson, Glenn Close, Alan Bates, Paul Scofield.

HAMLET
SONY. December, 1996. (Kenneth Branagh), Kenneth Branagh, Julie Christie, Billy Crystal, Gerard Depardieu, Charlton Heston, Derek Jacobi, Jack Lemmon, Rufus Sewell, Robin Williams, Kate Winslet.

HANA-BI
OFFICE KITANO. Sept., 1997. Japanese. (Takeshi Kitano) Beat Takeshi, Kayoko Kishimoto, Ren Osugi, Susumu Terajima.

THE HAND THAT ROCKS THE CRADLE
BUENA VISTA. January, 1992. (Curtis Hanson) Annabella Sciorra, Rebecca De Mornay, Matt McCoy.

THE HANDMAID'S TALE
CINECOM. March, 1990. (Volker Schlondorff) Natasha Richardson, Faye Dunaway, Aidan Quinn.

HAND OF FATE
LUMINOUS FILMS. June, 1999 (Scott Morgan) Neela Baba, Colette Baron Reid, Thubten Ngodup, Rita Rogers, Frank Andrews.

HANGFIRE
MOTION PICTURE CORP. OF AMERICA. January, 1991. (Peter Maris) Brad Davis, Jan Michael Vincent, Kim Delaney.

HANGIN' WITH THE HOMEBOYS
NEW LINE. May, 1991. (Joseph B. Vasquez) Doug E. Doug, Mario Joyner, John Leguizamo.

THE HANGING GARDEN
CINPLEX ODEON FILMS. Sept., 1997. Canadian. (Thom Fitzgerald) Chris Leavins, Kerry Fox, Seana McKenna, Peter MacNeill.

HANG THE DJ
ASKA FILM. Sept., 1998. Canadian. (Marco La Villa, Mauro La Villa). Junior Vasquez, Q-Bert, Roger Sanchez, A-Trak. Documentary.

HANNAH
STAR-FILM. Feb., 1997. Austrian. (Reinhard Schwabenitzky) Elfi Eschke, August Zirner, Jurgen Hentsch, Paul Herwig, Max Tidof.

HANS CHRISTIAN ANDERSEN'S THUMBELINA
WARNER BROS. March, 1994. (Don Bluth, Gary Goldman) Animated.

HAPPILY EVER AFTER
FIRST NATIONAL. May, 1993. (John Howley) Animated.

HAPPINESS
OCTOBER FILMS. May, 1998. (Todd Solondz) Jane Adams, Dylan Baker, Lara Flynn Boyle, Ben Gazzara, Jared Harris.

HAPPINESS IS IN THE FIELD
BAC FILMS. December, 1995. French. (Etienne Chatiliez) Michel Serrault, Eddy Mitchell.

HAPPINESS STREET
BEIJING FILM STUDIO. June, 1998. Chinese. (Li Shaohong) Song Dandan, Wang Xueqi, Lu Wenzheng, Gao Jun.

HAPPY BIRTHDAY
CINEMA SUPPORT FOUNDATION. Feb., 1999. Russian. (Larisa Sadilova) Gulya Stolyarova, Irina Prosyina, Eugene Turkina, Lyuba Starkova, Masha Kuzmina.

HAPPY BIRTHDAY, MR. MOGRABI
AVI MOGRABI. Feb., 1999. Israeli. (Avi Mograbi) Shachar Degal. Daoud Koutab, Ephraim Stan, Gidi Dar, Roni Pisker.

HAPPY END
SANDREW METRONOME. Aug., 1999. Swedish. (Christina Olofson) Par Ericson, Med Reventberg, Elin Gradin, Axel Widegren, Bengt Bostrom.

HAPPY GILMORE
UNIVERSAL. February, 1996. (Dennis Dugan) Adam Sandler, Christopher MacDonald, Julie Bowen, Carl Weathers.

HAPPY, TEXAS
MARKED ENTERTAINMENT. Jan., 1999. (Mark Illsley) Jeremy Northam, Steve Zahn, William H. Macy, Ally Walker, Illeana Douglas.

HAPPY TOGETHER
GOLDEN HARVEST/BLOCK 2. May, 1997. Hong Kong. (Waong Kar-wai) Leslie Cheung, Tony Leung Chiu-wai, Chang Chen.

HAPPY TOGETHER
SEYMOUR BORDE & ASSOC. May, 1990. (Mel Damski) Patrick Dempsey, Helen Slater.

HARAM SUARE
MEDUSA FILM. May, 1999. Italian-French-Turkish. (Ferzan Ozpetek) Marie Gillain, Alex Descas, Lucia Bose, Valeria Golina, Malick Bowens.

HARD
MPH PRODUCTION. June, 1998. (John Huckert) Noel Palomeria, Malcom Moorman, Charles Lanyer, Michael Waite, Arron Zeffron.

HARD CORE LOGO
CFP INTL. May, 1996. Canadian. (Bruce McDonald) Hugh Dillon, Keith Callum Rennie, John Pyper-Ferguson.

HARD MEN
ENTERTAINMENT FILM DISTRIBUTORS. Oct., 1996. British-French. (J.K. Amalou) Vincent Regan, Ross Boatman, Lee Ross.

HARD PROMISES
COLUMBIA. January, 1992. (Martin Davidson) Sissy Spacek, William Petersen, Brian Kerwin.

HARD RAIN
PARAMOUNT. Jan., 1998. (Mikael Salomon) Morgan Freeman, Christian Slater, Randy Quaid, Minnie Driver, Ed Asner.

HARD TARGET
UNIVERSAL. August, 1993. (John Woo) Jean Claude Van Damme, Lance Henriksen, Yancy Butler.

HARD TO KILL
WARNER BROS. February, 1990. (Bruce Malmuth) Steven Seagal, Kelly Le Brock, Bill Sadler.

THE HARD WAY
UNIVERSAL. March, 1991. (John Badham) Michael J. Fox, James Woods, Stephen Lang.

HARD–BOILED
GOLDEN PRINCESS/MILESTONE. April, 1993. Hong Kong. (John Woo) Chow Yun-fat, Bowie Lam, Philip Chan.

HARDSHIP TEST (HAERTETEST)
JUGENFILM. Feb., 1998. German. (Janek Rieke) Janek Reieke, Lisa Martinek, Gerhard Garber, Katrin Sass.

HARLEM DIARY: NINE VOICES OF RESILIENCE
DISCOVERY. October, 1995. (Jonathan Sacks) Jermaine Ashwood, Michael Cousins, Christina Head.

HARLEY DAVIDSON AND THE MARLBORO MAN
MGM. August, 1991. (Simon Wincer) Mickey Rourke, Don Johnson, Daniel Baldwin.

THE HARMONIUM IN MY MEMORY
ILSHIN INVESTMENT. May, 1999. South Korean. (Lee Young-jae) Lee Byung-heon, Jeon Do-yeon, Lee Mi-yeon, Jeon Mu-song, Choi Ju-bong.

THE HARMS CASE
INT'L FILM CIRCUIT, October, 1992. Yugoslavia (Slobodan Pesic) Franco Lasic, Damjana Luthar, Milica Tomic.

THE HARPIST
SCHLEMMER FILMS/JESTER PICTURES. May, 1997. German-British. (Hansjorg Thurn) Christien Anholt, Stephen McGann.

HARRIET THE SPY
PARAMOUNT. June, 1996. (Bronwen Hughes) Michelle Trachtenberg, Rosie O'Donnell, Vanessa Lee.

HARU
CINEQUANON. May, 1996. Japanese. (Yoshimitsu Morita) Eri Fukatsu, Masaki Uchino, Naho Toda.

HARVEST
GOLDHEART PICTURES. Apr., 1999. (Stuart Burkin) Mary McCormack, John Slattery, Jeffrey DeMunn.

THE HARVEST
ARROW. November, 1993. (David Marconi) Miguel Ferrer, Leilani Sarelle, Henry Silva, Harvey Fierstein.

HARVEST TIME
INTERARTES GMBH. Oct., 1998. German. (Stefan Schneider) Lucie Adelus, Jacques Bourgaux, Pascal Gravat, Gil Grillo, Katharine Sehnert.

HATHI
PRODUCTIONS LA FETE. Sept., 1998. Canadian. (Philippe Gautier) Jamedar Sabu Saab, Kawadi Makbul, Noorullah, Pyare Jan.

HAUNTED
OCTOBER FILMS. November, 1995. British. (Lewis Gilbert) Aidan Quinn, Kate Beckinsdale, Anthony Andrews.

THE HAUNTING
DREAMWORKS PICTURES. July, 1999. (Jan De Bont) Liam Neeson, Catherine Zeta-Jones, Owen Wilson, Lili Taylor, Bruce Dern.

THE HAUNTING OF MORELLA
CONCORDE. February, 1990. (Jim Wynorksi) David McCallum, Nicole Eggert.

HAVANA
UNIVERSAL. December, 1990. (Sydney Pollack) Robert Redford, Lena Olin, Alan Arkin, Raul Julia.

HAVANA QUARTET
LIDER FILMS. June, 1999. Spanish. (Fernando Colomo) Ernesto Alterio, Mirtha Ibarra, Javier Camara, Laura Ramos, Daisy Granados.

THE HAVEN
CFP DISTRIBUZIONE. Aug., 1997. Canadian. (Michel Poulette) Serge Dupire, Macha Grenon, Jacques Godin, Monique Spaziani.

THE HAWK
CASTLE HILL. December, 1993. British. (David Hayman) Helen Mirren, George Costigan, Rosemary Leach.

HEAD ABOVE WATER
FINE LINE FEATURES. Nov., 1996. (Jim Wilson), Harvey Keitel, Cameron Diaz, Craig Sheffer, Billy Zane.

HEAD ON
PALACE FILMS. May, 1998. Australian. (Ana Kokkinos) Alex Dimitriades, Paul Capsis, Julian Garner, Tony Nikolakopoulos.

HEADLESS BODY IN TOPLESS BAR
NORTHERN ARTS. February, 1996. (James Bruce) Jennifer MacDonald, Raymond J. Barry, Paul Williams, Taylor Nichols.

HEALING BY KILLING
NEW YORKER FILMS. April, 1998. Israeli. (Nitzan Aviram) documentary.

HEALTHY BABY GIRL
INDEPENDENT TELEVISION SERVICE. Jan., 1997. (Judith Helfand) Documentary.

HEAR MY SONG
MIRAMAX. December, 1991. British-Irish. (Peter Chelsom) Ned Beatty, Adrian Dunbar, Shirley Anne Field.

HEAR NO EVIL
20TH CENTURY FOX. March, 1993. (Robert Greenwald) Marlee Matlin, D.B. Sweeney, Martin Sheen.

HEARING VOICES
PHOENIX INT'L. November, 1991. (Sharon Greytak) Erika Nagy, Stephen Gatta, Tim Ahern.

HEART
FEATURE FILM CO. June, 1999. British. (Charles McDougall). Christorpher Eccleston, Saskia Reeves, Kate Hardie, Rhys Ifans, Anna Chancellor.

HEART AND SOULS
UNIVERSAL. August, 1993. (Ron Underwood) Robert Downey, Jr., Kyra Sedgwick, Charles Grodin.

HEART CONDITION
NEW LINE. February, 1990. (James D. Parriott) Bob Hoskins, Denzel Washington, Chloe Webb.

HEART OF LIGHT
ASA FILM AS. May, 1998. Danish. (Jacob Gronlykke) Rasmus Lyberth, Vivi Nielsen, Anda Kristiansen, Niels Platou.

HEART OF THE SUN
DANCING STONES FILM. Aug., 1998. Canadian. (Francis Damberger) Christianne Hirt, Shaun Johnston, Michael Riley.

HEARTS OF DARKNESS: A FILMMAKER'S APOCALYPSE
TRITON. November, 1991. (Fax Bahr) Documentary.

HEAT
WARNER BROS. December, 1995. (Michael Mann) Al Pacino, Robert De Niro, Val Kilmer, Jon Voight, Tom Sizemore.

HEAVEN
MIRAMAX FILMS. Sept., 1998. New Zealand. (Scott Reynolds) Martin Donovan, Danny Edwards, Richard Schiff, Joanna Going.

HEAVEN & EARTH
WARNER BROS. December, 1993. (Oliver Stone) Hiep Thi Le, Tommy Lee Jones, Joan Chen, Haing S. Ngor.

HEAVEN AND EARTH
TRITON. February, 1991. Japanese. (Haruki Kadokawa) Takaai Enoki, Masahiko Tsugawa.

HEAVEN BEFORE I DIE
BROTHERS IN ARMS. May, 1997. (Izidore K. Musallam) Andy Velasquez, Giancarlo Giannini, Joanna Pacula, Omar Sharif.

HEAVEN IS A PLAYGROUND
NEW LINE. October, 1991. (Randall Field) D.B. Sweeney, Michael Warren, Richard Jordan.

HEAVEN'S A DRAG
FIRST RUN. June, 1995. British. (Peter Mackenzie Litten) Thomas Arklie, Ian Williams, Tony Slattery.

HEAVENLY CREATURES
MIRAMAX. November, 1994. New Zealand. (Peter Jackson) Melanie Lynskey, Kate Winslet, Sarah Peirse.

HEAVEN'S BURNING
REP FILM DISTRIBUTORS. April, 1997. Australian. (Craig Lahiff) Russell Crowe, Youki Kudoh, Kenji Isomura, Ray Barrett.

HEAVY
CFP DISTRIBUTION. May, 1996. (James Mangold) Pruitt Taylor Vince, Shelley Winters, Deborah Harry, Evan Dando.

HEAVYWEIGHTS
BUENA VISTA. February, 1995. (Steven Brill) Aaron Schwartz, Tom McGowan, Ben Stiller, Shaun Weiss.

HE GOT GAME
BUENA VISTA. April, 1998. (Spike Lee) Denzel Washington, Ray Allen, Milla Jovovich, Rosario Dawson, Hill Harper, Zelda Harris.

THE HEIGHT OF THE SKY
GOOD GIRL FILMS. July, 1999. (Lyn Clinton) Jennifer Weedon, Jackie Stewart, Tom Crone, Grant Moninger, Evan Palazzo.

HEINRICH VON KLEIST'S THE PRINCE OF HOMBURG
ISTITUTO LUCE. March, 1997. Italian. (Marco Bellocchio) Andrea Di Stefano, Barbora Bobulova, Toni Bertorelli, Anita Laurenzi.

HELAS POUR MOI
CINEMA PARALLEL. March, 1994. Swiss-French. (Jean Luc Goddard) Gérard Depardieu, Laurence Masliah.

HELLRAISER: BLOODLINE
DIMENSION/TRANS ATLANTIC ENT. March 1996. (Alan Smithee) Bruce Ramsay, Valentina Vargas.

HELLRAISER III: HELL ON EARTH
DIMENSION. September, 1992. (Anthony Hickox) Doug Bradley, Terry Farrell, Paula Marshall.

HELL'S KITCHEN N.Y.C.
HK FILM CORP. Sept., 1998. (Cinciripini) Mekhi Phifer, Rosanna Arquette, William Forsythe, Angelina Jolie, Johnny Whitworth.

HEMINGWAY: A PORTRAIT
OGDEN ENTERTAINMENT. Sept., 1999. (Erik Canuel). Animated.

THE HEMP REVOLUTION
TARA. December, 1995. (Anthony Clarke) Documentary.

HENRY AND JUNE
UNIVERSAL. October, 1990. (Philip Kaufman) Fred Ward, Uma Thurman, Maria de Medeiros, Richard E. Grant.

HENRY FOOL
TRUE FICTION PICTURES/THE SHOOTING GALLERY. Sept., 1997. (Hal Hartley) Thomas Jay Ryan, James Urbaniak, Parker Posey, Maria Porter, James Saito, Kevin Corrigan, Liam Aiken.

HENRY JAMES' THE GHOSTLY RENTAL
NEW CONCORDE. May, 1999. (Mitch Marcus) Michael York, Andrew Bowen, Claudia Christian, Aideen O'Donnell.

HENRY: PORTRAIT OF A SERIAL KILLER
GREYCAT FILMS. January, 1990. (John McNaughton) Michael Rooker, Tracy Arnold, Tom Towles.

HERCULES
BUENA VISTA. June, 1997. (John Musker, Ron Clements), Tate Donovan, Josh Keaton, Roger Bart, Danny DeVito, James Woods.

THE HERD
NATIONAL FILM BOARD/ONTARIO CENTRE. Sept., 1998. Canadian. (Peter Lynch) Colm Feore, David Hemblen, Mark McKinney, Don McKellar, Jim Allodi. Documentary.

HERMAN
RKO. November, 1992. Norwegian. (Erik Gustavson) Anders Danielson Lie, Frank Robert, Elisabeth Sand.

HERO
COLUMBIA. October, 1992. (Stephen Frears) Dustin Hoffman, Geena Davis, Andy Garcia.

HEROES AND OTHER COWARDS
JUGENDFILM. Feb., 1999. German. (Dennis Satin) Ralf Bauer, Carin C. Tietze, Edgar M. Boehlke, Andreas Wisniewski, Peter Nottmeier.

HEROES IN THE TYROL
PROGRESS FILM. Feb., 1999. Austrian-Swiss-German. (Niki List) Christian Schmidt, Elke Winkens, Christian Pogats, I. Stangl, Gregor Seberg.

A HERO NEVER DIES
FILM CITY. Dec., 1998. Hong Kong. (Johnnie To) Leon Lai, Lau Ching-wan, Fiona Leung, Yo Yo Mung, Fong Ping.

HE SAID/SHE SAID
PARAMOUNT. February, 1991. (Ken Kwapis, Marisa Silver) Kevin Bacon, Elizabeth Perkins, Nathan Lane.

HEXED
COLUMBIA. January, 1993. (Alan Spencer) Arye Gross, Claudia Christian, Adrienne Shelly.

HHH: PORTRAIT OF HOU HSIAO-HSIEN
AMIP/HSU HSIAO MING FILM CORP. Sept., 1997. French-Taiwanese. (Olivier Assayas) Documentary.

HI COUSIN!
LEONOR FILMS. May, 1996. French-Algerian-Belgian-Luxembourgian. (Merzak Allouache) Gad Elmaleh.

HIDDEN AGENDA
HEMDALE. November, 1990. British. (Ken Loach) Frances McDormand, Brian Cox, Brad Dourif.

HIDE AND SEEK
ITVS. Jan., 1997. (Su Friedrich) Documentary. B & W.

HIDEAWAY
TRISTAR. March, 1995. (Brett Leonard) Jeff Goldblum, Christine Lahti, Alicia Silverstone, Jeremy Sisto.

HIDEOUS KINKY
AMLF. Oct., 1998. British-French. (Gillies MacKinnon) Kate Winslet, Said Taghmaoui, Bella Riza, Carrie Mullan, Pierre Clementi.

HIGH ART
OCTOBER FILMS. Jan., 1998. (Lisa Cholodenko) Ally Sheedy, Radha Mitchell, Patricia Clarkson, Tammy Grimes, Gabriel Mann, Bill Sage.

HIGHER LEARNING
COLUMBIA. January, 1995. (John Singleton) Omar Epps, Kristy Swanson, Michael Rapaport, Ice Cube.

HIGH HEELS
MIRAMAX. December, 1991. Spanish. (Pedro Almodovar) Victoria Abril, Marisa Paredes, Miguel Bose.

HIGHLANDER: THE FINAL DIMENSION
DIMENSION. January, 1995. Canadian-U.S. (Andy Morahan) Christopher Lambert, Mario Van Peebles.

HIGHLANDER 2: THE QUICKENING
INTERSTAR. November, 1991. (Russell Mulcahy) Christopher Lambert, Sean Connery, Virginia Madsen.

HIGH LONESOME: THE STORY OF BLUEGRASS MUSIC
TARA. April, 1994. (Rachel Liebling) Documentary.

HIGH SCHOOL II
ZIPPORAH. July, 1994. (Frederick Wiseman) Documentary.

HIGH SCHOOL HIGH
SONY PICTURES ENTERTAINMENT. October, 1996. (Hart Bochner), Jon Lovitz, Tia Carrere, Louise Fletcher, Mekhi Phifer.

HIGHWAY PATROLMAN
FIRST LOOK. November, 1993. Mexican. (Alex Cox) Roberto Sosa, Bruno Bichir, Vanessa Bauche.

HIGHWAY 61
SKOURAS. April, 1992. British-Canadian. (Bruce McDonald) Valerie Buhagiar, Don McKellar, Earl Pastko.

HIGHWAY TO HELL
HEMDALE. March, 1992. (Ate De Jong) Patrick Bergin, Adam Storke, Chad Lowe.

HILARY AND JACKIE
INTERMEDIA FILMS/FILM FOUR. Sept., 1998. British. (Anand Tucker) Emily Watson, Rachel Griffiths, James Frain.

HI-LIFE
LION'S GATE. Oct., 1998. (Roger Hedden): Katrin Cartlidge, Charles Durning, Daryl Hannah, Moira Kelly. Peter Reigert.

THE HI-LINE
BOYLE/TAYLOR PRODS. Jan., 1999. (Ron Judkins) Rachael Leigh Cook, Ryan Alosio, Tantoo Cardinal, Margot Kdder, Stuart Margolin.

THE HI-LO COUNTRY
GRAMERCY PICTURES. Dec., 1999. (Stephen Frears) Woody Harrelson, Billy Crudup, Patricia Arquette, Cole Hauser.

HIMALAYA
JACQUES PERRIN. Aug., 1999. French-Swiss. (Eric Valli) Thilen Lhondup, Lhapka Tsamchoe, Gurgon Kyap, Karm Tensing Nyama Lama.

HIS AND HERS
ALLIANCE INDEPENDENT FILMS. Jan., 1997. (Hal Salwen) Liev Schreiber, Caroleen Feeney, Michael Rispoli, Cynthia M. Watros.

HISTOIRE(S) DE CINEMA
GAUMONT/PERIPHERIA/CNC/FEMIS. May, 1997. French-Swiss. (Jean-Luc Godard) Documentary.

HIT AND RUNWAY
MIRADOR FILMS. Apr., 1999. (Christopher Livingston) Michael Parducci, Peter Jacobson, Judy Prescott, Kerr Smith, Joyt Richards.

HITCHCOCK, SELZNICK AND THE END OF HOLLYWOOD
AMERICAN MASTERS. Jan., 1999. (Michael Epstein). Documentary.

HITEBOYS
FOX SEARCHLIGHT. Aug., 1999. (Marc Levin) Danny Hoch, Dash Mihok, Mark Webber, Piper Perabo, Eugene Bird.

THE HITMAN
CANNON. October, 1991. (Aaron Norris) Chuck Norris, Michael Parks, Al Waxman.

THE HITMAN
FLEA MARKET. Aug., 1998. Hong Kong. (Tung Wai) Jet Li, Eric Tsang, Simon Yam, Gigi Leung, Keiji Sato.

HITTING THE GROUND
LIVING PICTURES. January, 1996. (David P. Moore) Neal Huff, Anney Giobbe, Rik Walter, Daintry Jensen.

HOCUS POCUS
BUENA VISTA. July, 1993. (Kenny Ortega) Bette Midler, Sarah Jessica Parker, Kathy Najimy, Omri Katz.

HOFFA
20TH CENTURY FOX. December, 1992. (Danny DeVito) Jack Nicholson, Danny DeVito, Armand Assante.

HOLD BACK THE NIGHT
FILM CONSORTIUM/FILMFOUR. May, 1999. British. (Phil Davis) Christine Tremarco, Stuart Sinclair Blyth, Sheila Hancock.

HOLD ME, THRILL ME, KISS ME
MAD DOG PICTURES. July, 1993. (Joel Hirshman) Adrienne Shelly, Sean Young, Max Parrish.

HOLD YOU TIGHT
GOLDEN HARVEST. Feb., 1998. Hong Kong. (Stanley Kwan) Chingmy Yau, Sunny Chan, Eric Tsang, Ko Yu-lun, Sandra Ng.

HOLLOW REED
SCALA. January, 1996. (Angela Pope) Martin Donovan, Joely Richardson, Ian Hart, Jason Flemyng, Sam Bould.

HOLLYWOOD MAVERICKS
ROXIE RELEASING. September, 1990. (Florence Dauman) Documentary.

HOLLYWOODISM: HOLY MAN
BUENA VISTA. Oct., 1998. (Stephen Herek) Eddie Murphy, Jeff Goldblum, Kelly Preston, Robert Loggia, Jon Cryer.

HOLY MATRIMONY
BUENA VISTA. April, 1994. (Leonard Nimoy) Patricia Arquette, Joseph Gordon Levitt, Armin Mueller Stahl.

HOLY SMOKE
MIRAMAX FILMS. Sept., 1999. (Jane Campion) Kate Winslet, Harvey Keitel, Pam Grier, Julie Hamilton, Sophie Lee.

HOMAGE
ARROW. October, 1995. (Ross Kagan Marks) Blythe Danner, Frank Whaley, Bruce Davison, Danny Nucci, Sheryl Lee.

HOMEBOYS ON THE BEACH
AFMD. June, 1999. French. (Djamel Bensalah) Jamel Debbouze, Stephane Soo Mongo, Lorant Deutsch, Julien Courbey.

HOME ALONE
20TH CENTURY FOX. November, 1990. (Chris Columbus) Macaulay Culkin, Joe Pesci, Daniel Stern.

HOME ALONE 2: LOST IN NEW YORK
20TH CENTURY FOX. November, 1992. (Chris Columbus) Macaulay Culkin, Joe Pesci, Brenda Fricker.

HOME ALONE 3
20TH CENTURY FOX. Dec., 1997. (Raja Gosnell) Alex D. Linz, Olek Krupa, Rya Kihlstedt, Lenny Von Dohlen, David Thornton.

HOMECOMING: LITTLE BUT TOUGH PART 2
MAFILM AKTIV STUDIO/DUNA TV, HUNNIA STUDIO. Feb., 1999. Hungarian. (Ferenc Grunwalsky) Sandor Gaspar, Agnes Csere, Janos Ban, Jacint Juhasz, Jozsef Szarvas Dorottya Udvaros.

HOME FOR THE HOLIDAYS
PARAMOUNT/POLYGRAM. November, 1995. (Jodie Foster) Holly Hunter, Robert Downey Jr., Anne Bancroft.

HOME FRIES
WARNER BROS. Sept., 1998. (Dean Parisot) Drew Barrymore, Luke Wilson, Catherine O'Hara, Jake Busey, Shelley Duvall, Kim Robillard.

HOMEGROWN
SONY PICTURES ENTERTAINMENT. April, 1998. (Stephen Gyllenhaal) Billy Bob Thornton, Hank Azaria, Kelly Lynch, Ryan Phillippe, Jon Bon Jovi, John Lithgow, Ted Danson.

A HOME OF OUR OWN
GRAMERCY. November, 1993. (Tony Bill) Kathy Bates, Edward Furlong, Soon-Teck Oh.

HOME PAGE
COPACETIC PICTURES/CINEMAX/ZDF-ARTE. Jan., 1999. (Doug Block). Documentary.

HOMETOWN BLUE
ARP. May, 1999. French. (Stephane Brize) Florence Vignon, Mathilde Seigner, Antoine Chappey, Philippe Duquesne, Jenny Alpha.

HOMEWARD BOUND: THE INCREDIBLE JOURNEY
BUENA VISTA. February, 1993. (DuWayne Dunham) Ben, Rattler, Tiki, Robert Hays.

HOMEWARD BOUND II: LOST IN SAN FRANCISCO
BUENA VISTA. March, 1996. (David R. Ellis) Robert Hayes, Kim Greist, Veronica Lauren, Kevin Chevalia, Max Perlich.

HOMICIDE
TRIUMPH. October, 1991. (David Mamet) Joe Mantegna, William H. Macy, Natalija Nogulich.

HOMO HEIGHTS
LEHMANN-MOORE PRODS. Feb., 1998. (Sara Moore) Quentin Crisp, Lea DeLaria, Stephen Sorrentino, David Fenley, Emil Herrera.

HONEY, I BLEW UP THE KID
BUENA VISTA. July, 1992. (Randal Kleiser) Rick Moranis, Marcia Strassman, Robert Oliveri.

HONEY, I SENT THE MEN TO THE MOON
COSTA BRAVA FILMS S.L. June, 1998. Spanish. (Marta Balletbo-Coll, Ana Simon Cerezo) Cookie Rufino, Claudia Carasso, Marta Balletbo-Coll.

HONEYMOON ACADEMY
TRIUMPH. May, 1990. (Gene Quintano) Kim Cattrall, Robert Hays, Leigh Taylor Young.

HONEYMOON IN VEGAS
COLUMBIA. August, 1992. (Andrew Bergman) Nicolas Cage, James Caan, Sarah Jessica Parker.

HONEYMOON TRIPS
WARNER BROS. ITALIA. December, 1995. Italian. (Carlo Verdone) Claudia Gerini, Cinzia Mascoli.

HOODLUMS
MGM. August, 1997. (Bill Duke), Laurence Fishburne, Tim Roth, Vanessa Williams, Andy Garcia, Cicely Tyson, Chi McBride.

HOOK
TRISTAR. December, 1991. (Steven Spielberg) Dustin Hoffman, Robin Williams, Julia Roberts.

HOOP DREAMS
FINE LINE. October, 1994. (Steve James) Documentary.

HOPE FLOATS
20TH CENTURY FOX. May, 1998. (Forest Whitaker) Sandra Bullock, Harry Connick Jr., Gena Rowlands, Mae Whitman, Michael Pare.

THE HORSE WHISPERER
BUENA VISTA. April, 1998. (Robert Redford) Robert Redford, Kristin Scott Thomas, Sam Neill, Dianne Wiest, Scarlett Johansson.

HORSEMAN ON THE ROOF
MIRAMAX/ZOE. French. (Jean-Paul Rappeneau) Juliette Binoche, Olivier Martinez, Isabelle Carre, Francois Cluzet.

THE HORSEPLAYER
GREYCAT FILMS. July, 1991. (Kurt Voss) Brad Dourif, Sammi Davis, M.K. Harris.

HORSES OF FORTUNE
FOR LIFE RECORDS. April, 1997. Japanese. (Kaizo Hayashi) Masatoshi Nagase, Yui Natsukawa, Tomoko Yamaguchi.

HOTEL ROOM
ALTA FILMS. Sept., 1998. Spanish-U.S.. (Cesc Gay) Barbara Boudon, Eric Kraus, Paris Kiely, Xaier Domingo.

HOT SHOTS!
20TH CENTURY FOX. July, 1991. (Jim Abrahams) Charlie Sheen, Lloyd Bridges, Cary Elwes.

HOT SHOTS! PART DEUX
20TH CENTURY FOX. May, 1993. (Jim Abrahams) Charlie Sheen, Lloyd Bridges, Richard Crenna, Valeria Golino.

THE HOT SPOT
ORION. October, 1990. (Dennis Hopper) Don Johnson, Virginia Madsen, Jennifer Connelly.

HOTEL SORRENTO
CASTLE HILL. May, 1995. Australian. (Richard Franklin) Joan Plowright, Caroline Goodall.

THE HOURS AND TIMES
ANTARCTIC. April, 1992. (Christopher Munch) David Angus, Ian Hart. B&W.

THE HOUSE
LES GRANDS FILMS CLASSIQUES. May, 1997. French-Portuguese-Lithuanian. May, 1997. (Sharunas Bartas) Francisco Nascimento.

HOUSE ARREST
MGM/UA. August, 1996. (Harry Winer) Jamie Lee Curtis, Kevin Pollack, Jeniffer Tilly, Christopher McDonald.

HOUSE OF AMERICA
MAYFAIR ENTERTAINMENT INTL. Jan., 1997. Welsh. (Marc Evans) Sian Phillips, Steven Mackintosh, Matthew Rhys, Lisa Palfrey.

HOUSE OF CARDS
MIRAMAX. June, 1993. (Michael Lessac) Kathleen Turner, Tommy Lee Jones, Asha Menina.

HOUSE OF SLEEPING BEAUTIES
HIROTO YOKOYAMA PRODS./TV TOKYO/TRIARTS. Feb., 1997. Japanese. (Hiroto Yokoyama) Yoshio Harada, Yuka Oonishi.

THE HOUSE OF THE SPIRITS
MIRAMAX. April, 1994. German-Danish-Portuguese. (Bille August) Jeremy Irons, Meryl Streep, Glenn Close.

THE HOUSE OF YES
MIRAMAX. Jan., 1997. (Mark Waters), Parker Posey, John Hamilton, Tori Spelling, Freddie Prinze, Jr., Genevieve Bujold.

HOUSE PARTY
NEW LINE. March, 1990. (Reginald Hudlin) Christopher Reid, Robin Harris.

HOUSE PARTY 2
NEW LINE. October, 1991. (Doug McHenry) Christopher Martin, Tisha Campbell, Martin Lawrence.

HOUSE PARTY 3
NEW LINE. January, 1994. (Eric Meza) Christopher Reid, Christopher Martin, David Edwards.

HOUSEGUEST
BUENA VISTA. January, 1995. (Randall Miller) Sinbad, Phil Hartman, Kim Greist, Stan Shaw.

HOUSEHOLD SAINTS
FINE LINE. September, 1993. (Nancy Savoca) Tracey Ullman, Vincent D'Onofrio, Lili Taylor.

HOUSESITTER
UNIVERSAL. June, 1992. (Frank Oz) Steve Martin, Goldie Hawn, Dana Delany.

HOW ANGELS ARE BORN
EMPORIO DE CINEMA/RIOFILME. Sept., 1996. Brazilian. (Murilo Salles) Priscilla Assum, Silvio Guindane, Larry Pine, Ryan Massey.

HOW I SPENT MY SUMMER VACATION
CINEMA GUILD. Nov., 1997. (John Fisher) RonReaco Lee, Deanna Davis, E. Roger Mitchell, Mike Ngaujah, Jade Janise Dixon.

HOW STELLA GOT HER GROOVE BACK
20TH CENTURY FOX. Aug., 1998. (Kevin Rodney Sullivan) Angela Bassett, Taye Diggs, Regina King, Whoopi Goldberg.

HOW THE WAR STARTED ON MY LITTLE ISLAND
HRT PRODUCTION. June, 1998. Croatian. (Vinko Bresan) Vlatko Dulic, Ljubomir Kerekes, Ivan Brkic, Predrag Vuovic-Predjo.

HOW TO BE LOUISE
VENUS DE MYLAR PRODS. September, 1990. (Anne Flournoy) Lea Floden, Bruce McCarthy.

HOW TO MAKE AN AMERICAN QUILT
UNIVERSAL. October, 1995. (Jocelyn Moorhouse) Elllen Burstyn, Winona Ryder, Maya Angelou, Kate Capshaw.

HOW TO MAKE LOVE TO A NEGRO WITHOUT GETTING TIRED
ANGELIKA. June, 1990. French. (Jacques W. Benoit) Issach De Bankole, Maka Kotto.

HOW TO MAKE THE CRUELEST MONTH
FUGUE STATE/MAGNET. Jan., 1998. (Kip Koenig) Clea DuVall, Gabriel Mann, Mary Kay Place, Marianne Jean-Baptiste.

HOW U LIKE ME NOW
SHAPIRO GLICKENHAUS. March, 1993. (Darryl Roberts) Darnell Williams, Salli Richardson, Daniel Gardner.

HUDSON HAWK
TRISTAR. May, 1991. (Michael Lehmann) Bruce Willis, Danny Aiello, Andie MacDowell.

THE HUDSUCKER PROXY
WARNER BROS. March, 1994. (Joel Coen) Tim Robbins, Jennifer Jason Leigh, Paul Newman.

HUGH HEFNER: ONCE UPON A TIME
I.R.S. October, 1992. (Robert Heath) Documentary.

HUGO POOL
NOMADIC PICTURES. Jan., 1997. (Robert Downey Sr.) Alyssa Milano, Patrick Dempsey, Cathy Moriarty, Malcolm McDowell.

HUMANITY
TADRART FILMS. May, 1999. (Bruno Dumont) Emmanuel Schotte, Severine Caneele, Philippe Tullier.

THE HUMAN RACE
TELL THE TRUTH PICTURES. June, 1998. (Bobby Houston) DOCUMENTARY.

THE HUMAN SHIELD
CANNON. May, 1992. (Ted Post) Michael Dudikoff, Tommy Hinkley, Hana Azoulay-Hasfari.

HUMAN TRAFFIC
METRODOME. June, 1999. British-Irish. (Justin Kerrigan) John Simm, Lorraine Pilkington, Shaun Parkes, Danny Dyer, Nicola Reynolds.

THE HUNCHBACK OF NOTRE DAME
BUENA VISTA. June, 1996. (Gary Trousdale, Kirk Wise) (voices) Tom Hulce, Demi Moore, Heidi Mollenhauer, Tony Jay.

HUNGER—ADDICTED TO LOVE
BUENA VISTA INTL. Feb., 1998. German. (Dava Vavrova) Catherine Flemming, Kai Wiesinger, Christiane Horbiger, Jurgen Schornagel.

HUNGER AND THIRST
CECCHI GOR. MAR., 1999. Italian. (Antonio Albanese) Antonio Albanese, Lorenza Indovina, Aisha Cerami, Lucia Guzzardi, Rosa Pianeta.

THE HUNT
HUNGRY EYE PICTURES. Feb., 1998. Dutch. (Niek Koppen) documentary.

THE HUNT FOR RED OCTOBER
PARAMOUNT. March, 1990. (John McTiernan) Sean Connery, Alec Baldwin, Scott Glenn.

THE HUNTED
UNIVERSAL. February, 1995. (J.F. Lawton) Christopher Lambert, John Lone, Joan Chen.

THE HUNTER
UIP. May, 1998. Turkish-Hungarian. (Erden Kiral) Jale Arikan, Ahmet Ugurlu, Fikret Kuskan.

HUNTING
SKOURAS. February, 1992. Australian. (Frank Howson) John Savage, Kerry Armstrong, Jeffrey Thomas.

THE HURDY-GURDY MAN
TIMBERLAKE. Feb., 1999. U.S.-Hungarian. (Gabe Von Dettre) Brad Dourif, Kathleen Gati, William Hickey, Wallace Shawn, Meat Loaf.

HURLYBURLY
FINE LINE. Sept., 1998. (Anthony Drazan) Sean Penn, Kevin Spacey, Robin Wright-Penn, Chazz Palminteri, Garry Shandling, Meg Ryan.

HURRICANE
MGM. January, 1997. (Morgan J. Freeman), Brendan Sexton III, Shawn Elliot, Jose Zuniga, David Roland Frank, Carlo Alban.

HUSBANDS AND WIVES
TRISTAR. September, 1992. (Woody Allen) Woody Allen, Judy Davis, Mia Farrow, Sydney Pollack.

HUSH
SONY PICTURES ENTERTAINMENT. March, 1998. (Jonathan Darby) Jessica Lange, Gwyneth Paltrow, Johnathon Schaech, Nina Foch.

HUSTLER WHITE
STRAND RELEASING. January, 1996. (Bruce LaBruce) Tony Ward, LaBruce, Kevin P. Scott.

HYENAS
KINO. August, 1995. Senegalese. (Friedrich Durrenmatt) Mansour Diouf, Ami Diakhate.

HYGIENE DE L'ASSASSIN
MFD. Feb., 1999. French. (Francois Ruggieri) Jean Yanne, Barbara Schulz, Sophie Broustal, Catherine Hiegel, Eric Prat.

HYPE
HELVEY/PRAY. January, 1996. (Doug Pray) Documentary.

I

I AM CUBA
MILESTONE. March, 1995. Cuban-Russian, 1964. (Mikhail Kalatozov) Documentary. B&W.

I AM MY OWN WOMAN
CINEVISTA. April, 1994. German. (Rosa von Praunheim) Lothar Berfelde, Ichgola Androgyn, Jens Taschner.

I AM TIRED OF STANDING, I LIE DOWN
COMITE DU FILM ETHNOGRAPHIQUE. Feb., 1997. French-Nigerian. (Jean Rouch) Damoure Zika, Lam Ibrahim Dia.

I CAN'T SLEEP
NEW YORKER. August, 1995. French. (Claire Denis) Katerina Golubeva, Richard Courcet, Vincent Dupont.

THE ICE RUNNER
BORDE. November, 1993. (Barry Samson) Edward Albert, Victor Wong, Olga Kabo.

THE ICE STORM
FOX SEARCHLIGHT. May, 1997. (Ang Lee), Sigourney Weaver, Kevin Kline, Joan Allen, Henry Czerny, Adam Hann-Byrd, Christina Ricci.

THE ICICLE THIEF
ARIES. August, 1990. Italian. (Maurizio Nichetti) Maurizio Nichetti, Caterina Sylos Labini.

I COME IN PEACE
TRIUMPH. September, 1990. (Craig R. Baxley) Dolph Lundgren, Brian Benben, Betsy Brantley.

I COULD READ THE SKY
ARTS COUNCIL OF ENGLAND/IRISH FILM BOARD/CHANNEL FOUR/ BRITISH FILM INSTITUTE/REAL WORLD RECORDS. Aug., 1999. British-Irish. (Nichola Bruce) Dermot Healy, Maria Doyle Kennedy, Brendan Coyle, Stephen Rea, Jake WIlliams.

I CRAVE ROCK & ROLL
VISTA PACIFIC. June, 1996. (Carmen Santa Maria) Carmen Santa Maria, Julie Gray, Jon Rashad Kamal.

I.D.
FILMS SUD, VIDEOCAM/PETROUCHKA FILMS/SOL'OEIL FILMS. Sept., 1998. Belgian-French-Congolese. (Mweze Ngangura) Gerard Essomba, Herbert Flack, Jean-Louis Daulne, Dominique Mesa.

AN IDEAL HUSBAND
PATHE/MIRAMAX. Apr., 1999. (Oliver Parker) Rupert Everett, Julianne Moore, Jeremy Northam, Cate Blanchett, Minnie Driver.

IDLE HANDS
SONY. Apr., 1999. (Rodman Flender) Devon Sawa, Seth Green, Elden Henson, Jessica Alba, Christopher Hart.

I DON'T BUY KISSES ANYMORE
SKOURAS. February, 1992. (Robert Marcarelli) Jason Alexander, Nia Peeples, Lainie Kazan.

I DON'T WANT TO TALK ABOUT IT
SONY PICTURES CLASSICS. September, 1994. Argentine. (Maria Luisa Bemberg) Marcello Mastroianni, Luisina Brando.

IF I NEVER SEE YOU AGAIN
CENTRO DE CAPACITACION. March, 1997. Mexican. (Juan Pablo Villasenor) Jorge Galvan, Justo Martinez, Max Kerlow.

IF LOOKS COULD KILL
WARNER BROS. March, 1991. (William Dear) Richard Grieco, Linda Hunt, Roger Rees.

IF LUCY FELL
SONY PICTURES. January, 1996. (Eric Schaeffer) Jessica Parker, Eric Schaeffer, Ben Stiller, Elle Macpherson.

I FOLLOW IN MY FATHER'S FOOTSTEPS
POLYGRAM. Apr., 1999. French. (Remi Waterhouse) Jean Yanne, Guillaume Canet, Laurence Cote, Yves Renier.

IF YOU ONLY UNDERSTOOD
LUNA LLENA. Jan., 1999. Cuban-Spanish. (Rolando Diaz). Documentary.

I GOT THE HOOK-UP
DIMENSION FILMS. May, 1998. (Michael Martin) Master P, A. J. Johnson, Gretchen Palmer, Frantz Turner, Tommy Lister, Jr.

I HAVE KILLED
CINEMATHEQUE FRANCAISE. March, 1997. French. (Roger Lion) Sessue Hayakawa, Huguette Duflos, Max Maxudian. B&W. Restored 1924 movie.

I JUST WASN'T MADE FOR THESE TIMES
PALOMAR. August, 1995. (Don Was) Documentary.

IKINAI
NIPPON HERALD/OFFICE KITANO. Aug., 1998. Japanese. (Hiroshi Himizu) Dankan, Nanako Okoucki, Toshinori Omi, Ippei Soda.

I KNOW WHAT YOU DID LAST NIGHT
SONY PICTURES ENTERTAINMENT. Oct., 1997. (Jim Gillespie) Jennifer Love Hewitt, Sarah Michelle Gellar, Freddie Prinze Jr., Anne Heche.

IL CIELO IN UNA STANZA
FILMAURO. Mar., 1999. Italian. (Carlo Vanzina) Elio Germano Gabriele Mainetti, Francesco Venditti, Alessandro Cianfione, Ricky Tognazzi.

I LIKE IT LIKE THAT
COLUMBIA. October, 1994. (Darnell Martin) Lauren Velez, Jon Seda, Jesse Borrego, Lisa Vidal, Griffin Dunne.

IL LADRO DI BAMBINI (STOLEN CHILDREN)
SAMUEL GOLDWYN. March, 1993. Italian. (Gianni Amelio) Enrico LoVerso, Valentina Scalici, Florence Darel.

I'LL BE HOME FOR CHRISTMAS
BUENA VISTA. Nov., 1998. (Arlene Sanford) Jonathan Taylor Thomas, Jessica Biel, Adam LaVorgna, Gary Cole, Eve Gordon.

I'LL DO ANYTHING
COLUMBIA. February, 1994. (James L. Brooks) Nick Nolte, Albert Brooks, Whittni Wright, Julie Kavner.

ILL GOTTEN GAINS
SPATS FILMS. Sept., 1998. (Joel Ben Marsden) Djimon Hounsou, Akousa Busia, De'Aundre Bonds, Eartha Kitt, Reg E. Cathey.

I'LL LOVE YOU FOREVER... TONIGHT
HEADLINER PRODS. July, 1993. (Edgar Michael Bravo) Paul Marius, Jason Adams, David Poynter. B&W.

I'LL MAKE YOU HAPPY
AMPLE FILMS. May, 1999. New Zealand. (Athina Tsoulis) Jodie Rimmer, Carl Bland, Ian Hughes, Michael Hurst, Jennifer Ward-Lealand.

ILLTOWN
Shooting Gallery. September, 1996. (Nick Gomez) Michael Rapaport, Lili Taylor, Adam Trese.

I LOATHE LOVE
REZO FILMS. April, 1997. French. (Laurence Ferreira Barbosa) Jeanne Balibar, Jean Quentin Chatelain, Laurent Lucas.

I LOVE TROUBLE
BUENA VISTA. June, 1994. (Charles Shyer) Julia Roberts, Nick Nolte, Saul Rubinek.

I LOVE YOU, I LOVE YOU NOT
AVALANCHE. Nov., 1997. (Billy Hopkins) Jeanne Moreau, Claire Danes, Jude Law, James Van Der Beck, Kris Park, Lauren Fox.

I LOVE YOU TO DEATH
TRISTAR. April, 1990. (Lawrence Kasdan) Kevin Kline, Joan Plowright, William Hurt, River Phoenix.

IMAGES OF THE WORLD AND THE INSCRIPTION OF WAR
GOETHE HOUSE. November, 1991. German. (Harum Farocki) Documentary.

IMAGINARY CRIMES
WARNER BROS. October, 1994. (Anthony Drazen) Harvey Keitel, Fairuza Balk, Kelly Lynch, Chris Penn.

I'M ALIVE AND I LOVE YOU
CINEMA PUBLC FILMS. Nov., 1998. French-Belgian-Hungarian. (Roger Kahane) Jerome Deschamps, Dorian Lambert, Agnes Soral, Yvette Merlin.

THE IMAX NUTCRACKER
IMAX CORP. Nov., 1997. (Christine Edzard) Miriam Margoyles, Heathcote Williams, Lotte Johnson, Benjamin Hall, Harriet Thorpe.

I'M LOSING YOU
LIONS GATE FILMS. Sept., 1998. (Bruce Wagner) Rosanna Arquette, Amanda Donohoe, Buck Henry, Frank Langella, Andrew McCarthy.

IMMORTAL BELOVED
COLUMBIA. December, 1994. (Bernard Rose) Gary Oldman, Jeroen Krabbe, Isabella Rossellini.

I'M NOT AFRAID OF LIFE
PATHE. Aug., 1999. French-Swiss. (Noemie Lvovsky) Magali Woch, Ingrid Molinier, Julie-Marie Parmentier.

I'M NOT RAPPAPORT
GRAMERCY. Nov., 1996. (Herb Gardner) Walter Matthau, Ossie Davis, Amy Irving, Martha Plimpton, Craig T. Nelson, Boyd Gaines.

THE IMPORTANCE OF BEING EARNEST
ECLECTIC CONCEPTS. May, 1992. (Kurt Baker) Wren T. Baker, Daryl Roach, Chris Calloway.

THE IMPORTED BRIDEGROOM
ASA COMMUNICATIONS. March, 1990. (Pamela Berger) Gene Troobnick, Avi Hoffman.

THE IMPOSTOR
MOJAME S.A./OSCAR KRAMER. Sept., 1997. Argentine. (Alejandro Maci) Antonio Birabent, Walter Quiroz, Bilan Blanco, Norman Briski

THE IMPOSTORS
FOX SEARCHLIGHT. May, 1998. (Stanley Tucci) Oliver Platt, Stanley Tucci, Teagle F. Bougere, Steve Buscemi, Billy Connolly.

IMPROMPTU
HEMDALE. April, 1991. (James Lapine) Judy Davis, Hugh Grant, Bernadette Peters, Mandy Patinkin.

IMPROPER CHANNELS
CROWN INT'L. May, 1992. Canadian. (Eric Till) Alan Arkin, Mariette Hartley, Monica Parker.

IMPULSE
WARNER BROS. April, 1990. (Sondra Locke) Theresa Russell, Jeff Fahey, George Dzundza.

IMUHAR: A LEGEND
M.P. PRODUCTION. Oct., 1998. French-Nigerian. (Jacques Dubuisson) Ibrahim Paris, Mohamed Ixa, Mohamed Ichika, Rhali, Atibou Aboubacar, Oumou Algabid.

IN ADVANCE OF THE LANDING
CINEPLEX ODEON. January, 1993. Canadian. (Dan Curtis) Documentary.

IN & OUT
PARAMOUNT. August, 1997. (Frank Oz), Kevin Kline, Joan Cusack, Matt Dillon, Debbie Reynolds, Wilford Brimley, Bob Newhart, Tom Selleck.

IN ALL INNOCENCE
BAC FILMS. Nov., 1998. French. (Pierre Jolivet) Gerard Lanvin, Virginie Ledoyen, Carole Bouquet, Guillaume Canet, Aurelie Verillon.

IN CHINA THEY EAT DOGS - DON'T THEY?
STEEN HERDEL. May, 1999. Danish. (Lasse Spang Olsen). Dejan Cukie, Kim Bodnia, Trine Dyrhol, Nikolaj Lie Kaas, Tomas Villum Jensen.

IN CUSTODY
SONY PICTURES CLASSICS. April, 1994. Indian. (Ismail Merchant) Shashi Kapoor, Om Puri, Shabana Azmi.

IN GOD'S HANDS
SONY PICTURES ENTERTAINMENT. April, 1998. (Zalman King) Patrick Shane Dorian, Matt George, Matty Liu, Shaun Thompson.

IN HEAVEN
FRAMES FILMPRODS.. Jan., 1999. Austrian. (Michael Bindlechner) Sylvie Testud, Xaver Hutter, Merab Ninidse.

IN LOVE AND WAR
NEW LINE. December, 1996. (Richard Attenborough), Sandra Bullock, Chris O'Donnell, Mackenzie Astin, Emilio Bonucci.

IN PRAISE OF OLDER WOMEN
SOGEPAQ. April, 1997. Spanish. (Manuel Lombardero) Juan Diego Botto, Miguel A. Garcia, Faye Dunaway, Carmen Elias.

IN SEARCH OF KUNDUN WITH MARTIN SCORCESE
COMPAGNIE PANOPTIQUE. Aug., 1998. French. (Michael Henry Wilson) documentary.

IN THE ARMY NOW
BUENA VISTA. August, 1994. (Daniel Petrie, Jr.) Pauly Shore, Lori Petty, David Alan Grier.

IN THE BLOOD
WHITE MOUNTAIN. April, 1990. (George Butler) Documentary.

IN THE COMPANY OF MEN
STEPHEN PEVNER/ATLANTIS ENTERTAINMENT. Jan., 1997. (Neil Labute) Aaron Eckhart, Stacy Edwards, Matt Malloy, Mark Rector.

IN THE HEAT OF PASSION
CONCORDE. January, 1992. (Rodman Flender) Sally Kirkland, Nick Corri, Jack Carter.

IN THE LAND OF THE DEAF
INT'L. FILM CIRCUIT. September, 1994. French. (Nicolas Philibert) Documentary.

IN THE LINE OF FIRE
COLUMBIA. July, 1993. (Wolfgang Petersen) Clint Eastwood, John Malkovich, Rene Russo.

IN THE MOUTH OF MADNESS
NEW LINE. February, 1995. (John Carpenter) Sam Neill, Julie Carmen, Jurgen Prochnow.

IN THE NAME OF THE FATHER
UNIVERSAL. December, 1993. Irish. (Jim Sheridan) Daniel Day-Lewis, Pete Postlethwaite, Emma Thompson.

IN THE NAVEL OF THE SEA
GMA FILMS/NEPTUNE FILMS. Feb., 1998. Philippine. (Marilou Diaz-Abaya) Jomari Yllana, Elizabeth Oropesa, Chin Chin Gutierrez.

IN THE SHADOW OF THE STARS
FIRST RUN FEATURES. August, 1991. (Irving Sarah, Allie Light) Documentary.

IN THE SOUP
TRITON. October, 1992. (Alexandre Rockwell) Steve Buscemi, Seymour Cassel, Jennifer Beals. B&W.

IN THE SPIRIT
CASTLE HILL. April, 1990. (Sandra Seacat) Marlo Thomas, Elaine May, Peter Falk.

IN THE WINTER DARK
GLOBE FILM. May, 1998. Australian. (James Bogle) Brenda Blethyn, Ray Barrett, Richard Roxburgh, Miranda Otto.

INCIDENT AT OGLALA
MIRAMAX. May, 1992. (Michael Apted) Documentary, narrated by Robert Redford.

INCOGNITO
WARNER BROS. Nov., 1997. (John Badham) Jason Patric, Irene Jacob, Ian Richardson, Simon Chandler, Rod Steiger, Ian Holm.

INCREDIBLY TRUE ADVENTURE OF TWO GIRLS IN LOVE, THE
FINE LINE. June, 1995. (Maria Maggenti) Laurel Holloman, Nicole Parker, Kate Stafford.

INDECENT PROPOSAL
PARAMOUNT. April, 1993. (Adrian Lyne) Robert Redford, Demi Moore, Woody Harrelson.

INDEPENDENCE DAY
20TH CENTURY FOX. June, 1996. (Roland Emmerich) Will Smith, Bill Pullman, Jeff Goldblum, Mary McDonnell.

THE INDIAN IN THE CUPBOARD
PARAMOUNT. July, 1995. (Frank Oz) Hal Scardino, Litefoot, Lindsay Crouse, Richard Jenkins.

THE INDIAN RUNNER
MGM. September, 1991. (Sean Penn) David Morse, Viggo Mortensen, Valeria Golino.

INDIAN SUMMER
BUENA VISTA. April, 1993. (Mike Binder) Alan Arkin, Elizabeth Perkins, Bill Paxton, Vincent Spano.

IN DREAMS
DREAMWORKS. Jan., 1999. (Neil Jordan) Annette Bening, Aidan Quinn, Robert Downey Jr., Paul Guilfoyle, Dennis Boutsikaris.

INEVITABLE GRACE
SILVERSTAR. September, 1994. (Alex Canawati) Maxwell Caulfield, Jennifer Nicholson, Tippi Hedren.

INFINITY
FIRST LOOK PICTURES. September, 1996. (Matthew Broderick) Matthew Broderick, Patricia Arquette.

THE INFORMANT
SHOWTIME PRESENTATION. Sept., 1997. Irish-US. (Jim McBride) Timothy Dalton, Cary Elwes, Anthony Brophy, Maria Lennon.

THE INKWELL
BUENA VISTA. April, 1994. (Matty Rich) Larenz Tate, Joe Morton, Suzzanne Douglas, Glynn Turman.

THE INNER CIRCLE
COLUMBIA. December, 1991. (Andrei Konchalovsky) Tom Hulce, Lolita Davidovich, Bob Hoskins.

INNOCENCE (MASUMIYET)
MAVI FILMCILIK. Sept., 1997. Turkish. (Zaki Demirkubuz) Guven Kirac, Haluk Bilginer, Derya Alabora.

THE INNOCENT
MIRAMAX. September, 1995. British. (John Schlesinger) Anthony Hopkins, Isabella Rossellini, Campbell Scott.

INNOCENT BLOOD
WARNER BROS. September, 1992. (John Landis) Ann Parillaud, Robert Loggia, Anthony LaPaglia.

THE INNOCENTS
STYOPA. July, 1999. (Katherine Griffin) Kama Lee, Katherine Griffin, Joe Kellogg, Brad Carroll, Monte Jenkins.

INN TROUBLE!
FEARLESS PRODS. June, 1996. (Cristina Rey) Christina Rey, Stephani Shope, Melissa Aronson.

INQUIETUDE
MADROGOA FILMES/GEMINI FILMS/WANDA FILMS/LIGHT NIGHT. May, 1998. Portuguese-French-Spanish-Swiss. (Manoel de Oliveira) Jose Pinto, Luis Miguel Cintra, Isabel Ruth, Leonor Silveira.

INSIDE
SHOWTIME. April, 1996. (Arthur Penn) Eric Stoltz, Nigel Hawthorne, Louis Gossett Jr., Ian Roberts.

INSIDE MONKEY ZETTERLAND
I.R.S. August, 1993. (Jefery Levy) Steven Antin, Patricia Arquette, Tate Donovan.

INSIDE/OUT
PARALLEL PICTURES/BALTIMORE FILM FACTORY. May, 1997. (Rob Tregenza) Frederic Pierrot, Stefania Rocca, Berangere Allaux.

INSOMNIA
COLUMBIA TRISTAR ESPANA. Feb., 1998. Spanish. (Chus Gutierrez) Cristina Marcos, Candela Pena, Ernesto Alterio, Maria Pujalte.

INSOMNIA
NORSK FILM/NORDIC SCREEN. May, 1997. Norwegian. (Erik Skjoldbjaerg) Stellan Skarsgard, Sverre Anker Ousdal.

INSPECTOR GADGET
BUENA VISTA. July, 1999. (David Kellogg) Matthew Broderick, Rupert Everett, Joely Fisher, Michelle Trachtenberg, Andy Dick.

INSTANT KARMA
MGM/UA. April, 1990. (Roderick Taylor) Craig Sheffer, David Cassidy, Chelsea Noble.

INSTINCT
BUENA VISTA. May, 1999. (Jon Turteltaub): Anthony Hopkins, Cuba Gooding Jr., Donald Sutherland, Maura Tierney, George Dzundza.

INTERGIRL
UNIV. OF MN. FILM CENTER. January, 1992. Russian-Swedish. (Pyotr Todorovski) Elena Yakovleva.

INTERNAL AFFAIRS
PARAMOUNT. January, 1990. (Mike Figgis) Richard Gere, Andy Garcia, Nancy Travis.

INTERSECTION
PARAMOUNT. January, 1993. (Mark Rydell) Richard Gere, Sharon Stone, Lolita Davidovich.

INTERVIEW WITH THE VAMPIRE
WARNER BROS. November, 1994. (Neil Jordan) Tom Crusie, Brad Pitt, Antonio Banderas, Stephen Rea.

INTERVISTA
CASTLE HILL. November, 1992. Italian. (Federico Fellini) Sergio Rubini, Maurizio Mein, Anita Ekberg.

IN THE BEGINNING THERE WAS UNDERWEAR
MEDUSA FILM. Feb., 1999. Italian. (Anna Negri) Teresa Saponangelo, Stefania Rocca, Bebo Storti, Filippo Timi, Monica Scattini,.

IN THE FLESH
CAPE TOWN FILMS. June, 1999. (Ben Taylor) Dane Ritter, Ed Corbin, Adele Phares, Philip Solomon, Adrian Roberts.

INTIMATE RELATIONS
FOX SEARCHLIGHT. June, 1996. British-Canadian. (Philip Goodhew) Julie Walters, Rupert Graves, Laura Sadler.

INTO MY HEART
MARS FILMS. Sept., 1998. (Sean Smith, Anthony Stark) Rob Morrow, Claire Forlani, Jake Weber, Jayne Brook.

IN TOO DEEP
DIMENSION FILMS. Aug., 1999. (Michael Rymer) Omar Epps, LL Cool J, Nia Long, Stanley Tucci, Hill Harper.

INTO THE SUN
TRIMARK. January, 1992. (Fritz Kiersch) Anthony Michael Hall, Michael Paré, Deborah Maria Moore.

INTO THE WEST
MIRAMAX. September, 1993. Irish. (Mike Newell) Gabriel Byrne, Ellen Barkin, Ciaran Fitzgerald.

INVASION OF PRIVACY
SENATOR. May, 1996. British. (Anthony Hickox) Mili Avital, Jonathan Schaech, Naomi Campbell.

INVENTING THE ABBOTTS
20TH CENTURY FOX. March, 1997. (Pat O'Connor), Joaquin Phoenix, Billy Crudup, Liv Tyler, Will Patton, Kathy Baker.

THE INVISIBLES
ZERO PICTURES. JAN., 1999. (Noah Stern) Michael Goorjian, Portia de Rossi, Terry Camilleri.

I ONLY WANT YOU TO LOVE ME
BAVARIA. April, 1994; originally released 1976. German. (Rainer Werner Fassbinder) Vitus Zeplichal, Elke Aberle.

I.Q.
PARAMOUNT. December, 1994. (Fred Schepisi) Tim Robbins, Meg Ryan, Walter Matthau, Stephen Fry.

IRAN IS MY HOMELAND
Feb., 1999. Iranian. (Parviz Kimiavi) Rehzad Khodaveysi, Saeed Pur-Samimi, Parviz Shahin-Khoo, Mehdi Faqih, Qasem-Pur-Sattar.

IRON AND SILK
PRESTIGE. February, 1991. (Shirley Sun) Mark Salzman, Pan Qingfu.

IRON EAGLE IV
NORSTAR. January, 1996. Canadian. (Sidney J. Furie) Louis Gossett Jr, Al Waxman, Jason Cadieux.

THE IRON HEEL OF THE OLIGARCHY
DEBOSHIR FILM. Sept., 1998. Russian. (Alexandre Bashirov) Alexander Bashirov, Rita Margo, Elena Yudanova, Inna Volkova.

IRON MAZE
CASTLE HILL. November, 1991. Japanese-U.S. (Hiroaki Yoshida) Jeff Fahey, Bridget Fonda, Hiroaki Murakami.

IRON WILL
BUENA VISTA. January, 1994. (Charles Haid) Mackenzie Astin, Kevin Spacey, David Ogden Stiers.

I SHOT ANDY WARHOL
SAMUEL GOLDWYN. January, 1996. (Mary Harron) Lili Taylor, Jared Harris, Lothaire Bluteau, Martha Plimpton.

THE ISLAND OF DR. MOREAU
NEW LINE. August, 1996. (John Frankenheimer) Marlon Brando, Val Kilmer, David Thewlis, Fairuza Balk, Ron Perlman.

ISLAND OF THE SHARKS
IMAX. Apr., 1999. (Howard Hall). Documentary.

THE ISLAND ON BIRD STREET
MOONSTONE ENT. Feb., 1997. Danish-British-German. (Soren Kragh-Jacobsen) Patrick Bergin, Jordan Kiziuk, Jack Warden.

ISLAND, ALICIA
BEAR HAND FILMS. May, 1998. (Ken Yunome) Jeff Miller, Jne Jepson, Cherly Aden, Ed Bicarri, Kim Beuche, Pony Wilde.

ISLE OF DARKNESS
NORSK FILM. May, 1998. Norwegian.(Trygve Allister Diesen) Sofie Grabol, Paul-Ottar Haga, Sina Langfeldt, Martin Slaatto.

ISLE OF LESBOS
DUCE FILMS INTL. Feb., 1997. (Jeff B. Harmon) Kirsten Holly Smith, Danica Sheridan, Sonya Hensley, Michael Dotson.

I STILL KNOW WHAT YOU DID LAST SUMMER
SONY. Nov., 1998. (Danny Cannon) Jennifer Love Hewitt, Freddie Prinze, Jr., Brandy, Mekhi Phifer, Muse Watson.

IT ALL STARTS TODAY
LES FILMS ALAIN SARDE/LITTLE BEAR/TF1 FILMS. Jan., 1999. French. (Bertrand Tavernier) Philippe Torreton, Mria Pitarresi, Nadia Kaci.

IT COULD HAPPEN TO YOU
TRISTAR. July, 1994. (Andrew Bergman) Nicolas Cage, Bridget Fonda, Rosie Perez.

THE ITEM
TRILLION ENTERTAINMENT. Jan., 1999. (Dan Clark) Dawn Marie Velasquez, Dan Clark, Dave Pressler, Dan Lake, Ron Fitzgerald.

I, THE WORST OF ALL
FIRST RUN. September, 1995. Argentine. (Maria Luisa Bemberg) Assumpta Serna, Dominque Sanda.

I THINK I DO
DANGER FILMWORKS & HOUSE OF PAIN. June, 1997. (Brian Sloan) Alexis Arquette, Christian Maelen, Maddie Corman.

IT RUNS IN THE FAMILY
MGM. September, 1995. (Bob Clark) Charles Grodin, Kieran Culkin, Mary Steenburgen, Christian Culkin.

IT'S A LONG ROAD
ALCO FILM/GREEK FILM CENTRE. Feb., 1998. Greek. (Pantelis Voulgaris) Dimitris Katalifos, Thanassis Vengos, Giorgos Armenis.

IT'S ALL BOB
HELKON MEDIA. June, 1999. German-Danish-Austrian. (Otto Alexander Jahrreiss) Martina Gedeck, Gregor Torzs, Dieter Landuris, Hasan Ali Mete, Tonio Arango.

IT'S ALL TRUE: BASED ON AN UNFINISHED FILM BY ORSON WELLES
PARAMOUNT. October, 1993. French-U.S. (Richard Wilson, Myron Meisel, Bill Krohn) Documentary.

IT'S ELEMENTARY: TALKING ABOUT GAY ISSUES IN SCHOOL
WOMEN'S EDUCATIONAL MEDIA. May, 1996. (Debra Chasnoff) Documentary.

IT'S HAPPENING TOMORROW
SACIS. April, 1994. Italian. (Daniele Luchetti) Paolo Hendel, Giovanni Guidelli, Ciccio Ingrassia.

IT'S IN THE WATER
HERD FILM CO. June, 1997. (Kelli Herd) Keri Jo Chapman, Teresa Garrett, Derrick Sanders, Timothy Vahle, Barbara Lasater.

IT'S MY PARTY
MGM/UA. January, 1996. (Randal Kleiser) Eric Roberts, Gregory Harrison, Lee Grant, Marlee Matlin, Paul Regina.

IT'S PAT
BUENA VISTA. August, 1994. (Adam Bernstein) Julia Sweeney, David Foley, Charles Rocket.

IT'S YOUR TURN, LAURA CADIEUX
ALLIANCE. Oct., 1998. Canadian. (Denise Filatrault) Ginette Reno, Pierette Robitaille, Denis Dubois, Adele Reinhardt, Mireille Thibault, Danielle Lorain.

IT TAKES TWO
WARNER BROS. November, 1995. (Andy Tennant) Kirstie Alley, Steve Guttenberg, Mary-Kate and Ashley Olsen.

IVAN AND ABRAHAM
NEW YORKER. March, 1994. French-Yiddish-Polish. (Yolande Zauberman) Roma Alexandrovitch. B&W.

IVO THE GENIUS
UIP. October, 1995. Italian. (Alessandro Benvenuti) Benvenuti, Francesca Neri, Davide Bechini.

I WANT YOU
POLYGRAM FILMED ENTERTAINMENT. Feb., 1998. British. (Michael Winterbottom) Rachel Weisz, Alessandro Nivola, Luka Petrusic.

I WAS A JEWISH SEX WORKER
PHILIP B. ROTH. June, 1996. (Philip B. Roth) Documentary.

I WOKE UP EARLY THE DAY I DIED
MUSE PRODS./CINEQUANON PICTURES INTL. Sept., 1998. (Aris Iliopulos) Billy Zane, Sandra Bernhard, Ron Perlman, Tippi Hedren.

I WONDER WHO'S KISSING YOU NOW
BUENA VISTA. Feb., 1999. Danish. (Henning Carlsen) Tommy Kenter, Marika Lagercrantz, Morten Grunwald, Lars Knutsen, Henrik Larsen.

J

JACK
BUENA VISTA. July, 1996. (Francis Ford Coppola) Robin Williams, Diane Lane, Brian Kerwin, Fran Drescher.

JACK & JILL
ALLIANCE. Sept., 1998. Canadian. (John Kalangis) John Kalangis, Shauna MacDonald, Kathryn Zenna, Scott Gibson, Tara Johnson.

JACK & SARAH
POLYGRAM. March, 1996. (Tim Sullivan) Richard E. Grant, Samantha Mathis, Judi Dench. Ian McKellen.

JACK BE NIMBLE
CINEVISTA. June, 1994. New Zealand. (Garth Maxwell) Alexis Arquette, Sarah Smuts Kennedy, Bruno Lawrence.

JACK FROST
WARNER BROS. Dec., 1998. (Troy Miller) Michael Keaton, Kelly Preston, Mark Addy, Joseph Cross.

JACK THE BEAR
20TH CENTURY FOX. April, 1993. (Marshall Herskovitz) Danny DeVito, Robert J. Steinmiller, Jr., Gary Sinise.

THE JACKAL
UNIVERSAL. Nov., 1997. (Michael Caton-Jones) Bruce Willis, Richard Gere, Sidney Poitier, Diane Venora, Tess Harper, J.K. Simmons

JACKIE BROWN
MIRAMAX. Dec., 1997. (Quentin Tarantino) Pam Grier, Samuel L. Jackson, Robert Forster, Bridget Fonda, Michael Keaton, Robert De Niro.

JACOB'S LADDER
TRISTAR. November, 1990. (Adrian Lyne) Tim Robbins, Elizabeth Pena, Danny Aiello.

JACQUOT
SONY PICTURES CLASSICS. June, 1993. French. (Agnes Varda) Philippe Maron, Edouard Joubeaud, Laurent Monnier.

JADE
PARAMOUNT. October, 1995. (William Friedkin) David Caruso, Linda Fiorentino, Chazz Palminteri, Michael Biehn.

THE JAGUAR
GAMOUNT BUENA VISTA INTL. Sept., 1996. French. (Francis Veber) Jean Reno, Patrick Gruel, Harrison Lowe, Patricia Velasquez.

JAKOB THE LIAR
SONY. Aug., 1999. (Peter Kassovitz) Robin Williams, Alan Arkin, Bob Balaban, Hannah Taylor Gordon, Michael Jeter.

JAM
UNITED SODA FILMS/CHEN YIWEN FILM PRODS./LITTLE MORE CO. Sept.n 1998. Taiwanese. (Chen Yiwen) Cai Xinghung, June Cai, Vina Xu, Gao Minjun, Jine Shijie.

JAMES AND THE GIANT PEACH
BUENA VISTA. April, 1996. (Henry Selick) (voices) Simon Callow, Richard Dreyfuss, Jane Leeves, Joanna Lumley.

THE JAMES GANG
POLYGRAM FILMED ENT. Aug., 1997. British. (Mike Barker) John Hannah, Helen McCrory, Jason Flemyng, Toni Collette.

JAMON JAMON
ACADEMY ENT. September, 1993. Spanish. (Bigas Lunas) Penelope Cruz, Anna Galiena, Javier Bardem.

JAM SESSION: OFFICIAL BOOTLEG OF KIKUJIRO
OFFICE KITANO. Aug., 1999. Japanese. (Makoto Shinozaki) . Documentary.

JANE: AN ABORTION SERVICE
ITVS. 1995. (Kate Kirtz, Nell Lundy) Documentary.

JANE AUSTEN'S MAFIA!
BUENA VISTA. July, 1998. (Jim Abrahams) Jay Mohr, Billy Burke, Christina Applegate, Pamela Gidley, Olympia Dukakis, Lloyd Bridges.

JANE EYRE
MIRAMAX. April, 1996. (Franco Zeffirelli) William Hurt, Charlotte Gainsbourg, Joan Plowright, Anna Paquin.

JANE STREET
BEADS & TRINKETS PRODS. June, 1996. (Charles Merzbacher) Mark Berlin, Jane Jensen, Christa Kirby.

JANICE BEARD
FILM CONSORTIUM. May, 1999. British. (Clare Kilner) Eileen Walsh, Rhys Ifans, Patsy Kensit, David O'Hara, Sandra Voe.

THE JAR
ARTISTIC LICENSE. September, 1995. Iranian. (Ebrahim Foruzesh) Behzad Khodaveisi, Fatemeh Azrah.

JASON GOES TO HELL: THE FINAL FRIDAY
NEW LINE. August, 1993. (Adam Marcus) John D. LeMay, Kane Hodder, Allison Smith.

JASON'S LYRIC
GRAMERCY. September, 1994. (Doug McHenry) Allen Payne, Jada Pinkett, Bokeem Woodbine, Forest Whitaker.

JAWBREAKER
SONY. Jan., 1999. (Darren Stein) Rose McGowan, Rebecca Gayeart, Julie Benz, Judy Greer, Chad Christ.

JEANNE AND THE PERFECT GUY
LES FILMS DE REQUIN. Feb., 1998. French. (Olivier Ducastel) Virginie Ladoyen, Mathieu Demy, Jacques Bonnaffe, Valerie Bonneton.

JEFFERSON IN PARIS
BUENA VISTA. March, 1995. (James Ivory) Nick Nolte, Greta Scacchi, Jean Pierre Aumont, Simon Callow.

JEFFREY
ORION CLASSICS. August, 1995. (Christopher Ashley) Peter Weber, Patrick Stewart, Michael T. Weiss.

JENIPAPO
BOKU/RAVINA/DUETO. September, 1995. (Monique Gardenberg) Patrick Bauchau, Marilia Pera.

JENNIFER EIGHT
PARAMOUNT. November, 1992. (Bruce Robinson) Andy Garcia, Uma Thurman, Lance Henriksen.

THE JERKY BOYS
BUENA VISTA. February, 1995. (James Melkonian) Johnny Brennan, Kamal Ahmed, Alan Arkin.

JEROME
JET FILM CO. Aug., 1998. (Thomas Johnston, David Elton, Eric Tignini) Drew Pillsbury, Wendie Malick, Scott McKenna.

JERRY MACGUIRE
SONY PICTURES ENTERTAINMENT. December, 1996. (Cameron Crowe), Tom Cruise, Cuba Gooding Jr. Renee Zellweger, Kelly Preston.

JESUS IS A PALESTINIAN
WARNER BROS.. Jan., 1999. Dutch. (Lodewijk Crijns) Hans Teeuwen, Dijn Blom, Kim van Kooten, Peer Mascini.

JESUS OF MONTREAL
ORION CLASSICS. May, 1990. Canadian-French. (Denys Arcand) Lothaire Bluteau, Catherine Wilkening.

JETSONS: THE MOVIE
UNIVERSAL. July, 1990. (David Michener) Animated.

JEW-BOY LEVI
ZERO FILM. Mar., 1999. German-Swiss-Austrian. (Didi Danquart) Bruno Cathomas, Caroline Ebner, Ulrich Noethen, Martina Gedeck, Bernd Michael Lade.

JEWS, MOVIES AND THE AMERICAN DREAM
ASSOCIATED PRODUCERS. Feb., 1998. Canadian. (Simcha Jacobovici) documentary with Bernard Avishai, Judith Balaban.

JFK
WARNER BROS. December, 1991. (Oliver Stone) Kevin Costner, Sissy Spacek, Tommy Lee Jones, Kevin Bacon.

JIMI HENDRIX AT THE ISLE OF WIGHT
ORIGINAL CINEMA. July, 1991. (Murray Lerner) Jimi Hendrix.

JIMMY HOLLYWOOD
PARAMOUNT. March, 1994. (Barry Levinson) Joe Pesci, Christian Slater, Victoria Abril.

JIMMY ZIP
INCENDIARY ARTS. Aug., 1999. (Robert McGinley) Brendan Fletcher, Ike Gingrich, Adrienne Frantz, Zia, John Truong,.

JINGLE ALL THE WAY
20TH CENTRY FOX. November, 1996. (Brian Levant), Arnold Schwarzenegger, Sinbad, Phil Hartman, Rita Wilson, Robert Conrad.

JINNAH
AKBAR AHMED. Sept., 1998. Pakistanian-British. (Jamil Dehlavi) Christopher Lee, James Fox, Maria Aitken, Shashi Kapoor, Richard Lintern.

JIN-ROH: THE WOLF BRIGADE
BANDAI VISUAL CO. May, 1999. Japanese. (Hiroyuki Okiura). Animated.

JIT
NORTHERN ARTS. March, 1993. Zimbabwe. (Michael Raeburn) Dominic Makuvachuma, Sibongile Nene.

J.L.G. BY J.L.G.
INDEPT./PUBLIC TH. January, 1995. French. (Jean Luc Godard) Documentary.

JOE & JOE
LITTLE HORSE THIEF. November, 1995. (David Wall) David Wysocki, Sean Patrick Brennan, Tracy Griffith.

JOE VERSUS THE VOLCANO
WARNER BROS. March, 1990. (John Patrick Shanley) Tom Hanks, Meg Ryan, Lloyd Bridges.

JOE'S APARTMENT
WARNER BROS. July, 1996. (John Payson) Jerry O'Connell, Megan Ward, Jim Sterling, Shiek Mahmud-Bey, Jim Turner.

JOE'S SO MEAN TO JOSEPHINE
ALLIANCE RELEASING. Feb., 1997. Canadian. (Peter Wellington) Eric Thal, Sarah Polley, Don McKellar, Waneta Storms.

JOE THE KING
49TH PARALLEL, FORENSIC/291 FILMS,LOWER EAST SIDE FILMS . Jan., 1999. (Frank Whaley) Noah Fleiss, Val Kilmer, Karen Young, Ethan Hawke, John Leguizamo.

JOEY
ROADSHOW. Nov., 1997. Australian. (Ian Barry) Jamie Croft, Alex McKenna, Rebecca Gibney, Ed Begley, Jr.

JOEY BREAKER
SKOURAS. May, 1993. (Steven Starr) Richard Edson, Cedella Marley, Fred Fondren.

JOEY TAKES A CAB
BANDWAGON PRODS. June, 1991. (Albert Band) Lionel Stander, Kathleen Freeman.

JOHANNA D'ARC OF MONGOLIA
WOMEN MAKE MOVIES. May, 1992. West German. (Ulrike Ottinger) Delphine Seyrig, Xu Re Huar, Irm Hermann.

JOHN LURIE AND THE LOUNGE LIZARDS LIVE IN BERLIN
TELECOM JAPAN. September, 1992. Japanese. (Garret Linn) Documentary.

JOHNNY MNEMONIC
TRISTAR. May, 1995. (Robert Longo) Keanu Reeves, Dolph Lundgren, Takeshi, Ice-T, Dina Meyer, Udo Kier.

JOHNNY SKIDMARKS
CINEPIX FILM PROPERTIES. Jan., 1998. (John Raffo) Peter Gallagher, Frances McDormand, John Lithgow, Geoffrey Lower.

JOHNNY STECCHINO
NEW LINE. October, 1992. Italian. (Roberto Benigni) Roberto Benigni, Nicoletta Braschi, Paolo Bonacelli.

JOHNNY SUEDE
MIRAMAX. August, 1992. (Tom DiCillo) Brad Pitt, Alison Moir, Calvin Levels.

JOHNS
FIRST LOOK/OVERSEAS FILMGROUP. January, 1996. (Scott Silver) Lukas Haas, David Arquette, Arliss Howard.

JOINT ADVENTURE
ELECTRIC MOUNTAIN. October, 1995. (John Foran) James Brinkley, David Haley, Biz Lyon.

JOSE RIZAL
GMA NETWORK. Feb., 1999. Philippine. (Marilou Diaz-Abaya) Cesar Montano, Joel Torre, Jaime Fabregas, Gloria Diaz, Gardo Versoza.

JOSH AND S.A.M.
COLUMBIA. November, 1993. (Billy Weber) Jacob Tierney, Noah Fleiss, Martha Plimpton.

THE JOURNEY OF AUGUST KING
MIRAMAX. November, 1995. (John Duigan) Jason Patric, Thandie Newton, Larry Drake, Sam Waterston.

JOURNEY OF HOPE
MIRAMAX. April, 1991. Swiss. (Xavier Koller) Necmettin Cobanoglu, Nur Surer, Emin Sivas.

THE JOURNEY TO PARIS
MARS FILMS. May, 1999., French. (Marc-Henri Dufresne) Olivier Broche, Francois Morel, Micheline Presle, Marina Tome, Valentin Morel.

JOURNEY TO SPIRIT ISLAND
GRIFFIN FILM ASSOCS. May, 1990. (Laszlo Pal) Bettina, Marie Antoinette Rodgers.

JOURNEY TO THE BEGINNING OF THE WORLD
MADRAGOA FILMS/GEMINI FILMS. May, 1997. Portuguese-French. (Manoel de Oliveira) Marcello Mastroianni, Jean Yves Gautier.

JOURNEY TO THE SUN
ISTINAI FILMLER & REKLAMAS/FABRICA. Feb., 1999. Turkish-Dutch-german. (Yesim Ustaoglu) Newroz Bax, Nazmi Qirix, Mizgin Kapazan, Nigar Aktar, Iskender Bagcilar.

JOURNEY TO WISDOM
NEW GENERATION CINEMA. May, 1997. Indian. (Jayaraj) Master Kumar, Vijaya Raghavan, Mini Nair, Unnikrishnan Namboothiri.

THE JOY LUCK CLUB
BUENA VISTA. September, 1993. (Wayne Wang) Tsai Chin, Kieu Chinh, Lauren Tom, Tamlyn Tomita.

THE JOYS OF SMOKING
VERGING PRODS. June, 1999. (Nik Katasapetses) Matthew Rozen, Steven Sorenson, Deborah Cordell, Carrie Mogan, Jon Prutow.

JUAN, I FORGOT, I DON'T REMEMBER
LA MEDIA LUNA. Mar., 1999. Mexican. (Juan Carlos Rulfo). Documentary.

JU DOU
MIRAMAX. March, 1991. Chinese. (Zhang Yimou) Gong Li, Baotian Li, Wei Li.

JUDAS KISS
KEY ENTERTAINMENT. Sept., 1997. (Sebastian Gutierrez) Simon Baker-Denny, Gil Bellows, Carla Gugino, Alan Rickman, Til Schweiger.

THE JUDAS PROJECT
RS ENTERTAINMENT. February, 1993. (James H. Barden) John O'Banion, Ramy Zada, Jeff Corey.

JUDE
POLYGRAM. June, 1996. British. (Michael Winterbottom) Christopher Eccleston, Kate Winslet.

JUDGE DREDD
BUENA VISTA. June, 1995. (Danny Cannon) Sylvester Stallone, Armand Assante, Rob Schneider, Jurgen Prochnow.

JUDGMENT IN FLAMES
GOLDEN NETWORK. May, 1998. Taiwanese. (James Chia-ming Liu) Rachel Chang, Yin Chiao-the, Jackson Lou.

JUDGMENT NIGHT
UNIVERSAL. October, 1993. (Stephen Hopkins) Emilio Estevez, Cuba Gooding Jr., Stephen Dorff.

JUDY BERLIN
CARUSO/MENDELSOHN. Jan., 1999. (Eric Mendelsohn) Barbara Barrie, Bob Dishy, Edie Falco, Carlin Glynn, Aaron Harnick.

JUHA
SPUTNIK OY. Feb., 1999. Finnish. (Aki Kaurismaki) Sakari Kuosmanen, Kati Outinen, Andre Wilms, Markku Peltola, Elina Salo.

JUICE
PARAMOUNT. January, 1992. (Ernest Dickerson) Omar Epps, Tupac Shakur, Jermaine Hopkins.

JULIA HAS TWO LOVERS
SOUTH GATE ENT. March, 1991. (Bashar Shbib) Daphna Kastner, David Duchovny, David Charles.

JULIAN PO
FINE LINE. Sept., 1997. (Alan Wade) Christain Slater, Robin Tunney, Michael Parks, Cherry Jones, Frankie R. Faison, Harve Presnell.

JULIEN DONKEY-BOY
FINE LINE. Sept., 1999. (Harmony Korine) Ewen Bremner, Chloe Sevigny, Werner Herzog, Evan Neumann, Joyce Korine.

JULIETTE OF THE HERBS
MABINOGION FILMS. Apr., 1999. (Tish Streeten). Documentary.

JULIO AND HIS ANGEL
ANGEL FILMS. Oct., 1998. Mexican. (Jorge Cervera, Jr.). Eduardo Saul Martinex, Jorge Cervera, Jr. Carmen del Valle, Cristobal Clark Cervera.

JUMANJI
TRISTAR. December, 1995. (Joe Johnston) Robin Williams, Bonnie Hunt, Jonathan Hyde, Kirsten Dunst, Bradley Pierce.

JUMP
(GIVEN) FILMS. Apr., 1999. (Justin McCarthy) Peter Appel, Jessica Hecht, James LeGros, Michael, McGlone, Amanda Peet.

JUMP THE GUN
FILM FOUR. Feb., 1997. British-South African. (Les Blair) Baby Cele, Lionel Newton, Michele Burgers, Thulani Nyembe.

JUMPIN AT THE BONEYARD
20TH CENTURY FOX. September, 1992. (Jeff Stanzler) Tim Roth, Alexis Arquette, Danitra Vance.

JUNGLE FEVER
UNIVERSAL. June, 1991. (Spike Lee) Wesley Snipes, Annabella Sciorra, Anthony Quinn, Ossie Davis.

JUNGLE 2 JUNGLE
BUENA VISTA. March, 1997. (John Pasquin), Tim Allen, Martin Short, JoBeth Williams, Lolita Davidovich, Sam Huntington, David Ogden Stiers.

JUNIOR
UNIVERSAL. November, 1994. (Ivan Reitman) Arnold Schwarzenegger, Danny DeVito, Emma Thompson.

JUNK MAIL
MOVIEMAKERS/NORSK FILM/ATLAS FILM. May, 1997. Norwegian. (Pal Sletaune) Robert Skjaerstad, Andrine Saether.

JUPITER'S WIFE
ARTISTIC LICENSE. August, 1995. (Michel Negroponte) Documentary.

JURASSIC PARK
UNIVERSAL. June, 1993. (Steven Spielberg) Sam Neill, Laura Dern, Richard Attenborough, Jeff Goldblum.

THE JUROR
COLLUMBIA. January, 1996. (Brian Gibson) Demi Moore, Alec Baldwin, Joseph Gordon-Levitt, Anne Heche.

JURY DUTY
TRISTAR. April, 1995. (John Fortenberry) Pauly Shore, Stanley Tucci, Abe Vigoda, Brian Doyle Murray.

JUST A LITTLE HARMLESS SEX
PHAEDRA CINEMA. June, 1999. (Rick Rosenthal) Alison Eastwood, Robert Mailhouse, Rachel Hunter, Kimberly Williams, Lauren Hutton.

JUST ANOTHER GIRL ON THE I.R.T.
MIRAMAX. March, 1993. (Leslie Harris) Ariyan Johnson, Kevin Thigpen, Ebony Jerido.

JUST CAUSE
WARNER BROS. February, 1995. (Arne Glimcher) Sean Connery, Laurence Fishburne, Blair Underwood.

JUST FRIENDS
SCINTILLATING PRODS. Dec., 1996. (Maria Burton) Anthony Palermo, Anita Barone, Barbara Alyn Woods, Hal Linden, Tim Bohn.

JUST LIKE A WOMAN
SAMUEL GOLDWYN. July, 1994. British. (Christopher Monger) Julie Walters, Adrian Pasdar, Paul Freeman.

JUST LIKE IN THE MOVIES
CABRIOLET. September, 1990. (Bram Towbin, Mark Halliday) Jay O. Sanders, Alan Ruck.

JUST MARRIED
MOANA-FILM/GMBH. Sept., 1998. German. (Rudolf Thome) Laura Maori Tonke, Herbert Frisch, Marquard Bohm, Johannes Herschmann, Valeska Hanel.

JUST THE TICKET
MGM. Feb., 1999. (Richard Wenk) Andy Garcia, Andie MacDowell, Richard Bradford, Laura Harris, Andre Blake.

JUST WRITE
CURB ENTERTAINMENT INTL. Sept., 1998. (Andrew Gallerani) Sherilyn Fenn, Jeremy Piven, JoBeth Williams, Wallace Shawn.

K

KAFKA
MIRAMAX. December, 1991. (Steven Soderberg) Jeremy Irons, Theresa Russell, Joel Grey, Ian Holm. B&W/Color.

KALIFORNIA
GRAMERCY. Sveptember, 1993. (Dominic Sena) Brad Pitt, Juliette Lewis, David Duchovny.

KAMA SUTRA: A TALE OF LOVE
TRIMARK. Sept., 1996. Indian. (Mira Nair) Indira Varma, Sarita Choudhury, Ramon Tikaram, Naveen Andrews, Devi Rekha.

KANSAS CITY
FINE LINE. June, 1996. French-U.S. (Robert Altman) Jennifer Jason Leigh, Miranda Richardson, Harry Belafonte.

KARMA LOCAL
KLLC PRODS.. Mar., 1999. Indian. (Dharshan Bhagat) Dharshan Bhagat, Josh Pais, Bairaj, Uppal, Mariusz Szczech.

KARNAVAL
MK2. Feb., 1999. French-Belgian-Swiss. (Thomas Vincent) Amar Ben Abdallah, Sylvia Testud, Clovis Cornillac, Martine Godart,.

KAZAAM
BUENA VISTA. July, 1996. (Paul M. Glaser) Shaquille O'Neal, Francis Capra, Ally Walker, Marshall Manesh.

KEATON'S COP
CANNON. March, 1990. (Bob Burge) Lee Majors, Abe Vigoda.

KEBAB CONNECTION
AMLF. May, 1998. French. (Hiner Saleem) Georges Corraface, Marina Kobakhidze, Stephanie Lagarde, Tuncel Kurtiz, Fatah Solanti.

KEEP COOL
GUANG XI FILM STUDIO. Sept., 1997. Chinese. (Zhang Yimou) Jiang Wen, Li Baotian, Qu Ying, Ge You, Zhang Yimou.

THE KEEPER
RADA. January, 1996. (Joe Brewster) Giancarlo Esposito, Regina Taylor, Isaach de Bankole.

KEEPERS OF THE FRAME
MOUNT PILOT PRODS. Mar., 1999. (Mark McLaughlin) Alan Alda, Laurence Austin, Stan Brakhage, Leonard Maltin, Roddy McDowall. Documentary.

KEEP THE ASPIDISTRA FLYING
FIRST INDEPENDENT. Sept., 1997. British. (Robert Bierman) Richard E. Grant, Helena Bonham Carter, Julian Wadham.

KEIHO
SHOCHIKU. Feb., 1999. Japanese. (Yoshimitsu Morita) Kyoka Suzuki, Shinichi Tsutsumi, Ittoku Kishibe, Hideko Yoshida, Mirai Yamamoto.

KENOMA
A.F. CINEMA E VIDEO. Sept., 1998. Brazilian. (Eliane Caffe) Jose Dumont, Enrique Diaz, Jonas Bloch, Mariana Lima, Matheus Natchergaelle.

KESWA, THE LOST THREAD
LES FILMS DE LA MOUETTE/MORGANE PROD./MPS. Oct., 1998. (Kalthoum Bornaz) Rim Turki, Nouna Noureddine, Ali Mosbah, Ahmed El Hafian.

THE KEY
TOHOKUSHINSHA FILM CO. March, 1998. Japanese. (Toshiharu Ikeda) Naomi Kawashima, Akira Emoto, Mikio Osawa, Kaori Tsuji.

KEYS TO TULSA
GRAMERCY. March, 1997. (Leslie Greig) Eric Stoltz, Cameron Diaz, Randy Graff, Mary Tyler Moore, James Coburn.

KHRUSTALIOV, MY CAR!
POLYGRAM FILM DISTRIBUTION. May, 1998. French-Russian. (Alexei Guerman) Y. Tsurilo, N. Ruslanova, M. Dementiev, A. Bachirov.

KICHIKU
ONI PROD. Feb., 1998. Japanese. (Kazuyoshi Kumakiri) Sumiko Mikami, Syunsuke Sawada, Shigeru Bokuda, Toshiyuki Sugihara.

KICK
BEYOND FILMS. May, 1999. Australian. (Lynda Heys) Russell Page, Rebecca Yates, Martin Henderson, Radha Mitchell, Paul Mercurio.

KICKBOXER 2
TRIMARK. June, 1991. (Albert Pyun) Sasha Mitchell, Peter Boyle.

KICKED IN THE HEAD
OCTOBER. May, 1997. (Matthew Harrison) Kevin Corrigan, Linda Fiorentino, Michael Rapaport, Lili Taylor, James Woods.

KICKING & SCREAMING
TRIMARK. November, 1995. (Noah Baumbach) Josh Hamilton, Sam Gould, Catherine Keller, Eric Stoltz, Olivia D'Abo.

THE KID FROM CHAABA
AFMD. Feb., 1998. French. (Christpher Ruggia) Bouzid Negnoug, Mohamed Fellag, Francois Morel, Amina Medjoubi, Nabil Ghalem.

A KID IN KING ARTHUR'S COURT
BUENA VISTA. August, 1995. (Michael Gottlieb) Thomas Ian Nichols, Joss Ackland, Art Malik.

KIDS
EXCALIBUR. July, 1995. (Larry Clark) Leo Fitzpatrick, Justin Pierce, Yakira Peguero.

KIDS IN THE HALL: BRAIN CANDY
PARAMOUNT. April, 1996. (Kelly Makin) David Foley, Bruce McCulloch, Kevin McDonald, Mark McKinney.

KIDS OF SURVIVAL THE ART AND LIFE OF TIM ROLLINS & K.O.S.
GELLER/GOLDFINE PRODS. April, 1996. (Daniel Geller, Danya Goldfine). Documentary.

KIDS RETURN
OFFICE KITANO. May, 1996. Japanese. (Takeshi Kitano) Masanobu Ando, Ken Kaneko.

KIKA
OCTOBER FILMS. May, 1994. Spanish. (Pedro Almodovar) Veronica Forque, Peter Coyote, Victoria Abril.

KIKI'S DELIVERY SERVICE
BUENA VISTA. June, 1998. (Hayao Miyazaki) Voices: Kirsten Dunst, Phil Hartman, Janeane Garofolo, Matthew Lawrence.

KIKUJIRO
SONY. May, 1999. Japanese. (Takeshi Kitano) Beat Takeshi, Yusuke Sekiguchi, Kayoko Kishimoto, Yuko Daike, Kazuko Yoshiyuiki.

KILLER
ARTCAM INTL./KADAM. May, 1998. French-Kazakh. (Darezhan Omirbaev) Talgat Assetov, Roksana Abouova.

KILLER: A JOURNAL OF MURDER
OLIVER STONE/SPELLING FILMS. January, 1996. (Tim Metcalfe) James Woods, Robert Sean Leonard, Lili Taylor.

THE KILLER CONDOM
ASCOT FILMVERLEIH. Feb., 1997. German. (Martin Walz) Udo Samel, Peter Lohmeyer, Marc Richter, Leonard Lansink.

KILLER STORY
HANMAC ENTERTAINMENT. Sept., 1998. South Korean. (Yeo Kyun-dong) Hwang Cine, Mun Seong-keun, Lee Kyeong-yeong.

KILLER TONGUE
SOGEPAQ INTL. May, 1996. Spanish-British. (Alberto Sciamma) Melinda Clarke, Jason Durr, Robert Englund.

KILLING ZOE
OCTOBER FILMS. August, 1994. (Roger Roberts Avary) Eric Stoltz, Julie Delpy, Jean-Hughes Anglade.

THE KILL–OFF
CABRIOLET. October, 1990. (Maggie Greenwald) Loretta Gross, Jackson Sims.

KILL THE MAN
SEATTLE PACIFIC INVESTMENTS/SUMMIT ENTERTAINMENT. Jan., 1999. (Tom Booker) Luke Wilson, Joshua Malina, Paula Devicq, Phil LaMarr, Phillip Rhys.

KIMBERLY
MOONSTONE. Sept., 1999. U.S.-German. (Frederic Golchan) Gabrielle Anwar, Sean Astin, Jason Lewis, Robert Mailhouse, Chris Rydell.

A KIND OF HUSH
CAPITOL FILMS. Sept., 1998. British. (Brian Stirner) Harley Smith, Marcella Plunkett, Ben Roberts, Paul Williams, Nathan Constance.

KINDERGARTEN COP
UNIVERSAL. December, 1990. (Ivan Reitman) Arnold Schwarzenegger, Penelope Ann Miller, Pamela Reed.

A KIND OF HUSH
CAPITOL FILMS. Sept., 1998. British. (Brian Stirner) Harley Smith, Marcella Plunkett, Ben Roberts, Paul Williams, Nathan Constance.

THE KING AND I
WARNER BROS. Mar., 1999. (Richard Rich) Miranda Richardson, Christiane Noll, Martin Vidnovic.

KING JAMES VERSION
FIRST RUN FEATURES. September, 1991. (Robert Gardner) Christina Braggs, Joan Pryor, Ellwoodson Williams.

KING OF COMEDY
STAR OVERSEAS. July, 1999. Hong Kong. (Li Lik-chi, Stepphen Chiau) Stephen Chiau, Karen Mok, Cecilia Cheung, Ng Mang-tat, Jackie Chan.

KING OF NEW YORK
NEW LINE. September, 1990. Italian-U.S. (Abel Ferrara) Christopher Walken, Laurence Fishburne.

KING OF THE BEGGARS
RIM. November, 1993. Chinese. (Gordon Chan) Stephen Chiau, Chang Min, Ng Man Tat.

KING OF THE HILL
GRAMERCY. August, 1993. (Steven Soberbergh) Jesse Bradford, Jeroen Krabbe, Lisa Eichhorn.

KING RALPH
UNIVERSAL. February, 1991. (David S. Ward) John Goodman, Peter O'Toole, John Hurt.

THE KINGDOM
OCTOBER FILMS. November, 1995. Swedish. (Lars Von Trier) Ernst Hugo Jaregard, Kirsten Rolffes, Ghita Norby, Udo Kier.

THE KINGDOM II
ZENTROPA. Sept., 1997. Danish. (Lars Van Trier) Ernst-Hugo Jaregard, Kirsten Rolffes, Holger Juul Hansen, Soren Pilmark.

THE KINGDOM OF ZYDECO
MUGSHOT. June, 1994. (Robert Mugge) Documentary.

KINGPIN
MGM/UA. June, 1996. (Peter and Bobby Farrelly) Woody Harrelson, Randy Quaid, Vanessa Angel, Bill Murray.

KINI & ADAMS
POLYGRAM. May, 1997. French. (Idrissa Ouedraogo) Vusi Kunene, David Mohloki, Nthati Moshesh, John Kani.

KIRIKOU AND THE SORCERESS
GEBEKA FILMS. Dec., 1998. French-Belgian-Luxembourgeois. (Michel Ocelot). Animated.

KISMET
HELKON. June, 1999. German. (Andreas Thiel) Steffen Wink, Fatih Akin, Jule Ronstedt, Axel Milberg, Lilo Wanders.

KISS & TELL
FILMWORKS, Burbank. May, 1996. (Jordan Alan) Lewis Arquette, Richmond Arquette, Justine Bateman.

KISS AND TELL
BASE PRODS. Aug., 1999. (John Brenkus) James McCauley, Bryan Callen, Kerr Smith, Daniel Cosgrove, Bridget Ann WhiteWimmer, Natalie Zea.

A KISS BEFORE DYING
UNIVERSAL. April, 1991. (James Dearden) Matt Dillon, Sean Young, Max von Sydow.

KISS, CUDDLE AND CELEBRATE
ALMA FILMS. July, 1998. German. (Peter Kern) documentary.

KISSES AND HUGS
CECCHI GORI. Jan., 1999. Italian. (Paolo Virzi) Francesco Paolantoni, Massimo Gambacciani, Piero Gremigni, Samuele Marzi.

KISS ME A KILLER
CONCORDE. April, 1991. (Marcus De Leon) Julie Carmen, Robert Beltran.

KISS ME, GUIDO
CAPITOL FILMS/KARDANA FILMS. Jan., 1997. (Tony Vitale) Nick Scotti, Anthony Barrile, Anthony DeSando, Craig Chester.

KISS OF DEATH
20TH CENTURY FOX. April, 1995. (Barbet Schroeder) David Caruso, Nicholas Cage, Samuel L. Jackson.

KISS OR KILL
OCTOBER. April, 1997. Australian. (Bill Bennett) Frances O'Connor, Matt Day, Chris Haywood, Barry Otto, Max Cullen.

KISS THE GIRLS
PARAMOUNT. September, 1997. (Gary Fleder), Morgan Freeman, Ashley Judd, Cary Elwes, Tony Goldwyn, Jay O. Sanders, Bill Nunn.

KISSING A FOOL
UNIVERSAL. Feb., 1998. (Doug Ellin) David Schwimmer, Jason Lee, Mili Avital, Bonnie Hunt, Vanessa Angel, Kari Wuhrer.

KITCHEN
GOLDEN HARVEST/AMUSE INC. Feb., 1997. Hong Kong-Japanese. (Yim Ho) Jason Chan, Yasuko Tomita, Law Kar-ying, Karen Mok.

KITCHEN PARTY
CINEPLEX ODEON FILMS. Sept., 1997. Canadian. (Gary Burns) Scott Speedman, Laura Harris, Gillian Barber, Kevin McNulty.

THE KKK BOUTIQUE AIN'T JUST REDNECKS
INDEPT./PUBLIC TH. March, 1995. (Camille Billops, James V. Hatch) Documentary.

KNIGHT MOVES
INTERSTAR. January, 1993. (Carl Schenkel) Christopher Lambert, Diane Lane, Tom Skerritt.

KNOCK OFF
TRISTAR PICTURES. Aug., 1998. (Tsui Hark) Jean-Claude Van Damme, Rob Schneider, Lela Rochon, Paul Sorvino, Carmen Lee.

KNOCKIN' ON HEAVEN'S DOOR
BUENA VISTA INTL. Nov., 1997. German. (Thomas Jahn) Til Schweiger, Jan Josef Liefers, Thierry van Werveke.

KNOWLEDGE OF HEALING
A T & C FILM AG. Sept., 1997. Swiss. (Franz Reichler) documentary with Dr. Tenzin Gyatso, Dr. Alfred Hassig, Dr. Isaac Ginsburg

KOKKURI
NIKKATSU CORP./HRS FUNAI CO. Sept., 1997. Japanese. (Takahisa Zeze) Ayumi Yamatsu, Hiroko Shimada, Moe Ishikawa, Rika Furukawa, Saki Aoshima.

KOLYA
MIRAMAX. September, 1996. Czech-British-French. (Jan Sverak) Zdenek Sverak, Andrej Chalimon, Libuse Safrankova.

KOMODO
SCANBOX ASIA PACIFIC. May, 1999. Australian. (Michael Lantieri) Jill Hennessy, Billy Burke, Kevin Zegers, Paul Gleeson, Nina Landis.

KORCZAK
NEW YORKER. April, 1991. Polish. (Andrzej Wajda) Wojtek Pszoniak, Ewa Dalkowska, Piotr Kozlowski.

THE KRAYS
MIRAMAX. November, 1990. British. (Peter Medak) Gary Kemp, Martin Kemp, Billie Whitelaw.

KRIPPENDORF'S TRIBE
BUENA VISTA. Feb., 1998. (Todd Holland) Richard Dreyfuss, Jenna Elfman, Natasha Lyonne, Gregory Smith, Elaine Stritch, Tom Poston.

K2
PARAMOUNT. May, 1992. British. (Franc Roddam) Michael Biehn, Matt Craven, Raymond J. Barry.

KUFFS
UNIVERSAL. January, 1992. (Bruce A. Evans) Christian Slater, Tony Goldwyn, Milla Jovovich.

KULL THE CONQUEROR
UNIVERSAL. August, 1997. (John Nicolella), Kevin Sorbo, Tia Carrere, Thomas Ian Griffith, Litefoot, Karina Lombard, Roy Brocksmith.

KUNDUN
BUENA VISTA. Dec., 1997. (Martin Scorcese) Tenzin Thuthob Tsarong, Gyurme Tethong, Tulku Jamyang Kunga Tenzin.

KURT GERRON'S KARUSSELL
TV-VENTURES. Feb., 1999. German. (Ilona Ziok). Documentary.

KUSAH HAKWAAN
ALASKAN NOMAD. July, 1999. (Sean Morris) Paul Asicksik, Don Savage, Gary Waid, Diane E. Benson, Kuth Ka.

L

LA BELLE NOISEUSE
MK2. October, 1991. French. (Jacques Ribette) Michel Piccoli, Jane Birkin, Emmanuelle Beart.

LA BOMBA
MEDUSA FILM. Apr., 1999. (Giulio Base) Alessandro Gassman, Enrico Brignano, Rocco Papaleo, Lola Pagnani, Vittorio Gassman.

LABYRINTH OF DREAMS
KSS FILMS PROD. Feb., 1997. Japanese. (Sogo Ishii) Rena Komine, Tadanobu Asano, Kotomi Kyono, Kirika Mano, Tomoka Kurotani. B&W.

LABYRINTH OF PASSION
CINEVISTA. January, 1990. Spanish. (Pedro Almodovar) Cecilia Roth, Imanol Arias, Antonio Banderas.

LA CARNADA
KUSI FILMS/ZDF ARTE/BRUSSELS AVE. May, 1999. Peruvian-German-belgian. (Marianne Eyde) Monica Sanchez, Gabriela Velasquez, Miguel Medina, Orlando Felices, Ana Cecilia.

LA CHASSE AUX PAPILLONS
NEW YORKER. October, 1993. French-German-Italian. (Otar Iosseliani) Narda Blanchet, Pierrett Pompom Bailhache.

L.A. CONFIDENTIAL
WARNER BROS. Arpil, 1997. (Curtis Hanson), Kevin Spacey, Russell Crowe, Guy Pearce, James Cromwell, David Strathairn, Kim Basinger.

LA DILETTANTE
GOUTTE D'OR. June, 1999. French. (Pascal Thomas) Catherine Frot, Bernard Verley, Barbara Schulz, Didier Bezace, Marie-Christine Barrault.

LA DISCRETE
MK2. August, 1992. French. (Christian Vincent) Fabrice Muchini, Judith Henry, Maurice Garrel.

THE LADY
SAHARA CULTURAL-FILM INSTITUTE/AMA. Feb., 1999. Iranian. (Dariush Mehrjui) Bita Farrahi, Khosro Shakibai, Ezzatollah Entezami.

LADYBIRD, LADYBIRD
SAMUEL GOLDWYN. December, 1994. British. (Ken Loach) Crissy Rock, Vladimir Vega, Ray Winstone.

LADYBUGS
PARAMOUNT. March, 1992. (Sidney J. Furie) Rodney Dangerfield, Jackée, Jonathan Brandis.

LA FEMME NIKITA
SAMUEL GOLDWYN. March, 1991. French. (Luc Besson) Anne Parillaud, Jean-Hughes Anglade, Jeanne Moreau.

LAIBACH: VICTORY UNDER THE SUN
INT'L FILM CIRCUIT. October, 1992. Yugoslavian (Goran Gajic).

THE LAKE
SONET. JAN., 1999. Swedish. (Hans Ake Gabrielsson) Regina Lund, Mats Rudal, Bjorn Gedda, Fredrik Hammar, Maria Lundquist.

LAKE PLACID
20TH CENTURY FOX. July, 1999. (David E. Kelley) Bill Pullman, Bridget Fonda, Oliver Platt, Brendan Gleeson, Betty White.

LAMB
CAPITOL ENT. February, 1995. British, 1986. (Colin Gregg) Liam Neeson, Hugh O'Connor, Ian Bannen.

LAMBADA
WARNER BROS. March, 1990. (Joel Silberg) J. Eddie Peck, Melora Hardin, Shabba-Doo.

THE LAND GIRLS
GRAMERCY PICTURES. Jan., 1998. (David Leland) Catherine McCormack, Rachel Weisz, Anna Friel, Steven Mackintosh.

LAND OF MILK AND HONEY
SHOWCASE. September, 1995. (Joseph Destein) Richard Panebiance, Lumi Cavazos, Roxana Zal.

THE LAND OF THE DEAF
GORKY FILMSTUDIO. Feb., 1998. Russian. (Valery Todorovsky) Chulpan Khamatova, Dina Korzun, Maxim Sukhanov, Nikita Tiunin.

LANDSCAPE IN THE MIST
NEW YORKER. September, 1990. Greek. (Theo Angelopoulos) Michalis Zeke, Tania Palaiologou.

L'ANGE
FIRST RUN FEATURES. March, 1991. French. (Patrick Bokanowski) Maurice Baquet, Jean Marie Bon.

LANGMUIR'S WORLD
ROGER R. SUMERHAYES. Jan., 1999. (Roger R. Summerhayes). Documentary.

LANI LOA: THE PASSAGE
FRANCIS FORD COPPOLA/WAYNE WANG. Sept., 1998. (Sherwood Hu) Angus MacFadyen, Carlotta Chang, Ray Bumatai, Chris Tashima.

LA PASSIONE
WARNER VISION INT'L. Nov., 1997. (John H. Hobbs) Shirley Bassey, Sean Gallagher, Thomas Orange, Paul Shane.

LARGER THAN LIFE
MGM/UA October, 1996. (Howard Franklin), Bill Murray, Janeane Garofalo, Matthew McConaughey, Keith David, Pat Hingle, Jeremy Piven.

LARKS ON A STRING
IFEX. February, 1991; originally released 1969. Czech. (Jiri Menzel) Vaclav Neckar, Rudolf Hrusinsky.

LA SCORTA
FIRST LOOK. May, 1994. Italian. (Ricky Tognazzi) Claudio Amendola, Enrico Lo Verso, Carlo Cecchi.

THE LASER MAN
ORIGINAL CINEMA. March, 1990. (Peter Wang) Marc Hayashi, Tony Leung.

LASSIE
PARAMOUNT. July, 1994. (Daniel Petrie) Thomas Guiry, Helen Slater, Jon Tenney, Lassie.

LAST ACTION HERO
COLUMBIA. June, 1993. (John McTiernan) Arnold Schwarzenegger, Austin O'Brien, Charles Dance.

THE LAST BEST SUNDAY
LAST BEST. June, 1999. (Don Most) Douglas Spain, Angela Bettis, William Lucking, Kim Darby, Daneil Beer,.

THE LAST BIG ATTRACTION
HOPWOOD. June, 1999. (Hopwood DePree) Hopwood DePree, Christine Elise, Victoria Haas, Richard Speight, Jr. Brenda Ballard.

THE LAST BOY SCOUT
WARNER BROS. December, 1991. (Tony Scott) Bruce Willis, Damon Wayans, Chelsea Field.

THE LAST BUS HOME
BEYOND FILMS. May, 1997. Irish. (Johnny Gogan) Annie Ryan, Brian O'Byrne, John Cronin, Barry Comerford, Anthony Brophy.

THE LAST BUTTERFLY
ARROW. August, 1993. Czech. (Karel Kachyna) Tom Courtenay, Brigitte Fossey, Ingrid Held.

LAST CALL
FUSION/WEINY/WOODWARD. October, 1995. (Rich Wilkes) Ben Afflek, French Stewart, Sam Rockwell.

LAST CALL
ROOS FILM S.A. Aug., 1999. Chilean. (Christine Lucas) Peter Coyote, Elizabeth Berkley, Garret Dillahunt, Elizabeth Rossa.

LAST CALL AT MAUD'S
MAUD'S PROJECT. March, 1993. (Paris Poirier) Documentary.

THE LAST CIGARETTE
NEW YORKER FILMS. Aug., 1999. (Kevin Rafferty). Documentary.

LAST DANCE
BUENA VISTA. April, 1996. (Bruce Beresford) Sharon Stone, Rob Morrow, Randy Quaid, Peter Gallagher, Jack Thompson.

THE LAST DANCE
EURO AMERICAN FILMS/PANAVAM. May, 1999. French-Indian. (Shaji Karun) Mohanlal, Suhasini, Mattanoor Shankara Marar, Kukku Parameshwaram, Venmani Haridas.

THE LAST DAYS
OCTOBER FILMS. Oct., 1998. (James Moll). Documentary.

THE LAST DAYS OF CHEZ NOUS
FINE LINE. February, 1993. Australian. (Gillian Armstrong) Lisa Harrow, Bruno Ganz, Kerry Fox.

THE LAST DAYS OF DISCO
GRAMERCY. April, 1998. (Whit Stillman) Chloe Sevigny, Kate Beckinsale, Chris Eigeman, Matt Keeslar, Mackenzie Astin.

THE LAST DAYS OF FRANKIE THE FLY
NU IMAGE. March, 1997. (Peter Markle) Dennis Hopper, Daryl Hannah, Michael Madsen, Kiefer Sutherland, Dayton Callie.

LAST EXIT TO BROOKLYN
CINECOM. May, 1990. West German-U.S. (Uli Edel) Stephen Lang, Jennifer Jason Leigh, Burt Young.

THE LAST GASP
CHANNEL 1 DRAMA. April, 1997. Swedish. (Ingmar Bergman) (director for TV: Mans Reutersward) Bjorn Granath, Ingvar Kjellson, Anna Von Rosen

THE LAST GOOD TIME
SAMUEL GOLDWYN. April, 1995. (Bob Balaban) Armin Mueller Stahl, Olivia d'Abo, Maureen Stapleton.

THE LAST KLEZMER
INDEPENDENT. August, 1994. (Yale Strom) Documentary.

LAST MAN STANDING
NEW LINE. September, 1996. (Walter Hill) Bruce Willis, Christopher Walken, Bruce Dern.

LAST NIGHT
CINEPLEX. May, 1998. Canadian. (Don McKellar) Don McKellar Sandra Oh, Callum Keith Rennie, Sarah Polley.

LAST OF THE DOGMEN
SAVOY. September, 1995. (Tab Murphy) Tom Berenger, Barbara Hershey, Steve Reevis.

LAST OF THE FINEST
ORION. March, 1990. (John Mackenzie) Brian Dennehy, Joe Pantoliano, Bill Paxton.

THE LAST OF THE HIGH KINGS
FIRST INDEPENDENT FILMS. Nov., 1996. Irish-British-Danish. (David Keating) Catherine O'Hara, Jared Leto, Christina Ricci.

THE LAST OF THE MOHICANS
20TH CENTURY FOX. September, 1992. (Michael Mann) Daniel Day-Lewis, Madeleine Stowe, Russell Means.

L.A. STORY
TRISTAR. February, 1991. (Mick Jackson) Steve Martin, Victoria Tennant, Richard E. Grant.

THE LAST PARTY
TRITON. August, 1993. (Mark Benjamin, Marc Levin) Robert Downey, Jr.

THE LAST SEDUCTION
OCTOBER FILMS. October, 1994. (John Dahl) Linda Fiorentino, Peter Berg, Bill Pullman. (Premiered on Showtime in July '94.)

THE LAST SEPTEMBER
TRIMARK. May, 1999. Irish-British-French. (Deborah Warner) Maggie Smith, Michael Gambon, Jane Birkin, Fiona Shaw, Lambert Wilson.

THE LAST SHOT
LES PIERIDES. Aug., 1999. Belgian. (Benoit Peeters) Florin Piersic, Jr., Manuela Servais, Mihai Dinvale, Pierre Arditi, Jean-Michel Jarre.

THE LAST STATION
DANIEL ZUTA FILMPRODUKTION/FILMEX ROMANIA/CDI. May, 1999. German-Romanian-Italian. (Bogdan (Dumitrescu) Dreyer) Sergio Rubini, Marion Kracht, Darel Visan.

LAST STOP PARADISE
MK2 DIFFUSION. Aug., 1998. French-Romanian. (Lucian Pintilie) Costel Cascaval, Dorina Chiriac, Gheorghe Visu, Victor Rebengiuc.

LAST SUMMER IN THE HAMPTONS
RAINBOW FILM. September, 1995. (Henry Jaglom) Victoria Foyt, Viveca Lindfors, Martha Plimpton, Roddy McDowall.

LAST SUPPER, THE
VAULT. October, 1995. (Stacy Title) Cameron Diaz, Ron Eldard, Annabeth Gish, Jonathan Penner, Courtney B. Vance.

THE LAST TIME I COMMITTED SUICIDE
KUSHNER-LOCKE CO./TAPESTRY FILMS. Jan., 1997. (Stephen Kay) Thomas Jane, Keanu Reeves, Tom Bower, Adrien Brody.

THE LAST YELLOW
SCALA PRODS./CAPITOL FILMS/HOLLYWOOD PARTNERS. Aug., 1999. British-German. (Julian Farino) Mark Addy, Charlie Creed-Miles, Samantha Morton, Kenneth Cranham, James Hooton.

LATCHO DROM
SHADOW DISTRIB. July, 1994. French. (Tony Gatlif) Documentary.

LATE AUGUST, EARLY SEPTEMBER
POLYGRAM. Sept., 1998., French. (Olivier Assayas) Mathieu Amalric, Virginie Ledoyen, Francois, Cluzet, Jeanne Balibar, Alex Descas.

LATE BLOOMERS
ONE MIND. January, 1996. (Julia Dyer, Gretchen Dyer) Connie Nelson, Dee Hennigan, Gary Carter.

LATE FOR DINNER
COLUMBIA. September, 1991. (W.D. Richter) Brian Wimmer, Peter Berg, Marcia Gay Harden.

LATE SHOW
CONSTANTIN FILM. Feb., 1999. German. (Helmut Dietl) Thomas Gottschalk, Harald Schmidt, Veronica Ferres, Jasmin Tabatabai, Olli Dittrich, Sabine Orleans.

LA TIGRA
INT'L FILM CIRCUIT. January, 1991. Ecuador (Camilo Luzuriaga) Lissette Cabrera, Rosanna Iturralde.

LATIN BOYS GO TO HELL
STRAND. June, 1997. U.S.-German-Spanish. (Ela Troyano) Irwin Ossa, John Bryant Davila, Jennifer Lee Simard, Alexis Artiles.

LAUGHING DEAD
ISHI ENTERTAINMENT. July, 1998. (Patrick Gleason) Patrick Gleason, John Hamond, Fern Finer Rico Cymone.

LAUTREC
LES FILMS DU LOSANGE. Aug., 1998. French-Spanish. (Roger Planchon) Regis Royer, Elsa Zylberstein, Anemone, Claude Rich.

LA VIE DE BOHEME
KINO. July, 1993. French-Finnish. (Aki Kurasmaki) Matti Pellonpaa, Evelyn Didi, Andre Wilms.

L.A. WITHOUT A MAP
DAN FILMS/EURO AMERICAN FILMS/MARIANNA FILMS. Sept., 1998. British-French-Finnish. (Mika Kaurismaki) David Tennant, Vinessa Shaw, Julie Delpy, Vincent Gallo, Cameron Bancroft.

LAW OF THE FRONTIER
UIP. January, 1996. Spanish. (Adolfo Aristarain) Pere Ponce, Achero Manas, Aitana Sanchez-Gijon.

LAWN DOGS
RANK FILM. Aug., 1997. British. (John Duigan) Sam Rockwell, Christopher McDonald, Kathleen Quinlan, Bruce McGill, Mischa Barton.

THE LAWNMOWER MAN
NEW LINE. March, 1992. (Brett Leonard) Jeff Fahey, Pierce Brosnan, Jenny Wright.

LAWNMOWER MAN 2: BEYOND CYBERSPACE
NEW LINE. January, 1996. (Farhad Mann) Patrick Bergen, Matt Frewer, Austin O'Brien.

LAWS OF GRAVITY
RKO. August, 1992. (Nick Gomez) Adam Trese, Peter Greene, Edie Falco.

LAYIN' LOW
SHOOTING GALLERY. Oct., 1996. (Danny Leiner) Jeremy Piven, Louise Lasser, Edie Falco, Frank John Hughes, Allana Ubach.

LEA
IVAN FILA FILMPRODUKTION/AVISTA FILM. Sept., 1996. German. (Ivan Fila) Lenka Vlasakova, Christian Redl, Hanna Schygulla.

LEAF ON A PILLOW
CHRISTINE HAKIM FILM. May, 1998. Indonesian. (Garin Nugroho) Kancil, Heru, Sugeng, Christine Hakim, Kabri Wali, Denny Christantra.

THE LEAFBLOWER
BLACK SHOE FILMS. March, 1998. (Dominic J. DeJoseph) Jon Hyrns, Marco Giudice, Charles Langley, Jeanne Foss, Paul Yates.

A LEAGUE OF THEIR OWN
COLUMBIA. July, 1992. (Penny Marshall) Tom Hanks, Geena Davis, Lori Petty, Madonna.

LEAP OF FAITH
PARAMOUNT. December, 1992. (Richard Pearce) Steve Martin, Debra Winger, Lukas Haas, Lolita Davidovich.

A LEAP OF FAITH
PARALLEL. January, 1996. (Jennifer McShane, Tricia Regan) Documentary.

THE LEARNING CURVE
MOTION PICTURE CORP. OF AMERICA. Aug., 1999. (Eric Schwab) Carmine Giovinazzo, Monet Mazur, Vincent Ventresca, Steven Bauer, Majandra Delfino.

LEATHER JACKET LOVE STORY
LEATHER JACKET PRODS. June, 1997. (David DeCoteau) Christopher Bradley, Sean Tataryn, Geoff Moody, Hector Mercado.

LEATHERFACE: TEXAS CHAINSAW MASSACRE III
NEW LINE. January, 1990. (Jeff Burr) Kate Hodge, Ken Foree, Viggo Mortensen.

LEAVE A LITTLE ONE
A LA SEPT/ARTE, AGAT FILMS & CIE. May, 1998. French. (Zaida Ghorab-Volta) Andree Damant, Aurelia Petit, Lise Payen.

LEAVING
SHOCHIKU CO. Feb., 1998. Japanese. (Masato Harada) Hitomi Sato, Yasue Sato, Yukiko Okamoto, Jun Murakami, Shin Yazawa.

LEAVING LAS VEGAS
MGM/UA. October, 1995. (Mike Figgis) Nicholas Cage, Elizabeth Shue, Julian Sands, Valerie Golino, Richard Lewis.

LEAVING NORMAL
UNIVERSAL. April, 1992. (Edward Zwick) Christine Lahti, Meg Tilly, Patrika Darbo.

LE DERRIERE
AMLF. Mar., 1999. French. (Valerie Lemercier) Valerie Lemercier, Claude Rich, Dieudonne, Marthe Keller, Patrick Catalifo.

LEFT LUGGAGE
TRIDENT. Feb., 1998. (Jeroen Krabbe) Laura Fraser, Isabella Rossellini, Maximilian Schell, Jeroen Krabbe, Marianne Sagebrecht.

LE GARCU
PAN-EUROPEENNE. October, 1995. French. (Maurice Pialat) Gerard Depardieu, Geralding Pailhas.

THE LEGACY: MURDER & MEDIA, POLITICS & PRISON
PORCH LIGHT. Jan., 1999. (Michael J. Moore). Documentary.

LEGEND OF WOLF MOUNTAIN
HEMDALE. November, 1992. (Craig Clyde) Bo Hopkins, Mickey Rooney, Robert Z'Dar.

LEGENDS OF THE FALL
TRISTAR. December, 1994. (Edward Zwick) Brad Pitt, Anthony Hopkins, Aidan Quinn, Julia Ormond.

LEILA
FARAZMAND. Feb., 1998. Iranian. (Dariush Mehrjui) Leila Hatami, Ali Mosaffa, Jamileh Sheikhi, Mohammad Reza Sharifinia.

THE LEMON SISTERS
MIRAMAX. August, 1990. (Joyce Chopra) Diane Keaton, Carol Kane, Kathryn Grody.

LENA'S DREAMS
OLYMPIA PICTURES/LENA'S FILM. April, 1997. (Heather Johnston) Marlene Forte, Gary Perez, Susan Peirez, Jeremiah Birkett.

L'ENFER
MK2. October, 1994. French. (Claude Chabrol) Emmanuelle Beart, Francois Cluzet, Nathalie Cardone.

LENINGRAD COWBOYS GO AMERICA
ORION CLASSICS. November, 1990. Finnish. (Aki Kaurismaki) Matti Pellonpaa, Heikki Keskinen.

LENNY BRUCE: SWEAR TO TELL THE TRUTH
WHYADUCK. Oct., 1998. (Robert B. Weide). Documentary.

LEO TOLSTOY'S ANNA KARENINA
WARNER BROS. March, 1997. (Bernard Rose), Sophie Marceau, Sean Bean, Alfred Molina, Mia Kirshner, James Fox, Fiona Shaw.

LEOLO
FINE LINE. April, 1993. French. (Jean Claude Lauzon) Gilbert Sicotte, Maxime Collin, Ginette Reno.

LEON THE PIG FARMER
CINEVISTA. September, 1993. British. (Vadim Jean, Gary Sinyor) Mark Frankel, Janet Suzman, Brian Glover.

LEPRECHAUN
TRIMARK. January, 1993. (Mark Jones) Warwick Davis, Jennifer Aniston, Ken Olandt.

LEPRECHAUN 2
TRIMARK. April, 1994. (Rodman Flender) Warwick Davis, Charlie Heath, Shevonne Durkin.

LES GRANDS DUCS
BAC FILMS. January, 1996. French. (Patrice Leconte) Phillipe Noiret, Michel Blanc.

LES LUMIERE DE BERLIN
LES FILMS DU LOSANGE. July, 1996. German. (Wim Wenders) Udo Kier, Nadine Buttner, Christoph Merg.

LES SANGUINAURES
LA SEPT ARTE/HAUT ET COURT PROD. Aug., 1997. French. (Laurent Cantet) Frederic Pierrot, Catherine Baugue.

L'ETAT SAUVAGE
INTERAMA. January, 1990. French (Francis Girod) Marie Christine Barrault, Claude Brasseur.

LETHAL WEAPON 3
WARNER BROS. May, 1992. (Richard Donner) Mel Gibson, Danny Glover, Joe Pesci, Rene Russo.

LETHAL WEAPON 4
WARNER BROS. July, 1998. Mel Gibson, Danny Glover, Joe Pesci, Rene Russo, Chris Rock, Jet Li, Steve Kahan, Kim Chan.

LET HIM HAVE IT
NEW LINE. December, 1991. British. (Peter Medak) Chris Eccleston, Paul Reynolds, Tom Courtenay.

LET'S GET LOST
PER HOLST FILM. Feb., 1998. Danish. (Jonas Elmer) Sidse Babett Knudsen, Bjarne Henriksen, Troels Lyby.

LET'S TALK ABOUT SEX
FINE LINE FEATURES. Sept., 1998. (Troy Beyer) Troy Beyer, Paget Brewster, Randi Ingerman, Joseph C. Phillips, Michaline Babich.

THE LETTER
MADRIAGIA FILMES. May, 1999. Portuguese-French-Spanish. (Manoel de Oliveira): Chiara Mastroianni, Pedro Abrunhosa, Antoine Chappey, Leonor Silveira, Francoise Fabian.

LETTER TO THE NEXT GENERATION
NEW DAY. May, 1990. (James Klein) Documentary.

LETTERS FROM THE PARK
FOX/LORBER. January, 1990. Cuban. (Tomas Futierrez) Victor Laplace, Ivonne Lopez.

LET THE DEVIL WEAR BLACK
TRIMARK. Jan, 1999. (Stacy Title) Jonathan Penner, Jacqueline Bisset, Mary-Louise Parker, Jamey Sheridan, Philip Baker Hall.

LET THERE BE LIGHT
ARZU FILMS. Oct., 1997. Turkish. (Reis Celik) Berhan Simsek, Tarik Tarcan, Sermin Karaali, Tuncel Kurtiz.

LET THERE BE LIGHT
AFMD. July, 1998. French. (Arthur Joffe) Helene de Fougerolles, Tcheky Karyo, Ticky Holgado.

LEVEL FIVE
LES FILMS DE L'ASTROPHORE/ARGOS FILMS/LA SEPT CINEMA/CANAL PLUS. Nov., 1996. French. (Chris Marker) Catherine Belkhodja, Kenji Tokitsu, Nagisa Oshima, Documentary.

LEVITATION
TENTH MUSE. April, 1997. (Scott D. Goldstein) Sarah Paulson, Ernie Hudson, Jeremy London, Ann Magnuson, Antonio Fargas.

LEWIS & CLARK & GEORGE
DAVIS ENTERTAINMENT CLASSICS & DARK MATTER PRODS. Jan., 1997. (Rod McCall) Rose McGowan, Salvator Xuereb.

LIABILITY CRISIS
FILMHAUS. June, 1995. (Richard Brody) Mirjana Jokovic, Jim Helsinger, Sheri Meg Seidman.

LIAR
MGM. August, 1997. (Jonas and Joshua Pate), Tim Roth, Chris Penn, Michael Rooker, Renee Zellweger, Ellen Burstyn, Rosanna Arquette.

LIAR LIAR
UNIVERSAL. March, 1997. (Tom Shadyac), Jim Carrey, Maura Tierney, Jennifer Tilly, Swoosie Kurtz, Amanda Donohoe.

LICENSE TO LIVE
DAIEI CO.. Feb., 1999. Japanese. (Kiyoshi Kurosawa) Hidetoshi Nishijima, Koji Yakusho, Shun Sugata, Lily, Kumiko Asou.

LICENSED TO KILL
DEEP FOCUS. Jan., 1997. (Arthur Dong) Documentary.

LIEBESTRAUM
MGM. September, 1991. (Mike Figgis) Kevin Anderson, Pamela Gidley, Kim Novak.

LIE DOWN WITH DOGS
MIRAMAX. June, 1995. (Wally White) Wally White, James Sexton, Randy Becker.

LIES
SHINCINE COMMUNICATIONS. Sept., 1999. South Korean. (Jang Sun Woo) Lee Sang Hyun, Kim Tae yeon, Jeon Hye Jin.

LIFE
UNIVERSAL. Apr., 1999. (Ted Demme) Eddie Murphy, Martin Lawrence, Obba Babatunde, Ned Beatty, Bernie Mac.

THE LIFE AND TIMES OF ALLEN GINSBERG
FIRST RUN. February, 1994. (Jerry Aronson) Documentary.

THE LIFE AND TIMES OF HANK GREENBERG
CIESLA FOUNDATION. June, 1999. (Aviva Kempner). Documentary.

LIFEBREATH
FIRST LOOK PICTURES. June, 1997. (P.J. Posner) Luke Perry, Francie Swift, Gia Carides.

LIFE IS A BLUFF
ZZ FILMS. May, 1997. German. (Peter Zingler) Mario Adorf, Elke Sommer, Ben Becker, Muriel Baumeister, Heinz Hoenig.

LIFE IS A LONG QUIET RIVER
MK2 PRODS. July, 1990. French. (Etienne Chatiliez) Benoit Magimel, Helene Vincent.

LIFE IS ALL YOU GET
SENATOR FILM. Feb., 1997. German. (Wolfgang Becker) Jurgen Vogel, Christiane Paul, Ricky Tomlinson, Christina Papamichou.

LIFE IS BEAUTIFUL
CECCHI GORI DISTRIBUZIONE. Dec., 1997. Italian. (Roberto Benigni) Roberto Benigni, Nicoletta Breaschi, Guistino Durano.

LIFE IS CHEAP ... BUT TOILET PAPER IS EXPENSIVE
SILVERLIGHT. August, 1990. Chinese. (Wayne Wang) Chan Kim Wan, Spencer Nakasako, Victor Wong.

LIFE IS SWEET
OCTOBER FILMS. October, 1991. British. (Mike Leigh) Alison Steadman, Jim Broadbent, Jane Horrocks.

LIFE IS THE MAIN THING
UFA FERNSEHPRODUKTION. May, 1999. German. (Connie Walther) Renee Soutenkijk, Hans-Werner Meyer, Huub Stapel, Isabel Trimborn, Rebecca Hessing.

LIFE IS WHISTLING
NIRVANA. JULY, 1999. Cuban-Spanish. (Fernando Perez) Luis Alberto Garcia, Coralia Veloz, Claudia Rojas, Bebe Perez, Isabel Santos.

A LIFE LESS ORDINARY
POLYGRAM/FOX SEARCHLIGHT. Oct., 1997. British. (Danny Boyle) Ewan McGregor, Cameron Diaz, Holly Hunter, Delroy Lindo, Ian Holm, Ian McNeice, Stanley Tucci, Dan Hedaya, Tony Shalhoub.

LIFE, LOVE & CELLULOID
RAINER WERNER FASSBINDER FOUNDATION. Feb., 1998. German. (Juliane Lorenz) documentary.

THE LIFE OF JESUS
TADRART FILMS. April, 1997. French. (Bruno Dumont) David Douche, Marjorie Cottreel, Genevieve Cottreel, Kader Chaatouf.

LIFE ON A STRING
KINO. January, 1992. German-Japanese-British-Mandarin. (Chen Kaige) Liu Zhongyuan, Huang Lei.

LIFE ON EARTH
A HAUT ET COURT DISTRIBUTION. May, 1998. French. (Abderrahmane Sissako) Abderrahmane Sissako, Nana Baby, Mohamed Sissako.

LIFE ON THE EDGE
FESTIVAL ENT. June, 1992. (Andrew Yates) Jeff Perry, Jennifer Holmes, Andrew Prine.

LIFE STINKS
MGM. July, 1991. (Mel Brooks) Mel Brooks, Lesley Ann Warren, Jeffrey Tambor.

THE LIFESTYLE
GOOD MACHINE. Apr., 1999. (David Schisgall). Documentary.

LIFE TASTES GOOD
LIFE TASTES GOOD PRODS. Jan. 1999. (Philip Kan Gotanda) Sab Shimono, Julia Nickson, Tamlyn Tomita, Greg Watanabe.

LIFE WITH MIKEY
BUENA VISTA. June, 1993. (James Lapine) Michael J. Fox, Christina Vidal, Nathan Lane.

LIGHT SLEEPER
FINE LINE. August, 1992. (Paul Schrader) Willem Dafoe, Susan Sarandon, Dana Delany.

LIGHTNING JACK
SAVOY. March, 1994. Australian. (Simon Wincer) Paul Hogan, Cuba Gooding Jr., Beverly D'Angelo.

LIKE A FISH OUT OF WATER
SOCIETE NOUVELLE DE DISTRIBUTION/CLT-UFA. May, 1999. French. (Herve Hadmar) Tcheky Karyo, Monica Bellucci, Dominque Pinon, Michel Muller, Mehmet Ulusoy.

LIKE IT IS
DANGEROUS TO KNOW. May, 1998. British. (Paul Oremland) Roger Daltrey, Dani Behr, Ian Rose, Steve Bell.

LIKE WATER FOR CHOCOLATE
MIRAMAX. February, 1993. Mexican. (Alfonso Arau) Lumi Cavazos, Marco Leonardi, Pegina Torne.

LILA LILI
GEMINI FILMS/LA SEPT CINEMA. Feb., 1999. French. (Marie Vermillard) Alexia Monduit, Genevieve Tenne, Simon Abkarian, Zinedine Soualem, Antoine Chappey.

LIMBO
SONY. May, 1999. (John Sayles) Mary Elizabeth Mastrantonio, David Strathairn, Vanessa Martinez, Kris Kristofferson.

LIMITE
MOMA. August, 1992. Brazilian, 1932. (Mario Peixoto) Silent. B&W.

THE LIMITS OF THERMAL TRAVELLING
BLUESTORM INTERNATIONAL. October, 1995. (Mark Bender) David Jacob Ryder, Cullen Douglas, Robin Krasny.

THE LINGUINI INCIDENT
ACADEMY ENTERTAINMENT. May, 1992. (Richard Shepard) Rosanna Arquette, David Bowie, Eszter Balint.

LIONHEART
UNIVERSAL. January, 1991. (Sheldon Lettich) Jean Claude Van Damme, Harrison Page, Deborah Rennard.

THE LION KING
BUENA VISTA. June, 1994. (Roger Allers, Rob Minkoff) Animated.

THE LION KING II: SIMBA'S PRIDE.
BUENA VISTA. Oct., 1998. (Darrell Rooney).Animated.

LIPSTICK CAMERA
TRIBORO. March, 1994. (Mike Bonifer) Brian Wimmer, Ele Keats, Corey Feldman.

LIQUID DREAMS
NORTHERN ARTS. April, 1992. (Mark Manos) Candice Daly, Richard Steinmetz, Juan Fernandez.

LISA
MGM/UA. April, 1990. (Gary Sherman) Cheryl Ladd, Staci Keanan, D. W. Moffett.

LISBON
ALTA FILMS. June, 1999. Spanish-Argentine. (Antonio Hernandez).

LISTEN
ORION PICTURES. September, 1996. (Gavin Wilding) Brooke Langton, Sarah Buxton, Gordon Currie.

LISTEN UP: THE LIVES OF QUINCY JONES
WARNER BROS. October, 1990. (Ellen Weissbrod) Documentary.

LITTLE BIG LEAGUE
COLUMBIA. June, 1994. (Andrew Scheinman) Luke Edwards, Timothy Busfield, John Ashton.

LITTLE BIRD
PRIMA FILM. Aug., 1997. Spanish. (Carlos Saura) Alejandro Martinez, Dafne Fernandez, Francisco Rabal, Manuel Bandera.

LITTLE BOY BLUE
JAZZ PICTURES. May, 1997. (Antonio Tibaldi) Ryan Phillippe, Nastassja Kinski, John Savage, Tyrin Turner, Jenny Lewis.

LITTLE BROTHERS
MK2 DIFFUSION. Feb., 1999. French. (Jacques Doillon) Stephanie Touly, Ilies Sefraoui, Mustapha Goumane, Nassim Izem, Rachid Mansouri.

LITTLE BUDDHA
MIRAMAX. May, 1994. (Bernardo Bertolucci) Keanu Reeves, Chris Isaak, Bridget Fonda, Ying Ruocheng.

LITTLE CITY
MIRAMAX. April, 1997. (Roberto Benabib), Jon Bon Jovi, Penelope Ann Miller, Josh Charles, Annabella Sciorra, JoBeth Williams.

LITTLE GIANTS
WARNER BROS. October, 1994. (Duwayne Dunham) Rick Moranis, Ed O'Neill, John Madden.

LITTLE GIRLS
ARENA FILMS. LA SEPT ARTE. Nov., 1998. French. (Noemie Lvovsky) Magalie Woch, Ingrid Molinier, Julie-Marie Parmentier, Camille Rousselet, Jean Luc Bideau.

THE LITTLE GIRL WHO SOLD 'THE SUN'
MAAG DAAN/WAKA FILMS/RENARDES PRODS. Feb., 1999. Senegalese-Swiss-French. (Dijibril Diop Mambety) Lissa Balera.

A LITTLE LIFE-OPERA
GREAT ROOT/FUJIAN FILM STUDIO. Feb., 1997. Hong Kong-Chinese. (Allen Fong) Winston Chao, Yang Kuei-mei, Zeng Jingping.

LITTLE MAN TATE
ORION. October, 1991. (Jodie Foster) Jodie Foster, Dianne Wiest, Adam Hann Byrd, Harry Connick, Jr.

LITTLE MEN
LEGACY. May, 1998. (Rodney Gibbons) Michael Caloz, Mariel Hemingway, Ben Cook, Ricky Mabe, Chris Sarandon, Gabrielle Boni.

LITTLE MIRACLES
SPANISH TELEVISION SERVICES. April, 1998. Argentine. (Eliseo Subiela) Julieta Ortega, Antonio Birabent, Monica Galan, Paco M.

LITTLE NEMO: ADVENTURES IN SLUMBERLAND
HEMDALE. August, 1992. Japanese. (Masami Hata, William T. Hurtz) Animated.

LITTLE NOISES
MONUMENT PICTURES. April, 1992. (Jane Spencer) Crispin Glover, Tatum O'Neal, Rik Mayall.

LITTLE ODESSA
FINE LINE. May, 1995. (James Gray) Tim Roth, Maximilian Schell, Edward Furlong.

A LITTLE PRINCESS
WARNER BROS. May, 1995. (Alfonso Cuaron) Liesel Matthews, Eleanor Bron, Liam Cunningham.

THE LITTLE RASCALS
UNIVERSAL. August, 1994. (Penelope Spheeris) Travis Tedford, Bug Hall, Brittany Ashton Holmes.

LITTLE TEACHERS
CECCHI GORI DISTRIBUZIONE. Aug., 1998. Italian. (Daniele Luchetti) Stefano Accorsi, Stefania Montorsi, Giorgio Pasotti.

LITTLE THIEVES, BIG THIEVES
ALEJANDRO SADERMAN PRODS., CNAC, CINEMATERIALES, POST HOUSE/LICHTBLICK/TNT AMERICA LATINA. Sept., 1998. Venezuelan-German-U.S. (Alejandro Saderman) Orlando Urdaneta, Daniel Lugo.

LITTLE TONY
WARNER BROS. May, 1998. Dutch. (Alex van Warmerdam) Annet Malherbe, Ariane Schluter, Alex van Warmerdam.

LITTLE TROPICANA
ICAIC/BMG INTL. Sept., 1998. Cuban-Spanish-German. (Daniel Diaz Torres) Peter Lohmeyer, Vladimir Cruz, Corina Mestre, Thais Vlades.

LITTLE VEGAS
I.R.S. RELEASING. November, 1990. (Perry Land) Anthony John Denison, Catherine O'Hara, Ann Francis.

LITTLE WOMEN
COLUMBIA. December, 1994. (Gillian Armstrong) Winona Ryder, Gabriel Byrne, Trini Alvarado.

LIVE FLESH
MGM/CIBY DISTRIBUTION/WARNER ESPANOLA. Sept., 1997. French-Spanish. (Pedro Almodovar) Javier Bardem, Francesca Neri.

LIVE IN PEACE
PEARL RIVER FILM STUDIO. June, 1998. Chinese. (Hu Bingliu) Pan Yu, Bai Xueyun, Sun Min, Wang Hong, Huang Jinchang.
"T.C." Carson, Lisa Arrindell, Blanche Baker.

LIVING DREAM
CELESTIAL MEDIA ORGANIZATION. May, 1996. Chinese. (Hu Xueyang) Jindao Xinxin, Zhang Mengxi.

THE LIVING END
OCTOBER FILMS. August, 1992. (Gregg Araki) Mike Dytri, Craig Gilmore, Darcy Marta.

LIVING IN OBLIVION
SONY PICTURES CLASSICS. July, 1995. (Tom DiCillo) Steve Buscemi, Catherine Keener, Dermot Mulroney.

LIVING IN PARADISE
3B PRODS./ALINEA FILM/EXPOSED FILMS/WFE. Sept., 1998. French-Belgian-Norwegian-Algerian. (Bourlem Guerdjou) Roschdy Zem, Fadila Belkebla, Omar Bekhaled, Farida Rahouadj.

THE LIVING MUSEUM
LIVING FILMWORKS. Jan. 1999. (Jessica Yu). Documentary.

LIVING OUT LOUD
NEW LINE CINEMA. Sept., 1998. (Richard LaGravenese) Holly Hunter, Danny DeVito, Queen Latifah, Martin Donovan, Elias Koteas.

LIVING PROOF: H.I.V. AND THE PURSUIT OF HAPPINESS
FIRST RUN. February, 1994. (Kermit Cole) Documentary.

LIVING TO DIE
PM ENTERTAINMENT. September, 1990. (Wings Hauser) Wings Hauser, Darcy DeMoss, Asher Brauner.

LIVIN' LARGE
SAMUEL GOLDWYN. September, 1991. (Michael Schultz) Terrence

LOBSTER MAN FROM MARS
ELECTRIC PICTURES. February, 1990. (Stanley Sheff) Tony Curtis, Deborah Foreman.

LOCH NESS
GRAMERCY. February, 1996. British. (John Henderson) Ted Danson, Joely Richardson, Ian Hom.

LOCKED UP TIME
ZEITGEIST. May, 1992. German. (Sibylle Schonemann) Documentary. B&W.

LOCK, STOCK AND TWO SMOKING BARRELS
POLYGRAM FILMED ENTERTAINMENT. July, 1998. British. (Guy Ritchie) Jason Flemyng, Dexter Fletcher, Nick Moran, Jason Statham.

THE LOCUSTS
MGM. August, 1997. (John Patrick Kelley), Kate Capshaw, Jeremy Davies, Vince Vaughn, Ashely Judd, Paul Rudd, Daniel Meyer.

LOLA + BILIDIKID
ZERO FILM. Feb., 1999. German. (Kutlug Ataman) Gandi Mukli, Erdal Yildiz, Baki Davrak, Inge Keller, Celal Perk.

LOLITA
AMLF. Sept., 1997. (Adrian Lyne) Jeremy Irons, Melanie Griffith, Frank Langella, Dominique Swain, Suzanne Shepherd.

LONDON
ZEITGEIST. September, 1994. British. (Patrick Keiller) Documentary.

LONDON KILLS ME
FINE LINE. August, 1992. British. (Hanif Kureishi) Justin Chadwick, Steven Mackintosh, Fiona Shaw.

LONE STAR
SONY PICTURES CLASSICS. March, 1996. (John Sayles) Chris Cooper, Elizabeth Pena, Joe Morton, Kris Kristofferson.

LONELY WOMAN SEEKS LIFE COMPANION
IFEX. March, 1990. Russian, (Vyacheslav Krishtofovich) Irina Kupchenko, Aleksandr Zbruyev

THE LONG DAY CLOSES
SONY PICTURES CLASSICS. May, 1993. British. (Terence Davies) Leigh McCormack, Marjorie Yates, Anthony Watson.

LONG DAY'S JOURNEY INTO NIGHT
CINEPLEX ODEON. Sept., 1996. Canadian. (David Wellington) William Hutt, Martha Henry, Tom McCamus, Peter Donaldson.

THE LONGEST SUMMER
TEAM WORK PRODUCTION HOUSE. Feb., 1999. Hong Kong. (Fruit Chan) Tony Ho, Sam Lee, Jo Kuk, Chan Sang, Pang Yick-wai,.

LONG HELLO AND SHORT GOODBYE
WARNER BROS.. June, 1999. German. (Rainer Kaufmann) Nicholette Krebitz, Marc Hosemann, Sunnyi Melles, Axel Milberg, Dietrich Hollinderbaumer.

THE LONG JOURNEY
GIAI PHONG FILMS STUDIO. Jan., 1998. Vietnamese. (Le Hoang) Moc Mien, Cong Minh, My Duyen.

A LONG JOURNEY TO GUADALUPE
INSTITUTO NACIONAL INDIGENISTA. Jan., 1997. Mexican. (Juan Francisco Urrusti) Documentary.

THE LONG KISS GOODNIGHT
NEW LINE. October, 1996. (Renny Harlin) Geena Davis, Samuel L. Jackson, G.D. Spradlin, Patrick Malahide.

LONG LIVE LIFE
BHAVE-SUKTHANKAR. Sept., 1998. Indian. (Sumitra Bhave, Sunil Sukthankar) Om Puri, Meeta Vashishta, Milind Gunaji, Uttara Baokar.

LONG LIVE THE QUEEN
CONCORDE FILMS. Sept., 1996. Dutch. (Esme Lammers) Monique van de Ven, Tiba Tossijn, Derek de Lint, Jack Wouterse.

LITHIUM
CARAVAN. Aug., 1999. Swedish. (David Flamhole) Agnieszka Doson, Fredrik Dolk, Johna Widerberg, Pierre Boutros, Yvonne Lombard.

LONG TIME SINCE
LUCIUS FILMS/BERGMAN LUSTIG. Sept., 1998. (Jay Anania) Paulina Porizkova, Julian Sands, Julianne Nicholson.

THE LONG WALK HOME
MIRAMAX. December, 1990. (Richard Pearce) Sissy Spacek, Whoopi Goldberg, Dwight Schultz.

THE LONG WAY HOME
MORIAH FILMS. Jan., 1997. (Mark Jonathan) Documentary.

LONG WEEKEND (O' DESPAIR)
DESPERATE PICTURES. June, 1990. (Gregg Araki) Bretton Vail, Maureen Dondanville.

LONGTIME COMPANION
SAMUEL GOLDWYN. May, 1990. (Norman Rene). Campbell Scott, Bruce Davison, Mark Lamos.

LOOK WHO'S TALKING NOW
TRISTAR. November, 1993. (Tom Ropelewski) John Travolta, Kirstie Alley, Olympia Dukakis.

LOOK WHO'S TALKING TOO
TRISTAR. December, 1990. (Amy Heckerling) John Travolta, Kirstie Alley, Elias Koteas.

LOOKING FOR PARADISE
MEDUSA. December, 1995. Italian. (Mario Monicelli) Margherita Buy, Lello Arena, Philippe Noiret.

LOOKING FOR RICHARD
FOX SEARCHLIGHT. January, 1996. (Al Pacino) Al Pacino, Harris Yulin, Penelope Allen, Alec Baldwin, Kevin Spacey, .

LOOSE CANNONS
TRISTAR. February, 1990. (Bob Clark) Gene Hackman, Dan Aykroyd, Dom DeLuise.

LOOSE ENDS
LUNA-FILM GmbH. June, 1996. German. (Sandra Nettlebeck) Regula Grauwiller, Jasmin Tabatabai, Natascha Bub.

LOOSE ENDS
FRAMELINE. Apr., 1999. German. (Sandra Nettelbeck) Regula Grauwiller, Jasmin Tabatabai, Natascha Bub, Andreas Herde.

LOOSE WOMEN
INMOTION ENTERTAINMENT. Nov., 1996. (Paul F. Bernard) Sherry Ham, Melissa Errico, Marialisa Costanzo, Corey Glover.

LORD OF ILLUSIONS
MGM/UA. August, 1995. (Clive Barker) Scott Bakula, Kevin J. O'Connor, Famke Janssen.

LORD OF THE FLIES
COLUMBIA. March, 1990. (Harry Hook) Balthazar Getty, Chris Furrh, Danuel Pipoly.

THE LORD'S LANTERN IN BUDAPEST
KREATIV MEDIA MUHELY/3J+1BT. Feb., 1999. Hungarian. (Miklos Jancso) Zoltan Mucsi, Peter Scherer, Miklos Jancso, Gyula Hernadi, Emese Vasvari.

LORENZO'S OIL
UNIVERSAL. December, 1992. (George Miller) Nick Nolte, Susan Sarandon, Zack O'Malley Greenburg.

LOS LOCOS
GRAMERCY. Aug., 1997. (Jean-Marc Vallee) Mario Van Pebbles, Melora Walters, Rene Auberjonois, Paul Lazar, Danny Trejo.

LOSER
EDGE CINEMA. March, 1996. (Kirk Harris) Harris, Jonathan Chaus, Norman Saleet, Peta Wilson.

LOS ENCHILADAS!
EXPAND PRODS. Jan., 1999. (Mitch Hedberg) Mitch Hedberg, Jana Johnson, Brian Malow, Dave Attell, Marc Maron.

LOSING CHASE
SHOWTIME. January, 1996. (Kevin Bacon) Helen Mirren, Kyra Sedgwick, Beau Bridges, Michael Yarmush.

LOSING ISAIAH
PARAMOUNT. March, 1995. (Stephen Gyllenhaal) Jessica Lange, Halle Berry, David Strathairn.

THE LOSS OF SEXUAL INNOCENCE
SONY. Jan., 1999. (Mike Figgis) Julian Sands, Saffron Burrows, Stefano Dionisi, Johnathan Rhys-Meyers, Kelly MacDonald.

LOST & FOUND
WARNER BROS. APR., 1999. (Jeff Pollack) David Spade, Sophie Marceau, Patrick Bruel, Artie Lange, Mitchell Whitfieldk.

LOST AND FOUND
ML PRODS. June, 1998. (Ron Burrus) Michael Landes, Hedy Burress, Dina Spybey, Lane Smith, Geoffrey Blake, Lenny Clarke, John Shea.

THE LOST GARDEN
THE LIFE AND CINEMA OF ALICE GUY-BLANCHE
NATIONAL FILM BOARD OF CANADA. November, 1995. Canadian. (Marquise LePage) Documentary.

LOST IN SPACE
NEW LINE CINEMA. April, 1998. (Stephen Hopkins) William Hurt, Mimi Rogers, Heather Graham, Gary Oldman, Matt LeBlanc.

LOST PARADISE
ALLAINCE. Aug., 1997. Japanese. (Yoshimitsu Morita) Koji Yakusho, Hitomi Kuroki, Akira Terao, Toshio Shiba, Tomoko Hoshino.

LOST PROPHET
ROCKVILLE PICTURES. June, 1992. (Michael de Avila) James Burton, Zandra Huston, Drew Morone. B&W.

THE LOST SON
BAC FILMS/UIP-THE FILM CONSORTIUM. Apr., 1999. British-French. (Chris Menges) Daniel Auteuil, Natassja Kinski, Katrin Cartlidge, Ciaran Hinds, Marianne Denicourt.

THE LOST WORDS
FILM CRASH. September, 1994. (Scott Saunders) Michael Kaniecki, Bob McGrath, Zelda Gergel.

THE LOST WORLD: JURASSIC PARK
UNIVERSAL. May, 1997. (Steven Spielberg), Jeff Goldblum, Julianne Moore, Pete Postlethwaite, Arliss Howard, Richard Attenborough.

LOUISE (TAKE 2)
INITIAL PRODS./STUDIO CANAL PLUS/CINE VALSE. June, 1998. French. Elodie Bouchez, Roschdy Zem, Gerald Thomassin.

LOVE AFFAIR
WARNER BROS. October, 1994. (Glenn Gordon) Warren Beatty, Annette Bening, Katharine Hepburn.

LOVE AFTER LOVE
RAINBOW. July, 1994. French. (Diane Kurys) Isabelle Huppert, Bernard Giraudeau, Hippolyte Girardot.

LOVE ALWAYS
CINEWEST. Nov., 1996. (Jude Pauline Eberhard) Marisa Ryan, Moon Zappa, James Victor, Michael Reilly Burke, Dough Hutchinson.

LOVE AND A .45
TRIMARK. November, 1994. (C.M. Talkington) Gil Bellows, Renee Zellweger, Rory Cochrane, Jeffrey Combs.

LOVE & CRIME
KINOPRODUCTION OY. Feb., 1999. Finnish. (Pekka Milonoff) Kai Lehtinen, Tiina Lymi, Tomi Salmela, Maija Junno Pekka Valkeejarvi.

LOVE AND DEATH ON LONG ISLAND
SKYLINE FILMS/IMAGEX. May, 1997. British-Canadian. (Richard Kwietniowski) John Hurt, Jason Priestly, Fiona Loewi.

LOVE AND HUMAN REMAINS
SONY PICTURES CLASSICS. June, 1995. Canadian. (Denys Arcand) Thomas Gibson, Cameron Bancroft, Ruth Marshall.

LOVE AND MURDER
HEMDALE/SOUTHPAW. November, 1991. Canadian. (Steven Hilliard Stern) Todd Waring, Kathleen Lasky, Ron White.

LOVE AT LARGE
ORION. March, 1990. (Alan Rudolph) Tom Berenger, Elizabeth Perkins, Anne Archer.

LOVE CASE
SMART EGG PICTURES. May, 1996. Italian. (Riccardo Sesani) Stephane Ferrara, Marina Giulia Cavalli.

LOVE CRIMES
MILLIMETER FILMS. January, 1992. (Lizzie Borden) Sean Young, Patrick Bergen, Arnetia Walker.

LOVED
CROSSLIGHT/MDP WORLDWIDE. June, 1997. (Erin Dignam) Robin Wright Penn, William Hurt, Amy Madigan, Lucinda Jenney.

LOVE FIELD
ORION. December, 1992. (Jonathan Kaplan) Michelle Pfeiffer, Dennis Haysbert, Stephanie McFadden.

LOVE FOOLS
SONET. Oct., 1998. Swedish. (Leif Magnusson) Tomas von Bromssen, Anna Wallander, Ia Langhammer, Mikael Persbrandt, Matar Samba.

LOVE FROM GROUND ZERO
SANDBOX FILMS. Oct., 1998. (Stephen Grynberg) Pruitt Taylor-Vince, Simon Baker-Denny, Jacqueline McKenzie, Kathryne Erbe.

LOVE GOD
JAMES SCHAMUS & TED HOPE. Jan., 1997. (Frank Grow) Will Keenan, Yukio Yamoto, Michael Laurence, Kimberli Ghee.

LOVE GO GO
CENTRAL MOTION PICTURE CORP./SPRING CINEMA AGENCIES/ZOOM HUNT INTL.. Sept., 1998. Taiwanese. (Chen Yu-hsun) Tang Na, Eli Shih, Chen Cheng-hsin, Liao Hui-jen, Huang Tsi-chiao.

LOVE HAPPENS
CURB ENTERTAINMENT. June, 1999. (Tony Cookson) Megyn Price, Ken Marino, Jenica Bergere, Ryan Bollman, Elizabeth Lackey.

LOVE INC.
QUIMERA FILMES. Feb., 1998. Brazilian. (Helvecio Ratton) Marco Nanini, Patricia Pillar, Alexandre Borges.

LOVE IN THE MIRROR
FACTORY/G.M.F. Sept., 1999. Italian. (Salvatore Maira) Anna Galiena, Peter Stormare, Simona Cavallari, Jacques Sernas, Maurizio Micheli.

LOVE IS ALL THERE IS
TRIDENT. May, 1996. (Renee Taylor) Lainie Kazan, Joseph Bologna, Barbara Carrera.

LOVE IS THE DEVIL
STRAND RELEASING (U.S.)/ARTIFICAL EYE (U.K.). May, 1998. British. (John Maybury) Derek Jacobi, Daniel Craig, Tilda Swinton.

LOVE JONES
NEW LINE. January, 1997. (Theodore Witcher), Larenz Tate, Nia Long, Isaiah Washington, Lisa Nicole Carson, Khalil Kain.

LOVE KILLS
TRIDENT. May, 1998. (Mario Van Peebles) Mario Van Peebles, Lesley Ann Warren, Daniel Baldwin, Donovan Leitch, Alexis Arquette.

THE LOVE LESSON
GREYTAK. Oct., 1996. (Sharon Greytak) Stephen Delot, Teresa Vicario, Ruth Hackett, Tara Milutis, Eve Annsol, John Reidy.

THE LOVE LETTER
DREAMWORKS. May, 1999. (Peter Ho-Sun) Kate Capshaw, Blythe Danner, Ellen DeGeneres, Geraldine McEwan, Julian Nicholson.

THE LOVE MACHINE
CRYSTAL PICTURES. Apr., 1999. (Gordon Ericksen) Marlene Forte, Gary Perez, Tomo Omori, Jun Suenaga, Elizabeth Wunsch.

THE LOVEMASTER
ROCKET PICTURES. Sept., 1997. (Michael Goldberg) Craig Shoemaker, Farrah Fawcett, Courtney Thorne-Smith, Harley Jane Kozak.

LOVE OR MONEY
HEMDALE. January, 1990. (Todd Hallowell) Timothy Daly, Michael Garin, Kevin McCarthy.

LOVE POTION NO. 9
20TH CENTURY FOX. November, 1992. (Dale Launer) Tate Donovan, Sandra Bullock, Mary Mara.

LOVERS
TOLODA & BAR-NOTHING. May, 1999. French. (Jean-Marc Barr) Elodie Bouchez, Sergei Trifunovic, Genevieve Page, Dragan Nicolic, Thibault de Montalembert.

THE LOVER
MGM. October, 1992. French. (Jean Jacques Annaud) Jane March, Tony Leung, Frederique Meininger.

LOVER GIRL
DREAM ENTERTAINMENT. Sept., 1997. (Lisa Addario, Joe Syracuse) Sandra Bernhard, Kristy Swanson, Tara Subkoff.

LOVERS
ARIES. March, 1992. Spanish. (Vicente Aranda) Victoria Abril, Jorge Sanz, Maribel Verdu.

LOVER'S KNOT
SHOWCASE ENTERTAINMENT. May, 1996. (Peter Shaner) Bill Campbell, Jennifer Grey, Tim Curry.

THE LOVERS OF THE ARCTIC CIRCLE
SOGETEL. July, 1998. Spanish. (Julio Medem) Najwa Nimri, Fele Martinez, Nancho Novo, Maru Valdiviesio, Peru Medem.

LOVE SCENES FROM PLANET EARTH
BUENA VISTA INTL. Feb., 1999. German. (Marc Rothemund) Christoph Waltz, Ann-Kathrin Kramer, Heio von Stetten, Michaela May, Anica Dobra, Dieter Landuris.

LOVE'S DEBRIS
MC4 AND IMALYRE/VTCOM. Oct., 1996. German-French. (Werner Schroeder) Documentary.

LOVE STINKS
INDEPENDENT ARTISTS. Sept. 1999. (Jeff Franklin) French Stewart, Bridgette Wilson, Bill Bellamy, Tyra Banks, Steve Hytner.

LOVE STORY WITH CRAMPS
CECCHI GORI. January, 1996. Italian. (Pino Quartullo) Sergio Rubini, Chiara Caselli, Debora Caprioglio, Rosella Falk.

LOVE TANGLES
AB FILMS DISTRIBUTION. Feb., 1998. French-Swiss-Spanish. (Olivier Peray) Bruno Putzulu, Smadi Wolfman, Vincent Elbaz.

LOVE! VALOUR! COMPASSION!
FINE LINE. January, 1997. (Joe Mantello), Jason Alexander, Randy Becker, Stephen Bogardus, John Glover, John Benjamin Hickey.

LOVE WILL TEAR US APART
TONY LEUNG PRODS.. May, 1999. Hong Kong. (Nelson Yu Lik-wai) Tony Leung Kar-fai, Lu Liping, Wang Ning, Rolf Chow.

LOVE WITHOUT PITY
ORION CLASSICS. May, 1991. French. (Eric Rochant) Hippolyte Girardot, Mireille Perrier, Yvan Attal.

LOVE YOUR MAMA
HEMDALE. March, 1993. (Ruby L. Oliver) Carol E. Hall, Audrey Morgan, Andre Robinson.

LOVE YOUR NEIGHBOR!
DELPHI FILMVERLEIH. May, 1999. German. (Detlev Buck) Moritz Bleibtreu, Lea Mornar, Heike Makatsch, Marc Hosemann, Heribert Sasse.

A LOW DOWN DIRTY SHAME
BUENA VISTA. November, 1994. (Keenen Ivory Wayans) Wayans, Charles S. Dutton, Jada Pinkett.

L.627
KINO. July, 1994. French. (Bertrand Tavernier) Didier Bezace, Jean Paul Comart, Cecile Garcia Fogel.

LUCIE AUBRAC
AMLF. Feb., 1997. French. (Claude Berri) Carole Bouquet, Daniel Auteuil, Patrice Chereau, John-Roger Milo, Eric Boucher.

LUCIGNOLO
CECCHI GORI. Mar., 1999. Italian. (Massimo Ceccherini) Massimo Ceccherini, Claudia Gernin, Alessandro Paci, Flavio Bucci, Cosetta Mercatelli.

LUCINDA'S SPELL
ZERO PICTURES. May, 1998. (Jon Jacobs) Jon Jacobs, Christina Fulton, Shannah Battz, Leon Herbert, Angie Green, Alex Koromzay.

LUCK OR COINCIDENCE
FILM 13/TF1 FILMS/UGC IMAGES/NEUILLY/SDA. Sept., 1998. French-Canadian. (Claude Lelouch) Alessandra Martines, Pierre Arditi, Marc Hollogne, Geoffrey Holder, Laurent Hilare.

LUCKY STAR
ALTA FILMS. May, 1997. Spanish-French-Italian. (Ricardo Franco) Antonio Resines, Maribel Verdu, Jordi Molla, Elvira Minguez.

LULU
ALLIANCE. May, 1996. Canadian. (Srinivas Krishna) Kim Lieu, Clark Johnson, Michael Rhoades.

LULU ON THE BRIDGE
CAPITOL FILMS. May, 1998. (Paul Auster) Harvey Keitel, Mira Sorvino, Willem Dafoe, Gina Gershon, Mandy Patinkin, Vanessa Redgrave.

LUMIERE AND COMPANY
CINETEVE. November, 1995. French. (Sarah Moon) Documentary.

LUMINOUS MOTION
FIONA FILMS. Aug., 1998. (Bette Gordon) Eric Lloyd, Deborah Kara Unger, Terry Kinney, Jamey Sheridan, James Berland.

LUNA PARK
NORTHERN ARTS. January, 1994. Russian. (Pavel Lounguine) Oleg Borisov, Andrei Goutine, Natalya Yegorova.

THE LUNATIC
TRITON. February, 1992. (Lol Creme) Julie T. Wallace, Paul Campbell, Reggie Carter.

LUST AND REVENGE
SEAWELL FILMS. March, 1996. Australian. (Paul Cox) Nicholas Hope, Gosia Dobrowolska, Claudia Karvan.

LUST FOR LIFE
ARTHAUS FILMVERLEIH. Feb., 1999. German. (Oskar Roehler) Jasmin Tabatabai, Richy Mueller, Gregor Toerzs, Nele Mueller-Stoefen, Eva Hassmann.

M

MAACHIS
PAN PICTURES. May, 1997. Indian. (Gulzar) Chandrachur Singh, Tabu, Om Puri.

MAC
SAMUEL GOLDWYN. February, 1993. (John Turturro) John Turturro, Michael Badalucco, Carl Capotorto.

MACADAM TRIBE
MERCURE DISTRIBUTION. May, 1996. Zairian-French. (Jose Laplaine) Lydia Ewande, Hassane Kouyate, Sidy Camara.

MACBETH IN MANHATTAN
AMBER WAVES. Mar., 1999. (Greg Lombardo) Gloria Reuben, David Lansbury, Nick Gregory, John Glover, Harold Perrineau.

MACK THE KNIFE
21ST CENTURY FILMS. February, 1990. (Menahem Golan) Raul Julia, Richard Harris, Julia Migenes.

MAD CITY
WARNER BROS. Oct., 1997. (Costa-Gavras) John Travolta, Dustin Hoffman, Mia Kirshner, Alan Alda, Robert Prosky, Blythe Danner.

MAD DOG AND GLORY
UNIVERSAL. March, 1993. (John McNaughton) Robert De Niro, Uma Thurman, Bill Murray, David Caruso.

MAD DOG TIME
MGM/UA. November, 1996. (Larry Bishop), Ellen Barkin, Gabriel Byrne, Richard Dreyfuss, Jeff Goldblum, Diane Lane, Gregory Hines.

MAD LOVE
BUENA VISTA. May, 1995. (Antonia Bird) Chris O'Donnell, Drew Barrymore, Matthew Lillard.

MADAME BOVARY
SAMUEL GOLDWYN. December, 1991. French. (Claude Chabrol) Isabelle Huppert, Jean Francois Balmer, Christophe Malavoy.

MADAME BUTTERFLY
FILMS DU LOSANGE. December, 1995. French. (Frederic Mitterand) Ying Huang, Richard Troxell.

MADE IN AMERICA
WARNER BROS. May, 1993. (Richard Benjamin) Whoopi Goldberg, Ted Danson, Will Smith.

MADELINE
SONY PICTURES ENTERTAINMENT. June, 1998. (Daisy von Scherler Mayer) Frances McDormand, Nigel Hawthorne, Hatty Jones.

MADHOUSE
ORION. February, 1990. (Tom Ropelewski) John Larroquette, Kirstie Alley, Alison LaPlaca.

THE MADNESS OF KING GEORGE
SAMUEL GOLDWYN. December, 1994. British. (Nicholas Hytner) Nigel Hawthorne, Helen Mirren, Ian Holm.

MAGIC IN THE WATER
TRISTAR. August, 1995. (Rick Stevenson) Mark Harmon, Joshua Jackson, Harley Jane Kozak.

THE MAGICAL WORLD OF CHUCK JONES
WARNER BROS. May, 1993. (George Daugherty) Documentary.

THE MAGNETIST'S FIFTH WINTER
COMUMBIA TRISTAR. Jan., 1999. Danish-Norwegian-Swedish. (Morten Henriksen) Ole Lemmeke, Rolf Lassgard, Johanna Sallstrom, Gard B. Eidsvold, Robert Skjaerstad.

THE MAHABHARATA
MK2. April. 1990. British-French. (Peter Brook) Robert Langton Lloyd, Antonin Stahly Vishwanadan.

MAIDEN WORK
EASTLINE. Oct., 1998. Chinese. (Wang Guangli) Ye You, Lou Ming, He Xiaipei, Meng Jinghiu, Liu Bo.

MAJOR LEAGUE: BACK TO THE MINORS
WARNER BROS. April, 1998. (John Warren) Scott Bakula, Corbin Bernsen, Dennis Haysbert, Takaaki Ishibashi, Jensen Daggett.

MAJOR LEAGUE 2
WARNER BROS. March, 1994. (David S. Ward) Charlie Sheen, Tom Berenger, Corbin Bernsen.

MAJOR PAYNE
UNIVERSAL. March, 1995. (Nick Castle) Damon Wayans, Karyn Parsons, William Hickey, Albert Hall.

MAKING A FILM FOR ME IS LIVING
October, 1995. Italian. (Enrica Antonioni) Michelangelo Antonioni, John Malkovich, Win Wenders. Documentary.

THE MAKING OF STEEL
BEIJING FILM STUDIO. May, 1998. Chinese. (Lu Xuechang) Zhu Hongmao, Zhe Jie, Yin Shoujie, Luo Jun, Tian Zhuangzhuang.

THE MAKING OF THE MAHATMA
NFDC. May, 1996. Indian-South African. (Shyam Benegal) Rajit Kapur, Pallavi Joshi, Keith Stevenson.

MALCOLM X
WARNER BROS. November, 1992. (Spike Lee) Denzel Washington, Angela Bassett, Al Freeman Jr., Spike Lee.

MALICE
COLUMBIA. October, 1993. (Harold Becker) Alec Baldwin, Nicole Kidman, Bill Pullman.

MALINA
INDEPENDENT. September, 1993. German. (Werner Schroeter) Isabelle Huppert, Mathieu Carriere, Can Togay.

MALLRATS
GRAMERCY. September, 1995. (Kevin Smith) Shannen Doherty, Jeremy London, Jason Lee.

MAMA
STUDIO RUSSIAN PROJECT/NTV-PROFIT FILM CO. May, 1999. Russian. (Denis Yevstigneev) Nonna Mordukova, Oleg Menshikov, Vladimir Mashkov, Alexei Kravchenko, Mikhail Krylov.

MAMA ROMA
MILESTONE. January, 1995. Italian, 1962. (Pier Paolo Pasolini) Anna Magnani, Ettore Garofalo, Franco Citti.

MAMA, THERE'S A MAN IN YOUR BED
MIRAMAX. April, 1990. French. (Coline Serreau) Firmine Richard, Pierre Vernier.

MAMBI
CARTEL/RIOS TV .Sept., 1998. Spanish. (Teodoro and Santiago Rios) Carlos Fuentes, Gretel Pequeno, Alvaro de Luna, Aitor Merino, Carlos Quintana.

THE MAMBO KINGS
WARNER BROS. February, 1992. (Arne Glimcher) Armand Assante, Antonio Banderas, Cathy Moriarty.

A MAN AND HIS DOG
GOUTTE D'OR DISTRIBUTION . Mar., 1999. Dutch. (Annette Apon) Ramsey Nasr, Viviane de Muynck, Monic Hendrickx, Nina Deuss, Truus te Selle.

MAN BITES DOG
ROXIE RELEASING. January, 1993. Belgian-French. (Remy Belvaux) Benoit Poelvoorde, Remy Belvaux, Andre Bonzel.

A MAN CALLED SARGE
CANNON. February, 1990. (Stuart Gillard) Gary Kroeger, Marc Singer.

THE MAN IN HER LIFE
STAR CINEMA. Feb., 1998. Philippine. (Carlos Siguion-Reyna) Rosanna Roces, Ricky Davao, Gardo Versoza, Alan Paule.

THE MAN IN THE IRON MASK
MGM. March, 1998. (Randall Wallace.) Leonardo DiCaprio, Jeremy Irons, John Malkovich, Gerard Depardieu, Gabriel Byrne

THE MAN IN THE MOON
MGM. October, 1991. (Robert Mulligan) Reese Witherspoon, Jason London, Sam Waterston.

A MAN IN UNIFORM
ALLIANCE. June, 1994. Canadian. (David Wellington) Tom McCamus, Brigitte Bako, Kevin Tighe.

THE MAN INSIDE
NEW LINE. October, 1990. (Bobby Roth) Jurgen Prochnow, Peter Coyote, Nathalie Baye.

MAN IS A WOMAN
POLYGRAM FILM DISTRIBUTION. March, 1998. French. (Jean-Jacques Zilbermann) Antoine de Caunes, Elsa Zylberstein.

A MAN OF NO IMPORTANCE
SONY PICTURES CLASSICS. December, 1994. British. (Suri Krishnamma) Albert Finney, Brenda Fricker, Michael Gambon.

MAN OF THE HOUSE
BUENA VISTA. March, 1995. (James Orr) Chevy Chase, Jonathan Taylor Thomas, Farrah Fawcett.

MAN OF THE STORY
ADOOR GOPALAKRISHNAN/NHK JAPANESE BROADCAST CORP. Sept., 1996. Indian-Japanese. (Adoor Gopalakrishnan) Viswanathan, Mini, Aranmula, Ponnamma, Urmila Unni, Vasu Narendra.

MAN OF THE YEAR
SEVENTH ART. February, 1996. (Dirk Shafer) Shafer, Vivan Paxton, Michael Ornstein, Bill Brochtrup.

MANOLITO GAFOTAS
FILMAX INTL. June, 1999. Spanish. (Miguel Albaladejo) Savid Sancheza del Rey, Adriana Ozores, Roberto Alvarez, Antonio Gamero.

MANSFIELD PARK
MIRAMAX. Aug., 1999. British-U.S. (Patricia Rozema) Embeth Davidtz, Jonny Lee Miller, Alessandro Nivola, Frances O'Connor, Harold Pinter.

MAN TROUBLE
20TH CENTURY FOX. July, 1992. (Bob Rafelson) Jack Nicholson, Ellen Barkin, Beverly D'Angelo.

THE MAN WHO DROVE WITH MANDELA
JEZEBEL PRODS. Aug., 1998. British. (Greta Schiller) documentary with Corin Redgrave.

THE MAN WHO KNEW TOO LITTLE
WARNER BROS. Oct., 1997. (Jon Amiel) Bill Murray, Peter Gallagher, Joanne Whalley, Alfred Molina, Richard Wilson, Geraldine James.

THE MAN WHO WOULD LIVE FOREVER
FINAL CUT PRODS./POINT OF NO RETURN PRODS.. Jan., 1999. Danish. (Torben Skjodt Jensen) Ghita Norby, Lars Simonsen, Anita Ekblad, Claus Flygare, Torben Zeller.

MAN WITH A GUN
OCTOBER FILMS. October, 1995. (David Wyles) Michael Madsen, Jennifer Tilly, Gary Busey, Robert Loggia.

MAN WITH A PLAN
BELLWEATHER FILMS. May, 1996. (John O'Brien) Fred Tuttle, Joe Tuttle, Bruce Lyndes.

THE MAN WITH RAIN IN HIS SHOES
HANDMADE FILMS/PARAGON ENTERTAINMENT CORP. Feb., 1998. Spanish-British. (Maria Ripoll) Douglas Henshall, Lena Headey.

THE MAN WITHOUT A FACE
WARNER BROS. August, 1993. (Mel Gibson) Mel Gibson, Nick Stahl, Margaret Whitton.

THE MAN WITHOUT A WORLD
MILESTONE. September, 1992. (Eleanor Antin) Pier Marton, Christine Berry, Anna Henriques. B&W.

MAN'S BEST FRIEND
NEW LINE. November, 1993. (John Lafia) Ally Sheedy, Lance Henriksen, Robert Costanzo.

THE MANDARIN
GRUPO NOVO DE CINEMA ETV. May, 1996. Brazilian. (Julio Bressane) Fernando Eiras, Giulia Gam, Gal Costa.

THE MANGLER
NEW LINE. March, 1995. (Tobe Hooper) Robert Englund, Ted Levine, Daniel Matmor.

MANHATTAN BY NUMBERS
INDEPENDENT. November, 1994. (Amir Naderi) Jonh Wojda, Branislav Tomich, Mary Chang.

MANHATTAN MURDER MYSTERY
TRISTAR. August, 1993. (Woody Allen) Diane Keaton, Woody Allen, Alan Alda, Anjelica Huston.

MANNEQUIN TWO ON THE MOVE
20TH CENTURY FOX. May, 1991. (Stewart Raffill) William Ragsdale, Kristy Swanson, Meshach Taylor.

MANNY & LO
SONY PICTURES CLASSICS. January, 1996. (Lisa Krueger) Mary Kay Place, Scarlett Johansson, Aleksa Palladino.

MAN OF THE CENTURY
SUN-TELEGRAM PICTURES. Mar., 1999. (Adam Abraham) Gibson Frazier, Susan Egan, Cara Buono, Brian Davies, Swight Ewell.

MANUFACTURING CONSENT: NOAM CHOMSKY AND THE MEDIA
ZEITGEIST. March, 1993. Canadian. (Mark Achbar, Peter Witonik) Documentary.

THE MAO GAME
RENAISSANCE ROAD. June, 1999. (Joshua Miller) Joshua Miller, Piper Laurie, Kirstie Alley, Jeffrey Tambor, Jodi Leesley.

MAP OF THE HUMAN HEART
MIRAMAX. April, 1993. British-French-Australian-Canadian. (Vincent Ward) Jason Scott Lee, Anne Parillaud.

A MAP OF THE WORLD
OVERSEAS FILMGROUP. Sept., 1999. (Scott Elliott) Sigourney Weaver, Julianne Moore, David Strathairn, Ron Lea, Arliss Howard.

MARARIA
ALTA FILMS. Oct., 1998. Spanish.(Antonio Jose Betancor) Carmelo Gomez, Ian Glen, Goya Toledo, Mirta Ibarra, Jose Manuel Cervino.

MARCELLO MASTROIANNI: I REMEMBER, YES I REMEMBER
MIKADO. May, 1997. Italian. (Anna Maria Tato) documentary.

MARCH OF HAPPINESS
GREEN APPLE FILMS/FORMOSA TV. May, 1999. Taiwanese. (Lin Cheng-sheng) Lim Giong, Hsiao Shu-shen, Leon Dai, Chen Kun-chang, Grace Chen.

MARIGOLDS IN FLOWER
LENFILM/STUDIO BARMALE/PK SLOVO/ROSKOMKINO. Feb., 1999. Russian. (Sergei Sneshkin) Era Siganshina, Marine Saloptshenko, Ksenya Rappoport, Julia Sharikova, German Orlov.

MARION
BAC FILMS. Jan., 1997. French. (Manuel Poirier) Coralie Tetard, Pierre Berriau, Elisabeth Commelin, Marie-France Pisier.

MARIUS AND JEANNETTE
DIAPHANA DISTRIBUTION. May, 1997. French. (Robert Guediguian) Ariane Ascaride, Gerard Meylan, Pascale Roberts.

MARK TWAIN'S AMERICA IN 3D
SONY PICTURES CLASSICS. June, 1998. (Stephen Low) DOCUMENTARY. Narrator: Anne Bancroft.

MARKED FOR DEATH
20TH CENTURY FOX. October, 1990. (Dwight H. Little) Steven Seagal, Basil Wallace, Keith David.

MARKUS AND DIANA
NORTHERN LIGHTS. Feb., 1997. Norwegian. (Svein Scharffenberg) Robert Reierskog, Herman Bernhoft, Laila Goody, Klaus Hagerup.

MARQUIS
A.Y. ALLIGATOR. July, 1991. Belgian-French. (Henri Xhonneux) Philippe Bizot, Bien de Moor.

MARQUIS
AMLF. Aug., 1997. French-Italian-Swiss-Spanish. (Vera Belmont) Sophie Marceau, Bernard Giraudeau, Lambert Wilson.

MARRIAGES
FILMAURO. Oct., 1998. Italian-French. (Cristina Comencini) Francesca Neri, Diego Abatantuono, Stefania Sandrelli, Claude Brasseur.

MARRIED TO IT
ORION. March, 1993. (Arthur Hiller) Stockard Channing, Robert Sean Leonard, Ron Silver.

THE MARRYING MAN
BUENA VISTA. April, 1991. (Jerry Rees) Alec Baldwin, Kim Basinger, Robert Loggia, Fisher Stevens.

MARS ATTACKS!
WARNER BROS. November, 1997. (Tim Burton), Jack Nicholson, Glenn Close, Annette Bening, Pierce Brosnan, Danny DeVito, Sarah Jessica Parker, Martin Short, Michael J. Fox, Natalie Portman.

MARTHA & ETHEL
SONY PICTURES CLASSICS. February, 1995. (Jyll Johnstone) Documentary.

MARTHA AND I
CINEMA FOUR. March, 1995. German. (Jiri Weiss) Marianne Sagebrecht, Michel Piccoli, Vaclov Chalupa.

MARTHA— MEET FRANK, DANIEL AND LAURENCE
FILM FOUR DISTRIBUTORS/MIRAMAX. March, 1998. British. (Nick Hamm) Monica Potter, Rufus Sewell, Tom Hollander, Joseph Fiennes.

MARTIANS GO HOME
TAURUS ENTERTAINMENT. April, 1990. (David Odell) Randy Quaid, Margaret Colin, Anita Morris.

MARVIN'S ROOM
MIRAMAX. November, 1996. (Jerry Zaks), Meryl Streep, Leonardo DiCaprio, Diane Keaton, Robert De Niro, Hume Cronyn.

MARY JANE'S NOT A VIRGIN ANYMORE
STATION WAGON PRODS. Jan., 1997. (Ruth Jacobson) Lisa Gerstein, Greg Cruikshank, Beth Allen, Chris Enright.

MARY SHELLEY'S FRANKENSTEIN
TRISTAR. November, 1994. (Kenneth Branagh) Kenneth Branagh, Robert De Niro, Helena Bonham Carter.

MASALA
STRAND. March, 1993. Canadian. (Srinivas Krishna) Saeed Jaffrey, Zohra Segal, Sakina Jaffrey.

MASCARA
PHAEDRA CINEMA. May, 1999. (Linda Kandel) Ione Skye, Lumi Cavazos, Amanda de Cadenet, Steve Schub, Steve Jones.

THE MASK
NEW LINE. July, 1994. (Chuck Russell) Jim Carrey, Cameron Diaz, Peter Riegert.

THE MASK OF ZORRO
SONY PICTURES ENTERTAINMENT. June, 1998. (Martin Campbell) Antonio Banderas, Anthony Hopkins, Catherine Zeta-Jones.

THE MASTER DETECTIVE LIVES DANGEROUSLY
SVENSK FILMINDUSTRI. Dec., 1996. Swedish. (Goran Carmback) Malte Forsberg, Josefin Arling, Totte Steneby, Victor Sandberg.

MASTERMINDS
SONY PICTURES ENTERTAINMENT. AUGUST, 1997. (Roger Christian), Patrick Stewart, Vincent Kartheiser, Brenda Fricker.

THE MATCH
UNIVERSAL, AUG., 1999. British-U.S. (Mick Davis) Max Beesley, Isla Blair, James Cosmo, Laura Fraser, Richard E. Grant.

THE MATCH FACTORY GIRL
KINO INT'L. November, 1992. Finnish. (Aki Kaurismaki) Kati Outinen, Elina Salo, Esko Nikkari.

THE MATCHMAKER
GRAMERCY. Sept., 1997. Irish-British-U.S. (Mark Joffee) Janeane Garofalo, David O'Hara, Milo O'Shea, Jay O. Sanders.

MATILDA
SONY PICTURES. July, 1996. (Danny DeVito) Mara Wilson, Danny DeVito, Rhea Perlman, Paul Reubens, Tracy Walter.

MATINEE
UNIVERSAL. January, 1993. (Joe Dante) John Goodman, Omri Katz, Cathy Moriarty, Simon Fenton.

THE MATING HABITS OF THE EARTHBOUND HUMAN
EARTHBOUND HUMAN PRODS. Sept., 1999. (Jeff Abugov) Mackenzie Astin, Carmen Electra, Markus Redmond, Lucy Liu.

THE MATRIX
WARNER BROS. Mar., 1999. (Wachowski Brothers) Keanu Reeves, Laurence Fishburne, Carrie-Anne Moss, Hugo Weaving.

A MATTER OF DEGREES
FOX/LORBER. September, 1991. (W. T. Morgan) Arye Gross, Judith Hoag, Tom Sizemore, Bruce Norris.

MATUSALEM II
MOTION INTERNATIONAL. Dec., 1997. Canadian. (Roger Cantin) Marc Labreche, Emile Proulx Cloutier, Steve Gendron.

MAVERICK
WARNER BROS. May, 1994. (Richard Donner) Mel Gibson, Jodie Foster, James Garner.

MA VIE EN ROSE
SONY PICTURES CLASSICS/HAUT & COURT, May, 1997. French-Belgian-British. (Alain Berliner) Michele Laroque, Helene Vincent.

MAX & BOBO
ARTEMIS. Jan. 1999. Belgian. (Frederic Fonteyne) Alfredo Pea, Jan Hamenecker.

MAXIMUM RISK
SONY PICTURES. September, 1996. (Ringo Lam) Jean Claude Van Damme, Natasha Henstridge, Zach Grenier.

MAY FOOLS
ORION CLASSICS. June, 1990. French. (Louis Malle) Michel Piccoli, Miou-Miou, Michel Duchaussoy.

MAYOR OEDIPUS
LATINA. May, 1996. Colombian-Mexican-Spanish. (Jorge Ali Triana) Jorge Perugorria, Angela Molina, Francisco Rabal.

MAZEPPA
MK2. December, 1993. French. (Bartabas) Miguel Bose, Bartabas, Brigitte Marty.

M. BUTTERFLY
WARNER BROS. October, 1993. (David Cronenberg) Jeremy Irons, John Lone, Barbara Sukowa.

MCBAIN
SHAPIRO GLICKENHAUS. September, 1991. (James Glickenhaus) Christopher Walken, Michael Ironside.

MCHALE'S NAVY
UNIVERSAL. April, 1997. (Bryan Spicer), Tom Arnold, Tim Curry, Dean Stockwell, David Alan Grier, Debra Messing, Ernest Borgnine.

ME & MY MATCHMAKER
WEXLER'S WORLD. January, 1996. (Mark Wexler) Documentary.

ME AND THE KID
ORION. October, 1993. (Dan Curtis) Danny Aiello, Alex Zuckerman, Joe Pantoliano, Cathy Moriarty.

ME AND THE MOB
ARROW. September, 1994. (Frank Rainone) James Lorinz, Tony Darrow, Vinny Pastore.

ME AND VERONICA
ARROW. September, 1993. (Don Scardino) Elizabeth McGovern, Patricia Wettig, Michael O'Keefe.

MEDICINE MAN
BUENA VISTA. February, 1992. (John McTiernan) Sean Connery, Lorraine Bracco, Jose Wilker.

MEETING DADDY
MIKE SAYLES AND MATT SALINGER. Oct., 1998. (Peter Gould) Josh Charles, Alexandra Wentworth, Lloyd Bridges, Beau Bridges.

MEETING PEOPLE IS EASY
SEVENTH ART RELEASING. Mar., 1999. British. (Grant Gee) Radiohead (Thom Yorke, Jonny Greenwood, Phil Selway, Ed O'Brien, Colin Greenwood.). Documentary.

MEETING VENUS
WARNER BROS. November, 1991. British. (Istvan Szabo) Glenn Close, Niels Arestrup, Erland Josephson.

MEET JOE BLACK
UNIVERSAL. Oct., 1998. (Martin Brest) Brad Pitt, Anthony Hopkins, Claire Forlani, Jake Weber, Marica Gay Harden.

MEET THE APPLEGATES
TRITON. February, 1991. (Michael Lehmann) Ed Begley Jr., Stockard Channing, Dabney Coleman.

MEET THE DEEDLES
BUENA VISTA. March 21, 1998. (Steve Boyum) Steve Van Wormer, Paul Walker, A.J. Langer, John Ashton, Dennis Hopper, Eric Braeden.

MEET THE FEEBLES
GREYCAT. February, 1995. New Zealand. (Peter Jackson) Puppets.

MEGA CITIES: 12 STORIES OF SURVIVAL
LOTUS FILM/FAMA FILM. Aug. 1998. Austrian-Swiss. (Michael Glawogger). Documentary.

MEIN KRIEG
LEISURE TIME. April, 1993. German. (Harriet Eder, Thomas Kufus) Documentary.

MEKTOUB
SHEM'S/PLAYTIME. Jan., 1998. Moroccan-French. (Nabil Ayouch) Rachid El Ouali, Amal Chabli, Mohamed Miftah, Faouzi Bensaidi.

MELTING POT
MELTING POT PRODS. (Tom Musca) Paul Rodriguez, CCH Pounder, Cliff Robertson.

MELVIN VAN PEEBLES' CLASSIFIED X
LES FILMS D'ICI/YEAH INC./ECOUTEZ VOIE/LA SEPT ARTE. Jan., 1998. French-U.S. (Mark Daniels) documentary.

MEMOIRS OF A RIVER
CASTLE HILL. March, 1992. Hungarian-French. (Judit Elek) Sandor Gaspar, Pal Hetenyi, Andras Stohl.

MEMORIA
FORMA INTL./CDEC. Feb., 1997. Italian. (Ruggero Gabbai) Documentary.

MEMORIES OF A MARRIAGE (WALTZING REGITZE)
NORDISK FILM. January, 1991. Danish. (Kaspar Rostrup) Frits Helmuth, Mikael Helmuth.

MEMORIES UNLOCKED
LIONS GATE. Aug., 1999. Canadian. (Jean Beaudin) James Hyndman, Pascale Bussieres. Pierre-Luc Brillant.

MEMOIRS OF AN INVISIBLE MAN
WARNER BROS. February, 1992. (John Carpenter) Chevy Chase, Daryl Hannah, Sam Neill.

MEMORY & DESIRE
NEWMARKET CAPITAL GROUP/GOLDWYN FILMS. May, 1998. New Zealander. (Niki Caro) Yuri Kinugawa, Eugene Nomura, Yoko Narahashi.

MEMPHIS BELLE
WARNER BROS. October, 1990. British. (Michael Caton Jones) Matthew Modine, Eric Stoltz, D.B. Sweeney.

ME MYSELF I
SONY. Sept., 1999. Australian-French. (Pip Karmel) Rachel Griffiths, David Roberts, Sandy Winton, Yael Stone, Shaun Loseby.

MEN
SHONDEROSA PRODS. & HILLMAN/WILLIAMS PRODS. May, 1997. (Zoe-Clarke Williams) Sean Young, John Heard, Dylan Walsh.

MEN AND WOMEN
APSARAS FILM & TV. Aug., 1999. Chinese. (Liu Bingjian) Yang Qing, Yu Bo, Zhang Kang, Yu Mengjie, Wei Jiangang.

MEN AT WORK
TRIUMPH. August, 1990. (Emilio Estevez) Charlie Sheen, Emilio Estevez, Leslie Hope.

MEN CRY BULLETS
IDIOT FILMS. March, 1998. (Hernandez) Steven Nelson, Honey Lauren, Jeri Lynn Ryan.

MEN BEHIND BARS
ADRIANA CHIESE ENTERPRISES. Sept., 1998. Italian. (Giancarlo Planta) Massimo De Francovich, Gianni Cavina, Chiara Muti, Said Taghnaoui, Franco Castellano.

MEN DON'T LEAVE
WARNER BROS. February, 1990. (Paul Brickman) Jessica Lange, Arliss Howard, Chris O'Donnell, Charlie Korsmo.

MEN IN BLACK
SONY PICTURES ENTERTAINMENT. June, 1997. (Barry Sonnenfeld), Tommy Lee Jones, Will Smith, Linda Fiorentino, Vincent D'Onofrio, Rip Torn, Tony Shalhoub.

MEN IN LOVE
CRYSTAL CLEAR COMMUNICATIONS. January, 1990. (Marc Huestis) Doug Self, Joe Tolbe.

MEN OF RESPECT
COLUMBIA. January, 1991. (William Reilly) John Turturro, Katherine Borowitz, Dennis Farina.

MEN OF THE PORT (LES HOMMES DU PORT)
LES FILM DU CYCLONE. April, 1996. Swiss-French. (Alain Tanner) Documentary.

MEN WITH GUNS
NORSTAR ENTERTAINMENT. Feb., 1998. Canadian. (Kari Skogland) Donal Logue, Gregory Sporleder, Callum Keith Rennie, Max Perlich.

MEN WITH GUNS
SONY PICTURES ENTERTAINMENT. August, 1997. (John Sayles), Federico Luppi, Damian Delgado, Dan Rivera Gonzalez. Tania Cruz.

MENACE II SOCIETY
NEW LINE. May, 1993. (The Hughes Brothers) Tyrin Turner, Jada Pinkett, Larenz Tate.

MENAGE A TROIS
MIRABELLA FILM. Feb., 1998. Russian. (Pyotr Todorovsky) Elena Yakovleva, Sergei Makovetsky, Yevgeni Sidikhin.

MENDEL
NORTHERN LIGHTS. Feb., 1997. Norwegian-Danish-German. (Alexander Rosler) Thomas Jungling Sorensen, Teresa Harder, Hans Kremer.

MENSAKA
ALTA FILMS. May, 1998. Spanish. (Salvador Garcia Ruiz) Gustavo Salmeron, Tristan Ulloa, Adria Collado, Laia Marull, Maria Esteve.

MERCI MON CHIEN
BAC FILMS. May, 1999. French. (Philippe Galland) Atmen Kelif, Jean Benguigui, Yolande Moreau, Laurent Olmedo, Abbes Zahmani, Geno Lechner, Faiza Kaddour.

MERCURY RISING
UNIVERSAL March, 1998. (Harold Becker) Bruce Willis, Alec Baldwin, Miko Hughes, Chi McBride, Kim Dickens, Bodhi Pine Elfman.

MERCY
INJOSHO. October, 1995. (Richard Shephard) John Rubinstein, Amber Kain, Sam Rockwell, Jane Lanier.

MERIDIAN (KISS OF THE BEAST)
JGM ENTERPRISES. April, 1990. (Charles Band) Sherilyn Fenn, Malcolm Jamieson.

MERMAIDS
ORION. December, 1990. (Richard Benjamin) Cher, Bob Hoskins, Winona Ryder.

MESSAGE IN A BOTTLE
WARNER BROS. Feb., 1999. (Luis Mandoki) Kevin Costner, Robin Wright Penn, Paul Newman, John Savage, Illeana Douglas.

MESSAGE TO LOVE
CASTLE MUSIC. February, 1996. (Murray Lerner) Documentary.

METAL AND MELANCHOLY
ARIEL. April, 1995. Spanish-Dutch. (Heddy Honigmann, Peter Delpeut) Documentary.

THE METEOR MAN
MGM. August, 1993. (Robert Townsend) Robert Townsend, Marla Gibbs, James Earl Jones.

METRO
BUENA VISTA. January, 1997. (Thomas Carter), Eddie Murphy, Michael Rapaport, Michael Wincott, Carmen Ejogo, Denis Arndt.

METROLAND
PANDORA. Aug., 1997. British-French. (Philip Saville) Christian Bale, Lee Ross, Emily Watson, Elsa Zylberstein, Rufus, Jonathan Aris.

METROPOLITAN
NEW LINE. August, 1990. (Whit Stillman) Carolyn Farina, Edward Clements, Christopher Eigeman.

MI VIDA LOCA (MY CRAZY LIFE)
SONY PICTURES CLASSICS. July, 1994. (Allison Anders) Agel Aviles, Seidy Lopez, Jacob Vargas.

MIAMI BLUES
ORION. April, 1990. (George Armitage) Fred Ward, Alec Baldwin, Jennifer Jason Leigh.

MIAMI RHAPSODY
BUENA VISTA. January, 1995. (David Frankel) Sarah Jessica Parker, Gil Bellows, Antonio Banderas.

MICHAEL
NEW LINE. December, 1996. (Nora Ephron), John Travolta, Andie MacDowell, William Hurt, Bob Hoskins, Robert Pastorelli.

MICKEY BLUE EYES
WARNER BROS. Aug., 1999. (Kelly Makin) Hugh Grant, James Caan, Jeanne Tripplehorn, Burt Young, James Fox.

MIDNIGHT
HAUT & COURT, LA SEPT-ARTE/VIDEOFILMES, RIOFILME. Aug., 1998. French-Brazilian. (Walter Salles, Daniela Thomas) Fernanda Torres, Luis Carlos Vasconcellos, Carlos Vereza.

A MIDNIGHT CLEAR
INTERSTAR. April, 1992. (Keith Gordon) Ethan Hawke, Arye Gross, Frank Whaley, Gary Sinise.

MIDNIGHT DANCERS
FIRST RUN. July, 1995. Filipino. (Mel Chionglo) Alex Del Rosario, Grandong Cervantes, Lawrence David.

MIDNIGHT EDITION
SHAPIRO GLICKENHAUS. April, 1994. (Howard Libov) Will Patton, Michael DeLuise, Sarabeth Tucek.

MIDNIGHT IN THE GARDEN OF GOOD AND EVIL
WARNER BROS. Nov., 1997. (Clint Eastwood) Kevin Spacey, John Cusack, Jack Thompson, The Lady Chablis, Alison Eastwood, Irma P. Hall.

MIDNIGHT TEST
GEMINI FILMS. Dec., 1998. French. (Daniele Dubroux) Francois Cuzet, Serge Riaboukine, Julie Depardieu.

A MIDSUMMER'S NIGHT DREAM
FILM FOUR. Oct., 1996. British. (Adrian Noble) Lindsay Duncan, Alex Jennings, Desmond Barrit, Barry Lynch, Osheen Jones.

A MIDWINTER'S TALE
CASTLE ROCK. February, 1996. (Kenneth Branagh) Richard Briers, Hetta Charnely, Joan Collins.

MIFUNE
SONY. Feb., 1999. Danish. (Soren Kragh-Jacobsen) Anders W. Berthelsen, Iben Hjejle, Jesper Asholt, Emil Tarding, Anders Hove.

MIGHTY APHRODITE
MIRAMAX. October, 1995. (Woody Allen) F. Murray Abraham, Allen, Claire Bloom, Mira Sirvino.

THE MIGHTY DUCKS
BUENA VISTA. October, 1992. (Stephen Herek) Emilio Estevez, Lane Smith, Heidi Kling.

MIGHTY JOE YOUNG
BUENA VISTA. Dec., 1998. (Ron Underwood) Charlize Theron, Bill Paxton, Rade Sherbedgia, Peter Firth, David Paymer.

MIGHTY MORPHIN POWER RANGERS: THE MOVIE
20TH CENTURY FOX. June, 1995. (Brian Spicer) Karen Ashley, Johnny Yong Bosch, Steve Cardenas.

MIGUEL/MICHELLE
FOREFRONT FILMS. Aug., 1998. Filipino. (Gil M. Portes) Romnick Sarmenta, Gloria Diaz, Ray Ventura, Cris Villanueva, Mylene Dizon.

MILK & MONEY
RKO PICTURES. Oct., 1996. (Michael Bergmann) Robert Petkoff, Calista Flockhart, Peter Boyle, Robert Vaughn, Dina Merrill.

MILK MONEY
PARAMOUNT. August, 1994. (Richard Benjamin) Melanie Griffith, Ed Harris, Michael Patrick Carter.

THE MILKY WAY
SANABEL PRODS. Aug., 1997. Israeli. (Ali Nassar) Muhammad Bakri, Suheil Haddad, Makram Khoury, Yussef Abu Warda.

THE MILL ON THE FLOSS
CARNIVAL FILMS. May, 1997. (Graham Theakston) Emily Watson, Ifan Meredith, James Frain, Bernard Hill, James Weber-Brown.

MILLER'S CROSSING
20TH CENTURY FOX. September, 1990. (Joel Coen) Gabriel Byrne, Marcia Gay Harden, Albert Finney.

A MILLION TO JUAN
SAMUEL GOLDWYN. May, 1994. (Paul Rodriguez) Paul Rodriguez, Ruben Blades, Polly Draper.

MIMIC
DIMENSION FILMS. Aug., 1997. (Guillermo Del Toro) Mira Sorvino, Jeremy Northam, Josh Brolin, Giancarlo Giannini, Charles S. Dutton.

MINA TANNENBAUM
NEW YORKER. March, 1995. French. (Martine Dugowson) Romane Bohringer, Elsa Zylberstein, Florence Thomassin.

MINBO—OR THE GENTLE ART OF JAPANESE EXTORTION
NORTHERN ARTS. October, 1994. Japanese. (Juzo Itami) Nobuko Miyamoto, Akira Takarada, Yasuo Daichi.

MIND THE GAP
MEDIOPOLIS FILM. Feb., 1997. German. (Elfi Mikesch) Documentary.

MINDWALK
TRITON. October, 1991. (Bernt Capra) Liv Ullman, Sam Waterston, John Heard.

THE MINISTER OF STATE
KINOTUOTANTO OY/MOVIEMAKERS/NORTHERN LIGHTS. Feb., 1997. Finnish-Swedish-Norwegian. (Paul-Anders Simma) Erik Kiviniemi, Bjorn Sundquist, Sara Margrethe Oskal.

THE MINUS MAN
TSG PICTURES. Jan., 1999. (Hampton Fancher) Owen Wilson, Brian Cox, Mercedes Ruehl, Janeane Garofalo, Dwight Yoakam.

A MINUTE OF SILENCE
REZO FILMS. Sept., 1998. French-German-Belgian. (Florent Emilio Siri) Benoit Magimel, Bruno Putzulu, Rudiger Voegler.

THE MIRACLE
MIRAMAX. July, 1991. British. (Neil Jordan) Beverly D'Angelo, Donald McCann, Niall Byrne.

MIRACLE ON 34TH STREET
20TH CENTURY FOX. November, 1994. (Les Mayfield) Richard Attenborough, Elizabeth Perkins.

MIRAMAR
RIOFILME. Sept., 1997. Brazilian. (Julio Bressane) Joao Rebello, Diogo Vilela, Louise Cardoso, Bio Nunes, Fernanda Torres.

THE MIRROR
ROOZ FILM. Aug., 1997. Iranian. (Jafar Panahi) Mina Mohammad Khani, Kadem Mojdehi.

THE MIRROR HAS TWO FACES
SONY PICTURES ENTERTAINMENT. November, 1997. (Barbra Streisand), Streisand, Jeff Bridges, Pierce Brosnan, George Segal.

MIRROR, MIRROR
ORPHANS ENTERTAINMENT. September, 1990. (Marina Sargenti) Karen Black, Rainbow Harvest.

THE MISADVENTURES OF MARGARET
TF1 INTL./GRANADA. Jan., 1998. British-French. (Brian Skeet) Parker Posey, Jeremy Northam, Craig Chester, Elizabeth McGovern.

THE MISADVENTURES OF MR. WILT
SAMUEL GOLDWYN. June, 1990. British (Michael Tuchner) Griff Rhys Jones, Mel Smith.

LES MISERABLES
SONY PICTURES ENTERTAINMENT. April, 1998. (Bille August) Liam Neeson, Geoffrey Rush, Uma Thurman, Claire Danes.

MISERY
COLUMBIA. November, 1990. (Rob Reiner) James Caan, Kathy Bates, Lauren Bacall.

MISFORTUNES OF BEAUTY
BAC FILMS . Aug., 1999. French. (John Lvoff) Arielle Dombasle, Maria de Medeiros, Thibault de Montalembert, Jean-Philippe Ecoffey.

MISPLACED
SUBWAY FILMS. October, 1990. (Louis Yansen) John Cameron Mitchell, Viveca Lindfors, Elzbieta Czyzewska.

MISS JULIE
MGM/UA. Sept., 1999. British. (Mike Figgis) Saffron Burrows, Peter Mullan, Maria Doyle Kennedy.

MISS MONDAY
LAKESHORE INTL. May, 1998. (Benson Lee) Andrea Hart, James Hicks, Alex Giannini, Louise Barrett, Julie Alanagh-Brighten.

MISS NOBODY
STUDIO FILMOWE "PERSPEKTYWA". Feb., 1997. Polish (Andrzej Wajda) Anna Wielgucka, Anna Mucha, Anna Powierza.

MISSION
QUINTE FIMPRODUKTION-ARTE-BLUEBERRRY FILMS. Feb., 1997. German. (Mirjam Quinte, Pete Danquart) Documentary.

MISSION: IMPOSSIBLE
PARAMOUNT. May, 1996. (Brian De Palma) Tom Cruise, Jon Voight, Emmanuelle Beart, Henry Czerny, Jean Reno.

MISSISSIPPI MASALA
SAMUEL GOLDWYN. February, 1992. (Mira Nair) Denzel Washington, Sarita Choudhury, Roshan Seth.

MISTAKEN IDENTITY
ALLEGRO. February, 1996. Canadian. (Gilles Noel) Michel Cote, Macha Grenon, Paul Doucet.

MISTER JOHNSON
AVENUE. March, 1991. British. (Bruce Beresford) Pierce Brosnan, Maynard Eziashi, Edward Woodward.

MISTRESS
RAINBOW/TRIBECA. August, 1992. (Barry Primus) Robert Wuhl, Martin Landau, Robert De Niro.

MIXED NUTS
TRISTAR. December, 1994. (Nora Ephron) Steve Martin, Madeleine Kahn, Robert Klein, Anthony LaPaglia.

MIXING NIA
ARROWHEAD PICTURES. April, 1998. (Alison Swan) Karyn Parsons, Eric Thal, Isaiah Washington, Diego Serrano, Rosalyn Coleman.

MO' BETTER BLUES
UNIVERSAL. August, 1990. (Spike Lee) Denzel Washington, Joie Lee, Wesley Snipes.

MO' MONEY
COLUMBIA. July, 1992. (Peter MacDonald) Damon Wayans, Marlon Wayans, Stacey Dash.

MOBSTERS
UNIVERSAL. July, 1991. (Michael Karbelnikoff) Christian Slater, Patrick Dempsey, Richard Grieco.

THE MODEL COUPLE
INDEPT. November, 1990. French. (William Klein) Anemone, Andre Dussolier.

A MODERN AFFAIR
TRIBE. September, 1995. (Vern Oakley) Lisa Eichhorn, Stanley Tucci, Tammy Grimes, Robert Joy.

MODERN LOVE
SVS/TRIUMPH. April, 1990. (Robby Benson) Robby Benson, Karla DeVito, Burt Reynolds.

THE MOD SQUAD
MGM. Mar., 1999. (Scott Silver) Claire Danes, Giovanni Ribisi, Omar Epps, Dennis Farina, Josh Brolin.

MODULATIONS
CALPIRINHA PRODS. Jan., 1998. (Lara Lee) DOCUMENTARY.

MOEBIUS
UNIVERSIDAD DE CINE. September, 1996. Argentine. (Gustavo Mosquera & students of the Universidad de Cine) Guillermo Angelelli, Roberto Carnaghi.

MOJAVE MOON
INITIAL ENTERTAINMENT GROUP. May, 1996. (Kevin Dowling) Danny Aiello, Anne Archer, Angelina Jolie.

MOLL FLANDERS
MGM/UA. March, 1996. (Pen Densham) Robin Wright, Morgan Freeman, Stockard Channing, John Lynch.

MOLOCH
LENFILM/ZERO FILM. May, 1999. Russian-German-French. (Alexander Sokurov) Elena Rufanova, Leonid Mosgovoi, Leonid Sokol, Elena Spiridonova, Vladimir Bogdanov.

MOM AND DAD SAVE THE WORLD
WARNER BROS. July, 1992. (Greg Beeman) Teri Garr, Jeffrey Jones, Jon Lovitz.

MOMMY'S A FOOL
DIORAMA. May, 1999. Spanish. (Santiago Lorenzo) Jose Luis Lago, Faustina Camacho, Eduardo Antuna, Cristina Marcos, Gines Garcia Millan.

MONDO
SHADOW DISTRIBUTION. Oct., 1996. French. (Tony Gatlif) Ovidiu Balan, Pierrette Fesch, Philippe Petit, Catherine Brun.\

MONEY FOR NOTHING
BUENA VISTA. September, 1993. (Ramon Menendez) John Cusack, Debi Mazar, Michael Madsen.

MONEY MAN
MILESTONE. January, 1993. (Philip Hass) Documentary.

MONEY TALKS
NEW LINE. July, 1997. (Brett Ratner), Chris Tucker, Charlie Sheen, Heather Locklear, Gerard Ismael, Paul Sorvino, Elise Neal.

MONEY TRAIN
COLUMBIA. November, 1995. (Joseph Ruben) Wesley Snipes, Woody Harrelson, Jennifer Lopez, Robert Blake.

THE MONEYTREE
BLACK SHEEP FILMS. April, 1992. (Alan Dienstag) Christopher Dienstag, Robbi Collins, Richard Roughgarden.

MONK DAWSON
DE WARRENNE PICTURES. May, 1997. British. (Tom Waller) John Michie, Ben Taylor, Paula Hamilton, Kate Steavenson-Payne.

MONKEY TROUBLE
NEW LINE. March, 1994. (Franco Amurri) Thora Birch, Harvey Keitel, Mimi Rogers.

MONSIEUR HIRE
ORION CLASSICS. April, 1990. French. (Patrice Leconte) Michel Blanc, Sandrine Bonnaire.

THE MONSTER
CFP DISTRIBUTION. April, 1996. Italian. (Roberto Benigni) Benigni, Michel Blanc, Nicoletta Braschi.

MONSTER IN A BOX
FINE LINE. May, 1992. (Nick Broomfield) Spalding Gray.

MONTANA
INITIAL ENTERTAINMENT GROUP. Jan., 1998. (Jennifer Leitzes) Kyra Sedgwick, Stanley Tucci, Robbie Coltrane, Robin Tunney.

A MONTH BY THE LAKE
MIRAMAX. September, 1995. British. (John Irvin) Vanessa Redgrave, Edward Fox, Uma Thurman.

MONUMENT AVE.
FILMLINE INTL./PHOENICIAN FILMS/CLINICA ESTETICO/ TRIBECO. Jan., 1998. (Ted Demme) Denis Leary, Jason Barry, Billy Crudup.

MOOKIE
AMLF. Dec., 1998. French. (Herve Palud) Jacques Villeret, Eric Cantona, Emiliano Suarez, Victor Sanchez Ramirez.

MOON LAKE
GREEN FOREST ADVERTISEMENT CO. May, 1996. Taiwanese. (Hu Chen-hsiang) Wang Yu-wen.

MOONLIGHT WHISPERS
NIKKATSU CORP. Aug., 1999. Japanese. (Akihiko Shiota) Kenji Mizuhashi, Tsugumi, Kota Kusano Kota Inoue.

MOON OVER BROADWAY
PENNEBAKER HEGEDUS FILMS/MCETTINGER FILMS. Sept., 1997. (Chris Hegedus, D.A. Pennebaker) Documentary.

MOONCALF
REZO FILMS May, 1998. French. (Claude Mourieras) Muriel Mayette, Frederic Pierrot, Vincent Deneriaz, Cedric Vieira, Julien Charpy.

MOONLIGHT AND VALENTINO
GRAMERCY. September, 1995. (David Anspaugh) Elizabeth Perkins, Kathleen Turner, Whoopi Goldberg.

MOONLIGHT SERENADE
SHOCHIKU CO./OFFICE TWO/ONE-FUJI TV/PONY CANYON. Feb., 1997. Japanese. (Masahiro Shinoda) Kyozo Nagatsuka, Hideyuki Kasahara.

MORE THAN YESTERDAY
MOVIMENTO, RHONE-ALPES CINEMA, LA SEPT CINEMA. Feb., 1999. French. (Laurent Achard) Martin Mihelich, Laetitia Legrix, Mireille Roussel.

MORNING GLORY
ACADEMY ENT. September, 1993. (Steven Hilliard Stern) Christopher Reeve, Deborah Raffin, Lloyd Bochner.

MORTAL KOMBAT
NEW LINE. August, 1995. (Paul Anderson) Linden Ashby, Cary Hiroyuki Tagawa, Christopher Lambert.

MORTAL KOMBAT: ANNIHILATION
NEW LINE CINEMA. Nov., 1997. (John R. Leonetti) Robin Shou, Talisa Sato, James Remar, Sandra Hess, Lynn Red Williams.

MORTAL PASSIONS
MGM/UA. January, 1990. (Andrew Lane) Zach Galligan, Krista Errickson.

MORTAL THOUGHTS
COLUMBIA. April, 1991. (Alan Rudolph) Demi Moore, Glenne Headley, Bruce Willis.

MOST WANTED
NEW LINE CINEMA. Oct., 1997. (David Glenn Hogan) Keenen Ivory Wayans, Jon Voight, Jill Hennessy, Paul Sorvino, Eric Roberts.

MOTEL
CINEMA LIBRE. November, 1995. Canadian. (Pascal Maeder) Anna Papdakos, Jerry Snell, Carlo d'Orlando.

MOTHER
PARAMOUNT. September, 1996. (Albert Brooks) Albert Brooks, Debbie Reynolds, Rob Morrow, Lisa Kudrow.

M/OTHER
SUNCENT CINEMAWORKS. MAY, 1999. Japanese. (Nobuhiro Suwa) Tomokazu Miura, Makiko Watanabe, Ryudai Takahashi.

A MOTHER ALONE
SUMATHI FILMS. Nov., 1997. Sri Lankan. (Sumitra Peries) Sangeetha Weeraratne, Tony Ranasinghe, Sanath Gunathilake.

MOTHER AND SON
ZERO FILM. Feb., 1997. German-Russian.(Aleksandr Sokurov) Alexei Ananischnov, Gudrun Geyer.

MOTHER CHRISTIAN
CINE 9. Sept., 1998. French. (Myriam Boyer) Myriam Boyer, Bruno Boeglin, Maryline Even, Clovis Cornillac, Lorraine Bouchet.

MOTHER'S BOYS
DIMENSION. March, 1994. (Yves Simoneau) Jamie Lee Curtis, Peter Gallagher, Luke Edwards.

MOTORAMA
TWO MOON RELEASING. January, 1993. (Barry Shils) Jordan Christopher Michael, Martha Quinn, Susan Tyrrell.

MOUNTAINS OF THE MOON
TRISTAR. February, 1990. (Bob Rafelson) Patrick Bergin, Iain Glen, Richard E. Grant.

THE MOUSE
EARLY MORNING FILMS. Oct., 1996. (Daniel Adams) John Savage, Angelica Torn, Charles Bailey-Gates, Irina Cashen, Tim Williams.

MOUSE HUNT
DREAMWORKS PICTURES. Dec., 1997. (Gore Verbinski) Nathan Lane, Lee Evans, Vicki Lewis, Maury Chaykin, Eric Christmas.

MOUTH TO MOUTH
MIRAMAX. November, 1995. Spanish. (Manual Gomez Periera) Javier Bardem, Aitana Sanchez-Gijon.

MOVING THE MOUNTAIN
OCTOBER FILMS. April, 1995. (Michael Apted) Documentary.

MR. AND MRS. BRIDGE
MIRAMAX. November, 1990. (James Ivory) Paul Newman, Joanne Woodward, Robert Sean Leonard.

MR. BASEBALL
UNIVERSAL. October, 1992. (Fred Schepisi) Tom Selleck, Ken Takakura, Aya Takanashi.

MR. DESTINY
BUENA VISTA. October, 1990. (James Orr) James Belushi, Michael Caine, Linda Hamilton.

MR. FIFTEEN BALLS
MEDUSA. Sept., 1998. Italian. (Francesco Nuti) Francesco Nuti, Sabrina Ferilli, Novello Novelli, Antonio Perocelli, Giulia Weber.

MR. FROST
TRIUMPH. November, 1990. British-French. (Philippe Setbon) Jeff Goldblum, Kathy Baker, Alan Bates.

MR. HOLLAND'S OPUS
BUENA VISTA. January, 1996. (Stephen Herek).Richard Dreyfuss. Glenne Headley, Jay Thomas, Olympia Dukakis.

MR. HOOVER & I
TURIN FILM. April, 1990. (Emile DeAntonio) Documentary.

MR. JEALOUSY
JOEL CASTLEBERG PRODS. Sept., 1997. (Noah Baumbach) Eric Stoltz, Annabella Sciorra, Chris Eigeman, Carlos Jacott, Marianne Jean-Baptiste, Brian Kerwin, Peter Bogdanovich.

MR. JONES
TRISTAR. October, 1993. (Mike Figgis) Richard Gere, Lena Olin, Anne Bancroft, Delroy Lindo.

MR. MAGOO
BUENA VISTA. Dec., 1997. (Stanely Tong) Leslie Nielsen, Kelly Lynch, Matt Keeslar, Ernie Hudson, Miguel Ferrer, Malcolm McDowell.

MR. NANNY
NEW LINE. October, 1993. (Michael Gottlieb) Hulk Hogan, Sherman Hemsley, Austin Pendleton.

MR. NAPHTALI
PATHE. Aug, 1999. French. (Olivier Schatzky) Elie Kakou, Gilbert Melki, Isabelle Ferron, Alice Evans, Jena-Marie Lamour.

MR. NICE GUY
NEW LINE CINEMA. May, 1997. Hong Kong. (Samo Hung) Jackie Chan, Richard Norton, Gabrielle Fitzpatrick, Miki Lee.

MR. RELIABLE: A TRUE STORY
POLYGRAM. May, 1996. Australian. (Nadia Tass) Colin Friels, Jacqueline McKenzie, Paul Sonkkila.

MR. SATURDAY NIGHT
COLUMBIA. September, 1992. (Billy Crystal) Billy Crystal, David Paymer, Helen Hunt, Julie Warner.

MR. SPECKMAN'S BOAT
CINEQUANON PICTURES INTL. May, 1996. (John Huddles) Jennifer Connelly, Edward Atterton, Jim True.

MRS. RETTICH, CZERNY AND ME
JUGENDFILM. May, 1998. German. (Markus Imboden) Iris Berben, Marina Gedeck, Jeanette Hain, Olli Dittrich, Thomas Heinze.

MR. UNIVERSE
ZEITGEIST. March, 1990. Hungarian. (György Szomjas) Laszlo Szabo, Mickey Hargitay.

MR. VINCENT
ALCHEMY PICTURES. Jan., 1997. (Robert Celestino) Frank John Hughes, Lisa LoCicero, Mimi Scott, Robert Bruzio, Shoshana Ami.

MR. WONDERFUL
WARNER BROS. October, 1993. (Anthony Minghella) Matt Dillon, Annabella Sciorra, Mary Louise Parker.

MR. WRITE
SHAPIRO GLICKENHAUS. May, 1994. (Charlie Loventhal) Paul Reiser, Jessica Tuck, Doug Davidson.

MR. WRONG
BUENA VISTA. February, 1996. (Nick Castle) Ellen deGeneres, Bill Pullman, Joan Cusack, Dean Stockwell.

MR. ZHAO
BEIJING ZHANG TIAN CULTURE & MEDIA CENTER/NAM KWONG DEVELOPMENT. Aug., 1998. Chinese. (Lu Yue) Shi Jingming, Zhang Zhihua, Chen Yinan, Jiang Wenli.

MRS. BROWN
MIRAMAX. May, 1997. British. (John Madden), Judi Dench, Billy Connolly, Geoffrey Palmer, Anthony Sher, Gerald Butler.

MRS. DALLOWAY
FIRST LOOK PICTURES. Sept., 1997. (Marleen Gorris) Vanessa Redgrave, Natascha McElhone, Rupert Graves, Michael Kitchen.

MRS. DOUBTFIRE
20TH CENTURY FOX. November, 1993. (Chris Columbus) Robin Williams, Sally Field, Pierce Brosnan.

MRS. PARKER AND THE VICIOUS CIRCLE
FINE LINE. November, 1994. (Alan Rudolph) Jennifer Jason Leigh, Campbell Scott, Matthew Broderick.

MRS. WINTERBOURNE
TRISTAR. April, 1996. (Richard Benjamin) Shirley MacLaine, Ricki Lake, Brendan Fraser, Miguel Sandoval, Loren Dean.

MUCH ADO ABOUT NOTHING
SAMUEL GOLDWYN. May, 1993. British. (Kenneth Branagh) Kenneth Branagh, Robert Sean Leonard, Emma Thompson.

MUGSHOT
MORTAL FILMS. April, 1996. (Matt Mahurin) Robert Knepper, Michael Williams, Robert Walker, Belinda Becker.

MUHAMMAD ALI, THE GREATEST
FILMS PARIS. November, 1990. (William Klein) Documentary.

MULAN
BUENA VISTA. May, 1998. (Barry Cook, Tony Bancroft) Ming-Na Wen, Lea Salonga, Eddie Murphy, B. D. Wong, Donny Osmond (voices).

MULHOLLAND FALLS
MGM/UA. April, 1996. (Lee Tamahori) Nick Nolte, Melanie Griffith, Chazz Palminteri, Michael Madsen, Chris Penn.

MULTIPLICITY
SONY PICTURES. July, 1996. (Harold Ramis) Michael Keaton, Andie MacDowell, Harris Yulin, Richard Masur.

MUMFORD
BUENA VISTA. Sept., 1999. (Lawrence Kasdan) Loren Dean, Hope Davis, Jason Lee, Alfre Woodard, Mary McDonnell.

THE MUMMY
UNIVERSAL PICTURES. May, 1999. (Stephen Sommers) Brendan Fraser, Rachel Weisz, John Hannah, Arnold Vosloo.

MUMU
MOSFILM. June, 1999. Russian. (Yuri Grymov) Lyudmilla Makasakova, Alexander Baluev, Vladimir Steklov

MUNCHIE
CONCORDE. May, 1992. (Jim Wynorski) Loni Anderson, Andrew Stevens, Jaime McEnnan.

MUPPET CHRISTMAS CAROL, THE
BUENA VISTA. December, 1992. (Brian Henson) Michael Caine, The Muppets.

MUPPETS FROM OUTER SPACE
SONY. July, 1999. (Tim Hill) Dave Goelz, Steve Whitmire, Bill Barretta, Jerry Nelson, Brian Henson.

MUPPET TREASURE ISLAND
WALT DISNEY. February, 1996. (Brain Henson) Tim Curry, Kevin Bishop, Billy Connolly, Jennifer Saunders.

MURATTI AND SAROTTI-THE HISTORY OF GERMAN ANIMATION FILM 1920-1960
ANIGRAF FILMPRODUKTION. Aug., 1999. German. (Gerd Gockell). Documentary.

MURDER AT 1600
WARNER BROS. April, 1997. (Dwight Little), Cast: Wesley Snipes, Diane Lane, Daniel Benzali, Dennis Miller, Alan Alda, Ronny Cox.

THE MURDER IN CHINA BASIN
GERARD FILMS. July, 1999. (Norman Gerard) Elizabeth Rossa, Chris Byrne, Jennifer Starr, Noel Harrison, Derek Sitter.

MURDER IN THE FIRST
WARNER BROS. January, 1995. (Marc Rocco) Christian Slater, Kevin Bacon, Gary Oldman.

MURDER MAGIC
METROPOLIS. May, 1994. (Windell Williams) Ron Cephas Jones, D. Ruben Green, Collette Wilson.

MURIEL'S WEDDING
MIRAMAX. March, 1995. Australian. (P.J. Hogan) Toni Collette, Rachel Griffiths, Bill Hunter.

MURMUR OF YOUTH
CENTRAL MOTION PICTURE. May, 1997. Taiwanese. (Lin Cheng-sheng) Rene Liu, Tseng Tsing, Tsai Chin Hsin, Lin Hsui.

MURMURING
DOCU FACTORY VISTA. March, 1996. South Korean. (Byun Young-joo) Documentary.

THE MUSE
USA FILMS. Aug., 1999. (Albert Brooks) Albert Brooks, Sharon Stone, Andie MacDowell, Jeff Bridges, Mark Feuerstein.

THE MUSIC OF CHANCE
I.R.S. June, 1993. (Philip Haas) Mandy Patinkin, James Spader, M. Emmet Walsh.

MUSIC OF THE HEART
MIRAMAX. Sept., 1999. (Wes Craven) Meryl Streep, Aidan Quinn, Angela Bassett, Cloris Leachman, Gloria Estefan.

THE MUSIC TELLS YOU
PENNEBAKER ASSOCS. June, 1992. (Chris Hegedus, D. A. Pennebaker) Branford Marsalis.

MUSICALS GREAT MUSICALS
ALTERNATE CURRENT, 13/WNET, TURNER CLASSIC MOVIES /NHK. U.S.-Japanese. Nov., 1996. (David Thompson) Cyd Charisse, Hugh Fordin, Stanley Donen, Andre Previn, Documentary - video.

THE MUTANTS
JBA. Feb., 1999. French-Portuguese. (Teresa Villaverde): Ana Moreira, Alexandre Pinto, Nelson Varela.

MUTE WITNESS
SONY PICTURES CLASSICS. September, 1995. British. (Anthony Waller) Marina Sudina, Evan Richards, Fay Ripley.

MY AMERICAN VACATION
SANTA MONICA PICTURES. Apr., 1999. (V V Dachin) Tsai Chin, Kim Miyori, Deborah Nishimura, Dennis Dun.

MY BEST FIEND
WERNER HERZOG FILMPRODUKTION/CAFE PRODUCTION/ ZEPHIR FILM. May, 1999. German. (Werner Herzog).

MY BEST FRIEND'S WEDDING
SONY PICTURES ENTERTAINMENT. June, 1997. (P.J. Hogan), Julia Roberts, Dermont Mulroney, Cameron Diaz, Rupert Everett.

MY BLUE HEAVEN
WARNER BROS. August, 1990. (Herbert Ross) Steve Martin, Rick Moranis, Joan Cusack.

MY BOYFRIEND'S BACK
BUENA VISTA. August, 1993. (Bob Balaban) Andrew Lowery, Traci Lind, Austin Pendleton, Paul Dooley.

MY BROTHER AND I
GREEK FILM CENTER-HYPERION-GREEK TELEVISION ERK-TONIKON-SPENTZOS FILM. May, 1998. Greek. (Antonis Kokkinos) Vangelis Germanos, Demosthenes Papadopoulos, Pemy Zouni.

MY COUSIN VINNY
20TH CENTURY FOX. March, 1992. (Jonathan Lynn) Joe Pesci, Marisa Tomei, Ralph Macchio.

MY DEAREST FRIENDS
CECCHI GORI DISTRIBUZIONE. April, 1998. Italian. (Alessandro Benvenuti) Alessandro Benvenuti, Eva Robin's, Athina Cenci.

MY DUBIOUS SEXDRIVE
SEAMLESS. October, 1995. (Lucy Phillips, Glen Scantlebury) Samantha Pendse, Ian Spencer.

MY FAMILY, MI FAMILIA
NEW LINE. May, 1995. (Gregory Nava) Jimmy Smits, Esai Morales, Eduardo Lopez Rojas.

MY FAMILY'S HONOR
3.B. PRODS./LA SEPT CINEMA. Feb., 1998. French. (Rachid Bouchareb) Seloua Hamse, Karole Rocher, Roschdy Zem.

MY FATHER, MY MOTHER, MY SISTER AND MY BROTHERS...
SND. July, 1999. French-Spanish. (Charlotte de Turckheim) Victoria Abril, Charlotte de Turckheim, Alain Bashung, Philip Giangreco, Marc Andreoni.

MY FATHER, THE HERO
BUENA VISTA. February, 1994. (Steve Miner) Gérard Depardieu, Katherine Heigl, Dalton James.

MY FATHER'S COMING
TARA RELEASING. November, 1991. German. (Monika Treut) Alfred Edel, Shelley Kastner, Annie Sprinkle.

MY FATHER'S GARDEN
MIRANDA PRODS. January, 1996. (Miranda Smith) Documentary.

MY FATHER'S GLORY
ORION CLASSICS. June, 1991. French. (Yves Robert) Philippe Caubere, Nathalie Roussel.

MY FAVORITE MARTIAN
BUENA VISTA. Feb., 1999. (Donald Petrie) Christopher Lloyd, Jeff Daniels, Elizabeth Hurley, Daryl Hannah, Wallace Shawn.

MY FAVORITE SEASON (MA SAISON PRÉFERÉE)
FILMOPOLIS. April, 1996. French. (André Téchiné) Catherine Deneuve, Daniel Auteuil.

MY FELLOW AMERICANS
WARNER BROS. December, 1995. (Peter Segal), Jack Lemmon, James Garner, Dan Aykroyd, John Heard, Sela Ward, Wilfred Brimley.

MY FRIEND JOE
PORTMAN ENTERTAINMENT GROUP. June, 1996. Irish-German. (Chris Bould) Schuyler Fisk, John Cleere.

MY FRIEND PAUL
FIVE POINTS PICTURES. Mar., 1999. (Jonathan Berman). Documentary.

MY GIANT
SONY PICTURES ENTERTAINMENT. March, 1997. (Michael Lehmann) Billy Crystal, Kathleen Quinlan, Gheorghe Muresan.

MY GIRL
COLUMBIA. November, 1991. (Howard Zieff) Dan Aykroyd, Jamie Lee Curtis, Anna Chlumsky, Macaulay Culkin.

MY GIRL 2
COLUMBIA. February, 1994. (Howard Zieff) Anna Chlumsky, Dan Aykroyd, Jamie Lee Curtis, Austin O'Brien.

MY HEART IS MINE ALONE
HELMER SANDERS. Feb., 1997. German. (Helma Sanders-Brahms) Lena Stolze, Cornelius Obonya, Oliver Grice, Thomas Ruffer.

MY HEROES HAVE ALWAYS BEEN COWBOYS
SAMUEL GOLDWYN. March, 1991. (Stuart Rosenberg) Scott Glenn, Kate Capshaw, Ben Johnson, Balthazar Getty.

MY LAST MAN
GAVIOLA PRODS. May, 1996. Chilean. (Tatiana Gaviola) Claudia DiGirolamo, Willy Semler, Liliana Garcia.

MY LIFE
COLUMBIA. November, 1993. (Bruce Joel Rubin) Michael Keaton, Nicole Kidman, Haing S. Ngor.

MY LIFE AND TIMES WITH ANTONIN ARTAUD
LEISURE TIME. July, 1995. French. (Gerard Mordillat) Sami Frey, Marc Barbe, Julie Jezequel.

MY LIFE'S IN TURNAROUND
ARROW. June, 1994. (Eric Schaeffer, Donald Lardner Ward) Eric Schaeffer, Donald Lardner Ward, John Sayles.

MY LIFE SO FAR
MIRAMAX. May, 1999. British. (Hugh Hudson): Colin Firth, Mary Elizabeth Mastrantonio, Rosemary Harris, Irene Jacob, Tcheky Karyo.

MY LITTLE BUSINESS
BAC FILMS. Aug., 1999. French. (Pierre Jolivet) Vincent Lindon, Francois Berleand, Roschdy Zem, Zabou Breitman, Albert Dray.

MY MOTHER'S CASTLE
ORION CLASSICS. July, 1991. French. (Yves Robert) Julien Ciamaca, Philippe Caubere.

MY NAME IS JOE
PARALLAX PICTURES/ROAD MOVIES VIERTE PROD. May, 1998. French-German-British. (Ken Loach) Peter Mullan, Louise Goodall.

MY NAME IS SARA
FILMAX. May, 1999. Spanish. (Dolores Payas) Elvira Minguez, Francois Eric Gendron, Jeannine Mestre, Elena Castells.

MY NEIGHBOR TOTORO
TROMA. May, 1993. Japanese. (Hayao Miyazaki) Animated.

MY NEW GUN
I.R.S. October, 1992. (Stacy Cochran) Diane Lane, James LeGros, Stephen Collins.

MY OWN PRIVATE IDAHO
NEW LINE. September, 1991. (Gus Van Sant) River Phoenix, Keanu Reeves, James Russo.

MY SECRET CACHE
TOHO CO. Feb., 1997. Japanese. (Shinobu Yaguchi) Naomi Nishida, Go Riju, Taketoshi Naito.

MY SON THE FANATIC
BBC FILMS. April, 1997. British. (Udayan Prasad) Om Puri, Rachel Griffiths, Stellan Skarsgard, Akbar Kurtha, Gopi Desai.

MYSTERY, ALASKA
BUENA VISTA. Oct., 1999. (Jay Roach) Russell Crowe, Hank Azaria, Mary McCormack, Burt Reynolds, Colm Meaney.

MYSTERY DATE
ORION. August, 1991. (Jonathan Wacks) Ethan Hawke, Teri Polo, B.D. Wong, Brian McNamara.

MYSTERY MEN
UNIVERSAL. July, 1999. (Kinka Usher) Hank Azaria, Janeane Garofalo, William H. Macy, Del Mitchell, Paul Reubens.

MYSTERY OF RAMPO, THE
SAMUEL GOLDWYN. May, 1995. Japanese. (Kazuyoshi Okuyama) Masahiro Motoki, Naoto Takenaka, Michiko Hada.

MYSTERY SCIENCE THEATER 3000
GRAMERCY. April, 1996. (Jim Mallon) Michael J. Nelson, Trace Beaulieu, Kevin Murphy.

MY SUMMER VACATION
ORTON PRODS. May, 1996. Canadian. (Sky Gilbert) Clinton Walker, Christofer Williamson.

THE MYTH OF FINGERPRINTS
SONY PICTURES CLASSICS. Jan., 1997. (Bart Freundlich) Arija Bareikis, Blythe Danner, Hope Davis, Laurel Holloman, Brian Kerwin.

MY TRUE SWEDISH FRIEND
CECCHI GORI. Jan., 1999. Italian. (Vincenzo Salemme) Vincenzo Salemme, Eva Harzigova, Carlo Buccirosso, Maurizio Casagrande, Nando Paone.

MY UNCLE'S LEGACY
IFEX. June, 1990. Serbo-Croatian. (Krsto Papic) Davor Janjic, Alma Prica.

MY WEST
CECCHI GORI. Dec., 1998. Italian. (Giovanni Veronesi) Leonardo Pieraccioni, Harvey Keitel, David Bowie, Sandrine Holt, Alessia Marcuzzi.

N

NADIA AND THE HIPPOS
DIAPHANA. May, 1999. French. (Dominique Cabrera) Ariane Ascaride, Marilyne Canto, Thierry Fremont, Philippe Fretun, Najd Hamou-Medja.

NADJA
OCTOBER FILMS. August, 1995. (Michael Almereyda) Elina Lowensohn, Peter Fonda, Suzy Amis, Martin Donovan. B&W.

NADRO
ARTEMESIA. Oct., 1998. French. (Ivana Massetti). Documentary.

NAKED
FINE LINE. December, 1993. British. (Mike Leigh) David Thewlis, Lesley Sharp, Katrin Cartlidge, Greg Cruttwell.

THE NAKED EYE (LA MIRADA DEL OTRO)
COLUMBIA TRISTAR ESPANA. Feb., 1998. Spanish. (Vicente Aranda) Laura Morante, Jose Coronado, Miguel Angel Garcia.

NAKED GUN 2½: THE SMELL OF FEAR
PARAMOUNT. June, 1991. (David Zucker) Leslie Nielsen, Priscilla Presley, Robert Goulet.

NAKED GUN 33 1/3: THE FINAL INSULT
PARAMOUNT. March, 1994. (Peter Segal) Leslie Nielsen, Priscilla Presley, O.J. Simpson, Fred Ward.

NAKED IN NEW YORK
FINE LINE. April, 1994. (Dan Algrant) Eric Stoltz, Mary Louise Parker, Tony Curtis, Ralph Macchio.

NAKED KILLER
RIM. March, 1995. Hong Kong. (Clarence Fok) Simon Yam, Chingmy Yau, Carrie Ng.

NAKED LUNCH
20TH CENTURY FOX. December, 1991. British-Canadian. (David Cronenberg) Peter Weller, Judy Davis, Ian Holm.

THE NAKED MAN
RIO FILM/MAC COMMUNICACOES. Aug., 1997. Brazilian. (Hugo Carvana) Claudio Marzo, Lucia Verisimo, Daniel Dantas.

NAKED OBSESSION
CONCORDE. January, 1991. (Dan Golden) William Katt, Rick Dean, Maria Ford.

NAKED SONGS: THE LIVE AND TIMES OF RICKY LEE JONES
WARNER REPRISE. Oct., 1996. (Ethan A. Russell) Documentary.

NAKED TANGO
NEW LINE. August, 1991. Argentinian-U.S. (Leonard Schrader) Vincent D'Onofrio, Mathilda May, Esai Morales.

THE NANNY
ISTITUTO LUCE. May, 1999. Italian. (Marco Bellocchio) Fabrizio Bentivoglio, Valeria Bruni Tedeschi, Maya Sansa, Jacqueline Lustig, Pier Giorgio Bellocchio.

NARROW MARGIN
TRISTAR. September, 1990. (Peter Hyams) Gene Hackman, Anne Archer, James B. Sikking.

THE NASTY GIRL
MIRAMAX. October, 1990. German. (Michael Verhoeven) Lena Stolze, Monika Baumgartner. Color/B&W.

NATIONAL LAMPOON'S LOADED WEAPON 1
NEW LINE. February, 1993. (Gene Quintano) Emilio Estevez, Samuel L. Jackson, Jon Lovitz.

NATIONAL LAMPOON'S SENIOR TRIP
NEW LINE. September, 1995. (Kelly Makin) Matt Frewer, Valeri Mahaffey, Thomas Chong.

NATURAL BORN KILLERS
WARNER BROS. August, 1994. (Oliver Stone) Woody Harrelson, Juliette Lewis, Robert Downey Jr.

THE NATURAL HISTORY OF PARKING LOTS
STRAND. October, 1990. (Everett Lewis) Charlie Bean, B. Wyatt.

NATURALLY NATIVE
RED-HORSE NATIVE. Jan., 1998. (Jennifer Wynne Farmer, Valerie Red-Horse) Valerie Red-Horse, Irene Bedard, Kimberly Norris Guerrero.

NATURE'S WARRIOR
SVENSK FILMINDISTRI. Feb., 1997. Swedish-Danish (Stefan Jarl) Robin Milldoff, John Belindo, Jan Malmsjo, Mikael Persbrandt.

NAVY SEALS
ORION. July, 1990. (Lewis Teague) Charlie Sheen, Michael Biehn, Rick Rossovich.

NECESSARY ROUGHNESS
PARAMOUNT. September, 1991. (Stan Dragoti) Scott Bakula, Hector Elizondo, Robert Loggia.

NEEDFUL THINGS
COLUMBIA. August, 1993. (Fraser Heston) Max von Sydow, Ed Harris, Bonnie Bedelia, J.T. Walsh.

THE NEGOTIATOR
WARNER BROS. July, 1998. (F. Gary Gray) Samuel L. Jackson, Kevin Spacey, David Morse, Ron Rifkin, John Spencer, J. T. Walsh.

NEIL SIMON'S "LOST IN YONKERS"
COLUMBIA. May, 1993. (Martha Coolidge) Mercedes Ruehl, Richard Dreyfuss, Irene Worth, Brad Stoll.

NEITHER EVE NOR ADAM
Phillipe Martin. Sept., 1996. French. (Jean Paul Civeyrac) Guillaume Verdier, Morgane Hainaux, Frederique Gagnol, Helene Chambon.

NELL
20TH CENTURY FOX. December, 1994. (Michael Apted) Jodie Foster, Liam Neeson, Natasha Richardson.

NEMESIS
IMPERIAL. January, 1993. (Albert Pyun) Olivier Gruner, Tim Thomerson, Cary Hiroyuki Tagawa.

THE NEPHEW
IRISH DREAMTIME/WORLD 2000 ENTERTAINMENT. May, 1998. Irish. (Eugene Brady) Hill Harper, Aislin McGuckin, Pierce Brosnan.

THE NEST (LIGDZA)
TRIS FILM STUDIO. April, 1996. Latvian. (Aivars Freimanis) Leonids Locenieks, Dace Bonate.

THE NET
COLUMBIA. July, 1995. (Irwin Winkler) Sandra Bullock, Jeremy Northam, Dennis Miller, Diane Baker.

NEVER BEEN KISSED
20TH CENTURY FOX. Mar., 1999. (Raja Gosnell) Drew Barrymore, David Arquette, Michael Vartan, Molly Shannon, John C. Reilly.

NEVER EVER
TRIMARK PICTURES. September, 1996. U.S.-British. (Charles Finch) Sandrine Bonnaire, Jane March.

NEVER LEAVE NEVADA
CABRIOLET. April, 1991. (Steve Swartz) Steve Swartz, Rodney Rincon. B&W.

NEVER MET PICASSO
MIGHTY REEL. June, 1996. (Stephen Kijak) Margot Kidder, Alexis Arquette, Georgia Ragsdale.

THE NEVERENDING STORY II: THE NEXT CHAPTER
WARNER BROS. February, 1991. German. (George Miller) Jonathan Brandis, Kenny Morrison, Clarissa Burt.

THE NEW AGE
WARNER BROS. September, 1994. (Michael Tolkin) Peter Weller, Judy Davis, Patrick Bauchau, Adam West.

NEW BLOOD
LIONS GATE/SCREENLAND PICTURES. May, 1999. British-Canadian. (Michael Hurst) John Hurt, Nick Moran, Carrie-Anne Moss, Shawn Wayans, Joe Pantoliano.

NEW DAWN
HAUT ET COURT . May, 1999. French. (Emilie Deleuze) Samuel Le Bihan, Marcial De Fonzo Bo, Catherine Vinatier.

THE NEW EVE
Gemini. Jan. 1999. French. (Catherine Corsini) Karin Viard, Pierre-Loup Rajot, Catherine Frot, Sergi Lopez, Mireille Roussel.

NEW JACK CITY
WARNER BROS. March, 1991. (Mario Van Peebles) Wesley Snipes, Ice T, Mario Van Peebles, Judd Nelson.

NEW JERSEY DRIVE
GRAMERCY. April, 1995. (Nick Gomez) Sharron Corley, Gabriel Casseus, Saul Stein.

NEW ROSE HOTEL
EDWARD R. PRESSMAN FILM CORP. Sept., 1998. (Abel Ferrara) Christopher Walken, Willem Dafoe, Asia Argento, Yoshitaka Amano, Annabella Sciorra, Gretchen Mol, John Lurie.

NEW SCHOOL ORDER
INDEPENDENT TELEVISION SERVICE. Jan., 1997. (Gini Reticker) Documentary.

NEWSIES
BUENA VISTA. April, 1992. (Kenny Ortega) Christian Bale, Robert Duvall, David Moscow, Trey Parker.

THE NEWTON BOYS
20TH CENTURY FOX. March, 1998. (Richard Linklater) Matthew McConaughey, Skeet Ulrich, Ethan Hawke, Vincent D'Onofrio, Julianna Margulies, Dwight Yoakam.

NEW WATERFORD GIRL
ODEON. Sept., 1999. Canadian. (Allan Moyle) Liane Balaban, Tara Spencer Nairn, Andrew McCarthy, Mary Walsh, Nicholas Campbell.

THE NEXT KARATE KID
COLUMBIA. August, 1994. (Christopher Cain) Noriyuki "Pat" Morita, Hilary Swank, Michael Ironside.

THE NEXT STEP
WAVELENGHT. March, 1996. (Christian Faber) Rick Negron, Kristin Moreau, Denise Faye.

NEXT STOP WONDERLAND
MIRAMAX. Jan., 1998. (Brad Anderson) Hope Davis, Alan Gelfant, Victor Argo, Jon Benjamin.

NEXT TIME
ALHONDIGA PICTURES. Aug., 1998. (Alan Fraser) Christian Campbell, Jonelle Allen.

NEXT YEAR ... WE'LL GO TO BED BY TEN
SACIS INTL. June, 1996. Italian. (Angelo Orlando) Angelo Orlando, Ricky Memphis, Ninetto Davoli

NIAGARA NIAGARA
SHOOTING GALLERY. Aug., 1997. (Bob Gosse) Robin Tunney, Henry Thomas, Michael Parks, Stephen Lang, John MacKay.

NICK OF TIME
PARAMOUNT. December, 1995. (John Badham) Johnny Depp, Christopher Walken, Charles S. Duffon, Peter Strauss.

NICO ICON
ROXIE. January, 1996. German. (Susanne Ofteringer) Documentary.

NIGHT AND DAY
INT'L FILM CIRCUIT. December, 1992. French. (Chantal Ackerman) Guilaine Londez, Thomas Langmann.

NIGHT AND THE CITY
20TH CENTURY FOX. October, 1992. (Irwin Winkler) Robert De Niro, Jessica Lange, Alan King, Jack Warden.

NIGHT ANGEL
FRIES ENT. September, 1990. (Dominique Othenin Girard) Isa Anderson, Karen Black, Debra Feuer.

A NIGHT AT THE ROXBURY
PARAMOUNT PICTURES. Sept., 1998. (John Fortenberry) Will Ferrell, Chris Kattan, Molly Shannon, Dan Hedaya, Richard Grieco.

NIGHTBREED
20TH CENTURY FOX. February, 1990. (Clive Barker) Craig Sheffer, David Cronenberg.

NIGHT FLIER
NEW LINE CINEMA. Feb., 1998. (Mark Pavia) Miguel Ferrer, Julie Entwisle, Dan Monahan, Merton H. Moss, John Bennes.

NIGHT MUSIC
SVENKA FILM INSTITUT. April, 1997. Swedish. (Georg af Klerker) Manne Gothson, Gabriel Alw. Restoration of 1918 feature.

NIGHT OF DESTINY
LES FILMS DU PLACE. Feb., 1999. French. (Abdelkrim Bahloul) Philippe Volter, Boris Terral, Gamil Ratib, Sonia Mankai, Marie-Jose Nat.

NIGHT OF THE DEMONS 2
REPUBLIC. May, 1994. (Brian Trenchard Smith) Cristi Harris, Bobby Jacoby, Merle Kennedy.

NIGHT OF THE FLOOD
ANTENNA. Oct., 1996. Canadian. (Bernar Hebert) Genevieve Rochette, Julie McClemens, Jacques Godin, Estelle Clareton.

NIGHT OF THE LIVING DEAD
COLUMBIA. October, 1990. (Tom Savini) Tony Todd, Patricia Tallman, Tom Towles.

NIGHT OF THE WARRIOR
TRIMARK. June, 1991. (Rafal Zielinski) Lorenzo Lamas, Anthony Geary, Arlene Dahl.

NIGHT ON EARTH
FINE LINE. May, 1992. (Jim Jarmusch) Gena Rowlands, Giancarlo Esposito, Roberto Benigni, Winona Ryder.

NIGHT SHAPES
PETER ROMMEL PRODS. Feb., 1999. German. (Andreas Dresen) Meriam Abbas, Dominique Horwitz, Oliver Bassler, Susanne Bornmann, Michael Gwisdek.

NIGHT TRAIN
ALTERNATIVE CINEMA CO. Sept., 1998. Irish. (John Lynch) John Hurt, Brenda Blethyn, Pauline Flanagan, Rynagh O'Grady, Peter Caffrey.

NIGHTWATCH
MIRAMAX FILMS. April, 1998. (Ole Bornedal) Ewan McGregor, Nick Nolte, Josh Brolin, Patricia Arquette, Alix Koromzay, Brad Dourif.

THE NIGHT WE NEVER MET
MIRAMAX. April, 1993. (Warren Leight) Matthew Broderick, Annabella Sciorra, Kevin Anderson.

NIGHT WIND
MARS FILMS. Jan., 1999. French-Swiss-Italian. (Philippe Garrel) Catherine Deneuve, Daniel Duval, Xavier Beauvois, Jacques Lasalle.

NIL BY MOUTH
SONY CLASSICS. May, 1997. British. (Gary Oldman) Ray Winstone, Kathy Burke, Charlie Creed-Miles, Laila Morse, Edna Dore.

NINA HAGEN = PUNK + GLORY
BLACK SUN FLOWER. Feb., 1999. German. (Peter Sempel). Documentary.

NINA TAKES A LOVER
TRIUMPH. March, 1995. (Alan Jacobs) Laura San Giacomo, Paul Rhys, Michael O'Keefe.

9 MILLIMETER
SONNET FILM. May, 1997. Swedish. (Peter Lindmark) Paolo Roberto, Rebecca Facey, Abou-Bakre Aalam.

NINE MONTHS
20TH CENTURY FOX. July, 1995. (Chris Columbus) Hugh Grant, Julianne Moore, Tom Arnold, Joan Cusack.

1999
SACRED POOLS. April, 1998. (Nick Davis) Dan Futterman, Jennifer Garner, Matt McGrath, Amanda Peet, Steven Wright, Sandrine Hold.

1999 MADELEINE
PLAYTIME/CLIMAX. Aug., 1999. French. (Laurent Bouhnik) Vera Briole, Manuel Blanc, Anouk Aimee, Jean-Michel Fete, Jean-Francois Galotte.

1991: THE YEAR PUNK BROKE
TARA. November, 1992. (Dave Markey) Documentary.

THE NINTH GATE
BAC FILMS/ARTISAN. Aug., 1999. French-Spanish. (Roman Polanski) Johnny Depp, Frank Langella, Lena Olin, Emmanuelle Seigner, Barbara Jefford.

NINTH STREET
Hodcarrier Films. Jan., 1999. (Tim Rebman) Don Washington, Devin Willmott, Nadine Griffith, Byron Myrick, Isaac Hayes.

NITRATE KISSES
STRAND. April, 1993. (Barbara Hammer) Documentary.

NIXON
BUENA VISTA. December, 1995. (Oliver Stone) Anthony Hopkins, Joan Allen, Powers Boothe, Ed Harris, Bob Hoskins.

NO DEPOSIT, NO RETURN
ISTITUTO LUCE. Feb., 1999. Italian. (Massimo Costa) Giancarlo Giannini, Silvia De Santis, Max Malatesta.

NO EASY WAY
PGFW. Oct., 1996. (Jeffrey Fine) Alan Boyce, Khandi Alexander, Brandon Hammond, Jermaine Montell, Christina Pickles.

NO ESCAPE
SAVOY. April, 1994. (Martin Campbell) Ray Liotta, Lance Henriksen, Stuart Wilson, Kevin Dillon.

NO FEAR, NO DIE
ART LOGIC. August, 1992. French. (Claire Denis) Isaach de Bankole, Alex Descas, Jean Claude Brialy.

NO LOOKING BACK
GRAMERCY/20TH CENTURY FOX. March, 1998. (Edward Burns) Lauren Holly, Edward Burns, Jon Bon Jovi, Blythe Danner.

NO MERCY
INCA FILMS. September, 1995. Spanish. (Francisco J. Lombardi) Diego Bertie, Adriana Davila, Jorge Chiarella.

NO NAMES ON THE DOORS
ALTERNATIVE FILM. Feb., 1997. Israeli. (Nadav Levitan) Mosku Alkaly, Avi Pnini, Dorit Lev Ari, Danny Bassan, Meir Swissa.

NO ONE WRITES TO THE COLONEL
PRODUCCIONES AMARANTA, GARDENIA PRODUCCIONES, TORNASOL/DMVB/INSTITUTO MEXICANO DE CINEMATOGRAFIA/ FONDO PARA LA PRODUCCION CINEMATOGRAFICA DE CALIDAD. Apr., 1999. Mexican-Spanish-French. (Arturo Ripstein) Fernando Lujan, Marisa Paredes, Salma Hayek.

NO PICNIC
GREAT JONES FILM GROUP. July, 1990. (Philip Hartman) David Brisbin, Myoshin.

NORTH BY NORTH
BBSA/DOLMENFILM. Feb., 1999. Hungarian. (Csaba Bollok) Laura Ruttkay, Zsolt Trill, Barnabas Marton, Nelli Szucs.

NORTHERN SKIRTS
POLYFILM. Sept., 1999. Austrian-German-Swiss. (Barbar Albert) Nina Proll, Edita Malovcic, Michael Tanczos, Tudor Chirila.

NO SCANDAL
CINE B/IMA. Sept., 1999. French. (Benoit Jacquot) Fabrice Luchini, Isabelle Huppert, Vincent Lindon, Vahina Giocante, Sophie Aubry.

NO SECRETS
I.R.S. MEDIA. May, 1991. (Dezso Magyar) Adam Coleman Howard, Amy Locane, Traci Lind.

NO SEX LAST NIGHT
PIERRE GRISE. January, 1996. French-U.S. (Sophie Calle) Documentary.

NO SKIN OFF MY ASS
STRAND. November, 1991. Canadian. (Bruce LaBruce) Bruce LaBruce, Klaus Von Brucker, G. B. Jones.

NOTES FOR A STORY
LIDER FILMS. Sept., 1998. Argentine-Spanish. (Jana Bokova) German Palacios, Silke, Ines Estevez, Hector Alterio.

NOTHING
TELEWIZJA POLSKA/KID FILM/AGENCJA PRODUKCJI FILMOWEJ/LODZKIE CENTRUM FILMOWE. Mar., 1999. Polish. (Dorota Kedzierzawska); Anita Kuskowska-Borkowska, Janusz Panasewicz.

NOTHING IN THE FRIDGE
COLUMBIA TRISTAR. Oct., 1998. Spanish. (Alvaro Fernandez Armero) Maria Esteve, Coque Malla, Roberto Alvarez, Laura Aparicio, Itziar Miranda.

NOT OF THIS WORLD
MIKADO. Mar., 1999. Italian. (Giuseppe Piccioni) Margherita Buy, Silvio Orlando, Carolina Freschi.

NOT ONE LESS
COLUMBIA. Sept., 1999. Chinese. (Zhang Yimou) Wei Minzhi, Zhang Huike, Tian Zhenda, Gao Enman.

NO TRAINS NO PLANES
WARNER BROS. Feb., 1999. Dutch. (Jos Stelling) Dirk van Dijck, Ellen ten Damme, Henri Garcin, Gene Bervoets, Dominique Horwitz.

NO WAY HOME
NORSTAR. Oct., 1996. (Buddy Giovinazzo) Tim Roth, James Russo, Deborah Unger, Bernadette Penotti, Larry Romano.

NOBODY LOVES ME
COBRA. November, 1995. German. (Doris Dorrie) Maria Schrader, Pierre Sanoussi-Bloiss, Michael von Au.

NOBODY WILL SPEAK OF US WHEN WE'RE DEAD
FLAMENCO. January, 1996. Spanish. (Augustin Diaz Yanes) Victoria Abril, Federico Luppi, Pilar Bardem.

NOBODY'S BUSINESS
Oct., 1996. (Alan Berliner) Documentary.

NOBODY'S FOOL
PARAMOUNT. December, 1994. (Robert Benton) Paul Newman, Jessica Tandy, Bruce Willis, Melanie Griffith.

NOBODY'S PERFECT
MOVIESTORE ENT. February, 1990. (Robert Kaylor) Chad Lowe, Gail O'Grady.

NOEL FIELD: THE FICTITIOUS SPY
DSCHOINT VERNTSCHR AG. Swiss. (Werner Schweizer) Documentary.

NOIR ET BLANC
GREYCAT FILMS. May, 1991. French. (Claire Devers) Francis Frappat, Jacques Martial.

NOISES OFF
BUENA VISTA. March, 1992. (Peter Bogdanovich) Michael Caine, Carol Burnett, John Ritter, Christopher Reeve.

NORMAL LIFE
FINE LINE. January, 1996. (John McNaughton) Ashley Judd, Luke Perry, Bruce Young, Jim True, Dawn Maxey.

NORTH
COLUMBIA. July, 1994. (Rob Reiner) Elijah Wood, Jon Lovitz, Bruce Willis, Alan Arkin.

THE NORTH END
MAVEX. Aug., 1997. (Frank Ciota) Frank Vincent, Tony Darrow, Freddie Fabucci, Lina Sivio, Mark Hartmann, Pater Marciano.

NORTH STAR
WARNER BROS. Oct., 1996. French-British-Norwegian-Itallian. (Nils Gaup) James Caan, Christopher Lambert, Catherine McCormack.

THE NORTHERNERS
INDEPENDENT. November, 1993. Dutch. (Alex van Warmerdam) Leonard Lucieer, Jack Vouterse.

NOSTRADAMUS
ORION CLASSICS. September, 1994. British-German. (Roger Christian) Tcheky Karyo, Amanda Plummer.

NOT AFRAID TO SAY...
UNTITLED PRODS./FREEWHEEL PRODS.. July, 1999. (Adam Vetri) Adam Vetri Chelsea Lago, Monica Trombetta, Jason Beck.

NOT LOVE, JUST FRENZY
ALTA FILMS. Sept., 1996. Spanish. (Alfonso Albacete, Miguel Bardem, David Menkes). Nancho Novo, Cayetana Guillen Cuervo.

NOT ME!
MALOFILM INT'L. May, 1996. Canadian. (Pierre Gang) Louise Portal, Isabelle Pasco, Patrice Godin.

NOT WITHOUT MY DAUGHTER
MGM. January, 1991. (Brian Gilbert) Sally Field, Alfred Molina, Sheila Rosenthal.

NOTEBOOKS ON CITIES AND CLOTHES
CONNOISSEUR. October, 1991. German. (Wim Wenders) Documentary.

NOTES FROM UNDERGROUND
WALKOW-GRUBER/RENEGADE. October, 1995. (Gary Alan Walkow) Henry Czerny, Sheryl Lee, Eammon Roche.

NOTHING BUT THE TRUTH
MARK STEVEN SHEPHERD. Oct., 1998. (Mark Steven Shepherd). Documentary.

NOTHING BUT TROUBLE
WARNER BROS. February, 1991. (Dan Aykroyd) Chevy Chase, Demi Moore, John Candy, Dan Aykroyd.

NOTHING SACRED
EX NIHILO FILMS. June, 1997. (David Elliot) Paul Provenza, Stephen Dunham, John Gloria, Shannon Day, Krista Taylor.

NOTHING TO LOSE
BUENA VISTA. July, 1997. (Steve Oedekerk), Martin Lawrence, Tim Robbins, John C. McGinley, Giancarlo Esposito, Kelly Preston.

NO VACANCY
ERNEST KOSKIN . Apr., 1999. (Marius Balchunas Ryan Bollman, Lolita Davidovich, Joaquim de Almeida, Olek Krupa, Gabriel Mann.

THE NOVEMBER MEN
NORTHERN ARTS. November, 1995. (Paul Williams) Leslie Bevis, James Andronica, Baeu Starr.

NOW AND THEN
NEW LINE. October, 1995. (Lesli Linka) Christina Ricci, Thora Birch, Gaby Hoffman.

NOW & THEN: FROM FROSH TO SENIORS
GELLER/GOLDFINE PRODS.. Sept., 1999. (Daniel Geller, Dayna Goldfine). Documentary.

NOWHERE FAST
CHILD HOODS. February, 1996. (Cinque Lee) Darnell Martin, Addison Cook, Gloria Toyum Park.

NOWHERE TO GO
KEVIN J. FOXE. March, 1998. (John Caire) Tricia Vessy, John Shea, Marianne Jean-Baptiste, Carroll Baker, Jacob Smith, Ryan Francis

NOWHERE TO RUN
COLUMBIA. January, 1993. (Robert Harmon) Jean Claude Van Damme, Rosanna Arquette, Kieran Culkin.

NUEBA YOL
KIT PARKER/D'PELICULA. February, 1996. Dominican. (Angel Muniz) Lusito Marti, Caridad Ravelo, Raul Carbonell.

NUNS ON THE RUN
20TH CENTURY FOX. March, 1990. British. (Jonathan Lynn) Eric Idle, Robbie Coltrane. Camille Coduri.

THE NUTCRACKER PRINCE
WARNER BROS. November, 1990. Canadian. (Paul Schibli) Animated.

THE NUTTY PROFESSOR
UNIVERSAL. June, 1996. (Tom Shadyac) Eddie Murphy, Jada Pinkett, James Coburn, Larry Miller, Dave Chappelle.

O

THE OAK
MK2. January, 1993. Romanian. (Lucian Pintilie) Maia Morgenstern, Razvan Vasilescu, Victor Rebengiuc.

O AMOR NATURAL
PIETER VAN HUYSTREE FILM & TV/NPS TV PROD. Feb., 1997. Dutch. (Heddy Honigmann) Documentary.

OBERWASSER - BY U BOAT TO AMERICA
NEUW BERLINER FILMGESELLSCHAFT. Sept., 1998. German. (Wolfram R. Bauer). Documentary.

THE OBJECT OF BEAUTY
AVENUE. April 1991. British. (Michael Lindsay Hogg) John Malkovich, Andie MacDowell.

THE OBJECT OF MY AFFECTION
20TH CENTURY FOX. April, 1998. (Nicholas Hytner) Jennifer Aniston, Paul Rudd, Alan Alda, Nigel Hawthorne, John Pankow, Tim Daly.

OBLIVION
FULL MOON. January, 1995. (Sam Irvin) Richard Joseph Paul, Jackie Swanson, Andrew Divoff.

OCCASIONAL COARSE LANGUAGE
ROADSHOW. Nov., 1998. Australian. (Brad Hayward Sara Browne, Astrid Grant, Nicholas Bishop.

OCEAN TRIBE
SEAREEL. April, 1997. (Will Geiger) Gregg Rainwater, Robert Caso, Troy Fazio, Mark Matheisen, Vaughn Roberts, Brian Brophy.

OCTOBER SKY
UNIVERSAL. Feb., 1999. (Joe Johnston) Jake Gyllenhaal, Chris Cooper, Laura Dern, Chris Owen, William Lee Scott.

THE OCTOPUS
BAC FILMS. Sept., 1998. French. (Guillaume Nicloux) Jean-Pierre Darroussin, Clotilde Courau, Stephane Boucher, Julie Delarme.

THE ODD COUPLE II
PARAMOUNT PICTURES. March, 1998. (Howard Deutch) Jack Lemmon, Walter Matthau, Christine Baranski, Barnard Hughes.

OI! WARNING
SCHLAMMTACHER-FILM. June, 1999. German. (Dominik and Bejamin Reding) Sascha Backhaus, Simon Goerts, Sandra Borgmann, Jens Veith, Britta Dirks.

THE OLD MAN AND THE SEA
OGDEN ENTERTAINMENT. Sept., 1999. (Alexander Petrov). Animated.

OLD MAN RIVER
PINK PLASTIC PRODS. Feb., 1999. (Allan Holzman). Documentary.

OFFICE SPACE
20TH CENTURY FOX. Feb., 1999. (Mike Judge) Ron Livingston, Jennifer Aniston, David Herman, Ajay Naidu, Diedrich Bader.

OF MICE AND MEN
MGM. October, 1992. (Gary Sinise) John Malkovich, Gary Sinise, Ray Walston, Sherilynn Fenn.

OFF THE MENU: THE LAST DAYS OF CHASEN'S
LOBO GRANDE PICTURES. April, 1997. (Shari Springer Berman) Documentary-16mm.

OFFICE KILLER
STRAND. Aug., 1997. (Cindy Sherman) Carol Kane, Molly Ringwald, Jeanne Tripplehorn, Barbara Sukowa, Michael Imperioli.

THE OGRE
UGC D.A. August, 1996. German-French-British. (Volker Schlondorff) John Malkovich, Armin Mueller-Stahl.

O.K. GARAGE
TALANA PRODS./RIALTO FILM. April, 1998. (Brandon Cole) John Turturro, Lili Taylor, Will Patton, Gemma Jones, Joe Maher.

OKOGE
CINEVISTA. April, 1993. Japanese. (Takehiro Nakajima) Misa Shimizu, Takehiro Murata, Takeo Nakahara.

OLD EXPLORERS
TAURUS. September, 1990. (William Pohlad) Jose Ferrer, James Whitmore, Jeffrey Gadbois.

THE OLD LADY WHO WALKED IN THE SEA
CFP. September, 1995. French. (Laurent Heynemann) Jeanne Moreau, Michael Serrault, Luc Thuillier.

OLEANNA
SAMUEL GOLDWYN. November, 1994. (David Mamet) William H. Macy, Debra Eisenstadt.

OLIVIER, OLIVIER
SONY PICTURES CLASSICS. February, 1993. French. (Agnieszka Holland) François Cluzet, Brigitte Rouan.

THE OLYMPIC SUMMER
NEW YORKER. August, 1994. German. (Gordian Maugg) Jost Gerstein, Verena Plangger. B&W.

ON BOARD
YENI SINEMACILIK. Apr., 1999. Turkish. (Serdar Akar) Erkan Can, Haldun Boysan, Yildiray Sahinler.

ONCE AROUND
UNIVERSAL. January, 1991. (Lasse Halstrom) Richard Dreyfuss, Holly Hunter, Danny Aiello.

ONCE UPON A CRIME
MGM. March, 1992. (Eugene Levy) John Candy, James Belushi, Sean Young, Cybill Shepherd.

ONCE UPON A FOREST
20TH CENTURY FOX. June, 1993. (Charles Grosvenor) Animated.

ONCE UPON A TIME IN CHINA
GOLDEN HARVEST. May, 1992. Hong Kong. (Tsui Hark) Jet Li, Yuen Biao, Jacky Cheung.

ONCE UPON A TIME IN CHINA PART 2
GOLDEN HARVEST. September, 1993. Hong Kong. (Tsui Hark) Jet Li, Rosamund Kwan, Mok Siucheung.

ONCE UPON A TIME...THIS MORNING
FIVE STARS. February, 1996. Thai. (Bhandit Rittakol) Jintara

ONCE UPON A TIME...WHEN WE WERE COLORED
REPUBLIC. January, 1996. (Tim Reid) Al Freeman, Jr., Phylicia Rashad, Polly Bergen, Richard Roundtree.

ONCE WERE WARRIORS
FINE LINE. February, 1995. New Zealand. (Lee Tamahori) Rena Owen, Temuera Morrison, Mamaengaroa KerrBell.

ONCE WE WERE STRANGERS
BACKPAIN PRODS. & ACQUARIO FILMS. Aug., 1997. (Emanuele Crialese) Vincenzo Amato, Jessica W. Gould, Ajay Naidu.

ON DEADLY GROUND
WARNER BROS. February, 1994. (Steven Seagal) Steven Seagal, Michael Caine, Joan Chen.

ONE AND A HALF
MEDIA ASIA. December, 1995. Hong Kong. (Lawrence Ah Mon) Zhang Fengyi, Carrie Ng, Paul Chen.

187
WARNER BROS. July, 1997. (Kevin Reynolds), Samuel L. Jackson, John Heard, Kelly Rowan, Clifton Gonzalez Gonzalez, Tony Plana.

ONE FALSE MOVE
I.R.S. May, 1992. (Carl Franklin) Bill Paxton, Cynda Williams, Billy Bob Thornton.

ONE FINE DAY
20TH CENTURY FOX. November, 1996. (Michael Hoffman), Michelle Pfeiffer, George Clooney, Mae Whitman, Alex D. Linz.

O-NEGATIVE
GRAMMY FILM CO. Nov., 1998. Thai. (Paiboon Damrongchaithan) Amita (Tata) Young, Shawekrit Yamnam, Ray MacDonald.

ONEGIN
SEVEN ARTS INTL.. Sept., 1999. British. (Martha Fiennes) Ralph Fiennes, Liv Tyler, Toby Stephens, Lena Heady, Martin Donovan.

ONE GOOD COP
BUENA VISTA. May, 1991. (Heywood Gould) Michael Keaton, Rene Russo, Anthony LaPaglia.

ONE HAND DON'T CLAP
RHAPSODY FILMS. August, 1991. (Kavery Dutta) Documentary.

101 DALMATIANS
BUENA VISTA. November, 1996. (Stephen Herek), Glenn Close, Jeff Daniels, Joely Richardson, Joan Plowright, Hugh Laurie.

100 PROOF
MAMMOTH PICTURES. Jan., 1997. (Jeremy Horton) Pamela Holden Stewart, Tara Bellando, Jack Stubblefield Johnson.

ONE MAN'S HERO
MGM. Sept., 1999. (Lance Hool) Tom Berenger, Joaquim De Almeida, Daniela Romo, Mark Moses, Stuart Graham.

ONE NIGHT STAND
NEW LINE. August, 1997. (Mike Figgis), Wesley Snipes, Nastassja Kinski, Ming-Na Wen, Robert Downey Jr., Kyle MacLachlan.

1–900
ZEITGEIST. September, 1995. Dutch. (Theo van Gogh) Ariane Schluter, Ad van Kempen.

1000 PIECES OF GOLD
GREYCAT. May, 1991. (Nancy Kelly) Rosalind Chao, Chris Cooper, Dennis Dun.

ONE TOUGH COP
STRATOSPHERE ENTERTAINMENT. Sept., 1998. (Bruno Barreto) Stephen Baldwin, Chris Penn, Mike McGlone, Gina Gershon, Paul Guilfoyle, Amy Irving, Victor Slezak, Luis Guzman.

ONE TRUE THING
UNIVERSAL PICTURES. Aug., 1998. (Carl Franklin) Meryl Streep, Rene Zellweiger, William Hurt, Tom Everett Scott, Lauren Graham.

ONE WAY OUT
ARROW PICTURES. April, 1996. (Kevin Lynn) Jack Swaltney, Jeff Monahan, Isabel Gillies, Annie Golden.

ONE WINTER BEHIND GOD'S BACK
MAGIC MEDIA/47EME PARALELLE/MAGELLAN PRODUCTION/ NEIKA FILMS. Feb., 1999. Hungarian-French-Belgian-Slovak. (Togay Can) Matej Matejka, David Szabo, Karoly Eperjes.

ONLY THE BRAVE
FIRST RUN. May, 1995. Australian. (Ana Kokkinos) Elena Mandalis, Dora Kaskanis, Maude Davey.

ONLY THE BRAVE
SCORPIO. August, 1994. Dutch. (Sonia Herman Dolz) Documentary.

ONLY THE LONELY
20TH CENTURY FOX. May, 1991. (Chris Columbus) John Candy, Ally Sheedy, Maureen O'Hara.

ONLY THE STRONG
20TH CENTURY FOX. August, 1993. (Sheldon Lettich) Mark Dacascos, Stacey Travis, Geoffrey Lewis.

THE ONLY THRILL
MOONSTONE. May, 1997. (Peter Masterson) Diane Keaton, Sam Shepard, Diane Lane, Robert Patrick, Tate Donovan.

ONLY YOU
TRISTAR. October, 1994. (Norman Jewison) Marisa Tomei, Robert Downey, Jr., Bonnie Hunt, Billy Zane.

ON THE BRIDGE
DIRECT CINEMA. October, 1993. (Frank Perry) Frank Perry. Sukkapat, Satisuk Phromisi. Martang Jantranee.

ON THE HEIGHTS ALL IS PEACE
MUSEO STORICO IN TRENTO, COMUNE DI ROVERETO, FONDAZIONE CADUTI IN GUERRA DI ROVERETO. Feb., 1999. Italian. (Yervant Gianikian, Angela Ricci Lucchi). Documentary.

ON THE ROPES
HIGHWAY FILMS/LEARNING CHANNEL. Jan., 1999. (Nanette Burstein). Documentary.

OPEN DOORS
ORION CLASSICS. March, 1991. Italian. (Gianni Amelio) Gian Maria Volonte, Ennio Fantastichini.

OPERATION DUMBO DROP
BUENA VISTA. July, 1995. (Simon Wincer) Danny Glover, Ray Liotta, Denis Leary, Doug E. Doug.

THE OPIUM WAR
EMEI FILM STUDIO. May, 1997. Chinese. (Xie Jin) Bao Guoan, Lin Liankun, Su Min, Sihung Lung, Bob Peck, Simon Williams, Shao Xin.

OPPORTUNITY KNOCKS
UNIVERSAL. March, 1990. (Donald Petrie) Dana Carvey, Robert Loggia, Todd Graff.

OPPOSITE SEX, THE (AND HOW TO LIVE WITH THEM)
MIRAMAX. March, 1993. (Matthew Meshekoff) Arye Gross, Courteney Cox, Kevin Pollak.

ORBIS PICTUS
CHARLIE'S. May, 1997. Slovak-Czech. (Martin Sulik) Dorotka Nvotova, Marian Labuda, Bozidara Turzonovova, Julius Satinsky.

ORDINARY HEROES
GOLDEN HARVEST. Feb., 1999. Hong Kong. (Ann Hui) Rachel Lee, Lee Kang-sheng, Anthony Wong, Tse Kwan-ho.

ORGAN
ORGAN VITAL PROD. Sept., 1996. Japanese. (Kei Fujiwara) Kimihiko Hasegawa, Kenji Nasa, Kei Fujiwara, Ryo Okubo.

ORGAZMO
OCTOBER FILMS. Sept., 1997. (Trey Parker) Trey Parker, Dian Bachar, Robyn Lynne, Michael Dean Jacobs, Ron Jeremy.

ORIGINAL GANGSTAS
ORION. April, 1996. (Larry Cohen) Fred Williamson, Jim Brown, Pam Grier, Paul Winfield.

ORLANDO
SONY PICTURES CLASSICS. June, 1993. British-Russian-French-Dutch. (Sally Potter) Tilda Swinton, Billy Zane, Lothaire Bluteau.

OSCAR
BUENA VISTA. April, 1991. (John Landis) Sylvester Stallone, Peter Riegert, Vincent Spano, Tim Curry.

OSCAR AND LUCINDA
FOX SEARCHLIGHT. Nov., 1997. (Gillian Armstrong) Ralph Fiennes, Cate Blanchett, Ciaran Hinds, Tom Wilkinson, Richard Roxburgh.

OSKAR AND JACK
JANE BALFOUR FILMS. April, 1996. German. (Frauke Sandig) Documentary.

OSKAR AND LENI
BASIS FILM. Feb., 1999. German. (Petra Katharina Wagner) Christian Redl, Anna Thalbach, Elisabeth Trissenaar, Reiner Heise, Nadja Engel.

OTHELLO
ROCKBOTTOM/UPTOWN FILMS. November, 1990. (Ted Lange) Ted Lange, Hawthorne James, Mary Otis.

OTHELLO
COLUMBIA. December, 1995. (Oliver Parker) Laurence Fishburne, Irene Jacob, Kenneth Branagh, Nathaniel Parker.

THE OTHER
MISR INTERNATIONAL. MAY, 1999. French-Egyptian. (Youssef Chahine) Nabila Ebeid, Mahmoud Hemeida, Hanane tork, Hani Salama, Lebleba.

THE OTHER CONQUEST
CARRASCO & DOMINGO FILMS/SECRETARIA DE DESARROLLO SOCIAL/CONACULTA/FONCA/IMCINE/TABASCO FILMS. May, 1999. Mexican. (Salvador Carrasco) Damian Delgado, Jose Carlos Rodriguez, Elpidia Carrillo, Inaki Aierra, Honorato Magaloni.

OTHER PEOPLE'S MONEY
WARNER BROS. October, 1991. (Norman Jewison) Danny DeVito, Gregory Peck, Penelope Ann Miller.

THE OTHER SHORE
POLYGRAM. May, 1997. French. (Dominique Cabrera) Claude Brasseur, Roschdy Zem, Marthe Villalonga, Agoumi.

THE OTHER SIDE OF SUNDAY
NORSK FILMDISTRIBUSJON. Nov., 1996. Norwegian. (Berit Nesheim) Marie Theisen, Bjorn Sundquist, Hildegunn Riise.

THE OTHER SIDE OF THE TRACKS
FRANCE 2/LITTLE BEAR. Oct., 1998. French. (Bertrand Tavernier). Documentary.

THE OTHER SISTER
BUENA VISTA. FEB. 1999. (Garry Marshall) Juliette Lewis, Diane Keaton, Tom Skerritt, Giovanni Ribisi, Poppy Montgomery.

OTHER STORIES
RIOFILME. May, 1999. Brazilian. (Pedro Bial) Paulo Jose, Walderez De Barros, Caca Carvalho, Chico Neto, Juca De Oliveira.

OTHER VOICES, OTHER ROOMS
GOLDEN EYE. October, 1995. (David Rocksavage) Lothaire Bluteau, Anna Thompson, David Speck.

OUR HAPPY LIVES
MARS FILMS. May, 1999. French. (Jacques Maillot) Marie Payen Cecile Richard Camille Japy, Sami Bouajila, Eric Bonicatto.

OUR INDIANS
RIOFILME. Feb., 1997. Brazilian. (Sylvio Back) Documentary.

OUR ISLAND IN THE SOUTH PACIFIC
SENATOR FILM. May, 1999. German. (Thomas Bahmann) Herbert Knaup, Andrea Sawitzki, Alexandra Maria Lara.

THE OUTFITTERS
PORCHLIGHT. Jan., 1999. (Reverge Anselmo) Danny Nucci, Del Zamora, Sarah lassez, Dana Delany, Jerry Haynes.

OUT FOR JUSTICE
WARNER BROS. April, 1991. (John Flynn) Steven Seagal, William Forsythe, Jerry Orbach.

OUT IN THE OPEN
PRODUCCIONES 800. March, 1997. Venezuelan-Canadian-French. (Luis Armando Roche) Roy Dupuis, Christian Vadim, Carlos Cruz.

OUTLAW
COLUMBIA TRISTAR. Apr., 1999. Italian. (Enzo Monteleone) Stefano Accorsi, Giovanni Esposito, Eilio Solfrizzi.

OUT OF DEPTH
REDBUS FILMS. May, 1999. British. (Simon Marshall) Sean Maguire, Danny Midwinter, Nicholas Ball, Phil Cornwall, Josephine Butler.

OUT OF SIGHT
UNIVERSAL PICTURES. June, 1998. (Steven Soderbergh) George Clooney, Jennifer Lopez, Ving Rhames, Don Cheadle, Dennis Farina.

OUT OF THE COLD
OLD TOWN. Aug., 1999. Estonian-Russian. (Sasha Buravsky) Keith Carradine, Mia Kirschner, Brian Dennehy, Judd Hirsch, Mercedes Ruehl.

THE OUT-OF-TOWNERS
PARAMOUNT. Mar., 1999. (Sam Weisman) Steve Martin, Goldie Hawn, Mark McKinney, John Cleese, Oliver Hudson.

OUT OF WORK
ANDERSON/GOLD FILMS. Jan., 1997. (Kelly Anderson) Documentary - 16mm.

OUT ON A LIMB
UNIVERSAL. September, 1992. (Francis Veber) Matthew Broderick, Jeffrey Jones, Heidi Kling.

THE OUTSIDE CHANCE OF MAXIMILLIAN GLICK
SOUTH GATE ENTERTAINMENT. January, 1990. Canadian. (Allan A. Goldstein) Noam Zylberman, Fairuza Balk.

OUTSIDE OZONA
SONY. Dec. 1998. (J. S. Cardone) Robert Forster, Kevin Pollak, Sherlyn Fenn, David Paymer, Penelope Ann Miller.

OUTSIDE PROVIDENCE
MIRAMAX. July, 1999. (Michael Corrente) Shawn Hatosy, Jon Abrahams, Tommy Bone, Jonathan Brandis, Jack Ferver.

THE OUTSKIRTS
Morning of the XXI Century Studio/Goskino of Russia. Oct., 1998. Russian. (Petr Lutsik) Yuri Dubrovin, Nikolai Olyalin, Alexei Pushkin, Alexei Vanin, Rimma Markova.

OUT TO SEA
20TH CENTURY FOX. June, 1997. (Martha Coolidge), Jack Lemmon, Walter Matthau, Dyan Cannon, Gloria De Haven, Brent Spine.

OUTBREAK
WARNER BROS. March, 1995. (Wolfgang Petersen) Dustin Hoffman, Renee Russo, Morgan Freeman.

OVEREXPOSED
CONCORDE. March, 1990. (Larry Brand) Catherine Oxenberg, David Naughton.

OVERSEAS
ARIES. November, 1991. French. (Brigitte Rouan) Nicole Garcia, Marianne Basler, Brigitte Rouan.

OVOSODO
CECCHI GORI DISTRIBUZIONE. Sept., 1997. Italian. (Paolo Virzi) Edoardo Gabbriellini, Malcolm Lunghi, Matteo Campus.

THE OX
CASTLE HILL/FIRST RUN FEATURES. August, 1992. Swedish. (Sven Nykvist) Stellan Skarsgård, Ewa Fröling.

THE OYSTER AND THE WIND
RIOFILME. Aug., 1997. Brazilian. (Walter Lima Jr.) Leandra Leal, Lima Duarte, Fernando Torres, Floriano Peixoto, Castrinho.

P

PCU
20TH CENTURY FOX. April, 1994. (Hart Bochner) Jeremy Piven, Chris Young, David Spade.

PACIFIC HEIGHTS
20TH CENTURY FOX. September, 1990. (John Schlesinger) Matthew Modine, Melanie Griffith, Michael Keaton.

THE PAGEMASTER
20TH CENTURY FOX. November, 1994. (Joe Johnston) Macauley Culkin, Christopher Lloyd, Ed Begley Jr.

PAIN IS...
Les Films d'Ici/Urbane Ltd./ZDF/Arte. Oct., 1998. French-German-British. (Stephen Dwoskin). Documentary.

PAINTED HERO
IRS. November, 1995. (Terry Benedict) Dwight Yokam, Michelle Joyner, Bo Hopkins, John Getz.

A PAINTING FOR LOVE
FARABI CINEMA FOUNDATION. May, 1999. Iranian. (Hosseinali Lialastani) Farrokh Nemati, Jahangir Almasi, Fateme Goudarzi, Jamshid Layegh.

PAINTING THE TOWN
PADDED CELL. May, 1992. (Andrew Behar) Richard Osterwell.

PALE SAINTS
NORSTAR ENTERTAINMENT/FREQUENCY FILMS. May, 1997. Canadian. (Joel Wyner) Sean Patrick Flanery, Michael Riley.

THE PALLBEARER
MIRAMAX. May, 1996. (Matt Reeves) David Schwimmer, Gwyneth Paltrow, Michael Rapaport, Toni Collette.

PALMER'S PICK-UP
WINCHESTER FILMS. Mar., 1999. (Christopher Coppola) Robert Carradine, Richard Hillman, Patrick Kilpatrick, Neil Guintoli.

PALOOKAVILLE
PLAYHOUSE INTERNATIONAL. Septmber, 1995. (Alan Taylor) William Forsythe, Vincent Gallo, Frances McDormand.

PALOMBELLA ROSSA
INT'L FILM CIRCUIT. January, 1991. Italian. (Nanni Moretti) Nanni Moretti, Silvio Orlando, Mariella Valentini.

THE PANAMA DECEPTION
EMPOWERMENT PROJECT. July, 1992. (Barbara Trent) Documentary.

THE PANDORA PROJECT
CINE/TEL. May, 1998. (Jim Wynorski, John Terlesky) Daniel Baldwin, Erika Eleniak, Richard Tyson, Tony Todd, Jeff Yagher, Bo Jackson.

PANTHER
GRAMERCY. May, 1995. (Mario Van Peebles) Kadeem Hardison, Bokeem Woodbine, Courtney B. Vance.

PAPARAZZI
FILMAURO. Jan., 1999. Italian. (Neri Parenti). Christian De Sica, Massimo Boldi, Diego Abatantuono, Roberto Brunetti, Nin D'Angelo.

THE PAPER
UNIVERSAL. March, 1994. (Ron Howard) Michael Keaton, Glenn Close, Marisa Tomei, Robert Duvall.

PAPERBACK HERO
POLYGRAM. Feb., 1999. Australian. (Antony J. Bowman) Claudia Karvan, Hugh Jackman, Angie Milliken.

PAPER MASK
CASTLE HILL. November, 1991. British. (Christopher Morahan) Paul McGann, Amanda Donohoe, Frederick Treves.

A PAPER WEDDING
CAPITOL ENT. June, 1991. French-Canadian. (Michel Brault) Genevieve Bujold, Manuel Aranguiz.

PARADISE
BUENA VISTA. September, 1991. (Mary Agnes Donoghue) Don Johnson, Melanie Griffith, Elijah Wood.

PARADISE FALLS
MECEO PRODS. Aug., 1998. (Nick Sercy) Sean Bridgers, Christopher Berry, Nick Searcy, Sonny Shroyer, Claire Eye.

PARADISE LOST:
THE CHILD MURDERS AT ROBIN HOOD HILLS
HBO. January, 1996. (Joe Berlinger) Documentary.

PARADISE ROAD
FOX SEARCHLIGHT. MArch, 1997. (Bruce Beresford), Glenn Close, Pauline Collins, Cate Blanchett, Frances McDormand, Julianna Margulies.

A PARALYZING FEAR:
THE STORY OF POLIO IN AMERICA
BELLEVUE FILMS. Feb., 1998. (Nina Gilden Seavey) Nina Dickens, Lillian Folley, Hermine Douglas, Alan Douglas, Anisa Dickens.

THE PARENT TRAP
BUENA VISTA. July, 1998. (Nancy Meyers) Lindsay Lohan, Dennis Quaid, Natasha Richardson, Elaine Hendrix, Lisa Ann Walter.

PARENTAL GUIDANCE
LES CINEMAS DE LA ZONE. May, 1996. French. (Lucile Hadzihalilovic) Sandra Sammartino, Michel Trillot.

PARIS
DOUBLE D COPYRIGHT FILMS. Aug., 1998. French. (Raymond Depardon) Sylvie Peyre, Luc Delahaye, Emilie Lafarge, Barbara Jung, Metilde Weyergans.

PARIS, FRANCE
ALLIANCE. February, 1994. Canadian. (Gerard Ciccoritti) Leslie Hope, Peter Outerbridge, Victor Ertmanis.

PARIS, MY LITTLE BODY IS AWEARY OF THIS GREAT WORLD
OGNON PICTURES/GALATEE FILMS. Aug., 1999. French. (Franssou Prenant) Manuel Cedron, Cecile Garcia Fogel, Franssou Prenant.

PARIS IS BURNING
OFF WHITE PRODS. March, 1991. (Jennie Livingston) Documentary.

PARK DAY
CLANDESTINE ENTERTAINMENT. Nov., 1998. (Sterling Macer, Jr.) Hill Harper, Monica Calhoun, Lande Scott, Brock Peters.

THE PARTY CRASHERS
CINEMA ARTS. Feb. 1999. (Phil Leirness) John Saxon, Max Parrish, Peter Murnik, Shawnee Smith, Phil Leirness.

PARTY GIRL
FIRST LOOK. June, 1995. (Daisy von Scherler Mayer) Parker Posey, Guillermo Diaz, Omar Townsend.

PARTY MONSTER
WORLD OF WONDER. Feb., 1998. (Fenton Bailey, Randy Barbato) DOCUMENTARY.

PARTY'S AT SAM'S
EDWARD & SHARON EBOCH/HARVEY & RUTH MARKOWITZ/ CHRIS EBOCH. Jan., 1997. (Douglas J. Eboch) Rick Fitzgerald, Michael Markowitz, Sinneman Brown.

PASSAGE
ETAMP FILM PRODS. Feb., 1997. Czech-French-Belgian. (Juraj Herz) Jacek Borkowski, Malgorzata Kozuchowska.

PASSED AWAY
BUENA VISTA. April, 1992. (Charlie Peters) Bob Hoskins, Pamela Reed, Maureen Stapleton.

PASSENGER 57
WARNER BROS. November, 1992. (Kevin Hooks) Wesley Snipes, Bruce Payne, Alex Datcher.

THE PASSENGERS
LES FILMS DU LOSANGE. Apr., 1999. French. (Jean-Claude Guiguet) Fabienne Babe, Philippe Garziano, Bruno Putzulu, Stephane Rideau, Gwenaelle Simon.

PASSION
REP. June, 1999. Australian-U.S. (Peter Duncan) Barbara Hershey, Richard Roxburgh, Emily Woof, Claudia Karvan, Simon Burke.

PASSION FISH
MIRAMAX. December, 1992. (John Sayles) Mary McDonnell, Alfre Woodard, David Strathairn.

PASSION IN THE DESSERT
FINE LINE. Aug., 1997. (Lavinia Currier) Ben Daniels, Michel Piccoli, Paul Meston, Kenneth Collard, Nadi Odeh.

THE PASSION OF AYN RAND
SHOWTIME. Jan., 1999. (Christopher Menaul) Helen Mirren, Eric Stoltz, Julie Delpy, Peter Fonda, Tom McCamus.

A PASSION TO KILL
APIX/RYSHER. November, 1994. (Rick King) Scott Bakula, Chelsea Field, Sheila Kelley, France Nuyen.

PASTIME
MIRAMAX. August, 1991. (Robin B. Armstrong) William Russ, Glenn Plummer, Noble Willingham.

PATCH ADAMS
UNIVERSAL. Dec., 1998. (Tom Shadyac) Robin Williams, Daniel London, Monica Potter, Philip Seymour Hoffman, Bob Gunton.

PATHS IN THE NIGHT
O-FILM/ZDF. May, 1999. German. (Andreas Kleinert) Hilmar Thate, Cornelia Schamus, Henriette Heinze.

PATRIOT GAMES
PARAMOUNT. June, 1992. (Phillip Noyce) Harrison Ford, Patrick Bergin, Anne Archer, Sean Bean.

PAUL BOWLES: THE COMPLETE OUTSIDER
FIRST RUN. September, 1994. (Catherine Warnow, Regina Weinreich) Documentary.

PAUL MCCARTNEY'S GET BACK
NEW LINE. October, 1991. British. (Richard Lester) Documentary.

PAUL MONETTE: THE BRINK OF SUMMER'S END
BRINK OF SUMMER'S END. Jan., 1997. (Monte Bramer) Documentary - 16mm.

PAULIE
DREAMWORKS PICTURES. April, 1998. (John Roberts) Gena Rowlands, Tony Shalhoub, Cheech Marin, Bruce Davison, Jay Mohr, Trini Alvarado, Buddy Hackett.

PAULINA
CINEMAMAS. March, 1998. (Vicky Funari) Paulina Cruz Suarez, Mathyselene Heredia Castillo, Mariam Manzano Duran.

PAYBACK
PARAMOUNT. Feb., 1999. (Brian Helgeland) Mel Gibson, Gregg Henry, Maria Bello, Deborah Kara Unger, David Paymer.

PEACEMAKER
FRIES. May, 1990. (Kevin S. Tenney) Robert Forster, Lance Edwards, Robert Davi.

THE PEBBLE AND THE PENGUIN
MGM/UA. April, 1995. (Russel Boland) (voices) Martin Short, Annie Golden, Tim Curry, James Belushi. Animated.

PECKER
FINE LINE. July, 1998. (John Waters) Edward Furlong, Christina Ricci, Mary Kay Place, Martha Plimpton, Mink Stole, Lili Taylor.

THE PELICAN BRIEF
WARNER BROS. December, 1993. (Alan J. Pakula) Julia Roberts, Denzel Washington, Sam Shepard.

THE PENKNIFE
BOS BROS. Oct., 1998. Dutch. (Ben Sombogaart) Olivier Tuinier, Genio de Groot, Adelheid Roosen, Verno Romney.

THE PEOPLE UNDER THE STAIRS
UNIVERSAL. November, 1991. (Wes Craven) Brandon Adams, Everett McGill, Wendy Robie.

PEOPLE WHO LOVE EACH OTHER
BLUE DAHLIA PROD., LE STUDIO CANAL PLUS, FRANCE 3 CINEMA, JCT PRODS./ARTEMIS PROD./SAMSA FILM/TORNASOL FILMS. June, 1999. French-Belgian-Luxembourgois. (Jean-Charles Tacchella) Richard Berry, Jacqueline Bisset, Jule Gayet, Bruno Putzulu, Marie Collins.

PEPE GUINDO
ALTA FILMS. Aug., 1999. Spanish. (Manuel Iborra) Fernando Fernan-Gomez, Veronica Forque, Antonio Resines, Jorge Sanz, Yael Barnatan.

PEP SQUAD
TROMA ENTERTAINMENT. May, 1998. (Steve Balderson) Jennifer Dreiling, Brooke Balderson, Amy Kelly, Adrian Pejol.

THE PEREZ FAMILY
SAMUEL GOLDWYN. May, 1995. (Mira Nair) Marisa Tomei, Alfred Molina, Anjelica Huston, Chazz Palminteri.

A PERFECT CANDIDATE
SEVENTH ART. April, 1996. (R.J. Cutler) Documentary.

THE PERFECT CIRCLE
PARNASSE INTL/SARAJEVO DOKUMENT. May, 1997. Bosnian-French. (Ademir Kenovic) Mustafa Nadarevic, Almedin Leleta.

THE PERFECT EDUCATION
SHOCHIKU CO. LTD. Aug., 1999. Japanese. (Ben Wada) Naoto Takenaka, Hijiri Kojima, Eriko Watanabe, Kazuki Kitamura, Asami Sawaki.

PERFECT LOVE!
FLACH PYRAMIDE INTL. May, 1996. French. (Catherine Breillat) Isabelle Renauld, Francis Renaud, Laura Saglio.

A PERFECT MURDER
WARNER BROS. May, 1998. (Andrew Davis) Michael Douglas, Gwyneth Paltrow, Vigo Mortensen, David Suchet, Sarita Choudhury.

THE PERFECT MURDER
MERCHANT IVORY PRODS. March, 1990. British-Indian. (Zafar Hai) Naseeruddin Shan, Stellan Skarsgård.

THE PERFECT WEAPON
PARAMOUNT. March, 1991. (Mark DiSalle) Jeff Speakman, John Dye, Mako.

A PERFECT WORLD
WARNER BROS. November, 1993. (Clint Eastwood) Kevin Costner, Clint Eastwood, Laura Dern, T.J. Lowther.

PERFECTLY NORMAL
4 SEASONS ENT. February, 1991. Canadian. (Yves Simoneau) Robbie Coltrane, Michael Riley.

PERFUMED BALL
RIO FILME. May, 1997. Brazilian. (Paulo Caldas, Lirio Ferreira) Duda Mamberti, Luiz Carlos Vasconcelos, Aramis Trindade, Chico Diaz.

PERMANENT MIDNIGHT
ARTISAN ENTERTAINMENT. Sept., 1998. (David Veloz) Ben Stiller, Elizabeth Hurley, Maria Bello, Owen Wilson, Lourdes Benedicto.

PERMANENT VACATION
ANTHOLOGY FILMS. September, 1990; release of 1980 film. (Jim Jarmusch) Chris Parker, Leila Gastil.

PERSONAL BELONGINGS
STEVEN BOGNAR. January, 1996. (Steven Bognar) Documentary.

THE PERSONALS
EDKO FILMS. Dec., 1998. Taiwanese. (Chen Kuo-fu) Rene Liu, Chen Chao-jung, Wu Pai, Chin Shih-chieh, Ku Pao-ming,.

PERSUASION
SONY PICTURES CLASSICS. October, 1995. British. (Roger Michell) Amanda Root, Ciaran Hinds, Susan Fleetwood.

THE PEST
TRISTAR/BUBBLE FACTORY. February, 1997. (Paul Miller), John Leguizamo, Jeffrey Jones, Edoardo Ballerini, Freddy Rodriguez.

PET SEMATARY II
PARAMOUNT. August, 1992. (Mary Lambert) Edward Furlong, Anthony Edwards, Clancy Brown.

PETER'S FRIENDS
SAMUEL GOLDWYN. December, 1992. British. (Kenneth Branagh) Hugh Laurie, Kenneth Branagh, Emma Thompson.

THE PHANTOM
PARAMOUNT. June, 1996. (Simon Wincer) Billy Zane, Kristy Swanson, Treat Williams, Catherine Zeta-Jones.

PHANTOM BEIRUT
GH FILMS, IDEA PRODS/OPTIMA. Oct., 1998. French-Lebanese. (Ghassan Salhab) Aouni Kawas, Darina Al Joundi, Rabih Mroue.

THE PHANTOM LOVER
MANDARIN FILMS. Nov., 1996. Hong Kong. (Ronny Yu) Leslie Cheung, Wu Chien-lien, Huang Lei, Liu Lin.

THE PHANTOM OF THE OPERA
HIRSCHFELD PRODS. June, 1991. (Darwin Knight) David Staller, Elizabeth Walsh.

THE PHANTOM OF THE OPERA
MEDUSA. Nov., 1998. Italian. (Dario Argento). Julian Sands, Asia Argento, Andrea Di Stefano, Nadia Rinaldi, Coralina Cataldi-Tassoni.

PHANTOM PAIN
WHITE STREAK. June, 1996. (Neil Matsumoto) Tina Alexis, Scott Reda, Holly Woodland.

PHAT BEACH
ORION. August, 1996. (Doug Ellin) Jermaine (Huggy) Hopkins, Brian Hooks, Gregg Vance.

PHENOMENON
BUENA VISTA. June, 1996. (Jon Turteltaub) John Travolta, Robert Duvall, Forest Whitaker, Kyra Sedgewick.

PHILADELPHIA
TRISTAR. December, 1993. (Jonathan Demme) Tom Hanks, Denzel Washington, Jason Robards.

THE PHILADELPHIA EXPERIMENT 2
TRIMARK. November, 1993. (Stephen Cornwell) Brad Johnson, Marjean Holden, Gerrit Graham.

PHOENIX
LAKESHORE ENTERTAINMENT. May, 1998. (Danny Cannon) Ray Liotta, Anthony La Paglia, Anjelica Huston, Daniel Baldwin, Jeremy Piven, Giancarlo Espositio.

PHOTOGRAPHER
SEVENTH ART. Dec., 1998. Polishi-French. (Darius Jablonski). Documentary.

THE PIANIST
MASSA D'OR PRODS./TORNASOL. Sept., 1998. Spanish. (Mario Gas) Jordi Molla, Pere Ponce, Paulina Galvez, Laurent Terzieff, Serge Reggiani.

THE PIANO
MIRAMAX. November, 1993. Australian-New Zealand-French. (Jane Campion) Holly Hunter, Harvey Keitel.

THE PICKLE
COLUMBIA. April, 1993. (Paul Mazursky) Danny Aiello, Dyan Cannon, Clotilde Courau.

PICTURE BRIDE
MIRAMAX. April, 1995. (Kayo Hatta) Youki Kudoch, Akira Takayama, Tamlyn Tomita.

PICTURES FROM A REVOLUTION
KINO INT'L. May, 1992. (Susan Meiselas, Richard O. Rogers, Alfred Guzzetti) Documentary.

PICTURES OF THE SOUL
ADAGIO SRL. October, 1995. Argentinian. (Diego Musiak) Jorge Diez, Maria Lura Leon, China Zorilla.

PIERRE AND MARIE
AMLF. March, 1997. French. (Claude Pinoteau) Isabelle Huppert, Philippe Noiret, Charles Berling, Christian Charmetant.

THE PIG'S RETRIBUTION
SUNCENT CINEMA WORKS. Aug. 1999. (Yohichi Sai) Yukiyoshi Ozawa, Yoshie Hayasaka, Michiko Ameku, Mayumi Ueda, Susumu Taira.

PIN GODS
ARC PICTURES. Sept., 1996. (Larry Locke) Documentary.

PIT AND THE PENDULUM
JGM/FULL MOON. May, 1991. (Stuart Gordon) Lance Henriksen, Rona De Ricci, Jonathan Fuller.

PIZZA, BOOZE, SMOKES
PALO Y A LA BOLSA CINE. Sept., 1998. Argentine. (Bruno Stagnaro) Hector Anglada, Jorge Sesan, Pamela Jordan.

PIZZA MAN
MEGALOMANIA PRODS. December, 1991. (J.D. Athens) Bill Maher, Annabelle Gurwitch, David McKnight.

PLAYBOYS
SAMUEL GOLDWYN. April, 1992. Irish. (Gillies MacKinnon) Albert Finney, Aidan Quinn, Robin Wright.

THE PLAYER
FINE LINE. April, 1992. (Robert Altman) Tim Robbins, Greta Scacchi, Whoopi Goldberg, Fred Ward.

THE PLAYERS CLUB
NEW LINE CINEMA. April, 1998. (Ice Cube) Lisa Raye, Bernie Mac, Monica Calhoun, A.J. Johnson, Ice Cube, Alex Thomas, Jamie Foxx.

PLAYING BY HEART
MIRAMAX. Dec., 1998. (Willard Carroll) Gillian Anderson, Angelina Jolie, Madeleine Stowe, Anthony Edwards, Ryan Phillippe.

PLAYING GOD
BUENA VISTA. Oct., 1997. (Andy Wilson) David Duchovny, Timothy Hutton, Angelina Joie, Michael Massee, Peter Stormare.

THE PLAY OF GOD
NEW GENERATION CINEMA. Oct., 1998. Indian. (Jayaraaj) Jatin Bora, Ashish Vidyarthi, Debashree Roy, Nipon Gowami, Mridhula Barua.

PLEASANTVILLE
NEW LINE CINEMA. Sept., 1998. (Gary Ross) Tobey Maguire, Jeff Daniels, Joan Allen, William H. Macy, J. T. Walsh, Reese Witherspoon.

THE PLOT AGAINST HARRY
NEW YORKER. January, 1990; made in 1969. (Michael Roemer) Martin Priest, Ben Lang. B&W.

PLUMP FICTION
LEGACY. May, 1998. (Bob Koherr) Tommy Davidson, Julie Brown, Paul Dinello, Sandra Bernhard, Dan Castellaneta, Colleen Camp.

PLUNKETT & MACLEANE
POLYGRAM/GRAMMERCY. Mar., 1999. (Jake Scott) Robert Carlyle, Jonny Lee Miller. Liv Tyler, Ken Stott, Michael Gambon.

THE PLUTONIUM CIRCUS
GREYCAT. February, 1996. (George Whittenberg Ratliff) Documentary.

POCAHONTAS
BUENA VISTA. June, 1995. (Mike Gabriel, Eric Goldberg) Animated.

POCO LOCO
SIGNS OF LIFE. October, 1995. (Deborah Koons) Susan Brecht, George Castillo, Sandra Chapin.

POETIC JUSTICE
COLUMBIA. July, 1993. (John Singleton) Janet Jackson, Tupac Shakur, Regina King.

POINT BREAK
20TH CENTURY FOX. July, 1991. (Kathryn Bigelow) Patrick Swayze, Keanu Reeves, Gary Busey.

POINT OF NO RETURN
WARNER BROS. March, 1993. (John Badham) Bridget Fonda, Gabriel Byrne, Dermot Mulroney.

POISON
ZEITGEIST. April, 1991. (Todd Haynes) Larry Maxwell, Susan Norman, Scott Renderer.

POISON IVY
NEW LINE. May, 1992. (Katt Shea) Sara Gilbert, Drew Barrymore, Tom Skerritt.

POLA X
PATHE. May, 1999. French-German-Japanese-Swiss. (Leos Carax) Guillaume Depardieu, Katerina Golubeva, Catherine Deneuve, Delphine Chuillot, Petruta Catana.

POLICE ACADEMY: MISSION TO MOSCOW
WARNER BROS. August, 1994. (Alan Metter) George Gaynes, Michael Winslow, David Graf.

POLICE STORY III: SUPERCOP
PACIFIC FILMS. October, 1993. Chinese. (Stanley Tong) Jackie Chan, Michelle Yeoh, Maggie Cheung.

POLISH WEDDING
FOX SEARCHLIGHT. July, 1998. (Theresa Connelly) Lena Olin, Gabriel Byrne, Claire Danes, Adam Trese, Mili Avital.

PONTIAC MOON
PARAMOUNT. November, 1994. (Peter Medak) Ted Danson, Mary Steenburgen, Ryan Todd, Eric Schweig.

POP & ME
RICHARD AND CHRIS ROE. Apr., 1999. (Chris Roe). Documentary.

POPCORN
STUDIO THREE. February, 1991. (Mark Herrier) Jill Schoelen, Tom Villard, Tony Roberts.

POPCORN
FIM PLUSS KFT. Feb., 1999. Hungarian. (Peter Gabor) Tamas J. Toth, Ferenc Karsai, Zsolt Gonda, Sarolta Zoldhegyi.

THE POPE MUST DIE
MIRAMAX. August, 1991. British. (Peter Richardson) Robbie Coltrane, Beverly D'Angelo, Herbert Lom.

THE PORNOGRAPHER
INTEGRITY PICTURES. Mar., 1999. (Doug Atchison) Michael DeGood, Craig Wasson, Monique Parent, Katheryn Cain, Todd Feder.

A PORNOGRAPHIC AFFAIR
FINE LINE FEATURES. Sept., 1999. Belgian-French. (Frederic Fonteyne) Nathalie Baye, Sergi Lopez.

PORT DJEMA
PARADISE FILMS. Feb., 1997. French-Italian-Greek. (Eric Heumann) Jean Yves Dubois, Nathalie Boutefeu, Christophe Odent.

PORTLAND STREET BLUES
EVERWIDE. Oct., 1998. Hong Kong. (Raymond Yip) Sandra Ng, Kristy Yeung, Alex Fong, Vincent Wan, Shu Q.

THE PORTRAIT OF A LADY
GRAMERCY. September, 1996. (Jane Campion) Nicole Kidman, John Malkovich, Barbara Hershey.

POSITIVE
FIRST RUN FEATURES. May, 1990. W. German. (Rosa von Praunheim) Documentary.

POSSE
GRAMERCY. May, 1993. (Mario Van Peebles) Mario Van Peebles, Charles Lane, Stephen Baldwin.

POSSESSED
ZENTROPA ENTERTAINMENTS/DRTV DANISH BROADCASTING CORP./SVT. May, 1999. Danish. (Anders Ronnow-Klarlund) Udo Kier, Ole Lemmeke, Kirsti Eline Torhaug, Ole Ernst, Neils Anders Thorn, Jesper Langberg.

POSSUMS
HSX FILMS/KUSHNER-LOCKE. June, 1998. (J. Max Burnett) Mac Davis, Cynthia Sikes, Gregory Coolidge, Andrew Prine.

POST COITUM, ANIMAL TRISTE
OGNON PICTURES/PINOU FILM. May, 1997. French. (Brigitte Rouan) Brigitte Rouan, Boris Terral, Patrick Chesnais, Nils Tavernier.

POSTCARDS FROM AMERICA
STRAND. July, 1995. (Steve McLean) Jim Lyons, Michael Tighe, Michael Imperioli.

POSTCARDS FROM THE EDGE
COLUMBIA. September, 1990. (Mike Nichols) Meryl Streep, Shirley MacLaine, Dennis Quaid, Gene Hackman.

THE POSTMAN
MIRAMAX. June, 1995. Italian-French. (Michael Radford) Massimo Troisi, Philippe Noiret.

THE POSTMAN
WARNER BROS. Dec., 1997. (Kevin Costner) Kevin Costner, Will Patton, Larenz Tate, Olivia Williams, James Russo.

POSTMAN BLUES
SUPLEX INC. Nov., 1998. Japanese. (Sabu) Shinichi Tsutsumi, Keiko Tohyama, Ren Ohsugi, Keisuke Horibe.

POST MORTEM
FILM TONIC. Aug., 1999. Canadian. (Louis Belanger) Gabriel Arcand, Sylvie Moreau, Helene Loiselle, Sarah Lecompte-Bergeron.

THE POSTWOMAN
VILNIS KALNAELLIS. May, 1996. Latvian. (Laila Pakalnina) Documentary.

POUSSE CAFE
BURNT MOUNTAIN FILMS. March, 1997. (Susan Winter) Anthony F. Hamilton, Dominic Hamilton-Little, Beatrix Ost.

POVERTY AND OTHER DELIGHTS
FUNFILM DIST. Nov., 1996. Canadian (Denys Arcand) Gaston Lepage, Benoit Briere, Chantal Baril, Roger Blay.

POVERTY OUTLAW
SKYLIGHT PICTURES. Jan., 1997. (Pamela Yates) Documentary - 16mm.

POWDER
BUENA VISTA. October, 1995. (Victor Salva) Mary Steenburgen, Sean Patrick Flannery, Lance Henriksen.

POWER 98
WARNERVISION FILMS. April, 1996. (Jaime Hellman) Eric Roberts, Jason Gedrick, Jennie Garth, Larry Drake.

THE POWER OF KANGWON PROVINCE
MIRACIN KOREA FILM CO. Sept., 1998. South Korean. (Hong Sang-soo) Baek Jong-hak, Oh Yun-hong, Kim Yu-seok, Chun Jae-hyun, Park Hyun-yeong.

THE POWER OF ONE
WARNER BROS. March, 1992. (John G. Avildsen) Stephen Dorff, Armin Mueller, Morgan Freeman.

PRACTICAL MAGIC
WARNER BROS. Oct., 1998. (Griffin Dunne) Sandra Bullock, Nicole Kidman, Dianne Wiest, Stockard Channing, Aidan Quinn.

PRAGUE STORIES
SIRENA FILM. Jan., 1999. Czech. (Artermio Benki, Michaela Pavlatova, Martin Sulik, Petr Vaclav, Vladimir Michalek): Laurence Cote, Arnaud Giovaninetti, Karel Roden, Theodora Remundova, Bozidara Turzonovova.

PRAYER OF THE ROLLERBOYS
CASTLE HILL. August, 1991. (Rick King) Corey Haim, Patricia Arquette, Christopher Collet.

PRAYING WITH ANGER
CINEVISTA/UNAPIX. September, 1993. Indian. (M. Night Shyamalan) M. Night Shyamalan, Mike Muthu.

THE PREACHER'S WIFE
BUENA VISTA. December, 1996. (Penny Marshall), Denzel Washington, Whitney Houston, Courtney Vance, Gregory Hines.

PRECIOUS
MIRAMAX. January, 1996. (Alexander Payne) Laura Dern, Swoosie Kurtz, Kurtwood Smith, Mary Kay Place.

PREDATOR 2
20TH CENTURY FOX. November, 1990. (Stephen Hopkins) Danny Glover, Gary Busey, Ruben Blades.

PREFONTAINE
BUENA VISTA. January, 1997. (Steve James), Jared Leto, R. Lee Ermey, Ed O'Neil, Amy Locane, Lindsay Crouse, Laurel Holloman.

PRELUDE TO A KISS
20TH CENTURY FOX. July, 1992. (Norman Rene) Alec Baldwin, Meg Ryan, Sydney Walker, Patty Duke.

PRESUMED INNOCENT
WARNER BROS. July, 1990. (Alan J. Pakula) Harrison Ford, Raul Julia, Bonnie Bedelia.

PRETTY WOMAN
BUENA VISTA. March, 1990. (Garry Marshall) Richard Gere, Julia Roberts, Hector Elizondo.

PREY OF THE JAGUAR
UNITED FILM DISTRIBUTORS. May, 1996. (David DeCoteau) Maxwell Caulfield, Linda Blair, Stacey Keach.

A PRICE ABOVE RUBIES
MIRAMAX. Jan., 1998. (Boaz Yakin) Rene Zellweiger, Christopher Eccleston, Glenn Fitzgerald, Allen Payne, Julianna Margulies.

THE PRICE OF KISSING
MDP WORLDWIDE. April, 1997. (Vincent DiPersio) Pauley P., Leon, Nicole Eggert, Jon Seda, Loretta Devine, Lou Rawls.

PRIDE DIVIDE
HORIZON UNLIMITED. June, 1997. (Paris Poirier) Camille Paglia, Kate Clinton, Michael Musto, Rose Troche, Documentary - video.

PRIEST
MIRAMAX. March, 1995. British. (Antonia Bird) Linus Roache, Tom Wilkinson, Cathy Tyson.

PRIMAL FEAR
PARAMOUNT. March, 1996. (Gregory Hoblit) Richard Gere, Laura Linney, John Mahoney, Alfre Woodard.

PRIMARY COLORS
UNIVERSAL. March, 1998. (Mike Nichols) John Travolta, Emma Thompson, Billy Bob Thornton, Kathy Bates, Adrian Lester, Larry Hagman, Diane Ladd.

PRIMARY MOTIVE
BLOSSOM PICTURES. July, 1992. (Daniel Adams) Judd Nelson, Justine Bateman, John Savage.

PRIME TARGET
BORDER/HERO FILMS. September, 1991. (David Heavener) David Heavener, Tony Curtis, Isaac Hayes.

PRINCE BRAT AND THE WHIPPING BOY
GEMINI/JONES. September, 1995. (Syd McCartney) Nic Knight, Truan Munro, George C. Scott.

THE PRINCE OF CENTRAL PARK
SEAGAL/NASSO. May, 1999. (John Leekley) Kathleen Turner, Danny Aiello, Cathy Moriarty, Frankie Nasso, Harvey Keitel.

THE PRINCE OF EGYPT
DREAMWORKS. Dec., 1998. (Brenda Chapman). Animated.

THE PRINCE OF TIDES
COLUMBIA. December, 1991. (Barbra Streisand) Nick Nolte, Barbra Streisand, Blythe Danner.

PRINCES IN EXILE
FRIES ENT. February, 1991. Canadian. (Giles Walker) Zachary Ansley, Stacie Mistysyn.

THE PRINCESS AND THE GOBLIN
HEMDALE. June, 1994. British-Hungarian. (Joszef Gemes) Animated.

PRINCESS CARABOO
TRISTAR. September, 1994. (Michael Austin) Phoebe Cates, Jim Broadbent, Wendy Hughes, Kevin Kline.

PRIVATE PARTS
PARAMOUNT. February, 1997. (Betty Thomas), Howard Stern, Robin Quivers, Mary McCormack.

THE PRISONER OF ST. PETERSBURG
INDEPT. November, 1990. Soviet-German. (Ian Pringle) Noah Taylor, Katja Teichmann. B&W.

PRISONERS OF THE SUN (BLOOD OATH)
SKOURAS. July, 1991. Australian. (Stephen Wallace) Bryan Brown, George Takei, Terry O'Quinn.

PRISONERS OF WAR
LAB 80. June, 1996. Italian. (Yervant Gianikian, Angela Ricci Lucchi) Documentary.

PRIVATE CONFESSIONS
SVERIGES TELEVISION. DRAMA. May, 1997. Swedish. (Liv Ullmann) Pernilla August, Max von Sydow, Samuel Froler.

PRIVATE LIVES
NEW LIFE. May, 1996. Icelandic. (Thrainn Bertelsson) Gottskalkur Dagur, Dora Takefusa, Olafur Egilsson.

PRIVATE WARS
NHK ENTERPRISES. Feb., 1997. Philippine. (Nick Deocampo) Documentary.

PRIVILEGE
ZEITGEIST. January, 1991. (Yvonne Rainer) Alice Spivak, Novella Nelson.

PROBLEM CHILD
UNIVERSAL. July, 1990. (Dennis Dugan) John Ritter, Jack Warden, Amy Yasbeck.

PROBLEM CHILD 2
UNIVERSAL. July, 1991. (Brian Levant) John Ritter, Jack Warden, Laraine Newman.

PROFESSOR ALBEIT
MEGAFILM/RTL KLUB. Feb., 1999. Hungarian. (Robert Koltai) Robert Koltai, Kata Dobo, Ferenc Kallai, Gabor Reviszky, Judit Hernadi.

PROGENY
FRIES FILM GROUP. May, 1998. (Brian Yuzna) Arnold Vasloo, Jillian McWhirther, Brad Dourif, Lindsay Crouse, Wilford Brimley.

THE PROGRAM
BUENA VISTA. September, 1993. (David S. Ward) Craig Sheffer, James Caan, Halle Berry, Omar Epps.

PROFESSION: NEO-NAZI
DRIFT. May, 1995. German. (Winfried Bonengal) Documentary.

THE PROFESSIONAL
COLUMBIA. November, 1994. (Luc Besson) Jean Reno, Gary Oldman, Natalie Portman, Danny Aiello.

PROJECT GRIZZLY
NATIONAL FILM BD OF CANADA. Sept., 1996. Canadian. (Peter Lynch).

THE PROMISE
FINE LINE. September, 1995. German. (Margarethe von Trotta) Corinna Harfouch, August Zirner.

THE PROMISE
SEAWELL FILMS. May, 1996. Belgian-French-Luxembourgian. (Jean-Pierre Dardenne) Jeremie Renier.

THE PROMPTER
WILDHAGEN PRODS. May, 1999. Norwegian. (Hilde Heier): Hege Schoyen, Sven Nordin, Philip Zanden, Sigrid Huun.

PROOF
FINE LINE. March, 1992. Australian. (Jocelyn Moorhouse) Hugo Weaving, Genevieve Picot, Russell Crowe.

THE PROPHECY
DIMENSION. September, 1995. (Gregory Widen) Christopher Walken, Elias Koteas, Eric Stoltz, Virginia Madsen.

THE PROPOSITION
POLYGRAM FILMS. March, 1998. (Lesli Linka Glatter) Kenneth Branagh, Madeleine Stowe, William Hurt, Neil Patrick Harris, Robert Loggia, Josef Sommer, Blythe Danner.

THE PROPRIETOR
WARNER BROS. October, 1996. (Ismail Merchant) Jeanne Moreau, Sean Young, Sam Waterston, Christopher Cazenove

THE PROS AND CONS OF BREATHING
LEISURE TIME. June, 1995. (Robert Munic) Joey Lauren Adams, Phillip Brock, Joey Dedeo.

PROSPERO'S BOOKS
MIRAMAX. November, 1991. British-Dutch. (Peter Greenaway) John Gielgud, Michael Clark, Michel Blanc.

PSYCHO
UNIVERSAL. Dec., 1998. (Gus Van Sant) Vince Vaughn, Anne Heche, Julianne Moore, Viggo Mortensen, William H. Macy.

PTERODACTYL WOMAN FROM BEVERLY HILLS
PTERO PICTURES. January, 1996. (Phillipe Mora) Beverly D'Angelo, Brad Wilson, Moon Zappa.

P. TINTO'S MIRACLE
WARNER SOGEFILMS. Dec., 1998. Spanish. (Javier Fesser) Luis Ciges, Silvia Casanova, Pablo Pinedo, Javier Aller, Emilio Gaviria.

THE PUBLIC EYE
UNIVERSAL. October, 1992. (Howard Franklin) Joe Pesci, Barbara Hershey, Stanley Tucci.

PUBLIC HOUSING
ZIPPORAH FILMS. Oct., 1997. (Frederick Wiseman) DOCUMENTARY.

PUDDLE CRUISER
BROKEN LIZARD. Oct., 1996. (Jay Chandrasekhar) Jay Chandrasekhar, Kevin Hefferman, Steve Lemme, Paul Soter.

PUERTO RICAN MAMBO, THE (NOT A MUSICAL)
CABRIOLET FILMS. March, 1992. (Ben Model) Luis Caballero.

PULP FICTION
MIRAMAX. October, 1994. (Quentin Tarantino) John Travolta, Samuel L. Jackson, Uma Thurman, Bruce Willis.

PUMP UP THE VOLUME
NEW LINE. August, 1990. (Allan Moyle) Christian Slater, Annie Ross, Ellen Greene.

PUNITIVE DAMAGE
RONIN FILMS. June, 1999. New Zealand. (Annie Goldson). Documentary.

PUNK LAWYER
CONCORDE FILM. Sept., 1996. Dutch. (Gerrit van Elst) Pierre Bokma, Margo Dames, Jaap Spijkers, Peter Oosthoek.

PUPPET MASTER
JGM ENTERPRISES. January, 1990. (David Schmoeller) Paul LeMat, Irene Miracle.

PUPS
TEAM OKUYAMA/TBD. Apr., 1999. (Ash) Cameron Van Hoy, Mischa Barton, Burt Reynolds.

PURE COUNTRY
WARNER BROS. October, 1992. (Christopher Cain) George Strait, Lesley Ann Warren, Isabel Glasser.

A PURE FORMALITY
SONY PICTURES CLASSICS. May, 1995. French. (Giuseppe Tornatore) Gérard Depardieu, Roman Polanski.

PURE LUCK
UNIVERSAL. August, 1991. (Nadia Tass) Martin Short, Danny Glover, Sheila Kelley.

PUSHING HANDS
CFP. June, 1995. Chinese. (Ang Lee) Sihung Lung, Lai Wang, Bo Z. Wang.

PUSHING TIN
20TH CENTURY FOX. Apr., 1999. (Mike Newell) John Cusack, Billy Bob Thornton, Cate Blanchett, Angelina Jolie, Vicki Lewis.

A PYROMANIAC'S LOVE STORY
BUENA VISTA. April, 1995. (Joshua Brand) William Baldwin, John Leguizamo, Sadie Frost, Erik Eleniak.

Q

Q&A
TRISTAR. April, 1990. (Sidney Lumet) Nick Nolte, Timothy Hutton, Armand Assante.

QUASIMODO D'EL PARIS
BAC FILMS. Mar., 1999. French. (Patrick Timsit) Patrick Timsit, Richard Berry, Melanie Thierry, Vincent Elbaz, Didier Flamand.

QUEENS LOGIC
NEW LINE. February, 1991. (Steve Rash) Kevin Bacon, Joe Mantegna, John Malkovich.

QUEEN MARGOT
MIRAMAX. December, 1994. (Patrice Chereau) Isabelle Adjani, Daniel Auteuil, Jean-Hugues Anglade.

THE QUEST
UNIVERSAL. April, 1996. (Jean Claude Van Damme) Jean Claude Van Damme, Roger Moore, James Remar.

QUEST FOR CAMELOT
WARNER BROS. April, 1998. (Frederick Du Chan) Jessalyn Gilsig, Andrea Corr, Cary Elwes, Bryan White, Gary Oldman, Eric Idle, Don Rickles, Jane Seymour, Celine Dion.

THE QUICK AND THE DEAD
TRISTAR. February, 1995. (Sam Raimi) Sharon Stone, Gene Hackman, Leonardo DiCaprio, Russell Crowe.

QUICK CHANGE
WARNER BROS. July, 1990. (Howard Franklin, Bill Murray) Bill Murray, Geena Davis, Randy Quaid.

QUICKSAND
LES FILMS DE LA LIANE. April, 1996. French. (Paul Carpita) Beppe Clericci, Daniel San Pedro, Ludiuine Vaillet.

QUIET DAYS IN HOLLYWOOD
WARNER BROS. May, 1997. German. (Josef Rusnak) Meta Golding, Chad Lowe, Bill Cusack, Natasha Gregson Wagner, Peter Dobson.

THE QUIET FAMILY
MYUNG FILM. Sept., 1998. South Korean. (Kim Ji-un) Song Kang-ho, Park In-hwan, N Mun-heui, Choe Min-sik, Lee Yeon-sung.

THE QUIET VILLAGE
VILLEALFA FILMPRODS/FINNISH BROADCASTING CO. Feb., 1997. Finnish. (Kari Vaananen) Taisto Reimaluoto, Sari Havas.

QUIGLEY DOWN UNDER
MGM. October, 1990. (Simon Wincer) Tom Selleck, Alan Rickman, Laura San Giacomo.

QUIZ SHOW
BUENA VISTA. September, 1994. (Robert Redford) John Turturro, Rob Morrow, Ralph Fiennes.

R

RACE THE SUN
SONY PICTURES. March, 1996. (Charles T. Kanganis) Halle Berry, James Belushi, Casey Affleck, Eliza Dushku.

THE RACE TO SAVE 100 YEARS
WARNER BROS./TURNER ENTERTAINMENT. March, 1998. (Scott Benson) DOCUMENTARY.

RACHEL'S DAUGHTERS
LIGHT-SARAF FILMS. Oct., 1997. (Allie Light, Irving Saraf) DOCUMENTARY.

RADIATION
RADIATION PICTURES. Jan., 1999. (Suki Stetson Hawley) Unai Fresnedo, Katy Petty, Ignacio Fernandez, Thalia Zedek, Chris Brokaw.

RADIO FLYER
COLUMBIA. February, 1992. (Richard Donner) Elijah Wood, Lorraine Bracco, Joseph Mazzello.

RADIO STORIES
INDEPENDENT. November, 1993; made in 1955. Spanish. (Jose Luis Saez de Heredia) Francisco Rabal, Margarita Andrey.

RADIOLAND MURDERS
UNIVERSAL. October, 1994. (Mel Smith) Mary Stuart Masterson, Brian Benben, Stephen Toblowsky.

RAFTERS
TELEVISO DE CATALUNYA, S.A. Feb., 1997. Spanish. (Carles Bosch) Documentary.

THE RAGE: CARRIE 2
MGM. Mar., 1999. (Katt Shea): Emily Bergl, Jason Lodon, Dylan Bruno, J. Smith-Cameron, Amy Irving.

A RAGE IN HARLEM
MIRAMAX. May, 1991. (Bill Duke) Forest Whitaker, Gregory Hines, Robin Givens.

THE RAGGEDY RAWNEY
L.W. BLAIR PRODS. February, 1990. British. (Bob Hoskins) Bob Hoskins, Dexter Fletcher.

RAGING ANGELS
MARK BORDE FILMS. November, 1995. (Alan Smithee) Sean Patrick Flannery, Dianne Ladd, Monet Mazur.

RANDOM ACTS OF VIOLENCE
GUTTER BROTHERS. July, 1999. (Drew Bell): Esteban Powell, A.J. Buckley, Alex Solowitz, Brain Klugman, Rainbow Borden.

THE RAIN KILLER
CONCORDE. September, 1990. (Ken Stein) Ray Sharkey, David Beecroft, Michael Chiklis.

RAIN WITHOUT THUNDER
ORION CLASSICS. February, 1993. (Gary Bennett) Betty Buckley, Jeff Daniels, Frederic Forrest.

RAINBOW
FIRST INDEPENDENT. July, 1996. Canadian-British. (Bob Hoskins) Dan Aykroyd, Saul Rubinek, Terry Finn.

RAINBOW FOR RIMBAUD
MICHELE RAY-GAVRAS. June, 1996. French. (Jean Teule) Laure Marsac, Robert MacLeod, Bernadette Lafont.

RAINING STONES
NORTHERN ARTS. March, 1994. British. (Ken Loach) Bruce Jones, Julie Brown, Gemma Phoenix.

THE RAINMAKER
PARAMOUNT. Nov., 1997. (Francis Ford Coppola) Matt Damon, Claire Danes, Jon Voight, Mary Kay Place, Mickey Rourke, Danny DeVito.

RAISE THE RED LANTERN
ORION CLASSICS. March, 1992. Hong Kong-Chinese-Mandarin. (Zhang Yimou) Gong Li, Jingwu Ma, Califei He.

RAISING CAIN
UNIVERSAL. August, 1992. (Brian DePalma) John Lithgow, Lolita Davidovich, Steven Bauer.

RAISING HEROES
DOPELGANGER FILMS. June, 1996. (Douglas Langway) Troy Sostillio, Henry White, Edmond Sorel.

RAIZING THE ASHES
ZEN PEACEMAKER ORGANIZATION/MICHAEL O'KEEFE. Sept., 1997. (Michael O'Keefe) DOCUMENTARY.

RAMBLIN' GAL
AQUARIUS. June, 1991. (Roberto Monticello, Lu Ann Horstman Person) Deborah Strang, Andrew Krawetz.

RAMBLING ROSE
NEW LINE. October, 1991. (Martha Coolidge) Laura Dern, Robert Duvall, Lukas Haas, Diane Ladd.

RAMPAGE
MIRAMAX. October, 1992. (William Friedkin) Michael Biehn, Alex McArthur, Nicholas Campbell.

RANSOM
BUENA VISTA. October, 1996. (Ron Howard), Mel Gibson, Rene Russo, Gary Sinise, Delroy Lindo, Lili Taylor, Liev Schreiber.

RAPA NUI
WARNER BROS. September, 1994. (Kevin Reynolds) Jason Scott Lee, Esai Morales, Sandrine Holt.

RAPID FIRE
20TH CENTURY FOX. August, 1992. (Dwight H. Little) Brandon Lee, Powers Boothe, Nick Mancuso.

THE RAPTURE
NEW LINE. October, 1991. (Michael Tolkin) Mimi Rogers, David Duchovny, Patrick Bauchau.

RASPAD
MK2. April, 1992. Soviet. (Mikhail Belikov) Sergei Shakurov, Tatiana Kochemasova.

RATCATCHER
PATHE PICTURES/BBC FILMS. May, 1999. British. (Lynne Ramsay) William Eadie, Tommy Flanagan, Mandy Matthews.

RATCHET
RATCHET PRODS. September, 1996. (John Johnson) Tom Gilroy, Margaret Welsh.

A RATHER ENGLISH MARRIAGE
WALL TO WALL TELEVISION. Nov., 1998. British. (Paul Seed) Albert Finney, Tom Courtenay, Joanna Lumley, John Light, Katie Carr.

RAVENOUS
20TH CENTURY FOX. Jan., 1999. (Antonio Bird) Guy Pearce, Robert Carlyle, Jeremy Davies, Jeffrey Jones, John Spencer.

RAW NERVE
A.I.P. STUDIOS. May, 1991. (David A. Prior) Glenn Ford, Ted Prior, Sandahl Bergman.

RAZOR BLADE SMILE
PALM PICTURES/MANGA LIVE. Oct., 1998. British. (Jake West) Eileen Daley, Christopher Adamson, Kevin Howarth, Jonathan Coote, David Warbeck.

REACH THE ROCK
GRAMMERCY. Oct., 1998. (William Ryan) William Sadler, Alessandro Nivola, Bruce Norris, Karen Sillas, Brooke Langton.

READY TO WEAR (PRET–A–PORTER)
MIRAMAX. December, 1994. (Robert Altman) Sophia Loren, Tim Robbins, Julia Roberts, Stephen Rea.

READY WILLING & ABLE
UNITED CREW FILMS. July, 1999. (Jenni Gold) Christopher Templeton, Rus Blackwell, Steve DuMouchel, Mike Kalvoda.

THE REAL MCCOY
UNIVERSAL. September, 1993. (Russell Mulcahy) Kim Basinger, Val Kilmer, Terence Stamp.

THE REAL MCCOY
KINOFINLANDIA. Finnish-British-Swdish-Indian.1999 (Pekka Lehto) Andy McCoy, Angela Nicoletti, Michael Monroe.

REALITY BITES
UNIVERSAL. February, 1994. (Ben Stiller) Winona Ryder, Ethan Hawke, Ben Stiller, Steve Zahn, Janeane Garofalo.

A REASONABLE MAN
PANDORA CINEMA. Aug., 1999. South African-French. (Gavin Hood Gavin Hood, Nigel Hawthorne, Janine Eser, Vusi Kunene, Ken Gampu.

A REASON TO BELIEVE
CASTLE HILL. September, 1995. (Douglas Tirola) Allison Smith, Jay Underwood, Danny Quinn.

RECIPES TO STAY TOGETHER
IMCINE/TELEVICINE/CONSTELACION FILMS PROD. March, 1997. Mexican. (Rafael Montero) Demian Bichir, Arcelia Ramirez.

RECKLESS
SAMUEL GOLDWYN. September, 1995. (Norman Rene) Mia Farrow, Scott Glenn, Mary Luois Parker, Tony Goldwyn.

RECOLLECTIONS OF THE YELLOW HOUSE
INVICTA. February, 1994. Portuguese. (Joao Cesar Monteiro) Manuela de Freira, Joao Cesar Monteiro.

RED
MIRAMAX. December, 1994. Polish. (Krzysztof Kieslowski) Irene Jacob, Jean-Louis Trintignant, Frederique Feder.

RED BLOODED 2
SC ENTERTAINMENT. May, 1996. Canadian. (David Blyth) Kari Salin, Kristoffer Ryan Winters, Burt Young.

RED CHERRY
MOONSTONE INT'L. January, 1996. Chinese. (Ye Ying) Guo Ke-Yu, Xiu Xiao-Li, Vladimir Mizmiroff.

RED CORNER
MGM. Oct., 1997. (Jon Avnet) Richard Gere, Bai Ling, Bradley Whitford, Byron Mann, Peter Donat, Robert Stanton, Tsai Chin.

REDEEM HER HONOR
STAR CINEMA. November, 1995. Filipino. (Marilou Diaz Albaya) Sharmaine Arnaiz, Chin Chin Gutierrez.

RED FIRECRACKER, GREEN FIRECRACKER
OCTOBER FILMS. April, 1995. Hong Kong. (He Ping) Ning Jing, Wu Gang, Zhao Xiaoruli.

THE RED RIBBON
VARAHONAR CO. Feb., 1999. Iranian. (Ebrahim Hatamikia) Azita Hajiyan, Parviz Parastuyi, Reza Kianian.

RED RIBBON BLUES
RED RIBBON. September, 1995. (Charles Winkler) Paul Mercurio, Debi Mazar, RuPaul, John Epperson.

RED ROCK WEST
ROXIE. January, 1994. (John Dahl) Nicolas Cage, Dennis Hopper, Lara Flynn Boyle.

RED SURF
ARROWHEAD ENT. June, 1990. (H. Gordon Boos) George Clooney, Doug Savant.

RED, WHITE & YELLOW
NORTHERN LIGHTS POST. Oct., 1998. (Marshall Dostal, Mark Littman). Documentary.

THE REF
BUENA VISTA. March, 1994. (Ted Demme) Denis Leary, Judy Davis, Kevin Spacey.

THE REFLECTING SKIN
PRESTIGE. June, 1991. British. (Philip Ridley) Viggo Mortensen, Lindsay Duncan, Jeremy Cooper.

REFLECTIONS IN THE DARK
CONCORDE. April, 1995. (Jon Purdy) Mimi Rogers, Billy Zane, John Terry.

THE REFRIGERATOR
AVENUE D. September, 1992. (Nicholas Tony Jacobs) Julia Mueller, David Simonds, Angel Caban.

REGARDING HENRY
PARAMOUNT. July, 1991. (Mike Nichols) Harrison Ford, Annette Bening, Bill Nunn, Mikki Allen.

REGENERATION
ARTIFICIAL EYE. May, 1997. British-Canadian. (Gillies MacKinnon) Jonathan Pryce, James Wilby, Jonny Lee Miller, Stuart Bunce.

THE REGGAE MOVIE
TRIMEDIA. September, 1995. (Randy Rovins) Documentary.

THE REGGAE MOVIE
UNITED ARTISTS THEATRES. May, 1996. (Randy Rovins) Documentary.

REGRET TO INFORM
SUN FOUNTAIN. Kam/ 1999. (Barbara Sonneborn). Documentary.

REGULAR GUYS
BUENA VISTA INTL. May, 1996. German. (Rolf Silber) Christoph M. Ohrt, Carin C. Tietze, Tim Bergmann.

RELAX... IT'S JUST SEX
ATLAS ENTERTAINMENT. Jan., 1998. (P.J. Castellaneta) Jennifer Tilly, Mitchell Anderson, Cynda Williams, Lori Petty, Serena Scott Thomas.

THE RELIC
PARAMOUNT. January, 1997. (Peter Hyams), Penelope Ann Miller, Tom Sizemore, Linda Hunt, James Whitmore, Clayton Rohner.

THE REMAINS OF THE DAY
COLUMBIA. November, 1993. British-U.S. (James Ivory) Anthony Hopkins, Emma Thompson, Christopher Reeve.

RENAISSANCE MAN
BUENA VISTA. June, 1994. (Penny Marshall) Danny DeVito, Gregory Hines, Lilo Brancato.

RENDEZVOUS IN PARIS
ARTIFICIAL EYE. August, 1996. French. (Eric Rohmer) Clara Bellar, Antoine Basler, Serge Renko.

THE REPLACEMENT KILLERS
SONY. Jan., 1998. (Antoine Fuqua) Chow Yun-Fat, Mira Sorvino, Michael Rooker, Jurgen Prochnow, Kenneth Tsang, Til Schweiger.

REPLY WITH PHOTO
SONET FILMS. Aug., 1999. Swedish-Latvian. (Una Celma) Samuel Froler, Baiba Broka, Lennart Jahkel, Eva-Lena Bjorkman

REPOSSESSED
NEW LINE. September, 1990. (Bob Logan) Linda Blair, Leslie Nielsen, Ned Beatty.

REQUIEM FOR A ROMANTIC WOMAN
TIME. May, 1999. German. (Dagmar Knoepfel) Janina Sachau, Sylvester Groth, Jeanette Hain, Felix von Manteuffel.

REQUIEM FOR DOMINIC
HEMDALE. April, 1991. Austrian. (Robert Dornhelm) Felix Mitterer, Victoria Schubert.

RESCUE ME
CANNON. December, 1993. (Arthur Allan Seidelman) Michael Dudikoff, Stephen Dorff, Ami Dolenz.

THE RESCUERS DOWN UNDER
BUENA VISTA. November, 1990. (Hendel Butoy, Mike Gabriel) Animated.

RESCUING DESIRE
PILGRIMS 4. May, 1996. (Adam Rodgers) Melinda Mullins, Tamara Tunie, Caitlin Dulany.

RESERVOIR DOGS
MIRAMAX. October, 1992. (Quentin Tarantino) Harvey Keitel, Tim Roth, Michael Madsen.

RESIDENT ALIEN
GREYCAT. October, 1991. (Jonathan Nossiter) Documentary.

RESISTANCE
ANGELIKA. November, 1994. Australian. (Paul Elliott, Hugh Keays Byrne) Lorna Lesley, Jennifer Claire, Bobby Noble.

RESTAURANT
PALISADES PICTURES. April, 1998. (Eric Bross) Adrien Brody, Elise Neal, David Moscow, Malcolm Jamal Warner.

RESTLESS
SCITECH CULTURE CO./CELESTIAL PICTURES. Nov., 1998. (Jule Gilfillan) Catherine Kellner, David Wu, Sarita Choudhury, Geng Le.

RESTORATION
MIRAMAX. December, 1995. (Michael Hoffman) Robert Downey, Jr., Sam Neill, David Thewlis, Polly Walker.

RETROACTIVE
ORION. May, 1997. (Louis Morneau) James Belushi, Kylie Travis, Shannon Whirry, Frank Whaley, M. Emmet Walsh, Jesse Borrego.

THE RETURN OF SUPERFLY
TRITON PICTURES. November, 1990. (Sig Shore) Nathan Purdee, Margaret Avery, David Groh.

RETURN OF THE IDIOT
CINEMART. Sept., 1999. Czech. (Sasa Gedeon) Pavel Liska, Tatiana Vilhelmova, Anna Geislerova, Jiri Langmajer, Jiri Machacek.

RETURN OF THE LIVING DEAD 3
TRIMARK. October, 1993. (Brian Yuzna) Mindy Clarke, J. Trevor Edmond, Kent McCord.

RETURN TO THE BLUE LAGOON
COLUMBIA. August, 1991. (William A. Graham) Milla Jovovich, Brian Krause, Lisa Pelikan.

RETURN TO PARADISE
POLYGRAM FILMS. July, 1998. (Joseph Ruben) Vince Vaughn, Anne Heche, Joaquin Phoenix, David Conrad, Vera Farmiga, Nick Sandow.

RETURN WITH HONOR
SANDERS & MOCK. Oct., 1998. (Freida Lee Mock, Terry Sanders) . Documentary.

REUNION
CASTLE HILL. March, 1991. French-German-British. (Jerry Schatzberg) Jason Robards, Christien Anholt, Samuel West.

REVENGE
COLUMBIA. February, 1990. (Tony Scott) Kevin Costner, Anthony Quinn, Madeleine Stowe.

REVERSAL OF FORTUNE
WARNER BROS. October, 1990. (Barbet Schroeder) Jeremy Irons, Glenn Close, Ron Silver.

REVOLUTION!
NORTHERN ARTS. November, 1991. (Jeff Kahn) Christopher Renstrom, Kimberly Flynn, Georg Osterman.

REWIND
ALTA FILMS. July, 1999. Spanish. (Nicolas Munoz) Daniel Guzman, Maria Adanez, Enrique Simon, Paz Gomez, Tristan Ulloa.

RHAPSODY IN AUGUST
ORION CLASSICS. December, 1991. Japanese. (Akira Kurosawa) Sachiko Murase, Hisashi Igawa, Richard Gere.

RHAPSODY IN BLOOM
BECKER ENTERTAINMENT. May, 1998. (Craig Saavedra) Penelope Ann Miller, Ron Silver, Craig Sheffer, Caroline Goodall.

RHYME & REASON
MIRAMAX. Feb., 1997. (Peter Spirer) Documentary.

RHYTHM THIEF
STRAND. November 1995. (Matthew Harrison) Jason Andrews, Eddie Daniels, Kevin Corrigan.

RICHARD III
MGM/UA. December, 1995. (Richard Loncraine) Ian McKellen, Annette Bening, Jim Broadbent, Robert Downey Jr.

RICH GIRL
STUDIO THREE FILM CORP. May, 1991. (Joel Bender) Jill Schoelen, Don Michael Paul, Paul Gleason.

RICH IN LOVE
MGM. March, 1993. (Bruce Beresford) Albert Finney, Kathryn Erbe, Kyle MacLachlan, Ethan Hawke.

THE RICH MAN'S WIFE
BUENA VISTA. September, 1996. (Amy Holden) Halle Berry, Christoper McDonald, Clive Owen, Peter Greene.

RICHIE RICH
WARNER BROS. December, 1994. (Donald Petrie) Macauley Culkin, John Larroquette, Edward Herrman.

RICHTER, THE ENIGMA
WARNER VISION. Sept., 1998. French. (Bruno Monsaingeon) Sviatoslav Richter. Documentary.

RICOCHET
WARNER BROS. October, 1991. (Russell Mulcahy) Denzel Washington, John Lithgow, Ice T.

RIDE
DIMENSION FILMS. March, 1998. (Millicent Shelton) Malik Yoba, Melissa De Sousa, John Witherspoon, Frendro Starr.

THE RIDE
WORLD WIDE PICTURES. March, 1998. (Michael O. Sajbel) Michael Biehn, Brock Pierce, Jennifer Blanc, Chris Owen, Clarence Felder.

RIDER OF THE FLAMES
PROGRESS FILM-VERLEIH. Jan., 1999. German. (Nina Grosse) Martin Feifel, Marianne Denicourt, Ulrich Matthes, Ulrich Muhe, Nina Hoss.

RIDE WITH THE DEVIL
USA FILMS. Aug., 1999. (Ang Lee) Skeet Ulrich, Tobey Maguire, Jewel, Jeffrey Wright, Simon Baker.

RIDICULE
POLYGRAM. April, 1996. French. (Patrice Leconte) Charles Berling, Jean Rochefort, Fanny Ardant.

RIDING THE RAILS
UYS-LOVELL. Jan., 1997. (Michael Uys, Lexy Lovell) Documentary.

RIEN SUR ROBERT
REZO FILMS. Feb., 1999. French. (Pascal Bonitzer) Fabrice Luchini, Sandrine Kiberlain, Valentina Cervi, Michel Piccoli, Bernadette Lafont.

RIFF–RAFF
FINE LINE. February, 1993. British. (Ken Loach) Robert Carlyle, Emer McCourt, Jimmy Coleman.

RIFT
CURB ENT. June, 1995. (Edward S. Barkin) William Sage, Timothy Cavanaugh, Jennifer Bransford.

RIKYU
CAPITOL ENT. January, 1991. Japanese. (Hiroshi Teshigahara) Rentaro Mikuni, Tsutomu Yamazaki.

THE RING
KADOKAWA SHOTEN PUBLISHING CO. July, 1999. Japanese. (Hideo Nakata) Nanko Matsushima, Hiroyuki Sanada, Miki Nakatani, Yuko Takeuchi, Hitomi Sato.

THE RING 2
KADOKAWA SHOTEN PUBLISHING CO. July, 1998. Japanese. (Hideo Nakata) Miki Nakatani, Hitomi Sato, Kyoko Fukada, Nanako Matsushima.

RINGMASTER
ARTISAN. Nov., 1998. (Neil Baramson) Jerry Springer, Jaime Pressly, Molly Hagan, Michael Dudikoff, Ashley Holbrook.

RIOT
PM ENTERTAINMENT GROUP. May, 1996. (Joseph Merhi) Gary Daniels, Sugar Ray Leonard, Paige Rowland.

RIPE
C&P PRODS. April, 1996. (Mo Ogrodnik) Monica Keena, Daisy Eagan, Gordon Currie, Ron Brice.

RISING SUN
20TH CENTURY FOX. July, 1993. (Philip Kaufman) Sean Connery, Wesley Snipes, Tia Carrere, Harvey Keitel.

RISK
SEVENTH ART. October, 1994. (Deirdre Fishel) Karen Sillas, David Ilku, Molly Price.

RITES OF PASSAGE
WORLD INTL.. June, 1999. (Victor Salva) Dean Stockwell, Jason Behr, Robert keith, Jaimz Woolvett, James Remar.

THE RIVER
CENTRAL MOTION PICTURE CORP. Feb., 1997. Taiwanese. (Tsai Ming-liang) Lee Kang-sheng, Miao Tien, Lu Hsiao-ling.

THE RIVER CHAO PHRAYA
TUSK PRODUCTION. Oct., 1996. Thai. (Sampson Williams) Eak Natilocksana, Krissana Rattanakul, Diyanuch Ongalor.

RIVER OF GRASS
STRAND. August, 1995. (Kelly Reichardt) Lisa Bowman, Larry Fessenden, Dick Russell.

RIVER RED
DRILLING FILMS. Jan., 1998. (Eric Drilling) Tom Everett Scott, David Moscow, Cara Buono, David Lowery, Denis O'Hare, Michael Kelly.

A RIVER RUNS THROUGH IT
COLUMBIA. October, 1992. (Robert Redford) Craig Sheffer, Brad Pitt, Tom Skerritt.

THE RIVER WILD
UNIVERSAL. September, 1994. (Curtis Hanson) Meryl Streep, Kevin Bacon, David Strathairn.

RIVERBEND
PRISM ENTERTAINMENT. March, 1990. (San Firstenberg) Steve James, Margaret Avery.

RIVIERA HOTEL
PIETER VAN HUYSTEE FILM & TV. Oct., 1998. Dutch. (Bernie Ijdis). Documentary.

ROAD KILL
RICMAR PRODS. Mar., 1999. (Matthew Leutwyler) Jennifer Rubin, Erik Palladino, Billy Jayne, Tony Denison, Jon Polito.

ROAD MOVIE
WARNER BROS. RECORDS. September, 1996. (Peter Care) Documentary with R.E.M.

ROAD SCHOLAR
SAMUEL GOLDWYN. July, 1993. (Roger Weisberg) Andrei Codrescu.

THE ROAD TO WELLVILLE
COLUMBIA. October, 1994. (Alan Parker) Anthony Hopkins, Matthew Broderick, Bridget Fonda, John Cusack.

ROADSIDE PROPHETS
FINE LINE. March, 1992. (Abbe Wool) John Doe, Adam Horovitz, David Anthony Marshall.

ROBERTA
MOVING PARTS. Jan. 1999. (Eric Mandelbaum) Kevin Corrigan, Daisy Rojas, Amy Ryan, Bill Sage, Brian Tarantina.

ROB ROY
MGM/UA. April, 1995. (Michael Caton Jones) Liam Neeson, Jessica Lange, John Hurt, Tim Roth.

ROBERT A. HEINLEN'S THE PUPPET MASTERS
BUENA VISTA. October, 1994. (Stuart Orne) Donald Sutherland, Eric Thal, Julie Warner, Keith David.

ROBERT ALTMAN'S JAZZ '34: REMEMBRANCES OF KANSAS CITY SWING
SANDCASTLE 5/CIBY 2000. September 1996. (Robert Altman) Harry Belafonte.

ROBIN HOOD: MEN IN TIGHTS
20TH CENTURY FOX. July, 1993. (Mel Brooks) Cary Elwes, Richard Lewis, Roger Rees.

ROBIN HOOD: PRINCE OF THIEVES
WARNER BROS. June, 1991. (Kevin Reynolds) Kevin Costner, Morgan Freeman, Alan Rickman.

ROBOCOP 2
ORION. June, 1990. (Irvin Kershner) Peter Weller, Nancy Allen, Tom Noonan.

ROBOCOP 3
ORION. November, 1993. (Fred Dekker) Robert John Burke, Nancy Allen, Rip Torn.

ROBOT CARNIVAL
STREAMLINE. February, 1991. Japanese. (Various directors) Animated.

ROBOT JOX
TRIUMPH. November, 1990. (Stuart Gordon) Gary Graham, Anne-Marie Johnson, Paul Koslo.

THE ROCK
BUENA VISTA. June, 1996. (Michael Bay) Sean Connery, Nicholas Cage, Ed Harris, Michael Biehn, William Forsythe

ROCK HUDSON'S HOME MOVIES
COUCH POTATO INC. April, 1993. (Mark Rappaport) Documentary.

ROCK–A–DOODLE
SAMUEL GOLDWYN. April, 1992. (Don Bluth) Animated.

ROCK SOUP
Z FILMS. April, 1992. (Lech Kowalski) Documentary.

THE ROCKETEER
BUENA VISTA. June, 1991. (Joe Johnston) Bill Campbell, Jennifer Connelly, Alan Arkin, Timothy Dalton.

ROCKETMAN
BUENA VISTA. Sept., 1997. (Stuart Gillard) Harland Williams, Jessica Lundy, William Sadler, Jeffrey DeMunn, Beau Bridges, Peter Onorati.

ROCKULA
CANNON. February, 1990. (Luca Bercovici) Dean Cameron, Toni Basil, Susan Tyrrell.

ROCKY V
MGM/UA. November, 1990. (John G. Avildsen) Sylvester Stallone, Talia Shire, Burt Young.

RODRIGO D: NO FUTURE
KINO INT'L. January, 1991. Colombian-Spanish. (Victor Manuel Gaviria) Ramiro Menese, Carlos Maria Resrepo.

ROGER CORMAN'S FRANKENSTEIN UNBOUND
20TH CENTURY FOX. November, 1990. (Roger Corman) John Hurt, Raul Julia, Jason Patric.

ROGUE TRADER
PATHE. June, 1999. British. (James Dearden) Ewan McGregor, Anna Friel, Yves Beneyton, Betsy Brantley, Carole Langrishe.

THE ROLLING STONES ROCK AND ROLL CIRCUS
ABKCO/Rolling Stones. September, 1996. (Michael Lindsay Hogg) The Rolling Stones.

ROMANCE
FLACH FILM, CB FILMS, ARTE-FRANCE CINEMA. Feb., 1999. French. (Catherine Brellat) Caroline Ducey, Sagamore Stevenin, Francois Berleand, Rocco Siffredi.

ROMEO & JULIA
KAUFMAN FILMS. February, 1992. (Kevin Kaufman) Bob Koherr, Ivana Kane, Patrick McGuinness.

ROMEO IS BLEEDING
GRAMERCY. February, 1994. (Peter Medak) Gary Oldman, Lena Olin, Annabella Sciorra, Juliette Lewis.

ROMPER STOMPER
ACADEMY ENT. June, 1993. Australian. (Geoffrey Wright) Russell Crowe, Daniel Pollock, Jacqueline McKenzie.

ROMY AND MICHELE'S HIGH SCHOOL REUNION
BUENA VISTA. April, 1997. (David Mirkin), Mira Sorvino, Lisa Kudrow, Janeane Garofalo, Alan Cumming, Julia Campbell, Mia Cottet.

RONIN
MGM. Aug., 1998. (John Frankenheimer) Robert De Niro, Jean Reno, Natascha McElhone, Stellan Skarsgard, Sean Bean, Skipp Sudduth.

THE ROOKIE
WARNER BROS. December, 1990. (Clint Eastwood) Clint Eastwood, Charlie Sheen, Raul Julia, Sonia Braga.

ROOKIE OF THE YEAR
20TH CENTURY FOX. July, 1993. (Daniel Stern) Thomas Ian Nichols, Gary Busey, Daniel Stern.

A ROOM FOR ROMEO BRASS
Alliance Atlantis. Aug., 1999. British. (Shane Meadows) Andrew Shim, Ben Marshall, Paddy Considine, Frank Harper, Julia Ford.

ROOMMATES
BUENA VISTA. Match, 1995. (Peter Yates) Peter Falk, D.B. Sweeney, Julianne Moore, Jan Rubes.

THE ROOSTER
CECCHI GORI. Oct., 1998. Italian. (Carlo Verdone) Carlo Verdone, Regina Orioli, Paolo Triestino, Ines Nobili, Enrica Rosso.

ROOSTERS
IRS. July, 1995. (Robert M. Young) Edward James Olmos, Sonia Braga, Maria Conchita Alonso.

ROSALIE GOES SHOPPING
FOUR SEASONS ENTERTAINMENT. February, 1990. W. German. (Percy Adlon) Marianne Sagebrecht, Brad Davis.

ROSENCRANTZ & GUILDENSTERN ARE DEAD
CINECOM. February, 1991. British. (Tom Stoppard) Gary Oldman, Tim Roth, Richard Dreyfuss.

ROSENZWEIG'S FREEDOM
SWR TELEVISION. Aug., 1999. German. (Liliane Targownik) Benjamin Sadler, Christoph Gareissen, Peter Roggisch, Gertrud Roll, Felix von Manteuffe.

ROSETTA
USA FILMS. May, 1999. Belgian-French. (Luc and Jean-Pierre Dardenne) Emilie Dequenne, Fabrizio Rongione, Anne Yernaux, Olivier Gourmet.

ROSEWOOD
WARNER BROS. February, 1997. (John Singleton), Jon Voight, Ving Rhames, Don Cheadle, Bruce McGill, Loren Dean, Esther Rolle.

ROSSINI: OR THE FATAL QUESTION, WHO SLEPT WITH WHOM
CONSTANTIN FILM. May, 1997. German. (Helmut Dietl) Goetz George, Mario Adorf, Heiner Lauterbach, Gudrun Landgrebe.

ROUGE OF THE NORTH
GREYCAT. December, 1991. Chinese. (Fred Tan) Hsia Wen Shi, Msu Ming, Kao Chich.

ROUNDERS
MIRAMAX. Aug., 1998. (John Dahl) Matt Damon, Edward Norton, John Turturro, Gretchen Mol, Famke Janssen, John Malkovich, Martin Landau.

ROUTE ONE/USA
INTERAMA. November, 1990. (Robert Kramer) Documentary.

ROUTE 9
MOTION PICTURE CORP. OF AMERICA/PFG ENTERTAINMENT . May, 1999. (David Mackay) Kyle MacLachlan, Peter Coyote, Roma Maffia, Miguel Sandoval, Wade Andrew Williams.

ROVER DANGERFIELD
WARNER BROS. August, 1991. (Jim George, Bob Seeley) Animated.

ROY COHN/JACK SMITH
STRAND. August, 1995. (Jill Godmilow) Ron Vawter.

RUBIN & ED
I.R.S. May, 1992. (Trent Harris) Crispin Glover, Howard Hesseman, Karen Black.

RUBY
TRIUMPH. March, 1992. (John Mackenzie) Danny Aiello, Sherilyn Fenn, Arliss Howard.

RUBY IN PARADISE
OCTOBER FILMS. October, 1993. (Victor Nunez) Ashley Judd, Bentley Mitchum, Todd Field.

RUDE AWAKENING
S.P.B. Films. March, 1996. (Steve Bilich) Denia Ridley, John Ellison, Glen B. Svendrowski, Euan McDonald.

RUDOLF THE RED-NOSED REINDEER: THE MOVIE
LEGACY. Oct., 1998. (Bill Kowalchuk). Animated.

RUDY
TRISTAR. October, 1993. (David Anspaugh) Sean Astin, Charles S. Dutton, Ned Beatty.

RUDYARD KIPLING'S THE JUNGLE BOOK
BUEN VISTA. December, 1995. (Stephen Sommers) Jason Scott Lee, Cary Elwes, Lena Headey, Sam Neill.

RUDYARD KIPLING'S THE SECOND JUNGLE BOOK: MOWGLI AND BALOO
SONY PICTURES ENTERTAINMENT. May, 1997. (Duncan McLachlan), James Williams, Bill Campbell, Roddy McDowall.

THE RUGRATS MOVIE
PARAMOUNT. Nov., 1998. (Norton Virgien, Igor Kovalyov. Animated.

RUN
BUENA VISTA. Feburary, 1991. (Geoff Burrowes) Patrick Dempsey, Kelly Preston, Ken Pogue.

RUNAWAY BRIDE
PARAMOUNT. July, 1999. (Garry Marshall) Julia Roberts, Richard Gere, Joan Cusack, Hector Elizondo, Rita Wilson.

THE RUN OF THE COUNTRY
COLUMBIA. September, 1995. British. (Peter Yates) Albert Finney, Matt Keeslar, Victoria Smurfit.

RUN OF THE HOUSE
ZOO PRODS. LTD. May, 1992. (James M. Felter) Alan Edwards, Lisa-Marie Felter, Harry A. Winter.

THE RUNESTONE
HYPERION PICTURES. February, 1992. (Willard Carroll) Peter Riegert, Joan Severance, Alexander Gudonov.

THE RUNNER
ASPECT RATIO FILMS. May, 1999. (Ron Moler): Ron Eldard, Courteney Cox, Joe Mantegna, Bokeem Woodbine, John Goodman.

RUSH
MGM. December, 1991. (Lili Fini Zanuck) Jason Patric, Jennifer Jason Leigh, Sam Elliott.

RUSH HOUR
NEW LINE CINEMA. Aug., 1998. (Brett Ratner) ackie Chan, Chris Tucker, Tom Wilkinson, Elizabeth Pena, Philip Baker Hall.

RUSHMORE
BUENA VISTA. Sept., 1998. (Wes Anderson) Jason Schwartzman, Bill Murray, Olivia Williams, Seymour Cassel, Brian Cox, Mason Gamble.

THE RUSSIA HOUSE
MGM. December, 1990. (Fred Schepisi) Sean Connery, Michelle Pfeiffer, Roy Scheider.

RUSSIAN MEAT
HRVATSKA RADIO TELEVISZIJA. Aug., 1998. Croation. (Luka Nola) Ivo Gregurevic, Barbara Nola, Goran Grgic, Kristijan Ugrina, Bojan Navojec.

RUSTEM'S NOTES WITH ILLUSTRATIONS
CENTER FOR FILM PRODUCTION, REPUBLIC OF KAZAKHSTAN r. Feb., 1999. Kazakhstani. (Ardak Armikulov) Erzhan Rustembekov, Assel Shaimukhammedova.

S

S.
FLANDERS IMAGE. June, 1999. Belgian. (Guido Henderickx) Natali Broods, Kristine van Pellicom, Inge Paulussen, Isnel Da Silveira, Katelijne Damen.

SABRINA
PARAMOUNT. December, 1995. (Sydney Pollack) Harrison Ford, Julia Ormond, Greg Kinnear, Nancy Marchand.

SACRED
OCEAN FILMS. May, 1999. Israeli-French. (Amos Gitai) Yael Abecassis, Yoram Hattab, Meital Barda, Uri Ran Klauzner, Yussef Abu Warda.

SACRED HEARTS
AMERICAN MONGREL.October, 1995. (Patrick O'Connor) Kelly Fritz, Doug Hubbel, Marlene May.

SAFE
SONY PICTURES CLASSICS. June, 1995. (Todd Haynes) Julianne Moore, Xander Berkeley, Peter Friedman.

SAFE MEN
ANDELL ENTERTAINMENT. Jan., 1998. (John Hamburg) Sam Rockwell, Steve Zahn, Paul Giamatti, Michael Schmidt.

SAFE PASSAGE
NEW LINE. December, 1994. (Robert Allan Ackerman) Susan Sarandon, Sam Shepard.

SAHARA
ROADSHOW. June, 1996. Australian-U.S. (Brian Trenchard-Smith) James Belushi, Jerome Ehlers, Paul Empson.

THE SAINT
PARAMOUNT. March, 1997. (Phillip Noyce), Val Kilmer, Elizabeth Shue, Rade Serbedzija, Valery Nikolaev, Henry Goodman.

SAINT EX
GUILD PATHE. Nov., 1996. British. (Anand Tucker) Bruno Ganz, Miranda Richardson, Janet McTeer, Ken Scott, Katrin Cartlidge.

SAINT LUCIFER
IMCINE/PRODUCCIONES NUEVO SOL PROD. April, 1997. Mexican. (Miguel Sabido) Rafael Cortes, Victor Perez.

THE SAINT OF FORT WASHINGTON
WARNER BROS. November, 1993. (Tim Hunter) Matt Dillon, Danny Glover, Rick Aviles.

SALLY MARSHALL IS NOT AN ALIEN
UIP. June, 1999. Australian-Canadian. (Mario Andreacchio) Helen Neville, Natalie Vansier, Thea Gumbert, Glenn McMillan, Danielle de Grossi.

SALMONBERRIES
ROXIE. March, 1994. German. (Percy Adlon) K.D. Lang, Rosel Zech, Chuck Connors.

SALT IN THE WOUND
FERNANDO COLOMO/MANDALA. May, 1996. Spanish-Argentine. (Alberto Lecchi) Juanjo Puigcorbe, Karra Elejalde.

SAMANTHA
ACADEMY ENT. November, 1992. (Stephen La Rocque) Martha Plimpton, Dermot Mulroney, Hector Elizondo.

SAMBA TRAORE
NEW YORKER. September, 1993. Burkina Faso. (Idrissa Ouedraogo) Bakary Sangare, Mariam Kaba.

SAMURAI FICTION
PONY CANYON/JUNGLE/DIGITAL GARAGE . May, 1999. Japanese. (Hiroyuki Nakano) Morio Kazama, Mitsuru Fukikoshi, Tomoyasu Hotei, Tamaki Ogawa, Mari Natsuki.

THE SANDLOT
20TH CENTURY FOX. April, 1993. (David Mickey Evans) Tom Guiry, Mike Vitar, Karen Allen, James Earl Jones.

SANKOFA
MYPHEDUH. April, 1994. German-Ghanian-Burkina Faso-U.S. (Haile Gerima) Oyafunmike Ogunlano.

THE SANTA CLAUSE
BUENA VISTA. November, 1994. (John Pasquin) Tim Allen, Judge Reinhold, Wendy Crewson.

SANTA FE
NULMGE. Nov., 1997. (Andrew Shea) Gary Cole, Lolita Davidovich, Tina Majorino, Sheila Kelley, Jere Burns, Pamela Reed

SARABANDE
RHOMBUS MEDIA PROD. Aug., 1997. Canadian. (Atom Egoyan) Yo-Yo Ma, Lori Singer, Arsinee Khanjian, Don McKeller, Jan Rubes.

SARAFINA!
BUENA VISTA. September, 1992. French-British-South African. (Darrell James Roodt) Leleti Khumalo, Whoopi Goldberg.

SATAN
RUSSIMPEX. June, 1992. Russian. (Viktor Aristov) Sergei Kuprianov, Svetlana Bragarnik, Veniamin Malotschevski.

THE SATIN SLIPPER
CANNON GROUP. September, 1994. French-Portuguese. (Manoel de Oliveira) Luis Miguel Cintra, Anne Consigny, Patricia Barzyk.

A SATURDAY ON EARTH
AFMD. May, 1996. French. (Diane Bertrand) Elsa Zylberstein, Eric Caravaca.

SAVAGE NIGHTS
GRAMERCY. February, 1994. French-Italian. (Cyril Collard) Cyril Collard, Romane Bohringer, Carlos Lopez.

SAVAGES
MEDUSA. January, 1996. Italian. (Carlo Vanzina) Enzo Greggio, Cinzia Leone, Leo Gullotta.

SAVE AND PROTECT
INT'L. FILM CIRCUIT. July, 1992. Russian. (Aleksandr Sokurov) Cecile Zervudacki, Robert Vaab.

SAVING PRIVATE RYAN
DREAMWORKS PICTURES/PARAMOUNT. July, 1998. (Steven Spielberg) Tom Hanks, Edward Burns, Tom Sizemore, Jeremy Davies, Adam Goldberg, Barry Pepper, Giovanni Ribisi, Matt Damon.

SAVIOR
FIRST INDEPENDENT. June, 1998. (Peter Antonijevic) Dennis Quaid, Nastassja Kinski, Stellan Skarsgard. Natasa Ninkovic.

SAY YOU'LL BE MINE
EAGLE BEACH PRODS. June, 1999. (Brad Kane) Nicky Katt, Libby Langdon, Daniel Lapaine, Megan Ward, Justine Bateman.

SCANNERS II: THE NEW ORDER
TRITON. June, 1991. Canadian. (Christian Duguay, David Hewlett) Yvan Ponton, Deborah Raffin.

SCARFIES
ESSENTIAL FILMS. May, 1999. New Zealand. (Robert Sarkies) Willa O'Neill, Neill Rea, Taika Cohen, Ashleigh Seagar, Charlie Bleakley.

THE SCARLET LETTER
BUENA VISTA. October, 1995. (Roland Joffe) Gary Oldman, Robert Duval, Demi Moore, Joan Plowright, Amy Wright.

SCARRED CITY
MILLENNIUM FILMS. May, 1998. (Ken Sanzel) Stephen Baldwin, Chazz Palminteri, Tia Carrere, Gary Dourdan, Michael Rispoli.

SCENERY
YAN CHEN. Jan., 1999. Chinese. (Zhao Jisong): Lin Peng, Sun Fengyiin, Zhao Yunyun.

SCENES FROM A MALL
BUENA VISTA. February, 1991. (Paul Mazursky) Bette Midler, Woody Allen.

SCENT OF A WOMAN
UNIVERSAL. December, 1992. (Martin Brest) Al Pacino, Chris O'Donnell, James Rebhorn.

SCENT OF GREEN PAPAYA, THE
FIRST LOOK. January, 1994. Vietnamese. (Tran Anh Hung) Tran Nu Yen Khe, Lu Man San, Truong Thi Loc.

THE SCENT OF THE NIGHT
FILMAURO. Sept., 1998. Italian. (Claudio Caligari) Valerio Mastandrea, Marco Giallini, Giorgio Tirabassi, Alessio Fugardi, Emanuel Bevilacqua.

SCHINDLER'S LIST
UNIVERSAL. December, 1993. (Steven Spielberg) Liam Neeson, Ben Kingsley, Ralph Fiennes. B&W.

SCHIZOPOLIS
POINT 406 LTD. May, 1996. (Steven Soderbergh) Steven Soderbergh, Betsy Brantley, David Jensen.

SCHOOL TIES
PARAMOUNT. September, 1992. (Robert Mandel) Brendan Fraser, Matt Damon, Andrew Lowery, Chris O'Donnell.

SCHPAAA
EUROPAFILM. Feb., 1999. Norwegian. (Erik Poppe) Maikel Andressen Abou-Zelof, Jalal Zahedjekta, Sharjil Arshed Vaseer, Mickael Marman.

SCISSORS
DDM FILM CORP. March, 1991. (Frank De Felitta) Sharon Stone, Steve Railsback, Ronny Cox.

SCORPION SPRING
ANANT SINGH/DISTANT HORIZON. October, 1995. (Brian Cox) Alfred Molina, Patrick McGaw, Esai Morales.

THE SCOTTISH TALE
POLHEMUS PICTURES. Jan., 1997. (Mackinlay Polhemus) Josiah Polhemus, Ann Boehlke, Robert Ross, Sandy Kenyon, Marcia Rodd.

THE SCOUT
20TH CENTURY FOX. September, 1994. (Michael Ritchie) Albert Brooks, Brendan Fraser, Dianne Wiest.

SCRAPBOOK
FRAGILE ENTERTAINMENT. Jan., 1999. (Kurt Kuenne) Justin Urich, Eric Balfour, Chadwick Palmatier, Keili Lefkowitz, Jed Rhein.

SCRATCH THE SURFACE
TARA FITZPATRICK/MILDRED PRODS. June, 1997. (Tara Fitzpatrick) Brooke Shields, Phoebe Cates, Whitney Houston. Documentary.

SCREAM
MIRAMAX. December, 1996. (Wes Craven), Neve Campbell, David Arquette, Courteney Cox, Matthew Lillard, Skeet Ulrich, Rose McGowan, Drew Barrymore.

THE SCREAM OF THE SILK
PRESIDENT FILMS. April, 1996. French-Swiss-Belgian. (Yvon Marciano) Marie Trintignant, Sergio Castellitto.

SCREAM 2
MIRAMAX. Dec., 1997. (Wes Craven) David Arquette, Neve Campbell, Courteney Cox, Sarah Michelle Gellar, Jamie Kennedy.

SCREAMERS
TRIUMPH. September, 1995. (Christian Duguay) Peter Weller, Roy Dupus, Charles Powell, Jennifer Rubin.

SCREENPLAY
SCREENPLAY LIMITED PARTNERS. July, 1999. (Adam Winston) Sean Gavigan, David Coburn, Kathryn Morris, Kristofer Linquist.

SEARCH AND DESTROY
OCTOBER FILMS. April, 1995. (David Salle) Griffin Dunne, Illeana Douglas, Christopher Walken.

THE SEARCH FOR ONE-EYED JIMMY
NORTHERN ARTS. June, 1996. (Sam Henry Kass) Nick Turturro, Steve Buscemi, Michael Baldalucco.

THE SEARCH FOR SIGNS OF INTELLIGENT LIFE IN THE UNIVERSE
ORION CLASSICS. September, 1991. (John Gailey) Lily Tomlin.

SEARCHING FOR BOBBY FISCHER
PARAMOUNT. August, 1993. (Steven Zaillian) Max Pomeranc, Joe Mantegna, Ben Kingsley, Joan Allen.

SEBASTIAN
MEFISTO FILM/MIRAMAR/NORDISK FILM. June, 1996. Norwegian-Swedish. (Svend Wam) Hampus Bjorck.

SECOND BEST
WARNER BROS. September, 1994. British. (Chris Menges) William Hurt, Chris Cleary Miles, Keith Allen.

THE SECOND CIRCLE
INT'L. FILM CIRCUIT. January, 1992. Russian. (Alexander Sokhurov, Kroeg Vitorj).

THE SECOND TIME
LUCKY RED. November, 1995. Italian-French. (Mimmo Calopresti) Nanni Moretti, Valeria Bruni Tedeschi.

THE SECOND WIFE
CECCHI GORI. Aug., 1998. Italian. (Ugo Chiti) Maria Grazia Cucinotta, Lazar Ristovski, Girogio Noe, Jessica Auriemma, Patrizia Corti.

THE SECRET ADVENTURES OF TOM THUMB
ZEITGEIST. April, 1994. British-French. (Dave Borthwick) Animation.

SECRET FRIENDS
BRIARPATCH. February, 1992. British. (Dennis Potter) Alan Bates, Gina Bellman, Frances Barber.

THE SECRET GARDEN
WARNER BROS. August, 1993. (Agnieszka Holland) Kate Maberly, Heydon Prowse, Maggie Smith.

THE SECRET LIFE OF ALGERNON
MARANO PRODS. Sept., 1997. Canadian. (Charles Jarrott) John Cullum, Carrie-Anne Moss, Charles Durning.

THE SECRET LIFE OF GIRLS
OVERSEAS FILM GROUP. June, 1999. (Holly Goldberg) Linda Hamilton, Eugene Levy, Majandra Delfino, Meagan Good.

THE SECRET RAPTURE
CASTLE HILL. April, 1994. British. (Howard Davies) Juliet Stevenson, Joanne Whalley Kilmer, Penelope Whilton.

SECRETS & LIES
FILM FOUR. June, 1996. French-British. (Mike Leigh) Timothy Spall, Brenda Blethyn, Phyllis Logan.

SECRETS OF THE HEART
AIETE FILMS-ARIANE FILMS. Feb., 1997. Spanish-French-Portuguese. (Montxo Armendariz) Andoni Erburu, Carmelo Gomez.

SECUESTRO: A STORY OF A KIDNAPPING
INDEPENDENT. January, 1994. Colombian-Spanish. (Camila Motta) Documentary.

SEE JULIE AGAIN
FILM TONIC. Oct., 1998. Canadian. (Jeanne Crepeau) Dominique Leduc, Stephanie Morgenstern, Marcel Sabourin, Muriel Dutil, Lucille Belair.

SEEKING THE CAFE BOB
CALICO DOG PRODS. April, 1996. (Jeff Stolhand) Christian Zimmerman, Michael Dalman, Roger Harrell.

SEIZE THE DAY (UZ)
BONTONFILM. April, 1996. Czech. (Zdenek Tyc) Radek Holub, Barbora Hrzanova.

SELECT HOTEL
CLIMAX. April, 1996. French. (Laurent Bouhnik) Julie Gayet, Jean-Michel Fete, Serge Blumental.

SELENA
WARNER BROS. March, 1997. (Gregory Nava), Jennifer Lopez, Edward James Olmos, Jon Seda, Constance Marie, Jacob Vargas.

SENSE AND SENSIBILITY
COLUMBIA. December, 1995. (Ang Lee) Emma Thompson, Alan Rickman, Kate Winslet, Hugh Grant, James Fleet.

SENSO UNICO
BENGAL TIGER PICTURES. June, 1999. Italian-Indian-British. (Aditya Bhattacharya) Lothaire Bluteau, Laila Rouass, Stefania Rocca.

SEPARATE LIVES
TRIMARK. September, 1995. (David Madden) James Belushi, Linda Hamilton, Vera Miles.

SERIAL MOM
SAVOY. April, 1994. (John Waters) Kathleen Turner, Sam Waterston, Ricki Lake, Mink Stole.

THE SERPENT'S KISS
BERRYER FILMS/PRESIDENT FILMS/FRANCE 2 CINEMA/RED PARROT. May, 1997. French-German-British. (Philippe Rousselot) Ewan McGregor, Greta Scacchi, Pete Postlethwaite.

SERPENT'S LAIR
KUSHNER-LOCKE. October, 1995. (Jeffrey Reiner) Jeff Fahey, Lisa B., Heather Medway, Anthony Palermo.

SERPENT'S PATH
DAIEI CO. Aug., 1999. Japanese. (Kiyoshi Kurosawa) Sho Aikawa, Teruyuki Kagawa.

THE SERVANT'S SHIRT
ANT CARRY THE MOUNTAIN FILMS. Feb., 1999. Indian-Dutch. (Mani Kaul) Pankaj Sudhir Mishra, Anu Joseph, Om Praksh Dwivedi.

SET ME FREE
FRANCE FILM. Feb., 199. Canadaian-Swiss-French. (Lea Pool) Karine Vanasse, Alexandre Merineau, Pascale Bussieres, Miki Manojiovic, Charlotte Christeler.

SET IT OFF
NEW LINE. October, 1996. (F. Gary Gray), Jada Pinkett, Queen Latifah, Vivica A. Fox, Kimberly Elise, John C. McGinley, Blair Underwood.

THE SETTLEMENT
DOGSMILE PICTURES/DAVIS ENTERTAINMENT/CINETEL FILMS . Apr., 1999. (Mark Steilen) John C. Reilly, William Fichtner, Kelly McGillis, David Rasche, Dan Castellaneta.

SEVEN
NEW LINE. September, 1995. (David Fincher) Morgan Freeman, Brad Pitt, Gwyneth Paltrow.

SEVENTEEN YEARS
KEETMAN LTD./XI'AN FILM STUDIO. Aug., 1999. Chinese-Italian. (Zhang Yuan) Liu Lin, Li Bingbing, Le Yeping, Liang Song, Li Jun.

7/25
PALMYLA MOON. May, 1999. Japanese. (Wataru Hayakawa) Isamu Hyuga, Mihoko Umetsu, Junya Nakano, Risa Miyanaga.

SEVEN YEARS IN TIBET
SONY PICTURES ENTERTAINMENT. September, 1997. (Jean-Jacques Annaud), Brad Pitt, David Thewlis, B.D. Wong, Mako.

THE SEVENTH COIN
HEMDALE. September, 1993. Israeli. (Dror Soref) Peter O'Toole, Navin Chowdhry, Alexandra Powers.

SEX AND ZEN
GOLDEN HARVEST. August, 1993. Hong Kong. (Michael Mak) Amy Yip, Isabella Chow, Lawrence Ng.

SEX, DRUGS AND DEMOCRACY
RED HAT PRODS. February, 1995. (Jonathan Blank) Documentary.

SEX, DRUGS, ROCK & ROLL
AVENUE. September, 1991. (John McNaughton) Eric Bogosian.

SEX IS
OUTSIDER PRODS. May, 1993. (Marc Huestis) Documentary.

THE SEX MONSTER
TRIMARK. May, 1999. (Mike Binder) Mariel Hemingway, Mike Binder, Renee Humphrey, Taylor Nichols, Missy Crider.

THE SEX OF THE STARS
FIRST RUN FEATURES. October, 1994. Canadian. (Paule Baillargeon) Denis Mercier, Marianne Coquelicot Mercier.

SEX, SHAME AND TEARS
TITAN & SPL.. Mar., 1999. Mexican. (Antonio Serrano) Demian Bichir, Susana Zabaleta, Monic Dionne, Jorge Salinas, Cecilia Suarez.

SEX: THE ANNABEL CHONG STORY
OMNI INTL. AND GREYCAT RELEASING. Jan., 1999. U.S.-Canadian. (Gough Lewis) Grace Quek, Annabel Chong.

S.F.W.
GRAMERCY. January, 1995. (Jefery Levy) Stephen Dorff, Reese Witherspoon, Jack Noseworthy.

SGT. BILKO
UNIVERSAL. March, 1996. (Jonathan Lynn) Steve Martin, Dan Ackroyd, Phil Hartman, Glenne Headly.

THE SHADE
FILMAKER. May, 1999. French. (Raphael Nadjari) Richard Edson, Lorie Marino, Barbara Haas, Jeff Ware.

THE SHADOW
UNIVERSAL. July, 1994. (Russell Mulcahy) Alec Baldwin, John Lone, Penelope Ann Miller.

SHADOW CONSPIRACY
BUENA VISTA. January, 1997. (George P. Cosmatos), Charlie Sheen, Donald Sutherland, Linda Hamilton, Stephen Lang, Ben Gazzara.

SHADOW BOXERS
SWERVE FILMS. June, 1999. (Katya Bankowsky) Lucia Rijker, Jill Matthews, Freddie Roach. Documentary.

SHADOW OF ANGELS
ALBATROS/ARTCOFILM. March, 1992. German. (Daniel Schmid) Ingrid Craven, Rainer Werner Fassbinder.

THE SHADOW OF CAIN
UIP. July, 1999. Spanish-Portuguese-Dutch. (Paco Lucio) Eusebio Poncela, Laia Marull, Jorge de Juan, Juan Erasmo Mochi.

SHADOW OF CHINA
NEW LINE. March, 1991. Japanese. (Mitsuo Yanagimachi) John Lone, Koichi Sato, Sammi Davis.

SHADOW OF THE PEPPER TREE
QUETZAL FILMS. Oct., 1996. Mexican-New Zealand-U.S. (Francesca Fisher, Taggart Siegel) Mayra Serbulo, Thom Vernon.

SHADOW OF THE WOLF
TRIUMPH. March, 1993. French-Canadian. (Jacques Dorfmann) Lou Diamond Phillips, Toshiro Mifune.

SHADOW PLAY
UFD. Sept., 1996. French. (Martine Dugowson) Helena Bonham Carter, Romane Bohringer, Marie Trintignant, Elsa Zylberstein.

SHADOWLANDS
SAVOY. December, 1993. British. (Richard Attenborough) Anthony Hopkins, Debra Winger.

SHADOWS AND FOG
ORION. March, 1992. (Woody Allen) Woody Allen, Mia Farrow, John Cusack, Lily Tomlin. B & W.

SHADOWZONE
JGM ENTERPRISES. January, 1990. (J.S. Cardone) Louise Fletcher, David Beecroft.

SHADY GROVE
DREAM HOME PICTURES. March, 1996. (Christian Moore) Richard (Dicko) Mather, Amy Grappell, Jubal Clark.

SHAKESPEARE IN LOVE
MIRAMAX/UNIVERSAL. Dec., 1998. (John Madden) Joseph Fiennes, Gwyneth Paltrow, Geoffrey Rush, Judi Dench, Simon Callow.

SHAKES THE CLOWN
I.R.S. March, 1992. (Bobcat Goldthwait) Bobcat Goldthwait, Julie Brown, Paul Dooley.

SHAKING THE TREE
CASTLE HILL. January, 1992. (Duane Clark) Arye Gross, Gale Hansen, Courteney Cox.

SHAKMA
QUEST ENT. October, 1990. (Hugh Parks, Tom Logan) Christopher Atkins, Amanda Wyss, Roddy McDowall.

SHALL WE DANCE
DAIEI/NTV NETWORK/HAKUHODO/NIPPAN. May, 1996. Japanese. (Masayuki Suo) Koji Yakusyo, Tamiyo Kusakari.

SHALLOW GRAVE
GRAMERCY. February, 1995. Scottish. (Danny Boyle) Kerry Fox, Christopher Eccleston, Ewan McGregor.

SHAMPOO HORNS
ELIAS QUEREJETA PC. Feb., 1997. Spanish. (Manuel Toledano) Jason Reeves, Cheyenne Besch, Jonathan Lawrence.

SHANGHAI TRIAD
SONY PICTURES CLASSICS. January, 1996. Chinese. (Zhang Yimou) Gong Li, Baotian Li, Xiaoxiao Wang.

SHARK SKIN MAN AND PEACH HIP GIRL
TOHOKUSHINSHA FILM CORP. Sept., 1998. Japanese. (Katsuhito Ishii) Tadanobu Asano, Sie Kohinata, Ittoku Kishibe, Susumu Tershima, Simie Shingyogi.

SHATTERED
MGM. October, 1991. (Wolfgang Petersen) Tom Berenger, Bob Hoskins, Greta Scacchi.

SHATTERED IMAGE
SEVEN ARTS PICTURES/SCHROEDER HOFFMAN. Aug., 1998. (Raul Ruiz) Anne Parillaud, William Baldwin, Lisanne Falk, Graham Greene.

THE SHAWSHANK REDEMPTION
COLUMBIA. September, 1994. (Frank Darabont) Tim Robbins, Morgan Freeman, Bob Gunton.

SHE GOOD FIGHTER
INDEPENDENT PRODS. Sept., 1996. Belgian. (Marc Punt) Dagmar Liekens, Sophie Winters, Tom van Landuyt, Carl Ridders.

SHE LIVES TO RIDE
ARTISTIC LICENSE. July, 1995. (Alice Stone) Documentary.

SHE'S ALL THAT
MIRAMAX. Jan., 1999. (Robert Iscove) Freddie Prinze Jr., Rachael Leigh Cook, Matthew Lillard, Paul Walker, Jodi Lyn O'Keefe.

SHE'S BEEN AWAY
BBC. December, 1990. British. (Peter Hall) Peggy Ashcroft, James Fox, Geraldine James.

SHE'S SO LOVELY
MIRAMAX. May, 1997. (Nick Cassavetes), Sean Penn, Robin Wright Penn, John Travolta, Harry Dean Stanton, Debi Mazar.

SHE'S THE ONE
FOX SEARCHLIGHT. September, 1996. (Edward Burns) Jennifer Aniston, Maxine Bahns, Cameron Diaz.

THE SHELTERING SKY
WARNER BROS. December, 1990. British-Italian. (Bernardo Bertolucci) Debra Winger, John Malkovich, Campbell Scott.

SHIKOKU
TOHO. Aug., 1999. Japanese. (Shunichi Nagasaki) Yui Natsukawa, Michitaka Tsutsui, Chiaki Kuriyama.

SHILOH
UTOPIA PICTURES/CARL BORACK. Oct., 1996. (Dale Rosenbloom) Michael Moriarty, Rod Steiger, Blake Heron, Scott Wilson.

SHINE
RONIN. January, 1996. Australian-British. (Scott Hicks) Armin Mueller-Stahl, Noah Taylor, Lynn Redgrave.

SHINING THROUGH
20TH CENTURY FOX. January, 1992. (David Seltzer) Michael Douglas, Melanie Griffith, Liam Neeson.

SHIPWRECKED
BUENA VISTA. March, 1991. Norwegian. (Nils Gaup) Stian Smestad, Gabriel Byrne, Louisa Haigh.

A SHOCK TO THE SYSTEM
CORSAIR PICTURES. March, 1990. (Jan Egleson) Michael Caine, Elizabeth McGovern, Swoosie Kurtz.

THE SHOOTER
DIMENSION. January, 1996. British-U.S.-Spanish-Czech. (Ted Kotcheff) Dolph Ludgren, Maruschka Detmers.

SHOOTING LILY
GOLIATH/WINDROCK ENTERTAINMENT. Oct., 1996. (Arthur Borman) Matt Winston, Amy Smallman, Roy Jenkins.

SHOOTING PORN
CARYN HORWITZ. May, 1997 (Ronnie Larsen) Gino Colbert, Chi Chi LaRue, Blue Blake, Bryan Kidd, Adam Rom. Documentary.

SHOPPING FOR FANGS
DE/CENTER COMMUNICATIONS. Feb., 1997. Canadian-U.S. (Quentin Lee, Justin Lin) Radmar Jao, Jeanne Chin, Clint Jung.

SHORES OF TWILIGHT (TA RODINA AKROYIALIA)
GREEK FILM CENTRE. Nov., 1998. Greek. (Efthimios Hatzis) Stefanos Iatridis, Anna-Maria Papaharalambous.

SHORT CUTS
FINE LINE. October, 1993. (Robert Altman) Matthew Modine, Jack Lemmon, Lily Tomlin, Tim Robbins.

SHORT TIME
20TH CENTURY FOX. May, 1990. (Gregg Champion) Dabney Coleman, Matt Frewer, Teri Garr.

SHOTGUN FREEWAY: DRIVES THROUGH LOST L.A.
SHOTGUN. December, 1995. (Morgan Neville, Harry Pallenberg) Documentary.

SHOT THROUGH THE HEART
ALLIANCE COMMUNICATIONS, HBO PICTURES, BBC FILMS. Nov., 1998. British-Canadian-Hungarian. (David Attwood) Vincent Perez, Linus Roache, Lia Williams, Lothaire Bluteau, Adam Kotz.

SHOUT
UNIVERSAL. October, 1991. (Jeffrey Hornaday) James Walters, John Travolta, Heather Graham.

THE SHOW
SAVOY. August, 1995. (Brian Robbins) Concert Documentary.

SHOWER
XI'AN FILM STUDIO/ZHANG PEIMIN. Sept., 1999. Chinese. (Zhang Yang) Zhu Xu, Pu Cunxin, Jiang Wu, Li Ding, Feng Shun.

A SHOW OF FORCE
PARAMOUNT. May, 1990. (Bruno Barreto) Amy Irving, Lou Diamond Phillips, Andy Garcia.

SHOWDOWN IN LITTLE TOKYO
WARNER BROS. August, 1991. (Mark L. Lester) Dolph Lundgren, Brandon Lee, Tia Carrere.

SHOWGIRLS
MGM/UA. September, 1995. (Paul Verhoeven) Elizabeth Berkley, Kyle MacLachlan, Gina Gershon.

SHUT UP AND LISTEN!
NORDIC SCREEN DEVELOPMENT. May, 1996. Norwegian. (Erik Gustavson) Bjorn Floberg, Kjersti Holmen, Keve Hjelm.

SHUT YER MOUTH!
WORD OF MOUTH! March, 1996. (Fraser Bresnahan) Colleen Quinn, Michael Louis Wells, Ben Bode.

SIAM SUNSET
UIP. May, 1999. Australian. (John Polson) Linus Roache, Victoria Hill, Danielle Cormack, Ian Bliss, Roy Billing.

SIBLING RIVALRY
COLUMBIA. October, 1990. (Carl Reiner) Kirstie Alley, Bill Pullman, Carrie Fisher, Scott Bakula.

SICILY!
PIERRE GRISE PRODS./MARTINE MARIGNAC/CENTRE NATIONAL DE LA CINEMATOGRAPHIE/ALIA FILM/ENZO PORCELLI/ISTITUTO LUCE. May, 1999. French-Italian. (Daniele Huillet).

SICK THE LIFE & DEATH OF BOB FLANAGAN, SUPERMASOCHIST
KIRBY DICK. Jan., 1997. (Kirby Dick) Kathe Burkhart, Kirby Dick, Rita Valencia, Bob Flanagan, Sheree Rose, Documentary.

SIDE OUT
TRISTAR. March, 1990. (Peter Israelson) C. Thomas Howell, Peter Horton, Courtney Thorne Smith.

SIDE STREETS
MERCHANT IVORY PRODS./CEO FILMS. Sept., 1998. (Tony Gerber) Valeria Golino, Shashi Kapoor, Leon, Art Malik, Shabana Azmi.

SIDEKICKS
TRIUMPH. April, 1993. (Aaron Norris) Jonathan Brandis, Chuck Norris, Beau Bridges.

SIESTAS & OLAS:
A SURFING JOURNEY THROUGH MEXICO
DAN-O SURF FILMS. Dec., 1997. DOCUMENTARY.

SILENCE BROKEN: KOREAN COMFORT WOMEN
DAI SIL. Mar., 1999. (Dai Sil Kim-Gibson) Han Seung Yun, Lee Kwang Sun, Hwang Jin Kyung. Docudrama.

SILENCE = DEATH
FIRST RUN FEATURES. May, 1990. West German. (Rosa von Praunheim) Documentary.

THE SILENCE OF THE LAMBS
ORION. February, 1991. (Jonathan Demme) Jodie Foster, Anthony Hopkins, Scott Glenn, Ted Levine.

SILENT FALL
WARNER BROS. October, 1994. (Bruce Beresford) Richard Dreyfuss, Linda Hamilton, John Lithgow.

SILENT TONGUE
TRIMARK. February, 1994. (Sam Shepard) Richard Harris, Alan Bates, River Phoenix, Dermot Mulroney.

THE SILENT TOUCH
CASTLE HILL. November, 1993. British-Polish-Danish. (Krzysztof Zanussi) Max von Sydow, Lothaire Bluteau.

THE SILK ROAD
TRIMARK. January, 1992. Japanese, 1988. (Junya Sato) Koichi Sato, Toshiyuki Nishida.

SILVERLAKE LIFE: THE VIEW FROM HERE
ZEITGEIST. March, 1993. (Tom Joslin, Peter Friedman) Documentary.

SILVIA PRIETO
LES ATELIERS DES ARCHES. Jan., 1999. Argentine. (Martin Rejtman) Rosario Blefari, Gabriel Fernandez Capello, Mirtha Busnelli, Valeria Bertucelli.

SIMON BIRCH
BUENA VISTA. Aug., 1998. (Mark Steven Johnson) Ian Michael Smith, Joseph Mazzello, Ashley Judd, Oliver Platt, David Strathairn.

SIMON MAGUS
HAROM NYUL STUDIO, MTV, EUROFILM STUDIO/ARTCAM INTL. . Feb., 1999. Hungarian-French. (Ildiko Enyedi) Peter Andorai, Julie Delarme, Peter Halasz.

SIMON SEZ
INDEPENDENT ARTISTS. Sept., 1999. (Kevin Elders Dennis Rodman, Dane Cook, Natalia Cigliuti, Filip Nicolic, John Pinette.

SIMPATICO
FINE LINE. Sept., 1999. (Matthew Warchus) Nick Nolte, Jeff Bridges, Sharon Stone, Catherine Keener, Albert Finney.

SIMPLE MEN
FINE LINE. October, 1992. (Hal Hartley) Robert Burke, William Sage, Karen Sillas.

A SIMPLE PLAN
PARAMOUNT. Sept., 1998. (Sam Raimi) Bill Paxton, Billy Bob Thornton, Brent Briscoe, Bridget Fonda, Jack Walsh, Chelcie Ross.

A SIMPLE TWIST OF FATE
BUENA VISTA. September, 1994. (Gillies MacKinnon) Steve Martin, Gabriel Byrne, Catherine O'Hara.

A SIMPLE WISH
UNIVERSAL. June, 1997. (Michael Ritchie), Martin Short, Mara Wilson, Robert Pastorelli, Amanda Plummer, Kathleen Turner.

SIMPLY IRRESISTIBLE
20TH CENTURY FOX. Feb., 1999. (Mark Tarlov) Sarah Michelle Gellar, Sean Patrick Flanery, Patricia Clarkson, Dylan Baker.

SING FASTER: THE STAGEHANDS' RING CYCLE
SING FASTER. Jan., 1999. (Jon Else). Documentary.

SINGLE ACTION
KINGSIZE. Sept., 1998. (Carlos Gallardo) Carlos Gallardo, Alejandra Prado, Miguel Gurza, Oscar Castaneda, Manuel Vela.

A SINGLE GIRL
CINEA. November, 1995. French. (Benoit Jacquot) Virginie Ledoyen, Benoit Magimel, Vera Briole.

SINGLE WHITE FEMALE
COLUMBIA. August, 1992. (Barbet Schroeder) Bridget Fonda, Jennifer Jason Leigh, Steven Weber.

SINGLES
WARNER BROS. September, 1992. (Cameron Crowe) Campbell Scott, Bridget Fonda, Kyra Sedgwick, Matt Dillon.

SIOUX CITY
I.R.S. September, 1994. (Lou Diamond Phillips) Lou Diamond Phillips, Salli Richardson, Melinda Dillon.

SIRENS
MIRAMAX. March, 1994. Australian-British. (John Duigan) Tara Fitzgerald, Hugh Grant, Elle McPherson.

SISTER ACT
BUENA VISTA. May, 1992. (Emile Ardolino) Whoopi Goldberg, Maggie Smith, Harvey Keitel, Kathy Najimy.

SISTER ACT 2:
BACK IN THE HABIT
BUENA VISTA. December, 1993. (Bill Duke) Whoopi Goldberg, Kathy Najimy, Barnard Hughes.

SISTER ISLAND
WILLIAM MORRIS AGENCY. June, 1996. (Avery Crounse) Kathleen York, Karen Black, Erin Buchanan.

SISTER MY SISTER
7TH ART. June, 1995. British. (Nancy Meckler) Julie Walters, Joely Richardson, Jodhi May.

SIX DAYS, SEVEN NIGHTS
BUENA VISTA. June, 1998. (Ivan Reitman) Harrison Ford, Anne Heche, David Schwimmer, Jacqueline Obradors, Temuera Morrison.

SIX DEGREES OF SEPARATION
MGM. December, 1993. (Fred Schepisi) Stockard Channing, Will Smith, Donald Sutherland.

SIX-STRING SAMURAI
PALM PICTURES. Feb., 1998. (Lance Mungia) Jeffrey Falcon, Justin McQuire, Stephane Gauger, John Sakisian, Gabrielle Pimenter.

THE 6TH MAN
BUENA VISTA. March, 1997. (Randall Miller), Marlon Wayans, Kadeem Hardison, David Paymer, Michaell Michele, Kevin Dunn.

6:3
BUDAPEST FILM. Feb., 1999. Hungarian. (Peter Timar) Karoly Eperjes, Ferenc Kallai, Tamas Cseh, Andras Kern, Attila Lote.

THE SIXTH SENSE
BUENA VISTA. July, 1999. (M. Night Shyamalan) Bruce WIllis, Toni Collette, Olivia Williams, Haley Joel Osment, Donnie Wahlberg.

SIX WAYS TO SUNDAY
PROPSPERITY ELECTRIC. Sept., 1997. (Adam Bernstein) Norman Reedus, Deborah Harry, Elina Lowensohn, Adrien Brody.

THE SIZE OF WATERMELONS
NORSTAR ENTERTAINMENT. May, 1996. Canadian. (Kari Skogland) Paul Rudd, Donal Logue, Marissa Ribisi.

SKIN OF MAN, HEART OF BEAST
WHY NOT PRODS./ARTE FRANCE CINEMA. Aug., 1999. French. (Angel, Agnes de Sacy) Serge Riaboukine, Bernard Blancan, Pascal Cervo, Maaike Jansen.

SKI PATROL
TRIUMPH. January, 1990. (Richard Correll) Roger Rose, T. K. Carter, Martin Mull.

SKI SCHOOL
MOVIESTORE ENT. January, 1991. Canadian. (Damian Lee) Dean Cameron, Tom Breznahan, Patrick Labyorteaux.

SKIN & BONE
FILM RESEARCH UNIT. June, 1996. (Everett Lewis) b. Wyatt, Alan Boyce, Garret Scullin.

THE SKY IS FALLING
STELLARQUEST. Mar., 1999. (Florrie Laurence) Dedee Pfeiffer, Teri Garr, Howard Hesseman, Eric Close, Laura Leighton,.

THE SLAB BOYS
CHANNEL 4 FILMS. May, 1997. British. (John Byrne) Robin Laing, Duncan Ross, Russell Barr, Bill Gardiner, Louise Berry.

SLACKER
ORION CLASSICS. July, 1991. (Richard Linklater) Richard Linklater, Rudy Basquez.

THE SLAMMER
MARIE-DOMINIQUE GIRODET. Aug., 1999. French. (Alain Robak) Claude Brasseur, Olivier Martinez, Bernard Le Coq.

SLAVES OF THE UNDERGROUND
FIRST LOOK PICTURES. Jan, 1997. (Kristine Peterson) Molly Gross, Marisa Ryan, Jason Bortz, Bob Neuwirth.

SLC PUNK
SONY. Jan., 1999. (James Merendino) Matthew Lillard, Michael Goorjian, Annabeth Gish, Jennifer Lien, Christopher McDonald.

THE SLEAZY UNCLE
QUARTET. February, 1991. Italian. (Franco Brusati) Vittorio Gassman, Giancarlo Giannini, Andrea Ferreol.

THE SLEEPWALKER
LA SONAMBULA. Sept., 1998. Argentine. (Fernando Spiner) Eusebio Ponce, Sofia Viruboff, Lorenzo Quintero, Norman Briski, Alejandro Urdapilleta.

SLEEP WITH ME
MGM/UA. September, 1994. (Rory Kelly) Eric Stoltz, Meg Tilly, Craig Sheffer, Adrienne Shelly.

THE SLEEPING CAR
TRIAX ENT. February, 1990. (Douglas Curtis) David Naughton, Judie Aronson.

SLEEPING WITH THE ENEMY
20TH CENTURY FOX. February, 1991. (Joseph Ruben) Julia Roberts, Patrick Bergin, Kevin Anderson.

SLEEPLESS IN SEATTLE
TRISTAR. June, 1993. (Nora Ephron) Tom Hanks, Meg Ryan, Ross Malinger, Rosie O'Donnell.

SLIDIN'-BRIGHT AND SHINY WORLD
NOVOTNY & NOVOTNY. Jan., 1999. Austrian. (Barbara Albert) Maria Kastner, Cornelia Stastny, Sandra Maria Schoner, Martina Poltl.

A SLIPPING-DOWN LIFE
DVC/RADDON. Jan. 1999. (Toni Kalem): Lili Taylor, Guy Pearce, John Hawkes, Sara Rue, Irma P. Hall.

SLING BLADE
MIRAMAX. August, 1996. (Billy Bob Thornton) Billy Bob Thornton, Dwight Yoakam, J.T. Walsh.

THE SLINGSHOT
SONY PICTURES CLASSICS. June, 1994. Swedish. (Ake Sandgren) Jesper Salen, Stellan Skarsgard, Basia Frydman.

SLIVER
PARAMOUNT. May, 1993. (Phillip Noyce) Sharon Stone, William Baldwin, Tom Berenger.

SLUMBER PARTY MASSACRE III
CONCORDE. September, 1990. (Sally Mattison) Keely Christian, Brittain Frye.

SMALL SOLDIERS
DREAMWORKS. July, 1998. (Joe Dante) Kirsten Dunst, Gregory Smith, Jay Mohr, Phil Hartman, Kevin Dunn, Denis Leary.

SMALL TIME
KUSHNER-LOCKE CO.,/WORKIN' MAN FILMS. Nov., 1996. (Jeffrey Reiner) Glen Plummer, Patrick Cupo, Ernie Reyes.

SMALL TIME
PANORAMA. November, 1991. (Norman Loftis) Richard Barboza, Carolyn Kinebrew, Scott Ferguson.

A SMILE LIKE YOURS
PARAMOUNT. August, 1997. (Keith Samples), Greg Kinnear, Lauren Holly, Joan Cusack, Jay Thomas, Jill Hennessy.

SMILLA'S SENSE OF SNOW
FOX SEARCHLIGHT. Feb., 1997. German-Danish-Swedish. (Bille August) Julia Ormond, Gabriel Byrne, Richard Harris.

SMOKE
MIRAMAX. June, 1995. (Wayne Wang) Harvey Keitel, William Hurt, Forest Whitaker.

SMOKE SIGNALS
MIRAMAX. Jan., 1998. (Chris Eyre) Adam Beach, Evan Adams, Irene Bedard, Gary Farmer, Tantoo Cardinal, Cody Lightning, Simon Baker.

SNAKE EYES
PARAMOUNT/BUENA VISTA INTL. Aug., 1998. (Brian De Palma) Nicolas Cage, Gary Sinise, John Heard, Carla Gugino, Stan Shaw.

SNAKE SKIN JACKET
GERARD FILMS. May, 1997. (Norman Gerard) Silas Cooper, Jennifer Starr, Rupert Green, Patricia Place, Spencer Scofield.

SNAKES AND LADDERS
LIVIA FILMS. Sept., 1996. Irish-German. (Trish McAdam) Pom Boyd Gina Moxley, Sean Hughes, Paudge Behan, Pierce Turner.

SNAPPED
ILLVILLE PICTURES. Apr., 1999. (Jesse Feigelman) Gaby Hoffman, Johnny Zander, David Wheir, Seymour Cassel.

THE SNAPPER
MIRAMAX. November, 1993. British. (Stephen Frears) Colm Meaney, Tina Kellegher, Ruth McCabe.

SNEAKERS
UNIVERSAL. September, 1992. (Phil Alden Robinson) Robert Redford, Sidney Poitier, River Phoenix.

SNIDE & PREJUDICE
BOMBASTIC PICTURES. May, 1997. (Philippe Mora) Angus MacFadyen, Rene Auberjonois, Brion James, Sam Bottoms.

SNIPER
TRISTAR. January, 1993. (Luis Llosa) Tom Berenger, Billy Zane, J. T. Walsh.

SNOW
WINTER LIGHT FILMS. April, 1998. (Eric Tretbar) Shane Barach, Rose Mailutha, Lara Miklasevics, Erika Remillard, John Crozier

SNOW FALLING ON CEDARS
UNIVERSAL. Sept., 1999. (Scott Hicks) Ethan Hawke, James Cromwell, Richard Jenkins, James Rebhorn, Sam Shepard.

SO I MARRIED AN AXE MURDERER
TRISTAR. July, 1993. (Thomas Schlamme) Mike Myers, Nancy Travis, Anthony LaPaglia.

SOAPDISH
PARAMOUNT. June, 1991. (Michael Hoffman) Sally Field, Kevin Kline, Robert Downey Jr., Whoopi Goldberg.

SOCIETY
ZECCA CORP. February, 1992. (Brian Yuzna) Bill Warlock, Connie Danese, Ben Slack.

SOFIE
ARROW. May, 1993. Danish, 1993. (Liv Ullmann) Karen Lise Mynster, Ghita Norby, Erland Josephson.

SOFT FRUIT
FOX SEARCHLIGHT/20TH CENTURY FOX. June, 1999. Australian. (Christina Andreef) Jeanie Drynan, Linal Haft,Genevieve Lemon.

SOLDIER
WARNER BROS. Sept., 1998. (Paul Anderson) Kurt Russell, Jason Scott Lee, Connie Nielsen, Sean Pertwee, Michael Chiklis.

A SOLDIER'S DAUGHTER NEVER CRIES
OCTOBER FILMS. July, 1998. (James Ivory) Kris Kristofferson, Barbara Hershey, Leelee Sobieski, Jesse Bradford, Dominique Blanc.

SOLO
SONY PICTURES CLASSICS. August, 1996. (Norberto Barba) Mario Van Peebles, Barry Corbin, Bill Sadler.

SOLO FOR CLARINET
SENATOR FILM. Oct., 1998. German. (Nico Hofmann) Gotz George, Corinna Harfouch, Tim Bergmann.

SOLOVKI POWER
MOSFILM. January, 1991. Soviet. (Marina Goldovskaya) Documentary.

SOLOMON AND GAENOR
FILMFOUR DISTRIBUTORS. Feb., 1999. British. (Paul Morrison) Ioan Gruffudd, Nia Roberts, Sue Jones Davies, William Thomas.

SOLO SHUTTLE
PSYCHOLOGY NEWS. July, 1999. British-French. (David Cohen) Virginie Aster, Jean Yves Berteloot, John Shrapnel, Alex Jennings, Sean Hughes.

SO MAMBO
MEDUSA. Aug., 1999. Italian. (Luca Pellegrini Luca Bizzarri, Paolo Kessisoglu, Luciana Littizzetto, Maddalena Maggi.

SOMEBODY IS WAITING
REDHEAD FILMS. Nov., 1996. (Martin Donovan) Gabriel Byrne, Nastassja Kinski, Johnny Whitworth, Rebecca Gayheart.

SOMEBODY UP THERE LIKES ME
LONG SHOW PICTURES. June, 1996. Hong Kong. (Patrick Leung) Aaron Kwok, Carmen Lee, Sammo Hung.

SOME KINDA LOVE
OFFICE SHIROUS. Oct., 1996. Japanese. (Shunichi Nagasaki) Koji Tamaki, LaSalle Ishii, Kaori Mizushima, Shinya Tsukamoto.

SOME NUDITY REQUIRED
ONLY CHILD. Jan., 1998. (Odette Springer, Johanna Demetrakas) DOCUMENTARY.

SOME PREFER CAKE
UP ALL NIGHT PRODS. June, 1997. (Heidi Arnesen) Kathleen Fontaine, Tara Howley, Desi del Valle, Leon Acord, Machiko Saito.

SOMETHING MORE
ALLIANCE ATLANTIS. Sept., 1999. Canadian. (Rob King) Michael Goorjian, Chandra West, David Lovgren, Thomas Cavanaugh, Jennifer Beals.

SOMETHING ORGANIC
HAUT & COURT. Sept., 1998. French-Canadian. (Bertrand Bonello) Romane Bohringer, Laurent Lucas, Charlotte Laurier.

SOMETHING TO TALK ABOUT
WARNER BROS. August, 1995. (Lasse Hallstrom) Julia Roberts, Dennis Quaid, Robert Duvall, Kyra Sedgwick.

SOMETHING TO DO WITH THE WALL
FIRST RUN FEATURES. February, 1991. (Marilyn Levine, Ross McElwee) Documentary.

SOMETIME IN AUGUST
(Caio Ribeiro) Michael Medeiros, Sylva Kelegian, Glenn English, Terry Keane, Lois Markle.

SOMEWHERE IN THE CITY
SIDESHOW INC. June, 1997. (Ramin Niami) Sandra Bernhard, Ornella Muti, Robert John Burke, Peter Stormare, Bai Ling.

SOMMERSBY
WARNER BROS. February, 1993. (Jon Amiel) Richard Gere, Jodie Foster, Bill Pullman.

SON–IN–LAW
BUENA VISTA. July, 1993. (Steve Rash) Pauly Shore, Carla Gugino, Lane Smith.

SONNY BOY
TRIUMPH. October, 1990. (Robert Martin Caroll) David Carradine, Brad Dourif, Paul L. Smith.

SON OF MARY
HI KHANEH HOUSE OF CHILDREN'S LITERATURE & ARTS . Feb., 1999. Iranian. (Hamid Jebelli) Mohsen Falsafin, Rafik Dergabrilian, Hadi Na'iinizade, Seyyed Ali, Seyyad Mehdi.

SON OF THE PINK PANTHER
MGM. August, 1993. (Blake Edwards) Robert Benigni, Herbert Lom, Claudia Cardinale.

SON OF THE SHARK
7TH ARTS. March, 1995. French-Belgian. (Agnes Merlet) Ludovic Vandendaele, Erick DaSilva, Sandrine Blancke.

THE SOONG SISTERS
GOLDEN HARVEST. Feb., 1997. Hong Kong. (Mabel Cheung Yuen-ting) Michelle Yeoh, Maggie Cheung, Vivian Wu, Winston Chao.

SOUL ACHE
EL MECANISMO ENCANTADO/ARTCAM INTL./AXELOTIL FILMS . June, 1999. Spanish-French-Italian. (Fernando Merinero) Martxelo Rubio, Bruno Buzzi, Juan Potau, Nathalie Sesena, Angelica Reverte.

SOUL FOOD
20TH CENTURY FOX. September, 1997. (George Tilman Jr.), Vanessa L. Williams, Vivica A. Fox, Nia Long, Michael Beach, Mekhi Phifer.

THE SOUL GUARDIANS
POLYVISION. Sept., 1998 South Korean. (K. C. Park) Ahn Sung-ki, Shin Hyeon-jun, Chu Sang-mi, Oh Hyeon-chul.

SOUL IN THE HOLE
HBO. January, 1996. (Danielle Gardner) Documentary.

SOUL SQUARE
DISTRIBUTION CO. Sept., 1998. Argentine. (Fernando Diaz) Alejandro Gance, Vera Fogwill, Olga Zubarry, Norman Briski.

SOULTAKER
ACTION INT'L. PICTURES. October, 1990. (Michael Rissi) Joe Estevez, Vivian Schilling.

SOUND MAN
MOUNTAINAIR FILMS. Aug., 1998. (Steven Ho) Wayne Pere, Eliane Chappuis, William Forsythe, Wes Studi, Nick Stahl, John Koyama.

SOUR GRAPES
SONY. April, 1998. (Larry David) Steven Weber, Craig Bierko, Matt Keeslar, Karen Sillas, Robyn Peterman, Viola Harris, Orlando Jones.

SOUTH
AMIP/PARADISE FILMS/CHEMAH I.S. May, 1999. French-Belgian. (Chantal Akerman). Documentary.

SOUTH CENTRAL
WARNER BROS. September, 1992. (Steve Anderson) Glenn Plummer, Byron Keith Minns, Lexie D. Bigham.

SOUTHIE
AMERICAN WORLD PICTURES. June, 1998. (John Shea) Donnie Wahlberg, Rose McGowan, Anne Meara, James Cummings.

SOUTH PARK
PARAMOUNT/WARNER BROS. June, 1999. (Trey Parker).Animated.

SOUTHPAW
BOARD SCANNAN NA HEIREANN. Jan., 1999. Irish. (Liam McGrath). Documentary.

SPACE AVENGER
MANLEY PRODS. May, 1990. (Richard W. Haines) Robert Prichard, Mike McCleric.

SPACE IS THE PLACE
RHAPSODY. September, 1993. (John Coney) Sun Ra.

SPACE JAM
WARNER BROS. November, 1996. (Joe Pytka), Michael Jordan, Wayne Knight, Theresa Randle.

SPACE TRUCKERS
GOLDCREST. Oct., 1997. (Stuart Gordon) Dennis Hooper, Stephen Dorff, Debi Mazar, Charles Dance George Wendt, Shane Rimmer.

SPACED INVADERS
BUENA VISTA. April, 1990. (Patrick Read Johnson) Douglas Barr, Royal Dano, Ariana Richards.

SPANK!
PALACE. June, 1999. Australian. (Ernie Clark) Robert Mammone, Vice Poletto, Victoria Dixon-Whittle, Mario Gamma, Lucia Mastrantone.

SPANISH FLY
MIRAMAX. May, 1998. (Daphna Kastner) Daphna Kastner, Toni Canto, Martin Donovan, Marianne Sagebrecht, Maria de Medeiros.

THE SPANISH PRISONER
SWEETLAND FILMS. Sept., 1997. (David Mamet) Campbell Scott, Rebecca Pidgeon, Steve Martin, Ricky Jay, Ben Gazzara.

SPANKING THE MONKEY
FINE LINE. July, 1994. (David O. Russell) Jeremy Davies, Alberta Watson, Carla Gallo.

SPAWN
NEW LINE. July, 1997. (Mark A.Z. Dippe), John Leguizamo, Michael Jai White, Martin Sheen, Theresa Randle, Melinda Clarke.

SPEAKING IN STRINGS
COUNTERPOINT FILMS. Jan., 1999. (Paola di Florio). Documentary.

SPEAKING PARTS
ZEITGEIST. February, 1990. Canadian (Atom Egoyan) Michael McManus, Arsinee Khanjian.

SPEAK LIKE A CHILD
BFI PRODS./BBC FILMS/LEDA SERENE. Sept., 1998. British. (John Akomfrah) Cal Macaninch, Daniel Newman, Richard Mylan, Fraser Ayres, Rachel Fielding.

SPECIAL EFFECTS
NOVA/WGBH BOSTON. June, 1996. (Ben Burtt) Documentary.

THE SPECIALIST
WARNER BROS. October, 1994. (Luis Llosa) Sylvester Stallone, Sharon Stone, James Woods, Eric Roberts.

THE SPECIALIST
Intermedia Arc. Feb., 1999. French. (Eyal Sivan).

SPECIES
MGM/UA. July, 1995. (Roger Donaldson) Ben Kingsley, Michael Madsen, Alfred Molina, Forrest Whitaker.

SPECIES II
MGM. April, 1998. (Peter Medak) Michael Madsen, Natasha Henstridge, Marg Helgenberger, Mykelti Williamson, George Dzundza.

SPEECHLESS
MGM. December, 1994. (Ron Underwood) Michael Keaton, Geena Davis, Christopher Reeve, Bonnie Bedelia.

SPEED
20TH CENTURY FOX. June, 1994. (Jan De Bont) Keanu Reeves, Dennis Hopper, Sandra Bullock.

SPEED 2: CRUISE CONTROL
20TH CENTURY FOX. June, 1997. (Jan De Bont), Sandra Bullock, Jason Patric, Willem Dafoe, Temuera Morrison, Brian McCardie.

SPEEDWAY JUNKY
MAGIC ENTERTAINMENT. Feb., 1999. Israeli-U.S. (Nickolas Perry) Jesse Bradford, Jordan Brower, Jonathan Taylor Thomas, Daryl Hannah.

SPEEDY BOYS
CARGO CULT PRODS.. Jan., 1999. (James Herbert) Andy Liedilato, Carter Davis, Aline Nari, Alessandra Palma, Kari Malievich.

SPIN THE BOTTLE
CINEBLAST!. Mar., 1999. (Jamie Yerkes): Mitchell Riggs, Kim Winter, Jessica Faller, Heather Goldenhersch, Holter Graham.

THE SPIRIT AND MYSTERY OF FLAMENCO
CINEMATHEQUE DE LA DANSE. April, 1996. Spanish. Antonio, Pilar Lopez and the Ballet Espanol.

SPIRIT OF 76, THE
COLUMBIA. October, 1990. (Lucas Reiner) David Cassidy, Olivia D'Abo, Geoff Hoyle.

SPIRITS RISING
RAMONA S. DIAZ. April, 1996. (Ramona S. Diaz) Documentary narrated by William Consul.

THE SPITFIRE GRILL
COLUMBIA. September, 1996. (Lee David Zlotoff) Alison Elliott, Ellen Burstyn, Marcia Gay Harden, Will Patton.

SPLENDOR
SUMMIT ENTERTAINMENT/ NEWMARKET CAPITAL GROUP. Jan., 1999. (Gregg Araki) Kathleen Robertson, Johnathon Schaech, Matt Keeslar, Kelly Macdonald, Eric Mabius.

SPLIT
JANE BALFOUR. September, 1993. (Andrew Weeks, Ellen Fisher Turk) Documentary.

THE SPLIT
ALFA FILM/ICELANDIC FILM CORP./ARTCAM INTL./TNS PRODS./SCARABEE FILM PRODS.. May, 1999. Icelandic-Turkish. (Canan Gerede) Bennu Gerede, Mahir Gunsiray, Baltasar Kormakur, Rebecca Haas, Sibel Baykam.

SPLIT SECOND
INTERSTAR. May, 1992. British. (Tony Maylam) Rutger Hauer, Kim Cattrall, Michael J. Pollard.

SPONTANEOUS COMBUSTION
TAURUS ENTERTAINMENT. February, 1990. (Tobe Hooper) Brad Dourif, Cynthia Bain.

SPRUNG
TRIMARK. May, 1997. (Rusty Cundieff), Tisha Campbell, Rusty Cundieff, Paula Jai Parker, Joe Torry, John Witherspoon, Jennifer Lee.

SPY HARD
BUENA VISTA. May, 1996. (Rick Friedberg) Leslie Nielsen, Nicollette Sheridan, Charles Durning, Marcia Gay Harden.

SQUANTO: A WARRIOR'S TALE
BUENA VISTA. October, 1994. (Xavier Koller) Adam Beach, Sheldon Peters Wolfchild, Eric Schweig.

SQUEEZE
MIRAMAX. April, 1996. (Robert Patton-Spruill) Tyrone Burton, Eddie Cutanda, Phuong Duong, Geoffrey Rhue.

STACCATO PURR OF THE EXHAUST
SKUNKBOY INK. January, 1996. (L.M. Meza) Ron Garcia, Michelle Beauchamp, Dennis Brooks, Kristina Haddad.

STADIUM COUP
ALTA FILMS. Aug., 1999. Spanish-Italian-Colombain. (Sergio Cabrera) Emma Suarez, Nicolas Montero, Cesar Mora, Raul Sender, Andrea Giordana.

STAG
CINEPIX FILM PROPERTIES/RAMPAGE ENTERTAINMENT. April, 1997. Canadian. (Gavin Wilding) Andrew McCarthy, John Stockwell.

STAGES
PAUL THOMPSON FILMS. November, 1990. (Randy Thompson) Ron Reid, Dan Lishner.

STANDING ON FISHES
STANDING ON FISHES. Mar., 1999. (Meredith Scott Lynn, Bradford Tatum) Bradford Tatum, Meredith Scott Lynn, Jason Priestley, Lauren Fox.

STAND-INS
OVERSEAS FILMGROUP. Oct., 1997. (Harvey Keith) Daphne Zuniga, Costas Mandylor, Missy Crider, Charlotte Chatton, Sammi Davis

STAND TALL
WORLD TOUR PRODS. Jan., 1997. (Mark Nalley) Darryl Bassani, Documentary.

STANLEY & IRIS
MGM/UA. February, 1990. (Martin Ritt) Jane Fonda, Robert De Niro, Swoosie Kurtz.

STARGATE
MGM. October, 1994. (Roland Emmerich) Kurt Russell, James Spader, Jaye Davidson, Viveca Lindfors.

STAR KID
TRIMARK. Jan., 1998. (Manny Coto) Joseph Mazzello, Joey Simmrin, Alex Daniels, Arthur Burghardt, Brian Simpson, Corinne Bohrer.

STAR MAKER
MIRAMAX. March, 1996. Italian. (Guiseppe Tornatore) Serio Castellitto, Tiziana Lodato.

STAR MAPS
FOX SEARCHLIGHT. Jan., 1997. (Miguel Arteta) Doughlas Spain, Efrain Figueroa, Kandeyce Jensen, Martha Velez, Lysa Flores.

STARLIGHT
ASTRAL. Nov., 1996. Canadian. (Jonathon Kay) Rae Dawn Chong, Billy Wirth, Willie Nelson, Jim Byrnes, Alex Diakun.

STARRY NIGHT
YELLOW HAT. Aug., 1999. U.S.-British. (Paul Davids) Abbott Alexander, Lisa Waltz, Lou Wagner, Sally Kirkland.

STAR SISTERS
FILMLANCE INTL. Feb., 1999. Swedish. (Tobias Falk) Teresa Niva, Vania Panes Lundmark, Fanny Kivimaki, Tintin Anderzon.

STAR TIME
NORTHERN ARTS. April, 1993. (Alexander Cassini) John P. Ryan, Michael St. Gerard, Maureen Teefy.

STAR TREK: FIRST CONTACT
PARAMOUNT. November, 1996. (Jonathan Frakes), Patrick Stewart, Jonathan Frakes, Brent Spiner, LeVar Burton, Alfre Woodward.

STAR TREK GENERATIONS
PARAMOUNT. November, 1994. (David Carson) Patrick Stewart, Malcolm McDowell, William Shatner.

STAR TREK: INSURRECTION
PARAMOUNT. Dec., 1998. (Jonathan Frakes) Patrick Stewart, Jonathan Frakes, Brent Spiner, LeVar Burton, Gates McFadden.

STAR TREK VI: THE UNDISCOVERED COUNTRY
PARAMOUNT. December, 1991. (Nicholas Meyer) William Shatner, Leonard Nimoy, Christopher Plummer.

THE STARS FELL ON HENRIETTA
WARNER BROS. September, 1995. (James Keach) Robert Duvall, Aidan Quinn, Frances Fisher.

STARSHIP TROOPERS
SONY. Oct., 1997. (Paul Verhoeven).Cast: Casper Van Dien, Dina Meyer, Denise Richards, Jake Busey, Neil Patrick Harris.

STARTING PLACE
INTERAMA. April, 1995. French-Vietnamese. (Robert Kramer) Documentary.

STARVING ARTISTS
PANAORAMA ENTERTAINMENT. Jan., 1999. (Allan Piper) Allan Piper, Bess Wohl, Joe Smith, Sandi Carroll.

STAR WARS: EPISODE I - THE PHANTOM MENACE
20TH CENTURY FOX. May, 1999. (George Lucas) Qui-Gon Jinn, Ewan McGregor, Natalie Portman, Jake Lloyd, Pernilla August.

STATE OF GRACE
ORION. September, 1990. (Phil Joanou) Sean Penn, Ed Harris, Gary Oldman, Robin Wright.

THE STATION
ARIES. January, 1992. Italian. (Sergio Rubini) Sergio Rubini, Margherita Buy, Ennio Fantastichini.

STAY TUNED
WARNER BROS. August, 1992. (Peter Hyams) John Ritter, Pam Dawber, Jeffrey Jones.

STEAL AMERICA
TARA RELEASING. April, 1992. (Lucy Phillips) Clara Bellino, Charlie Homo, Diviana Ingravallo.

STEAL BIG, STEAL LITTLE
SAVOY. September, 1995. (Andrew Davis) Andy Garcia, Rachel Ticotin, Alan Arkin.

STEALING BEAUTY
FOX SEARCHLIGHT. June, 1996. (Bernardo Bertolucci) Liv Tyler, Sinead Cusack, Donal McCann, Jeremy Irons.

STEEL
WARNER BROS. August, 1997. (Kenneth Johnson), Shaquille O'Neal, Annabeth Gish, Judd Nelson, Richard Roundtree.

STEEL & LACE
FRIES/PARAGON ARTS. November, 1990. (Ernest Farino) Clare Wren, Bruce Davison, David Naughton.

STEFANO QUANTESTORIE
ITALTOONS. November, 1994. Italian. (Maurizio Nichetti) Maurizio Nichetti, James Spencer Thierree.

STELLA
BUENA VISTA. February, 1990. (John Erman) Bette Midler, Trini Alvarado, John Goodman, Stephen Collins.

STELLA DOES TRICKS
BRITISH FILM INSTITUTE/CHANNEL 4 TV. Nov., 1996. British. (Coky Giedroyc) Kelly MacDonald, James Bolam, Hans Mathieson.

STEPHEN KING'S GRAVEYARD SHIFT
PARAMOUNT. October, 1990. (Ralph S. Singleton) David Andrews, Stephen Macht, Brad Dourif.

STEPHEN KING'S SLEEPWALKERS
COLUMBIA. April, 1992. (Mick Garris) Brian Krause, Alice Krige, Mädchen Amick.

STEPHEN KING'S THINNER
PARAMOUNT. October, 1996. (Tom Holland), Robert John Burke, Joe Mantegna, Michael Constantine, Lucinda Jenney, Kari Wuhrer.

STEPMOM
SONY. Nov., 1998. (Chris Columbus) Julia Roberts, Susan Sarandon, Ed Harris, Jena Malone, Liam Aiken.

STEPPING OUT
PARAMOUNT. October, 1991. (Lewis Gilbert) Liza Minnelli, Shelley Winters, Ellen Greene, Bill Irwin.

THE STEPS OF THE PALAIS
LA COMEDIE NOUVELLE. May, 1997. French. (Bernard Dartigues) Philippe Caubere.

STICKS AND STONES
GOLDBAR INTL. Sept., 1996. (Neil Tolkin) Justin Isfeld, Max Goldblatt, Chauncey Leopardi, Jordan Brower, Gary Busey.

STIGMATA
MGM. Sept., 1999. (Rupert Wainwright) Patricia Arquette Gabriel Byrne, Jonathan Pryce, Nia Long, Thomas Kopache.

STILL CRAZY
COLUMBIA TRISTAR FILMS/SONY. Oct., 1998. British. (Brian Gibson) Stephen Rea, Billy Connolly, Jimmy Nail, Timothy Spall, Bill Nighy.

STIR OF ECHOES
ARTISAN. July, 1999. (David Koepp) Kevin Bacon, Kathryn Erbe, Illeana Douglas, Kevin Dunn, Conor O'Farrell, Jennifer Morrison.

STONE COLD
COLUMBIA. May, 1991. (Craig R. Baxley) Brian Bosworth, Lance Henriksen, William Forsythe.

THE STONECUTTER
FOOTPRINT FILMS. March, 1998. (Stephen Erickson) Michael Cavalieri, Trisha Melynkov, Harold Cannon, Karin Argoud-Morrisey.

STONEWALL
STRAND RELEASING. July, 1996. (Nigel Finch) Guillermo Diaz, Frederick Weller, Duane Boutte.

STOP! OR MY MOM WILL SHOOT
UNIVERSAL. February, 1992. (Roger Spottiswoode) Sylvester Stallone, Estelle Getty, JoBeth Williams.

STOREFRONT HITCHCOCK
ORION PICTURES. April, 1998. (Jonathan Demme) DOCUMENTARY.

THE STORY OF A BAD BOY
SWEET FILMS. June, 1999. (Tom Donaghy) Jeremy Hollingworth, Christian Camargo, Stephen Lang, Julie Kavner, Lauren Ward.

THE STORY OF BOYS AND GIRLS
ARIES. August, 1991. Italian. (Pupi Avati) Felice Andreasi, Angiola Baggi, Davide Bechini.

THE STORY OF COMPUTER GRAPHICS
ACM/SIGGRAPH. Aug., 1999. (Frank Foster). Documentary.

THE STORY OF QIU JU
SONY PICTURES CLASSICS. April, 1993. Chinese-Mandarin. (Zhang Yimou) Gong Li, Lei Lao Sheng, Liu Pei Qi.

STORYVILLE
20TH CENTURY FOX. August, 1992. (Mark Frost) James Spader, Jason Robards, Joanne Whalley Kilmer.

STOWAWAYS
MOTION INTL. Aug., 1997. Canadian-Swiss. (Denis Chouinard) Ovidiu Balan, Moussa Maaskri, Simona Maicanescu.

STRAIGHT OUT OF BROOKLYN
SAMUEL GOLDWYN. May, 1991. (Matty Rich) George T. Odom, Lawrence Gilliard Jr.

THE STRAIGHT STORY
BUENA VISTA. May, 1999. French-U.S., (David Lynch) Richard Farnsworth, Sissy Spacek, Jane Galloway Heitz, Everett McGill, Jennifer Edwards-Hughes.

STRAIGHT TALK
BUENA VISTA. April, 1992. (Barnet Kellman) Dolly Parton, James Woods, Griffin Dunne.

STRANGE DAYS
20TH CENTURY FOX. October, 1995. (Kathryn Bigelow) Ralph Fiennes, Angela Bassett, Juliette Lewis, Tom Sizemore.

STRANGE FITS OF PASSION
BEYOND FILMS. May, 1999. Australian. (Elise McCredie) Michela Noonan, Mitchell Butel, Samuel Johnson, Steve Adams, Anni Finsterer.

STRANGE PLANET
NEW VISION. May, 1999. Australian. (Emma-Kate Croghan). Claudia Karvan, Naomi Watts, Alice Garner, Tom Long, Aaron Jeffrey.

THE STRANGER
NATL. FILM DEVELOPMENT. May, 1992. Indian. (Satyajit Ray) Deepankar De, Mamata Shankar, Utpal Dutt.

A STRANGER AMONG US
BUENA VISTA. July, 1992. (Sidney Lumet) Melanie Griffith, Eric Thal, John Pankow.

A STRANGER IN THE KINGDOM
WHISKEYJACK PICTURES/KINGDOM COME PICTURES. Aug., 1998. (Jay Craven) David Lansbury, Ernie Hudson, Martin Sheen.

STRANGERS IN BEIJING (HUN ZAI BEIJING)
SOUTHERN FILM CO. April, 1996. Chinese. (He Qun) Zhang Guoli, Ju Xuem, Xi Meijuan.

STRANGERS IN GOOD COMPANY
FIRST RUN/CASTLE HILL. May, 1991. Canadian. (Cynthia Scott) Alice Diabo, Constance Garneau.

STRANGER THAN FICTION
MOONSTONE. May, 1999. (Eric Bross) Mackenzie Astin, Todd Field, Dina Meyer, Natasha Gregson Wagner.

STRANGE TIMES
AZERKINOVIDEO CO. Feb., 1997. Azerbaijani. (Hussein Mekhtiev) Ayan Mirkasimova, Alladin Abbasov.

STRAPLESS
MIRAMAX. May, 1990. British. (David Hare) Blair Brown, Bruno Ganz, Bridget Fonda.

STRAWBERRY AND CHOCOLATE
MIRAMAX. January, 1995. Cuban. (Tomas Guiteerz Alea) Juan Carlos Tabio, Jorge Perugorria, Vladimir Cruz.

STRAWBERRY FIELDS
INDEPENDENT TELEVISION SERVICE. March, 1997. (Rea Tajiri) Suzy Nakamura, James Sie, Heather Yoshimura, Marilyn Tokuda.

STRAYDOGS
SANDREW METRONOME. Jan., 1999. Swedish. (Daniel Alfredson) Michael Legge, Sarah Jane Potts, Kevin Knapman, Mark Bagnall, Axel Widegren.

STRAYS
VIN DIESEL. Jan., 1997. (Vin Diesel) Vin Diesel, Joey Dedio, T.K. Kirkland, Mike Epps, E. Valentino Morales, Suzanne Lanza.

THE STREET: A FILM WITH THE HOMELESS
CINEMA LIBRE. June, 1997. Canadian. (Daniel Cross) Documentary.

STREET ASYLUM
ORIGINAL CINEMA. April, 1990. (Greggory Brown) Wings Hauser, Alex Cord, G. Gordon Liddy.

STREET CORNER JUSTICE
SUNSET FILMS INTERNATIONAL. September, 1996. (Chuck Bail) Marc Singer, Steve Railsback, Kim Lankford.

STREET FIGHTER
UNIVERSAL. December, 1994. (Steven E. de Souza) Jean Claude Van Damme, Raul Julia, Ming-Na Wen.

STREET HUNTER
CDGP/21ST CENTURY FILMS. November, 1990. (John A. Gallagher) Steve James, Reb Brown, John Legiuzamo.

STREET KNIGHT
CANNON. March, 1993. (Albert Magnoli) Jeff Speakman, Christopher Neame, Lewis Van Bergen.

STREET OF NO RETURN
THUNDER FILMS. August, 1991. French-Portuguese. (Samuel Fuller) Keith Carradine, Valentina Vargas, Bill Duke.

STREET SOLDIERS
ACADEMY ENTERTAINMENT. March, 1991. (Lee Harry) Jun Chong, Jeff Rector.

STREETS
CONCORDE. January, 1990. (Katt Shea Ruben) Christina Applegate, David Mendenhall, Kay Lenz.

STRICTLY BALLROOM
MIRAMAX. February, 1993. Australian. (Baz Luhrmann) Paul Mercurio, Tara Morice, Bill Hunter.

STRICTLY BUSINESS
WARNER BROS. November, 1991. (Kevin Hooks) Tommy Davidson, Halle Berry, Joseph C. Phillips.

STRICTLY PROPAGANDA
FIRST RUN. October, 1993. German. (Wolfgang Kissel) Documentary.

STRIKE!
MIRAMAX. Aug., 1998. (Sarah Kernochan) Lynn Redgrave, Gaby Hoffman, Kirsten Dunst, Monica Keena, Heather Matarazzo.

STRIKE IT RICH
MILLIMETER. January, 1990. British. (James Scott) Robert Lindsay, Molly Ringwald, John Gielgud.

STRIKING BACK
OCTOBER FILMS/MUSIC. Oct., 1998. Taiwanese. (Fu Shan-Fong) Neil Peng, Ku Jung-Kao, Tsan Cheng-Chun, Huang Shih-Wei, Fan Jui-Chun.

STRIKING DISTANCE
COLUMBIA. September, 1993. (Rowdy Herrington) Bruce Willis, Sarah Jessica Parker, Dennis Farina.

STRIP JACK NAKED
FRAMELINE. June, 1991. British. (Ron Peck) Documentary.

STRIPPED AND TEASED: TALES FROM LAS VEGAS WOMEN
BAL-MAIDEN. Nov., 1998. (Amie Williams). Documentary.

STRIPTEASE
SONY PICTURES. June, 1996. (Andrew Bergman) Demi Moore, Armand Assante, Ving Rhames, Robert Patrick.

STRUGGLES IN STEEL
ITVS. January, 1996. (Tony Buba, Raymond Henderson) Documentary. Color/B&W.

STUART BLISS
PERILOUS PICTURES. Jan., 1998. (Neil Grieve) Michael Zelniker, Dea Lawrence, Hoke Howell, Derek McGrath, Ania Suli, Mark Fite.

STUART SAVES HIS FAMILY
PARAMOUNT. April, 1995. (Harold Ramis) Al Franken, Laura San Giacomo, Vincent D'Onofrio.

THE STUNT WOMAN
GOLDEN HARVEST. Feb., 1997. Hong Kong. (Ann Hui) Michelle Yeoh, Sammo Hung, Jimmy Wong, Ken Lo, Mang Hoi, Richard Ng.

THE STUPIDS
NEW LINE. August, 1996. (John Landis) Tom Arnold, Jessica Lundy, Bug Hall, Alex McKenna, Jenny McCarthy.

SUBURBAN COMMANDO
NEW LINE. October, 1991. (Burt Kennedy) Hulk Hogan, Christopher Lloyd, Shelley Duvall.

THE SUBURBANS
IGNITE ENTERTAINMENT. Jan., 1999. (Donal Lardner Ward) : Craig Bierko, Amy Brenneman, Antonio Fargas, Will Ferrell, Tony Guma.

SUBURBIA
SONY PICTURES CLASSICS. Oct., 1996. (Richard Linklater), Jayce Bartok, Amie Carey, Micky Katt, Ajay Naidu, Steve Zahn.

THE SUBSTANCE OF FIRE
MIRAMAX. October, 1996. (Daniel Sullivan) Ron Rifkin, Sarah Jessica Parker, Tony Goldwyn, Timothy Hutton.

THE SUBSTITUTE
ORION. April, 1996. (Robert Mandel) Tom Berenger, Ernie Hudson, Diane Venora, Marc Anthony, William Forsythe.

SUCH A LONG JOURNEY
RED SKY. Sept., 1998. Canadian-British. (Sturla Gunnarsson) Roshan Seth, Soni Razdan, Om Puri, Naseeruddin Shah, Ranjit Chowdhry.

SUCH IS LIFE
SVENSK FILMINDUSTRI. Oct., 1996. Swedish. (Colin Nutley) Helena Bergstrom, Lena Nyman, Sverre Anker Ousdal.

SUCKERFISH
GLASS EYE. Mar., 1999., (Brien Burroughs) Dan Donovan, Tim Orr, Gerri Lawlor, Kurt Bodden.

SUDDEN DEATH
UNIVERSAL. December, 1995. (Peter Hyams) Jean Claude Van Damme, Powers Boothe, Raymond J. Barry.

SUDDEN MANHATTAN
HOMEGROWN PICTURES. April, 1996. (Adrienne Shelly) Shelly, Tim Guinee, Roger Rees, Louis Lasser.

SUGAR HILL
20TH CENTURY FOX. February, 1994. (Leon Ichaso) Wesley Snipes, Michael Wright, Theresa Randle.

SUGAR TOWN
OCTOBER FILMS. Jan., 1999. (Allison Anders, Kurt Voss) Jade Gordon, Michael Des Barres, John Taylor, Martin Kemp.

SUICIDE KINGS
LIVE ENTERTAINMENT. Sept., 1997. (Peter O'Fallon) Christopher Walken, Denis Leary, Henry Thomas, Sean Patrick Flanery.

SUICIDE, THE COMEDY
ALIBI ENTERTAINMENT. Aug., 1999. (Glen Freyer) Jamie Harris, Alison Eastwood, Brian Klugman, Josh Fardon, Walter Olkewicz.

SUITS
TENAFLY FILM CO. Jan., 1999. (Eric Weber) Robert Klein, Tony Hendra, Larry Pine, Paul Lazar, Randy Pearlstein.

THE SUM OF US
SAMUEL GOLDWYN. March, 1995. Australian. (Kevin Dowling, Geoff Burton) Jack Thompson, Russell Crowe.

THE SUMMER HOUSE
SAMUEL GOLDWYN. December, 1993. British. (Waris Hussein) Jeanne Moreau, Joan Plowright, Julie Walters.

SUMMER OF SAM
BUENA VISTA. May, 1999. (Spike Lee) John Leguizamo, Adrien Brody, Mira Sorvino, Jennifer Esposito, Anthony LaPaglia.

SUMMER OF THE MONKEY
BWE. Sept., 1998. Canadian. (Michael Anderson): Michael Ontkean, Leslie Hope, Wilford Brimley.

A SUMMER'S TALE
LES FILMS DU LOSANGE. May, 1996. French. (Eric Rohmer) Melvil Poupaud, Amanda Langlet, Aurelia Nolin.

SUMMER VACATION: 1999
NEW YORKER. March, 1990. Japanese. (Shusuke Kaneko) Eri Miyajima, Temeke Otakara.

SUNBURN
SWEETLAND FILMS. July, 1999. (Nelson Hume) Cillian Murphy, Paloma Baeza, Barry Ward, Michael Liebmann.

SUNDAY
DOUBLE A FILMS. Jan., 1997. (Jonathan Nossiter) David Suchet, Lisa Harrow, Jared Harris, Larry Pine, Joe Grifasi, Arnold Barkus.

SUNDAY DRIVE
KAIJU THEATER CO. Sept., 1998. Japanese. (Hisashi Saito) Shinya Tsukamoto, Miako Dadano, Takumi Tanji.

SUNDAY'S CHILDREN
CASTLE HILL. April, 1994. Swedish. (Daniel Bergman) Henrik Linnos, Thommy Berggen, Lena Enare.

SUNSET PARK
SONY PICTURES. April, 1996. (Steve Gomer) Rhea Perlman, Fredro Starr, Carol Kane, Terrence Dashon Howard.

SUNSETS
COUSIN'S FILM. Feb., 1997. (Michael Idemoto) Josh Brand, Nicholas Constant, Michael Idemoto. B&W.

SUNSHINE
ALLIANCE ATLANTIS. Sept., 1999. Hungarian-German-Canadian-Austraian. (Istvan Szabo) Ralph Fiennes, Rosemary Harris, Rachel Weisz, Jennifer Ehle, Molly Parker, Deborah Kara Unger.

THE SUN SISTERS
GBVI. April, 1997. French. (Jeannot Szwarc) Marie-Anne Chazal, Thierry Lhermitte, Clementine Celarie.

THE SUPER
20TH CENTURY FOX. October, 1991. (Rod Daniel) Joe Pesci, Vincent Gardenia, Madolyn Smith Osborne.

SUPER 8 1/2
STRAND. March, 1995. Canadian. (Bruce La Bruce) Bruce La Bruce, Liza LaMonica, Chris Teen.

SUPERLOVE
PLAYTIME. Apr., 1999. French. (Jean-Claude Janer) Gregoire Colin, Isabelle Carre, Carmen Maura, Luis Rego, Marthe Villalonga.

SUPER MARIO BROS.
BUENA VISTA. May, 1993. (Rocky Morton, Annabel Jankel) Bob Hoskins, John Leguizamo, Dennis Hopper.

THE SUPER-WIFE
ATLAS INTL. June, 1996. German. (Soenke Wortmann) Veronica Ferres, Joachim Krol, Thomas Heinze.

SUPERCOP
MIRAMAX/DIMENSION. July, 1996. Chinese. (Stanley Tong) Jackie Chan, Michelle Khan, Maggie Cheung.

SUPERMARKET WOMAN
JUZO ITAMI FILMS. June, 1997. Japanese. (Juzo Itami) Nobuko Miyamoto, Masahiko Tsugawa.

SUPERSTAR: THE LIFE AND TIMES OF ANDY WARHOL
ARIES FILMS. February, 1991. (Chuck Workman) Documentary.

SURE FIRE
STRAND. October, 1993. (Jon Jost) Tom Blair, Robert Ernst, Kristi Hager.

SURF NINJAS
NEW LINE. August, 1993. (Neal Israel) Ernie Reyes Jr., Rob Schneider, Leslie Nielsen.

SURVEILLANCE
XIAOXIANG FILM. Feb., 1997. Chinese. (Huan Jianxin) Feng Gong, Jiang Shan, Teng Rujun, Zhang Xiaotong, Niu Zhenhua.

SURVIVING PICASSO
WARNER BROS. September, 1996. (James Ivory) Anthony Hopkins, Natascha McElhone, Julianne Moore, Joss Ackland.

SURVIVING THE GAME
NEW LINE. April, 1994. (Ernest Dickerson) Ice T, Rutger Hauer, Gary Busey, F. Murray Abraham.

SUTURE
SAMUEL GOLDWYN. March, 1994. (Scott McGehee, David Siegel) Dennis Haysbert, Mel Harris, Sab Shimono. B&W.

SUZANNE FARRELL: ELUSIVE MUSE
SEAHORSE FILMS. Oct., 1996. (Deborah Dickson) Suzanne Farrell, Jacques d'Amboise, Maria Calegari, Arthur Mitchell, Maurice Bejart.

SUZIE WASHINGTON
FILMLADEN. Sept., 1998. Austrian. (Florian Flicker) Birgit Doll, August Zirner, Karl Ferdinand Kratzl, Wolfram Berger, Nina Proll.

SWAN LAKE–THE ZONE
ZEITGEIST. September, 1991. Soviet-Swedish-Canadian-U.S. (Yuri Illienko) Viktor Solovyov.

THE SWAN PRINCESS
NEW LINE. November, 1994. (Richard Rich) Animated.

THE SWAN PRICESS: ESCAPE FROM CASTLE MOUNTAIN
LEGACY. July, 1997. (Richard Rich) Michelle Nicastro, Douglas Sills, Jake Williamson, Christy Landers, Donald Sage MacKay.

SWEET AGONY
Feb., 1999. Iranian. (Ali Reza Davudnezhad) Reza Davudnezhad, Mona Davudnezhad, Mohammad Reza Davudnezhad, Ehteram Habibian, Shojo-o-Din Habibian.

A SWEET SCENT OF DEATH
MIRADOR/IVANIA/LOLA/FONDO PARA LA PRODUCCION CINEMATOGRAFICA DE CALIDAD, ALEPH MEDIA, IMCINE, INCAA, VIA DIGITAL. Mar., 1999. Mexican-Spanish-Argentine. (Gabriel Retes) Karra Elejalde, Ana Alvarez, Diego Luna, Hector Alterio.

THE SWEET HEREAFTER
FINE LINE FILMS. May, 1997. Canadian. (Atom Egoyan) Ian Holm, Sarah Polley, Bruce Greenwood, Tom McCamus.

SWEETIE
AVENUE. January, 1990. Australian. (Jane Campion) Genevieve Lemon, Karen Colston.

SWEET JANE
NEO MOTION PICTURE. Oct., 1997. (Joe Gayton) Samantha Mathis, Joseph Gordon-Levitt, Bud Cort, Mary Woronov, William McNamara.

SWEET NOTHING
WARNER BROS. September, 1996. (Gary Winick) Michael Imperioli, Mira Sorvino, Paul Calderon.

SWEET POWER
RIOFILME. Jan., 1997. Brazilian. (Lucia Murat) Marisa Orth, Antonio Fagundes, Tuca Andrada, Sergio Mamberti, Otavio Augusto.

SWEET TALKER
7 ARTS/NEW LINE. May, 1991. Australian. (Michael Jenkins) Bryan Brown, Karen Allen, Bill Kerr.

SWEET THING
JAM PICTURES. June, 1999. (Mark David). Jeremy Fox, Amalia Stifter, Ev Lunning, Jr., Steven Bruton, Evan Greenwalt.

SWEET UNDERGROUND
FOURTH DENSITY PRODS.. Apr., 1999. (Dorsay Alavi) Matthew Flint, Kevin Walls, Cindy Adkins, Alex Demir, Tracy Grant.

SWEPT FROM THE SEA
SONY PICTURES. Sept., 1997. British. (Beeban Kidron) Vincent Perez, Rachel Weisz, Ian McKellen, Joss Ackland, Kathy Bates.

SWIMMING WITH SHARKS
TRIMARK. April, 1995. (George Huang) Kevin Spacey, Frank Whaley, Michelle Forbes.

SWING
TAPESTRY/KUSHNER-LOCKE. Apr., 1999. British. (Nick Mead) Hugo Speer, Lisa Stansfield, Paul Usher, Tom Bell, Rita Tushingham.

SWING KIDS
BUENA VISTA. March, 1993. (Thomas Carter) Robert Sean Leonard, Christian Bale, Frank Whaley.

SWINGERS
MIRAMAX. September, 1996. (Doug Liman) John Favreau, Vince Vaughn.

SWITCH
WARNER BROS. May, 1991. (Blake Edwards) Ellen Barkin, Jimmy Smits, JoBeth Williams.

SWITCHBACK
PARAMOUNT. Oct., 1997. (Jeb Stuart) Dennis Quaid, Danny Glover, Jared Leto, R. Lee Ermey, Ted Levine, William Fichtner.

SWOON
FINE LINE. September, 1992. (Tom Kalin) Daniel Schlachet, Craig Chester, Ron Vawter. B&W.

SYDNEY
SAMUEL GOLDWYN. January, 1996. (Paul Thomas Anderson) Philip Baker Hall, Gwyneth Paltrow.

SYNTHETIC PLEASURES
CAIPIRINHA. September, 1995. (Lara Lee) Documentary.

T

TAAFE FANGA
TAARE FILMS. April, 1997. Mali-German. (Adama Drabo) Fanta Berete, Ramata Drabo, Ibrahim S. Koita, Helene Diarra.

TAEKWONDO
MS FILMS/KEYWECKSHIDE. Sept, 1998. Polish-South Korean. (Moon Seung-wook) Ahn Sung-ki, Pawel Burczyk, Ewa Gawryluk.

TAIGA
NEW YORKER. March, 1993. Mongolian. (Ulrike Ottinger). Documentary.

TAKE A NUMBER
40 CREDITORS AND A DEFERRAL. March, 1997. (Fritzi Horstman) Frederikla Kesten, Josh Carmichael, Jon Kean, Tim Bohn.

TAKING CARE OF BUSINESS
BUENA VISTA. August, 1990. (Arthur Hiller) James Belushi, Charles Grodin, Anne DeSalvo.

TAKING OF BEVERLY HILLS, THE
COLUMBIA. October, 1991. (Sidney J. Furie) Ken Wahl, Matt Frewer, Harley Jane Kozak.

A TALE OF SPRINGTIME
ORION CLASSICS. July, 1992. French. (Eric Rohmer) Anne Teyssedre, Hugues Quester, Florence Darel.

A TALE OF THE WIND
CAPI FILMS. January, 1991. Dutch-French. (Joris Ivens, Marceline Loridan) Joris Ivens, Han Zenxiang.

A TALE OF WINTER
MK2. April, 1994. French. (Eric Rohmer) Charlotte Very, F. Van Dren Driessche, Michel Voletti.

TALENT FOR THE GAME
PARAMOUNT. April, 1991. (Robert M. Young) Edward James Olmos, Lorraine Bracco, Jeff Corbett.

TALES FOM THE CRYPT PRESENTS BORDELLO OF BLOOD
UNIVERSAL. August, 1996. (Gilbert Adler) Dennis Miller, Erika Eleniaki, Angie Everhart, Chris Sarandon.

TALES FROM THE CRYPT PRESENTS DEMON KNIGHT
UNIVERSAL. January, 1995. (Ernest Dickerson) Billy Zane, William Sadler, Jada Pinkett, Brenda Bakke.

TALES FROM THE DARKSIDE: THE MOVIE
PARAMOUNT. May, 1990. (John Harrison) Christian Slater, Rae Dawn Chong, Deborah Harry.

TALES FROM THE HOOD
SAVOY. May, 1995. (Rusty Cundieff) Clarence Williams III, Joe Torry, Wings Hauser, Corbin Bernsen.

TALKIN' DIRTY AFTER DARK
NEW LINE. August, 1991. (Topper Carew) Martin Lawrence, Jedda James, Mark Curry.

TALKING TO STRANGERS
BALTIMORE. December, 1991. (Rob Tregenza) Ken Gruz, Marvin Hunter, Dennis Hunter.

TALK OF ANGELS
MIRAMAX FILMS. OKCT., 1998. (Nick Hamm) Polly Walker, Vincent Perez, Franco Nero, Marisa Paredes, Leire Berrocal.

THE TALL GUY
MIRAMAX. September, 1990. British. (Mel Smith) Jeff Goldblum, Emma Thompson, Rowan Atkinson.

TALL TALE
BUENA VISTA. March, 1995. (Jeremiah Chechik) Nick Stahl, Patrick Swayze, Scott Glenn, Oliver Platt.

TAMARO: STONES AND ANGELS. MARIO BOTTA AND ENZO CUCCHI
IMAGOFILM LUGANO. June, 1999. Swiss. (Villi Hermann). Documentary.

TANGIER- LEGEND OF A CITY
PETER GOEDEL FILMPRODUKTION. Feb., 1998. (Peter Goedel) Armin Muller-Stahl, Martin Kluge, Ulrich Klaus Gunther, Paul Bowles.

THE TANGO LESSON
SONY CLASSICS. Aug., 1997. British. (Sally Potter) Sally Potter, Pablo Veron, Gustavo Naveira, Fabian Salas, David Toole.

THE TANGO PLAYER
DEFA STUDIOS. November, 1993. German. (Roland Graf) Michael Gwisdek, Corinna Harfouch.

TANK GIRL
MGM/UA. March, 1995. (Rachel Talalay) Lori Petty, Malcolm McDowell, Ice-T, Naomi Watts.

TANO DA MORIRE
LUCKY RED DISTRIBUZIONE. Aug., 1997. Italian. (Roberta Torre) Ciccio Guarino, Enzo Paglino, Mimma D. De Rosalia, Maria Aliotta.

THE TARGET
UFD. Feb., 1997. French-Swiss-Spanish. (Pierre Courrege) Daniel Russo, Sagamore Stevenin, Anemone, Hippolyte Girardot.

TARZAN
BUENA VISTA. June, 1999. (Kevin Lima, Chris Buck). Animated.

TARZAN AND THE LOST CITY
WARNER BROS. April, 1998. (Carl Schenkel) Casper Van Dien, Jane March, Steven Waddington, Winston Ntshona, Rapulana Seiphemo.

THE TASTE OF CHERRIES
CIBY 2000. May, 1997. Iranian. (Abbas Kiarostami) Homayon Ershadi, Abdolrahman Bagheri.

TATIE DANIELLE
PRESTIGE. May, 1991. French. (Etienne Chatiliez) Tsilla Chelton, Catherine Jacob, Isabelle Nanty.

TATTOO BOY
GOTHAM/OREGON.October, 1995. (Larry Turner) C.J. Barkus, Amanda Tirey, Matthew James.

THE TAVERN
FOOTE SPEED PRODS.. July, 1999. (Walter Foote) Cameron Dye, Kevin Geer, Carlo Alban, Kym Austin, Margaret Cho.

TAXI BLUES
MK2. January, 1991. Soviet-French. (Pavel Lounguine) Piotr Mamonov, Piotr Zaitchenko.

TAXI DANCER
POWERS PRODS. Sept., 1998. (Sharon Powers) Darlene Reynolds, Bel Hernandez, Robert Nelson, Takayo Fischer, Leigh Kelly.

TAXMAN
COUNTERCLOCK PICTURES. May, 1998. (Avi Nesher) Joe Pantoliano, Wade Dominguez, Elizabeth Berkley, Michael Chiklis.

TEACHING MRS. TINGLE
DIMENSION FILMS. Aug., 1999. (Kevin Williamson) Helen Mirren, Katie Holmes, Jeffrey Tambor, Barry Watson, Marisa Coughlan.

TEARS OF STONE
TELEPICTURE MARKETING. May, 1996. Icelandic. (Hilmar Oddsson) Throstur Leo Gunnarsson, Ruth Olafsdottir.

TEA WITH MUSSOLINI
UIP/MGM. Mar., 1999. Italian-British. (Franco Zeffirelli) Cher, Judi Dench, Joan Plowright, Maggie Smith, Lily Tomlin.

TED
CHRONIC FILMWORKS. Jan., 1999. (Gary Ellenberg) Daniel Passer, Edie McClurg, Richard Fancy, Jeff Corey, Paul Provenza.

TED & VENUS
DOUBLE HELIX. December, 1991. (Bud Cort) Bud Cort, Jim Brolin, Kim Adams, Carol Kane.

TEENAGE MUTANT NINJA TURTLES
NEW LINE. March, 1990. (Steve Barron) Judith Hoag, Elias Koteas.

TEENAGE MUTANT NINJA TURTLES II: THE SECRET OF THE OOZE
NEW LINE. March, 1991. (Michael Pressman) Paige Turco, David Warner, Michelan Sisti.

TEENAGE MUTANT NINJA TURTLES III
NEW LINE. March, 1993. (Stuart Gillard) Elias Koteas, Paige Turco, Sab Shimono.

THE TEMP
PARAMOUNT. February, 1993. (Tom Holland) Timothy Hutton, Lara Flynn Boyle, Faye Dunaway.

TELLING LIES IN AMERICA
ALLIANCE. Aug., 1997. (Guy Ferland) Kevin Bacon, Brad Renfro, Maximilian Schell, Calista Flockhart, Paul Dooley.

TELLING YOU
MIRAMAX. Aug., 1998. (Robert DeFranco) Peter Facinelli, Dash Mihok, Jennifer Love Hewitt, Frank Medrano, Richard Libertini.

TEMPTATION
MGN FILMES/SIC/SKY LIGHT CINEMA. Aug., 1998. Portuguese-Brazilian. (Joaquim Leitao) Joaquim de Almeida, Cristina Camara, Diogo Infante, Ana Bustorff, Sofia Leite.

TEMPTATION OF A MONK
NORTHERN ARTS. December, 1994. Chinese. (Clara Law) Joan Chen, Wu Hsinkuo, Zhang Fengyi.

TEMPTING HEART
MEDIA ASIA. May, 1999. Hong Kong-Japanese. (Sylvia Chang) Takeshi Kaneshiro, Gigi Leung, Karen Mok, Elaine Jin.

TEN THINGS I HATE ABOUT YOU
BUENA VISTA. Mar., 1999. (Gil Junger) Heath Ledger, Julia Stiles, Joseph Gordon-Levitt, Larisa Oleynik, David Krumholtz.

TERMINAL BLISS
CANNON. March, 1992. (Jordan Alan) Timothy Owen, Luke Perry, Estee Chandler.

TERMINAL CITY RICOCHET
FESTIVAL FILMS. February, 1991. Canadian. (Zale Dalen) Peter Breck, Jello Biafra.

TERMINAL VELOCITY
BUENA VISTA. September, 1994. (Deran Serafian) Charlie Sheen, Nastassja Kinski, James Gandolfini.

TERMINATOR 2: JUDGMENT DAY
TRISTAR. July, 1991. (James Cameron) Arnold Schwarzenegger, Linda Hamilton, Robert Patrick.

TERMINI STATION
NORTHERN ARTS. May, 1991. Canadian. (Allan King) Colleen Dewhurst, Megan Follows, Gordon Clapp.

TERRA NOVA
DENDY FILMS. Aug., 1998. Australian. (Paul Middleditch) Jeanette Cronin. Paul Kelman, Trent Atkinson, Angela Punch McGregor.

THANK GOD HE MET LIZZIE
REP. May, 1997. Australian. (Cherie Nowlan) Richard Roxburgh, Cate Blanchett, Frances O'Connor, Linden Wilkinson, John Gaden.

THE TERRITORY
INT'L FILM CIRCUIT. August, 1990. French. (Raul Ruiz) Isabelle Weingarten, Rebecca Pauly.

TERROR FIRMER
TROMA TEAM. May, 1999. (Lloyd Kaufman) Will Keenan, Alyce LaTourelle, Trent Haaga, Debbie Rochon, Sheri Wenden.

THE TERRORIST
MODERNE GALLERIE/INDIAN IMAGE PRODS. Sept., 1998. Indian. (Santosh Sivan) Ayesha Dharkar, Vishnu Vardhan, Bhanu Prakash.

TERROR 2000
LEISURE TIME. November, 1994. German. (Christoph Schlingensief) Peter Kern, Margit Carstensen, Udo Kier.

THE TERROR WITHIN II
CONCORDE. January, 1991. (Andrew Stevens) Andrew Stevens, Stella Stevens, Chick Vennera.

TETSUO: THE IRON MAN
ORIGINAL CINEMA. April, 1992. Japanese, 1989. (Shinya Tsukamoto) Tomoroh Taguchi, Nobu Kanaoko, Shinya Tsukamoto.

TEXAS TENOR: THE ILLINOIS JACQUET STORY
RHAPSODY FILMS. November, 1992. (Arthur Elgort) Documentary.

TEXASVILLE
COLUMBIA. September, 1990. (Peter Bogdanovich) Jeff Bridges, Cybill Shepherd, Timothy Bottoms.

TGV
FLACH FILM, LES FILMS DE LA SAGA/LES FILMS DU CROCODILE . Oct., 1998. French-Senegalese. (Moussa Toure) Makena Diop, Al Hamdou Traore, Bernard Giraudeau, Philippine Leroy-Beaulieu.

THANK YOU AND GOODNIGHT!
ARIES FILMS. January, 1992. (Jan Oxenberg) Documentary.

THAT DARN CAT
BUENA VISTA. February, 1997. (Bob Spiers), Christina Ricci, Doug E. Doug, Dean Jones, George Dzundza, Peter Boyle, Michael McKean.

THAT NIGHT
WARNER BROS. August, 1993. (Craig Bolotin) C. Thomas Howell, Juliette Lewis, Eliza Duschku.

THAT OLD FEELING
UNIVERSAL. March, 1997. (Carl Reiner), Bette Midler, Dennis Farina, Paula Marshall, Gail O'Grady, David Rasche, Danny Nucci.

THAT'S IT
MIKADO. Nov., 1998. Italian. (Gabriele Muccino) Giorgio Pasotti, Barbora Bobulove, Claudkio Santamaria, Ginevra Colonna, Enrico Silvestrin.

THAT'S LIFE
MEDUSA. Dec., 1998. Italian. (Aldo Baglio, Giovanni Storti, Giacomo Poretti, Massimo Venier) Aldo Baglio, Giovanni Storti, Giacomo Poretti, Marina Massironi, Antonio Catania.

THAT THING YOU DO
20TH CENTURY FOX. October, 1996. (Tom Hanks) Liv Tyler, Johnathon Schaech, Steve Zahn, Ethan Embry, Tom Hanks.

THAT'S ADEQUATE
SOUTH GATE ENTERTAINMENT. January, 1990. (Harry Hurwitz) Tony Randall, James Coco, Bruce Willis.

THAT'S ENTERTAINMENT! III
MGM. May, 1994. (Bud Friedgen, Michael J. Sheridan) Gene Kelly, Cyd Charisse, Lena Horne, Howard Keel.

THEIR LAST LOVE AFFAIR
DAEWANO CINEMA NETWORK. Aug., 1997. South Korean. (Lee Myung-Sae) Kang Soo-Yeon, Kim Kap-Soo, Kim Hak-Soo.

THELMA AND LOUISE
MGM. May, 1991. (Ridley Scott) Susan Sarandon, Geena Davis, Harvey Keitel, Brad Pitt.

THEODORE REX
NEW LINE. June, 1996. (Jonathan Betuel) Whoopi Goldberg, Armin Mueller-Stahl, Juliet Landau.

THERE GOES MY BABY
ORION. September, 1994. (Floyd Mutrux) Dermot Mulroney, Rick Schroder, Kelli Williams, Noah Wyle.

THERE GOES THE NEIGHBORHOOD
PARAMOUNT. November, 1992. (Bill Phillips) Jeff Daniels, Catherine O'Hara, Dabney Coleman.

THERE'S NO FISH FOOD IN HEAVEN
STORM ENTERTAINMENT. Oct., 1998. (Eleanor E. Gaver) Fairuza Balk, Noah Taylor, Debi Taylor, Tea Leoni, James LeGros.

THERE'S NOTHING OUT THERE
VALKHN FILM. January, 1992. (Rolfe Kanefsky) Craig Peck, Wendy Bednarz, Mark Collver.

THERE'S SOMETHING ABOUT MARY
20TH CENTURY FOX. June, 1998. (Peter Farrelly, Bobby Farrelly) Cameron Diaz, Matt Dillon, Ben Stiller, Lee Evans, Chris Elliott.

THEREMIN: AN ELECTRONIC ODYSSEY
ORION CLASSICS. August, 1995. (Steven M. Martin) Documentary.

THEY COME AT NIGHT
REFUGE PRODS. Sept., 1998. (Lindy Laub) Elpidia Carrillo, Barbara Williams, Trevor O'Brien, Sabrina Weiner, Romeo Romero Fabian.

THIEVES
STUDIO CANAL PLUS. May, 1996. French. (Andre Techine) Daniel Auteuil, Catherine Deneuve, Laurence Cote.

THIEVES QUARTET
HEADLINER. June, 1994. (Joe Chappelle) Phillip Van Lear, Joe Guastaferro, Michele Cole.

A THIN LINE BETWEEN LOVE AND HATE
NEW LINE. April, 1996. (Martin Lawrence) Lawrence, Lynn Whitfield, Regina King, Bobby Brown, Della Reese.

THE THIN RED LINE
20TH CENTURY FOX. Dec., 1998. (Terence Malick) Sean Penn, Adrien Brody, Jim Caviezel, Ben Chaplin, George Clooney.

THE THIEF
NTV-PROFIT/PRODS. LE PONT. Aug., 1997. Russian. (Pavel Chukhrai) Vladimir Mashkov, Ekatarina Rednikova, Misha Philipchuk.

THE THING CALLED LOVE
PARAMOUNT. August, 1993. (Peter Bogdanovich) River Phoenix, Samantha Mathis, Dermot Mulroney.

THINGS I NEVER TOLD YOU
EDDIE SAETA/CARBO FILMS. February, 1996. U.S.-Spanish. (Isabel Coixet) Lili Taylor, Andrew McCarthy, Debi Mazar.

THINGS TO DO IN DENVER WHEN YOU'RE DEAD
MIRAMAX. December, 1995. (Gary Fleder) Andy Garcia, Christopher Walken, Treat Wiliams.

THINK BIG
CONCORDE. March, 1990. (Jon Turteltaub) Peter Paul, David Paul, Martin Mull.

THE THIRD MIRACLE
SONY. Sept., 1999. (Agnieszka Holland) Ed Harris, Anne Heche, Armin Mueller-Stahl, Charles Haid, Michael Rispoli.

THE THIRD PAGE
MAVI FILMCILIK CO. Aug., 1999. Turkish. (Zeki Demirkubuz) Ruhi Sari, Basak Kuklukaya, Cengiz Sezici, Serdar Orcin, Emrah Elciboga.

THE THIRTEENTH FLOOR
COLUMBIA PICTURES. May, 1999. (Josef Rusnak) Craig Bierko, Armin Mueller-Stahl, Gretchen Mol, Vincent D'Onofrio.

THE 13TH WARRIOR
BUENA VISTA. Aug., 1999. (John McTiernan) Antonio Banderas, Diane Venora, Dennis Storhoi, Vladimir Kulich, Omar Sharif.

35 MILES FROM NORMAL
TERN. Jan., 1997. (Mark Schwahn) Gabriel Olds, Alan Tudyk, Kellie Overbey, Jennifer Crystal, G. Riley Mills, Ethan Suplee.

30, STILL SINGLE: CONTEMPLATING SUICIDE
TEAM LAN. Mar., 1999. (Gregory J. Lanesky) Christopher May, Terry Gatens, Jill Zimmerman, Jill Kneeland, Rachel Reenstra.

THIRTY-TWO SHORT FILMS ABOUT GLENN GOULD
SAMUEL GOLDWYN. April, 1994. Canadian. (Francois Girard) Colm Feore, Katya Lada, Don McKellar.

35 UP
SAMUEL GOLDWYN. January, 1992. British. (Michael Apted) Documentary.

THIS BOY'S LIFE
WARNER BROS. April, 1993. (Michael Caton Jones) Robert De Niro, Ellen Barkin, Leonardo DiCaprio.

THIS IS CUBA
ASPECT RATIO/UNA CHICA ENT. February, 1996. (Chris Hume) Documentary

THIS IS MY FATHER
FILMLINE INTL./HUMMINGBIRD COMMUNICATION. Aug., 1998. (Paul Quinn) Aidan Quinn, James Caan, Stephen Rea, John Cusack.

THIS IS MY LIFE
20TH CENTURY FOX. February, 1992. (Nora Ephron) Julie Kavner, Samantha Mathis, Dan Aykroyd.

THIS SPACE BETWEEN US
TSBU/LLC. June, 1999. (Matthew Leutwyler) Jeremy Sisto, Vanessa Marcil, Poppy Montgomery, Clara Bellar, Erik Palladino.

THIS WORLD, THEN THE FIREWORKS
ORION CLASSICS. Jan., 1997. (Michael Oblowitz) Billy Zane, Gina Gershon, Sheryl Lee, Rue McClanahan, Seymour Cassel.

THE THOMAS CROWN AFFAIR
MGM. July, 1999. (John McTiernan) Pierce Brosnan, Rene Russo, Denis Leary, Ben Gazzara, Frankie Faison.

A THOUSAND ACRES
BUENA VISTA. September, 1997. (Jocelyn Moorhouse), Michelle Pfeiffer, Jessica Lange, Jason Robards, Jennifer Jason Leigh.

THE THOUSAND WONDERS OF THE UNIVERSE
UGC. May, 1997. Canadian-French. (Jean-Michel Roux) Tcheky Karyo, Julie Delpy, Feodor Atkine, Maria De Medeiros, Chick Ortega.

THRANE'S METHOD
SPERANZA FILMS/UNNI STRAUME. Feb. 1999. Norwegian. (Unni Straume) Bjorn Sundquist, Petronella Barker, Nils O. Oftebro, Kai Remlov, Hege Schoyen.

3 A LA MODE
MIRAMAX. August, 1994. French. (Remy Duchemin) Jean Yanne, Ken Higelin, Florence Darel.

THREE BRIDGES OVER THE RIVER
GEMINI/MADRAGOA. Feb., 1999. French-Portuguese. (Jean-Claude Biette) Jeanne Balibar, Mathieu Amalric, Thomas Badek, Andre Baptista, Sara Paz.

THREE BROTHERS
AMLF. January, 1996. French. (Didier Bourdon, Bernard Campan) Bourdon, Campan, Pascal Legitimus.

THREE BUSINESSMEN
EXTERMINATING ANGEL. Oct., 1998. (Alex Cox) Miguel Sandoval, Alex Cox, Robert Wisdom, Isabel Ampudia.

THREE FRIENDS
SAMSUNG ENTERTAINMENT. Oct., 1996. South Korean. (Yim Soon-Rye) Kim Hyun-Sung, Lee Jang-Won, Jung Hee-Suk.

THREE KINGS
WARNER BROS. Sept., 1999. (David O. Russell) George Clooney, Mark Wahlberg, Ice Cube, Spike Jonze, Nora Dunn.

THREE LIVES AND ONLY ONE DEATH
GEMINI FILMS. May, 1996. French. (Raoul Ruiz) Marcello Mastroianni, anna Galiena, Marisa Paredes.

THREE MEN AND A LITTLE LADY
BUENA VISTA. November, 1990. (Emile Ardolino) Tom Selleck, Steve Guttenberg, Ted Danson.

THE THREE MUSKETEERS
BUENA VISTA. November, 1993. (Stephen Herek) Kiefer Sutherland, Chris O'Donnell, Charlie Sheen.

3 NINJAS
BUENA VISTA. August, 1992. (Jon Turtletaub) Victor Wong, Michael Treanor, Max Elliott Slade.

3 NINJAS: HIGH NOON ON MEGA MOUNTAIN
SONY. April, 1998. (Sean McNamara) Hulk Hogan, Loni Anderson, Jim Varney, Mathew Botuchis, Michael J. O'Laskey II, J.P. Roeske.

3 NINJAS KICK BACK
TRISTAR. May, 1994. (Charles T. Kanganis) Victor Wong, Max Elliott Slade, Sean Fox.

3 NINJAS KNUCKLE UP
TRISTAR. March, 1995. (Simon S. Sheen) Victor Wong, Charles Napier, Michael Treanor, Max Elliot Slade.

THREE OF HEARTS
NEW LINE. April, 1993. (Yurek Bogayevicz) William Baldwin, Kelly Lynch, Sherilyn Fenn.

THREE SEASONS
OCTOBER FILMS. Jan., 1999. (Tony Bui) Don Duong, Nguyen Ngoc Hiep, Tran Manh Cuong, Harvey Keitel, Zoe Bui.

THREE STORIES
IGOR TOLSTUNOV. Feb., 1997. Russian-Ukrainian. (Kira Muratova) Sergej Makovecij, Renata Litvinova, Oleg Tabakov.

THREE WISHES
SAVOY. October, 1995. (Martha Coolidge) Patrick Swayze, Mary Elizabeth Mastranonio, Seth Mumy.

301, 302
MORNING CALM. September, 1995. South Korean. (Chul-Soo Park) Eun-Jin Pang, Sin-Hye Hwang.

THREESOME
TRISTAR. April, 1994. (Andrew Fleming) Stephen Baldwin, Lara Flynn Boyle, Josh Charles.

THRILL RIDE: THE SCIENCE OF FUN
SONY PICTURES CLASSICS. July, 1997. (Ben Stassen) Harry Shearer, Documentary.

THROUGH THE OLIVE TREES
MIRAMAX. February, 1995. Iranian. (Abbas Kiarostami) Tahereh Ladania, Mohamad Ali Kershavarz.

THROUGH THE WIRE
ORIGINAL CINEMA. April, 1990. (Nina Rosenblum) Documentary.

THROWING DOWN
NIGHT LIGHT. October, 1995. (Lawrence O'Neill) Jeffrey Donovan, Kevin Pinassi, Colleen Werthmann.

THUG LIFE IN D.C.
HBO. Feb., 1999. (Marc Levin). Documentary.

THUNDERHEART
TRISTAR. April, 1992. (Michael Apted) Val Kilmer, Sam Shepard, Graham Greene.

THURSDAY
GRAMERCY PICTURES. Sept., 1998. (Skip Woods) Thomas Jane, Aaron Eckhart, Paulina Porizkova, James Le Gros, Paula Marshall.

TIE-DIED: ROCK-AND-ROLL'S MOST DEADICATED FANS
I.S.A. September, 1995. (Andrew Behar) Documentary.

TIE ME UP! TIE ME DOWN!
MIRAMAX. April, 1990. Spanish. (Pedro Almodovar) Victoria Abril, Antonio Banderas.

THE TIE THAT BINDS
BUENA VISTA. September, 1995. (Wesley Strick) Daryl Hannah. Keith Carradine, Moira Kelly, Vincent Spano.

TIES TO RACHEL
COUNTERPRODUCTIONS. March, 1997. (Jon Resnik) Adrian Pasdar, George Dickerson, Joanna Adler, Arthur Bridgers.

TIGRERO: A FILM THAT WAS NEVER MADE
ARROW. December, 1994. Finnish-German-Brazilian. (Mika Kaurismaki) Samuel Fuller, Jim Jarmusch.

'TIL CHRISTMAS
GOOD MACHINE. May, 1996. (Jon Sherman) Dan Futterman, Susan Floyd, Nadia Dajani.

'TIL DEATH DO US PART
AGAT FILMS. November, 1995. French. (Robert Guediguian) Ariane Ascaride, Jacques Boudet.

'TIL THERE WAS YOU
PARAMOUNT. April, 1997. (Scott Winant), Jeanne Tripplehorn, Dylan McDermott, Sarah Jessica Parker, Jennifer Aniston, Ken Olin.

TILAI
NEW YORKER. October, 1990. Burkina Faso. (Idrissa Ouedraogo) Rasmane Ouedraogo, Ina Cisse.

TIM BURTON'S THE NIGHTMARE BEFORE CHRISTMAS
BUENA VISTA. October, 1993. (Henry Selick) Stop-action animation.

TIME INDEFINITE
FIRST RUN FEATURES. May, 1993. (Ross McElwee) Documentary.

TIMELESS, BOTTOMLESS, BAD MOVIE
MIRACIN KOREA. Oct., 1998. South Korean. (Jang Sun-Woo) Kwok Hyok-Sin, Jang Nam-Kyoung, Ducky Kim.

THE TIME OF THE BRAVE
COLUMBIA TRISTAR. Dec., 1998. Spanish. (Antonio Mercero) Gabino Diego, Leonor Watling, Adriana Ozores, Luis Cuenca, Hector Colome.

TIME OF THE GYPSIES
COLUMBIA. February, 1990. Serbo-Croatian. (Emir Kusturica) Davor Dujmovic, Bora Todorovic.

THE TIME OF YELLOW GRASS (VREMYA JHOLTOI TRAVY)
TADJIKFILM STUDIO. April, 1996. Tajakistani. (Mairiam Yusupova) R. Makarov.

TIME REGAINED
GEMINI. May, 1999. French-Italian. (Raoul Ruiz) Catherine Deneuve, Emmanuelle Beart, Vincent Perez, John Malkovich, Pascal Greggory.

A TIME TO KILL
WARNER BROS. June, 1996. (Joel Schumacher) Sandra Bullock, Samuel L. Jackson, Matthew McConaughey.

A TIME TO LOVE
3 EMME CINEMATOGRAFICA/HUNGRY EYE LOWLANDS/NOE . Aug., 1999. Italian-British-French. (Giacomo Campiotti) Ciaran Hinds, Ignazio Oliva, Juliet Aubrey, Natacha Regnier, Natalia Piatti.

TIME WILL TELL
I.R.S. May, 1992. British. (Delcan Lowney) Documentary.

TIMEBOMB
MGM. September, 1991. (Avi Nesher) Michael Biehn, Patsy Kensit, Tracy Scoggins, Robert Culp.

TIMECOP
UNIVERSAL. September, 1994. (Peter Hyams) Jean Claude Van Damme, Mia Sara, Ron Silver.

TIMELESS
TGOM. July, 1996. (Chris Hart) Peter Byrne, Melissa Duge, Michael Griffiths.

TIMISOARA: DECEMBER 1989
SAHIAFILM. September, 1995. Romanian. (Bose O. Pastina) Documentary, B&W.

TIN CUP
WARNER BROS. July, 1996. (Ron Shelton) Kevin Costner, Rene Russo, Cheech Marin, Linda Hart, Don Johnson.

TITANIC
PARAMOUNT/20TH CENTURY FOX. Oct., 1997. (James Cameron) Leonardo DiCaprio, Kate Winslet, Billy Zane, Kathy Bates, Frances Fisher, Gloria Stuart, Bill Paxton, Bernard Hill.

TITO AND ME
KINO. August, 1993. Yugoslav-French. (Goran Markovic) Dimitrie Vojnov, Lozar Ristovski.

TO BE OR NOT TO BE
FARABI CINEMA. Feb., 1999. Iranian. (Kianoosh Ayyari) Asal Badi'ie, Farhad Sharifi, Hossein Ilbeygi, Maryam Bubani, Nur-Ali Lotfin.

TODAY OR NEVER
REMSTAR. Oct., 1998. Canadian. (Jean Pierre Lefebvre) Marcel Sabourin, Jean-Pierre Ronfard, Claude Blanchard, Julie Menard, Micheline Lanctot.

TO DIE FOR
COLUMBIA. September, 1995. (Gus Van Sant) Nicole Kidman, Matt Dillon, Joaquin Phoenix, Casey Affleck.

TOGETHER ALONE
FRAMELINE. September, 1992. (P.J. Castellaneta) Todd Stites, Terry Curry. B&W.

TO GILLIAN ON HER 37TH BIRTHDAY
SONY PICTURES ENTERTAINMENT. September, 1996. (Michael Pressman), Peter Gallagher, Claire Danes, Kathy Baker, Michelle Pfeiffer.

TO HAVE AND TO HOLD
SOUTHERN STAR GROUP. April, 1996. Australian. (John Hillcoat) Tcheky Karyo, Rachel Griffiths, Steve Jacobs.

THE TOILERS AND THE WAYFARERS
OUTSIDER. December, 1995. (Keith Froelich) Matt Klemp, Ralf Schirg, Andrew Woodhouse, Michael Glen.

TOKYO DECADENCE
NORTHERN ARTS. April, 1993. Japanese. (Ryu Murakami) Miho Nikaido, Tenmei Kano, Yayoi Kusama.

TOKYO LULLABY
SHOCHIKU SATELLITE CINEMA. Sept., 1997. Japanese. (Juni Ichikawa) Kyozo Nagatsuka, Kaori Momoi, Mitsuko Baisho.

TO LIVE
SAMUEL GOLDWYN. November, 1994. Chinese. (Zhang Yimou) Ge You, Gong Li, Niu Ben.

TO LOVE
NIKKATS CORP. Aug., 1997. Japanese. (Kei Kumai) Miki Sakai, Atsuro Watabe, Kyoko Kishida, Keiju Kobayashi, Joe Shishido.

TOM AND JERRY: THE MOVIE
MIRAMAX. July, 1993. (Phil Roman) Animated.

TOM AND HUCK
BUENA VISTA. December, 1995. (Peter Hewitt) Jonathan Taylor Thomas, Brad Renfro, Eric Schweig, Charles Rocket.

TOM & VIV
MIRAMAX. December, 1994. British. (Brian Gilbert) Willem Dafoe, Miranda Richardson, Rosemary Murphy.

TOMBSTONE
BUENA VISTA. December, 1993. (George P. Cosmatos) Kurt Russell, Val Kilmer, Dana Delany, Michael Biehn.

TOMMY BOY
PARAMOUNT. March, 1995. (Peter Segal) Chris Farley, David Spade, Brian Dennehy, Bo Derek, Rob Lowe.

TOMORROW NEVER DIES
MGM. Dec., 1997. (Roger Spottiswoode) Pierce Brosnan, Jonathan Pryce, Michelle Yeaoh.

TOMORROW NIGHT
CIRCUS KING. Jan., 1998. (Louis C.K.) Chuck Sklar, Martha Greenhouse, Heather Morgan, Rick Shapiro, J.B. Smoove.

TOM'S MIDNIGHT GARDEN
HYPERION. June, 1999. British. (Willard Carroll) Greta Saachi, James Wilby, Joan Plowright, Anthony Way, David Bradley.

TOO BEAUTIFUL FOR YOU
ORION CLASSICS. March, 1990. French. (Bertrand Blier) Gérard Depardieu, Josiane Balasko, Carole Bouquet.

TOO LATE
MKL MK2 DIFFUSION. May, 1996. French-Romanian. (Lucian Pintilie) Razvan Vasilescu, Cecilia Barbora, Victor Rebengiuc.

TOO MUCH SUN
NEW LINE. January, 1991. (Robert Downey) Andrea Martin, Eric Idle, Robert Downey, Jr.

TOO TIRED TO DIE
DREAM SEARCH ENTERTAINMENT. Jan., 1998. (Wonsuk Chin) Takeshi Kaneshiro, Mira Sorvino, Jeffrey Wright, Michael Imperioli.

TOP DOG
MGM/UA. April, 1995. (Aaron Norris) Chuck Norris, Clyde Kusatsu, Michele Lamar Richards.

TOPLESS WOMEN TALK ABOUT THEIR LIVES
JOHN SWIMMER. May, 1997. New Zealand. (Harry Sinclair) Danielle Cormack, Joel Tobeck, Ian Hughes, Willa O'Neill, Shimpal Lelisi.

TOPSY-TURVY
OCTOBER FILMS/PATHE. Sept., 1999. British. (Mike Leigh) Jim Broadbent, Allan Corduner, Lesley Manville, Eleanor David, Ron Cook.

TO RENDER A LIFE
AGEE FILM PROJ. November, 1992. (Ross Spears) Documentary.

TORN APART
CASTLE HILL. April, 1990. (Jack Fisher) Adrian Pasdar, Cecilia Peck, Barry Primus.

TORRENTS OF SPRING
MILLIMETER. February, 1990. Italian-French. (Jerzy Skolimowski) Timothy Hutton, Nastassja Kinski.

TO SLEEP WITH ANGER
SAMUEL GOLDWYN. October, 1990. (Charles Burnett) Danny Glover, Paul Butler, Mary Alice.

TOTAL ECLIPSE
FINE LINE. November, 1995. (Agnieska Holland) Leonardo DiCaprio, David Thewlis, Dominique Blanc.

TOTAL RECALL
TRISTAR. June, 1990. (Paul Verhoeven) Arnold Schwarzenegger, Rachel Ticotin, Sharon Stone.

TOTALLY CONFUSED
MURRAY SHUMAN. June, 1998. (Gary Rosen, Greg Pritikin) Greg Pritikin, Gary Rosen, Jackie Katzman, Heather Donaldson.

TOTALLY F**D UP**
STRAND. August, 1994. (Gregg Araki) James Duval, Roko Belic, Susan Behshid.

TO THE ENDS OF TIME
TOTEM PICTURES. Oct., 1996. (Markus Rothkrantz) Joss Ackland, Christine Taylor, Tom Schultz, Sarah Douglas, Michael Silverback.

TO THE HORIZON AND BEYOND
PROGRESS. Feb., 1999. German. (Peter Kahane) Wolfgang Stumph, Corinna Harfouch, Nina Petri, Gudrun Okras, Heinrich Schafmeister.

TO THOSE WHO LOVE
ALTA. Oct., 1998. Spanish-French. (Isabel Coixet) Julio Nunez, Patxi Freitez, Olalla Moreno, Monica Bellucci, Christopher Thompson.

TOTO LE HEROS
TRITON. March, 1992. Belgian-French-German. (Jaco Van Dormael) Michel Bouguet, Jo De Backer, Thomas Doget.

TOUCH
MGM/UA. February, 1997. (Paul Schrader), Bridget Fonda, Christopher Walken, Skeet Ulrich, Tom Arnold, Gina Gershon, Lolita Davidovich, Paul Mazursky, Janeane Garofalo.

TOUCH ME
DEVIN ENTERTAINMENT. May, 1997. (H. Gordon Boos) Amanda Peet, Michael Vartan, Peter Facinelli, Kari Wuhrer, Erica Gimpel.

TOUCH OF A STRANGER
RAVENSTAR PICTURES. September, 1990. (Brad Gilbert) Shelley Winters, Anthony Nocerino.

TOUKI–BOUKI
INT'L. FILM CIRCUIT. February, 1991. French-Senegalese. (Djibril Diop Mambety) Magaye Niang, Mareme Niang.

TOUS LES MATINS DU MONDE (ALL THE MORNINGS OF THE WORLD)
OCTOBER FILMS. November, 1992. French. (Alain Corneau) Jean Pierre Marielle, Gerard Depardieu, Anne Brochet.

TO WALK WITH LIONS
KINGSBOROUGH GREENLIGHT. June, 1999. Canadian-British-Kenyan. (Carl Schultz) Richard Harris, John Michie, Ian Bannen, Kerry Fox, High Quarshie.

TO WONG FOO, THANKS FOR EVERYTHING! JULIE NEWMAR
UNIVERSAL. September, 1995. (Beeban Kidron) Wesley Snipes, Patrick Swayze, John Leguizamo.

TOYS
20TH CENTURY FOX. December, 1992. (Barry Levinson) Robin Williams, Joan Cusack, Michael Gambon.

TOY SOLDIERS
TRISTAR. April, 1991. (Daniel Petrie, Jr.) Sean Astin, Wil Wheaton, Keith Coogan, Louis Gossett, Jr.

TOY STORY
BUENA VISTA. November, 1995. (William Reeves) (voices) Tom Hanks, Tim Allen, Don Rickles, Jim Varney.

TRACES OF RED
SAMUEL GOLDWYN. November, 1992. (Andy Wolk) James Belushi, Lorraine Bracco, Tony Goldwyn.

TRADING MOM
TRIMARK. May, 1994. (Tia Brelis) Sissy Spacek, Anna Chlumsky, Aaron Michael Metchik, Maureen Stapleton.

TRAILER CAMP
ARTISTIC LICENSE. January, 1996. (Jenni Olson) Compilation.

TRAIN OF SHADOWS: THE SPECTER OF LE THUIT
GRUP CINEMA ART/FILMS 59. May, 1997. Spanish. (Jose Luis Guerin) Juliette Gaultier, Ivon Orvain, Anne Celine Auche.

TRAINSPOTTING
MIRAMAX. January, 1996. British. (Danny Boyle) Ewan McGregor, Ewen Bremmer, Jonny Lee Miller.

TRAIN TO PAKISTAN
NATIONAL FILM DEVELOPMENT CORP. OF INDIA. Feb., 1999. Indian. (Pamela Rooks) MohanAgashe, Xirmal Pandey, Rajit Kapur, Smriti Mishra, Divya Dutta.

TRAMWAY TO MALVARROSA
SOGETEL/LOLA. June, 1997. Spanish. (Jose Luis Garcia Sanchez) Liberto Rabal, Jorge Merino, Ariadna Gil.

TRANCEFORMER: A PORTRAIT OF LARS VON TRIER
AB MEMFIS FILM. Sept., 1997. Swedish. (Stig Bjorkman) Documentary.

TRANS
YID PRADER/DOWN HOME PICTURES. Sept., 1998. (Julian Goldberger) Tyan Daugherty, Justin Lakes, Jon Daugherty, MIchael Gulnac, Stephanie David.

TRAP FOR A CAT
PRODUCCIONESJOTA Y JOROPODO. Sept., 1998. Venezuelan. (Manuel de Pedro) Amado Zambrano, Alejandro Faillace, Gregorio Milano. Yasmin Hernandez, Alberto Alcala.

TRAPPED IN PARADISE
20TH CENTURY FOX. December, 1994. (George Gallo) Nicolas Cage, Jon Lovitz, Dana Carvey.

TRAPS
FILMOPOLIS. December, 1995. Australian. (Pauline Chan) Sami Frey, Saskia Reeves, Jacqueline McKenzie.

TRAPS
CINEART. Sept., 1998. Czech. (Vera Chytilova): Miroslav Donutil, Zuzana Stivinova, Tomas Hanak.

THE TRAVELER FROM THE SOUTH
IRIB/CHANNEL TWO. Iranian. (Parviz Shahbazi) Reza Moghadam, Ghamar Nassiri Jozani.

TRAVELING COMPANION (COMPAGNA DI VIAGGIO)
ISTITUTO LUCE. April, 1996. Italian. (Peter Del Monte) Michel Piccoli, Asia Argento, Lino Capolicchio.

TRAVELING SAINTS
INSTITUTO MEXICANO DE CINEMATOGRAFIA. Jan., 1999. Mexican. (Alejandro Springall) Dolores Heredia, Demian Bichir, Alberto Estrella, Roberto Cobo, Ana Bertha Espin.

TREASURE ISLAND
KING PICTURES. Jan., 1999. (Scott King) Lance Baker, Nick Offerman, Jonah Blechman, Pat Healy, Suzy Nakamura.

THE TREATY OF CHANCE
PIERRA GRISE. July, 1999. French. (Patrick Mimouni) Eliane Pin Carringhton, Nini Crepon, Laurent Chemda, Bruno Anthony de Trigancei.

TREE OF BLOOD
MERCURE DISTRIBUTION. May, 1996. French-Guinea Bissau-Tunisian-Portuguese. (Flora Gomes) Ramiro Naka.

THE TREE OF LIFE
IRIB CHANNEL 2, MOHAMMAD-REZA, SARHANGI. Sept., 1998. Iranian. (Farhad Mehranfar) Anis Shakoori, Omid Amiri, Adeleh Shaoori, Jian Amir Rezvani.

TREES LOUNGE
ORION. October, 1996 (Steve Buscemi) Steve Buscemi, Elizabeth Bracco, Anthony LaPaglia, Debi Mazar.

TREMORS
UNIVERSAL. January, 1990. (Ron Underwood) Kevin Bacon, Fred Ward, Finn Carter.

THE TRENCH
ENTERTAINMENT FILM DISTRIBUTORS. May, 1999. British-French. (William Boyd) Paul Nichols, Daniel Craig, Julian Rhind-Tutt, Danny Dyer, James D'Arcy.

TRESPASS
UNIVERSAL. December, 1992. (Walter Hill) Bill Paxton, William Sadler, Ice T, Ice Cube.

T-REX: BACK TO THE CRETACEOUS
IMAX. Oct., 1998. (Brett Leonard) Peter Horton, Liz Stauber, Kari Coleman, Laurie Murdoch, Tuck Milligan.

TRIAL BY JURY
WARNER. September, 1994. (Heywood Gould) Joanna Whalley-Kilmer, Armand Assante, Gabriel Byrne.

THE TRIAL
ANGELIKA. November, 1993. British. (David Jones) Kyle MacLachlan, Alfred Molina, Anthony Hopkins.

TRIAL AND ERROR
NEW LINE. May, 1997. (Jonathan Lynn), Michael Richards, Jeff Daniels, Charlize Theron, Jessica Steen, Austin Pendleton, Rip Torn.

TRICK
FINE LINE/GOOD MACHINE. Jan., 1999. (Jim Fall) Christian Campbell, John Paul Pitoc, Tori Spelling, Steve Hayes.

A TRICK OF THE LIGHT
WIM WENDERS/HOCHSCHULE. Sept., 1996. German. (Wim Wenders) Udo Kier, Nadine Buttner, Christoph Merg, Otto Kuhnle.

THE TRIGGER EFFECT
GRAMERCY. June, 1966. (David Koepp) Kyle MacLachlan, Elisabeth Shue, Dermot Mulroney.

TRIPLE BOGEY ON A PAR 5 HOLE
POE PRODS. March, 1992. (Amos Poe) Eric Mitchell, Daisy Hall, Jesse McBride.

TRIPPIN'
ROGUE PICTURES. May, 1999. (David Raynr) Deon Richmond, Donald Adeosun Faison, Maia Campbell, Guy Torry, Aloma Wright.

TROJAN EDDIE
FILM FOUR INT'L. August, 1996. British. (Gillies MacKinnon) Richard Harris, Stephen Rea, Brendan Gleeson.

TROIKA
GUARDEZ-BIEN. Nov., 1998. (Jennifer Montgomery) Jenny Bass, Lev Shekhtman, Marina Shterenberg, Valery Manenti, Vitali Baganov.

TROLL IN CENTRAL PARK
WARNER BROS. October, 1994. (Don Bluth, Gary Goldman) Animated.

TROMEO & JULIET
TROMA, NY. May, 1996. (Lloyd Kaufman) Will Keenan, Jane Jensen, Debbie Rochon.

TROUBLE-SHOOTERS
BANDAI VISUAL. June, 1999. Japanese. (Masato Harada) Koji Matoba, Leo Morimoto, Hiroko Fukuda, Hajime Asoh.

TROUBLESOME CREEK: A MIDWESTERN
WEST CITY. January, 1996. (Jeanne Jordan) Documentary.

TRUE BELIEVERS: THE MUSICAL FAMILY OF ROUNDER RECORDS
DAKIN. April, 1995. (Robert Mugge) Documentary.

TRUE BLUE
MIRAMAX. September, 1996. British. (Ferdinand Fairfax) Johan Leysen, Dominic West, Dylan Baker.

TRUE COLORS
PARAMOUNT. March, 1991. (Herbert Ross) John Cusack, James Spader, Imogen Stubbs, Mandy Patinkin.

TRUE FRIENDS
2ND GENERATION FILMS. Jan., 1998. (James Quattrochi) James Quattrochi, Loreto Mauro, Rodrigo Botero, Kyle Gibson.

TRUE IDENTITY
BUENA VISTA. August, 1991. (Charles Lane) Lenny Henry, Frank Langella, Charles Lane.

TRUE LIES
20TH CENTURY FOX. July, 1994. (James Cameron) Arnold Schwarzenegger, Jamie Lee Curtis, Bill Paxton.

TRUE LOVE AND CHAOS
NEW VISION. March, 1997. Australian.(Stavros Andonis Efthymiou) Miranda Otto, Naveen Andrews, Hugo Weaving, Noah Taylor.

TRUE MOMENTS
SANDREW. Aug., 1998. Swediah-Finnish-Danish. (Lena Koppel) Lena Endre, Krister Henriksson, Arne Ukskula, Anita Bjork, Oyana Lugn-Rodriguez.

TRUE ROMANCE
WARNER BROS. September, 1993. (Tony Scott) Christian Slater, Patricia Arquette, Dennis Hopper.

TRULY, MADLY, DEEPLY
SAMUEL GOLDWYN. May, 1991. British. (Anthony Minghella) Juliette Stevenson, Alan Rickman, Michael Maloney.

THE TRUMAN SHOW
PARAMOUNT. April, 1998. (Peter Weir) Jim Carrey, Laura Linney, Noah Emmerich, Natascha McElhone, Holland Taylor, Ed Harris

TRUST
FINE LINE/NEW CINEMA. July, 1991. (Hal Hartley) Adrienne Shelly, Martin Donovan, Merritt Nelson.

TRUSTING BEATRICE
CASTLE HILL. January, 1993. (Cindy Lou Johnson) Mark Evan Jacobs, Irene Jacob, Charlotte Moore.

THE TRUTH ABOUTH CATS & DOGS
20TH CENTURY FOX. April, 1996. (Michael Lehmann) Uma Thurman, Janeane Garofalo, Ben Chaplin, Jamie Foxx.

TRUTH OR CONSEQUENCES, N.M.
SONY PICTURES ENTERTAINMENT. April, 1997. (Kiefer Sutherland), Vincent Gallo, Mykelti Williamson, Kiefer Sutherland, Kevin Pollak.

TRUTH OR DARE
MIRAMAX. May, 1991. (Alek Keshishian) Madonna.

TSAHAL
NEW YORKER. January, 1995. Israeli-French. (Claude Lanzmann) Documentary.

TUMBLEWEEDS
FINE LINE. Jan., 1999. (Gavin O'Connor) Janet McTeer, Kimberly J. Brown, Gavin O'Connor, Jay O'Sanders, Lois Smith.

THE TUNE
OCTOBER FILMS. September, 1992. (Bill Plympton) Animated.

TUNE IN TOMORROW
CINECOM. October, 1990. (Jon Amiel) Barbara Hershey, Keanu Reeves, Peter Falk.

TUNNU'S TINA
NATIONAL FILM DEVT CORP/DOORDARSHAN. Feb., 1997. Indian. (Paresh Kamdar) Sunil Barve, Rajeshwari, Renuka Shahane.

TUPAMAROS
SPECOGNA FILM PROD., TAG/TRAUM/BIOGRAPHY FILM. Feb., 1997. German-Swiss. (Heidi Specogna) Documentary.

TURBO: A POWER RANGERS MOVIE
20TH CENTURY FOX. March, 1997. (David Winning, Shuki Levy), Jason David Frank, Steve Cardenas, Johnny Yong Bosch.

TURBULENCE
MGM/UA. December, 1996. (Robert Butler), Ray Liotta, Lauren Holly, Brendan Gleeson, Hector Elizondo, Ben Cross, Rachel Ticotin.

THE TURKISH BATH - HAMAM
FILMAURO DIST. April. 1997. Italian-Turkish-Spanish. (Ferzan Ozpetek) Alessandro Gassman, Francesca d'Aloja, Carlo Cecchi.

TURTLE BEACH
WARNER BROS. May, 1992. Australian. (Stephen Wallace) Greta Scacchi, Joan Chen, Jack Thompson.

TWELFTH NIGHT
FINE LINE. September, 1996. British-U.S. (Trevor Nunn) Helena Bonham Carter, Richard E. Grant, Nigel Hawthorne.

12 MONKEYS
UNIVERSAL/ATLAS/CLASSICO. January, 1996. (Terry Gilliam) Bruce Willis, Madeleine Stowe, Brad Pitt.

12 STOREYS
BRINK CREATIVE/SPRINGROLL ENTERTAINMENT/ZHAO WEI FILMS. May, 1997. Singaporean. (Eric Khoo) Jack Neo, Koh Boon-pin.

TWENTY BUCKS
TRITON. October, 1993. (Keva Rosenfeld) Brendan Fraser, Linda Hunt, Christopher Lloyd, Elisabeth Shue.

THE 24 HOUR WOMAN
ARTISAN. Jan., 1999. (Nancy Savoca) Rosie Perez, Marianne Jean-Baptiste, Patti LuPone, Karen Duffy, Diego Serrano.

24 NIGHTS
CYNICAL BOY. Mar., 1999. (Kieran Turner) Kevin Isola, Aida Turturro, Stephen Mailer, David Burtka, Mary Louise Wilson.

TWENTYFOURSEVEN
OCTOBER FILMS. Sept., 1997. British. (Shane Meadows) Bob Hoskins, Danny Nussbaum, James Hooton, Darren O. Campbell.

29TH STREET
20TH CENTURY FOX. November, 1991. (George Gallo) Danny Aiello, Anthony LaPaglia, Lainie Kazan.

TWENTY–ONE
TRITON. October, 1991. British. (Don Boyd) Patsy Kensit, Jack Shepherd, Patrick Ryecart.

TWENTY PEACHES IN A BOX
SIDE SHOW FILMS. Jan., 1999. (Carlos Hamill) Cindy Peters, Talitha Peters, Giorgio della Terza, Michele Markarian.

TWILIGHT
PARAMOUNT. March, 1998. (Robert Benton) Paul Newman, Susan Sarandon, Gene Hackman, Reese Witherspoon, Stockard Channing, James Garner, Giancarlo Esposito.

THE TWILIGHT OF THE GOLDS
SHOWTIME NETWORKS. Dec., 1996. (Ross Marks) Jennifer Beals, Jon Tenney, Faye Dunaway, Brendan Fraser, Garry Marshall.

TWILIGHT HIGHWAY
SHOOTING GALLERY. November, 1995. (Laurie Taylor-Williams) Sandy Baron, D.V. De Vincentis.

THE TWILIGHT OF THE ICE NYMPHS
ALLIANCE. Aug., 1997. Canadian. (Guy Maddin) Pascale Bussieres, Nigel Whitmey, Shelley Duvall, Frank Gorshin, Alice Krige.

TWIN DRAGONS
DIMENSION. APR., 1999. Hong Kong. (Tsui Hark) Jackie Chan, Maggie Cheung, Nina Li Chi, Anthony Chan, Philip Chan.

TWIN FALLS IDAHO
SONY. Jan. 1999. (Michael Polish) Michael Polish, Mark Polish, Michele Hicks, Jon Gries, Patrick Bauchau.

TWIN PEAKS: FIRE WALK WITH ME
NEW LINE. August, 1992. (David Lynch) Sheryl Lee, Moira Kelly, Ray Wise.

TWIN TOWN
GRAMERCY. Feb., 1997. British. (Kevin Allen) Llyr Evans, Rhys Ifans, Dougray Scott, Dorien Thomas, William Thomas.

TWISTED
DONS QUIXOTE. July, 1996. (Seth Michael) David Norona, Keivyn McNeil Graves, Anthony Crivelo.

TWISTED JUSTICE
SEYMOUR BORDE. March, 1990. (David Heavener) David Heavener, Erik Estrada.

TWISTED OBSESSION
IVE. August, 1990. French-Italian. (Fernando Trueba) Jeff Goldblum, Miranda Richardson, Anemone.

TWISTER
WARNER BROS. May, 1996. (Jan De Bont) Helen Hunt, Bill Paxton, Cary Elwes, Jami Gertz, Lois Smith.

TWO BITS
MIRAMAX. August, 1996. (James Foley) Jerry Barone, Mary Elizabeth Mastrantonio, Al Pacino, Joe Grifasi, Joanna Merlin.

2 BY 4
ELECTRIC HEAD. Jan., 1998. (Jimmy Smallhorne) Jimmy Smallhorne, Chris O'Neill, Bradley Fitts, Joe Holyoake, Terrence McGoff.

TWO DADS AND ONE MOM
AMLF. May, 1996. French. (Jean-Marc Longval) Arielle Dombasle, Smain, Antoine de Caunes.

2 DAYS IN THE VALLEY
MGM/UA. September, 1996. (John Herzfeld) Danny Aiello, Jeff Daniels, Teri Hatcher, James Spader, Glenne Headly.

TWO EVIL EYES
TAURUS. October, 1991. Italian. (George Romero, Dario Argento) Adrienne Barbeau, Harvey Keitel, Madeleine Potter.

TWO FRIENDS
MILESTONE FILMS. April, 1996. Autralian. (Jane Campion) Kris Bedenko, Emma Coles (originally debuted in 1986).

TWOGETHER
BORDE. February, 1994. (Andre Chiaramonte) Nick Cassavetes, Brenda Bakke, Jeremy Piven.

TWO GIRLS AND A GUY
FOX SEARCHLIGHT. Aug., 1997. (James Toback) Robert Downey Jr., Heather Graham, Natasha Gregson Wagner, Angel David.

TWO HANDS
BEYOND FILMS/AUSTRALIAN FILM FINANCE CORP. Jan., 1999. Australian. (Gregor Jordan) Heath Ledger, Rose Byrne, Bryan Brown, David Field.

TWO IF BY SEA
WARNER BROS. January, 1996. (Bill Bennett) Sandra Bullock, Denis Leary, Stephen Dillane, Yaphet Kotto.

THE TWO JAKES
PARAMOUNT. August, 1990. (Jack Nicholson) Jack Nicholson, Harvey Keitel, Meg Tilly.

TWO MUCH
BUENA VISTA. March, 1996. (Fernando Trueba) Antonio Banderas, Melanie Griffith, Daryl Hannah, Danny Aiello.

TWO SMALL BODIES
CASTLE HILL. April, 1994. German. (Beth B.) Fred Ward, Suzy Amis.

TWO STREAMS
DEZENOVE SOM E IMAGENS. Aug., 1999. Brazilian. (Carlos Reichenbach) Carlos Alberto Riccelli, Beth Goulart, Ingra Liberato, Vanessa Goulart, Luciana Brasil.

TWO WOMEN
ARTA. Feb., 1999. Iranian. (Tahmineh Milani). Niki Karimi, Marila Zare'i, Mohammad Reza Forutan.

THE TYPEWRITER, THE RIFLE & THE MOVIE CAMERA
BRITISH FILM INSTITUTE/INDEPENDENT FILM CHANNEL. January, 1996. (Adam Simon) Documentary.

U

THE UGLY
ESSENTIAL FILMS. May, 1997. New Zealand (Scott Reynolds) Paolo Rotondo, Rebecca Hobbs, Jennifer Ward-Lealand, Roy Ward.

ULEES'S GOLD
ORION CLASSICS. January, 1997. (Victor Nunez), Peter Fonda, Patricia Richardson, Jessica Biel, J. Kenneth Campbell.

UN AIR DE FAMILLE
CANAL PLUS. May, 1996. French. (Cedric Klapisch) Jean-Pierre Bacri, Agnes Jaoui, Jean-Pierre Darroussin.

UNBECOMING AGE
CASTLE HILL. April, 1993. (Deborah Ringel) Diane Salinger, John Calvin, Wallace Shawn.

THE UNBELIEVABLE TRUTH
MIRAMAX. July, 1990. (Hal Hartley) Adrienne Shelly, Robert Burke, Christopher Cooke, Gary Sauer.

THE UNBORN
CONCORDE. April, 1991. (Rodman Flender) Brooke Adams, Jeff Hayenga, James Karen, K Callan.

UNCLE MOSES
NATL CTR FOR JEWISH FILM. November, 1991. Yiddish. (Origianally released 1932). (Sidney Goldin, Aubrey Scotto) Maurice Schwartz, Zvee Scooler. B&W.

UN COEUR EN HIVER (A HEART IN WINTER)
OCTOBER FILMS. June, 1993. French. (Claude Sautet) Daniel Auteuil, Emmanuelle Beart, André Dussollier.

UNCONDITIONAL LOVE
HORNE ENTERTAINMENT, INC. Feb., 1999. (Steven Rush) John Kennedy Horne, Tracey Ross, Henry Silva, Miles O'Keefe.

UNDER CALIFORNIA: THE LIMIT OF TIME
IMCINE/SINCRONIA. Jan., 1999. Mexican. (Carlos Bolado) Damian Alcazar, Jesus Ochoa.

UNDER ONE ROOF
CASTLE HILL. March, 1994. Portuguese. (Paulo Thiago) Norma Bengell, Maria Zilda Bethlem.

UNDER SIEGE
WARNER BROS. October, 1992. (Andrew Davis) Steven Seagal, Tommy Lee Jones, Gary Busey.

UNDER SIEGE 2: DARK TERRITORY
WARNER BROS. July, 1995. (Geoff Murphy) Steven Seagal, Eric Bogosian, Katherine Heigl, Everett McGill.

UNDERSTANDING JANE
SCALA. Nov., 1998. British. (Caleb Lindsay) Kevin McKidd, Amelia Curtis, John Simon, Louisa Milwood Haigh, Carl Proctor.

UNDER SUSPICION
COLUMBIA. February, 1992. British. (Simon Moore) Liam Neeson, Laura San Giacomo, Kenneth Cranham.

UNDER THE LIGHTHOUSE
SILVER TURTLE. Apri., 1997. Australian. (Graeme Rattigan) Jack Thompson, Jacqueline McKenzie, Naomi Watts, Aden Gillett.

UNDER THE SKIN
TORNASOL FILMS. Sept., 1996. Spanish-Peruvian-German. (Francisco J. Lombardi) Ana Risueno, Jose Luis Ruiz Barahona.

UNDER THE SKIN
BFI FILMS. Aug., 1997. British. (Carine Adler) Samantha Morton, Claire Rushbrook, Rita Tushingham, Mark Womack.

UNDER THE SUN
SVENSK FILMINDUSTRI. Dec., 1998. Swedish. (Colin Nutley) Rolf Lassgard, Helena Bergstrom, Johan Widerberg, Gunilla Roor, Jonas Falk.

UNDER WESTERN EYES
NOVEMBER FILMS. Feb., 1997. Israeli. (Joseph Pitchadze) Eyal Schehter, Liat Glick, Ezra Kafri, Carmel Betto, Gidon Shemer.

UNDERCOVER BLUES
MGM. September, 1993. (Herbert Ross) Kathleen Turner, Dennis Quaid, Fiona Shaw.

THE UNDERNEATH
GRAMERCY. April, 1995. (Steven Soderbergh) Peter Gallagher, Alison Elliott, William Fichtner.

UNDERTOW
CAPSTONE. September, 1992. (Thomas Mazziotti) Peter Dobson, Burtt Harris, Greg Mullavey.

UNFORGETTABLE
MGM. February, 1996. (John Dahl) Ray Liotta, Linda Fiorentino, Peter Coyote, Christopher MacDonald.

THE UNIVERSAL SOLDIER: THE RETURN
SONY. Aug., 1999. (Mic Rodgers) Jean-Claude Van Damme, Michael Jai White, Heidi Schanz, Xander Berkeley, Justin Lazard.

THE UNPREDICTABLE NATURE OF THE RIVER
CANAL PLUS. November, 1995. French. (Bernard Giraudeau) Giraudeau, Richard Bohringer, Anna Galiena.

UNDER HEAVEN
BANNER ENTERTAINMENT. Jan., 1998. (Meg Richman) Joely Richardson, Aden Young, Molly Parker, Kevin Phillip.

UNFORGIVEN
WARNER BROS. August, 1992. (Clint Eastwood) Clint Eastwood, Gene Hackman, Morgan Freeman, Richard Harris.

UNIVERSAL SOLDIER
TRISTAR. July, 1992. (Roland Emmerich) Jean Claude Van Damme, Dolph Lundgren, Ally Walker.

THE UNKNOWN CYCLIST
TRIDENT RELEASING. June, 1998. (Bernard Salzman) Lea Thompson, Vincent Spano, Danny Nucci, Stephen Spinella.

UNLAWFUL ENTRY
20TH CENTURY FOX. June, 1992. (Jonathan Kaplan) Kurt Russell, Ray Liotta, Madeleine Stowe.

UNMADE BEDS
CHELSEA PICTURES. Aug., 1997. (Nicholas Barker) Aimee Copp, Michael De Stefano, Brenda Monte, Mikey Russo.

UNSTRUNG HEROES
BUENA VISTA. September, 1995. (Diane Keaton) John Turturro, Andie MacDowell, Michael Richards.

UNTAMED HEART
MGM. February, 1993. (Tony Bill) Christian Slater, Marisa Tomei, Rosie Perez.

UNTIL THE END OF THE WORLD
WARNER BROS. December, 1991. German-French-Australian. (Wim Wenders) William Hurt, Solveig Dommartin.

THE UNVEILING
MIASMA FILMS. June, 1998. DOCUMENTARY

UNZIPPED
MIRAMAX. August, 1995. (Douglas Keeve) Documentary.

UP CLOSE AND PERSONAL
BUENA VISTA. March, 1996. (Jon Avnet) Robert Redford, Michelle Pfeiffer, Stockard Channing, Joe Mantegna.

THE UPRISING
CINEMA SERVICE. Aug., 1999. South Korean-French. (Park Kwang-su) Lee Jung-jae, Shim Eun-ha, Myung Kay-nam, Frederic Andrau, Kang Shin-il.

UPSIDE DOWN
AND WHATABOUT US/DE CUERNOS AL ABISMO FILMS. July, 1999. (Mario Mandujano) Chantal Chamandy, Alex Furth, Francisco Lorite.

UPSTATE
SHOOTING GALLERY. Oct., 1997. (Steven O'Connor) Jonah Bay, Julie Kessler, Hugh O'Gorman, Cheyann Benedict.

URANUS
PRESTIGE. August, 1991. French. (Claude Berri) Philippe Noiret, Gérard Depardieu, Michel Blanc.

URBAN FEEL
URBAN FEEL PRODS. Feb., 1999. Israeli. (Jonathan Sagall) Dafna Rechter, Scharonn Alexander, Jonathan Sagall.

URBAN LEGEND
TRISTAR. Sept., 1998. (Jamie Blanks) Jared Leto, Alicia Witt, Rebecca Gayheart, Michael Rosenbaum, Loretta Devine.

U.S. MARSHALS
WARNER BROS. March, 1998. (Stuart Baird) Tommy Lee Jones, Wesley Snipes, Robert Downey, Jr., Kate Nelligan, Joe Pantoliano, Irene Jacob.

USED PEOPLE
20TH CENTURY FOX. December, 1992. (Beeban Kidron) Shirley MacLaine, Marcello Mastroianni, Kathy Bates.

THE USUAL SUSPECTS
GRAMERCY. August, 1995. (Bryan Singer) Gabriel Byrne, Kevin Spacey, Chazz Palminteri, Giancarlo Esposito, Stephen Baldwin, Suzy Amis.

U-TURN
SONY PICTURES ENTERTAINMENT. August, 1997. (Oliver Stone), Sean Penn, Nick Nolte, Jennifer Lopez, Powers Boothe, Claire Danes.

UTZ
FIRST RUN FEATURES. February, 1993. British-Italian-German. (George Sluizer) Armin Muller Stahl.

V

THE VAGRANT
MGM. May, 1992. (Chris Walas) Bill Paxton, Michael Ironside, Colleen Camp, Marc McClure.

VALERIE FLAKE
I.E. FILMS. Jan., 1999. (John Putch) Susan Traylor, Jay Underwood, Christina Pickles, Peter Michael Goetz, Rosemay Forsyth.

VALLEY OF ABRAHAM
INDEPENDENT. December, 1993. Portuguese-French-Swiss. (Manoel de Oliveira) Leonor Silveira, Cecil Sanz De Alba.

VAMPIRA: ABOUT SEX, DEATH, AND TAXES
GREEN BIRD OY. Oct., 1996. (Mika J. Ripatti) Maila Nurmi/Vampira.

VAMPIRE IN BROOKLYN
PARAMOUNT. October, 1995. (Wes Craven) Eddie Murphy, Angela Bassett, Allen Payne, Kadeem Hardison.

VAMPIRES
CTV INTL. April, 1998. (John Carpenter) James Woods, Daniel Baldwin, Sheryl Lee, Thomas Ian Griffith, Tim Guinee, Maximilian Schell.

VAN GOGH
SONY PICTURES CLASSICS. October, 1992. French. (Maurice Pialat) Jacques Dutronc, Alexandra London.

THE VANISHING
TARA. October, 1990. Dutch. (George Sluizer) Bernard Pierre Donnadieu, Gene Bervoets.

THE VANISHING
20TH CENTURY FOX. February, 1993. (George Sluizer) Jeff Bridges, Keifer Sutherland, Nancy Travis.

VANYA ON 42ND STREET
SONY PICTURES CLASSICS. October, 1994. (Louis Malle) Wallace Shawn, Julianne Moore, Brooke Smith, Larry Pine.

VARSITY BLUES
PARAMOUNT. Jan., 1999. (Brian Robbins) James Van Der Beek, Jon Voight, Paul Walker, Ron Lester, Scott Cann.

VEGAS IN SPACE
TROMA. December, 1993. (Phillip R. Ford) Doris Fish, Miss X, Ginger Quest.

VEGAS VACATION
WARNER BROS. February, 1997. (Stephen Kessler), Chevy Chase, Beverly D'Angelo, Randy Quaid, Ethan Embry, Marisol Nichols.

THE VELOCITY OF GARY
CINEVILLE. Sept., 1998. (Dan Ireland) Salma Hayek, Vincent D'Onofrio, Thomas Jane, Olivia d'Abo, Chad Lindberg, Lucky Luciano.

VENIAL SINS
JOSE MARIA LARA PC/ALOKATU PC. Sept., 1998. Spanish. (Ramon Barea) Elena Irureta, Ane Gabarain, Loli Astoreka, Aitzpea Goenaga, Itziar Lazkano.

THE VENICE PROJECT
TERRA FILM-JUNE 99-OZANIT. Sept., 1999. Austrian. (Robert Dornhelm) Lauren Bacall, Dennis Hopper, Linus Roache, Ben Cross, Stuart Townsend.

VENICE/VENICE
RAINBOW. October, 1992. (Henry Jaglom) Nelly Alard, Henry Jaglom, Suzanne Bertish.

VENUS BEAUTY INSTITUTE
PYRAMIDE. Jan., 1999. French. (Tonie Marshall) Nathalie Baye, Bulle Ogier, Samuel LeBihan.

VERONICO CRUZ
CINEVISTA. January, 1990. Argentinian-British. (Miguel Pereira) Juan Jose Camero, Gonzalo Morales.

VERTICAL REALITY
WARREN MILLER. October, 1994. (Kurt Miller, Peter Speek) Documentary.

VERY BAD THINGS
POLYGRAM FILMS. Sept., 1998. (Peter Berg) Christian Slater, Cameron Diaz, Daniel Stern, Jeanne Tripplehorn, Jon Favreau.

A VERY BRADY SEQUEL
PARAMOUNT. August, 1996. (Arlene Sanford) Shelley Long, Gary Cole, Tim Matheson, Christopher Daniel Barnes.

A VERY OLD MAN WITH ENORMOUS WINGS
ORIGINAL CINEMA. December, 1990. Spanish. (Fernando Birri) Fernando Birri, Asdrubal Melendez.

VIA APPIA
STRAND. August, 1992. German. (Jochen Hick) Peter Senner, Yves Jansen, Guilherme de Padua.

VIA SATELLITE
SCREEN VISION NZ. NOV., 1998. NEW ZEALAND. (Anthony McCarten) Danielle Cormack, Rima Te Wiata, Jodie Dorday.

VICTOR...WHILE IT'S TOO LATE
PYRAMIDE. Nov., 1998. French. (Sandrine Veysset) Jeremy Chaix, Lydia Andrei, Mathieu Lane

VICTORY
MIRAMAX. May, 1997. British-French-German. (Mark Peploe) Willem Dafoe, Sam Neill, Irene Jacob, Rufus Sewell, Jean Yanne, Ho Yi.

VIETNAM, TEXAS
TRIUMPH. June, 1990. (Robert Ginty) Robert Ginty, Haing S. Ngor.

THE VIGIL
COME AS YOU ARTS. Sept., 1998. Canadian. (Justin MacGregor) Damon Johnson, Donny Lucas, Allan Franz, Trevor White.

VIGO: PASSION FOR LIFE
FILMFOUR DISTRIBUTORS. May, 1999. British-Japanese-French. (Julien Temple) Romane Bohringer, James Frain, Jim Carter, Diana Quick, William Scott-Masson.

VILLAGE OF THE DAMNED
UNIVERSAL. April, 1995. (John Carpenter) Christopher Reeve, Kirstie Alley, Linda Kozlowski.

VINCENT & THEO
HEMDALE. November, 1990. French-British. (Robert Altman) Tim Roth, Paul Rhys, Johanna Ter Steege.

VIOLET'S VISIT
DONNA FILMS. June, 1997. Australian. (Richard Turner) Rebecca Smart, Graham Harvey, David Franklin, Caleb Packham, May Lloyd.

VIRTUAL SEXUALITY
COLUMBIA TRISTAR. Apr., 1999. British. (Nick Hurran) Laura Fraser, Rupert Penry-Jones, Luke de Lacey, Kieran O'Brien, Marcelle Duprey.

VIRTUOSITY
PARAMOUNT. August, 1995. (Brett Leonard) Denzel Washington, Kelly Lynch, Russell Crowe.

VISION OF LIGHT
KINO INT'L. April, 1993. (Arnold Glassman, Todd McCarthy, Stuart Samuels) Documentary.

VISIT TO A GREEN PLANET (LA BELLE VERTE)
STUDIO CANAL PLUS. August, 1996. French. (Coline Serreau) Coline Serreau, Vincent Lindon.

THE VISITORS
MIRAMAX. July, 1996. French. (Jean-Marie Poire) Christian Clavier, Jean Reno, Valerie Lemercier.

VITAL SIGNS
20TH CENTURY FOX. April, 1990. (Marisa Silver) Adrian Pasdar, Diane Lane, Jimmy Smits.

VIVA EROTICA
GOLDEN HARVEST. Feb., 1997. Hong Kong. (Derek Yee) Leslie Cheung, Karen Mok, Law Kar-ying, Shu Qi, Tsui Kam-kong.

VIVID
SC ENTERTAINMENT. May, 1996. Canadian. (Evan Georgiades) Stephen Shellen, Kari Salin, Ilene Kristen.

V. I. WARSHAWSKI
BUENA VISTA. July, 1991. (Jeff Kanew) Kathleen Turner, Jay O. Sanders, Charles Durning.

VOICES
AVENUE PICTURES. September, 1995. (Malcolm Clarke) Jeremy Northam, Tushka Bergen, Allan Corduner.

VOICES FROM THE FRONT
FRAMELINE. March, 1992. (Robyn Hutt) Documentary.

VOICES UNHEARD
B PRODUCTIONS. Apr., 1998. Beth B. Documentary.

VOL-AU-VENT
WINCHESTER FILMS & TV SALES. June, 1996. British. (John McKenzie) Dennis Waterman, Julia McKenzie, Lisa Coleman.

VOLCANO
20TH CENTURY FOX. April, 1997. (Mick Jackson), Tommy Lee Jones, Anne Heche, Gaby Hoffman, Don Cheadle, Jacquelin Kim, Keith David.

THE VOLCANO
OTTOKAR RUNZE FILMHERSTELLUNG. Aug., 1999. German. (Ottokar Runze) Nina Hoss, Meret Becker, Christian Nickel, Udo Samel.

VOLERE, VOLARE
FINE LINE. February, 1993. Italian. (Maurizio Nichetti, Guido Manuli) Maurizio Nichetti.

VOYAGER
CASTLE HILL. January, 1992. German-French. (Volker Schlondorff) Sam Shepard, Julie Delpy, Barbara Sukowa.

VOYAGES
MK2 DIFFUSION. May, 1999. French. (Emmanuel Finkiel) Shulamit Adar, Liliane Rovere, Esther Gorintin, Nathan Cogan, Moscu Alcalay.

VOYEUR
PRESTIGE. August, 1991. Dutch. (Alex Van Warmerdam) Alex Van Warmerdam, Olga Zuiderhoek.

W

WAALO FENDO: WHERE THE EARTH FREEZES
AMKA FILMS PRODS. SA. Sept. 1998. Senegalese-Swiss. (Mohammed Soudani) Saidou Moussa Ba, Bara Ngom, Souleymane Ndiaye.

WAG THE DOG
NEW LINE CINEMA. Dec., 1998. (Barry Levinson) Dustin Hoffman, Robert De Niro, Anne Heche, Woody Harrelson, Denis Leary.

WAGONS EAST!
TRISTAR. August, 1994. (Peter Markle) John Candy, Richard Lewis, John C. McGinley.

WAIT AND SEE
SHOCHIKU. Feb., 1999. Japanese. (Shinji Somai) Koichi Sato, Yuki Saito, Tsutomu Yamazaki, Jyunko Fuji.

WAIT FOR ME IN HEAVEN
MD WAX/COURIER. October, 1990. Spanish. (Antonio Mercero) Jose Soriano, Chus Lampreave.

WAITING FOR A TENOR
SVENSK FILMINDUSTRI. Aug., 1998. Swedish. (Lisa Ohlin) John Hison Kjellgren, Krister Henriksson, Lena B. Erikson.

WAITING FOR GUFFMAN
SONY PICTURES CLASSICS. August, 1996. (Christopher Guest) Christopher Guest, Eugene Levy, Fred Willard.

WAITING FOR THE LIGHT
TRIUMPH. November, 1990. (Christopher Monger) Shirley MacLaine, Teri Garr, Clancy Brown.

WAITING FOR THE MAN
PANORAMA ENTERTAINMENT CORP. Jan., 1997. (John Covert) John Harriman, Daniel Gately, Kendra James, Elyse Mirto.

WAITING TO EXHALE
20TH CENTURY FOX. December, 1995. (Forest Whitaker) Whitney Houston, Angela Bassett, Lela Rochon.

WAIT UNTIL SPRING, BANDINI
ORION CLASSICS. June, 1990. Belgian-French-Italian. (Dominique Deruddere) Joe Mantegna, Faye Dunaway.

WAKE UP LOVE
LIDER FILM. Feb., 1997. Argentine. (Eliseo Subiela) Dario Grandinetti, Soledad Silveyra, Juan Leyrado, Marilyn Solaya.

A WALK IN THE CLOUDS
20TH CENTURY FOX. August, 1995. (Alfonse Arau) Keanu Reeves, Aitana Sanchez-Gijon, Anthony Quinn.

WALKING AND TALKING
MIRAMAX. January, 1996. (Nicole Holofcener) Catherine Keener, Anne Heche, Todd Field.

THE WALKING DEAD
SAVOY. February, 1995. (Preston A. Whitmore II) Allen Payne, Eddie Griffin, Joe Morton.

A WALK ON THE MOON
MIRAMAX. Jan., 1999. (Tony Goldwyn) Diane Lane, Liev Schreiber, Anny Paquin, Viggo Mortensen, Tovah Feldshuh.

WALLACE & GROMIT
NORTHERN ARTS. April, 1996. (Nick Park). Animated.

WALLOWITCH & ROSS: THIS MOMENT
KARMIC RELEASE LTD. Jan., 1999. (Richard Morris). Documentary.

THE WAR
UNIVERSAL. November, 1994. (Jon Avnet) Elijah Wood, Kevin Costner, Mare Winningham, Lexi Randall.

THE WAR AT HOME
Buena Vista. November, 1996. (Emilio Estevez) Emilio Estevez, Kathy Bates, Charlie Sheen, Kimberly Williams.

THE WAR BETWEEN US
ATLANTIS. February, 1996. Canadian. (Anne Wheeler) Shannon Lawson, Mieko Ouchi, Robert Wisden, Ian Tracey.

THE WAR IN THE HIGHLANDS
CAB PRODS. Feb., 1999. Swiss-French-Belgian. (Francis Reusser) Marion Cotillard, Yann Tregouet, Francois Marthouret.

WAR OF THE BUTTONS
WARNER BROS. September, 1995. (John Roberts) Gregg Fitzgerald, John Coffey, Colm Meaney.

THE WAR ROOM
OCTOBER FILMS. November, 1993. (D.A. Pennebaker) Documentary.

WAR ZONE
FILM FATALE INC./HANK LEVINE FILM. Feb., 1998. (Maggie Hadleigh-West) DOCUMENTARY.

THE WAR ZONE
FILM FOUR. Jan. 1999. British. (Tim Roth) Ray Winstone, Tilda Swubton, Lara Belmont, Freddie Cunliffe, Kate Ashfield.

WARLOCK
TRIMARK. January, 1991. (Steve Miner) Julian Sands, Richard E. Grant, Lori Singer.

WARLOCK: THE ARMAGEDDON
TRIMARK. September, 1993. (Tony Hickox) Julian Sands, Chris Young, Paula Marshall.

WARRIORS OF VIRTUE
MGM. April, 1997. (Ronny Yu), Angus Macfadyen, Mario Yedidia, Marley Shelton, Chao-Li Chi, Dennis Dun, Jack Tate, Doug Jones.

WASHINGTON SQUARE
BUENA VISTA. August, 1997. (Agnieszka Holland), Jennifer Jason Leigh, Albert Finney, Ben Chaplin, Maggie Smith, Judith Ivey.

WASHINGTON WOLVES
ALTA FILMS. Aug., 1999. Spanish. (Mariano Barroso) Javier Bardem, Eduardo Fernandez, Jose Sancho, Ernesto Alterio, Antonio San Juan.

THE WASTE LAND
ILLUMINATIONS TELEVISION. May, 1996. British. (Deborah Warner) Fiona Shaw.

WASTED
CONCORDE FILM. Feb., 1997. Dutch. (Ian Kerkhof) Fem van den Elzen, Tygo Gernandt, Hugo Metsers III, Mike Libanon.

WATANI: A WORLD WITHOUT EVIL
MH FILMS. June, 1999. French. (Med Hondo) Patrick Poivey, Coumba Awa Tall, Mboup Massyla, Anne Jolivet, James Campbell.

WATARI-GAWA: THE RIVER OF RECONCILIATION
WATARI-GAWA. February, 1996. Japanese. (Duk-Chui Kim, Yasduyuki Moli) Documentary.

WATCHING THE DETECTIVE
YAGI JUNICHI. Oct., 1998. Japanese. (Yagi Junichi) Oki Eiji, Mabuchi Haruko, Ozawa Miki, Nakamura Horyu, Kato Kanami.

WATCH IT
SKOURAS. March, 1993. (Tom Flynn) Peter Gallagher, Lili Taylor, John C. McGinley.

THE WATERBOY
BUENA VISTA. Nov., 1998. (Frank Coraci) Adam Sandler, Kathy Bates, Henry Winkler, Fairuza Balk, Jerry Reed.

THE WATERDANCE
SAMUEL GOLDWYN. May, 1992. (Neal Jimenez, Michael Steinberg) Eric Stoltz, Helen Hunt, Wesley Snipes.

WATERLAND
FINE LINE. October, 1992. British. (Stephen Gyllenhaal) Jeremy Irons, Ethan Hawke, Sinead Cusack.

THE WATERMELON WOMAN
DANCING GIRLS PROD. February, 1996. (Cheryl Dunye) Guin Turner, Valerie Walker, Lisa Marie Bronson.

WATERWORLD
UNIVERSAL. July, 1995. (Kevin Reynolds) Kevin Costner, Dennis Hopper, Jeanne Tripplehorn, Tina Majorino.

WAX MAX
ITALIAN INT'L. FILM. April, 1997. Italian-French. (Sergio Stivaletti) Robert Hossein, Romina Mondello, Riccardo Serventi Longhi.

WAX, OR THE DISCOVERY OF TELEVISION AMONG THE BEES
JASMINE TEA. August, 1992. (David Blair) David Blair, Meg Savlov.

WAYNE'S WORLD
PARAMOUNT. February, 1992. (Penelope Spheeris) Mike Myers, Dana Carvey, Rob Lowe.

WAYNE'S WORLD 2
PARAMOUNT. December, 1993. (Stephen Surjik) Mike Myers, Dana Carvey, Christopher Walken.

THE WAY TO A WOMAN'S HEART
FANTASIAFILMI OY. Feb., 1997. Finnish. (Pekka Parikka) Timo Torikka, Satu Silvo, Peter Franzen, Tom Wentzel, Merja Larivaara.

WE ALL FALL DOWN
COLUMBIA TRISTAR FILMS ITALIA. April, 1997. (Davide Ferrario) Valerio Mastandrea, Carlo Monni, Benedetta Mazzini.

WEDDING BAND
I.R.S. MEDIA. March, 1990. (Daniel Raskov) William Katt, Joyce Hyser.

WEDDING BAND
BIRD WOLF. Jan., 1999. (Martin Guigni) Deborah Gibson, Joey Scherr, Martin Gyigui, Kelly Bishop, Les Shenkel.

THE WEDDING BANQUET
SAMUEL GOLDWYN. August, 1993. (Ang Lee) Ah Leh Gua, Sihung Lung, Mitchell Lichtenstein.

WEDDING BELL BLUES
BERGMAN LUSTIG. Oct., 1996. (Dana Lustig) Illeana Douglas, Paulina Porizkova, Julie Warner, John Corbett, Jonathan Penner.

THE WEDDING GIFT
MIRAMAX. July, 1994. British. (Richard Loncraine) Julie Walters, Jim Broadbent, Thora Hird.

WEDDING MOON
COTUDIC. Oct., 1998. Tunisian. (Taieb Louhichi) Mess Hattou, Mohamed Hedi Moumen, Rym Riahi.

WEDNESDAY'S CHILD
WRITE ANGLES PRODS. July, 1999. (Brad Marlowe) Sommer Knight, David King, Brandon Hiott, Todd Surber, Tom Polanski.

WEEKEND AT BERNIE'S II
TRISTAR. July, 1993. (Robert Klane) Andrew McCarthy, Jonathan Silverman, Barry Bostwick.

A WEEK IN THE LIFE OF A MAN
ZEBRA. Sept., 1999. Polish. (Jerzy Stuhr) Jerzy Stuhr, Gosia Dobrowolska, Danuta Szaflarska.

WEININGER'S LAST NIGHT
CINEPOOL/WEGA FILM. July, 1991. Austrian. (Paulus Manker) Paulus Manker, Hilde Sochor.

WELCOME HOME ROXY CARMICHAEL
PARAMOUNT. October, 1990. (Jim Abrahams) Winona Ryder, Jeff Daniels, Laila Robbins.

WELCOME SAYS THE ANGEL
SILVER SHADOW. February, 1996. (Phillipe Dib) Jon Jacobs, Ayesha Hauer, Leroy Jones, Marian O'Brien.

WELCOME TO OBLIVION
CONCORDE. February, 1990. (Augusto Tomayo) Dack Rambo, Meshach Taylor.

WELCOME TO SARAJEVO
FILM FOUR DIST. May, 1997. British-U.S. (Michael Winterbottom) Stephen Dillane, Woody Harrelson, Marisa Tomei, Emira Nusevic.

WELCOME TO THE DOLLHOUSE
SUBURBAN PICTURES. September, 1995. (Todd Solondz) Heather Matarazzo, Daria Kalinina, Matthew Faber.

WELCOME TO WOOP WOOP
METROMEDIA ENTERTAINMENT GROUP. May, 1997. Australian-British. (Stephan Elliott) Jonathon Schaech, Rod Taylor, Susie Porter.

WE'RE BACK: A DINOSAUR'S STORY
UNIVERSAL. November, 1993. (Dick Zondag, Ralph Zondag, Phil Nibblink, Simon Wells) Animated.

WE'RE TALKIN' SERIOUS MONEY
CINETEL. May, 1992. (James Lemmo) Dennis Farina, Leo Rossi, Fran Drescher.

WES CRAVEN'S NEW NIGHTMARE
NEW LINE. October, 1994. (Wes Craven) Robert Englund, Heather Langenkamp, Miko Hughes, John Saxon.

WESTERN
DIAPHANA. May, 1997. French. (Manuel Poirier) Sergi Lopez, Sacha Bourdo, Elizabeth Vitali, Marie Matheron, Basile Siekoua.

WHAT ABOUT BOB?
BUENA VISTA. May, 1991. (Frank Oz) Bill Murray, Richard Dreyfuss, Julie Hagerty.

WHAT BECOMES OF THE BROKEN HEARTED?
POLYGRAM. May, 1999. New Zealand. (Ian Mune) Temuera Morrison, Clint Eruera, Nancy Brunning, Pete Smith, Lawrence Makoare.

WHAT DO WOMEN LAUGH ABOUT?
COLUMBIA TRISTAR. April, 1997. Spanish. (Joaquin Oristrell) Veronica Forque, Candela Pena, Adriana Ozores, Jordi Bosch.

WHAT DREAMS MAY COME
POLYGRAM FILMS. Sept., 1998. (Vincent Ward) Robin Williams, Cuba Gooding Jr., Annabella Sciorra, Max von Sydow.

WHAT HAPPENED WAS...
SAMUEL GOLDWYN. September, 1994. (Tom Noonan) Noonan, Karen Sillas.

WHAT'S EATING GILBERT GRAPE
PARAMOUNT. December, 1993. (Lasse Hallstrom) Johnny Depp, Leonardo DiCaprio, Juliette Lewis.

WHAT'S LOVE GOT TO DO WITH IT
BUENA VISTA. June, 1993. (Brian Ibson) Angela Bassett, Laurence Fishburne, Vanessa Bell Calloway.

WHEN IT'S OVER
PAPA FILMS. April, 1998. (Richard Mancuso) Troy Ruptash, Vincent Caruso, Renee Rizzo, Shoshana Ami, John Fell, Patrick Ferraro.

WHEN A MAN LOVES A WOMAN
BUENA VISTA. April, 1994. (Luis Mandoki) Andy Garcia, Meg Ryan, Lauren Tom, Tina Majorino.

WHEN NIGHT IS FALLING
OCTOBER FILMS. November, 1995. (Patricia Rozema) Rachael Crawford, Pascale Bussieres, Henry Czerny.

WHEN SATURDAY COMES
GUILD FILM. February, 1996. British. (Maria Giese) Sean Bean, Emily Lloyd, Pete Postlethwaite.

WHEN THE DEAD START SINGING
JADRAN. Aug., 1999. Croation. (Krsto Papic) Ivo Gregurevic, Ivica Vidovic, Mirjana Majurec.

WHEN THE EAST MEETS THE WEST
BEJING FILM STUDIO. Nov., 1998. Chinese. (Ding Yinnam). Wang Zhuxia, Zhu Xu, Du Ruiqiu, Rachel Dworsky.

WHEN THE STARS MEET THE SEA
MERCURE DISTRIBUTION. May, 1996. French. (Raymond Rajaonarivelo) Jean Rabenjamina, Barbara Razanajao.

WHEN TRUMPETS FADE
HBO NYC. June, 1998. (John Irvin) Ron Eldard, Zak Orth, Frank Whaley, Dylan Bruno, Martin Donovan, Timothy Olyphant.

WHEN WE WERE KINGS
UFA NON-FICTION/USA January, 1996. (Leon Gast) Documentary.

WHERE ANGELS FEAR TO TREAD
FINE LINE. February, 1992. British. (Charles Sturridge) Helena Bonham Carter, Rupert Graves.

WHERE'S MARLOWE?
PARAMOUNT. Oct., 1998. (Daniel Pyne) Miguel Ferrer, Mos Def, John Livingston, Allison Dean, John Slattery.

WHERE THE DAY TAKES YOU
NEW LINE. September, 1992. (Marc Rocco) Dermot Mulroney, Sean Astin, Balthazar Getty, Lara Flynn Boyle.

WHERE THE HEART IS
BUENA VISTA. February, 1990. (John Boorman) Dabney Coleman, Uma Thurman, Joanna Cassidy.

WHERE THE RIVERS FLOW NORTH
CALEDONIA. January, 1994. (Jay Craven) Rip Torn, Tantoo Cardinal, Bill Raymond, Michael J. Fox.

WHERE TRUTH LIES
SILVERLINE PICS. April, 1996. (William H. Molina) John Savage, Kim Cattral, Malcolm McDowell, Cadice Daly.

WHICH SIDE EDEN
LUMAR PRODS. Sept., 1999. Czech-U.S. (Vojtech Jasny). Vladimir Pucholt, Ingrid Timkova, Adam Davidson.

WHILE YOU WERE SLEEPING
BUENA VISTA. April, 1995. (Jon Turtletaub) Sandra Bullock, Bill Pullman, Peter Gallagher, Peter Boyle.

WHISPERING CORRIDORS
CINE 2000. Oct., 1998. South Korean. (Park Ki-Hyung) Lee Mi-Youn, Park Yong-Su, Lee Yong-Nyuh, Kim Yoo-Suk.

WHISPERS IN THE DARK
PARAMOUNT. August, 1992. (Christopher Crowe) Annabella Sciorra, Jamey Sheridan, Alan Alda.

WHITE
MIRAMAX. June, 1994. Polish. (Krzysztof Kieslowski) Zbigniew Zamachowski, Julie Delpy, Janusz Gajos.

THE WHITE BALLOON
OCTOBER FILMS. January, 1996. Iranian. (Jafar Panahi) Aida Mohammadkhani, Mohsen Kalifi, Anna Boukowska.

WHITE FANG
BUENA VISTA. January, 1991. (Randal Kleiser) Ethan Hawke, Klaus Maria Brandauer, Seymour Cassel.

WHITE FANG 2: THE MYTH OF THE WHITE WOLF
BUENA VISTA. April, 1994. (Ken Olin) Scott Bairstow, Charmaine Craig, Al Harrington.

THE WHITE FEAST (BELY PRAZNIK)
MOSFILM STUDIO. April, 1996. Russian. (Vladimir Naumov) Innokenti Smoktunovsky.

WHITE HUNTER, BLACK HEART
WARNER BROS. September, 1990. (Clint Eastwood) Clint Eastwood, Jeff Fahey, George Dzundza.

WHITE MAN'S BURDEN
SAVOY. October, 1995. (Desmond Nakano) John Travolta, Harry Belafonte, Kelly Lynch, Margaret Avery.

WHITE MEN CAN'T JUMP
20TH CENTURY FOX. March, 1992. (Ron Shelton) Wesley Snipes, Woody Harrelson, Rosie Perez.

WHITE PALACE
UNIVERSAL. October, 1990. (Luis Mandoki) Susan Sarandon, James Spader, Eileen Brennan.

WHITE SANDS
WARNER BROS. April, 1992. (Roger Donaldson) Willem Dafoe, Mary Elizabeth Mastrantonio, Mickey Rourke.

WHITE SQUALL
BUENA VISTA. January, 1996. (Ridley Scott) Jeff Bridges, Caroline Goodall, John Savage, Scott Wolf, Jeremy Sisto.

THE WHITE SUIT
ZILLION FILMS. May, 1999. Yugoslav. (Lazar Ristovski) Lazar Ristovski, Radmila Shchogolyeva, Dragan Nikolic.

WHO IS HENRY JAGLOM?
CALLIOPE. December, 1995. (Alex Rubin, Jeremy Workman) Documentary.

WHO IS THE MONSTER...YOU OR ME?
DAVID A. HESS PRODS. September, 1995. German. (David A. Hess). Documentary.

THE WHOLE OF THE MOON
CFP INTL. April, 1996. New Zealand-Canadian. (Ian Mune) Toby Fisher, Nikki Si'Ulepa, Pascale Bussieres.

THE WHOLE TRUTH
CINEVISTA. October, 1992. (Dan Cohen, Jonathan Smythe) Dyan Kane, Dan Cohen, Jim Willig.

THE WHOLE WIDE WORLD
KUSHNER-LOCKE. January, 1996. (Dan Ireland) Vincent D'Onofrio, Renee Zellweger, Harve Presnell.

WHO PLUCKED THE FEATHERS OFF THE MOON?
CINE VALSE/ARTE FRANCE CINEMA/CRRAV. May, 1999. French. (Christine Carriere) Jean-Pierre Darroussin, Garance Clavel, Elsa Dourdet.

WHORE
TRIMARK. October, 1991. (Ken Russell) Theresa Russell, Antonio Fargas, Benjamin Mouton.

WHO'S THE CABOOSE?
PILOT SEASON PRODS. June, 1999. (Sam Seder) Sarah Silverman, Sam Seder, Andy Dick, H. Jon Benjamin, David Cross.

WHO'S THE MAN?
NEW LINE. April, 1993. (Ted Demme) Doctor Dre, Ed Lover, Badja Djola.

WHY DO FOOLS FALL IN LOVE
WARNER BROS. Aug., 1998. (Gregory Nava) Halle Berry, Vivica A. Fox, Lela Rochon, Larenz Tate, Paul Mazursky, Little Richard.

WHY ME?
TRIUMPH. April, 1990. (Gene Quintano) Christopher Lambert, Christopher Lloyd, Kim Greist.

WHY NOT ME?
UFD. Jan., 1999. French-Spanish-Swiss. (Stephane Guisti) Amira Casar, Julie Gayet, Bruno Putzulu.

WICKED
FRANKENSTEIN ENTERTAINMENT. Jan., 1998. (Michael Steinberg) Julia Stiles, William R. Moses, Patrick Muldoon, Vanessa Zima.

WICKED CITY
STREAMLINE. October, 1993. Japanese. (Carl Macek) Animated.

WIDE AWAKE
MIRAMAX. FEB., 1998. (M. Night Shyamalan) Joseph Cross, Timothy Reifsnyder, Dana Delaney, Denis Leary, Camryn Manheim.

WIDE SARGASSO SEA
FINE LINE. April, 1993. Australian. (John Duigan) Karina Lombard, Nathaniel Parker, Rachel Ward.

WIDOW'S PEAK
FINE LINE. May, 1994. British. (John Irvin) Mia Farrow, Joan Plowright, Natasha Richardson.

WIGSTOCK: THE MOVIE
SAMUEL GOLDWYN. June, 1995. (Barry Shils) Documentary.

WILBUR FALLS
VEXATIOUS FILMS. Sept., 1998. (Juliane Glantz) Danny Aiello, Sally Kirkland, Shanee Edwards, Jeff Daurey, Cheril Hayres.

WILD AMERICA
WARNER BROS. June, 1997. (William Dear), Jonathan Taylor Thomas, Devon Sawa, Scott Bairstow, Frances Fisher.

WILD AT HEART
SAMUEL GOLDWYN. August, 1990. (David Lynch) Nicolas Cage, Laura Dern, Willem Dafoe.

WILD BILL
MGM/UA. December, 1995. (Walter Hill) Jeff Bridges, Ellen Barkin, John Hurt, Diane Lane, David Arquette.

WILD BILL: HOLLYWOOD MAVERICK
TURNER. January, 1996. (Todd Robinson) Documentary.

THE WILD BUNCH: AN ALBUM IN MONTAGE
WARNER BROS. Nov., 1996. (Paul Seydor) (voices) Nick Redman, Walon Green, Newell Alexander, Edmond O'Brien, Documentary.

WILDE
POLYGRAM FILMED ENT. Aug., 1997. British. (Brian Gilbert) Stephen Fry, Jude Law, Vanessa Redgrave, Jennifer Ehle.

WILDER NAPALM
TRISTAR. August, 1993. (Glenn Gordon Caron) Debra Winger, Dennis Quaid, Arliss Howard.

WILDFIRE: FEEL THE HEAT
PRIMESCO COMMUNICATIONS. July, 1999. (Mike Slee). Documentary.

WILD HEARTS CAN'T BE BROKEN
BUENA VISTA. May, 1991. (Steve Miner) Gabrielle Anwar, Michael Schoeffling, Cliff Robertson.

WILD MAN BLUES
FINE LINE. Aug., 1997. (Barbara Kopple) Documentary.

WILD ORCHID
TRIUMPH. April, 1990. (Zalman King) Mickey Rourke, Jacqueline Bisset, Carre Otis.

THE WILD REEDS
STRAND. May, 1995. French. (Andre Techine) Elodie Bouchez, Gael Morel, Stephane Rideau.

WILDSIDE
BALBOA 2/ICELANDIC FILM CORP.. May, 1998. Danish-Icelandic. (Simon Staho) Nikolaj Coster Waldau, Mads Mikkelsen, Nukaka.

WILD THINGS
SONY. (John McNaughton) Kevin Bacon, Matt Dillon, Neve Campbell, Theresa Russell, Denise Richards, Daphne Rubin-Vega.

WILD WEST
SAMUEL GOLDWYN. November, 1993. British. (David Attwood) Naveen Andrews, Sarita Choudhury, Ronny Jhutti.

WILD WHEELS
TARA RELEASING. August, 1992. (Harrold Blank) Documentary.

WILD WILD WEST
WARNER BROS. June, 1999. (Barry Sonnenfeld) Will Smith, Kevin Kline, Salma Hayek, Ted Levine, M. Emmet Walsh.

WILLIAM SHAKESPEARE'S ROMEO & JULIET
20TH CENTURY FOX. October, 1996. (Baz Luhrmann), Leonardo DiCaprio, Claire Danes, Brian Dennehy, John Leguizamo, Paul Sorvino, Diane Venora.

WILLIAMSTOWNE
WOODLEAF. Nov., 1998. (Richard Horian) Deni Delory, Richard Horian, Lynn Britt, Brian Heath, Adisa Bankole.

WILL IT SNOW AT CHRISTMAS?
OGNON PICTURES. May, 1996. French. (Sandrine Veysset) Daniel Duval, Jessica Martinez, Alexandre Roger.

WIND
TRISTAR. September, 1992. (Carroll Ballard) Matthew Modine, Jennifer Grey, Cliff Robertson.

WINDHORSE
SHADOW DISTRIBUTION. Sept., 1998. (Paul Wagner) Dadon, Jampa Kelsang, Richard Chang, Taije Silverman, Lu Yu.

THE WIND IN THE WILLOWS
GOOD TIMES. January, 1996. British. (Dave Unwin) (voices) Alan Bennett, Michael Palin, Rik Mayall.

WINDOW SHOPPING
WORLD ARTISTS. April, 1992. French. (Chantal Akerman) Miriam Boyer, John Berry, Delphine Seyrig.

WINDOW TO PARIS
SONY PICTURES CLASSICS. February, 1995. French-Russian. (Yuri Mamin) Agnes Soral, Sergei Dontsov, Viktor Mikhailov.

THE WIND'S ECHO IN ME
KYUNGSUNG UNIV. DEPT OF THEATRE & CINEMA PROD. May, 1997. South Korean. (Jean Soo Il) Cho Jae Hyun, Kim Myung Jo.

THE WIND WILL CARRY US
MK2 DIFFUSION. Sept., 1999. French-Iranian. (Abbas Kiarostami) Behzad Dourani.

WING COMMANDER
20TH CENTURY FOX. Mar., 1999. (Chris Roberts) Freddie Prinze, Jr., Saffron Burrows, Matthew Lillard, Tcheky Karyo.

WINGS OF COURAGE
SONY PICTURES CLASSICS. February, 1996. (Jean-Jacques Annaud) Craig Sheffer, Tom Hulce, Elizabeth McGovern, Val Kilmer; IMAX 3-D.

WINGS OF THE DOVE
MIRAMAX. Sept., 1997. British. (Iain Softley), Helena Bonham Carter, Linus Roache, Alison Elliott, Elizabeth McGovern.

THE WINNER
NORTSAR/MDP WORLDWIDE. September, 1996. (Alex Cox) Vincent D'Onofrio, Rebecca DeMornay, Delroy Lindo.

THE WINSLOW BOY
SONY. Apr., 1999. (David Mamet) Nigel Hawthorne, Jeremy Northam, Rebecca Pidgeon, Gemma Jones, Guy Edwards.

WINTER FLOWERS
FILMFABRIK. Feb., 1997. German. (Kadir Sozen) Menderes Samancilar, Meral Yuzgulec, Gandi Mukli, Cengiz Sezici.

THE WINTER GUEST
FINE LINE. Aug., 1997. British. (Alan Rickman) Phyllida Law, Emma Thompson, Gary Hollywood, Arlene Cockburn, Sheila Reid.

THE WINTER IN LISBON
CASTLE HILL. March, 1992. Spanish-French-Portuguese. (Jose Antonio Zorrilla) Dizzy Gillespie, Christian Vadim.

WINTER STORIES
BEHAVIOUR DISTRIBUTION. Feb., 1999. Canadian. (Francois Bouvier) Joel Drapeau-Dalpe, Denis Bouchard, Luc Guerin\.

THE WISDOM OF CROCODILES
ENTERTAINMENT FILM DISTRIBUTORS. Nov., 1998. British. (Po Chih Leong) Jude Law, Elina Lowensohn, Timothy Spall, Kerry Fox.

WISECRACKS
ALLIANCE. June, 1992. Canadian. (Gail Singer) Documentary.

WISHMAN
CURB ESQUIRE. July, 1993. (Michael Marvin) Paul LeMat, Geoffrey Lewis, Brion James.

THE WITCHES
WARNER BROS. February, 1990. (Nicolas Roeg) Anjelica Huston, Jasen Fisher, Mai Zetterling.

WITH FRIENDS LIKE THESE...
ROBERT GREENHUT/PARKWAY/QUADRANT. Feb., 1998. (Philip Messina) Adam Arkin, Beverly D'Angelo, Elle Macpherson, Amy Madigan, Laura San Giacomo.

WITH HONORS
WARNER BROS. April, 1994. (Alex Keshishian) Joe Pesci, Brendan Fraser, Moira Kelly, Josh Hamilton.

WITH OR WITHOUT YOU
MOUNT CURVE AND WARDENCLYFFE ENTERTAINMENT. April, 1998. (Wendell Jon Andersson) Kristoffer Winters, Marisa Ryan.

WITH OR WITHOUT YOU
MIRAMAX. Sept., 1999. British. (Michael Winterbottom) Christopher Eccleston, Dervla Kirwan, Yvan Attal.

WITHOUT EVIDENCE
MFD LTD. March, 1996. (Gill Dennis) Scott Plank, Anna Gunn, Andrew Prine, Angelina Jolie, Paul Perri.

WITHOUT LIMITS
WARNER BROS. March, 1998. (Robert Towne) Billy Crudup, Donald Sutherland, Monica Potter, Jeremy Sisto, Matthew Lillard, Billy Burke.

WITHOUT YOU I'M NOTHING
M.C.E.G. May, 1990. (John Boskovich) Sandra Bernhard.

WITTGENSTEIN
ZEITGEIST. September, 1993. British. (Derek Jarman) Karl Johnson, Michael Gough, Clancy Chassay.

WITTSTOCK, WITTSTOCK
KRUSCHKE FILM & VIDEO PROD. Feb., 1997. German. (Volker Koepp) Documentary.

WIVES III
NORSK FILMDISTRIBUSJON. May, 1996. Norwegian. (Anja Breien) Froydis Armand, Katja Medboe, Anne Marie Ottersen.

WOLF
COLUMBIA. June, 1994. (Mike Nichols) Jack Nicholson, Michelle Pfeiffer, James Spader.

A WOMAN, HER MEN AND HER FUTON
INTERPERSONAL FILMS. July, 1992. (Mussef Sibay) Jennifer Rubin, Lance Edwards, Michael Cerveris.

WOMAN HUMAN DEMON
JASMINE TEA. September, 1992. Chinese. (Huang Shuqin) Xu Houli, Li Baotian.

A WOMAN OF THE NORTH
HUNGRY EYE LOWLAND. Sept., 1999. Dutch-Italian. (Frans Weisz) Johanna Ter Steege, Massimo Ghini, Anthony Calf.

A WOMAN'S TALE
ORION CLASSICS. December, 1991. Australian. (Paul Cox) Sheila Florance, Gosia Dobrowolska, Norman Kaye.

WOMEN FROM THE LAKE OF SCENTED SOULS
YELLOW LINE. February, 1994. Chinese. (Xie Fie) Siquin Gaowa, Wu Yujuan, Lei Luosheng.

THE WONDERFUL HORRIBLE LIFE OF LENI RIEFENSTAHL
KINO. March, 1994. German-British-French. (Ray Muller) Documentary.

THE WONDERFUL ICE CREAM SUIT
BUENA VISTA. Jan., 1998. (Stuart Gordon) Joe Mantegna, Esai Morales, Edward James Olmos, Clifton Gonzalez, Gregory Sierra.

WONDERLAND
RHINESTONE. Jan., 1997. (John O'Hagan) Documentary – 16mm.

WONDERLAND
UNIVERSAL. May, 1999. British. (Michael Winterbottom) Shirley Henderson, Gina McKee, Molly Parker, Ian Hart.

WOO
NEW LINE. April, 1998. (Daisy V.S. Mayer) Jada Pinket Smith, Tommy Davidson, Duane Martin, Michael Ralph, Darrel M. Heath.

THE WOOD
PARAMOUNT. July, 1999. (Rick Famuyiwa) Omar Epps, Sean Nelson, Taye Diggs, Trent Cameron, Richard T. Jones.

THE WOODEN MAN'S BRIDE
ARROW. February, 1995. Chinese. (Huang Jianxin) Chang Shih, Wang Lan, Ku Paoming.

WORK
DISTRICT PICTURES. March, 1996. (Rachel Reichmann) Cynthia Kaplan, Sonja Sohn, Peter Sprague.

WORKAHOLIC
CONCORDE/CASTLE ROCK TURNER. May, 1996. German. (Sharon von Wietersheim) Christiane Paul, Tobias Moretti.

WORLD AND TIME ENOUGH
STRAND. August, 1995. (Eric Mueller) Matt Guidry, Gregory G. Giles.

THE WOUNDS
COBRA FILM DEPT./PANDORA. Sept., 1998. Serbian-French. (Srdjan Dragojevic) Dusan Pekic, Milan Maric, Dragan Bjelogrlic.

WRESTLING ERNEST HEMINGWAY
WARNER BROS. December, 1993. (Randa Haines) Robert Duvall, Richard Harris, Shriley MacLaine.

WRESTLING WITH ALLIGATORS
PORTMAN PRODS./HOMEGROWN PICTURES. Jan., 1998. (Laurie Weltz) Aleksa Palladino, Koely Richardson, Claire Bloom.

WRONGFULLY ACCUSED
WARNER BROS. Aug., 1998. (Pat Proft) Leslie Nielson, Richard Crenna, Kelly Le Brock, Melinda McGraw, Michael York.

WYATT EARP
WARNER BROS. June, 1994. (Lawrence Kasdan) Kevin Costner, Dennis Quaid, Gene Hackman.

X

X,Y
AFMD January, 1996. French-Belgian. (Jean-Paul Lielenfeld) Clementine Celarie, Patrick Braoude, Jenny Cleve.

THE X-FILES
20TH CENTURY FOX. June, 1998. (Rob Bowman) David Duchovny, Gillian Anderson, Martin Landau, Armin Mueller-Stahl, Blythe Danner, Mitch Pileggi, William B. Davis.

Y

YEAR OF THE COMET
COLUMBIA. April, 1992. (Peter Yates) Penelope Ann Miller, Tim Daly.

YEAR OF THE GUN
TRIUMPH. November, 1991. (John Frankenheimer) Andrew McCarthy, Valeria Golino, Sharon Stone.

YEAR OF THE HORSE
SHAKEY PICTURES. May, 1997. (Jim Jarmusch) documentary.

YEARNING FOR A LIFE
SVENSK FILMINDUSTRI. Feb., 1999. Swedish. (Christer Engberg) Lotta Ornryd, Mattias Barthelsson, Nina Morin.

YEAR'S LOVE
ENTERTAINMENT FILM DISTRIBUTORS. Feb., 1999. British. (David Kane) Kathy Burke, Jennifer Ehle, Ian Hart, Douglas Henshall, Catherine McCormack.

YELLOW
PUBLIC WORKS FILMS. March, 1997. (Chris Chan Lee) Michael Chung, Burt Bulos, John Cho, Jason Tobin, Angie Suh, Mia Suh.

THE YEN FAMILY
FUJISANKEI COMMUN. INT'L. August, 1991. Japanese. (Yojiri Takita) Kaori Momoi, Takeshi Kaga.

YESTERDAY'S WINE
CHINA FILM EXPORT & IMPORT CORP. May, 1996. Chinese. (Xia Gang) Liu Yan, Shao Bing, Guo Yuan.

YOU KNOW MY NAME
TNT. Jan., 1999. (John Kent Harrison) Sam Elliott, Arliss Howard, Carolyn McCormick, James Gammon, R. Lee Erney.

YOUNG GUNS II
20TH CENTURY FOX. August, 1990. (Geoff Murphy) Emilio Estevez, Lou Diamond Phillips, Christian Slater.

YOU OR ME
AXIS PLUSZ/MTV. Feb., 1999. Hungarian. (Tamas Sas) Gabi Gubas, Attila Kiraly, Viktor Bodo, Karina Kecskes.

YOUR BLACK HAIR AND MY HAND
VANKE FILMS CO./SHANGHAI FILM STUDIO. Sept., 1996. (Lee Xin) inston Chao, Shang Haiming, Wang Yanan.

YOUR FRIENDS & NEIGHBORS
GRAMERCY PICTURES. July, 1998. (Neil LaBute) Amy Brenneman, Aaron Eckhart, Catherine Keener, Nastassja Kinski, Jason Patric, Ben Stiller.

YOU SO CRAZY
SAMUEL GOLDWYN. April, 1994. (Thomas Schlamme) Martin Lawrence.

YOU'RE LAUGHING
ISTITUTO LUCE. Aug., 1998. Italian-Spanish-French. (Paolo and Vittorio Taviani) Antonio Albanese, Sabrina Ferilli, Luca Zingaretti.

YOUTH WITHOUT GOD
CANAL PLUS DISTRIBUTION. April, 1996. French-Belgian. (Catherine Corsini) Marc Barbe, Roland Amstuz.

YOU'VE GOT MAIL
WARNER BROS. Dec., 1998. (Nora Ephron): Tom Hanks, Meg Ryan, Parker Posey, Greg Kinnear, Jean Stapleton.

Y2K
PM ENTERTAINMENT GROUP. May, 1999. (Richard Pepin) Louis Gossett, Jr., Jaimz Woolvett, Ed O'Ross, Sarah Chalke.

YURI
DAVID LAMPING CO. May, 1996. South Korean. (Yoonho Yang) Shinyang Park, Eunjung Lee, Youngdong Moon.

YUSHO-RENAISSANCE
JEANS FACTORY. Jan., 1999. Japanese. (Hiroyuki Oki). Toshiko Taniuchi, Ken Morimoto, Riko Kondo, Sawako Goda, Yuko Fukunaga.

Z

ZACHARIA FARTED
WINDOWSHOT. Sept., 1998. Canadian. (Michael Rohl) Colin Cunningham, Benjamin Ratner, Madison Graie.

ZEBRAHEAD
TRIUMPH. October, 1992. (Anthony Drazan) Michael Rapaport, N'Bushe Wright, Ray Sharkey.

ZENTROPA
PRESTIGE. May, 1992. Danish-French-German-Swedish. (Lars Von Trier) Jean Marc Barr, Barbara Sukowa, Udo Kier.

THE ZERO EFFECT
COLUMBIA. Jan., 1998. (Jake Kasdan), Bill Pullman, Ben Stiller, Ryan O'Neal, Kim Dickens, Angela Featherstone.

ZERO PATIENCE
CINEVISTA. March, 1994. Canadian. (John Greyson) John Robinson, Normand Fauteux, Dianne Heatherington.

ZEUS AND ROXANNE
MGM. January, 1997. (George Miller), Steve Guttenberg, Kathleen Quinlan, Arnold Vosloo, Dawn McMillan, Miko Hughes.

ZOMBIE AND THE GHOST TRAIN
FIRST RUN. August, 1994. Finnish. (Mika Kaurismaki) Silu Sepala, Marjo Leinonen, Matti Pellonpaa.

ZONE 39
BEYOND FILMS. May, 1996. Australian. (John Tatoulis) Peter Phelps, Caroline Bock, William Zappa.

ZONZON
MK2 DIFFUSION. Sept., 1998. French. (Laurent Bouhnik) Pascal Greggory, Gael Morel, Jamel Debbouze.

ZORBA AND LUCKY
CECCHI GOR. DEC., 1998. Italian. (Enzo D'Alo).

INTERNATIONAL FILM & TV FESTIVALS AND MARKETS

JANUARY

BRUSSELS INTERNATIONAL FILM FESTIVAL
(32) 2-227-3980. FAX: (32) 2-218-1860.
email: infoffb@netcity.be
GENERAL DELEGATE
Christrian Thomas

CINEMART
c/o International Film Festival Rotterdam, P.O. Box 21696, AR Rotterdam, 3001, The Netherlands. (31) 10-890-9090. FAX: (31) 10-890-9091. www.iffrotterdam.nl
email: cinemart@iffrotterdam.nl
COORDINATOR
Ido Abram

FESTIVAL INTERNATIONAL DE PROGRAMMES AUDIOVISUELS
(33) 1-4489-9999. FAX: (33) 1-4489-9960.
www.persa.wonadoo.fr/fipa email: fipa@wanadoo.fr
PRESIDENT
Marie-France Pisier

FILMFESTIVAL MAX OPHULS PREIS
Mainzertstr. 8, Saarbrucken, 66111, Germany. (49) 681-936-7421. FAX: (49) 681-936-7429.
www.saarbruecken.de/filmhaus.htm email: filmfestsb@aol.com
DIRECTOR
Christel Drawer

GOTEBORG FILM FESTIVAL
(46) 31-410-546. FAX: (46) 31-410-063.
www.goteborg.filmfestival.org email: goteborg@filmfestival.org
DIRECTOR
Gunnar Bergdahlm

INTERNATIONAL FILM FESTIVAL ROTTERDAM
(31) 10-890-9090. FAX: (31) 10-890-9091.
www.iffrotterdam.nl email: tiger@iffrotterdam.nl
DIRECTOR
Simon Field

KIDFILM/USA FILM FESTIVAL/ DALLAS
6116 N. Central Expwy., Ste. 105, Dallas, TX 75206. (214) 821-6300. FAX: (214) 821-6364. www.usafilmfestival.com

MIDEM MUSIC MARKET
c/o Reed Midem Organization Ltd., 125 Park Ave, 24th Flr., New York, NY 10017. (212) 370-7470. FAX: (212) 370-7471. c/o Reed Midem Organisation Ltd., Walmar House, 296 Regent St., London W1R 6AB, UK. (44) 207-528-0086. FAX: (44) 207-895-0949. www.midem.com

NATIONAL ASSOCIATION OF TV PROGRAM EXECUTIVES/ PROGRAM CONFERENCE & EXHIBITION (NATPE)
(310) 453-4440. FAX: (310) 453-5258. www.natpe.org

THE NEW YORK FESTIVALS
186 5th Ave., 7th Flr., New York, NY 10010. (914) 238-4481. FAX: (914) 238-5040. www.nyfests.com

NORTEL PALM SPRINGS INTERNATIONAL FILM FESTIVAL
(760) 322-2930. FAX: (760) 322-4087. www.psfilmfest.org
email: cprater@psfilmfest.org
EXECUTIVE DIRECTOR
Craig Prater (January)

PREMIERS PLANS-FESTIVAL D'ANGERS
(European Films Only)
(33)1-4271-5370. FAX: (33)1-4271-0111.
www.anjou.com/premiersplans
FESTIVAL DIRECTOR
Claude-Eric Poiroux

SOLOTHURN FILM FESTIVAL
(41) 32-625-8080. FAX: (41) 32-623-6410.
www.filmtage-solothurn.ch email: filmtage@cuenet.ch
DIRECTOR
Kummer Ivo

SUNDANCE FILM FESTIVAL
Park City, UT. (801) 328-FILM. FAX: (801) 575-5175.
www.sundance.org email: institute@sundance.org
V.P.
Nicole Guillemet

FEBRUARY

AMERICAN FILM MARKET (AFM)
(310) 446-1000. FAX: (310) 446-1600. www.afma.com
email: info@afma.com
E.V.P.
Jonathan Wolf

BERLIN INTERNATIONAL FILM FESTIVAL
(49) 30-2592-0202. FAX: (49) 30-2592-0299. www.berlinale.de
email: info@berlinale.de
EXECUTIVE DIRECTOR
Moritz Hadeln

CINEQUEST THE SAN JOSE FILM FESTIVAL
(408) 995-6305. FAX: (408) 995-5713. www.cinequest.org
email: sjfilmfest@aol.com
PROGRAMMING DIRECTOR
Mike Rabehl

CLERMONT FERRAND SHORT FILM FESTIVAL
(33) 47-391-6573. FAX: (33) 47-392-1193.
www.clermont-filmfest.com
CO-DIRECTOR
Roger Gonin

FANTASPORTO-OPORTO INTERNATIONAL FILM FESTIVAL
(351) 2-507-3880. FAX: (351) 2-550-8210.
www.caleida.pt/fantasporto email: fantas@caleida.pt
DIRECTOR
Mario Dorminsky

FILM ALTERNATIVE/BIG MUDDY FILM FESTIVAL
(618) 453-1482. FAX: (618) 453-2264.
email: bigmuddy@siu.edu

FILM SOCIETY OF MIAMI
(305) 377-3456. FAX: (305) 577-9768.
www.filmsocietyofmiami.com
FESTIVAL DIRECTOR
Nat Chediak

FRIENDS OF THE GERMAN FILM ARCHIVE & INTERNATIONAL FORUM OF NEW CINEMA
(49) 30-2548-9246. FAX: (49) 30-261-5025. www.fdk-berlin.de
email: forum@fdk-berlin.de
DIRECTOR
Ulrich Gregor

INFOCOMM JAPAN
11242 Waples Mill Rd.,Ste. 200, Fairfax, VA 22030. (703) 273-7200, (800) 659-7469. FAX: (81) 3-3241-4999.
www.infocomm.org. email: infocomm@jij.co.jp

MONTE CARLO TELEVISION FESTIVAL
(377) 9310-4060. FAX: (377) 9350-7014.

PORTLAND INTERNATIONAL FILM FESTIVAL
(503) 221-1156. FAX: (503) 294-0874. www.nwfilm.org
email: info@nwfilm.org

SMPTE ADVANCED MOTION IMAGING CONFERENCE
(914) 761-1100. FAX: (914) 761-3115. www.smpte.org
email: mktg@smpte.org
MARKETING COORDINATOR
Linda Alexander

UCLA ENTERTAINMENT SYMPOSIUM
(310) 825-0971, (310) 206-1121. FAX: (310) 825-1372.
www.law.ucla.edu

MARCH

ANN ARBOR FILM FESTIVAL
(734) 995-5356. FAX: (734) 995-5396. www.aafilmfest.org
email: vicki@honeyman.org
DIRECTOR
Vicki Honeyman

BRADFORD FILM FESTIVAL
(44) 127-420-3345. FAX: (44) 127-477-0217.
www.nmsi.ac.uk/nmpft email: w.lawrence@nmsi.ac.uk
HEAD OF CINEMA
Bill Lawrence

BRUSSELS INTERNATIONAL FESTIVAL OF FANTASY, THRILLER & SCIENCE-FICTION FILMS
(32) 2-201-1713. FAX: (32) 2-201-1469. www.bifff.org
email: peymey@skypro.be
CONTACT
Bozzo Freddy

CHICAGO LATINO CINEMA
(312) 431-1330. FAX: (312) 344-8030.

CINEMA DU REEL
(33) 1-4478-4421, (33) 1-4478-4516. FAX: (33) 1-4478-1224.
www.bpi.fr email: cinereel@bpi.fr
CONTACT
Suzette Glenadel

CINEMATECA URUGUAYA
(598) 408-2460. FAX: (598) 409-4572. www.cinemateca.org.uy
email: cinemuy@chasque.apc.org
DIRECTOR
Manuel Carril

CLEVELAND INTERNATIONAL FILM FESTIVAL
(216) 623-3456. FAX: (216) 623-0103. www.clevelandfilm.org
email: cfs@clevelandfilm.org
EXECUTIVE DIRECTOR
David W. Wittkowsky

FESTIVAL DE FILMS DE FRIBOURG
(41) 26-322-2232. FAX: (41) 26-322-7950. www.fiff.ch
email: info@fiff.ch
DIRECTOR
Knaebel Martial

LAON INTERNATIONAL FILM FESTIVAL FOR YOUNG PEOPLE
(33) 3-2379-3937. FAX: (33) 3-2379-3932.
email: festival.cinema.laon@wanadoo.fr
ADMINISTRATOR
Fabienne Pechard

LONDON LESBIAN & GAY FILM FESTIVAL
(44) 207-815-1323. FAX: (44) 207-633-0786.
email: carol.coombes@bfi.org.uk
EXECUTIVE DIRECTOR
Adrian Wootton

SAN FRANCISCO INTERNATIONAL ASIAN AMERICAN FILM FESTIVAL
(415) 863-0814. FAX: (415) 863-7428.
www.naatanet.org/festival email: festival@naatanet.org
FESTIVAL DIRECTOR
Brian Lau

SANTA BARBARA INTERNATIONAL FILM FESTIVAL
(805) 963-0023. FAX: (805) 962-2524. www.sbfilmfestival.com
email: info@sbfilmfestival.com
PROGRAMMER
Cynthia Felando

SANTA CLARITA INTERNATIONAL FILM FESTIVAL
(805) 257-3131. FAX: (805) 257-8989. www.sciff.org
email: pattemitch@col.com
EXECUTIVE DIRECTOR
Chris Shoemaker

SEDONA INTERNATIONAL FILM FESTIVAL WORKSHOP
P.O. Box 2515, Sedona, AZ 86339. (800) 780-ARTS.
(520) 282-0747. FAX: (520) 282-5358.
www.sedona.net/scp/festival email: scp@sedona.net

SHOWEST
(310) 657-7724. FAX: (310) 657-4758. www.showest.com
email: showest@aol.com
CHAIRMAN
Milton Moritz

U.S. INTERNATIONAL FILM & VIDEO FESTIVAL
(630) 834-7773, (630) 834-7774. FAX: (630) 834-5565.
www.filmfestawards.com
email: filmfestinfo@filmfestawards.com
CHAIRMAN
J. W. Anderson

VIEWPOINT 99, INTERNATIONAL DOCUMENTARY FILM FESTIVAL
(32) 9-225-0845. FAX: (32) 9-233-7522.
www.cinebel.com/studioskoop email: studio.skoop@net7.be
PROGRAMMER
Cis Bierinckx

THE WILLIAM S. PALEY TELEVISION FESTIVAL
(212) 621-6755. FAX: (212) 621-6765. www.mtv.org

WOMEN IN THE DIRECTOR'S CHAIR INTERNATIONAL FILM & VIDEO FESTIVAL
941 W. Lawrence Ave., Ste. 500, Chicago, IL 60640. (773) 907-0610. FAX: (773) 907-0381. www.widc.org email: widc@widc.org

APRIL

ASPEN SHORTSFEST
(970) 925-6882. FAX: (970) 925-1967. www.aspenfilm.org
email: shortsfest@aspenfilm.org
GENERAL MANAGER
Jennifer Swanson

BAC FILM & VIDEO FESTIVAL
(718) 625-0080. FAX: (718) 625-3294.
email: baca195@aol.com

DUBLIN FILM FESTIVAL
(353) 1-679-2937. FAX: (353) 1-679-2939. www.iol.ie/dff
email: dff@iol.ie

HONG KONG INTERNATIONAL FILM FESTIVAL (HKIFF)
(852) 2734-2903. FAX: (852) 2366-5206.

HUMBOLDT INTERNATIONAL FILM FESTIVAL
(707) 826-4113. FAX: (707) 826-4112.
www.humboldt.edu/~theatre/ filmfest.html
email: filmfest@axe.humboldt.edu
CONTACT
Marcelle Pecot

THE INTERNATIONAL COMMUNICATIONS FILM & VIDEO COMPETITION
(312) 425-9400. FAX: (312) 425-0944.
www.chicago.ddbn.com/filmfest email: filmfest@wwa.com
DIRECTOR
Michael Kutza

MIP-DOC
(44) 207-528-0086. FAX: (44) 207-895-0949.

MINNEAPOLIS/ST. PAUL INTERNATIONAL FILM FESTIVAL
(612) 627-4431, (612) 627-4432. FAX: (612) 627-4111.
www.ufilm.org email: filmsoc@tc.umn.edu
DIRECTOR
Al Milgrom

MIP-TV
c/o Reed Midem Organization Ltd., 125 Park Ave, 24th Flr., New York, NY 10017. (212) 370-7470. FAX: (212) 370-7471.
c/o Reed Midem Organisation Ltd., Walmar House, 296 Regent St., London W1R 6AB, UK. (44) 207-528-0086. FAX: (44) 207-895-0949. www.midem.com

NATIONAL ASSOCIATION OF BROADCASTERS
(202) 775-4970. FAX: (202) 429-5343. www.nab.org
email: register@nab.org
MARKETING ASSISTANT
Laura Cary

NEW ENGLAND FILM & VIDEO FESTIVAL
(Open to New England Residents Only)
(617) 536-1540. FAX: (617) 536-3576. www.bfvf.org
email: info@bfvf.org
FESTIVAL CO-DIRECTOR
Devon Damonte

PHILADELPHIA FESTIVAL OF WORLD CINEMA
(215) 895-6593. FAX: (215) 895-6562. www.libertynet.org/pfwc

SAN FRANCISCO INTERNATIONAL FILM FESTIVAL
(415) 929-5000. FAX: (415) 921-5032. www.sfiff.org
email: sfiff@sfiff.org
ARTISTIC DIRECTOR
Peter Scarlet

SINGAPORE INTERNATIONAL FILM FESTIVAL
(65) 738-7567. FAX: (65) 738-7578. www.filmfest.org.sg
email: filmfest@pacific.net.sg
FESTIVAL PROGRAMMER
Philip Cheah

TURIN INTERNATIONAL GAY & LESBIAN FILM FESTIVAL
(39) 011-534-888. FAX: (39) 011-535-796.
www.space.tin.it/cinema/gminerba
email: glfilmfest@assioma.com
DIRECTOR
Giovanni Minerba

USA FILM FESTIVAL/DALLAS
6116 N. Central Expwy., Ste., 105, Dallas, TX 75206. (214) 821-6300. FAX: (214) 821-6364. www.usafilmfestival.com

WORLDFEST-HOUSTON INTERNATIONAL FILM FESTIVAL
(713) 965-9955. FAX: (713) 965-9960. www.worldfest.org

YOSEMITE FILM FESTIVAL
40637 Hwy. 41, Oakhurst, CA 93644. (559) 683-4636.
www.yosemitefilm.com
CONTACT
Peggy Kukulus

MAY

FESTIVAL INTERNATIONAL DU FILM (CANNES)
(33) 1-4561-6605. FAX: (33) l4561-9494. (212) 832-8860. FAX: (212) 755-0629. email: gilles.jacob@festival-cannes.fr.
GENERAL DELEGATE
Gilles Jacob

MAUI FILM FESTIVAL
P.O. Box 669, Paia, HI 96779. (808) 579-9996. FAX: (808) 579-9552. www.mauifilmfestival.com
email: mauifilmfestival@mauifilmfestival.com
CONTACT
Donne Dawson

MUNICH INTERNATIONAL DOCUMENTARY FILM FESTIVAL
(49) 89-470-3237. FAX: (49) 89-470-6611.

PRO VISION INTERNATIONAL, INC.
213 Congress Ave., Ste., 282, Austin, TX 78701. (512) 476-8999. FAX: (512) 476-2441. email: pvi100@yahoo.com
CEO
Frances Jones

NATIONAL EDUCATIONAL MEDIA NETWORK
(510) 465-6885. Fax: (510) 465-2835. www.nemn.org
email: nemn@nemn.org
CONTACT
Cathy Phoenix

QUINZAINE DES REALISATEURS (DIRECTOR'S FORTNIGHT)
(Independent Section of the Cannes Film Festival)
(33) 1-4489-9999. FAX: (33) 1-4489-9960.
email: quinzain@club-internet.fr
GENERAL DELEGATE, DIRECTOR'S FORTNIGHT
Marie Pierre Mascia

SAGUARO FILM FESTIVAL
(602) 970-8711. FAX: (480) 945-3339.
www.extracheese.com/afs email: afs@extra_cheese.com
FESTIVAL DIRECTOR
Durrie Parks

SEATTLE INTERNATIONAL FILM FESTIVAL
(206) 464-5830. FAX: (206) 264-7919. www.seattlefilm.com
email: mail@seattlefilm.com
FESTIVAL DIRECTOR
Darryl Macdonald

YORKTON SHORT FILM & VIDEO FESTIVAL
(306) 782-7077. FAX: (306) 782-1550.
www.yorktonshortfilm.org email: info@yorktonshortfilm.org

JUNE

ADRIATICOCINEMA
(39) 0541-26-399. FAX: (39) 0541-24-227.
email: adriaticocinema@comune.rimini.it

ANNECY INTERNATIONAL ANIMATED FILM FESTIVAL
(33) 4-5010-0900. FAX. (33) 4-5010-0970. www.annecy.org
email: info@annecy.org
PRESIDENT
Dominique Puthod

BANFF TELEVISION FESTIVAL
(403) 678-9260. FAX: (403) 678-9269. www.banfftvfest.com
email: info@banfftvfest.com
PRESIDENT & CEO
Pat Ferris

BITE THE MANGO FILM FESTIVAL
(44) 127-420-3300. FAX: (44) 127-477-0217.
www.bitethemango.ac.uk email: filmfest@nmsi.ac.uk
HEAD OF CINEMA
Bill Lawrence

BRADFORD ANIMATION FESTIVAL
c/o National Museum of Photography, Film & Television, Pictureville Cinema, Bradford, BD1 1NQ, England. (44) 127-420-3345. FAX: (44) 127-477-0217. www.nmsi.ac.uk
email: filmfest@nmsi.ac.uk
HEAD OF CINEMA
Bill Larwence

BUREAU OF THE INTERNATIONAL FILM FESTIVALS/ "FESTIVAL OF FESTIVALS"
(812) 237-0304. FAX: (812) 394-5870.
DIRECTOR
Alexander Momontov

CHICAGO ALT.FILM FILM FESTIVAL
3430 N. Lake Shore Dr., Ste. 19N, Chicago, IL 60657. (773) 525-4559. FAX: (773) 327-8669.
FOUNDER & DIRECTOR
Dennis Neal Vaughn

CINEMA EXPO INTERNATIONAL
(212) 246-6460. FAX: (212) 265-6428. www.cinemaexpo.com
email: sunshine@maestro.com
CONVENTION MANAGER
Andrew Sunshine

CINEVISION INTERNATIONAL FILM FESTIVAL
(43) 512-580-723. FAX: (43) 512-581-762.
www.pirolkultur.at/cinema

FLORIDA FILM FESTIVAL
(407) 629-1088. FAX: (407) 629-6870.
www.floridafilmfestival.com email: filmfest@gate.net
DIRECTOR OF PROGRAMMING
Matthew Curtis

HONG KONG INTERNATIONAL FILM & TV MARKET (FILMART 2000)
(852) 2584-4333. FAX: (852) 2824-0249.
www.hkfilmart.tdc.org.hk email: hktdc@tdc.org.hk
MANAGER
Johnson Yip

THE HUDSON VALLEY FILM FESTIVAL
40 Garden St., Poughkeepsie, NY 12601. (914) 473-0318. FAX: (914) 473-0082. www.sandbook.com/hvfo
email: hvfo@vh.net
FESTIVAL DIRECTOR
Aslihan Coker

INDEPENDENT FEATURE PROJECT
104 W. 29th St., 12th Flr., New York, NY 10001. (212) 465-8200. FAX: (212) 465-8525. www.ifp.org email: ifpny@ifp.org

INFOCOMM INTERNATIONAL
11242 Waples Mill Rd., Ste. 200, Fairfax, VA 22030. (703) 273-7200. FAX: (703) 278-8082. www.infocomm.org
CONTACT
Bob Brown

MARIN COUNTY NATIONAL SHORT FILM FESTIVAL
(415) 499-6400. FAX: (415) 499-3700.
MANAGER
Jim Farley

MUNICH FILM FESTIVAL
(49) 89-381-9040. FAX: (49) 89-381-9047.
CONTACT
Eberhard Huwff

SAN FRANCISCO INTERNATIONAL LESBIAN & GAY FILM FESTIVAL
(415) 703-8650. FAX: (415) 861-1404. www.frameline.org
email: info@frameline.org
CONTACT
Michael Lumpkin

SHOWBIZ WEST EXPO REED EXHIBITION COMPANIES
(203) 840-5556, (203) 840-5688. FAX: (203) 840-9556, (203) 840-9688.

SYDNEY FILM FESTIVAL
(61) 2-9660-3844. FAX: (61) 2-9692-8793.
www.sydfilm-fest.com.au email: info@sydfilm-fest.com.au

JULY

BRISBANE INTERNATIONAL FILM FESTIVAL
c/o Pacific Film & Television Commission, III George St.,Level 15, Brisbane, Queensland 4000, Australia. (61) 7-3220-0333. FAX: (61) 7-3220-0400. www.pftc.com.au
EXECUTIVE ASSISTANT
Megan Rowe

JUST FOR LAUGHS! THE MONTREAL INTERNATIONAL COMEDY FESTIVAL
(514) 845-3155. FAX: (514) 845-4140. www.hahaha.com

PALM SPRINGS INTERNATIONAL SHORT FILM FESTIVAL
(760) 322-2930. FAX: (760) 322-4087. www.psfilmfest.org
email: cprater@psfilmfest.org
EXECUTIVE DIRECTOR
Craig Prater

WINE COUNTRY FILM FESTIVAL
(707) 996-2536. FAX: (707) 996-6964.
www.winecountryfilmfest.com email: wcfilmfest@aol.com
DIRECTOR
Stephen Ashton

AUGUST

MONTREAL WORLD FILM FESTIVAL
(514) 848-3883. FAX: (514) 848-3886.
www.ffm-montreal.org

ODENSE INTERNATIONAL FILM FESTIVAL
(45) 66-131-372. FAX: (45) 65-914-318. www.filmfestival.dk
email: filmfestival@post.odkomm.dk

SEPTEMBER

A.J. PRODUCTIONS
(New York Independent Film Festival)
1335 N. La Brea Ave.,Ste. 2197, Hollywood, CA 90028. (323) 876-0975. FAX: (323) 876-0975.
www.hollywoodindependents.com email: jaa@simplyweb.net
PROGRAMMING DIRECTOR
John Greenlow

ASPEN FILMFEST
(970) 925-6882. FAX: (970) 925-1967. www.aspenfilm.org
email: filmfest@aspenfilm.org
GENERAL MANAGER
Jennifer Swunson

FILMMAKERS SYMPOSIUM
(732) 528-6660. Direct line: (800) 222-7719.
email: filmrose@aol.com
EXECUTIVE DIRECTOR
Chuck Rose

HOLLYWOOD INDEPENDENT FILM FESTIVAL
c/o Hollywood Independents, 1335 N. La Brea Ave., Ste. 2197, Hollywood, CA 90028. (323) 876-0975. FAX: (323) 876-0975.
www.hollywoodindependents.com email: jaa@simplyweb.net
PRESIDENT
Jorge Ameer

INDEPENDENT FEATURE FILM MARKET
(212) 465-8200. FAX: (212) 465-8525. www.ifp.org

INFOCOMM ASIA
(Fall 2001, takes place every 2 years)
11242 Waples Mill Rd., Ste. 200 Fairfax, VA 22030.
(703) 273-7200, (800) 659-7469. FAX: (703) 273-5924.
www.infocomm.org

INFOCOMM EUROPE AT PHOTOKINA
(703) 273-7200, (800) 659-7469. FAX: (703) 273-5924.
www.infocomm.org
CONTACT
Bob Brown

L.A. INTERNATIONAL SHORT FILM FESTIVAL
(213) 427-8016. www.lashortsfest.com
email: info@lashortsfest.com
FOUNDER & FESTIVAL DIRECTOR
Robert Arentz

LAGUNA BEACH FILM FESTIVAL
P.O. Box 4444, Laguna Beach, CA 92652. (949) 494-1313.
www.lagunafilmfestival.org email: info@lagunafilmfestival.org
FESTIVAL CHAIRMAN
John Fazio

NEW YORK FILM FESTIVAL
THE FILM SOCIETY OF LINCOLN CENTER
(212) 875-5638. FAX: (212) 875-5636. www.filmlinc.com
email: sbensman@filmlinc.com

POST/LA EXPO
(323) 654-6530. FAX: (323) 654-2954. www.postlaexpo.com

TELLURIDE FILM FESTIVAL
(603) 433-9202. FAX: (603) 433-9206.
www.telluridefilmfestival.com email: Tellufilm@aol.com
CONTACT
Stella Pence

TEMECULA VALLEY INTERNATIONAL FILM FESTIVAL
(909) 699-6267. FAX: (909) 308-1414. www.tviff.com
FESTIVAL DIRECTOR
Jo Moulton

TORONTO INTERNATIONAL FILM FESTIVAL
(416) 967-7371. FAX: (416) 967-9477. www.bell.ca/filmfest

VANCOUVER INTERNATIONAL FILM FESTIVAL
(604) 685-0260. FAX: (604) 688-8221. www.viff.org
email: viff@viff.org
FESTIVAL DIRECTOR
Alan Franey

OCTOBER

AFI/LOS ANGELES INTERNATIONAL FILM FESTIVAL
(323) 856-7707. FAX: (323) 462-4049. www.afifest.com
email: afifest@afionline.org

CHICAGO INTERNATIONAL CHILDREN'S FILM FESTIVAL
(773) 281-9075. FAX: (773) 929-5437. www.facets.org
email: kidsfesf@facets.org
FESTIVAL DIRECTOR
Rebekah Cowing

CHICAGO INTERNATIONAL FILM FESTIVAL
(312) 425-9400. FAX: (312) 425-0944.
www.chicago.ddbn.com/filmfest email: filmfest@com
FOUNDER & ARTISTIC DIRECTOR
Michael Kutza

DENVER INTERNATIONAL FILM FESTIVAL
(303) 595-3456. FAX: (303) 595-0956. www.denverfilm.org
email: dfs@denverfilm.org
DIRECTOR
Ron Henderson

DUBLIN THEATRE FESTIVAL
(353) 1-677-8439. FAX: (353) 1-679-7709.
www.iftn.ie/dublinfestival emall: dubfest@iol.ie
DIRECTOR
Fergus Linehan

FILMFESTIVAL MANNHEIM- HEIDELBERG
Collini Center Galerye, Mannheim, 68161, Germany. (49) 621-102-943. FAX: (49) 621-291-564.

FORT LAUDERDALE INTERNATIONAL FILM FESTIVAL
(954) 760-9898. FAX: (954) 760-9099.
www.ftlaudfilmfestival.com email: brofilm@aol.com
CONTACT
Gregory Von Hausch

THE HAMPTONS INTERNATIONAL FILM FESTIVAL
(516) 324-4600. FAX: (516) 324-5116. www.hamptonsfest.org
EXECUTIVE DIRECTOR
Denise Kasell

HEARTLAND FILM FESTIVAL
(317) 464-9405. FAX: (317) 635-4201.
www.heartlandfilmfest.org email: hff@pop.iquest.net
ARTISTIC DIRECTOR
Jeff Sparks

HOT SPRINGS DOCUMENTARY FILM FESTIVAL
(501) 321-4747. FAX: (501) 321-0211. www.DocuFilmInst.org
email: hsdff@docufilminst.org
CONTACT
Gretchen Taylor

INDEPENDENT FILMMAKERS COMPETITION
(323) 737-3292. FAX: (323) 737-2842. www.wsbrec.org

MILL VALLEY FILM FESTIVAL
THE FILM INSTITUTE OF NORTHERN CALIFORNIA
(415) 383-5256. FAX: (415) 383-8606. www.finc.org
email: finc@well.com
EXECUTIVE DIRECTOR
Mark Fishkin

MIPCOM
c/o Reed Midem Organization Ltd., 125 Park Ave, 24th Flr., New York, NY 10017. (212) 370-7470. FAX: (212) 370-7471.
c/o Reed Midem Organisation Ltd., Walmar House, 296 Regent St., London W1R 6AB, UK. (44) 207-528-0086. FAX: (44) 207-895-0949. www.midem.com

MIPCOM JR.
c/o Reed Midem Organization Ltd., 125 Park Ave, 24th Flr., New York, NY 10017. (212) 370-7470. FAX: (212) 370-7471.
c/o Reed Midem Organisation Ltd., Walmar House, 296 Regent St., London W1R 6AB, UK. (44) 207-528-0086. FAX: (44) 207-895-0949. www.midem.com

THE MURPHY'S CORK FILM FESTIVAL
(353) 21-271-711. FAX: (353) 21-275-945.
www.corkfilmfest.org email: ciff@indigo.ie
FESTIVAL DIRECTOR
Mick Hannigan

NEW ORLEANS FILM & VIDEO FESTIVAL
225 Baronne St., Ste. 1712, New Orleans, LA 70112. (504) 523-3818. FAX: (504) 529-2430.www.neworleansfilmfest.com
email: neworleansfilmfest@worldnet.att.net
EXECUTIVE DIRECTOR
Carol Gniady

SHOWBIZ EAST EXPO REED EXHIBITION COMPANIES
383 Main Ave., Norwalk, CT 06851. (203) 840-5556. FAX: (203) 840-9556.
CONTACT
Steven Kalman

SHOWEAST
(212) 246-6460. FAX: (212) 265-6428. www.showeast.com
email: sunshine@maestro.com
CONVENTION MANAGER
Mitch Neuhauser

VERMONT INTERNATIONAL FILM FESTIVAL
(802) 660-2600. FAX: (802) 860-9555. www.vtiff.org
email: viff@together.net
EVENTS COORDINATOR
Jennie Bedusa

YAMAGATA INTL. DOCUMENTARY FILM FESTIVAL
(81) 3-3266-9704. FAX: (81) 3-3266-9700.
www.city.yamagata.yamagata.jp/yidff
DIRECTOR
Yano Kazuyuki

NOVEMBER

BRITISH FILM FESTIVAL
2775 Market St.,Ste. 303, San Francisco, CA 94114-1825.
(415) 437-6789. FAX: (415) 487-9750.
www.grin.net/~britfilms email: britfilms@grin.net
MANAGING DIRECTOR
Simon Overton

THE CHICAGO LESBIAN & GAY INTERNATIONAL FILM FESTIVAL
(773) 293-1447. FAX: (773) 293-0575.
www.chicagofilmmakers.org/reeling
email: reeling@chicagofilmmakers.org
EXECUTIVE DIRECTOR
Brenda Webb

HAWAII INTERNATIONAL FILM FESTIVAL
(808) 528-3456. FAX: (808) 528-1410. www.hiff.org
email: hiffinfo@hiff.org
FESTIVAL DIRECTOR & DIRECTOR OF PROGRAMMING
Christian Gaines

LONDON FILM FESTIVAL
(44) 207-815-1323. FAX: (44) 207-633-0786.
email: sarahlutton@bfi.org.uk
FESTIVAL DIRECTOR
Adrian Wootton

NORTHWEST FILM & VIDEO FESTIVAL
(503) 221-1156. FAX: (503) 294-0874. www.nwfilm.org
email: info@nwfilm.org

THE OJAI FILM SOCIETY
10942 Encino Dr., Oak View, CA 93022. (805) 649-4000.
www.ojai.net/film email: stevo@ix.netcom.com
FESTIVAL CO-CHAIR & ARTISTIC DIRECTOR
Steve Grumette

WORLDFEST-FLAGSTAFF INTERNATIONAL FILM FESTIVAL
2700 Post Oak Blvd., Ste. 1798, Houston, TX 77056. (713) 965-9955. FAX: (713) 965-9960. www.worldfest.org

DECEMBER

CINE VEGAS INTERNATIONAL FILM FESTIVAL
c/o Blo Towers Plaza, 3745 Las Vegas Blvd., Ste. 204, Las Vegas, NV 89109. (704) 477-7530. FAX: (704) 477-7533.
www.cinevegas.com email: cinevegas@aol.com
FESTIVAL COORDINATOR
Amy Carrelli

CINEASIA
(212) 246-6460. FAX: (212) 265-6428. www.cineasia.com
email: sunshine@maestro.com

Production Companies

Histories of the Motion Picture Studios 636

Motion Picture Producers & Distributors 645

Non-Theatrical Producers & Distributors 704

HISTORIES OF THE MAJOR MOTION PICTURE STUDIOS

COLUMBIA PICTURES (SONY PICTURES ENTERTAINMENT, INC.)

Columbia Pictures can trace its beginnings to the CBC Films Sales Co., formed in 1920 by Harry Cohn, Jack Cohn and Joe Brandt, all of whom had previously worked together at Universal Studios. CBC was set up to make a series of shorts known as Screen Snapshots, showing the off-screen activities of movie stars to publicize their current pictures. Soon the new company expanded to produce westerns and other comedy shorts and in 1922 produced its first feature, "More To Be Pitied Than Scorned." In 1924, the owners renamed their company Columbia Pictures.

Two years later, Columbia had advanced to the point where it began to open film exchanges of its own instead of selling films outright to theatres for a flat fee and established a studio with two stages and a small office building. Sam Briskin was hired as general manager. In 1929, it produced its first all-talking feature, "The Donovan Affair." This low-budget murder mystery was directed by Frank Capra. By this time, the company had opened a home office in New York where Jack Cohn functioned as vice president and treasurer, while Harry ran the production operation on the West Coast.

In 1931, Brandt sold his interest in Columbia and retired. The next year, Harry Cohn assumed the title of president, while retaining his post as production chief. In 1935, Columbia purchased a 40-acre ranch in Burbank for location filming (later expanded to 80 acres). The company's first big artistic success was in 1934 with Capra's "It Happened One Night," which was not only the top box office draw of 1934, but a winner of five major Academy Awards including Best Picture. Capra followed this with such hits as "Mr. Deeds Goes to Town" (1936), "Lost Horizon" (1937), "You Can't Take It With You" (1938) and "Mr. Smith Goes to Washington" (1939).

Throughout the 40s Columbia prospered and by the end of the decade, it could claim to be one of the industry's major studios. Unlike the other studios, Columbia did not own any theatres and was not affected by the industry's Consent Decrees which forced those studios to divest themselves of their exhibition properties. Commercial hits of the period included "Gilda" (1946), "The Jolson Story" (1946) and "Jolson Sings Again" (1949).

In 1951, Columbia diversified into television by forming Screen Gems, a wholly owned subsidiary set up to make programs and commercials. Founder Harry Cohn died in 1958. The successor management—headed by veterans of the company, Abe Schneider and Leo Jaffe—made major investments in British film production and released "Lawrence of Arabia" (1962), "A Man for All Seasons" (1966) and the musical "Oliver!" (1968). Other hits of the 60's were "Guess Who's Coming to Dinner" (1967) and "To Sir With Love" (1967). The success of these and others was attributable to Mike Frankovich, who became production head in 1954 and was succeeded by Stanley Schneider, whose father, Abe, headed the company at the time. Another son of Abe, Bert, and Bob Rafelson co-produced "Easy Rider" in 1969, one of the biggest hits in Columbia's history.

At the beginning of the 70s, Herbert Allen Jr., a former Wall Street banker, bought control of Columbia and took over as president and CEO. Allen brought in new management headed by Alan Hirschfield and David Begelman, who produced such hits as "Shampoo" (1975) and "Close Encounters of the Third Kind" (1977). Begelman's successor as production chief was Frank Price (who had previously headed Universal Television) and under his regime the company produced such successful films as "Kramer vs. Kramer" (1979), "Tootsie" (1982) and "Ghostbusters" (1984). In 1982, Columbia was purchased by the Coca-Cola Company. Under its aegis Columbia, Home Box Office and CBS, Inc. joined forces to finance a new production company, TriStar Pictures. At the start, it was emphasized that the new company would be separate from Columbia, with TriStar using Columbia's distribution. Price departed in 1985 and in 1986 David Puttnam, an independent British producer, was signed as chairman. Succeeding him was Dawn Steel, who was named president. In 1989, TriStar was made a unit of Columbia Pictures with Jeff Sagansky, president of TriStar, reporting to Ms. Steel.

Columbia Pictures Entertainment was formed in 1987 by Coca-Cola to restructure its entertainment business. CPE consisted of two film production companies: Columbia Pictures and TriStar Pictures; two television arms: Columbia Pictures Television, Merv Griffin Enterprises and Loews Theatre Management Corp.

In September 1989, Columbia Pictures Entertainment was purchased by the Sony Corporation of Japan. Sony previously acquired CBS Records in 1987. Producers Jon Peters and Peter Guber were brought in as co-chairmen. In 1991, Peters resigned from his position as co-chairman, the company was renamed Sony Pictures Entertainment, Inc. and Mark Canton left Warner Bros. to become the new chairman of Columbia Pictures. In June 1994, Fred Bernstein was put in charge of the motion picture units at Columbia Pictures, TriStar Pictures, Sony Pictures Classics and Triumph Releasing Corporation. Later that summer, the marketing and distribution arms of these divisions were consolidated under the direction of Sid Ganis as president. In September 1994, Peter Guber announced his resignation as Sony chairman, with Alan J. Levine named as his successor. Sony was forced to write off $3.2 billion in 1995, but the Japanese parent company vowed to maintain its Hollywood commitment. In September of 1996, Canton was removed as chairman of Columbia Pictures, followed in October of that year by the resignation of Levine, who was replaced by John Calley, formerly of MGM/UA. Mr. Canton's removal was accompanied by that of Lisa Henson and Barry Josephson, Columbia Pictures presidents; Marc Platt was ousted as was his successor Robert Cooper, TriStar Pictures president along with Stacey Snider, Tristar production president, Alan Levine, Sony Pictures chairman, and Fred Bernstein, Columbia TriStar president. This was a rather strange turn of events, as the deposed team was responsible for Sony's record $1.3 billion in domestic box office for 1997, having developed such movies as "Jerry Maguire," "Anaconda," "The Fifth Element" and "My Best Friend's Wedding."

Calley reorganized and restructured Sony Pictures Entertainment, closing the TriStar Motion Picture Group and bringing the remaining executives over to Columbia Pictures which became Sony Pictures Entertainment's principal production arm. SPE also resurrected a past label, Screen Gems, to make films in the $4-5 million range.

In 1998, Jeff Sagansky left Columbia to join the newest network, Pax TV. Sony Pictures Classics, the art film distributor arm of Sony Corp., despite a profitable 1998, came under criticism for its co-presidents' insistence on earning a profit on each of their releases and failing to take on more commercial fare. Although its revenues for the first seven months of 1998, of $20 million, were twice its 1997 grosses, SPC was surpassed in 1995 by Miramax, a younger arthouse, but one that has taken more financial risks.

After a two-year legal battle, Sony lost its claim to the movie rights for the lucrative James Bond franchise. In a settlement with MGM, Sony gave up its claim for a meager $5 million.

In early 1999, Sony Pictures Entertainment signed a groundbreaking deal with 30 screenwriters stating that in exchange for one film each over the next four years, each writer will receive up-front fees as well as 2% of gross receipts.

On October 3, 1999, Sony bade a final farewell to its co-founder, Akio Morita who died at the age of 78.

Currently, Sony Pictures Entertainment, still helmed by Chairman & CEO John Calley, includes the unified production studio, Columbia Pictures, Screen Gems, Sony Pictures Classics (specializing in arthouse films), producers of third-party product (e.g., Phoenix, Centropolis, Jim Henson Productions), and global motion picture production operations. SPE's releasing arms include Sony Pictures Releasing (U.S.) and Columbia TriStar Film Distributors International

In 2000, Sony continued to struggle, releasing several expensive features that generated little box office interest. What Planet Are You From? cost $50 million and grossed only $6.5 million, while I Dreamed of Africa cost $40 million and brought in $6.5 million. Even the highly anticipated summer films, The Patriot and Hollow Man underperformed at the box office, barely breaking even. John Calley, now 70, has been able to slow the outrageous spending and losses that once plagued the studio but has yet to improve market share (currently 9%) or produce the blockbusters needed to return Sony to its former prominence.

In spite of Monday morning box office woes, Sony Pictures Entertainment has increased overall sales 55% since Calley took over in 1996, in large part due to its pay-tv, video and tv content businesses.

RECENT COLUMBIA/SPE RELEASES

1990:	Awakenings, Misery, Postcards From the Edge.
1991:	Boyz N the Hood, City Slickers, The Prince of Tides.
1992:	Bram Stoker's Dracula, A League of Their Own, A River Runs Through It.
1993:	In the Line of Fire, Last Action Hero, The Remains of the Day.
1994:	Little Women, The Shawshank Redemption, Wolf.
1995:	The Net, Sense and Sensibility.
1996:	The Cable Guy, Donnie Brasco, The Fan, Jerry Maguire.
1997:	Air Force One, Anaconda, The Devil's Own, The Fifth Element, Men in Black.
1998:	Can't Hardly Wait, I Know What You Did Last Night, My Giant, Wild Things.
1999:	Big Daddy, Muppets From Space, Blue Streak, Hanging Up, Girl Interrupted.
2000:	The Patriot, Hollow Man, Random Hearts, 28 Days, I Dreamed of Africa, What Planet Are You From?

RECENT SONY PICTURES CLASSICS RELEASES

1995:	Shanghai Triad, Safe, Celluloid Closet, Crumb.
1996:	Beautiful Thing, Welcome To the Dollhouse, The Flower of My Secret.
1997:	In the Company of Men, The Myth of Fingerprints, Ma Vie En Rose.
1998:	The Governess, The Opposite of Sex, Henry Fool.
1999:	Run Lola Run, The Dreamlife of Angels, The Winslow Boy, Sweet and Lowdown.
2000:	Crouching Tiger Hidden Dragon, Bossa Nova, Trixie, Groove, Pollock.

THE WALT DISNEY COMPANY

In 1923, Walt Disney set up an animation studio with his brother Roy. Five years later, he introduced his most famous creation, Mickey Mouse, in a cartoon called "Steamboat Willie." It was an immediate hit and Disney began his series of Silly Symphony cartoons, based on musical themes, the first of which was called "The Skeleton Dance." From 1929 through 1931, Disney distributed his products through Columbia Pictures. In 1932, distribution was through United Artists with about 20 cartoons per year—half of them featuring Mickey Mouse and the others in the Silly Symphony series. Production cost of the cartoons was about $50,000 each. UA paid Disney 60% of rentals received from exhibitors, and his gross income at the time was in the neighborhood of one and a half million dollars per year.

Disney's contract with UA expired in 1937. He switched over to RKO, for whom he produced his first feature-length cartoon, "Snow White and the Seven Dwarfs" followed by "Pinnochio" (1940), "Fantasia" (1940), "Dumbo" (1941), "Bambi" (1942), "Cinderella" (1950) and "Peter Pan" (1953), all released by RKO.

RKO's financial troubles, which led to its demise in 1958, caused Walt Disney Productions to break with it in 1953 and form its own national distribution unit, Buena Vista. Buena Vista's first release was "The Living Desert" (1953), winner of the Academy Award for feature documentary and an outgrowth of the True-Life Adventure shorts started in 1948. Disneyland in Anaheim, California, opened in 1955.

Rising costs in the production of animation films caused Disney to concentrate on live-action features, such as "20,000 Leagues Under the Sea" (1954) which took in over $11 million in domestic rentals, and "Mary Poppins" (1964) which made more than $45 million.

Walt Disney died in 1966. Roy Disney's death in 1971 left no surviving Disney family members at the studio's helm. Walt Disney World in Central Florida (near Orlando) opened in 1971. In 1983, Ron Miller, Walt's son-in-law, was made chief executive and started Touchstone Pictures, a subsidiary designed to make adult-oriented films. In 1984, Touchstone delivered "Splash." In the same year, a drive for new leadership was spearheaded by Roy Disney, son of Walt's brother of the same name. Frank Wells, former vice chairman of Warner Bros. and Michael Eisner, president of Paramount, were hired in 1984 with Eisner as chairman, Wells as president and Disney serving as vice chairman. Early in 1990, the Company announced a massive, ten-year expansion agenda that would add hundreds of new rides and shows to its existing theme parks, and provide for the building of additional attractions in Southern California and Florida. Euro-Disneyland opened near Paris in 1992.

Disney continued to do well in its motion picture division with "Pretty Woman," "Dick Tracy" and new division Hollywood Pictures' "Arachnophobia" and "The Hand That Rocks the Cradle." The 1991 animated feature "Beauty and the Beast" took in over $145 million in the U.S., and became the first animated feature nominated for Best Picture. This success was followed by 1992's "Aladdin" which became the first Disney release to gross more than $200 million in the U.S. In 1993, Disney purchased the highly successful independent distributor Miramax, which would continue to operate as a separate company.

1994 saw the death of Frank Wells. "The Lion King" became the highest grossing film in Disney history. Jeffrey Katzenberg, crucial to the revitalization of the company's animation department, resigned as chairman to join Steven Spielberg and David Geffen in their own entertainment company, DreamWorks SKG. David Hoberman was named president of Disney's motion picture divisions. However, his departure after eight months threw the weight of responsibilities over to new chairman of the motion picture group, Joe Roth. The year ended with Disney becoming the first distributor to achieve annual box office revenues of over $1 billion.

The big entertainment news of 1995 was the company's $19 billion purchase of Capital Cities/ABC. Michael Eisner named Creative Artists Agency chairman Michael Ovitz as president of the Walt Disney Company. Ovitz was removed as chairman in November of 1996 (with a severance package rumored to be in excess of $90 million, much to the ire of Disney stock-holders.)

Three years later, the dispute between Jeffrey Katzenberg, the former Disney animation chairman, and Michael Eisner, was still bubbling. Katzenberg was allegedly promised 2% share of revenues from projects begun while still at Disney. Mr. Eisner disputed the claim. In November of 1997, Disney attorneys admitted that Katzenberg was owed the money under terms of his employment contract. The pact was thrown out of court, and handed over to a "rent-a-judge." In light of Mr. Ovitz's settlement in 1996, many speculated that Disney would make a preemptive settlement offer rather than risk the rent-a-judge's decision for an amount that would upset Disney stockholders. Mr. Katzenberg's lawsuit was for $500 million.

Miramax's past two years were good ones, with the Oscar wins in 1997 for "The English Patient" and for "Good Will Hunting" a year later. Dimension also fared well in 1998, increasing its revenue from $14 million in 1993, to $120 million in 1998. In 1997, Dimension made up 45% of Miramax's total grosses with only 3 releases: "Scream 2," "Operation Condor," and "Mimic." Despite its success, Miramax lost some of its top executives in 1997, and chairmen Bob and Harvey Weinstein had to entrust their key personnel with additional duties. President Richard Sands was promoted to chairman, making him the only executive to have the title besides the Weinsteins.

Miramax scored again in 1998 with "Shakespeare in Love" which was a boxoffice and critical success.

In July of 1999, Disney agreed to settle the suit brought by its former studio chief, Jeffrey Katzenberg, who claimed over $500 million in damages for bonuses he said he was owed. Leaks about the settlement put the figure paid to Katzenberg between $100 million to close to $250 million.

Other financial woes are plaguing the company. In spite of box office gross exceeding $500 million in the summers of 1998 and 1999, Disney as a whole has been in a two year slump, during which earnings have dropped 21% through the fiscal third quarter of 1999 (ending June 30) and shares have lost an annual average of 1.3%. Eisner has been struggling ever since company president Frank Wells died in a helicopter crash in 1994. Eisner has yet to choose a second-in-command from the ranks of Disney's talented executives. However the motion picture division is one of Disney's most profitable businesses with 1999 box office revenue up by $150 million.

As a result of the drop in revenue, Eisner initiated a review of capital spending. In spite of the studio's profitability, cuts will be widespread. Eisner plans to slash development deals and offload hundreds of millions of dollars in costs, including staff and production overhead at Miramax and Disney.

Personnel changes at Disney in 1999 included Peter Schneider's promotion to President of Walt Disney Pictures and Robert Iger's selection to head up the newly streamlined operations of Buena Vista International.

In 2000, Peter Schneider began to make his presence felt. Schneider was one of the executives responsible for "Mulan," "Tarzan," "The Lion King" and "Beauty & The Beast" and now wants to make Disney even more family friendly with dramas such as "Disney's The Kid" and "Remember the Titans." Schneider is also keen to make the most of Disney's franchises, encouraging synergy among the divisions, as evidenced by the upcoming films "Pirates of the Caribbean" and "Country Bears," based on Disneyland rides; "Recess" and "The Tigger Movie" which derive from animated series and the stage production of "The Lion King." Disney will continue to produce adult-oriented fare with Jerry Bruckheimer and others, but recognizes that the road to profit is through multiple-division branding and family product.

Also in 2000, Nina Jacobsen became sole president of the Buena Vista Motion Picture Group after Todd Garner left to join Joe Roth and Rob Moore at Revolution.

RECENT DISNEY RELEASES

1990:	Arachnophobia, Dick Tracy, Pretty Woman.
1991:	Beauty and the Beast, Billy Bathgate, Father of the Bride.
1992:	Aladdin, The Mighty Ducks, Sister Act.
1993:	Cool Runnings, The Nightmare Before Christmas, Tombstone, What's Love Got to Do With It.
1994:	Ed Wood, The Lion King, The Santa Clause, When a Man Loves a Woman.
1995:	Crimson Tide, Pocahontas, Toy Story.
1996:	The Hunchback of Notre Dame, Ransom, The Rock.
1997:	ConAir, George of the Jungle, Hercules, Jungle 2 Jungle
1998:	Flubber, Starship Troopers, George of the Jungle, Mr. Magoo.
1999:	Tarzan, Inspector Gadget, The Sixth Sense, The Insider, Toy Story 2.
2000:	Dinosaur, Keeping the Faith Disney's The Kid, Coyote Ugly, Gone in Sixty Seconds, Unbreakable.

RECENT MIRAMAX/DIMENSION RELEASES

1992:	Reservoir Dogs.
1993:	Farewell My Concubine, Like Water for Chocolate.
1994:	Bullets Over Broadway, The Crow, Pulp Fiction.
1995:	Muriel's Wedding, The Postman.
1996:	The English Patient, Scream, Shine, Sling Blade, Trainspotting.
1997:	Copland, Mimic, She's So Lovely, The House of Yes, Wings of the Dove, Scream 2.
1998:	Good Will Hunting, Jackie Brown.
1999:	An Ideal Husband, Music of the Heart, Princess Mononoke, She's All That, The Faculty, In Too Deep.
2000:	Down to You, The Yards, Scary Movie, Scream 3.

DREAMWORKS SKG

Dreamworks SKG was founded in 1994 by director Steven Spielberg, former Disney executive Jeffrey Katzenberg, and record mogul David Geffen. Dreamworks started out with a few dreamy deals including a 10-year, $1 billion HBO licensing agreement with HBO; a $100 million programming partnership with ABC; a $50 million animation studio co-founded with Silicon Graphics; and a $30 million joint venture with Microsoft to produce interactive software. The first release for the infant studio was "The Peacemaker" in September 1997, starring George Clooney. In a surprise move, Dreamworks devised a new distribution paradigm, opting for self-distribution, rather than relying on one of the major studios' distribution arms, and by attempting to book the film theatre-by-theatre in order to optimize grosses. The fledgling company managed to silence many of its critics, with the success of its movie releases. "Antz," proved the highest grossing non-Disney animation film, and the first post-Disney animation film for Mr. Katzenberg. The summer of 1998 brought "Deep Impact" and "Saving Private Ryan" which were the company's first real blockbusters. The company had more of a problem dealing with the development of their new headquarters at Playa Vista, near L.A. Int'l. Airport. The project, announced in December 1995, went stale when Dreamworks began having disagreements with Playa Capital, the owners of the site since 1997. Playa Capital wanted to share some of the proposed studio lot, but Dreamworks opposed the idea. In October 1998, the two reached an agreement in which Playa Capital surrendered its claim for part of the property.

However, on July 1, 1999, Dreamworks announced that they were pulling out of the deal and will, temporarily, continue to work out of their offices in Universal City.

Jeffrey Katzenberg settled his $500 million suit against Disney for an undisclosed amount somewhere between $100 and $250 million.

DreamWorks enjoyed a good year at the box office in 2000, with two films in the top ten highest grossing movies of the year. Gladiator had an astounding $35 million opening weekend, DreamWorks' strongest to date.

DreamWorks also landed a three-picture distribution deal with Woody Allen who ended his longtime relationship with Jean Doumanian's Sweetland Films.

DREAMWORKS RELEASES

1997:	Amistad, The Peacemaker, Mouse Hunt.
1998:	Saving Private Ryan, Small Soldiers, Deep Impact, Antz.
1999:	Prince of Egypt, American Beauty, The Haunting, The Love Letter.
2000:	Almost Famous, Meet the Parents, Gladiator, What Lies Beneath, The Legend of Bagger Vance.

METRO-GOLDWYN-MAYER/ UNITED ARTISTS, INC.

Metro-Goldwyn-Mayer, Inc. was originally founded by exhibitor Marcus Loew. In 1910, after several years of expansion, Loew organized Loew's Consolidated Enterprises, succeeded the next year by Loew's Theatrical Enterprises. In 1920, Loew's acquired the Metro Pictures Corporation, which later turned out such films as "The Prisoner of Zenda," "Scaramouche" and "The Four Horsemen of the Apocalypse."

In 1924, Loew and his associates, Nicholas and Joseph Schenk and Adolph Zukor acquired the Goldwyn Company (founded in 1917), and Loew's became the owner of the merged Metro-Goldwyn stock. Loew's then acquired Louis B. Mayer Pictures and the services of Mayer, Irving Thalberg and J. Robert Rubin. The company was renamed Metro-Goldwyn-Mayer.

In 1936 and 1937, legal control of the entire production and distribution organization was vested in Loew's, with Metro-Goldwyn-Mayer used merely as a trade name. On February 6, 1952, the consent decree against Loew's, Inc. provided for a divorce between the producing and distributing phases of the corporation and its domestic exhibition activities and interests. Among notable pictures in the company's history have been "Ben Hur" (silent), "The Thin Man," "Mutiny on the Bounty," "Goodbye Mr. Chips," "Mrs. Miniver," "The Wizard of Oz," "Gone With the Wind," "Meet Me in St. Louis," "King Solomon's Mines," "Ben Hur" (sound), "Doctor Zhivago," "2001: A Space Odyssey" and many more.

In 1973, the company ceased its own distribution and licensed domestic distribution to United Artists and foreign distribution to CIC. In June 1980, the motion picture operations of MGM, Inc. were sold to stockholders as Metro-Goldwyn-Mayer Film Co. United Artists was purchased by the Metro-Goldwyn-Mayer Film Co. in 1981 with the former company becoming a wholly-owned subsidiary of the latter. In 1983, the name of the parent company was changed to MGM/UA Entertainment Co.

In 1986, Turner Broadcasting System purchased MGM/UA and sold the UA portion to Tracinda Corporation along with MGM motion picture and television production, distribution and the home entertainment division. The MGM lot and lab were sold by Turner to Lorimar-Telepictures. Turner retained only the MGM film library. During this period, MGM-UA produced "Moonstruck," "Rain Man" and "A Fish Called Wanda."

Pathe Communications Corporation acquired MGM/UA in November 1990 with Giancarlo Parretti as chairman. The new company was now renamed MGM-Pathe. In 1991, Parretti was removed as chairman with control given to Alan Ladd Jr., and MGM-Pathe was given a $145 million loan from Credit Lyonnais, allowing them to start film distribution after months of inactivity. Due to loans and transactions totalling $885 million, Pathe was $395 million in debt to Credit Lyonnais. In 1992, Credit Lyonnais bought up 98.5% of MGM, thereby officially disposing of Parretti. Following this move, the company was again renamed Metro-Goldwyn-Mayer, Inc. In July of 1993, Alan Ladd Jr. was replaced by former Paramount Pictures chairman Frank G. Mancuso. In 1994, the distribution arm was once again bearing the title MGM/UA and the revived studio had a major hit with the science-fiction film "Stargate." 1995 proved that Metro-Goldwyn-Mayer was again a major force with a number of critical and financial successes such as "Get Shorty" and "Leaving Las Vegas." Although "The Birdcage" was a big hit, in early 1996 MGM was the target of yet another bidding war. In late July of 1996 MGM was purchased (again) by Kirk Kerkorian and a consortium of investors, including Australian television magnate Kerry Packer, for $1.3 billion. In 1997, MGM purchased the movie-related business of John Kluge's Metromedia Group, including Orion Pictures.Less than two years after buying MGM for the third time, Kerkorian has put MGM on the auction block again. Faced with a cash crisis, MGM froze television production and made cutbacks in the number of features planned for release.

In October of 1997, MGM Inc. announced Goldwyn Films, a division specializing in film production, that will take on horror pics, oddball comedies and off-beat movies. Not to be confused with Samuel Goldwyn Co., the reincarnation of the company was swallowed up first by Metromedia, then by MGM.

In the last two years, MGM has continued to struggle, despite the box office success of "Armageddon" and "Tomorrow Never Dies." By the spring of 1999 however, things were beginning to look up. As part of a plan to revitalize the ailing studio, MGM announced a company-wide restructuring under the new leadership of Alex Yemenidjian, the new chairman & CEO. Through the Orion and PolyGram acquisitions, MGM now has the world's largest film library with over 5,000 titles. MGM also won its legal battle with Sony over the rights to the James Bond franchise, negotiated an early termination of its Home Video contract with Warner and signed a multi-picture deal with Miramax.

In October, 1999, MGM posted the results of its first profitable quarter in over three years. A $750 million equity offering is expected to provide funding for new film and television production initiatives while the company turns an eye toward expansion in cable and satellite.

2000 saw the profits continue, with 3rd quarter results showing improved cash flow and exceeding expectations. Much of the credit goes to MGM's film library and aggressive licensing to television and home video and DVD sales though MGM's own distribution channels. MGM also closed several movie channel deals worldwide for which they can provide current and future content through their film library and new product.

MGM has slated 20 films for 2001 release under new head of production, Alex Gartner and new distribution head, Ian Sutherland.

RECENT MGM RELEASES

1990:	Blue Steel.
1991:	The Indian Runner, Thelma & Louise,
1992:	The Lover, Of Mice and Men.
1993:	Benny & Joon, Six Degrees of Separation.
1994:	Stargate, That's Entertainment III.
1995:	Get Shorty, Goldeneye, Leaving Las Vegas.
1996:	The Birdcage.
1997:	Hoodlum, Hurricane, Tomorrow Never Dies, Warriors of Virtue.
1998:	The Parent Trap, Armageddon, Mulan, The Horse Whisperer, Six Days Seven Nights.
1999:	Flawless, The World Is Not Enough, Tea With Mussolini, Stigmata, The Thomas Crown Affair.
2000:	Things You Can Tell Just By Looking At Her, Supernova, Original Sin, Hannibal.

PARAMOUNT PICTURES

Adolph Zukor formed the Engadine Corporation in 1912, which evolved into Famous Players Film Company. W. W. Hodkinson, from General Film Company, formed Paramount Pictures Corporation in 1914, distributing Zukor products and the products of the Jesse L. Lasky Feature Play Company and others. Famous Players-Lasky Corp. was incorporated in 1916. In 1917, twelve production companies merged with it and the corporation integrated production and distribution by acquiring a national distribution system through a merger with Artcraft Pictures and Paramount Pictures. Famous Players-Lasky began acquiring theatres in 1919 with Southern Enterprises, Inc. (135 theatres); followed in later years by New England Theatres, Inc. (50 theatres); the Butterfield Theatre Circuit (70 theatres) and Balaban & Katz (50 theatres). Theatres in the West and Midwest were acquired later.

Paramount's first great star was Mary Pickford. B.P. Schulberg was named head of production in 1925. In April 1927, the corporate name was changed to Paramount Famous Lasky Corporation, and in April of 1930 it became Paramount Publix Corporation, which declared bankruptcy in 1933. Lasky and Schulberg left the company at this point. In 1935, it was reorganized under the name of Paramount Pictures. During this period, the studio's greatest asset was Mae West, whose outrageous hits, "She Done Him Wrong" and "I'm No Angel," caused much furor among censors.

The company regained its footing in the late 1930s and 1940s with such popular stars as Bing Crosby, Bob Hope, Ray Milland and Dorothy Lamour, as well as high-profile films from notable directors Ernst Lubitsch, Preston Sturges, Billy Wilder and Cecil B. DeMille. The 1940s saw such blockbuster hits as "For Whom the Bell Tolls," "Going My Way" and "Samson and Delilah." In 1949, as a result of the Consent Decree, Paramount split into two companies: Paramount Pictures Corp. for production and distribution, and United Paramount Theatres for theatre operation. After WWII, Paramount introduced a new process called VistaVision to compete with 20th Century Fox's Cinema Scope. The first film in the process was the Bing Crosby-Danny Kaye hit musical "White Christmas," followed by Cecil B. DeMille's 1956 remake of "The Ten Commandments."

Paramount merged with Gulf & Western Industries in 1966, with Paramount as a subsidiary retaining its own management. Robert Evans was brought in as production head under Charles Bludhorn, head of Gulf & Western. Bludhorn expanded theatrical film production and increased the company's investment in TV production (an area Paramount had been slow to move into). Evans had great success with "Love Story" (1970) and two Francis Ford Coppola pictures, "The Godfather" (1972) and "The Godfather, Part II" (1974).

With the departure of Evans in 1975, the company moved ahead under Barry Diller as CEO and later under Frank Mancuso, promoted from vice president of distribution to chairman of Paramount Pictures in 1984. The decade of the 1980s brought the company many successes including the "Star Trek" series, the "Indiana Jones" films, "Fatal Attraction," and "Top Gun." Ned Tanen left Universal Pictures to become president of Paramount. In 1989, Gulf and Western changed its name to Paramount Communications, Inc. and Davis began streamlining Paramount Communications in order to focus on entertainment and publishing.

In 1991, Mancuso was replaced by former NBC head Brandon Tartikoff, who resigned in 1992 to be replaced by Sherry Lansing. In the winter of 1994, Viacom Inc. purchased the company for $9.75 billion. Viacom head Sumner Redstone appointed Jonathan Dolgen, formerly of Sony, to oversee entertainment at both Paramount and Viacom. Earlier in 1994, the studio soared at the box office with "Forrest Gump" which became the highest grossing movie in Paramount history. In 1996, Viacom president and CEO Frank Biondi was dismissed with no replacement. That summer, "Mission: Impossible," a remake of the classic television show, became a smash hit, taking in $75 million over the six-day Memorial Day weekend.

Viacom entered 1997 in a slump and with investor confidence low, for the most part due to the poor fortunes of the Viacom-owned Blockbuster Video chain.

In March 1998, James Cameron's "Titanic" grosses reached a record $1 billion plus, worldwide. Although "Titanic's" revenues more than covered the $200 million production cost, the hard fact remains that the already phenomenal cost of movie production keeps going up.

Paramount released several successful films in 1999, though it is unlikely that they will break their record $1 billion in box office reached in 1998.

Parent company Viacom's fortunes improved dramatically in 1999. Viacom decided to sell a minority stake in the Blockbuster video chain in 1999 with plans to shed the rest over the next year. Viacom agreed to buy TV network CBS in an enormous deal valued at about $35 billion. The acquisition is the biggest media transaction in history and will catapult Viacom to the second-largest entertainment firm in the world (behind Time Warner). Chairman Sumner Redstone, who controls 67% of Viacom's voting stock through his privately held company, National Amusements, will remain as chairman and CEO of the combined firm. CBS president Mel Karmazin will become president and COO.

Like the other studios, Paramount spent 2000 streamlining its operations, ridding itself of costly production deals and creating synergy between broadcast, cable and motion picture divisions for multi-franchise content.

RECENT PARAMOUNT RELEASES

1990:	Ghost, The Godfather Part III, The Hunt for Red October.
1991:	The Addams Family, Flight of the Intruder, The Naked Gun 2 1/2: The Smell of Fear.
1992:	Juice, Patriot Games, Wayne's World.
1993:	Addams Family Values, The Firm, What's Eating Gilbert Grape.
1994:	Clear and Present Danger, Forrest Gump.
1995:	Braveheart, Clueless, Congo.
1996:	Mission: Impossible, Star Trek: Resurrection Day.
1997:	Event Horizon, Face/Off, The Flood, Howard Stern's Private Parts, Kiss the Girls, The Saint, Titanic (with Fox).
1998:	Deep Impact, The Truman Show.
1999:	Runaway Bride, Double Jeopardy, The General's Daughter, Angela's Ashes.
2000:	Wonder Boys, The Next Best Thing, Mission Impossible 2, Shaft, The Original Kings of Comedy, Rules of Engagement.

TWENTIETH CENTURY FOX

Twentieth Century Fox Film Corporation was started by William Fox, a pioneer in the arcade and nickelodeon business. Fox became a member of the exhibition firm of Fox, Moss and Brill and established the Greater New York Film Rental Company. In 1913, he organized the Box Office Attraction Company, acquiring the services of Winfield Sheehan. On February 1, 1915, the Fox Film Corporation was founded, combining production, exhibition and distribution under one name and with film exchanges in a dozen cities.

In 1917, Fox Films moved into its Sunset Studio in Hollywood. In 1926, Fox introduced Movietone, a sound-on-film process developed by Theodore Case and Earl I. Sponable.

In 1929, Fox began a series of reorganizations and financial deals, principally the purchase by Fox Films of Loew's, Inc. By order of the courts, Fox's ownership of Loew's was later dissolved and various banking interests acquired control of Loew's. During these reorganizations, William Fox's connections with the company were discontinued. Sidney R. Kent became the company's president.

In 1935, The Fox Film Corporation merged with Twentieth Century Pictures, headed by Joseph M. Schenck, and the company assumed its present corporate name. This merger brought Darryl F. Zanuck into the company as vice president in charge of production. Schenck became chairman of the board and continued in that position until his resignation in June 1942, when Wendell L. Wilkie took over the post. Zanuck remained as production head until 1956, when Buddy Adler succeeded him. Upon Adler's death, Robert Goldstein and then Peter G. Levathes took over studio reins. Spyros P. Skouras, a leading theatre operator, became president. On July 25, 1962, Darryl F. Zanuck was elected president and Skouras was named chairman of the board, a position he held until 1969. Richard D. Zanuck was named executive vice president in charge of worldwide production. The Zanucks turned an ailing company into an industry leader. In 1969, Darryl Zanuck was made chairman of the board and CEO and Richard Zanuck was made president.

In 1971, 20th Century Fox Film Corporation weathered a trying proxy fight which had the resounding effect of giving the company added resolve. A new managerial team was elected by the Board of Directors which saw Dennis C. Stanfill succeeding Richard Zanuck as president of the company. Shortly thereafter, Stanfill was elevated to the position of chairman of the board of directors and the studio's CEO. In 1972, Fox's East Coast offices were consolidated with the West Coast offices.

In 1981, Fox merged with a company owned by Marvin Davis. In 1985, Davis sold the company to Rupert Murdoch's News Corporation and Fox, Inc. was formed, consolidating the principal operating units: Twentieth Century Fox Film Corporation, Fox Television Stations, Inc. and Fox Broadcasting Company. In the summer of 1989, revamping signalled a new emphasis on motion pictures. The company appointed Joe Roth, an independent producer and director, as chairman of its major film-making unit and renamed it the Fox Film Corporation, marking the first time a film director had run a major studio since Ernst Lubitsch headed Paramount Pictures in 1935. Roth's first picture for Fox, "Die Hard 2," proved to be a hit in the summer of 1990. This was followed by the gigantic success of "Home Alone" which went on to become the second highest grossing film in the studio's history following 1977's "Star Wars." At that time, the science-fiction epic had dethroned the company's previous record-holder, "The Sound of Music."

Roth announced his resignation in December of 1992. His replacement, Peter Chernin, was a Fox television executive. In 1994, Fox released the James Cameron film "True Lies" which reportedly cost in excess of $100 million to produce. In 1996, "Independence Day" became one of the top-grossing films in history. In the Winter of 1996-97, George Lucas' ground-breaking "Star Wars" trilogy was re-released theatrically, with new state-of-the-art special effects footage added, and all three immediately broke box-office records (again). The 1997 release of James Cameron's "Titanic" was delayed from its scheduled July release until the Fall of 1997, ostensibly due to extensive special effects re-shooting. With this feature Cameron broke the "Waterworld" record by setting a new negative cost record rumored to be in excess of $200 million. Late in the year, Fox threatened Disney's monopoly on animated musicals, with its own mega-budgeted animated feature release, "Anastasia."

In 1998, Fox, Inc. went public. 20th Century Fox and Fox 2000 now operate under the supervision of Bill Mechanic, chairman of Fox Filmed Entertainment.

In late 1999, Fox Filmed Entertainment promoted Tom Rothman to President of 20th Century Fox Film Group, a newly created executive post charged with overseeing production operations Twentieth Century Fox and Fox 2000. Elizabeth Gabler replaced Laura Ziskin as head of Fox 2000, which despite failing box office, will continue to produce around 15 pictures per year.

After 1998's record year, box office revenue continued to be healthy in 1999, largely driven by the summer release of "Star Wars Episode 1: The Phantom Menace" which, by Labor Day, had grossed $421 million. It was, however, the only superhit of the year.

2000 brought the blockbusters Big Momma's House and X-Men, though midsummer's Me Myself and Irene proved to be a disappointment in spite of Jim Carrey's leading role. Earnings for the quarter ending September 30th were $119 million (EBITDA) versus $62 million for the previous year, showing a nice rebound after the post-Titanic doldrums. Fox continues to reap strong returns from its television product. Currently, the company is the largest producer of programming for the U.S. market.

RECENT FOX RELEASES

1990: Die Hard 2, Edward Scissorhands, Home Alone.

1991: Barton Fink, Point Break, Sleeping With the Enemy.

1992: Hoffa, Home Alone 2: Lost in New York, White Men Can't Jump.

1993: Hot Shots! Part Deux, Mrs. Doubtfire, Rising Sun.

1994: Nell, Speed, True Lies.

1995: Die Hard With a Vengeance, Mighty Morphin Power Rangers.

1996: Broken Arrow, Independence Day.

1997: Alien Resurrection, Anastasia, Great Expectations, Picture Perfect, Speed II: Cruise Control, Titanic (with Paramount), Volcano.

1998: The X-Files, Bulworth, Hope Floats, Something About Mary, Dr. Dolittle, Ever After

1999: Star Wars Episode 1: The Phantom Menace, Anna and the King, Fight Club.

2000: The Beach, Big Momma's House, Me Myself and Irene, X-Men, Men of Honor.

UNIVERSAL PICTURES

Universal Pictures was formed in 1912, when exhibitor Carl Laemmle amalgamated Bison 101, Nestor, Powers and several other organizations, including his own Imp firm. Laemmle had earlier founded Laemmle Film Service and released his first Independent Motion Picture Company feature "Hiawatha" in 1909. Universal launched the star system by hiring Florence Lawrence for $1,000 a week and billing her as "Queen of the Screen." Universal acquired a studio in 1914. In 1915, production was moved to its present site, Universal City. Contracted stars included Wallace Reid, Lon Chaney, Mary Pickford, Rudolph Valentino and Boris Karloff. "Foolish Wives" ("the first million-dollar feature"), "The Hunchback of Notre Dame," "All Quiet On the Western Front" and others were filmed in the decades that followed. On March 16, 1920, Laemmle and R. H. Cochrane assumed complete control of the company.

In 1936, Universal named new management, with J. Cheever Cowdin as chairman of the board and Nate J. Blumberg as president beginning in 1938. Under the new management, Universal embarked upon the policy of developing star values and such stars as Deanna Durbin, Abbott & Costello, Maria Montez, Donald O'Connor and others were put under contract.

In 1946, the company underwent its second transformation, eliminating the production of all so-called "B" pictures, westerns and serials. This followed a merger and acquisition of the assets of International Pictures Corp. of Leo Spitz and William Goetz, who became production heads and the Universal-International trademark emerged. Universal also completed a distribution deal with the J. Arthur Rank organization for the American distribution of British pictures produced by Rank. 1946 also saw the emergence of United World Pictures, a wholly-owned Universal subsidiary, to handle the production and distribution of non-theatrical films including the Bell and Howell Film Library and Castle Films.

1950 saw the resignation of Cowdin with Blumberg assuming full command. Alfred E. Daff, who had been foreign sales manager, assumed the top post in the foreign distribution set-up and then became director of world sales. In 1951, Decca Records acquired approximately 28% of Universal's common stock to make it the largest single stockholder in the company. In 1952, Decca Records became the controlling stockholder of Universal. Milton R. Rackmil, president of Decca Records, was made a member of the Universal board and subsequently elected president of Universal in July, 1952.

In 1962, MCA consolidated with Decca and made Universal Pictures Company the theatrical film producing division of MCA, Inc. In 1964, the creation of the Universal City Studios image started with the separate motion picture and television arms. That same year, the company began its profitable Universal Studios Tour. In 1966, Universal Pictures became a division of Universal City Studios, Inc., a subsidiary of MCA, Inc. The company entered a successful period of high-profile hits including "Thoroughly Modern Millie," "Airport," "American Graffiti," "The Sting," "Earthquake" and Steven Spielberg's "Jaws," which in 1975 became the highest grossing movie to that date.

In 1982, Universal released Steven Spielberg's "E.T.: The ExtraTerrestrial," which became the top-grossing film of all time, racking up over $228 million in film rentals in the domestic market alone. Other recent success have included the "Back to the Future" series, "Field of Dreams," "Born on the Fourth of July," and "Fried Green Tomatoes."

1990 saw two major events in the studio's recent history. A fire swept through the backlot in Universal City destroying acres of sets and causing millions of dollars worth of damage. MCA Inc. was purchased by the Matsushita Electrical Industrial Company for an estimated $6.6 billion, the most expensive sale of an American company to the Japanese in history. In 1993, Spielberg's "Jurassic Park" grossed over $300 million, placing it as the second highest grossing film of all time right behind "E.T." Spielberg was also responsible for "Schindler's List," the first black-and-white Academy Award winner for Best Picture in 33 years.Seagram Co. purchased 80% of MCA Inc. in 1995 for $5.7 billion, with Seagram's president & CEO Edgar Bronfman Jr. serving as acting chairman of the entertainment company. With this change of ownership, Lew Wasserman stepped down and was named chairman emeritus, and Sid Sheinberg ended his 22-year reign as president. In the summer of 1995, Universal released "Waterworld," which holds the dubious distinction of being the most expensive movie ever made, with estimates of its cost ranging as high as $175 million. In spite of critical drubbings and a lackluster domestic box-office, Waterworld went on to earn money for the company in the international market. "The Lost World," Steven Spielberg's sequel to his mega-hit "Jurassic Park," opened Memorial Day weekend to a record-breaking $90.2 million at approximately 6000 screens (nearly one-quarter of the screens in the United States). Universal also purchased art house distributor October Films in 1997.

The departure of Steven Spielberg and Amblin Entertainment, placed the burden on Ron Howard and partner Brian Grazer's Imagine Entertainment, as Universal Pictures' major provider. Although the history between Universal and Imagine goes back some ten years, and although the company has accounted for more than $2.6 billion in grosses, Universal's need for Imagine to put out box office hits has deepened in Mr. Spielberg's absence. To fill the hole left by Mr. Spielberg, Universal has also signed production deals with Will Smith, Penny Marshall, Mike Nichols and Danny Devito. Universal announced a plan to increase its annual output from 12 films in 1997, to somewhere between 20 and 25, by year 2000.

Universal went through some executive cuts in April 1998. Although there were no explanations offered for the restructuring, speculation arose that the changes were the by-product of Edgar Bronfman Jr.'s, dissatisfaction with Universal's performance in 1997-98.

Universal's lagging sales and string of disappointing films in 1998 (such as "Meet Joe Black" and "Babe: Pig in the City") resulted in Universal posting more than $130 million in losses. Universal's film business turned the corner in 1999 thanks to the success of its releases such as "The Mummy," "Notting Hill" and "American Pie." The company's box office grosses for 1999 (as of October) have totaled about $775 million compared to 1998's $315 million. In addition, the studio's market share has grown from 2.4 percent in 1998 to 12.9 percent this year–without adding extra movies to its roster.

In 2000, merger-mania hit Universal. In a three-way deal worth $34 billion, Seagram (Universal's 92% owner) was acquired by French companies Vivendi and Canal Plus to create a multinational media giant. The merger was approved by the EC, simplifying the process that has plagued the AOL-TimeWarner merger. The new company, Vivendi Universal, will be chaired by Jean-Marie Messier (Vivendi), Pierre Lescure (Canal Plus) and Edgar Bronfman Jr. (Seagram) who offered the Studio executives his assurance that film production would be business-as-usual despite the merger.

Meanwhile, Brian Grazer and Ron Howard's Imagine Entertainment signed on for another five years with Universal after a brief flirtation with DreamWorks, guaranteeing the box-office health of Universal in the near future.

RECENT UNIVERSAL RELEASES

1990:	Back to the Future Part III, Kindergarten Cop.
1991:	Backdraft, Fried Green Tomatoes, Jungle Fever.
1992:	Beethoven, Far and Away, Scent of a Woman.
1993:	Jurassic Park, Schindler's List.
1994:	The Flintstones, Radioland Murders, The River Wild.
1995:	Apollo 13, Babe, Casper, Waterworld.
1996:	Dragonheart, Flipper, The Nutty Professor.
1997:	Dante's Peak, For Richer For Poorer, The Jackal, Leave It to Beaver, Liar, Liar, The Lost World.
1998:	BASEketball, Out of Sight, Primary Colors, Mercury Rising, Meet Joe Black.
1999:	The Mummy, Notting Hill, America Pie, The Bone Collector, The Best Man, EDtv.
2000:	Meet the Parents, The Nutty Professor II: The Klumps, Erin Brokovich, U-571, Billy Elliot, How the Grinch Stole Christmas, The Family Man, Head Over Heels.

WARNER BROS.

Warner Bros. Pictures, Inc. may be said to have its origins in the 90-seat Cascade Theatre set up by Harry Warner and his three brothers, Sam, Albert and Jack in New Castle, PA, in 1905. The brothers soon branched out into distribution, establishing film exchanges in Pennsylvania and Virginia. In 1913, they moved into film production with Warner Features. Warner Features' first production was 1918's "My Four Years in Germany." In 1920-22 they averaged only two or three features per year. Warner Bros. was incorporated in 1923 to produce as well as distribute and release 14 pictures, including the first of the famous Rin-Tin-Tin series. Scripts were written by Darryl F. Zanuck, an ambitious writer who soon worked his way up to become the company's production chief under Jack Warner. Harry was president; Albert, treasurer; and Sam shared production responsibilities with Jack. Zanuck stayed until 1933 and was succeeded by Hall Wallis, who held the post for the next decade.

In 1925, Warner acquired Vitagraph, Inc., which operated 34 exchanges in the U.S. and Canada, and two other concerns with foreign exchanges. That same year, the company began its experiments with sound, collaborating with Western Electric to produce a sound-on-disc process (called Vitaphone) for synchronized film sound.

The first Vitaphone program premiered in August 1926, including some musical shorts and the feature "Don Juan" with John Barrymore backed by a full musical and sound-effects track. Owing to this success, the studio released the feature "The Jazz Singer" in October 1927, with dialogue and certain musical numbers in sound and in 1928, "the first 100% all-talking picture"—"Lights of New York," a one-hour feature that broke boxoffice records. In 1927, Sam Warner died.

The new sound technology brought Warner Bros. to the forefront of the industry. It further expanded its theatre holdings and studio facilities, acquiring the Stanley Company of America theatre circuit in 1928, First National Pictures which had a 135-acre studio and back lot, along with exchanges and theatres, and a number of music publishing companies. Those acquisitions greatly helped in the production of the Warner Bros. musicals including "Forty-Second Street," the "Gold Diggers" series, "Footlight Parade" and others. Along with the other motion picture companies, Warner Bros. suffered in the early days of the Depression. Sales of some assets and theatres, along with drastic cuts in production costs, enabled the company to recover and to take advantage of the boom in the 1940s.

In 1953, the company completed the reorganization it was forced to undergo by the government's Consent Decree. Stockholders approved a plan to separate the company into two entities: the theatres were sold to Fabian Enterprises, Inc., and the company was renamed Stanley Warner Corporation. The "new" production-distribution company remained Warner Bros. Pictures, Inc. In 1956, Harry and Albert sold their shares in the company to an investment group headed by Serge Semenenko and Charles Allen Jr. Jack retained his shares, remaining the largest single stockholder and becoming president of the company. The Warner pre-1948 film library of 850 features and 1,000 shorts was sold to United Artists in 1956.

On July 15, 1967, a subsidiary of Seven Arts Productions Limited (a Canadian-based company headed by Eliot Hyman) acquired substantially all the assets and business of Warner Bros. Pictures, Inc. The company subsequently was called Warner Bros.-Seven Arts Limited. In 1969, Warner Bros.-Seven Arts was acquired by Kinney National Service, Inc., headed by Steven J. Ross, and changed its name in 1971 to Warner Communications, Inc. The studio reverted to the original name of Warner Bros. and appointed Ted Ashley as studio chief. The studio's successes during this period included "Superman," "The Exorcist" and "All the President's Men." Robert A. Daly succeeded Ashley as Warner Bros. chairman and CEO in 1980.

In 1989, Warner Communications was acquired by Time, Inc. in an $18 billion merger that created one of the largest communications and entertainment companies in the world. Time-Warner, as the new company is called, consists of Warner and its subsidiaries, Time Publishing, Home Box Office, Cinemax, HBO Video and American Television & Communications Corp. John Peters and Peter Guber were instrumental in aiding Warner to rebound from a two-year box office slump. In the summer of 1989, Peters and Guber produced "Batman," which brought in domestic rentals of over $150 million, making it the fourth top-grossing film of all time to that date.

In early 1991, the company announced a partnership with several European entertainment companies to produce 20 films. Time-Warner continues to hold a 50% interest in Cinamerica Limited Partnership, a company that includes Mann Theatres and Festival Theatres in California, and Trans-Lux Theatres in the East. In October 1991, two Japanese companies, Toshiba Corp. and C. Itoh & Co., paid $500 million each for a combined 12.5% stake in the company. In May 1993, the company created a new division, Warner Bros. Family Entertainment, to release movies aimed at the children's market including the hit "Free Willy." In the autumn of 1995, Time–Warner began negotiations for the $7.3 billion purchase of the Turner Broadcasting System. These negotiations were the subject of intense FTC scrutiny in 1996, due to the 20% stake cable giant TCI held in Turner, but were finally approved by Warner Bros. stockholders on October 10, 1996. Although Turner-owned New Line Cinema was originally to be auctioned off, in May of 1997 the company was removed from the sale shelf, with no plans for its future by Time-Warner, but with its release schedule and creative autonomy intact.

After 18 stagnant months, New Line scored big with the release of "The Wedding Singer." The success was due to the new formula of releasing quirky, non-studio material such as, "Wag the Dog" and "Boogie Nights." The company is also concentrating on producing movies with potential ancillary value. New Line's arthouse division, Fine Line Features, is going through changes of its own, under the leadership of its new president, Mark Ordesky.

In April of 1998, New Line announced the launching of Fine Line's international and distribution division, Fine Line International, headed by Mr. Odesky and New Line International president, Rolf Mittweg.

In 1998, New Line's domestic ticket sales climbed 42%, and the studio's 8% market share put it ahead of majors like Universal Pictures, Dreamworks, and MGM for a sixth-place finish at the U.S. box office. New Line grossed over $200 million with "Austin Powers: The Spy Who Shagged Me," continuing its boxoffice success.

Sara Risher celebrated her 25th year with New Line Cinema by creating a new in-house production company called ChickFlicks

In July, 1999, Robert Daly and Terry Semel stunned the entertainment world by telling Time Warner Chairman Gerald Levin and other directors of the studio's parent company that they would not renew their contracts after their 19 year tenure with the company.

Effective October, 1999, Barry Meyer, executive vice president and COO of Warner Bros., was promoted to chairman and CEO, and Alan Horn, chairman and CEO of Castle Rock Entertainment, became president and COO. 1999 box office was favorable, with four films surpassing the $100 million domestic box office mark: "You've Got Mail," "Analyze This," "The Matrix" and "Wild Wild West."

In 2000, Time-Warner agreed to an acquisition by AOL. The merger is being held up by various regulatory concerns in Washington DC and Brussels. Gerald Levin will be the CEO of the newly merged concern that will likely provide the film entertainment group with new opportunities for cable and online distribution.

Both Warner and New Line enjoyed box office success in 2000, with the phenomenal grosses of "The Perfect Storm" and the impressive opening of "The Cell." With 2000's "Pokemon: The Movie" and "The Powerpuff Girls" and "Harry Potter" in the pipeline, Warner is trying to achieve synergy with other Time-Warner owned units. Offering numerous opportunities for tv and consumer-product merchandising, these will allow Warner to make the most of its distribution channels throughout the AOL-Time-Warner empire.

RECENT WARNER BROS. RELEASES

1990: GoodFellas, Reversal of Fortune, The Witches.
1991: JFK, New Jack City, Robin Hood.
1992: Batman Returns, The Bodyguard, Malcolm X, Unforgiven.
1993: Falling Down, Free Willy, The Fugitive.
1994: Ace Ventura: Pet Detective, Disclosure, Natural Born Killers.
1995: Ace Ventura: When Nature Calls, Batman Forever, The Bridges of Madison County.
1996: Eraser, Executive Decision, Space Jam, A Time to Kill, Twister.
1997: Batman and Robin, Conspiracy Theory, Contact, Father's Day, L.A. Confidential.
1998: The Negotiator, Lethal Weapon 4, A Perfect Murder, City of Angels, You've Got Mail.
1999: The Matrix, Deep Blue Sea, Iron Giant, Three Kings, The Green Mile.
2000: The Perfect Storm, Any Given Sunday, The Art of War, Space Cowboys, Pokemon, Get Carter.

RECENT NEW LINE/FINE LINE RELEASES

1992: Glengarry Glen Ross.
1993: Menace II Society, Short Cuts, Teenage Mutant Ninja Turtles III.
1994: Above the Rim, The Mask.
1995: Don Juan DeMarco, Mortal Kombat, Seven.
1996: The Grass Harp, The Island of Doctor Moreau, Last Man Standing, Michael.
1997: Austin Powers, Crash, Dark City, Mortal Kombat II: Annihilation, Spawn, Boogie Nights.
1998: Lost In Space, The Wedding Singer, Woo, Wag the Dog.
1999: Austin Powers: The Spy Who Shagged Me, The Bachelor, Magnolia.
2000: Frequency, The Cell, Dancer in the Dark, Saving Grace.

MOTION PICTURE PRODUCERS & DISTRIBUTORS

See also, Index: Film Distributors in Key Cities, Non-Theatrical Motion Picture Companies, Exhibition Circuits & Services.

A BAND APART

7966 Beverly Blvd., Los Angeles, CA 90048. (323) 951-4600. FAX: (323) 951-4601.
WRITER & DIRECTOR & PARTNER
Quentin Tarantino
PRODUCER & PARTNER
Lawrence Bender
PRODUCERS
John Baldecchi
Laura Bickford
SENIOR V.P., PRODUCTION
Julie Kirkham
EXECUTIVE PRODUCER, TV
Kevin Brown
V.P., PRODUCTION
Christian D'Andrea
V.P., DEVELOPMENT
Nicole Pennington
STORY EDITOR
Janet Jeffries
OFFICE MANAGER
Jeff Fishman
PRODUCTION ASSISTANT
Matt Krinsky

ABANDON ENTERTAINMENT

135 W. 50th St., Ste. 2305, New York, NY 10020. (212) 246-4445. FAX: (212) 397-8361. www.abandonent.com
email: abandonent@abandonent.com
PRESIDENT & CEO
Marcus Ticotin
PRESIDENT, ABANDON PICTURES
Karen Lauder
MANAGER, MEDIA VENTURES
Deborah Marinoff

FRANK ABATEMARCO PRODUCTIONS

4500 Wilshire Blvd., 3rd Flr., Los Angeles, CA 90010. (323) 954-4560. FAX: (323) 954-4550. email: fabatemarco@hill-fields.com
PRODUCER & WRITER
Frank Abatemarco
MANAGER, DEVELOPMENT
Erik Adams

ABILENE PICTURES

2401 Colorado Ave., Bldg. A, Ste. 1072, Santa Monica, CA 90404. (310) 586-8716.
DIRECTOR
Gregory Hoblit
V.P., DEVELOPMENT
Beverly Graf
ASSOCIATE PRODUCER
Patricia Graf

ABOUT FACE PRODUCTIONS

626 Santa Monica Blvd., Ste. 303, Santa Monica, CA 90401-1066. (310) 278-6886. FAX: (310) 457-4315.
PRODUCER & DIRECTOR
Nicholas Hondrogen
BUSINESS AFFAIRS
George Bennett
CONTACT
Edwin Oro

AB'-STRAKT PICTURES

100 N. Crescent Dr., Beverly Hills, CA 90210. (310) 385-6611. (310) 385-4306. email: gailmu@yahoo.com
PRODUCER
Gail Mutrux
V.P., PRODUCTION
Valerie Dean

AC WORKS

10862 Washington Blvd., Culver City, CA 90232. (310) 204-7811. FAX: (310) 204-7801. email: acwrks@aol.com
OWNER & PRODUCER
Alex Chorches

ACAPPELLA PICTURES

8271 Melrose Ave., Ste. 101, Los Angeles, CA 90046. (323) 782-8200. FAX: (323) 782-8210.
PRESIDENT
Charles Evans Jr.
V.P., DEVELOPMENT & PRODUCTION
Benjamin Sztajnkrycer
STORY EDITOR
Scott Stein
EXECUTIVE ASSISTANT
Jason Amos

ACT III PRODUCTIONS

100 N. Crescent Dr., Beverly Hills, CA 90210. (310) 553-3636. FAX: (310) 553-3928.
CHAIRMAN & CEO, ACT III COMMUNICATIONS
Norman Lear
PRESIDENT
John Baskin
V.P., TV & MOTION PICTURES
Rachel Davidson

ACTION AMERICA ENTERTAINMENT

5073 Avenida Hacienda, Tarzana, CA 91356-4222. (818) 881-1515. FAX: (818) 888-7977.
email: actionamerica@bigfoot.com
PRODUCERS
Robert Kessler
Robin Lombardo
ASSISTANTS
Cheryl Campbell
Noah Hall

MICHAEL ADDIS FILMS (GORGON)

620 S. La Jolla Ave., Los Angeles, CA 90048-4819. (323) 931-8076. email: mikeaddis@loop.com
WRITER & DIRECTOR
Michael Addis
DIRECTOR, DEVELOPMENT
Phil Shuster

ORLY ADELSON PRODUCTIONS

12304 Santa Monica Blvd., Ste. 115, Los Angeles, CA 90025. (310) 442-2012. FAX: (310) 442-2013.
PRESIDENT
Orly Adelson
DEVELOPMENT ASSISTANT
Jonathan Eskanes

AFRA-FILM ENTERPRISES, INC.

137 S. Robertson Blvd., Ste. 254, Beverly Hills, CA 90211. (323) 882-6193. FAX (323) 882-6103
email: afrafilm@aol.com
PRESIDENT
Anatoly A. Fradis
DEVELOPMENT EXECUTIVE
Felix Kleiman

MINDY AFFRIME PRODUCTIONS

1429 Avon Park Terrace, Los Angeles, CA 90026. (323) 661-4481. FAX: (323) 644-0680. email: minaffrime@aol.com
PRESIDENT & PRODUCER
Mindy Affrime

AGAMEMNON FILMS, INC.

650 N. Bronson Ave., Ste. B-225, Los Angeles, CA 90004. (323) 960-4066.
PRESIDENT
Fraser C. Heston
VICE PRESIDENT
John Stronach
PRODUCER
Alex Butler
DEVELOPMENT
Timothy Colvin

ALCHEMY ENTERTAINMENT

73 Market St., Venice, CA 90291. (310) 396-5937.
PARTNER & WRITER & DIRECTOR
Andy Tennant
PARTNER & PRODUCER
Jon Jashni
PARTNER & PRODUCER
Wink Mordaunt

ALCON ENTERTAINMENT, LLC

Lantana Center, 3000 W. Olympic Blvd., Santa Monica, CA 90404. (310) 315-4725. FAX: (310) 315-4734.
email: Alcontent@aol.com
CO-PRESIDENT & CO-FOUNDER
Broderick Johnson
CO-PRESIDENT & CO-FOUNDER
Andrew A. Kosove
PRODUCER
Christi Moore-Brantley
V.P., PRODUCTION
Kira Davis
V.P., DEVELOPMENT
Steven P. Wegner
PRODUCTION EXECUTIVE
Derek Guiley
EXECUTIVE ASSISTANTS
Christopher Fealy
Chris Alexander

ALIVE FILMS

3264 S. Kihei, Kihei, HI 96753. (808) 891-0022. FAX: (808) 879-2734. email: alivewow@maui.net
CHAIRMAN
Shep Gordon

ALL GIRL PRODUCTIONS

4024 Radford Ave., Bung. 20, Studio City, CA 91604-2190. (818) 655-6000. FAX: (818) 655-8380.
ACTRESS & PRODUCER
Bette Midler
PRODUCER
Bonnie Bruckheimer
EXECUTIVE V.P.
Yvette Taylor
SENIOR V.P.
Julia Eisenman
DEVELOPMENT ASSISTANT
Laura Mueller

ALLIANCE ATLANTIS COMMUNICATIONS, INC.

(Creator and distributor of filmed entertainment)
121 Bloor St. E., Ste. 1500, Toronto, ON, Canada M4W 3M5. (416) 967-1174. FAX: (416) 960-0971.
808 Wilshire Blvd., Third Flr., Los Angeles, CA 90401. (310) 899-8000. FAX: (310) 899-8100 www.allianceatlantis.com
email: allianceatlantis@allianceatlantis.com
CHAIRMAN & CEO
Michael MacMillan
PRESIDENT, MOTION PICTURE PRODUCTION
Seaton McLean
CHAIRMAN, MOTION PICTURE GROUP
Victor Loewy
PRESIDENT, MOTION PICTURE DISTRIBUTION
Patrice Theroux
EXECUTIVE V.P., MOTION PICTURE PRODUCTION
Bill House
SENIOR V.P., ACQUISITIONS & DEVELOPMENT
Charlotte Mickie
SENIOR V.P., MOTION PICTURE PROD. & ACQUISITIONS
Ted East
SENIOR V.P., MKTG. & COMM., MOTION PICTURE DIST.
Jill Lieberman
PRESIDENT, ODEON FILMS
Bryan Gliserman
PRESIDENT, VIVA FILM
Guy Gagnon
V.P., ACQUISITIONS & SALES, VIVA FILM
Patrick Roy
PRESIDENT, PICTURES INTERNATIONAL
Mark Horowitz
V.P., MARKETING, MOTION PICTURE DISTRIBUTION
Grace Cianciotta
DIRECTOR OF PUBLICITY, MOTION PICTURE DIST.
Alyson Dewar
MANAGER, MARKETING, MOTION PICTURE DISTRIBUTION
Alex Wermester

Toronto - TMP The Music Publisher, 121 Bloor St. E., Ste. 1400, Toronto, ON, Canada M4W 3M5. (416) 967-1174. FAX: (416) 960-0971.

Montréal - Alliance Vivafilm, 5 Pl. Ville Marie, Ste. 1435, Montréal, Canada H3B 2G2. (514) 878-2282. FAX: (514) 878-2419.

Shannon - Alliance Atlantis Television International, Block 1, Unit C, Shannon Business Park, Shannon, Co. Clare, Ireland. (3536) 147 2329. FAX: (3536) 147 2228.

London - Company Pictures, 184-192 Drummond St., 2nd. Fl., London NW1 3HP, England. (44207) 391-6900. FAX: (44207) 383-0404.

Australia - Alliance Atlantis Releasing PTY, 401 Darling St., Ste. 2, Balmain, Sydney NSW 2041, Australia. (6129) 810-8922. FAX: (6129) 810-8966.

ALLIED STARS

10202 W. Washington Blvd., Lean Bldg., #423, Culver City, CA 90232-3195. (310) 244-5188. FAX: (310) 244-6499.
SENIOR V.P., PRODUCTION
Melissa Henning
V.P., DEVELOPMENT
Kelly Jones

ALPHAVILLE

5555 Melrose Ave., DeMille Bldg., 2nd Flr., Hollywood, CA 90038-3197. (323) 956-4803. FAX: (323) 862-1616. email: firstname@aville.com
PRODUCER & PARTNER
Sean Daniel
PRODUCER & PARTNER
Jim Jacks
PRESIDENT, PRODUCTION
Caldecot Chubb
CREATIVE EXECUTIVE
Jennifer Moyer

ALTAR ROCK FILMS, INC.

(Independent motion picture & TV production company.)
29 Greene Street, New York, NY 10013. (212) 965-9444. FAX: (212) 965-9520. www.altarrockfilms/com
CHAIRMAN
John Johnson
PRESIDENT
George Belshaw
SENIOR V.P.
Terry J. Field
Jonathan M. Judge
EXECUTIVE V.P.
Charles R. Merzbacher
ASSOCIATE PRODUCER & CASTING DIRECTOR
Kim Murray
DIRECTOR, DEVELOPMENT
Cassandra Del Viscio

AMAZING MOVIES

(Producer and distributor of feature films worldwide.)
7471 Melrose Ave., Ste. 7, Los Angeles, CA 90046. (323) 852-1396. FAX: (323)658-7265. www.amazingpiz.com
email: amazingmov@aol.com
PRESIDENT
Douglas C. Witkins
DIRECTOR OF OPERATIONS
Orly Ravid

AMC ENTERTAINMENT, INC.

(For theatres listing see American Multi-Cinema, Inc. in Theatre Circuits section.)
106 W. 14th St., Kansas City, MO 64105. (816) 221-4000.
www.amctheatres.com
CHAIRMAN, PRESIDENT & CEO
Peter C. Brown
CFO
Craig R. Ramsey
SENIOR V.P., TREASURY & ASSET MANAGEMENT
James V. Beynon
EXECUTIVE V.P., NORTH AMERICAN OPERATIONS
John D. McDonald
PRESIDENT & COO OF AMERICAN MULTI-CINEMA, INC.
Philip M. Singleton

AMALGAMATED INCORPORATED

2045 S. Barrington Dr., Los Angeles, CA 90025. (310) 447-7000. FAX: (310) 445-9191.
CONTACTS
Erik Feig
Dawn Ebert-Byrnes

AMC FILM MARKETING, INC.

(Motion picture distributor)
21700 Oxnard St., Ste. 640, Woodland Hills, CA 91367.(818) 587-6400. FAX:. (818) 587-6498.
AMC FILM MARKETING PRESIDENT
Richard M. Fay

AMEN RA FILMS
9460 Wilshire Blvd., Ste. 400, Beverly Hills, CA 90212. (310) 246-6510. FAX: (310) 550-1932.
email: firstname@amenrafilms.com
ACTOR & PRODUCER
Wesley Snipes
PRESIDENT & PRODUCER
Kimiko Fox
SENIOR V.P. & PRODUCER
Victor McGauley
COMPTROLLER
Carmen Baker
CREATIVE EXECUTIVE
Julian Chang Zolkin
PHYSICAL PRODUCTION
Glennis Bastien
HUMAN RESOURCES
Trudy Snipes Baylock
HUMAN RESOURCES, EAST COAST
Sandra Farrior
SPECIAL PROJECTS
Rachelle Thomas

AMERICAN ENTERTAINMENT CO.
5225 Wilshire Blvd., #615, Los Angeles, CA 90036. (323) 939-6746. FAX: (323) 939-6747.
PRESIDENT & PRODUCER
Bill Paxton
V.P., DEVELOPMENT
Tom Huckabee
CREATIVE ASSOCIATES
Jim Young
Mike Culbert

AMERICAN FILMWORKS
(Independent motion picture & TV producer)
2118 Wilshire Blvd., Ste. 485, Santa Monica, CA 90403. (310) 288-0569. FAX: (310) 288-0578. email: AmFilm@aol.com
PRESIDENT & PRODUCER
Bruce Gilbert

AMERICAN FIRST RUN STUDIOS
(Production and distribution)
14225 Ventura Blvd., Sherman Oaks, CA 91423. (818) 981-4950. FAX: (818) 501-6224.
CHAIRMAN
Max Keller
PRESIDENT
Micheline Keller

AMERICAN NEW WAVE FILMS
7775 Sunset Blvd., Ste. 150, Hollywood, CA 90046. (323) 850-1700. FAX: (323) 850-1788.
WRITER & DIRECTOR & PRODUCER
Norman Thaddeus Vane
LINE PRODUCER
Rheinhardt Schreiner
PRODUCTION COORDINATOR
Gus Ramos

AMERICAN WORLD PICTURES
21700 Oxnard St., Ste. 660, Woodland Hills, CA 91367. (818) 715-1480. FAX: (818) 715-1081. email: awpics@earthlink.net
PRESIDENT
Mark L. Lester
PRESIDENT, PRODUCTION
Dana Dubousky
SENIOR V.P., DISTRIBUTION
Therese Linden Kohn
V.P., PRODUCTION & CREATIVE
Brian Etting

AMERICAN ZOETROPE
5225 Wilshire Blvd., Ste. 204, Los Angeles, CA 90036. (310) 899-8000, (310) 899-8123. FAX: (323) 935-6185.
www.zoetrope.com
1350 Ave. of the Americas, 24th Flr., New York, NY 10019. (212) 708-0400. FAX: (212) 708-0475.
916 Kearny St., San Francisco, CA 94133.
PRESIDENT
Linda Reisman (New York)
CEO
Jay Shoemaker
SENIOR V.P., TV & PRODUCER
Tara McCann
V.P., PRODUCTION & ACQUISITIONS
Bobby Rock
CREATIVE EXECUTIVE, TV
Audie Soichet
PRODUCTION
Susan Paley Abramson (New York)

AM PRODUCTIONS & MANAGEMENT
8899 Beverly Blvd., Ste. 713, Los Angeles, CA 90048. (310) 275-9081. FAX: (275) 275-9082. email: bramam@aol.com
ACTOR & EXECUTIVE PRODUCER
Ann-Margret
ACTOR & DIRECTOR & EXECUTIVE PRODUCER
Burt Reynolds
EXECUTIVE PRODUCER
Alan Margulies
EXECUTIVE PRODUCER & WRITER
Roger Smith

AMSELL ENTERTAINMENT, INC.
(Motion picture, TV & video distributor)
12001 Ventura Pl., Ste. 404, Studio City, CA 91604. (818) 766-8500. FAX: (818) 766-7873. email: amsellent@aol.com
PRESIDENT
Alan Solomon

CRAIG ANDERSON PRODUCTIONS
9696 Culver Blvd., Ste.208, Culver City, CA 90232. (310) 841-2555. FAX: (310) 841-5934. email: CAPPix@aol.com
EXECUTIVE PRODUCER
Craig Anderson
EXECUTIVE V.P., DEVELOPMENT
Phil Kruener
CREATIVE EXECUTIVE
Chris St. George
PRODUCTION SUPERVISOR
Marty E. Schwartz

ANGEL ARK PRODUCTIONS
12711 Ventura Blvd., Ste. 330, Studio City, CA 91604. (818) 508-3338. FAX: (818) 508-2009.
CREATIVE PARTNERS
Jason Alexander
Jenny Birchfield-Eick
Michael A. Jackman
V.P., TV
Christopher May

ANGRY DRAGON ENTERTAINMENT
10202 W. Washington Blvd., Culver City, CA 90232. (310) 244-6996. FAX:(310) 244-0996.
PRESIDENT
Dean Cain
CREATIVE EXECUTIVE
Abe Abdelhadi
V.P., DEVELOPMENT
Mike Carr

ANGRY FILMS, INC.
10202 W. Washington Blvd., Poitier Bldg., #3206, Culver City, CA 90232. (310) 244-7590. FAX: (310) 244-2060.
email: firstname-lastname@spe-sony.com
PRODUCER
Don Murphy
VICE PRESIDENT
Richard Benattar

APATOW PRODUCTIONS
1438 N. Gower St., Bldg. 35, Ste. 557, Los Angeles, CA 90028. (323) 860-7825. FAX: (323) 860-7849.
WRITER & PRODUCER
Judd Apatow
VICE PRESIDENT
Mia Apatow

A PLUS ENTERTAINMENT
15030 Ventura Blvd., Ste. 762, Sherman Oaks, CA 91403. (818) 994-9831. FAX: (818) 994-9837. www.aplusent.com
email: aplusent@earthlink.net
PRESIDENT & CEO
Emilio Ferrari
V.P., PRODUCTION
Monika S.
V.P., ACQUISITION
Gregg Ratinoff
HEAD, DEVELOPMENT
Georginia Saksa

APOSTLE PICTURES
The Ed Sullivan Theater, 1697 Broadway, Ste. 906, New York, NY 10019. (212) 541-4323. FAX: (212) 541-4339.
ACTOR & DIRECTOR & PRODUCER
Denis Leary
PRESIDENT, MOTION PICTURES & TV
Jim Serpico
CREATIVE EXECUTIVE
Tom Sellitti

APPLEDOWN FILMS, INC.

9687 W. Olympic Blvd., Beverly Hills, CA 90212. (310) 552-1833. FAX: (310) 552-1331.
PRODUCER & WRITER
Larry Spiegel
PRODUCER
Judy Goldstein

AQUARIUS RELEASING, INC./AQUARIUS MEDIA CORP.

(Distribution, exhibition & production.)
P.O. Box 590 Englewood, N.J. 07631. (201) 541-1912. FAX: (201) 541-2365.
CEO
Terry Levene
SECRETARY & TREASURER
Sarie Berenstein
PUBLICITY & ADVERTISING DEPARTMENT
Wayne Weil
Irving Russell (NY & Philadelphia branch office)

ARAMA ENTERTAINMENT

(Motion picture producer & distributor)
18034 Ventura Blvd., #435, Encino, CA 91316. (818) 788-6400. FAX: (818) 990-9344. www.aramaent.com
PRESIDENT & CHAIRMAN
Shimon Arama
PRODUCER
Don Schneider

MARK ARCHER ENTERTAINMENT

1910 St. Joe Ctr. Rd., Ste. 22, Fort Wayne, IN 46825. (219) 486-8831. FAX: (219) 486-8971.
www.markarcherentertainment.com
email: markarcherentertainment@worldnet.att.net
PRESIDENT
Mark Archer
V.P., PRODUCTION & OPERATIONS
Jonathan Brouwer

ARCIMAGE FILMS

12358 Deerbrook Lane, Los Angeles, CA 90049. (310) 440-9596. FAX: (310) 440-2096.
PRODUCERS
Elizabeth Karl
John Roach
John Faunce
EXECUTIVE CONSULTANT
Carol Dreschler

ARIES ENTERTAINMENT, INC.

13033 Ventura Blvd., Ste. C, Studio City, CA 91604. (818) 385-1236. FAX: (818) 385-1392. email: ariesent@hotmail.com
PRESIDENT
Norbert Meisel

ARROW ENTERTAINMENT

(Motion picture, TV & video producer & distributor)
25 W. 45th St., Ste. 707, New York, NY 10036. (212) 398-9511. FAX: (212) 398-9558. www.arrowfilms.com
email: arrowent1@aol.com
PRESIDENT
Dennis Friedland
V.P., BUSINESS & LEGAL AFFAIRS
John Cusimano
ACQUISITION
Kate Gradd
INTERNATIONAL SALES
Tom Conroy

ARTHOUSE ENTERTAINMENT

9350 Wilshire Blvd., Ste. 328, Beverly Hills, CA 90212. (310) 247-9119. FAX: (310) 247-9974.
email: arthouseent@mindspring.com
PARTNERS
Laina Cohn
Morgan Sackett

ARTISAN ENTERTAINMENT

2700 Colorado Ave., 2nd Flr., Los Angeles, CA 90404. (310) 449-9200. www.artisanent.com
CEO
Amir Malin
CO-PRESIDENT & COO
Ken Schapiro
CO-PRESIDENT
Bill Block
EXECUTIVE V.P., CORPORATE DEVELOPMENT & CHIEF STRATEGIC OFFICER/PRESIDENT, DIGITAL MEDIA
Nicolas Van Dyk
PRESIDENT, HOME ENTERTAINMENT
Steve Beeks
PRESIDENT, FAMILY HOME ENTERTAINMENT
Glenn Ross
PRESIDENT, HOME ENTERTAINMENT SALES & MARKETING
Jeff Fink
PRESIDENT, DOMESTIC THEATRICAL DISTRIBUTION
Steve Rothenberh
EXECUTIVE V.P.
Patrick Gunn
EXECUTIVE V.P., WORLDWIDE MARKETING
Amorette Jones
EXECUTIVE V.P., PHYSICAL PRODUCTION
Andrew Golov
EXECUTIVE V.P., PRODUCTION
Caitlin Scanlon
EXECUTIVE V.P. & CFO
James Keegan
EXECUTIVE V.P., ARTISAN TELEVISION
Gary Rubin
S.V.P., NATIONAL PUBLICITY & CORPORATE COMMUNICATIONS
Paul Pflug
S.V.P., THEATRICAL MARKETING
LeAnne Gayner
S.V.P., ASSET MANAGEMENT
Kathleen Laychak
S.V.P., STRATEGIC MARKETING & BUSINESS DEVELOPMENT
Dominic Ianno
S.V.P., MARKETING, ARTISAN HOME ENTERTAINMENT
Hosea Belcher
S.V.P., SALES & DISTRIBUTION, ARTISAN HOME ENTERTAINMENT
Tim Fournier
S.V.P., RENTAL SALES & DISTRIBUTION, ARTISAN HOME ENTERTAINMENT
Jed Grossman

ARTISTIC LICENSE FILMS

250 W. 57th St., #606, New York, NY 10107. (212) 265-9119. FAX: (212) 262-9299.www.artlic.com email: artlic@artlic.com
PRESIDENT
Sande Zeig
MANAGING DIRECTOR
Vicky Waldron
NATIONAL SALES MANAGER
Steve Fagan
DISTRIBUTION ASSOCIATE
Anne Crozat
FINANCIAL DIRECTOR
Nora Coblence

THE ARTISTS' COLONY

7421 Beverly Blvd., Ste. 13, Los Angeles, CA 90036. (323) 930-7900. FAX: (323) 930-7919. www.theartisitscolony.com
email: las@theartistscolony.com
PRODUCER
Lloyd A. Silverman
DIRECTOR, URBAN MARKETS
Julian A. Bernard
DIRECTOR, DEVELOPMENT
Steve Grill
EXECUTIVE ASSISTANT
Caelyn Smith

ASTRON FILMS CORPORATION

(Writers, producers, directors, independent financiers of films.)
360 W. 22 St., New York, NY 10011. (212) 989-6089. FAX: (212) 627-5191.
PRESIDENT & CHAIRMAN
Jack O'Connell
CREATIVE DIRECTOR
Patricia Kay Williams

THE ASYLUM

6671 Sunset Blvd, Bldg. 1593, Hollywood, CA 90028. (323) 463-6575. FAX: (323) 463-6299.
email: asylumthe@aol.com
PARTNERS
David Michael Latt
David Rimawi
Sherri Strain
V.P., ACQUISITIONS
Karl Hirsch

ATA TRADING CORP.

(Distribution)
P.O. Box 307, Massapequa Park, NY 11762. (516) 541-5336. FAX: (516) 541-5336. email: atatr@optonline.net
PRESIDENT
Harold G. Lewis
DIRECTOR OF SALES
Luci Lo Russo

ATKINSON WAY FILMS
6121 Santa Monica Blvd., Ste. 100, Los Angeles, CA 90038. (323) 465-3350. FAX: (323) 465-3344. www.atkinsonway.com
PRODUCERS
Sam Waterston
Beth Colt
V.P., TALENT & DIRECTOR, DEVELOPMENT
Andrew Myler

ATLANTIC STREAMLINE
1323A Third St., Santa Monica, CA 90401. (310) 319-9366. FAX: (310) 319-9235. www.atlanticstreamline.com
email: info@atlanticstreamline.com
CEO & PRESIDENT
Marco Weber
SENOR, V.P., PRODUCTION & FINANCE
Fran Lucci
WRITER & DIRECTOR
Andy J. Hurst

ATLAS ENTERTAINMENT
9169 Sunset Blvd., Los Angeles, CA 90069. (310) 724-7350. FAX: (310) 724-7345.
PRODUCER & PARTNER
Charles Roven
MANAGER & PRODUCER & PARTNER
Todd Smith
V.P., FINANCE
Dianne Gunn
PRODUCERS
Kelley Smith-Wait
Richard Suckle
EXECUTIVE V.P., PRODUCTION
Douglas Segal
ASSOCIATE PRODUCER
Alan Glazer
STORY EDITORS
Tom Brennan
Gloria Fan

ATMAN ENTERTAINMENT
1326 S. Stanley Ave., Los Angeles, CA 90019. (323) 938-9772. FAX: (323) 938-9773. email: rbell74020@aol.com
PRODUCER
Ross Grayson Bell

AUGUST ENTERTAINMENT
838 N. Fairfax Ave., Los Angeles, CA 90046. (323) 658-8888. FAX: (323) 658-7654.
PRESIDENT
Gregory Cascante
EXECUTIVE V.P. & CFO
Elizabeth Davis
V.P., OPERATIONS
Colleen McNichols

AURORA PRODUCTIONS
8642 Melrose Ave., Ste. 200, Los Angeles, CA 90069. (310) 854-6900. FAX: (310) 854-0583. email: auroraprod@aol.com
PRESIDENT
William Stuart
DIRECTOR, DEVELOPMENT
Nancy Best

AUTOMATIC PICTURES
5225 Wilshire Blvd., Ste. 525, Los Angeles, CA 90038.
email:fbeddor@earthlink.net
PRODUCER
Frank Beddor
CREATIVE EXECUTIVE
Liz Cavalier
ASSISTANT
Matthew Lloyd

AVALANCHE ENTERTAINMENT
506 Santa Monica Blvd., Ste. 322, Santa Monica, CA 90401. (310) 395-3660. FAX: (310) 395-8322.
PRESIDENT & PRODUCER
Richard Hull
DIRECTOR, DEVELOPMENT
Anthony Ross

AVENUE PICTURES
11111 Santa Monica Blvd., Ste. 525, Los Angeles, CA 90025. (310) 996-6800. FAX: (310) 473-4376.
www.avenue-entertainment.com email: avepx@aol.com
CHAIRMAN & CEO
Cary Brokaw
SENIOR V.P. & CFO
Sheri Halfon
CONTROLLER
Judy Geletko

AVIATOR FILMS, LLC
4150 Riverside Dr., #201, Burbank, CA 91505. (818) 558-5880. FAX: (818) 556-2899.
PARTNERS
Anthony Edwards
Dante di Lorento
STORY EDITOR
Jane Ridley
ASSOCIATE
Frank Pavich

AVNET-KERNER CO.
3815 Hughes Ave., Culver City, CA 90232. (310) 838-2500. FAX: (310) 204-4208.
PRODUCERS
Jon Avnet
Jordan Kerner
SENIOR V.P., DEVELOPMENT & PRODUCTION
Paul Neesan
SENIOR V.P., DEVELOPMENT & PRODUCTION
Lisa Lindstrom

AXELSON-WEINTRAUB PRODUCTIONS
4421 Riverside Dr., Burbank, CA 91505. (818) 954-8661. FAX: (818) 954-0468. email: aw-prods@earthlink.net
EXECUTIVE PRODUCER & DIRECTOR
John Axelson
EXECUTIVE PRODUCER
Barbara Weintraub
CREATIVE ASSOCIATE
Miranda Liu

THE BADHAM CO.
3344 Clerendon Road, Beverly Hills, CA 90210. (818) 990-9495. FAX: (818) 981-9163. www.badhamcompany.com
email: development@badhamcompany.com
DIRECTOR & PRODUCER
John Badham
CO-PRODUCER & DEVELOPMENT
Cammie Crier-Herbert

BAER ENTERTAINMENT GROUP
9229 Sunset Blvd., Ste. 401, Los Angeles, CA 90069. (310) 777-3680. FAX: (310) 777-3685.
PRODUCER
Thomas Baer
PARTNER
Micheal Steinhardt
DIRECTOR, DEVELOPMENT
Mario Acosta

BAKULA PRODUCTIONS, INC.
5555 Melrose Ave., Hollywood, CA 90038. (323) 960-4005.
CEO & PRODUCER
Scott Bakula
PRESIDENT & PRODUCER
Tom Spiroff
CREATIVE EXECUTIVE
Ron Cortes

BALLPARK PRODUCTIONS
P.O. Box 508, Venice, CA 90294. (310) 827-1328. FAX: (310) 577-9626.
PRODUCER
Michael Schiffer
V.P., DEVELOPMENT
Sally Allen

BALLYHOO, INC.
6738 Wedgewood Pl., Los Angeles, CA 90068. (323) 874-3396. FAX: (323) 883-0265. email: mbesman@aol.com
PRODUCER
Michael Besman

BALTIMORE/SPRING CREEK PICTURES, LLC
4000 Warner Blvd., Burbank, CA 91522. (818) 954-1210. FAX: (818) 954-2737. www.Levinson.com
DIRECTOR & WRITER & PRODUCER
Barry Levinson
PRODUCER
Paula Weinstein
CFO & BUSINESS AFFAIRS
Amy Solan
EXECUTIVE V.P.
Len Amato
EXECUTIVE V.P.
Robin Forman
VICE PRESIDENT
Vanessa Coifman
STORY EDITOR
Naketha Mattocks

BANDEIRA ENTERTAINMENT
8447 Wilshire Blvd., Ste. 212, Beverly Hills, CA 90211. (323) 866-3535. FAX: (323) 866-3599.
PRODUCER
Beau Flynn
DIRECTOR, DEVELOPMENT
Christine Johnson
STORY EDITOR
Cathy Twigg

BANNER ENTERTAINMENT
8265 Sunset Blvd., Ste. 200, Los Angeles, CA 90046. (323) 848-2880. FAX: (323) 848-2255.
PRESIDENT
Mickey Liddell

ALAN BARNETTE PRODUCTIONS
100 Universal City Plaza, Bldg. 2352, Rm. 100, Universal City, CA 91608. (818) 733-0993.
EXECUTIVE PRODUCER
Alan Barnette
DIRECTOR, DEVELOPMENT
Carol Paciorek

BARNHOLTZ ENTERTAINMENT
31770 Cottontail Lane, Malibu, CA 90265-2624. (310) 457-7484. FAX: (310) 589-2681. email: bbarnholtz@aol.com
PRESIDENT
Barry Barnholtz
CFO
Murray Gilden
DIRECTOR, ACQUISITIONS
Katherine Miller
SENIOR V.P., BUSINESS AFFAIRS
Matthew Fladell
LEGAL AFFAIRS
Irina Piyevsky

BARNSTORM FILMS
73 Market St., Venice, CA 90291. (310) 396-5937. FAX: (310) 450-4988.
PRODUCER & DIRECTOR
Tony Bill
PRODUCER
Helen Bartlett

BARWOOD FILMS
330 W. 58th St., Ste. 301, New York, NY 10019. (212) 765-7191. FAX: (212) 765-6988.
OWNER & ACTRESS & PRODUCER & DIRECTOR
Barbara Streisand
PRESIDENT
Cis Corman
V.P., DEVELOPMENT
Evan Cohen
STORY EDITOR
Jane Mendle

BATJAC PRODUCTIONS, INC.
9595 Wilshire Blvd., #610, Beverly Hills, CA 90212-2506. (310) 278-9870. FAX: (323) 272-7381.
PRESIDENT
Michael A. Wayne

THE BAUER COMPANY
9465 Wilshire Blvd., Ste. 308, Beverly Hills, CA 90212. (310) 247-3880. FAX: (310) 247-3881.
PRODUCERS
Martin R. Bauer
Cory Concoff
Robert Marsala
DEVELOPMENT EXECUTVE
Ben Tappan

BAUMGARTEN/PROPHET ENTERTAINMENT
1640 S. Sepulveda Blvd., #218, Los Angeles, CA 90025. (310) 996-1885. FAX: (310) 996-1982.
email: bpeproduction@aol.com
PRODUCER & PARTNER
Craig Baumgarten
MANAGER & PARTNER
Melissa Prophet
PRODUCER & HEAD, PRODUCTION
Adam Merims
MANAGER
Jessica Berlinski
OFFICE MANAGER
Dee Mattel

CAROL BAUM PRODUCTIONS
8899 Beverly Blvd., Ste. 721, Los Angeles, CA 90048. (310) 550-4575. FAX: (310) 550-2088.
PRODUCER
Carol Baum

BAY FILMS
2110 Broadway, Santa Monica, CA 90404. (310) 829-7799. FAX: (310) 829-7099.
DIRECTOR & PRODUCER
Michael Bay
VICE PRESIDENT
Jennifer Klein
CREATIVE EXECUTIVE
Matthew Cohan
STORY EDITOR
Scott Windhauser

BAYLEY SILLECK PRODUCTIONS, INC.
(Large format film production)
148 Waverly Pl., New York, NY 10014. (212) 645-0745. FAX: (212) 691-1299. email: Bsilleck@aol.com
CONTACT
Bayley Silleck

BEACON COMMUNICATIONS, LLC
120 Broadway, Ste. 200, Santa Monica, CA 90401. (310) 260-7000. FAX: (310) 260-7050
CHAIRMAN
Armyan Bernstein
PRESIDENT
Marc Abraham
COO
Thomas Bliss
EXECUTIVE V.P., BUSINESS & LEGAL AFFAIRS
Paul Green
SENIOR V.P., DEVELOPMENT & PRODUCTION
Suzann Ellis
SENIOR V.P., DEVELOPMENT & PRODUCTION
Eric Newman
SENIOR V.P., PRODUCTION
Nancy Rae Stone
V.P., FINANCE
Cindy McWethy
DIRECTOR, HUMAN RESOURCES & ADMINISTRATION
Merry Rose

THE BEDFORD FALLS CO.
409 Santa Monica Blvd., Penthouse, Santa Monica, CA 90401. (310) 394-5022. FAX: (310) 394-5825.
EXECUTIVE PRODUCER & WRITER & DIRECTOR
Marshall Herskovitz
EXECUTIVE PRODUCER & WRITER & DIRECTOR
Edward Zwick
PRESIDENT
Richard Solomon
SENIOR V.P., PRODUCTION
Lisa Moiselle
DIRECTOR, DEVELOPMENT
Robin Budd

BEL-AIR ENTERTAINMENT
4000 Warner Blvd., Bldg. 66, Burbank, CA 91522. (818) 954-4040. FAX: (818) 954-2838.
CHAIRMAN & CEO
Steve Reuther
COO
Philip Elway
EXECUTIVE V.P., PRODUCTION
Allyn Stewart
SENIOR V.P., PRODUCTION
John Schimmel
SENIOR V.P., PRODUCTION
Keri Selig
V.P., PRODUCTION ADMINISTRATION
Kirk Borcherding
V.P., POST-PRODUCTION
Carol Dantuono
V.P., BUSINESS & LEGAL AFFAIRS
Ann L. Duval
CREATIVE EXECUTIVE
Heather Courtney
STORY EDITOR
Leslie Goott

BELISARIUS PRODUCTIONS
5555 Melrose Ave., Clara Bow Bldg., #204, Los Angeles, CA 90038-3197. (323) 956-8660. FAX: (323) 862-0250.
WRITER & EXECUTIVE PRODUCER & DIRECTOR
Donald P. Belisario
CO-EXECUTIVE PRODUCER
Chas. Floyd Johnson

CO-EXECUTIVE PRODUCER & WRITER
Ed Zuckerman
PRODUCERS
David Bellisario
Dana Coen
Avery Drewe
Mark M. Horowitz
Mark Saracene
Julie Watson
ASSOCIATE PRODUCER
Megan Mecena
CONSULTING PRODUCER
Stephen Zito
SCRIPT COORDINATOR
Shari Ramsey
STORY EDITORS
Jonathan Kaplan
Paul Levine

BENDER-SPINK

1149 N. Poinsettia Pl., West Hollywood, CA 90046. (323) 845-1640. FAX: (323) 512-5347.
email: bender_spink@hotmail.com
EXECUTIVES
Chris Bender
J.C. Spink
Charlie Gogolak
Roy Lee
Jim Valdes
EXECUTIVE ASSISTANTS
Sarah Almazol
George Collins
Nicole Harb
Bryan O'Donnell

ROBERT BENEDETTI PRODUCTIONS, INC.

2533 6th St., Santa Monica, CA 90405-3707. (310) 664-0912.
FAX: (310) 664-0932. email: Benedetti1@aol.com
PRESIDENT
Robert Benedetti

BERG/SACCANI ENTERTAINMENT

7421 Beverly Blvd., Los Angeles, CA 90036. (323) 930-9935.
FAX: (323) 930-9934. email: info@berg-saccani.com
PARTNERS
Jon Berg
David Donegan
Damien Saccani

RICK BERMAN PRODUCTIONS

5555 Melrose Ave., Cooper Bldg., Ste. 232, Los Angeles, CA 90038. (323) 956-5037. FAX: (323) 862-1076.
EXECUTIVE PRODUCER
Rick Berman
ASSISTANT
Joanna Fuller
SUPERVISOR, STAR TREK PROJECTS
Dave Rossi

FRED BERNER FILMS

401 Fifth Ave., Fifth Flr., New York, NY 10016. (212) 592-0673.
FAX: (212) 592-0696.
PRESIDENT
Fred Berner
DIRECTOR, CREATIVE AFFAIRS
Elaine Frontain Bryant
CREATIVE ASSOCIATE
Ann C. Young

RICK BIEBER PRODUCTIONS

3000 W. Olympic Blvd., Bldg. 4, Ste. 1314, Santa Monica, CA 90404. (310) 246-3886. FAX: (310) 315-4800.
CONTACTS
Rick Bieber
Sharon Holmes
Judit Maull

BIG BANG FILMS

P.O. Box 1746, Studio City, CA 91614-0746. (818) 909-6325.
FAX: (818) 909-6325. email: gayne1024@aol.com
PRESIDENT
Matthew Gayne

BIG TOWN PRODUCTIONS

6201 Sunset Blvd., #80, Los Angeles, CA 90028-8704. (323) 962-8099. FAX: (323) 962-8029.
ACTOR & PRODUCER
Bill Pullman
V.P., DEVELOPMENT & PRODUCER
Ruth Fainberg
ASSISTANT
Elizabeth Hill

BLACK & BLU ENTERTAINMENT

10202 W. Washington Blvd., Lean Bldg. 333, Culver City, CA 90232. (310) 244-8833. www.hollywoodlitsales.com
PRODUCERS
Todd Black
Jason Blumenthal
SENIOR V.P.
Brian Morewitz
V.P., DEVELOPMENT
Chrissy Blumenthal
DIRECTOR, INTERNET LITERATURE ACQUISITIONS
Howard Meibach
STORY EDITOR
Erica Kane
CREATIVE ASSISTANTS
Jeff Forsyth
Lindsey Williams
OFFICE MANAGER
Kathy Rowe

BLEECKER STREET FILMS

1438 N. Gower Street, Box 22, Los Angeles, CA 90028. (323) 993-7386. FAX: (323) 993-7387.
PRESIDENT
Lois Bonfiglio
DEVELOPMENT ASSOCIATE
Simone Study

BLUE RELIEF, INC.

301 N. Canon Dr., Ste. 205, Beverly Hills, CA 90210. (310) 275-7900. FAX: (310) 724-5820.
DIRECTOR & PRODUCER
Diane Keaton
PRODUCER
Bill Robinson
ASSISTANTS
Erin Corzine

BLUE TULIP PRODUCTIONS

1658 10th St., Santa Monica, CA 90404. (310) 752-7900.
FAX: (310) 752-7920.
PRODUCERS
Jan De Bont
Lucas Foster

BLUE WOLF PRODUCTIONS, INC.

39 Mesa St., Ste. 201, San Francisco, CA 94129. (415) 451-8890. FAX: (415) 561-6650.
CONTACTS
Robin Williams
Marsha Williams
Daniel Spencer
Cyndi Margolis
Jennifer Garces Cerchiai

BOARDWALK ENTERTAINMENT

210 E. 39th St., New York, NY 10016. (212) 679-3800. FAX: (212) 679-3816. email: Boardwalk@infohouse.com
CHAIRMAN
Alan Wagner
PRESIDENT
Susan Wagner

CAROL BODIE ENTERTAINMENT

9465 Wilshire Blvd., Ste. 420, Beverly Hills, CA 90212. (310) 247-8181. FAX: (310) 247-8555. email: entcbe@aol.com
PRODUCER & CEO
Carol Bodie
COO
Steven Dubin
EXECUTIVE ASSISTANT
Jennifer Choi
ASSISTANT
Sara Giller

BONA FIDE PRODUCTIONS

8899 Beverly Blvd., Ste. 804, Los Angeles, CA 90048. (310) 273-6782. FAX: (310) 273-7821.
PRODUCERS
Albert Berger
Ron Yerxa
STORY EDITOR
Kristin Landholt

BONEYARD ENTERTAINMENT

863 Park Ave., Ste. 11E, New York, NY 10021. (212) 628-8600.
FAX: (212) 628-8615.
PRESIDENT & CEO
Daniel J. Victor
EXECUTIVE V.P.
Richard M. Victor

BOXING CAT PRODUCTIONS

11500 Hart St., North Hollywood, CA 91605. (818) 765-4870. FAX: (818) 765-4975.
PRODUCER & ACTOR
Tim Allen
PRODUCER
Brian Reilly
DIRECTOR, DEVELOPMENT
Matt Carroll

BREGMAN PRODUCTIONS

859 N. Hollywood Way, PMB 462, Burbank, CA 91505. (818) 954-9988. FAX: (818) 954-9989.
PRODUCERS
Martin Bregman
Michael Bregman

BRILLSTEIN-GREY ENTERTAINMENT

9150 Wilshire Blvd., Ste. 350, Beverly Hills, CA 90212. (310) 275-6135. FAX: (310) 275-6180.
CONSULTANT
Bernie Brillstein
CHAIRMAN & CEO
Brad Grey
PRESIDENT, BGTV
Kevin Reilly
CFO
Steve Blume
SENIOR EXECUTIVE V.P.
Sandy Wernick
CO-HEAD, MOTION PICTURE DIVISION
Matthew Baer
V.P., MOTION PICTURES
Laura Hopper
V.P., MOTION PICTURES
Denise Steward
CO-HEAD, BGTV
Jonathan Liebman
CO-HEAD, BGTV
Marc Gurvitz
CO-HEAD, BGTV
Peter Traugott
SENIOR V.P., TV
Susie Fitzgerald
V.P., PRODUCTION, TV
Tony Carey
DIRECTOR, DEVELOPMENT
Becky Clements
DIRECTOR, DEVELOPMENT
Marianne Cracchiolo
DIRECTOR, BUSINESS AFFAIRS
Amy Weiss
COORDINATOR, TV
Lisa Goldsmith
MANAGER, TV
Sean White

BRISTOL CITIES

5555 Melrose Ave., Swanson Bldg., Rm. 105, Los Angeles, CA 90038. (323) 956-3513. FAX: (323) 862-1172.
email: BrstlCty@aol.com
PRODUCERS
Jane Leeves
Peri Gilpin
V.P., CREATIVE AFFAIRS
Doug Collins

BROOKSFILMS, LTD.

9336 W. Washington Blvd., Culver City, CA 90232. (310) 202-3292. FAX: (310) 202-3225.
PRESIDENT
Mel Brooks
V.P., PRODUCTION SERVICES
Leah Zappy
DEVELOPMENT
Jennifer Yale

JERRY BRUCKHEIMER FILMS

1631 10th St., Santa Monica, CA 90403. (310) 664-6260. FAX: (310) 664-6261. www.jbfilms.z.com
PRODUCER
Jerry Bruckheimer
PRESIDENT
Mike Stenson
SENIOR V.P.
Chad Oman
DIRECTOR OF PRODUCTION
Kristie Anne Groelinger

THE BUBBLE FACTORY

8840 Wilshire Blvd., 3rd Flr., Beverly Hills, CA 90211. (310) 358-3000. FAX: (310) 358-3299.
PARTNERS
Sid Sheinberg
Bill Sheinberg
Jon Sheinberg
CONSULTANT, BUSINESS AFFAIRS
Gerald S. Barton
SENIOR V.P., PRODUCTION
Gerard Bocaccio
SENIOR V.P., PRODUCTION
Tom Prince
V.P., FINANCE & OPERATIONS
Kevin D. Forester
DIRECTOR, DEVELOPMENT
Gwen Osborne
MANAGER, MEDIA & CONSUMER PRODUCTS
Cory M. Lidschin
OFFICE MANAGER
Kimberly Gross

BUENA VISTA PICTURES

(see The Walt Disney Company.)

BUNGALOW 78 PRODUCTIONS

5555 Melrose Ave., Lasky Bldg. 200, Los Angeles, CA 90038. (323) 956-4440. FAX: (323) 862-2090.
EXECUTIVE PRODUCER & WRITER
Barry Kemp
PRESIDENT., FEATURE PRODUCTION
Devorah Moos-Hankin
DIRECTOR, DEVELOPMENT, FEATURE PRODUCTION
Bess Walkes
EXECUTIVE ASSISTANT
Jill Bowles

BURRUD PRODUCTIONS

16351 Gothard St., Unit D, Huntington Beach, CA 92647. (714) 842-8422. FAX: (714) 842-0433. www.burrud.com
email: burrudprod@aol.com
PRESIDENT & CEO
John Burrud
PRODUCER
Gita Patel
EXECUTIVE V.P., BUSINESS AFFAIRS
Stanley H. Green
V.P., PRODUCTION
Drew Horton
V.P., ADMINISTRATION & SALES
Linda Karabin
V.P., POST-PRODUCTION
Kurt Porter

BUTCHERS RUN FILMS

8978 Norma Pl., West Hollywood, CA 90069. (310) 246-4630. (310) 246-1033.
ACTOR & PRODUCER & DIRECTOR
Robert Duvall
PRODUCER
Rob Carliner
DIRECTOR, DEVELOPMENT
Adam Prince

CANAL + (U.S.)

301 N. Canon Drive, Ste. 207, Beverly Hills, CA 90210. (310) 247-0994. FAX: (310) 247-0998.
email: canalplus@cplus-us.com
CHAIRMAN & PRESIDENT & CEO
Pierre Lescure
CO-PRESIDENT
Stephane Sperry
CFO
Robert Chamberlin
V.P., BUSINESS AFFAIRS
Arnaud Duteil
DIRECTOR, CONTRACT ADMINISTRATION
Barbara DiNallo

THE CANTON COMPANY

4000 Warner Blvd., Bldg. 81, Ste. 200, Burbank, CA 91522. (818) 954-2130. FAX: (818) 954-2967.
CONTACTS
Mark Canton
Barbara Kalish
Anna DeRoy
Nathan Kahane
Chris Carter
Ben Hurvitz
Matthew Bakal

CAPELLA FILMS, INC.

9242 Beverly Blvd., Ste. 280, Beverly Hills, CA 90210-3710. (310) 247-4700. FAX: (310) 247-4701.
PRESIDENT
David Korda
PRESIDENT, CAPELLA INTERNATIONAL
Jean-Louis Rubin
CFO
Craig Arrington
EXECUTIVE V.P.
Alessandra McAliley

CAPPA PRODUCTIONS

445 Park Ave., New York, NY 10022. (212) 906-8800.
DIRECTOR
Martin Scorsese
PRODUCER
Barbara De Fina
DIRECTOR, DEVELOPMENT
Shira Levin

CASTLE HILL PRODUCTIONS, INC.

1414 Ave. of the Americas, New York, NY, 10019. (212) 888-0080. FAX: (212) 644-0956. email: castlehillinc@sprintmail.com
8899 Beverly Blvd. Ste. 407 Los Angeles, CA 90048. (310)) 858-0034. FAX: (310) 858-6934.
PRESIDENT
Julian Schlossberg
PRESIDENT, MARKETING & DISTRIBUTION
Mel Maron
VICE PRESIDENT
Milly Sherman
V.P., TELEVISION SALES
Barbara Karmel
DIRECTOR, ADVERTISING AND PUBLICITY
Steve Hadden
DIRECTOR, THEATRICAL DISTRIBUTION
Ivory Harris

CASTLE ROCK ENTERTAINMENT

335 N. Maple Dr., Ste. 135, Beverly Hills, CA 90210-3867. (310) 285-2300. FAX: (310) 285-2345.
PRODUCER & DIRECTOR
Rob Reiner
PRESIDENT, CASTLE ROCK TV
Glenn Padnick
PRODUCER & DIRECTOR
Andrew Scheinman
PRESIDENT, CASTLE ROCK PICTURES
Martin Shafer
COO
Greg Paul
PRESIDENT, CASTLE ROCK PICTURES
Liz Glotzer
EXECUTIVE V.P., PRODUCTION MANAGEMENT
Jeffrey Stott
CREATIVE EXECUTIVE
Brady Thomas
SENIOR V.P., BUSINESS & LEGAL AFFAIRS
David Goodman
SENIOR V.P., CASTLE ROCK TV
Robin Green
SENIOR V.P., PRODUCTION
Steven Rabiner
SENIOR V.P., BUSINESS & LEGAL AFFAIRS
Jessica Roddy
V.P., ADMINISTRATION
Carlos Perez
CREATIVE EXECUTIVE
Gaylyn Fraiche
DIRECTOR, FINANCIAL ADMINISTRATION
James Campbell
DIRECTOR, BUSINESS AFFAIRS ADMINISTRATION
Margo Meyer

CECCHI GORI PICTURES

11990 San Vicente Blvd., Ste. 200, Los Angeles, CA 90049. (310) 442-4777. FAX: (310) 442-9507. www.cecchigori.com
PRESIDENT
Gianni Nunnari
GENERAL COUNSEL
Claire Ambrosio
RESEARCH & DEVELOPMENT COORDINATOR
Paula Kahlenberg
CFO
Roland Lilavois
EXECUTIVE ASSISTANT
Marina Salvo

CENTROPOLIS ENTERTAINMENT

10202 W. Washington Blvd., Culver City, CA 90232. (310) 244-4300. FAX: (310) 244-4360. www.centropolis.com
PARTNERS
Roland Emmerich
Dean Devlin
Ute Emmerich
PRESIDENT
William Fay
SENIOR V.P.
Peter Winther
HEAD, BUSINESS DEVELOPMENT
Philippe Maigret
V.P., DEVELOPMENT
Marc Roskin

CHARTOFF PRODUCTIONS

1250 Sixth St., Ste. 101, Santa Monica, CA 90401. (310) 319-1960.
CEO & PRESIDENT
Robert Chartoff
EXECUTIVE V.P.
Lynn Hendee

CHERRY ALLEY PRODUCTIONS

1250 Sixth St., Ste. 200, Santa Monica, CA 90401. (310) 458-8886.
CEO
Goldie Hawn
PRESIDENT
Teri Schwartz
V.P., PRODUCTION
Philip E. Thomas

THE CINEMA GUILD

130 Madison Ave., 2nd Fl., New York, NY 10016-7038. (212) 685-6242. FAX: (212) 685-4717. www.cinemaguild.com
email: thecinemag@aol.com
PRESIDENT
Philip S. Hobel
V.P. & GENERAL MANAGER
Gary Crowdus
VICE PRESIDENT
Mary Ann Hobel

CINEMANSON MARKETING & DISTRIBUTION

1414 Ave. of the Americas, New York, NY 10019-2514. (212) 832-2806. FAX: (212) 832-2825. email: cinemanson@aol.com
PRESIDENT
Arthur Manson

CINEMA SEVEN PRODUCTIONS

154 W. 57th St., Ste. 112, New York, NY 10019. (212) 315-1060. FAX: (212) 315-1085. email: cin7prod@aol.com
144 S. Beverly Dr., Ste. 603, Beverly Hills, CA 90212. (310) 247-1444. FAX: (310) 247-1477.
PRESIDENT
Elliot Kastner
PRODUCER
Dillon Kastner
SENIOR V.P.
George Pappas
HEAD, PRODUCTION
Pasquale Botta (NY)
HEAD, DEVELOPMENT
James Deyarmin
HEAD, PRODUCTION
Julius Orthiguero (CA)

CINERGI PICTURES ENTERTAINMENT, INC.

2308 Broadway, Santa Monica, CA 90404-2916. (310) 315-6000. FAX: (310) 828-0443.
CHAIRMAN & CEO
Andrew Vajna
SENIOR V.P., FINANCE
Samuel Falconello

CINETEL FILMS, INC.

(Motion picture and TV distribution)
8255 Sunset Blvd., Los Angeles, CA 90046. (323) 654-4000. FAX: (213) 650-6400.
PRESIDENT & CEO
Paul Hertzberg
EXECUTIVE V.P
Lisa Hansen
CFO
Nick Gorenc
V.P., INTERNATIONAL DISTRIBUTION
Marcy Rubin

CINETEL PICTURES

PRESIDENT
Lisa Hansen

CINEVILLE INTERNATIONAL
225 Santa Monica Blvd., Santa Monica, CA 90401. (310) 394-4699. FAX: (310) 394-3052. email: cineville@aol.com
OWNER
Christopher Henkel
PRESIDENT
Carl-Jan Colpaert
DIRECTOR, DEVELOPMENT
Annabelle Frankl
DIRECTOR, OPERATIONS
Bob Joyce

CINEVISTA, INC.
(Distribution and sales.)
2044 Prairie Ave., Miami Beach, FL 33139. (305) 532-3400. (800) 341-CINE. FAX (305) 532-0047. www.cinevistavideo.com
PRESIDENT
Rene Fuentes-Chao
VICE PRESIDENT
Susan Morin

CLASSIC FILMS
6427 Sunset Blvd., Hollywood, CA 90028. (323) 962-7855. FAX: (323) 962-8028. email: brro@aol.com
PRESIDENT
Brian Rosen

COHEN PICTURES
7966 Beverly Blvd., Los Angeles, CA 90048. (323) 951-4250. FAX: (323) 655-1594. email: bobby_cohen@yahoo.com
PRODUCER
Bobby Cohen
ASSISTANT
Wittney Horton

HERMAN COHEN PRODUCTIONS/ COBRA MEDIA, INC.
650 N. Bronson Ave., Ste. 116, Hollywood, CA 90004. (323) 466-3388. (323) 653-4875
PRESIDENT
Herman Cohen
EXECUTIVE V.P.
Didier Chatelain

COLUMBIA PICTURES
(see Sony Pictures Entertainment, Inc.)

CONSTANTIN FILM DEVELOPMENT, INC.
9200 Sunset Blvd., Ste. 730, Los Angeles, CA 90069. (310) 247-0300. FAX: (310) 2467-0305.
PRODUCTION EXECUTIVE
Mitch Horwitz
CONTACTS
Bernd Eichinger
Lisa Kregness
Robert Kulzner
Marsha Metz
Cynthia Pruett
Elizabeth Wang Lee

CONTEMPTIBLE ENTERTAINMENT
9333 Wilshire Blvd., Beverly Hills, CA 90210. (310) 385-4183. FAX: (310) 385-6633. email: contempt63@aol.com
DIRECTOR & WRITER & PRODUCER
Neil LaBute
DIRECTOR, DEVELOPMENT
Melissa Brantley

CONTINENTAL FILM GROUP LTD.
1001 Park St., Sharon, PA 16146-3090. (724) 981-3456. FAX: (724) 981-2668.
Los.Angeles: 15131 Mulholland Dr., Bel Air, CA 90077 (818) 907-0938.
PRESIDENT & CEO
Amin Q. Chaudhri
V.P. IN CHARGE OF DEVELOPMENT
Asha N. Chaudhri
ASSISTANT TO THE PRESIDENT & CEO
Maraline A. Kubik
BOARD OF DIRECTORS
Amin Q. Chaudhri
Robert Holof

CONUNDRUM ENTERTAINMENT
325 Wilshire Blvd., Ste. 201, Santa Monica, CA 90401. (310) 319-2800. FAX: (310) 319-2808.
CONTACTS
Bobby Farrelly
Peter Farrelly
Bradley Thomas
Mark Charpentier
Clemens Franek

THOMAS CRAVEN FILM CORP.
5 W. 19th St., New York, NY 10011. (212) 463-7190. FAX: (212) 627-4761.
PRESIDENT
Michael Craven
VICE PRESIDENT
Ernest Barbieri

WES CRAVEN FILMS
11846 Ventura Blvd., Ste. 208, Studio City, CA 91604. (818) 752-0197. FAX: (818) 752-1789.
DIRECTOR & PRODUCER
Wes Craven
PRESIDENT & PRODUCER
Marianne Maddalena
PRESIDENT, PRODUCTION
Rene Garcia
V.P., DEVELOPMENT
Alix Taylor
CREATIVE EXECUTIVE
Richard Schulman
ASSISTANTS
Suzanne Santry
Collin Fowler

CROWN INTERNATIONAL PICTURES, INC.
8701 Wilshire Blvd., Beverly Hills, CA 90210. (310) 657-6700. FAX: (310) 657-4489. www.crownintlpictures.com
PRESIDENT & CEO
Mark Tenser
SENIOR V.P.
Scott E Schwimer
CONTROLLER
Willie De Leon
DIRECTOR, PUBLICITY & ADVERTISING
Lisa Agay
PRODUCERS
Marilyn J. Tenser
Scott E Schwimer
CONTROLLER
Willie De Leon
PRODUCER
Marilyn J. Tenser

CRUSADER ENTERTAINMENT
132B Lasky Dr., Beverly Hills, CA 90212. (310) 248-6360. FAX: (310) 248-6370.
CHAIRMAN
Howard Baldwin
CO-PRESIDENT
Karen Baldwin
CO-PRESIDENT
Andrew Reif
PRODUCER
Stuart Benjamin
V.P., FINANCE & LEGAL AFFAIRS
Nick Ruta
CREATIVE EXECUTIVE
Todd Slater
CREATIVE ASSISTANT
Tom Brainard

CRYSTAL PYRAMID PRODUCTIONS
7323 Rondel Ct., San Diego, CA 92119-1530. (619) 644-3000. www.crystalpyramid.com email: cpp@newuniquevideos.com
CEO
Mark Schulze
COO
Patty Mooney
V.P., PRODUCTION
Michael Sterner

CRYSTAL SKY, LLC
1901 Ave. of the Stars, Ste. 605, Los Angeles, CA 90067. (310) 843-0223. FAX: (310) 553-9895.
email: office@crystal-sky.com
CHAIRMAN
Hank Paul
CO-CHAIRMAN
Dorothy Koster
PRESIDENT
Steven Paul
SENIOR EXECUTIVE V.P.
Andrew Hersh
SENIOR V.P., FINANCE
Joe Inga
V.P., PRODUCTION & DEVELOPMENT
Patrick Ewald

CURB ENTERTAINMENT
3907 W. Alameda Ave., Ste. 200, Burbank, CA 91505. (818) 843-8580. FAX: (818) 566-1719. email: curbfilm@earthlink.net
PRESIDENT
Carole Curb
CHAIRPERSON
Mike Curb

C/W PRODUCTIONS
5555 Melrose Ave., Hollywood, CA 90038. (323) 956-8150. FAX: (323) 862-1250.
CONTACTS
Paula Wagner
Christopher Hanada
Darren Miller
Nick Roe
Gaye Hirsch
Missy Bania
Jane Whitney
Tanner Kling

DANJAQ, LLC
2401 Colorado Ave., Ste. 330, Santa Monica, CA 90404. (310) 449-3185. FAX: (310) 449-3189.
CO-CHAIRMAN
Dana Broccoli
PRESIDENT & CEO
Michael Wilson
COO
David Pope
V.P., PRODUCTION & DEVELOPMENT
Barbara Broccoli

DARK HORSE ENTERTAINMENT
100 Universal City Plaza, John Ford Bldg., Ste. 3G, Universal City, CA 91608. (818) 777-5830. FAX: (818) 866-5939. www.dhrose.com
PRESIDENT & PRODUCER
Mike Richardson
V.P., PRODUCTION
Steven Gilder

DAVIS ENTERTAINMENT CO.
2121 Ave. of the Stars, Ste. 2900, Los Angeles, CA 90067. (310) 556-3550. FAX: (310) 556-3688 & (310) 282-8775.
CHAIRMAN, DAVIS ENTERTAINMENT CO., TV
John A. Davis
PRESIDENT, SERIES TV
Paul Spadone
PRESIDENT, DAVIS ENTERTAINMENT FEATURES
Teddy Zee
EXECUTIVE V.P., ADMINISTRATION
Brooke Brooks
EXECUTIVE V.P., PRODUCTION
Wyck Godfrey
CREATIVE EXECUTIVE
Lil Phillips
DIRECTOR, DEVELOPMENT, TV
Amy Palmer

DAYBREAK PRODUCTIONS
100 Universal City Plaza, Bung. 4172, Universal City, CA 91608. (818) 777-0278. FAX: (818) 866-0285.
PRODUCER
Charles Gordon
PRESIDENT
Marc Sternberg

DESTINATION CINEMA, INC.
(Large-format production & distribution)
4155 Harrison Blvd., Ste. 210, Ogden, UT 84403. (801) 392-2001. FAX: (801) 392-6703. www.destinationcinema.com
PRESIDENT, FILM DISTRIBUTION
Ed Capelle
PRESIDENT, THEATER OPERATIONS
Bob Perkins

DIGITAL DOMAIN
300 Rose Ave., Venice, CA 90291. (310) 314-2800. FAX: (310) 314-2888. www.d2.com
CEO & PRODUCER
Scott Ross
SENIOR V.P., FEATURE VFX PRODUCTIONS
Nancy Bernstein
SENIOR V.P., BUSINESS AFFAIRS & GENERAL COUNSEL
Brad Call
SENIOR V.P., COMMERICAL PRODUCTION
Ed Ulbrich
V.P., FEATURE FILM DEVELOPMENT
Kevin K. Cooper
CREATIVE EXECUTIVE
Jonathan Howard

DIMENSION FILMS
(see Miramax Films)

DINAMO ENTERTAINMENT
1537 Pontius Ave., 2nd Flr., Los Angeles, CA 90025. (310) 473-1311. FAX: (310) 473-8233. email: dinamo@earthlink.net
PRESIDENT
Morrie Eisenman
DIRECTOR, CREATIVE AFFAIRS
Jim Zaphiriou

DINO DE LAURENTIIS COMPANY
100 Universal City Plaza, Bung. 5195, Universal City, CA 91608. (818) 777-2111. FAX: (818) 866-566.
CONSULTANT
Dino De Laurentiis
PRESIDENT & PRODUCER
Martha De Laurentiis
BUSINESS AFFAIRS
Scott Browning

DI NOVI PICTURES
3110 Main St., Ste. 220, Santa Monica, CA 90405. (310) 581-1355. FAX: (310) 399-0499.
PRODUCER
Denise Di Novi
PRESIDENT
Ed McDonnell

DISCOVERY PICTURES
(Large-format film production)
7700 Wisconsin Ave., Bethesda, MD 20814-1999. (301) 986-1999. FAX: (301) 986-4827. www.discovery.com

THE WALT DISNEY COMPANY
500 S. Buena Vista St., Burbank, CA 91521. (818) 560-1000. FAX: (818) 840-5737. www.disney.com
CHAIRMAN & CEO
Michael D. Eisner
VICE CHAIRMAN. OF THE BOARD
Roy E. Disney
SENIOR. EXECUTIVE V.P. & CCO
Sanford Litvack
EXECUTIVE V.P., CORP. AFFAIRS
John F. Cooke
SENIOR V.P., PLANNING & CONTROL
John J. Garand
V.P. & CORPORATE SECRETARY
Marsha L. Reed

THE WALT DISNEY MOTION PICTURES GROUP
500 South Buena Vista St., Burbank, CA 91521. (818) 560-1000.
CHAIRMAN, WALT DISNEY STUDIOS
Peter Schneider
CHMN., WALT DISNEY MOTION PICTURES GROUP
Richard Cook
PRESIDENT, BUENA VISTA INT'L.
Mark Zoradi
PRESIDENT, MUSIC
Kathy Nelson
PRESIDENT, BUENA VISTA PICTURES DISTRIBUTION
Chuck Viane
CO-PRESIDENTS, BUENA VISTA PICTURES MARKETING
Geoffrey Ammer
Oren Aviv
EXECUTIVE V.P., BUSINESS AFFAIRS
Bernardine Brandis
EXECUTIVE V.P., ACQUISITIONS, DEVEL. & NEW BUSINESS
Susan Lyne
PRESIDENT, PRODUCTION MANAGEMENT
Bruce Hendricks
SENIOR V.P. & CFO, WALT DISNEY STUDIOS
Dean Hallett
SENIOR V.P., CHARACTER VOICES & DUBBING
Jeffrey Miller
SENIOR V.P., MUSIC BUSINESS & LEGAL AFFAIRS
Scott Holtzman
SENIOR V.P., VISUAL EFFECTS & PRODUCTION
Art Repola
V.P., MOTION PICTURE PRODUCTION
Jerry Ketcham

BUENA VISTA PICTURES DISTRIBUTION, INC.
3900 W. Alameda Ave., #2400, Burbank, CA 91521. (818) 567-5000. FAX: (818) 972-9447
PRESIDENT
Chuck Viane
SENIOR V.P., GENERAL COUNSEL
Robert Cunningham
SENIOR V.P., NON-THEATRICAL SALES
Linda Palmer
SENIOR V.P., OPERATIONS
Gary Weaver

SENIOR V.P., GENERAL SALES MANAGER
Rod Rodriguez
SENIOR V.P., SPECIAL EVENTS
Lylle Breier
V.P., EASTERN DIVISION
Phil Fortune
V.P., NONTHEATRICAL
Nancy Kleuter
V.P., FINANCE
Deborah Morrison
V.P., SOUTHWESTERN DIVISION
Jim Nocella
V.P., WESTERN DIVISION
Pat Pade
V.P., MIDWESTERN DIVISION
Rick Rice

BUENA VISTA PICTURES DISTRIBUTION CANADA, INC.

1235 Bay Street, Ste. 502, Toronto, ON M5R 3K4. (416) 964-9275.
V.P., CANADA
Anthony Macina

BUENA VISTA PICTURES MARKETING

500 South Buena Vista St., Burbank, CA 91521. (818) 560-1000.
CO-PRESIDENT BUENA VISTA PICTURES MARKETING
Geoff Ammer
CO-PRESIDENT BUENA VISTA PICTURES MARKETING
Oren Aviv
SENIOR V.P., PUBLICITY
Heidi Trotta
SENIOR V.P., PROMOTIONS & FIELD OPERATIONS
Brett Dicker
SENIOR V.P., MEDIA
Kristy Frudenfeld
SENIOR V.P., WALT DISNEY ANIMATION CREATIVE
Fred Tio
SENIOR V.P., RESEARCH
Dana Lombardo
V.P., MEDIA OPERATIONS
Nina Anderson
V.P., CREATIVE FILM SERVICES
Jim Gallagher
Dave Singh
V.P., PUBLICITY
Denise Greenawalt
V.P. PUBLICITY
Mae Joyce
V.P., PRINT ADVERTISING
Whitney Cookson
V.P., EAST COAST PUBLICITY
Charlie Nelson
V.P., NATIONAL PROMOTIONS
Cherise McVicar
V.P., FIELD MARKETING
Georgia O'Connor
V.P., CREATIVE PRINT
John Sabel
V.P., CREATIVE FILM SERVICES
Constance Wells

BUENA VISTA MOTION PICTURES GROUP

WALT DISNEY PICTURES & TOUCHSTONE PICTURES
500 South Buena Vista St., Burbank, CA 91521. (818) 560-1000.
CHAIRMAN, THE WALT DISNEY STUDIOS
Peter Schneider
CHAIRMAN, WALT DISNEY MOTION PICTURES GROUP
Richard Cook
PRESIDENT, WALT DISNEY FEATURE ANIMATION, WALT DISNEY TELEVISION ANIMATION & BUENA VISTA THEATRICAL GROUP
Thomas Schumacher
PRESIDENT, BUENA VISTA MOTION PICTURES GROUP
Nina Jacobson
PRESIDENT, THEATRICAL MUSIC
Kathy Nelson
EXECUTIVE V.P., WALT DISNEY MOTION PICTURES GROUP
Bernardine Brandis
PRESIDENT, MOTION PICTURE PRODUCTION
Bruce Hendricks
SENIOR V.P., LEGAL AFFAIRS, BUENA VISTA MOTION PICTURES GROUP
Steve Bardwill
SENIOR V.P., BUSINESS & LEGAL AFFAIRS, WALT DISNEY FEATURE ANIMATION & BUENA VISTA THEATRICAL GROUP
Kevin W. Breen
SENIOR V.P., CREATIVE AFFAIRS, WALT DISNEY FEATURE ANIMATION
Pam Coats
SENIOR V.P., WALT DISNEY FEATURE ANIMATION
Tim Engel
SENIOR V.P., BUSINESS & LEGAL AFFAIRS, MUSIC
Scott R. Holtzman
SENIOR V.P., PRODUCTION, WALT DISNEY FEATURE ANIMATION
Phil Lofaro
SENIOR V.P., WALT DISNEY PICTURES & TELEVISION POST-PRODUCTION
David McCann
SENIOR V.P., BUSINESS & LEGAL AFFAIRS BUENA VISTA MOTION PICTURES GROUP
Phillip Muhl
SENIOR V.P., CREATIVE AFFAIRS, BUENA VISTA THEATRICAL GROUP
Stuart Oken
SENIOR V.P., FEATURE CASTING, BUENA VISTA MOTION PICTURES GROUP
Marcia S. Ross
EXECUTIVE V.P., PRODUCTION, BUENA VISTA MOTION PICTURES GROUP
Mark Vahradian
SENIOR V.P., PRODUCTION, BUENA VISTA MOTION PICTURES GROUP
Jason Reed
V.P., PRODUCTION, BUENA VISTA MOTION PICTURES GROUP
Jeffrey Clifford
V.P., PRODUCTION, BUENA VISTA MOTION PICTURES GROUP
Karen Glass
V.P., PRODUCTION FINANCE, WALT DISNEY FEATURE ANIMATION
Bob Bacon
SENIOR V.P., BUSINESS AFFAIRS
Doug Carter
V.P., LEGAL AFFAIRS
Sherri Feldman
V.P., PARTICIPATIONS & RESIDUALS
Michele Gazica
V.P., BUSINESS & LEGAL AFFAIRS
Steven W. Gerse
V.P., CREDIT & TITLE ADMINISTRATION
Stephanie Harris
SENIOR V.P., LABOR RELATIONS, WALT DISNEY PICTURES & TELEVISION
Robert W. Johnson
SENIOR V.P., CORPORATE NEW TECHNOLOGY
Bob Lambert
V.P. & GENERAL MANAGER, BUENA VISTA THEATRICAL GROUP
Alan Levey
V.P., CASTING, BUENA VISTA MOTION PICTURES GROUP
Donna Morong
V.P., FINANCE, WALT DISNEY FEATURE ANIMATION
Duncan Orrell-Jones
SENIOR V.P., HUMAN RESOURCES & ADMINISTRATION, WALT DISNEY STUDIOS
Marjorie Randolph
V.P., BUSINESS AFFAIRS
Howard Safenowitz
SENIOR V.P., WALT DISNEY FEATURE ANIMATION FLORIDA
Clark Spencer
SENIOR V.P., MOTION PICTURE PRODUCTION FINANCE
Paul Steinke

CREATIVE EXECUTIVES
DIRECTOR, PRODUCTION, BUENA VISTA MOTION PICTURES GROUP
Kristin Burr
DIRECTOR, PRODUCTION, BUENA VISTA MOTION PICTURES GROUP
Doug Short
DIRECTOR, PRODUCTION, BUENA VISTA MOTION PICTURES GROUP
Brigham Taylor
CREATIVE EXECUTIVE, BUENA VISTA MOTION PICTURE GROUP
Michael Haynes

LEGAL AFFAIRS
V.P., MUSIC BUSINESS & LEGAL AFFAIRS
Sylvia J. Krask
SENIOR ATTORNEYS
Ann Bowman
Carol McDermott
Lee Parnell
Joe Quigley
Paige Wright
ATTORNEYS
David Trygstad
Elizabeth Lynch
DIRECTOR, BUSINESS AFFAIRS
Kal Walthers
ATTORNEY, MUSIC, BUSINESS & LEGAL AFFAIRS
Don Welty

BUENA VISTA PRODUCTIONS
500 South Buena Vista St., Burbank, CA 91521. (818) 560-5000. FAX: (818) 560-1930.
PRESIDENT
Angela Shapiro
SENIOR V.P., PROGRAMMING & DEVELOPMENT
Holly Jacobs
SENIOR V.P., CURRENT PROGRAMMING
Mary Kellogg-Joslyn
V.P., DEVELOPMENT
Karen Glass
V.P., PRODUCTION
Carlos Torres

BUENA VISTA INTERNATIONAL
500 S. Buena Vista St., Burbank, CA 91521 (818) 560-1000.
PRESIDENT
Mark Zoradi
EXECUTIVE V.P. & GENERAL MANAGER
Lawrence Kaplan
PRESIDENT, WALT DISNEY INTERNATIONAL LATIN AMERICA
Diego Lerner
SENIOR V.P. MARKETING
Ignacio Darnaude
SENIOR V.P., PUBLICITY
Teri Ritzer
SENIOR V.P., DISTRIBUTION
Anthony Marcoly
SENIOR V.P., VOICE & DUBBING
Jeffrey Miller
SENIOR V.P., DIST. & GENERAL MANAGER, EUROPE
Stuart Salter
SENIOR V.P. & GENERAL MANAGER, GERMANY BVI-BVHE
Wolfgang Braun
V.P. & MANAGER, SWEDEN
Eric Broberg
SENIOR V.P., & GENERAL MANAGER, UK
Daniel Battsek
V.P., GENERAL MANAGER, FRANCE
Jean-Francois Camilleri
V.P. & GENERAL MANAGER, SOUTH KOREA
S.I. Kim
V.P., & GENERAL MANAGER, AUSTRIA
Ferdinand Morawetz
SENIOR V.P. & GENERAL MANAGER, ITALY
Paul Zonderland
V.P. & GENERAL MANAGER, SPAIN
Javier Vassalo
V.P. & GENERAL MANAGER, NETHERLANDS
Eline Danker
V.P. SALES & MARKETING, ASIA
Jeff Forman
V.P. FINANCE, BVI-BVHE
Jerome LeGrand
GENERAL MANAGER, SWITZERLAND
Roger Crotti
GENERAL MANAGER, JAPAN
Dick Sano
GENERAL MANAGER, TAIWAN
Rudy Tseng

BUENA VISTA HOME ENTERTAINMENT INTERNATIONAL
350 South Buena Vista St., Burbank, CA 91521. (818) 560-1000.
PRESIDENT
Mark Zoradi
SENIOR V.P., OPTIONS & LOGISTICS
Craig Komblau
V.P., ANTI-PIRACY
Judy Denenholz
V.P., TECHNICAL SERVICES
Steve Muckerheide
SENIOR V.P., MARKETING
Robyn Miller
SENIOR V.P., BUSINESS & LEGAL AFFAIRS
Brett Chapman
V.P., ADMINISTRATION AND OPERATIONS
Chris Menosky
V.P., PRODUCTION
Anita Puglisi
V.P., FINANCE
Tim Brasher
PRESIDENT, EUROPE, MIDDLE EAST & AFRICA
Stuart Warrener
SENIOR V.P., EUROPEAN OPERATIONS
Diana Rivera
V.P., EUROPEAN BUSINESS & LEGAL AFFAIRS
Rosemary Bloom
V.P., EUROPEAN FINANCE
Ian Bull
V.P., EUROPEAN SALES & MARKETING
David Hollander
SENIOR V.P., LATIN AMERICA & CARIBBEAN
Diego Lerner
V.P., SALES & MARKETING, ASIA/PACIFIC
Denise Anker
V.P., BUSINESS DEVEL. & FINANCE, ASIA/PACIFIC
Tim Sullivan
SENIOR V.P., RETAIL MARKETING & MERCHANDISING
Kelley Avery
SENIOR V.P., BUSINESS & LEGAL AFFAIRS
Rick Clair
SENIOR V.P., FINANCE
Mitch Koch
SENIOR V.P., SALES & DISTRIBUTION
Dennis Maguire
SENIOR V.P., MARKETING
Dennis Rice
V.P., RETAIL MARKETING & MERCHANDISING, N. AMERICA
Michael Aufricht
V.P., SALES PLANNING & ADMINISTRATION
Kevin Brennan
V.P., BRAND MARKETING
Bob Chapek
V.P., MARKETING & SERVICES
Randy Erickson
V.P., INFORMATION SERVICES
Tamara Gallagher
V.P., FINANCE & PLANNING
Kimberly Harold
SENIOR V.P., N. AMERICA MEDIA, RESEARCH, PROMOTIONS, & PUBLIC RELATIONS
Mary Kincaid
V.P., BUSINESS & LEGAL AFFAIRS
James Krauss
V.P., PROGRAMMING
Eleanor Richman
V.P., ACQUISITIONS
Anne Sterling
V.P., OPERATIONS & LOGISTICS
Michael Tofolo
V.P., NATIONAL ACCOUNTS/CANADIAN MARKETS
Bob Topping
V.P. & GENERAL MANAGER
Des Walsh

BUENA VISTA HOME ENTERTAINMENT
350 S. Buena Vista St., Burbank, CA 91521. (818) 560-1000.
SENIOR V.P. & GENERAL MANAGER OF NORTH AMERICA
Mitch Koch

BUENA VISTA PAY TELEVISION
500 South Buena Vista St., Burbank, CA 91521. (818) 560-1000. FAX: (818) 557-6504. www.disneychannel.com
PRESIDENT
Janice Marinelli
SENIOR V.P. & GM, PAY TV
Dan Cohen
SENIOR V.P., BUSINESS & LEGAL AFFAIRS
Lori Bernstein
V.P., DISTRIBUTION & BUSINESS AFFAIRS
Bill Rogers

DISNEY CHANNEL
3800 West Alameda Ave., Burbank, CA 91505. (818) 569-7500. FAX: (818) 845-8249. www.disneychannel.com
PRESIDENT, DISNEY/ABC CABLE NETWORKS & PRESIDENT, DISNEY CHANNEL
Anne Sweeney
EXECUTIVE V.P., MARKETING, DISNEY/ABC CABLE NETWORKS
Eleo Hensleigh
EXECUTIVE V.P., BUSINESS & LEGAL AFFAIRS, DISNEY CHANNEL
Frederick Kuperberg
GENERAL MANAGER & EXEC. V.P., PROG. & PROD.
Rich Ross
SENIOR V.P., NATIONAL ACCOUNTS
Benjamin Pyne
SENIOR V.P. & GEN. MGR., CHILDRENS PROGRAMMING
Jonathan Barzilay

BUENA VISTA TELEVISION
500 S. Buena Vista St., Burbank, CA 91521. (818) 560-5000. FAX: (818) 566-7412.
PRESIDENT, BUENA TELEVISION
Janice Marinelli
PRESIDENT, BUENA VISTA PRODUCTIONS
Angela Shapiro
EXECUTIVE V.P., SALES
Tom Cerio
EXECUTIVE V.P., AD SALES
Howard Levy
SENIOR V.P. & GENERAL SALES MANAGER
John Bryan
SENIOR V.P. & GENERAL MANAGER, PAY TV & DIST.
Dan Cohen
SENIOR V.P., WESTERN REGION
Jed Cohen
SENIOR V.P., AD SALES, MIDWEST
Jim Engleman

SENIOR V.P., PROG. & DEV., BUENA VISTA PRODS.
Holly Jacobs
SENIOR V.P., CURRENT PROG., BUENA VISTA PRODS.
Mary Kellogg-Joslyn
SENIOR V.P., STRATEGIC RESEARCH
Lloyd Komesar
SENIOR V.P., FINANCE
Tom Malanga
SENIOR V.P. & GENERAL SALES MANAGER, WEST
Jim Packer
SENIOR V.P., MARKETING
Sal Sardo
V.P., BUSINESS AFFAIRS
Lori Bernstein
V.P., AFFILIATE RELATIONS
Sandra Brewer
V.P., OPERATIONS & SALES DEVELOPMENT
Helen Faust
V.P., DEVELOPMENT, BUENA VISTA PRODUCTIONS
Karen Glass
V.P., PUBLICITY
Kim Harbin
V.P., CREATIVE SERVICES
Mike Henry
V.P., PRINT ADVERTISING
Jimmy Lee
V.P., AD SALES, EAST
Norman Lesser
V.P., RESEARCH & AD SALES
Noreen McGrath
V.P., MIDWEST REGION
David McLeod
V.P., OPERATIONS & AD SALES
Eddie Meister
V.P., GENERAL SALES MANAGER EAST
Chris Oldre
V.P., SOUTHWEST REGION
Steven Orr, Jr.
V.P., SALES SERVICE & ADMINISTRATION
Teri Owen
V.P., RESEARCH
Julie Piepenkotter
V.P. DISTRIBUTION & BUSINESS AFFAIRS
Bill Rogers
V.P., AD SALES EAST
Irv Schulman
V.P., SYNDICATION DISTRIBUTION
Christopher Stefanidis
V.P., AD SALES EAST
Cathy Thomas
V.P., PRODUCTION, BUENA VISTA PRODUCTIONS
Carlos Torres

WALT DISNEY IMAGINEERING

1401 Flower Street, Glendale, CA 91221. (818) 544-6500. FAX: (818) 544-5080.
VICE CHMN. & PRINCIPAL CREATIVE EXECUTIVE
Martin Sklar
PRESIDENT, WDI, DISNEYLAND INTERNATIONAL
James Thomas
EXECUTIVE V.P., MASTER PLANNING, ARCH. & DESIGN
Wing Chao
EXECUTIVE V.P., ENGINEERING & PRODUCTION
Gilbert Decker
EXECUTIVE V.P., STORY, SCRIPT, MEDIA
Thomas Fitzgerald
EXECUTIVE V.P., WDI
Donald Goodman
EXECUTIVE V.P., RESEARCH & DEVELOPMENT
Eric Haseltine
SENIOR V.P., WDI
Tony Baxter
SENIOR V.P & EXECUTIVE PRODUCER
Barry Braverman
SENIOR V.P & SHOW PRODUCER
John De Santis
SENIOR V.P., CREATIVE MGMT. & HUMAN RESOURCES
Ronni Fridman
SENIOR V.P., GENERAL MANAGER (CA)
Timur Galen
SENIOR V.P., WDI
John Hench
SENIOR V.P., WDI
Eric Jacobson
SENIOR V.P., CREATIVE EXECUTIVE
Stephen Kirk
SENIOR V.P., ENGINEERING
Thomas McCann
SENIOR V.P., PRE-DEVELOPMENT
Douglas Moreland
EXECUTIVE CONCEPT ARCHITECT & V.P.
Christopher Carradine
PROJECT V.P., WDI (FL)
John Blitch
V.P., BUSINESS PLANNING & DEVELOPMENT
Lynn Carrigan
TECHNICAL V.P.
Alan Cross
EXECUTIVE DESIGNER V.P.
Timothy Delaney
V.P., FACILITIES DEVELOPMENT
Thomas Dunlap
V.P., DEVELOPMENT MANAGEMENT
Bryan Elliott
V.P., EXECUTIVE PRODUCTION DESIGNER
Ronald Ferrante
V.P., DESIGN & PRODUCTION
Orlando Ferrante
V.P., CREATIVE
Laurence Gertz
V.P., SHOW QUALITY STANDARD
George Head
V.P., A&E
Arthur Henderson
V.P., RESORTS DEVELOPMENT
Robert Holland
V.P., DISNEY FELLOW
Alan Kay
V.P., REAL ESTATE DEVELOPMENT & OPERATIONS
Matthew Kelly
V.P., FINANCE
David King
V.P., PROJECTS
Arthur Kishiyama
V.P., CREATIVE
Kathryn Klatt
V.P., PROJECT MANAGEMENT
Paul La France
V.P., EXECUTIVE PRODUCTION DESIGNER
Oscar Lange, Jr.
V.P., EXECUTIVE PRODUCER
Kathryn Mangum
V.P., OPERATIONS & BUSINESS AFFAIRS
Thomas Markes
V.P., PLANNING INFRASTRUCTURE
Harold McIntyre
V.P., INFORMATION SERVICES
Jeffrey Mirich
V.P., DESIGN & PRODUCTION
Michael Morris
V.P., EXECUTIVE PRODUCER
Thomas Morris
V.P., EXEC. DESIGNER, RESEARCH & DEVELOPMENT
Andrew Ogden
V.P., EXECUTIVE PRODUCTION DESIGNER
John Olson
V.P., EXECUTIVE PRODUCER
Paul Osterhout
V.P., SENIOR ENGINEERING & PRODUCTION
Hurt Pritz
V.P., GENERAL MANAGER CELEBRATION
Perry Reader
V.P., EXECUTIVE DESIGNER
Joseph Rohde
V.P., PROJECT MANAGEMENT
Alan Rose
V.P., ADVANCED TECHNOLOGY RESEARCH
Eric Rosenthal
V.P., EXECUTIVE SHOW PRODUCER
Frederick Rothschild
V.P., A&FE MANAGEMENT, TDR
Craig Russell
V.P., CREATIVE DEVELOPMENT, TPP
John Solomon
V.P., GENERAL COUNSEL
Peter Steinman
V.P., PROJECT MANAGEMENT
David Todd
V.P., PROJECT
John Verity
V.P., ONLINE & ADVANCED MEDIA
Scott Watson
V.P. SENIOR ENGINEERING
Michael Withers
V.P., PROJECT CONSTRUCTION MANAGEMENT
Walter Wrobleski

DISTANT HORIZON

8282 Sunset Blvd., Ste. A, Los Angeles, CA 90046. (323) 848-4140. FAX: (323) 848-4144. www.distant-horizone.com
PRESIDENT
Anant Singh

MAUREEN DONLEY PICTURES

914 Westwood Blvd., Ste. 591, Los Angeles, CA 90024. (310) 441-0834 FAX: (310) 441-1595. email: mcd@mdpix.com
PRODUCER
Maureen Donley
DIRECTOR, DEVELOPMENT
Lauren Sands

DONNER/SHULER DONNER PRODS.

c/o Warner Bros., 4000 Warner Blvd., Bldgs. 102 & 103, #4, Burbank, CA 91522-0001. (818) 954-3961. FAX: (818) 954-4908.
PRODUCER & DIRECTOR
Richard Donner
PRODUCER
Lauren Shuler Donner

JEAN DOUMANIAN PRODUCTIONS

595 Madison Ave., Ste. 2200, New York, NY 10022. (212) 486-2626. FAX: (212) 688-6236.
PRESIDENT
Jean Doumanian
EXECUTIVE V.P.
John Logigian
DIRECTOR, DEVELOPMENT
Adam Schlesinger
STORY EDITORS
Kimberly Jose
Marcus Witte

DREAMWORKS SKG

100 Universal City Plaza, Bldg. 477, Universal City, CA 91608. (818) 733-7000.
650 Madison Ave., 22nd Flr., New York, NY 10022.
PRINCIPALS
Steven Spielberg
Jeffrey Katzenberg
David Geffen
CO-HEAD, MOTION PICTURE DIVISION
Laurie MacDonald
CO-HEAD, MOTION PICTURE DIVISION
Walter Parkes
HEAD, THEATRICAL DISTRIBUTION
Jim Tharp
HEAD, MARKETING & PUBLIC RELATIONS
Terry Press

DREYFUSS/JAMES PRDOUCTIONS

1041 Formosa Ave., Pickford Bldg., Rm. 110, West Hollywood, CA 90046. (323) 850-3140. FAX: (323) 850-3141.
OWNER & EXECUTIVE PRODUCER
Richard Dreyfuss
OWNER & EXECUTIVE PRODUCER
Judith James
DIRECTOR, DEVELOPMENT
Greg Szimonisz

EASTMAN KODAK COMPANY

343 State St., Rochester, NY 14650. (716) 724-4000.
815 W. Van Buren, Ste. 320, Chicago, IL 60607 (312) 492-1423
6700 Santa Monica Blvd., Hollywood, CA 90038. (323) 464-6131.
360 W. 31 St., New York, NY 10001. (212) 631-3450.
4 Concourse Pkwy., Ste. 300, Atlanta, GA 30328. (800) 800-8398. www.kodak.com
CHAIRMAN & CEO
George M.C. Fisher
PRESIDENT
Daniel A. Carp
PRESIDENT, ENTERTAINMENT IMAGING
Joerg D. Agin

EAST WEST CAPITAL ASSOCIATES

10900 Wilshire Blvd., Ste. 950, Los Angeles, CA 90024. (310) 209-6155. FAX: (310) 209-6160.
PRODUCER
Gary Adelson

EDMONDS ENTERTAINMENT

1635 N. Cahenga Blvd., 5th Flr., Los Angeles, CA 90028. (323) 860-1550. FAX: (323) 860-1554.
PRESIDENT & CEO
Kenneth Edmonds
PRESIDENT & CEO
Tracey E. Edmonds
SENIOR V.P., FILM
Bridget D. Davis
V.P., E2 FILMWORKS
Patrik-Ian Polk
V.P., DEVELOPMENT TV
Sheila Ducksworth
STORY EDITOR, E2 FILMWORKS
Jimmy Tsai
LINE PRODUCER, E2 FILMWORKS
Carol Shine

BLAKE EDWARDS CO.

10345 W. Olympic Blvd., Los Angeles, CA 90064-2524. (310) 234-0989 FAX: (310) 234-9179.
CHAIRMAN
Blake Edwards

EGG PICTURES

5555 Melrose Ave., Jerry Lewis Bldg. Annex, Los Angeles, CA 90038. (323) 956-8400. FAX: (323) 862-1414.
ACTOR & DIRECTOR & PRODUCER
Jodie Foster
PRESIDENT
Meg LeFauve
VICE PRESIDENT
Lisa Buono
EXECUTIVE ASSISTANT
Erin O'Donnell
DEVELOPMENT ASSISTANT
Lorielle Mallue

EL DORADO PICTURES

725 Arizona Ave., Ste. 100, Santa Monica, CA 90401. (310) 458-4800. FAX: (310) 458-4802.
PRODUCERS
Alec Baldwin
Jon Cornick
ASSOCIATE PRODUCER
T. Vincent

EL NORTE PRODUCTIONS

8701 W. Olympic Blvd., Los Angeles, CA 90035. (310) 360-1194. FAX: (310) 360-1199.
DIRECTOR & PRODUCER
Gregory Nava
V.P., DEVELOPMENT & PRODUCER
Darlene Caamano
V.P., TV
Barbara Martinez Jitman
DEVELOPMENT & PRODUCTION ASSISTANT
Laura Flores

ENTERTAINMENT DATA, INC.

2210 Wilshire Blvd., Ste. 744, Santa Monica, CA 90403. (310) 456-3143.
PRESIDENT
Edward Coe

ENTERTAINMENT PRODUCTIONS, INC.

P.O. Box 554, Malibu, CA 90265. (310) 456-3143. FAX: (310) 456-8950.
PRESIDENT & PRODUCER
Edward Coe

EQUINOX ENTERTAINMENT, LTD.

15030 Ventura Blvd., #815, Sherman Oaks, CA 91403. (818) 788-2500. FAX: (818) 528-1488.
EXECUTIVE PRODUCER & PRODUCER
Mark Michopoulos
CO-PRODUCER
Bob Manning
DIRECTOR, OPERATIONS
Ben Carpenter
DIRECTOR, DEVELOPMENT
Alex Ellis
DIRECTOR, RESEARCH & ACQUISITIONS
Mandy Goldberg
DIRECTOR, CREATIVE AFFAIRS
Tim Mathos
DIRECTOR, PRODUCTION
Amy Segal
DIRECTOR, BUSINESS AFFAIRS
Samantha Wagner
DIRECTOR, FINANCE & MARKETING & DISTRIBUTION
Lauren Worth
STORY EDITOR
Nick Andraos
ASSOCIATE PRODUCER & DIRECTOR, TALENT & CASTING
Ryan Sahlberg
EXECUTIVE ASSISTANTS
Lisa Logan
Jennifer Mancini
ASSISTANT STORY EDITOR
Evan Cartwright
ASSISTANT, TALENT & CASTING
Sara Palmer
ASSISTANT, DEVELOPMENT
C.J. Pillsbury
ASSISTANT, RESEARCH & ACQUISITIONS
Max Shepherd

ETERNITY PICTURES, INC.

169 Pier Ave., Second Flr., Santa Monica, CA 90405. (310) 452-7313. FAX: (310) 452-4006. email: etpic@aol.com
PRODUCER
Willi E. Baer
PRODUCER
Carmen M. Miller

THE ROBERT EVANS CO.

5555 Melrose Ave., Lubitsch Bldg. #117, Los Angeles, CA 90038-3197. (323) 956-8800. FAX: (323) 862-0070.
CHAIRMAN
Robert Evans
PRESIDENT
Christine Forsyth-Peters
EXECUTIVE V.P.
Robin Guthrie
DIRECTOR, DEVELOPMENT
Cyntha Matzger
STORY EDITOR
Samuel Dowe-Sanders
DEVELOPMENT ASSISTANT
James Smith

FACE PRODUCTIONS

335 N. Maple Dr., Ste. 135, Beverly Hills, CA 90210. (310) 285-2300. FAX: (310) 285-2386.
ACTOR & PRODUCER
Billy Crystal
V.P., DEVELOPMENT
Samantha Sprecher
STORY EDITOR
Annette Mathews
ASSISTANT
Carol Sidlow

EDWARD S. FELDMAN CO.

2600 W. Olive Ave., Ste. 748, Burbank, CA 91521-7254. (818) 972-3304. FAX: (818) 973-3309. email: esfeldman@aol.com
PRESIDENT & PRODUCER
Ed Feldman
CREATIVE ASSOCIATE
Winship Cook

FGM ENTERTAINMENT

8670 Wilshire Blvd., Ste. 301, Beverly Hills, CA 90211. (310) 358-1370. FAX: (310) 358-1380.
PRODUCER & PRESIDENT
Frank Mancuso Jr.
LINE PRODUCER
Vikki Williams

FIFTY CANNON ENTERTAINMENT, LLC

10390 Santa Monica Blvd., Ste. 350, Los Angeles, CA 90025. (310) 552-1518. FAX: (310) 552-2310. www.50cannon.com
CHAIRMAN
Mike Newell
PRESIDENT
Cameron Jones
V.P., MOTION PICTURE PRODUCTION
Brent Travers
DIRECTOR, CREATIVE AFFAIRS
William Butler-Sloss

54TH STREET PRODUCTIONS

10880 Wilshire Blvd., Ste. 1840, Los Angeles, CA 90024. (310) 445-5484.
PRINCIPAL
Lindsay Conner

FILMCOLONY, LTD.

7966 Beverly Blvd., 3rd Flr., Los Angeles, CA 90048. (323) 951-4650. FAX: (323) 951-4660.
PRESIDENT & PRODUCER
Richard N. Gladstein
SENIOR V.P., PRODUCTION & CO-PRODUCER
Gary Binkow
DIRECTOR, DEVELOPMENT
Stacy Zand

FILMOPOLIS

P.O. Box 4867, Carson, CA 90749. (310) 914-1776. FAX: (978) 334-5539.
CEO & V.P. SALES
Ray Kavandi
PRESIDENT
Zachary Lovas
V.P., PRODUCTION
Jason Lovas

FILMS AROUND THE WORLD, INC.

60 East 42nd St. Ste. 630, New York, NY 10165 (212) 599-9500. FAX: (212) 599-6040.
PRESIDENT
Alexander W. Kogan, Jr.

FILMWORLD INTERNATIONAL, INC.

304 N. Edinburgh Ave., Los Angeles, CA 90048. (323) 655-7705. FAX: (323) 655-7706. www.filmworldinc.com
email: fworld@filmworldinc.com
CHAIRMAN
Menahem Golan
PRESIDENTS
Evgeny Afineevsky
Abraham M. Daniels
Daniel De Liege

FINE LINE FEATURES

(see New Line Cinema)

WENDY FINERMAN PRODUCTIONS

10201 W. Pico Blvd., Los Angeles, CA 90035. (310) 369-8808. FAX: (310) 369-8800.
140 W. 57th St., Ste. 10D, New York, NY 10019. (212) 586-6000. FAX: (212) 586-7600.
PRODUCER
Wendy Finerman
PRESIDENT, PRODUCTION
Greg Mooradian
CREATIVE EXECUTIVE
Jennifer Goldstein
Tiffany Ericksen
V.P., PRODUCTION
David Stephanou

FINNEGAN-PINCHUK COMPANY

(Motion picture producers)
27420 Avenue Scott, Santa Clarita, CA 91355-3450. (818) 508-5614. FAX: (818) 313-9746. email: FINNPINC@aol.com
EXECUTIVE PRODUCERS
Patricia Finnegan
William Finnegan
Sheldon Pinchuk

FIRST KISS PRODUCTIONS

8383 Wilshire Blvd., Ste. 446, Beverly Hills, CA 90211. (323) 951-1220. FAX: (323) 951-1240.
ACTRESS & PRODUCER
Alicia Silverstone
MANAGER & PRODUCER
Carolyn Kessler
CREATIVE EXECUTIVE
Matt Miranda

FIRST LIGHT

9720 Wilshire Blvd., 4th Flr., Beverly Hills, CA 90212. (310) 777-3105. FAX: (310) 777-5243.
DIRECTOR
Kathryn Bigelow
DIRECTOR, DEVELOPMENT
Erin Lacey

FIRST LOOK PICTURES/OVERSEAS FILM GROUP

(Film distribution and acquisition)
8800 Sunset Blvd., Ste. 302, Los Angeles, CA 90069. (310) 855-1199. FAX: (310) 855-0719. www.ofg.com
PRESIDENT & CO-CHAIRMAN
Robert Little
CO-CHAIRMAN
Ellen Little
CEO & CO-CHAIRMAN
Chris Cooney
COO
Bill Lischak
SENIOR V.P., DISTRIBUTION AND MARKETING
M J Peckos
V.P., BUSINESS & LEGAL AFFAIRS
Doug McClure

FIRST RUN FEATURES

153 Waverly Pl., New York, NY 10014. (800) 229-8575. FAX: (212) 989-7649. email: info@firstrunfeatures.com
PRESIDENT
Seymour Wishman
VICE PRESIDENT
Marc A. Mauceri

FLOWER FILMS, INC.

9220 Sunset Blvd., #309, Los Angeles, CA 90069. (310) 285-0200. FAX: (310) 285-0827.
PARTNERS
Drew Barrymore
Nancy Juvonen
V.P., DEVELOPMENT
Stephanie Savage
CREATIVE EXECUTIVE
Linda McDonough

FORTIS FILMS

8581 Santa Monica Blvd., Ste. 1, West Hollywood, CA 90069. (310) 659-4533. FAX: (310) 659-4373.
OWNER
Sandra Bullock
PRESIDENT & CEO
John Bullock
EXECUTIVE V.P.
Gesine Bullock
PRODUCTION EXECUTIVE
Maggie Biggar
DIRECTOR, DEVELOPMENT
Lillian Dean

FORTY ACRES & A MULE FILMWORKS

124 Dekalb Ave., Brooklyn, NY 11217. (718) 624-3703. FAX: (718) 624-2008.
8899 Beverly Blvd. Ste. 401, Los Angeles, CA 90048 (310) 276-2116. FAX (310) 276-2164.
CEO
Spike Lee
PRESIDENT, PRODUCTION
Sam Kitt
DIRECTOR, DEVELOPMENT
Andre Hereford

44 BLUE PRODUCTIONS, INC.

4040 Vineland Ave., Ste. 105, Studio City, CA 91604. (818) 760-4442. FAX: (818) 760-1509.
email: fortyfourblu@earthlink.net
PRESIDENT & EXECUTIVE PRODUCER
Rasha Drachkovitch
SENIOR PRODUCER
Lasta Drachkovitch
PRODUCER
Dick Noonan
ASSOCIATE PRODUCER
David R. Hale

FORWARD PASS, INC.

12233 W. Olympic Blvd., Ste. 340, Los Angeles, CA 90064. (310) 571-3443.
WRITER & PRODUCER & DIRECTOR
Michael Mann
V.P., DEVELOPMENT & PRODUCTION
Michael Schulman
V.P., BUSINESS AFFAIRS
Nancy Peardon

FOUNTAINBRIDGE FILMS

10202 W. Washington Blvd., Crawford Bldg., Culver City, CA 90232. (310) 244-8080. FAX: (310) 244-8484.
ACTOR & PRODUCER
Sean Connery
PRESIDENT & PRODUCER
Rhonda Tollefson
CREATIVE EXECUTIVE
Lynette Ramirez
ASSISTANT
Joanna Butan

1492 PICTURES

10201 W. Pico Blvd., Bldg.86, 2nd Flr., Los Angeles, CA 90035 (310) 369-2368.
WRITER & DIRECTOR & PRODUCER & PARTNER
Chris Columbus
PRESIDENT & PRODUCER & PARTNER
Michael Barnathan
PRODUCER & PARTNER
Mark Radcliffe
ASSOCIATE PRODUCER
Paula DuPre-Pesmen
V.P., CREATIVE AFFAIRS
Jennifer Blum
V.P., CREATIVE AFFAIRS
James Mulay

FOX, INC.

(Fox Inc. is the parent company of Fox Broadcasting Co., Fox Television Stations Inc. & Fox Filmed Entertainment, which includes Twentieth Century Fox Film Corporation and Fox 2000)
10201 W. Pico Blvd., Los Angeles, CA 90035. (310) 369-1000.
1211 Ave. of the Americas 16th Flr., New York, NY 10036. (212) 556-8600. FAX: (212) 556-8606. www.newscorp.com
www.fox.com
14755 Preston Rd., Ste. 420, Dallas, TX 75240. (972) 392-0101. FAX: (972) 392-1007.
6320 Canoga Ave., Ste. 430, Woodland Hills, CA 91367 (818) 702-7200. (818) 702-7289
33 Bloor St E., Ste. 1106, Toronto, ON M4W 3H1. (416) 921-0001. FAX: (416) 921-9062.
CHAIRMAN & CEO, NEWS CORPORATION
Rupert Murdoch
CHAIRMAN & CO-COO, FOX NEWS CORP.
Peter Chernin
CO-COO
Chase Carey
SENIOR EXECUTIVE V.P. & CFO
David F. DeVoe
SENIOR EXECUTIVE V.P. & GENERAL COUNSEL
Arthur M. Siskind

FOX FILMED ENTERTAINMENT

CHAIRMEN
Tom Rothman
Jim Gianopulos
SENIOR V.P. & CHAIRMAN, TWENTIETH CENTURY FOX DOMESTIC FILM GROUP
Tom Sherak
PRESIDENT, WORLDWIDE MARKETING
Robert Harper
EXECUTIVE V.P.
Greg Gelfan
SENIOR V.P. & CFO
Simon Bax

TWENTIETH CENTURY FOX

PRESIDENT, TWENTIETH CENTURY FOX FILM GROUP
Tom Rothman
PRESIDENT, PRODUCTION
Hutch Parker
EXECUTIVE V.P., POST-PRODUCTION
Theodore Gagliano
SENIOR V.P., PRODUCTION
Peter Rice
SENIOR V.P., PRODUCTION
Fred Baron
V.P., FEATURE PRODUCTION
Kimberly Cooper
V.P., ACQUISITIONS & PRODUCTION
Robert Aaronson
V.P., ACQUISITIONS
Roseanne Korenberg

MARKETING

EXECUTIVE V.P., & GENERAL SALES MANAGER
Richard Myerson
EXECUTIVE V.P., INTERNATIONAL SALES & DISTRIBUTION
Julian Levin
EXECUTIVE V.P., MARKETING, MEDIA & RESEARCH
Nancy Utley
EXECUTIVE V.P., INTERNATIONAL MARKETING
Scott Neeson
SENIOR V.P., MARKETING & DISTRIBUTION
Bruce Pfander
SENIOR V.P., MARKETING & CREATIVE ADVERTISING
Anthony Sella
SENIOR V.P., MARKETING & CREATIVE ADVERTISING
Greg McClatchy
SENIOR V.P., MEDIA & CO-OP ADVERTISING
Steve Siskind
SENIOR V.P., PUBLICITY & PROMOTIONS
Jeffrey Godsick
V.P., NATIONAL PUBLICITY
Carol Sewell
V.P., NATIONAL PUBLICITY
Debbie Miller
V.P., PROMOTIONAL PROGRAMMING
Tom Grane
V.P., ADVERTISING & MARKETING
Laura Carillo
V.P., ADVERTISING & MKTG. & CREATIVE ADVERTISING
Christopher Pawlak
V.P., MARKET RESEARCH
Pam Levine-Katz
V.P., PROMOTIONS & INTERNATIONAL MARKETING
Ron Rubin

DISTRIBUTION

PRESIDENT, DOMESTIC DISTRIBUTION
Bruce Snyder
EXECUTIVE V.P., INTL. SALES & DISTRIBUTION
Julian Levin
V.P., WORLDWIDE NONTHEATRICAL SALES
Harvey Applebaum
V.P., CREATIVE ADVERTISING & INTL. THEATRICAL DIST.
Jim Darbinian
V.P., EXHIBITOR SERVICES
Branden Miller
EXEC. DIRECTOR EXHIBITOR SERVICES
Jill Amerman
V.P., DISTRIBUTION, MID WESTERN DIVISION
Bob Kaplowitz
V.P., DISTRIBUTION, WESTERN DIVISION
Bert Livingston
V.P., DISTRIBUTION, ATLANTIC DIVISION
Ron Polon

V.P., DISTRIBUTION, EASTERN DIVISION
Henri Frankfurter
GENERAL MANAGER, CANADA
Barry Newstead

ADMINISTRATION

EXECUTIVE V.P., DEPUTY GENERAL COUNSEL
Lyman Gronemeyer
EXECUTIVE V.P., LEGAL AFFAIRS
Robert Cohen
EXECUTIVE V.P., BUSINESS AFFAIRS
Steven Bersch
SENIOR V.P., LEGAL AFFAIRS & ASST. GENERAL COUNSEL
Michael Doodan
SENIOR V.P., LEGAL & BUSINESS AFFAIRS
Jamie Samson
SENIOR V.P., BUSINESS AFFAIRS
Daniel Ferleger
SENIOR V.P., BUSINESS AFFAIRS
Mark Resnick
SENIOR V.P., BUSINESS AFFAIRS
Lance Grode
SENIOR V.P., PERSONNEL
Leslee Perlstein
SENIOR V.P., FINANCE
Peter Cyffka
V.P., CONTROLLER
Matt Dubil
V.P., BUSINESS AFFAIRS
Victoria Rosselini
V.P., CORPORATE COMMUNICATIONS
Florence Grace
V.P., LEGAL AFFAIRS
William Petrasich
V.P., LEGAL AFFAIRS
Joan Hansen
V.P., LEGAL AFFAIRS
James Taylor
V.P., FINANCE
Mark Rosenbaum
V.P., FINANCE, DOMESTIC
Todd Greenfield

INTERNATIONAL

EXECUTIVE V.P., INTERNATIONAL SALES & DISTRIBUTION
Julian Levin
SENIOR V.P., INTERNATIONAL MARKETING
Scott Neeson
SENIOR V.P., EUROPE/NEAR EAST & AFRICA
Jorge Canizares

FOX STUDIO OPERATIONS

SENIOR V.P., FOX STUDIO OPERATIONS
Gary Ehrlich

FOX 2000

PRESIDENT
Elizabeth Gabler
SENIOR V.P.
Carla Hacken
V.P., PRODUCTION
Ashely Kramer

FOX SEARCHLIGHT

PRESIDENT
Lindsay Law
EXECUTIVE V.P., BUSINESS AFFAIRS
Joseph De Marco
SENIOR V.P., PRODUCTION
Claudia Lewis
SENIOR V.P., DOMESTIC DISTRIBUTION
Robert M. Cheren
SENIOR V.P., ACQUISITIONS
Tony Safford
V.P., MARKETING & PUBLICITY
Valerie Van Galder
V.P., CREATIVE ADVERTISING
Samantha Hart
V.P., ACQUISITONS
Rosanne Korenberg
V.P., PRODUCTION
Joe Pichirallo

FOX ANIMATION STUDIOS

PRESIDENT
Chris Meldandri
GENERAL MANAGER
John McKenna
SENIOR V.P., PRODUCTION
Kevin Bannerman
SENIOR V.P., PHYSICAL PRODUCTION
Chuck Richardson
V.P., PRODUCTION
Melissa Cobb
PRODUCER & DIRECTOR
Gary Goldman
PRODUCER & DIRECTOR
Don Bluth

FOX LICENSING & MERCHANDISING

SENIOR V.P., WORLDWIDE PROMOTIONS
Steve Ross
SENIOR V.P., LEGAL & BUSINESS AFFAIRS
Jamie Samso
V.P., NATIONAL PROMOTIONS, FEATURE FILM & VIDEO
Michael Tomlin
V.P., WORLDWIDE PROMOTIONS & TELEVISION
Pierre Steele
V.P., LICENSING & MERCHANDISING
Michael Malone
V.P., FINANCE & ADMINISTRATION
Lisa Turchan

FOX STUDIO AUSTRALIA

PRESIDENT
Kim Williams

TWENTIETH CENTURY FOX TELEVISION

CO-PRESIDENT
Sandy Grushnow
CO-PRESIDENT
Gary Newman
CO-PRESIDENT
Dana Walden
CFO & EXECUTIVE V.P.
Robert Barron
EXECUTIVE V.P., PRODUCTION & FINANCE
Charlie Goldstein
EXECUTIVE V.P., BUSINESS & LEGAL AFFAIRS
Howard Kurtzman
SENIOR V.P., TV PRODUCTION, DRAMA
Janie Kleiman
SENIOR V.P., TV PRODUCTION, COMEDY
Joel Hornstock
SENIOR V.P., TV POST PRODUCTION
Edward Nassour
SENIOR V.P., TALENT & CASTING
Marcia Schulman
SENIOR V.P., DRAMA
Scott Vila
SENIOR V.P., COMEDY
Brad Johnson
V.P., MEDIA RELATIONS
Steven Melnick

FOX HOME ENTERTAINMENT

PRESIDENT, NORTH AMERICA, FOX HOME ENTERTAINMENT
Bob DeLellis
EXEC. V.P., PHYSICAL DISTRIBUTION & INFORMATION SERVICES
Ben Means
EXECUTIVE V.P., MARKETING & SALES
Mike Dunn
SENIOR V.P., NATIONAL SALES, MASS MERCHANTS
Ray Gagnon
SENIOR V.P., LATIN AMERICA, INTERNATIONAL HOME ENTERTAINMENT
Jane Pemberton
SENIOR V.P., RETAIL OPERATIONS
Simon Swart
SENIOR V.P., PROGRAM ACQUISITION
Stephen Poe
V.P., OPERATIONS
Nadine Holt

FOX INTERACTIVE

PRESIDENT
Jon Richmond
EXEC. DIRECTOR, PRODUCT DEVELOPMENT
Paul Provenzano
V.P., WORLDWIDE PROMOTIONS
Scott Marcus
V.P., SALES, INTERACTIVE
Dave Reich

FRANCHISE PICTURES INC.

8228 Sunset Blvd., Ste. 305, Los Angeles, CA 90046. (323) 822-0730. FAX: (323) 822-2165.
CHAIRMAN
Elie Samaha
PRESIDENT & CEO
Andrew Stevens
PRESIDENT, FILM MUSIC & SENIOR V.P., PRODUCTION
Mark McGarry
PRESIDENT, DEVELOPMENT
Tracee Stanley
EXECUTIVE V.P.
Andrew Kramer
SENIOR V.P. & CFO
Hans Turner
V.P., DEVELOPMENT
Dawn Miller
V.P., DEVELOPMENT
Emily Cummins

FRIENDLY PRODUCTIONS
10201 W. Pico Blvd., Bldg. 41, Los Angeles, CA 90035. (310) 369-3973. FAX: (310) 369-7436.
PRODUCER
David T. Friendly
CONTACTS
David W. Higgins
Noessa Higa
Michael McGahey
Kori Nelson
DEVELOPMENT & SECURITY
Sparky Friendly

CHUCK FRIES PRODUCTIONS, INC.
(Motion picture distribution)
1880 Century Park East, Ste. 315, Los Angeles, CA 90067. (323) 203-9520. FAX: (323) 203-9519.
CHAIRMAN OF THE BOARD, PRESIDENT & CEO
Charles W. Fries

FULL MOON UNIVERSE
1645 N. Vine St., 9th fl., Hollywood, CA 90028. (323) 468-0599. FAX: (323) 468-0598. www.fullmoonpictures.com
CHAIRMAN & CEO
Charles Band
E.V.P., PRODUCTION
Albert Band

FURTHUR FILMS
100 Universal City Plaza, Bldg. 1320/4E, Universal City, 91608. (818) 777-6700. FAX: (818) 866-1278.
825 8th Ave., 30th Flr., New York, NY 10019. (212) 33301421. FAX: (212) 333-8163.
PRODUCER
Michael Douglas
PRODUCER
Allison Segan
V.P., CREATIVE AFFAIRS
Marcy Drogin
VICE PRESIDENT
Jackie Levine
CREATIVE EXECUTIVE
Adam Fratto
STORY EDITOR
James LaVigne

GENDECE FILM CO.
999 No. Doheny Dr., Ste. 411, Los Angeles, CA 90069. (310) 271-8596.
PRODUCER & PARTNER & WRITER
Brian Gendece
PARTNER & MUSIC DIRECTOR
Bob Esty

GENERAL MEDIA INTERNATIONAL
(Formerly Penthouse Films International)
11 Penn Plaza., 12th Flr., New York, NY 10001. (212) 702-6000. FAX: (212) 702-6262.
CHAIRMAN & CEO
Bob Guccione
VICE CHAIRMAN., PRESIDENT & COO
John Prebich
V.P., INTERNET OPERATIONS
G. VanDerLuen

GEORGE STREET PICTURES
4000 Warner Blvd., Bldg. 81, Rm. 203, Burbank, CA 91522. (818) 954-4361. FAX: (818) 954-3682.
PRINCIPAL
Chris O'Donnell
PRESIDENT
Bing Howenstein
STORY EDITOR
P.J. Byrne

GHOULDARDI FILM COMPANY
c/o New Line Cinema, 116 North Robertson Blvd., 2nd Fl., Los Angeles, CA 90048. (310) 854-5811. FAX: (310) 854-1824.
WRITER, DIRECTOR
Paul Thomas Anderson
PRODUCER
Joanne Sellar

GMR PRODUCTIONS, INC.
1333 6th Ave., Venice, CA 90291. (310) 401-1400. FAX: (310) 401-1200. email: ginares@earthlink.net
PRODUCER
Gina Resnick

GOAT CAY PRODUCTIONS, INC.
P.O. Box 38, New York, NY 10150. (212) 421-8293. FAX: (212) 421-8294. email: goatcay@earthlink.net
PRESIDENT & PRODUCER & ACTOR
Sigourney Weaver

THE GOATSINGERS
179 Franklin St., 6th Flr., New York, NY 10013. (212) 966-3045. FAX: (212) 966-4362.
PRESIDENT
Harvey Keitel
PARTNER
Peggy Gromley

FREDERIC GOLCHAN PRODUCTIONS
1043 Maybrook Dr., Beverly Hills, CA 90210 (310) 854-1133. FAX: (310) 854-9028. email: FGFilm@aol.com
PRESIDENT
Frederic A. Golchan
ASSISTANT TO THE PRESIDENT
Nanette Julian

GOLDEN HARVEST FILMS, INC.
(For additional company information, please see Hong Kong & Singapore under the World Market section.)
9891 Santa Monica Blvd., Beverly Hills, CA 90212. (310) 203-0722. FAX: (310) 556-3214.
V.P., PRODUCTION
Roberta Chin

GOLDEN QUILL
8899 Beverly Blvd., Ste. 702, Los Angeles, CA 90048. (310) 274-5016 & (212) 387-9656. FAX: (310) 274-5028.
DIRECTOR & PRODUCER
Arthur Hiller

THE GOLDSTEIN CO.
1644 Courtney Ave., Los Angeles, CA 90046. (310) 659-9511. FAX: (310) 659-8779.
PRODUCER
Gary W. Goldstein

SAMUEL GOLDWYN FILMS, LLC
9570 W. Pico Blvd., Ste. 400, Los Angeles, CA 90035. (310) 860-3100. FAX: (310) 860-3195.
1133 Broadway, Ste. 1101, New York, NY 10010. (212) 367-9435. FAX: (212) 367-0853
CHAIRMAN & CEO
Samuel Goldwyn, Jr.
PRESIDENT & COO
Meyer Gottlieb
DIRECTOR OF ACQUISITIONS (NY)
Tom Quinn
STORY EDITORS
Chris Rowe
Julie Huey
DEVELOPMENT & ACQUISITIONS COORDINATOR
Tasha Cronin

GOOD MACHINE
417 Canal, St., 4th Flr., New York, NY 10013. (212) 343-9230. FAX: (212) 343-9645. www.goodmachine.com
CO-CHAIRMAN
Ted Hope
CO-CHAIRMAN
James Schamus
SENIOR V.P., DEVELOPMENT
Anne Carey
V.P., PRODUCTION
Anthony Bregman
V.P., OPERATIONS
Noreen Ward
V.P., SALES
Glen Basner
DIRECTOR, PRODUCTION
Ross Katz
DIRECTOR, DEVELOPMENT
Cielo Cerezo

GOOD MACHINE INTERNATIONAL
(Film production & sales)
417 Canal St., 4th Flr., New York, NY 10013. (212) 343-9230. FAX: (212) 343-9645. www.goodmachine.com
PRESIDENT
Daivd Linde

GORDON FILMS, INC.
(Motion picture producer and distributor)
119 W. 57th St., New York, NY 10019. (212) 757-9390. FAX: (212) 757-9392.
PRESIDENT
Richard Gordon
VICE PRESIDENT
Joseph R. Cattuti

GOTHAM PICTURES
1114 Lachman Lane, Pacific Palisades, CA 90272. (310) 306-0120. FAX: (310) 656-3610. www.resolutionprod.com
PARTNERS
Greg McMurray
Rhonda Gunner

GRACIE FILMS

10202 W. Washington Blvd., Poitier Bldg., Culver City, CA 90232. (310) 244-4222. FAX: (310) 244-1530.
10201 W. Pico Blvd., Los Angeles, CA 90035.
PRODUCER & WRITER & DIRECTOR
James L. Brooks
PRESIDENT
Richard Sakai
PRESIDENT, MOTION PICTURES
Julie Ansell
EXECUTIVE V.P.
Denise Sirkot

GRAINY PICTURES

75 Main St., Cold Spring, NY 10516. (914) 265-2241. FAX: (914) 265-2543. www.grainypictures.com
email: info@grainypictures.com
CO-PRESIDENT
Janet Pierson
CO-PRESIDENT
John Pierson

GRANADA FILM

5225 Wilshire Blvd., Ste. 603, Los Angeles, CA 90036. (323) 692-9940. FAX: (323) 692-9944.
email: grandafilmsusa@pacificnet.net
The London Television Centre, Upper Ground, London SE1 9LT.
PRODUCER
Janette Day
HEAD, FILM
Pippa Cross
DEVELOPMENT
Rebecca Hodgson

GRANDVIEW PRODUCTIONS

(Large-format motion picture producer)
1016 Fairway Rd., Santa Barbara, CA 93108. (805) 565-3759.
FAX: (805) 565-3769, Toll-free fax: (877) 722-0361.
email: gv@delinet.com
CONTACT
Michael Cook

GREENESTREET FILMS, INC.

9 Desbrosses St., 2nd Flr., New York, NY 10013. (212) 343-1049. FAX: (212) 343-0774.
www.greenestreetfilms.com
email: general@gstreet.com
PARTNER & CEO
John Penotti
PARTNER & CREATIVE EXECUTIVE
Fisher Stevens
PARTNER & CFO
Bradley Yonover
GENERAL MANAGER
Debbie Johnson
HEAD, DEVELOPMENT
Jamie Gordon
HEAD, PRODUCTION
Tim Williams
ASSOCIATE, DEVELOPMENT
Courtney Potts

GREEN MOON PRODUCTIONS

3110 Main St., Ste. 205, Santa Monica, CA 90405. (310) 450-6111. FAX: (310) 450-1333.
email: name@greenmoon.com
PRODUCER & DIRECTOR & ACTOR
Melanie Griffith
PRODUCER & ACTOR
Antonio Banderas
PRESIDENT
Diane Sillan Isaacs
V.P., CREATIVE AFFAIRS
Lourdes Diaz
DIRECTOR, DEVELOPMENT
Sam Gagliani
DEVELOPMENT ASSISTANT
Catherine Satterwhite

GREYCAT FILMS

PMB 531, 2250 E. Tropicana Ave., Ste. 19, Las Vegas, NV 89109. (702) 737-0670. FAX: (702) 734-3628.
email: Greycat@lvcm.com
CO-PRESIDENTS
David Whitten
Suzanne Bowers Whitten

GUN FOR HIRE PRODUCTIONS

609 Greenwich St., New York, NY 10014. (212) 905-2300. FAX: (212) 905-2324.
1200 Dundas St. E., Toronto, Ontario, Canada M4M 1S3. (416) 462-3555. FAX: (416) 462-9089.
1874 West Ave., Miami Beach, Fl 33139. (305) 604-1486. FAX: (305) 604-0486.
1875 Boundary Rd., Vancouver, B.C., Canada V5M 3Y8. (604) 638-8750. FAX: (604) 638-8755.
PRESIDENT
C.J. Follini
SENIOR V.P.
David Tuttle

HALSTED PICTURES

15 Brooks Ave., Unit B, Venice, CA 90291. (310) 450-7804. FAX: (310) 450-8174.
PRODUCER
Dan Halsted
CREATIVE EXECUTIVE
David Scheer
STORY EDITOR
Ryan Lewis

HARPO FILMS, INC.

345 N. Maple Dr., Ste. 315, Beverly Hills, CA 90210. (310) 278-5559.
110 N. Carpenter, Chicago, IL 60607. (312) 633-1000.
CHAIRMAN & CEO
Oprah Winfrey
PRESIDENT
Kate Forte
DIRECTOR, MEDIA & CORPORATE RELATIONS
Lisa Halliday
DIRECTOR, DEVELOPMENT, TV
Susan Heyer
DIRECTOR, DEVELOPMENT, FEATURES
Valerie Scoon
DIRECTOR, PRODUCTION
Tim Tortora

HARRAH'S FILM CORP.

(Large-format motion picture production)
25613 Dollar St., #1, Hayward, CA 94544. (510) 881-4989.
FAX: (510) 881-0448.
CONTACT
Jerry Harrah

HAVOC, INC.

16 W. 19th St., 12th Flr., New York, NY 10011. (212) 924-1629 & (212) 924-1629. FAX: (212) 924-3105.
PRODUCER & DIRECTOR & WRITER & ACTOR
Tim Robbins

HEEL & TOE FILMS

650 N. Bronson Ave., Bronson Bdlg., Ste. 200, Hollywood, CA 90004. (323) 960-4591. FAX: (323) 960-4592.
WRITER & PRODUCER & DIRECTOR
Paul Attanasio
PRODUCER
Katie Jacobs
SENIOR V.P., PRODUCTION
Ned Gusick
ASSISTANTS
Jules Bianchi
Stephen Schuster
Brandon Noonan

JIM HENSON PICTURES

1416 N. La Brea Ave., Hollywood, CA 90028. (323) 802-1500. FAX: (323) 802-1825. www.henson.com
CONTACT
Lisa Henson
PRODUCTION
Kristine Belson
V.P., PRODUCTION & ADMINISTRATION
Louis N. Phillips
CREATIVE EXECUTIVE
Rob Valois
ASSISTANTS
Melissa Eaton
Gabriel Gonzales
Kevin Kelly
Aaron Merrell

HOFFLUND POLONE

9465 Wilshire Blvd., Ste. 820, Beverly Hills, CA 90212. (310) 859-1971. FAX: (310) 859-7250.
PARTNERS
Judy Hofflund
Gavin Polone
PRODUCTION EXECUTIVE
Vivian Cannon

HOGAN MOORHOUSE PICTURES

1250 6th St., Ste. 305, Santa Monica, CA 90401. (310) 319-9299. FAX: (310) 319-1889.
DIRECTOR & WRITER
P.J. Hogan
DIRECTOR & WRITER
Jocelyn Moorhouse
SENIOR V.P., PRODUCTION
Liza Moore
EXECUTIVE ASSISTANTS
Holly Brix
Cori Carlson

HOME BOX OFFICE, INC.

(A premium cable service, motion picture production company and subsidiary of Time Warner, Inc.)
1100 Ave. of the Americas, New York, NY 10036. (212) 512-1000. FAX: (212) 512-5517. www.hbo.com
2049 Century Park East, Ste. 4100, Los Angeles, CA 90067-3215. (310) 201-9200. FAX: (310) 207-9310.
PRESIDENT & CEO
Jeff Bewkes
PRESIDENT & CEO, TIME WARNER SPORTS
Seth Abraham
PRESIDENT, HBO ORIGINAL PROGRAMMING
Chris Albrecht
PRESIDENT, U.S. NETWORK GROUP
John Bilock
PRESIDENT, HBO FILMS
Collin Calender
PRESIDENT, HBO HOME VIDEO
Henry McGee
PRESIDENT, HBO INTERNATIONAL
Steve Rosenberg
PRESIDENT, FILM PROGRAMMING, VIDEO & ENTERPRISES
Steve Cheffer
PRESIDENT, HBO ENTERPRISES
Charles Schreger

HBO FILMS

SENIOR V.P., HBO FILMS
Kerith Putnam
V.P., CASTING, HBO FILMS
Carrie Frazier
V.P., HBO FILMS
Kary Antholis
V.P., HBO FILMS
Jonathan Krauss

ORIGINAL PROGRAMMING/HBO INDEPENDENT PRODUCTIONS/HBO DOWNTOWN PRODUCTIONS

EXECUTIVE V.P., ORIGINAL PROGRAMMING
Sheila Nevins
EXECUTIVE V.P., BUS. & PLANNING, HBO INDPT. PRODS.
Russel Schwartz
SENIOR V.P., ORIGINAL PROGRAMMING & SENIOR V.P., HBO DOWNTOWN PRODUCTIONS
Nancy Geller
SENIOR V.P., ORIGINAL PROGRAMMING, WEST COAST
Carolyn Strauss
SENIOR V.P., ORIGINAL PROGRAMMING, WEST COAST
Anne Thomopoulos
V.P., ORIGINAL PROGRAMMING, DOCUMENTARIES
Nanacy Abraham
V.P., ORIGINAL PROGRAMMING, COMEDY SERIES, LATE NIGHT & SPECIALS
Sarah Condon
V.P., ORIGINAL PROGRAMMING, PLANNING & OPERATIONS
Susan Ennis
V.P., PRODUCTION, HBO DOWNTOWN PRODUCTIONS
John Fisher
V.P., ORIGINAL PROGRAMMING, HBO FAMILY CHANNEL
Dolores Morris
V.P., ORIGINAL PROGRAMMING, PRODUCTION
Bruce Richmond
VP., ORIGINAL PROGRAMMING, PRODUCTION
Michael Hill

HBO/TIME WARNER SPORTS

SENIOR V.P., & EXECUTIVE PRODUCER, HBO SPORTS/TVKO
Ross Greenburg
SENIOR V.P., TVKO MARKETING & DISTRIBUTION
Mark Taffet
SENIOR V.P. & CFO, TIME WARNER SPORTS
Barbara Thomas
COO, HBO PROPERTIES
Pam Lester
V.P. & SENIOR PRODUCER, HBO SPORTS
Rick Bernstein
V.P., PROGRAM BUSINESS AFFAIRS, TW SPORTS
Kery Davis
V.P., SPORTS PRODUCTION, HBO SPORTS
David Harmon

CORPORATE COMMUNICATIONS

EXECUTIVE V.P., CORPORATE COMMUNICATIONS
Richard Plepler
SENIOR V.P., MEDIA RELATIONS
Quentin Schaffer
V.P., MEDIA RELATIONS
Nancy Lesser

TALENT RELATIONS

V.P., TALENT RELATIONS & SPECIAL EVENTS
Arthur Badavas
V.P., SPECIAL EVENTS & TALENT
Eileen Rivard

FILM PROGRAMMING

EXECUTIVE V.P., FILM ACQUISITIONS
Leslie Jacobson
V.P., FILM PROGRAMMING
Doris Casap
V.P., CREATIVE AFFAIRS, FILM DEVELOPMENT
Robert Conte
V.P., FILM PROGRAMMING
Perry Scheider

BUSINESS AFFAIRS

EXECUTIVE V.P., BUSINESS AFFAIRS
Hal Akselrad
SENIOR V.P., BUS. AFFAIRS & PRODUCTION, EAST COAST
Bruce Grivetti
SENIOR V.P., BUS. AFFAIRS & PRODUCTION, WEST COAST
Michael Lombardo
SENIOR V.P., BUS. AFFAIRS & PRODUCTION, WEST COAST
Glenn Whitehead
V.P., BUSINESS AFFAIRS, FILM ACQUISITION
Royce Battleman
V.P., PRODUCTION
Bill Chase
V.P., BUSINESS AFFAIRS, EAST COAST
Agnes Letterese
V.P., PRODUCTION, HBO PICTURES
Jay Roewe
V.P., SPORTS PRODUCTION
John Micale
V.P., BUSINESS AFFAIRS, EAST COAST
Sharon Werner
V.P., BUSINESS AFFAIRS, WEST COAST
Beth White
V.P., BUSINESS AFFAIRS, WEST COAST
Suzanne Young
V.P., ORIGINAL PROG., PROD. & CREATIVE OPERATIONS
Carmi Zlotnik

LEGAL

EXECUTIVE V.P. & GENERAL COUNSEL
John Redpath
SENIOR V.P. & CHIEF COUNSEL, FILM PROGRAMMING
George Cooke
SENIOR V.P. & CHIEF COUNSEL, ORIGINAL PROGRAMMING
Viviane Eisenberg
SENIOR V.P. & CHIEF COUNSEL, SALES & MARKETING
Tom Woodbury
V.P. & CHIEF COUNSEL, NETWORK OPERATIONS & INTL.
Linda Bogin
V.P., SENIOR COUNSEL, SALES & MARKETING
Michelle Gersen
V.P. & SENIOR COUNSEL, WEST COAST
Jeffrey Guthrie
V.P. & CHIEF COUNSEL, LITIGATION
Andrea Pollack
V.P. & SENIOR COUNSEL, WEST COAST
Molly Wilson
V.P. & SENIOR COUNSEL
Martine Shahar

MARKETING & CREATIVE SERVICES

EXECUTIVE V.P., MARKETING
Eric Kessler
SENIOR V.P., SUBSCRIBER MKTG. & SPECIAL MARKETS
Olivia Smashum
SENIOR V.P. & GENERAL MANAGER, CREATIVE SERVICES
Chris Spencer
SENIOR V.P., ADVERTISING & PROGRAM PROMOTION, ORIGINAL PROGRAMMING
Roberta Mell
V.P., ON-AIR, ORIGINAL PROGRAMMING
Sue Bailey
V.P., ON-AIR, THEATRICAL PROG. & BRAND IMAGE
Mark Davidson
V.P., ON-AIR, SPECIAL MARKETS
Che Che Mata
V.P., OPERATIONS
Patrick Manturi
V.P., INTERACTIVE VENTURES
Sarah Cotsen

V.P., MARKETING RESEARCH
Pam Flanagan
V.P., MARKET STRATEGY & ANALYSIS
Roger Strong
V.P., HBO DIRECT
Lisa Gussack

PROGRAM PLANNING
SENIOR V.P., HBO/CINEMAX PROGRAM PLANNING
Dave Baldwin
V.P., HBO SCHEDULING & ADMINISTRATION
Amy Feldman
V.P., CINEMAX SCHEDULING
Jill Champtaloup
V.P. AUDIENCE RESEARCH
Jan Pasquale
V.P., PRIMARY PROGRAMMING RESEARCH
Kathleen Carroll
V.P., NETWORK PROGRAMMING OPERATIONS
Janet Schwartz

HOME VIDEO
SENIOR V.P. & CFO HOME VIDEO
Angelo D'Amelio
V.P., MARKETING, HBO HOME VIDEO
Cynthia Rhea

HBO INTERNATIONAL
EXECUTIVE V.P., HBO INTERNATIONAL
Bill Hooks
SENIOR V.P., SALES & MARKETING, HBO ASIA
James Marturano
SENIOR V.P., PROGRAMMING, HBO ASIA
Mack Perryman
SENIOR V.P., HBO INTERNATIONAL, LONDON
Michael Spinelle
MANAGING DIRECTOR, HBO HUNGARY
George Douglas
PRESIDENT & CEO, HBO ASIA
Charles "Dan" Murrell
MANAGING DIRECTOR, HBO CZECH/SLOVAK REPUBLICS
Jitka Rombova
V.P., HBO INTERNATIONAL
Robert Sender
MANAGING DIRECTOR, HBO ROMANIA
Pavel Stantchev
MANAGING DIRECTOR, HBO POLAND
Slawomir Suss

TECHNOLOGY/STUDIO & BROADCAST OPERATIONS
SENIOR V.P., STUDIO & BROADCAST OPERATIONS
Dom Serio
SENIOR V.P., TECHNOLOGY OPERATIONS
Bob Zitter
V.P., BROADCAST OPERATIONS
Charles Cataldo
V.P., PRODUCTION ENGINEERING
Andres Colpa
V.P., TECHNOLOGY
Craig Cuttner
V.P., STUfDIO OPERATIONS
Ralph Fumante
V.P., TECHNOLOGY OPERATIONS
Barbara Jaffe
V.P., BROADCAST ENGINEERING
Elmer Musser
V.P., NETWORK QUALITY CONTROL, OPERATIONS
Debbie Pritchett

INFORMATION TECHNOLOGY
SENIOR V.P., INFORMATION TECHNOLOGY
Michael Gabriel
V.P., CUSTOMER INFORMATION SERVICES
Abraham Cytryn
V.P., APPLICATION DEV., NETWORK PROGRAMMING
Elizabeth Flanigan
V.P., INFORMATION TECHNOLOGY INFRASTRUCTURE
James Flock
V.P., TECHNOLOGY SERVICES
Bruce Probst

FINANCE
E.V.P, FINANCE, INFORMATION TECHNOLOGY & BUSINESS AFFAIRS CFO
Bill Nelson
CFO
Eric Levin
SENIOR V.P. & CONTROLLER
Rob Roth
V.P. & ASSISTANT CONTROLLER, WEST OCAST
Rich Battaglia
V.P. & ASST. CONTROLLER, CASH & REVENUE OPER.
Scott McElhone
V.P., FINANCIAL ANALYSIS
Keith Owitz
V.P. & ASST. CONTROLLER, WORLDWIDE ACCT. SERVICES
Gregory Sneed
V.P. & ASST. CONTROLLER, FINAN. OPER. & REPORTING
Joe Tarulli
V.P., CASH & REVENUE OPERATIONS
Anne Marie Mirabella

HUMAN RESOURCES
EXECUTIVE V.P., HUMAN RESOURCES & ADMINISTRATION
Shelley Fischel
V.P., FACILITIES MANAGEMENT
Dana Magee Grassi
V.P., REAL ESTATE & ADMINISTRATION
Michael Morrin
V.P., COMPENSATION & BENEFITS
Elly Silverman
V.P., HUMAN RESOURCES & FACILITIES, WEST COAST
Mary Lou Thomas

AFFILIATE OPERATIONS
EXECUTIVE V.P., AFFILIATE RELATIONS
Bob Grassi
SENIOR V.P. & GEN. MGR., LOS ANGELES/SAN FRANCISCO
Janice Aull
SENIOR V.P., & GEN. MGR., NEW YORK/PHILDELPHIA
Steve Davidson
SENIOR V.P. & GENERAL MANAGER, CHICAGO/DENVER
Jerry Flavin
SENIOR V.P. & GENERAL MANAGER, DALLAS
Sandra Mitchell
SENIOR V.P. & GENERAL MANAGER, ATLANTA
Gail Sermersheim
V.P., AFFILIATE OPERATIONS, ATLANTA
Dan Fobas
V.P., AFFILIATE OPERATIONS, DENVER
John High
V.P., AFFILIATE OPERATIONS, SAN FRANCISCO
Nancy Hom
V.P., AFFILIATE OPERATIONS, NEW YORK
Matthew Kasman
V.P., AFFILIATE OPERATIONS, PHILADELPHIA
Jim McLoughlin
V.P., AFFILIATE OPERATIONS, CHICAGO
Jane Moyer
V.P., SALES & MARKETING OPERATIONS
Sue Casey
V.P., SPECIAL MARKETS
John Hagerty
V.P., SPECIAL MARKETS
Ken Kinderman
V.P., AFFILIATE SPECIAL PROJECTS
Les Read
V.P., DIRECT BROADCAST
John Ovrutsky

HORSESHOE BAY PRODUCTIONS

710 Wilshire Blvd., Ste. 600, Santa Monica, CA 90401. (310) 587-0797. FAX: (310) 899-4259.
PRODUCER
Gary S. Foster
WRITER & DIRECTOR & PRODUCER
Mark Steven Johnson
PRESIDENT, PRODUCTION
Julia Dray
DIRECTOR, DEVELOPMENT
Erik Baiers
CREATIVE ASSOCIATES
Brian Olson
Karen Peterkin
Kirsten L. Crabtree
Amberwren Briskey-Choen

PETER HYAMS PRODUCTIONS, INC.

1453 Third St. Promenade, Ste. 315, Santa Monica, CA 90401-2397. (310) 393-1553. FAX: (310) 393-1554.
email: jdubbs@ix.netcom.com
DIRECTOR & WRITER
Peter Hyams
DIRECTOR, DEVELOPMENT
Jonathan Wilson

HYDE PARK ENTERTAINMENT

2500 Broadway St., Santa Monica, CA 90404. (310) 449-3191. FAX: (310) 449-3356.
CO-CHAIRMAN & CO-CEO
Ashok Amritraj
CO-CHAIRMAN & CO-CEO
David Hoberman
V.P., ACQUISITIONS
Todd Lieberman
V.P., PRODUCTION
Cookie Carosella
V.P., FINANCE
Joe D'Angelo

ICON PRODUCTIONS, INC.

(Motion picture production)
5555 Melrose Ave., Los Angeles, CA 90038 (323) 956-2100.
FAX: (323) 862-2121.
PRESIDENT
Bruce Davey
PRESIDENT OF TELEVISION
Jim Lemley
PRODUCER
Steve McEveety
PRESIDENT, FEATURE FILMS
Karen Glasser

IFM FILM ASSOCIATES, INC.

1328 E. Palmer Ave., Glendale, CA 91205. (818) 243-4976.
FAX: (818) 550-9728. email: ifmfilm@aol.com
PRESIDENT
Antony I. Ginnane
EXECUTIVE V.P.
Ann Lyons
V.P., INTERNATIONAL
Anthony J. Lyons
SALES EXECUTIVE
David Maklout

IMAGEMOVERS

100 Universal City Plaza, Bldg. 484, Universal City, CA 91608.
(818) 733-8313. FAX: (818) 733-8333.
WRITER & DIRECTOR & PRODUCER
Robert Zemeckis
PRODUCER
Steve Starkey
PRODUCER
Jack Rapke
CREATIVE EXECUTIVE
Bennett Schneir
HEAD, CREATIVE AFFAIRS
Jennifer Perini

IMAGINE ENTERTAINMENT

9465 Wilshire Blvd., 7th Flr., Beverly Hills, CA 90212. (310)
858-2000. FAX: (310) 858-2020.
www.imagine-entertainment.com
CO-CHAIRMAN
Brian Grazer
CO-CHAIRMAN
Ron Howard
CO-CHAIRMAN, IMAGINE FILMS
Karen Kehela
PRESIDENT, ENTERTAINMENT
Michael Rosenberg
SENIOR V.P., ADMINISTRATION & OPERATIONS
Robin Barris
SENIOR V.P., MOTION PICTURES
Maureen Peyrot
SENIOR V.P., MOTION PICTURES
Jim Whitaker
V.P., MOTION PICTURES
Kim Roth
DIRECTOR, DEVELOPMENT
Suzy Barbieri
DIRECTOR, DEVELOPMENT
David Bernardi
CREATIVE EXECUTIVE
Sarah Bowen
DIRECTOR, FINANCE
Christy Sterling
STORY EDITOR
Beth Babyak

IMAX CORPORATION

3003 Exposition Blvd., Santa Monica, CA 90404. (310) 255-
5500. FAX: (310) 255-5501. www.imax.com
SENIOR V.P., FILM & DISTRIBUTION
Andrew Gellis
V.P., FILM OPERATIONS
Patrick Murray
DIRECTOR, FILM DEVELOPMENT
Wendi Mirabella

IMMORTAL ENTERTAINMENT

1650 21 St., Santa Monica, CA 90404. (310) 582-8300. FAX:
(310) 582-8301.
OWNER
Happy Walters
HEAD, FILM PRODUCTION
Matt Weaver
VICE PRESIDENT
Scott Nemes
HEAD, TV
Cambi Clark

INDELIBLE PICTURES

1041 N. Formosa, Writers Bldg. 314, Los Angeles, CA 90046.
(323) 850-2822. FAX: (323) 850-2835.
PRODUCER
Art Linson
PRODUCER
Cean Chaffin
DIRECTOR & PRODUCER
David Fincher
PRODUCER
John Linson
EXECUTIVE
John Dorsey
V.P., ADMINISTRATION
Patti Roberts Nelson
DEVELOPMENT
Kareem Elseify

INDUSTRY ENTERTAINMENT

955 S. Carrillo Dr., 3rd Flr., Los Angeles, CA 90048. (323)
954-9000. FAX: (323) 954-9009.
CO-CHAIRMAN
Keith Addis
CO-CHAIRMAN
Nick Wechsler
COO
Lynwood Spinks
EXECUTVE V.P., PRODUCTION
Julia Chasman
PRODUCTION EXECUTIVES
Michael Gruskoff
Jono Hart
David Carmel
Marc A. Evans
STORY EDITOR
Jeff Sommerville
BUSINESS & LEGAL AFFAIRS
Aaron Michiel

INFINITY FILMWORKS

(Motion picture production of large-format features)
19405 Bilmoor Pl., Tarzana, CA 91356. (818) 881-3288. FAX:
(818) 881-8873. email: nsnitee@earthlink.net
CONTACT
Keith Melton

INITIAL ENTERTAINMENT GROUP

3000 W. Olympic Blvd., Ste. 1550, Santa Monica, CA 90404.
(310) 264-1813. FAX: (310) 315-1723.
PRESIDENT & CEO
Graham King
COO
Colin Cotter
V.P., CREATIVE AFFAIRS
David A. Jones

INTERAMA, INC.

(Motion picture, television, non-theatrical and video distribution)
301 W. 53rd St., Ste. 19E, New York, NY 10019. (212) 977-
4836. FAX: (212) 581-6582. email: InteramaNY@aol.com
PRESIDENT
Nicole Jouve

INTERMEDIA FILMS

9348 Civic Center Dr., Ste. 250, Beverly Hills, CA 90210. (310)
777-0007. FAX: (310) 777-0008.
email: info@intermediafilm.com.uk
CO-CHAIRMAN
Guy East
CO-CHAIRMAN
Nigel Sinclair
PRESIDENT, WEST COAST OPER. & SENIOR V.P., BUS &
LEGAL AFFAIRS.
Kathy Goodman
PRESIDENT, WORLDWIDE MARKETING & DISTRIBUTION
Jere Hausfater
SENIOR V.P., PRODUCTION
Julie Golden
V.P., CREATIVE AFFAIRS
Karen Belanger

INTERNATIONAL FILM CIRCUIT

(Motion picture distributor)
419 Park Ave. South, 20th Flr., New York, NY 10016 (212) 686-
6777. FAX: (212) 545-9931. www.winstartelevid.com
PRESIDENT
Wendy Lidell

INTERSCOPE COMMUNICATIONS, INC.

10900 Wilshire Blvd., Ste. 1400, Los Angeles, CA 90024. (310) 208-8525. FAX: (310) 208-1764.
CHAIRMAN & CEO
Ted W. Field
PRESIDENT & COO
Scott Kroopf
PRODUCERS
Tom Engelman
Erica Huggins
PRODUCTION EXECUTIVES
Monica Mullens
Will Stubbs
SENIOR V.P., BUSINESS & LEGAL
David Boyle
STORY EDITOR & ADMINISTRATOR
Derek Wilkins

IRISH DREAMTIME

2450 Broadway, Ste. E-5021, Santa Monica, CA 90404. (310) 449-3411. FAX: (310) 586-8138.
PRODUCER & PARTNER
Pierce Brosnan
PRODUCER & PARTNER
Beau St. Clair
V.P., DEVELOPMENT
Angelique Higgins
CREATIVE EXECUTIVE
Cynthia Palormo
PRODUCTION EXECUTIVE
Amanda Scarano

ITALTOONS CORP.

(Motion picture and TV production and distribution)
32 W. 40 St., Ste. 2L, New York, NY 10018. (212) 730-0280. FAX: (212) 730-0313. www.italtoons.com
email: salesinfo@italtoons.com
PRESIDENT
Giuliana Nicodemi
GENERAL MANAGER
Ken Priester
PRODUCER
Luisa Rivosecchi

IWERKS ENTERTAINMENT

4520 Valerio St., Burbank CA 91505. (818) 841-7766. FAX: (818) 840-7462. www.iwerks.com
email: dougy@iwerks.com
FOUNDER & CTO & CEO
Don Iwerks
EXECUTIVE PRODUCER
Douglas Yellin
FILM TECHNICAL DIRECTOR
Scott Shepley
POST-PRODUCTION COORDINATOR
Greg Meader

JALEM PRODUCTIONS, INC.

(Motion picture production.)
141 El Camino, #201, Beverly Hills, CA 90212. (310) 278-7750.
PRESIDENT
Jack Lemmon

JERSEY FILMS

10351 Santa Monica Blvd., Ste. 200, Los Angeles, CA 90025. (310) 203-1000. FAX: (310) 203-1010.
CO-CHAIRMAN
Danny DeVito
CO-CHAIRMAN
Michael Shamberg
CO-CHAIRMAN
Stacey Sher
PRESIDENT, TV
John Landgraf
SENIOR V.P., PRODUCTION
Pamela Abdy
V.P., SPECIAL PROJECTS
Carla Santos Shamberg
CREATIVE EXECUTIVE
Adrienne Biddle
STORY EDITOR
Sindy Lin
ASSISTANT STORY EDITOR
David Kurs
MANAGER, FINANCE
Monica Dotten

JUMBO PICTURES, INC.

161 Ave. of the Americas, 15th Flr., New York, NY 10013. (212) 337-0077. FAX: (212) 337-0437.
CREATOR & PRESIDENT
Jim Jinkins
EXECUTIVE V.P. & PRODUCER
David Campbell
V.P., FINANCE
Ellie Copeland
V.P., ADMINISTRATION
Bedleem Fortunato
V.P., ANIMATION
Jack Spillum
PRODUCER, ANIMATION
Melanie Grisanti

JUNCTION ENTERTAINMENT

500 S. Buena Vista St., Animation 1-B, Burbank, CA 91521-1616. (818) 560-2800. FAX: (818) 841-3176.
PRODUCER & DIRECTOR
Jon Turtletaub
PRESIDENT & PRODUCER
Christina Steinberg
CREATIVE EXECUTIVE
Victor H. Constantinto
DIRECTOR, DEVELOPMENT
Nikki Reed
CREATIVE ASSOCIATES
Dominique Fichera
Karim Zreick

JUST SINGER ENTERTAINMENT

4242 Tujunga Ave., Studio City, CA 91604. (818) 506-2400. FAX: (818) 506-2409.
EXECUTIVE PRODUCER
Sheri Singer
V.P., DEVELOPMENT
Georgene Smith

MARTY KATZ PRODUCTIONS

1250 6th St., Ste. 205, Santa Monica, CA 90401. (310) 260-8501. FAX: (310) 260-8502.
PRODUCER
Marty Katz
V.P., DEVELOPMENT
Frederick Levy
DEVELOPMENT ASSOCIATE
Campbell Katz

KENNEDY-MARSHALL COMPANY

1351 4th St., 4th Flr., Santa Monica, CA 90401. (310) 656-8400. FAX: (310) 656-8430.
PRESIDENT, PRODUCTION
Zanne Devine
DEVELOPMENT EXECUTIVE
Mark Ross
STORY EDITOR
Nancy Covello
PRODUCER
Kathleen Kennedy
PRODUCER & DIRECTOR
Frank Marshall

KILLER FILMS, INC.

380 Lafayette St., #302, New York, NY 10003. (212) 473-3950. FAX: (212) 473-6152. www.killerfilms.com
email: killer@killerfilms.com
PRODUCERS
Pamela Koffler
Christine Vachon
HEAD, PRODUCTION
Katie Roumel
DIRECTOR, DEVELOPMENT
Bradford Simpson
PRODUCTION ASSOCIATE
Jon Marcus
DEVELOPMENT
Jocelyn Hayes
INTERNATIONAL
Laird Adamson
COORDINATOR
Daniel Wagner

KINGSGATE FILMS, INC.

10201 W. Washington Blvd., Frankovich Bldg., Ste. 108, Culver City, CA 90232-3195. (310) 244-7004. FAXL (310) 244-6918.
email: Kingsgate1@earthlink.net
ACTOR & PRODUCER
Nick Nolte
PRODUCER
Greg Shapiro
EXECUTIVE ASSISTANT
Heather Edison

KINGS ROAD ENTERTAINMENT, INC.
3489 Cahuenga Blvd., W., Ste. D, Hollywood, CA 90068. (323) 512-5045. FAX: (323) 512-5156.
CHAIRMAN
David Dube

KINO INTERNATIONAL CORP.
333 W. 39th St., Suite 503, New York, NY 10018. (212) 629-6880. www.kino.com
PRESIDENT
Donald Krim

THE KOCH CO.
2791 Ellison Dr., Beverly Hills, CA 90210. (818) 954-7964. email: TheKochCo@aol.com
PRODUCER
Howard W. Koch Jr.

THE KONIGSBERG-SMITH CO.
7919 Sunset Blvd., 2nd Flr., Los Angeles, CA 90046. (323) 845-1000. FAX: (323) 845-1020.
EXECUTIVE PRODUCER
Frank Konigsberg
PRODUCER
Drew Smith

KOPELSON ENTERTAINMENT
2121 Ave. of the Stars, Ste. 1400, Los Angeles, CA 90067. (310) 369-7500. FAX: (310) 369-7501.
1211 Ave. of the Americas, 16th Flr., New York, NY 10036. (212) 556-8565.
PRODUCER & CO-CHAIRPERSON
Arnold Kopelson
PRODUCER & CO-CHAIRPERSON
Anne Kopelson
PRESIDENT, PRODUCTION
Stephen J. Brown
PRESIDENT, CREATIVE AFFAIRS
Nana Greenwald
EXECUTIVE V.P., PRODUCTION
Matthew Gross
V.P CREATIVE AFFAIRS
Sherryl Clark
CREATIVE EXECUTIVE
Lara Wood
STORY EDITORS
William Lung
Mark Stein

KOUF-BIGELOW PRODUCTIONS
10061 Riverside Dr., PMB #1024, Toluca Lake, CA 91602. (818) 508-1010. FAX: (818) 508-1079.
WRITER & DIRECTOR & PRODUCER
Jim Kouf
PRODUCER
Lynn Bigelow-Kouf

KUSHNER-LOCKE CO.
11601 Wilshire Blvd., 21st Flr., Los Angeles, CA 90025. (310) 481-2000. FAX: (310) 481-2101. www.kusher-locke.com email: kl@kushner-locke.com
CO-CHAIRMAN
Donald Kushner
CO-CHAIRMAN
Peter Locke
PRESIDENT & COO
Bruce Lilliston
CFO
Brett Robinson
EXECUTIVE V.P., BUSINESS AFFAIRS
Richard Marks
EXECUTIVE V.P., PRODUCTION & FEATURE FILMS
Adam Moos
EXECUTIVE V.P., OPERATIONS & FINANCE
Steve Rosen
V.P., POST-PRODUCTION
Bob Wenokur
V.P., BUSINESS AFFAIRS
Jerry Rubin
V.P., FEATURES
Dana Scanlan
DIRECTOR, HUMAN RESOURCES
Marshall Walker

THE LADD COMPANY
9465 Wilshire Blvd., Ste. 910, Beverly Hills, CA 90210. (310) 777-2060. FAX: (310) 777-2061.
PRESIDENT
Alan Ladd Jr.
PRODUCER
Kellianne Ladd
CREATIVE EXECUTIVES
Natalia Chydzik
Peter Bisanz

LAKESHORE ENTERTAINMENT CORP.
5555 Melrose Ave., Gloria Swanson Bldg., Hollywood, CA 90038. (323) 956-4222. FAX: (323) 862-1190.
CO-CHAIRMAN & CEO
Thomas Rosenberg
CO-CHAIRMAN
Ted Tannebaum
COO
Eric Reid
PRESIDENT, LAKESHORE ENTERTAINMENT
Gary Lucchesi
PRESIDENT, LAKESHORE INTERNATIONAL
Peter Rogers
EXECUTIVE V.P. & HEAD, PRODUCTION
Richard Wright
SENIOR V.P., BUSINESS & LEGAL AFFAIRS
Robert Benun
V.P., PHYSICAL PRODUCTION
Andre Lamal
V.P., FINANCE
Renee Mancuso
V.P., DEVELOPMENT
Robert McMinn
EXECUTIVE DIRECTOR, BUSINESS & LEGAL AFFAIRS
Christine Buckley
DIRECTOR, ACQUISITIONS
Bic Tran
OFFICE MANAGER
Kjose Elliot
STORY EDITOR
Chris Brown

LANDSCAPE ENTERTAINMENT
12400 Wilshire Blvd., Ste. 1200., Los Angeles, CA 90025. (310) 395-7233. FAX: (310) 447-7501.
PRESIDENT
Judy Ranan
V.P., TV
Barbara Bloom

LARGER THAN LIFE PRODUCTIONS
100 Universal City Plaza, Bldg. 6111, Universal City, CA 91608. (818) 777-4004. FAX: (818) 866-5677.
PARTNERS
Gary Ross
Jane Sindell
PRODUCER
Allison Thomas
ASSOCIATE PRODUCER
Robin Bissell
CREATIVE EXECUTIVES
Marc Berliner
Bryan Brucks

LARGO ENTERTAINMENT
(Foreign distribution company for motion pictures)
2029 Century Park East, Ste. 4125, Los Angeles, CA 90067. (310) 203-0055. FAX: (310) 203-0254.
PRESIDENT
Mike Shinohara
SENIOR V.P., ACQUISITIONS & BUSINESS AFFAIRS
Chris Taylor
CONTROLLER/TRESAURER
James R. Ewing

LEADING PICTURES, INC.
8981 Sunset Blvd., Ste. 311, West Hollywood, CA 90069. (310) 385-0951. FAX: (310) 385-9408. www.alistpictures.com
PRODUCER & PRESIDENT
Anthony Esposito
DIRECTOR, DEVELOPMENT
Danielle Probst
LEGAL AFFAIRS
Marty Barab
FINANCIAL EXECUTIVE
Raymond Lee

LEISURE TIME FEATURES
(Motion picture distribution)
40 Worth St., Rm. 709, New York, NY 10013. (212) 267-4501. FAX: (212) 267-4501. email bpleisure@aol.com www.leisurefeat.com
PRESIDENT
Bruce Pavlow

LEVY-GARDNER-LAVEN PRODUCTIONS, INC.
9595 Wilshire Blvd., Ste. 610, Beverly Hills, CA 90212. (310) 278-9820. FAX: (310) 278-2632.
PRESIDENT
Jules V. Levy
SECRETARY, TREASURER & V.P.
Arthur Gardner

THE ROBERT LEWIS COMPANY

(Motion picture production & distribution)
8755 Shoreham Dr, Ste. 303, Beverly Hills, CA 90069 (310) 854-3714. FAX: (310) 659-6932
PRESIDENT
Robert Lewis

LIBERTY LIVEWIRE CORPORATION

520 Broadway, 5th Flr., Santa Monica, CA 90401. (310) 434-7000. FAX: (310) 434-7001.
FOUNDER & CEO
David Beddow
PRESIDENT & COO
Robert Walston
EXECUTIVE V.P. & CFO
Jeffrey Marcketta
EXECUTIVE V.P. & CTO
Gavin Schutz
EXECUTIVE V.P. & GENERAL COUNSEL
Marcus Evans

LIGHTHOUSE PRODUCTIONS

120 El Camino Dr., Ste. 212, Beverly Hills, CA 90212. (310) 859-4923. FAX: (310) 859-7511. email: lighthouse@jfr.com
PRODUCERS
Michael Phillips
Juliana Maio
John Frank Rosenblum

LIGHTMOTIVE, INC.

10351 Santa Monica Blvd., #402, Los Angeles, CA 90025. (310) 282-0660. FAX: (310) 282-0990.
PARTNERS
Roland Joffe
Alain Goldman
CREATIVE DIRECTOR
Ethan Markowitz

LIGHTSTORM ENTERTAINMENT

919 Santa Monica Blvd., Santa Monica, CA 90401. (310) 656-6100. FAX: (310) 566-6102.
CHAIRMAN & CEO
James Cameron
PRESIDENT
Rae Sanchini
CO-PRESIDENT
Jon Landau
DIRECTOR, DEVELOPMENT
Jay Sanders
DIRECTOR, PRODUCTION SERVICES
Geoff Burdick
V.P., DEVELOPMENT
Stacy Maes

LION ROCK PRODUCTIONS

2450 Broadway, Ste. 590, Santa Monica, CA 90404-3061. (310) 449-3000.
DIRECTOR & PRODUCER
John Woo
PRODUCER
Terrence Chang
SENIOR V.P.
Caroline Bruce
VICE PRESIDENT
Suzanne Zizzi
CREATIVE EXECUTIVE
Annie Hughes

LIONS GATE FILMS PRODUCTION

5750 Wilshire Blvd., Ste. 501, Los Angeles, CA 90036. (323) 692- 7300. FAX: (323) 692-7396. www.lionsgatefilms.com
PRESIDENT, MOTION PICTURES
Mark Urman
PRESIDENT, LIONS GATE FILMS RELEASING
Tom Ortenberg
PRESIDENT, PRODUCTION
Michael Paseornek
VICE PRESIDENT.
Lauren McLaughlin
V.P., MARKETING
Amanda Sherwin
DIRECTOR, PRODUCTION
Ernie Barabarash
DIRECTOR OF PUBLICITY
Jennifer Morgerman
DIRECTOR OF BUSINESS AFFAIRS
Jodi Murphy
DIRECTOR OF ACQUISITIONS & DEVELOPMENT
Sarah Lash
NATIONAL PRINT CONTROLLER
Hank Truxillo
MANAGER, ADVERTISING
Debbie Laurence
REGIONAL PUBLICITY MANAGER
Beth English
POST-PRODUCTION SUPERVISOR
Phil Stilman
COORDINATOR
Frank Minerva

SI LITVINOFF PRODUCTIONS

2825 Woodstock Rd., Los Angeles, CA 90046. (323) 848-6907. FAX: (323) 848-6908. email: slitvinoff@aol.com
PRODUCER
Si Litvinoff
CREATIVE AFFAIRS
Paul Madden

LIVEPLANET

517 N. Robertson Blvd., Ste. 200, West Hollywood, CA 90048. (310) 786-2930. FAX: (310) 786-2931.
PARTNERS
Ben Affleck
Matt Damon
Chris Moore
Sean Bailey
CREATIVE EXECUTIVES
Jeff Balis
Stefan Frank

LONGBOW PRODUCTIONS

4181 Sunswept Dr., Ste. 100, Studio City, CA 91604-2335. (818) 762-6600. email: mail@longbowfilms.com
CHAIRMAN
Richard Kughn
PARTNER
Sharon Cicero
PARTNER
Ronnie D. Clemmer
PARTNER
Bill Pace
V.P., DEVELOPMENT
Marla White
DEVELOPMENT ASSISTANTS
Jonathan Foster
Matthew Clemmer

LOVE SPELL ENTERTAINMENT

10202 W. Washington Blvd., Gable Bldg., #103, Culver City, CA 90232. (310) 244-6040. FAX: (310) 244-0740.
PRESIDENT
Jennifer Love Hewitt
V.P., DEVELOPMENT & PRODUCTION
Jill Gillbert
DIRECTOR, DEVELOPMENT
Kim Kovac

LOWER EAST SIDE FILMS

443 Broadway, 5th Flr., New York, NY 10013. (212) 966-0111. FAX: (212) 966-0555. email: lesfilms@aol.com
PRESIDENT
John Leguizamo
PRODUCER
Kathy DeMarco

L-SQUARED ENTERTAINMENT

(Producer of large-format and traditional motion pictures)
530 Wilshire Blvd., 4th Flr., Santa Monica, CA 90401. (310) 587-2100. FAX: (310) 587-2121. www.lsqr.com
email: michaelr@lsqr.com
CEO & CO-FOUNDER
Michael V. Lewis
CHAIRMAN & CO-FOUNDER
Brett Leonard

LUCASFILM, LTD.

(Motion picture production)
P.O. Box 2009, San Rafael, CA 94912. (415) 662-1800. FAX: (415) 662-2437. www.lucasfilms.com
CHAIRMAN OF THE BOARD
George W. Lucas, Jr.
PRESIDENT
Gordon Radley
V.P. & GENERAL MANAGER, LICENSING
Howard Roffman
GENERAL MANAGER, THX
Monica Dashwood

LUCASARTS ENTERTAINMENT COMPANY

P.O. Box 10307, San Rafael, CA 94912. (415) 472-3400. FAX: (415) 444-8488. www.lucasarts.com
PRESIDENT
Simon Jeffery
DIRECTOR, SALES & MARKETING
Mary Bihr

LUCAS DIGITAL, LTD.
P.O. Box 2459, San Rafael, CA 94912. (415) 258-2000. FAX: (415) 448-9550. www.ilm.com
PRESIDENT
Jim Morris
V.P. & GENERAL MANAGER, SKYWALKER SOUND
Gloria Borders

LUCID MEDIA
7120 Alcove Ave., North Hollywood, CA 91605. (818) 764-8580. www.loop.com email: macbravo@loop.com
PRESIDENT
Marino Colmano

LUX PICTURES, INC.
120 Mildred Ave., Venice, CA 90291. (310) 301-0101. FAX: (310) 301-0153. email: info@luxpix.com
EXECUTIVE PRODUCER
James Magowan
PRODUCER
Martin Kistler
ASSOCIATE PRODUCER
Mark Ching
NEW BUSINESS DEVELOPMENT
Fiona Banister

MACGILLIVRAY FREEMAN FILMS
(Producer and distributor of large-format films)
P.O. Box 206, Laguna Beach, CA 92652. (949) 494-1055. FAX: (949) 494-2079. email: macgfree@aol.com
www.macfreefilms.com
CONTACT
Lori Rick

MAD CHANCE
4000 Warner Blvd., Bung. 3, Burbank, CA 91522. (818) 954-3803. FAX: (818) 954-3447.
email: madchance@sprintmail.com
PRODUCER
Andrew Lazar
CO-PRODUCER
Jody Hedien
V.P., PRODUCTION
Doug Davison
DIRECTOR, CREATIVE AFFAIRS
Far Shariat
CREATIVE ASSISTANT
Sean Wicks

MAELSTROM ENTERTAINMENT LLC
8733 Sunset Blvd., Ste. 202, West Hollywood, CA 90069. (310) 360-9945. FAX: (310) 652-0318.
CEO
Aaron Granath
EXECUTIVE DIRECTOR
Ruth Sutherland

MALIBU BAY FILMS
(Television and motion picture production)
P.O. Box 17244, Beverly Hills, CA 90209-3244. (310) 278-5056. FAX: (310) 278-5058. www.adnysidaris.com
PRESIDENT
Andrew Sidaris

MALPASO PRODUCTIONS
4000 Warner Blvd., Bldg. 81, Burbank, CA 91522-0811. (818) 954-3367. FAX: (818) 954-4803.
PRODUCER & ACTOR & DIRECTOR
Clint Eastwood
DIRECTOR, DEVELOPMENT
Melissa Rooker
EDITOR
Joel Cox

MANDALAY PICTURES
5555 Melrose Ave., Lewis Bldg., Hollywood, CA 90038. (323) 956-2400. FAX: (323) 862-2266.
CHAIRMAN
Peter Guber
VICE CHAIRMAN
Paul Schaeffer
PRESIDENT
Adam Platnick
EXECUTIVE V.P., BUSINESS AFFAIRS
Darrell Walker
EXECUTIVE V.P. & CFO
John Zabel
EXECUTIVE V.P., PRODUCTION
Karen Teicher
SENIOR V.P., POST-PRODUCTION
Chantal Feghali
SENIOR V.P., BUSINESS DEVELOPMENT
Randy Hermann
SENIOR V.P., PRODUCTION
Ori Marmur
SENIOR V.P., CORPORATE OPERATIONS
Shelly Riney
SENIOR V.P., PRODUCTION ADMINISTRATION
David Zelon
V.P., BUSINESS & LEGAL AFFAIRS
Barry Littman
V.P., FINANCE & CONTROLLER
Robert Spallina
V.P., BUSINESS AFFAIRS ADMINISTRATION
Michelle DiRaffaele
DIRECTOR, DEVELOPMENT
Tracy Andreen

MANDY FILMS, INC.
9201 Wilshire Blvd., #206, Beverly Hills, CA 90210. (310) 246-0500. FAX: (310) 246-0350.
PRESIDENT
Leonard Goldberg
V.P., DEVELOPMENT & PRODUCTION
Amanda Goldberg
V.P., DEVELOPMENT
Martina Lynne Papinchak
DEVELOPMENT ASSISTANT
Beau Blanchard

MANIFEST FILM COMPANY
1247 Euclid St., Santa Monica, CA 90404. (310) 899-5554. FAX: (310) 899-5553. email: manifilm@aol.com
PRODUCER & PARTNER
Lisa Henson
PRODUCER & PARTNER
Janet Yang
SENIOR V.P.
Naomi Despres

LAURENCE MARK PRODUCTIONS
10202 W. Washington Blvd., Poitier Bldg., Ste. 3111, Culver City, CA 90232. (310) 244-5239.
PRESIDENT & PRODUCER
Laurence Mark
PRESIDENT, PRODUCTION
Jonathan King
PRESIDENT, TV
Ilene Amy Berg
V.P., CREATIVE AFFAIRS
John McNamara
PRODUCTION OFFICE MANAGER
Petra Alexandria

MARVEL CHARACTERS, INC.
10474 Santa Monica Blvd., Ste. 206, Los Angeles, CA 90025. (310) 234-8991. FAX: (310) 234-8162. www.marvel.com
CHAIRMAN EMERITUS
Stan Lee
PRESIDENT & CEO, MARVEL STUDIOS
Avi Arad
PRESIDENT, MARVEL CHARACTER GROUP
Rick Ungar
SENIOR V.P., MARVEL STUDIOS
Kevin Feige
EXECUTIVE DIRECTOR, CREATIVE DEVELOPMENT
Carlos Lopez
DIRECTOR, DEVELOPMENT
Matt Sullivan

MATERIAL
4000 Warner Blvd., Bldg. 139, Rm. 27, Burbank, CA 91522. (818) 954-1551. FAX: (818) 954-5299.
PRODUCER
Jorge Saralegui
SENIOR V.P., PRODUCTION
Channing Dungey
VICE PRESIDENT
Percy Zuletta

THE MATTHAU COMPANY, INC.
11661 San Vicente Blvd., Ste. 609, Los Angeles, CA 90049. (818) 838-1000.
PRESIDENT
Charles Matthau
PRESIDENT, MANAGEMENT DIVISION
Michael McDavitt
OPERATIONS
Jason Cooper
DIRECTOR, BUSINESS AFFAIRS
Kristina Jeffers
DIRECTOR, CREATIVE AFFAIRS
Lana Morgan

MAVERICK ENTERTAINMENT

9348 Civic Center Dr., Mezzanine., Beverly Hills, CA 90210. (310) 276-6177. FAX: (310) 276-9477.
CONTACTS
Madonna
Guy Oseary
Caresse Henry
Gary Ventimigila
CREATIVE EXECUTIVE
Daniel Rosenfeld

MAYSVILLE PICTURES

4000 Warner Blvd., Bldg. 81, Rm. 117, Burbank, CA 91522. (818) 954-4840. FAX: (818) 954-4860.
CEO & PARTNER
George Clooney
CEO & PARTNER
Steven Soderbergh
PRESIDENT
Ben Cosgrove
VICE PRESIDENT
Kevin Field
V.P., TV DEVELOPMENT
Pam Oas Williams
COORDINATION PRODUCER
Amy Minda Cohen

MDP WORLDWIDE

1925 Century Park East, Ste. 1700, Los Angeles, CA 90067. (310) 226-8300. FAX: (310) 226-8350.
email: info@behaviourww.com
CHAIRMAN & CEO
Mark Damon
PRESIDENT & COO
Richard Kiratsoulis
V.P. & CFO
Matthew Carson
DIRECTOR OF FINANCE
Devin Cutler
V.P., INTERNATIONAL SALES & ACQUISITIONS
Reiko Bradley

BARRY MENDEL PRODUCTIONS

100 Universal City Plaza, Bung. 5163, Universal City, CA 91608. (818) 733-3076. FAX: (818) 733-4070.
CONTACTS
Barry Mendel
Jennifer Simpson
ASSISTANTS
Beth Irizarry
Heather Magee
Jason Miller

MERCHANT-IVORY

250 W. 57th St., Ste. 1825, New York, NY 10107. (212) 582-8049. FAX: (212) 459-9201. www.merchantivory.com
CO-PRESIDENT & PRODUCER
Ismail Merchant
CO-PRESIDENT & DIRECTOR
James Ivory
EXECUTIVE V.P. & EXECUTIVE PRODUCER
Richard Hawley
PRODUCTION COORDINATOR
Marla L. Shelton
DIRECTOR, DEVELOPMENT
Mary Murphy

RICARDO MESTRES PRODUCTIONS

500 S. Buena Vista St. Anim. Bldg., 2E8/2E5, Burbank, CA 91521. FAX: (818) 953-4238.
PRODUCER
Ricardo Mestres
CREATIVE EXECUTIVE
Ben Sussman

METRO-GOLDWYN-MAYER

Headquarters: 2500 Broadway St., Santa Monica, CA 90404-3061. (310) 449-3000. FAX: (310) 449-3100. www.mgm.com
1350 Ave. of the Americas, New York, NY 10019. (212) 708-0300. FAX: (212) 708-0337.
CHAIRMAN. OF THE BOARD & CEO
Alex Yemenidjian
VICE CHAIRMAN
Christopher McGurk
SENIOR. EXECUTIVE V.P. & CFO
Daniel J Taylor
SENIOR EXECUTIVE V.P. & SECRETARY
William A. Jones
PRESIDENT, WORLDWIDE THEATR. DIST., MGM DIST. CO.
Larry Gleason
PRESIDENT, WORLDWIDE MTKG., MGM DIST. CO.
Gerry Rich
PRESIDENT, WORLDWIDE TELEVISION DISTRIBUTION
James Griffiths
PRESIDENT, MGM HOME ENTERTAINMENT & CONSUMER PRODUCTS GROUP
Richard Cohen
EXEC. V.P., MGM MUSIC
Anita Camarato
EXEUTIVE V.P., FINANCE & CORP. DEVELOPMENT
Charles E. Cohen
SENIOR V.P., LABOR RELATIONS
Mark Crowley
SENIOR V.P., WORLDWIDE PUBLICITY
Amanda Lundberg
EXECUTIVE V.P., ADMINISTRATION
Richard Parness
EXECUTIVE V.P., DEPUTY GENERAL COUNSEL
Jay Rakow
SENIOR V.P., CORP. COMM. & INVESTOR RELATIONS
Craig Parsons
EXECUTIVE V.P., STUDIO FINANCE OPERATIONS
Daniel J. Rosett
SENIOR V.P., INFORMATION SERVICES
Kim Spenchian
V.P., TAXES
Deborah J. Arvesen

MGM PICTURES

2500 Broadway St., Santa Monica, CA 90404. (310) 449-3000. FAX: (310) 449-3100.
PRESIDENT, MGM PICTURES
Michael Nathanson
SENIOR EXECUTIVE V.P., BUSINESS AFFAIRS FOR MGM
Darcie Denkert
PRESIDENT, PRODUCTION FOR MGM PICTURES /UA
Robert E. Relyea
EXECUTIVE V.P., FINANCIAL OPERATIONS
Daniel J Rosett
SENIOR V.P., LABOR RELATIONS
Mark Crowley
SENIOR V.P., PRODUCTION
Jeff Coleman
SENIOR V.P., BUSINESS AFFAIRS ADMINISTRATION
Luba Keske
SENIOR V.P., BUSINESS AFFAIRS
Marla E. Levine
SENIOR V.P., PRODUCTION
Elizabeth Carroll
DIRECTOR, CREATIVE AFFAIRS
Kim Ciliberto

MGM DISTRIBUTION COMPANY

1350 Ave. of the Americas, New York, NY 10019-4870. (212) 708-0300.

11111 Santa Monica Blvd., 3rd Flr., Los Angeles, CA 90025. (310) 444-1600. FAX: (310) 312-3372. FAX (Sales): (310) 444-1698.

CANADA

720 King St. West, Ste. 611, Toronto, ON, Canada M5V 2T3. Tel: (416) 703-9579. FAX: (416) 504-3821.
EXECUTIVE V.P., GENERAL SALES MANAGER
Erik Lomis
SENIOR V.P., EASTERN SALES MANAGER
William Lewis
SENIOR V.P., WESTERN SALES MANAGER
Mike Bisio
V.P., CANADIAN DIVISION MANAGER
Marisa Contardi
V.P., NONTHEATRICAL SALES
Jan Sirridge
V.P. DOMESTIC DISTRIBUTION
Derek Mclay

PUERTO RICO

Citibank Tower, 10th Flr., 252 Ponce de Leon Ave., Hato Rey, Puerto Rico 00918. Tel: (787) 751-5122. FAX: (787) 751-5188.

UNITED KINGDOM

Glenthorne House, Hammersmith Grove, London W6 0ND. Tel: (44181) 563-8383, ext. 233. FAX: (44181) 563-9014.

UNITED ARTISTS INTERNATIONAL

10 Steven Mews London, England W1P 1PP 011-44-171-33-8877.
CEO
Wendy Palmer
COO
Francois Thos
EXECUTIVE V.P.
Fiona Mitchell

THE MILTON I. MORITZ COMPANY, INC.

856 Malcolm Ave., Garden Ste., Los Angeles, CA, 90024. (310) 470-9122. FAX: (310) 475-5614.
PRESIDENT
Neal H. Moritz

MIRACLE ENTERTAINMENT

8730 Sunset Blvd., Penthouse East, West Hollywood, CA 90069. (310) 360-7490. FAX: (310) 360-7499.
PRODUCERS
Richard G. Abramson
Martin Landau

MIRACLE PICTURES

1625 Olympic Blvd., Ste. 200, Santa Monica, CA 90404. (310) 392-3011. FAX: (310) 392-2021.
PRESIDENT
A. Kitman Ho
V.P., DEVELOPMENT & PRODUCTION
Laurie Hansen
V.P., DEVELOPMENT & PRODUCTION
Andrew D. Spaulding

MIRAGE ENTERPRISES

10202 W. Washington Blvd., Lean Bldg., Culver City, CA 90232-3195. (310) 244-2044. FAX: (310) 244-0044.
PRODUCER & DIRECTOR
Sydney Pollack
PRODUCERS
William Horberg
David Rubin
Geoff Stier
OFFICE MANAGER
Jenny McLaren

MIRAMAX FILMS CORP.

(Subsidiaries: Dimension Films, Shining Excalibur Pictures)
375 Greenwich St., New York, NY 10013. (212) 941-3800. FAX: (212) 941-3949. www.miramax.com
8439 Sunset Blvd., West Hollywood, CA 90069. (323) 822-4100. FAX: (323) 822-4128.
CHAIRMEN
Bob Weinstein
Harvey Weinstein
EXECUTIVE V.P., FINANCE & OPERATIONS
Bahman Naraghi
PRESIDENT, MIRAMAX (LOS ANGELES)
Mark Gill
EXECUTIVE V.P.
Charles Layton
SENIOR V.P., BUSINESS & LEGAL AFFAIRS
Vicky Cherkas
SENIOR V.P., LEGAL AFFAIRS
Andrew Herwitz
S.V.P
Michael Luisi
V.P., HUMAN RESOURCES
Paula Simonetti

PRODUCTION

CO-PRESIDENT, PRODUCTION
Bob Osher
CO-PRESIDENT, PRODUCTION
Meryl Poster
EXECUTIVE V.P., DEVELOPMENT
Colin Vaines
EXECUTIVE V.P., PRODUCTION
Jon Gordon
EXECUTIVE V.P., PRODUCTION & DEVELOPMENT
Julie Goldstein
EXECUTIVE V.P., PHYSICAL PRODUCTION
Kevin Hyman
SENIOR V.P., PRODUCTION FINANCE
John Hadity
SENIOR V.P., POST-PRODUCTION
Scott Martin
PRESIDENT, MOTION PICTURE MUSIC
Randy Spendlove

ACQUISITIONS

EXECUTIVE V.P., ACQUISITIONS & CO-PRODUCTIONS
Agnes Mentre
SENIOR V.P., ACQUISITIONS & CO-PRODUCTIONS
Andreio Herwitz
SENIOR V.P., ACQUISITIONS & CO-PRODUCTIONS
Jason Blum

DISTRIBUTION

CHAIRMAN, WORLDWIDE DISTRIBUTION
Rick Sands
EXECUTIVE V.P., INTERNATIONAL MARKETING
Stephen Klain
SENIOR V.P., DOMESTIC DISTRIBUTION
Mike Rudnitsky
SENIOR V.P., DELIVERY SERVICES
Glaister Kerr

MARKETING & PUBLICITY

PRESIDENT, PUBLICITY & CORPORATE COMMUNICATIONS
Marcy Granata
EXECUTIVE V.P., MARKETING & NEW VENTURES
David Brooks
SENIOR V.P., MARKETING
Lorin Prince
SENIOR V.P., MARKETING
Dabid Kaminow
SENIOR V.P., PUBLICITY, WEST COAST
Janet Hill
SENIOR V.P., PUBLICITY
Terri Kane
SENIOR V.P., PUBLICITY
Gina Gardini

DIMENSION FILMS

PRESIDENT
Brad Weston
SENIOR V.P., PRODUCTION & DEVELOPMENT
Andrew Rona

HOME VIDEO

EXECUTIVE V.P.
Kevin Kasha
SENIOR V.P., VIDEO BROADCAST & POST PRODUCTION
Shannon McIntosh

THE MIRISCH CORPORATION OF CALIFORNIA

100 Universal City Plaza, Bldg. 507 #2C, Universal City, CA 91608-1085. (818) 777-1271. FAX: (818) 866-1422.
PRODUCERS
Marvin E. Mirisch
Walter Mirisch

MOJO FILMS

9021 Melrose Ave., Ste. 302, Los Angeles, CA 90069. (310) 248-6070. FAX: (310) 385-0475.
PRODUCER & DIRECTOR
Gary Fleder
V.P., PRODUCTION & DEVELOPMENT
Amber Stevens
STORY EDITOR
Joe Culella

MONTAGE ENTERTAINMENT

2118 Wilshire Blvd., #297, Santa Monica, CA 90403-5784. (310) 966-0222. FAX: (310) 966-0223.
PRODUCER
David Peters
PRODUCER
Bill Ewart
DIRECTOR, DEVELOPMENT
Jim Mercurio

THE MONTECITO PICTURE COMPANY

1482 E. Valley Road, Ste. 477, Montecito, CA 93108. (805) 565-8590. FAX: (805) 565-8661.
9465 Wilshire Blvd., Ste. 920, Beverly Hills, CA 90212. (310) 247-9880.
PARTNERS
Ivan Reitman
Tom Pollock
DEVELOPMENT & CASTING EXECUTIVE & PRODUCER
Michael Chinich
PRODUCER
Joe Medjuck
PRODUCER
Dan M. Goldberg
PRODUCER & EDITOR
Sheldon Khan

MOONSTONE ENTERTAINMENT

P.O. Box 7400, Studio City, CA 91614; 3539 Laurel Canyon, Studio City, CA 91604. (818) 985-3303. FAX: (818) 985-3009.
PRESIDENT
Ernst Stroh
EXECUTIVE V.P.
Yael Stroh
VICE PRESIDENT
Luz Moretti
CONTROLLER
Greg Majerus
DIRECTOR
Michael Kasher
EXECUTIVE DIRECTOR
Dana Williams

MORESS-NANAS-HART ENTERTAINMENT

14945 Ventura Blvd., Ste. 228, Sherman Oaks, CA 91403. (818) 379-9516. FAX: (818) 379-9517.
email: mnhent@earthlink.net
1102 18th Ave. South, Nashville, TN 37212. (615) 329-9945.
PRODUCER & PERSONAL MANAGER
Scott Hart
PRODUCER & PERSONAL MANAGER
Stan Moress
PRODUCER & PERSONAL MANAGER
Herb Nanas

MORGAN CREEK PRODUCTIONS

4000 Warner Blvd., Bldg. 76, Burbank, CA 91522. (818) 954-4800. FAX: (818) 954-4811.
CHAIRMAN & CEO
James G. Robinson
CFO
Howard Kaplan
PRESIDENT, PRODUCTION
Jonathan A. Zimbert
SENIOR V.P., DEVELOPMENT
Joe Martino
V.P., DEVELOPMENT
Hilary Galanoy
HEAD, WORLDWIDE MARKETING
Brian Robinson
INTERNATIONAL
Lawrence Steven Meyers
HEAD OF PUBLICITY
Greg Mielcarz

MOSTOW/LIEBERMAN

100 Universal City Plaza, Bung. 4111, Universal City, CA 91608. (818) 777-4444. FAX: (818) 866-1328.
PARTNERS
Hal Lieberman
Jonathan Mostow
Richard Silverman

MOTION PICTURE CORP. OF AMERICA (A METROMEDIA ENTERTAINMENT GROUP CO.)

(Motion picture producer and distributor)
1401 Ocean Ave., #301, Santa Monica, CA 90401. (310) 319-9500. FAX: (310) 319-9501.
PRESIDENT
Brad Krevoy
SENIOR V.P., PRODUCTION & DEVELOPMENT
Tim Foster
V.P., PRODUCTION & DEVELOPMENT
Adam Richman

THE MOUNT COMPANY

(Motion picture & TV production)
6363 Sunset Blvd. Ste. 500, Los Angeles, CA 90028. (323) 769-3434. FAX: (323) 468-8307.
www.hollywoodbroadcasting.com
PRESIDENT
Thomas Mount
CREATIVE EXECUTIVE
Patrick Olmstead
HEAD OF TELEVISION & CABLE DIVISION
Rodman Gregg

MOVING PICTURES

375 Greenwich St., New York, NY 10013. (212) 219-4545. FAX: (212) 219-4546.
PARTNER
Demi Moore
PARTNER & PRESIDENT
Daneen Conroy
SENIOR V.P., DEVELOPMENT & PRODUCTION
Andrea Asimow
CREATIVE EXECUTIVE
Danielle Gaydos

MOVING PICTURES, LTD.

3487 W. 2100 South, Ste. 132, Salt Lake City, UT 84119. (801) 973-0632. FAX: (801) 973-0380. www.movingpics.net
CONTACT
Troy Parkinson

MOZARK PRODUCTIONS

4024 Radford Ave., Bldg. 5, #104, Studio City, CA 91604. (818) 655-5779. FAX: (818) 655-5129.
email: mozark@ix.netcom.com
EXECUTIVE PRODUCER & WRITER
Linda Bloodworth-Thomason
EXECUTIVE PRODUCER & DIRECTOR
Harry Thomason

MR. MUDD

5225 Wilshire Blvd., Ste. 604, Los Angeles, CA 90036. (323) 932-5656. FAX: (323) 932-5666.
PRODUCER & DIRECTOR
John Malkovich
PRODUCER
Lianne Halfon
PRODUCER
Russ Smith
HEAD, PRODUCTION
Aileen Argentini
CREATIVE ASSOCIATE
Shannon Clark

MTV FILMS

5555 Melrose Ave., Modular Bldg. 213, Los Angeles, CA 90038. (323) 956-8023. FAX: (323) 862-1386 & (323) 862-8020. www.mtv.com
GEN. MGR., MTV NETWORKS & PRESIDENT, MTV PRODS.
Van Toffler
HEAD, MTV FILMS & SENIOR V.P., MTV
David M. Gale
PRODUCTION MANAGER, MTV FILMS
Momita Sengupta
STORY EDITOR
Gregg Goldin
CREATIVE EXECUTIVE
Susan Lewis
PRODUCTION EXECUTIVE
Troy Craig Poon

MUSE PRODUCTIONS, INC.

15 Brooks Ave., Unit B, Venice, CA 90921. (310) 306-2001. FAX: (310) 574-2614.
www.musefilm.com
PRESIDENT & PRODUCER
Chris Hanley
PRESIDENT & DIRECTOR
Roberta Hanley

MUTANT ENEMY, INC.

P.O. Box 900, Beverly Hills, CA 90213-0900. (310) 579-5180. FAX: (310) 579-5380.
CEO
Joss Whedon
CREATIVE EXECUTIVE
Tom Plotkin
DIRECTOR, DEVELOPMENT
George Snyder

MUTUAL FILM COMPANY

650 N. Bronson Ave., Clinton Bldg., Los Angeles, CA 90004. (323) 871-5690. FAX: (323) 871-5689.
PRINCIPALS
Marc Gordon
Gary Levinsohn
PRESIDENT, PRODUCTION
Betsy Bees
CFO
Kathleen Amundson
PRODUCTION EXECUTIVES
Tania Landau
Suzanne Patmore
MUTUAL FILM INTERNATIONAL
Pamela Pickering
OPERATIONS & ADMINISTRATION, MUTUTAL FILM INTL.
Lesly Gross
CONTROLLER
Al Haferkamp
INTERNATIONAL SERVICING
Jennifer P. Shepard

NASSO PRODUCTIONS

5824 12th Ave., Brooklyn, New York 11219. (718) 854-1561. FAX: (718) 972-2355.
PRESIDENT & PRODUCER
Julius R. Nasso

NATIONAL GEOGRAPHIC

1145 17th St. N.W., Washington, DC 20036. (202) 775-6147. FAX: (202) 775-6590. www.nationalgeographic.com/main.html

NATIONAL LAMPOON

(Motion pictures & TV production)
A subsidiary of J2 Communications, 10850 Wilshire Blvd., Ste. 1000, Los Angeles, CA 90024. (310) 474-5252. FAX: (310) 474-1219. www.nationallampoon.com
PRESIDENT & CEO
Jim Jimirro
V.P., MARKETING
Duncan Murray
CFO
Chris Trunkey
EDITOR IN CHIEF, NATIONAL LAMPOON.COM
Scott Rubin

MACE NEUFELD PRODUCTIONS

10202 W. Washington Blvd., Steward Bldg., Ste. 220, Culver City, CA 90232-3195. (310) 244-2555. FAX: (310) 244-0255.
PRINCIPAL
Mace Neufeld

ASSOCIATE PRODUCER
Elisabeth Kern
V.P., DEVELOPMENT
Kel Symons
DIRECTOR, DEVELOPMENT
David Engel
CREATIVE EXECUTIVE
Jeff Kirschenbaum

NEW CONCORDE CORP.

(Motion picture & TV production & distribution)
11600 San Vicente Blvd., Los Angeles, CA 90049. (310) 820-6733. FAX: (310) 207-6816. www.concorde-newhorizons.com
PRESIDENT & CEO
Roger Corman
PRESIDENT, NEW HORIZONS HOME VIDEO
Gary Jones
PRODUCER
Catherine Corman
SENIOR V.P. & PRODUCER
Julie Corman
V.P., DEVELOPMENT
Frances Doel
V.P., FINANCE
Goly Jamshidi
V.P., BUSINESS DEVELOPMENT
Doug Lowell
DIRECTOR, PRODUCTION
Damian Akhavi

NEW CRIME PRODUCTIONS

555 Rose Ave., Venice, CA 90291. (310) 396-2199. FAX: (310) 396-4249. email: newcrime@aol.com
WRITER & PRODUCER & ACTOR
John Cusack
WRITER & PRODUCER
Steve Pink
WRITER & PRODUCER
D.V. DeVincentis
VICE PRESIDENT
Grace Loh

NEW LINE CINEMA CORPORATION

888 Seventh Ave., 20th Flr., New York, NY 10106. (212) 649-4900. FAX: (212) 649-4966. www.newline.com
116 North Robertson Blvd., 2nd Fl., Los Angeles, CA 90048. (310) 854-5811. FAX: (310) 854-1824.
CHAIRMAN & CEO
Robert K. Shaye
PRESIDENT & COO
Michael Lynne
CFO
Stephen D. Abramson
PRESIDENT, FINE LINE FEATURES
Mark Ordesky
PRESIDENT, NEW MEDIA
James Rosenthal
SENIOR EXECUTIVE V.P., FINANCE
Michael Spatt
SENIOR EXECUTIVE V.P., BUSINESS & LEGAL AFFAIRS
Benjamin Zinkin
EXECUTIVE V.P., FINANCE
Tracy Schefler
EXECUTIVE V.P., ROYALTY & CONTRACTS
Susannah Juni
EXECUTIVE V.P., ADMINISTRATION
Marsha Hook Haygood
SENIOR V.P.
Judd Funk
SENIOR V.P., TELEVISION & ANCILLARY
Frank Buquicchio
SENIOR V.P., FINANCIAL OPERATIONS
David Eichler
SENIOR V.P., CORPORATE
Raymond Landes
SENIOR V.P.
Amy Goodman
V.P., BUSINESS AFFAIRS & ADMINISTRATION
Sonya Thompson
V.P., BUSINESS & LEGAL AFFAIRS
Suzanne Rosencranz

THEATRICAL DISTRIBUTION

EXECUTIVE V.P., FINELINE DISTRIBUTION
Steve Friedlander
SENIOR V.P., SALES ADMINISTRATION
David Keith
SENIOR V.P., EASTERN DIVISION MANAGER
Johnathan Beal
SENIOR V.P., SOUTHEASTERN DIVISION MANAGER
Don Osley
SENIOR V.P., SOUTHERN DIVISION MANAGER
John Trickett
SENIOR V.P., WESTERN DIVISION MANAGER
Larry Levy
V.P., NATIONAL PRINT CONTROL
Gisela Corcoran

INTERNATIONAL DISTRIBUTION

PRESIDENT
Rolf Mittweg
EXECUTIVE V.P., EUROPE SUP.
Camela Galano
SENIOR V.P., SALES & ADMINISTRATION
Nestor Nieves
SENIOR V.P., INTL.. DISTRIBUTION & CONTRACTS
Ralpho Borgos
V.P., INTERNATIONAL MARKETING
Teri Grochowski

MARKETING

CO-CHAIRMAN, WORLDWIDE THEATRICAL MARKETING
Rolf Mittweg
CO-CHAIRMAN, WORLDWIDE THEATRICAL MARKETING
Robert Friedman
PRESIDENT, THEATRICAL MARKETING
Joe Nimzicki
EXECUTIVE V.P., MEDIA & COOPERATIVE ADVERTISING
Robert Kobus
EXECUTIVE V.P., PUBLICITY
Mary Donovan
SENIOR V.P., CORP. PUBLICITY
Steve Elzer
SENIOR V.P., NATIONAL PROMOTIONS
Mary Goss
SENIOR V.P., FIELD & INTERACTIVE
Elissa Greer
V.P., CREATIVE SERVICES
Luise Hollowell
V.P., CREATIVE SERVICES
Helene Steel
SENIOR V.P., COOPERATIVE ADVERTISING
Susan Russell

PRODUCTION

CHAIRPERSON
Sara Risher
PRESIDENT & COO
Michael de Luca
SENIOR EXECUTIVE V.P.
Richard Saperstein
SENIOR EXECUTIVE V.P., PRODUCTION ADMINISTRATION
Carla Fry
EXECUTIVE V.P., PRODUCTION
Claire Rudnick-Polstein
EXECUTIVE V.P., PRODUCTION
Lynn Harris
SENIOR V.P., PRODUCTION
Jay Stern
SENIOR V.P., PRODUCTION FINANCE
Paul Prokop
PRESIDENT, MUSIC
Toby Emmerich
SENIOR V.P.'S, MUSIC
Dana Sano
Paul Broucek
SENIOR V.P., PRODUCTION & DEVELOPMENT
Amy Henkels
SENIOR V.P., POST-PRODUCTION
Richard Keeley
SENIOR V.P., POST-PRODUCTION
Sara King

TELEVISION DISTRIBUTION

PRESIDENT
Robert Friedman
EXECUTIVE V.P., TV INTERNATIONAL
Diane Keating
EXECUTIVE V.P., DISTRIBUTION
David Spiegelman
EXECUTIVE V.P., LICENSING & MERCHANDISING
David Imhoff
SENIOR V.P., SALES ADMINISTRATION
Vicky Gregorian
V.P., PRODUCTION & DEVELOPMENT
Laura Armstrong

HOME VIDEO

PRESIDENT
Stephen Einhorn
SENIOR V.P., FINANCE
Rita Chiapetta-Thibault

INFORMATION DISTRIBUTION

EXECUTIVE V.P., INFORMATION SERVICES
Karen Zimmer

NEWMAN/TOOLEY FILMS

101 S. Robertson Blvd., #203, Los Angeles, CA 90048. (310) 777-8733. FAX: (310) 777-8730.
email: newmantooley@earthlink.net
PRODUCER & CO-CHAIRMAN
Vincent G. Newman
PRODUCER & CO-CHAIRMAN
Tucker Tooley
PRODUCER
Ronene A. Ettinger
DIRECTOR, PRODUCTION & DEVELOPMENT
Nancy Lanham
EXECUTIVE ASSISTANT
Ryan Egno
EXECUTIVE ASSISTANT
Micha Walker

NEWMARKET CAPITAL GROUP

202 N. Canon Dr., Beverly Hills, CA 90210. (310) 858-7472. FAX: (310) 858-7473.
PARTNERS
Chris Ball
William Tyrer
CFO
Rene Cogan
STORY EDITOR
John Crye
ACCOUNTING
Kenneth Kim
BUSINESS AFFAIRS
Cindy Kirven
DEVELOPMENT
Scott Leclau
SPECIAL PROJECTS
Debra Pollack
ACQUISITIONS
Linda Hawkins
Aaron Ryder

NEW REGENCY PRODUCTIONS

10201 W. Pico Blvd., Bldg. 12, Los Angeles, CA 90035. (310) 369-8300. FAX: (310) 969-0470. www.newregency.com
PRODUCER
Arnon Milchan
PRESIDENT & CEO
David Matalon
PRESIDENT, PRODUCTION
Sanford Panitch
EXECUTIVE V.P. & CFO
Louis Santer
EXECUTIVE V.P., BUS. & LGL. AFFRS. & GEN. COUNSEL
William S. Weiner
SENIOR V.P., PRODUCTION
Peter Cramer
SENIOR V.P., FEATURE PRODUCTION
Bonnie Daniels
SENIOR V.P., PHYSICAL PRODUCTION
Thomas Imperanto
SENIOR V.P., POST-PRODUCTION
Elissa Loparco
V.P., PRODUCTION
Kara Francis
V.P., ACQUISITIONS
Alexandra Milchan
PRODUCTION SUPERVISOR
Carole Nix
CREATIVE ASSOCIATE
Michelle Brattson

NEWSTAR MEDIA, INC.

8955 Beverly Blvd., Los Angeles, CA 90040. (310) 786-1600. FAX: (310) 246-6544. www.newstarmedia.com
CFO
John Brady
PRESIDENT, NEWSTAR TELEVISION
Ron Ziskin
V.P., DEVELOPMENT
Dave Collins

NEW YORKER FILMS

(Motion picture distribution)
16 W. 61 St., 11th Flr., New York, NY 10023. (212) 247-6110. FAX: (212) 307-7855. www.newyorkerfilms.com
PRESIDENT
Daniel Talbot

NICKELODEON MOVIES

5555 Melrose Ave., Lubitsch Bldg., #119, Hollywood, CA 90038. (323) 956-8663. FAX: (323) 862-1663.
1515 Broadway, 37th Flr., New York, NY 10036. (212) 258-7500.
PRESIDENT
Albie Hecht
SENIOR V.P.
Julia Pistor
V.P., ANIMATION
Share Stallings
SENIOR PRODUCER, ANIMATION
Ramsey Naito
EXECUTIVE DIRECTOR, DEVELOPMENT, LIVE ACTION
Ricki Spector
CREATIVE EXECUTIVE
Damon Ross

NO PRISONERS

2260 S. Centinela Ave., Los Angeles, CA 90064. (310) 979-9097. FAX: (310) 979-7097. www.noprisoners.com
email: info@noprisoners.net
CEO & PRODUCER
Todd Moyer
PRESIDENT & COO
Bruce Martin
CREATIVE EXECUTIVE
Michael Abbott
DIRECTOR
Barnaby Jackson
DIRECTOR
Nic Mathieu
VISUAL EFFECTS SUPERVISOR
Chris Brown
CONTROLLER
Jim McCarthy

NORTHERN ARTS ENTERTAINMENT

(Motion picture producers and distributors)
Northern Arts Studios,Williamsburg, MA 01096-0763. (413) 268-9301. FAX: (413) 268-9309.
CHAIRMAN
John Lawrence Re
PRESIDENT
David Mazor
V.P., ACQUISITIONS
Ava Lazar
DIRECTOR, FOREIGN ACQUISITIONS
Andrew Weeks

NORWOOD ENTERTAINMENT GROUP

1438 N. Gower St., Bldg. 35, Los Angeles, CA 90028. (323) 860-7448.
PRINCIPALS
Willie R. Norwood Sr.
Sonja B. Norwood
DIRECTOR, SPECIAL PROJECTS
Jihad Scott
EXECUTIVE ASSISTANT
Portia Hodge

NOVA LARGE FORMAT FILMS

125 Western Ave., Boston, MA 02134. (617) 300-4391. FAX: (617) 300-1003. www.pbs.org/nova

NUANCE PRODUCTIONS

345 N. Maple Dr., Ste. 208, Beverly Hills, CA 90210. (310) 247-1870. FAX: (310) 247-8150. email: nuancepr@pacbell.net
PARTNER
Paul Reiser
PARTNER
Arthur Spivak
V.P., TV DEVELOPMENT
Vernon Sanders
DEVELOPMENT ASSOCIATE
Catherine Cobb

NWAVE PICTURES

(Digital production specializing in large-format and ride films)
3000 West Olympic Blvd., Santa Monica, CA 90404. (310) 264-4268. www.nwave.com
CONTACT
Charlotte Huggins

LYNDA OBST PRODUCTIONS

5555 Melrose Ave., Bldg. 210, Hollywood, CA 90038. (323) 956-8744. FAX: (323) 862-2287.
PRODUCER
Lynda Obst
SENIOR V.P., PHYSICAL PRODUCTIONS
Elizabeth Hooper
SENIOR V.P., DEVELOPMENT
Marc Rosen
V.P., DEVELOPMENT
Mandy Safavi
CREATIVE EXECUTIVE
Kellie Bryce

OCEAN PICTURES

10201 W. Pico Blvd., Bldg. 12, Rm. 123, Los Angeles, CA 90035. (310) 369-0093. FAX: (310) 369-7742.
DIRECTOR & WRITER & PRODUCER
Harold Ramis
PRODUCER
Trevor Albert
CREATIVE EXECUTIVE
Lisa Ullman
DIRECTOR, DEVELOPMENT
Suzanne Herrington
DEVELOPMENT ASSISTANTS
Laurel Ward
Kym Bye

OCELOT FILMS, INC.

179 So. Detroit St., Los Angeles, CA 90036. (323) 934-5353. FAX: (323) 934-5354. email: ocelotfilm@mindspring.com
PRODUCER
D.J. Paul

OCTOBER FILMS

(See USA Films)

OFFROAD ENTERTAINMENT

5555 Melrose Ave., Drier #209, Hollywood, CA 90038. (323) 956-4425. FAX: (323) 862-1120.
PRODUCER
Steven L. Bernstein
DIRECTOR, DEVELOPMENT
Pat Bernard
STORY DEPARTMENT
Lucy Baxter

OLMOS PRODUCTIONS, INC.

2020 Ave. of the Stars, Ste. 500, Century City, CA 90067. (310) 557-7010. FAX: (310) 557-6276.
email: stephen.b.hunt@abc.com
CHAIRMAN
Edward James Olmos
PRESIDENT, DEVELOPMENT
Sandy Martin
PRODUCERS
Nick Athas
Danny Haro
OFFICE MANAGER
Javier Varon

OMEGA ENTERTAINMENT, LTD.

(Motion picture & TV production and distribution)
8760 Shoreham Dr., Los Angeles, CA 90069. (310) 855-0516. FAX: (310) 652-2044. www.omegapic.com
PRESIDENT & CEO
Nico Mastorakis
V.P., SALES
Carole Mishkind
EXECUTIVE V.P.
Isabelle Mastorakis Thompson
V.P., PRODUCTION
Christy L. Pokarney
EXECUTIVE ASSISTANT
Bill Cunningham

OMNIBUS

500 S. Buena Vista, Animation Bldg., 2E/2-4, Burbank, CA 91521-1755. (818) 560-3611. FAX: (818) 972-2841.
PRODUCER
Rob Schiedlinger

100% ENTERTAINMENT

200 N. Larchmont Blvd., Los Angeles, CA 90004. (323) 461-6360. FAX: (323) 461-6330. www.100percent.com
email: 100percent@iname.com
PRESIDENT
Stanley Isaacs

ON STILTS PRODUCTIONS

(310) 391-6053. email: PStelzer@aol.com
PRODUCER
Peter Stelzer

OPEN DOOR ENTERTAINMENT

115 Brooks Ave., Venice, CA 90291. (310) 577-9911. FAX: (310) 577-9900. email: kai@opendoorkai.com
ODE, ul. Forteczna 11 m.3, 01 430 Warsaw, Poland. TEL: 48-601-366-767. FAX: 48-22395470.
CEO & PRESIDENT & PRODUCER
Kai P. Schoenhals
CFO
Robert Scherer
ASSOCIATE
Stanislaw Dziedzic

ORACLE ENTERTAINMENT

P.O. Box 15965, Beverly Hills, CA 90209. (310) 281-0855.
PRODUCER & PARTNER
Glen Cote
PRODUCER & PARTNER
Michael Sibay

ORBIT ENTERTAINMENT GROUP

714 N. La Brea Ave., Hollywood, CA 90038. (323) 525-2626. FAX: (323) 525-2627. email: orbit@orbiteg.com
PARTNER & PRESIDENT & DIRECTOR
Dror Soref
PARTNER & CO-CEO & EXECUTIVE PRODUCER
Lee Nelson
V.P., ORBIT PICTURES
Kevin Moretson
EXECUTIVE PRODUCERS
Lynne Pateman

ORIGINAL FILM

2045 S. Barrington Ave., Los Angeles, CA 90025. (310) 445-9000. FAX: (310) 445-9191.
PRODUCER & OWNER
Neal Moritz
PRESIDENT, TV
Mark Rossen
SENIOR V.P., PRODUCTION
Stokely Chaffin
SENIOR V.P., PRODUCTION
Brad Luff
V.P., PRODUCTION
Heather Zeegen
CREATIVE EXECUTIVE
Justin Rosenblatt
DIRECTOR, TV
Brian Gefsky
DIRECTOR, DEVELOPMENT
Jennifer Tuthill
DEVELOPMENT ASSISTANTS
Amanda Cohen
Gretchen Douglas
Jennifer Grandy
Russ Brown
PRODUCTION ASSISTANT & RUNNER
Jonah Barnes

ORIGINAL VOICES, INC.

2617 Third St., Santa Monica, CA 90405-4108. (310) 392-3479. FAX: (310) 392-3489. email: ovoices@aol.com
CEO
David Kirkpatrick
PRESIDENT, PRODUCTION
Paul Harvey
DEVELOPMENT EXECUTIVE
Martin Svab
BUSINESS AFFAIRS
Angela Bond

ORPHEUS FILMS

114 West Valerio St., Ste. 1, Santa Barbara, CA 93101.
P.O. Box 736, State College, PA 16804.
www.orpheusfilms.com
email: info@orpheusfilms.com
PRESIDENT & DIRECTOR & WRITER
Isaiah Violante
V.P. & EXECUTIVE PRODUCER
T. Stevens
WRITER
Edward Peterlin
PRODUCER
Evan Harder

OUTERBANKS ENTERTAINMENT

8000 Sunset Blvd., 3rd Flr., Los Angeles, CA 90046. (323) 654-3700. FAX: (323) 6554-3797.
email: firstname@outerbanks-ent.com
WRITER & DIRECTOR & PRODUCER
Kevin Williamson
V.P., PRODUCTION & DEVELOPMENT
Sherry Carnes
HEAD, PRODUCTION
Gina Fortunato
PRODUCTION ASSISTANT
Sarah Kucserka
OFFICE ASSISTANT
Mitch Ryan
ASSISTANT
Jennifer Breslow

OUTLAW PRODUCTIONS
9155 Sunset Blvd., West Hollywood, CA 90069. (310) 777-2000. FAX: (310) 777-2010. www.outlawfilm.com
email: outlaw@outlawfilm.com
PRODUCER
Robert Newmyer
PRODUCER
Jeffrey Silver
PRESIDENT, PRODUCTION
Scott Strauss
ASSOCIATE PRODUCER
Susan Novick
CREATIVE EXECUTIVE
Brad Ley

OUT OF THE BLUE ENTERTAINMENT
10202 W. Washington Blvd., Astair Bldg., Ste.1200, Culver City, CA 90232-3195. (310) 244-7811. FAX: (310) 244-1539.
CONTACTS
Sid Ganis
Alex Siskin
David Levine
Jennifer Todhunter
Mike Johnson
Marissa Kamin

OVERBROOK ENTERTAINMENT
100 Universal City Plaza, Bldg. 6111, Universal City, CA 91608-1002. (818) 777-2224. FAX: (818) 866-5440.
PARTNER
Will Smith
PARTNER
James Lassiter
GENERAL MANAGER
Dale Ottley
EXECUTIVE V.P., MUSIC
John Dukakis
EXECUTIVE V.P., TV
David Tochterman
EXECUTIVES, MOTION PICTURES
Glendon Palmer
So Yun Roe
Lori Zuker

OXYGEN MEDIA
75 Ninth Ave., New York, NY 10011. (212) 651-2000. FAX: (212) 651-2099. www.oxygen.com
PRESIDENT & CEO
Geraldine Laybourne
CO-FOUNDER
Marcy Carsey
CO-FOUNDER
Tom Werner
CO-FOUNDER
Caryn Mandabach
CO-FOUNDER
Oprah Winfrey
COO
Lisa Hall
PRESIDENT, CONVERGENCE
Geoffrey Darby
SENIOR V.P., PROGRAMMING & DEVELOPMENT
Jude Brennan
SENIOR V.P., FINANCE
Susan Kolar
GENERAL COUNSEL
Dan Taitz

O/Z FILMS
10202 W. Washington Blvd., Frankovitch Bldg., Ste. 115B, Culver City, CA 90232. (310) 244-6380. FAX: (310) 842-7530.
PRODUCERS
Nick Osbourne
Jeffrey Zarnow
MANAGER
Trevor Engelson

PACIFIC DATA IMAGES
3101 Park Blvd., Palo Alto, CA 94306. (650) 846-8100. FAX: (650) 846-8101.
HEAD, PDI
Aron Warner
V.P., SENIOR VISUAL EFFECTS SUPERVISOR
Richard Chung
CREATIVE DIRECTOR
John Bell
DIRECTOR, ANIMATION
Larry Bafia
DESIGNER & DIRECTOR
Cliff Boule
VISUAL EFFECTS SUPERVISOR
Henry LaBounta

PACIFIC MOTION PICTURES
8899 Beverly Blvd., Ste. 501, Los Angeles, CA 90048. (310) 275-4368. FAX: (310) 275-4187.
email: info@pmp.ca
1380 Burrad St., 3rd Flr., Vancouver, BC V6V 2H3 Canada.
PRESIDENT
Matthew O'Connor
PRESIDENT, CREATIVE AFFAIRS
Tom Row
DEVELOPMENT ASSISTANT
Amanda James

PACIFICA ENTERTAINMENT, INC.
335 N. Maple Dr., Ste. 235, Beverly Hills, CA 90210. (310) 285-9696. FAX: (310) 285-9691. email:info@pacificafilms.com
PRESIDENT
Moritz Borman
SENIOR V.P., BUSINESS AFFAIRS
Linda Benjamin
V.P., DEVELOPMENT
Chris Dubrow

PALOMAR PICTURES
5657 Wilshire Blvd., 5th Flr., Los Angeles, CA 90036. (323) 525-2900. FAX: (323) 525-2912.
PRESIDENT
Joni Sighvatsson
PRODUCER & CO-PRESIDENT & CEO
Jonathan Ker
COO
Kim MacKaye
EXECUTIVE PRODUCER
Tasmin Priggi
HEAD, PRODUCTION
Skot Bright

PARADOX PRODUCTIONS, INC.
11846 Ventura Blvd., Ste. 202, Studio City, CA 91604. (818) 623-2855. FAX: (818) 623-2856.
DIRECTOR & PRESIDENT
John Pasquin
V.P., PRODUCTION
Kimberly Brent
STORY EDITOR
Monica Gelardo

PARAMOUNT PICTURES
(see Viacom, Inc.)

PARKWAY PRODUCTIONS
10202 W. Washington Blvd., Astaire Bldg., Ste. 2210, Culver City, CA 90232. (310) 244-4040. FAX: (310) 244-0240.
DIRECTOR
Penny Marshall
PRESIDENT
Sean Corrigan
PRODUCER
Amy Lemisch
V.P., DEVELOPMENT
Jessica Cox

PATCHWORK PRODUCTIONS
1663 Euclid St., Santa Monica, CA 90404. (310) 288-7488. FAX: (310) 288-7445.
PRODUCERS
Penney Finkelman Cox
Sandra Rabins
Jay Rifkin
Hans Zimmer
DEVELOPMENT EXECUTIVE
Craig Berenson
DEVELOPMENT EXECUTIVE
Elizabeth Hackett

PATRIOT PICTURES
2029 Century Park East, Ste. 298, Los Angeles, CA 90069. (310) 551-7340. FAX: (310) 552-2727.
CHAIRMAN & CEO
Michael Mendelsohn
DIRECTOR, DEVELOPMENT
Chris Hammond

DANIEL L. PAULSON PRODUCTIONS
10880 Wilshire Blvd., Ste. 1101, Los Angeles, CA 90024. (310) 234-5270. FAX: (310) 234-5059.
PRESIDENT
Daniel L. Paulson
V.P., CREATIVE AFFAIRS
Bob Chmiel
DIRECTOR, ADMINISTRATION
Steve A. Kennedy

PB MANAGEMENT/AFT PRODUCTIONS

6523 W. 6th St., Los Angeles, CA 90048. (323) 653-7284. FAX: (323) 653-5285. email: capnett@hotmail.com
PRESIDENT
Paul Bennett
V.P., DEVELOPMENT
Barbara Caplan

PEAK PRODUCTIONS

1533 S. Main St., Winston-Salem, NC 27127. (336) 770-1331. FAX: (336) 770-1339. email: pollockd@ncarts.edu
PRESIDENT
Dale Pollock

ZAK PENN'S COMPANY

10201 W. Pico, Bldg. 31, Rm. 303, Los Angeles, CA 90035. (310) 369-7360. FAX: (310) 969-0249.
WRITER & PRODUCER
Zak Penn
DEVELOPMENT
Joe Pescatella

PERMUT PRESENTATIONS

9150 Wilshire Blvd., Ste. 247, Beverly Hills, CA 90212. (310) 248-2792. FAX: (310) 248-2797.
PRODUCER & PRESIDENT
David Permut
V.P., PRODUCTION
Steven A. Longi

LESTER PERSKY PRODUCTIONS

9910 Tower Lane, Beverly Hills, CA 90210-2129. (310) 278-1995. FAX: (310) 278-1910. email: lesterprod@aol.com
PRESIDENT & EXECUTIVE PRODUCER
Lester Persky
V.P. & PRODUCER
Tomlinson Dean
CONTROLLER
Camille Pollock
DIRECTOR, DEVELOPMENT
Jonah A. Nelson

PETERS ENTERTAINMENT

4000 Warner Blvd., Bldg. 15, Burbank, CA 91522. (818) 954-2441. FAX: (818) 954-4976.
CHAIRMAN
Jon Peters
EXECUTIVE V.P.
Brian D. Manis

PET FLY PRODUCTIONS

12754 Ventura Blvd., Ste. D, Studio City, CA 91604. (818) 752-1212. FAX: (818) 752-1215.
WRITER & EXECUTIVE PRODUCER & DIRECTOR
Danny Bilson
WRITER & EXECUTIVE PRODUCER
Paul De Meo
PRESIDENT
Joe Lauer
PRODUCTION ASSOCIATE
Lisa Beard

DANIEL PETRIE JR. & CO.

440 Coldwater Canyon Ave., Ste. 202, Studio City, CA 91604. (818) 623-1600. FAX: (818) 623-1606.
DIRECTOR & WRITER & PRODUCER
Daniel Petrie Jr.
ASSOCIATE
Scott Killinger

STEPHEN PEVNER, INC.

248 W. 73rd St., 2nd Flr., New York, NY 10023. (212) 496-0474. FAX: (917) 441-6675. email: spevner@aol.com
PRODUCER
Stephen Pevner

PFEFFER FILM

500 S. Buena Vista Blvd., Animation Bldg., 2F-8, Burbank, CA 91521. (818) 560-3177. FAX: (818) 843-7485.
PRODUCER
Rachel Pfeffer
VICE PRESIDENT
Jess Siegler

PFILMCO, INC.

169 Pier Ave., Second Flr., Santa Monica, CA 90405-5311. (310) 452-2557. FAX: (310) 452-4006.
PRODUCER
Andrew Pfeffer
DEVELOPMENT ASSISTANT
Emily Mullen

PHAEDRA CINEMA

(Motion picture distributor)
3440 Wilshire Blvd., Ste 603, Los Angeles CA 90010. (213) 380-9323. FAX: (213) 380-9334. www.phaedracinema.com
PRESIDENT
Gregory Hatanaka
EXECUTIVE V.P.
Roseann Cherenson
SENIOR V.P., CO-PRODUCTIONS & CREATIVE SERVICES
Taka Arai
SALES, THEATRICAL
Christa Hamilton
ACQUISITIONS
Alicia Hollinger

PHASE I PRODUCTIONS

429 Santa Monica Blvd., Ste. 610, Santa Monica, CA 90401. (310) 842-8401. FAX: (310) 280-0415.
email: phase1prod@earthlink.net
PARTNER
Joe Wizan
PARTNER
Don Schneider
PRESIDENT
Steve Wizan
V.P., CREATIVE AFFAIRS
Dru A. Ransom

PHIL ALDEN ROBINSON

100 Universal City Plaza, Bung. 4132, Universal City, CA 91608-1085. (818) 777-5055. FAX: (818) 866-1575.
WRITER & DIRECTOR & PRODUCER
Phil Alden Robinson

PHOENIX PICTURES

10202 W. Washington Blvd., Frankovich Bldg., Culver City, CA 90232. (310) 244-6100. FAX: (310) 839-8915.
CHAIRMAN & CEO
Mike Medavoy
PRESIDENT & COO
Arnold Messer
EXECUTIVE V.P., BUSINESS & LEGAL AFFAIRS
Lindsey Bayman
V.P., CONTROLLER
Judith Garinger
DIRECTOR, DEVELOPMENT
Brad Fischer
SENIOR V.P., DEVELOPMENT, PHOENIX PICS. DEVEL CO.
Eric Paquette
DIRECTOR, BUSINESS & LEGAL AFFAIRS
Scott Douglas Sebasty

PICO CREEK PRODUCTIONS

409 Santa Monica Blvd., Penthouse, Santa Monica, CA 90401. (310) 394-7522. FAX: (310) 394-5825.
DIRECTOR & ACTOR
Peter Horton
HEAD, DEVELOPMENT
Julie Robinson

PICTURE THIS ENTERTAINMENT

(International Distributor)
7471 Melrose Ave., Ste. 7, Los Angeles, CA 90046. (323) 852-1398. FAX: (323) 658-7265. www.picturethisent.com
email: highlandcp@aol.com
PRESIDENT
Douglas C Witkins

PIRATES COVE ENTERTAINMENT, INC.

9255 Sunset Blvd., Ste. 1000, Los Angeles, CA 90069. (310) 288-2000. FAX: (310) 288-2000.
EXECUTIVE PRODUCER
Paul Stupin
DIRECTOR, DEVELOPMENT
Nicole Ranadive

PLATINUM STUDIOS, LLC

9744 Wilshire Blvd., Ste. 400, Beverly Hills, CA 90212. (310) 276-3900. FAX: (310) 276-2799.
email: info@platinumstudios.com
CHAIRMAN
Scott Mitchell Rosenberg
SENIOR V.P., CREATIVE AFFAIRS
Gregory Noveck
V.P., BUSINESS & LEGAL AFFAIRS
Deborah Chiaramonte
DIRECTOR, CREATIVE AFFAIRS
Paul Benjamin
DIRECTOR, ON-LINE PRODUCTION
Andy Walton
BUSINESS DEVELOPMENT
Blake Morrison

PLATONIC FILMS, INC.

29 Greene St., New York, NY 10013. (212) 633-2000. FAX: (212) 965-0812. www.platonicfilms.com
email: ksegalla@platonicfilms.com
PRESIDENT
Kevin Segalla
CREATIVE EXECUTIVE
Benjamin Patton

MARC PLATT PRODUCTIONS

100 Universal City Plaza, Bung. 5184, Universal City, CA 91608. (818) 777-1122. FAX: (818) 866-6353.
CONTACTS
Marc Platt
Christian McLaughlin
Dan Teebor
Joey Levy
Gregory Lessans
Abby Wolf
Adam Siegal
TELEVISION
Moe Jelline

PLURABELLE FILMS

10125 W. Washington Blvd., Ste. 117, Culver City, CA 90232. (310) 244-6782. FAX: (310) 244-0590.
CONTACTS
Gabriel Byrne
Amy Singer
Christina Giffen

MARTIN POLL FILMS, LTD.

(Motion picture and TV production.)
P.O. Box 17137, Beverly Hills, CA 90209. (323) 876-8873. FAX: (323) 876-8892.
PRESIDENT
Martin Poll
EXECUTIVE V.P.
Shirley Mellner

PORCHLIGHT ENTERTAINMENT

11777 Mississippi Ave., Los Angeles, CA 90025. (310) 477-8400. FAX: (310) 477-555. www.porchlight.com
email: distribution@porchlight.com
PRESIDENT & CEO
Bruce D. Johnson
EXECUTIVE V.P. & CFO
William T. Baumann
PRODUCER
Andrea Tompkins
SENIOR V.P., FILMED ENTERTAINMENT
Joe Broido
V.P., POST-PRODUCTION
Tom Gleason
V.P. & PRODUCER, CHILDREN'S PROGRAMMING
Fred Schaefer
HEAD, ACQUISITIONS
Zac Reeder

PORT STREET FILMS (SPOOKY HOUSE)

1041 N. Formosa, Writers Bldg., Ste. 12, W. Hollywood, CA 90046. (323) 850-2555.
ACTOR & PRODUCER
John Larroquette
DEVELOPMENT & PRODUCTION
LeeAnn Lambright

PRAIRIE FILMS

9333 Wilshire Blvd., Beverly Hills, CA 90210. (310) 385-4141. FAX: (310) 385-4306.
PRODUCER
Lynn Arost
PRODUCER
Jessica Lange
DIRECTOR, DEVELOPMENT
Damon Gambutto

PRAY FOR RAIN PICTURES, INC.

Manhattan Beach Studios, 1600 Rosecrans Ave., Media Center, Manhattan Beach, CA 90266. (310) 727-3350. FAX: (310) 727-3351. www.toendallwars.com
OWNER
David L. Cunningham

OTTO PREMINGER FILMS, LTD.

(Motion picture and TV production and distribution)
17 Seth Canyon Dr., Mt. Kisco, NY 10549-9804. (914) 242-5112. FAX: (914) 666-4553. email: OPFILMS@aol.com
PRESIDENT
Hope B. Preminger
VICE PRESIDENT
Valerie Robins

EDWARD R. PRESSMAN FILM CORP.

(Film production)
130 S. El Camino Dr., Beverly Hills, CA 90210. (310) 271-8383. FAX: (310) 271-9497.
130 West 57th St., Ste. 3B, New York, NY 10019. (212) 489-3333. FAX: (212) 489-2103. www.pressman.com
PRESIDENT
Edward R. Pressman
SENIOR V.P., PRODUCTION
Alessandro Camon
CFO & CO-COO
Greg Woertz
V.P., MARKETING
Emily Zalenski

PRINCIPAL LARGE FORMAT

(Large-format (Imax) production)
Picture House, 65 Hopton St., London, SE1 9LR, UK.
44 (0) 207 928-9287. FAX: 44 (0) 207 928-9886.
www principalmedia.com
email: phil.streather@principalmedia.com
CONTACT
Phil Streather

PRIVILEGED COMMUNICATIONS

1240 Amherst Ave., Ste.702, Los Angeles, CA 90025. (310) 820-1101. FAX: (310) 820-3255. www.thebasket.net
email: lester310@earthlink.net
PRESIDENT
Matt Kohn
DIRECTOR, DEVELOPMENT
Sharon Lester

PROMARK ENTERTAINMENT GROUP

(International distribution and production)
3599 Cahuenga Blvd. W., 3rd Flr., Los Angeles, CA 90068. (323) 878-0404. FAX: (323) 878-0486.
email: Promark@promarkgroup.com
PRESIDENT
Jonathan M. Kramer
V.P., PRODUCTION
Steve Beswick
DIRECTOR, INTERNATIONAL SALES & OPERATIONS
Eric Bernstein
DIRECTOR, DISTRIBUTION SERVICES
Patrick Caneday

PROPAGANDA FILMS

940 N. Mansfield Ave., Los Angeles, CA 90038-3197. (323) 462-6400. FAX: (323) 463-7874. www,propagandafilms.com
902 Broadway, Ste. 1603, New York, NY 10010. (212) 982-1700.
PRESIDENT
Rick Hess
COO
Trevor Macy
CFO
Severin White
HEAD, MANAGEMENT DIVISION
Beth Holden
GENERAL COUNSEL
Lisa Franklin

PRUFROCK PICTURES

335 N. Maple Dr., Ste. 135, Beverly Hills, CA 90210. (310) 285-2360. FAX: (310) 888-3595.
ACTRESS & PRODUCER
Meg Ryan
PRESIDENT
Nina R. Sadowsky
CREATIVE EXECUTIVE
Kevin Donahue
V.P., DEVELOPMENT
Ali Woodward
STORY EDITOR
Michael Patrick

PUNCH PRODUCTIONS

1926 Broadway, #305, New York, NY 10023. (212) 595-8800.
email: maureenf@punch21.com
11661 San Vicente Blvd., Los Angeles, CA 90049. (310) 442-4888.
OWNER
Dustin Hoffman
PARTNER
Jay Cohen
PRESIDENT
Lee Gottsegen
V.P., PRODUCTION
Laura Gheradi
PRODUCER
Murray Schisgal
DIRECTOR, DEVELOPMENT
Heather Waterman

PURE ARTS
8840 Wilshire Blvd., Ste. 200, Beverly Hills, CA 90211. (310) 203-8000. FAX: (310) 358-3256.
email: postmaster@pure-arts.com
PARTNERS
Alan Somers
Mark Teitlebaum
MANAGING PARTNER
Alan David
PRESIDENT.
Chris E. Henze
MANAGER & EXECUTIVE
Brian M. Inerfled
MANAGER & EXECUTIVE
David Yoo

QUINCE PRODUCTIONS, INC.
12400 Ventura Blvd., #371, Studio City, CA 91604. (323) 436-0677. FAX: (323) 436-0246.
PRESIDENT & EXECUTIVE PRODUCER
Edward Asner

QUINCY JONES MEDIA GROUP, INC.
3800 Barham Blvd., 5th Flr., Los Angeles, CA 90068. (323) 874-2009. FAX: (323) 874-3364.
CEO
Quincy Jones
PRESIDENT
Joel Simon
VICE PRESIDENT
Jill Tanner

RADIANT PRODUCTIONS
914 Montana Ave., 2nd Flr., Santa Monica, CA 90403. (310) 656-1400. FAX: (310) 656-1408.
DIRECTOR & PRODUCER
Wolfgang Petersen
PRESIDENT & PRODUCER
Gail Katz
VICE PRESIDENT
Samuel Dickerman
HEAD, TV
Rosemary Tarquino
DIRECTOR, DEVELOPMENT
Susan Stein
STORY EDITOR
David Markus
DEVELOPMENT ASSISTANT
Veronica Becker

RAINBOW FILM CO./RAINBOW RELEASING
9165 Sunset Blvd., Ste. 300, Los Angeles, CA 90069. (310) 271-0202. FAX: (310) 271-2753. www.rainbowfilms.com
email: rainbow@icnt.net
PRESIDENT
Henry Jaglom
PRODUCER & DEVELOPMENT
Judith Wolinsky
DIRECTOR, DEVELOPMENT
Sharon Lester
DEVELOPMENT
Lauren Beck

RAINCITY, INC.
(310) 578-2114. FAX: (310) 578-2248.
DIRECTOR
Alan Rudloph
PRODUCER
David Blocker

RAINMAKER PRODUCTIONS, INC.
P.O. Box 5780, Beverly Hills, CA 90209-5780. (800) 858-0520. FAX: (800) 858-0520. email: nealedel@hotmail.com
PRESIDENT & PRODUCER
Neal Edelstein
HEAD, DEVELOPMENT & PRODUCER
Gaye Pope

RANKIN/BASS PRODUCTIONS
24 W. 55 St., New York, NY 10019. (212) 582-4017.
PRESIDENT & CEO
Arthur Rankin, Jr.
SENIOR V.P., PRODUCTION & DEVELOPMENT
Peter Bakalian

MARTIN RANSOHOFF PRODUCTIONS, INC.
400 S. Beverly Dr., Ste. 308, Beverly Hills, CA 90212. (310) 551-2680. FAX: (310) 551-2094.
PRODUCER
Martin Ransohoff
VICE PRESIDENT
Bob Robinson
CREATIVE ASSISTANT & OPERATIONS
Heather Bowles

RASTAR PRODUCTIONS
10202 W. Washington Blvd., Hepburn West, Culver City, CA 90232-3195. (310) 244-7871. FAX: (310) 244-2331.
CHAIRMAN
Ray Stark
PRESIDENT
Marykay Powell
V.P., ADMINISTRATION
Janet Garrison
CONSULTANTS
Don Safran
Michael Sudmeier

RAT ENTERTAINMENT/RAT TV
9060 Santa Monica Blvd., Ste. 350, Los Angeles, CA 90069. (310) 248-6040. FAX: (310) 858-8921.
DIRECTOR & PRODUCER
Brett Ratner
HEAD, FEATURE DEVELOPMENT
Alyss Dixson
HEAD, TV DEVELOPMENT
Geoff Silverman
CREATIVE EXECUTIVE
John Cheng

RECORDED PICTURE COMPANY
7001 Melrose Ave., Los Angeles, CA 90038. (323) 937-0733. FAX: (323) 936-4913.
24 Hanway St., London W1P 9DD. Tel: 0171-6362251.
PRODUCER & CHAIRMAN
Jeremy Thomas
HEAD, DEVELOPMENT
Hercules Bellville
SENIOR V.P. & HEAD, DEVELOPMENT
Alexandra Stone
BUSINESS AFFAIRS EXECUTIVE
Florence Larsonneur
HEAD, FINANCE
Stephan Mallmann
HEAD, BUSINESS AFFAIRS
Peter Watson

RED BIRD PRODUCTIONS
725 Arizona Ave., Ste. 200, Santa Monica, CA 90049. (310) 394-9654.
PRESIDENT & ACTOR & DIRECTOR & PRODUCER
Debbie Allen

REDEEMABLE FEATURES
427 Broadway, 2nd Flr., New York, NY 10013. (212) 334-6398. FAX: (212) 343-8269. www.redeemable.com
email: info@redeemable.com
PARTNERS
Ira Deutchman
Greg Johnson
Peter Newman
V.P., CREATIVE AFFAIRS
Melissa Chesman

RED HOUR FILMS
193 N. Robertson Blvd., Beverly Hills, CA 90211. (310) 289-2565. FAX: (310) 289-5988.
WRITER & DIRECTOR & PRODUCER
Ben Stiller
FEATURES
Stuart Cornfeld
TV
Erin Simon Berenson
CREATIVE EXECUTIVE
Rhoades Rader
PRODUCTION EXECUTIVE
Alan Griswold

RED MULLET, INC.
1532 N. Hayworth Ave., #9, Los Angeles, CA 90046. (323) 874-3372.
DIRECTOR & PRODUCER
Mike Figgis
PRODUCER
Annie Stewart

RED WAGON PRODUCTIONS
10202 W. Washington Blvd., Hepburn W. Bldg., Culver City, CA 90232-3195. (310) 244-4466. FAX: (310) 244-1480.
PRODUCER & PRESIDENT
Douglas Z. Wick
PRODUCER
Lucy Fisher
CREATIVE EXECUTIVE
Tara Mark

REGENT ENTERTAINMENT, INC.

1401 Ocean Ave., Ste. 300, Santa Monica, CA 90401. (310) 260-3333. FAX: (310) 260-3343.
www.regententertainment.com
email: jschenck@regententertainment.com
PARTNERS
Paul Colichman
Peter Dekom
Mark R. Harris
Stephen P. Jarchow
PRESIDENT, REGENT INTERNATIONAL
Gene L. George
V.P., ACQUISITIONS & THEATRICAL DISTRIBUTION
John Lambert
V.P., DEVELOPMENT
Jeff Schenck

REHME PRODUCTIONS

1145 Gayley Ave., Ste. 301, Los Angeles, CA 90024. (310) 824-3371. FAX: (310) 824-5459.
PRINCIPAL
Robert Rehme
EXECUTIVE V.P. & PRODUCER
Nick Grillo
DIRECTOR, DEVELOPMENT
Darin Mark

RENAISSANCE PICTURES

100 Universal City Plaza, Bldg., 5166, Universal City, CA 91608. (818) 777-0088. FAX: (818) 866-0223.
DIRECTOR & EXECUTIVE PRODUCER
Sam Raimi
EXECUTIVE PRODUCER
Robert Tapert
PRESIDENT, TV
Patrick Moran
V.P., CURRENT PRODUCTION
Mike McDonald
BUSINESS MANAGER
Sue Binder

RENFIELD PRODUCTIONS

1041 N. Formosa Ave., Writer's Bldg. 321, West Hollywood, CA 90046. (323) 850-3905. FAX: (323) 850-3907.
PRODUCER & PRESIDENT
Michael Finnell
V.P., DEVELOPMENT
John Morgan
DIRECTOR
Joe Dante

REPERAGE

1041 N. Formosa Ave., Writer's Bldg., Ste. 307, .West Hollywood, CA 90046. (323) 2675. FAX: (323) 850-2688.
email: jjala@mindspring.com
DIRECTOR & PRODUCER & WRITER
Jean-Jacques Annaud
EXECUTIVE PRODUCER
Alisa Tager
CREATIVE EXECUTIVE
Melissa Savage

REVEAL ENTERTAINMENT

100 Universal Plaza, Bldg. 5171, Universal City, CA 91608. (818) 733-9818. FAX: (818) 733-9808.
CONTACTS
Brad Silberling
Barry Isaacson
Valeska Ramet
Minor Childers
Todd Hofacker

REVELATIONS ENTERTAINMENT

301 Arizona Ave., Ste. 303, Santa Monica, CA 90401. (310) 394-3131. FAX: (310) 394-3133. www.revelationsent.com
email: mccreary@revelationsent.com
ACTOR & DIRECTOR & PRODUCER & PRESIDENT
Morgan Freeman
CEO
Lori McCreary
COO & PRODUCER
Anne Marie Gillen
DIRECTOR, DEVELOPMENT
Janet M. Harrison
DIRECTOR, ACCOUNTING
Meg Madison
BUSINESS CONSULTANT
Stuart Hammer
MANAGEMENT CONSULTANT
Geanne Frank
PUBLICIST, BIZCUIT (P.R. FOR MORGAN FREEMAN)
Tonya Jones

REVOLUTION MEDIA MANAGEMENT

1776 Broadway #1400, New York, NY 10019. (212) 265-8360. FAX: (212) 253-8361. email: fogbow@mindspring.com
EXECUTIVE PRODUCER
Bradley Latham

RGH/LIONS SHARE PICTURES, INC.

(Foreign film distribution, co-production, insurance financing)
8831 Sunset Blvd., Ste. 300, West Hollywood, CA 90069. (310) 652-2893. FAX: (310) 652-6237. www.lionsharepictures.com
email: lionshare@pacbell.net
PRESIDENT
Adriana Shaw
CO-CHAIRS
Eric Lozil
Billy Blake

RIVER ONE FILMS

1619 Broadway, Ste. 1109, New York, NY 10019. (212) 956-2455. FAX: (212) 956-1519.
email: BillyGith@riveronefilms.com
PRESIDENT & PRODUCER
Thomas J. Mangan IV
V.P. & PRODUCER
William E. Githens

RKO PICTURES

1875 Century Park East, Ste. 2140, Los Angeles, CA 90067. (310) 277-0707. FAX: (310) 226-2490.
3 East 54th St., 12th fl., New York, NY 10022. (212) 644-0600. FAX: (212) 644-0384. www.rko.co
email: RKOPIX@ix.netcom.com
CHAIRMAN & CEO
Ted Hartley
VICE CHAIRMAN
Dina Merrill
PRESIDENT, PRODUCTION, RADIO PICTURES
Ron Gell
EXECUTIVE V.P.
Arthur Horan
V.P., TV DEVELOPMENT
David Marcoi
V.P., DEVELOPMENT
Julia Halperin
V.P. & ASSISTANT GENERAL COUNSEL
Heather Carmen
V.P., FINANCE & ADMINISTRATION
Laurel Lees-Gonzalez
HEAD OF SALES & MARKETING
June Shelley

AMY ROBINSON PRODUCTIONS

250 W. 57th St., Ste. 2217, New York, NY 10107. (212) 262-5500. FAX: (212) 262-4940.
PRODUCER
Amy Robinson
DEVELOPMENT
Victoria Asness

ROBSON ENTERTAINMENT

270 N. Cannon Dr., #1338, Beverly Hills, CA 90210. (310) 246-4688. FAX: (310) 247-8882.
PRODUCER
Sybil A. Robson

ROLLINS & JOFFE, INC.

860 Birchwood Dr., Los Angeles, CA 90024. (310) 278-7711. FAX: (310) 278-7719.
PRESIDENT
Charles Joffe
PRODUCER
Jack Rollins

ROSCOE ENTERPRISES, INC.

3000 W. Olympic Blvd., Ste. 2276, Santa Monica, CA 90404. (310) 449-4066. FAX: (310) 264-4158.
PRINCIPALS
Hans Brockmann
Francois Duplat
MANAGING DIRECTOR
Alexandra Schultze

HOWARD ROSENMAN PRODUCTIONS

635A Westbourne Dr., Los Angeles, CA 90069. (310) 659-2100. email: BIGzR@aol.com
PRESIDENT
Howard Rosenman

HERBERT ROSS, HERA PRODUCTIONS

9255 Sunset Blvd., Ste. 901, Los Angeles, CA 90069. (310) 278-4201 & (213) 960-4964. FAX: (310) 278-5330.
DIRECTOR & PRODUCER
Herbert Ross

ROUNDTABLE INK
6161 Santa Monica Blvd., Ste. 202, Hollywood, CA 90038. (323) 466-4646. FAX: (323) 466-464o.
email: rtink@pacbell.net
PRODUCER & PRESIDENT & CEO
Gina Mathews

ROXIE RELEASING
3125 16th St., San Francisco, CA 94103. (415) 431-3611. FAX: (415) 431-2822. www.roxie.com
CEO
Bill Banning
CO-PRESIDENT, ACQUISITIONS AND PROGRAMMING
Elliot Lavine
CO-PRESIDENT, DISTRIBUTION
Rick Norris
CFO & V.P., OPERATIONS
Charles Ferris

ROYAL PICTURES
(Motion picture distributor)
19619 E. 17 Pl., Aurora, CO 80011. (303) 367-4948. FAX: (303) 343-6010.
GENERAL MANAGER
James Lowry

RSO FILMS
122 E. 42nd St., #810, New York, NY 10168. (212) 975-0700.
CHAIRMAN
Robert Stigwood

SCOTT RUDIN PRODUCTIONS
5555 Melrose Ave., DeMille Bldg., #100, Los Angeles, CA 90038. (323) 956-4600. FAX: (323) 862-0262.
120 W. 45th St., 10th. Flr., New York, NY 10036. (212) 704-4600.
PRODUCER
Scott Rudin
SENIOR V.P.
Scott Aversano
VICE PRESIDENT.
Eric Steel
PRODUCTION EXECUTIVE
Mark Roybal
DIRECTOR, DEVELOPMENT
Jose M. Calleja Jr.
DIRECTOR, DEVELOPMENT
Ian Mcgloin
DEVELOPMENT
John Delaney

RYSHER ENTERTAINMENT
(For production information call Paramount)
2425 Olympic Blvd., Ste. 6040W, Santa Monica, CA 90404. (310) 309-5200.
PRESIDENT & CEO
Tim Helfet
SENIOR V.P., BUSINESS & LEGAL AFFAIRS
Frank Stewart

SABAN ENTERTAINMENT
10960 Wilshire Blvd., Los Angeles, CA 90024. (310) 235-5100. FAX: (310) 235-5102.
CHAIRMAN & CEO
Haim Saban
PRESIDENT, SABAN INTERNATIONAL SERVICES
Stan Golden
PRESIDENT, PRODUCTION
Shuki Levy
SENIOR V.P., ANIMATION
Dana Booton
SENIOR V.P., SPECIAL PROJECTS PRODUCTION
Mark Pinsker
SENIRO V.P., PHYSICAL PRODUCTION
Rodd Feingold
V.P., BUSINESS & LEGAL AFFAIRS
Stacy Lifton

SAMUEL GOLDWYN FILMS
9570 W. Pico Blvd., Ste. 400, Los Angeles, CA 90035. (310) 860-3100. FAX: (310) 860-3195.
1133 Broadway, Ste. 1101, New York, NY 10010. (212) 367-9435. FAX: (212) 367-0853.
CHAIRMAN & CEO
Samuel Goldwyn Jr.
PRESIDENT & COO
Meyer Gottlieb
DIRECTOR, ACQUISITIONS (NY)
Tom Quinn
STORY EDITORS
Julie Huey
Chris Rowe
DEVELOPMENT & ACQUISITIONS COORDINATOR
Tasha Cronin

SAMUELSON PRODUCTIONS
10401 Wyton Dr., Los Angeles, CA 90024-2527. (310) 208-1000. FAX: (310) 208-2809.
www.oscarwilde.com
email: petersam@idt.net
13 Manette St., London W1V 5LB. Tel: 44207 439 4900. FAX: 44207 439 4901.
email: SamuelsonP@aol.com
PARTNERS
Peter Samuelson
Marc Samuelson
ASSOCIATE PRODUCER
Rachel Cuperman
CONTROLLER
Saryl Hirsch

SANFORD/PILLSBURY PRODUCTIONS
506 Santa Monica Blvd., Ste. 210, Santa Monica, CA 90401. (310) 393-5225. FAX: (310) 393-8665.
PRODUCER
Sarah Pillsbury
PRODUCER
Midge Sanford
CREATIVE DIRECTOR
Rebecca Baldwin

SARABANDE PRODUCTIONS
530 Wilshire Blvd., Ste. 308, Santa Monica, CA 90401. (310) 395-4842. FAX: (310) 395-7079.
PRESIDENT
David Manson
EXECUTIVE V.P.
Arla Sorkin Manson
DEVELOPMENT ASSOCIATE
David Strohmeyer

ARTHUR SARKISSIAN PRODUCTIONS
9465 Wilshire Blvd., Ste. 980, Beverly Hills, CA 90212. (310) 385-1486. FAX: (310) 385-1489.
PRODUCER
Arthur Sarkissian
PRESIDENT
David J. Wally

SATURN FILMS
9000 Sunset Blvd., #911, West Hollywood, CA 90069. (310) 887-0900. FAX: (310) 248-2965.
www.saturnfilms.com
PRESIDENT & PRODUCER
Nicolas Cage
V.P., CREATIVE AFFAIRS
Norm Golightly
STORY EDITOR
Clarke Anderson

EDGAR J. SCHERICK ASSOCIATES, INC.
1950 Sawtelle Blvd., Ste. 282, Los Angeles, CA 90025. (310) 996-2376. FAX: (310) 996-2392.
EXECUTIVE PRODUCER & PRESIDENT
Edgar J. Scherick

PAUL SCHIFF PRODUCTIONS
1741 Ivar Ave., Hollywood, CA 90028. (323) 462-6400.
PRESIDENT & PRODUCER
Paul Schiff
SENIOR V.P., PRODUCTION
Matt Berenson

DEBORAH SCHINDLER PRODUCTIONS
110 W. 57th St., Ste. 401, New York, NY 10019. (212) 265-7760. FAX: (212) 581-3617.
PRODUCER
Deborah Schindler
DIRECTOR, LITERARY AFFAIRS
Mark James
DIRECTOR, DEVELOPMENT
Suzie Moldavon
STORY EDITOR
Cathy Lao

JOEL SCHUMACHER PRODUCTIONS
4000 Warner Blvd., Bldg. 81, Rm. 207, Burbank, CA 91522-1332. (818) 954-2508. FAX: 9818) 954-2509.
OWNER
Joel Schumacher

SCOTT FREE PRODUCTIONS

634 N. La Peer Dr., West Hollywood, CA 90069. (310) 360-2250. FAX: (310) 360-2251.
CO-CHAIRMAN
Ridley Scott
CO-CHAIRMAN
Tony Scott
PRESIDENT
Lisa Elizey
V.P., PRODUCTION
Zach Schiff-Abrams
STORY EDITOR
Rene Brar

SCREEN GEMS

10202 W. Washington Blvd., SPP Bldg., Rm. 207, Culver City, CA 90232. (310) 244-8555. FAX: (310) 244-2037.
EXECUTIVE V.P., PRODUCTION & ACQUISITIONS
Clint Culpepper
V.P., PRODUCTION
Stacy Kolker
V.P., ACQUISITIONS
Benedict Carver

SEGUE PRODUCTIONS, INC.

11150 Santa Monica Blvd., Ste. 1200, Los Angeles, CA 90025. (310) 312-1828. FAX: (310) 312-1868.
CHAIRMAN & PRESIDENT
Kip Hagopian

DYLAN SELLERS PRODUCTIONS

4000 Warner Blvd., Burbank, CA 91522. (818) 954-4929.
PRODUCER
Dylan Sellers

SEVEN ARTS PICTURES

7080 Hollywood Blvd., Ste. 201, Hollywood, CA 90028. (323) 464-0225. FAX: (323) 464-8305.
CHAIRMAN
Peter M. Hoffman
PRODUCER & PARTNER
Colleen Camp
PRODUCER & PARTNER
Neil Canton
PRODUCER & PARTNER
Susan Hoffman
PRESIDENT, PRODUCTION
Eric Sandys
CREATIVE EXECUTIVES
Victor Teran
Kate Hoffman
Brette Krinick

SEVENTH ART RELEASING

7551 Sunset Blvd., Ste. 104, Los Angeles, CA 90046. (323) 845-1455. FAX: (213) 845-4717. www.7thart.com
PRINCIPAL
Udy Epstein
V.P., THEATRICAL DISTRIBUTION
Oren Bitan
V.P., DEVELOPMENT
Shelley Spevakow
V.P., WORLDWIDE PRODUCTION
Janice Van Vawagner
DIRECTOR, DEVELOPMENT & ACQUISITIONS
Erica Blitz

SHADY ACRES ENTERTAINMENT

100 Universal City Plaza, Bldg. 5225, 2nd Flr., Universal City, CA 91608. (818) 777-4446. FAX: (818) 866-6612.
CONTACTS
Michael Bostick
Jim Brubaker
Ginny Durkin
Tom Shadyac
Winston Stromberg
Gina Warendorp
Jason Wilson
Jordan Wolfe
Brook Worley

SHINING EXCALIBUR PICTURES

(see Miramax Films.)

SHOELACE PRODUCTIONS, INC.

16 W. 19th St., 12th Flr., New York, NY 10011. (212) 243-2900. FAX (212) 243-2973.
ACTOR & PRODUCER
Julia Roberts
PRESIDENT, PRODUCTION & DEVEL. & PRODUCER
Deborah Schindler
V.P., DEVELOPMENT
Suzanne Weinert

SHONKYTE PRODUCTIONS, INC.

11935 Kling St., #10, Valley Village, CA 91607. (818) 505-1332. FAX: (818) 505-1411. www.seanyoung.org
email: syspi@seanyoung.com
CEO & ACTRESS & PRODUCER & DIRECTOR
Sean Young
V.P. & PRODUCER & DEVELOPEMENT
Stephany Hurkos
V.P. & PRODUCER & DEVELOPMENT
Robert Lujan

THE SHOOTING GALLERY, INC.

609 Greenwich St., New York, NY 10013. (212) 905-2000. FAX: (212) 905-2221. www.shootinggallery.com
10877 Wilshire Blvd., Ste. 1800, Los Angeles, CA 90024. (310) 443-1926. FAX: (310) 443-1976.
CHAIRMAN & CEO
Larry Meistrich
PRESIDENT
Stephen Carlis
COO & GENERAL COUNSEL
Jonathan Marshall, Esq.
PRESIDENT, PRODUCTION
Andrew Given
PRESIDENT, SHOOTING GALLERY FILMS
Eamonn Bowles
PRESIDENT, SHOOTING GALLERY INTERNATIONAL
Steven Bickel
CO-PRESIDENT, SHOOTING GALLERY INTERACTIVE
Joe DiMartino
CO-PRESIDENT, SHOOTING GALLERY INTERACTIVE
Joseph Tedeschi
PRESIDENT, SHOOTING GALLERY PRODUCTIONS
Tim Clawson
PRESIDENT, SHOOTING GALLERY TELEVISION
Josh Kane
PRESIDENT, SHOOTING GALLERY MUSIC
Phil Carson
SENIOR V.P.
Brandon Rosser

SHOWSCAN ENTERTAINMENT

(Film production & entertainment/simulation attractions; for a listing of Showscan sites, see Specialty Exhibition section)
6033 W. Century Blvd.,Ste. 400, Los Angeles, CA 90045-6410. (310) 412-8464. FAX: (310) 412-8565. www.showscan.com
PRESIDENT & CEO
Dennis Pope
SENIOR V.P.
Russell Chesley
SENIOR V.P.
Mike Ellis
V.P., WORLDWIDE SALES & MARKETING
Ernest M. Bakenie
V.P., SHOWSCAN STUDIOS
Jeanne Lucas
V.P., HUMAN RESOURCES & CORPORATE SERVICES
Patti Gordon
MANAGER, BUSINESS AFFAIRS
Vivian T. Patrick

SHUTT-JONES PRODUCTIONS

100 Universal City Plaza, John Ford Bldg., Ste. 4H, Universal City, CA 91608. (818) 777-9619. FAX: (818) 866-5006.
email :shuttjonesproduction@unistudio.com
PRODUCERS
Buffy Shutt
Kathy Jones
V.P., DEVELOPMENT
Martin Navis
OPERATIONS MANAGER
Michael Frances
STORY EDITOR
Ken Holdren

CHARLES SHYER, INC.

3000 W. Olympic Blvd., Bldg. 3, Ste. 2410, Santa Monica, CA 90404. (310) 315-4747. FAX: (310) 315-4746.
WRITER & PRODUCER & DIRECTOR
Charles Shyer

SILVERFILM PRODUCTIONS, INC.

(Motion picture production)
510 Park Ave., #9B, New York, NY 10022. (212) 355-0282. FAX: (212) 421-8254.
PRESIDENT
Raphael Silver
VICE PRESIDENT
Joan Micklin Silver

SILVERLIGHT ENTERTAINMENT

4000 Warner Blvd., Bldg. 139, 1st Flr., Burbank, CA 91522-1391. (818) 954-7067. FAX: (818) 954-7859.
www.silverlightent.com email: silvlite@aol.com
(Music Prod.): 15490 Ventura Blvd., #220, Sherman Oaks, CA 91403. (818) 981-4400. FAX: (818) 981-4418.
PARTNER & CEO
Stephen Drimmer
PARTNER & PRESIDENT
Heidi Robart
MANAGER, DEVELOPMENT
Herman Michael Torres

SILVERLINING PRODUCTIONS

(Feature film, large-format and television production)
217 Forbes Ave., San Anselmo, CA 94960. (415) 256-9700.
FAX: (415) 256-9677.
CONTACT
Laurel Ladevich

SILVER LION FILMS

(Motion picture production)
701 Santa Monica Blvd., Ste. 240, Santa Monica, CA 90401.
(310) 393-9177. FAX: (310) 458-9372.
PRODUCERS
Lance Hool
Conrad Hool

SILVER PICTURES

4000 Warner Blvd., Bldg. 90, Burbank, CA 91522-0001. (818) 954-4490. FAX: (818) 954-3237.
CHAIRMAN
Joel Silver
CFO
Steve Richard
SENIOR V.P., PRODUCTION
Dan Cracchiolo
V.P., PRODUCTION
Susan Levin
V.P., OPERATIONS
Pam Martin

SINGLE CELL PICTURES

1016 N. Palm Ave., West Hollywood, CA 90069. (310) 360-7600. FAX: (310) 360-7011.
www,singlecellpictures.com
PRODUCER
Michael Stipe
PRODUCER
Sandy Stern
VICE PRESIDENT
Farley Ziegler

SITTING DUCKS PRODUCTIONS

1532 Micheltorena St., Los Angeles, CA 90026. (323) 660-0861. FAX: (323) 660-6021.
EXECUTIVE PRODUCER
Michael Bedard
EXECUTIVE PRODUCER
Elizabeth Daro
DEVELOPMENT EXECUTIVE
Ray Shenusay

SKYFISH PRODUCTIONS

10100 Santa Monica Blvd., Los Angeles, CA 90067. (310) 229-4439. (310) 552-4557.
ACTRESS & PRODUCER
Kim Basinger

SKYLARK ENTERTAINMENT, INC./R & R FILMS

12405 Venice Blvd., Ste. 237, Los Angeles, CA 90066. (310) 390-2659. FAX: (310) 390-2759.
email: skylarkent@hotmail.com
PRESIDENT & PRODUCER
Jacobus Rose
CREATIVE EXECUTIVE
John Ross

SKYLARK FILMS, LTD.

1123 Pacific St., Ste. G, Santa Monica, CA 90405-1525. (310) 396-5753. FAX: (310) 396-5753. email: skyfilm@aol.com
PRODUCER
Bradford Pollack
DEVELOPMENT ASSOCIATE & STORY EDITOR
Jasan Pagni
DEVELOPMENT ASSOCIATE & STORY ANALYST
Annelouise Verboan

SKYLINE PARTNERS

10550 Wilshire Blvd., Ste. 304, Los Angeles, CA 90024. (310) 470-3363. FAX: (310) 470-0060.
email: fkuehnert@earthlink.net
MANAGING PARTNER & PRODUCER
Fred Kuehnert
PARTNER & PRODUCER
Mark V. Tchelistscheff
EXECUTIVE PRODUCER
Robert Birmingham
PRODUCER
Tim Versaci
DIRECTOR & WRITER & PRODUCER
Gary Chason

SKY POND PRODUCTIONS

(Motion picture production-post production)
12163 W. Sunset Blvd., Los Angeles, CA 90049. (310) 476-0618. FAX: (310) 476-9492.
PRESIDENT
John Amicarella

SLADEK ENTERTAINMENT CORP.

8306 Wilshire Blvd., #510, Beverly Hills, CA 90211. (323) 934-9268. FAX: (323) 934-7362. email: dansladek@aol.com
CEO & PRODUCER
Daniel Sladek
PRODUCER
Chris Taaffe

SLOANE/BORDEN PICTURES

4220 W. Newdale Drive, Los Angeles, CA 90027. (323) 665-7700.
PARTNERS
Morgan Sloane
Michael Sweney Borden

ALAN SMITHEE FILMS

7510 Sunset Blvd., Ste. 525, Hollywood, CA 90046. (323) 850-8926. www.smithee.com/films email: SmitheeFilms@aol.com
DIRECTOR
Fred Smythe
ASSOCIATE DIRECTOR
Michael Runstrom

SNAPDRAGON FILMS, INC.

13428 Maxella Ave., #293, Marina del Rey, CA 90292. (310) 822-2505. FAX: (310) 822-7054.
DIRECTOR & PRODUCER & WRITER
Bonnie Palef

SNEAK PREVIEW ENTERTAINMENT, INC.

1604 Vista del Mar St., Hollywood, CA 90028. (323) 962-0295.
FAX: (323) 962-0372.
CHAIRMAN & CEO & PRODUCER
Steven J. Wolfe
PRESIDENT & WRITER
Lynette Prucha
DIRECTOR, DEVELOPMENT
Michael J. Roth
EXECUTIVE ASSISTANTS
Jon Cohen
Mark Tucker

SNL STUDIOS

5555 Melrose Ave., Dressing Rm. #105, Los Angeles, CA 90038-3197. (323) 956-5729. FAX: (323) 862-8605.
CHAIRMAN
Lorne Michaels
COO
Jack Sullivan
PRESIDENT
Richard Feldman
PRESIDENT
Marci Klein
DIRECTOR, DEVELOPMENT
Mallory Eisenstein

SNOW LEOPARD PRODUCTIONS

4727 La Villa Marina, Ste. C, Marina del Rey, CA 90292. (310) 827-1220. FAX: (310) 821-5251. email: www.snowleopard.net
PRODUCER & CO-OWNER
C'esca Lawrence
PRODUCER & CO-OWNER
Dan Tursi
V.P., CREATIVE AFFAIRS
Jan Monroe
DIRECTOR, DEVELOPMENT
Tim Merritt

SOLO ONE PRODUCTIONS

8205 Santa Monica Blvd., #1279, Los Angeles, CA 90046-5912. (323) 658-8748. FAX: (323) 658-8749.
email: Solo1productions@aol.com
ACTRESS & PRODUCER
Marlee Matlin
PRODUCER
Jack Jason

SONY PICTURES ENTERTAINMENT, INC.

10202 W. Washington Blvd., Culver City, CA 90232. (310) 244-4000. FAX: (310) 244-2626. www.spe.sony.com
550 Madison Ave., New York, NY 10022, (212) 833-8500.
CHAIRMAN & CEO
John Calley
CO-PRESIDENT & COO
Mel Harris
CO-PRESIDENT, DIGITAL ENTERTAINMENT
Yuki Nozoe
EXECUTIVE V.P., CAO
Beth Berke
EXECUTIVE V.P., CORPORATE COMMUNICATIONS
Jerry Giaquinta
EXECUTIVE V.P., GENERAL COUNSEL & CORP. SECRETARY
Ronald Jacobi
EXECUTIVE V.P.
Yair Landau
EXECUTIVE V.P. & CFO
Bedi A. Singh
SENIOR V.P., HUMAN RESOURCES
Suzanne Criley
SENIOR V.P. & TREASURER
Joe Kraft
VICE PRESIDENT
Karen L. Halby
ASSISTANT SECRETARIES
Robert Eichorn
Jared Jussim
Leah Weil
ASSISTANT TREASURERS
Lynne R. Shulim
Michael Winchester

COLUMBIA TRISTAR MOTION PICTURE GROUP

10202 W. Washington Blvd., Culver City, CA 90232. (310) 244-8000. FAX: (310) 244-2626; Advertising: (310) 244-1369; Marketing: (310) 244-1369; Media: (310) 244-1766; Research: (310) 244-1300; Promotions: (310) 244-1746; Publicity: (310) 244-1363; International Publicity: (310) 244-1421; Legal: (310) 244-1358.
CHAIRMAN
Amy Pascal
VICE-CHAIRMAN (CTMPG)
Gareth Wigan
PRESIDENT (CTMPG)
Kenneth Lemberger
EXECUTIVE V.P. (CTMPG)
Paul Smith

COLUMBIA PICTURES

10202 W. Washington Blvd., Culver City, CA 90232. (310) 244-4000. FAX: (310) 244-2626; Advertising: (310) 244-1369; Marketing: (310) 244-2198; Media: (310) 244-1766;. Research: (310) 244-1330; International Publicity: (310) 244-1421; Columbia Legal: (310) 244-1358.
550 Madison Ave., New York, NY 10022-3211. (212) 833-8833. FAX: (212) 833-8844.
PRESIDENT
Amy Pascal
PRESIDENT, PRODUCTION
Peter Schlessel
EXECUTIVE V.P., PRODUCTION
Amy Baer
EXECUTIVE V.P., PRODUCTION
Doug Belgrad
EXECUTIVE V.P., PRODUCTION
Michael Costigan
EXECUTIVE V.P., PRODUCTION
Matt Tolmach
SENIOR V.P., PRODUCTION
Andrea Giannetti
SENIOR V.P., PRODUCTION
Lori Goldklang-Furie
SENIOR V.P., PRODUCTION
Carrie Richman
PRESIDENT, SPE WORLDWIDE MARKETING
Robert Levin
EXECUTIVE V.P., WORLDWIDE PUBLICITY
Blaise Noto
SENIOR V.P., PUBLICITY
Michelle Abbrecht
SENIOR V.P., N. AMERICAN THEATRICAL MARKETING
Christine Birch
SENIOR V.P., PUBLICITY
Andre Caraco
SENIOR V.P., MEDIA
Cherie Crane
SENIOR V.P., CREATIVE ADVERTISING
Neil Dick
SENIOR V.P., WORLDWIDE MARKETING SERVICES
Joseph Foley
SENIOR V.P., PUBLICITY
Jamie Geller Hawtof
SENIOR V.P., CREATIVE ADVERTISING
Josh Goldstine
SENIOR V.P., PUBLICITY
Dennis P. Higgins
SENIOR V.P., PROMOTIONS
George Leon
SENIOR V.P., PUBLICTY
Susan Levin

SONY PICTURES CLASSICS

550 Madison Ave., 8th Flr.., New York, NY 10022. (212) 833-8833.
CO-PRESIDENTS
Michael Barker
Tom Bernard
Marcie Bloom
SENIOR V.P., ACQUISITIONS
Dylan Leiner
SENIOR V.P., OPERATIONS
Grace Murphy
V.P., ADVERTISING & PUBLICITY
Carmelo Pirrone
V.P., SALES
Tom Prassis
VICE PRESIDENT
Derval Whelan

SCREEN GEMS

10202 W. Washington Blvd., Culver City, CA 90232. (310) 244-4000.
EXECUTIVE V.P., ACQUISITIONS & PRODUCTION
Clinton Culpepper
EXECUTIVE V.P., MARKETING
Valerie Van Galder
V.P., ACQUISITIONS (CTMPG & CTHV)
Benedict Carver
V.P., PRODUCTION
Stacy Kolker
V.P., PUBLICITY
Tracy McArdle
VICE PRESIDENT
Linda Meadows

SONY PICTURES RELEASING

10202 W. Washington Blvd., Culver City, CA 90232. (310) 244-4000. FAX: (310) 244-1362.
555 Madison Ave., 9th Flr., New York, NY 10022-3301. (212) 833-7623. FAX: (212) 833-6783.
12770 Merit Dr., #705, Lock Box 90, Dallas, TX 75251-1219. (972) 770-4200. FAX: (972) 770-4201.
3400 Riverside Dr., 11th Flr., Burbank, CA 91505-4627. (818) 972-0244. FAX: (818) 972-0077.
PRESIDENT, WORLDWIDE SALES & DISTRIBUTION, COLUMBIA PICTURES
Jeffrey Blake
EXECUTIVE V.P. & GENERAL SALES MANAGER
Rory Bruer
SENIOR V.P. & ASSISTANT GENERAL SALES MANAGER
David Garel
EXECUTIVE V.P., WORLDWIDE DIST. OPERATIONS
Mark L. Zucker
V.P., EASTERN DIVISION
Jim Amos
V.P., SALES ADMINISTRATION
Craig Bartlet
V.P., BRANCH OPERATIONS
Al Cameron
V.P., EXHIBITOR RELATIONS
Ann-Elizabeth Crotty
V.P., PRINT OPERATIONS
Mike Jones
V.P., ACQUISITIONS/REPERTORY SALES
Michael Schlesinger
GENERAL MANAGER, CANADA
Michael Skewes
V.P., WESTERN DIVISION
Adrian Smith
V.P., DISTRIBUTION SERVICES
Conrad K. Steely
V.P., SOUTHERN DIVISION MANAGER
Terry Tharpe
V.P., CENTRAL DIVISION MANAGER
Sherman Wood

COLUMBIA TRISTAR FILM DISTRIBUTORS INT'L.
10202 W. Washington Blvd., Culver City, CA 90232. (310) 244-4000. FAX: (310) 244-2626.
EXECUTIVE V.P., WORLDWIDE MARKETING
Nigel Clark
EXECUTIVE V.P.
S. Anthony Manne
SENIOR V.P., SALES & DISTRIBUTION
Ralph Alexander, Jr.
SENIOR V.P., INTERNATIONAL MARKETING
Martin Bachmann
SENIOR V.P., EUROPE, MIDDLE EAST & AFRICA
Lester McKellar
SENIOR V.P., PUBLICITY & PROMOTIONS
Susan van der Werff
V.P., MARKETING, WORLDWIDE
Mimi Burri
V.P., DISTRIBUTION
Sal Ladestro
V.P., & MANAGING DIRECTOR, FILM PRODUCTS, ASIA
Barbara Robinson
V.P., INTERNATIONAL OPERATIONS
Jonathan Sands
V.P., INTERNATIONAL PRINT SERVICES
Beverly Starr
V.P., MARKETING, LATIN AMERICA
Vittorio Tamburini

COLUMBIA TRISTAR TELEVISION GROUP
9336 W. Washington Blvd., Culver City, CA 90232. (310) 202-1234.
PRESIDENT
Len Grossi
EXECUTIVE V.P., MEDIA RELATIONS
Justin Pierce

COLUMBIA TRISTAR TELEVISION
9336 W. Washington Blvd., Culver City, CA 90232. (310) 202-1234.
PRESIDENT, NETWORK PRODUCTION
Helene Michaels
EXECUTIVE V.P., PROGRAMMING
Jeanie Breadley
EXECUTIVE V.P., PRODUCTION
Edward Lammi
EXECUTIVE V.P., BUSINESS AFFAIRS
Don Loughery
EXECUTIVE V.P., DRAMA DEVELOPMENT
Sarah Timberman
EXECUTIVE V.P., MOVIES & MINISERIES
Helen Verno
SENIOR V.P., MEDIA RELATIONS/PROMOTIONS
Paula Askanas
SENIOR V.P., MUSIC
Robert Hunka

COLUMBIA TRISTAR TELEVISION DISTRIBUTION
10202 W. Washington Blvd., Culver City, CA 90232. (310) 244-4000.
PRESIDENT
Steve Mosko
EXECUTIVE V.P., ADVERTISING SALES
Bo Argentino

COLUMBIA TRISTAR INTERNATIONAL TELEVISION
10202 W. Washington Blvd., Culver City, CA 90232. (310) 244-4000.
PRESIDENT, CTIT
Michael Grindon

COLUMBIA TRISTAR HOME VIDEO
10202 W. Washington Blvd., Culver City, CA 90232. (310) 244-4000. FAX: (310) 244-2626.
PRESIDENT
Ben Feingold
EXECUTIVE V.P., BUSINESS AFFAIRS
Robin Russell

THE CULVER STUDIOS
9336 W. Washington Blvd., Culver City, CA 90232. (310) 202-1234.
PRESIDENT, STUDIO OPERATIONS & ADMINISTRATION
Jack Kindberg
SENIOR V.P., STUDIO ADMINISTRATION
Rick Garcia
SENIOR V.P., OPERATIONS, THE CULVER STUDIOS
Jan Kelly
V.P., STUDIO ADMINISTRATION
Sherrie Butler
V.P., CORPORATE SECURITY
Mike Cantrell
V.P., WESTSIDE PROD. SERV., SONY PICTURES STUDIOS
Earl Capello
V.P., LOGISTICS
Paul Casella
V.P., STUDIO OPERATIONS, SONY PICTURES STUDIOS
Barbara Francuz
V.P., ADMINISTRATION SERVICES
Lucienne Hassler

SONY PICTURES STUDIOS POST-PRODUCTION FACILITIES
PRESIDENT, DIGITAL POST-PRODUCTION FACILITIES
Michael Kohut
SENIOR V.P., SOUND, VIDEO & PROJECTION
Richard Branca
SENIOR V.P., THEATRICAL & TV SOUND EDITORIAL
Tom McCarthy
V.P., POST-PRODUCTION
Patricia Furnare
V.P., POST-PRODUCTION SOUND ENGINEERING
Mark Koffman

SONY DIGITAL STUDIOS DIVISION
10202 W. Washington Blvd., Culver City, CA 90232. (310) 244-4000. FAX: (310) 244-2626.
SENIOR V.P., WORLDWIDE PRODUCT FULFILLMENT
Brunella Lisi
V.P., STRATEGIC TECHNOLOGIES
William Hausch

IMAGEWORKS
9050 W. Washington Blvd., Culver City, CA 90232. (310) 840-8000. FAX (310) 840-8100.
PRESIDENT
Ken Ralston
EXECUTIVE V.P., GENERAL MANAGER
Tim Sarnoff
SENIOR V.P., PRODUCTION
Jenny Fulle
V.P., TECHNOLOGY
George Joblove
SENIOR V.P., ANIMATION PRODUCTION
Barry Weiss
VICE PRESIDENT
Debbie Denise
V.P., OPERATIONS
Thomas Hershey
V.P., TECHNICAL FILM SERVICES
John Nicolard
V.P./CONTROLLER
Mark Rudoloph
V.P., DIGITAL PRODUCTION
Stanley Szymanski
V.P., TECHNICAL OPERATIONS
William Villarreal
EXEC. PRODUCER, COMMERCIAL DIVISION
Tracy Hauser

FAMILY ENTERTAINMENT GROUP
9050 W. Washington Blvd., Culver City, CA 90232. (310) 202-3704. FAX: (310) 202-3722.
PRESIDENT
Sander Schwartz
SENIOR V.P., PRODUCTION
Stacey Attanasio
SENIOR V.P., & GENERAL MANAGER
Gary A. Hirsch
V.P., BUSINESS AFFAIRS
Michael Helfand
V.P., CREATIVE AFFAIRS
Bob Higgins
V.P., MARKETING
David Palmer

SONY PICTURES ENTERTAINMENT INTERNATIONAL OFFICES

ARGENTINA
Buena Vista Columbia TriStar Films of Argentina S.A., Ayacucho 537, 1026 Buenos Aires. Tel: (541) 954-3820. FAX: (541) 954-3819.

AUSTRALIA
Columbia Tristar Films Pty Ltd., One Market St., Sydney, NSW 2000. Tel: (612) 9272-2900. FAX: (612) 9272-2991.

63 Tope St., South Melbourne, Victoria 3205. Tel: (613) 9686-3866. FAX: (613) 9686-3966.

Unit 4B, 200 Newmarket Rd., New Market, Queensland 4051. Tel: (617) 3356-5255. FAX: (617) 3856-0198.

1st Flr., Westcentre, 1260 Hay St., West Perth, Western Australia 6005. Tel: (619) 321-8600. FAX: (619) 321-8100.

AUSTRIA
Columbia TriStar Filmverleih G.m.b.H., Wallgasse 21/1/9, Vienna A-1062. Tel: (431) 597-1515. FAX: (431) 597-1517.

Mailing address: Postfach 99, A-1062 Vienna, Austria.

BELGIUM
N.V. Columbia TriStar Fox Films S.A., Rue de Geneve 10, 1140 Evere. Tel: (322) 702-3511. FAX: (322) 702-3515.

BRAZIL
Columbia TriStar Buena Vista Film Do Brasil, Ltda., Edificio Plaza Centenario, Av. Da Nacoes Unidas, 12.995, 12th andar, Vila Almeida, Sao Paulo SP04578.000. Tel: (5511) 5505-3886. FAX: (5511) 5505-3857.

CHINA
Sony Pictures Entertainment/China, Inc., Rm. 50530 Beijing Friendship Hotel, No. 3 Bai Shi Qiao Rd., Haidian District, Beijing 100873. Tel: (8610) 6849-8600. FAX: (8610) 6849-8628.

COLOMBIA
Columbia TriStar Buena Vista Films of Colombia, Ltda., Carrera 13A, No. 97-23, Bogota. Tel: (571) 610-0149. FAX: (571) 610-0125.

Mailing address: Apartado Aereo 3892, Bogota, Colombia.

FRANCE
Columbia TriStar Films S.A., 131 Ave. de Wagram, 75017 Paris. Tel: (331) 4440-6000. FAX: (331) 4440-6201.

Mailing address: BP 135, 75821 Paris, France cedex 17.

GERMANY
Columbia TriStar Film GmbH, Ickstattstrasse, 80469 Munich. Tel: (4989) 230-370. FAX: (4989) 264-380.

Mailing address: Postfach 14 06 49, 80456 Munich, Germany.

HOLLAND
Columbia TriStar Fox Films B.V., "Authumn" Building, Overschiestraat 184-L, 1062 X.K. Amsterdam. Tel: (3120) 346-2060. FAX: (3120) 346-2061.

Mailing address: P.O. Box 533, 1000 AM Amsterdam, The Netherlands.

HONG KONG
Edko Columbia TriStar Films, 1212 Tower 2, Admiralty Center, 18 Harcourt Rd., Hong Kong. Tel: (852) 2529-3898. FAX: (852) 2865-4155.

INDIA
Columbia TriStar Films of India, Ltd., Metro House, 1st Flr., Mahatma Gandhi Rd., Mumbai. Tel: (9122) 201-4264. FAX: (9122) 201-4321.

Mailing address: P.O. Box 390, Mumbai 400 001, India.

ITALY
Columbia TriStar Film Italia, S.R.L., Via Palestro N. 24, 00185 Rome. Tel: (396) 494-1196. FAX: (396) 446-9936.

JAPAN
Sony Pictures Entertainment, Japan, Hamamatsucho-TS Building, 2-8-14 Hamamatsu-cho, Minato-ku, Tokyo 105. Tel: (813) 5473-8368. FAX: (813) 5473-8370.

MALAYSIA
Buena Vista Columbia TriStar Films (Malaysia) Sdn. Bhd., Ste. 15-03, 15th Flr., Menara Keck Seng, 203 Jalan Bukit Bintang, 55100 Kuala Lumpur. Tel: (603) 466-3322. FAX: (603) 466-0777.

MEXICO
Buena Vista Columbia TriStar Films de Mexico, S.A., Edificio Plaza Refroma, Prolong, Paseo de la Reforma #600, Penthouse Cuerpo D. Col. Santa Fe Pena Blanca, Mexico, D.F. 0120. Tel: (525) 258-2700.

NEW ZEALAND
Columbia TriStar NZ Limited, Level 1, 19 Hargraves St., College Hill, Ponsonby, Auckland. Tel: (649) 302-2223. FAX: (649) 302-2887.

PHILIPPINES
Columbia Pictures Industries, Inc., Rms. 307-308, Philippine President Lines Bldg., 1000 United Nationas Ave., Manila. Tel: (632) 522-3198. FAX: (632) 5221-3684.

Mailing address: P.O. Box 3373, Manila, Philippines.

PORTUGAL
Columbia TriStar and Warner Films de Portugal LDA, Rua Barata Salgueiro, 30, 1200 Lisbon. Tel: (3511) 316-0968. FAX: (3511) 316-1548.

PUERTO RICO
Columbia TriStar Films of Puerto Rico, Colgate Palmolive Buiding, Ste. 300, Metro Office Park, Guaynabo, Puerto Rico 00968-1705. Tel: (787) 793-1500. FAX: (787) 793-2859.

SINGAPORE
Buena Vista Columbia TriStar Films (Singapore) Pte. Ltd., 30 Merchant Rd., #04-21/23, Riverside Point, Singapore 058282. Tel: (65) 438-5595. FAX: (65) 438-4133.

SOUTH KOREA
Columbia TriStar Films of Korea, Inc., 8th Flr., Kyungahm Building 157-27 Samsung-dong, Kangnam-gu, Seoul, 135-090. Tel: (822) 563-4000. FAX: (822) 539-1221.

SPAIN
Columbia TriStar Films de Espana, S.A., Edificio Megapolis, Hernandez de Tejada, 3, 28027 Madrid. Tel: (341) 377-7100. FAX: (341) 377-7128.

SWEDEN
Columbia TriStar Films (Sweden) AB, Hornsbruksgatan 19, Stockholm. Tel: (468) 658-1140. Tel: (468) 658-1140. FAX: (468) 841-204.

Mailing address: P.O. Box 9501, S-102 74 Stockholm.

SWITZERLAND
20th Century Fox Columbia TriStar Film Corp., Route des Acacias 52, 1227 Carouge, Geneva. Tel: (4122) 343-3315. FAX: (4122) 343-9255.

TAIWAN
Columbia TriStar Films of China Ltd., City Hero Plaza, 8F-A, No. 59, Chung-hua Rd., Section 1, Taipei 100. Tel: (8862) 314-8286. FAX: (9962) 381-4492.

THAILAND
Columbia TriStar Buena Vista (Thailand) Ltd., Level 6, Gaysorn Plaza, Ploenchit Rd., Patumwan, Bangkok, 10330. Tel: (662) 656-1857. FAX: (662) 656-1866.

UNITED KINGDOM
European Supervisor's Office and U.K. Operations Sony Pictures London House, 25 Golden Square, London W1R 6LU. Tel: (44171) 533-1111, (44171) 533-1000. FAX: (44171) 528-1266.

SPECTROMEDIA ENTERTAINMENT

(Motion picture and TV production)
P.O. Box 2397, Oxnard, CA 93034-2397. (805) 984-3525. FAX: (805) 984-5527. www.goldcoasthandbook.com
email: spectromedia@earthlink.net
PRESIDENT
William Byron Hillman
VICE PRESIDENT
Henry Hiller
ACQUISITIONS
Rob Hill

SOUTH FORK PICTURES

1101 Montana Ave., Ste. B, Santa Monica, CA 90403. (310) 395-7779. FAX: (310) 395-2575.
email: SFPics@earthlink.net
OWNER
Robert Redford
PRESIDENT
Michael Nozik
SENIOR V.P., DEVELOPMENT & PRODUCTION
Miranda de Pencier
STORY EDITOR
Linda Davis

SPANKY PICTURES, INC.

1041 N. Formosa Ave, Writer's Bldg., Ste. 7, West Hollywood, CA 90046. (323) 850-2788. FAX: (323) 850-2745.
email: spankypics@earthlink.net
1010 N. Orlando, Los Angeles, CA 90069. (323) 654-3033. FAX: (323) 654-8058.
CO-CHAIRMAN
Ted Demme
V.P., DEVELOPMENT
Tracy Falco

SPIKINGS ENTERTAINMENT

19016 Pacific Coast Hwy., Malibu, CA 90265. (310) 456-8039. FAX: (310) 456-1598.
PRESIDENT & OWNER
Barry P. Spikings

SPIRIT DANCE ENTERTAINMENT

1023 N. Orange Dr., Los Angeles, CA 90038-2317. (323) 512-7988. FAX: (323) 512-7996.
PRESIDENT
Forest Whitaker
V.P., TV PRODUCTION
Lenny Brown
V.P., FILM PRODUCTION
Tajamika Paxton
V.P., MUSIC
Damon Whitaker
PROMOTIONS & A&R
Awkmel Toomes
STORY EDITOR
Robert Wheaton
DEVELOPMENT ASSISTANT, FILM
Cathy Thomas

SPYGLASS ENTERTAINMENT GROUP

500 S. Buena Vista St., Burbank, CA 91521-1855. (818) 560-3458.
CO-CHAIRMAN & CEO
Gary Barber
CO-CHAIRMAN & CEO
Roger Birnbaum

CFO
Paul Schwake
PRESIDENT, PRODUCTION
Jonathan Glickman
EXECUTIVE V.P.
Drew Larner
SENIOR V.P., PHYSICAL PRODUCTION
Ned Dowd
V.P., PRODUCTION
Claudia Sachs
V.P., PRODUCTION
Derek Evans
V.P., BUSINESS & LEGAL AFFAIRS
Paul Neinstein
VP., POST-PRODUCTION
Rebekah Rudd

STAMPEDE ENTERTAINMENT

10345 W. Olympic Blvd., 3rd Flr., Los Angeles, CA 90064. (310) 264-4229.
PARTNER & PRESIDENT
Nancy Roberts
PARTNERS
Ron Underwood
S.S. Wilson
Brent Maddock
STORY EDITOR
Greg Stevens

STATE STREET PICTURES

10201 W. Pico Blvd., Los Angeles, CA 90064. (310) 369-5099. FAX: (310) 369-8613.
PRODUCER
Robert Teitel
DIRECTOR
George Tillman Jr.
CREATIVE EXECUTIVE
Poppy Hanks

STEAMROLLER PRODUCTIONS

1041 N. Formosa Ave., The Writer's Bldg., Ste. 11, West Hollywood, CA 90046.
CHAIRMAN
Steven Seagal
PRESIDENT & COO
Phillip Goldfine

THE HOWARD STERN PRODUCTION COMPANY

10 E. 44th St., New York, NY 10017. (212) 867-1200. FAX: (212) 867-2434.
PRESIDENT
Howard Stern
AGENT
Don Buchwald

STIEFEL ENTERTAINMENT

9255 Sunset Blvd., Ste. 610, Los Angeles, CA 90069. (310) 275-3377. FAX: (310) 275-8774.
CHAIRMAN & PRODUCER
Arnold Stiefel

STONE VS. STONE

189 Franklin St., 3rd Flr., New York, NY 10013. (212) 941-1200. FAX: (212) 941-4115.
PRODUCER & WRITER
Robert Stone
PRODUCER & WRITER
Webster Stone

STRAND RELEASING/NEW OZ PRODUCTIONS

1460 4th St., Ste. 302, Santa Monica, CA 90401. (310) 395-5002. FAX: (310) 395-2502. www.strandreleasing.com
email: strand@strandreleasing.com
CO-PRESIDENTS
Jon Gerrans
Marcus Hu
NEW OZ PRODUCTIONS
Victor Syrmis

STRATOSPHERE ENTERTAINMENT

(Film distributor)
767 Fifth Ave., Ste. 4700, New York, NY 10153. (212) 605-1010. FAX: (212) 813-0300. www.stratosphereent.com
email: stratent@aol.com
EXECUTIVE V.P., PRODUCTION & ACQUISITIONS
Ronna Wallace
V.P., BUSINESS AFFAIRS
Angela Schapiro
PRODUCTION ACQUISITIONS
Francois Martin

STUDIO HOME ENTERTAINMENT

(Production, finance and distribution)
11846 Ventura Blvd., Ste. 300, Studio City, CA 91604. (818) 762-0005. FAX: (818) 762-0006.
PRESIDENT
Clem Gatmailtan

SUMMIT ENTERTAINMENT

1630 Stewart St., Ste. 120, Santa Monica, CA 90404. (310) 309-8400. FAX: (310) 828-4132.
PRESIDENT & CEO
Patrick Wachsberger
COO
Bob Hayward
SENIOR V.P.
David Garrett
SENIOR V.P., PRODUCTION & ACQUISITIONS
Modi Wiczyk
DIRECTOR, DEVELOPMENT
Miranda Thompson

SUNDANCE INSTITUTE

8857 W. Olympic Blvd., Ste. 300, Beverly Hills, CA 90211. (310) 360-1981. FAX: (310) 360-1969. www.sundance.org
email: la@sundance.org
EXECUTIVE DIRECTOR
Kenneth Brecher
V.P. & CO-DIRECTOR, SUNDANCE FILM FESTIVAL
Nicole Guillemet
CO-DIRECTOR, PROGRAMMING, SUNDANCE FILM FEST.
Geoffrey Gilmore
DIRECTOR, FEATURE FILM PROGRAM
Michelle Satter
ASSISTANT TO ARTISTIC DIRECTOR, THEATRE
Debby Stover
DIRECTOR, INTERNATIONAL PROGRAM
Patricia Boero
ASSOCIATE DIRECTOR, FILM FESTIVAL PROGRAMMING
John Cooper
ASSOCIATE DIRECTOR, FEATURE FILM PROGRAM
Lynn Auerbach
SENIOR PROGRAMMER & ASSOC. DIR., SPEC. PROJ.
Rebecca Yeldham

SWARTWOUT ENTERPRISES, INC.

(Motion picture production specializing in giant screen films)
P.O. Box 20667, Sedona, AZ 86341. (520) 284-3813. FAX: (520) 284-3571. www.supervue.com
CONTACT
Dave Swartwout

TAPESTRY FILMS, INC.

9328 Civic Center Dr., Beverly Hills, CA 90210. (310) 275-1191. FAX: (310) 275-1266.
email: tapestryfilms@tapestryfilms.com
PRODUCER & PARTNER
Peter Abrams
PRESIDENT, PRODUCTION
Jennifer Gibgot
PRODUCER & PARTNER
Robert L. Levy
V.P. & PRODUCER
Jonathan Komack-Martin
PRODUCERS
Louise Rosner
Natan Zahavi
V.P., PRODUCTION
Andrew Panay
POST-PRODUCTION SUPERVISOR
Sherwood Jones
STORY EDITOR
Michelle Castillo
BUSINESS AFFAIRS
Alicia Hopkins

TAURUS ENTERTAINMENT CO.

5831 Sunset Blvd., Hollywood, CA 90028. (323) 860-0807. FAX: (323) 860-0834. www.taurus-entertainment.com
CHAIRMAN
Stanley Dudelson
PRESIDENT & CEO
James Dudelson
PRESIDENT & COO
Robert Dudelson
V.P., PRODUCTION
Ana Klavell
DIRECTOR, DEVELOPMENT
Alex Fayvil

TAYLOR MADE FILMS

225 Santa Monica Blvd., Ste. 610, Santa Monica, CA 90401. (310) 899-6739. FAX: (310) 899-5715.
email: tmadefilms@aol.com
PRESIDENT & PRODUCER
Geoffrey Taylor

TEAM TODD

9021 Melrose Ave., Ste. 301, Los Angeles, CA 90069. (310) 248-6001. FAX: (310) 385-8072. email: TeamTodd@aol.com
PRODUCERS
Jennifer Todd
Suzanne Todd
VICE PRESIDENT
Pamela Post
PRODUCTION ASSISTANT
Frank Johnson
DEVELOPMENT ASSISTANTS
Julie Ragland
Lauren Tabach-Bank

TELLING PICTURES

121 Ninth St., San Francisco, CA 94103. (415) 864-6714. FAX: (415) 864-4364. www.tellingpix.com
email: tellingpix@aol.com
PRODUCER & DIRECTOR
Rob Epstein
PRODUCER & DIRECTOR
Jeffrey Friedman
PRODUCER, PARAGRAPH 175
Michael Ehrenzweig

TEN THIRTEEN PRODUCTIONS

P.O. Box 900, Beverly Hills, CA 90213. (310) 369-1130.
EXECUTIVE PRODUCER
Chris Carter
PRESIDENT & EXECUTIVE PRODUCER
Frank Spotnitz
VICE PRESIDENT
Mary Astadourian

BOB THOMAS PRODUCTIONS, INC.

(Motion picture and TV producer)
60 E. 42 St., New York, NY 10165. (212) 221-3602.
2 Franklin Ct., Montville, NJ 07045. (973) 335-9100.
PRESIDENT
Robert G. Thomas

3 ARTS ENTERTAINMENT

9460 Wilshire Blvd., 7th Flr., Beverly Hills, CA 90212. (310) 888-3200. FAX: (310) 888-3210.
888 7th Ave., Ste. 3402, New York, NY 10106. (212) 262-6565.
CONTACTS
Dave Becky (New York)
Nick Frenkel (New York)
Jeff Goldenberg
Howard Klein
Raelle Koota (New York)
Molly Madden
David Miner (New York)
Daniel Rappaport
Dave Rath
Michael Rotenberg
Mark Schulman
Lainie Sorkin
Erwin Stoff
Kara Welker-Ryder (New York)

3 RING CIRCUS FILMS

1857 Taft Ave., Hollywood, CA 90028. (323) 957-3800. FAX: (323) 957-7210. email: filmcircus@aol.com
PRESIDENT
Jeff Boortz
CEO
John Sideropoulos
CFO
David Kovacs
HEAD, FILM
Johnny Wow
HEAD, DEVELOPMENT
Drew Fleming

THREE STRANGE ANGELS, INC.

2450 Broadway St., Santa Monica, CA 90404. (310) 449-3425. FAX: (310) 449-8858.
PRODUCER
Lindsay Doran
ASSISTANT
Jinyi Chong

TIDEWATER ENTERTAINMENT, INC.

320 Mount Holyoke Ave., Pacific Palisades, CA 90272. (310) 459-8711. FAX: (310) 459-0149.
PRESIDENT
Bill Unger

TIG PRODUCTIONS, INC.

4000 Warner Blvd., Burbank, CA 91522. (818) 954-4500. FAX: (818) 954-4882.
CREATIVE EXECUTIVE
Soraya Delawari
PRODUCTION EXECUTIVE
Lynee Whiteford
DEVELOPMENT EXECUTIVE
Gregory Avellone
DEVELOPMENT ASSISTANT
Magaly Doty

THE STEVE TISCH CO.

3815 Hughes Ave., Culver City, CA 90232-2715. (310) 838-2500. FAX (310) 204-2713.
CHAIRMAN
Steve Tisch
CONTROLLER & BUSINESS AFFAIRS
Kim Skeeters
PRODUCTION ASSISTANT
William Driver

TOTEM PRODUCTIONS

8009 Santa Monica Blvd., Los Angeles, CA 90046. (323) 650-4994. FAX: (323) 650-1961. email: totempro@aol.com
CO-CHAIRMAN
Tony Scott

TOUCHSTONE PICTURES

(see Walt Disney Company)

TRIBECA PRODUCTIONS

375 Greenwich St., 8th Flr., New York, NY 10013. (212) 941-4000. FAX: (212) 941-4044. www.tribecafilm.com
PARTNER
Robert De Niro
PARTNER
Jane Rosenthal
PRESIDENT, PRODUCTION
Brad Epstein
V.P., DEVELOPMENT
Hardy Justice
V.P., OPERATIONS & FINANCE
Trina Wyatt
DIRECTOR, DEVELOPMENT
Scott Neustadter

TRICOR ENTERTAINMENT

1613 Chelsea Rd., Ste. 329, San Marino, CA 91108-1821. (818) 763-0699. FAX: (626) 441-0033.
PARTNER
Craig Darian
PARTNER
Howard Kazanjian
DEVELOPMENT EXECUTIVE
Ron Mencer

TRIDENT RELEASING

(Sales agents for motion pictures and TV)
8401 Melrose Pl., 2nd Flr., Los Angeles, CA 90069. (323) 655-8818. FAX: (323) 655-0515. www.tridentreleasing.com
email: info@tridentreleasing.com
PRESIDENTS
Jean Ovrum
Victoria Plummer

TRILOGY ENTERTAINMENT GROUP

2450 Broadway St. Penthouse, Ste. 675, Santa Monica, CA 90404-3061. (310) 449-3095. FAX: (310) 449-3195.
email: name@trilogyent.com
FOUNDERS
Pen Densham
John Watson
PRESIDENT & COO
Guy McElwaine
PRESIDENT, TV
Mark Stern
V.P., PRODUCTION
Nora O'Brien
CREATIVE EXECUTIVE
Finley Glaize
DIRECTOR, PRODUCTION & ADMINISTRATION
Jennifer Hare
STORY EDITOR
Kelly Stuart

TRIMARK PICTURES

(a division of Trimark Holdings, Inc.)
4553 Glencoe Avenue, Ste. 200, Marina del Rey, CA 90292.
(310) 314-2000. FAX: (310) 392-0252. www.trimarkpictures.com
CHAIRMAN
Mark Amin
EXECUTIVE V.P., CAO
Cami Winikoff
CFO
Jeff Gonzalez
SENIOR V.P., INTERNATIONAL SALES
Sergei Yershov
SENIOR V.P., SPECIALIZED THEATRICAL
Dennis O'Connor
SENIOR V.P., WORLDWIDE TELEVISION
Andy Reimer
SENIOR V.P., PRODUCTION
Robin Schorr
SENIOR V.P., HOME VIDEO
Ron Schwartz
SENIOR V.P., PHYSICAL OPERATIONS
Richard Jordan
V.P., PRODUCTION
Darin Spillman
V.P., TELEVISION PRODUCTION
Peter Marshall
V.P., ACQUISITIONS
Guy Stodel
V.P., THEATRICAL DISTRIBUTION
Suzanne Leroy
V.P., PUBLICITY
Marina Bailey
V.P., WORLDWIDE THEATRICAL MARKETING
Erin O' Neil
V.P., WORLDWIDE HOME VIDEO MARKETING
Tracy Ames

CINEMANOW

(A subsidiary of Trimark Holdings, Inc.)
CEO
Curt Marvis
EXECUTIVE V.P.
Bruce Eisen

TRISTAR PICTURES

(see Sony Pictures Entertainment)

TROMA ENTERTAINMENT, INC.

(Producer and distributor)
733 Ninth Ave., New York, NY 10019. (212) 757-4555. FAX: (212) 399-9885.www.troma.com
12952 Washington Blvd.,Los Angeles, CA 90066. (310) 827-6360. FAX: (310) 827-0412.
PRESIDENT
Lloyd Kaufman
VICE PRESIDENT
Michael Herz
DIRECTOR, LOS ANGELES OPERATIONS
Scott McKinley
ASSISTANT DIRECTOR OF LOS ANGELES OPERATIONS
Adam Jahnke
ACQUISITIONS
Christina Hibbs
PRODUCTION
Doug Sakmann
DIRECTOR OF INTERNATIONAL SALES
Michael Dwyer
DIRECTOR OF BUSINESS & LEGAL AFFAIRS
Eric Przybisiki
DIRECTOR OF DOMESTIC SALES & LEGAL AFFAIRS
Bradley Buchanan
MARKETING & PROMOTIONS
Megan Powers
Josh Petraglia
WEBMASTER/MANAGER OF TROMAVILLE.COM
Malcom Kahraman
SALES MANAGER OF TROMA TEAM VIDEO
Michael Butler
DVD PRODUCTION MANAGER
Ronni Thomas
OPERATIONS/PRODUCTION MANAGER
Greg Thurik

THE TURMAN-MORRISSEY COMPANY

10202 W. Washington Blvd., Poitier Bldg. 1111, Culver City, CA 90232-3195. (310) 244-4943. FAX: (310) 244-2332.
PARTNERS
John Morrissey
Lawrence Turman
VICE PRESIDENT
Fiona Mackenzie
CREATIVE EXECUTIVE
Devon Terrill
CREATIVE EXECUTIVE & OFFICE MANAGER
Mathew Waldman

TWENTIETH CENTURY FOX FILM CORPORATION

(see Fox, Inc.)

UFLAND PRODUCTIONS

534 21st St., Santa Monica, CA 90402. (310) 656-3031. FAX: (310) 656-3073. email: ufland@aol.com
PRODUCERS
Harry J. Ufland
Mary Jane Ufland

UNITED ARTISTS FILMS, INC.

2500 Broadway, Santa Monica, CA 90404-3061. (310) 449-3000. FAX: (310) 586-8358.
10 Stephen Mews, London W1P 1PP, United Kingdom. Tel: 44-171-333-8877.
CEO
Wendy Palmer
SENIOR EXECUTIVE V.P.
Fiona Mitchell
CFO
Francois Thos
V.P., ACQUISITIONS & PRODUCTION
Tom Strudwick

UNITED ARTISTS PICTURES

(see Metro-Goldwyn-Mayer Inc.)

UNIVERSAL STUDIOS, INC.

100 Universal City Plaza, Universal City, CA 91608. (818) 777-1000. FAX: (818) 733-1506. www.unistudios.com
445 Park Ave., New York, NY 10022. (212) 759-7500.
95 Broadway, Boston, MA 02166 (617)426-8760 FAX: (617)426-5057.
7502 Greenville Ave., Ste. 200, P.O. Box 650572, Dallas, TX 75265-0572 (214) 361-4730 FAX: 361-5074.
PRESIDENT & COO
Ron Meyer
EXECUTIVE V.P.
Helene S. Runtagh
EXECUTIVE V.P. & GENERAL COUNSEL
Karen Randall
EXECUTIVE V.P., HUMAN RESOURCES
Kenneth L. Kahrs
SENIOR V.P. & CFO
William A. Sutman
SENIOR V.P., CORPORATE COMM. & PUBLIC AFFAIRS
Doborah S. Rosen
SENIOR V.P., INTELLECTUAL PROPERTY COUNSEL
Maren Christensen
SENIOR V.P., GLOBAL REAL ESTATE & FACILITIES
George H. Garfield, Jr.
SENIOR V.P., LABOR RELATIONS
Keith Gorham
SENIOR V.P., CORPORATE MARKETING & PARTNERSHIPS
Stephanie Sperber
V.P., EMPLOYMENT COUNSEL
Nestor Barrero
V.P., LABOR RELATIONS
Stephanie A. Caprielian
V.P., WORLDWIDE ANTI-PRIVACY
Karen Elliott
V.P., CORPORATE COMMUNICATIONS & PUBLIC AFFAIRS
Susan Nahley Fleishman
V.P., EXTERNAL COMMUNICATIONS
Iris Gelt
V.P., DIRECTOR OF TAXES
H. Steven Gordan
V.P., GOVERNMENTAL AFFAIRS
Ann M. O'Connor
V.P., DOMESTIC TAX COUNSEL
Mark Palotay
V.P., FINANCE & ADMINISTRATION - CANADA
Eric Pertsch
V.P., CONTROLLER
Terry Reagan
V.P., GLOBAL STRATEGIC SOURCING
Rick Roberts
V.P., CORPORATE DEV. & STRATEGIC PLANNING
Diana Schulz
V.P., REAL ESTATE FOR EUROPE, MIDDLE EAST & AFRICA, GLOBAL REAL ESTATE GROUP
Denis Taylor
V.P., FACILITIES, HEALTH SAFETY & ENVIRONMENT
David Thomas
CIO
Bruce Wilson

UNIVERSAL STUDIOS ONLINE
PRESIDENT
Kenton Low
V.P., BUSINESS-TO-BUSINESS
Lisa Tormino
V.P., ONLINE SERVICES
Eileen Vessella
V.P., EMERGING TECHNOLOGIES
Peter Marx

UNIVERSAL STUDIOS OPERATION GROUP
PRESIDENT & GENERAL MANAGER
Jim Watters
EXECUTIVE V.P., STUDIO OPERATIONS & ADMINISTRATION
Michael J. Connor
SENIOR V.P., BUSINESS AND LEGAL AFFAIRS
Jerrold E Blair
SENIOR V.P., FINANCE
Dave Clark
SENIOR V.P., TECHNICAL SERVICES
Michael Daruty
SENIOR V.P., POST-PRODUCTION
Ed Zeier
V.P., PRODUCTION SERVICES
Dave Beanes
V.P., TECHNICAL OPERATIONS
Michael Fitzgerald
V.P., FACILITY SERVICES
Mark Lyrum
V.P., DUPLICATION & DISTRIBUTION
Ann Leirer
V.P., SOUND
Bill Varney
V.P., REAL ESTATE SERVICES
Brad Wilson

UNIVERSAL PICTURES
100 Universal City Plaza, Universal City, CA 91608. (818) 777-1000. FAX: (818) 733-1440.
CHAIRMAN
Stacey Snider
PRESIDENT
Rick Finkelstein
EXECUTIVE V.P.
Jon Gumpert
EXECUTIVE V.P., BUSINESS & LEGAL AFFAIRS
James M. Horowitz
CFO
Frederick Huntsberry
GROUP INFORMATION OFFICER
Paul Rasmusson
SENIOR V.P., INTERNATIONAL OPERATIONS
Jim Burk
SENIOR V.P., HUMAN RESOURCES
Laura R. Kessler
SENIOR V.P.
Mark Kristol
SENIOR V.P., TECHNOLOGY
Jerry Pierce
V.P.,INTERNATIONAL OPERATIONS
Allen Clement
CONTROLLER, FEATURE FILM & HOME VIDEO, FILMED ENTERTAINMENT ACCOUNTING GROUP
Janice Etzkorn
V.P., BUSINESS DEVELOPMENT & STRATEGIC PLANNING
Michael Joe
V.P., GROUP CONTROLLER, FILMED ENTERTAINMENT
Dan Martinez
V.P., WORLDWIDE MARKETING FINANCE
Denise Monden
V.P., LEGAL AFFIARS
Julie Spielberg
V.P., LEGAL AFFAIRS
Anthony Zummo, III
V.P., PLANING & ULTIMATES
Alan Youngstein
V.P., CONTROLLER, FILMED ENTERTAINMENT ACCOUNTING GROUP
Michelle Stratton
CONTROLLER, TELEVISION, FILMED ENTERTAINMENT ACCOUNTING GROUP
Debbie Stratz

UNIVERSAL PICTURES PRODUCTION
PRESIDENT, PRODUCTION
Kevin Misher
EXECUTIVE V.P., PRODUCTION
Allison Brecker
EXECUTIVE V.P., PRODUCTION
Ron Lynch
EXECUTIVE V.P., PRODUCTION
Mary Parent
EXECUTIVE V.P., PRODUCTION
Scott Stuber
SENIOR V.P., MUSIC
Harry Garfield
SENIOR V.P., PHYSICAL PRODUCTION
Andrew Given
SENIOR V.P., PRODUCTION
Leonard Kornberg
SENIOR V.P., LEGAL AFFAIRS
Mary Ledding
SENIOR V.P., PRODUCTION TECHNOLOGY
John Swallow
SENIOR V.P., MUSIC & BUSINESS AFFAIRS
Philip Cohen
V.P., FEATURE CASTING
Joanna Colbert
V.P., PRODUCTION RESOURCES
Tony Grana
V.P., PRODUCTION
Eric Hughes
V.P., PRODUCTION FINANCE
Bret Johnson
V.P., STORY DEPARTMENT
Romy Kaufman
V.P., PHYSICAL PRODUCTION
Kool Marder
V.P. & CONTROLLER
Carlos Penera
V.P., PARTICIPATIONS
Joseph Randazzo
V.P., ANIMATION PRODUCTION & CREATIVE AFFAIRS
Douglas Wood
V.P., NATIONAL PROMOTIONS
Jamie Sykes
V.P., PHYSICAL PRODUCTION
Deborah Johnson
V.P., PRODUCTION
Jennifer Fox

UNIVERSAL PICTURES MARKETING
PRESIDENT
Mark Shmuger
EXECUTIVE V.P., MARKETING
Edward Egan
EXECUTIVE V.P., NATIONAL PUBLICITY
Terry Curtin
SENIOR V.P., MARKETING & NATIONAL PROMOTIONS
Pamela Blum
SENIOR V.P., SPECIAL PROJECTS
Hollace Davids
SENIOR V.P., MEDIA & CO-OP ADVERTISING
Anthy Evergates-Price
SENIOR V.P., CREATIVE ADVERTISING
Adam Fogelson
Samantha Hart
William Loper
SENIOR V.P., NATIONAL PUBLICITY
Jeffrey Sakson
SENIOR V.P., CREATIVE ADVERTISING OPERATIONS
Dan Wolfe
SENIOR V.P., NATIONAL PROMOTIONS
Beth Goss
V.P., NON-THEATRICAL SALES
Phyllis Bagdadi
V.P., CREATIVE SERVICES
Julie Berk
V.P., MARKET RESEARCH
Chuck Gaylord
V.P., MARKETING STRATEGY
Elizabeth Gelfan
V.P., NATIONAL PUBLICITY
Stephanie Kluft
V.P., EAST COAST PUBLICITY
Scott Levine
V.P., NATIONAL PUBLICITY
Michael Moses
V.P., PLANNING & FINANCE
Charlotte Reith
V.P., FIELD OPERATIONS
Greg Sucherman
V.P., NATIONAL PROMOTIONS
Jamie Sykes
V.P., CREATIVE ADVERTISING OPERATIONS
Dan Wolfe
V.P., FINANCE
David Yuratich

UNIVERSAL PICTURES INTERNATIONAL MARKETING
PRESIDENT, INTL. THEATRICAL MKTG., DIST. & OPER.
Nadia Bronson
V.P., INTERNATIONAL ADVERTISING & PROMOTION
Stacy Barger
V.P., INTERNATIONAL PUBLICITY
Thomas Castaneda

V.P., INTERNATIONAL MARKETING
Elizabeth Gaynes

UNIVERSAL PICTURES DISTRIBUTION
PRESIDENT
Nikki Rocco
EXECUTIVE V.P., NATIONAL SALES MANAGER
Nick Carpou
EXECUTIVE V.P., NATIONAL SALES MANAGER
Mark Gaines
SENIOR V.P., DISTRIBUTION & MARKETING
Alan Sutton
V.P., GENERAL MANAGER, UNIVERSAL FILMS CANADA
Eugene Amodeo
V.P., NATIONAL EXHIBITOR RELATIONS
Steve Ellman
V.P., DIVISION MANAGER
Jack Finn
V.P., DIVISION MANAGER
Albert Quaedvlieg
V.P., DIVISION MANAGER
Dave Richoux

UNIVERSAL STUDIOS HOME VIDEO
PRESIDENT, UNIVERSAL STUDIOS HOME VIDEO
E.V.P & GEN. MGR., UNIVERSAL MUSIC & VIDEO DIST.
Craig Kornblau
CFO, UNIVERSAL STUDIOS HOME VIDEO & SENIOR V.P., DIRECT ACCT. MGMT., UNIVERSAL MUSIC & VIDEO DIST.
Lawrence Hariton
SENIOR V.P., MARKETING
Ken Graffeo
SENIOR V.P., SALES & DISTRIBUTION, VIDEO
Richard Longwell
SENIOR V.P., CREATIVE SOURCES
Linda Turner

UNIVERSAL FAMILY & HOME ENTERTAINMENT
PRESIDENT
Louis A. Feola
EXECUTIVE V.P., UNIVERSAL CARTOON STUDIOS
Nancy Steingard
EXECUTIVE V.P., DIRECT-TO-VIDEO PROGRAMMING
Suzie Peterson
SENIOR V.P., BUSINESS AFFAIRS
Robert W. Rubin
SENIOR V.P., CARTOON STUSIOS
Tom Ruzicka

UNIVERSAL TELEVISION & NETWORKS
CHAIRMAN
Blair Westlake
EXECUTIVE V.P. & CFO
Beverly Thelander
EXECUTIVE V.P. & GROUP STRATEGIC DIRECTOR
Peter Schoenfeld
EXECUTIVE V.P., BUSINESS & LEGAL AFFAIRS
Philip Schuman
SENIOR V.P., BUSINESS & LEGAL AFFAIRS
Andrea Melville
SENIOR V.P., BUSINESS DEVELOPMENT
Dan Marks
SENIOR V.P., FINANCE
Brian Kesterson
SENIOR V.P., LEGAL AFFAIRS
Richard Silliman
SENIOR V.P., SALES ADMINISTRATION & DISTRIBUTION
Von Johnson
SENIOR V.P., MARKETING
Karin Timpone

UNIVERSAL INTERNATIONAL TELEVISION
EXECUTIVE V.P.
Steve Jarmus

UNIVERSAL STUDIOS NETWORKS
PRESIDENT
Tony Garland

UNIVERSAL WORLDWIDE TELEVISION
PRESIDENT, PRODUCTION
Ned Nalle
EXECUTIVE V.P., DRAMATIC PRODUCTION
Dan Filie

UNIVERSAL STUDIOS RECREATION GROUP
CHAIRMAN & CEO
Tom Williams
CFO
Michael Corcoran
PRESIDENT, INTERNATIONAL & HEAD OF GLOBAL BUSINESS AFFAIRS
Glenn J. Gumpel
PRESIDENT, INTL. NEW BUSINESS DEVELOPMENT
Frank Stanek
PRESIDENT, NEW BUSINESS & DEVELOPMENT
Chris Gorog

UNIVERSAL STUDIOS HOLLYWOOD
PRESIDENT & COO
Larry Kurzwell

UNIVERSAL STUDIOS ORLANDO
PRESIDENT & COO
Felix Mussenden

UNIVERSAL STUDIOS JAPAN
EXECUTIVE V.P. & COO
Bob Gault

UNIVERSAL STUDIOS PORT AVENTURA
MANAGING DIRECTOR
B.J. Fair

UPA PRODS. OF AMERICA
8460 Wilshire Blvd., Beverly Hills, CA 90211 (310) 659-6004 FAX: (310) 659-4599.
PRESIDENT
Eric Ellenbogen

USA FILMS
(Formerly Gramercy Pictures)
(Motion picture production and distribution)
100 N. Crescent Dr., Garden Level, Beverly Hils, CA 90210. (310) 385-4400. FAX: (310) 385-4404. www.usafilms.com
65 Bleeker St., New York, NY 10012. (212) 539-4000. FAX: (212) 539-4099.
CHAIRMAN
Scott Greenstein
PRESIDENT
Russell Schwartz
EXECUTIVE V.P., BUSINESS & LEGAL AFFAIRS
Avy Eschenasy
EXECUTIVE V.P., MARKETING
Steve Flynn
EXECUTIVE V.P., DISTRIBUTION
Jack Foley
SENIOR V.P., NATIONAL SALES
Linda Ditrinco
SENIOR V.P., ACQUISITIONS
Steven Raphael
SENIOR V.P., PUBLICITY
Adriene Bowles
V.P., CREATIVE ADVERTISING
Blair Green
SENIOR V.P., BUSINESS AFFAIRS
Howard Meyers
SENIOR V.P., PRODUCTION
Randy Ostrow

VANGUARD DOCUMENTARIES
(Television and film production)
135 E. 65 St., 4th Flr., New York, NY 10021. (212) 517-4333. FAX: (212) 734-3609. email: tv_producers@email.msn.com
PRESIDENT
Charles Hobson

VALHALLA MOTION PICTURES
3575 Cahuenga Blvd. W., Ste. 415, Los Angeles, CA 90068-1343. (323) 969-4300. FAX: (323) 969-4301.
email: vmp@valhallamotionpics.com
CHAIRMAN & CEO
Gale Anne Hurd
CFO
Julie Thomson
PRESIDENT
Barbara Boyle
V.P., DEVELOPMENT
Kelly Campbell
DIRECTOR, DEVELOPMENT
Tracy Mercer

VENTANAROSA PRODUCTIONS
9000 Sunset Blvd., Ste. 814, Los Angeles, CA 90069. (310) 860-0899. FAX: (310) 860-0895.
CHAIRPERSON
Salma Hayek
PRESIDENT
Ricka Fisher
DIRECTOR, DEVELOPMENT
Jose Tamez

VERDON-CEDRIC PRODUCTIONS
9350 Wilshire Blvd., Ste. 303, Beverly Hills, CA 90212. (310) 274-7253.
PRODUCER & DIRECTOR & WRITER & ACTOR
Sidney Poitier

VIACOM, INC.

(Viacom merged with CBS in September, 1999)
1515 Broadway, New York, NY 10036, (212) 258-6000, FAX: (212) 258-6175. www.viacom.com
CHAIRMAN OF THE BOARD & CEO OF VIACOM, INC.
CHAIRMAN, PRESIDENT & CEO NATIONAL AMUSEMENTS INC.
Sumner M. Redstone
CHAIRMAN & CEO, VIACOM ENTERTAINMENT GROUP
Jonathan Dolgen
PRESIDENT & COO
Mel Karmazin

PARAMOUNT PICTURES

5555 Melrose Ave., Los Angeles, CA 90038. (213) 956-5000.
CHAIRMAN & CEO, VIACOM ENTERTAINMENT GROUP
Jonathan Dolgen
EXECUTIVE V.P., PARAMOUNT PICTURES
William Berstein
SENIOR V.P., & CFO
Mark Badagliacca
SENIOR V.P. & TREASURER
Alan J. Bailey
SENIOR V.P., FINANCIAL PLANNING
Stephanie Love
SENIOR V.P., ADMINISTRATION
Rosemary DiPietra
SENIOR V.P. & DEPUTY GENERAL COUNSEL
David Friedman
SENIOR V.P., HUMAN RESOURCES
William A. Hawkins
SENIOR V.P., INDUSTRIAL RELATIONS
Stephen Koppekin
SENIOR V.P. & GENERAL COUNSEL
Rebecca L. Prentice
SENIOR V.P. & GENERAL COUNSEL
J. Jay Rakow
SENIOR V.P., FINANCE
Stephen P. Taylor
SENIOR V.P., INFORMATION SYSTEMS & CIO
H. Edgar Trainor
V.P., INFORMATION PROCESSING & INFORMATION SYS.
S.R. (Stan) Balcomb
V.P., SYSTEMS DEVELOPMENT
Diana N. Browne
V.P., GROUP ACCOUNTING
Chact S. Chu
V.P., CONTRACT ACCOUNTING
Carmen Desiderio
V.P., FINANCIAL PLANNING
Stephanie Love
V.P., FINANCE
Michael Masters
V.P., TREASURY MANAGEMENT
Steve Nagan
V.P., ADMINISTRATION
Rosemary DiPietra
V.P. & ASSOCIATE GENERAL COUNSEL
David C. Friedman
V.P., LEGAL & HUMAN RESOURCES
Louis Gutierrez
V.P., RESIDUALS
Kathleen Hoops
V.P., HUMAN RESOURCES & LEGAL
Louis Guttierez
V.P., EMPLOYEE RELATIONS & SENIOR COUNSEL, EMPLOYEE RELATIONS
Rina Walluck
V.P., LABOR RELATIONS
Louis Shore
V.P., MOTION PICTURE CONTROLLER
Carolyn F. Scott
EXEC. DIRECTOR, GROUP FINANCIAL REPORTING
Stephen Hendry
EXEC. DIRECTOR, EMPLOYMENT & DEVELOPMENT
Cassandra Thomas
EXEC. DIRECTOR, CONTRACT ACCOUNTING
Vicente P. Ching

MOTION PICTURE GROUP

CHAIRMAN
Sherry Lansing
VICE-CHAIRMAN
Robert Friedman
PRESIDENT, WORLDWIDE MARKETING
Arthur Cohen
PRESIDENT, WORLDWIDE VIDEO
Eric Doctorow
PRESIDENT, MOTION PICTURE GROUP
John Goldwyn
PRESIDENT, MOTION PICTURE DISTRIBUTION
Wayne Lewellen
PRESIDENT, WORLDWIDE PAY TELEVISION
Jack Waterman
SENIOR V.P., BUSINESS AFFAIRS
Richard Fowkes
SENIOR V.P., BUSINESS AFFAIRS
Rochel Blachman
SENIOR V.P., LEGAL AFFAIRS
Karen Magid
SENIOR V.P., MUSIC LEGAL AFFAIRS
Linda Wohl
SENIOR V.P., LEGAL
Alan Heppel
SENIOR V.P., MUSIC BUSINESS AFFAIRS
Kevin Koloff
SENIOR V.P., INTELLECTUAL PROPERTIES
Scott Martin
V.P., INTERNATIONAL (London)
Michael O'Sullivan
V.P., MUSIC
Linda Springer
DISTRICT MANAGER, MOTION PICTURE DISTRIBUTION
Donald Wallace
DISTRICT MANAGERS
Mike Share
Robert Box

DOMESTIC DISTRIBUTION DIVISION, MOTION PICTURE GROUP

PRESIDENT, DISTRIBUTION
Wayne Lewellen
EXECUTIVE V.P., ELECTRONIC CINEMA
Gino Campagnola
EXECUTIVE V.P., SALES OPERATIONS
Steve Rapaport
SENIOR V.P., ASSISTANT GENERAL COUNSEL
Paul Springer
SENIOR V.P. AND GENERAL SALES MANAGER
Clark Woods
V.P. SOUTHERN DIVISION
Royce Brimage
V.P., EASTERN DIVISION
Mike Share
V.P., WESTERN DIVISION
Robert Weiss
SENIOR V.P., CANADIAN DIVISION
Chris Sullivan
V.P., SALES ADMINISTRATION
John Hersker
EXEC. DIRECTOR, EXHIBITOR RELATIONS
Mark Mulcahy

DISTRICT BRANCHES AND MANAGERS, MOTION PICTURE GROUP

EASTERN

1633 Broadway, 11th Flr., New York, NY 10019.
DISTRICT MANAGER, NEW YORK
Pam Araujo

SOUTHERN

12222 Merit Drive, Ste. 1700, Dallas, TX 75251.
BRANCH MANAGER, DALLAS/NEW ORLEANS/OKLAHOMA CITY/MEMPHIS
Don Wallace

PUERTO RICO

Miramar Plaza Building, 954 Ponce de Leon Avenue, Ste. 201, San Juan, PR 00907.
BRANCH SALES MANAGER
Nestor Rivera

WESTERN

15260 Ventura Boulevard, Ste. 1140, Sherman Oaks, CA 91403.
BRANCH MANAGER, LOS ANGELES
Bob Box

MONTREAL

1255 University Street, Ste. 921, Montreal, QC H3B 3W4.
BRANCH SALES MANAGER
Lise Bertrand

TORONTO

146 Bloor Street West, Toronto, ON, Canada M5S 1M4.
BRANCH SALES MANAGER, TORONTO
Bob Cowan
BRANCH SALES MANAGER, ST. JOHN/WINNIPEG
Jean White

HOME VIDEO DIVISION, MOTION PICTURE GROUP

PRESIDENT, WORLDWIDE VIDEO
Eric Doctorow
EXECUTIVE V.P., SALES & MARKETING
Jack Kanne

MARKETING DIVISION, MOTION PICTURE GROUP
PRESIDENT, WORLDWIDE MARKETING
Arthur Cohen
EXECUTIVE V.P., NATIONAL ADVERTISING/PROMOTION
Thomas Campanella
EXECUTIVE V.P., CREATIVE SERVICES, ADVERTISING
James P. Gibbons
EXECUTIVE V.P., MARKETING/CREATIVE AFFAIRS
Nancy Goliger
EXECUTIVE V.P., WORLDWIDE PUBLICITY
Nancy Kirkpatrick
EXECUTIVE V.P., CREATIVE AVERTISING
Lucia Ludovico
SENIOR V.P., MARKETING, SPECIAL PROJECTS
Maren Moebius
SENIOR V.P., CREATIVE ADVERTISING
William Rus
SENIOR V.P., MEDIA DIRECTOR
Susan Wrenn
SENIOR V.P., MARKETING ADMINSTRATION
Leslie H. Anderson
SENIOR V.P., WORLDWIDE MARKETING PARTNERSHIPS
Lisa Di Marzio
V.P., SPECIAL PROJECTS
Allison Jackson
V.P., NATIONAL PUBLICITY
Susan Ciccone
V.P., INTERNATIONAL MARKETING
John Rentsch
V.P., BROADCASTING PRODUCTION
Shaylee Dunn
V.P., PRINT PRODUCTION
John Barry
V.P., NATIONAL PUBLICITY
Greg Brilliant
V.P., PLANNING, NATIONAL ADVERTISING
Suki Yamashita
EXEC. DIRECTOR, MARKETING ADMINISTRATION & MEDIA
Fred Manny
EXEC. DIRECTOR, NATIONAL PROMOTIONS
Susan M. Kelly
EXEC. DIRECTOR, SPOT BROADCASTING
Nicky Shapiro

PRODUCTION DIVISION, MOTION PICTURE GROUP
PRESIDENT, MOTION PICTURE PRODUCTION
Michelle Manning
EXECUTIVE V.P., PRODUCTION
Karen Rosenfelt
EXECUTIVE V.P., FEATURE PROD. MGMT., WORLDWIDE
Fred T. Gallo
EXECUTIVE V.P., PRODUCTION
Donald Granger
EXECUTIVE V.P., PRODUCTION
Brian Witten
PRESIDENT, MOTION PICTURE DIVISION, BVI
Thomas K. Levine
PRESIDENT, MUSIC
Burt Berman
V.P., TELEVISION MUSIC
David Grossman
V.P., CREATIVE AFFAIRS
Bradley Kessell
V.P., MUSIC
Linda Springer
V.P., MUSIC CLEARANCE
Eldridge Walker
V.P., PRODUCTION FINANCE
Brain Wensel
EXEC. DIRECTOR, MUSIC PROD. & CREATIVE AFFAIRS
Steve Londo

POST-PRODUCTION DIVISION, MOTION PICTURE GROUP
EXECUTIVE V.P., POST-PRODUCTION
Paul Haggar
V.P., POST-PRODUCTION
John Wiseman
V.P., POST-PRODUCTION FACILITIES
John Bloechle
V.P., WORLDWIDE TECHNOLOGY
Laverne Williams

PARAMOUNT DIGITAL ENTERTAINMENT
PRESIDENT
Leonard Washington

PARAMOUNT STUDIO GROUP
PRESIDENT
Earl Lestz
SENIOR V.P., VIDEO OPERATIONS
Tom Bruehl
SENIOR V.P., FACILITIES OPERATIONS
Rae Ann Del Pozzo
SENIOR V.P., PLANNING & DEVELOPMENT
Christine Essel
SENIOR V.P., STUDIO ADMINISTRATION
Larry A. Owens
V.P., STUDIO PROTECTION
Thomas G. Hays
V.P., PLANNING & CONSTRUCTION
Michael Romano
V.P., LEGAL SERVICES
Nathan Smith

PARAMOUNT TELEVISION GROUP
CHAIRMAN, PARAMOUNT TELEVISION GROUP
Kerry Mc Cluggage
EXECUTIVE V.P. & CAO, TELEVISION GROUP
Steve Goldman
EXECUTIVE V.P., BUSINESS AFFAIRS/FINANCE
Robert Sheehan
EXECUTIVE V.P., MARKETING & MEDIA RELATIONS
John A. Wentworth
SENIOR V.P., RESEARCH
Mike Mellon
SENIOR V.P., MEDIA RELATIONS
Michelle Hunt

PARAMOUNT DOMESTIC TELEVISION DIVISION
CO-PRESIDENTS, DOMESTIC TELEVISION
Joel Berman
Frank Kelly
PRESIDENT, DISTRIBUTION
John Nogawski
EXECUTIVE V.P., MARKETING
Michael Mischler
EXECUTIVE V.P., CURRENT PROGRAMMING
Bobbee Gabelmann
EXECUTIVE V.P., BUSINESS AFFAIRS & LEGAL
Bruce Pottash
SENIOR V.P., OFF-NETWORK SALES
Dennis Emerson
SENIOR V.P., BUSINESS AFFAIRS & LEGAL
Robert Mendez
SENIOR V.P., GENERAL SALES MANAGER
Mark Dvornik
SENIOR V.P., ADVERTISING & PROMOTION
David Lafountaine
V.P., SALES SPECIAL PROJECTS
Dawn Abel
V.P., PROGRAMMING
Linda Carrasquillo
V.P., PROGRAMMING
Lou Dennig
V.P., PROGRAMMING
Terry Wood
V.P., PROGRAMMING
John Kohler
V.P., DEVELOPMENT
Clancy Collins
V.P., BUSINESS AFFAIRS ADMINISTRATION
Lynn Fero
V.P., ADVERTISING & PROMOTION
Gary Holland
V.P., SALES ADMINISTRATION & PROGRAM LINEUPS
Lisa Fimiani
SENIOR V.P., CABLE SALES
Robert Friedman
V.P., WESTERN DIVISION MANAGER
Stan Justice
V.P., BUSINESS AFFAIRS - LEGAL
Peter Kane
V.P., OFF-NETWORK & SPECIAL PROJECTS
Cynthia Lieberman
V.P.s, LEGAL
Cynthia Teele
David Theodosopoulos
V.P., CREATIVE SERVICES & DESIGN
David Thomas
V.P., WESTERN REGIONAL MANAGER
Rob Wussler
V.P., RESEARCH
Christopher Gerondale

PARAMOUNT NETWORK TELEVISION
PRESIDENT, NETWORK TELEVISION
Garry Hart
EXECUTIVE V.P., CREATIVE AFFIARS
Tom Mazza
EXECUTIVE V.P., BUSINESS AFFAIRS
Jake Jacobson
SENIOR V.P., ADVERTISING, PUBLICITY & PROMOTION
Trisha Cardoso
SENIOR V.P., COMEDY DEVELOPMENT
Dan Fauci
SENIOR V.P., POST-PRODUCTION
Hal Harrison

SENIOR V.P., DRAMA DEVELOPMENT
Kathy Lingg
EXECUTIVE V.P., LEGAL, NETWORK TV
Milinda McNeely
SENIOR V.P., TALENT & CASTING
Helen Mossler
V.P., TELEVISION MOVIES & MINISERIES
Tom Russo
SENIOR V.P., PRODUCTION
Reid Shane
SENIOR V.P., CURRENT PROGRAMS
Steve Stark
V.P., TELEVISION MUSIC
David Grossman
V.P., CURRENT PROGRAMS
Marshall Coben
V.P., CURRENT PROGRAMS NETWORK
Brett King
V.P., BUSINESS AFFAIRS NETWORK TV
J.R. McGinnis
V.P., COMEDY DEVELOPMENT
Rose Catherine Pinkney
V.P., BUSINESS AFFAIRS
Sandra Delaney
DIRECTOR OF BUSINESS
Craig Wagner
V.P., PRODUCTION FINANCE
Mark Weissman

FAMOUS MUSIC PUBLISHING

10635 Santa Monica Blvd., #300, Los Angeles, CA 90025.
CHAIRMAN & CEO
Irwin A. Robinson
PRESIDENT
Ira Jaffe
EXECUTIVE V.P., ADMINISTRATION (NY)
Sidney Herman

VIACOM NEW MEDIA

EXECUTIVE V.P. & GENERAL MANAGER
Paul Meyer

VIACOM CONSUMER PRODUCTS

PRESIDENT
Andrea Hein
SENIOR V.P., BUSINESS DEVELOPMENT & FINANCE
Michael Goldman
SENIOR V.P., DOMESTIC LICENSING
Terri Helton
SENIOR V.P., INTERNATIONAL LICENSING
Jonathon Zill
V.P., SALES
Howard Berk

VIEW ASKEW PRODUCTIONS, INC.

3 Harding Rd., Red Bank, NJ 07701. (732) 842-6933. FAX: (732) 842-3772. www.viewaskew.com
email: tooaskew@aol.com
PRESIDENT
Kevin Smith
VICE PRESIDENT
Scott Mosier
DEVELOPMENT EXECUTIVE
Kim Loughran

VILLAGE ROADSHOW PICTURES

3400 Riverside Dr., Ste. 900, Burbank, CA 91505. (818) 260-6000. FAX: (818) 260-6001.
CHAIRMAN & CEO
Bruce Berman
PRESIDENT, PRODUCTION
Bernie Goldmann
COO
Steve Krone
CFO
Reid Sullivan
EXECUTIVE V.P., WORLDWIDE FEATURE PRODUCTION
Michael Lake
SENIIOR V.P., PRODUCTION
Matt Berman
SENIOR V.P.
Dana Goldberg
SENIOR V.P., INTERNATIONAL ACQUISITIONS
Robert Meyers
CREATIVE EXECUTIVE
Jordanna Fraiberg
DIRECTOR, BUSINESS & LEGAL AFFAIRS
Kevin Berg
DIRECTOR, BUSINESS & LEGAL AFFAIRS
Joel Goldstein
STORY EDITOR
David Glaubke

JON VOIGHT ENTERTAINMENT

1901 Ave. of the Stars, Ste. 605, Los Angeles, CA 90067. (310) 843-0223. FAX: (310) 553-9895.
email: p.ewald@crystal-sky.com
PRESIDENT
Jon Voight
V.P., PRODUCTION & DEVELOPMENT
Patrick Ewald
DEVELOPMENT ASSOCIATE
Dave Molendyk

JEFF WALD ENTERTAINMENT, INC.

3000 W. Olympic Blvd., Bldg. 2, Ste. 1400, Santa Monica, CA 90404. (310) 264-4156. FAX: (310) 264-4157.
PRESIDENT & CHAIRMAN
Jeff Wald
SENIOR V.P.
Steven Thomas

VINCENT WARD FILMS, INC.

1134 N. Gardner St., West Hollywood, CA 90046. (323) 850-5703. FAX: (323) 850-5743.
email: vincentward@earthlink.net
PRODUCER & DIRECTOR
Vincent Ward
DIRECTOR, DEVELOPMENT
Carmen Lynne

WARNER BROS. INC.

(A subsidiary of Time Warner, Inc.)
4000 Warner Blvd., Burbank, CA 91522. (818) 954-6000.
1325 Ave. of the Americas, 29th Flr., New York, NY 10019 (212) 636-5100. FAX: (212) 636-5236. www.warnerbros.com
45 Braintree Hill Office Park, Ste. 301, Boston, MA 02184-8743. (617) 848-2250. FAX: (617) 849-6270.
8144 Walnut Hill Ln., Ste. 920, Dallas, TX 75231-4316. (214) 691-6101. FAX: (214) 696-1154.
CHAIRMAN & CEO
Barry M. Meyer
PRESIDENT & COO
Alan Horn
EXECUTIVE V.P., ADMIN. & STUDIO OPERATIONS
Gary Credle
EXECUTIVE V.P., INTERNATIONAL
Richard J. Fox
EXECUTIVE V.P., MARKETING & PLANNING
Sanford E. Reisenbach
EXECUTIVE V.P., TELEVISION
Bruce Rosenblum
EXECUTIVE V.P. & GENERAL COUNSEL
John A. Schulman
EXECUTIVE V.P. & CFO
Edward A. Romano
EXECUTIVE V.P., SPECIAL PROJECTS
Stephen Ross
EXECUTIVE V.P., NEW MEDIA
Kevin Tsujihara
SENIOR V.P., CHIEF CORPORATE COMM. OFFICER
Barbara Brogliatti
ASSISTANT TO CHAIRMAN & V.P., CORPORATE SERVICES
Marisa O'Neil

WARNER BROS. ADMINISTRATION & CORP. SERVICES

EXECUTIVE V.P., CTO
Chris Cookson
SENIOR V.P. & CONTROLLER
Reginald Harpur
SENIOR V.P., BUSINESS DEVELOPMENT, ASIA PACIFIC
Ellen Eliasoph
SENIOR V.P., REAL ESTATE PLANNING
Dan Garcia
SENIOR V.P., CORPORATE MARKETING & ADVERTISING
Yelena Garofalo
SENIOR V.P. & CIO
James L. Halsey
SENIOR V.P., CORP. BUS. AFFRS. & DEP. GEN. COUNSEL
Gary Meisel
SENIOR V.P. & ASSISTANT GENERAL COUNSEL
Zazi Pope
SENIOR V.P. & DEPUTY GENERAL COUNSEL
Sheldon Presser
SENIOR V.P., INDUSTRIAL RELATIONS
Alan Raphael
SENIOR V.P., WORLDWIDE CORPORATE PROMOTIONS
Bob Schneider
SENIOR V.P., STUDIO & PRODUCTION AFFAIRS
Lisa Rawlins
SENIOR V.P., INTERNATIONAL BUSINESS AFFAIRS
Eric Senat
SENIOR V.P., TV FINANCIAL MANAGEMENT
Laura Valan

SENIOR V.P., WORLDWIDE HUMAN RESOURCES
Kiko Washington
V.P., CORPORATE STRATEGIC PLANNING & DEV.
Doug Regan
V.P., CORPORATE COMMUNICATIONS
Scott Rowe
V.P., CLIP & STILL LICENSING
Judith Singer

WARNER BROS. PICTURES PRODUCTION

PRESIDENT, WORLDWIDE PRODUCTION
Lorenzo di Bonaventura
EXECUTIVE V.P., PRODUCTION
Robert Guralnick
EXECUTIVE V.P., PRODUCTION
Kevin McCormick
EXECUTIVE V.P., WORLDWIDE FEATURE PRODUCTION
Steven Papazian
SENIOR V.P, CASTING
Lora Kennedy
SENIOR V.P., PRODUCTION
Courtenay Valenti
SENIOR V.P., PRODUCTION
Jeff Robinov
SENIOR V.P., FEATURE PRODUCTION
William Young
V.P., THEATRICAL PRODUCTION
Polly Cohen
SENIOR V.P., POST-PRODUCTION
Marc Solomon
V.P., PRODUCTION
Basil Iwanyk
V.P., PRODUCTION
Lionel Wigram
V.P., FEATURE PRODUCTION
Mark Scoon
V.P., POST-PRODUCTION
Fred Talmadge

WARNER BROS. PICTURES MARKETING

PRESIDENT, DOMESTIC MARKETING
Brad Ball
EXECUTIVE V.P., SPECIAL PROJECTS, PUBLICITY
Joe Hyams
EXECUTIVE V.P., DOMESTIC MARKETING
Dawn Taubin
EXECUTIVE V.P., WORLDWIDE CREATIVE ADV. PROJECTS
Joel Wayne
SENIOR V.P., NEW MEDIA
Don Buckley
SENIOR V.P., CREATIVE ADVERTISING
Jim Frederick
SENIOR V.P., CREATIVE ADVERTISING
Massey Rafani
SENIOR V.P., MKTG. STRATEGY DOMESTIC & INTL.
Richard Del Belso
SENIOR V.P., MARKETING RESEARCH
Daniel P. Rosen
SENIOR V.P., WORLDWIDE MEDIA
Lynn Whitney
V.P., PUBLICITY
John Dartigue
V.P., PUBLICITY
Juli Goodwin
V.P., PUBLICITY
Mark Reina
V.P., CREDIT & TITLE ADMINISTRATION
Norma Fuss
V.P., ADVERTISING & PUBLICITY SERVICES
Drew Giordano
V.P., FIELD PUBLICITY & NATIONAL PROMOTION
Ernie Johnston
V.P., ADMINISTRATION, DOMESTIC MARKETING
Dennis Tange

WARNER BROS. DOMESTIC DISTRIBUTION

PRESIDENT, DOMESTIC THEATRICAL DISTRIBUTION
Daniel R. Fellman
SENIOR V.P., NONTHEATRICAL SALES
Jeff Crawford
SENIOR V.P. & GENERAL SALES MANAGER
Jeff Goldstein
SENIOR V.P. & GENERAL COUNSEL
Connie Minnett
SENIOR V.P., ADMINISTRATION
Howard Welinsky
V.P., CANADIAN DISTRICT MANAGER
Florent Boulet
V.P., FINANCIAL ADMINISTRATION & OPERATIONS
Bonnie Fallone
V.P., PRINT CONTROL
Nancy Sams
V.P., SALES OPERATIONS
Richard A. Schiff
V.P., SYSTEMS & DEVELOPMENT
Don Tannenbaum

WARNER BROS. PICTURES INTERNATIONAL DISTRIBUTION

SENIOR V.P., EUROPE, MIDDLE EAST & AFRICA
Ivan Cheah
SENIOR V.P., LATIN AMERICA
Redo Farah
SENIOR V.P., INTERNATIONAL MARKETING
Sue Kroll
SENIOR V.P., INTERNATIONAL DISTRIBUTION
Veronica Kwan-Rubinek
SENIOR V.P., EUROPEAN ADVERTISING & PUBLICITY
Julian Senior
SENIOR V.P., INTERNATIONAL OPERATIONS & FINANCE
Angelina Speare
V.P., ASIA
John Alonte
V.P., OPERATIONS EUROPE
David Brander
V.P., INTERNATIONAL DISTRIBUTION
Nancy Carson
V.P., INTERNATIONAL MARKETING
Ling Chan
V.P., EASTERN EUROPE & MIDDLE EAST
Jacques Dubois
V.P., INTERNATIONAL DISTRIBUTION
Monque Esclavissat
V.P., MEDIA EUROPE
Con Gornell
MANAGING DIRECTOR, JAPAN
Bill Ireton
V.P., INTERNATIONAL MEDIA
Gina Kilberg
V.P., INTERNATIONAL PUBLICITY
Mic Kramer
V.P., INTERNATIONAL OPERATIONS
Lisa Mundt
V.P., OPERATIONS, ASIA/PACIFIC & LATIN AMERICA
Jack Nguyen
V.P., INTERNATIONAL PROMOTIONS
Juliana Olinka
V.P., EUROPEAN SALES
Sarig Peker
V.P., INTERNATIONAL MARKET RESEARCH
Barbara Shuler
V.P., INTERNATIONAL ADVERTISING & PUBLICITY SERVICES
Francine Velarde
V.P., INTERNATIONAL FINANCE
David Williamson

WARNER BROS. PICTURES BUSINESS/LEGAL AFFAIRS

EXECUTIVE V.P., WORLDWIDE BUSINESS AFFAIRS
Steve Spira
SENIOR V.P. & GEN. COUNSEL, BUS. & LEGAL AFFAIRS
David Sagal
SENIOR V.P., BUSINESS AFFAIRS
Patti Connolly
SENIOR V.P. & GENERAL COUNSEL
Jeremy Williams
V.P., ASSOCIATE GENERAL COUNSEL
Eileen Hale
V.P., BUSINESS AFFAIRS
Jodi Levinson
V.P. & GENERAL COUNSEL
Pam Kirsh
V.P. & GENERAL COUNSEL, INTL. DISTRIBUTION
Steven Mertz
V.P., LEGAL
Jack Sattinger
V.P., BUSINESS AFFAIRS
Virginia Tweedy
V.P., CONTINENTAL FINANCE
Chris Young

WARNER BROS. PICTURES MUSIC

PRESIDENT, MUSIC
Gary LeMel
EXECUTIVE V.P., MUSIC
Doug Frank
SENIOR V.P., BUSINESS AFFAIRS MUSIC
Keith Zajic

WARNER HOME VIDEO

PRESIDENT
Warren Lieberfarb
EXEC. V.P., WORLDWIDE FINANCE, LOGIS. & SYSTEMS
Ed Byrnes
EXECUTIVE V.P., NORTH AMERICA, AUSTRALIA & NEW ZEALAND
Jim Cardwell

EXECUTIVE V.P., WORLDWIDE BUSINESS AFFAIRS, LEGAL & HUMAN RESOURCES
Marsha King
SENIOR V.P., WORLDWIDE FINANCE & STRAT. PLANNING
John Avagliano
SENIOR V.P., BUSINESS AFFAIRS & GENERAL COUNSEL
Beth Baier
SENIOR V.P., S. AMERICA & MANAGING DIR. FOR SPAIN
Alex de Muns
SENIOR V.P., VIDEO ON DEMAND & PAY-PER-VIEW
Jeffrey Calman
SENIOR V.P., INTERNATIONAL PLANNING & OPERATIONS
Mark Gillions
SENIOR V.P. & GENERAL MANAGER, CANADA
Gord Edwards
SENIOR V.P., US MARKETING
Mark Horak
SENIOR V.P., WORLDWIDE MARKETING & DEVELOPMENT
Tom Lesinski
SENIOR V.P., SALES
John Quinn
SENIOR V.P. & CO-MANAGING DIRECTOR, EUROPE, MIDDLE EAST & AFRICA
Ron Sanders
SENIOR V.P. & CO-MANAGING DIRECTOR, EUROPE, MIDDLE EAST & AFRICA
Gerry Weber
V.P., CREDIT CUSTOMER OPERATIONS
Jerry Brandt
V.P., INTERNATIONAL MARKETING
Jeff Brown
V.P., FAMILY & SPECIAL INTEREST MARKETING
Dan Capone
V.P., REGIONAL
Philippe Cardon
V.P., RENTAL SALES
Patrick Connor
V.P., SELL-THROUGH SALES
Trevor Drinkwater
V.P., WORLDWIDE PUBLICITY
Pamela Godfrey
V.P., EDITORIAL & PROGRAMMING
Mike Finnegan
V.P., DOMESTIC FINANCE
Keith Hillyer
V.P., WORLDWIDE HUMAN RESOURCES
Joy Hoshino
V.P., INTERNATIONAL MARKETING
Brian Jamieson
V.P., ANTI-PIRACY
Molly Kellogg
V.P., BUSINESS & LEGAL AFFAIRS, EUROPE
Irus Knobloch
V.P., CONTROLLER
Mike Kory
V.P., FIELD SALES COMMUNICATIONS & PROMOTIONS
Frank Kraus
V.P., SPECIAL PROJECTS
Howard Livingston
V.P., FINANCIAL PLANNING & ANALYSIS
Mukul Mehta
V.P., RETAIL DIRECT
Dan Miron
V.P., SALES & PLANNING ADMINISTRATION
Ken Mueller
V.P., DVD MARKETING
Steve Nickerson
V.P., NEW MEDIA APPLICATIONS & OPERATIONS
Lewis Ostrover
V.P., DVD MARKET DEVELOPMENT-WORLDWIDE
John Powers
V.P., WORLDWIDE CREATIVE SERVICES
John Richards
V.P., OPERATIONS
Edwards Ross
V.P., CREATIVE SERVICES
Ardis Rubenstein
V.P., FEATURES MARKETING
Mike Saksa
V.P., PROMOTIONS
Mimi Slavin
V.P., INTERNET MARKETING
Jim Wuthrich
V.P., ASIA PACIFIC
Francis Yam

WARNER BROS. CONSUMER PRODUCTS

PRESIDENT, WORLDWIDE CONSUMER PRODUCTS
Dan Romanelli
PRESIDENT, WORLDWIDE LICENSING & STUDIO STORES
Geroge Jones
EXECUTIVE V.P., WORLDWIDE CONSUMER PRODUCTS
Randy Blotky
EXECUTIVE V.P., WORLDWIDE MARKETING & RETAIL BUSINESS DEVELOPMENT
Rob Gruen
EXECUTIVE V.P., MERCHANDISING, STUDIO STORES
Audrey Schlaepfer
EXECUTIVE V.P., STUDIO STORES OPERATIONS
Peter Lynch
EXECUTIVE V.P., INTERNATIONAL LICENSING
Mark Matheney
SENIOR V.P., DC COMICS PROMOTIONS & ADVERTISING
Joel Ehrlich
SENIOR V.P. & MANAGING DIRECTOR EUROPE, MIDDLE EAST & AFRICA
Dave Evans
SENIOR V.P., TOYS
Ron Hayes
SENIOR V.P., PUBLICITY & LIVE EVENTS
Karine Joret
SENIOR V.P., RETAIL BUSINESS DEVELOPMENT
Gwilym McGrew
SENIOR V.P., NORTH AMERICAN SALES
Karen McTier
SENIOR V.P., STUDIO STORES OPERATIONS
Michele Patton
SENIOR V.P., BUSINESS & LEGAL AFFAIRS
Gary Simon
SENIOR V.P., APPAREL FOR LIC. & STUDIO STORES
Karen Weiss
V.P., INTL. STUDIO STORES SALES & PLANNING
Wendy Bachelis
V.P., SOURCING
Jon Brewer
V.P., ADULT MERCHANDISING
Sally Brooks
V.P., APPAREL, U.S. SALES
Patti Buckner
V.P., CREATIVE DESIGN, STUDIO STORES
Ruth Clampett
V.P., ONLINE MARKETING & MERCHANDISING
Dave Clark
V.P., MARKETING, THEATRICAL & DC PROPERTIES
Suzie Domnick
V.P., TOYS, GIFTS, STATIONARY, UK
Paul Flett
V.P., BRAND ASSURANCE
Kim Furzer
V.P., MARKETING, CREATIVE SERVICES & BRAND ASSURANCE, EUROPE, MIDDLE EAST & AFRICA
Mara Gardner
V.P., FINANCE
Nairi Gardiner
V.P., TOYS & THEME PARK LICENSING
Kelly Gilmore
V.P., MARKETING LOONEY TUNES & CARTOON NETWORK PROPERTIES
Tom Gowan
V.P., CREATIVE SERVICES
Brenda Guttman
V.P., WORLDWIDE PUBLISHING
Michael Harkavy
V.P., PROMOTIONS & BRANDED FOODS
Dave Hedrick
V.P., PAN-CHINA & S.E. ASIA
Bernard Kam
V.P., KIDS MERCHANDISING
Wendy Klarik
V.P., LICENSING, LATIN AMERICA
Claudio Ludovisi
V.P., INTERNATIONAL OPERATIONS
Bruce Marshall
V.P., PLANNING & ALLOCATION
Bill Martin
V.P., U.S. SALES
Dave Rupert
V.P., VISUAL PRESENTATION & STORE DESIGN
Tom Sandonato
V.P., STUDIO LICENSING
Michelle Sucillon
V.P., RETAIL INFORMATION SYSTEMS
Roxane Suurvarik
V.P., DIRECT MARKETING
Marcia Tabler
V.P., GALLERY
Mark Taliani
V.P., LOGISTICS
Michael Tillman
V.P., MERCHANDISING, HARD GOODS
Cynthia Tosches
V.P., FINANCE
Linda Van Wagner

WARNER BROS. TELEVISION
PRESIDENT
Peter Roth
EXECUTIVE V.P.
Craig Hunegs
EXECUTIVE V.P., NETWORK PRODUCTION
Andrew Ackerman
EXECUTIVE V.P., DEVELOPMENT
Steve Pearlman
SENIOR V.P., COMEDY DEVELOPMENT, ALTERNATIVE PROGRAMMING
Tom Campbell
SENIOR V.P., BUSINESS AFFAIRS
Karen Cease
SENIOR V.P., ADMINISTRATION
Geriann Geraci McIntosh
SENIOR V.P., CURRENT PROGRAMMING
Trent Jones
SENIOR V.P., LABOR RELATIONS
Hank Lachmund
SENIOR V.P., MOVIES & MINI-SERIES
Gregg Maday
SENIOR V.P., PUBLICITY, ADVERTISING & PROMOTION
Sharan Magnuson
SENIOR V.P., TALENT & CASTING
Barbara Miller
SENIOR V.P., BUSINESS AFFAIRS
Roni Mueller
SENIOR V.P., STUDIO GENERAL COUNSEL
Marjorie Neufeld
SENIOR V.P., CURRENT PROGRAMMING
David Sacks
SENIOR V.P., DRAMA & COMEDY PRODUCTION
Judith Zaylor
V.P., NETWORK PRODUCTION
Lewis Abel
V.P., MOVIES & MINI-SERIES
Jim Botko
V.P., DRAMA DEVELOPMENT
Leonard Goldstein
V.P., PUBLICITY
Phil Gonzales
V.P., BUSINESS AFFAIRS
Gary Gradinger
V.P., NETWORK PRODUCTION
Henry Johnson
V.P., CASTING
Geraldine Leder
V.P., CASTING
John Levey
V.P., NETWORK PRODUCTION
Lisa Lewis
V.P., TELEVISION MUSIC
Roxanne Lippel
V.P., TALENT
Irene Mariano
V.P., POST-PRODUCTION
Blake McCormick
V.P., NETWORK PRODUCTION
Partick Newcomb
V.P., BUSINESS AFFAIRS
Brett Paul
V.P., NETWORK PRODUCTION
Ellen Rauch
V.P., CASTING
Mark Saks
V.P., CASTING
Tony Sepulveda
V.P., PRODUCTION CONTROL & ESTIMATING
Christina Smith
V.P., LABOR RELATIONS
Sam Wolfson

WARNER BROS. ANIMATION
PRESIDENT
Jean MacCurdy
SENIOR V.P. & GEN. MGR., TELEVISION ANIMATION
Andy Lewis
SENIOR V.P., CLASSIC ANIMATION
Kathleen Helpie-Shipley
SENIOR V.P., CREATIVE AFFAIRS, TELEVISION ANIMATION
Linda Steiner
V.P., CLASSIC ANIMATION
Lorri Bond
V.P., PRODUCTION, FEATURE ANIMATION
Dennis Edwards
V.P., CREATIVE AFFAIRS, TELEVISION ANIMATION
Christopher Keenan

TELEPICTURES PRODUCTIONS
PRESIDENT, PRODUCTION
Jim Paratore
EXECUTIVE V.P., LEGAL & BUSINESS AFFAIRS
Alan Saxe
SENIOR V.P., NEW MEDIA & CURRENT PROGRAMMING
David Auerbach
SENIOR V.P., DEVELOPMENT
Stephanie Drachkovitch
SENIOR V.P., PROGRAMMING & DEVELOPMENT
Hilary Estey-McLoughlin
SENIOR V.P., PRODUCTION
Kevin Fortson
V.P., DEVELOPMENT
Lisa Hackner-Goldberg
SENIOR EXECUTIVE PRODUCER, REALITY PROGRAMMING
Lisa Gregorisch-Dempsey

TELEPICTURES DISTRIBUTION
SENIOR V.P., GENERAL SALES MANAGER
Bill Marcus
V.P., CENTRAL SALES MANAGER
Bill Hague
V.P., SOUTHEASTERN SALES
Chuck Self

WARNER BROS. INTERNATIONAL THEATRES
PRESIDENT
Millard Ochs
EXECUTIVE V.P.
Chris Adelmann
SENIOR V.P., WORLDWIDE OPERATIONS
David Pearson
SENIOR V.P., ARCHITECTURAL DESIGN
Ira Stiegler
V.P., I.S., OPERATIONAL FINANCE & ADMINISTRATION
David Bent
V.P., BUSINESS & LEGAL AFFAIRS
James Birch
V.P., INTERNATIONAL FILM RELATIONS
Peter Dobson
V.P., FINANCE
Paul Miller

WARNER BROS. STUDIO FACILITIES
PRESIDENT
Jon Gilbert
SENIOR V.P., POST-PRODUCTION SERVICES
Norman Barnett
SENIOR V.P., LABOR RELATIONS & BUSINESS AFFAIRS
Jeff Nagler
SENIOR V.P., PRODUCTION SERVICES
Ron Stein
SENIOR V.P., FINANCE & PLANNING
Leisa Wu
V.P., STUDIO PROTECTION
Scott Nelson
V.P., CONSTRUCTION MANAGEMENT
Jason Parker
V.P., POST-PRODUCTION SERVICES
Barry Snyder
V.P., STUDIO DESIGN & CONSTRUCTION SERVICES
Kirk Solomon

WARNER BROS. NEW MEDIA
SENIOR V.P., EMERGING TECHNOLOGY
Chuck Dages
V.P., BUSINESS DEVELOPMENT
John Calkins
V.P., BUSINESS & LEGAL AFFAIRS
Clarissa Weirick

NTERNATIONAL OFFICES, DISTRIBUTORS & MGRS.

ARGENTINA
Warner Bros./Fox, Tucuman 1938, 1050 Buenos Aires. Tel:(5411) 4372 6094. FAX: (5411) 112 030.
GENERAL MANAGER
Griselda Fortunalo

AUSTRALIA
c/o Village Roadshow Corp. Ltd., 206 Bourke St., Melbourne VIC 3001, Australia. Tel: (613) 9667 6666. FAX: (613) 9663 1972.
GENERAL MANAGING DISTRIBUTION
Kathryn Carroll

AUSTRIA
Warner Bros. Ges. M.B.H., Zieglergasse 10, 1070 Vienna, Austria. Tel: (431) 523 86 2626. FAX: (431) 523 86 2631.
V.P., & MANAGING DIRECTOR
Wilhelm Geike (Germany)

BELGIUM
Warner Bros., Boulevard Brand Whitlock 42, 1200 Brussels, Belgium. Tel: (322) 735 4242. FAX: (322) 735 4919.
GENERAL MANAGER
Anny Schmit

BOLIVIA
c/o Manfer Films, S.R.L., Avenida Montes 768, 4to. Piso, Edificio Giovanni de Col, La Paz, Bolivia. Tel: (591) 233 3722. FAX: (591) 811 2922.
AGENT
Licnio Manay

BRAZIL
Fox-Warner Brazil, Calcados dos Cravos 141, Centro Commercial Alphaville, Barueri, Sao Paolo CEP 06543-000, Brazil. Tel: (5511) 7296 1400. FAX: (5511) 7295 1143.
GENERAL MANAGER
Marcos Oliviera

BULGARIA
c/o Alexandra Films, 17 Najcho Tsanov St., Sofia 1000, Bulgaria. Tel: (3592) 980 6040. FAX: (3592) 9810 0715.
MANAGING DIRECTOR
Christo Dermenjiev

CHILE
Associacion Fox/Warner, Huerfanos 786, Oficina 210, Santigo, Chile. Tel: (562) 639 1515. FAX: (562) 639 7921.
GENERAL MANAGER
Pedro Jux

CHINA
Warner New Asia, Rm. 1908 Scitech Tower, 22 Jianguomenwai Ave., Beijing, China. 100004. Tel: (8610) 6515 9992. FAX: (8610) 6515 9994.
SENIOR V.P., BUSINESS DEVELOPMENT, ASIA PACIFIC
Ellen Eliasoph

COLOMBIA
c/o Cine Colombia, S.A., Carrera 13 No. 38-85, Santa Fe de Bogota, Colombia. Tel: (571) 287-7005. FAX: (571) 287-5139.
PRESIDENT
Munir Falah

CROATIA
c/o Intercom-Issa d.o.o., Nova Ves 18, 10000 Zagreb, Croatia. Tel: (3851) 466 7983. FAX: (3851) 466 7982.
GENERAL MANAGER
Gvozden Vldovic

CYPRUS
c/o Islanders Overseas Ltd., Nikou Demetriou, 4, Larnaca, Cyprus. Tel: (3574) 627 320. FAX: (3574) 628 921.
MANAGING DIRECTOR
Elias Antypas

CZECH REPUBLIC
Warner Czech Republic, NA porici 30, 5th Flr., 110 00 Prague 1, Czech Republic. Tel: (420) 22173 2401. FAX: (420) 22173 2501.
MANAGING DIRECTOR
Dr. Ladislav Stastny

DENMARK
c/o Sandrew Metronome Denmark A/S, Sondermarksvej 16, DK 2500 Copenhagen/Valby, Denmark. Tel: (45) 3615 9500. FAX: (45) 3615 9525.
GENERAL MANAGER
Loke Havn

DOMINICAN REPUBLIC
c/o Cinema Centro Dominicano, S.A., Edificio Cinema Centro, Avendia George Washington #457, Santo Domingo, Republic Dominicana. Tel: (809) 685 2373. FAX: (809) 686 2642.
PRESIDENT
Victor Carrady

ECUADOR
c/o Productora Filmica Nacional, Del Ecaudor C. Ltda., Cordova #1015 y 9 De Octubre, Guayaquil, Ecuador. Tel: (5934) 564 455. FAX: (5934) 306 218.
PRESIDENT
Carlos Espinosa

EGYPT
c/o United Motion Pictures, 7, 26 July Street, P.O. Box 923, Cairo, Egypt. Tel: (202) 591 2477. FAX: (202) 591 2829.
MANAGING DIRECTOR
Antoine Zeind

ESTONIA
c/o Motion Picture Distribution of Estonia, Parnu mnt. 45, Tallinn 10119, Estonia. Tel: (3726) 313 569. FAX: (37266) 77899.
MANAGER
Aldo Tammsaar

FINLAND
c/o Sandrew Metronome Distribution Finland OY, 3rd Flr., Kaisaniemenkatu 1B a 69, 00100 Helsinki, Finland. Tel: (3589) 8624-5806. FAX: (3589) 8624 5810.
GENERAL MANAGER
Leif Lindblad

FRANCE
Warner Bros., 67, Avenue de Wagram, 75017 Paris, France. Tel: (331) 4401 4999. FAX: (331) 4054 7193.
MANAGING DIRECTOR
Francis Boespflug

GERMANY
Warner Bros. Film GmbH, Jarrestrasse 4, D-22303, Hamburg, Germany. Tel: (4940) 226 500. FAX: (4940) 2265 0149.
V.P., & MANAGING DIRECTOR
Wilhelm Geike

GREECE
Warner Roadshow Distributors Greece, Marinou Antypa 47, 141 21 Neo Irakleio, Athens, Greece. Tel: (301) 2720 025. FAX: (301) 2793 003.
MANAGING DIRECTOR
Lily Papdopoulos

HOLLAND
Warner Bros. (Holland) B. V., De Boelelaan 16 3H, 1083 HJ Amsterdam, The Netherlands. Tel: (3120) 541 1211. FAX: (3120) 644 9001.
GENERAL MANAGER
Wilco Wolfers

HONG KONG
Warner Bros. (Far East) Inc., 34/F Oxford House, Taikoo Pl., 979 Kings Rd., Quarry Bay, Hong Kong. Tel: (852) 3128 1200. FAX: (852) 3128 1210.
GENERAL MANAGER
Erlina Suharjono
V.P., ASIA
John Alonte

HUNGARY
c/o Intercom, Bacskai u. 28-36, Budapest 1145, Hungary. Tel: (361) 467 1400. FAX: (361) 252 2736.
V.P., INTERNATIONAL DISTRIBUTION & EXHIBITION
Andras Kalman

ICELAND
c/o Samfilm, Alfabakka 8, 109 Rekjavik, Iceland. Tel: (354) 587 8900. FAX: (354) 587 8910.
CEO
Arni Samuelsson

INDIA
Warner Bros. (Far East) Inc., Eros Cinema Bldg., 42 M. Karve Rd., Bombay, India 400020. Tel: (9122) 285 6557. FAX: (9122) 285 0984.
MANAGING DIRECTOR
Blaise J. Fernandes

INDONESIA
c/o P.T. Satyra Perkasa Esthetika Film, JL. K.H. Wahid Hasylm No. 96, 1st Flr. Jakarta 10310, Indonesia. Tel: (6221) 3190 7330. FAX: (6221) 3190 7344.
WARNER REPRESENTATIVE
TBD

IRELAND
Warner Bros. Distributors Ltd., 1st Flr. 9 Town Yard Lane, Malahide, County Dublin, Ireland. Tel: (3531) 845 1844. FAX: (3731) 845 1858.
MANAGING DIRECTOR
Nigel Sharrocks (based in the UK)

ISRAEL
c/o Noah Films, 10 Glickson St., 3rd Flr., Tel Aviv 63567. Tel: (9723) 5266-331. FAX: (9723) 6202 435.
MANAGING DIRECTOR
Chilik Michaeli

ITALY
Warner Bros. Italia S.p.A., Via Varese, 16/B, 00185 Rome, Italy. Tel: (3906) 490 891. FAX: (3906) 446 2981.
MANAGING DIRECTOR
Paolo Ferrari

JAMAICA
c/o Russgram Investments Ltd., 1A South Camp Rd., Kingston, Jamaica. Tel: (876) 928 1240. FAX: (876) 928 5632.
PRESIDENT
Douglas Graham

JAPAN
Warner Bros. Theatrical Distribution Japan, a division of TWEJ, 1-2-4 Hamamatsucho, Minato-ku, Tokyo 105-0013 Japan. Tel: (813) 5472 8000. FAX: (813) 5472 8031.
MANAGING DIRECTOR
William Ireton

KENYA
c/o Fox Theatres (EA) Ltd., 20th Century Plaza, Mam Ngina Street, Box 40067, Nairobl Kenya. Tel: (254) 222-6981. FAX: (254) 222-7957.
CHIEF EXECUTIVE
Anil Kapila

KOREA
Warner Bros. Korea, Inc., M Building, 6th Flr., 221-5 Nonhyun-Dong, Kangnam-ku, Seoul, Korea 135-010. Tel: (822) 547 0181. FAX: (822) 547-8396.
GENERAL MANAGER
HS Park

LATVIA
c/o Baltic Cinema SIA, Muitas lela 1, LV-1010 Riga, Latvia. Tel: (371) 783 0519. FAX: (371) 783 0520.
MANAGING DIRECTOR
Atis Amolins

LEBANON
c/o Joseph Chacra & Son, Kazandjian Bldg., Horsh Tabet, Shamoun St., Sin El-Fil Beirut, Lebanon. Tel: (9611) 510 784. FAX: (9611) 510 785.
OWNER
Joseph Chacra

MALAYSIA
Warner Bros (M) SDN. BHD., C-12-1, 12th Flr., Block C, Megan Phileo Ave. #12, Jaian Yap Kwan Seng, 50450 Kuala Lumpur, Malaysia. Tel: (603) 2166 9933. FAX: (603) 2166 6099.
GENERAL MANAGER
Kong Lee Chok

MEXICO
c/o Videocine, S.A. de C.V., Benito Juarez No. 7, Col. Del Carmen, Coyoacan, 04100 Mexico, D.F. Tel: (525) 659 5929. FAX: (525) 554 7493.
MANAGING DIRECTOR
Eckhardt Von Damm

NEW ZEALAND
c/o Roadshow Film Distributors (N.Z.) Ltd., Level 8, 82 Symonds St., Auckland, New Zealand. Tel: (649) 377 9669. FAX: (649) 377 9449.
GENERAL MANAGER
Lisa Hubbard

NORWAY
c/o Sandrew Metronome Norge A/S, Grensen 15, N-0180 Oslo, Norway. Tel: (47) 2282 7800. FAX: (47) 2282 7810.
GENERAL MANAGER
Frida Ohrvik

PANAMA
Warner Bros. (South) Inc., Avenida Balboa, Centro Commercial Balboa Plaza, Quinto Piso, Oficina 504, Panama. Tel: (507) 284 2608. FAX: (507) 263 9161.
MANAGER
Miquel Joseph

PERU
Warner Bros. (South) Inc./20th Century Park, Av. Carnaval Y Moreyra, No. 290, #21, San Isidro, Lima 27. Tel/FAX: (5114) 412 568. FAX: (5114) 413 888.
GENERAL MANAGER
Jorge Licetti

PHILIPPINES
Warner Bros. (Far East), 4th Flr. Ramon Magsaysay, Award Foundation Center, 1680 Roxas Blvd., Manila, Philippines. Tel: (632) 526 5741. FAX: (632) 521 2673.
GENERAL MANAGER
Francis Soliven

POLAND
Warner Bros. Poland, ul. Okrezna 9, 02-916 Warszawa, Poland. Tel: (4822) 651 7920. FAX: (4822) 642 0082.
MANAGING DIRECTOR
Arkadiusz Praglowski

PORTUGAL
Columbia TriStar & Warner Filmes De Portugal Limitada, Rua Barata Salguiero 30-6 Dt., 1200 Lisbon. Tel: (3511) 316 6400. FAX: (3511) 316 1548.
GENERAL MANAGER
Antonio Avelar Gomes

PUERTO RICO
Warner Bros. (South) Inc.,Edificio Pesquera, Calle Del Parque 601, Ofna 605, Santurce 00910. Tel: (809) 725 5795. FAX: (809) 725 7275.
ACTING GENERAL MANAGER
Redo Farah

ROMANIA
c/o Intercom Film, Str. Srcului, #14-A, Etaj 1, Apt. 7, Sector 2, COD 70221 - Bucharest, Romania. Tel: (401) 210 5359. FAX: (401) 210 7699.
MANAGING DIRECTOR
Andrea Comanici

RUSSIA
c/o Caro Premier, 2, Pushkinskaya Sq., Moscow 103006, Russia. Tel: (7095) 200 6544. FAX: (7095) 209 6283.
GENERAL DIRECTOR
Alexei Ryazantsev

SCANDINAVLA REGIONAL
Warner Bros., Sweden AB, Floragatan 4 B, S-114 31 Stockholm, Sweden. Tel: (468) 762 1700. FAX: (468) 24 5642.
SCANDANAVIAN SUPERVISOR
Peter Jansson

SINGAPORE
Warner-Golden Village, 68 Orchard Rd., #07-10/14, Plaza Singapura, Singapore 238839. Tel: (65) 334 3766. FAX: (65) 334 8397.
GENERAL MANAGER
Gerald Dibbayawan

SLOVAKIA
c/o Continental Film, s.r.o., Fialkove udolie 14, 811 01 Bratisiava, Slovakia. Tel: (4217) 5441 0783. FAX: (4217) 5441 2383.
MANAGING DIRECTOR
Anton Drobny

SLOVENIA
c/o Ljubljanski Kinematografi d.d., Nazorjeva 2, 1000 Ljubljana, Slovenia. Tel: (38661) 219 564. FAX: (38661) 219 524.
GENERAL MANAGER
Sergej Racman

SOUTH AFRICA
c/o Nu Metro Distribution, Ground Flr., Gallo House, 6 Hood Ave., Rosebank 2196, Johannesburg, South Africa. Tel: (2711) 880 7040. FAX: (2711) 442 7030.
MANAGING DIRECTOR
Robert Pagan

SPAIN
Warner Sogefilms A.I.E., Cardenal Marcelo Spinola, 8. Planta 2a, 28016 Madrid, Spain. Tel: (3491) 768 8800. FAX (3491) 768 6829.
GENERAL MANAGER
Luis Hernandez

SWEDEN
c/o Sandrew Metronome Distribution Sverige AB, Florsgatan 4, P.O. Box 5612, S-114 86 Stockholm, Sewden. Tel: (468) 762 1700. FAX: (468) 10 3850.
GENERAL MANAGER
Staffan Wallhem

SWITZERLAND
Warner Bros. (Transatlantic), Inc., Basierstrasse 52, 8048 Zurich, Switzerland. Tel: (411) 495 7777. FAX: (411) 495 7795.
GENERAL MANAGER
Leo Baumgartner

TAIWAN
Warner Bros. (Far East) Inc., 13 F, #59, Section 1, Chung-Hwa Road,Taipei 100 Taiwan, R.O.C.. Tel: (8862) 2311 3238. FAX: (8862) 2311 8526.
GENERAL. MANAGER
Eric Shih

THAILAND
Warner Bros. (Far East) Inc./20th Century-Fox Thailand, 6th Flr., Rm. 603, South East Insurance Building, 315 Silom Road, Bangkok 10500 Thailand. Tel: (662) 631 1218. FAX: (662) 236 4834.
GENERAL. MANAGER
Henry Tran

TRINIDAD
c/o United International Pictures, Film Center, St. James, Port of Spain, Trinidad, W.I. Tel: (868) 622 4671. FAX: (868) 622 2517.
MANAGING DIRECTOR
Anthony King

TURKEY
Warner Bros. Film & Video San. Tic. A.S., Topcu Cad, Uygun Is Merkezi No. 2/6, 80090 Taksim, Istanbul, Turkey. Tel: (90212) 237 2000. FAX: (90212) 237 2600.
MANAGING DIRECTOR
Haluk Kaplanoglu

UNITED KINGDOM
Warner Bros. Distributors Ltd., Warner House 98 Theobald's Road, London WC1X 8WB, England. Tel: (4420) 7984 5200. FAX: (4420) 7984 5211.
MANAGING DIRECTOR
Nigel Sharrocks
SENIOR V.P., EUROPE, MIDDLE EAST & AFRICA
Ivan Cheah

URUGUAY
c/o Horacio Hermida Limitida, Moviecenter, Montevideo Shopping Center, Luis Alberto de Herrera 1290, 11300 Montevideo, Uruguay. Tel: (5982) 628 9077. FAX: (5982) 628 9078.
MANAGER
Cecilla Hermida de Ara

VENEZUELA
c/o Distribuidora Difox C.A., Edificio Teatro Las Palmas, 4o Piso, Avenida Las Palmas Los Caobos, Caracas 1050, Venezuela. Tel: (582) 782 2922. FAX: (582) 781 7586.
WARNER REPRESENTATIVE
Augusto Bogni

YUGOSLAVIA
c/o Tuckvision, Valikomoravska 11-15, 11000 Belgrade, Serbia, Yugoslavia. Tel: (38111) 424 666. FAX: (38111) 413 177.
MANAGING DIRECTOR
Zvonimir Djordevic

MD WAX/COURIER FILMS
(Distributor)
1560 Broadway, Ste. 706, New York, NY 10036. (212) 302-5360. FAX: (212) 302-5364.
PRESIDENT
Morton D. Wax

WEED ROAD PICTURES
4000 Warner Blvd., Bldg. 81, Ste. 115, Burbank, CA 91522. (818) 954-3771. FAX: (818) 954-3061.
email: weedroad@earthlink.net
PRODUCER
Akiva Goldsman
EXECUTIVE V.P.
Varina Bleil
DIRECTOR, DEVELOPMENT
Stephanie Gisondi
ASSISTANTS
Zack Adler
Anthony Vlasto

WEST GLEN COMMUNICATONS, INC.
(Televsion production and distribution.)
1430 Broadway, 9th Fl., New York, NY 10018. (212) 921-2800. FAX: (212) 944-9055. www.westglen.com
PRESIDENT
Stanley Zeitlin
THEATRICAL DISTRIBUTION MANAGER
Cathy Boje

WHITE WOLF PRODUCTIONS
2932 Wilshire Blvd., Ste. 201, Santa Monica, CA 90403. (310) 829-7500. FAX: (310) 586-0717.
PRESIDENT
David S. Ward

WILD CHILD ENTERTAINMENT, LTD.
(Producer of large-format motion pictures)
69 Church St., Seymour, CT 06483-2611. (203) 888-2405. FAX: (203) 888-2405. www.wildchildent.com
email: WildChildEnt@compuserve.com

WILDWOOD ENTERPRISES, INC.
1101 Montana Ave., Ste. E, Santa Monica, CA 90403. (310) 395-5155. FAX: (310) 395-3975.
OWNER
Robert Redford
PRESIDENT
Michael Nozik
CREATIVE EXECUTIVE
Per Saari
DIRECTOR, PRODUCTION
Brad Simonsen

WINKLER FILMS, INC.
211 S. Beverly Dr., #200, Beverly Hills, CA 90212. (310) 858-5780. FAX: (310) 858-5799.
CEO, PRODUCER & DIRECTOR
Irwin Winkler
PRESIDENT
Rob Cowan

WINSOME PICTURES, INC.
843 S. Sierra Bonita Ave., Los Angeles, CA 90036-4703. (323) 934-9943. email: winpix@usa.net
WRITER & PRODUCER
Ross LaManna
EXECUTIVE V.P., BUSINESS AFFAIRS
Lynn LaManna
V.P., DEVELOPMENT
Kathleen Rose

WINSTAR TELEVISION & VIDEO
(Formerly Fox Lorber Associates, Inc; TV & video distribution)
419 Park Ave. S., 20th Flr., New York, NY 10016. (212) 686-6777. FAX: (212) 685-2625. www.winstartelevid.com
PRESIDENT
Al Cattabiani
CO-CHAIRMAN
Richard Lorber
EXECUTIVE V.P. & GENERAL MANAGER, INTL. SALES
Sheri Levine
SENIOR DIRECTOR, MARKETING
Paul Freehauf
DIRECTOR, INTERNATIONAL SALES
Linda saetre
SENIOR V.P., ACQUISITIONS
Krysanne Katsoolis
DIRECTOR, MARKETING & CREATIVE SERVICES
Kimberly Rubin

RALPH WINTER PRODUCTIONS
1201 W. Fifth St., Maryland Bldg., M215, Los Angeles, CA 90017. (213) 534-3654. FAX: (213) 534-3078.
email: rwinter195@aol.com
PRODUCER
Ralph Winter

WITT-THOMAS FILMS
4000 Warner Blvd., Producers 3, Rm. 20, Burbank, CA 91522. (818) 954-2545. FAX: (818) 954-2660.
PRODUCERS
Paul Junger Witt
Tony Thomas
Edward L. McDonnell
DIRECTOR, DEVELOPMENT
Tony Witt

THE WOLPER ORGANIZATION
4000 Warner Blvd., Bldg. 14, Rm. X, Burbank, CA 91522-0001. (818) 954-1421. FAX: (818) 954-1593.
CHAIRMAN
David L. Wolper
PRESIDENT & EXECUTIVE PRODUCER
Mark M. Wolper
V.P., DEVELOPMENT
Kevin Nicklaus
STORY EDITOR
Mura Hussain

WORKING TITLE FILMS
(Film production)
9720 Wilshire Blvd., Beverly Hills, CA 90212. (310) 777-3100. FAX: (310) 777-5243.
CHAIRMEN
Tim Bevan
Eric Fellner

WORLD FILM SERVICES, INC.
630 Fifth Ave., Ste. 1505, New York, NY 10111. (212) 632-3456. FAX: (212) 632-3457.
CEO
John Heyman
VICE PRESIDENT
Pamela Osowski
CANADA
Roy Krost

WORLDVIEW ENTERTAINMENT, INC.
The Killiam Collection, 145 W 55th St., Ste. 7-D, New York, NY 10019. (212) 247-8464. FAX: (212) 925-2314.
email: birnhak@aol.com
CHAIRMAN & CEO
Sandra J. Birnhak
PRESIDENT
Glenn E. Shealey

WYCHWOOD PRODUCTIONS
940 N. Mansfield Ave., Hollywood, CA 90038. (323) 462-6400. FAX: (323) 465-6709.
DIRECTOR & PRODUCER
Simon West
V.P., DEVELOPMENT
Jib Polhemus

THE WYLE/KATZ COMPANY
4000 Warner Blvd., Bldg.138, Ste. 1201, Burbank, CA 91522. (818) 954-7440. FAX: (818) 954-1846.
PRODUCER
James Katz
ACTOR & PRODUCER
Noah Wyle
DIRECTOR, DEVELOPMENT
Marlene Noble

WYMAN/SULLIVAN PRODUCTIONS

144 S. Beverly Dr., #505, Beverly Hills, CA 90212. (310) 858-7111. FAX: (310) 858-0852.
email: bradlauren@wyman-management.com
PRESIDENT, PRODUCTION
Tim Sullivan
PRESIDENT, PRODUCTION
Brad Wyman
DIRECTOR, DEVELOPMENT
Karen Jacobs

YAK YAK PICTURES

4000 Warner Blvd., Bldg. 138, Rm. 1202, Burbank, CA 91522. (818) 954-6264. FAX: (818) 954-1614.
DIRECTOR & PRODUCER
Mimi Leder
V.P., DEVELOPMENT
Jill Arthur
CREATIVE EXECUTIVE
A.J. Marcantonio
ASSISTANT
Bob Merrick

YORKTOWN PRODUCTIONS, INC.

3000 Olympic Blvd., Bldg. 2, Ste. 2465, Santa Monica, CA 90404. (310) 264-4155. FAX: (310) 264-4167.
DIRECTOR & PRODUCER
Norman Jewison
CREATIVE EXECUTIVE
Dianne Hatlestad

SAUL ZAENTZ FILM CENTER

2600 Tenth St., Berkeley, CA 94710. (510) 486-2100. FAX: (510) 486-2115.
www.zaentz-filmcenter.com
PRESIDENT
Saul Zaentz
GENERAL MANAGER
Steve Shurtz
MANAGER
Scott Roberts

THE ZANUCK COMPANY

(Producer of theatrical motion pictures)
9465 Wilshire Blvd., Beverly Hills, CA 90212. (310) 274-0261. FAX: (310) 273-9217.
PARTNERS
Richard D. Zanuck
Lili Fini Zanuck

ZEITGEIST FILMS LTD.

(Distributor of independent films)
247 Centre St., 2nd Flr., New York, NY 10013. (212) 274-1989. FAX: (212) 274-1644. www.zeitgeistfilm.com
email: mail@zeitgeistfilm.com
CO-PRESIDENTS
Emily Russo
Nancy Gerstman

ZIDE/PERRY ENTERTAINMENT

9100 Wilshire Blvd., Ste. 615 E., Beverly Hills, CA 90212. (310) 887-2999. FAX: (310) 887-2995. www.inzide.com
email: inzide@inzide.com
PRODUCER & MANAGER
Warren Zide
PRODUCER
Craig Perry
MANAGER
Steve Freedman
MANAGER & DIRECTOR, LITERARY ACQUISITIONS
Jennifer Frankel
DIRECTOR, DEVELOPMENT
Sheila Hanahan

ZOLLO PRODUCTIONS, INC.

257 W. 52nd St., 2nd Flr., New York, NY 10019. (212) 957-1300. FAX: (212) 957-1315.
www.members.aol.com/zpi/index.html
email: zpi@aol.com
PRODUCERS
Nicholas Paleologos
Frederick Zollo
V.P., CREATIVE AFFAIRS
Bostic Beard

ZUCKER PRODUCTIONS

1351 Fourth St., Ste. 300, Santa Monica, CA 90401. (310) 656-9200. FAX: (310) 656-9220.
DIRECTOR
Jerry Zucker
PRODUCER
Janet Zucker

ZUCKER/NETTER PRODUCTIONS

1411 Fifth St., Ste. 402, Santa Monica, CA 90401. (310) 394-1644. FAX: (310) 899-6722.
PRODUCER & DIRECTOR & WRITER
David Zucker
PRESIDENT
Gil Netter
VICE PRESIDENT
Lawrence Grey

NON-THEATRICAL MOTION PICTURE COMPANIES

Following is a list of producers, distributors and film libraries handling educational, entertainment and advertising pictures for non-theatrical distribution to schools, clubs, civic organizations, and teaching groups, as well as television.

THE AHERN GROUP
3700 Malden Ave., Baltimore, MD 21211. (410) 367-9660. FAX: (410) 367-9661. email: videoahern@aol.com
PRESIDENT/TREASURER
Donald A'Hern

BUENA VISTA NON-THEATRICAL
3900 W. Alameda Ave., #2400, Burbank, CA 91521. (818) 567-5058. FAX: (818) 557-0797.
S.V.P., NON-THEATRICAL
Linda Palmer

CAMERON PRODUCTIONS
222 Minor Ave. N., Seattle, WA 98109. (206) 623-4103. FAX: (206) 623-7256. email: cameron.productions@worldnet.att.net
PRESIDENT
R. Scott Cameron

CAROUSEL FILMS, INC.
260 Fifth Ave., New York, NY 10001. (212) 683-1660, (800) 683-1660. FAX: (212) 683-1662. email: carousel@pipeline.com
URL: http://www.carouselfilms.com
PRESIDENT
David Dash

CAVALCADE PRODUCTIONS, INC.
P.O. Box 2480, Nevada City, CA 95959-1948. Tel/FAX: (530) 477-0701. email: cavpro@nccn.net URL: http://www.nccn.net/~cavpro
PRODUER/DIRECTOR
Bruce McCulley

CIFEX CORPORATION
One Peconic Hills Ct., Southampton, NY 11968-1618. (631) 283-9454, FAX: (631) 283-4210. email: cifex@prodigy.net
PRESIDENT
Gerald J. Rappaport

CONTINENTAL FILM PRODUCTIONS CORP.
4315 North Creek Rd.,P.O. Box 5126 Chattanooga, TN 37406. (423) 622-1193. FAX: (423) 629-0853. email: cfpc@chattanooga.net. URL: http://www.continentalfilm.com
PRESIDENT
James L. Webster

CRAVEN FILM CORPORATION
5 W. 19 St., 3rd floor, New York, NY 10011-4216. (212) 463-7190. FAX: (212) 627-4761. email: TCFC@aol.com
PRESIDENT
Michael Craven

CUSTOM FILMS/VIDEO, INC.
11 Cob Dr., Westport, CT 06880. (203) 226-0300. FAX: (203) 227-9435.

FILMS FOR EDUCATORS/FILMS FOR TV
420 E. 55th St., Ste. 6-U, New York, NY 10022. (212) 486-6577. FAX: (212) 980-9826.
PRESIDENT
Harlan B. DeBell

GOLDSHOLL FILM GROUP
420 Frontage Rd., Northfield, IL 60093. (847) 446-8300. FAX: (847) 446-8320.
PRESIDENT
Harry Goldsholl

HANNA-BARBERA CARTOONS
15303 Ventura Blvd., Ste. 1400, Sherman Oaks, CA 91403. (818) 977-7500. FAX: (818) 997-7510.
PRESIDENT
Jean MacCurdy

HARDCASTLE FILMS & VIDEO
7319 Wise Ave., St. Louis, MO 63117. (314) 647-4200. FAX: (314) 647-4201.
DIRECTOR
Jeff Hardcastle

HUGH & SUZANNE JOHNSTON, INC.
16 Valley Rd., Princeton, NJ 08540. (609) 924-7505. email: suzanneandhugh@earthlink.net
PRESIDENT
Hugh Johnston

LEE MENDELSON FILM PRODUCTIONS, INC.
330 Primrose Rd., Ste 310, Burlingame, CA 94010. (650) 342-8284. FAX: (650) 342-6170.
PRESIDENT
Lee Mendelson

NFL FILMS, INC.
330 Fellowship Rd., Mt. Laurel, NJ 08054. (856) 778-1600. FAX: (856) 722-6779.
PRESIDENT
Steve Sabol

PACE FILMS, INC.
411 E. 53rd St., New York, NY 10022. (212) 755-5486.

PENFIELD PRODUCTIONS, INC.
35 Springfield St., Agawam, MA 01001. (413) 786-4454. FAX: (413) 789-4240.
PRESIDENT
Brook Ashby

PLAYHOUSE PICTURES
1401 N. La Brea Ave., Hollywood, CA 90028. (323) 851-2112. FAX: (323) 851-2117.
PRESIDENT
Ted Woolery

SWAIN FILM & VIDEO
1404 South Tuttle Ave., Sarasota, FL 34239. (941) 365-8433. FAX: (941) 365-5359. email: swain@excelonline.com
PRESIDENT
Tony Swain

SWANK MOTION PICTURES, INC.
201 S. Jefferson Ave., St. Louis, MO 63103. (314) 534-6300. FAX: (314) 289-2187. URL: http://www.swank.com
PRESIDENT
Tim Swank

T.H.A. MEDIA DISTRIBUTORS LTD.
1200 W. Pender St., Ste. #307, Vancouver, B.C., Canada V6E 2S9. (604) 687-4215. FAX: (604) 688-8349 email: tha@thamedia.com
PRESIDENT
Tom Howe

TR PRODUCTIONS, INC.
1031 Commonwealth Ave., Boston, MA 02215-1094. (617) 783-0200. FAX: (617) 783-4844.
PRESIDENT
Ross Benjamin

TEL-AIR INTEREST, INC.
2040 Sherman St., Hollywood, FL 33020. (954) 924-4949. FAX: (954) 924-4980. email: telair@aol.com
PRESIDENT
Grant H. Gravitt, Jr.

WEST GLEN COMMUNICATIONS, INC.
1430 Broadway, 9th floor, New York, NY 10018. (212) 921-2800. FAX: (212) 944-9055.
PRESIDENT
Stan Zeitlan

WEXLER FILM PRODUCTIONS, INC.
801 N. Seward St., Los Angeles, CA 90038-3601. (213) 462-6671. FAX: (213) 462-6349.

Production Services

Advertising and Publicity 706
Animation 712
Casting Directors 721
Consultants and Technical Advisors 724
Costume and Prop Rentals 726
Entertainment Lawyers 730
Film Preservation,
Processing and Repair 735
Film Stock 736
Financial Services 737
Market Research and Analysis 741
Sound Studios and Services 742
Special Effects 746
Stock Shots 753
Studio & Editing Equipment Rentals 755
Subtitles and Captions 759
Talent Agencies 760

ADVERTISING & PUBLICITY

BOB ABRAMS AND ASSOCIATES
2030 Prosser Ave., Los Angeles, CA 90025. (310) 475-7739. FAX: (310) 475-7739.
Bob Abrams

ADMARKETING, INC.
1801 Century Park East, Ste. 2000, Los Angeles, CA 90067. (310) 203-8400. FAX: (310) 277-7621. www.admarketing.com
PRESIDENT
Jack Roth

ADSPOSURE ADVERTISING SPECIALTIES
209 W. Alameda Ave., Ste. 102, Burbank, CA 91502. (818) 559-6304. FAX: (818) 563-6423.
www.adsposure.com email: mimivh@webtv.net
PRESIDENT
Mimi Van Horn

AMBERGATE ASSOCIATES
3000 W. Olympic Blvd., Santa Monica, CA 90404. (310) 264-3970. FAX (310) 264-7973. www.ambergate.net
CONTACT
Eddie Kalish

AMERICAN ASSOCIATION OF ADVERTISING AGENCIES, INC. (A.A.A.A.)
130 Battery St., Ste. 330, San Francisco, CA 94111. (415) 291-4999. FAX: (415) 291-4995.
www.aaaa.org email: jerryg@aaaa.org
EXECUTIVE V.P.
Jerry L. Gibbons

AMOROSANO ASSOCIATES
535 W. 40th St., San Pedro, CA 90731. (310) 548-8400. FAX: (310) 548-1735. email: amorprla@aol.com
CONTACT
Ken Amorosano

THE ANGELLOTTI COMPANY
12413 Ventura Court, Ste. 200, Studio City, CA 91604. (818) 506-7887. FAX: (818) 506-8822. email: Tony@angelco.clrs.com
PRESIDENT
Tony Angellotti
V.P. & SENIOR PUBLICIST
Karen Fried

ANT FARM
910 N. Sycamore Ave., Los Angeles, CA 90038. (323) 850-0700. FAX: (323) 850-0777.

APOGEE PRODUCTIONS
10000 Riverside Dr., Ste. 6, Toluca Lake, CA 91602. (818) 762-6556. FAX: (818) 762-6559.
email: ricko@apogeeproductions.com
PRESIDENT
Rick Ouellette

THE ARENAS GROUP
(specializing in the Hispanic market)
8010 Hollywood Blvd., Los Angeles, CA 90046. (323) 650-0656. FAX: (323) 650-5737. www.arenasgroup.com
PRESIDENT
Santiago Pozo

ASTHER/GOULD ADVERTISING, INC.
5900 Wilshire Blvd., 31st Flr., Los Angeles, CA 90036. (323) 931-4151. FAX: (323) 931-4548.

AXIS MEDIA
289 S. Robertson Blvd., Ste. 489, Beverly Hills, CA 90211. (310) 478-4944. FAX: (310) 478-3036. www.axismedia.com
CONTACT
Sean Olson

JANE AYER PUBLIC RELATIONS, INC.
3204 Ocean Park Blvd., Ste. 240, Santa Monica, CA 90405. (310) 581-1330. FAX: (310) 581-1335. email: japr@aol.com

N.W. AYER & PARTNERS
Worldwide Plaza, 825 Eighth Ave., New York, NY 10019-7498. (212) 474-5000. FAX: (212) 474-5400.
CEO
Mary Lou Quinlan

BABLOVE AGENCY, INC.
2980 N. Campbell St., Ste. 190, Tucson, AZ 85719, (520) 322-9060.

BACKER, SPIELVOGEL, BATES INC.
2010 Main St., Ste. 700, Irvine, CA 92614. (714) 261-0330. FAX: (714) 261-6565.

BAKER, WINOKUR, RYDER
405 S. Beverly Dr., 5th Flr., Beverly Hills, CA 90212. (310) 277-6200.
250 W. 57th St., #1610, New York, NY 10017. (212) 582-0700. FAX: (212) 582-0490.

BALLARD COMMUNICATIONS
1850 E. Flamingo Rd., Ste. 120, Las Vegas, NV 89119. (702) 836-3000, (800) 864-2792. FAX: (702) 836-3003.

BARCLAY COMMUNICATIONS
3550 N. Central, Ste. 915, Phoenix, AZ 85012. (602) 277-3550. FAX: (602) 277-1217. email: Barclay@netzone.com

BARTEL DESIGN GROUP
2820 Glendale Blvd., Los Angeles, CA 90039. (323) 662-6869. FAX: (323) 662-2026.
www.barteldesign.com email: jane@barteldesign.com
PRESIDENT & CREATIVE DIRECTOR
Jane Bartel

BBDO LOS ANGELES
10960 Wilshire Blvd., #1600, Los Angeles, CA 90024. (310) 444-4500. FAX: (310) 444-7581.

BBDO WORLDWIDE
1285 Ave. of the Americas, New York, NY 10019. (212) 459-5000.

BEAR ADVERTISING, INC.
32121 Lindero Canyon Rd., Ste. 200, Westlake Village, CA 91361. (818) 865-6464. FAX: (818) 865-6499.

BENDER, GOLDMAN & HELPER
11500 W. Olympic Blvd., Ste. 655, Los Angeles, CA 90064. (310) 473-4147.
400 Madison Ave., New York, NY 10017. (212) 371-0798. FAX: (212) 754-4380.

WALTER F. BENNETT COMMUNICATIONS
7111 Valley Green Rd., Ste. 220, Fort Washington, PA 19034. (215) 836-2727. FAX: (215) 836-2726.
PRESIDENT
Robert H. Straton

BIEDERMAN, KELLY & SHAFFER, INC.
475 Park Ave. South, New York, NY 10016. (212) 213-5500. FAX: (212) 213-4775.
CHAIRMAN
Barry Biederman

MARION BILLINGS PUBLICITY, LTD.
250 W. 57th St., #2420, New York, NY 10107. (212) 581-4493.

BLOCK-KORENBROT PUBLIC RELATIONS
8271 Melrose Ave., Rm. 115, Los Angeles, CA 90046. (323) 655-0593. FAX: (323) 655-7302. email: classicpr@aol

MICHELLE BOLTON & ASSOCIATES
100 S. Doheny Dr., #420, Los Angeles, CA 90048. (310) 273-4030. FAX: (310) 273-2640.
CONTACT
Michelle Bolton

BOZELL WORLDWIDE
40 W. 23rd St., New York, NY 10010. (212) 727-5000. FAX: (212) 645-9262. email: dbell@newyork.com
PRESIDENT & CEO
David A. Bell

BRAGMAN HYMAN CAFARELLI
9171 Wilshire Blvd., Penthouse, Beverly Hills, CA 90210. (310) 274-7800. FAX: (310) 274-7838.
email: dharris.bnc@mcimail.com
V.P., ENTERTAINMENT MARKETING
Debi Farkas Harris

BRAMSON & ASSOCIATES
7400 Beverly Blvd., Los Angeles, CA 90036. (323) 938-3595. FAX: (323) 938-0852.

THE BROKAW COMPANY
9255 Sunset Blvd., #804, Los Angeles, CA 90069. (310) 273-2060. FAX: (310) 276-4037. email: brokawc@aol.com
PARTNERS
David Brokaw
Sanford Brokaw

BUMBLE WARD & ASSOCIATES
6426 W. 82nd St., Los Angeles, CA 90045. (310) 645-8517. FAX: (310) 645-3001

LEO BURNETT COMPANY, INC.
35 W. Wacker, Chicago, IL 60601. (312) 220-5959. FAX: (312) 220-3299.
10900 Wilshire Blvd., Ste. 700, Los Angeles, CA 90024. (310) 443-2000. FAX: (310) 208-5984.
CHAIRMAN & CEO
Richard Fizdale
PRESIDENT
Jim Oats

BURSON-MARSTELLER
230 Park Ave. South, New York, NY 10003-1566. (212) 614-4000. FAX: (212) 598-6942.
1800 Century Park East Ste. 200, Los Angeles, CA 90067. (310) 226-3000. FAX: (310) 226-3030.
CHAIRMAN
Harold Burson

JON BYK ADVERTISING, INC.
140 S. Barrington Ave., Los Angeles, CA 90049. (310) 476-3012. FAX: (310) 476-3016. www.bykadertising.com
VICE PRESIDENT
Tim Byk

CAPSTONE FILM CO.
29 W. 74th St., Ste. 3B, New York, NY 10023. (212) 362-9828. FAX: (212) 362-9828.
PRESIDENT
Ed Cruea

THE CATANIA GROUP
(Advertising, publicity and trailers)
520 Washington Blvd., Ste. 641, Marina Del Rey, CA 90292. (310) 535-5815. FAX: (310) 473-2704.
email: catania@ix.netcom.com
PRESIDENT
Cirina Catania

CITIGATE, ALBERT, FRANK LAW, INC.
850 3rd Ave., New York, NY 10022. (212) 755-6841.
CHAIRMAN
Gary Goldstein
PRESIDENT
James H. Feeney

CLEIN & WHITE, INC.
8584 Melrose Ave., 2nd Flr., W. Hollywood, CA 90069. (310) 659-4141. FAX: (310) 659-3995.
HEAD OF PUBLICITY
Heather Burgett

CLICK ACTIVE MEDIA
2701 Ocean Park Blvd., Ste. 205, Santa Monica, CA 90405. (310) 581-4000. FAX: (310) 581-4004.
www.clickmedia.com email: bizdev@clickmedia.com
OFFICE MANAGER
Ty Donaldson

CLOCK-WISE
2661 S. Gravenstein Hwy., Unit 102, Sabastopol, CA 95472. (800) 969-8463, (707) 823-1382. FAX: (707) 823-8251.
www.clockwise.com email: jcl@sonic.net
PRESIDENT
Jon Liebling

CMG WORLDWIDE
10500 CrossPoint Blvd., Indianapolis, IN 46256. (317) 570-5000. FAX: (317) 570-5500.
CHARIMAN & CEO
Mark Roesler

COMMUNICATIONS PLUS, INC.
102 Madison Ave. S., New York, NY 10016. (212) 686-9570.

CONSOLIDATED ADVERTISING DIRECTORS, INC.
8060 Melrose Ave., Ste. 300, Los Angeles, CA 90046. (323) 653-8060. FAX: (323) 655-9452.
PRESIDENT
Mitchell Neal

CREATIVE PRODUCTIONS
1850 Redondo Ave., Ste. 104, Long Beach, CA 90804. (562) 985-1363. FAX: (562) 985-1365.
www.creativeproductions.com email: cpnow@aol.com
PRESIDENT & OWNER
Deborah Castro

CREATIVE RESOURCE MAVEN
P.O. Box 191183, Dallas, TX 75219. (972) 438-4085. FAX: (972) 438-5090.

AARON D. CUSHMAN & ASSOCIATES, INC.
35 E. Wacker Dr., Ste. 850, Chicago, IL 60601. (312) 263-2500. FAX: (312) 263-1197.
380 Lexington, Ste. 1700. New York, NY 10168. (212) 856-0100. FAX: (212) 551-1001.

D'ARCY, MASIUS, BENTON & BOWLES
1675 Broadway, New York, NY 10019-5809. (212) 468-3622. FAX: (212) 468-4385.
6500 Wilshire Blvd., Los Angeles, CA 90048. (323) 658-4500. FAX: (323) 658-4592.
CEO (L.A.)
Patrick Sherwood

DAVISELEN ADVERTISING, INC.
865 S. Figueroa St., 12th Flr., Los Angeles, CA 90017. (213) 688-7000. FAX: (213) 688-7288.
PRESIDENTS
Mark Davis
Bob Elen

DAZU MERCHANDISING, INC.
10859 Burbank Blvd., North Hollywood, CA 91605. (818) 506-9200. FAX: 9818) 752-9675. email: dazumerch@earthlink.net
PRESIDENT
Ruben Mamann

DENNIS DAVIDSON & ASSOCIATES, INC.
5670 Wilshire Blvd., Ste. 700, Los Angeles, CA 90036. (323) 954-5858. FAX: (323) 954-5850.
1776 Broadway, New York, NY 10019. (212) 246-0500. FAX: (212) 246-8918.
PRESIDENT (CA)
Melanie Hodal
CONTACTS (NY)
Jeremy Walker
Mary Flanagan

DDB NEEDHAM WORLDWIDE, INC.
437 Madison Ave., New York, NY 10022. (212) 415-2000. FAX: (212) 415-3591.
CHAIRMAN & CEO
Keith Reinhard
PRESIDENT, NY
Ken Kaes

SAMANTHA DEAN & ASSOCIATES
36 W. 44th St., Ste. 1401, New York, NY 10036. (212) 391-2675. FAX: (212) 391-4913.

DENTSU, INC.
120 Broadway, Ste. 220, Santa Monica, CA 90401. (310) 899-1113. FAX: (310) 899-0113.

DOREMUS & COMPANY
200 Varick St., 11th & 12th Flrs., New York, NY 10014. (212) 366-3000. FAX: (212) 366-3632.
12100 Wilshire Blvd., Ste. 400, Los Angeles, CA 90025. (310) 207-3210. FAX: (310) 207-5444. email: cparsons@pondel.com
CONTACT (CA)
Craig A. Parsons
PRESIDENT
Carl Anderson
EXECUTIVE V.P., WORLDWIDE CREATIVE DIRECTOR
Rebecca Tudor-Foley

LARRY DORN ASSOCIATES, INC.
(Product placements)
5820 Wilshire Blvd., Ste. 306, Los Angeles, CA 90036. (323) 935-6266. FAX: (323) 935-9523.
PRESIDENT
Larry Dorn
CONTACTS
Linda Dorn-Wallerstein
Lucy Kohn

E SQUARED
215 N. Larchmont Blvd., Los Angeles, CA 90004. (323) 467-9808. FAX: (323) 467-9806.
DIRECTOR OF ACCOUNTS
John Ellis

EDELMAN PUBLIC RELATIONS WORLDWIDE
5670 Wilshire Blvd., #1500, Los Angeles, CA 90036. (323) 857-9100. FAX: (323) 857-9117.
www.edelman.com email: gdrucker@la.edelman.com
CONTACT
George Drucker

MAX EISEN
234 W. 44th St., New York, NY 10036. (212) 391-1072. FAX: (212) 391-4004.

1124 DESIGN ADVERTISING, INC.
323 Culver Blvd., Playa Vista, CA 90293. (310) 822-7855. FAX: (310) 821-1972. email: artsimms@1124design.com
CEO
Art Simms

EMA MULTIMEDIA, INC.
1800 Ave. of the Stars, Ste. 430, Los Angeles, CA 90067. (310) 277-7379.. FAX: (310) 277-7378.
www.emamulti.com email: pace@emamulti.com
CREATIVE DIRECTOR & CEO
Michael Pace

JOHN EMMERLING PRODUCTION
415 Madison Ave., New York, NY 10017. (212) 753-4700. FAX: (212) 753-4996.

ENCORE INTERNATIONAL GROUP
280 S. Beverly Dr., Penthouse, Beverly Hills, CA 90212. (310) 246-0688. FAX: (310) 246- 9038.
CONTACT
Jerry Pam

ENTERTAINMENT COMMUNICATIONS NETWORK
4370 Tujunga Ave., 2nd Flr., Studio City, CA 91604. (818) 752-1400.

EURO RSCG TATHAM
980 N. Michigan Ave., Chicago, IL 60611. (312) 337-4400. FAX: (312) 337-5930.
CHAIRMAN & CHIEF CREATIVE OFFICER
Robert H. Welke

FELDMAN PUBLIC RELATIONS
9220 Sunset Blvd., #230, Los Angeles, CA 90069. (310) 859-9062.
CONTACT
Brenda Feldman

FOOTE, CONE & BELDING COMMUNICATIONS, INC.
101 E. Erie Street, Chicago, IL 60611-2897. (312) 425-7000. FAX: (312) 425-5010.
Los Angeles: (310) 312-7000.
CHAIRMAN & CEO
Bruce Mason

B. D. FOX & FRIENDS, INC. ADVERTISING
1111 Broadway, Santa Monica, CA 90401. (310) 394-7150. FAX: (310) 393-1569. www.bdfox.com
PRESIDENT & CEO
Brian D. Fox.

FRIES MULTIMEDIA, INC.
1828 Broadway, Santa Monica, CA 90404. (310) 586-6999. FAX: (310) 586-6899. email: dyfries@aol.com
PRESIDENT
Dyanne Fries

GELFOND, GORDON ASSOCIATES
11500 Olympic Blvd., Ste. 350, Los Angeles, CA 90064. (310) 478-3600. FAX: (310) 477-4825. email: ggelfond@aol.com
PRESIDENT
Gordon Gelfond

GERBER ADVERTISING AGENCY
209 S.W. Oak St., Portland, OR 97204. (503) 221-0100. FAX: (503) 228-5315.
PRESIDENT & CEO
Duncan Strang

GOLIN/HARRIS COMMUNICATIONS
601 W. 5th St., 4th Flr., Los Angeles, CA 90071. (213) 623-4200. FAX: (213) 895-4745.
500 N. Michigan Ave., Chicago, IL 60611. (312) 729-4000.
CHAIRMAN
Al Golin
PRESIDENT & CEO
Rich Jernstedt
GENERAL MANAGER, L.A.
Fred Cook

GOOD WAG MERCHANDISING, INC.
80 8th Ave., Ste. 303, New York, NY 10011. (212) 807-5728. FAX: (212) 242-4287.

GREY ADVERTISING, INC.
777 Third Ave., New York, NY 10017. (212) 546-2000. FAX: (212) 546-1495.
6100 Wilshire Blvd., 9th Flr., Los Angeles, CA 90048. (323) 936-6060.
CHAIRMAN & CEO (NY)
Edward H. Meyer
PRESIDENT & COO (L.A.)
John Crosson
PRESIDENT & CHIEF CREATIVE OFFICER (L.A.)
Peter Mooney

GREY ENTERTAINMENT & MEDIA
875 Third Ave., New York, NY 10022. (212) 303-2400. FAX: (212) 418-3950.
3400 Riverside Dr., Ste. 150, Burbank, CA 91505. (818) 525-3000. FAX: (818) 525-3050.
EXECUTIVE V.P.
Kris Coontz

GS ENTERTAINMENT MARKETING GROUP
522 N. Larchmont Blvd., Los Angeles, CA 90004. (323) 860-0270. FAX: (323) 860-0279.
CONTACT
Steven Zeller

GUTTMAN ASSOCIATES
118 S. Beverly Dr., Ste. 201, Beverly Hills, CA 90212. (310) 246-4600. FAX: (310) 246-4601.

HANSON & SCHWAM
9350 Wilshire Blvd., Ste. 315, Beverly Hills, CA 90212. (310) 248-4488. FAX: (310) 248-4499.

HILL & NOLTON
466 Lexington Ave., New York, NY 10017. (212) 885-0300.

BERNARD HODES ADVERTISING
555 Madison Ave., New York, NY 10022. (212) 758-2600. FAX: (212) 751-6278.
Los Angeles: (310) 575-4000. FAX: (310) 450-7208.
VICE PRESIDENT
Susan Edwards

NATHALIE HOFFMAN & ASSOCIATES
429 Santa Monica Blvd., Ste. 620, Santa Monica, CA 90401. (310) 656-3430. FAX: (310) 656-3425.
email: entlawla@aol.com

THE HOLLYWOOD-MADISON GROUP
11684 Ventura Blvd., Ste. 258, Studio City, CA 91604. (818) 762-8008. FAX: (818) 762-8089.
www.hollywood-madison.com
email: info@hollywood-madison.com
CONTACT
Jonathan Holiff

HORIZON MEDIA, INC.
1801 Century Park East, Ste. 480, Los Angeles, CA 90067. (310) 282-0909. FAX: (310) 277-9692.

HUTCHINS/YOUNG & RUBICAM
400 Midtown Tower, Rochester, NY 14604. (716) 546-6480. FAX: (716) 325-0360.
PRESIDENT & CEO
M.A. Sapos

IMAGINARY FORCES
6526 Sunset Blvd., Hollywood, CA 90028. (323) 957-6888. FAX: (323) 957-9577. www.imaginaryforces.com

INDEPENDENT MEDIA WEST, INC.
10100 Santa Monica Blvd., Ste. 270, Los Angeles, CA 90067. (310) 556-2455. FAX: (310) 556-2164.

INFOMERCIAL SOLUTIONS, INC.
5512 Meadow Vista Way, Agoura Hills, CA 91301. (818) 879-1140. FAX: (818) 879-1148. www.infomercialsolutions.com
CONTACT
David Schwartz

INTER/MEDIA ADVERTISING
15910 Ventura Blvd., Ste. 1010, Encino, CA 91435. (818) 995-1455.

INTERNATIONAL COMMUNICATIONS GROUP, INC.
1925 Century Park East, Ste. 1850, Los Angeles, CA 90067. (310) 557-2585. FAX: (310) 557-3009. www.icg-media.com
CONTACT
Andrew Butcher

INTERNATIONAL MEDIA & ADVERTISING GROUP IN ENTERTAINMENT (I.M.A.G.E.)
P.O. Box 20105, Raleigh, NC 27619. (919) 875-1185. FAX: (919) 875-1196. www.ImageMediaGroup.com
PRESIDENT & CEO
Chris Johnson

INTERNET IMPACT
P.O. Box 10207, Beverly Hills, CA 90213. (310) 962-7949.
www.internetimpact.com
SENIOR CONSULTANT
Ty Dehkhoda

JENSEN COMMUNICATIONS, INC.
230 E. Union St., Pasadena, CA 91101. (626) 585-9575. FAX: (626) 564-8920.

KAISER COMMUNICATIONS, INC
15928 Ventura Blvd., Ste. 117, Encino, CA 91436. (818) 380-0140. FAX: (818) 380-0147.
PRESIDENT
David Kaiser

KAISER MCEUEN, INC.
1631 Pontius Ave., Los Angeles, CA 90025. (310) 479-8999. FAX: (310) 479-8006.

KAUFER MILLER COMMUNICATIONS
1750 112th Ave., NE, Ste. D-154. Bellevue, WA 98004. (206) 450 - 9965. FAX: (206) 450-9963. email: marketing@kmcomm.com
V.P., MARKETING
Rusty Citron

HENRY J. KAUFMAN & ASSOCIATES, INC.
2233 Wisconsin Ave. N.W., Washington, DC 20007. (202) 333-0700.
PRESIDENT & CEO
Michael G. Carberry

KETCHUM COMMUNICATIONS, INC.
340 Main St., 2nd Flr., Venice, CA 90291. (310) 314-9000.

LANDIN MEDIA, INC.
3033 N. 44 St., #375, Phoenix, AZ 85018-7229. (602) 348-9225. FAX: (602) 553-4090.
PRESIDENT & CEO
Larry L. Cummings

BILL LANESE ADVERTISING & PUBLIC RELATIONS
33 New Montgomery, Ste. 1200, San Francisco, CA 94105. (415) 543-8000. FAX: (415) 543-7765.
1809 7th Ave. Ste. 1008, Seattle, WA 98101. (206) 343-8000. FAX: (206) 682-2877.

LEE & ASSOCIATES, INC.
145 S. Fairfax Ave., Los Angeles, CA 90036. (323) 938-3300. FAX: (323) 938-3305.
CONTACT
Leo Pearlstein

LEVINSON ASSOCIATES
(International marketing support)
1440 Veteran Ave., Ste. 650, Los Angeles, CA 90024. (323) 663-6940. FAX: (323) 663-2820. email: leviinc@aol.com
PRESIDENT
Robert S. Levinson
CONTACT
Jed Leland, Jr.

LIPPIN GROUP INC.
6100 Wilshire Blvd., #400, Los Angeles, CA 90048. (323) 965-1990. FAX: (323) 965-1993.
PRESIDENT
Richard Lippin

TED LOR ENTERTAINMENT MARKETING
(Consultant)
4465 Nogales Dr., Tarzana, CA 91356. (818) 776-8035. FAX: (818) 776-8108. email: tedlor@aol.com
PRESIDENT
Eugene Cofsky

THE LYON GROUP, INC.
P.O. Box 158, Malibu, CA 90265. (310) 456-3199. FAX: (310) 456-8019. email: LyonGrp@aol.com

MACY & ASSOCIATES
515 Boccaccio Ave., Venice, CA 90291. (310) 821-5300. FAX: (310) 821-8178. www.macyinc.com

MARCUS ADVERTISING, INC.
Landmark Center, 25700 Science Park Dr., Cleveland, OH 44122. (216) 292-4700. FAX: (216) 831-6189.
CHAIRMAN & CEO
Donald M. Marcus

MARKETING COMMUNICATIONS SERVICES
5217 Oliva Ave., Lakewood, CA 90712. (562) 630-8439. FAX: (562)-546-3018.
PRESIDENT
Bill Ormsby

MARKHAM/NOVELL COMMUNICATIONS, LTD.
4311 Wilshire Blvd., Ste. 419, Los Angeles, CA 90010. (323) 634-5434. FAX: (323) 634-5420. email: mnovella@aol.com
SENIOR V.P.
Patricia O'Brien Fine
211 E. 43rd St., Ste. 1102, New York, NY 10017. (212) 687-1765, (800) 762-4761. FAX: (212) 687-1978.
CONTACT
Arthur Novell

MARLIN ENTERTAINMENT GROUP
767 3rd Ave., 14th Flr., New York, NY 10017. (212) 888-5890. FAX: (212) 888-5896.

MATSON ADVERTISING
1304 Desoto Ave., Ste. 400, Tampa, FL 33606. (813) 254-8610. FAX: (813) 253-0858.
www.matsonadagency.com email: matson@gte.net

McCANN-ERICKSON, INC.
750 Third Ave., New York, NY 10017. (212) 697-6000.
6300 Wilshire Blvd., Ste. 2100, Los Angeles, CA 90048. (323) 655-9420.
CHAIRMAN
John Dooner
PRESIDENT, NORTH AMERICA
Don Dillon

MINDSHARE MEDIA
369 San Miguel Dr., Newport Beach, CA 92660. (949) 222-6490. FAX: (949) 717-6463. www.msmedia.com

DAVID MIRISCH
2824 La Costa Ave., Rancho La Costa, CA 92009. (760) 632-7770. FAX: (760) 632-5408. www.davidmirisch.com

MOMENTUM INTERNATIONAL MARKETING MANAGEMENT
P.O. Box 5889, Sherman Oaks, CA 91413. (818) 752-4500. FAX: (818) 752-4554.

MOROCH & ASSOCIATES
3625 N. Hall St., #1200, Dallas, TX 75219. (214) 520-9700. FAX: (214) 520-6464.
CHAIRMAN
Tom Moroch

MOTION PICTURE PLACEMENT
(Product placement and promotional tie-ins)
10 Universal City Plaza, Ste. 2000, Universal City, CA 91608. (310) 858-1173. FAx: (818) 754-0048.
email: JHenrie@msn.com
PRINCIPAL
Joel Henrie

JULIAN MYERS PUBLIC RELATIONS
2040 Ave. of the Stars, 4th Flr., Century City, CA 90067. (310) 557-1525. FAX: (310) 557-0133. email: jmyerspr@soca.com
CEO & OWNER
Julian Myers

MYRIAD ENTERTAINMENT
8170 Beverly Blvd., Ste. 106, Los Angeles, CA 90048. (213) 651-5001. FAX: (213) 651-3323. email: myriad-la@msn.com
VICE PRESIDENT
Steven Jensen

NATIONWIDE ADVERTISING SERVICE, INC.
15303 Ventura Blvd., Ste. 1050, Sherman Oaks, CA 91403. (818) 906-3313.

NEALE ADVERTISING ASSOCIATES
10201 Riverside Dr., Ste. 200, Toluca Lake, CA 91602. (818) 508-7003. FAX: (818) 508-3141. email: Neale9@idt.net
PRESIDENT
Ted Neale

NEW WAVE ENTERTAINMENT
2660 W. Olive Ave., Burbank, CA 91505. (818) 295-5000. FAX: (818) 295-5001.
PRESIDENT
Allan Haines

OGILVY & MATHER, INC.
309 W. 49th St., New York, NY 10019. (212) 237-4000. FAX: (212) 237-5123.
11766 Wilshire Blvd., Ste. 900, Los Angeles, CA 90025. (310) 996-0400. FAX: (310) 996-0492.
CHAIRMAN EMERITUS
Charlotte Beers

OLMOS MARKETING
1551 4th Ave., Ste. 503, San Diego, CA 92101. (619) 238-1239. FAX: (619) 238-9878. email: elichavez@aol.com
PRESIDENT
Elida Chavez

DALE C. OLSON & ASSOCIATES
7420 Mulholland Dr., Los Angeles, CA 90046. Tel/FAX: (323) 876-9331. email: dolson2000@aol.com
PRESIDENT
Dale Olson

PARROT COMMUNICATIONS INTERNATIONAL, INC.
2917 N. Ontario St., Burbank, CA 91504. (818) 567-4700. FAX: (818) 567-4699.
www.parrotmedia.com email: info@parrotmedia.com
PRESIDENT & CEO
Robert Mertz

PASADENA ADVERTISING
51 W. Dayton St., Ste. 100, Pasadena, CA 91105. (626) 584-0011. FAX: (626) 584-0907.
www.pasadenaadv.com email: accts@pasadenaadv.com

PLA MEDIA WEST
11959 Hatteras St., North Hollywood, CA 91607. (818) 761-7171. FAX: (818) 761-7175.
www.plamedia.com email: plamediaw@aol.com
1303 16th Ave., South Nashville, TN 37212. (615) 327-0100. FAX: (615) 320-1061.

PMK, INC.
955 Carrillo Dr., Ste. 200, Los Angeles, CA 90048. (213) 954-4000. FAX: (213) 954-4011.
1775 Broadway, New York, NY 10019. (212) 582-1111. FAX: (212) 582-6666.

THE POLLACK PR MARKETING GROUP
1901 Ave. of the Stars, Ste. 1040, Los Angeles, CA 90067. (310) 556-4443. FAX: (310) 286-2350.
PRESIDENT
Noemi Pollack.

PORTER/NOVELLI
10960 Wilshire Blvd., #800, Los Angeles, CA 90024. (310) 444-7000.
437 Madison Ave., 12th Flr., New York, NY 10022. (212) 872-8000.

P.O.V.
12248 Santa Monica Blvd., Ste. B, Los Angeles, CA 90025. (310) 207-8584. FAX: (310) 207-8524. email: 1pov@earthlink.net
PRESIDENT
Duane Meltzer

PR NEWSWIRE
865 S. Figueroa St., Ste. 2310, Los Angeles, CA 90017. (800) 321-8169, (213) 626-5500. FAX: (213) 488-1152. www.prnewswire.com email: lisa_lamprich@prnewswire.com
NATIONAL MARKET MANAGER, ENTERTAINMENT
Lisa Lamprich

PUBLIC RELATIONS ASSOCIATES
557 Norwich Dr., Los Angeles, CA 90048. (310) 659-0380. FAX: (310) 659-5270.

PUBLICITY WEST
2155 Ridgemont Dr., Los Angeles, CA 90046. (213) 654-3816. FAX: (213) 654-3816.

THE RALEIGH GROUP
1223 Wilshire Blvd., Ste. 502, Santa Monica, CA 90403. (310) 209-0990

REGBERG & ASSOCIATES, INC.
10850 Wilshire Blvd., Ste. 301, Los Angeles, CA 90024. (310) 475-5735. FAX: (310) 470-3101.
PRESIDENT
Scott Regberg

RESPONSE MARKETING
32123 W. Lindero Canyon Rd., 3rd Flr., Westlake Village, CA 91364. (818) 224-2050. www.responsemarketing.com email: info@responsemarketing.com
PRESIDENT
Robert Haukoos

RNF MEDIA CORPORATION, INC.
9440 Santa Monica Blvd., Ste 710, Beverly Hills, CA 90210. (310) 273-2912. FAX: (310) 276-8950.

ROGERS & COWAN
1888 Century Park East, Ste. 500, Los Angeles, CA 90067-1709. (310) 201-8800. FAX: (310) 552-0412.
475 Park Ave. S., 32nd Flr., New York, NY 10016. (212) 779-3500. FAX: (212) 447-9630.

STAN ROSENFIELD PUBLIC RELATIONS, LTD
2029 Century Park East, Ste. 1240, Los Angeles, CA 90067. (310) 286-7474. FAX: (310) 286-2255.
375 Greenwich St., Ste. 700, New York, NY 10013. (212) 941-3999. FAX: (212) 941-3997.

RUDEHONEY DESIGN GROUP
30181 Cuthbert Rd., Ste. 100, Malibu, CA 90265. (310) 589-9640. FAX: (310) 589-2585. www.rudehoney.com
V.P., SALES
Frank Celecia

SAATCHI & SAATCHI ADVERTISING
375 Hudson St., New York, NY 10014-3620. (212) 463-2000. FAX: (212) 463-9855.
CEO, WORLDWIDE
Kevin Roberts
CHAIRMAN & CEO, NORTH AMERICA
Jennifer Lang

SAATCHI & SAATCHI/THE SAATCHI ENTERTAINMENT GROUP
3501 Sepulveda Blvd., Torrance, CA 90505. (310) 214-6000. FAX: (310) 214-6160.
PRESIDENT
Scott Gilbert

SAGON-PHIOR GROUP
13425 Ventura Blvd., 2nd Flr., Sherman Oaks, CA 91423. (818) 380-0280. FAX: (818) 380-0325.

SAM COMMUNICATIONS
5252 Coldwater Canyon. Ste. 208, Sherman Oaks, CA 91401. (818) 762-0068. FAX: (818) 506-8571.

SCREENVISION CINEMA NETWORK
6601 Center Dr. West, Ste. 500, Los Angeles, CA 90045. (310) 342-8240.
597 5th Ave., 7th Flr., New York, NY 10017. (212) 752-5774. FAX: (212) 752-0086.

NANCY SELTZER & ASSOCIATES
1775 Broadway, New York, NY 10019. (212) 307-0117. FAX: (212) 307-0182.

SGI MARKETING
18034 Ventura Blvd., Ste. 275, Encino, CA 91316. (818) 343-3669.
PRESIDENT
Brian Scott

SIMONS MICHELSON ZIEVE, INC.
900 Wilshire Dr., Troy, MI 48084-1600. (313) 362-4242. FAX: (313) 362-2014.
CHAIRMAN
Morton Zieve

SOUTH BAY STUDIOS
20434 S. Santa Fe Ave., Long Beach, CA 90810. (310) 762-1360.
CONTACT
Dana Bromley

SMOKE & MIRRORS PUBLIC RELATIONS
10200 Culver Blvd., Culver Citry, CA 90232. (310) 204-4404. FAX: (310) 204-4408.
OWNER
Rochelle Winters

THE SPARK FACTORY
1601 Colorado Ave., Santa Monica, CA 90640. (310) 829-4549. FAX: (310) 829-4539.
PRODUCER
Robert Teimowitz

SPELLING COMMUNICATIONS
1180 S. Beverly Dr., Ste. 601, Los Angeles, CA 90035. (310) 277-8811. FAX: (310) 277-8106.
www.spellcom.com email: info@spellcom.com
CEO
Daniel Spelling

SPLASH RADIO
8391 Beverly Blvd., Ste. 310, Los Angeles, CA 90048. (323) 655-5495. FAX: (323) 655-1011. www.splashradio.com
PRESIDENT
Eric Poole

SSA PUBLIC RELATIONS
16027 Ventura Blvd., Ste. 206, Encino, CA 91436. (818) 501-0700. FAX: (818) 501-7216. www.ssapr.com
245 5th Ave., Ste. 903, New York, NY 10016. (212) 679-4750. FAX: (212) 679-4725.
PRESIDENT
Steve Syatt

STUDIO CITY
3330 Cahuenga Blvd., Los Angeles, CA 90068. (818) 557-7777. FAX: (818) 557-6777. www.studiocity.com
PRESIDENT
Stu Weiss

SUDLER & HENNESSEY, INC.
1633 Broadway, New York, NY 10019. FAX: (212) 969-5991. FAX: (212) 969-5991.
CHAIRMAN & CEO
Jed Beitler
PRESIDENT
Barbara Renta

TAFFETDESIGN, INC.
530 Wilshire Blvd., Ste. 200, Santa Monica, CA 90401. (310) 451-7444. FAX: (310) 451-7421 www.taffetdesign.com
CREATIVE DIRECTOR
Jill Taffet

TANZANITE PRODUCTIONS
2118 Wilshire Blvd., Ste. 176, Santa Monica, CA 90403. (310) 281-8139. FAX: (310) 828-0427.
SENIOR V.P., SALES & DEVELOPMENT
Maria Laing

TARGET ENTERPRISES
16501 Ventura Blvd., Ste. 515, Encino, CA 91436. (818) 905-0005. FAX: (818) 905-1444.

T.G.I.F. PRODUCTIONS
310 Washington Blvd., Ste. 106, Marina Del Rey, CA 90292. (310) 314-1111. FAX: (310) 314-1115. www.tgifproductions.com
CONTACT
Grant Simmons

30SIXTY DESIGN, INC.
2801 Cahunega Blvd. West, Los Angeles, CA 90068. (323) 850-5311.

J. WALTER THOMPSON COMPANY
466 Lexington Ave., New York, NY 10017. (212) 210-7000. FAX: (212) 210-6889.
6500 Wilshire Blvd., Ste. 2100, Los Angeles, CA 90048. (323) 951-1500.
CHAIRMAN & CEO
Chris Jones

TIERNEY & PARTNERS
200 S. Broad St., Philadelphia, PA 19102. (215) 790-4100. FAX: (215) 790-4363.
PRESIDENT & CEO
Brian P. Tierney
S.V.P., MEDIA DIRECTOR
Molly K. Watson

TIGERMARK—THE DISPLAY SOURCE, INC.
188 W. Techonology, Ste. D, Irvine, CA 92618. (714) 557-7779, (800) 972-3022. FAX: (714) 557-7837.
PRESIDENT
Marie L. Titolo

TMG INTERNATIONAL
499 N. Canon Dr., Penthouse, Beverly Hills, CA 90210. (310) 887-7077. FAX: (310) 887-7078.

TOTAL CREATIVE
8360 Melrose Ave., 3rd Flr., Los Angeles, CA 90069. (323) 655-2300. FAX: (323) 655-9159.

TRACY-LOCKE ADVERTISING, INC.
200 Crescent Ct., Box 50129, Dallas, TX 75250. (214) 969-9000.
PRESIDENT & CEO
Bruce Orr

TRI-ELITE ENTERTAINMENT, LTD.
9244 Wilshire Blvd., Beverly Hills, CA 90212. (310) 285-9743. FAX: (310) 285-9770.
PRESIDENT
Jarvee E. Hutcherson

TUCKER WAYNE/LUCKIE & CO.
1100 Peachtree St., N.E., Ste. 1800, Atlanta, GA 30309. (404) 347-8700. FAX: (404) 347-8800.
CHAIRMAN & CEO
Knox Massey, Jr.
PRESIDENT
Sidney L. Smith

VANGUARD PRODUCTIONS
PO Box 931497, Hollywood, CA 90093. (310) 772-8212.
DIRECTOR, PROMOTION & PUBLICITY
Maverick

VISTA GROUP
805 S. San Fernando Blvd., Burbank, CA 91502. (818) 840-6789. FAX: (818) 840-6880. www.vistagroupusa.com
DIRECTOR OF CLIENT SERVICES
Eric Dahlquist, Jr.

WANG & WILLIAMS
11400 W. Olympic Blvd., 2nd Flr., Los Angeles, CA 90064. (310) 312-0061. FAX: (310) 312-0082.
CONTACT
Ming Wang

MORTON D. WAX PUBLIC RELATIONS
1560 Broadway, New York, NY 10019. (212) 302-5360. FAX: (212) 302-5364.
email: mortwax@worldnet.att.net
PRESIDENT
Morton D. Wax

WESTERN PRODUCT PLACEMENT
8544 Sunset Blvd., Los Angeles, CA 90069. (310) 659-5711. FAX: (310) 659-0271.
DIRECTOR OF ACCOUNT SERVICES
Jason R. Ballance
DIRECTOR OF BUSINESS DEVELOPMENT
David M. Mansfield

WOLF GROUP
1350 Euclid Ave., Cleveland, OH 44115. (216) 241-2141. FAX: (216) 479-2437.
PRESIDENT & EXECUTIVE CREATIVE DIRECTOR
Jerry Preyss
V.P., DIRECTOR OF BROADCAST PRODUCTION
Ginny Carmichael

WORD OF MOUTH CREATIVE
19 W. 21st St., Ste. 1105, New York, NY 10010. (212) 924-8359. FAX: (212) 924-8426.
PRESIDENT
Olivia Olkowski

WORTH MENTIONING PUBLIC RELATIONS
8231 De Longpre Ave., Ste. 1, West Hollywood, CA 90046. (323) 656-6545.

YOUNG & RUBICAM, INC.
285 Madison Ave., New York, NY 10017-6486. (212) 210-3000. FAX (212) 490-9073.
CHAIRMAN & CEO
Edward Vick

ZERO 2 60
121 W. 27th St., New York, NY 10001. (212) 807-7123.

ANIMATION

ANIMATION EQUIPMENT

CATALINA GRAPHIC FILMS
27001 Agoura Rd., Ste. 100, Alabasas Hills, CA 91301. (818) 880-8060. FAX: (818) 880-1144.

CHARACTER BUILDERS, INC.
1476 Manning Parkway, Powell, OH 43065. (614) 885-2211. FAX: (614) 885-3873. www.cbuilders.com
EXECUTIVE PRODUCER
Leslie Hough

CHROMACOLOUR INTERNATIONAL
1410 28th St. N.E., Calgary, Alberta T2A 7W6, Canada. (403) 250-5880. FAX: (403) 250-7194.

CINEMA ENGINEERING COMPANY
7243 Atoll Ave., Ste. A, North Hollywood, CA 91605. (818) 765-5340. FAX: (818) 765-5349. www.cinema-engineering.com
PRESIDENT
Richard Bennett

DISNEY-MGM STUDIOS
Box 10200, Film-TV Dept., Bungalow 2, Lake Buena Vista, FL 32830. (407) 560-5736. FAX: (407) 824-5168.
VICE PRESIDENT
Bob Allen

FAX ANIMATION COMPANY
5625 Melrose Ave., Hollywood, CA 90038. (323) 466-3561. FAX: (323) 871-2193. www.alangordon.com
CONTACT
Grant Loncks

GLOCOM PRODUCTS, INC.
(Digital asset management)
23945 Calabasas Rd., Calabasas, CA 91302. (818) 591-2177. FAX: (818) 591-2150. www.glocom.com
V.P., BUSINESS DEVELOPMENT
Harsh Deshpande

INTERGRAPH COMPUTER SYSTEMS
1 Madison Industrial Park, Hunstville, AL 35894. (800) 763-0242. FAX: (205) 730-6445. www.intergraph.com

LINKER SYSTEMS
13612 Onkayha Circle, Irvine, CA 92620. (949) 552-1904. FAX: (949) 552-6985. www.linker.com
CONTACT
Toni Poper

OCS/PIXEL MAGIC
10635 Riverside Dr., Toluca Lake, CA 91602. (818) 760-0862. FAX: (818) 760-0483. www.pixelmagicfx.com
VICE PRESIDENT
Ray McIntyre Jr.

OPTICAL EFFECTS & PHOTOGRAPHY, CEL, CLAY AND DIGITAL ANIMATION

AARDMAN ANIMATIONS
Gas Ferry Rd., Bristol, Avon BS1 6UN. Tel: (0117) 984 8485. FAX: (0117) 984-8486. www.aardman.com
FOUNDERS
David Sproxton
Peter Lord
CONTACT
Lisa Murphy

AARGH! ANIMATION, INC.
(Hand drawn cel and stop-motion animation)
8137 LK Crowell Circle, Ste. 101, Orlando, FL 32836. (407) 307-3190. FAX: (407) 370-2602. www.storyboards-east.com
DIRECTOR
Dave Kallaher

ABBY LOU ENTERTAINMENT
1411 Edgehill Pl., Pasadena, CA 91103. (818) 795-7334. FAX: (818) 795-4013. email: ALE@Full-Moon.com
PRESIDENT & CEO
George LaFave

ACME FILMWORKS
6525 Sunset Blvd., Garden Ste. 10, Hollywood, CA 90028. (323) 464-7805. FAX: (323) 464-6614.
www.awm.com/acmefilmworks email: ron@awm.com
EXECUTIVE PRODUCER
Ron Diamond

ACORN ENTERTAINMENT
1800 N. Vine St., Ste. 305, Hollywood, CA 90028. (818) 340-5272. www.acornentertainment.com
PRESIDENT
Thad Weinlein

ALICE ENTERTAINMENT
2986 Baseline Ave., Santa Ynez, CA 93460. (805) 688-1523. FAX: (805) 688-7934. email: aliceranch@aol.com
1539 Sawtelle Blvd., Ste. 4, Los Angeles, CA 90025. (310) 231-1050. FAX: (310) 231-1159.
PRESIDENT & CEO
Alice Donenfeld

DAVID ALLEN PRODUCTIONS
(Stop-motion animation & puppets)
918 W. Oak St., Burbank, CA 91506. (818) 845-9270. FAX: (818) 567-4954.
CONTACT
Chris Endicott

ANGEL FILMS
(Computer generated)
967 Highway 40, New Franklin, MO 65274-9778. (573) 698-3900. FAX: (573) 698-3900. email: AngelFilm@aol.com
PRESIDENT
Arlene Hulse
CEO & CFO
Joyce L. Chow
V.P., PRODUCTION
Matthew P. Eastman

ANIMAL MAKERS
12473 Gladstone Ave., Unit A, Lake View Terrace, CA 91342. (818) 838-3440. FAX: (818) 838-3441.
www.animalmakers.com email: jim@animalmakers.com

ANIMATICS & STORYBOARDS, INC.
(Live action and animated storyboards, animatics and web animation)
8137 Lake Crowell Circle, Ste. 102, Orlando, FL 32836. (407) 370-2673. FAX: (407) 370-2602.
PRESIDENT
Mark Simon

ANIME COMICS & MOVIES
590 Hewitt Dr., Orlando, FL 32807. (407) 282-5564. FAX: (407) 384-0340. www.animecomics.com
PRESIDENT
Nahid Avaregan

ANIMOTION
501 W. Fayette St., Syracuse, NY 13204. (315) 471-3533. FAX: (315) 471-2730. email: animotion@aol.com
CONTACTS
David Hicock
Larry Royer

ARC SCIENCE SIMULATIONS
306 N. Washington Ave., Box 1955, Loveland, CO 80537. (970) 667-1168. FAX: (970) 667-1105. www.arcscience.com
PRESIDENT
Tom Ligon

ASTRALTECH, INC.
2101 Rue Ste. Catherine Ouest, Montreal, Quebec, H3HY 1M6. (514) 939-5060. FAX: (514) 939-5070.
email: belleros@astral.com
PRESIDENT
Hubert Harel
DIRECTOR, MARKETING, SALES & CUSTOMER SERVICE
Paul Bellerose

ATOMIX, INC.
1800 N. Vine St., Ste. 310, Hollywood, CA 90028. (310) 962-4745. FAX: (323) 962-3206. www.tomix.com
PRESIDENT & CEO
Chris Mitchell

BACKGROUND ANIMATION
720 N. Franklin, Ste. 400, Chicago, IL 60610. (312) 664-4580.
EXECUTIVE PRODUCER
Harriet Katz

BAER ANIMATION COMPANY, INC.
(Specialists in integrating animation with live-action and CGI)
7743 Woodrow Wilson Dr., Los Angeles, CA 90046-1211. (323) 874-9122. FAX: (323) 874-7690. www.baeranimation.com
PRESIDENT
Jane Baer
VICE PRESIDENT
Hope Parker

BAGDASARIAN PRODUCTIONS
1192 E. Mountain Dr., Montecito, CA 93108. (805) 969-3349. FAX: (805) 969-7466.
CHAIRMAN & CEO
Ross Bagdasarian

BBC WORLDWIDE AMERICAS
747 3rd Ave., New York, NY 10017. (212) 705-9300.
VICE PRESIDENT
Rick Siggelkow

BIFROST LASERFX
(3D animation and laser animation)
6733 Sale Ave., West Hills, CA 91307. (818) 704-0423. FAX: (818) 704-4629. email: howshore@aol.com

BLACK LOGIC
305 E. 46th St., New York, NY 10017. (212) 980-9200. FAX: (212) 754-4622. www.blacklogic.com
V.P., MARKETING
Alfie Schloss

BLUE RIVER DIGITAL
(Oxberry computer controlled animation cameras)
401 S. Flower St., Burbank, CA 91502. (818) 951-1664. FAX: (818) 951-1664. www.brdllc.com
CO-FOUNDER
Steven Benson

BLUE SKY STUDIOS
(Digital and visual effects for motion pictures & commercials)
One South Rd., Harrison, NY 10528. (914) 381-8400. FAX: (914) 381-9790. www.vifx.com email: lee@bluesky.com
ACTING EXECUTIVE PRODUCER
Carol Laufer

BLUR STUDIO, INC.
1130 Abbot Kinney Blvd., Venice, CA 90291. (310) 581-8848. FAX: (310) 581-8850. www.blur.com email: cat@blur.com
EXECUTIVE PRODUCER
Cat Chapman

BOBTOWN
2003 Canyon Drive, Hollywood, CA 90068. (323) 462-6116.
PRESIDENT
John Lamb

BOHBOT ENTERTAINMENT
41 Madison Ave., 26th Flr., New York, NY 10010. (212) 213-2700. FAX: (212) 685-8332.
PRESIDENT & CEO
Allen J. Bohbot

BOYINGTON FILM PRODUCTIONS
5907 W. Pico Blvd., Los Angeles, CA 90035. (323) 933-7500. FAX: (323) 930-3255.
OWNER
Paul Boyington

BROADWAY VIDEO DESIGN
1619 Broadway, 10th Flr., New York, NY 10019. (212) 265-7600.
V.P., SALES
Bob Koch

BRYANT & JOHNSEN, INC.
13351-D Riverside Dr., Ste. 607, Sherman Oaks, CA 91423. (818) 557-7495. FAX: 9818) 764-4949.

BUENA VISTA IMAGING
500 S. Buena Vista St., Burbank, CA 915221. (818) 560-5284. www.stu-ops.disney.com

BUZZCO ASSOCIATES, INC.
(2D animation)
33 Bleecker St., New York, NY 10012. (212) 473-8800. FAX: (212) 473-8891.
www.buzzzco.com email: info@BUZZZCO.com
CONTACT
Candy Kugel

CALABASH ANIMATION
657 W. Ohio St., Chicago, IL 60610. (312) 243-3433. FAX: (312) 243-6227.
EXECUTIVE PRODUCER
Monica Kendall

CALICO WORLD ENTERTAINMENT
10200 Riverside Dr., Ste. 203, North Hollywood, CA 91602. (818) 755-3800. FAX: (818) 755-4643.
EXECUTIVE DIRECTOR
Tom Burton

THE CALVERT GROUP
5050 Tujunga Ave., Ste. 5, North Hollywood, CA 91601. (818) 760-8700.
PRESIDENT
Fred Calvert

CELLULOID STUDIOS
(Animation and mixed media)
2128 15th St., Denver, CO 80202. (303) 595-3152. FAX: (303) 595-4908. www.celluloidstudios.com
PRESIDENT
Olivier Katz
EXECUTIVE PRODUCER
Jan Jonson
DIRECTOR
Jeff Jurich
DIRECTORS & DESIGNERS
Roch Moyer
Eric Stoh
Brian Larson
DESIGNERS
Jimmy Helton
Steve Hidinger

CHARACTER BUILDERS, INC.
1476 Manning Pkwy., Powell, OH 43065. (614) 885-2211. FAX: (614) 885-3873.
www.cbuilders.com email: cbuilders@cbuilders.com
PRODUCER
Leslie Hough

CHILDREN'S MEDIA PRODUCTIONS
(producer and distributor)
P.O. Box 40400, Pasadena, CA 91114. (626) 797-5462. FAX: (626) 797-7524. email: childrensmedia@yahoo.com
CONTACT
C. Ray Carlson

CHIODO BROTHERS PRODUCTIONS, INC.
110 W. Providencia Ave., Burbank, CA 91502. (818) 842-5656. FAX: (818) 848-0891.
PRESIDENT
Stephen Chiodo

CHYRON CORP.
5 Hub Dr., Melville, NY 11747. (516) 845-2000. FAX: (516) 845-3895. www.chyron.com
V.P., NORTH AMERICAN SALES
Rich Hidju

CINAR FILMS (US), INC.
1055 Rene Levesque Blvd. E., Montreal, Quebec, Canada H2L 4S5. (514) 843-7070. FAX: (514) 843-7080.
www.cinar.com email: info@cinar.com
PUBLICITY & PROMOTION COORDINATOR
Katina Katadotis

CINEMOTION PICTURES
7275 Mulholland Dr., Los Angeles, CA 90068. (323) 874-1566. FAX: 9323) 874-51225.
EFFECTS SUPERVISOR
Max Anderson

CINEVOX ENTERTAINMENT
9000 Sunset Blvd., Ste. 1010, Los Angeles, CA 90069. (310) 273-1460. FAX: (310) 273-9420.
HEAD OF INTERNATIONAL
Sigrid Ann Davison

CLICK 3XLA
2415 Michigan Ave., Santa Monica, CA 90404. (310) 264-5511. FAX: (310) 264-5512. www.click3x.com
DIRECTOR, BUSINESS DEVELOPMENT
Paul Scott

COLOSSAL PICTURES
2800 3rd. St., San Francisco, CA 94107. (415) 643-1799.
PRESIDENT
Drew Takahashi

CONSOLIDATED FILM INDUSTRIES (CFI)
(Digital)
959 Seward St., Hollywood, CA 90038. (323) 960-7444. FAX: 9323) 962-8746. www.cfi-hollywood.com
V.P., SALES & MARKETING
Adam Chuck

CPC ENTERTAINMENT
840 N. Larabee St., Ste. 2322, Los Angeles, CA 90069. (310) 652-8194. FAX: (310) 652-4998.
email: 7415.1117@compuserve.com
353 W. 57th St., Ste. 2411, New York, NY 10019. (212) 554-6447. FAX: (310) 652-4998.
PRODUCER & DIRECTOR
Peggy Chase

CREATIVE CHARACTER ENGINEERING
16110 Hart St., Van Nuys, CA 91406. (818) 901-0507. FAX: (818) 901-8417.
CREATIVE DIRECTOR
Andrew Clement

CREATIVE INTERESTS
146 Main St., Ste. 205, Los Altos, CA 94022. (415) 948-5650. FAX: (415) 948-1315.

CREATIVE VISIONS MIAMI, INC.
260 Crandon Blvd., Ste. 32-160, Key Biscayne, FL 33149. (305) 880-7228. FAX: (954) 989-7268. email: tarzan@safari.net

CRUSE & COMPANY
7000 Romaine St., Hollywood, CA 90038. (323) 851-8814. FAX: (323) 851-8788.

CURIOUS PICTURES
(Computer animation, cel and stop-motion animation)
440 Lafayette, New York, NY 10003. (212) 674-1400. FAX: (212) 674-0081.
www.curiouspictures.com email: rwink5@curiouspictures.com
1360 Mission St., Ste. 201, San Francisco, CA 94103. (415) 437-1400. FAX: (415) 437-1408.
PRESIDENT
Steve Oakes
EXECUTIVE PRODUCER
David Starr

CYBER F/X
615 Ruberta Ave., Glendale, CA 91201. (818) 246-2911. FAX: (818) 246-3610. www.cyberfx3-D.com
PRESIDENT
Dick Cavdek

CYCLOTRON
220 E. 42nd St., Ste. 2-S, New York, NY 10017. (212) 687-8989. FAX: (212) 818-0655. www.strangequark.com
MANAGING DIRECTOR
Angela Bowen

DADDY-O PRODUCTIONS
22616 Erwin St., Woodland Hills, CA 91367. (818) 598-8784.
CONTACT
Tom McLaughlin

DANGER PRODUCTIONS
305 San Anselmo Ave., Ste. 203, San Anselmo, CA 94960. (415) 256-8850.
CONTACT
Ken Pontac

DIC ENTERTAINMENT, L.P.
303 N. Glen Oaks Blvd., Burbank, CA 91502. (818) 955-5400. FAX: (818) 955-5696.
PRESIDENT
Andy Heyward

DIGISCOPE DIGITAL VISUAL EFFECTS
2308 Broadway, Santa Monica, CA 90404. (310) 315-6060. FAX: (310) 828-5856. www.digiscope.com
PRESIDENT
Mary Stuart

DIGITAL CONSORTIUM
(510)-276-4841. www.digitalconsortium.com

DIGITAL CREATIVE
1112 N. Tamarind Ave., Hollywood, CA 90038. (800) 94M-EDIA. (323) 993-9570. FAX: (323) 962-3446.
email: webmaster@digitalcreative.com
PRESIDENT
Brian Patterson

DIGITAL DOMAIN
300 Rose Ave., Venice, CA 90291. 9310) 314-2800. FAX: (310) 314-2888.
PRESIDENT
Scott Ross

DIGITAL QUEST
Box 341635, Los Angeles, CA 90034. (310) 815-4870. FAX: (310) 287-3734.
DIRECTOR, INTERACTIVE
Casey Gelvin

WALT DISNEY FEATURE ANIMATION
500 S. Buena Vista St., Burbank, CA 91521. (818) 560-1000. FAX: (818) 560-8899.
P.O. Box 10200, Lake Buena Vista, FL 32830. (407) 560-4968.

WALT DISNEY TELEVISION ANIMATION
5200 Lankershim Blvd., North Hollywood, CA 91601. (818) 754-7100. FAX: (818) 752-9835.
PRESIDENT
Peter Schneider

DLT ENTERTAINMENT, LTD.
31 W. 56th St., New York, NY 10019. (212) 245-4680. FAX: (212) 315-1132.

DNA PRODUCTIONS, INC.
5950 Cedar Springs Rd., Ste. 250, Dallas, TX 75235. (214) 352-4696. FAX: (214) 352-4696. email: dnahelix@dnahelix.com
CONTACT
Keith Alcorn

DREAM QUEST IMAGES
(Character animation, live action photography, digital visual effects)
2635 Park Center Dr., Simi Valley, CA 93065. (805) 578-3100. FAX: (805) 583-4673. email: talent@dqimages.com
DIRECTOR OF PUBLIC AFFAIRS
Mary Reardon
V.P. & GENERAL MANAGER
Andrew Millstein

DREAM THEATER
21345 Lassen St., Ste. 200, Chatsworth, CA 91311. (818) 773-4979. FAX: (818) 773-8314.
www.dreamtheater.com email: darren@dreamtheater.com
MANAGER
Darren Chuckry

DREAMWORKS SKG FEATURE ANIMATION
1000 Flower St., Glendale, CA 91201. (818) 733-7000. FAX: (818) 733-3036.
FEATURE ANIMATION
Bonne Radford

DUCK SOUP STUDIOS
(Animation for commercials, film and TV titles, multimedia; 2 and 3 D computer animation, cel, character design, digital compositing, digital ink & paint)
2205 Stoner Ave., Los Angeles, CA 90064. (310) 478-0771. FAX: (310) 478-0773. www.ducksoupla.com
EXECUTIVE PRODUCER
Mark Medernach

DYNACS DIGITAL STUDIOS
(Game engines, 2 and 3D effects and animation)
572 E. Green St., Ste. 204, Pasadena, CA 91101. (626) 449-7385. FAX: (626) 449-7432. www.dynacs.com
PRESIDENT
Javier Benavente

ELECTRIC MACHINE ENTERTAINMENT
1930 Purdue Ave., Ste. 6, Los Angeles, CA 90025. (310) 330-8841. FAX: (310) 477-7292. email: emeprods@aol.com
CONTACT
Clive Milton

EMA MULTIMEDIA
1800 Ave. of the Stars, Ste. 430, Los Angeles, CA 90067. (310) 277-7379. FAX: (310) 277-7378.
www.emamulti.com email: pace@emamulti.com
CREATIVE DIRECTOR & CEO
Michael Pace

ENCORE ENTERPRISES
25510 Stanford Ave., Ste. 101, Valencia, CA 91355. (805) 295-0677. FAX: (805) 295-0680. email: encore@ecom.net
PRESIDENT
Bill Hutten

ENGINEERING ANIMATION, INC.
2321 N. Loop Dr., Ames, IA 50010. (515) 296-9908. FAX: (515) 296-7025. www.eai.com
DIRECTOR, BUSINESS DEVELOPMENT
Robert Coshland

ENOKI FILMS U.S.A., INC.
16501 Ventur Blvd., Ste. 306, Encino, CA 91436. (818) 907-6503.
V.P., DISTRIBUTION
Ricky Ames

EXPLOSIVE STUDIOS
31455 West St., South Laguna Beach, CA 92677. (949) 499-9964. FAX: (949) 499-9964.
www.toothandclaw.com email: exstudios@aol.com
ART DIRECTOR
Mark Pacella

EYEMARK ENTERTAINMENT
10877 Wilshire Blvd., Los Angeles, CA 90024. (310) 446-6000. FAX: (310) 446-6066.
PRESIDENT
Ed Wilson

FANTASY II FILM EFFECTS
504 S. Varney St., Burbank, CA 91502. (818) 849-1413. FAX: (818) 848-2824.
CONTACT
Leslie Huntley

RUSS FARBER
(Blue screen, camera motion control)
19324 Oxnard St., Tarzana, CA 91356. (818) 882-8220.
email: jfmusic@primenet.com

FARMHOUSE FILMS, INC.
4399 Irvine Ave., Studio City, CA 91604. (818) 760-8700.
PRESIDENT
Fred Calvert

FILM ROMAN, INC.
12020 Chandler Blvd., Ste. 200, North Hollywood, CA 91607.
(818) 761-2544.
CHAIRMAN/FOUNDER
Phil Roman
PRESIDENT
David Pritchard

FILM VENTURES INTERNATIONAL
1640 S. Sepulveda Blvd., Ste. 520, Los Angeles, CA 90025.
(310) 479-6755. FAX: (310) 479-3475.

FLAMDOODLE ANIMATION, INC.
6 Cuesta Lane, Santa Fe, NM 87505. (505) 982-3132. FAX:
(505) 466-3475. email: staff@flamdoodle.com
PRESIDENT
Jeff LaFlamme

FLEISCHER STUDIOS, INC.
10160 Cielo Dr., Beverly Hills, CA 90210. (310) 276-7503. FAX:
(310) 276-1559. email: stanhandmans@msn.com
PRESIDENT
Richard Fleischer

FLIP YOUR LID ANIMATION STUDIOS
(Character design, 2 and 3D animation, compositing)
650 N. Bronson Ave., Ste. 223, Hollywood, CA 90004. (323)
960-1306. FAX: (323) 461-4202. email: jay@flipyourlid.com
CREATIVE DIRECTOR & ANIMATOR
Jay Jacoby

FLYING FOTO FACTORY, INC.
P.O. Box 1166, Durham, NC 27702. (919) 682-3411. FAX: (919)
688-7886. www.flyingfoto.com
V.P., SALES & MARKETING
Kathy Bennett

FOX ANIMATION STUDIOS
2747 E. Camelback Rd., Phoenix, AZ 85016. (602) 808-4600.
EXECUTIVE V.P.
Steve Brian

F-STOP, INC.
120 S. Buena Vista St., Burbank, CA 91505. (818) 843-7867.
FAX: (818) 842-7706.

GALAXIE ENTERTAINMENT CO.
Box 8523, Universal City, CA 91618-8523. (818) 362-6005.
CONTACT
Dave Gregory

GALAXY WORLD, INC.
216 S. Jackson St., Glendale, CA 91205. (818) 265-5600. FAX:
(818) 265-1200.
PRODUCTION MANAGER
Jonathan Kang

JIM GAMBLE PUPPET PRODUCTIONS
6777 Vallon Dr., Rancho Palos Verdes, CA 90275. (310) 541-
1921. FAX: (310) 541-2195. www.jimgamble.com

GEAR PRODUCTIONS/GEAR CGI
7621 Melrose Ave., 2nd Flr., Los Angeles, CA 90046. (323)
653-0099. FAX: (323) 653-0919. www.gearprod.com
EXECUTIVE PRODUCER
David Kim

GRACIE FILMS
10202 W. Washington Blvd., Sidney Poitier Bldg., #2221,
Culver City, CA 90232. (310) 244-4222. FAX: (310) 244-1530.
CONTACT
Maria Kavanaugh

GREATEST TALES
22477 MacFarlane Dr., Woodland Hills, CA 91364. (818)
225-9545.
PRESIDENT
Fred Ladd

GREEN GRASS BLUE SKY COMPANY
10700 Ventura Blvd., Studio City, CA 91604. (818) 763-4182.
FAX: (818) 763-4625. email: frankcatalano@msn.com
WRITER & PRODUCER
Frank Catalano

HALLMARK ENTERTAINMENT
1235 Ave. of the Americas, 21st Flr., New York, NY 10019. (212)
977-9001. FAX: (212) 977-9049.
S.V.P., WORLDWIDE MARKETING
Donna Cornwell

HANDS-ON BROADCAST
124 W. 24th St., Ste. 6B, new York, NY 10011. 9212) 924-5036.
FAX: (212) 604-9036.
www.jobopts.com email: bgspeed@aol.com
PRESIDENT
Lorraine Rebe

HANNA-BARBERA PRODUCTIONS
15303 Ventura Blvd., #1400, Sherman Oaks, CA 91403. (818)
977-7500.
PRESIDENT
Fred Seibert

HBO ANIMATION
2049 Century Park East, Ste. 4100, Los Angeles, CA 90067.
(310) 229-1100. www.hbo.com
VICE PRESIDENT
Catherine Winder

HEARST ENTERTAINMENT, INC.
1640 S. Sepulveda Blvd., 4th Flr., Los Angeles, CA 90025.
(310) 478-1700. FAX: (310) 478-2203.
235 E. 45th St., New York, NY 10017. (212) 455-4000. FAX:
(212) 983-6379.
PRESIDENT
William Miller

HEART OF TEXAS PRODUCTIONS
3006 Bee Caves Rd., Ste. A-340, Austin, TX 78746. (512) 329-
8262.
PRESIDENT
Don Smith

JIM HENSON PRODUCTIONS
c/o Raleigh Studios, 5358 Melrose Ave., West Bldg., 3rd Flr.,
Hollywood, CA 90038. (323) 960-4096. FAX: (323) 960-4935.
CONTACT
Nicole Chiasson

HOUSE OF MOVIES MOTION CAPTURE STUDIOS, LLC
5318 McConnell Ave., Los Angeles, CA 90066. (310) 306-
6131. FAX: (310) 306-1351. www.moves.com
EXECUTIVE PRODUCER
Jarrod Phillips

HUBLEY STUDIO
2575 Palisade Ave., Riverdale, NY 10463. (718) 543-5958.
Faith Hubley

HYPERION STUDIOS
111 N. Maryland Ave., Ste. 200, Glendale, CA 91206. (818)
244-4704. FAX: (818) 244-4713.
PRESIDENT
Tom Wilhite

ICE TEA PRODUCTIONS
160 E. 38 St., #15-G, New York, NY 10016. (212) 557-8185.
PRESIDENT
Richard Durkih

IF/X PRODUCTION, INC.
5103 Gloria Ave., Encino, CA 91436. (818) 501-1822. FAX:
(818) 501-4526. email: ifx@aol.com
PRESIDENT
George Daugherty

ILLUVATAR, LLC
Box 639, Westminster, CA 92684. (714) 373-4228.
www.illuatar.com email: info@illuvatar.com
CEO
Bill Bescanceney

IMAGICA USA, INC.
5320 McConnell Ave., Los Angeles, CA 90066. (310) 305-
8081. FAX: (310) 305-7563. email: ius@imagicausa.com
CONTACT
Christopher Reyna

IMAGINATION FACTORY
9340 Eton Ave., Chatsworth, CA 91311. (818) 993-4448.
PRESIDENT
Stanford Blum

INDUSTRIAL LIGHT & MAGIC (ILM)
Box 2459, San Rafael, CA 94912. (415) 258-2000.
PRESIDENT
Jim Morris

THE INK TANK
2 W. 47th St., New York, NY 10036. (212) 869-1630. FAX: (212) 764-4169
EXECUTIVE PRODUCER
Brian O'Connell

IN-SIGHT PIX
321 Hampton Dr., Venice, CA 90291. (310) 399-0858. FAX: (310) 399-1334.
PRODUCER
Nicole Tidwell

INVISION ENTERTAINMENT
3000 Ocean Park Blvd., Ste. 3045, Santa Monica, CA 90405. 9310) 452-3555. FAX: (310) 452-1550.
EXECUTIVE V.P.
Michael Hack

ITC ENTERTAINMENT
9100 Wilshire Blvd., 600 West, Beverly Hills, CA 90212. (310) 724-8100. FAX: (310) 274-7849.
PRESIDENT & CEO
Jules Haimovitz

ITZAWRAP, INC.
(2d Animation)
P.O. Box 993, Homewood, IL 60430. (708) 335-3538. FAX: (708) 335-3999. email: jdmc@juno.com
EXECUTIVE PRODUCER
Christine McClenahan

JETLAG PRODUCTIONS
15315 Magnolia Blvd., Ste. 310, Sherman Oaks, CA 91403. (818) 385-3400. FAX: (818) 385-1610.
PRESIDENT
Jean Chalopin

J.J. SEDELMAIER PRODUCTIONS, INC.
199 Main St., 10th Flr., White Plains, NY 10601. (914) 949-7979. FAX: (914) 949-7989. email: sedelmaier@aol.com
PRESIDENT &DIRECTOR
J.J. Sedelmaier

JONSEISA PRODUCTIONS INTERNATIONALE, INC.
(Pre-production animation concept and character design)
500 Redondo Ave., Ste. 203, Long Beach, CA 90814. (562) 987-4474.

JUMBO PICTURES
161 6th Ave., 15th Flr., New York, NY 10013. (212) 337-0077. FAX: (212) 337-0437.
PRESIDENT
Jim Jinkins
EXECUTIVE V.P.
David R. Campbell

JIM KEESHEN PRODUCTIONS
1950 Sawtelle Blvd., Ste. 220, Los Angeles, CA 90025. (310) 478-7230. FAX: (310) 478-5142.
www.jfkproductions.com email: animatics@aol.com
PRESIDENT
Jim Keeshan

KENIMATION ANIMATION SERVICES
1424 N. Wilcox Ave., Hollywood, CA 90028-8124. (323) 462-2679. FAX: (323) 462-2684. email: kenru@thegrid.net
CONTACT
Ken Rudolph

KLASKY CSUPO, INC.
1139 N. Highland Ave., Hollywood, CA 90038. (323) 957-4183. FAX: (323) 462-6745. email: kccomm@earthlink.net
EXECUTIVE PRODUCER
Liz Seidman

GENE KRAFT PRODUCTIONS
(Animation for film & tv)
29 Calvados, Newport Beach, CA 92657. (714) 721-0609.

THE KRISLIN COMPANY
23901 Calabasas Road, Ste. 1051, Calabasas, CA 91302. (818) 222-0555.
PRESIDENT
Walt Kubiak

KURTZ & FRIENDS
2312 W. Olive Ave., Burbank, CA 91506. (818) 841-8188. FAX: (828) 841-6263.
PRESIDENT
Bob Kurtz
PRODUCER
Boo Kurtz-Lopez

L.A. ANIMATION
23501 Park Sorrenta, Ste. 207, Calabasas, CA 91302. (818) 224-4888. FAX: (818) 224-4148.
PRESIDENT
Lyn Henderson

LAMB & COMPANY
650 3rd Ave. South, 17th Flr., Minneapolis, MN 55402. (612) 333-8666. FAX: (612) 333-9173.
www.lamb.com email: larry@lamb.com
CONTACT
Larry Lamb

LANDMARK ENTERTAINMENT GROUP
5200 Lankershim Blvd., North Hollywood, CA 91601. (818) 753-6700. FAX: (818) 753-6767.

LEPREVOST CORPORATION
6781 Wildlife Rd., Malibu, CA 90265. (310) 457-3742. FAX: (310) 457-6142. email: leprevost@aol.com
V.P., MARKETING
John H. LePrevost

JERRY LIEBERMAN PRODUCTIONS
76 Laight Street, New York, NY 10013. (212) 431-3452. FAX: (212) 941-8976.
Jerry Lieberman

LIBERTY INTERNATIONAL ENTERTAINMENT, INC.
(Specials and series animation)
1990 Westwood Blvd., Penthouse, Los Angeles, CA 90025. (310) 479-6755. FAX: (310) 474-7455.
CEO
Irv Hollender

LINKER SYSTEMS
13612 Onkayha Circle, Irvine, CA 92620. (949) 552-1904. FAX: (949) 552-6985. www.linker.com
CONTACT
Toni Poper

LION'S DEN ANIMATION, INC.
(Cartoon production)
P.O. Box 7368, Northridge, CA 91327. (818) 894-4955.
VICE PRESIDENT
Milton Gray

WILLIAM LITTLEJOHN PRODUCTIONS, INC.
23425 Malibu Colony Dr., Malibu, CA 90265. (310) 456-8620. FAX: (310) 456-2978.

LIVE WIRE PRODUCTIONS & VFX
(visual effects animation and compositing)
28631 S. Western Ave., Ste. 101, Rancho Palos Verdes, CA 90275. (310) 831-6227. FAX: (310) 547-3456.
VISUAL EFFECTS PRODUCER
Kristen Simmons

WARREN LOCKHART PRODUCTIONS, INC.
P.O. Box 11629, Marina Del Rey, CA 90295. (310) 306-4661. FAX: (310) 301-0536. email: WarrenLockhartFilms@compuserve.com
PRESIDENT
Warren L. Lockhart

LUMENI PRODUCTIONS, INC.
(Digital and film, titles, graphics, effects)
1632 Flower St., Glendale, CA 91201. (818) 956-2200. FAX: (818) 956-3298. email: lumeni@aol.com
CONTACT
Patricia Malin

MANGA ENTERTAINMENT
727 N. Hudson St., Ste. 100, Chicago, IL 60610. (312) 751-0020. FAX: (312) 751-2483.
www.manga.com/manga email: manga@manga.com
CEO
Marvin Gleicher

MARVEL FILMS ANIMATION
1440 S. Sepulveda Blvd., Los Angeles, CA 90025. (310) 444-8644. FAX: (310) 444-8168.
PRESIDENT
Avi Arad

MATINEE ENTERTAINMENT
345 N. Maple Dr., Ste. 285, Beverly Hills, CA 90210. (310) 246-9044. FAX: (310) 246-9066.
PRESIDENT
Michael I. Yanover

MATTHEWS PRODUCTIONS
P.O. Box 74, Cedar Glen, CA 92321. FAX: (909) 867-5068.
PRODUCER
John Clark Matthews

MAX INK CAFE
2700 Pacific Ave., Venice, CA 90291. (310) 827-5351. FAX: (310) 827-5651.
www.MaxInkCafe.com email: info@MaxInkCafe.com
EXECUTIVE PRODUCER
Jennifer A. Champagne

MEDIALAB PRODUCTIONS
301 N. Canon Dr., Ste. 228, Beverly Hills, CA 90210. (310) 247-0994. www.medialab3d.com
SENIOR V.P, CREATIVE AFFAIRS
Carole Kirschner

MEDIAMAX PRODUCTIONS
9538 Brighton Way, Beverly Hills, CA 90210. (310) 285-0550.
PRESIDENT
Frederick Ittah

MEGA ENTERTAINMENT
156 W. 95th St., Ste. B, New York, NY 10025. (212) 678-4421. FAX: (212) 865-3411. email: mega-int@msn.com
MARKETING & SALES
Nancy Oster

BILL MELENDEZ PRODUCTIONS
439 N. Larchmont Ave., Los Angeles, CA 90004. (323) 463-4101. FAX: (323) 469-0195.
PRESIDENT
Bill Melendez

LEE MENDELSON FILM PRODUCTIONS
330 Primrose Rd., Ste. 310, Burlingame, CA 94010. (415) 342-8284. FAX: (415) 342-6170.
CONTACT
Glenn Mendelson

METROLIGHT STUDIOS
5724 W. 3rd St., Ste. 400, Los Angeles, CA 90036-3078. (323) 932-0400. FAX: (323) 932-8440.
www.metrolight.com email: info@metrolight.com
PRESIDENT
James W. Kristoff

METROPOLIS DIGITAL
12 S. 1st St., 11th Flr., San Jose, CA 95113. (408) 286-2900. (408) 286-2970.
www.metrosd.com email: degrande@metrosd.com
EXECUTIVE PRODUCER
Ken DeGrande

MGM ANIMATION, INC.
1545 26th St., 2nd Flr., Santa Monica, CA 90404. (310) 449-3250. FAX: (310) 449-3251.
EXECUTIVE PRODUCER
Jonathan Dern

MILNE FX
(Design and isual effects)
4411 W. Olive Ave., Burbank, CA 91505. (818) 840-1705. FAX: (818) 840-8994. email: milnefx@pacbell.net

MODERN CARTOONS
228 Main St., Ste. 12, Venice, CA 90291. (310) 396-9066.
PRODUCER
Aaron Slavin

MONKEY BOY PRODUCTIONS
(2 and 3D cel animation)
6381 Hollywood Blvd., Ste. 570, Hollywood, CA 90028. (323) 466-6539. FAX: (323) 466-6565.
www.mobopro.com email: info@mobopro.com
CONTACT
Bernie Gallardo

MOON MESA MEDIA
14945 Ventura Blvd., Ste. 300, Sherman Oaks, CA 91408. (818) 528-1455. FAX: (818) 528-1467.
PRESIDENT
Sheryl Hardy

MORGAN CREEK PRODUCTIONS
4000 Warner Blvd., Bldg. 76, Burbank, CA 91522. (818) 954-4800.
CONTACT
Brian Robinson

MORNING SUN ANIMATION GROUP, INC.
8642 Melrose Ave., Ste. 200, Los Angeles, CA 90069. (310) 854-3510. FAX: (310) 854-1881. email: smsla@earthlink.net
CONTACT
Alexis Wallrich

MOTION CITY FILMS
501 Santa Monica Blvd., Ste. A, Santa Monica, CA 90401. (800) 719-2812. www.motioncity.com
email@witt@motioncity.com
PRODUCER & DIRECTOR
Jerry Witt

M3D STUDIOS, INC.
15820 Arminta St., Van Nuys, CA 91406. (818) 785-6662. FAX: (818) 785-6810.
www.m3dstudios.com email: m3d@m3dstudios.com
CEO
Marcel Nottea

MTM ENTERPRISES
12700 Ventura Blvd., Studio City, CA 91604. (818) 755-2400.
CEO
Anthony D. Thomopolous

MTV ANIMATION
1633 Broadway, 31st Flr., New York, NY 10019. (212) 654-3600. FAX: (212) 654-4701.

MUSIVISION
185 E. 85th St., New York, NY 10028. (212) 860-4420.
CONTACT
Fred Kessler

NELVANA COMMUNICATIONS, INC.
4500 Wilshire Blvd., 1st Flr., Los Angeles, CA 90010. (323) 549-4222. FAX: (323) 549-4232.

NEST ENTERTAINMENT
6100 Colwell Blvd., Irving, TX 75039. (214) 402-7100. FAX: (214) 402-7181.

NETTER DIGITAL ENTERTAINMENT, INC.
5125 Lankershim Blvd., North Hollytwood, CA 91601. (818) 753-1990. FAX: (818) 753-7655.
BUISINESS DIRECTOR
Jason Netter

NEW HOLLYWOOD, INC.
1302 N. Cahuenga Blvd., Hollywood, CA 90028. (323) 466-3686. email: newhollywood@hotmail.com
CONTACT
Ozzie Zornizer

NEW WORLD ANIMATION
3340 Ocean Park Blvd., Santa Monica, CA 90405. (310) 444-8113.
PRESIDENT
Rick Unger

NICKELODEON
1515 Broadway, New York, NY 10036. (212) 258-7500.

NICKTOONS ANIMATION
4040 Vineland Ave., Ste. 105, Studio City, CA 91604. (818) 753-3255.

OCS/PIXEL MAGIC
10635 Riverside Dr., Toluca Lake, CA 91602. (818) 760-0862. FAX: (818) 760-0483. www.pixelmagicfx.com
VICE PRESIDENT
Ray McIntyre

OCULUS
220 E. 42nd Str., 28th Flr., New York, NY 10036. (212) 338-0501. FAX: (212) 818-0655.

ODYSSEY PRODUCTIONS
4413 Ocean Valley Lane, San Diego, CA 92130. (858) 793-1900. FAX: (858) 793-1942.

OPTICAM, INC.
(Cel animation, motion control downshooter, photo-rotos animation camera service)
810 Navy St., Santa Monica, CA 90405. (310) 396-4665, (800) 345-6394. FAX: (310) 452-0040. email: opcam@aol.com
CONTACT
Annette Buehre

ORBIT PRODUCTIONS
915 14th St., Modesto, CA 95354. (209) 529-4835. FAX: (209) 571-2307.
www.orbitproductions.com email: kevin@orbitproductions.com
CONTACT
Kevin Orbit

OVATION/ANIMATION
9 Caccamo St., Westport, CT 06880. (203) 227-9346.
CONTACT
Art Petricone

PACHYDERM ENTERTAINMENT
8899 Beverly Blvd., Ste. 502, Los Angeles, CA 90048. (310) 777-8387. FAX: (310) 777-8381.

PACIFIC DATA IMAGES
(3D character animation, visual effects)
3101 Park Blvd., Palo Alto, CA 94306. (650) 846-8100. FAX: (650) 846-8101. www.pdi.com email: info@pdi.com
DIRECTOR, MARKETING
Julie Haddon

PARAGON ENTERTAINMENT
11300 W. Olympic Blvd., Ste. 800, Los Angeles, CA 90064. (310) 478-7272. FAX: (310) 479-2314.
CEO
Jon Slan

PERENNIAL PICTURES FILM CORP.
2102 E. 52nd St., Indianapolis, IN 46205. (317) 253-1519.
PRESIDENT
Jerry Reynolds

PHOENIX ENTERTAINMENT
2222 Linstromeberg Rd., Beaufort, MO 63013. (573) 484-4599.
CHAIRMAN & CEO
Ed Ascherman

PINNACLE EFX
2334 Elliott Ave., Seattle, WA 98121. (206) 441-9878. FAX: (206) 728-2266.

PITTARD SULLIVAN
3535 Hayden Ave., Culver City, CA 90232. (310) 845-1000. FAX: (310) 845-1001.
www.pittardsullivan.com

PIXAR ANIMATION STUDIOS
(computer animation)
1001 W. Cutting Blvd., Ste. 200, Richmond, CA 94804. (510) 236-4000. (510) 236-0388.
www.pixar.com
EXECUTIVE V.P.
Ed Catmull

PIXEL LIBERATION FRONT
150 W. 28th St., Ste. 1003, New York. NY 10001. (212) 604-0203. FAX: (212) 604-0204.

PLAYHOUSE PICTURES
(2 and 3D animation)
1401 N. La Brea Ave., Hollywood, CA 90028. (323) 851-2112. FAX: (323) 851-2117. email: playpix@aol.com
PRESIDENT & PRODUCER
Ted Woolery
DIRECTORS
Sam Cornwell
Todd Shaller
Gerry Woolery

P.O.P. ANIMATION
730 Arizona, Santa Monica, CA 90401. (310) 393-4699. FAX: (310) 393-4799. www.popstudios.com
EXECUTIVE PRODUCER
Carl Seibert

PORCHLIGHT ENTERTAINMENT
11828 LaGrange Ave., Los Angeles, CA 90025. (310) 477-8400.
PRESIDENT
Bruce Johnson
EXECUTIVE V.P. & CFO
William T. Bauman
V.P., POST-PRODUCTION
Tom Gleason
V.P., ANIMATION
Fred Schaefer

PROTOZOA, INC.
2727 Mariposa, Ste. 100, San Francisco, CA 94110. (415) 522-6500. FAX: (415) 522-6522.
www.protozoa.com
email: info@protozoa.com
EXECUTIVE PRODUCER
Jane White

PULSE ENTERTAINMENT
2444 Wilshire Blvd., Ste. 303, Santa Monica, CA 90403. (310) 264-8320. FAX: (310) 264-8321. email: pulse@loop.com
CEO
Ron Layton

PUPPET STUDIO
(Puppets)
c/o The Taft Building, 1680 Vine St., Ste. 506, Hollywood, CA 90028. (323) 461-1415. FAX: (323) 461-1415.
email: steve@thepuppetstudio.com
CONTACT
Steve Sherman

PYROS CORPORATION
3197 Airport Loop Dr., Costa Mesa, CA 92626. (714) 708-3400. FAX: (714) 708-3500. www.pyros.com

QUANTEL, LTD.
28 Thorndal Circle, Dariend, CT 06820. (203) 656-3100. FAX: (203) 656-3459. www.quantel.com

R & B FILMS
7001 Melrose Ave., Hollywood, CA 90038. (323) 933-5703. FAX: (323) 933-4911.

RAINMAKER DIGITAL PICTURES
(2 and 3D visual effects)
175 E. Olive Ave., Ste. 405, Burbank, CA 91502. (818) 526-1500. FAX: (818) 953-5051. www.rainmaker.com
email: info@rainmaker.com
50 West 2nd Ave., Vancouver, B.C. V5Y 1B3. (604) 874-8700. FAX: (604) 874-1719.
PRESIDENT (CA)
Peter Sternlicht
PRESIDENT (CANADA)
Bob Scarabelli

RANKIN/BASS
24 W. 55th St., New York, NY 10019. (212) 582-4017. FAX: (212) 582-0937.

R/C MODELS
803 Channel St., San Pedro, CA 90731. (310) 833-9166. FAX: (310) 833-9167. www.rcmodelsusa.com

REALITY CHECK, INC.
(Motion graphics and design, 3D)
723 N. Cahuenga Blvd., Hollywood, CA 90038. (323) 465-3900. FAX: (323) 465-3600. www.realityx.com
email: andrew@realityx.com
PRESIDENT
Andrew Heimbold

REEL EFFECTS
28 W. 38th St., 2nd Flr., New York, NY 10018. (212) 768-9300. FAX: (212) 768-0438. www.reimedia.com

REMBRANDT FILMS
BallyHack Rd., Brewster, NY 10509. (914) 279-4158.
PRESIDENT
Adam Snyder

REMOTE CONTROL PRODUCTIONS
1547 14th St., Santa Monica, CA 90404. (310) 260-3172. FAX: (310) 260-3172. email: jweiss@rcprods.com
PRODUCER
Karla Murray

RENEGADE ANIMATION
204 N. San Fernando Rd., Burbank, CA 91502. (818) 556-3395. FAX: (818) 556-3398.
EXECUTIVE PRODUCER
Ashley Postlewaite
ANIMATION DIRECTOR
Darrell Van Citters

REZN8 PRODUCTIONS, INC.
6430 Sunset Blvd., Hollywood, CA 90028. (323) 957-2161. FAX: (323) 464-8912. www.rezn8.com

RICK REINERT PICTURES, INC.
32107 Lindero Canyon Rd., Ste. 224, Westlake Village, CA 91361. (818) 889-8977. FAX: (818) 889-9097.
PRESIDENT
Rick Reinert
ART DIRECTOR
Dave Bennett

RHYTHM & HUES
5404 Jandy Place, Los Angeles, CA 90066. (310) 448-7500. FAX: (310) 448-7600.
www.rhythm.com email: suze@rhythm.com
ADVERTISING & PUBLICITY DIRECTOR
Suzanne Datz

RICH ANIMATION STUDIO
333 N. Glenoaks Blvd., 3rd Flr., Burbank, CA 91502. (818) 846-0166.
CONTACT
Tom Tobin

ROARING MOUSE ENTERTAINMENT
1388 Cheswick Pl., Westlake Village, CA 91361. (310) 589-5029. FAX: (310) 589-4829.

RUBY-SPEARS PRODUCTIONS
710 S. Victory Blvd., #201, Burbank, CA 91502. (818) 840-1234. FAX: (818) 840-1258. email: rubyspears@earthlink.net
PRESIDENT
Joe Ruby

SABAN ENTERTAINMENT
10960 Wilshire Blvd., Ste. 2400, Los Angeles, CA 90024. (310) 235-5100. FAX: (310) 235-5102.
PRESIDENT
Haim Saban

SCHOLASTIC PRODUCTIONS
555 Broadway, New York, NY 10012. (212) 343-7500. FAX: (212) 343-7570. www.scholastic.com

SCHWARTZBERG & COMPANY
12700 Ventura Blvd., 4th Flr., Studio City, CA 91604. (818) 508-1833. FAX: (818) 508-1253.

J.J. SEDELMAIER PRODUCTIONS, INC.
199 Main St., 10th Flr., White Plains, NY 10601. (914) 949-7979. FAX: (914) 949-7989. email: sedelmaier@aol.com
PRESIDENT & DIRECTOR
J.J. Sedelmaier

7TH LEVEL, INC.
900 Allen Ave., Glendale, CA 91201. (818) 547-1955. FAX: (818) 246-5198.
S.V.P., OPERATIONS
Veronica Murdock

SHANGHAI MORNING SUN ANIMATION CO., LTD.
8642 Melrose Ave., Ste. 200, Los Angeles, CA 90069. (310) 854-3510. FAX: (310) 854-1881.
CONTACT
Faith DeVeaux

SHERER DIGITAL ANIMATION
(3D animation)
71-956B Magnesia Falls Dr., Rancho Mirage, CA 92270. (760) 346-7234. FAX: (760) 340-3170. www.shererdesign.com
PRESIDENT & CEO
Steve Sherer

SILVERLINE PICTURES
11846 Ventura Blvd., Ste. 100, Studio City, CA 91604. (818) 752-3730.
PRESIDENT
Axel Munch
CEO
Leman Cetiner

SIM EX DIGITAL STUDIOS
(Computer animation, graphics and digital effects)
3250 Ocean Park Blvd., Ste. 100, Santa Monica, CA 90405. (310) 664-9500. FAX: (310) 664-9977. www.simexds.com
EXECUTIVE PRODUCER
Michelle Gannes

SINGLE FRAME FILMS
(Stop motion, training, consultation)
437-1/2 N. Genessee Ave., Los Angeles, CA 90036. (323) 655-2664.
CONTACT
Gary Schwartz

SIX FOOT TWO PRODUCTIONS
(Oxberry animation stand)
1011 Magnolia Ave., Larkspur, CA 94939. (415) 925-9909. FAX: (415) 925-9922.
www.sixfoottwo.com email: animate@sixfoottwo.com
EXECUTIVE PRODUCER
Suzanne Atherly
DIRECTORS
Robbin Atherty
Tom Annolt
Steve Bellin

SKYVIEW STUDIOS
541 N. Fairbanks, Ste. 2200, Chicago, IL 60611. (312) 670-2020. FAX: (312) 670-3010.

SMITHGROUP COMMUNICATIONS
(Animation for films, commercial and theatrical trailers)
614 SW 11th Ave., Ste. 405, Portland, OR 97205. (513) 224-1905. FAX: (503) 224-5548. email: smithgrp@smithgrp.com
PRESIDENT
Phil Bevans
OPERATIONS MANAGER/PRODUCER
Gretchen Stevenson

ELAN SOLTES FX & DESIGN
2745 Angelo Dr., Los Angeles, CA 90077. (310) 858-3170. FAX: (310) 278-2356. email: elanfx@earthlink.net
CONTACT
Elan Soltes

SONY PICTURES IMAGEWORKS
9050 W. Washington Blvd., Culver City, CA 90232. (310) 840-8000. FAX: (310) 840-8100.
www.spiw.com email: don@spimageworks.com
EXECUTIVE DIRECTOR OF PUBLICITY, PROMOTIONS & ADVERTISING
Don Levy

LEONARD SOUTH PRODUCTIONS
11108 Huston St., North Hollywood, CA 91601. (818) 760-8383. FAX: (818) 766-8301.

SPECTAK PRODUCTIONS, INC.
(Laser special effects)
222 N. Sepuleda Blvd., Ste. 2000, El Segundo, CA 90245. (310) 335-2038.

MICHAEL SPORN ANIMATION, LTD.
632 Broadway, 4th Flr., New York, NY 10012. (212) 228-3372.
PRESIDENT
Michael Sporn

SPUMCO, INC.
5625 Melrose Ave., 2nd Flr., Hollywood, CA 90038. (323) 462-2943. FAX: (323) 957-1128. www.spumco.com
email: spumcoinc@aol.com
PRESIDENT
John Kricfalusi

ST PRODUCTIONS
(Cel, dimensional, stop motion and CGI, Oxberry and stop motion)
2041 Manning St., Burbank, CA 91505. (818) 846-3939. FAX: (818) 846-2530. email: stprods@earthlink.net
CONTACT
Sam Longoria

STARGATE FILMS, INC.
1103 W. Isabel St., Burbank, CA 91506. (818) 972-1100. FAX: (818) 972-9411. www.stargatefilms.com
VICE PRESIDENT
Larry Detwiler

STARTOONS INTERNATIONAL
P.O. Box 1232, Homewood, IL 60430. (708) 335-3535. FAX: (708) 339-3999. email: star2ns@aol.xom.
EXECUTIVE PRODUCER
Christine McClenahan
PRESIDENT
Jon McClenahan
VICE PRESIDENT
Ravi Yanamadula

DAVID STIPES PRODUCTIONS, INC.
45409 Gingham Ave., Lancaster, CA 93535. (818) 243-1442.
PRESIDENT
David Stipes III

STOKES/KOHNE ASSOCIATES, INC.
742 Cahuenga Blvd., Hollywood, CA 90038. (323) 468-2340. FAX: (323) 468-2345. email: djkohne@aol.com
CONTACT
Dan Kohne

STORYOPOLIS
116 N. Robertson Blvd., Plaza A, Los Angeles, CA 90048. (310) 358-2525.
PRESIDENT
Fonda Snyder

BERT STRATFORD PRODUCTIONS
221 W. 57th St., 10th Flr., New York, NY 10019. (212) 757-2211. FAX: (212) 757-2213.

STREAMLINE PICTURES
8624 Wilshire Blvd., Beverly Hills, CA 90211. (310) 659-7690. FAX: (310) 899-9471.
PRESIDENT
Carl Macek
DIRECTOR OF MARKETING
Fred Patten

STRIBLING PRODUCTIONS
6528 Camellia Ave., N. Hollywood, CA 91606. (818) 509-0748. FAX: (818) 509-1966.
PRESIDENT
Mike Stribling

STUDIO PRODUCTIONS
(2 and 3D animation, main titles, graphic design, compositing)
650 N. Bronson Ave., Ste. 223, Hollywood, CA 90004. (323) 856-8048. FAX: (323) 461-4702.
EXECUTIVE PRODUCER
Steve Soffer

SUNBOW ENTERTAINMENT
100 Fifth Ave., New York, NY 10011. (212) 886-4900. FAX: (212) 366-4242. email: cj-kettler@sunbow.com
CFO
Andrew Karpen
PRESIDENT
C.J. Kettler

SUPERCOLOR
979 N. La Brea Ave., Hollywood, CA 90038. (323) 874-2188. FAX: (323) 436-0588. www.supercolorimaging.com
GENERAL MANAGER
Marie Shieh

TAPE HOUSE TOONS
222 E. 44th St., 10th Flr., New York, NY 10017. (212) 557-9611. www.tapehouse.com
EXECUTIVE PRODUCER
Rob Issen

TAWEEL LOOS & CO. ENTERTAINMENT
CBS Studio Center, 4024 Radford Ave., Studio City, CA 91604. (818) 655-6155. FAX: (818) 655-6254.
OWNERS
George Taweel
Rob Loos

THRESHOLD ENTERTAINMENT
1649 11th St., Santa Monica, CA 90404. (310) 452-8899. FAX: (310) 452-0736.

TLC ENTERTAINMENT/THE MINI-MOVIE STUDIO
c/o CBS Studios, 4024 Radford Ave., Studio City, CA 91604. (818) 760-6155. FAX: (818) 760-6254. email: TLCE@aol.com
CONTACT
George Taweel

TMS/KYOKUICHI CORPORATION
15760 Ventura Blvd., Ste. 700, Encino, CA 91436. (818) 905-8881. FAX: (818) 905-0815.
L.A. DIRECTOR OF OPERATIONS
Andrew Berman

TOEI ANIMATION CO., LTD.
444 W. Ocean Blvd., Ste. 1000, Long Beach, CA 90802. (310) 901-2444.
VICE PRESIDENT
Mary Jo Winchester

TOON MAKERS, INC.
16007 Knapp St., North Hills, CA 91343. (818) 895-2995. FAX: (818) 893-4888. email: cartoonmkr@aol.com
EXECUTIVE PRODUCER & CEO
Rocky Solotoff

THE TOONIVERSAL COMPANY, INC.
6324 Variel Ave., Ste. 318, Woodland Hills, CA 91367. (818) 884-2374. FAX: (818) 884-2259.
PRESIDENT
Igor Meglic

TROON, LTD.
914 Colorado Ave., Santa Monica, CA 90401. (310) 394-3946. FAX: (310) 394-1224. email: troon@troon.com

TURNER FEATURE ANIMATION
611 B. Brand Blvd., 5th Flr., Glendale, CA 91203. (818) 553-5500. FAX: (818) 553-4930.

TWILIGHT ENTERTAINMENT FILMS
c/o Todd Calhoun, P.O. Box 76196, Los Angeles, CA 90076. (213) 387-6267.
PRODUCER, ACTOR & FOUNDER
Todd Calhoun

UPA PRODUCTIONS OF AMERICA
8640 Wilshire Blvd., Beverly Hills, CA 90211. (310) 659-6004. FAX: (310) 659-4599.
PRESIDENT
Hank Saperstein

UNITED MEDIA
330 Primrose Rd., Ste. 310, Burlingame, CA 94010. (415) 342-8284.
DIRECTOR
Lee Mendelson

UNIVERSAL CARTOON STUDIOS
100 Universal City Plaza, Universal City, CA 91608. (818) 777-1000.
PRESIDENT
Jeff Segal

VIDE-U PRODUCTIONS
9976 W. Wanda Dr., Beverly Hills, CA 90210. (310) 276-5509. FAX: (310) 276-1183. email: brad3845@aol.com
CONTACT
Bradley Freeman

VIEW STUDIO, INC.
6715 Melrose Ave., Hollywood, CA 90038. (323) 965-1270. FAX: (323) 965-1277. email: info@viewstudio.com
DIRECTOR, MARKETING
Kim Bajorek

VIEWPOINT DATALABS
13348 Beach Ave., Marina Del Rey, CA 90292. (31) 305-1981. FAX: (310) 305-8582. www.viewpoint.com
ACCOUNT EXECUTIVE
Steve Skinner

VIEWPORT IMAGES
109 N. Naomi St., Burbank, CA 91505. (818) 559-8705. FAX: (818) 559-5453.
PRESIDENT
John Howard

WILL VINTON STUDIOS
(Dimensional computer animation and claymation)
1400 N. W. 22nd Ave., Portland, OR 97210. (503) 225-1130. FAX: (503) 226-3746.
CONTACT
Susan Conklin

VIRTUALMAGIC ANIMATION
(Digital ink, paint & compositing for 2-D animation)
4640 Lankershim Blvd., Ste. 201, North Hollywood, CA 91602. (818) 623-1866. FAX: 9818) 623-1868.
www.virtualmagicusa.com email: jan@virtualmagicusa.com
DIRECTOR, BUSINESS DEVELOPMENT & MARKETING
Jan Nagel

VISUAL CONCEPT ENGINEERING
(Digital effects and motion control)
13300 Ralston Ave., Sylmar, CA 91342-7608. (818) 367-9187. FAX: (818) 362-3490. www.vce.com
PRESIDENT
Peter Kuran

VISUAL IMPULSE PRODUCTIONS (V.I.P.)
(3D and effects; interactive solutions)
10850 Wilshire Blvd., Ste. 380, Los Angeles, CA 90024. (310) 441-2556. FAX: (310) 441-2558.

WARNER BROS. CLASSIC ANIMATION
15303 Ventura Blvd., Ste. 1200, Sherman Oaks, CA 91403. (818) 977-8534. FAX: (818) 977-8252.

WARNER BROS. FEATURE ANIMATION
500 N. Brand St., Ste. 1800, Glendale, CA 91203-1923. (818) 977-7600, (800) 286-0868. FAX: (818) 977-7111.
PRESIDENT
Max Howard

WARNER BROS. TELEVISION ANIMATION
15303 Ventura Blvd., Ste. 1200, Sherman Oaks, CA 91403. (818) 977-8700.
PRESIDENT
Jean MacCurdy

WHAMO ENTERTAINMENT
1850 S. Sepulveda Blvd., Ste. 201, Los Angeles, CA 90025. (310) 477-0338.
CHAIRMAN & CEO
Myles Spector

WILD BRAIN, INC.
2650 18th St., Sam Francisco, CA 94110. (415) 553-8000. FAX: (415) 553-8009.
www.wildbrain.com email: jeff@wildbrain.com
CEO
Jeff Fino

FRED WOLF FILMS
4222 W. Burbank Blvd., Burbank, CA 91505. (818) 846-0611.
PRESIDENT
Fred Wolf

WORLD EVENTS PRODUCTIONS, LTD.
4935 Lindell Blvd., Saint Louis, MO 63108. (314) 454-6475. FAX: (314) 454-6428.
www.wep.com email: world_events@mail.KPLR.com
MANAGING DIRECTOR
Kevin Harlan

XAOS
(Visual effects and animation)
444 De Haro St., Ste. 211, San Francisco, CA 94107. (415) 558-9267. FAX: (415) 558-9160.
PRESIDENT
Arthur Schwartzberg
EXECUTIVE PRODUCER
Christina Scmidlin

MIKE YOUNG PRODUCTIONS
20335 Ventura Blvd., Ste. 225, Woodland Hills, CA 91364. (818) 999-0062. FAX: (818) 999-0172.
CONTACT
Liz Young

ZEN ENTERTAINMENT
1620 26th St. Ste. 250, Santa Monica, CA 90404. (310) 315-4166. FAX: (310) 315-4171.
CONTACT
Peter Keefe

ZOOM CARTOONS ENTERTAINMENT
(Animation studio, 2 and 3D)
c/o Los Angeles Center Studios, 1201 W. 5th St., Ste. M-3000, Los Angeles, CA 90017. (213) 202-5959. FAX: (213) 202-5960. www.zoomcartoons.com
PRESIDENT & EXECUTIVE PRODUCER
Susan Deming Berstein

CASTING DIRECTORS

ABA PICTURE VEHICLES & CASTING SERVICEF
8306 Wilshire Blvd., PMB 900, Beverly Hills, CA 90212. (310) 323-9028. FAX: (310) 323-3144.
CEO
Antoinette Meier

ACADEMY CASTING
(Union & non-union principals and extras)
7437 Balboa Blvd., Van Nuys, CA 91406. (818) 781-8233. FAX: (818) 781-8233.

ACCESS CASTING
16209 Victory Blvd., Ste. 225, Van Nuys, CA 91406. (818) 908-9213. FAX: (818) 884-9886.
CASTING DIRECTOR
Joseph Grant

AKIMA'S CASTING & PRODUCTIONS SERVICES
Box 7088, Van Nuys, CA 91409. (818) 988-9168.
CASTING DIRECTOR
Akima Castaneda

SANDY ALLISON
1759 Orchid Ave., Los Angeles, CA 90028. (323) 874-3631.

AMERICAN INDIANS IN FILM
(Casting of Native Americans)
65 N. Allen Ave., Ste. 105, Pasadena, CA 91106. (626) 578-0344. FAX: (626) 449-2735.
CEO
Sonny Skyhawk

HOWARD ANDERSON WEST
(Screen tests for casting)
5418 McConnell Ave., Los Angeles, CA 90066. (310) 823-5511. FAX: (310) 832-5501.
CONTACT
Jack Edgerton

ANDERSON/MCCOOK/WHITE CASTING, INC.
451 N. La Cienega Blvd., Ste. 2, Los Angeles, CA 90048. (310) 659-5535. FAX: (310) 659-5007.
PRESIDENT
Nancy McCook

DEBORAH AQUILA
Feature Casting, Paramount Pictures, 5555 Melrose Ave., Bob Hope Bldg. #206, Los Angeles, CA 90038. (310) 956-5444. FAX: (310) 862-1371.

ARTZ & COHEN CASTING
5225 Wilshire Blvd., Ste. 624, Los Angeles, CA 90036. (323) 938-1043. FAX: (323) 938-1046.
CONTACT
Mary Gail Artz

RISE BARISH CASTING
21920 Lamplighter Lane, Malibu, CA 90265. (310) 456-9018. FAX: (310) 456-9718.

BARTON G. CREATIVE PRODUCTIONS
400 N.E. 67th St., Miami, FL 33138. (305) 576-8888. FAX: (305) 751-0040.

FRAN BASCOM & ASSOCIATES
3400 Riverside Dr., Ste. 765, Burbank, CA 91505. (818) 972-8339. FAX: (818) 972-0295.

PAMELA BASKER
Warner Bros. Casting, 300 Television Plaza, Bldg. 140, Room #148, Burbank, CA 91505. (818) 954-4291. FAX: (818) 954-2748.

ANNETTE BENSON
11601 Wilshire Blvd., 21st Flr., Los Angeles, CA 90025. (310) 481-2000.

TERRY BERLAND CASTING
2050 S. Bundy Dr., Los Angeles, CA 90025. (310) 571-4141. FAX: (310) 820-5408.

BOSTON CASTING
JFK P.O. Box 9067, Boston, MA 02114. (617) 437-6600. FAX: (617) 437-6677.
DIRECTORS
Angela Peri
Lisa Lobel

BRAMSON & ASSOCIATES
7400 Beverly Blvd., Los Angeles, CA 90036. (310) 938-3595. FAX: (310) 938-0852.

BROWN/WEST CASTING
7319 Beverly Blvd., Ste. 10, Los Angeles, CA 90036. (323) 938-2575. FAX: (323) 938-2755.

BUCK/EDELMAN CASTING CO.
4045 Radford Ave., Ste. B, Studio City, CA 91604. (818) 506-7328.

CATHI CARLTON CASTING
(310) 820-9200.

THE CASTING COMPANY
7461 Beverly Blvd., Penthouse, Los Angeles, CA 90036-2704. (323) 938-0700.

THE CASTING CREW, INC.
1948 Tyler St., Hollywood, FL 33020. (954) 927-2329. FAX: (954) 927-2371

CASTING SOCIETY OF AMERICA
606 N. Larchmont Blvd., #4B, Los Angeles, CA 90004. (323) 463-1925. FAX: (323) 463-5753.
DIRECTORS
Julie Alter, Maureen Arata, Simon Ayer, Lisa Beach, Juel Bestrop, Susan Bluestein, Jacklynn Briskey, Jackie Burch, Irene Cagen, Marta Carlson, Ferne Cassel, Alice Cassidy, Fern Champion, Ellen Chenoweth, Andrea Cohen, Barbara Cohen, Mary Colquhoun, Leslee Dennis, Dick Dinman, Dorian Dunas, Howard Feuer, Nancy Foy, Gerald Franks, Carrie Frazier, Jean Sarah Frost, Risa Bramon Garcia, Melinda Gartzman, Alixe Gordon, Harriet Greenspan, Tory Herald, Vicki Huff, Steven Jacobs, Amy Klein, Nancy Klopper, Allison Kohler, Carol Lewis, Terry Liebling, Lisa London, Jackie Margey, Valorie Massalas, Lisa Mionie, Patrick Mock, Roger Mussneden, Robin Nassif, Mark Paladini, Linda Phillips Palo, Pamela Rack, Joe Reich, Gretchen Rennell, Eleanor Ross, Renee Rousselot, Julie Selzer, Bill Shepard, Jennifer Shull, Margaret Simkin, Catherine Stroud, Joel Thurm, Mark Tillman, Rosemary Weldon, Susan Wieder, Geri Windsor, Liz Woodman, Ronnie Yeskel, Debra Zane, Gary Zuckerbroad.

CASTING 2000/STARCAST 2000
3760 Cahuenga Blvd. W., Universal City, CA 91604. (818) 754-8868. FAX: (818) 754-5986.

CCDA: COMMERCIAL CASTING DIRECTORS ASSOCIATES
c/o Big House Studios, 4420 Lankershim Blvd., North Hollywood, CA 91602. (818) 752-7100. FAX: (818) 752-7101.
PRESIDENT
Jeff Gerrard

CENTRAL CASTING
1700 W. Burbank Blvd., Burbank, CA 91506. (818) 562-2799. FAX: (818) 260-9806.

CIRCUIT RIDER TALENT & MANAGEMENT
(Bookings, casting, career management)
120 Walton Ferry Rd., Hendersonville, TN 37075. (615) 824-1947, (800) 420-8568. FAX: (615) 264-0462.
email: dotwool@bellsouth.net
PRESIDENT
Linda Dotson

BARBARA CLAMAN CASTING
10834 Burbank Blvd., North Hollywood, CA 91601. (818) 755-9235.

MARGIE CLARK CASTING
9636 Heather Rd., Beverly Hills, CA 90210. (310) 859-2807. FAX: (310) 858-0926.

LORI COBE CASTING
2005 Palo Verde Ave., Ste. 306, Long Beach, CA 90815. (562) 938-9088.

ANNELISE COLLINS CASTING
(310) 586-1936. FAX: (310) 586-1100.
email: anneliscast@earthlink.net

COMMUNICATIONS CORP. OF AMERICA
(Specializing in teens, pre-teens and young adults)
2501 N. Sheffield Ave., Chicago, IL 60614. (773) 348-0001. FAX: (773) 472-7398.
EXECUTIVE PRODUCER
Fred Strauss

COPELAND CREATIVE TALENT
(Talent for commercials, industrials)
4140-1/2 Grand Ave., Des Moines, IA 50312. (515) 271-5970. FAX: (515) 277-0770. email: copetalent@aol.com
CONTACT
Deb Copeland

PATRICK CUNNINGHAM, CSA
c/o Casting Society of America (CSA), 606 N. Larehmont Blvd., Ste. 4B, Los Angeles, CA 90004. (323) 463-1925. (323) 222-1656. FAX: (323) 225-7815. email: pscrox@aol.com

BILL DANCE CASTING
(323) 878-0668.

RICHARD DELANCY & ASSOCIATES
4741 Laurel Canyon Blvd., Ste. 100, Valley Village, 91607. (818) 760-3110.
www.delancy.com email: rdelancy@juno.com

DIPRIMA CASTING
(TV commericals and real people)
1688 Meridian Ave., Ste. 418, Miami Beach, FL 33139. (305) 672-9232. FAX: (305) 672-9020. email: diprima@aol.com
CASTING DIRECTOR
Barbara DiPrima

DIVISEK CASTING & ASSOCIATES
6420 Wilshire Blvd., LL 100, Los Angeles, CA 90048. (323) 655-7766. FAX: (323) 822-2199.

PAM DIXON
P.O. Box 672, Beverly Hills, CA 90213. (818) 954-3928.

DONNA ECKHOLDT
20th Century Fox, 10201 W. Pico Blvd., Trailer 730, Los Angeles, CA 90035. (310) 369-4501. FAX: (310) 369-8926.

DONOVAN/FOLEY CASTING
12716 Riverside Dr., Ste. 100, North Hollywood, CA 91607. (818) 985-9902. FAX: (818) 753-9322.

MICK DOWD/TOM REUDY CASTING
5724 W. 3rd St., Ste. 508, Los Angeles, CA 90036. (323) 665-1776, (323) 954-0007. FAX: (323) 913-9379.

ALICE ELLIS CASTING
Box 1828, Venice, CA 90294. (310) 314-1488. FAX: (310) 3147-2649.
CASTING DIRECTOR
Alice Ellis

ENTERTAINMENT PARTNERS
2835 N. Naomi St., Burbank, CA 90510-7836. (818) 955-6000. FAX: (818) 845-6507. www.ep.services.com
CONTACT
Albeth Grass

STEVEN ERDEK/STACEY HERMAN CASTING
2050 S. Bundy Dr., Los Angeles, CA 90025. (310) 820-9200. FAX: (310) 820-5408.
OWNER
Steven Erdek

THE ERICKSON AGENCY
8201 Greensboro Dr., Ste. 214, McLean, VA 22102. (703) 356-0040, (703) 356-4251. FAX: (703) 442-0055.
www.ericksonagency.com email: talent@ericksonagency.com

EXTRAS NETWORK CASTING
(323) 851-9577. FAX: (323) 851-4410. www.extrasnet.com
CASTING DIRECTOR
John Laccetti

THE FLASHCAST COMPANIES, INC.
c/o Centrum Towers, 3575 Cahuenga Blvd. W., Ste. 120, Los Angeles, CA 90068. (800) 273-9008. FAX: (818) 760-6792.
www.flashcastkids.com

MEGAN FOLEY CASTING
12716 Riverside Dr., Ste. 100, N. Hollywood, CA 91607. (818) 755-9455. FAX: 9818) 753-9322.

FOUR SISTERS CASTING
(818) 755-1815. FAX: (818) 755-1642.
email: filmcast@pacbell.net
CONTACT
Thomas Daniels

EDDIE FOY, III, CASTING
3003 W. Olive Ave., Burbank, CA 91505. (818) 841-3003. FAX: (818) 954-8609.
DIRECTOR, PUBLICITY
Melissa Cummings

JEFF GERRARD CASTING
Big House Studios, 4420 Lankershim Blvd., N. Hollywood, CA 91602. (818) 752-7100. FAX: (818) 752-7101.

DANNY GOLDMAN & ASSOCIATES CASTING
1006 N. Cole Ave., Los Angeles, CA 90038. (323) 463-1600. FAX: (323) 463-3139.

JEFF GREENBERG
Paramount, 5555 Melrose Ave., Marx Brothers Bldg., #102, Los Angeles, CA 90038. (323) 956-4886. FAX: (323) 862-1368.

AARON GRIFFITH CASTING
(Casting for independent feature films)
8440 Santa Monica Blvd., Ste. 200, Los Angeles, CA 90069. (323) 654-0033.

IRIS GROSSMAN
Turner Netowrk Television, Inc., 1888 Century Park East, 14th Flr., Los Angeles, CA 90067. (310) 551-6352. FAX: (310) 551-6383.

ROBERT HARBIN
c/o Twentieth Century Fox, 10201 W. Pico Blvd., Los Angeles, CA 90035. (310) 369-3847. FAX: (310) 369-1914.

PATTI HAYES
(323) 933-0116. FAX: (323) 934-5199.
email: pattisan@jetcafe.org

HISPANIC TALENT CASTING OF HOLLYWOOD
(323) 934-6465. email: billhooey@aol.com

JANET HIRSHENSON
(Feature films and television)
7461 Beverly Blvd., Penthouse, Los Angeles, CA 90036. (323) 938-0700.

BETH HOLMES CASTING
11331 Ventura Blvd., Ste. 201, Studio City, CA 91604. (818) 752-8100.

THE HOLLYWOOD MADISON GROUP
11684 Ventura Blvd., Ste. 258, Studio City, CA 91604. (818) 762-8008. FAX: (818) 762-8089. www.hollywood-madison.com
CONTACT
Jonathan Holiff

II JAM PRODUCTIONS
(Sports casting)
12531 Chanute St., Pacoima, CA 91331. (310) 246-8267. FAX: (818) 834-4515. email: nmiguel@aol.com
COORDINATOR
Nigel Miguel

DONNA ISAACSON
20th Century Fox, 10201 W. Pico Blvd., Bldg. 12, Room 201, Los Angeles, CA 90035. (310) 369-1824. FAX: (310) 369-1469.

ALEC ISBELL CASTING
6605 Hollywood Blvd., Ste. 225, Los Angeles, CA 90028. (323) 860-0373. FAX: (323) 860-0377.

JAG ENTERTAINMENT
4265 Hazeltine Ave., Sherman Oaks, CA 91423. (818) 905-5511. FAX: (818) 501-4911.
PRESIDENT
Jo-Ann Geffen

JOHNSON/LIFF CASTING
1501 Broadway, Ste. 1400, New York, NY 10036. (212) 391-2680. FAX: (212) 840-0691.

EILEEN KNIGHT
12009 Guerin St., Studio City, CA 91604. (818) 752-1994.

DEBORAH KURTZ CASTING
1345 Abbot Kinney Blvd., Venice, CA 90291. (310) 452-6800.

ROSS LACY CASTING
9899 Santa Monica Blvd., Ste. 270, Beverly Hills, CA 90212. (310) 358-7558. FAX: (310) 393-4806. email: rmmlacy@aol.com

LEAR CASTING
1112 S. 3rd. St., Las Vegas, NV 89104. (702) 385-9000. FAX: (702) 474-6352.

JOHN LEVEY
c/o Warner Bros., 300 Television Plaza, Bldg. 140, Rm. 138, Burbank, CA 91505. (818) 954-4080.

LIBERMAN PATTON CASTING
4311 Wilshire Blvd., Ste. 606, Los Angeles, CA 90010. (323) 525-1381.

LIEN COWEN CASTING
7461 Beverly Blvd., Ste. 203, Los Angeles, CA 90036. (323) 937-0411.

MACDONALD-BULLINGTON CASTING
1645 N. Vine St., 9th Flr., Hollywoood, CA 90028. (323) 468-0599. FAX: (323) 468-0598.

MAGIC CASTING, INC.
1660 Cougar Ridge Rd., Buellton, CA 93427. (805) 688-3702.

MALI FINN CASTING
c/o MGM/UA 2500 Broadway, Ste. E-5014, Santa Monica, CA 90404. (310) 586-8220. FAX: (310) 586-8221.

MAMBO KASTING
8679 W. Olympic Blvd., Los Angeles, CA 90035. (310) 657-6108. email: mambo2@idt.net
CASTING DIRECTOR
Orlette Ruiz

MAXANN'S CASTING CO.
(Principal and extras casting for features, TV movies, commercials and music videos)
Box 4137, Rock Hill, DC 29732. (803) 328-3420. FAX: (803) 328-2173.
CEO & CASTING DIRECTOR
Maxann Crotts
CASTING ASSISTANTS
Genna Delp
Robin Carlan

MEDIA ACCESS OFFICE IEDD
(Casting liaison office for performers with disabilities)
4640 Lankershim Blvd., North Hollywood, CA 91602. (818) 752-1196. FAX: (818) 505-7317. email: GCastane@edd.ca.gov

ANN MILLER CASTING
P.O. Box 5273, North Hollywood, CA 91616. (818) 506-8922. FAX: (818) 506-8922.

MIMI WEBB MILLER
171 Pier Ave., Santa Monica, CA 90405. (310) 452-0863.

NANCY NAYOR
c/o Universal Studios, 100 Universal City Plaza, Bldg. 507/3A, Universal City, CA 91608. (818) 777-3566. FAX: (818) 866-3319.

NEVADA CASTING GROUP, INC.
100 Washington St., Ste. 100, Reno, NV 89503. (702) 322-8187. FAX: (702) 322-0161.

DAVID O'CONNOR CASTING COMPANY
1017 W. Washington Blvd., Ste. 2A, Chicago, IL 60607. (312) 226-9112. FAX: (312) 226-9921.

LORI OPENDEN
c/o NBC Network, 3000 W. Alameda Ave., Ste. 231, Burbank, CA 91523. (818) 840-3774. FAX: (818) 840-4412.

JESSICA OVERWISE
17250 Sunset Blvd., Ste. 304, Pacific Palisades, CA 90272. (310) 459-2686. FAX: (310) 459-0961.
email: jessica01@aol.com

PAGANO/MANWILLER CASTING
c/o 20th Century Fox, 10201 W. Pico, Trailer 776, Los Angeles, CA 90035. (310) 369-3153. FAX: (310) 369-3572.

MARVIN PAIGE CASTING
P.O. Box 69964, West Hollywood, CA 90069. (818) 760-3040.

PARADOXE CASTING
P.O. Box 691037, West Hollywood, CA 90069. (310) 552-8257.

LINDA PHILLIPS PALO
225 Santa Monica Blvd., 7th Flr., Santa Monica, CA 90401. (310) 394-4699. FAX: (310) 394-3052.

CAMILLE H. PATTON
Witt-Thomas Prods., 1438 N. Gower St., Bldg. 35, Ste. 155, Los Angeles, CA 90028. (323) 960-8276. FAX: (323) 960-8311.

PRIME CASTING
(Extras casting)
7060 Hollywood Blvd., #1025, Hollywood, CA 90028. (323) 962-0377, (323) 962-0378. FAX: (323) 466-4166.
email: Extracast@aol.com
CASTING DIRECTOR
Peter Alwazzan

KATHY LEIGH PRYOR
P.O. Box 458113, San Antonio, TX 78280. (210) 692-3664. FAX: (210) 647-4119.

R & M CASTING
451 N. La Cienega Blvd., Los Angeles, CA 90048. (310) 939-3388.

RAINBOW CASTING
12501 Chandler Blvd., #204, N. Hollywood, CA 91607. (818) 752-2278. FAX: (818) 752-6580.
OWNER
Terry Zarchi

REAL PEOPLE CASTING
4732-D Villa Marina, Marina Del Rey, CA 90292. (310) 827-9498.

REEL SOUTHERN CASTING
(Theatrical, commerical and music)
c/o CRTM-123 Walton Ferry Rd., Hendersonville, TN 37075. (800) 420-8568. FAX: (615) 264-0462.
email: dotwool@bellsouth.net
PRESIDENT
Linda Dotson

CHARLES ROSEN CASTING
2633 34th St., Santa Monica, CA 90405. (310) 314-3348.

DONNA ROSENSTEIN
c/o ABC Entertainment, 2040 6th Ave., 5th Flr., Century City, CA 90067. (310) 557-6532. FAX: (310) 557-6928.

GABRIELLE SCHARY CASTING
1418 Abbot Kinney Blvd., Venice, CA 90291. (310) 450-0835.

TINA SEILER CASTING
P.O. Box 46321, Los Angeles, CA 90046. (818) 382-7929.

LILA SELIK CASTING
(Commercials, films, tv, industrials)
1551 S. Robertson Blvd., Ste. 202, Los Angeles, CA 90035. (310) 556-2444. FAX: (310) 556-3266.

AVA SHEVITT
Village Studio, 519 Broadway, Santa Monica, CA 90401. (310) 656-4600. FAX: (310) 656-4610.

SHOOTING FROM THE HIP CASTING
c/o Second Story Studios, 13107 Ventura Blvd., Studio City, CA 91604. (818) 783-8900. FAX: (818) 783-3831.
CASTING DIRECTOR
Francene Selkirk

SLATE PLEASE CASTING
(Low budget features)
4047 Radford Ave., Studio City, CA 91604. (818) 785-9568. FAX: (818) 785-7965.
OWNER
Shancy Pierce

MARY JO SLATER CASTING
2425 Colorado, Ste. 204, Santa Monica, CA 90404. (310) 449-3685. FAX: (310) 449-3685.
CONTACTS
Tim Michals
Camila Rhodes

DON SLATON CASTING
2323 Delaware St., Ste. 1, Huntington Beach, CA 92648. (714) 969-4348. FAX: (714) 969-4348. email: gatbar1@aol.com

RON SMITH'S CELEBRITY LOOK-ALIKES
(Celebrity impersonators)
7060 Hollywood Blvd., #1215, Hollywood, CA 90028. (323) 467-3030. FAX: (323) 467-6720.

LYNN STALMASTER, & ASSOCIATES
500 S. Sepulveda Blvd., Ste. 600, Los Angeles, CA 90049. (310) 552-0983.

STUART STONE CASTING
2050 N. Bundy Dr., Los Angeles, CA 90025. (323) 650-4463. FAX: (310) 820-5408. email: stonecast1@aol.com

STUDIO TALENT GROUP
1328 12th St., Ste. 3, Santa Monica, CA 90401. (310) 393-8004. FAX: (310) 393-2473. email: stgactor@gte.net
PRESIDENT
Phillip L. Brock

MARK TAPER FORUM CASTING
601 W. Temple St., Ste. 112, Los Angeles, CA 90012. (323) 972-7374. FAX: (323) 972-7645.

SUSAN TYLER CASTING
c/o 2nd Story Studio, 13107 Ventura Blvd., Studio City, CA 91604. (818) 506-0400.

VOICECASTER
1832 W. Burbank Blvd., Burbank, CA 91506-1348. (818) 841-5300. FAX: (818) 841-2085.
MANAGING DIRECTOR
Lisa Dyson

WISE & ASSOCIATES, C.S.A.
18034 Ventura Blvd., Ste. 403, Encino, CA 91316. (818) 343-8936. FAX: (818) 345-1792. email: castwise@aol.com
PRESIDENT
Peter Wise

KEITH WOLFE CASTING
1438 N. Gower, Ste. 39, Hollywood, CA 91605. (323) 469-5595. FAX: (323) 957-1872.

LORI WYMAN CASTING
16499 N.E. 19th Ave., Ste. 203, North Miami Beach, FL 33162. (305) 354-3901. FAX: (305) 354-3970.

Consultants & Technical Advisors

A & C HARBOUR LITES, LTD.
(Marine consultants)
8819 Dehaviland Ave., Los Angeles, CA 90045. (310) 641-9566. FAX: (310) 641-9566. email: captsetu1@aol.com
PRESIDENT
Seth Chase

ACCOMMODATING IDEAS, INC.
(Sign-language consultants)
11650 Riverside Dr., Ste. 4, North Hollywood, CA 91602. (818) 752-3320. FAX: (818) 752-3323.

ADVANCED FIRE & RESCUE SERVICES
10044 Columbus Ave., Mission Hills, CA 91345. (818) 837-7336, (661) 299-4801. FAX: (661) 298-3069.
CONTACTS
Craig Sanford
Mark Pedro

AERIAL FOCUS PRODUCTIONS
(Aerial, skydiving, base jumps, hang gliding)
8 Camino Verde, Santa Barbara, CA 93103. (805) 962-9911. FAX: (805) 962-9536.
www.aerialfocus.com email: aerialfcs@aol.com

ALEXANDER TECHNIQUE/ACTOR'S MOVEMENT SPECIALIST
(Movement choreography)
P.O. Box 3194, Beverly Hills, CA 90212. (310) 277-0009. FAX: (310) 277-0009. email: jeanlouis@aol.com
DIRECTOR OF TRAINING
Jean-Louis Rodrigue

AVIATION IN ENTERTAINMENT CONSULTANTS
(Airline & military aircraft, pilots, procedure)
21521 Hummingbird St., Trabuco Canyon, CA 92679. (714) 888-0550. FAX: (714) 888-0099.
PRESIDENT
John T. Durkin

BEE PEOPLE UNLIMITED
(Insect handlers, trainers and research services)
P.O. Box 343, Claremont, CA 91711. (909) 869-7690, (800) 924-3097. FAX: (909) 869-7391.
CONTACTS
Gregg Manston
Debra Copple

BIGGS-ADAMS
(Union labor consultant)
8019 Corbin Ave., Canoga Park, CA 91306. (818) 349-4057. FAX: (818) 993-8642.

BLACKSTONE MAGIK ENTERPRISES, INC.
(Magic technical advisers, consultants)
12800 Puesta Del Sol, Redlands, CA 92373. (909) 792-1227. FAX: (909) 794-2737. www.BlackstoneMagik.com

BOOZ, ALLEN & HAMILTON, INC.
(Strategy, reorganization for companies)
Four Wood Hollow Road, Parsippany, NJ 07054-2814. (973) 630-7600.

BRAVO HELICOPTERS
(Aerial technical advisers)
3401 Airport Dr., Torrance, CA 90505. (310) 325-9565, (800) 77F-LYNN. FAX: (310) 325-9856. www.bravoair.com
OWNER & CHIEF PILOT
Robin Petgrave

BRIGHT & ASSOCIATES
(Identity design & consultants)
4223 Glencoe Ave., Ste. A-223, Marina Del Rey, CA 90292. (310) 305-2565. FAX: (310) 305-2566.

BROADCAST BUSINESS CONSULTANTS, LTD.
(Talent payment and negotiations)
317 Madison Ave., New York, NY 10017. (212) 687-3525. FAX: (212) 949-9143.

PAUL BRONSTON, M.D.
(Medical adviser)
1 Jib St., #202, Marina Del Rey, CA 90292. (310) 301-9426. FAX: (310) 823-2433.

BUDGETS BY DESIGN
(Schedules & budgets)
428 Spencer St., Glendale, CA 91202. (818) 507-4449. FAX: (818) 507-4464.
www.budgetsbydesign.com email: budgets@earthlink.net
CONTACT
Robert Schneider

CALIFORNIA HISTORICAL GROUP WWII LIVING HISTORY ASSOCIATION
(World War II technical advice)
P.O. Box 1950, Costa Mesa, CA 92628. (714) 641-3421, (310) 479-5943. FAX: (714) 546-9035.
www.wgn.net/~roberte/chg email: roberte@wgn.net
CHAIRMAN
Stan Wolcott

CALIFORNIA SAILING ACADEMY
(Boating advisor)
14025 Panay Way, Marina Del Rey, CA 90292. (310) 821-3433. FAX: (310) 821-4141. email: rufus@ucla.edu
PRESIDENT
Paul Miller

CALL THE COPS
(Police tactics, homicide procedures)
P.O. Box 911, Agoura Hills, CA 91376. (661) 245-2677, (818) 595-5125. FAX: (661) 245-2677. www.call-the-cops.com
CONTACT
Randy Walker

RICHARD G. CASTANON, M.D., F.A.C.S.
(Medical adviser)
17822 Beach Blvd., Ste. 325, Huntington Beach, CA 92647. (714) 842-2596. FAX: (714) 841-5413.

THE CHARTER CONNECTION
(Marine coordination & consulting)
5015 Pacific Ave., Marina Del Rey, CA 90292. (310) 827-4105. FAX: (310) 827-0381.
CONTACT
Bertram McCann

CHEQUERED FLAG INTERNATIONAL, INC.
(Classic european cars, technical advisers)
4128 Lincoln Blvd., Marina Del Rey, CA 90292. (310) 827-8665. FAX: (310) 821-1272.

CONSULTANTS FOR TALENT PAYMENT, INC.
(Talent payment and residuals)
22 W. 27 St., New York, NY 10001. (212) 696-1100. FAX: (212) 545-0607.

COUNCIL OF CONSULTING ORGANIZATIONS
521 Fifth Ave., 35th Flr., New York, NY 10175. (212) 697-8262.

DALE SYSTEM, INC.
(Security consultants)
1101 Stewart Ave., Garden City, NY 11530. (516) 794-2800. FAX: (516) 542-1063.
250 W. 57 St., New York, NY 10107. (212) 586-1320.
2440 Whitney Ave., Hamden, CT 06518. (203) 288-7933.
PRESIDENT
Harvey M. Yaffe

CURT DECKERT ASSOCIATES, INC.
(Technical management consultants, optical technology research & development)
18061 Darmel Pl., Santa Ana, CA 92705. (714) 639-0746. FAX: (714) 639-0746.
www.cdeckert.com email: cdeckert@wdc.net

JOSEF DOLEZAL, CZECH SLOVAK CONSULTING SVCS.
(Consulting services for Czech Rep. & Eastern Europe)
9025 Wilshire Blvd., Ste. 301, Beverly Hills, CA 90211. (310) 281-8042. FAX: (310) 281-8021.

ELECTROFEX
(Entertainment industry electronics support)
1146 N. Central, Ste. 231, Glendale, CA 91202. (818) 775-3838. email: bat2@flash.net

DONALD M. FAXON
(Historic architecture & transportation adviser)
365 Mariposa Ave., Unit D, Sierra Madre, CA 91024. (626) 355-1826.

FIRE PROTECTION SPECIALISTS/DAN GOLD
(Fire & rescue advice)
260 S. Lake Ave., Ste. 169, Pasadena, CA 91101. (800) 327-1239, (310) 502-9389. email: FranMC@aol.com
CONTACTS
Dan Gold
Fran Couzens

FLORIDA FILM CARS/CLASSIC VEHICLE RENTALS
(Advisers for vehicles for film)
4691 University Dr., Ste. 204, Coral Springs, FL 33067. (954) 340-3013, (800) 746-9140.

NINA FOCH STUDIOS
(Creative consultant)
P.O. Box 1884, Beverly Hills, CA 90213. (310) 553-5805. FAX: (310) 553-6149.
CONTACT
Maud Valot

DODI FROMSON
(Art consultant)
P.O. Box 49808, Los Angeles, CA 90049. (310) 451-1110.

GARY GANG STABLES
(Western period livestock, firearms)
13801 Gladstone, Sylmar, CA 91342. (818) 362-4648.

GOLDEN PARASHOOT ENTERTAINMENT
(Skydiving, hang gliding and aerial stunts)
30251 Golden Lantern, Ste. E-518, Laguna Niguel, CA 92677. (949) 644-1212. FAX: (949) 644-6565.

IRA A. GREENBERG, PH.D/GROUP HYPNOSIS CENTER
(Hypnosis for problem solving: actors, writers and directors)
8939 S. Sepulveda Blvd., Ste. 318, Los Angeles, CA 90045. (310) 568-0022. FAX: (310) 568-0011.

LARTEC SYSTEMS
(Studio design and wiring)
4201 W. Burbank Blvd., Burbank, CA 91505. (818) 972-1070. FAX: (818) 845-2414.

LENA PRODUCTION SERVICES
(Initial budgets, breakdowns and invoicing)
11700 Iowa Ave., Ste. 203, Los Angeles, CA 90025. (310) 207-5362. FAX: (310) 826-5362.

LEXINGTON SCENERY & PROPS
(Scenery design and fabrication)
10443 Arminta St., Sun Valley, CA 91352-4109. (818) 768-5768. FAX: (818) 768-4217.
www.lexingtonscenery.com email: lexscene@earthlink.net
OWNERS
John Wright, Frank Bencivengo

LIN-DEL ASSOCIATES
(Consultants on period props)
13601 Ventura Blvd., Ste. 359, Sherman Oaks, CA 91423. (310) 453-0193, (516) 374-0173. FAX: (310) 453-0193.

WARREN LOCKHART CONSULTING
(Film & TV production consultants)
4333 Admiralty Way, Ste. 10BP on the Promenade, Marina Del Rey, CA 90292. (310) 821-1414. FAX: (310) 301-0536.
email: WarrenLockhartFilms@compuserve.com
CONTACT
McKenzie Allen

MARSHALL/PLUMB RESEARCH ASSOCIATES
(Legal research, script clearances)
4150 Riverside Dr., # 209, Burbank, CA 91505. (818) 848-7071.

MEDIA CITY TELEPRODUCTION
(Technical advisers for TV production)
2525 N. Naomi St., Burbank, CA 91504. (818) 848-5800. FAX: (818) 848-6454.
www.mediacitystudios.com email: tvburbank@aol.com
V.P., SALES & MARKETING
Ellen Elledge

MIRIMAR ENTERPRISES
(Script consultants)
P.O. Box 4621, N. Hollywood, CA 91607. (818) 784-4177. FAX: (818) 990-3439.

LARRY MOSS SPEECH & DIALECT SERVICES
(Dialect, diction & speech)
855 3rd St., Ste. 305, Santa Monica, CA 90403. (310) 395-4284.

PANPIPES MAGICKAL MARKETPLACE
(Occult technical advisers)
1641 N. Cahuenga Blvd., Hollywood, CA 90028. (323) 462-7078. FAX: (323) 462-6700.
GENERAL MANAGER & PRACTITIONER
George H. Derby

PROFESSIONAL FORCE SECURITY CONSULTANTS
(Police technical adviser)
(800) 662-7372. FAX: (800) 662-7372.
email: rjnla@earthlink.net
PRESIDENT
Ron Boyd

SANTA ANITA PARK
(Technical advisers, horse racing)
285 W. Huntington Dr., Arcadia, CA 91007. (626) 574-6394. FAX: (626) 574-5074.
www.santaanita.com email: santaanita@aol.com

KATHRYN SEGURA'S PHD ANIMALS
(Animal rentals)
(818) 508-8353. FAX: (818) 508-6732.
email: phdanimals@aol.com

SECOND LINE SEARCH
(Stock footage researchers)
1926 Broadway, New York, NY 10023. (212) 787-7500.

THE SIGN LANGUAGE COMPANY
(Sign Language Consultants, Interpreters & Tutors)
14203 Califa St., Van Nuys, CA 91401. (818) 782-6002. FAX: (818) 994-3214. www.signlanguage.to
email: scriptla@aol.com
CONTACT
Bill Pugin

THRILLSEEKERS UNLIMITED, INC.
(Extreme sports for film, TV and S.A.G. stuntpersons)
3172 N. Rainbow Blvd., Ste. 321, Las Vegas, NV 89108. (702) 699-5550, (305) 531-9670 (Miami Beach).
www.thrillnet.com email: thrillrich@msn.com
CEO & DIRECTOR OF OPERATIONS
Rich Hopkins

II JAM PRODUCTIONS
(Locations/casting for Belize)
12531 Chanute St., Pacoima, CA 91331. (310) 246-8267. FAX: (818) 834-4515. email: nmiguel@aol.com
COORDINATOR
Nigel Miguel

MADEMOISELLE IRENE UJDA
(Period re-enactment & historical consultant)
2546-1/2 Corralitas Dr., Los Angeles, CA 90039. (323) 664-0227, (310) 244-8028.

U.S. FILM FORCE
(Military & government coordination, technical advice)
8306 Wilshire Blvd., Ste. 2659, Beverly Hills, CA 90211. (323) 468-0282. FAX: (323) 651-0380. email: filmforce@aol.com
PRESIDENT
David Georgi

MICHAEL WIESE PRODUCTIONS
11288 Ventura Blvd., Ste. 821, Studio City, CA 91604. (818) 379-8799. FAX: (818) 986-3408.
www.earthlink.net/~mwp email: kenlee@earthlink.net

THE WING GALLERY
13520 Ventura Blvd., Sherman Oaks, CA 91423. (818) 981-9464. Fax: (818) 981-2787. www.winggallery.com
OWNER
Mark Dietrich

Costume & Prop Rentals

ABC COSTUME SHOP
3704 N.E. 2nd Ave., Miami, FL 33137. (305) 573-5657. FAX: (305) 573-5758.

ABRAHAM RUGS GALLERY
525 N. La Cienega Blvd., Los Angeles, CA 90048. (310) 652-6520. (800) 222-RUGS. FAX: (310) 652-6594.

ACCU-CAST/ACCU-DENT
(Prosthetic grade alginates, fast to slow setting for prop duplication)
85-F Industrial Way, Buellton, CA 93427. (805) 686-4672, (800) 344-5457. FAX: (805) 688-7928. www.accucast-alginate.com
CONTACT
Lucinda Baker

ACTION SETS & PROPS/WONDERWORKS
7231 Remmet Ave., Canoga Park, CA 91303. (818) 992-8811. FAX: (818) 347-4330. www.wonderworksweb.com
PRESIDENT
Brick Price

ADAM'S STAINED GLASS
1426 4th St., Santa Monica, CA 90401. (310) 451-9390. FAX: 9310) 451-9386.
CONTACT
Adam Gritlefeld

ADELE'S OF HOLLYWOOD
5034 Hollywood Blvd., Los Angeles, 90027. (310) 663-2231. FAX: (310) 663-2232.

AERO MOCK-UPS
13110 Saticoy St., Ste. C, North Hollywood, CA 91605. (818) 982-7327. FAX: 9818) 982-0122. www.aeromockups.com
PRESIDENT
Richard Chan

AGAPE UNIFORM COMPANY
3606 W. Washington Blvd., Los Angeles, CA 90018. (323) 731-0690.

AIM PROMOTIONS
37 35th Ave., #11, Astoria, NY 11101. (718) 729-9288.

AIR HOLLYWOOD
(Aircraft props)
1811 W. Magnolia Blvd., Burbank, CA 91506. (818) 557-1516. FAX: (818) 557-0056. www.airhollywood.com
PRESIDENT
Talaat Captan

AIRPOWER AVIATION RESOURCES
(Antique, civilian and military aircraft)
702 Paseo Vista, Thousand Oaks, CA 91360. (818) 499-0307. FAX: (805) 498-0357. www.airpower-aviation.com
CONTACT
Michael Patlin

ALLAN UNIFORM RENTAL SERVICE, INC.
121 E. 24 St., 7th Flr., New York, NY 10010. (212) 529-4655.

ALL EFFECTS COMPANY, INC.
(Breakaway props)
17614 Lahey St., Granada Hills, CA 91344. (818) 366-7658. FAX: (818) 366-3768. www.allfx.com

ALMOST CHRISTMAS PROPSHOP
(Holiday decorations, animated Santas, elves and sleighs)
3630 Holdridge Ave., Los Angeles, CA 90016. (310) 839-0921. FAX: (310) 839-7512. www.christmaslights.com
CONTACT
Cathy Christmas

ALTERED ANATOMY, INC.
7125 Laurel Canyon Blvd., Ste. A, North Hollywood, CA 91605. (818) 765-1992. FAX: (818) 765-5147.

ALTMAN LUGGAGE
135 Orchard St., New York, NY 10002. (212) 254-7275.

AMERICAN COSTUME CORP.
(Period wardrobe, 1770-1970)
12980 Raymer St., North Hollywood, CA 91605. (818) 764-2239. FAX: (818) 765-7614.
PRESIDENT
Janet Stout

ANA SPECIAL EFFECTS
(Glass and props)
7021 Hayvenhurst Ave., Van Nuys, CA 91406. (818) 909-6999.

ANATOMORPHEX
(Animation creatures and characters, makeup effects, hero props and statues)
8210 Lankershim Blvd., Ste. 14, North Hollywood, CA 91605. (818) 768-2880. FAX: (818) 768-4808. www.anatomorphex.com

ANIMAL MAKERS
12473 Gladstone Av.e, Unit A, Lake View Terrace, CA 91342. (818) 838-3440, (818) 838-359. FAX: (818) 838-3441. www.animalmakers.com

ANIMAL OUTFITS FOR PEOPLE CO.
2255 Broadway, New York, NY 10024. (212) 877-5085.

ANTIQUARIAN TRADERS
9031 W. Olympic Blvd., Beverly Hills, CA 90211. (310) 247-3900. FAX: (310) 247-8864. www.antiquariantraders.com
email: antiques@antiquariantraders.com

ANTIQUE & CLASSIC VEHICLES
811 Union St., Brooklyn, NY 11215. (718) 788-3400.
CONTACT
Leonard Shiller

ANTIQUE GUILD
8800 Venice Blvd., Los Angeles, CA 90034. (310) 838-3131. FAX: (310) 287-2486.

ARTS & CRAFTERS, INC.
175 Johnson St., Brooklyn, NY 11201. (718) 875-8151.

AQUAVISION
(Marine props and fabrication)
256 Loma Ave., Long Beach, CA 90803. (562) 433-2863. ww.aquavision.net

BEDFELLOWS
12250 Ventura Blvd., Sherman Oaks, CA 91604. (818) 985-0500. FAX: (818) 985-0617.

BIGGER THAN LIFE, INC.
(Inflatables, sets and props)
1327 Fayette St., El Cajon, CA 92020. (619) 449-9988, (800) 383-9980. FAX: (619) 449-8299. www.biggerthanlife.com
CONTACT
Mark Hassett

BRILES WING & HELICOPTER, INC.
16303 Waterman Dr., Van Nuys, CA 91406. (818) 994-1445. FAX: (818) 994-1447. www.briles.rotor.com
CONTACT
Mike Guest

THE BRUBAKER GROUP
10560 Dolcedo Way, Los Angeles, CA 90077. (310) 472-4766.

PAT BRYMER CREATIONS
(Custom fantasy walk arounds)
136 N. Avenue 61, Ste. 102, Los Angeles, CA 90042-4263. (323) 259-0400. FAX: (323) 259-0358. www.pbcreations.com

BUENA VISTA STUDIOS
500 S. Buena Vista St., Burbank, CA 91521. (818) 560-1056.

CAGEY COSTUME SOURCE
1109 Francis Marion Dr., Wilmington, NC 28412. (910) 270-4720.
COSTUME DESIGNER
Gloria Glynn

CAL-EAST IMPORTS
(Specializing in wigs)
232 S. Beverly Dr., #211, Beverly Hills, CA 90212. (310) 270-4720. FAX: (310) 278-4761.

CALIFORNIA ART PRODUCTS CO.
(Custom fiberglass products)
11111 Chandler Blvd., North Hollywood, CA 91601. (818) 762-4276. FAX: (818) 762-9826.
CONTACT
Patrick Berberian

CALIFORNIA SAILING ACADEMY
(Antique marine props)
14025 Panay Way, Marina Del Rey, CA 90292. (310) 821-3433. FAX: (310) 821-4141. www.sailingacademy.com
PRESIDENT
Paul Miller

CALIFORNIA SURPLUS MART
6263 Santa Monica Blvd., Hollywood, CA 90038. (323) 465-5525.

CAMERA READY CARS
11161 Slater Ave., Fountain Valley, CA 92708. (714) 444-1700.

CELEBRITY EYEWORKS
c/o Independent Studio Services, 11907 Wichs St., Sun Valley, CA 91352. (818) 764-0840.
CONTACT
Michael Hirsch

CENTRAL PROPERTIES
514 W. 49th St., 2nd Flr., New York, NY 10019. (212) 265-7767. FAX: (212) 582-3746.

CENTRE FIREARMS CO, INC.
10 W. 37 St., New York, NY 10018. (212) 244-4040, (212) 244-4044. FAX: (212) 947-1233.

CHARISMA DESIGN STUDIO, INC.
(Custom props, mechanical or steel, glass, foam, plastics, full-sgn services)
13227 San Fernando Rd., Sylmar, CA 91342. (818) 364-8383. FAX: (818) 364-8386. www.charismadesign.com
CONTACT
Ben Baron

CINEMAFLOAT
1624 W. Ocean Front, Newport Beach, CA 92663. (714) 675-8888.

C.J.S. FILM STUDIOS
2005 N. 103rd Ave., Avondale, AZ 85323. (602) 264-2539. FAX: (602) 936-7015.

CLASSIC CAR SUPPLIERS
1905 Sunset Plaza Dr., W. Hollywood, CA 90069. (310) 657-7823.

CLASSIC CARS LEASING CO.
500 Park Ave., New York, NY 10022. (212) 752-8080.

CONTEMPORARY ART RESOURCE
(Custom fine props)
1035 N. Myra Ave., Los Angeles, CA 90029. (323) 665-7566.

CONTINENTAL SCENERY
7802 Clybourn Ave., Sun Valley, CA 91352. (323) 461-4139.

COOPER FILM CARS
132 Perry, New York, NY 10014. (212) 929-3909.

COSTUME ARMOUR, INC.
2 Mill St., Cornwall, NY 12518. (914) 534-9120.

COSTUME COLLECTION
7119 Fair Ave., North Hollywood, CA 91605. (818) 503-0544. FAX: (818) 764-6719.

THE COSTUME PLACE
3117 Hamilton Way, Los Angeles, CA 90029. Tel/FAX: (323) 661-2597.
CONTACT
Betty St. Clair

COSTUME RENTALS CO.
11149 Vanowen St., North Hollywood, CA 91605. (818) 753-3700. FAX: (818) 753-3737.
CONTACT
Buffy Snyder

ELIZABETH COURTNEY COSTUMES
4019 Tujunga Ave., Studio City, CA 91604. (818) 763-8615.

CREATIVE COSTUME CO.
242 West 36th St., 8th Flr., New York, NY 10018. (212) 564-5552. FAX: (212) 564-5613.

CUSTOM CHARACTERS
621 Thompson Ave., Glendale, CA 91201-2032. (818) 507-5940. FAX: (818) 507-1619.

DAVID'S OUTFITTERS, INC.
36 W. 20 St., New York, NY 10011. (212) 691-7388.

DES CARTES CATERING
(Antique style food-cart rentals)
5499 W. Washington Blvd., Los Angeles, CA 90016. (323) 935-6995. FAX: (323) 9358-6205. www.cartparty.com
CONTACT
Michael Damico

DESERT PROPS
42848 150th St. East, Lancaster, CA 93535. (805) 946-6426. FAX: (805) 946-0454. www.waldhaus.com
MANAGER
Rady Czajkowski

THE WALT DISNEY STUDIOS
500 S. Buena Vista St., Burbank, CA 91521. (818) 560-0044.

DOMSEY INTERNATIONAL SALES CORP.
431 Kent Ave., Brooklyn, NY 11211. (718) 384-6000.

DOZAR OFFICE FURNITURE
9937 Jefferson Blvd., Ste. 100, Culver City, CA 90232. (310) 559-9292. FAX: (310) 559-9009.

E. C. 2 COSTUMES
4019 Tujunga Ave., Studio City, CA 91604. (818) 506-7695. FAX: (818) 506-0772.
MANAGER
Worthy Meacham

E=MC^2
(Television, video and computer props)
710 Ivy St., Glendale, CA 91204. (818) 243-2424. FAX: (818) 243-5126. www.emc2visfx.com
CONTACT
Bob Morgenroth

EASTERN COSTUME
7243 Coldwater Canyon, N. Hollywood, CA 91605. (818) 982-3611. www.easterncostume.com

EAVES-BROOKS COSTUME CO., INC.
21-07 41st Ave., Long Island City, NY 11101. (718) 729-1010.

ECLECTIC ENCORE PROPERTIES, INC.
620 W. 26 St., 4th Flr., New York, NY 10001. (212) 645-8880. FAX: (212) 243-6508.
James Gill

ELLIS PROPS & GRAPHICS
169 N. La Brea Ave., Los Angeles, CA 90036. (323) 933-7334. FAX: (323) 930-1268.

ENVIRION VISION
3074 Whaleneck Dr., Merrick, NY 11566. (516) 378-2250.

ERA AVIATION
6160 Carl Brady Dr., Anchorage, AK 99502. (907) 248-4422, (800) 478-1947. FAX: (907) 266-8383. www.era-aviation.com
CONTACT
Lee Ann McDonald

EXECUTIVE YACHT MANAGEMENT, INC./FILM SERVICES DIVISION
(Picture and camera boats)
644 Venice Blvd., Marina Del Rey, CA 90291-4801. (310) 306-2555. FAX: (310) 306-1147.

EXTREME MARINE PRODUCTION SERVICES
3419 Via Lido, Ste. 145, Newport Beach, CA 92663. (562) 596-7105. FAX: (562) 596-7125.
CONTACT
Linda Flewitt

EXTREME SPORTS FOR FILMING
3419 Via Lido, Ste. 145, Newport Beach, CA 92663. (562) 596-7105. FAX: (562) 596-7125.
PRESIDENT
Miles Flewitt

EYES ON MAIN
3110 Main St., #108, Santa Monica, CA 90405. (310) 399-3302. FAX: (310) 399-7682.

LARRY FIORITTO'S SPECIAL EFFECTS SERVICES
(Pyrotechnics, weather, rigging)
1067 E. Orange Grove, Burbank, CA 91501. (818) 954-9829.
CONTACT
Larry Fioritto

FUN ANTIQUES & COLLECTIBLES
1101 First Ave., New York, NY 10021. (212) 838-0730. FAX: (212) 838-3617.
www.fun-antiques.com email: george@fun-antiques.com

GARY GANG STABLES
13801 Gladstone, Sylmar, CA 91342. (818) 362-4648.

PETER GEYER ACTION PROPS & SETS
(Breakaways, including rubber)
8235 Lankershim Blvd., Ste. G, N. Hollywood, CA 91605. (818) 768-0070.

GLENDALE COSTUMES
746 W. Doran St., Glendale, CA 91203. (818) 244-1161. FAX: (818) 244-8576.
CONTACT
Tim Deitlein

GLOBAL EFFECTS, INC.
(Spacesuits and armor)
7119 Laurel Canyon Blvd., Unit 4, North Hollywood, CA 91605. (818) 503-9273. FAX: (818) 503-9459.

GRAPHIC ILLUSIONS/HOLLYWOOD 2000
(Custom computer props)
4200 Verdant, Unit C, Los Angeles, CA 90039. (818) 840-8333.
CONTACT
Joe Martinez

GREGORY'S TUX SHOP
12051 Magnolia Blvd., North Hollywood, CA 91607. (818) 980-5480. FAX: (818) 980-5084. www.tuxedosonline.com
CONTACT
Vrej Gregorian

GROSH SCENIC RENTALS, INC.
4114 Sunset Blvd., Los Angeles, CA 90029. (323) 662-1134. FAX: (323) 664-7526.

HAND PROP ROOM, INC.
5700 Venice Blvd., Los Angeles, CA 90019. (323) 931-1534. FAX: (323) 931-2145.

HOLLYWOOD BREAKAWAY
416 S. Victory Bld., Burbank, CA 91502. (818) 845-2779. FAX: (323) 466-2942.

HOLLYWOOD CENTRAL PROPS
9171 San Fernando Rd., Sun Valley, CA 91352-1414. (818) 394-4504. FAX: (818) 394-4509.
V.P. & GENERAL MANAGER
Rick Caprarelli

HOLLYWOOD GLASS COMPANY
5119 Hollywood Blvd., Los Angeles, CA 90027. (323) 665-8829. FAX: (323) 661-7261.

HOLLYWOOD PICTURE VEHICLES/THE BOSEWS COLLECTION
1028 N. LaBrea Ave., Hollywood, CA 90038. (323) 466-2277. FAX: (323) 466-6541.
CONTACT
Michael Fox

HOLLYWOOD TOYS & COSTUMES
6600 Hollywood Blvd., Hollywood, CA 90028. (323) 464-4444. FAX: (323) 464-4644. www.hollywoodtoys.com

HOUSE OF COSTUMES, LTD.
166 Jericho Turnpike, Mineola, NY 11501. (516) 294-0170.

HOUSE OF PROPS
(Fine arts prop rentals)
1117 Gower St., Hollywood, CA 90038. (323) 463-3166. FAX: (323) 463-8302.
CONTACT
Norman Balos

IMAGE ENGINEERING, INC.
733 N. Reese Place, Burbank, CA 91505. (818) 840-1444.
CONTACT
Peter Chesney

IN COSTUME
37 W. 20 St., New York, NY 10011. (212) 255-5502. FAX: (212) 255-3788.

INDEPENDENT STUDIO SERVICES
11907 Wicks St., Sun Valley, CA 91352. (818) 764-0840, (818) 768-6320.

INTERNATIONAL COSTUME
1423 Marcellina Ave., Torrance, CA 90501. (310) 320-6392. FAX: (310) 320-3054. www.internationalcostume.com

IT'S A WRAP
3315 W. Magnolia Blvd., Burbank, CA 91505. (818) 567-7366. www.movieclothes.com

IWASAKI IMAGES OF AMERICA
(Food Replicas)
20460 Gramercy Pl., Torrance, CA 90501. (310) 328-7121. FAX: (310) 618-0876. www.iwasaki-images.com
email: iwasaki@iwasaki-images.com

IZQUIERDO STUDIOS
118 W. 22 St., New York, NY 10011. (212) 807-9757.

JULES & JIM CUSTOM ARTWORK
(Design and artwork for props and set dressing)
14740 Cumpston St., Sherman Oaks, CA 91411. (818) 7803278. FAX: (818) 780-3278.

KREISS COLLECTION
8619 Melrose Ave., Los Angeles, CA 90069-5010. (310) 657-3990.

KUTTNER PROP RENTALS, INC.
601 W. 26th St., 3rd Flr., New York 10001. (212) 242-7969. FAX: (212) 247-1293.
CONTACT
Barbara Genest

L.A. EYEWORKS
7407 Melrose Ave., Los Angeles, CA 90046. (323) 653-8255. FAX: (323) 653-8176. email: laeyeworks@earthlink.net

LEXINGTON SCENERY & PROPS
10443 Arminta St., Sun Valley, CA 91352. (818) 768-5768. FAX: (818) 768-4217.

LILLIAN COSTUME CO. OF L.I., INC.
226 Jericho Turnpike, Mineola, NY 11501. (516) 746-6060.

MADE IN L.A.
(Custom screen graphic movie props)
4200 Verdant St., Ste. C, Los Angeles, CA 90039. (818) 840-8333. FAX: (818) 551-9178.
CONTACT
Joe Martinez

THE MANNEQUIN GALLERY
P2021 W. Burbank Blvd., Burbank, CA 91506. (818) 845-5084. FAX: 9818) 842-6054.
CONTACT
Shelley Freeman

MED + RENT, INC.
11677 Sheldon St., Sun alley, CA 91352. (818) 252-0700. FAX: (818) 252-0705. www.medrent.com
GENERAL MANAGER
Andrew Corcia

MODERN PROPS
5500 W. Jefferson Blvd., Los Angeles, CA 90016. (323) 934-3000. FAX: (323) 934-3155. www.modernprops.com

MOTION PICTURE COSTUMES & SUPPLIES, INC.
6844 Lankershim Blvd., North Hollywood, CA 91605. (818) 764-8191. FAX: (818) 764-9430.
PRESIDENT
Michelle Archer

MOTION PICTURE MARINE
616 Venice Blvd., Marina Del Rey, CA 90291. (310) 822-1100. FAX: (310) 822-2679. www.motionpicturemarine.com

MUSIC PROP SERVICES
(Musical instruments for film & television)
1609 Cahuenga Blvd., Hollywood, CA 90028. (323) 466-5120.

NATIONAL HELICOPTER SERVICE
16800 Roscoe Blvd., Van Nuys, CA 91406. (818) 345-5222. FAX: (818) 782-0466. www.nationalhelicopter.com
CONTACT
Richard Hart

NAUTICAL HERITAGE FILM SERVICES
1064 Calle Negocio, Ste. B, San Clemente, CA 92673. (800) 432-2201. FAX: (562) 594-9242.
CONTACT
Michael Neipris

NEOTEK, INC.
(Electronic and surveillance equipment)
1121 Chestnut St., Burbank, CA 91506. (818) 840-8225. FAX: (818) 840-8301. www.neotekinc.com

NIGHTS OF NEON
7442 Varna Ave., North Hollywood, CA 91605. (818) 982-3592. FAX: (818) 503-1090.

NORCOSTCO, INC.
3606 W. Magnolia Blvd., Burbank, CA 91505. (818) 567-0753, (800) 220-6915. FAX: (818) 567-1961.
GENERAL MANAGER
Wayne Thornton

OMEGA CINEMA PROPS
5857 Santa Monica, Blvd., Los Angeles, CA 90038. (310) 466-8201. FAX: (310) 461-3643.

OUR SECRET CREATIONS
(Custom cubic zirconia and jewelry rentals)
246 S. Robertson Blvd., Beverly Hills, CA 90211. (310) 358-8404. FAX: (310) 358-0179.

PALACE COSTUME & PROP COMPANY
835 N. Fairfax Ave., Los Angeles, CA 90046. (323) 651-5458. FAX: (323) 658-6860. www.palacecostume.com
CONTACT
Seo Alanzo

PARAMOUNT COSTUME DEPARTMENT
5555 Melrose Ave., Backlot Operations, Hollywood, CA 90038. (323) 956-5288. FAX: (323) 956-2342.

PERIOD PROPS
235 W. Olive Ave., Burbank, CA 91502. (818) 848-PROP. (818) 41S-ERVE. FAX: (818) 843-4745.

PETERSEN AVIATION
7155 Valjean Ave., Van Buys, CA 91406. (818) 989-2300, (800) 451-7270. FAX: (818) 902-9386. www.petersenaviation.com
CONTACT
Ken Curry

PICTURE CARS, EAST, INC.
72 Huntington St., Brooklyn, NY 11231. (718) 852-2300.

PROP-ART
(Custom props, including sculpture, mechanized devices)
6189 Sylvan Dr., Simi Valley, CA 93063. Tel/FAX: (805) 583-4773.

PROP MASTERS, INC.
912 W. Isabel St., Burbank, CA 91506. (818) 846-3915, (818) 846-3957. FAX: (818) 846-1278.

PROP SERVICES WEST, INC.
915 N. Citrus Ave., Los Angeles, CA 90038. (323) 461-3371. FAX: (323) 461-4571.

PROPS DISPLAYS & INTERIORS, INC.
132 W. 18th St., New York, NY 10011. (212) 620-3840. FAX: (212) 620-5472.

PROPS FOR TODAY
330 W. 34th St. New York, NY 10001. (212) 244-9600. FAX: (212) 244-1053. email: prophouse@aol.com

QUARTERMASTER UNIFORM COMPANY
5057 W. Pico Blvd., Los Angeles, CA 90019. (323) 692-0092. FAX: (323) 692-0494. www.qmuniforms.com

R/C MODELS
803 Channel St., San Pedro, CA 90731. (310) 833-9166. FAX: (310) 833-9167. www.rcmodelsusa.com

ROCK & WATER CREATIONS, INC.
(Ponds, watrerfalls and boulders)
815 5th St., Filmore, CA 93015. (805) 524-5600. FAX: (805) 524-7339.
PRESIDENT
Roger Embury

RUBIE'S COSTUME CO., INC.
120-08 Jamaica Ave., Richmond Hill, Queens, NY 11418. (718) 846-1008.

SCENIC HIGHLIGHTS
4640 Sperry St., Los Angeles, CA 90039. (818) 956-3610. FAX: (818) 956-3616.

SCHOEPFER STUDIOS
138 W. 31 St., New York, NY 10001. (212) 736-6939.

SETS & PROPS BY FOAM-TEC, INC.
11107 Randall St., Sun Valley, CA 91352. (818) 504-7303. FAX: (818) 504-7314.

SHAKEY'S WIGS
6364 Hollywood Blvd., Hollywood, CA 90028. (323) 461-8481.

SHELLY'S APPAREL WAREHOUSE
2089 Westwood Blvd., Los Angeles, CA 90025. (310) 475-1400. FAX: (310) 470-6125.

SOMPER FURS
301 N. Canon Dr., Beverly Hills, CA 90210. (310) 273-5262. FAX: (310) 273-7270.

SONY PICTURES STUDIOS WARDROBE
10202 W. Washington Blvd., Culver City, CA 90232. (310) 280-7260. FAX: (310) 244-1408.

SPORTSROBE
8654 Hayden Place, Culer City, CA 90232. (310) 559-3999. FAX: (310) 559-4767.

STEFAN WILCOX
(Props & weapons master)
c/o Wilcox Cinema Props, P.O. Box 1331, Studio City, CA 91614. (818) 990-9057.

STICKS & STONES
(Specialty props, costume design, custom build only; make-up effects and puppets)
12990 Branford St., Ste. M, Arleta, CA 91331. (818) 252-2088. FAX: (818) 252-2087.
email: jemrtb@ecom.net
CONTACTS
Rob Burman
Jennifer E. McManus

STUDIO PICTURE VEHICLES
(Transportation: police vehicles, armored trucks, ambulances, taxis)
5418 Fair Ave., North Hollywood, CA 91601. (818) 765-1201, (818) 781-4223. FAX: (818) 506-4789.

THE STUDIO WARDROBE DEPARTMENT
1357 N. Highland Ave., Hollywood, CA 90038. (323) 467-9455.
CONTACT
Rick Pickrone

THE SWORD & THE STONE
(Period clothing & armour)
723 N. Victory Ave., Burbank, CA 91502. (818) 562-6548. FAX: (818) 564-6549. www.swordandstone.com

TRIANGLE SCENERY/DRAPERY/LIGHTING CO.
1215 Bates Ave., Los Angeles, CA 90029. (323) 662-8129.

MIKE TRISTANO WEAPONS & SPECIAL EFFECTS
(Prop weapons, blank firing weapons, on-set weapons handlers and armorer)
14431 Ventura Blvd., Ste. 185, Sherman Oaks, CA 91423. (818) 888-6970. FAX: (818) 888-6447.

20TH CENTURY FOX/FOX PRODUCTION SERVICES: WARDROBE
10201 W. Pico Blvd., Bldg. 99, Los Angeles, CA 90035. (310) 369-1897. FAX: (310) 369-2487.
CONTACT
Mike Vogh

20TH CENTURY FOX/FOX PRODUCTION SERVICES: PROPS
10201 W. Pico Blvd., Bldg. 99, Room 342, Los Angeles, CA 90035. (310) 369-2775. FAX: (310) 369-3183.
CONTACT
Randy Torpin

20TH CENTURY PROPS
(WWII submarine and F-18 fighter jet for rent)
11651 Hart St., North Hollywood, CA 91605-5802. (818) 759-1190. FAX: (818) 759-0081. www.20thcenturyprops.com

UNITED AMERICAN COSTUME
12980 Raymer St., North Hollywood, CA 91605. (818) 764-2239. FAX: (818) 765-7614.
MANAGER
Janet Stout

UNIVERSAL FACILITIES RENTAL
100 Universal City Plaza, #480-3, Universal City, CA 91608. (818) 777-3000, (800) 892-1979. FAX: (818) 733-1579.

USHIST HISTORICAL RESOURCES
(Civil War, Indian Wars, Cowboy costumes)
Box 26957, Phoenix, AZ 85068-6957. (602) 331-4945. FAX: (602) 331-8592.
CONTACT
Terrance C. Leavey

VISUAL SERVICES
40 W. 72 St., New York, NY 10023. (212) 580-9551.

WARNER BROS. STUDIOS, FACILITIES/WIG RENTALS
4000 Warner Blvd., Burbank, CA 91522. Costumes: (818) 954-1297. Wigs: (818) 954-2151.
CONTACT
Tracy Balsz

WEAPONS SPECIALISTS, LTD.
33 Greene St., 1-W, New York, NY 10013. (212) 941-7696. (800) 878-7696. FAX: (212) 941-7654.
CONTACT
Rick Washburn

WEIRD STUFF DESIGNERS
6040 N. 26th Ave., Phoenix, AZ 85019. (602) 973-5224. FAX: (602) 973-4404.

WESTERN COSTUME CO.
11041 Van Owen St., North Hollywood, CA 91605. (818) 760-0900. FAX: (818) 508-2190.

WONDERWORKS
7231 Remmet Ave., #F, Canoga Park, CA 91303. (818) 992-8811. FAX: (818) 347-4330.

ADRIA ZIMMERMAN
5 Park Village Ct., Greensboro, NC 27455. (910) 288-4736. FAX: (910) 288-4736.

Entertainment Lawyers

AKIN, GUMP, STRAUSS, HAUER & FELD
2029 Century Park East, Ste. 2600, Los Angeles, CA 90067. (310) 229-1000. FAX: (310) 229-1001.
ATTORNEYS
David A. Braun

AKRE, BRYAN & MAILAN, LP
444 S. Flower St., 20th Flr., Los Angeles, CA 90071. (213) 623-1100. FAX: (213) 623-1533. www.akrelaw.com
ATTORNEY
David Symons

ALSCHULER, GROSSMAN, STEIN & KAHAN, LLP
2049 Century Park East, Ste. 3900, Los Angeles, CA 90067. (310) 277-1226. FAX: (310) 552-6077.
ATTORNEY
John Schwimmer

ARMSTRONG, HIRSCH, JACKOWAY, TYERMAN & WERTHEIMER
1888 Century Park East, 18th Flr., Los Angeles, CA 90067-1722. (310) 553-0305. FAX: (310) 553-5036.
ATTORNEYS
Allan L. Alexander
Karl R. Asuten
Ronald J. Bass
Joseph D'Onofrio
Alan Epstein
Howard A. Fishman
Andrew Gulker
Robert Getman
George T. Hayum
Geraldine S. Hemmerling
Barry L. Hirsch
James R. Jackoway
Jonathan D. Kaufelt
Chris F. Kerns
James C. Mandelbaum
David J. Matlof
Marcy Morris
Michael M. Mulrooney
Jeffrey Oblath
Paul Reese
Scott Stein
Robert Stulberg
Barry Tyerman
Robert Wallerstein
Eric Weissler
Alan S. Wetheimer

ARNOLD & PORTER
777 S. Figueroa St., 44th Flr., Los Angeles, CA 90017-2513. (213) 243-4000. FAX: (213) 243-4199.

ARTISAN LEGAL
1925 Century Park East, Ste. 500, Los Angeles, CA 90067. (310) 289-5447. FAX: (310) 289-5486. URL: www.yourcounselor.com

ASHERSON, KLEIN & DARBININ
9150 Wilshire Blvd., Ste. 210, Beverly Hills, CA 90212. (310) 247-6070. (310) 278-8454.
GENERAL PARTNERS
Neville Asherson
Anna Darbinin

BARAB, KLINE & COATE, LLP
9606 Santa Monica Bld., 3rd Flr., Beverly Hills, CA 90210. (310) 859-6644. FAX: (310) 859-6650.
MANAGING PARTNER
Martin Barab

STEPHEN BARON
1299 Ocean Ave., Ste. 312, Santa Monica, CA 90401. (310) 260-6060. FAX: (310) 260-6061.

BEHR & ABRAMSON
2049 Century Park East, Ste. 2690, Los Angeles, CA 90067. (310) 556-9200. FAX: (310) 556-9227.

BELDOCK, LEVINE & HOFFMAN
99 Park Ave., Ste. 1600, New York, NY 10016-1503. (212) 490-0400. FAX: (212) 557-0565.

BERGER, KAHN, SHAFTON, MOSS, FIGLER, SOMON & GLADSTONE
4215 Glencoe Ave., 2nd Flr., Marina Del Rey, CA 92092. (310) 821-9000. FAX: (310) 578-6178.
DIRECTOR, ENTERTAINMENT DEPARTMENT
Leon Gladstone

BERKOWITZ & ASSOCIATES
468 N. Camden Dr., Ste. 200, Beverly Hills, CA 90210. (310) 276-9031. FAX: (310) 276-9272.
CONTACT
Barbara Berkowitz

BERTON & DONALDSON
9595 Wilshire Blvd., Ste. 711, Beverly Hills, CA 90212-2507. (310) 271-5123. FAX: (310) 271-4760.
ATTORNEYS
Stuart Berton
Michael C. Donaldson
Mark Litwak
Michael E. Morales

BIENSTOCK & CLARK
3250 Ocean Park Blvd., Ste. 350, Santa Monica, CA 90405. (310) 314-8660. FAX: (310) 314-8662.

BLAIN & ASSOCIATES
8447 Wilshire Blvd., Ste. 107, Beverly Hills, CA 90211. (323) 951-7150. FAX: (323) 951-7159.
ATTORNEYS
Tony Blain
Alexander Greenfield
Marc Primo

BLANC, WILLIAMS, JOHNSTON & KRONSTADT
1900 Ave. of the Stars, Ste. 1700, Los Angeles, CA 90067. (310) 552-2500. FAX: (310) 552-1191.
ATTORNEY
Harley Williams

BLOOM, HERGOTT, COOK, DIEMER & KLEIN
150 S. Rodeo Dr., 3rd Flr., Beverly Hills, CA 90212.
ATTORNEYS
Jacob A. Bloom
Stephen F. Breimer
Steven L. Brookman
Eric M. Brooks
Melanie Cook
John Diemer
David B. Feldman
Candice S. Hanson
Alan S. Hergott
Thomas F. Hunter
Tina J. Kahn
Deborah L. Klein
Patricia M. Knapp
Roger Patton
Stuart Rosenthal
Robin Roth
MIchael Schenkman
Richard D. Thompson
David E. Weber

CHRISTENSEN, MILLER, FINK, JACOBS, GLASER, WEIL & SHAPIRO
2121 Ave. of the Stars, Ste. 1800, Los Angeles, CA 90067. (310) 553-3000. FAX: (310) 556-2920.
ATTORNEYS
Patricia Glaser
Robert Shapiro

CODIKOW, CARROLL, GUIDO & GROSSMAN
9113 Sunset Blvd., Los Angeles, CA 90069-3106. (310) 271-0241. FAX: (310) 271-0775.
ATTORNEYS
Rosemary Carroll
David Codikow

COUNTRYMAN & MCDANIEL
5933 W. Century Blvd., Ste. 1111, Los Angeles, CA 90045. (310) 342-6500. FAX: (310) 342-6505.
ATTORNEYS
Byron Countryman
Michael McDaniel

COWAN, DEBAETS, ABRAHAMS & SHEPPARD
40 W. 57th St., New York, NY 10019. (212) 974-7474. FAX: (212) 974-8474.
ATTORNEYS
Philip M. Cowan
Timothy K. DeBaets

DEL, SHAW, BLYE & MOONVES
2029 Century Park East, Ste. 3910, Los Angeles, CA 90067-3025. (310) 772-2000. FAX: (310) 772-2777.
ATTORNEY
Nina Shaw

JUDITH C. DORNSTEIN
1888 Century Park East, Ste. 1100, Los Angeles, CA 90067. (310) 286-9896. FAX: (310) 553-2510.

ERICKSON & HALLORAN
1620 26th St., Ste. 2060 N., Santa Monica, CA 90404. (310) 453-0700. FAX: (310) 453-0706.
ATTORNEY
Gunnar Erickson

ERVIN, COHEN & JESSUP
9401 Wilshire Blvd., 9th Flr., Beverly Hills, CA 92012. (310) 273-6333. FAX: (310) 859-2325.
ATTORNEY
Gary Freedman

ESQ. MANAGEMENT
Box 16194, Beverly Hills, CA 90209. (310) 252-9879.
PERSONAL MANAGER & ATTORNEY
Patricia Lee

FRAGOMEN, DEL REY & BERNSEN
12121 Wilshire Blvd., Ste. 1001, Los Angeles, CA 90025. (310) 820-3322. FAX: (310) 820-2702.

FRANKFURT, GARBUS, KLEIN & SELZ, P.C.
488 Madison Ave., 9th Flr., New York, NY 10022. (212) 980-0120. FAX: (212) 593-9175. www.fgks.com
ENTERTAINMENT PARTNERS
Lisa E. Davis
Jill N. Goldstein
Richard B. Heller
Richard Hofstetter
Candice Kersh
Stewart Kleinman
Brain Murphy
Amy Cibinic Ondreyka
Edward Rosenthal
Thomas Selz
Gerald E. Singleton
Michael Williams
Maura Wogan

FREDERICKS & VONDERHORST
12121 Wilshire Blvd., Ste. 950, Los Angeles, CA 90025. (310) 820-3600. FAX: (310) 820-1832.
email: fredrickslaw@earthlink.net
CONTACT
Mark Binder

FREEDMAN & TAITELMAN, LLP
6420 Wilshire Blvd., Ste. 200, Los Angeles, CA 90048. (323) 653-4900. FAX: (323) 653-4910.
ATTORNEY
Michael A. Taitelman

GAGE, FRASIER & TEEPLE
9255 Towne Centre Dr., Ste. 500, San Diego, CA 92121. (858) 622-7878. FAX: (858) 622-0411.
PARTNER
Ben Gage

GARVIN, DAVIS & BENJAMIN, LLP
9200 Sunset Blvd., Penthouse 25, Los Angeles, CA 90069. (310) 278-7300. FAX: (310) 278-7306. email: lhb@gdblaw.net
CONTACT
Linda H. Benjamin, Esq.

GENDLER & KELLY
9113 Sunset Blvd., Los Angeles, CA 90069. (310) 281-2552. FAX: (310) 275-1999.
ATTORNEYS
Michael Gendler
Kevin M. Kelly

GERDES & ASSOCIATES
2029 Century Park East, Ste. 2750, Los Angeles, CA 90067. (310) 385-9501. FAX: (310) 858-6703.
ATTORNEY
Ted Gerdes

GIBSON, DUNN & CRUTCHER, LLP
2029 Century Park East, Ste. 4000, Los Angeles, CA 90067. (310) 552-8500. FAX: (310) 551-8741.

GIPSON, HOFFMAN & PANCIONE
1901 Ave. of the Stars, Ste. 1100, Los Angeles, CA 90067. (310) 556-4660. FAX: (310) 556-8945.
ATTORNEYS
Robert Gipson
G. Raymond Gross
John McHale
Mara Morner Ritt
Peter Pancione
Randy Paul
Julia Ross
Kenneth Sidle
Robert Steinberg

GLICKFELD, FIELDS & JAFFE
9460 Wilshire Blvd., 5th Flr., Beverly Hills, CA 90212. (310) 550-7222. FAX: (310) 550-6222.
ATTORNEY
Michael Glickfeld

GRAKAL, ROOT & ROSENTHAL, LLP
1541 Ocean Ave., Ste. 200, Santa Monica, CA 90401. (310) 260-1055. FAX: (310) 260-1058.
ATTORNEY
Richard Rosenthal

JEFFREY L. GRAUBERT
2029 Century Park East, Ste. 2700, Los Angeles, CA 90067. (310) 788-2650. FAX: (310) 788-2657.

GREENBERG, GLUSKER, FIELDS, CLAMAN & MACHTINGER, LLP
1900 Ave. of the Stars, Ste. 2100, Los Angeles, CA 90067. (310) 553-3610. FAX: (310) 553-0687.
ATTORNEYS
Bertram Fields
Leonard S. Machtiger

HALL, DICKLER, KENT, FRIEDMAN & WOOD
2029 Century Park East, Ste. 3760, Los Angeles, CA 90067. (310) 203-810. FAX: (310) 203-8559.

HANSEN, JACOBSEN, TELLER, HOBERMAN, NEWMAN & WARREN, HERTZ & GOLDRING
450 N. Roxbury Dr., 8th Flr., Beverly Hills, CA 90210. (310) 271-8777. FAX: (310) 276-8310.

HEENAN BLAIKIE
9401 Wilshire Blvd., Ste. 1100, Beverly Hills, CA 90212-2924. (310) 275-3600. FAX: (310) 724-8340.
ATTORNEYS
Jeffrey Berkowitz
Dan Black
Brad Fenscer
Jody Simon
Larry Verbit

GARY D. HERZOG
1632 N. Formosa, Ste. 107, Los Angeles, CA 90046. (323) 876-5920. FAX: (323) 876-6061.

IRELL & MANELLA, LLP
1800 Ave. of the Stars, Ste. 900, Los Angeles, CA 90067-4276. (310) 277-1010. FAX: (310) 203-7199.
ENTERTAINMENT ATTORNEYS
Lois Scali
Joan Lesser
Lee Liedecke
Molly MacIsaac Coleman
Phil Miller
David Nimmer
Heather Sachs
Clark Siegal
Juliet Youngblood
Ed Zeldow

ISAACMAN, KAUFMAN & PAINTER
8484 Wilshire Blvd., Ste. 850, Beverly Hills, CA 90211. (323) 782-7700. FAX: (323) 782-7744.
email: ikpaint@worldnet.att.net
ATTORNEY
Neil Fischer

IVERSON, YOAKUM, PAPIANO & HIRSCH
624 S. Grand Ave., 27th Flr., Los Angeles, CA 90017. (213) 624-7444. (213) 629-4563.
PARTNER
Neil Papiano
ENTERTAINMENT ATTORNEYS
Adam Burke
Lara Citrano

JACOBSON & COLFIN, P.C.
156 5th Ave., Ste. 434, New York, NY 10010. (212) 691-5630. FAX: (212) 645-5038. www.thefirm.com
ATTORNEYS
Bruce E. Colfin
Jeffrey E. Jacobson

JEFFER, MANGELS, BUTLER & MARMARO
2121 Ave. of the Stars, 10th Flr., Los Angeles, CA 90067. (310) 203-8080. FAX: (310) 203-0567. www.jmbm.com
ENTERTAINMENT ATTORNEYS
Neil O. Andrus
Michael S. Sherman

JOHNSON & RISHWAIN, LLP
12121 Wilshire Blvd., Ste. 1201, Los Angeles, CA 90025. (310) 826-2410. FAX: (310) 826-5450. www.jandrlaw.com
ATTORNEY
Neville L. Johnson

KATTEN, MUCHIN & ZAVIS
1999 Ave. of the Stars, Ste. 1400, Los Angeles, CA 90067. (310) 788-4400. FAX: (310) 788-4471. www.kmz.com
ENTERTAINMENT PARTNERS
Kristin Acterhof
Ivy Kagan Bierman
Marsha A. Boysaw
Steve Cochran
Susan A. Grode
Joyce S. Sun
Melvin L. Katten
Valerie E. Kincaid
Zia F. Modabber
Michael P. Murphy
DeAnne H. Ozaki
Melvin E. Pearl
Charles M. Stern
M. Kenneth Suddleson
Gail Migdal Title
Joel R. Weiner

KATZ, GOLDEN & SULLIVAN, LLP
10850 Wilshire Blvd., Ste. 600, Los Angeles, CA 90024. (310) 470-7777. FAX: (310) 470-7481.
ATTORNEY
Steven B. Katz

KEHR, SCHIFF & CRANE
12400 Wilshire Blvd., Ste. 1300, Los Angeles, CA 90025-1030. (310) 820-3455. FAX: (310) 820-4414.

KENOFF & MACHTINGER
1999 Ave. of the Stars, Ste. 1250, Los Angeles, CA 90067. (310) 552-0808. FAX: (310) 277-0653.
PARTNERS
Jay S. Kenoff
Leaonard S. Machtinger

JEFFREY G. KICHAVEN
1801 Century Park East, Ste. 2500, Los Angeles, CA 90067. (310) 556-1444. FAX: (310) 556-0444.

KINSELLA, BOESCH, FUJIKAWA & TOWLE
1901 Ave. of the Stars, Ste. 700, Los Angeles, CA 90067. (310) 201-2000. FAX: (310) 284-6018.

KIRSCH & MITCHELL
2029 Century Park East, Ste. 2750, Los Angeles, CA 90067. (310) 785-1200. FAX: (310) 286-9573.

KIRTLAND & PACKARD
1900 Ave. of the Stars, 26th Flr., Los Angeles, CA 90067. (310) 552-9700. FAX: (310) 552-0957.

KLEINBERG, LOPEZ, LANGE, BRISBIN & CUDDY, LLP
2049 Century Park East, Ste. 3180, Los Angeles, CA 90067. (310) 286-9696. FAX: (310) 286-6445.

LEONARD, DICKER & SCHREIBER
9430 Olympic Blvd., Ste. 400, Beverly Hills, CA 90212. (310) 551-1987. FAX: (310) 277-8050.

LEWIS, D'AMATO, BRISBOIS & BISGAARD
221 N. Figueroa, Ste. 1200, Los Angeles, CA 90012. (213) 250-1800. FAX: (213) 250-7900.
ATTORNEY
Robert Lewis

LICHTER, GROSSMAN, NICHOLS & ADLER
9200 Sunset Blvd., Ste. 1200, Los Angeles, CA 90069. (310) 205-6999.

LOEB & LOEB, LLP
10100 Santa Monica Blvd., Ste. 2200, Los Angeles, CA 90067. (310) 282-2000. FAX: (310) 282-2192.
345 Park Ave., New York, NY 10154. (212) 407-4000. FAX: (212) 407-4990. www.loeb.com
ATTORNEYS
Leah Antonio-Ketcham
Harold D. Berkowitz
David Byrnes
John J. Dellaverson
Craig Emannuel
Keith Fleer
John T. Frankenheimer
Jim Goodkind
Phillip Graves
Michael A. Myerson
Randolf Mendelsohn
Stephen Mick
Miles Mogulescu
Nigel Graham Pearson
Steen Pena
Saul Rittenberg
Myron Slobodien
Rebel Steiner
Irwin Tenenbaum
Don Thornburgh
Jonathan Wight
Susan Z. Williams

LOWY & ZUCKER
9107 Wilshire Blvd., Ste. 650, Beverly Hills, CA 90210. (310) 275-9999. FAX: (310) 275-1683. www.lowyzucker.com
ATTORNEYS
Steven Lowy
Andrew Zucker

MANATT, PHELPS & PHILLIPS, LLP
11355 W. Olympic Blvd., Los Angeles, CA 90064. (310) 312-4000. FAX: (310) 312-4224.
ATTORNEYS
Gerald A. Margolis
Laurence M. Marks
L. Lee Phillips

MAYOR, GLASSMAN, GAINES & RAPORE, LLP
11726 San Vicente Blvd., Ste. 400, Los Angeles, CA 90049-5006. (310) 207-0007. FAX: (310) 207-3578.

MAZIE & SILVERMAN
468 N. Camden Dr., Ste. 300, Beverly Hills, CA 90210. (310) 285-5346. FAX: (310) 285-5347.
MANAGING PARTNER
Mark Mazie

CAROL L. MCKELVY
1925 Century Park East., Ste. 2000, Los Angeles, CA 90067. (310) 277-2236. FAX: (310) 551-2022.

MENES LAW CORPORATION
1801 Century Park East, Ste. 1560, Los Angeles, CA 90067. (310) 277-4895. FAX: (310) 556-5695.

MITCHELL, SILERBERG & KNUPP, LLP
11377 W. Olympic Blvd., Los Angeles, CA 90064. (310) 312-2000. FAX: (310) 312-3100. www.msk.com
ATTORNEYS
Phillip Davis
Harold Friedman
Roger Sherman

MORRISON & FOERSTER
555 W. 5th St., Ste. 3500, Los Angeles, CA 90013. (213) 892-5200. FAX: (213) 892-5454. www.mofo.com

RICHARD A. MORSE II
MGM Plaza, 2450 Broadway, Ste. 550, Santa Monica, CA 90404. (310) 315-6325. FAX: (310) 315-6301.

MYMAN, ABELL, FINEMAN & GREENSPAN
11777 San Vicente Blvd., Ste. 880, Los Angeles, CA 90049. (310) 820-7717. FAX: (310) 207-2680.

NELSON, GUGGENHEIM, FELKER & LEVINE, LLP
10880 Wilshire Blvd., Ste. 2070, Los Angeles, CA 90024-4101. (310) 441-8000. FAX: (310) 441-8010.
ATTORNEYS
George M. Davis
Warren D. Davis
Corinne Farley
Patti C. Felker
Michael R. Fuller
Alfred Guggenheim
Jared E. Levine
Peter Martin Nelson
Fred Toczek

LOUISE NEMSCHOFF
1801 Ave. of the Stars, 6th Flr., Los Angeles, CA 90067. (310) 274-4627. FAX: (310) 274-5039.

NOVIAN & NOVIAN, LLP
1801 Century Park East, Ste. 1201, Los Angeles, CA 90067. (310) 553-1222. FAX: (310) 553-0222.
CONTACT
Farhad Novian

JAAK OLESK
270 N. Canon Dr., Ste. 203, Beverly Hills, CA 90210. (310) 288-0693. FAX: (310) 288-0863.

O'MELVENY & MYERS
1999 Ave. of the Stars, Ste. 700, Los Angeles, CA 90067. (310) 553-6700. FAX: (310) 246-6779. www.omm.com

ORRICK, HERRINGTON & SUTCLIFFE
777 S. Figueroa, Ste. 3200, Los Angeles, CA 90017. (213) 629-2020. FAX: (213) 612-2499. www.orrick.com
666 5th Ave., New York, NY 10103. (212) 506-5000.
Washington Harbour, 3050 K. St. N.W., Washington, DC 20007. (202) 339-8400. FAX: (202) 339-8500.
ATTORNEY
Jeffrey White

PASCOTTO & GALLAVOTTI
1800 Ave. of the Stars, Ste. 900, Los Angeles, CA 90067. (310) 203-7515. FAX: (310) 284-3021.
ATTORNEY
Alvaro Pascotto

PILLSBURY, MADISON & SUTRO
725 S. Figueroa, Ste. 1200, Los Angeles, CA 90017. (213) 488-7100. FAX: (213) 629-1033.

PROSKAUER ROSE, LLP
2049 Century Park East, Ste. 3200, Los Angeles, CA 90067-3206. (310) 557-2900. FAX: (310) 557-2193. www.proskauer.com
ENTERTAINMENT ATTORNEYS
Howard D. Behar
Sandra A. Crawshaw
Paul H. Epstein
William M. Hart
Jeffrey A. Horwitz
Carla M. Miller
Charles B. Ortner
Lawrence I. Weinstein

RICHMAN, LAWRENCE, MANN, CHIZEVER, PHILLIPS & DUBOFF
9601 Wilshire Blvd., Penthouse, Beverly Hills, CA 90210. (310) 274-8300. FAX: (310) 274-2831. www.richmanlaw.com

HUGH DUFF ROBERTSON
4727 Wilshire Blvd., Ste. 605, Los Angeles, CA 90010-3875. (323) 939-8900. FAX: (323) 939-5544.

ROSENFELD, MEYER & SUSMAN, LLP
9601 Wilshire Blvd., 4th Flr., Beverly Hills, CA 90210-5288. (310) 858-7700. FAX: (310) 271-6430. www.rmslaw.com
ENTERTAINMENT ATTORNEYS
Greg S. Bernstein
Renee A. Farrell
Krista Helfferich
Lawrence Kartiganer
Marvin B. Meyer
Jerry Nagin
Allen E. Susman
Melissa Tapie

RUBIN, BAUM, LEVIN
20 Rockefeller Plaza, 29th Flr., New York, NY 10112. (212) 698-7700. FAX: (212) 698-7825.

SEYFARTH, SHAW, FAIRWEATHER & GERALDSON
2029 Century Park East, Ste. 3300, Los Angeles, CA 90067-3063. (310) 277-7200. FAX: (310) 201-5219. www.seyfarth.com

SHELDON & MAK, INC.
225 S. Lake Ave., 9th Flr., Pasadena, CA 91101. (626) 796-4000. FAX: (626) 795-6321. www.usip.com
ATTORNEY
Daniel J. Coplan

SHEPPARD, MULLIN, RICHTER & HAMPTON
333 S. Hope St., 48th Flr., Los Angeles, CA 90071. (213) 620-1780. www.smrh.com

SHUMAKER, SRAGOW & STECKBAUER, LLP
300 S. Grand Ave., Ste. 1400, Los Angeles, CA 90071-3124. (213) 229-2868. FAX: (213) 629-4520.

SIDLEY & AUSTIN
555 W. 5th St., Ste. 4000, Los Angeles, CA 90013-1010. (213) 896-6000. FAX: (213) 896-6600.

SKADDEN, ARPS, SLATE, MEAGHER & FLOM, LLP
300 S. Grand Ave., Ste. 3400, Los Angeles, CA 90071. (213) 687-5000. www.sasmf.com

SLOSS LAW OFFICE
170 5th Ave., Ste. 800, New York, NY 10010. (212) 627-9898. FAX: (212) 627-6498. www.slosslaw.com

SOMMER & BEAR
9777 Wilshire Blvd., Ste. 512, Beverly Hills, CA 90212. (310) 858-4989. FAX: (310) 858-0775.
ATTORNEY
Paul Sommer

STANBURY & FISHELMAN, INC.
9200 Sunset Bld., Penthouse 30, Los Angeles, CA 90069-3607. (310) 278-1800. FAX: (310) 278-1802.
email: stanfish@msn.com
ATTORNEY
Bruce C. Fishelman

STANKEVICH-GOCHMAN, LLP
9777 Wilshire Blvd., Ste. 550, Beverly Hills, CA 90212. (310) 859-8825. FAX: (310) 859-8830.
ATTORNEY
Mark Stankevich

STERN, NEUBAUER, GREENWALD & PAULY
1299 Ocean Ave., 4th Flr., Santa Monica, CA 90401. (310) 451-8001. FAX: (310) 395-5965.

KATHY L. TANNEN
Box 55004, Sherman Oaks, CA 91413. (818) 501-7517. FAX: (818) 501-2053.

THELEN, REID & PRIEST, LLP
333 S. Grand Ave., 34th Floor, Los Angeles, CA 90071-3193. (213) 621-9800. FAX: (213) 623-4742.
40 West 57th St., New York, NY 10019. (212) 603-2000. FAX: (212) 603-2001. www.thelenreid.com
ENTERTAINMENT ATTORNEYS
Ezra J. Doner
Michael S. Elkin
Andrew P. Kransdorf
H. Joseph Mello
J. Michael Parish
Karen Young

TISDALE & NICHOLSON
2049 Century Park East, Ste. 755, Los Angeles, CA 90067. (310) 286-1260. FAX: (310) 286-2351.

TROOP, STEUBER, PASICH, REDDICK & TOBEY, LLP
2029 Century Park East, 24th Flr., Los Angeles, CA 90067. (310) 728-3739. FAX: (310) 728-2200. www.trooplaw.com

HARRIS TULCHIN & ASSOCIATES
11377 W. Olympic Blvd., 2nd Flr., Los Angeles, CA 90064. (310) 914-7979. FAX: (310) 914-7927. www.medialawyer.com
ATTORNEYS
Paul D. Fix
Harris Tulchin

LAWRENCE J. TURNER
9200 Sunset Blvd., Ste. 701, Los Angeles, CA 90069. (310) 273-4858. FAX: (310) 273-1869.

SUZANNE VAUGHAN
6848 Firmament Ave., Van Nuys, CA 91406. (818) 988-5599. FAX: (818) 988-5577. www. suzyesq.com

A. CHANDLER WARREN, JR.
7715 Sunset Blvd., Ste. 208, Los Angeles, CA 90046. (323) 876-6400. FAX: (323) 876-3170.

WEIL, GOTSHAL & MANGES
767 5th Ave., New York, NY 10053. (212) 735-4553. FAX: (212) 735-4502.
2882 San Hill Rd., Ste. 280, Menlo Park, CA 94025. (650) 926-6200. FAX: (650) 854-3713.

WEINSTEIN & HART
9777 Wilshire Blvd., Ste. 1009, Beverly Hills, CA 90212. (310) 274-7157. FAX: (310) 274-1437.
email: joehartlaw@worldnet.att.net
ATTORNEY
Joseph Hart

WEISSMAN, WOLF, BERGMAN, COLEMAN & SILVERMAN
9665 Wilshire Blvd., Ste. 900, Beverly Hills, CA 90212. (310) 858-7888.

WILSON, ELSER, MOSKOWITZ, EDELMAN & DICKER LLP
1055 W. 7th St., Ste. 2700, Los Angeles, CA 90017. (213) 624-3044. FAX: (213) 624-8060. www.wemed.com

WOLF, RIFKIN & SHAPIRO
11400 W. Olympic Blvd., 9th Flr., Los Angeles, CA 90064. (310) 478-4100. FAX: (310) 478-4100.
ENTERTAINMENT ATTORNEY
Michael Leventhal

ROBERT J. YOUNG
11664 National Blvd., Ste. 441, Los Angeles, CA 90064. (3100 820-2988. FAX: (310) 820-8466.

HELEN YU
1901 Ave. of the Stars, 20th Flr., Los Angeles, CA 90067. (310) 286-7667. FAX: (310) 286-7473. email: helenyu@earthlink.net

ZIFFREN & ZIFFREN
2049 Century Park East, Ste. 1100, Los Angeles, CA 90067. (310) 286-9971.
ATTORNEYS
Leo G. Ziffren
Lester Ziffren

ZIFFREN, BRITTENHAM, BRANCA & FISCHER
1801 Century Park West, Los Angeles, CA 90067. (310) 552-3388. FAX: (310) 553-7068.
ATTORNEYS
John G. Branca
Paul Brindze
Harry M. Brittenham
Samuel Fischer
Clifford Gilbert-Lurie
Kathleen Hallberg
Dennis Luderer

Film Preservation, Processing, Repair & Storage

AFD/PHOTOGRAD FILM COATING LAB
1015 N. Cahuenga Blvd., Hollywood, CA 90038. (323) 469-8141. FAX: (323) 469-1888.

ALLIED/VAUGHN'S NEW INDEPENDENTS LAB
(Negative conforming and 16 to 35mm blow-ups)
6305 N. O'Connor Road, Bldg. 4, #111, Irving, TX 75039. (972) 869-0100. FAX: (972) 869-2117.
email: toni.bifano@allied-digital.com

ALPHA CINE LABORATORY INC.
1001 Lenora St., Seattle, WA 98121. (206) 682-8230. FAX: (206) 682-6649. email: jean@alphacine.com
CONTACTS
Roberta Ukura
Jean Fee

AMERICAN ARCHIVES, INC.
2636 North Ontario, Burbank, CA 91504. (818) 558-6995. FAX: (818) 558-7791.

ASTRO COLOR LAB
61 W. Erie St., Chicago, IL 60610. (312) 280-5500.

AVALON STAGES
6918 Tujunga Ave., N. Hollywood, CA 91605. (818) 508-0505. FAX: (818) 508-5581.

BENTON FILM FORWARDING CO.
150 Great Southwest Pkwy., Atlanta, GA 30336. (404) 699-2020. FAX: (404) 699-5588.
CONTACT
Lucy Benton

BONDED FILM STORAGE
550 Main St., Fort Lee, NJ 07024. (201) 944-3700.

BONDED SERVICES
3205 Burton Ave., Burbank, CA 91504. (818) 848-9766.

BRAMBLES INFORMATION MANAGEMENT
P.O. Box 128, Sun Valley, CA 91352. (800) 310-DATA. FAX: (818) 504-6918.
CONTACT
Reed E. Irvin

CHACE PRODUCTIONS, INC.
(Sound restoration and remastering)
201 S. Victory Blvd., Burbank, CA 91502. (818) 842-8346. FAX: (818) 843-8353. www.chace.com
PRESIDENT
Robert Heiber
GENERAL MANAGER
Allan Falk

CINE MAGNETICS FILM & VIDEO
100 Business Park Dr., Armonk, NY 10504. (914) 273-7500.

CINE MOTION PICTURE SERVICE LAB
377 Court St., Bldg. 3, Plymouth, MA 02360. (508) 746-3085.
email: cinelab@aol.com

CINEFILM/CINETRANSFER
2156 Faulkner Rd., N.E., Atlanta, GA 30324. (404) 633-1448, (800) 633-1448. FAX: (404) 633-3867.

CONSOLIDATED FILM INDUSTRIES (CFI)
959 N. Seward St., Hollywood, CA 90038. (323) 462-3161. FAX: (323) 460-4885.

CONTINENTAL FILM LABS, INC.
1998 NE 150 St., N. Miami, FL 33181. (305) 949-4252, (800) 327-8396. FAX: (305) 949-3242.
CONTACT
Vincent Hogan

7675 Currency Drive, Orlando, FL 33181. (407) 856-8958. FAX: (407) 856-4070.
CONTACT
A. J. Robbins

CREST NATIONAL VIDEO FILM LABS
(35mm & 16mm lab services, negative processing and prints, color correction, film, video and audio restoration)
1141 N. Seward St., Hollywood, CA 90038. (323) 466-0624, (323) 462-6696. FAX: (323) 461-8901.

DU ART FILM LABORATORIES
245 W. 55 St., New York, NY 10019. (212) 757-4580.

DELUXE LABORATORIES, INC.
(Full service film lab.)
1377 N. Serrano Ave., Hollywood, CA 90027. (323) 462-6171, (800) 2DE-LUXE. FAX: (323) 461-0608. www.deluxe-ent.com
V.P., SALES & MARKETING
David Hagberg

DELTA PRODUCTIONS
3333 Glendale Blvd., Ste. 3, Los Angeles, CA 90039. (323) 663-8754. FAX: (323) 663-3460.

FILM CRAFT LAB
(Processing, repair, transfers)
23815 Industrial Park Drive, Farmington Hills, MI 48335. (248) 474-3900. FAX: (248) 474-1577.
SALES REPRESENTATIVE
Patrice Heath

FILM PRESERVE
2 Depot Plaza, #202-B, Bedford Hills, NY 10507. (914) 242-9838. FAX: (914) 242-9854.
Robert A. Harris

FILM TECHNOLOGY COMPANY, INC.
726 N. Cole Ave., Hollywood, CA 90038. (323) 464-3456. FAX: (323) 464-7439.

FILMACK STUDIOS
1327 S. Wabash Ave., Chicago, IL 60605. (312) 427-3395, (800) FILMACK. FAX: (312) 427-4866.
OWNER
Robert Mack

FILMLIFE INC. AMERICAN FILM REPAIR INSTITUTE
(Preservation, repair and storage)
P.O. Box 604, Lake Worth, FL 33460. (973) 835-4200.
CHAIRMAN & CEO
Marvin A. Bernard
SENIOR V.P., PRODUCTION
Jeremy D. Bernard
COMPUTER GRAPHICS V.P., DESIGN ENGINEER
Rachel D. Bernard
V.P. WORLD-WIDE OPERATIONS
Milton Miller

FILMTREAT INTERNATIONAL CORP.
(Film preservation, restoration and repair)
42-24 Orchard St., Long Island City, NY 11101. (718) 784-4040. FAX: (718) 784-4766
CONTACTS
Y. W. Mociuk
Sam Borodinsky

FILMTREAT WEST CORP.
10810 Cantara St., Sun Valley, CA 91352. (818) 771-5390.

FORDE MOTION PICTURE LABS
306 Fairview Ave. N., Seattle, WA 98109. (206) 682-2510.

FORT LEE FILM STORAGE & SERVICE
1 Mt. Vernon, St., Ridgefield Park, NJ 07660. (201) 440-6200. FAX: (201) 440-5799.
EXECUTIVE V.P.
Patricia Miller

FOTO-KEM FOTO-TRONICS, FILM-VIDEO LAB
(Preservation, processing, repair, storage, transfer)
2800 W. Olive Ave., Burbank, CA 91505. (818) 846-3101. FAX: (818) 841-2130.
V.P., SALES
Steve Van Anda

FOUR MEDIA COMPANY
2813 W. Alameda Ave., Burbank, CA 91505. (818) 840-7000. FAX: (818) 840-7195.

GUFFANTI FILM LABORATORIES, INC.
630 Ninth Ave., New York, NY 10036. (212) 265-5530.

HIGHLAND LABORATORIES
747 Front St., #202, San Francisco, CA 94111. (415) 981-5010.

HOLLYWOOD FILM & VIDEO, INC.
6060 Sunset Blvd., Hollywood, 90028. (323) 464-2181. FAX: (323) 464-0893.

HOLLYWOOD FILM CO.
826 Seward St., Hollywood, CA 90038. (323) 462-1971, (323) 462-3284. FAX: (323) 263-9665.

HOLLYWOOD VAULTS, INC.
(Film preservation, off-site storage)
Vault: 742 N. Seward St., Hollywood, 90038. (323) 461-6464. FAX: (323) 461-6479.
Office: 1780 Prospect Ave., Santa Barbara, CA 93103. (805) 569-5336. FAX: (805) 569-1657.
www.hollywoodvaults.com email: vault@hollywoodvaults.com
PRESIDENT
David Wexler

FRANK HOLMES LABORATORIES
6609 Santa Monica Blvd., Hollywood, CA 90038. (323) 461-8078.

ICS SERVICES, INC.
920 Allen Ave., Glendale, CA 91201. (818) 242-3839. FAX: (818) 242-1566. www.members.aol.com/INTERCINE
email: Intercine@aol.com

IRON MOUNTAIN RECORDS MANAGEMENT
6190 Boyle Ave., Vernon, CA 90058-3952. (323) 466-9271. FAX: (323) 467-8068.

LASER-PACIFIC MEDIA CORP.
809 N. Cahuenga Blvd., Hollywood, CA 90038. (323) 462-6266. FAX: (323) 464-3233.

KEN LIEBERMAN LABORATORIES, INC.
(Custom prints and transparencies)
118 W. 22 St., New York, NY 10011. (212) 633-0500. FAX: (212) 675-0500. email: lieberman@lieberman-labs.com
CONTACT
Ken Lieberman

LIPSNER-SMITH COMPANY
4700 Chase, Lincolnwood, IL 60646-1689. (847) 677-3000, FAX: (847) 677-1311, (800) 784-6733.
www.rtico.com email: sales@rtico.com
6 Swan Wharf, Waterloo Road, Uxgridge UB8 2RA, England. (01895) 252191. FAX: (01895) 274692.
email: rtiuk@cix.compulink.co.uk

LUCASFILM, LTD.
P.O. Box 2009, San Rafael, CA 94912. (415) 662-1800.

MAGNO SOUND, INC.
729 Seventh Ave., New York, NY 10019. (212) 302-2505. FAX: (212) 819-1282.

MAGNO VISUALS
115 W. 45 St., New York, NY 10036. (212) 575-5162, (212) 575-5159. FAX: (212) 719-1867.

MILLENNIUM FILM WORK SHOP
66 E. 4 St., New York, NY 10003. (212) 673-0090.

MOTION PICTURE LABORATORIES, INC.
781 S. Main St., Memphis, TN 38106. (901) 774-4944, (800) 467-5675.

PACIFIC TITLE ARCHIVES
4800 San Vicente Blvd., Los Angeles, CA 90019. (323) 938-3711. FAX: (323) 938-6364.
CONTACT
David Weeden
561 Mateo St., Los Angeles, CA 90013. (213) 617-8650. FAX: (213) 617-7876.
10717 Vanowen St., N. Hollywood, CA 91605. (818) 760-4223. FAX: (818) 760-1704.
900 Grand Central Ave., Glendale, CA 91201. (818) 547-0090. FAX: (818) 548-7990.
CONTACT
Dan Gentile

PHOTOVISION, LOS ANGELES
221 N. Westmoreland Ave., Los Angeles, CA 90004. (213) 380-2980. FAX: (213) 739-6984.

PRODUCERS COLOR SERVICE
2921 E. Grand Blvd., Detroit, MI 48202. (313) 874-1112.

PRODUCERS FILM CENTER
948 N. Sycamore Ave., Hollywood, 90038. (323) 851-1122.

RGB COLOR LAB
816 N. Highland Ave., Los Angeles, CA 90038. (323) 469-1959.

RAINMAKER DIGITAL PICTURES
175 E. Olive Ave., Ste. 405, Burbank, CA 91502. (818) 526-1500. FAX: (818) 953-5051. email: info@rainmaker.com
50 West 2nd Ave., Vancouver, B.C. V5Y 1B3. (604) 874-8700. FAX: (604) 874-1719.
PRESIDENT (CA)
Peter Sternlicht
PRESIDENT (CANADA)
Bob Scarabelli

SPECTRUM MOTION PICTURE LAB
399 Gundersen Dr., Carol Stream, IL 60188. (708) 665-4242, (800) 345-6522.

SPORTS FILM LAB
361 W. Broadway, South Boston, MA 02127. (617) 268-8388. FAX: (617) 268-8390.

TECHNICOLOR, INC.
Professional Film Division, 4050 Lankershim Blvd., North Hollywood, CA 91608. (818) 769-8500.
321 W. 44 St., New York, NY 10036. (212) 582-7310.

TRACKWISE, INC.
(Preservation and repair)
123 W. 18 St., New York, NY 10011. (212) 627-7700.
MANAGER
Fran Bowen

FILM STOCK

DR. RAWSTOCK
6916 Santa Monica Blvd., Ste. A, Los Angeles, CA 90038. (323) 960-1781. FAX: (323) 960-1780. email: filmsell@aol.com
PRESIDENT
Lowell Kay

EASTMAN KODAK COMPANY
343 State St., Rochester, NY 14650-0310. (716) 724-4000.
6700 Santa Monica Blvd., Hollywood, CA 90038. (323) 464-6131. FAX: (323) 468-1568.
360 W. 31 St., New York, NY 10001. (212) 631-3450.
4 Concourse Pkwy., Ste. 300, Atlanta, GA 30328. Information: (800) 800-8398; MP Film Orders: (800) 621-FILM.
CHAIRMAN & CEO
George M.C. Fisher
PRESIDENT & COO
Daniel Carp
PRESIDENT, ENTERTAINMENT IMAGING
Joerg D. Agin
COO, PROFESSIONAL MOTION IMAGING
Richard P. Aschman

FILM EMPORIUM
(Kodak and Ilford; video and audio tape)
274 Madison Ave., New York, NY 10016. (800) 371-2555. FAX: (212) 683-2740. www.filmemporium.com
CEO
Laird R. Criner

FUJI PHOTO FILM U.S.A., INC.
555 Taxter Rd., Elmsford, NY 10523. (914) 789-8100. (800) 755-3854. FAX: (770) 789-8295.
1285 Hamilton Pkwy., Itasca, IL 60143. (800) 877-0555, (630) 773-7200. FAX: (630) 773-6266.
1628 W, Crobsy Rd., Ste. 100, Carrollton, TX 75006. (800) 927-3854, (214) 466-9200. FAX: (214) 446-1329.
2450 Satellite Blvd., Duluth, GA 30136. (800) 366-3854, (770) 813-5100. FAX: (770) 813-5166.

ILFORD IMAGING U.S.A., INC..
W. 70 Century Rd., Paramus, NJ 07653. (201) 265-6000.

RAW STOCK
1133 Broadway, 5th Flr., New York, NY 10010. (212) 255-0445.

RESEARCH TECHNOLOGY, INC.
4700 Chase Ave., Lincolnwood, IL 60646. (847) 677-3000.

STEADI SYSTEMS
1014 N. Highland Ave., Los Angeles, CA 90038. (323) 993-3031. FAX: (323) 461-8915. www.steadi.com

STUDIO FILM & TAPE, INC.
1215 N. Highland, Hollywood, CA 90038. (323) 769-0300, (800) 824-3130. FAX: (323) 463-2121.
630 Ninth Ave., New York, NY 10036. (212) 977-9330, (800) 444-9330. FAX: (212) 586-2420.
101 W. Kinzie St., 1st Flr., Chicago, IL 60610. (312) 467-0070, (800) 467-0070. FAX: (312) 467-0074.

SUPER8 SOUND
2805 W. Magnolia Blvd., Burbank, CA 91505. (818) 848-5522.

FINANCIAL SERVICES

PROJECT FINANCING

AFRA FILM ENTERPRISES, INC.
137 S. Robertson Blvd., Ste. 254, Beverly Hills, CA 90211-2831. (310) 785-6671. FAX: (310) 785-6683.
PRESIDENT
Anatoly A. Fradis

ALLEGRA PARTNERS
515 Madison Ave., 29th Flr., New York, NY 10022. (212) 826-9824. FAX: (212) 759-2561.

ALLIED ENTERTAINMENT GROUP
14930 Ventura Blvd., Ste. 340, Sherman Oaks, CA 91403. (818) 728-9900. FAX: (818) 728-9903.
PRESIDENT
Emilio Ferrari

AMBERGATE ASSOCIATES
3000 W. Olympic Blvd., Santa Monica, CA 90404. (310) 264-3970. FAX: (310) 264-7973. www.ambergate.net
CONTACT
Eddie Kalish

AUSTRALIAN FILM COMMISSION
Level 4, 150 William St., Woolloomooloo, NSW 2011, Australia. (61 2) 9321 6444. FAX: (61 2) 9357 3737.
email: info@afc.gov.au

BANK OF AMERICA NT & SA/COMMERCIAL BANKING ENTERTAINMENT OFFICE
2049 Century Park East, #200, Los Angeles, CA 90067. (310) 785-6077. FAX: (310) 785-6100.
BUSINESS DEVELOPMENT
Paul L. Backus

BANK OF CALIFORNIA
Entertainment Division, 9401 Wilshire Blvd., 6th Flr., Beverly Hills, CA 90212. (310) 273-7200. FAX: (310) 273-9030.

BANK OF NEW YORK
530 Fifth Ave., New York, NY 10036. (212) 852-4099.

BANK SUMITOMO
777 S. Figueroa, Ste. 2600, Los Angeles, CA 90017. (213) 955-0800. FAX: (213) 623-6832.

BANKERS TRUST CO.
Entertainment Division, 300 S. Grand Ave., 41st Flr., Los Angeles, CA 90071. (213) 620-8200. FAX: (213) 620-8484.

BANQUE PARIBAS
2029 Century Park East, #3900, Los Angeles, CA 90067. (310) 551-7399. FAX: (310) 556-3145. email: rene_turin@paribas.com
ENTERTAINMENT COORDINATOR
Rene Turin

BEAR, STEARNS & CO., INC.
1999 Ave. of the Stars, Ste. 3200, Los Angeles, CA 90067-6100. (310) 201-2600. FAX: 9310) 201-2755.

BRIMSTONE ENTERTAINMENT
106 Sunridge St., Top Flr., Playa Del Rey, CA 90203. (310) 406-0670. FAX: (310) 821-7060.

BRITISH COLUMBIA PRODUCTION FINANCING
2225 W. Broadway, Vancouver, BC, Canada, V6K 2E4. (604) 736-7997. FAX: (604) 736-7290.

BRITISH CONNECTION
11955 Missouri Ave., Ste. 10, Los Angeles, CA 90025. (310) 820-7280. FAX: (310) 820-3286.
PRESIDENT
Judy Hevenly

CALIFORNIA UNITED BANK
16030 Ventura Blvd., Ste. 650, Encino, CA 91436-4487. (818) 379-1249. FAX: (818) 907-9132.
SENIOR MARKETING DIRECTOR
Steve Ellis

CAPELLA FILMS, INC. & CONNEXION AMERICAN MEDIA
9242 Beverly Blvd., Ste. 280, Beverly Hills, CA 90210. (310) 247-4700. FAX: (310) 247-4701.

CHASE SECURITIES, INC./ENTERTAINMENT GROUP
c/o The Chase Manhattan Bank, 1800 Century Park East, #400, Los Angeles, CA 90067. (310) 788-5600. FAX: (310) 788-5628.
CONTACT
Ken Wilson

CITICORP
725 S. Figueroa St., Los Angeles, CA 90025. (310) 575-4808. FAX: (310) 575-1890

CITY NATIONAL BANK
Entertainment Division, 400 N. Roxbury Dr., 4th Flr., Beverly Hills, CA 90210. (310) 888-6200. FAX: (310) 888-6157.
www.cityweb.cityntl.com

COMERICA BANK, CALIFORNIA
10900 Wilshire Blvd., 3rd Flr., Los Angeles, CA 90024. (310) 824-5700.

CREATIVE MANAGEMENT AGENCY, INC.
1 Penn Plaza, Ste. 1910, New York, NY 10119. (212) 239-0804. FAX: (212) 239-9417.
PRESIDENT & CPA
Rick Gould

FILM CAPITAL CORP.
555 S. Sunrise Way, Palm Springs, CA 92264. (760) 778-5574. FAX: (760) 778-5319. www.filmcapitalcorporation.com
CONTACT
Marlene Mendoza

FILM FINANCES, INC.
9000 Sunset Blvd., Ste. 1400, Los Angeles, CA 90069. (310) 275-7323. FAX: (310) 275-1706.
www.filmfinances.com email: ffl@ffl.com
PRESIDENT
Richard Soames

FINANCIAL MANAGEMENT ADVISORS, INC.
1900 Ave. of the Stars, Ste. 900, Los Angeles, CA 90067. (310) 229-2940. FAX: (310) 229-2950. www.fma-inc.com
SENIOR V.P. & PORTFOLIO MANAGER
Robert A. Kahn

FINANCIAL NETWORK INVESTMENT CORP.
3807 Wilshire Blvd., Ste. 1040, Los Angeles, CA 90010. (818) 547-1733. FAX: (818) 547-0388.

FIRST CHARTER BANK, N.A.
Entertainment Division, 265 N. Beverly Drive, Beverly Hills, CA 90210. (310) 278-7200. FAX: (310) 278-9543.

FLASHPOINT ENTERTAINMENT FINANCING
67 Pall Mall, London SW1 Y 5PA, U.K. (44-171) 930-9315. FAX: (44-171) 930-9316. www.flashpointuk.com
PARTNERS
David Forrest
Beau Rogers

FOUNDRY FILM PARTNERS
140 West 57th Street, Ste. 5B, New York City, NY 10019.
email: foundry@foundrycom.com
CONTACT
John Ein
Robert Greenhut

GERARD KLAUER MATTISON & CO.
529 5th Ave., 2nd Flr., New York, NY 10017. (212) 885-4000.

LEWIS HORWITZ ORGANIZATION
1840 Century Park East, Los Angeles, CA 90067. (310) 275-7171. FAX: (310) 275-8055.
PRESIDENT
Lewis Horwitz

IMPERIAL BANK
Entertainment Banking, 9777 Wilshire Blvd., Beverly Hills, CA 90212. 310) 281-2400. FAX: (310) 281-2476.
PRESIDENT
Morgan Rector

INITIAL ENTERTAINMENT GROUP
6380 Wilshire Blvd., Ste. 1600, Los Angeles, CA 90048. (323) 658-5603. FAX: (323) 658-5605. www.initial-ent.com

KRAMER & KASLOW
2029 Century Park East, Ste. 1700, Los Angeles, CA 90067. (310) 553-3838. FAX: (310) 553-3939.

THE LOCHLAND GROUP, LLC
8733 Sunset Blvd., Ste. 202, W. Hollywood, CA 90069. (310) 652-2647. FAX: (310) 652-0318.
PRESIDENT
Aaron Granath
EXECUTIVE DIRECTOR
Ruth Sutherland

MARATHON NATIONAL BANK
Entertainment Division, 11150 W. Olympic Blvd., Los Angeles, CA 90064. (310) 996-9100. FAX: (310) 996-9113.

MERCANTILE NATIONAL BANK
Entertainment Industries Division, 1840 Century Park East, 2nd Flr., Los Angeles, CA 90067. (310) 277-2265.

MERLIN FILM GROUP
16 Upper Pembroke Street, Dublin 2, Ireland. (353 1) 676 4373. FAX: (353 1) 676 4368. e-mail: info@merlin.ie
8831 Sunset Blvd., Ste. 201, W. Hollywood, CA 90069. (310) 854 0707. FAX: (310) 854 0757.
CONTACT
Norman Siderow

MORGAN & LASKY
170 McAulay Pl., Laguna Beach, CA 92651. (949) 494-8298. FAX: (949) 494-8958.
CONTACT
Michael Lasky

MOUNTAINTOP PRODUCTIONS
3400 Ave. of the Arts, Ste. A110, Costa Mesa, CA 92626. (714) 540-1989. FAX: (714) 540-1967. email: mountaintop@earthlink.net

NATEXIS BANQUE-BFCE
660 S. Figueroa St., Ste. 1400, Los Angeles, CA 90017. (213) 627-8677. FAX: (213) 627-2761.
V.P., GROUP MANAGER
Bennett Pozil

NATWEST GROUP/COUTTS
150 S. Rodeo Drive, Ste. 120, Beverly Hills, CA 90210. (310) 777-6500. FAX: (310) 777-6509.
SENIOR V.P.
Hal Sadoff

NEUBERGER & BERMAN
1999 Ave. of the Stars, Ste. 1950, Los Angeles, CA 90067. (310) 843-4949. FAX: (310) 843-4944. www.nb.com
SENIOR DIRECTOR
W. Chip Eggers

NEWMARKET CAPITAL GROUP
202 N. Canon Drive, Beverly Hills, CA 90210. (310) 858-7472. FAX: (310) 858-7473.
CONTACTS
William A Tyrer
Chris J. Ball

NEXT WAVE FILMS
(Financing and support for independent filmmakers)
2510 7th Street, Ste. E, Santa Monica, CA 90405. (310) 392-1720. FAX: (310) 399-3455. email: launch@nextwavefilms.com
PRESIDENT
Peter Broderick
DIRECTOR, POST-PRODUCTION & FINANCE
Mark Stolaroff

OCEAN CAPITAL CORP.
6500 Wilshire Blvd., Ste. 500, Los Angeles, CA 90048. (323) 653-3600. FAX: (323) 653-3834.

OPPENHEIMER & CO.
10880 Wilshire Blvd., Los Angeles, CA 90024. (310) 446-7100. FAX: (310) 446-7411.

PACIFIC CENTURY BANK
16030 Ventura Blvd., Encino, CA 91436. (818) 379-1252. FAX: (818) 379-1620.
CONTACT
David Henry

PLATINUM FILM INVESTMENTS
2269 Chestnut St., Ste. 315, San Francisco, CA 94123. (415) 885-0100. FAX: (415) 292-4464.
email: platinum@sprynet.com

THE PULLMAN GROUP
1370 Ave. of the Americas, New York, NY 10019. (212) 750-0210. FAX: (212) 750-0464. www.pullmanco.com
MANAGING DIRECTOR
David Pullman

REGENT ENTERTAINMENT, INC.
1401 Ocean Ave., Ste. 300, Santa Monica, CA 90401. (310) 260-3333. FAX: (310) 260-3343. www.regententertainment.com

D. R. REIFF & ASSOCIATES
41 W. 83rd St., New York, NY 10024. (212) 877-1099.

RUBEN, ALBERT G., & CO.
48 W. 25th St., 12th Flr., New York, NY 10010. (212) 627-7400.

SALIBELLO & BRODER
6500 Wilshire Blvd., Ste. 560, Los Angeles, CA 90048. (323) 966-2500. FAX: (323) 966-2501. email: sandbla@aol.com
SENIOR MANAGER
Johnny Joseph

SANTA MONICA BANK
1888 Century Park East, Ste. 915, Los Angeles, CA 90067. (310) 556-7727. FAXL (310) 286-1030.
email: kwhiting@smbank.com
CONTACT
Ken Whiting

SCHRODER & CO.
10877 Wilshire Blvd., Ste. 500, Los Angeles, CA 90024. (310) 443-0500. FAX: (310) 443-0589.

SCHULZE & ASSOCIATES
1701 Lake Ave., Ste. 255, Glenview, IL 60025. (847) 998-4500. FAX: (847) 998-4502. email: schulze@interaccess.com

SG COWEN
202 N. Canon Dr., Beverly Hills, CA 90210. (310) 276-3555. FAX: (310) 276-0583.

THE SHINDLER PERSPECTIVE
Box 8633, Calabasas, CA 91372-8633. (818) 223-8345. FAX: (818) 223-8372. email: shindler@aol.com
CONTACT
Marty Shindler

SILICON VALLEY BANK
Entertainment Division, 10585 Santa Monica Blvd., Ste. 135, Los Angeles, CA 90025. (310) 234-3580. FAX: (310) 234-3589.
email: pwyckoff@svbank.com
CONTACT
Paul Wyckoff

SMITH AFFILIATED CAPITAL CORP.
880 3rd Ave., 8th Flr., New York. NY 10022. (212) 644-9440. FAX: (212) 644-1979.

ST PRODUCTIONS
2041 Manning St., Burbank, CA 91505. (818) 846-3939. FAX: (818) 846-2530. email: stprods@earthlink.net
CONTACT
Sam Longoria

STEREO VISION ENTERTAINMENT
11166 Burbank Blvd., North Hollywood, CA 91601. (818) 760-7007. FAX: (818) 760-7774.
CONTACT
Tammi Harrison

TRIDENT FILM FINANCING
P.O. Box 388, Burbank, CA 91503. (818) 382-4568.

TRUST COMPANY OF THE WEST
865 S. Figueroa, Ste. 1800, Los Angeles, CA 90017. (213) 244-0000. FAX: (213) 224-0741.

2 MATCH WORLD SALES
18 Bruton Pls., Berkeley Square, Mayfair, London W1X 7AA, England. (44 207) 493-3345. FAX: (44 207) 493-3997.
CEO
Marie Hoy

UNION BANK OF CALIFORNIA ENTERTAINMENT GROUP
Communications/Media Division, 445 S. Figueroa, 15th Flr., Los Angeles, CA 90071. (213) 236-7001. FAX: (213) 236-5747.
SENIOR V.P. & MANAGER
Joseph Woolf

VOLPE, BROWN, WHELAN & CO.
1 Maritime Plaza, 11th Flr., San Francisco, CA 94111. (415) 956-8120. FAX: (415) 986-6754.

THE WALDEN GROUP
750 Battery St., Ste. 700, San Francisco, CA 94111. (415) 391-7225. FAX: (415) 391-7262.

WESTERN SECURITY BANK
Entertainment Division, 4100 W. Alameda Ave., Burbank, CA 91505. (323) 849-3200.

J.C. WILLIAMSON ENTERTAINMENT, INC.
460 S. Bedford Dr., Beverly Hills, CA 90212. (310) 273-5079. FAX: (310) 273-2589.
CONTACT
Geoffrey Talbot

COMPLETION BONDS & INSURANCE

AIU MEDIA & ENTERTAINMENT
80 Pine St., 8th Flr., New York, NY 10005. (212) 770-7353. FAX: (212) 809-4577. www.aig.com
CONTACT
Stuart Kohn

ALBERT G. RUBEN INSURANCE SERVICES, INC.
10880 Wilshire Bld., 7th Flr., Los Angeles, CA 90024. (310) 234-6800. FAX: (310) 446-7839.
SENIOR V.P.
John A. Hamby

48 W. 25th St., 12th Flr., New York, NY 10010-2703. (212) 627-7400. FAX: (212) 633-1457. www.aon.com

Pinewood Studios, Pinewood Rd., Iver, Bucks SL0 0NH, England. (44 175) 365-8200. FAX: (44 175) 365-3152.

AON/RUBEN-WINKLER ENTERTAINMENT INSURANCE
20 Bay St., Toronto, ONT M5J 2N9, Canada. (416) 868-2460. FAX: (416) 868-2469. www.aon.ca

LLOYD S. BERKETT AGENCY
11150 W. Olympic Bld., Ste. 1100, Los Angeles, CA 90064. (310) 857-5757. FAX: (310) 857-5750.
PRESIDENT & CEO
Jeff Burkett

C&S INTERNATIONAL INSURANCE BROKERS, INC.
20 Vesey St., Ste. 500, New York. NY 10007. (212) 406-4499. FAX: (212) 406-7588.
PRESIDENT
Deborah Kozee

CHUBB GROUP INSURANCE
801 S. Figueroa St., 24th Flr., Los Angeles, CA 90017. (213) 612-0880. FAX: (213) 612-5731.
MANAGER, ENTERTAINMENT
David Seaman

CINEMA COMPLETIONS INTERNATIONAL
4040 Vineland Ave., Ste. 204, Studio City, CA 91604. (818) 505-5858. FAX: (818) 505-5890. email: info@cnacci.com
PRESIDENT & CEO
Donna Smith

COLONY WEST FINANCIAL & INSURANCE
(Property & liability)
17602 17th St., Ste. 102, Tustin, CA 92680. (714) 542-4870. FAX: (714) 542-4871. www.colony-west.com
CONTACT
Matthew Chamberlain

DEWITT STERN GROUP, INC.
420 Lexington Ave., Ste. 2720, New York, NY 10170. (212) 867-3550. FAX: (212) 983-6483.

ENTERTAINMENT BROKERS INTERNATIONAL
(International production insurance, contract coverage)
10940 Wilshire Blvd., 17th Flr., Los Angeles, CA 90024. (310) 824-0111. FAX: (310) 824-5733.
PARTNER
Martin Rodgers

ENTERTAINMENT COALITION
(Completion bonds, entertainment insurance)
10 Universal City Plaza, 28th Flr., Universal City, CA 91608. (818) 505-5900. FAX: (818) 505-5999.
PRESIDENT & CEO
Donna Smith

INTERNATIONAL FILM GUARANTORS
10940 Wilshire Blvd., Ste. 2010, Los Angeles, CA 90024. (310) 208-4500. FAX: (310) 443-8998.
PRESIDENT & COO
Steve Mangel

9 Hanover St., London W1R 9HF. (0171) 493-4686. FAX: (0171) 496-4696.
CONTACT
Malcolm Burgess

ENTERTAINMENT GROUP INSURANCE & ADMINISTRATORS/NEAR NORTH ENTERTAINMENT INSURANCE SERVICES
(Production & cast insurance, medical & employee benefits)
1840 Century Park East, 5th Flr., Los Angeles, CA 90067. (310) 712-4507. FAX: 9310) 556-4773. www.egabenefits.com
CONTACT
Jeff Copans

FILM BOND INTERNATIONAL
415 N. Camden Dr., Beverly Hills, CA 90210. (310) 275-5577. FAX: (310) 275-9967.
39 Broadway, 17th Flr., New York, NY 10006. (212) 785-3456. FAX: (212) 785-6677.

FILM FINANCES SERVICES
9000 Sunset Blvd., Ste. 1400, Los Angeles, CA 90069. (310) 275-7323. FAX: (310) 275-1706. www.ffi.com

Film Finances Ltd., 14/15 Conduit Street, London, England W1R 9TG. (44 171) 629-6557. FAX: (44 171) 491-7530.

Film FInances Canada Ltd., 1100 Rene-Levesque Blvd., Ste. 1350, Montreal, Quebec H3B 4N4. (514) 875-6763. FAX: (514) 876-3987.

Film Finances Canada Ltd., 104 Yorkville Ave., Ste. 300, Toronto, Ontario M5R 1B9. (416) 929-6763. FAX: (416) 964-3987.

Film Finances. FW Thring Building, Box 205, Fox Studios Australia, Driver Ave., Moore Park, New South Wales 1363. Australia. (61 2) 8353-2600. FAX: (61 2) 8353-2601. email: filmfin@samsonprod.com.au

Film Finances France, 20 Rue Therese, 75001 Paris. (33 1) 40-20-00-05. FAX: (331) 40-20-00-06.

Film Finances Italia S.P.A., Via Panama 124, 00198 Rome. (39 06) 884-2061. FAX: (39 06) 474-0123.

GELFAND, NEWMAN & WASSERMAN
11500 W. Olympic Blvd., Ste. 404, Los Angeles, CA 90064. (310) 473-2522. FAX: (310) 478-8392. www.gnwinsurance.com

GENERAL INSURANCE CONSULTANTS
18757 Burbank Blvd., Ste. 230, Tarzana, CA 91356. (818) 776-1400. FAX: (818) 776-0900.
SENIOR V.P. & DIRECTOR, CREATIVE ENTERTAINMENT DIVISION
Michael Locelso, LL.B.

GULF INSURANCE GROUP
4600 Fuller Dr., Irving, TX 75038. (972) 650-2800. FAX: (972) 650-3682.

JOHN WILLIAM HART III INSURANCE AGENCY
12100 Wilshire Blvd., Ste. M70, Los Angeles, CA 90025. (310) 207-5432. FAX: (310) 207-8526.
CONTACT
John Hart

EVELYN HUDSON INSURANCE
(Low budget & independent production liability insurance)
1373 Westwood Blvd., Ste. 201, Los Angeles, CA 90024. (310) 477-0568. FAX: (310) 477-0569.
OWNER & BROKER
Evelyn Hudson

INFINITI PACIFIC INSURANCE SERVICE
5373 Tripple Crown Dr., Bonsall, CA 92003. (803) 419-1007. FAX: 9760) 945-6503. email: aaic@cts.com
PRESIDENT
Richard Glaser

INTERNATIONAL FILM GUARANTORS
10940 Wilshire Blvd., Ste. 2010, Los Angeles, CA 90024. (310) 208-4500. FAX: (310) 443-8998. email: smangel@nnng.com
PRESIDENT & COO
Steven Mangel

LA XCESS INSURANCE BROKERS, INC.
6280 Manchester Blvd., Ste. 345, Buena Park, CA 90621. (714) 562-8500. FAX: (714) 562-9200. www.laxcess.com
V.P. & CIC
Richard Rutkin

ALLEN LAWRENCE & ASSOCIATES
(Entertainment insurance)
7033 Owensmouth Ave/. Canoga Park, CA 91303. (714) 562-8500. FAX: (714) 562-0141.
PRESIDENT
Allen Lawrence

MANAGEMENT BROKERS INSURANCE AGENCY
(Group & individual life & disability)
9301 Wilshire Blvd., Ste. 206, Beverly Hills, CA 90210. (310) 278-5943. FAX: (310) 278-6285.
PRESIDENT
Richard Horowitz

MAROEVICH, O'SHEA & COGHLAN INSURANCE BROKERS
425 Market St., 10th Flr., San Francisco, CA 94105. (415) 957-0600. FAX: (415) 957-0577. www.maroevich.com
VICE PRESIDENT
Steve Elkins

MARSH RISK & INSURANCE SERVICES
777 S. Figueroa St. Ste. 2200, Los Angeles, CA 90017. (213) 624-5555. FAX: (213) 346-5928. www.jhmarshmc.com
ENTERTAINMENT INSURANCE
Julie Umphries

MARSHALL ENTERTAINMENT INSURANCE, INC.
2000 Universal Studios Plaza, Ste. 625, Orlando, FL 32819. (407) 363-1537. FAX: (407) 352-3308. www.marshallentertainment.com

THE MOTION PICTURE BOND COMPANY
1901 Avenue of the Stars, #2000, Los Angeles, CA 90067. (310) 551-0371. FAX: (310) 551-0518.
email: filmbonds@aol.com

NEAR NORTH INSURANCE BROKERAGE, INC.
Entertainment Division, 1840 Century Park East, Ste. 1100, Los Angeles, CA 90067-2112. (310) 556-1900. FAX: (310) 556-4702. www.nnng.com
SENIOR V.P.
David Oliver

777 Third Ave., 17th Flr., New York, NY 10017. 9212) 935-7373. FAX: (212) 702-3333.

PERCENTERPRISES COMPLETION BONDS, INC.
1901 Ave. of the Stars, Ste. 2000, Los Angeles, CA 90067. (310) 551-0371. FAX: (310) 551-0518.
email: lephraim@aol.com
PRESIDENT & COO
Joe Hobel

PETERSEN INTERNATIONAL UNDERWRITERS
23929 Valenca Blvd. Ste. 215, Valencia, CA 91355. (661) 254-0006. FAX: (661) 254-0604. www.peterseninternational.com

REYNOLDS & REYNOLDS, INC.
300 Walnut St., Ste. 200, Des Moines, IA 50309-2244. (515) 243-1724. FAX: (515) 243-6664.
email: info@reynolds-reynolds.com
PRESIDENT
Stan Reynolds

SPEARE & COMPANY INSURANCE
11620 Wilshire Blvd., Ste. 900, Los Angeles, CA 90025. (310) 914-9300. FAX: (310) 914-9398.
EXECUTIVE V.P.
Tom Alper

TAYLOR & TAYLOR ASSOCIATES, INC.
90 Park Ave., 3rd Flr., New York, NY 10016. (212) 490-8511. FAX: (212) 490-7236.

MAURICE TAYLOR INSURANCE BROKERS, INC.
Box 29127, Los Angeles, CA 90029-0127. (323) 662-9110. FAX: (323) 660-0749.
PRESIDENT
Maurice Taylor

TRAVELERS INSURANCE CO.
c/o Securities Dept., One Tower Sq., Hartford, CT 06183. (860) 277-0111.

UNITED AGENCIES, INC.
350 W. Colorado Blvd., Ste. 220, Pasadena, CA 91105-1855. (800) 800-5880. FAX: (626) 577-1346.
www.unitedagencies.com
CONTACT
Jeff Galineau

USI ENTERTAINMENT INSURANCE SERVICES
14140 Ventura Blvd., Ste. 300, Sherman Oaks, CA 91423-2750. (818) 971-5469. FAX: (818) 704-4699.
SENIOR V.P.
Greg Jones

THE WATKINS GROUP/TWG, LTD.
6709 La Tijera Blvd., Ste. 350, Los Angeles, CA 90045. (323) 782-8991. FAX: (323) 291-4026.
SENIOR PARTNER
Cedric Watkins II

MARKET RESEARCH & ANALYSIS

A.C. NIELSEN COMPANY
150 N. Martingale Rd., Schaumburg, IL 60173.
731 Wilshire Blvd., #940, Los Angeles, CA 90010. (310) 966-4900.
299 Park Ave., New York, NY 10171. (212) 708-7500.

A.C. NIELSEN COMPANY— EDI
(Provides daily box-office information for exhibition and distribution. On-line access to data.)
8350 Wilshire Blvd., #210, Beverly Hills, CA 90211. (323) 658-8300.
PRESIDENT
Marcy Polier
SENIOR V.P.
Philip Garfinkle

AMERICAN MARKETING ASSOCIATION
(310) 568-5713.

BJK&E MEDIA GROUP
40 W. 23rd St., New York, NY 10010. (212) 727-5000.

BRAMSON & ASSOCIATES
7400 Beverly Blvd., Los Angeles, CA 90036. (323) 938-3595.

ROBERT A. BRILLIANT, INC.
(TV, film & promotion research)
13245 Riverside Dr., #530, Sherman Oaks, CA 91423. (818) 386-6600. FAX: (818) 990-9007. email: rabinc@earthlink.net.
PRESIDENT
Robert Brilliant

CERTIFIED MARKETING SERVICES, INC. (CMS)
Route 9, Kinderhook, NY 12106. (518) 758-6405.

CERTIFIED REPORTS, INC. (CRI) EAST
(Theatre checking open, blind and trailer checking nationwide.)
7 Hudson St., Kinderhook NY 12106. (518) 758-6400. FAX: (518) 758-6451.
CHAIRMAN OF BOARD
Jack J. Spitzer
PRESIDENT
Bill Smith
EXECUTIVE V.P.
Bryan Zweig
VICE PRESIDENT
Elizabeth Stevens

CERTIFIED REPORTS, INC. (CRI) WEST
PO Box 208670, Northridge CA 91325. (818) 727-0929. FAX: (818) 727-7426.
VICE PRESIDENT
Elizabeth Stevens

CINEMA CONSULTANTS GROUP
(International sales and marketing)
9903 Santa Monica Blvd., PMB 831, Beverly Hills, CA 90212-1671. (310) 470-2295. FAX: (310) 470-2975.
email: Goldmanmf@aol.com
PRESIDENT
Michael F. Goldman

CINEMASCORE
8524 Sahara Blvd., P.O. Box 173, Las Vegas, NV 89117. (702) 255-9963.

CONSUMERS PERSPECTIVE
1456 Canfield Ave., Los Angeles, CA 90035. (310) 556-3006. FAX: (310) 556-3002.

DALE SYSTEM, INC., THEATRE DIVISION
1101 Stewart Ave., Garden City, NY 11530. (516) 794-2800. FAX: (516) 542-1063.

EXHIBITOR RELATIONS CO., INC.
116 N. Robertson Blvd., Ste. 606, Los Angeles CA 90048. (310) 657-2005. FAX: (310) 657-7283.
PRESIDENT
Paul Dergarabedian

THE GALLUP ORGANIZATION
47 Hulfish St., Princeton, NJ 08542. (609) 924-9600. FAX: (609) 924-0228.

HANOVER SECURITY REPORTS
952 Manhattan Beach Blvd., Ste. 250, Manhattan Beach CA 90266. (310) 545-9891. (800) 634-5560. FAX: (310) 545-7690.
EXECUTIVE V.P.
Nancy Stein

HISPANIC ENTERTAINMENT SPECIALIST
3726 Laurel Canyon Blvd., Studio City, CA 91604. (818) 766-9100. FAX: (818) 766-9201.

IMAGE ANALYSTS ALL-MEDIA
P.O. Box 1587, Santa Monica, CA 90406. (310) 458-0503.

INTERNATIONAL RESEARCH & EVALUATION,
21098 IRE Control Ctr., Eagan, MN 55121-0098. (612) 888-9635. FAX: (612) 888-9124.
CONTACT
Rick Kenrick

PAUL KAGAN ASSOCIATES, INC.
(Research and analysis of entertainment, communications and media industries.)
126 Clock Tower Place, Carmel, CA 93923-8734. (408) 624-1536. FAX: (408) 625-3225.
www.pkbaseline.com email: info@kagan.com
PRESIDENT
Paul Kagan

KINDERHOOK RESEARCH, INC.
(Distributor & exhibitor open and blind checking; industry research; housekeeping/integrity surveys.)
P.O. Box 589, Kinderhook, NY 12106. (518) 758-1492. FAX: (518) 758-9896.
PRESIDENT
Andrea Koppel

McCANN-ERICKSON, INC.
6420 Wilshire Blvd., Los Angeles, CA 90048. (323) 655-9420.

MOMENTUM INTERNATIONAL
(Media & entertainment consulting services)
P.O. Box 5889, Sherman Oaks, CA 91413. (818) 752-4500. FAX: (818) 752-4554.

CHARLES A. MOSES
3211 W. Alameda Ave., Ste. A, Burbank, CA 91505-4412. (818) 848-0513. FAX: (818) 848-4977.

OPINION RESEARCH CORP. INTL.
P.O. Box 183, Princeton, NJ 08542-0183. (609) 924-5900. FAX: (609) 908-5103.

JOAN PEARCE RESEARCH ASSOCS.
8111 Beverly Blvd., #308, Los Angeles, CA 90048. (323) 655-5464. FAX: (323) 655-4770.

PREMIER DATA VISION (P.D.I.)
(Collects and distributes ShowTime information; ShowTime packaging and resale; Ad-Gen–theatre directories)
1536 Cole Blvd., Ste. 340, Golden, CO 80401.
PRESIDENT & CEO
Blaine Newton
DIRECTOR, RESEARCH & DEVELOPMENT
Gordon Hoak

PROFESSIONAL RESEARCH ASSOCIATES
6255 Sunset Blvd., #1515, Los Angeles, CA 90028. (323) 466-6124.

R. SELTZER ASSOCIATES
15445 Ventura Blvd., #14, Sherman Oaks, CA 91413. (818) 888-8450. FAX: (818) 888-8446.

VIDEO MONITORING SERVICES OF AMERICA
6430 W. Sunset Blvd., #504, Los Angeles, CA 90028. (323) 993-0111.

WABASH ASSOCIATES
70 E. Lake St., 16th Flr., Chicago, IL 60601. (312) 251-1920. FAX: (312) 251-1921.
CONTACTS
Barry A. Schain
Daniel Porter

Sound Studios & Services

AB AUDIO DESIGN STUDIOS
(sound design and original music)
3765 Marwick Ave., Long Beach, CA 90808. (562) 429-1042. FAX: (562) 429-2401. www.abaudio.com
email: sound@abaudio.com
PRESIDENT
Arlan H. Boll
STUDIO MANAGER
Linda Rippee

A & J RECORDING STUDIOS, INC.
225 W. 57 St., New York, NY 10019. (212) 247-4860.

ADVANTAGE AUDIO
1026 Hollywood Way, Burbank, CA 91505. (818) 566-8555.
email: tammy@advantageaudio.com
PRESIDENT
Bill Koepnick
VICE PRESIDENT
Jim Hodson
STUDIO MANAGER
Tammy Crosby

ALL POST, INC.
1133 N. Hollywood Way, Burbank, CA 91505. (818) 556-5700. FAX: (818) 556-5748.
SENIOR V.P., SALES & SERVICE
Ben "Ponz" Ponzio

ASSOCIATED PRODUCTION MUSIC
6255 Sunset Blvd., Ste. 820, Hollywood, CA 90028. (323) 461-3211, (800) 543-4276. FAX (323) 461-9102.
www.apmmusic.com
PRESIDENT
Bill Brooks
WEST COAST SALES DIRECTOR
Tia Sommer
EAST COAST SALES DIRECTOR
Marla Mauer

ASTRALTECH, INC.
2101 St. Catherine West, Montreal, Quebec, H3H 1M6. (514) 939-5060. FAX: (514) 939-5070.
email: belleros@astral.com
PRESIDENT
Hubert Harel
VICE PRESIDENT
Michel Deslisle
DIRECTOR, MARKETING, SALES & CUSTOMER SERVICE
Paul Bellerose

THE AUDIO DEPARTMENT
119 W. 57 St., 4th Flr., New York, NY 10019. (212) 586-3503.

AUDIO MECHANICS
(Sound restoration and noise reduction)
6735 Forest Lawn Dr., #200, Los Angeles, CA 90068. (323) 874-4422. FAX: (323) 874-8413. www.audiomechanics.com
email: info@audiomechanics.com

AUDIO SERVICES COMPANY
353 West 48th St., New York, NY 10036. (212) 977-5150. FAX: (212) 262-5150.
www.audioservicesco.com email: mtopham@msn.com
PRESIDENT
Marva Topham
VICE PRESIDENT
Ron Topham

AVID TECHNOLOGY
Metropolitan Technology Park, One Park West, Tewksbury, MA 01876. (508) 640-6789. FAX: (508) 640-1366.
115 N. 1st St., Ste. 208, Burbank, CA 91502. (818) 557-2520. FAX: (818) 557-2558.

THE BAKERY RECORDING STUDIO
10709 Burbank Blvd., North Hollywood, CA 91601. (818) 508-7800. FAX: (818) 508-7122. email: chrisaustin@bakerystudio.com
PRESIDENT
Andre Watterman
STUDIO MANAGER & CONTACT
Chris Austin

BLUEFIELD MUSIC DESIGN
1006 E. Cooper St., Aspen, CO 81611. (970) 925-2202. FAX: (970) 825-2202. www.clazzax.com email: dblue@rof.net
PRESIDENT
David Bluefield

WALLY BURR RECORDING
1126 Hollywood Way, #203, Burbank, CA 91505. (818) 845-0500.

CAPITOL STUDIOS
1750 N. Vine St., Hollywood, CA 90028. (323) 871-5001. FAX: (323) 871-5058. email: paula@capitolstudios.com
STUDIO DIRECTOR
Paula Salvatore

CHACE PRODUCTIONS, INC.
(Sound restoration and remastering, stereo conversion for DVD)
201 S. Victory Blvd., Burbank, CA 91502. (818) 842-8346. FAX: (818) 843-8353.
PRESIDENT
Robert Heiber
CFO
Louis Fiore

CINESOUND
915 N. Highland Ave., Hollywood, CA 90038. (323) 464-1155. FAX: (323) 464-1820.

CLAY DIGITAL SOUND
3151 Cahuenga Blvd. West, Ste. 105, Los Angeles, CA 90068. (818) 769-8778. FAX: (323) 876-1132.

CONCEPT PLUS
1132 Vine St., Hollywood, CA 90038. (323) 466-2066. FAX: (323) 466-2717. email: onstott@faithlink.net
VICE PRESIDENT
Brad Onstott

CORELLI-JACOBS RECORDING, INC.
25 W. 45 St., New York, NY 10036. (212) 382-0220. FAX: (212) 382-0220.
CONTACT
Andrew Jacobs

CREATIVE MEDIA RECORDING
(Audio post-production for video)
11105 Knott Ave., Ste. G, Cypress, CA 90630. (714) 892-9469.
email: KeenanCM@worldnet.att.net
OPERATIONS DIRECTOR
Tim Keenan
STUDIO MANAGER
Linda Keenan

CRESCENDO STUDIOS
615 Battery St., San Francisco, CA 94111. (415) 834-0580. FAX: (415) 834-0599.
DIRECTOR OF OPERATIONS
Cindy McSherry

DB SOUND & MUSIC
(Film & television sound editing)
4176 Arch Street, Ste. 310, Studio City, CA 91604-3295.
Tel/FAX: (818) 753-4954. email: bondelev@usc.edu
PRESIDENT
David J. Bondelevitch

DIGITAL MASTERS
13848 Ventura Blvd., 2nd Flr., Sherman Oaks, CA 91423. (818) 386-9172. FAX: (818) 386-9646. email: digitalm@earthlink.net
CONTACT
Galen Walker

DIGITAL THEATER SYSTEMS
(Digital sound)
5171 Clareton Dr., Agoura Hills, CA 91301. (818) 706-3525, (800) 959-4109. FAX: (818) 706-1868.
www.dtsonline.com email: info@dtsonline.com
CHAIRMAN & FOUNDER
Terry Beard
VICE CHAIRMAN & CEO
Dan Slusser
EXECUTIVE V.P.
Jon Kirchner
DIRECTOR, WORLDWIDE SALES
Jim Murray

DIRECTORS SOUND & EDITORIAL SERVICE
1150 W. Olive Ave., Burbank, CA 91506. (818) 843-0950. FAX: (818) 843-0357.

DISNEY I.D.E.A.S. AT THE DISNEY MGM STUDIOS
Roy O. Disney Production Ctr., Lake Buena Vista, FL 32830. (407) 560-5600. FAX: (407) 560-5483.
CONTACT
Jamie Fuehner

DOLBY LABORATORIES, INC.
3375 Barham Blvd., Los Angeles, CA 90068. (323) 845-1880. FAX: (415) 863-1373.
CONTACT
Karen Greshler

100 Portrero Ave., San Francisco, CA 94103. (415) 558-0200.
175 S. Hill Court, Brisbane, CA 94005. (415) 715-0200.
1350 Ave. of the Americas, 28th Flr., New York, NY 10019-4703. (212) 767-1700.

ECHO SOUND SERVICES, INC.
4119 Burbank Blvd., Burbank, CA 91505. (818) 841-4114. FAX: (818) 841-5038.
CONTACTS
Joe Melody
Russ Tinsley

EDS DIGITAL STUDIOS
3575 Cahuenga Blvd. West, Ste. 675, Los Angeles, CA 90068. (323) 850-1165. FAX: (323) 850-6151.

EFX
919 N. Victory Blvd., Burbank, CA 91502. (818) 843-4762. FAX: (818) 843-4029. www.efx.com
PRESIDENT
Rick Stevens
VICE PRESIDENT
John O'Connor
STUDIO MANAGER
Lisa Ramirez

ALAN ETT MUSIC GROUP
12711 Ventura Blvd., Ste. 110, Studio City, CA 91604. (818) 955-7010. FAX: (818) 955-7088.
PRESIDENT
Alan Ett
VICE PRESIDENT
Scott Liggett
CONTACT
Jim Faraci

FIESTA SOUND
1655 S. Compton Ave., Los Angeles, CA 90021. (213) 748-2057. FAX: (213) 748-5388.
CONTACT
R. G. Robeson

FOUR MEDIA COMPANY
2813 W. Alameda Ave., Burbank, CA 91505-4455. (818) 840-7100. FAX: (818) 846-5197. www.4mc.com
CEO
Robert T. Walston
HUMAN RESOURCES
Kristi Kleckner

GNOME PRODUCTIONS
3610 W. Magnolia Blvd., Burbank, CA 91505. (818) 558-5088. FAX: (818) 558-5817. www.magnoliastudios.com/~gnome
email: gnome@magnoliastudios.com
CONTACT
Bruce Nazarian

GRM PRODUCTIONS
5914 Tuxedo Terrace, Los Angeles, CA 90068. (323) 462-3220. FAX: (323) 462-0656. email: glandress@aol.com
PRESIDENT
George Landress

JOHN HILL MUSIC
116 E. 37th St., New York, NY 10016. (212) 683-2273. FAX: (212) 683-2546.
CONTACT
Rosemary Rogers

IF/X DIGITAL, INC.
3522 Knobhill Dr., Sherman Oaks, CA 91423. (818) 501-1822. FAX: (818) 501-4526. www.IFX.com email: IFXdig@aol.com
PRESIDENT
George Daugherty

INTERLOCK STUDIOS
6520 Sunset Blvd., Los Angeles, CA, 90028. (323) 469-3986. FAX: (323) 469-8507.
CEO
Michael Perricone
PRESIDENT
Jim Henderson
OPERATIONS MANAGER
Kim Welsh

INTERSOUND, INC.
8746 Sunset Blvd., Los Angeles, CA 90069. (310) 652-3741. FAX: (310) 854-7290.
www.netcom.com/~ispost email: admin@wedubem.com
PRESIDENT
Kent Harrison Hayes

INTERWEAVE ENTERTAINMENT
22723 Berdon St., Woodland Hills, CA 91367. (818) 883-1920. FAX: (818) 883-9650.
www.interweaveinc.com email: iweinc@earthlink.net
CONTACT
Lynne Weaver

KILLER MUSIC
30 Kewen Place, San Marino, CA 91108. (626) 792-0540. FAX: (626) 792-0545.
PRESIDENT
Ron Hicklin

LARSON SOUND CENTER
4109 W. Burbank Blvd., Burbank, CA 91505. (818) 845-4100. FAX: (818) 845-2414.

LASER PACIFIC MEDIA CORP., SOUND SERVICES
809 N. Cahuenga Blvd., Los Angeles, CA 90038. (323) 462-6266. FAX: (323) 466-5047.
www.laserpacific. com email: info@laserpacific.com
PRESIDENT
Emory Cohen
EXEC. V.P,. SALES & MARKETING
Leon Silverman
DIRECTOR, SOUND SERVICES
Ed Fassl

540 N. Hollywood Way, Burbank, CA 91505. (818) 842-0777, (323) 462-6266. FAX: (818) 566-9834.
VICE PRESIDENT, OPERATIONS
Steve Mitchell

823 N. Seward Ave., Hollywood, CA 90038. (323) 469-4040, (323) 462-6266. FAX: (323) 466-5047.
GENERAL MANGER
Ethan Bush

LITTLE GEMSTONE MUSIC/24 CARAT PRODUCTIONS
(Sound recording, motion picture soundtracks)
P.O. Box 1703, Fort Lee, NJ 07024. (201) 488-8562.
Kevin D. Noel

LOOK, INC.
168 5th Ave., New York, NY 10010. (212) 627-3500. FAX: (212) 633-1980.
Jeanne Look

LUCASFILM, LTD. (THX DIVISION)
P.O. Box 10327, San Rafael, CA 94912. (415) 492-3900. FAX: (415) 492-3973.
DIRECTOR
Kurt Schwenk
DIRECTOR, THEATRE ALIGNMENT
Tim Schafbuch
DIRECTOR, CUSTOMER RELATIONS
Tim Schafbuch
MANAGERS, INT'L SALES
Lawrence Cervantes
Martin Dew

MAD DOG STUDIOS & SOUTH LAKE STAGE
291-293 S. Lake St., Burbank, CA 91502. (818) 557-0100. FAX: (818) 557-6383. email: mdogstudio@aol.com
OWNERS
Dusty Wakeman
Michael Dumas
STUDIO MANAGER
Mark Harvey

LEE MAGID, INC.
P.O. Box 532, Malibu, CA 90265. (323) 463-5998. FAX: (310) 457-8891.
PRESIDENT
Lee Magid
VICE PRESIDENT
Adam Magid

CHRIS MANY MUSIC/SILVERSTORM STUDIOS
907 S. Victory Blvd., Burbank, CA 91508. (818) 953-5126. FAX: (818) 953-5140.
PRESIDENT
Chris Many
STUDIO MANAGER
Jim Kee

MARCLAND INTERNATIONAL COMMUNICATIONS
P.O. Box 3100, Burbank, CA 91508. (818) 557-6677. FAX: (818) 567-0568.
www.marcland.com email: info@marcland.com
CEO
Alfredo Marco Fulchignoni

MCA MUSIC MEDIA STUDIOS
5161 Lankershim Blvd., Ste. 201, North Hollywood, CA 91601. (818) 777-9200. FAX: (818) 777-9235.

MEDIA CITY SOUND
(Film, TV and editorial mixing)
12711 Ventura Blvd., Ste. 110, Studio City, CA 91604. (818) 508-3311. FAX: (818) 508-3314.
PRESIDENT
Alan Ett
SENIOR V.P.
Scott Liggett
VICE PRESIDENT, OPERATIONS
Donna Walker

MOVIE TECH STUDIOS
832 N. Seward St., Hollywood, CA 90038. (323) 467-8491. FAX: (323) 467-8471.

MUSIC ROOM PICTURES, PRODUCTIONS & PUBLISHING
P.O. Box 219, Redondo Beach, CA 90277. (310) 316-4551. FAX: (310) 540-3532. email: MRP@aol.com
PRESIDENT
John Reed

NT AUDIO'S HOLLYWOOD TELECINE FACILITY
(Sound and post-production)
1833 Centinela Ave., Santa Monica, CA 90404. (310) 828-1098. FAX: (310) 828-9737.
www.ntaudio.com email: kk@ntaudio.com
PRESIDENT
Tom McCormick
OPERATIONS MANAGER
Jon Seifert

NAMRAC MUSIC/SOUCI MUSIC
15456 Cabrito Rd., Van Nuys, CA 91406. (818) 787-6436. FAX: (818) 787-3981.
PRESIDENT
Tommy R. Skeeter

NOVASTAR DIGITAL SOUND
6430 Sunset Blvd., #103, Hollywood, CA 90028. (323) 467-5020. FAX: (323) 957-8707.
www.novastarpost.com email: bsky@novastarpost.com
V.P. & GENERAL MANAGER
Bob Sky
MANAGER, CLIENT SERVICES/SCHEDULING
Scott Sonderegger

PARAMOUNT RECORDING STUDIOS
6245 Santa Monica Blvd., Hollywood, CA 90038. (323) 465-4000. FAX: (323) 469-1905.
www.teaminfinity.com/Paramount.html
email: calrocker@earthlink.net
CONTACTS
Adam L. Beilenson
Michael Kerns

PLUS THREE POST
3610 W. Magnolia Blvd., Burbank, CA 91505. (818) 558-5088. FAX: (818) 558-5817.

RALEIGH SOUND
650 N. Bronson Ave., Hollywood, CA 90004. (323) 960-4720. FAX: (323) 871-5629.
CONTACT
Keith Stephenson

RUSSIAN HILL RECORDING
1520 Pacific Ave., San Francisco, CA 94109. (415) 474-4520. FAX: (415) 474-7190. email: russian@rhrnet.com
STUDIO MANAGER
Lucrezia Conklin

RYDER SOUND SERVICES, INC.
1147 N. Vine St., Hollywood, CA 90038. (323) 469-3511. FAX: (323) 461-8057.

SCREENMUSIC STUDIOS
11700 Ventura Blvd., Studio City, CA 91604. (818) 753-6040. FAX: (818) 508-4870. email: jkaufman@earthlink.net
COO
Jay R. Kaufman

SEVEN TORCH MUSIC
12932 Huston St., Sherman Oaks, CA 91423. (818) 789-7568. FAX: (818) 784-2570.
www.7torch.home.ml.org email: steverino@earthlink.net
PRESIDENT
Steven Orich
CONTACT
Judy Halpert

SKYVIEW FILM & VIDEO
541 N. Fairbanks, Ste. 2200, Chicago, IL 60611. (312) 670-2020. FAX: (312) 670-3010.
PRESIDENT
Jack Tohtz
STUDIO MANAGER
Bill Reis
SALES
Al Nolan-Cohn

SONY PICTURES STUDIOS
10202 W. Washington Blvd., Culver City, CA 90232. (310) 244-5722. FAX: (310) 244-4152.
email: richard_branca@spe.sony.com
S.V.P., SOUND, PROJECTION & VIDEO
Richard Branca

SOUND MASTER AUDIO/VIDEO
10747 Magnolia Blvd., Los Angeles, CA 91601. (323) 650-8000.

SOUND THINKING MUSIC RESEARCH
1534 N. Moorpark Rd., #333, Thousand Oaks, CA 91360. (805) 495-3306. FAX: (805) 495-3306.
www.success.edu/ncginell email: cginell@gte.net
CONTACT
Cary Ginell

SOUNDCASTLE RECORDING STUDIO
2840 Rowena Ave., Los Angeles, CA 90039. (323) 665-5201. FAX: (323) 662-4273.
CONTACT
Candace Corn

SOUNDSCAPE PRODUCTIONS
3614 Overland Ave., Los Angeles, CA 90034. (310) 202-9989. FAX: (310) 202-6088. email: dubscape@pacbell.net
CHIEF ENGINEER
Gregg Hall

SOUNDELUX/SOUNDELUX MEDIA LABS
7060 Hollywood Blvd., 7th Flr., Hollywood, CA 90028. (323) 463-3855. FAX: (323) 463-1977.
www.soundelux.com email: cmeister@soundelux.com
PRESIDENT
Charlie Meister

SOUNDELUX SHOWORKS
4401 Vineland Rd., Ste. 117, Orlando, FL 32811. (407) 345-1555. FAX: (407) 345-0014.
CONTACTS
John Miceli
Tony Miceli

SOUNDZ NU
95 Madison Ave., New York, NY 10016. (212) 684-7222. FAX: (212) 689-5084.
PRESIDENT
Elvis Herbert
VICE PRESIDENT
Adam Charity

SOUTHERN LIBRARY OF RECORDED MUSIC
4621 Cahuenga Blvd., Toluca Lake, CA 91602. (818) 752-1530. FAX: (818) 508-0213.
PRESIDENT
Ralph Peer II
MANAGER
Roy Kohn

STARDUST FILM, INC.
(Production sound for motion pictures)
7510 Sunset Blvd., #240, Hollywood, CA 90046. (310) 288-7889. FAX: (818) 763-5886.
www.stardustfil.com email: pvm@stardustfilm.com
PRESIDENT
Peter V. Meiselmann, C.A.S.

STUDIO 56
7000 Santa Monica Blvd., Hollywood, CA 90038. (323) 464-7747.

STUDIO M PRODUCTIONS UNLIMITED
4032 Wilshire Blvd., #403, Los Angeles, CA 90010. (213) 389-7372, (888) 389-7372. FAX: (213) 389-3299.
www.mandy.com/stuoo1.html
email: studiom@pacbell.net
8715 Waikiki Station, Honolulu, HI 96830. (808) 734-3345, (888) 734-3345. FAX: (808) 521-0919.
OWNER
Senator Mike Michaels, C.A.S.

SUNSET SOUND RECORDERS
6650 Sunset Blvd., Hollywood, CA 90028. (323) 469-1186. FAX: (323) 465-5579. www.sunsetsound.com
CONTACT
Craig Hubler

SUPERLOOPERS
(Looping)
P.O. Box 341678, Los Angeles, CA 90034. (310) 839-0895, (310) 649-3332. FAX: (310) 839-0896. email: tcp823@aol.com
PRESIDENT
DeVera Marcus
CONTACT
Norman Marcus

TODD-AO/EDITWORKS
3399 Peachtree Rd. N.E., Ste. 200, Atlanta, GA 30326. (404) 237-9977. FAX: (404) 237-3923.
V.P., SALES & MARKETING
Mike Hoff

TODD-AO STUDIOS
900 N. Seward St., Hollywood, CA 90038. (323) 962-4000. FAX: (323) 466-2327.
PRESIDENT
Christopher Jenkins

TODD-AO STUDIOS EAST
259 W. 54th St., New York, NY 10019. (212) 265-6225. FAX: (212) 247-5206.
PRESIDENT & GENERAL MANAGER
Stephen Castellano

TODD-AO STUDIOS WEST
3000 Olympic Blvd., Bldg. One, Santa Monica, CA 90404. (310) 315-5000. FAX: (310) 315-5018.
PRESIDENT
Richard Hassanein

TOM THUMB MUSIC/ RUTH WHITE FILMS
(Divisions of Rhythms Productions) Box 34485, Los Angeles, CA 90034-0485. (310) 836-4678.
PRESIDENT
Ruth White
EXECUTIVE PRODUCER
David White
ART DIRECTOR
Lotte Cherin

ULTRA STEREO LABS, INC.
18730 Oxnard St., Ste. 208, Tarzana, CA 91356. (818) 609-7405. FAX: (818) 609-7408.
181 Bonetti Dr., San Luis Obispo, CA 93401. (805) 549-0161. FAX: (805) 549-0163.

UNIVERSAL STUDIOS
100 Universal City Plaza, Universal City, CA 91608. (818) 777-0169. FAX: (818) 866-1494. www.universalstudios.com/studio
email: TamiLozano@unistudios.com
DIRECTOR, SOUND FACILITIES
Tami Hulcher

VOICES
16 E. 48th St., New York, NY 10017. (212) 935-9820. FAX: (212) 755-1150.
CONTACT
Richard Leonai

WARNER BROS. STUDIOS FACILITIES
4000 Warner Blvd., Burbank, CA 91522. (818) 954-3000. FAX: (818) 954-2677. www.wbsf.com email: wbsf@warnerbros.com
CONTACT
Tracy Balsz

WARNER HOLLYWOOD STUDIOS
1041 N. Formosa, Los Angeles, CA 90046. (323) 850-2500. FAX: (323) 850-2839.

WAVES SOUND RECORDERS
1956 N. Cahuenga Blvd., Hollywood, CA 90048. (323) 466-6141. FAX: (323) 466-3751.

WEST PRODUCTIONS, INC.
(Full service post-production audio for TV and film)
2921 W. Olive Ave., Burbank, CA 91505. (818) 841-4500. FAX: (818) 567-1820.
PRESIDENT
David Rawlinson
CEO
David West

WESTLAKE AUDIO
7265 Santa Monica Blvd., Los Angeles, CA 90046. (323) 851-9800. FAX: (323) 851-9386.
8447 Beverly Blvd., Los Angeles, CA 90048. (323) 654-2155.
OWNER
Glen Phoenix
STUDIO MANAGER
Steve Burdick

WORKSHIRT MUSIC
P.O. Box 3945, Hollywood, CA 90078. (323) 466-6046.
OWNER
Chris Anderson

ZACUTO AUDIO
1316 3rd St., Ste. 109, Santa Monica, CA 90401. (310) 394-4932. FAX: (310) 458-7802.
www.zacuToaudio.com email: zacz@earthlink.net
PRESIDENT
Gary Zacuto
STUDIO MANAGER
Martin Royer

SAUL ZAENTZ FILM CENTER
2600 Tenth St., Berkeley, CA 94710. (510) 486-2100, (800) 227-0466. FAX: (510) 486-2115. www.zaentz-filmcenter.com
email: filmweb@zaentz-filmcenter.com
CONTACT
Steve Shurtz

Special Effects

A & A SPECIAL EFFECTS
7021 Hayvenhurst Ave., Van Nuys, CA 91406. (818) 909-6999. FAX: (818) 782-0635.

A.D.2, INC.
(Miultimedia design and production)
2118 Wilshire Blvd., Ste. 205, Santa Monica, CA 90403. (310) 394-8379. FAX: (310) 451-0966. www.ad2.com
PRESIDENT
Brad Mooberry

ADVANCED CAMERA SYSTEMS
16117 Cohasset St., Van Nuys, CA 91406-2908. (818) 989-5222. FAX: (818) 994-8405.

ADVANCED FIRE & RESCUE SERVICES
10044 Columbus Ave., Mission Hills, CA 91345. (818) 837-7336, (661) 299-4801. FAX: (661) 298-3069.
CONTACTS
Craig Sanford
Mark Pedro

ALIAS/WAVEFRONT
11835 W. Olympic Blvd., Ste. 350, Los Angeles, CA 90064. (310) 914-1566. FAX: (310) 914-1580. www.aw.sgi.com

ALL EFFECTS COMPANY, INC.
7915 Ajay Dr., Sun Valley, CA 91352. (818) 768-2000. FAX: (818) 768-2312.

DAVID ALLEN PRODUCTIONS
918 W. Oak St., Burbank, CA 91506. (818) 845-2970. FAX: (818) 567-4954.
CONTACT
David Allen

ALTERIAN STUDIOS
1107 S. Mountain Ave., Monrovia, CA 91016. (626) 932-1488. FAX: (626) 932-1494.
PRESIDENT
Tony Gardner

AMALGAMATED DYNAMICS
(Special make-up and creature effects design)
20100 Plummer St., Chatsworth, CA 91311. (818) 882-8638. FAX: (818) 882-7327.
OWNERS
Alec Gillis
Tom Woodruff, Jr.

ANATOMORPHEX
8210 Lankershim, Ste. 14, North Hollywood, CA 91605. (818) 768-2880. FAX: (818) 768-4808.
CONTACTS
Robert Devine
James Clark

HOWARD A. ANDERSON CO.
100 Universal City Plaza, #504-3, Universal City, CA 19608. (818) 777-2402, (818) 777-2779. FAX: (818) 733-1118.
5418 McConnell Ave., Los Angeles, CA 90066. (805) 823-5511. FAX: (805) 823-5501.

ANIMUS FILMS
2 W. 47th St., New York, NY 10036. (212) 391-8716.

APA STUDIOS
500 S. Lakeview Dr., Lake Helen, FL 32744. (904) 228-2144. FAX: (904) 228-2155. www.A-P-A.com

ARTEFFEX
5419 Clean St., North Hollywood, CA 91601. (818) 506-5358. FAX: (818) 506-3171.
CONTACT
Dann O'Quinn

AVAILABLE LIGHT, LTD.
1125 Flower S. St., Burbank, CA 91502. (818) 842-2109. FAX: (818) 842-0661. email: avlight@availablelightltd.com
OWNER & PRESIDENT
John VanVliet
OWNER & CFO
Katherine Kean

BALSMEYER & EVERETT, INC.
459 W. 15th St., New York, NY 10011. (212) 627-3430. FAX: (212) 989-6528. www.balsmeyer-everett.com
email: randyb@balsmeyer-everett.com
3000 W. Olymbpic Blvd., Santa Monica, CA 90404. (310) 264-4115. FAX: (31) 264-4116.

BANNED FROM THE RANCH ENTERTAINMENT
2048 Broadway, Santa Monica, CA 90404. (310) 449-1313. FAX: (310) 449-1315.
CONTACT
Casey Cannon

BIFROST LASERFX
6733 Sale Ave., West Hills, CA 91307. (818) 704-0423. FAX: (818) 704-4629. email: bifrost@earthlink.com

BIGGER THAN LIFE, INC.
1327 Fayette St., El Cajon, CA 92020. (800) 383-9980. FAX: (619) 449-8299.
www.biggerthanlife.com email: bgrnlife@ix.netcom.com
PRESIDENT
R.T. "Dick" Dickson
CEO
Mark Bachman
MARKETING MANAGER
Connie Clark

BILLY SKY PRODUCTIONS
1739 Berkeley St., Ste. 101, Santa Monica, CA 90404. (310) 264-7800. FAX: (310) 828-2404.
www.bigskypost.com email: staff@bigskypost.com
OPERATIONS MANAGER
Michael Davis

BIOVISION
44-460 Indian Wells Lane, Indian Wells, CA 92210. (760) 341-5007, (888) bio-vision. FAX: (760) 773-4004.
www.biovisionsp.com email: sportscenter@earthlink.net
DIRECTOR & CEO
Ken Kline

BLACKSTONE MAGIK ENTRPRISES, INC.
12800 Puesta Del Sol, Redlands, CA 92373-7408.
www.blackstone.org

BLUE SKY/VIFX
5333 McConnell Ave., Los Angeles, CA 90066. (310) 822-8872. FAX: (310) 821-1012. www.vifx.com
One South Rd., Harrison, NY 10528. (914) 381-8400. FAX: (914) 381-9790.

BLUR STUDIO, INC.
1130 Abbot Kinney Blvd., Venice, CA 90291. (310) 581-8848. FAX: (310) 581-8850. www.blur.com email: cat@blur.com
EXECUTIVE PRODUCER
Cat Chapman

BODYTECH
13659 Victory Blvd., Ste. 145, Van Nuys, CA 91401. (818) 385-0633.

BOOM BOOM EFFECTS
17402 Chase St., Northridge, CA 91325. (818) 345-7703. FAX: (818) 365-0882.

BRANAM ENTERPRISES, INC.
20675 Bahama St., Chatsworth, CA 91311. (818) 709-8787. FAX: (818) 717-9898. email: branam@gte.net
PRESIDENT
Joe Branam
CONTACT
Randy Beckman

BROOKLYN MODEL WORKS
60 Washington Ave., Brooklyn, NY 11205. (718) 834-1944. FAX: (718) 596-8934. email: bromowo@inch.com
PRESIDENT
John Kuntzsch

THE BRUBAKER GROUP
10560 Dolcedo Way, Los Angeles, CA 90077. (310) 472-4766.

BUENA VISTA IMAGING
(Post-production visual effects)
500 S. Buena Vista St., Burbank, CA 91521-5073. (818) 560-5284. FAX: (818) 563-0532.
EXECUTIVE DIRECTOR
John Chambers

BURMAN STUDIOS, INC.
(Special make-up effects and prosthetics)
4706 W. Magnolia Blvd., Burbank, CA 91505. (818) 980-6587. FAX: (818) 980-6589.
CONTACT
Bari Dreiband-Burman

CACIOPPO PRODUCTION DESIGN, INC.
928 Broadway, Ste. 1204, New York, NY 10010. (212) 777-1828. FAX: (212) 777-1847.

CALICO ENTERTAINMENT
9340 Eton Ave., Chatsworth, CA 91311-5879. (818) 407-5200. FAX: (818) 407-5323.
PRESIDENT & CEO
Tom Burton

THE CHARACTER SHOP, INC.
9033 Owensmouth Ave., Canoga Park, CA 91304-1417. (818) 718-0094. FAX: (818) 718-0967.
CONTACT & PRESIDENT
Rick Lazzarini

CHIODO BROS. PRODUCTIONS, INC.
110 W. Providencia Ave., Burbank, CA 91502. (818) 842-5656. FAX: (818) 848-0891.
PRESIDENT
Stephen Chiodo

CIMMELLI, INC.
16 Walter St., Pearl River, NY 10965. (914) 735-2090.

CINEMA ENGINEERING COMPANY
7243 Atoll Ave., Ste. A, N. Hollywood, CA 91605-4105. (818) 765-5340. FAX: (818) 765-5349. email: CineEng@aol.com

CINENET (CINEMA NETWORK, INC.)
1350 Los Angeles Ave., 3rd Flr., Simi Valley, CA 93065. (805) 527-0093. FAX: (805) 527-0305. www.cinenet.com

CINESITE, INC.
(Visual effects, digital mastering, film scanning and recording)
1017 N. Las Palmas Ave., Los Angeles, CA 90038. (323) 468-5742. FAX: (323) 468-4483. www.cinesite.com
New York: (212) 631-3414. FAX: (212) 631-3436.
London: (0171) 973-4000. FAX: (0171) 973-4040.
DIRECTOR OF MARKETING
Rita Cahill

CINEVISION ENTERTAINMENT
1111 S. Victory Blvd., Burbank, CA 91502. (818) 566-4917. FAX: (818) 566-6639.
PRESIDENT
Philip Jones

CINNABAR
2840 N. Hollywood Way, Burbank, CA 91505. (818) 842-8190. FAX: (818) 842-0563.
www.cinnabar.com email: info@cinnabar.com
CONTACTS
Doug Morris
Ann Mitchell

CIS HOLLYWOOD
(Visual effects, 2D and 3D digital effects, all-format compositing)
1144 N. Las Palmas Ave., Hollywood, CA 90038. (323) 463-8811.
CEO
Joseph Matza
NEW BUSINESS DEVELOPMENT
Joni Jacobsen
EXECUTIVE PRODUCER
C. Marie Davis

THE COMPUTER FILM COMPANY
8522 National Blvd., Ste. 103, Culver City, CA 90232. (310) 838-3456. FAX: (310) 838-1713. www.cfla.com email: info@cfla.com
PRESIDENT
Donald R. Fly

CREATIVE CHARACTER ENGINEERING
16110 Hart St., Van Nuys, CA 91406. (818) 901-0507. FAX: (818) 901-8417. email: andyCCE@earthlink.com
CREATIVE DIRECTOR
Andrew Clement

CREATIVE EFFECTS, INC.
760 Arroyo Ave., San Fernando, CA 91340-2222. (818) 365-0655. FAX: (818) 365-0651.

THE CREATIVE GROUP
305 E. 46th St., 12th Flr., New York, NY 10017. (212) 935-0145. FAX: (212) 838-0853.
PRESIDENT
Linda Ardigo

CRUSE & COMPANY, INC.
7000 Romaine St., Hollywood, CA 90038. (323) 851-8814. FAX: (323) 851-8788.

CUBENA RESEARCH CORP./DIGITAL RESOLUTION
6860 Lexington Ave., Hollywood, CA 90038. (323) 460-4111. FAX: (323) 463-2483.
V.P., MARKETING & SALES
John Haggar

DAVE'S MARINE SERVICES, INC.
1438 W. 14th St., Long Beach, CA 90813. (562) 437-4772. FAX: (562) 503-0848.
CONTACT
David W.L. Hilchey

DAY SHADES
6859 Leetsdale Dr., Ste. 202, Denver, CO 80224. (303) 399-8889. FAX: (303) 399-8881.
CONTACT
Craig T. Jones

DE LA MARE ENGINEERING, INC.
1908 1st St., San Fernando, CA 91340-2610. (818) 365-9208. FAX: (818) 365-8775.

DIGISCOPE
2308 Broadway, Santa Monica, CA 90034. (310) 315-6060. FAX: (310) 828-5856.
www.digiscope.com email: m_stuart@digiscope.com
CONTACT
Mary Stuart

DIGITAL DOMAIN
300 Rose Ave., Venice, CA 90291. (310) 314-2800. FAX: (310) 314-2888.
PRESIDENT
Scott Ross

DIGITAL MAGIC COMPANY
3000 W. Olympic Blvd., 2nd Flr., Santa Monica, CA 90404. (310) 315-4720. FAX: (310) 315-4721.

DIMENSION 3
(Stereoscopic film & video)
5240 Medina Rd., Woodland Hills, CA 91364-1913. (818) 592-0999.. FAX: (818) 592-0987.
www.3dcompany.com email: mr3d@3dcompany.com
PRESIDENT
Daniel Symmes

DISNEY I.D.E.A.S. AT THE DISNEY MGM STUDIOS
Roy O. Disney Production Center, Lake Buena Vista, FL 32830. (407) 560-5600. FAX: (407) 560-5483.
CONTACT
Jamie Fuehner

WALT DISNEY IMAGINEERING
1401 Flower St., P.O. Box 25020, Glendale, CA 91221-5020. (818) 544-6500.

DISNEY-MGM STUDIOS
PO Box 10200, Film-TV Dept., Bung. 2, Lake Buena Vista, FL 32830. (407) 560-5736. FAX: (407) 827-5168.

THE WALT DISNEY STUDIOS
500 S. Buena Vista St., Burbank, CA 91521. (818) 560-1000.
CONTACT
Tony Richards

DREAM QUEST IMAGES
(Character animation, live action photography, digital visual effects)
2635 Park Center Dr., Simi Valley, CA 93065. (805) 578-3100. FAX: (805) 583-4673. email: talent@dqimages.com
DIRECTOR OF PUBLIC AFFAIRS
Mary Reardon

DREAM THEATER
21345 Lassen St., Ste. 200, Chatsworth, CA 91311. (818) 773-4979. FAX: (818) 773-4970.
www.dreamtheater.com email: darren@dreamtheater.com
CONTACT
Darren Chuckry

DYNACS DIGITAL STUDIOS
572 E. Green St., Ste. 204, Pasadena, CA 91101. (818) 449-7385, (818) 725-3899. FAX: (818) 449-7432.
www.dynacsdigital.com email: javiben@dynacs.com
PRESIDENT
Javier E. Benavente

E=MC^2, INC.
(Visual effects)
710 W. Ivy Street, Glendale, CA 91204. (818) 243-2424. FAX: (818) 243-5126.
CONTACT
Bob Morgenroth

EDS DIGITAL STUDIOS
3575 Cahuenga Blvd. W., Ste. 675, Los Angeles, CA 90068. (323) 850-1165. FAX: (323) 850-6151.

EDITEL LOS ANGELES
729 N. Highland Ave., Hollywood, CA 90038-3437. (323) 931-1821. FAX: (323) 931-7771.

EFEX SPECIALISTS
43-17 37th St., Long Island City, NY 11101. (718) 937-2417.

EFFECTIVE ENGINEERING
6727 Flanders Dr., Ste. 106, San Diego, CA 92121. (619) 450-1024. FAX: (619) 452-3241.
www.effecteng.com/mlipsky email: mlipsky@effecteng.com
CONTACT
Mark Lipsky

THE EFFECTS HOUSE
111 8th Ave., Ste. 914, New York, NY 10011. (212) 924-9150. FAX: (212) 924-9193.

EFILM
1146 N. Las Palmas, Hollywood, CA 90038. (323) 463-7041. FAX: (323) 465-7342. www.efilm.com email: info@efilm.com
CONTACT
David Hays

ELECTRIC MACHINE ENTERTAINMENT
1930 Purdue Ave., Ste. 6, Los Angeles, CA 90025. (310) 330-8841. FAX: (310) 473-7317. email: emeinc@earthlink.net
CONTACT
Clive Milton

ELECTROFEX
1146 N. Central, Ste. 231, Glendale, CA 91202. (818) 775-3838. email: bat2@flash.net

ENCORE VISUAL EFFECTS
702 Arizona Ave., Santa Monica, CA 90401. (310) 656-7663. FAX: (310) 656-7699. www.encorevideo.com
6344 Fountain Ave., Hollywood, CA 90028. (323) 466-7663. FAX: (323) 467-5539. email: jwarren@encorevideo.com
CONTACT
Jan Warren

ENERGY FILM LIBRARY
12700 Ventura Blvd., 4th Flr., Studio City, CA 91604. (818) 508-1444, (800) IMAGERY. FAX: 818-508-1293.
CONTACT
Joan Sargent

EUE/SCREEN GEM PRINTS
222 E. 44th St., New York, NY 10017. (212) 867-4030.

F-STOP, INC.
120 S. Buena Vista St., Burbank, CA 91505. (818) 843-7867. FAX: (818) 842-7706.

FX ZONE—SPECIAL EFFECTS
Jamboree Center, One Park Plaza, 6th Flr., Irvine, CA 92614. (714) 852-7375. FAX: (714) 434-2776.
CONTACT
Jeff T. Miller

FANTASY II FILM EFFECTS
504 S. Varney St., Burbank, CA 91502. (818) 843-1413. FAX: (818) 848-2824.
CONTACT
Leslie Huntley

RUSS FARBER
19324 Oxnard St., Tarzana, CA 91356-1123. (818) 882-8220. FAX: (818) 708-8113. email: jfmusic@primenet.com

FILM EAST
9 E. Stow Rd., Ste. A, Marlton, NJ 08053. (609) 810-1090. FAX: (609) 810-1077. www.filmeast.com

FILM TECHNICAL SERVICES/SPECIAL EFFECTS
11118 Ventura Blvd., Studio City, CA 91604. (818) 508-1094.

FILMTRIX, INC.
P.O. Box 715, N. Hollywood, CA 91603-0715. (818) 980-3700. FAX: (818) 980-3703. email: filmtrix@aol.com
CONTACT
Kevin Pike

FINE ART PRODUCTIONS/TICHIE SURACI PICTURES
67 Maple St., Newburgh, NY 12550-4034. (914) 542-1585. FAX: (914) 561-5866.
www.geopages.com/Hollywood/1077 email: rs7.fap@mhv.net

FINE LINE GRAPHICS
P.O. Box 441, Madison, OH 44057. (216) 428-7332. FAX: (216) 428-7332. email: finelinegr@aol.com
CEO
Rick Fike

LARRY FIORITTO'S SPECIAL EFFECTS SERVICES
(Pyrotechnics, weather, rigging)
1067 E. Orange Grove, Burbank, CA 91501. (818) 954-9829.
CONTACT
Larry Fioritto

525 POST PRODUCTION
6424 Santa Monica Blvd., Hollywood, CA 90038. (323) 525-1234. FAX: (323) 467-1589.
www.525post.com email: irichards@525post.com

FLAT EARTH
4405 Riverside Dr., Ste. 205, Burbank, CA 91505. (818) 563-6419. FAX: (818) 563-5218. email: flatearth@aol.com
97 Wooster St., 6th Flr., New York, NY 10012. (212) 750-7029. FAX: (212) 343-3178.
CONTACT
Michael Schertz

4-WARD PRODUCTIONS
2801 Hyperion Ave., Studio 104, Los Angeles, CA 90027. (323) 660-2430. FAX: (323) 660-2445.

FX & DESIGN
(Visual effects)
2745 Angelo Dr., Los Angeles, CA 90077-2101. (310) 858-3170. FAX: (310) 278-2356. email: elanfx@earthlink.net
OWNER
Elan Soltes

GALAXIE ENTERTAINMENT CO.
P.O. Box 8523, Universal City, CA 91618. (818) 362-6005. email: galaxie@loop.com
CONTACT
Dave Gregory

JOHN GATI FILM EFFECTS, INC.
6456 83rd Pl., Middle Village, NY 11379. (718) 894-5753.

GEAR PRODUCTIONS
(3D animation, digital effects)
6404 Hollywood Blvd., Ste. 424, Hollywood, CA 90028. (323) 466-GEAR. FAX: (323) 466-0546. www.gearprod.com
PRESIDENT
David Kim

PETER GEYER ACTION PROPS & SETS
8235 Lankershim Blvd., Ste. G, North Hollywood, CA 91605. (818) 768-0070.

GILDERFLUKE & COMPANY, INC.
205 S. Flower St., Burbank, CA 91502. (818) 546-1618. FAX: (818) 546-1619. www.gilderfluke.com
CONTACT
Doug Mobley

GLOBUS STUDIOS, INC.
44 W. 24th St., New York, NY 10010. (212) 243-1008.

RICHARD HAAS PHOTO IMAGERY, LTD.
P.O. Box 8385, Universal City, CA 91618. (818) 248-8696, (818) 417-2064. FAX: (818) 549-0616.

HANSARD ENTERPRISES, INC.
P.O. Box 469, Culver City, CA 90232. (310) 840-5660. FAX: (310) 840-5662. email: hansard@earthlink.net.
CONTACT
William Hansard

HBO STUDIO PRODUCTIONS
120-A E. 23rd St., New York, NY 10010. (212) 512-7800. FAX: (212) 512-7788. email: hsp@hsptv.com
CONTACT
Judy Glassman

HFWD VISUAL EFX
5634 Melrose Ave., Hollywood, CA 90038. (323) 962-2225. FAX: (323) 962-2220.
www.hfwd-vfx.com email: HFWDefx@aol.com
CONTACTS
Jayelle Sargent
Gretchen Shronts
Celia Falkin

JIM HENSON'S CREATURE SHOP
(Animatronix)
2821 Burton Ave., Burbank, CA 91504. (818) 953-3030. FAX: (818) 953-3039. email: mbritton@la.creatureshop.henson.com
CONTACT
Matt J. Britton

HOLLYWOOD DIGITAL
6690 Sunset Blvd., Hollywood, CA 90028. (323) 465-0101.
FAX: (323) 469-8055.

HOLOGRAPHIC STUDIOS
240 E. 26th St., New York, NY 10010. (212) 686-9397.

HUNTER GRATZNER INDUSTRIES, INC.
4107 Redwood Ave., Los Angeles, CA 90088. (310) 578-9929.
FAX: (310) 578-7370. email: hgimodels@aol.com
PARTNERS
Matthew Gratzner
Ian Hunter
Shannon Blake Gans

IF/X DIGITAL, INC.
3522 Knobhill Dr., Sherman Oaks, CA 91423. (818) 501-1822.
FAX: (818) 501-4526. www.IFX.com email: IFXdig@aol.com
PRESIDENT
George Dougherty

ILLUSIONS
(Mechanical and pyrotechnics effects)
21205 Georgetown Dr., Santa Clarita, CA 91350. (661) 296-9620. FAX: (661) 296-9621. email: illusions24@prodigy.net
CONTACT
Dave Simmons

IMAGE CREATORS, INC.
2712 6th St., Santa Monica, CA 90405. (310) 392-3583. FAX: (310) 396-6972.
www.image creators. com email: creators@flash.net
OWNER & CEO
Fred Spencer
CFO
Karen Brooks

IMAGE ENGINEERING, INC.
736 N. Reese Place, Burbank, CA 91506. (818) 840-1444.

IMAGINE THAT
28064 Avenue, Unit K, Valencia, CA 91355. (805) 294-0061.

INDUSTRIAL F/X PRODUCTIONS, INC.
5103 Gloria St., Encino, CA 91436. (818) 501-1822. FAX: (818) 501-4526.

INDUSTRIAL LIGHT & MAGIC (ILM)
P.O. Box 2459, San Rafael, CA 94912. (415) 258-2000.
www.ilm-jobs.com
PRESIDENT
Jim Morris

INTELLIGENT MEDIA, INC.
1350 Abbot Kinney Blvd., Ste. 203, Venice, CA 90291. (310) 581-8840. FAX: (310) 581-8844.
www.intelligentmedia.com email: mail@intelligentmedia.com
PRESIDENT
Ron Marbolis

INTERNATIONAL CREATIVE EFFECTS
401 S. Flower St., Burbank, CA 91502. (818) 840-8338. FAX: (818) 840-8023.
www.primenet.com/nicefx email: icefx@primenet.com
CHAIRMAN
Lawrence E. Benson

INTROVISION INTERNATIONAL
1011 N. Fuller Ave., Hollywood, CA 90046. (323) 969-1930.
FAX: (323) 969-9360.

JEX FX
47 Paul Dr., #9, San Rafael, CA 94903. (415) 499-9477. FAX: (415) 499-0911. www.jexfx.com

STEVE JOHNSON'S X/FX, INC.
320 S. Flower St., Burbank, CA 91502. (818) 504-2177. FAX: (818) 531-1525.

THE JONES EFFECTS STUDIO
26007 Huntington Lane, Ste. 9, Santa Clarita, CA 91355-2746.
(805) 294-9159. FAX: (805) 294-9689.
CONTACT
Andrew Jones

KNB EFX GROUP, INC.
(Make-up effects, dummies)
20830 Dearborn St., Chatsworth, CA 91311. (818) 341-1484.
CONTACT
Greg Nicotero

GENE KRAFT PRODUCTIONS
29 Calvados, Newport Beach, CA 92657. (714) 721-0609.
OWNER
Gene Kraft

L.A. VIDEOGRAMS
3203 Overland Ave., Ste. 6157, Los Angeles, CA 90034. (310) 836-9224. email: LExplore1@aol.com
CONTACT
Larry Rosen

LASER-PACIFIC MEDIA CORP.
540 N. Hollywood Way, Burbank, CA 91505. (818) 842-0777, (213) 462-6266. FAX: (818) 566-9834.
809 N. Cahuenga Blvd., Hollywood, CA 90038. (213) 462-6266.
FAX: (213) 464-3233. www.laserpacific.com
email: info@laserpacific.com

LEXINGTON SCENERY & PROPS
10443 Arminta St., Sun Valley, CA 91352-4109. (818) 768-5768.
FAX: (818) 768-4217. www.lexingtonscenery.com
email: lexscene@lexingtonscenery.com

LIBERTY STUDIOS, INC.
238 E. 26th St., New York, NY 10010. (212) 532-1865.

LINKER SYSTEMS
13612 Onkayha Circle, Irvine, CA 92620. (949) 552-1904. FAX: (949) 552-6985. www.linker.com email: linker@linker.com

LIVE WIRE PRODUCTIONS & VFX
28631 S. Western Ave., Ste. 101, Rancho Palos Verdes, CA 90275-0800. (310) 831-6227.
VISUAL EFFECTS PRODUCER
Kris Simmons

LOWTECH
11825 Major St., Ste. 8, Culver City, CA 90230. (310) 398-7094.

LUCASFILM, LTD.
(see Industrial Light & Magic)

LUMENI PRODUCTIONS, INC.
1632 Flower Street, Glendale, CA 91201-2357. (818) 956-2200. FAX: (818) 956-3298. email: lumeni@aol.com

MAGICAL MEDIA INDUSTRIES, INC.
12031 Vose St., North Hollywood, CA 91605. (818) 765-6150.

MAKEUP & EFFECTS LABORATORIES, INC. (M.E.I.)
7110 Laurel Canyon Blvd., Unit E, N. Hollywood, CA 91605.
(818) 982-1483. FAX: (818) 982-5712.

MAKEUP & MONSTERS
1012 Fair Oaks, #271, South Pasadena, CA 90130. (818) 886-6587. FAX: (818) 709-6587. email: afryt4u@earthlink.net

MANHATTAN TRANSFER/EDIT/DIGITAL
545 5th Ave., New York, NY 10017. (212) 687-4000. FAX: (212) 687-2719. email: info@mte.com
CONTACTS
Joanne Gross, Steve Coffey

PAUL MANTELL STUDIO
16 Yale Ave., Jersey City, NJ 07304. (212) 966-9038.

THE MARK YURKIW GROUP
(Live action effects, models)
180 Carick St., New York, NY 10014. (212) 229-0742.
CEO
Mark Yurkiw
PRODUCTION MANAGER
Ed Wood

MASS-ILLUSION
30 Riverview Rd., Lenox, MA 01240. (413) 637-4500. FAX: (413) 637-0054. email: diane@mass-illusion.com
EXECUTIVE PRODUCER
Diane Pearlman

MASTERSFX, INC
10312 Norris Ave., Unit D, Arleta, CA 91331. (818) 834-3000.
www.mastersfx.com email: mastersfx@prodigy.net
PRESIDENT
Todd Masters

MATTE WORLD DIGITAL
24 Digital Dr., Ste. 6, Novato, CA 94949. (415) 382-1929. FAX: (415) 382-1999.
www.matteworld.com email: info@matteworld.com
CONTACT
Krystyna Demkowicz

MAX INK CAFE
3015 Ocean Front Walk, Studio 2, Venice, CA 90291. (310) 827-5351. FAX: (310) 827-5651.
www.mediacap.com email: info@mediacap.com
VICE PRESIDENT
Bob Skibinski

MCCOURRY & ROBIN, INC.
22647 Ventura Blvd., Ste. 240, Woodland Hills, CA 91364.
(888) 932-8113. FAX: (818) 386-2113.

MEDIA FABRICATORS, INC.
5067 W. Washington Blvd., Los Angeles, CA 90016. (323) 937-3344. FAX: (323) 937-1142. www.mediafab.com
email: info@mediafab.com
PRESIDENT
Barry Fluster

MEDIALAB PRODUCTIONS/MEDIALAB STUDIO L.A.
301 N. Canon Dr., Ste. 228, Beverly Hills, CA 90210.
www.medialab3d.com
S.V.P., CREATIVE AFFAIRS
Carole Kirschner
2130 N. Hollywood Way, Burbank, Ca 91505. (818) 973-2037. FAX: (818) 973-2033. email: medialave@4mc.com
EXECUTIVE PRODUCER
Mackenzie Waggaman

MELROSE TITLES & OPTICAL EFFECTS
(323) 469-2070. FAX: (323) 469-7088.

METROLIGHT STUDIOS
5724 W. 3rd St., Ste. 400, Los Angeles, CA 90036. (323) 932-0400. FAX: (323) 932-8440.
PRESIDENT
James W. Kristoff

BILL MILLAR
116 S. Buena Vista St., Burbank, CA 91505. (818) 848-3300. FAX: (818) 848-3301.

MILLER IMAGING INTERNATIONAL, INC.
2401 West Olive Ave., Burbank, CA 91506. (818) 972-1440. FAX: (818) 972-2098.
www. millercd.com email: info@millercd.com
CONTACT
Steve Miller

MODUS EFX PRODUCTIONS
11535 Tuxford St., Sun Valley, CA 91352. (818) 771-0016. FAX: (818) 771-0017.

MONSTER MECANIX
13958 Huston St., Sherman Oaks, CA 91423. (818) 995-0271.
CONTACT
Jurgen Heimann

MOTION CITY FILMS
1847 Centinela Ave., Santa Monica, CA 90404. (310) 264-4870. FAX: (310) 264-4871.
www.motioncity.com email: witt@motioncity.com
CONTACT
Jerry Witt

MOVIE TECH STUDIOS
832 N. Seward St., Hollywood, CA 90038. (213) 467-8491. FAX: (213) 467-8471.
Ewing M. "Lucky" Brown

NETWORK ART SERVICE
630 S. Mariposa St., Burbank, CA 91506. (818) 843-5078. FAX: (818) 843-2528.

NOVOCOM
5401 Beethoven St., Playa Vista, CA 90066-7016. (310) 448-2500 FAX: (310) 448-2525. www.novo.com
CONTACT
Tami Clark

OCS/FREEZE FRAME/PIXEL MAGIC
10635 Riverside Dr., Toluca Lake, CA 91602. (818) 760-0862. FAX: (818) 760-0483.
CONTACTS
Ray McIntyre Jr.
Dave Fiske

JAMES O'NEIL & ASSOCIATES
725 N. Western Ave., Ste. 109, Los Angeles, CA 90029. (323) 464-2995. FAX: (323) 464-2994.
Jim O'Neil

OPTIC NERVE STUDIOS
9818 Glenoaks Blvd., Sun Valley, CA 91352. (818) 771-1007. FAX: (818) 771-1009. email: JohnVulich@aol.com
PRESIDENT
John Vulich

OWEN MAGIC SUPREME
734 N. McKeever Ave., Azusa, CA 91702. (626) 969-4519. FAX: (626) 969-4614.

PACIFIC DATA IMAGES
3101 Park Blvd., Palo Alto, CA 94306. (650) 846-8100. FAX: (650) 846-8101. www.pdi.com email: info@pdi.com
CONTACT
Judy Conner

PACIFIC ENTERTAINMENT GROUP
(Scenic blacklight, 3D special effects)
100 S. Doheny Dr., Ste. 402, Los Angeles, CA 90048. (310) 278-2800. FAX: (310) 274-0400.
OPERATIONS DIRECTOR
Jim Beatty

PACIFIC TITLE/MIRAGE
6350 Santa Monica Blvd., Los Angeles 90038. (323) 464-0121. email: ksmith@pactitle.com

PACIFIC TITLE MIRAGE STUDIO
1149 N. Gower, Los Angeles, CA 90038. (323) 769-3700. FAX: (323) 769-3701.

PERFORMANCE WORLD SPECIAL EFFECTS
416 S. Victory Blvd., Burbank, CA 91502. (818) 845-2704. FAX: (818) 846-1145.
PRESIDENT
Jerry Williams

PERPETUAL MOTION PICTURES
24730 Tibbets Avenue, Ste. 160, Valencia, CA 91355-3449. (805) 294-0788. FAX: (805) 294-0786. email: rmpmp@aol.com
CONTACT
Richard Malzahn

PINNACLE EFX
2334 Elliot Ave., Seattle, WA 98121. (206) 441-9878. FAX: (206) 728-2266.
EXECUTIVE PRODUCER
Karen Olcott

POLAR TECHNOLOGIES USA
(Snow making, any temperature)
P.O. Box 1515, Folsom, CA 95763. (916) 677-4484. FAX: (916) 677-4485.
PRESIDENT & MANAGING DIRECTOR
Steve Carey
V.P. & DIRECTOR OF OPERATIONS
Joe Ippolito

POST EDGE
1111 Lincoln Rd., Ste. 700, Miami Beach, FL 33139. (305) 674-0700. FAX: (305) 674-8900.
400 Hollywood Blvd., Ste. 180-N, Hollywood, FL 33021. (954) 894-9900. FAX: (954) 894-8600.

PYROS PICTURES
1201 Dove St., Ste. 550, Newport Beach, CA 92660. (949) 833-0334. FAX: (949) 833-8655.
www.pyrospictures.com email: gpyros@pyros.com

QUANTEL
28 Thorndale Circle, Darien, CT 06820. (203) 656-3100. FAX: (203) 656-3459. www.quantel.com

R/C MODELS
803 Channel St., San Pedro, CA 90731. (310) 833-4700. FAX: (310) 833-9167.

RAINMAKER DIGITAL PICTURES
175 E. Olive Ave., Ste. 405, Burbank, CA 91502. (818) 526-1500. FAX: (818) 953-5051. email: info@rainmaker.com
50 West 2nd Ave., Vancouver, B.C. V5Y 1B3. (604) 874-8700. FAX: (604) 874-1719.
PRESIDENT (CA)
Peter Sternlicht
PRESIDENT (CANADA)
Bob Scarabelli

RANDO PRODUCTIONS
1829 Dana St., Glendale, CA 91201. (818) 552-2900. FAX: (818) 552-2388.
CONTACT
Joe Rando

REEL EFX
5539 Riverton Ave., N. Hollywood, CA 91601. (818) 762-1710.

REELISTIC FX
(Rentals, pyrotechnics, miniatures, motion controlled gimbals and flying devices)
21318 Hart St., Canoga Park, CA 91312. (818) 346-2484. FAX: (818) 346-2710.
PRESIDENT
John Gray

RHYTHM & HUES STUDIOS
5404 Jandy Pl., Los Angeles, CA 90066. (310) 448-7500. FAX: (310) 448-7600. www.rhythm.com email: suze@rhythm.com
ADVERTISING & PUBLICITY DIRECTOR
Suzanne Datz

ROARING MOUSE ENTERTAINMENT
1800 Bridgegate St., Ste. 103, Westlake Village, CA 91361. (805) 373-8131. FAX: (805) 373-8133.

S.O.T.A. FX
7338 Valjean Ave., Van Nuys, CA 91406. (818) 780-1003. FAX: (818) 780-4315.

SAFARI ANIMATION & EFFECTS
10845 Van Owen St., Unit E, North Hollywood, CA 91605. (818) 762-5203. FAX: (818) 762-3709.

SCENIC TECHNOLOGIES
6050 S. Valley View Blvd., Las Vegas, NV 89118. (702) 942-4774. FAX: (702) 942-4775. www.prg.com
CONTACT
Robert Mealmear

SCHWARTZBERG & COMPANY
12700 Ventura Blvd., 4th Flr., Studio City, CA 91604. (818) 508-1833. FAX: (818) 508-1253.

SCREAMING MAD GEORGE, INC.
11750 Roscoe Blvd., Ste. 11, Sun Valley, CA 91352. (818) 767-8587. FAX: (818) 768-3968.

SIDESHOW PRODUCTIONS
31364 Via Colinas, Ste. 106, Westlake Village, CA 91362. (818) 879-1996. FAX: (818) 879-1603.

SIGHT EFFECTS
321 Hampton Rd., Venice, CA 90291. (310) 392-0999. FAX: (310) 392-7112.
PRODUCER
Jeff Blodgett

SINGLE FRAME FILMS
437-1/2 N. Genesee Ave., Los Angeles, CA 90036. (323) 655-2664.
CONTACT
Gary Schwartz

SLAGLE MINIMOTION, INC.
39 E. Walnut St., Pasadena, CA 91103. (626) 584-4088. FAX: (626) 584-4099.

SOLDIERS OF LIGHT PRODUCTIONS
P.O. Box 16354, Encino, CA 91416-6354. (818) 345-3866.

SONY PICTURES IMAGEWORKS
9050 W. Washington Blvd., Culver City, CA 90232. (310) 840-8000. FAX: (310) 840-8100.
www.spiw.com email: don@spimageworks.com
CONTACT
Don Levy

SPECIAL EFFECTS SYSTEMS
P.O. Box 220-399, Santa Clarita, CA 91322-0399. (805) 251-1333, (323) 462-2301. FAX: (805) 255-1723.
CONTACT
Christina Knipe

SPECIAL EFFECTS UNLIMITED, INC.
1005 Lillian Way, Los Angeles, CA 90038. (323) 466-3361. FAX: (323) 466-5712.
CONTACT
Lorraine Fadden

SPECTAK PRODUCTIONS
222 N. Sepulveda Blvd., Ste. 2000, El Segundo, CA 90245. (310) 335-2038.

STAGE 18
18 Leonard St., Norwalk, CT 06850. (203) 852-8185. FAX: (203) 838-3126.

STICKS & STONES
(Specialty props, costume design, custom build only; make-up effects and puppets)
12990 Branford St., Ste. M, Arleta, CA 91331. (818) 252-2088. FAX: (818) 252-2087. email: jemrtb@ecom.net
CONTACT
Rob Burman
Jennifer E. McManus

DAVID STIPES PRODUCTIONS, INC.
685 Glenandale Ter., Glendale, CA 91206. (818) 243-1442.
CONTACT
David Stipes III

STOKES/KOHNE ASSOCIATES, INC.
742 Cahuenga Blvd., Hollywood, CA 90038. (323) 468-2340. FAX: (323) 468-2345.

STUDIO PRODUCTIONS
650 N. Bronson Ave., Ste. 223, Hollywood, CA 90004. (323) 856-8048. FAX: (323) 461-4202. email: Vizualman@aol.com
EXECUTIVE PRODUCER
Steve Soffer

SUNSET POST, INC.
1813 Victory Blvd., Glendale, CA 91201. (818) 956-7912. FAX: (818) 545-7586.

T.E.S.T. KREASHENS
26536 Golden Valley Rd., Ste. 612, Saugus, CA 91350. (805) 251-6466. FAX: (805) 251-1153.

T & T OPTICAL EFFECTS
1619 1/2 S. Victory Blvd., Glendale, CA 91201. (818) 241-7407. FAX: (818) 241-7207.

TANZINITE PRODUCTIONS
2118 Wilshire Blvd., Ste. 176, Santa Monica, CA 90403. (310) 281-8139. FAX: (310) 828-0427.
SENIOR V.P., SALES & DEVELOPMENT
Maria Laing

TECHNICREATIONS
2328 N. Batavia, Ste. 106, Orange, CA 92865. (714) 282-8423. FAX: (714) 282-7853. www.netpage.com/technicreations.html
email: tcreate@deltanet.com
CONTACT
Terry Carrigan

THIRD DIMENSION EFFECTS
427 W, Alameda Ave., Burbank, CA 91506-3201. (818) 842-5665. FAX: (818) 842-9132.

TITLE HOUSE INC./TITLE HOUSE DIGITAL EFFECTS
(Digital visual effects, titles and optical effects)
738 N. Cahuenga Blvd., Los Angeles, CA 90038. (323) 469-8171. FAX: (323) 469-0377.
PRESIDENT
Keith Allan
VICE PRESIDENT
Mark Allan
DIRECTOR OF SALES
Ridge Blackwell
EXECUTIVE PRODUCER
Mark Shore

TODD-AO DIGITAL IMAGES
6601 Romaine St., Hollywood, CA 90038. (323) 962-4141. FAX: (323) 466-7903.
PRESIDENT
Brian Jennings

TRIBAL SCENERY
3216 Vanowen St., Burbank, CA 91505. (818) 558-4045.

TRI-ESS SCIENCES, INC.
1020 W. Chestnut St., Burbank, CA 91506. (818) 848-7838. FAX: (818) 848-3521. email: pyro@tri-sss.com
CONTACT
Kim Greenfield

MIKE TRISTANO WEAPONS & SPECIAL EFFECTS
(Weapon effects, blood hits, dust hits, spark hits, make-up effects, blood effects)
14431 Ventura Blvd., Ste. 185, Sherman Oaks, CA 91423. (818) 888-6970. FAX: (818) 888-6447.

TWO HEADED MONSTER
6161 Santa Monica Blvd., Ste. 100, Los Angeles, CA 90038. (323) 957-5370. FAX: (323) 957-5371.
email:thmonster@aol.com
CONTACT
Ruth Schiller

ULTIMATE EFFECTS
642 Sonora Ave., Glendale, CA 91201. (818) 547-4743.

UNITEL VIDEO
729 N. Highland Ave., Los Angeles, CA 90038. (323) 878-5800. FAX: (323) 931-7771 www.univid.com
515 W. 57th St., New York, NY 10019. (212) 265-3600. FAX: (212) 765-5801.

THE VIDEO AGENCY
10900 Ventura Blvd., Studio City, CA 91604. (818) 505-8300. FAX: (818) 505-8370. email: TVA@pacbell.net
CONTACT
Jeffrey Goddard

VIDEO POST & TRANSFER, INC.
(Film to tape transfer, video online editing, audio, broadcast design, 3D animation, visual effects)
2727 Inwood Rd., Dallas, TX 75235. (214) 350-2676. FAX: (214) 352-1427. email: roberth@videopost.com
DIRECTOR OF MARKETING
Robert Haasz

VIEW POINT STUDIOS
162 Columbus Ave., Boston, MA 02116. (617) 338-1113. FAX: (617) 423-1481. www.viewpointstudios.com
email: imendez@viewpointstudios.com
BROADCAST MARKET COORDINATOR
Liz Mendez

VIEW STUDIO, INC.
6715 Melrose Ave., Hollywood, CA 90038. (323) 965-1270. FAX: (323) 965-1277.
EXECUTIVE PRODUCER
Henry Kline

VIEWPOINT DATA LABS
625 S. State Street, Orem, UT 84058. (801) 229-3000. FAX: (801) 229-3300. email: vpia@viewpoint.com
4223 Glencoe Ave., Ste. C-100, Los Angeles, CA 90292. (310) 578-6997, (888) 773-7276. FAX: (310) 578-9867.
www.viewpoint.com
CONTACT
Steve Skinner

VIEWPORT IMAGES
109 N. Naomi St., Burbank, CA 91505. (818) 559-8705. FAX: (818) 559-5453.
PRESIDENT
John Howard

VISION ART DESIGN & ANIMATION
3025 Olympic Blvd., Santa Monica, CA 90404. (210) 264-5566. FAX: (310) 264-5572.

VISUAL CONCEPT ENGINEERING (VCE)
13300 Ralston Ave., Sylmar, CA 91342-7608. (818) 367-9187. FAX: (818) 362-3490. www.vce.com email: vceinc@aol.com
CONTACT
Peter Kuran

VISION CREW UNLIMITED
5939 Rodeo Rd., Los Angeles, CA 90016. (310) 558-0450. FAX: (310) 558-0437.
www.visioncrew.com email: visioncrew@visioncrew.com
EXECUTIVE PRODUCER
Evan Jacobs

VISUAL FX.COM
8129 Willow Glen Rd., Los Angeles, CA 90046. (323) 650-0772. FAX: (323) 650-7209.
www.visualfx.com email: rohaver@earthlink.com

VISUAL IMPULSE PRODUCTIONS (V.I.P.)
(3D and effects; interactive solutions)
10850 Wilshire Blvd., Ste. 380, Los Angeles, CA 90024. (310) 441-2556. FAX: (310) 441-2558.

DON WAYNE MAGIC EFFECTS
(Magic illusions)
10929 Hartsook St., N. Hollywood, CA 91601. (818) 763-3192. FAX: (818) 985-4953. email: donwayneinc@earthlink.net

WILDFIRE, INC. LIGHTING & VISUAL EFFECTS
5200 W. 83rd St., Los Angeles, CA 90045. (310) 645-7787, (800) 937-8065. FAX: (310) 645-9009.
CONTACT
Richard Gleen

STAN WINSTON STUDIO
7032 Valjean Ave., Van Nuys, CA 91406. (818) 782-0870.

WONDERWORKS, INC.
7231 Remmet Ave., Canoga Park, CA 91303. (818) 992-8811. FAX: (818) 347-4330.
www.wonderworks.web.com email: WndrWrksEt@aol.com

STEVE WRIGHT DIGITAL FX, INC.
2206 Carnegie Lane, Ste. A, Redondo Beach, CA 90278. (310) 374-4164. FAX: (310) 374-7574. email: swdfx@cyberverse.com
CONTACT
Steve Wright

WUNDERFILM DESIGN
7700 W. Sunset Blvd., Los Angeles, CA 90046. (323) 845-4100. FAX: (323) 845-4101. email: jerry@wunderfilm.com
OWNER
Jerry Jaskulski

XAOS
(Special effects design and production)
444 De Haro St., Ste. 211, San Francisco, CA 94107. (415) 558-9267. FAX: (415) 558-9160.
PRESIDENT
Arthur Schwartzberg
EXECUTIVE PRODUCER
Marcus McWaters

X-STREAM POST (LAUBE-ROTH, INC.)
7025 Santa Monica Blvd., Hollywood, CA 90038. (323) 464-7337. FAX: (323) 856-9934. email: Xstreampo@aol.com
PRESIDENT
Greg Laube
CONTACT
Sherry Howell

Y.L.S. PRODUCTIONS
P.O. Box 34, Los Alamitos, CA 90720. (562) 430-2890. FAX: (562) 596-9563.

KEVIN YAGHER PRODUCTIONS
6615 Valjean Ave., Van Nuys, CA 91406. (818) 374-3210. FAX: (818) 374-3214.

GENE YOUNG EFFECTS
517 W. Windsor Street, Glendale, CA 91204. (818) 243-8593.

Stock Shots

ACADEMY OF MOTION PICTURE ARTS & SCIENCES
(Motion picture stills)
333 S. La Cienega Blvd., Beverly Hills, CA 90211. (310) 247-3020, (310) 247-3000. FAX: (310) 657-5193.

AMERICAN FILM INSTITUTE LIBRARY
2021 N. Western Ave., Los Angeles, 90027. (323) 856-7600.

AMERICAN STOCK PHOTOGRAPHY
6255 Sunset Blvd., #716, Los Angeles, CA 90028. (323) 469-3900. FAX: (323) 469-3909.

ARCHIVE FILMS/ARCHIVE PHOTOS
530 W. 25th St., New York, NY 10001. (212) 822-7800, (800) 876-5115. FAX: (212) 645-2137.
www.archivefilms.com email: sales@archivefilms.com
V.P., SALES
Eric Rachlis

ASSOCIATED MEDIA IMAGES, INC.
650 N. Bronson, Ste. 300, Los Angeles, 90004. (323) 871-1340. FAX: (323) 469-6048.

THE BBC WORLDWIDE AMERICAS/THE BBC LIBRARY
3500 W. Olive Ave., Ste. 110, Burbank, CA 91505. (818) 840-9770, (800) 966-5424. FAX: (818) 840-9779.
email: lals@bbcfootage.com

BEST SHOT, INC.
4726 N. Lois Ave., Ste. A, Tampa, FL 33614. (813) 877-2118. FAX: (813) 874-3655.
www.cyberspy.com/bestshot email: bestshot@cyberspy.com
CONTACT
Peter Klein

BLOOMING PARADISE PRODUCTIONS
5202 Edgewood Pl. #B, Los Angeles, CA 90019. Tel/FAX: (323) 937-0432.

THE BRIDGEMAN ART LIBRARY INTERNATIONAL
65 E. 93rd St., New York, NY 10128. (212) 828-1238. FAX: (212) 828-1255.
www.bridgeman.co.uk email: lori@bridgemanart.com
PICTURE MANAGER
Lori Bridgeman

BRITANNICA FILMS
310 S. Michigan, Chicago, IL 60604. (312) 347-7400, ext. 6512, (800) 554-9862.

BUDGET FILMS
4427 Santa Monica Blvd., Los Angeles, 90029. (323) 660-0187. FAX: (323) 660-5571.

BUENA VISTA IMAGING (DISNEY)
(Nature, scenics, aerials, contemporary cities)
500 S. Buena Vista St., Burbank, 91521. (818) 560-1270. FAX: (818) 842-9454.
CONTACT
Ben F. Hendicks, Jr.

CAMEO FILM LIBRARY, INC.
10760 Burbank Blvd., North Hollywood, 91601. (818) 980-8700. FAX: (818) 980-7113.
LIBRARIANS
Marilyn Chielens
Steve Vrabel

CHERTOK ASSOCIATES, INC.
100 S. Main St., New City, NY 10956. (914) 639-4238.

DICK CLARK MEDIA ARCHIVES
3003 W. Olive Ave., Burbank, CA 91505. (818) 841-3003. FAX: (818) 954-8609.

CLASSIC IMAGES
1041 N. Formosa Ave., W. Hollywood, CA 90046. (323) 850-2980, (800) 949-CLIP. FAX: (323) 850-2981.
www.classicimg.com email: sales@classicimg.com
PRESIDENT
Marcie Alexander

THE CLIP JOINT FOR FILM
833-B N. Hollywood Way, Burbank, CA 91505. (818) 842-2525. FAX: (818) 842-2644.

LARRY DORN ASSOCIATES, INC.
(Film and video libraries; world backgrounds, Cessna aircraft)
5820 Wilshire Blvd., #306, Los Angeles, CA 90036. (323) 935-6266. FAX: (323) 935-9523.
STOCK FOOTAGE LIBRARIAN
Linda Dorn Wallerstein

EASTMAN KODAK COMPANY
343 State St., Rochester, NY 14650. (800) 242-2424.

ENERGY FILM LIBRARY
12700 Ventura Blvd., 4th Flr., Studio City, 91604. (818) 508-1444, (800) IMAGERY. FAX: (818) 508-1293.
www.digital-energy.com email: rob@digital-energy.com
DIRECTOR OF LIBRARY SALES, WEST COAST
Joan Sargent
404 Park Ave. S., Ste. 1304, New York, NY 10016. (212) 686-4900. (800) IMAGERY. FAX: (212) 686-4998.
DIRECTOR OF LIBRARY SALES, EAST COAST
Larry K. Aubrey

F.I.L.M. ARCHIVES, INC.
432 Park Ave. S., New York, NY 10016. (212) 696-2616. FAX: (212) 696-0021.
www.fastimages.com email:fastimages@compuserve.com

FILM & VIDEO STOCK SHOTS, INC.
10442 Burbank Blvd., N. Hollywood, CA 91601-2217. (888) 4-FOOTAGE, (818) 760-2098. FAX: (818) 760-3294.
email: stockshot@earthlink.net
PRESIDENT
Stephanie Siebert

FILM BANK
425 S. Victory Blvd., Burbank, CA 91502. (818) 841-9176. FAX: (818) 567-4235.
www.filmbank.com email: filmbank@primenet.com
PRESIDENT
Paula Lumbard
SALES REPRESENTATIVES
Carol Martin
Barry Dagestino

GORDY COMPANY MEDIA LIBRARY
6255 Sunset Blvd., #1800, Los Angeles, CA 90028. (323) 856-3500. FAX: (323) 962-3054.

GREAT WAVES FILM LIBRARY
483 Mariposa Dr., Ventura, CA 93001-2230. (805) 653-2699.

HALCYON DAYS PRODUCTIONS
1926 Broadway, #302, New York, NY10023. (212) 724-2626. FAX: (212) 724-4239.

HOLLYWOOD NEWSREEL SYNDICATE, INC.
1622 N. Gower St., Hollywood, CA 90028. (323) 469-7307. FAX: (323) 469-8251.

THE IMAGE BANK/THE IMAGE BANK WEST
111 Fifth Ave., New York, NY 10003. (212) 539-8300. FAX: (212) 539-8370.
2400 Broadway, #220, Santa Monica, CA 90404. (310) 264-4850. FAX: (310) 453-1482.

INTERNATIONAL COLOR STOCK, INC.
3841 N.E. 2nd Ave., Ste. 304, Miami, FL 33137-3639. (305) 573-5200. email: ins@mindspring.com
CONTACT
R. Taylor

INTERVIDEO, INC.
1500 W. Burbank Blvd., Burbank, CA 91506-1309. (818) 843-3624, (800) 843-3626. FAX: (818) 843-6884.
PRESIDENT
Richard Clark
SALES
Regina Hamilton

JALBERT PRODUCTIONS, INC.
775 Park Ave., Huntington, NY 11743. (516) 351-5878.

KESSER STOCK LIBRARY
21 S.W. 15th Rd., Miami, FL 33129. (305) 358-7900, (800) 785-3843. FAX: (305) 358-2209.
www.kesser.com
email: kesser@icanect.net

CLAY LACY AVIATION, INC.
7435 Valjean Ave., Van Nuys, CA 91406. (818) 989-2900. FAX: (818) 909-9537. www.claylacy.com
ADMINISTRATIVE DIRECTOR
Tina Gossman

LIBRARY OF MOVING IMAGES, INC.
6671 Sunset Blvd., #1581, Hollywood, CA 90028. (323) 469-7499. FAX: (323) 469-7559.
OWNER
Michael Peter Yakaitis

MACGILLIVRAY FREEMAN FILMS
P.O. Box 205, Laguna Beach, CA 92652. (714) 494-1055. FAX: (714) 494-2079.
STOCK LIBRARIAN
Robert Walker

MUSEUM OF NATURAL HISTORY FILM ARCHIVES
Central Park W. at 79th St., New York, NY 10024. (212) 769-5419.

NBC NEWS ARCHIVES
30 Rockefeller Plaza, Rm. 280-E, New York, NY 10112. (212) 664-3797. FAX: (212) 957-8917.

NATIONAL GEOGRAPHIC FILM LIBRARY
1145 17th St. N.W., Washington, DC 20036. (202) 857-7659. (202) 775-6167. FAX: 202) 429-5755.
NATIONAL SALES MANAGER
Sally Russell

4370 Tujunga Ave., Ste. 300., Studio City, CA 91604. (818) 506-8300. FAX: (818) 506-8200.
CONTACT
Robyn Paul

1251 6th Ave., 17th Flr., New York, NY 10020. (212) 221-5842. FAX: (212) 221-5815.
CONTACT
Erica Sashin

PALISADES WILDLIFE LIBRARY
1205 S. Ogden Dr., Los Angeles, CA 90019. (323) 931-6186.

PARAMOUNT PICTURES STOCK FOOTAGE LIBRARY
5555 Melrose Ave., Hollywood, CA 90038. (323) 956-5510, (888) 264-9009. FAX: (323) 862-1833, (888) 264-9011
www.Paramountstock.com email: Pat Harris@Paramount.com
HEAD LIBRAIAN
Pat Harris

PASSPORT INTERNATIONAL PRODUCTIONS
10520 Magnolia Blvd., North Hollywood, CA 91601. (818) 760-1500. FAX: (818) 760-1532. email: passport4@earthlink.com
V.P., OPERATIONS
Jeanette Pugliese

PRODUCERS LIBRARY SERVICE
1051 N. Cole Ave., Hollywood, CA 90038. (323) 465-0572. FAX: (323) 465-1671.
www.filmfootage.com email: stockftg@primenet.com
OWNER
Jeff Goodman

PYRAMID FILM & VIDEO
2801 Colorado Ave., Santa Monica, 90404. (310) 828-7577. FAX: (310) 453-9083.
www.pyramidmedia.com email: info@pyramidmedia.com
PRESIDENT
Randy Wright

A RETROSPECT FILM ARCHIVE
11693 San Vicente Blvd., #111, Los Angeles, CA 90049. (310) 471-1906, (415) 948-7526. FAX: (310) 471-1430.
www.nettwork@hotmail.com
DIRECTOR
Patrick Netter

REUTERS NEWMEDIA, INC.
1700 Broadway, 15th Flr., New York, NY 10019. (212) 603-3850. FAX: (212) 397-3003.

RO-MA STOCK IMAGES
(Backgrounds, skylines, wildlife, nature)
1003 S. Los Robles Ave., Pasadena, CA 91106-4332. (818) 799-7733. FAX: (818) 799-6622.
www.eyecatchingimages.com
email: romastock@aol.com
PRESIDENT
Robert Marien

SECOND LINE SEARCH
1926 Broadway, 5th Flr., New York, NY 10023. (212) 787-7500. FAX: (212) 787-7636. email: clips@secondline.com
CONTACT
Eileen Kelly

THE SOURCE STOCK FOOTAGE
150 S. Camino Seco, Ste. 119A, Tucson, AZ 85710. (520) 298-4810. FAX: (520) 290-8831. www.sourcefootage.com
email: Requests@sourcefootage.com
LIBRARY MANAGER
Don French

SPECTRAL COMMUNICATIONS
178 S. Victory Blvd., #106, Burbank, CA 91502. (818) 840-0111. FAX: (818) 840-0618.

THE STOCK HOUSE
6922 Hollywood Blvd., Ste. 621, Los Angeles, 90028. (323) 461-0061. FAX: (323) 461-2457.
V.P., OPERATIONS
Allison Hopeland

UCLA FILM & TELEVISION ARCHIVE
1015 N. Cahuenga Blvd., Hollywood, CA 90038. (323) 466-8559. FAX: (323) 461-6317.
CONTACT
Howard Hays

UNIVERSAL STOCK FOOTAGE LIBRARY
100 Universal City Plaza, Bldg. 99, Rm. 213, Universal City, 91608. (818) 777-3000. FAX: (818) 733-1579.
www.universalstudios.com email: jzwilli@unistudios.com
HEAD LIBRARIAN
John Willison

VIDEO TAPE LIBRARY, LTD.
1509 N. Crescent Heights Blvd. #2, Los Angeles, 90046. (323) 656-4330. FAX: (323) 656-8746.
www.videotapelibrary.com email: vtl@earthlink.net
PRESIDENT
Melody St. John

WISH YOU WERE HERE FILM & VIDEO
105 W. Alameda Ave., Ste. 217, Burbank, CA 91502. (818) 569-5876. FAX: (818) 569-5880.
email: noborders@wywhstock.com

STUDIO & EDITING EQUIPMENT RENTALS

ADDRESS ONE POST
662 N. Van Ness Ave., Ste. 201, Los Angeles, CA 90004. (310) 838-7783. FAX: (323) 960-4961.
CONTACT
Tess Thompson

AFTERSHOCK DIGITAL
8222 Melrose Ave., Ste. 304, Los Angeles, CA 90046. (323) 658-5700. FAX: (323) 658-5200.
www.aftershockdigital.com email: edit@aftershockdigital.com
CONTACT
Fritz Feick

AMERICAN FILM & TAPE, INC.
9823 Mason Ave., Ste. 12, Chatsworth, CA 91311. (818) 885-6641. FAX: 9818) 885-6217.
MANAGER
Al Landsdale

AMERICAN ZOETROPE
916 Kearny St., San Francisco, CA 94133. (415) 788-7500. FAX: (415) 989-7910.
CEO
Jay Shumacher
FACILITIES COORDINATOR
James Levine

ANCHOR EDITORIAL
1542 15th St., Santa Monica, CA 90404. (310) 656-9400. FAX: 9310) 656-9401.

ARCHION
4235 Marellen Ave., Ste. 302, Studio City, CA 91604. (818) 655-2222. FAX: (818) 655-2233. www.archion.com
CEO
Reuben Lima

ASC AUDIO VIDEO CORP.
4400 Vanowen St., Burbank, CA 91505. (818) 843-7004. FAX: (818) 842-8945.

AUTHENTIC DESIGN
(Digital imaging)
Box 310, Malibu, CA 90265. (818) 707-0007.
email: authentic@earthlink.net
OWNER
Stephen Morales

AVAILABLE LIGHT, LTD.
1125 Flower St., Burbank, CA 91502. (818) 842-2109.
CEO
Katherine Kean
PRESIDENT
John Van Vliet
POST PRODUCTION SUPERVISOR
Gretchen Weiland

AVID TECHNOLOGY
115 N. 1st St., Ste. 208, Burbank, CA 91502. (818) 557-2520. FAX: (818) 557-2558. www.avid.com
Corporate: Avid Technology, Inc., Avid Technology Park, One Park West, Weksebury, MA 01876. (978) 640-6789. FAX: (978) 640-1366.
PRESIDENT & CEO
David Krall
SENIOR V.P. & ACTING CFO
Ethan E. Jacks
SENIOR V.P. & GENERAL MANAGER, DIGIDESIGN
David Froker
SENIOR V.P., WORLDWIDE SALES
Chas Smith
CTO, V.P. & GENERAL MANAGER, INTERNET SOLUTIONS GROUP
Mike Rockwell
V.P., WORLDWIDE PRODUCT MARKETING
Rob Kobrin
V.P. & GENERAL MANAGER, MEDIA SOLUTIONS GROUP
Joe Bentivegna
V.P. & GENERAL MANAGER, SOFTIMAGE
David Pritchard

BABYLON POST
901 N. Seward St., Hollywood, CA 90038. (323) 460-4088. FAX: (323) 460-6312. email: babylonpost@earthlink.net
OWNER
Robin Fellows

BAYPOST COMPANY
8380 Melrose Ave., Ste. 210, Los Angeles, CA 90069. (323) 653-2777. FAX: (323) 653-1531. www.baypost.com

BIG TIME PICTURE COMPANY
12210-1/2 Nebraska Ave., Los Angeles, CA 90025. (310) 207-0921. FAX: 9310) 826-0071. email: bigtimepic@earthlink.net

BLUEFIELD MUSIC DESIGN
1006 E. Cooper Ave., Aspen, CO 81611. (970) 925-2202. FAX: (970) 925-2202.
OWNER
David Bluefield

BOTTOM LINE STUDIOS
5729 Cahuenga Blvd., North Hollywood, CA 91601. (818) 762-9918. email: bottln@ix.netcom.com
PRODUCER & DIRECTOR, DEVELOPMENT
Patrick Donahue

BOUQUET POST
881 Alma Real Dr., Ste. T-8, Pacific Palisades, CA 90272. (310) 573-7394, Ext. 144. FAX: (310) 573-2025.
www.bouquet.com email: info@bouquet.com
SALES MANAGER
Matt Radecki

CALIBAN FILMWORKS
662 N. Robertson Blvd., W. Hollywood, CA 90069. (310) 289-2727. FAX: (310) 289-2728.
www.calibanfilms.com email: bernice@calibanfilms.com
PRODUCTION MANAGER
Bernice Briggs

CALIFORNIA COMMUNICATIONS, INC. (CCI DIGITAL)
2921 W. Alameda Ave., Burbank, CA 91505. (818) 562-6300. FAX: 9818) 562-8222. www.ccidigital.com
PRESIDENT
Rick Morris

CEG POST
(Features, AVID, sound)
1901 Ave. of the Stars, Los Angeles, CA 90067. (310) 229-3505. FAX: 9310) 229-3508.

CHASE PRODUCTIONS, INC.
201 S. Victory Blvd., Burbank, CA 91502. (818) 842-8346. FAX: (818) 842-8353. www.chace.com
MANAGING PARTNER
Robert Heiber

BOB CHENOWETH RENTALS
1015 N. Cahuenga Blvd., Hollywood, CA 90038. (562) 691-1652. FAX: (562) 690-8362. email: cheoweth1@aol.com

CHRISTY'S EDITORIAL FILM & VIDEO SUPPLY
3625 W. Pacific Ave., Burbank, CA 91505. (818) 845-1755. FAX: (818) 845-756. www.christys.net

CINESITE DIGITAL STUDIOS
1017 N. Las Palmas, Ste. 300, Los Angeles, CA 90038. (323) 468-4400. FAX: (323) 468-4404. www.cinesite.com
V.P. & HEAD OF PRODUCTION
Gil Gagnon

CINEVISION EDITORIAL, INC.
1111 S. Victory Blvd., Burbank, CA 91502. (818) 566-4917. FAX: (818) 566-6639.
PRESIDENT
Philip Jones

CONCEPT PLUS
(Fairlight MXK 3 digital audio)
1132 Vine St., Hollywood, CA 90038. (323) 466-2066. FAX: (323) 466-2717.
CONTACT
Jan Jebson

CREATIVE WEST
937 N. Cole Ave., Ste. 3-4, Los Angeles, CA 90038. (323) 464-8697. FAX: 9323) 464-8699.

CREST NATIONAL DIGITAL MEDIA COMPLEX
1141 N. Seward St., Hollywood, CA 90038. (323) 462-6696. FAX: (323) 462-5039. www.crestnational.com
FILM ACCOUNT EXECUTIVE
Peter Dana

HAL DENNIS PRODUCTIONS
6314 La Mirada Ave., Hollywood, CA 90038. (323) 467-7146. FAX: (323) 467-7235.

DES
4142 Lankershim Blvd., North Hollywood, CA 91602-2829. (818) 508-8200. FAX: (818) 508-8222.
www.digitalediting.com email: jbuchignani@digitalediting.com
DIRECTOR, SALES & EDITORIAL DIVISION
Jeff Buchignani

DIGITAL MAGIC COMPANY
3000 W. Olympic Blvd., Bldg. One, 2nd Flr., Santa Monica, CA 90404. (310) 315-9505. FAX: (310) 315-9545. www.4mc.com
CONACT
Bill Frazee

DIGITAL QUEST
3000 S. Robertson, Ste. 295, Los Angeles, CA 90034. (310) 815-4870. FAX: (310) 287-3734.
www.dqpost.com email: info@dqpost.com
DIRECTOR, POST-PRODUCTION
Casey Gelvin, email: casey@dqpost.com
DIRECTOR, TECHNICAL & CREATIVE
John Chi, email: john@dqpost.com
DIRECTOR, MARKETING & MEDIA
Anne Gelvin, email: anne@dqpost.com
DIRECTOR, TRAINING & RESOURCES
Mark Tarver, email: mark@dqpost.com

DIGITAL TELEVISION EQUIPMENT, INC.
2445 Capital St., Ste. 105, Fresno, CA 93721. (559) 445-0255. FAX: (559) 445-0252.

WALT DISNEY STUDIOS POST-PRODUCTION SERVICES
500 S. Buena Vista St., Burbank, CA 91521. (818) 560-1000. www.stu-ops.disney.com

D-VISION SYSTEMS, INC.
600 W. Fulton, Chicago, IL 60601. (312) 382-7710. FAX: (312) 382-1427.

EAGLE EYE FILM COMPANY
10825 Burbank Blvd., North Hollywodd, CA 91601. (818) 506-6100. FAX: 9818) 506-4313. www.eagleeyedigital.com
CONTACT
Shane Wilhoite

EAST COAST POST
110 Leroy St., 8th Flr., New York, NY 10014. (212) 807-9828. FAX: (212) 691-9148. www.eastcoastpost.com
DIRECTOR
Kristen Flynn

EDIT POINT POST PRODUCTION SYSTEMS
620 N. Victory Blvd., Burbank, CA 91502. (818) 841-7336. FAX: 9818) 841-7378.

EFILM
1146 N. Las Palmas Ave., Hollywood, CA 90038. (323) 463-7041. FAX: (323) 465-7342. www.efilm.com
V.P.
David Hays

ELECTRIC PICTURE SOLUTIONS
3752 Cahuenga Blvd. W., Studio City, CA 91604. (818) 766-5000. FAX: (818) 623-7547.
www.picturesolutions.com email: info@picturesolutions.com
EDITOR & PRESIDENT
David Pincus

ENTERPRISE IMAGE
(AID nonlinear, Sony, Tascam)
2731 N. Hollywood Way, Burbank, CA 91505. (818) 840-8480. FAX: (818) 558-6238. www.enterpriseimage.com
GENERAL MANAGER
David Harrelson

ENTERTAINMENT POST
(SyncSound dailies)
3575 Cahuenga Blvd. W., Ste. 103, Los Angeles, CA 90068. (323) 876-5800. FAX: 9323) 876-5849.
GENERAL MANAGER
Glenn Jepson

FAST MULTIMEDIA
15029 Woodinville-Redmond Dr., Woodinville, WA 98072. (425) 354-2002. FAX: (425) 354-2005. www.fastmultimedia.com

FILMWERKS DIGITAL
(Post-production services, 2D & 3D effects, new media)
3000 W. Olympic Blvd., Santa Monica, CA 90404. (310) 264-3978. www.filmwerks.com email: filmwerks@filmswerks.com
CONTACT
Jenn Dewey

FPC, INC.
6677 Santa Monica Blvd., Hollywood, CA 90038. (323) 468-5774. FAX: (323) 468-5771. www.fpcfilm.com
CEO
Kenneth Knaus

FRONTIER POST
6525 Sunset Blvd., Ste. 201, Los Angeles, CA 90028. (323) 460-2970. FAX: (323) 460-2971. email: skip@sc.net

GELULA & CO.
8421 Wilshire Blvd., Ste. 205, Beverly Hills, CA 90211. (323) 651-1167. FAX: (323) 651-3612. www.gelula.com
PRESIDENT
Elio Zarmati

GOING POSTAL PRODUCTIONS
315 Washington Blvd., Ste. 2, Marina Del Rey, CA 90292. (310) 823-9362. FAX: (310) 823-9562. www.goingpostalprod.com
PRESIDENT & SENIOR EDITOR
Wes Rubinstein

GOOD EDIT
417 Canal St., 3rd Flr., New York, NY 10013. (212) 966-8616. FAX: (212) 966-8592.
MANAGER
Janell Fletcher

GUN FOR HIRE PRODUCTION CENTER
110 Leroy St., New York, NY 10014. (212) 414-1557. FAX: (212) 741-6457. www.gfhpc.com
V.P., SALES
Dave Tuttle

HAMMER FILMS
6311 Romaine St., Ste. 7316, Hollywood, CA 90038. (323) 463-9156. FAX: (323) 463-8130.
FACILITY COORDINATOR
Jennifer Fong

HARLEY'S HOUSE
1855 Centinela Ave., Santa Monica, CA 90404. (310) 829-4255. FAX: (310) 828-5944. www.harleyshouse.com
SENIOR PRODUCER
Michael Raimondi

HOLLYWOOD FILM COMPANY
3294 E. 26th St., Los Angeles, CA 90023. (323) 261-3700. FAX: (323) 263-9665.
CONTACT
Vincent Carabello

JKR PRODUCTIONS, INC.
12140 W. Olympic Blvd., Ste. 21, Los Angeles, CA 90064. (310) 826-3666.
CONTACT
Jim Ruxin

LASER PACIFIC MEDIA CORP.
540 N. Hollywood Way, Burbank, CA 91505. (818) 842-0777. FAX: (818) 566-9834. www.laserpacific.com
809 N. Cahuenga Blvd., Los Angeles, CA 90038. (323) 462-2266. FAX: (323) 464-6005.
CHAIRMAN & CEO
James R. Parks
PRESIDENT & COO
Emory Cohen
DIRECTORS
Ronal Zimmerman
Thomas Gordon
Craig Jacobsen
EXECUTIVE V.P.
Leon Silverman
SENIOR V.P., ENGINEERING
Randolph Blim
V.P. & GENERAL MANAGER
Jane Swearingen
CFO & CORPORATE SECRETARY
Robery McClain
V.P., OPERATIONS, BURBANK
Steve Mitchell
MANAGER, OPERATIONS, BURBANK
David Boito
MANAGER, FILM & VIDEO LIBRARY SERVICES, BURBANK
Brian House
DIRECTOR, OPERATIONS, HOLLYWOOD
Margie Gladden
MANAGER, FILM & VIDEO LIBRARY SERVICES, HOLLYWOOD
Dale Brown
MANAGER, OPERATIONS, HOLLYWOOD
Dave Carlson
MANAGER, SCHEDULING, HOLLYWOOD
Rob Smith
MANAGER, DIGITAL MASTERING & RESTORATION SERVICES, HOLLYWOOD
Diane Zaelke

LOST PLANET PRODUCTIONS
(Digital nonlinear online, motion graphics, dupes)
28310 Roadside Dr., Ste. 234, Agoura Hills, CA 91301. (818) 597-1726. FAX: (818) 597-1389. www.lost-planet.com
PRESIDENT
Marvin Whisman

MAGIC FILM & VIDEO WORKS
2721 W. Burbank Blvd., Burbank, CA 91505. (818) 845-8781. FAX: (818) 845-4392.

MAGNO SOUND & VIDEO
729 7th Ave., New York, NY 10019. (212) 302-2505. FAX: (212) 819-1282. www.magnosoundandvideo.com
V.P.
David Friedman

MATCHFRAME VIDEO
610 N. Hollywood Way, Ste. 101, Burbank, CA 91505. (818) 840-6800. FAX: (818) 840-2726. email: info@mfv.com
DIRECTOR, POST-PRODUCTION SERVICES
Michael Levy

MONTAGE GROUP, LTD.
527 W. 34th St., 6th Flr., New York, NY 10001. (212) 714-9600. FAX: (212) 714-9896.

MONTANA EDIT
1131 Montana Ave., Santa Monica, CA 90403. (310) 451-9933. FAX: 9310) 451-0606.
www.montanaedit.com email: info@montanaedit.com
GENERAL MANAGER
Janee Thiel

MOVIE TECH STUDIOS
832 N. Seward St., Hollywood, CA 90038. (323) 461-8491. FAX: (323) 467-8471. www.movietech.com
PRESIDENT & CEO
Ewing M. Brown

MY YOU ME PRODUCTIONS
2050 S. Bundy Dr., Ste. 104, West Los Angeles, CA 90025. (310) 820-1772. FAX: 9310) 820-1332.
CONTACT
Richard Heene

NATIONAL VIDEO CENTER
460 W. 42nd St., New York, NY 10036. (212) 279-2000. FAX: (212) 947-6439. www.nationalvideocenter.com
EXECUTIVE DIRECTOR
Bob Shavelson

NEW HOLLYWOOD, INC.
1302 N. Caheunga Blvd., Hollywood, CA 90028. (323) 466-3686. email: newhollywood@hotmail.com
CONTACT
Ozzie Zornizer

NEWEDIT, INC.
8300 Beverly Blvd., Los Angeles, CA 90048. (323) 653-3575. FAX: (323) 653-8855.
CONTACT
Stan Cassio

NITELITE EDITORIAL
12711 Ventura Blvd., Ste. 350, Studio City, CA 91604. (310) 839-0707. FAX: 9310) 839-0149. www.nitelite.org
EXECUTIVE PRODUCER
Harry Lowell

NT AUDIO VIDEO FILM LABS
1804 Ivar St., Hollywood, CA 90028. (323) 957-4200. FAX: (323) 957-4212. www.ntaudiovideofilmlabs.com
CONTACT
Clarisse Sirianni

ON-TIME OFF-LINE VIDEO
1800 Stanford St., Santa Monica, CA 90404. (310) 828-5662. FAX: (310) 829-9876. www.otolvideo.com
CONTACT
Nancy Altidor

PACIFIC OCEAN POST
730 Arizona Ave., Santa Monica, CA 90401. (310) 458-3300. FAX: (310) 394-6852.

PACIFIC TITLE & ART STUDIO
6350 Santa Monica Blvd., Hollywood, CA 90038. (323) 464-0121.

PACIFIC TITLE DIGITAL
1149 N. Gower St., Hollywood, CA 90038. (323) 769-3700. FAX: (323) 769-3701. www.pactitle.com

PADDED CELL PRODUCTIONS
3401 Pacific Ave., Ste. 18, Marina Del Rey, CA 90292. (310) 301-9555. FAX: (310) 823-5999.
email: paddedcell@mediaone.net
CEO
Rich Lewis

PASADENA PRODUCTION STUDIOS
39 E. Walnut St., Pasadena, CA 91103. (626) 584-4090. FAX: 9626) 584-4099. www.danwolfe.com
TRAFFIC MANAGER
Carrie Harfman

PELICAN PICTURES
210 Baronne St., Ste. 1347, New Orleans, LA 70112. (504) 524-8097. FAX: (504) 522-4751. www.pelicanpictures.com
ASSOCIATE PRODUCER
Bobbie Westerfield

PLANET VIDEO
11040 Santa Monica Blvd., Ste. 360, Los Angeles, CA 90025. (310) 473-2154. FAX: 9310) 473-5752. www.thelec.com
CONTACT
David Connor

POST CONSULTANTS GROUP
23900 Haynes St., West Hills, CA 91307. (818) 999-2924. FAX: (818) 316-0550.
PRESIDENT
Brian Murray

POST LOGIC STUDIOS
1800 N. Vine St.,M Ste. 100, Hollywood, CA 90028. (323) 461-7887. FAX: (323) 461-7790. www.postlogic.com
2049 Broadway, Santa Monica, CA 90404. (310) 315-955. FAX: (310) 315-3073.
DIRECTOR, SALES & MARKETING
Michael Gresch

POST PRODUCTION PLAYGROUND
1618 Broadway, 5th Flr., New York, NY 10019. (212) 399-0409.
CONTACT
Eitan Hakami

POST TIME
28206 W. Foothill Blvd., Castaic, CA 91384. (805) 257-2020. FAX: (805) 257-4018.
POSTPRODUCTION SUPERVISOR
Brad Arensman

PRECISION POST
3019 Pico Blvd., Santa Monica, CA 90405. (310) 829-5684. FAX: (310) 315-1757. email: precpost@aol.com
CONTACT
Joseph Arnao

PRIME POST
3500 Caheunga Blvd. W., Los Angeles, CA 90068. (323) 878-0782. FAX: 9323) 878-2781.
www.primepost.com email: info@primepost.com
GENERAL MANAGER
Brigitte Prouty

QUARTERMOON @ NATIONAL
1200 Post Rd., E., Westport, CT 06880. (203) 227-7887. FAX: (203) 454-7576. www.quartermoon.com
CREATIVE DIRECTOR
Gary Balionis

RALEIGH STUDIOS
5300 Melrose Ave., Hollywood, CA 90038. (323) 466-3111. FAX: 9323) 871-5600. www.raleighstudios.com
GENERAL MANAGER
Mary Fry

RED CAR LOS ANGELES
c/o Bergamot Studios, 2415 Michigan Ave., Santa Monica, CA 90404. (310) 828-7500. FAX: (310) 828-1245.

ROUNDABOUT ENTERTAINMENT
3915 Burbank Blvd., Burbank, CA 91505. (818) 842-9300. FAX: (818) 842-9301.
www.roundabout.com email: rndbt@westworld.com

RUNWAY EDITING SERVICES
c/o Santa Monica Airport, 3159 Donald Douglas Loop South, Santa Monica, CA 90405. (310) 636-2000. FAX: (310) 572-6296.

SKYVIEW STUDIOS
541 N. Fairbanks Ct., Ste. 2200, Chicago, IL 60611. (312) 670-2020. FAX: (312) 670-4520. www.skyview.com

SONY PICTURES STUDIOS
10202 W. Washington Blvd., Culver City, CA 90232. (310) 244-5523. FAX: (310) 204-2123. email: steve_cohen@spe.sony.com
V.P., SALES & DEVELOPMENT
Steven Cohen

SONY PICTURES DIGITAL STUDIOS DIVISION
10202 W. Washington Blvd., Culver City, CA 90232. (310) 244-4000. FAX: (310) 244-2626.
PRESIDENT
Ken Williams

SONY PICTURES STUDIOS POST-PRODUCTION FACILITIES
10202 W. Washington Blvd., Culver City, CA 90232. (310) 244-5722. FAX: (310) 244-2303.

LEONARD SOUTH PRODUCTIONS
11108 Huston St., North Hollywood, CA 91601. (818) 760-8383. FAX: (818) 766-8301.

RICK SPALLA VIDEO & HOLLYWOOD NEWSREEL
301 W. 45th St., Ste. 3-L, New York, NY 10036. (212) 764-4646.

STEENBECK, INC.
9554 Vassar Ave., Chatsworth, CA 91311. (818) 998-4033. FAX: 9818) 998-6992. email: steenbeck@compuserve.com
GENERAL MANAGER
Bob Campos

TEKTRONIX
5161 Lankershim Blvd., Ste. 100, North Hollywood, CA 91601. (818) 760-1699.

3 POINT DIGITAL
3300 N. San Fernando Blvd., Burbank, CA 91504. (818) 729-3000. FAX: (818) 729-3001. www.3pd.com
MARKETING DIRECTOR
Scott Taylor

TODD-AO/EDITWORKS
3399 Peachtree Rd. N.E., Ste. 200, Atlanta, GA 30326. www.editworks.com email: info@editworks.com
DIRECTOR, SALES & MARKETING
Beth Helmer

TOTAL DIGITAL PRODUCTIONS
1550 Flower St., Glendale, CA 91201. (818) 241-9792. FAX: 9818) 241-9796. www.total-digital.com
DIRECTOR, SPECIAL PROJECTS
Adrian Urrea

TWO HEADED MONSTER
725 Arizona Ave., Ste. 103, Santa Monica, CA 90401. (310) 319-5370. FAX: (310) 319-5380.

UNITEL VIDEO
(Digital transfers)
729 N. Highland Ave., Hollywood, CA 90038. (323) 931-1821. FAX: (323) 931-1398. www.unitelvideo.com

UNIVERSAL STUDIOS
100 Universal City Plaza, Bldg. 2313, Rm. 101, Universal City, CA 91608. (818) 777-4728. FAX: (818) 866-0763. www.universalstudios.com/studio
CONTACT
Keith Alexander

WARNER BROS. STUDIOS FACILITIES
4000 Warner Blvd., Burbank, CA 91522. (818) 954-2515. FAX: (818) 954-2677. www.wbsf.com
CONTACT
Tracy Balsz

WARNER HOLLYWOOD STUDIOS, STUDIO SERVICES
1041 N. Formosa Ave., W. Hollywood, CA 90046. (323) 850-2641. FAX: (323) 850-3550.
DIRECTOR, STUDIO SERVICES
Donna Jesse

WEST PRODUCTIONS, INC.
2921 W. Olive Ave., Burbank, CA 91505. (818) 841-4500. FAX: (818) 567-1820. www.westprod.com

WESTAR PRODUCTIONS, LLC
244 E. Union Turnpike, Wharton, NJ 07885. (973) 989-8403. FAX: (973) 989-8413. www.westarllc.com

XZACTO POST & ILLUSION
9306 Beatties Ford Rd., Ste. 3, Huntersville, NC 28078. (704) 398-8888. FAX: (704) 392-5133.
www.xzacto.com
PRESIDENT
Ben Griffith, Jr.

THE SAUL ZAENTZ FILM CENTER
2600 10th St., Berkeley, CA 94710. (510) 486-2100. FAX: (510) 486-2115.

SUBTITLES & CAPTIONS

BERLITZ TRANSLATION CENTER
525 Broadway, Ste. 300, Santa Monica, CA 90401. (310) 260-7100. FAX: (310) 260-7185.

CAPTION CENTER
(Closed captions, subtitles, dual-languge captioning)
610 N. Hollywood Way, Ste. 350, Burbank, CA 91505. (818) 562-3344. FAX: (818) 562-3388.
MARKETING REPRESENTATIVE
Michelle Maddalena

125 Western Ave., Boston, MA 02134. (617) 492-9225. FAX: (617) 582-0590. www.wgbh.org/caption
MARKETING REPRESENTATIVE
Liz Cavano

475 Park Ave. S., 10th Flr., New York, NY 10016. (212) 223-4930. FAX: (212) 688-2181.
MARKETING DIRECTOR
Susan Schneider

CAPTIONMAX
(Closed-captioning/foreign language captioning)
708 N. 1st St., Ste. 238, Minneapolis, MN 55401. (800) 822-3566. FAX: (612) 341-2345. www.captionmax.com

CAPTIONS, INC.
(Closed-captions, subtitles, translations)
5744 San Fernando Rd., Glendale, CA 91202. (818) 500-7301. FAX: (818) 500-7023.
SALES MANAGER
Robert Troy

619 W. 54th St., 5th Flr., New York, NY 10019. (212) CAP-TION. FAX: (212) 262-4855.
CONTACT
John Baxter

541 N. Fairbanks Ct., Ste. 2030, Chicago, IL 60611. (773) CAP-TION. FAX: (773) 527-0948.
CONTACT
Marko Iglendza

CINETYP, INC.
(Foreign language and theatrical captions)
843 Seward St., Hollywood, CA 90038. (323) 463-8569. FAX: (323) 463-4129. www.cinetyp.com email: cinetyp@aol.com
CEO & PRESIDENT
John H. Bell
PRODUCTION MANAGER
Dave Margolis

CREST NATIONAL DIGITAL MEDIA COMPLEX
(Foreign language dubbing and subtitling)
1000 N. Highland Ave., Hollywood, CA 90038. (323) 860-1300. FAX: (323) 466-7128. www.crestnational.com
EXECUTIVE V.P., SALES & MARKETING
John Walker

FOREIGN LANGUAGE GRAPHICS
12517 Chandler Blvd., #102, Valley Village, CA 91607. (818) 753-9584. FAX: (818) 753-9617. www.ISItrans.com

GELULA & CO., INC.
(Subtitles for theatrical, home video & DVD releases)
8421 Wilshire Blvd., Ste. 205, Beverly Hills, CA 90211. (323) 651-1167. FAX: (323) 651-3612. email: info@gelula.com
PRESIDENT
Elio Zarmatti

GLOBAL LANGUAGE SERVICES
2027 Las Lunas, Pasadena, CA 91107. (626) 792-0862, (626) 792-0576. FAX: (818) 792-8793. www.aebi@hss.caltech.edu
CONTACT
Dr. Andreas Aebi

INTEX AUDIOVISUALS
(Foreign language adaptations, 58 languages)
9021 Melrose Ave., Ste. 205, Los Angeles, CA 90069. (310) 275-9571. FAX: (310) 271-1319.

LANGUAGE SERVICES, INTERNATIONAL
804 Main St., Venice, CA 90291. (310) 399-1790. FAX: (310) 399-1901. www.language.net
CONTACT
Melanie Goodman

LASER VIDEO TITRES, INC.
375 Greenwich St., New York, NY 10013. (212) 343-1910. FAX: (212) 965-1338.
CHAIRMAN
Denis Auboyer

LINGUATHEQUE OF L.A.
13601 Ventura Blvd., #102, Sherman Oaks, CA 91423. (818) 995-8933. FAX: (818) 995-1228.
CONTACT
Karen Delaney

MARCLAND INTERNATIONAL COMMUNICATIONS
P.O. Box 3100, Burbank, CA 91508. (818) 557-6677. FAX: (818) 567-0568. www.marcland.com
CEO
Alfredo Marco Fulchignoni

MASTERWORDS
(Subtitles, dialogue, continuity)
1512 11th St., #205, Santa Monica, CA 90401-2907. (310) 390-1033. FAX: (310) 394-7954.

NATIONAL CAPTIONING INSTITUTE
(Closed-captioning, subtitling)
303 N. Glenoaks Blvd., Ste. 200, Burbank, CA 91502. (818) 238-0068. FAX: (818) 238-4266. www.ncicap.org/nci
MARKETING DIRECTOR
Doug Roberts

545 5th Ave., Ste. 1101, New York, NY 10017. (212) 557-7011. FAX: (212) 557-6975. email: mail@ncicap.org
V.P., MARKETING
Betty Hallman

1900 Gallows Rd., Ste. 3000, Vienna, VA 22182. (703) 917-7600. FAX: (703) 917-9853.

PACIFIC TITLE & ART STUDIO
6350 Santa Monica Blvd., Los Angeles, CA 90038. (323) 464-0121. FAX: (323) 938-6364.

P.F.M. DUBBING INTERNATIONAL
(Produces and dubs american English versions of foreign language films)
1007 Montana Ave., Ste. 306, Santa Monica, CA 90403. (310) 451-6068. FAX: (310) 451-6058.
PRESIDENT
Andre Guimond

JOY RENCHER'S EDITORIAL SERVICE
738 Cahuenga Blvd., Hollywood, CA 90038. (323) 463-9836. FAX: (323) 469-0377.

STS FOREIGN LANGUAGE SERVICES
(Foreign language translations, subtitling, voice-overs)
P.O. Box 10213, Burbank, CA 91510. (818) 508-1454. email: STSMedia@aol.com

SOFTNI SUBTITLING & DUBBING INTERNATIONAL
11444 W. Olympic Blvd., #200, Los Angeles, CA 90064. (310) 312- 9558. FAX: (310) 445-8800. www.softni.com
PRESIDENT
Jose M. Salgado

TITLE HOUSE, INC.
738 N. Cahuenga Blvd., Los Angeles, CA 90038. (323) 469-8171. FAX: (323) 469-0377.

TITRA CALIFORNIA, INC.
(Laser subtitles)
733 Salem St., Glendale, CA 91203. (818) 244-3663. FAX: (818) 244-6205. www.titra.com email: lalaser@aol.com
MANAGING DIRECTOR
Daniele Allen

285 W. Broadway, Ste. 560, New York, NY 10013. (212) 334-6927. FAX: (212) 334-6935. email: raoulny@aol.com
CONTACT
Ted Hicks

VITAC
44605 Lankershim Blvd., Ste. 250, N. Hollywood, CA 91602. (818) 755-0410. FAX: (818) 755-0411. email: vitacla@aol.com
PRESIDENT
Joseph Karlovits
GENERAL MANAGER & V.P., SALES
Deborah Schuster

WORDS IN PICTURES
1028 S. Alfred, Los Angeles, CA 90035. (323) 655-9221. FAX: (323) 655-3350.

TALENT AGENCIES

ABRAMS ARTISTS AGENCY
9200 Sunset Blvd., 11th Flr., Los Angeles, CA 90069. (310) 859-0625. FAX: (310) 276-6193.
PRESIDENT, MOTION PICTURES, TV & COMMERCIALS
Harry Abrams
MOTION PICTURES/TV
David Ginsberg
Marni Goldman
Maani Golesorkhi
Joe Rice
Shani Rosenzweig
Lara Smolev
YOUTH DIVISION
Wendi Green
BUSINESS AFFAIRS
Brian Chough
Larry Israel
Nathan Schwam

275 7th Ave., 26th Flr., New York, NY 10001. (646) 486-4600. FAX: (646) 486-0100.
PRESIDENT, MOTION PICTURES
Harry Abrams
THEATRICAL/MOTION PICTURES/TV
Robert Atterman
TV/MOTION PICTURES/THEATRICAL
Craig Cohen
THEATRICAL/MOTION PICTURES/TV
Jill McGrath

ABRAMS, RUBALOFF & LAWRENCE
8075 W. 3rd, Ste. 303, Los Angeles, CA 90048. (323) 935-1700. FAX: (323) 932-9901.

ABOVE THE LINE AGENCY
(Literary agents)
9200 Sunset Blvd., #804, Los Angeles, CA 90069. (310) 859-6115.
OWNER
Rima Greer
VICE PRESIDENT
Bruce Bartlett

ACME TALENT & LITERARY
6310 San Vicente Blvd., Ste. 520, Los Angeles, CA 90048. (323) 954-2263. FAX: (323) 954-2262.
AGENT & COO
Adam Lieblein
TALENT/FEATURE FILM
Rodney Ferrell

ACTORS ETC., INC.
2620 Foutainview, Ste. 210, Houston, TX 77057. (713) 785-4495. FAX: (713) 785-2641. www.actorsetc.com
AGENTS
Denise Coburn
Taylor Martin

BRET ADAMS LTD.
448 W. 44th St., New York, NY 10036. (212) 765-5630. FAX: (212) 265-2212.

THE AGENCY
1800 Ave. of the Stars, #400, Los Angeles, CA 90067. (310) 551-3000. FAX: (310) 551-1424.
CHAIRMAN
Jerry Zeitman
TALENT
Frank Gonzales
LITERARY
Tiffany Bartlett
Nick Mechanic
TV PACKAGING
Lynn Rosenberg

AGENCY FOR THE PERFORMING ARTS, INC.
9200 Sunset Blvd., Ste. 900, Los Angeles, CA 90069. (310) 273-0744. FAX: (310) 888-4242.
CHAIRMAN & CEO
Roger Vorce
PRESIDENT
Jim Grosnell
SENIOR V.P., PERSONAL APPEARANCE
Troy Blakely
SENIOR V.P., HEAD, LITERARY
Lee Dinstman
SENIOR V.P., PACKAGING & LITERARY
Jim Kellem
SENIOR V.P., MOTION PICTURE & TV TALENT
Gary Rado
HEAD, MOTION PICTURES & LITERARY
David Saunders

AGENCY 2 TALENT AGENCY
2425 San Diego Ave., Ste. 211, San Diego, CA 92110-2876. (619) 291-9556. FAX: (619) 291-4952.
www.showbizdatabase.com/A2
AGENTS
Lois Ringe, Terry Ringe

AGENTS FOR THE ARTS
203 W. 23rd St., 3rd Flr., New York, NY 10011. (212) 229-2562. FAX: (212) 463-9313.
OWNER
Carole J. Russo

AKO PRODUCTIONS
20531 Plummer St., Chatsworth, CA 91311. (818) 998-0443. FAX: (818) 998-2537.
GENERAL MANAGER
A.E. Sullivan

ALLIANCE TALENT, INC.
9171 Wilshire Blvd., Ste. 441, Beverly Hills, CA 90210. (310) 858-10190.

THE ALPERN GROUP
4400 Coldwater Canyon, Ste. 125, Studio City, CA 91604. (818) 752-1877. FAX: (818) 752-1859.

CARLOS ALVARADO AGENCY
8455 Beverly Blvd., Ste. 406, Los Angeles, CA 90048-3416. (323) 655-7978.
OWNER/AGENT
Mona Lee Schilling

MICHAEL AMATO THEATRICAL AGENCY
1650 Broadway, Ste. 307, New York, NY 10019. (212) 247-4456.
PRESIDENT
Michael Amato

AMBROSIO-JOHNSTON MANAGEMENT
2317 W. Olive Ave., Burbank, CA 91506. (818) 566-9996. FAX: (818) 566-9998.
OWNER/TALENT & LITERARY
Louis J. Ambrosio
OWNER/TALENT & LITERARY
Marisa A. Johnston

AMG-RENAISSANCE
(Literary)
9465 Wilshire Blvd., Beverly Hills, CA 90212. (310) 858-5365. FAX: (310) 860-8000.
PRESIDENT
Joel Gotler
PARTNERS
Irv Schwartz
Alan Nevins

AMERICAN INTERNATIONAL TALENT AGENCY
303 W. 42nd St., Ste. 608, New York, NY 10036. (212) 245-8888. FAX: (212) 245-8926.

AMSEL, EISENSTADT & FRAZIER, INC.
5757 Wilshire Blvd. #510, Los Angeles, CA 90036. (323) 939-1188. FAX: (323) 939-0630.
CO-OWNERS/THEATRICAL AGENTS
Michael Eisenstadt
John Frazier
LITERARY
Doug Brodax

BEVERLY ANDERSON
1501 Broadway, New York, NY 10036. (212) 944-7773. FAX: (212) 944-1034.
OWNER & PRESIDENT
Beverly Anderson

ANDREADIS TALENT AGENCY, INC.
(Talent & commercial)
119 W. 57th St., Ste. 711, New York, NY 10019. (212) 315-0303. FAX: (212) 315-0311.
OWNER & AGENT
Barbara Andreadis

ANIMANAGEMENT
(Literary, specializing in new media, composers, producers, writers & directors)
245 E. Olive Ave., Ste. 400, Burbank, CA 91502. (818) 526-7600. FAX: (818) 526-7606.
CHAIRMAN & CEO
Aaron Berger
PRESIDENT
B. Paul Husband

ARIA MODEL & TALENT MANAGEMENT
1017 W. Washington, Ste. 2-C, Chicago, IL 60607. (312) 243-9400. FAX: (312) 243-9020. www.ariamodel.com
OWNERS
Mary Boncher
Marie Anderson Boyd

ARTIST MANAGEMENT AGENCY
835 5th Ave., Ste. 411, San Diego, CA 92101. (619) 233-6655. FAX: (619) 233-5332.
PRESIDENT
Nanci Washburn

ARTIST NETWORK
8438 Melrose Pl., Los Angeles, CA 90039. (323) 651-4244. FAX: (323) 651-4699.
CONTACT
Debra Hope

THE ARTISTS AGENCY
(Literary & talent)
10000 Santa Monica Blvd., Ste. 305, Los Angeles, CA 90067. (310) 277-7779. FAX: (310) 785-9338.

ASSOCIATED BOOKING CORP.
1995 Broadway, New York, NY 10023. (212) 874-2400.

RICHARD ASTOR
250 W. 57th St., New York, NY 10107. (212) 581-1970

ATKINS & ASSOCIATES
303 S. Crescent Heights Blvd., Los Angeles, CA 90048. (323) 658-1025. FAX: (323) 852-4709.

BADGLEY/CONNOR
9229 Sunset Blvd., #311, Los Angeles, CA 90069. (310) 278-9313. FAX: (310) 278-4128.

RICHARD BAUMAN & ASSOC.
5757 Wilshire Blvd., Ste. 473, Los Angeles, CA 90036. (323) 857-6666. FAX: (323) 857-0368.
250 W. 57th St., #2223, New York, NY 10019. 757-0098. (212) 757-0098. FAX: (212) 489-8531.

BENNETT AGENCY
150 S. Barrington Ave., Ste. 1, Los Angeles, CA 90049. (310) 471-2251. FAX: (310) 471-2254.

THE SARA BENNETT AGENCY
6404 Hollywood Blvd. Ste. 316, Hollywood, CA 90028. (323) 965-9666.

BERZON TALENT AGENCY
336 E. 17th St., Costa Mesa, CA 92627. (714) 631-5936. www.berzon.com email: marian@berzon.com

BLOOM AT FORD
8826 Burton Way, Beverly Hills, CA 90211. (310) 859-9300.

J. MICHAEL BLOOM & ASSOC.
9255 Sunset Blvd., Ste. 710, Los Angeles, CA 90069. (310) 275-6800. FAX: (310) 275-6941.

THE BOHRMAN AGENCY
8489 W. 3rd St., Los Angeles, CA 90048. (323) 653-6701. FAX: (323) 653-6702.

BONTALENT, INC.
146 Great Oak Dr., Hapstead, NC 82443. (910) 270-9413. FAX: (910) 270-9490.
PRESIDENT
John Bonitz

BORINSTEIN ORECK BOGART AGENCY
8271 Melrose Ave., Ste. 110, Los Angeles, CA 90046. (323) 658-7500. FAX: (323) 658-8866.

THE BRANDT COMPANY
15250 Ventura Blvd., #720, Sherman Oaks, CA 91403. (818) 783-7747. FAX: (818) 784-6012. email: brandtco@aol.com
CONTACT
Geoffrey Brandt

BRESLER KELLY & ASSOCIATES
11500 W. Olympic Blvd., #510, Los Angeles, CA 90064. (818) 905-1155.

BREVARD TALENT GROUP, INC.
405 Palm Springs Blvd., Indian Harbour Beach, FL 32937. (407) 773-1355. FAX: (407) 773-1842. email: brevtalent@aol.com
PRESIDENT
Traci Danielle

CURTIS BROWN, LTD.
10 Astor Pl., 3rd Flr., New York, NY 10003. (212) 473-5400.

BURKETT TALENT AGENCY
27001 La Paz Rd., #418, Mission Viejo, CA 92691. (949) 830-6300. FAX: (949) 830-6399. email: nancy@burketttalent.com
AGENT
Nancy Burkett
Jackie Ashman

DOTT BURNS TALENT AGENCY
478 Severn, Tampa, FL 33606. (813) 251-5882. FAX: (813) 253-2363

IRIS BURTON AGENCY
P.O. Box 15306, Beverly Hills, CA 90219. (310) 288-0121. FAX: (310) 274-4882.

CAA/CREATIVE ARTISTS AGENCY
9830 Wilshire Blvd., Beverly Hills, CA 90212. (310) 288-4545. FAX: (310) 288-4800.
PRESIDENT
Richard Lovett
CO-CHAIR
Lee Gabler
CO-CHAIR
Rick Nicita
AGENTS
Dan Adler
Jenna Alexander
Steve Alexander
Rowena Arguelles
Dennis Ashley
Ronald Baird
Stan Barnett
Martin Baum
Adam Berkowitz
Jane Berliner
Glenn Bickel
Robert Bookman
Michael Camacho
John Campisi
Joe Cohen
Erin Culley-LaChapelle
Jill Cutler
Christopher Dalston
Jimmy Darmody
Matthew DelPiano
Teri Dickerson
Joshua Donan
Daryl Eaton
Rodney Essig
Tony Etz
Craig Gering
Risa Gertner
Debra Goldfarb
Boz Graham
Brain Greenbaum
Scott Greenberg
Jeff Gregg
Michael Gruber
Alix Hartley
Kimberly Hodgert
Jared Hoffman
Rand Holston
Laurie Horowitz
John Huie
Kevin Huvane
Jeffrey Jacobs
Mara Jacobs
Nancy Jones
Adam Kanter
Carole Kinzel
Courtney Kivowitz
Adam Krentzman
Rich Kurtzman
Scott Landis
James Lefkowitz
John Lesher
Jon Levin
Peter Levine
Josh Lieberman
Rob Light
Brett Loncar
Brain Loucks
Bryan Lourd
Victoria Metzger
Peter Micelli
Ted Miller
Darin Murphy
Tracey Murray
Clay Myers
Andrea Nelson
Michael Nilon
Robert Norman
Emanuel Nunez
David O'Connor
Rob Paris
Brian Pike
Michael Piranian
Jeremy Plager
Gwenn Potiker
John Ptak
Alan Rautbort
Jennifer Rawlings

Michael Rizzo
Mitch Rose
Joe Rosenberg
Michael Rosenfeld
Sonya Rosenfeld
Rick Roskin
Jonathan Ruiz
Carin Sage
Steve Seidel
Larry Shapiro
Brian Siberell
Chris Simonian
Shari Smiley
Steve Smooke
Matthew Snyder
Steve Specktor
Martin Spencer
Tracy Steinsapir
Ken Stovitz
David Styne
Elizabeth Swofford
Steve Tellez
David Tenzer
Jim Toth
Jessica Tuchinsky
Bruce Vinokur
Jamie Waldron
John Ward
Kathy White
Patrick Whitesell
Cynthia Whittington
Sally Willcox
Michael Wimer

THE CAMPBELL AGENCY
3906 Lemmon Ave., Ste. 200, Dallas, TX 75219. (214) 522-8991.

WILLIAM CARROLL AGENCY
139 N. San Fernando Blvd., Ste. A, Burbank, CA 91502. (818) 848-9948. FAX: (818) 845-1769.

CARSON ADLER AGENCY, INC.
250 W. 57th St., Ste. 808, New York, NY 10107. (212) 307-1842. FAX: (212) 541-7008.
PRESIDENT
Nancy Carson
SENIOR AGENTS
Bonnie Deroski, Shirley Faison

CASSELL-LEVY, INC.
843 N. Sycamore Ave., Los Angeles, CA 90038. (323) 461-3971. FAX: (323) 461-1134.

CAVALERI & ASSOCIATES
405 Riverside Dr., Ste. 200, Burbank, CA 91506. (818) 955-9300. FAX: (818) 955-9399.
Ray Cavaleri

CENTURY ARTISTS, LTD.
3511 Sealedge Lane, Santa Barbara, CA 93109. (310) 395-3800. FAX: (310) 393-7988.

THE CHASIN AGENCY
8899 Beverly Blvd., Ste. 716, Los Angeles, CA 90048. (310) 278-7505. FAX: (310) 275-6685.

CINEMA TALENT AGENCY
8033 W. Sunset Blvd., Ste. PMB 808. Los Angeles, CA 90046. (323) 656-1937. FAX: (323) 654-4678.

CIRCLE TALENT AGENCY
433 N. Camden Dr., #400, Beverly Hills, CA 90210. (310) 285-1585.

CIRCUIT RIDER TALENT & MANAGEMENT
123 Walton Ferry Rd., Hendersonville, TN 37075. (615) 824-1947. FAX: (615) 264-0462. email: dotwool@bellsouth.net.com
PRESIDENT
Linda S. Dotson
SENIOR AGENT
Doreen Patten

W. RANDOLPH CLARK COMPANY
13415 Ventura Blvd., Ste. 3, Sherman Oaks, CA 91423. (818) 385-0583. FAX: (818) 385-0599.
PRESIDENT
W. Randolph Clark
V.P., TALENT
Arlene Tsurutani

CLINC TALENT AGENCY
843 N. Sycamore Ave., Los Angeles, CA 90038. (323) 461-3971. FAX: (323) 461-1134.
PRESIDENT
Leanna Levy
SENIOR AGENTS
Richard Ohanesian

COAST TO COAST TALENT GROUP, INC.
4942 Vineland Ave., Ste. 200, North Hollywood, CA 91601. (818) 762-6278. FAX: (818) 762-7049.

COLLEEN CLER AGENCY
178 S. Victory Blvd., #108, Burbank, CA 91502. (818) 841-7943. FAX: (818) 841-4541.
CONTACT
Colleen Cler

COLOURS TALENT AGENCY
8344-1/2 W. 3rd St., Los Angeles, CA 90048. (323) 658-7072.

COMMERCIALS UNLIMITED, INC.
9601 Wilshire Blvd., #620, Los Angeles, CA 90210. (310) 888-8788. FAX: (310) 888-8712.

CONTEMPORARY ARTISTS, LTD. TALENT AGENCY
1317 5th St., #200, Santa Monica, CA 90401. (310) 395-1800. FAX: (310) 394-3308.

COPELAND CREATIVE TALENT
4140 1/2 Grand Ave., Des Moines, IA 50312. (515) 271-5970. FAX: (515) 277-0770.
email: copetalent@aol.com
OWNER
Debra Copeland

CORALIE JR. AGENCY
4789 Vineland Ave., #100, N. Hollywood, CA 91602. (818) 766-9501.
AGENT, ACTORS & ACTRESSES
Stuart Edward
LITERARY AGENT
Gary Dean

THE COSDEN AGENCY
3518 Cahuenga Blvd. W., Ste. 216, Los Angeles, CA 90068. (323) 874-7200.

THE CRAIG AGENCY
8485 Melrose Pl., Ste. E, Los Angeles, CA 90069. (323) 655-0236. FAX: (323) 655-1491.

CUNNINGHAM, ESCOTT, DIPENE & ASSOC.
10635 Santa Monica Blvd., Los Angeles, CA 90025-4900. Commercial: (310) 475-2111; Children's: (310) 475-3336. FAX: (310) 475-1929.
257 Park Ave. S., New York, NY 10010. Commerical: (212) 477-1666; Children's: (212) 477-6622. FAX: (212) 979-2011.
One East Superior St., Ste. 505, Chicago, IL 60611. (312) 944-5600. FAX: (312) 944-5694.

DADE/SCHULTZ ASSOCS.
12302 Sarah St., Studio City, CA 91604. (818) 760-3100. FAX: (818) 760-1395.

D.D.K.
9744 Wilshire Blvd., Ste. 203, Beverly Hills, CA 90212. (310) 274-9356.
16 W. 22nd St., 7th Flr., New York, NY 10010. (212) 727-7820.

DH TALENT AGENCY
1800 N. Highland Ave., Ste. 300, Los Angeles, CA 90028. (323) 962-6643.

DIAMOND ARTISTS AGENCY, LTD.
215 N. Barrington Ave., Los Angeles, CA 90049. (310) 472-7579. FAX: (310) 472-2687.

DOUGLAS, GORMAN, ROTHACKER & WILHELM
1501 Broadway, Ste. 703, New York, NY 10036. (212) 382-2000.

DURKIN ENTERTAINMENT GROUP
(Talent management)
127 Broadway, Ste. 210, Santa Monica, CA 90401. (310) 458-5377. FAX: (310) 458-5337.
email: debbied@castnet.com
CONTACT
Debbie Durkin

DUVA-FLACK ASSOCIATES, INC.
200 W. 57th St., Ste. 1008, New York, NY 10019. (212) 957-9600. FAX: (212) 957-9606.

DYTMAN & ASSOCIATES
9200 Sunset Blvd., Ste. 809, Los Angeles, CA 90069. (310) 274-8844.

ELITE CASTING
2820 Eagle St., New Orleans, LA 70118. (504) 861-0245.

ENDEAVOR TALENT AGENCY, LLC
9701 Wilshire Blvd., 10th Flr., Beverly Hills, CA 90212. (310) 248-2000. FAX: (310) 248-2020.
CFO
Edward McKenna Jr.
BUSINESS AFFAIRS
Rick Olshansky

AGENTS
Marty Adelstein
Sergio Aguero
Adriana Alberghetti
Bonnie Bernstein
Chris Donnelly
Andy Elkin
Ariel Emaniel
Sandy Epstein
Leanne Fader Coronel
Stuart Fry
David Greenblatt
Ari Greenburg
Greg Hodes
Greg Horangic
Rick Lefitz
Brian "Buddy" Lipson
David Lonner
Brad Mendelsohn
Jaime Misher
Bryant Mulligan
Jonathan Perry
Sean E. Perry
Roger Pliakas
Steve Rabineau
Philip Raskind
Stephanie Ritz
Doug Robinson
Lon Rosen
Rich Rosen
Dawn Saltzman
Greg Spiegel
Jason Spitz
Darren Statt
Tom Strickler
Brain Swardstrom
Adam Venit
Kevin Volchok
Will Ward
Richard Weitz
Shelley Zimmerman

ENTERTAINMENT ENTERPRISES
1680 Vine St., Ste. 519, Los Angeles, CA 90028. (323) 462-6001, (323) 462-6002. FAX: (323) 462-6003.

EPSTEIN-WYCKOFF & ASSOCIATES
311 W. 43rd St., Ste. 304, New York, NY 10036. (212) 586-9110. FAX: (212) 586-8019.

CAROL FAITH AGENCY
280 South Beverly Dr., Ste. 411, Beverly Hills, CA 90212. (310) 274-0776. FAX: (310) 274-2670. email: carolatcfa@aol.com
PRESIDENT
Carol Faith

E. FARRELL/C. COULTER TALENT AGENCY
P.O. Box 15189, North Hollywood, CA 91615. (818) 765-0400. FAX: (818) 765-0153.

FAVORED ARTISTS
122 S. Robertson Blvd., #202, Los Angeles, CA 90048. (310) 247-1040. FAX: (310) 247-1048.
AGENTS
Amy Mackie, Peter Albers
230 W. 55th St., Ste. 29-D, New York, NY 10019. (212) 245-6960. FAX: (212) 333-7420.

FERRAR MAZIROFF ASSOCIATES
8430 Santa Monica Blvd., Ste. 220, West Hollywood, CA 90069. (323) 654-2601. FAX: (323) 654-2979.

THE FIELD-COCH AGENCY, INC.
12725 Ventura Blvd., Ste. D, Studio City, CA 91604. (818) 980-2001. FAX: (818) 980-0754.

FILM ARTISTS ASSOCIATES
13563 Ventura Blvd., 2nd Flr., Sherman Oaks, CA 91423. (818) 386-9669. FAX: (818) 386-9363.
CEO
Cris Dennis
PRESIDENT
Penrod Dennis

FILM MUSIC ASSOCIATES
6525 W. Sunset Blvd., 3rd Flr., Hollywood, CA 90028. (323) 463-1070. FAX: (323) 463-1077.
SENIOR AGENTS
John Tempereau, Michael Horner

FLASHCAST COMPANIES, INC.
(Computerized casting service specializing in children and infants)
3575 Cahuenga Blvd. W., Ground Floor, Universal City, Los Angeles, CA 90068. (800) 273-9008, (323) 661-5795, (818) 760-7986. FAX: (818) 760-6792. www.flashcastkids.com
PRESIDENT & CEO
Carl Carranza

FLICK EAST-WEST TALENTS, INC.
9057 Nemo St., Ste. A, W. Hollywood, 90069. (310) 247-1777. FAX: (310) 858-1357.
Carnegie Hall Studio 1110, 881 Seventh Ave., New York, NY 10019. (212) 307-1850.

FOLKLORE PRODUCTIONS, INC.
1671 Appian Way, Santa Monica, CA 90401. (310) 451-0767. FAX: (310) 458-6005. www.rootsworld.com/folklore/
email: 71222.2600@compuserve.com

FRONTIER BOOKING INTERNATIONAL
1560 Broadway, Ste. 1110, New York, NY 10036. (212) 221-0220.

THE GAGE GROUP
9255 Sunset Blvd., Ste. 515, Los Angeles, CA 90069. (310) 859-8777. FAX: (310) 859-8166.
315 W. 57 St., Ste. 4H, New York, NY 10019. 541-5250. FAX: (212) 956-7466.

GARBER TALENT AGENCY
2 Pennsylvania Plaza, Ste. 1910, New York, NY 10121. (212) 292-4910.

DALE GARRICK INTL. AGENCY
8831 Sunset Blvd., #402, Los Angeles, CA 90069. (310) 657-2661.

GEDDES AGENCY
8430 Santa Monica Blvd. #200, W. Hollywood, CA 90069. (323) 848-2700.
PRINCIPAL
Ann Geddes
AGENTS
Anne Margaret Tower
Glenn Hughes III
AGENT, LITERARY
Dana Wright

DON GERLER TALENT AGENCY
3349 Cahuenga Blvd. West, Ste. 1, Los Angeles, CA 90068. (323) 850-7386. FAX: (323) 850-7490.

THE GERSH AGENCY
232 N. Canon Dr., Beverly Hills, CA 90210. (310) 274-6611. FAX: (310) 274-4035.
AGENTS
Phil Gersh, David Gersh, Nancy Nigrosh, Maryann Kellt, Lee Keele, Jim Lefkowitz, Richard Arlook
130 W. 42nd St., #2400, New York, NY 10036. (212) 997-1818. FAX: (212) 391-8459.
AGENTS
David Guc, Scott Yoselow

THE GILCHRIST TALENT GROUP
630 Ninth Ave., Ste. 800, New York, NY 10036. (212) 692-9166.

GILLA ROOS, LTD. (DDK)
3800 Barham Blvd., Sute. 303, CA 90068. (310) 274-9356. FAX: (310) 274-3604.

GOLD/MARSHAK/LIEDKE ASSOCIATES
3500 W. Olive, Ste. 1400, Burbank, CA 91505. (818) 972-4300. FAX: (818) 955-6411.

THE GOLDEY COMPANY
1156 S. Carmelina, Los Angeles, CA 90049. (310) 447-6611. FAX: (310) 447-6616.

GORFAINE/SCHWARTZ AGENCY, INC.
13245 Riverside, Ste. 450, Sherman Oaks, CA 91423. (818) 461-9600. FAX: (818) 461-9622.

GOTHIC ARTIST AGENCY
699 Bay St., Santa Monica, CA 90405. (310) 581-9102. FAX: (310) 581-9383. email: megaent@aol.com
PRESIDENT
Diane Anderson

MARY GRADY AGENCY
4444 Lankershim Blvd., Ste. 207, North Hollywood, CA 91602. (818) 766-4414. FAX: (818) 766-3860.

GREENE & ASSOCIATES
9229 W. Sunset Blvd., Ste. 301, Los Angeles, CA 90069. (310) 288-2100. FAX: (310) 274-3835.

LARRY GROSSMAN & ASSOCIATES
211 S. Beverly Dr., St.e 206, Beverly Hills, CA 90212. (310) 550-8127. FAX: (310) 550-8129.

BUZZ HALLIDAY & ASSOCIATES
8899 Beverly Blvd., Ste. 715, Los Angeles, CA 90048. (310) 275-6028. FAX: (310) 275-8514.

HAMILBURG AGENCY
292 S. La Cienega, Ste. 312, Beverly Hills, CA 90211. (310) 657-1501.

VAUGHN D. HART
8899 Beverly Blvd., Ste. 815, Los Angeles, CA 90048. (310) 273-7887. FAX: (310) 273-7924.

MICHAEL HARTIG
156 Fifth Ave., New York, NY 10010. (212) 929-1772.

BEVERLY HECHT AGENCY
12001 Ventura Pl., Ste. 320, Studio City, CA 91604. (818) 505-1192. FAX: (818) 505-1590.

HENDERSON/HOGAN AGENCY
247 S. Beverly Dr., #102, Beverly Hills, CA 90212. (310) 274-7815. FAX: (310) 274-0751.
850 Seventh Ave., New York, NY 10019. (212) 765-5190. (212) 586-2855.

THE HOUSE OF REPRESENTATIVES
400 S. Beverly Dr., Ste. 101, Beverly Hills, CA 90212. (310) 772-0772. FAX: (310) 772-0998.

HOWARD TALENT WEST
11712 Moorpark St., Ste. 205B, Studio City, CA 91604. (818) 766-5300. FAX: (818) 760-3328. email: me10u90@wavenet.com

H.W.A. TALENT REPRESENTATIVES
1964 Westwood Blvd., Ste. 400, Los Angeles, CA 90025. (310) 446-1313.
36 E. 22nd St., 3rd Flr., New York, NY 10010. (212) 529-4555.

IFA TALENT AGENCY
8730 Sunset Blvd., #490, Los Angeles, CA 90069. (310) 659-5522. FAX: (310) 659-3344.

INNOVATIVE ARTISTS
1999 Ave. of the Stars, Ste. 2850, Los Angeles, CA 90067-6082. (310) 553-5200. FAX: (310) 557-2211.
141 5th Ave., Ste. 3S, New York, NY 10010. (212) 253-6900. FAX: (212) 253-1198.
OWNER
Scott Harris

INTERNATIONAL CREATIVE MANAGEMENT
8942 Wilshire Blvd., Beverly Hills, CA 90211. (310) 550-4000. FAX: (310) 550-4100.
CHAIRMAN & CEO
Jeffrey Berg
CO-PRESIDENT & VICE CHAIRMAN
Ed Limato
CO-PRESIDENT
Nancy Josephson
CFO
Robert Murphy
SENIOR V.P. & GENERAL COUNSEL
Richard Levy, Esq.
EXEC. V.P., MOTION PICTURE TALENT
Jack Gilardi
EXEC. V.P., HEAD WORDLWIDE TV
Bob Sanitsky
SENIOR V.P., INTERNATIONAL OPERATIONS
Ken Kamins
SENIOR V.P., MOTION PICTURE TALENT
Toni Howard
SENIOR V.P., HEAD, MOTION PICTURE LITERARY
Robert Newman
S,V,P., HEAD, MOTION PICTURE TALENT
Eddy Yablans
S,V,P., MOTION PICTURE PRODUCTION
Paul Hook
SENIOR V.P., MOTION PICTURE TALENT
Martha Luttrell
SENIOR V.P., MOTION PICTURE TALENT
Risa Shapiro
SENIOR V.P., TV TALENT
Sylvia Gold
SENIOR V.P., TV TALENT
Leigh Brillstein
SENIOR V.P., FINANCE & ADMINISTRATIONS
Don Cannon
SENIOR V.P., HEAD, MOTION PICTURE BUSINESS AFFAIRS
Pam Brockie
SENIOR V.P., CORPORATE COMMUNICATIONS
Stacy Ivers
V.P. & HEAD, TV TALENT
Ron West
V.P., TV PROGRAMMING
Scott Arnovitz
V.P. & HEAD, TV SYNDICATION
Steve Wohl
V.P. & HEAD COMEDY & WEST COAST CONCERTS
Steve Levine
V.P., MOTION PICTURE TALENT
Joe Funicello
V.P., TV LITERARY
Dianne Fraser
V.P., TV BUSINESS AFFAIRS
Janet Kaye
HEAD, MOTION PICTURES/SUBSIDIARY RIGHTS
Ron Bernstein
HEAD, TV LITERARY
Matt Solo
HEAD, TV, LONG FORM PACKAGING
Carrie Stein
HEAD, NEWS & BROADCASTING
Babette Perry
HEAD, TV BUSINESS AFFAIRS
Michael Tenzer
HEAD, VOICE OVER
Jeff Danis
HEAD, COMMERCIALS/ON CAMERA
Karen Sellars
MOTION PICTURE TALENT
Jason Barrett
Tracy Brennan
Steve Chasman
Steve Dontanville
Richard Konigsberg
MOTION PICTURE BUSINESS AFFAIRS
George Ruiz
MOTION PICTURE PRODUCTION BUSINESS AFFAIRS
Michael Runnels
MOTION PICTURE LITERARY
Patty Detroit
Barbara Dreyfus
Michael Eisner
Todd Feldman
Jeff Gorin
Doug McLaren
Barbara Mandel
Jeff Shumway
Ben Smith
Lars Theriot
David Unger
Jeanne Williams
Tracy Brim
Mark Finkel
Jon Greyson
MOTION PICTURE PRODUCTION
Craig Bernstein
Tom Marquardt
Kerstin Meyer
STORY EDITOR
Emily Greines
TV TALENT
Tom Burke
Brett Carella
Andy Cohen
Lisa Gallant
Brain Mann
Scott Simpson
TV PROGRAMMING
Cal Boyington
Catherine Gottlieb
Matt Minneypenny
TV PACKAGING
Bob Levinson
Tanya Lopez
TV LITERARY
Kevin Crotty
Nancy Etz
Jill Holwager
Scott Seidel
Steve Simons
NEW YORK OFFICE
40 W. 57th St., New York, NY 10019. (212) 556-5600. FAX: (212) 556-5665.
VICE CHAIR, ICM HOLDINGS, INC.
Sam Cohn
CO-HEAD, LITERARY
Esther Newberg
CO-HEAD LITERARY
Amanda Urban
HEAD, COMMERCIALS/VOICE OVERS
Steve Arcieri
HEAD, EAST COAST MUSIC
Terry Rhodes
MOTION PICTURES/LITERARY
Leora Bloch
MOTION PICTURES
Boaty Boatwright
Andrea Eastman
Elaine Goldsmith-Thomas
Paul Martino
Scott Schacter
Bart Walker
Scott Wexler
BUSINESS AFFAIRS
Maarten Kooij
David Scherler
Helen Shabason

JACKMAN & TAUSSIG ENTERTAINMENT
1815 Butler Ave., Ste. 120, Los Angeles, CA 90025. (310) 478-6641. FAX: 9310) 444-8935.

JACKSON ARTISTS CORP.
7251 Lowell Dr., Overland Park, Ste. 200, KS 66204. (913) 384-6688. FAX: (913) 384-5353.
CEO
Dave Jackson
SENIOR AGENTS
Jean Newland
Tom Zang

JAN J. AGENCY
365 W. 34 St., New York, NY 10001. (212) 967-5265.

THE GEORGE JAY AGENCY
6269 Selma Ave., Hollywood, CA 90028. (323) 466-6665. FAX: (323) 462-6197.
AGENTS
George Jay
Anthony Freeman

JORDAN, GILL & DORNBAUM
156 Fifth Ave., #711, New York, NY 10010. (212) 463-8455. FAX: (212) 691-6111.

KAPLAN-STAHLER-GUHMER AGENCY
8383 Wilshire Blvd., #923, Beverly Hills, CA 90211. (323) 653-4483. email: TKSA@aol.com
PARTNERS
Mitchell T. Kaplan
Elliot J. Stahler
Robert Guhmer

KAZARIAN AND SPENCER AND ASSOCIATES, INC.
11365 Ventura Blvd., #100, Studio City, CA 91604. (818) 769-9111. FAX: (818) 769-9840.

KELMAN/ARLETTA AGENCY
7813 Sunset Blvd., Los Angeles, CA 90046. (323) 851-8822. FAX: (323) 851-4923.

TYLER KJAR AGENCY
10643 Riverside Dr., Toluca Lake, CA 91602. (818) 760-0321.
PRESIDENT
Tyler Kjar
SENIOR AGENTS
Brandon Kjar
Candy Potter
Julie Edwards

THE ERIC KLASS AGENCY
144 S. Beverly Dr., Beverly Hills, CA 90212. (310) 274-9169.

PAUL KOHNER AGENCY
9300 Wilshire Blvd., #555, Beverly Hills, CA 90212. (310) 550-1060. FAX: (310) 276-1083.

THE KRAFT-BENJAMIN AGENCY
345 N. Maple Dr., Ste. 385, Beverly Hills, CA 90210. (310) 247-0123. FAX: (310) 247-0066. email: kbagency@aol.com
CONTACTS
Richard Kraft
Lyn Benjamin
Laura Engel

THE KRASNY OFFICE
1501 Broadway, Ste. 1303, New York, Ny 10036. (212) 730-8160. FAX: (212) 768-9379.

L.A. TALENT
8335 Sunset Blvd., 2nd Flr., Los Angeles, CA 90069. (323) 656-3722. FAX: (323) 650-4272.
www.lamodels.com email: general@lamodels.com

CANDACE LAKE AGENCY
9229 Sunset Blvd., Ste. 320, Los Angeles, CA 90069. (310) 247-2115. FAX: (310) 247-2116.

LALLY TALENT AGENCY
630 Ninth Ave., Ste. 800, New York, NY 10036. (212) 974-8718.

STACEY LANE TALENT AGENCY
13455 Ventura Blvd., Ste. 240, Sherman Oaks, CA 91423. (818) 501-2668.

SUSAN LANE MODEL & TALENT AGENCY, INC.
14071 Windsor Pl., Santa Ana, CA 92705. (714) 731-1420. FAX: (714) 731-5223.
PRESIDENT & CEO
Susan Lane
MANAGING DIRECTOR
Grace Berukoff
ASSISTANT DIRECTOR
Sharon Moiseiff

THE LANTZ OFFICE
888 Seventh Ave., #2500, New York, NY 10106. (212) 586-0200. FAX: (212) 262-6659.

LIONEL LARNER, LTD.
119 W. 57th St., Ste. 1412, New York, NY 10019. (212) 246-3105. FAX: (212) 956-2851.

JACK LENNY ASSOCIATES
9454 Wilshire Blvd., Ste. 600, Beverly Hills, CA 90212. (310) 271-2174. FAX: (310) 271-3540.

BUDDY LEE ATTRACTIONS, INC.
38 Music Square E., Nashville, TN 37203. (615) 244-4336. FAX: (615) 726-0429. email: blanash@aol.com
PRESIDENT
Tony Conway
SENIOR V.P.
John Sachel
VICE PRESIDENTS
Paul Lohr
Kevin Neal

THE LEVIN AGENCY
8484 Wilshire Blvd., Ste. 745, Beverly Hills, CA 90211. (323) 653-7073. FAX: (323) 653-0280.

ROBIN LEVY & ASSOCIATES
9220 Sunset Blvd., Ste. 305, Los Angeles, CA 90069. (310) 278-8748. FAX: (310) 278-8767.

TERRY LICHTMAN COMPANY
1246 Moorpark St., Studio City, CA 91604. (818) 655-9898. FAX: (818) 655-9899.

THE ROBERT LIGHT AGENCY
6404 Wilshire Blvd., Ste. 900, Los Angeles, CA 90048. (323) 651-1777. FAX: (323) 651-4933. email: rlatalent@aol.com

KEN LINDNER & ASSOCIATES, INC.
2049 Century Park East., Ste. 2750, Los Angeles, CA 90067. (310) 277-9223. FAX: (310) 277-5806.

LOOK TALENT
166 Geary St., San Francisco, CA 94108. (415) 781-2841. FAX: (415) 781-5722.

LOVELL & ASSOCIATES
7095 Hollywood Blvd., Los Angeles, CA 90028. (323) 462-1672.

JANA LUKER TALENT AGENCY
1923 1/2 Westwood Blvd., Ste. 3, Los Angeles, CA 90025. (310) 441-2822. FAX: (310) 441-2820.
PRESIDENT
Jana Luker
SENIOR AGENT
Kathy Keeley

LYNNE & REILLY AGENCY
10725 Vanowen St., Ste. 113, North Hollywood, CA 91605. (323) 850-1984.

THE LYONS/SHELDON AGENCY
800 S. Robertson Blvd., Los Angeles, CA 90035. (310) 652-8778. FAX: (310) 652-8772.

SANDRA MARSH MANAGEMENT
9150 Wilshire Blvd., #220, Beverly Hills, CA 90210. (310) 285-0303. FAX: (310) 285-0218.

MARTIN & DONALDS TALENT AGENCY, INC.
1915-A Hollywood Blvd., Hollywood, FL 33020. (954) 921-2427. FAX: (954) 921-7635.

JOHNNIE MARTINELLI ATTRACTIONS, INC.
888 Eighth Ave., New York, NY 10019. (212) 586-0963. FAX: (212) 581-9362.
PRESIDENT
John Martinelli
TALENT DEVELOPMENT
Hyun Mi Lee

MARGE McDERMOTT
216 E. 39th St., New York, NY 10016. (212) 889-1583.

MCQUEENEY MANAGEMENT, INC.
10279 Century Woods Dr., Los Angeles, CA 90067. (310) 277-1882. FAX: (310) 788-0985.
OWNER/AGENT
Patricia McQueeney

MEDIA ARTISTS GROUP
8383 Wilshire Blvd., Ste. 954, Beverly Hills, CA 90211-2408. (323) 658-5050. FAX: 9213) 658-7871.

METROPOLITAN TALENT AGENCY
4526 Wilshire Blvd., Los Angeles, CA 90010. (323) 857-4500. FAX: (323) 857-4599. www.mta.com
PRESIDENT
Christopher Barrett

MIRAMAR TALENT AGENCY
7400 Beverly Dr., Ste. 220, Los Angeles, CA 90036. (323) 934-0700.

THE MIRISCH AGENCY
(Specializing in below-the-line talent)
10100 Santa Monica Blvd., #700, Los Angeles, CA 90067. (310) 282-9940. FAX: (310) 282-0702. email: mirischagy@aol.com
PRESIDENT
Lawrence A. Mirisch
SENIOR AGENTS
Penny Key
Robin Schreer
Jamie Allen
Cecilia Bank
Ann Murtha

MITCHELL AGENCY, INC.
323 Geary St., Ste. 302, San Francisco, Ca 94102. (514) 395-9475. FAX: (415) 395-9301.
VICE PRESIDENT
John J. Erlendson

PATTY MITCHELL AGENCY
4605 Lankershim Blvd., Ste. 408, N. Hollywood, CA 91602. (818) 508-6181.

MONTANA ARTISTS
625 Montana Ave., 2nd Flr., Santa Monica, CA 90403. (310) 576-3456. FAX: (310) 576-7840.

H. DAVID MOSS & ASSOCIATES
733 N. Seward St., Penthouse, Hollywood, CA 90038. (323) 465-1234. FAX: (323) 465-1241.

MOTION ARTISTS, INC.
1400 N. Hayworth Ave., Ste. 36, Los Angeles, CA 90046. (323) 851-7737. FAX: (323) 851-7649.
PRESIDENT
Philip Mittell

NATIONWIDE ENTERTAINMENT SERVICES
2756 N. Green Valley Pkwy., #449, Las Vegas, NV 89014. (702) 451-8090. www.EntertainmentServices.com
PRESIDENT
A.J. Sagman
AGENTS
S. Rosenthal
Deb Manning

OMNIPROP, INC. TALENT AGENCY WEST
10700 Ventura Blvd., 2nd Flr., Studio City, 91604 (818) 980-9267. FAX: (818) 980-9371.
55 W. Old Country Rd., Hicksville, NY 11801. (516) 937-6011. FAX: (516) 937-6209.

OPPENHEIM-CHRISTIE ASSOCIATES
13 E. 37 St., New York, NY 10016. (212) 213-4330.

FIFI OSCARD AGENCY
24 W. 40th St., New York, NY 10018. (212) 764-1100.

DOROTHY DAY OTIS & ASSOCIATES
499 N. Canon Dr., Ste. 313, Beverly Hills, CA 902120. (310) 887-7028. FAX: (310) 887-7009.

OTTO MODEL & TALENT AGENCY
1460 N. Sweetzer Ave., West Hollywood, CA 90069. (323) 650-2200. FAX: (323) 650-1134. www.ottomodels.com
OWNER
Sal Reyes

PAKULA/KING & ASSOCIATES
9229 Sunset Blvd., Ste. 315, Los Angeles, CA 90069. (310) 281-4868. FAX: (310) 281-4866.

DOROTHY PALMER TALENT AGENCY, INC.
235 W. 56th St., Ste. 24-K, New York, NY 10019. (212) 765-4280.

PARADIGM A TALENT & LITERARY AGENCY
10100 Santa Monica Blvd., 25th Flr., Los Angeles, CA 90067. (310) 277-4400. FAX: (310) 277-7820.
200 W. 57th St., Ste. 900, New York, NY 10019. (212) 246-1030.
AGENTS
Ken Gross
Bernard Weintraub
Gary Pearl
Stu Robinson
Doug Brodex
Kerry Jones
Lucy Stille

PINE MOUNTAIN TALENT AGENCY
1042 Willow Creek Rd., Ste A-111-125, Prescott, AZ 86301. (520) 771-1380. FAX: (520) 445-4090.

THE PLAYERS TALENT AGENCY
8770 Shoreham Dr., Ste. 2, West Hollywood, CA 90069. (310) 289-8777. FAX: (310) 289-8779.

RICHARD POIRIER MODEL & TALENT AGENCY
3575 Cahuenga Blvd., W., Ste. 254, Los Angeles, CA 90068. (323) 969-9990. FAX: (323) 850-3382.

PREMIER TALENT AGENCY
3 E. 54th St., New York, NY 10022. (212) 758-4900. FAX: (212) 755-3251.

PREMIERE ARTISTS AGENCY
8899 Beverly Blvd., #510, Los Angeles, CA 90048. (310) 271-1414. FAX: (310) 205-3981.

JIM PREMINGER AGENCY
1650 Westwood, Ste. 201, Los Angeles, CA 90024. (310) 475-9491. FAX: (310) 470-2934.
AGENTS
Jim Preminger
Harvey Harrison
Monica Riordan

PROGRESSIVE ARTISTS AGENCY
400 S. Beverly Dr., Ste. 216, Beverly Hills, CA 90212. (310) 553-8561. FAX: (310) 553-4726.

GORDON RAEL COMPANY
9229 Sunset Blvd., Ste. 310, Los Angeles, CA 90069. (310) 285-0572.

RENAISSANCE
(310) 858-5365. FAX: (310) 858-5389.
email: renaissance@earthlink.net
PARTNERS
Alan Nevins
Irv Schwartz
Joel Gotler

THE RICHLAND AGENCY
11777 San Vicente Blvd., Ste. 702, Los Angeles, CA 90049. (310) 571-1833. FAX: (310) 571-1834.

THE ROBERTS COMPANY
10345 W. Olympic Blvd., Penthouse, Los Angeles, CA 90064. (310) 552-7800. FAX: (310) 552-9324.

THE MARION ROSENBERG OFFICE
8428 Melrose Pl., Ste. B, Los Angeles, CA 90069. (323) 653-7383. FAX: (323) 653-9268.
AGENT
Matthew Lesher

THE ROTHMAN AGENCY
9465 Wilshire Blvd., Ste. 840, Beverly Hills, CA 90212. (310) 247-9898. FAX: (310) 247-9888.

THE SANDERS AGENCY, LTD.
8831 Sunset Blvd., Ste. 304, Los Angeles, CA 90069. (310) 652-1119. FAX: (310) 652-7810.
1204 Broadway, Ste. 306, New York, NY 10001. (212) 779-3737. email: snadersla@aol.com
AGENTS
Honey Sander
Gretchen Osmond
Steven Cumins
Tony Petrilli
Ron Digman
Aaron Wiener
TV & MP, EQUITY, NY
Barbara Sanders
Leo Simard

THE SAVAGE AGENCY
6212 Banner Ave., Los Angeles, CA 90038. (323) 461-8316. FAX: (323) 461-2417.

IRV SCHECTER COMPANY
9300 Wilshire Blvd., #400, Beverly Hills, CA 90212. (310) 278-8070. FAX: (310) 278-6058. email: iscagency@aol.com
AGENTS
Irv Schechter
Victorya Michaels
Debbee Klein
Don Klein
Charlotte Savavi
Debra Lieb
Andrea Simon
Michael Magules

SCHULLER TALENT
276 Fifth Ave., New York, NY 10001. (212) 532-6005.

WILLIAM SCHILL AGENCY
250 W. 57th St., Ste. 2402, New York, NY 10107. (212) 315-5919. FAX: 9212) 397-7366.

DON SCHWARTZ & ASSOC.
6922 Hollywood Blvd., #508, Los Angeles, CA 90028. (323) 464-4366. FAX: (323) 464-4661.

SEVEN SUMMITS PICTURES & MANAGEMENT
8447 Wilshire Blvd., Ste. 206, Beverly Hills, CA 90211. (323) 655-0101.

DAVID SHAPIRA ASSOCIATES, INC.
15301 Ventura Blvd., Ste. 345, Sherman Oaks, CA 91403. (818) 906-0322. FAX: (818) 783-2562.
AGENTS
David Shapira
Diane Pinter
Doug Warner
Bobby Litman
Dede Binder

SILVER, MASSETTI & SZATMARY, LTD.
8730 Sunset Blvd., Ste. 480, Los Angeles, CA 90069. (310) 289-0909. FAX: (310) 289-0990.
PARTNERS
Monty Silver
Donna Massetti
Marilyn Szatmary

RICHARD SINDELL & ASSOCIATES
8271 Melrose Ave., Ste. 202, Los Angeles, CA 90046. (323) 653-5051.

MICHAEL SLESSINGER & ASSOCIATES
8730 Sunset Blvd., Ste. 270 W., Los Angeles, CA 90069. (310) 657-7113. FAX: (310) 657-1756.
PRESIDENT/AGENT
Michael Slessinger

SUSAN SMITH & ASSOCIATES
121 N. San Vicente Blvd., Beverly Hills, CA 90211. (310) 852-4777. FAX: (323) 658-7170.
AGENTS
Peter Donaldson
Joanne Roberts
Lisa Helsing.

SCOTT STANDER & ASSOCIATES
13701 Magnolia Blvd., #201, Sherman Oaks, CA 91423. (818) 905-7000. FAX: (818) 990-0582.
AGENTS
Scott Stander
Ruth Webb

SUITE A. MANAGEMENT
1728 S. La Cienega Blvd., Ste. A, Los Angeles, CA 90035. (310) 558-3820. FAX: (310) 558-4440.
OWNER
Lloyd D. Robinson

THE SUN AGENCY
8961 Sunset Blvd., Ste. V, Los Angeles, CA 90069. (310) 888-8737. FAX: (310) 888-7721.

SUTTON, BARTH & VENNARI, INC.
145 S. Fairfax Ave., #310, Los Angeles, CA 90036. (323) 938-6000. FAX: (323) 935-8671.
PARTNERS
Vic Sutton
Rita Vennari

TALENT GROUP, INC.
6300 Wilshire Blvd., Ste. 2110, Los Angeles, CA 90048. (323) 852-9559. FAX: 9213) 852-9579.

TALENT TREK AND NASHVILLE
2021 21st Ave. S., Ste. 102, Nashville, TN 37212.
PARNTERS
Jaunell Walker
Charlotte Dennison
AGENTS
Evelyn Foster
Sharon D. Smith

THE TANTLEFF OFFICE
375 Greenwich St., Ste. 700, New York, NY 10013. (212) 941-3939. FAX: (212) 941-3948.

TISHERMAN AGENCY, INC.
6767 Forest Lawn Dr., Ste. 101, Los Angeles, CA 90068. (323) 850-6767. FAX: (323) 850-7340. www.tishermanagency.com

TURNING POINT MANAGEMENT TALENT AGENCY
6601 Center Dr. W., Ste. 500, Los Angeles, CA 90445.(310) 348-8171. FAX: 9310) 348-0174.
AGENT
Cheryl Downs

TWENTIETH CENTURY ARTISTS
4605 Lankershim Blvd., Ste. 305, North Hollywood, CA 91602. (818) 980-5118.
PRESIDENT
Diane Davis
ADULT THEATRICAL MP, TV, STAGE, CHOREOGRAPHERS, STAGE DIRECTORS
Jae Ross
ADULT THEATRICAL MP, TV LITERARY, TV DIRECTORS
David Ankrum
ADULT THEATRICAL MP, TV CHILDREN (6 AND UP) THEATRICAL MP, TV, VIDEO, INDUSTRIALS
Richard Devin

UNITED TALENT AGENCY
9560 Wilshire Blvd., #500, Beverly Hills, CA 90212. (310) 273-6700. FAX: (310) 247-1111.
PRESIDENT, CHAIRMAN & BOARD MEMBER
James Berkus
PARTNER & AGENT
Dan Aloni
PARTNER, AGENT & BOARD MEMBER
Peter Benedek
PARTNER, AGENT & BOARD MEMBER
Gary Cosay
PARTNER, AGENT & BOARD MEMBER
Nick Stevens
PARTNER, AGENT & BOARD MEMBER
Jeremy Zimmer
PARTNER & AGENT
Chris Harbert
PARTNER & AGENT
J.J. Harris
PARTNER & AGENT
Tracey Jacobs
PARTNER & AGENT
John Lesher
PARTNER & AGENT
Sue Naegle
PARTNER & AGENT
David Schiff
PARTNER & AGENT
Cynthia Shelton-Droke
PARTNER & AGENT
Jay Sures
AGENTS
Allison Band
Elana Barry
Blair Belcher
Marty Bowen
Andrew Cannava
Garret Chau
Chris Coelen
Howard Cohen
Pamela Cole
David DeCamillo
James Degus
Shana Eddy
Donna Fazzari
Charlie Ferraro
Wayne Fitterman
Peter Franciosa
Richard Green
Lisa Hallerman
Al Hassas
Jason Heyman
Adam Isaacs
Lisa Jacobsen
Alex Kerr
Keya Khayatian
Robert Kim
Gleb Klioner
David Kramer
Billy Lazarus
Martin Lesak
Leslie Maskin
Hayden Meyer
Billy Rose
Madeline Ruan
Clar Ryu
Larry Salz
Howard Sanders
Eluse Scherz
Ruthanne Secunda
Sharon Sheinwold
Stephen Small
Kevin Stoper

ANNETTE VAN DUREN AGENCY
(Representing writers and animators)
11684 Ventura Blvd., #235, Los Angeles, CA 91604. (818) 752-6000. FAX: (818) 7523-6985. email: avdagency@aol.com

SHIRLEY WILSON AGENCY
5410 Wilshire Blvd., Ste. 227, Los Angeles, CA 90036. (323) 857-6977. FAX: (323) 857-6980.

WARDLOW & ASSOCIATES
1501 Main St., #204, Venice, CA 90291. (310) 452-1292. FAX: (310) 452-9002.
PRINCIPAL & OWNER
David Wardlow
LITERARY
Jeff Ordway

DONNA WAUHOB AGENCY
(SAG franchised agent, literary agent)
3135 Industrial Rd., Ste. 204, Las Vegas, NV 89109-1122. (702) 733-1017. FAX: (702) 733-1215. email: dwahob@wizard.com

WILLIAM MORRIS AGENCY
151 El Camino Dr., Beverly Hills, CA 90212. (310) 859-4000. FAX: (310) 859-4462.
1325 Ave. of the Americas, New York, NY 10019. (212) 586-5100. FAX: (212) 246-3583.
2100 West End Ave., Ste. 100, Nashville, TN 37203. (615) 963-3000. FAX: (615) 963-3090.
CHAIRMAN
Norman Brokaw
VICE CHAIRMAN
Kerry Katzman
CEO
Walt Zifkin
PRESIDENT & CO-CEO
Jim Wiatt
COO
Steven Kram
CFO
Irv Weintraub
WORLDWIDE HEAD, COMMERICALS
Rick Hersh
WORLDWIDE HEAD, TV
Sam Haskell
WORLDWIDE HEAD, MOTION PICTURES
Bill Douglas
WORLDWIDE CO-HEAD, MOTION PICTURES
John Burnham
WORLDWIDE CO-HEAD, MOTION PICTURES
Dave Wirtschafter
HEAD, WILLIAM MORRIS INDEPENDENT
Cassian Elwes
NORTH AMERICAN HEAD, MOTION PICTURE TALENT
Hylda Queally
WEST COAST HEAD, MOTION PICTURE TALENT
Lee Stollman
HEAD, MOTION PICTURE WRITERS
Alan Gasmer
HEAD, MOTION PICTURE DIRECTORS
Todd Harris
HEAD, TV DIRECTORS
Steven Glick
HEAD, TV. TALENT
John Kimble
HEAD, TV CREATIVE DEVELOPMENT
Greg Lipstone
CO-HEAD, TV LITERARY
Lenny Noveck
CO-HEAD, TV LITERARY
Jeffrey S. Robin
HEAD, BUSINESS AFFAIRS
Mike Simpson
AGENTS, MOTION PICTURE
Nicole David
Leonard Hirshan
Rena Ronson
Fred Westheimer
AGENTS, MOTION PICTURE TALENT
Julie Colbert
Ames Cushing
John Fogelman
George Freeman
Alicia Fordon
Eric Handler
Scott Henderson
Scott Lambert
Joel Lubin
Randi Michel
Gaby Morgerman
Joanne Wiles
Lisa Wong
AGENTS, MOTION PICTURE LITERARY
Sara Bottfeld
Rob Carlson
Chris Fenton
Amy Ferris
Jenny Fritz
Sophie Holodnik
Ramses Ishak
David Lubliner
Gregory McKnight
Michael Sheresky
Robert Stein
Dan Strone
AGENTS, TV
Bill Douglas
John Ferriter
Sol Leon
Paul Nagle
Carey Nelson-Burch
Chris Newman
Richard Rogers
Lee Rosenberg
Adam Sher
Ray Solley
Suzy Unger
Steve Weiss
AGENTS, TV TALENT
Holly Baril
Jennifer Craig
Jenny Delaney
Jonathan Howard
Jeff Kolodny
Lisa Lieberman
Gayle Nachlis
Marc Schwartz
Jeff Witjas
AGENTS, TV LITERARY
Ann Blanchard
Rober Golenberg
Aaron Kaplan
Renee Kurtz
Cori Wellins

WORLD CLASS SPORTS
880 Apollo St., El Segundo, CA 90245. (310) 535-9120. FAX: (310) 535-9128.
SENIOR AGENTS
Andrew Woolf
Don Franken

WRITERS & ARTISTS AGENCY
924 Westwood Blvd., Ste. 900, Los Angeles, CA 90024. (310) 824-6300.
PRESIDENT & FOUNDER
Joan Scott
PARTNER & HEAD OF TALENT
Norman Aladjem
PARTNER
Marti Blumenthal
HEAD, LITERARY
Jim Stein
V.P., BUSINESS AFFAIRS
Dina Appleton
LITERARY AGENTS
Rick Berg
Angela Cheng
Carel Cutler
Richard Freeman
Dave Phillips
TALENT
David Brownstein
Sarah Clossey
Todd Eisner
Jason Gutman
Chris Schmidy
Don Spradlin

NEW YORK OFFICE
19 W. 44 St., #1000, New York, NY 10036. (212) 391-1112. FAX: (212) 398-9877.
PARTNER & HEAD, NY OFFICE
William Craver
AGENTS, LITERARY
Nicole Graham
Tom Heller
AGENTS, TALENT
Jeff Berger
Cris Criswell
Linda Jacobs Kalodner
James Suskin

The Exhibition Industry

Theatre Circuits .771

Circuit Theatres by State 819

Circuit Theatres by Market 831

Independent Theatres 848

Specialty Exhibitors 876

Specialty Exhibitor Equipment 878

Theatre Equipment 879

Concession Suppliers 896

Screening Rooms 900

Preview and Policy Trailers 901

Buying & Booking 902

Distributors in Key Cities 904

Exhibitor Organizations 905

EXHIBITION FACTS

For complete Industry facts including Exhibition, Production, Employment and Ratings, please see the Statistics section of this book beginning on page 9.

BASIC FACTS

Number of U.S. Screens: 37,185
Number of Indoor Screens: 36,448
Number of Drive-In Screens: 737
Percentage of U.S. Screens Owned by Top Ten Circuits: 50.1%
Average Screens Per Theatre, Top Ten Circuits: 9.2
Average Admission Price: $5.08
Age Group with Highest Admission Percentage: 16-20 year olds (20%)
Age Group with Lowest Admission Percentage: 50-59 year olds (7%)

ADMISSIONS

	Gross ($ millions)	Admissions (millions)	Per week (millions)
1999	7,448.0	1,465.2	28.2
1998	6,949.0	1480.7	28.5
1997	6,365.9	1,387.7	26.7
1996	5,911.5	1,338.6	25.7
1995	5,493.5	1,262.6	24.3
1994	5,396.2	1,291.7	24.8
1993	5,154.2	1,244.0	23.9
1992	4,871.0	1,173.2	22.6
1991	4,803.2	1,140.6	21.9
1990	5,021.8	1,188.6	22.9
1985	3,749.4	1,056.1	20.3
1980	2,748.5	1,021.5	19.6
1975	2,114.8	1,032.8	19.9
1970	1,429.2	920.6	17.7
1960	984.4	1,304.5	25.1
1950	1,379.0	3,017.5	58.0

THE TOP 10 U.S. THEATRE CIRCUITS, 1999

Circuit	U.S. Theatres	U.S. Screens	% of All U.S. Screens	% of Top 10
Regal Cinemas	431	4464	12.0	24.0
Carmike	360	2424	6.5	13.0
Loews Cineplex	241	1956	5.3	10.5
United Artists	226	1685	4.5	9.0
AMC	188	2611	7.0	14.0
Cinemark	188	2180	5.9	11.7
National Amusements	109	1121	3.0	6.0
Hoyts	105	889	2.4	4.8
General Cinema	93	784	2.1	4.2
Kerasotes	90	521	1.4	2.8

THEATRE CIRCUITS

ABSHER ENTERPRISES, INC.

4 theatres, 26 screens.
409 North Arnold Ave., Prestonburg, KY 41653. (606) 886-6397. FAX: (606) 886-0848.
OWNER
J. Absher

THEATRES

River Fill 10 Cinemas	94 Pike St.	Pikeville	KY	41501	10	564
Strand Theatre	203 S. Lake Dr.	Prestonsburg	KY	41653	2	564
Showplace Cinema	Somerset Mall	Somerset	KY	42501	9	541
Southside Cinemas	275 Southside Mall Rd.	South Williams	KY	41503	5	564

ALLEN THEATRES, INC.

22 theatres, 79 screens.
P.O. Drawer 1500, 208B West Main St., Farmington, NM 87401. (505) 325-9313. FAX: (505) 326-2647.
PRESIDENT
Larry F. Allen
VICE PRESIDENT
Lane E. Allen
SECRETARY-TREASURER
Boyd F. Scott
FILM BUYER
Larry F. Allen

THEATRES

Fiesta Twin	23 W. Main	Cortez	CO	81321	2	790
Cinema 5	3199 N. White Sands	Alamogordo	NM	88310	5	790
Mall Cinema	2322 W. Pierce	Carlsbad	NM	88220	3	790
Hilltop	Hilltop Shopping Center	Clovis	NM	88101	2	634
North Plains 4	2809 N. Prince	Clovis	NM	88101	4	634
Allen 8	1819 20th St.	Farmington	NM	87401	8	790
Animas	4601 E. Main	Farmington	NM	87402	4	790
Apache Drive-In	1411 W. Apache	Farmington	NM	87401	2	790
Cameo	734 W. Broadway	Farmington	NM	87401	1	790
Centennial	3030 E. Main	Farmington	NM	87402	2	790
Aztec Twin	911 W. Aztec	Gallup	NM	87301	5	790
El Morro	207 W. Coal	Gallup	NM	87301	1	790
Rio West Twin	1300 W. Frontage	Gallup	NM	87301	2	790
Broadmoor	Broadmoor Shopping Center	Hobbs	NM	88240	1	790
Cinema 3	1609 Joe Harvey Blvd.	Hobbs	NM	88240	3	790
Cinema 8	700 Telshor	Las Cruces	NM	88011	8	765
Telshor	2811 N. Telshor	Las Cruces	NM	88011	12	765
Video 4	1005 S. El Paseo	Las Cruces	NM	88011	4	765
Tower Twin	101 N. Ave. A	Portales	NM	88130	2	634
Cinema 4	4501 N. Main	Roswell	NM	88201	4	790
Del Norte Twin	2810 B N. Main	Roswell	NM	88201	2	790
Park Twin	1717 S. Union	Roswell	NM	88203	2	790

AMC ENTERTAINMENT, INC.

188 theatres, 2611 screens in U.S.; 203 theatres, 2911 screens worldwide (Japan: 5 theatres, 79 screens; Hong Kong 1 theatre, 11 screens; Portugal: 1 theatre, 20 screens; Canada 5 theatres, 122 screens; Spain 2 theatre, 48 screens; France: 1 theatre, 20 screens.)
Headquarters: 106 West 14th St., Ste. 2200, Kansas City, MO 64105. (816) 221-4000. FAX: (816) 480-4617.
CHAIRMAN & CEO
Peter C. Brown
PRESIDENT, AMC, INC.
Philip M. Singleton
PRESIDENT, AMC FILM MARKETING
Richard M. Fay

THEATRES

AMC Laguna Village 10	5835 W. Ray Rd.	Chandler	AZ	85226	10	753
AMC Arrowhead 14	7700 W. Arrowhead Dr.	Glendale	AZ	85308	14	753
AMC Three Fountains 4	1350 S. Longmore	Mesa	AZ	85202	4	753
AMC Mesa Grand 24	1645 S. Stapley	Mesa	AZ	85204	24	753
AMC Ahwatukee 24	4915 E. Ray Rd.	Phoenix	AZ	85044	24	753
AMC Arizona Center 24	455 N. 3rd St.	Phoenix	AZ	85004	24	753
AMC Bell Plaza 8	3301 E. Bell Rd.	Phoenix	AZ	85032	8	753
AMC Deer Valley 30	3033 W. Agua Fria Freeway	Phoenix	AZ	85027	30	753
AMC Town & Country 6	2087 E. Camelback Rd.	Phoenix	AZ	85016	6	753
AMC Esplande 14	2515 E. Camelback	Phoenix	AZ	85016	14	753
AMC Burbank 14	140 E. Palm Ave.	Burbank	CA	91502	14	803
AMC Media Center 8	201 E. Magnolia Blvd.	Burbank	CA	91501	8	803
AMC Media Center North 6	770 N. First St.	Burbank	CA	91501	6	803
AMC Chino Town Square 10	5501 Philadelphia St.	Chino	CA	91710	10	803
AMC Covina 30	1414 N. Azusa Ave.	Covina	CA	91722	30	803
AMC Wiegand Plaza 8	220 N. El Camino Real	Encinitas	CA	92024	8	825
AMC Fullerton 20	1001 S. Lemon	Fullerton	CA	92832	20	803
AMC Puente Hills 20	1560 S. Azusa Ave	Industry	CA	91748	20	803
AMC La Jolla Village 12	8657 Villa La Jolla Dr.	La Jolla	CA	92037	12	825
AMC Marina Pacifica 12	6346 E. Pacific Coast Hwy.	Long Beach	CA	90803	12	803
AMC Pine Square 16	245 Pine Ave #100	Long Beach	CA	90802	16	803
AMC Century 14	10250 Santa Monica Blvd.	Los Angeles	CA	90067	14	803
AMC Milpitas 10	577 E. Calaveras Blvd.	Milpitas	CA	95035	10	807
AMC Montebello 10	1475 N. Montebello Blvd.	Montebello	CA	90640	10	803
AMC Norwalk 20	12300 E. Civic Center Dr.	Norwalk	CA	90651	20	803
AMC Ontario Mills 30	4549 Mills Circle	Ontario	CA	91764	30	803
AMC 30 At The Block	20 City Blvd.	Orange	CA	92868	30	803
AMC Old Pasadena 8	42 Miller Alley	Pasadena	CA	91103	8	803

AMC Fashion Valley 18	7037 Friars Rd.	San Diego	CA	92108	18	825
AMC Mission Valley 20	1640 Camino Del Rio	San Diego	CA	92108	20	825
AMC Palm Promenade 24	770 Dennery Rd.	San Diego	CA	92154	24	825
AMC Kabuki 8	1881 Post St.	San Francisco	CA	94115	8	807
AMC Van Ness 14	1000 Van Ness Ave.	San Francisco	CA	94109	14	807
AMC Saratoga 14	700 El Paseo De Saratoga	San Jose	CA	95130	14	807
AMC Main Place 6	2800 N. Main St.	Santa Ana	CA	92701	6	803
AMC Mercado 20	3111 Mission College Blvd.	Santa Clara	CA	95054	20	807
AMC Santa Monica 7	1310 3rd St.	Santa Monica	CA	90401	7	803
AMC Sunnyvale Six Theatres	2604 Town Center Lane	Sunnyvale	CA	94086	6	807
AMC Rolling Hills 20	2591 Airport Dr.	Torrance	CA	90505	20	803
AMC Vallejo Plaza Six	3465 Sonoma Blvd.	Vallejo	CA	94590	6	807
AMC Promenade 16	21801 Oxnard St.	Woodland Hills	CA	91367	16	803
AMC Seven Hills 10	18605 E. Hampden Ave.	Aurora	CO	80013	10	751
AMC Tiffany Square 6	6805 Corporate Dr.	Colorado Springs	CO	80919	6	752
AMC Tiffany Plaza 6	7400 East Hampden Ave.	Denver	CO	80231	6	751
AMC Highlands Ranch 24	103 Centennial Rd.	Highlands Ranch	CO	80126	24	751
AMC Westminster Promenade 24	10655 Westminster Blvd.	Westminster	CO	80030	24	751
AMC Union Station 9	50 Massachusetts Ave.	Washington	DC	20002	9	511
AMC Aventura 24	19501 Biscayne Blvd.	Aventura	FL	33180	24	528
AMC Mizner Park 8	301 Plaza Real	Boca Raton	FL	33432	8	548
AMC Regency - Bdn 20	2496 Brandon Blvd.	Brandon	FL	33511	20	539
AMC Celebration 2	651 Front St.	Celebration	FL	34747	2	534
AMC Clearwater 5	20505 US Highway 19 North	Clearwater	FL	33764	5	539
AMC Countryside 6	2591 State Rd.	Clearwater	FL	33761	6	539
AMC Tri-City 8	5140 East Bay Dr.	Clearwater	FL	33764	8	539
AMC Cocowalk 16	3015 Grand Ave.	Coconut Grove	FL	33133	16	528
AMC Ridge Plaza 8	9200 State Rd. 84	Davie	FL	33324	8	528
AMC Volusia Square 8	2455 Volusia Ave.	Daytona	FL	32114	8	534
AMC Coral Ridge 10	3401 N.E. 26th Ave.	Fort Lauderdale	FL	33306	10	528
AMC Oaks 6	6309 Newberry Rd.	Gainsville	FL	32605	6	592
AMC Sheridan Plaza 12	4999 Sheridan St.	Hollywood	FL	33021	12	528
AMC Regency 24	9451 Regency Square Blvd.	Jacksonville	FL	32225	24	561
AMC Pleasure Island 24	1500 Buena Vista Dr.	Lake Buena Vista	FL	32830	24	534
AMC Merchants Walk 10	3615 S. Florida Ave.	Lakeland	FL	33803	10	539
AMC Lake Square 12	10401-015 US Hwy 441 South	Leesburg	FL	34788	12	534
AMC Merritt 6	163 Merritt Square Mall	Merritt Island	FL	32952	6	534
AMC Merritt Square 7/12	777 E. Merritt Island Causeway	Merritt Island	FL	32952	6	534
AMC Kendall T and C 10	8400 Mills Dr.	Miami	FL	33183	10	528
AMC Mall Of Americas 14	7795 W. Flager	Miami	FL	33144	14	528
AMC South Dade 8	18591 S. Dixie Hwy.	Miami	FL	33157	8	528
AMC Merchants Crossing 16	15201 N. Cleveland Ave.	N. Ft. Myers	FL	33903	16	571
AMC Fashion Island 16	18741 Biscayne Blvd.	N. Miami Beach	FL	33180	16	528
AMC West Oaks 14	9415 W. Colonial Dr.	Ocoee	FL	34761	14	534
AMC Woodlands Square 20	3128 Tampa Rd.	Oldsmar	FL	34677	20	539
AMC Orange Park 24	1910 Wells Rd.	Orange Park	FL	32073	24	561
AMC Fashion Village 8	735 Herndon Ave.	Orlando	FL	32803	8	534
AMC Highland Lakes 12	801 Dorscher Rd.	Orlando	FL	32818	12	534
AMC Sarasota 6	8201 S. Tamiami Trail	Sarasota	FL	34238	6	539
AMC Sarasota East 7/12	8027 Beneva Rd.	Sarasota	FL	34238	6	539
AMC Seminole 8	8100 Seminole Mall	Seminole	FL	33772	8	539
AMC Sunset Place 24	5701 Sunset Dr.	South Miami	FL	33143	24	528
AMC Crossroads Center 8	2190 Tyrone Blvd.	St. Petersburg	FL	33710	8	539
AMC Tyrone Square 6	6901 22nd Ave	St. Petersburg	FL	33710	6	539
AMC Tallahassee Mall 20	2415 N. Monroe St	Tallahassee	FL	32303	20	530
AMC Old Hyde Park 7	1609 Swann Ave.	Tampa	FL	33606	7	539
AMC Veterans Expressway 24	9302 Anderson Rd.	Tampa	FL	33634	24	539
AMC Indian River 24	6200 20th St.	Vero Beach	FL	32966	24	548
AMC Mansell Crossing 14	7730 N. Point Pkwy.	Alpharetta	GA	30202	14	524
AMC Buckhead Backlot 6	3340 Peachtree Rd.	Atlanta	GA	30326	6	524
AMC Galleria 8 Atl	1 Galleria Pkwy.	Atlanta	GA	30339	8	524
AMC Phipps Plaza 14	3500 Peachtree Rd.	Atlanta	GA	30326	14	524
AMC North Dekalb Mall 16	2042 Lawrenceville Hwy.	Decatur	GA	30033	16	524
AMC Barrett Commons 24	2600 Cobb Place Lane	Kennesaw	GA	30144	24	524
AMC Colonial 18	825 Lawrenceville-Suwanee Rd.	Lawrenceville	GA	30245	18	524
AMC Southlake Pavilion	7065 Mount Zion Circle	Morrow	GA	30260	24	524
AMC Northlake 8	4043 La Vista Rd.	Tucker	GA	30084	8	524
AMC South Barrington 30	170 Studio Dr.	South Barrington	IL	60010	30	602
AMC Cantera 30	28250 Deihl Rd.	Warrenville	IL	60555	30	602
AMC Town Center 20	11701 Nall Rd.	Leawood	KS	66211	20	616
AMC Studio 30	12075 S. Stangline Rd.	Olathe	KS	66062	24	616
AMC Oak Park Plaza 6	9747 Quivira	Overland Park	KS	66215	6	616
AMC Galleria 8 - N.O.	One Galleria Blvd.	Metairie	LA	70001	8	622
AMC Mountain Farms 4	Mountain Farms Mall	Hadley	MA	01035	4	543
AMC Academy 6	6228 Greenbelt Rd.	Greenbelt	MD	20770	6	511
AMC Academy 8	6198 Greenbelt Rd.	Greenbelt	MD	20770	8	511
AMC Country Club Mall 6	1280 Volke Rd.	Lavale	MD	21502	6	511
AMC Rivertowne 12	6081 Oxon Hill Rd.	Oxon Hill	MD	20745	12	511
AMC City Place 10	8661 Colesville Rd.	Silver Spring	MD	20901	10	511
AMC Bel-Air Centre 10	10100 E. 8 Mile Rd.	Detroit	MI	48234	10	505
AMC Eastland Mall 5	C300 Eastland Center	Harper Woods	MI	48225	5	505
AMC Elmwood Plaza 8	936 Mall Dr.	Lansing	MI	48917	8	551
AMC Laurel Park 10	17310 Laurel Pk Dr.	Livonia	MI	48152	10	505
AMC Wonderland 6	30009 Plymouth Rd.	Livonia	MI	48150	6	505
AMC Livonia 20	19500 Haggerty Rd.	Livonia	MI	48152	20	505
AMC Abbey 8	32800 Concord Dr.	Madison Heights	MI	48071	8	505
AMC Meridian Mall 6	1999 Central Park Dr.	Okemos	MI	48864	6	551
AMC Southfield City 12	23275 Greenfield Rd.	Southfield	MI	48075	12	505
AMC Sterling Center 10	44625 Schoenherr Rd.	Sterling Heights	MI	48313	10	505
AMC Forum 30	44681 Mound Rd.	Sterling Heights	MI	48314	30	505
AMC Creve Coeur 12	10465 Olive Blvd.	Creve Coeur	MO	63141	12	609
AMC West Olive 16	12657 Olive St.	Creve Coeur	MO	63141	16	609
AMC Village 6	100 Village Square Dr.	Hazelwood	MO	63042	6	609
AMC Independence 20	19200 E. 39th St.	Independence	MO	64057	20	616
AMC Barrywoods 24	8101 Roanridge Rd.	Kansas City	MO	64151	24	616
AMC Crown Center 6	2450 Grand Ave.	Kansas City	MO	64108	6	616
AMC Metro North Plaza 6	220 Metro North Dr.	Kansas City	MO	64155	6	616
AMC Parkway 22	8600 Ward Pkwy.	Kansas City	MO	64114	22	616
AMC Crestwood 10	#0248 Crestwood Plaza	St. Louis	MO	63126	10	609

AMC Esquire 7	6706 Clayton Rd.	St. Louis	MO	63117	7	609
AMC Galleria 6	#30 St. Louis Galleria	St. Louis	MO	63117	6	609
AMC Carolina Pavilions 22	9541 South Blvd.	Charlotte	NC	28273	22	517
AMC Concord Mills 24	8421 Concord Mills Blvd.	Concord	NC	28027	24	517
AMC Oak View 24	3555 S. 140th Plaza	Omaha	NE	68144	24	652
AMC Millside 4	Rt 130 N. & Haines Mill Rd	Delran	NJ	08075	4	504
AMC Deptford 8	1740 Clements Bridge Rd	Deptford	NJ	08096	8	504
AMC Hamilton 24	325 Sloan Ave.	Hamilton	NJ	08619	24	504
AMC Marlton 8	800 N. Route 73	Marlton	NJ	08053	8	504
AMC Rockaway 7/12	Rockaway Conv. Cntr	Rockaway	NJ	07866	6	501
AMC Maple Ridge 8	4276 Maple Rd	Amherst	NY	14226	8	514
AMC Empire 25	234 W. 42nd St.	New York	NY	10036	25	501
AMC Eastland Centre 8	2596 S. Hamilton Rd.	Columbus	OH	43232	8	535
AMC Lennox Town Center 24	777 Kinnear Rd.	Columbus	OH	43212	24	535
AMC Easton 30	275 Easton Towne Center	Columbus	OH	43219	30	535
AMC Dublin Village 18	6700 Village Pkwy.	Dublin	OH	43017	18	535
AMC Westerville 6	100 Westerville Mall	Westerville	OH	43081	6	535
AMC Quail Springs Mall 24	2501 W. Memorial	Oklahoma City	OK	73134	24	650
AMC Southroads 20	4923 E. 41st St.	Tulsa	OK	74135	20	671
AMC Tilghman 8	4608 Broadway	Allentown	PA	18104	8	504
AMC Woodhaven 10	1336 Bristol Pike	Bensalem	PA	19020	10	504
AMC Neshaminy 24	3900 Rockhill Dr.	Bensalem	PA	19020	24	504
AMC Colonial Commons 9	5114 Jonestown Rd.	Harrisburg	PA	17112	9	566
AMC Wonderland 4	2265 Lincoln Hwy.	Lancaster	PA	17605	4	566
AMC Hampden Center 8	4902 Carlisle Pike	Mechanicsburg	PA	17055	8	566
AMC Granite Run 8	1067 W. Baltimore Pike	Media	PA	19063	8	504
AMC Andorra 8	Ridge & Henry Avenues	Philadelphia	PA	19128	8	504
AMC Orleans 8	2274 Bleigh St.	Philadelphia	PA	19152	8	504
AMC 309 Cinema 9	Routes 309 & 63	Spring House	PA	19477	9	504
AMC Marple 10	400 S. State St.	Springfield	PA	19064	10	504
AMC Painters Crossing 9	112 Wilmington Pike	West Chester	PA	19382	9	504
AMC Green Oaks 8	5727 Hwy 20	Arlington	TX	76016	8	623
AMC Grand 24	10110 Technology Blvd.	Dallas	TX	75220	24	623
AMC Glen Lakes 8	9450 N. Central Expy	Dallas	TX	75231	8	623
AMC Palace 9	220 E. 3rd St.	Fort Worth	TX	76102	9	623
AMC Hulen 10	6330 Hulen Bend Blvd.	Fort Worth	TX	76132	10	623
AMC Sundance West 11	304 Huston St.	Fort Worth	TX	76102	11	623
AMC Stonebriar	2601 Preston Rd.	Frisco	TX	74034	24	671
AMC Grapevine Mills 30	3150 Grapevine Mills Pkwy	Grapevine	TX	76051	30	623
AMC Highland Park 4	32 Highland Park Village	Highland Park	TX	75205	4	623
AMC Studio 30	2949 Dunvale	Houston	TX	77063	30	618
AMC Meyer Park 16	4730 W. Belfort	Houston	TX	77035	16	618
AMC Commerce Park 8	15719 N. Freeway	Houston	TX	77090	8	618
AMC Gulf Pointe 30	11801 S. Sam Houston Pkwy.	Houston	TX	77089	30	618
AMC Willowbrook 24	17145 Tomball Pkwy.	Houston	TX	77064	24	618
AMC Deerbrook Mall 24	20131 Highway 59	Humble	TX	77338	24	618
AMC Katy Mills 20	5000 Katy Mills Circle	Katy	TX	77494	20	618
AMC Mesquite 30	19919 I.H. 635	Mesquite	TX	75149	30	623
AMC Rivercenter 9	849 E. Commerce St.	San Antonio	TX	78205	9	641
AMC Huebner Oaks 24	11075 1H 10 West	San Antonio	TX	78230	24	641
AMC First Colony 24	3301 Town Center Blvd	Sugarland	TX	77478	24	618
AMC Courthouse Plaza 8	2150 Clarendon Blvd.	Arlington	VA	22201	8	511
AMC Skyline 12	5141 Leesburg Pike	Falls Church	VA	22041	12	511
AMC Hampton Towne Center 24	60 Towne Center Way	Hampton	VA	23666	24	544
AMC Lynnhaven Mall Upper Level 5	701 Lynnhaven Pkwy.	Virginia Beach	VA	23452	5	544
AMC Lynnhaven 8	2736 N. Mall Dr.	Virginia Beach	VA	23452	8	544
AMC Potomac Mills 15	2700 Potomac Mills Circle	Woodbridge	VA	22192	15	511
AMC SeaTac North	31600 20th Ave.	Federal Way	WA	98003	6	819
AMC Seatac 6 South	2000 S. Seatac Mall	Federal Way	WA	98003	6	819
AMC River Park Square 20	808 W. Main	Spokane	WA	99201	14	881
AMC Narrows Plaza 8	2208 Mildred St.	Tacoma	WA	98466	8	819

B & B THEATRES

27 Theatres, 114 Screens.

Box 171, 114 West 2nd, Salisbury, MO 65281. (660) 388-5219. Kansas Office: Box 388, 210 N. Washington, Iola, KS 66749. (316) 365-5701. FAX: (316) 365-2753.

PRESIDENT & FILM BUYER
Robert Bagby
CO-CHAIRMAN
Elmer Bills
CO-CHAIRMAN
Sterling Bagby

THEATRES

Burford Theatre	118 S. Summit St.	Arkanas City	KS	67005	3	678
Chanute Cinema	309 E. Main	Chanute	KS	66720	2	603
Coffeyville Cinema	210 W. 10th St.	Coffeyville	KS	67337	2	671
Dodge City Village 8	Village Sq. Mall, 2601 Central	Dodge City	KS	67801	8	678
Independence Cinema	121 Laurel St.	Independence	KS	67301	4	671
Iola Cinema	202 S. Washington	Iola	KS	66749	2	603
Iola 54 Drive-In	1300 2200 St.	Gas City	KS	66749	1	603
McPherson Cinema 4	316 N. Main St.	McPherson	KS	67460	4	678
Winfield Cinema	1007 Main St.	Winfield	KS	67156	3	678
Bolivar Cinema 4	800 E. Aldrich Rd.	Boliver	MO	65613	4	619
Brookfield Cedar Cinema	127 E. Brooks St.	Brookfield	MO	64628	1	616
Grand 6	2880 N. Grand Dr.	Chillicothe	MO	64601	6	616
Festus Eight	1522 Pkwy	Festus	MO	63028	8	609
Fulton Cinema	613 Court St.	Fulton	MO	65251	2	604
Hannibal Cinema 5	#7 Northport Shopping Center	Hannibal	MO	63401	5	717
Lake West Cinema 5	1651 Hwy. 0, Bldg. C-1	Gravois Mills	MO	65037	5	604
Harrisonville Cinema 6	2727 Cantrell Rd.	Harrisonville	MO	64701	6	616
Ritz 4 Theatre	925 S. Jefferson	Lebanon	MO	65536	4	619
Liberty Cinema 12	2101 W. Kansas	Liberty	MO	64069	12	616
Marshall Cinema	114-120 E. North St.	Marshall	MO	65340	3	616
Moberly Five & Drive	3000 N. Morley	Moberly	MO	65270	6	604
Monett Plaza Five	507 Plaza Dr.	Monett	MO	65708	5	619
Neosho Six	1601 Malcolm Mosby Dr.	Neosho	MO	64850	6	603
Lyric Theatre	110 W. 2nd St.	Salisbury	MO	65281	1	604
Waynesville Cinema 8	City Rte 66	Waynesville	MO	65583	8	619
Airline Drive-In	1800 W. Highland	Ponca City	OK	74604	1	650
Ponca Plaza Twin	1417 E. Hartford	Ponca City	OK	74604	2	650

CARMIKE CINEMAS

360 theatres, 2,424 screens.

1301 First Ave., P.O. Box 391, Columbus, GA 31902-0391. (706) 576-3400. FAX: (706) 576-3441.

CHAIRMAN
C. L. Patrick
PRESIDENT & CEO
Michael W. Patrick
SENIOR V.P., FINANCE, TREASURER & CFO
Martin Durant
SENIOR V.P., FILM
Anthony J. Rhead
SENIOR V.P., OPERATIONS
Fred Van Noy
SENIOR V.P., REAL ESTATE
P. Lamar Fields
SENIOR V.P., CONCESSIONS & ASSISTANT SECRETARY
H. Madison Shirley
V.P., ADVERTISING
Marilyn Grant
SENIOR V.P., GENERAL COUNSEL & SECRETARY
F. Lee Champion, III
ASSISTANT V.P. & CONTROLLER
Philip Smitley
DIRECTOR, HUMAN RESOURCES
Sadie Marshall

THEATRES

Carmike 6	5804 Weaver Rd.	Anniston	AL	36202	6	646
Carmike Plaza 6	3416 McClellan Blvd.	Anniston	AL	36201	6	646
Carmike Wynnsong 16	2111 E. University Ave	Auburn	AL	36831	16	522
Carmike 10	3443 Loma Ridge Dr.	Birmingham	AL	35216	10	630
Carmike Summit 16	321 Summit Blvd.	Birmingham	AL	35243	16	630
Carmike Wynnsong 12	500 Commons Dr.	Birmingham	AL	35209	12	630
Carmike Town Square 3	Towne Square Shopping Center	Cullman	AL	35055	3	630
Carmike Century Cinema 8	607 14th St.	Decatur	AL	35602	8	691
Carmike Circle West 4	3120 Ross Clark	Dothan	AL	36303	4	606
Carmike Capri 4	Cox Creek Hwy.	Florence	AL	35631	4	691
Carmike Hickory Hills 6	1946 Florence Ave.	Florence	AL	35630	6	691
Carmike 10	1359 Old Monrovia Rd.	Huntsville	AL	35806	10	691
Carmike 14	4900 Government Blvd.	Mobile	AL	36616	14	686
Carmike Springdale	3020 Springdale	Mobile	AL	36606	11	686
Carmike Wynnsong 16	785 Schillinger Rd.	Mobile	AL	36694	16	686
Carmike 8	1755 Eastern Blvd.	Montgomery	AL	36117	8	698
Carmike Wynnsong 10	3975 Eastern Blvd.	Montgomery	AL	36118	10	698
Carmike Eastdale 8	1001 Eastdale Mall	Montgomery	AL	36117	8	698
Carmike Movies 2	708 E. Main St.	Prattville	AL	36067	2	698
Carmike Martin 3	Northgate Shopping Center, Route 1	Talladega	AL	35161	3	630
Carmike Bama 6	2600 McFarland	Tuscaloosa	AL	35405	6	620
Carmike Oaks 7	2250 Harrison	Batesville	AR	72501	7	693
Carmike Sugar Creek 10	#10 Sugar Creek Center	Bell Vista	AR	72714	10	670
Carmike Cinema	3 Faulkner Plaza	Conway	AR	72032	6	693
Carmike 14	5716 Townson Ave.	Fort Smith	AR	72906	14	670
Carmike Harrison 8	617 Hwy 62 & 65	Harrison	AR	72601	8	619
Carmike Central City 10	909 Higdon Ferry Rd.	Hot Springs	AR	71901	10	693
Carmike Wynnsong 10	12200 Westhaven Dr.	Little Rock	AR	72211	10	693
Carmike Village 5	729 East Hwy. 62	Mountain Home	AR	72653	5	619
Carmike 7	4000 McCaine Blvd.	N. Little Rock	AR	72231	7	693
Carmike Pines Mall 8	2901 Pines Mall Dr.	Pine Bluff	AR	71601	8	693
Carmike Stage	625 E. Main St.	Aspen	CO	81612	3	751
Carmike Chapel Hills 10-15	1701 Briargate Blvd.	Colorado Springs	CO	80920	6	752
Carmike 10	1550 Pulsar Dr.	Colorado Springs	CO	80935	10	752
Carmike Chapel Hills 9	1701 Briargate Blvd	Colorado Springs	CO	80920	9	752
Carmike 10	3636 Manhattan	Fort Collins	CO	80526	10	751
Carmike Mall 3	51027 Hwy 6 & 24	Glenwood Springs	CO	81601	3	751
Carmike 7	590 24 1/2 Rd.	Grand Junction	CO	81502	7	773
Carmike 5	2495 W. 28th	Greeley	CO	80631	5	751
Carmike Chief Plaza 4	813 Lincoln	Steamboat Springs	CO	80477	4	751
Carmike Ski Time Square 1	Unit G-105 Ski Time Square	Steamboat Springs	CO	80477	1	751
Carmike 14	US Route 13 Dover Mall	Dover	DE	19901	14	504
Carmike Royal Palm	2507 53rd Ave.	Bradenton	FL	34203	20	539
Carmike Amelia Island 7	1132 14th St.	Fernandina Beach	FL	32035	7	561
Carmike Palm Cinema 3	4226 Old Hwy. 37	Lakeland	FL	33812	3	539
Carmike 10	4049 W. 23rd St	Panama City	FL	32405	10	656
Carmike Mall 4	2218 N. Cove Blvd.	Panama City	FL	32405	4	656
Carmike 10	161 E. Nine Mile Rd.	Penasacola	FL	32534	10	686
Carmike Lake Walden Cinema	220 W. Alexander	Plant City	Fl.	33566	8	539
Carmike Lakeshore 8	901 US Hwy. 27	Sebring	FL	33870	8	539
Carmike Hillsboro West 8	3306 W. Hillsboro Ave.	Tampa	FL	33614	8	539
Carmike Cont'l Mugs & Movies 2	880 Cypress Gardens Blvd.	Winterhaven	FL	33880	2	539
Carmike University 8	4080 Goldenrod Rd.	Winter Park	FL	32792	8	534
Carmike Wynnsong 16	2700 Ledo Rd.	Albany	GA	31707	16	525
Carmike 2	1610-D Vienna Rd.	Americus	GA	31709	2	522
Carmike 12	1575 Lexington Rd.	Athens	GA	30605	12	524
Carmike Martin	222 Wallace C. Bryan Pkwy	Calhoun	GA	30701	3	524
Carmike 16	5 Reinhardt College Pkwy.	Canton	GA	30114	16	524
Carmike Plaza	N. Tennessee St.	Cartersville	GA	30120	8	524
Columbus Square	3100 Macon Rd.	Cloumbus	GA	31907	8	522
Carmike Peachtree 8	3131 Manchester Expy.	Columbus	GA	31909	8	522
Carmike Hollywood Connection	1683 Whittlesey Rd.	Columbus	GA	31904	10	522
Carmike 7	5301 Sidney Simons Blvd.	Columbus	GA	31904	7	522
Carmike Conyers 8	1605 Hwy. 138	Conyers	GA	30208	8	524
Carmike Martin 3	901 E. 16th Ave.	Cordele	GA	31015	3	525
Carmike 9	1250 E. Walnut Ave.	Dalton	GA	30722	9	575
Carmike Martin Twin	Bownes Mill Rd.	Douglas	GA	31534	2	525
Carmike 8	2103 Verterans	Dublin	GA	31040	8	503
Carmike Capri Twin	Village Shopping Center	Fitzgerald	GA	31750	2	525
Carmike Wynnsong 10	7290 Ingersol St.	Fort Benning	GA	31905	10	522

Carmike Southgate 5	532 Battlefield Pkwy.	Fort Oglethorpe	GA	30742	5	575
Carmike 4	1671 N. Expressway	Griffin	GA	30223	4	524
Carmike LaGrange 6 Theatre	1510 Lafayette Park	LaGrange	GA	30241	6	524
Carmike 6	2400 N. Columbia St.	Milledgeville	GA	31061	6	503
Carmike 10	87 Newnan Station	Newnan	GA	30236	10	524
Carmike Wynnsong 11	1150 Shawnee St.	Savannah	GA	31419	11	507
Carmike 10	511 Stephenson	Savannah	GA	31416	10	507
Carmike 12	1905 Scenic Hwy.	Snellville	GA	30278	12	524
Carmike 9	610 Brannen St.	Statesboro	GA	30459	9	507
Carmike 6	216 Virginia Ave	Tifton	GA	31794	6	525
Carmike Wynnsong 12	2416 Jomar Court	Cedar Rapids	IA	52404	12	637
Carmike 7	5245 Northland Cedar Rapids	Cedar Rapids	IA	52410	7	637
Carmike Collins Rd.	1462 Twixtown	Cedar Rapids	IA	52410	5	637
Carmike Lindale Mall	255 Collins Rd.	Cedar Rapids	IA	52410	6	637
Carmike Mall Bluffs	1751 Madison	Council Bluffs	IA	51502	5	652
Carmike Southridge	6720 S.E. 14th Ave.	Des Moines	IA	50320	12	679
Carmike Cobblestone 9	8501 Hickman Rd.	Des Moines	IA	50322	9	679
Carmike Kennedy Mall 6	555 J.F.Kennedy Rd.	Dubuque	IA	52002	6	637
Carmike Cinema Center 8	75 J.F. Kennedy Rd.	Dubuque	IA	52002	8	637
Carmike Wynnsong 16	5233 N.W. 84th St.	Johnston	IA	50131	16	679
Carmike Southern Hills 12	4400 Sergeant Rd.	Sioux City	IA	51106	12	624
Carmike Plaza 2	2939 B Hamilton Blvd.	Sioux City	IA	51104	2	624
Carmike Starlite	4031 Poleline	Chubbuck	ID	83202	7	758
Carmike Rio 1	271 Broadway	Idaho Falls	ID	83405	1	758
Carmike University 4	120 N. Farm Rd.	Moscow	ID	83843	4	881
Carmike Alameda Plaza 3	1010 Yellowstone	Pocatello	ID	83201	3	758
Carmike Holiday 3	26 S. Center	Rexburg	ID	83440	3	758
Carmike Westwood Theatre	2 E. Main	Rexburg	ID	83440	1	758
Carmike Twin	306 University	Macomb	IL	61455	2	717
Carmike 20	103410 Dibold Rd.	Fort Wayne	IN	46825	20	509
Carmike Seth Childs 12	2610 Farm Bureau	Manhattan	KS	66502	12	605
Carmike Plaza	600 US 31 W. Bypass	Bowling Green	KY	42101	6	736
Carmike Greenwood	2625 Scotsville Rd.	Bowling Green	KY	42101	6	736
Carmike Cinema	1000 E. Cumberland Gap Pkwy.	Corbin	KY	40701	4	557
Carmike Cinema 4	1594 Houstonville Rd.	Danville	KY	40422	4	541
Cinema 4	N.E. Side of Hwy. Across from Village Cntr.	Grays Knob	KY	40829	4	557
Carmike Martin 5	4000 Fort Campbell Blvd.	Hopkinsville	KY	42241	5	659
Carmike 10	3151 Mapleleaf	Lexington	KY	40509	10	541
Carmike Martin 4	25 Madison Square Dr.	Madisonville	KY	42431	4	649
Carmike Cinema 4	1579 US Hwy. 68	Marysville	KY	41056	4	515
Carmike Cinema 4	900 US Hwy. 25	Middlesboro	KY	40965	4	557
Carmike Alexandria	3820 Alexandria Mall Dr.	Alexandria	LA	71301	6	644
Carmike 10	501 Acadiana Mall Circle	Lafayette	LA	70503	10	642
Carmike North Shores 6	160 Airport Dr.	Slidell	LA	70460	6	622
Carmike Sun & Surf 8	14301 Coastal Hwy.	Ocean City	MD	21842	8	576
Carmike Copper 5	1703 West Memorial Dr.	Houghton	MI	49931	5	553
Carmike Wynnsong 15	15630 Cedar Ave.	Apple Valley	MN	55124	15	613
Carmike Sterling	1403 First Ave.	Austin	MN	55912	3	611
Carmike State 3	35 Washington Ave.	Hutchinson	MN	55350	3	613
Carmike Cinema 4	220 Stadium Rd.	Mankato	MN	56002	4	737
Carmike Mall 4	11640 Mankato Mall	Mankato	MN	56002	4	737
Carmike Wynnsong 16	2430 Hwy. 10	Moundsview	MN	55112	16	613
Carmike Cinema 3	1 N. German St.	New Ulm	MN	56073	3	737
Carmike Oakdale	1188 Helmo Ave.	Oakdale	MN	55128	20	613
Carmike Apache Theatre	801 Apache Mall	Rochester	MN	55903	4	611
Carmike Barclay Square	1300 Salem Rd.	Rochester	MN	55903	6	611
Carmike Kandi 6	1605 S. 1st St.	Wilmar	MN	56201	6	613
Carmike University 8	727 N. Charles	Warrensburg	MO	64093	8	616
Carmike 7	2255 Overland Ave.	Billings	MT	59102	7	756
Carmike Wynnsong 10	2456 Central Ave	Billings	MT	59102	10	756
Carmike Ellen 1	1611 S. 11th Ave.	Bozeman	MT	59715	1	754
Carmike Rialto 1	1611 S. 11th Ave.	Bozeman	MT	59715	1	754
Carmike Campus	1611 S. 11th Ave.	Bozeman	MT	59715	8	754
Carmike Plaza 6	3100 Harrison Ave.	Butte	MT	59701	6	754
Carmike 10	1601 Marketplace Dr.	Great Falls	MT	59404	10	755
Carmike Cine 4	1108 9th St.	Great Falls	MT	59405	4	755
Carmike Village 2	900 13th Ave.	Great Falls	MT	59403	2	755
Carmike Circus Twin	3010 N. Montana	Helena	MT	59601	2	766
Carmike Gaslight 3	5 W. Broadway	Helena	MT	59601	3	766
Carmike 10	3640 Mullan Rd.	Missoula	MT	59802	10	762
Carmike Cine 3	3601 Brooks	Missoula	MT	59601	3	766
Carmike Village 6	3804 S. Reserve	Missoula	MT	59801	6	762
Carmike 10	299-1 Swannonoa River Rd.	Asheville	NC	28805	10	567
Carmike Chalet	290 Boone Heights Dr.	Boone	NC	28607	3	517
Carmike Appalachian	559 W. King St.	Boone	NC	28607	2	517
Carmike Cinema	P.O. Box 2047	Carolina Beach	NC	28428	4	550
Carmike Ram	136 E. Rosemary	Chapel Hill	NC	27514	3	560
Carmike Plaza Twin	Dunn Plaza Shopping Center	Dunn	NC	28334	2	560
Carmike 7	2000 Avondale Dr.	Durham	NC	27704	7	560
Carmike Willowdale 8	3823 Guess Rd.	Durham	NC	27705	8	560
Carmike Wynnsong 15	1807 Martin Luther King Blvd.	Durham	NC	27707	15	560
Carmike Kingsway 4	258 L. W. Kings	Eden	NC	27288	4	518
Carmike Wynnsong 7	3039 Boone Trail	Fayetteville	NC	28304	7	560
Carmike 12	Freeway @ Morgaton Rd.	Fayetteville	NC	28309	12	560
Carmike Marketfair	1916 Skibo Rd.	Fayetteville	NC	28314	15	560
Carmike Cinema 4	Tri City Mall	Forest City	NC	28043	4	567
Carmike Berkeley 4	3101 Cashwell	Goldsboro	NC	27530	4	560
Carmike 12	1685 E. Fire Tower Rd.	Greenville	NC	27858	12	545
Carmike Carolina 4	Carolina E. Convenience Center	Greenville	NC	27834	4	545
Carmike 18	4822 Koger Blvd.	Greensboro	NC	27407	18	518
Carmike Cinema 6	Hwy. 70, McCotter Blvd.	Havelock	NC	28532	6	545
Carmike 12	2000 S.E. Catawba Valley Blvd.	Hickory	NC	28603	12	517
Carmike 8	2705 N. Main St.	High Point	NC	27262	8	518
Carmike 6	Western Blvd.	Jacksonville	NC	28541	6	545
Carmike Brynn Marr 3	Brynn Marr Shopping Center	Jacksonville	NC	28541	3	545
Carmike 7	1038 Henderson	Jacksonville	NC	28541	7	545

Carmike Plaza Twin	Plaza Shopping Center	Kinston	NC	28501	2	545
Carmike Westgate Twin	Westgate Shopping Center	Lenoir	NC	28645	2	517
Carmike Cinema 8	234 Talbert Blvd	Lexington	NC	27292	8	518
Carmike Cinema 8	1700 N. Aspen St.	Lincolnton	NC	28092	8	517
Carmike Cinema 3	1311 Arendell St.	Morehead City	NC	28557	3	545
Carmike Morehead Twin	1311 Arendell St	Morehead City	NC	28557	2	545
Carmike Park Place 16	9525 Chapel Hill Rd.	Morrisville	NC	27560	16	560
Carmike Cinema Triple	2500 Neuse Blvd.	New Bern	NC	28561	3	545
Carmike Blueridge 14	600 Blueridge Rd.	Raleigh	NC	27606	14	560
Carmike 15	5501 Atlantic Springs Rd.	Raleigh	NC	27658	15	560
Carmike Golden East 4	100 N. Wesleyan Blvd.	Rocky Mount	NC	27804	4	560
Carmike Kendale Cinema 2	2738 Industrial Dr.	Sanford	NC	27331	2	560
Carmike Cinema 4	414 S. Lafayette St.	Shelby	NC	28150	4	517
Carmike Mall 4	2201 - 4 E. Dixson Blvd.	Shelby	NC	28150	4	517
Carmike Cinema 4	215 Turner St.	Southern Pines	NC	28387	4	560
Carmike Town & Country 2	Town & Country Shopping Center	Southern Pines	NC	28387	2	560
Carmike Gateway 4	1203 Free Nancy Rd.	Statesville	NC	28677	4	517
Carmike Cinema 7	Washington Square Mall	Washington	NC	27889	7	545
Carmike 16	111 Cinema Dr.	Wilmington	NC	28403	16	550
Carmike 6	5335 Oleander Dr.	Wilmington	NC	28406	6	550
Carmike Parkwood 3	Parkwood Shopping Center	Wilson	NC	27893	3	560
Carmike Wynnsong 16	1501 Hanes Mall Blvd	Winston-Salem	NC	27103	16	518
Carmike 10	3640 Renolda Rd.	Winston-Salem	NC	27106	10	518
Carmike Plaza	639 Kirkwood Plaza	Bismarck	ND	58502	3	687
Carmike Midco	2700 State St.	Bismarck	ND	58502	8	687
Carmike Lake 3 Theatre	25 Fourth St.	Devils Lake	ND	58301	3	724
Carmike 3	Hwy 22 & I-94	Dickinson	ND	58601	3	687
Carmike Midco 10	2306 32nd Ave.	Grand Forks	ND	58208	10	724
Carmike Columbia 4	3100 32nd Ave.	Grand Forks	ND	58208	4	724
Carmike South 8-12	2400 10th St.	Minot	ND	58701	5	687
Carmike North 1-7	2400 10th St.	Minot	ND	59701	7	754
Carmike Conestoga 4	3404 W. 13th St.	Grand Island	NE	68802	4	722
Carmike Island Twin	2228 N. Webb Rd.	Grand Island	NE	68802	2	722
Carmike Imperial 3	3207 W. 12th St.	Hastings	NE	68902	3	722
Carmike Hilltop Theatre	5307 2nd Ave.	Kearney	NE	68848	4	722
Carmike Mall 3	1100 S. Dewey	North Platte	NE	69101	3	740
Carmike Monument Mall 6	2302 Frontage Rd.	Scottsbluff	NE	69361	6	759
Carmike Village 2	1402 E. 20th St.	Scottsbluff	NE	69361	2	759
Carmike 2	418 W. Main	Artesia	NM	88210	2	790
Carmike 8	1875 Cinema Dr	Olean	NY	14706	8	514
Carmike Cinema	3315 N. Ridge	Ashtabula	OH	44004	6	510
Carmike Findlay 6	1800 Tiffin Ave.	Findlay	OH	45840	6	547
Carmike Kingsgate 4	1300 Park Ave.	Mansfield	OH	44906	4	510
Carmike Plaza 8	2314 Milan Rd.	Sandusky	OH	44871	8	510
Carmike Ohio Valley Mall 9	700 Banfield Ave.	St. Clairsville	OH	43950	9	554
Carmike Cinema 6	100 Mall Dr.	Steubenville	OH	43952	6	554
Carmike 5	2600 W. Broadway	Ardmore	OK	73402	5	657
Carmike Eastland	Eastland Center	Bartlesville	OK	74003	4	671
Carmike Dunkin Theatre	207 E. Broadway	Cushing	OK	74023	1	650
Carmike 6	1501 Plato Rd.	Duncan	OK	73533	6	627
Carmike Video Twin	3517 Lahoma Rd.	Enid	OK	73702	2	650
Carmike 8	7102 N. W. Cache Rd.	Lawton	OK	73507	8	627
Carmike 6	2812 W. Shawnee Bypass	Muskogee	OK	74401	6	671
Carmike North Park 4	800 E. Prospect	Ponca City	OK	74601	4	650
Carmike Cinema Center 8	3031 N. Harrison	Shawnee	OK	74802	8	650
Carmike Hornbeck	125 N. Bell	Shawnee	OK	74802	2	650
Carmike 10	1909 N. Perkins Rd.	Stillwater	OK	74076	10	650
Carmike 16	1700 Catasouque	Allentown	PA	18103	16	504
Carmike 8	600 Logan Valley Mall	Altoona	PA	16602	8	574
Carmike Park Hills Plaza	West Plank Rd.	Altoona	PA	16602	7	574
Carmike Plaza 6	6800 Big Beaver Blvd.	Beaver Falls	PA	15010	6	508
Carmike Cinema	900 Chambersburg Mall	Chambersburg	PA	17201	4	511
Carmike Laurel Mall 4	University Dr.	Connellsville	PA	15425	4	508
Carmike Cranberry Mall 5	Route 257 & 332	Cranberry	PA	16319	5	508
Carmike Cranberry 8	Route 19 & Freedom Rd.	Cranberry Township	PA	16066	8	508
Carmike 12	401 Vine St.	Delmont	PA	15626	12	508
Carmike 5	Dubois Mall	Dubois	PA	15801	5	574
Carmike 15	Westmoreland Mall, Route 30	Greensburg	PA	15601	15	508
Carmike Fox 6 Theatre	Carlisle St., N. Hanover Plaza	Hanover	PA	17331	6	566
Carmike Hermitage Plaza 8	2461 E. State St	Hermitage	PA	16148	8	536
Carmike Sunbury 4	Route 11 & 15	Hummels Wharf	PA	17831	4	577
Carmike Cinema 4	Indiana Mall	Indiana	PA	15701	4	508
Carmike Cinema 4	Franklin Village Mall	Kittanning	PA	16201	4	508
Carmike M. v. Monaca 7 Theatre	Route 18 Wal-Mart Plaza	Monaca	PA	15061	7	508
Carmike Galleria 6	1500 Washington Rd.	Mt. Lebanon	PA	15228	6	508
Carmike 10	700 Ft. Couch Rd., S. Hills Village	Pittsburgh	PA	15241	10	508
Carmike Southland 9	629 Clairton Blvd.	Pleasant Hills	PA	15236	9	508
Carmike Coventry 8	650 W. Schuylkill Rd.	Pottstown	PA	19464	8	504
Carmike Fox 2 Theatre	Route 61 North, Fairlane Village	Pottsville	PA	17901	2	577
Carmike Wyomissing 8	800 Berkshire Blvd.	Reading	PA	19610	8	504
Carmike Fairgrounds 5	3050-88 N. 5th St. Hwy.	Reading	PA	19605	5	504
Carmike State Twin	128 1/2 W. College	State College	PA	16801	2	574
Carmike 5	116 Heister Rd.	State College	PA	16801	5	574
Carmike Cinema 6	501 Benner Pike	State College	PA	16801	6	574
Carmike Movies 1	407 E. Beaver Ave.	State College	PA	16801	1	574
Carmike 6	1372 W. Main St.	Uniontown	PA	15401	6	508
Carmike Cinema 3 Theatre	500 Hyde Park Rd.	Vandergrift	PA	15656	3	508
Carmike Washington 8	342 Oak Spring Rd.	Washington	PA	15301	8	508
Carmike Maxi-Saver 12	2001 Mountain View Dr.	West Mifflin	PA	15122	12	508
Carmike 3	130 Laurens St.	Aiken	SC	29802	3	520
Carmike James Island 8	1743 Central Park Rd.	Charleston	SC	29412	8	519
Carmike Astro	403 College Ave.	Clemson	SC	29631	3	567
Carmike Wynnsong	5320 Forest Dr.	Columbia	SC	29206	10	546
Carmike 14	122 Afton Court	Columbia	SC	29212	14	546
Carmike Magnolia 3	Magnolia Mall I-20	Florence	SC	29501	3	570
Carmike 7	50 Antrim Dr.	Greenville	SC	29606	7	567
Carmike Crosscreek Mall 3	420-40 72 Bypass	Greenwood	SC	29646	3	567

Carmike Twin	118 West Carolina	Hartsville	SC	29550	2	570
Carmike Broadway 16	1175 Celebrity Circle	Myrtle Beach	SC	29578	16	570
Carmike Dunes Cinema 8	4501 N. Kings Hwy	Myrtle Beach	SC	29577	8	570
Carmike Briarcliffe Cinema 6	Hwy 17 N. #10177	N. Myrtle Beach	SC	29582	10	570
Carmike Camelot 4	2016 Columbia Rd., K Mart Shopping Center	Orangeburg	SC	29116	4	546
Carmike Cinema 7	2150 Cherry Rd.	Rock Hill	SC	29731	7	517
Carmike 7	1985 Eastmain St.	Spartanburg	SC	29307	7	567
Carmike Wynnsong 7	1640 Reidville Rd.	Spartanburg	SC	29306	7	567
Carmike Movies 3	1016 Broad St	Sumter	SC	29151	3	546
Carmike Palmetto 2	Palmetto Plaza	Sumter	SC	29150	2	546
Carmike Midco	3315 6th Ave.	Aberdeen	SD	57401	9	725
Carmike Rushmore 7	350 E. Disk	Rapid City	SD	57709	7	764
Carmike 7	230 Knollwood Dr.	Rapid City	SD	57709	7	764
Carmike Empire 6	3800 S. Louise	Sioux Falls	SD	57105	6	725
Carmike West Mall 7	2101 W. 41st St.	Sioux Falls	SD	57105	7	725
Carmike 7	3404 Gateway	Sioux Falls	SD	57186	7	725
Carmike Yankton Mall 5	2101 Broadway Ave.	Yankton	SD	57078	5	725
Carmike Bell Forge 10	5400 Bell Forge Lane	Antioch	TN	37013	10	659
Carmike Hickory 8	901 Bell Rd.	Antioch	TN	37011	8	659
Carmike Plaza	146 Decatur Pike	Athens	TN	37303	2	575
Carmike Wynnsong 10	2210 Gunbarrel Rd.	Chattanooga	TN	37421	10	575
Carmike Bijou 7	215 Broad St.	Chattanooga	TN	37402	7	575
Carmike 8	1955 Madison St.	Clarksville	TN	37040	8	659
Carmike 5	2801 Guthrie Hwy.	Clarksville	TN	37040	5	659
Carmike Village 2	Village Shopping Center	Cleveland	TN	37320	2	575
Carmike Highland	1181 S. Jefferson	Cookeville	TN	38503	10	659
Carmike Varsity	705 N. Dixie Ave	Cookeville	TN	38501	2	659
Carmike Capri Twin	Woodmere Mall, Hwy. 127	Crossville	TN	38557	2	557
Carmike 9	528 Green Village Shopping Center	Dyersburg	TN	38024	9	640
Carmike Eastridge 6	5086 S. Terrace	Eastridge	TN	37412	6	575
Carmike Galleria 10	1730 Galleria Rd.	Franklin	TN	37064	10	659
Carmike Thoroughbred 20	633 Frazier Dr.	Franklin	TN	37064	20	659
Carmike Rivergate 8	800 Two Mile Pkwy.	Goodlettsville	TN	37070	8	659
Carmike Capri Twin	11 Bypass	Greenville	TN	37744	2	531
Carmike Hermitage	4426 Lebanon Rd.	Hermitage	TN	37076	8	659
Carmike Northgate 8	622 Northgate Mall	Hixson	TN	37343	8	575
Carmike Johnson City 14	1805 N. Roan St.	Johnson City	TN	37601	14	531
Carmike Fort Henry 5	2101 Fort Henry Dr.	Kingsport	TN	37664	5	531
Carmike Commons 6	227 N. Peters Blvd.	Knoxville	TN	37923	6	557
Carmike Movies 7	175 N. Seven Oaks	Knoxville	TN	37922	7	557
Carmike 10	5020 Millertown Pike	Knoxville	TN	37917	10	557
Carmike Wynnsong 16	200 N. Peters Rd.	Knoxville	TN	37923	16	557
Carmike Movies 2	2108 Jacksboro Hwy.	Lafollette	TN	37766	2	557
Carmike Martin 3	1447 S.W. Main	Lebanon	TN	37087	3	659
Carmike Foothills	507 Foothills Plaza	Maryville	TN	37801	12	557
Carmike College Square 6	2250 E. Morris	Morristown	TN	37816	6	557
Carmike Wynnsong	2626 Cason Square Blvd.	Murfreesboro	TN	37133	16	659
Carmike Bellevue 8	120 Bell Forest Circle	Nashville	TN	37221	8	659
Carmike Wynnsong 10	721 Myatt Dr.	Nashville	TN	37115	10	659
Carmike Cinema 3 Theatre	Hwy. 27 North	Oneida	TN	37841	3	557
Carmike Cinema 1	718 S. Main St.	Springfield	TN	37172	1	659
Carmike Park Central	3234 S. Clack St.	Abilene	TX	79606	6	662
Carmike Cinema 5	916 W. University Dr.	Denton	TX	76201	5	623
Carmike 20	3003 S. Expressway	Edinburg	TX	78539	20	636
Carmike 16	9480 Gateway Blvd.	El Paso	TX	79924	16	765
Carmike Rolling Hills 4	6219 Wesley St.	Greenville	TX	75401	4	623
Carmike Cinema 3	1708 S. Jackson	Jacksonville	TX	75766	3	709
Carmike Cinema 4	1500 Brazos Mall	Lake Jackson	TX	77566	4	618
Carmike 10	201 Tall Pines Rd.	Longview	TX	75605	10	709
Carmike Northloop 6	2531 Judson Rd.	Longview	TX	75606	6	709
Carmike Cinema 4	Lufkin Mall	Lufkin	TX	75902	4	709
Carmike Towne Square 4	460 N. Timberland Dr.	Lufkin	TX	75902	4	709
Carmike Angelina Twin	3051 John Reddit	Lufkin	TX	75901	2	709
Carmike 7 & 8	Northview Plaza Shopping Center	Nacogdoches	TX	75961	2	709
Carmike 6	Northview Plaza Shopping Center	Nacogdoches	TX	75961	6	709
Carmike Pines Theatre	340 N. 14th St.	Silsbee	TX	77656	1	692
Carmike Sikes 10	238 Sikes Center	Wichita Falls	TX	76308	10	627
Carmike Century City 6	4105 Maplewood	Wichita Falls	TX	76308	6	627
Carmike Cache Valley 3	1221 N. 200	Logan	UT	84323	3	770
Carmike Wynnsong 12	4925 N. Edgewood Dr.	Provo	UT	84604	12	770
Carmike Cottonwood Mall 4	4890 Highland Dr.	Salt Lake City	UT	84117	4	770
Carmike Villa Theatre	3092 S. Highland Dr.	Salt Lake City	UT	84106	1	770
Carmike 12	1600 W. Fox Park Dr.	West Jordan	UT	84088	12	770
Carmike Hollywood Conn. 16	3217 S. Decker Lake Dr.	West Valley City	UT	84119	15	770
Carmike 6	1803 Seminole Trail	Charlottesville	VA	22901	6	584
Carmike Riverside Twin	3250 Riverside Center	Danville	VA	24541	2	573
Carmike Plaza Twin	2905 Riverside Dr.	Danville	VA	24543	2	573
Carmike 8	801 Lakeside Dr.	Lynchburg	VA	24501	4	573
Carmike River Ridge 4	3405 Candlers Mt. Rd.	Lynchburg	VA	24502	4	573
Carmike 10	1100 Alverser Dr.	Midlothian	VA	23113	10	556
Carmike 10	4494 Electric Rd.	Roanoke	VA	24014	10	573
Carmike Valley 8	1700 Apperson Dr.	Salem	VA	24153	8	573
Carmike 4	222 Monticello	Williamsburg	VA	23185	4	544
Carmike Williamsburg 7	5251-18 John Tyler Hwy.	Williamsburg	VA	23185	7	544
Carmike Apple Blossom 6	1850 Apple Blossom Dr.	Winchester	VA	22601	6	511
Carmike Cinema Center 6	601 E. Jubal Early Dr.	Winchester	VA	22601	6	511
Carmike 12	1331 N. Central Pkwy.	Kennewick	WA	99336	12	810
Carmike Oakwood 12	4800 Golf Rd.	Eau Claire	WI	54701	12	702
Carmike Valley Theatre	4400 Hwy. 16	Lacrosse	WI	54603	6	702
Carmike University Square 4	62 University Square Mall	Madison	WI	53715	4	669
Carmike Mariner 4	Mariner Mall Hill & 28th St.	Superior	WI	54880	4	676
Carmike Huntington Mall	700 Huntington Mall	Barboursville	WV	25504	6	564
Carmike 8	Mercer Mall	Bluefield	WV	24701	8	559
Carmike Meadowbrook	2205 Meadowbrook Mall	Bridgeport	WV	26330	6	598
Carmike Mall 8	9540 Mall Rd.	Morganton	WV	26505	8	508
Carmike Frontier	1400 Del Range Blvd.	Cheyenne	WY	82009	6	759
Carmike Cole Square	517 Cole Square Shopping Center	Cheyenne	WY	82601	3	767

CENTRAL STATES THEATRE CORP.

22 theatres, 79 screens.
505 Fifth Ave., Insurance Exchange Bldg., Des Moines, IA 50309. (515) 243-5287. (515) 243-5892.
PRESIDENT & TREASURER
Myron Blank
V.P. & ASSISTANT SECRETARY
Jacqueline Blank
GENERAL MANAGER
Arthur Stein, Jr.
SECRETARY & ASSISTANT TREASURER
R. D. Jackson

THEATRES

Central States Mall 6	550 S. Gear Ave	Burlington	IA	52601	6	682
Cinema 4	6301 University Ave.	Cedar Falls	IA	50613	4	637
Capri III	218 6th Ave.	Clinton	IA	52732	3	682
Cinema I	214 6th Ave.	Clinton	IA	52732	1	682
Coral Ridge 10	1451 Coral Ridge Ave.	Coralville	IA	52241	10	637
Council Bluffs Drive-In	1130 W. South	Council Bluffs	IA	51501	2	652
Co Ed II	119 W. Broadway	Fairfield	IA	52556	2	631
Co Ed II	3100 23rd St.	Fairfield	IA	52556	2	631
Central States Cinema 4	1417 Central	Ft. Dodge	IA	50501	4	679
Campus III	Old Capitol Mall	Iowa City	IA	52240	3	637
The Cinemas	1600 Sycamore St.	Iowa City	IA	52240	2	637
Cinema II	1670 Sycamore St.	Iowa City	IA	52240	2	637
Cinema V Mason City	100 S. Federal	Mason City	IA	50401	5	611
Cinema West	4710 4th St.	Mason City	IA	50401	8	611
Central States Capitol II	116 1st St.	Newton	IA	50208	2	679
Capri V	229 E. Main St.	Ottumwa	IA	52501	5	631
Pella Cinemas	708 Main St.	Pella	IA	50219	3	679
Center 6	30 Center Mall	Columbus	NE	68601	6	652
Cinema III	742 E. 23rd St.	Fremount	NE	68025	3	652
World II	2318 Central Ave.	Kearney	NE	68847	2	722
Kearney Drive-In	2813 Ave. North	Kearney	NE	68847	1	722
Cinema III	120 S. 3rd	Norfolk	NE	68701	3	624

CENTURY THEATRES

63 theatres, 659 screens.
150 Pelican Way, San Rafael CA 94901. (415) 448-8400. (415) 448-8358. www.centurytheatres.com
CEO
Raymond W. Syufy
PRESIDENT
Joseph Syufy
COO
David Shesgreen
CFO
Michael Dittmann
EXECUTIVE V.P., BUSINESS AFFAIRS
Mike Plymesser
SENIOR V.P., OPERATIONS
William Hulme
SENIOR V.P., BUSINESS AFFAIRS
Andrew McCullough
SENIOR V.P., FILM
Shauna King
SENIOR V.P., CORPORATE ANALYSIS
Robert McCleskey
SENIOR V.P., CORPORATE DEVELOPMENT
Victor Castillo
V.P., HUMAN RESOURCES
Kim Ramsay-Parikh
V.P., MARKETING
Nancy M. Klasky
V.P., CONSTRUCTION
Blair Walker
V.P.'s, CONCESSIONS
Lisa Rahn
Bob Shimmin
V.P., FACILITIES & PROJECTION
Phil Hacker
V.P., PURCHASING
Chris Duffie
V.P., INFORMATION SERVICES
Damian Wardle

THEATRES

Century 16 Anchorage	301 E. 36th Ave.	Anchorage	AK	99503	16	743
Glendale Drive-In	5650 N. 55th Ave.	Glendale	AZ	85301	9	753
Scottsdale 6 Drive-In	8101 E. Mckellips	Scottsdale	AZ	85256	6	753
Century Park Tucson	1055 W. Grant Rd.	Yucson	AZ	85705	16	789
Century El Con	3601 E. Broadway	Tucson	AZ	85716	20	789
Century Gateway	770 N. Kolb Rd.	Tucson	AZ	85710	12	789
Hyatt Cinema 3	1304 Bayshore Hwy	Burlingame	CA	94010	3	807
Solano Drive-Ins 2	1611 Solano Way	Concord	CA	94520	2	807
Century Laguna 16	9349 Big Horn Blvd.	Elk Grove	CA	95758	16	862
Century Folsom 14	261 Iron Point Rd.	Folsom	CA	95630	14	862
Cinedome Fremont 8	39153 Fremont Dr.	Fremont	CA	94538	8	807
Century Larkspur	500 Larkspur Landing Cir.	Larkspur	CA	94925	4	807
Century Cinema 16	1500 N. Shoreline Blvd.	Mountain View	CA	94043	16	807
Cinedome Napa 8	825 Pearl St.	Napa	CA	94559	8	807
Cinedome Newark 7	6000 New Park Mall	Newark	CA	94560	7	807
Century No. Hollywood 8	12827 Victory Blvd.	North Hollywood	CA	91606	8	803
Century Stadium Promenade 25	1701 West Katella Ave.	Orange	CA	92868	25	803
Century Pinole 10	1491 Fitzgerald Dr.	Pinole	CA	94564	10	807
Century Pleasant Hill	2314 Monument Blvd.	Pleasant Hill	CA	94523	5	807
Century Park Redwood 12	557 E. Bayshore	Redwood City	CA	94063	12	807
Century Roseville 14	1555 Eureka	Roseville	CA	95661	14	862
Century Stadium 21	1600 Ethan Way	Sacramento	CA	95825	2	862
Cinedome 9	6233 Garfield Ave.	Sacramento	CA	95841	9	862

Sacramento Drive-In	9616 Oates Dr.	Sacramento	CA	95827	6	862
Century Stadium 14	1590 Ethan Way	Sacramento	CA	95825	12	862
Downtown Plaza	445 Downtown Plaza	Sacramento	CA	95814	7	862
Northridge	350 Northridge Shopping Ctr.	Salinas	CA	93906	8	828
Century Park	10 Simas St	Salinas	CA	93901	7	828
Cinema 21 San Francisco	2141 Chestnut St.	San Francisco	CA	94123	1	807
Empire Cinema 3	85 West Portal Ave.	San Francisco	CA	94127	3	807
Presidio 1	2340 Chestnut St.	San Francisco	CA	94123	1	807
Century Plaza 10	410 Noor Ave.	S. San Francisco	CA	94080	10	807
Capitol Drive-In	3630 Hillcap Ave	San Jose	CA	95136	6	807
Century Capitol 16	3690 Hillcap Ave.	San Jose	CA	95136	16	807
Century Berryessa	1155 N. Capitol Ave.	San Jose	CA	95132	10	807
Century 21	3161 Olsen Dr.	San Jose	CA	95117	1	807
Century 22	3162 Olsen Ave.	San Jose	CA	95117	3	807
Century 23	3164 Olsen Ave.	San Jose	CA	95117	2	807
Century 24	741 Winchester Blvd.	San Jose	CA	95129	2	807
Century 25	1694 Saratoga Ave.	San Jose	CA	95117	2	807
Century 25 Union City	32100 Union Landing Rd.	Union City	CA	94587	25	807
Cinedome Vallejo 8	1190 Admiral Callaghan Lane	Vallejo	CA	94591	8	807
Century Ventura 16	2875 Elba St.	Ventura	CA	93003	16	803
Century Downtown 10	555 East Main St.	Ventura	CA	93001	10	803
Century 16 Aurora	14300 E. Alameda Ave.	Aurora	CO	80012	16	751
Century Rio	4901 Pan American Fwy	Albuquerque	NM	87109	24	790
Cinedome Henderson	851 So. Boulder Hwy.	Henderson	NV	89015	12	839
Las Vegas Drive-In	4150 West Carey Ave.	Las Vegas	NV	89032	5	839
Rancho Santa Fe	5101 N. Rainbow Dr.	Las Vegas	NV	89130	16	839
Suncoast	9090 Alta Dr.	Las Vegas	NV	89144	16	839
Century Desert	2606 S. Lamb Blvd.	Las Vegas	NV	89121	16	839
Cinedome Las Vegas	3200 S. Decatur Blvd.	Las Vegas	NV	89102	12	839
Century Orleans 12	4500 Tropicana Ave.	Las Vegas	NV	89103	12	839
Century Park Lane 16	210 E. Plum Lane	Reno	NV	89502	16	811
Riverside 12	11 N. Sierra St	Reno	NV	89501	12	811
Century Sparks	1250 Victorian Ave	Sparks	NV	89431	14	811
El Rancho Drive-In 4	555 El Rancho Dr.	Sparks	NV	89431	4	811
Century Eastport 16	4040 S.E. 82nd Ave.	Portland	OR	97266	16	820
Stadium 14 Sioux Falls	2400 South Carolyn	Sioux Falls	SD	57106	14	725
Century Abilene 12	3818 John Knox Dr.	Abilene	TX	79606	12	662
Century Corpus Christi	6685 South Padre Island Dr.	Corpus Christi	TX	78412	16	600
Odessa 12	4221 Preston Smith Rd.	Odessa	TX	79762	12	633
Century Salt Lake	125 East 3300	Salt Lake City	UT	84115	16	770

CHAKERES THEATRES

19 theatres, 61 screens.
222 N. Murray St., Box 1200, Springfield, OH 45501. (937) 323-6447. FAX: (937) 325-1100.
PRESIDENT & CEO
Michael H. Chakeres
V.P. & COO
Philip H. Chakeres
V.P.
Harry N. Chakeres
DIRECTOR OF ADVERTISING
Paul Ramsey
FILM BUYER
Fred Schweitzer
COMPTROLLER
Elden L. Paden

THEATRES

Chakeres Franklin Square 6	161 Franklin Square Shopping Center	Frankfort	KY	40604	6	541
Chakeres Brighton Park	114 Brighton Park Boulevard	Frankfort	KY	40603	2	541
Chakeres University Cinema	159 East Main St.	Morehead	KY	40351	1	541
Skyvue Drive-In	5909 Lexington Rd.	Winchester	KY	40391	2	541
Chakeres Bellefontaine Cinema 8	888 East Sandusky St.	Bellefontaine	OH	43311	8	542
Chakeres Celina 5	116 N. Main St.	Celina	OH	45822	5	542
Chakeres Lake Drive-In	8477 State Route 703	Celina	OH	45822	1	542
Chakeres Melody 49 Drive-In	State Route 49	Dayton	OH	45322	2	542
Chakeres Kettering Cinema 2	1441 E. Dorothy Lane	Dayton	OH	45429	2	542
Chakeres Skyborn Drive-In	Route 235 & Haddix Rd.	Fairborn	OH	45324	1	542
Chakeres Scioto Breeze Drive-In	State Route 23	Lucasville	OH	45648	2	564
Chakeres Park Layne Drive-In	2550 S. Dayton-Lakeview Rd.	New Carlisle	OH	45344	1	542
Chakeres Sidney 3	101 W. Poplar	Sidney	OH	45365	3	542
Chakeres Melody Cruise-In	4025 East National Rd.	Springfield	OH	45505	2	542
Chakeres Upper Valley 5	1475 Upper Valley Pike	Springfield	OH	45504	5	542
Chakeres Cinema 10	3115 East National Rd.	Springfield	OH	45505	10	542
Chakeres Urbana 1 & 2	216 South Main St.	Urbana	OH	43078	2	542
Chakeres Wilmington Plaza 5	1276 Romback Ave.	Wilmington	OH	45177	5	515
Chakeres Wilmington Drive-In	1129 N. Route 134	Wilmington	OH	45177	1	515

CINEMA GRILL

27 theatres, 72 screens.
P.O. Box 28467, Atlanta, GA 30358. (404) 250-9536. www.cinemagrill.com
PRESIDENT
James Duffy
FILM BUYER
Ken Stolts

THEATRES

Terrace Cinema Grill	28845 S. Western Rancho	Palos Verdes	CA	90275	5	803
Aurora Cinema Grill	13682 E. Alameda Ave.	Aurora	CO	80012	3	751
Aloma Cinema Grill	2155 Aloma Ave.	Winter Park	FL	32792	2	534
North Springs Cinema Grill	7270 Roswell Rd.	Atlanta	GA	30328	2	524
Oglethorpe Cinema Grill	7804 Abercorn Ext.	Savannah	GA	29212	3	546
Greenbriar Cinema Grill	1289 W. 86th St.	Indianapolis	IN	46260	2	527
Northwood Cinema Grill	6069 Stellhorn Rd.	Ft. Wayne	IN	46815	2	509
Turfland Mall Cinema Grill	Lane Ave.	Harrodsburg	KY	40504	2	541
Town East Cinema Grill	7700 E. Kellogg	Wichita	KS	67207	4	678
Annapolis Cinema Grill	81-C Forrest Plaza	Annapolis	MD	21401	2	512
Suburban World Cinema Grill	3022 Hennipen Ave.	Minneapolis	MN	30222	1	524
Yorktown Cinema Grill	3313 Hazelton Rd.	Edina	MN	55495	3	613

Eastland Cinema Grill	5423 Central Ave.	Charlotte	NC	28212	3	517
Raleighwood Cinema Grill	6609 Falls of the Neuse Rd.	Raleigh	NC	27615	2	560
Longleaf Cinema Grill	4310 Shipyard Blvd.	Willmington	NC	28403	3	550
Fargo Cinema Grill	630 1st Ave.	Fargo	ND	58102	3	724
Covedale Cinema Grill	4990 Glenway Ave.	Cincinnati	OH	45240	2	515
Mt. Lookout Cinema Grill	3187 Linwood Ave.	Cincinnati	OH	45208	2	515
Centrum Cinema Grill	2781 Euclid Hts. Blvd.	Cleveland	OH	44106	3	510
Harrisburg Cinema Grill	1090 Union Deposit Rd.	Harrisburg	PA	17111	2	566
American Cinema Grill	446 King Ave.	Charleston	SC	29410	2	519
Terrace Cinema Grill	315 Mohican St.	Knoxville	TN	37919	2	557
Westchase Cinema Grill	4749 Westheimer Rd.	Houston	TX	77042	5	618
Greenbrier Cinema Grill	1401 Grennbrier Pkwy.	Chesapeake	VA	23320	4	544
Star City Cinema Grill	5002 Airport Rd.	Roanoke	VA	24012	2	573
Aurora Cinema Grill	13000 Linden Ave.	Seattle	WA	98133	3	819
Fox Bay Cinema Grill	334 Silver Springs Dr.	Whitefish	WI	53217	3	617

CINEMARK USA, INC.

188 U.S. theatres, 2,180 U.S. screens; Foreign holdings: 64 theatres, 570 screens; TOTAL: 244 theatres, 2537 screens.
3900 Dallas Pkwy., Ste. 500, Plano, TX 75093. (972) 665-1000. FAX: (972) 665-1004. URL: http:www.cinemark.com
188 theatres, 2180 screens
CHAIRMAN & CEO
Lee Roy Mitchell
PRESIDENT
Alan Stock
EXECUTIVE V.P.
Tandy Mitchell
SENIOR V.P., OPERATIONS
Robert Carmony
V.P., GENERAL COUNSEL
Mike Cavalier
V.P., PURCHASING
Walter Hebert
V.P., MARKETING & COMMUNICATIONS
Randy Hester
V.P., CONSTRUCTION
Don Harton
PRESIDENT, CINEMARK DE MEXICO
Ken Higgins
V.P., REAL ESTATE
Margaret Richards
V.P., M. I. S.
Philip Wood

CINEMARK INTERNATIONAL
PRESIDENT
Tim Warner
V.P., HEAD FILM BUYER & HEAD OF MARKETING
Ken Higgins
V.P., CONSTRUCTION
Juan Maldonado
V.P., OPERATIONS
Steve Zuehlke
V.P., CONCESSIONS
Maria Angles
DIRECTOR, ADVERTISING & MARKETING
Diane Feffer
ENGINEER
Don McShane
V.P. & DIRECTOR, REAL ESTATE
John Hathaway
DIRECTOR, REAL ESTATE, BRAZIL
Joel Resnick
DIRECTOR, PROMOTIONS & MARKETING
James Meredith

THEATRES

Tinseltown Benton	17314 I-30	Benton	AR	72015	14	693
Cinemark 6 Theatres	HWY 65 @ I-40	Conway	AR	72032	6	693
Tandy Movies	4188 E. McCain	Little Rock	AR	72117	10	693
The Movies 4	4055 Stockton Hill Rd.	Kingman	AZ	86401	4	753
Cinemark Sierra Vista	2175 El Mercado Loop	Sierra Vista	AZ	85635	10	789
Movies 10	34491 Date Palm Dr.	Cathedral City	CA	92234	10	804
Tinseltown 14	801 East Ave.	Chico	CA	95926	14	868
Cinemark Movies 8- Chino	5546 Philadelphia St.	Chino	CA	91710	8	803
Blackhawk	4175 Blackhawk Plaza Circle	Danville	CA	94526	7	807
Movies	136 N. 11th Ave.	Hanford	CA	93230	4	866
Movies 8 Hanford Mall	1669 W. Lacey Blvd.	Hanford	CA	93230	8	866
Movies 12 Lancaster	44790 Valley Central Way	Lancaster	CA	93534	12	803
Movies 1-4	43821 15th St.	Lancaster	CA	93534	4	803
Cinemark 22	2600 West Ave. I	Lancaster	CA	93536	22	803
Movies 8 Palmdale	2210 Palmdale Blvd.	Palmdale	CA	93550	8	803
Movies 10	1247 W. Ave P	Palmdale	CA	93551	10	803
Movies 8	359 Park Marina Circle	Redding	CA	96001	8	868
Movies 10	980 Old Alturas Rd.	Redding	CA	96003	10	868
Movies 14	3300 N. Naglee Rd.	Tracy	CA	95376	14	862
Cinemark Victor Valley 10	14470 Bear Valley Rd.	Victorville	CA	92392	10	803
Movies 10	12353 Mariposa Rd.	Victorville	CA	92392	10	803
County Fair Movies 5	1579 A East St.	Woodland	CA	95776	5	862
Yuba City 8	1410 Whyler Rd.	Yuba City	CA	95993	8	862
Tinseltown USA	1545 E. Cheyenne Mountain Blvd.	Colorado Springs	CO	80906	20	752
Cinemark At Fort Collins	4721 South Timberline Rd.	Fort Collins	CO	80525	16	751
Tinseltown Pueblo	4140 N. Frwy	Pueblo	CO	81008	14	752
Movies 10	1796 West Newport Pike	Wilmington	DE	19804	10	504
Tinseltown USA	4535 Southside Blvd.	Jacksonville	FL	32216	20	561
Festival Bay	5150 Orlando Dr.	Orlando	FL	32819	20	534
Movies 8	2810 Sharer #31	Tallahassee	FL	32303	8	530
Movies 10	157 Banks Station	Fayetteville	GA	30214	10	524
Tinseltown	134 Pavilion Pkwy.	Fayetteville	GA	30214	17	524
Movies 12	1317 Buckeye Ave.	Ames	IA	50010	12	679
Varsity II	2412 Lincoln	Ames	IA	50010	2	679
North Grand 5	2801 Grand Ave.	Ames	IA	50010	5	679
Movies 10	1600 N. State, Rte. 50	Bourbonnais	IL	60914	10	602

Movies 8	3101 Hennepin Rd.	Joliet	IL	60435	8	602
Movies 10	2601 Plainfield Rd.	Joliet	IL	60435	10	602
Cinemark 10	1001 W. North Ave.	Melrose Park	IL	60160	10	602
Tinseltown	320 South Lincoln Way	North Aurora	IL	60542	17	602
Cinemark at Seven Bridges	6500 Route 53	Woodridge	IL	60517	17	602
Greentree	717 State Rd. 141	Clarksville	IN	47129	4	529
Greentree	757 A State Rd. 131	Clarksville	IN	47129	10	529
Greenwood	1848 E. Stop 13 Rd.	Indianapolis	IN	46227	8	527
Washington	10455 E. Washington	Indianapolis	IN	46229	8	527
University Park 6	6424 Grape Rd.	Mishawaka	IN	46545	6	588
Movies 14	910 West Edison	Mishawaka	IN	46545	14	588
Cinemark -Merriam	5500 Antioch	Merriam	KS	66202	20	616
Town Cinema	400 Winchester Ave.	Ashland	KY	41101	10	564
Man O'war Movies 8	133 N. Locust Hill Dr.	Lexington	KY	40509	8	541
Lexington Green Movies	200 Lexington Green Circle	Lexington	KY	40503	8	541
Movies 10	425 Codell Dr.	Lexington	KY	40509	10	541
Tinseltown	4400 Towne Center Dr.	Louisville	KY	40241	19	529
Kentucky Oaks	5161 Hinkleville Rd.	Paducah	KY	42001	12	632
Richmond Mall	404 Richmond Mall	Richmond	KY	40475	8	541
Tinseltown	10955 N. Mall Dr.	Baton Rouge	LA	70810	10	716
Cinema 10	4700 Milhaven Rd.	Monroe	LA	71203	10	628
Tinseltown	8400 Millicent Way	Shreveport	LA	71105	17	612
Tinseltown USA	220 Blanchard St.	West Monroe	LA	71291	17	628
Cinemark 20	3728 Rivertown Pkwy	Grandville	MI	49418	20	563
Movies 16	28600 Dequindre Rd.	Warren	MI	48092	16	505
Movies 8	1850 Adams St.	Mankato	MN	56001	8	737
The Palace Cinemark 14	500 Nichols Rd.	Kansas City	MO	64112	14	616
Cinemark 16	15171 Community Rd.	Gulfport	MS	39503	16	746
Tinseltown USA	411 Riverwind Dr.	Pearl	MS	39208	17	718
Movies 8	1001 Barnes Crossing Rd.	Tupelo	MS	38804	8	673
Randolph Cinema	400 Randolph Mall	Asheboro	NC	27203	5	518
Brassfield Cinema	2101 New Garden Rd.	Greensboro	NC	27410	10	518
Movies 10	9508 Northeast Ct	Matthews	NC	28105	10	517
Tinseltown USA	305 Faith Rd.	Salisbury	NC	28146	14	517
Movies 8	3205 L St.	Omaha	NE	68107	8	652
Movies 16	711 Evesham, Lionshead Plaza	Somerdale	NJ	08083	16	504
Movies 8	4591 San Mateo	Albuquerque	NM	87109	8	790
Movies West	9201 Coors Rd.	Albuquerque	NM	87114	8	790
Tinseltown	2291 Buffalo Rd.	Rochester	NY	14624	17	538
Movies 10	2613 W. Henrietta Rd.	West Brighton	NY	14623	10	538
Carnation Cinema	2500 W. State St.	Alliance	OH	44601	5	510
Tinseltown USA	7401 Market St.	Boardman	OH	44512	7	536
Cinema 5	1234 N. Mall St.	Bowling Green	OH	43402	5	547
Movies 4	3911 Everhard Rd.	Canton	OH	44709	4	510
Movie 12	2570 Bethel Rd.	Columbus	OH	43220	12	535
Movies 10	5275 Westpointe Plaza Dr.	Columbus	OH	43228	10	535
Movies 16	323 Stoneridge Lane	Gahanna	OH	43240	16	535
Movies 12	3773 Ridge Mill Dr.	Hillard	OH	43026	12	535
Cinemark 15	8161 Macedonia Commons Blvd	Macedonia	OH	44056	15	510
Cinema 10	498 N. Lexington-Springmill	Mansfield	OH	44906	10	510
Movies 10	6284 Dressler Rd.	North Canton	OH	44720	10	510
Tinseltown	4720 Mega St.	North Canton	OH	44720	15	510
Richland III	575 Stumbo Rd.	Ontario	OH	44906	3	510
Miami Valley	987 E. Ash St.	Piqua	OH	43536	6	542
Movies 10	5500 Milan Rd.	Sandusky	OH	44870	10	510
Cinemark 24	6001 Canal Rd.	Valley View	OH	44125	24	510
Movies 10	27613 Chardon Rd.	Willoughby Hills	OH	44092	10	510
Movies 10	4108 Burbank Rd.	Wooster	OH	44691	10	510
Movies 8	469 Boardman/Poland Rd.	Youngstown	OH	44512	8	536
Colony Square	3535 N. Maple Ave.	Zanesville	OH	43701	10	596
North Hills	1106 J.A. Richardson Loop	Ada	OK	74820	6	657
Cinema 8	3812 South Elm Place	Broken Arrow	OK	74011	8	671
Tinseltown 20	6001 N. M.L.K. Blvd.	Oklahoma City	OK	73111	20	650
Cinema 8	1112 E. Charles Page Blvd.	Sand Springs	OK	74063	8	671
Movies 8	6808 S. Memorial #310	Tulsa	OK	74133	8	671
The Tulsa by Cinemark	10802 E. 71st St.	Tulsa	OK	74133	17	671
Movies 5	1600 N. Riverside	Medford	OR	97501	5	813
Tinseltown	651 Medford Center	Medford	OR	97501	15	813
Movies 12	2850 Gateway Mall	Springfield	OR	97477	12	801
Cinemark 17	2900 Gateway	Springfield	OR	97477	17	801
White City	7501 Crater Lake Hwy	White City	OR	97503	6	813
Movies 17	1910 Rotunda Dr.	Erie	PA	16509	17	516
Millcreek Cinema	5800 Peast St., Millcreek Mall	Erie	PA	16509	6	516
Cinemark 20	40 Glenmaura National Blvd.	Moosic	PA	18507	20	577
Movies 8	4488 Ladson Rd.	Summerville	SC	29485	8	519
Tinseltown	755 West Main St	Oakridge	TN	37830	14	557
Cinemark 16	9100 Canyon Dr.	Amarillo	TX	79119	16	634
Tinseltown	2815 E. Division St.	Arlington	TX	76011	9	623
Barton Creek	2224-B Walsh Tarlton Rd.	Austin	TX	78746	10	635
Dollar Cinema 8	3407 Wells Branch Pkwy.	Austin	TX	78728	8	635
Tinseltown	5501 IH 35	South Austin	TX	78744	17	635
Tinseltown	3855 Interstate 10	Beaumont	TX	77705	15	692
Movies 10	3471 Old Hwy 77	Brownsville	TX	78520	10	636
Cinemark 16	2370 N. Expressway	Brownsville	TX	78521	16	636
Cinema 6	1643 W. Henderson	Cleburne	TX	76031	6	623
Movies 16	1401 E. Bypass	College Station	TX	77845	16	625
Dollar Cinema	5858 S. Padre Is. Dr.	Corpus Christi	TX	78412	7	600
Tinseltown	5218 Silverberry	Corpus Christi	TX	78416	16	600
Cinema IV	1803 W. 77th	Corsicana	TX	75110	4	623
Cinemark 17	11819 Webb Chapel Rd.	Dallas	TX	75234	17	623
Movies 8	2205 Ave. F	Del Rio	TX	78840	8	641
Tinseltown	11855 Gateway Blvd.	East El Paso	TX	79936	20	765
Hollywood USA	4040 S. Shiloh Rd.	Garland	TX	75041	15	623
Movies 16	220 Westchester Pkwy	Grand Prairie	TX	75052	15	623
Tinseltown	911 State Hwy. 114	Grapevine	TX	76051	17	623
Movies 10	629 N. 13th St.	Harlingen	TX	78550	10	636
Cinemark	601 S. Expressway 83	Harlingen	TX	78550	16	636
Tinseltown	12920 N.W. Freeway	Houston	TX	77040	16	618
Tinseltown Westchase	3600 W. Sam Houston Pkwy.	Houston	TX	77042	24	618
Tinseltown	11450 East Freeway	Jacinto City	TX	77029	17	618
Cinemark 19	1030 W. Grand Pkwy.	Katy	TX	77449	19	618

Movies 14	3250 W. Plesant Run Rd.	Lancaster	TX	75146	14	623
Movies 12	5412 San Bernardo	Laredo	TX	78041	12	749
Movies 12	2400 S. Stemmons	Lewisville	TX	75067	12	623
Cinemark 8	420 Oak Bend Dr.	Lewisville	TX	75056	8	623
Movies 16	5721 58th St.	Lubbock	TX	79423	17	651
Tinseltown 17	2535 82nd St.	Lubbock	TX	79423	17	651
Movies 17	100 W. Nolana Loop	McAllen	TX	78504	17	636
Main Place	1800 South 16th	McAllen	TX	78501	6	636
Movies 14	1701 S. Central Expwy.	McKinney	TX	75069	14	623
Tinseltown	2422 E. Expwy. 83	Mission	TX	78572	17	636
Movies 8	1225 N. East Loop 286	Paris	TX	75460	8	623
Hollywood USA	2101 E. Beltway 8	Pasadena	TX	77503	20	618
Tinseltown	15436 FM 1825	Pflugerville	TX	78660	20	635
Movies 8	500 N. Jackson	Pharr	TX	78577	8	636
Town Centre	1001 I-27 Hwy N. #70	Plainview	TX	79072	6	651
Movies 10	1818 Coit Rd.	Plano	TX	75075	10	623
Tinseltown	3800 Dallas Pkwy.	Plano	TX	75093	20	623
Cinemark 24	7201 Central Expwy.	Plano	TX	75025	24	623
Movies 8	7560 N.E. Loop 820	N. Richland Hills	TX	76180	8	623
Rockwall 8	497 I-30	Rockwall	TX	75032	8	623
Rosenberg 8	5101 Ave. H	Rosenberg	TX	77471	8	618
Movies 8	2132 N. Mays, Ste. 800	Round Rock	TX	78664	8	635
Tinseltown 14	4425 Sherwood Way	San Angelo	TX	76904	14	661
Dollar Movies	5063 Loop 410 N.W.	San Antonio	TX	78229	16	641
Movies 9	4100 New Braufels Ave	San Antonio	TX	78223	9	641
Cinema 7	2510 Texoma Pkwy.	Sherman	TX	75090	7	657
Midway Movies	4800 Texoma Pkwy.	Sherman	TX	75090	5	657
Cinema 6	2900 W. Washington	Stephenville	TX	76401	6	623
Temple 5	4105 S. 31st St.	Temple	TX	76502	5	625
Temple 6	3111 S. 31st St.	Temple	TX	76502	6	625
Movies 12	3912 Hampton Rd.	Texarkana	TX	75503	12	612
Movies 12	10000 Emmet F. Lowry Expwy.	Texas City	TX	77591	12	618
Salem Cinema	5912 Navarro	Victoria	TX	77904	6	626
Playhouse Cinema	1207 Sam Houston Dr.	Victoria	TX	77901	4	626
Cinema IV	7002 N.E. Zac Lentz Pkwy.	Victoria	TX	77904	4	626
Cinema 18	20915 Gulf Freeway	Webster	TX	77598	18	618
Movies 10	2113 W. Expressway 83	Weslaco	TX	78596	10	636
Tinseltown	1600 Lake Robbins Dr.	Woodlands	TX	77380	17	618
Tinseltown	720 W. 1500 North	Layton	UT	84041	17	770
Tinseltown	1010 Newgate Mall	Ogden	UT	84405	14	770
Village Cinema	1776 Park Ave.	Park City	UT	84060	3	770
Movies 8	2424 N. University Pkwy.	Provo	UT	84604	8	770
Cinemark 16	1200 Town Center Blvd.	Provo	UT	84601	16	770
Movies 10	2227 S. Highland Dr.	Salt Lake City	UT	84106	10	770
Movies 9	9539 S. 7th St.	Sandy	UT	84070	9	770
Cinemark 24	7301 S. Jordon Landing	West Jordon	UT	84088	24	770
Valley Fair	3601 S. 2700 West	West Valley City	UT	84119	9	770
Tinseltown	3004 Linden Dr.	Bristol	VA	24201	14	531
Movies 10	4300 Portsmouth Blvd.	Chesapeake	VA	23321	10	544
Movies 10	3700 Candlers Mountain Blvd.	Lynchburg	VA	24502	10	573
Cinemark at Military Circle	880 N. Military Hwy.	Norfolk	VA	23502	18	544
Tinseltown USA	7101 70th Court	Kenosha	WI	53142	14	617

CITY CINEMAS

7 theatres, 27 screens.

950 Third Ave., 30th Fl., New York, NY 10022. (212) 521-9400. FAX: (212) 521-9420.

CHAIRMAN
James J. Cotter
PRESIDENT & CEO
Robert Smerling
V.P. & GENERAL MANAGER
Richard Einiger

THEARES

Angelika Film Center	18 W. Houston St.	New York City	NY	10012	6	501
Cinema 1, 2 & 3	1001 3rd Ave.	New York City	NY	10022	3	501
Eastside Playhouse	919 3rd Ave.	New York City	NY	10022	1	501
East 86th St. Cinemas	210 E. 86th St.	New York City	NY	10028	4	501
Murray Hill Cinemas	160 E. 34th St.	New York City	NY	10016	4	501
Sutton 1 & 2	205 E. 57th St.	New York City	NY	10022	2	501
Village East Cinemas	181-189 2nd Ave.	New York City	NY	10003	7	501

CINEMA ENTERTAINMENT CORP.

19 theatres, 159 screens.

Box 1126, St. Cloud, MN 56302. (320) 251-9131. FAX: (320) 251-1003.

PRESIDENT
Bob Ross
VICE PRESIDENT
Anthony D. Tillemans
SECRETARY
Dave Ross
TREASURER
George Becker
OPERATIONS MANAGER
Noelle Hanson
FILM BUYER
Dwight Gunderson

THEATRES

CEC Crossroads 12	2450 Crossroads Blvd.	Waterloo	IA	50702	12	637
CEC Mall Cinema 7	2510 Bridge Ave.	Albert Lea	MN	56007	7	611
CEC Amigo 9	5240 Highway 2	Bemidji	MN	56619	9	613
CEC Cinema 6	320 Minnesota Ave.	Breckenridge	MN	56520	6	724
CEC Cinema 6	200 Western Ave.	Faribault	MN	55021	6	613
CEC Lakes 10	4351 Stebner Rd.	Hermantown	MN	55811	10	676
CEC Cinema 8	4191 Haines Rd.	Hermantown	MN	55811	8	676
CEC Marshall 6	230 W. Lyon	Marshall	MN	56258	6	613
CEC Safari 7	925 S. 30th Ave.	Moorhead	MN	56560	7	724
CEC Cinema 6	7 S. Enterprise Dr.	Mountain Iron	MN	55768	6	676
CEC Cinema Arts 3	612 S. 2nd St.	St Cloud	MN	56301	3	613
CEC Parkwood 18	1533 Frontage Rd.	Waite Park	MN	56387	18	613

CEC Crossroads 6	230 N.E. 3rd Ave.	Waite Park	MN	56387	6	613
CEC Winona 7	70 W. 2nd St.	Winona	MN	55987	7	702
CEC Century 10	3931 9th Ave.	Fargo	ND	58103	10	724
CEC West Acres 14	4101 17th Ave.	Fargo	ND	58103	14	724
CEC Hudson Cinema 9	1920 Crestview Dr.	Hudson	WI	54016	9	613
CEC Lake 7	1769 County Highway SS	Rice Lake	WI	54868	7	613
CEC Mariner Mall 8	Mariner Mall	Superior	WI	54880	8	676

CINEMAGIC THEATRES

4 theatres, 28 screens.
Midwest Theatres Corporation, 5425 84th Ave. North, Brooklyn Park, MN 55443. (763) 781-8858. FAX: (763) 537-4492.
PRESIDENT, COO & FILM BUYER
Steven L. Tripp
CFO & BUSINESS DEVELOPMENT
Bryan J. Sieve

THEATRES

Great Lakes Cinema 7	1698 Exchange St.	Okoboji	IA	51355	7	624
CineMagic 7 Theatres	1301 18th Ave.	Austin	MN	55912	7	611
Century 7 Theatres	766 Century Ave.	Hutchinson	MN	55350	7	613
CineMagic Stadium 7 Theatres	2521 Hwy. 25	Menomonie	WI	54751	7	613

CINEMASTAR LUXURY THEATERS, INC.

7 theatres, 87 screens. 1 Mexican theatre, 10 screens. TOTAL: 8 theatres, 79 screens reported.
12230 El Camino Real, Ste. 320, San Diego, CA 92130. (619) 509-2777. FAX: (619) 509-9426. www.cinemastar.com
CHAIRMAN & CEO
Jack Crosby
CO-PRESIDENT & CEO
Paul Hobby
V.P. & CFO
Don Harnois
V.P., OPERATIONS
Clay Colbert
FILM BUYER
Allen Elrod
CORPORATE CONSTRUCTION MANAGER
Al Zlotnik
DIRECTOR OF ADVERTISING & MARKETING
Dan Cahill
DIRECTOR OF INTERNATIONAL OPERATIONS
John Prock

THEATRES

CinemaStar Galaxy 6 Cinemas	5256 S. Mission Rd.	Bonsall	CA	92003	6	825
CinemaStar Chula Vista 10	555 Broadway	Chula Vista	CA	91910	10	825
CinemaStar Mission Marketplace 13	431 College Blvd.	Oceanside	CA	92054	13	825
CinemaStar Perris Plaza 10	1688 N. Perris Blvd.	Perris	CA	92571	10	803
CinemaStar University Village 10	1201 University Ave.	Riverside	CA	92507	10	803
CinemaStar Mission Grove 18	121 East Alessandro	Riverside	CA	92508	18	803
CinemaStar Empire 20	450 N.E St.	San Bernardino	CA	92401	20	803

CLARK THEATRES

5 theatres, 12 screens.
P.O. Box 310570, Enterprise, AL 36331-0570. (334) 347-1129. FAX: (334) 347-8242.
OWNER
Mack Clark, Jr.
GENERAL MANAGER
Walter C. (Charlie) Andrews

THEATRES

Clark Theatre on the Square	Court Square	Andalusia	AL	36420	3	698
Clark Cinemas I & II	608 Boll Weevil Cir.	Enterprise	AL	36330	2	606
Clark Cinemas III & IV	621 Boll Weevil Cir.	Enterprise	AL	36330	2	606
College Cinemas I, II & III	501 Pl. Dr, Ste. 137	Enterprise	AL	36330	3	606
Clark Twin Cinemas	Hwy 231 & Andrews Ave.	Ozark	AL	36360	2	606

CLASSIC CINEMAS

18 theatres, 84 screens.
(A division of Tivoli Enterprises, Inc.) 603 Rogers St. Downers Grove, IL 60515-3770. (630) 968-1600. FAX: (630) 968-1626. www.classiccinemas.com
PRESIDENT
Willis Johnson
V.P.
Christopher Johnson
SECRETARY
Shirley Johnson
FILM BUYER
Lou Michael

THEATRES

CC Cinema 12 Theatre	100 Besinger Dr.	Carpentersville	IL	60110	12	602
CC Tivoli Theatre	5021 Highland Ave.	Downers Grove	IL	60515	1	602
CC Casino Cinema	250 S. Grove Ave.	Elgin	IL	60120	3	602
CC Elk Grove Theatre	1050 Town Center	Elk Grove	IL	60007	6	602
CC York Theatre	150 N. York Rd.	Elmhurst	IL	60126	5	602
CC Fox Lake Theatre	115 Lakeland Plaza	Fox Lake	IL	60020	5	602
CC Lindo Theatre	115 South Chicago Ave.	Freeport	IL	61032	6	610
CC Tradewinds Theatre	1452 Irving Park Rd.	Hanover Park	IL	60103	2	602
CC Barrington Square Theatre	2330 West Higgins Rd.	Hoffman Estates	IL	60195	6	602
CC Meadowview Theatre	55 Meadowview Center	Kankakee	IL	60901	3	602
CC Paramount	213 N. Schuyler Ave.	Kankakee	IL	60901	5	602
CC Ogden 6 Theatre	1227 East Ogden Ave.	Naperville	IL	60563	6	602
CC Lake Theatre	1022 Lake St.	Oak Park	IL	60301	7	602
CC Park Forest Theatre	340 Main St.	Park Forest	IL	60466	5	602
CC Arcada Theatre	105 E. Main St.	St. Charles	IL	60174	1	602
CC Foxfield Theatre	151 Fieldgate	St. Charles	IL	60174	7	602
CC Sterling Theatre	402 Locust St.	Sterling	IL	61081	2	682
CC Woodstock Theatre	209 Main St.	Woodstock	IL	60098	2	602

CLEARVIEW CINEMA CORP.

64 theatres, 297 screens.
97 Main St., Chatham, NJ 07928 (973) 377-4646. FAX (973) 377-4303.
PRESIDENT
Charles Goldwater
V.P., THEATRE OPERATIONS
Cynthia Cronkhite
V.P., FACILITIES & CONSTRUCTION
Steven Ventor
V.P., FILM
Craig Zeltner
FILM BUYERS
Rosemarie Devery
Mary Shefford

THEATRES

Clearview Greenwich 1 & 2	356 Greenwich Ave.	Greenwich	CT	06830	2	501
Clearview Middlebrook Cinema 10	Middlebrook Shopping Center	Asbury Park	NJ	07712	10	501
Clearview Bergenfield Cinema Quad	58 S. Washington Ave.	Bergenfield	NJ	07621	5	501
Clearview Bernardsville Cinema 3	5 Mine Brook Rd.	Bernardsville	NJ	07924	3	501
Clearview Caldwell Cinema 4	317 Bloomfield Ave.	Caldwell	NJ	07006	4	501
Clearview Cinema 23 Fiveplex	Route 23.	Cedar Grove	NJ	07009	5	501
Clearview Chester Cinema 6	Rte. 206 & Rte. 24.	Chester	NJ	07930	6	501
Clearview Allwood Cinema 6	96 Market St.	Clifton	NJ	07012	6	501
Clearview Closter Cinema 4	130 Closter Plaza	Closter	NJ	07624	4	501
Clearview Edison Cinema	1655 Oak Tree Rd.	Edison	NJ	08820	8	501
Clearview Emerson Cinema Quad	344 Kinderkamack Rd.	Emerson	NJ	07630	4	501
Clearview Mansfield Cinema 15	1965 Route 57	Hackettstown	NJ	07840	15	501
Clearview Kinnelon 11	25 Kinnelon Rd.	Kinnelon	NJ	07405	11	501
Clearview Colony 3 Theatre	21 East Mount Pleasant Ave.	Livingston	NJ	07039	3	501
Clearview Madison Cinema 4	Lincoln Pl.	Madison	NJ	07940	4	501
Clearview Strathmore Cinema 4	1055 Rte. 34	Matawan	NJ	07747	4	501
Clearview Millburn Cinemas	350 Millburn Ave.	Millburn	NJ	07041	4	501
Clearview Clairidge Cinemas	486 Bloomfield Ave.	Montclair	NJ	07042	5	501
Clearview Screening Zone	544 Bloomfield Ave.	Montclair	NJ	07042	2	501
Clearview Headquarters 10 Theatres	72 Headquarters Plaza	Morristown	NJ	07960	10	501
Clearview Parsippany 12 Cinema	3165 Rte. 46	Parsippany	NJ	07054	12	501
Clearview Red Bank Cinemas	36 White St.	Red Bank	NJ	07701	2	501
Clearview Warner Quad	190 E. Ridgewood Ave.	Ridgewood	NJ	07450	4	501
Clearview Succasunna 10 Cinema	21 Sunset Blvd.	Succasunna	NJ	07876	10	501
Clearview Beacon Hill 5	343 Springfield Ave.	Summit	NJ	07901	4	501
Clearview Tenafly Cinema	4 1/2 Railroad Ave.	Tenafly	NJ	07670	4	501
Clearview Bellevue 3	260 Bellevue Ave	Upper Montclair	NJ	07043	3	501
Clearview Washington Township	249 Pascack Rd.	Washington Twnsp.	NJ	07675	3	501
Clearview Wayne Preakness	Preakness Shop. Cntr.; Hamburg Turnpike	Wayne	NJ	07470	4	501
Clearview West Milford Theatre	35 D. Marshall Hill Rd.	West Milford	NJ	07480	4	501
Clearview Woodbridge Cinemas	Rte. 1 & Gill Ln.	Woodbridge	NJ	07095	4	501
Clearview Babylon Cinemas	34 Main St.	Babylon	NY	11702	3	501
Clearview Grand Ave	Grand Ave. Shopping Center	Baldwin	NY	11572	5	501
Clearview Bedford Playhouse	Route 22.	Bedford	NY	10506	3	501
Clearview Bronxville 3	84 Kraft Ave	Bronxville	NY	10708	3	501
Clearview Cobble Hill Cinema	265 Court St. At Butler St.	Brooklyn	NY	11231	5	501
Clearview Franklin Square Theatre	989 Hempstead Turnpike	Franklin Square	NY	11530	15	501
Clearview Squire Cinemas	115 Middle Neck Rd.	Great Neck	NY	11361	7	501
Clearview Larchmont Playhouse	1975 Palmer Ave.	Larchmont	NY	10538	3	501
Clearview Mamaroneck Playhouse 4	243 Mamaroneck Ave.	Mamaroneck	NY	10543	4	501
Clearview Manhasset 3	430 Plandome Rd.	Manhasset	NY	11030	3	501
Clearview Mt Kisco Cinemas	144 Main St.	Mount Kisco	NY	10549	4	501
Clearview New City Cinema 6	202 S. Main St.	New City	NY	10956	6	501
Clearview Cinema 304	164 N. Main St.	New City	NY	10956	2	501
Clearview Herricks Twin	Herricks Rd.	New Hyde Park	NY	11598	2	501
Clearview 59th St Cinema	235/239 East 59th St	New York	NY	10022	1	501
Clearview 62nd & Broadway	1871 Broadway	New York	NY	10023	1	501
Clearview Beekman	1254 Second Ave	New York	NY	10021	1	501
Clearview Central Plaza 4	2630 Central Park Ave.	New York	NY	10710	4	501
Clearview Chelsea	260 West 23rd St	New York	NY	10011	9	501
Clearview Chelsea West	333 West 23rd St	New York	NY	10011	3	501
Clearview First & 62nd	400 East 62nd St	New York	NY	10021	6	501
Clearview Metro Twin	2626 Broadyway	New York	NY	10025	2	501
Clearview Olympia	2770 Broadway	New York	NY	10025	2	501
Clearview Park & 86th St.	125 East 86th St.	New York	NY	10028	2	501
Clearview Waverly Twin	323 Sixth Ave.	New York -	NY	10014	2	501
Clearview Ziegfeld	141 West 54th St	New York	NY	10019	1	501
Clearview Port Washington Cinemas	116 Main St.	Port Washington	NY	11030	7	501
Clearview Soundview 6	7-9 Soundview Market Place; Shore Rd.	Port Washington	NY	11050	6	501
Clearview Roslyn Theatre	20 Tower Pl.	Roslyn	NY	11030	4	501
Clearview Rye Ridge Cinema	1 Rye Ridge Plaza	Rye	NY	10573	2	501
Clearview Cinema 100 Twin	93 Knollwood Rd.	White Plains	NY	10607	2	501
Clearview Bala Theater	157 Bala Ave.	Bala Cynwyd	PA	19004	3	504
Clearview Anthony Wayne 5	109 W. Lancaster Ave	Wayne	PA	19087	5	504

COLORADO CINEMAS

9 theatres, 81 screens.
6696 S. Parker Rd., Aurora, CO 80076. (303) 766-7900. FAX: (303) 766-9865.
PRESIDENT & CEO
Haydn Silleck
V.P. & COO
Cliff Godfrey

THEATRES

Olde Town 14	5550 Wadsworth Blvd.	Arvada	CO	80002	14	751
Arapahoe Crossing 16	6696 S. Parker Rd.	Aurora	CO	80016	16	751
Arapahoe Village 4	2480 Arapahoe Ave.	Boulder	CO	80302	4	751
Basemar Twin	2490 Baseline Rd.	Boulder	CO	80305	2	751
Cherry Creek 8	3000 E. 1st Ave.	Denver	CO	80206	8	751
Bergen Park 7	1204 Bergen Pkwy.	Evergreen	CO	80439	7	751
Cinema Saver 6	2525 Worthington Circle	Ft. Collins	CO	80526	6	751
Bowles Crossing 12	8035 W. Bowles Ave.	Littleton	CO	80123	12	751
Colony Square 12	1164 Dryer Rd.	Louisville	CO	80027	12	751

COMING ATTRACTIONS, INC.

14 theatres, 82 screens.
1644 Ashland St., Ashland, OR 97520. (541) 488-1021. FAX: (541) 482-9290.
OWNER & CEO
John C. Schweiger
SENIOR V.P. & CFO
Larry McLennan
V.P. & GENERAL MANAGER
Don Immenschuh

THEATRES

Crescent City Cinema	375 M St.	Crescent City	CA	95531	8	802
Ashland Steet Cinema	1644 Ashland St.	Ashland	OR	97520	6	813
Varsity Theatre	166 E. Main St.	Ashland	OR	97520	5	813
Astoria Gateway Cinema	1875 Marine Dr.	Astoria	OR	97103	7	820
Egyptian	229 S. Broadway	Coos Bay	OR	97420	3	801
Florence Cinema	1930 Hwy. 101	Florence	OR	97439	4	801
Forest Grove Cinema 7	2828 Pacific Ave.	Forest Grove	OR	97116	7	820
Movies 6	1111 N.E. D St.	Grants Pass	OR	97526	6	813
Southgate Cinemas	1625 S.W. Ringuette St.	Grants Pass	OR	97527	4	813
Pelican Cinema	2643 Biehn St.	Klamath Falls	OR	97601	10	813
McMinnville Cinema 8	2725 N.E. Tanger Dr.	McMinnville	OR	97128	8	820
Pony Village Cinema	1611 Virginia	North Bend	OR	97459	4	801
Harvard Cinema	3161 W. Harvard Ave.	Roseburg	OR	97470	3	801
Roseburg Cinema 7	1750 N.W. Hughwood	Roseburg	OR	97470	7	801

CONSOLIDATED THEATRES

14 theatres, 99 screens.
(A subsidiary of Pacific Theatres) 1601 Kapiolani Blvd., #1250, Honolulu, HI 96814. (808) 952-5800. FAX: (808) 952-5805.
PRESIDENT
Phil Shimmin

THEATRES

Pearlridge West	98-1005 Moanalua Rd.	Aiea	HI	96701	16	744
Kaahumanu	275 Kaahumanu Ave.	Kahului	HI	96732	6	744
Aikahi Twins	25 Kaneohe Bay Dr.	Kailua	HI	96734	2	744
Keauhou Cinemas	78-6831 Alii Dr.	Kailua-Kona	HI	96740	7	744
Koolau	47-260 Hui Iwa St.	Kaneohe	HI	96744	10	744
Kapolei	890 kamokila Blvd.	Kapolei	HI	96707	16	744
Kukui Mall	1819 S. Kihei Rd.	Kihei	HI	96753	4	744
IMAX Theatre	325 Seaside Ave.	Honolulu	HI	96815	3	744
Kahala	4211 Waialae Ave.	Honolulu	HI	96816	8	744
Koko Marina	7192 Kalanianaole Hwy.	Honolulu	HI	96825	8	744
Varsity Twins	1106 University Ave.	Honolulu	HI	96826	2	744
Waikiki	2284 Kalakaua Ave.	Honolulu	HI	96815	1	744
Waikiki Twins	333 Seaside Ave.	Honolulu	HI	96815	2	744
Mililani	95-1249 Meheula Pkwy.	Mililani	HI	96825	14	744

CROWN THEATRES

11 theatres, 105 screens.
64 N. Main St., South Norwalk, CT 06854. (203) 846-8800. FAX: (203) 846-9828.
PRESIDENT
Daniel M. Crown
SENIOR EXECUTIVE V. P. & COO
Milt Daly
EXECUTIVE V.P. & CFO.
David Clifford
EXECUTIVE V.P. & GENERAL COUNSEL
Glenn Garfinkel
DIRECTOR OF OPERATIONS
Chris Dugger
CONTROLLER
Catherine Nonnenmacher
DIRECTOR ADVERTISING
Steve Gould
DIRECTOR OF SPECIAL PROJECTS
Thomas Becker

THEATRES

Crown Plaza	2 Railroad Ave	Greenwich	CT	06830	3	501
Crown Royale 6	542 Westport Ave.	Norwalk	CT	06851	6	501
Crown Regent	64 N. Main St.	South Norwalk	CT	06850	8	501
Crown Majestic 6	118 Summer St.	Stamford	CT	06901	6	501
Crown Landmark Square 9	5 Landmark Square	Stamford	CT	06901	9	501
Crown Marquis 16 Theater	100 Quarry Rd.	Trumbull	CT	06611	16	501
Crown Palace 17	3300 New Park Ave.	West Hartford	CT	06107	17	533
Crown Grand 18	179-50 N.W. 57th Ave.	Hialeah	FL	33015	18	528
Crown Harbour Center IX	Rt, 2 at Patuxent Blvd.	Annapolis	MD	21401	9	512
Crown Annapolis Mall	Annapolis Mall	Annapolis	MD	21401	11	512
Crown Eastport Cinemas	Eastport Shopping Center	Annapolis	MD	21401	2	512

DANBARRY CINEMAS

4 theatres, 46 screens.
105 West 4th St., Ste. 1000, Cincinnati, OH 45202. (513) 784-1521. FAX: (513) 784-1554.
OWNERS
Daniels J. Heilbrunn
Barry A. Kohn
GENERAL MANAGER
Tom Sanders.

THEATRES

Danbarry Dollar Saver Cinemas	5190 Glenncrossing Way	Cincinnati	OH	45238	12	515
Danbarry Dollar Saver Cinemas	8300 Lyons Ridge Dr.	Dayton	OH	45458	12	515
Danbarry Dollar Saver Cinemas	7650 Waynetowne Blvd.	Huber Heights	OH	45424	12	542
Danbarry Cinemas Middletown	3479 Dixie Hwy.	Middletown	OH	45005	10	515

DEANZA LAND & LEISURE CORP.

7 theatres, 29 screens.
1615 Cordova St., Los Angeles, CA 90007. (323) 734-9951. FAX: (323) 734-2531.
PRESIDENT
William H. Oldknow
SENIOR V.P.,
Gerald T. Oldknow

THEATRES

De Anza Quad	1401 S. Alvernon Way	Tucson	AZ	85711	4	789
Van Buren Blvd.	3035 Van Buren Blvd.	Arlington	CA	92503	3	803
Mission Quad	4407 State St.	Montclair	CA	91763	4	803
Rubidoux Triple	3770 Opal St.	Riverside	CA	92509	3	803
South Bay Triple	2170 coronado Ave.	San Diego	CA	92154	3	825
Starlight Six-Plex	2000 Moreland Ave.	Atlanta	GA	30316	6	524
Redwood Six-Plex	3688 S. Redwood Rd.	West Valley	UT	84119	6	770

DICKINSON THEATRES, INC.

24 theatres, 196 screens.
5913 Woodson Rd., Mission, KS 66202. (913) 432-2334. FAX: (913) 432-9507.
PRESIDENT & CEO
John Hartley
V.P., OPERATIONS
Brett Miller
V.P., HEAD FILM BUYER
Ron Horton
CFO
Cheryl Ballieu

THEATRES

Flinthills 8	1614 Industrial Rd.	Emporia	KS	66801	8	605
Sequoyah 9	1118 Fleming	Garden City	KS	67846	9	678
Fox 2 Hays	1202 Main St.	Hays	KS	67601	2	678
Mall Hays Theatre	2925 Vine St.	Hays	KS	67601	8	678
Mall 8 Hutchinson	1500 E. 11th St.	Hutchinson	KS	67504	8	678
Mall 4 Hutchinson	1500 E. 11th St.	Hutchinson	KS	67501	4	678
Plaza 6 Leavenworth	3400 S. 4th St.	Leavenworth	KS	66048	6	616
Great Mall 16	20060 W. 151st St.	Olathe	KS	66061	16	616
Central Mall 8	2259 S. 9th St.	Salina	KS	67402	8	678
Midstates 2	2450 S. 9th St.	Salina	KS	67401	2	678
Sunset 2	1221 W. Crawford	Salina	KS	67401	2	678
Westglen 18	16301 Midland Dr.	Shawnee	KS	66217	18	616
Northrock 6	3242 N. Rock Rd.	Wichita	KS	67225	6	678
Northrock 14	3151 Penstemon	Wichita	KS	67226	14	678
Belton 8	1207 E. North Ave.	Belton	MO	64012	8	616
Noland Fashion Square 6	13520 40 Hwy.	Independence	MO	64055	6	616
Red Bridge 4	11118 Holmes Rd.	Kansas City	MO	64131	4	616
Eastglen 16	1451 N.E. Douglas St.	Lee's Summit	MO	64086	16	616
Owasso 10	12601 E. 86th St.	Owasso	OK	74055	10	671
Arrowhead Mall 6	Arrowhead Shopping Center	Muskogee	OK	74401	6	671
Starworld 20	10301 S. Memorial Dr.	Tulsa	OK	74133	20	671
Showest 3	West Historic Rte 66	Weatherford	OK	73096	3	650
66 Twin Driv-In	West Historic Rte 66	Weatherford	OK	73096	2	650
Central Mall 10	3100 Hwy. 365	Port Arthur	TX	77642	10	692

DIPSON THEATRES, INC.

13 theatres, 38 screens.
210 Main St. East, Room 111, 2nd Floor, Batavia, NY 14020; P.O. Box 579, Batavia, NY 14021. (716) 343-2700.
PRESIDENT
Michael Clement
V.P./SECRETARY
Bryan Spokane
TREASURER
Henry Janes

THEATRES

Cinema 1 & 2	210-2 Main St.	Batavia	NY	14020	2	514
Mall 2	6 Alva Pl. West	Batavia	NY	14020	2	514
Amherst Theatre	3500 Main St.	Buffalo	NY	14226	3	514
North Park	1428 Hertel Ave.	Buffalo	NY	14216	1	514
Market Arcade Film & Arts Center	639 Main St.	Buffalo	NY	14203	8	514
Heights Theatre	210 14th St.	Elmira	NY	14903	1	565
Elmira 3	111 College Ave	Elmira	NY	14002	3	565
Hornell 3	191 Main St	Hornell	NY	14843	3	565
Lakewood Cinema 6	171-3 Fairmount Ave.	Lakewood	NY	14750	6	514
Chautauqua 2	500 Chautauqua Mall	Lakewood	NY	14750	2	514
Salamanca 2	100 Main St.	Salamanca	NY	14779	2	514
Eastern Hills Cinema	4545 Transit Rd.	Williamsville	NY	14221	3	514
Bradford 2	123 Main St.	Bradford	PA	16701	2	514

DOUGLAS THEATRE CO.

13 theatres, 84 screens.
1300 P St., Lincoln NE 68501. (402) 474-4909. FAX: (402) 474-4914. www.dougtheatres.com
CHAIRMAN
Russell Brehm
CEO & PRESIDENT
David Livingston
V.P.
Doborah Brehm
FILM BOOKER
Frank Rhodes

THEATRES

South Cinema 7	1311 S. Fort Crook Rd.	Bellevue	NE	68005	7	652
Southroads 4	Southroads Mall, 1001 Fort Crook Rd.	Bellevue	NE	68005	4	652
Cinema Twin	210 N. 13th St.	Lincoln	NE	68508	2	722
Douglas 3	1300 P St.	Lincoln	NE	68508	3	722
East Park 6	East Park Plaza, 220 N. 66th	Lincoln	NE	68505	6	722

Edgewood 3	5220 S. 56th St.	Lincoln	NE	68516	3	722
The Lincoln	1145 P St.	Lincoln	NE	68508	3	722
Plaza 4	201 N. 12th St.	Lincoln	NE	68508	4	722
South Pointe Cinema	2920 Pine Lake Rd.	Lincoln	NE	68516	6	722
Starship 9	1311 Q St.	Lincoln	NE	68508	9	722
Cinema Center Complex	2828 S. 82nd Ave.	Omaha	NE	68124	8	652
Q Cinema 9	5505 S. 120th St.	Omaha	NE	68137	9	652
20 Grand	14304 W. Maple Rd.	Omaha	NE	68164	20	652

EASTERN FEDERAL CORP.

20 theatres, 180 screens.

901 East Boulevard, Charlotte, NC 28203-5203. (704) 377-3495. FAX: (704) 358-8427.

PRESIDENT
Ira S. Meiselman
V.P. & TREASURER
Goeorge A. Royster, Jr.
SECRETARY
James I. Stewart
FILM BUYER
Curtis Fainn
V.P., OPERATIONS
Scott Baldwin
ADVERTISING COORDINATOR
Nancy Herron
SENIOR ENGINEER
James Trippe
REAL ESTATE
William Wilson

THEATRES

Sun Plaza Stadium	427 Mary Esther Cutoff	Fort Walton	FL	32549	8	686
Royal Park Stadium	3702 Newberry Rd.	Gainesville	FL	32607	16	592
Regency Eleven	1515 W. 23rd St.	Panama City	FL	32406	11	656
Port Orange Six	1015 Eagle Lake Trail	Port Orange	FL	32129	6	534
Village Green	9410 South US 1 Hwy.	Port St Lucie	FL	34986	6	548
Miracle Theatre	1815 Thomasville Rd.	Tallahassee	FL	32303	5	530
Movies @ Governor's Square	1501 Governor's Square Blvd	Tallahassee	FL	32301	12	530
Movies at Timberlyne 6	120 Banks St.	Chapel Hill	NC	27514	6	560
Plaza Theatre	141 Elliott Rd.	Chapel Hill	NC	27514	5	560
Delta Six Theatre	8800 W.T. Harris Blvd.	Charlotte	NC	28212	6	517
Manor Theatre	607 Providence Rd.	Charlotte	NC	28207	3	517
Movies at Crownpoint 12	9630 Monroe Rd.	Charlotte	NC	28270	12	517
Starlight Stadium	11240 N. US Hwy 29	Charlotte	NC	28262	15	517
Movies at the Lake	20310 Chartwell Center Dr.	Cornelius	NC	28031	12	517
Movies at Franklin Square	3778 East Franklin Blvd	Gastonia	NC	28056	14	704
Town & Country Four	3525 Fayetteville Rd.	Lumberton	NC	28359	4	570
North Pointe	4660 Brownsboro Rd.	Winston-Salem	NC	27106	5	518
Starlight Cinema	141 Interstate Blvd	Anderson	SC	29621	14	567
Movies at Mt. Pleasant	963 Houston-Northcutt Blvd.	Charleston	SC	29464	12	519
Movies at Polo Road	9700 Two Notch Rd.	Columbia	SC	29223	8	546

EDWARDS THEATRES

75 theatres, 760 screens.

300 Newport Center Dr., Newport Beach, CA 92660. (949) 640-4600. FAX: (949) 721-7170.

CO-CHAIRMAN & CEO
W. James Edwards III
SNEIOR V.P. & CFO
John C. Fuller
V.P, OPERATIONS
Kevin Frabotta
EXECUTIVE V.P. & HEAD FILM BUYER
Chris S. LeRoy

THEATRES

Edwards Aliso Viejo Stadium 20	26701 Aliso Creek Rd.	Aliso Viejo	CA	92656	20	803
Edwards Alhambra Place 5	100 Bay State St.	Alhambra	CA	91801	5	803
Edwards Atlantic Palace 10	700 West Main St.	Alhambra	CA	91801	10	803
Edwards Anaheim Hills 14	8032 E. Santa Ana Canyon Rd.	Anaheim Hills	CA	92808	14	803
Edwards Foothill Center 10	854 E. Alosta	Azusa	CA	91702	10	803
Edwards Bakersfield 14	9000 G. Ming Ave.	Bakersfield	CA	93311	14	800
Edwards Brea Plaza 5	453 Associated Rd.	Brea	CA	92821	5	803
Edwards Brea Stadium 22	155 West Birch St.	Brea	CA	92821	22	803
Grand Palace Stadium Calabasas	4767 Commons Way	Calabasas	CA	91302	6	803
Edwards Camarillo 12	680 Ventura Blvd.	Camarillo	CA	93010	12	803
Edwards Cerritos 10	12761 Towne Center Dr.	Cerritos	CA	90701	10	803
Edwards Corona 15	351 West Rincon St.	Corona	CA	91720	15	803
Edwards Triangle Square 8	1870 Harbor Blvd.	Costa Mesa	CA	92627	8	803
Edwards Cinema Center 4	2701 E. Harbor Blvd.	Costa Mesa	CA	92626	4	803
Edwards South Coast Village 3	1561 W. Sunflower Ave.	Costa Mesa	CA	92704	3	803
Edwards Town Center 4	3199 Park Center Dr.	Costa Mesa	CA	92626	4	803
Edwards Metro Pointe 12	901 South Coast Dr.	Costa Mesa	CA	92626	12	803
Edwards Flower Hill 4	2430 Via De La Valle	Del Mar	CA	92014	4	825
Edwards Rancho San Diego 15	2951 Jamacha Rd.	El Cajon	CA	92020	15	825
Edwards El Monte 8	10661 Valley Blvd.	El Monte	CA	91731	8	803
Edwards El Toro 5	23633 El Toro Rd.	El Toro	CA	92630	5	803
Edwards Fairfield Stadium 16	1549 Gateway Blvd.	Fairfield	CA	94533	16	862
Edwards Fresno Stadium 21	7750 N. Blackstone Ave.	Fresno	CA	93720	21	866
Edwards Fresno IMAX	7768 N. Black Stone Ave.	Fresno	CA	93720	1	866
Edwards Charter Center 5	7822 Warner Ave.	Huntington Beach	CA	92648	5	803
Edwards Pierside 6	300 Pacific Coast Hwy.	Huntington Beach	CA	92648	6	803
Edwards Woodbridge 5	4626 Barranca Pkwy.	Irvine	CA	92604	5	803
Edwards University Town Center 6	4245 Campus Dr.	Irvine	CA	92715	6	803
Edwards Westpark 8	3755 Alton Pkwy.	Irvine	CA	92606	8	803
Edwards Irvine Spectrum 21 + IMAX	65 Fortune Dr.	Irvine	CA	92618	22	803
Edwards Park Place 10	3031 Michelson Dr.	Irvine	CA	92612	10	803

Edwards Marketplace Stadium 10	13782 Jamboree Rd.	Irvine	CA	92602	10	803
Edwards La Verne 12	1950 Foothill Blvd.	La Verne	CA	91750	12	803
Edwards South Coast Laguna 2	156 S. Coast Hwy	Laguna Beach	CA	92651	2	803
Edwards Ocean Ranch 7	32401 Golden Lantern	Laguna Niguel	CA	92656	7	803
Edwards Rancho Niguel 8	25471 Rancho Niguel Rd.	Laguna Niguel	CA	92677	8	803
Edwards Long Beach 26	7501 Carson Blvd	Long Beach	CA	90808	26	803
Edwards Trabuco Hills	27765 Santa Margarita Pkwy.	Mission Viejo	CA	92691	5	803
Edwards Kaleidoscope Stadium 10	Crown Valley Pkwy.	Mission Viejo	CA	92691	10	803
Edwards Towngate 8	12625 Frederick	Moreno Valley	CA	92553	8	803
Edwards Newport 6	300 Newport Center Dr.	Newport Beach	CA	92660	6	803
Edwards Island 7	999 Newport Center Dr.	Newport Beach	CA	92660	7	803
Edwards Lido	5459 Via Lido	Newport Beach	CA	92663	1	803
Edwards Ontario Palace 22 + IMAX	4900 E. 4th St.	Ontario	CA	91764	22	803
Edwards Ontario Mountain Village 14	N. Mountain Ave.	Ontario	CA	91764	14	803
Edwards Poway 10	13475 Poway Rd.	Poway	CA	92064	10	825
Edwards Rancho Santa Margarita	30632 Santa Margarita Pkwy.	Rncho S. Margarita	CA	92688	6	803
Edwards Jurupa Stadium 14	8032 Limonite Ave	Riverside	CA	92509	14	803
Edwards Del Mar Highlands 8	12905 El Camino Real	San Diego	CA	92130	8	825
Edwards Mira Mesa Stadium 18	10733 Westview Pkwy.	San Diego	CA	92126	18	825
Edwards Fremont 4	On Monterey St.	San Luis Obispo	CA	93403	4	855
Edwards Mission 3	1025 Montery St.	San Luis Obispo	CA	93401	3	855
Edwards San Marcos Stadium 18	1180 West San Marcos	San Marcos	CA	92069	18	825
Edwards Hutton Center 8	9 Hutton Centre Dr.	Santa Ana	CA	92707	8	803
Edwards Valencia Stadium 21	Majic Mountain Pkwy.	Santa Clarita	CA	91355	21	803
Edwards Canyon Country 10	18800 Soledad Canyon Rd.	Santa Clarita	CA	91355	10	803
Edwards Valencia IMAX	24201 Valencia Blvd.	Santa Clarita	CA	91355	1	803
Edwards Santa Maria	101 Freeway At Stowell Rd.	Santa Maria	CA	93454	10	855
Edwards Simi Valley Plaza 10	1457 Los Angeles Ave.	Simi Valley	CA	93065	10	803
Edwards El Paso Stadium Cinema	8630 South Garfield	South Gate	CA	90280	20	803
Edwards Temecula Stadium 15	40750 Winchester Rd.	Temecula	CA	92591	15	803
Edwards Temple 4	Rosemead At Las Tunas	Temple City	CA	91780	4	803
Edwards Tustin Marketplace	2961 El Camino Real	Tustin	CA	92782	6	803
Edwards West Covina 18	265 South Glendora Ave.	West Covina	CA	91790	18	803
Edwards Westminster 10	6721 Westminster Blvd.	Westminster	CA	92683	10	803
Edwards Westminster Mall 4	1044 Westminster Mall	Westminster	CA	92683	4	803
Edwards Grand Teton Stadium 14	2702 S. 25th St.	Ammon	ID	83401	14	758
Edwards Boise Stadium 21	7701 Overland Rd.	Boise	ID	83704	21	757
Edwards Boise IMAX	7703 Overland Rd.	Boise	ID	83709	2	757
Edwards Nampa Stadium 14	2001 N. Cassia St.	Nampa	ID	83651	14	757
Edwards Greenway Palace 24	3839 Westlayan	Houston	TX	77027	24	618
Edwards Houston Marq*E 23 + IMAX	7620 Kati Freeway	Houston	TX	77024	23	618

F & F/VALUE THEATRES

9 theatres, 41 screens.
707 Skokie Blvd., Ste. 400, Northbrook, IL 60062. (847) 480-0330. FAX: (847) 480-1649.
PRESIDENT
Robert Fink
DIRECTOR OF OPERATIONS/FILM BUYER
Larry D. Hanson
FILM BOOKER
Bene Stein

THEATRES

Arlington Theatres	53 S. Evergreen St.	Arlington Heights	IL	60005	6	602
Harlem Carners Theatre	7340 W. 87th St.	Bridgeview	IL	60455	6	602
Buffalo Grove Theatres	120 McHenry Rd.	Buffalo Grove	IL	60089	5	602
Davis Art Theatre	4614 N. Lincoln Ave.	Chicago	IL	60625	1	602
Davis Theatre	4614 N. Lincoln Ave	Chicago	IL	60625	3	602
Morton Grove Theatre	7300 W. Dempster	Morton Grove	IL	60053	4	602
Bremen Theatres	15926 Oak Park Ave	Tinley Park	IL	60477	6	602
Delavan Theatre	405 E. Walworth Ave.	Delavan	WI	53147	2	617
Giant 41 Drive-In	7701 S. 27th St.	Franklin	WI	53132	4	617
Geneva Theatre	244 Broad St.	Lake Geneva	WI	53147	4	617

FRIDLEY THEATRES

36 theatres, 87 screens.
1321 Walnut St. Des Moines, IA 50309. (515) 282-9287. FAX: (515) 282-8310.
OWNER
R. L. Fridley
FILM BUYER
Brian Firdley

THEATRES

Algona Theatre	216 E. State St.	Algona	IA	50511	1	611
The Springwood 9	2829 S. Ankeny Blvd.	Ankeny	IA	50021	9	679
Atlantic	28 W. Fifth St	Atlantic	IA	50022	2	652
Boone Theatre	818 Story St.	Boone	IA	50036	1	679
Carroll 5 Theatre	407 N. Main St.	Carroll	IA	51401	5	679
American	108 E. Main	Cherokee	IA	51012	1	624
Clarion	115 N.E. 1st. Ave.	Clarion	IA	50525	1	679
Strand Theatre	309 West Adams St.	Creston	IA	50801	1	679
Viking 3	111 N. Mechanic	Decorah	IA	52101	3	637
Riviera Theatre	2209 Main.	Emmetsburg	IA	50536	1	624
Grand 3 Theatre	1031 Central Ave.	Estherville	IA	51334	3	737
Cinema Theatre and Home Video	921 Main St	Grinnell	IA	50112	2	679
Humota	515 Sumner Ave	Humboldt	IA	50548	1	679
Paramount 3	105 S. 1st St.	Indianola	IA	50125	3	679
Metropolitan 2 Theatres	515 Washington Ave.	Iowa Falls	IA	50126	2	679
Sierra Theatre	212 E. State St	Jefferson	IA	50129	1	679
Village 1 & 2 Theatre	212 E. Robinson	Knoxville	IA	50138	2	679
Capri Theatre	117 N. Center St.	Lake City	IA	51449	1	679
Castle Theatre	112 E. Main	Manchester	IA	52057	1	637
Plaza 5 Theatre	2500 S. Center St.	Marshalltown	IA	50158	5	679
Orpheum Twin	220 E. Main St.	Marshalltown	IA	50158	2	679
Temple 2	115 N. Main St.	Mt. Pleasant	IA	52641	2	682
Plaza 4	1903 Park Ave.	Muscatine	IA	52761	4	682

Camelot	1114 6th St.	Nevada	IA	50201	1	679
Paramount Theatre	26 S. Fredrick Ave.	Oelwein	IA	50662	2	637
Penn Centre Twin	216 2nd Ave.	Oskaloosa	IA	52577	2	679
Grand 3 Theatre	1312 2nd St.	Perry	IA	50220	3	679
Copper Creek 9	1325 Copper Creek Dr.	Pleasant Hill	IA	50317	9	679
Grand Theatre	410 Coolbaugh	Red Oak	IA	51566	1	652
Spencer 3	504 Grand Ave.	Spencer	IA	51301	3	624
Vista 3	712 Lake Ave.	Storm Lake	IA	50588	3	624
State Theatre	123 E. Washington St.	Washington	IA	52353	1	637
Webster Theatre	610 2nd St	Webster City	IA	50595	1	679
Grand	316 W. 3rd St.	Grand Island	NE	68801	1	722
Rivoli3	528 W. 2nd St.	Hastings	NE	68902	3	722
Cinema 3	224 W. View Plaza	McCook	NE	69001	3	722

GENERAL CINEMA THEATRES

93 theatres, 784 screens.

(A subsidiary of GC Companies, Inc.) 1300 Boylston St., Chestnut Hill, MA 02467. (617) 264-8000. FAX: (617) 277-8875.

CHAIRMAN
Paul Del Rossi
PRESIDENT
Frank Stryjewski
CFO
Gail Edwards
SENIOR V.P., FILM
Alan DeLemos
V.P., CONSTRUCTION
Douglas Alexander
SENIOR V.P., MARKETING
Page Thompson
V.P., REAL ESTATE
John Selden
DIRECTOR, HUMAN RESOURCES
Brenna Jones
DIRECTOR, PUBLIC RELATIONS
Brian Callaghan
DIRECTOR, PURCHASING
Tammy Diorio

THEATRES

GC Beverly Connection	100 N. La Cienega Blvd.	Beverly Hills	CA	90048	6	803
GC Birdcage Centre	6075 Sunrise Blvd.	Citrus Heights	CA	95610	6	862
GC Dublin Place 6 Cinemas	7000 Amador Plaza Rd.	Dublin	CA	94568	6	807
GC Glendale Central Cinema 5	501 N. Orange	Glendale	CA	91203	5	803
GC Hollywood Galaxy	7021 Hollywood Blvd.	Hollywood	CA	90069	6	803
GC Redondo Cinema 3	1509 Hawthorne Blvd.	Redondo Beach	CA	90278	3	803
GC Galleria at South Bay	1815 Hawthorne Blvd	Redondo Beach	CA	90278	16	803
GC Sherman Oaks Cinema	14424 Milbank St.	Sherman Oaks	CA	91403	7	803
GC Avco Cinema	10840 Wilshire Blvd.	Westwood	CA	90024	4	803
GC Mazza Gallerie	5300 Wisconsin Ave.	Washington	DC	20015	7	511
GC Christiana Mall	215 Christiana Mall	Newark	DE	19702	5	504
GC Parkway Pointe	3101 Cobb Pkwy.	Atlanta	GA	30339	15	524
GC Ford City 14	7601 S. Cicero Ave	Chicago	IL	60652	14	602
GC City North 14	2600 N. Western Ave.	Chicago	IL	60647	14	602
GC Deerbrook	180 So Waukegan Rd.	Deerfield	IL	60015	4	602
GC Yorktown	Yorktown Shopping Ctr.	Lombard	IL	60148	17	602
GC Premium Cinema at the Yorktown	Yorktown Shopping Ctr	Lombard	IL	60148	1	602
GC Lincoln Mall	4647 Lincoln Mall Dr.	Matteson	IL	60443-2333	3	602
GC Randhurst	101 E. Euclid Ave	Mt. Prospect	IL	60056	16	602
GC Northbrook	1525 Lake Cook Rd.	Northbrook	IL	60062	14	602
GC Lakehurst	601 Lakehurst Rd.	Waukegan	IL	60085	12	602
GC Greenwood Park 14	461 South Greenwood Park Dr.	Greenwood	IN	46142	14	527
GC Castleton Square	6135 E. 86th St.	Indianapolis	IN	46250	3	527
GC Eastgate Mall 6	7150 E. Washington St.	Indianapolis	IN	46219	6	527
GC Clearwater Crossing 12	4016 E. 82nd St.	Indianapolis	IN	46250	12	527
GC Lafayette Sq.	Southeast Parking Lot	Indianapolis	IN	46254	3	527
GC Southlake Mall Cinema	2475 Southlake Mall	Merrillville	IN	46410	9	602
GC County Seat Cinema 1-6	2849 Calumet	Valpariaiso	IN	46383	6	602
GC Fenway Theatre	201 Brookline Ave.	Boston	MA	02115	13	506
GC Braintree	121 Grandview Rd.	Braintree	MA	02184	10	506
GC Burlington 10	20 South Ave.	Burlington	MA	01803	10	506
GC Chestnut Hill	27 Boylston St.	Chestnut Hill	MA	02167	5	506
GC Framingham 16	Rt. 9 & 30, Shoppers World	Framingham	MA	01701	16	506
GC Premium Cinema at Framingham	22 Flutie Pass	Framingham	MA	01701	1	506
GC N. Dartmouth Mall	Rt. 6 & Faunce Corner RD.	N. Dartmouth	MA	02747	12	521
GC Tyngsboro	440 Middlesex Rd.	Tyngsboro	MA	01879	12	506
GC Columbia City 3	10205 Wincopin Circle	Columbia	MD	21044	3	512
GC Owings Mills 17	10100 Mill Run Circle	Owings Mills	MD	21117	17	512
GC Towson Commons 8	435 York Rd.	Towson	MD	21204	8	512
GC Security Square 8	1717 Rolling Rd.	Woodlawn	MD	21207	8	512
GC Maine Mall Cinemas	413 Maine Mall Rd.	S. Portland	ME	04106	7	500
GC Mall Of America Cinema 14	401 South Ave.	Bloomington	MN	55425	14	613
GC Centennial Lakes 8	7311 France Ave.	Edina	MN	55435	8	613
GC Har Mar Cinema 11	2100 N. Snelling	Roseville	MN	55113	11	613
GC Shelard Park	411 Ford Rd.	St. Louis Park	MN	55426	5	613
GC Bridgewater Commons 7	400 Commons Way	Bridgewater	NJ	08807	7	501
GC Clifton Commons 16	405 Route 3	Clifton	NJ	07014	16	501
GC Deptford Mall 6	Deptford Center Rd.	Deptford	NJ	08096	6	504
GC Rutgers Cinemas	1030 Easton Ave.	Somerset	NJ	08873	6	501
GC Essex Green Cinema	1 Prospect Ave.	West Orange	NJ	07052	9	501
GC University 8	4100 Maple Rd.	Amherst	NY	14226	8	514
GC Bay Plaza Cinemas	2210 Bartow Ave.	Bronx	NY	10475	13	501
GC Walden Galleria	6 Walden Galleria	Cheektowaga	NY	14225	12	514
GC McKinley Mall	634 McKinley Mall	Hamburg	NY	14219	6	514
GC Marketplace Mall Cinema	100 Miracle Mile	Rochester	NY	14623	7	538
GC Pittsford Plaza Cinema	3349 Monroe Ave.	Rochester	NY	14618	6	538
GC West Market Plaza Cinema	3879 Medina Rd.	Akron	OH	44313	7	510

GC Ridge Park Sq Cinema	4788 Ridge Rd.	Brooklyn	OH	44144	8	510
GC Westland 8	4265 Shoppers Lane	Columbus	OH	43228	8	535
GC Plaza Cinemas Chapel Hill	500 Howe Rd.	Cuyahoga Falls	OH	44221	8	510
GC Midway Mall Cinemas	2650 Midway Mall	Elyria	OH	44035	8	510
GC Erie Commons Cinema 8	8057 Plaza Blvd	Mentor	OH	44060	8	510
GC Parmatown Cinema	8141 W. Ridgewood Dr.	Parma	OH	44129	5	510
GC Westgate Mall Cinema	3200 Linden Rd.	Rocky River	OH	44116	6	510
GC Westwood Town Center	21653 Center Ridge Rd.	Rocky River	OH	44116	8	510
GC Franklin Mills 14	Franklin Mills Mall	Philadelphia	PA	19154	14	504
GC Plymouth Meeting 12	Plymouth Meeting Mall	Plymouth Meeting	PA	19462	12	504
GC Lehigh Valley Cinema 8	740 Lehigh Valley Mall	Whitehall	PA	18052	8	504
GC Wyoming Valley Mall 1-4	East End Blvd.	Wilkes Barre	PA	18702	4	577
GC Wyoming Valley Mall 5-7	East End Blvd.	Wilkes Barre	PA	18702	3	577
GC Citadel Mall 6	2072 Sam Rittenburg	Charleston	SC	29407	6	519
GC Columbia Mall Cinema 1-8	7201/802 Two Notch	Columbia	SC	29223	8	546
GC Dutch Square 14	800 Bush River Rd.	Columbia	SC	29210	14	546
GC Northwoods Mall Cinema	2150 Northwoods Blvd	N. Charleston	SC	29406	8	519
GC Arlington Park	1111 W. Arbrook Blvd.	Arlington	TX	76015	8	623
GC Barton Creek Square	2901 Capital of Texas Highway	Austin	TX	78746	14	635
GC Furneaux Creek	2656 Old Denton Rd.	Carrollton	TX	75007	7	623
GC Galleria	13350 Dallas Pkwy.	Dallas	TX	75240	5	623
GC Cielo Vista Cinema 4-10	7700-A Viscount Blvd.	El Paso	TX	79925	6	765
GC Sunland Park Mall Cinema	750 sunland Park Dr.	El Paso	TX	79912	6	765
GC The Park Cinema 6	200 S. Alto Mesa Dr.	El Paso	TX	79912	6	765
GC Meyerland Plaza	100 Meyerland Plaza Shopping Center	Houston	TX	77096	8	618
GC Irving Mall 14	Hwy 183 & Beltline	Irving	TX	75062	14	623
GC Janaf Plaza 8 Cinemas	6 Janaf Shopping Center	Norfolk	VA	23502	8	544
GC Springfield Mall	195 So. Franconia Rd.	Springfield	VA	22150	10	511
GC Everett Mall {In the Mall}	In The Mall Adjacent To The Bon	Everett	WA	98205	3	819
GC Everett Mall {Mall Village}	So. End of Everett Mall Village	Everett	WA	98205	7	819
GC Renton Village 8	25 S.Grady Way	Renton	WA	98058	8	819
GC Aurora Cinema Grill	13000 Linden Ave.	Seattle	WA	98133	3	819
GC Pacific Place 11	600 Pine St.	Seattle	WA	98101	11	819
GC Cinerama	2100 4th Ave	Seattle	WA	98121	1	819
GC Kitsap Mall 8 Cinemas	10055 N.W. Kitsap Mall	Silverdale	WA	98383	8	819
GC Mayfair Mall	2500 N. Mayfair Rd.	Wauwatosa	WI	53226	18	617

GKC THEATRES

37 theatres, 273 screens.
755 Apple Orchard St., Springfield IL 62703. (217) 528-4981. FAX: (217) 528-6490.
CHAIRMAN
George G. Kerasotes
PRESIDENT
Beth Kerasotes
CFO & EXECUTVE VICE PRESIDENT, FINANCE
Jeffrey A. Cole
EXECUTIVE V.P., FILM & MARKETING
Bryan Jeffries
V.P., CONCESSION
Krystal LaReese
V.P., CONSTRUCTION & DEVELOPMENT
Matt Heissinger
DIRECTOR OF MARKETING
James G. Whitman
V.P., OPERATIONS
Eileen Grace

THEATRES

GKC American Cinemas	4690 N. Oracle Rd.	Tucson	AZ	85704	6	789
GKC Parkway Cinemas	2103 N. Veterans Pkwy	Bloomington	IL	61704	8	675
GKC Palace Cinemas	415 Detroit Dr.	Bloomington	IL	61704	9	675
GKC Country Fair 5	113 S. Mattis Ave.	Champaign	IL	61820	5	648
GKC Beverly 18	910 Meijer Dr.	Champaign	IL	61821	18	648
GKC Strand	2360 S. Mt Zion Rd.	Decatur	IL	62521	10	648
GKC Market Square	2160 Sycamore Rd.	Dekalb	IL	60115	12	602
GKC Campus Cinema	1015 Blackhawk	Dekalb	IL	60115	4	602
GKC Hickory Point Cinema	US Highway 51	Forsyth	IL	62535	8	648
GKC Wanee Twin Cinema	106 S. Main St.	Kewanee	IL	61443	2	682
GKC Lincoln Cinemas	215 S. Kickapoo St	Lincoln	IL	62656	2	648
GKC Orpheum Cinema	515 W. Gore Rd.	Morris	IL	60450	10	602
GKC University	1010 S. Main St	Normal	IL	61761	6	675
GKC College Hills Cinema	1503 E. College Ave	Normal	IL	61761	4	675
GKC Roxy Cinema	827 La Salle St.	Ottawa	IL	61350	6	602
GKC Landmark 12	3225 N. Dries Lane	Peoria	IL	61604	12	675
GKC Westlake 5	2601 Westlake St.	Peoria	IL	61615	5	675
GKC Peru Mall 8 Cinema	3940 Route 251	Peru	IL	61354	8	602
GKC Crescent Twin	313 W. Madison St.	Pontiac	IL	61764	2	602
GKC Apollo Twin Cinema	455 S. Main St.	Princeton	IL	61356	2	682
GKC Sauk Valley Cinema	4110 E. 30th St.	Sterling	IL	61081	8	682
GKC Sunnyland 10	Washington Rd.	Washington	IL	61571	10	675
GKC Capri Cinemas	205 Dry Branch Dr	Crawfordsville	IN	47933	8	527
GKC Encore Park 8 Cinema	2701 Cassopolis St.	Elkhart	IN	46514	8	588
GKC Royal Knights 3	101 South Second	Alpena	MI	49707	3	583
GKC State Cinema 5	206 N. 2nd St.	Alpena	MI	49707	5	583
GKC Towne Cinema 8	15375 South Helmer Rd.	Battle Creek	MI	49015	8	563
GKC Lakeview Square 10 Cinema	5775 Beckley Rd.	Battlecreek	MI	49015	10	563
GKC Big Rapids 4 Cinemas	213 S. Michigan	Big Rapids	MI	49307	4	540
GKC Birchwood 10	4350 24th St.	Fort Gratiot	MI	48059	10	505
GKC Plaza Cinema	1700 N. Wisner St.	Jackson	MI	49202	7	551
GKC Lyric Cinema 4	208 S. James St.	Ludington	MI	49431	4	540
GKC Royal 10	1351 O'dovero Dr.	Marquette	MI	49855	10	553
GKC Fashion Square Mall 10	4511 Fashion Square	Saginqaw	MI	48604	10	513
GKC Varsity Cinema	1098 W. 3 Mile Rd.	Sault Ste Marie	MI	49783	10	540
GKC Grand Traverse Cinema 9	3200 S. Airport Rd.	Traverse City	MI	49684	9	540
GKC Horizon 10	3587 Market Place Circle	Traverse City	MI	49684	10	540

GEORGIA THEATRE COMPANY II

21 theatres, 177 screens.
2999 Piedmont Rd., Atlanta, GA 30305. (404) 264-4542. FAX: (404) 233-8184.
CHAIRMAN & PRESIDENT
William J. Stembler
VICE-CHAIRMAN
John H. Stembler
V.P., OPERATIONS
Scott Bagwell
V.P., FILM
Clifford "Kip" Smiley, Jr.
VICE PRESIDENT
John Stemdler, Jr.
SECRETARY
Dennis Merton

THEATRES

GTC Beechwood Stadium 11	196 Alps Rd.	Athens	GA	30606	11	524
GTC Masters 7	2824 Washington Rd.	Augusta	GA	30909	7	520
GTC Glynn Place 11	200 Mall Blvd.	Brunswick	GA	31525	11	561
GTC Mall 8 Theatre	1004 Bankhead Hwy.	Carrollton	GA	30117	8	524
GTC Newton Twin Cinema	US 278	Covington	GA	30014	2	524
GTC Evans 12 Cinema	4365 Towne Center Dr.	Evans	GA	30809	12	520
GTC Hollywood 14	659 N.W. Green Hill Circle	Gainesville	GA	30501	14	524
GTC Lakeshore Mall Cinema	1285 W. Washington St.	Gainesville	GA	30501	4	524
GTC Town Center 10	700 Gwinnett Dr.	Lawrenceville	GA	30045	10	524
GTC Park 12 Cobb	2925 Gordy Pkwy.	Marietta	GA	30066	12	524
GTC Moultrie Twin	Business 319	Moultrie	GA	31768	2	525
GTC Rome VII Cinema	2535 Shorter Ave.	Rome	GA	30161	7	524
GTC Kings Bay Cinemas	201 City Smitty Dr.	St Marys	GA	31558	10	561
GTC Island Cinemas 7	500 Sea Island Rd.	St Simons	GA	31522	7	561
GTC Gateway Cinemas	US 19 South	Thomasville	GA	31792	7	530
GTC Valdosta Mall	1700 Norman Dr.	Valdosta	GA	31602	6	530
GTC Ashley Cinemas	2812 N. Ashley St.	Valdosta	GA	31601	8	530
GTC Parkway 6 Cinema	821 Richard B Russell Pkwy.	Warner Robins	GA	31063	6	503
GTC Galleria 10 Cinema	2980 Watson Blvd.	Warner Robins	GA	31093	10	503
GTC Waycross Mall Cinema 7	2260 Brunswick Hwy.	Waycross	GA	31503	7	561
GTC Cherokee 16	2295 Towne Lake Pkwy.	Woodstock	GA	30189	16	524

GOODRICH QUALITY THEATERS, INC.

35 theatres, 298 screens.
4417 Broadmoor S.E., Kentwood, MI 49512. (616) 698-7733. FAX: (616) 698-7220. www.gqti.com
PRESIDENT & SECRETARY
Robert Emmett Goodrich
V.P. & GENERAL MANAGER
William T. McMannis
CFO
Ross Pettinga
FILM BUYER
Wanda J. Holst
CONTROLLER
Ronald B. Muscott
OPERATIONS MANAGER
Martin S. Betz
MARKETING MANAGER
Matthew Johnson
MICHIGAN DISTRICT MANAGER
Reed L. Simon
KANSAS, MISSOURI, INDIANA & ILLINOIS DISTRICT MANAGER
Philipp Carter

THEATRES

Randall 16	550 N. Randall Rd.	Batavia	IL	60510	16	602
Kendall 10	95 5th St.	Oswego	IL	60543	10	602
Willow Knolls 14	4100 W. Willow Knolls Dr.	Peoria	IL	61615	14	675
Savoy 16	232 W. Burwash	Savoy	IL	61874	16	648
Applewood 9	1704 E. 60th	Anderson	IN	46013	9	527
Huntington 7	350 Hauenstein Rd.	Huntington	IN	46750	7	509
Eastside 10	300 Farabee Dr.	Lafayette	IN	47905	10	582
Lafayette 7	3525 McCarty Ln.	Lafayette	IN	47904	7	582
Wabash Landing 9	300 E. State St.	Lafayette	IN	47906	9	582
Portage 9	5935 US Route 6	Portage	IN	46368	9	602
Pittsburg 8	202 Centennial Dr.	Pittsburg	KS	66762	8	603
Branson 4	1840 W. 76 Hwy.	Branson	MO	65616	4	619
Forum 8	1209 Forum Katy Pkwy.	Columbia	MO	65203	8	604
Capital 8	3550 Country Club Dr.	Jefferson City	MO	65109	8	604
Capital 4	3600 Country Club Dr.	Jefferson City	MO	65109	4	604
Springfield 8	3200 E. Montclair St.	Springfield	MO	65806	8	619
Town & Country 6	2711 N. Kansas	Springfield	MO	65803	6	619
Quality 16	3686 Jackson Rd.	Ann Arbor	MI	48103	16	505
West Columbia 7	2500 W. Columbia	Battle Creek	MI	49015	7	563
Bay City 8	4101 Wilder Rd.	Bay City	MI	48706	8	513
Cadillac 5	202 S. Mitchell St.	Cadillac	MI	49601	5	540
Canton 6	435 Ford Rd.	Canton	MI	48187	6	505
Hampton 6	888 N. Pine Rd.	Essexville	MI	48732	6	513
Grand Haven 9	17220 Hayes St.	Grand Haven	MI	49417	9	563
Hastings 4	213 W. State St.	Hastings	MI	49058	4	563
Holland 7	500 Waverly Rd.	Holland	MI	49423	7	563
Jackson 10	1501 N. Wisner	Jackson	MI	49202	10	551
Kalamazoo 10	820 Maple Hill Dr.	Kalamazoo	MI	49009	10	563
Lansing Mall 6	921 Mall Dr.	Lansing	MI	48917	6	551
Ada Lowell 5	2175 W. Main St.	Lowell	MI	49331	5	563
Novi Town Center 8	26085 Town Center Dr.	Novi	MI	48375	8	505
Oxford 7	48 S. Washington	Oxford	MI	48371	7	505
Krafft 8	2725 Krafft Rd.	Port Huron	MI	48060	8	505
Saginaw 8/The Quad	3250 Kabobel	Saginaw	MI	48604	12	513
Three Rivers 6	120 Enterprise Dr.	Three Rivers	MI	49093	6	563

GREATER HUNTINGTON THEATRE CORP.

4 theatres, 21 screens.
P.O. Box 1957, 401 11th St., Ste. 805, Huntington, WV 25720-1957. (304) 523-0185. FAX: (304) 525-1153. www.ourshowtimes.com
CHAIRMAN
Jack S. Hyman
PRESIDENT
Derek Hyman

THEATRES

Park Place Stadium II	600 Washington St.	Charleston	WV	25301	11	564
Camelot Theatre 2	1030 4th Ave.	Huntington	WV	25701	2	564
Cinema 4	1021 4th Ave.	Huntington	WV	25701	4	564
Keith Albee Theatre 4	925 4th Ave.	Huntington	WV	25701	4	564

HARKINS THEATRES

20 theatres, 205 screens.
7511 E. McDonald Dr., Scottsdale, AZ 85258. (480) 627-7777. (480) 443-0950.
PRESIDENT & CEO
Dan Harkins
EXECUTIVE VICE PRESIDENT
Wayne Kullander
CFO
Greta Newell
V.P., OPERATIONS
Time Spain
Mike Bowers
V.P. & GENERAL COUNSEL
Dave Farren
DIRECTOR, MARKETING SERVICES
Randall Blaum
DIRECTOR, HUMAN RESOURCES
Gina Browning
FILM BUYER
Lou Lencioni

THEATRES

Flagstaff 11	1959 S. Woodlands Village Blvd.	Flagstaff	AZ	86001	11	753
Poca Fiesta 4	1020 West Southern Ave.	Mesa	AZ	85202	4	753
Fiesta 5	1520 S. Longmoor	Mesa	AZ	85202	5	753
Superstition Sprgs 25	6950 East Superstition Springs Blvd.	Mesa	AZ	85220	25	753
Arrowhead 18	16046 N. Arrowhead Fountain Center Dr.	Peoria	AZ	85345	18	753
Arcadia 8	3975 E. Thomas Rd.	Phoenix	AZ	85018	8	753
Bell Towne Centre 8	302 E. Greenway Pkwy.	Phoenix	AZ	85022	8	753
Christown 11	5707 N. 19th Ave.	Phoenix	AZ	85015	11	753
Desert Sky Mall 6	In Desert Sky Mall	Phoenix	AZ	85033	6	753
Metro 12	9615-A Metro Pkwy.	Phoenix	AZ	85051	12	753
Paradise Valley Mall 7	4550-168 E. Cactus Rd.	Phoenix	AZ	85032	7	753
Southwest Plaza 8	6601 West Thomas Rd.	Phoenix	AZ	85033	8	753
Prescott Valley 14	7202 Pav Way.	Prescott Valley	AZ	86314	14	753
Camelview 5	7001 E. Highland Ave.	Scottsdale	AZ	85251	5	753
Fashion Square 7	7014 E. Camelback Rd.	Scottsdale	AZ	85253	7	753
Shea 14	7354 E. Shea Blvd.	Scottsdale	AZ	85260	14	753
Sedona 6	2081 Highway 89A	Sedona	AZ	86336	6	753
Arizona Mills 24	5000 Arizona Mills Circle	Tempe	AZ	85282	24	753
Centerpoint 11	730 S. Mill Ave.	Tempe	AZ	85281	11	753
Valley Art Theatre	505 S. Mill Ave.	Tempe	AZ	85821	1	753

HOYTS CINEMAS CORPORATION

105 theatres, 889 screens.
One Exeter Plaza, Boston, MA 02116-2836. (617) 646-5700. FAX: (617) 262-0707.
CEO
Paul Johnson
CFO
Terence Moriarty
SENIOR EXECUTIVE V.P., FILM
Jud Parker
SENIOR V.P., OPERATIONS & MARKETING
Daniel Vieira
SENIOR V.P., DEVELOPMENT
Hal Cleveland

THEATRES

Hoyts Cinema 12	325 E. Main St.	Branford	CT	06405	12	533
Hoyts Dayville 3	Route 12 & 101	Dayville	CT	06241	3	533
Hoyts Enfield 12	90 Elm St.	Enfield	CT	06082	12	533
Hoyts Groton 6	Groton Shoppers Mart	Groton	CT	06340	6	533
Hoyts Manchester 6	308 Broad St.	Manchester	CT	06040	6	533
Hoyts Meriden 10	61 Pomeroy Ave	Meriden	CT	06450	10	533
Hoyts Mystic Village 3	Route 27, Old Mystic Village	Mystic	CT	06355	3	533
Hoyts New Canaan Playhouse 2	89 Elm St.	New Canaan	CT	06840	2	501
Hoyts Norwich Twin	109 Salem Turnpike	Norwich	CT	06360	2	533
Hoyts Saybrook 6	210 Main St.	Old Saybrook	CT	06475	6	533
Hoyts Stonington 10	85 Voluntown Rd.	Pawcatuck	CT	06379	10	533
Hoyts Saybrook Twin	166 Main St.	Saybrook	CT	06475	2	533
Hoyts Simsbury 8	530 Bushy Hill Rd.	Simsbury	CT	06070	8	533
Hoyts Waterbury 12	495 Union St.	Waterbury	CT	06705	12	533
Hoyts Waterford 9	123 Cross Rd.	Waterford	CT	06385	9	533
Hoyts Willimantic 6	1 Jillson Square	Willimantic	CT	06226	6	533
Hoyts Wilton 4	Wilton Campus Center	Wilton	CT	06897	4	501
Hoyts Acton 4	Rt. 2A	Acton	MA	01718	4	506
Hoyts Bellingham Cinema 14	Exit 18 Off Of 495	Bellingham	MA	02019	14	506
Hoyts Solomon Pond 15, Berlin	Exit 25B Off Tr. 290	Berlin	MA	01503	15	506
Hoyts Westgate Theatre	Off Rt. 27	Brockton	MA	02043	7	506
Hoyts Buzzards Bay Theatre	105 Main St.	Buzzards Bay	MA	02532	4	506
Hoyts East Bridgewater	6 Carriage Crossing	East Bridgewater	MA	02324	6	506
Hoyts Harwich 6	Route 137	East Harwich	MA	02645	6	506
Hoyts Falmouth 6	Route 28	Falmouth	MA	02540	6	506

Hoyts Airport 8	Rte. 132	Hyannis	MA	02601	8	506
Hoyts Cape Cod Mall Cinema 12	769 Route 132	Hyannis	MA	02601	12	506
Hoyts Independence Mall 14	off of Route 3	Kingston	MA	02364	14	506
Hoyts Berkshire Mall 10	Route 8 and Old State Rd.	Lanesboro	MA	01237	10	532
Hoyts Mashpee 6	Routes 28 and 151	Mashpee	MA	02649	6	506
Hoyts Nickelodeon Cinema	742 Nathan Ellis Hwy	N. Falmouth	MA	02556	4	506
Hoyts North Weymouth	789 Bridge St.	N. Weymouth	MA	02189	10	506
Hoyts Salisbury 6	201 Elm St.	Salibury	MA	01952	6	506
Hoyts Sharon 8	Interstate 95	Sharon	MA	02067	8	506
Hoyts South Dennis 12	Patriot Square Mall, 2-6 Enterprise Rd.	South Dennis	MA	02660	12	506
Hoyts Silver City 10	2 Galleria Mall Dr.	Taunton	MA	02780	10	521
Hoyts Westborough 12	231 Turnpike Rd.	Westborough	MA	01581	12	506
Hoyts Bowie Crossing 14	15200 Major Lansdale Blvd.	Bowie	MD	20716	14	511
Hoyts Frederick 10	1301 West Patrick St.	Frederick	MD	21701	10	511
Hoyts West Ridge 6	West Ridge Square, Route 40	Frederick	MD	21701	6	511
Hoyts Hunt Valley 12	11511 McCormick Rd.	Hunt Valley	MD	21030	12	512
Hoyts West Nursery 14	1591 W. Nursery Rd.	Linthicum	MD	21090	14	512
Hoyts Salisbury 6	317 E. Main St.	Salisbury	MD	21801	6	576
Hoyts Salisbury 10	2312 N. Salisbury Blvd.	Salisbury	MD	21801	10	576
Hoyts Cranberry Mall 9	400 N. Center St.	Westminster	MD	21157	9	512
Hoyts Auburn 10	746 Center St.	Auburn	ME	04210	10	500
Hoyts Augusta 10	23 Market Place Dr.	Augusta	ME	04330	10	500
Hoyts Bangor 10	557 Stillwater Ave.	Bango	ME	04401	10	537
Hoyts Biddeford 8	420 L. Alfred Rd.	Biddeford	ME	04005	8	500
Hoyts Brunswick 10	19 Gurnet St.	Brunswick	ME	04011	10	500
Hoyts Maine Coast 2	Route 1A	Ellsworth	ME	04605	2	537
Hoyts Falmouth 10	206 US Route 1	Falmouth	ME	04105	10	500
Hoyts Aroostook Centre 8	830 Main St.	Presque Isle	ME	04769	8	552
Hoyts Clarks Pond 8	333 Clarks Pond Rd.	South Portland	ME	04106	8	500
Hoyts Waterville 6	250 Kenedy Memorial Dr.	Waterville	ME	04901	6	500
Hoyts Bedford Mall 7	Bedford Mall	Bedford	NH	03110	7	506
Hoyts Concord 10	282 Loudon Rd.	Concord	NH	03301	10	506
Hoyts Gilford 8	9 Old Lake Shore Rd.	Gilford	NH	03246	8	506
Hoyts Hooksett 8	100 Technology Dr.	Hooksett	NH	03106	8	506
Hoyts Key 6	121 Key Rd.	Keene	NH	03431	6	506
Hoyts Manchester 9	1279 South Willow St.	Manchester	NH	03103	9	506
Hoyts Nashua Mall 4	Everett Turnpike & Broad St	Nashua	NH	03063	4	506
Hoyts Newington 12	45 Gosling Rd.	Newington	NH	03801	12	506
Hoyts Portsmouth 5	581 Lafayette Rd.	Portsmouth	NH	03801	5	506
Hoyts Dover	20 Tri City Plaza	Somersworth	NH	03878	4	506
Hoyts Tri City Quad	20 Tri City Plaza	Somersworth	NH	03867	4	506
Hoyts Colony 4 Brant Beach	3401 Long Beach Island Blvd	Beach Haven	NJ	08008	4	501
Hoyts Colonial 4	Bay Ave & Center St.	Beach Haven	NJ	08008	4	501
Hoyts Beach Haven 4	Herbert Ave & Long Beach Blvd	Beach Haven	NJ	08008	4	501
Hoyts Moorlyn 4	820 Boardwalk	Ocean City	NJ	08226	4	504
Hoyts Pennsauken 10	5107 East Route 70	Pennsauken	NJ	08109	10	504
Hoyts Crossgates 12	120 Washington Ave.	Albany	NY	12203	12	532
Hoyts Crossgates 18	120 Washington Ave.	Albany	NY	12203	18	532
Hoyts Binghamton 12	900 Front St	Binghamton	NY	13901	12	502
Hoyts Camillus 10	Route 5 Camillus Mall	Camillus	NY	13031	10	555
Hoyts Cicero 13	5865 East Circle Dr.	Cicero	NY	13039	13	555
Hoyts Great Northern 10	Route 481 & 31	Clay	NY	13041	10	555
Hoyts Clifton Park 8	Clifton Country Mall	Clifton Park	NY	12065	8	532
Hoyts Shoppingtown 10	3649 Erie Blvd	Dewitt	NY	13214	10	555
Hoyts Fishkill 10	Route 9	Fishkill	NY	12524	10	501
Hoyts Elmira 10	3300 Chambers Rd.	Horseheads	NY	14845	10	565
Hoyts Ithaca 10	40 Catherwood Rd.	Ithaca	NY	14850	10	555
Hoyts Ithaca 4	2 Cinemas Dr.	Ithaca	NY	14850	4	555
Hoyts Hudson Valley Mall	Hudson Valley Mall	Kingston	NY	12401	12	501
Hoyts Latham 10	800 New Loudon Rd.	Latham	NY	12110	10	532
Hoyts Sangertown 9	Commercial Dr.	New Hartford	NY	13413	9	526
Hoyts Champlain Centre 8	60 Smithfield Blvd.	Plattsburgh	NY	12901	8	523
Hoyts Galleria 12	790 South Rd.	Poughkeepsie	NY	12601	12	501
Hoyts Aviation 7	Aviation Mall Rd.	Queensbury	NY	12804	7	532
Hoyts Route 9 Cinema 5	Rte. 9	Queensbury	NY	12804	5	532
Hoyts East Greenbush 8	279 Troy Rd.	Rensselaer	NY	12144	8	532
Hoyts Greece Ridge 12	176 Greece Ridge Center Dr.	Rochester	NY	14626	12	538
Hoyts Wilton Mall 8	3065 Route 50	Saratoga Springs	NY	12866	8	532
Hoyts Carousel Center 19	9586 Carousel Center	Syracuse	NY	13290	19	555
Hoyts Riverside 8	Riverside Mall	Utica	NY	13502	8	526
Hoyts Salmon Run Mall 8	Arsenal St. Rd.	Watertown	NY	13601	8	549
Hoyts Saucon Valley 10	3696 Route 378	Bethlehem	PA	18015	10	504
Hoyts East Harrisburg 14	1500 Caughey Dr.	Harrisburg	PA	17112	14	566
Hoyts Hazleton 10	400 Laurel Mall	Hazleton	PA	18201	10	577
Hoyts Providence 16	Providence Place Mall	Providence	RI	02903	16	521
Hoyts Nickelodeon 6	222 College St.	Burlington	VT	05401	6	523
Hoyts Newport Showplace 3	123 E. Main St.	Newport	VT	05855	3	523
Hoyts South Burlington 9	10 Fayette Rd.	South Burlington	VT	05403	9	523
Hoyts Showcase 5	1214 Williston Rd.	South Burlington	VT	05403	5	523
Hoyts Martinsburg 10	9050 Foxcroft Ave.	Martinsburg	WV	25401	10	511

KERASOTES THEATRES

90 theatres, 521 screens.

Kerasotes Building, 104 N. 6th St., Springfield, IL 62701. (217) 788-5200. FAX: (217) 788-5207. www.kerasotes.com

PRESIDENT & CEO
Anthony L. Kerasotes
EXECUTIVE V.P. & COO
Dean L. Kerasotes
HEAD FILM BUYER
Pat Rembusch
CFO
Jim Debruzzi
DIRECTOR, REAL ESTATE
Robert Gallivan
DIRECTOR, OPERATIONS
Tim Johnson
DIRECTOR, TECHNICAL SERVICES & PURCHASING
Fred Walraven
ADVERTISING MANAGER
Barry Tester

THEATRES

Plaza Cinema 3	300 Main St., Ste 460	Keobuk	IA	52632	3	717
Toler 2	711 W. Washington	Benton	IL	62812	2	632
Showplace 12	1221 W. Boughton Rd.	Bolingbrook	IL	60440	12	602
University Place 8	1370 E. Main St.	Carbondale	IL	62902	8	632
Varsity Theatre 3	418 South Illinois	Carbondale	IL	62902	3	632
Fox Eastgate 3	712 East Walnut	Carbondale	IL	62902	3	632
Illinois Theatre	126 S. Locust	Centralia	IL	62801	2	609
Will Rogers Theatre	705 Monroe St.	Charleston	IL	61920	2	648
Village Mall Cinema	2917 N. Vermilion	Danville	IL	61834	6	648
Eastgate Cinema	625 Lewis & Clark Blvd	East Alton	IL	62024	6	609
Showplace 12	6633 Center Grove Rd.	Edwardsville	IL	62025	12	609
Sandburg Mall Cinema	1150 West Carl Sandburg	Galesburg	IL	61401	2	682
West Cinema	42 S. Prairie St	Galesburg	IL	61401	2	682
Cottonwood Cinema	300 Cottonwood Mall	Glen Carbon	IL	62025	3	609
Nameoki	30 Nameoki Village S.C.	Granite City	IL	62040	2	609
Cinema 4	5 Main St.	Harrisburg	IL	62946	4	632
Lory Theatre	810 Main St.	Highland	IL	62249	2	609
Times Theatre	231 East State St.	Jacksonville	IL	62651	2	648
Illinois Theatre	204 N. Mauvaisterne	Jacksonville	IL	62651	2	648
Stadium Theatre	117 E. Pearl	Jerseyville	IL	62052	2	609
Lake in the Hills 12	311 N. Randall Rd.	Lake in the Hills	IL	60102	12	602
Illinois Theatre	124 N. Lafayette St.	Macomb	IL	61455	2	717
Illinois Center	3107 Civic Circle Blvd	Marion	IL	62959	8	632
Showplace 8	2509 Hurst Dr.	Mattoon	IL	61938	8	648
Showplace 8	400 Potomac	Mt Vernon	IL	62864	8	632
Showplace 12	1124 Edgewater	Pekin	IL	61554	12	675
Paris Theatre	119 N. Central Ave.	Paris	IL	61944	2	581
Quincy Showcase 6	300 N. 33rd St.	Quincy	IL	62301	6	717
Quincy Mall Cinema	3429 Quincy Mall	Quincy	IL	62301	3	717
Showplace 16	8301 East State St.	Rockford	IL	61125	16	610
Colonial Village Cinema	4228 Newburg Rd.	Rockford	IL	61125	5	610
North Towne Cinema	890 West Riverside Blvd.	Rockford	IL	61130	6	610
Movies at Machesney	890 W. Riverside Blvd.	Rockford	IL	61130	10	610
Cine Theatre	400 N. Central St.	Roxana	IL	62084	1	609
Showplace	1320 S. MacArthur Blvd.	Springfield	IL	62704	8	648
Esquire Theatre	1320 S. MacArthur Blvd.	Springfield	IL	62704	4	648
Parkway Pointe	1320 S. MacArthur Blvd.	Springfield	IL	62704	8	648
White Oaks Cinema	1320 S. MacArthur Blvd.	Springfield	IL	62704	5	648
Cinema	117 W. Main Cross	Taylorville	IL	62568	2	648
Showplace 8	555 N. Lakeview Pkwy.	Vernon Hills	IL	60061	8	602
Mounds Mall	1834 Mounds Rd.	Anderson	IN	46015	2	527
Showplace 4	2101 State Rd. 9	Anderson	IN	46015	4	527
College Mall Cinema	1351 College Mall Rd.	Bloomington	IN	47402	4	527
Showplace 11	1351 College Mall Rd.	Bloomington	IN	47408	11	527
Showplace West 12	2929 West Third St.	Bloomington	IN	47408	12	527
Columbus Cinema 5	1865 National Highway	Columbus	IN	47202	5	527
Commons Cinema	395 Courthouse Center	Columbus	IN	47202	2	527
Stadium 16	5600 Pearl Dr.	Evansville	IN	47719	16	649
Showplace 16	4325 S. Meridian	Indianapolis	IN	46217	16	527
ShowPlace 12	6102 N. Rural St.	Indianapolis	IN	46220	12	527
Kokomo Mall Cinema	1530 East Blvd.	Kokomo	IN	46902	8	527
Markland Mall Cinema	1201 S. Reed Rd.	Kokomo	IN	46902	5	527
LaPorte Cinema	608 Colfax	LaPorte	IN	46350	4	602
Showplace 12	713 B. Theatre Dr.	Marion	IN	46952	12	527
Marquette Cinema	430 St. John Rd.	Michigan City	IN	46361	3	602
Dunes Plaza Cinema	100 Dunes Plaza, Rt. 20	Michigan City	IN	46361	6	602
Showplace 7	3401 W.Community Dr.	Muncie	IN	47308	7	527
Muncie Mall	3201 Granville Ave.	Muncie	IN	47308	3	527
Northwest Plaza Cinema	1907 W. McGalliard	Muncie	IN	47308	8	527
Castle Theatre	221 S. Main St	New Castle	IN	47362	1	527
Eastwood Cinema	663 E. Main St.	Peru	IN	46970	2	527
Princeton Theatre	301 W. Broadway	Princeton	IN	47670	4	649
Dollar Cinema	600 Commerce Rd.	Richmond	IN	47374	10	542
Cinema 11	4713 E. National Rd.	Richmond	IN	47375	11	542
Showplace 16	875 Deercreek Dr.	Schererville	IN	46375	16	602
Scottsdale Cinema	1290 Scottsdale Mall	South Bend	IN	46614	6	588
Showplace 16	450 Chippewa Dr	South Bend	IN	46614	16	588
Honey Creek West	3131 S. Third St. Place	Terra Haute	IN	47802	8	581
ShowPlace 12	3153 S. Third St. Place	Terre Haute	IN	47802	12	581
Plaza Cinema 2	635 Niblock Rd.	Vincennes	IN	47591	2	581
Showplace 3	529 Main St.	Vincennes	IN	47591	3	581
Indiana Theatre 2	419 E. Main St.	Washington	IN	47501	2	581
Showplace 16 Coon Rapids	10051 Woodcrest Dr.	Coon Rapids	MN	55433	16	613
Showplace 16	5567 Bishop Ave.	Inver Grove Heights	MN	55077	16	613
Town Plaza Cinema 5	2136 William St.	Cape Girardeau	MO	63702	5	632
Town & Country Cinema	1618 Business 60	Dexter	MO	63841	2	632
Showplace 4	838 Valley Creek	Farmington	MO	63640	4	609
Kennett Cinema 1	224 First St.	Kennett	MO	63857	1	632
Movies	300 W. Main St.	Park Hills	MO	63601	2	609
Showplace 8	3225 S. Westwood	Poplar Bluff	MO	63902	8	632
Meramec Cinema	1-44 S. Service Rd.	Sullivan	MO	63080	2	609
Cinemas 10	877 Washington Blvd.	Hamilton	OH	45013	10	515
Showplace 8	Main St.	Hamilton	OH	45013	8	515

KRIKORIAN PREMIERE THEATRES, LLC

4 theatres, 43 screens.

131 Palos Verdes Blvd., Redondo Beach, CA 90277. (310) 791-8688. FAX: (310) 791-1997. www.krikoriantheatres.com

PRESIDENT & CEO
George Krikorian
DIRECTOR, CORPORATE DEVELOPMENT
Dale Davison
DIRECTOR, FILM
Lou Lencioni
DIRECTOR, OPERATIONS
Neal Meyer

THEATRES

Downey	8200 3rd St.	Downey	CA	90241	10	803
Redlands	340 N. Eureka St.	Redlands	CA	92373	14	803
San Clemente	641-B Camino De Los Mares	San Clemente	CA	92673	7	803
Manrovia Cinema 12	410 S. Myrtle Ave.	Monrovia	CA	91016	12	803

LAEMMLE THEATRES

11 theatres, 36 screens.
11523 Santa Monica Blvd., Los Angeles, CA 90025. (310) 478-1041. FAX: (310) 478-4452.
CHIEF OFFICERS
Robert Laemmle
Gregory Laemmle

THEATRES

Laemmle Music Hall	9036 Wilshire Blvd.	Beverly Hills	CA	90211	3	803
Laemmle's Paseo Camarillo	390 Lantana	Camarillo	CA	93010	3	803
Laemmle's Town Center 5	17200 Ventura Blvd.	Encino	CA	91316	5	803
Laemmle's Regent Showcase	614 N. La Brea Ave.	Hollywood	CA	90036	1	803
Laemmle's Grande	345 S. Figueroa St.	Los Angeles	CA	90071	4	803
Laemmle Sunset 5	8000 Sunset Blvd.	Los Angeles	CA	90046	5	803
Laemmle's Royal	11523 Santa Monica Blvd.	Los Angeles	CA	90025	1	803
Laemmle's Colorado	2588 E. Colorado Blvd.	Pasadena	CA	91107	1	803
Laemmle's Playhouse 7	673 E. Colorado	Pasadena	CA	91103	7	803
Laemmle's Monica 4	1332 Second St.	Santa Monica	CA	90401	4	803
Laemmle's Westlake Village Twin	4711 Lakeview Canyon Rd.	Westlake Village	CA	91361	2	803

LAKES & RIVERS CINEMAS

8 theatres, 41 screens.
3989 Central Ave. N.E., Box 48, Columbia Heights, MN 55421. (763) 781-8858. FAX: (763) 781-0510.
PRESIDENT
James H. Payne
SECRETARY & CASHIER
Shiloy Ziemann
GENERAL MANAGER
Alex Avila
FILM BUYER
Steve Tripp

THEATRES

Washington Square 5	121 W. Front St.	Detroit Lakes	MN	56501	5	724
Fair Lakes 5	1201 N. State St.	Fairmont	MN	56031	5	737
Westridge Cinema 5	2001 W. Lincoln Ave.	Fergus Fails	MN	56537	5	724
Cedar Mall Cinema 6	1929 S. Cedar St.	Owatonna	MN	55060	6	613
Red Wing Cinema 5	160 Tyler Rd.	Red Wing	MN	55066	5	613
Northland Cinema 5	1635 Oxford St.	Worthington	MN	56187	5	725
Watertown Cinema 5	1111 14th St.	Watertown	SD	57201	5	725
Falls Cinema 5	200 N. Washington	St. Croix Falls	WI	54024	5	613

JACK LOEKS THEATRES

10 theatres, 95 screens.
1400 28th St., S.W., Grand Rapids, MI 49509. (616) 532-6302. FAX: (616) 532-3660.
CHAIRMAN
John D. Loeks
PRESIDENT, CEO & COO
John D. Loeks, Jr.
VICE PRESIDENTS
Ron Van Timmeren
Roger Lubs
Steve Forythe
CFO
Nancy Hagan

THEATRES

Jack Loeks Celebration! Cinema	1468 Cinema Way	Benton Harbor	MI	49022	14	588
Jack Loeks Studio 28	1350 SW. 28th St.	Grand Rapids	MI	49509	20	563
Jack Loeks Alpine 4	3219 N.W. Alpine Ave.	Grand Rapids	MI	49544	4	563
Jack Loeks Plaza 2	6235 South Westnedge	Kalamazoo	MI	49002	2	563
Jack Loeks Celebration Cinema	200 East Edgewood Blvd.	Lansing	MI	48911	18	551
Jack Loeks Celebration Cinema	4935 E. Pickard	Mt. Pleasant	MI	48858	11	513
Jack Loeks Cinema 4	816 E. Preston	Mt Pleasant	MI	48858	4	513
Jack Loeks Getty Drive-In	920 E. Summit	Muskegon	MI	49441	4	563
Jack Loeks Cinema Carousel	4289 Grand Haven Rd.	Muskegon	MI	49441	16	563
Jack Loeks Plaza 1 and 2	3450 Henry St.	Muskegon	MI	49441	2	563

LOEKS STAR THEATRES

10 theatres, 156 screens.
(Loeks Michigan Theatres, Inc., general partner, and Star Theatres, Inc., general partner.) 3020 Charlevoix Dr. S.E., Grand Rapids, MI 49546. (616) 940-0866. FAX: (616) 940-0046.
PRESIDENT
Barrie Loeks
CHAIRMAN
Jim Loeks
COO & V.P.
Kenyon Shane
V.P., OPERATIONS
Bob Kleinhans
TREASURER
Jay Laninga
V.P., TECHNICAL
Jon Karell
V.P., ADVERTISING & PROMOTION
Krys Bylund
FILM BUYER
Lisa Ermitinger

THEATRES

Great Lakes Crossing	4300 Baldwin Rd.	Auburn Hills	MI	48326	25	505
Star Gratiot	35705 Gratiot Ave.	Clinton Twp.	MI	48035	21	505
Star Fairlane	18900 Michigan Ave.	Dearborn	MI	48126	21	505
Star Grand Rapids	3000 Alpine Ave.	Grand Rapids	MI	49544	18	563
Star Holland	12270 James St.	Holland	MI	49424	8	563
Star Lincoln Park	1748 Dix Rd.	Lincoln Park	MI	48146	8	505
Star John R	32289 John R Rd.	Madison Heights	MI	48071	15	505
Star Rochester	200 Barclay Circle	Rochester Hills	MI	48307	10	505
Star Southfield	25333 W. 12 Mile	Southfield	MI	48034	20	505
Star Taylor	22265 Eureka Rd.	Taylor	MI	48180	10	505

LOEWS CINEPLEX ENTERTAINMENT CORP.
(LOEWS THEATRES, SONY THEATRES, CINEPLEX ODEON, MAGIC JOHNSON THEATRES, STAR THEATRES)

241 theatres, 1,956 screens (includes 4 IMAX)

Corp. Headquarters: 711 Fifth Ave., New York, NY 10022-3109. (212) 833-6200. Canadian Headquarters: 1303 Yonge St., Toronto, Ontario M4T 2Y9. (416) 323-6600.

LCE CORPORATE PRESIDENT & CEO
Lawrence Ruisi
SENIOR V.P. & CFO
John J. Walker
SENIOR V.P. & GENERAL COUNSEL
John C. McBride, Jr.
V.P., FINANCE/CONTROLLER
Joseph Sparacio
V.P., INVESTOR RELATIONS & STRATEGIC PLANNING
Mindy Tucker
PRESIDENT
Travis Reid
EXECUTIVE V.P.
Michael P. Norris
EXECUTIVE V.P.
Robert J. Lenihan
EXECUTIVE V.P. & GENERAL COUNSEL
Seymour Smith
SENIOR V.P., MARKETING
Marc J. Pascucci
SENIOR V.P., FILM BUYER
Steve Bunnell
SENIOR V.P., REAL ESTATE
Terrence L. Jackson
SENIOR V.P., CONSTRUCTION & DESIGN
John Faltings
V.P., ASSET MANAGEMENT
Joel Kwinter
V.P., AUDITING
Robert Cohen
V.P., FINANCE
Bryan Berndt
V.P. & DEPUTY GENERAL COUNSEL
David Badain
V.P., CONCESSIONS
Fred Gable
V.P., FILM
Phil Groves
V.P., HUMAN RESOURCES & ADMINISTRATION
Peter Fournier
V.P., IS
Jim Fagerstrom
V.P., IMAX THEATRES
Mary Jane Dodge
V.P., LEGAL AFFAIRS
Felicia Buebel
DIVISIONAL S.V.P., OPERATIONS, EAST COAST
Brian Blatchey
DIVISIONAL V.P., OPERATIONS, MIDWEST
Roger Smith
DIVISIONAL V.P., OPERATIONS, WEST COAST
Len Westenberg
V.P., PURCHASING
Thomas Hogan
V.P., REAL ESTATE
Alan Benjamin
V.P., REAL ESTATE
Kenneth Benjamin
V.P., SAFETY/SECURITY
Gerry Cieremans
CINEPLEX ODEON CANADA CHAIRMAN & CEO
Allan Karp
SENIOR V.P., FINANCE
Gordon Nelson
SENIOR V.P., FILM & PROGRAMMING
Tony Cianciotta
LOEWS CINEPLEX INTERNATIONAL PRESIDENT
J. Edward Shugrue
EXECUTIVE V.P.
Irwin Cohen
GENERAL MANAGER DESIGN & CONSTRUCTION
Sam DiMichelle

THEATRES

Catalina	2320 N. Campbell Ave.	Tucson	AZ	85719	6	789
Crossroads	4811 E. Grant Rd.	Tucson	AZ	85712	6	789
El Dorado	5925 E. Broadway Blvd.	Tucson	AZ	85711	6	789
Foothills	7401 La Cholla Blvd.	Tucson	AZ	85741	15	789
Beverly Center 13	8522 Beverly Blvd.	Los Angeles	CA	90048	13	803
Century Plaza Cinemas 4	2040 Ave. Of The Stars	Los Angeles	CA	90067	4	803
Fairfax Cinemas 3	7907 Beverly Blvd.	Los Angeles	CA	90048	3	803

Magic Johnson Theatre	4020 Marlton Ave.	Los Angeles	CA	90008	15	803
Marina	13455 Maxella Ave.	Marina Del Rey	CA	90292	6	803
Metreon	101 Fourth St.	San Francisco	CA	94103	16	807
Broadway Cinemas 4	1441 3rd St. Promenade	Santa Monica	CA	90401	4	803
Danbury 10	4-6 International Dr.	Danbury	CT	06810	10	501
Community 1 & 2	1424 Post Rd.	Fairfield	CT	06430	2	501
Plainville	220 New Britain Rd.	Plainville	CT	06062	20	533
Avalon 2	5612 Connecticut Ave. Northwest	Washington	DC	20015	2	511
Cinema 1	5100 Wisconsin Ave.	Washington	DC	20016	1	511
Dupont 5	1350 19th St. Northwest	Washington	DC	20036	5	511
Foundry 7	1055 Thomas Jefferson St. Northwest	Washington	DC	20007	7	511
Inner Circle 3	2301 M St., Northwest	Washington	DC	20037	3	511
Janus 3	1660 Connecticut Ave. Northwest	Washington	DC	20036	3	511
Outer Circle	4849 Wisconsin Ave. Northwest	Washington	DC	20016	2	511
Uptown 1	3426 Connecticut Ave. Northwest	Washington	DC	20008	1	511
Wisconsin Ave Cinemas 6	4000 Wisconsin Ave., Northwest	Washington	DC	20016	6	511
Sand Lake 7	835 Sand Lake Rd.	Orlando	FL	32809	7	534
Magic Johnson Greenbrier	2841 Greenbrier Pkwy.	Atlanta	GA	30331	12	524
8th St. Marketplace	390 S. 8th St.	Boise	ID	83706	2	757
Town Square Cinemas	130 N. Milwaukee	Boise	ID	83704	6	757
Northgate Cinema 6	6950 W. State St.	Boise	ID	83703	6	757
Nampa Cinemas 6	2104 Caldwell Blvd.	Nampa	ID	83651	6	757
Ridge Plaza 8	960 W. Dundee Rd.	Arlington Hts.	IL	60004	8	602
Bloomingdale 6	324 W. Army Trail Rd.	Bloomingdale	IL	60108	6	602
Stratford 4	804 Stratford Square	Bloomingdale	IL	60108	4	602
River Oaks 6	132 River Oaks Centre	Calumet City	IL	60409	6	602
River Oaks 2	70 River Oaks Center	Calumet City	IL	60409	2	602
River Oaks 2	300 River Oaks Dr.	Calumet City	IL	60409	2	602
600 North Michigan	600 N. Michigan Ave.	Chicago	IL	60611	9	602
62nd & Western	2258 W. 62nd St.	Chigaco	IL	60636	10	602
900 North Michigan 2	900 N. Michigan Ave.	Chicago	IL	60611	2	602
Chatham 14	210 87th St.	Chicago	IL	60620	14	602
Esquire 6	58 E. Oak St.	Chicago	IL	60611	6	602
Fine Arts 4	418 S. Michigan Ave.	Chicago	IL	60605	4	602
Lawndale 10	3330 W. Roosevelt Rd.	Chicago	IL	60624	10	602
Lincoln Village 1-6	6341 N. McCormick Blvd.	Chicago	IL	60659	6	602
Lincoln Village 7-9 3	6101 N. Lincoln Ave.	Chicago	IL	60659	3	602
McClurg Court 3	330 E. Ohio St.	Chicago	IL	60611	3	602
Pipers Alley 4	1608 N. Wells	Chicago	IL	60610	4	602
Webster Place	1471 W. Webster Ave.	Chicago	IL	60614	11	602
Commons 4	222 Commons Dr.	Chicago Ridge	IL	60415	4	602
Chicago Ridge 6	500 Chicago Ridge Mall	Chicago Ridge	IL	60415	6	602
Crestwood	13221 Rivercrest Dr.	Crestwood	IL	60445	18	602
Grove Cinemas 6	1620 75th St.	Downers Grove	IL	60517	6	602
Evanston 5	1716 Central Ave.	Evanston	IL	60201	5	602
Hillside Square 6	4500 Frontage Rd.	Hillside	IL	60162	6	602
Hillside Mall 3	4541 Harrison Rd.	Hillside	IL	60162	3	602
Quarry 14	9201 63rd St.	Hodgkins	IL	60525	14	602
River Run 8	16621 Torrence Ave.	Lansing	IL	60438	8	602
Westridge Court 8	352 S. Route 59	Naperville	IL	60540	8	602
Golf Mill 3	9210 N. Milwaukee Ave.	Niles	IL	60714	3	602
Golf Glen 6	9180 W. Golf Rd.	Niles	IL	60016	6	602
Norridge 10	4520 N. Harlem Ave.	Norridge	IL	60706	10	602
North Riverside 6	7501 W. Cermak Rd.	N. Riverside	IL	60546	6	602
Oakbrook 4	300 Oakbrook Plaza	Oak Brook	IL	60521	4	602
Oakbrook 3	2020 Spring Rd.	Oakbrook	IL	60521	3	602
Orland Square 1-6	49 Orland Sq. Dr.	Orland Park	IL	60462	6	602
Orland Square 7-10 4	82 Orland Sq. Dr.	Orland Park	IL	60462	4	602
Rolling Meadows 9	1701 Algonquin Rd.	Rolling Meadows	IL	60008	9	602
Streets of Woodfield	601 N. Martingale Rd.	Schaumburg	IL	60173	20	602
Gardens 7	175 Old Orchard Center	Skokie	IL	60077	7	602
Streamwood 14	1500 Buttita Dr.	Streamwood	IL	60107	14	602
Rivertree Court 8	701 N. Milwaukee	Vernon Hills	IL	60061	8	602
Rice Lake Square 10	301 Rice Lake Square	Wheaton	IL	60187	10	602
Woodridge 18	10000 Woodward Ave.	Woodridge	IL	60517	18	602
Greenwood 9	733 Loews Blvd.	Greenwood	IN	46142	9	527
Cherry Tree 10	9529 E. Washington St.	Indianapolis	IN	46229	10	527
College Park 14	3535 W. 86th St.	Indianapolis	IN	46268	14	527
Lafayette 8	4751 Century Plaza	Indianapolis	IN	46254	8	527
Merrillville 10	2360 E. 79th Ave.	Merrillville	IN	46410	10	602
Midtown 3	711 12th St.	Ashland	KY	41101	3	564
South Park 1-6	163 Canary Rd.	Lexington	KY	40503	6	541
Copley Place 11	100 Huntington Ave.	Boston	MA	02116	11	506
Nickelodeon 5	606 Commonwealth Ave	Boston	MA	02215	5	506
Cheri 4	50 Dalton St.	Boston	MA	02115	4	506
Harvard Square 5	10 Church St.	Cambridge	MA	02138	5	506
Fresh Pond 10	168 Alewife Brk Pkwy	Cambridge	MA	02138	10	506
Liberty Tree Mall	100 Independence Way	Danvers	MA	01923	20	506
Harbour Mall 1-8	Rts. 81 & 24	Fall River	MA	02721	8	521
Leominster 1-12	Searstown Shopping Center	Leominster	MA	01453	12	506
Methuen	90 Pleasant St.	Methuen	MA	21844	20	660
Natick 6	1398 Worcester	Natick	MA	01760	6	506
Assembly Sq. 12	35 Middlesex Ave.	Somerville	MA	02145	12	506
Rotunda 2	711 W. 40th St.	Baltimore	MD	21211	2	512
White Marsh	8141 Honeygo Blvd.	Baltimore	MD	21236	16	512
Center Park 8	4001 Powder Mill Rd.	Beltsville	MD	20705	8	511
Montgomery Mall 3	7101 Democracy Blvd.	Bethesda	MD	20817	3	511
Columbia Palace 9	8805 Centre Park Dr.	Columbia	MD	21045	9	512
Rio 14	9811 Washingtonian Ctr.	Gaithersburg	MD	20878	14	511
Germantown 6	12926 Middlebrook Rd.	Germantown	MD	20874	6	511
Glen Burnie 7	7480 Baltimore Annapolis	Glen Burnie	MD	21060	7	512
Lexington Park Six	21882 FDR Blvd.	Lexington Park	MD	20653	6	511
Marlow 6	3899 Branch Ave.	Marlow Heights	MD	20748	6	511
Valley Center 9	9616 Reistertown Rd.	Owings Mills	MD	21117	9	512
White Flint 5	11301 Rockville Pike	Rockville	MD	20895	5	511
Timonium 3	2131 York Rd.	Timonium	MD	21093	3	512
Waldorf South 5	195 Smallwood Village Ctr.	Waldorf	MD	20601	5	511
St. Charles Towne Center 9	11115 Mall Circle	Waldorf	MD	20601	9	511
Wheaton Plaza 11	11160 Veirs Mill Rd.	Wheaton	MD	20902	11	511

Wheaton Plaza 4	11160 Viers Mill Rd.	Wheaton	MD	20902	4	511
Great Lakes	4300 Baldwin Rd.	Auburn Hills	MI	48326	25	505
Gratiot	35705 Gratiot Ave.	Clinton Township	MI	48043	21	505
Fairlane Town Center	18900 Michigan Ave.	Dearborn	MI	48126	21	505
Grand Rapids	3000 Alpine Ave.	Grand Rapids	MI	49544	18	563
Holland	12270 James St.	Holland	MI	49424	8	563
Lincoln Park	1748 Dix Rd.	Lincoln Park	MI	48146	8	505
John R	32289 John R. Rd.	Madison Heights	MI	48071	15	505
Rochester Hills	200 Barclay Circle	Rochester Hills	MI	48307	10	505
Southfield	25333 W. 12 Mile Rd.	Southfield	MI	48034	20	505
Taylor	22265 Eureka Rd.	Taylor	MI	48180	10	505
Edina 4	3911 W. 50th St.	Edina	MN	55424	4	612
Westwind 3	4721 Hwy 101	Minnetonka	MN	55345	3	616
Willow Creek 8	9900 Shelard Pkwy.	Plymouth	MN	55441	8	618
Merrimack 5	192 Loudon Rd.	Concord	NH	03301	5	506
Lebanon 1-6	Rt. 4 - Miracle Mile	Lebanon	NH	03766	6	523
Cinema Centre 5	35 Kennedy Mall	Brick	NJ	08723	5	501
Brick Plaza	3 Brick Plaza	Bricktown	NJ	08723	10	501
Cherry Hill Theatre	2121 Route 38	Cherry Hill	NJ	08002	24	504
East Hanover 12	145 Route 10	East Hanover	NJ	07936	12	501
Monmouth Mall 15	Route 35 & 36	Eatontown	NJ	07724	15	501
Showboat Quad 4	725 River Rd.	Edgewater	NJ	07020	4	501
Menlo Park 12	390 Menlo Park Mall/U.S.Route1	Edison	NJ	04405	12	501
Freehold Metroplex 14	101 Trotters Way	Freehold	NJ	07728	14	501
Newport Centre 11	30-300 Mall Dr.	Jersey City	NJ	07303	11	501
Mountain Side 10	1021 Route 22	Mountainside	NJ	07092	10	501
New Brunswick	15 US Hwy #1	New Brunswick	NJ	08903	18	501
Newark Metroplex 6	360-394 Springfield Ave.	Newark	NJ	07103	6	501
Paramus Route 4	260 E. Route 4	Paramus	NJ	07652	10	501
Route Seventeen 3	S-85 Route 17	Paramus	NJ	07652	3	501
Interstate 2	235 Interstate Shopping Ctr.	Ramsey	NJ	07446	2	501
Ridgefield Park 12	75 Challenger Rd.	Ridgefield Park	NJ	07660	12	501
Meadow Six 6	800 Plaza Dr.	Secaucus	NJ	07094	6	501
Plaza Eight 8	495 Harmon Meadow Blvd.	Secaucus	NJ	07094	8	501
Seacourt 10	635 Bay Ave.	Toms River	NJ	08753	10	501
Wayne	67 Willowbrook Blvd.	Wayne	NJ	07470	14	501
Bay Terrace 6	211-01 26th Ave.	Bayside	NY	11360	6	501
Alpine 7	6817 5th Ave.	Brooklyn-	NY	11220	7	501
Fortway 5	6722 Fort Hamilton Pkwy	Brooklyn	NY	11219	5	501
Kings Plaza 6	5201 Kings Plaza	Brooklyn	NY	11234	6	501
Kingsway 5	946 Kings Highway	Brooklyn-	NY	11223	5	501
Elmwood 4	57-02 Hoffman Dr.	Elmhurst	NY	11373	4	501
City Cinema	183-15 Horace Harding Ex Pwy	Fresh Meadows	NY	11365	5	501
Fresh Meadows 5	190-02 Horace Harding Blvd.	Fresh Meadows	NY	11365	7	501
Roosevelt Field 8	Roosevelt Field Mall	Garden City	NY	11530	8	501
Glen Cove 6	5 School St.	Glen Cove	NY	11542	6	501
Shore 8	37 Wall St.	Huntington	NY	11743	8	501
Whitman 1	290-4 Whitman Mall, Route 110	Huntington Station	NY	11746	1	501
Oakdale Mall 1-3	Oakdale Mall	Johnson City	NY	13790	3	502
Smith Haven Mall 4	15 Smith Haven Mall	Lake Grove	NY	11755	4	501
Nassau Metroplex 10	3585 Hempstead Tpke.	Levittown	NY	11756	10	501
Mattituck 8	Route 25	Mattituck	NY	11952	8	501
Galleria Metroplex 10	1 Galleria Dr.	Middletown	NY	10940	16	501
Nanuet 5	420 Nanuet Mall	Nanuet	NY	10954	5	501
19th St. East 6	890 Broadway	New York	NY	10003	6	501
42nd St. East Walk	247 W. 42nd St.	New York	NY	10036	13	501
72nd St. East 1	1230 3rd Ave. 72nd St.	New York	NY	10021	1	501
84th St. Theatre 6	2310 Broadway	New York	NY	10024	6	501
Astor Plaza 1	1515 Broadway	New York	NY	10036	1	501
Coronet Cinemas	993 3rd Ave	New York	NY	10022	2	501
Kips Bay Theatre	550 2nd Ave.	New York	NY	10016	15	501
Lincoln Square 12	1998 Broadway	New York	NY	10023	12	501
Magic Johnson Theatre - Harlem	125th @ Frederick Douglass Blvd.	New York	NY	10027	9	501
New York Twin 2	1271 2nd Ave. 66th St.	New York	NY	10021	2	501
Orpheum 7	1538 3rd Ave. 86th St.	New York	NY	10028	7	501
State Theatre 4	1540 Broadway	New York	NY	10036	4	501
Village Theatre Vii 7	66 3rd Ave. 11th St.	New York	NY	10003	7	501
Worldwide Cinemas	340 W. 50th St	New York	NY	10019	6	501
Fantasy 5	18 N. Park Ave.	Rockville Center	NY	11570	5	501
Rockville Centre 2	340 Sunrise Highway	Rockville Center	NY	11570	2	501
Rotterdam Square Mall 6	93 W. Campbell Rd.	Schenectady	NY	12306	6	532
Stony Brook 15	2196 Nesconset Highway	Stony Brook	NY	11790	15	501
Sony Town Square 9	2425 Vestal Pkwy	Vestal	NY	13850	9	502
Webster Twelve 12	2190 Empire Blvd.	Webster	NY	14580	12	538
Hamptons Arts 2	2 Brook Rd.	West Hampton	NY	11978	2	501
Loews Palisades Center	4403 Palisades Center Dr.	West Nyack	NY	10994	21	501
Rosevelt Raceway 10	1025 Corporate Dr.	Westbury	NY	11590	10	501
Magic Johnson Randall Park Mall	20801 Miles Rd.	N. Randall	OH	44128	12	510
Richmond Town Square	631 Richmond Rd.	Richmond Heights	OH	44143	20	510
North Versailles	200 Loews Dr.	N. Versailles	PA	15137	20	508
Stroud Mall Seven 7	Rte 611-160 Stroud Mall	Stroudburg	PA	18360	7	577
Waterfront Theatre	300 W. Waterfront Dr.	West Homestead	PA	15120	22	508
Lincoln Square 10	800 Lincoln Square	Arlington	TX	76011	10	623
20 & 287 6	4930 Little Rd.	Arlington	TX	76016	6	623
Keystone	13933 N. Central Expressway	Dallas	TX	75243	16	623
Cityplace 14	2600 N. Haskell	Dallas	TX	75204	14	623
City View 8	4728 Bryant Irvin Rd.	Ft. Worth	TX	76132	8	623
Easton Commons 8	8580 Highway 6	Houston	TX	77095	8	618
Memorial City 8	502 Memorial City Mall	Houston	TX	77024	8	618
Magic Johnson Northline Mall	100 Northline Mall	Houston	TX	77022	12	618
River Oaks Plaza 12	1450 W. Gray St	Houston	TX	77019	12	618
Sharpstown Center	535 Sharpstown Ctr.	Houston	TX	77036	8	618
Spectrum 9	2660 Augusta Dr.	Houston	TX	77057	9	618
West Oaks Mall 7	1000 W. Oaks Mall	Houston	TX	77082	7	618
Chisholm 5	300 Chisholm Place	Plano	TX	75075	5	623
Preston Park 6	1900 Preston Park Blvd.	Plano	TX	75075	6	623
Spring 10	20115 Holzwarth Rd.	Spring	TX	77388	10	618
Fountains	11225 Fountain Lake Dr.	Stafford	TX	77477	18	618

Southwest 6	12002 Southwest Freeway	Stafford	TX	77477	6	618
Bay Area 6	20005 Gulf Freeway	Webster	TX	77598	6	618
Layton Hills Cinemas	728 W. 1425 North	Layton Hills	UT	84041	9	770
Trolley North 3	1000 N. 500 East	N.Salt Lake City	UT	84054	3	770
Cinedome 2 Theatre	1481 W. Riverdale Rd.	Ogden	UT	84405	2	770
University 4	959 S. 700 East St.	Orem	UT	84097	4	770
Broadway Centre 6	111 E. Broadway	Salt Lake City	UT	84111	6	770
Crossroads Cinemas 3	50 S. Main	Salt Lake City	UT	84144	3	770
Holladay Center Cinemas 6	1945 E. 4800 South	Salt Lake City	UT	84117	6	770
Trolley Corners 3	515 S. 700 East	Salt Lake City	UT	84102	3	770
Trolley Sq. Mall Cinemas 4	523 Trolley Square	Salt Lake City	UT	84102	4	770
Southtowne Cinemas 10	282 W. 10600 South	Sandy	UT	84070	10	770
Midvalley Cinemas 6	5766 S. 1900 W.	Taylorsville	UT	84118	12	770
Pentagon City 6	1100 S. Hayes St.	Arlington	VA	22202	6	511
Shirlington 7	2772 S. Randolph St.	Arlington	VA	22206	7	511
Worldgate 9	13025 Worldgate Dr.	Herndon	VA	22070	9	511
Manassas Mall 7	8300 Sudley Rd.	Manassas	VA	20109	7	511
Fairfax Square 8	8065 Leesburg Pike	Vienna	VA	22182	8	511
Tacket's Mill 4	2230-A Tackett's Mill Dr.	Woodbridge	VA	22192	4	511
Factoria Cinemas 8	3505 Factoria Blvd	Bellevue	WA	98006	8	819
Cascade Cinemas	200 Cascade Mall Dr.	Burlington	WA	98233	14	819
Totem Lake 3	12232 N.E. Totem Lake Way	Kirkland	WA	98033	3	819
Kirkland Park Pl. 6	404 Park Place	Kirkland	WA	98034	6	819
Lakewood Mall 6	10509 Gravelly Lake Dr. Southwest	Lakewood	WA	98499	12	819
Grand Cinemas	18421 Alderwood Mall Pkwy.	Lynnwood	WA	98037	8	819
Redmond Town Center 8	16451 N.E. 74th St.	Redmond	WA	98052	8	819
City Centre	1420 5th Ave.	Seattle	WA	98101	2	819
Meridian 16	1501 7th Ave.	Seattle	WA	98101	16	819
Northgate	410 N.E. Northgate Wayt.	Seattle	WA	07136	1	819
Oak Tree Cinemas	10006 Aurora Ave.	Seattle	WA	98133	6	819
Uptown Cinemas	511 Queen Anne Ave	Seattle	WA	98109	3	819
Tacoma Central 6	3102 S.23rd St.	Tacoma	WA	98405	6	819
Tacoma Mall Twin 2	4302 Tacoma Mall Blvd.	Tacoma	WA	98409	2	819
Tacoma South 5	7601 Hosmer St.	Tacoma	WA	98408	5	819
Southcenter 1	15700 SouthCenter Pkwy.	Tukwila	WA	98188	1	819
Lewis & Clark 7	15820 Tukwila Int'l Blvd.	Tukwila	WA	98188	7	819
Woodinville 12	17640-138 Pl.	Woodinville	WA	98072	12	819

MJR THEATRES, INC.

6 theatres, 79 screens.
13691 West Eleven Mile Rd., Oak Park, MI 48237. (248) 548-8282. FAX: (248) 548-4706.
PRESIDENT
Michael R. Mihalich
V.P., FILM BUYER
Candi Mihalich
V.P., OPERATIONS
Dennis Redmer
DIRECTOR OF PROMOTIONS
Robin Hansen

THEATRES

Adrian Cinema	3150 N. Adrian Hwy.	Adrian	MI	49221	10	547
Allen Park Cinema	6601 Allen Rd.	Allen Park	MI	48101	5	505
Brighton Town Square Cinema	8200 Murphy Dr.	Brighton	MI	48116	16	505
Chesterfield Crossing	50675 Gratiot Ave.	Chesterfield	MI	48051	12	505
Southgate Cinemas	15651 Trenton Rd.	Southgate	MI	48195	20	505
Waterford Cinema	7501 Highland Rd.	Waterford	MI	48327	16	505

MALCO THEATRES, INC.

32 theatres, 224 screens.
5851 Ridgeway Center Pkwy., Memphis, TN 38120. (901) 761-3480. FAX: (901) 681-2044. www.malco.com
CHAIRMAN
Richard Lightman
PRESIDENT & CEO
Stephen Lightman
EXECUTIVE V.P.
Herbert Levy
SENIOR V.P., OPERATIONS
James Tashie
SENIOR V.P., ADVERTISING
Robert Levy
CFO & TREASURE
Bill Blackburn
V.P. & DISTRICT MANAGER
James Lloyd
V.P. & HEAD FILM BUYER
Jeff Kaufman
DISTRICT MANAGER
Don Burchett
V.P., TECHNICAL SUPPORT
Mike Thompson
AREA MANAGER
Alan Denton
DIRECTOR OF CONCESSIONS
Larry Etter
PROMOTIONS & MARKETING
Julie Kellyman

THEATRES

Malco Trio	Hwy. 18 E. At I-55	Blytheville	AR	72315	3	640
Malco Razorback 6	2035 N. College	Fayetteville	AR	72701	6	670
Malco Mall Twin	4201 N. College	Fayetteville	AR	72701	2	670
Malco Quartet	3212 S. 70th St.	Fort Smith	AR	72903	4	670
Malco Mall Trio	5111 Rogers Ave.	Fort Smith	AR	72904	3	670
Malco Cinema 14	2001 E. Highland Dr.	Jonesboro	AR	72401	14	734
Malco Paragould Twin	Plaza West Shopping Center	Paragould	AR	72450	2	734
Malco Sunset Cinema 9	2940-G West Sunset	Springdale	AR	72762	9	670

Malco Plaza Twin	429 Park Plaza	Owensboro	KY	42303	2	649
Malco Cinema 12	5333 Frederica St.	Owensboro	KY	42303	12	649
Malco Trio	1045 E. Malone	Sikeston	MO	63801	3	632
Malco Cinema 3	Hwy. 45 N.	Columbus	MS	39703	3	673
Malco Leigh Mall	Hwy. 45 N.	Columbus	MS	39701	1	673
Malco Twin	219 Alabama St.	Columbus	MS	39701	2	673
Malco Varsity Twin	401 Main St.	Columbus	MS	39703	2	673
Malco DeSoto Cinema 16	7130 Malco Blvd.	Southaven	MS	38671	16	640
Malco Cinema 10	861 Cliff Gookin Blvd.	Tupelo	MS	38801	10	673
Malco Stage Cinema 12	7930 Stage Rd.	Barlett	TN	38134	12	640
Malco Trinity Commons	704 Gernantown Pkwy.	Cordova	TN	38018	9	640
Malco Forest Hill	3180 Village Shops Dr.	Germantown	TN	38138	8	640
Malco Cinema 8	2891 45 Bypass N.	Jackson	TN	38305	8	639
Malco Appletree Cinema 12	6000 Appletree Dr.	Memphis	TN	38115	12	640
Malco Bartlett Cinema 10	2809 Bartlett Blvd.	Memphis	TN	38134	10	640
Malco Collierville Towne Cinema 16	380 Market Blvd.	Memphis	TN	38017	16	640
Malco Highland Quartet	3473 Poplar Ave.	Memphis	TN	38111	4	640
Malco Majestic Theatre	7051 Malco Crossing	Memphis	TN	38115	20	640
Malco Ridgeway 4	5853 Ridgeway Center Pkwy.	Memphis	TN	38120	4	640
Malco Southwest Drive-In	4233 Highway 61	Memphis	TN	38109	2	640
Malco Studio on the Square	2105 Court St.	Memphis	TN	38104	5	640
Malco Summer Drive-In	5310 Summer Ave.	Memphis	TN	38122	4	640
Malco Winchester Court Cinema	6740 Winchester Rd.	Memphis	TN	38115	8	640
Malco Wolfchase Galleria	2766 N. Germantown Pkwy.	Memphis	TN	38133	8	640

MANN THEATRES OF MINNESOTA

13 theatres, 78 screens.
711 Hennepin Ave. 3rd Flr., Minneapolis, MN 55403. (612) 332-3303. FAX: (612) 332-3305.
PRESIDENT
Stephen Mann
VICE PRESIDENT
Benjie Mann
FILM BUYER & BOOKER
Neil O'Leary

THEATRES

Movies 10 at Westgate	1301 Excelsior Rd.	Baxter	MN	56425	10	613
Westport Theatre	Hwy. 371 & K-Mart Dr.	Baxter	MN	55425	3	613
Apache 6 Theatre	2101 37th Ave.	Columbia Heights	MN	55421	6	613
Cottage View Drive-In	9338 E. Point Douglas Rd.	Cottage Grove	MN	55016	1	613
Eagan Cinema 9	1225 Town Centre Dr.	Eagan	MN	55123	9	613
Grand Rapids Cinema	113 S. 21st St.	Grand Rapids	MN	55744	8	676
Irongate Cinema 3	990 W. 41st St.	Hibbing	MN	55746	3	676
Hopkins Cinema 6	1118 Main St.	Hopkins	MN	55343	6	613
Maple Grove Cinema 10	13644 80th Circle	Maple Grove	MN	55369	10	613
Plymouth Cinema 12	3400 Vicksburg Ln.	Plymouth	MN	55447	12	613
St. Louis Park Cinema	5400 Excelsior Blvd.	St. Louis Park	MN	55416	6	613
Grandview 1 & 2 Theatres	1830 Grand Ave.	St. Paul	MN	55105	2	613
Highland 1 & 2 Theatres	760 S. Cleveland Ave.	St. Paul	MN	55116	2	613

MARCUS THEATRES CORPORATION

49 theatres, 480 screens.
250 E. Wisconsin Ave., Ste. 1650, Milwaukee, WI 53202-4222. (414) 905-1500. FAX: (414) 905-2189.
CHAIRMAN
Steve Marcus
PRESIDENT
Bruce J. Olson
EXECUTIVE V.P. & FILM BUYER
Michael Kominsky
V.P. & BOOKER
Michael Ogrodowski
V.P. & FILM BOOKER
Rick Neals
VICE PRESIDENT
Don Perkins
VICE PRESIDENT
Mark Gramz
DIRECTOR, CONCESSIONS & PURCHASING
Patrick Striebel
DIRECTOR, ADVERTISING & MARKETING
Michael Tiemeyer
DIRECTOR, COMMUNICATIONS & PROMOTIONS
Carlo Petrick
FILM BOOKER
Dave Stawicki

THEATRES

Marcus Addison	I 355 At Lake & 53	Addison	IL	60101	21	602
Marcus Chicago Heights	1301 Hiltop Ave	Chicago Heights	IL	60411	14	602
Marcus Elgin Fox Theatre	111 S. Randall Rd.	Elgin	IL	60123	14	602
Marcus Gurnee Cinema	6144 Grand Ave., Gurnee Milts Mall	Gurnee	IL	60031	20	602
Marcus Orland Park Cinemas	16350 South LaGrange Rd.	Orland Park	IL	60462	14	602
Marcus Apple Valley Theatres	7200 W. 147th St	Apple Valley	MN	55124	6	613
Marcus Cambridge Cinema 5	123 Second Ave	Cambridge	MN	55008	5	613
Marcus Elk River 17	Elk River Mall	Elk River	MN	55330	17	613
Marcus Hastings Theater	1325 S. Frontage Rd.	Hastings	MN	55033	9	613
Marcus Cinema Oakdale North	5677 Hadley Ave N.	Oakdale	MN	55128	16	613
Marcus Rosemount Theater	15280 Carrousel Way	Rosemount	MN	55068	8	613
Marcus Cinema Shakopee	1116 Shakopee Town Sq.	Shakopee	MN	55379	11	613
Marcus Cinemas Crosswoods	200 Hutchinson Ave.	Columbus	OH	43235	17	535
Marcus Cinema Pickerington	1776 Hill Rd.	Pickerington	OH	43147	16	535
Marcus Valley Value Cinemas	1401 Valley Fair Mall	Appleton	WI	54915	6	658
Marcus Hollywood Cinemas	513 N. Westhill Blvd.	Appleton	WI	54914	11	658
Marcus Stadium Cinemas	1237 Lombardi Ave.	Ashwaubenon	WI	54304	4	658
Marcus Bay Park	755 Willard Dr.	Ashwaubenon	WI	54304	16	658
Marcus Wisconsin Theatres	236 Front St.	Beaver Dam	WI	53916	4	617

Marcus Tower Cinema	20075 Watertower Blvd.	Brookfield	WI	53045	8	617
Marcus Westpoint Cinema	20241 W. Bluemound Rd.	Brookfield	WI	53045	8	617
Marcus Rivoli Budget Theatre	W. 62 N. 567 Washington Ave.	Cedarburg	WI	53012	1	617
Marcus Hillside Cinema	2950 Kettle Ct.	Delafield	WI	53018	14	617
Marcus Marc Cinemas 8 Green Bay	1815 E. Main St.	Green Bay	WI	54302	8	658
Marcus King Cinemas	216 South 17th St.	LaCrosse	WI	54601	3	702
Marcus Cinema Theatres	2032 Ward Ave.	LaCrosse	WI	54601	8	702
Marcus Eastgate Cinemas	5202 High Crossing Blvd.	Madison	WI	53704	16	669
Marcus Point Cinemas	7825 Big Sky Dr.	Madison	WI	53719	16	669
Marcus Westgate Cinemas	340 Westgate Mall	Madison	WI	53711	3	669
Marcus Main St. Cinema	N88 W. 15377 Main St.	Menomonee Falls	WI	53051	5	617
Marcus Menomonee Falls	W180 N9393 Premier Lane	Menomonee Falls	WI	53051	12	617
Marcus North Shore Cinema	11700 N. Port Washington	Mequon	WI	53092	11	617
Marcus Northtown Cinema	7440 N. 76th St.	Milwaukee	WI	53223	8	617
Marcus Prospect Mall	2239 N. Prospect Ave	Milwaukee	WI	53202	3	617
Marcus Southtown Cinema	2906 S. 108th St	Milwaukee	WI	53227	4	617
Marcus Southgate Theatre 10	3330 S. 30th St.	Milwaukee	WI	53215	10	617
Marcus Cedar Creek Cinema	10101 Market St.	Mosinee	WI	54455	10	705
Marcus South Towne Cinemas	2305 West Broadway	Monona	WI	53713	5	669
Marcus Ridge Cinema	5200 S. Mooreland Rd.	New Berlin	WI	53151	20	617
Marcus South Shore	7261 South 13th St.	Oak Creek	WI	53154	16	617
Marcus Value Cinema Oak Creek	6912 S. 27th St.	Oak Creek	WI	53154	8	617
Marcus Cinema Ten	340 South Koeller Rd.	Oshkosh	WI	54901	10	658
Marcus Regency Cinemas	5230 Durand Ave	Racine	WI	53406	8	617
Marcus Westgate 5 Racine	5101 Washington Ave.	Racine	WI	53406	5	617
Marcus Campus Theatre	103 Watson St.	Ripon	WI	54971	1	658
Marcus Cinema Sheboygan	3226 Kohler Memorial D.	Sheboygan	WI	53081	14	617
Marcus Westown	2440 E. Moreland Blvd	Waukesha	WI	53186	8	617
Marcus Crossroad Cinemas	306 South 18th Ave.	Wausau	WI	54401	4	705

MARQUEE CINEMAS

8 theatres, 52 screens.
552 Ragland Rd., Beckley, WV 25801. (304) 255-4036. FAX: (304) 252-0526.
PRESIDENT & CEO
Curtis E. McCall
EXECUTIVE V.P.
James M. Cox
CFO
Cindy Ramsden
V.P., PERSONNEL
Toni Y. McCall
V.P., REAL ESTATE DEVELOPMENT
David Beauregard
DIRECTOR, OPERATIONS
Craig D. Worth
DIRECTOR, MARKETING
Robin A. Shumate

THEATRES

Marquee-Highland 7 Cinemas	1628 Happy Valley Rd.	Glasgow	KY	42142	7	736
Marquee-Park Plaza Cinemas	201 Park Plaza	Hilton Head Island	SC	29928	5	507
Marquee-Southpoint Cinemas	58 Southpoint Blvd.	Fredericksburg	VA	22407	9	511
Marquee-Showplace 7	1408 N. Eisenhower Dr.	Beckley	WV	25801	7	559
Marquee-Southridge Cinemas	331 Southridge Blvd	Charleston	WV	25309	12	564
Marquee-Seneca Showcase	Greenbier Valley Mall	Lewisburg	WV	24901	2	559
Marquee-Crossroads	22 Crossroads Mall	Mt Hope	WV	25880	6	559
Marquee-Nicholas Showplace	300 Merchants Walk Plaza	Summersville	WV	26651	4	564

METROPOLITAN THEATRES CORP.

17 theatres, 59 screens.
8727 West Third St., Los Angeles CA 90048. (310) 858-2800 FAX: (310) 858-2860.
CEO
Bruce C. Corwin
PRESIDENT
David Corwin
V.P., PLANNING & DEVELOPMENT
Bill Hughes
V.P., FILM MARKETING
Alan Stokes
V.P., OPERATIONS & CONCESSIONS
Ralph Breland

THEATRES

Calexico 10 Theatre	2441 Scaroni Rd.	Calexico	CA	92231	10	771
Cinema Twin	6050 Hollister Ave.	Goleta	CA	93117	2	855
Fairview Twin	251 N. Fairview	Goleta	CA	93117	2	855
Camino Real Cinemas	7040 Marketplace Dr.	Goleta	CA	93117	6	855
Park Theatre	6564 Pacific Blvd.	Huntington Park	CA	90255	2	803
Vine Twin Theatre	1722 1st St.	Livermore	CA	94550	2	807
Campus Theatre	1020 N. Vermont Ave.	Los Angeles	CA	90029	1	803
Orpheum Theatre	842 S. Broadway St.	Los Angeles	CA	90014	1	803
Palace Theatre	630 S. Broadway St.	Los Angeles	CA	90014	2	803
Teatro Fiesta	305-100 E. 4th St.	Santa Ana	CA	92701	2	803
Arlington Theatre	1317 State St.	Santa Barbara	CA	93101	1	855
Fiesta 5 Theatre	916 State St.	Santa Barbara	CA	93101	5	855
Metro 4 Theatre	618 State St.	Santa Barbara	CA	93101	4	855
Paseo Nuevo Cinemas	8 W. De La Guerra Place	Santa Barbara	CA	93101	4	855
Plaza De Oro Twin	371 S. Hitchcock Way	Santa Barbara	CA	93105	2	855
Riviera Theatre	2044 Alameda Padre Serra	Santa Barbara	CA	93103	1	855
MetroLux 12 Theatre	1380 N. Denver Ave.	Love Land	CO	80537	12	751

MINI THEATRES

58 theatres, 203 screens.
31 W. Main St., Ste. 310, Patchogue, NY 11772. (631) 758-3456. FAX: (631) 207-0794.
PARTNERS
Marty Goldman
Harold Lager

THEATRES

Diamond State Drive-In	Route Box 13	Felton	DE	19943	1	504
Colonial	615 Main St.	Laconia	NH	03246	5	506
Weirs Drive-In	Route 3	Laconia	NH	03246	4	506
Bay Drive-In	Route Box 26	Alexandria Bay	NY	13607	2	549
Norma Jean	136 Perth Plaza	Amsterdam	NY	12010	7	532
Hollywood Drive-In	9270 Route 66	Averill Park	NY	12018	1	532
Fingerlakes Drive-In	Clark St. Rd.	Auburn	NY	13021	1	555
Movieplex	Fingerlakes Mall	Auburn	NY	13021	8	555
Malta Drive-In	Rural Route 9	Ballston Spa	NY	12020	1	532
Movietime	Walmart Plaza	Canandaigua	NY	14424	10	538
American		Canton	NY		3	549
Movieplex Carmel	150 Route 52	Carmel	NY	10512	8	501
Crandell	Main St.	Chatham	NY	12037	1	532
Park Theater		Cobleskill	NY		1	532
Movieplex		Dunkirk	NY		8	514
Movieplex Hudson	350 Fairview Ave.	Hudson	NY	12534	8	532
Hunter Theater	Main St.	Hunter	NY	12442	1	532
Movieplex		Geneva	NY		8	538
Glen Drive-In	Lake George Rd.	Glens Falls	NY	12801	2	532
Greenville Drive-In	Route Box #32	Greenville	NY	12083	1	532
Tamarac Cafe	Route Box #28	Inlet	NY	13360	1	532
Movieplex Johnstown	236 N. Comrie Ave.	Johnstown	NY	12095	9	532
Palace	26 Main St.	Lake Placid	NY	12946	3	523
Town Hall	Shady Ave.	Lowville	NY	13367	1	549
Plaza	10 Pearl St.	Malone	NY	12953	1	523
56 Auto Drive-In	Andrews St.	Massena	NY	13662	1	549
Movieplex Massena	Haven Shopping Plaza	Massena	NY	13662	8	549
Hathaway Drive-In	Route Box #67	N. Hoosick	NY	12133	1	532
Cinema Twin	Ogdensburg Mall	Ogdensburg	NY	13669	2	549
Strand	Main St.	Old Forge	NY	13420	4	526
Oneonta Cinema	47 Chestnut St.	Oneonta	NY	13820	2	526
Crystal Cinema		Painted Post	NY		8	565
Roxy	20 Main St.	Potsdam	NY	13676	2	549
Thousand Island		Thousand Isl. Park	NY		1	549
State Theater		Tupper Lake	NY		1	523
Valleybrook Drive-In		Unadilla	NY		1	526
Cinema Greenfield	229 Mohawk Trail	Greenfield	MA	01301	6	543
Cinema North Adams	Route Box # 8	N. Adams	MA	01247	6	532
Tower South Hadley	19 College St.	South Hadley	MA	01075	2	543
New Art Provincetown	214 Commercial St.	Provincetown	MA	02657-0212	2	506
Island	Circuit Ave.	Oaks Bluff	MA	02557	1	506
Capawock	Main St.	Vineyard Haven	MA	02568	1	506
Strand	Oak Bluffs Ave.	Oaks Bluff	MA	02557	1	506
Gourcester Cinema	74 Essex Ave.	Gloucester	MA	01930	3	506
Cinemagic		Salisbury	MA		9	506
Route 1		N. Attelboro	MA		2	506
Bijou		Fairhaven	MA		1	521
Cinemagic 12		Saco	ME		12	500
Pier	3 Beach St.	Narragansett	RI	02882	3	521
Campus	17 Columbia St.	Wakefield	RI	02879	3	521
Empire	17 Water St.	Portsmouth	RI	02871	1	521
Park	848 Park Ave.	Cranston	RI	02910	4	521
Plaza	Rutland Plaza	Rutland	VT	05701	9	523
Westway	Westway Plaza	West Rutland	VT	05777	4	523
Movieplex	Kocher Dr.	Bennington	VT	05201	3	532

MUVICO THEATERS

11 theatres, 187 screens.

3101 N. Federal Highway, 6th Floor, Ft. Lauderdale, FL 33306. (954) 564-6550. FAX: (954) 564-6553.

PRESIDENT
A. Hamid Hashemi
CFO
Michael F. Whalen
SENIOR V.P., DEVELOPMENT
Michael Melvin
SENIOR V.P., FILM BUYER
Jerry Gruenberg
VICE PRESIDENT, OPERATIONS
Deane Hashemi
DIRECTOR OF MARKETING
Randi Emerman
DIRECTOR, FOOD & BEVERAGE
Mark Uolko
DIRECTOR, OPERATION
Chuck DeWitt
VICE PRESIDENT, REAL ESTATE
Barry Ruzat
VICE PRESIDENT, CONSTRUCTION
John Townsend
DIRECTOR, PURCHASING
Merrill Goldstein

THEATRES

Muvico Palace 20	3200 Airport Rd.	Boca Raton	FL	33431	20	548
Muvico Paradise 24	15601 Sheridan St.	Davie	FL	33331	24	528
Muvico Hialeah 14	780 W. 49th St.	Hialeah	FL	33012	14	528
Muvico IMAX Theatre	9101 International Dr	Orlando	FL	32819	1	534
Muvico Pointe 20 Theatres	9101 International Dr.	Orlando	FL	32819	20	534
Muvico Palm Harbor 10	37912 US Highway 19N	Palm Harbor	FL	34684	10	539
Muvico Pompano 18	2315 N. Federal Highway	Pompano Beach	FL	33062	18	528
Muvico Baywalk 20	101 3rd Ave. North	St. Petersburg	FL	33701	20	539
Muvico Majestic 20	1600 E. 8th Ave.	Tampa	FL	33605	20	539
Muvico Starlight 20	18002 Highwood Preserve Pkwy	Tampa	FL	33647	20	539
Muvico Parisian 20	550 Rosemary St.	W. Palm Beach	FL	33401	20	548

NATIONAL AMUSEMENTS, INC.

109 U.S. theatres, 1121 U.S. screens; 16 U.K. theatres, 211 U.K. screens; 7 South American theatres, 84 South American screens; Total: 124 theatres, 1,352 screens.

200 Elm St., P.O. Box 9126, Dedham, MA 02026. (781) 461-1600. FAX: (781) 326-1306.

PRESIDENT
Shari E. Redstone
EXECUTIVE V.P.
Shari E. Redstone
SENIOR V.P., FINANCE & TREASURER
Jerome Magner
SENIOR V.P., OPERATIONS
William J. Towey
SENIOR V.P., FILM BOOKING
George Levitt
V.P. & GENERAL COUNSEL
Thaddues Jankowski
V.P., INTERNATIONAL OPERATIONS
John Bilsborough
V.P., REAL ESTATE, LATIN AMERICA
William J. Moscarelli
V.P., FILM INTERNATIONAL
Mark Walukevich
V.P., CONSTRUCTION
Peter J. Brady
V.P., FINANCE & ADMINISTRATION
Richard Sherman
V.P., CONCESSIONS
James Hughes
V.P., MIS
Stephen Sohles
V.P., OPERATIONS
James Murray
ASSISTANT V.P. & DEPUTY GENERAL COUNSEL
Patricia Reeser
ASSISTANT V.P., SALES & MARKETING
John Zawalich
ASSISTANT V.P., CORPORATE COMMUNICATIONS
Dana L.B. Wilson

THEATRES

Showcase Berlin	19 Frontage Rd.	Berlin	CT	06037	12	533
Showcase Bridgeport @Blackrock	286 Canfield Ave.	Bridgeport	CT	06605	12	501
Showcase Cinemas @ Black Rock	286 Canfield St.	Bridgeport	CT	06605	12	501
S/C East Hartford	936 Silver Lane	East Hartford	CT	06118	14	533
Showcase East Windsor	140 Bridge St.	East Windsor	CT	06088	12	533
Fairfield Cinemas	40 Black Rock Tnpk.	Fairfield	CT	06430	9	501
Showcase Cinemas Buckland Hills	99 Red Stone Rd.	Manchester	CT	06045	16	533
Showcase Milford	230 Cherry St.	Milford	CT	06460	5	533
Milford Quad	1201 Boston Post Rd.	Milford	CT	06460	4	533
Showcase Cinemas 5	230 Cherry St.	Milford	CT	06460	5	533
Showcase North Haven	550 Universal Dr.	N. Haven	CT	06473	15	533
Showcase Orange	100 Marsh Hill Rd.	Orange	CT	06477	8	533
Showcase Southington	1821 Meriden Waterbury Tnpk.	Southington	CT	06489	12	533
Super Cinemas Davenport	6219 Brady St.	Davenport	IA	52806	10	682
Showcase Cinemas 53 Davenport	3601 East 53rd St.	Davenport	IA	52806	18	682
Showcase Cinemas Milan	107 West 10th Ave.	Milan	IL	61264	11	682
Moline Super Saver Cinemas	2018 36th Ave.	Moline	IL	61265	6	682
River Falls Cinemas	951 E. Hwy 131	Clarksville	IN	47129	10	529
Showcase Erlanger	3220 Meadow Lane	Erlanger	KY	41018	9	515
Florence Cinemas	7685 Florence Mall Rd.	Florence	KY	41042	9	515
Stonybrook Cinemas	2745 S. Hurstbourne Pkwy.	Louisville	KY	40220	20	529
Showcase Cinemas Louisville	3408 Bardstown Rd.	Louisville	KY	40218	13	529
Kenwood Drive-In	7001 Southside Dr.	Louisville	KY	40214	1	529
Allston Cinema	214 Harvard Ave.	Allston	MA	02134	2	506
Quincy	1585 Hancock St.	Boston	MA	02169	8	506
Circle Cinemas	399 Chesnut Hill Ave.	Brookline	MA	02136	7	506
Showcase Cinemas Dedham	950 Providence Hwy.	Dedham	MA	02026	12	506
Showcase Lawrence 1-6	141 Winthrop Ave	Lawrence	MA	01843	6	506
Showcase Cinemas Lawrence 7-14	141 Winthrop Ave	Lawrence	MA	01843	8	506
Showcase Cinemas Lowell	32 Reiss Ave.	Lowell	MA	01851	14	506
North Attleboro	640 S. Washington St.	N. Attleboro	MA	02760	12	521
Showcase Cinemas Randolph	Rte 139	Randolph	MA	02368	16	506
Showcase Cinemas Revere	565 Squire Rd.	Revere	MA	02151	20	506
Seekonk 1-8	800 Fall River Ave.	Seekonk	MA	02771	10	521
Seekonk 9-10	775 Fall River Ave.	Seekonk	MA	02771	2	521
Showcase Seekonk	Rt 114A	Seekonk	MA	02771	10	521
White City Cinemas	50 Boston Turnpike	Shrewsbury	MA	01545	3	506
Springfield Cinemas	1060 Wilbraham Rd.	Springfield	MA	01128	12	543
S/C Cinemas At Eastfield Mall	1655 Boston Rd.	Springfield	MA	01129	16	543
S/C West Springfield 16-19	895 Riverdale St.	West Springfield	MA	01089	4	543
S/C West Springfield 1-15	864 Riverdale St.	West Springfield	MA	01089	15	543
Showcase Cinemas Woburn	25 Middlesex Canal Pkwy.	Woburn	MA	01801	14	506
Worcester North	135 Brooke St.	Worcester	MA	01606	18	506
Showcase Auburn Hills	2150 N. Opdyke Rd.	Auburn Hills	MI	48326	14	505
Showcase Pontiac 6-12	2405 S. Telegraph Rd.	Bloomfield Hills	MI	48302	7	505
Showcase Pontiac 1-5	2400 S. Telegraph Rd.	Bloomfield Hills	MI	48302	5	505
Showcase Flint East	5205 E. Court St.	Burton	MI	48509	14	513
Courtland Center Cinemas	4226 E. Court St.	Burton	MI	48509	6	513
Miracle Twin Drive-In	G6383 E. Court St.	Burton	MI	48509	2	513
Showcase Dearborn	24105 Michigan Ave.	Dearborn	MI	48124	8	505
Cinema 10 Flint	4425 Lennon Rd.	Flint	MI	48507	10	513
Showcase Flint West	1591 South Graham Rd.	Flint Township	MI	48532	14	513
Showcase Grand Rapids	5100 28th St.	Grand Rapids	MI	49512	10	563
Beacon East Cinemas	19305 Vernier Rd.	Harper Woods	MI	48225	4	505
Showcase Sterling Heights	35100 Van Dyke	Sterling Heights	MI	48312	15	505
Showcase Westland	6800 N. Wayne Rd.	Westland	MI	48185	8	505

Quo Vadis Cinemas	7420 N. Wayne Rd.	Westland	MI	48185	6	505
Showcase Ann Arbor	4100 Carpenter Rd.	Ypsilanti	MI	48197	20	505
Salem-Tri	451 South Broadway	Salem	NH	03079	3	506
Atco Multiplex	178 White Horse Pike	Atco	NJ	08004	14	504
Edgewater Multiplex Cinemas	339 River Rd.	Edgewater	NJ	07020	14	501
Hazlet Multiplex	2821 Highway 35	Hazlet	NJ	07730	12	501
All-Jersey Multiplex	104-180 Foundry St.	Newark	NJ	07105	12	501
Amboy Multiplex	US 9 & Route 35	Sayreville	NJ	08872	14	501
Concourse Plaza Multiplex	214 East 161st St.	Bronx	NY	10451	10	501
Whitestone Multiplex	2505 Bruckner Blvd.	Bronx	NY	10465	14	501
Linden Blvd. Multiplex	2784 Linden Blvd.	Brooklyn	NY	11208	14	501
Commack Multiplex	100 Long Island Expressway	Commack	NY	11725	15	501
Greenburgh Multiplex Cinemas	320 Saw Mill River Rd.	Elmsford	NY	10523	10	501
Farmingdale Multiplex	1001 Broad Hollow Rd.	Farmingdale	NY	11735	14	501
All Westchester Saw Mill Multi	151 Saw Mill River Rd.	Hawthorne	NY	10532	10	501
Broadway Multiplex	955 Broadway Mall	Hicksville	NY	11801	12	501
Brookhaven Multiplex	440 Long Island Expressway	Medford	NY	11763	14	501
Green Acres Cinemas	610 West Sunrise Hwy.	Valley Stream	NY	11581	6	501
Sunrise Multiplex	760 W. Sunrise Hwy.	Valley Stream	NY	11582	14	501
College Point Multiplex	28-55 Ulmer St.	Whitestone	NY	11357	12	501
Cross County Multiplex	Two South Dr.	Yonkers	NY	10704	10	501
Dayton Mall Cinemas	2700 Miamisburg	Centerville	OH	45459	1	515
Showcase Cross Pointe 12	6751 Loop Rd.	Centerville	OH	45459	12	515
Centerville Cinemas	965 Miamisburg	Centerville	OH	45459	6	515
Showcase Western Hills	5870 Harrison Ave.	Cincinnati	OH	45248	14	515
Showcase Eastgate	4701 Eastgate Blvd.	Cincinnati	OH	45245	7	515
Showcase Cincinnati	1701 Showcase Dr.	Cincinnati	OH	45237	12	515
Kenwood Towne Centre	7875 Montgomery Rd.	Cincinnati	OH	45236	5	515
Showcase Springdale	12064 Springfield Pike	Cincinnati	OH	45246	10	515
Northgate Cinemas	9727 Colerain Ave.	Cincinnati	OH	45239	7	515
S/C Spring Meadows, Toledo	1301 East Mall Dr.	Holland	OH	43528	10	547
Showcase Huber Heights 16	7737 Waynetown Blvd.	Huber Heights	OH	45424	16	542
Oakley Drive-In	5033 Madison Rd.	Madisonville	OH	45227	1	515
Showcase Kings Island	5937 Kings Island Dr.	Mason	OH	45040	12	515
Showcase Maumee	1360 Conant St., Route 20	Maumee	OH	43537	18	547
Showcase Cinemas Milford	500 Rivers Edge Dr.	Milford	OH	45150	16	515
275 East Cinemas	5874 Montclair Blvd.	Milford	OH	45150	4	515
Franklin Park 6	5801 Monroe St.	Toledo	OH	43623	6	547
Franklin Park Cinemas	5235 Monroe St.	Toledo	OH	43623	5	547
North Towne Mall 5	343 New Towne Square	Toledo	OH	43612	5	547
Southwyck Mall 3	102 Southwyke Shopping Center	Toledo	OH	43614	3	547
Showcase Toledo	3500 Seccer Rd.	Toledo	OH	43606	5	547
Showcase Cinemas Miamisburgh	195 Mall Woods Dr.	West Carrollton	OH	45449	16	542
Showcase Cinemas East	3455 Wm. Penn Hwy.	Pittsburgh	PA	15235	10	508
Showcase Cinemas West	Park Manor Dr.	Pittsburgh	PA	15205	12	508
Showcase Cinemas North - Pitt	9700 Mcknight Rd.	Pittsburgh	PA	15237	11	508
Super Saver Cinemas 8	8000 McKnight Rd.	Pittsburgh	PA	15237	8	508
Apple Valley Cinemas	445 Putnam Pike	Greenville	RI	02828	8	521
Warwick	1200 Quaker Lane	Warwick	RI	02886	15	521
Mt. Vernon Multiplex	7940 Richmond Hwy.	Alexandria	VA	22306	10	511
Centervill Multiplex	6201 Multiplex Dr.	Centerville	VA	22121	12	511
Lee Highway Multiplex	8223 Lee Hwy.	Merrifield	VA	22116	14	511
Reston Multiplex	11940 Market St.	Reston	VA	20195	11	511

O'NEIL THEATRES, INC.

15 theatres, 136 screens.
1926 C Corporate Square Dr., Slidell, LA 70458. (504) 641-4720. FAX: (504) 641-5726. www.movie-info.com
PRESIDENT
Tim O'Neil, Jr.
VICE PRESIDENT
Tim O'Neil III
SECRETARY & TREASURER
Betty O'Neil
OFFICE OPERATIONS
C. Jean Johnson
FIELD OPERATIONS
Steven L. Moss

THEATRES

O'Neil Riviera 12 Cinema	110 Riviera Blvd.	Foley	AL	36535	12	686
O'Neil Promenade Cinema 12	2399 Cobbs Ford Rd.	Prattville	AL	36066	12	698
O'Neil Westbrook Cinema 12	314 Flat Rock Place	Westbrook	CT	06498	12	533
O'Neil Destin Cinema 10	759 Hwy 98 East	Destin	FL	32541	10	686
O'Neil Taft Hollywood Cinema 12	7001 Taft St.	Hollywood	FL	33024	12	528
O'Neil Edgewater Cinema 10	473 B Bechrich Rd.	Panama City Beach	FL	32407	10	656
O'Neil Avondale Cinema 16	3604 Memorial Dr.	Decatur	GA	30030	16	524
O'Neil Holiday Square Cinema 10	201 N. Hwy 190	Covington	LA	70448	10	622
O'Neil Crowley Cinema IV	2304 N. Parkerson	Crowley	LA	70526	4	642
O'Neil Causeway Place Cinema 4	1631 N. Causeway Blvd.	Mandeville	LA	70448	4	622
O'Neil Movies 8 Slidell	139 Gause Blvd.	Slidell	LA	70458	8	622
O'Neil Market Place Cinema 12	651 Business Loop I-35 North	New Braunfels	TX	78130	12	641
O'Neil Broadacres Cinema	6661 Hwy 49 North	Hattiesburg	MS	39401	6	710
O'Neil River Ridge Cinema 4	733 Cooper Rd.	Picayune	MS	39466	4	622
O'Neil Choctaw Cinema 4	310 Hwy 90	Waveland	MS	39576	4	622

PACIFIC THEATRES

34 theatres, 296 screens.
(also owns Consolidated Amusement, Hawaii) 120 N. Robertson Boulevard, Los Angeles, CA 90048. (310) 657-8420.
BOARD CHAIRMAN
Michael R. Forman
CEO
Christopher Forman
CFO
John Hunter
EXECUTIVE V.P., HEAD FILM BUYER
Chan Wood

THEATRES

Bakersfield Valley Plaza 16	2000 Wible Rd.	Bakersfield	CA	93304	16	800
Ceres Drive-In	1651 Whitmore Ave.	Ceres	CA	95307	2	862
Winnetka	9201 Winnetka Ave.	Chatsworth	CA	91311	21	803
Commerce 14	950 Goodrich Blvd.	City of Commerce	CA	90022	14	803
Vineland Drive-In 4	443 N. Vineland Ave.	City of Industry	CA	91715	4	803
Cinema Corte Madera	41 Tamal Vista Blvd.	Corte Madera	CA	94925	1	807
Beach Cities Stadium 16	831 Nash St.	El Segundo	CA	90245	16	803
Pacific's Woodward Park D.I.	7150 N. Abby	Fresno	CA	93710	4	866
Warners 2	6714 Pacific Blvd.	Huntington Park	CA	90255	2	803
Grossmont Trolley 8	8555 Fletcher Pkwy.	La Mesa	CA	91942	8	825
Grossmont Center 8	5500 Grossmont Center Dr.	La Mesa	CA	91942	8	825
Regency 8	2650 E. Carson St.	Lakewood	CA	90712	8	803
Lakewood Center Stadium 16	5200 Faculty Ave.	Lakewood	CA	90712	16	803
Lakewood Center South 9	4821 Del Amo Blvd.	Lakewood	CA	90712	9	803
Pacific Crest	1262 Westwood Blvd.	Los Angeles	CA	90024	1	803
Manhattan Village	3560 Sepulveda Blvd.	Manhattan Beach	CA	90266	6	803
Sequoia	25 Throckmorton St.	Mill Valley	CA	94941	2	807
Sweetwater	1920 Sweetwater Rd.	National City	CA	91950	9	825
Northridge Cinemas	19401 Parthenia St.	Northridge	CA	91324	10	803
Northridge Fashion Center	9400 N. Shirley Ave.	Northridge	CA	91324	10	803
Rowland Plaza	44 Rowland Way	Novato	CA	94947	8	807
Ontario 10	2560 Archibald Ave.	Ontario	CA	91761	10	803
Hastings Pacific	355 N. Rosemead Blvd.	Pasadena	CA	91107	8	803
Hastings Ranch	467 N. Rosemead Blvd.	Pasadena	CA	91107	3	803
Petaluma	1363 N. Mcdowell Blvd.	Petaluma	CA	94954	8	807
Rohnert Park 16	555 Rohnert Park Expressway	Rohnert Park	CA	94928	16	807
Inland Center 5	787 Inland Center Dr.	San Bernardino	CA	92408	5	803
Cinerama 6	5831 University Ave.	San Diego	CA	92115	6	825
Pacific Carmel Mountain 12	11620 Carmel Mt. Rd.	San Diego	CA	92128	12	825
Town Square Stadium 14	4665 Clairemont Dr.	San Diego	CA	92117	14	825
Gaslamp Stadium 15	701 5th Ave.	San Diego	CA	92101	15	825
Northgate	7000 Northgate Dr.	San Rafael	CA	94903	15	807
Regency	280 Smith Ranch Rd.	San Rafael	CA	94903	6	807
Marin	101 Caledonia St.	Sausalito	CA	94965	3	807

THE PATRIOT CINEMAS, INC.

5 theatres, 22 screens.
800 Hingham Str., Rockland, MA 02370. (781) 982-2244. FAX: (781) 982-5511.
PRESIDENT
Philip J. Scott
VICE PRESIDENT
David A. Kiolbasa
VICE PRESIDENT
Edith L. Scott
FILM BOOKER & BUYER
David A. Scott

THEATRES

Patriot Cinemas, Loring Hall	65 Main St.	Hingham	MA	02043	1	506
Patriot Cinemas, Museum Place	2 E. India Sq.	Salem	MA	01970	3	506
Patriot Cinemas, Cameo Theatre	14 Columbian St.	S. Weymouth	MA	02190	2	506
Patriot Cinemas, Nickelodeon 6	One Temple St.	Portland	ME	04101	6	500
Patriot Cinemas, E. Providence 10	60 Newport Ave.	E. Providence	RI	02916	10	521

POLSON THEATRES

8 theatres, 15 screens.
P.O. Box 999, Polson, MT 59860. (406) 883-5603. FAX: (406) 883-5639.
OWNER
Howard Pickerill
HEAD FILM BUYER
Gary Dupuis

THEATRES

River Cinemas	526 Main St.	Salmon	ID	83467	2	758
Big Sky Cinemas	560 N. Montana	Dillon	MT	59725	2	754
Valley Cinemas	200 2nd Ave.	Glasgow	MT	59230	2	755
Havre Cinemas	328 2nd St.	Havre	MT	59501	2	755
Showboat Cinemas	416 Main St.	Polson	MT	59860	2	762
Entertainer Cinema	410 Main St.	Ronan	MT	59864	1	762
Mountain Cinemas	6475 Hwy 93	Whitefish	MT	59937	2	762
Prairie Cinemas	314 Main St.	Wolf Point	MT	59201	2	687

R/C THEATRES MANAGEMENT CORP.

24 theatres, 153 screens.
231 W. Cherry Hill Ct., Box 1056, Reisterstown, MD 21136. (410) 526-4774. FAX: (410) 526-6871.
PRESIDENT, CHAIRMAN & CEO
J. Wayne Anderson
EXECUTIVE V.P., COO
Dennis R. Daniels
SENIOR V.P.
David G. Phillips
DIRECTOR OF FILM
Scott R. Cohen
CONTROLLER
Richard A. Hershel
SENIOR FILM BUYER
Jan S. Anderson
CFO
Jeffrey D. Weeks
DIVISION MANAGERS
Philip Ridenour (MD, PA)
David Knight (VA & NC)

THEATRES

OceanWalk 10	300 N. Atlantic Ave.	Daytona Beach	FL	32118	10	534
Parkside 16	7200 US Hwy. 19	Pinellas Park	FL	33781	16	539
Carrolltown Movies 6	6405 W. Hemlock Rd.	Eldersburg	MD	21784	6	512
Westview 16	Rte. 85 & Buckystown Pike	Frederick	MD	21701	16	511
Frostburg Cinemas 3	10701 New Georges Creek Rd.	Frostburg	MD	21532	3	511
Hagerstown Cinemas 10	Leitersburg Pike	Hagerstown	MD	21740	10	511
Valley Mall Movies 16	17301 Valley Mall Rd.	Hagerstown	MD	21740	16	511
Long Meadow Cinemas	1553 N. Potomac Ave.	Hagerstown	MD	21742	3	511
White Marlin Movies 5	12641 Ocean Gateway	Ocean City	MD	21842	5	576
M.J. Mall Cinemas 8	250 Noble Blvd.	Carlisle	PA	17013	8	566
Majestic 3	29 Carlisle St.	Gettysburg	PA	17325	3	566
Culpeper Movies 4	210 S. Main St.	Culpeper	VA	22701	4	511

MANAGED THEATRES

Hollywood Cinemas	5509 Oregon Ave.	Arbutus	MD	21227	4	512
Eastpoint Movies	7938 Eastern Blvd.	Baltimore	MD	21224	10	512
Easton Movies	Marlboro Rd.	Easton	MD	21601	4	512
Hatteras Movies	Hwy. 12	Avon	NC	27915	4	544
Corolla Movies	815 E-Ocean Trail	Corolla	NC	27927	4	544
Kitty Hawk Twin	3850 N. Croatan Hwy	Kitty Hawk	NC	27949	2	544
Market Place	110 N. Croatan Hwy	Kitty Hawk	NC	27949	2	544
Cineplex Movies	2423 S. Croatan Hwy.	Nags Head	NC	27959	4	544
Hanover Movies	380 Eisenhower Dr.	Hanover	PA	17331	9	566
Fox East	4350 Perknomen Ave.	Reading	PA	19606	4	504
Covington Movies	139 N. Maple Ave.	Covington	VA	24426	3	579
State Cinema 3	12W. Nelson St.	Lexington	VA	24450	3	573

REGAL CINEMAS, INC.

431 theatres, 4,464 screens, 6 IMAX.
7132 Commercial Park Dr., Knoxville, TN. 37918. (865) 922-1123. FAX: (865) 922-3188.
CHAIRMAN, PRESIDENT & CEO
Mike Campbell
EXECUTIVE V.P., COO
Greg Dunn
SENIOR V.P. & CFO
Amy Miles
SENIOR V.P. & CIO
J.E. Henry
SENIOR V.P., GENERAL COUNSEL & SECRETARY
Peter Brandow
SENIOR V.P., HUMAN RESOURCE COUNSEL
Randy Smith
SENIOR V.P., PURCHASING
Rob Del Moro
SENIOR V.P. & HEAD FILM BUYER
Denise Gurin
SENIOR V.P., OPERATIONS
Mike Levesque
SENIOR V.P., CONSTRUCTION
Ron Reid
SENIOR V.P., MARKETING & ADVERTISING
Richard Westerling
V.P., OPERATIONS, NORTH
Fred Buffum
V.P., THEATRE EQUIPMENT
Ray Dunlap
V.P., OPERATIONS, WEST
Curtis Ewing
V.P., CONTROLLER
Macon Fields
V.P., TECHNICAL SERVICES
Roger Frazee
V.P., ADVERTISING
Rich Given
V.P., SYSTEMS & DEVELOPMENT
Charlie Gooden
V.P., SECURITY & QUALITY CONTROL
Leon Hurst
V.P., TECH INFORMATION SYSTEMS
Todd King
V.P., CONSTRUCTION
Ronald Kooch
V.P., OPERATIONS, SOUTH
Bill Koontz
V.P., HUMAN RESOURCES
Jackie McClure
V.P., OPERATIONS, CENTRAL
Mark Reis
V.P., REAL ESTATE & PROPERTY MANAGEMENT
John Roper
V.P., ASSISTANT HEAD FILM BUYER
Barry Steinberg

THEATRES

Regal Dimond Center 9 Cinemas	800 E. Dimond Blvd.	Anchorage	AK	99515	9	743
Regal Fireweed 7 Cinemas	661 E. Fireweed Lane	Anchorage	AK	99503	7	743
Regal Totem 8 Theatres	3131 Muldoon Rd.	Anchorage	AK	99504	8	743
Regal Goldstream 16	1855 Airport Rd.	Fairbanks	AK	99701	16	745
Regal Kambe Theatre 3	215 S. Willow St.	Kenai	AK	99611	3	743
Regal Festival 18	7001 Crestwood Blvd.	Birmingham	AL	35210	18	630
Regal Galleria 10	3200 Galleria Circle	Birmingham	AL	35216	10	630
Regal 16 - Trussville	5895 Trussville Crossing Pkwy.	Birmingham	AL	35235	16	630
Regal Wildwood 14 Cinemas	275 Lakeshore Pkwy.	Birmingham	AL	35209	14	630
Regal River Oaks Cinema 8	2203 S.W. Family Security Place	Decatur	AL	35603	8	691
Regal Rainbow Cinema 8	948 Rainbow Dr.	Gadsden	AL	35902	8	630
Regal Hollywood 18-Huntsville	3312 South Memorial Pkwy.	Huntsville	AL	35802	18	691

Regal Madison Square 12	5905 University Dr.	Huntsville	AL	35806	12	691
Regal Brook Highland 10	5255 Hwy 280 South	Inverness	AL	35242	10	630
Regal Movies 4	1007 Hwy 78 West	Jasper	AL	35501	4	630
Regal Fox 12	900 Skyland Blvd.	Tuscaloosa	AL	35405	12	620
Regal Fiesta Square 16	3033 N. College	Fayetteville	AR	72703	16	670
Regal Rogers Mall 6	100 Dixieland Rd.	Rogers	AR	72756	6	670
Regal Deer Valley 16	4204 Lone Tree Way	Antioch	CA	94509	16	807
Regal Rancho Del Rey 16	1025 Tierra Del Rey	Chula Vista	CA	91910	16	825
Regal Diamond Bar Cinema 8	2751 Diamond Bar Blvd.	Diamond Bar	CA	91765	8	803
Regal Hacienda Crossing	5000 Dublin Blvd.	Dublin	CA	94568	20	807
Regal Hacienda Crossing IMAX	5000 Dublin Blvd.	Dublin	CA	94568	1	807
Regal Parkway Plaza 18	405 Parkway Plaza	El Cajon	CA	92020	18	825
Regal Foothill Towne Center 22	26602 Towne Center Dr.	Foothill Ranch	CA	92610	22	803
Regal Garden Grove 16	9741 Chapman Ave.	Garden Grove	CA	92841	16	803
Regal Hemet Cinema 12	2369 West Florida Ave.	Hemet	CA	92545	12	803
Regal La Habra 16	1351 W. Imperial Hwy.	La Habra	CA	90631	16	803
Regal Lake Elsinore Cinema 8	32260 Mission Trail	Lake Elsinore	CA	92530	8	803
Regal Moorpark 8	543 Los Angeles Ave.	Moorpark	CA	93021	8	803
Regal Oceanside 16	401 Mission Ave.	Oceanside	CA	92054	16	825
Regal Galaxy 8	4200 Rosewood	Pleasanton	CA	94588	8	807
Regal Terrace Cinema 6	28901 S. Western Ave.	Rancho Palos	CA	90732	6	803
Regal The Ave. 13	550 Deep Valley Dr.	Rolling Hills Estates	CA	90274	13	803
Regal Natomas Marketplace 16	3561 Truxel Rd.	Sacramento	CA	95834	16	862
Regal Del Rosa 8	1895 N. Del Rosa Ave.	San Bernardino	CA	92404	8	803
Regal Civic Center Plaza 16	2751 Papo Canyon Rd.	Simi Valley	CA	93063	16	803
Regal Whittwood Cinema 10	10228 Scott Lane	Whittier	CA	90603	10	803
Regal Peoples Plaza Cinema 17	1100 Peoples Plaza	Newark	DE	19702	17	504
Regal Brandywine Town Center 16	3200 Brandywine Pkwy.	Wilmington	DE	19803	16	504
Regal Shadowood 16	9889 W. Glades Rd.	Boca Raton	FL	33434	16	548
Regal Bonita Springs 12	25251 S. Tamiami Trail	Bonita Springs	FL	34134	12	571
Regal Boynton 8 Cinema	2290 N. Congress Ave.	Boynton Beach	FL	33426	8	548
Regal Bradenton 8 Cinemas	7150 Cortez Rd.	Bradenton	FL	34210	8	539
Regal Desoto Square Mall 6 Cinemas	303-301 Blvd W.	Bradenton	FL	34205	6	539
Regal Oakmont 8	4801 Cortez Rd.	Bradenton	FL	34210	8	539
Regal Coralwood 10 Cinemas	2301 Del Prado Blvd.	Cape Coral	FL	33904	10	571
Regal Mayfair 10	3390 Mary St.	Coconut Grove	FL	33134	10	528
Regal Magnolia Place 16	9645 Westview Dr.	Coral Springs	FL	33076	16	528
Regal Crystal River Mall 9	1801 N.W. US Hwy. 19	Crystal River	FL	34428	9	539
Regal Delray Beach 18	1668 S. Federal Hwy.	Delray Beach	FL	33483	18	548
Regal Las Olas 23	300 S.W. First Ave.	Fort Lauderdale	FL	33301	23	528
Regal Belltower 20	13499 Belltower Dr.	Ft. Meyers	FL	33907	20	571
Regal Cypress Creek Station 16	6415 N. Andrews Ave.	Fort Lauderdale	FL	33334	16	528
Regal Gainesville Cinema 14	3101 S.W. 35th Blvd.	Gainesville	FL	32608	14	592
Regal Lake Worth 8 Cinemas	5881 Lake Worth Rd.	Greenacres City	FL	33463	8	548
Regal Oakwood 18	2800 Oakwood Blvd.	Hollywood	FL	33020	18	528
Regal Citrus Cinemas 6	2635 East Gulf To Lake Hwy.	Inverness	FL	34450	6	539
Regal Beach Boulevard 18	14051 Beach Blvd.	Jacksonville	FL	32250	18	561
Regal Jacksonville Cinema 10	6681 103rd St.	Jacksonville	FL	32210	10	561
Regal The Ave.s 20	9525 Phillips Hwy.	Jacksonville	FL	32256	20	561
Regal Jupiter 18	204 N. US 1	Jupiter	FL	33477	18	548
Regal Cinema Key West 6	3338 N. Roosevelt Blvd.	Key West	FL	33040	6	528
Regal Osceola Square East 6	1821 Armstrong Blvd.	Kissimmee	FL	34741	6	534
Regal Osceola Square West 6	3827 West Vine St.	Kissimmee	FL	34741	6	534
Regal Lake Mary Cinema 10	3580 N. Hwy 17-92	Lake Mary	FL	32746	10	534
Regal Eagle Ridge Mall 12	955 Eagle Ridge Dr. & Hwy. 27	Lake Wales	FL	33853	12	539
Regal Largo Mall 8	10500 Ulmerton Rd.	Largo	FL	33771	8	539
Regal Hollywood 20-Northgate	3979 Van Dyke Rd.	Lutz	FL	33549	20	539
Regal Oaks 10	1800 W. Hibiscus Blvd.	Melbourne	FL	32901	10	534
Regal Kendall 9	12090 S.W. 88th St.	Miami	FL	33186	9	528
Regal Palace 18	11865 S.W. 26th St.	Miami	FL	33175	18	528
Regal South Beach Cinema 18	1100 Lincoln Rd.	Miami Beach	FL	33139	18	528
Regal Miami Lakes 17	6711 Main St.	Miami Lakes	FL	33014	17	528
Regal Hollywood 20-Naples	6006 Hollywood Dr.	Naples	FL	34101	20	571
Regal Pavilion 10	833 Vanderbilt Beach Rd.	Naples	FL	34108	10	571
Regal Hollywood 16-Ocala	2801 S.W. 27th Ave.	Ocala	FL	34474	16	534
Regal Southchase Cinema 7	12441 S. Orange Blossom Trail	Orlando	FL	32837	7	534
Regal UC7 Cinema	12255 University Blvd.	Orlando	FL	32817	7	534
Regal Waterford Lakes	541 N. Alafaya Trail	Orlando	FL	32828	20	534
Regal Ormond Beach Cinema 12	215 Williamson Blvd.	Ormond Beach	FL	32174	12	534
Regal Oviedo Marketplace 22	1500 Oviedo Marketplace Blvd.	Oviedo	FL	32765	22	534
Regal Palm Bay 10	160 Malabar Rd.	Palm Bay	FL	32907	10	534
Regal Roxy 10 Cinemas	1553 Palm Bay Rd.	Palm Bay	FL	32905	10	534
Regal Westfork Plaza 13	15977 West Pines Blvd.	Pembroke Pines	FL	33027	13	528
Regal Cordova Cinemas 3	5020 Bayou Blvd.	Pensacola	FL	32504	3	686
Regal Cordova Mall Cinemas 4	5100 N. 9th Ave.	Pensacola	FL	32504	4	686
Regal Town Center 16-Port Charlotte	1441 Tamiami Trail	Port Charlotte	FL	33948	16	571
Regal Embassy 6	9510 US 19 North	Port Richey	FL	34668	6	539
Regal Hollywood 18-Port Richey	6701 Cinema Dr.	Port Richey	FL	34668	18	539
Regal Royal Palm Beach 18	1003 State Rd. 7	Royal Palm Beach	FL	33411	18	548
Regal Crossings Cinema 10	5521 Fruitville Rd.	Sarasota	FL	34232	10	539
Regal Hollywood 20	1993 Main St.	Sarasota	FL	34236	20	539
Regal Parkway 8 Cinemas	6300 N. Lockwood Ridge Rd.	Sarasota	FL	34243	8	539
Regal Spring Hill 8 Cinemas	2955 Commercial Way	Spring Hill	FL	34606	8	539
Regal Mall St Augustine 6	2121 US 1 South	St Augustine	FL	32086	6	561
Regal Regency Square 8	2448 S. Federal Hwy.	Stuart	FL	34994	8	548
Regal Sawgrass 23	2600 N.W. 136th Ave.	Sunrise	FL	33323	23	528
Regal Britton 8	3938 Dale Mabry Hwy.	Tampa	FL	33611	8	539
Regal Citrus Park 20	7999 Citrus Park Town Center Mall	Tampa	FL	33625	20	539
Regal University 16	12332 University Mall Ct.	Tampa	FL	33612	16	539
Regal Venetian 6	1735 S. Tamiami Trail	Venice	FL	34293	6	539
Regal Winter Park Village 20	510 N. Orlando Ave.	Winter Park	FL	32789	20	534
Regal Spring Lake 10	920 Springlake Square N.W.	Winter Haven	FL	33881	10	539
Regal Augusta Village Cinema 12	1323 Augusta West Pkwy.	Augusta	GA	30909	12	520
Regal Augusta Exchange 20	1144 Agerton Lane	Augusta	GA	30909	20	520
Regal 22 @ Austell	2480 E.W. Connector Rd.	Austell	GA	30106	22	524
Regal Mall of Georgia 20	3333 Buford Dr.	Buford	GA	30518	20	524
Regal Mall of Georgia IMAX	3333 Buford Dr.	Buford	GA	30518	2	524
Regal Hollywood 24 @ North I-85	3265 N.E. Expressway Access	Chamblee	GA	30341	24	524

Regal Arbor Place Mall 18	6600 Douglas Blvd.	Douglasville	GA	30135	18	524
Regal Medlock Crossing 18	9700 Medlock Bridge Rd.	Duluth	GA	30097	18	524
Regal Town Center 16-Kennesaw	2795 Town Center Dr.	Kennesaw	GA	30144	16	524
Regal Covington Square Cinema 8	2244 Panola Rd.	Lithonia	GA	30058	8	524
Regal Colonial Mall 8	3653 Eisenhower Pkwy.	Macon	GA	31206	8	503
Regal Rivergate Cinema 14	245 Tom Hill Senior Blvd.	Macon	GA	31210	14	503
Regal Delk 10	2854 Delk Rd.	Marietta	GA	30067	10	524
Regal Cinema 10	1050 Powder Springs Rd.	Marietta	GA	30064	10	524
Regal Peachtree Corners 10	6135 Peachtree Pkwy.	Norcross	GA	30092	10	524
Regal Riverdale Cinema 14	274 Hwy. 138	Riverdale	GA	30274	14	524
Regal Eisenhower Square 6	1100 Eisenhower Dr.	Savannah	GA	31406	6	507
Regal Savannah 10	1132-34 Shawnee Ave.	Savannah	GA	31401	10	507
Regal Victory Square Cinema 9	3001 Skidway Rd.	Savannah	GA	31414	9	507
Regal Snellville Oaks 14	2125 E. Main St.	Snellville	GA	30078	14	524
Regal Coeur D Alene 5 Cinema	3555 N. Government Way	Coeur D'Alene	ID	83814	5	881
Regal Showboat 5 Cinemas	5725 Pioneer Dr.	Coeur D'Alene	ID	83814	5	881
Regal Liberty Theatre	611 Main St.	Lewiston	ID	83501	1	881
Regal Orchards Tri Cinema	3323 10th Ave.	Lewiston	ID	83501	3	881
Regal Showplace 16	5000 W. Route 14	Crystal Lake	IL	60014	16	602
Regal Lake Zurich 12	755 S. Rand Rd.	Lake Zurich	IL	60047	12	602
Regal Lincolnshire 20	300 Parkway Dr.	Lincolnshire	IL	60069	20	602
Regal Round Lake Beach 18	550 E. Rollins Rd.	Round Lake Beach	IL	60073	18	602
Regal Charlestowne Mall 18	3740 E. Main St.	St. Charles	IL	60174	18	602
Regal Shiloh Crossing 18	10400 E. US 36	Avon	IN	46123	18	527
Regal Village Park Cinema 12	2222 E. 146th St.	Carmel	IN	46032	17	527
Regal Coldwater Crossing 8	211 W. Washington Center Rd.	Fort Wayne	IN	46825	8	509
Regal Coventry 13	5495 Coventry Lane	Fort Wayne	IN	46804	13	509
Regal Georgetown Square 1 & 2	6414 E. State Blvd.	Fort Wayne	IN	46815	2	509
Regal Glenbrook Cinema 3	4201 Coldwater Rd.	Fort Wayne	IN	46805	3	509
Regal Holiday 6	931 Northcrest Shoping center	Fort Wayne	IN	46805	6	509
Regal Turfway Park Cinema 10	7650 Turfway Rd.	Florence	KY	41042	10	515
Regal Hamburg Pavilion 16	1949 Starshoot Rd.	Lexington	KY	40509	16	541
Regal Bossier Corners Cinema 9	2800 Shad Rd.	Bossier City	LA	71111	9	612
Regal Southpark Mall Cinema 6	8924 Jewella Rd.	Shreveport	LA	71118	6	612
Regal Springfield Plaza 16	1250 Saint James Ave.	Springfield	MA	01118	16	543
Regal Bel Air Cinema 14	409 Constant Friendship Blvd.	Abingdon	MD	21009	14	512
Regal Holiday Cinema 2	100 Baughmans Lane	Frederick	MD	21702	2	511
Regal Rockville Center 13	199 E. Montgomery Ave.	Rockville	MD	20850	13	511
Regal Frenchtown Square Mall 8	2121 N. Monroe St.	Monroe	MI	48161	8	505
Regal Eagan 16	2055 Cliff Rd.	Eagan	MN	55122	16	613
Regal Brooklyn Center 20	6420 Camden Ave.	Minneapolis	MN	55430	20	613
Regal Kansas City 18 Cinemas	8201 N.E. Birmingham Rd.	Kansas City	MO	64161	18	616
Regal Hollywood Cinemas 14	1640 Hendersonville Rd.	Asheville	NC	28803	14	567
Regal Boone Cinema 7	210 New Market St. Centre	Boone	NC	28607	7	517
Regal Stonecrest at Piper Glen 22	7824 Rea Rd.	Charlotte	NC	28277	22	517
Regal Omni Cinema 8	3729 Sycamore Dairy Rd.	Fayetteville	NC	28303	8	560
Regal Greensboro Cinema 7	4631 High Point Rd.	Greensboro	NC	27409	7	518
Regal Oak Hollow Mall 7	931 Eastchester Dr.	High Point	NC	27265	7	518
Regal Mayberry Cinema 5	840 Fowler Rd.	Mount Airy	NC	27030	5	518
Regal Wilson Cinema 6	1705 Montgomery Dr.	WIlson	NC	27895	6	560
Regal Burlington 20	250 Bromley Blvd.	Burlington	NJ	08016	20	504
Regal Town Center Plaza 15	319 Route 130	East Windsor	NJ	08520	15	504
Regal Hudson Mall 7	Route 440	Jersey City	NJ	07305	7	501
Regal Marlboro Cinema 8	12 Route 9	Morganville	NJ	07751	8	501
Regal Columbia Park	3115 Kennedy Blvd.	N. Bergen	NJ	07047	12	501
Regal Commerce Center 18	2399 Route 1	N. Brunswick	NJ	08902	18	501
Regal Pohatcong 12	1246 Highway 22	Phillipsburgh	NJ	08865	12	501
Regal Hadley Theatre 16	1000 Corporate Court	South Plainfield	NJ	07080	16	501
Regal Cross Keys Cinema 12	151 American Blvd.	Turnersville	NJ	08012	12	504
Regal Cumberland Mall 14	3849 S. Delsea	Vineland	NJ	08360	14	504
Regal Sunset Station 13 Theatre	1301-A W. Sunset Rd.	Henderson	NV	89014	13	839
Regal Boulder Station 11 theatre	4111 Boulder Hwy.	Las Vegas	NV	89121	11	839
Regal Colonnade 14	8880 S. Eastern Ave.	Las Vegas	NV	89123	14	839
Regal Texas Station 18	2101 N. Texas Star Ln.	Las Vegas	NV	89030	18	839
Regal Village Square 18	9400 W. Sahara Ave.	Las Vegas	NV	89117	18	839
Regal Kaufman Astoria Cinema 14	35-01 37th St.	Astoria	NY	11101	14	501
Regal Court St. 12	108 Court St.	Brooklyn	NY	11201	12	501
Regal Elmwood Center 16	2001 Elmwood Ave.	Buffalo	NY	14207	16	514
Regal Culver Ridge Plaza 16	2255 Ridge Rd.	Irondequoit	NY	14622	16	538
Regal New Roc City 18	33 Le Count Place	New Rochelle	NY	10801	18	501
Regal New Roc City IMAX	33 Le Count Place	New Rochelle	NY	10801	2	501
Regal Battery Park City 16	102 N. End Ave.	New York	NY	10281	16	501
Regal Hollywood 12	720 Builders Way	Niagara Falls	NY	14304	12	514
Regal Quaker Crossing 18	3450 Amelia Dr.	Orchard Park	NY	14127	18	514
Regal Henrietta Cinema 18	525 Marketplace Dr.	Rochester	NY	14623	18	538
Regal Ronkonkoma Cinema 9	565 Portion Rd.	Ronkonkoma	NY	11779	9	501
Regal Staten Island 16	2474 Forest Ave.	Staten Island	NY	10303	16	501
Regal Eastview Mall 13	70 Eastview Mall Dr.	Victor	NY	14564	13	538
Regal Transit Center 18	6707 Transit Rd.	Williamsville	NY	14221	18	514
Regal Transit Center IMAX	6707 Transit Rd.	Williamsville	NY	14221	1	514
Regal Independence 10	1210 Independence Ave.	Akron	OH	44310	10	510
Regal Interstate Park Cinema 18	1089 Interstate Pkwy.	Akron	OH	44312	18	510
Regal Montrose Movies 12	4020 Medina Rd.	Akron	OH	44333	12	510
Regal Lake Cinema 8	588 W. Tuscarawas Ave.	Barberton	OH	44203	8	510
Regal Hollywood 20 @ Fairfield Comm.	2651 Fairfield Commons	Beavercreek	OH	45431	20	542
Regal Brookgate Saver 5	5837 Smith Rd.	Brookpark	OH	44142	5	510
Regal Hickory Ridge Cinema 8	1055 Pearl Rd.	Brunswick	OH	44212	8	510
Regal 6	2077 Western Ave.	Chilicothe	OH	45601	6	535
Regal Shawnee Square Cinema 4	144 Consumer Dr.	Chilicothe	OH	45601	4	535
Regal Central Parke Cinema 11	4600 Smith Rd.	Cincinati	OH	45212	11	515
Regal Severance Town Center 14	3492 Mayfield Rd.	Cleveland Heights	OH	44118	14	510
Regal Georgesville Square 16	1800 Georgesville Square Dr.	Columbus	OH	43228	16	535
Regal Northtowne Cinema 9	1500 N. Clinton St.	Defiance	OH	43512	9	547
Regal Delaware Square Movies 5	1141 S. Columbus Pike	Delaware	OH	43015	5	535
Regal Cobblestone Square 20	5500 Abbe Rd.	Elyria	OH	44035	20	510
Regal Garfield Mall Movies 5	12686 Rockside Rd.	Garfield Heights	OH	44125	5	510
Regal Hudson Cinema 10	5339 Darrow Rd.	Hudson	OH	44236	10	510

Regal River Valley Mall 10	1635 River Valley Circle	Lancaster	OH	43130	10	535
Regal Lima Center Cinema 3	2720 Elida Rd.	Lima	OH	45805	3	558
Regal Cinema 7	1450 N. Cable Rd.	Lima	OH	45805	7	558
Regal Sheffield Centre 10	100 Sheffield Centre	Lorain	OH	44055	10	510
Regal Lafayette Center Cinema 7	430 Pike St.	Marietta	OH	45750	7	597
Regal Southland Cinema 7	1415 Marion-Waldo Rd.	Marion	OH	43302	7	535
Regal Mayfield Heights 10	1345 SOM Center Rd.	Mayfield Heights	OH	44124	10	510
Regal Medina 16 @ Huntington St.	200 W. Reagan Pkwy.	Medina	OH	44256	16	510
Regal Great Lakes Mall 9	7850 Mentor Ave.	Mentor	OH	44060	9	510
Regal Middleberg Town Square 12	18348 Bagley Rd.	Middleburg Heights	OH	44130	12	510
Regal Towne East Cinema 5	2835 Cincinnati-Dayton Rd.	Middletown	OH	45044	5	515
Regal New Towne Cinema 8	400 Mill Ave.	New Philadelphia	OH	44663	8	510
Regal Boulevard Center 14	24 Boulevard Center	Niles	OH	44446	14	536
Regal Movie World 6	930 Great East Plaza	Niles	OH	44446	6	536
Regal Great Northern Movies 7	26315 Brook Park Rd.	N. Olmsted	OH	44070	7	510
Regal Consumer Square 14	6530 Tussing Rd.	Reynoldsburg	OH	43068	14	535
Regal Solon Commons Cinema 16	6185 Enterprise Pkwy.	Solon	OH	44139	16	510
Regal Tiffin Movies 4	870 W. Market St. Ste #3	Tiffin	OH	44883	4	547
Regal Westlake Promenade 11	30147 Detroit Rd.	Westlake	OH	44145	11	510
Regal Willoughby Commons 16	36655 Euclid Ave.	Willoughby	OH	44094	16	510
Regal Austintown Plaza 10	6020 Mahoning Ave.	Youngstown	OH	44515	10	536
Regal Cinemasouth Cinema 10	7420 South Ave.	Youngstown	OH	44512	10	536
Regal Kickingbird Cinemas 8	1225 E. Danforth Rd.	Edmond	OK	73083	8	650
Regal Crossroads Mall 16	1211 E. I-240	Oklahoma City	OK	73149	16	650
Regal Windsor Hills Cinema 10	4625 N.W. 23rd St.	Oklahoma City	OK	73127	10	650
Regal Albany 7 Cinemas	1350 S.E. Waverly Dr.	Albany	OR	97321	7	820
Regal Westgate 5 Theatres	3950 S.W. Cedar Hills Blvd.	Beaverton	OR	97005	5	820
Regal Mountain View 4 Cinema	63455 N. Hwy. 97	Bend	OR	97701	4	821
Regal Old Mill 10	680 Powerhouse Dr.	Bend	OR	97702	10	821
Regal Pilot Butte 6 Theatres	2717 N.E. Hwy. 20	Bend	OR	97702	6	821
Regal Clackamas Towne Center 5	12000 S.E. 82nd	Clackamas	OR	97266	5	820
Regal Cornelius 9 Cinemas	200 N. 26th	Cornelius	OR	97113	9	820
Regal Ninth St. 4 Cinemas	1750 N.W. 9th St.	Corvallis	OR	97330	4	801
Regal State Theatre	219 S.W. 3rd St.	Corvallis	OR	97333	1	801
Regal Whiteside Theatre	361 S.W. Madison Ave.	Corvallis	OR	97333	1	801
Regal Cinema World 8 Valley River	1087 Valley River Way	Eugene	OR	97401	8	801
Regal McDonald Theatre	1010 Willamette St.	Eugene	OR	97401	1	801
Regal West 11th Movieland	808 Seneca St.	Eugene	OR	97402	6	801
Regal Stark St. 10	2929 N.E. Kane Dr.	Gresham	OR	97030	10	820
Regal Evergreen Parkway	2625 N.W. 188th	Hillsboro	OR	97124	13	820
Regal Movies On TV 16	2929 S.W. 234	Hillsboro	OR	97123	16	820
Regal Trail Indoor	Ste. 106A-131	Hood River	OR	97031	1	820
Regal Trail Drive-In	1655 Tucker Rd.	Hood River	OR	97031	1	820
Regal Lincoln City 6	3755 Southeast High School Dr.	Lincoln City	OR	97367	6	820
Regal Newport Tri	Ste. A Box #270	Newport	OR	97365	3	820
Regal Hilltop 9 Cinema	325 Beavercreek Rd.	Oregon City	OR	97045	9	820
Regal 82nd Ave. 6 Cinemas	9600 S.E. 82nd Ave.	Portland	OR	97266	6	820
Regal Broadway Metro 4 Theatres	1000 S.W. Broadway	Portland	OR	97205	4	820
Regal Division St.	16603 S.E. Division St.	Portland	OR	97236	13	820
Regal Eastgate 3 Cinemas	2025 S.E. 82nd Ave.	Portland	OR	97216	3	820
Regal Fox Tower 10	846 S.W. Park Ave.	Portland	OR	97205	10	820
Regal Koin Center 6 Cinemas	222 S.W. Columbia	Portland	OR	97205	6	820
Regal Lloyd Center 10 Cinema	1510 N.E. Multnomah Blvd.	Portland	OR	97232	10	820
Regal Lloyd Mall 8 Cinema	2320 Lloyd Center Mall	Portland	OR	97232	8	820
Regal Washington Square 4 Cinema	10125 S.W. Washington Sq. Rd.	Portland	OR	97223	4	820
Regal Lancaster 4	831 Lancaster Dr.	Salem	OR	97301	4	820
Regal Movieland 7	501 Marion St.	Salem	OR	97301	7	820
Regal Santiam 11	365 Lancaster Dr.	Salem	OR	97301	11	820
Regal Sherwood 10	15995 Tualatin Sherwood Rd.	Sherwood	OR	97140	10	820
Regal Tigard 11 Cinemas	11626 S.W. Pacific Hwy.	Tigard	OR	97223	11	820
Regal Wilsonville 9 Cinema	29300 S.W. Town Center Loop	Wilsonville	OR	97070	9	820
Regal Moraine Pointe Cinema 10	300 Moraine Pointe Plaza	Butler	PA	16001	10	508
Regal Plymouth Meeting 10	1011 W. Ridge Pike	Conshohocken	PA	19428	10	504
Regal Downingtown Cinema 16	100 Quarry Rd.	Downingtown	PA	19335	16	504
Regal Barn Plaza 14	1745 Easton Rd.	Doylestown	PA	18901	14	504
Regal Northampton Cinema 11	3720 Easton-Nazareth Hwy.	Easton	PA	18047	11	504
Regal Edgmont Square 10	4777 W. Chester Pike	Edgmont	PA	19073	10	504
Regal Huntington Valley 14	2020 County Line Rd.	Huntington Valley	PA	19006	14	504
Regal Manor 16	1246 Millersville Pike	Lancaster	PA	17603	16	566
Regal Lionville Cinemas 12	120 Eagleview Blvd.	Lionville	PA	19341	12	504
Regal Marketplace @ Oaks 24	180 Mill Rd.	Oaks	PA	19456	24	504
Regal Richland Crossing 12	185 N.W. End Blvd.	Quakertown	PA	18955	12	504
Regal Warrington Crossing 22	140 Easton Rd.	Warrington	PA	18976	22	504
Regal Queensgate Cinemas 10	2081 Springwood Rd.	York	PA	17403	10	566
Regal West Manchester Mall 13	1800 Loucks Rd.	West Manchester	PA	17404	13	566
Regal Aiken Mall Cinema 8	300 E. Gate Dr.	Aiken	SC	29802	8	520
Regal North Charleston 10	2055 Eagle Landing Blvd.	Charleston	SC	29406	10	519
Regal Columbia Cinema 7	3400 Forest Dr.	Columbia	SC	29204	7	546
Regal Hollywood 20-Greenville	1025 Woodruff Rd.	Greenville	SC	29607	20	567
Regal Pelham Road 10	3558 Pelham Rd.	Greenville	SC	29615	10	567
Regal Inlet Square 12	10125 Hwy. 17 Bypass #12F	Murrells Inlet	SC	29576	12	519
Regal Pottery 6	3135 Outlet Blvd.	Myrtle Beach	SC	29577	6	570
Regal Charles Towne Square 18	2401 Mall Dr.	N. Charleston	SC	29406	18	519
Regal Galleria Mall 8	590 Galleria Mall Blvd.	Rock Hill	SC	29731	8	517
Regal Converse Cinemas 6	1200 E. Main St.	Spartanburg	SC	29302	6	567
Regal Westgate Mall Cinema 8	205 Blackstock Rd.	Spartanburg	SC	29302	8	567
Regal Hamilton Place 10-17	2000 Hamilton Place Blvd.	Chattanooga	TN	37421	8	575
Regal Hamilton Place Mall 9	2100 Hamilton Place Mall	Chattanooga	TN	37421	9	575
Regal Indian Lake Cinema 10	120 Indian Lake Blvd.	Henderson	TN	37075	10	659
Regal Courtyard Cinema 8	3445 Lebannon Rd.	Hermitage	TN	37076	8	659
Regal Northgate Crossing 6	5131 Old Hixson Pike	Hixson	TN	37343	6	575
Regal Jackson Cinema 10	71 Conrad Dr.	Jackson	TN	38305	10	639
Regal Downtown West Cinema 8	1640 Downtown West Blvd.	Knoxville	TN	37919	8	557
Regal East Town Crossing 8	4762 Centerline Dr.	Knoxville	TN	37917	8	557
Regal Farragut Towne Square 10	11847 Kingston Pike	Knoxville	TN	37922	10	557
Regal Knoxville Center 10	3051 B Knoxville Center Mall	Knoxville	TN	37924	10	557
Regal West Town Mall 9	7600 Kingston Pike Ste. 1520	Knoxville	TN	37919	9	557
Regal Bellevue Cinema 12	7741 Hwy. 70 South	Nashville	TN	37221	12	659

Regal Green Hills 16	3815 Greenhills Village Dr.	Nashville	TN	37215	16	659
Regal Hollywood 27-Nashville	719 Thompson Lane	Nashville	TN	37204	27	659
Regal Nippers Corner Cinema 10	15534 Old Hickory Blvd.	Nashville	TN	37211	10	659
Regal Opry Mills 20	570 Opry Mills Dr.	Nashville	TN	37214	20	659
Regal Opry Mills IMAX	470 Opry Mills Dr.	Nashville	TN	37214	1	659
Regal Tullahoma Cinema 8	Highway 41A	Tullahoma	TN	37388	8	659
Regal Arbor 7 Cinemas	10000 Research Blvd. #147	Austin	TX	78759	7	635
Regal Gateway 16	9700 Stonelake Blvd.	Austin	TX	78759	16	635
Regal Lakecreek 8	13729 U.S. Hwy. 183	Austin	TX	78750	8	635
Regal Lakeline Mall 9	11200 Lakeline Mall Dr.	Austin	TX	78613	9	635
Regal Lincoln 6 Theatres	6404 IH-35 North	Austin	TX	78752	6	635
Regal Metropolitan 14	901 Little Texas Lane	Austin	TX	78745	14	635
Regal Northcross 6	2525 Anderson Lane	Austin	TX	78757	6	635
Regal Riverside 8 Cinema	2410 E. Riverside Dr.	Austin	TX	78741	8	635
Regal Village 4	2700 W. Anderson Lane	Austin	TX	78757	4	635
Regal Westgate 11 Theatres	4477 S. Lamar Blvd.	Austin	TX	78745	11	635
Regal Live Oak 18	7901 Pat Booker Rd.	Live Oak	TX	78233	18	641
Regal Alamo Quarry 14	255 E. Basse Rd.	San Antonio	TX	78209	14	641
Regal Century Plaza 8 Cinema	1918 S.W. Military Dr.	San Antonio	TX	78221	8	641
Regal Cielo Vista 18	2828 Cinema Ridge	San Antonio	TX	78238	18	641
Regal Crossroads 6 Theatres	4522 Fredericksburg Rd.	San Antonio	TX	78201	6	641
Regal Embassy 14 Theatres	13707 Embassy Row	San Antonio	TX	78216	14	641
Regal Fiesta 16 Theatres	12631 Vance Jackson	San Anotnio	TX	78230	16	641
Regal Galaxy 14 Theatres	2938 N.E. Loop 410	San Antonio	TX	78218	14	641
Regal Northwest 14 Theatres	7600 I-H10 West	San Antonio	TX	78230	14	641
Regal Northwoods 14	17640 Henderson Pass	San Antonio	TX	78232	14	641
Regal Rolling Oaks 6 Theatre	6909 N. Loop 1604 East	San Antonio	TX	78247	6	641
Regal Westlakes 9 Theatres	1255 S.W. Loop 410	San Antonio	TX	78227	9	641
Regal Windsor Mall 5 Theatre	7900 IH-35 North	San Antonio	TX	78218	5	641
Regal Ballston Common 12	671 N. Glebe Rd.	Arlington	VA	22203	12	511
Regal Capri 2	702 University Blvd.	Blacksburg	VA	24062	2	573
Regal Downtown Mall 6	200 W. Main St.	Charlottesville	VA	22902	6	584
Regal Seminole Square Cinema 4	2306 India Dr.	Charlottesvile	VA	22901	4	584
Regal Greenbrier Cinema 13	600 Jarman Rd.	Chesapeake	VA	23320	13	544
Regal Greenbrier Cinema 4	1401 Greenbriar Pkwy.	Chesapeake	VA	23320	4	544
Regal Chester Cinemas 6	13025 Jefferson Davis Hwy.	Chester	VA	23831	6	556
Regal New River Valley 11	400 New River Rd.	Christiansburg	VA	24073	11	573
Regal Southpark Cinema 6	374 Southpark Mall	Colonial Heights	VA	23834	6	556
Regal Longwood Village Cinema 3	Milwood Rd.	Farmville	VA	23901	3	556
Regal Armory Drive Cinema 3	1363 Armory Dr.	Franklin	VA	23851	3	544
Regal Fredericksburg 15	3301 Plank Rd. Route 3W	Fredericksburg	VA	22401	15	511
Regal Spotsylvania Mall 4	130 Spotsylvania Mall	Fredericksburg	VA	22407	4	511
Regal Virginian 4	4200 Lafayette Blvd. US 1	Fredericksburg	VA	22401	4	511
Regal Virginia Center 20	10091 Jeb Stuart Pkwy.	Glen Allen	VA	23060	20	556
Regal Riverdale Plaza 12	1044 Von Schilling Dr.	Hampton	VA	23666	12	544
Regal Harrisonburg 14	381 University Blvd.	Harrisonburg	VA	22801	14	569
Regal Valley Mall Cinemas 4	1925 E. Market St.	Harrisonburg	VA	22801	4	569
Regal York River Crossing 8	2226 York Crossing Dr.	Hayes	VA	23072	8	544
Regal Tally Ho 2	19 W. Market St.	Leesburg	VA	20175	2	511
Regal Genito Cinema 9	11000 Hull St. Rd.	Midlothian	VA	23112	9	556
Regal Kiln Creek Cinema 20	100 Regal Way	Newport News	VA	23602	20	544
Regal MacArthur Center 18	300 Monticello Ave. Ste. 330	Norfolk	VA	23510	18	544
Regal Main Gate 10	Bldg. CD12 NEX Mall Complex	Norfolk	VA	23503	10	544
Regal Crater Cinema 8	25 Crater Circle	Petersburg	VA	23803	8	556
Regal Cloverleaf Cinema 8	7201 Midlothian Pike	Richmond	VA	23225	8	556
Regal Ridge Cinema 7	1510 E. Ridge Rd.	Richmond	VA	23229	7	556
Regal Westhampton Cinema 2	5706 Grove Ave.	Richmond	VA	23226	2	556
Regal Willow Lawn Cinema 4	1601 Willow Lawn Dr.	Richmond	VA	23230	4	556
Regal Aquia 10	2850 Jefferson Davis Hwy.	Stafford	VA	22554	10	511
Regal Staunton Mall Cinema 6	US Route 11 South	Staunton	VA	24401	6	556
Regal Countryside 20	45980 Regal Plaza	Sterling	VA	20165	20	511
Regal Columbus 12	104 Constitution Dr.	Virginia Beach	VA	23463	12	544
Regal Pembroke Cinema 8	4576-76 Virginia Beach Blvd.	Virginia Beach	VA	23462	8	544
Regal Strawbridge Marketplace 12	2133 General Booth Blvd.	Virginia Beach	VA	23454	12	544
Regal Surf & Sand 8	941 Laskin Rd.	Virginia Beach	VA	23451	8	544
Regal Southshore 4 Mall	1017 Boone St.	Aberdeen	WA	98520	4	819
Regal Auburn 17 Theatres	1101 Super Mall Way Ste. 901	Auburn	WA	98001	17	819
Regal Crossroads 8 Cinema	1200 156th Ave.	Bellevue	WA	98004	8	819
Regal Galleria 11	550 106th Ave.	Bellevue	WA	98004	11	819
Regal Bellis Fair 6 Cinema	#5 Bellis Fair Pkwy.	Bellingham	WA	98226	6	819
Regal Sehome 3 Cinemas	3300 Fielding Ave.	Bellingham	WA	98225	3	819
Regal Sunset Square Cinema 6	1135 E. Sunset Dr.	Bellingham	WA	98226	6	819
Regal Tall Firs 10	20751 State Route 410	Bonny Lake	WA	98390	10	819
Regal Redwood Plaza 4 Cinema	1500 N.W. Riddell Rd.	Bremerton	WA	98310	4	819
Regal Cinema 3	2100 N. National Ave.	Chehalis	WA	98532	3	819
Regal Everett 9	830 S.E. Everett Mall Way	Everett	WA	98208	9	819
Regal Gig Harbor 3	5401 Olympic Dr.	Gig Harbor	WA	98335	3	819
Regal Issaquah 9 Theatre	1490 N.W. 11th Ave.	Issaquah	WA	98027	9	819
Regal Three Rivers Mall 5	1301 Grade St.	Kelso	WA	98626	5	820
Regal Clearwater Cinemas 3	325 N. Johnson	Kennewick	WA	99336	3	810
Regal Columbia Center 3	704 Columbia	Kennewick	WA	99336	3	810
Regal Columbia Mall 8	701 Columbia Center	Kennwick	WA	99336	8	810
Regal Kent 6 Theatres	10116 S.E. 256th	Kent	WA	98031	6	819
Regal Lakewood Cinema 15	2410 84th St. South	Lakewood	WA	98499	15	819
Regal Longview Theatre 1	1433 Commerce Ave.	Longview	WA	98632	1	820
Regal Triangle Quad Cinemas	1228 Washington Way	Longview	WA	98632	4	820
Regal Alderwood 7	3501 184th St. Southwest	Lynnwood	WA	98037	7	819
Regal Alderwood Village 12	3815 196th St. Southwest	Lynnwood	WA	98036	12	819
Regal Marysville 14	9811 State Ave.	Marysville	WA	98270	14	819
Regal Mount Lake 9	6009 S.W. 244th St.	Mt. Lake Terrace	WA	98043	9	819
Regal Capital Mall 4	302 Capital Mall	Olympia	WA	98502	4	819
Regal Lacey 8 Theatres	4431 Martin Way	Olympia	WA	98516	8	819
Regal South Sound Cinema 10	1435 Olney Ave.	Port Orchard	WA	98366	10	819
Regal Poulsbo 10	P.O. Box 1012	Poulsbo	WA	98370	10	819
Regal Longston Place 14	13317 Meridian St. East	Puyallup	WA	98375	14	819
Regal Puyallup 6 Cinemas	1200 Fourth St.	Puyallup	WA	98371	6	819
Regal South Hill Cinema 6	3500 S. Meridian	Puyallup	WA	98373	6	819
Regal Bella Botega 11 Cinema	8890 N.E. 161st Ave.	Redmond	WA	98052	11	819

Regal East Valley 13 Cinema	3751 E. Valley Hwy.	Renton	WA	98055	13	819
Regal Metro 4 Cinemas	2588 N. Columbia Center Blvd.	Richland	WA	99352	4	810
Regal Uptown Triplex Theatre	1300 Jadwin Ave.	Richland	WA	99352	3	810
Regal Silverdale 4 Theatres	9923 Clear Cr. Rd.	Silverdale	WA	98383	4	819
Regal Eastside 2 Cinemas	4209 E. Pacific Ave.	Spokane	WA	99202	2	881
Regal Lincoln Heights 4 Cinema	2930 E. 27th Ave.	Spokane	WA	99203	4	881
Regal Newport Road 8	10404 N. Newport Rd.	Spokane	WA	99218	8	881
Regal Northtown Mall 12	4750 N. Division St.	Spokane	WA	99207	12	881
Regal Spokane Valley 12	14706 E. Indiana Ave.	Spokane	WA	99216	12	881
Regal Parkway Plaza 12	5910 S. 180th St.	Tukwila	WA	98188	12	819
Regal Cascade 16 Cinemas	1101 S.E. 160th Ave.	Vancouver	WA	98684	16	820
Regal City Center 12	801 C St.	Vancouver	WA	98660	12	820
Regal Vancouver Plaza 10 Cinema	7800 N.E. Fourth Plain	Vancouver	WA	98662	10	820
Regal Cinema 99 11	9010 N.E. Hwy 99	Vancouver	WA	98665	11	820
Regal College Ave. 16	W3091 Van Roy Rd.	Appleton	WI	54915	16	658
Regal Towne Square Cinema 6	P.O. Box 1325	Parkersburg	WV	26102	6	597
Regal Grand Central Mall 12	P.O. Box 6086	Vienna	WV	26105	12	597

ROGERS CINEMA, INC.

5 theatres, 27 screens.
407 S. Maple, P.O. Box 280, Marshfield, WI 54449. (715) 387-3437. FAX: (715) 387-2165.
OWNER & PRESIDENT
Paul J. Rogers
GENERAL MANAGER
Ted Rosenfeldt

THEATRES

Rogers Cinema 7	419 S. Central	Marshfield	WI	54449	7	705
Grand Theatre 4	208 Wolf River Plaza	New London	WI	54961	4	658
Rogers Cinema 5	2825 S. Church St.	Stevens Point	WI	54481	5	705
Rosa Theatre 4	218 S. Main	Waupaca	WI	54981	4	658
Rogers Cinema 7	220 E. Grand Ave.	Wisconsin Rapids	WI	54494	7	705

SIGNATURE THEATRES

30 theatres, 202 screens.
1600 Broadway, Oakland, CA 94612. (510) 268-9498. FAX: (510) 268-9843. www.signatiretheatres.com
OWNER, CHAIRMAN, & PRESIDENT
Philip Harris III
OWNERS
Philip Harris, Sr.
Douglas Stephens
FILM BUYER
Bill Herting

THEATRES

Signature Festival Cinemas 10	1160 W. Branch St.	Arroyo Grande	CA	93420	10	855
Signature Auburn Twin	536 Grass Valley Highway	Auburn	CA	95604	2	862
Signature State Twin Theatre	985 Lincoln Way	Auburn	CA	95604	2	862
Signature Regency Cinemas, 6-Plex	1600 Willow Ave.	Clovis	CA	93612	6	866
Signature Holiday Cinema	101 F. St.	Davis	CA	95616	6	862
Signature Stadium 5	420 G St.	Davis	CA	95616	5	862
Signature Manchester Stadium	2055 E. Shields Ave.	Fresno	CA	93726	16	866
Signature Jackson Cinemas	201 Shopping Dr.	Jackson	CA	95642	4	862
Contra Costa Cinemas 5	555 Center Ave.	Martinez	CA	94553	5	807
Signature Mann Festival Cinemas	3969 Mchenry Ave.	Modesto	CA	95356	10	862
Signature Placerville 8	337 Placerville Dr.	Placerville	CA	95667	8	862
Crow Canyon Cinemas 6	2525 San Ramon Valley Blvd.	San Ramon	CA	94583	6	807
Signature Santa Cruz Cinema 9	1405 Pacific Ave.	Santa Cruz	CA	95060	9	828
Signature Riverfront Twin	155 S. River St	Santa Cruz	CA	95060	2	828
Sonora Plaza Cinema	800 East Mono Way	Sonora	CA	95370	5	862
Signature Festival Cinemas, 4-Plex	6436 Pacific Ave.	Stockton	CA	95207	4	862
Signature Regency Cinemas, 4-Plex	7809 Etna Lane	Stockton	CA	95207	4	862
Signature Holiday Cinemas 8	6262 West Lane	Stockton	CA	95210	8	862
Stockton Royal	1825 Pacific Ave.	Stockton	CA	95207	4	862
Turlock Stadium 14	2323 W. Main St.	Turlock	CA	95380	14	862
Signature Ukiah 6	612 State St.	Ukiah	CA	95482	6	807
Signature Sequoia Mall 12	3355 S. Mooney Blvd	Visalia	CA	93277	12	866
Signature Stadium 10	120 S. Bridge St	Visalia	CA	93279	10	866
Festival Cinemas 5	1450 N. California Blvd.	Walnut Creek	CA	94596	5	807
Signature Dole Cannery	735 B Iwilei Rd.	Honolulu	HI	96817	18	744
Signature Pearl Highlands 12	1000 Kam Hwy	Pearl City	HI	96782	12	744
Signature Midway Drive-In	3115 Hwy 40 West	Columbia Falls	MT	59901	1	762
Signature Gateway Cinema	1275 Highway 2 West	Kalispell	MT	59901	6	762
Signature Liberty Theatre	120 1st Ave. East	Kalispell	MT	59901	1	762
Signature Strand Theatre	120 2nd St. East	Kalispell	MT	59901	1	762

SILVER CINEMAS, INC.

(Silver Cinemas and Landmark Theatres are divisions of Silver Cinemas, Inc.)
78 theatres, 331 screens.
4004 Beltline Rd., Ste. 205, LB 18, Addison, TX 75001 (972) 503-9851. FAX: (972) 503-9013.
PRESIDENT & CEO
Larry Hohl
CFO
Tom Adrus
SENIOR V.P., OPERATIONS
Mike Mullen
GENERAL COUNSEL
Paul Ledbetter
DIRECTORS OF OPERATIONS
Alan Blangy
Maureen McNamara
Kevin O'Neil
DIRECTOR OF CONCESSIONS
Kathi Gillman
DIRECTOR OF MIS
Brian Wonder
DIRECTOR OF HUMAN RESOURCES
Paula Taylor

LANDMARK THEATRES

Albany Twin	1115 Solano Ave.	Albany	CA	94706	2	807
Act 1 and 2	2128 Center St.	Berkeley	CA	94704	2	807
California Theatre	2113 Kittredge St.	Berkeley	CA	94704	3	807
Shattuck Cinemas	2230 Shattuck Ave.	Berkeley	CA	94704	8	807
U.C. Theatre	2038 University Ave.	Berkeley	CA	94704	1	807
Fine Arts	8556 Wilshire Blvd.	Beverly Hills	CA	90211	1	803
Cove Theatre	7730 Girard Ave	La Jolla	CA	92037	1	825
La Jolla Village Cinemas	8879 Villa La Jolla Dr.	La Jolla	CA	92037	4	825
Westside Pavilion Cinemas	10800 Pico Blvd.	Los Angeles	CA	90064	4	803
Nuart Theatre	11272 Santa Monica Blvd.	Los Angeles	CA	90025	1	803
Guild Theatre	949 El Camino Real	Menlo Park	CA	94025	1	807
Park Theatre	1275 El Camino Real	Menlo Park	CA	94025	1	807
Piedmont Theatre	4186 Piedmont Ave.	Oakland	CA	94611	3	807
Aquarius Theatre	430 Emerson St.	Palo Alto	CA	94301	2	807
Palo Alto Square Theatre	3000 El Camino Real	Palo Alto	CA	94306	2	807
Hillcrest Cinemas	3965 5th Ave.	San Diego	CA	92103	5	825
Ken Theatre	4061 Adams Ave.	San Diego	CA	92116	1	825
Bridge Theatre	3010 Geary Blvd.	San Francisco	CA	94118	1	807
Clay Theatre	2261 Fillmore	San Francisco	CA	94115	1	807
Embarcadero Center Cinemas	1 Embarcadero Center; Promenade Level	San Francisco	CA	94111	5	807
Lumiere Theatre	1572 California St.	San Francisco	CA	94109	3	807
Opera Plaza Cinema	601 Van Ness Ave.	San Francisco	CA	94102	4	807
NuWilshire Theatre	1314 Wilshire Blvd.	Santa Monica	CA	90403	2	803
Rialto Theatre	1023 Fair Oaks Ave.	South Pasadena	CA	91030	1	803
Esquire Theatre	590 Downing St.	Denver	CO	80219	2	751
Mayan Theatre	110 Broadway	Denver	CO	80203	3	751
Chez Artiste	4150 E. Amherst Ave.	Denver	CO	80222	3	751
Landmark Century Centre Cinema	2828 N. Clark St.	Chicago	IL	60657	7	602
Canal Place Cinema	333 Canal St.	New Orleans	LA	70130	4	622
Kendall Square Cinema	1 Kendall Square	Cambridge	MA	02139	9	506
Embassy Cinema	16 Pine St.	Waltham	MA	02154	6	506
Maple 3	4135 W. Maple Rd.	Bloomfield	MI	48301	3	505
Main Art Theatre	118 N. Main St.	Royal Oak	MI	48067	3	505
Lagoon Cinema	1320 Lagoon Ave.	Minneapolis	MN	55408	5	613
Uptown Theatre	2906 Hennepin Ave.	Minneapolis	MN	55408	1	613
Plaza Frontenac	210 Plaza Frontenac	St. Louis	MO	63131	6	609
Tivoli Theatre	6350 Delmar	Universal City	MO	63130	3	609
Dobie Theatre	2021 Guadalupe	Austin	TX	78705	4	635
Inwood Theatre	5458 W. Lovers Ln.	Dallas	TX	75209	3	623
Greenway 3 Theatre	5 Greenway Plaza	Houston	TX	77046	3	618
River Oaks Theatre	2009 W. Gray	Houston	TX	77019	3	618
Broadway Market Cinemas	401 Broadway	Seattle	WA	98102	4	819
Crest Cinema Center	16505 5th Ave., N.E.	Seattle	WA	98155	2	819
Egyptian Theatre	801 E. Pine	Seattle	WA	98122	1	819
Guild 45th Theatre	2115 N. 45th	Seattle	WA	98103	2	819
Harvard Exit Theatre	807 E. Roy	Seattle	WA	98102	2	819
Metro Cinemas	4500 8th Ave. N.E. #200	Seattle	WA	98105	2	819
Neptune Theatre	1303 N.E. 45th	Seattle	WA	98105	1	819
Seven Gables Theatre	911 N.E. 50th St.	Seattle	WA	98105	2	819
Varsity Theater	4329 University Way N.E.	Seattle	WA	98105	3	819
Downer Theatre	2689 Downer Ave.	Milwaukee	WI	53211	2	617
Oriental Theatre	2230 N. Farwell Ave.	Milwaukee	WI	53202	3	617

SILVER CINEMAS THEATRES

Cinema-Superstition Mall	6555-1002 E. Southern	Mesa	AZ	85206	8	753
Super Saver Cinema Bell Rd.	2710 W. Bell Rd., Ste. 1125	Phoenix	AZ	85053	8	753
Super Saver Cinema - Rossmoor Cntr.	12343 Seal Beach Blvd.	Seal Beach	CA	90740	7	803
Super Saver Cinema - Norwalk S.C.	13917 Pioneer Blvd.	Norwalk	CA	90650	8	803
Super Saver Cinema - Citadel Crossing	901 N. Academy	Colorado Springs	CO	80909	8	752
Silver Cinemas 10	6000 Aurora	Des Moines	IA	50322	10	679
Renaissance Place	1850 2nd St.	Highland Park	IL	60035	6	602
Super Saver Cinema - Joliet	3340 Mall Loop Dr.	Joliet	IL	60431	6	602
Washington Square Cinema 4	314 N. Franklin St.	Bastrop	LA	71220	4	628
Trackside 5 Cinema	200 Cumberland St.	Bogalusa	LA	70427	5	622
Chalmette Cinema 9	8700 W. Judge Perez Dr.	Chalmette	LA	70043	9	622
Cinema City 8	2440 Veterans Blvd.	Kenner	LA	70062	8	622
La Place Movies 7	1324 W. Airline Hwy.	LaPlace	LA	70068	7	622
Silver Cinema Macomb Mall	32233 Gratiot Ave.	Roseville	MI	48066	6	505
Super Saver Cinema - Westwood	2809 S. 125th Ave.	Omaha	NE	68144	8	652
South Hills 8	838 S. Rd., South Hills Mall	Poughkeepsie	NY	12601	8	501
Super Saver Cinema - Elmwood	2050 Elmwood Ave.	Buffalo	NY	14207	8	514
North Park Cinema 7	12100 N. May Ave.	Oklahoma City	OK	73120	7	650
Dollar Movies 5	1219 Garth Brooks Blvd.	Yukon	OK	73099	5	650
East Pointe Village 12	8300 Gateway East	El Paso	TX	79907	12	765
Montwood 7	2200 N. Yarbrough	El Paso	TX	79925	7	765
Ethan Allen Cinema 4	1170 N. Ave.,	Burlington	VT	05401	4	523
Budget Cinemas - East Town Mall	2350 E. Mason St.	Green Bay	WI	54302	6	658
Budget Cinemas - South 6	1475 S. 108th St.	Greenfield	WI	53228	6	617
Budget Cinemas - East Towne	96 East Towne Mall	Madison	WI	53704	4	669
Market Square Theatres	6604 Odana Rd.	Madison	WI	53719	5	669

SOCAL CINEMAS, INC.

9 theatres, 76 screens.
13 Corporate Plaza, Newport Beach, CA 92660. (949) 640-2370.
PRESIDENT
Bruce Sanborn
GENERAL MANAGER
Gary Richardson

THEATRES

Socal Cinemapolis 13 Cinemas	5635 E. La Palma	Anaheim	CA	92807	13	803
Socal Blue Jay	27315 N. Bay Rd.	Blue Jay	CA	92317	4	803
Socal Plaza Camino Real	2385 Marron Rd.	Carlsbad	CA	92008	4	825
Movie Experience 12 Spectrum	3750 Grand	Chino	CA	91710	12	803
Socal Laguna Hills Mall Cinema	24155 Laguna Hills Mall Rd.	Laguna Hills	CA	92653	3	803
Movie Experience 17 at California Oaks	41090 California Oaks Rd.	Murrieta	CA	92562	17	803
Socal Downtown Centre Cinema	888 Marsh St.	San Luis Obispo	CA	93401	7	855
Movie Experience 10 at Tower Plaza	27531 Ynez Rd.	Temecula	CA	92591	10	803
Socal Temeku Cinema	26463 Ynez Rd.	Temecula	CA	92591	6	803

SPINELLI CINEMAS

5 theatres, 18 screens.
400 Central Ave., Dover, NH 03820. (603) 749-2555. FAX: (603) 749-0195.
PRESIDENT
Michael Spinelli

THEATRES

Spinelli-Barrington 6	Route 125	Barrington	NH	03825	6	506
Spinelli Royal Twin	25 Green Square	Berlin	NH	03750	2	523
Spinelli-Strand Theatre	20 3rd St.	Dover	NH	03820	3	506
Spinelli-Merideth Cinema	Route 25	Merideth	NH	03253	3	506
Spinelli-Lilac Mall 4	Route 125	Rochester	NH	03867	4	506

STAR CINEMAS (AGT ENTERPRISES, INC.)

7 theatres, 56 screens.
AGT Enterprises, Inc., P.O. Box 317, Prairie Du Chien, WI 53821. (608) 326-5449. FAX: (608) 326-5382.
OWNERS
Bill Adamany
Bill Adamany, Jr.

THEATRES

Star Cinema	Highway 18 & PD	Fitchburg	WI	53719	14	669
Star Cinema 12	242 Village Walk Lane	Johnson Creek	WI	53038	12	617
Hilldale Theatre	702 N. Midvale Blvd.	Madison	WI	53705	2	669
Star Cinema Prairie Du Chien	Hwy 18 South	Prairie Du Chien	WI	53821	6	637
Star Cinema	115 N. Webb Ave.	Reedsburg	WI	53959	6	669
Star Cinema	1010 Maple	Sparta	WI	54656	6	702
Desert Star Cinema	I-90/94 & Hwy 12	Wisconsin Dells	WI	53940	10	669

STARNET CINEMAS

8 theatres, 49 screens.
2870 University Blvd. W., Jacksonville, FL 32217. (904) 731-9616. FAX: (904) 739-2752.
Booking Office: 4407 Highlands Dr., McKinney, TX 75070. (972) 529-6535.
PRESIDENT, COMPTROLLER, FILM BUYER
Robert Fulford
V.P. & GENERAL MANAGER OF OPERATIONS
William J. Homer

THEATRES

Atlantic Theatre	751 Atlantic Blvd.	Atlantic Beach	FL	32233	8	561
Belleview Cinemas	10845 S.E. Hwy 441	Belleview	FL	34420	2	534
Pabio Theatres	1970 S. Third St.	Jacksonville	FL	32250	9	561
St. Johns Theatre	4530 St. Johns Ave.	Jacksonville	FL	32210	8	561
Lakeland Square 10 Cinemas	3606 US Hwy 98 North	Lakeland	FL	33809	10	539
Marianna Cinemas	4341 Lafayette St.	Marianna	FL	32446	2	656
Palatka Mall Cinemas	400 Hwy 19 North	Palatka	FL	32177	4	561
Bainbridge Mall Cinemas	1400 E. Shotwell St.	Bainbridge	GA	31717	6	530

SYNDICATE THEATRES, INC.

5 theatres, 13 screens.
55 1/2 E. Court St., Franklin, IN 46131. (317) 736-7144. FAX (317) 736 4299.
CHAIRMAN
Trueman T. Rembusch
PRESIDENT & FILM BUYER
Michael Rembusch
BOOKER
Nancy Gilliland

THEATRES

Gibson Theatre	106 Main St.	Batesville	IN	47006	1	515
Canary Creek Cinemas	870 Mallory Pkwy.	Franklin	IN	46131	8	527
Huntington Drive-In Theatre	1291 Condit St.	Huntington	IN	46750	1	509
13-24 Drive-In Theatre	St. RD. 13 N., 106 W. Market St.	Wabash	IN	46992	1	509
Eagles Theatre	106 W. Market St.	Wabash	IN	46992	1	509

THEATRE MANAGEMENT, INC. (TMI THEATRES)

8 theatres, 49 screens.
P.O. Box 2076, Deland, FL 32721. (904) 736-6830. FAX: (904) 738-2596.
PRESIDENT
Clint DeMarsh
VICE PRESIDENT
Frank DeMarsh

THEATRES

Beacon Theatres	12961 Cortez Blvd.	Brooksville	FL	34613	10	539
Victoria Square 6	1798 S. Woodland Blvd.	DeLand	FL	32721	6	534
Beacon 12 Theatre	1401 S. Dixie Freeway	New Smyrna Bch.	FL	32168	12	534
Showcase Cinemas	2411 E. Graves Ave.	Orange City	FL	32763	2	534
Penn Cinemas	147 N. Mian St.	Butler	PA	16003	2	508
Pioneer Drive-In Theatre	1985 N. Main St.	Butler	PA	16003	3	508
Meadville Cinemas	952 Park Ave.	Meadville	PA	16335	4	516
Beacon 10 Theatres	1121 Broad St.	Sumter	SC	29150	10	546

TRANS-LUX

14 theatres, 66 screens.
433 Paseo de Peralta, Santa Fe, NM 87501. (505) 989-9300 www.transluxmovies.com
VICE PRESIDENT
Bryan Mercer
OPERATIONS MANAGER
Nick Sanchez
OPERATIONS SUPERVISOR
Ron Lujan
HUMAN RESOURCES COORDINATOR
Gini Mercer
MARKETING DIRECTOR
Jennifer Montano

THEATRES

Trans-Lux Desert Sky Cinema	70 W. Duvall Mine Rd.	Sahuarita	AZ	85629	6	789
Trans-Lux Lake Dillon Cinema	135 Main St, Dillon Center	Dillon	CO	80435	4	751
Trans-Lux Skyline Cinema	312 US Highway 6	Dillon	CO	80435	6	751
Trans-Lux High Five Cinemas	900 Translux Dr.	Durango	CO	81301	5	790
Trans-Lux Gaslight Cinemas	102 E. Fifth St.	Durango	CO	81301	2	790
Trans-Lux Metrolux 12	1380 N. Denver Ave.	Loveland	CO	80537	12	751
Trans Lux Dream Catcher Cinema	33771 S. US Hwy 285	Espanola	NM	87532	6	790
Trans-Lux High Society Cinema	1718 17th St.	Los Alamos	NM	87544	3	790
Trans-Lux Starlight Cinema	2226 Sun Ranch Village Loop	Los Lunas	NM	87031	8	790
Trans-Lux Grand Illusion Theatre	1610 Llano St.	Santa Fe	NM	87505	1	790
Trans-Lux Jean Cocteau Cinema	418 Montezuma	Santa Fe	NM	87501	1	790
Trans-Lux Loma Theatre	107 Manzanares Ave.	Socorro	NM	87801	1	790
Trans-Lux Storyteller Cinemas	110 Old Talpa Canon Rd.	Taos	NM	87571	7	790
Trans-Lux Fox Theatre	505 South 20th St.	Laramie	WY	82070	4	751

UNITED ARTISTS THEATRE CIRCUIT, INC.

226 theatres, 1,685 screens.

9110 E. Nichols Ave., Ste. 200, Englewood, CO 80112. (303) 792-3600. Western Region: 11801 McCree Rd., Dallas, TX 75238. Eastern Region: Route 73 & 130 N., Pennsasken, PA 08110.

DIRECTOR, PRESIDENT & CEO
Kurt Hall
DIRECTOR, E.V.P.
Michael Pade
EXECUTIVE V.P., GENERAL COUNSEL & SECRETARY
Ralph Hardy
EXECUTIVE V.P.s
Raymond Nutt
Neal Pinsker
Bruce Taffet
SENIOR V.P.
Steven J. Koets

THEATRES

UA Cinema 150	Asher & University	Little Rock	AR	72204	1	693
Breckenridge Village	1200 Breckenridge Dr.	Little Rock	AR	72205	12	693
Cameo 3 Theatre	111 N. Jackson St.	Magnolia	AR	71753	3	612
Lakewood Village Theatre	2939 Lakewood Village Dr.	N. Little Rock	AR	72216	8	693
Christown Mall Cinema	1546 W. Montebello	Phoenix	AZ	85015	6	753
Metro Park Theatre	10201 N. Metro Pkwy.	Phoenix	AZ	85051	8	753
UA Scottsdale Pavilions	9090 E. Indian Bend Rd.	Scottsdale	AZ	85250	11	753
UA Sonora Village	15512 N. Pima Rd.	Scottsdale	AZ	85260	10	753
UA East Hills 10 Theatre	3100 Mall View Rd.	Bakersfield	CA	93306	10	800
UA 7 Berkeley	2274 Shattuck Ave.	Berkeley	CA	94704	7	807
UA Mission Oaks	5001 Verdugo Way	Camarillo	CA	93012	11	803
UA Los Cerritos	435 Los Cerritos	Cerritos	CA	90803	11	803
El Rey Theatre	230 W. 2nd St.	Chico	CA	95926	1	868
UA Sunrise Cinema 4	5926 Sunrise Mall	Citrus Heights	CA	95610	4	862
UA 8 Clovis	2301 Villa Ave.	Clovis	CA	93612	8	866
UA Sierra Vista Theatre	801 Santa Anna Ave.	Clovis	CA	93612	6	866
Cinema 6	200 Metro Center	Colma	CA	94014	6	807
Movies @ Emery Bay	6330 Christie Ave.	Emeryville	CA	94608	10	807
Broadway Faire 10	3351 W. Shaw Ave.	Fresno	CA	93711	10	866
Del Oro	165 Mill St.	Grass Valley	CA	95945	3	862
Grass Valley Cinema	11399 Sutton Way	Grass Valley	CA	95945	2	862
Hayward Cinema 6	24800 Hasperian Blvd.	Hayward	CA	94515	6	807
UA La Canada	1919 Verdugo Blvd.	La Canada	CA	91011	8	803
UA Movies Long Beach	6601 Pacific Coast Hwy.	Long Beach	CA	90803	6	803
UA Coronet	10889 Wellworth Ave.	Los Angeles	CA	90024	3	803
UA 6 Marina Del Rey	4335 Glencoe Ave.	Marina Del Rey	CA	90291	6	803
UA Merced Movies 4	301 W. Main St.	Merced	CA	95341	4	866
UA Regency Theatre	635 Fairfield Dr.	Merced	CA	95340	7	866
UA State Monterey	417 Alvarado St	Monterey	CA	93940	3	828
UA Movies 6	6355 Bellingham Ave.	N. Hollywood	CA	91606	6	803
UA Movies 6	64 W. Colorado Blvd.	Pasadena	CA	91105	6	803
UA 6 Riverside	3600 Park Sierra Dr.	Riverside	CA	92505	6	803
Olympus Pointe	520 N. Sunrise Ave.	Roseville	CA	95661	12	862
Laguna Village Theatre	8755 Center Pkwy. Dr.	S. Sacramento	CA	95823	12	862
UA Arden Fair	1739 Arden Way	Sacramento	CA	95815	6	862
Movies @ Horton Plaza	475 Horton Plaza	San Diego	CA	92101	14	825
UA Twin Stonestown	501 Buckingham Way	San Francisco	CA	94132	2	807
Alexandria Theatre	5400 Geary Blvd.	San Francisco	CA	94121	3	807
UA Coronet Theatre	3575 Geary Blvd.	San Francisco	CA	94118	1	807
UA Galaxy 4	1285 Sutter St.	San Francisco	CA	94123	4	807
Metro Theatre	2055 Union St.	San Francisco	CA	94123	1	807
Vogue Theatre	3290 Sacramento St.	San Francisco	CA	94115	1	807
Santa Rosa Theatre	620 Third Ave.	Santa Rosa	CA	95404	6	807
UA 5 Santa Rosa	547 Mendocino	Santa Rosa	CA	95401	5	807
UA 5 Thousand Oaks	382 W. Hillcrest Dr.	Thousand Oaks	CA	91360	5	803
Village 4	2525 Arapahoe Ave.	Boulder	CO	80306	4	751
Broadmoor Theatre	c/o Broadmoor Hotel	Colorado Springs	CO	80936	1	752
Continental Theatre	3635 S. Monaco Blvd.	Denver	CO	80237	6	751
UA Colorado Center	1970 S. Colorado Blvd.	Denver	CO	80222	9	751
Denver Pavilions	500 16th St.	Denver	CO	80202	15	751
UA Greenwood Plaza	8141 E. Arapahoe Rd.	Denver	CO	80111	12	751
Campus West	1325 W. Elizabeth	Fort Collins	CO	80522	2	751
Denver West Village 12	14225 W.Colfax	Golden	CO	80401	12	751
Teller Arms Twin	2401 N. Ave.	Grand Junction	CO	81502	2	773
Colorado West 4 Cinema	2424 Highway 6 & 50	Grand Junction	CO	81505	4	773
Cooper Twin Theatre	2333 W. 28th St.	Greeley	CO	80631	2	751
Bittersweet Theatre	3760 W. 10th St.	Greeley	CO	80634	4	751
UA Meadows 12	9355 Park Meadows Dr.	Littleton	CO	80124	12	751
Twin Peaks 10	1250 S. Hover Rd.	Longmont	CO	80501	10	751
Thornton Town Center	10001 Grant St.	Thornton	CO	80229	10	751
UA Darien Playhouse	1077 Post Rd.	Darien	CT	06820	2	501
UA Movies @ Wekiva	2141 N. Semoran Blvd.	Apopka	FL	32703	8	534
UA Movies @ Boynton	244 N. Congress Ave.	Boynton Beach	FL	33426	9	548

UA Movies @ Clearwater	27419 US Hwy. 19 North	Clearwater	FL	33721	8	539
Movies @ Regency Square	9333 Atlantic Blvd.	Jacksonville	FL	32211	12	561
Movies @ Orange Park	8635 Blanding Blvd.	Jacksonville	FL	32244	7	561
UA Cinema 90	Hwy. 90 West	Lake City	FL	32055	6	561
UA Movies @ Lauderhill	7800 W. Commercial Blvd.	Lauderhill	FL	33321	13	528
Santa Rosa Cinema	300 Mary Esther Blvd.	Mary Esther	FL	32569	10	686
UA Movies @ The Falls	9000 S.W. 136th St.	Miami	FL	33176	7	528
UA Cinemas West	1919 S.W. 27th Ave.	Ocala	FL	34478	5	534
MVS Marketplace	822-4 Saxon Blvd.	Orange City	FL	32763	8	534
Movies @ Florida Mall	1001 Florida Mall Ln.	Orlando	FL	32809	7	534
UA Promenade Plaza	9930 Alternate A1A.	Palm Bch Gardens	FL	33410	8	548
Movies @ Pembroke Pines	11350 Pines Blvd.	Pembroke Pines	FL	33026	9	528
University 11 Theatre	7171 N. Davis Hwy.	Pensacola	FL	32504	11	686
UA Seminole Towne Center	430 Towne Center Circle	Sanford	FL	32771	10	534
UA Searstown Mall	3550 S. Washington Ave.	Titusville	FL	32780	10	534
UA Okee Square	2027 Okeechobee Blvd.	West Palm Beach	FL	33401	8	548
UA North Point Market	6500 N. Point Pkwy.	Alpharetta	GA	30202	8	561
Lenox Square Theatre	3393 Peachtree Rd.	Atlanta	GA	30326	6	524
Midtown 8 Theatre	931 Monroe Dr.	Atlanta	GA	30308	8	524
Tara 4 Theatre	2345 Cheshire Bridge Rd.	Atlanta	GA	30324	4	524
UA Perimeter Pointe	1155 Mt. Vernon Hwy.	Atlanta	GA	30338	10	524
Shannon 8 Theatre	4600 Jonesboro Rd.	Union City	GA	30291	8	524
UA Circle Center	49 W. Maryland St.	Indianapolis	IN	46204	9	527
Galaxy 14	8105 E. 96th Ave.	Indianapolis	IN	46256	14	527
UA Eagle Highlands	3901 Shore Dr.	Indianapolis	IN	46254	10	527
Westgate Cinema	323 MacArthur Dr.	Alexandria	LA	71301	8	644
Siegen Village Cinema 10	7166 Siegen Ln.	Baton Rouge	LA	70809	10	716
UA Citiplace	2610 Citiplace Dr.	Baton Rouge	LA	70808	12	716
Southland Cinema 4	3030 W. Park Ave.	Houma	LA	70364	4	622
Northgate 8	100 Castle St.	Lafayette	LA	70501	8	642
Westwood Theatre	2421 W. Congress St.	Lafayette	LA	70506	1	642
Ammassador 10	2315 Kaliste Saloom Rd.	Lafayette	LA	70508	10	642
Oak Park Cinemas 6	2145 Oak Park Blvd.	Lake Charles	LA	70601	6	643
UA Lake Charles	3416 Derek Dr.	Lake Charles	LA	70605	10	643
Lee Hills Theatre	1350 Boone St.	Leesville	LA	71446	6	644
Bayou Landing Cinema 6	1000 Parkview Dr.	New Iberia	LA	70562	6	642
Vista Village Cinema	1020 Creswell Ln.	Opelousas	LA	70570	4	642
UA Westview Mall	5824 Baltimore National Pike	Baltimore	MD	21228	9	512
United Artists Theatre	7272 Wisconsin Ave.	Bethesda	MD	20817	10	511
UA Snowden Square	9161 Commerce Center Dr.	Columbia	MD	21046	14	512
Movies @ Marley Station	7880 S. Governor Ritchie	Glen Burnie	MD	21061	8	512
UA W. River Theatre	30170 Grand River Ave.	Farmington	MI	48024	9	505
MVS @ Portage	6600 Ring Rd.	Portage	MI	49001	10	563
UA Commerce Township 14	3033 Spring Vale Dr.	Walled Lake	MI	48390	14	505
Movies @ Brookdale Square	5810 Shingle Creek	Brooklyn Center	MN	55430	8	613
UA Burnsville II	14300 Buckhill Rd.	Burnsville	MN	55306	4	613
Movies @ Eden Prairie W.	1076 Eden Prairie Center	Eden Prairie	MN	55344	5	613
Movies @ Maplewood I	3091 White Bear Ave.	Maplewood	MN	55109	6	613
Movies @ Maplewood II	1793 Beam Ave.	Maplewood	MN	55109	6	613
Movies @ Pavilions Place	1655 W. County Rd.	Roseville	MN	55113	7	613
UA Woodbury	1470 Queens Dr.	Woodbury	MN	55125	10	613
Biloxi 10 Theatre	2681 C.T. Switzer Dr.	Biloxi	MS	39531	10	746
Westbrook Cinema	454 Brookway Blvd	Brookhaven	MS	39601	4	718
UA Clinton Center 10	201 Clinton Center Dr.	Clinton	MS	39056	10	718
UA Parkway Place	1075 Pkwy.	Flowood	MS	39208	10	718
Singing River Theatre	2800 Hwy. 90	Gautier	MS	39553	4	746
Singing River Cinema	2800 Hwy. 90	Gautier	MS	39553	5	746
Cinema I-82	Abraham Shopping Center	Greenville	MS	38701	4	647
Highland Park 3 Thearte	Highland Park Shopping Center	Greenwood	MS	38930	3	647
UA Turtle Creek	1000 Turtle Creek Dr.	Hattiesburg	MS	39402	9	710
Sawmill Square	910 Sawmill Rd.	Laurel	MS	39440	5	710
Camelia Cinema	1005 Delware Ave.	McComb	MS	39648	4	718
Bonita Lakes	1680 Bonita Lakes Circle #G	Meridian	MS	30301	9	524
Natchez Mall Cinema	350 John R. Junkin Dr.	Natchez	MS	39120	4	718
Cinema 4	Hwy. 6 Oxford Mall	Oxford	MS	38655	4	640
Movies @ Northpark	250 Ring Rd.	Ridgeland	MS	39157	14	718
Pemberton Square Cinemas	3505 Pemberton Blvd.	Vicksburg	MS	39180	4	718
Eastgate Cinemas	East Gate Shopping Center	Albemarle	NC	28001	5	517
Beaucatcher Cinemas	321 Haw Creek Ln.	Ashville	NC	28805	7	567
UA Movies @ Biltmore Square	800 Brevard Rd.	Ashville	NC	28806	6	567
Carolina Mall Cinemas	120 Country Club Dr.	Concord	NC	28025	8	517
UA Towne Square 10	2600 Timber Dr.	Garner	NC	27529	10	560
Litchfield Cinemas	301 N. Berkeley Blvd.	Goldsboro	NC	27532	4	560
Four Seasons Cinema	1800 7th Ave.	Hendersonville	NC	28793	4	567
Crown 6 Cinemas	Hwy. 70	Hickory	NC	28601	6	517
Cinema IV	Intersection NC 211 & US 301A	Lumberton	NC	28350	4	550
College Rd. Cinemas	632 S. College Rd.	Wilmington	NC	28403	6	550
UA Moorestown	Rt. 38 & Lenola Rd.	Moorestown	NJ	08057	7	504
Eric Pennsauken Theatre	Rt. 73 & 130 North	Pennsauken	NJ	08110	11	504
Movies @ Marketfair	3521 US Rt. 1	Princeton	NJ	08540	9	504
UA Washington Township	121 Tuckahoe Rd.	Sewell	NJ	08080	14	504
Coronado 6 Theatre	6401 Uptown Blvd.	Albuquerque	NM	87110	6	790
UA Cottonwood Mall	10000 Coors Blvd.	Albuquerque	NM	87114	9	790
UA Four Hills 10	13120 Central	Albuquerque	NM	87123	10	790
UA @ Highridge Theatre	12921 School Rd.	Albuquerque	NM	87112	8	790
UA De Vargas Center 6	562 N. Guadalupe	Santa Fe	NM	87501	6	790
UA North Theatre	4250 Cerrillos Rd.	Santa Fe	NM	87505	6	790
UA South	4250 Cerrillos Rd.	Santa Fe	NM	87504	6	790
UA Green Valley Cinemas	4500 E. Sunset Rd.	Henderson	NV	89014	8	839
UA Rainbow Promenade	2321 N. Rainbow Blvd.	Las Vegas	NV	89108	10	839
Showcase Mall	3769 S. Las Vegas Blvd.	Las Vegas	NV	89109	8	839
Bayside 4 Theatre	38-39 Bell Blvd.	Bayside	NY	11361	4	501
Marboro Theatre 4	68-17 Bay Pkwy.	Brooklyn	NY	11204	4	501
Movies @ Sheepshead Bay	3907 Shore Pkwy.	Brooklyn	NY	11235	9	501
Coram 12 Theatre	Rte. 25 & 112	Coram	NY	11727	12	501
Movieworld Douglston	242-02 61st Ave.	Douglaston	NY	11362	7	501
Easthampton Cinema	30 Main St.	East Hampton	NY	11937	6	501
Meadowbrook Theatre	2549 Hempstead Tpke.	East Meadow	NY	11554	6	501
UA Farmingdale	20 Michael Ave.	Farmingdale	NY	11735	10	501
Brandon Cinemas	70-20 Austin St.	Forest Hills	NY	11375	2	501

Midway 9 Cinemas	108-22 Queens Blvd.	Forest Hills	NY	11375	9	501
UA Hampton Bays	119 W. Montauk Hwy.	Hampton Bays	NY	11946	5	501
Astoria 6 Theatre	2860 Steinway St.	Long Island City	NY	11103	6	501
Lynbrook 6 Theatre	321 Merrick Rd.	Lynbrook	NY	11563	6	501
Cortlandt Town Center	3131 E. Main St.	Mohegan Lake	NY	15047	11	508
UA Cinema East	1629 1st Ave.	New York	NY	10028	1	501
Gemini Theatre	1210 2nd Ave.	New York	NY	10021	3	501
United Artist Union Square	850 Broadway	New York	NY	10003	14	501
Crossbay 1 Theatre	94-11 Rockaway Blvd.	Ozone Park	NY	11417	3	501
Crossbay Theatre	92-10 Rockaway Blvd.	Ozone Park	NY	11417	7	501
Movies @ Patchogue	600 Sunrise Hwy	Patchogue	NY	11772	13	501
UA Smithtown	2 E. Main St.	Smithtown	NY	11787	1	501
Southampton Theatre	43 Hill St.	Southampton	NY	11968	4	501
UA Hylan Plaza	107 Mill Rd.	Staten Island	NY	10306	5	501
Movies @ Staten Island	141-145 E. Service Rd.	Staten Island	NY	10304	14	501
UA Westbury	7000 Brush Hollow Rd	Westbury	NY	11950	12	501
UA Cinema 150	7500 Jericho Turnpike	Woodbury	NY	11797	1	501
Movieland Yonkers 6	2548 Central Park Ave.	Yonkers	NY	10710	6	501
Movies @ Jefferson Valley	650 Lee Blvd.	Yorktown Heights	NY	10598	8	501
Camp Hill Twin Theatre	1800 Camp Hill Shopping Mall	Camp Hill	PA	17011	2	566
UA 6 Capital City Cinema	3594 Capital City Mall	Camp Hill	PA	17011	6	566
UA East Whiteland	593 W. Lancaster Ave.	E.Whiteland	PA	19355	9	504
Movies @ Schuylkill	Rt 61 & I-81	Frackville	PA	17931	4	577
Eric Macdade Mall	Macdade Blvd. & South Ave.	Holmes	PA	19043	4	504
UA King of Prussia	300 Goddard Blvd.	King of Prussia	PA	19406	16	504
UA Oxford Valley	403 Middletown Blvd.	Langhorne	PA	19047	10	504
Main St.	3720-40 Main St.	Manayuk	PA	19127	6	504
UA Montgomeryville	Rte. 202, 309 & 463	Montgomeryville	PA	18936	7	504
Movies @ Lycoming Mall	Junction of 147 & 220	Muncy	PA	17756	4	577
UA @ Cheltenham Square	2385 Cheltenham Square	Philadelphia	PA	19150	8	504
UA Grant Plaza	1619 Grant Ave.	Philadelphia	PA	19115	9	504
Riverview Plaza Theatre	1400 S. Columbus Blvd.	Philadelphia	PA	19147	17	504
Sameric IV Theatre	1908 Chestnut St.	Philadelphia	PA	19103	4	504
UA Scranton 8	933 Scranton-Carbondale Hwy.	Scranton	PA	18508	8	577
UA Steamtown Mall	301 Lackawanna Ave.	Scranton	PA	18508	8	577
UA Theatres 69th St.	53 S. 69th St.	Upper Darby	PA	19082	9	504
Market Place Cinemas	Marketplace Shopping Center	Anderson	SC	29623	6	567
Capri Cinema 3	840 S. Irby St.	Florence	SC	29504	3	570
Julia Cinemas IV	1110 S. Irby St.	Florence	SC	29504	4	570
Bijou Theatre	2035 Wade Hampton Blvd.	Greenville	SC	29615	8	567
Haywood Cinemas	303 Haywood Rd.	Greenville	SC	29607	10	567
UA Cinema 10	Mall of Abilene #1344	Abilene	TX	79605	10	662
UA Amarillo 14	8275 Amarillo Blvd.	Amarillo	TX	79106	14	634
UA Bowen 8 Theatre	4255 S. Bowen	Arlington	TX	76015	8	623
UA Bedford 10 Theatre	2000 Forum Pkwy.	Bedford	TX	76021	10	623
UA Cinema 6 Theatre	4701 S. Staples St.	Corpus Christi	TX	78411	6	600
UA Cine 1 & 2 Theatre	5540 Yale Blvd.	Dallas	TX	75206	2	623
Galaxy Theatre	11801 Mc Cree Rd.	Dallas	TX	75238	9	623
United Artists Theatre	9330 N. Central Expwy	Dallas	TX	75231	8	623
UA Golden Triangle 4	2201 S. I-35 East	Denton	TX	76205	4	623
UA Golden Triangle 5	2201 S. I-35 East	Denton	TX	76205	5	623
UA Eastchase	8301 Ederville	Fort Worth	TX	76120	9	623
UA Fossil Creek	6100 N. Freeway	Fort Worth	TX	76137	11	623
UA Hulen 10 Theatre	4920 S. Hulen	Fort Worth	TX	76132	10	623
Las Vegas Trail 8 Theatre	8300 I-30 West	Fort Worth	TX	76108	8	623
UA Northstar 8 Theatre	1146 Beltline Rd.	Garland	TX	75042	8	623
UA Grand Prairie	510 Westchester	Grand Prairie	TX	75052	10	623
MacArthur Marketplace	8505 Walton Blvd.	Irving	TX	75063	16	623
North Creek 10	7807 San Dario	Laredo	TX	78041	10	749
UA Lakepointe 10	1600 S. Stemmons Freeway	Lewisville	TX	75057	10	623
UA Fairfax Towne Center	12110 W. Ox Rd.	Fairfax	VA	22033	10	511
UA Chesterfeild Towne Center	11500 Midothian Turnpike	Richmond	VA	23235	9	556
West Tower Cinemas	8998 West Broad St.	Richmond	VA	23294	10	556

WALLACE THEATER CORPORATION

65 theatres, 466 screens.
(Incorporating Hollywood Theatres)
919 S.W. Taylor St., Ste. 800, Portland, OR 97205. (503) 221-7090. FAX: (503) 796-0229.
PRESIDENT
Walt Aman
CEO
Scott C. Wallace
SENIOR V.P., OPERATIONS
Timothy G. Wood
SENIOR V.P., DEVELOPMENT
Tim Reed
V.P., OPERATIONS, MIDWEST
Steve Guffey
V.P., OPERATIONS, WESTERN U.S. & PACIFIC RIM
Brett Havlik
V.P., CONCESSION & PURCHASING
Robert Perkins
V.P. & HEAD FILM BUYER
Steve Friedstrom
V.P., MARKETING & ADVERTISING
David L. Lyons
CONTROLLER
Lawrence T. Reid

THEATRES

WTC- Stadium/Mobile 18	1230 Satchell Paige Dr.	Mobile	AL	36606	10	686
WTC- New Barstow Cinema 6	1503 E. Main St.	Barstow	CA	92311	6	803
WTC- New Malibu Cinema 2	3822 Crosscreek Rd.	Malibu	CA	90265	2	803
WTC- Town Center Cinema 3	218 Town Center	Santa Maria	CA	93454	3	855
WTC- Santa Paula Cinema 7	550 W. Main St.	Santa Paula	CA	93060	7	803
WTC- New Stateline Cinema 1	1093 Park Ave.	South Lake Tahoe	CA	95729	1	862
WTC- Guam Megaplex Cinemas	235 Pas St.	Tamuning	GU	96911	14	—
WTC- Waiakea Cinema 3	88 Kanoelehua Ave.	Hilo	HI	96720	3	744
WTC- Prince Kuhio Cinema 9	111 E. Puainako St.	Hilo	HI	96720	9	744
WTC- Kress Cinema 4	174 Kamehameha Ave.	Hilo	HI	96720	4	744

WTC- Restaurant Row 9	500 Ala Moana Blvd.	Honolulu	HI	96813	9	744
WTC- Maui Mall Cinema 12	70 E. Kahnumanu Ave.	Kahului	HI	96732	12	744
WTC- Keolu Center Cinema 4	1090 Keolu Dr.	Kailua	HI	96734	4	744
WTC- Kailua Cinema 2	345 Hahani St.	Kailua	HI	96734	2	744
WTC- Enchanted Lake Cinema 3	1060 Keolu Dr.	Kailua	HI	96734	3	744
WTC- Kona Marketplace 2	75-5725 Ali'I Dr.	Kailua-Kona	HI	96740	2	744
WTC- Coconut Marketplace 2	4-484 Kuhio Highway	Kapa'a	HI	96746	2	744
WTC- Wharf Cinema 3	658 Front St.	Lahaina	HI	96761	3	744
WTC- Front St. Cinema 4	900 Front St.	Lahaina	HI	96761	4	744
WTC- Lai'e Cinema 2	55-510 Kamehameha Hwy #18	Lai'e	HI	96792	2	744
WTC- Maunaloa Town Cinema 3	1 Maunaloa Highway	Maunaloa	HI	96770	3	744
WTC- Village Cinema 3	4805 West 10th St.	Great Bend	KS	67530	3	678
WTC- Westside Cinema 4	1016 W. 6th St.	Junction City	KS	66441	4	605
WTC- Plaza Cinema 6	2339 South Iowa St.	Lawrence	KS	66046	6	616
WTC- Southwind Cinema 12	3433 Iowa St.	Lawrence	KS	66046	12	616
WTC- Southgate Cinema 4	1104 S. Kansas Ave.	Liberal	KS	67901	4	678
WTC- Fox Whitelakes Cinema 4	320 S.W. Croix	Topeka	KS	66611	4	605
WTC- West Ridge Cinema 6	1801 S.W. Wanamaker	Topeka	KS	66604	6	605
WTC- West Ridge Cinema 8	1727 S.W. Wanamaker	Topeka	KS	66604	8	605
WTC- Stadium Cinema 14	2800 Goodwin Pointe Dr.	Columbia	MO	65201	14	604
WTC- Joplin Cinema 6	1110 East 7th St.	Joplin	MO	64801	6	603
WTC- Northstar Cinema 14	201 N. Northpark Lane	Joplin	MO	64801	14	603
WTC- Forum Cinema 4	1101 E. 18th St.	Rolla	MO	64502	4	638
WTC- Plaza Cinema 8	2219 N. Belt Hwy	St. Joseph	MO	64506	8	638
WTC- Union Station Cinema 10	900 St Louis Union Station	St. Louis	MO	63103	10	609
WTC- Northgate Cinema 10	2571 N. Carson St.	Carson City	NV	89706	10	811
WTC- New Cinema 50	2226 Highway 50	Carson City	NV	89706	2	811
WTC- Horizon Stadium 8	50 West Hwy. 50	Stateline	NV	89449	8	811
WTC- Indian Mound Cinema 11	771 S. 30th St.	Heath	OH	43506	11	547
WTC- Movies Cinema 6	2350 S.E. Washington Blvd.	Bartlesville	OK	74005	6	671
WTC- Cache Cinema 8	4908 N.W. Cache Rd.	Lawton	OK	73505	8	627
WTC- Heritage Plaza 5	351 N. Air Dept	Midwest City	OK	73110	5	650
WTC- Spotlight Cinema 14	1100 N. Interstate Dr.	Norman	OK	73072	14	650
WTC- Brixton Square Cinema 8	7101 N.W. Expressway	Oklahoma City	OK	73132	8	650
WTC- Crossroads Cinema 8	7400 S. Prospect	Oklahoma City	OK	73149	8	650
WTC- Penn Square Cinema 10	2100 Penn Square	Oklahoma City	OK	73118	10	650
WTC- Movies Cinema 6	4901 N. Kickapoo	Shawnee	OK	74801	6	650
WTC- Palace Cinema 12	4107 S. Yale	Tulsa	OK	74135	12	671
WTC- Woodland Hills Cinema 6	8220 E. 66th St.	Tulsa	OK	74133	6	671
WTC- Eastland Mall Cinema 6	14002 E. 21st St.	Tulsa	OK	74134	6	671
WTC- Star Cinema 12	4455 Dowlen Rd.	Beaumont	TX	77706	12	692
WTC- Movies Cinema 14	301 W. Rendon-Crowley Rd.	Burleson	TX	76028	14	623
WTC- Medallion Cinema 5	125 Medallion Center	Dallas	TX	75214	5	623
WTC- Town Center Cinema 8	4200 S. Freeway	Fort Worth	TX	76115	8	623
WTC- Movies Cinema 8	1301 William D. Tate	Grapevine	TX	76051	8	623
WTC- Killeen Stadium Cinema 14	2501 E. Central Texas Expressway	Killeen	TX	76543	10	625
WTC- Cinema 4	2100 S. WS Young Dr.	Killeen	TX	76541	4	625
WTC- Movies Cinema 9	720 US Hwy 259	Longview	TX	75603	9	709
WTC- Tall City Cinema 10	4915 W. Loop 250 North	Midland	TX	79707	10	633
WTC- Cine 4	3207 Cuthbert	Midland	TX	79701	4	633
WTC- Permian Palace Cinema 11	4101 E. 42nd St.	Odessa	TX	79762	11	633
WTC- Cinema 7	4325 John Ben Shepperd Pkwy.	Odessa	TX	79762	7	633
WTC- Tyler Rose Cinema 14	1250 S.W. Loop 323	Tyler	TX	75701	14	709
WTC- Movies Cinema 6	2747 East 5th St.	Tyler	TX	75701	6	709
WTC- Jewel Cinema 16	7200 Woodway Dr.	Waco	TX	76712	16	625

WEHRENBERG THEATRES, INC.

26 theatres, 246 screens.

12800 Manchester Rd., St. Louis, MO 63131. (314) 822-4520. FAX: (314) 822-8032.

PRESIDENT
Ronald P. Krueger
V.P. & CFO
Charles Nicks
V.P., FILM BUYER
Doug Whitford
DIRECTOR OF FACILITIES.
Bill Menke
DIRECTOR OF OPERATIONS
Ronald Krueger II
DIRECTOR OF CONCESSIONS
Larry Mattson

THEATRES

Wehrenberg Greentree 3	1800 South Milton Rd.	Flagstaff	AZ	86002	3	753
Wehrenberg University Plaza 2	1300 South Plaza Way	Flagstaff	AZ	86001	2	753
Wehrenberg Frontier Village 10	1771 Highway 69	Prescott	AZ	86302	10	753
Wehrenberg St. Clair Cinema 10	50 Ludwig Dr	Fairview Height	IL	62208	10	609
Wehrenberg Cape West 14	247 Siemers Dr.	Cape Girardeau	MO	63703	14	632
Wehrenberg West Park 4	157 West Park Mall	Cape Girardeau	MO	63701	4	632
Wehrenberg Chesterfield 4 Cinema	595 Chesterfield Center	Chesterfield	MO	63017	4	609
Wehrenberg Clarkson 6 Cinema	1785 Clarkson Rd.	Chesterfield	MO	63017	6	609
Wehrenberg Eureka 6 Cinema	99 Hilltop Village Center	Eureka	MO	63025	6	609
Wehrenberg Jamestown 14	209 Jamestown Mall	Florissant	MO	63034	14	609
Wehrenberg O'Fallon 15 Cinema	1320 Central Park Dr.	O'Fallon	MO	62269	15	609
Wehrenberg Osage Village 5	Factory Outlet Village	Osage Beach	MO	65065	5	619
Wehrenberg Ronnies 20 Cinema	5320 S. Lindbergh Blvd	Sappington	MO	63126	20	609
Wehrenberg Battlefield Mall 6	2825 South Glenstone	Springfield	MO	65804	6	619
Wehrenberg Campbell 16	4005 South Ave.	Springfield	MO	65807	16	619
Wehrenberg Northwest 9 Cinema	300 Northwest Plaza	St. Ann	MO	63074	9	609
Wehrenberg St. Charles 18	1830 S. 1st Capital Rd.	St. Charles	MO	63303	18	609
Wehrenberg Arnold 14	1912 Richardson Rd.	St. Louis	MO	63131	14	609
Wehrenberg Des Peres 14	1215 Des Peres Rd.	St. Louis	MO	63131	14	609
Wehrenberg Halls Ferry 14 Cinema	2845 Target Dr.	St. Louis	MO	63136	14	609
Wehrenberg Keller 8 Cinema	4572 Lemay Ferry Rd.	St. Louis	MO	63129	8	609
Wehrenberg Kenrick 8 Cinema	7505 Watson Rd.	St. Louis	MO	63119	8	609
Wehrenberg Lindbergh 8 Cinema	7545 S. Lindbergh Blvd	St. Louis	MO	63125	8	609
Wehrenberg Mid Rivers 14 Cinema	I-70 & Midrivers Mall Rd.	St. Louis	MO	63125	14	609
Wehrenberg North Twin Drive-In	9425 Lewis & Clark Blvd.	St. Louis	MO	63136	2	609
Wehrenberg Westport Cinema	910 Westport Plaza	St. Louis	MO	63141	2	609

W. F. CINEMA HOLDINGS, L.P. (MANN THEATRES)

29 theatres, 169 screens.

P.O. 20077, Encino, CA 91416-0077; 16530 Ventura Blvd., Ste. 500, Encino, CA, 91436. (818) 784-6266. FAX: (818) 784-8717.

SENIOR V.P., FILM
Ben Barbosa
CFO
John Waterman
V.P., INFORMATION SERVICES
Steve Broudy
V.P., HUMAN RESOURCES
Jason Hebert
DIRECTOR, MARKETING
Martin Griego
DIRECTOR, CONCESSIONS
Sally Basada
DIRECTOR, PURCHASING
Aimee Litel-White
DIRECTOR, REAL ESTATE
Joanne McClellan

THEATRES

Mann Agoura Hills 8	29045 Agoura Rd.	Agoura Hills	CA	91301	8	803
Mann 6 Puente Hills 6	17640 E. Castleton St.	City of Industry	CA	91748	6	803
Mann Culver Plaza 6	9919 Washington Blvd.	Culver City	CA	90232	6	803
Mann Glendale Exchange 10	128 N. Maryland Ave.	Glendale	CA	91206	10	803
Mann Glendale Marketplace 4	144 S. Brand Blvd.	Glendale	CA	91206	4	803
Mann 9 Granada Hills	16830 Devonshire St.	Granada Hills	CA	91344	9	803
Mann Chinese 1	6925 Hollywood Blvd.	Hollywood	CA	90028	1	803
Mann Village 1	961 Broxton Ave.	Los Angeles	CA	90024	1	803
Mann Bruin 1	948 Broxton Ave.	Los Angeles	CA	90024	1	803
Mann National 1	10925 Lindbrook Dr.	Los Angeles	CA	90024	1	803
Mann Westwood Quad	1050 Gayley Ave.	Los Angeles	CA	90024	4	803
Mann Regent 1	1045 Broxton Ave.	Los Angeles	CA	90024	1	803
Mann Plaza 1	1067 Glendon Ave.	Los Angeles	CA	90024	1	803
Mann Festival Westwood 1	10887 Lindbrook Dr	Los Angeles	CA	90024	1	803
Mann 6 Huntington Oaks	650 W. Huntington Dr.	Monrovia	CA	91016	6	803
Mann 7 Hazard Center	7510 Hazard Ctr. Dr.	San Diego	CA	92108	7	825
Mann Criterion 6	1313 Third St. Promenade	Santa Monica	CA	90401	6	803
Mann 6 Simi Valley	3050 Cochran St.	Simi Valley	CA	93065	6	803
Mann 9 Valley West	8632 Ventura Blvd.	Tarzana	CA	91356	9	803
Mann 9 Janss Marketplace	255 N. Moorpark Rd.	Thousand Oaks	CA	91360	9	803
Mann Del Amo 9	3550 Carson St.	Torrance	CA	90503	9	803
Mann 10 Valencia	23415 W. Cinema Dr.	Valencia	CA	91355	10	803
Mann Plant 16	7876 Van Nuys Blvd.	Van Nuys	CA	91402	16	803
Mann 6 Buenaventura	1440 Eastman Ave.	Ventura	CA	93003	6	803
Mann Westlake Village 8	180 Promenade Way	Westlake Village	CA	91362	8	803
Mann Crossroads Commons 6	2985 Pearl St.	Boulder	CO	80301	6	751
Mann 6 Tamarac Square	7777 E. Hampden Ave.	Denver	CO	80231	6	751
Mann 6 Green Mountain	12344 W. Alameda Pkwy.	Lakewood	CO	80228	6	751
Mann Southwest Plaza 5	8501 Bowles Ave.	Littleton	CO	80123	5	751

WILDWOOD THEATRES

5 theatres, 54 screens.

557 Cottonwood Ave,. Hartland, WI 53029.. FAX: (262) 369-1990. FAX: (262) 369-1650.

COMPANY OFFICERS
Brad Porchetta
Anthony Groh
Hank Furlong
Michael Furlong

THEATRES

Palm Valley 14	1325 Litchfield Rd.	Goodyear	AZ	85338	14	753
Luxury 10	2799 Cranston Rd.	Beluit	WI	53511	10	669
Movies 10	3100 Deerfield Dr.	Janesville	WI	53546	10	669
Rock Theatres 9	1620 Newport Rd.	Janesville	WI	53546	9	669
Capitol Cinemas 11	1275 Capitol Dr.	Pewaukee	WI	53072	11	617

CIRCUIT THEATRES BY STATE

ALABAMA

CARMIKE—ANNISTON: Plaza 6; AUBURN: Wynnsong 16; BIRMINGHAM: Carmike 10, Summit 16, Wynnsong 12; CULLMAN: Town Square 3; DECATUR: Century Cinema 8; DOTHAN: Circle West 4; FLORENCE: Capri 4, Hickory Hills 6; HUNTSVILLE: Carmike 10; MOBILE: Carmike 14, Springdale 6, Wynnsong 16; MONTGOMERY: Carmike 8, Eastdale 8, Wynnsong 10; PRATTVILLE: Movies 2; TALLADEGA: Martin 3; TUSCALOOSA: Bama 6.

CLARK—ANDALUSIA: Clark Theatre on the Square 3; ENTERPRISE: Clark Cinema I & II, Clark Cinema III & IV, College Cinema I, II & III; OZARK: Twin Cinemas.

O'NEIL—FOLEY: Riviera 12 Cinema; PRATTVILLE: Promenade Cinema 12.

REGAL—BIRMINGHAM: Festival 18, Galleria 10, Regal 16, Wildwood 14; DECATUR: River Oaks 8; GADSDEN: Rainbow 8; HUNTSVILLE: Hollywood 18, Madison Square 12; INVERNESS: Brook Highland 10; JASPER: Movies 4; TUSCALOOSA: Fox 12.

WALLACE—MOBILE: Stadium/Mobile 18.

ALASKA

CENTURY—ANCHORAGE: Century 16.

REGAL—ANCHORAGE: Diamond Center 9, Fireweed 7, Totem 8; FAIRBANKS: Goldstream 9; KENAI: Kambe 3.

ARIZONA

AMC—CHANDLER: Laguna Village 10; GLENDALE: Arrowhead 14; MESA: Three Fountains 4, Mesa Grand 24; PHOENIX: Ahwautukee 24, Arizona Center 24, Bell Plaza 8, Deer Valley 30, Town & Country 6, Esplanade 14.

CENTURY—ANCHORAGE: Century 16; GLENDALE: Glendale 9 Drive-In; SCOTTSDALE: Scottsdale 6 Drive-In; TUCSON: Century Gateway 12, Century 20 El Con.

CINEMARK—KINGMAN: The Movies 4; SIERRA VISTA: Cinemark Sierra Vista 10.

DEANZA—TUSCON: DeAnza 4.

GKC—TUCSON: American Cinemas 6.

HARKINS—FLAGSTAFF: Flagstaff 11; MESA: Fiesta 5, Poca Fiesta 4, Superstition Springs 25; PEORIA: Arrowhead 18; PHOENIX: Arcadia 8, Bell Towne Centre 8, Christown Luxury 11, Desert Sky Mall 6, Metrocenter 12, Paradise Valley Mall 7, Southwest 8; SCOTTSDALE: Camelview 5, Fashion Square 7, Shea 14; SEDONA: Sedona 6; TEMPE: Arizona Mills 24, Centerpoint 11, Valley Art Theatre.

LOEWS CINPLEX—TUCSON: Catalina 6, Crossroads 6, El Dorado 6, Foothills 15.

SILVER—MESA: Superstition Springs 8; PHOENIX: Super Saver Cinema Bell Canyon Road 8.

TRANS-LUX—SAHUARITA: Desert Sky Cinema 6.

UA—PHOENIX: Metro Park 8, Christown Mall 6; SCOTTSDALE: Sonora Village 10, Scottsdale Pavillion 11.

WEHRENBERG —FLAGSTAFF: Greentree 3, University Plaza 2; PRESCOTT: Frontier Village 10.

WILDWOOD—GOODYEAR: Palm Valley 14.

ARKANSAS

CARMIKE—BATESVILLE: Oaks 7; BELL VISTA: Sugar Creek 10; CONWAY: Cinema 6; FT. SMITH: Carmike 14; HARRISON: Harrison 8; HOT SPRINGS: Central City 10; LITTLE ROCK: Wynnsong 10; MOUNTAIN HOME: Village 5; N. LITTLE ROCK: Carmike 7; PINE BLUFF: Pines Mall 8.

CINEMARK—BENTON: Tinseltown Benton 14; CONWAY: Cinema 6; LITTLE ROCK: Tandy Movies 10.

MALCO—BLYTHEVILLE: Malco Trio; FAYETTEVILLE: Mall Twin, Razorback 6; FT. SMITH: Mall Trio, Malco Quartet; JONESBORO: Malco Cinema 14, PARAGOULD: Paragould Twin; SPRINGDALE: Sunset Cinema 9.

REGAL—FAYETTEVILLE: Fiesta Square 16; RODGERS: Mall 6.

UA—LITTLE ROCK: Cinema 150 (1), Breckenridge Village 12; MAGNOLIA: Cameo 3; N. LITTLE ROCK: Lakewood Village 8.

CALIFORNIA

AMC—BURBANK: Burbank 14, Media Center 8, Media Center 6; CHINO: Chino Town Square 10; COVINA: Covina 30; ENCINITAS: Wiegand Plaza 8; FULLERTON: Fullerton 20; INDUSTRY: Puente Hills 20; LA JOLLA: La Jolla 12; LONG BEACH: Marina Pacifica 12, Pine Square 16; LOS ANGELES: Century 14; MILPITAS: Milpitas 10; MONTEBELLO: Montebello 10; NORWALK: Norwalk 20; ONTARIO: Ontario Mills 30; ORANGE: The Block 30; PASADENA: Old Pasadena 8; SAN DIEGO: Fashion Valley 18, Mission Valley 20, Palm Promenade 24; SAN FRANCISCO: Van Ness 14, Kabuki 8; SAN JOSE: Saratoga 14; SANTA ANA: Mainplace 6; SANTA CLARA: Mercado 20; SANTA MONICA; Santa Monica 7; SUNNYVALE: Sunnyvale 6; TORRANCE: Rolling Hills 20; VALLEJO: Vallejo Plaza 6; WOODLAND HILLS: Promenade 16.

CENTURY—BURLINGAME: Hyatt Cinema Triplex; CONCORD: Solano 2 Drive-In; ELK GROVE: Laguna 16; FOLSOM: Folsom 14; FREMONT: Cinedome 8; LARKSPUR: Century Larkspur; MOUNTAIN VIEW: Cinema 16; NAPA: Cinedome 8; NEWARK: Cinedome 7; NORTH HOLLYWOOD: Century 8; ORANGE: Stadium 25; PINOLE: Century 10; PLEASANT HILL: Century 5; REDWOOD: Century Park 12; ROSEVILLE: CENTURY 14; SACRAMENTO: Century Stadium 21, Cinedome 9, Sacramento Drive-In, Century Stadium 14, Downtown Plaza 7; SALINAS: Northridge 8, Century Park 7; SAN FRANCISCO: Cinema 21, Empire 3, Presidio; SAN JOSE: Capitol Drive-In, Century Capitol 16, Century Berryessa, Century 21-25; S. SAN FRANCISCO: Century Plaza 10; UNION CITY: Century 25; VALLEJO: Cinedome 8; VENTURA: Century 16, Century 10.

CINEMA GRILL—PALOS VERDES: Terrace Cinema Grill 5.

CINEMARK—CATHEDRAL CITY: Movies 10; CHICO: Cinemark Movies 8, Tinseltown 14; DANVILLE: Blackhawk 7; HANFORD: Movies 4, Movies 8; LANCASTER: Movies 1-4, Movies 12, Cinemark 22; PALMDALE: Movies 8, Movies 10; REDDING: Movies 8, Movies 10; TRACY: Movies 14; VICTORVILLE: Movies 10, Victor Valley 10; WOODLAND: County Fair Movies 5; YUBA CITY: Yuba City 8.

CINEMASTAR LUXURY—BONSALL: Galaxy 6; CHULA VISTA: Chula Vista 10; OCEANSIDE: Mission Marketplace 13; PERRIS: Perris Plaza 10; RIVERSIDE: Mission Grove 14, University Village 10; SAN BERNARDINO: Empire 20.

COMING ATTRACTIONS—CRESCENT CITY: Crescent City Cinema 8.

DEANZA—ARLINGTON: Van Buren Boulvard; MONTCLAIR: Mission Quad; RIVERSIDE: Rubidoux 3; SAN DIEGO: South Bay 3.

EDWARDS—ALHAMBRA: Alhambra Place 5, Atlantic Palace 10; ALISO VIEJO: Aliso Viejo Stadium 20; ANAHEIM: Anaheim Hills 14; AZUSA: Foothill Center 10; BAKERSFIELD: Bakersfield 14; BREA: Brea Plaza 5, Brea Stadium 12; CALABASAS: Calabasas 6; CAMARILLO: Camarillo Palace 12; CERRITOS: Cerritos 10; CORONA: Corona 15; COSTA MESA: Cinema Center 4, Metro Pointe Stadium 12, South Coast Plaza 3, Town Center 4, Triangle Square 8; DEL MAR: Flower Hill 4; EL CAJON: Rancho San Diego 15; EL MONTE: El Monte 8; EL TORO: El Toro 5; FAIRFIELD: Fairfield 16; FRESNO: Fresno 21; HUNTINGTON BEACH: Charter Center 5, Pierside 6; IRVINE: Irvine Spectrum 21 (1 Imax 3D screen), Marketplace Stadium 10, Park Place 10, University Town Center 6, Westpark 8, Woodbridge 5; LA VERNE: La Verne 12; LAGUNA BEACH: South Coast Laguna 2; LAGUNA NIGUEL: Ocean Ranch 7, Rancho Niguel 8; LONG BEACH: Long Beach 26; MISSION VIEJO: Trabuco Hills 5, Kaleidoscope Stadium 10; MORENO VALLEY: Towngate 8; NEWPORT BEACH: Newport 6, Island 7, Lido; ONTARIO: Ontario Mountain 14, Ontario Palace 22; POWAY: Poway 10; RANCHO SANTA MARGARITA: Rancho Santa Margarita 6; RIVERSIDE: Jurupa 14; SAN DIEGO: Del Mar Highlands 8, Mira Mesa Stadium 18; SAN LUIS OBISPO: Fremont 4, Mission 3; SAN MARCOS: San Marcos 18; SANTA ANA: Hutton Center 8; SANTA CLARITA: Canyon Country 10, Valencia 22; SANTA MARIA: Santa Maria 10; SIMI VALLEY: Simi Valley Plaza 10; SOUTH GATE: El Paso Stadium Cinema 20; TEMECULA: Temecula Stadium 15; TEMPLE CITY: Temple 4; TUSTIN: Tustin Market Place 6; WEST COVINA: West Covina 18; WESTMINSTER: Westminster 10, Westminster Mall 4.

GENERAL CINEMA—BEVERLY HILLS: Beverly Connection 6; CITRUS HEIGHTS: Birdcage Centre 6; DUBLIN: Dublin Place 6; GLENDALE: Central Cinema 5; HOLLYWOOD: Hollywood Galaxy 6; REDONDO BEACH: Galleria at South Bay 16, Cinema 3; SHERMAN OAKS: Cinema 7; WESTWOOD: Avco Cinema 4.

KRIKORIAN PREMIERE—DOWNEY: Downey 10; REDLANDS: Redlands 14; SAN CLEMENTE: San Clemente 7; Manrovia 12.

LAEMMLE—BEVERLY HILLS: Music Hall 3; CAMARILLO: Paseo Camarillo 3; ENCINO: Town Center 5; HOLLYWOOD: Regent Showcase; LOS ANGELES: Grande 4, Sunset 5, Royal; PASADENA: Colorado, Playhouse 7; SANTA MONICA: Monica 4; WESTLAKE VILLAGE: Westlake Village Twin.

LOEWS CINEPLEX—LOS ANGELES: Beverly Center 13, Century Plaza 4, Fairfax 3; MARINA DEL REY: Marina 6; SAN FRANCISCO: Metreon 17; SANTA MONICA: Broadway 4.

LANDMARK—ALBANY: Albany Twin; BERKELEY: Act I & II, California 3, Shattuck 8, U. C. Theatre; BEVERLY HILLS: Fine Arts; LA JOLLA: Cove , La Jolla Village 4; LOS ANGELES: Nuart, Westside Pavilion Cinemas 4; MENLO PARK: Guild, Park; OAKLAND: Piedmont; PALO ALTO: Aquarius 2, Palo Alto Square; SAN DIEGO: Hillcrest 5, Ken; SAN FRANCISCO: Bridge, Clay, Embarcadero Center 5, Lumiere 3, Opera Plaza 4; SANTA MONICA: NuWilshire Theatre; SOUTH PASADENA: Rialto.

METROPOLITAN—CALEXICO: 10 Theatre; GOLETA: Cinema Twin, Fairview Twin, Camino Real Cinemas 6; HUNTINGTON PARK: Park Theatre; LIVERMORE: Vine Twin; LOS ANGELES: Campus, Orpheum, Palace 2; SANTA ANA: Teatro Fiesta; SANTA BARBARA: Arlington Theatre, Fiesta 5, Metro 4, Paseo Nuevo Cinemas, Plaza De Oro Twin, Riviera Theatre.

PACIFIC—Drive-in theatres: CERES: Ceres 2; FRESNO: Woodward Park 4; INDUSTRY: Vineland 4; **Walk-In theatres:** BAKERSFIELD: Valley Plaza 16; CHATSWORTH: Winnetka 21; COMMERCE: Commerce 14; CORTE MADERA: Cinema Corte Madera; EL SEGUNDO: Beach Cities Cinema 16; HUNTINGTON PARK: Warners 2; LA MESA: Grossmont Center 10, Trolley 8; LAKEWOOD: Regency 8, Center Stadium 16, Center South 9; LOS ANGELES: Crest 1; MANHATTAN BEACH: MANHATTAN VILLAGE 6; MILL VALLEY: Sequoia 2; NATIONAL CITY: Sweetwater 9; NORTHRIDGE: Northridge 10, Northbridge Fashion Center 10; NOVATO: Rowland Plaza 8; ONTARIO: Ontario 10; PASADENA: Hastings Pacific 8, Hastings Ranch 3; PETALUMA: Petaluma 8; ROHNERT PARK: Rohnert Park 16; SAN BERNARDINO: Inland Cinema 5; SAN DIEGO: Carmel Mountian 12, Cinerama 6, Gaslamp 15, Town Square 14; SAN RAFAEL: Northgate Cinemas 15, Regency 6; SAUSALITO: Marin 3.

REGAL—ANTIOCH: Deer Valley 16; CHULA VISTA: Rancho Del Rey 16; DIAMOND BAR: Diamond Bar 8; DUBLIN: Haceinda Crossing 20 & IMAX; EL CAJON: Parkway Plaza 18; FOOTHILL RANCH: Foothill Town Center 22; GARDEN GROVE: Garden Grove 16; HEMET: Hemet 12; LA HABRA: La Habra 16; LAKE ELSINORE: Lake Elsinore 8; MOORPARK: Moorpark 8; OCEANSIDE: Oceanside 16; PLEASANTON: Galaxy 8; RANCHO PALOS VERDES: Terrace Cinema 6; ROLLING HILLS ESTATES: The Avenue 13; SACRAMENTO: Natomas Marketplace 16; SAN BERNARDINO: Del Rosa 8; SIMI VALLEY: Civic Center 16; WHITTIER: Whittwood Cinema 10.

SIGNATURE—ARROYO GRANDE: Festival Cinemas 10; AUBURN: Auburn 2, State 2; CLOVIS: Regency Cinemas 6; DAVIS: Holiday 6, Stadium 5; FRESNO: Manchester Stadium 16; JACKSON: Jackson 4; MARTINEZ: Contra Costa Cinemas 5; MODESTO: Mann Festival Cinemas 10; PLACERVILLE: Placerville 8; SAN RAMON: Crow Canyon Cinemas 6; SANTA CRUZ: Santa Cruz 9, Riverfront Twin; SONORA: Cinema 5; STOCKTON: Festival Cinemas 4, Regency Cinemas 4, Holiday 8, Royal 4; TURLOCK: Stadium 14; UKIAH: Ukiah 6; VISALIA: Sequoia Mall 12, Stadium 10; WALNUT CREEK: Festival Cinemas 5.

SILVER—SEAL BEACH: Super Saver Cinema - Rossmoor Cntr.; NORWALK: Super Saver Cinema - Norwalk Shopping Center.

SOCAL—ANAHEIM: Cinemapolis 13; BLUE JAY: Blue Jay 4; CARLSBAD: Plaza Camino Real 4; CHINO: Movie Experience Spectrum 12; LAGUNA HILLS: Laguna Hills Mall Cinema 3; MURRIETA: Movie Experience at Cal Oaks 17; SAN LUIS OBISPO: Downtown Center 7; TEMECULA: Movie Experience 10 at Tower Plaza, Temeku Cinema 6.

UA—BAKERSFIELD: UA East Hills 10; BERKELEY: UA 7 Berkeley; CAMARILLO: UA Mission Oaks 11; CERRITOS: UA Los Cerritos 11, CHICO: El Rey 1; CITRUS HEIGHTS: Sunrise 4; CLOVIS: UA 8 Clovis, UA Sierra Vista 6; COLMA: Cinema 6; EMERYVILLE: Movies @ Emery Bay 10; FRESNO: Broadway Faire 10; GRASS VALLEY: Grass Valley Cinema 2, Del Oro 3; HAYWARD: UA Hayward 6; LA CANADA: UA La Canada 8; LONG BEACH: UA Movies Long Beach 6; LOS ANGELES: UA Coronet 3; MARINA DEL REY: UA 6 Marina Del Rey; MERCED: UA 4 Merced, UA Regency 7; MONTEREY: UA State Monterey 3; NORTH HOLLYWOOD: UA Movies 6; PASADENA: UA Movies 6; RIVERSIDE: UA Park Sierra 6; ROSEVILLE: Olympus Pointe 12; SACRAMENTO: Arden Fair 6; SAN DIEGO: Horton Plaza 14; SAN FRANCISCO: UA Twin Stonestown, Alexandria 3, Coronet Theatre 1, Galaxy 4, Metro Theatre 1, Vogue Theatre 1; SANTA ROSA: Santa Rosa 6, UA 5 Santa Rosa; SOUTH SACRAMENTO: Laguna Village Theatre 12; THOUSAND OAKS: UA 5 Thousand Oaks.

WALLACE—BARSTOW: New Barstow Cinema 6; MALIBU: New Malibu Cinemas 2; SANTA MARIA: Town Center Cinemas 3; SANTA PAULA: Santa Paula Cinema 7; SOUTH LAKE TAHOE: New Stateline Cinema 2.

W.F. CINEMA—AGOURA HILLS: Agoura Hills 8; CITY OF INDUSTRY: Puente Hills 6; CULVER CITY: Culver Plaza 6; GLENDALE: Exchange 10; Glendale Marketplace 4; GRANADA HILLS: Granada Hills 9; HOLLYWOOD: Chinese; LOS ANGELES: Village, Bruin, Westwood Quad, Regent, Plaza, Festival Westwood; MONROVIA: Huntington Oaks 6-plex; SAN DIEGO: Hazard Center 7; SANTA MONICA: Criterion 6; SIMI VALLEY: Simi Valley 6; TARZANA: Valley West 9; THOUSAND OAKS: Janss Marketplace 9; TORRANCE: Del Amo 9; VALENCIA: Valencia 10; VAN NUYS: Plant 16; VENTURA: Buenaventura 6; WESTLAKE: Village 8.

COLORADO

ALLEN—CORTEZ: Fiesta Twin.

AMC—AURORA: Seven Hills 10; COLORADO SPRINGS: Tiffany Square 6; DENVER: Tiffany Plaza 6; HIGHLANDS RANCH: Highlands Ranch 24; WESTMINSTER: Westminster Promenade 24.

CARMIKE—ASPEN: Stage 3; COLORADO SPRINGS: Carmike 10, Chapel Hills 9, Chapel Hills 10-15; FT. COLLINS: Carmike 10; GLENWOOD SPRINGS: Mall 3; GRAND JUNCTION: Carmike 7; GREELEY: Carmike 5; STEAMBOAT SPRINGS: Chief Plaza 4, Ski Time Square.

CENTURY—AURORA: Aurora 16.

CINEMA GRILL—AURORA: Cinema Grill 3.

CINEMARK—COLORADO SPRINGS: Tinseltown USA 20; FORT COLLINS: Cinemark at Fort Collins; PUEBLO: Tinseltown USA 14.

COLORADO CINEMAS—ARVADA: Olde Town 14; AURORA: Arapahoe Crossing 16; BOULDER: Arapahoe Village 4. Basemar Twin; DENVER: Cherry Creek 8; EVERGREEN: Bergen Park 7; FT. COLLINS: Cinema Saver 6; LITTLETON: Bowles Crossing 12; LOUISVILLE: Colony Square 12.

LANDMARK—DENVER: Chez Artiste 3, Esquire 2, Mayan 3.

METROPOLITAN—LOVELAND: Metrolux 12.

SILVER—COLORADO SPRINGS: Super Saver Cinema - Citadel Crossing 8.

TRANS-LUX—DILLON: Lake Dillon Cinema 4, Skyline Cinema 6; DURANGO: High Five Cinemas, Gaslight Cinemas 2; LOVE LAND: Metrolux 12.

UA—BOULDER: Village 4; COLORADO SPRINGS: Broadmoor Theatre; DENVER: Colorado Center 9, Continental 6, Denver Pavillions 15, UA Greenwood Plaza; FT. COLLINS: Campus West 2; GOLDEN: Denver West 12; GRAND JUNCTION: Colorado West 4, Teller Arms Twin 2; GREELEY: Cooper Twin 2, Bittersweet 4; LITTLETON: Meadows 12; LONGMONT: Twin peaks 10; THORNTON: Thornton Town Center 10.

W.F. CINEMA—BOULDER: Crossroads 6; DENVER: Tamarac Square 6; LAKEWOOD: Green Mountain 6, LITTLETON: Southwest Plaza 5.

CONNECTICUT

CLEARVIEW—GREENWICH: Greenwich Cinemas 2.

CROWN—GREENWICH: Plaza 3; NORWALK: Regent 8, Royale 6; STAMFORD: Landmark Square 9, Majestic 6; TRUMBULL: Marquis 16; WEST HARTFORD: Palace 17.

HOYTS—BRANFORD: Cinema 12; DAYVILLE: Dayville 3; ENFIELD: Enfield 12; GROTON: Groton 6; MANCHESTER: Manchester Cinemas 6; MERIDEN: Meriden 10; MYSTIC: Mystic Village 3; NEW CANAAN: Playhouse 2; NORWICH: Norwich 2; PAWCATUCK: Stonington 10; SAYBROOK: Saybrook Cinemas 2, Saybrook Cinemas 6; SIMSBURY: Simsbury 8; WATERBURY: Waterbury 12. WATERFORD: Waterford 9; WILLIMANTIC: Willimantic 6; WILTON: Wilton 4.

LOEWS CINEPLEX—DANBURY: Danbury 10; FAIRFIELD: Community 1 & 2 (2); PLAINVILLE: Plainville 20.

NATIONAL AMUSEMENTS—BERLIN: Showcase Cinemas 12; BRIDGEPORT: Bridgeport @ Black Rock 12, Cinemas @ Black Rock 12; E. HARTFORD: Showcase East Hartford 14; E. WINDSOR: Showcase East Windsor 12; FAIRFIELD: Fairfield Cinemas 9; MANCHESTER: Showcase Cinemas Buckland Hills 16; MILFORD: Showcase Cinemas 5, Showcase Milford 5, Milford Quad; NORTH HAVEN: Showcase North Haven 15; ORANGE: Showcase Orange 8; SOUTHINGTON: Showcase Southington 12.

O'NEIL—WESTBROOK: Westbrook 12.

UA—DARIEN: UA Darien Playhouse 2.

DELAWARE

CARMIKE—DOVER: Carmike 14.

CINEMARK—WILMINGTON: Movies 10.

GENERAL CINEMA—NEWARK: Christiana Mall 5.

MINI—FELTON: Diamond State Drive-In.

REGAL—NEWARK: Peoples Plaza 17; WILMINGTON: Brandywine Town Center 16.

DISTRICT OF COLUMBIA

AMC—WASHINGTON: Union Station 9.

GENERAL CINEMA—WASHINGTON: Mazza Gallerie 7.

LOEWS CINEPLEX—WASHINGTON: Avalon 2, Cinema 1, Dupont 5, Foundry 7, Inner Circle 3, Janus 3, Outer Circle 2, Uptown 1, Wisconsin 6.

FLORIDA

AMC—AVENTURA: Aventura 24; BOCA RATON: Mizner Park 8; BRANDON: Regency 20; CELEBRATION: Celebration 2; CLEARWATER: Clearwater 5, Countryside 6, Tri-City 8; COCONUT GROVE: Cocowalk 16; DAVIE: Ridge Plaza 8; DAYTONA: Volusia Square 8; FT. LAUDERDALE: Coral Ridge 10; FT. MYERS: Merchants Crossing 16; GAINESVILLE: Oaks 6; HOLLYWOOD: Sheridan Plaza 12; JACKSONVILLE: Regency 24; LAKE BUENA VISTA: Pleasure Island 24; LAKELAND: Merchants Walk 10; LEESBURG: Lake Square 12; MERRITT ISLAND: Merritt 6, Merritt Square 7-12; MIAMI: Fashion Island 16, Kendall 10, Mall of the Americas 14, South Dade 8, Sunset Place 24; OCOCEE: West Oaks 14; OLDSMAR: Woodlands Square 20; ORANGE PARK: Orange Park 24; ORLANDO: Fashion Village 8, Highland Lakes 12; SARASOTA: Sarasota 6, Sarasota 7-12; SEMINOLE: Seminole 8; ST. PETERSBURG: Crossroads 8, Tyrone Square 6; TALLAHASSEE: Tallahassee 20; TAMPA: Old Hyde Park 7, Veterans Expressway 24; VERO BEACH: Indian River 24.

CARMIKE—BRADENTON: Royal Palm 20; FERNANDINA BEACH: Amelia Island 7; LAKELAND: Palm Cinema 3; PANAMA CITY: Carmike 10, Mall 4; PENSACOLA: Carmike 10; PLANT CITY: Lake Waldon; SEBRING: Lakeshore 8; TAMPA: Hillsboro West 8; WINTER PARK: University 8; WINTER HAVEN: Continental Mugs & Movies.

CINEMA GRILL—WINTER PARK: Aloma Cinema Grill.

CINEMARK—JACKSONVILLE: Tinseltown USA 20; ORLANDO: Festival Bay 20; TALLAHASSEE: Movies 8.

CROWN—HIALEAH: Grand 18.

EASTERN FEDERAL—FT. WALTON BEACH: Sun Plaza Stadium 8; GAINESVILLE: Royal Park Stadium 16; PANAMA CITY: Regency 11; PORT ORANGE: Port Orange 6; PORT ST. LUCIE: Village Green 6; TALLAHASSEE: Miracle 5, Movies at Governor's Square 12.

LOEWS CINEPLEX—ORLANDO: Sand Lake 7.

MUVICO—BOCA RATON: Palace 20; DAVIE: Paradise 24; HIALEAH: Hialeah 14; ORLANDO: Pointe 20 Theatres; PALM HARBOR: Palm Harbor 10; POMPANO BEACH: Pompano 18; ST. PETERSBURG: Baywalk 20; TAMPA: Majestic 20, Starlight 20; W. PLAM BEACH: Parisian 20.

O'NEIL—DESTIN: Destin Cinema 10; HOLLYWOOD: Taft-Hollywood Cinema 12; PANAMA CITY BEACH: Edgewater Cinema 10.

R/C THEATRES—DAYTONA BEACH: OceanWalk 10; PINELLAS PARK: Parkside 16.

REGAL—BOCA RATON: Shadowood 12; BONITA SPRINGS: Bonita Springs 12; BOYNTON BEACH: Boynton 8; BRADENTON: Bradenton 8, DeSoto Square 6, Oakmont 8; CAPE CORAL: Coralwood 10; COCONUT GROVE: Mayfair 10; CORAL SPRINGS: Magnolia Place 16; CRYSTAL RIVER: Crystal River Mall 9; DELRAY BEACH: Delray 18; FT. LAUDERDALE: Cypress Creek Station 16, Las Olas 23; FT. MYERS: Bell Tower 20; GAINESVILLE: Gainesville Cinema 14; GREENACRES: Lake Worth 8; HOLLYWOOD: Oakwood 18; INVERNESS: Citrus 6; JACKSONVILLE: Beach Boulevard 18, Jacksonville 10, The Avenues 20; JUPITER: Jupiter 18; KEY WEST: Key West 6; KISSIMMEE: Osceola Square East 6, Osceola Square West 6; LAKE MARY: Lake Mary 10; LAKE WALES: Eagle Ridge Mall 12; LARGO: Largo Mall 8; LUTZ: Hollywood 20 Northgate; MELBOURNE: Oaks 10; MIAMI: Bay Harbor 4, Kendall 9, Palace 18; MIAMI BEACH: Byron Carlyle 7, South Beach 18; MIAMI LAKES: Miami Lakes 17; NAPLES: Hollywood 20, Pavilion 10, Towne Centre 6; NORTH MIAMI BEACH: California Club 6; OCALA: Hollywood 16; ORLANDO: Southchase 7, UC 7, Waterford Lakes 20; ORMOND BEACH: Ormond Beach 12; OVIEDO: Oviedo Marketplace 22; PALM BAY: Palm Bay 10, Roxy 10; PEMBROKE PINES: Westfork Plaza 13; PENSACOLA: Cordova 3, Cordova Mall 4; PORT CHARLOTTE: Port Charlotte Town Center 16; PORT RICHEY: Embassy 6, Hollywood 18; ROYAL PALM BEACH: Royal Palm Beach 18; SARASOTA: Crossings 10, Hollywood 20, Parkway 8; SPRING HILL: Spring Hill 8; ST. AUGUSTINE: Mall 6; STUART: Regency Square 8; SUNRISE: Sawgrass 23; TAMPA: Britton 8, Citrus Park 20, University 16; VENICE: Venetian 6; WINTER HAVEN: Springlake 10; WINTER PARK: Winter Park Village 20.

STARNET—ATLANTIC BEACH: Atlantic 8; BELLEVIEW: Bellewview 2; JACKSONVILLE: Pablo 9, St. Johns Theatre; LAKELAND: Lakeland Square 10; MARIANNA: Marianna 2; PALATKA: Palatka Mall Cinemas 4.

TMI—BROOKSVILLE: Beacon Theatres 10; DELAND: Victoria 6; NEW SMYRNA BEACH: Beacon 12; ORANGE CITY: Showcase 2.

UA—APOPKA: Wekiva 8; BOYNTON BEACH: Boynton 9; CLEARWATER: Clearwater 8; JACKSONVILLE: Regency 12, Orange Park 7; LAKE CITY: Cinema 90 (6); LAUDERHILL: Lauderhill 13; MARY ESTHER: Santa Rosa 10; MIAMI: The Falls 7; OCALA: Cinemas West 5; ORANGE CITY: Market Place 8; ORLANDO: Florida Mall 7; PALM BEACH GARDENS: Promenade Plaza 8; PEMBROKE PINES: Pembroke Pines 9; PENSACOLA: University 11; SANFORD: Seminole Town Center 10; TITUSVILLE: Searstown Mall 10; WEST PALM BEACH: Okee Square 8.

GEORGIA

AMC—ALPHARETTA: Mansell Crossing 14; ATLANTA: Buckhead Backlot 6, Galleria 8, Phipps Plaza 14; DECATUR: North Dekalb 16; KENNESAW: Barret Commons 24; LAWRENCEVILLE: Colonial 18; MORROW: Southlake Pavillion 24; TUCKER: Northlake 8.

CARMIKE—ALBANY: Carmike Wynnsong 16; AMERICUS: Cinema 2; ATHENS: Carmike 12; CALHOUN: Martin 3; CANTON: Carmike 16; CARTERSVILLE: Plaza 8; COLUMBUS: Carmike 7, Columbus Square 8, Hollywood, Peachtree 8; CONYERS: Conyers 8; CORDELE: Martin 3; DALTON: Carmike 9; DOUGLAS: Martin Twin; DUBLIN: Carmike 8; FITZGERALD: Capri Twin; FT. BENNING: Wynnsong 10; FT. OGLETHORPE: Southgate 5; GRIFFIN: Carmike 4; LA GRANGE: LaGrange 6; MILLEDGEVILLE: Carmike 6; NEWNAN: Carmike 10; SAVANNAH: Carmike 10, Wynnsong 11; SNELLVILLE: Carmike 12; STATESBORO: Cinema 9; TIFTON: Cinema 6.

CINEMA GRILL—ATLANTA: North Springs Cinema Grill; SAVANNAH: Oglethorpe Cinema Grill.

CINEMARK—FAYETTEVILLE: Movies 10, Tinseltown 17.

DEANZA—ATLANTA: Starlight 6.

GENERAL CINEMA—ATLANTA: Parkway Pointe 15.

GEORGIA THEATRE—ATHENS: Beechwood Stadium 11; AUGUSTA: Masters 7; BRUNSWICK: Glynn Place 11; CARROLLTON: Mall 8; COVINGTON: Newton Twin Cinema; EVANS: Evans 12; GAINESVILLE: Hollywood 14, Lakeshore Cinema 4; LAWRENCEVILLE: Town Center 10; MARIETTA: Park 12 Cobb; MOULTRIE: Moultrie Twin; ROME: Rome VII; ST. MARY'S: Kings Bay 9; ST. SIMONS: Island Cinema 7; THOMASVILLE: Gateway 7; VALDOSTA: Ashley Cinema 8, Valdosta Mall 6; WARNER-ROBINS: Galleria 10, Parkway Cinemas 6; WAYCROSS: Mall Cinema 7; WOODSTOCK: Cherokee 16.

LOEWS CINEPLEX—ATLANTA: Magic Johnson Greenbriar 12.

O'NEIL—DECATUR: Avondale Mall Cinema 16.

REGAL—AUGUSTA: Augusta Village 12, Exchange 20; AUSTELL: 22 @ Austell; BUFORD: Mall of Georgia 20; CHAMBLEE: Hollywood 24 @ North I-85; DOUGLASVILLE: Arbor Place Mall 18; DULUTH: Medlock Crossing 18; KENNESAW: Town Center 16; LITHONIA: Covington Square 8; MACON: Macon 8, Rivergate 14; MARIETTA: Delk 10, Cinema 10; NORCROSS: Peachtree Corners 10; RIVERDALE: Riverdale 14; SAVANNAH: Eisenhower Square 6, Victory Square 9, Savannah 10; SNELLVILLE: Snellville Oaks 14.

STARNET—BAINBRIDGE: Bainbridge Mall 6.

SUPER SAVER—ROSWELL: Roswell 10.

UA—ALPHARETTA: North Point Market 8; ATLANTA: Lenox Square 6, Midtown 8, Perimeter Pointe 10, Tara 4; UNION CITY: Shannon 8.

HAWAII

CONSOLIDATED—AIEA: Pearlridge West 16; KAHULUI: Kaahumanu 6; KAILUA: Aikahi Twins; KAIHUA KONA: Keauhou Cinemas 7; KANEOHE: Koolau 10; KAPOLEI: Kapolei 16; KIHEI: Kukui Mall 4; HONOLULU: Kahala 8, Koko Marina 8, Varsity Twins, Waikiki, Waikiki Twins; MILILANI: Mililani 14.

SIGNATURE—HONOLULU: Dole Cannery 18; PEARL CITY: Pearl Highlands 12.

WALLACE—HILO: Kress 4, Prince Kuhio 9, Walakia 3; HONOLULU: Restaurant Row 9; KAHULUI: Maui Mall 12; KAILUA: Kailua 2, Enchanted Lake 3, Keolu Center 4; KAILUA-KONA: Kona Marketplace 2; KAPA'A: Coconut Marketplace 2; LAHAINA: Wharf Cinema 3, Front Street 4; LAI'E: Lail'e 2; MAUNALOA: Town Cinema 3.

IDAHO

CARMIKE—CHUBBUCK: Starlite 7; IDAHO FALLS: Rio Theatre; MOSCOW: University 4; POCATELLO: Alameda Plaza 3; REXBURG: Holiday 3, Westwood.

EDWARDS—AMMON: Grand Teton 14; BOISE: Boise Stadium 21; NAMPA: Nampa Stadium 14.

LOEWS CINEPLEX—BOISE: 8th Street Market 2, Northgate 6, Town Square 6; NAMPA: Nampa 6.

POLSON—SALMON: River Cinema 2.

REGAL—COEUR D'ALENE: Coeur D'Alene 5, Showboat 5, LEWISTON: Liberty, Orchards Tri Cinema.

ILLINOIS

AMC—SOUTH BARRINGTON: South Barrington 30; WARRENVILLE: Cantera 30.

CARMIKE—MACOMB: Cinema Twin.

CINEMARK—BOURBONNAIS: Movies 10; JOLIET: Movies 8, Movies 10; MELROSE PARK: Cinemark 10; N. AURORA: Tinseltown 17; WOODRIDGE: Cinemark @ Seven Bridges.

CLASSIC—CARPENTERSVILLE: Cinema 12; DOWNERS GROVE: Tivoli; ELGIN: Casino 3; ELK GROVE: Elk Grove 6; ELMHURST: York 5; FOX LAKE: Fox Lake 5; FREEPORT: Lindo 6; HANOVER PARK: Tradewinds 2; HOFFMAN ESTATES: Barrington Square 6; KANKAKEE: Meadowview 3, Paramount 5; NAPERVILLE: Ogden 6; OAK PARK: Lake 7; PARK FOREST: Park Forest 5; ST. CHARLES: Arcada, Foxfield 7; STERLING: Sterling 2; WOODSTOCK: Woodstock 2.

F & F/VALUE—ARLINGTON HEIGHTS: Arlington Cinema 6; BRIDGEVIEW: Harlem Corners 6; BUFFALO GROVE: Buffalo Grove 5; CHICAGO: Davis Art Theatre; Davis 3; MORTON GROVE: Morton Grove Theatres 4; TINLEY PARK: Bremen Theatres 6.

GKC—BLOOMINGTON/NORMAL: University 6, College Hills 4, Palace 9, Parkway 8; CHAMPAIGN: Beverly 18, Country Fair 5; DEKALB: Campus Cinemas 4, Market Square 10; FORSYTH/DECATUR: Hickory Point 8, Strand 10; KEWANEE: Wanee 2; LINCOLN: Lincoln 4; MORRIS: Orpheum 10; OTTAWA: Roxy 6; PEORIA/WASHINGTON: Sunnyland 10, Landmark Mall 12, Westlake Cinemas 5, Sunnydale 10; PERU: Peru Mall 8; PONTIAC: Crescent 2; PRINCETON: Apollo 2; STERLING: Sauk Valley 8.

GENERAL CINEMA—CHICAGO: Ford City 14, City North 14; DEERFIELD: Deerbrook 4; LOMBARD: Yorktown, Premium Cinema at the Yorktown; MATTESON: Lincoln Mall 3; MT. PROSPECT: Randhurst; NORTHBROOK: Northbrook 14; WAUKEGAN: Lakehurst.

GOODRICH QUALITY—BATAVIA: Randall 16; OSWEGO: Kendall 10; PEORIA: Willow Knolls 14; SAVOY: Savoy 16.

KERASOTES—BENTON: Toler 2; BOLINGBROOK: Showplace 12; CARBONDALE: Fox Eastgate 3, University Plaza 8, Varsity 3; CENTRALIA: Illinois 2; CHARLESTON: Will Rogers 2; DANVILLE: Village Mall Cinema 6; EAST ALTON: Eastgate 6; EDWARDSVILLE: Showplace 12; GALESBURG: West 2, Sandburg Mall 2; GLEN CARBON: Cottonwood Cinema; GRANITE CITY: Nameoki 2; HARRISBURG: Cinema 4; HIGHLAND: Lory 2; JACKSONVILLE: Times 2, Illinois 2; JERSEYVILLE: Stadium 2; LAKE IN THE HILLS: Lake in the Hills 12; MACOMB: Illinois 2; MARION: Illinois Center 8; MATTOON: Showplace 8; MT. VERNON: Showplace 8; PARIS: Paris 2; PEKIN: Showplace 12; QUINCY: Quincy Mall 3, Quincy Showcase 6; ROCKFORD: Colonial Village 5, Machesney Park 10, North Towne 6, Showplace 16; ROXANA: Cine; SPRINGFIELD: Esquire 4, Showplace 8, White Oaks Cinema 5, Parkway Pointe 8; TAYLORVILLE: Cinema 2; VERNON HILLS: Showplace 8.

LANDMARK—CHICAGO: Century Centre 7.

LOEWS CINEPLEX—ARLINGTON HEIGHTS: Ridge Plaza 1-8 (8); BLOOMINGDALE: Stratford 1-4 (4), Bloomingdale 6; CALUMET CITY: River Oaks 1-6, River Oaks 7-8, River Oaks 9-10; CHICAGO: Chatham 14, Esquire 6, Fine Arts 4, Lawndale 10, Lincoln 7-9, Lincoln Village 1-6, McClurg 3, 900 North Michigan Ave. 2, Pipers Alley 4, 600 North Michigan Ave. 9, 62nd & Western 10; Webster Place 11; CHICAGO RIDGE: Chicago Ridge 6, Commons 4; CRESTWOOD: Crestwood 18; DOWNERS GROVE: Grove Cinema 6; EVANSTON: Evanston 5; HILLSIDE: Hillside Mall 3, Hillside Square 6; HODGKINS: Quarry Cinemas 14; LANSING: River Run 8; NAPERVILLE: Westridge Court 8; NILES: Golf Glen 1-6, Golf Mill 1-3 (3); NORRIDGE: Norridge 10; NORTH RIVERSIDE: North Riverside 6; OAKBROOK: Oakbrook 5-7 (3), Oakbrook 1-4 (4); ORLAND PARK: Orland 1-6, Orland 7-10; ROLLING MEADOWS: Rolling Meadows 9; SCHAUMBERG: Streets of Woodfield 5-9; SKOKIE: Gardens 7; STREAMWOOD: Streamwood 14; VERNON HILLS: Rivertree Court 8; WHEATON: Rice Lake 10; WOODRIDGE: Woodridge 18.

MARCUS—ADDISON: Addison 20; CHICAGO HEIGHTS: Chicago Heights 14; ELGIN: Elgin Fox 14; GURNEE: Gurnee 20; ORLAND PARK: Orland Park 14.

NATIONAL AMUSEMENTS—MILAN: Showcase 11; MOLINE: Super Saver 6.

REGAL—CRYSTAL LAKE: Showplace 16; LAKE ZURICH: Lake Zurich 12; LINCOLNSHIRE: Lincolnshire 20; ROUND LAKE BEACH: Round Lake Beach 18; ST. CHARLES: Charlestowne Mall 18.

SILVER—HIGHLAND PARK: Renaissance Place 6; JOLIET: Super Saver Cinema 6.

WEHRENBERG—FAIRVIEW HEIGHTS: St. Clair 10.

INDIANA

CARMIKE—FORT WAYNE: Carmike 20.

CINEMA GRILL—INDIANAPOLIS: Greenbriar Cinema Grill ; FT. WAYNE: Northwood Cinema Grill 2.

CINEMARK—CLARKSVILLE: Greentree 4, Greentree 10; INDIANAPOLIS: Greenwood 8, Washington 8; MISHAWAKA: Movies 14, University Park 6.

GKC—CRAWFORDSVILLE: Capri 8; ELKHART: Encore Park Cinemas 8.

GENERAL CINEMA—GREENWOOD: Greenwood Park 14; INDIANAPOLIS: Castleton Square 3, Clearwater Crossing 12, Eastgate Mall 6, Lafayette Square 5; MERRILLVILLE: Southlake Mall Cinema 9; VALPARISO: County Seat 6.

GOODRICH QUALITY—ANDERSON: Applewood 9; HUNTINGTON: Huntington 7; LAFAYETTE: Eastside 10, Lafayette 7, Wabash Landing 9; PORTAGE: Portage 9.

KERASOTES—ANDERSON: Showplace 4, Mounds Mall 2; BLOOMINGTON: College Mall 4, Showplace West 12, Showplace 11; COLUMBUS: Columbus Center 5, Columbus Cinema 2; EVANSVILLE: Showplace 16; INDIANAPOLIS: Showplace 12, Showplace 16; KOKOMO: Kokomo Mall 8, Markland Mall 5; .LA PORTE: La Porte 4; MARION: Showplace 12; MICHIGAN CITY: Dunes Plaza 6, Marquette 3; MUNCIE: Showplace 7, Muncie Mall 3, Northwest Plaza 8; NEW CASTLE: Castle; PERU: Eastwood 2; PRINCETON: Princeton 4; RICHMOND: Cinema 11, Dollar Cinema 10; SCHERERVILLE: Showplace 16; SOUTH BEND: Scottsdale 6, Showplace 16 ; TERRE HAUTE: Honey Creek 8, Showplace 12; VINCENNES: Plaza 2, Showplace 3; WASHINGTON: Indiana 2.

LOEWS CINEPLEX—GREENWOOD: Greenwood 9; INDIANAPOLIS: Cherry Tree 10, College Park 14, Lafayette Square 8; MERRILLVILLE: Merrillville 10.

NATIONAL AMUSEMENTS—CLARKSVILLE: River Falls 10.

REGAL—AVON: Shiloh Crossing 18; CARMEL: Village Park 12; FT. WAYNE: Coldwater Crossing 8, Coventry 13, Georgetown 1 & 2, Glenbrook 3, Holiday 1 & 2, Holiday 6.

SYNDICATE—BATESVILLE: Gibson; FRANKLIN: Canary Creek 8; HUNTINGTON: Huntington Drive-In; WABASH: Eagles, 13-24 Drive-In.

UA—INDIANAPOLIS: Circle Center 9, Eagle Highlands 10, Galaxy 14.

IOWA

CARMIKE—CEDAR RAPIDS: Carmike 7, Collins Road 5, Lindale Mall 6, Wynnsong 12; COUNCIL BLUFFS: Mall Bluffs 5; DES MOINES: Cobblestone 9, Southridge 12; DUBUQUE: Cinema Center 8, Kennedy Mall 6; JOHNSTON: Wynnsong 16; SIOUX CITY: Plaza 2, Southern Hills 12.

CENTRAL STATES—BURLINGTON: Mall 6; CEDAR FALLS: Cinema 4; CLINTON: Capri III, Cinema I; CORALVILLE: Coral Ridge 10; COUNCIL BLUFFS: Drive-In 2; FAIRFIELD: CoEd 2; Co Ed II; FT. DODGE: Cinema 4; IOWA CITY: Cinema 2, Campus 3, The Cinemas 2; MASON CITY: Cinema V, Cinema West 8; NEWTON: Capitol 2; OTTUMWA: Capri V; PELLA: Palla Cinemas 3.

CINEMA ENTERTAINMENT—WATERLOO: Crossroads 12.

CINEMAGIC—OKOBOJI: Great Lakes 7.

CINEMARK—AMES: Movies 12, North Grand 5, Varsity II.

FRIDLEY—ALGONA: Algona; ANKENY: Springwood 9; ATLANTIC: Atlantic 2; BOONE: Boone; CARROLL: Carroll 5; CHEROKEE: American; CLARION: Clarion; CRESTON: Strand; DECORAH: Viking 3; EMMETSBURG: Riviera; ESTHERVILLE: Grand 3; GRINNELL: Cinema 2; HUMBOLDT: Humota; INDIANOLA: Paramount 3; IOWA FALLS: Metropolitan 2; JEFFERSON: Sierra; KNOXVILLE: Village 2, LAKE CITY: Capri; MANCHESTER: Castle; MARSHALLTOWN: Orpheum 2, Plaza 5; MT. PLEASANT: Temple 2; MUSCATINE: Plaza 4; NEVADA: Camelot; OELWEIN: Paramount 2; OSKALOOSA: Penn Centre Twin; PERRY: Grand 3; PLEASANT HILL: Copper Creek 9; RED OAK: Grand; SPENCER: Spencer 3; STORM LAKE: Vista 3; WASHINGTON: State; WEBSTER CITY: Webster.

KERASOTES—KEOKUK: Plaza Cinema 3.

NATIONAL AMUSEMENTS—DAVENPORT: Super Cinemas Davenport 10, Showcase Cinema Davenport 53 (18).

SILVER—DES MOINES: Silver 10.

KANSAS

AMC—LEAWOOD: Town Center 20; OLATHE: Studio 30; OVERLAND PARK: Oak Park Plaza 6.

B & B—ARKANSAS CITY: Buford 3; CHANUTE: Chanute 2; COFFEYVILLE: Coffeyville 2; DODGE CITY: Village 8; INDEPENDENCE: Independence 4; IOLA: Iola 2; GAS CITY: Iola 54 Drive-In; McPHERSON: McPherson 4; WINFIELD: Winfield 3.

CARMIKE—MANHATTAN: Seth Childs 6.

CINEMA GRILL—WICHITA: Town East Cinema Grill.

CINEMARK—MERNAM: Cinemark 20.

DICKINSON—EMPORIA: Flinthills 8; GARDEN CITY: Sequoyah 9; HAYS: Fox 2, Mall Hayes 4; HUTCHINSON: Mall 4, Mall 8; LEAVENWORTH: Plaza 6; OLATHE: Great Mall 16; SALINA: Central Mall 8, Midstates 2, Sunset 2; SHAWNEE: WestGlen 18; WICHITA: Northrock 6, Northrock 14.

GOODRICH—PITTSBURG: Pittsburg 8.

WALLACE—GREAT BEND: Village 3; JUNCTION CITY: Westside 4; LAWRENCE: Plaza 6, Southwind 12; LIBERAL: Southgate 4; TOPEKA: Fox Whitelake 4, West Ridge 6, West Ridge 8.

KENTUCKY

ABSHER ENTERPRISES—PIKEVILLE: Riverfill 10; PRESTONBURG: Strand 2; SOMERSET: Showplace 9; SOUTH WILLIAMS: Southside Cinemas 5.

CARMIKE—BOWLING GREEN: Greenwood 6, Plaza 6; CORBIN: Cinema 4; DANVILLE: Cinema 4; GRAYS KNOB: Cinema 4; HOPKINSVILLE: Martin 5; LEXINGTON: Carmike 10; MADISONVILLE: Martin 4; MAYSVILLE: Cinema 4; MIDDLESBORO: Cinema 4.

CHAKERES—FRANKFORT: Brighton Park 2, Franklin Square 6; MOREHEAD: University Cinema; WINCHESTER: Skyvue Drive-In 2.

CINEMA GRILL—HARRODSBURG: Turfland Mall Cinema Grill.

CINEMARK—ASHLAND: Town Cinema 10; LEXINGTON: Man O' War 8, Movies 10, Lexington Green 8; LOUISVILLE: Tinseltown 19; PADUCAH: Kentucky Oaks 12; RICHMOND: Richmond Mall Cinema 8.

LOEWS CINEPLEX—ASHLAND: Midtown 1-3 (3); LEXINGTON: South Park 1-6 (6).

MALCO—OWENSBORO: Cinema 12, Plaza Twin.

MARQUEE—GLASGOW: Highland 7.

NATIONAL AMUSEMENTS—ERLANGER: Showcase 9; FLORENCE: Cinemas 9; LOUISVILLE: Showcase 13, Showcase 20, Kenwood Drive-In.

REGAL—FLORENCE: Turfway Park 10; LEXINGTON: Hamburg Pavilion 16.

LOUISIANA

AMC—METAIRIE: Galleria 8.

CARMIKE—ALEXANDRIA: Alexandria 6; LAFAYETTE: Carmike 10; SLIDELL: North Shores 6.

CINEMARK—BATON ROUGE: Tinseltown 10; MONROE: Cinema 10; SHREVEPORT: Tinseltown 17; WEST MONROE: Tinseltown USA 17.

LANDMARK—NEW ORLEANS: Canal Place Cinema 4.

O'NEIL—COVINGTON: Holiday Square 12; CROWLEY: Crowley 4; MANDEVILLE: Causeway Place 4; SLIDELL: Movies 8.

REGAL—BOSSIER CITY: Bossier Corners 9; SHREVEPORT: Southpark Mall 8.

SILVER—BASTROP: Washington Square 4; BOGALUSA: Trackside 5; CHALMETTE: Chalmette 9; KENNER: Cinema City 8; LaPLACE: Movies 7.

UA—ALEXANDRIA: Westgate 8; BATON ROUGE: UA Citiplace 12, Siegen Village 10; HOUMA: Southland 4; LAFAYETTE: Ambassador 10; Northgate 8, Westwood 1; LAKE CHARLES: Oak Park 6, UA Lake Charles 10; LEESVILLE: Lee Hills 6; NEW IBERIA: Bayou Landing 6; OPELOUSAS: Vista Village 4.

MAINE

GENERAL CINEMA—PORTLAND: Maine Mall 7.

HOYTS—AUBURN: Auburn 10; AUGUSTA: Augusta 10; BANGOR: Bangor Mall 10; BIDDEFORD: Biddeford 8; BRUNSWICK: Brunswick 10; ELLSWORTH: Maine Coast 2; FALMOUTH: Falmouth 10; PORTLAND: Clarks Pond 8; PRESQUE ISLE: Aroostock Centre 8; WATERVILLE: Waterville 6.

MINI—SACO: Cinemagic 12.

PATRIOT—PORTLAND: Nickelodeon 6.

MARYLAND

AMC—GREENBELT: Academy 8, Academy 6; LAVALE: Country Club 6; OXON HILL: Rivertowne 12; SILVER SPRING: City Place 10.

CARMIKE—OCEAN CITY: Sun & Surf 8.

CINEMA GRILL—ANNAPOLIS: Annapolis Cinema Grill 2.

CROWN—ANNAPOLIS: Annapolis Mall 11, Harbour Center 9, Eastport 2.

GENERAL CINEMA—COLUMBIA: Columbia City 3; OWINGS MILLS: Owings Mills 17; TOWSON: Towson Commons 8; WOODLAWNL: Security Square 8.

HOYTS—BOWIE: Bowie Crossing 14; FREDERICK: Frederick 10, West Ridge 6; HUNT VALLEY: Hunt Valley 12; LINTHICUM: West Nursery 14; SALISBURY: Salisbury 10; WESTMINSTER: Cranberry Mall 9.

LOEWS CINEPLEX—BALTIMORE: Rotunda 2, White Marsh 16; BELTSVILLE: Center Park 8; BETHESDA: Montgomery Mall 3; COLUMBIA: Columbia Palace 9; GAITHERSBURG: Rio Cinemas 14; GERMANTOWN: Germantown 6; GLEN BURNIE: Glen Burnie 7; LEXINGTON PARK: Lexington Park 6; MARLOW HEIGHTS: Marlow 6; OWINGS MILLS: Valley Centre 9; ROCKVILLE: White Flint 5; TIMONIUM: Timonium 3; WALDORF: Waldort South 5, St. Charles Town Centre 9; WHEATON: Wheaton Plaza 11, Wheaton 4.

R/C THEATRES—ARBUTUS: Hollywood 4; BALTOMORE: Eastpoint 10; EASTON: Easton 4; ELDERSBURG: Carrolltowne 6; FREDERICK: Westview 16; FROSTBURG: Frostburg 3; HAGERSTOWN: Hagerstown 10, Long Meadow Triple, Valley Mall 16; OCEAN CITY: White Marlin Movies 5.

REGAL—ABINGDON: Bel Air 14; FREDERICK: Holiday 2; ROCKVILLE: Rockville Center 13.

UA—BALTIMORE: Westview Mall 9; BETHESDA: UA 10; COLUMBIA: Snowden Square 14; GLEN BURNIE: Marley Station 8.

MASSACHUSETTS

AMC—HADLEY: Mountain Farms 4.

GENERAL CINEMA—BOSTON: Fenway 13; BRAINTREE: Braintree 10; BURLINGTON: Burlington 10; CHESTNUT HILL: Chestnut Hill 5; FRAMINGHAM: Framingham 16, Premium Cinema at Framingham; N. DARTMOUTH: North Dartmouth Mall 12; TYNGSBORO: Tyngsboro 12.

HOYTS—ACTON: Acton 4; BELLINGHAM: Bellingham 14; BERLIN: Solomon Pond 15; BROCKTON: West Theatre 7; BUZZARDS BAY: Buzzards Bay Theatre 4; EAST BRIDGEWATER: East Bridgewater 6; FALMOUTH: Falmouth 6; HARWICH: Harwich 6; HYANNIS: Airport Cinema 8, Cape Cod Mall 12; KINGSTON: Independence Mall 14; LANESBORO: Berkshire Mall 10; MASHPEE: Mashpee 6; NORTH FALMOUTH: Nickelodeon 4; NORTH WEYMOUTH: North Weymouth 10; SALISBURY: Salisbury 6; SHARON: Sharon 8; SOUTH DENNIS: South Dennis 12; TAUNTON: Silver City 10; WESTBOROUGH: Westborough 12.

LANDMARK—CAMBRIDGE: Kendall Square 9; WALTHAM: Embassy Cinema 6.

LOEWS CINEPLEX—BOSTON: Cheri 1-4 (4), Copley Place 11, Nickelodeon 1-5; CAMBRIDGE: Fresh Pond 10, Harvard Square 1-5 (5); DANVERS: Liberty Tree Mall 20; FALL RIVER: Harbour Mall 1-8 (8); LEOMINSTER: Leominster 1-12 (12); METHUEN: Methuen 20; NATICK: Natick 1-6 (6); SOMERVILLE: Assembly Square 1-12 (12).

MINI—FAIRHAVEN: Bijou 1; GLOUCESTER: Gloucester 3; GREENFIELD: Cinema 6; MARTHA'S VINEYARD: Capawock 1, Island 1, Strand 1; NORTH ADAMS: Cinema 6; NORTH ATTLEBORO: Route 1; OAKS BLUFF: Island, Strand; PROVINCETOWN: New Art 2; SALISBURY: Cinemagic 9; SOUTH HADLEY: Tower 2; VINEYARD HAVEN: Capawock.

NATIONAL AMUSEMENTS—ALLSTON: Allston 2; BOSTON: Quincy 8; BROOKLINE: Circle 7; DEDHAM: Showcase 12; LAWRENCE: Showcase 1-6, Showcase 7-14; LOWELL: Showcase 14; NORTH ATTLEBOROUGH: North Attleborough 12; RANDOLPH: Showcase 16; REVERE: Showcase 20; SEEKONK: Showcase 10, Showcase 1-8; Showcase 9-10; SHREWSBURY: White City 3; SPRINGFIELD: Springfield 12, Showcase at Eastfield Mall 16; W. SPRINGFIELD: Showcase 16-19, Showcase 1-15; WOBURN: Showcase 14; WORCESTER: Worester North 18.

PATRIOT—HINGHAM: Loring Hall; SALEM: Museum Place 3; SOUTH WEYMOUTH: Cameo 2.

REGAL—SPRINGFIELD: Springfield Plaza 16.

MICHIGAN

AMC—DETROIT: Bel-Air Centre 10; HARPER WOODS: Eastland 5; LANSING: Elmwood 8; LIVONIA: Laurel Park 10; Livonia 20, Wonderland 6; MADISON HEIGHTS: Abbey 8; OKEMOS: Meridian 6; SOUTHFIELD: Southfield City 12; STERLING HEIGHTS: Sterling Center 10, Forum 30.

CARMIKE—HOUGHTON: Copper 5.

CINEMARK—GRANDVILLE: Cinemark 20; WARREN: Movies 16.

GKC—ALPENA: Royal Knight 3, State 5; BATTLE CREEK: Lakeview Square 11, Towne 8; BIG RAPIDS: Big Rapids 4; FORT GRATIOT: Birchwood 10; JACKSON: Plaza 7; LUDINGTON: Lyric 4; MARQUETTE: Royal 10; SAGINAW: Fashion Square 10; SAULT STE. MARIE: Varsity 10; TRAVERSE CITY: Grand Traverse 9, Horizon 10.

GOODRICH QUALITY—ANN ARBOR: Quality 16; BATTLE CREEK: W. Columbia 7; BAY CITY: Bay City 8; CADILLAC: Cadillac 5; CANTON: Canton 6; ESSEXVILLE: Hampton 6;

GRAND HAVEN: Grand Haven 9; HASTINGS: Hastings 4; HOLLAND: Holland 7; JACKSON: Jackson 10; KALAMAZOO: Kalamazoo 10; LANSING: Lansing Mall 6; LOWELL: Ada-Lowell 5; NOVI: Novi Town Center 8; OXFORD: Oxford 7; PORT HURON: Krafft 8; SAGINAW: Saginaw 8, The Quad; THREE RIVERS: Three Rivers 6.

JACK LOEKS—BENTON HARBOR: Celebration 16; GRAND RAPIDS: Studio 28 (18), Alpine 4; KALAMAZOO: Plaza 2; LANGSING: Celebration 18; MT. PLEASANT: Celebration 11, Celebration 4; MUSKEGON: Cinema Carousel 10, Getty 4 Drive-In, Plaza 1 & 2.

LOEKS STAR—AUBURN HILLS: Great Lakes Crossing 25; CLINTON TOWNSHIP: Star Gratiot 21; DEARBORN: Star Fairlane 21; GRAND RAPIDS: Star Grand Rapids 18; HOLLAND: Star Holland 8; LINCOLN PARK: Star Lincoln Park 8; MADISON HEIGHTS: Star John R 15; ROCHESTER HILLS: Star Rochester 10; SOUTHFIELD: Star Southfield 20; TAYLOR: Star Taylor 10.

LOEWS CINEPLEX—AUBURN HILLS: Great Lakes 25; CLINTON TOWNSHIP: Gratiot 21; DEARBORN: Fairlane Town Center; GRAND RAPIS: Grand Rapids 18; HOLLAND: Holland 8; LINCOLN PARK: Lincoln Park 8; MADISON HEIGHTS: John R 15; ROCHESTER HILLS: Rochester Hills 10; SOUTHFIELD: Southfield 20; TAYLOR: Taylor 10.

LANDMARK—BLOOMFIELD: Maple 3, ROYAL OAK: Main Art Theatre 3.

MJR—ADRIAN: Adrian 10; ALLEN PARK: Allen Park 5; BRIGHTON: Brighton Town Square 16; CHESTERFIELD: Chesterfield Crossing 12; SOUTHGATE: Southgate 20; WATERFORD: Waterford 16.

NATIONAL AMUSEMENTS—AUBURN HILLS: Showcase Auburn Hills 14; BLOOMFIELD HILLS: Showcase Pontiac 1-5, Showcase Pontiac 6-12; BURTON: Showcase Flint East, Courtland Center 6, Miracle Twin Driv-In; DEARBORN: Showcase Dearborn 8; FLINT: Cinema 10; FLINT TOWNSHIP: Showcase Flint West 14; GRAND RAPIDS: Showcase Grand Rapids 10; HARPER WOODS: Beacon East 4; STERLING HEIGHTS: Showcase Sterling Heights 15; WESTLAND: Quo Vadis 6, Showcase Westland 8; YPSILANTI: Showcase Ann Arbor 20.

REGAL—MONROE: Frenchtown Square Mall 8.

SILVER—ROSEVILLE: Macomb Mall 6.

UA—FARMINGTON: UA West River 9; PORTAGE: Movies 10; WALLED LAKE: Commerce Township 14.

MINNESOTA

CARMIKE—APPLE VALLEY: Wynnsong 15; AUSTIN: Sterling 3; HUTCHINSON: State 3; MANKATO: Cinema 4, Mall 4; MOUNDS VIEW: Wynnsong 16; NEW ULM: Cinema 3; OAKDALE: Oakdale 20; ROCHESTER: Apache 4, Barclay Square 6; WILMAR: Kandi 6.

CINEMA GRILL—MINNEAPOLIS: Suburban World Cinema Grill; Rdina: Yorktown Cinema Grill 3.

CINEMA ENTERTAINMENT—ALBERT LEA: Mall 7; BEMIDJI: Amigo 9; BRECKENRIDGE: Cinema 6; FARIBAULT: Cinema 6; HERMANTOWN: Lakes 10, Cinema 8; MARSHALL: Marshall 6; MOORHEAD: Safari 7; MOUNTAIN IRON: Cinema 6; ST. CLOUD: Cinema Arts 3; WAITE PARK: Parkwood 18, Crossroads 6; WINONA: Cinema 7.

CINEMAGIC—AUSTIN: CineMagic 7; HUTCHINSON: Century 7.

CINEMARK—MANKATO: Movies 8.

GENERAL CINEMA—BLOOMINGTON: Mall of America 14; EDINA: Centennial Lakes 8; ROSEVILLE: Har Mar 11; ST. LOUIS PARK: Shelard Park 5.

KERASOTES—COON RAPIDS: Showplace 16; INVERGROVE HEIGHTS: Showplace 16.

LAKES & RIVERS—DETROIT LAKES: Washington Square 5; FAIRMONT: Fair Lakes 5; FERGUS FALLS: Westride 5; OWATONNA: Cedar Mall 6; RED WING: Red Wing 5; WORTHINGTON: Northland 5.

LANDMARK—MINNEAPOLIS: Lagoon 5, Uptown.

LOEWS CINEPLEX—EDINA: Edina 4; MINNETONKA: Westwind 3; PLYMOUTH: Willow Creek 8.

MANN OF MN—BAXTER: Westport 3, Movies 10 at Westgate; COLUMBIA HEIGHTS: Apache 6; COTTAGE GROVE: Cottage View Drive-In; EAGAN: Eagan 9; GRAND RAPIDS: Grand Rapids 8; HIBBING: Irongate 3; HOPKINS: Hopkins 6; MAPLE GROVE: Maple Grove 10; PLYMOUTH: Plymouth 12; ST. LOUIS PARK: St. Louis Park 6; ST. PAUL: Grandview 2, Highland 2.

MARCUS—APPLE VALLEY: Apple Valley 6; CAMBRIDGE: Cambridge 5; ELK RIVER: Elk River 17; HASTINGS: Hastings 9; OAKDALE: Oakdale North 16; ROSEMOUNT: Rosemount 8; SHAKOPEE: Shakopee 11.

REGAL—EAGAN: Eagan 16.

UA—BROOKLYN CENTER: Movies at Brookdale 8; BURNSVILLE: UA Burnsville II (4); EDEN PRAIRIE: Movies at Eden Prairie West 5; MAPLEWOOD: Movies at Maplewood I (6), Movies at Maplewood II (6); ROSEVILLE: Movies at Pavillon Place 7; WOODBURY: UA Woodbury 10.

MISSISSIPPI

CINEMARK—GULFPORT: Cinemark 16; PEARL: Tinseltown USA 17; TUPELO: Movies 8.

MALCO—COLUMBUS: Cinema 3, Malco Twin, Leigh Mall, Varsity Twin; SOUTHAVEN: Desoto 16; TUPELO: Malco 10.

O'NEIL—HATTIESBURG: Broadacres 6; PICAYUNE: River Ridge 4; WAVELAND: Choctow 4.

UA—BILOXI: Biloxi 10; BROOKHAVEN: Westbrook 4; CLINTON: UA Clinton 10; FLOWOOD: UA Parkway Place 10; GAUTIER: Singing River Theatre 4, Singing River 5; GREENVILLE: Cinema I-82 (4), GREENWOOD: Highland Park 3; HATTIESBURG: UA Turtle Creek 9; LAUREL: Sawmill Square 5; McCOMB: Camelia 4; MERIDIAN: Bonita Lakes 9; NATCHEZ: Natchez Mall 4; OXFORD: Cinema 4; RIDGELAND: Movies at Northpark 14; VICKSBURG: Pemberton Square 4.

MISSOURI

AMC—CREVE COEUR: Creve Coeur 12, West Olive 16; HAZELWOOD: Village 6; INDEPENDENCE: Independence 20; KANSAS CITY: Barry Woods 24, Crown Center 6, Metro North 7-12, Parkway 22; ST. LOUIS: Esquire 7, Crestwood 10, Galleria 6.

B & B—BOLIVAR: Bolivar 4; BROOKFIELD: Brookfield Cedar; CHILLICOTHE: Grand 6; FESTUS: Festus 8; FULTON: Fulton 2; GRAVOIS MILLS: Lake West 5; HANNIBAL: Hannibal 5; HARRISONVILLE: Harrisonville 6; LEBANON: Ritz 4; LIBERTY: Liberty 12; MARSHALL: Marshall 3; MOBERLY: Five and Drive; MONETT: Plaza 5; NEOSHO: Neosho 6; SALISBURY: Lyric; WAYNESVILLE: Waynesville 8.

CARMIKE—WARRENSBURG: University 8.

CINEMARK—KANSAS CITY: The Palace Cinemark 14.

DICKINSON—BELTON: Belton 8; INDEPENDENCE: Noland Fashion Square 6; KANSAS CITY: Red Bridge 4; LEE'S SUMMIT: EastGlen 16;

GOODRICH—BRANSON: Branson 4; COLUMBIA: Forum 8; JEFFERSON CITY: Capital 4, Capital 8; SPRINGFIELD: Town & Country 6, Springfield 8.

KERASOTES—CAPE GIRARDEAU: Town Plaza 5; DEXTER: Town & Country 2; FARMINGTON: Showplace 4; KENNETT: Kennett; PARK HILLS: Movies 2; POPLAR BLUFF: Showplace 8; SULLIVAN: Meramec 2.

LANDMARK—ST. LOUIS: Plaza Frontenac 6; UNIVERSAL CITY: Tivoli 3.

MALCO—SIKESTON: Malco Trio.

REGAL—KANSAS CITY: Kansas City 18.

WALLACE—COLUMBIA: Stadium 14; JOPLIN: Joplin 6, Northstar 14; ROLLA: Forum 4; ST. JOSEPH: Plaza 8; ST. LOUIS: Union Station 10.

WEHRENBERG—CAPE GIRARDEAU: Cape West 14; West Park 4; CHESTERFIELD: Chesterfield 4; Clarkson 6; EUREKA: Eureka 6;FLORISSANT: Jamestown 14; O'FALLON: O'Fallon 15; OSAGE BEACH: Osage Village 5; SAPPINGTON: Ronnies 20; SPRINGFIELD: Battlefield Mall 6, Campbell 16; ST. ANN: Northwest 9; ST. CHARLES: St. Charles 18; ST. LOUIS: Arnold 14, Des Peres 14, Halls Ferry 14, Keller 8, Kenrick 8, Lindbergh 8, Mid Rivers 14, North Twin Drive-In, Westport 2.

MONTANA

CARMIKE—BILLINGS: Carmike, Wynnsong 10; BOZEMAN: Campus 8, Ellen, Rialto; BUTTE: Plaza 6; GREAT FALLS: Carmike 10, Cine 4, Village Twin; HELENA: Circus Twin, Gaslight 3; MISSOULA: Carmike 10, Cine 3, Village 6.

POLSON—DILLON: Big Sky 2; GLASGOW: Valley Cinemas; HAVRE: Havre 2; POLSON: Showboat 2; RONAN: Entertainer; WHITEFISH: Mountain 2; WOLF POINT: Prairie 2.

SIGNATURE—KALISPELL: Gateway 5, Liberty, Strand; COLUMBIA FALLS: Midway Drive-In.

NEBRASKA

AMC—OMAHA: Oakview 24.

CARMIKE—GRAND ISLAND: Conestoga 4, Island 2; HASTINGS: Imperial 3; KEARNEY: Hilltop 4; NORTH PLATTE: Mall 3; SCOTTSBLUFF: Monument Mall 8, Village 2.

CENTRAL STATES—COLUMBUS: Center 6; FREMONT: Cinema 3; KEARNEY: World 2, Drive-In; NORFOLK: Cinema 3.

CINEMARK—OMAHA: Movies 8.

DOUGLAS—BELLEVUE: South 7, Southroads 4; LINCOLN: Cinema Twin, East Park 6, Douglas 3, Edgewood 3, Lincoln 3, Plaza 4, Starship 9, South Pointe Cinema 6; OMAHA: Cinema Center Complex 8, Q Cinema 9, Grand 20.

FRIDLEY—GRAND ISLAND: Grand; HASTINGS: Rivoli 3; McCOOK: Cinema 3.

SILVER—OMAHA: Super Saver Westwood 8.

NEVADA

CENTURY—HENDERSON: Cinedome 12; LAS VEGAS: Cinedome 12, Century Desert 16, Century Rancho Santa Fe, Century Orleans 12, Las Vegas Drive-In, Suncoast 16; RENO: Century Park Lane 16, Riverside 12; SPARKS: Century 12 Sparks, El Rancho Drive-In 4.

REGAL—HENDERSON: Sunset Station 13; LAS VEGAS: Boulder Station 11, Colonnade 14, Texas 18; Village Square 18.

UA—HENDERSON: UA Green Valley 8; LAS VEGAS: UA Raibow Promenade 10, Showcase Mall 8.

WALLACE—CARSON CITY:Northgate 10, New Cinema 2; STATELINE: Horizon Stadium 8.

NEW HAMPSHIRE

HOYTS—BEDFORD: Bedford 7; CONCORD: Concord 10; GILFORD: Gilford 8; HOOKSETT: Hooksett 8; KEENE: Key 6; MANCHESTER: Manchester 9; NASHUA: Nashua Mall 4; NEWINGTON: Newington Mall 12; PORTSMOUTH: Portsmouth 5; SOMERSWORTH: Dover 4, Tri City Quad.

LOEWS CINEPLEX—CONCORD: Merrimack 5; LEBANON: Lebanon 1-6 (6).

MINI—LACONIA: Colonial 5, Weirs Drive-In 4.

NATIONAL AMUSEMENTS—SALEM: Salem Tri.

SPINELLI CINEMAS—Barrington: Barrington 6; BERLIN: Royal Twin; DOVER: Strand 3; MERIDETH: Merideth 3; ROCHESTER: Lilac Mall 4.

NEW JERSEY

AMC—DELRAN: Millside 4; DEPTFORD: Deptford 8; HAMILTON: Hamilton 24; MARLTON: Marlton 8; ROCKAWAY 6;

CINEMARK—SOMERDALE: Somerdale Movies 16.

CLEARVIEW—ASBURY PARK: Middlebrook 10; BERGENFIELD: Bergenfield 4; BERNARDSVILLE: Bernardsville 3; CALDWELL: Caldwell 4; CEDAR GROVE: Cinema 23 (5); CHESTER: Chester Cinema 6; CLIFTON: Allwood 6; CLOSTER: Closter 4; EDISON: Edison 8; EMERSON: Emerson Quad; HACKETTSTOWN: Mansfield 15; KINNELON: Kinnelon 11; LIVINGSTON: Colony 3; MADISON: Madison 4; MATAWAN: Strathmore 4; MILLBURN: Millburn 4; MONTCLAIR: Clairidge 5, Screening Zone 2; MORRISTOWN: Headquarters 10; PARSIPPANY: Cinema 12; RED BANK: Red Bank 2; RIDGEWOOD: Warner Quad; SUCCASUNNA: Succasunna 10; SUMMIT: Beacon Hill 5; TENAFLY: Tenafly 4; UPPER MONTCLAIR: Bellevue 4; WASHINGTON: Washington Township 3; WAYNE: Wayne Preakness 4; WEST MILFORD: West Milford 4; WOODBRIDGE: Woodbridge 4.

GENERAL CINEMA—BRIDGEWATER: Bridgewater Commons 7; CLIFTON: Clifton Commons 16; DEPTFORD: Deptford Mall 6; SOMERSET: Rutgers 6; WEST ORANGE: Essex Green 9.

HOYTS—BEACH HAVEN PARK: Beach Haven Cinema 4, Colonial Cinema 4, Colony 4 Brant Beach 4; OCEAN CITY: Moorlyn 4; PENNSUAKEN: Pennsuaken 10.

LOEWS CINEPLEX—BRICK: Cinema Centre 5; BRICKTOWN: Brick Plaza 10; CHERRY HILL: Cherry Hill 24; EAST HANOVER: East Hanover 12; EATONTOWN: Monmouth Mall 15; EDGEWATER: Showboat Quad (4); EDISON: Menlo Park 12; FREEHOLD: Freehold Metroplex 14; JERSEY CITY: Newport Centre 11; MOUNTAINSIDE: Mountainside 10; NEW BRUNSWICK: New Brunswick 18; NEWARK: Newark Metroplex 6; PARAMUS: Paramus Route 4 (10), Route 17 (3); RAMSAY: Interstate 2; RIDGEFIELD PARK: Ridgefield Park 12; SECAUCUS: Meadow 6, Plaza 8; TOMS RIVER: Seacourt 10; WAYNE: Wayne 14.

NATIONAL AMUSEMENTS—ATCO: Multiplex 14; EDGEWATER: Multiplex 14; HAZLET: Hazlet Multiplex 12; NEWARK: All Jersey Multiplex 12; SAYERVILLE: Amboy Multiplex 14.

REGAL—BURLINGTON: Burlington 20; EAST WINDSOR: Town Centre Plaza 15; JERSEY CITY: Hudson Mall 7; MORGANVILLE: Marlboro 8; NORTH BERGEN: Columbia Park 12; NORTH BRUNSWICK Commerce Center 18; PHILLIPSBURGH: Pohatcong 12; SOUTH PLAINFIELD: Hadley 16; TURNERSVILLE: Cross Keys 12VINELAND: Cumberland Mall 14.

UA—MOORESTOWN: Moorestown 7; PENNSAUKEN: Pennsauken 11; PRINCETON: Marketfair 9; SEWELL: Washington Township 14.

NEW MEXICO

ALLEN—ALAMOGORDO: Cinema 5; CARLSBAD: Mall Cinema 3; CLOVIS: Hilltop Twin, North Plains 4; FARMINGTON: Allen 8, Animas 4, Apache Twin Drive-In, Cameo, Centennial Twin; GALLUP: Aztec 5, El Morro, Rio West Twin; HOBBS: Broadmoor, Cinema 3; LAS CRUCES: Cinema 8, Telshor 12, Video 4; PORTALES: Tower Twin; ROSWELL: Cinema 4, Del Norte Twin, Park Twin.

CARMIKE—ARTESIA: Cinema 2.

CENTURY—ALBUQUERQUE: Century Rio 24.

CINEMARK—ALBUQUERQUE: Movies 8, Movies West 8.

TRANS-LUX—ESPANOLA: DreamCatcher 6; LOS ALAMOS: High Society 3; LOS LUNAS: Starlight 8; SANTA FE: Grand Illusion, Jean Cocteau; SOCORRO: Loma; TAOS: Storyteller 7.

UA—ALBUQUERQUE: Coronado 6, Cottonwood 9, UA Four Hills 10, UA at High Ridge 8; SANTA FE: UA De Vargas Center 6, UA North Theatre 6, UA South 6.

NEW YORK

AMC—AMHERST: Maple Ridge 8; NEW YORK: Empire 25.

CARMIKE—OLEAN: Carmike 8.

CINEMARK—ROCHESTER: Tinseltown USA 17; WEST BRIGHTON: Movies 10.

CITY CINEMAS—NEW YORK: Angelika Film Center 6, Cinema 1, 2 & 3, Eastside Playhouse, 86th St. East Cinemas 4, Murray Hill 4, Sutton 1 & 2, Village East Cinemas 7.

CLEARVIEW—BABYLON: Babylon 3; BALDWIN: Grand Ave. 5; BEDFORD: Bedford Playhouse; BRONXVILLE: Bronxville 3; BROOKLYN: Cobble Hill 5; FRANKLIN SQUARE: Franklin Square 15; GREAT NECK: Squire 7; LARCHMONT: Larchmont Playhouse 3; MAMARONECK: Mamaroneck Playouse 4; MANHASSET: Manhasset 3; MT. KISCO: Mt. Kisco Cinemas; NEW YORK: 59th St. East, 62nd & Broadway, Beekman, Chelsea 9, Chelsea West 3, First & 62nd St., Metro Twin, Olympia 2, Park & 86th St.; Waverly Twin, Ziegfeld Theatre, Cinema 304, New City 6, Herricks Twin, Central Plaza 4; NEW HYDE PARK: Herricks 4; PORT WASHINGTON: Port Washington 7, Soundview 6; ROSLYN: Roslyn 4; RYE: Rye Ridge 2; WHITE PLAINS: Cinema 100 2.

DIPSON—BATAVIA: Cinemas 2, Mall 2; BUFFALO: Amherst 3, North Park, Market Arcade Film & Arts Center; ELMIRA: Elmira 3, Heights; HORNELL: Hornell 3; LAKEWOOD: Chautauqua 2, Lakewood 6; SALAMANCA: Salamanca 2, WILLIAMSVILLE: Eastern Hills 3.

GENERAL CINEMA—AMHERST: University 8; BRONX: Bay Plaza 13; CHEEKTOWAGA: Walden Galleria 12; HAMBURG: McKinley Mall; ROCHESTER: Marketplace 7, Pittsford Plaza 6

HOYTS—ALBANY: Crossgates 12, Crossgates 18; BINGHAMTON: Binghamton 12; CAMILLUS: Camillus 10; CICERO: Cicero 13; CLAY: Great Northern 10; CLIFTON PARK: Clifton Park 8; DEWITT: Shoppingtown 10; FISHKILL: Fishkill 10; HORSEHEADS: Elmira 10; ITHACA: Ithaca 4, Ithaca 10; KINGSTON: Hudson Valley Mall 12; LATHAM: Latham 10; NEW HARTFORD: Sangertown Square 9; PLATTSBURGH: Champlain Centre 8; POUGHKEEPSIE: Galleria 12; QUEENSBURY: Aviation 7, Route 9 Cinemas 5; RENSSELAER: East Greenbush 8; ROCHESTER: Greece Ridge 12; SARATOGA SPRINGS: Wilton Mall 8; SYRACUSE: Carousel Center Mall 19; UTICA: Riverside 8; WATERTOWN: Salmon Run Mall 8.

LOEWS CINEPLEX—BAYSIDE: Bay Terrace 6; BROOKLYN: Alpine 7, Fortway 5, Kings Plaza Simplex 6, Kingsway 5; ELMHURST: Elmwood 4; FRESH MEADOWS: Cinema 5, Fresh Meadows 7; GARDEN CITY: Roosevelt Field 8; GLEN COVE: Glen Cove 6; HUNTINGTON: Shore 8; HUNGTINGTON STATION: Whitman 1; JOHNSON CITY: Oakdale Mall 1-3; LAKE GROVE: Smith Haven Mall 4; LEVITTOWN: Nassau Metroplex 10; MATTITUCK: Mattituck 8; MIDDLETOWN: Galleria Metroplex 16; NANUET: Nanuet 5; NEW YORK: Astor Plaza 1, Coronet 1 & 2, 84th St 6, Kips Bay 15, 42nd St. W., Lincoln Square 12 & IMAX, Magic Johnson Theatre - Harlem, New York Twin, 19th St. East 6, Orpheum 7, 72nd St. 1, State 4, Village VII (7), Worldwide Cinemas 6; NEW BRUNSWICK: New Brunswick 18; ROCKVILLE CENTRE: Fantasy 5, Rockville Centre 2; SCHENECTADY: Rotterdam Square Mall 6; STONY BROOK: Stony Brook 15; VESTAL: Sony Towne Square 9; WEBSTER: Wesbster Twelveplex; W. HAMPTON BEACH: Hampton Arts 2; WEST NYACK: Loews Palisades Center; WESTBURY: Roosevelt Raceway 10.

MINI—AUBURN: Fingerlakes Drive-In, Movieplex 8; ALEXANDRIA BAY: Bay Drive-In; AVERILL PARK: Hollywood Drive-In; CANANDAIGUA: Movieplex 10; CANTON: American 3; CARMEL: Movieplex 8; CHATHAM: Crandell Cinema; COBBLESKILL: Park; DUNKIRK: Movieplex 8; GENEVA: Movieplex 8; GLENS FALLS: Glen Twin Drive-In; GREENVILLE: Greenville Drive-In; HUDSON: Movieplex 8; HUNTER: Hunter;

INLET: Tamarack Cafe; JOHNSTOWN: Movieplex 9; LAKE PLACID: Palace 3; LITTLE FALLS: Valley Twin; LOWVILLE: Town Hall, Valleybrook Drive-In; MADISON: Norma Jean 7; MALONE: Plaza; MALTA: Malta Drive-In; MASSENA: Movieplex 8, 56 Auto Drive-In; NORTH HOOSICK: Hathaway Drive-In; OGDENSBURG: Cinema Twin; OLD FORGE: Strand; ONEONTA: Oneonta 2; PAINTED POST: Crystal 8; POTSDAM: Roxy 2; SCHROON LAKE: Strand; THOUSAND ISLAND PARK: Thousand Island; TUPPER LAKE: State; UNADILLA: Unadilla Drive-In

NATIONAL AMUSEMENTS—BRONX: Concourse Plaza 10, Whitestone 14; BROOKLYN: Linden Blvd. Multiplex 14; COMMACK: Commack Multiplex 15; ELMSFORD: Greenburgh Multiplex 10; FARMINGDALE: Multiplex 14; HAWTHORNE: Saw Mill Multiplex 10; HICKSVILLE: Broadway Multiplex 12; MEDFORD: Brookhaven 14; VALLEY STREAM: Green Acres 6, Sunrise Multiplex 14; WHITESTONE: College Point 12; YONKERS: Cross Country Multiplex 10.

REGAL—ASTORIA: Kaufman Astoria Cinema 14; BROOKLYN: Court Street 12; BUFFALO: Elmwood Center 16; IRONDEQUOIT: Culver Ridge Plaza 16; NEW ROCHELLE: New Roc City 18; NEW YORK: Battery Park City 16; NIAGARA FALLS: Hollywood 12; ORCHARD PARK: Quaker Crossing 18; ROCHESTER: Henrietta 18; RONKONKOMA: Ronkonkoma 9; STATEN ISLAND: Staten Island 16; VICTOR: Eastview Mall 13; WILLIAMSVILLE: Transit Center 18.

SILVER—BUFFALO: Super Saver Cinema Elmwood 8; POUGHKEEPSIE: South Hills 8.

UA—BAYSIDE: Bayside 4; BROOKLYN: Marboro 4, Movies at Sheepshead Bay 9; CORAM: Coram 12; DOUGLASTON: Movieworld Douglaston 7; EASTHAMPTON: Easthampton 6; EAST MEADOW: Meadowbrook 6; FARMINGDALE: Farmingdale 10; FOREST HILLS: Brandon 2, Midway 9, HAMPTON BAY: Hampton Bays 5; LONG ISLAND CITY: Astoria 6; LYNBROOK: Lynbrook 6; MOHEGAN LAKE: Cortlandt Town Center 11; NEW YORK: UA Cinema East Theatre, Gemini 3, AU Union Sqaure 14; OZONE PARK: Crossbay I 3, Crossbay 7; PATCHOGUE: Patchogue 13; SMITHTOWN: UA Smithtown; SOUTHAMPTON: Southampton 4; STATEN ISLAND: Hylan Plaza 5, Staten Island 14; WESTBURY: UA Westbury 12; WOODBURY: Cinema 150 (1); YONKERS: Movieland Yonkers 6; YORKTOWN HEIGHTS: Jefferson Valley 8.

NORTH CAROLINA

AMC—CHARLOTTE: Carolina Pavilion 22; CONCORD: Concord Mills 24.

CARMIKE—ASHEVILLE: Carmike 10; BOONE: Apalachian Twin, Chalet 3; CAROLINA BEACH: Cinema 4; CHAPEL HILL: Ram 3; DUNN: Plaza Twin; DURHAM: Carmike 7, Willowdale 8, Wynnsong 15; EDEN: Kingsway 4; FAYETTEVILLE: Carmike 12, Marketfair 15, Wynnsong 7; FOREST CITY: Cinema 4; GOLDSBORO: Berkeley 4; GREENSBORO: Carmike 18; GREENVILLE: Carmike 12, Carolina 4; HAVELOCK: Cinema 6; HICKORY: Carmike 12; HIGH POINT: Carmike 8; JACKSONVILLE: Bryn Marr 3, Carmike 7, Cinema 6; KINSTON: Plaza Twin; LENOIR: Westgate Twin; LEXINGTON: Cinema 8; LINCOLNTON: Cinema 8; MOREHEAD CITY: Cinema 3, Morehead Twin; MORRISVILLE: Park Place 16; NEW BERN: Cinema 3; RALEIGH: Blueridge 14, Carmike 15; ROCKY MOUNT: Golden East 4; SANFORD: Kendale 2; SHELBY: Cinema 4, Mall 4; SOUTHERN PINES: Cinema 4, Town & Country 2; STATESVILLE: Gateway 4; WASHINGTON: Cinema 7; WILMINGTON: Carmike 6, Carmike 16; WILSON: Parkwood 3; WINSTON-SALEM Carmike 10, Wynnsong 16.

CINEMA GRILL—CHARLOTTE: Eastland Cinema Grill 3; RALEIGH: Raleighwood Cinema Grill 2; WILLMINGTON: Longleaf Cinema Grill 3.

CINEMARK—ASHEBORO: Randolph 5; GREENSBORO: Brassfield 10; MATTHEWS: Movies 10; SALISBURY: Tinseltown USA 14.

EASTERN FEDERAL—CHAPEL HILL: Movies at Timberlyne 6, Plaza 5; CHARLOTTE: Delta 6, Manor 3, Movies at Crownpoint 12, Starlight Stadium 15; CORNELIUS: Movies at the Lake 12; GASTONIA: Movies at Franklin Square 14; LUMBERTON: Town & Country 4; WINSTON-SALEM: North Point 5.

R/C THEATRES—AVON: Hatteras; COROLLA: Corolla 4; KITTY HAWK: Kitty Hawk 2, Market Place 2; NAGS HEAD: Cineplex 4.

REGAL—ASHEVILLE: Hollywood 14; BOONE: Boone 7; CHARLOTTE: Stonecrest at Piper Glen 22; FAYETTEVILLE: Omni 8; GREENSBORO: Greensboro 7; HIGH POINT: Oak Hollow Mall 7; MOUNT AIRY: Mayberry 5; WILSON: Wilson 6.

UA—ALBEMARLE: Eastgate 5; ASHEVILLE: Beaucatcher 7, UA Movies at Biltmore Square 6; CONCORD: Carolina Mall 8; GARNER: Garner Towne Square 10; GOLDSBORO: Litchfield 4; HENDERSONVILLE: Four Seasons 4; HICKORY: Crown 6; LUMBERTON: Cinemas IV; WILMINGTON: College Road 6.

NORTH DAKOTA

CARMIKE—BISMARK: Midco 8, Plaza 3; DEVIL'S LAKE: Lake 3 Theatre 3; DICKINSON: Cinema 3; GRAND FORKS: Columbia 4, Midco 10; MINOT: North 7, South 5.

CINEMA GRILL—FARGO: Fargo Cinema Grill 3.

CINEMA ENTERTAINMENT—FARGO: West Acres 12, Century 10.

OHIO

AMC—COLUMBUS: Eastland Centre 8; Lennox Town Center 24 24, Easton 30; DUBLIN: Dublin Village 18; WESTERVILLE: Westerville 6.

CARMIKE—ASHTABULA: Cinema 6; FINDLAY: Findlay 6; MANSFIELD: Kingsgate 4; SAINT CLAIRSVILLE: Ohio Valley Mall 9; SANDUSKY: Plaza 8; STEUBENVILLE: Cinema 6.

CHAKERES—BELLFONTAINE: Bellefontaine 8; CELINA: Celina 5, Lake Drive-In; DAYTON: Kettering 2, Melody 49 Drive-In 2; FAIRBORN: Skyborn Drive-In; LUCASVILLE: Scioto Breeze Drive-In 2; NEW CARLISLE: Park Layne Drive-In; SIDNEY: Sidney 3; SPRINGFIELD: Cinemas 10, Upper Valley 5, Melody Cruise-In 2; URBANA: Urbana 2; WILMINGTON: Plaza Cinemas 5, Wilmington Drive-In.

CINEMA GRILL—CINCINNATI: Covedale Cinema Grill 2, Mt. Cinema Grill 2; CLEVELAND: Centrum Cinema Grill 3.

CINEMARK—ALLIANCE: Carnation 5; BOARDMAN: Tinseltown USA 7; BOWLING GREEN: Cinema 5; CANTON: Movies 4; COLUMBUS: Movies 10; Movies 12; GAHANNA: Movies 16; HILLIARD: Movies 12; MACEDONIA: Cinemark 15; MANSFIELD: Cinema 10; NORTH CANTON: Movies 10, Tinseltown 15; ONTARIO: Richland III; PIQUA: Miami Valley 6; SANDUSKY: Movies 10; VALLEY VIEW: Cinemark 24; WILLOUGHBY HILLS: Movies 10; WOOSTER: Movies 10; YOUNGSTOWN: Movies 8; ZANESVILLE: Colony Square 10.

DANBARRY CINEMA—CINCINNATI: Dollar Saver 12; DAYTON: Dollar Saver 12; HUBER HEIGHTS: Dollar Saver 12; MIDDLETOWN: Cinemas Middletown 10.

GENERAL CINEMA—AKRON: West Market Plaza 7; BROOKLYN: Ridge Park Square 8;CUYAHOGA FALLS: Plaza Cinemas Chapel Hill 8; ELYRIA: Midway Mall 8; MENTOR: Erie Commons 8; PARMA: Parmatown 5; ROCKY RIVER: Westgate Mall 6, Westwood Town Center 8.

KERASOTES—HAMILTON: Cinema 10, Showplace 8.

LOEWS CINEPLEX—NORTH RANDALL: Magic Johnson Randall Park Mall 12; RICHMOND HEIGHTS: Richmond Town Square 20.

MARCUS—COLUMBUS: Crosswoods 17; PICKERINGTON: Pickerington 16.

NATIONAL AMUSEMENTS—CENTERVILLE: Centerville 6, Dayton Mall, Showcase Cross Point 12; CINCINNATI: Kenwood Towne Centre 5, Northgate 7, Showcase Cincinnati 12, Showcase Eastgate 7, Showcase Western Hills 14, Showcase Springdale 10; HOLLAND: Showcase Spring Meadows, Toledo 10; HUBER HEIGHTS: Showcase 16; MADISONVILLE: Oakley Drive-In; MASON: Showcase Kings Island 12; MAUMEE: Showcase Maumee 18; MILFORD: 275 East 4. Showcase Milford 16; TOLEDO: Franklin Park 6, Franklin Park 6, North Towne Mall 5, Showcase Toledo 5, Southwyck 3; WEST CARROLLTON: Showcase Miamisburgh 16.

REGAL—AKRON: Independence 10, Interstate Park 18, Montrose 12; BARBERTON: Lake 8; BEAVERCREEK: Hollywood 20 at Fairfield Comm. 20; BROOK PARK: Brookgate Saver 5; BRUNSWICK: Hickory Ridge 8; CHILLICOTHE: Regal 6, Shawnee Square 4; CINCINNATI: Central Parke 11; CLEVELAND HEIGHTS: Severance Town Center 14; COLUMBUS: Georgeville Square 16; DEFIANCE: Northtowne 9; DELAWARE: Delaware Square 5; ELYRIA: Cobblestone Square 20; GARFIELD HEIGHTS: Garfield Mall 5; HUDSON: Hudson 10; LANCASTER: River Valley Mall 10; LIMA: Lima Center 3, Cinema 7; LORAIN: Sheffield Centre 10; MARIETTA: Lafayette Center 7; MARION: Southland 7; MAYFIELD HEIGHTS: Mayfield Heights 10; MEDINA: Medina 16 at Huntington St. 16; MENTOR: Great Lakes Mall 9; MIDDLEBURG HEIGHTS: Middleburg Town Square 12; MIDDLETOWN: Towne East 5; NEW PHILADELPHIA: New Towne Cinema 8; NILES: Boulevard Centre 14, Movie World 6; NORTH OLMSTED: Great Northern 7; REYNOLDSBURG: Consumer Square 14; SOLON: Solon Commons 16; TIFFIN: Tiffin 4; WESTLAKE: Westlake Promenade 11; WILLOUGHBY: Willoughby Commons 16; YOUNGSTOWN: Austintown Plaza 10, Cinemasouth 10.

WALLACE—HEATH: Indian Mound 11.

OKLAHOMA

AMC—OKLAHOMA CITY: Quail Springs Mall 24; TULSA: Southroads 20.

B & B—PONCA CITY: Airline Drive-In, Plaza Twin.

CARMIKE—ARDMORE: Carmike 5; BARTLESVILLE: Eastland 4; CUSHING: Dunkin; DUNCAN: Carmike 6; ENID: Video Twin; LAWTON: Carmike 8; MUSKOGEE: Carmike 6; PONCA CITY: North Park 4; SHAWNEE: Cinema Center 8, Hornbeck; STILLWATER: Carmike 10.

CINEMARK—ADA: North Hills 6; BROKEN ARROW: Cinema 8; OKLAHOMA CITY: Tinseltown 20; SAND SPRINGS: Cinema 8; TULSA: Movies 8, The Tulsa by Cinemark 17.

DICKINSON—OWASSO: Owasso 10; MUSKOGEE: Arrowhead Mall 6; TULSA: Starworld 20; WEATHERFORD: Showest 3, 66 Twin Drive-In.

REGAL—EDMOND: Kickingbird 8; OKLAHOMA CITY: Crossroads Mall 16, Windsor Hills 10.

SILVER—OKLAHOMA CITY: North Park Mall 7; YUKON: Dollar Movies 5.

WALLACE—BARTLESVILLE: Movies 6; LAWTON: Cache 8; MIDWEST CITY: Heritage Plaza 5; NORMAN: Spotlight 14; OKLAHOMA CITY: Brixton Square 8, Crossroads 8, Penn Square 10; SHAWNEE: Movies 6; TULSA: Eastland Mall 6, Palace 12, Woodland Hills 6.

OREGON

CENTURY—PORTLAND: Century Eastport 16.

CINEMARK—MEDFORD: Movies 5, Tinseltown 15; SPRINGFIELD: Movies 12, Cinemark 17; WHITE CITY: White City 6.

COMING ATTRACTIONS—ASHLAND: Ashland Street 6, Varsity 5; ASTORIA: Astoria Gateway 7; COOS BAY: Egyptian 3; FLORENCE: Florence 4; FOREST GROVE: Forest Grove 7; GRANTS PASS: Southgate 4, Movies 6; KLAMATH FALLS: Pelican 6; MCMINNVILLE: McMinnville 8; NORTH BEND: Pony Village 4; ROSEBURG: Harvard 3, Roseburg Cinema 7.

REGAL—ALBANY: Albany 7; BEAVERTON: Westgate 5; BEND: Mountain View 4; Old Mill 10; Pilot Butte 6; CLACKAMAS: Clackamas Towne Center 5; CORNELIUS: Cornelius 9; CORVALLIS: Ninth Street 4, State, Whiteside; EUGENE: Cinema World 8 Valley River, West 11th Movieland 6, McDonald; GRESHAM: Stark Street 10; HILLSBORO: Evergreen Parkway 13, Movies on TV 16; HOOD RIVER: Trail Indoor, Trail Drive-In; LINCOLN CITY: Lincoln City 6; NEWPORT: Newport Tri 3; OREGON CITY: Hilltop 9; PORTLAND: 82nd Ave. 6, Broadway Metro 4, Division Street 13, Eastgate 3, Fox Tower 10; Koin Center 6, Lloyd Center 10, Lloyd Mall 8, Washington Square 4; SALEM: Lancaster 4, Movieland 7, Santiam 11; SHERWOOD: Sherwood 10; TIGARD: Tigard 11; WILSONVILLE: Wilsonville 9.

PENNSYLVANIA

AMC—ALLENTOWN: Tilghman 8; BENSALEM: Neshaminy 24, Woodhaven 10; HARRISBURG: Colonial Commons 9; LANCASTER: Wonderland 4; MECHANICSURG: Hampden Center 8; MEDIA: Granite Run 8; PHILADELPHIA: Adnorra 8, Orleans; SPRINGFIELD: Marlpe 10; SPRINGHOUSE: 309 Cinema 9; WESTCHESTER: Painters Crossing 9.

CARMIKE—ALLENTOWN: Carmike 16; ALTOONA: Carmike 8, Park Hills Plaza 7; BEAVER FALLS: Plaza 6; CHAMBERSBURG: Cinema 4; CONNELLSVILLE: Lauel Mall 4; CRANBERRY: Cranberry Mall 5; CRANBERRY TOWNSHIP: Cranberry 8; DELMONT: Carmike 12; DUBOIS: Cinema 5; GREENSBURG: Carmike 15; HANOVER: Fox 6; HERMITAGE: Hermitage Plaza 8; HUMMELS WHARF: Sunbury 4; INDIANA: Cinema 4; KITTANING: Cinema 4; MONACA: Movie World 7; MOUNT LEBANON: Galleria 6; PITTSBURGH: Carmike 10; PLEASANT HILLS: Southland 9; POTTSTOWN: Coventry 8; POTTSVILLE: Fox 2: READING: Fairgrounds 5, Wyomissing 8; STATE COLLEGE: Cinema 5, Cinema 6, State Twin, The Movies 1; UNIONTOWN: Carmike 6; VANDERGRIFT: Cinema 3; WASHINGTON: Washington Mall 8; WEST MIFFLIN: Maxi-Saver 12.

CINEMA GRILL—HARRISBURG: Harrisburg Cinema Grill 2.

CINEMARK—ERIE: Millcreek Cinema 6, Movies 17; MOOSIC: Cinemark 20.

CLEARVIEW—BALA CYNWYD: Bala 3; WAYNE: Anthony Wayne 5.

DIPSON—BRADFORD: Bradford 2.

GENERAL CINEMA—PHILADELPHIA: Franklin Mills 14, PLYMOUTH MEETING: Plymouth Meeting 12; WHITEHALL: Leigh Valey Cinema 8; WILKES-BARRE: Wyoming Valley Mall 4, Wyoming Valley Mall 3.

HOYTS—BETHLEHEM: Saucon Valley 10; HARRISBURG: East Harrisburg 14; HAZELTON: Hazelton 10.

LOEWS CINEPLEX—NORTH VERSAILLES: North Versailles 20; STROUDSBURG: Stroud Mall 7; WEST HOMESTEAD: Waterfront 22.

NATIONAL AMUSEMENTS—PITTSBURGH: Showcase Cinemas West 12, Showcase Cinemas East 10, Showcase Cinemas North 11, Super Saver Cinema 8.

R/C THEATRES—CARLISLE: M.J. Mall 8; GETTYSBURG: Majestic 3, HANOVER: Hanover 9; READING: Fox East 4.

REGAL—BUTLER: Moraine Pointe 10; CONSHOHOCKEN: Plymouth Meeting 10; DOWNINGTOWN: Downingtown 16; DOYLESTOWN: Barn Plaza 14; EASTON: Northampton 11; EDGEMONT: Edgmont Square 10; HUNTINGDON VALLEY: Huntingdon Valley 14; LANCASTER: Manor 16; LIONVILLE: Lionville 12; OAKS: Marketplace at Oaks 24; QUARKERTOWN: Richland Crossing 12; WARRINGTON: Warrington Crossing 22; YORK: Queensgate 10, WEST MANCHESTER: West Manchester Mall 13.

TMI—BUTLER: Penn 2, Pioneer Drive-In 3, MEADVILLE: Meadville 4.

UA—CAMP HILL: Camp Hill Twin, UA Capital City 6; E. WHITELAND: UA East Whiteland 9; FRACKVILLE: Movies at Schuylkill 4; HOLMES: Eric Macdade Mall 4; KING OF PRUSSIA: UA King of Prussia 16; LANGHORNE: UA Oxford Valley 10; MANYUNK: Main Street 6; MONTGOMERYVILLE: Montgomeryville 7; MUNCY: Lycoming Mall 4; PHILADELPHIA: UA at Cheltenham Square 8, Grant Plaza 9, Riverview Plaza 17, Sameric 4; SCRANTON: Scranton 8, Steamtown Mall 8; UPPER DARBY: 69th Street 9.

RHODE ISLAND

HOYTS—PROVIDENCE: Providence 16.

MINI—BLOCK ISLAND: Empire 2; CRANSTON: Park 4; NARRAGANSETT: Pier 3; WAKEFIELD: Campus 3.

NATIONAL AMUSEMENTS—GREENVILLE: Apple Valley 8; WARWICK: Warwick 15.

PATROT—EAST PROVIDENCE: Cinema 10.

SOUTH CAROLINA

CARMIKE—AIKEN: Cinema 3; CHARLESTON: James Island 8; CLEMSON: Astro 3; COLUMBIA: Carmike 14, Wynnsong 10; FLORENCE: Magnolia 3; GREENVILLE: Carmike 7; GREENWOOD: Crosscreek 3; HARTSVILLE: Cinema Twin; MYRTLE BEACH: Broadway 16, Dunes 8; NORTH MYRTLE BEACH: Briarcliffe 10; ORANGEBURG: Camelot 4; ROCK HILL: Cinema 7; SPARTANBURG: Carmike 7, Wynnsong 7; SUMTER: Movies 3, Palmetto 2.

CINEMA GRILL—CHARLESTON: American Cinema Grill 2.

CINEMARK—SUMMERVILLE: Movies 8.

EASTERN FEDERAL—ANDERSON: Starlight 14; CHARLESTON: Movies at Mt. Pleasant 12; COLUMBIA: The Movies at Polo Road 8.

GENERAL CINEMA—CHARLESTON: Citadel Mall 6; COLUMBIA: Columbia Mall 8, Dutch Square 14; NORTH CHARLESTON: Northwoods Mall 8.

MARQUEE—HILTON HEAD ISLAND: Park Plaza Cinema 5.

REGAL—AIKEN: Aiken Mall 8; CHARLESTON: North Charleston 10; COLUMBIA: Columbia 7; GREENVILLE: Pelham Road 10, Hollywood 20; MURRELS INLET: Inlet Square 7; MYRTLE BEACH: Pottery 6; NORTH CHARLESTON: Charles Towne Square 18; ROCK HILL: Galleria Mall 8; SPARTANBURG: Converse 6, Westgate Mall 8.

TMI—SUMTER: Beacon 10.

UA—ANDERSON: Market Place 6; FLORENCE: Capri 3, Julia 4; GREENVILLE: Bijou 8, Haywood 10.

SOUTH DAKOTA

CARMIKE—ABERDEEN: Midco 9; RAPID CITY: Carmike 7, Rushmore 7; SIOUX FALLS: Carmike 7, Empire 6, West Mall 7; YANKTON: Yankton Mall 5.

CENTURY—SIOUX FALLS: Stadium 14 Sioux Falls.

LAKES & RIVERS—WATERTOWN: Falls Cinema 5.

TENNESSEE

CARMIKE—ANTIOCH: Belle Forge 10, Hickoey 8; ATHENS: Plaza 2; CHATTANOOGA: Bijou 7, Wynnsong 10; CLARKSVILLE: Carmike 8, Cinema 5; CLEVELAND: Village 2; COOKEVILLE: Highland 10, Varsity 2; CROSSVILLE: Capri 2; DYERSBURG: Carmike 9; EAST RIDGE: Eastridge 6; FRANKLIN: Galleria 10, Thoroughbred 20; GOODLETTSVILLE: Rivergate 8; GREENVILLE: Capri 2; HERMITAGE: Hermitage 4; HIXSON: Northgate 8; JOHNSON CITY: Johnson City 14; KINGSPORT: Ft. Henry 5; KNOXVILLE: Carmike 10, Commons 6, Movies 7, Wynnsong 16; LAFOLETTE: Movies 2; LEBANON: Martin 3; MARYVILLE: Foothills 12; MORRISTOWN: College Square 6; MURFREESBORO: Wynnsong; NASHVILLE: Bellevue 8, Wynnsong 10; ONEIDA: Cinema 3; SPRINGFIELD: Cinema 1.

CINEMA GRILL—KNOXVILLE: Terrace Cinema Grill 2.

CINEMARK—OAKRIDGE: Tinseltown 14.

MALCO—BARLETT: Stage 12; CORDOVA: Trinity Commons 9; GERMANTOWN: Forest Hill 8; JACKSON: Cinema 8; MEMPHIS: Appletree 12, Bartlett 10, Collierville 16, Highland Quartet, Majestic 20, Ridgeway 4, Southwest Twin Drive-In, Studio on the Square, Summer Four Drive-In, Winchester Court 8, Wolfchase Galleria 8.

REGAL—CHATTANOOGA: Hamilton Place 9, Hamilton Place 10-17; HENDERSONVILLE: Indian Lake 10; HERMITAGE: Courtyard 8; HIXSON: Northgate Crossing 6; JACKSON: Jackson 10; KNOXVILLE: Downtown West 8, East Towne Crossing 8, Farragut Towne Square 10, Knoxville Center 10, West Town Mall 9; NASHVILLE: Bellevue 12, Green Hills 16, Nippers Corner 10, Hollywood 27, Opry Mills 20; TULLAHOMA: Tullahoma 8.

TEXAS

AMC—ARLINGTON: Green Oaks 8; DALLAS: Glen Lakes 8, Grand 24; FT. WORTH: Palace 9, Hulen 10, Sundance West 11; FRISCO: Stonebriar 24; GRAPEVINE: Grapevine Mills 30; HIGHLAND PARK: Highland Park Village 4; HOUSTON: Commerce Park 8, Gulf Pointe 30, Meyer Park 16, Studio 30, Willowbrook 24; HUMBLE: Deerbrook 24; KATY: Katy Mills 20; MESQUITE: Mesquite 30; SAN ANTONIO: Rivercenter 9, Huebner Oaks 24; SUGARLAND: First Colony 24.

CARMIKE—ABILENE: Park Central 6; DENTON: Cinema 5; EDINBURG: Carmike 20; EL PASO: Carmike 16; GREENVILLE: Rolling Hills 4; JACKSONVILLE: Cinema 3; LAKE JACKSON: Cinema 4; LONGVIEW: Carmike 10, Northloop 6; LUFKIN: Angelina Twin, Cinema 4, Towne Square 4; NACODOCHES: Carmike 6, Carmike 2; SILSBEE: Pines 1; WICHITA FALLS: Century City 6, Sikes 10.

CENTURY—ABILENE: Century Abilene 12; CORPUS CHRISTI: Century Corpus Christi 16; ODESSA: Odessa 12.

CINEMA GRILL—HOUSTON: Westchase Cinema Girll 5.

CINEMARK—AMARILLO: Cinemark 16; ARLINGTON: Tinseltown 9; AUSTIN: Barton Creek 10, Tinseltown 17, Dollar Cinema 8; BEAUMONT: Tinseltown 15; BROWNSVILLE: Movies 10, Cinemark 16; CLEBURNE: Cinema 6; COLLEGE STATION: Movies 16; CORPUS CHRISTIE: Tinseltown 16, Dollar Cinemas 7; CORSICANA: Cinema 4; DALLAS: Cinemark 17; DEL RIO: Movies 8; EAST EL PASO: Tinseltown 20; GARLAND: Hollywood USA 15; GRAND PRAIRIE: Movies 16; GRAPEVINE: Tinseltown 17; HARLINGEN: Cinema 16, Movies 10; HOUSTON: Tinseltown 16, Tinseltown 24; JACINTO CITY: Tinseltown 17; KATY: Cinemark 19; LANCASTER: Movies 14; LAREDO: Movies 12; LEWISVILLE: Movies 12, Cinemark 8; LUBBOCK: Movies 16, Tinseltown 17; MC ALLEN: Main Place Movies 17; MC KINNEY Movies 14; MISSION: Tinseltown 17; PARIS: Movies 8; PASADENA: Hollywood USA 20; PFLUGERVILLE: Tinseltown 20; PHARR: Movies 8; PLAINVIEW: Town Centre 6; PLANO: Cinemark 24, Movies 10, Tinseltown 20; RICHLAND HILLS: Movies 8; ROCKWALL: Rockwall 8; ROSENBERG: Rosenberg 8; ROUND ROCK: Movies 8; SAN ANGELO: Tinseltown 14; SAN ANTONIO: Dollar Movies 16, Movies 9; SHERMAN: Cinema 7, Midway Movies 5; STEPHENVILLE: Cinema 6; TEMPLE: Temple 5, Temple 6; TEXARKANA: Movies 12; TEXAS CITY: Movies 12; VICTORIA: Cinema 4, Playhouse Cinema 4, Salem Cinema 6: WESLACO: Cinema 18; WESLACO: Movies 10; WOODLANDS: Tinseltown 17.

DICKINSON—PORT ARTHUR: Central Mall 10.

EDWARDS—HOUSTON: Greenway Plaza 24, Houston Marquee 23.

GENERAL CINEMA—ARLINGTON: Arlington Park 8; AUSTIN: Barton Creek 14; CARROLLTON: Furneaux Creek 7; DALLAS: Galleria 5; EL PASO: Cielo Vista Mall 6, The Park 6, Sunland Park Mall 6; HOUSTON: Meyerland 8; IRVING: Irving Mall 14.

LANDMARK—AUSTIN: Dobie 4; DALLAS: Inwood 3; HOUSTON: Greenway 3, River Oaks 3.

LOEWS CINEPLEX—ARLINGTON: Lincoln Square 10, 20 & 287 (6); DALLAS: Cityplace 14, Keystone Park 16; FT. WORTH: City View Eightplex; HOUSTON: Easton Commons 8, Magic Johnson Northline 12, Memorial City 8, River Oaks 12, Sharpstown Centre 8, Spectrum 9, West Oaks Mall 7; PLANO: Chisholm Plano 5, Preston Park Sixplex; SPRING: Spring Tenplex; STAFFORD: Foutnains 18, Southwest Sixplex; WEBSTER: Bay Area Sixplex.

O'NEIL—NEW BRAUNFELS: Marketplace Cinema 12.

REGAL—AUSTIN: Arbor 7, Gateway 16, Lakecreek 8, Lakeline 9, Lincoln 6, Metropolitian 14, Northcross 6, Riverside 8, Village 4, Westgate 11; LIVE OAK: Live Oak 18; SAN ANTONIO: Alamo Quarry 14, Century Plaza 8, Cielo Vista 18, Crossroads 6, Embassy 14, Fiesta 16, Galaxy 14, Northwest 14 Theatres, Northwest 14, Rolling Oaks 6, Westlakes 9, Windsor Mall 5.

SILVER—EL PASO: East Pointe Village 12, Montwood 7.

UA—ABILENE: Cinema 10; AMARILLO: Amarillo 14; ARLINGTON: Bowen 8; BEDFORD: Bedford 10; CORPUS CHRISTI: Cinema 6; DALLAS: Cine 1 & 2, Galaxy 9; UA Theatre 8; DENTON: UA Golden Triangle 4, UA Golden Triangle 5; FT. WORTH: Eastchase 9, Fossil Creek 11, Hulen 10, Las Vegas Trail 8; GARLAND: Northstar 8; GRAND PRAIRIE: Grand Prairie 10; IRVING: Macarthur Marketplace 16; LAREDO: North Creek 10; LEWISVILLE: UA Lakepointe 10.

WALLACE—BEAUMONT: Star 12; BURLSEON: Movies 14; DALLAS: Medallion 5; FORT WORTH: Town Center 8; GRAPEVINE: Movies 8; KILLEEN: Cinema 4, Kileen Stadium 14; LONGVIEW: Movies 9; MIDLAND: Cine 4, Tall City 10; ODESSA: Cinema 7, Permian Palace 11; TYLER: Movies 6, Tyler Rose 14; WACO: Jewel 16.

UTAH

CARMIKE—LOGAN: Cache Valley 3; PROVO: Wynnsong 12; SALT LAKE CITY: Cottonwood Mall 4, Villa; WEST JORDAN: Carmike 12; WEST VALLEY CITY: HW Connection 15.

CENTURY—SALT LAKE CITY: Century 16.

CINEMARK—LAYTON: Tinseltown 17; OGDEN: Tinseltown 14; PARK CITY: Village 3; PROVO: Movies 8, Cinemark 16; SALT LAKE CITY: Movies 10; SANDY: Movies 9; WEST JORDAN: Cinemark 24; WEST VALLEY CITY: Valley Fair 9.

DEANZA—WEST VALLEY: Redwood 6.

LOEWS CINEPLEX—LAYTON HILLS: Layton Hills 9; NORTH SALT LAKE CITY: Trolley North 3; OGDEN: Cinedome 2; OREM: University 4; SALT LAKE CITY: Broadway Centre 6, Crossroads Cinemas 3, Holladay Centre 6, Trolley Croners 3, Trolley Square Mall 4; SANDY: Southtowne 10; TAYLORSVILLE: Midvalley 12.

VERMONT

HOYTS—BURLINGTON: Nickelodeon 6; NEWPORT: Showplace 3; SOUTH BURLINGTON: Showcase 5, South Burlington 9.

MINI—BENNINGTON: Movieplex 3; RUTLAND: Plaza 9, Westway 4.

SILVER—BURLINGTON: Ethan Allen 4.

VIRGINIA

AMC—ARLINGTON: Courthouse Plaza 8; FALLS CHURCH: Skyline 12, HAMPTON: Hampton Towne Center 24; VIRGINIA BEACH: Lynnhaven 5, Lynnhaven 8; WOODBRIDGE: Potomac Mills 15.

CARMIKE—CHARLOTTESVILLE: Carmike 6; DANVILLE: Plaza Twin, Riverside 3; LYNCHBURG: Carmike 8, River Ridge 4; MIDLOTHIAN: Carmike 10; ROANOKE: Carmike 10; SALEM: Valley 8; WILLIAMSBURG: Carmike 4, Williamsburg 7; WINCHESTER: Apple Blossom 6, Cinema Center 6.

CINEMA GRILL—CHESAPEAKE: Greenbrier Cinema Grill 4; ROANOKE: Star City Cinema Grill 2.

CINEMARK—BRISTOL: Tinseltown 14; CHESAPEAKE: Movies 10; LYNCHBURG: Movies 10; NORFOLK: Cinemark at Military Circle 18.

GENERAL CINEMA—NORFOLK: Janaf Plaza 8; SPRINGFIELD: Springfield Mall 10.

LOEWS CINEPLEX—ARLINGTON: Pentagon City 6, Shirlington 7; HERNDON: Worldgate 9; MANASSAS: Manassas Mall 7; VIENNA: Fairfax Square 8; WOODBRIDGE: Tacket's Mills 4.

MARQUEE—FREDERICKSBURG: Southpoint Cinema 9.

NATIONAL AMUSEMENTS—ALEXANDRIA: Mount Vernon Multiplex 10; CENTREVILLE: Centreville Multiplex 12; MERRIFIELD: Lee Highway Multiplex 14; RESTON: Reston Multiplex 11.

R/C THEATRES—COVINGTON: Covington 3; CULPEPER: Culpeper Movies 3; LEXINGTON: State 3.

REGAL—ARLINGTON: Ballston Common 12; BLACKSBURG: Capri 2; CHARLOTTESVILLE: Downtown Mall 6, Seminole Square 4; CHESAPEAKE: Greenbriar 4; Greenbriar 13, CHESTER: Chester 6; CHRISTIANSBURG: New River Valley 11; COLONIAL HEIGHTS: Southpark 6; FARMVILLE: Longwood Village 3; FRANKLIN: Armory Drive 3; FREDERICKSBURG: Fredericksburg 15, Virginian 4, Spotsylvania Mall 4; GLEN ALLEN: Virginia Center 14; HAMPTON: Riverdale Plaza 12; HARRISONBURG: Harrisonburg 14, Valley Mall 4; HAYES: York River Crossing 8; LEESBURG: Tally Ho 2; MIDLOTHIAN: Genito 9; NEWPORT NEWS: Kiln Creek 20; NORFOLK: MacArthur Center 18, Main Gate 10; PETERSBURG: Crater 8; RICHMOND: Cloverleaf 8, Ridge 7, Westhampton 2, Willow Lawn 4; STAFFORD: Aquia 10; STAUNTON: Staunton Mall 6; STERLING: Countryside 20; VIRGINIA BEACH: Columbus 12, Pembroke 8, Strawbridge Marketplace 12, Surf & Sand 8.

UA—FAIRFAX: Fairfax Town Center 10; RICHMOND: Chesterfield Towne Center 9, West Tower 10.

WASHINGTON

AMC—FEDERAL WAY: SeaTac North 6, SeaTac South 6; SPOKANE: River Park Square 20; TACOMA: Narrows Plaza 8.

CARMIKE—KENNEWICK: Carmike 12.

CINEMA GRILL—SEATTLE: Aurora Cinema Grill 3.

GENERAL CINEMA—EVERETT: Everett Mall Village 7, Everett Mall 3; RENTON: Renton Village 8; SEATTLE: Aurora 3, Cinerama, Pacific Place 11; SILVERDALE: Kitsap Mall 8.

LANDMARK—SEATTLE: Broadway Market 4, Crest 4, Egyptian, Guild 45th 2, Harvard Exit 2, Metro 10, Neptune, Seven Gables, Varsity 3.

LOEWS CINEPLEX—BELLEVUE: Factoria Cinemas 8, BURLINGTON: Cascade Mall 14; KIRKLAND: Kirkland Parkplace 6, Totem Lake 3; LAKEWOOD: Lakewood Mall 12; LYNNWOOD: Grand Cinemas Alderwood 8; REDMOND: Redmond Town Center 8; SEATTLE: City Centre Cinemas 2, Meridian 16, Northgate 1, Oak Tree Cinemas 6, Uptown Cinemas 3; TACOMA: Tacoma Central 6, Tacoma Mall Twin, Tacoma South Cinemas 5; TUKWILA: Lewis & Clark 7, Southcenter 1; WOODINVILLE: Woodinville 12.

REGAL—ABERDEEN: Southshore Mall 4; AUBURN: Auburn 17; BELLEVUE: Crossroads 8, Galleria 11; BELLINGHAM: Bellis Fair 6, Sehome 3, Sunset Square 6; BONNY LAKE: Tall Firs 10; BREMERTON: Redwood Plaza 4; CHEHALIS: Cinema 3; EVERETT: Everett 9; GIG HARBOR: Gig Harbor 3; ISSAQUAH: Issaquah 9; KELSO: Three Rivers Mall 5; KENNEWICK: Clearwater 3, Columbia Center 3, Columbia Mall 8; KENT: Kent 6; LAKEWOOD: Lakewood 15; LONGVIEW: Longview, Triangle 4; LYNNWOOD: Alderwood 7, Alderwood Village 12; MARYSVILLE: Marysville 14; MT. LAKE TERRACE: Mount Lake 9; OLYMPIA: Capitol Mall 4, Lacey 8; PORT ORCHARD: South Sound 10; POULSBO: Poulsbo 10; PUYALLUP: Puyallup 6, Longston Place 14, South Hill Mall 6; REDMOND: Bella Botega 11; RENTON: East Valley 13; RICHLAND: Metro 4, Uptown Triplex; SILVERDALE: Silverdale 4; SPOKANE: Eastside 2, Lincoln Heights 4, Newport Road 8, Northtown Mall 12, Spokane Valley 12; TUKWILA: Parkway Plaza 12; VANCOUVER: Cascade 16, Cinema 11, City Center 12, Vancouver Plaza 10.

WEST VIRGINIA

CARMIKE—BARBOURSVILLE: Huntington Mall 6; BLUEFIELD: Cinema 8; BRIDGEPORT: Meadowbrook 6; MORGANTOWN: Mall 8.

GREATER HUNTINGTON—CHARLESTON: Park Place Stadium 11; HUNTINGTON: Camelot 2, Cinema 4, Keith Albee 4.

HOYTS—MARTINSBURG: Martinsburg 10.

MARQUEE—BECKLEY: Showplace Cinemas 7; CHARLESTON: Southridge 12; LEWISBURG: Seneca 2; MT. HOPE: Crossroads 6, SUMMERSVILLE: Nicholas Showplace 4.

REGAL—PARKERSBURG: Towne Square 6; VIENNA: Grand Central Mall 12.

WISCONSIN

CARMIKE—EAU CLAIRE: Oakwood 10; LACROSSE: Valley 6; MADISON: University Square 4; SUPERIOR: Mariner 4.

CINEMA GRILL—WHITEFISH: Fox Bay Cinema Grill 3.

CINEMA ENTERTAINMENT—HUDSON: Hudson 9; RICE LAKE: Lake 7; SUPERIOR: Mariner Mall 8.

CINEMAGIC—MENOMONIE: CineMagic Stadium 7.

CINEMARK—KENOSHA: Tinseltown USA 14.

F & F/VALUE—DELAVAN: Delavan 2; FRANKLIN: Giant Drive-In 4; LAKE GENEVA: Geneva 4.

GENERAL CINEMA—WAUWATOSA: Mayfair Mall 18.

LANDMARK—MILWAUKEE: Downer 2, Orenital 3.

LAKES & RIVERS—SAINT CROIX FALLS: Falls 5.

MARCUS—APPLETON: Hollywood 11, Valley Fair 6; ASHWAUBENON: Stadium 4, Bay Park 16; BEAVER DAM: Wisconsin 4; BROOKFIELD: Tower 8, Westpoint 8; CEDARBURG: Rivoli; DELAFIELD: Hillside 14; GREEN BAY: Marc 8, LA CROSSE: Cinema 8, King 3; MADISON: Eastgate 16, Point 16, Westgate 3; MENOMONEE FALLS: Menomonee Falls 12, Main Street 5; MEQUON: North Shore 11: MILWAUKEE: Northtown 8, Prospect 3, Southgate 10; Southtown 4; MOSINEE: Cedar Creek 10; MONONA: South Towne 5; NEW BERLIN: Ridge 20; OAK CREEK: South Shore 16, Value Cinema Oak Creek 8; OSHKOSH: Cinema 10; RACINE: Regency Mall 8, Westgate 5; RIPON: Campus; SHEBOYGAN: Sheboygan 14; WAUSAU: Crossroads 4; WAUKESHA: Westown 8.

REGAL—APPLETON: College Avenue 16.

ROGERS—MARSHFIELD: Cinema 7; NEW LONDON: Grand 4; STEVENS POINT: Cinema 5; WAUPALA: Rosa Theatre 4; WISCONSIN RAPIDS: Cinema 7.

SILVER—GREEN BAY: East Town Mall 6; GREENFIELD: South 6; MADISON: East Towne 4, Market Square 5.

STAR CINEMAS—FITCHBURG: Star 14; JOHNSON CREEK: Star 12; MADISON: Hilldale 2; PRAIRIE DU CHIEN: Star Prairie Du Chein 6; REEDSBURG: Star 6; SPARTA: Star 6; WISCONSIN DELLS: Desert Star 10.

WILDWOOD—BELOIT: Luxury 10; JANESVILLE: Movies 10, Rock 9; PEWAUKEE: Capitol 11.

WYOMING

CARMIKE—CHEYENNE: Cole Square 3, Frontier 6.

TRANS-LUX—LARAMIE: Fox Theatre 4.

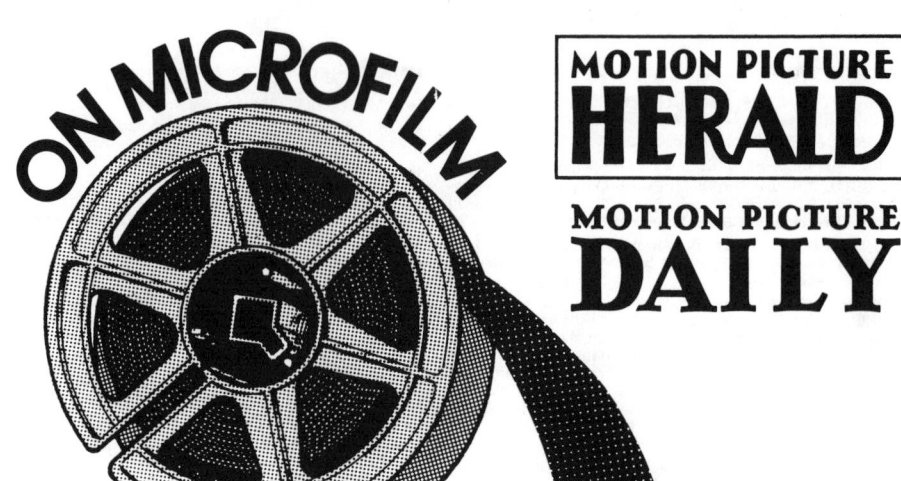

Circuit Theatres in the Top 50 U.S. Markets

Listed are national circuit theatres and major regional circuit theatres in the 50 largest U.S. metropolitan markets. The hierarchy used to sort this list is as follows: Market size then alphabetically by circuit name, state (for markets including cities in more than one state), municipality and theatre name. Smaller regional circuits, independent theatres and major national circuits with only one theatre in a market have been excluded. Market regions are determined by broadcast coverage of major television, radio and cable stations and distribution of major newspapers (designated market areas). For futher market information, please see the DMA codes in the Circuit Theatres section of this book.

The top 50 U.S. markets, in order of decreasing size:

1. New York
2. Los Angeles
3. Chicago
4. Philadelphia
5. San Francisco/Oakland/San Jose
6. Boston
7. Dallas/Ft. Worth
8. Washington, DC
9. Detroit
10. Atlanta
11. Houston
12. Seattle/Tacoma
13. Tampa/St. Petersburg/Sarasota
14. Minneapolis/St. Paul
15. Cleveland
16. Miami/Ft. Lauderdale
17. Phoenix
18. Denver
19. Sacramento/Stockton/Modesto
20. Pittsburgh
21. Orlando/Daytona Beach/Melbourne
22. St. Louis
23. Portland, OR
24. Baltimore
25. San Diego
26. Indianapolis
27. Hartford & New Haven
28. Charlotte
29. Raleigh/Durham
30. Kansas City
31. Nashville
32. Cincinnati
33. Milwaukee
34. Columbus, OH
35. Salt Lake City
36. San Antonio
37. Birmingham
38. Memphis
39. Norfolk/Virginia Beach
40. New Orleans
41. West Palm Beach/Ft. Pierce
42. Buffalo
43. Oklahoma City
44. Greensboro/High Point/Winston Salem
45. Louisville
46. Albuquerque/Sante Fe
47. Las Vegas
48. Jacksonville
49. Dayton
50. Austin

NEW YORK CITY

AMC

Empire 25	New York	NY
Rockaway 7/12	Rockaway	NJ

CITY CINEMAS

Angelika Film Center	New York City	NY
Cinema 1, 2 & 3	New York City	NY
East 86th St. Cinemas	New York City	NY
Eastside Playhouse	New York City	NY
Murray Hill Cinemas	New York City	NY
Sutton 1 & 2	New York City	NY
Village East Cinemas	New York City	NY

CLEARVIEW

Greenwich 1 & 2	Greenwich	CT
Middlebrook Cinema 10	Asbury Park	NJ
Bergenfield Cinema Quad	Bergenfield	NJ
Bernardsville Cinema 3	Bernardsville	NJ
Caldwell Cinema 4	Caldwell	NJ
Cinema 23 Fiveplex	Cedar Grove	NJ
Chester Cinema 6	Chester	NJ
Allwood Cinema 6	Clifton	NJ
Closter Cinema 4	Closter	NJ
Edison Cinema	Edison	NJ
Emerson Cinema Quad	Emerson	NJ
Mansfield Cinema 15	Hackettstown	NJ
Kinnelon 11	Kinnelon	NJ
Colony 3 Theatre	Livingston	NJ
Madison Cinema 4	Madison	NJ
Strathmore Cinema 4	Matawan	NJ
Millburn Cinemas	Millburn	NJ
Clairidge Cinemas	Montclair	NJ
Screening Zone	Montclair	NJ
Headquarters 10 Theatres	Morristown	NJ
Parsippany 12 Cinema	Parsippany	NJ
Red Bank Cinemas	Red Bank	NJ
Warner Quad	Ridgewood	NJ
Succasunna 10 Cinema	Succasunna	NJ
Beacon Hill 5	Summit	NJ
Tenafly Cinema	Tenafly	NJ
Bellevue 3	Upper Montclair	NJ
Washington Township	Washington Township	NJ
Wayne Preakness	Wayne	NJ
West Milford Theatre	West Milford	NJ
Woodbridge Cinemas	Woodbridge	NJ
Babylon Cinemas	Babylon	NY
Grand Ave.	Baldwin	NY
Bedford Playhouse	Bedford	NY
Bronxville 3	Bronxville	NY
Cobble Hill Cinema	Brooklyn	NY
Franklin Square Theatre	Franklin Square	NY
Squire Cinemas	Great Neck	NY
Larchmont Playhouse	Larchmont	NY
Mamaroneck Playhouse 4	Mamaroneck	NY
Manhasset 3	Manhasset	NY
Mt Kisco Cinemas	Mount Kisco	NY
Cinema 304	New City	NY
New City Cinema 6	New City	NY
Herricks Twin	New Hyde Park	NY
Central Plaza 4	New York	NY
59th St Cinema	New York	NY
62nd & Broadway	New York	NY
Beekman	New York	NY
Chelsea	New York	NY
Chelsea West	New York	NY
First & 62nd	New York	NY
Metro Twin	New York	NY
Olympia	New York	NY
Park & 86th St.	New York	NY
Ziegfeld	New York	NY
Waverly Twin	New York	NY
Port Washington Cinemas	Port Washington	NY
Soundview 6	Port Washington	NY
Roslyn Theatre	Roslyn	NY
Rye Ridge Cinema	Rye	NY
Cinema 100 Twin	White Plains	NY

CROWN

Plaza	Greenwich	CT
Royale 6	Norwalk	CT
Regent	South Norwalk	CT
Landmark Square 9	Stamford	CT
Majestic 6	Stamford	CT
Marquis 16 Theater	Trumbull	CT

GENERAL CINEMA

Bridgewater Commons 7	Bridgewater	NJ
Clifton Commons 16	Clifton	NJ
Rutgers Cinemas	Somerset	NJ
Essex Green Cinema	West Orange	NJ
Bay Plaza Cinemas	Bronx	NY

HOYTS

New Canaan Playhouse 2	New Canaan	CT
Wilton 4	Wilton	CT
Beach Haven 4	Beach Haven	NJ
Colonial 4	Beach Haven	NJ
Colony 4 Brant Beach	Beach Haven	NJ
Fishkill 10	Fishkill	NY
Hudson Valley Mall	Kingston	NY
Galleria 12	Poughkeepsie	NY

LOEWS CINEPLEX

Danbury 10	Danbury	CT
Community 1 & 2	Fairfield	CT
Cinema Centre 5	Brick	NJ
Brick Plaza	Bricktown	NJ
East Hanover 12	East Hanover	NJ
Monmouth Mall 15	Eatontown	NJ
Showboat Quad 4	Edgewater	NJ
Menlo Park 12	Edison	NJ
Freehold Metroplex 14	Freehold	NJ
Newport Centre 11	Jersey City	NJ
Mountain Side 10	Mountainside	NJ
New Brunswick	New Brunswick	NJ
Newark Metroplex 6	Newark	NJ
Paramus Route 4	Paramus	NJ
Route Seventeen 3	Paramus	NJ
Interstate 2	Ramsey	NJ
Ridgefield Park 12	Ridgefield Park	NJ
Meadow Six 6	Secaucus	NJ
Plaza Eight 8	Secaucus	NJ
Seacourt 10	Toms River	NJ
Wayne	Wayne	NJ
Bay Terrace 6	Bayside	NY
Alpine 7	Brooklyn	NY
Fortway 5	Brooklyn	NY
Kings Plaza 6	Brooklyn	NY
Kingsway 5	Brooklyn	NY
Elmwood 4	Elmhurst	NY
City Cinema	Fresh Meadows	NY
Fresh Meadows 5	Fresh Meadows	NY
Roosevelt Field 8	Garden City	NY
Glen Cove 6	Glen Cove	NY
Shore 8	Huntington	NY
Whitman 1	Huntington Station	NY
Smith Haven Mall 4	Lake Grove	NY
Nassau Metroplex 10	Levittown	NY
Mattituck 8	Mattituck	NY
Galleria Metroplex 10	Middletown	NY
Nanuet 5	Nanuet	NY
Coronet Cinemas	New York	NY
Astor Plaza 1	New York	NY
84th St. Theatre 6	New York	NY
New York Twin 2	New York	NY
Orpheum 7	New York	NY
72nd St. East 1	New York	NY
Village Theatre 7	New York	NY
19th St. East 6	New York	NY
Lincoln Square 12	New York	NY
State Theatre 4	New York	NY
Kips Bay Theatre	New York	NY
Magic Johnson Theatre - Harlem	New York	NY
42nd St. E Walk	New York	NY
Worldwide Cinemas	New York	NY
Fantasy 5	Rockville Center	NY
Rockville Centre 2	Rockville Center	NY
Stony Brook 15	Stony Brook	NY
Hamptons Arts 2	West Hampton	NY
Loews Palisades Center	West Nyack	NY
Rosevelt Raceway 10	Westbury	NY

MINI

Movieplex Carmel	Carmel	NY

NATIONAL AMUSEMENTS

S/C Bridgeport @ Black Rock	Bridgeport	CT
S/C Cinemas @ Black Rock	Bridgeport	CT
Fairfield Cinemas	Fairfield	CT
Edgewater Multiplex Cinemas	Edgewater	NJ
Hazlet Multiplex	Hazlet	NJ
All-Jersey Multiplex	Newark	NJ
Amboy Multiplex	Sayreville	NJ
Concourse Plaza Multiplex	Bronx	NY
Whitestone Multiplex	Bronx	NY
Linden Blvd. Multiplex	Brooklyn	NY
Commack Multiplex	Commack	NY
Greenburgh Multiplex Cinemas	Elmsford	NY
Farmingdale Multiplex	Farmingdale	NY
All Westchester Saw Mill Multi	Hawthorne	NY
Broadway Multiplex	Hicksville	NY
Brookhaven Multiplex	Medford	NY
Green Acres Cinemas	Valley Stream	NY
Sunrise Multiplex	Valley Stream	NY
College Point Multiplex	Whitestone	NY
Cross County Multiplex	Yonkers	NY

REGAL

Hudson Mall 7	Jersey City	NJ
Marlboro Cinema 8	Morganville	NJ
Columbia Park	North Bergen	NJ
Commerce Center 18	North Brunswick	NJ
Pohatcong 12	Phillipsburgh	NJ
Hadley Theatre 16	South Plainfield	NJ
Kaufman Astoria Cinema 14	Astoria	NY
Court St. 12	Brooklyn	NY
New Roc City 18	New Rochelle	NY
New Roc City IMAX	New Rochelle	NY
Battery Park City 16	New York	NY
Ronkonkoma Cinema 9	Ronkonkoma	NY
Staten Island 16	Staten Island	NY

SILVER CINEMAS

South Hills 8	Poughkeepsie	NY

UNITED ARTISTS

UA Darien Playhouse	Darien	CT
Bayside 4 Theatre	Bayside	NY
Marboro Theatre 4	Brooklyn	NY
Movies @ Sheepshead Bay	Brooklyn	NY
Coram 12 Theatre	Coram	NY
Movieworld Douglston	Douglaston	NY
Easthampton Cinema	East Hampton	NY
Meadowbrook Theatre	East Meadow	NY
UA Farmingdale	Farmingdale	NY
Brandon Cinemas	Forest Hills	NY
Midway 9 Cinemas	Forest Hills	NY
UA Hampton Bays	Hampton Bays	NY
Astoria 6 Theatre	Long Island City	NY
Lynbrook 6 Theatre	Lynbrook	NY
Gemini Theatre	New York	NY
UA Cinema East	New York	NY
United Artist Union Square	New York	NY
Crossbay 1 Theatre	Ozone Park	NY
Crossbay Theatre	Ozone Park	NY
Movies @ Patchogue	Patchogue	NY
UA Smithtown	Smithtown	NY
Southampton Theatre	Southampton	NY
Movies @ Staten Island	Staten Island	NY
UA Hylan Plaza	Staten Island	NY
UA Westbury	Westbury	NY
UA Cinema 150	Woodbury	NY
Movieland Yonkers 6	Yonkers	NY
Movies @ Jefferson Valley	Yorktown Heights	NY

LOS ANGELES

AMC

Burbank 14	Burbank	CA
Media Center 8	Burbank	CA
Media Center North 6	Burbank	CA
Chino Town Square 10	Chino	CA
Covina 30	Covina	CA
Fullerton 20	Fullerton	CA
Puente Hills 20	Industry	CA
Marina Pacifica 12	Long Beach	CA
Pine Square 16	Long Beach	CA
Century 14	Los Angeles	CA
Montebello 10	Montebello	CA
Norwalk 20	Norwalk	CA
Ontario Mills 30	Ontario	CA
30 At The Block	Orange	CA
Old Pasadena 8	Pasadena	CA
Main Place 6	Santa Ana	CA
Santa Monica 7	Santa Monica	CA
Rolling Hills 20	Torrance	CA
Promenade 16	Woodland Hills	CA

CENTURY

No. Hollywood 8	North Hollywood	CA
Stadium Promenade 25	Orange	CA
Downtown 10	Ventura	CA
Ventura 16	Ventura	CA

CINEMA GRILL

Terrace Cinema Grill	Palos Verdes	CA

CINEMARK

Cinemark Movies 8- Chino	Chino	CA
Cinemark 22	Lancaster	CA
Movies 1-4	Lancaster	CA
Movies 12 Lancaster	Lancaster	CA
Movies 10	Palmdale	CA
Movies 8 Palmdale	Palmdale	CA
Cinemark Victor Valley 10	Victorville	CA
Movies 10	Victorville	CA

CINEMASTAR LUXURY

Perris Plaza 10	Perris	CA
Mission Grove 18	Riverside	CA
University Village 10	Riverside	CA
Empire 20	San Bernardino	CA

DEANZA LAND & LEISURE CORP.

Van Buren Blvd.	Arlington	CA
Mission Quad	Montclair	CA
Rubidoux Triple	Riverside	CA

EDWARDS

Alhambra Place 5	Alhambra	CA
Atlantic Palace 10	Alhambra	CA
Aliso Viejo Stadium 20	Aliso Viejo	CA
Anaheim Hills 14	Anaheim Hills	CA
Foothill Center 10	Azusa	CA
Brea Plaza 5	Brea	CA
Brea Stadium 22	Brea	CA
Grand Palace Stadium Calabasas	Calabasas	CA
Camarillo 12	Camarillo	CA
Cerritos 10	Cerritos	CA
Corona 15	Corona	CA
Cinema Center 4	Costa Mesa	CA
Metro Pointe 12	Costa Mesa	CA
South Coast Village 3	Costa Mesa	CA
Town Center 4	Costa Mesa	CA
Triangle Square 8	Costa Mesa	CA
El Monte 8	El Monte	CA
El Toro 5	El Toro	CA
Charter Center 5	Huntington Beach	CA
Pierside 6	Huntington Beach	CA
Irvine Spectrum 21 + IMAX	Irvine	CA
Marketplace Stadium 10	Irvine	CA
Park Place 10	Irvine	CA
University Town Center 6	Irvine	CA
Westpark 8	Irvine	CA
Woodbridge 5	Irvine	CA
La Verne 12	La Verne	CA
South Coast Laguna 2	Laguna Beach	CA
Ocean Ranch 7	Laguna Niguel	CA
Rancho Niguel 8	Laguna Niguel	CA
Long Beach 26	Long Beach	CA
Kaleidoscope Stadium 10	Mission Viejo	CA
Trabuco Hills	Mission Viejo	CA
Towngate 8	Moreno Valley	CA
Island 7	Newport Beach	CA
Lido	Newport Beach	CA
Newport 6	Newport Beach	CA
Ontario Mountain Village 14	Ontario	CA
Ontario Palace 22 + IMAX	Ontario	CA
Jurupa Stadium 14	Riverside	CA
Rancho Santa Margarita	Rancho S. Margarita	CA
Hutton Center 8	Santa Ana	CA
Canyon Country 10	Santa Clarita	CA
Valencia IMAX	Santa Clarita	CA
Valencia Stadium 21	Santa Clarita	CA
Simi Valley Plaza 10	Simi Valley	CA
El Paso Stadium Cinema	South Gate	CA
Temecula Stadium 15	Temecula	CA
Temple 4	Temple City	CA
Tustin Marketplace	Tustin	CA
West Covina 18	West Covina	CA
Westminster 10	Westminster	CA
Westminster Mall 4	Westminster	CA

GENERAL CINEMA

Beverly Connection	Beverly Hills	CA
Glendale Central Cinema 5	Glendale	CA
Hollywood Galaxy	Hollywood	CA
Galleria at South Bay	Redondo Beach	CA
Redondo Cinema 3	Redondo Beach	CA
Sherman Oaks Cinema	Sherman Oaks	CA
Avco Cinema	Westwood	CA

KRIKORIAN PREMIERE

Downey	Downey	CA
Manrovia Cinema 12	Monrovia	CA
Redlands	Redlands	CA
San Clemente	San Clemente	CA

LOEWS CINEPLEX

Beverly Center 13	Los Angeles	CA
Century Plaza Cinemas 4	Los Angeles	CA
Fairfax Cinemas 3	Los Angeles	CA
Magic Johnson Theatre	Los Angeles	CA
Marina	Marina Del Rey	CA
Broadway Cinemas 4	Santa Monica	CA

LAEMMLE

Music Hall	Beverly Hills	CA
Paseo Camarillo	Camarillo	CA
Town Center 5	Encino	CA
Regent Showcase	Hollywood	CA
Sunset 5	Los Angeles	CA
Grande	Los Angeles	CA
Royal	Los Angeles	CA
Colorado	Pasadena	CA
Playhouse 7	Pasadena	CA
Monica 4	Santa Monica	CA
Westlake Village Twin	Westlake Village	CA

LANDMARK

Fine Arts	Beverly Hills	CA
Nuart Theatre	Los Angeles	CA
Westside Pavilion Cinemas	Los Angeles	CA
NuWilshire Theatre	Santa Monica	CA
Rialto Theatre	South Pasadena	CA

METROPOLITIAN

Park Theatre	Huntington Park	CA
Campus Theatre	Los Angeles	CA
Orpheum Theatre	Los Angeles	CA
Palace Theatre	Los Angeles	CA
Teatro Fiesta	Santa Ana	CA

PACIFIC

Winnetka	Chatsworth	CA
Commerce 14	City of Commerce	CA
Vineland Drive-In 4	City of Industry	CA
Beach Cities Stadium 16	El Segundo	CA
Warners 2	Huntington Park	CA
Lakewood Center South 9	Lakewood	CA
Lakewood Center Stadium 16	Lakewood	CA
Regency 8	Lakewood	CA
Pacific Crest	Los Angeles	CA
Manhattan Village	Manhattan Beach	CA
Northridge Cinemas	Northridge	CA
Northridge Fashion Center	Northridge	CA
Ontario 10	Ontario	CA
Hastings Pacific	Pasadena	CA
Hastings Ranch	Pasadena	CA
Inland Center 5	San Bernardino	CA

REGAL

Diamond Bar Cinema 8	Diamond Bar	CA
Foothill Towne Center 22	Foothill Ranch	CA
Garden Grove 16	Garden Grove	CA
Hemet Cinema 12	Hemet	CA
La Habra 16	La Habra	CA
Lake Elsinore Cinema 8	Lake Elsinore	CA
Moorpark 8	Moorpark	CA
Terrace Cinema 6	Rancho Palos	CA
The Ave.. 13	Rolling Hills Estates	CA
Del Rosa 8	San Bernardino	CA
Civic Center Plaza 16	Simi Valley	CA
Whittwood Cinema 10	Whittier	CA

SILVER CINEMAS

SS Cinema - Norwalk S.C.	Norwalk	CA
SS Cinema - Rossmoor Cntr.	Seal Beach	CA

SOCAL

Cinemapolis 13 Cinemas	Anaheim	CA
Blue Jay	Blue Jay	CA
12 Spectrum	Chino	CA
Laguna Hills Mall Cinema	Laguna Hills	CA
17 at California Oaks	Murrieta	CA
10 at Tower Plaza	Temecula	CA
Temeku Cinema	Temecula	CA

UNITED ARTISTS

Mission Oaks	Camarillo	CA
Los Cerritos	Cerritos	CA
La Canada	La Canada	CA
Movies Long Beach	Long Beach	CA
Coronet	Los Angeles	CA
6 Marina Del Rey	Marina Del Rey	CA
Movies 6	N. Hollywood	CA
Movies 6	Pasadena	CA
6 Riverside	Riverside	CA
5 Thousand Oaks	Thousand Oaks	CA

WALLACE

New Barstow Cinema 6	Barstow	CA
New Malibu Cinema 2	Malibu	CA
Santa Paula Cinema 7	Santa Paula	CA

W.F. CINEMA HOLDINGS

Agoura Hills 8	Agoura Hills	CA
6 Puente Hills 6	City of Industry	CA
Culver Plaza 6	Culver City	CA
Glendale Exchange 10	Glendale	CA
Glendale Marketplace 4	Glendale	CA
9 Granada Hills	Granada Hills	CA
Chinese 1	Hollywood	CA
Bruin 1	Los Angeles	CA
Festival Westwood 1	Los Angeles	CA
National 1	Los Angeles	CA
Plaza 1	Los Angeles	CA
Regent 1	Los Angeles	CA
Village 1	Los Angeles	CA
Westwood Quad	Los Angeles	CA
6 Huntington Oaks	Monrovia	CA
Criterion 6	Santa Monica	CA
6 Simi Valley	Simi Valley	CA
9 Valley West	Tarzana	CA
9 Janss Marketplace	Thousand Oaks	CA
Del Amo 9	Torrance	CA
10 Valencia	Valencia	CA
Plant 16	Van Nuys	CA
6 Buenaventura	Ventura	CA
Westlake Village 8	Westlake Village	CA

CHICAGO

AMC

South Barrington 30	South Barrington	IL
Cantera 30	Warrenville	IL

CINEMARK

Movies 10	Bourbonnais	IL
Movies 10	Joliet	IL
Movies 8	Joliet	IL
Cinemark 10	Melrose Park	IL
Tinseltown	North Aurora	IL
Cinemark at Seven Bridges	Woodridge	IL

CLASSIC

Cinema 12 Theatre	Carpentersville	IL
Tivoli Theatre	Downers Grove	IL
Casino Cinema	Elgin	IL
Elk Grove Theatre	Elk Grove	IL
York Theatre	Elmhurst	IL
Fox Lake Theatre	Fox Lake	IL
Tradewinds Theatre	Hanover Park	IL
Barrington Square Theatre	Hoffman Estates	IL
Meadowview Theatre	Kankakee	IL
Paramount	Kankakee	IL
Ogden 6 Theatre	Naperville	IL
Lake Theatre	Oak Park	IL
Park Forest Theatre	Park Forest	IL
Arcada Theatre	St. Charles	IL
Foxfield Theatre	St. Charles	IL
Woodstock Theatre	Woodstock	IL

F & F/VALUE

Arlington Theatres	Arlington Heights	IL
Harlem Carners Theatre	Bridgeview	IL
Buffalo Grove Theatres	Buffalo Grove	IL
Davis Art Theatre	Chicago	IL
Davis Theatre	Chicago	IL
Morton Grove Theatre	Morton Grove	IL
Bremen Theatres	Tinley Park	IL

GENERAL CINEMA

City North 14	Chicago	IL
Ford City 14	Chicago	IL
Deerbrook	Deerfield	IL
Premium Cinema at the Yorktown	Lombard	IL
Yorktown	Lombard	IL
Lincoln Mall	Matteson	IL
Randhurst	Mt. Prospect	IL
Northbrook	Northbrook	IL
Lakehurst	Waukegan	IL
Southlake Mall Cinema	Merrillville	IN
County Seat Cinema 1-6	Valpariaiso	IN

GKC

Campus Cinema	Dekalb	IL
Market Square	Dekalb	IL
Orpheum Cinema	Morris	IL
Roxy Cinema	Ottawa	IL
Peru Mall 8 Cinema	Peru	IL
Crescent Twin	Pontiac	IL

GOODRICH QUALITY

Randall 16	Batavia	IL
Kendall 10	Oswego	IL
Portage 9	Portage	IN

KERASOTES

Showplace 12	Bolingbrook	IL
Lake in the Hills 12	Lake in the Hills	IL
Showplace 8	Vernon Hills	IL
LaPorte Cinema	LaPorte	IN
Dunes Plaza Cinema	Michigan City	IN
Marquette Cinema	Michigan City	IN
Showplace 16	Schererville	IN

LOEWS CINEPLEX

Ridge Plaza 8	Arlington Hts.	IL
Bloomingdale 6	Bloomingdale	IL
Stratford 4	Bloomingdale	IL
River Oaks 1-6	Calumet City	IL
River Oaks 7-8 2	Calumet City	IL
River Oaks 9-10 2	Calumet City	IL
900 North Michigan 2	Chicago	IL
McClurg Court 3	Chicago	IL
Lincoln Village 1-6	Chicago	IL
Lincoln Village 7-9 3	Chicago	IL

Fine Arts 4	Chicago	IL
Pipers Alley 4	Chicago	IL
Esquire 6	Chicago	IL
Webster Place 8	Chicago	IL
600 North Michigan	Chicago	IL
Lawndale 10	Chicago	IL
Chatham 14	Chicago	IL
Commons 4	Chicago Ridge	IL
Chicago Ridge 6	Chicago Ridge	IL
62nd & Western	Chicago	IL
Crestwood	Crestwood	IL
Grove Cinemas 6	Downers Grove	IL
Evanston 5	Evanston	IL
Hillside Square 6	Hillside	IL
Hillside Mall 3	Hillside	IL
Quarry 14	Hodgkins	IL
River Run 8	Lansing	IL
Westridge Court 8	Naperville	IL
Golf Mill 3	Niles	IL
Golf Glen 6	Niles	IL
Norridge 10	Norridge	IL
North Riverside 6	North Riverside	IL
Oakbrook 4	Oak Brook	IL
Oakbrook 3	Oakbrook	IL
Orland Square 1-6	Orland Park	IL
Orland Square 7-10 4	Orland Park	IL
Rolling Meadows 9	Rolling Meadows	IL
Streets of Woodfield	Schaumburg	IL
Gardens 7	Skokie	IL
Streamwood 14	Streamwood	IL
Rivertree Court 8	Vernon Hills	IL
Rice Lake Square 10	Wheaton	IL
Woodridge 18	Woodridge	IL
Merrillville 10	Merrillville	IN

MARCUS

Addison	Addison	IL
Chicago Heights	Chicago Heights	IL
Elgin Fox Theatre	Elgin	IL
Gurnee Cinema	Gurnee	IL
Orland Park Cinemas	Orland Park	IL

REGAL

Showplace 16	Crystal Lake	IL
Lake Zurich 12	Lake Zurich	IL
Lincolnshire 20	Lincolnshire	IL
Round Lake Beach 18	Round Lake Beach	IL
Charlestowne Mall 18	St. Charles	IL

SILVER CINEMAS

Renaissance Place	Highland Park	IL
SS Cinema - Joliet	Joliet	IL

PHILADELPHIA

AMC

Millside 4	Delran	NJ
Deptford 8	Deptford	NJ
Hamilton 24	Hamilton	NJ
Marlton 8	Marlton	NJ
Tilghman 8	Allentown	PA
Neshaminy 24	Bensalem	PA
Woodhaven 10	Bensalem	PA
Granite Run 8	Media	PA
Andorra 8	Philadelphia	PA
Orleans 8	Philadelphia	PA
309 Cinema 9	Spring House	PA
Marple 10	Springfield	PA
Painters Crossing 9	West Chester	PA

CARMIKE

Carmike 14	Dover	DE
Carmike 16	Allentown	PA
Carmike Coventry 8	Pottstown	PA
Carmike Fairgrounds 5	Reading	PA
Carmike Wyomissing 8	Reading	PA

CINEMARK

Movies 10	Wilmington	DE
Movies 16	Somerdale	NJ

CLEARVIEW

Bala Theater	Bala Cynwyd	PA
Anthony Wayne 5	Wayne	PA

GENERAL CINEMA

Christiana Mall	Newark	DE
Deptford Mall 6	Deptford	NJ
Franklin Mills 14	Philadelphia	PA
Plymouth Meeting 12	Plymouth Meeting	PA
Lehigh Valley Cinema 8	Whitehall	PA

HOYTS

Moorlyn 4	Ocean City	NJ
Pennsauken 10	Pennsauken	NJ
Saucon Valley 10	Bethlehem	PA

LOEWS CINEPLEX

Cherry Hill Theatre	Cherry Hill	NJ

MINI

Diamond State Drive-In	Felton	DE

NATIONAL AMUSEMENTS

Atco Multiplex	Atco	NJ

R/C

Fox East	Reading	PA

REGAL

Peoples Plaza Cinema 17	Newark	DE
Brandywine Town Center 16	Wilmington	DE
Burlington 20	Burlington	NJ
Town Center Plaza 15	East Windsor	NJ
Cross Keys Cinema 12	Turnersville	NJ
Cumberland Mall 14	Vineland	NJ
Plymouth Meeting 10	Conshohocken	PA
Downingtown Cinema 16	Downingtown	PA
Barn Plaza 14	Doylestown	PA
Northampton Cinema 11	Easton	PA
Edgmont Square 10	Edgmont	PA
Huntington Valley 14	Huntington Valley	PA
Lionville Cinemas 12	Lionville	PA
Marketplace @ Oaks 24	Oaks	PA
Richland Crossing 12	Quakertown	PA
Warrington Crossing 22	Warrington	PA

UNITED ARTISTS

UA Moorestown	Moorestown	NJ
Eric Pennsauken Theatre	Pennsauken	NJ
Movies @ Marketfair	Princeton	NJ
UA Washington Township	Sewell	NJ
UA East Whiteland	E.Whiteland	PA
Eric Macdade Mall	Holmes	PA
UA King of Prussia	King of Prussia	PA
UA Oxford Valley	Langhorne	PA
Main St.	Manayuk	PA
UA Montgomeryville	Montgomeryville	PA
Riverview Plaza Theatre	Philadelphia	PA
Sameric IV Theatre	Philadelphia	PA
UA @ Cheltenham Square	Philadelphia	PA
UA Grant Plaza	Philadelphia	PA
UA Theatres 69th St.	Upper Darby	PA

SAN FRANCISCO/OAKLAND/SAN JOSE

AMC

Milpitas 10	Milpitas	CA
Kabuki 8	San Francisco	CA
Van Ness 14	San Francisco	CA
Saratoga 14	San Jose	CA
Mercado 20	Santa Clara	CA
Sunnyvale Six Theatres	Sunnyvale	CA
Vallejo Plaza Six	Vallejo	CA

CENTURY

Hyatt Cinema 3	Burlingame	CA
Solano Drive-Ins 2	Concord	CA
Cinedome Fremont 8	Fremont	CA
Larkspur	Larkspur	CA
Cinema 16	Mountain View	CA
Cinedome Napa 8	Napa	CA
Cinedome Newark 7	Newark	CA
Pinole 10	Pinole	CA
Pleasant Hill	Pleasant Hill	CA
Park Redwood 12	Redwood City	CA
Plaza 10	S. San Francisco	CA
Cinema 21 San Francisco	San Francisco	CA
Empire Cinema 3	San Francisco	CA
Presidio 1	San Francisco	CA
Capitol Drive-In	San Jose	CA
Century 21	San Jose	CA
Century 22	San Jose	CA
Century 23	San Jose	CA
Century 24	San Jose	CA
Century 25	San Jose	CA
Berryessa	San Jose	CA
Capitol 16	San Jose	CA
25 Union City	Union City	CA
Cinedome Vallejo 8	Vallejo	CA

CINEMARK

Blackhawk	Danville	CA

GENERAL CINEMA

Dublin Place 6 Cinemas	Dublin	CA

LANDMARK

Albany Twin	Albany	CA
Act 1 and 2	Berkeley	CA
California Theatre	Berkeley	CA
Shattuck Cinemas	Berkeley	CA

U.C. Theatre	Berkeley	CA
Guild Theatre	Menlo Park	CA
Park Theatre	Menlo Park	CA
Piedmont Theatre	Oakland	CA
Aquarius Theatre	Palo Alto	CA
Palo Alto Square Theatre	Palo Alto	CA
Bridge Theatre	San Francisco	CA
Clay Theatre	San Francisco	CA
Embarcadero Center Cinemas	San Francisco	CA
Lumiere Theatre	San Francisco	CA
Opera Plaza Cinema	San Francisco	CA

LOEWS CINEPLEX

Metreon	San Francisco	CA

METROPOLITIAN

Vine Twin Theatre	Livermore	CA

PACIFIC

Cinema Corte Madera	Corte Madera	CA
Sequoia	Mill Valley	CA
Rowland Plaza	Novato	CA
Petaluma	Petaluma	CA
Rohnert Park 16	Rohnert Park	CA
Northgate	San Rafael	CA
Regency	San Rafael	CA
Marin	Sausalito	CA

REGAL

Deer Valley 16	Antioch	CA
Hacienda Crossing	Dublin	CA
Hacienda Crossing IMAX	Dublin	CA
Galaxy 8	Pleasanton	CA

SIGNATURE

Contra Costa Cinemas 5	Martinez	CA
Crow Canyon Cinemas 6	San Ramon	CA
Ukiah 6	Ukiah	CA
Festival Cinemas 5	Walnut Creek	CA

UNITED ARTISTS

UA 7 Berkeley	Berkeley	CA
Cinema 6	Colma	CA
Movies @ Emery Bay	Emeryville	CA
Hayward Cinema 6	Hayward	CA
Alexandria Theatre	San Francisco	CA
Metro Theatre	San Francisco	CA
UA Coronet Theatre	San Francisco	CA
UA Galaxy 4	San Francisco	CA
UA Twin Stonestown	San Francisco	CA
Vogue Theatre	San Francisco	CA
Santa Rosa Theatre	Santa Rosa	CA
UA 5 Santa Rosa	Santa Rosa	CA

BOSTON

GENERAL CINEMA

Fenway Theatre	Boston	MA
Braintree	Braintree	MA
Burlington 10	Burlington	MA
Chestnut Hill	Chestnut Hill	MA
Framingham 16	Framingham	MA
Premium Cinema at Framingham	Framingham	MA
Tyngsboro	Tyngsboro	MA

HOYTS

Acton 4	Acton	MA
Bellingham Cinema 14	Bellingham	MA
Solomon Pond 15, Berlin	Berlin	MA
Westgate Theatre	Brockton	MA
Buzzards Bay Theatre	Buzzards Bay	MA
East Bridgewater	East Bridgewater	MA
Harwich 6	East Harwich	MA
Falmouth 6	Falmouth	MA
Airport 8	Hyannis	MA
Cape Cod Mall Cinema 12	Hyannis	MA
Independence Mall 14	Kingston	MA
Mashpee 6	Mashpee	MA
Nickelodeon Cinema	North Falmouth	MA
North Weymouth	North Weymouth	MA
Salisbury 6	Salibury	MA
Sharon 8	Sharon	MA
South Dennis 12	South Dennis	MA
Westborough 12	Westborough	MA
Bedford Mall 7	Bedford	NH
Concord 10	Concord	NH
Gilford 8	Gilford	NH
Hooksett 8	Hooksett	NH
Key 6	Keene	NH
Manchester 9	Manchester	NH
Nashua Mall 4	Nashua	NH
Newington 12	Newington	NH
Portsmouth 5	Portsmouth	NH
Dover	Somersworth	NH
Tri City Quad	Somersworth	NH

LANDMARK

Kendall Square Cinema	Cambridge	MA
Embassy Cinema	Waltham	MA

LOEWS CINEPLEX

Copley Place 11	Boston	MA
Nickelodeon 5	Boston	MA
Cheri 4	Boston	MA
Harvard Square 5	Cambridge	MA
Fresh Pond 10	Cambridge	MA
Liberty Tree Mall	Danvers	MA
Leominster 1-12	Leominster	MA
Natick 6	Natick	MA
Assembly Sq. 12	Somerville	MA
Merrimack 5	Concord	NH

MINI

Gourcester Cinema	Gloucester	MA
Route 1	N. Attelboro	MA
Island	Oaks Bluff	MA
Strand	Oaks Bluff	MA
New Art Provincetown	Provincetown	MA
Cinemagic	Salisbury	MA
Capawock	Vineyard Haven	MA
Colonial	Laconia	NH
Weirs Drive-In	Laconia	NH

NATIONAL AMUSEMENTS

Allston Cinema	Allston	MA
Quincy	Boston	MA
Circle Cinemas	Brookline	MA
S/C Cinemas Dedham	Dedham	MA
S/C Cinemas Lawrence 7-14	Lawrence	MA
S/C Lawrence 1-6	Lawrence	MA
S/C Cinemas Lowell	Lowell	MA
S/C Cinemas Randolph	Randolph	MA
S/C Cinemas Revere	Revere	MA
White City Cinemas	Shrewsbury	MA
S/C Cinemas Woburn	Woburn	MA
Worcester North	Worcester	MA
Salem-Tri	Salem	NH

PATRIOT

Loring Hall	Hingham	MA
Cameo Theatre	S. Weymouth	MA
Museum Place	Salem	MA

SPINELLI

Barrington 6	Barrington	NH
Strand Theatre	Dover	NH
Merideth Cinema	Merideth	NH
Lilac Mall 4	Rochester	NH

DALLAS/FT. WORTH

AMC

Green Oaks 8	Arlington	TX
Glen Lakes 8	Dallas	TX
Grand 24	Dallas	TX
Hulen 10	Fort Worth	TX
Palace 9	Fort Worth	TX
Sundance West 11	Fort Worth	TX
Grapevine Mills 30	Grapevine	TX
Highland Park 4	Highland Park	TX
Mesquite 30	Mesquite	TX

CARMIKE

Cinema 5	Denton	TX
Rolling Hills 4	Greenville	TX

CINEMARK

Tinseltown	Arlington	TX
Cinema 6	Cleburne	TX
Cinema IV	Corsicana	TX
Cinemark 17	Dallas	TX
Hollywood USA	Garland	TX
Movies 16	Grand Prairie	TX
Tinseltown	Grapevine	TX
Movies 14	Lancaster	TX
Cinemark 8	Lewisville	TX
Movies 12	Lewisville	TX
Movies 14	McKinney	TX
Movies 8	N. Richland Hills	TX
Movies 8	Paris	TX
Cinemark 24	Plano	TX
Movies 10	Plano	TX
Tinseltown	Plano	TX
Rockwall 8	Rockwall	TX
Cinema 6	Stephenville	TX

GENERAL CINEMA

Arlington Park	Arlington	TX
Furneaux Creek	Carrollton	TX
Galleria	Dallas	TX
Irving Mall 14	Irving	TX

LANDMARK

Inwood Theatre	Dallas	TX

LOEWS CINEPLEX

Lincoln Square 10	Arlington	TX
20 & 287 6	Arlington	TX
Keystone	Dallas	TX
Cityplace 14	Dallas	TX
City View 8	Ft. Worth	TX
Preston Park 6	Plano	TX
Chisholm 5	Plano	TX

UNITED ARTISTS

UA Bowen 8 Theatre	Arlington	TX
UA Bedford 10 Theatre	Bedford	TX
Galaxy Theatre	Dallas	TX
UA Cine 1 & 2 Theatre	Dallas	TX
United Artists Theatre	Dallas	TX
UA Golden Triangle 4	Denton	TX
UA Golden Triangle 5	Denton	TX
Las Vegas Trail 8 Theatre	Fort Worth	TX
UA Eastchase	Fort Worth	TX
UA Fossil Creek	Fort Worth	TX
UA Hulen 10 Theatre	Fort Worth	TX
UA Northstar 8 Theatre	Garland	TX
UA Grand Prairie	Grand Prairie	TX
MacArthur Marketplace	Irving	TX
UA Lakepointe 10	Lewisville	TX

WALLACE

Movies Cinema 14	Burleson	TX
Medallion Cinema 5	Dallas	TX
Town Center Cinema 8	Fort Worth	TX
Movies Cinema 8	Grapevine	TX

WASHINGTON, DC

AMC

Union Station 9	Washington	DC
Academy 6	Greenbelt	MD
Academy 8	Greenbelt	MD
Country Club Mall 6	Lavale	MD
Rivertowne 12	Oxon Hill	MD
City Place 10	Silver Spring	MD
Courthouse Plaza 8	Arlington	VA
Skyline 12	Falls Church	VA
Potomac Mills 15	Woodbridge	VA

CARMIKE

Apple Blossom 6	Winchester	VA
Cinema Center 6	Winchester	VA

HOYTS

Bowie Crossing 14	Bowie	MD
Frederick 10	Frederick	MD
West Ridge 6	Frederick	MD
Martinsburg 10	Martinsburg	WV

LOEWS CINEPLEX

Janus 3	Washington	DC
Outer Circle	Washington	DC
Avalon 2	Washington	DC
Cinema 1	Washington	DC
Dupont 5	Washington	DC
Foundry 7	Washington	DC
Wisconsin Ave. Cinemas 6	Washington	DC
Uptown 1	Washington	DC
Inner Circle 3	Washington	DC
Center Park 8	Beltsville	MD
Montgomery Mall 3	Bethesda	MD
Rio 14	Gaithersburg	MD
Germantown 6	Germantown	MD
Lexington Park Six	Lexington Park	MD
Marlow 6	Marlow Heights	MD
White Flint 5	Rockville	MD
Waldorf South 5	Waldorf	MD
St. Charles Towne Center 9	Waldorf	MD
Wheaton Plaza 11	Wheaton	MD
Wheaton Plaza 4	Wheaton	MD
Pentagon City 6	Arlington	VA
Shirlington 7	Arlington	VA
Worldgate 9	Herndon	VA
Manassas Mall 7	Manassas	VA
Fairfax Square 8	Vienna	VA
Tacket's Mill 4	Woodbridge	VA

MARQUEE

Southpoint Cinemas	Fredericksburg	VA

NATIONAL AMUSEMENTS

Mt. Vernon Multiplex	Alexandria	VA
Centerville Multiplex	Centerville	VA
Lee Highway Multiplex	Merrifield	VA
Reston Multiplex	Reston	VA

R/C THEATRES

Westview 16	Frederick	MD
Frostburg Cinemas 3	Frostburg	MD
Hagerstown Cinemas 10	Hagerstown	MD
Long Meadow Cinemas	Hagerstown	MD
Valley Mall Movies 16	Hagerstown	MD
Culpeper Movies 4	Culpeper	VA

REGAL

Holiday Cinema 2	Frederick	MD
Rockville Center 13	Rockville	MD
Ballston Common 12	Arlington	VA
Fredericksburg 15	Fredericksburg	VA
Spotsylvania Mall 4	Fredericksburg	VA
Virginian 4	Fredericksburg	VA
Tally Ho 2	Leesburg	VA
Aquia 10	Stafford	VA
Countryside 20	Sterling	VA

UNITED ARTISTS

United Artists Theatre	Bethesda	MD
UA Fairfax Towne Center	Fairfax	VA

DETROIT

AMC

Bel-Air Centre 10	Detroit	MI
Eastland Mall 5	Harper Woods	MI
Laurel Park 10	Livonia	MI
Livonia 20	Livonia	MI
Wonderland 6	Livonia	MI
Abbey 8	Madison Heights	MI
Southfield City 12	Southfield	MI
Forum 30	Sterling Heights	MI
Sterling Center 10	Sterling Heights	MI

CINEMARK

Movies 16	Warren	MI

GKC

GKC Birchwood 10	Fort Gratiot	MI

GOODRICH

Quality 16	Ann Arbor	MI
Canton 6	Canton	MI
Novi Town Center 8	Novi	MI
Oxford 7	Oxford	MI
Krafft 8	Port Huron	MI

LANDMARK

Maple 3	Bloomfield	MI
Main Art Theatre	Royal Oak	MI

LOEKS STAR

Great Lakes Crossing	Auburn Hills	MI
Star Gratiot	Clinton Twp.	MI
Star Fairlane	Dearborn	MI
Star Lincoln Park	Lincoln Park	MI
Star John R	Madison Heights	MI
Star Rochester	Rochester Hills	MI
Star Southfield	Southfield	MI
Star Taylor	Taylor	MI

LOEWS CINEPLEX

Great Lakes	Auburn Hills	MI
Gratiot	Clinton Township	MI
Lincoln Park	Lincoln Park	MI
John R	Madison Heights	MI
Rochester Hills	Rochester Hills	MI
Southfield	Southfield	MI
Taylor	Taylor	MI

MJR

Allen Park Cinema	Allen Park	MI
Brighton Town Square Cinema	Brighton	MI
Chesterfield Crossing	Chesterfield	MI
Southgate Cinemas	Southgate	MI
Waterford Cinema	Waterford	MI

NATIONAL AMUSEMENTS

S/C Auburn Hills	Auburn Hills	MI
S/C Pontiac 1-5	Bloomfield Hills	MI
S/C Pontiac 6-12	Bloomfield Hills	MI
S/C Dearborn	Dearborn	MI
Beacon East Cinemas	Harper Woods	MI
S/C Sterling Heights	Sterling Heights	MI
Quo Vadis Cinemas	Westland	MI
S/C Westland	Westland	MI
S/C Ann Arbor	Ypsilanti	MI

REGAL

Frenchtown Square Mall 8	Monroe	MI

SILVER CINEMAS

Macomb Mall	Roseville	MI

UNITED ARTISTS

UA W. River Theatre	Farmington	MI
UA Commerce Township 14	Walled Lake	MI

ATLANTA

AMC

Mansell Crossing 14	Alpharetta	GA
Buckhead Backlot 6	Atlanta	GA
Galleria 8 Atl	Atlanta	GA
Phipps Plaza 14	Atlanta	GA
North Dekalb Mall 16	Decatur	GA
Barrett Commons 24	Kennesaw	GA
Colonial 18	Lawrenceville	GA
Southlake Pavilion	Morrow	GA
Northlake 8	Tucker	GA

CARMIKE

Carmike 12	Athens	GA
Martin	Calhoun	GA
Carmike 16	Canton	GA
Plaza	Cartersville	GA
Conyers 8	Conyers	GA
Carmike 4	Griffin	GA
LaGrange 6 Theatre	LaGrange	GA
Carmike 10	Newnan	GA
Carmike 12	Snellville	GA

CINEMA GRILL

North Springs Cinema Grill	Atlanta	GA

CINEMARK

Movies 10	Fayetteville	GA
Tinseltown	Fayetteville	GA

DEANZA LAND & LEISURE

Starlight Six-Plex	Atlanta	GA

GENERAL CINEMA

Parkway Pointe	Atlanta	GA

GEORGIA THEATRE

Beechwood Stadium 11	Athens	GA
Mall 8 Theatre	Carrollton	GA
Newton Twin Cinema	Covington	GA
Hollywood 14	Gainesville	GA
Lakeshore Mall Cinema	Gainesville	GA
Town Center 10	Lawrenceville	GA
Park 12 Cobb	Marietta	GA
Rome VII Cinema	Rome	GA
Cherokee 16	Woodstock	GA

LOEWS CINEPLEX

Magic Johnson Greenbrier	Atlanta	GA

O'NEIL

Avondale Cinema 16	Decatur	GA

REGAL

22 @ Austell	Austell	GA
Mall of Georgia 20	Buford	GA
Mall of Georgia IMAX	Buford	GA
Hollywood 24 @ North I-85	Chamblee	GA
Arbor Place Mall 18	Douglasville	GA
Medlock Crossing 18	Duluth	GA
Town Center 16-Kennesaw	Kennesaw	GA
Covington Square Cinema 8	Lithonia	GA
Cinema 10	Marietta	GA
Delk 10	Marietta	GA
Peachtree Corners 10	Norcross	GA
Riverdale Cinema 14	Riverdale	GA
Snellville Oaks 14	Snellville	GA

UNITED ARTISTS

Lenox Square Theatre	Atlanta	GA
Midtown 8 Theatre	Atlanta	GA
Tara 4 Theatre	Atlanta	GA
UA Perimeter Pointe	Atlanta	GA
Shannon 8 Theatre	Union City	GA

HOUSTON

AMC

Commerce Park 8	Houston	TX
Gulf Pointe 30	Houston	TX
Meyer Park 16	Houston	TX
Studio 30	Houston	TX
Willowbrook 24	Houston	TX
Deerbrook Mall 24	Humble	TX
Katy Mills 20	Katy	TX
First Colony 24	Sugarland	TX

CARMIKE

Cinema 4	Lake Jackson	TX

CINEMA GRILL

Westchase Cinema Grill	Houston	TX

CINEMARK

Tinseltown	Houston	TX
Tinseltown Westchase	Houston	TX
Tinseltown	Jacinto City	TX
Cinemark 19	Katy	TX
Hollywood USA	Pasadena	TX
Rosenberg 8	Rosenberg	TX
Movies 12	Texas City	TX
Cinema 18	Webster	TX
Tinseltown	Woodlands	TX

EDWARDS

Greenway Palace 24	Houston	TX
Houston Marq*E 23 + IMAX	Houston	TX

GENERAL CINEMA

Meyerland Plaza	Houston	TX

LANDMARK

Greenway 3 Theatre	Houston	TX
River Oaks Theatre	Houston	TX

LOEWS CINEPLEX

Easton Commons 8	Houston	TX
Memorial City 8	Houston	TX
Magic Johnson Northline Mall	Houston	TX
River Oaks Plaza 12	Houston	TX
Sharpstown Center	Houston	TX
Spectrum 9	Houston	TX
West Oaks Mall 7	Houston	TX
Spring 10	Spring	TX
Fountains	Stafford	TX
Southwest 6	Stafford	TX
Bay Area 6	Webster	TX

SEATTLE/TACOMA

AMC

Sea Tac 6 South	Federal Way	WA
Sea Tac North	Federal Way	WA
Narrows Plaza 8	Tacoma	WA

CINEMA GRILL

Aurora Cinema Grill	Seattle	WA

GENERAL CINEMA

Everett Mall {In the Mall}	Everett	WA
Everett Mall {Mall Village}	Everett	WA
Renton Village 8	Renton	WA
Aurora Cinema Grill	Seattle	WA
Cinerama	Seattle	WA
Pacific Place 11	Seattle	WA
Kitsap Mall 8 Cinemas	Silverdale	WA

LANDMARK

Broadway Market Cinemas	Seattle	WA
Crest Cinema Center	Seattle	WA
Egyptian Theatre	Seattle	WA
Guild 45th Theatre	Seattle	WA
Harvard Exit Theatre	Seattle	WA
Metro Cinemas	Seattle	WA
Neptune Theatre	Seattle	WA
Seven Gables Theatre	Seattle	WA
Varsity Theater	Seattle	WA

LOEWS CINEPLEX

Factoria Cinemas 8	Bellevue	WA
Cascade Cinemas	Burlington	WA
Totem Lake 3	Kirkland	WA
Kirkland Park Pl. 6	Kirkland	WA
Lakewood Mall 6	Lakewood	WA
Grand Cinemas	Lynnwood	WA
Redmond Town Center 8	Redmond	WA
City Centre	Seattle	WA
Uptown Cinemas	Seattle	WA
Oak Tree Cinemas	Seattle	WA
Northgate	Seattle	WA
Meridian 16	Seattle	WA
Tacoma Central 6	Tacoma	WA
Tacoma Mall Twin 2	Tacoma	WA
Tacoma South 5	Tacoma	WA
Southcenter 1	Tukwila	WA
Lewis & Clark 7	Tukwila	WA
Woodinville 12	Woodinville	WA

REGAL

Southshore 4 Mall	Aberdeen	WA
Auburn 17 Theatres	Auburn	WA
Crossroads 8 Cinema	Bellevue	WA
Galleria 11	Bellevue	WA
Bellis Fair 6 Cinema	Bellingham	WA
Sehome 3 Cinemas	Bellingham	WA

Sunset Square Cinema 6	Bellingham	WA
Tall Firs 10	Bonny Lake	WA
Redwood Plaza 4 Cinema	Bremerton	WA
Cinema 3	Chehalis	WA
Everett 9	Everett	WA
Gig Harbor 3	Gig Harbor	WA
Issaquah 9 Theatre	Issaquah	WA
Kent 6 Theatres	Kent	WA
Lakewood Cinema 15	Lakewood	WA
Alderwood 7	Lynnwood	WA
Alderwood Village 12	Lynnwood	WA
Marysville 14	Marysville	WA
Mount Lake 9	Mt. Lake Terrace	WA
Capital Mall 4	Olympia	WA
Lacey 8 Theatres	Olympia	WA
South Sound Cinema 10	Port Orchard	WA
Poulsbo 10	Poulsbo	WA
Longston Place 14	Puyallup	WA
Puyallup 6 Cinemas	Puyallup	WA
South Hill Cinema 6	Puyallup	WA
Bella Botega 11 Cinema	Redmond	WA
East Valley 13 Cinema	Renton	WA
Silverdale 4 Theatres	Silverdale	WA
Parkway Plaza 12	Tukwila	WA

TAMPA/ST. PETERSBURG/SARASOTA

AMC

Regency - Bdn 20	Brandon	FL
Clearwater 5	Clearwater	FL
Countryside 6	Clearwater	FL
Tri-City 8	Clearwater	FL
Merchants Walk 10	Lakeland	FL
Woodlands Square 20	Oldsmar	FL
Sarasota 6	Sarasota	FL
Sarasota East 7/12	Sarasota	FL
Seminole 8	Seminole	FL
Crossroads Center 8	St. Petersburg	FL
Tyrone Square 6	St. Petersburg	FL
Old Hyde Park 7	Tampa	FL
Veterans Expressway 24	Tampa	FL

CARMIKE

Royal Palm	Bradenton	FL
Palm Cinema 3	Lakeland	FL
Lake Walden Cinema	Plant City	FL
Lakeshore 8	Sebring	FL
Hillsboro West 8	Tampa	FL
Cont'l Mugs & Movies 2	Winterhaven	FL

MUVICO

Palm Harbor 10	Palm Harbor	FL
Baywalk 20	St. Petersburg	FL
Majestic 20	Tampa	FL
Starlight 20	Tampa	FL

R/C

Parkside 16	Pinellas Park	FL

REGAL

Bradenton 8 Cinemas	Bradenton	FL
Desoto Square Mall 6 Cinemas	Bradenton	FL
Oakmont 8	Bradenton	FL
Crystal River Mall 9	Crystal River	FL
Citrus Cinemas 6	Inverness	FL
Eagle Ridge Mall 12	Lake Wales	FL
Largo Mall 8	Largo	FL
Hollywood 20-Northgate	Lutz	FL
Embassy 6	Port Richey	FL
Hollywood 18-Port Richey	Port Richey	FL
Crossings Cinema 10	Sarasota	FL
Hollywood 20	Sarasota	FL
Parkway 8 Cinemas	Sarasota	FL
Spring Hill 8 Cinemas	Spring Hill	FL
Britton 8	Tampa	FL
Citrus Park 20	Tampa	FL
University 16	Tampa	FL
Venetian 6	Venice	FL
Spring Lake 10	Winter Haven	FL

STARNET

Lakeland Square 10 Cinemas	Lakeland	FL

TMI

Beacon Theatres	Brooksville	FL

UNITED ARTISTS

UA Movies @ Clearwater	Clearwater	FL

MINNEAPOLIS/ST. PAUL

CARMIKE

Wynnsong 15	Apple Valley	MN
State 3	Hutchinson	MN
Wynnsong 16	Moundsview	MN
Oakdale	Oakdale	MN
Kandi 6	Wilmar	MN

CINEMA GRILL

Yorktown Cinema Grill	Edina	MN

CINEMA ENTERTAINMENT

Amigo 9	Bemidji	MN
Cinema 6	Faribault	MN
Marshall 6	Marshall	MN
Cinema Arts 3	St Cloud	MN
Crossroads 6	Waite Park	MN
Parkwood 18	Waite Park	MN
Hudson Cinema 9	Hudson	WI
Lake 7	Rice Lake	WI

CINEMAGIC

Century 7 Theatres	Hutchinson	MN
CineMagic Stadium 7 Theatres	Menomonie	WI

GENERAL CINEMA

Mall Of America Cinema 14	Bloomington	MN
Centennial Lakes 8	Edina	MN
Har Mar Cinema 11	Roseville	MN
Shelard Park	St. Louis Park	MN

KERASOTES

Showplace 16 Coon Rapids	Coon Rapids	MN
Showplace 16	Inver Grove Heights	MN

LAKES & RIVERS

Cedar Mall Cinema 6	Owatonna	MN
Red Wing Cinema 5	Red Wing	MN
Falls Cinema 5	St. Croix Falls	WI

LANDMARK

Lagoon Cinema	Minneapolis	MN
Uptown Theatre	Minneapolis	MN

MANN THEATRES OF MINNESOTA

Movies 10 at Westgate	Baxter	MN
Westport Theatre	Baxter	MN
Apache 6 Theatre	Columbia Heights	MN
Cottage View Drive-In	Cottage Grove	MN
Eagan Cinema 9	Eagan	MN
Hopkins Cinema 6	Hopkins	MN
Maple Grove Cinema 10	Maple Grove	MN
Plymouth Cinema 12	Plymouth	MN
St. Louis Park Cinema	St. Louis Park	MN
Grandview 1 & 2 Theatres	St. Paul	MN
Highland 1 & 2 Theatres	St. Paul	MN

MARCUS

Apple Valley Theatres	Apple Valley	MN
Marcus Cambridge Cinema 5	Cambridge	MN
Elk River 17	Elk River	MN
Hastings Theater	Hastings	MN
Marcus Cinema Oakdale North	Oakdale	MN
Rosemount Theater	Rosemount	MN
Marcus Cinema Shakopee	Shakopee	MN

REGAL

Eagan 16	Eagan	MN
Brooklyn Center 20	Minneapolis	MN

UNITED ARTISTS

Movies @ Brookdale Square	Brooklyn Center	MN
UA Burnsville II	Burnsville	MN
Movies @ Eden Prairie W.	Eden Prairie	MN
Movies @ Maplewood I	Maplewood	MN
Movies @ Maplewood II	Maplewood	MN
Movies @ Pavilions Place	Roseville	MN
UA Woodbury	Woodbury	MN

CLEVELAND

CARMIKE

Cinema	Ashtabula	OH
Kingsgate 4	Mansfield	OH
Plaza 8	Sandusky	OH

CINEMA GRILL

Centrum Cinema Grill	Cleveland	OH

CINEMARK

Carnation Cinema	Alliance	OH
Movies 4	Canton	OH
Cinemark 15	Macedonia	OH
Cinema 10	Mansfield	OH
Movies 10	North Canton	OH
Tinseltown	North Canton	OH
Richland III	Ontario	OH
Movies 10	Sandusky	OH
Cinemark 24	Valley View	OH
Movies 10	Willoughby Hills	OH
Movies 10	Wooster	OH

GENERAL CINEMA

West Market Plaza Cinema	Akron	OH
Ridge Park Sq. Cinema	Brooklyn	OH
Plaza Cinemas Chapel Hill	Cuyahoga Falls	OH
Midway Mall Cinemas	Elyria	OH
Erie Commons Cinema 8	Mentor	OH
Parmatown Cinema	Parma	OH
Westgate Mall Cinema	Rocky River	OH
Westwood Town Center	Rocky River	OH

LOEWS CINEPLEX

Magic Johnson Randall Park Mall	North Randall	OH
Richmond Town Square	Richmond Heights	OH

REGAL

Independence 10	Akron	OH
Interstate Park Cinema 18	Akron	OH
Montrose Movies 12	Akron	OH
Lake Cinema 8	Barberton	OH
Brookgate Saver 5	Brookpark	OH
Hickory Ridge Cinema 8	Brunswick	OH
Severance Town Center 14	Cleveland Heights	OH
Cobblestone Square 20	Elyria	OH
Garfield Mall Movies 5	Garfield Heights	OH
Hudson Cinema 10	Hudson	OH
Sheffield Centre 10	Lorain	OH
Mayfield Heights 10	Mayfield Heights	OH
Medina 16 @ Huntington St.	Medina	OH
Great Lakes Mall 9	Mentor	OH
Middleberg Town Square 12	Middleburg Heights	OH
New Towne Cinema 8	New Philadelphia	OH
Great Northern Movies 7	North Olmsted	OH
Solon Commons Cinema 16	Solon	OH
Westlake Promenade 11	Westlake	OH
Willoughby Commons 16	Willoughby	OH

MIAMI/FT. LAUDERDALE

AMC

Aventura 24	Aventura	FL
Cocowalk 16	Coconut Grove	FL
Ridge Plaza 8	Davie	FL
Coral Ridge 10	Fort Lauderdale	FL
Sheridan Plaza 12	Hollywood	FL
Kendall T and C 10	Miami	FL
Mall Of Americas 14	Miami	FL
South Dade 8	Miami	FL
Fashion Island 16	North Miami Beach	FL
Sunset Place 24	South Miami	FL

CROWN

Grand 18	Hialeah	FL

MUVICO

Paradise 24	Davie	FL
Hialeah 14	Hialeah	FL
Pompano 18	Pompano Beach	FL

O'NEIL

Taft Hollywood Cinema 12	Hollywood	FL

REGAL

Mayfair 10	Coconut Grove	FL
Magnolia Place 16	Coral Springs	FL
Cypress Creek Station 16	Fort Lauderdale	FL
Las Olas 23	Fort Lauderdale	FL
Oakwood 18	Hollywood	FL
Cinema Key West 6	Key West	FL
Kendall 9	Miami	FL
Palace 18	Miami	FL
South Beach Cinema 18	Miami Beach	FL
Miami Lakes 17	Miami Lakes	FL
Westfork Plaza 13	Pembroke Pines	FL
Sawgrass 23	Sunrise	FL

UNITED ARTISTS

UA Movies @ Lauderhill	Lauderhill	FL
UA Movies @ The Falls	Miami	FL
Movies @ Pembroke Pines	Pembroke Pines	FL

PHOENIX

AMC

Laguna Village 10	Chandler	AZ
Arrowhead 14	Glendale	AZ
Mesa Grand 24	Mesa	AZ
Three Fountains 4	Mesa	AZ
Ahwatukee 24	Phoenix	AZ
Arizona Center 24	Phoenix	AZ
Bell Plaza 8	Phoenix	AZ
Deer Valley 30	Phoenix	AZ
Esplande 14	Phoenix	AZ
Town & Country 6	Phoenix	AZ

CENTURY

Glendale Drive-In	Glendale	AZ
Scottsdale 6 Drive-In	Scottsdale	AZ

CINEMARK

The Movies 4	Kingman	AZ

HARKINS

Flagstaff 11	Flagstaff	AZ
Fiesta 5	Mesa	AZ
Poca Fiesta 4	Mesa	AZ
Superstition Sprgs 25	Mesa	AZ
Arrowhead 18	Peoria	AZ
Arcadia 8	Phoenix	AZ
Bell Towne Centre 8	Phoenix	AZ
Christown 11	Phoenix	AZ
Desert Sky Mall 6	Phoenix	AZ
Metro 12	Phoenix	AZ
Paradise Valley Mall 7	Phoenix	AZ
Southwest Plaza 8	Phoenix	AZ
Prescott Valley 14	Prescott Valley	AZ
Camelview 5	Scottsdale	AZ
Fashion Square 7	Scottsdale	AZ
Shea 14	Scottsdale	AZ
Sedona 6	Sedona	AZ
Arizona Mills 24	Tempe	AZ
Centerpoint 11	Tempe	AZ
Valley Art Theatre	Tempe	AZ

SILVER CINEMAS

Cinema-Superstition Mall	Mesa	AZ
Super Saver Cinema Bell Rd.	Phoenix	AZ

UNITED ARTIST

Christown Mall Cinema	Phoenix	AZ
Metro Park Theatre	Phoenix	AZ
UA Scottsdale Pavilions	Scottsdale	AZ
UA Sonora Village	Scottsdale	AZ

WEHRENBERG

Greentree 3	Flagstaff	AZ
University Plaza 2	Flagstaff	AZ
Frontier Village 10	Prescott	AZ

WILDWOOD

Palm Valley 14	Goodyear	AZ

DENVER

AMC

Seven Hills 10	Aurora	CO
Tiffany Plaza 6	Denver	CO
Highlands Ranch 24	Highlands Ranch	CO
Westminster Promenade 24	Westminster	CO

CARMIKE

Carmike Stage	Aspen	CO
Carmike 10	Fort Collins	CO
Carmike Mall 3	Glenwood Springs	CO
Carmike 5	Greeley	CO
Chief Plaza 4	Steamboat Springs	CO
Ski Time Square 1	Steamboat Springs	CO

CENTURY

Century 16 Aurora	Aurora	CO

CINEMARK

Cinemark At Fort Collins	Fort Collins	CO

COLORADO CINEMAS

Olde Town 14	Arvada	CO
Arapahoe Crossing 16	Aurora	CO
Arapahoe Village 4	Boulder	CO
Basemar Twin	Boulder	CO
Cherry Creek 8	Denver	CO
Bergen Park 7	Evergreen	CO
Cinema Saver 6	Ft. Collins	CO
Bowles Crossing 12	Littleton	CO
Colony Square 12	Louisville	CO

LANDMARK

Chez Artiste	Denver	CO
Esquire Theatre	Denver	CO
Mayan Theatre	Denver	CO

METROPOLITIAN

MetroLux 12 Theatre	Love Land	CO

TRANS-LUX

Lake Dillon Cinema	Dillon	CO
Skyline Cinema	Dillon	CO
Metrolux 12	Loveland	CO
Fox Theatre	Laramie	WY

UNITED ARTIST

Village 4	Boulder	CO
Continental Theatre	Denver	CO
Denver Pavilions	Denver	CO
UA Colorado Center	Denver	CO
UA Greenwood Plaza	Denver	CO
Campus West	Fort Collins	CO
Denver West Village 12	Golden	CO
Bittersweet Theatre	Greeley	CO
Cooper Twin Theatre	Greeley	CO
UA Meadows 12	Littleton	CO
Twin Peaks 10	Longmont	CO
Thornton Town Center	Thornton	CO

W.F. CINEMA HOLDINGS

Mann Crossroads Commons 6	Boulder	CO
Mann 6 Tamarac Square	Denver	CO
Mann 6 Green Mountain	Lakewood	CO
Mann Southwest Plaza 5	Littleton	CO

SACRAMENTO/STOCKTON/MODESTO

CENTURY

Laguna 16	Elk Grove	CA
Folsom 14	Folsom	CA
Roseville 14	Roseville	CA
Stadium 14	Sacramento	CA
Stadium 21	Sacramento	CA
Cinedome 9	Sacramento	CA
Downtown Plaza	Sacramento	CA
Sacramento Drive-In	Sacramento	CA

CINEMARK

Movies 14	Tracy	CA
County Fair Movies 5	Woodland	CA
Yuba City 8	Yuba City	CA

EDWARDS

Fairfield Stadium 16	Fairfield	CA

GENERAL CINEMA

Birdcage Centre	Citrus Heights	CA

PACIFIC

Ceres Drive-In	Ceres	CA

REGAL

Natomas Marketplace 16	Sacramento	CA

SIGNATURE

Auburn Twin	Auburn	CA
State Twin Theatre	Auburn	CA
Holiday Cinema	Davis	CA
Stadium 5	Davis	CA
Jackson Cinemas	Jackson	CA
Mann Festival Cinemas	Modesto	CA
Placerville 8	Placerville	CA
Sonora Plaza Cinema	Sonora	CA
Festival Cinemas, 4-Plex	Stockton	CA
Holiday Cinemas 8	Stockton	CA
Regency Cinemas, 4-Plex	Stockton	CA
Stockton Royal	Stockton	CA
Turlock Stadium 14	Turlock	CA

UNITED ARTIST

UA Sunrise Cinema 4	Citrus Heights	CA
Del Oro	Grass Valley	CA
Grass Valley Cinema	Grass Valley	CA
Olympus Pointe	Roseville	CA
Laguna Village Theatre	S. Sacramento	CA
UA Arden Fair	Sacramento	CA

WALLACE

New Stateline Cinema 1	South Lake Tahoe	CA

PITTSBURG

CARMIKE

Plaza 6	Beaver Falls	PA
Laurel Mall 4	Connellsville	PA
Cranberry Mall 5	Cranberry	PA
Cranberry 8	Cranberry Township	PA
Carmike 12	Delmont	PA
Carmike 15	Greensburg	PA
Cinema 4	Indiana	PA
Cinema 4	Kittanning	PA
M. V. Monaca 7 Theatre	Monaca	PA
Galleria 6	Mt. Lebanon	PA
Carmike 10	Pittsburgh	PA
Southland 9	Pleasant Hills	PA
Carmike 6	Uniontown	PA
Cinema 3 Theatre	Vandergrift	PA
Washington 8	Washington	PA
Maxi-Saver 12	West Mifflin	PA
Mall 8	Morganton	WV

LOEWS CINEPLEX

North Versailles	North Versailles	PA
Waterfront Theatre	West Homestead	PA

NATIONAL AMUSEMENTS

S/C Cinemas East	Pittsburgh	PA
S/C Cinemas North - Pitt	Pittsburgh	PA
S/C Cinemas West	Pittsburgh	PA
Super Saver Cinemas 8	Pittsburgh	PA

REGAL

Moraine Pointe Cinema 10	Butler	PA

TMI

Penn Cinemas	Butler	PA
Pioneer Drive-In Theatre	Butler	PA

UNITED ARTISTS

Cortlandt Town Center	Mohegan Lake	NY

ORLANDO/DAYTONA BEACH/MELBOURNE

AMC

Celebration 2	Celebration	FL
Volusia Square 8	Daytona	FL
Pleasure Island 24	Lake Buena Vista	FL
Lake Square 12	Leesburg	FL
Merritt 6	Merritt Island	FL
Merritt Square 7/12	Merritt Island	FL
West Oaks 14	Ocoee	FL
Fashion Village 8	Orlando	FL
Highland Lakes 12	Orlando	FL

CARMIKE

University 8	Winter Park	FL

CINEMA GRILL

Aloma Cinema Grill	Winter Park	FL

CINEMARK

Festival Bay	Orlando	FL

EASTERN FEDERAL

Port Orange Six	Port Orange	FL

LOEWS CINEPLEX

Sand Lake 7	Orlando	FL

MUVICO

IMAX Theatre	Orlando	FL
Pointe 20 Theatres	Orlando	FL

R/C

OceanWalk 10	Daytona Beach	FL

REGAL

Osceola Square East 6	Kissimmee	FL
Osceola Square West 6	Kissimmee	FL
Lake Mary Cinema 10	Lake Mary	FL
Oaks 10	Melbourne	FL
Hollywood 16-Ocala	Ocala	FL
Southchase Cinema 7	Orlando	FL
UC 7 Cinema	Orlando	FL
Waterford Lakes	Orlando	FL
Ormond Beach Cinema 12	Ormond Beach	FL
Oviedo Marketplace 22	Oviedo	FL
Palm Bay 10	Palm Bay	FL
Roxy 10 Cinemas	Palm Bay	FL
Winter Park Village 20	Winter Park	FL

STARNET

Belleview Cinemas	Belleview	FL

TMI

Victoria Square 6	DeLand	FL
Beacon 12 Theatre	New Smyrna Bch.	FL
Showcase Cinemas	Orange City	FL

UNITED ARTISTS

UA Movies @ Wekiva	Apopka	FL
UA Cinemas West	Ocala	FL
MVS Marketplace	Orange City	FL
Movies @ Florida Mall	Orlando	FL
UA Seminole Towne Center	Sanford	FL
UA Searstown Mall	Titusville	FL

ST. LOUIS

AMC

Creve Coeur 12	Creve Coeur	MO
West Olive 16	Creve Coeur	MO
Village 6	Hazelwood	MO
Crestwood 10	St. Louis	MO
Esquire 7	St. Louis	MO
Galleria 6	St. Louis	MO

B & B

Festus Eight	Festus	MO

KERASOTES

Illinois Theatre	Centralia	IL
Eastgate Cinema	East Alton	IL
Showplace 12	Edwardsville	IL
Cottonwood Cinema	Glen Carbon	IL
Nameoki	Granite City	IL
Lory Theatre	Highland	IL
Stadium Theatre	Jerseyville	IL
Cine Theatre	Roxana	IL
Showplace 4	Farmington	MO
Movies	Park Hills	MO
Meramec Cinema	Sullivan	MO

LANDMARK

Plaza Frontenac	St. Louis	MO
Tivoli Theatre	Universal City	MO

WALLACE

Union Station Cinema 10	St. Louis	MO

WEHRENBERG

St. Clair Cinema 10	Fairview Height	IL
Chesterfield 4 Cinema	Chesterfield	MO
Clarkson 6 Cinema	Chesterfield	MO
Eureka 6 Cinema	Eureka	MO
Jamestown 14	Florissant	MO
O'Fallon 15 Cinema	O'Fallon	MO
Ronnies 20 Cinema	Sappington	MO
Northwest 9 Cinema	St. Ann	MO
St. Charles 18	St. Charles	MO
Arnold 14	St. Louis	MO
Des Peres 14	St. Louis	MO
Halls Ferry 14 Cinema	St. Louis	MO
Keller 8 Cinema	St. Louis	MO
Kenrick 8 Cinema	St. Louis	MO
Lindbergh 8 Cinema	St. Louis	MO
Mid Rivers 14 Cinema	St. Louis	MO
North Twin Drive-In	St. Louis	MO
Westport Cinema	St. Louis	MO

PORTLAND, OR

CENTURY

Century Eastport 16	Portland	OR

COMING ATTRACTIONS

Astoria Gateway Cinema	Astoria	OR
Forest Grove Cinema 7	Forest Grove	OR
McMinnville Cinema 8	McMinnville	OR

REGAL

Albany 7 Cinemas	Albany	OR
Westgate 5 Theatres	Beaverton	OR
Clackamas Towne Center 5	Clackamas	OR
Cornelius 9 Cinemas	Cornelius	OR
Stark St. 10	Gresham	OR
Evergreen Parkway	Hillsboro	OR
Movies On TV 16	Hillsboro	OR
Trail Drive-In	Hood River	OR
Trail Indoor	Hood River	OR
Lincoln City 6	Lincoln City	OR
Newport Tri	Newport	OR
Hilltop 9 Cinema	Oregon City	OR
82nd Ave.. 6 Cinemas	Portland	OR
Broadway Metro 4 Theatres	Portland	OR
Division St.	Portland	OR
Eastgate 3 Cinemas	Portland	OR
Fox Tower 10	Portland	OR
Koin Center 6 Cinemas	Portland	OR
Lloyd Center 10 Cinema	Portland	OR
Lloyd Mall 8 Cinema	Portland	OR
Washington Square 4 Cinema	Portland	OR
Lancaster 4	Salem	OR
Movieland 7	Salem	OR
Santiam 11	Salem	OR
Sherwood 10	Sherwood	OR
Tigard 11 Cinemas	Tigard	OR
Wilsonville 9 Cinema	Wilsonville	OR
Three Rivers Mall 5	Kelso	WA
Longview Theatre 1	Longview	WA
Triangle Quad Cinemas	Longview	WA
Cascade 16 Cinemas	Vancouver	WA
Cinema 99 11	Vancouver	WA
City Center 12	Vancouver	WA
Vancouver Plaza 10 Cinema	Vancouver	WA

BALTIMORE

CINEMA GRILL

Annapolis Cinema Grill	Annapolis	MD

CROWN

Annapolis Mall	Annapolis	MD
Eastport Cinemas	Annapolis	MD
Harbour Center IX	Annapolis	MD

GENERAL CINEMA

Columbia City 3	Columbia	MD
Owings Mills 17	Owings Mills	MD
Towson Commons 8	Towson	MD
Security Square 8	Woodlawn	MD

HOYTS

Hunt Valley 12	Hunt Valley	MD
West Nursery 14	Linthicum	MD
Cranberry Mall 9	Westminster	MD

LOEWS CINEPLEX

Rotunda 2	Baltimore	MD
White Marsh	Baltimore	MD
Columbia Palace 9	Columbia	MD
Glen Burnie 7	Glen Burnie	MD
Valley Center 9	Owings Mills	MD
Timonium 3	Timonium	MD

R/C

Hollywood Cinemas	Arbutus	MD
Eastpoint Movies	Baltimore	MD
Easton Movies	Easton	MD
Carrolltown Movies 6	Eldersburg	MD

REGAL

Bel Air Cinema 14	Abingdon	MD

UNITED ARTISTS

UA Westview Mall	Baltimore	MD
UA Snowden Square	Columbia	MD
Movies @ Marley Station	Glen Burnie	MD

SAN DIEGO

AMC

Wiegand Plaza 8	Encinitas	CA
La Jolla Village 12	La Jolla	CA
Fashion Valley 18	San Diego	CA
Mission Valley 20	San Diego	CA
Palm Promenade 24	San Diego	CA

CINEMASTAR

Galaxy 6 Cinemas	Bonsall	CA
Chula Vista 10	Chula Vista	CA
Mission Marketplace 13	Oceanside	CA

DEANZA LAND & LEISURE

South Bay Triple	San Diego	CA

EDWARDS

Flower Hill 4	Del Mar	CA
Rancho San Diego 15	El Cajon	CA
Poway 10	Poway	CA
Del Mar Highlands 8	San Diego	CA
Mira Mesa Stadium 18	San Diego	CA
San Marcos Stadium 18	San Marcos	CA

LANDMARK

Cove Theatre	La Jolla	CA
La Jolla Village Cinemas	La Jolla	CA
Hillcrest Cinemas	San Diego	CA
Ken Theatre	San Diego	CA

PACIFIC

Grossmont Center 8	La Mesa	CA
Grossmont Trolley 8	La Mesa	CA
Sweetwater	National City	CA
Cinerama 6	San Diego	CA
Gaslamp Stadium 15	San Diego	CA
Pacific Carmel Mountain 12	San Diego	CA
Town Square Stadium 14	San Diego	CA

REGAL

Rancho Del Rey 16	Chula Vista	CA
Parkway Plaza 18	El Cajon	CA
Oceanside 16	Oceanside	CA

UNITED ARTISTS

Movies @ Horton Plaza	San Diego	CA

W.F. CINEMA HOLDINGS

Mann 7 Hazard Center	San Diego	CA

INDIANAPOLIS

CINEMA GRILL

Greenbriar Cinema Grill	Indianapolis	IN

CINEMARK

Greenwood	Indianapolis	IN
Washington	Indianapolis	IN

GENERAL CINEMA

Greenwood Park 14	Greenwood	IN
Castleton Square	Indianapolis	IN
Clearwater Crossing 12	Indianapolis	IN
Eastgate Mall 6	Indianapolis	IN
Lafayette Sq.	Indianapolis	IN

GKC

Capri Cinemas	Crawfordsville	IN

GOODRICH

Applewood 9	Anderson	IN

KERASOTES

Mounds Mall	Anderson	IN
Showplace 4	Anderson	IN
College Mall Cinema	Bloomington	IN
Showplace 11	Bloomington	IN
Showplace West 12	Bloomington	IN
Columbus Cinema 5	Columbus	IN
Commons Cinema	Columbus	IN
ShowPlace 12	Indianapolis	IN
Showplace 16	Indianapolis	IN
Kokomo Mall Cinema	Kokomo	IN
Markland Mall Cinema	Kokomo	IN
Showplace 12	Marion	IN
Muncie Mall	Muncie	IN
Northwest Plaza Cinema	Muncie	IN
Showplace 7	Muncie	IN
Castle Theatre	New Castle	IN
Eastwood Cinema	Peru	IN

LOEWS CINEPLEX

Greenwood 9	Greenwood	IN
Cherry Tree 10	Indianapolis	IN
College Park 14	Indianapolis	IN
Lafayette 8	Indianapolis	IN

REGAL

Shiloh Crossing 18	Avon	IN
Village Park Cinema 12	Carmel	IN

SYNDICATE

Canary Creek Cinemas	Franklin	IN

UNITED ARTISTS

Galaxy 14	Indianapolis	IN
UA Circle Center	Indianapolis	IN
UA Eagle Highlands	Indianapolis	IN

HARTFORD & NEW HAVEN

CROWN

Palace 17	West Hartford	CT

HOYTS

Cinema 12	Branford	CT
Dayville 3	Dayville	CT
Enfield 12	Enfield	CT
Groton 6	Groton	CT
Manchester 6	Manchester	CT
Meriden 10	Meriden	CT
Mystic Village 3	Mystic	CT
Norwich Twin	Norwich	CT
Saybrook 6	Old Saybrook	CT
Stonington 10	Pawcatuck	CT
Saybrook Twin	Saybrook	CT
Simsbury 8	Simsbury	CT
Waterbury 12	Waterbury	CT
Waterford 9	Waterford	CT
Willimantic 6	Willimantic	CT

LOEWS CINEPLEX

Plainville	Plainville	CT

NATIONAL AMUSEMENTS

S/C Berlin	Berlin	CT
S/C East Hartford	East Hartford	CT
S/C East Windsor	East Windsor	CT
S/C Cinemas Buckland Hills	Manchester	CT
Milford Quad	Milford	CT
S/C Cinemas 5	Milford	CT
S/C Milford	Milford	CT
S/C North Haven	North Haven	CT
S/C Orange	Orange	CT
S/C Southington	Southington	CT

O'NEIL

Westbrook Cinema 12	Westbrook	CT

CHARLOTTE

AMC

Carolina Pavilions 22	Charlotte	NC
Concord Mills 24	Concord	NC

CARMIKE

Appalachian	Boone	NC
Chalet	Boone	NC
Carmike 12	Hickory	NC
Westgate Twin	Lenoir	NC
Cinema 8	Lincolnton	NC
Cinema 4	Shelby	NC
Mall 4	Shelby	NC
Gateway 4	Statesville	NC
Cinema 7	Rock Hill	SC

CINEMA GRILL

Eastland Cinema Grill	Charlotte	NC

CINEMARK

Movies 10	Matthews	NC
Tinseltown USA	Salisbury	NC

EASTERN FEDERAL

Delta Six Theatre	Charlotte	NC
Manor Theatre	Charlotte	NC
Movies at Crownpoint 12	Charlotte	NC
Starlight Stadium	Charlotte	NC
Movies at the Lake	Cornelius	NC

REGAL

Boone Cinema 7	Boone	NC
Stonecrest at Piper Glen 22	Charlotte	NC
Galleria Mall 8	Rock Hill	SC

UNITED ARTISTS

Eastgate Cinemas	Albemarle	NC
Carolina Mall Cinemas	Concord	NC
Crown 6 Cinemas	Hickory	NC

RALEIGH/DURHAM

CARMIKE

Ram	Chapel Hill	NC
Plaza Twin	Dunn	NC
Carmike 7	Durham	NC
Willowdale 8	Durham	NC
Wynnsong 15	Durham	NC
Carmike 12	Fayetteville	NC
Marketfair	Fayetteville	NC
Wynnsong 7	Fayetteville	NC
Berkeley 4	Goldsboro	NC
Park Place 16	Morrisville	NC
Carmike 15	Raleigh	NC
Blueridge 14	Raleigh	NC
Golden East 4	Rocky Mount	NC
Kendale Cinema 2	Sanford	NC
Cinema 4	Southern Pines	NC
Town & Country 2	Southern Pines	NC
Parkwood 3	Wilson	NC

CINEMA GRILL

Raleighwood Cinema Grill	Raleigh	NC

EASTERN FEDERAL

Movies at Timberlyne 6	Chapel Hill	NC
Plaza Theatre	Chapel Hill	NC

REGAL

Omni Cinema 8	Fayetteville	NC
Wilson Cinema 6	Wilson	NC

UNITED ARTISITS

UA Towne Square 10	Garner	NC
Litchfield Cinemas	Goldsboro	NC

KANSAS CITY

AMC

Town Center 20	Leawood	KS
Studio 30	Olathe	KS
Oak Park Plaza 6	Overland Park	KS
Independence 20	Independence	MO
Barrywoods 24	Kansas City	MO
Crown Center 6	Kansas City	MO
Metro North Plaza 6	Kansas City	MO
Parkway 22	Kansas City	MO

B & B

Brookfield Cedar Cinema	Brookfield	MO
Grand 6	Chillicothe	MO
Harrisonville Cinema 6	Harrisonville	MO
Liberty Cinema 12	Liberty	MO
Marshall Cinema	Marshall	MO

CARMIKE

University 8	Warrensburg	MO

CINEMARK

Merriam	Merriam	KS
The Palace Cinemark 14	Kansas City	MO

DICKINSON

Plaza 6 Leavenworth	Leavenworth	KS
Great Mall 16	Olathe	KS
Westglen 18	Shawnee	KS
Belton 8	Belton	MO
Noland Fashion Square 6	Independence	MO
Red Bridge 4	Kansas City	MO
Eastglen 16	Lee's Summit	MO

LOEWS CINEPLEX

Westwind 3	Minnetonka	MN

REGAL

Kansas City 18 Cinemas	Kansas City	MO

WALLACE

Plaza Cinema 6	Lawrence	KS
Southwind Cinema 12	Lawrence	KS

NASHVILLE

CARMIKE

Martin 5	Hopkinsville	KY
Bell Forge 10	Antioch	TN
Hickory 8	Antioch	TN
Carmike 5	Clarksville	TN
Carmike 8	Clarksville	TN
Highland	Cookeville	TN
Varsity	Cookeville	TN
Galleria 10	Franklin	TN
Thoroughbred 20	Franklin	TN
Rivergate 8	Goodlettsville	TN
Hermitage	Hermitage	TN
Martin 3	Lebanon	TN
Wynnsong	Murfreesboro	TN
Bellevue 8	Nashville	TN
Wynnsong 10	Nashville	TN
Cinema 1	Springfield	TN

REGAL

Indian Lake Cinema 10	Henderson	TN
Courtyard Cinema 8	Hermitage	TN
Bellevue Cinema 12	Nashville	TN
Green Hills 16	Nashville	TN
Hollywood 27-Nashville	Nashville	TN
Nippers Corner Cinema 10	Nashville	TN
Opry Mills 20	Nashville	TN
Opry Mills IMAX	Nashville	TN
Tullahoma Cinema 8	Tullahoma	TN

CINCINNATI

CARMIKE

Cinema 4	Marysville	KY

CHAKERES

Wilmington Drive-In	Wilmington	OH
Wilmington Plaza 5	Wilmington	OH

CINEMA GRILL

Covedale Cinema Grill	Cincinnati	OH
Mt. Lookout Cinema Grill	Cincinnati	OH

DANBARRY

Dollar Saver Cinemas	Cincinnati	OH
Dollar Saver Cinemas	Dayton	OH
Cinemas Middletown	Middletown	OH

KERASOTES

Cinemas 10	Hamilton	OH
Showplace 8	Hamilton	OH

NATIONAL AMUSEMENTS

S/C Erlanger	Erlanger	KY
Florence Cinemas	Florence	KY
Centerville Cinemas	Centerville	OH
Dayton Mall Cinemas	Centerville	OH
S/C Cross Pointe 12	Centerville	OH
Kenwood Towne Centre	Cincinnati	OH
Northgate Cinemas	Cincinnati	OH
S/C Cincinnati	Cincinnati	OH
S/C Eastgate	Cincinnati	OH
S/C Springdale	Cincinnati	OH
S/C Western Hills	Cincinnati	OH
Oakley Drive-In	Madisonville	OH
S/C Kings Island	Mason	OH
275 East Cinemas	Milford	OH
S/C Cinemas Milford	Milford	OH

REGAL

Turfway Park Cinema 10	Florence	KY
Central Park Cinema 11	Cincinati	OH
Towne East Cinema 5	Middletown	OH

SYNDICATE

Gibson Theatre	Batesville	IN

MILWAUKEE

CINEMA GRILL

Fox Bay Cinema Grill	Whitefish	WI

CINEMARK

Tinseltown USA	Kenosha	WI

F & F/VALUE

Delavan Theatre	Delavan	WI
Giant 41 Drive-In	Franklin	WI
Geneva Theatre	Lake Geneva	WI

GENERAL CINEMA

Mayfair Mall	Wauwatosa	WI

LANDMARK

Downer Theatre	Milwaukee	WI
Oriental Theatre	Milwaukee	WI

MARCUS

Wisconsin Theatres	Beaver Dam	WI
Tower Cinema	Brookfield	WI
Westpoint Cinema	Brookfield	WI
Rivoli Budget Theatre	Cedarburg	WI
Hillside Cinema	Delafield	WI
Main St. Cinema	Menomonee Falls	WI
Menomonee Falls	Menomonee Falls	WI
North Shore Cinema	Mequon	WI
Northtown Cinema	Milwaukee	WI
Prospect Mall	Milwaukee	WI
Southgate Theatre 10	Milwaukee	WI
Southtown Cinema	Milwaukee	WI
Ridge Cinema	New Berlin	WI
South Shore	Oak Creek	WI
Value Cinema Oak Creek	Oak Creek	WI
Regency Cinemas	Racine	WI
Westgate 5 Racine	Racine	WI
Cinema Sheboygan	Sheboygan	WI
Westown	Waukesha	WI

SILVER CINEMAS

Budget Cinemas - South 6	Greenfield	WI

STAR CINEMA

Star Cinema 12	Johnson Creek	WI

WILDWOOD

Capitol Cinemas 11	Pewaukee	WI

COLUMBUS, OH

AMC

Eastland Centre 8	Columbus	OH
Easton 30	Columbus	OH
Lennox Town Center 24	Columbus	OH
Dublin Village 18	Dublin	OH
Westerville 6	Westerville	OH

CINEMARK

Movie 12	Columbus	OH
Movies 10	Columbus	OH
Movies 16	Gahanna	OH
Movies 12	Hillard	OH

GENERAL CINEMA

Westland 8	Columbus	OH

MARCUS

Cinemas Crosswoods	Columbus	OH
Cinema Pickerington	Pickerington	OH

REGAL

Regal 6	Chilicothe	OH
Shawnee Square Cinema 4	Chilicothe	OH
Georgesville Square 16	Columbus	OH
Delaware Square Movies 5	Delaware	OH
River Valley Mall 10	Lancaster	OH
Southland Cinema 7	Marion	OH
Consumer Square 14	Reynoldsburg	OH

SALT LAKE CITY

CARMIKE

Cache Valley 3	Logan	UT
Wynnsong 12	Provo	UT
Cottonwood Mall 4	Salt Lake City	UT
Villa Theatre	Salt Lake City	UT
Carmike 12	West Jordan	UT
Hollywood Conn. 16	West Valley City	UT

CENTURY

Century Salt Lake	Salt Lake City	UT

CINEMARK

Tinseltown	Layton	UT
Tinseltown	Ogden	UT
Village Cinema	Park City	UT
Cinemark 16	Provo	UT
Movies 8	Provo	UT
Movies 10	Salt Lake City	UT
Movies 9	Sandy	UT
Cinemark 24	West Jordan	UT
Valley Fair	West Valley City	UT

LOEWS CINEPLEX

Layton Hills Cinemas	Layton Hills	UT
Trolley North 3	N.Salt Lake City	UT
Cinedome 2 Theatre	Ogden	UT
University 4	Orem	UT
Broadway Centre 6	Salt Lake City	UT
Holladay Center Cinemas 6	Salt Lake City	UT
Crossroads Cinemas 3	Salt Lake City	UT
Trolley Corners 3	Salt Lake City	UT
Trolley Sq. Mall Cinemas 4	Salt Lake City	UT
Southtowne Cinemas 10	Sandy	UT
Midvalley Cinemas 6	Taylorsville	UT

SAN ANTONIO

AMC

Huebner Oaks 24	San Antonio	TX
Rivercenter 9	San Antonio	TX

CINEMARK

Movies 8	Del Rio	TX
Dollar Movies	San Antonio	TX
Movies 9	San Antonio	TX

O'NEIL

Market Place Cinema 12	New Braunfels	TX

REGAL

Live Oak 18	Live Oak	TX
Fiesta 16 Theatres	San Anotnio	TX
Alamo Quarry 14	San Antonio	TX
Century Plaza 8 Cinema	San Antonio	TX
Cielo Vista 18	San Antonio	TX
Crossroads 6 Theatres	San Antonio	TX
Embassy 14 Theatres	San Antonio	TX
Galaxy 14 Theatres	San Antonio	TX
Northwest 14 Theatres	San Antonio	TX
Northwoods 14	San Antonio	TX
Rolling Oaks 6 Theatre	San Antonio	TX
Westlakes 9 Theatres	San Antonio	TX
Windsor Mall 5 Theatre	San Antonio	TX

BIRMINGHAM

CARMIKE

Carmike 10	Birmingham	AL
Summit 16	Birmingham	AL
Wynnsong 12	Birmingham	AL
Town Square 3	Cullman	AL
Martin 3	Talladega	AL

REGAL

Regal 16 - Trussville	Birmingham	AL
Festival 18	Birmingham	AL
Galleria 10	Birmingham	AL
Wildwood 14 Cinemas	Birmingham	AL
Rainbow Cinema 8	Gadsden	AL
Brook Highland 10	Inverness	AL
Movies 4	Jasper	AL

MEMPHIS

CARMIKE

Carmike 9	Dyersburg	TN

MALCO

Malco Trio	Blytheville	AR
DeSoto Cinema 16	Southaven	MS
Stage Cinema 12	Barlett	TN
Trinity Commons	Cordova	TN
Forest Hill	Germantown	TN
Appletree Cinema 12	Memphis	TN
Bartlett Cinema 10	Memphis	TN
Collierville Towne Cinema 16	Memphis	TN
Highland Quartet	Memphis	TN
Majestic Theatre	Memphis	TN
Ridgeway 4	Memphis	TN
Southwest Drive-In	Memphis	TN
Studio on the Square	Memphis	TN
Summer Drive-In	Memphis	TN
Winchester Court Cinema	Memphis	TN
Wolfchase Galleria	Memphis	TN

UNITED ARTISTS

Cinema 4	Oxford	MS

NORFOLK/VIRGINIA BEACH

AMC

Hampton Towne Center 24	Hampton	VA
Lynnhaven 8	Virginia Beach	VA
Lynnhaven Mall Upper Level 5	Virginia Beach	VA

CARMIKE

Carmike 4	Williamsburg	VA
Williamsburg 7	Williamsburg	VA

CINEMA GRILL

Greenbrier Cinema Grill	Chesapeake	VA

CINEMARK

Movies 10	Chesapeake	VA
Cinemark at Military Circle	Norfolk	VA

GENERAL CINEMA

Janaf Plaza 8 Cinemas	Norfolk	VA

R/C

Hatteras Movies	Avon	NC
Corolla Movies	Corolla	NC
Kitty Hawk Twin	Kitty Hawk	NC
Market Place	Kitty Hawk	NC
Cineplex Movies	Nags Head	NC

REGAL

Greenbrier Cinema 13	Chesapeake	VA
Greenbrier Cinema 4	Chesapeake	VA
Armory Drive Cinema 3	Franklin	VA
Riverdale Plaza 12	Hampton	VA
York River Crossing 8	Hayes	VA
Kiln Creek Cinema 20	Newport News	VA
MacArthur Center 18	Norfolk	VA
Main Gate 10	Norfolk	VA
Columbus 12	Virginia Beach	VA
Pembroke Cinema 8	Virginia Beach	VA
Strawbridge Marketplace 12	Virginia Beach	VA
Surf & Sand 8	Virginia Beach	VA

NEW ORLEANS

AMC

Galleria 8 - N.O.	Metairie	LA

CARMIKE

North Shores 6	Slidell	LA

LANDMARK

Canal Place Cinema	New Orleans	LA

O'NEIL

Holiday Square Cinema 10	Covington	LA
Causeway Place Cinema 4	Mandeville	LA
Movies 8 Slidell	Slidell	LA
River Ridge Cinema 4	Picayune	MS
Choctaw Cinema 4	Waveland	MS

SILVER CINEMAS

Trackside 5 Cinema	Bogalusa	LA
Chalmette Cinema 9	Chalmette	LA
Cinema City 8	Kenner	LA
La Place Movies 7	LaPlace	LA

UNITED ARTISTS

Southland Cinema 4	Houma	LA

WEST PALM BEACH/FT. PIERCE

AMC

Mizner Park 8	Boca Raton	FL
Indian River 24	Vero Beach	FL

EASTERN FEDERAL

Village Green	Port St Lucie	FL

MUVICO

Palace 20	Boca Raton	FL
Parisian 20	W. Palm Beach	FL

REGAL

Shadowood 16	Boca Raton	FL
Boynton 8 Cinema	Boynton Beach	FL
Delray Beach 18	Delray Beach	FL
Lake Worth 8 Cinemas	Greenacres City	FL
Jupiter 18	Jupiter	FL
Royal Palm Beach 18	Royal Palm Beach	FL
Regency Square 8	Stuart	FL

UNITED ARTISTS

UA Movies @ Boynton	Boynton Beach	FL
UA Promenade Plaza	Palm Bch Gardens	FL
UA Okee Square	West Palm Beach	FL

BUFFALO

AMC

Maple Ridge 8	Amherst	NY

CARMIKE

Carmike 8	Olean	NY

DIPSON

Cinema 1 & 2	Batavia	NY
Mall 2	Batavia	NY
Amherst Theatre	Buffalo	NY
Market Arcade Film & Arts Center	Buffalo	NY
North Park	Buffalo	NY
Chautauqua 2	Lakewood	NY
Lakewood Cinema 6	Lakewood	NY
Salamanca 2	Salamanca	NY
Eastern Hills Cinema	Williamsville	NY
Bradford 2	Bradford	PA

GENERAL CINEMA

University 8	Amherst	NY
Walden Galleria	Cheektowaga	NY
McKinley Mall	Hamburg	NY

MINI

Movieplex	Dunkirk	NY

REGAL

Elmwood Center 16	Buffalo	NY
Hollywood 12	Niagara Falls	NY
Quaker Crossing 18	Orchard Park	NY
Transit Center 18	Williamsville	NY
Transit Center IMAX	Williamsville	NY

SILVER CINEMAS

Super Saver Cinema - Elmwood	Buffalo	NY

OKLAHOMA CITY

AMC

Quail Springs Mall 24	Oklahoma City	OK

B & B THEATRES

Airline Drive-In	Ponca City	OK
Ponca Plaza Twin	Ponca City	OK

CARMIKE

Dunkin Theatre	Cushing	OK
Video Twin	Enid	OK
North Park 4	Ponca City	OK
Cinema Center 8	Shawnee	OK
Hornbeck	Shawnee	OK
Carmike 10	Stillwater	OK

CINEMARK

Tinseltown 20	Oklahoma City	OK

DICKINSON

66 Twin Driv-In	Weatherford	OK
Showest 3	Weatherford	OK

REGAL

Kickingbird Cinemas 8	Edmond	OK
Crossroads Mall 16	Oklahoma City	OK
Windsor Hills Cinema 10	Oklahoma City	OK

SILVER CINEMAS

North Park Cinema 7	Oklahoma City	OK
Dollar Movies 5	Yukon	OK

WALLACE

Heritage Plaza 5	Midwest City	OK
Spotlight Cinema 14	Norman	OK
Brixton Square Cinema 8	Oklahoma City	OK
Crossroads Cinema 8	Oklahoma City	OK
Penn Square Cinema 10	Oklahoma City	OK
Movies Cinema 6	Shawnee	OK

GREENSBORO/HIGH POINT/WINSTON SALEM

CARMIKE

Kingsway 4	Eden	NC
Carmike 18	Greensboro	NC
Carmike 8	High Point	NC
Cinema 8	Lexington	NC
Carmike 10	Winston-Salem	NC
Wynnsong 16	Winston-Salem	NC

CINEMARK

Randolph Cinema	Asheboro	NC
Brassfield Cinema	Greensboro	NC

EASTERN FEDERAL

North Pointe	Winston-Salem	NC

REGAL

Greensboro Cinema 7	Greensboro	NC
Oak Hollow Mall 7	High Point	NC
Mayberry Cinema 5	Mount Airy	NC

LOUISVILLE

CINEMARK

Greentree	Clarksville	IN
Greentree	Clarksville	IN
Tinseltown	Louisville	KY

NATIONAL AMUSEMENTS

River Falls Cinemas	Clarksville	IN
Kenwood Drive-In	Louisville	KY
Showcase Cinemas Louisville	Louisville	KY
Stonybrook Cinemas	Louisville	KY

ALBUQUERQUE

ALLEN THEATRES

Fiesta Twin	Cortez	CO
Cinema 5	Alamogordo	NM
Mall Cinema	Carlsbad	NM
Allen 8	Farmington	NM
Animas	Farmington	NM
Apache Drive-In	Farmington	NM
Cameo	Farmington	NM
Centennial	Farmington	NM
Aztec Twin	Gallup	NM
El Morro	Gallup	NM
Rio West Twin	Gallup	NM
Broadmoor	Hobbs	NM
Cinema 3	Hobbs	NM
Cinema 4	Roswell	NM
Del Norte Twin	Roswell	NM
Park Twin	Roswell	NM

CARMIKE

Carmike 2	Artesia	NM

CENTURY

Century Rio	Albuquerque	NM

CINEMARK

Movies 8	Albuquerque	NM
Movies West	Albuquerque	NM

TRANS-LUX

High Five Cinemas	Durango	CO
Gaslight Cinemas	Durango	CO
Dream Catcher Cinema	Espanola	NM
High Society Cinema	Los Alamos	NM
Starlight Cinema	Los Lunas	NM
Grand Illusion Theatre	Santa Fe	NM
Jean Cocteau Cinema	Santa Fe	NM
Loma Theatre	Socorro	NM
Storyteller Cinemas	Taos	NM

UNITED ARTISTS

Coronado 6 Theatre	Albuquerque	NM
UA @ Highridge Theatre	Albuquerque	NM
UA Cottonwood Mall	Albuquerque	NM
UA Four Hills 10	Albuquerque	NM
UA De Vargas Center 6	Santa Fe	NM
UA North Theatre	Santa Fe	NM
UA South	Santa Fe	NM

LAS VEGAS

CENTURY

Cinedome Henderson	Henderson	NV
Century Desert	Las Vegas	NV
Century Orleans 12	Las Vegas	NV
Cinedome Las Vegas	Las Vegas	NV
Las Vegas Drive-In	Las Vegas	NV
Rancho Santa Fe	Las Vegas	NV
Suncoast	Las Vegas	NV

REGAL

Sunset Station 13 Theatre	Henderson	NV
Boulder Station 11 theatre	Las Vegas	NV
Colonnade 14	Las Vegas	NV
Texas Station 18	Las Vegas	NV
Village Square 18	Las Vegas	NV

UNITED ARTISTS

UA Green Valley Cinemas	Henderson	NV
Showcase Mall	Las Vegas	NV
UA Rainbow Promenade	Las Vegas	NV

JACKSONVILLE

AMC

Regency 24	Jacksonville	FL
Orange Park 24	Orange Park	FL

CARMIKE

Amelia Island 7	Fernandina Beach	FL

CINEMARK

Tinseltown USA	Jacksonville	FL

GEORGIA

Glynn Place 11	Brunswick	GA
Kings Bay Cinemas	St. Marys	GA
Island Cinemas 7	St. Simons	GA
Waycross Mall Cinema 7	Waycross	GA

REGAL

Beach Boulevard 18	Jacksonville	FL
Jacksonville Cinema 10	Jacksonville	FL
The Avenue 20	Jacksonville	FL
Mall St Augustine 6	St Augustine	FL

STARNET

Atlantic Theatre	Atlantic Beach	FL
Pabio Theatres	Jacksonville	FL
St. Johns Theatre	Jacksonville	FL
Palatka Mall Cinemas	Palatka	FL

UNITED ARTISTS

Movies @ Orange Park	Jacksonville	FL
Movies @ Regency Square	Jacksonville	FL
UA Cinema 90	Lake City	FL
UA North Point Market	Alpharetta	GA

DAYTON

CHAKERES

Bellefontaine Cinema 8	Bellefontaine	OH
Celina 5	Celina	OH
Lake Drive-In	Celina	OH
Kettering Cinema 2	Dayton	OH
Melody 49 Drive-In	Dayton	OH
Skyborn Drive-In	Fairborn	OH
Park Layne Drive-In	New Carlisle	OH
Sidney 3	Sidney	OH
Cinema 10	Springfield	OH
Melody Cruise-In	Springfield	OH
Upper Valley 5	Springfield	OH
Urbana 1 & 2	Urbana	OH

CINEMARK

Miami Valley	Piqua	OH

DANBARRY

Dollar Saver Cinemas.	Huber Heights	OH

KERASOTES

Cinema 11	Richmond	IN
Dollar Cinema	Richmond	IN

NATIONAL AMUSEMENTS

S/C Huber Heights 16	Huber Heights	OH
S/C Cinemas Miamisburgh	West Carrollton	OH

REGAL

Hollywood 20 @ Fairfield Comm.	Beavercreek	OH

AUSTIN

CINEMARK

Barton Creek	Austin	TX
Dollar Cinema 8	Austin	TX
Tinseltown	Pflugerville	TX
Movies 8	Round Rock	TX
Tinseltown	South Austin	TX

GENERAL CINEMA

Barton Creek Square	Austin	TX

LANDMARK

Dobie Theatre	Austin	TX

REGAL

Arbor 7 Cinemas	Austin	TX
Gateway 16	Austin	TX
Lakecreek 8	Austin	TX
Lakeline Mall 9	Austin	TX
Lincoln 6 Theatres	Austin	TX
Metropolitan 14	Austin	TX
Northcross 6	Austin	TX
Riverside 8 Cinema	Austin	TX
Village 4	Austin	TX
Westgate 11 Theatres	Austin	TX

INDEPENDENT THEATERS

ALASKA

Theatre Name	Address	City	State	Zip	Screens
Bear Tooth Theatre Pub	1230 W. 27th Ave	Anchorage	AK	99503	2
Capri Cinema	3425 E. Tudor Rd.	Anchorage	AK	99507	1
Homer Family Theatre	106 W. Main St.	Homer	AK	99603	1
Glacier Cinema	9091 Cinema Dr.	Juneau	AK	99801	5
Ketchikan Coliseum Theatre	405 Mission St.	Ketchikan	AK	99901	2
Orca Twin Theatre	Mile 19.5 Kalifornski	Soldotna	AK	99669	2
Mat-Su 3 Cinema	2430 Parks Hwy.	Wasilla	AK	99654	3

ALABAMA

Theatre Name	Address	City	State	Zip	Screens
Playhouse Cinema 3	1236 Cherokee Rd.	Alexander City	AL	35010-3917	3
Clark 3 Theatres	109 O'Neal Court	Andalusia	AL	36420	3
Strand Theatre	116 S. Main St.	Atmore	AL	36502	1
Alabama Theatre	1817 Third Ave. N.	Birmingham	AL	35203	1
McWane Center IMAX	205 19th St. N.	Birmingham	AL	35203	1
Sand Mountain Twin Drive-In	10480 U.S. Hwy. 431	Boaz	AL	35956-3120	2
Northside Cinema 1 & 2	3489 Ross Clark Circle	Dothan	AL	36303	10
Cinemas I and II	Enterprise Shopping Center	Enterprise	AL	36330	2
Cinemas III and IV	Westgate Center	Enterprise	AL	36330	2
College Cinema	College Plaza Shopping Ctr.	Enterprise	AL	36330	3
Hamilton 4 Cinemas	2718 Gault Ave. N.	Fort Payne	AL	35967	4
Theatre of Gadsden	310 N. 27th. St.	Gadsden	Al	35904	1
Blue Moon Drive-In	4690 US Hwy. 43	Guin	AL	35563	1
Havala Drive-In	Hwy. 195 E.	Haleyville	AL	35565	1
Dixie Cinema 3	225 Bexar Ave. E.	Hamilton	AL	35570	3
Sumter Theatre	16 Franklin St.	Livingston	AL	35470	1
IMAX Dome Gulf Coast Exploreum	65 Government St.	Mobile	AL	36602	1
Our Place Theatre	1 Teen Trail Dr.	Monroeville	AL	36460	1
Capri Theatre	1045 E. Fairview Ave.	Montgomery	AL	36106	1
LA Getaway Cinema	25050 Canal Rd.	Orange Beach	AL	36561	1
Clark Twin Cinema	Martindale Plaza	Ozark	AL	36360	2
Holiday Twin Cinema	1507 E. Willow St.	Scottsboro	AL	35768	2
Thomasville Theatre	24 W. Front St. S.	Thomasville	AL	36784	1
Continental Cinema 5	350 Hwy. 231 N.	Troy	AL	36081	5

ARKANSAS

Theatre Name	Address	City	State	Zip	Screens
Main Theatre	2075 Main St.	Berryville	AR	72616	1
Savage Theatre	20 N. Broadway Ave.	Booneville	AR	72927	1
Silver Screen Theatre	100 Cinema Blvd.	Cabot	AR	72023	4
Gateway Twin Theatres	Hwy. 65 S.	Clinton	AR	72031	2
Rialto Theatre	113 E. Cedar St.	El Dorado	AR	71730	3
112 Drive-In	3352 N. Hwy. 112	Fayetteville	AR	72703	1
Broadway Cinema	1101 E. Broadway St.	Forest City	AR	72335	2
Phoenix Village Twin	4600 Towson Ave. #105	Fort Smith	AR	72901	2
Lakeland Twin Cinema	Hwy 25 S. and 6th St.	Heber Springs	AR	72543	2
Behind The Mall 4 Cinema	4501 Central Ave.	Hot Springs	AR	71901	4
Hollywood 12 Cinema	2407 E. Parker Rd.	Jonesboro	AR	72401	12
IMAX @ Aerospace Education Center	3301 E. Roosevelt Rd.	Little Rock	AR	72206	1
Market St. Bargain Cinema	1521 Merrill Dr.	Little Rock	AR	72211	1
Ritz 2 Theatre	213 S. Main St.	Malvern	AR	72104	2
Silver Screen Twin Theatre	1200 Pine Ave.	Mena	AR	71953	2
Hollywood Cinema 6	Dearman Dr.	Monticello	AR	71655	6
Twinlake Tri Cinema	1606 Hwy. 62 E.	Mountain Home	AR	72653	3
Plaza Twin Cinema	Paragould Plaza Shopping Ctr.	Paragould	AR	72450	2
Paris Cinema	26 W. Walnut St.	Paris	AR	72855	1
Cinema City Twin	5259 Hwy. 67 S.	Pocahontas	AR	72455	2
Pickwood 11 Theatres	3800 W. Main	Russellville	AR	72801	11
Valley Cinema Trio	Hwy. 64 E.	Russellville	AR	72801	3
Searcy Cinema 8	3001 E. Race St.	Searcy	AR	72149	8
Stuttgart Twin Cinema	806 W. 22nd St., #F	Stuttgart	AR	72160-6504	2
Maxie Theatre	Hwy 63	Trumann	AR	72472	1
Wynne Twin Cinema	1915 N. Falls Blvd.	Wynne	AR	72396	2

ARIZONA

Theatre Name	Address	City	State	Zip	Screens
Mall Cinema 3	1226 E. Florence Blvd.	Casa Grande	AZ	85222	3
Cottonwood's Big Show	1389 E. Hwy 89A	Cottonwood	AZ	86326	1
Apache Drive-In	112 S. Broad St.	Globe	AZ	85501	1
Globe 2 Theatre	141 N. Broad St.	Globe	AZ	85501	2
Palm Valley Cinema	I-10 and Litchfield	Goodyear	AZ	85338	14
Movies Havasu 6	180 Swanson Ave.	Lake Havasu City	AZ	86403	6
Fountain Morenci Theatre	Morenci Plaza	Morenci Plaza	AZ	85540	1
Mesa Theatre	42 S. Lake Powell Blvd.	Page	AZ	86040	1
Fountain Cinema 1 Theatre	1914 W. Thatcher Blvd.	Safford	AZ	85546-3318	1
Town Square Theatre	1210 W. Cleveland	Saint Johns	AZ	85936	1
Flicker Shack Theatre	W. Hwy. 89A	Sedona	AZ	86336	1

Theatre Name	Address	City	State	Zip	Screens
Winchester 2 Theatre	1850 White Mountain Blvd.	Showlow	AZ	85901	2
R & M Cinema	300 E. Wilcox Dr.	Sierra Vista	AZ	85635	3
Uptown 3 Theatres	4341 S. State Hwy. 92	Sierra Vista	AZ	85650	3
El Rio Theatre	Springerville	Springerville	AZ	85938	1
Arizona Mills IMAX	5000 Arizona Mills Circle	Tempe	AZ	85283	1
Tempe Cinemas	1825 E. Elliot Rd.	Tempe	AZ	85284	4
Silver Screen Twin Cinemas	Hwy. 160 E., Junction 264	Tuba City	AZ	86045	2
De Anza Drive-In - Tucson	1401 S. Alvernon Way	Tucson	AZ	85711	4
Loft 2 Cinemas	3233 E. Speedway Blvd.	Tucson	AZ	85716-3933	2
The Screening Room	127 E. Congress St.	Tucson	AZ	85701-1707	1
Grand Canyon IMAX Theatre	Hwy. 64 @ Box 1397	Tusayan	AZ	86023	1
Saguaro	176 E. Wickenburg Way	Wickenburg	AZ	85358	1
Rex Allen Theatre	150 N. Railroad Ave.	Willcox	AZ	85643-2132	2
Mandarin Cinema	3142 S. Arizona Ave.	Yuma	AZ	85364	4
Plaza 5 Theatres	1560 S. 4th Ave.	Yuma	AZ	85364	5

CALIFORNIA

Theatre Name	Address	City	State	Zip	Screens
Niles Theatre	127 S. Main St.	Alturas	CA	96101	1
Brookhurst 4 Cinema	2299 West Ball Rd.	Anaheim	CA	92804	4
Angels Theatre	1228 S. Main St.	Angels Camp	CA	95222	1
Aptos Twin	122 Rancho Del Mar Center	Aptos	CA	95003	2
Arcata Theatre	1036 G St.	Arcata	CA	95521	1
Minor Theatre	1015 H St.	Arcata	CA	95521	3
Fair Oaks Theatre	1007 Grand Ave.	Arroyo Grande	CA	93420	1
Cinema Showcase Fox Cineplex	60 West Ramsey	Banning	CA	92220	3
Skyline Drive-In	31175 Old Hwy. 58	Barstow	CA	92311	1
Elmwood 3	2966 College Ave.	Berkeley	CA	94705	3
Fine Arts Cinema	2451 Shattuck Ave.	Berkeley	CA	94704	2
Pacific Film Archive	2575 Bancroft @ Bowditch	Berkeley	CA	94720-2250	1
Renaissance Oaks Theatre	1875 Solano Ave.	Berkeley	CA	94707	2
Village Theatre	40789 Village Dr.	Big Bear Lake	CA	92315	2
Village Theatres North	602 Pine Knot Ave.	Big Bear Lake	CA	92315	3
Bishop Twin	237 N. Main St.	Bishop	CA	93514	2
Allstars Cinema 2 Blythe	691 West Hobson Way	Blythe	CA	92225-1512	2
Sonoma Cinemas	200 Siesta Way	Boyes Hot Springs	CA	95431	4
Delta Cinemas	641 1st St.	Brentwood	CA	94513-1322	2
Parks Plaza	515 McMurray Rd.	Buellton	CA	93427	5
Mt. Burney Theatre	37030 Main St.	Burney	CA	96013	1
Plaza 4 Theatres	2501 S. Winchester Blvd.	Campbell	CA	95008	4
41st Ave. Playhouse	1475 41st Ave.	Capitola	CA	95010	3
Resort Theatre Crossroads	2 Crossroads Blvd.	Carmel	CA	93923	2
Carpinteria Plaza Theatre	4916 Carpinteria Ave.	Carpinteria	CA	93013	1
Chabot Cinema	2853 Castro Valley Blvd.	Castro Valley	CA	94546-5505	1
Desert IMAX Theatre	68-510 E. Palm Canyon Dr.	Cathedral City	CA	92234	1
Pageant Theatre	351 E. 6th St.	Chico	CA	95928	1
Movie Experience	Hwy. 71 & Grand Ave.	Chino	CA	91710	11
Vogue	226 3rd Ave.	Chula Vista	CA	91915	1
Clearlake Twin	3380 Washington St.	Clearlake	CA	95422	2
Clover Cinemas	121 E. 1st St.	Cloverdale	CA	95425	4
Coalinga Cinemas	122 W. Elm Ave.	Coalinga	CA	93210	2
Colfax Theatre	49 S. Main St.	Colfax	CA	95713	1
Colusa Theatre	513 Market St.	Colusa	CA	95932	1
Brenden Concord 14	1985 Willow Pass Rd.	Concord	CA	94520	14
Rodger's Theatre	1217 Solano St.	Corning	CA	96021	1
Village Coronado	820 Orange	Coronado	CA	92118	1
Fox Theatre - Covina	211 N. Azusa Ave.	Covina	CA	91722	3
Crescent City Cinema	375 M St.	Crescent City	CA	95531	8
Red's Showcase Twin Cinemas	395 G St.	Cresent City	CA	95531	2
Oaks Cinema 5	21275 Stevens Creek Blvd.	Cupertino	CA	95014	5
Family Twin Cinema	9823 Walker St.	Cypress	CA	90630	2
Ave. Theatre	11022 Downey Ave.	Downey	CA	90241	2
Eagle Rock	2700 Colorado Blvd.	Eagle Rock	CA	90041-1048	4
Aero Drive-In	1470 Broadway	El Cajon	CA	92021-5128	1
Fox 3 Theatres	139 S. 7th St.	El Centro	CA	92243	3
Old Town Music Hall	140 Richmond St.	El Segundo	CA	90245	1
La Paloma	471 S. Coast Hwy.	Encinitas	CA	92024-3530	1
Del Norte Plaza Movies 8	362 W. Del Norte Pkwy.	Escondido	CA	92027	8
Broadway Cinema 8	1223 Broadway St.	Eureka	CA	95501	8
Broadway Movies 6	3300 Broadway	Eureka	CA	95502	6
Movies Bayshore Mall	3300 Broadway	Eureka	CA	95501	6
Sunrise Drive-In	8149 Greenback Lane	Fair Oaks	CA	95628	1
Fall River	43118 Hwy 299 E.	Fall River	CA	96028	1
Towne Theatre-Fillmore	338 Central Ave.	Fillmore	CA	93015	1
Coast Cinemas	167 S. Franklin St.	Fort Bragg	CA	95437	4
NAZ 8 Cinemas	39400 Argonaut Way	Fremont	CA	94538	8
NAZ Cinema	37411 Fremont Blvd.	Fremont	CA	94536-3704	1
Garberville Theatre	766 Redwood St.	Garberville	CA	95542	1
Four Star Cinema	12111 Valley View St.	Garden Grove	CA	92845	4
Gardena Cinema	14948 Crenshaw Blvd.	Gardena	CA	90248	1
Platinum Theatres	353 E. 10th St.	Gilroy	CA	95020	7
Sierra Cinemas	840 E. Main St.	Grass Valley	CA	95945	4
Metro 4 Cinemas	123 E. 7th St.	Hanford	CA	93230	4
Raven Theatre and Film Center	115 N. St.	Healdsburg	CA	95448-3805	5
Granada Discount Theatre	336 5th St.	Hollister	CA	95023	1
Premiere Cinemas 5	581-A McCray St.	Hollister	CA	95023	5
Egyptian Theatre	6712 Hollywood Blvd.	Hollywood	CA	90028	1
Silent Movie Theatre	611 N. Fairfax Ave.	Hollywood	CA	90036	1
Vista	4473 Sunset Blvd.	Hollywood	CA	90020	1
California 3 Theatres	6528 Pacific Blvd.	Huntington Park	CA	90255	3

Theatre Name	Address	City	State	Zip	Screens
California Theatre	6528 Pacific Blvd.	Huntington Park	CA	90255	3
Metropolitan Park Twin	6504 Pacific Blvd	Huntington Park	CA	90255-4106	2
Rustic Theatre	54290 N. Circle Dr.	Idyllwild	CA	92549	1
Motor Vu Twin Drive-In	Hwy. 86	Imperial	CA	92251	2
Studio Cinema 3	827 Palm Ave.	Imperial Beach	CA	91932-1505	3
Movies	2335 Hwy. 86	Imperial Valley	CA	92251	6
Resort Theatre Metro 8 Theatre	81725 Hwy. 111	Indio	CA	92201	8
Reel Joy Theatre	219 Broadway St.	King City	CA	93930-2830	1
Renaissance Park Theatre	3519 Golden Gate Way	Lafayette	CA	94549	1
Lakeport Auto Movies	52 Soda Bay Rd.	Lakeport	CA	95453	1
Lakeport Cinema 5	52 Soda Bay Rd.	Lakeport	CA	95453	5
Valley Cinema	2570 West Lodi Ave.	Lodi	CA	95240	3
Movies Gemini	1028 N. H St..	Lompoc	CA	93436	2
Movies Of Lompoc	220 W. Barton	Lompoc	CA	93436	4
Art Theatre	2025 W. 4th St.	Long Beach	CA	90814-1001	1
Akarakian Highland 3 Theatre	5604 Figueroa St.	Los Angeles	CA	90042	3
California Science Center Imax	700 State Dr.	Los Angeles	CA	90037	1
Los Feliz 3	1822 N. Vermont Ave.	Los Angeles	CA	90027-4213	3
Metropolitan Campus	1020 N. Vermont Ave.	Los Angeles	CA	90029-2620	2
Metropolitan Orpheum	842 S. Broadway	Los Angeles	CA	90014	1
Metropolitan Palace	630 S. Broadway	Los Angeles	CA	90014	1
New Beverly Cinema	7165 Beverly Blvd	Los Angeles	CA	90036	1
University Cinema	USC	Los Angeles	CA	90007	3
Los Gatos	41 N. Santa Cruz Ave.	Los Gatos	CA	95030	2
Madera 6 Cinema	1140 N. Gateway Dr.	Madera	CA	93637	6
Minaret Cinemas	437 Old Mammoth Rd.	Mammoth Lakes	CA	93546	2
Plaza Theatre	569 Old Mammoth Rd.	Mammoth Lakes	CA	93546	1
Marketplace Stadium 10	1321 W. Yosemite Ave.	Manteca	CA	95336	10
Marysville Drive-In Theatre	5575 Chestnut Rd.	Marysville	CA	95901	2
Brenden Theatres 18	1021 10th St..	Modesto	CA	95354	18
Mission Drive-In Montclair	10798 Ramona Ave..	Montclair	CA	91763	1
Rio Theatre	20396 Bohemian Hwy.	Monte Rio	CA	95462	1
Dream Theatre	301 Prescott Ave	Monterey	CA	93940	2
Resort Theatre Galaxy 6	290 Del Monte Center	Monterey	CA	93940	6
Resort Theatres Osio	350 Alvarado St.	Monterey	CA	93940	6
Rheem Theatre	350 Park St.	Moraga	CA	94556	4
Canyon Springs Cinema 7	12125 Day St.	Moreno Valley	CA	92557	7
Uptown Cinemas 4	1350 Third St.	Napa	CA	94559	4
Harbor Drive-In	3200 D Ave..	National City	CA	91950-1392	1
Magic Theatre Nevada City	107 Argall Way	Nevada City	CA	95959	1
Nevada Theatre	401 Broad St.	Nevada City	CA	95959	1
Plaza Theatre	23710 Lyons Ave.	Newhall	CA	91321	1
Oakdale Cinema 2	832 N. Yosemite	Oakdale	CA	95361	2
Met Cinemas	40015 Hwy. 49	Oakhurst	CA	93644	5
Grand Lake Theatre	3200 Grand Ave.	Oakland	CA	94610	4
Jack London Cinema	100 Washington	Oakland	CA	94607	9
Paramount	2025 Broadway	Oakland	CA	94612	1
Parkway Theater	1834 Park Blvd.	Oakland	CA	94606	2
Star Theatre	402 N. Coast Hwy.	Oceanside	CA	92054	1
Ojai Playhouse	145 E. Ojai Ave	Ojai	CA	93023	1
Granada Theatre	303 N. Euclid Ave.	Ontario	CA	91761	1
Ultrascreen Theatre	1 Mill Circle	Ontario	CA	91764	1
Captain Bloods Village Theatre	1140 N. Tustin Ave.	Orange	CA	92867	2
Orinda Theatre	Orinda Exit At Hwy 24	Orinda	CA	94563	3
Feather River Cinema	2690 Feather River Blvd.	Oroville	CA	95965	6
Resort Theatre Lighthouse 4	525 Lighthouse Ave.	Pacific Grove	CA	93950	4
Seavue Theatre	520 Palmetto Ave.	Pacifica	CA	94044	2
Resort Theatre Cinema 10	72840 Hwy. 111	Palm Desert	CA	92260	10
Resort Theatre Cinema 3	72745 Hwy. 111	Palm Desert	CA	92260	3
Palm Springs Festival of Arts	2300 E. Baristo Rd.	Palm Springs	CA	92262-7128	2
Resort Theatre Courtyard 10	789 E. Tahquitz Canyon Way	Palm Springs	CA	92262	10
Stanford Theatre	221 University Ave.	Palo Alto	CA	94301	1
Bianchi Theatres	7770 E. Rosecrans Ave	Paramount	CA	90723	2
Paramount Theatres 7	7770 Rosecrans Ave.	Paramount	CA	90723	7
Academy 6 Theater	1003 E. Colorado Blvd.	Pasadena	CA	91106	6
Oakcreek Cinemas	1920 Creston Rd..	Paso Robles	CA	93446	3
Park Cinemas Paso Robles	1100 Pine St..	Paso Robles	CA	93446	6
Brenden 16 Theatre	4085 Century Blvd	Pittsburg	CA	94565	16
Arena Theatre	245 Main St.	Point Arena	CA	95468	1
Galaxy 9	631 N. Indiana	Porterville	CA	93257	9
Ramona Twin Cinemas	626 Main St.	Ramona	CA	92065-2044	2
Resort Theatre Rancho 16	72-777 Dinah Shore Dr.	Rancho Mirage	CA	92270	16
Krikorian Redlands Cinema 14	340 N. Eureka St.	Redlands	CA	92373	14
Ridgecrest Cinema	1631 N. Triangle Dr.	Ridgecrest	CA	93555	5
Canyon Crest	5225 Canyon Crest Dr	Riverside	CA	92507	1
Marketplace Cinema 6	4040 Vine St	Riverside	CA	92507	6
Van Buren Drive-In	3035 Van Buren	Riverside	CA	92503	3
Harding Plaza Cinema	212 Harding Blvd.	Roseville	CA	95678	1
Crest Theatre	1013 K St.	Sacramento	CA	95814	2
Esquire Imax Theatre	1211 K St.	Sacramento	CA	95814	1
Reading Entertainments Tower 3 Theatre	2508 Landpark Dr.	Sacramento	CA	95818	3
Skyview 2 Drive-In	201 Harrison Rd.	Salinas	CA	93902	2
Sterling Cinema	2373 N. Sterling Ave.	San Bernadino	CA	92404	6
Carousel Mall	155 Carousel Mall	San Bernadino	CA	92401	4
Tanforan Discount Cinemas	400 Tanforan Park	San Bruno	CA	94066	4
Reuben H. Fleet Space Theater	Balboa Park	San Diego	CA	92101	1
South Bay Drive In	2170 Coronado Ave.	San Diego	CA	92154	3
4 Star	2200 Clement St	San Francisco	CA	94121	3
Alliance Francaise	1345 Bush St.	San Francisco	CA	94109	1
Balboa Twin	36th & Balboa	San Francisco	CA	94121	2
Campus All-Male Theatre	220 Jones St.	San Francisco	CA	94102	1

Theatre Name	Address	City	State	Zip	Screens
Castro Theatre	429 Castro St.	San Francisco	CA	94114	1
Citibank Cinemax	Beach St. & the Embarcadero	San Francisco	CA	94133	1
St. Francis 1 & 2	965 Market St.	San Francisco	CA	94103	2
Tearoom Male	145 Eddy St.	San Francisco	CA	94102	1
The Red Vic Theatre	1727 Haight	San Francisco	CA	94117	1
The Roxie Theatre	3117 16th at Valencia	San Francisco	CA	94103	1
Victoria Theatre	2961 16th St.	San Francisco	CA	94103	2
Resort Theatre Metro 12	1599 S. San Jacinto Ave.	San Jacinto	CA	92583	12
Almaden Cinema Five	2306 Almaden Rd.	San Jose	CA	95125	5
Camera 3	288 S. Second St.	San Jose	CA	95113	3
Camera One	366 S. First St.	San Jose	CA	95113	1
Cine 16 at the Agenda Lounge	399 S. First St.	San Jose	CA	95113	1
Hackworth IMAX Dome	201 S. Market St.	San Jose	CA	95113	2
Towne 3	1433 The Alameda	San Jose	CA	95126	3
Palm Theatre 2	817 Palm St.	San Luis Obispo	CA	93401	2
Sunset Drive-In	255 Elks Lane	San Luis Obispo	CA	93401	1
Palm Theatre	1705 Palm Ave.	San Mateo	CA	94402	1
Rafael Film Center	1118 Fourth St.	San Rafael	CA	94901	3
Metropolitan Fiesta Twin	305 E. 4th St.	Santa Ana	CA	92701	2
IMAX Pictorium	2401 Agnew Rd.	Santa Clara	CA	95054	1
Del Mar Star Cinema 4	1124 Pacific Ave.	Santa Cruz	CA	95060-4415	4
Nickelodeon 4 Theatres	210 Lincoln St.	Santa Cruz	CA	95060	4
Rio Theatre	1205 Soquel Ave	Santa Cruz	CA	95062	1
Eros Cinema	1191 E. Santa Clara St.	Santa Jose	CA	95116	1
Hiway Drive-In	3170 Santa Maria Way	Santa Maria	CA	93455	1
Aero	1328 Montana Ave.	Santa Monica	CA	90403	1
Airport Cinema 8	409 Aviation Way	Santa Rosa	CA	95403	8
Santee Drive-In	10990 Woodside Ave.	Santee	CA	92071-2833	2
Scotts Valley 6 Cinemas	226 Mount Hermon Rd.	Scotts Valley	CA	95066	6
Bay Theatre	340 Main St.	Seal Beach	CA	90740	1
Sebastopol Cinema 9	6868 McKinley St.	Sebastopol	CA	95472	9
Selma Cinema	2705 Cinema Way	Selma	CA	93662	6
Sebastiani Theatre	476 1st St. E.	Sonoma	CA	95476	1
Cameo Cinema	1340 Main St.	St. Helena	CA	94574	1
Cobblestone Cinema Tahoe City	475 N. Lake Blvd.	Tahoe City	CA	96145	2
Hitching Post Theatre	Corner Green & F St.	Tehachapi	CA	93561	4
Valley Cinema	2710 Geer Rd.	Turlock	CA	95380	4
Smith's Ranch Drive-In	4584 Adobe Rd.	Twentynine Palms	CA	92277	1
Brenden Vacaville 16	531 Davis St.	Vacaville	CA	95688	16
Mooney Drive-In	26672 S. Mooney Blvd.	Visalia	CA	93291	2
Fox Theatre	15 Maple St.	Watsonville	CA	95076	3
Green Valley Cinema 6	1125 S.Green Valley Rd.	Watsonville	CA	95076	6
Trinity Theatre	Downtown Trinity	Weaverville	CA	96093	1
Rubidoux Drive-In	3770 Opal St.	West Riverside	CA	92509	1
Akarakian Whittier Village 9 Cinemas	7038 Greenleaf Ave.	Whittier	CA	90602	9
Santa Fe Springs Plaza	13469 Telegraph Rd.	Whittier	CA	90605	3
Noyo Theatre 3	57 E. Commercial St.	Willits	CA	95490	3
Opus	236 W. Sycamore St.	Willows	CA	95988	0
Empire Theatre	6742 Wofford Heights Blvd.	Wofford Heights	CA	93285	1
State Cinema 3	322 Main St.	Woodland	CA	95695	3
Sutter Cinema 3	754 Plumas St.	Yuba City	CA	95991	3
Cinema 6	56401 29 Palms Hwy.	Yucca Valley	CA	92284	4

COLORADO

Theatre Name	Address	City	State	Zip	Screens
Ski Hi 5	7089 W. Hwy 60	Alamosa	CO	81101	5
Resort Theatre Isis	406 E. Hopkins Ave.	Aspen	CO	81611	1
Sands Theatre	211 Clayton St.	Brush	CO	80723-2103	1
Crystal Theatre	427 Main St.	Carbondale	CO	81623	1
Movieland Cinemas	218 E. Valley Rd, Ste 300	Carbondale	CO	81623	5
Wells Theatre	170 E. 1st S.	Cheyenne Wells	CO	80810	1
Kimballs Twin Peak Theatres	115 E. Pikes Peak Ave.	Colorado Springs	CO	80903	2
88 Drive-In Theatre	E. 88th Ave. & Rosemary St.	Commerce City	CO	80022	1
Allen Fiesta Theatre	21 W. Main St.	Cortez	CO	81321	2
West 2 Theatres	29 E. Victory Way	Craig	CO	81625	2
Majestic 3 Theatres	507 Red Lady Ave.	Crested Butte	CO	81224	3
Egyptian Theatre	452 Main St.	Delta	CO	81416-1825	1
Tru Vu Drive-In	1001 Hwy. 92	Delta	CO	81416	1
Phipps IMAX-Denver Museum	2001 Colorado Blvd.	Denver	CO	80205	1
Rocket Drive-In	26126 Hwy. 160	Durango	CO	81301	1
Riverwalk Theatre	34253 US Hwy. 6	Edwards	CO	81632	4
Stanley Village 3 Theatres	543 Big Thompson Ave.	Estes Park	CO	80517-9651	3
Holiday Twin Drive-In	2206 S. Overland Trail	Fort Collins	CO	80522	2
Cover Theatre	314 Main St.	Ft. Morgan	CO	80701-2109	2
Wilshire Twin Theatre	1020 26th Ave	Greeley	CO	80631	2
Flick Twin Theatres	909 N. Wisconsin	Gunnison	CO	81230	2
Lincoln Theatre	245 E. Ave	Limon	CO	80828	1
Vali Theatre	139 Adams St.	Montevista	CO	81144	3
Liberty Theatre	418 N. Pagosa Blvd.	Pagosa Springs	CO	81147	1
Paradise	215 Grand Ave.	Paonia	CO	81428	0
Storyville Cinema	135 W. First St.	Salida	CO	81201	1
Cinderella City Drive-In	3400 S. Platte River Dr.	Sheridan	CO	80236	2
Capitol Theatre	149 E. 9th Ave	Springfield	CO	81073	1
Fox Theatre	423 W. Main St.	Trinidad	CO	81082	1
Movie Picture Show House	3600 E. Main St.	Trinidad	CO	81082	2
Cliff Theatre	420 Main St.	Wray	CO	80758-1725	1

Theatre Name	Address	City	State	Zip	Screens

CONNECTICUT

Theatre Name	Address	City	State	Zip	Screens
Bantam Cinema	115 Bantam Lake Rd.	Bantam	CT	06750	2
Bethel Cinema	269 Greenwood Ave.	Bethel	CT	06801	4
Entertainment Bloomfield Cinema 8	863 Park Ave.	Bloomfield	CT	06002	8
Gallery Cinemas	396 Old Hartford Rd.	Colchester	CT	06415	6
Elm 1 and 2 Theatres	924 S. Quaker Lane	Elmwood	CT	06110	2
Webster Theatre	31 Webster St.	Harford	CT	06114	1
Atheneum Cinema	600 Main St.	Hartford	CT	06103	1
Cine Studio Theatre	300 Summit St.	Hartford	CT	06106	1
Hoyts Cinema City 4	235 Brainard Rd.	Hartford	CT	06114	4
Real Art Ways Theatre	56 Arbor St.	Hartford	CT	06106	1
State Theatre	80 Main St.	Jewett City	CT	06350	2
Madison Art Cinemas	761 Boston Post Rd.	Madison	CT	06443	2
Mansfield Drive-In	Junction Rtes. 31 & 32	Mansfield	CT	06250	3
Destinta Metro Square 12	200 Main St.	Middletown	CT	06457	12
Cine 1-2-3-4	371 Middletown Ave.	New Haven	CT	06513	4
York Square Cinema 3	55 Broadway	New Haven	CT	06511	3
Bank St. Theatre	46 Bank St.	New Milford	CT	06776	2
Edmond Town Hall Theatre	45 Main St.	Newtown	CT	06470-2134	1
Niantic Cinema	279 Main St.	Niantic	CT	06357	4
Garden Cinemas Norwalk	26 Isaac St.	Norwalk	CT	06850	3
IMAX Maritime Aquarium Norwalk	10 N. Water St.	Norwalk	CT	06854	1
Southington Twin Drive-In	935 Meriden Waterbury Tpk.	Plantsville	CT	06479	2
Pleasant Valley Drive-In	Rte. 181 off Rte. 84	Pleasant Valley	CT	06063	1
Entertainment Seymour Plaza	814 Derby Ave.	Seymour	CT	06483	12
Strand Theatre	165 Main St.	Seymour	CT	06483	1
Sono Cinema Theatre	17 Washington St.	South Norwalk	CT	06854	1
State Cinema	990 Hope St.	Springdale	CT	06907	1
Stanford Flicks	Stanford University	Stanford	CT	06901	1
Village Cinema	118 Suffield Village Shopping	Suffield	CT	06078	1
Cinerom Digital Movieplex Torrington	89 Farley Place	Torrington	CT	06790	6
Holiday Cinemas 10	117 Sharon Rd.	Waterbury	CT	06702	10
Country Cinema	523 Main St.	Watertown	CT	06795	1
Forest Theatre	2 Forest Rd.	West Haven	CT	06513	1
Cinerom Digital Movieplex	Mallory Brook Plaza Rte 44	Winsted	CT	06098	9
Gilson Theatre	354 Main St.	Winsted	CT	06098	2

WASHINGTON, D.C.

Theatre Name	Address	City	State	Zip	Screens
American Film Institute	Kennedy Center	Washington	DC	20566	1
Ford's Theatre	511 10th St. N.W.	Washington	DC	20004	1
National Gallery of Art	3rd St. & Constitution	Washington	DC	20565	1
National Geographic Center	1600 M St.	Washington	DC	20036	1
Johnson IMAX @ Smithsonian NMNH	10th & Constitution Ave N.W.	Washington	DC	20560	1
Langley IMAX @ Smithsonian NASM	6th & Independence Ave S.W.	Washington	DC	20560	2
Studio Theatre	1333 P St. N.W.	Washington	DC	20005	1

DELAWARE

Theatre Name	Address	City	State	Zip	Screens
Clayton Theatre	900 Main St.	Dagsboro	DE	19939	1
Everett Theatre	47 W. Main St.	Middletown	DE	19709	1
F & G Cinema Art House	401 Newark Shopping Center	Newark	DE	19711	1
F & G Cinema Center 3	401 Newark Shopping Center	Newark	DE	19711	3
Midway Movies, Rehoboth	29 Midway Shopping Center	Rehoboth Beach	DE	19971-9801	14

FLORIDA

Theatre Name	Address	City	State	Zip	Screens
StarNet Belleview Cinemas	10845 S.E. Hwy. 441	Belleview	FL	34420	2
Premier At Muvico Palace 20	3200 Airport Rd	Boco Raton	FL	33431	4
R L R Boynton Cinema	9764 S. Military Trail	Boynton Beach	FL	33436	8
Favorite Cinemas Lake Howell	1271 Semoran Blvd.	Casselberry	FL	32707	8
Clearwater Cinema Cafe	24095 U.S. Hwy. 19 N.	Clearwater	FL	33763	2
Clewiston Theatre	100 E. Sugarland Hwy.	Clewiston	FL	33440	1
Absinthe House Cinematheque	235 Alcazar Ave.	Coral Gables	FL	33134	1
Astor Art Cinema	4120 Laguna St.	Coral Gables	FL	33146	1
Bill Cosford Cinema	University of Miami - Memorial Bldg	Coral Gables	FL	33146	1
Coral Springs Movie	2340 University Dr.	Coral Springs	FL	33065	5
Crestview III Theatre	789 N. Ferdon Blvd.	Crestview	FL	32536	3
Joylan Drive-In	U.S. 301	Dade City	FL	33525	1
Daytona 6	278 N. Nova Rd.; Daytona Mall	Daytona Beach	FL	32114-3444	6
R L R Deerfield Cinema 5	2205 W. Hillsboro Blvd.	Deerfield Beach	FL	33442	5
Movies of Delray	7421 W. Atlantic Ave.	Delray Beach	FL	33446	5
Blockbuster IMAX	401 S.W. 2nd St.	Fort Lauderdale	FL	33312	1
Cinema Cafe	1455 S.E. 17th St.	Fort Lauderdale	FL	33316	2
Galleria 4 Cinemas	2630 E. Sunrise Blvd.	Fort Lauderdale	FL	33304	4
Swap Shop Drive-In	3291 W. Sunrise Blvd.	Fort Lauderdale	FL	33311	11
Northside Drive-In	2521 N. Tamiami Trail	Fort Meyers	FL	33903	1
Suds-n-Cinema Picture Show	174 S.E. Miracle Strip Pkwy	Fort Walton Beach	FL	32548	1
South Pointe	6111 S. Pointe Blvd	Ft. Meyers	FL	33919	6
Hippodrome State Theatre	25 S.E. 2nd Place St.	Gainesville	FL	32601-6596	1
Clay Theatre	326 Walnut St.	Green Cove Spr	FL	32043-3442	2
Gulf Breeze Theatre	1175 Gulf Breeze Pkwy	Gulf Breeze	FL	32561	4
Favorite Cinema Hialeah	4650 W. 17th Court	Hialeah	FL	33012	8
Hobe Sound Cinema	8959 S.E. Bridge Rd	Hobe Sound	FL	33455	2
Tavernier Twin Cinema	201 Nautilus Dr.	Islamorada	FL	33036	2
Gazebo Cinema N'Drafthouse	5566 Fort Caroline Rd.	Jacksonville	FL	32277	1
Playtime 3 Drive-In	6300 Blanding Rd.	Jacksonville	FL	32244-2816	3

Theatre Name	Address	City	State	Zip	Screens
San Marco Theatre	1996 San Marco Blvd.	Jacksonville	FL	32207	1
StarNet Cinemas St. Johns 8	4530 St. Johns Ave	Jacksonville	FL	32210	8
StarNet Cinemas Pablo 9	1970 3rd St. S.	Jacksonville Beach	FL	32250	9
IMAX Theatre 1 & 2	Mail Code:DNPS	Kennedy Space Ctr	FL	32899	2
Rialto Villages Town Square	1105 Alonzo Ave.	Lady Lake	FL	32159	8
Movies of Lake Worth	7380 Lake Worth Rd.	Lake Worth	FL	33460	6
Trail Drive-In	3438 Lake Worth Rd.	Lake Worth	FL	33461	1
Lakeland Square 10 Cinema	3606 U.S. Hwy. 98	Lakeland	FL	33809	10
Polk Theatre	127 S. Florida Ave	Lakeland	FL	33801	1
Silver Moon Drive-In Theatre	4100 U.S. Hwy. 92	Lakeland	FL	33801	2
Inverrary Cinema 5	5570 W. Oakland Park Blvd.	Lauderhill	FL	33311	5
Enzian Cinema Cafe	1300 S. Orlando Ave.	Maitland	FL	32751	1
Marathon Community Theatre	5101 Overseas Hwy.	Marathon	FL	33050	1
Marco Movies 4	599 S. Collier Blvd.	Marco Island	FL	34145	4
StarNet Marianna Cinemas	4341 S. Lafayette	Marianna	FL	32446	2
Le Jeune Cinema 6	782 N.W. LeJeune Rd	Miami	FL	33126	6
Valentino Super Discount	8524 S.W. 8th St.	Miami	FL	33144	3
Alliance Cinema	927 Lincoln Rd.	Miami Beach	FL	33139	1
Naples Drive-In Twin Theatre	7700 E. Davis Blvd.	Naples	FL	34104	2
StarNet Cinemas Atlantic 8	751 Atlantic Blvd.	Neptune Beach	FL	32233	8
Twin Cities Cinema	1047 E. John C. Simes Pkwy.	Niceville	FL	32578	2
Ocala Drive-In	4850 S. Pine Ave.	Ocala	FL	34480	1
West Orange 5	1575 Maguire Rd.	Ocoee	FL	34761	5
Conway 2	2900 Curry Ford Rd.	Orlando	FL	32806	2
Horizons Pavillion	Walt Disney World	Orlando	FL	32819	1
Orlando Science Center	777 E. Princeton St.	Orlando	FL	32803	1
Universal Studios Florida	1000 Universal Studios Plaza	Orlando	FL	32819	2
Picture Show 3	229 St. Joe Plaza Dr.	Palm Coast	FL	32164	3
Naval Aviation Memorial IMAX	NAS Pensacola	Pensacola	FL	32508	1
Pensacola Silver Screen	7280 Plantation Rd.	Pensacola	FL	32504	5
Ruskin Drive-In	5011 U.S. Hwy. 41	Ruskin	FL	33572	1
Island Cinema	535 Tarpon Bay Rd.	Sanibel	FL	33957	2
Burns Court Cinema	506 Burns Lane	Sarasota	FL	34236	3
IMAX Theatre at Sunset Place	5701 Sunset Dr.	South Miami	FL	33143	1
Pot Belly's Cinema Plus	36 Granada St.	St Augustine	FL	32084	3
World Golf Village IMAX	1 World Golf Place	St. Augustine	FL	32092	1
Popcorn Palace	1110 10th St.	St. Cloud	FL	34769	1
28th St. Drive-In	4990 N. 28th St.	St. Petersburg	FL	33714	1
Beach Theatre	315 Corey Ave.	St. Petersburg Bch.	FL	33706	1
NS Varsity Theatre	1833 W. Tennessee St.	Tallahassee	FL	32304-3356	3
Tamarac Cinema 5	10036 W. McNab Rd.	Tamarac	FL	33321	5
Buccaneer Palace Cinemas Bar & Grill	8625 W. Hillsborough Ave.	Tampa	FL	33615	2
Funlan Drive-In	2302 E. Hillsborough Ave.	Tampa	FL	33610	3
IMAX Dome at MOSI	4801 E. Fowler Ave.	Tampa	FL	33617	1
Palace Cinema Brew Pub	8625 W. Hillsborough Ave.;	Tampa	FL	33615-3810	2
Tampa Pitcher Show	14416 N. Dale Mabry Hwy.	Tampa	FL	33624	1
Tampa Theatre	711 Franklin St.	Tampa	FL	33602	1
Maxi's Cinema Pub	300 N. Washington Ave.	Titusville	FL	32796	1
Silver Screen Cinema Cafe	12795 Forest Hill Blvd.	Wellington	FL	33414	2
Carefree Theatre	2000 S. Dixie Hwy.	West Palm Beach	FL	33401	1
Aloma Cinema Grill	2155 Aloma Ave.	Winter Park	FL	32792	2
Zephyrhills Cinema 6	6848 Gall Blvd.	Zephyrhills	FL	33541	6
Home Twin Theatre	38521 5th Ave.	Zephyrillis	FL	33540	2

GEORGIA

Theatre Name	Address	City	State	Zip	Screens
Alps Cinema	191 Alps Rd.	Athens	GA	30606	2
Cinefest Theatre	66 Courtland Ave.	Atlanta	GA	30303	1
High Museum of Art	1280 Peachtree St.	Atlanta	GA	30309	2
North Springs Cinema Grill	7270 Roswell Rd. N.E.	Atlanta	GA	30328-0724	2
Smith IMAX @ Fernbank Museum	767 Clifton Rd. N.E.	Atlanta	GA	30307	1
Starlight Drive-In Theatre	2000 Moreland Ave.	Atlanta	GA	30316	6
StarNet Bainbridge Cinemas	1400 E. Shotwell St	Bainbridge	GA	31717	3
Bald Mountain Cinema 3	1650 Backyard Lane	Blairsville	GA	30512	3
Blue Ridge Twin Theatres	Hwy. 5-400 bypass	Blue Ridge	GA	30513	2
Swan Drive-In	Doxol St.	Blue Ridge	GA	30513	1
MNM Movies 8	4300 Hwy. 20 N.E. Lake Lanier	Buford	GA	30518	8
Carmike Plaza 8 Theatre	N. Tennessee	Cartersville	GA	30120	8
Commerce Drive-In	2367 Hwy. 441	Commerce	GA	30529	3
Conyers Salem Gate Cinema	1490 Old Salem Rd.	Conyers	GA	30208	3
MNM Movies 400	415 Atlanta Hwy.	Cumming	GA	30040	12
Plaza Cinema	1223 Creekwood Pass	Dallas	GA	30132	1
Douglasville Cinema 3	5975 Fairburn Rd.	Douglasville	GA	30134	3
East Town Twin Cinema	East Town Center	Ellijay	GA	30540	2
Mom & Pop's Westside Cinema 2	Hwy. 80	Garden City	GA	31405	2
Brice City Cinema 2	603 Maxwell St., Hwy. 84	Hinesville	GA	31313	2
Strand Cinema Twin	169 W. Cherry St.	Jesup	GA	31545	2
GTC Town Center Value 10	700 Gwinnett Dr.	Lawrenceville	GA	30045	10
Amstar Cinemas 16	5996 Zebulon Rd.	Macon	GA	31210	16
Blackwell Theatre	3378 Canton Rd.	Marietta	GA	30066	2
Movies at Berry Square	2820 Martha Berry Hwy. N.E.	Rome	GA	30165-8631	6
Village Theatres	836 Turner McCall Blvd.	Rome	GA	30161	4
StarTime Roswell Town Center	608 Holcomb Bridge Rd.	Roswell	GA	30076-1591	10
Cinema Grill Savannah	Inside Oglethorpe Mall	Savannah	GA	31419	1
Toccoa Cinema 3	Hwy. 17	South Toccoa	GA	30577	3
Rama Twin Theatres	1707 Watson Blvd.	Warner Robins	GA	31093	2

Theatre Name	Address	City	State	Zip	Screens

HAWAII

Theatre Name	Address	City	State	Zip	Screens
Honokaa Peoples Theatre	Mamane St.	Honokaa	HI	96727	1
IMAX Polynesia	55-370 Kamehameha Hwy.	Laie	HI	96762	1
Naalehu Theatre	Downtown Naalehu	Naalehu	HI	96772	1
Waimea Theatre	P.O. Box 903	Waimea	HI	96796	1

IOWA

Theatre Name	Address	City	State	Zip	Screens
Lyric Theatre	431 E. Main St.	Belmond	IA	50421	1
Charles Theatre	409 N. Main St.	Charles City	IA	50616	1
American Theatre	108 E. Main St.	Cherokee	IA	51012	1
Lake Theatre Clear Lake	4 N. 4th St.	Clear Lake	IA	50428	1
Capri III Theatre	218 6th Ave. S.	Clinton	IA	52732-4306	3
Clinton Cinema 1	214 6th Ave. S.	Clinton	IA	52732-4306	1
Omni 4 Theatres	300 W. Broadway	Council Bluffs	IA	51503	4
Viking Theatre	111 N. Mechanic St.	Decorah	IA	52101	3
Cinema 4 Crawford County	309 Chamberlin Dr.	Denison	IA	51442-2803	4
Merle Hay Mall Cinema	3800 Merle Hay Rd.	Des Moines	IA	50310	1
Varsity Theatre Des Moines	1207 25th St.	Des Moines	IA	50311	1
Operahouse Theatre Dewitt	716 6th Ave.	Dewitt	IA	52742	1
Grand Theatre	1148 Edgington Ave.	Eldora	IA	50627	1
Co-Ed Theater	119 W. Broadway St.	Fairfield	IA	52556	2
Forest Theatre	215 N. Clark	Forest City	IA	50436	1
Windsor Theatre	103 N. Federal St.	Hampton	IA	50441	1
Paramount 3 Theatres Indianola	105 S. 1st St.	Indianola	IA	50125	3
Bijou @ University of Iowa	152 Iowa Memorial Union	Iowa City	IA	52240	1
Englert Theatre	221 E. Washington St.	Iowa City	IA	52240	2
Mills Theatre	216 W. Main	Lake Mills	IA	50450	1
Royal Twin	33 S.W. Central Ave.	Le Mars	IA	51031	2
South Central Iowa Theatre	208 N. Main St.	Leon	IA	50144	1
61 Drive-In Maquoketa	Hwy. 61 S.	Maquoketa	IA	52060	1
Voy 3-plex Theatre	207 S. Main St.	Maquoketa	IA	52060-3037	3
Temple Theater	115 N. Main St.	Mt Pleasant	IA	52641	2
Plaza 4 Theatres Muscatine	1903 Park Ave. #73	Muscatine	IA	52761-5400	4
Plaza Theatre	1903 Park Ave. #73	Muscatine	IA	52761	4
Great Lakes Cinema 5	1698 Exchange St.	Okaboji	IA	51355	5
Watts Theatre	714 Main St.	Osage	IA	50461	1
Lyric Theatre Osceola	118 S. Fillmore St.	Osceola	IA	50213	1
Penn Center 2	216 W. 2nd Ave.	Oskaloosa	IA	52577	2
Coppercreek Cinema	1355 Coppercreek Dr.	Pleasant Hill	IA	50317	1
Rialto	324 N. Main St.	Pocahontas	IA	50574	1
Iowa Theatre	923 3rd Ave.	Sheldon	IA	51201	1
Page Theatre	715 W. Sheridan Ave.	Shenandoah	IA	51601	1
Riviera Twin	714 4th St.	Sioux City	IA	51101	2
Spencer Theatre	504 S. Grand Ave.	Spencer	IA	51301	3
Vista 3 Theatres	712 Lake Ave.	Storm Lake	IA	50588	3
Hardacre Theatre	112 E. 5th St.	Tipton	IA	52772-1731	1
Waverly Palace Theatre	90 E. Bremer Ave.	Waverly	IA	50677	3
Billy Joes Pitcher Show	1701 25th St.	West Des Moines	IA	50266	1
New Strand Theatre	111 E. 3rd St.	West Liberty	IA	52776	1
Iowa Theatre	121 John Wayne Dr.	Winterset	IA	50273	1

IDAHO

Theatre Name	Address	City	State	Zip	Screens
Century Cinema 5	Alfresco Rd.	Burley	ID	83318	5
Spud Too Theatre	190 N. Main St.	Driggs	ID	83422	1
Blue Fox	116 W. Main St.	Grangeville	ID	83530	10
Liberty Theatre	110 N. Main	Hailey	ID	83333-8410	1
Coeur d'Alene Discount Cinemas	300 Central	Hayden Lake	ID	83814	6
Paramount Theatre	2085 Niagara St.	Idaho Falls	ID	83404	1
Kenworthy 1	508 S. Main	Moscow	ID	83843	1
Nuart 1	516 S. Main	Moscow	ID	83843	1
River City Cinemas	1311 W. Seltice Way	Post Falls	ID	83854	6
River Cinemas	526 Main St.	Salmon	ID	83467	2
Cinema 4 West	401 Oak St.	Sandpoint	ID	83864	4

ILLINOIS

Theatre Name	Address	City	State	Zip	Screens
Arlington Theatre	53 S. Evergreen	Arlington Heights	IL	60005	6
Catlow Theatre	116 W. Main St.	Barrington	IL	60010	1
Bac Skyview 2 Drive-In	5700 N. Belt W	Belleville	IL	62223	2
Lincoln Theatre	103 E. Main St.	Belleville	IL	62220	1
Old Red Barn 2	305 N. Hard Rd.	Benld	IL	62009	2
Bensenville 2 Theater	9 S. Center St.	Bensenville	IL	60106	2
Garden Theatre	62 N. Main St.	Canton	IL	61520	2
Marvel Theatre	228 W. Main St.	Carlinville	IL	62626	2
New Art Theatre	125 W. Church St.	Champaign	IL	61820	1
3 Penny Theatre Chicago	2424 N. Lincoln Ave.	Chicago	IL	60614	2
Brew & View	3145 N. Sheffield	Chicago	IL	60657	2
Davis Art	4614 N. Lincoln Ave	Chicago	IL	60625	1
Davis Theatre	4614 N. Lincoln Ave.	Chicago	IL	60625	4
Facets Multimedia Theatre	1517 W. Fullerton Ave.	Chicago	IL	60614	1
Film Center - Art Institute	280 S. Columbus	Chicago	IL	60603	1
Henry Crown MSI OMNIMAX	57th St. & Lake Shore Dr.	Chicago	IL	60637	1
Logan Theatre	2646 N. Milwaukee Ave	Chicago	IL	60647	4
Music Box	3733 N. Southport	Chicago	IL	60613	2
Patio Theatre	6008 W. Irving Park	Chicago	IL	60634	1

Theatre Name	Address	City	State	Zip	Screens
Portage 1 & 2 Theatre	4050 N. Milwaukee	Chicago	IL	60626	2
Village North Theatre	6746 N. Sheridan Rd.	Chicago	IL	60626	4
Village Theatre	1548 N. Clark St.	Chicago	IL	60610	4
Town Theatre	1029 N. Second St.	Chillicothe	IL	61523	2
Des Plaines Cinema 1-2	1476 Miner St.	Des Plaines	IL	60016	2
Plaza Cinemas 3	1315 N. Galena Ave	Dixon	IL	61021	3
Palace Theatre Elmwood	122 W. Main St.	Elmwood	IL	61529-9608	1
Geneseo Central Theatre	111 N. State St.	Geneseo	IL	61254	1
Glen Ellyn Art Theatre	540 Crescent Blvd.	Glen Ellyn	IL	60137	4
Glenwood Theatre	18255 S. Halsted	Glenwood	IL	60425	1
Pictorium IMAX	Six Flags Great America	Gurnee	IL	60637	1
Highland Park Theatre	Central Ave. and Sheridan Rd.	Highland Park	IL	60035	4
Hinsdale Theatre	29 E. 1st St.	Hinsdale	IL	60521	1
Lorraine	324 E. Main St.	Hoopeston	IL	60942	2
South County Cinema	2199 S. Main	Jacksonville	IL	62650	5
Hilltop Drive-In	1800 Maple Rd.	Joliet	IL	60432	1
La Grange Theatre	80 S. Lagrange Rd.	La Grange	IL	60525	4
Skyview Drive-In	Rte. 66 N.	Litchfield	IL	62056	2
Hi-Lite Indoor Theatre	Rte. 2 Box 126	Montgomery	IL	60538	1
Hi-Lite Thirty Drive-In	Montgomery Rd & Hill Ave.	Montgomery	IL	60538	2
Morton Cinema 5	Field Shopping Ctr.	Morton	IL	61550	5
Normal Theatre	209 W. North St.	Normal	IL	61761-2533	1
Arcadia Theatre	238 E. Main St.	Olney	IL	62450	3
Roseland Theatre	507 W. 3rd St.	Pana	IL	62557	1
Pickwick Theatre	5 S. Prospect Ave.	Park Ridge	IL	60068	4
Midway Drive-In Theatre	Old Rte 2	Prairieville	IL	61021	1
Hub Triplex Theatres	416 Lincoln Hwy.	Rochelle	IL	61068	3
Storefront Cinema	711 N. Main St.	Rockford	IL	61103	1
Princess Theatre	116 E. Lafayette	Rushville	IL	62681	1
WoW 7 Cinema	34th & Newvick Ave	Sandwich	IL	60548	7
Times Theatres	222 Main St.	Savanna	IL	61074	2
Skokie Theatre	7924 Lincoln Ave.	Skokie	IL	60076	1
Sycamore Theatre	420 W. State St.	Sycamore	IL	60178	3
Liberty Theatre	210 S. 4th St.	Vandalia	IL	62471	1
Princess Theatre	213 W. Walnut	Watseka	IL	60970-1260	1
Belvidere 4	2145 Belvedere Rd.	Waukegan	IL	60085	4
Cascade Drive-In	21 W. 741 N. Ave.	West Chicago	IL	60185	1
Wilmette Theatre	1122 Central Ave.	Wilmette	IL	60091	2
Mar Theatre	121 S. Main St.	Wilmington	IL	60481	1
Countryside Cinema 1 & 2	550 Countryside Dr.	Yorkville	IL	60560	2

INDIANA

Theatre Name	Address	City	State	Zip	Screens
Alex Theatre	407 N. Harrison St.	Alexandria	IN	46001	1
State Theatre	1303 Meridian St.	Anderson	IN	46016	1
Devon Theatre	107 W. Mill St.	Attica	IN	47918	1
Great Escape 7	2929 Great Escape Dr.	Bedford	IN	47421	7
Starlite Drive-In	7630 S. Old State Rd. 37	Bloomington	IN	47403	1
Brookville Theatre	16 W 5th St.	Brookville	IN	47012	1
Corydon Cinemas	2025 Edsel Lane N.W.	Corydon	IN	47112	4
Strand 2 Theatre	122 S. Green St.	Crawfordsville	IN	47933	2
Crown Theatre	19 N. Court St.	Crown Point	IN	46307	1
Lakeside Cinema	612 E. Lake Shore Dr.	Culver	IN	46511	2
Showplace Cinema East	1801 Morgan Center Dr.	Evansville	IN	47715	12
Showplace Cinema North	4200 N. Third Ave.	Evansville	IN	47708	9
Showplace Cinema South	950 S. Hebron Ave.	Evansville	IN	47714	7
Showplace Village North	4200 N. Third Ave	Evansville	IN	47710	4
Cinema Center Fort Wayne	437 E. Berry St.	Fort Wayne	IN	46802	1
Kerasotes Gateway 3 Cinema	1533 Goshen Rd.	Fort Wayne	IN	46808	3
Northwood Cinema Grill	6069 Stellhorn Rd.	Fort Wayne	IN	46885-5042	2
Southtown Cinema 3	7800 S. Anthony Blvd.	Fort Wayne	IN	46816	3
Fowler Theatre	111 E. 5th St.	Fowler	IN	47944	0
Auburn Garrett Drive-In	1014 State Rd. 8	Garrett	IN	46738	1
Silver Screen Cinema	111 S. Randolph St.	Garrett	IN	46738	1
Star Theatre	453 E. Line St	Geneva	IN	46740	1
Linway Plaza Cinema 9	514 W. Lincoln Ave.	Goshen	IN	46526	9
Greenfield Cinemas	2347 W. Main St.	Greenfield	IN	46140	6
Northgate Cinema	1051 N. State St.	Greenfield	IN	46140	1
Village Cinema 1 and 2	122 W. Main St.	Greenfield	IN	46140	2
Kennedy Theatre	6735 Kennedy Ave.	Hammond	IN	46323	1
Town Theatre	8616 Kennedy Ave.	Highland	IN	46322	1
Art Theatre	230 Main St.	Hobart	IN	46342	1
Huntington Drive-In	1291 Condit St.	Huntington	IN	46750	1
Cinema Grill	1289 W. 86th St.	Indianapolis	IN	46260	2
Encore Moviez	9100 Rockville Rd.	Indianapolis	IN	46234	6
Hollywood Bar and Film 3	247 S. Meridian	Indianapolis	IN	46225	3
IMAX 3D @ White River State Park	650 W. Washington St.	Indianapolis	IN	46204	1
South Keystone Art & Classics Theatre	4044 S. Keystone Ave.	Indianapolis	IN	46227	2
Speedway 1 and 2 Theatres	5694 Crawfordsville	Indianapolis	IN	46224	2
Tibbs Drive-In	480 S. Tibbs Ave	Indianapolis	IN	46224	3
Astra Theatre 1 and 2	517 Main St.	Jasper	IN	47546	2
Jasper 8	256 Brucke Strasse	Jasper	IN	47546	8
Melody Drive-In Theatre	7055 S. U.S. Hwy. 35	Knox	IN	46534-8210	2
Walnut Theatre	352 Walnut St.	Lawrenceburg	IN	47025	1
Linton Cinema 3	Linton Shopping Center	Linton	IN	47441	3
Skyline Drive-In	1353 N. State Rd 17	Logansport	IN	46947	2
State Cinemas	321 E. Market St.	Logansport	IN	46947	2
Madison 6	744 Jefferson	Madison	IN	47250	6

Theatre Name	Address	City	State	Zip	Screens
Ohio Theatre	105 E. Main St.	Madison	IN	47250	2
Showplace Cinema 2	1910 Morton Ave.	Martinsville	IN	46151	2
Monon Theatre	421 N. Market St	Monon	IN	47959	1
Monticello Drive-In	100 Rickey Rd	Monticello	IN	47960	2
Mooresville Movies 8	300 S. Bridge Crossing	Mooresville	IN	46151	8
Nappanee Theatre	154 N. Main St.	Nappanee	IN	46550-1938	1
Skyview Drive-In	1126 County Rd 500 S.	New Castle	IN	47362	2
Showplace Newburgh Cinema 2	7 Robin Hill Rd.	Newburgh	IN	47630	2
Village West Theatre	119 W. Main St.	Plainfield	IN	46168	1
Rees Cinema	100 N. Michigan St.	Plymouth	IN	46563-2133	1
Showland Theatre	2475 N. Oak Rd.	Plymouth	IN	46563	3
Tri-Way Drive-In	4400 Michigan Rd.	Plymouth	IN	46563	2
Ritz Theatre	202 N. Meridian St	Portland	IN	47371	2
Times 2 Theatre	618 Main St.	Rochester	IN	46975	2
CFS Holiday Drive-In	Jct. Hwy. 66 & 231	Rockport	IN	47635	1
Ritz Theatre	201 W. Ohio St.	Rockville	IN	47872	0
Princess Theatre	330 N. Main St.	Rushville	IN	46173	1
Scott Theatre	31 E. Wardell St	Scottsburg	IN	47170	1
Great Escape 8	357 Tanger Blvd, Ste. 401	Seymour	IN	47274	8
Skyline Drive-In	Hwy. 421 E.	Shelbyville	IN	46176	1
Pickwick Theatre	108 W. Main St.	Syracuse	IN	46567	1
Mel's Back to the 50s Drive-In	On State Rd. 39	Thorntown	IN	46071	1
49'er Drive-In Theatre	N. State Rd. 49	Valparaiso	IN	46383	1
Carmike Hollywood Connection 7	2500 Morthland Dr., Rte. 30	Valpraiso	IN	46383	7
13-24 Drive-In	106 W. Market St.	Wabash	IN	46992	2
Eagles Theatre	106 W. Market St.	Wabash	IN	46992	1
Lake 1 & 2 Theatre	Main St.	Warsaw	IN	46580	2
North Pointe Cinemas	1410 Mariner Dr.	Warsaw	IN	46580	6
Hoosier Theatre	1335 119th St.	Whiting	IN	46394	1
Airline Drive-In	2870 E. State Rd 32	Winchester	IN	47394	2

KANSAS

Burford Theatre	118 S. Summit St.	Arkansas City	KS	67005	4
Royal Theatre	612 Commercial St.	Atchison	KS	66002	3
Augusta Theatre	523 State St.	Augusta	KS	67010	1
Solomon Valley Cinema 2	1124 N. Hwy. 14	Beloit	KS	67420	2
Burlington 2 Cinema	326 Neosho St.	Burlington	KS	66839	2
Chanute Twin Cinema	309 E. Main St.	Chanute	KS	66720	2
Rex	519 Court St.	Clay Center	KS	67432	2
Coffeyville Cinema	210 W. 10th St	Coffeyville	KS	67337	2
Colby Twin & Arcade	355 N. Franklin	Colby	KS	67701	2
Derby Plaza Theatre	1300 N. Nelson Dr.	Derby	KS	67037	5
Cinema Circle	106 Kincaid St.	Dodge City	KS	67801	2
Dodge City Village 8	2601 Central	Dodge City	KS	67801	8
Dodge Theatre	108 Gunsmoke	Dodge City	KS	67801	1
South Drive-In	1019 McArt Dr.	Dodge City	KS	67801	2
Star-Vu Drive-In	R.R. 1	El Dorado	KS	67042	1
Fox Theatre	113 S. Main St.	Fort Scott	KS	66701	2
Fredonia Cinema	407 N. 6th St.	Fredonia	KS	66736	2
Sherman Theatre	1203 Main St.	Goodland	KS	67735	1
Bannister Mall	12208 S. 71 Hwy.	Grandview	KS	64030	4
Cinema 4	2925 Vine	Hays	KS	67601	4
Hoxie Theatre	162 S. Queen Ave.	Hoxie	KS	67740	1
WDP & Moscelene Carey IMAX Dome	1100 N. Plum	Hutchinson	KS	67501	1
Independence Square	121 W. Laurel St	Independence	KS	67301	4
Iola Theatre	202 S. Washington St.	Iola	KS	66749	1
Blvd. Drive-In	1051 Merriam Lane	Kansas City	KS	66103	1
Kingman Theatre	237 N. Main St.	Kingman	KS	67068	1
State	617 Broadway St.	Larned	KS	67550	1
Liberty Hall Cinema	644 Massachussets St.	Lawrence	KS	66044	1
Landing 4 Theatres	225 Delaware	Leavenworth	KS	66048	4
Astro	820 Center St.	Marysville	KS	66508	3
Mc Pherson Cinema	318 N. Main St.	Mc Pherson	KS	67460	4
Fine Arts	5909 Johnson Dr.	Mission	KS	66202	2
ROYALE 8	604 S.E. 36th St.	Newton	KS	67114	8
Norton Theatre	215 E. Main St.	Norton	KS	67654	2
Palace	101 Center Ave.	Oakley	KS	67748	0
Midway Drive-In	29591 W. 327th Old Hwy.	Osawatomie	KS	66064	1
Plaza Theatre	209 S. Main	Ottawa	KS	66067	2
Goodrich Glenwood 4	9100 Metcalf	Overland Park	KS	66212	4
Parsons Cinema	1818 Parsons Plaza	Parsons	KS	67357	0
Majestic Theatre	724 4th St	Phillipsburg	KS	67661	2
Seneca	301 Main St.	Seneca	KS	66538	2
Trailridge Theatres	7456 Nieman Rd.	Shawnee	KS	66203	3
Palace Theatre West	Kellogg and Ridge Rd.	Wichita	KS	67209	7
Palace Theatres East	E. Kellogg & Greenwich Rd.	Wichita	KS	67207	10
Pawnee Plaza Theatre	Pawnee Plaza	Wichita	KS	67211	4
Royale Cinemas East 6	320 N. Rock Rd.	Wichita	KS	67206	6
Royale Theatres Cinemas West	9035 W. Central	Wichita	KS	67212	4
Royale Towne East Square Mall 4	Crnr of Douglas & Armour-	Wichita	KS	67207	4
Royale Towne East Square Mall 2	Towne East Mall-Upper Level	Wichita	KS	67207	2
Royale Towne West Square 5	4600 W. Kellog Dr.	Wichita	KS	67209	5
Town East Mall Twin	7700 E. Kellog Dr.	Wichita	KS	67207	2
Warren Theatre	21st and Tyler	Wichita	KS	67205	16
Winfield Cinema	1007 Main St.	Winfield	KS	67156	3

Theatre Name	Address	City	State	Zip	Screens

KENTUCKY

Theatre Name	Address	City	State	Zip	Screens
Bardstown Twin Theatre	Bardstown Shopping Plaza	Bardstown	KY	40004	2
Marianne Theatre	607 Fairfield Ave.	Bellevue	KY	41073	1
Campbellsville Twin Cinema	Elmhurst Plaza	Campbellsville	KY	42718	2
Cinema 3 Theatres Central City	105 N. First St.	Central City	KY	42330-1501	3
Rohf Opera House	39 E. Pike St.	Cynthiana	KY	41031	1
American Theatres	1231 Woodland Dr.	Elizabethtown	KY	42701	8
Franklin Drive-In	6250 Nashville Rd.	Franklin	KY	42134	1
Georgetown Drive-In	8200 State Rd. 64	Georgetown	KY	47122	2
Theatres of Georgetown	Inside Factory Stores of Am. Mall	Georgetown	KY	40324	7
Marquee-Highland 7	1628 Happy Valley Rd.	Glasgow	KY	42141	7
Mall Cinema - Hartford	U.S. Hwy. 231 S.	Hartford	KY	42347	2
Fugate's Cinema	Lower Second Creek	Hazard	KY	41701	5
Hillside Theater	410 Morton Blvd	Hazard	KY	41701	4
Oldham 8 Theatres	410 S. 1st St.	La Grange	KY	40031	8
Kentucky Theatre	214 E. Main St.	Lexington	KY	40507	2
Turfland Mall Cinemas 2	2025 Harrodsburg Rd.	Lexington	KY	40504	2
Regency 7	1808 Hwy. 192 W.	London	KY	40741	7
Broadway Cinemas	12th & Broadway	Louisville	KY	40203	2
Dixie Dozen Cinemas	6801 Dixie Hwy.	Louisville	KY	40258	12
Filmworks Baxter Ave. 8 Theatres	1250 Bardstown Rd.	Louisville	KY	40204	8
Louisville Science Center IMAX	727 W. Main St.	Louisville	KY	40202-2681	1
Village 8	4014 Dutchman Lane	Louisville	KY	40207	8
Cardinal Drive-In	Hwy 45 S.	Mayfield	KY	42066	1
Cheri	1008 Chestnut St.	Murray	KY	42071	7
Movies 5 - Mayo Plaza	Mayo Plaza	Paintsville	KY	41240	5
Sipp Theatre	Main St.	Paintsville	KY	41240	1
Bourbon Drive-In	U.S. 68 at Jackstown Rd.	Paris	KY	40361	1
Riverfill 10	94 Pike St.	Pikeville	KY	41501	10
Strand 2	102 S. Lake Dr.	Prestonsburg	KY	41653-1915	2
Capitol Theatre 3	203 W. Main St	Princeton	KY	42445	3
University Cinemas 2 Richmond	616 Eastern Bypass	Richmond	KY	40475	2
Showplace 9	Hwy. 27- Somerset Mall	Somerset	KY	42501	9
Southside 5	390 Southside Mall	South Willamson	KY	41503	5
Sky View Drive-In	Celina Rd.	Tomkinsville	KY	42167	1
Whitesburg Cinema	Whitesburg Plaza	Whitesburg	KY	41858	2
Movies 5	Hwy. 25W c/o Radio Shack	Williamsburg	KY	40769	5
Movies 9	40 Winchester Plaza	Winchester	KY	40391	9

LOUISIANA

Theatre Name	Address	City	State	Zip	Screens
Amite Cinemas 4	809 W. Oak St.	Amite	LA	70422	4
Broadmoor Cinema 4	9810 Florida Blvd.	Baton Rouge	LA	70815-1130	4
Oak Cinema 8	15365 George O'Neal Rd.	Baton Rouge	LA	70817	8
The Queen Cinema	231 W. Walnut Ave.	Eunice	LA	70535	3
Show Theatres 2	16829 E. Main St.	Galliano	LA	70354	2
Palace Theatre 10	801 CM Fagan Dr.	Hammond	LA	70403	10
Palace Theatre 20	1200 Elmwood Park Blvd.	Harahan	LA	70123	20
Acadiana Mall 5	5725 Johnston St.	Lafayette	LA	70503	5
Charles Cinema 3 Theatre	115 W. Sale Rd.	Lake Charles	LA	70605	3
Lake Cinema Quad	1030 9th St.	Morgan City	LA	70380-1920	4
Downtown Joy	1200 Canal St.	New Orleans	LA	70112	5
Entergy IMAX Theater	1 Canal St.	New Orleans	LA	70130	1
Movie Pitchers	3941 Bienville St.	New Orleans	LA	70119	4
Prytania Theatre	5339 Prytania St.	New Orleans	LA	70115	1
State Palace Theatre	1108 Canal St.	New Orleans	LA	70112	1
St. Landry Cinema	1277 Heather Dr.	Opelousas	LA	70570	4
Sci-Port IMAX Dome	820 Clyde Fant Pkwy.	Shreveport	LA	71101	1
Nicholls Twin Cinema	506 St. Mary Hwy.	Thibodaux	LA	70301	2

MASSACHUSETTS

Theatre Name	Address	City	State	Zip	Screens
Agawam Twin Cinemas Theatre	866 Suffield St.	Agawam	MA	01001	2
Stage II Cinema Pub	109 Main St.	Amesbury	MA	01913-2823	2
Amherst Theatre	30 Amity St.	Amherst	MA	01002	1
Capitol Theatre	204 Massachussetts Ave.	Arlington	MA	02174	6
Triboro Cinema	P.O. Box 2666	Attleboro Falls	MA	02763	10
Belmont Studio	376 Trapelo Rd.	Belmont	MA	02178	1
Cabot St. Cinema	286 Cabot St.	Beverly	MA	01915	1
Boston Public Library	666 Boylston St.	Boston	MA	02117	1
Immersion Theater	Central Wharf	Boston	MA	02110	1
Museum of Fine Arts Film Screenings	465 Huntington Ave.	Boston	MA	02115	1
Omni Theatre, Museum of Science	1 Science Park	Boston	MA	02114	1
Coolidge Corner Theatre	290 Harvard Ave.	Brookline	MA	02146	2
Brattle Theatre	40 Brattle St.	Cambridge	MA	02138	2
Harvard Film Archive	24 Qunicy St., Harvard University	Cambridge	MA	02141	1
Last Strand Cinema & Drafthous	58 High St.	Clinton	MA	01510	1
Hollywood Hits Discount	7 Hutchinson Dr.	Danvers	MA	01923	7
Dedham Community Theatre	580 High St.	Dedham	MA	02026	2
Wellfleet Drive-In	Rte. 6	Eastham	MA	02663	1
Edgartown Cinema	65 Main St.	Edgartown	MA	02539	2
Cinema World	432 John Fitch Hwy.	Fitchburg	MA	01420	10
Zeotrope Theatre	Rt. 140, 34 E. Centeral St.	Franklin	MA	02038	3
Gardner Cinemas	34 Parker St.	Gardner	MA	01440	6
Mohawk Drive-In	Rte. 2	Gardner	MA	01440	1
Gloucester Cinema 3	74 Essex Ave.	Gloucester	MA	01930	3
Triplex Cinema	70 Railroad St.	Great Barrington	MA	01230	4

Theatre Name	Address	City	State	Zip	Screens
Greenfield Cinemas	Rte. 2, The Mohawk Trail	Greenfield	MA	01301	6
Chunky's Haverhill Cinema & Pub	371 Lowell Ave.	Haverhill	MA	01832	2
Patriot/Loring Theatres	65 Main St.	Hingham	MA	02043	1
Leicester Drive-In	1675 Main St. - Rte. 9	Leicester	MA	01524	1
Lexington Flick	1794 Massachussetts Ave.	Lexington	MA	02173	2
Littleton Flick	225 Great Rd.	Littleton	MA	01460	2
BrewHouse Pub Cinema	205 Cabot St.	Lowell	MA	01854	3
Entertainment Cinemas	689 Boston Post Rd.	Marlboro	MA	01752	7
Marlboro's 1-2-3	481 Boston Post Rd.	Marlboro	MA	01752	3
Marlboro Cinema	689 Boston Post Rd. & Rte. 20	Marlboro	MA	01752-3791	7
Fine Arts Theatre	19 Summer St.	Maynard	MA	01754	3
Mendon Drive-In	35 Milford St.	Mendon	MA	01756	1
Elm DraughtHouse Theatre	35 Elm Ct.	Millbury	MA	01527	1
Gaslight Theater	1 Union St.	Nantucket	MA	02554	1
Cinema 140	376 Hathaway Rd.	New Bedford	MA	02740	2
Newburyport Screening Room	82 State St.	Newburyport	MA	01950	1
North Adams Cinema 8	Rte. 8, Curran Hwy.	North Adams	MA	01247	8
Academy of Music Theatre	274 Main St.	Northampton	MA	01060	1
Pleasant St. Theatre	27 Pleasant Theatre	Northampton	MA	01060	2
Berkshire Museum Little Theatr	39 South St.	Pittsfield	MA	01201	1
Patriot/Museum Place Cinemas	Museum Place Mall	Salem	MA	01970	4
Somerville Theatre	55 Davis Square	Somerville	MA	02144	5
Tower Theatre	Village Commons	South Hadley	MA	01075	2
Wellfleet Cinemas	51 Rte. 6	South Wellfleet	MA	02663	4
Leominster Tri-Town	52 S. Nelson Rd.	Sterling	MA	01564	1
Cinema Pub Theatres	807 Washington St.	Stoughton	MA	02072	1
Entertainment Stoughton Cinema	807 Washington St.	Stoughton	MA	02072	1
Capawock Theatre	Main St. Ext.	Vineyard Haven	MA	02568	1
Casino Theatre	121 Main St.	Ware	MA	01082	1
West Boylston Cinema	101 W. Boylston	West Boylston	MA	01583	5
West Newton Cinema	1296 Washington St.	West Newton	MA	02165	3
Pittsfield Cinema Center	West Housatonic St.-Rte. 20	West Pittsfield	MA	01201	10
Patriot/Cameo Theatre	14 Columbian Square	Weymouth	MA	02188	2
Images Cinema	50 Spring St.	Williamstown	MA	01267	1

MARYLAND

Bengies Drive-In Theatre	3417 Eastern Blvd.	Baltimore	MD	21220-2147	1
Charles	1711 N. Charles St.	Baltimore	MD	21201	1
Imax Maryland Science Center	Light St. & Key Hwy	Baltimore	MD	21230-3899	1
Senator Theatre	5904 York Rd.	Baltimore	MD	21212	1
Bethesda Theatre Cafe	7719 Wisconsin Ave.	Bethesda	MD	20817	1
P and G Chester 5 Theatre	21 Washington Square	Chester Town	MD	21620	5
Hoff Theatre	University of Maryland	College Park	MD	20742	1
National Archives	8601 Adelphi Rd.	College Park	MD	20740	1
Elkton Movies 4	Rte. 40	Elkton	MD	21921	4
Silver Screen Cinema Beltway 6	Beltway Plaza Shopping Center	Fullerton	MD	21234	6
Kentland Stadium 8	629 Center Point Way	Gaithersburg	MD	20878	8
P and G Old Greenbelt	129 Center Way	Greenbelt	MD	20770	1
Laurel Cinema Cafe	312 Main St.	Laurel	MD	20707	1
Garrett 8	19741 Garrett Hwy.	Oakland	MD	21550	8
Fox White Marlin 5	12641 Ocean Gateway Unit 200	Ocean City	MD	21842	5
Olney 9 Cinemas	RT. 108 & Spartan RD.	Olney	MD	20832	9
Apex Calvert Village 5	Calvert Village Shopping Center	Prince Frederick	MD	20678	5

MAINE

Movie City Cinema	268 Odlin Rd.	Bangor	ME	04401	1
Colonial Theatre	163 High St.	Belfast	ME	04915	3
Magic Lantern Movie Theater	69 Main St.	Bridgton	ME	04009	2
Evening Star	149 Main St.	Brunswick	ME	04001	1
Alamo Theatre	379 Main St.	Bucksport	ME	04416	1
State	79 Main St.	Calais	ME	04619	3
Narrow Gauge Cinemas	Front St.	Farmington	ME	04938	4
Century Theatre	8 Hall St.	Ft. Kent	ME	04743	1
Temple	Market Square	Houlton	ME	04730	2
Leavitt Fine Arts Theatre 1	41 Main St.	Ogunquit	ME	03907	1
Keystone Theatre Cafe	504 Congress St.	Portland	ME	04101	4
Patriot/Nickelodeon Cinema 1-6	1 Temple St.	Portland	ME	04101	6
Strand Cinema	339 Main St.	Rockland	ME	04861	2
Saco Drive-In	969 Portland Rd. Rte. 1	Saco	ME	04072	1
Spinelli-Sanford Cinemas	277A Main St.	Sanford	ME	04073	4
Flagship Cinemas 7	US Rte. 1	Thomaston	ME	04861	7
Railroad Square Cinema	17 Railroad Square	Waterville	ME	04901	3
Wells Five Star Cinema	75 Wells Plaza	Wells	ME	04090	7
Chunky's Cinema Pub	765 Roosevelt Trail	Windham	ME	04062	2
Windham Five Star Cinema	795 Roosevelt Trail, Box 400	Windham	ME	04062	5
York Beach Theatre	6 Beach St.	York Beach	ME	03909-6237	1

MICHIGAN

MJR Adrian Cinemas	3150 N. Adrian Hwy.	Adrian	MI	49221	10
New Bohm 3 Theatre	201 S. Superior	Albion	MI	49224	3
MJR Allen Park Cinema	6601 Allen Rd.	Allen Park	MI	48101	5
Alma Cinemas 4	3002 W. Monroe	Alma	MI	48801	4
Strand Theatre	217 E. Superior	Alma	MI	48801	1
Michigan Theatre	603 E. Liberty St.	Ann Arbor	MI	48107	1
MJR Fox Village Theatre	375 N. Maple Rd.	Ann Arbor	MI	48103	4

Theatre Name	Address	City	State	Zip	Screens
State Theatre	233 S. State St.	Ann Arbor	MI.	48104	2
State Theatre	913 Washington Ave.	Bay City	MI.	48708	1
Gem Theatre	120 N. Ross.	Beaverton	MI.	48612	1
Bellaire Theatre	219 N. Bridge St.	Bellaire	MI.	49615	1
Cinema Hollywood	12280 Dixie Hwy.	Birch Run	MI.	48415	6
Birmingham Theatre	211 S. Woodward Ave	Birmingham	MI.	48009	8
MJR Brighton Cinemas	8487 W. Grand River	Brighton	MI.	48116	9
Strand Theatre	101 S. State St.	Caro	MI.	48723	1
Cass Theatre	6711 Houghton St.	Cass City	MI.	48726	1
Cinema III	107 Antrim St.	Charlevoix	MI.	49720	3
Eaton 3	235 S. Cochran St.	Charlotte	MI.	48813	3
Kingston 5	406 N. Main St.	Cheboygan	MI.	49721	5
MJR Chesterfield Crossing 12	50675 Gratiot Ave.	Chesterfield	MI.	48051	12
Ideal Theatre	607 McEwan	Clare	MI.	48617	1
Clinton Theatre	130 W. Michigan Ave.	Clinton	MI.	49236	1
Clio Cinema	2151 W. Vienna Rd.	Clio	MI.	48420	4
Capri Drive-In	1455 W. Chicago Rd.	Coldwater	MI.	49036	1
Coldwater Cinema	414 N. Willowbrook Rd.	Coldwater	MI.	49036	7
Loma 3 Theatres	219 N. Paw Paw Ave.	Coloma	MI.	49038	3
Ford Wyoming Drive-In	10400 Ford Rd.	Dearborn	MI.	48126	9
Henry Ford IMAX	20900 Oakwood Blvd.	Dearborn	MI.	48124	1
Ford Tel Theatre	23830 Ford Rd.	Dearborn Heights	MI.	48126	2
Fox Theatre	600 Civic Center Dr.	Detroit	MI.	48226	1
IMAX Dome Theatre	John Rd.	Detroit	MI.	48202	1
Norwest 1-2	17630 Grand River.	Detroit	MI.	48227	2
Redford Theatre	17360 Lahser Rd.	Detroit	MI.	48219	1
Renaissance Center Theatres	400 Renaissance Center #200	Detroit	MI.	48243	4
5 Mile Drive-In	28190 M 152	Dowagiac	MI.	49047	1
Elk Rapids Cinema Theatre	205 River St.	Elk Rapids	MI.	49629	1
Willow Creek Cinema 8	2701 3rd Ave N.	Escanaba	MI.	49829	8
Farmington Civic 2 Theatre	3332 Grand River	Farmington	MI.	48335	2
Fenton Cinema	291 Alloy Dr.	Fenton	MI.	48430	8
Magic Bag Theatre	22920 Woodward Ave.	Ferndale	MI.	48220	1
Garden Theatre	301 Main St.	Frankfort	MI.	49635	1
Fremont Twin Cinema	West Main Shopping Center	Fremont	MI.	49412	2
Gaylord Cinema Downtown	115 E. Main St.	Gaylord	MI.	49735	2
Gaylord West 6	115 E. Main St.	Gaylord	MI.	49735	6
Grand Theatre	22 Washington St.	Grand Haven	MI.	49417	1
Sun Theatre	316 Bridge St.	Grand Ledge	MI.	48837	1
Greenville Cinemas	1500 N. Lafayette	Greenville	MI.	48838	5
Harbor Beach Community Theatre	105 N. Huron Ave.	Harbor Beach	MI.	48441	1
Alco Theatre	410 E. Main St.	Harrisville	MI.	48740	1
Hartford Theatre 8	2941 State Rd. 83	Hartford	MI.	49057	8
Sunset Drive-In	69017 Red Arrow Hwy	Hartford	MI.	49057	1
Hillman Theatre	430 N. State St.	Hillman	MI.	49746	1
Knickerbocker Theatre	86 E. 8th St.	Holland	MI.	49423	1
Cherrybowl Drive-In	9812 Honor Hwy.	Honor	MI.	49640	1
Ionia Theatre	209 W. Main St.	Ionia	MI.	48846	1
Plaza	Riverside Plaza	Iron River	MI.	49935	1
Lapeer Cinema 6	1650 DeMille Rd.	Lapeer	MI.	48446	6
Courtyard Cinema	248 S. Huron St	Mackinaw City	MI.	49701	5
Vogue Theatre	383 River St.	Manistee	MI.	49660	2
Riverside Cinemas 3	6746 S. River Rd.	Marine City	MI.	48039	3
Bogar Theatre	223 E. Michigan	Marshall	MI.	49068	1
Midland Cinema 10	6540 Cinema Dr.	Midland	MI.	48640	10
Denniston Cinema 1 and 2	6495 N. Monroe St.	Monroe	MI.	48161	2
Ready 4 Theatre	420 E. Main St.	Niles	MI.	49120	4
M-89 Cinema	392 Cross Oaks Mall	Otsego	MI.	49078	6
Owosso Cinemas	314 Comstock St.	Owosso	MI.	48867	5
Strand Theatre	115 E. Michigan	Paw Paw	MI.	49079	1
Gaslight 5	302 Petoskey	Petoskey	MI.	49770	5
Penn Theatre	760 Penniman Ave	Plymouth	MI.	48170	1
Rogers Theatre	245 N. 3rd Ave.	Rogers City	MI.	49779	1
Roscommon	200 N. Main	Roscommon	MI.	48653	0
Michigan 3 Theatres	210 Center	South Haven	MI.	49090	3
South Lyon Cinema	126 E. Lake St.	South Lyon	MI.	48178	1
MJR Southgate Cinema 20	15651 Trenton Rd.	Southgate	MI.	48195	20
Shores Theatre	23495 Greater Mack Ave	St Clair Shores	MI.	48080	2
Strand Theatre	217 W. Chicago	Sturgis	MI.	49091	1
Southland 4	#24 Southland Ctr; 23000 Eureka Rd	Taylor	MI.	48180	4
Vickers Theatre	6 N. Elm St.	Three Oaks	MI.	49128	1
Riviera Theatre	50 N. Main St.	Three Rivers	MI.	49093	1
Romeo Theatre	66120 Van Dyke.	Washington	MI.	48095	2
MJR Waterford Cinema 11	7501 Highland Rd.	Waterford Twp.	MI.	48327	11
State Wayne Theatre	35310 Michigan Ave.	Wayne	MI.	48184	4
West Branch Cinema	210 W. Houghton Ave.	West Branch	MI.	48661	2
Northstar 3 Theatres	8171 White Hall Rd.	Whitehall	MI.	49461	3
Sun Theatre	150 W. Grand River Ave	Williamston	MI.	48895	1

MINNESOTA

Rialto Theatre Aitkin	220 N. Minnesota Ave.	Aitkin	MN	56431	1
Midway Mall	2910 S. Broadway St.	Alexandria	MN	56308	0
Andover Cinema 10	1836 Bunker Lake Blvd.	Andover	MN	55304	10
Imation Imax Theatre	12000 Zoo Blvd.	Apple Valley	MN	55124-4623	1
Demarce	1320 Atlantic	Benson	MN	56215	1
Blackduck Theater	Main St.	Blackduck	MN	56630	1

Theatre Name	Address	City	State	Zip	Screens
Blaine 65 Drive-In	Central Ave. and 101st	Blaine	MN	55434	2
Buffalo Cinema	100 First Ave.	Buffalo	MN	55313	2
Chaska Cinema	511 Walnut St. N.	Chaska	MN	55318	4
Premier Theatres	904 Hwy. 33 S..	Cloquet	MN	55720	6
Heights Theatre	3951 N.E. Central Ave.	Columbia Heights	MN	55421	1
Grand Theatre	124 E. 2nd	Crookston	MN	56716-1711	2
Delano Theatre	W. Hwy. 12	Delano	MN	55328	5
Washington Square Theatre	121 W. Front St	Detroit Lakes	MN	56501	5
Duluth Omnimax Theatre	301 Harbor Dr..	Duluth	MN	55802	1
East Bethel 10 Theatres	18635 N.E. Ulysses	East Bethel	MN	55011	10
Cinema Grill Minneapolis	3313 Hazelton Rd.	Edina	MN	55435	3
State	238 E. Sheridan St.	Ely	MN	55731	1
Excelsior Dock Cinema 3	26 Water St.	Excelsior	MN	55331	3
Fair Lakes Cinema 5	1201 N. State St.	Fairmont	MN	56031	5
Westridge 5	2001 W. Lincoln Ave	Fergus Falls	MN	56537	5
Mann Irongate 3 Theatres	990 W. 41st St	Hibbing	MN	55746	3
Kee Civic Theatre	108 N. Main St.	Kiester	MN	56051	1
Lakeville 18	County Rd. 70 & 35 West	Lakeville	MN	55044	18
Hollywood Theater	210 N. Sibley Ave.	Litchfield	MN	55352	3
Falls Cinema 3	115 S.E. 1st St.	Little Falls	MN	56345	3
Madelia Theatre	117 W. Main St.	Madelia	MN	56062-1439	1
Grand Madison	310 6th Ave	Madison	MN	56256	2
Plaza Twin Cinemas	1847 Larpenteur Ave..	Maplewood	MN	55019	2
Historic Suburban World Theatre	3022 Hennepin Ave..	Minneapolis	MN	55408	1
Hudson South Side Cinema 9	1920 Crestview Dr.	Minneapolis	MN	55125	9
Oak St. Cinema	309 S.E. Oak St.	Minneapolis	MN	55414	1
Pkwy. Theatre	4814 Chicago Ave.	Minneapolis	MN	55417	1
St Anthony Main	115 S.E. Main St..	Minneapolis	MN	55414	5
U Film Society	2331 University Ave. S.E., Ste. 130B	Minneapolis	MN	55414	1
Walker Art Center	725 Vineland Place	Minneapolis	MN	55403	1
Plaza Theatre	Southtown Mall	Montevideo	MN	56345	3
Monti 4 Theatre	137 E. Broadway	Monticello	MN	55362	4
Morris	12 E. 6th St.	Morris	MN	56267	0
New Hope Cinema Cafe	2749 Winnetka Ave N.	New Hope	MN	55427	5
Family Theatre	628 Main	North Branch	MN	55056	2
North Branch Cinema	38573 Tanger Dr.	North Branch	MN	55056	2
Cedar Mall Cinema 6	1929 Cedar Ave. S.	Owatonna	MN	55060	6
Park Theatre, Park Rapids	107 S. Main St.	Park Rapids	MN	56470-1515	2
Koronis Cinema	209 Washburne Ave.	Paynesville	MN	56362	2
Red Wing Cinema 5	160 Tyler Rd. N.	Red Wing	MN	55066	5
Redwood Falls Twin	230 E. Second St.	Redwood Falls	MN	56283-1604	2
Roseville 4 Theaters	1211 Larpenteur Ave. W.	Roseville	MN	55113	4
Main St. Theatre	319 Main St.	Sauk Centre	MN	56378	4
IMAX Cinema	One Valleyfair Dr.	Shakopee	MN	55379	1
Shakopee Town Theater	1116 Shakopee Town Sq.	Shakopee	MN	55379	6
St Paul Student Center	2017 Buford Ave.	St Paul	MN	55108	1
Princess Theatre-Community Center	505 S. 1st Ave.	St. James	MN	56081-1727	1
Science Museum of Minnesota	30 E. 10th	St. Paul	MN	55101	1
St. Peter 5	621 S. Minnesota Ave.	St. Peter	MN	56082	5
Staples Theatre	204 N.E. 4th St.	Staples	MN	56479	1
Waconia	101 W. 1st St.	Waconia	MN	55387-1319	6
Cozy Twin Theatre	223 S. Jefferson St.	Wadena	MN	56482	2
Gopher	907 Broadway	Wheaton	MN	56296	1
White Bear Township Theatre	1180 County Rd. J	White Bear	MN	55110	17
Woodbury Cinema Cafe	1750 Weir Dr..	Woodbury	MN	55125	5
Northland 5	1635 Oxford St.	Worthington	MN	56187	5

MISSOURI

Theatre Name	Address	City	State	Zip	Screens
Princess Theatre	Hwy. 39	Aurora	MO	65605	1
El Teatro Real	117 S. 15th St..	Bethany	MO	64424	2
Blue Springs Cinema	1901 N. Hwy 7	Blue Springs	MO	64015	8
Bolivar Cinema 4	800 E. Aldrich Rd, Ste. 10	Bolivar	MO	65613	4
Ozarks Discovery IMAX Theater	3562 Shepherd of the Hills Expressway	Branson	MO	65616	1
Cedar Theatre	127 E. Brooks St.	Brookfield	MO	64628	1
Starlite Drive-In	Rt 2, Box 2670	Cadet	MO	63630	1
Ritz	311 N. Main	Cameron	MO	64429	2
Grand 6	2880 Grand Ave.	Chillicothe	MO	64601	6
Crest Theater	112 N. Washington	Clinton	MO	64735	3
Melba Theatre	300 S. Main St.	De Soto	MO	63020	1
Festus 8 Theatres	1522 Pkwy. W.	Festus	MO	63028	8
Fulton Cinema	613 Court St..	Fulton	MO	65251	2
Hannibal Cinema 5	7 Northport Shopping Center	Hannibal	MO	63401	5
Cinema 6 Harrisonville	2727 Cantrell Rd..	Harrisonville	MO	64701	6
Englewood Theatre	10917 Winner Rd.	Independence	MO	64052	1
Independence Square Cinema 4	114 W. Maple	Independence	MO	64050	4
KC Area Drive-In 8	110 W. Maple	Independence	MO	64050	8
Twin Drive-In Theatre	1320 N. 71 By-Pass	Independence	MO	64137	2
Ramada 4 Theatres	1614 Jefferson St.	Jefferson City	MO	65109	4
MALL 5 Theatres	101 N. Rangeline Rd..	Joplin	MO	64801-4118	5
Chouteau Theater	2815 N.E. Vivion Rd.	Kansas City	MO	64119	4
I-70 Four Screen Drive-In	8701 E. Hwy 40	Kansas City	MO	64129	4
Sprint IMAX @ Kansas City Zoo	6800 Zoo Dr.	Kansas City	MO	64132	1
Tivoli Manor Square	4050 Pennsylvania	Kansas City	MO	64111	3
Kirkwood Cinema	338 S. Kirkwood Rd.	Kirkwood	MO	63122	2
Lebanon Ritz 4 Theatre	925 S. Jefferson	Lebanon	MO	65536	4
Liberty Cinema 12	2101 W. Kansas	Liberty	MO	64068	12

Theatre Name	Address	City	State	Zip	Screens
Macon Cinema	2218 U.S. Hwy. 63	Macon	MO	63552	4
Uptown	104 N. Kansas Ave.	Marceline	MO	64658	1
Marshall Cinema	114-120 E. N. St.	Marshall	MO	65340	2
Missouri Theatre	118 N. Main St.	Maryville	MO	64468	0
Moberly 5 and Dr.	3000 N. Morley	Moberly	MO	65270	5
Monett Plaza 5	507 Plaza Dr.	Monett	MO	65708	5
Lyric Theatre	110 W. 2nd St.	Salisury	MO	65281	1
State Fair	1400 S. Limit	Sedalia	MO	65301	4
Owen Drive-In	1 Owen Dr.	Seymour	MO	65746	1
Palace Theatre	2220 W. Chesterfield Blvd	Springfield	MO	65807	9
St. Andrews 3	2025 Golfway Dr.	St. Charles	MO	63301	3
Arch Odyssey	707 N. 1st St.	St. Louis	MO	63102	1
Chase Park Plaza Cinemas	212 N. Kingshwy. Blvd	St. Louis	MO	63108	5
Hi-Pointe Cinema	1001 McCausland Ave.	St. Louis	MO	63117	1
Omnimax @ St. Louis Science Center	5050 Oakland Ave.	St. Louis	MO	63110	1
Mid Rivers Mall Cinema	1220 Mid Rivers Mall	St. Peters	MO	63376	1
Mainstreet	1316 Main St.	Trenton	MO	64683	1
Great Eight Cinema	Prairie Dell Rd.	Union	MO	63084	8
Belle Starr Playhouse and Cinema	112 E. Booneslick	Warrenton	MO	63383	1
Roxy Theatre	319 Van Buren St.	Warsaw	MO	65355	2
Cinema 1 Plus 1	1160 Clock Tower Plaza	Washington	MO	63090	2
Capitol Theatre	507 Mary Dr.	Waterloo	MO	62298	1
Waynesville Cinema 5	City Rte. 66	Waynesville	MO	65583	5
Glass Sword Cinema	Bypass 63 S.	West Plains	MO	65775	3

MISSISSIPPI

Theatre Name	Address	City	State	Zip	Screens
Delta Theatre	11 3rd St.	Clarksdale	MS	39194	1
Hardy Court Cinema	25 Hardy Court Shopping Center	Gulfport	MS	39507	9
Cloverleaf Cinema Three	5912 Hwy 49 N. D-16	Hattiesburg	MS	39401	3
Broadcountry Cinema III	1 Block off Hwy. 49	Magee	MS	39111	3
The Movie Reel	720 Coulter Dr.	New Albany	MS	38652	4
Southaven Cinema	2010 Stateline Rd. W.	Southaven	MS	38671	8
Plaza Theatre	K Mart Plaza	Yazoo City	MS	39194	2

MONTANA

Theatre Name	Address	City	State	Zip	Screens
Washoe	305 S.Main St.	Anaconda	MT	59711	1
Campus Square 8	1611 S. 11th Ave.	Bozeman	MT	59715	8
Big Sky Cinemas	560 N. Montana St.	Dillon	MT	59725	2
Majestic Theatre	215 Dewey Ave.	Eureka	MT	59917	1
Valley Cinemas	600 S. 2nd Ave.	Glasgow	MT	59230	2
Roxy Twin	120 2nd St. N.	Hamilton	MT	59840	2
Havre Cinemas	328 2nd St.	Havre	MT	59501	2
Dome Theatre	Mineral Ave.	Libby	MT	59923	1
Empire	106 N. 2nd Ave.	Livingston	MT	59047	2
Wilma Theater	131 S.Higgins Ave.	Missoula	MT	59802	0
Showboat	416 Main St.	Polson	MT	59860	2
Entertainer	17 S.W. 4th Ave.	Ronan	MT	59864	1
Centre	211 S. Central	Sidney	MT	59270	1
Yellowstone IMAX Theatre	101 S. Canyon St.	West Yellowstone	MT	59758	1
Mountain	6475 U.S. Hwy 93 S.	Whitefish	MT	59937	2
Prairie Cinemas	316 Main St.	Wolf Point	MT	59201	2

NORTH CAROLINA

Theatre Name	Address	City	State	Zip	Screens
Earl Theatre	127 E. Main St.	Ahoskie	NC	27910	4
Badin Rd. Drive-In	2411 Badin Rd.	Albemarle	NC	28001	1
Eastgate Cinemas	823 Hwy. 24	Albemarle	NC	28001	5
Biltmore Square 6	800 Brevard Rd.	Asheville	NC	28806	6
Fine Arts Theatre	36 Biltmore Ave.	Asheville	NC	28801	2
R/C Hatteras Movies 4	Hatteras Island Plaza Hwy. 12	Avon	NC	27915	4
Belmont Drive-In	314 McAdenville Rd.	Belmont	NC	28012	1
Co-Ed Theatre	101 W. Main St.	Brevard	NC	28712	1
Church St. Cinema Twin	1887 S. Church St.	Burlington	NC	27215	2
Plaza Cinema Burlington	2137 N. Church St.	Burlington	NC	27215	2
Cinema 4	Fed Point Station Shopping Center	Carolina Beach	NC	28428	4
Crossroads 20	501 Caitboo Ave.	Cary	NC	27511	20
UA Imperial Cinema	800 E. Maynard Rd.	Cary	NC	27511	6
Carolina Theatre	1088 E. Franklin St.	Chapel Hill	NC	27514	1
Chelsea Theatre	1129 Weaver Dairy Rd.	Chapel Hill	NC	27514	3
Movies @ Timberlyne	120 Banks St.	Chapel Hill	NC	27514	6
Plaza Theatre	141 Elliott Rd.	Chapel Hill	NC	27514	5
UNC Student Union Auditorium	Frank Porter Graham St	Chapel Hill	NC	27514	1
Varsity Theatre	123 E. Franklin St.	Chapel Hill	NC	27514	2
Arboretum 12 Cinema	8008 Providence Rd.	Charlotte	NC	28277	12
Carmike Town Cinema 6	8640 University City Blvd.	Charlotte	NC	28213	6
Carmike University Place 6	8925 JM Keynes Dr.	Charlotte	NC	28262	6
Delta Six Theatre	8800 E. Harris Blvd. @ Albemarle Rd.	Charlotte	NC	28212	6
GC Southpark Cinema	4400 Sharon Rd.	Charlotte	NC	28211	3
Manor Theatre	607 Providence Rd.	Charlotte	NC	28207	2
Movies @ Crownpoint	9630 Monroe Rd. @ Sardis Rd. N.	Charlotte	NC	28270	12
Observer Omnimax Theatre	301 N. Tryon St.	Charlotte	NC	28202	1
Park Terrace 6	4289 Park Rd.	Charlotte	NC	28209	6
Phillips Place Stadium	5970 Fairview Rd.	Charlotte	NC	28209	10
Starlight Stadium	Hwy 29 N. @ Blockbuster Pavilion Blvd.	Charlotte	NC	28262	12
Carolina Mall Cinemas	120 Country Club Dr. N.E.	Concord	NC	28205	8

Theatre Name	Address	City	State	Zip	Screens
Movies @ The Lake	I-77 Exit 28	Cornelius	NC	28031	12
R/C Corolla Movies 4	Monteray Plaza; 815 E. Ocean Trail	Corolla	NC	27927	4
Carolina Theatre	309 W. Morgan St.	Durham	NC	27701	2
Starlite Drive-In Theatre	2523 E. Club Blvd.	Durham	NC	27704-3533	1
Cinema VI	5065 Calhoun Memorial Hwy.	Easley	NC	29640	6
Eden Drive-In	106 Fireman Club Rd.	Eden	NC	27288	2
Taylor Theatre	208 S. Broad St.	Edenton	NC	27932	2
Gateway Cinemas	Southgate Shopping Center	Elizabeth City	NC	27909	2
GC Cross Creek Cinema 3	216 Cross Creek Mall	Fayetteville	NC	28303	3
GC Cross Pointe 6 Cinemas	5075 Morganton Rd.	Fayetteville	NC	28304	6
Sycamore Cinema 5	828 Shannon Dr.	Fayetteville	NC	28302	5
UA Garner Town Square	2600 Timber Dr.	Garner	NC	27529	10
Cinema 4	2132 Goforth Ave.	Gastonia	NC	28054	4
Movies @ Franklin Square	3778 E. Franklin Blvd.	Gastonia	NC	28056	14
Graham Cinema	119 N. Main	Graham	NC	27253	1
Carousel Cinemas	1305 Battleground Ave	Greensboro	NC	27403	15
GC Four Seasons Cinema 4	650 Four Season Mall	Greensboro	NC	27407	4
Quaker Cinemas 1 & 2	615 Dolly Madison Rd.	Greensboro	NC	27410	2
Market Place Cinema	907 W Beckford Dr.	Henderson	NC	27536	4
Westchester Cinema	2200 Westchester Dr.	High Point	NC	27262	2
Starmount Crossing 5	209 Winston Rd.	Jonesville	NC	28642	5
Gem Theatre	111 W. 1st St.	Kannapolis	NC	28081	1
Countryside Cinema 3 Kernersville	631 N. Main St.	Kernersville	NC	27284	3
Bessemer City Drive-In	1365 Bessemer City Rd.	Kings Mountain	NC	28086	1
R/C Kitty Hawk	3850 N. Croatan Hwy.	Kitty Hawk	NC	27949	2
R/C Marketplace	110 N. Croatan Hwy.	Kitty Hawk	NC	27949	2
Lexington Cinema 8	235 Talbert Blvd.	Lexington	NC	27292	8
Louisburg Theatre 2	109 West Nash St.	Louisburg	NC	27549	2
Town & Country Four	3525 Fayetteville Rd.	Lumberton	NC	28359	4
Pioneer Theatre	113 Budleigh St.	Manteo	NC	27954	1
Carmike Festival 10	10404 E. Independence	Matthews	NC	28105	10
Union Square Cinema 8	1911 Dickerson Blvd.	Monroe	NC	28110	8
AmStar Cinemas 14	206 Norman Station Blvd.	Mooresville	NC	28117	14
R/C Cineplex	2423 S. Croatan Pkwy.	Nags Head	NC	27959	4
Southgate Cinema 6	2806 Trent Rd.	New Bern	NC	28560	6
State Cinema	117 N. College Ave.	Newton	NC	28658	2
Colony Theatres	5438 Six Forks Rd.	Raleigh	NC	27609	2
GC Pleasant Valley Promenade	6240 Glenwood Ave.	Raleigh	NC	27612	7
NC State University Cinema	Witherspoon Student Center	Raleigh	NC	27695	1
Raleigh Grand Cinema	4840 Grove Barton Rd.	Raleigh	NC	27613	14
Raleighwood Cinema	6609 Falls of Neuse	Raleigh	NC	27615	2
Rialto Theatre	1620 Glenwood Ave.	Raleigh	NC	27605	1
Studio	2526-111 Hillsborough St.	Raleigh	NC	27607	2
Rockingham Theatre	205 Gilmer St.	Reidsville	NC	27320	1
Roanoke Cinemas	1722 E. 10th St.	Roanoke City	NC	27870	3
Plaza Cinema 4	1305 E. Broad Ave	Rockingham	NC	28379	4
Sunset Drive-In	US 74 West	Shelby	NC	28150	1
Howell Theatre	141 S. 3rd St.	Smithfield	NC	27577	2
Surf Cinema	4836 Long Beach Rd	Southport	NC	28461	4
Quin Theatre	E. Sylva Shopping Center	Sylva	NC	28779	2
Bel-Air Drive-In	5153 Reidsville Rd.	Walkertown	NC	27051	1
Cinema Theatre	623 Madison St.	Whiteville	NC	28472	3
GC Hanes Mall Cinema 4	180 Hanes Mall Circle	Winston Salem	NC	27103	4
NorthPoint 5	4660 Brownsboro Rd.	Winston Salem	NC	27106	5
University Plaza 1 & 2	University Plaza Shopping Ctr.	Winston-Salem	NC	27105	2

NORTH DAKOTA

Belfield	113 1st Ave N.W.	Belfield	ND	58622	1
Fargo Theatre	314 Broadway	Fargo	ND	58102	1
Grand Theatre	312 Main St.	Williston	ND	58801	7
Lake Park Drive-In	Hwy. 2 N.	Williston	ND	58801	1

NEBRASKA

Geju-Alliance Theatre	410 Box Butte Ave.	Alliance	NE	69301	3
State Theatre	1221 J. St.	Auburn	NE	68305	1
Cinema Theatre	615 Court St.	Beatrice	NE	68310	2
Douglas South Cinema 7	1311 S. Fort Crook Rd.	Bellevue	NE	68002	7
Douglas Southroads 4	1001 Fort Crook Rd. N.	Bellevue	NE	68005	4
Blair Twin	West Hwy. 30	Blair	NE	68008	2
Main St. Blair Three	West Hwy. 30	Blair	NE	68008	3
Eagle Theatre	244 Main St.	Chadron	NE	69337	4
Central States Center 6	3100 23rd St	Columbus	NE	68601	6
Rialto Theatre	202 E. 8th St.	Cozad	NE	69130	1
Isis Theatre	139 W. 13th St.	Crete	NE	68333	2
River Twin Cinema	1715 Stone	Falls City	NE	68355	2
Central States Cinema 3	742 E. 23rd St.	Fremont	NE	68025	3
Fremont 4	866 E. 23rd St.	Fremont	NE	68025	4
Grand Island	316 W. 3rd St.	Grand Island	NE	68801	1
Lied IMAX Theater	1330 N. Burlington Ave.	Hastings	NE	68902-1286	1
Rivoli Theatre	528 W. 2nd St.	Hastings	NE	68901	1
Majestic Theatre	5th and Lincoln	Hebron	NE	68370	2
Cinema Twin	201 N. 13th St	Lincoln	NE	68508	2
Douglas Theatre	1300 P St.	Lincoln	NE	68501	3
East Park	E. Park Plaza Mall	Lincoln	NE	68505	6
Edgewood 3 Theatre	5220 S.56th St.	Lincoln	NE	68516	3

Theatre Name	Address	City	State	Zip	Screens
Joyo	6102 Havelock Ave.	Lincoln	NE	68507-1233	1
Mary Riepma Ross Film Theatre	12th & R. St.	Lincoln	NE	68588	1
Plaza 4 Theatre	201 N. 12th St.	Lincoln	NE	68508	4
Southpointe Cinema	2920 Pine Lake Rd.	Lincoln	NE	68516	6
Star Ship 9	1311 Q St.	Lincoln	NE	68508	9
Stuart Theatre	140 N. 13th St.	Lincoln	NE	68508	1
The Lincoln	1145 P St.	Lincoln	NE	68508	3
Cinema 3	224 Westview Plaza	McCook	NE	69001-4414	3
Pioneer Theater	110 S. 11th St.	Nebraska City	NE	68410	3
Kings Theatre	1000 Riverside Blvd.	Norfolk	NE	68701	4
Douglas 20 Grand	14304 W Maple Rd.	Omaha	NE	68164	20
Douglas Cinema Center Complex	2828 S.82nd Ave	Omaha	NE	68124	8
Douglas Q Cinema 9	5505 S.120th St.	Omaha	NE	68137	9
Dundee Theatre	4952 Dodge St.	Omaha	NE	68132	1
Lozier IMAX Theatre	3701 10th St.	Omaha	NE	68107	2
Super Saver Cinema 8-Westwood	2809 S. 125th Ave, Ste. 297	Omaha	NE	68144	8
Ritz Theatre	134 S.6th St.	Plattsmouth	NE	68048	1
Rivoli Theatre	533 Main St.	Seward	NE	68902	1

NEW HAMPSHIRE

Claremont Cinema Center	345 Washington St.-Rte. 11	Claremont	NH	03743	6
Ioka Theatre 1	55 Water St.	Exeter	NH	03833-2440	1
Hampton Cinema 6	321 Lafayette Rd.	Hampton	NH	03842	6
The Nugget Theatre	S. Main St.	Hanover	NH	03755	4
Colonial Theatre NH	95 Main St.	Keene	NH	03431	1
Colonial 5 Theatres	615 Main St.	Laconia	NH	03246-3447	5
Lakes Region Cinema 3	1387 Lake Shore Rd.	Laconia	NH	03246-2264	3
Jax Jr Cinemas	33 Main St.	Littleton	NH	03561	2
Cinema 8 Apple Tree Mall	16 Orchard View Dr.	Londonderry	NH	03053-3366	8
Mt. Valley	Rte. 16 302	N. Conway	NH	03860	7
Brandt Cinema 3	300 Main St.	Nashua	NH	03060	3
Premiere 8	Post Rd. Plaza Rte. 101A	Nashua	NH	03054	8
North Conway Twin	Main St. N. Conway Village	North Conway	NH	03860	2
Chunky's Pelham Cinema & Pub	150 Bridge St.	Pelham	NH	03076	5
Plymouth Theatre	39 Main St.	Plymouth	NH	03264	2
The Music Hall Theatre 1	28 Chestnut St.	Portsmouth	NH	03801	1
Meadows Drive-In	Rte. 135	Woodsville	NH	03785	1

NEW JERSEY

Atlantic Cinema 5	82 First Ave.	Atlantic Highland	NJ	07716	5
Montgomery Cinema	Rte. 206 S.	Belle Mead	NJ	08502	6
Clearview Bergenfield 5	58 S.Washington Ave.	Bergenfield	NJ	07621	5
Berkeley Cinema	450 Springfield Ave.	Berkeley Heights	NJ	07922	1
Darress Theatre	615 Main St.	Boonton	NJ	07005	1
Roberts Theatre Brook Theatre	10 Hamilton St.	Boundbrook	NJ	08805	1
Beach Cinema	110 Main St.	Bradley Beach	NJ	07720	1
Hoyts Cape May Beach 4	711 Beach Ave.	Cape May	NJ	08204	4
Roberts Theatres Chatham Theatre	Sunpike Rd.	Chatham	NJ	07928	1
Clearview Chester Cinema 6	Rte. 206	Chester	NJ	07930	6
Clifton Quad	1136 Main St.	Clifton	NJ	07013	4
Cranford Theatre	25 North Ave.	Cranford	NJ	07016	5
Dunellen Theatre	458 North Ave	Dunellen	NJ	08812	1
MEGA Movies at Brunswick Square	755 Rte. 18	East Brunswick	NJ	08816	13
East Windsor Cinemas	Rte. 130 S.E. Windsor	East Windsor	NJ	08520	2
Clearview Edison 8 Theatre	1655 Oak Tree Rd.	Edison	NJ	08818	8
Clearview Emerson Quad	344 Kinderkamack Rd.	Emerson	NJ	07630	4
Hyway 6 Theatres	2218 Broadway	Fairlawn	NJ	07410	6
Cinema Plaza 6	Rte.s 202 and 31	Flemington	NJ	08822	6
Galaxy Theatre	7000 Blvd. East	Guttenberg	NJ	07093	3
Mall Theatre	215 Mountain Ave.	Hackettstown	NJ	07840	2
Destinta Hamilton 12	2465 S. Broad St.	Hamilton	NJ	07644	12
Hawthorne Quad	300 Lafayette Ave.	Hawthorne	NJ	07506	4
Hoboken Cinema	5 Marine View Plaza	Hoboken	NJ	07030	2
Hudson St. Cinemas	5 Marine View Plaza	Hoboken	NJ	07030	2
Movies Under the Stars	1 Hudson Place	Hoboken	NJ	07030	1
Clearview Woodbridge 5 Theatre	675 Rte. 1	Iselin	NJ	08830	5
Kodak OMNI Theater	251 Phillip St.	Jersey City	NJ	07305-4699	1
Lincoln Cinemas	838 Kearny Ave	Kearny	NJ	07032	6
Clearview Kinnelon 11	25 Kinnelton Rd.	Kinnelon	NJ	07405	11
Linden 5 Plex	400 Northwood Ave.	Linden	NJ	07036	5
Hoyts Manahawkin 10	733 Rte. 72E	Manahawkin	NJ	08050	10
Reading Cinema Manville 12	180 N. Main St.	Manville	NJ	08835	12
Maplewood Theatre	155 Maplewood Ave.	Maplewood	NJ	07040	6
Roberts Theatres Wellmont	5 Seymour St.	Montclair	NJ	07042	3
Harwan Theatre	9 S. Blackhorse Pike	Mt. Ephraim	NJ	08059	1
Rutgers University Film	Rutgers University	New Brunswick	NJ	08903	2
Newton Theatre	234 Spring St.	Newton	NJ	07860	2
Hoyts Bayshore 8	Lincoln Blvd & Bayshore Rd.	North Cape May	NJ	08204	8
Tilton 9 Theatre	331 Tilton Rd.	Northfield	NJ	08225	9
Franklin Triplex	510 Franklin Ave.	Nutley	NJ	07068	3
Hoyts Ocean City Strand 5	9th and Boardwalk	Ocean City	NJ	08226	5
Clearview Middlebrook Galleria	Middlebrook Shopping Plaza	Ocean Township	NJ	07712	10
Cinema 35	65 E. State Rte. 4.	Paramus	NJ	07652	2
Paramus Picture Show	35 Plaza	Paramus	NJ	07652	1
Clearview Parsippany Cinema 12	3165 Rte. 46	Parsippany	NJ	07054	12

Theatre Name	Address	City	State	Zip	Screens
Broadway Theatre	47 S. Broadway	Pitman	NJ	08071	1
Hoyts Towne 14 Theatres	6733 Blackhorse Pike	Pleasantville	NJ	08232	14
Market Fair 9	3521 US Rte. 1	Princeton	NJ	08540	9
Princeton Garden	160 Nassau St.	Princeton	NJ	08542	2
Ramsey Theatre	125 E. Main St.	Ramsey	NJ	07068	1
Rialto Theatre-Ridgefield Park	Main St.	Ridgefield Park	NJ	07660	1
Creative Entertainment New Park Cinema	23 W. Westfield Ave	Roselle Park	NJ	07204	5
Williams Center Cinemas 2	1 Williams Plaza	Rutherford	NJ	07070	2
Loews Meadows 6	800 Plaza Dr.	Secaucus	NJ	07094	6
Hoyts Somers Point 4	20 MacArthur Blvd.	Somers Point	NJ	08204	4
Sparta Theatre	25 Centre St.	Sparta	NJ	07871	2
Hoyts Stone Harbor 5	271 96th St.	Stone Harbor	NJ	08247	5
Clearview Succasunna Cinema 10	Rocksbury Mall	Succasunna	NJ	07876	10
Teaneck 4 Theatre	503 Cedar Lane	Teaneck	NJ	07666	4
Clearview Tenafly Cinema 4	4 1/2 Railroad Ave	Tenafly	NJ	07670	4
Union Sevenplex	990 Stuyvesant Ave	Union	NJ	07083	7
Summit Quad Theatres	1214 Summit Ave.	Union City	NJ	07087	4
Bargain Cinema Echelon Mall	3012 Echelon Mall	Voorhees	NJ	08043	4
Ritz Sixteen	900 Haddonfield-Berlin Rd.	Voorhees	NJ	08043	16
Washington Theatre	165 E. Washington Ave	Washington	NJ	07882	3
Clearview Washington Township	249 Pascack Rd.	Washington Twnsip	NJ	07675	3
Valley View Twin Theatre	777 Hamburg Tnpke.	Wayne	NJ	07470	2
Mayfair 3-Plex	6405 Park Ave.	West New York	NJ	07093	3
Rialto Theatre of Westfield	250 E. Broad St.	Westfield	NJ	07090	5
Pascack 6	182 Center St.	Westwood	NJ	07675	6
Westwood Cinema Corp	182 Center St.	Westwood	NJ	07675	6

NEW MEXICO

Tombaugh IMAX Dome Theatre	New Mexico Hwy 2001	Alamogordo	NM	88310	1
Dynamax Theatre	1801 Mountain Rd. N.W.	Albuquerque	NM	87104	1
Guild Art Theatre	3405 Central Ave. N.E.	Albuquerque	NM	87106-1431	1
Lobo Theatre	3013 Central Ave. N.E.	Albuquerque	NM	87106	1
Southwest Film Center	3601 University Blvd S.E.	Albuquerque	NM	87106	1
Fiesta Drive-In 3	401 W. Fiesta Dr.	Carlsbad	NM	88220-5454	3
Deming Cinema 3 Theatre	Village Square Shopping Center	Deming	NM	88030	3
Trans Lux Dream Catcher	33771 S. Hwy. 285	Espanola	NM	87532	6
El Morro Theatre	207 W. Coal Ave.	Gallup	NM	87301-6305	1
West Theatre Grants	118 W. Santa Fe Ave.	Grants	NM	87020-2528	1
Fountain Theatre - Mesilla Valley	2469 Calle de Guadalupe	Mesilla	NM	88046	1
El Raton 85 Drive-In	115 N. 1st St.	Raton	NM	87740-3859	1
Sierra Cinema	721 Mechem Dr #D	Ruidoso	NM	88345-6911	3
The Screen	1600 St Michael's Dr.	Santa Fe	NM	87505	1
Pecos Theatre	219 4th	Santa Rosa	NM	88435	1
Cinematheque At Plan B	1050 Old Pecos Trail	Sante Fe	NM	87501-4562	1
El Sol Theatre	404 N. Bullard St.	Silver City	NM	88061	1
Gila Theatre	415 N. Bullard St.	Silver City	NM	88061	1
Real West Cinema II	11585 Hwy. 180 E.	Silver City	NM	88061-7780	2
El Cortez Theatre	415 Main St.	Truth/Consequence	NM	87901-2842	1
Odeon Theatre Tucumcari	123 S. 2nd St.	Tucumcari	NM	88401-2281	1

NEVADA

Cinema 8	3025 E. Desert Inn Rd.	Las Vegas	NV	89121	8
IMAX 3D Simulator @ Caesars Palace	3500 Las Vegas Blvd. S.	Las Vegas	NV	89109	1
Luxor IMAX Theatre	3900 Las Vegas Blvd. S.	Las Vegas	NV	89119	1
Omnimax Theater	3570 Las Vegas Blvd. N.	Las Vegas	NV	89109	1
Paradise Dollar Theatre	3330 E. Tropicana	LAS VEGAS	NV	89121	6
Laughlin Stadium 9	1955 S. Casino Dr.	Laughlin	NV	89029	9
Virgin River Cinema	22 Main St.	Mesquite	NV	89024	4
Ironwood Stadium Cinema 8	1760 Hwy 395	Minden	NV	89423	8
Pahrump Theatre	1301 E. Cal Vada Blvd.	Pahrump	NV	89401	1

NEW YORK

Norma Jean Madison	1036 Madison Ave.	Albany	NY	12208	7
Spectrum 7	290 Delaware Ave.	Albany	NY	12209	7
Castle Cinema	W. State Rd.	Allegany	NY	14706	1
Screening Room Cinema Cafe	3131 Sheridan Dr	Amherst	NY	14226	1
University Cinema	4100 Maple Rd.	Amherst	NY	14226	5
Norma Jean's Amsterdam Theatre	136 Perth Plaza, Rte. 30	Amsterdam	NY	12010	10
Riverfront Cinemas	Main St. and Rte. 30	Amsterdam	NY	12010	7
Grandview Drive-In	Rte. 5 and Lake St.	Angola	NY	14006	2
Auburn Movieplex 8	Grant Ave. Plaza, Rte. 5	Auburn	NY	13021	8
Fingerlake Mall Cinemas	Rte. 5 & 20	Auburn	NY	13022-7580	4
Hollywood Drive-In	9254 NY 66	Averill Park	NY	12018	1
Avon Park Theatre	71 Genesee St.	Avon	NY	14414	1
Vintage Drive-In	1520 Rte. 15	Avon	NY	14414	3
Tri-County Cinema	Rte. 31 Baldwinsville	Baldwinsville	NY	13027	2
Dipson Batavia Mall Cinema	6 Alva Pl. W.	Batavia	NY	14020	2
Bellmore Movies	222 Pettit Ave.	Bellmore	NY	11710	1
Five Star Theatres Bellmore Playhouse	525 Bedford Ave.	Bellmore	NY	11710	5
Mid Island Triplex	Hempstead Tnpke.	Bethpage	NY	11801	2
Elmira Drive-In	Rt 352	Big Flats	NY	14814	1
Strand Theatre	Main St.	Brockport	NY	14420	3
American Theatre	1450 East Ave.	Bronx	NY	10462-7502	7
Brooklyn Heights Cinema	70 Henry St.	Brooklyn	NY	11201-1727	2

Theatre Name	Address	City	State	Zip	Screens
Canarsie Triplex	9310 Ave. L @ E. 93rd St.	Brooklyn	NY	11236-4807	3
Kent Theatre	1170 Coney Island Ave	Brooklyn	NY	11230-2912	4
Rose Cinemas	30 Lafayette Ave.	Brooklyn	NY	11217	1
Screen Arts Pavilion Theatre	188 Prospect Park West	Brooklyn	NY	11215	6
Dipson Market Arcade Film & Arts	639 Main St.	Buffalo	NY	14203	8
Pfeifer Theatre	681 Main St.	Buffalo	NY	14203	1
Super Saver Cinema 8	2050 Elmwood Ave.	Buffalo	NY	14207	8
Callicoon Theatre	Acacemy St.	Callicoon	NY	12723	1
Norma Jean Movietime Cinema	Wal-Mart Plaza	Canandiagua	NY	14424	10
Community Theatre	373 Main St.	Catskill	NY	12414	2
Crandell Theatre	46-48 Main St.	Chatham	NY	12037	1
Appletree Theatres	34 Appletree Business Park	Cheektowaga	NY	14227	6
Buffalo Drive-In Theatre	3085 Harlem Rd.	Cheektowaga	NY	14225-2563	2
Chester 4 Cinema	Rte. 17 M Quickway Plaza	Chester	NY	10918	4
Chester Cinema 6	Rte.17	Chester	NY	10918	6
Clinton Cinema	2 Fountain St.	Clinton	NY	13323	1
Movieland of Coram	1850 Rt 112	Coram	NY	11727	8
Queen City Plaza I & II Corona	10314 Roosevelt Ave.	Corona	NY	11368-2395	2
Plaza 6 Cinema - Cortland	Tompkins & Glenwood	Cortland	NY	13045	6
Hi Way Drive-In	Rte. 9 West	Coxsackie	NY	12037	1
Dansville Star Theatre	144 Main St.	Dansville	NY	14437	1
Delevan Drive-In	Rte. 16	Delevan	NY	14042	1
Dunkirk Cinemas	10520 Bennett Rd.	Dunkirk	NY	14048	8
Aurora Theatre	673 Main St.	East Aurora	NY	14052	1
Cinema Saver	19 Madison Ave	Endicott	NY	13760	4
North Shore Tower Cinemas	27-10 Grand Central Pkwy.	Floral Park	NY	11005-1109	2
Cinemart Cinemas	106-03 Metropolitan Ave.	Forest Hills	NY	11375	5
Geneseo Square Theatres	Rte. 20-A, Lakeville Rd.	Geneseo	NY	14454	6
Geneva Cinema 5	495 Exchange St.	Geneva	NY	14456	5
Geneva Movieplex 8	371 Hamilton St.	Geneva	NY	14456	8
Jericho Drive-In	Rte. 9 West	Glenmont	NY	12077	1
Glen Drive-In	Rte. 9	Glens Falls	NY	12801	1
Village Cinema Greenport	211 Front St.	Greenport	NY	11944	1
Greenville Drive-In	Rte. 32	Greenville	NY	12083	1
Palace Hamburg	31 Buffalo St.	Hamburg	NY	14075	1
Capra Cinema	93 West Front St	Hancock	NY	13783	1
Harrison Cinema	221 Harrison Ave.	Harrison	NY	10528	1
Village 7 Cinemas	145 N. Franklin	Hempstead	NY	11550	7
Fairview 3	160 Fairview Ave	Hudson	NY	12534	3
Hudson Movieplex	Rte. 9 Fairview Ave.	Hudson	NY	12534	8
Courthouse Theatre	122 Main St.	Hudson Falls	NY	12839	1
Hunter Theatre	Main St.	Hunter	NY	12442	1
Cinema Arts Centre	423 Park Ave.	Huntington	NY	11740	3
Hyde Park Drive-In	Off Rte. 9 at Hyde Park	Hyde Park	NY	12538	1
Roosevelt Cinemas	Rte. 9	Hyde Park	NY	12538	3
Islip 3	410 West Main St.	Islip-	NY	11751-3411	3
Queen City Jackson Triplex Theatre	82nd St.	Jackson Heights	NY	11373-1304	3
Holiday Twin Theatre	Rte. 30 @ Arterial Hwy.	Johnstown	NY	12095	2
Johnstown Movieplex 9	Pyramid Mall- Rte. 30A	Johnstown	NY	12095	9
Main St. Cinemas	72-66 Main St.	Kew Garden Hills	NY	11367-2421	6
Kew Gardens Cinemas	81-05 Lefferts Blvd.	Kew Gardens	NY	11415	5
Palace Theatre	26 Main St.	Lake Placid	NY	12946-1302	4
Flix Superplex Movie Theatre	4901 Transit Rd.	Lancaster	NY	14086	10
Lindenhurst Theatre	20 E. Montauk Hwy.	Lindenhurst	NY	11757	1
Dipson Lockport Mall 8	5737 S. Transit Rd.	Lockport	NY	14094	8
Palace Theatre Lockport	2 East Ave.	Lockport	NY	14094	1
Transit Drive-In	6655 Transit Rd.	Lockport	NY	14094	3
Park Ave. Twin Theatre	179 E. Park Ave.	Long Beach	NY	11572	2
West Wayne Theatre	Rte. 31 - West Wayne Plaza	Macedon	NY	14502	1
Cinema Plaza	10 Pearl St.	Malone	NY	12953	1
Malta Drive-In	Rte. 9	Malta	NY	12010	1
Malverne Cinema 4	350 Hempstead Ave.	Malverne	NY	11598	4
Emelin Theatre	Library Lane	Mamaroneck	NY	10543	1
Manlius Art Cinema	135 E. Seneca St.	Manlius	NY	13104	1
Massena Movieplex	Rte.s 37 and 420	Massena	NY	13662	8
Movieland of Mastic	1708 Montauk Hwy.	Mastic	NY	11950	8
Hollywood Theatre	2221 Brewerton Rd.	Mattydale	NY	13211	3
Sunset Drive-In, Middleport	Telegraph Rd.	Middleport	NY	14105	3
Bargain Cinema Middletown Discount	128 Dolson Ave.	Middletown	NY	10940	5
Middletown Twin Drive-In	Rte. 6 West & 17 M	Middletown	NY	10940	2
Moviehouse	Main St.	Millerton	NY	12546	1
Midway Drive-In	2785 NYS Rte. 48	Minetto	NY	13115	1
Montauk Movies	3 Edgemere Rd.	Montauk	NY	11954	1
Mall Quad Cinema	State Hwy. 42	Monticello	NY	12701	4
IMAX Theatre @ Palisades Ctr	4270 Palisades Center Dr.	New Nyack	NY	10994	1
New Paltz Theatre	Rte. 299	New Paltz	NY	12561	4
Destinta New Windsor 12	Rte. 94 and Union Ave.	New Windsor	NY	12553	12
Anthology Film Archives	2nd Ave. & 2nd St.	New York	NY	10008	1
CC Cinema 3 Theatres	1001 Third Ave.	New York	NY	10022	3
Cinema Classics	332 E. 11th St.	New York	NY	10003	1
Cinema Village	22 E. 12st.	New York	NY	10003-4403	1
City Cinemas 1, 2, 3rd Ave.	1001 Third Ave.	New York	NY	10022	3
Coliseum Theatre	703 W. 181 St.	New York	NY	10033	4
Crown/City Cinemas Gotham	969 Third Ave.	New York	NY	10022	1
Film Forum	209 E. Houston St.	New York	NY	10014-4837	3
Guild	33 W. 50th St.	New York	NY	10020	1
IMAX @ Museum of Natural History	Central Park West at 79th St.	New York	NY	10024	1
Jewish Museum	5th Ave. at 92nd St.	New York	NY	10128	1

Theatre Name	Address	City	State	Zip	Screens
Lincoln Plaza Cinemas	30 Lincoln Plaza	New York	NY	10023-7103	3
Locus Media	594 Broadway	New York	NY	10012	1
Museum of Modern Art	11 W. 53rd St.	New York	NY	10019	2
Nova Cinemas	3589 Broadway	New York	NY	10031-3218	3
Paris Theatre	4 W. 58th St.	New York	NY	10019-2515	1
Quad Cinema	34 W. 13th St.	New York	NY	10011-7911	4
Screening Room	54 Varick St.	New York	NY	10013	1
Walter Reade Theatre	Lincoln Center Plaza	New York	NY	10023-6548	4
Whitney Museum of American Art	945 Madison Ave.	New York	NY	10021	1
Newark Showplace 5	Main & Union St.	Newark	NY	14513	5
Four Seasons Cinema 6	2429 Military Rd.	Niagara Falls	NY	14304	6
Hathaway's Drive-In	Rte. 67	North Hoosick	NY	12133	1
Northport Theatre	250 Main St.	Northport	NY	11768	1
Colonia Theater	35 S. Broad St.	Norwich	NY	13815	3
Oceanside Twin	2743 Long Beach Rd.	Oceanside	NY	11572	2
Strand	Main	Old Forge	NY	13420	1
Glenwood Movieplex 9 of Oneida	Rt 5 & 46	Oneida	NY	13421	9
Southside Oneonta Mall	47 Chestnut St.	Oneonta	NY	13820	4
Oswego Cinema 7	138 West 2nd St.	Oswego	NY	13126	7
Crystal Cinemas	94 Victory Hwy.	Painted Post	NY	14870	8
Plaza Twin Cinema	314 Flatbush Ave.	Park Slope	NY	11238	2
Central Twin	99 Central Ave.	Pearl River	NY	10965	2
Paramount Center	1008 Brown St.	Peekskill	NY	10566	1
Pelham Picture House	175 Wolf's Lane	Pelham	NY	10803	1
Lake St. Plaza Theatres-Penn Yan	230A Lake St. Plaza	Penn Yan	NY	14527	3
Silver Lake Drive-In	Rte. 39, Chapman Rd.	Perry	NY	14530	1
Strand Theatre	25 Brinkerhoff St.	Plattsburgh	NY	12901	2
Port Jefferson Cinemas	1068 Rte. 112	Port Jefferson Stn	NY	11776	7
Roxy Theatre	20 Main St.	Potsdam	NY	13676	2
Overlook Drive-In	12601 Overlook Rd.	Poughkeepsie	NY	12538	1
New York Hall of Science	Flushing Meadows-Corona Park	Queens	NY	10029	1
Lyceum Annex	Rte. 9	Red Hook	NY	12571	1
Lyceum Cinemas	Rte. 9	Red Hook	NY	12571	7
Upstate Film Theatre	26 Montgomery St.	Rhinebeck	NY	12572	2
Queen City Ridgewood Theatre	55-27 Myrtle Ave.	Ridgewood	NY	11385-3550	6
Riverhead Music Hall	Peconic Ave.	Riverhead	NY	11901	1
Cinema Theatre Rochester	957 S. Clinton Ave.	Rochester	NY	14620	1
Dryden Theatre [George Eastman House]	900 East Ave.	Rochester	NY	14607	1
Little Theatres	240 East Ave.	Rochester	NY	14604	5
Strasenburgh Planetarium	657 East Ave.	Rochester	NY	14607	1
Rome Cinemas 8	1222 Erie Blvd West	Rome	NY	13440	8
West Rome Drive-In 2	Rt 69	Rome	NY	13440	2
Rosendale Theatre	Main St.	Rosendale	NY	12472	1
Sag Harbor Cinema	90 Main St.	Sag Harbor	NY	11963	1
Berkeley Cinema	1 Berkeley Square	Saranac Lake	NY	12983	1
Off Broadway Theatre	Congress Plaza	Saratoga Springs	NY	12866	1
Orpheum Theatre	Main St	Saugerties	NY	12477	4
Sayville Theatre	103 Railroad Ave.	Sayville	NY	11715	4
Fine Arts Theatres	365 Central Ave.	Scarsdale	NY	10583	1
Proctors Theatre	432 State St.	Schenectady	NY	12301	2
Scotia Cinema	Rte. 5	Scotia	NY	12302	1
Maveli Twin Cinema 59	Kennedy Mall	Spring Valley	NY	10977	2
Joylan	11 W. Main St.	Springville	NY	14141	1
Atrium Cinema	680 Arthur Kill Rd.	Staten Island	NY	10308-1106	9
Lafayette Theatre	Rte. 59	Suffern	NY	10901	1
Sunnyside Center Cinema 5	Queens Blvd. and 43rd St.	Sunnyside	NY	11104	5
Bristol Omnitheatre	500 S. Franklin St.	Syracuse	NY	13202	1
Landmark Theatre	362 S. Salina St.	Syracuse	NY	13202	1
Palace Theatre - Syracuse	2384 James St.	Syracuse	NY	13206	1
Westcott Cinema	524 Westcott St.	Syracuse	NY	13210	2
State Theatres	1 Block Ave.	Tupper Lake	NY	12986	1
Warsaw Cinema	23 S. Main	Warsaw	NY	14569	1
Warwick 3 Drive-In	Rte. 94 & Warwick Tnpke.	Warwick	NY	10990	3
New York Public Library	20	West 53rd St.	NY	10019	1
South Bay Cinemas	495 W Montauk Hwy.	West Babylon	NY	11704	5
Westhampton Beach Performing Arts	2 Brook Rd., Rte. 31	West Hampton Bch	NY	11978	1
Westbury Theatre	Norther State Pkwy.	Westbury	NY	11030	2
Windham Theatre	11 Vets Rd.	Windham	NY	12496	1
Wolcott Palace Theatre	61 E. Main St.	Wolcott	NY	14590	1
Tinker St. Cinema	132 Tinker St.	Woodstock	NY	12498	2

OHIO

Ada Theatre	215 S. Main St.	Ada	OH	45810	1
Gardner Student Center	University of Akron	Akron	OH	44325	1
Highland Theatre	826 Market St.	Akron	OH	44303	1
Linda Theatre	1745 Goodyear Blvd.	Akron	OH	44305	1
Starlite Drive-In Theatre	2255 Beechmont Ave.	Amelia	OH	45103	1
Amherst	260 Church St.	Amherst	OH	44001	1
Ashland Square Cinemas	214 Center St.	Ashland	OH	44805	3
Ashtabula Cinemas	3409 N. Ridge Rd. West	Ashtabula	OH	44004	4
Athena Cinema	20 S. Court St.	Athens	OH	45701-2810	3
Atlas Avon Lake 4	33487 Lake Rd.	Avon Lake	OH	44012	4
Magic City Drive-In	5602 Cleveland	Barberton	OH	44203	2
West Theatre	1017 Wooster Rd. West	Barberton	OH	44203	1
Midway Theatre	210 W. Plane St.	Bethel	OH	45106	1
Blanchester Cinemas	115 E. Main St.	Blanchester	OH	45107	3
Shannon Theatre	S. Main St.	Bluffton	OH	45817	1

Theatre Name	Address	City	State	Zip	Screens
Cla-Zel Theatre	127 N. Main St.	Bowling Green	OH	43402	1
Brunswick Cinema	1480 Pearl Rd.	Brunswick	OH	44212	4
Bryan Theatre	140 S. Lynn St.	Bryan	OH	43506	3
Palace Theatre	605 Market Ave. N.	Canton	OH	44702	1
Chakeres Lake Drive-In	8477 State Rte. 703	Celina	OH	45822-0270	1
Chagrin Cinema	8200 E. Washington St.	Chagrin Falls	OH	44022	15
Esquire 6 Theatres	320 Ludlow Ave.	Cincinnati	OH	45220	6
Mariemont 3 Theatres	6906 Wooster Rd.	Cincinnati	OH	45227	3
Mount Lookout Cinema Grill	3187 Linwood Ave	Cincinnati	OH	45208	2
Parkland Theatre	6548 Parkland Ave.	Cincinnati	OH	45233	1
Robert D. Lindner Omnimax	1301 Western Ave.	Cincinnati	OH	45203	1
Super Saver Cinemas 8	601 Forest Fair Dr.	Cincinnati	OH	45240	8
Super Saver Eastgate 8 Theatre	4450 Eastgate Blvd.	Cincinnati	OH	45245	8
Circle Cinema Down	117 Pickney St.	Circleville	OH	43113	2
Atlas Cinemas Colony 5	13116 Shaker Square	Cleveland	OH	44120	5
Cleveland Cinematheque	1141 E. Blvd	Cleveland	OH	44104	1
Great Lakes Science Center Omnimax	601 Erieside Ave.	Cleveland	OH	44114-1021	1
Mayfield Drive-In	Rt. 322 at Mayfield Rd.	Cleveland	OH	44114	1
Memphis 3 Drive-In	10543 Memphis	Cleveland	OH	44144	3
Palace Theatre	Playhouse Square Center	Cleveland	OH	44115	1
Tower City 11	230 Huron Rd.	Cleveland	OH	44113	11
Cedar Lee Theatres	2163 Lee Rd.	Cleveland Heights	OH	44118	6
40 East Drive-In	8659 E. Main St.	Columbus	OH	43068	1
Drexel	2254 E. Main St.	Columbus	OH	43209	3
Drexel Grandview	1247 Grandview Ave.	Columbus	OH	43212	1
Marcus Cinemas & IMAX - Crosswoods	200 Hutchinson Ave.	Columbus	OH	43235	17
South Drive-In	3050 S. High St.	Columbus	OH	43207	1
Studio 35 Cinema	3055 Indianola Ave.	Columbus	OH	43202	1
Conneaut Plaza Theatre	348 W Main Rd.	Conneaut	OH	44030	1
Chakeres Kettering Cinema 2	1441 E. Dorothy Lane	Dayton	OH	45430	2
Huber Heights Movie Palace	5589 Old Troy Pike	Dayton	OH	45424-5702	1
New Neon Movies	130 E. 5th St.	Dayton	OH	45402	1
Kingman Drive-In	229 Cheshire Rd.	Delaware	OH	43015	1
Strand Theatre I, II, III	28 E. Winter St.	Delaware	OH	43015	3
Englewood Cinema	320 W. National Rd.	Englewood	OH	45322	1
Atlas Lakeshore 7	22624 Lake Shore Blvd	Euclid	OH	44123	7
Paramount Cinema	301 S. Front St.	Fremont	OH	43420	4
Spring Valley 7	1284 Jackson Pike	Gallipolis	OH	43110	7
Garretsville Cinema	8009 State St.	Garretsville	OH	44231	2
Byjo Theatre	20 N. Main	Germantown	OH	45327	1
Wayne Cinema	538 S. Broadway St.	Greenville	OH	45331-1927	2
Star Cinema 8-Grove City	2384 Stringtown Rd.	Grove City	OH	43123	8
Holiday Auto Theatre	1816 Old Oxford Rd.	Hamilton	OH	45013	1
Star Cinema	211 Harry Saunder Rd.	Hillsboro	OH	45133	6
Elder Theatre	106 W. Pike St.	Jackson Center	OH	45334	1
Kent Cinema Theatre	175 E. Main St.	Kent	OH	44240	2
University Plaza 7	140 Cherry St	Kent	OH	44240	7
Kenton Theatre 3	221 West Franklin St.	Kenton	OH	43326	3
Detroit Theatre	16407 Detroit Ave	Lakewood	OH	44107	2
Lancaster Cinema	1516 Sheridan Dr.	Lancaster	OH	43130-3503	3
Colony Square Cinemas 1 & 2	726 E. Main St.	Lebanon	OH	45036-1900	2
State Theatre	69 S. Main St.	London	OH	43140	1
Lorain Palace Civic Center	617 Broadway	Lorain	OH	44052	1
Scioto Breeze Drive-In	State Rte. 23	Lucasville	OH	45648	2
Atlas Mapletown 3	15716 Broadway	Maple Heights	OH	44137	3
Southgate Cinemas 5	5390 Northfield Rd.	Maple Heights	OH	44137	5
Marysville Cinemas	121 S. Main St.	Marysville	OH	43040	3
McArthur	112 N. Market St	McArthur	OH	45651	2
Medina Twin Theatre	139 W Liberty St.	Medina	OH	44256	2
Atlas Cinemas Diamond Ctr 12	9555 Diamond Center Dr.	Mentor	OH	44060	12
Van-Del Drive-In	19986 Lincoln Hwy	Middle Point	OH	45863	1
Movies 10-Nelsonville	14333 US 33 S.	Nelsonville	OH	45764	10
Quaker Cinemas	158 West High Ave	New Philadelphia	OH	44668-3841	4
Posh Virginia Theatre	119 N. Main	North Baltimore	OH	45872	1
Hi-Rd. Drive-In	8059 State Rd. 68	North Kenton	OH	43326	1
Auto Rama Drive-In	33395 Lorian Rd.	North Ridgeville	OH	44039	2
Apollo	19 E. College St.	Oberlin	OH	44074	1
Sundance Kid Drive-In	4500 Navarre Ave.	Oregon	OH	43616	1
Orr Twin Cinema	415 N. Main St.	Orrville	OH	44667	2
Cinema 20	1469 Menter Ave.	Painesville	OH	44077	20
Cinema Twenty	Painesville Shopping Center	Painesville	OH	44077	1
Parma 3 Theatres	5826 Ridge Rd.	Parma	OH	44129	3
Marcus Cinemas - Pickerington	1776 Hill Rd. N	Pickerington	OH	43147	17
Midway Twin Drive-In	2736 State Rte. 59	Ravenna	OH	44266	2
Salem Twin Cinema	2350 E. State St.	Salem	OH	44460-2577	2
Cedar Point Cinema	1 Cedar Point Dr.	Sandusky	OH	44870	1
Act 1 Cinema	11165 Reading Rd.	Sharonville	OH	45241	1
Chakeres Melody Cruise In	4025 E. National Rd.	Springfield	OH	45505	2
Starlight Drive-In	Rt. 127 & Rt. 119	St. Henry	OH	45883	1
Lynn Auto Theatre	9735 State Rte. 250 N.W.	Strasburg	OH	44680	2
Strongsville Cinema	14767 Pearl Rd.	Strongsville	OH	44136	4
Fox Woodville 4	3725 Williston Rd.	Toledo	OH	43616	4
Ultra Savers Salem Mall	5200 Salem Ave.	Trotwood	OH	45426	4
Mayflower 4 Theatres	9 W Main St.	Troy	OH	45373	4
Movies 5 - Troy	11 W. Main St.	Troy	OH	45373-3211	5
Ridgeway Drive-In	10709 Lincoln Hwy	Van Wert	OH	45891	1
Twin Cinemas	10709 Lincoln Hwy	Van Wert	OH	45891	2

Theatre Name	Address	City	State	Zip	Screens
Dixie Drive-In	6201 N. Dixie Dr.	Vandalia	OH	45377	1
Blue Sky Drive-In	959 Broad St.	Wadsworth	OH	44281	1
Great Oaks Cinema	251 Great Oaks Trail	Wadsworth	OH	44281	2
Wapa Theatre	15 Willipie St..	Wapakoneta	OH	45895-1968	1
Elm Rd. Twin Drive-In	1895 Elm Rd..	Warren	OH	44483	2
Starview Drive-In.	Rte. 20	West Norwalk	OH	44857	1
Wheelersburg 6.	8805 Ohio River Rd.	Wheelersburg	OH	45694	6
IMAX Theatre at the USAF	Gate 28B.	Wright Patterson AFB	OH	45433	1
Little Art Theatre	247 Xenia Ave	Yellow Springs	OH	45387	1
Sunrise Cinemas.	195 Sunrise Center	Zanesville	OH	43701	3

OKLAHOMA

Theatre Name	Address	City	State	Zip	Screens
Heritage Park Theatre	3917 N. Main	Altus	OK	73521	5
Rialto Twin Theatre	516 Flynn St	Alva	OK	73717	2
Carmike 5.	2600 Broadway St..	Ardmore	OK	73401	5
Carmike Eastland 4.	P.O. Box 3069	Bartlesville	OK	74003	4
Rivoli	106 S. Main	Blackwell.	OK	74631	1
Valley View Theatre.	2505 Valley View Dr.	Chickasha	OK	73018	6
Washita Twin.	509 Chickasha Ave.	Chickasha	OK	73023	2
Carmike Dunkin 1	207 E. Broadway	Cushing	OK	74023	1
Carmike 6.	1501 Plato Rd	Duncan	OK	73533	6
Tiffany Cinema	110 S. Bickford Ave..	El Reno.	OK	73036-2720	1
Heritage Park Theatre Elk City.	2708 W 3rd St.	Elk City	OK	73644	4
Carmike Video 2	3517 Lahoma Rd	Enid	OK	73702	2
Beacon Drive-In	2404 S. Division.	Guthrie	OK	73044	1
McCurtain Cinema	Rte. 3 Box 138.	Idabel	OK	74745	2
Carmike 8.	7102 N.W. Cache.	Lawton	OK	73507	8
Vaska Theatre.	1902 N.W. Ferris Ave	Lawton	OK	73505	1
Cinema 69	1116 S. George Nigh Expressway	McAlester	OK	74502	4
Carmike 6.	2612 West Shawnee Bypass	Muskogee	OK	74401	6
Dickinson Arrowhead Mall 6	501 N. Main, Space #102-	Muskogee	OK	74401	6
OmniDome Theatre.	2100 N.E. 52nd St..	Oklahoma City.	OK	73111	1
Silver Cinemas North Park 7	12100 N. May Ave	Oklahoma City.	OK	73120	7
Winchester Drive-In.	6930 S. Western	Oklahoma City.	OK	73139	1
Orpheum Theatre	210 W. 7th.	Okmulgee	OK	74447	2
Airline Drive-In	1800 W Highland	Ponca City.	OK	74601	1
Carmike North Park 4	800 Prospect Ave.	Ponca City.	OK	74601	4
Ponca Plaza Twin	1417 E. Hartford	Ponca City.	OK	74604	2
Poteau Cinema	2214 N. Broadway	Poteau	OK	74953	0
Cinema Centre 8.	3031 N. Harrison	Shawnee.	OK	74801	8
Hornbeck/Penthouse Twin	125 N. Bell.	Shawnee.	OK	74801-6901	2
Carmike 10.	P.O. Box 277	Stillwater.	OK	74074	10
Admiral Drive-In	7355 E. Easton St..	Tulsa.	OK	74115	2
Dickinson Starworld 20	10301 S. Memorial Dr.	Tulsa.	OK	74133	20
Dickinson 66 Twin Drive-In.	P.O. Box 556	Weatherford	OK	73096	2
Dickinson Showest 3.	P.O. Box 556, Rte. 66	Weatherford	OK	73096	3
Picture Show Theatre	119 W Main.	Wilburton	OK	74578	2
Silver Cinemas Dollar Movies 5	1219 Garth Brooks Rd.	Yukon	OK	73099	5

OREGON

Theatre Name	Address	City	State	Zip	Screens
Ashland St Cinemas	1644 Ashland St.	Ashland.	OR	97520	6
Varsity Theatre	166 E. Main St.	Ashland.	OR	97520	5
Astoria Gateway Cinema.	1875 Marine Dr	Astoria	OR	97103	7
Columbian Theatre	1102 Marine Dr..	Astoria	OR	97103	2
Fifth Ave. Cinemas	510 Southwest Hall	Beaverton	OR	97005	1
Desert Theatre	68 N. Broadway	Burns	OR	97720	1
Egyptian	229 S. Broadway	Coos Bay	OR	97420	3
Avalon Cinema Corvallis	160 N.W. Jackson Ave..	Corvallis	OR	97330-4827	1
Cottage Grove Cinemas	1205 Hwy. 99 N.	Cottage Grove.	OR	97424	2
Fox Theatre Dallas OR	166 S.E. Mill St..	Dallas	OR	97338-1908	1
Motor-Vu Drive-In Dallas	315 S.E. Fir Villa Rd.	Dallas	OR	97338-9200	1
Bijou Arts Cinemas	492 E. 13th Ave	Eugene	OR	97401	2
Florence Cinema.	1930 Hwy 101	Florence	OR	97439	4
Forest Grove Cinema 7	2828 Pacific Ave.	Forest Grove	OR	97116	7
Forest Theatre	1911 Pacific Ave.	Forest Grove	OR	97116	1
Grants Pass Movies Six.	1111 N.E. D St.	Grants Pass	OR	97526	6
Rogue Cinema	143 S.E. H St.	Grants Pass	OR	97526	1
Southgate Cinemas.	1625 S.W. Ringuette St	Grants Pass	OR	97527	4
Mt. Hood Theatre	401 E. Powell Blvd.	Gresham	OR	97030	1
Hermiston Cinema	355 W Theatre St.	Hermiston	OR	97838	5
Skylight.	107 Oak St	Hood River	OR	97031	2
Pelican Cinema.	2626 Biehn St.	Klamath Falls	OR	97601	6
Lake Twin Cinema.	106 N. State St	Lake Oswego	OR	97034	2
Kuhn Theatre	668 S. Main St.	Lebanon	OR	97355-3337	1
Motor-Vu Drive-In Lebanon	S. Santiam Hwy..	Lebanon	OR	97355	1
Bijou	1624 N.E. Hwy. 101	Lincoln City	OR	97367	1
Mac Cinema	711 N. Hwy 99 W.	McMinnville	OR	97128	3
McMinnville 8	2725 N.E. Tanger Dr.	McMinnville	OR	97128	8
Moonlight Theatre	433 N.E. 3rd St.	McMinnville	OR	97128	4
Southside Cinema.	1221 S. Riverside Ave	Medford.	OR	97501	4
Milwaukie Theatre.	11011 S.E. Main St	Milwaukie	OR	97222	2
Oak Grove 8 Cinemas.	16100 S.E. McLaughlin Blvd.	Milwaukie	OR	97222	8
99 West Twin.	Hwy. 99W	Newberg	OR	97132	2
99 West Drive-In	Portland Rd.	Newberg	OR	97132	3
Cameo Theatre	304 E. First	Newberg	OR	97132	1

Theatre Name	Address	City	State	Zip	Screens
Pony Village Cinema	Pony Village Shopping Center	North Bend	OR	97459	4
Centre Theatre	205 S.W. 1st	Ontario	OR	97914	1
Pix Theatre	358 S.Oregon St	Ontario	OR	97914	1
The Reel Theatre 8 Ontario	477 S.E. 13th St.	Ontario	OR	97914	8
Pendleton Cinemas	410 Southwest First St	Pendleton	OR	97801	3
Avalon Theatre	3451 S.E. Belmont St.	Portland	OR	97214	2
Bagdad Theatre	3702 S.E. Hawthorne Blvd.	Portland	OR	97214	1
Cine Magic Theatre	2021 S.E. Hawthorne Blvd.	Portland	OR	97214	1
Cinema 21	616 N.W. 231st Ave.	Portland	OR	97209	1
Clinton St. Cinema	2522 S.E. Clinton St.	Portland	OR	97202	1
Kennedy School Theatre	5736 N.E.. 33rd St	Portland	OR	97060	2
Laurelhurst Theatre	2735 E. Burnside	Portland	OR	97222	4
Mission Theatre	1624 N.W. Glisan	Portland	OR	97209	1
Moreland Theatre	6712 S.E. Milwaukie Ave.	Portland	OR	97202	1
Northwest Film Center	1219 S.W. Park Ave.	Portland	OR	97205	2
OMNIMAX @ Oregon Museum	1945 S.E. Water Ave.	Portland	OR	97214-3354	1
Roseway Theatre	7229 N.E. Sandy Blvd.	Portland	OR	97213	1
St Johns 1 & 2 Theatre	8704 N. Lombard St.	Portland	OR	97203	2
Redmond Theatre	1535 S.W. Odem Medo Way	Redmond	OR	97756	0
Harvard Cinema	3161 W. Harvard Ave	Roseburg	OR	97470	3
Roseburg Cinema 7	1750 N.W. Hughwood	Roseburg	OR	97470	7
Salem Cinema	445 High St. S.E.	Salem	OR	97301-3615	1
Cannes Cinema Center	1026 12th Ave	Seaside	OR	97138-7946	4
Palace Theatre	Oak & Water St.	Silverton	OR	97381	1
Columbia Theatre St. Helens	212 S. First St.	St. Helens	OR	97051	1
Star Cinema	350 N. 3rd Ave.	Stayton	OR	97383-1726	1
Rio Theatre	1439 Main St.	Sweet Home	OR	97386-1618	1
Cascade Cinema	802 W 6th St	The Delles	OR	97058	2
Columbia Cinema	2727 W 7th St	The Delles	OR	97058	4
Tigard Joy Theatre	11959 S.W. Pacific Hwy	Tigard	OR	97223	1
Edgefield Powerstation Theatre	2126 S.W. Halsey	Troutdale	OR	97060	1
Tualatin Twin	8345 Nyberg Rd.	Tualatin	OR	97062	2
Woodburn Drive-In	1970 Molalla Rd.	Woodburn	OR	97071	1

PENNSYLVANIA

Theatre Name	Address	City	State	Zip	Screens
19th St. Theatre	527 N. 19th St.	Allentown	PA	18104	1
Ambridge Family Theatre	645 Merchant St.	Ambridge	PA	15003	1
Pitt	134 E. Pitt St.	Bedford	PA	15522	1
Cinemagic Bellevue Theater	609 Lincoln	Bellevue	PA	15202	2
Berwick Theatre	110 E. Front St.	Berwick	PA	18603	1
Boyd Theatre	30 West Broad St.	Bethlehem	PA	18018	1
Cinema Center Bloomsburg	1879 New Berwick Hwy.	Bloomsburg	PA	17815	12
State Theatre	61 N. Reading Ave.	Boyertown	PA	19512	1
Dipson Bradford I and II	123 Main St.	Bradford	PA	16701	2
Destinta Chartiers 20	1025 Washington Pike	Bridgeville	PA	15017	20
Star City Cinemas - S. Fayette 14	100 Hickory Grade Rd.	Bridgeville	PA	15017	14
Penn Cinemas	147 N. Main St.	Butler	PA	16003	2
Pioneer Drive-In	1985 N. Main St.	Butler	PA	16003	3
R/C Theatres MJ Mall Cinemas 8	250 Noble Blvd.	Carlisle	PA	17013	8
Cheswick Quads	1500 Pittsburgh	Cheswick	PA	15024	6
Destinta Theatre Clarion 7	Clarion Mall	Clarion	PA	16214	7
Ritz Twin	111 E. Market	Clearfield	PA	16830	2
Angela Twin Theatres	113 E. Phillips St.	Coaldale	PA	18218	2
Starlite Drive-In State Colleg	1100 Benner Pike	College State	PA	16801	1
Columbia Drive-In	4061 Columbia Ave	Columbia	PA	17512	1
Dallas Theatre	18 E. Main St.	Dallastown	PA	17313	1
Haar's Drive-In	185 Hogan Rd.	Dillsburg	PA	17019	1
County Theatre	20 E. State St.	Doylestown	PA	18901	2
Pocono Cinema & Coffee Shop	88 S. Courtland St.	East Stroudsburg	PA	18301	3
Starlite Drive-In	3440 Freemansburg Ave.	Easton	PA	18405	1
Gateway Cinema Center	Rte. 11	Edwardsville	PA	18704	1
Movietown Theatre	700 N. Hanover St	Elizabethtown	PA	17022	0
Emmaus Cinema	19 S. 4th St.	Emmaus	PA	18049	1
Main 2 Theatres	128 E. Main	Ephrata	PA	17522	2
Plaza Cinemas	800 West Erie Plaza	Erie	PA	16505	4
Reel Ent. Plaza Theatre	800 W.Erie Plaza	Erie	PA	16505	4
Bargain Cinema Eynon Plaza	Rte. 6 Eynon Plaza	Eynon	PA	18403	4
R/C Majestic	29 Carlisle St.	Gettysburg	PA	17325	3
Glen Theatre	37 Manchester St.	Glen Rock	PA	17327	1
Hamburg Strand Movie	234 State St.	Hamburg	PA	19526	1
Grass/Rite Aid IMAX	222 Market St.	Harrisburg	PA	17101	1
Harrisburg Cinema Grill	I-83 & Union Deposit Rd	Harrisburg	PA	17111	1
Movies Theatre Hellertown	1154 Main St.	Hellertown	PA	18055	1
Cocoaplex Cinema	1130 Cocoa Ave	Hershey	PA	17033	7
Cinema 6	Rte. 6 Plaza	Honesdale	PA	18431	6
Bargain Cinema Village Mall	Blair Mill Rd.	Horsham	PA	19044	2
Huntingdon Cinema Clifton 5	717 Washington St.	Huntingdon	PA	16652	5
Regency	Regency Mal	Indiana	PA	15701	2
Lamp Theatre	220 Main St.	Irwin	PA	15642	1
Merlin	212 Old York Rd.	Jenkintown	PA	19046	2
Bel Air Cinemas	848 Scalp Ave	Johnstown	PA	15904	4
Richland Mall Cinemas 12	3200 Elton Rd.	Johnstown	PA	15904	12
Westwood Plaza Theatre	Westwood Plaza	Johnstown	PA	15905	3
Family Drive-In Theatre	Rte. 6 E.	Kane	PA	16735	1
Strand Theatre	32 N. White Oak St.	Kutztown	PA	19530	2
Howard 2 Theatres	Rte 72 & Quentin Rd.	Lebanon	PA	17042	2

Theatre Name	Address	City	State	Zip	Screens
Cinema 3	500 Hyde Park Rd.	Leechburg	PA	15656	3
Mahoning Valley 8 Cinema	246 N. 6th St.	Lehighton	PA	18235	8
Miller Cinema 6	46 W. Market St.	Lewistown	PA	17044	6
Roxy Theatre Lock Haven	314 E. Main St.	Lock Haven	PA	17745	1
Foxmoor Cinema 7	Foxmoor Factory Outlet Center.	Marshall Creek	PA	18335	7
Tri-State Drive-In	Rte.s 6 & 209	Matamoras	PA	18336	1
Tristate Indoor	Rte.s 6 & 209	Matamoras	PA	18336	2
Meadville Cinemas	952 Park Ave.	Meadville.	PA	16335	4
Little Theatre Mechanicsburg	South York Extention	Mechanicsburg	PA	14604	1
Elks Theatre	Emaus.	Middletown	PA	17057	1
Point Of View Cinema	121 West Frederick St.	Millersville	PA	17551	1
Dependable Drive-In	Moon Clinton Rd.	Moon Township	PA	15108	3
Dollar Twin Theatre	Pennsbury Plaza Phase 2	Morrisville	PA	19067	2
Cinemagic Denis 4 Theatres	685 Washington Rd	Mt. Lebanon	PA	15228	4
Narberth Theatre	129 N. Narberth Ave.	Narberth	PA	19072	2
Westgate Cinema	2000 West State St.	New Castle	PA	16101	7
West Shore Theatre	317 Bridge St.	New Cumberland.	PA	17070	1
Newtown	120 N. State St.	Newtown	PA	18940	1
Cumberland Drive-In	715 Centerville Rd.	Newville	PA	17241	1
Destinta Plaza East 22	1701 Lincoln Hwy.	North Versailles	PA	15137	22
Roxy Theatre	2004 Main St.	Northampton	PA	18067	1
Oaks Theatre	310 Allegheny River Blvd.	Oakmont	PA	15139	1
Shankweiler Drive-In	Rte. 309.	Orefield	PA	18069	1
Cinema Center of Palmyra	2 N. Londonberry Square	Palmyra.	PA	17078	12
Cinematropolis Penn Hills	76 Federae Dr.	Penn Hills	PA	15235-3314	4
Cinemagic 3 At Penn.	3925 Walnut St.	Philadelphia	PA	19104-3608	3
Devon Theatre	6333 Frankford Ave. at Levick St.	Philadelphia	PA	19154	1
GC Franklin Mills	903 Franklin Mills Circle	Philadelphia	PA	19154	10
Ritz East	2nd St between Chestnut and Walnut	Philadelphia	PA	19106	2
Ritz Theatres Ritz at the Bourse	400 Ramstead St.	Philadelphia	PA	19106-0025	5
Ritz Theatres Ritz Five	214 Walnut St.	Philadelphia	PA	19106-3904	5
Roxy Theater	2023 Sanson St.	Philadelphia	PA	19103	2
Tuttleman Omniverse Theatre	20th and Pkwy.	Philadelphia	PA	19130	1
Rowland Theatre Philipsburg	125 N. Front St.	Philipsburg	PA	16866	1
Colonial Theatre	227 Bridge St.	Phoenixville.	PA	19460	1
Carnegie Museum of Art	4400 Forbes Ave	Pittsburgh	PA	15213-4080	1
Cinema 4	3075 W. Liberty Ave.	Pittsburgh	PA	15216	4
Harmer Cinemas 4	2583 Freeport Rd.	Pittsburgh	PA	15238	4
Harris Theatre	809 Liberty Ave.	Pittsburgh	PA	15222	1
Melwood Screening Room	477 Melwood Ave	Pittsburgh	PA	15213	1
Penn Hills	76 Federal Dr.	Pittsburgh	PA	15220	4
Plaza Theater 2	4765 Liberty Ave.	Pittsburgh	PA	15224-2039	2
Rangos Omnimax Theater	One Allegheny Ave.	Pittsburgh	PA	15212	1
Regent Square Theatre	1035 S. Braddock Ave.1	Pittsburgh	PA	15218	1
Waterworks Cinema 10	923 Freeport Rd.	Pittsburgh	PA	15238	10
USA Grand Slam Cinemas	240-S.West End Blvd.	Quakertown	PA	18951	6
Fox East Theatre	4350 Perkiomen Ave	Reading	PA	19606	4
Premier Cinemas Reading 4	3225 5th St. Hwy	Reading	PA	19605	4
Cinema 356	718 S. Pike Ave.	Sarver	PA	16055	4
Ritz Theatre	222 Wyoming Ave.	Scranton	PA	18503	1
Sellersville	24 W. Temple Ave.	Sellersville.	PA	18960	1
Palace Theatre	Rte. 601 N.	Somerset	PA	15501	1
Broad Theatre	24 W. Broad St.	Souderton	PA	18964	1
Cinemagic Manor Theatres	1729 Murray Ave.	Squirrel Hill	PA	15217	4
Cinemagic Squirrel Hill Theatre	5824 Forward Ave.	Squirrel Hill	PA	15217	6
Diamond Theatre	19 N. Michael St	St Marys	PA	15857	2
Keystone	601 Main St.	Towanda	PA	18848-1613	1
Bargain Cinema Trexler Mall	Rte. 222 Trexler Mall	Trexlertown	PA	18087	3
Galaxy Drive-In	Rte. 66 N.	Vandergrift	PA	15690	1
Becky's Drive-In Theatre	4548 Lehigh Dr.	Walnutport.	PA	18088	1
Watson Theatre	131 Main St.	Watsontown	PA	17777	1
Waynesboro Theatre	75 Main St.	Waynesboro	PA	17268	1
Arcadia Theater	50 Main St.	Wellsboro	PA	16901	4
Key Theatre	29 West Broad St.	West Hazleton.	PA	18201	1
Bargain Cinema Kendig Square	2600 N. Willow St.	Willow St.	PA	17504	6
Yeadon	541 Church Lane	Yeadon	PA	19050	1
Bargain Cinema Delco Cinema 5	1201 Carlisle Rd.	York	PA	17404	5

RHODE ISLAND

Theatre Name	Address	City	State	Zip	Screens
Park Cinemas	848 Park Ave	Cranston	RI	02910	3
Patriot/East Providence	60 Newport Ave.	East Providence	RI	02914	10
Holiday Cinemas	105 Chase Lane	Middletown	RI	02842	1
Starcase Triplex Theatres	283 W Main Rd.	Middletown	RI	02842	3
Narragansett 2 Theatres	3 Beach St.	Narragansett	RI	02882	2
Jane Pickens Theatre	49 Touro St.	Newport	RI	02840	1
Opera House 4 Theatres	19 Touro St.	Newport	RI	02840	4
Tri Boro Cinema 12	Rte. 95	North Attleborough	RI	02760	12
Rustic Drive-In	Louisquisset Pike	North Smithfield.	RI	02896	3
Avon Cinemas	260 Thayer St.	Providence	RI	02906	1
Cable Car	204 S.Main	Providence	RI	02903	1
Castle Cinemas 1 and 2	1030 Chalkstone Ave	Providence	RI	02908	2
IMAX Theatre	9 Providence Place	Providence	RI	02903	1
Campus Cinemas	17 Columbia St.	Wakefield	RI	02879	2
Woonsocket Cinema	1900 Diamond Hill Rd.	Woonsocket.	RI	02895	8

Theatre Name	Address	City	State	Zip	Screens

SOUTH CAROLINA

Theatre Name	Address	City	State	Zip	Screens
Village 4 Theatres	E. Shockley Ferry Rd.	Anderson	SC	29624	4
Hiway 21 Drive-In Beaufort	55 Parker Dr.	Beaufort	SC	29906-8317	1
Dusty Bend Cinema	2504 Broad St.	Camden	SC	29020-2238	1
American Theatre	446 King St.	Charleston	SC	29407	2
Imax Theater	360 Concord St	Charleston	SC	29401	1
Roxy Theatre Charleston	245 E. Bay St.	Charleston	SC	29401-2631	1
South Windemere	94 Folly Rd.	Charleston	SC	29407-7551	2
Terrace	1956 Maybank Hwy.	Charleston	SC	29412-2126	1
Columbiana Grande	1250 Bower Pkwy.	Columbia	SC	29120	12
Dutch Mall 14	Dutch Square Shopping Ctr.	Columbia	SC	29210	14
Movies @ Polo Rd.	9700 Two Notch Rd.	Columbia	SC	29223	8
St Andrews Cinema 5	527 St Andrews Rd.	Columbia	SC	29210	5
Colony 2 Theatre	315 W. Main St.	Easley	SC	29640	2
Easley Cinemas 8	5065 Calhoun Memorial Hwy.	Easley	SC	29640	8
Coffee Underground Theatre	1 E. Coffee St.	Greenville	SC	29601	1
Movies By Haywood Mall	635 Haywood Dr.	Greenville	SC	29607	6
REI Greenwood Cinema 10	SC 72 Bypass	Greenwood	SC	29646	10
Northridge 10	435 William Hilton Pkwy.	Hilton Head	SC	29926	10
Marquee-Park Plaza	201 Park Plaza	Hilton Head Island	SC	29928	5
Crown Cinema	1041 W. Meeting St.	Lancaster	SC	29720-2205	2
Pastime Pavilion 8	929 N. Lake Dr.	Lexington	SC	29072	8
Monetta Drive-In Theatre	Hwy I and Batesburg	Monetta	SC	29105	1
Mt. Pleasant Cinema	1001 Johnnie Dodds Blvd.	Mount Pleasant	SC	29464-3106	3
Palmetto Grande 16	1891 N. Hwy. 17.	Mount Pleasant	SC	29464	16
Movies @ Mt Pleasant	963 Houston-Northcutt Blvd.	Mt Pleasant	SC	29464	10
IMAX Discovery Theater	1195 Celebrity Circle	Myrtle Beach	SC	29577	1
Seneca Cinema 8	675 Hwy. 123 Bypass	Seneca	SC	29678	8
TMI Beacon Theatre	1121 Broad St.	Sumter	SC	29150	2
Union Square Cinema	719 N. Duncan Bypass.	Union	SC	29379-8605	2
Ivanhoe Cinema 4	320 Ivanhoe Rd.	Walterboro	SC	29488	4

SOUTH DAKOTA

Theatre Name	Address	City	State	Zip	Screens
Showcase Cinema 5	City Plaza	Brookings	SD	57006	5
Mac Cinema	311 Main	Mobridge	SD	57601	1
State 123	123 W. Capitol Dr.	Pierre	SD	57501	3
Stargate Theatre	919 E. N St	Rapid City	SD	57701	2
Northern Hills	1830 N. Main St.	Spearfish	SD	57783	6
Coyote Theatre	10 E. Main St.	Vermillion	SD	57069	2
Vermillion Theatre	4 W. Main St.	Vermillion	SD	57069	1
Watertown 5	1111 14th St S.E.	Watertown	SD	57201	5
Kramer IMAX Theatre	Winnipeg St. @ Wascana Dr.	Regina	SK	S4P 3M3	1

TENNESSEE

Theatre Name	Address	City	State	Zip	Screens
American Cinema of Athens	Whiteway Shopping Center	Athens	TN	37303	1
Hollywood 20 Cinema	6711 Stage Rd.	Bartlett	TN	38134	20
Tri-Cities Cinema	354 Shadowtown Rd.	Blountville	TN	37617	7
Twin City Drive-In	2512 Volunteer Pkwy.	Bristol	TN	37620	2
IMAX 3D @ Tennessee Aquarium	201 Chestnut St.	Chattanooga	TN	37401	1
Cleveland Cinema	300 Grove Ave. S.W.	Cleveland	TN	37311	2
Shadybrook 11 Cinemas	1907 Shadybrook St.	Columbia	TN	38401	11
Broadway Drive-In	3020 Hwy. 70 E.	Dickson	TN	37055	1
Dunlap Drive-In	Hwy 127 S.	Dunlap	TN	37327	1
Eastridge 6	P.O. Box 9967	Eastridge	TN	37412	6
Bonnie Kate Theatre	115 S. Sycamore St.	Elizabethton	TN	37643	2
R & R Franklin Cinema	419 Main St.	Franklin	TN	37064	1
Court Theatre	155 Court Sq.	Huntingdon	TN	38344	1
Hollywood Cinema 12	575 Vann Dr.	Jackson	TN	38305	12
Real to Reel	130 W. Springbrook Dr.	Johnson City	TN	37604	2
Halls Cinema	3800 Neal Rd.	Knoxville	TN	37918	7
Lafayette Cinema	204 College St.	Lafayette	TN	37083	1
Hi Way 50 Drive-In	1584 Fayetteville Hwy.	Lewisburg	TN	37047	1
O'Neil Old Hickory Cinema 16	109 N. Gallatin Pkwy.	Madison	TN	37115	16
Three Star	1360 Sparta St.	Mc Minnville	TN	37110	5
Star Cinema 12	5117 Old Summer Rd.	Memphis	TN	38122	12
Union Planters IMAX	3050 Central Ave.	Memphis	TN	38111	1
Ritz Theatre	1109 S. Main St	Milan	TN	38358-2725	3
R & R Campus Twin	726 S. Tennessee Blvd.	Murfreesboro	TN	37130	2
Watkins-Belcourt Theatre	2102 Belcourt Ave	Nashville	TN	37212	2
Newport Cinema 4	424 Heritage Blvd.	Newport	TN	37821	4
Paree Twin Cinema	1115 Mineral Wells Ave.	Paris	TN	38242	2
Rogersville Cinema 4	1287 E. Main St	Rogersville	TN	37857	4
Southgate	Hwy 69	Savannah	TN	38372	6
Movies on the Pkwy.	713 Winfield Dunn Pkwy.	Sevierville	TN	37876	5
Mi-De-Ga Theatre	106 W. Court Sq.	Waverly	TN	37185	2

TEXAS

Theatre Name	Address	City	State	Zip	Screens
Westwood Twin Theatre	3440 N. 1st	Abilene	TX	79603	2
Cinema 1 & 2	109 E. Holland Ave	Alpine	TX	79830	2
Alvin Premier 5	325 E. House St.	Alvin	TX	77511	5
Noret Showplace 4	3440 Bell St Ste. 300	Amarillo	TX	79109	4
Park Plaza Cinema 4	1632 New York Ave	Arlington	TX	76010	4
Premier Cinema 6	435 Forum 303 Mall	Arlington	TX	76010	6
Cinema 4	218 Wood St.	Athens	TX	75751	4
Paramount Theatre	713 Congress Ave	Austin	TX	78701	1
Texas Union Theatre	UT Campus	Austin	TX	78701	1
Cinema 4 Theatre	1801 East FM 700	Big Spring	TX	79720	4

Theatre Name	Address	City	State	Zip	Screens
Ritz	401 S. Main	Big Spring	TX	79721	3
Star Theatre	College Park Shopping Ctr.	Big Spring	TX	79720	2
Majestic 6 Theatre	Hwy. 121 S.	Bonham	TX	75476	6
Tri-Lakes 4 Theatre	415 N. Breckenridge Ave.	Breckenridge	TX	76424	4
Schulman College Park 6	2002 E. 29th St	Bryan	TX	77802	6
Carthage Twin Theatre	1120 W Panola St	Carthage	TX	75633	2
Lone Star Four Theatre	Gateway Shopping Center	Childress	TX	79201	4
Commerce Cineplex	University Shopping Center	Commerce	TX	75428	4
Pine Hollow Cinema 6	2000 I 45 N.	Conroe	TX	77305	6
Silver Cinemas Five Points	4147 Five Points Rd.	Corpus Christi	TX	78410	5
Granada Movie Grill-Greenville	3524 Greenville Ave.	Dallas	TX	75206	1
Granada Movie Grill-Prestonwood	Beltline & Prestonwood	Dallas	TX	75248	4
Lakewood Theatres	1825 Abrams Pkwy.	Dallas	TX	75214	1
TI Founders IMAX	1318 Second Ave.	Dallas	TX	75210	1
Plaza 3 Theatre	1510 Hwy 51 S.	Decatur	TX	76234	3
Eagle Pass Cinema 3	455 S. Bibb Ave	Eagle Pass	TX	78852	3
Showcase 3 Cinema Inc.	904 West Loop	El Campo	TX	77437	3
Omni Theater	1501 Montgomery St.	Fort Worth	TX	76107	1
Ridglea Theatre	6025 Camp Bowie Blvd	Fort Worth	TX	76116	1
Wedgwood Village 4 Theater	5298 Trail Lake Dr.	Fort Worth	TX	76133	4
IMAX 3D @ Moody Gardens	One Hope Blvd.	Galveston	TX	77554	1
Premiere Cinema	8902 Seawall Blvd.	Galveston	TX	77554	7
Ganado Theatre	120 South St.	Ganado	TX	77962	1
Walnut Theatre	3310 W. Walnut St.	Garland	TX	75042	1
National Theatre	522 Oak St.	Graham	TX	76450-3039	3
Brazos Cinema and Drive-In	West Pearl St.	Granbury	TX	76048	4
Driftwood Theatre 6	1201 Old Cleburne Rd.	Granbury	TX	76048	6
Majestic 8 Theatres	1401 Joe Ramsey Blvd.	Greenville	TX	75402-7602	8
Hempstead Theater	740 12th St.	Hempstead	TX	77445	6
Circle Plaza Cinema 3	1401 Lone Star St.	Henderson	TX	75653	3
Moovies Six	400 N. 25 Mile Ave.	Hereford	TX	79045	6
Texas Theatre	107 S. Waco St	Hillsboro	TX	76645-3326	2
Angelika Film Center	500 Texas St.	Houston	TX	77002	8
Imax Space Center Houston	1601 Nasa Rd.	Houston	TX	77058	1
Museum of Fine Arts Houston	1001 Bissonnet	Houston	TX	77005	1
Rice Media Center	2030 University Blvd	Houston	TX	77030	1
Wind Chimes Cinema 8	13155 Westheimer Rd.	Houston	TX	77077	8
Wortham Imax	One Hermann Circle Dr.	Houston	TX	77030	2
Cinema 10 Theatre	3027 11 St.	Huntsville	TX	77340	10
Belaire Theatre	404 E. Pipline Rd.	Hurst	TX	76054	4
Everest Theatre	700 Plymouth Park	Irving	TX	75061-1947	2
Plaza Theatres	110 Plaza Dr.	Kerrville	TX	78028	6
Four Star Cinema	2100 S. W.S. Young Dr	Kilgore	TX	75663	4
Pleasant Run Movies 7	1450 W Pleasant Run Rd	Lancaster	TX	75146	7
Science Spectrum Omnimax	2579 S. Loop 289, Ste. 250	Lubbock	TX	79423	1
Showplace 6 Theatres	6707 S. University	Lubbock	TX	79413-6303	6
Marble Theatre	218 Main St.	Marble Falls	TX	78645	1
Marshall Cinema	1901 E. Travis St.	Marshall	TX	75670	5
Brazos Cinema	2801 Hwy 180 E.	Mineral Wells	TX	76068	3
Silver Cinemas Missouri City 6	2420 Texas Pkwy.	Missouri City	TX	77459	6
Southside Cinema 5	1706 S. Jefferson Ave.	Mt Pleasant	TX	75455	5
Walnut 6 Theatres	694 S. Walnut Ave.	New Braunfels	TX	78130	6
Orange Cinema	3330 Bowling Lane	Orange	TX	77630	2
Schulman Dogwood 6	501 E. Palestine Rd	Palestine	TX	75801	6
Southmore Cinema 6	2233 E. Southmore Ave	Pasadena	TX	77502	6
Ellis Theatre	217 S. Main St.	Perryton	TX	79070	2
Studio Movie Grill	4721 W. Park. #100	Plano	TX	75075	8
Island Cinema 4	1004 Padre Blvd.	S.Padre Island	TX	78597	4
Alameda Theatre	314 Houston St.	San Antonio	TX	78205	1
IMAX Alamo Rivercenter	217 Alamo Plaza	San Antonio	TX	78205	1
Cinema 5	905 Hwy. 80	San Marcos	TX	78666	5
Lone Star Theaters - Starplex	1250 Wonderworld Dr.	San Marcos	TX	78666	12
Noret Cinema I & II	1907 College Ave.	Snyder	TX	79549	2
Tower Drive-In Theatre	Rt. 1 Box 15	Tule	TX	79547	1
Forum Theatres 6	Hwy. 90 E.	Uvalde	TX	78801	6
Encore 6 Cinemas	1105 Wooded Acres at Valley Mills	Waco	TX	76710	6
Movies at Buffalo Creek	507 N. Hwy. 77, Bldg. 1300	Waxahachie	TX	75165	4
Texas Theater	110 West Main	Waxahachie	TX	75165	1
Weatherford Theatres	111 College	Weatherford	TX	76086	5
Nasa Dollar 8 Theatres	20833 Gulf Fwy.	Webster	TX	77598	8

UTAH

Towne Cinemas 1 and 2	120 W. Main St.	American Fork	UT	84003	2
Wayne Theatre	111 E. Main St.	Bicknell	UT	84715	1
Capital Theatre	53 S. Main St.	Brigham City	UT	84302-2526	2
Walker Cinema IV	1776 S. Hwy. 89	Brigham City	UT	84302-4110	4
Reel Theatre I	94 S.Main St	Heber City	UT	84032	1
Reel Theatre II	115 N. Main	Heber City	UT	84032	1
Kaysville Theatre	21 N. Main St.	Kaysville	UT	87047	3
Cinefour	2297 N. Main	Logan	UT	84321	4
Movies 5	2450 N. Main	Logan	UT	84341	5
Utah Theatre	18 W. Center	Logan	UT	84321	1
Reel Theatre Magna	8325 W. 3500 S.	Magna	UT	84044	5
Slickrock Cinema 3	580 Kane Creek Blvd.	Moab	UT	84532	3
North Pointe Theatre	1610 N. Washington Blvd.	North Ogden	UT	84414	4
Reel Theatre	151 12th St.	Ogden	UT	84401	6
Scera Theatre	745 S. State St.	Orem	UT	84057	1
Huish Theatre	98 W. Utah Ave.	Payson	UT	84651	1
Water Gardens Cinema 6	912 W. Garden Dr.	Pleasant Grove	UT	84062	6
King Coal Theatre	1171 E. Main St.	Price	UT	84501	2

Theatre Name	Address	City	State	Zip	Screens
Academy Cinema	56 N. University Ave	Provo	UT	84601	1
Pioneer Twin Drive-In	1250 S. State St.	Provo	UT	84606-6432	2
Huish Reel Theatre	131 N. Main	Richfield	UT	84701	1
Reel Theatre Richfield	1150 Hwy. 89 S..	Richfield	UT	84701	2
Roosevelt Twin Theatre	21 S. 200 E..	Roosevelt	UT	84066	2
Avalon Theatre	3605 S.State St.	Salt Lake City	UT	84115	1
Brewvies 2 Theatre	677 S. 200 W.	Salt Lake City	UT	84101	2
Redwood Drive-In	3700 S.Redwood Rd.	Salt Lake City	UT	84119	1
Starship Cinema 5	4100 W 5400 S	Salt Lake City	UT	84118	5
Starship Gateway 8	206 S. 625 West	Salt Lake City	UT	84104	8
Starship Sandy Mall 4	9400 S. 800 East	Salt Lake City	UT	84094	4
Tower Theatre	876 E. 900 S..	Salt Lake City	UT	84105	1
Megaplex 17 - Jordon Commons	9400 S. State St.	Sandy	UT	84070-3213	17
Spanish 8 Theatre	790 Expressway Lane	Spanish Fork	UT	84660	8
Zion Canyon Cinemax	145 Zion Park Blvd.	Springdale	UT	84767	1
Art City Drive-In	720 N. Main St.	Springville	UT	84653	1
Ritz Theatre	111 N. Main St.	Tooele	UT	84074	2
Vernal Cinemas	40 E. Main St.	Vernal	UT	84078	4

VIRGINIA

Theatre Name	Address	City	State	Zip	Screens
Abingdon Cinemall	721 E. Main St.	Abingdon	VA	24210	8
Foxchase 2 & 3	Foxchase Shopping Center	Alexandria	VA	22314	2
Hoyts Potomac Yards 16	3575 Jefferson Davis Hwy.	Alexandria	VA	22305	16
Arlington Cinema Draft House	2903 Columbia Pike	Arlington	VA	22204	1
Idle Hour	Belle Haven Rd..	Belle Haven	VA	23306	1
Lyric Theatre Blacksburg	135 College Ave.	Blacksburg	VA	24060	1
Valley Cinema	2275 Beech Ave.	Buena Vista	VA	24416	2
Jefferson 2	110 E. Main St.	Charlottesville	VA	22902	2
Vinegar Hill Theatre	220 W. Market St.	Charlottesville	VA	22903	1
Island Roxy	4074 S.Main St.	Chincoteague	VA	23336	1
Starlite Drive-In Christiansbg	365 Starlite Dr.	Christiansburg	VA	24073	1
Coeburn 3	501 W. Front St.	Coeburn	VA	24230	3
R/C Covington Movies 3	139 N. Maple Ave.	Covington	VA	24426	3
Ballou Park Theatre	150 Tunstall Rd.	Danville	VA	24541	2
Cinema Arts Theatre	Rte. 236 and Pickett Rd	Fairfax	VA	22031	6
UA Fairfax Town Center	12110 Fair Towne Center	Fairfax	VA	22033	10
University Mall Theatres	10659 Braddock Rd.	Fairfax	VA	22032	3
Fork Union Drive-In	Rte. 612	Fork Union	VA	23055	1
Marquee-Southpoint 9	5800 Southpoint Blvd.	Fredricksburg	VA	22407	9
Royal Cinemas	117 E. Main St.	Front Royal	VA	22630	3
Twin County Cinema III	957 E. Stuart Dr.	Galax	VA	24333	1
Twin Theatre	957 E. Stuart Dr.	Galax	VA	24333	3
Hillside 2 Cinema	Rte 14	Gloucester	VA	23061	2
Virginia Air & Space Ctr IMAX	600 Settlers Landing Rd.	Hampton	VA	23669	1
The Court Square Theatre	Kelley St.	Harrionburg	VA	22801	2
Grafton-Stovall Theatre	800 S. Main St.	Harrisonburg	VA	22801	2
R/C State Theatre	12 W Nelson St	Lexington	VA	24450	3
Hoyts Manassas Cinema 14	11380 Bulloch Dr.	Manassas	VA	20109	12
Manassas Cinemas	8890 Mathis Ave.	Manassas	VA	22210	4
Movie Town 5	Rte. 825	Martinsville	VA	24112	5
Naro Expanded Cinema	1507 Colley Ave.	Norfolk	VA	23517	1
Roseland Theatre	48 Market St.	Onancock	VA	23417	1
Commodore Theatre	421 High St.	Portsmouth	VA	23704	1
Plaza Theatre	3237 Tyre Neck Rd.	Portsmouth	VA	23703	3
Radford Plaza Cinema Twin	7472 Lee Hwy.	Radford	VA	24141	2
Radford Theatre	1043 Norwood St.	Radford	VA	24141	1
Byrd Theatre	2908 W. Cary St.	Richmond	VA	23222	1
Ethyl IMAX Dome	2500 W. Broad St.	Richmond	VA	23220	1
Features Dinner Cinema	8099 West Broad	Richmond	VA	23294	4
Southgate Cinemas	5955 Midlothian Tpke.	Richmond	VA	23225	2
Grandin Theatre	1310 Grandin Rd. S.W..	Roanoke	VA	24015	4
Star City Cinema Grill	5002 Airport Rd.	Roanoke	VA	24019	2
Town Center Cinemas	21800 Town Ctr Plaza	Sterling	VA	20164	3
Cinema Cafe	758 Independence Blvd..	Virginia Beach	VA	23455	3
Family Channel IMAX 3D Theater	717 General Booth Blvd	Virginia Beach	VA	23451	1
Warrenton Movies 5	627 Frost Ave.	Warrenton	VA	20186	5
Williamsburg Theatre Merchant's Square	424 W Duke Of Gloucester St.	Williamsburg	VA	23185	4
Delco Cinemas Twin	170 Delco Plaza	Winchester	VA	22601	2
Millwald Triple Theatre	205 W. Main St.	Wytheville	VA	24382	3

VERMONT

Theatre Name	Address	City	State	Zip	Screens
Bennington Movieplex	Rte. 67 @ Northside Dr.	Bennington	VT	05201	3
Cinema 7 Bennington	319 Northside Dr..	Bennington	VT	05201	7
Brattleboro 6	Putney Rd.	Brattleboro	VT	05304	6
Latchis Theater	48 Main St.	Brattleboro	VT	05301	3
Sunset Drive-In	Porters Point Rd.	Colchester	VT	05446	4
Marquis	Main street	Middlebury	VT	05753	2
Capitol Theatre	100 State St	Montpelier	VT	05602	5
Bijou Cineplex 4	Rte. 100	Morrisville	VT	05661	4
Plaza Movieplex	143 Merchants Row	Rutland	VT	05701	9
Stowe Cinema 3 Plex	Rte. 108 Mountain Rd.	Stowe	VT	05672	3
Spinelli-West Dover Cinema	Rte. 100 N- Mountain Park Plaza	W. Dover	VT	05356	3
Flick Mad River	Winter Park, Rte. 100	Waitsfield	VT	05673	2
Westway Cinemas	Westway Mall Rte. 4A	West Rutland	VT	05777	4

Theatre Name	Address	City	State	Zip	Screens

WASHINGTON

Theatre Name	Address	City	State	Zip	Screens
Olympic Theater	107 N. Olympic Ave.	Arlington	WA	98223	1
Valley Drive-In	401 49th St. N.E.	Auburn	WA	98002	6
Lynwood Theatre	4569 Lynwood Center Rd.	Bainbridge	WA	98110	1
Bainbridge Cinemas	403 N. Madison Ave.	Bainbridge Island	WA	98110	6
Pickford Cinema	1416 Cornwall Ave.	Bellingham	WA	98225	2
Charleston Cinema	333 N. Callow Ave	Bremerton	WA	98312-4010	1
Liberty Theatre	315 N.E. 4th Ave.	Camas	WA	98607	1
Mount St Helens Cinedome	1238 Mount St. Helens Way N.E.	Castle Rock	WA	98611	1
Ruby	135 E. Woodin Ave.	Chelan	WA	98816	1
Cheney Cinema	421 Second St.	Cheney	WA	99004	2
Alpine Theatre	112 N. Main	Colville	WA	99114	1
Sunset	102 N. Columbia	Connell	WA	99326	1
Village Cinema	515 River Dr.	Coulee Dam	WA	99116	1
Columbia Cinema	470 Grant Rd.	E. Wenatchee	WA	98801	1
Roxy Theatre	115 Marshell Ave.	Eatonville	WA	98328	1
Edmonds Theater	415 Main St.	Edmonds	WA	98020	1
Chalet Theatre	1721 Wells	Enumclaw	WA	98022	1
Enumclaw Cinema	258 Roosevelt Ave. E.	Enumclaw	WA	98022-8215	1
Lee Theatre	347 Basin St.,N.W.	Ephrata	WA	98823	1
Everett Cosmopolitan Theatre	1908 Hewitt Ave.	Everett	WA	98201	1
Everett Theatre	2911 Colby Ave.	Everett	WA	98204	1
Puget Park Drive-In	128th S.W. and I-5 S.	Everett	WA	98208-6422	1
The Clyde, Langley	213 1st St.	Langley	WA	98260	1
Neptune Theatre	801 Oceanbeach Blvd. S.	Long Beach	WA	98631	2
Kelso Theatre Pub	214 S. Pacific	Longview	WA	98632	1
Mossyrock	106 E.State St.	Mossyrock	WA	98564	1
Cinema 5 Mount Vernon	1900 Continental Place	Mount Vernon	WA	98273	5
Lincoln Theater	712 1st St.	Mount Vernon	WA	98273	1
Roxy Theater	120 S. Washington	Newport	WA	99156	1
Blue Fox Drive-In	1403 N. Monroe Landing Rd.	Oak Harbor	WA	98277	2
Plaza Cinema 3, Oak Harbor	1321 S.W. Barlow St.	Oak Harbor	WA	98277	3
Capital Mall Cinemas	302 Capitol Mall.	Olympia	WA	98501	4
Capitol Theatre	206 5th Ave. S.E.	Olympia	WA	98501	1
Omak Cinema	108 N. Main St.	Omak	WA	98841	1
Deer Park Cinemas	96 Deerpark Rd.	Port Angeles	WA	98362	5
Plaza Twin Cinema	567 Bay St.	Port Orchard	WA	98366	1
Rodeo Drive-In	7369 State Hwy. 3 W	Port Orchard	WA	98367	3
Rose Theatre	235 Taylor St.	Port Townsend	WA	98368	2
Uptown Theatre	826 P St.	Port Townsend	WA	98368	1
Cordova 1	N. 135 Grand	Pullman	WA	99163	1
Raymond	323 3rd St.	Raymond	WA	98577	1
Roxy Theater	504 S. Third St.	Renton	WA	98055	2
The New Ritz Theatre	107 E. Main Ave.	Ritzville	WA	99169	1
Roslyn Theatre	101 Dakota St.	Roslyn	WA	98941	1
Admiral Twin Theatre	2343 California Ave. S.	Seattle	WA	98116	2
Des Moines Cinema	22333 Marina View Dr.	Seattle	WA	98198	1
Frye Art Museum Auditorium	704 Terry Ave.	Seattle	WA	98104	1
Grand Illusion Theatre	1403 N.E. 50th St.	Seattle	WA	98402	1
Laser Fantasy Theater	In the Pacific Science Center	Seattle	WA	98109	1
Little Theatre	608 19th Ave. E	Seattle	WA	98112	1
Media Arts Center	117 Yale Ave. N.	Seattle	WA	98109	1
Pacific Science Center IMAX Theatres	200 Second Ave. N.	Seattle	WA	98109	2
Seattle Omnidome	Pier 59 Waterfront Park	Seattle	WA	98101	1
Shelton Cinema	517 W Franklin	Shelton	WA	98584	2
Garland Dollar Theatre	924 W. Garland	Spokane	WA	99201	1
Imax Theatre	507 N. Howard St.	Spokane	WA	99201	2
Art Cinema at the Met	901 W Sprague	Sprague	WA	99004	1
Stanwood Cinemas	6996 265th St. N.W.	Stanwood	WA	98292	5
Blue Mouse Theatre	2611 N. Proctor	Tacoma	WA	98407	1
Grand Cinema Tacoma	606 S. Fawcett Ave.	Tacoma	WA	98402	3
Kiggins Theatre	1011 Main St.	Vancouver	WA	98660	1
Vashon Theatre	99 S.W. 178th	Vashon	WA	98070	1
Liberty Cinemas	1 S. Mission	Wenatchee	WA	98801	1
Mercy 6 Plex	17 E. Valley Mall Blvd.	Yakima	WA	98907	6
Uptown Plaza	202 E. Chestnut	Yakima	WA	98901	4
Yakima Cinema	1305 N. 16th Ave	Yakima	WA	98907	10

WISCONSIN

Theatre Name	Address	City	State	Zip	Screens
Amery Theatre	118 N. Keller Ave	Amery	WI	54001	1
Palace Theatre	823 5th Ave	Antigo	WI	54409	1
Baraboo Theatre	136 4th Ave	Baraboo	WI	53913	1
Wildwood Prairie 5	2950 Prairie	Beloit	WI	53511	5
Wildwood's Luxury 10	2799 Cranston Rd.	Beloit	WI	53511	10
Plaza Theatre Burlington	448 Milwaukee Ave.	Burlington	WI	53105	4
Chilton Theatre	26 N. Madison St.	Chilton	WI	53014	1
Cornell Theatre	214 Main St.	Cornell	WI	54732	1
Delavan Twin	405 E. Walworth	Delavan	WI	53115	2
Dodge Theatre	205 N. Iowa St.	Dodgeville	WI	53533	1
Durand Theatre	111 E. Main St.	Durand	WI	54736	1
Cameo Budget Twin Theatres	315 S. Barstow St.	Eau Claire	WI	54701	2
Gemini Drive-In	Interstate 94	Eau Claire	WI	54701	1
London Square Six	3109 Mall Dr.	Eau Claire	WI	54701	6
Fond Du Lac Theatre 8	1131 W. Scott St.	Fond Du Lac	WI	54937	8
Forest Mall Cinema I & II Fond du Lac	755 W. Johnson St.	Fond du Lac	WI	54935	2
Riverpoint Cinemas	8617 N. Port Washington	Fox Point	WI	53217	4
Hartford Theatres	2941 Hwy. 83 S.	Hartford	WI	53027	8
Park Theatre	116 E. 1st St.	Hayward	WI	54843	1
Wildwood Movies 10	3100 Deerfield Dr.	Janesville	WI	53546	10
Wildwood Rock Cinema 9	1620 Newport Ave.	Janesville	WI	53545	9

Theatre Name	Address	City	State	Zip	Screens
Academy Theatres 5 Kenosha	7310 57th Ave.	Kenosha	WI	53142	5
Keno Family Drive-In	9102 Sheridan Rd.	Kenosha	WI	53143	1
Market Square 4 Cinema	8600 Sheridan Rd.	Kenosha	WI	53143	4
Orpheum Kenosha	5819 Sixth Ave.	Kenosha	WI	53140-4105	4
Hollywood Theatre	123 S.5th St	La Crosse	WI	54601	1
Rivoli Theatre	117 N. Fourth St.	La Crosse	WI	54601	1
Miner Theatre	116 E. Miner Ave.	Ladysmith	WI	54848	1
Geneva 4 Theatre	244 Broad St.	Lake Geneva	WI	53147	4
Showboat of Lyons	2565 Hwy. 120	Lake Geneva	WI	53147	6
Grantland Theater	218 S. Madison St.	Lancaster	WI	53813	1
Hilldale Theatre	702 N. Midvale Blvd.	Madison	WI	53705	2
Orpheum I & II Theatres	216 State St.	Madison	WI	53703	2
Strand Theatre	315 N. 8th St.	Manitowoc	WI	54220	6
GKC Pine Tree Cinema	2727 Cahill Rd.	Marinette	WI	54143	9
Mariner 2	2000 Ella Court	Marinette	WI	54143	2
Rogers 7 Cinema	419 S. Central Ave.	Marshfield	WI	54449	7
State Cinema 4	639 Broadway St. S.	Menomonie	WI	54751	4
Avalon	2473 S. Kinnickinnic Ave	Milwaukee	WI	53207	1
Humphrey IMAX Dome Theater	710 W. Wells	Milwaukee	WI	53233	1
Spector Spring Mall	4200 S. 76th St.	Milwaukee	WI	53220	1
Times Cinema	5906 W. Vliet St.	Milwaukee	WI	53208	1
Mineral Point Opera House	139 High St.	Mineral Point	WI	53565	1
Goetz Sky Vue Drive-In	1936 Hwy. 69 N.	Monroe	WI	53566	1
Goetz Theatres 3	1704 11th St.	Monroe	WI	53566	3
Montello Theatre	30 E. Montello St.	Montello	WI	53949-9701	1
Muskego Movie-Plex	Racine Ave & Chance Dr.	Muskego	WI	53150	2
Rogers Grand Cinema	319 W. N. Water St.	New London	WI	54961	4
New Richmond 6	1261 Heritage Dr.	New Richmond	WI	54017	6
Wildwood Capitol Cinema 12	1275 Capitol Dr.	Pewaukee	WI	53072	12
Avalon Cinema	95 E. Main St.	Platteville	WI	53818	3
Portage Theatre	322 W. Wisconsin St.	Portage	WI	53901-2138	7
Bonham Theatre & Video	564 Water St.	Praire du Sac	WI	53578	3
Center Cinema -Richland Center	192 S. Central Ave.	Richland Center	WI	53581-2332	2
Marcus Cedar Creek Cinema	10101 Market St.	Rothschild	WI	54474	10
Crescent Pitcher Show	220 S. Main St.	Shawano	WI	54166-2746	1
Shawano Cinema I, II, III	1494 E. Green Bay St.	Shawano	WI	54166	3
Marc Cinemas - Sheboygan	3226 Kohler Memorial Dr.	Sheboygan	WI	53081	10
Palace Theatre	238 Walnut St.	Spooner	WI	54801	2
Gard Theatre	111 E. Jefferson St.	Spring Green	WI	53588	1
St. Croix Falls 5	200 N. Washington Ave	St. Croix Falls	WI	54024	5
Cinema Cafe 5	255 E. Main St.	Stoughton	WI	53589-1722	5
Donna Theatre	239 N. 3rd Ave.	Sturgeon Bay	WI	54235-0006	1
Towne Cinema Watertown	302 E. Main St.	Watertown	WI	53094-3749	3
Rogers Rosa Theatre	218 S. Main	Waupaca	WI	54981	2
Rosebud Cinema Drafthouse	6823 W North Ave.	Wauwatosa	WI	53213	1
Paradise Theatre	2014 Pkwy. Dr.	West Bend	WI	53095	1
West Bend Cinema	125 N. Main St.	West Bend	WI	53095	3
Fox-Bay Cinema Grill	334 E. Silver Spring Dr.	Whitefish Bay	WI	53217	3
Theatres of Whitehater	151 S. Pearson Lane	Whitewater	WI	53190	1
Big Sky Twin Drive-In	Hwy. 16	Wisconsin Dells	WI	53965	1
Rogers Cinema-Wisconsin Rapids	220 E. Grand Ave.	Wisconsin Rapids	WI	54494-4361	7
Elroy Theatre	E. 731 Plum Valley Rd.	Wonewoc	WI	53968-9203	1

WEST VIRGINIA

Theatre Name	Address	City	State	Zip	Screens
Raleigh Mall Cinemas	RT 21, By-Pass	Beckley	WV	25801	2
Park Place Stadium Cinemas	600 Washington St. E.	Charleston	WV	25301	7
Elkins Cinema 6	Tygart Valley Mall	Elkins	WV	26241	6
Tygart Valley Cinema 7	Rte. 250 Box S	Fairmont	WV	26554	7
Ritz Theatre Hinton	211 Ballengee St.	Hinton	WV	25951-2318	1
Camelot Theatre	30 4th Ave	Huntington	WV	25701	2
Cinema 4 Theatre Huntington	401 11th St.	Huntington	WV	25701-2218	4
Keith Albee 4	925 4th Ave.	Huntington	WV	25701	4
Lewis Theatre	113 N. Court St.	Lewisburg	WV	24901-1101	1
Berkeley Plaza Theatre	Berkeley Plaza	Martinsburg	WV	25401	7
Valley Cinema 3	3 New Martinsville Plaza	New Martinsville	WV	26155	3
Mountaineer Cinemas	126 Academy Dr.	Ripley	WV	25271	2
Shepherdstown Opera House	131 W. German St.	West Virginia	WV	25443	1
Weston 4 Theatres	Market Place Plaza, Rte. 33	Weston	WV	26452	4
Greenbrier Hotel Cinema	300 West Main St.	White Sulphur Spr.	WV	24986	1

WYOMING

Theatre Name	Address	City	State	Zip	Screens
American Theatre - Casper	119 S. Center St.	Casper	WY	82601-2521	1
Fox Movie Palace	150 W. 2nd St.	Casper	WY	82601-2411	3
Rialto Theatre - Casper	100 E. 2nd St.	Casper	WY	82601-2502	1
Big Horn Cinema	2525 Big Horn Ave.	Cody	WY	82414	2
Mesa Theatre	104 N. 3rd St.	Douglas	WY	82633-2135	1
Cinemajik Valley 4 Cinemas	45 E. Aspen Grove Rd.	Evanston	WY	82930	4
Movieworks Cinema 4	860 S. Hwy. 89	Jackson	WY	83001	4
Grand Theatre - Lander	250 W. Main St.	Lander	WY	82520-3128	1
Movies 3	1720 Edinburgh St.	Rawlins	WY	82301	3
Acme Theatre	312 E. Main St.	Riverton	WY	82501-4338	1
Gem Theatre	119 S. 3rd St. E.	Riverton	WY	82501-4325	1
Centennial Theatres	36 E. Alger St.	Sheridan	WY	82801-3912	6
The Ritz Theatre - Thermopolis	309 Arapahoe St.	Thermopolis	WY	82443-2705	1
Wyoming Theatre	126 E. 20th Ave.	Torrington	WY	82240-2812	1
Cinema West Theatre	609 10th St.	Wheatland	WY	82201-2923	1
Cottonwood Twin Cinemas	101 Pleasant View Dr.	Worland	WY	82401-9777	2

Specialty & Large Format Exhibitors

Specialty exhibitors show non-theatrical films, usually in a proprietary format and occasionally involving mechanical simulations or special viewing devices in conjunction with the film, to non-theatrical audiences (usually museum-goers and amusement park attendees). However, traditional exhibitors are installing limited numbers of specialty screens in multiplexes. For equipment & services, please see the section of this book entitled Specialty Exhibitor Equipment & Services.

IMAX CORPORATION

IMAX leases IMAX projection systems and distributes films to specially designed theatres worldwide. Subsidiaries include: Sonics Associates, Inc., David Keighley Productions/70MM Inc., and Digital Projection International
2525 Speakman Drive, Sheridan Science and Technology Park, Mississauga, Ontario, L5K 1B1 Canada. (905) 403-6500. FAX: (905) 403-6450. www.imax.com
email: info@imax.com
CO-CHAIRMAN & CO-CEO
Richard Gelfond
CO-CHAIRMAN & CO-CEO
Bradley J. Wechsler
COO
John Davison
EXECUTIVE V.P., TECHNOLOGY
Michael Gibbon
EXECUTIVE V.P. & PRESIDENT, NETWORK GROUP
Mary Pat Ryan
EXECUTIVE V.P., WORLDWIDE SALES & MARKETING
Udo von Karhan
SENIOR V.P., FILM PRODUCTION
David Keighley
SENIOR V.P., FILM
Andrew Gellis
SENIOR V.P.,OPERATIONS
Brian Weisfeld
V.P., MARKETING & G.M., JAPAN AND ASIA PACIFIC
Michel Farache

U.S. IMAX THEATRES

(Most American IMAX theatres are independently owned and operated. Theatres marked with an asterisk have IMAX 3D capability.)

ALABAMA—BIRMINGHAM: IMAX Dome John W. Woods Theater; HUNTSVILLE: Spacedome IMAX Theater; MOBILE: J.L. Bedsole IMAX Dome.
ARIZONA—TEMPE: IMAX Theatre at Arizona Mills*; TUSAYAN: Grand Canyon IMAX Theater.
ARKANSAS—LITTLE ROCK: IMAX Theater.
CALIFORNIA—CATHEDRAL CITY: The KESQ-TV3 Desert IMAX Theatre*; DUBLIN: Regal IMAX Theatres*; FRESNO: Edwards IMAX Theatre*; IRVINE: Edwards IMAX Theatre*; LOS ANGELES: California Science Center IMAX Theater*, Back to the Future - the Ride (Universal Studios), Universal Studios IMAX Theatre (Citywalk); ONTARIO: Edwards IMAX Theatre*; SACRAMENTO: Esquire IMAX Theatre*; SAN DIEGO: Reuben H. Fleet Space Theater & Science Center; SAN FRANCISCO: Sony IMAX Theatre at Metreon*; SAN JOSE: The Hackworth IMAX Dome Theatre; SANTA CLARA: Pictorium IMAX Theater*; VALENCIA: Edwards IMAX Theater*.
COLORADO—DENVER: Lawrence Phipps IMAX Theater, United Artists IMAX Theatre.
CONNECTICUT—NORWALK: IMAX The Maritime Aquarium.
DISTRICT OF COLUMBIA—WASHINGTON: Langley Theater, Samuel C. Johnson Theater*.
FLORIDA—FORT LAUDERDALE: Blockbuster IMAX 3D Theater*; JACKSONVILLE: World Golf Village IMAX Theater; KENNEDY SPACE CENTER: IMAX Theater*, IMAX Theatre; MIAMI: IMAX Theatre at Sunset Place*; ORLANDO: Muvico IMAX Theater*, Back to the Future - the Ride; PENSACOLA: IMAX Theatre (National Museum of Naval Aviation); TAMPA: IMAX Dome Theater (Museum of Science and Industry).
GEORGIA—ATLANTA: Rankin M. Smith, Jr. IMAX Theater; MILL CREEK: Regal IMAX Theater*.
HAWAII—HONOLULU: The Waikiki IMAX Theatre*; LAIE: IMAX POLYNESIA.
IDAHO—BOISE: Edwards IMAX Theatre*.
ILLINOIS—ADDISON: Marcus IMAX Theatre*; CHICAGO: Henry Crown Space Center OMNIMAX Theatre, Navy Pier IMAX Theater*; GURNEE: Pictorium*; LINCOLNSHIRE: CityPark 20 & IMAX Theater*; WOODRIDGE: Cinemark IMAX Theatre*.
INDIANA—INDIANAPOLIS: IMAX 3D Theatre*.
KANSAS—HUTCHINSON: W.D.P. & Moscelene Carey IMAX Dome Theater (Kansas Cosmosphere & Space Center).
KENTUCKY—LOUISVILLE: IMAX Theater.
LOUISIANA—NEW ORLEANS: Entergy IMAX Theater*; SHREVEPORT: IMAX Dome Theatre.
MARYLAND—BALTIMORE: IMAX Theater.
MASSACHUSETTS—BOSTON: Mugar Omni Theater.
MICHIGAN—DEARBORN: IMAX Theatre*; DETROIT: IMAX Dome Theater.
MINNESOTA—DULUTH: Duluth OMNIMAX Theatre; MINNEAPOLIS: Imation IMAX Theatre*; SHAKOPEE: IMAX Cinema; SAINT PAUL: William L. McKnight-3M Omnitheater.
MISSOURI—BRANSON: Ozarks Discovery IMAX Theatre; KANSAS CITY: Sprint IMAX Theatre; ST. LOUIS: OMNIMAX Theater.
MONTANA—W. YELLOWSTONE: Yellowstone IMAX Theatre.
NEBRASKA—HASTINGS: Lied IMAX Theater; OMAHA: Lozier IMAX Theatre.*
NEVADA—LAS VEGAS: Luxor IMAX Theater*, Race for Atlantis Simulator Ride*.
NEW JERSEY—JERSEY CITY: Kodak IMAX Dome Theater.
NEW MEXICO—ALAMOGORDO: Clyde W. Tombaugh Space Theater.
NEW YORK—BUFFALO: Regal IMAX Theatre*; NEW ROCHELLE: Regal IMAX Theatre*; NEW YORK CITY: Sony IMAX at Lincoln Square*, Museum of Natural History; ROCHESTER: Cinemark IMAX Theatre*; SYRACUSE: Bristol Omnitheatre; WEST NYACK: IMAX Theatre at Palisades Center*.
NORTH CAROLINA—CHARLOTTE: Observer OMNIMAX Theatre.
OHIO—CINCINNATI: Robert D. Lindner Family OMNIMAX Theater; CLEVELAND: Cleveland Clinic Foundation OMNIMAX Theater; COLUMBUS: Marcus IMAX Theatre at Crossroads*; DAYTON: IMAX Theater; SANDUSKY: IMAX Cinema.
OKLAHOMA—TULSA: Cinemark IMAX Theatre*.
OREGON—PORTLAND: OMNIMAX Theater.
PENNSYLVANIA—HARRISBURG: Grass/Rite-Aid IMAX Theater*; KING OF PRUSSIA: IMAX Theatre & United Artists*; PHILADELPHIA: Tuttleman Omniverse Theater; PITTSBURGH: Rangos OMNIMAX Theater.
RHODE ISLAND—PROVIDENCE: Feinstein IMAX Theatre*.
SOUTH CAROLINA—MYRTLE BEACH: IMAX Discovery Theatre; CHARLESTON: Charleston IMAX Theatre*.
TENNESSEE—CHATTANOOGA: IMAX 3D Theater*; MEMPHIS: Union Planters IMAX Theater; NASHVILLE: Regal IMAX Theatre*.
TEXAS—DALLAS: Cinemark IMAX Theatre*, TI Founders IMAX Theater; FORT WORTH: Omni Theatre (Fort Worth Museum of Science & History); GALVESTON: IMAX 3D Theater*; HOUSTON: Space Center Theater, Wortham IMAX Theater, Edwards IMAX Theatre*; LUBBOCK: OMNIMAX Theater; SAN ANTONIO: Alamo IMAX Theater.
VIRGINIA—HAMPTON: IMAX Theater; RICHMOND: Ethyl Universe Planetarium/Space Theatre; VIRGINIA BEACH: The Family Channel IMAX 3D Theater*.
WASHINGTON—SEATTLE: Boeing IMAX Theater*, Seattle Omnidome, Eames IMAX Theatre; SPOKANE: IMAX Theatre.
WISCONSIN—MILWAUKEE: Humphrey IMAX Dome Theater.

SHOWSCAN ENTERTAINMENT

6033 W. Century Blvd., Ste. 400, Los Angeles, CA 90045-6410. (310) 412-8464. FAX: (310) 412-8565. www.showscan.com
PRESIDENT & CEO
Dennis Pope
SENIOR V.P.
Russell Chesley
SENIOR V.P.
Mike Ellis
V.P., WORLDWIDE SALES & MARKETING
Ernest Bakenie
V.P., SHOWSCAN STUDIOS
Jeanne Lucas
V.P., HUMAN RESOURCES & CORPORATE SERVICES
Patti Gordon
MANAGER, BUSINESS AFFAIRS
Vivian T. Patrick

U.S. & MEXICO SHOWSCAN LOCATIONS

CALIFORNIA—SAN JOSE: United Artists Pavilion Starport: UNIVERSAL CITY: Emaginator at Universal Studios CityWalk.
COLORADO—DENVER: United Artists Park Meadows Starport.
INDIANA—INDIANAPOLIS: Sega City at Circle Center.
MARYLAND—BALTIMORE: United Artists Golden Ring Starport.
MASSACHUSETTS—BOSTON: Jillian's Billiards Club.
NEVADA—LAS VEGAS: Excalibur Hotel & Casino (2 screens); PRIMM: Buffalo Bills (2 screens).
NEW MEXICO—ALBUQUERQUE: United Artists Cottonwood Mall Starport.
NEW YORK—SYRACUSE: Regal Cinema Funscape II.
TEXAS—AUSTIN: Sega City at Lakeline Mall Starport; DALLAS: United Artists Jupiter Road.
VIRGINIA—CHESAPEAKE: Regal Cinemas Funscape I.
MEXICO—MEXICO CITY: Renio Aventura.

EUROPEAN SHOWSCAN LOCATIONS

AUSTRIA—GRAZ: Kino Centre; SALZBURG: Motion Ride Cinema.
BELGIUM—LIBIU: Euro Space Center.
ENGLAND—CAMBRIDGE: Duxford/War Museum; TYNE: Newcastle (International Center for Life).
FRANCE—POITIERS: Futurscope; MAIZIERES LES METZ: Walibi Schtroumpf.
GERMANY—MUNICH: Bavaria Film Tour, Olympic Spirit; POTSDAM: Babelsberg Studio Tour.
ITALY—VERONA: Gardaland.
SPAIN—MADRID: Parque de Atracciones; CANARY ISLANDS: Loro Parque.

MIDDLE EASTERN SHOWSCAN LOCATIONS

EGYPT—CAIRO: Giroland.
KUWAIT—KUWAIT CITY: Sha'ab Leisure Park.
SAUDI ARABIA—JEDDAH: Wonderland.
SOUTH AFRICA—SUN CITY: Sun City/Ster-Kinekor.
UNITED ARAB EMIRATES—ABU DHABI: Hill Fun City.

ASIA SHOWSCAN LOCATIONS

CHINA—SHANGHAI: Ping An (2 screens); SHENZHEN: Nanguo; XIANGYANG: Chonqing; BEIJING: Beijing Train Station; GUILIN: Guilin Park.
INDONESIA—SURABAYA: Subentra.
JAPAN—HYOGO: Himegi Central Park; KAGAWA: Reoma World; KANAGAWA: Hakone; KITAKYUSHE: Space World; KYOTO: Uzamasa; LAKE HAMANA, SHIZUOKA: PAL PAL; MIYAZAKI: MHI Ocean Dome (2 screens); NAGOYA: Sea Train Land; OSAKA: Asia & Pacific Trade Center; Expoland; Hirakata Park, Kasumi; SAITAMA: Seibu Unesco Village; TOKYO: Namco, Tokyo Science Museum; TOKYO HARBOUR: Water Science Pavilion; YOKAHAMA: Yokahama Dream Land.
KOREA—JEONJU CITY: Muju Resort; KYONGGI-DO: Everland; KYUNG-NAM: Tongdo Fantasia; PUSAN: Lotte Sky Plaza; SEOUL: Lotte World.
SINGAPORE—SENTOSA: Fantasy Island.
TAIWAN—FUNG YENG CITY: Formosan Aboriginal Cultural Village; HSTINTSU SHIEN: Leofoo Village.

NEW ZEALAND & AUSTRALIA SHOWSCAN LOCATIONS

AUSTRALIA—SYDNEY: Darling Harbour.
NEW ZEALAND—QUEENSTOWN: Helicopter Line.

SPECIALTY EXHIBITOR SERVICES & EQUIPMENT

The companies below provide equipment, construction, sound, projectors, etc. for large format and ride film exhibition.

BIG SCREEN PICTURES, LLC
(Marketing, distribution and financing)
635 Byram Lake Rd., Bedford Corners, NY 10549.
email: mcannold@aol.com
CONTACT
Mitchell Cannold

BOSTON LIGHT AND SOUND, INC.
(Designers, consultant and system integrators of projection and sound systems as well as 3-D systems)
290 N. Bacon St., Boston, MA 02135-1990. (617) 787-3131.
FAX: (617) 787-4257. www.blsi.com
CONTACT
C. Chapin Cutler, Jr.

CHRISTIE, INC.
(Projection equipment and accessories)
10550 Camden Dr., Cypress, CA 90630. (714) 236-8610. FAX: (714) 229-3185. www.christieinc.com
MARKETING DIRECTOR
Craig M. Sholder

CINEGRAND
(Large format theater development & operation)
1105 Quail St., Newport Beach, CA 92660. (310) 273-8831.
FAX: (310) 273-8874. www.cinegrand.com
email: linda@cineGRAND.com
CONTACT
Linda Nelson

CINEMA SYSTEMS
1405 San Marino, San Marino, CA 91108. (626) 405-7006.
FAX: (626) 309-5098.
CONTACT
Tuen-Ping Yang

DIGITAL THEATRE SYSTEMS
(Sound)
5171 Clareton Dr., Agoura Hills, CA 91301. (818) 706-3525.
FAX: (818) 706-1868. www.dtsonline.com
CONTACT
Bill Hunter

DOLBY LABORATORIES, INC.
(Sound)
100 Potrero Ave., San Francisco, CA 94103. (415) 558-0200.
FAX: (415) 863-1373. www.dolby.com email: info@Dolby.com
CONTACT
Robert Warren

EVANS & SUTHERLAND
(StarRider digital theatres, DigiStar II digital planetarium projection system)
600 Komas Dr., Salt Lake City, UT 84108. (801) 588-1000.
FAX: (801) 588-4520. www.es.com email: jpanek@es.com
CONTACT
Jeri Panek

HARRAH'S THEATRE EQUIPMENT CO.
(Sound, projection, seating, draperies, design services)
25613 Dollar St., #1, Hayward, CA 94544. (510) 881-4989.
FAX: (510) 881-0448.
CONTACT
Jerry Harrah

IWERKS ENTERTAINMENT
(Provider of high-tech entertainment systems, support services and software for ride simulation and specialty venue attractions)
4520 W. Valerio St., Burbank, CA 91505. (818) 841-7766. FAX: (818) 840-6192. www.iwerks.com
CONTACT
David Ervin

LARGE FORMAT CINEMA ASSOCIATION
8436 Colonial Dr., Stockton, CA 95209-2319. (209) 477-2726.
FAX: (209) 951-8113.
PHD ADMINISTRATOR
Wayne Narron

MAGNUM CINEMA
(Destination theatre. Napa Valley Imax Theatre)
1811 Grand Ave., Ste. F, San Rafael, CA 94901. (415) 454-4912. FAX: (415) 454-8553.
CEO
Ted Cochran

MEDIA TECHNOLOGY SOURCE, INC.
(Theatre equipment, installation, support services)
1802 Victory Blvd., Glendale, CA 91201. (818) 247-8667. FAX: (818) 247-3508.
10501 Florida Ave. S., Minneapolis, MN 55438. (612) 829-0161. (800) 227-3587. FAX: (612) 829-0166.
PRESIDENT
Phil Rafson
E.V.P.
John P. Ayotte
CONTACT
Jerry Van de Rydt

MEGASYSTEMS
(Technical solutions for large format theatres)
435 Devon Park Dr., The 500 Building, Wayne, PA 19087.
(610) 225-7200. FAX: (610) 225-7258. www.megasystem.com
CONTACT
ZeeAnn Mason

PACIFIC TITLE/MIRAGE STUDIO
6350 Santa Monica Blvd., Hollywood, CA 90038. (323) 464-0121. FAX: (323) 461-8325. www.pactitle.com

PETER CRANE ASSOC.
(Consultants, theatre development)
110 W. Mariposa, San Clemente, CA 92672. (949) 492-0958.
FAX: (949) 498-5518. email: Mike4film@aol.com

STRONG INTERNATIONAL
(Special venue projection equipment)
4350 McKinley St., Omaha, NE 68112. (402) 453-4444. FAX: (402) 453-7238. www.Strong-Cinema.com
CONTACTS
Ray Boegner

XAOS, INC.
444 De Haro St., San Francisco, CA 94107. (415) 558-9267.
FAX: (415) 558-9160.
CONTACT
Marcus McWaters

XENOTECH, INC.
1915 Orangewood Ave., 2nd Flr., Orange, CA 92868. (714) 939-5560. FAX: (714) 939-5561. email: jlynch3d@aol.com
CONTACT
Jim Lynch

THEATRE EQUIPMENT & SERVICES

ACOUSTIC AND NOISE CONTROL WALL COVERINGS

ACOUSTIPLEAT CO.
592 Old Sherman Hill Rd., Woodbury, CT 06798. (203) 577-2026. email: acoustiplt@aol.com
PRESIDENT
Diana Peterson

ALPRO ACOUSTICS
600 St. George Ave., #A, New Orleans, LA 70121-1117. (504) 733-3836. FAX: (504) 733-3851.
PRESIDENT
Maura Hawkins
DIRECTOR OF MANUFACTURING
Michael Sergi

AVL SYSTEMS, INC.
5540 S.W. 6th Place, Ocala, FL 34474. (800) ACUSTIC. FAX: (352) 854-1278. www.avlonline.com email: info@avlonline.com
PRESIDENT
J. Philip Hale

BREJTFUS ENTERPRISES, INC.
410 S. Madison Drive, Suite #3, Tempe, AZ, 85050. (480) 731-9899. FAX: (480) 731-9469. www.brejtfus.com
email: info@brejtfus.com
PRESIDENT
Michael Regan
NATIONAL SALES MANAGER
John Sterling

DECOUSTICS CINE-LINE
65 Disco Road, Toronto, Ontario M9W1M2. (800) 387-3809
FAX: (416) 675-5546. www.decoustics.com
email: sales@decoustics.com
V.P., SALES
John Balog

ECONO-PLEAT/EAST WEST CARPET MILLS
11143 West Washington Blvd., Culver City, CA 90232. (310) 559-RUGS (7847). FAX: (310) 559-6357.
CONTACT
Larry Sperling

G&S ACOUSTICS (GOLTERMAN & SABO), INC.
3555 Scarlet Oak Blvd., St. Louis, MO 63122. (800) 737-0307.
FAX: (314) 781-3836. www.golterman.com
email: ned@golterman.com
VICE PRESIDENT
Ned Golterman

KINETICS NOISE CONTROL
6300 Irelan Place, Dublin, OH 43017-3257. (614) 889-0480.
FAX: (614) 889-0540. www.kineticsnoise.com
PRESIDENT & CEO
Virgil Temple
SALES
Jill Skaggs

LBI/BOYD WALLCOVERINGS
2275 Auto Centre Dr., Glendora, CA 91740. (909) 596-0987.
FAX: (909) 592-1700. www.lbiboyd.com
VICE PRESIDENT
Michael Lyngle

MBI PRODUCTS
5309 Hamilton Avenue, Cleveland OH 44114. (216) 431-6400
FAX: (216) 431-9000. www.mbiproducts.com
email: sales@mbiproducts.com
VICE PRESIDENT
Christopher Kysela
SALES MANAGER
Charlie Splain

MDC WALLCOVERINGS
1200 Arthur Ave., Elk Grove, IL 60007. (847) 437-4000. FAX: (847) 437-4064. www.mdcwallcoverings.com
EXECUTIVE ASSISTANT
Nancy Camarano

MELDED FABRICS, INC
1000 Quail St., Newport Beach, CA 92660. (562) 407-3067, (800) 535-6091. www.meldedfabrics.com
email: mfiusal@aol.com
CONTACT
Jeff Anderson

O'BRIEN PARTITION COMPANY
5301 E. 59th Street, Kansas City, MO 64130. (800) 821-3595.
FAX: (816) 363-7034. www.obrienwalls.com
CEO
Ed Newcomer

PNC WEST, INC.
835 W. Fairway Dr., Chandler, AZ 85225. (480) 917-1999. FAX: (480) 917-1899. email: PNCWest@email.msn.com
PRESIDENT
Cheryl Van Meter

SOUNDFOLD
9200 North State Rt. 48, Centerville, OH 45458. (800) 782-8018, (800) 885-5115. FAX: (937) 885-5100.
www.soundfold.com email: kpierson@soundfold.com
VICE PRESIDENT
Thomas Miltner

TROY SOUNDWALL SYSTEMS
3420 South Malt Ave., Commerce, CA 90040. (800) 987-3306.
email: tsws95@aol.com
V.P., MARKETING & SALES
Bruce C. Holden

WHISPER WALLS
10957 E. Bethany Dr., Aurora, CO 80014. (303) 671-6696.
FAX: (303) 671-0606. www.whisperwalls.com
email: sales@whisperwalls.com
GENERAL MANAGER
Brad Enter

AISLE AND WALL LIGHTING

APPLIED LIGHTING SYSTEMS
407 Old County Rd., Belmont, CA 94002-2547. (650) 595-5496. FAX: (650) 595-5197. email: cnemaservcs@aol.com
OWNER
Rodolfo Luppi

ATLAS SPECIALTY LIGHTING
7304 N. Florida Avenue, Tampa, FL 33604. (813) 238-6481.
FAX: (813) 238-6656. www.asltg.com
email: alicia@asltg.com
MANAGERS
Ralph Felton, Jr.
Bob Ray

AURA LIGHTING PRODUCTS
779 North Benson Ave., Upland, CA 91786-5836. (909) 985-3864. (800) 942-8880. FAX: (909) 985-5938.
PRODUCTION MANAGER
Rolando Flores

CELESTIAL LIGHTING PRODUCTS
14009 Dinard Ave., Santa Fe Springs, CA 90670. (800) 233-3563, (562) 802-8811. FAX: (562) 802-2882.
email: JPNunez@msn.com
NATIONAL SALES MANAGER
Jaime Nunez

CINEMA LIGHTING & INSTALLATION
6088 Sunningdale Dr., Hudsonville, MI 49426. (616) 669-5018.
FAX: (616) 669-5011. www.cinemalighting.com
CEO
Kirk Campbell

DAVID TYSON LIGHTING, INC.
P.O. Box 1932, Callahan, FL 32011. (800) 385-3148. FAX: (800) 385-3149.
CONTACT
Donna Tyson

DECOLITE PRODUCTS
21610-3 Lassen Street, Chatsworth, CA 91311.
CONTACT
Herb Beatus

EAST COAST LAMP SALES, INC.
8 Vernon Valley Road, East Northport, NY 11731. (631) 754-5655. FAX: (631) 754-2213.
PRESIDENT
James Kelly
VICE PRESIDENT
Thomas Kelly

HIGH END SYSTEMS, INC
2217 W. Braker Lane, Austin, TX 78758. (512) 836-2242. FAX: (512) 837-5290. www.highend.com
email: bruce_jordahl@highend.com
MARKETING DIRECTOR
Nils Thorjussen

ILLUMILITE, INC.
1270 Rangeley Dr., Colorado Springs, CO 80921. (719) 488-2379. FAX: (719) 488-2561.
PRESIDENT
Jana DeWitt

LEHIGH ELECTRIC PRODUCTS
6265 Hamilton Blvd., Allentown, PA 18106. (610) 395-3386. FAX: (610) 395-7735.
www.lehighdim.com
PRESIDENT
Lloyd Jones

LIGHTING AND ELECTRONIC DESIGN (LED)
141 Cassia Way, Units B & C, Henderson, NV 89014. (800) 700-5483. FAX: (888) 223-6599. www.ledlinc.com
email: led@ledlinc.com
OWNER
Janie Lynn

LIGHTWORKS
3345 W. Hunting Park Ave., Philadelphia, PA 19132. (215) 223-9200. FAX: (215) 227-7332.
CONTACT
Peter Altman

LINSEY-FAIRBANKS, INC.
1670 Maywood Ave, Upland, CA 91784. (909) 982-0467 FAX: (909) 982-7036. email: jlolfi@aol.com
PRESIDENT
George Mackey

MICA LIGHTING COMPANY, INC.
717 S. State College Blvd., Bldgs. K&L, Fullerton, CA 92831. (714) 738-8448. FAX: (714) 738-7748. www. micalighting.com
email: micalighting@earthlink.net
PRESIDENT
Gayle von Eissler
V.P., OPERATIONS
Francisco Briseno

MICROLITE LIGHTING CONTROL
1150 Powis Rd., West Chicago, IL 60185. (630) 876-0500. FAX: (630) 876-0580. www.microlite.net
NATIONAL ACCOUNTS & MARKETING MANAGER
Tom Scheu

PASKAL LIGHTING
6820 Romaine St., Los Angeles, CA 90038-2433. (323) 466-5233. FAX: (213) 466-1071. www.paskal.com
OWNER & PRESIDENT
Evan Green

PERMLIGHT, INC
422 W. 6th St., Tustin, CA 92780. (714) 508-0729. FAX: (714) 508-0920. www.Permlight.com
email: permlight@permlight.com
PRESIDENT
James F. George

TEMPO INDUSTRIES, INC.
1961 Mcgaw Ave., Irvine, CA92614. (949) 442-1601. FAX: (949) 442-1609. email: mail@tempoindustries.com
PRESIDENT
Gregory Smith

TIVOLI INDUSTRIES, INC.
(Aisle & step lighting)
1513 East St. Gertrude Place, Santa Ana, CA 92705. (714) 957-6101. FAX: (714) 957-1501. www.tivolilighting.com
email: Tivoli@targettiusa.com
MARKETING MANAGER
Marie Paris

TUBE LIGHTING PRODUCTS
1050 Pioneer Way, Ste. G, El Cajon, CA 92020. (619) 442-0577. FAX: (619) 442-0578.
GENERAL MANAGER
Paul Hamwey

VISTA MANUFACTURING, INC.
8086 F.M. 2449., Ponder, TX 76259. (940) 479-2787. FAX: (940) 479-8139. www.vistamfg.com
email: vistamfg2@sprynet.com
MANAGER
Tod E. Tieszen

ARCHITECTURE, DESIGN AND CONSTRUCTION

ARROWSTREET, INC.
212 Elm Street, Somerville, MA 02144. (617) 623-5555 FAX: (617) 776-1619. www.arrowstreet.com
email: info@arrowstreet.com
PRINCIPAL
John Cole

BEHR BROWERS ARCHITECTS, INC.
340 N. Westlake Blvd., #250, Westlake Village, CA 91362. (805) 496-1101 FAX: (805) 494-1421. www.behrbrowers.com
email: BBAIncArch@aol.com
EXECUTIVE DIRECTORS
Rossana Behr

BENCHMARK DESIGN GROUP
456 Osceola Ave., Jacksonville Beach, FL 32250. (904) 246-5060 FAX: (904) 246-9008. www.benchmark.com
email: bncmkdsn@bellsouth.net
PRESIDENT
Mark Carroll

BIRTCHER CONSTRUCTION
275 E. Baker St., Costa Mesa, CA 92626. (949) 629-4300 FAX: (949) 629-4310. www.birtcherconst.com
email: ayoungquist@birtcherconst.com
PRESIDENT
Andy Youngquist

BLAIR DESIGN & CONSTRUCTION
12021 Plano Rd., Ste. 175, Dallas, TX 75243. (972) 889-0600. FAX: (972) 889-0660.
V.P., OPERATIONS
James B. Reed

CLASSIC INDUSTRIES
(Architectural metal fabrication)
905 E. Broad St., Forney, TX 75126. (972) 564-2192. FAX: (972) 564-2190. www.classicusa.com
V.P., SALES
Gary Byrd

CONSTRUCTION SOLUTIONS/STADIUM SEATING
6799 Great Oaks Dr., Memphis, TN 38138. (901) 753-4009. FAX: (901) 752-0720.
OWNER
Scott Reading

DIMENSIONAL INNOVATIONS
(Thematic architectural elements & signage)
3421 Merriam Lane, Overland Park, KS 66203. (913) 384-3488. FAX: (913) 384-3477. www.dimin.com
PROJECT DEVELOPMENT
Curt Baxter
Greg Powers

FIRST IMPRESSIONS
12564 N.E. 14th Ave, N. Miami, FL 33161. (305) 891-6121. (800) 305-7545. FAX: (305) 891-7103.
email: fidm-designt@worldnet.att.net
MARKETING
RoseAnne Keighley

HENRY ARCHITECTS
6203 Dayton Avenue N., Seattle, WA 98103. (206) 784-6964. FAX: (206) 784-0873.
PRESIDENT
Rob Henry

IWERKS ENTERTAINMENT
(Specialized theatre manufacturing)
4520 W. Valerio St., Burbank, CA 91505. (818) 841-7766. FAX: (818) 841) 7847. www.iwerks.com
COO
Don Stults
CFO
Jeff Dahl
V.P., MARKETING
Christina Frueh

JOHNSON/MCKIBBEN ARCHITECTS
965 Slocum Street, Dallas, TX 75207. (214) 745-7070. FAX: (214) 745-1515. www.web2.airmail.net/jma1
email: mail@johnsonmckibben.com
PRESIDENT
Michael L. Johnson

KMD ARCHITECTS
222 Vallejo Street, San Francisco, CA 94111. (415) 398-5191. FAX: (415) 394-7158. www.kmd-arch.com
SR. PROJECT ARCHITECT
Howard McNenny

LARGO CONSTRUCTION
555 Street Rd., Bensalem, PA 19020. (215) 245-0300. (800) 272-2432. FAX: (215) 638-7933. email: largoconst@aol.com
V.P., THEATRE DIVISION
Jeffrey W. Spence

MESBUR & SMITH ARCHITECTS
148 Kenwood Ave.,Ste. 100, Toronto, Ontario M6C 253. (416) 656-5751 FAX: (416) 656-5615. www.mesbursmith.com
email: mail@mesbursmith@on.aibn.com
PARTNER
David Mesbur
PARTNER
Harold Smith

MHB PARADIGM DESIGN
550 3 Mile Rd., N.W., Grand Rapids, MI 49544. (616) 785-5656. FAX: (616) 785-5657. www.mhbparadigm.com
email: paradigm@mhbparadigm.com
PRESIDENT
Richard A. Murphy

OAKVIEW CONSTRUCTION, INC.
1981 G Ave., Box 450, Red Oak, IA 51566. (712) 623-4927. FAX: (712) 623-5497.www.oakviewconst.com
CHAIRMAN
Richard Bulkeley

PCNY USA
(Theatre construction)
4038 Victory Blvd., Staten Island, NY 10314. (718) 698-5050. FAX: (718) 370-8373.
email: anyone@pcnyusa.com
PRESIDENT
Anthony Pepe

P.P.R. ENTERPRISES
(Concession design)
890 Mariner St., Brea, CA 92821. (714) 529-7863. FAX: (714) 529-1418. email: pprpoul@pacbell.net
PRESIDENT
Poul Rasmussen
VICE PRESIDENT
Peter Rasmussen

PACIFIC CONCESSIONS, INC.
(Concession design)
1250 Bayhill Drive, Ste. 301, San Bruno, CA 94066. (650) 871-8711. FAX (650) 871-7480.
email: info@pacificconcessions.com
PRESIDENT
Alan Kates

PROCTOR COMPANIES
(Concession design)
10497 W. Centennial Rd., Littleton, CO 80127-4218. (303) 973-8989, (800) 221-3699. FAX: (303) 973-8884.
www.proctorco.com
PRESIDENT
Bruce Proctor

RTAS LLC
(Insulated concrete forms)
9730 South 700 East, #100, Sandy, UT 84070. (801) 523-2480. FAX: (801) 816-9645. email: rtas@citystreet.com
PRESIDENT
Michael D. Schwab

TK ARCHITECTS
106 W. 11th St., Suite 1900, Kansas City, MO 64105. (816) 842-7552. FAX: (816)-842-1302. www.tkarch.com
email: tkapo@tkarch.com
VICE PRESIDENT
Tamra Knapp

TOTAL THEATRE DESIGN
21 South St., Washingtonville, NY 10992. (914) 496-9125. FAX: (914) 496-1692. email: bho@frontiernet.net
PRINCIPAL
Harvey Berg

VERTEX CONSTRUCTION, LLC
(General contractor)
1275 81st St., Brooklyn, NY 11228. (718) 761-3500. FAX: (718) 491-2834.
CONTACT
Anthony Pepe

WPH ARCHITECTURE
513 NW 13th Ave., #300, Portland, OR 97209. (503) 827-0505. FAX: (503) 827-0506. www.wphpc.com
MARKETING DIRECTOR
Gwen Millius

ASSISTIVE LISTENING SYSTEMS

ASSOCIATED HEARING INSTRUMENTS
6976 Market St., Upper Darby, PA 19082-2308. (610) 352-0600. FAX: (610) 352-2469. email: asshearing@aol.com
VICE PRESIDENT
Gary Bond

AUDEX, ASSISTIVE LISTENING SYSTEMS
710 Standard Street, Longview, TX 75604. (800) 237-0716. FAX:(903) 295-0310. www.audex.com
email: cbeatty@iamerica.net
PRESIDENT
Charles Beatty

NADY SYSTEMS, INC.
6701 Shellmound Street, Emeryville, CA 94608. (510) 652-2411. FAX: (510) 652-5075.
CONTACT
Toby Nady

PHONIC EAR
3880 Cypress Drive, Petaluma, CA 94954. (800) 227-0735. FAX: (707) 769-9624. www.phonicear.com
email: marketing@phonicear.com
V.P., MARKETING
Rick Pimentel

SENNHEISER ELECTRONIC CORP.
1 Enterprise Dr., Old Lyme, CT 06371. (860) 434-9190. FAX: (860) 434-1759. www.sennheiserusa.com
DIRECTOR OF MARKETING
Joe Ciandelli

SOUND ASSOCIATES, INC.
424 West 45th Street, New York, NY 10036. (212) 757-5679. FAX: (212) 265-1250. www.soundassociates.com
V.P., OPERATIONS
Mark Annunziato

WILLIAMS SOUND CORP.
10399 W. 70th Street, Eden Prairie, MN 55344. (612) 943-2252. FAX: (612) 943-2174. www.williamsound.com
email: info@williamssound.com
PRESIDENT
Jim Broz

BOX OFFICE, CONCESSION AND ACCOUNTING SYSTEMS

This listing incorporates both hardware and software.

AAMI-TDS (THEATRON)
P.O. Box 4142, Seal Beach, CA 90740. (562) 434-1627. FAX: (562) 434-9948. www.theatronsystems.com
CHAIRMAN
R. Hoffman

AASI-TDS (SYSTEMS) (THEATRON)
P.O. Box 70575, Reno, NV 71647. (562) 434-9947 FAX: (818) 705-6878. www.theatron.com
VICE PRESIDENT
L. Ratgauz

AASI- TDS-NV
P.O. Box 70575-0575, Reno, NV 89570. (775) 825-3273.
MANAGING DIRECTOR
M. E. Johnston

AMERICAN EXPRESS
200 Vesey St., 34th Flr., New York, NY 10285-3405. (888) 851-5392. FAX: (888) 851-5392. www.americanexpress.com
email: ruth.tolles@aext.com
VICE PRESIDENT
Ruth Tolles

AUTOMATICKET
(A Division of CEMCORP) 110 Industry Lane, P.O. Box 296, Forest Hill, MD 21050. (410) 879-3022. FAX: (410) 838-8079.
www.hurleyscreen.com
email: info@hurleyscreen.com
V.P., OPERATIONS
Gorman White Jr.

CARDLOGIX
16 Hughes St., Irvine, CA 92618. (949) 380-1312 FAX: (949) 380-1428. www.cardlogix.com
email: sales@cardlogix.com
V.P. MARKETING
Bruce Ross
V.P., SALES
Emil Nastri

EIMS, INC.
8801 State Highway 16, Suite A, Gig Harbor, WA 98332.
(253) 857-6411 FAX: (253) 857-6461. www.eims-inc.com
email: eims@eims-inc.com
SECRETARY-TREASURERS
Deborah Von Ditter
Michael Von Ditter
Kevin Kendrick

FPL ENERGY SERVICES
(Utility expense management)
9250 W. Flagler St., Dept. IBS-GO, Miami, FL 33174. (305) 552-4128. FAX: (305) 552-4955.
ACCOUNTS MANAGER
Morton Friedrich

ICON INTERNATIONAL
949 South Coast Dr., #300, Costa Mesa, CA 92626. (714) 444-5600. FAX: (714) 444-5650. www.iconsoftware.com
V.P., SALES
Gary Brown

INDIANA CASH DRAWER COMPANY
P.O. Box 236, Shelbyville, IN 46176-0236.
(317) 398-6643. FAX: (317) 392-0958.
www.icdpos.com
SALES & MARKETING MANAGER
Catherine Woods

MARS SEQUEL THEATER MANAGEMENT SYSTEM/ AOL MOVIEFONE
333 Westchester Ave., White Plains,NY 10604. (914) 872-0333. FAX: (914) 872-0066. www.mars-tms.com
SALES COORDIATOR
Tonette Earl

MCALLISTER ASSOCIATES, INC.
(Computer Systems)
247 Main St., Reading, MA 01867. (781) 942-0700. FAX: (781) 942-0240. www.midware.com e
mail: dick1@frontiernet.net
PRESIDENT
Dick McAllister

MERRILL LYNCH
701 B St., #2400, San Diego, CA 92101. (619) 699-3721. FAX: (619) 236-8162. www.fc.ml.com/benter_group
FINANCIAL CONSULTANT, FCM
Brad Benter

OMNITERM DATA TECHNOLOGY, LTD.
2785 Skymark Ave., #11, Mississauga Ontario L4W 4Y3. (905) 629-4757 FAX: (905) 629-8590.
www.omniterm.com email: info@omniterm.com
PRESIDENT
Ed Coman

PACER/CATS
3701 Wilshire Blvd., #1050, Los Angeles, CA 90010. (213) 639-6132. FAX: (213) 382-6106. www.pacercats.com
email: lpryor@ticketmaster.com
EXECUTIVE V.P.
Del Banjo
CFO
Janet Evans

RDS DATA GROUP
101 Donly Dr., South, Simcoe, Ontario, Canada N3Y 4L5.
(519) 428-2400. FAX: (519) 428-9441, (519) 428-0131.
www.rdsdata.com email: info@rdsdata.com
V.P., SALES & MARKETING
Brad DePoorter
ACCOUNT MANAGER
Jeff Simpson

RETRIEVER SOFTWARE
1978 South Garrison St., Ste. 101, Lakewood, CO 80227.
(303) 969-0096. FAX: (303) 969-9852. www.retriever-pos.com
PRESIDENT
Ed Kearney
MANAGER, TECHNICAL SERVICES
David Miller

TICKETING SYSTEMS.COM
1153 Inspiration Lane, Escondido, CA 92025. (760) 480-1002.
FAX: (760) 480-6830. www.ticketingsystems.com
PRESIDENT
Bruce L. Hall

TICKETPRO SYSTEMS
870 Mercury Dr, S.E., Lawrenceville, GA 30045. (770) 682-5485. FAX: (770) 682-8397. www.ticketpro.org
email: ticketpro@bellsouth.net
CEO
John Shaw
SYSTEMS INTEGRATOR
Willie Vandenheuvel

CARPETS

BRINTONS U.S. AXMINSTER
1856 Artistry Lane, Greenville, MS 38701. (662) 332-1581.
FAX: (662) 332-1594. www.brintons.net
SENIOR V.P., SALES
Jeff Coveny
SALES
John Sawyer

CINEMA SERVICES
407 Old County Rd., Belmont, CA 94002. (650) 595-5496.
FAX: (650) 595-5197.
OWNER
Rodolfo Luppi

DURKAN PATTERNED CARPET
405 Virgil Drive, Dalton, GA 30720. (706) 278-7037. FAX: (706) 279-8451. www.durkancpt.com email: sales@durkancpt.com
SALES COORDINATING MANAGER
Karen Lawson

KONETA/LRV
(Rubber matting)
P.O. Box 150, Wapakoneta, OH 45895. (419) 739-4200. FAX: (419) 739-4247. www.konetalrv.com
email: sales@konetalrv.com
SALES MANAGER
Dave Rose

MASLAND CARPETS, INC.
P.O. Box 11467, Mobile, AL 36671. (800) 633-0468, (334) 675-9080. FAX: (334) 675-8330. www.maslandcarpets.com
NATIONAL ACCOUNTS MANAGER
Jay Loughran

MILLIKEN CARPET
201 Lukken Industrial Drive West, LaGrange, GA 30240. (706) 880-5154. FAX: (706) 880-5888. www.millikencarpet.com
COMMUNICATIONS MANAGER
Dean Gaffney

OMEGA PATTERN WORKS, INC./ARTISANS, INC.
P.O. Box 1059 Calhoun, GA 30703. (800) 241-4908. FAX: (706) 602-3569.
CUSTOMER SERVICE
Joyce Maxwell

CONCESSION EQUIPMENT

ACORTO, INC.
1287 120th Ave. Northeast, Bellevue, WA 98005. (425) 453-2800. FAX: (425) 453-2167. www.acorto.com
email: info@acorto.com

ALL-STAR CARTS AND VEHICLES, INC.
1565 Fifth Industrial Ct., Bayshore, NY 11706. (800) 831-3166.
FAX: (516) 666-1319. www.allstarcarts.com
VICE PRESIDENT
Bob Kronrad

AUTOMATIC BAR CONTROLS/WUNDER-BAR
790 Eubanks Rd., Vacaville, CA 95688. (707) 448-5151. FAX: (707) 448-1521. www.wunderbar.com
NATIONAL ACCOUNT MANAGERS
Wally Stern
Bob McBride
CONTACT
John Rodrigues

BEAVER MACHINE CORP.
1341 Kerrisdale Blvd., Newmarket ON L3Y 7V1. (800) 265-6772, (905) 836-4700. FAX: (905) 836-4737.
www.beavervending.com email: sales@beavervending.com
EXECUTIVE SECRETARY
Nancy Calderone

BLODGETT ADVANCED COOKING & TECHNOLOGY/ MAYTAG
10500 Metric Dr., #110, TX 75243. (214) 379-6048. FAX: (214) 340-0916. www.blodgett.com
DIRECTOR OF MARKETING
Ralph Bellinger

C. CRETORS & COMPANY
3243 N. California Avenue, Chicago, IL 60618. (800) 228-1885.
FAX: (773) 588-7141. www.cretors.com
V.P., OPERATIONS
Van Neathery
V.P., SALES & MARKETING
Gino Nardulli
MARKETING DIRECTOR
Beth Cretors

CHART INDUSTRIES/MVE
3505 County Road, 42 West, Burnsville, MN 55306. (800) 247-4446. FAX: (952) 882-5185. www. chart-inc.com
SALES
Gary Fowler

CINEMA SUPPLY CO.
502 S. Market St., Millersburg, PA 17061. (800) 437-5505. FAX: (717) 692-3073. email: cinemasupply.com
OPERATIONS MANAGER
Van Troutman
SALES MANAGER
Gina DiSanto

CONCESSION SUPPLY COMPANY
1016 Summit Street, Toledo, OH 43697. (419) 241-7711.
OWNER & PRESIDENT
Robert Brockway

FAWN VENDORS
8040 University Blvd., Des Moines, IA 50305. (800) 548-1982. FAX: (515) 274-9256. www.fawnvendors.com
NATIONAL ACCOUNTS MANAGER
Gary Bahr

FRYWORKS
2225 E. 28th St., Ste. 507, Signal Hill, CA 90806. (562) 997-9699. FAX: (562) 997-9279. www.fryworks.com
VICE PRESIDENT
Earl Keegan

FUNACHO
2165 Central Parkway, Cincinati OH 45214. (800) 386-2246. FAX: (513) 352-5122. www.funacho.com
email: sales@funacho.com
PRESIDENT
Michael Grause

GABRIELLA IMPORTS
(Espresso & cappuccino machines)
5100 Prospect Ave., Cleveland, OH 44103. (216) 432-3651. FAX: (216) 432-3654. www.gabimports.com
email: info@gabimports.com
OWNER & PRESIDENT
Douglas Friedman

GLOBAL CUP
Av. President Juarez, #139-B, Tlalnepantla, Mexico 54090. (525) 365-1674. FAX: (525) 365-1674.
CONTACT
Alfonso Ruelas

GOLD MEDAL PRODUCTS
10700 Medallion Dr., Cincinnati, OH 45214-4807. (513) 769-7676, (800) 543-0862. FAX: (513) 769-8500, (800) 542-1496. www.gmpopcorn.com
email: goldme19@eos.net
NATIONAL SALES DIRECTOR
Chris Petroff

HOSHIZAKI NORTH EASTERN
(Ice machines, refrigerators/freezers)
20 Drexel Dr., Bayshore, Long Island 11706. (800) 281-5249. FAX: (631) 582-2882. www.hoshizak.com
SALES MANAGER
Roseann Michalowski
ACCOUNT MANAGER
Nick Tippert

IMI CORNELIUS, INC.
One Cornelius Place, Anoka, MN 55303. (800) 238-3600. FAX: (612) 422-3226. www.cornelius.com
SALES & MARKETING
David Storey

INTEGRATED FOOD SYSTEMS
11705 Gold Park Lane, Gold River, CA 95670. (916) 852-0556. FAX: (916) 852-0626. www.ifs-corp.com
email: fmathes@ifs-corp.com
CONTACT
Forest A. Mathes

JARCO INDUSTRIES
125 Laser Court, Hauppauge, NY 11788. (631) 851-9100. FAX: (631) 851-9101. www.concessionstands.com
PRESIDENT & CEO
Jeffrey Stein

KRISPY KIST MACHINE COMPANY
(A Subsidiary of C. Cretors)
3243 N. California Avenue, Chicago, IL 60618. (800) 228-1885. FAX: (773) 588-7141. www.cretors.com
V.P., OPERATIONS
Van Neathery
V.P., SALES & MARKETING
Gino Nardulli

LANCER CORP., INC.
6655 Lancer Blvd., San Antonio, TX, 78219. (800) 729-1500. FAX: (210) 310-7242. www.lancercorp.com
CONTROLLER
Mark Frerich

MAINSTREET MENU SYSTEMS
1375 N. Barker Rd., Brookfield, WI 53045. (262) 782-6000. FAX: (262) 782-6515. www.mainstreetmenu.com
MARKETING MANAGER
Dawn Baumeister

METROPOLITAN PROVISIONS
(Snack bar equipment)
16639 Gale Ave., City of Industry, CA 91745. (626) 330-1414. FAX: (626) 330-1455.
SALES DIRECTOR
Ron Naslund

MICHAELO ESPRESSO, INC.
3801 Stone Way, N., Seattle, WA 98103-8005. (206) 548-9000. FAX (206) 695-4951. www.michaelo.com
DISTRICT SALES MANAGER
Bob Cappelletti

MULTIPLEX COMPANY
250 Old Ballwin Road, Ballwin, MO 63021-4800. (636) 256-7777. FAX (636) 527-4313. www.multiplex-beverage.com
email: markg@multiplex-beverage.com
V.P., CORPORATE BUSINESS DEVELOPMENT
Mark Giroux

NATIONAL CINEMA SUPPLY CORP.
14499 North Dale Mabry Highway, Suite 201, Tampa, FL 33618. (813) 962-2772. FAX: (813) 962-3620.
OWNER & CEO
Daniel P. Miller
PRESIDENT
Barney Bailey

BRANCHES
National Cinema Supply, (Sales) P.O. Box 206, Castaic, CA 91310-0206. (888) 900-1984, (661) 257-1984. FAX: (805) 257-1660. email: GABrucejr@compuserve.com
REGIONAL SALES MANAGER
George A. Bruce, Jr.

National Cinema Supply, (Sales) 99 Limestone Rd.,P.O. Box 549, Ridgefield, CT 06877. (203) 438 3405, (203) 438-1274. FAX: (203) 438-1419, (203) 438-1542.
email: WWBeatty@Compuserve.com
V.P. & GENERAL SALES MANAGER
Walter Beatty, Jr.
MARKETING ASSISTANT
Karen Raymond

National Cinema Supply, (Food Service) 8404 Sunstate St., Tampa, FL 33634. (800) 749-4469, (813) 884-0445. FAX: (813) 884-0544.
REGIONAL SALES MANAGER
Greg Thomas

National Cinema Supply, (Food Service) Capital City Supply, 2140 B Jackson Pkwy NW, Atlanta, GA 30318 (404) 792-8424 FAX: (404) 792-1424. email: Ffisher@aol.com
OPERATIONS MANAGER
John Holloway

National Cinema Supply, (Food Service) 8246 Marshall Dr., Lenexa, KS 66214. (800) 457-3357; (913) 492-0966. FAX: (913) 492-1477. email: riaynes@ncskc.com
V.P., NEW BUSINESS & DEVELOPMENT
Rob Jaynes
TECHNICAL SALES
Troy Fickle
SALES REPRESENTATIVE
Edward Jones

National Cinema Supply, (Technical service) 15700 W. Ten Mile Rd., Suite 209, Southfield, MI 48075 (248) 552-0461. FAX: (248) 552-0114. email: JimFox3@Compuserve.com
V.P., OPERATIONS
Jim Fox
National Cinema Supply, (Sales & food service) 5854 Highland Ridge Drive, Cincinnati, OH 45232. (800) 543-0418; (513) 242-6801. FAX: (513) 242-6931. email: DReidy@Compuserve.com
VICE PRESIDENT
Barbara Cammack
REGIONAL SALES MANAGER
Mitchell Bryson

National Cinema Supply, (Sales) 10 Cutter Mill Road, Suite 201, Great Neck, NY 11021 (516) 498-9058 FAX: (516) 498-9059. email: Billnorthacker@Compuserve.com
REGIONAL SALES MANAGER
William Northacker

OMI INDUSTRIES
P.O. Box 310, 4768 U.S. Highway 30N, Ontario, OH 44862 (419) 683-1233. FAX (419) 683-1050.
PRESIDENT
Paul Otterbacher

PACIFIC CONCESSIONS, INC.
1250 Bayhill Dr., # 301, San Bruno, CA 94066. (650) 871-8711. FAX (650) 871-7480. email: info@pacificconcessions.com
PRESIDENT
Alan Kates

PACKAGING CONCEPTS
(Popcorn bags)
4971 Fyler Ave., St. Louis, MO 63139. (314) 481-1155. FAX: (314) 481-6567. www.packaging conceptsinc.com
PRESIDENT
John Irace
ART DIRECTOR
Linda Naughton

PACKAGING DYNAMICS
3900 W. 43rd St., Chicago, IL 60632. (773) 254-8000. FAX: (773) 254-8204. www.bagcraft.com
DIRECTOR, CONSUMER PRODUCTS
Nancy Chico

PIONEER SALES & MARKETING: HUNT-WESSON
(Concession equipment)
P.O. Box 292605, Lewisville, TX 75029. (972) 436-2355. FAX: (972) 436-5813. email: rvulpit@email.msn.com
PRESIDENT
Russ Vulpitta

PRIME TICKET, INC.
(Concession supplies)
1131 Shine Ave., #106, Myrtle Beach, SC 29577. (843) 839-3138. FAX: (843) 839-3173. email: pticketinc.com
PRESIDENT
Keith Black

PROCTOR COMPANIES
(Concession design)
10497 W. Centennial Rd., Littleton, CO 80127-4218. (303) 973-8989. FAX: (303) 973-8884. www.proctorco.com
PRESIDENT
Bruce Proctor
V.P., SALES & MARKETING
Kurt Connolly

PROMOTIONAL MANAGEMENT GROUP, INC.
(Concession containers & supplies)
1800 Baltimore Ave., Kansas City, MO 64108. (816) 221-3833. FAX: (816) 221-6166.
E.V.P., SALES & MARKETING
James McGuinness

ROBINSON/KIRSHBAUM INDUSTRIES, INC.
8915 S. La Cienega Blvd. Unit F, Inglewood, CA 90301. (310) 645-4993. FAX (310) 645-2034. email: rkindstry@aol.com
EXECUTIVE VICE PRESIDENT
Bruce Kirshbaum

ROLL-A-GRILL CORP.
12 First Street, Pelham, NY 10803. (914) 738-4333, (800) 468-4681. FAX (914) 738-2186.

ROUNDUP FOOD EQUIPMENT
180 Kehoe Blvd., Carol Stream, IL 60188. (800) 253-2991. FAX: (630) 784-1650. www.ajantunes.com
MARKETING
Thomas Krisch.

SANI-SERV
2020 Production Drive, Indianapolis, IN 46241. (317) 247-0460. FAX: (317) 247-5130. www.saniserv.com
SALES & MARKETING
Steve Dowling

SERVER PRODUCTS, INC.
P.O. Box 530, Menomonee Falls, WI 53052. (800) 558-8722, (262) 251-7100. FAX: (262) 251-2688. www.serverproducts.com
email: pumps@excpc.com
SALES
Carol Neuser

STAR MANUFACTURING INTERNATIONAL
10 Sunnen Dr., P.O. Box 43129, St. Louis, MO 63143. (314) 781-2777. FAX: (314) 781-3636. www.star-mfg.com
CEO
Frank Ricchio

STEIN INDUSTRIES
22 Sprague Ave., Amityville, NY 11701-0536. (516) 789-2222. FAX: (516) 789-8888. email: steinincone@aol.com
OWNER
Andrew Stein

TAYLOR COMPANY
750 N. Blackhawk Blvd., Rockton, IL 61072. (815) 624-8333. FAX: (815) 624-8000. www.taylor-company.com
PRESIDENT
Clark Wangaard

TURBOCHEF TECHNOLOGIES
10500 Metric Dr., #128, Dallas TX 75243. (214) 341-9471 FAX: (214) 340-8477. www.turbochef.com
email: rbellinger@turbochef.com
DIRECTOR, BUSINESS DEVELOPMENT
Ralph Bellinger

WILSHIRE CORP.
2401 N. Palmer Drive, Schaumburg, IL 60196. (847) 397-4600. FAX: (847) 397-0250.
SALES
Robert Wonder

WINPAK TECHNOLOGIES, INC.
85 Laird Dr., Toronto, Ont., Canada M4G 3T8. (416) 421-1700. FAX: (416) 421-7957. URL: www.winpak.com
V.P., SALES & MARKETING
Louis de Bellefeuille

WESNIC/HINES III
(Site furnishings)
6000 Bowdendale Ave., Jacksonville, FL 32216. (904) 733-8444. FAX: (904) 733-3736. www.wesnic.com
DIRECTOR OF MARKETING
Bill Gilbert

CROWD CONTROL

ALVARADO MANUFACTURING
12660 Colony St., Chino, CA 91710. (909) 591-8431. FAX: (909) 628-1403. www.alvaradomanufacturing.com
email: alvaradomfg@compuserve.com
MARKETING MANAGER
Peter Nichols

BRASS SMITH, INC.
3880 Holly Street, Denver, CO 80207. (800) 662-9595. FAX: (303) 331-8444. www.brasssmith.com
email: bsi@brasssmith.com
SALES MANAGER
Benny Martinez

CROWN INDUSTRIES, INC.
155 North Park Street, East Orange, NJ 07017. (800) GO-CROWN. FAX: (973) 672-7536. www.gocrown.com
email: support@gocrown.com
PRESIDENT
Hugh Loebner

LAVI INDUSTRIES
27810 Hopkins Ave., Valencia, CA 91355-3409. (800) 624-6225. FAX: (661) 257-4938. www.lavi.com
email: RudyL@lavi.com
SALES
Rudy Leufroy

LAWRENCE METAL PRODUCTS, INC.
P.O. Box 400-M, Bay Shore, NY 11706. (800) 441-0019. FAX: (631) 666-0336. www.lawrencemetal.com
email: service@lawrencemetal.com
PRESIDENT
David Lawrence
CORPORATE OFFICER
Betty Castro

CURTAINS AND DRAPERY

AUTOMATIC DEVICES COMPANY
2121 S. 12th St. Allentown, PA 18103-4751. (610) 797-6000. FAX: (610) 797-4088. www.automaticdevices.com
PRESIDENT
John Samuels

CINEMA SERVICES
407 Old Country Road, Belmont, CA 94002. (650) 595-5496. FAX: (650) 595-5197. email: cnmaservcs@aol.com
OWNER
Rudolfo Luppi

CLOUD INDUSTRIES, INC.
P.O. Box 11717, Kansas City, MO 64138. (816) 737-0798. FAX: (816) 737-0571.
OWNER & PRESIDENT
Mary Shoemaker
V.P., SALES
Chuck Shoemaker

HALGO SPECIALTIES COMPANY
16760 Stagg Street, Suite 209, Van Nuys, CA 91406. (818) 786-4436, (818) 366-0744. FAX (818) 780-3486.
email: halgoone@aol.com
PRESIDENT
Norman Dean Goldstein

NOVELTY SCENIC STUDIOS
40 Sea Cliff Ave., Glen Cove, NY 11542. (718) 895-8668. FAX: (516) 674-2213.
VICE PRESIDENT
Leslie Kessler

S & K THEATRICAL DRAPERIES
7313 Varna Ave., North Hollywood, CA 91605-4009. (818) 503-0596. FAX: (818) 503-0599. www.sktheatrical.com

TRIANGLE SCENERY DRAPERY & LIGHTING
1215 Bates Ave., Los Angeles, CA 90029-2203. (323) 662-8129. FAX: (323) 662-8120. www.tridrape.com
OWNER & PRESIDENT
Terry Miller

DIGITAL SOUND SYSTEMS

DIGITAL TECHNOLOGY SYSTEMS, INC.
3707 Fifth Ave., San Diego, CA 92103. (619) 542-1966.
CONTACT
Ronald Vale

DIGITAL THEATER SYSTEMS
5171 Clareton Dr., Agoura Hills, CA 91301. (818) 706-3525. FAX: (818) 706-1868. www.dtsonline.com
email: cinemamarketing@dtsonline.com
GENERAL MANAGER, CINEMA
Andrea Nee

DOLBY LABORATORIES
100 Potrero Ave., San Francisco, CA 94103-4886. (415) 558-0200. FAX: (415) 863-1373. www.dolby.com
MANAGER
Robert S. Warren

MARQUEE TECHNICAL SERVICES
740 Fallowfield Dr., Loganville, GA 30052 (800) 339-1662
FAX: (770) 554-9844. www.marqueetech.com
email: marqueetch@amindspring.net
PRESIDENT
Scott Meader
VICE PRESIDENT
Robin Meader

SONY CINEMA PRODUCTS CORPORATION
10950 West Washington Blvd., Ste.200, Culver City, CA 90232. (310) 244-5777. FAX: (310) 244-2024. www.sdds.com
V.P., INDUSTRY RELATIONS
Dan Taylor
CONTACT
Sonia Ffrench

THX
(A Division of Lucasfilm) P.O. Box 10327, San Rafael, CA 94912. (415) 492-3900. FAX: (415) 492-3999. www.thx.com
CONTACT
Kurt Schwenk

EXHIBITOR SERVICES

DIGITAL SPARKS
1207 Bridgeway, Suite I, Sausalito, CA 94965. (415) 332-5555
FAX: (415) 332-5010. www.digitalsparx.com
email: jon@digitalsparx.com
CEO
Jon Stern

MAROEVICH, OSHEA & COGHLAN
(Insurance)
425 Market St., # 1030, San Francisco, CA 94105. (415) 957-0600. (800) 951-0600. FAX: (415) 957-0577.
www.maroevich.com
V.P., ENTERTAINMENT
Steve Elkins

MEDIA SALLES
(European exhibition statistics)
Via Soperga 2, 20127 Milano, Italy. (39-2) 6698 4405. FAX: (392)669 1574. www.mediasalles.it
email: inforcinema@mediasalles.it
COORDINATOR OF PROMOTIONAL EVENTS
R. Gioffre
SECRETARY GENERAL
Elisabetta Brunella

MOVIEAD CORP.
(Distributor of advertising and concession print materials)
3500 N. Andrews Ave. Extension., Pompano Beach, FL 33064. (800) 329-4989. FAX: (954) 784-0700. www.Movieq.com
email: info@movieq.com
PRESIDENT
Emil Noah

NATIONAL CINEMA NETWORK, INC.
1300 East 104th St., #100, Kansas City, MO 64131. (800) SCREEN-1. FAX: (816) 942-8418. www.NCNinc.com
PRESIDENT
Chuck Battey
SENIOR V.P., SALES
Janice Meyers

TECHNICOLOR ENTERTAINMENT
(Distribution of promotional materials)
40 Rockwood Pl., Englewood, NJ 07631. (201) 871-7900. FAX: (201) 871-7914.
PRESIDENT
Peter Koplik
TREASURER
Ronald Seitenback
BRANCHES
National Screen Service, 3655 Lenawee Ave., Los Angeles, CA 90016. (310) 836-1505. FAX: (310) 836-9878.
V. P., FILM DISTRIBUTION
Mitchell Wilen
National Screen Service, 1800 Baltimore Ave., Kansas City, MO 64108. (816) 842-5893. FAX: (816) 842-4553.
MANAGER
Eric Allen

REYNOLDS AND REYNOLDS
(Insurance)
The Plaza, Suite 200, 300 Walnut St., Des Moines, IA 50309. (800) 767-1724. FAX: (515) 243-6664.
email: info@reynolds-reynolds.com
MANAGER, THEATER DEPT.
Sandra Bell

THEATRE SERVICE NETWORK
(Consultants)
P. O. Box 190, Yorkville, IL 60560. (630) 553-0588. FAX: (630) 553-0594.

WILLIAM TUFT CORP.
(Insurance)
P. O. Box 10167, Peoria, IL 61612-0167. (309) 674-2673, (309) 691-6356. FAX: (309) 691-8340.

MARQUEES, SIGNS AND DISPLAYS

ACE AUDIO VISUAL
33-49 55th St., Woodside, NY 11377. (800) 468-7667. FAX: (718) 899-1995.

ADAPTIVE MICRO SYSTEMS
7840 N. 86th St., Milwaukee, WI 53224. (414) 357-2020. FAX: (414) 357-2029. www.adaptivedisplays.com
SALES MANAGER
Bill Kern

AXIS ANIMATED GRAPHIC SYSTEMS LLSC
2313 N. Valley Street, Burbank CA 91505. (818) 557-7523
FAX: (818) 557-0160. email: rmclellan1@earthlink.net
CONTACT
Robert McLelland

BASS INDUSTRIES
380 N.E. 67th St., Miami, FL 33138-6024. (305) 751-2716, (800) 346-8575. FAX: (305) 756-6165. www.bassind.com
email: sales@bassind.com
OWNER
Robert Baron
ASSISTANT TO OWNER
Terry Pratt

BUX-MONT SIGNS
221 Horsham Road, Horsham, PA 19044. (215) 675-1040.
FAX: (215) 675-4443. www.buxmontflagpoles.com
email: buxmont@bellatlantic.net
OWNER
William Sweigart

CHANGE AD-LETTER COMPANY
20954 Currier Road, Walnut, CA 91789. (909) 598-1996. FAX: (909) 598-2251.
OWNER
Beverly Greene

CINEMA CONCEPTS
2030 Powers Ferry Road #214, Atlanta, GA 30339. (770) 956-7460. FAX: (770) 956-8358. www.cinemaconcepts.com
email: info@cinemaconcepts.com
CEO
Stewart D. Harnell

CUSTOM COLOR CORP.
300 W. 19th Terrace, Kansas City, MO 64108. (816) 474-3200. FAX: (816) 842-1498. www.customcolor.com
CONTACT
Brian Bailey

DAKTRONICS, INC.
331 32nd Avenue, Brookings, SD 57006. (605) 697-4000. FAX: (605) 697-4700. www.daktronics.com
V.P., SALES
Frank Kurtenbach

DATA DISPLAY
5004 Veteran's Memorial Hwy., Holbrook, NY 11741. (631) 218-2130. FAX: (631) 218-2140. www.data-display.com
OWNER
Kevin Neville

DURA ENGRAVING CORP.
48-15 32nd Place, Long Island City, NY 11101. (718) 706-6400. FAX: (718) 786-2863. www.duracorp.com
VICE PRESIDENT
Art Forst

FAST-AD, INC.
220 S. Center Street, Santa Ana, CA. 92703. (714) 835-9353. FAX: (714) 835-4805.
PRESIDENT
Guy Barnes

GAMMA TECHNOLOGIES
6959 N.W. 82nd Ave., Miami, FL 33166. (305) 477-7567. FAX: (305) 477-7637. www.gamma-tech.com
PRESIDENT
Shai Dinari

GEMINI, INC.
103 Mensing Way, Cannon Falls, MN 55009. (800) 538-8377, (800) LETTERS. FAX: (507) 263-4887, (800) 421-1256. www.signletters.com email: sales@signletters. com
CONTACT
Sandra Reagan

ICON IDENTITY SOLUTIONS
5058 Rt. 13 North, at the PA Turnpike, Bristol, PA 19007. (215) 781-8500. FAX: (215) 781-0400.
EXECUTIVE V.P.
Steven Weiler

IMAGE NATIONAL
444 E. Amity Rd., Boise, ID, 83716. (208) 345-4020. FAX: (208) 336-9886. www.imagenational.com
GENERAL MANAGER
Doug Bender Douglas

ISLAND DISPLAY CORP.
95 K Hoffman Lane South, Central Islip, NY 11722. (516) 234-9628. FAX (516) 234-9463.
Christine Araujo

JUST IMAGINE EXHIBITS
(Exhibits & moving posters)
5145 Dumont Pl., Woodland Hills, CA 91364. (800) 688-3772, (818) 704-6250. FAX: (818) 704-6270.
PRESIDENT
Steve Cohen

KULLMAN INDUSTRIES
Woodbridge, NJ (732) 636-1813.
CONTACT
Joel Petrocy

MAINSTREET MENU SYSTEMS
1375 N. Barker Rd., Brookfield, WI 53045. (262) 782-6000. FAX: (262) 782-6515. www.mainstreetmenu.com
MARKETING MANAGER
Dawn Baumeister

MULTIMEDIA, INC.
(Electronic message displays)
3300 Monier Circle, Ste. 150, Rancho Cordova, CA 95742. (916) 852-4220. FAX: (916) 852-8325. www.multimedialed.com
SALES
George White

NRD, INC.
(Luminous exit signs)
2937 Alt Blvd., Grand Island, NY 14072. (716) 773-7634. FAX: (716) 773-7744. www.nrdinc.com
VICE PRESIDENT
Larry Keating

POBLOCKI AND SONS
922 S. 70th St., West Allis, WI 53214. (414) 453-4010. FAX: (414) 453-3070. www.poblocki.com
MANAGER, DISPLAYS & DIRECTORIES
Mike Musser

READERVISION, INC.
1231 Shields Rd., Kernersville, NC 27284. (336) 992-1338. FAX: (336) 992-1343. www.readervision.com
VICE PRESIDENT
Skip Boswell

SCHULT DESIGN AND DISPLAY
318 Cedar, Pleasant Hill, MO 64080. (800) 783-8998. FAX: (816) 540-4790. www.schult.com email: sales@schult.com
PRESIDENT
Robert Schult

SIGNATURE TECHNOLOGIES
31 Village Green, Burlington, VT 05401. (800) 545-7976. FAX: (802) 863-6663.
CONTACT
Mary Skelton

SIMPLY DONE SOFTWARE
7815 Beverly Blvd., Castle Rock, CO 80104. www.sdsof.com
email: info@sdsoft.com
PARTNERS
Michael Boltz
Randy Quade

SUNNYWELL DISPLAY SYSTEMS
730 Stimson Avenue, City of Industry, CA 91745. (626) 369-7359. FAX: (626) 369-5739. www.sunnywell.com
email: sunnywell@earthlink.net
HEAD OF SALES
Tina Finch

TRANS-LUX CORP.
(LED displays)
110 Richards Ave., Norwalk, CT 06854. (203) 853-4321. FAX: (203) 855-8636. www.trans-lux.com
email: sales@trans-lux.com
V.P., CORPORATE SALES
Gene Coyne

WAGNER ZIP CHANGE, INC.
3100 Hirsch St., Melrose Park, IL 60160. (800) 323-0744. FAX: (800) 243-4924. www.wagnerzip.com
email: sales@wagnerzip.com
VICE PRESIDENT
Gary Delaquila

MISCELLANEOUS EQUIPMENT

ADVANCED THERMAL TECHNOLOGIES
(Desiccant dehumidification equipment)
2102 Riverfront Drive, #120, Little Rock, AR 72202. (501) 666-4288 FAX: (501) 666-6270. www.advancedthermal.com
email: advancedth@aol.com
V.P., MARKETING & NATIONAL ACCOUNTS
Jeffrey Bushey

ANDACTION CORP.
(Digital projection systems & displays)
5050 Amestoy Ave., Encino, CA 91316. (818) 645-2769. FAX: (818) 475-1688. www.andaction.com
CEO
Craig Winter

BRADLEY FIXTURES CORP.
(Bathroom fixtures)
W142 N9101 Fountain Blvd., Menomonee Falls, WI 53051. (262) 251-6000. FAX: (414) 251-0128.
www.bradleycorp.com
MARKETING
Jessica Drexler

CADDY CUPHOLDER
(Cup holders)
10501 Florida Ave. South, Minneapolis, MN 55438. (800) 845-0591, (952) 828-0030. FAX: (952) 829-0166.
www.mediatechsrc.com
MANAGING DIRECTOR
Peter Bergin

CAWLEY COMPANY
(Name badges)
1544 N. 8th St., Manitowoc, WI 54221. (800) 822-9539. FAX: (920) 682-5520. www.thecawleycompany.com
SALES REPRESENTATIVE
Debbie Schimmel

CINEMA PRODUCTS INTERNATIONAL
1015 Fifth Avenue No., Nashville, TN 37219. (800) 891-1031
FAX: (615) 248-2725. www.cinprod.com
email: sales@cinprod.com
OWNER
Ron Purtee
CONTROLLER
Elizabeth Langley

CINETRANSFORMER
(Mobile theaters & special promotions)
Sinaloa, #106, Colonia, Roma, Mexico, DF 06700, Mexico.
(525) 533-0730/0732. FAX: (525) 207-0124.
www.cinetransformer.com email: cinetran@avantel.net
CONTACT
Julio Fernandez

CREDIT CARD CENTER
(ATM Sales, Service, Processing)
4850 Rhawn St., Philadelphia, PA 19136. (215) 335-2773. FAX:
(215) 335-3002. www.ccc-atm.com
PRESIDENT
Andy Kallok

28A Baiting Place Rd., Farmingdale, NY 11735. (631) 391-9838. FAX: (631) 391-9836. email: dlsend@msn.com
ENTERTAINMENT INDUSTRY DIRECTOR
Len Sendroff

CREST-TALMADGE
(Janitorial supplies)
1590 Rollins Road, Burlingame, CA 94010. (650) 692-7378.
FAX: (650) 692-8059.
VICE PRESIDENT
Mark Talmadge

DURAFORM
(Waste containers)
1435 S. Santa Fe Avenue, Compton, CA 90221. (310) 761-1640, (800) 823-1121. FAX: (310) 761-1646.
www.duraformcpi.com email: duraform@earthlink.net
CUSTOMER SERVICES MANAGER
Betty Prosser

FANTASY ENTERTAINMENT
(Self-service photo kiosks)
8 Commercial St., Hudson, NH 03051. (603) 324-3240. FAX:
(603) 879-9203. www.fantasyent.com
email: mbouley@fantasyent.com
SALES
Mary Bouley

FIELD CONTAINER CO., LP
(Popcorn containers, theatre trays)
1501 Industrial Park Dr., Tuscaloosa, AL 35401. (205) 333-0333. FAX: (205) 333-9862.
V.P., SALES
Richard Burklew
REGIONAL SALES MANAGER
Dennis Maccagnone

GLASSFORM
(Fibreglass furnishings)
10639 Roselle St., Ste. A, San Diego, CA 92121. (800) 842-1121, (800) 995-8322. FAX (630) 761-8859.
www.Glassform.net email: Glassform@aol.com
SALES MANAGER
Cyndi Gardner

GOLDBERG BROTHERS, INC.
(Film shipping, booth & lobby equipment)
8000 E. 40th Ave., Denver, CO 80207, P. O. Box 17048,
Denver, CO 80217. (303) 321-1099. FAX: (303) 388-0749.
EXECUTIVE VICE PRESIDENT
Randall Urlik

HOLLYWOOD SOFTWARE, INC.
(Theatrical distribution software)
1604 N. Cahuenga Blvd., Ste. 115, Hollywood, CA 90028.
(323) 463-2144. FAX: (323) 463-1319.
CEO
Dave Gajda

KOALA CORP.
(Child care products)
11600 East 53rd Ave., Unit D, Denver, CO 80239-2312 (800)
666-0363. FAX: (303) 574-9000. www.koalabear.com
DISTRIBUTOR/SALES MANAGER
Angela Larry

LENNOX INDUSTRIES
(Air-conditioning)
2100 Lake Park Blvd., Richardson, TX 75080. (972) 497-5000.
FAX: (972) 497-5112. www.davelennox.com
V.P., NATIONAL MARKETING
Mike Belloli

MAH COMMUNICATION, INC.
(Single source payphones)
151 Kalmus Dr., Ste., J-7, Costa Mesa, CA 92626, (714) 966-9164. FAX: (714) 966-8538.
email: MAHCOMM@aol.com
ACCOUNTS MANAGERS
Kathy Perez
Susan Atwell

MANUTECH COMPANY
(Vacuum cleaners and leaf blowers)
P.O. Box. 51295, 2080 Sunset Drive, Pacific Grove, CA 93950.
(800) 676-2569. FAX: (831) 655-8967. www.manutech.com
OWNER
Angelo Villucci

MIRACLE RECREATION EQUIPMENT COMPANY
(Playground equipment)
P.O. Box 420, Monett, MO 65708-0420. (417) 235-6917. FAX:
(417) 235-6816. www.miraclerecreation.com

MODULAR HARDWARE
(Restroom & Toilet partition equipment)
P.O. Box 1889, Cortaro, AZ 85652, 6765 W. Ina Rd., Tucson,
AZ 85743. (800) 533-0042. FAX: (800) 533-7942.
www.modularhardware.com
email: sales@modularhardware.com
PRESIDENT
Robert Hotch

NAMCO CYBERTAINMENT
(Amusement equipment)
877 Supreme Dr., Bensenville, IL 60106. (630) 238-2200. FAX:
(630) 238-0560. www.funcrafters.com
email: aorban@funcrafters.com
V.P., BUSINESS DEVELOPMENT
George Smith
SENIOR ACCOUNT EXECUTIVE
Sam Dando

NATION GLASS & GATE SERVICES, INC.
(N.G.&G. FACILITY SERVICES)
(Emergency repairs & security renovations)
2416 S. Kearney St., Denver, CO 80222. (303) 757-3097. FAX:
(303) 691-2052. www.nationalglass.com
WESTERN REGIONAL SALES MANAGER
Kit Filbey

NOVAR CONTROLS CORP.
(Air-conditioning)
3333 Copley Rd., Copley, OH 44321. (330) 670-1010. FAX:
(330) 670-1029. www.novar.com email: emsdl@aol.com
VICE PRESIDENT
Dean I. Lindstrom

P&O NEDLLOYD
(Global transporation for fixtures & fittings)
1 Meadowlands Plaza, 12th Flr., East Rutherford, NJ 07073.
(201) 896-3231. FAX: (201) 896-3252. www.ponl.com
LOGISTICS MANAGER
Alex Tate

RAXXESS
(Studio furniture & equipment) 261 Buffalo Ave., Paterson, NJ
07503. (973) 523-5105. FAX: (973) 523-5106.
www.raxxess.com
PRESIDENT
Hyman Teller

SHEFFIELD SYSTEMS
(Payphones)
5601 West 120 St., Alsip, IL 60803. (708) 489-6800. FAX: (708)
489-0256.
V.P., SALES & MARKETING
James E. DeShazer

SMART PRODUCTS
(Children's safety products)
2330 Toomey Ave., Charlotte, NC 28203. (800) 343-3635. FAX:
(704) 377-4247. www.smartproducts.com
email: kwood55890@aol.com
NATIONAL SALES MANAGER
Jeff Mirgan
SALES REPRESENTATIVE
Kim Wood

SPECTRA CINE, INC.
(Light measuring equipment)
3607 W. Magnolia Blvd., Burbank, CA 91505. (818) 954-9222.
FAX (818) 954-0016.
www.spectracine.com
PRESIDENT
Nasir J. Zaidi

TRANE CO.
(Air-conditioning & chilling systems)
2550 Corporate Exchange Dr., #200, Columbus, OH 43231. (614) 899-5100.FAX: (614) 882-5456. www.tranenet.com
CONTACT
Ida Gallant

TVP–THEATRE & VIDEO PRODUCTS
(Cinema-studio equipment)
921 N.E. 79th St., Miami, FL 33138. (305) 754-9136. FAX: (305) 759-0863. www.tvpmiami.com
email: tvpmiami@tvpmiami.com
CONTACT
Richard Fowler

UNIVERSAL CINEMA SERVICES
(Theatre equipment & supplies)
1205 Corporate Dr., East, Arlington, TX 76006. (817) 633-2180. FAX: (817) 633-2190. email: custserv@goUCS.com
PRESIDENT
Jack Panzeca
EXECUTIVE VICE PRESIDENT
Stan Lamb

WING ENTERPRISES
(Ladder manufacturer)
1325 W. Industrial Circle, Springville, UT 84663. (800)453-1192. FAX: (801) 489-3685. www.ladders.com
NATIONAL SALES
Greg Boyer

WOLFE MERCHANDISING
(Customized p.o.p. displays)
6 Dohme Ave., Toronto, Ont., Canada M4B 1Y8. (416) 752-5599. FAX: (416) 752-8746. www.wolfe-intl.com
ACCOUNTS EXECUTIVE
Kurt Budnick

PROJECTION ROOM AND FILM HANDLING EQUIPMENT

AVASK
75 West Forest Ave., Englewood, NJ 07631. (201) 567-7300. FAX: (201) 569-6285.
PRESIDENT
Robert Bredin
VICE PRESIDENT
Les Kaplan

BALLANTYNE OF OMAHA/STRONG INTERNATIONAL
4350 McKinley St., Omaha, NE 68112. (402) 453-4444. FAX: (402) 453-7238. www.strong-cinema.com; www.ballantyne-omaha.com
PRESIDENT
John Wilmers
VICE PRESIDENT
Ray Boegner

BARTCO COMPANY
(Film cleaning)
924 N. Formosa, Hollywood, CA 90046. (323) 851-5411. FAX: (323) 851-5411.
PRESIDENT
LeRoy Bartels

BIG SKY INDUSTRIES
259 Center St., Phillipsburg, NJ 08865. (908) 454-6344. FAX: (908) 454-6373. www.bigskyindustries.net
OWNER & PRESIDENT
Mark Smith

CINEMA PRODUCTS INTL.
1015 5th Ave., North, Nashville, TN 37219. (800) 891-1031. FAX: (615) 248-2725. www.cinprod.com
email: ron@cinprod.com
PRESIDENT
Ron Purtee
SALES
Dave Bevilacque

CLOUD INDUSTRIES, INC.
P.O. Box 11717, Kansas City, MO 64138. (816) 737-0798. FAX: (816) 737-0571.
OWNER & PRESIDENT
Mary Shoemaker
V.P., SALES
Chuck Shoemaker

EVS BROADCAST EQUIPMENT
16 rue du Bois Sain Jean, Ougree Liege, Belgium B-4102. (324) 361-7000. FAX: (324) 361-7099.
CONTACT
Jean-Francois Nivart

GOLDBERG BROTHERS, INC.
8000 East 40th Ave., Denver, CO 80207. (303) 321-1099. FAX: (303) 388-0749. www.goldbergbrothers.uswestdex.com
email: goldbroinc@aol.com
EXECUTIVE VICE PRESIDENT
Randy Urlik
CUSTOMER SERVICE
Victoria Adams

HANOVIA
100 Chestnut St., Newark, NJ 07105-1192. (973) 589-4300. FAX: (973) 589-4430.
CONTACT
Dennis Priscandero

INTERNATIONAL CINEMA EQUIPMENT
100 N.E. 39th St., Miami, FL 33137-3632. (305) 573-7339. FAX: (305) 573-8101. www.iceco.com email: iceco@aol.com
PRESIDENT & OWNER
Steven Krams

KELMAR SYSTEMS, INC.
284 Broadway, Huntington Station, NY 11746-1497. (631) 421-1230. FAX: (631) 421-1274. www.kelmarsystems.com
PRESIDENT
Andrew Marglin

KINETRONICS
1778 Main St., Sarasota, FL 34236. (800) 624-3204, (941) 951-2432. FAX: (941) 955-5992. www.kinetronics.com
email: info@kinetronics.com
DIRECTOR OF SALES
Mark Bosworth

LAVEZZI PRECISION, INC.
999 Regency Dr., Glendale Heights, IL 60139-2281. (630) 582-1238. FAX: (630) 582-1238. www.lavezzi.com
email: lpi@lavezzi.com

LEN-D ENTERPRISES
6080 Okeechobee Blvd., West Palm Beach, FL 33417. (561) 682-3500. FAX: (561) 682-3777.
email: Lenenterprises@yahoo.com
PRESIDENT
Leondard Dickstein

LINSEY-FAIRBANKS, INC.
(Dimmers)
1670 Maywood Ave., Upland, CA 91784. (909) 982-0467. FAX: (909) 982-7036. email: jlolfi@aol.com
PRESIDENT
George Mackey

LUTRON ELECTRONICS
(Visual & environmental controls)
7200 Suter Rd., Coopersburg, PA 18036. (610) 282-3800. FAX: (610)282-6437. www.lutron.com
CONTACT
David Eisenhauer

MARBLE COMPANY, INC.
P.O. Box 160030, Nashville, TN 37212. (800) 759-5905. FAX: (615) 227-7008. www.marbleco.com email: randy@drivein.net
CONTACT
Randy Bauch

NATIONAL CINEMA SERVICE
P.O. Box 10799, New Orleans, LA 70181. (504) 734-0707. FAX: (504)734-0700. www.ncservice.com
PRESIDENT
Charles Achee

NEUMADE PRODUCTS CORP.
30-40 Pecks Lane, Newton, CT 06470. (203) 270-1100. FAX: (203) 270-7778. www.Neumade.com
VICE PRESIDENT
Walter Browski

NORCON COMMUNICATIONS, INC.
(Intercoms)
510 Burnside Avenue, Inwood, NY 11096. (516) 239-0300. FAX: (516) 239-8915.

ODYSSEY PRODUCTS, INC.
5845 Oakbrook Parkway, Suite G, Norcross, GA 30093. (770) 825-0243. FAX (770) 825-0245. www.odyssey-products.com
email: odysseyproducts@mindspring.com
PRESIDENT
Eve Miller

PLASTIC REEL CORP. OF AMERICA
40 Triangle Blvd., Carlstadt, NJ 070072. (800) 772-4748. FAX: (201) 933-9468.
VICE PRESIDENT
Pat Baccarella

SPECO
709 N. 6th St., Kansas City, KS 66101. (913) 321-3978. FAX: (913) 321-7439. email: info@speco-usa.com
PRESIDENT
George Higginbotham
VICE PRESIDENT
Jaren Higginbotham

SYSTEMS & PRODUCTS ENGINEERING COMPANY
709 N. 6th St., Kansas City, KS 66101-3031. (800) 633-5913. FAX: (913) 321-7439. email: info@speco-usa.com
PRESIDENT
George Higginbotham

TECHNOLOGY INTERNATIONAL
(CE Marking for European film markets)
P.O. Box 1246, Midlothian, VA 23113. (804) 897-5334. FAX: (804) 897-8585. www.techintl.com email: pcaran@techintl.com
CEO
Penny Caran
SALES DIRECTOR
Wayland Stephenson

TECO
1122 Industrial Drive, Mathews, NC 28105. (704) 847-4455. FAX: (704) 845-1709.
PRESIDENT
Bob Saunders

TOUCH CONTROLS, INC.
520 Industrial Way, Fallbrook, CA 92028. (760) 723-7900. FAX: (760) 723-7910. www.touchcontrol.com
DIRECTOR OF MARKETING
Dory Clemens

EDWARD H. WOLK, INC.
921 S. Jefferson St., Chicago, IL 60607. (312) 939-2720. FAX: (312) 939-0654. www.edwolk.com
email: sales@edwolk.com
GENERAL MANAGER
Norm Lauterbach

XETRON DIVISION/NEUMADE PRODUCTS
30-40 Pecks Lane, Newton, CT 06470. (203) 270-1100. FAX: (203) 270-7778. www.Neumade.com
VICE PRESIDENT
Walter Browski

PROJECTORS

BALLANTYNE OF OMAHA/STRONG INTERNATIONAL
4350 McKinley St., Omaha, NE 68112. (402) 453-4444. FAX: (402) 453-7238. www.strong-cinema.com;
www.ballantyne-omaha.com
PRESIDENT
John Wilmers
VICE PRESIDENT
Ray Boegner

BIG SKY INDUSTRIES
259 Center St., Phillipsburg, NJ 08865. (908) 454-6344. FAX: (908) 454-6373. www.bigskyindustries.net
OWNER & PRESIDENT
Mark Smith

CHINA FILM EQUIPMENT CORP.
189 Gentry Street, Pomona, CA 91767. (909) 392-2247. FAX: (909) 596-5289.
CONTROLLER
Patrick Tao

CHRISTIE, INC.
10550 Camden Dr., Cypress, CA 90630-4600. (714) 236-8610. FAX: (714) 229-3185. www.christieinc.com
SALES MANAGER
Scott Freidberg

CINEMA FILM SYSTEMS/RENTEC, INC.
779 N. Benson Ave., Upland, CA 91786-5836. (909) 931-9318. FAX: (909) 949-8815. www.cinemafilmsystems.com
email: CFS.Sales@cinemasystems.com
SALES & MARKETING
Greg Johnson

CINEMECCANICA U.S., INC.
8753 Lion Street, Rancho Cucamonga, CA 91730. (909) 481-5842. FAX (909) 481-5845. www.cinemec.com
V.P., OPERATIONS
Thomas H. Brenner

IWERKS ENTERTAINMENT
(Projection systems) 4520 W. Valerio St., Burbank, CA 91505. (818) 841-7766. FAX: (818) 841) 7847. www.iwerks.com
COO
Don Stults
CFO
Jeff Dahl
V.P., MARKETING
Christina Frueh

KINOTON
(A Division of Boston Light & Sound)
290 N. Beacon St., Boston, MA 02135. (617) 787-3131. FAX: (617) 787-4257. www.blsi.com/kinoton email: johng@blsi.com
SALES MANAGER
John Galucci

KNEISLEY ELECTRIC
P.O. Box 4692., Toledo, OH 43610. (419) 241-1219. FAX: (419) 241-9920.
PRESIDENT
Harry Ewell

MEDIA TECHNOLOGY SOURCE, INC.
10501 Florida Ave. S., Minneapolis, MN 55438. (952) 829-0161, (800) 227-3587. FAX: (952) 829-0166.
1802 Victory Blvd., Glendale, CA 91201.
818) 247-8667. FAX: (818) 247-3508.
www.mediatechsrc.com
EXECUTIVE V.P.
John P. Ayotte

MEGASYSTEMS
(Large-format film projectors and theatre design)
P.O. Box 4186, St. Augustine, FL 32085. (904) 829-5702. FAX: (904) 829-5707. www.megasystem.com
CONTACT
Carrie Horn

PANASONIC
(Projectors & broadcast equipment)
3330 Cahuenga Blvd., West, Los Angeles, CA 90068. (323) 437-3597. FAX: (323) 436-3660.
www.panasonic.com/broadcast
NATIONAL SALES MANAGER
Steve Abend

STRONG INTERNATIONAL
4350 McKinley St., Omaha, NE 68112. (402) 453-4444. FAX: (402) 453-7238. www.strong-cinema.com
www.ballantyne-omaha.com
PRESIDENT
John Wilmers
VICE PRESIDENT
Ray Boegner

WESTAR/INTERNATIONAL CINEMA EQUIPMENT CO.
100 North East 39th St., Miami, FL 33137. (305) 573-7339. FAX: (305) 573-8101. www.iceco.com email: iceco@aol.com
OWNER
Steven Krams

PROJECTOR LAMPS AND LENSES

ATLAS SPECIALTY LIGHTING
7304 N. Florida Ave., Tampa, FL 33606. (813) 238-6481. FAX: (813) 238-6656.
OWNER/MANAGER
Ralph Felten, Jr.

CINEMA XENON INTERNATIONAL
261 Valley Vista Dr., Camarillo, CA 93010. (888) 669-7271
FAX: (805) 389-9611. www.cinexenon.com
email: cinexenon@aol.com
PRESIDENT
Dick Stockton
VICE PRESIDENT
Dean DeNegri

GOLDBERG BROTHERS, INC.
8000 E. 40th Avenue, Denver, CO 80207. (303) 321-1099. FAX: (303) 388-0749. www.goldbergbrothers.com
email: goldborginc@aol.com
SALES MANAGER
Victoria Adams

BERN LEVY ASSOCIATES
(Lens cleaning) 21 Whippoorwill Lane, Palmyra, VA 22963. (804) 589-2171. FAX: (804) 589-2172.
Bern Levy

EG&G OPTO-ELECTRONICS
2175 Mission College Blvd., Santa Clara, CA 95054. (408) 565-0870. FAX: (408) 565-0703. www.egginc.com
email: earl@egginc.com
SALES MANAGER
Donna Reina
SALES DIRECTOR
Don Rushforth

L.P. ASSOCIATES, INC.
6650 Lexington Avenue, Hollywood, CA 90038. (323) 462-4714. FAX: (323) 462-7584.
CORPORATE OFFICER
Leonard Pincus

OSRAM SYLVANIA, INC.
100 Endicott St., Danvers MA 01923. (978) 777-1900. FAX: (978) 750-2630. www.sylvania.com
CONTACT
John Dawsey

SCHNEIDER OPTICS, INC.
285 Oser Ave., Hauppauge, NY 11788. (631) 761-5000. FAX: (631) 761-5090. www.schneideroptics.com
email: info@schneideroptics.com
SENIOR VICE PRESIDENT
Dwight Lindsey

SPECIAL OPTICS
315 Richard Mine Road, Wharton, NJ 07885.
(973) 366-7289. FAX: (973) 366-7407.
www.specopt.com email: specopt@aol.com
SALES ASSISTANT
Steven Morales

SUPERIOR QUARTZ PRODUCTS WEST
(Projection lamps)
P.O. Box 8826, Newport Beach, CA 92658. (714) 502-9999, (949) 720-1441. FAX: (949) 720-9455. www.sqpuv.com
PRESIDENT
Richard W. Wind
SALES MANAGER
Ernest E. Estrada

SUPERIOR QUARTZ PRODUCTS, INC.
Route 519, P.O. Box 618, Phillipsburg, NJ 08865-0833. (908) 454-1700. FAX: (908) 454-4154.
V.P., SALES
Dennis Losco, Jr.

VANTAGE LIGHTING, INC.
175 Paul Drive, San Rafael, CA 94903-2041. (800) 445-2677. (415) 507-0402. FAX: (415) 507-0502. URL: www.vanltg.com
PRESIDENT
Marc Allsman

SCREENS AND FRAMES

SOUTHWEST CINEMA PRODUCTS
(Screen cleaning)
P.O. Box 690356, Tulsa, OK 74169-0356. (918) 627-8111. FAX: (918) 627-9199.
CONTACT, TULSA
Dennis Hall

HARKNESS HALL
10 Harkness Blvd., Fredericksburg VA 22401. (540) 370-1590 FAX: (540) 370-1592. www.harknesshall.com
email: info@harknesshall.com
SALES MANAGERS
Joe Ward
Fred Fisher

MPO VIDEOTRONICS
1167 Lawrence Dr., Newbury Park, CA 91320. (805) 499-8513. FAX: (805) 499-8206. www.mpo-video.com
SALES
Rick Ayeroff

HURLEY SCREEN CORP.
(A Subsidiary of CEMCORP)
110 Industry Lane, P.O. Box 296, Forest Hill, MD 21050. (410) 838-0036. FAX: (410) 838-8079. www.hurleyscreen.com
email: info@hurleyscreen.com
V.P., OPERATIONS
Gorman W. White, Jr.

INTERNATIONAL CINEMA EQUIPMENT
100 N.E. 39th St., Miami, FL 33137-3632. (305) 573-7339. FAX: (305) 573-8101. www.iceco.com email: iceco@aol.com
PRESIDENT & OWNER
Steven Krams

KLIPSCH PROFESSIONAL
8900 Keystone Crossing, #1220, Indianapolis, IN 46240. (317) 581-3185. FAX: (317) 574-3870. www.klipsch.com
COMMUNICATIONS
Christine Pile

MARCEL DESROCHERS, INC.
(Screens, masking motors)
1440, Raoul Charrette, Joliette, Quebec, Canada J6E 8S7. (450) 755-3795. FAX: (450) 755-3122. www.mdicinema.com
PRESIDENT
Marcel Desrochers
SALES
Maryse Granger

NICK MULONE & SONS, INC.
100 Highland Ave., Cheswick, PA 15024. (724) 274-3221. FAX: (724) 274-4808.
OWNER
Nick Mulone

SELBY PRODUCTS, INC.
(Drive-in screens)
P.O. Box 267, Richfield, OH 44286-0267. (330) 659-6631, (800) 647-6224. FAX: (330) 659-4112.
CONTACT
Jerry Selby

STEWART FILMSCREEN CORP.
1161 Sepulveda Blvd., Torrance, CA 90502-2797. (310) 784-5300. FAX: (310) 326-6870. www.stewartfilm.com
VICE PRESIDENT
Don Stewart

TECHNIKOTE SCREEN CORP.
63 Seabring St., Brooklyn, NY 11231-1697. (718) 624-6429. FAX: (718) 624-0129.
CONTACT
Mitchell M. Schwam

SEATING AND RE-UPHOLSTERY

AMERICAN SEATING COMPANY
901 Broadway Ave. NW, Grand Rapids, MI 49504-4499. (616) 732-6895. FAX: (616) 732-6502. www.americanseating.com
email: contract@amseco.com
NATIONAL SALES MANAGER, AUDITORIUM PRODUCTS
Jim VanStee

ASSIGNED SEATING & MANUFACTURING GROUP, INC.
P.O. Box 3206, S. El Monte, CA 91715. (626) 454-4599. FAX: (626) 454-4590. email: seatman1@pacbell.net
PRESIDENT
Chuck Kaplan

CALIFORNIA SEATING & REPAIR COMPANY, INC.
12455 Branford Street, Suite 21, Arleta, CA 91331. (818) 890-7328. FAX: (805) 581-0226. email: deltatyme@aol.com
CONTACT
Tim McMahan

CAMATIC SEATING
2606 Julianne, Belton TX 76513. (254) 939-9392. FAX: (254) 939-9368. www.camatic.com email: garyknight@vvm.com
VICE PRESIDENT
Gary Knight

CY YOUNG INDUSTRIES, INC.
(Public seating) #711 E. 14th Ave., North Kansas City, MO 64116. (800) 729-2610, (816) 474-1776. FAX: (816) 474-1900. www.cyyoungind.com
PRESIDENT & CEO
Rick Young

FIGUERAS INTERNATIONAL SEATING
Crta. Parets a Bigues, km 77, Llica de Munt, Barcelona 08186 34-93-844-5050. FAX: 34-93-844-5064. www.figueras.com
email: tyfigueras@mail.cinet.com
CONTACT
Jordi Chaparro

GRAMMER CINEMA SEATING
Brakerstrasse 1, Bielefeld, Germany D-33729. (49 521) 977-2600. FAX: (49 521) 977-2650.
CONTACT
Agatha Florkemeier

HUSSEY SEATING COMPANY
38 Dyer St. Ext., N. Berwick, ME 03906. (207) 676-0234. FAX: (207) 676-2222. www.husseyseating.com
email: rbilodeau@husseyseating.com
NEW BUSINESS DEVELOPMENT MANAGER
Ron Bilodeau

IRWIN SEATING COMPANY
P.O. Box 2429, Grand Rapids, MI 49501-2429. (616) 574-7400. FAX: (616) 574-7411. www.irwinseating.com
email: dsales@irwin-seat.com
V.P., SALES
Bruce Cohen

LINO SONEGO & C.S.R.L.
Via Resel, 51, 31010 Pianzano di Godega, Italy. (0438) 430 026. FAX: (0438) 430 287. www.linosonego.it
email: info@linosonego.it
GENERAL DIRECTOR
Fabio Sonego
CUSTOMER SERVICE
Viviana Favero

MAG-TECH ENVIRONMENTAL INC.
(Seat cleaning)
710 Season Heather Ct., Ballwin, MO 63021. (636) 394-0414. FAX: (636) 394-0516.
VICE PRESIDENT
Don Waldman

MANKO SEATING CO.
(Seat covers)
50 W. 36th St., New York, NY 10018-8002. (212) 695-7470. FAX: (212) 563-0840.
CONTACT
Norman Manko

PREMIER SEATING COMPANY
4211 Shannon Drive, Baltimore, MD 21213. (888) 456-7328. FAX: (410) 488-9969. www.premierseating.com
email: info@premierseating.com
CONTACT
Paul Wenger

QUINETTE GALLAY
15 rue de la Nouvelle France, 33100 Montreuil, France. (331) 4988 6333. FAX: (331) 4858 2286.
email: quinettegallay@dial.oleane.com
PRESIDENT
Yves Caucheteux
EXPORT DEPARTMENT
Brigitte Berty

SEATING CONCEPTS, INC.
4901-600 Morena Blvd., San Diego, CA 92117. (858) 581-5715. FAX: (858) 581-5725. www.seatingconcepts.com
email: sales_seatingconcepts@compuserve.com
GENERAL MANAGER & VICE PRESIDENT
James Walsh

SERIES, USA
12570 SW 69th Ave., Ste. 103, Tigard, OR 97223. (503) 639-7480. FAX: (503) 639-7430. www.series.com.co
email: gstantonQ@series.com.co
PRESIDENT
Mauricio Olarte
V.P., SALES
Gaylord Stanton

UNIVERSAL SEATING/BASS INDUSTRIES
380 NE 67 St., Miami, FL 33138. (800) 346-8575. FAX: (305) 756-6165. URL: www.bassind.com email: sales@bassind.com
PRESIDENT
Robert M. Baron
VICE PRESIDENT
Paul Baron

VISTEON
26090 23 Mile Road, Chesterfield, MI 48051. (800) 762-6390. FAX: (941) 723-2669. www.visteon.com
NATIONAL SALES MANAGER
Thomas M. O'Hara

SECURITY SERVICES

ALCOPS INCORPORATED
6701 West 64th Street, Overland Park, KS 66202. (913) 362-0104. FAX: (913) 362-5859. www.alcops.com
OWNER
Mickey Gitlin

DALE SYSTEM, INC., THEATRE DIVISION
1101 Stewart Ave, Garden City, NY 11530-4808. (516) 794-2800. FAX: (516) 542-1063. www.dalesysteminc.com
email: dalesys@aol.com
PRESIDENT
Harvey Yaffe

DATA QUEST INVESTIGATIONS, LTD.
667 Boylston St., Ste. 200, Boston, MA 02116. (617) 437-0030. (800) 292-9797. FAX: (617) 437-0034.
www.dataquestonline.net email: rbubas@dataquestonline.net
PRESIDENT
Russ Bubas
VICE PRESIDENT
Tracey Bubas

WORLDWIDE SAFE & VAULT
1746 N.W. 82nd Ave., Miami, FL 33126. (305) 477-9266. FAX: (305) 477-9744. www.worldwidesafe.com
OWNER & PRESIDENT
Scott Hirsch

SOUND EQUIPMENT

BGW SYSTEMS
P.O. Box 5042, Hawthorne, CA 90251-5042. (310) 973-8090, (800) 468-AMPS. FAX: (310) 676-6713. www.bgw.com email: sales@bgw.com
PRESIDENT
Barbara Wachner
SALES MANAGER/AUDIO
Joe Demeo

COMPONENT ENGINEERING
4237 24th Ave., West, Seattle, WA 98119. (206) 284-9171. FAX: (206) 286-4462. www.componentengineering.com
PRESIDENT
Bill Purdy
OPERATIONS
Brian Long

EPRAD, INC.
6979 Wales Rd., Northwood, OH. (419) 666-3266. FAX: (419) 666-8109. www.eprad.com
OWNER & MANAGER
Ted Stechschulte
CONTACT
Ted Lewandowski

INTL. ELECTRICAL WIRE/CABLE
P.O. Box 958184 Hoffman Estates, IL 60195. (800) 323-0210, (630) 289-2210. FAX: (630) 860-0305.
email: iewcinc@earthlink.net
SALES MANAGER
Kevin McClure

LOWELL MANUFACTURING CO.
(Speakers, racks & cabinets)
100 Integram Dr., Pacific MO 63069. (636) 257-3400 FAX: (636) 257-6606. www.lowellmfg.com
PRESIDENT
John J. Lowell

LUCASFILM, LTD.
P.O. Box 10327, San Rafael, CA 94912. (415) 492-3900. FAX: (415) 492-3999. www.thx.com
GENERAL MANAGER
Monica Dashwood

MEDIA TECHNOLOGY SOURCE, INC.
10501 Florida Ave. S., Minneapolis, MN 55438. (612) 829-0161. (800) 227-3587. FAX: (612) 829-0166.
1802 Victory Blvd., Glendale, CA 91201. (818) 247-8667. FAX: (818) 247-3508. www.mediatechsrc.com
PRESIDENT
Phil Rafson
EXECUTIVE V.P.
John P. Ayotte

MONSTER CABLE
(Cabling)
50 Park Pl., Brisbane, CA 94005. (415) 840-2000. FAX: (415) 468-0311.
PRESIDENT
Noel Lee

PANASTEREO, INC.
(Premium sound products & panalogic devices)
5945 Peachtree Corners East, Norcross, GA 30071. (770) 449-3833. FAX: (770) 449-6728. www.panastereo.com
email: info@panastereo.com
PRESIDENT
Norman Schneider
V.P., SALES/OPERATIONS
Robin Klamforth

PROJECTED SOUND, INC.
(Drive-in sound equipment)
469 Avon Ave., Plainfield, IN 46168-1001. (317) 839-4111. FAX: (317) 839-2476.
CONTACT
Tom Hilligoss

QSC AUDIO
(Amplifier manufacturing)
1675 Macarthur Blvd., Costa Mesa, CA 92626. (714) 754-6175. FAX: (714) 754-6174. www.qscaudio.com
MARKETING MANAGER, CINEMA
Barry Ferrell
MARKETING SERVICES MANAGER
John Subbiondo

SMART DEVICES, INC.
(Sound components & systems)
5945 Peachtree Corners East, Norcross, GA 30071. (770) 449-6698. FAX: (770) 449-6728. www.smartdev.com
email: smart@america.net
CEO
Norman Schneider
OPERATIONS MANAGER
Robin Klamforth

SONICS ASSOCIATES
2111 Parkway Office Circle, Birmingham, AL 35244. (205) 733-0500. FAX: (205) 733-0569. www.sonics.com
DIRECTOR OF SALES
David Millard
CONTACT
Jennifer Alexander

STAGE ACCOMPANY USA
8917 Shore Court, Bay Ridge, NY 11209. (800) 955-7474. FAX: (800) 955-9564. www.StageAccompany.com
email: SA@StageAccompany.com
PRESIDENT
Marcel Vantuyn

THX
(A Division of Lucasfilm)
P.O. Box 10327, San Rafael, CA 94912. (415) 492-3900. FAX: (415) 492-3999. www.thx.com
DIRECTOR OF THX OPERATIONS
Kurt Schwenk

YAMAHA ELECTRONICS
P.o. Box 6660, Buena Park, CA 90622. (714) 522-9105. FAX: (714) 670-0108.
ADVERTISING SALES PROMOTIONAL MANAGER
Doan Hoff

SOUND REINFORCEMENT

ASHLY AUDIO, INC.
847 Holt Rd., Webster, NY 14580-9103. (716) 872-0010. (800) 828-6308. FAX: (716) 872-0739. www.ashley.com
MARKETING MANAGER
Jim Stachowski

BGW SYSTEMS, INC.
P.O. Box 5042, Hawthorne, CA 90251. (310) 973-8090. (800) 468-AMPS. FAX: (310) 676-6713. www.bgw.com
email: sales@bgw.com
PRESIDENT
Barbara Wachner

CREST AUDIO, INC.
100 Eisenhower Dr., Paramus, NJ 07652-1401. (201) 909-8700. FAX: (201) 909-8744.
CONTACT
John V. Lee

CROWN INTERNATIONAL
P.O. Box 1000, Elkhart, IN 46515. (219) 294-8200. FAX: (219) 294-8329. www.crownintl.com
CONTACT
Scott Robbins

HAFLER PROFESSIONAL
546 S. Rockford Drive, Tempe, AZ 85281. (888) 423-5371. FAX: (480) 894-1528. www.hafler.com
MANAGING DIRECTOR
Jerry Cave

HIGH PERFORMANCE STEREO
64 Bowen St., Newton, MA 02459-1820. (617) 244-1737. FAX: (617) 244-4390. www.hps4000.com
FOUNDER & PRESIDENT
John Allen

KAWASHO INTL.
44 Montgomery St., Ste. 1010, San Francisco, CA 94104. (415) 445-0203. FAX: (415) 391-7241.
SALES MANAGER
Michiyo Fontaine

PEAVEY ELECTRONICS
711A Street, Meridian, MS 39301. (601) 483-5376. FAX: (601) 486-1154. www.peavey.com
OWNER
Hartley D. Peavey

QSC AUDIO PRODUCTS
1675 Macarthur Blvd., Costa Mesa, CA 92626-1440. (714) 754-6175. FAX: (714) 754-6174. www.qscaudio.com
email: info@qscaudio.com
MARKETING MANAGER, CINEMA
Barry Ferrell

SMART THEATRE SYSTEMS
5945 Peachtree Corners E, Norcross, GA 30071-1337. (770) 449-6698, (800) 457-6278. FAX: (770) 449-6728.
www.smartdev.com email: smart@america.net
VICE PRESIDENT
Robin Klamforth

SOUNDCRAFT USA
1449 Donelson Pike, Nashville, TN 37217. (615) 360-0471. FAX: (615) 360-0273. www.soundcraft.com
DIRECTOR OF OPERATIONS
Ken DeBelius

ULTRA STEREO LABS
181 Bonetti Dr., San Luis Obispo, CA 93401-7310. (805) 549-0161. FAX: (805) 549-0163. www.uslinc.com
VICE PRESIDENT
Felicia Cashin

SPEAKERS

ALLEN PRODUCTS CO., INC.
1635 E. Burnett St., Signal Hill, CA 90806. (562) 424-1100. FAX: (562) 424-3520. www.allenproducts.com
email: info@allenproducts.com
PRESIDENT
Paul Allen
CUSTOMER SUPPORT
Mike Capelle

CERWIN-VEGA
555 E. Easy Street, Simi Valley, CA 93065. (805) 584-9332. FAX: (805) 583-0865. /www.cerwin-vega.com
MANAGER, PROFESSIONAL SALES
Rich Mandella

COMMUNITY LIGHT & SOUND, INC.
333 East Fifth Street, Chester, PA 19013. (610) 876-3400. FAX: (610) 874-0190. URL: www.loudspeakers.net

EASTERN ACOUSTIC WORKS
One Main Street, Whitinsville, MA 01588. (508) 234-6158. FAX: (508) 234-8251. www.eaw.com
email: mmayfield@eaw.com
CONTACT
Mark Mayfield

EAW, INC.
One Main Street, Whitinsville, MA 01588. (508) 234-6158. FAX (508) 234-8251. www.eaw.com email: mmayfield@eaw.com
DIRECTOR OF CINEMA PRODUCTS
Mark Mayfield

ELECTRO-VOICE
(Subsidiary of Telex Comm.)
600 Cecil St., Buchanan, MI 49107-1799. (616) 695-6831. FAX: (616) 695-1304. www.electrovoice.com
CONSULTANT
Jim Long

EVI AUDIO
(Subsidiary of Telex Comm.)
600 Cecil St., Buchanan, MI 49107. (616) 695-6831. FAX: (616) 695-1304. www.EVIAudio.com
email: monte.wise@telex.com
SALES & MARKETING MANAGER
Monte Wise

FRAZIER, INC.
3030 Kintan St., Dallas, TX 75226. (214) 741-7136. FAX: (214) 939-0328.
CONTACT
J. E. Mitchell

IRA TEC/PRO AUDIO
(Speaker &audio repair)
42 Armstrong Dr., Mustang, OK 73064. (405) 324-5311. FAX: (405) 376-3998. www.iratec@yahoo.com
OWNER
Ira Rastampour

JBL PROFESSIONAL
8400 Balboa Blvd., Northridge, CA 91329. (818) 894-8850, (818) 894-4351. FAX: (818) 830-7865. www.jblpro.com
email: cgoodsel@harman.com
PRESIDENT
Mark Terry

KLIPSCH LLC
P.O. Box 688, 137 County Road 278, Hope, AR 71801-0688. (870) 777-6751. FAX: (870) 777-6753. www.klipsch.com
PRESIDENT
Fred Klipsch

MILLER & KREISEL SOUND CORP.
10391 Jefferson Blvd., Culver City, CA 90232. (310) 204-2854 FAX: (310) 202-8782. www.mksound.com
email: cminto@mksound.com
MARKETING MANAGER
Lynn Shubert

MISCO/MINNEAPOLIS SPEAKER CO., INC.
3806 Grand Avenue South, Minneapolis, MN 55409-1287. (612) 825-1010. FAX: (612) 825-7010. www.miscospeakers.com
email: info@miscospeakers.com
GENERAL MANAGER
Dan Digre
SALES/PRODUCTION
Gail Boyum

PEAVEY ELECTRONICS
711A Street, Meridian, MS 39301. (601) 483-5376.
OWNER
Hartley D. Peavey

SERIES USA
2000 Island Blvd., #710, Aventura, FL 33160. (305) 705-9035. FAX: (305) 705-9035. www.series@seriescom.co
PRESIDENT
Mauricio Olarte

SOUND RELATED TECHNOLOGIES
(Cinema speaker systems)
2680 Production Dr., Ste. 101, Virginia Beach, VA 23454. (757) 463-4300. FAX: (757) 498-3231. www.hydrosonic.com
V.P., SALES & MARKETING
Sean C. Bowers

STAGE DESIGN

CALIFORNIA STAGE & LIGHTING
3211 MacArthur Blvd., Santa Ana, CA 92704-6001. (714) 966-1852. FAX: (714) 966-0104. www.csl4lights@aol.com
OWNER
Jimmy Ray Hutton

GROSH SCENIC RENTALS, INC
4114 Sunset Blvd., Hollywood, CA 90029. (323) 662-1134. FAX: (323) 664-7526. www.grosh.com
SALES MANAGER
Leona Bethel

LIBERTY THEATRICAL DECOR
22313 Meekland Av., Hayward, CA 94541. (510) 889-1951. FAX: (510) 889-1602. email: libertyrig@aol.com
OWNER
Don Nethercott

THEATRE CLEANING AND MAINTENANCE

A&B COMPANY
6536 Fulton Ave., Van Nuys, CA 91401. (818) 985-7768. FAX: (818) 763-7914.
CONTACT
Michael Fuss

AMPAC THEATRE CLEANING SERVICES
P.O. Box 421, Monterey, CA 93942. (831) 372-3728. FAX: (831) 373-3490.
CONTACT
Arnold Meltzer

BUBBA SCRUBBA GUM REMOVAL SVC
1050 Katella Ave., #G, Orange, CA 92867. (714) 633-5228. FAX: (714) 633-5799. www.bubbascrubba.com
CONTACT
Dennis Lira

CINCOM–THE MEGAPLEX CINEMA SPECIALISTS
P.O. Box 2533, Salem, NH 030079. (603) 893-4403. FAX: (603) 893-1667. www.cincom.net
PRESIDENT
Matthew W. Sinopoli
DIRECTOR OF OPERATIONS
Charles A. Hyatt

CLEAN NET USA
50 W. Big Beaver #130, Troy, MI 48084. (248) 680-6750. FAX: (248) 680-0880. www.cleannetusa@erols.com
email: ckrawczyk@aol.com
REGIONAL DIRECTOR
Carl Krawczyk

COLGATE-PALMOLIVE COMPANY
191 E. Hanover Ave., Morristown, NJ 07962. (973) 631-9000 FAX: (973) 292-6021. www.colpalipd.com
MARKETING MANAGER
Barbara E. Kiefel

JOHNSON KWICK BAG
5245 Goldenwood Dr., Inglewood, CA 90302. (310) 419-5885. FAX: (310) 419-5885. www.kwickbag.com
CEO
Jaimy Johnson

MAG-TECH ENVIRONMENTAL INC.
(Seats, screens, drapery & masking cleaning)
710 Season Heather Ct., Ballwin, MO 63021. (314) 394-0414. FAX: (314) 394-0506. www.goofydee5.com
OWNERS
Donald Waldman
Lee Waldman
Darlene Waldman

NATIONAL MAINTENANCE SUPPLY
99 Limestone Red., Ridgefield, CT 06877. (203) 438-1274. FAX: (203) 438-1274, (203) 438-1542. www.ncsco.com
V.P. & GENERAL SALES MANAGER
Walter Beatty

PREMIER CHEMICAL PRODUCTS
5408 N. 59th St., Ste. A, Tampa FL 33610. (813) 740-8611 FAX: (813) 740-8218. www.premierchemical.com
email: rfgreene@aol.com
PRESIDENT
Randall F. Greene

PRO STAR INDUSTRIES
1590-A North Harvey Mitchell Pkwy., Bryan, TX 77803. (800) 262-7104, (979) 779-9399. FAX: (979) 779-7616.
www.prostarindustries.com
CONTACT
Dory Howell

PROTOCOL
(Janitorial supplies and equipment) 1370 Mendota Heights Rd., Mendota Heights, MN 55120. (800) 227-5336. FAX: (651) 454-9542. www.air-serb.com
CONTACT
Jaime Karalis

RED ROSE SALES/MARKETING
(Janitorial supplies)
P.O. Box 9869, Las Vegas, NV 89193. (919) 269-6060. FAX: (919) 269-7739. email: redroseinc@aol.com
OFFICE MANAGER
Lisa Strickland

RMS SERVICE AND ELECTRONICS, INC.
45 W. 45th St., 3rd Flr., New York, NY 10019. (212) 586-4900. FAX: (212) 586-5069. www.rmsservice.com
CONTACT
Roger Getzoff

THEATRE SERVICES
610 Parkview Lane, Richardson, TX 75080. (972) 690-0615. FAX: (972) 699-7355. www.tsc-usa.com email: tsc@airmail.net
OWNER & PRESIDENT
David Stuck

THEATRE SPECIALTY COMPANY, INC.
P.O. Box 2126, Loveland, CO 80538. (970) 669-5407. FAX: (970) 669-1829.
CONTACT
Dave Sizemore

BOB WELLS THEATRE PAINTING
1823 Cordova Ave., Cincinnati, OH 45239-4963. (513) 522-9026.
CONTACT
Bob Wells

THEATRE EQUIPMENT DEALERS

AMERICAN CINEMA EQUIPMENT, INC.
(Motion picture equipment) 1927 N. Argyle St., Portland, OR 97217. (503) 285-7015. FAX: (503) 285-6765.
www.cinequip.com email: doug1@cinequip.com
PRESIDENT
Scott R. Hicks
NATIONAL SALES MANAGER
Doug Sabin

ASC THEATRE EQUIPMENT SALES
7027 Twin Hills, Dallas, TX 75231. (214) 265-9303. FAX: (214) 691-8949. email: royl@asccompanies.com
SALES
Roy Lisenbe

BIG SKY INDUSTRIES
259 Center St., Phillipsburg, NJ 08865. (908) 454-6344 FAX: (908) 454-6373.
OWNER & PRESIDENT
Mark Smith

BOSTON LIGHT AND SOUND
290 N. Beacon St., Boston MA 02135. (617) 787-3131. FAX: (617) 787-4257. www.blsi.com email: info@blsi.com
PROJECTION SALES MANAGER
Tony Lazzaro

CARDINAL SOUND & MOTION PICTURE SYSTEMS, INC.
10219 Southard Drive, Beltsville, MD 20705-2126. (301) 595-8811. FAX: (301) 595-5985.
email: nrockman@cardinalsound.com
OFFICE MANAGER
Catherine Rockman

CINEMA EQUIPMENT, INC.
12441 S.W. 130th St., Miami, FL 33186. (305) 232-8182. FAX: (305) 232-8172. www.cinemaequipment.com
PRESIDENT & OWNER
William Younger

F.F. & E. ENTERPRISES, INC.
7502 Greenville Avenue, Suite 400, Dallas, TX 75231. (214) 369-1034. FAX: (214) 369-1768. www.ffeenterprises.com
CONTACT
Randy Taylor

HARRAH'S THEATRE EQUIPMENT COMPANY
25613 Dollar St., Unit 1, Hayward, CA 94544-2535. (510) 881-4989. FAX: (510) 881-0448.
OWNER
Jerry Harrah

MEGASYSTEMS
(Large-format film products & services)
435 Devon Park Dr. (The 500 Bldg.), Wayne, PA 19087. (610) 225-7200. FAX: (610) 225-7258.
PRESIDENT
Hilary Grinker

THEATRE & VIDEO PRODUCTS
(Cinema equipment)
921 N.E. 79th St., Miami, FL 33138. (305) 754-9136. FAX: (305) 759-0863. www.tvpmiami.com
CONTACT
Richard Fowler

UNIVERSAL CINEMA SERVICES
1205 Corporate Dr., E., Arlington, TX 76006. (817) 633-2180. FAX: (817) 633-2190. www.goucs.com
CEO
Jack Panzeca

TICKETS AND TICKET STOCK

AMLON TICKET
254 Helicopter Circl,. Corona, CA 92880. (909) 278-8888. FAX: (909) 278-8891. email: amlon@pe.net
SALES
Jason Rogers

DILLINGHAM TICKET COMPANY
781 Ceres Ave., Los Angeles, CA 90021-1515. (213) 627-6916. FAX: (213) 623-2758.
SALES REPRESENTATIVE
Michael O'Keefe

ECI–WWW.TICKETING SYSTEMS
1153 Inspiration Ln., Escondido, CA 92025. (760) 480-1002. FAX: (760) 480-6830. www.ticketingsystems.com
email: brucehall@ticketingsystems.com
PRESIDENT
Bruce Hall
SALES MANAGER
Ronn Hall

GLOBE TICKET & LABEL CO.
300 Constance Dr., Warminster, PA 18974. (800) 523-5968. FAX: (215) 956-2490.
SALES MANAGER
Michael Nawn
SALES REPRESENTATIVE
Michael Quinn

PREMIER SOUTHERN TICKET COMPANY
(Thermal ticket stock)
7911 School Road, Cincinnati, OH 45249. (800) 331-2283. FAX: (513) 489-6867. www.premiersouthern.com
MARKETING MANAGER
Doug Smith

NATIONAL TICKET COMPANY
P.O. Box 547, Shamokin, PA 17872-0547. (570) 672-2900. FAX: (570) 672-2999. www.nationalticket.com
email: ticket@nationalticket.com
V.P., SALES
William A. Alter

PRACTICAL AUTOMATION
45 Woodmont Road, Milford, CT 06460. (203) 882-5640. FAX: (203) 882-5648. www.practicalautomation.com
email: pa@practicalautomation.com
CUSTOMER SERVICE MANAGER
Richard Banzaca

RADIANT SYSTEMS, INC
3925 Brookside Pkwy., Alpharetta, GA 30022. (770) 576-6000. FAX: (770) 754-7790. www.radiantsystems.com
email: cchapin@radiantsystems.com
DIRECTOR, GLOBAL SOLUTIONS
Craig Chapin

RDS DATA GROUP, INC.
101 Donly Drive South, Simcoe Ontario N3Y 4LS. (519) 428-2500. FAX: (519) 428-9441. www.rdsdata.com
email: info@rdsdata.com
V.P., MARKETING & SALES
Brad De Porter

TICKETING SYSTEMS.COM
1153 Inspiration Lane, Escondido, CA 92025. (760) 480-1002. FAX: (760) 480-6830. www.ticketingsystems.com
PRESIDENT
Bruce L. Hall

TICKET USA, LLC
(International software trading)
P.O. Box 2023, 102 Rose Lane, Darien, CT 06820. (203) 316-8391. FAX: (203) 316-8391. www.ticket-international.com
email: USA@ticket-international.com
CONTACT
Andreas Fuchs

TICKET PRO SYSTEMS
870 Mercury Drive S.E., Lawrenceville, GA 30045. (770) 682-5485. FAX: (770) 682-8397. www.ticketpro.org
email: ticketpro@bellsouth.net
CONTACT
John W. Shaw

V.A.S.T. INC.
11772 Sorrento Valley Rd., #212, San Diego, CA 92121. (858) 350-0510. FAX: (858) 350-0515. email: vastinc@pacbell.net
PRESIDENT
Jeffrey Mitchell

WELDON WILLIAMS & LICK, INC.
P.O. Box 168, Fort Smith, AR 72902-0168. (800) 242-4995. FAX: (501) 783-7050. www.wwlinc.com
CONTACTS
Steve Lensing
Greg. W. Slayline

UNIFORMS

FASHION SEAL UNIFORMS
P.O. Box 4002, Seminole, FL 33775. (727) 397-9611. FAX: (727) 391-5401. www.superioruniformgroup.com
NATIONAL ACCOUNTS
George Mulroy

FLAVOR WEAR
28425 S. Cole Grade Road, Valley Center, CA 92082. (800) 647-8372, (760) 749-1332. FAX: (760) 749-6164. www.flavorwear.com email: flavorwr@ix.netcom.com
CONTACT
Lawrence Schleif

HANOVER UNIFORM COMPANY
529 W. 29th St., Baltimore, MD 21211-2988. (800) 541-9709. FAX: (410) 235-6071. www.hanoveruniform.com
email: jmintz@hanoveruniform.com
CONTACT
John Mintz

PRIORITY MANUFACTURING, INC.
571 N.W. 29th Street, Miami, FL 33127. (305) 576-3000. FAX: (305) 576-2672. www.customuniforms.com

UNIFORMS TO YOU
5600 W. 73rd St., Chicago, IL 60638. (800) 864-3676. FAX: (800)864-3888. www.uty.com
V.P., NATIONAL SALES
Bill Riesner

Proctor
CONCESSION
STANDS AND
EQUIPMENT

CONCESSION SUPPLIERS

BEVERAGES

BOYD COFFEE COMPANY
19730 NE Sandy Blvd., Portland, OR, 97230. (503) 666-4545. FAX: (503) 669-2223. email: dougm@boyds.com, larryd@boyds.com, larryw@boyds.com www.buycoffee@boyds.com
SENIOR V. P., SALES & MARKETING
Doug McKay
SENIOR V.P., DIRECTOR SALES & DISTRIBUTION
Larry Downs
SENIOR V. P., NATIONAL ACCOUNTS
Larry Winkler

BRAD BARRY CO./CAFFE D'VITA CAPPUCCINO
1245 E. Watson Center Road, Building A, Carson, CA, 90745. (310) 522-8848. FAX: (310) 522-8844.
HEAD OF SALES
Frank Abbadessa

CHINA MIST TEA COMPANY
7435 E. Tierra Buena Lane, Scottsdale, AZ 85260. (800) 242-8807. FAX: (480) 443-8384. www.chinamist.com
HEAD OF SALES
Wally Hankins

THE COCA-COLA COMPANY
One Coca-Cola Plaza, Atlanta, GA 30313. (404) 676-7945. FAX: (404) 676-3605. email: kschulte@na.ko.com
THEATRE MARKETING ASSET MANAGER
Krista L. Schulte

DR. PEPPER/SEVEN-UP
5301 Legacy Dr., Plano, TX 75024. (972) 673-7781. FAX: (972) 673-7115. www.drpepper.com
www.seven-up.com
ASST. MANAGER OF CONVENTIONS
Jason Stripling

GEHL'S GUERNSEY FARMS, INC.
P. O. Box 1004, Germantown, WI 53022-8204. (414) 251-8570. FAX: (414) 251-9318. www.gehls.com
HEAD OF SALES
Tracey Propst

HUNT WESSON
1645 West Valencia Drive, Fullerton, CA 92833. (714) 578-6141. FAX: (714) 578-6505.
NATIONAL BEVERAGE DIRECTOR
Deborah Harris

ICEE USA
4701 Airport Dr., Ontario, CA 91761. (909) 390-4233. FAX: (909) 390-6804.
CONTACT
Suzie Swisher

JUICY WHIP, INC.
15845 Business Center Dr., Irwindale, CA, 91706. (626) 338-5339. FAX: (626) 814-8016.
PRESIDENT
Gus Stratton

NATIONAL ICEE CORP.
160 Novner Dr., Cincinnati, OH 45215. (513) 771-0630. FAX: (513) 771-3826. email: hstabler@icee.com
HEAD OF SALES
Harry Stabler

NATIVE PLANET FOODS
8900 E. Chaparral Road, Ste. 1000, Scottsdale, AZ 85250. (480) 367-5588. (480) 367-5516. FAX: (480) 367-5676.
CONTACT
Kathy Gallivun

PARROT ICE DRINK
13738 FM 529, Houston, TX 77041. (713) 896-8798. FAX: (713) 896-6676.
CONTACT
Mike Mitchell

PEPSI-COLA COMPANY
700 Andersonhill Road, Purchase, NY 10577. (914) 253-3017. FAX: (914) 249-8224. email: peter.leyh@pepsi.com
SENIOR NAT'L ACCT. SALES MANAGER ENT. ACCOUNTS
Peter Leyh

RIO SYRUP COMPANY, INC.
2311 Chestnut Street, St. Louis, MO 63103. (800) 325-7666. FAX: (314) 436-7707. E-mail: snocones@riosyrup. www.riosyrup.com
HEAD OF SALES
Phillip Tomber

V.C.I BEVERAGE CO.
6050 East Hanna Ave., Indianapolis, IN 46203. (888) 473-7446. FAX: (317) 791-0522.
CONTACT
Bob Labrador

VICTOR PRODUCTS CO.
P.O Drawer 7910, Richmond, VA 23223. (804) 643-9091. FAX: (804) 648-3601. www.victorproducts.com
HEAD OF SALES
Mitchell Zinder

CANDY & CONFECTIONS

ADAMS & BROOKS
1915 South Hoover St., P. O. Box 7303, Los Angeles, CA 90007. (213) 749-3226. FAX: (213) 746-7614.
PRESIDENT
John Brooks
CONTACT
Russell Case

AMERICAN INTERNATIONAL CONCESSION PRODUCTS CORP.
P. O. Box 379, Malverne, NY, 11565. (631) 420-1868. FAX: (631) 420-4042.
20 Dubon Court, Farmingdale, NY 11735. (800) 401-2427. www.plantsweets.com
PRESIDENT
Paul Sciortino
VICE PRESIDENT
Chris Sciortino

AMERICAN LICORICE COMPANY
2477 Liston Way, Union City, CA, 94587. (510) 487-5500. FAX: (510) 487-2517. email: mikemactn@aol.com
3701 W. 138 Place, Alsip, IL 60803. (708) 371-1414. FAX: (708) 371-0231.
www.redvines.com or www.sourpunch.com
HEAD OF SALES (CA)
Mike MacDonald
CONTACT (IL)
Will Miller

BANNER CANDY MFG. CORP.
700 Liberty Avenue, Brooklyn, NY, 11208. (718) 647-4747. FAX: (718) 647-7192.
11439 Dillon Way, Dublin, CA 94568. (925) 551-3311. FAX: (925) 551-7758.
PRESIDENT
Peter Stone
HEAD OF SALES
Libby Maurl

DIPPIN' DOTS
5101 Charter Oak Drive, Paducha, KY 42001. (270) 443-8994. FAX: (270) 443-8997.
CONTACT
Marilyn Phillips

EURO-AMERICAN BRANDS, INC.
15 Prospect Street, Paramus NJ 07652. (201) 368-2624. FAX: (201) 368-2512. www.euroamericanbrands.com
SALES
Linda Wette

FOLZ VENDING COMPANY
3401 Lawson Blvd., Oceanside, NY 11572. (516) 678-6005. FAX: (516) 678-3644.
CONTACT
Debbie Pugliese

THE FOREIGN CANDY COMPANY, INC.
451 Black Forest Road, Hull, IA 51239. (800) 831-8541. FAX: (800) 832-8541. www.megawarheads.com
SALES
Mike Fisher

GHIRARDELLI CHOCOLATE COMPANY
2 Oak Way, Berkeley Heights, NJ 07922. (908) 898-0023. FAX: (908) 0040. email: pmazzatta@ghirardellilindt.com
CONTACT
Patricia Mazzatta

HERMAN GOELITZ CANDY CO., INC.
2400 N. Watney Way, Fairfield, CA 94533. (707) 428-2800. FAX: (707) 423-4436. www.jellybelly.com
PRESIDENT
Russ Albers

GOLDENBERG CANDY CO.
7701 State Road, Philadelphia, PA 19136. (215) 335-4500. FAX: (215) 335-4510. www.goldenbergcandy.com
VICE PRESIDENT
Mindy Goldenberg

HARIBO OF AMERICA, INC.
1825 Woodlawn Drive, Ste. 204, Baltimore, MD 21207. (410) 265-8890. FAX: (410) 265-8898. www.haribo.com

HENRY HEIDE INC.
14 Terminal Rd., New Brunswick, NJ 08901. (732) 846-2400, (800) 233-2143. FAX: (732) 846-8109.

HERSHEY FOODS
14 East Choclate Avenue, Hershey, PA 17033. (717) 534-5494. FAX: (717) 534-8718. www.hersheys.com
CONTACT
Michelle Bentley

JUDSON-ATKINSON CANDY CO.
P. O. Box 200669, San Antonio, TX 78220-0669. (800) 962-3984. FAX: (210) 359-8392.
CONTACT
Ken Deecken

JUST BORN, INC.
1300 Stefko Blvd., Bethlehem, PA 18017-6620. (800) 445-5787, (610) 867-7568. FAX: (610) 867-5537.
www.justborn.com
V. P., SALES & MARKETING
Greg Barrett

MCLANE COMPANY
4747 McLane Pkwy., Temple, TX 76504. (254) 771-7500. FAX: (254) 771-7200.
CONTACT
Joe Digesare

M&M MARS
800 High Street, Hackettstown, NJ 07840. (908) 852-1000. FAX: (908) 850-2734. www.m-ms.com
CONTACT
Michelle Sellin

NESTLE USA
3450 Dulles Drive, Mira Loma, CA 91752. (800) 367-4449. FAX: (909) 361-0755. www.nestlenewbiz.com
CATEGORY SALES DEVELOPMENT MANAGER
Mike Mosher

NEW ENGLAND CONFECTIONARY
254 Massachusetts Avenue, Cambridge, MA 02139. (617) 876-4700. FAX: (617) 876-2356. www.necco.com
CONTACT
Charley Blood

PROMOTION IN MOTION CO., INC./FERRARA PAN CANDY
3 Reuten Drive, Closter, NJ 07624. (201) 784-5800. FAX: (201) 784-1010. email: jscudillo@promotioninmotion.com
www.promotioninmotion.com
HEAD OF SALES
Joesph Edwards

SARNOW CANDY
1001 South Oyster Bay Road, Bethpage, NY 11741. (516) 576-9800. FAX: (516) 576-0730. email: bsmith@sarnowcandy.com
www.sarnowcandy.com
V. P., OF SALES & OPERATIONS
Bill Smith

TOOTSIE ROLL INDUSTRIES, INC.
7401 South Cicero Ave., Chicago, IL 60629. (800) 877-7655. (773) 838-3400. FAX: (312) 838-3569.(773) 838-3569.
www.tootsie.com
SALES MANAGER
Robert Immen

W.L. MITCHELL & ASSOCIATES
1132 N. California St., Burbank, CA 91505. (818) 845-9793. FAX: (818) 954-0859.
CONTACT
Bill Mitchell

ICE CREAM & FROZEN DAIRY PRODUCTS

ALTA-DENA CERTIFIED DAIRY
17637 Valley Blvd., La Puente, CA 91744. (800) 535-1369. FAX: (626) 854-4287. www.altadenadairy.com
DIRECTOR OF MARKETING
Roland Dickens

DREYER'S GRAND ICE CREAM
5929 College Avenue, Oakland, CA 94618. (510) 652-8187. FAX: (510) 450-4592. www.dreyers.com
V. P., OF SALES
Tom Delaplane

GOOD HUMOR
909 Packerland Dr., Green Bay, WI 54303. (920) 499-5151. FAX: (920) 497-6582. www.goodhumor.com
V. P., OF SALES
Gary Doyle

HAAGEN-DAZS
17043 E. Green Drive, City of Industry, CA 91745. (626) 935-6017. FAX: (626) 965-3889. www.haagendazs.com
CONTACT
Randy Tripp

NESTLE ICE CREAM
30003 Bainbridge Rd., Solon, OH 44139. (440) 349-5757. FAX: (440) 498-7892.
CONTACTS
Kelly Atkins
Cindy Temple

MEAT PRODUCTS

BIL MAR FOODS, INC.
8300 96th Avenue, Zeeland, MI, 49464. (616) 875-7711. FAX: (616) 875-7591.
PRESIDENT
George Chivari

DUBUQUE FOODS, INC.
10550 New York Ave., Urbandale, IA 50322. (515) 334-0500. FAX: (515) 334-0600.
DISTRICT MANAGER
Steve Anderson

EISENBERG GOURMET BEEF FRANKS
3531 N. Elston Avenue, Chicago, IL 60618. (773) 588-2882. FAX: (773) 588-0810.
PRESIDENT
Marvin Eisenberg

HOFFY
2731 S. Soto St., Los Angeles, CA 90023. (323) 267-4600. FAX: (323) 261-7350.
V. P., OF SALES
Mike Polini

KRAFT FOODS/OSCAR MAYER
185 Technology Dr. West, Irvine, CA 92618. (949) 453-3621. FAX: (949) 453-3754.
CONTACT
Howard Gasser

SARA LEE/BALL PARK FRANKS
900 N. Branch Street, Chicago, IL 60622. (800) 654-3650. FAX: (312) 274-8241.
CONTACT
Mark Zittel

PAPER & PLASTIC GOODS

AFFILIATED PAPER COMPANIES, INC.
3195 Danville Blvd., #2, Alamo, CA 94507. (925) 855-1065. FAX: (925) 855-1490. URL: http://apclink.com
HEAD OF SALES
George Van Fossen

AMERICAN CAN CO.
Kesslerville Road, Easton, PA 18042. (215) 258-5371.

CREATIVE PACKAGING
334-D Pleasant St., Belmont, MA 24478. (617) 489-0303. FAX: (617) 489-6690.
CONTACT
Carl Erickson

DART CONTAINER CORPORATION
500 Hogsback Road, Mason, MI 48854. (800) 248-5960. FAX: (517) 676-3883.

DEAN PICKLE & SPECIALTY PRODUCTS
10255 W. Higgins Road, 5th Floor, Rosemont, IL 60018. (847) 375-8413. FAX: (847) 375-8404.
CONTACT
Mike Trabbold

FIELD CONTAINER CO. LP
1501 Industrial Park Drive, Tuscaloosa, AL 35401. (205) 333-0333. FAX: (205) 333-9862.
V. P., OF SALES
Richard Burklew

INTL. PAPER FOODSERVICE
3 Paragon Dr., Montvale, NJ 07645. (201) 391-1776. FAX: (201) 307-6125.
CONTACT
Luz Tarra

MAUI CUP
52585 Dequinder Road, Rochester, MI 48307. (248) 652-0557. FAX: (248) 652-0577.
CONTACT
Stephanie Adams

MCLANE COMPANY
4747 McLane Pkwy., Temple, TX 76504. (254) 771-7500. FAX: (254) 771-7200.
CONTACT
Joe Digesare

PACKAGING CONCEPTS
4971 Fyler Ave., St. Louis, MO 63139. (314) 481-1155. FAX: (314) 481-6567.
CONTACT
Anthony W. Irace

PACKAGING DYNAMICS BAGCRAFT DIVISION
3900 West 43rd Street, Chicago, IL, 60632. (773) 254-8000. FAX: (773) 254-8204. www.bagcraft.com
CONSUMER PRODUCT SPECIALIST
Colleen Wills
V. P., OF SALES
Stan Kerman

PACTIVE CORPORATION
14505 Proctor Ave, Industry, CA 91746. (626) 968-3801. FAX: (626) 961-9625.
SALES MANAGER
Cathy Donahoe

ROYAL PAPER CORP.
8940 Sorensen Avenue, Santa Fe Springs, CA 90670. (562) 903-9030. FAX: (562) 903-9229.
CONTACT
Marianne Abi Aad

SOLO CUP
1700 Old Deerfield Road, Highland Park, IL 60035. (847) 831-4800. FAX: (847) 831-0421. URL: www.solocup.com

SOUTHFIELD/J.G. CLARK COMPANY
1171 West Center St,. Marion, OH 43302. (800) 274-4882. (205) 333-0333. FAX: (740) 387-0012. (205) 333-9862.
CONTACT
Richard Burklew

SWEETHEART CUP CO.
10100 Reistertown Road, Owings Mills, MD 21117. (410) 363-1111. www.sweetheart.com
SALES & MARKETING V.P.
Mike Hastings

W.N.A./CUPS ILLUSTRATED, INC.
2155 W. Longhorn Drive, Lancaster, TX 75134. (800) 334-CUPS. FAX: (972) 224 3067.
www.cupsillustrated.com
SALES
Tina Daniel

WINCHESTER CARTON
P. O. Box 597, Eutaw, AL 35462. (205) 372-3337. FAX: (205) 372-9226.
PRESIDENT
Dan Williams

WINPAK TECHNOLOGIES INC.
85 Laird Drive, Toronto, Ontario, Canada M4G 3T8. (416) 421-1700. FAX: (416) 421-7957.
CONTACT
Louis de Bellefeuille

ZENITH SPECIALTY BAG COMPANY, INC.
17625 E. Railroad Street, Industry, CA 91748. (626) 912-2481. FAX: (626) 810-5136. www.zsb.com
VICE PRESIDENT OF SALES
Ron Anderson

POPCORN & POPPING OILS

AMERICAN POPCORN COMPANY
P. O. Box 178, Sioux City, IA, 51102. (712) 239-1232. FAX: (712) 239-1268. email: email@jollytime.com
www.jollytime.com
VICE PRESIDENT
Gary Smith

CARGILL
P. O. Box 5693, Minneapolis, MN 55440. (800) 323-6232. FAX: (612) 742-5503. www.cargrill.com
SALES MANAGER
Mark Overland

CENTRAL SOYA COMPANY, INC.
Packaged Oil Products, 1946 West Cook Road, Fort Wayne, IN 46818. (800) 788-6336. (219) 425-5100. FAX: (219) 425-5753.
www.centralsoya.com
SALES COORDINATOR
Jerre Conrad

ELLIS POPCORN COMPANY, INC.
101 East Poplar Street, Murray, KY 42071. (502) 753-5451. FAX: (502) 753-7002. www.ellispopcorn.com
SALES MANAGER
Dave Roberts

GREAT WESTERN PRODUCTS COMPANY
30290 US Highway 72, Hollywood, AL 35752. (800) 239-2143. FAX: (256) 574-2116.
PRESIDENT
Scott Martin

MCLANE COMPANY
4747 McLane Pkwy., Temple, TX 76504. (254) 771-7500. FAX: (254) 771-7200.
CONTACT
Joe Digesare

MORRISON FARMS POPCORN
RR 1, Box 50A, Clearwater, NE 68726. (402) 887-5335. FAX: (402) 887-4709. URL: http//www.nebraskapopcorn.com
PRESIDENT
Frank Morrison

ODELL'S
1325 Airmotive Way, Ste. 290, Reno, NV 89502. P.O. Box 11336, Reno, NV 89510-1336. (775) 323-8688. FAX: (775) 323-6532. www.popntop.com
SENIOR SALES MANAGER
Arthur Anderson

PREFFERRED POPCORN LLC
1132 9th Road, Chapman, NE 68827. (308) 986-2526. FAX: (308) 986-2626.
CONTACT
Norm Krug

RAMSEY POPCORN CO., INC.
5645 Clover Valley Road NW, Ramsey, IN 47166. (812) 347-2441. FAX: (812) 347 3336.
www.ramseypopcorn.com
PRESIDENT
Wilfred Sieg, Jr.

T. MILLER POPCORN CO.
PO Box 493, Trenton, MO 64683. (660) 359-6958. FAX: (660) 359-6037.
CONTACT
Joseph A. DiGirolamo

VENTURA FOODS
731 N. Railroad Ave., Opelousas, LA 70570. (800) 551-9080. FAX: (318) 942-3773. www.venturafoods.com
PRESIDENT
Jack Davis

VOGEL POPCORN CO.
2301 Washington Street, Hamburg, IA 51640. (800) 831-5818. FAX: (712) 382-1357.
2683 250th Street, Lake View, IA 51450. (712) 657-8561. FAX: (712) 657-2152.
www.vogelpopcorn.com
PRESIDENT
Roger Morey

WEAVER POPCORN COMPANY, INC.
130 E. Main Street, Van Buren, IN 46991. (800) 227-6159, (765) 934-2101. FAX: (765) 934-4052.
www.popweaver.com
PRESIDENT
Michael Weaver

W.L. MITCHELL & ASSOCIATES
1132 N. California St., Burbank, CA 91505. (818) 845-9793. FAX: (818) 954-0859.
CONTACT
Bill Mitchell

WORD POPCORN CO.
P. O. Box 466, Hwy 72 East, Hollywood, AL 35752. (800) 633-5091. FAX: (256) 574-2116.
PRESIDENT
Scott Martin

WRIGHT POPCORN & NUT CO.
150 Potrero Ave., San Francisco, CA 94103. (415) 861-0912. FAX: (415) 861-6745. www.wrightpopcorn.com

SNACK FOODS

CORN POPPERS
PO Box 620156, San Diego, CA 92162. (619) 231-2617. FAX: (619) 231-2985. www.cornpopers.com
EXEC. DIRECTOR OF SALES
Joe Alves

DEAN PICKLE & SPECIALTY PRODUCTS
10255 W. Higgins Road, 5th Floor, Rosemont, IL 60018. (847) 375-8413. FAX: (847) 375-8404.
NATIONAL ACCOUNTING SALES MANAGER
Mike Trabbold

FUNACHO
2165 Central Pkwy., Cincinnati, OH 45214. (800) 386-2246. FAX: (513) 352-5122.
CONTACT
Casey Basil

GOLD MEDAL PRODUCTS
10700 Medallion Drive, Cincinnati, OH 45241. (513) 769-7676. FAX: (513) 769-8500.
V. P., SALES
John Evans
DIRECTOR, THEATRE SALES
Roberta Wood

HOT COOKIES PRODUCTIONS
5924 SW 68th St., South Miami, FL 33143. (305) 667-5577. FAX: (305) 666-5335.
CONTACT
Larry Berrin

J & J SNACKS
5353 Downey Road, Vernon, CA 90058. (323) 581-0171. FAX: (323) 583-4732. www.jjsnacks.com
HEAD OF SALES
Michael Kulka

KIM & SCOTT'S GOURMET PRETZELS
2107 W. Carroll St., Chicago, IL 60612. (312) 243-9971. FAX: (312) 243-9972.
CONTACT
Gail Henderson

THE MINUTEMAID CO.
PO Box 2079, Houston, TX 77252. (713) 888-5000. FAX: (713) 888-5959. www.minutemaid.com
PRESIDENT
Don Knauss

NABISCO INC.
13244 Trail Hollow Dr., Houston, TX 77079. (713) 827-2286. FAX: (713) 827-8257.
CONTACT
Julie Gordon

THE NUTTY BAVARIAN
37 Skyline Drive, #2106, Lake Mary, FL 32746. (407) 444-6322. FAX: (407) 444-6335.
CONTACT
David Brent

RICOS
621 S. Flores, San Antonio, TX 78204. (210) 222-1415. email: nachos@ricos.com www.RICOS.com
PRESIDENT
Frank Liberto
VICE PRESIDENT
Tony Liberto

SNACKWORKS, INC.
8101 Orion Ave. #6, Van Nuys, CA 91406. (818) 780-8711. FAX: (818) 780-8817.
CONTACT
Bryan Freeman

SQUARE H BRANDS
2731 S. Soto Street, Los Angeles, CA 90023. (323) 267-4600. FAX: (323) 261-7350.
V. P., OF SALES
Mike Palini

TASTE OF NATURE
400 S. Beverly Dr. #214, Beverly Hills, CA 90212. (310) 396-4433. FAX: (310) 396-4432.
CONTACT
Scott Samet

WYANDOT, INC.
135 Wyandot Avenue, Marion, OH 43302. (740) 383-4031. FAX: (740) 382-5584. www.wyandotsnacks.com
PRESIDENT
Nick Chilton

Screening Rooms

All major studios, producers and distributors have screening rooms at their home offices in Hollywood and New York for their own use. Most also have screening room facilities at local distribution offices. Major circuits also lease theatres as screening rooms.

AMPAS: ACADEMY LITTLE THEATRE & SAMUEL GOLDWYN THEATRE
8949 Wilshire Blvd., 3rd Flr., Beverly Hills, CA 90211-1972. (310) 247-3000. FAX: (310) 859-9619.
THEATRE OPERATIONS
Michael Angel

THE CHARLES AIDIKOFF SCREENING ROOM
150 S. Rodeo Dr., #140, Beverly Hills, CA 90212. (310) 274-0866. FAX: (310) 550-1794.
CO-OWNERS
Charles Aidikoff
Gregg Aidikoff

CHARLES AJAR PROJECTOR CO., INC.
10510 Burbank Blvd., North Hollywood, CA 91601. (818) 980-1948. FAX: (818) 980-7273. email: upcajar@aol.com
OWNER
Tammy Ajar

AMERICAN FILM INSTITUTE
2021 N. Western Ave., Los Angeles, CA 90027. (323) 856-7600. FAX: (323) 467-4578. www.afionline.org
COORDINATOR OF COMMUNICATIONS
Eva Langsdorff

ASTRO FILM & VIDEO
61 W, Erie St., Chicago, IL 60610. (312) 280-5500. FAX: (312) 280-5510. www.astro-labs.com
PRODUCTION MANAGER
Jan Cooper

BIG TIME PICTURE COMPANY
12210-1/2 Nebraska Ave., Los Angeles, CA 90025. (310) 207-0921. FAX: (310) 826-0071.
OWNER
Susan Klos

BROADWAY SCREENING ROOM
1619 Broadway, 5th Flr., New York, NY 10019. (212) 307-0990. FAX: 212-307-5727.
MANAGER
Nina Wallace

CHICAGO FILMMAKERS
5243 N. Clark, 2nd Flr., Chicago, IL 60640. (773) 293-1447. FAX: (773) 293-0575. www.chicagofilmmakers.org
EXEC. DIRECTOR
Brenda Webb

THE CLIP JOINT FOR FILM
833-B N. Hollywood Way, Burbank, CA 91505. (818) 842-2525. FAX: (818) 842-2644.

CONSOLIDATED FILM INDUSTRIES
959 Seward St., Hollywood, CA 90038. (323) 960-7444. FAX: (323) 962-8746. www.cfi-hollywood.com
SALES
Mike Papadaki

DIRECTORS GUILD OF AMERICA
7920 W. Sunset Blvd., Los Angeles, CA 90046. (310) 289-2000. FAX: (310) 289-2029. www.dga.org
THEATRE OPERATIONS MANAGER
Jennifer Clark

DISNEY-MGM STUDIOS
PO Box 10200, Film-TV Dept, Bungalow 2, Lake Buena Vista, FL 32830-0200. (407) 560-5736. FAX: (407) 827-5168.

EXPLORATORIUM, MCBEAN THEATER
3601 Lyon St., San Francisco, CA 94123. (415) 563-7337. FAX: (415) 561-0307. www.exploratorium.com
DIRECTOR
Liz Kein

LEONARD H. GOLDENSON THEATRE
5230 Lankershim Blvd., N. Hollywood, CA 91601-3109. (818) 754-2825. FAX: (818) 761-8524.
THEATRE MANAGER
Vicky Campobasso

HARMONY GOLD PREVIEW HOUSE
7655 Sunset Blvd., Los Angeles, CA 90046. (323) 851-4900. FAX: (323) 851-5599.
THEATRE MANAGER
Bachmai Luu

HOLLYWOOD NEWSREEL SYNDICATE, INC.
1622 N. Gower St., Los Angeles, CA 90028. (323) 469-7307. FAX: (323) 469-8251.
PRESIDENT
Rick Spalla

LOS ANGELES COUNTY MUSEUM OF ART
5905 Wilshire Blvd., Los Angeles, CA 90036. (323) 857-6111. FAX: (323) 857-6125. www.lacma.org
email: ibirnie@lacma.org
DIRECTOR
Ian Bernie

LOS ANGELES THEATRE
615 S. Broadway, Los Angeles, CA 90014. (213) 629-2939. FAX: (213) 629-2999.

MAGNO SOUND SCREENING ROOM
729 Seventh Ave., New York, NY 10019. (212) 302-2505. FAX: (212) 819-1282. www.magnosoundandvideo.com
DIRECTOR
Sally Barajaas

NAVESYNC SOUND
306 W. 38th St., 5th Flr., New York, NY 10018. (212) 244-7177. FAX: (212) 244-5495.
RENTAL MANAGER
Mike McCann

OCEAN AVENUE SCREENING ROOM
1401 Ocean Ave., Ste. 301, Santa Monica, CA 90401. (310) 576-1831. FAX: (310) 319-9501.

OCCIDENTAL STUDIOS
201 N. Occidental Blvd., Los Angeles, CA 90026. (213) 384-3331. FAX: (213) 384-2684.www.occidentalstudios.com
FACILITIES MANAGER
Scott Eberlein

PACIFIC FILM ARCHIVE
2625 Durant Ave., Berkeley, CA 94720-2250. (510) 642-1412. FAX: (510) 642-4889.
THEATRE OPERATIONS MANAGER
Dennis Love

RALEIGH STUDIOS
5300 Melrose Ave., Hollywood, CA 90038. (323) 466-3111. FAX: (323) 871-5600.
DIRECTOR
Mike Donahue

TECHNICOLOR
321 W. 44 St., New York, NY 10036. (212) 582-7310. FAX: (212) 265-9089.
SECRETARY DAILIES DEPARTMENT
Arlyne Smith

TRIBECA FILM CENTER
375 Greenwich St., New York, NY 10013-2338. (212) 941-4000. FAX: (212) 941-3997. www.tribecafilm.com
DIRECTOR
Barry Manasch

VYNYL
1650 Schrader, Hollywood, CA 90028. (323) 465-7449. FAX: (323) 465-9644. www.vynyl.com
PRESIDENT
Marc Smith

WARNER HOLLYWOOD STUDIOS
1041 Formosa Ave., West Hollywood, CA 90046. (323) 850-2581. FAX: (323) 850-3535.
VICE PRESIDENT
Robert Wiender

WRITERS GUILD THEATER
135 S. Doheny Dr., Beverly Hills, CA 90211. (310) 550-1000, 205-2502. FAX: (323) 782-4808. www.wga.org
DIRECTOR
Phil Haggood

SAUL ZAENTZ CO. FILM CENTER
2600 Tenth St., Berkeley, CA 94710. (510) 549-2500. FAX: (510) 227-0466. email: shurtzs@aol.com
DIRECTOR
Steve Shurtz

PREVIEW & POLICY TRAILERS

HOWARD A. ANDERSON, CO.
5161 Lankershim Blvd., #120, North Hollywood, CA 91601. (818) 623-1111. FAX: (818) 623-7761.
PRESIDENT & CEO
Howard Anderson III

BLOOMFILM
P.O. Box 461802 (323) 850-5575. FAX: (323) 850-7304. email: bloomfilm@attglobal.net
PRESIDENT
Jon Bloom

CINEMA CONCEPTS THEATRE SERVICE COMPANY, INC.
2030 Powers Ferry Rd., Suite 214, Atlanta, GA 30339. (770) 956-7460, (800) SHOWADS. FAX: (770) 956-8358.
URL: http://www.cinemaconcepts.com
PRESIDENT
Stewart Harnell

THE CREATIVE WEST
937 N. Cole, Suite 3 & 4, Hollywood, CA 90038 (323) 464-8697. FAX: (323) 464-8699. email: creativewest@earthlink.net
PRESIDENT
Steve Shearsby

CRUSE & CO.
7000 Romaine St., Hollywood, CA 90038. (323) 851-8814. FAX: (323) 851-8788.

FILMACK STUDIOS
1327 S. Wabash Ave., Chicago, IL 60605-2574. (312) 427-3395. (800) FILMACK. FAX: (312) 427-4866.
OWNER
Robert Mack

GLASS/SCHOOR FILMS
706 N. Citrus Ave., Los Angeles, CA 90038-3402. (323) 525-1155. FAX: (323) 525-1150.
PRESIDENT
Edward Glass

HOLLYWOOD NEWSREEL SYNDICATE, INC.
1622 N. Gower St., Los Angeles, CA 90028. (323) 469-7307. FAX: (323) 469-8251.
PRESIDENT
Rick Spalla

INTERMISSION PRODUCTIONS
6179 Knoll Wood Road, Suite 306, Willowbrook, IL 60514. (630) 654-0200. FAX: (630) 887-0380. email: allswell@citizen-welles.com
PRESIDENT
Barbara Schueren

JKR PRODUCTIONS, INC.
12140 W. Olympic Blvd., Suite 21, Los Angeles, CA 90064. (310) 826-3666.
PRESIDENT
James Rukin

KALEIDOSCOPE FILMS, INC.
8447 Wilshire Blvd., Suite 300, Beverly Hills, CA 90211. (323) 866-7000. FAX: (323) 866-7001.

LOBBY PREVIEWS
1953 Lakeshore Dr., Muskegon, MI 49441. (800) 861-7675. FAX: (231) 722-3124. URL: http://www.pelicanproductions.com
PRESIDENT
Joe Edick

LUMENI PRODUCTIONS
1632 Flower St., Glendale, CA 91201-2357. (818) 956-2200. FAX: (818) 956-3298.
PRESIDENT
Tony Valdez

METROLIGHT STUDIOS
5724 West 3rd St., Suite 400, Los Angeles, CA 90036. (323) 932-0400. FAX: (323) 932-8440.
PRESIDENT
Jim Kristoff

NATIONAL SCREEN SERVICE GROUP INC.
3655 Lenawee Ave., Los Angeles, CA 90016. (310) 836-1505. FAX: (310) 836-9878.
PRESIDENT
Peter Koplik

40 Rockwood Pl., Englewood, NJ 07631. (201) 871-7900. FAX: (201) 871-7914.

PIKE PRODUCTIONS, INC.
11 Clarke Street, Box 300, Newport, RI 02840. (401) 846-8890. FAX (401) 847-0070.
OWNER
James A. Pike

QUARTERMOON PRODUCTIONS
12 Morand Lane, Wilton, CT 06897. (203) 227-7887. email: qmoongb@earthlink.net
CONTACT
Gary Balionis

BIG SCREEN IDEAS
5455 Wilshire Blvd., Suite 1902, Los Angeles, CA 90036. (323) 935-2200. FAX: (323) 935-2022.
PRESIDENT
Tony Silver

SMITHGROUP COMMUNICATIONS, INC.
267 SE 33rd Avenue, Portland, OR 97214. (503) 239-4215. FAX: (503) 239-1570.
email: smithgrp@smithgrp.com
PRESIDENT
Phil Bevans

SSI ADVANCED POST SERVICES
7155 Santa Monica Blvd., Los Angeles, CA 90046. (323) 874-9344. FAX: (323) 850-7189.
URL: http://www.ssi-post.com
CONTACT
Stuart Bartell

LEONARD SOUTH PRODUCTIONS
11108 Huston St., N. Hollywood, CA 91601. (818) 760-8383. FAX: (818) 760-8301.
PRESIDENT
Leonard South

HERBERT L. STROCK PRODUCTIONS
6311 Romaine St., Suite 7113, Los Angeles, CA 90038. (323) 461-1298. FAX: (323) 465-9317.
CONTACT
Herbert L. Strock

VIDE-U PRODUCTIONS
9976 Westwanda Dr., Beverly Hills, CA 90210. (310) 276-5509. FAX: (310) 276-1185. URL: http://www.acmetoys.com
PRESIDENT
Bradly Fridman

WEST GLEN COMMUNICATIONS
1430 Broadway, 9th floor, New York, NY 10018. (212) 921-2800. FAX: (212) 944-9055. email: info@westglen.com
URL: http://www.westglen.com
PRESIDENT
Stan Zeltlin

WILLMING REAMS ANIMATION
325 East Ramsey Rd., San Antonio, TX 78216. (210) 342-2141. FAX: (210) 342-1523. email: wranim8@aol.com.
URL: http://www.wranim8.com
PRESIDENT
Denise White

BUYING AND BOOKING SERVICES

ASHURST AGENCY
215 Huntcliff Court, Fayetteville, GA 30214. (770) 461-9851. FAX: (770) 719-1565.
OWNER
Annette Ashurst

CALIFORNIA BOOKING
Box 11, Agoura, CA 91376. (818) 991-8593. FAX: (818) 991-8898.
OWNER
Carol Combs

CINEMA BOOKING SVC. OF NEW ENGLAND
P.O. Box 920827, Needham, MA 02492. (781) 986-2122. email: stadav@aol.com
PRESIDENT
Stanton Davis

CINEMA SERVICE
10300 N. Central Expwy #172, Dallas, TX 75231 (214) 692-7555. FAX: (214) 692-7559. email: csc@flexcomp.com
PRESIDENT
Tim Patton

COMPLETE BOOKING SERVICE
1819 Sabrina Ct., Charlotte, NC 28210. (704) 643-1522. FAX: (704) 554-0570.
OWNER
Gary Vanderhorst

CONTINENTAL FILM SERVICE
17463 Meadowview Dr., Middletown, CA 95461. (707) 987-8266. FAX: (707) 987-8270.
OWNERS
Richard Gambogi
Jeanette Gambogi

CO-OPERATIVE THEATRES OF OHIO, INC.
6263 Mayfield Rd., Suite 214, Mayfield Heights, OH 44124. (440) 461-2700. FAX: (440) 461-6411.
PRESIDENT
John Knepp
BOOKER
Frances Volan

CREATIVE ENTERTAINMENT CONSULTANTS
1600 Broadway, Suite 307, New York, NY 10019. (212) 333-7770. FAX: (212) 333-7904.
PRESIDENT
Nick Guadagno

EDDY G. ERICKSON BOOKING SERVICE
3405 Jubilee Trail, Dallas, TX 75229. (214) 352-3821.
OWNER
Eddy G. Erickson

FILM SERVICE THEATRE GROUP
Ivy Place II, 4700 South 900 East, Suite 41-D, Salt Lake City, UT 84117-4938. (801) 281-9694. FAX: (801) 281-9764.
PRESIDENT
David Sharp

FLORIN-CREATIVE FILM SERVICES
125 North Main Street, Port Chester, NY 10573. (914) 937-1603. FAX: (914) 937-8496.
PRESIDENT
Steven Florin

GUYETT BOOKING SERVICE
P.O. Box 6346, Shawnee Mission, KS 66206. (913) 648-5189.
FILM BUYER & BOOKER
Harold P. Guyett

INDEPENDENT FILM SERVICES
8900 State Line Rd., Suite 405, Leawood, KS 66206. (913) 381-5555. FAX: (913) 381-5552. email: indepfilm@earthlink.net
OWNER
Bradford Bills

INDEPENDENT THEATRE BOOKING
4523 Park Road, #A-105, Charlotte, NC 28209. (704) 529-1200. FAX: (704) 529-1201. email: dmovie@mindspring.com
PRESIDENT & FILM BUYER
Steve Smith
MANAGER, OPERATIONS
Bryan Smith

JANE M. KLOTZ BOOKING
9801 Tribonian Drive, Fort Washington, MD 20744. (301) 567-1775. FAX: (301) 567-1775. email: GramJ40@aol.com
OWNER & BOOKER
Jane M. Klotz

LESSER THEATRE SERVICE
110 Greene Street, Suite 701, New York, NY 10012. (212) 925-4776. FAX: (212) 941-6719.
PRESIDENT
Ron Lesser
FILM BUYER
Rob Lawinski
OFFICE MANAGER
Sabrina Canalini

MJR THEATRE SERVICE, INC.
13691 West Eleven Mile Rd., Oak Park, MI 48237. (248) 548-8282. FAX: (248) 548-4706.
www.mjrtheatres.com
PRESIDENT
Michael R. Mihalich

MARCUS THEATRES CORPORATION
250 E. Wisconsin Avenue, Milwaukee, WI 53202. (414) 905-1500. FAX: (414) 272-0872.
PRESIDENT
Bruce Olson
EXECUTIVE VICE PRESIDENT/FILM BUYER
Michael Kominsky

MESCOP, INC.
P.O. Box 303, Sussex, WI 53089. (262) 251-6808. FAX: (262) 251-9033.
PRESIDENT & BUYER
James Florence
BOOKER
Patricia B. Florence

MORRIS PROJECTS, INC.
1551 Oak Street, Sarasota, FL 34236. (941) 364-8662. FAX: (941) 364-8478. email: sfsfilm@ij.net
URL: http://www.filmsoceity.org
MANAGING DIRECTOR
Dick Morris
VICE PRESIDENT
Kelly Sanders

MOTION PICTURE COUNSELING
301 Mt. Shasta Dr., San Rafael, CA 94903-1029. (415) 491-1234.
OWNER
Ronald Litvin

NORRIS BOOKING AGENCY
P.O. Box 350052, Jacksonville, FL 32235. (904) 641-0019. FAX: (904) 641-0019.
OWNER
Rex Norris

NORTHWEST DIVERSIFIED ENTERTAINMENT
348 West Olympic Place #101, Seattle, WA 98119. (206) 352-4004. FAX: (206) 352-4008.
PRESIDENT
Benjamin L. Hannah
FILM BUYERS
Victoria Hawker
Bruce Goodnow
John Teegarden

PHILBIN CINEMA SERVICE, INC.
4700 S. 900 E., Suite 9B, Holladay, UT 84117-4938. (801) 263-3725.
OWNER
Tom Philbin

R/C THEATRES BOOKING SERVICE
231 West Cherry Hill Ct., Box 1056, Reisterstown, MD 21136. (410) 526-4774. FAX: (410) 526-6871.
PRESIDENT & CEO
J. Wayne Anderson
PRESIDENT, FILM
Scott R. Cohen
V.P., FILM
Jan S. Anderson

ROXY MANAGEMENT COMPANY, INC.
2004 Main Street, Northampton, PA 18067-5514. (610) 262-7699. FAX: (610) 262-6459.
URL: http://www.roxytheatrenorthhampton.com
PRESIDENT
Richard C. Wolfe
VICE PRESIDENT
Lee J. Stein

THEATRE MANAGEMENT ASSOC.
53 Carlton Pl., Passaic, NJ 07055. (973) 471-3002. FAX: (973) 471-3004.
PRESIDENT
Rudy DeBlasio
VICE PRESIDENT
Rick Sullivan

THEATRE SERVICE NETWORK
P.O. Box 190, 211 S. Bridge St., Yorkville, IL 60560. (630) 553-0588. FAX: (630) 553-0594.
PRESIDENT
Buck Kolkmeyer
VICE PRESIDENT
Kara Walker
EXECUTIVE VICE PRESIDENT
Steve Felperin

TRIANGLE THEATRE SERVICE, INC.
1170 Broadway, New York, NY 10001. (212) 679-6400. FAX: (212) 679-6461.
OWNER
Richard Dollinger

TRI-STATE THEATRE SERVICE, INC.
Film Arts Building, 636 Northland Rd., Cincinnati, OH 45240-3221. (513) 851-5700. FAX: (513) 851-5708.
email: tristatetheatre@cs.com
PRESIDENT
Florence Groner
VICE PRESIDENT
Steve Zeiser

TURBYFILL BOOKING SERVICE
P.O. Box 16126, Jacksonville, FL 32245. (904) 725-7590.
OWNER
Beverly Turbyfill

TWIN STATES BOOKING SERVICE
3600 Johnny Cake Lane, Charlotte, NC 28226. (704) 554-5949. FAX: (704) 554-6519.
OWNERS
R.T. Belcher
Mark Belcher

UNITED THEATRE SERVICE
P.O. Box 1649, Bothell, WA 98041. (425) 488-0944. FAX: (425) 488-9318. email: happybooker@wa.freei.net
BOOKER
Dorothea Mayes

WILSON THEATRE SERVICE
22035 167th St., Big Lake, MN 55309-9637. (612) 263-3800. FAX: (612) 263-3805.
OWNER
Jim Wilson

Distributors in Key Cities

ATLANTA

BUENA VISTA PICTURES DISTRIBUTION, INC.
5950 Live Oak Pkwy., Ste. 175, Norcross, GA 30093. (770) 246-8930.

NEW LINE CINEMA DISTRIBUTION, INC.
4501 Circle 75 Parkway, Ste. A1270, Atlanta, GA 30339. (770) 952-0056. FAX: (770) 952-9152.

BOSTON

CINEMA BOOKING SERVICE OF NEW ENGLAND
39 Church St., Boston, MA 02116. FAX: (617) 426-2274.

CINEMA FILM CONSULTANTS INC.
1245 Hancock St. Ste. 11 Quincy, MA 02169. (617) 479-0138.

UNIVERSAL FILM EXCHANGES, INC.
95 Broadway., Boston, MA 02116. (617) 426-8760.

WARNER BROS. DISTRIBUTING CORP.
45 Braintree Hill, Office Park 301, Braintree, MA 02184. (781) 848-2550.

ZIPPORAH FILMS
1 Richdale Ave. #4, Cambridge, MA 02140. (617) 576-3603. FAX: (617) 864-8006. email: zfilms@world.std.com

CHICAGO

BEACON FILMS
1560 Sherman Ave., #100, Evanston, IL 60201. (800) 323-5448.

BUENA VISTA DISTRIBUTION CO. INC.
9700 W. Higgins Rd. Ste 550, Rosemont, IL 60018. (847) 696-0900.

DALLAS

BUENA VISTA DISTRIBUTION
10000 N. Central Expressway, #850, Dallas, TX 75231. (214) 363-9494.

NEW LINE CINEMA DISTRIBUTION, INC.
6060 N. Central Expwy., Ste. 602, Dallas, TX 75206. (214) 696-0755. FAX: (214) 360-9465.

PARAMOUNT FILM DISTRIBUTING CORP.
12222 Merit Dr., Ste. 1700, Dallas, TX 75251. (972) 387-4400.

SONY PICTURES RELEASING
12770 Merit Dr., Ste. 702, Dallas, TX 75251. (972) 770-4220.

TWENTIETH CENTURY FOX FILM CORP.
14755 Preston Rd., Ste. 420, Dallas, TX 75240. (972) 392-0101.

UNIVERSAL FILM EXCHANGE, INC.
7502 Greenville Ave., Ste 200, Dallas, TX 75231. (214) 360-0022.

WARNER BROS. DISTRIBUTING CORP.
8144 Walnut Hill Ln., Ste. 500, Dallas, TX 75231. (214) 691-6101.

LOS ANGELES

***BUDGET FILMS**
4427 Santa Monica Blvd., Los Angeles, CA 90029. (323) 660-0187.

BUENA VISTA PICTURES DISTRIBUTION CO. INC.
350 S. Buena Vista St., Burbank, CA 91521-1226. (818) 560-2300. FAX: (818) 563-4456. Non-theatrical: (818) 567-5058.

CROWN INTERNATIONAL PICTURES, INC.
8701 Wilshire Blvd., Beverly Hills, CA 90211. (310) 657-6700.

***DIRECT CINEMA**
P.O. Box 10003, Santa Monica, CA 90410. (310) 636-8200. FAX: (310) 636-8228. email: directcinema@ATTMAIL.com

***EM GEE FILM LIBRARY**
6924 Canby Ave., Ste. 103, Reseda, CA 91335. (818) 881-8110. FAX: (818) 981-5506. email: mglass@worldnet.att.net

NEW LINE FEATURES DISTRIBUTION, INC.
116 N. Robertson Blvd., Ste. 200, Los Angeles, CA 90048. (310) 854-5811. FAX: (310) 854-1824.

IND. ARTISTS/LEGACY RELEASING
8446 Melrose Place, Los Angeles, CA 90069 (323) 852-9778 FAX: (323) 852-1088

MGM DISTRIBUTION CO.
2500 Broadway St., Santa Monica, CA 90404. (310) 449-3350.

NEW LINE CINEMA DISTRIBUTION, INC.
16027 Ventura Blvd., Ste. 506, Encino, CA 91436. (818) 380-7300. FAX: (818) 995-6049.

PYRAMID MEDIA
P.O. Box 1048, Santa Monica, CA 90406-1048. (310) 828-7577.

TOHO COMPANY, LTD.
2029 Century Park E., Ste. 1150, Los Angeles, CA 90067. (310) 277-1081. FAX: (310) 277-6351.

TWENTIETH CENTURY FOX FILM CORP.
6320 Canoga Ave., #430, Woodland Hills, CA 91367. (818) 702-7282.

WARNER BROS. DISTRIBUTING CORP.
15821 Ventura Blvd., Ste. 525, Encino, CA 91436. (818) 784-7494.

MIAMI

CINEVISTA, INC.
2044 Prairie Ave., Miami Beach, FL 33139 (305) 532-3400. FAX: (305) 532-0047.

NEW YORK

BUENA VISTA DISTRIBUTION CO.
477 Madison Ave., New York, NY 10022. (212) 593-8900.

***CAROUSEL FILM, INC.**
250 5th Ave,. Ste 204, New York, NY 10001. (212) 683-1660.

***CINEMA GUILD**
130 Madison Ave., 2nd Flr., New York, NY 10016. (212) 685-6242. email: TheCinemaG@aol.com

***CORINTH FILMS**
34 Gansevoort St., New York, NY 10014. (212) 463-0305.

NEW LINE FEATURES DISTRIBUTION, INC.
888 7th Ave., 19th Flr., New York, NY 10106. (212) 649-4800.

***FIRST RUN/ICARUS**
153 Waverly Place, New York, NY 10014. (212) 243-0600.

INDEPENDENT FEATURE PROJECT
104 W. 29th St., 12th Flr., New York, NY 10001. (212) 465-8200. FAX: (212) 465-8525. www.ifp.org

KINO INTERNATIONAL
333 W. 39th St., Ste. 503, New York, NY 10018. (212) 629-6880. FAX: (212) 714-0871.

MGM DISTRIBUTION CO.
1350 Ave. of the Americas, New York, NY 10019. (212) 708-0300. FAX: (212) 245-1481.

MIRAMAX FILMS
375 Greenwich St., New York, NY 10013. (212) 941-3800.

***MUSEUM OF MODERN ART FILM LIBRARY**
11 W. 53rd St., New York, NY 10019. (212) 708-9433.

***NEW YORKER FILMS**
16 W. 61st St., 11th Flr., New York, NY 10023. (212) 247-6110.

SONY PICTURES RELEASING
550 Madison Ave., New York, NY 10022. (212) 833-8500.

TOHO INTERNATIONAL
1501 Broadway, Ste. 2005, New York, NY 10036. (212) 391-9058.

TWENTIETH CENTURY FOX FILM CORP.
1211 Ave. of the Americas, New York, NY 10036. FAX: (212) 556-2400.

ST. LOUIS

***SWANK MOTION PICTURES**
201 S. Jefferson Ave., St. Louis, MO 63103. (800) 876-5577. FAX: (314) 289-2192. www.swank.com.

SAN FRANCISCO

KIT PARKER FILMS
(also 16mm) 1801 Catalina St., Sand City, CA 93955. (831) 393-0303, (800) 538-5838. FAX: (831) 393-0304.

SEATTLE

NORTHWEST DIVERSIFIED ENTERTAINMENT
348 W. Olympic Pl., #101, Seattle, WA 98119. (206) 352-4004.

WASHINGTON, DC

KEY THEATRE ENTERPRISES
1325-1/2 Wisconsin Ave., NW, Washington, DC 20007. (202) 965-4401. FAX: (202) 965-4416.

EXHIBITOR ORGANIZATIONS

INTERNATIONAL THEATRE EQUIPMENT ASSOCIATION

244 W. 49th St., New York, NY 10019. (212) 246-6460. FAX: (212) 265-6428. www.ita.com
PRESIDENT
Terri Westhafer
VICE PRESIDENT
Dwight Lindsey
SECRETARY
Mark Mayfield
TREASURER
Jerry Van de Rydt
EXECUTIVE DIRECTOR
Robert H. Sunshine

LARGE FORMAT CINEMA ASSOCIATION

8436 Cikibuak Dr., Stockton, CA 95298-2319. (209) 477-2726. FAX: (209) 951-8113.
PHD ADMINISTRATOR
Wayne Narron

NATIONAL ASSOCIATION OF CONCESSIONAIRES

(Organized 1944.)
35 E. Wacker Dr., Ste. 1816, Chicago, IL 60601. (312) 236-3858. FAX: (312) 236-7809. www.naconline.org
EXECUTIVE DIRECTOR
Charles A. Winans
PRESIDENT
Skip Stefansen
PRESIDENT ELECT
Gary Horvath
CHAIRMAN OF THE BOARD
Norman Chesler
DIRECTOR, COMMUNICATIONS
Susan Cross
VICE PRESIDENTS
Bruce Proctor
Peter Leyh
Nancy Kjelman, CCM
TREASURER
R. Evan Gordon
DIRECTORS, DIVERSIFIED OPERATORS
Phil Noyes
Guy Procopio
Sis Greco
Randy Ziegler
DIRECTOR, THEATRE CONCESSION OPERATORS
Bruce Taffett
DIRECTOR, EQUIPMENT MANUFACTURERS
David Tomber, CCM
DIRECTOR, SUPPLIERS
Ralph Ferber
DIRECTOR, JOBBERS/DISTRIBUTORS
Libby Mauro
DIRECTORS-AT-LARGE
Maria Angles, Chris Bigelow, Phil Blavat, Robert Scribner, Mike Mosher, Krista Schulte, Robert Scribner, Carmen Torzon.
REGIONAL VICE PRESIDENTS
Jeff Dodge CCM, Larry Etter, John Evans, Jr., Dan Gray, Brian Hobbs, Ron KruegerII, Frank Liberto, Ron Naslund, Sheila Parisien CCM, Damian Piza Velazquez CCM, Robert Perkins, Bill Wells ACE.
LIFETIME HONORARY MEMBERS, BOARD OF DIRECTORS
Larry Blumenthal, Sydney Spiegel, Van Myers
COUNCIL OF PAST PRESIDENTS
Andrew S. Berwick, Jr., Shelley Feldman, Doug Larson, Julian Lefkowitz, Jack Leonard, Philip L. Lowe, Phillip M. Lowe, Edward S. Redstone, Vernon B. Ryles, Jr., Vince Pantuso, Bill Rector, David Scoco.

NATIONAL ASSOCIATION OF THEATRE OWNERS, INC.

4605 Lankershim Blvd., Ste. 340, N. Hollywood, CA 91602. (818) 506-1778. FAX: (818) 506-0269.
PRESIDENT
John Fithian
CHAIRMAN OF THE BOARD
Barry Lawson Loeks
CHAIRMAN, FINANCE COMMITTEE & TREASURER
Steve Marcus
SECRETARY
Ayron Pickerill
VICE PRESIDENT & EXECUTIVE DIRECTOR
Mary Ann Grasso
EXECUTIVE COMMITTEE
J. Wayne Anderson (Reisterstown, MD), Michael Campbell (Knoxville, TN), James Edwards, III (Newport Beach, CA), John Fithian (N. Hollywood, CA), Jerome Forman (Los Angeles, CA), Kurt Hall (Englewood, CO), Philip Harris, III (Oakland, CA), Barrie Lawson Loeks (Rye, NY), Steve Marcus (Milwaukee, WI), Lee Roy Mitchell (Plano, TX), Judson Parker (Boston, MA), Ayron Pickerill (Polson, MT), Shari Redstone (Dedham, MA), Travis Reid (New York, NY), Philip Singleton (Kansas City, MO), William Stembler (Atlanta, GA).
BOARD OF DIRECTORS
J. Wayne Anderson (Reisterstown, MD), Thomas Becker (South Norwalk, CT), Byron Berkley (Kilgore, TX), Joost Bert (Brusssels, Belgium), Myron N. Blank (Des Moines, IA), Matt Brandt (N. Hollywood, CA), Peter Brown (Kansas City, MO), H. Donald Busch (Philadelphia, PA), Bill Campbell (Sheridon, NY), Michael Campbell (Knoxville, TN), Hal Cleveland (Boston, MA), Irwin A. Cohen (Toronto, Canada), Irwin R. Cohen (Reisterstown, MD), Scott Cohen (Reisterstown, MD), Bruce Corwin (Los Angeles, CA), David Corwin (Los Angeles, CA), Daniel Crown (New York, NY), Milt Daly (South Norwalk, CT), Dennis Daniels (Reisterstown, MD), Dale Davison (Concord, CA), Rob Del Moro (Knoxville, TN), Greg Dunn (Knoxville, TN), James Edwards, III (Newport Beach, CA), Randi Emerman (Ft. Lauderdale, FL), John Fithian (N. Hollywood, CA), Jerome Forman (Los Angeles, CA), Richard Fox (Boca Raton, FL), William Freedman (Los Angeles, CA), A. Alan Friedberg (Boston, MA), Jack Fuller, Jr. (Columbia, SC), Darrell Gabel (Lander, WY), Robynn Gabel (Lander, Wyoming), Marvin J. Goldman (Bethseda, MD), Charles Goldwater (Chatham, NJ), Robert Goodrich (Grand Rapids, MI), Jerome Gordon (Hampton, VA), Malcolm Green (Boston, MA), Patrick Greene (Circleville, OH), Kurt Hall, (Englewood, CO), Larry Hanson (Northbrook, IL), Dan Harkins (Scottsdale, AZ), Philip Harris (Oakland, CA), Hamid Hashemi (Ft. Lauderdale, FL), Jan Herring (Bent Mountain, VA), Bryan Jeffries (Springfield, IL), Richard Herring (Bent Mountain, VA), Willis Johnson (Downers Grove, IL), Allen Karp (Toronto, Canada), Beth Kerasotes (Springfield, IL), George Kerasotes (Springfield, IL), Dan Klusmann (Bozeman, MT), Edgar Knudson (Dedham, MA), Ronald Krueger (St. Louis, MO), Ronald Krueger II (St. Louis, MO), George Lefont (Atlanta, GA), Chris LeRoy (Los Angeles, CA), Ron Leslie (Los Angeles, CA), Barrie Lawson Loeks (Rye, NY), Jim Loeks (Rye, NY), John Loeks Jr. (Grand Rapids, MI), Jeff Logan (Mitchell, SD), Jerome Magner (Dedham, MA), George Mann (Oakland, CA), Bess Joyner (Warsaw, IN), Steve Marcus (Milwaukee, WI), John McDonald (Kansas City, MO), William McMannis (Grand Rapids, MI), Ira Meiselman (Charlotte, NC), Lee Roy Mitchell (Plano, TX), James Murray (Dedham, MA), R.A. "Skeet" Noret (Lubbock, TX), Mike Norris (New York, NY), Bruce Olson (Milwaukee, WI), Mark O'Meara (Fairfax, VA), Millard Ochs (Burbank, CA), Richard Orear (Kansas City, MO), Judson Parker (Boston, MA), Nicki Pappas Perakos (Orange, CT), Sperie Perakos (New Britain, CT), Ayron Pickerill (Polson, MT), Howard Pickerill (Polson, MT), Neal Pinsker (Englewood, CO), Shari Redstone (New York, NY), Sumner Redstone (Dedham, MA), Travis Reid (New York, NY), Ron Reid (Knoxville, TN), Michael Rembusch (Franklin, IN), Joel Resnick (Plano, TX), Lawrence Ruisi (New York, NY), John Saag (Louisville, KY), Bruce Sanborn (Newport Beach. CA), Kenyon Shane (Grand Rapids, MI), Philip Singleton (Kansas City, MO), T. G. Soloman (New Orleans, LA), Arthur Stein, Jr. (Des Moines, IA), William Stembler (St. Simon Island, GA), Alan Stock (Plano, TX), H. Aubrey Stone, Jr. (Charlotte, NC), Herman Stone, Sr. (Charlotte, NC), Bruce Taffet (Englewood, CO), Bob Tankersley (Denver, CO), Rand Thornsley (Anchorage, AK), William Towey (Dedham, MA), Peter Walch (Switzerland), Tim Warner (Plano, TX), Richard Westerling (Knoxville, TN), Roy B. White (Naples, FL), Russell Wintner (Pepper Pike, OH), Tim Wood (Portland, OR).

ARIZONA THEATRE OWNERS ASSOCIATION

7111 N. 10th Ave., Phoenix, AZ 85201. (602) 331-3788.
PRESIDENT
Brian Deveny
CHAIRMAN
Zoe Lefferts

NATO OF CALIFORNIA/NEVADA

116 N. Robertson Blvd., Ste. 708, Los Angeles, CA 90048. (310) 652-1093. FAX: (310) 657-4758.
PRESIDENT
Milton Moritz
CHAIRMAN
Phil Harris

NATO OF COLORADO AND WYOMING
P.O. Box C, 36 E. Alger, Sheriddan, WY 82801. (307) 672-5797. FAX: (603) 388-1546
PRESIDENT
Bill Campbell
CHAIRMAN
Darrell Gabel (Wyoming)

CONNECTICUT ASSOCIATION OF THEATRE OWNERS
64 North Main St., South Norwalk, CT 06854. (203) 795-1060. FAX: (203) 795-1061.
PRESIDENT
Milt Daly
VICE PRESIDENT
Ted Maliglowka

NATO OF FLORIDA
P.O. Box 2076, DeLand, FL 32720. (904) 736-6830. FAX: (904) 738-2596.
PRESIDENT
Jon C. Wray, Sr.

NATO OF GEORGIA
2161 Merchants Way, Duluth, GA 30096. (770) 623-5852.
PRESIDENT
Jeff Molbey

NATO OF IDAHO
P.O. Box 338, Parma, ID 83660. (208) 722-5446.
PRESIDENT
Al Wagner

NATO OF ILLINOIS
603 Rogers St., Downers Grove, IL 60515. (630) 968-1600 ext. 119. FAX: (630) 968-1626.
PRESIDENT
Willis Johnson

THEATRE OWNERS OF INDIANA
6919 E. 10th Street, Ste. B-5, Indianapolis, IN 46219-4811. (317) 357-3660. FAX: (317) 357-3379.
CORP. SECRETARY & GENERAL MANAGER
Ann L. Craft

UNITED MOTION PICTURE ASSOCIATION OF KANSAS & MISSOURI
8900 State Line Rd., Ste. 405, Leawood, KS 66206. (913) 381-5555. FAX: (913) 381-5552.
EXECUTIVE SECRETARY
Brad Bills

NATO OF MICHIGAN
121 W. Allegan, Lansing, MI 48933. (517) 482-9806.
PRESIDENT
Bob Schwick

MID-ATLANTIC NATO
(Maryland, Virginia, Washington, D.C.)
P.O. Box 1830, Hampton, VA 23669-0830. (757) 722-5275. FAX: (757) 722-5276.
EXECUTIVE DIRECTOR
Jerome Gordon
CHAIRMAN
William J. Headley (Ballou Park Theater)
PRESIDENT (Maryland)
Peter J. Carney (Bethesda Theater Cafe)
PRESIDENT (Virginia)
William J. Headley (Ballou Park Theater)
PRESIDENT (District of Columbia)
Ted Pedas (Circle Management Co.)

MID-STATES NATO
(Kentucky, Ohio, Tennessee, West Virginia,)
3982 Powell Rd., Powell, OH 43065. (740) 881-5541. FAX: (740) 881-5390.
EXECUTIVE DIRECTOR
Belinda Judson

MONTANA ASSOCIATION OF THEATRE OWNERS
P.O. Box 868, Shelby, MT 59474. (406) 434-2181.
PRESIDENT
Larry Flesch

THEATRE OWNERS OF NEW ENGLAND
One Exeter Plaza, 6th Flr., Boston, MA 02116-2836. (617) 424-8663. FAX: (617) 262-0707.
EXECUTIVE DIRECTOR
Carl Goldman

NATO OF NEW JERSEY
250 E. Broad St., Westfield, NJ 07090. (908) 232-7100. FAX: (908) 232-7340.
PRESIDENT
Jesse Sayegh

NATO OF NEW YORK STATE
244 West 49th St., Ste. 200, New York, NY 10019. (212) 246-6460. FAX: (212) 265-6248.
EXECUTIVE DIRECTOR
Robert H. Sunshine

NATO OF NORTH & SOUTH CAROLINA
4523 Park Rd., Ste. A105, Charlotte, NC 28209. (704) 529-1200.
PRESIDENT
George Royster
VICE PRESIDENT
Steve Smith

NATO OF PENNSYLVANIA
128 Chestnut Street, Ste. 303, Philadelphia, PA 19106. (215) 238-0633. FAX: (215) 238-0683.
PRESIDENT & EXECUTIVE DIRECTOR
H. Donald Busch

SOUTH CENTRAL STATES NATO
(Arkansas, Louisiana, Oklahoma, Texas)
c/o Loews Theatre, 800 Lincoln, TX 76011. (817) 228-1690.
P.O. Box 200815, Arlington, TX 76006-0815.
EXECUTIVE DIRECTOR
Rein Rabakukk
PRESIDENT (Louisiana)
Nels Offerdahl

NATO OF WISCONSIN & UPPER MICHIGAN
P.O. Box 146, Sussex, WI 53089. (262) 532-0017.
PRESIDENT
Paul J. Rogers

MOTION PICTURE EXHIBITORS OF WASHINGTON & ALASKA & OREGON
12040 - 98 Ave. N.E., Ste. 101, Kirkland, WA 98034. (206) 823-9456. FAX: (206) 823-2022.
PRESIDENT
Bruce Humphrey
EXECUTIVE DIRECTOR
Bruce Gardiner

Professional and Government Organizations

Motion Picture Organizations 908

Guilds and Unions 915

State and City Film Commissions 921

Federal Government Offices and Film and Media Services 929

The Press 931

MOTION PICTURE ORGANIZATIONS

ACADEMY OF MOTION PICTURE ARTS AND SCIENCES
(Organized June, 1927. Membership: approx. 6,000.)
8949 Wilshire Blvd., Beverly Hills, CA 90211. (310) 247-3000.
Library: 333 S. La Cienega Blvd., Beverly Hills, CA 90211.
(310) 247-3020.
PRESIDENT
Robert Rehme
FIRST V.P.
Alan Bengman
VICE PRESIDENTS
Sid Ganis
Kathy Bates
SECRETARY
Donald C. Rogans
EXECUTIVE DIRECTOR
Bruce Davis
LEGAL COUNSEL
John B. Quinn
BOARD OF GOVERNORS
Dede Allen, John Bailey, Kathy Bates, Ed Begley, Jr., Alan Bergman, Charles Berstein, Jon N. Bloom, Richard Edlund, Jonathan Erland, June Foray, John Frankenheimer, Sid Ganis, Samuel Goldwyn, Jr., Douglas Greenfield, Conrad L. Hall, Don Hall, Arthur Hamilton, Cheryl Boone Isaacs, Ray Kanin, Hal Kanter, Marvin Levy, William C. Littlejohn, Carol Littleton, Michael Mann.

ALLIANCE OF MOTION PICTURE AND TELEVISION PRODUCERS
(Membership: Major studios, independent production companies and film processing laboratories.)
15503 Ventura Blvd., Encino, CA 91436-3140. (818) 995-3600. FAX: (818) 382-1798. www.mpaa.org
PRESIDENT
J. Nicholas Counter III
S.V.P., LEGAL & BUSINESS AFFAIRS
Carol A. Lombardini
V.P., LEGAL AFFAIRS
Helayne Antler

AMERICAN CINEMATHEQUE
(Organized 1984. Celebrates the moving picture in all its forms through public film and video exhibition.)
1800 N. Highland Ave., Ste. 717, Hollywood, CA 90028. (323) 461-2020. FAX: (323) 461-9737. Program Information: (213) 466-FILM. www.americancinematheque.com
email: amcin@msn.com
CO-CHAIRMEN
Peter J. Dekom
Mike Medavoy
PRESIDENT
Henry Shields, Jr.
DIRECTOR
Barbara Zicka Smith
CHAIRMAN EMERITUS
Sydney Pollack
BOARD OF DIRECTORS
Peter Bart, Bill Block, Charles Champlin, Sanford Climan, Wendi L. Doyle, John S. Farrand, Rick Finkelstein, David Geffen, Brian Grazer, Buck Henry, Godfrey Isaac, Anne Keshen, Kenneth Kleinberg, Leonard Levy, Robert Mayson, Buddy Morra, Peter Morton, George E. Moss, Rick Nicita,Sanford P. Paris, Norman J. Pattiz, Michael John Pittas, Elisabeth Pollon, Arnold Rifkin, Lloyd E. Rigler, James G. Robinson, Sigurjon "Joni" Sighvatsson, Steve Tisch, Stephen Unger, J. Kendall Whiting, Saul Zaentz.

THE AMERICAN FILM INSTITUTE
(A national trust dedicated to advancing and preserving the art of the moving image.)
2021 N. Western Ave., P.O. Box 27999, Los Angeles, CA 90027. (323) 856-7600. FAX: (323) 467-4578.
The John F. Kennedy Center for the Performing Arts, Washington, D.C. 20566. (202) 416-7815. FAX: (202) 659-1970. www.afionline.org
FOUNDING DIRECTOR
George Stevens, Jr.
AFI CEO
Jean Picker Firstenberg
CO-DIRECTOR & COO
James Hindman
BOARD OF TRUSTEES
CHAIRMAN
Tom Pollock
VICE CHAIRMEN
Mark Canton, Michael Nesmith, Howard Stringer
HONORARY TRUSTEE
Harrison Ford
BOARD MEMBERS
Merv Adelson, Debbie Allen, Gilbert Amelio, Jon Avnet, Robert M. Bennett, Jeff Berg, Allen J. Bernstein, James Billington, Richard Brandt, John Calley, Mark Canton, Peter Chernin, John F Cooke, Martha Coolidge, Robert A. Daly, Suzanne de Passe, John DiBiaggio, Bill Duke, Roger Enrico, Michael Forman, Richard Frank, Stephen O. Frankfurt, Charles W. Fries, Ina Ginsburg, David Greenblatt, Philip Guarascio, Suzanne Lloyd Hayes, Lawrence Herbert, Robert Iger, Gene F. Jankowski, Robert L. Johnson, Fay Kanin, Jerry Katzman, Kathleen Kennedy, James V. Kinsey, Patricia Kingsley, Sherry Lansing, Warren N. Lieberfarb, Marsha Mason, Barry M. Meyer, Ron Meyer, Leslie Moonves, Janet H. Murray, Michael Nesmith, Mace Neufeld, Rick Nicita, Daniel Petrie., Frederick S. Pierce, Tom Pollock, Tony Ponturo, Robert G Rehme, Kelly A. Rose, Jill Sackler, Robert Shaye, Vivian Sobchack, Steven Spielberg, Howard Stringer, Liener Temerlin, David L. Wolper, Robert C. Wright, Alex Yemenidjian, Bud Yorkin.

AMERICAN FILM MARKETING ASSOCIATION (AFMA)
(Organized 1980. Membership: 170 companies engaged in the production and sale of independently produced films and TV programs to the international market. Produces the American Film Market every February.)
10850 Wilshire Blvd., 9th Flr., Los Angeles, CA 90024. (310) 446-1000. FAX: (310) 446-1600. www.afma.com
email: info@afma.com
CHAIRMAN OF BOARD
Kathy Morgan
PRESIDENT
Jean Prewitt
EXECUTIVE V.P.
Jonathan Wolf
V.P., RESEARCH & PUBLICATIONS
William A. Anderson
V.P., COLLECTIONS & EUROPEAN POLICY
Janet Gagnon
V.P., FINANCE & ACCOUNTING
Robert Newman
BOARD OF DIRECTORS
Mark Amin (Trimark Pictures), Steve Bickel (The Shooting Gallery), Talaat Captan (Green Communications), Sharyon Cobe (Kushner-Locke Co.), Roger Corman (New Concorde), Mark Damon (MDP Worldwide), Pierre David (World International Network, LLC), Peter Elson (Global Cinema Group, LLC), Herb Fletcher (Crown International Pictures), Michael Goldman (Cinema Consultants Group), Tim Hill (Team Communication), Lewis Horwitz (The Lewis Horwitz Organization), Norman Katz (The Norkat Company, Ltd.), lloyd Kaufman (Troma Entertainment, Inc.), Brad Krevoy (Motion Picture Corporation of America), Todd Leavitt (Tulip Media, Ltd.), Avi Lerner (Nu Image), Robert Meyers (Village Roadshow Pictures International), Barbara Mudge (Worldwide Entertainment, LLC), Jean Ovrum (Trident Releasing, Inc.), Steven Paul (Crystal Sky, LLC), Lawrence Safir (Safir Films, Ltd.), Rick Sands (Miramax International), June Shelley (RKO Pictures), Willaim Shields (Independent). Alternates: Peter Rogers (Lakeshore International), Michael Werner (Fortissimo Film Sales/Lighthouse Entertainment), Lisa Wilson (Franchise Pictures, LLC).

AMERICAN HUMANE ASSOCIATION
(Organized 1877. Liaison with the television and motion picture industry as supervisors of animal action in television and motion picture production.)
15366 Dickens St., Sherman Oaks, CA 91403. (818) 501-0123. www.ahafilm.org e-mail: ahawest@aol.com
National Headquarters: 63 Inverness Dr. E., Englewood, CO 80112. (303) 792-9900.
NATIONAL PRESIDENT
Tim O'Brien
DIRECTOR, WESTERN REGIONAL OFFICE
Gini Barrett

AMERICAN SOCIETY OF COMPOSERS, AUTHORS AND PUBLISHERS (ASCAP)
(Organized February 13, 1914. Membership: 100,000 Songwriters and Music Publishers.)
New York: One Lincoln Plaza, New York, NY 10023. (212) 621-6000. FAX: (212) 724-9064.
Los Angeles: 7920 Sunset Blvd., Ste. 300, Hollywood, CA 90046. (323) 883-1000. FAX: (323) 883-1049.
Nashville: Two Music Square W., Nashville, TN 37203. (615) 742-5000. FAX: (615) 742-5020.
Miami: 209 Ninth St., Ste. #2, Miami Beach, FL 33139. (305) 673-3446. FAX: (305) 673-2446.
Chicago: 1608 W. Belmont Ave., Ste. 200, Chicago, IL 60657. (773) 472-1157. FAX: (773) 471-1158.
Atlanta: PMB 400, 541 Tenth St., N.W., Atlanta, GA 30318-5713. (404) 635-1758. FAX: (404) 627-2404.
Licensing Office: 3350 Cumberland Circle, Ste. 1890, Atlanta, GA 30339.
PRESIDENT & CHAIRMAN
Marilyn Bergman
CEO
John A. LoFrumento
COO
Al Wallace
CFO
Jim Collins
VICE CHAIRMEN
Cy Coleman
Jay Morgenstern
SECRETARY
Arthur Hamilton
TREASURER
Arnold Broido
COUNSEL
I. Fred Koenigsberg
BOARD OF DIRECTORS
Marilyn Bergman, John Bettis, Freddy Bienstock, Joanne Boris, Leon J. Brettler, Arnold Broido, John Cacavas, Cy Coleman, Hal David, John L. Eastman, Nicholas Firth, Arthur Hamilton, Donna Hilley, Jimmy Jam, Dean Kay, Leeds Levy, Johnny Mandel, Jay Morgenstern, Stephen Paulus, David Raksin, David Renzer, Irwin Z. Robinson, Jimmy Webb, Doug Wood.

ASSOCIATION OF FILM COMMISSIONERS INTERNATIONAL
(Organized 1975. Acts as a liaison between the visual communications industry and local governments or organizations to facilitate on-location production, to stimulate economic benefit for member governments.)
7060 Hollywood Blvd., Ste. 614, Los Angeles, CA 90028. (213) 462-6092. FAX: (213) 462-6091.
PRESIDENT
Ward Emling (Mississippi Film Commission)

ASSOCIATION OF INDEPENDENT VIDEO & FILMMAKERS, INC. (AIVF)
(AIVF is a membership organization serving independent film- and videomakers. AIVF also publishes *The Independent Film and Video Monthly*, a publication dedicated to the media field.)
304 Hudson St., 6th Flr. N, New York, NY 10013. (212) 807-1400. FAX: (212) 463-8519. www.aivf.org
email: info@aivf.org
EXECUTIVE DIRECTOR
Elizabeth Peters
PROGRAM & INFORMATION SERVICES DIRECTOR
Michelle Coe
MEMBERSHIP DIRECTOR
LaTrice Dixon
EDITOR-IN-CHIEF, *The Independent*
Pat Thompson
MANAGING EDITOR, *The Independent*
Paul Power
ADVERTISING DIRECTOR, *The Independent*
Laura Davis
EDITORIAL ASSISTANT, *The Independent*
Scott Castle
BOARD OF DIRECTORS
Loni Ding, Lee Lew-Lee, Graham Leggat, Peter Lewnes, Rick Linklater, Diane Markrow, Jim McKay, Rob Moss, Robert Richter, Valerie Soe, Bart Weiss.

BMI (BROADCAST MUSIC, INC.)
320 W. 57 St., New York, NY 10019. (212) 586-2000. FAX: (212) 245-8986. www.bmi.com email: newyork@bmi.com
V.P., WRITER/PUBLISHER RELATIONS, NEW YORK
Charlie S. Feldman
8730 Sunset Blvd., 3rd Flr., West, Los Angeles, CA 90069. (310) 659-9109. FAX: (310) 657-6947. email: losangeles@bmi.com
V.P., WRITER/PUBLISHER RELATIONS, LOS ANGELES
Rick Riccobono
10 Music Square E., Nashville, TN 37203. (615) 401-2000. FAX: (615) 401-2707. email: nashville@bmi.com
V.P., WRITER/PUBLISHER RELATIONS, NASHVILLE
Roger Sovine
5201 Blue Lagoon Dr., Ste. 310, Miami, FL 33126. (305) 266-3636. FAX: (305) 266-2442. email: miami@bmi.com.
CONTACT
Diane Almodovar
255 Ponce de Leon, East Wing, Ste. 262, Royal Bank Center, Hato Rey, PR 00917. (787) 754-6490. FAX: (787) 753-6765. email: latin@bmi.com
CONTACT
Joey Mercado
84 Harley House, Marylebone Rd., London NW1 5HN, England. (44 171) 935-2037. FAX: (44 171) 224-1046. email: london@bmi.com
CHAIRMAN OF THE BOARD
Phil Jones
PRESIDENT & CEO
Frances W. Preston

COMMUNICATION COMMISSION OF THE NATIONAL COUNCIL OF THE CHURCHES OF CHRIST IN THE USA
475 Riverside Dr., Room 852, New York, NY 10115. (212) 870-2574. FAX: (212) 870-2030. www.nccusa.org
email: dave@nccusa.org.
CHAIRMAN
Eric Shafer
DIRECTOR OF ELECTRONIC MEDIA
David W. Pomeroy

COUNCIL ON INTERNATIONAL NON-THEATRICAL EVENTS (C.I.N.E.)
(Organized 1957. CINE selects and enters tv documentaries, theatrical short subjects, educational, religious, scientific film and tv products in 120 international film & video competitions.)
1001 Connecticut Ave. N.W., Ste. 625, Washington, DC 20036. (202) 785-1136. (202) 785-1137. FAX: (202) 785-4114.
PRESIDENT
Vivian Schiller
CHAIRMAN
Dr. Frank Frost
EXECUTIVE DIRECTOR
Donna Chiffely

ENTERTAINMENT INDUSTRIES FOUNDATION
11132 Ventura Blvd., Ste. 401, Studio City, CA 91604-3156. (818) 760-7722. FAX: (818) 760-7898. www.eifoundation.org
PRESIDENT & CEO
Lisa Paulsen
CFO
Merrily Newton
E.V.P.
Danielle M. Guttman

FILM SOCIETY OF LINCOLN CENTER
(Organized 1969. Sponsors The New York Film Festival and publishes *Film Comment* magazine.)
70 Lincoln Center Plaza, New York, NY 10023-6595. (212) 875-5610. FAX: (212) 875-5636. www.filminc.com
CHAIRMAN
Ira M. Resnick
PRESIDENT
Henry McGee
EXECUTIVE VICE-PRESIDENT
Joanne Koch
EXECUTIVE PRODUCER, SPECIAL EVENTS
Wendy Keys
ADMINISTRATIVE DIRECTOR
Claudia Bonn

FILM/VIDEO ARTS
(Organized 1968. Provides independents with training, equipment rental and editing services.)
50 Broadway, 21st Flr., New York, NY 10004. (212) 673-9361. FAX: (212) 324-3318. www.fva.com
EXECUTIVE DIRECTOR
Eileen Newman
HEAD OF DEVELOPMENT & PUBLIC RELATIONS
Duana C. Butler
HEAD OF EDUCATION
Marguerite Ruscito
EQUIPMENT MANAGER
Shari Smith

THE FOUNDATION OF MOTION PICTURE PIONEERS, INC.
244 W. 49 St., Ste. 200, New York, NY 10019. (212) 247-3178. FAX: (212) 265-6428.
PRESIDENT
Travis Reid
CHAIRMAN OF BOARD
Mitch Goldman
EXECUTIVE V.P.
Wayne Lewellen
VICE PRESIDENTS
Jeff Blake
Michael Campbell
Jerry Forman
Larry Gleason
Kurt Hall
Allen Karp
Hank Lightstone
Barrie Lawson Loeks
Michael Patrick.
Nikki Rocco
TREASURER
Jack Foley
SECRETARY
Robert Sunshine

FRENCH FILM OFFICE/UNIFRANCE FILM INTERNATIONAL
424 Madison Ave., 8th Flr., New York, NY 10017. (212) 832-8860. FAX: (212) 755-0629. www.unifrance.org
EXECUTIVE DIRECTOR FOR THE U.S.
Catherine Verret

FRIARS CLUB
57 E. 55 St., New York, NY 10022. (212) 751-7272. FAX: (212) 355-0217. www.friarsclub.com
ABBOT
Alan King
DEAN
Freddie Roman
PRIOR
Sally Jessy Raphael
SCRIBE
Stewie Stone
TREASURER
David B. Cornstein
EXECUTIVE DIRECTOR
Jean-Pierre L. Trebot
HONORARY OFFICERS
ABBOT EMERITUS
Milton Berle
DEAN EMERITUS
Jack L Green
SCRIBE EMERITUS
Frank Military
CHAMBERLAIN
David W Tebet
BARD
Tony Martin
PROCTORS
Billy Crystal
Buddy Hackett
JESTER
Sid Caesar
HERALD
Paul Anka
MONITOR
Richard Lewis
TROUBADOUR
Tony Bennett
SQUIRE
Soupy Sales
HISTORIAN
Bernard M. Kamber
MONK
Robert Merrill
SAMARITAN
Norman King
KNIGHT
Danny Aiello
KNIGHT
Gene Baylos
KNIGHT
Tom Jones

FRIARS CLUB OF CALIFORNIA, INC.
9900 Santa Monica Blvd., Beverly Hills, CA 90212. (310) 553-0850. FAX: (310) 286-7906. www.friarsclub-ca.org
CHAIRMAN
Larry King
PRESIDENT
Irwin M. Schaeffer
FIRST V.P.
Stan King
SECOND V.P.
Lawrence J. Stern
SECRETARY
Elizabeth Sampson

THE INDEPENDENT FEATURE PROJECT
(Organized 1979. Non-profit organization that provides information and support services to independent filmmakers.)
104 W. 29th St., 12th Flr., New York, NY 10001-5310. (212) 465-8200. FAX: (212) 465-8525. www.ifpny@ifp.org
email: ifpny@ifp.org
EXECUTIVE DIRECTOR
Michelle Byrd
MARKETING DIRECTOR
Milton Tabbot
BOARD OF DIRECTORS
Doro Bachrach, Michael Barker, Richard Brick, Kathleen Dore, Maggie Greenwald, Ted Hope, Peter Howe, Tom Kalin, Elliott Kanbar, Jeff Lipsky, Sheila Nevins, Richard Pena, Rosie Perez, Richard P. Rubinstein, Sandra Schulberg, Thomas Selz, Nancy Sher, Raphael Silver, John Sloss, Stacy Spikes, Susan A. Stover, Catherine Tait, Irwin Young.

INDEPENDENT FEATURE PROJECT/MIDWEST
633 E. Congress Ave., Rm. 505, Chicago, IL 60605. (312) 435-1825. FAX: (312) 435-1828. www.ifp.org
PRESIDENT
Dan Moore
EXECUTIVE DIRECTOR
Rebecca Cowing

INDEPENDENT FEATURE PROJECT/NORTH
450 N. Third St. #490, Minneapolis, MN 55401. (612) 338-0871. FAX: (612) 338-4747. www.ifpnorth.org
MEMBERSHIP/EDUCATION DIRECTOR
Patrice Snead
MEMBERSHIP DIRECTOR
Chris Dotson
EXECUTIVE DIRECTOR
Jane Minton
BUSINESS DIRECTOR
Rita Pucci
PR & MARKETING DIRECTOR
Kelly Nathe

INDEPENDENT FEATURE PROJECT/SOUTH
927 Lincoln Rd., Ste. 119, Miami Beach, FL 33139. (305) 534-7171. FAX: (305) 532-9710.
www.ifp.org; www.alliance-cinema.org
EXECUTIVE DIRECTOR
Joanne Butcher
BOARD MEMBERS
Jamin O'Brien
Rhonda Mitrani

INDEPENDENT FEATURE PROJECT/WEST
(Organized 1980. Publishes *Filmmaker: The Magazine of Independent Film*, a co-publication of IFP/West & IFP.)
1964 Westwood Blvd., Ste. 205, Los Angeles, CA 90025. (310) 465-4379. FAX: (310) 441-5676.
email: dearifpwest@earthlink.net
EXECUTIVE DIRECTOR
Dawn Hudson
MANAGING DIRECTOR
Michael Harrison
MARKETING COORDINATOR
Michelle Bryant
EXECUTIVE ASSISTANTS
ErinCorzine
Sheilah Aragon
ACCOUNTANT
Monique White
DIRECTOR OF DEVELOPMENT
Sean McManus
MEMBERSHIP MANAGER
Kristi Lomas
DIRECTOR OF PROGRAMMING
Alexander F. Nohe
PUBLICITY
Laura Kim
Amy Lillard
Annalee Paulo
MARKETING CONSULTANT
Jamie McGurk
INDEPENDENT SPIRITS AWARDS PRODUCER
Diana Zahn

INTERNATIONAL DOCUMENTARY ASSOCIATION
(Organized 1982.)
1201 W. 5th St., Ste. M320, Los Angeles, CA 90017-1461. (213) 534-3600. FAX: (213) 534-3610. www.documentary.org
email: info@documentary.org
PRESIDENT
David Haugland
V.P.
Marina Goldovskaya
SECRETARY
Richard Propper
TREASURER
Mitchell Block
LEGAL COUNSEL
Michael C. Donaldson
EXECUTIVE DIRECTOR
Grace Ouchida

BOARD OF DIRECTORS
Sven Berkemeier, Lyn Goldfarb, Barbara Leigh-Gregson, Carol Munday Lawrence, Lisa Leeman, John Mason, Joan Owens, Steven Poster, Mary Schaffer, Richard Trank, Thelma Vickroy

REGIONAL MEMBERS
Len McClure (Hong Kong), Michael Rabiger (Chicago), Andre Singer (London), Frederick Wiseman (Boston).

JAPAN SOCIETY/FILM CENTER
(Organized 1907. Promotes Japanese culture through exhibiting Japanese films and films on Japan.)
333 E. 47 St., New York, NY 10017. (212) 832-1155. FAX: (212) 715-1262. www.jpnsoc.org e-mail: gen@jpnsoc.org
DIRECTOR, FILM CENTER
Dr. Kyoko Hirano
FILM PROGRAM ASSISTANT
Robert Lazzaro

MOTION PICTURE AND TELEVISION FUND
23388 Mulholland Dr., Woodland Hills, CA 91364. (800) 876-8320.
Bob Hope Health Center, 335 N. La Brea Ave., Los Angeles, CA 90036. (323) 634-3850.
Santa Clarita Health Center, 25751 McBean Pkwy., #210, Valencia, CA 91355. (661) 284-3100.
Toluca Lake Health Center, 4323 Riverside Dr., Burbank, CA 91505. (818) 556-2700.
Westside Health Center, 1950 Sawtelle Blvd., Ste.. 130, Los Angeles, CA 90025. (310) 996-9355.
Woodland Hills Health Center, 23388 Mulholland Dr., Woodland Hills, CA 91364. (818) 876-1050.
Samuel Goldwyn Foundation Children's Center, 2114 Pontius Ave., Los Angeles, CA 90025. (310) 445-8993.
PRESIDENT & CEO
David B. Tillman, M.D.
CHAIRMAN
Roger L. Mayer
VICE CHAIRS
Robert Blees
Irma Kalish
Michael Wayne
TREASURER
Raymond Kurtzman
SECRETARY
Gloria M. Palazzo

MOTION PICTURE ASSOCIATION OF AMERICA, INC./ MOTION PICTURE ASSOCIATION
15503 Ventura Blvd., Encino, CA 91436. (818) 995-6600. FAX: (818) 382-1799. Anti-Piracy Hot Line: 1-800-NO-COPYS.
1600 Eye St. N.W., Washington, D.C. 20006. (202) 293-1966. FAX: (202) 293-7674.
PRESIDENT & CEO/CHAIRMAN & CEO, MPA
Jack Valenti
EXECUTIVE V.P. & COO
William Murray
Simon Bresky
SENIOR VICE PRESIDENTS
Fritz Attaway
John J. Collins
Bethlyn Hand
Vans Stevenson
VICE PRESIDENTS
Paul Egge
Marsha Kessler
Nancy Thompson

CALIFORNIA OFFICE
V.P. & DIRECTOR, FINANCE WORLDWIDE ANTI-PIRACY
Mark Howe
S.V.P., WORLD-WIDE ANTI-PIRACY
Ken Jacobsen
V.P. & DEPUTY, GENERAL COUNSEL
Gregory P. Goeckner
V.P. & DIRECTOR, LEGAL AFFAIRS
Marc Litvack
DIR., PROGRAM ADMINISTRATION, U.S. ANTI-PIRACY
Mary Callahan
S. MANAGER FINANCE, WORLD-WIDE ANTI-PIRACY
Alex Hawkins

WASHINGTON OFFICE
PRESIDENT & CEO
Jack Valenti
S.V.P., GOVERNMENT RELATIONS
Fritz Attaway
S.V.P., & GENERAL COUNSEL
Bonnie Richardson
V.P., CABLE COPYRIGHT COLLECTION DISTRIBUTION
Marsha Kessler
V.P., ADMINISTRATION
Nancy Thompson
DIRECTOR, STATE LEGISLATION
Karin Krueger
DIRECTOR, DOMESTIC TAX
Angela Hoyt
V.P., STATE LEGISLATION
Vans Stevenson
DIRECTOR, DOMESTIC CABLE COPYRIGHT
Sandra Pope
DIRECTOR, INTERNATIONAL COPYRIGHT
Jane Saunders
DIRECTOR, PUBLIC AFFAIRS
Richard Taylor
DIRECTOR, ADMINISTRATION
Kathy Grant
DOMESTIC COUNSEL
Dan Robbins
EUROPE, MIDDLE EAST & AFRICA OPERATIONS:
V.P., SENIOR COUNSEL/V.P., FOREIGN TAX & COMMERCIAL AFFAIRS
Barbara Rosenfeld
V.P., COPYRIGHT AFFAIRS
Axel Aus der Muhlen
S.V.P. & CFO
John J. Collins
V.P., CONTROLLER & ASSISTANT TREASURER
Tom Igner
V.P., MIS
Paul Egge
V.P., FINANCE
Don McLellan
S.V.P., ADMINISTRATION
Bethlyn J. Hand
DIRECTOR, BENEFITS
Kari Hollinger
V.P., ADMINISTRATION/ASSOC. DIR., ADVERTISING
Marilyn Gordon
V.P. & GENERAL MANAGER, CA GROUP
Melissa Patack
V.P., WORLDWIDE HOME VIDEO
Thomas Molter
V.P., THEATRE
Allyson Rosen
V.P., WORLDWIDE MARKET RESEARCH
Robin Patino
DIRECTOR, TITLE REGISTRATION BUREAU
Mitchell Schwartz, Director
CHAIRMAN, CLASSIFICATION & RATING ADMIN.
Joan Graves
S.V.P. & DIRECTOR, ADVERTISING
Bethlyn J. Hand
V.P. ADMINISTRATION/ASSOCIATE DIR., ADVERTISING
Marilyn Gordon
DEPUTY DIRECTOR, EU AFFAIRS
Harvey Rouse
DIRECTOR, INT'L. RELATIONS
Brian Grzelkowski
S.V.P., LATIN AMERICA
Steve Solot
V.P., LATIN AMERICA
Sean Spencer
SENIOR V.P., AUSTRALIA & ASIA
Michael Connors
V.P., ASIA PACIFIC
Jeffrey Hardee
EXECUTIVE DIRECTOR
Richard O'Neill
SENIOR V.P., ROME
Marc Spiegel
PRESIDENT, CMOPA., MONTREAL
Douglas Frith

MUSEUM OF MODERN ART, DEPT. OF FILM & VIDEO
(Organized May, 1935.)
11 W. 53th St., New York, NY 10019. (212) 708-9500.
FAX: (212) 708-9531.
CHIEF CURATOR
Mary Lea Bandy
SENIOR CURATOR & COORDINATOR OF EXHIBITIONS
Laurence Kardish
CIRCULATING FILM LIBRARIAN
William Sloan
CURATOR: ARCHIVES FILM COLLECTIONS
Stephen Higgins
SENIOR RESEARCHER
Charles Silver

NATIONAL ALLIANCE FOR MEDIA ARTS & CULTURE
(NAMAC distributes a newletter to the media arts and information network.) 346 Ninth St., San Francisco, CA 94103.
(415) 431-1391. FAX: (415) 431-1392. www.namac.org
e-mail: namac@namac.org
NATIONAL DIRECTOR
Helen DeMichiel

NATIONAL ASIAN AMERICAN TELECOMMUNICATIONS ASSOCIATION (NAATA)
(NAATA supports and distributes Asian Pacific American media productions through national public television broadcasts.)
346 Ninth St., 2nd Flr., San Francisco, CA 94103. (415) 863-0814. FAX: (415) 863-7428. www.naatanet.org
email: naata@naatanet.org
EXECUTIVE DIRECTOR
Eddie Wong
MEDIA FUND & PROGRAMMING DIRECTOR
Donald Young
FESTIVAL DIRECTOR
Chi-Hui Yang
DISTRIBUTION DIRECTOR
Julie Hatta

NATIONAL ASSOCIATION OF THEATRE OWNERS, INC.
(For the NATO board, a complete list of state and regional NATO offices and Directors-at-Large please see Exhibitor Organizations.)
4605 Lankershim Blvd., Ste. 340, N. Hollywood, CA 91602.
(818) 506-1778. FAX: (818) 506-0269. email: nato@chq.com
PRESIDENT
John Fithian
CHAIRMAN
Barrie Lawson Loeks
CHAIRMAN, FINANCE COMMITTEE & TREASURER
Steve Marcus
SECRETARY
Ayron Pickerill
V.P. & EXECUTIVE DIRECTOR
Mary Ann Grasso

NATIONAL BOARD OF REVIEW OF MOTION PICTURES, INC.
(Organized March, 1909. Publisher of *Films in Review.*)
245 E. 72nd St., New York, NY 10021. (212) 628-1594.
PRESIDENT
Lois Balon
EDITOR
Robin Little

NATIONAL FILM PRESERVATION FOUNDATION
(Organized 1997)
870 Market St., Ste. 1113, San Francisco, CA 94102. (415) 392-7291. FAX: (415) 392-7293. www.filmpreservation.org
email: info@filmpreservation.org
DIRECTOR
Annette Melville
BUSINESS MANAGER
Beverly Belben
COMMUNICATIONS MANAGER
Rolanda Chu Foerster
DEVELOPMENT DIRECTOR
Cecelia . McCoy
BOARD OF DIRECTORS
Roger L. Mayer (Chairman), Celeste Bartos, John F. Cooke, Laurence Fishburne, I. Michael Heyman, The Hon. Robert W. Kastenmeier, John Ptak, Robert G. Rehm, Martin Scorsese, James H. Billington (ex officio, The Librarian of Congress).

NATIONAL MUSIC PUBLISHERS' ASSOCIATION, INC./ THE HARRY FOX AGENCY, INC.
(NMPA represents music publishing companies. The Harry Fox Agency was founded in 1927 and represents more than 15,000 music publishers).
711 Third Ave., 8th Fl., New York, NY 10017. (212) 370-5330.
FAX: (212) 953-2384. www.nmpa.org
PRESIDENT & CEO
Edward P. Murphy
EXECUTIVE V.P. & COO
Robert Shaw

NEW YORK FOUNDATION FOR THE ARTS INC
155 Ave. of the Americas, 14th Flr., New York, NY 10013. (212) 366-6900. FAX: (212) 366-1778. www.nyfa.org
EXECUTIVE DIRECTOR
Theodore Berger
PROGRAM DIRECTOR
Penelope Dannenberg

NEW YORK STATE COUNCIL ON THE ARTS (NYSCA)
915 Broadway, 8th Flr., New York, NY 10010. (212) 387-7000.
FAX: (212) 387-7168. www.nysca.org
email: nysca@interport.net
ASSOCIATE, ELECTRONIC MEDIA & FILM PROGRAM
Claude Meyer
DIRECTOR, INDIVIDUAL ARTISTS PROGRAM
Don Palmer
DIRECTOR, ELECTRONIC MEDIA & FILM PROGRAM
Karen Helmerson

NEW YORK WOMEN IN FILM & TELEVISION
6 E. 39th St., 12th Flr., New York, NY 10016-0112.
(212) 679-0870. FAX: (212) 679-0899. www.nywift.org
email: staff@nywift.org
PRESIDENT
Marcie Setlow
V.P., COMMUNICATIONS
Stephanie Seligman
V.P., DEVELOPMENT
Carey Graeber
V.P., MEMBERSHIP
Jancy Ball
V.P., PROGRAMMING
Lynn Holst
V.P., SPECIAL EVENTS
Mary Jane Louaver
SECRETARY
Sara Stuart
TREASURER
Merle Kallas
DEVELOPMENT
Kate B. Wood
Denise Kasell
MEMBERSHIP
Nicole Betancourt
Dorothy Rompalske
PROGRAMMING
Linda Lee Alexander
Joann McFarlane
SPECIAL EVENTS
Cynthia Griffin
Susan Steiger
CHAPTERS
Arizona, Atlanta, Austin, Colorado, Dallas, Florida, Houston, Los Angeles, Maryland, New England, New Orleans, New York, Seattle, Washington D.C., Africa, Europe, Australia, New Zealand.

SESAC, INC.
(A music licensing organization.)
55 Music Square East, Nashville, TN 37203. (800) 826-9996.
FAX: (615) 329-9627. www.sesac.com
CHAIRMEN
Freddie Gershon
Ira Smith
Stephen Swid
PRESIDENT & COO
Bill Velez
S.V.P., WRITER/PUBLISHER RELATIONS
Pat Rogers

SOCIETY OF COMPOSERS & LYRICISTS
400 S. Beverly Dr., Ste. 214, Beverly Hills, CA 90212. (310) 281-2812. FAX: (818) 990-0601. www.filmscore.org
PRESIDENT
Richard Bellis
V.P.S
Alf Clausen
Garry Schyman
SECRETARY/TREASURER
Christopher Farrell
ADVISORY BOARD
Alan Bergman, Marilyn Bergman, Elmer Bernstein, Bill Conti, Jerry Goldsmith, James Newton Howard, Quincy Jones, Peter Matz, Alan Menken, David Raksin, Lalo Schifrin, Marc Shaiman, Howard Shore, Alan Silvestri, Patrick Williams, Hans Zimmer.
BOARD OF DIRECTORS
Lori Barth, Richard Bellis, Charles Bernstein, Bruce Broughton, Jay Chattaway, Alf Clausen, Harvey Cohen, Ray Colcord, James Di Pasquale, Christopher Farrell, Lorraine Feather, Dan Foliart, Craig Stuart Garfinkle, Ron Grant, Arthur Hamilton, Christopher Klatman, Michael McCuistion, Jim McVey, Peter Rodgers Melnick, Marc Parmet, Garry Schyman, Alex Shapiro, Dennis Spiegel Mark Watters, Gary Woods, Chris Young.

SOCIETY OF MOTION PICTURE AND TELEVISION ENGINEERS
(Organized 1916. Membership: 9,700.)
595 W. Hartsdale Ave., White Plains, NY 10607-1824. (914) 761-1100. FAX: (914) 761-3115.
EXECUTIVE DIRECTOR
Frederick C. Motts
MARKETING COORDINATOR
Linda Alexander
DIRECTOR OF PUBLICATIONS
David M. Juhren
PRODUCTION/GRAPHICS SUPERVISOR
Mathew V. Kuriakose
MANAGING EDITOR
MaryAnn Frusciante
ASSISTANT EDITOR
Jermaine Hall

UNITED STATES CATHOLIC CONFERENCE, DEPARTMENT OF COMMUNICATION—OFFICE FOR FILM & BROADCASTING
1011 First Ave., Ste. #1300, New York, NY 10022. (212) 644-1880. FAX: (212) 644-1886. email: ofb@email.msn.com
DIRECTOR, OFFICE FOR FILM & BROADCASTING
Gerri Pare

VARIETY CLUBS INTERNATIONAL
(Organized October 10, 1927. Membership: 15,000.)
1560 Broadway, Ste. 1209, New York, NY 10036. (212) 695-3818. FAX: (212) 695-3851.
PRESIDENT
Peter J. Barnett
CHAIRMAN OF THE BOARD
Tony Hatch
INTERNATIONAL CHAIRMAN
Monty Hall, O.C.
PAST PRESIDENTS
Jarvis Astaire, Monty Hall, O.C., Robert R. Hall, Q.C., Salah M. Hassanein, Eric D. Morley, Ralph W. Pries, John Ratcliff, Stanley J. Reynolds, John H. Rowley, Joseph Sinay.
VICE PRESIDENTS
Maureen Arthur-Ruben
Peter S. Drummond
Tom Fenno
Michael R. Forman
Frederick M. Friedman
Tony Hasham
Julia Morley
George Pitman
Marsha Rae Ratcliff
Jody Reynolds
Bruce Rosen
Ory Slonim, Adv.
Frank Strean
John R. Weber, Sr.
TREASURER
Bernard Myerson
PRESIDENT'S COUNCIL
Samuel Z. Arkoff, Monty Berman, MBE, Sir Trevor Chinn, CVO, Lou Lavinthal, Frank Mancuso, Grahame Mapp, A.M., Hank Milgram, Carl L. Patrick, Ric R. Roman, Zollie Volchok.
INTERNATIONAL COUNSELOR
Robert R. Hall, Q.C.
AMBASSADORS
Rob T. Allen, Beatrice Arthur, Lloyd Barr, F.C.A., Kevin Barry, Alvin Blechman, Fran Blechman, Michael Caine, Sydney Chertkoff, Q.C., Sean Connery, Raymond Curtis, Penny Docherty, Nick Faldo, Stephen Gottlieb, Ilene Graf, Hortense Grant, Marjorie Grant, C.K. Greidinger, Billy Hicks, Sr., Don Ho, Paul Hogan, Richard O Jacobson, Gordon Josie, David Lapidus, Peter Legge, Hank Lightstone, Milton H. London, Dame Vera Lynn, Ian Martens, Pauline McFetridge, Roger Moore, James Murray, Jeff Newman, O.A.M., Gregory Peck, Ronald S Pennock M.D., Emma Samms, Neil Sinclair, Barbara Stewart, Robert Thorpe, Gina Tolleson, Chaim Topell, Jackie Trent, Louis Trepel, Stuart Wagstaff, John D Webber, James West, James Whittell.
MEDICAL ADVISOR
Michael LaCorte, M.D.
MEDIA RELATIONS
Peter Legge
EXECUTIVE DIRECTOR
Rosalie F Sochinski

VARIETY CLUB TENTS
TENT No. 1: Variety Club of Pittsburgh, Penn Center West One, Ste. 411, Pittsburgh, PA 15276/ (412) 747-2680.
TENT No. 4: Variety Club of St. Louis, 2200 Westport Plaza Dr., St. Louis, MO 63146. (314) 543-0543.
TENT No. 5: Variety Club of Detroit, 30161 Southfield Rd., Ste. 301, Southfield, MI 48076. (248) 258-5511.
TENT No. 7: Variety Club of Buffalo, 193-195 Delaware Ave., Buffalo, NY 14202. (716) 854-7577.
TENT No. 8: Variety Club of Greater Kansas City, 8340 Mission Rd., Ste. B4, Prairie Village, KS 66206. (913) 341-2315.
TENT No. 10: Variety Club of Indiana, 6919 E. 10th St., Ste. B5, Indianapolis, IN 46219. (317) 359-1650.
TENT No. 12: Variety Children's Association, Mayo Box 727, 420 Delaware St., S.E., Minneapolis, MN 55455-0374. (612) 624-6900.
TENT No. 13: Variety Club Philadelphia, 1520 Locust St., Ste. 900, Philadelphia, PA 19102. (215) 735-0803.
TENT No. 14: Variety Club of Wisconsin, 212 W. Wisconsin Ave, Ste. 420, Milwaukee, WI 53203. (414) 298-9991.
TENT No. 15: Variety Club of Iowa, 505 Fifth Ave., Ste. 310, Des Moines, IA 50309. (515) 243-4600.
TENT No. 16: Variety Club of Nebraska, 9100 F. St., Omaha, NE 68127. (402) 331-4313.
TENT No. 17: Variety Club of Northern Texas, 6060 N. Central Expwy., Ste. 308, Dallas, TX 75206. (214) 368-7449.
TENT No. 20: Variety Club of Memphis, 3294 Poplar St., Memphis, TN 38111. (901) 323-2220.
TENT NO. 21: Variety Club of Georgia, 72 Marietta St, 4th Flr., Atlanta, GA 30303. (404) 526-5229.
TENT No. 23: Variety Club of New England, P.O. Box 1289, Saugus, MA 01906. (617) 437-9500.
TENT No. 25: Variety Club of Southern California, 8455 Beverly Blvd., Ste. 501, Los Angeles, CA 90048. (323) 655-1547.
TENT No. 26: Variety Club of Illinois, 1 IBM Plaza, Ste. 2800, Chicago, IL 60611. (312) 822-0660.
TENT No. 27: Variety Club of Western Michigan, P.O. Box 2293, Grand Rapdis, MI 49501. (616) 836-3159.
TENT No. 28: Variety Club of Ontario, 37 King St. East, Ste. 300, Toronto, Ont. M5C 1E9 Canada. (416) 367-2828.
TENT No. 29: Variety Club of Mexico, Heriberto Frias #1145, Col. Del Valle, Mexico D.F. 03100, Mexico. 525 559-1024.
TENT No. 32: Variety Club of Northern California, 582 Market St., Ste. 101, San Francisco, CA 94104. (415) 781-3894.
TENT No. 34: Variety Club of Houston, 1415 N. Loop West, #215, Houston, TX 77008. (713) 426-5437.
TENT No. 35: Variety Club of New York, 350 5th Ave., Ste. 1234, New York, NY 10118. (212) 760-2777.
TENT No. 36: Variety Club of Great Britain, Variety Club House, 93 Bayham St., London NW1 OAG, U.K. (207) 428-8100.
TENT No. 37: Variety Club of Colorado, 9210 E. Berry Ave., Englewood, CO 80111. (303) 841-8167.
TENT No. 39: Variety Club of Southern Nevada, 3F Sunset Way, Ste. A-12, Henderson, NV 89014. (702) 383-8466..
TENT No. 41: Variety Club of Ireland, Room 25, Central Hotel Chambers, Dame Court, Dublin 2, Ireland. (31) 671-8469.
TENT NO. 45: Variety Club of New Orleans, 4132 S. Carrolton Ave., New Orleans, LA 70119. (504) 486-3255.
TENT No. 46: Variety Club of the Pacific Northwest, 911 Pine St., #807, Seattle, WA 98101. (206) 812-1159.
TENT No. 47: Variety Club of British Columbia, 4300 Still Creek Dr., Burnaby, B.C., V5C, 6C3, Canada. (604) 320-0505.
TENT No. 50: Variety Club of Hawaii, P.O. Box 1180, Honolulu, HI 96744. (808) 955-5106.
TENT No. 51: Variety Club of Israel, 26 Yimiyahu St., Tel Aviv, 62594 Israel. (23) 546-7715.
TENT No. 52: Variety Club of Jersey, Maufant Variety Youth Centre, Grand Route de St. Martin, Jersey, St. Saviour, JE2 6JT Channel Islands. 44 1534 856-937.
TENT No. 54: Soleil d'enfance, 46 Rue de Seine, Paris, France 75006. 33 144 07-2828.
TENT No. 56: Variety Club of New South Wales, 707 Darling St., Rozelle, NSW 2039, Australia. 612 9555-1688.
TENT No. 58: Variety Club of Manitoba, 611 Wellington Crescent, Winnipeg, R3M 0A7 Manitoba, Canada. (204) 982-1058.
TENT No. 60: Variety Club of Utah, 2500 Emigration Canyon, Salt Lake City, UT 84108. (801) 582-0700.
TENT No. 61: Variety Club of Southern Alberta, Ste. 201, 1509 11th Ave., S.W., Calgary, Alberta T3C 0N1, Canada. (403) 228-6168.
TENT No. 63: Variety Club of Northern Alberta, 5th Flr., Liberty Bldg., #505, 1050006 Jasper Ave., Edmonton, Alberta T5J 1Z7, Canada. (780) 448-9544.
TENT No. 65: Variety Club of The Palm Beaches, 2875 S. Ocean Blvd., Ste. 200, Unit 7, Palm Beach, FL 33480. (561) 585-5561.
TENT No. 66: Variety Club of the Desert, 1729 E. Palm Canyon Dr, Ste.103, Palm Springs, CA 92264. (760) 320-1177.
TENT No. 68: Variety Club of New Zealand, P.O. Box 17276, Greelane, Auckland 1005, New Zealand. 64 9520-4111.
TENT No. 70: Variety Club of Orlando, 3905 El Rey Rd., Orlando, FL 32808. (407) 298-2980 Ext. 310.

TENT No. 71: Variety Club of Ottawa, 2428 Greys Creek Rd., Greely, Ontario K4P 1N2, Canada. (613) 821-3606.
TENT No. 72: Variety Club of South Dakota, Children's Care Hospital and School, 2501 E. 26th St., Sioux Falls, SD 57105. (605) 336-1840 Ext. 2325.
TENT No. 73: Variety Club of The Caribbean (Barbados), c/o Ercil Walcott, Summerland House, Prospect, St. James, Barbados. (246) 432-2395.
TENT No. 74: Variety Club of Western Australia, P.O. Box 534, West Perth, Western Australia, 6872, Australia. 618 9388 3480.
TENT No. 75: Variety Club of South Australia, 540 South Rd., Kurralta Park, Adelaide, South Australia, 5037, Australia. 618 8293 8744.
TENT No. 76: Variety Club of Queensland, 18 Brisbane Rd., Labrador, Queensland 4215 Australia. 617 5537 6376.
TENT No. 77: Variety Club of Victoria, 1st Flr., 322 Glenferrie Rd., Malvern, Victoria 3144, Australia. 613 9804 3355.
TENT No. 78: Variety Club of Tasmania, 1/57 King St., P.O. Box 893, Sandy Bay, Tasmania 7005, Australia. 613 6223 1886.
TENT No. 79: Variety Club of Italy, c/o Ivan Scinardo, La Cittadella dell'Oasi, Via Conte Ruggerio, #73, Troina 94018, Sicily, Italy. 39 935 653 966.
TENT No. 80: Variety Club of South Africa, c/o Ster-Kinekor Films, P.O. Box 76461, Wendywood 2144, South Africa. 27 11 445-7760.

WILL ROGERS MEMORIAL FUND

1640 Marengo St., Ste. 406, Los Angeles, CA 90033-1036. (888) 994-FUND. FAX: (323) 223-0035. www.wrinstitute.org
PRESIDENT
Erik Lomis
CHAIRMAN OF THE BOARD
Wayne Lewellen
HONORARY CHAIRMEN
Salah M. Hassanein, Frank G. Mancuso, Bernard Myerson, Burton Stone
EXECUTIVE OFFICERS
Michael Pade
Bruce Snyder
Chuck Viane
TREASURER
Steve Rapaport
SECRETARY
Richie M. Fay
EXECUTIVE DIRECTOR
Todd Vradenburg
EXECUTIVE COMMITTEE
Gino Campnagnola, Michael L. Campbell, Nick Carpou, Richard Cook, Bruce C. Corwin, Frank M. Dwyer, Tom Elefante, Daniel R. Fellman, Jerome A Forman, Mark Gaines, Mitchell Goldman, Jeff Goldstein, Kurt C. Hall, Mort Hock, Bob Lenihan, Hank Lightstone, Rick Myerson, Michael W. Patrick, Allen M. Pinsker, Dr. Martin S. Quigley, D. Barry Reardon, Sumner Redstone, Robert Rehme, Travis Reid, Nikki Rocco, Rick Sands, Tom Sherak, William Soady, Jay Swerdlow, Clark Woods.

WOMEN IN COMMUNICATIONS

1244 Ritchie Hwy., Ste. 6, Arnold, MD 21012-1887. (410) 544-7442. FAX: (410) 544 4640. www.womcom.org
email: womcom@aol.com
EXECUTIVE DIRECTOR
Patricia Troy

GUILDS AND UNIONS

ACTORS' EQUITY ASSOCIATION
(AAAA AFL CIO CLC)
(Organized May 26, 1913. Membership: 40,000.)
National/Eastern Regional Office: 165 W. 48th St., New York, New York 10036. (212) 869-8530; FAX (212) 719-9815.
Central Regional Office: 203 N. Wabash Ave., Ste. 1700, Chicago, IL 60601. (312) 641-0393; FAX (312) 641-6365.
Western Regional Office: 5757 Wilshire Blvd., Ste. One, Los Angeles, CA 90036. (323) 634-1750. FAX (323) 634-1777.
San Francisco Office: 235 Pine Street, Ste. 1200, San Francisco, CA 94104. (415) 391-3838. FAX (415) 391-0102.
Orlando Office: 10319 Orangewood Blvd., Orlando, FL 32821. (407) 345-8800. FAX (407) 345-1222. www.actorsequity.org
PRESIDENT
Patrick Quinn
FIRST V.P.
Mark Zimmerman
SECOND V.P.
Jean-Paul Richard
THIRD V.P.
Alan Hall
CENTRAL REGIONAL V.P.
Madeleine Fallon
WESTERN REGIONAL V.P.
Carol Swarbrick
EASTERN REGIONAL V.P.
Arne Gundersen
SECRETARY & TREASURER
Conard Fowkes
COUNSEL
Spivak, Lipton, Watanabe, Spivak (NY)
Taylor, Roth, Bush & Geffner (L.A.)

AMERICAN CINEMA EDITORS
(Organized November 28, 1950. Membership: 500.)
100 Universal City Plaza, Bldg. 2282, Rm. 234, Universal City, CA 91608. www.ace-filmeditors.org
PRESIDENT
Mark Goldblatt
V.P.
Tina Hirsch
SECRETARY
Christopher Cooke
TREASURER
Ed Abroms

AMERICAN FEDERATION OF MUSICIANS (AFL-CIO)
(Organized October, 1896. Membership: 150,000.)
1501 Broadway, New York, NY 10036. (212) 869-1330. FAX: (212) 764-6134.
PRESIDENT
Steve Young
V.P.
Harold Bradley, 11 Music Circle, Nashville, TN 37212.
CANADIAN V.P.
David Jandrisch, 75 The Donway West, Ste. 1010, Don Mills, Ontario, Canada M3C 2E9.
SECRETARY-TREASURER
Tom Lee
EXECUTIVE BOARD
Thomas C. Bailey, Edward Ward, Tammy Kirk, Tim Shea, Kenneth B. Shirk

AMERICAN GUILD OF MUSICAL ARTISTS, INC.
(AAAA AFL CIO,)
(Organized 1936. Membership: 5,500.)
1727 Broadway, New York, NY 10019-5284. (212) 265-3687. FAX: (212) 262-9088.
PRESIDENT
Linda Mays
FIRST V.P.
Burman Timberlake
SECOND V.P.
James Odom
THIRD V.P.
John Colman
FOURTH V.P.
George Scott
FIFTH V.P.
Donna Marie Covert
TREASURER
Lynn A. Lundgren
NATIONAL EXECUTIVE SECRETARY
Alan S. Gordon
COUNSEL
Cohen, Weiss & Simon
MEMBERSHIP SUPERVISOR
Carl Saloga
RECORDING SECRETARY
Candace Itow
NATIONAL MANAGER OF ADMIN. & OPERATIONS
Gerry Angel

CANADA: Susan Wallace, 260 Richmond St. E., Toronto, Ontario M5A 1P4. (416) 867-9165. CHICAGO: Barbara J. Hillman, Cornfield & Feldman, 343 S. Dearborn St., 13th Flr., Chicago, IL 60604. (312) 922-2800. NEW ENGLAND: Robert M. Segal, 11 Beacon St., Boston, MA 02108. (617) 742-0208. NEW ORLEANS: Rosemary LeBoeuf, 4438 St. Peter St., New Orleans, LA 70119. (504) 486-9410. NORTHWEST: Carolyn C. Carpp, 11021 NE 123rd Lane, Apt. C114, Kirkland, WA 98034. (206) 820-2999. PHILADELPHIA: Gail Lopez-Henriquez, 400 Market St., Philadelphia, PA 19106. (215) 925-8400. PITTSBURGH: Frank Kerin, 223 Thompson Run, Pittsburgh, PA 15232. (412) 798-0550. SAN FRANCISCO: Harry Polland, Donald Tayer, Carol Birnhak, 235 Pine St., Suite 1100, San Francisco, CA 94104. (415) 986-4060. TEXAS: Benny Hopper, 3915 Fairlakes Dr., Dallas, TX 75228. (214) 279-4720. WASHINGTON DC: Eleni Kallas, 16600 Shea Lane, Gaithersburg, MD 20877. (301) 869-8266.

AMERICAN GUILD OF VARIETY ARTISTS
(AAAA AFL-CIO)
(Organized July 14, 1939. Registered Membership: 78,000.)
184 Fifth Ave., New York, NY 10010. (212) 675-1003.
4741 Laurel Canyon Blvd., #208, N. Hollywood, CA 91607. (818) 508-9984. FAX: (818) 508-3029. email: AGVANY@aol.com
PRESIDENT
Rod McKuen
EXECUTIVE SECRETARY-TREASURER
Frances Gaar
EXECUTIVE V.P.
David J. Cullen
HONORARY PRESIDENT
Phyllis Diller
HONORARY FIRST V.P.
Rip Taylor
REGIONAL V.P.S
Emelise Aleandri
Bobby Brookes
Mary Lynn Cullen
Susanne Doris
Larry Dorn
John Eaden
Wayne Hermans
Elaine Jacovini
Dee Dee Knapp-Brody
Paula Lane
Judy Little
Tina Marie
Stafford Mills
Victoria Reed
Dorothy Stratton
Dorothy Zuckerman

AMERICAN SOCIETY OF CINEMATOGRAPHERS
1782 N. Orange Dr., Hollywood, CA 90028. (323) 876-5080. FAX: (323) 882-6391.
PRESIDENT
Victor J. Kemper
FIRST V.P..
Steven B. Poster
SECOND V.P.
Laszlo Kovacs
THIRD V.P.
Russell P. Carpenter
TREASURER
Howard A. Anderson, Jr.
SECRETARY
John Hora
SERGEANT AT ARMS
Dean R. Cundey

ART DIRECTORS, HOLLYWOOD
LOCAL 876 (See IATSE).

ASSOCIATED ACTORS AND ARTISTS OF AMERICA (AAAA-AFL-CIO)
(Organized July 18, 1919. Membership: 93,000.)
165 W. 46 St., New York, NY 10036. (212) 869-0358. FAX: (212) 869-1746.
PRESIDENT
Theodore Bikel
V.P.S
Carl Harns
Rod McKuen
Kendall Orsatti
Seymour Rexite
Paul Borghese
TREASURER
Thomas Jamerson

ASSOCIATED MUSICIANS OF GREATER NEW YORK LOCAL 802 AFM (NEW YORK)
(Organized August 27, 1921. Membership: 15,000.)
322 W. 48 St., New York, NY 10036-1308. (212) 245-4802. FAX: (212) 489-6030.
PRESIDENT
William Moriarity
FINANCIAL V.P.
Mary Landolfi
RECORDING V.P.
Erwin Price

ASSOCIATION OF TALENT AGENTS
(Organized April, 1937. Official organization of Hollywood talent agents.)
9255 Sunset Blvd., Ste. 930, Los Angeles, CA 90069. (310) 274-0628. FAX: (310) 274-5063.
www.agentassociation.com email: agentassoc@aol.com
EXECUTIVE DIRECTOR
Karen Stuart
FIRST V.P.
Sandy Bresler
V.P.S
T. J. Escott
Sheldon Sroloff
Sonjia Warren Brandon
SECRETARY & TREASURER
Martin Gage

AUTHORS GUILD, INC.
(Membership: 8,200.)
330 W. 42 St., 29th Flr., New York, NY 10036-6902. (212) 563-5904. FAX: (212) 564-8363. www.authorsguild.org
email: staff@authorsguild.org
PRESIDENT
Letty Cottin Pogrebin
V.P.
James Gleick
SECRETARY
Pat Cummings
TREASURER
Peter Petre
EXECUTIVE DIRECTOR
Paul Aiken

THE AUTHORS LEAGUE OF AMERICA, INC.
(Membership: 15,000.)
Authors League, 330 W. 42 St., 29th Flr., New York, NY 10036. (212) 564-8350.
PRESIDENT
Leddy Pogrebin
ADMINISTRATOR
Paul Aiken

BROADCASTING STUDIO EMPLOYEES
LOCAL 782 (See IATSE)

DIRECTORS GUILD OF AMERICA, INC. (DGA)
7920 Sunset Blvd., Los Angeles, CA 90046. (310) 289-2000. FAX: (310) 289-2029.
110 W. 57 St., New York, NY 10019. (212) 581-0370. FAX: (212) 581-1441.
400 N. Michigan Ave., Ste. 307, Chicago, IL 60611. (312) 644-5050. FAX: (312) 644-5776.
330 N. Federal Highway, Hollywood, FL 33020. (954) 927-3338. FAX: (954) 923-8737.
PRESIDENT
Jack Shea
NATIONAL V.P.
Edwin Sherin
V.P.S
Larry Auerbach
Paris Barclay
Wiilliam M. Brady
Martha Coolidge
John Frankenheimer
Max A. Schindler
SECRETARY & TREASURER
Gilbert Cates
NATIONAL EXECUTIVE DIRECTOR
Jay D. Roth
Martha Coolidge
John Frankenheimer
Max A. Schindler
SECRETARY & TREASURER
Gilbert Cates
EXECUTIVE DIRECTOR
Jay D. Roth

THE DRAMATISTS GUILD OF AMERICA, INC.
1501 Broadway, Ste. 701, New York, NY 10036. (212) 398-9366. FAX: (212) 944-0420. www.dramaguild.com
PRESIDENT
John Weidman
V.P.
Marsha Norman
SECRETARY
Arthur Kopit
TREASURER
Christopher Durang
EXECUTIVE DIRECTOR
Christopher C. Wilson
COUNSEL
Cahill, Gordon & Reindel

EPISCOPAL ACTORS GUILD OF AMERICA, INC.
(Organized 1923. 700 members.)
One E. 29 St., New York, NY 10016. (212) 685-2927. FAX: (212) 782-8793.
EXECUTIVE SECRETARY
Mart Hulswit
PRESIDENT
Barnard Hughes
V.P. AND WARDEN
Rev. Frederic Brunson
V.P.S
Robert Aberdeen
Peter Harris
Cliff Robertson
Eugene Smith

EXHIBITION EMPLOYEES
LOCAL 829 (See IATSE)

FILM EXCHANGE EMPLOYEES, BACK ROOM, LOCALS (IATSE)
(See IATSE)

FILM EXCHANGE EMPLOYEES, FRONT OFFICE
LOCAL F-45 (See IATSE)

FIRST AID EMPLOYEES
LOCAL 767 (IATSE) (See IATSE)

HOLLYWOOD ENTERTAINMENT LABOR COUNCIL
(Organized September, 1947.)
c/o SAG (Yvette Foley) 5757 Wilshire Blvd., 8th Flr., Los Angeles, CA 90036. (323) 549-6613. FAX: (323) 549-6603.
PRESIDENT
Leonard Chassman
FIRST V.P.
Scott Roth
SECOND V.P.
Paul Petersen
THIRD V.P.
G. Lynd Bingham
SECRETARY-TREASURER
H. O'Neil Shanks

INTERNATIONAL ALLIANCE OF THEATRICAL STAGE EMPLOYEES & MOVING PICTURE TECHNICIANS, ARTISTS AND ALLIED CRAFTS OF THE U.S., ITS TERRITORIES, AND CANADA (AFL-CIO, CLC)
(Organized nationally, July 17, 1893; internationally, October 1, 1902. The Alliance comprises approximately 500 local unions covering the United States,its territories, Canada and Hawaii, P.R. & VI.) 1515 Broadway, Ste. 601, New York, NY 10036-5741. (212) 730-1770. FAX: (212) 921-7699.
INTERNATIONAL PRESIDENT
Thomas C. Short
GENERAL SECRETARY & TREASURER
Michael W. Proscia
FIRST V.P.
John J. Nolan
SECOND V.P.
Edward C. Powell
THIRD V.P.
Daniel J. Kerins
FOURTH V.P.
Rudy N. Napoleone
FIFTH V.P.
Carmine A. Palazzo

SIXTH V.P.
Jean Fox
SEVENTH V.P.
Timothy Magee
EIGHTH V.P.
James Wood
NINTH V.P.
Michael J. Sullivan
TENTH V.P.
Michael Barnes
ELEVENTH V.P.
J. Walter Cahill
INTERNATIONAL TRUSTEES
Albert A. Burns
Ron Cunningham
C. Faye Harper
AFL-CIO DELEGATES
Stephen R. Flint
Nancy Manganelli-Bues
CLC DELEGATE
C. Gus Bottas

IATSE PRODUCTION

AFFILIATED PROPERTY CRAFTSMEN LOCAL 44 (IATSE-AFL-CIO), HOLLYWOOD
12021 Riverside Dr., N. Hollywood, CA 91607 (818) 769-2500. FAX: (818) 769-1739. www.local44.org
SECRETARY
Walter Keske
BUSINESS AGENT
Ronald Cunningham
Walter Keske

ART DIRECTORS, LOCAL 876 (IATSE), HOLLYWOOD
11969 Ventura Blvd., #200, Studio City, CA 91604. (818) 762-9995. FAX: (818) 762-9997. www.artdirectors.org

COSTUME DESIGNERS GUILD LOCAL 892
13949 Ventura Blvd., Ste. 309, Sherman Oaks, CA 91423. (818) 905-1557. FAX: (818) 905-1560.
SECRETARY
Dan Moore

FIRST AID EMPLOYEES, LOCAL 767 (IATSE), LOS ANGELES
2611 Taffrail Lane, Oxnard CA 93035-1766. (805) 984-7918. FAX: (310) 523-3691.
SECRETARY
Eddie R. Clark

MOTION PICTURE COSTUMERS, LOCAL 705 (IATSE), HOLLYWOOD
1427 N. La Brea Ave., Hollywood, CA 90028. (323) 851-0220. FAX: (323) 851-9062.
SECRETARY
Paul DeLucca

MOTION PICTURE CRAFTS SERVICE LOCAL 80 (IATSE), HOLLYWOOD
2520 W. Olive, Burbank, CA 91505. (818) 526-0700. FAX: (818) 526-0719.
BUSINESS REPRESENTATIVE
Tom Davis

MOTION PICTURE & VIDEO EDITORS GUILD, LOCAL 700 (IATSE), LOS ANGELES
7715 Sunset Blvd., Ste. 200, Hollywood, CA 90046. (323) 876-4770. FAX: (323) 876-0861. www.editorsguild.com
EXECUTIVE DIRECTOR
Ronald G. Kutak
SECRETARY
Diane Adler

MOTION PICTURE EDITORS GUILD, LOCAL 700 (IATSE), NEW YORK
165 W. 46 St., Suite 900, New York, NY 10036. (212) 302-0700. FAX: (212) 302-1091. www.editorsguild.com
NATIONAL PRESIDENT
Don Cambern
ASST. EXECUTIVE DIRECTOR
Lorraine Seidel

MOTION PICTURE SCREEN CARTOONISTS, LOCAL 839 (IATSE), HOLLYWOOD
4729 Lankershim Blvd., N. Hollywood, CA 91602-1864. (818) 766-7151. FAX: (818) 506-4805.
SECRETARY
Jeffrey Massie

MOTION PICTURE SCRIPT SUPERVISORS AND PRODUCTION OFFICE COORDINATORS, LOCAL 161
630 9th Ave., #1103, New York, NY 10036. (212) 977-9655. FAX: (212) 977-9609.
BUSINESS MANAGER
Alan Myers

MOTION PICTURE SET PAINTERS, LOCAL 729 (IATSE), HOLLYWOOD
1811 W. Burbank Blvd., Burbank, CA 91506-1314. (818) 842-7729. FAX: (818) 846-3729.
BUSINESS DIRECTOR & SECRETARY
George A. Palazzo

MOTION PICTURE STUDIO ELECTRICAL LIGHTING TECHNICIANS, LOCAL 728 (IATSE)
14629 Nordhoff St., Panorama City, CA 91402. (818) 891-0728. FAX: (818) 891-5288.
BUSINESS REPRESENTATIVE SECRETARY
Norman Glasser

MOTION PICTURE STUDIO ART CRAFTSMEN, (ILLUSTRATORS AND MATTE ARTISTS) LOCAL 790 (IATSE), HOLLYWOOD
13949 Ventura Blvd., Ste. 301, Sherman Oaks, CA 91423. (818) 784-6555. FAX: (818) 784-2004.
SECRETARY
Camille Abbot

MOTION PICTURE STUDIO GRIPS, LOCAL 80 (IATSE), HOLLYWOOD
2520 W. Olive, Burbank, CA 91505. (818) 526-0700. FAX: (818) 526-0719.
SECRETARY
Rick Schurke

MOTION PICTURE STUDIO MECHANICS, LOCAL 476 (IATSE), CHICAGO
6309 N. Northwest Hwy., Chicago, IL 60631. (773) 775-5300. FAX: (773) 775-2477.
SECRETARY
J. Paul Oddo

MOTION PICTURE STUDIO TEACHERS AND WELFARE WORKERS, LOCAL 884 (IATSE) HOLLYWOOD
P.O. Box 461467, Los Angeles, CA 90046. (213) 650-3792.
SECRETARY
Craig Schoenfeld

PRODUCTION OFFICE COORDINATORS & ACCOUNTANTS GUILD LOCAL 717
1159 Chandler Blvd., North Hollywood, CA 91601. (818) 509-7871. FAX: (818) 506-1555.
BUSINESS AGENT
Lainie Miller

PUBLICISTS, LOCAL 818 (IATSE), HOLLYWOOD
13949 Ventura Blvd., Ste. 302, Sherman Oaks, CA 91423. (818) 905-1541. FAX: (818) 905-6944.
SECRETARY
Jess Garcia
BUSINESS AGENT
Marlene Mattaschiam

RADIO AND TELEVISION BROADCAST ENGINEERS, LOCAL 1212
230 W. 41st St., New York, NY 10036. (212) 354-6770. FAX: (212) 819-9517. www.ibew1212.org
BUSINESS MANAGER
Peter Quaranta

SCENIC & TITLE ARTISTS, LOCAL 816 (IATSE), LOS ANGELES
11969 Ventura Blvd., Ste. 204, Studio City, CA 91604. (818) 487-8161. FAX: (818) 487-8261. www.artist816.org
SECRETARY
Lisa Frazza
BUSINESS AGENT
Gavin J. Koon

SCRIPT SUPERVISORS, LOCAL 871 (IATSE), HOLLYWOOD
1159 Chandler Blvd., North Hollywood, CA 91601. (818) 509-7871. FAX: (818) 506-1555.
BUSINESS AGENT
Lainie Miller

SET DESIGNERS AND MODEL MAKERS, LOCAL 847 (IATSE), HOLLYWOOD
13949 Ventura Blvd., Ste. 301, Sherman Oaks, CA 91423. (818) 784-6555. FAX: (818) 784-2004.
SECRETARY
Suzanne Feller-Otto

STORY ANALYSTS, LOCAL 700 (IATSE), HOLLYWOOD
(See Motion Picture Editors Guild, Local 700)

STUDIO MECHANICS, LOCAL 479 (IATSE), ATLANTA
P.O. Box 78757, Atlanta, GA 30357. 404-885-9134. FAX: (404) 367-0240. www.iatse479.com
SECRETARY
Suzanne L. Carter
BUSINESS AGENT
Michael Akins

STUDIO MECHANICS, LOCAL 812 (IATSE), DETROIT
20017 Van Dyke, Detroit, MI 48234. (313) 368-0825. FAX: (313) 368-1151.
SECRETARY
John Connelly

STUDIO MECHANICS, LOCAL 52 (IATSE), NEW YORK
326 W. 48 St., New York, NY 10036. (212) 399-0980. FAX: (212) 315-1073. www.iatselocal52.org
SECRETARY
John R. Ford

STUDIO MECHANICS, LOCAL 477 (IATSE), N. MIAMI
10705 N.W. 33th St., Ste. 110, Miami, FL 33172. (305) 594-8585. FAX: (305) 597-9278.
SECRETARY
George Cerchiai
BUSINESS AGENT
Michael McCarthy

STUDIO MECHANICS, LOCAL 209 (IATSE), OHIO
1468 West 9th St., Rm. 435, Cleveland, OH 44113. (216) 621-9537. FAX: (216) 621-3518.
BUSINESS AGENT
Peter Lambros
SECRETARY
Kenneth McCahan

STUDIO MECHANICS, LOCAL 480 (IATSE), SANTA FE
P.O. Box 1563 Santa Fe NM 87506-5633. (505) 473-5100. FAX: (505) 505 424-0100. www.iatse480.com
SECRETARY
J R Pollard
BUSINESS AGENT
Stephen Mullen

STUDIO MECHANICS, LOCAL 484 (IATSE), TEXAS
440 Louisiana, Ste. 480, Houston, TX 77002. (713) 229-8357. FAX: (713) 229-8138.
SECRETARY
Janelle V. Flanagan

THEATRICAL WARDROBE ATTENDANTS, LOCAL 768 (IATSE), LOS ANGELES
13949 Ventura Blvd., Ste. 307, Sherman Oaks, CA 91423. (818) 789-8735. FAX: (818) 789-1928.
SECRETARY
Mary B. Seward
BUSINESS AGENT
Dorothy Priest FAX: (626) 905-6297

THEATRICAL WARDROBE UNION, LOCAL 764 (IATSE), NEW YORK
545 W. 45th St., 2nd Flr., New York, NY 10036. (212) 957-3500. FAX: (212) 957-3232.
SECRETARY/TREASURER
Jenna Krempel
BUSINESS REPRESENTATIVE
James Hurley

EXHIBITION

EXHIBITION EMPLOYEES, LOCAL 829 (IATSE), NEW YORK
150 E. 58 St., New York, NY 10022. (212) 752-4427. FAX: (212) 826-2275.
SECRETARY
John V. McNamee, Jr.

OPERATORS LOCAL 150 (IATSE), LOS ANGELES
1545 N. Verdugo Rd., Ste. 9, Glendale, CA 91208. (818) 240-5644. FAX: (818) 240-6196.
SECRETARY
Teri L. McClintock

MOTION PICTURE PROJECTIONISTS & VIDEO TECHNICIANS, LOCAL 110 (IATSE), CHICAGO
230 W. Monroe St., Ste. 2511, Chicago, IL 60606. (312) 443-1011. FAX: (312) 443-1012.
SECRETARY
Al. Brenkus

MOTION PICTURE PROJECTIONISTS, VIDEO TECHNICIANS, & THEATRE EMPLOYESS, LOCAL 306 (IATSE), NEW YORK
723 Seventh Ave., 11th Flr., New York, NY 10019. (212) 764-6270, (212) 719-3122. FAX: (212) 302-6369. www.local306.org
SECRETARY
Joel Deitch
BUSINESS REPRESENTATIVE
Michael Goldberg

STAGE EMPLOYEES, LOCAL 4 (IATSE), BROOKLYN
2917 Glenwood Rd., Brooklyn, NY 11210. (718) 252-8777. FAX: (718) 421-5605.
SECRETARY
Terence Ryan

STAGE EMPLOYEES, LOCAL 2 (IATSE), CHICAGO
20 N. Wacker Dr., Ste. 1032, Chicago, IL 60606. (312) 236-3457. FAX: (312) 236-0701.
SECRETARY
Thomas J. Cleary

STAGE EMPLOYEES, LOCAL 33 (IATSE), LOS ANGELES
1720 W. Magnolia Blvd., Burbank, CA 91506-1871. (818) 841-9233. FAX: (818) 567-1138. www.ia33.org
SECRETARY
Joseph F. Doucette, Jr.

STAGE EMPLOYEES, LOCAL 1 (IATSE), NEW YORK
320 W. 46 St., New York, NY 10036. (212) 333-2500. FAX: (212) 586-2437. www.iatse-local1.org
SECRETARY
Frank Dwyer

THEATRE EMPLOYEES, LOCAL B-46 (IATSE), CHICAGO
230 W. Monroe St., Ste. 2511, Chicago, IL 60606. (312) 443-1011. FAX: (312) 443-1012.
SECRETARY
Al Brenkus

THEATRE EMPLOYEES, LOCAL B-183 (IATSE), NEW YORK
319 W. 48th St., New York, NY 10036. (212) 586-9620. FAX: (212) 586-7106.
SECRETARY
Mary A. Huff

TREASURERS AND TICKET SELLERS, LOCAL 750 (IATSE), CHICAGO
446 N. Edgewood, LaGrange Park, IL 60525. (708) 579-9381. FAX: (708) 352-9085.
SECRETARY
Gene McElwain

TREASURERS AND TICKET SELLERS, LOCAL 857 (IATSE), LOS ANGELES
13949 Ventura Blvd., Ste. 303, Sherman Oaks, CA 91423. (818) 990-7107. FAX: (818) 990-8287.
SECRETARY
Deirdre Floyd

TREASURERS AND TICKET SELLERS, LOCAL 751 (IATSE), NEW YORK
1500 Broadway, Rm. 2011, New York, NY 10036. (212) 302-7300. FAX: (212) 944-8687.
SECRETARY
Gene McElwain

INTERNATIONAL BROTHERHOOD OF ELECTRICAL WORKERS (AFL-CIO, CFL)
(Organized November 28, 1891. Membership: over one million.)
1125 15th St. N.W., Washington, DC 20005. (202) 833-7000.
INTERNATIONAL PRESIDENT
John J. Barry
INTERNATIONAL SECRETARY/TREASURER
Edwin D. Hill

DISTRICT OFFICES
ALABAMA: Melvin Horton, 100 Concourse Pkwy., Ste. 300, Brimingham, AL 35244.
CALIFORNIA: Michael Mowrey, 2500 Venture Oaks Way, Ste. 250, Sacramento, CA 95833-3287.
CANADA: Donald Louds, 1450 Meyerside Dr., Ste. 300, Mississuga, Ontario L5T 2N5.
IDAHO: Jon F. Walters, 330 Shoup Ave., Ste. 204, P.O. Box 51216, Idaho Falls, ID 83405.
ILLINOIS: Jeremiah J. O'Conner, 8174 Cass Ave., Darien, IL 60561.
MASSACHUSETTS: Frank J. Carroll, 100 Grandview Rd., Ste. 111, Braintree, MA 02184.
MISSOURI: William C. Eads, 300 South Jefferson, Ste.300, Springfield, MO 65806.
OHIO: Paul J. Witte, 7710 Reading Rd., Ste. 9, Cincinnati, OH 45237.
OKLAHOMA: Orville A. Tate, Jr., 4400 Will Rogers Pkwy., Ste. 309, Oklahoma City, OK 73108.
PENNSYLVANIA: Lawrence E. Rossa, 500 Cherrington Pkwy., Ste. 325, Coraopolis, PA 15108.
TENNESSEE: Carl Lansden, 5726 Marlin Rd., Ste. 500, Chattanooga, TN 37411-4043.

IBEW, LOCAL 349 (FILM)
1657 N.W. 17th Ave., Miami, FL 33125. (305) 325-1330. FAX: (305) 325-1521.
BUSINESS MANAGER
Art Fernandez

IBEW, LOCAL 40 (FILM)
5643 Vineland Ave., North Hollywood, CA 91601. (818) 762-4239.
www.local40.com email: local40@earthlink.net
BUSINESS MANAGER
Rick DesJardins

INTERNATIONAL SOUND TECHNICIANS OF THE MOTION PICTURE BROADCAST AND AMUSEMENT INDUSTRIES
LOCAL 695 (See IATSE)

LABORATORY TECHNICIANS
LOCALS 683, 702 and 780 (See IATSE)

MAKE-UP ARTISTS & HAIR STYLISTS
LOCALS 706 and 798 (See IATSE)

MOTION PICTURE COSTUMERS
LOCAL 705 (See IATSE)

MOTION PICTURE CRAFTS SERVICE
LOCAL 727 (See IATSE)

MOTION PICTURE & VIDEO EDITORS
LOCALS 771 and 776 (See IATSE)

MOTION PICTURE HOME OFFICE EMPLOYEES
LOCAL H-63 (See IATSE)

MOTION PICTURE SCREEN CARTOONISTS
LOCAL 839 (See IATSE)

MOTION PICTURE SET PAINTERS
LOCAL 729 (See IATSE)

MOTION PICTURE STUDIO ELECTRICAL TECHNICIANS
LOCAL 728 (See IATSE)

PRODUCER-WRITERS GUILD OF AMERICA PENSION PLAN
1015 N. Hollywood Way, Burbank, CA 91505. (818) 846-1015, (800) 227-7863. FAX: (818) 566-8445.
INTERIM ADMINISTRATOR
Dianne White

PRODUCERS GUILD OF AMERICA
(Founded 1950. Membership: 500.)
6363 Sunset Blvd., Ninth Flr., Los Angeles, CA 90028. (323) 960-2590. FAX :(323) 960-2591. email: thepga@pacbell.net
PRESIDENT
Thom Mount
V.P., MOTION PICTURES
Hawk Koch
V.P., TELEVISION
Marian Rees
SECRETARY
Charles Floyd Johnson
TREASURER
Joel Freeman
EXECUTIVE DIRECTOR
Vance Van Patten

PROFESSIONAL MUSICIANS, LOCAL 47, (AFM, AFL-CIO)
(Organized October 30, 1894. Membership: 10,000.)
817 N. Vine St., Hollywood, CA 90038. (213) 462-2161. FAX: (213) 461-5260, (213) 466-1289, (213) 461-3090.
PRESIDENT
Bill Peterson
VICE PRESIDENT
Hal Espinosa
SECRETARY
Serena Kay Williams
TREASURER
Richard Totusek
TRUSTEES
Vince Trombetta, Abe Most, Irving Bush
DIRECTORS
William (Buddy) Collette
Art Davis
Vince DiBari
Lyle (Spud) Murphy
Jay Rosen
Ann Stockton

PROJECTIONISTS, IATSE & MPMO LOCALS
(See IATSE)

PUBLICISTS GUILD, INC.
LOCAL 818 (See IATSE)

RADIO & TELEVISION SOUND EFFECTS
LOCAL 844 (See IATSE)

SCENIC ARTISTS
LOCAL 816 (See IATSE)

SCREEN ACTORS GUILD (AAAA-AFL-CIO)
(Organized July 1933. Membership: 96,000.)
5757 Wilshire Blvd., Los Angeles, CA 90036-3600. (323) 954-1600, (323) 549-6652. FAX: (323) 549-6656, (323) 549-6603.
PRESIDENT
William Daniels
RECORDING SECRETARY
Karen Austin
TREASURER
F.J. O'Neil
FIRST V.P.
Sumi Haru (Hollywood)
SECOND V.P.
Lisa Scarola (New York)
THIRD V.P.
Richard Herd (Hollywood)
FOURTH V.P.
Eileen Henry (New York)
FIFTH V.P.
Mary Seibel (Chicago)
SIXTH V.P.
Chuck Dorsett (San Francisco)
SEVENTH V.P.
Laird Stuart (Florida)
EIGHTH V.P.
D.J. Sullivan (Regional Branches)
NINTH V.P.
Gary Epp (Hollywood)
TENTH V.P.
Maureen Donnelly (New York)
ELEVENTH V.P.
David Jolliffe (Hollywood)
TWELFTH V.P.
Larry Keith (New York)
NATIONAL EXECUTIVE DIRECTOR
Ken Orsatti
ASSOCIATE NATIONAL EXECUTIVE DIRECTOR
John McGuire
HOLLYWOOD EXECUTIVE DIRECTOR
Leonard Chassman
DIRECTOR, COMMUNICATIONS
Greg Krizman
COUNSEL
Leo Geffner
DIRECTOR, FINANCE
Gerald Wilson
DIRECTOR OF ADMINISTRATION
Clinta Dayton

DISTRICT OFFICES
ARIZONA: Don Livesay, 1616 East Indian School Rd., Ste. 330, Phoenix, AZ 85016. (602) 265-2712. FAX: (602) 264-7571.
BOSTON: Dona Sommers, 11 Beacon St., Rm. 512, Boston, MA 02108. (617) 742-2688. FAX: (617) 742-4904.
CHICAGO: Eileen Willenborg, One E. Erie St., Ste. 650, Chicago, IL 60611. (312) 573-8081. FAX: (312) 573-0318.
CLEVELAND: Stephen Hatch, 1030 Euclid Ave., Ste. 429, Cleveland, OH 44115. (216) 579-9305. FAX: (216) 781-2257.
COLORADO: Susan Gurule, Devon Nance, 950 S. Cherry Street, Ste. 502, Denver, CO 80246. (303) 757-6226. FAX: (303) 757-1769.
DALLAS: Ken Freehill, 6060 N. Central Expressway, Ste. 302, LB 604, Dallas, TX 75206. (214) 363-8300. FAX: (214) 363-5386.
DETROIT: Barbara Honner, 27770 Franklin Road, Southfield, MI 48034. (248) 355-3105. FAX: (248) 355-2879.
FLORIDA: Hollis Batchelor, 7300 N. Kendall Dr., Ste. 620, Miami, FL 33156. (305) 670-7677. FAX: (305) 670-1813.; Joel Binford, 646 W. Colonial Dr., Orlando, FL 32804. (407) 649-3100. FAX: (407) 649-7222.
GEORGIA: Melissa Goodman, 455 E. Paces Ferry Rd., NE, #334, Atlanta, GA 30305. (404) 239-0131. FAX: (404) 239-0137.
HAWAII: Brenda Ching, 949 Kapiolani Blvd., Ste. 105, Honolulu, HI 96814. (808) 596-0388. FAX: (808) 593-2636.
HOLLYWOOD: Ken Orsatti, Leonard Chassman, 5757 Wilshire Blvd., Los Angeles, CA 90036. (213) 954-1600. FAX: (323) 549-6603.
HOUSTON: Jack Dunlop, 2400 Augusta Dr., Ste. 264, Houston, TX 77057. (713) 972-1806. FAX: (713) 780-0261.
MINNEAPOLIS/ST. PAUL: Colleen Aho, 708 N. First St., Ste. 333, Minneapolis, MN 55401. (612) 371-9120. FAX: (612) 372-9119.
NASHVILLE: Randall Himes, 1108 17th Ave. S, P.O. Box 121087, Nashville, TN 37212. (615) 327-2944. FAX: 615) 329-2803.
NEVADA: Bobbi Hughes, 3900 Paradise Rd., Ste. 206, Las Vegas, NV 89109. (702) 737) 8818. FAX: (702) 737-8851.
NEW YORK: John McGuire, John Sucke, 1515 Broadway, 44th Flr., New York, NY 10036. (212) 944-1030. FAX: (212) 944-6774.
NORTH CAROLINA: Patti Pocsik, 311 N. Second St, Ste. 2, Wilmington, NC 28401. (910) 762-1889. FAX: (910) 762-0881.
PHILADELPHIA: John Kailin, 230 South Broad St., 10th Flr., Philadelphia, PA 19102. (215) 545-3150. FAX: (215) 732-0086.
PORTLAND: Stuart Pemble-Belkin, 3030 S.W. Moody, Ste. 104, Portland, OR 97201. (503) 279-9600. FAX: (503) 279-9603.

PUERTO RICO: Jose Luis Rey, 530 Ponce de Leon Ave., Ste. 312, San Juan, Puerto Rico 00901. (787) 289-7832 ext. 3212. FAX: (787) 289-8732.
ST. LOUIS: Jackie Dietrich, 1310 Papin St., Ste. 103, St. Louis, MO 63103. (314) 231-8410. FAX: (314) 231-8412.
SAN DIEGO: Tom Doyle, 7827 Convoy Court, Ste. 400, San Diego, CA 92111. (858) 278-7695. FAX: (858) 278-2505.
SAN FRANCISCO: Frank DuCharme, 235 Pine St., 11th Flr., San Francisco, CA 94104. (415) 391-7510. FAX: (415) 391-1108.
SEATTLE: Joan Kalhorn, 601 Valley St., Ste. 100, Seattle, WA 98109. (206) 270-0493. FAX: (206) 282-7073.
WASHINGTON DC/BALTIMORE: Patricia O'Donnell, 4340 East West Highway, Ste. 204, Bethesda, MD 20814. (301) 657-2560. FAX: (301) 656-3615.

SCRIPT SUPERVISORS & SCREEN COMPOSERS OF AMERICA

2451 Nichols Canyon Rd., Los Angeles, CA 90046-1798. (323) 876-6040. FAX: (323) 876-6041.
PRESIDENT
Herschel Burke Gilbert
V.P.
John Parker
SECRETARY
Frank DeVol
TREASURER
Nathan Scott

SCREEN WRITERS' GUILD, INC.

(See Writers Guild of America)

SCRIPT SUPERVISORS

LOCAL 871 (See IATSE)

SET DESIGNERS AND MODEL MAKERS

LOCAL 847 (See IATSE)

SOCIETY OF MOTION PICTURE ART DIRECTORS

LOCAL 876 (See IATSE)

THE SONGWRITERS GUILD OF AMERICA

1500 Harbor Blvd., Weehawken, NJ 07087-6732. (201) 867-7603. FAX: (201) 867-7335. www.songwriters.org
1560 Broadway, Room 1306, New York, NY 10036. (212) 768-7902. FAX: (212) 768-9048. email SGANews@aol.com
6430 Sunset Blvd., Ste. 705, Hollywood, CA 90028. (323) 462-1108. FAX: (323) 462-5430. email: LASGA@aol.com
1222 16th Avenue South, Ste. 25, Nashville, TN 37212. (615) 329-1782. FAX: (615) 329-2623.
email: SGANash@aol.com
PRESIDENT
George David Weiss
EXECUTIVE DIRECTOR
Lewis M. Bachman

STAGE EMPLOYEES

LOCALS 1, 2, 4 and 33 (See IATSE)

STORY ANALYSTS

LOCAL 854 (See IATSE)

STUDIO GRIPS

LOCAL 80 (See IATSE)

STUDIO MECHANICS

LOCALS 52 and 476 (See IATSE)

STUDIO PROJECTIONISTS

LOCAL 165 (See IATSE)

STUDIO PROPERTY CRAFTSMEN

LOCAL 44 (See IATSE)

STUNTMEN'S ASSOCIATION

(Organized 1961.)
10660 Riverside Dr., 2nd Flr., Ste. E, Toluca Lake, CA 91602. (818) 766-4334. FAX: (818) 766-5943. www.stuntmen.com
PRESIDENT
Fred Lerner

THEATRE AUTHORITY, INC.

(Organized May 21, 1934.)
729 Seventh Ave., 11th Flr., New York, NY 10019. (212) 764-0156. FAX: (212) 764-0158.
EXECUTIVE DIRECTOR
Helen Leahy
PRESIDENT
Tony Roberts
FIRST V.P.
John H. Sucke
SECOND V.P.
Terry Walker
THIRD V.P.
Robert J. Bruyr
FOURTH V.P.
Rod McKuen
RECORDING SECRETARY
Thomas H. Jamerson
TREASURER
Joan Greenspan
REPRESENTATIVE
Frances Garr
ADVISORY COMMITTEE
Jane Alexander, Julie Andrews, Lucie Arnaz, Harry Belafonte, Theodore Bikel, Ellen Burstyn, Billy Davis Jr., Hugh Downs, Patty Duke, Richard Dysart, Hector Elizondo, Barbara Feldon, John Forsythe, Barry Gordon, Robert Goulet, Eileen Heckart, Charlton Heston, Celeste Holm, Bob Hope, Barnard Hughes, Jack Jones, Alan King, Robert Klein, Werner Klemperer, Angela Lansbury, Ron Liebman, Patti Lupone, Marilyn McCoo, Ed McMahon, Ann Miller, Jerry Orbach, Estelle Parsons, Gregory Peck, Jane Powell, Tony Randall, Lou Rawls, Lynn Redgrave, Debbie Reynolds, Barbra Streisand, Nancy Wilson.

THEATRE EMPLOYEES

LOCALS B-46 and B-183 (See IATSE)

THEATRICAL WARDROBE ATTENDANTS

LOCALS 764, 768 and 769 (See IATSE)

WRITERS GUILD OF AMERICA, EAST, INC.

555 W. 57th St., New York, NY 10019. (212) 767-7800. FAX: 212) 582-1909. www.wgaeast.org
PRESIDENT
Herb Sargent
EXECUTIVE DIRECTOR
Mona Mangan

WRITERS GUILD OF AMERICA, WEST, INC.

7000 W. 3rd St., Los Angeles, CA 90048. (323) 951-4000. FAX: (323) 782-4800.
PRESIDENT
John Wells
V.P.
Daniel Petrie, Jr.
EXECUTIVE DIRECTOR
John McLean

STATE & CITY FILM COMMISSIONS

ALABAMA

ALABAMA FILM OFFICE
401 Adams Ave., Montgomery, AL 36130. (800) 633-5898, (334) 242-4195. FAX: (334) 242-2077.
www.telefilm-south.com/Alabama/Alabama.html
FILM LIAISON
Courtney Murphy

CITY OF MOBILE FILM OFFICE
150 South Royal Street, P. O. Box 1827, Mobile, AL 36693. (334) 208-7305. FAX: (334) 208-7659.
DIRECTOR:
Eva Golson

ARIZONA

ARIZONA FILM COMMISSION
3800 N. Central Ave., Bldg. D, Phoenix, AZ 85012. (602) 280-1380, (800) 523-6695. FAX: (602) 280-1384.
DIRECTOR
Linda Peterson Warren

CITY OF PHOENIX FILM OFFICE
200 W. Washington, 10th fl., Phoenix, AZ 85003. (602) 262-4850. FAX: (602) 534-2295
PROGRAM MANAGER
Luci Fontanilla

CITY OF SCOTTSDALE
3939 Civic Center Blvd., Scottsdale, AZ 85251. (480) 312-7828. FAX: (480) 312-7011
FILM LIAISON
Leslie Diamond

APACHE JUNCTION CHAMBER OF COMMERCE
P.O. Box 1747, Apache Junction, AZ 85217-1747. (602) 982-3141, (800) 252-3141. FAX: (602) 982-3234.
email: chamber@ciapache-jct.az.us
www.goldcanyon.com.ajfc
DIRECTOR
Carolyn A. Doty

COCHISE COUNTY FILM COMMISSION
1415 W. Melody Lane, Building B, Bisbee, AZ 85603. (520) 432-9454. FAX: (520) 432-9656.
email: lsmall@cochisecounty.com
www.arizonaguide.com/cochise
DIRECTOR
Linda M. Small

COTTONWOOD FILM COMMISSION
1010 S. Main Street, Cottonwood, AZ 86326. (520) 634-7593. FAX: (520) 634-7594.
DIRECTOR
Peter A. Sesow

FLAGSTAFF FILM COMMISSION
1300 S. Milton Rd., Suite 125, Flagstaff, AZ 86001. (520) 779-7658, (800) 595-7658. FAX: (520) 556-0940.
email: marcied@gfec.org
DIRECTOR
Marcie Delmotte

GLOBE/MIAMI FILM COMMISSION
1360 North Broad Street, U.S. 60, P.O. Box 2539, Globe, AZ 85502. (520) 425-4495, (800) 804-5623. FAX: (520) 425-3410.
DIRECTOR
Gerald Kohlbeck

KINGMAN FILM COMMISSION
P. O. Box 1150, Kingman, AZ 86402. (520) 753-5100. FAX: (520) 753-1049.
DIRECTOR
Beverly J. Liles

NAVAJO NATION FILM OFFICE
Highway 264, P. O. Box 2310, Window Rock, AZ 86515. (520) 871-7351. FAX: (520) 871-7355.
email: navflmof@cia-g.com
www.cia-g.com/~navflmof
DIRECTOR
Karen Bedonie

PAGE/LAKE POWELL FILM COMMISSION
644 N. Navajo Drive, P.O. Box 727, Page, AZ 86040. (520) 645-2741. FAX: (520) 645-3181.
email: chamber@page-lakepowell.com
DIRECTOR
Joan Nevills Staveley

CITY OF PRESCOTT
P.O. Box 2059, Prescott, AZ 86302. (520) 445-3500. FAX: (520) 776-6255.
DIRECTOR
Greg Fister

SAFFORD/GRAHAM COUNTY REGIONAL FILM OFFICE
1111 Thatcher Boulevard, Safford, AZ 85546. (520) 428-2511, (888) 837-1841. FAX: (520) 428-0744.
DIRECTOR
Sheldon Miller

SEDONA FILM COMMISSION
P.O. Box 2489, Sedona, AZ 86339. (520) 204-1123. FAX: (520) 204-1064.
DIRECTOR
Frank Miller

TUCSON FILM OFFICE
166 W. Alameda, P. O. Box 27210, Tucson, AZ 85726-7210. (520) 791-4000. FAX: 520-791-5413.
email: shall1@ci.tucson.az.us
DIRECTOR
Shelli Hall

WICKENBURG FILM COMMISSION
216 North Frontier Street, Wickenburg, AZ 85390. (520) 684-5479. FAX: (520) 684-5470. email: wburgcoc@primenet.com
www.wickenburgchamber.com
DIRECTOR
Julie Brooks

YUMA FILM COMMISSION
850 West 32nd Street, Suite 6, Yuma, AZ 85364. (520) 341-1616. FAX: (520) 341-1685.
DIRECTOR
Yvonne Taylor

ARKANSAS

ARKANSAS FILM OFFICE
One State Capitol Mall, 4th floor, Little Rock, AR 72201. (501) 682-7676. FAX: (501) 682-FILM. email: jglass@1800ARKANSAS.com
FILM & VIDEO PROMOTIONS SPECIALIST
Joe Glass

CALIFORNIA

ANTELOPE VALLEY FILM OFFICE
44933 North Fern Avenue, Lancaster, CA 93534. (661) 723-6090. FAX: (661) 723-5914. email: peast@city.lancaster.ca.us
www.avfilm.com
DIRECTOR
Pauline East

BERKELEY FILM OFFICE
2015 Center Street, Berkeley, CA 94704-1204. (510) 549-7040, (800) 847-4823. FAX: (510) 644-2052.
email: bconvis@ix.netcom.com
www.berkeleycvb.com
DIRECTOR
Barbara Hillman

BIG BEAR LAKE FILM OFFICE
39707 Big Bear Boulevard, P.O. Box 10000, Big Bear Lake, CA 92315. (909) 878-3040. FAX: (909) 866-6766.
email: bblfilm@citybigbearlake.com
www.citybigbearlake.com/film.html
DIRECTOR
Ranee Ruble

CALIFORNIA FILM COMMISSION
7080 Hollywood Blvd., Suite 900, Hollywood, CA 90028. (800) 858-4PIX. FAX: (323) 860-2972. email: filmca@commerce.ca.gov
DIRECTOR
Patti Stolkin Archuletta

CHICO CHAMBER/BUTTE COUNTY FILM COMMISSION
300 Salem Street, Chico, CA 95928. (530) 891-5556 x 326, (800) 852-8570. FAX: (530) 891-3613.
email: ccsusan@aol.com
DIRECTOR
Susan Peterson

CATALINA ISLAND FILM COMMISSION
313 Beacon Street, P.O. Box 217, Avalon, CA 90704. (310) 510-7646. FAX: 310-510-1646. email: bureau@catalinas.net
www.catalinas.net
DIRECTOR
Shirley Davy

CITY OF SAN DIEGO
San Diego Film Commission, 1010 Second Ave, #1500, San Diego, CA 92101-4912. (619) 234-3456. FAX: (619) 234-4631.
FILM COMMISSIONER
Cathy Anderson

CITY OF SAN FRANCISCO
San Francisco Film and Video Arts Commission, 1 Dr. Carlton B. Goodlett Place, Rm. #473, San Francisco, CA 94102. (415) 554-6244. FAX: (415) 554-6503
DIRECTOR
P.J. Johnston

CITY OF SAN JOSE
San Jose Film & Video Commission, 333 W. San Carlos St., Suite 1000, San Jose, CA 95110. (408) 295-9600, (800) SAN-JOSE. FAX: (408) 295-3937. email: jokane@sanjose.org
www.sanjose.org
EXECUTIVE DIRECTOR
Joe O' Kane

CITY OF WEST HOLLYWOOD
8300 Santa Monica Boulevard, West Hollywood, CA 90069-4314. (323) 848-6489. FAX: (323) 848-6561.
email: wehofilm@ci.west-hollywood.ca.us
www.ci.west-hollywood.ca.us/
DIRECTOR
Terry S. House

CLOVIS FILM OFFICE
325 Pollasky Avenue, Clovis, CA 93612. (209) 299-7273. FAX: (209) 299-2969. email: cfodir@aol.com
www.c-f-o.com
DIRECTOR
Michael D. Long

COUNTY OF LOS ANGELES
Entertainment Industry Development Corp., Los Angeles Film Office, 7083 Hollywood Blvd., Suite 500, Hollywood, CA 90028. (323) 957-1000. FAX: (323) 962-4966.
PRESIDENT
Cody Cluff

EL DORADO/TAHOE FILM COMMISSION
542 Main Street, Placerville, CA 95667. (530) 626-4400, (800) 457-6279. FAX: (530) 642-1624. email: filmtaho@calweb.com
www.calweb.com/~filmtaho
DIRECTOR
Kathleen Dodge

EUREKA! HUMBOLDT FILM COMMISSION
1034 Second Street, Eureka, CA 95501-0541. (707) 443-5097, (800) 346-3482. FAX: (707) 443-5115.
email: redwoodvis@aol.com
www.redwoodvisitor.org
DIRECTOR
Don Leonard

FRESNO FILM COMMISSION
808 M Street, Fresno, CA 93721. (800) 788-0836, (559) 233-0836. FAX: (559) 445-0122. email: tourfresno@aol.com
DIRECTOR
Brian Ziegler

IMPERIAL COUNTY FILM COMMISSION
940 West Main Street, Suite 208, El Centro, CA 92243. (760) 339-4290, (800) 345-6437. FAX: (760) 352-7876.
DIRECTOR
Cindy Stillman

THE INLAND EMPIRE FILM COMMISSION
301 E. Vanderbilt Way, Suite 100, San Bernardino, CA 92408. (909) 890-1090, (800) 500-4367. FAX: (909) 890-1088.
email: sdavis@ieep.com, rshandil@ieep.com
www.filminlandempire.com
DIRECTOR
Sheri Davis

KERN COUNTY BOARD OF TRADE
2101 Oak Street, P. O. Bin 1312, Bakersfield, CA 93302. (805) 861-2367, (800) 500-KERN. FAX: (805) 861-2017.
email: tourism@lightspeed.net
DIRECTOR
Ann Gutcher

LAKE COUNTY MARKETING PROGRAM
875 Lakeport Boulevard, Lakeport, CA 95453. (707) 263-9544, (800) 525-3743. FAX: (707) 263-9564.
email: info@lakecounty.com
www.lakecounty.com
DIRECTOR
Wilda Shock

LASSEN COUNTY FILM COMMISSION
810 Nevada Street, Susanville, CA 96130. (530) 257-6098. FAX: (530) 257-5929. email: lkoppelman@filmlassen.org
www.filmlassen.org
DIRECTOR
Lillian Koppelman

LONG BEACH OFFICE OF SPECIAL EVENTS
333 W. Ocean Blvd., 13th Floor, Long Beach, CA 90802. (562) 570-5333. FAX: (562) 570-5335.
DIRECTOR
Jo Ann Burns

MADERA COUNTY FILM COMMISSION
41729 Highway 41, Oakhurst, CA 93644. (559) 683-4636. FAX: (559) 683-5697. email: ysvb@sierratel.com

MALIBU CITY FILM COMMISSION
23555 Civic Center Way, Malibu, CA 91360. (310) 456-2489 x-236. FAX: (310) 456-5799. email: kcollins@ci.malibu.ca.us
www.ci.malibu.ca.us
DIRECTOR
Kimberly Collins

MENDOCINO COUNTY FILM OFFICE
332 N. Main Street, Fort Bragg, CA 95437. (707) 961-6303, (800)-726-2780. FAX: (707) 964-2056.
email: chamber@mcn.org
DIRECTOR
Cammie King Conlon

OAKLAND FILM COMMISSION
250 Frank H. Ogawa Plaza, #3315, Oakland, CA 94612. (510) 238-4734. FAX: (510) 238-2226.
DIRECTOR
Ami Zins

MONTEREY COUNTY
Monterey County Film Commission, P.O. Box 111, Monterey, CA 93942-0111. (831) 646-0910. FAX: (831) 655-9244.
email: mryfilm@aol.com; www.filmmonterey.org
EXECUTIVE DIRECTOR
Karen Nordstrand

ORANGE COUNTY FILM COMMISSION
2 Park Plaza, Suite 100, Irvine, CA 92614. (949) 476-2242, (800) 628-8033. FAX: (949) 476-0513.
email: dhausdorfer@ocbc.org
www.ocbc.org
DIRECTOR
Debi Hausdorfer

PALM SPRINGS DESERT RESORTS CVB/FILM OFFICE
69-930 Highway 111, Suite 201, Rancho Mirage, CA 92270. (760) 770-9000, (800) 96-RESORTS. FAX: (760) 770-9001.
email: lenaz@desert-resorts.org
www.desert-resorts.com
DIRECTOR
Lena Zimmerschied

PASADENA FILM OFFICE
175 North Garfield Avenue, Pasadena, CA 91109. (626) 744-3964. FAX: (626)-744-4785. email: apenn@ci.pasadena.ca.us
www.filmpasadena.com
email: jbrice@ci.pasadena.ca.us
DIRECTOR
Ariel Penn

PLACER COUNTY FILM OFFICE
175 Fulweiler Avenue, Auburn, CA 95603-4543. (530) 889-4016, (800)-427-6463 (In CA). FAX: (530) 889-4095.
www.placer.org
DIRECTOR
Beverly Lewis

REDDING/SHASTA COUNTY FILM COMMISSION
777 Auditorium Drive, Redding, CA 96001. (530)-225-4100, (800) 874-7562. FAX: (530) 225-4354.
DIRECTOR
Sherry Ferguson

RIDGECREST FILM COMMISSION
100 West California Avenue, Ridgecrest, CA 93555. (760) 375-8202, (800)-847-4830. FAX: (760) 371-1654.
email: racvb@ridgenet.net
www.ridgenet.net/~filmcomm/
DIRECTOR
Ann Gutcher

SACRAMENTO FILM COMMISSION
1303 J Street, Suite 600, Sacramento, CA 95814. (916) 264-7777. FAX: (916) 264-7788. email: lsteffens@gw.sacto.org
www.sacramentocvb.org
DIRECTOR
Lucy Steffens

SAN BENITO FILM COUNCIL
615-C San Benito Street, Hollister, CA 95023. (408) 637-5315. FAX: (408) 637-1008. email: SBCCC@HollOnline.com
www.sbccc.org
DIRECTOR
Neal Hinds

SAN LUIS OBISPO COUNTY FILM COMMISSION
1037 Mill Street, San Luis Obispo, CA 93401. (805) 541-8000. FAX: (805) 543-9498. email: slocvcb@slonet.org
www.sanluisobispocounty.com
DIRECTOR
Jonni Biaggini

SANTA BARBARA FILM COMMISSION
12 East Carrillo St., Santa Barbara, CA 93101. (805) 966-9222. FAX: (805)-966-1728. email: egenolio@filmsantabarbara.com
DIRECTOR
Elizabeth Melley Genolio

SANTA CLARITA VALLEY FILM & ENTERTAINMENT BUREAU
23920 Valencia Boulevard, Suite 100, Santa Clarita, CA 91355-2175. (800) 4FILMSC, (661) 259-4787. FAX: (661) 259-7304. email: scv4afci@hotmail.com
DIRECTOR
April Aston

SANTA CRUZ COUNTY FILM COMMISSION
701 Front Street, Santa Cruz, CA 95003. (831) 425-1234, (800) 833-3494. FAX: (831) 425-1260.
email: mjessee@santacruzca.org
www.santacruzca.org
DIRECTOR
Malei Jessee

SANTA MONICA MOUNTAINS
401 West Hillcrest Dr., Thousand Oaks, CA 91360. (805) 370-2308. FAX: (805) 370-1851. email: alice_allen@nps.gov
www.nps.gov/samo
DIRECTOR
Alice Allen

SONOMA COUNTY FILM COMMISSION
401 D College Ave. - EconDevBoard, Santa Rosa, CA 95401. (707) 524-7347. FAX: (707) 524-7231.
email: cdeprima@sonoma-county.org
www.sonoma-county.org/film
DIRECTOR
Catherine DePrima

TEMECULA VALLEY FILM COUNCIL
27740 Jefferson Avenue, Suite 100, Temecula, CA 92590. (909) 699-6267. FAX: (909) 699-0387.
DIRECTOR
Sunny Poulson Thomas

TRI-VALLEY FILM AND VIDEO
260 Main Street, Pleasanton, CA 94566. (925) 846-8910, (888) 874-9253. FAX: (925) 846-9502. email: alison@trivalleycvb.com
www.trivalleycvb.com
DIRECTOR
Alison Levelis

TUOLUMNE COUNTY FILM COMMISSION
P. O. Box 4020, Sonora, CA 95370. (209) 533-7796, (800) 446-1333. FAX: (209) 533-0956.
DIRECTOR
Nanci Sikes

VALLEJO/SOLANO COUNTY FILM COMMISSION
495 Mare Island Way, Vallejo, CA 94590. (707) 642-3653, (800) 4-VALLEJO. FAX: (707) 644-2206. email: film@visitvallejo.com
www.visitvallejo.com/film
DIRECTOR
Jim Reikowsky

VENTURA COUNTY FILM COUNCIL
1601 Carmen Dr., # 215, Camarillo, CA 93010. (805) 384-1800. FAX: (805) 384-1805. email: bobcooper@edc-vc.com
www.edc-vc.com
DIRECTOR
Bob Cooper

COLORADO

COLORADO MOTION PICTURE & TV COMMISSION
1625 Broadway, Suite 1700, Denver, CO 80202. (303) 620-4500, (800) SCO-UTUS. FAX: (303) 620-4545. email:
staff@coloradofilm.org; www.coloradofilm.org
DIRECTOR
Michael Klein

BOULDER COUNTY FILM COMMISSION
2440 Pearl St., Boulder, CO 80302. (303) 442-1044. FAX: (303) 938-8837.
DIRECTOR
Shelly Helmerick

CLEAR CREEK COUNTY FILM COMMISSION
P. O. Box 100, Idaho Springs, CO 80452. (303) 567-4660, (800) 88-BLAST. FAX: (303) 567-0967.
email: ccctb@sundownnet.com
www.colotourism.com
DIRECTOR
Barbara McKenna Boyer

COLORADO SPRINGS FILM COMMISSION
Colorado Springs Convention & Visitors Bureau, 104 S. Cascade Ave., #104, Colorado Springs, CO 80903. (719) 635-7506 x131. FAX: (719) 635-4968.
DIRECTOR
Edwina Foreman

FORT COLLINS/LARIMER COUNTY FILM OFFICE
420 S. Howes Street, Suite 101, P. O. Box 1998, Fort Collins, CO 80522-1998. (970) 482-5821, (800) 274-3678. FAX: (970) 493-8061. email: ftcollin@ftcollins.com
www.ftcollins.com
DIRECTOR
Rita Greene

FORT MORGAN AREA FILM COMMISSION
Sandy Schneider-Engle, 710 East Railroad Avenue, P.O. Box 100, Fort Morgan, CO 80701. (970) 867-4310. FAX: (970) 867-3039. email: ssengle@twol.com
DIRECTOR
Jim Reikowsky

FREMONT/CUSTER COUNTY FILM COMMISSION
403 Royal Gorge Boulevard, Canon City, CO 81212. (719) 275-2331, (800) 876-7922. FAX: (719) 275-2332.
DIRECTOR
George R. Turner

GREELEY/WELD COUNTY FILM COMMISSION
902 7th Avenue, Greeley, CO 80631. (970) 352-3566, (800) 449-3866. FAX: (970) 352-3572.
DIRECTOR
Sarah MacQuiddy

MAYOR'S OFFICE OF ART, CULTURE & FILM
Ronald F. Pinkard, 303 W. Colfax Avenue #615, Denver, CO 80204. (303) 640-2686. FAX: (303) 640-2737.
DIRECTOR
Ronald F. Pinkard

NORTHWEST COLORADO FILM COMMISSION /YAMPA VALLEY FILM
Box 772305, Steamboat Springs, CO 80477. (970) 879-0882. FAX: (970) 879-2543. email: sevans@cmn.net
www.steamboat-chamber.com/community
DIRECTOR
Sandy Evans

SOUTHWEST COLORADO FILM COMMISSION
295-A Girard, Durango, CO 81301. (970) 247-9621. FAX: (970) 247-9513. email: swctr@frontier.net
www.swcolotravel.org
DIRECTOR
Jane Zimmerman

TRINIDAD FILM COMMISSION
136 West Main Street, Trinidad, CO 81082. (719) 846-9412, (800) 748-1970. FAX: (719) 846-4550.
email: forjobs@iguana.ruralnet.net
www.tsjc.cccoes.edu/tri-film/tri-film.htm

CONNECTICUT

CONNECTICUT FILM OFFICE
505 Hudson St., Hartford, CT 06106. (860) 270-8084. FAX: (860) 270-8077.
DIRECTOR
Katherine Ray

DANBURY FILM OFFICE
P.O. Box 406, Danbury, CT 06813. (203)-743-0546, (800) 841-4488. FAX: (203) 790-6124.
DIRECTOR
Elizabeth Engelhard

SOUTHEASTERN CONNECTICUT FILM OFFICE
PO Box 89 - 470 Bank St c/o CT Mystic & More, New London, CT 06320. (888) 657-FILM, (860) 444-2206. FAX: (860) 442-4257. email: moretwosee@aol.com
DIRECTOR
Philip Hanson

DELAWARE

DELAWARE FILM OFFICE
Delaware Tourism Office, 99 Kings Highway, Dover, DE 19901. (302) 739-4271. FAX: (302) 739-5749.
FILM COMMISSIONER
Jennifer Hastings

DISTRICT OF COLUMBIA

MAYOR'S OFFICE OF TV & FILM
410 Eighth St., NW., Washington, D.C. 20004. (202) 727-6608/6607. FAX: (202) 727-3787.
DIRECTOR
Crystal Palmer

FLORIDA

FORT LAUDERDALE AREA/BROWARD COUNTY
Motion Picture & TV Office, Broward Economic Development Council, 200 E. Las Olas Blvd., Suite 1850, Fort Lauderdale, FL 33301. (954) 524-3113. FAX: (954) 524-3167.
email: BEDC@safari.net
DIRECTOR
Elizabeth Wentworth

CITY OF JACKSONVILLE
Jacksonville Film & TV Office, 220 E. Bay St., Suites 405-407, Jacksonville, FL 32202. (904) 630-2522. FAX: (904) 630-1485.
www.coj.net/film
DIRECTOR
Todd Roobin

FLORIDA KEYS & KEY WEST FILM COMMISSION
1201 White Street, Suite 102, Key West, FL 33040-3328. (305) 293-1800, (800) Film Keys. FAX: (305) 296-0788.
email: keysfilm@aol.com
www.filmkeys.com
DIRECTOR
Rita Brown

METRO ORLANDO FILM & TELEVISION COMMISSION
200 East Robinson Street, Suite #600, Orlando, FL 32801. (407) 422-7159. FAX: (407) 841-0694.
email: addyl@business-orlando.org
www.film-orlando.org
DIRECTOR
Katherine Ramsberger

MIAMI-DADE COUNTY
Miami-Dade Mayor's Office of Film and Entertainment, 111 Northwest 1st Street, Suite 2540, Miami, FL 33128. (305) 375-3288. FAX: (305) 375-3266.
DIRECTOR
Jeff Peel

NORTHWEST FLORIDA/OKALOOSA-WALTON FILM COMMISSION
P.O. Box 609, Ft. Walton Beach, FL 32549-0609. (850) 651-7131 x-226, (800) 322-3319. FAX: (850) 651-7149.
www.destin-fwb.com
DIRECTOR
Dawn Rinehart

OCALA/MARION COUNTY FILM COMMISSION
Chamber of Commerce, 110 East Silver Springs Blvd., Ocala, FL 34470. (352) 629-8051, x225. FAX: (352) 629-7651.
DIRECTOR
Jude Hagin

ORLANDO/CENTRAL FLORIDA FILM & TV OFFICE
200 E. Robinson St., Suite 600, Orlando, FL 32801-1950. (407) 422-7159. FAX: (407) 841-9069. email: filminfo@film-orlando.org; www.film-orlando.org
DIRECTOR
Katherine Ramsberger

PALM BEACH COUNTY FILM & TV COMMISSION
1555 Palm Beach Lakes Blvd., Suite 414, West Palm Beach, FL 33401. (800) 745-FILM, (561) 233-1000. FAX: (561) 683-6957. www.pbfilm.com
FILM COMMISSIONER
Chuck Elderd

SOUTHWEST FLORIDA FILM COMMISSION
2180 W. First St., #306, Fort Myers, FL 33901-3219. (941) 338-3161, (800) 330-3161. FAX: (941) 338-3227.
DIRECTOR
Beverly Fox

SPACE COAST FILM COMMISSION
8810 Astronaut Boulevard, Cape Canaveral, FL 32920. (407) 868-1126, (800) 93-OCEAN. FAX: (407) 868-1139.
email: bkingfilm@aol.com
www.film-space-coast.com
DIRECTOR
Bonnie King

TAMPA/HILLSBOROUGH COUNTY FILM COMMISSION
400 North Tampa Street, Suite 1010, Tampa, FL 33602. (813) 223-1111 Ext. 58, (800) 826-8358. FAX: (813) 229-6616.
email: eemerald@thcva.com
www.thcva.com
DIRECTOR
Edie Emerald

GEORGIA

GEORGIA FILM & VIDEOTAPE OFFICE
285 Peachtree Center Avenue, NW, Suite 1000, Atlanta, GA 30303. (404) 656-3591. FAX: (404) 651-9063. email: Film@itt.state.ga.us; www.Georgia-on-my-mind.org
DIRECTOR
Greg Torre

SAVANNAH FILM COMMISSION
P.O. Box 1027, Savannah, GA 31402. (912) 651-3696. FAX: (912) 238-0872. email: JSelf@milkyway.ci.savannah.ga.us
DIRECTOR
Jay M. Self

HAWAII

BIG ISLAND FILM OFFICE
25 Aupuni Street, Room 219, Hilo, HI 96720. (808) 961-8366, (808) 326-2663 Kona. FAX: (808) 935-1205.
email: film@bigisland.com
filmbigisland.com
DIRECTOR
Marilyn Killeri

HAWAII FILM OFFICE
P.O. Box 2359, Honolulu, HI 96804. (808) 586-2570. FAX: (808) 586-2572.
MANAGER
Georgette T. Deemer

HONOLULU FILM OFFICE
530 S. King St., Room 306, Honolulu, HI 96813. (808) 527-6108. FAX: (808) 527-6102. email: info@filmhonolulu.com
URL: http://www.filmhonolulu.com
DIRECTOR
Walea L. Constantinau

KAUAI FILM COMMISSION
4280-B Rice Street, Lihue, HI 96766. (808) 241-6390. FAX: (808) 241-6399. email: info@filmkauai.com
URL: http://www.filmkauai.com
DIRECTOR
Judy Drosd

MAUI FILM OFFICE
200 S. High Street, 6th Floor, Wailuku, Maui, HI 96793. (808) 243-7710. FAX: (808) 243-7995. email: prpub@msn.com
DIRECTOR
Amy Kastens

IDAHO

IDAHO FILM BUREAU
700 W. State St., Box 83720, Boise, ID 83720, (800) 942-8338. FAX: (208) 334-2631.
DIRECTOR
Peg Owens

ILLINOIS

CITY OF CHICAGO FILM OFFICE
One North LaSalle, Suite 2165, Chicago, IL 60602. (312) 744-6415. FAX: (312) 744-1378.
DIRECTOR
Richard M. Moskal

ILLINOIS FILM OFFICE
100 W. Randolph, Suite 3-400, Chicago, IL 60601. (312) 814-3600. FAX: (312) 814-8874.
DIRECTOR
Ron Ver Kuilen

INDIANA

INDIANA DEPARTMENT OF COMMERCE
1 N. Capitol Ave., Suite 700, Indianapolis, IN 46204-2288. (317) 233-8829. FAX: (317) 233-6887.
www.a1.com/derringer/filmcomm.html
DIRECTOR
Jane Rulon

IOWA

CEDAR RAPIDS AREA FILM COMMISSION
119 First Avenue SE, P.O. Box 5339, Cedar Rapids, IA 52406-5339. (319) 398-5009 x-127, (800) 735-5557 x-127. FAX: (319) 398-5089. email: visitors@fyiowa.infi.net
www.cedar-rapids.com/iowa/cvb/
DIRECTOR
Josh Schamberger

IOWA FILM OFFICE
200 E. Grand Ave., Des Moines, IA 50309. (515) 242-4726. FAX: (515) 242-4859, www.state.ia.us/film
DIRECTOR
Wendol Jarvis

KANSAS

KANSAS FILM COMMISSION
700 SW Harrison St., Suite 1300, Topeka, KS 66603-3712. (785) 296-4927. FAX: (785) 296-6988. TTY: (785) 296-3487.
FILM COMMISSIONER
Vicky Henley

KANSAS III FILM COMMISSION/LAWRENCE CVB
734 Vermont, Lawrence, KS 66044. (785) 865-4411. FAX: (785) 865-4400.
DIRECTOR
Judy Billings

WICHITA CONVENTION & VISITORS BUREAU
100 South Main, Suite 100, Wichita, KS 67202. (316) 265-2800, (800) 288-9424. FAX: (316) 265-0162.
DIRECTOR
Gene Countryman

KENTUCKY

KENTUCKY FILM COMMISSION
Capitol Plaza Tower, 500 Mero St., 22nd floor, Frankfort, KY 40601. (800) 345-6591. FAX: (502) 564-7588.
DIRECTOR
Jim Toole

LOUISIANA

CITY OF NEW ORLEANS FILM AND VIDEO COMMISSION
1515 Poydras St., New Orleans, LA 70112. (504) 565-8104. FAX: (504) 565-0801.
CONTACT
Kimberly Carbo

JEFF DAVIS PARISH FILM COMMISSION
P.O. Box 1207, Jennings, LA 70546-1207. (318) 821-5534. FAX: (318) 821-5536. www.jeffdavis.org
DIRECTOR
Jack Giovo

LOUISIANA FILM COMMISSION
P.O. Box 44320, Baton Rouge, LA 70804-4320. (225) 342-8150. FAX: (225) 342-7988. www.lafilm.org.
DIRECTOR
Peter Loop II

SHREVEPORT-BOSSIER FILM COMMISSION
P.O. Box 1761, Shreveport, LA 71166. (318) 222-9391, (800) 551-8682. FAX: (318) 222-0056. email: filmcom@prysm.net
DIRECTOR
Betty Jo LeBrun

MAINE

MAINE FILM OFFICE
Station 59, Augusta, ME 04333-0059. (207) 287-5703. FAX: (207) 287-8070. www.filminmaine.com
DIRECTOR
Lea Girardin

MARYLAND

BALTIMORE FILM COMMISSION
34 Market Place, Suite 200, Baltimore, MD 21202. (410) 396-4550. FAX: (410) 727-5850.
email: baltfilm@orion.ci.baltimore.md.us
DIRECTOR
Rose Greene

MARYLAND FILM OFFICE
217 E. Redwood St., 9th floor, Baltimore, MD 21202. (410) 767-6340, (800) 333-6632. FAX: (410) 333-0044.
DIRECTOR
Michael Styer

MASSACHUSETTS

MASSACHUSETTS FILM OFFICE
10 Park Plaza, Suite 2310, Boston, MA 02116. (617) 973-8800. FAX: (617) 973-8810.
DIRECTOR
Robin Dawson

MICHIGAN

MICHIGAN FILM OFFICE
201 N. Washington Sq., Lansing, MI 48913. (517) 373-0638, (800) 477-3456. FAX: (517) 373-0059. email: lockwoodj@michigan.org
DIRECTOR
Janet Lockwood

MINNESOTA

MINNEAPOLIS OFFICE OF FILM/VIDEO/RECORDING
323M City Hall - 350 S. 5th Street, Minneapolis, MN 55415. (612) 673-2947. Pager: (612) 818-1221. FAX: (612) 673-2011.
email: janet.zahn@ci.minneapolis.mn.us
DIRECTOR
Janet Zahn

MINNESOTA FILM BOARD
401 N. Third St., Suite 460, Minneapolis, MN 55401. (612) 332-6493. FAX: (612) 332-3735.
EXECUTIVE DIRECTORS
Randy Adamsick, Kelly Heikkila
DIRECTOR OF PRODUCTION
Eric Mueller

MISSISSIPPI

CITY OF COLUMBUS
Columbus Film Commission, P.O.Box 789, Columbus, MS 39703. (662) 329-1191, (800) 327-2686. FAX: (662) 329-8969.
DIRECTOR
Tom Uphold

CITY OF NATCHEZ
Natchez Film Commission, P.O. Box 1485, Natchez, MS 39121. (601) 446-6345, (800) 647-6724. FAX: (601) 442-0814.
DIRECTOR
Laura Godfrey

GREENWOOD CONVENTION & VISITORS BUREAU
P. O. Drawer 739, Greenwood, MS 38935-0739. (601) 453-9197, (800) 748-9064. FAX: (601) 453-5526.
email: gcvb@netdoor.com
DIRECTOR
Suzy Gordon

MISSISSIPPI FILM OFFICE
550 High St., Walter Sillers Blsg., Suite 1100, Jackson, MS 39205-0849. (601) 359-3297. FAX: (601) 359-5048.
DIRECTOR
Ward Emling

TUPELO FILM COMMISSION
399 East Main Street, P.O. Box 47, Tupelo, MS 38802-0047. (601) 841-6521, (800) 533-0611. FAX: (601) 841-6558.
email: tour20@tsixroads.com
/www.tupelo.net
DIRECTOR
Linda Butler

VICKSBURG FILM COMMISSION
P.O. Box 110, Vicksburg, MS 39180 USA. (601) 636-9421, (800 221-3536. FAX: (601) 636-9475.
DIRECTOR
Al Elmore

MISSOURI

KANSAS CITY, MISSOURI FILM OFFICE
10 Petticoat Lane, Suite 250, Kansas City, MO 64106-2103. (816) 221-0636, (800) 889-0636. FAX: (816) 221-0189.
email: patti@kcfilm.co; www.kcfilm.com
DIRECTOR
Patti Watkins

MISSOURI FILM OFFICE
301 West High, Room 720, P.O. Box 118, Jefferson City, MO 65102. (573) 751-9050. FAX: (573) 751-7384.
www.ecodev.state.mo.us/film
MANAGER
Richard Smreker

SAINT LOUIS FILM OFFICE
#1 Metropolitan Sq., #1100, Saint Louis, MO 63102. (314) 992-0609. FAX: (314) 421-0394. email: gfilminfo@stlfilm.com
www.stlfilm.com
DIRECTOR
James Leonis

MONTANA

CITY OF BILLINGS FILM LIAISON OFFICE
P.O. Box 31177, Billings, MT 59107. (406) 245-4111, (800) 711-2630. FAX: (406) 245-7333.
DIRECTOR
John Brewer

CITY OF BUTTE FILM LIAISON OFFICE
1000 George St., Butte, MT 59701. (406) 723-3177 FAX: (406) 723-1215
FILM LIAISON TO STATE COMMISSIONER
Connie Kenney

GREAT FALLS REGIONAL FILM LIAISON
P.O. Box 2127, Great Falls, MT 59403. (406) 761-4434, (800) 735-8535. FAX: (406) 761-6129.
FILM COMMISSIONER
Lisa Goff

MONTANA FILM OFFICE
1424 Ninth Ave., Helena, MT 59620. (406) 444-3762, (800) 553-4563. FAX: (406) 444-4191. email: montanafilm@visitmt.com
www.montanafilm.com
DIRECTOR
Lonie Stimac

NEBRASKA

NEBRASKA FILM OFFICE
P.O. Box 98907, 700 S. 16th St., Lincoln, NE 68509-4666. (402) 471-3680, (800) 228-4307. FAX: (402) 471-3026. www.filmnebraska.org
DIRECTOR
Laurie J. Richards

OMAHA FILM COMMISSION
6800 Mercy Rd., Suite 202, Omaha, NE 68106. (402) 444-7736. FAX: (402) 444-4511.
DIRECTOR
Julie Ginsberg

NEVADA

NEVADA ECONOMIC DEVELOPMENT COMMISSION
3770 Howard Hughes Pkwy., Suite 295, Las Vegas, NV 89109. (702) 486-7150, (702) 791-0839 (after hours and holidays). FAX: (702) 486-7372.
MOTION PICTURE DIVISION/C.E.D.
Robert Hirsch

NEVADA FILM OFFICE-LAS VEGAS
555 East Washington, Suite 5400, Las Vegas, NV 89101-1078. (702) 486-2711, (877) 638-3456. FAX: (702) 486-2712. email: lvnfo@bizopp.state.nv.us
www.nevadafilm.com
DIRECTOR
Charles Geocaris

NEVADA FILM OFFICE - RENO/TAHOE
108 E. Proctor Street, Carson City, NV 89701. (800) 336-1600, (775) 687-1814. FAX: (775) 687-4450.
email: rhbird@bizopp.state.nv.us
www.nevadafilm.com
DIRECTOR
Robin Holabird

NEW HAMPSHIRE

NEW HAMPSHIRE FILM & TELEVISION BUREAU
Box 1856, 172 Pembroke Rd., Concord, NH 03302-1856. (603) 271-2598. FAX: (603) 271-6784, URL: www.visitnh.gov
DIRECTOR
Laura Simoes

NEW JERSEY

NEW JERSEY MOTION PICTURE & TV COMMISSION
P.O. Box 47023, 153 Halsey St., 5th floor, Newark, NJ 07101. (973) 648-6279. FAX: (973) 648-7350. email: njfilm@nj.com
www.nj.com/njfilm
DIRECTOR
Joseph Friedman

NEW MEXICO

CITY OF ALBUQUERQUE
Albuquerque TV & Film Office, Albuquerque Convention & Visitor's Bureau, Box 26866, Albuquerque, NM 87125. (505) 842-9918, (800) 733-9918. FAX: (505) 247-9101.
email: barnhill@abqcvb.org
DIRECTOR OF TOURISM SERVICES
Shannon Barnhill

NEW MEXICO FILM OFFICE
P.O. Box 20003, Santa Fe, NM 87504-5003. (505) 827-9810, (800) 545-9871. FAX: (505) 827-9799. www.filmnm.com
DIRECTOR
Nancy Everist

LAS CRUCES FILM COMMISSION
211 North Water Street, Las Cruces, NM 88001. (505) 541-2444, (800) FIESTAS. FAX: (505) 541-2164.
DIRECTOR
Ted Scanlon

SANTA FE FILM OFFICE
201 W. Marcy Street, Santa Fe, NM 87501. (505) 984-6760, (800) 984-9984. FAX: (505) 984-6679.
email: kmadden@ci.santa-fe.nm.us
www.santafe.org
DIRECTOR
Kathy Madden

NEW YORK

CITY OF NEW YORK MAYOR'S OFFICE OF FILM, THEATRE & BROADCASTING
1697 Broadway, 6th floor, New York, NY 10019. (212) 489-6710. FAX: (212) 307-6237. FAXBACK SVC: (212) 262-8825.
www.ci.nyc.ny.us/html/filmcom/
COMMISSIONER
Patricia Reed Scott

HUDSON VALLEY FILM & VIDEO OFFICE, INC.
40 Garden Street, Poughkeepsie, NY 12601. (914) 473-0318. FAX: (914) 473-0082. email: hvfo@vh.net
www.sandbook.com/hvfo
DIRECTOR
Nancy Cozean

NASSAU COUNTY FILM OFFICE
1550 Franklin Ave., Rm. 207, Mineola, NY 11501. (516) 571-4160. FAX: (516) 571-4161.
email: debfilm@aol.com
DIRECTOR
Debra Markowitz

NEW YORK STATE GOVERNOR'S OFFICE FOR MOTION PICTURE & TELEVISION DEVELOPMENT
633 Third Ave., 33rd fl, New York, NY 10017. (212) 803-2330. FAX: (212) 803-2339. email: NYFILM@empire.state.ny.us
DEPUTY COMMISSIONER & DIRECTOR
Pat Swinney Kaufman

ROCHESTER/FINGER LAKES FILM & VIDEO OFFICE
126 Andrews Street, Rochester, NY 14604-1102. (716) 546-5490. FAX: (716) 232-4822. email: rochfilm@frontiernet.net
www.filmrochester.org
DIRECTOR
June Foster

SARATOGA COUNTY FILM COMMISSION
28 Clinton Street, Saratoga Springs, NY 12866. (518) 584-3255, (800) 526-8970. FAX: (518) 587-0318.
email: info@saratoga.org
www.saratoga.org
DIRECTOR
Linda G. Toohey

SUFFOLK COUNTY MOTION PICTURE & TV OFFICE
Dennison Bldg., 2nd fl, 100 Veterans Memorial Hwy., NY 11788. (516) 853-4800, (800) 762-GROW. FAX: (516) 853-4888.
COMMISSIONER
Alice A. Amrhein

NORTH CAROLINA

CHARLOTTE REGION FILM OFFICE
112 S. Tryon Street, Suite 900, Charlotte, NC 28284. (800) 554-4373, (704) 347-8942. FAX: (704) 347-8981.
email: MKelso@Charlotteregion.com
www.Charlotteregion.com
DIRECTOR
Marcie Oberndorf-Kelso

DURHAM CONVENTION & VISITORS BUREAU
101 East Morgan Street, Durham, NC 27701. (919) 687-0288. (800) 446-8604. FAX: (919) 683-9555.
email: jill@durham-cvb.com; DCVB.Durham.NC.US
DIRECTOR
Jill Melnick

NORTH CAROLINA FILM COMMISSION
301 N. Wilmington St., 4317 Mail Service Center, Raleigh, NC 27699. (919) 733-9900, (800) 232-9227. FAX: (919) 715-0151.
www.telefilm-south.com
DIRECTOR
William Arnold

WESTERN NORTH CAROLINA FILM COMMISSION
P.O. Box 1258, Arden, NC 28704. (828) 687-7234. FAX: (828) 687-7552. email: WNCREDC@MAILBOX.IOA.COM
www.haywood.cc.nc.us/wncedc
DIRECTOR
Mary Nell Webb

WILMINGTON REGIONAL FILM COMMISSION
1223 North 23rd Street, Wilmington, NC 28405. (910) 343-3456. FAX: (910) 343-3457.
email: commish@wilmington-film.com
www.wilmington-film.com
DIRECTOR
Mark L. Stricklin

WINSTON-SALEM PIEDMONT TRIAD FILM COMMISSION
601 West Fourth Street, Winston-Salem, NC 27101. (336) 728-9237. FAX: (336) 721-2209.
email: film@winstonsalem.com
www.winstonsalem.com/film
DIRECTOR
Dianna Costello

NORTH DAKOTA

NORTH DAKOTA FILM OFFICE
604 E. Boulevard Ave., Bismarck, ND 58505. (701) 328-2525, (800) 328-2871. FAX: (701) 328-4878. email: phertz@state.nd.us
FILM COMMISSIONER
Pat Hertz

OHIO

GREATER CINCINNATI FILM COMMISSION
602 Main St., Suite 712, Cincinnati, OH 45202. (513) 784-1744. FAX: (513) 768-8963.
email: info@film-cincinnati.org
EXECUTIVE DIRECTOR
Lori Holladay

GREATER CLEVELAND MEDIA DEVELOPMENT CORP.
825 Terminal Tower, Cleveland, OH 44113. (216) 623-3910, (888) 746-FILM. FAX: (216) 736-7792.
email: info@clevelandfilm.com
www.clevelandfilm.com
DIRECTOR
Christopher Carmody

OHIO FILM COMMISSION
77 S. High St., 29th Floor, Columbus, OH 43216-1001. (614) 466-2284, (800) 230-3523. FAX: (614) 466-6744.
MANAGER
Steve Cover

OKLAHOMA

OKLAHOMA FILM COMMISSION
440 S. Houston, Suite 304, Tulsa, OK 74127. (800) 766-3456, (918) 581-2660. FAX: (918) 581-2244.
www.otrd.state.ok.us/filmcommission
DIRECTOR
Robert M. Davis

OREGON

OREGON FILM & VIDEO OFFICE
One World Trade Center, 121 S.W. Salmon St., Suite 1205, Portland, OR 97204. (503) 229-5832. FAX: (503) 229-6869.
email: shoot@oregonfilm.org
ASSISTANT DIRECTOR
Veronica Rinard

PENNSYLVANIA

GREATER PHILADELPHIA FILM OFFICE
Land Title Bldg., 100 S. Broad St., Suite 600, Philadelphia, PA 19110, (215) 686-2668. FAX: (215) 686-3659. email: mail@film.org; www.film.org
EXECUTIVE DIRECTOR
Sharon Pinkenson

PENNSYLVANIA FILM OFFICE
Department of Commerce, 200 N. 3rd St., Suite 901, Harrisburg, PA 17101. (717) 783-3456. FAX: (717) 772-3581.
DIRECTOR
Timothy D. Chambers

PITTSBURGH FILM OFFICE
223 Fourth Avenue, Suite 1300, Pittsburgh, PA 15222. (412) 261-2744, (888) 744-3456. FAX: (412) 471-7317.
email: info@pghfilm.org
DIRECTOR
Dawn Keezer

RHODE ISLAND

PROVIDENCE FILM COMMISSION
400 Westminster Street, 6th Floor, Providence, RI 02903. (401) 273-3456. FAX: (401) 351-9533.
email: provfilm@providenceri.com
www.providenceri.com/film
DIRECTOR
Eric B. Olin

RHODE ISLAND FILM & TV OFFICE
1 W. Exchange St., Providence, RI 02903. (401) 222- 2601. FAX: (401) 273-8270, www.rifilm.com.
DIRECTOR
Richardson Smith

SOUTH CAROLINA

SOUTH CAROLINA FILM OFFICE
P.O. Box 7367, Columbia, SC 29202. (803) 737-0490. FAX: (803) 737-3104
DIRECTOR
Jeff Monks

SOUTH DAKOTA

SOUTH DAKOTA FILM COMMISSION
711 E. Wells Ave., Pierre, SD 57501-3369. (605) 773-3301. FAX: (605) 773-3256. email: garyk@goed.state.sd.us.
FILM OFFICE COORDINATOR
Gary Keller

TENNESSEE

TENNESSEE FILM, ENTERTAINMENT & MUSIC COMMISSION
Rachel Jackson Bldg., 320 Sixth Ave. N., 7th floor, Nashville, TN 37243-0790. (615) 741-3456, (877) 818-3456. FAX: (615) 741-5554. www.state.tn.us/film.
EXECUTIVE DIRECTOR
Anne Pope

EAST TENNESSEE FILM COMMISSION
601 W. Summit Hill Dr., Knoxille, TN 37902-2011. (865) 632-8762. FAX: (865) 523-2071. email: etfc@kacp.com
EXECUTIVE DIRECTOR
Mona May

MEMPHIS-SHELBY CO. FILM/TAPE/MUSIC COMMISSION
Beale St. Landing, 245 Wagner Pl., Suite 4, Memphis, TN 38103-3815. (901) 527-8300. FAX: (901) 527-8326.
EXECUTIVE DIRECTOR
Linn Sitler

NASHVILLE MAYOR'S OFFICE OF FILM
117 Union Street, Nashville, TN 37201-1301. (615) 862-4700. FAX: (615) 862-6025. email: kym_jackson@metro.nashville.org
www.nashville.net/~cinevent
DIRECTOR
Kym Gerlock Jackson

TEXAS

AMARILLO FILM OFFICE
1000 S. Polk St., Amarillo, TX 79101. (806) 374-1497. FAX: (806) 373-3909.
DIRECTOR
Jutta Matalk

AUSTIN FILM OFFICE
201 E. Second Street, Austin, TX 78701. (512) 404-4562, (800) 926-2282 x-4562. FAX: (512) 404-4564.
DIRECTOR
Gary Bond

EL PASO FILM COMMISSION
One Civic Center Plaza, El Paso, TX 79901. (915) 534-0698, (800) 351-6024. FAX: (915) 534-0687.
email: sgaines@elpasosvb.com.
FILM COMMISSIONER
Susie Gaines

HOUSTON FILM COMMISSION
901 Bagby, Houston, TX 77002. (800) 365-7575, (713) 227-3100 x615. FAX: (713) 223-3816. www.neosoft.com/~yfsfilms.
DIRECTOR
Rick Ferguson

IRVING TEXAS FILM COMMISSION
6309 N. O'Connor Rd., Suite 222, Irving, TX 75039-3510. (972) 869-0303, (800) 247-8464. FAX: (972) 869-4609.
DIRECTOR
Ellen Mayers

DALLAS/FORT WORTH REGIONAL FILM COMMISSION
P.O. Box 610246, DFW Airport, TX 75261. (972) 621-0400, (800) 2FILM99. FAX: (972) 929-0916. email: 2filmdfwtexas@ntc-dfw.org
DIRECTORS
Roger Burke
Sarah Bruce Craft

SAN ANTONIO FILM COMMISSION
P.O. Box 2277, San Antonio, TX 78230. (210) 270-8700. FAX: (210) 270-8782.
DIRECTORS
Kathy Rhodes
Kaye Cruz

TEXAS FILM COMMISSION
P.O. Box 13246, Austin, TX 78711. (512) 463-9200. FAX: (512) 463-4114. email: film@governor.state.texas.us
www.governor.state.tx.us/film
EXECUTIVE DIRECTOR
Tom Copeland

UTAH

CENTRAL UTAH FILM COMMISSION
100 E. Center St., Suite 3200, Provo, UT 84606. (801) 370-8100, (800) 222-8824. FAX: (801) 370-8105.
email: ucadm.marilyn@state.ut.us
www.utahvalley.org/film
DIRECTOR
Marilyn Toone

KANAB/KANE COUNTY FILM COMMISSION
78 S 100 E., Kanab, UT 84741. (435) 644-5033, (800) SEE-KANE. FAX: (435) 644-5923. www.kaneutah.com
DIRECTOR
Donna Casebolt

MOAB TO MONUMENT VALLEY FILM COMMISSION
50 East Center, #1, Moab, UT 84532. (435) 259-6388. FAX: (435) 259-6399.
EXECUTIVE DIRECTOR
Kari Murphy

NORTHERN UTAH FILM COMMISSION
160 N. Main, Logan, UT 84321. (435) 752-2161, (800) 882-4433. FAX: (435) 753-5825. email: btr@sunrem.com
www.bridgerland.com
DIRECTOR
Maridene A. Hancock

PARK CITY FILM COMMISSION
P.O. Box 1630, Park City, UT 84060. (800) 453-1360. FAX: (435) 649-4132, (435) 649-6100. URL: www.parkcityfilm.com
COMMISSIONER
Mary Bradley

UTAH FILM COMMISSION
324 South State, Suite 500, Salt Lake City, UT 84114. (801) 538-8740. FAX: (801) 538-8886.
EXECUTIVE DIRECTOR
Leigh von der Esch

VERMONT

VERMONT FILM BUREAU
Agency of Development and Community Affairs, 134 State St., VT 05601-1471. (802) 828-33847. FAX: (802) 828-3233. email: ggerdel@dca.state.vt.us
DIRECTOR
J. Gregory Gerdel

VIRGINIA

CITY OF VIRGINIA BEACH - SPECIAL EVENTS & FILM
1000 19th Street, Virginia Beach, VA 23451. (757) 437-4800. FAX: (757) 437-4737. email: eomalley@city.virginia-beach.va.us
www.virginia-beach.va.us
DIRECTOR
Elizabeth T. O'Malley

METRO RICHMOND CVB & FILM OFFICE
550 East Marshall Street, Richmond, VA 23219. (804) 782-2777, (800) 370-9004. FAX: (804) 780-2577.
email: KThompson@richmondva.org
www.richmondva.org
DIRECTOR
Kendal Thompson

PETERSBURG REGIONAL FILM OFFICE
29 South Market Street, Petersburg, VA 23803. (804) 733-2403. FAX: (804) 861-6780. email: kroy@erols.com
DIRECTOR
Kenneth W. Roy

VIRGINIA FILM OFFICE
901 E. Byrd St., Richmond, VA 23219. (804) 371-8204. FAX: (804) 371-8177. email: vafilm@vedp.state.va.us
www.film.virginia.org
DIRECTOR
Rita McClenny
LOCATION MANAGER
Andrew Edmonds

WASHINGTON STATE

CITY OF SEATTLE - MAYOR'S FILM OFFICE
600 Fourth Avenue - 2nd Floor, Seattle, WA 98104-1826. (206) 684-5030. FAX: (206) 684-0379.
www.ci.seattle.wa.us/filmoffice
DIRECTOR
Donna James

WASHINGTON STATE FILM OFFICE
2001 6th Ave., Suite 2600, Seattle, WA 98121. (206) 956-3200. FAX: (206) 956-3205.
DIRECTOR
Suzy Kellett

WEST VIRGINIA

WEST VIRGINIA FILM OFFICE
State Capitol Complex, Building 6, Rm. 525, Charleston, WV 25305. (304) 558-2234. FAX: (304) 558-1189, (800) 982-3386.
DIRECTOR
Mark McNabb

WISCONSIN

GREATER MILWAUKEE CVB
510 West Kilbourn Avenue, Milwaukee, WI 53203. (414) 273-2879, (888) 571-2879. FAX: (414) 273-5596.
DIRECTOR
Patti Gorsky

WISCONSIN FILM OFFICE
201 W. Washington Ave., 2nd floor, P.O. Box 7976, Madison, WI 53707-7976. (608) FILM-WIS, (800) FILM-WIS. FAX: (608) 266-3403.
email: wisconsin@mail.state.wi.us.
www.film.state.wi.us
DIRECTOR
Stanley Solheim

WYOMING

WYOMING BUSINESS COUNSEL FILM OFFICE
214 W. 15th St., Cheyenne, WY 82002-0240. (800) 458-6657, (307) 777-3400. FAX: (307) 777-6904.
email: info@wyoming.org
MANAGING DIRECTOR
Michell Phelan

JACKSON HOLE FILM COMMISSION
P.O. Box E, Jackson, WY 83001. (307) 733-3316. FAX: (307) 733-5585.
DIRECTOR
Deborah Supowit

CASPER AREA FILM COMMISSION
538 SW Wyoming Boulevard, P. O. Drawer 848, Mills, WY 82644. (307) 235-9325. FAX: (307) 235-9611.
email: kellye@trib.com
DIRECTOR
Kelly Eastes

CHEYENNE AREA FILM OFFICE
309 West Lincolnway, Cheyenne, WY 82001. (307) 778-3133. (800) 426-5009. FAX: (307) 778-3190. www.cheyenne.org
email: lisa@cheyenne.org
DIRECTOR
Lisa Thorson

U.S. TERRITORIES & PROTECTORATES

PUERTO RICO FILM COMMISSION
355 F. D. Roosevelt Ave., Fomento Bldg., Suite 106, San Juan, PR 00918. (787) 758- 4747, ext. 2250-2255. FAX: (787) 756-5706. www.prfilm.com

U.S. VIRGIN ISLANDS FILM PROMOTION OFFICE
78 Contant 1-2-3, St. Thomas, U.S.V.I. 00804. (340) 774-8784, (340) 775-1444. FAX: (340) 774-4390.
DIRECTOR
Manny Centeno

FEDERAL GOVERNMENT OFFICES AND FILM & MEDIA SERVICES

EXECUTIVE DEPARTMENTS

DEPARTMENT OF AGRICULTURE
VIDEO, TELECONFERENCE AND RADIO DIVISION
1400 Indepedence Ave., 1614 South Bldg., USDA, Washington, DC 20250-1300. (202) 720-6072. FAX: (202) 720-5773.
DIRECTOR
Larry Quinn

DEPARTMENT OF COMMERCE
OFFICE OF PUBLIC AFFAIRS—MEDIA SECTION
Office of the Secretary, 14th St. & Constitution Ave., Rm. 5056, Washington, DC 20230. (202) 482-3140. FAX: (202) 482-2639.
PRODUCER & DIRECTOR
J.R. Olivero

INTERNATIONAL TRADE ADMINISTRATION—OFFICE OF SERVICE INDUSTRIES
Information Industries Division—International Trade in Film & Recorded Music, 14th St. and Constitution Ave., Rm. H-1124, Washington, DC 20230. (202) 482-4781. FAX: (202) 482-2669.
SENIOR INTERNATIONAL TRADE SPECIALIST
John Siegmund

NATIONAL TELECOMMUNICATIONS AND INFORMATION ADMINISTRATION
Main Commerce Bldg., 1401 Constitution Ave., Washington, DC 20230. (202) 482-1840. FAX: (202) 482-1635.
ASST. SECRETARY, COMMUNICATIONS & INFORMATION
Gregory Rohde

NATIONAL TECHNICAL INFORMATION SERVICE
5285 Port Royal Rd., Springfield, VA 22161. (800) 553-6847. FAX: (703) 605-6900.
ACTING DIRECTOR
Ron Lawson

DEPARTMENT OF DEFENSE
SPECIAL ASSISTANT (AUDIOVISUAL)
Office of the Assistant Secretary of Defense (Public Affairs), The Pentagon, Room 2E789, Washington, DC 20301. (703) 695-2936. FAX: (703) 695-1149.
HEAD OF DIVISION
Philip M. Strub

AUDIOVISUAL RESEARCH DIVISION
Office of the Assistant Secretary of Defense (Public Affairs), The Pentagon, Room 2E765, Washington, DC 20301. (703) 695-0168. FAX: (703) 697-3501.
BRANCH CHIEF
Jim Kout

MILITARY SERVICES
SECRETARY OF THE AIR FORCE
Office of Public Affairs, The Pentagon, Room 4A120, Washington, DC 20330-1000. (703) 697-2769. FAX: (703) 693-9601.
CHIEF OF DIVISION
Lt. Col. Bob Williams

SECRETARY OF THE ARMY
Media Relations Division, Army Public Affairs, 1500 Army Pentagon, Room 2E641, Washington, DC 20310-1500, (703) 697-2564. FAX: (703) 697-2159.
CHIEF OF DIVISION
Col. Ed F. Veiga

DEPARTMENT OF THE NAVY
Chief of Information, 1200 Navy Pentagon, Room 4A686, Washington, DC 20350-1200. (703) 697-4627. FAX: (703) 692-9046.
CHIEF OF INFORMATION
Rear Admiral Thomas J. Jurkowsky

HEADQUARTERS, U.S. MARINE CORPS.
Media Branch Public Affairs Division, Code PAM, The Pentagon, Washington, DC 20380. (703) 614-8010. FAX: (703) 697-5362.
DIRECTOR
BGen. General John F. Sattler

DEPARTMENT OF EDUCATION
OFFICE OF PUBLIC AFFAIRS
Audiovisual Division, 400 Maryland Ave. SW, 7th Fl., Washington, DC 20202. (202) 401-1576. FAX: (202) 401-3130.
AUDIOVISUAL OFFICER
Sherry Sweitzer

OFFICE OF SPECIAL EDUCATION AND REHAB. SERVICES
Office of the Asst. Secretary, 330 C St. SW, Ste. 3006, Sweitzer Bldg., Washington, DC 20202-2500. (202) 205-5465. FAX: (202) 205-9252.
BRANCH CHIEF, CAPTIONING
Judith Hewmann

DEPARTMENT OF ENERGY
OFFICE OF PUBLIC AFFAIRS—MEDIA & MP DIVISION
Forrestal Bldg.,1000 Independence Ave. SW, PA5, Room IE206, Washington, DC 20585. (202) 586-6250. FAX: (202) 586-7303.
DIRECTOR
Chet Gray

DEPARTMENT OF HEALTH AND HUMAN SERVICES
OFFICE OF PUBLIC AFFAIRS
200 Independence Ave. SW, Room 647D, Washington, DC 20201. (202) 690-7850. FAX: (202) 690-5673.
DIRECTOR OF COMMUNICATIONS
Campbell Garnett

ADMINISTRATION FOR CHILDREN & FAMILY
370 L'Enfant Promenade SW, 7th floor, Washington, DC 20447. (202) 401-9215. FAX: (202) 205-9688.
DIRECTOR
Michael Kharfen

HEALTH CARE FINANCING ADMINISTRATION
200 Independence Ave. SW, Room 314G, Washington, DC 20201. (202) 690-6113. FAX: (202) 690-6262.
ADMINISTRATOR
Nancy Ann De Parle

SOCIAL SECURITY ADMIN. OFFICE OF PUBLIC AFFAIRS
4200 West High Rise, 6401 Security Blvd., Baltimore, MD 21235. (410) 965-1720. FAX: (410) 965-3903.
DIRECTOR
Deputy Com. Phil Gambino

DEPARTMENT OF HOUSING AND URBAN DEV.
OFFICE OF PUBLIC AFFAIRS
HUD Bldg., 451 7th St. SW, Rm. 10132, Washington, DC 20410. (202) 708-0980. FAX: (202) 619-8153.
DEPUTY ASSISTANT SECRETARY TV & RADIO
Lisa MacSpadden

DEPARTMENT OF THE INTERIOR
OFFICE OF COMMUNICATIONS, DEPARTMENT OF NEWS & INFORMATION CENTER
1849 C St. NW, Washington, DC 20240. (202) 501-9649. FAX: (202) 219-1436.
INFORMATION OFFICER
Steve Brooks

DEPARTMENT OF JUSTICE
AUDIOVISUAL SERVICES
10th St. & Pennsylvania Ave., Rm. 1313, Washington, DC 20530. (202) 514-4387. FAX: (202) 514-6741.
SUPERVISOR
Jody Antol

DEPARTMENT OF LABOR
AUDIOVISUAL AND PHOTOGRAPHIC SERVICES BRANCH
Audiovisual Division, 200 Constitution Ave. NW, N6311, Washington, DC 20210. (202) 693-5041. FAX: (202) 693-4692.
DIRECTOR
Meg Ingold
EXECUTIVE PRODUCER
Stan Hankin

DEPARTMENT OF STATE
INTERNATIONAL COMM. AND INFORMATION POLICY
Department of State, Rm. 4826, 2201 C St. NW, Washington, DC 20520. (202) 647-5212. FAX: (202) 647-5957.
DEPUTY ASST. SECRETARY
Malcolm R. Lee

OFFICE OF INTERNATIONAL TRADE CONTROL
Department of State, Office of Defense Trade Control, SA1, Room 1304G, 82401E, 2401 E. St., NW, Washington, DC 20037. (202) 663-2714. FAX: (202) 261-8264.
DIRECTOR
William Lowell

OFFICE OF PRESS RELATIONS
Department of State, Rm. 2109-A, Washington, DC 20520. (202) 647-0874. FAX: (202) 647-0244.
DIRECTOR OF STAFF
Adam Ereli

BUREAU OF EDUCATIONAL & CULTURAL AFFAIRS
301 4th Street SW, Rm. 849, Washington, DC 20547. (202) 619-5053. FAX: (202) 619-5068. email: cstearns@pd.state.gov
PUBLIC AFFAIRS OFFICER
Catherine Stearns

INTERNATIONAL BROADCASTING BUREAU OF FEDERAL GOVERNMENT
Public Affairs, Voice of America, 330 Independence Ave., SW, Rm. 3349, Washington, DC 20547. (202) 619-2538. FAX: (202) 619-1241.
DIRECTOR
Joesph O'Connell

DEPARTMENT OF TRANSPORTATION
FEDERAL HIGHWAY ADMINISTRATION AUDIOVISUAL AND VISUAL AIDS
400 7th St. SW, Rm. 4429, HMS51, Washington, DC 20590. (202) 366-0481. FAX: (202) 366-7079.
MULTI MEDIA SPECIALIST
Colonel Giles

NATIONAL HIGHWAY AND TRAFFIC SAFETY ADMINISTRATION
Public Affairs, Audiovisual Section, 400 7th St. SW, Rm. 5232, Washington, DC 20590. (202) 366-9550. FAX: (202) 366-5962.
PUBLIC AFFAIRS SPECIALIST
Tina Foley

U.S. COAST GUARD MOTION PICTURE & TELEVISION LIAISON OFFICE
10880 Wilshire Blvd., Ste. 1210, Los Angeles, CA 90024. (310) 235-7817. FAX: (310) 235-7851.
LIAISON OFFICERS
Lt. Cmdr. Scott Loftus, CWO Alastair Worden, CWO Dan Waldschmidt

U.S. COAST GUARD MEDIA RELATIONS BRANCH
2100 2nd St. SW, Washington, DC 20593. (202) 267-1587. FAX: (202) 267-4307.
CHIEF OF DEPARTMENT
Cmdr. Jim MacPherson

U.S. COAST GUARD AUDIOVISUAL BRANCH
2100 2nd Street, SW, Rm. 3403, G-IPA-1, Washington, DC 20593. (202) 267-0923. FAX: (202) 267-4645.
IMAGERY BRANCH
CWO Ron Mench

DEPARTMENT OF TREASURY
OFFICE OF PUBLIC AFFAIRS
1500 Pennsylvania Ave. NW, Rm. 3442, Washington, DC 20220. (202) 622-2920. FAX: (202) 622-2808.
ASSISTANT SECRETARY
Michelle A. Smith

EXECUTIVE AGENCIES

BROADCAST BOARD OF GOVERNORS
WORLDNET TELEVISION AND FILM SERVICE
330 Independence Ave., SW, Washington, DC 20237. (202) 401-8494. FAX: (202) 690-4952.
DIRECTOR
Marie Skiba

ENVIRONMENTAL PROTECTION AGENCY
AUDIOVISUAL DIVISION
401 M St. SW, North Conference, Washington, DC 20460. (202) 260-6735. FAX: (301) 585-7976.
DIRECTOR
Rolando Hernadez

FEDERAL COMMUNICATIONS COMMISSION
(For an expanded listing, please see the section entitled Federal Communications Commission beginning on page 628).
1919 M St. NW, Washington, DC 20554. (202) 418-0200. FAX: (202) 418-0999. URL: http://www.fcc.gov

FEDERAL TRADE COMMISSION
Press Office, 6th St. and Pennsylvania Ave. NW, Washington, DC 20580. (202) 326-2180. FAX: (202) 326-3676.
CHAIRMAN
Robert Pitofsky

LIBRARY OF CONGRESS
COPYRIGHT OFFICE
Madison Bldg., Rm. 403, Washington, DC 20540. (202) 707-8350. FAX: (202) 707-8366.
REGISTER OF COPYRIGHTS
Marybeth Peters

COPYRIGHT CATALOGING DIVISION
Madison Bldg., Rm. 513, Washington, DC 20540. (202) 707-8040. FAX: (202) 707-8049.
CHIEF OF DIVISION
Walter D. Sampson

MOTION PICTURE, BROADCASTING AND RECORDED SOUND DIVISION
Madison Bldg., Rm. 338, Washington, DC 20540. (202) 707-5840. FAX: (202) 707-2371.
CHIEF OF DIVISION
David Francis

NATIONAL AERONAUTICS & SPACE ADMINISTRATION
NASA VIDEO LIBRARY
Code AP32, Bldg. 423, Johnson Space Center, Houston, TX 77058. (281) 483-2973. FAX: (281) 483-2848.
SUPERVISOR
Gloria Sanchez

NATIONAL ARCHIVES AND RECORDS ADMINISTRATION
MOTION PICTURE, SOUND AND VIDEO BRANCH
8601 Adelphi Rd., College Park, MD 20740. (301) 713-7060. FAX: (301) 713-6904
DIVISION DIRECTOR
Robert Richardson

NATIONAL ARCHIVES LIBRARIES
7th St. & Pennslyvania Ave. NW, Rm. 104, Washington, DC 20408. (202) 501-5700. FAX: (202) 208-6938.
DIRECTOR
Nancy Smith

NATIONAL ENDOWMENT FOR THE ARTS
MEDIA ARTS PROGRAM
1100 Pennsylvania Ave. NW, Rm. 726, Washington, DC 20506. (202) 682-5452. FAX: (202) 682-5721.
MEDIA ARTS DIRECTOR
Laura Welsh

NATIONAL ENDOWMENT FOR THE HUMANITIES
HUMANITIES PROJECTS IN MEDIA—DIVISION OF PUBLIC PROGRAMS
1100 Pennsylvania Ave. NW, Rm. 426, Washington, DC 20506. (202) 606-8267. FAX: (202) 606-8557.
DIRECTOR OF THE DIVISION OF PUBLIC PROGRAMS
Nancy Rogers

SECURITIES AND EXCHANGE COMMISSION
DIVISION OF CORPORATE FINANCE
450 5th St. NW, Washington, DC 20549. (202) 942-8088.
Radio, Television, and Telegraph
450 5th St. NW, Washington, DC 20549-0406. (202) 942-1800. FAX: (202) 942-9525.
ASSISTANT DIRECTOR
James Daly

MOTION PICTURES
450 5th St. NW, Washington, DC 20549-0406. (202) 942-1800.
ASSISTANT DIRECTOR
James Daly

SMITHSONIAN INSTITUTION
FILM ARCHIVES
Archives Division, National Air and Space Museum, Washington, DC 20560. (202) 357-4721. FAX: (202) 786-2835.
FILM ARCHIVIST
Mark Taylor

SMITHSONIAN PRODUCTIONS
National Museum of American History, Rm. BB40, Washington, DC 20560. (202) 357-2984. FAX: (202) 357-1565.
DIRECTOR
Paul Johnson

U.S. INTERNATIONAL TRADE COMMISSION
OFFICE OF THE SECRETARY
500 E Street, Rm. 112, Washington, DC 20436. (202) 205-2000. FAX: (202) 205-2104.
SECRETARY
Donna R. Koehnke

MILITARY FILM LIAISONS

OFFICE, CHIEF OF PUBLIC AFFAIRS
10880 Wilshire Blvd., Suite 1250, 12th Floor, Los Angeles, CA 90024-4101. (310) 235-7621. FAX: (310) 235-6075.
CHIEF OF PUBLIC AFFAIRS
Ann. K. Canham Ross
TECHNICAL ADVISOR
Deputy Chief of Public Affairs—Maj. Andres Ortegon

MARINE CORPS PUBLIC AFFAIRS
10880 Wilshire Blvd., Ste. 1230, Los Angeles, CA 90024. (310) 235-7272. FAX: (310) 235-7274.
DIRECTOR
Major T.V. Johnson

U. S. AIR FORCE, MOTION PICTURE AND TELEVISION LIAISON OFFICE
10880 Wilshire Blvd., Ste. 1240, Los Angeles, CA 90024. (310) 235-7522. FAX: (310) 235-7500.
CHIEF, ENTERTAINMENT LIAISON
Charles E. Davis

U. S. COAST GUARD, MOTION PICTURE AND TELEVISION OFFICE
10880 Wilshire Blvd., Ste. 1210, Los Angeles, CA 90024. (310) 235-7817. FAX: (310) 235-7851.
LIAISON OFFICERS
Lt. Cmdr. Scott Luftus, CWO Alastair Worden, CWO Dan Waldschmidt

TRADE PUBLICATIONS

ACADEMY PLAYERS DIRECTORY
(Tri-Annual) Academy of Motion Picture Arts & Sciences, 8949 Wilshire Blvd., Beverly Hills, CA 90211-1972. (310) 247-3000. FAX: (310) 550-5034. www.playersdirectory.com
EDITOR
Keith W. Gonzales

ADVERTISING AGE
(Weekly) 740 N. Rush St., Chicago, IL 60611. (312) 649-5200.
771 3rd Ave., New York, NY 10017. (212) 210-0100.
CHAIRMAN
Keith Crain
PUBLISHING DIRECTOR
Joe Cappo
PUBLISHER
Ed Erhardt
PRESIDENT & EDITOR-IN-CHIEF
Rance Crain

THE AMERICAN CINEMATOGRAPHER
(Monthly) Published by American Society of Cinematographers, Inc., P.O. Box 2230, Hollywood, CA 90078. (323) 969-4333. FAX: (323) 876-4973.
PUBLISHER
Jim McCullaugh
EDITOR
Stephen Pizzello
ASSOCIATE EDITOR
Rachael Bosley
ASSISTANT EDITOR
Douglas Bankston
CIRCULATION MANAGER
Saul Molina

ANNUAL INDEX TO MOTION PICTURE CREDITS
(Annual compilation of feature film credits) Academy of Motion Picture Arts and Sciences, 8949 Wilshire Blvd., Beverly Hills, CA 90211. (310) 247-3000. FAX: (310) 859-9619.
EXECUTIVE DIRECTOR
Bruce Davis
EDITOR
Byerly Woodward

AV GUIDE: THE LEARNING MEDIA NEWSLETTER
(Monthly) 380 East Northwest Highway, Ste. 200 Des Plaines, IL 60016-2282. (847) 298-6622. FAX: (847) 390-0408.
PUBLISHER
H. S. Gillette
EDITOR
Natalie Ferguson
CIRCULATION DIRECTOR
Linda Lambdin

BILLBOARD
(Weekly) 5055 Wilshire Blvd., Los Angeles, CA 90036-4396. (323) 525-2300. FAX: (323) 525-2394.
1515 Broadway, New York, NY 10036. (212) 764-7300. FAX: (212) 536-5358.
49 Music Square W., Nashville, TN 37203. (615) 321-4290. FAX: (615) 320-0454.
50-51 Bedford Row, London WC1R 4LR. (01 71) 822-8300. FAX: (01 71) 242-9136.
PRESIDENT & PUBLISHER
Howard Lander
EDITOR-IN-CHIEF
Timothy White
MANAGING EDITOR
Susan Nunziata
ASSOCIATE PUBLISHER, MARKETING & SALES
Gene Smith

BOXOFFICE
155 S. El Molino Ave., Ste. #100, Pasadena, CA 91101. (626) 396-0250. FAX: (626) 396-0248. Published by RLD.
P.O. Box 25485, Chicago, IL 60625. (773) 338-7007. FAX: (773) 338-1884. www.boxoffice.com
email: editorial@boxoffice.com
PUBLISHER
Robert L. Dietmeier
EDITOR-IN-CHIEF
Kim Williamson
NATIONAL AD DIRECTOR
Robert M. Vale

BROADCASTING & CABLE—THE NEWS WEEKLY OF TELEVISION AND RADIO
(Weekly) 1627 K St., NW, Washington, DC 20036. (202) 463-3711. FAX: (202) 463-3742.
245 W. 17 St., New York, NY 10011. (212) 645-0067. FAX: (212) 337-7028.
5700 Wilshire Blvd., #120, Los Angeles, CA 90036. (323) 549-4100. FAX: (323) 937-4240.
GROUP PUBLISHER
Lawrence Oliver
GROUP EDITOR-IN-CHIEF
Donald V. West

BROADCASTING & CABLE YEARBOOK
(Annual) R. R. Bowker, 121 Chanlon Rd., New Providence, NJ 07974. (908) 464-6800. FAX: (908) 771-7704.
MANAGING DIRECTOR
Owen O'Donnell
MANAGING EDITOR
Caroline Buckley
SENIOR EDITOR
Edin Herrera

CELEBRITY SERVICE INTERNATIONAL
Publisher of Celebrity Bulletin (daily), Celebrity Service International Date Book (bi-monthly) and Celebrity Service International Contact Book (semi-annual). 250 W 57th St., Ste. 819 New York, NY 10107. (212) 757-7979. FAX: (212) 582-7701.
8833 Sunset Blvd., Ste. 401 Los Angeles, CA 90069. (310) 652-1700. FAX: (310) 652-9244.
EDITOR, CELEBRITY BULLETIN (NY)
Bill Murray
EDITOR, CELEBRITY BULLETIN (LA)
Todd Longwell
OWNER
Vicki Bagley
MANAGING DIRECTOR
Mark Kerrigan

COMING ATTRACTIONS
(Monthly) Connell Communications Inc., 86 Elm St., Peterborough, NH 03458. (603) 924-7271. FAX: (603) 924-7013.
EXECUTIVE PUBLISHER
Jim Connell

CINEFEX
(Quarterly) P.O. Box 20027, Riverside, CA 92516. (800) 434-3339. (909) 781-1917. FAX: (909) 788-1793.
www.cinefex.com email: circulation@cinefex.com
PUBLISHER
Don Shay
EDITOR
Jody Duncan

COSTUME DESIGNERS GUILD DIRECTORY
(Annual) c/o Costume Designers Guild, 13949 Ventura Blvd., #309, Sherman Oaks, CA 91423. (818) 905-1557. FAX: (818) 905-1560. email: cdgia@email.msn.com

DAILY VARIETY
(Daily) 5700 Wilshire Blvd., Ste. 120, Los Angeles, CA 90036. (213) 857-6600. FAX: (213) 857-0494.
SPECIAL EDITIONS EDITOR
Pat Superstein
MANAGING EDITORS
Jim Gray
Todd Cunningham
NATIONAL SALES MANAGERS
Wayne Roche
Robin Dunn
PRODUCTION MANAGER
Bob Butler

EDITOR & PUBLISHER
(Weekly) 770 Broadway, New York, NY 10003. (212) 675-4380. FAX: (212) 929-1259.
VICE PRESIDENT & PUBLISHER
Dennis O'Neill
EXECUTIVE EDITOR
Steve Yahn

ELECTRONIC MEDIA
(Weekly) 6500 Wilshire Blvd., Ste. 2300, Los Angeles, CA 90048. (323) 370-2432. FAX: (323) 653-4425.
VICE PRESIDENT, PUBLISHER & EDITORIAL DIRECTOR
Chuck Ross
EDITOR
Tom Gilbert

ELECTRONICS NOW
(Monthly) 275 G. Marcus Blvd., Hauppauge, NY 11788. (631) 592-6720. FAX: (631) 592-6723.
www.gernsback.com
PUBLISHER
Larry Steckler

FILM & VIDEO MAGAZINE
(Monthly) Organized 1983. 6310 San Vincente Blvd., Ste. 510, Los Angeles, CA 90048. (323) 653-8053. FAX: (323) 653-8190.
1201 Seven Locks Rd., Ste. 300, Potomac, MD 20854. (800) 777-5006.
PUBLISHER & EDITOR-IN-CHIEF
Peter Caranicas
SENIOR EDITOR
Ed Eberle

FILM JOURNAL INTERNATIONAL
(Monthly) 244 W. 49 St., Ste. 200, New York, NY 10019. (212) 246-6460. FAX: (212) 265-6428.
PUBLISHER & EDITOR
Robert H. Sunshine
ASSOCIATE PUBLISHER
Jimmy Sunshine
MANAGING EDITOR
Kevin Lally
ASSOCIATE EDITORS
Ed Kelleher
Mitch Neuhauser
DIRECTOR OF ADVERTISING & SALES
Jim Merck
WEST COAST EDITOR
Peter Henne
CIRCULATION MANAGER
Joan Masella

HOLLYWOOD CREATIVE DIRECTORY
(Annual) 3000 West Olympic Blvd.,Ste. 2525, Santa Monica, CA 90404. (800) 815-0503. (310) 315-4815. FAX: (310) 315-4816. www.hollywoodcreative.com
email: hcd@hcdonline.com

THE HOLLYWOOD REPORTER
(Daily) 5055 Wilshire Blvd., Los Angeles, CA 90036. (323) 525-2000. (323) 525-2068 (editorial). FAX: (323) 525-2377 (editorial), (323) 525-2372 (advertising), (323) 525-2390 (special issues).
1515 Broadway, New York, NY, 10036. (212) 536-5344, (212) 536-5325 (editorial). FAX: (212) 536-5345.
733 15th St., N.W. Ste. 510, Washington, DC 20005. (202) 737-2828. FAX: (202) 737-3833.
50-51 Bedford Row, London WC1R 4LR England. (01 71) 822-8301. FAX: (01 71) 242-9137.
www.hollywoodreporter.com
PUBLISHER & EDITOR-IN-CHIEF
Robert J. Dowling
EDITOR
Anita M. Busch
DEPUTY EDITOR
Howard Burns

I.A.T.S.E. OFFICIAL BULLETIN
(Quarterly) 1515 Broadway, Ste. 601, New York, NY 10036. (212) 730-1770. FAX: (212) 921-7699.
EDITOR
Michael W. Proscia
ASSISTANT EDITOR
Mary Ann Kelly

INSIDE FILM MAGAZINE
(Bi-monthly) 8421 Wilshire Blvd., Penthouse, Beverly Hills, CA 90211. (213) 852-0434. www.insidefilm.com
PUBLISHER & EDITOR
Susan Royal
ASSISTANT EDITOR
Dawn Brooks

INTERNATIONAL DOCUMENTARY ASSOCIATION
1201 West 5th Street, Ste. M320, Los Angeles, CA 90017-2015. (213) 534-3600. FAX: (213) 534-3610.
www.documentary.org email: info@documentary.org
EDITOR
Jessica Rath

INTERNATIONAL CINEMATOGRAPHERS GUILD MAGAZINE
(Monthly) 7715 Sunset Blvd., Ste. 300, Hollywood, CA 90046. (323) 876-0160. FAX: (323) 878-1180.
www.cameraguild.com
EDITOR-IN-CHIEF
George Spiro Dibie, ASC
EDITOR
Andrew Thompson

INTERNATIONAL MOTION PICTURE ALMANAC
(please see Quigley Publishing Company for complete listing)
(Annual) Editorial & Sales: P.O. Box 1952, La Jolla, CA 92038-1952. (858) 459-1159. FAX: (858) 459-1590.
email: QUIGLEYPUB@aol.com
PUBLISHER
Martin S. Quigley
EDITORIAL DIRECTOR
Tracy Stevens

INTERNATIONAL TELEVISION & VIDEO ALMANAC
(please see Quigley Publishing Company for complete listing)
(Annual) Editorial & Sales: P.O. Box 1952, La Jolla, CA 92038-1952. (858) 459-1159. FAX: (858) 459-1590.
email: QUIGLEYPUB@aol.com
PUBLISHER
Martin S. Quigley
EDITORIAL DIRECTOR
Tracy Stevens

MARKEE— REGIONAL AMERICA'S MAGAZINE FOR FILM AND VIDEO PRODUCTION
366 E Graves Ave. Ste. D., Orange City, FL 32763. (904) 774-8881. FAX: (904) 774-8908.
www.markeemag.com
PUBLISHER
Janet Karcher
EDITOR
John Hutchinson

MEDIA WEEK
(Weekly) BPI Communications. 770 Broadway, New York, NY 10003. (646) 654-5250. FAX: (646) 654-5367. (646) 654-5368.
www.mediaweek.com
EDITOR IN CHIEF
Sid Holt
EDITOR
William F. Gloede
EXECUTIVE EDITOR
Brian Moran
MANAGING EDITOR
Dwight Cunningham

MILLIMETER MAGAZINE
(Monthly) Intertec Publishing. Prime Media. 5 Penn Plaza, 13th Flr., New York, NY 10001. (212) 613-9700. Fax: (212) 563-3028.
6700 Fallbrook Ave., Ste. 222, West Hills, CA 91307. (818) 763-2874. FAX: (818) 763-2894.
www.millimeter.com
email: cynwt@aol.com
PUBLISHER
Jud Alford
EDITOR
Cynthia Wisehart

PACIFIC COAST STUDIO DIRECTORY
(3 times per year) P.O. Box V, Pine Mountain, CA 93222-0022. (661) 242-2722. FAX: (661) 242-2724.
PUBLISHER
Jack Reitz

PERFORMANCE MAGAZINE
(Weekly) 2049 Century Park E., Ste. 1100, Los Angeles, CA 90067. (310) 552-3118. FAX: (310) 286-1990.
PUBLISHER
Pete Clay
SENIOR EDITOR
Stann Findelle
MANAGING EDITOR
Jane Cohen

PRODUCER'S MASTERGUIDE
(60 E. 8th St., 34st Flr., New York, NY 10003. (212) 777-4002. FAX: (212) 777-4101.
www.producers.masterguide.com
PUBLISHER
Shmuel Bension

QUIGLEY PUBLISHING COMPANY
Publishers of International Motion Picture Almanac (Annual) and International Television and Video Almanac (Annual).
Corporate: 9 Railroad Way, Larchmont, NY 10538. (914) 834-2348. FAX: (914) 834-2194.
Editorial & Sales: P.O. Box 1952, La Jolla, CA 92038-1952. (858) 459-1159. FAX: (858) 459-1590.
email: QUIGLEYPUB@aol.com1
PRESIDENT AND PUBLISHER
Martin Quigley
VICE PRESIDENT
Katherine D. Quigley
VICE PRESIDENT & EDITORIAL DIRECTOR
Tracy Stevens
ASSOCIATE EDITORS
Aaron Dior Pinkham
Melinda Lu Campbell
CONSULTANTS
Tanya Brooks
Isaiah Violante
Jonathan Rubin

CANADIAN BUREAU
Deborah Tiffen, Editor. Box 720, Port Perry, ONT L9L 1A6, Canada. (905) 986-0050.

U.K. BUREAU
Nimra Hanif, 68 Kensington Hgts., Campden Hill Rd, London W87 BD England (011 44 0207) 229-5229.

THE REEL DIRECTORY
(Annual) P.O. Box 866, Cotati, CA 94931. (707) 584-8083.
www.reeldirectory.com
PUBLISHER & EDITOR
Bonnie Carroll

SMPTE JOURNAL (SOCIETY OF MOTION PICTURE AND TELEVISION ENGINEERS)
(Monthly) 595 West Hartsdale Ave., White Plains, NY 10607. (914) 761-1100. FAX: (914) 761-3115.
www.smpte.org
DIRECTOR OF MARKETING & COMMUNICATIONS
Linda Alexandre

SCREEN ACTOR/CALL SHEET
(Bi-Monthly) 5757 Wilshire Blvd., Los Angeles, CA 90036. (213) 549-6652. FAX: (213) 549-6656.
PRESIDENT
William Daniels

SHOOT
(Weekly) 770 Broadway, New York, NY 10003. (646) 654-5500. FAX: (646) 654-5354.
5055 Wilshire Blvd., Los Angeles, CA 90036. (323) 525-2262. FAX: (323) 525-0275.
PUBLISHER
Roberta Griefer
EDITOR
Bob Goldrich

TV GUIDE
(Weekly) News America Publications, Inc., 100 Matsonford Rd., Radnor, PA 19088. (610) 293-8500.
EDITOR-IN-CHIEF
Steven Reddicliffe
PRESIDENT & CEO
Joseph Kiener
PUBLISHER & SENIOR VICE PRESIDENT
Dick Porter
MANAGING EDITOR, PROGRAMMING
Steve Sonsky

TAPE/DISC BUSINESS
(Monthly) Knowledge Industry Publications, Inc., 701 Westchester Ave., White Plains, NY 10604-3098. (914) 328-9157. FAX: (914) 684-1518.
EDITOR
Tom O'Reilly
CIRCULATION MANAGER
James De Rose

TELEVISION & CABLE FACTBOOK
(Annual) Warren Communications News, Inc., 2115 Ward Court, N.W., Washington, DC 20037. (202) 872- 9200. FAX: (202) 293-3435.
www.warren-news.com
EDITOR & PUBLISHER
Albert Warren
MANAGING EDITOR
Michael C. Taliaferro
EDITORIAL DIRECTOR
Richard Kochl

TELEVISION DIGEST WITH CONSUMER ELECTRONICS
(Weekly) Warren Communications News, Inc., 2115 Ward Court, N.W., Washington, DC 20037. (202) 872-9200. FAX: (202) 293-3435. www.warren-news.com
EDITOR & PUBLISHER
Albert Warren
EDITORIAL DIRECTOR
David Lachenbruch
EXECUTIVE EDITOR
Dawson B. Nail
SENIOR EDITOR & EXECUTIVE PUBLISHER
Paul Warren
SENIOR EDITOR & ASSOCIATE PUBLISHER
Daniel Warren

TELEVISION QUARTERLY
(Quarterly) National Academy of Television Arts & Sciences, 111 W. 57 St., Ste. 1020, New York, NY 10019. (212) 586-8424. FAX: (212) 246-8129.
EDITOR
Federick A. Jacobi
ADVERTISING
Trudy Wilson

VARIETY
(Weekly) Cahners Business Information, 245 W. 17 St., New York, NY 10011. (212) 337-7002. FAX: (212) 337-6956.
5700 Wilshire Blvd., Ste. #120, Los Angeles, CA 90036, (323) 857-6600. FAX: (323) 965-4469.
Washington: (202) 463-3705. FAX: (202) 463-3744.
Italy: Lungotevere Flaminio 22, Rome. (39-6) 3936-6413.
England: 6 Bell Yard, London WC2A 2JR. (44171) 520-5222 FAX: (44171) 520-5217
Madrid: (34 91) 766-1356. FAX: (34 91) 383-8671.
Sydney:(612) 9422 8630. FAX: (612) 9418-7784.
Latin America: (598-99) 688-419. FAX: (598-2) 9000609.
www.variety.com
CAHNERS CEO
Marc Teren
CAHNERS PRESIDENT & COO
Brian Nairn
GROUP VICE PRESIDENT, PUBLISHER
Charles C. Koones
VICE PRESIDENT, EDITOR-IN-CHIEF
Peter Bart
MANAGING EDITORS
Steven Gaydos
Elizabeth Guider
EUROPEAN EDITOR
Adam Dawtrey

VIDEO STORE MAGAZINE
(Weekly) 201 E. Sandpointe Ave., Ste.. 600, Santa Ana, CA 92707. (714) 513-8400, (800) 854-3112. FAX: (714) 513-8402. www.videostoremag.com
www.hive4media.com
PRESIDENT OF PUBLICATIONS & PUBLISHER
Don Rosenberg
EDITOR-IN-CHIEF
Thomas K. Arnold
MARKET RESEARCH DIRECTOR
Judith McCourt

VIDEO SYSTEMS MAGAZINE
(Monthly) 9800 Metcalf Ave., Overland Park, KS 66212-2215. (913) 341-1300. FAX: (913) 967-1898.
PUBLISHER
Judd Alford
GROUP VICE PRESIDENT
John Torrey
MARKETING MANAGER
Emily Griste
SENIOR AD PRODUCTION COORDINATOR
Julia Gilpin

VIDEO WEEK
(Weekly) Warren Publishing, Inc. 276 5th Avenue, Rm 1002, New York, NY 10001. (212) 686-5410. FAX: (212) 889-5097.
EDITOR
Paul Gluckman

GREAT BRITAIN

BROADCAST
(Published weekly) EMAP Media Ltd., 33-39 Bowling Green Lane, London, EC1R ODA. (44171) 505 8014. FAX: (440207) 505 8050.
EDITOR
Steve Clarke

IMAGE TECHNOLOGY
Journal of the BKSTS–The Moving Image Society, Unit 5 Walpole Court, Ealing Studios, Ealing Green, London, W5 5ED England. (44171) 242-8400. FAX: (44171) 405 3560.
MANAGING EDITOR
Jim Slater

KEMPS FILM, TV & VIDEO HANDBOOK
(Annual) Reed Information Services, Windsor Court, East Grinstead House, East Grinstead, West Sussex, RH19 1XA England. (44171) 580-9486. FAX: (44171) 636-7379.
www.kftv.com
PUBLISHER
Richard Woolley
EDITOR
Claire Crossfield

SCREEN INTERNATIONAL
(Published weekly) Published by EMAP Media, 33-39 Bowling Green Lane, London EC1R 0DA, England. (440207) 505-8096.
www.screendaily.com
MANAGING EDITOR
Leo Barraclough

TELEVISUAL
(Published monthly) Centaur Communications, St. Giles House, 50 Poland St., London, W1V 4AX. (44207) 970-6666. (44207) 439-4222. FAX: (44207) 970-6733. www.televisual.com
PUBLISHER
Morag Armand Addey
EDITOR
Mundy Ellis

CANADA

FILM CANADA YEARBOOK
Box 720, Port Perry, Ontario, L9L 1A6, Canada. (905) 986-0050. FAX: (905) 986-1113. www.filmcanadayearbook.com
email: deborah@filmcanadayearbook.com
EDITOR
Deborah Tiffin

FRANCE

LE FILM FRANCAIS
(Weekly) 103 Blvd. St. Michel, Paris, France, 75005. (331) 4329 4090. FAX: (331) 4329 1405.
PUBLISHER
Claude Pommereau
EDITOR
Marie-Claude Arbaudie

THE WORLD MARKET

CANADA

YEAR IN REVIEW 936

PRODUCTION COMPANIES 938

PRODUCTION SERVICES 952

DISTRIBUTION COMPANIES 957

EXHIBITORS AND EXHIBITION SERVICES 963

TRADE ASSOCIATIONS 967

GOVERNMENT AGENCIES 970

GREAT BRITAIN

MOTION PICTURE YEAR IN REVIEW 972

EXHIBITION CIRCUITS 973

PRODUCERS AND DISTRIBUTORS 976

PRODUCTION SERVICES:
ANIMATION—STUDIO FACILITIES 987

TRADE ORGANIZATIONS & GOVERNMENT UNITS 999

EUROPE, LATIN AMERICA, ASIA AND THE PACIFIC

GUIDE TO EUROPEAN MULTIPLEXES 1002

THE MOTION PICTURE INDUSTRY, A–Z 1007

CANADIAN YEAR IN REVIEW

BY DEBORAH TIFFIN

Telefilm Canada, as part of its program of investment in feature films between April 1, 1999 and March 31, 2000, backed "Law of Enclosures," co-produced by Pluck Inc. (Toronto) and Buffalo Gal Productions (Winnipeg); "Desire," co-produced by Subjective Eye (Toronto), Buffalo Gal Productions (Winnipeg) and Bioskop Film (Germany); "Possible Worlds," co-produced by The East Side Film Company (Toronto) and In Extremis Images (Montreal); "Ginger Snaps," Water Pictures (Toronto); "Love Come Down," The Film Works (Toronto); "The Perfect Son," New Real Films/Perfect Son Productions (Toronto); "waydowntown," Burns Films Ltd. (Calgary); "La moitié gauche du frigo," Quatre Par Quatre Films (Montreal); "St. Jude and Possible Worlds," The East Side Film Company (Toronto); "Parsley Days," a.d. pictures (Halifax), and "Marine Life," Marine Life Productions (Vancouver). All were screened at the Toronto International Film Festival (TIFF) in September.

TIFF celebrated its 25th Anniversary in September 2000, and marked the occasion with "Preludes"—10 original short films. Directors David Cronenberg, Atom Egoyan, Mike Jones, Jean Pierre Lefebvre, Don McKellar, Jeremy Podeswa, Guy Maddin, Patricia Rozema, Michael Snow and Anne Wheeler, along with crews and suppliers donated their time, services and materials to create 10 distinctive and unique tributes to the Festival.

The Perspective Canada series offered a record 15 world premier feature films, with six filmmakers having the world premiere of their debut feature films in the program. The winner of the CITY-TV Award for Best Canadian First Feature Film went to Philippe Falardeau's "La moitié gauche du frigo." From the Perspective Canada Series, the winner of the Toronto City Award for Best Canadian Feature Film went to Gary Burn's "waydowntown." The Benson & Hedges Film People's Choice Award went to Ang Lee's "Crouching Tiger, Hidden Dragon" (Taiwan), with Rob Stitch's "The Dish" (Australia) in second place, Paul Cox's "Innocence" (Australia) and Stephen Daldry's "Billy Elliot" (UK) tied for third.

British Columbia's production tally for 1999 marked a record $1.07 billion in film and television spending - a 32% increase over the 1998 total of $808 million. Foreign production figures (including 22 feature films) totaled $664 million (a 50% increase). Domestic activity (including 32 feature films) accounted for $405 million (a 14% increase).

The Ontario Film Development Corp. (OFDC) reported its own new record in production spending in 1999, totaling $934 million. This marks an upturn of $190.8 million (25.7%) from 1998 totals. Domestic productions account for 53% of the volume (an increase of 24%); foreign productions 47% (an increase of 27.6%, which includes 21 feature film projects). The increase is largely due to domestic television production activity, while the number of domestic feature film projects decreased to 17 (from 21 in 1998). An OFDC spokesman suggested that a combination of factors contributed to this decline: less funding for development and pre-production support, changes in the Ontario Film and Television Tax Credit program, and weak marketing and distribution opportunity for Canadian product. A reorganization of the OFDC was unveiled in May, changing the landscape of the Ontario tax credit regime. The provincial government budget forecasted an investment of $30 million over 5 years to create the new Ontario Media Development Fund, mandated to assume the current functions of the OFDC, as well as enhance the development of new interactive digital media projects, and spur a move to shift a greater proportion of location shooting in the province beyond the borders of the Greater Toronto area.

The Montreal Film and Television Commission reported a production spending total of $725.4 million for 1999. This represents a growth rate of only 5%, compared to a 20% average over the last five years. Foreign production accounted for $213.4 million (a 6% increase), and domestic production totaled $512 million.

While the hot-button issue of "runaway productions" continued to garner attention south of the border, Canadian industry representatives such as Adam Knelman Ostry of the OFDC continued to put the issue in perspective. In Playback, on Feb. 7, Ostry was quoted: "U.S. production in Canada, let alone Ontario, only represents about 2% to 3% of the U.S. industry. Also, U.S. production activity in Canada constitutes, by and large, principal photography, so it only represents 25% to 50% of any given production budget."

Telefilm announced in September that financing for co-productions was reported to have totaled $571.3 million by the end of August. Feature films represented $188.6 million of this total ($105.9 million—56%—from Canadian sources). The UK led the field in feature film co-productions: 12 projects totaling $98.2 million (64% Canadian). France followed with 9 feature film co-productions totaling $59.2 million (51% Canadian). Feature-length animation co-productions totaled $14.4 million.

Alliance Atlantis Corporation (AAC) reported an increase in revenues to $771.6 million for the year ending March 3, a 21.8% increase over last year's earnings of $633.4 million. A new three-year agreement was signed with Spain's Telecinco, giving the company all rights to AAC's Le Monde genre division. AAC extended its "first-look" production and development arrangement with the UK's Natural Nylon Entertainment to 2001, and expanded it to include television development and production. Other agreements include ongoing first-look arrangements with Serendipity Point Films (Toronto), Max Films (Montreal), Coote/Hayes Productions (Australia), Company Pictures (UK), a non-exclusive arrangement with L.A. based producer Andras Hamoi, as well as an ongoing production partnership with Germany's Kinowelt Medien Ag, and a recent three year distribution deal with Artisan Entertainment in the UK which expands on the present Canadian distribution deal. At the end of May, Playback, in an interview with head of motion picture production Seaton McLean, reported AAC's intent to invest as much as $750,000 in new development projects. In March, AAC folded Alliance Atlantis Equicap into a new joint venture with Sentinel Hill to form Sentinel Hill Alliance Atlantis Equipcap (the company is privately held and will be managed by Sentinel Hill). The new, larger company will be increasingly active in gap and structured financing, pursuing a larger share of the Canadian market.

In January, Lions Gate Entertainment (LGE) embarked on a wave of change beginning with an announcement of a new $49 million CDN financing arrangement with a group that included Seattle-based Paul Allen (Vulcan Ventures) and two European broadcasters (SBS Broadcasting SA and Tele-Munchen). The deal is expected to generate new acquisitions (targets included production and distribution companies, and film libraries) and production, as well as facilitating more European partnerships. Frank Giustra stepped down as CEO March 21 to be replaced by Jon Feltheimer. Giustra will focus on mergers and acquisitions, and occupy a "non-executive chair". On June 6, the company acquired Trimark Holdings (production/distribution and a valuable library) in a $50 million CDN deal. In September, LGE entered into a 50/50 joint venture with Toronto financier MediaVentures to form CineGate Production Management services. The deal is expected to result in $300 million in production by March 2001.

According to Feltheimer the arrangement "will create opportunities to identify and acquire funded projects that may be attractive for distribution."

Equinox Entertainment (the film division of La Compagne France Film) announced major expansion in April, operating divisions in film and TV production, theatrical and domestic TV distribution, and home video. In May the company announced sub-distribution deals for the Quebec market with Paramount Classics (English and French) and Buena Vista Pictures.

In September, International Keystone Entertainment announced the acquisition of Red Sky Entertainment, and intends to shift the focus to the distribution of more commercial films. Seville Pictures announced 15 theatrical releases, beginning September 2000. The company turned a profit in fiscal 2000, and plans to enter into international sales in the coming year.

Exhibitors Galaxy Entertainment, Famous Players, and Alliance Atlantis Communications announced a strategic alliance that will see new "state-of-the-art" theatres and the refurbishment of existing venues in midsize Canadian cities. Galaxy has plans to build 20 new complexes across Canada by 2002. Imax Corporation announced that its British subsidiary, Digital Projection International, is developing a design for digital projectors in anticipation of a complete changeover of the estimated 75,000 existing 35mm film projectors, which they are predicting may begin late in 2001. It is belived that, while digital production may lag, the new projection systems may soon be the exclusive delivery system for 35mm product.

The last weeks of 1999 marked the beginning of a turbulent period for Montreal-based Cinar Corporation. Recommendations made in a report by the outgoing SODEC president, Pierre Lampron, identifying irregularities in public financing of Quebec Film & TV productions, were reviewed by the Quebec Department of Revenue. A federal RCMP investigation into Canadian content tax claims by Cinar (and other producers) was launched, as well as internal reviews, coordinated by Canadian Heritage in the Ministries of Revenue, Justice & Finance. In the interim, Cinar continued to negotiate new acquisition, distribution and co-production agreements in China, the U.S. and Mexico. The Heritage Department auditors' report, released in February, called for "better coordination", particularly in the areas of risk-analysis and overlapping jurisdictions. The report was viewed with some skepticism by industry associations in Quebec. In a joint statement, they demanded greater transparency in the funding process and the granting of tax credits.

In March, class-action suits, filed in the U.S. and later in Canada on behalf of investors, suggested that Cinar had violated securities laws by falsely representing scripts written by US citizens as being of Canadian origin in order to obtain tax credit benefit, resulting in an artificial inflation of financial results. Cinar's year-end reporting was delayed, and a statement released Feb. 18 anticipated greater implications of the tax credit investigation than originally expected. This news was followed on March 8 by a suspension in trading on both the NASDAQ and Toronto exchanges as the ongoing tax credit investigation revealed that $179 million CDN had been invested without the knowledge of the board of directors. The subsequent announcement of an administrative leave for founders Ronald A. Weinberg and Micheline Charest as well as their resignation from their co-executive officer positions, saw Barrie Usher named as the new president and CEO and the formation of a new management committee. In June, the Ontario Securities Commission widened the scope of its temporary cease-trading order, due to a failure by the company to meet a statutory filing deadline of 1999 financial statements, resulting from the continuing tax-credit investigation. Company shares were suspended on the TSE on Aug. 30th, with de-listing to follow in one year's time if revised financial statements dating back to 1997 were not produced. NASDAQ de-listed the company in a July hearing, due to a failure to produce the required financial reports. It was announced that Charest and Weinberg had been asked to step down from the board and that their employment was terminated on Aug. 17th.

At the 20th Anniversary of the Genie Awards in January, the award for Best Motion Picture went to "Sunshine," by Robert Lantos and Andras Hamori; the award for best performance by an Actor in a Leading Role was won by Bob Hoskins for "Felicia's Journey"; best performance by an Actress in a Leading Role went to Sylvie Moreau in "Post Mortem"; best Original Screenplay was won by Louis Bélanger for "Post Mortem" and the Adapted Screenplay - award was given to Atom Egoyan for "Felicia's Journey."

PRODUCTION COMPANIES

ABATON PICTURES, INC.
214 Rusholme Rd., Toronto, ON M6H 2Y8. (416) 537-2641. FAX: (416) 537-2995.
PRESIDENT
Ian McDougall

ABRAMS MEDIA, INC.
560 Main St. Ste. 120, Building A, Saint John NB E2K 1J5. (506) 633-6038. FAX: (506) 633-7493.
email: abrams@sonoptic.com
CONTACT
Greg Abrams

ACCENT ENTERTAINMENT CORPORATION
666B Queen St. W., 2nd Fl., Toronto, ON M6J 1E5. (416) 867-8700. FAX: (416) 867-1764.
PRESIDENT
Susan Cavan

THE ACE FILM COMPANY, INC.
1152 Mainland St., Ste. 400, Vancouver, BC V6B 4X2. (604) 682-0001. FAX: (604) 682-7346. www.acefilm.com
EXECUTIVE PRODUCER
Parker Jefferson
DIRECTOR/CINEMATOGRAPHER
Allen G. Jones

ACPAV
1050 boul. René-Lévesque est, bur. 200, Montréal, QC H2L 2L6. (514) 849-2281. FAX: (514) 849-9487.
PRODUCERS
Marc Daigle
René Gueissaz
Bernadette Payeur

ACROLET INTERNATIONAL
155 Topcliffe Cres., Fredericton, NB E3B 4P8. (506) 457-1793. FAX: (506) 454-6757.
CONTACT
Semra N. Yuksel

A.K.A. CARTOON
200 - 220 Cambie St., Vancouver, BC V6B 2M9. (604) 682-6652. FAX: (604) 682-6259. email: vincent@akacartoon.com
EXECUTIVE PRODUCER & DIRECTOR
Danny Antonucci
PRODUCER & ACCOUNTANT
Ruth Vincent
PRODUCER
Christine Danzo

ALLAN KING ASSOCIATES LIMITED
965 Bay St., #2409, Toronto, ON M5S 2A3. (416) 964-7284. FAX: (416) 964-7997.
PRESIDENT
Allan King
VICE PRESIDENT
Colleen Murphy
EXECUTIVE ASSISTANT
Elisa Suppa

ALLIANCE ATLANTIS COMMUNICATIONS, INC.
Head Office: 121 Bloor St. E., Ste. 1500, Toronto, ON M4W 3M5. (416) 967-1174. FAX: (416) 960-0971.
www.allianceatlantis.com
email: allianceatlantis@allianceatlantis.com

HEAD OFFICE
CHAIRMAN & CEO
Michael MacMillan
EXECUTIVE VICE PRESIDENT AND CFO
W. Judson Martin
CHAIRMAN, MOTION PICTURE GROUP
Victor Loewy
PRESIDENT, MOTION PICTURE PRODUCTION
Seaton McLean
PRESIDENT, TELEVISION DISTRIBUTION
Ted Riley
PRESIDENT, MOTION PICTURE DISTRIBUTION
Patrice Théroux
EXECUTIVE V.P.,TELEVISION PRODUCTION
Steve Ord
EXECUTIVE V.P.,TELEVISION PRODUCTION
Christine Shipton
S.V.P., PRODUCTION, MOVIES & MINI-SERIES, TELEVISION
Ian McDougall
S.V.P., PRODUCTION, SERIES, TELEVISION
Mary Kahn
S.V.P., COMMUNICATIONS
Alexandra Brown
PRESIDENT, TELEVISION PRODUCTION, LOS ANGELES
Peter Sussman
PRESIDENT, CITADEL ENTERTAINMENT, LLC, LOS ANGELES
Judy Ranan
BRANCH OFFICES

Montréal: Alliance Vivafilm, 5 Place Ville Marie, Ste. 1435 Montréal, QC H3B 2G2. (514) 878-2282. FAX: (514) 878-2419.

Vancouver: Two Bentall Centre, 555 Burrard St., Vancouver, BC V7X 1M7. (604) 687-3798. FAX: (604) 687-3958.

Los Angeles: Alliance Atlantis Entertainment Inc., 808 Wilshire Blvd., Santa Monica, CA 90401-1810. (310) 899-8000. FAX: (310) 899-8100.

Shannon: Alliance Atlantis Television International, Block 1, Unit C, Shannon Business Park, Shannon, Co. Clare, Ireland. (011) 35361472329. FAX: (011) 35361472228.

London: Company Pictures, 184-192 Drummond St., 2nd. Fl., London NW1 3HP, England. (011) 44 171 291 6900. FAX: (011) 44 171 383-0404.

Australia: Alliance Atlantis Releasing PTY, 65 Military Rd., Ste. 4, Neutral Bay, N.S.W. 2089, Australia. (011) 6129 953-2999. FAX: (011) 6129 953-3248.

AMERIMAGE-SPECTRA
822 rue Sherbrooke est, Montréal, QC H2L 1K4. (514) 525-7833. FAX: (514) 525-8033.
PRODUCERS
Alain Simard
Pierre L. Touchette

ANAID PRODUCTIONS, INC.
318, 8925 - 51 Ave., Edmonton, AB T6E 5J3. (780) 413-9285. FAX: (780) 465-0580. email: anaid@compusmart.ab.ca
CONTACT
Margaret Mardirossian

ANIGRAPH PRODUCTIONS LIMITED
P.O. Box 13490, Stn. A, St. John's, NF A1B 4B8. (709) 722-2820. FAX: (709) 739-4801. email: anigraph@avalon.nf.ca
PRESIDENT
C. Anne MacLeod
PRODUCER
Paul G. MacLeod

ANNETTE COHEN PRODUCTIONS LIMITED
25 Imperial St., #500, Toronto, ON M5P 1C1. (416) 483-8018, Ext. 230. FAX: (416) 483-9763.
PRESIDENT
Annette Cohen

ANNEX ENTERTAINMENT
332 Dupont St., Toronto, ON M5R 1V9. (416) 929-3939. FAX: (416) 921-1325. email: annex@interlog.com
PRODUCERS
Paul Wynn
Richard Borchiver

THE "A" PICTURE COMPANY
212 James St., Ottawa, ON K1R 5M7. (613) 230-9769. FAX: (613) 230-6004.
CONTACT
Ramona Macdonald

AQUILA FILM & VIDEO, INC.
48 Proctor Blvd., Hamilton, ON L8M 2M4. (905) 545-4773.
DIRECTOR/CAMERAMAN
Jim Aquila, csc

AQUILON FILM, INC.
Box 370, Victoria Stn., Westmount, QC H3Z 2V8. (514) 985-2597. FAX: (514) 982-6894.
PRESIDENT
Werner Volkmer

ARMEDIA COMMUNICATIONS
Box 257, Stn. C, Toronto, ON M6J 3P4. (905) 889-0076. FAX: (905) 889-0078. email: armedia@canada.com
CONTACT
David Mazmanian

ARTCORE PRODUCTIONS, LTD.
2024 Glenada Cr., Oakville, ON L6H 4M6. (905) 338-3642. FAX: (905) 338-8642. email: artcore@pathco.com
CONTACT
Vlad Kabelik

ARTHUR HOLBROOK PRODUCTIONS, INC.
2705 Arbutus Rd., Victoria, BC V8N 1W8. (250) 477-5057. FAX: (250) 477-5447. email: holbrook@islandnet.com
CONTACT
Arthur Holbrook

ARTO-PELLI MOTION PICTURES, INC.
124 Cumberland St., 3rd Fl., Toronto, ON M5R 1A6. (416) 928-0164. FAX: (416) 928-3399.
PRODUCER
Stavros C. Stavrides

ARTS ET IMAGES PRODUCTIONS
370 Short St., Sherbrooke, QC J1H 2E2. (819) 822-4131. FAX: (819) 822-4132. email: aipi@interlinx.qc.ca
EXECUTIVE PRODUCER & DIRECTOR
Mario Desmarais
LINE PRODUCER
Madeleine Audet
DIRECTOR
Marcel Jean

ART YOUNG VIDEO PRODUCTIONS
8387 - 13th Ave., Burnaby, BC V3N 2G8. (604) 526-8897. FAX: (604) 526-8814. email: artyoung@telus.net
CONTACT
Art Young

THE ASHLAND ENTERTAINMENT AND LEARNING COMPANY
2 Berkeley St., Ste. 300, Toronto, ON M5A 2W3. (416) 368-5633. FAX: (416) 368-2227.
PRESIDENT
Brian Ash
OPERATIONS MANAGER
Mike Ball

ASKA FILM PRODUCTIONS, INC.
1600 ave. de Lorimier, Ste. 211, Montréal, QC H2K 3W5. (514) 521-7103. FAX: (514) 521-6174. email: askafilm@login.net
CONTACTS
Claude Gagnon
Yuri Yoshimura-Gagnon

ASSOCIATED PRODUCERS
110 Spadina Ave., 10th Fl., Ste. 1001, Toronto, ON M5V 2K4. (416) 504-6662. FAX: (416) 504-6667.
CONTACTS
Elliott Halpern
Simcha Jacobovici
Jack Rabinovitcha

ASTERISK PRODUCTIONS, LTD.
977 Hampshire Rd., Victoria, BC V8S 4S3. (250) 480-5256. FAX: (250) 480-5299. www.asterisk.bc.ca
email: asterisk@islandnet.com
CONTACTS
David Springbett
Heather MacAndrew

ASTRAL MEDIA, INC.
Maison Astral, 2100, rue Sainte-Catherine Ouest, bur. 1000, Montréal, QC H3H 2T3. (514) 939-5000. FAX: (514) 939-1515.
CHAIRMAN
André Bureau, O.C.
PRESIDENT/CEO
Ian Greenberg
VICE PRESIDENT
Sidney Greenberg
VICE PRESIDENT, FINANCE
Claude Gagnon
VICE PRESIDENT, DEVELOPMENT
Jacques Parisien
VICE PRESIDENT, HUMAN RESOURCES
Arnold Chiasson
GENERAL COUNSEL & SECRETARY
Monique Ryan
COMMUNICATIONS CONSULTANT
David Novek

ATLANTIC MEDIAWORKS
469 King St., Fredericton NB E3B 1E5. (506) 458-8806. FAX: (506) 452-2700. email: amw@nbnet.nb.ca
CONTACTS
Bob Miller
Daphne Curtis

AUDACINE, INC.
68 Hamilton St., Toronto, ON M4M 2C8. Tel. & FAX: (416) 778-4562.
PRESIDENT
Mary Jane Gomes

AVANTI PICTURES CORPORATION
#410 - 425 Carrall St., Vancouver, BC V6B 6E3. (604) 609-0339. FAX: (604) 609-0336. www.avantipics.com
email: avantipc@axionet.com
PRODUCER/DIRECTOR
Tony Papa

BAR HARBOUR FILMS, INC.
67 Riverdale Ave., Toronto, ON M4K 1C2. (416) 778-4491. FAX: (416) 778-4144.
WRITER/DIRECTOR
Martin Harbury

BARNA-ALPER PRODUCTIONS, INC.
366 Adelaide St. W., Ste. 700, Toronto, ON M5V 1R9. (416) 979-0676. FAX: (416) 979-7476.
CONTACT
Laszlo Barna

BERYT PRODUCTIONS, INC.
8111 Yonge St., Ste. 1503, Thornhill, ON L3T 4V9. (905) 764-6872. FAX: (905) 764-3615.
PRESIDENT/PRODUCER
Eliza Haddad
ASSOCIATE PRODUCER
Kathryn Kearn

BIG STAR MOTION PICTURES, LTD.
13025 Yonge St., Ste. 201, Richmond Hill, ON L4E 1Z5. (905) 773-8670. FAX: (905) 773-3153. email: bigstar@pathcom.com
PRESIDENT/EXECUTIVE PRODUCER
Frank A. Deluca
VICE PRESIDENT/EXECUTIVE PRODUCER
Giacomo Moncada

BIRDSONG COMMUNICATIONS
806 Victoria Ave., Regina, SK S4N 0R6. (306) 359-3070. FAX: (306) 525-1204. email: birdsong.ltd@sk.sympatico.ca
PRESIDENT
Don List
PRODUCER
Rodger Ross

DAROLD BLACK
2116 Palliser Dr. S.W., Calgary, AB T2V 3S1. Tel. & FAX: (403) 251-5568.

BLACKWATCH COMMUNICATIONS
1410 Stanley, Ste. 606, Montreal, QC H3A 1P8. (514) 844-6655. FAX: (514) 844-6886.
CEO
William R. Mariani
EXECUTIVE VICE PRESIDENT
Pierre Colas
CFO
Ronald W. Price
CONTROLLER
John Talbot
V.P. BUSINESS & LEGAL AFFAIRS
Charlene Paling

BLACKWATCH PRODUCTIONS
643 de Courcelle, Ste. 306, Montreal, QC H4C 3C5. (514) 933-7575. FAX: (514) 933-5545.
PRESIDENT
Kim Berlin
CONTROLLER
Lise Chapdelaine
EXECUTIVE ASSISTANT
Franca Visconti

BLOKLAND PICTURES CORPORATION
217 St. George St., Unit 44, Toronto, ON M5R 3S7. (416) 975-9259. FAX: (416) 975-8214. email: admin@blokland.com
WRITER/DIRECTOR
Jim Blokland

BLUEMOON PRODUCTIONS, INC.
2 Berkeley St., Ste. 400, Toronto, ON M5A 2W3. (416) 955-1855. FAX: (416) 955-0989. www.bluemoonproductions.com
email: bluemoon@inforamp.net
EXECUTIVE PRODUCERS
John Crampton
June Weber

BLUE SKY PRODUCTIONS, INC.
1619 Hampshire Rd., Victoria, BC V8R 5T4. (250) 598-4563.
email: cellulloyd@home.com
CONTACTS
Lloyd Chesley
James Fry

BONGARD FILMS, INC.
59 Mutual St., Toronto, ON M5B 2A9. (416) 368-4593.
PRODUCER/DIRECTOR
Ralph Bongard

BOOTLEG FILMS
177 Shaw St., Toronto, ON M6J 2W6. (416) 588-0608. FAX: (416) 588-0489. email: bootleg@interlog.com
CONTACTS
Milan Cheylov
Lori Lansens

BRADSHAW MACLEOD & ASSOCIATES/ALBERTA FILM-WORKS
1310 - 11TH St. S.W., Calgary, A.B. T2R 1G6. (403) 777-9900. FAX: (403) 777-9914. email: afw@cadvision.com
EXECUTIVE PRODUCER/PRODUCER
Doug MacLeod
PRODUCER
Tom Dent-Cox
PRODUCER/DIRECTOR
Randy Bradshaw

BRAVURA PRODUCTIONS, LTD.
One Benvenuto Pl., Ste. 220, Toronto, ON M4V 2L1. (416) 964-7490. FAX: (416) 960-3247.
PRESIDENT
Bruce Martin

BREAKTHROUGH FILMS AND TELEVISION, INC.
179 Mavety St., Toronto, ON M6P 2M1. (416) 766-6588. FAX: (416) 769-1436. email: business@breakthroughfilms.com
DIRECTORS/PRODUCERS
Ira Levy
Peter Williamson

BRIAN BOBBIE PRODUCTIONS, LTD.
759 Pape Ave., 2nd Floor, Toronto, ON M4K 3T2. (416) 466-6350. FAX: (416) 466-9271. email: people@bbpl.com
CONTACTS
Brian Bobbie
Janice Bobbie

BRIDGE FILM PRODUCTIONS, INC.
44 Charles St. W., Ste. 2518, Toronto, ON M4Y 1R7. (416) 927-0663.
CONTACT
Brigitte Berman

BROADCAST PRODUCTIONS, INC.
77 Huntley St., Ste. 2522, Toronto, ON M4Y 2P3. (416) 961-1776. FAX: (905) 309-0999.
PRESIDENT
Brian E. Purdy

BUCK PRODUCTIONS
543 Richmond St. W., Ste. 125, Toronto, ON M5V 1Y6. (416) 362-3330. FAX: (416) 362-3336. www.buckproductions.com
EXECUTIVE PRODUCER
Sean Buckley

BUFFALO GAL PICTURES, INC.
490 - 70 Arthur St., Winnipeg, MB R3B 1G7. (204) 956-2777. FAX: (204) 956-7999. email: bgal@mb.sympatico.ca
PRESIDENT
Phyllis Laing

CADENCE ENTERTAINMENT, INC.
92 Lonsdale Ave., 2nd Fl., North Vancouver, BC V7M 2E1. (604) 984-8877. FAX: (604) 984-8870.
email: cadence@cadence-ent.com
CONTACTS
Scott Kennedy
Bill Thumm
Daegan Fryklind

CAMBIUM FILM & VIDEO PRODUCTIONS, LTD.
18 Dupont St., Toronto, ON M5R 1V2. (416) 964-8750. FAX: (416) 964-1980.
EXECUTIVE PRODUCER
Arnie Zipursky
GENERAL MANAGER & GENERAL COUNSEL
Annette Frymer
V.P. PRODUCTION
Hasmi Giakoumis
CREATIVE DEVELOPMENT OFFICER
Dan Fill

CAMERA ONE FILMS LIMITED
1 Metcalfe St., Toronto, ON M4X 1R5. Tel. & FAX: (416) 921-6588. email: epetras@niagarac.on.ca
PRODUCER/DIRECTOR
Elias Petra

CANADIAN WILDERNESS VIDEOS & PRODUCTIONS
1010 Larch Pl., Canmore, AB T1W 1S7. (403) 678-3795. FAX: (403) 678-3796. email: crvideo@agt.net
PRODUCER/DIRECTOR/CAMERA
Eric Langshaw

CANAMEDIA PRODUCTIONS, LTD.
1670 Bayview Ave., Ste. 408, Toronto, ON M4G 3C2. (416) 483-7446. FAX: (416) 483-7529.
PRESIDENT
Les Harris
SECRETARY/TREASURER
Jane Harris
VICE PRESIDENT, DISTRIBUTION, NORTH AMERICA
David W. Jackson
INTERNATIONAL SALES EXECUTIVE
Michèle Dal Cin

CAROL REYNOLDS PRODUCTIONS, INC.
2 Bloor St. W., Ste. 1740, Toronto, ON M4W 3E2. (416) 926-1661. FAX: (416) 926-1668.
PRESIDENT
Carol A. Reynolds

CATALYST ENTERTAINMENT, INC.
67 Mowat Ave., Ste. 200, Toronto, ON M6K 3E3. (416) 533-6767. FAX: (416) 533-2070.
email: catalyst@catalysttoronto.com
CEO
Charles Falzon

CELLAR DOOR PRODUCTIONS
3 Malahu Dr., Charlottetown, PEI C1A 8A5. (902) 628-3880. FAX: (902) 628-2088. email: productions@isn.net
PRESIDENT
Gretha Rose
VICE PRESIDENT, BUSINESS AFFAIRS, MARKETING & DISTRIBUTION
Lawrie Rotenberg
ASSOCIATE PRODUCER
Angela Campbell

CHRISTOPHER CHAPMAN, LTD.
R.R. 3, Uxbridge, ON L9P 1R3. (905) 852-9136.
PRESIDENT
Christopher Chapman

CHESLER/PERLMUTTER PRODUCTIONS, INC.
129 Yorkville Ave., Ste. 200, Toronto, ON M5R 1C4. (416) 927-0016. FAX: (416) 960-8447.
CO-CHAIRMAN
David M. Perlmutter

CHRONICLE PICTURES
1657 Barrington St., Ste. 515, Halifax, NS B3J 2A1. (902) 425-4885. FAX: (902) 425-4851. email: chronpic@istar.ca
PRODUCERS
Craig Cameron
Evangelo Kioussis
Scott Simpson

CINAK LTÉE
1313, Chemin Guthrie, Saint-Armand, QC J0J 1T0. (450) 248-3295.
PRÉSIDENT
Jean-Pierre Lefebvre

CINAR CORPORATION
1055 boul. René Lévesque est , Montréal, QC H2L 4S5. (514) 843-7070. FAX: (514) 843-7080.
CHAIRMAN & CEO
Barry Usher
PRESIDENT, CINAR ENTERTAINMENT
Peter Moss

CINEFILE PRODUCTIONS, INC.
424 Dufferin St., Fredericton, NB E3B 3A7. (506) 455-5666. FAX: (506) 455-5667. email: cinefile@sprint.ca
PRESIDENT
Barry Cameron

CINEFLIX, INC.
5505 St-Laurent Blvd., Ste. 3008, Montréal, QC H2T 1S6. (514) 278-3140. FAX: (514) 270-3165.
PRODUCER
Glen Salzman

CINEGRAPHE PRODUCTIONS
820 rue De Rougemont, Sainte-Foy, QC G1X 2M5. (418) 652-3345. FAX: (418) 652-3353. email: cinegraf@mediom.qc.ca
CONTACTS
Nicholas Kinsey
Andrée Tousignant

CINÉ-GROUPE
1151 Alexandre-Desève St., Montréal, QC H2L 2T7. (514) 524-7567. FAX: (514) 524-7354. email: distribution@cinegroupe.ca
SENIOR VICE PRESIDENT
Bill Gray
VICE PRESIDENT, DEVELOPMENT
Marie-Claude Beauchamp

CINEMA ESPERANCA INTERNATIONAL, INC.
96 Spadina Ave., Ste. 301, Toronto, ON M5V 2J6. (416) 703-5000, (877) 525-3776. FAX: (416) 703-5002.
email: jakeprod@on.aibn.com
CHAIRMAN/PRESIDENT/CEO
André Bennett

CINÉMAREVIE CO-OP LTÉE
146, chemin Canada, Edmundston NB E3V 1V9. (506) 736-6837. FAX: (506) 739-6929.
CONTACT
Rodolphe Caron

CINEMAX FILMS, INC.
2222 W. 33rd Ave., Vancouver, BC V6M 1C2. (604) 266-9690.
PRODUCER/PRODUCTION MANAGER
Don McLean

CINEMILLENNIUM, INC.
400 Walmer Rd., Park Towers E., Ste. 2323, Toronto, ON M5P 2X7. (416) 961-2001. (011) 36-20-931-8000. FAX: (416) 961-2003. email: cinemail@ican.net
CONTACT
Bob Schulz

CINEMOD INTERNATIONAL, INC.
944 Scarlett Rd., Toronto, ON M9P 2V6. (416) 241-5908. FAX: (416) 241-0235.
CONTACT
Domenic Ubaldino

CINENOVA PRODUCTIONS
468 King St. W., 6th Fl., Toronto, ON M5V 1L8. (416) 363-2600. FAX: (416) 363-2609.
CHAIRMAN/CEO
David Lint
PRESIDENT
Jane Armstrong

CINE QUA NON FILMS
5266 boul. St-Laurent, Montréal, QC H2T 1S1. (514) 271-4000. FAX: (514) 271-4005.
PRODUCER
Michel Ouellette
DIRECTOR/PRODUCER
Bernar Hébert
HEAD PROJECT COORDINATOR AND DEVELOPMENT
Valérie Chartrand

CINEROUTES PRODUCTIONS, INC.
259 Erskine Ave., Toronto, ON M4P 1Z6. (416) 486-4830.
CONTACT
Anthony Azzopardi

CINEVIDEO, INC.
1320 Graham Blvd., Ste. 200, Montréal, QC H3P 3C8. (514) 272-5077. FAX: (514) 272-3154.
PRESIDENT/PRODUCER
Justine Héroux
ADMINISTRATOR
Marcel Bergeron

CINIMAGE FILMS, INC.
140 Champlain St., Ste 101, Dieppe, NB E1A 1N8. (506) 386-1616. FAX: (506) 855-7025. email: cinimage@nb.sympatico.ca
CONTACTS
Monique LeBlanc
Michael LeBlanc

CITE AMERIQUE CINEMA TELEVISION
5800 boul, St-Laurent, 2nd Fl., Montréal, QC H2T 1T3. (514) 278-8080. FAX: (514) 278-4000.
PRESIDENT
Lorraine Richard

CLARENCE SQUARE PICTURES
49 Spadina Ave., Ste. 100, Toronto, ON M5V 2J1. (416) 971-6281. FAX: (416) 971-7925.
email: clarencesquare@hotmail.com
CONTACTS
Jeffrey Berman
Richard D'Alessio
Christina Ford

CLEARWATER FILMS LIMITED
1255 Yonge St., Ste. 100, Toronto, ON M4T 1W6. (416) 929-7232. FAX: (416) 929-7225.
PRESIDENT
G. Chalmers Adams

COCHRAN ENTERTAINMENT, INC.
Ground Fl., Purdy's Wharf Two, 1969 Upper Water St., Halifax, NS B3J 3R7. (902) 421-9777. FAX: (902) 425-8659.
email: hello@cochran.com
PRESIDENT
Andrew Cochran
VICE PRESIDENT, MARKETING
Maureen Wheller
VICE PRESIDENT, BUSINESS AFFAIRS
Randy Dewell
MANAGER OF INTERNATIONAL SALES
Marisa Ma, New York (212) 965-4671

CODLESSCO, LTD.
19 Waterford Bridge Rd., St. John's, NF A1E 1C5. (709) 738-4355. FAX: (709) 738-4360. www.mediatouch.com/untoldstory
PRODUCER
Marian Frances White

COMMUNICATIONS CLAUDE HÉROUX
4984, place de la Savane, Ste. 100, Montréal, QC H4P 1Z6. (514) 738-3737. FAX: (514) 738-3290.
email: cheroux@aol.com
PRESIDENT
Claude Héroux
VICE PRESIDENT, PRODUCTION
Caroline Héroux

CONDOR PRODUCTIONS
Apt. 511, 110 The Esplanade, Toronto, ON M5E 1X9. (416) 362-1740.
PRESIDENT/PRODUCER
Vladimir Bondarenko

CONNECTIONS PRODUCTIONS
236, boul. St. George, bureau 406, Moncton NB E1C 1W1. (506) 382-3984. FAX: (506) 382-3980.
email: coprod@nbnet.nb.ca
CONTACTS
François Savoie
Michael Savoie

CONQUERING LION PICTURES
18 Gloucester Lane, 4th Fl., Toronto, ON M4Y 1L5. (416) 967-1055. FAX: (416) 923-8580. email: slate@interlog.com
PRESIDENT
Clement Virgo
VICE PRESIDENT
Damon D'Oliveira

COOTE COMMUNICATIONS VIDEO/PLUS
2511 Merrington Cres., Mississauga, ON L5K 2B8. (905) 855-1249.
PRESIDENT
G. Morgan Coote
VICE PRESIDENT
Donald C. Coote
SECRETARY-TREASURER
Morgan Coote

COYOTE FILMS, LTD.
1423 Howe St., Vancouver, BC V6Z 1R9. (604) 685-1417.
PRESIDENT
Ken Kuramoto

CRAWLEY FILMS LIMITED
P.O. Box 11069, Stn. H, Nepean, ON K2H 7T8. (613) 825-2479. FAX: (613) 825-9300.
CONTACT
Bill Stevens Jr.

CREATIVE ATLANTIC COMMUNICATIONS LIMITED
2085 Maitland St., Halifax, NS B3K 2Z8. (902) 423-1989. FAX: (902) 423-3711. email: creative.atlantic@ns.sympatico.ca
CONTACTS
Janice Evans
Greg Jones

CREDO ENTERTAINMENT CORPORATION
120 Sherbrooke St., Winnipeg, MB R3C 2B4. (204) 989-8188. FAX: (204) 989-8187, www.credocorp.com
PRESIDENT
Derek Mazur

CRESCENT ENTERTAINMENT
177 W. 7th Ave., Ste. 200, Vancouver, BC V5Y 1L8. (604) 668-8300. FAX: (604) 668-8304.
CONTACTS
Harold Tichenor
Gordon Mark
Jayme Pfahl
Arvi Liimatainen

CRONE FILMS, LTD.
8175 Pasco Rd., W. Vancouver, BC V7W 2T5. (604) 921-6500.
CONTACTS
Robert Crone, csc
David Crone

CROSSROADS CHRISTIAN COMMUNICATIONS, INC.
P.O. Box 5100, 1295 North Service Rd., Burlington, ON L7R 4M2. (905) 332-6400. FAX: (905) 332-6655.
www.crossroads.ca
PRESIDENT
David Mainse

CRYSTAL FILMS, INC.
P.O. Box 66586, Stoney Creek, ON L8G 5E5. (905) 273-6855. FAX: (905) 273-7202. www.reelstunts.on.ca
email: crystal@odyssey.on.ca
WRITER/PRODUCER/DIRECTOR
Randy Butcher
PRODUCER
Bob Tuli

CURLCOM PRODUCTIONS, LTD.
7 Avon Ct., Whitby, ON L1N 3H2. (905) 428-6466. FAX: (905) 666-8316.
PRESIDENT
E.G. (Ted) Curl

CYCLOPS COMMUNICATIONS CORPORATION
44 Gibson Ave., Toronto, ON M5R 1T5. (416) 926-8981. FAX: (416) 926-9878. email: cyclopscorp@sprint.ca
PRESIDENT
Samuel C. Jephcott

DARIUS FILMS
533 College St., Toronto, ON M6G 1A8. (416) 922-0007. FAX: (416) 928-3066. email: darius@darius.com
PRESIDENT/PRODUCER
Nicholas Tabarrok
PRODUCTION
Shasha Marusich

DAVID PAPERNY FILMS
1908 Tolmie St., Vancouver, BC V6R 4C2. (604) 228-1960. FAX: (604) 228-1911. email: paperny@axionet.com
PRODUCERS/DIRECTORS
David Paperny
Audrey Mehler
PRODUCER
Cal Shumiatcher

DECODE ENTERTAINMENT, INC.
512 King St. E., Ste. 104, Toronto, ON M5A 1M1. (416) 363-8034. FAX: (416) 363-8919.
CONTACT
John A. Delmage
Steven DeNure
Neil Court

DEE ANDERSON PRODUCTIONS
11 Mansfield Park Court, Ashburn, ON L0B 1A0. (905) 985-7761.
PRESIDENT/PRODUCER
Dee Anderson

DELANEY & FRIENDS CARTOON PRODUCTIONS
105 West 3rd Ave., Vancouver, BC V5Y 1E6. (604) 877-8585. email: delaney@axion.net
PRESIDENT
Chris Delaney
VICE PRESIDENT, DESIGN
John Delaney
MARKETING & BUSINESS DEVELOPMENT
Carolyn Paul

DEVINE ENTERTAINMENT CORPORATION
2 Berkeley St., Ste. 504, Toronto, ON M5A 2W3. (416) 364-2282. FAX: (416) 364-1440. email: devinent@interlog.com www.devine-ent.com
CONTACTS
David Devine
Richard Mozer

SIMON CHRISTOPHER DEW
35 Spruce St., Toronto, ON M5A 2H8. (416) 923-3432. FAX: (416) 923-6007. email: dew@christopher.net

DINOSAUR SOUP PRODUCTIONS
9353 - 50th St., Ste. 13, Edmonton, AB T6B 2L5. (780) 461-9465. FAX: (780) 461-0657. email: dinosoup@telusplanet.net
PRESIDENT/PRODUCER
Gerri Cook
VICE PRESIDENT/PRODUCER/MARKETING
Steve Moore

DISTANT SHORE PRODUCTIONS
126 Owens Rd., Saint John, NB E2N 1K7. Tel./FAX: (506) 672-0183. Cell: (506) 639-0072. email: diver15@nbnet.nb.ca
CONTACT
Darrell Bainbridge

LES DISTRIBUTIONS ROZON
2101 boul. St-Laurent, Montréal, QC H2X 2T5. (514) 845-3155. FAX: (514) 845-4140.
PRESIDENT
Gilbert Rozon
GENERAL MANAGER, TV/FILM
Pierre Girard

DMB PRODUCTIONS
10159 -108 St., Edmonton, AB T6J 1L1. (780) 448-0211. FAX: (780) 425-7235. email: lstewart@dmbproduction.com
PRESIDENT/DIRECTOR
David Benson
SENIOR PRODUCER
Laurie Stewart

DMU
897 Runnymede Rd., Toronto, ON M6N 3W3. (416) 766-1282. FAX: (416) 767-8561.
CONTACT
Domenic Ubaldino

DOCUMENTARY PRODUCTIONS, LTD.
1418 - 133A St., Surrey, BC V4A 6A2. (604) 535-8215. FAX: (604) 535-8265.
CONTACT
Jack McGaw

DOMINO FILM & TELEVISION INTERNATIONAL, LTD.
4002 Grey Ave., Montréal, QC H4A 3P1. (514) 484-0446. FAX: (514) 484-0468.
PRESIDENT
Jeanne Ritter

DOOMSDAY STUDIOS LIMITED
212 James St., Ottawa, ON K1R 5M7. (613) 230-9769. FAX: (613) 230-6004.
CONTACT
Ramona Macdonald

DORMONT STUDIOS, INC.
79 Orchard Park Blvd., Toronto, ON M4L 3E3. (416) 698-4482. Montréal: (514) 221-2300; Vancouver: (604) 730-0860; Los Angeles: (310) 496-3113.
www.autoplayer.com/peterb/index.html
email: dormont@hotmail.com
CINEMATOGRAPHER
Peter Benison, csc

DOTCOM VIDEO PRODUCTIONS
141 Hardisty St., Thunder Bay, ON P7C 3G7. (807) 623-5338. FAX: (807) 622-8497.
MANAGER
Peggy Garriock

DREAMSCAPE VIDEO PRODUCTIONS
645 Manning Ave., Toronto, ON M6G 2W2. (416) 534-7464. FAX: (416) 535-4477.
VIDEO PRODUCER/DIRECTOR
Brock Fricker

DREAMSMITH ENTERTAINMENT, INC.
795 Main St., Ste. 303, Moncton, NB EIC IE9. (506) 854-1057. Cell: (506) 866-8446 (Timothy); Cell: (506) 545-5744 (James). FAX: (506) 388-4162. email: tmhogan@nbnet.nb.ca
email: hoganwj@nbnet.nb.ca

DUFFERIN GATE PRODUCTIONS
20 Butterick Rd., Toronto, ON M8W 3Z8. (416) 255-2260. FAX: (416) 255-7488. email: dgpmail@interlog.com
PRESIDENT
Patrick Whitley
VICE PRESIDENT
Rose Lam

EDWARD LEE PRODUCTIONS
15225 - 104th Ave., Ste. 310, Surrey, BC V3R 6Y8. (604) 589-5270. FAX: (604) 588-1555. www.leevideo.com
email: leeproductions@sprint.ca
OWNER
Edward Lee
EDITOR
Richard Lee

EGO FILM ARTS
80 Niagara St., Toronto, ON M5V 1C5. (416) 703-2137. FAX: (416) 504-7161. email: egofilms@netcom.ca
CONTACTS
Simone Urdl
Atom Egoyan

ELLIS VISION INCORPORATED
1300 Yonge St., Ste. 300, Toronto, ON M4T 1X3. (416) 924-2186. FAX: (416) 924-6115. email: vision@ellisent.com
CHARIMAN
Ralph C. Ellis
PRESIDENT
Stephen Ellis

EPITOME PICTURES INC.
220 Bartley Dr., North York, ON M4A 1G2. (416) 752-7627. FAX: (416) 752-7837.
EXECUTIVE OFFICER
Linda Schuyler

EQUUS FILM PRODUCTIONS INC.
174 Fulton Ave., Toronto, ON M4K 1Y3. (416) 429-7399.
CONTACTS
Keith Lock, Leslie Padorr

ESPRIT FILMS LIMITED
2 Lake St., St. Catharines, ON L2R 5W6. (905) 685-8336.
PRESIDENT
Deborah Cartmer

EYELIGHT INC.
382 Breithaupt St., Kitchener, ON N2H 5H9. (519) 743-2600. FAX: (519) 743-3562.
PRESIDENT
Ron Repke

LA FABRIQUE D'IMAGES LIMITEE
318 rue Sherbrooke est, Montréal, QC H2X 1E6. (514) 282-1505. FAX: (514) 282-8784. www.fabimages.com
email: fabinfo@fabimages.com
PRODUCERS
Denis Martel
Christiane Hamelin
Michel Raymond
Claude Landry
Louis Morin
Christiane Ciupka
Martin Ulrich

DIRECTORS
Alain DesRochers
Christian Duguay
Jacques Fournier
Marc S. Grenier
Jean-François Pouliot
Jean François Rivard
Jean-Michel Ravon
Jason Hreno
Claude Brie
Michel Pelletier
J. Wesley Jones

F & F PRODUCTIONS INC.
215 Glen Rd., Toronto, ON M4W 2X2. (416) 967-3696. FAX: (416) 967-4722.

THE FACTORY
4593 de l'Esplanade, Montréal, QC H2T 2Y6. (514) 284-0722. FAX: (514) 282-0833. email: factory film@hotmail.com
PRODUCER
Derek Lebrero

FIDDLEHEAD ENTERTAINMENT INC.
Frontiers of Construction, P.O. Box 1306, Moncton, NB E1C 8T6. (506) 854-1057. FAX: (506) 388-4162.
CONTACTS
Sam Grana
W. James Hogan

FILM ARTS INC.
1177 Yonge St., Ste. 608, Toronto, ON M4T 2Y4. (416) 924-4839. FAX: (416) 924-6054. email: haigfilm@home.com
CONTACT
Don Haig

FILM CREW PRODUCTIONS
2345 Smith St., Regina, SK S4P 2P7. (306) 777-0160. FAX: (306) 352-8558. email: filmcrew@sk.sympatico.ca
EXECUTIVE PRODUCER
Michael Snook

FILM EAST INC.
P.O. Box 5574, St. John's, NF A1C 5W4. (709) 753-8500. FAX: (709) 579-8090.
CONTACTS
Paul Pope
Jennice Ripley
John Doyle

FILMLINE INTERNATIONAL INC.
410 St-Nicolas St., Ste. 10, Montréal, QC H2Y 2P5. (514) 288-5888. FAX: (514) 288-8083. email: filmline@sprint.ca
CONTACT
Nicolas Clermont

FILM ONE PRODUCTIONS
397 Donlands Ave., Toronto, ON M4J 3S2. (416) 696-9823. FAX: (416) 696-7901.
CONTACT
Jalal Merhi

LES FILMS ISATIS
866 du Coteau, St-Foy, QC G1X 292. (418) 653-7876. FAX: (418) 653-8089.
CONTACT
Jean Bourgault

LES FILMS VISION 4 INC.
4446, boul. St-Laurent, 7th Fl., Montréal, QC H2W 1Z5. (514) 499-0972. FAX: (514) 844-5498. email: telefiction@login.net
PRODUCERS
Claude Veillet
Jacques Bonin

THE FILM WORKS, LTD.
77 Mowat Ave., Ste. 114, Toronto, ON M6K 3E3. (416) 538-2666. FAX: (416) 538-0169.
CONTACTS
Eric Jordan
Paul Stephens
Victor Solnicki

FIREWORKS ENTERTAINMENT/CANWEST ENTERTAINMENT INC.
111 George St., 3rd Fl., Toronto, ON M5A 2N4. (416) 360-4321. FAX: (416) 364-4388.
CHAIRMAN & CEO
Jay Firestone
PRESIDENT & COO
Adam Haight
CFO
Blake Tohana
SENIOR VICE PRESIDENT, BUSINESS & LEGAL AFFAIRS
John Robinson

FISHTALES PRODUCTIONS
470 Euclid Ave., Toronto, ON M6G 2S9. Tel. & FAX: (416) 964-0003.
PRINCIPAL
Honey Fisher

FOLKUS ATLANTIC INC.
Silicon Island, Ste. 205, 70 Crescent St., Sydney, NS B1S 2Z7. (902) 562-5107. FAX: (902) 539-3363. www.folkus.com
email: folkus@atcon.com
CONTACT
Joan Weeks

FORCE FOUR ENTERTAINMENT
310 - 1152 Mainland St., Vancouver, BC V6B 4X2. (604) 669-4424. FAX: (604) 669-4535. www.forcefour.com
email: tv@forcefour.com
PRESIDENT
Hugh Beard
PRODUCTION MANAGER/PRODUCER
Debra Beard
SENIOR PRODUCER
John Ritchie
DIRECTOR, PROGRAM DEVELOPMENT
Rob Bromley

FOREVERGREEN TELEVISION & FILM PRODUCTIONS
181 Carlaw Ave., Ste. 230, Toronto, ON M4M 2S1. (416) 778-9944. FAX: (905) 628-1769. email: foreverg@icom.ca
PRESIDENT
Alan Aylward
VICE PRESIDENT
Jonathan Welsh

FORWARD FOCUS PRODUCTIONS, LTD.
784 Thurlow St., Ste. 31, Vancouver, BC V6E 1V9. Tel & FAX: (604) 681-4677.
PRESIDENT
Mary Anne McEwen

FREEDOM FILMS INC.
38 McGee St., Toronto, ON M4M 2K9. (416) 778-1358. FAX: (416) 778-1819. www.freedom2be.com
email: freedomfilm@hotmail.com
PRESIDENT
Aaron Goldman

FUNDAMENTALLY FILM INC.
46 Sherbourne St., Ste. 300, Toronto, ON M5A 2P7. (416) 947-5999. FAX: (416) 860-3855. www.fundamentallyfilm.com
email: info@fundamentallyfilm.com
CONTACT
Joe Green

FUNDY PRODUCTION ASSOCIATES
31 Highfield Rd., Douglas NB E3A 7P7. (506) 450-8006. FAX: (506) 450-8006. email: fpa@youngmonkey.ca
CONTACT
Doug Sutherland

GALAFILM INC.
5643, rue Clark, #300, Montréal, QC H2T 2V5. (514) 273-4252. FAX: (514) 273-8689. email: galafilm@galafilm.ca
PRESIDENT
Arnie Gelbart
PRODUCERS
Ian Whitehead
Richard Elson
Anna Poskal

GEMINI FILM PRODUCTIONS, LTD.
163 Queen St. E., Ste. 200, Toronto, ON M5A 1S1. (416) 862-9031.
PRODUCER/DIRECTOR
Edie Yolles

GFT ENTERTAINMENT
(Includes GFT Kingsborough Films & GFT/Paquinm Entertainment)
124 Merton St., Ste. 407, Toronto, ON M4S 2Z2. (416) 487-0377. FAX: (416) 487-6141.
PRESIDENT
Gary Howsam
PRESIDENT - GFT KINGSBOROUGH FILMS
Pieter Kroonenburg
PRESIDENT - GFT/PAQUIN ENTERTAINMENT
Gilles Paquin

LEN GILDAY, CSC
R.R.#1, B-46, Bowen Island, BC V0N 1G0. (604) 947-2388. FAX: (604) 947-2389.

GORDFILM INC.
5633 Chancellor Blvd., Vancouver, BC V6T 1E4. (604) 224-6470. FAX: (604) 224-4267.
CONTACT
Ken Gord

GORICA PRODUCTIONS
295 Silverbirch Ave., Toronto, ON M4E 3L6. (416) 324-1332. FAX: (416) 324-9594. email: gorica@interlog.com
PRESIDENT
Felice Gorica

GREAT NORTH PRODUCTIONS INC.
3720 - 76 Ave., Edmonton, AB T6B 2N9. (780) 440-2022. FAX: (780) 440-3400.
CONTACTS
Patricia Phillips
Brenda Hennig

GREEN LION PRODUCTIONS
20223 rue Lakeshore, Baie d'Urfe, QC H9X 1P9. (514) 457-5555. FAX: (514) 457-3255.
PRODUCER
Catherine Mullins

GREGORIAN FILMS, LTD.
P.O. Box 71040, 3552 W. 41st. Ave., Vancouver, BC V6N 1W0. Tel. & FAX: (604) 266-1617. email: ckpitts@telus.net
CONTACT
Charles K. Pitts

GREYSTONE INTERNATIONAL INC.
490 Adelaide St. W., Ste. 100, Toronto, ON M5V 1T2. (416) 504-6059. FAX: (416) 504-4843.
CONTACTS
G. Philip Jackson
Daniel D'or

GROUPE CINEMAGINAIRE INTERNATIONAL
5144 boul. Saint-Laurent, Montréal, QC H2T 1R8. (514) 272-5505. FAX: (514) 272-9841.
PRESIDENT & PRODUCER
Denise Robert
VICE PRESIDENT & PRODUCER
Daniel Louis

GRYPHON PRODUCTIONS, LTD.
P.O. Box 93009, 5331 Headlands Dr., Wets Vancouver, BC V7W 3C0. (604) 921-7627. FAX: (604) 921-7626.
CONTACT
Peter Von Puttkamer

HBW FILM CORP./RIVERWOOD PRODUCTIONS
2526 Battleford Ave. S.W., Ste. 225, Currie Barracks, Calgary, AB T3E 7J4. (403) 228-1900. FAX: (403) 228-1110.
email: hbwflmtv@ultralink.com
PRINCIPAL
Helene B. White

HEARTLAND MOTION PICTURES INC.
1102 - 8th Ave., 3rd Fl., Regina, SK S4R 1C9. (306) 777-0888. FAX: (306) 586-3537.
CONTACT
Stephen Onda

HEROIC FILM COMPANY
324 Markham St., Toronto, ON M6G 2K9. (416) 944-3433. FAX: (416) 944-3703. email: waterpix@interlog.com
EXECUTIVE PRODUCERS
Karen Lee Hall
John May
Suzanne Bolch

HIGH ROAD PRODUCTIONS INC.
571 Jarvis St., Toronto, ON M4Y 2J1. (416) 961-8370. FAX: (416) 929-3077.
CONTACTS
Paul Jay
David M. Ostriker

HOT GLACIER FILMS
33 Eastmount Ave., TH2, Toronto, ON M4K IV3. (416) 461-8895. email: hotglac@interlog.com
PRODUCER/DIRECTOR
David Gilmour Martin

HOTSHOTS
215 Glen Rd., Toronto, ON M4W 2X2. (416) 967-3696. FAX: (416) 967-4722.
DIRECTOR/CAMERAMAN
D. Evans

THE IDEA FACTORY!
18520 Stony Plain Rd., Edmonton, AB T5S 1A8. (780) 439-3985 . FAX: (780) 439-4051. email: info@ideafactory.ab.ca
PRESIDENTS
Drew Martin
VICE PRESIDENT, PRODUCTION
Lindsay Speer

IDEACOM INTERNATIONAL INC.
1000 Amherst, Ste. 300, Montréal, QC H2L 3K5. (514) 849-6966. FAX: (514) 849-0776. email: ideacom@istar.ca
CONTACTS
Jacques Nadeau
Josette D. Normandean

IMAX CORPORATION
2525 Speakman Dr., Sheridan Park, Mississauga, ON L5K 1B1. (905) 403-6500. FAX: (905) 403-6450.
CHAIRMAN & CO-C.E.O
Bradley J. Wechsler
VICE-CHAIRMAN & CO-CEO
Richard L. Gelfond
S.V.P., FILM
Andy Gellis
PRODUCERS
Graeme Ferguson
Roman Kroitor
Toni Myers
DIRECTOR, FILM TECHNOLOGY
Gord Harris
CAMERA RENTAL
Claude Richard

IMX COMMUNICATIONS
1190 Barrington Ave., 4th Fl., Halifax, NS B3H 2R4. (902) 422-4000. FAX: (902) 422-4427. email: imx@imx.ca
PRESIDENT/EXECUTIVE PRODUCER
Chris Zimmer
VICE PRESIDENT, BUSINESS AFFAIRS
John Kelly
VICE PRESIDENT, FINANCIAL
Dana Landry
VICE PRESIDENT, OPERATIONS & DEVELOPMENT
Jan Miller

INDEPENDENT PICTURES INC.
18 Gloucester Lane, 4th Fl., Toronto, ON M4Y 1L5. (416) 960-6310. FAX: (416) 960-8463.
PRESIDENT
Peter O'Brian

INDO CANADIAN FILMS INTERNATIONAL
4500 boul. de Maisonneuve O., bur 21, Montréal, QC H3Z 1L7. (514) 935-6888. FAX: (514) 935-8588..
email: indocdn.films@ibm.net
PRESIDENT
Gotham Hooja

INFORMACTION FILMS INC.
67 rue Ste-Catherine o., Ste. 500, Montréal, QC H2X 1Z7. (514) 284-0441. FAX: (514) 845-0631.
CONTACT
Nathalie Barton

INFRAME PRODUCTIONS INC.
1744 William St., Ste. 400, Montréal, QC H3J 1R4. (514) 935-7025. FAX: (514) 935-9238.
CONTACT
Nick Papadopoli

INSIGHT PRODUCTION COMPANY, LTD.
489 King St. W., Ste. 401, Toronto, ON M5V 1K4. (416) 596-8118. FAX: (416) 596-8270.
EXECUTIVE PRODUCERS
John M. Brunton
Barbara Bowlby

INTERCOM FILMS LIMITED
34 Colin Ave., Toronto, ON M5P 2B9. (416) 483-3862. FAX: (416) 483-1106.
PRESIDENT
Gilbert W. Taylor

INTERNATIONAL ROCKETSHIP, LTD.
1338 W. 6th Ave., Ste. 203, Vancouver, BC V6H 1A7. (604) 738-1778. FAX: (604) 738-0009.
PRODUCER
Julie Moreton

INTREPID FILMS INC./PETER LHOTKA
254 E. 18th St., North Vancouver, BC V7L 2X6. Tel. & FAX: (604) 987-5581. email: lhotka@npsnet.com
PRODUCER
Peter Lhotka

INVESTIGATIVE PRODUCTIONS INC.
862 Richmond St. W., Ste. 201, Toronto, ON M6J1C9. (416) 703-5580. FAX: (416) 703-1691. email: ipi@inforamp.net
PRESIDENT
Peter Raymont

JOHN McGREEVY PRODUCTIONS
36 Roxborough St. E., Toronto, ON M4W 1V6. (416) 922-8625. FAX: (416) 922-8624.
PRESIDENT
John McGreevy

JOHN M. ECKERT PRODUCTIONS LIMITED
385 Carlton St., Toronto, ON M5A 2M3. (416) 960-4961.
CONTACT
John M. Eckert

JOHN VAINSTEIN & ASSOCIATES
173 Heward Ave., Toronto, ON M4M 2T6. (416) 465-9535.

JOHN WALKER PRODUCTIONS, LTD.
730 Euclid Ave., 3rd Fl., Toronto, ON M6G 2T9. (416) 532-7442. FAX: (416) 532-8199. email: walk@interlog.com

JOHN WATSON & PEN DENSHAM'S INSIGHT PRODUCTIONS INC.
193 Gowan Ave., Toronto, ON M4J 2K7. (416) 423-4409.
CONTACT
Ann Mayall

JORDAN-BASTOW PRODUCTIONS INC.
2227 Victoria Dr., Vancouver, BC V5N 4K7. (604) 255-9373.
CONTACT
Gretchen Jordan-Bastow

JUST ONE STEP AT A TIME PRODUCTIONS INC.
118 Castlefield Ave., Toronto, ON M4R 1G4. Tel. & FAX: (416) 484-9671. email: josat@interlog.com
WRITER/DIRECTOR
Peter Gerretsen

JUTUL FILMS INC.
47 Amiens Rd., West Hill, ON M1E 3S7. (416) 282-4304. FAX: (416) 282-1767. email: jutul@interlog.com
CONTACT
Per-Inge Schei

KARVONEN FILMS
2001 - 91 Ave., Edmonton, AB T6P 1L1. (780) 467-7167. FAX: (780) 467-7162. email: films@karvonenfilms.com
PRESIDENT
Albert Karvonen
VICE PRESIDENT
Pirkko Karvonen

KATHERINE SMALLEY PRODUCTIONS
368 Brunswick Ave., Toronto, ON M5R 2Y9. (416) 961-8907. FAX: (416) 324-8253.
PRESIDENT
Katherine Smalley

KEATLEY MACLEOD PRODUCTIONS
2656 Eastbrook Parkway, Burnaby, BC V5C 5W8. (604) 291-9789. FAX: (604) 291-9759. email: coldsquad@uniserve.ca
PRESIDENT
Julia Keatley
SECRETARY
Matt MacLeod

KERRIGAN PRODUCTIONS INC.
3877 av. Draper, Montréal, QC H4A 2N9. (514) 486-8456.
PRODUCER/DIRECTOR
Bill Kerrigan

KONO FILMS, LTD.
81 Claremont Ave., Winnipeg, MB R2H 1W1. (204) 237-5649. FAX: (204) 237-1563. email: konosite@home.com
PRESIDENT
Charles Konowal

KRIZSAN FILM PRODUCTIONS
23 Fairbank St., Dartmouth, NS B3A 1B9. (902) 456-0948. FAX: (902) 466-8689. email: krizsan@ns.sympatico.ca
CONTACTS
Les Krizsan, csc, Corinne Lange

KUPER PRODUCTIONS, LTD.
301 Forest Hill Rd., Toronto, ON M5P 2N7. (416) 782-4553. FAX: (416) 782-4425.
CREATIVE DIRECTOR
Jack Kuper

L&A MOTION PICTURES
155 Marlee Ave., Ste. 1207, Toronto, ON M6B 4B5. (416) 783-5159. FAX: (416) 783-7684. email: tluppino@istar.ca
EXECUTIVE PRODUCER
Istvan Luppino

LAISSEZ-FAIRE FILMS INC.
Pier 32, Granville Island, 330-1333 Johnston St., Vancouver, BC V6H 3R9. (604) 689-0880. FAX: (604) 689-3036.
WRITER/PRODUCER
Terry Mercer
PRODUCER
Paxton Robertson

LAWRENCE HERTZOG PRODUCTIONS LIMITED
87 Barton Ave., Toronto, ON M6G 1P7. Tel. & FAX: (416) 531-4670. email: hertzog@interlog.com

LAWRENCE MARSHALL PRODUCTIONS
3348 Bayview Ave., Unit A, North York, ON M2M 3R9. (416) 590-0315. FAX: (416) 590-0317. email: lmp@inforamp.net
PRESIDENT
Lawrence Marshall

LIGHTBOX STUDIOS INC.
422 Dundas St. E., Toronto, ON M5A 2A8. (416) 929-1948. FAX: (416) 323-9295.
CONTACT
Mary Young

LINDISFARNE PRODUCTIONS INC.
22791-125 A Ave., Maple Ridge, BC V2X 0N4. Tel. & FAX: (604) 463-3977, Pager: (604) 450-3142.
WRITER/PRODUCER
Fred Keating

LINDUM FILMS INC.
67 Marjory Ave., Toronto, ON M4M 2Y2. (416) 461-2305. FAX: (416) 461-4311.
WRITER/DIRECTOR/PRODUCER
Peter Blow

LIONS GATE ENTERTAINMENT CORP.
2 Bloor St. W., Ste. 1901, Toronto, ON M4W 3E2. (416) 944-0104. FAX: (416) 944-2212. www.lionsgate-ent.com
PRESIDENT
Jeff Sackman

Vancouver: Ste. 3123 - 3 Bentall Centre, 595 Burrard St., P.O. Box 49139, Vancouver, BC V7X 1J1. (604) 609-6100. FAX: (604) 609-6149.

Quebec: 3600 boul. Thimens, St. Laurent, QC H4R 1V6. (514) 336-9696. FAX: (514) 336-6606.

New York: 561 Broadway, Ste. 12B, New York, NY 10012. (212) 966-4670. FAX: (212) 966-2544.
PRESIDENT OF PRODUCTION
Michael Paseornek

Los Angeles: 5750 Wilshire Blvd., Ste. 501, Los Angeles, CA 90036. (323) 692-7300. FAX: (323) 692-7373.

LOCKWOOD FILMS (LONDON), INC..
12569 Boston Drive, R.R. 41, London, ON N6H 5L2. Tel. & FAX: (519) 657-3994. email: mark.mccurdy@sympatico.ca
PRODUCER
Nancy C. Johnson
DIRECTOR/PRODUCER
Mark K. McCurdy
PRODUCER/PROGRAM DEVELOPMENT
Nancy Johnson

I. GEORGE LOMAGA
1906 Bough Beeches Blvd., Mississauga, ON L4W 2J7. (905) 629-9207. FAX: (905) 629-9138.

LONG SHOT PICTURES
3273 Homewood Lane, London, ON N6P 1K1. (519) 671-7111. FAX: (519) 652-7617. www.longshotpictures.com
email: greg@longshotpictures.com
CONTACT
Greg Bierbaum

LORENZO ORZARI PRODUCTIONS
6 Libersan, Montréal, QC H9A 2B5. Tel. & FAX: (514) 685-6170. email: lorzari@odyssee.net
WRITER/PRODUCER/DIRECTOR
Lorenzo Orzari

LOTEN MEDIA, INC.
35 High Park Ave., Ste. 1701, Toronto, ON M6P 2R6. (416) 598-4699. FAX: (416) 205 1258.
email: loten-media@on.aibn.com
CONTACTS
Wendy Loten
Walter Cudlip

MACFARLANE FILM PRODUCTIONS, LTD.
27 Stonehedge Hollow, Unionville, ON L3R 3Y9. (416) 477-8798. FAX: (416) 477-7507. email: macfarlane@globalserve.net
PRESIDENT
Duncan MacFarlane

MAINFRAME ENTERTAINMENT
2025 West Broadway, Ste. 500, Vancouver, BC V6J 1Z6. (604) 714-2600. FAX: (604) 714-2641. email: jules@reboot.com
EXECUTIVE PRODUCERS
Mark Ralston, Ian Pearson
PRODUCER
Ace Fipke

MAISON PREMIER PLAN, INC.
1600 de Lorimier, Montréal, QC H2K 3W5. (514) 521-1984. FAX: (514) 521-7081.
PRÉSIDENT
Pierre Valcour

MAKIN' MOVIES, INC.
265 Albany Ave., Toronto, ON M5R 3C7. (416) 516-1833. FAX: (416) 516-8474.
CONTACT
Maureen Judge

MARANO PRODUCTIONS, INC.
435 - 4th Ave. S.W., Ste. 450, Calgary, AB T2P 3A8. (403) 294-1457. FAX: (403) 265-0796. email: maranopod@telusplanet.net
PRODUCER
Nancy Marano

MASSEY PRODUCTIONS, LTD.
249 East St. James Rd., North Vancouver, BC V7N 1L3. (604) 990-9044. FAX: (604) 990-9066.
PRODUCER
Raymond Massey

MAX FILMS/MAX FILMS TELEVISION
500 Sherbrooke St. E., Montréal, QC H2L 1K1. (514) 282-8444. FAX: (514) 282-9222. email: info@maxfilms.ca
PRESIDENT
Roger Frappier
PRODUCERS
Luc Vandal
Jean Lemire

MAX MEDIA, LTD.
849 Barker St., Fredericton, NB E3A 3K4. (506) 472-0006. FAX: (506) 472-1496.
CONTACT
Kevin Matthews

THE MAY STREET GROUP
Film, Video & Animation Ltd., 1274 May St., Victoria, BC V8V 2T2. (250) 380-6656. FAX: (250) 380-6670.
PRESIDENT
Hilary Jones-Farrow

MEDIA CONCEPTS, INC.
Meadow Bank, Cornwall RR#2, Charlottetown, PE C0R 1H0. Mailing address: P.O. Box 2703, Charlottetown, PE C1A 8C3. (902) 892-7359. FAX: (902) 368-3798.
email: mconcept@isn.net
PRODUCER
Jack McAndrew

MEMORIA
200 - 690 St. Joseph St., Winnipeg, MB R2H 3E2. (204) 233-1189. FAX: (204) 233-0811.
CONTACT
Romeo Jacobucci

MENTOR PICTURES, LTD.
32 Marlwood Dr., Halifax, NS B3M 3H2. (902) 445-2740.
DIRECTOR
Michael Greer

MICROTAINMENT PLUS INTERNATIONAL
1 Atlantic Ave., Ste. 103, Toronto, ON M6K 3E7. (416) 537-5004. FAX: (416) 537-8984. email: mail@microtainment.com
CHAIRMAN
Garry Blye
PRESIDENT
Mark Shekter

MILAGRO FILMS
425 rue Guy, Ste. 201, Montréal, QC H3J 1S9. (514) 939-9969. FAX: (514) 933-2260. email: milagrofilms@altavista.com
PRODUCER
Jean-Marc Felio
DIRECTOR, DEVELOPMENT & SALES
Tom Philpott
CFO
Kamel Benameur

MILLBROOK PRODUCTIONS, INC.
329 Canada St., Fredericton, NB E3A 4A3. (506) 457-1967. Cell: (506) 461-0228. FAX: (506) 457-1900.
email: bdennis@millbrookstudios.com
CONTACT
Bruce Dennis

MINDS EYE PICTURES
2201 - 11th Ave., 3rd Fl., West Wing, Regina, SK S4P 0J8. (306) 359-7618. FAX: (306) 359-3466.
email: mindseye@sk. sympatico.ca
CHAIRMAN & CEO
Kevin DeWalt
PRESIDENT, CREATIVE AFFAIRS
Rob King
VICE PRESIDENT, OPERATIONS
Ken Krawczyk
VICE PRESIDENT, DEVELOPMENT
Josh Miller

MOBIUS ENTERTAINMENT CORP.
839 Churchill Row, Ste. 21, Fredericton, NB E3B 1R1. (506) 454-9555. FAX: (506) 454-3338. email: bittman980@home.com
PRESIDENT
Roman Bittman
PRODUCER
Marilyn Belec

MONGREL
3755 West 6th Ave., Ste. 109, Vancouver, BC V6R 1T9. (604) 222-3312. FAX: (604) 222-4436. email: dobrien@direct.ca
CONTACT
Duncan O'Brien

MOONDOG FILM COMPANY, INC.
78 Frizzell Ave., Toronto, ON M4J 1E3. (416) 461-7681. FAX: (416) 461-8729. Website: www.moondogfilm.com

MORAG PRODUCTIONS
P.O. Box 52, Stn. C, St. John's, NF A1C 5H5. (709) 739-0447. FAX: (709) 739-0467. email: morag@nf.sympatico.ca
PRODUCER/DIRECTOR
Barbara Doran

MORTIMER & OGILVY PRODUCTIONS LIMITED
1431 Howe St., Vancouver, BC V6Z 1R9. (604) 408-1693. FAX: (604) 254-2462.
PRODUCER
Sharon McGowan
PRODUCER/WRITER
Peggy Thompson

MOUNTAIN PRODUCTIONS
193 Sunhill Estates, Sherwood Park, AB T8A 4R7. (780) 922-6834. FAX: (780) 922-7683. email: bowden@connect.ab.ca
PRESIDENT/PRODUCER/DIRECTOR
Bowden J. Zachara, B.Sc.
AUDIO
Edward A. Zachara

THE MOVIE FACTORY
Mount Allison University, Unit #756, Sackville, NB E4L IB3. (506) 536-2953. email: testgem@mta.ca
CONTACT
Timothy St-Germain

MY COUNTRY PRODUCTIONS, INC.
3 Hillcrest Ave., Toronto, ON M4X 1W1. (416) 961-6031. FAX: (416) 961-9833. email: efrank@istar.ca
CONTACT
Elsa Franklin

NELVANA
(Including Nelvana Enterprises Inc., Nelvana Communications) 32 Atlantic Ave., Toronto, ON M6K 1X8. (416) 588-5571. FAX: (416) 588-5588. www.nelvana.com
CO-CEOs
Patrick Loubert
Michael Hirsh
Clive Smith
S.V.P., FINANCE & CFO
Sally Moyer Kent
S.V.P., PRODUCTION
Stephen Hodgins
V.P., GENERAL COUNSEL & CORPORATE SECRETARY
J. Harriet Reisman
V.P., PRODUCTION
Patricia Burns
V.P., BUSINESS AFFAIRS
Suzanne Cross
V.P., PRODUCTION & INFORMATION TECHNOLOGIES
Scott Dyer
V.P. & CONTROLLER
Christine Nalborczyk
V.P. & TREASURER
John Vandervelde
PRESIDENT, NELVANA COMMUNICATIONS
Toper Taylor
EXECUTIVE V.P., WORLDWIDE MERCHANDISING, NELVANA COMMUNICATIONS
Sidney Kaufman

BRANCHES

London: 22 Kingly Court, London, UK W1R 5LE. (011) 44-207-287-2770. FAX: (011) 44-207-287-2740.
email: cathyl@uk.nelvana.com
CONTACT
Cathy Laughton

Paris: 55, rue de Bretagne, Paris, France 75003. (33) 1-42 71 01 44. FAX: (33) 1 42 71 08 28.
CONTACT
Emmanuéle Petry

NEW AND IMPROVED FILMS, INC.
P.O. Box 5581, Stn. C, St. John's, NF A1C 5W4. (709) 739-0270. email: dmcgee@mirror.det.mun.ca
PRESIDENT
Debbie McGee

NEW BRUNSWICK FILMMAKERS' CO-OPERATIVE
P.O. Box 1537, Fredericton, N.B. E3B 4Y1. (506) 455-1632. FAX: (506) 457-2006. www.brunet.net/nbfilm/
email: nbfilmco-op@brunnet.net
CONTACTS
Tony Merzetti
Cathie LeBlanc

NEW CITY PRODUCTIONS
1380 Burrard St., 3rd Fl., Vancouver, BC V6Z 2H3. (604) 642-5400. FAX: (604) 642-5440.
PRESIDENT
Colleen Nystedt
VICE PRESIDENT, PRODUCTION
Christopher Courtney

NEW COMMUNICATION CONCEPTS, LTD.
5-23260 Dyke Rd., Richmond, BC V6V 1E2. (604) 520-0272. FAX: (604) 526-3351.
PRESIDENT
Keith Cutler

90th PARALLEL FILM & TELEVISION PRODUCTIONS
112 Parliament St., Toronto, ON M5A 2Y8. (416) 364-9090. FAX: (416) 364-0580.
PRESIDENT & PRODUCER
Gordon S. Henderson

NOMADIC PICTURES
3911 Trasimene Cr. S.W., Calgary, AB T3E 7J6. (403) 217-8751. FAX: (403) 217-0534.
PRODUCERS
Mike Frislev
Chad Oakes

NORFLICKS PRODUCTIONS
260 Richmond St. W., Ste. 607, Toronto, ON M5V 1W5. (416) 351-7558. FAX: (416) 205-1258. www.norflicks.com
PRESIDENT
Richard Nielson
V.P., DEVELOPMENT & BUSINESS AFFAIRS
Michael Ulster
V.P., PRODUCTION
Lana Pitkin

NORFOLK INTERNATIONAL
160 Bloor St. E., Ste. 1220, Toronto, ON M4W 1B9. (416) 921-5100. FAX: (416) 921-8800.
email: office@norfolk-international.com
PRESIDENT
William MacAdam
V.P., DEVELOPMENT
Jeffrey Round

NORSTAR FILMED ENTERTAINMENT, INC.
86 Bloor St. W., 4th Fl., Toronto, ON M5S 1M5. (416) 961-6278. FAX: (416) 961-5608.
CHAIRMAN & CEO
Peter R. Simpson
VICE PRESIDENT, FINANCE & OPERATIONS
Jim Woodside
VICE PRESIDENT, DEVELOPMENT
Carrie Paupst
DIRECTOR, SALES & OPERATIONS
Agapy Kapouranis
DIRECTOR, PRODUCTION & BUSINESS AFFAIRS
A. Daphne Park

NORTH AMERICAN PICTURES, LTD.
808 Nelson St., Ste. 2105, Vancouver, BC V6Z 2H2. (604) 681-2165. FAX: (604) 681-5538. email: group@nar.bc.ca
CHAIRMAN & CEO
Lloyd A. Simandl

OASIS PICTURES, INC.
6 Pardee Ave., Ste. 104, Toronto, ON M6K 3H5. (416) 588-6821. FAX: (416) 588-7276. www.oasispictures.com
email: info@oasispictures.com
PRESIDENT
Peter Emerson
DIRECTOR, PRODUCTION & DEVELOPMENT
Michael Sather

OCTOBER FILMS, INC.
67 Brookfield St., Toronto, ON M6J 3A8. (416) 532-6253.
CONTACT
Bruno Lazaro Pacheco

O'MARA & RYAN
2897 Bellevue Ave., West Vancouver, BC V7V 1E7. (604) 926-9155. FAX: (604) 926-9152.
CONTACTS
James O'Mara
Kate Ryan

OMNI FILM PRODUCTIONS, LTD.
(and Water Street Pictures Ltd.), 111 Water St., Ste. 204, Vancouver, BC V6B 1A7. (604) 681-6543. FAX: (604) 688-1425. email: omni@omnifilm.com
PRESIDENT/EXECUTIVE PRODUCER
Michael Chechik

OMNI PRODUCTIONS & ENTERTAINMENT GROUP, INC.
43 Colborne St., Concourse Level, Toronto, ON M5E 1E3. (416) 862-7100. FAX: (416) 862-5578.
PRESIDENT
Ben Abbassi

ONE REEL VISION
8 Admiral Circle, Grimsby, ON L3M 5C7. (905) 646-2108. FAX: (905) 646-8803. email: wkelly@onereelvision.com
PRESIDENT
Larry McGean

OPTIMA PRODUCTIONS, INC.
1253 McGill College, Rm. 452, Montréal, QC H3B 2Y5. (514) 397-9988. FAX: (514) 954-1237.
PRESIDENT
Jean Zaloum
DIRECTOR
Alain Zaloum

THE ORIGINAL MOTION PICTURE COMPANY
37 Sussex Ave., Toronto, Ont. M5S 1J6. (416) 368-4039. FAX: (416) 977-5264. email: sifilms@inforamp.net
CONTACT
John Board

PACIFIC MOTION PICTURES
1380 Burrard St., 3rd Fl., Vancouver, BC V6Z 2H3. (604) 602-7300. FAX: (604) 642-5442/
CEO
Tony Allard
PRESIDENT
Matthew O'Connor
CREATIVE AFFAIRS
Tom Rowe

THE PARTNERS' FILM COMPANY LIMITED
53 Ontario St., Toronto, ON M5A 2V1. (416) 869-3500. FAX: (416) 869-3365. www.partnersfilm.com
email: mail@partnersfilm.com
PRESIDENT
Donald McLean
GENERAL MANAGER
Ross McLean

PATTERSON-PARTINGTON TV PRODUCTIONS
250 Ferrand Dr., Ste. 402, Toronto, ON M3C 3G8. (416) 696-9633, (800) 350-2999. FAX: (416) 696-9640.
CONTACTS
Carol Patterson
Lawrence Partington

PAX PRODUCTIONS
3779 de Bullion, Montréal, QC H2W 2C9. (514) 844-7077. FAX: (514) 844-2265. email: paxprod@ibm.net
CONTACT
Tanya Tree

PEACE ARCH ENTERTAINMENT GROUP, INC.
302 - 1132 Hamilton St., Vancouver, BC V6B 2S2. (604) 681-9308. FAX: (604) 681-3299.
CONTACT
Tim Gamble

PEGASUS PRODUCTIONS, LTD.
11313 - 123 St., Edmonton, AB T5M 0G. (780) 452-8719.
email: pegasusproductions@compuserve.com
CONTACT
Marke Slipp

PETER ROWE PRODUCTIONS, INC.
Pyman Studios, 2196 Dunwin Dr., Mississauga, ON L5L 1C7. (905) 608-1666. FAX: (905) 608-2171.
email: peterowe@interlog.com

PETERSEN PRODUCTIONS, INC.
122 Powell St., Vancouver, BC V6A 1G1. (604) 669-8890. FAX: (604) 662-8013.
PRESIDENT
Curtis Petersen

PHALANX FILMWORKS, INC.
2 Moberly Ave., Toronto, ON M4C 4A8. (416) 690-9981.
ASSISTANT DIRECTOR
Michael Bowman

PHANTOM PRODUCTIONS, INC.
1010 Tamarack Dr., Bathurst NB E2A 4H4. (506) 547-8984. FAX: (506) 546-7448.
CONTACT
Tony Larder

PICTURE PLANT, LTD.
P.O. Box 2465, Halifax, NS B3J 3E4. (902) 455-3901. FAX: (902) 455-5704. www.pictureplant.com
email: pixplant@istar.ca
PRESIDENT
William MacGillivray
VICE PRESIDENT
Terry Greenlaw

PIKA PRODUCTIONS, INC.
258 Wallace Ave., Ste. 104, Toronto, ON M6P 3M9. (416) 535-7402. FAX: (416) 535-1839. email: tapestry@idirect.com
EXECUTIVE PRODUCER/PRODUCER
Mary Young Leckie

PITCAIRN PICTURES, INC.
Box 497, Lion's Bay, BC V0N 2E0. Tel. & FAX: (604) 921-8899.

THE PLAYERS FILM CO.
77 Mowat Ave., Ste. 400, Toronto, ON M6K 3E3. (416) 516-9110. FAX: (416) 516-9113.
EXECUTIVE PRODUCER/PRESIDENT
Philip Mellows

PLUCK, INC.
18 Gloucester Lane, 4th Fl., Toronto, ON M4Y 1L5. (416) 967-1055. FAX: (416) 923-8580. email: slate@interlog.com
PRESIDENT
John Greyson

POINT OF VIEW FILM, INC.
3216 W. 2nd Ave., Vancouver, BC V6K 1K8. (604) 734-5035. FAX: (604) 737-0123.

POPE PRODUCTIONS, LTD.
198 Water St., Ste. 400, Box 5278, St. John's, NF A1C 5W1. (709) 722-7673. FAX: (709) 738-7285. email: ppope@nfld.com
CONTACT
Paul Pope

POSTMODERN PRODUCTIONS
80 Carlton St., Ste. 110, Toronto, ON M5B 1L6. (416) 924-0005. FAX: (416) 413-1620. email: postmod@total.net
EXECUTIVE PRODUCER
Susan Papp

POWER PICTURES
80 Ward St., Toronto, ON M6H 4A6. (416) 531-6141, FAX: (416) 531-7664.
PRESIDENT & CEO
Julian Marks

PRAIRIE DOG PRODUCTIONS, LTD.
10 Huntly Ct., St. Albert, AB T8N 6M7. (780) 459-0619.
PRESIDENT
Ron E. Scott

PRIMITIVE FEATURES
585 Bloor St. W., Toronto, ON M6G 1K5. (416) 531-3087. FAX: (416) 531-4961. email: office@primitive.net
PRODUCER
Michael McMahon
DIRECTOR
Kevin McMahon
ASSOCIATE PRODUCER
Kristina McLaughlin
NEW MEDIA PRODUCER
Ian Kelso

LES PRODUCTIONS DE L'OEIL ENR.
860 Gohier, St-Laurent, QC H4L 3J2. (514) 744-1944. email: mario.bonenfant@zoo.net
CONTACT
Mario Bonenfant

LES PRODUCTIONS DORÉNAVANT, INC.
140, rue Champlain, Pièce 101, Dieppe, NB EIC IN8. (506) 383-9642, Cell: (506) 866-5285. FAX: (506) 383-9836. email: dorenav@nbnet.nb.ca
CONTACT
Michelle Marcil

LES PRODUCTIONS DU PHARE EST, INC.
140, rue Botsford, bureau 20, CP 517, Moncton, NB EIC 8L9. (506) 857-9941. FAX: (506) 857-1806. email: pharest@nbnet.nb.ca
CONTACTS
Cécile Chevrier
Gilles Losier

LES PRODUCTIONS GRANA PRODUCTIONS, INC.
145 Alexander Ave., Moncton, NB E1E 4N6. (506) 388-5333. FAX: (506) 383-5881.
CONTACT
Sam Grana

PRODUCTIONS GRAND NORD QUEBEC, INC.
La Maison Premier Plan, Ste. 392, 1600 ave. de Lorimier, Montréal, QC H2K 3W5. (514) 521-7433. FAX: (514) 522-3013.
CONTACT
Ian McLaren

PRODUCTIONS LA FÊTE, INC.
387 rue Saint-Paul O., Montréal, QC H2Y 2A7. (514) 848-0417. FAX: (514) 848-0064. email: info@lafete.com
PRESIDENT
Rock Demers
PRODUCER
Ina Fichman

PRODUCTIONS LIBRES, INC.
14 rue Church, bureau 200, Moncton, NB E1C 4Y9. (506) 853-7889. FAX: (506) 854-5272. email: libres@nbnet.nb.ca
CONTACT
Jacques G. Levesque

PRODUCTIONS MATCH TV/PRODUCTIONS NEOFILMS
5162 Saint-Laurent, bur 200, Montréal, QC H2T 1R8. (514) 270-4660. FAX: (514) 270-4465.
email: neomatch@neomatch.com
PRODUCERS
Philippe Dussault
Anne-Marie Hetu

LES PRODUCTIONS PRISMA, INC.
1035 Ave. Laurier ouest, 3ième étage, Outremont, QC H2V 2L1. (514) 277-6686. FAX: (514) 277-8910.
PRESIDENT/PRODUCTEUR EXÉCUTIF
Claude Godbout

LES PRODUCTIONS SOVIMAGE
1035 Ave. Laurier ouest, 1er étage, Outremont, QC H2V 2L1. (514) 277-6123. FAX: (514) 277-1139.
PRESIDENT/PRODUCER
Vincent Garbriele
PRODUCERS
Claudette Viau
Sophie Deschénes,
André Dupuy

LES PRODUCTIONS TELE-ACTION
1324 rue Sainte-Catherine est, Montréal, QC H2L 2H5. (514) 524-1118. FAX: (514) 524-2041.
PRODUCER
Claudio Luca

LES PRODUCTIONS VIA LE MONDE (DANIEL BERTOLINO) INC.
326 o. rue St-Paul, Montréal, QC H2Y 2A3. (514) 285-1658. FAX: (514) 285-1970.
CONTACTS
Daniel Bertolino
Catherine Viau

LES PRODUCTIONS VIDEOFILMS LIMITEE
296 o. rue St-Paul, bur. 400, Montréal, QC H2Y 2A3. (514) 844-8611. FAX: (514) 844-4034. email: prodfilm@mlink.net
CONTACT
Robert Ménard

PROGRAMMED COMMUNICATIONS LIMITED
1155 boul. Réne Lévesque o., Ste. 2901, Montréal, QC H3B 2L5. (514) 397-9091. FAX: (514) 397-9345.

PROSCENIUM FILMS
65 Hilton Ave., Toronto, ON M5R 3E5. (416) 538-3103.
PRODUCER
Brian Avery

PROTOCOL ENTERTAINMENT, INC.
1200 Bay St., 7th Fl., Toronto, ON M5R 2A5. (416) 966-2711. FAX: (416) 920-4424.
PRESIDENT
Steve Levitan
CHAIRMAN
Paul Bronfman

PRYCELESS PRODUCTIONS, LTD.
59 Pine Cr., Toronto, ON M4E 1L3. (416) 699-6322. FAX: (416) 699-6168.
PRODUCER
Craig Pryce

P.S. FILMS
100 - 873 Beatty St., Vancouver, BC V6B 2M6. (604) 681-5650. FAX: (604) 681-5664.
CONTACTS
Pat O'Brien
Shel Piercy
Dan Carriere

PTV PRODUCTIONS
585 Bloor St. W., 2nd Fl., Toronto, ON M6G 1K5. (416) 531-0100. FAX: (416) 531-3500.
PRESIDENT
Andrea Nemtin
UK DIRECTOR
Bill Nemtin

PUDDLE DUCK PRODUCTIONS, LTD.
2329 W. 14th Ave., Vancouver, BC V6K 2W2. (604) 734-1103. FAX: (604) 734-1150. email: puddlesbri@aol.com
PRESIDENT
Brian Schecter

RADICAL SHEEP PRODUCTIONS, INC.
258 Wallace Ave., Ste. 201, Toronto, ON M6P 3M9. (416) 539-0363. FAX: (416) 539-0496.
CONTACT
Robert Mills

RAYMOND INTERNATIONAL
238 Davenport Rd., Ste. 122, Toronto, ON M5R 1J6. (416) 485-3406. FAX: (416) 487-3820.
PRESIDENT
Bruce Raymond

PETER RAYMONT
862 Richmond St. W., Ste. 201, Toronto, ON M6J 1C9. (416) 703-5580. FAX: (416) 703-1691. Email: ipi@inforamp.net

R.C. PRODUCTIONS
132 ave. Kingsley, Dollard des Ormeaux, QC H9B 1M9. (514) 683-2527.
DIRECTEUR DE PHOTOGRAPHIE
Robert Chammas

REBELFILMS, INC.
494 Euclid Ave., Ste. 3, Toronto, ON M6G 2S9. (416) 963-8692. FAX: (416) 963-8368. email: rebelj@compuserve.com
CONTACT
Jeremy Podeswa

RED SNAPPER FILMS, LTD.
2125 Brunswick St., Halifax, NS B3K 2Y4. (902) 422-2427. FAX: (902) 492-2125. email: redsnap@supercity.ns.ca
PRODUCER/DIRECTOR
Lulu Keating

REQUISITE PRODUCTIONS
56 The Esplanade, Ste. 503, Toronto, ON M5E 1A7. (416) 955-9097. FAX: (416) 955-4556. email: req@interlog.com
PRODUCER/DOP
Nicholas de Pencier
PRODUCER/DIRECTOR
Jennifer Baichwal

RHOMBUS MEDIA, INC.
489 King St. W., Ste. 102, Toronto, ON M5V 1L3. (416) 971-7856. FAX: (416) 971-9647. email: rhombus@total.net
CONTACTS
Niv Fichman
Barbara Willis Sweete
Larry Weinstein
Sheena Macdonald
Daniel Iron

ROSE FILMS, INC.
Head Office & Production Office: C.P. 40, Saint-Paul d'Abbotsford, QC J0E 1A0. (450) 379-5304. FAX: (450) 379-5742.
CONTACTS
Claude Fournier
Marie-José Raymond

ROSEFIRE FILM, INC.
77 Huntley St., Ste. 812, Toronto, ON M4Y 2P3. (416) 925-6258.
WRITER/DIRECTOR
David Sobelman

ROWAN RIDGE PRODUCTIONS
175 Chamberlain Rd., Quispamsis, NB E2G 1B7. (506) 847-3185. FAX: (506) 847-3185. email: connell@nbnet.nb.ca
CONTACT
Lynn & Connell Smith

R.S.M. PRODUCTIONS INTERNATIONALES, INC.
720 Montpellier, Ste. 912, Ville St. Laurent, QC H4L 5B5. (514) 748-2678. FAX: (514) 748-7560.
PRODUCER/DIRECTOR
Rafik M. Murad

SAHARA FILMWORKS
6000 Yonge St., Ste. 505, Toronto, ON M2M 3W1. (416) 733-8770. FAX: (416) 733-2488. email: sahara@netcom.ca
PRESIDENT/PRODUCER
Adam B. Christie
VICE PRESIDENT/PRODUCER
Lee Hoverd

SAJO PRODUCTIONS, INC.
Box 888, Gibsons Landing, BC V0N 1V0. Tel. & Fax.: (604) 886-3639. email: devadas@uniserve.com
PRESIDENT/PRODUCER
Robert Nichol

SALTER STREET FILMS LIMITED
1668 Barrington St., Ste. 500, Halifax, NS B3J 2A2. (902) 420-1577. FAX: (902) 425-8260. email: salter@salter.com
PRESIDENT & COO
Catherine Tait
CHAIRMAN & CEO
Michael Donovan

SARRAZIN/COUTURE PRODUCTIONS, INC.
42 Bernard Ave., Toronto, ON M5R 1R2. (416) 324-9254. FAX: (416) 324-1262. email: cousar@interlog.com
CONTACTS
Pierre Sarrazin
Suzette Couture

SAWYER ARTS
163 Germain St., Saint John NB E2L 2G1. (506) 642-7372. FAX: (506) 642-7442.
CONTACT
Ken Furlong

S. BANKS GROUP, INC.
174 Johnston Ave., Toronto, ON M2N 1H3. (416) 224-0296. FAX: (416) 224-8542.
PRESIDENT
Sydney Banks

SCHULZ FILMS, INC.
400 Walmer Rd., Park Towers E., Ste. 2323, Toronto, ON M5P 2X7. (416) 961-2001. FAX: (416) 961-2003.
email: cinemail@ican.net
CONTACT
Bob Schulz

SCREENLIFE INCORPORATED
144 Front St. W., Ste. 310, Toronto, ON M5J 2L7. (416) 260-2099. FAX: (416) 260-2042.
CONTACT
Michael Maclear

SCREEN SIREN PICTURES
450 - 380 West 1st Ave., Vancouver, BC V5Y 3T7. (604) 687-7591. FAX: (604) 687-4937. email: trishdol@istar.ca
PRESIDENT/PRODUCER
Trish Dolman

SCREENWRITE DEVELOPMENT INC.
42 Fulton Ave., Toronto, ON M4K 1X5. (416) 422-3288. FAX: (416) 422-2699.
CONTACT
Allan Magee

SEA TO SKY ENTERTAINMENT/POLO PRODUCTIONS
Box 3640, Garibaldi Highlands, BC V0N 1T0. Tel. & FAX: (604) 898-5930. email: apolo@mountain-inter.net
DIRECTORS
Adriane Polo
Mark McConchie
Kathy Daniels

SELWYN ENTERPRISES INC.
1863 West 16 Ave., Vancouver, BC V6J 2M3. (604) 731-5257. email: selwyn_jacob@bc.sympatico.ca
EXECUTIVE PRODUCER
Joan Jacob

SEVILLE PICTURES INC.
147 St. Paul St. W., 2nd fl., Montréal, QC H2Y 1Z5. (514) 841-1910. FAX: (514) 847-8030.
PRESIDENT
John Hamilton

SHAFTESBURY FILMS
264B Adelaide St. E., Toronto, ON M5A 1N1. (416) 363-1411. FAX: (416) 363-1428. email: mailbox@shaftesbury.org
CHAIRMAN
Christina Jennings
PRESIDENT
Jonathan Barker
VICE PRESIDENTS
Laura Harbin
Scott Garvie

SHAVICK ENTERTAINMENT
116 East 2nd Ave., Vancouver, BC V5T 3B5. (604) 874-4300. FAX: (604) 874-4305. email: mail@shavickentertainment.com
CEO
James Shavick
PRESIDENT
Shawn Williamson
V.P., PRODUCTION & DEVELOPMENT
Van Arragon

SHAWNA MCPEEK PRODUCTIONS INC.
74 Indian Rd. Cres., Toronto, ON M6P 2G1. (416) 538-7732. Cell: (416) 520-4666. FAX: (416) 534-2224.

SLEEPING GIANT PRODUCTIONS, LTD.
260 Richmond St. W., Ste. 100, Toronto, ON M5V 1W5. (416) 351-9240. FAX: (416) 351-9241.
PRESIDENT/EXECUTIVE PRODUCER
Jim Hanley
EXECUTIVE VICE PRESIDENT
Paul McConvey

SLINGSHOT PRODUCTIONS INC.
1253 McGill College, Rm. 452, Montréal, QC H3B 2Y5. (514) 397-9988. FAX: (514) 954-1237.
email: Alain.Zaloum@sympatico.ca
DIRECTOR
Alain Zaloum

SOAPBOX PRODUCTIONS INC.
312 Stevens Dr., N. Vancouver, BC V7S 1C6. (604) 913-0101. FAX: (604) 913-0102. email: norchard@home.com
EXECUTIVE PRODUCER
Nick Orchard

SOMA: FILM & VIDEO
R.R. #1, Box-26, Bowen Island, BC V0N 1G0. (604) 947-0044. FAX: (604) 947-0049.
PRESIDENT
Deepak Sahasrabudhe
VICE PRESIDENT
Susan Millar

SPECTRUM FILMS
79 Lippincott St., Toronto, ON M5S 2P2. (416) 515-1077. www.the-wire.com/spectrum email: spectrum@the-wire.com
CONTACTS
Holly Dale
Janis Cole

SPHINX PRODUCTIONS
24 Mercer St., Toronto, ON M5V 1H3. (416) 971-9131. FAX: (416) 971-6014. email: mann@criterionco.com
CONTACT
Ron Mann

STARGATE PICTURES
530 Richmond St. W., Rear Bldg., Toronto, ON M5V 1Y4. (416) 504-5335. FAX: (416) 504-4545.
PRESIDENT
Wayne Trickett
VICE PRESIDENT
Robin Trickett

STONEHAVEN PRODUCTIONS
1310 rue Larivière, Montréal, QC H2L 1M8. (514) 527-2131. FAX: (514) 522-8599. email: stonehaven@stonehaven.ca
PRESIDENT
Michael C. Taylor

STORNOWAY PRODUCTIONS INC.
160 Bloor St. E., Ste. 1220, Toronto, ON M4W 1B9. (416) 923-1104. FAX: (416) 923-1122.
CONTACTS
Kitson Vincent
Martha Fusca

SULLIVAN ENTERTAINMENT INC.
110 Davenport Rd., Toronto, ON M5R 3R3. (416) 921-7177. FAX: (416) 921-7538.
PRESIDENT
Kevin Sullivan

SUMMERHILL ENTERTAINMENT INC.
56 Shaftesbury Ave., Toronto, ON M4T 1A3. (416) 967-6503. FAX: (416) 967-1292.
EXECUTIVE PRODUCERS
Ronald Lillie
William Johnston

SUNDOG FILMS
530 Richmond St. W., Rear Bldg., Toronto, ON M5V 1Y4. (416) 504-5335. FAX: (416) 504-4545.
CONTACT
Robin Trickett

SUNRISE FILMS LIMITED
352 Walmer Rd., Toronto, ON M5R 2Y4. (416) 929-7900. FAX: (416) 929-9900. email: sunrise@interlog.com
CONTACT
Paul Saltzman

SUSSEX PRODUCTIONS, LTD.
37 Sussex Ave., Toronto, Ont. M5S 1J6. (416) 368-4039. FAX: (416) 977-5264. email: sifilms@inforamp.net
CONTACT
John Board

TELEFICTION/LES FILMS VISION 4
4446 boul. Saint-Laurent, 7th Fl., Montréal, QC H2W 1Z5. (514) 499-0972. FAX: (514) 844-5498.
email: info@telefiction.com
CHAIRMAN & CEO
Claude Veillet
PRESIDENT
Jacques Bonin

TELEGENIC PRODUCTIONS
20 Holly St., Ste. 300, Toronto, ON M4S 3B1. (416) 484-8000. FAX: (416) 484-8001.
HEAD OF PRODUCTION
Jamie Wynne

TELESCENE FILM GROUP INC.
5705 Ferrier St., Ste. 200, Montréal, QC H4P 1N3. (514) 737-5512. FAX: (514) 737-7945.
PRESIDENT & CEO
Robin Spry
EXECUTIVE V.P. & COO
Paul Painter
EXECUTIVE V.P., TELESCENE FILM GROUP INC. (U.S.)
Bruce Moccia
EXECUTIVE V.P., TELESCENE ENTERTAINMENT INC.
Michael Yudin
S.V.P., SALES & MARKETING
Jennifer Chrein
V.P., FINANCE
Daniel Proulx
DIRECTOR OF BUSINESS & LEGAL AFFAIRS & SECRETARY
Claire Benoît
HEAD OF CREATIVE AFFAIRS
Anita Simand
HEAD OF PRODUCTION
Diane Arcand

TEL VISION
795, rue Main, 4e étage, Moncton, NB E1C 1E9. (506) 857-1090. FAX: (506) 857-0352. email: telvision@nbnet.nb.ca
CONTACT
Jean-Claude Bellefeuille

THEATRIFILM PRODUCTIONS INC.
34 Colin Ave., Toronto, ON M5P 2B9. (416) 483-3862. FAX: (416) 483-1106.
PRESIDENT
Gilbert W. Taylor

THOMEGA ENTERTAINMENT INC.
409 - 135 21st St., Saskatoon, SK S7K 0B4. (306) 244-5503. FAX: (306) 244-5504. email: anthonyjohn@sk.sympatico.ca
CONTACT
Anthony Towstego

THREE BLONDES INC.
72 Rusholme Rd., Toronto, ON M6J 3H6. (416) 537-8348. FAX: (416) 534-6542.
CONTACT
Annette Mangaard

TOPSAIL ENTERTAINMENT
1583 Hollis St., 2nd Fl., Halifax, NS B3J 1V4. (902) 421-1326. FAX: (902) 423-0484. email: contact@topsailentertainment.com
PRESIDENT/EXECUTIVE PRODUCER
Michael Volpe
EXECUTIVE PRODUCERS
Barry Cowling
Terry Fulmer
DIRECTOR OF CREATIVE DEVELOPMENT
Greg Morris
DIRECTOR OF PRODUCTION
Edward Peill

TRANSMAR FILMS INC.
26 rue des Robin E., Caraquet, NB E1W 1A7. (506) 727-6232. Cell: (506) 727-8524. FAX: (506) 727-6867.
email: tmar@nbnet.nb.ca
CONTACT
Rodrigue Jean

TRIAD COMMUNICATIONS, LTD.
2751 Oxford St., Vancouver, BC V5K 1N5. (604) 253-3990. FAX: (604) 253-0770.
CONTACT
Roland Loughhead

TRICORD PICTURES
141 Drakefield Rd., Markham, ON L3P 1G9. (905) 472-0445. FAX: (905) 472-0448. email: windborn@istar.ca
CONTACT
Karen Pascal

TRI MEDIA PRODUCTION SERVICES
5112 Prince St., 2nd Fl., Halifax, NS B3J 1L3. (902) 422-8816. FAX: (902) 422-8819. email: trimedia@netcom.ca
PRESIDENT/EXECUTIVE PRODUCER
F. Whitman Trecartin

TRINOME-INTER
1310 Alexandre-DeSeve, bur. 2, Montréal, QC H2L 2V1. (514) 527-9070. FAX: (514) 597-1571. www.trinome.com
email: courrier@trinome.com
EXECUTIVE PRODUCER
Pierre Blais
V.P., RESEARCH & DEVELOPMENT
Jean Tourangeau

TRIPTYCH MEDIA INC.
788 King St. W., 2nd fl., Toronto, ON M5V 1N6. (416) 703-8866. FAX: (416) 703-8867. email: trip@triptych.on.ca
PRODUCERS
Robin Cass
Louise Garfield
Anna Stratton
HEAD OF DEVELOPMENT
Carolyn Drebin

TROIKA PRODUCTIONS
404 - 999 Canada Pl., Vancouver, B.C. V6C 3E2. (604) 990-9020. FAX: (604) 990-9021. email: troika@ultranet.ca
PRESIDENT/PRODUCER
Walter Daroshin

TSUNAMI ENTERTAINMENT
25 Polson St., Toronto, ON M5A 1A4. (416) 463-2366. FAX: (416) 463-9001. email: omegpic1@aol.com
CHAIRMAN & CEO
Ken Nakamura
PRESIDENT & CFO
Mark Burman
V.P., ACQUISITIONS & DEVELOPMENT
Susan Wichmann

TUSTIAN FILM PRODUCTIONS
10754 - 72nd Ave., Edmonton, AB T6E 1A1. (780) 433-5136. FAX: (780) 433-5136. email: tustianfilms@netscape.net
CONTACT
Jim Tustian, csc

TWIN DRAGON FILM PRODUCTIONS, LTD.
6347 Yonge St., North York, ON M2M 3X7. (416) 229-1280. FAX: (416) 229-2425. www.twin-dragon.com
PRESIDENT
Michael McNamara
VICE PRESIDENT
Martin McNamara

UNIVERSAL HORIZONS TV PRODUCTIONS CORP.
P.O. Box 375, Stn. P, Toronto, ON M5S 2S9. (416) 260-7544. FAX: (416) 260-0417.
CONTACT
Ezz E. Gad

UP FRONT ENTERTAINMENT INC.
49 Spadina Ave., Ste. 302, Toronto, ON M5V 2J1. (416) 595-5850. FAX: (416) 595-5851. email: bbarde@upfront.ca
PRESIDENT
Barbara Barde

UPSTART PICTURES
230 Ashdale Ave., Toronto, ON M4L 2Y9. (416) 462-9699. FAX: (416) 405-8774. email: sberger@globalserve.net
PRODUCER
Susan Berger

URDLWEISS PRODUCTIONS
80 Niagara St., Toronto, ON M5V 1C5. (416) 703-7317. FAX: (416) 504-7161. email: urdlweis@netcom.ca
PRODUCERS
Simone Urdl
Jennifer Weiss

VANTAGE COMMUNICATIONS INC.
5657 Spring Garden Rd., Ste. 604, Halifax, NS B3J 3R4. (902) 423-2243. FAX: (902) 425-7866.
CEO
Lori Covert

VENT D'EST INC.
1750 rue Saint-André, Rm. 3028, Montréal, QC H2L 3T8. (514) 523-3163. FAX: (514) 523-4424. email: ventdest@videotron.ca
CINÉASTE/SCÉNARISTE/RÉALISATEUR
Richard Boutet

VERSEAU INTERNATIONAL INC.
225 rue Roy est, bur. 200, Montréal, QC H2W 1M5. (514) 848-9814. FAX: (514) 848-9908.
PRESIDENT
Aimee Danis

VIDEO KLIPS
92, 47 Ave. E., Edmundston NB E3V 3C4. (506) 739-5811. FAX: (506) 739-1091.

VIDEOGRAPHE
4550 rue Garnier, Montréal, QC H2J 3S7. (514) 521-2116. FAX: (514) 521-1676. email: production@videographe.qc.ca
CONTACT
Pierre Brault

VINTAGE VISUALS
210 Canvasback Pl., Salt Spring Island, BC V8K 2W5. (250) 537-8512.
PARTNERS
George C. Koller
Wendy M. Ennion

VISION FILM PRODUCTIONS INC.
#5 - 356 W. 15th Ave., Vancouver, BC V5Y 1Y2. (604) 732-4506. FAX: (604) 732-4306. email: thodgson@sprint.ca
PRODUCER
Trevor Hodgson

VISUAL SERVICES
705 - 258 Argyle Ave., Ottawa, ON K2P 1B9. (613) 236-8364. FAX: (613) 236-0472. email: pjd@cyberus.ca
PRODUCER/DIRECTOR/RESEARCHER
Peter Dudley

W. WASIK FILMS & VIDEOS
293 Blue Heron Dr. , Oshawa, ON L1G 6X7. (905) 576-1030. FAX: (905) 576-7364.
PRESIDENT
Walter Wasik

WEST WIND PICTURES
2345 Smith St., Regina, SK S4P 2P7. (306) 777-0160. FAX: (306) 352-8558. email: filmcrew@sk.sympatico.ca
EXECUTIVE PRODUCER
Michael Snook

Ontario: 489 College St., Ste. 301, Toronto, ON M6G 1A5. 416-975-2571. FAX: 416-975-8511. email: cdonnelly@sympatico.ca
EXECUTIVE PRODUCER
Clark Donnelly

WHITE PINE PICTURES
862 Richmond St. W., Ste. 201, Toronto, ON M6J1C9. (416) 703-5580. FAX: (416) 703-1691. www.whitepinepictures.com
CONTACTS
Peter Raymont
Lindalee Tracey
Maria Pimentel

WHITING COMMUNICATIONS, LTD.
2402 St. John's St., Ste. 10, Port Moody, BC V3H 2B1. (604) 931-1366. FAX: (604) 931-1499. email: whitcom@istar.ca
CONTACT
Glynnis Whiting

DAVID WINNING
Groundstar Entertainment Corp., 918 - 16 Ave. N.W., Ste. 4001, Calgary, AB T2M 0K3. (403) 284-2889/Vancouver: (604) 944-8407. FAX: (403) 282-7797. www.davidwinning.com

WONDERMENT ENTERTAINMENT INTERNATIONAL INC.
400 Walmer Rd., Park Towers E., Ste. 2323, Toronto, ON M5P 2X7. (416) 961-2001. FAX: (416) 961-2003.
CONTACT
Bob Schulz

YALETOWN ENTERTAINMENT CORP.
1431 Howe St., Vancouver, BC V6Z 1R9. (604) 669-3543. FAX: (604) 669-5149.
PRESIDENT/EXECUTIVE PRODUCER
Mike Collier

YELLOWKNIFE FILMS, LTD.
5021 53rd St., Yellowknife, NT X1A 1V5. (867) 873-8610. FAX: (867) 873-9405. email: ykfilms@theEdge.ca
CONTACT
Alan Booth

YORKTOWN PRODUCTIONS, LTD.
18 Gloucester Lane, Toronto, ON M4Y 1L5. (416) 923-2787, FAX: (416) 923-8580.
PRESIDENT
Norman Jewison
PRODUCTION
Michael Jewison

ZEITGEIST PRODUCTIONS
312 Stevens Dr. , N. Vancouver, BC V7S 1C6. (604) 913-0101. FAX: (604) 913-0102. email: norchard@home.com
EXECUTIVE PRODUCERS
Nick Orchard
Rick Drew

PRODUCTION SERVICES

STUDIO FACILITIES

AGINCOURT STUDIOS
P.O. Box 9, Station "O", Toronto, ON M4A 2M9. (416) 332-5272. FAX: (416) 332-5301.
DIRECTOR OF PRODUCTION
Sam Dynes

ALLARCOM STUDIOS
(100' x 150' soundstage/support facilities)
5305 Allard Way, Edmonton, AB T6H 5X8. (780) 438-8466. FAX: (780) 438-8495.
CONTACT
Doug Steeden

THE ANNEX STUDIOS, LTD.
176 Bedford Rd., Toronto, ON M5R 2K9. Studio: (416) 922-8270. FAX: (416) 922-7100.
PRESIDENT
Ed Zemla
STUDIO MANAGER, BOOKINGS
Rohan Roopnarine

THE BRIDGE STUDIOS
(6 soundstages on 15 acres/production offices/wardrobe/props/mill & workshop)
2400 Boundary Rd., Burnaby, BC V5M 3Z3. (604) 482-2000. FAX: (604) 482-2007. www.bridgestudios.com

CARDINAL STUDIO
43 Railside Rd., Don Mills, ON M3A 3L9. (416) 447-9126. FAX: (416) 444-9524.
PRESIDENT
William Hullah

THE CHURCH @ BERKELEY/MOXI STUDIOS
315 Queen St. E., Toronto, ON M5A 1S7. (416) 361-9666. FAX: (416) 361-1849. email: sskinner@sympatico.ca
CONTACT
Shannon Skinner; (416) 405-8809

CINÉ CITÉ MONTRÉAL
(5 studios/production offices/costume & set construction workshops/wardrobe & dressing rooms/honeywagon & vehicle rentals/rifle range/adjacent airstrip.)
4801, rue Leckie, B-121, Saint-Hubert, QC J3Z 1H6. (450) 926-2463. FAX: (450) 926-3937. www.cinecitemontreal.com

CINESPACE STUDIOS
345 Carlaw Ave., Ste. 100, Toronto, ON M4M 2T1. (416) 406-4000. FAX: (416) 469-5975.
CONTACTS
Sherrie Cameron
Nick Mirkopoulos

CINEVILLAGE
65 Heward Ave., Bldg. C, Toronto, ON M4M 2T5. (416) 461-8750. FAX: (416) 466-9612.
CONTACT
Renato Dumlao

DANFORTH STUDIOS, INC.
490 Adelaide St. W., Ste. 100, Toronto, ON M5V 1T2. (416) 504-6059. FAX: (416) 504-4843.
CONTACTS
G. Philip Jackson
Daniel D'or

ELECTROPOLIS MOTION PICTURE STUDIOS, INC.
(Four waterfront studios/production offices/art department/make up/wardrobe rooms/actor suites/extra rooms/green room/30,000 sq. ft. carp shop/floodability/ship mooring capability/tallest soundstage in North America.)
5091 Terminal Rd., Halifax, NS B3J 3Y1. (902) 429-1971. FAX: (902) 429-1471. www.electropolis-studios.com

FREEDOM STUDIOS, INC.
38 McGee St., Toronto, ON M4M 2K9. (416) 778-1358. FAX: (416) 778-1819. www.freedomstudiosinc.com
email: freedomstudios@hotmail.com
OWNER
Aaron Goldman
STUDIO MANAGER
Jocelyn Paris

HOOPLA INCORPORATED
(Casting facility.)
366 Adelaide St. E., Ste. 129, Toronto, ON M5A 3X9. (416) 364-9901. FAX: (416) 364-6788.

LIONSGATE STUDIOS
(Seven sound stages/long term & temporary offices/support services)
555 Brooksbank Ave., N. Vancouver, BC V7J 3S5. (604) 983-5555. FAX: (604) 983-5554. www.lionsgatestudios.com
GENERAL MANAGER
Peter Leitch

THE MASONIC TEMPLE
888 Yonge St., Toronto, ON M4W 2J2. (416) 332-5272. FAX: (416) 332-5301.
DIRECTOR OF PRODUCTION
Sam Dynes

THE POWER PLANT RECORDING STUDIOS
25 Toronto St., Barrie, ON L4N 1T8. (705) 725-1604. FAX: (705) 725-1347.

ROGERS PRODUCTIONS
(60 x 60 studio with cyc/support facilities & services.)
333 Bloor St. E., 7th Fl., Toronto, ON M4W 1G9. (416) 935-4758, (416) 935-4754. FAX: (416) 935-4777.
email: ccrosbie@rci.rogers.com
EXTERNAL CLIENT RELATIONS
Charles Crosbie
SALES & PROMOTIONS
Adam B. Christie

SOUND STROKES STUDIOS
Recording and Production House, 154A Main St. N., Markham, ON L3P 1Y3. (905) 472-3168. FAX: (905) 472-4928.
www.soundstrokes.com
email: soundstrokes@soundstrokes.com
CONTACTS
Cory Paganini
Andrew V. Paganini

STUDIOASIS MEDIA CORPORATION
(3 studios/production offices/dressing rooms/wardrobe & makeup rooms/carpentry shop/scissor lift/truck & mobile bays/screening.)
793 Pharmacy Ave., Scarborough, ON M1L 3K2. (416) 285-1111. FAX: (416) 285-9617. email: studio@studioasis
STUDIO MANAGER
Gord Brodie
OPERATIONS MANAGER
Gary Butler
SALES & MARKETING
Mike Kelly

TORONTO FILM STUDIOS
(16 film/TV stages (1,500 - 24,500 sq. ft.). Full services & support. Airplane cabin/cockpit/air traffic control/full prison set/luxury New York City apartment set.)
629 Eastern Ave., Toronto, ON M4M 1E4. (416) 406-1235. FAX: (416) 406-6964. www.torontofilmstudios.com
email: tfs@rosecorp.com
CONTACT
Ken Ferguson

TOUR TECH EAST
170 Thornhill Dr., Dartmouth, NS B3B 1S3. (902) 468-2800. FAX: (902) 468-8833. www.tourtecheast.com
PRESIDENT
Peter Hendrickson

VANCOUVER FILM STUDIOS
3505 E. 11th Ave., Vancouver, BC V5M 2B8. (604) 434-1191. FAX: (604) 434-1166. www.vfstudios.com

WALLACE AVENUE STUDIOS INC.
258 Wallace Ave., Ste. 100, Toronto, ON M6P 3M9. (416) 537-3471. FAX: (416) 532-3132. www.wallacestudios.com
V.P., MARKETING
Lillyann Goldstein
STUDIO COORDINATOR
Paula Pimpao

WSM STUDIOS INC.
(TV Series, documentaries, animation & post production.)
RR#3 King St. N., Alliston, ON L9R 1V3. (705) 434-2291, (888) 714-4790 (Canada only). FAX: (705) 434-2292.
www.wsmstudios.com email: rmorton@sportymorty.com
CONTACTS
Robert Morton
Stephen Milne

POST PRODUCTION FACILITIES

ADELAIDE FILM
(Negative cutter)
77 Howard St., Unit 1401, Toronto, ON M4X 1J9. Tel. & FAX: (416) 929-6054.
CONTACT
Kristina Nikolic

AIRWAVES SOUND DESIGN, LTD.
25 E. 2nd Ave., 2nd Fl., Vancouver, BC V5T 1B3. (604) 875-0114. FAX: (604) 876-1087.
PRESIDENT
Alex Downie
PRODUCTION MANAGER
Leanne Dennis
SOUND DESIGNER
Gael MacLean

ALCHEMY
(Original music-to-picture scoring and sound design.)
850 Adelaide St. W., Toronto, ON M6J 2T1. (416) 703-4385. email: alchemy@wiznet.ca
CONTACT
Gary Justice

ALPHA CINE MOTION PICTURE LABORATORY
A Division of Command Post & Transfer Corp., 916 Davie St., Vancouver, BC V6Z 1B8. (604) 688-7757. FAX: (604) 688-0127. www.compt.com
CONTACT
Rick Cooper

ALTIMAGE INC.
(Audio-visual/computer graphics/video editing.)
721 Walker Ave., Ste. 100, Montréal, QC H4C 2H5. (514) 935-5418. FAX: (514) 935-4008.
PRESIDENT
William Lee

ASTRALTECH INC.
An Astral Communications Company, 2101 rue Sainte-Catherine ouest, bureau 300, Montréal, QC H3H 1M6. (514) 939-5060. FAX: (514) 939-5070.
PRESIDENT, ASTRAL TECHNICAL SERVICES GROUP
Sidney Greenberg
PRESIDENT/GENERAL MANAGER
Hubert Harel
VICE PRESIDENT, OPERATIONS
Michel Delisle

AXYZ
425 Adelaide St. W., Toronto, ON M5V 1S4. (416) 504-0425. FAX: (416) 504-0045. email: js@axyzfx.com
OWNER/SENIOR EDITOR
Bruce Copeman
GENERAL MANAGER
John Stollar

BARBARA SWIFT NEGATIVE CUTTING SERVICE
181 Carlaw Ave., Ste. 256, Toronto, ON M4M 2S1. (416) 462-0395. FAX: (416) 462-0612.

BLACK & WHITE FILM FACTORY
(Full black & white service/16mm colour reversal/film to video transfer.)
40 Cawthra Ave., Toronto, ON M6N 5B3. (416) 763-0750. FAX: (416) 763-0847.
LAB MANAGER
Dragan Stojanovic

BLACKMAN
(Audio post - TV and film.)
4004 97th St., Ste. 32, Edmonton, AB T6E 6N1. (780) 435-5859. FAX: (780) 436-6234. email: pblack9976@aol.com
PRESIDENT
Perry Blackman

BROCK SOUND POST AUDIO
(Post audio for video/original music & sound effects for films & TV. Video editing services (see Dreamscape).)
576 Manning Ave., Toronto, ON M6G 2V9. (416) 534-7464. FAX: (416) 535-4477.
MANAGER/ENGINEER
Brock Fricker

CASABLANCA SOUND SERVICES INC.
(Sound & picture editing - features, MOWs, television.)
22 Boston Ave., Toronto, ON M4M 2T9. (416) 461-2550. FAX: (416) 461-9709.
TECHNICAL DIRECTOR
Tom Virostek
STUDIO MANAGER
Robert Hrycyna

CHANNELS AUDIO & POST PRODUCTION
697 Sargent Ave., Winnipeg, MB R3E 0A8. (204) 786-5578. FAX: (204) 772-5191.
ENGINEERS
John Schritt
Howard Rissin
Greg Boboski

CINAR STUDIOS
(Dubbing/audio & video recording & mixing/re-packaging/special effects.)
1207 rue St-André, Montréal, QC H2L 3S8. (514) 843-9000. FAX: (514) 843-9587.

CINE-BYTE IMAGING INC.
(High resolution scanning/film recording and video out to film.)
543 Richmond St. W., Ste. 220, P.O. Box 107, Toronto, ON M5V 1Y6. (416) 504-1010. FAX: (416) 504-9910.
email: info@cinebyte.com
PRESIDENT
Alan Bak

CINE GROUPE POST PRODUCTION INC.
(Dubbing studio/sound recording & mixing/film & video editing.)
1151 Alexandre-DeSéve St., Montréal, QC H2L 2T7. (514) 524-7567. FAX: (514) 524-7354.
email: postprod@cinegroupe.ca
CONTACT
André-Gilles Gagné

COAST MOUNTAIN
(Editing - commercials/documentaries/music videos. Offline.)
1168 Hamilton St., Ste. 305, Vancouver, BC V6B 2S2. (604) 682-6578. FAX: (604) 682-3548.
email: edit@coastmtnpost.com
EDITORS
Deb Tregale
Ian Jenkins
Melanie Snagg
Viggo Der Merwe

COMET POST PRODUCTION
(Independent filmmakers rates.)
1040 Hamilton St., Ste. 207, Vancouver, BC V6B 2R9. (604) 689-8063. FAX: (604) 689-8163. email: village@direct.ca
PRESIDENT
Fredrik Thorsen

C.O.R.E. DIGITAL PICTURES
(Compositing, CGI, 2D/3D Animation, Visual Effects Supervision.)
488 Wellington St. W., Ste. 600, Toronto, ON M5V 1E3. (416) 599.2673. FAX: (416) 599.1212. www.coredp.com
email: info@coredp.com
EXECUTIVE PRODUCERS
Shane Kinnear (Film)
Kirsten Marshall (TV)
CORPORATE COMMUNICATIONS
Stephanie Allen

COTE POST PRODUCTION LTEE./LTD.
218, rue St-Paul o., Montréal, QC H2Y 1Z9. (514) 284-0674. FAX: (514) 284-6712.
PRÉSIDENT
Bob Côté

CRUNCH RECORDING
(Post audio/music production - commercials/feature films.)
157 Princess St., 3rd Fl., Toronto, ON M5V 1S4. (416) 504-0425. FAX: (416) 504-0045.
CONTACT
Joe Serafini
Steve Pecile

CRUSH INC.
(Design & post - commercials/film/broadcast.)
439 Wellington St. W., 3rd Fl., Toronto, ON M5V 1E7. (416) 345-1936. FAX: (416) 345-1965. email: joann@crushinc.com
MANAGING DIRECTOR/EXECUTIVE PRODUCER
Jo-ann Cook
PRODUCER
Nancy McCreight
PRODUCER/CLIENT SERVICES
Patty Bradley

DAVE
(Commercial audio/TV series/MOWs/Imax films/audio & video duplication & distribution.)
49 Ontario St., Toronto, ON M5A 2B1. (416) 364-1422. FAX: (416) 364-7400.
GENERAL MANAGER, AUDIO
Peter Mann
EXECUTIVE PRODUCER, VIDEO
Michael Lambermont
SALES & MARKETING
Cathy MacMillan

DELUXE TORONTO
Laboratory: 380 Adelaide St. W., Toronto, ON M5V 1R7. (416) 364-4321.
Post Production Services: 424 Adelaide St. E., Toronto, ON M5A 1N4. (416) 364-4321.
PRESIDENT
Cyril R. Drabinsky
EXECUTIVE V.P. & GENERAL MANAGER
Des Henry
EXECUTIVE V.P. & GENERAL MANAGER, SOUND & VIDEO
Tom Allwood
V.P., LABORATORY OPERATIONS
Joe Micek
V.P., SALES
Stan Ford
V.P., SALES & SERVICES
Paul Norris
V.P., VIDEO SALES & OPERATIONS
Rod Haykin

DESCHAMPS RECORDING STUDIOS
(Audio post - TV/radio/corp. video.)
314 Dundas St. W., Toronto, ON M5T 1G5. (416) 977-5050. FAX: (416) 977-6945.
CONTACT
Claude Deschamps
John de Nottbeck

EDITCOMM INC.
(Complete video production center.)
100 Lombard St., Ste. 104, Toronto, ON M5C 1M3. (416) 864-1780. FAX: (416) 864-1664. www. editcomm.com
email: editcomm@ editcomm.com
PRESIDENT
Derek Baker-Lodge
VICE PRESIDENT/GENERAL MANAGER
Bob Chuter
OPERATIONS MANAGER
Neil Williamson
OFFICE MANAGER
Linda Pope
VIDEO EDITOR
Stephen Granger

EXCLUSIVE FILM & VIDEO SERVICES INC.
(Full service Super-8)
50 Portland St., Toronto, ON M5V 2M7. (416) 598-2700. FAX: (416) 598-2910.
CONTACT
Margaret Wagner

EYES POST GROUP
(Post & effects - commercials/TV/MOWs/features/documentaries/ music videos.)
320 King St. E., Toronto, ON M5A 1K6. (416) 363-3073. FAX: (416) 363-6335. email: diane@eyespostgroup.com
PRESIDENT
Izhak Hinitz
VICE PRESIDENT
Diane Cuthbert
DIRECTOR OF OPERATIONS
Joe Scrivo
SALES
Gary Robichaud

THE FEARLESS FILM & VIDEO CORPORATION
141 Bathurst St., Ste. 202, Toronto, ON M5V 2R2. (416) 504-9694. FAX: (416) 504-9693.
PRESIDENT
Al Maciulis
SENIOR EDITOR
Andrew Mandziuk
COORDINATOR
Carolyn Foster

FLASHCUT EDITING
504 Wellington St. W., 3rd Fl., Toronto, ON M5V 1E3. (416) 977-2401. FAX: (416) 977-4910.
GENERAL MANAGER
Mary Beth Odell
EXECUTIVE PRODUCERS
Gord Koch
Pamela Swedko

FRANCONT FILM & VIDEO CONFORM CO.
48 Stewart St., Toronto, ON M5V 1H6. (416) 504-6400. FAX: (416) 703-0675.

FREELANCE F/X
(Special effects graphics/digital compositing/animation.)
45 Charles St. E., Lower level, Toronto, ON M4Y 1S2. (416) 922-9760. FAX: (416) 922-9964.
PRESIDENT
Todd Morgan

GRAYSON MATTHEWS
(Music & sound design.)
468 Queen St. E., Toronto, ON M5A 1S7. (416) 681-9330. FAX: (416) 681-9331. www.graysonmatthews.com
email: elizabeth@graysonmatthews.com
CONTACTS
Elizabeth Taylor
Dave Sorbara
Tom Westin

GREAT BIG MUSIC
(Music & sound design.)
483 Eastern Ave., Toronto, ON M4M 1C2. (416) 461-3915. FAX: (416) 461-4405.
PRESIDENT
Tom Thorney
PRODUCERS
Tim Thorney
Carl Lenox

GRIFFITHS GIBSON & RAMSAY PRODUCTIONS
(Music & sound design/audio post.)
201 W. 7th Ave., Vancouver, BC V5Y 1L9. (604) 873-3811. FAX: (604) 873-5880. www.ggrp.com
CONTACTS
Brian Griffiths
Miles Ramsay
Gord Lord
Peter Clarke

JAVA POST PRODUCTION
2345 Smith St., Regina, SK S4P 2P7. (306) 777-0160. FAX: (306) 352-8858. email: javapost@sk.sympatico.ca
POST SUPERVISOR
Jack Tunnicliffe

KEEN MUSIC VOICE & SOUND DESIGN
(Music/voice/sound design.)
119 Spadina Ave., 7th Fl., Toronto, ON M5V 2L1. (416) 977-9845. FAX: (416) 977-4412.
DIRECTORS
Thomas Neuspiel
John Tucker
PRODUCTION MANAGER
Ophira Eisenberg

KITCHEN SYNC DIGITAL AUDIO
(Sound editing, Mixing, Voice-over.)
45 Charles St. E., Lower level, Toronto, ON M4Y 1S2. (416) 926-1444. FAX: (416) 926-0259.
CONTACT
Russell Walker

KRYSTAL MUSIC & SOUND DESIGN
(Audio production/original music - film, TV, commercials.)
317 Adelaide St. W., Ste. 401, Toronto, ON M5V 2P9. (416) 217-0488. FAX: (416) 217-0484. email: dkrystal@interlog.com
PRESIDENT
David Krystal
PRODUCTION CO-ORDINATOR
Natalie Hodgins

LONESOME PINE STUDIOS
260 King St. E., Ste. 507, Toronto, ON M5A 1K3. (416) 368-6525. FAX: (416) 360-1789.
CONTACT
Robert Armes

MAGNETIC NORTH
(Post production for film & TV.)
70 Richmond St. E., Ste. 100, Toronto, ON M5C 1N8. (416) 365-7622. FAX: (416) 365-2188. www.magpost.com
email: sales@magpost.com
COO
K. Bruce Grant
VICE PRESIDENT & GENERAL MANAGER VIDEO SERVICES
Tony Mearakker
VICE PRESIDENT & GENERAL MANAGER AUDIO SERVICES
David Greene
SALES & MARKETING MANAGER
Ross Robertson
OPERATIONS MANAGER
Peter Armstrong
SALES REPRESENTATIVE
Peter Campbell

MANTA EASTERN SOUND
A Division of Command Post & Transfer Corp., 311 Adelaide St. E., Toronto, ON M5A 1N2. (416) 863-9316. FAX: (416) 863-1448. www.compt.com
VICE PRESIDENT/GENERAL MANAGER
Kevin Evans
VICE PRESIDENT/OPERATIONS MANAGER
Sy Potma

MASTER'S
306 Rexdale Blvd., Ste. 7, Toronto, ON M9W 1R6. (416) 741-1312. FAX: (416) 741-1894.
email: mastersworkshop@canada.com
CREATIVE DIRECTOR
Tim Archer
GENERAL MANAGER
Andy Parisien

McCLEAR DIGITAL
(Music, audio post & recording studios.)
225 Mutual St., Toronto, ON M5B 2B4. (416) 977-9740. FAX: (416) 977-7147. www.mcclear.com
email: instudio@mcclear.com
BOOKINGS
Pamela Brookes
Karen Murphy
GENERAL MANAGER
Rob Yale

MCS RECORDING STUDIOS
(Recording & mixing audio for radio/TV/ industry. Audio duplication/distribution/music production.)
Media Communication Services Limited, 550 Queen St. E., Ste. G-100, Toronto, ON M5A 1V2. (416) 361-1688. FAX: (416) 361-5088. www.mcsrecording.com
PRESIDENT
Wm. (Bill) Walker

MEDALLION/PFA FILM-VIDEO-AUDIO
(Full lab services, component digital film transfer, on-line editorial, audio-post mixing - long form TV and film.)
A Division of Command Post & Transfer Corp., 111 Peter St., 9th Fl., Toronto, ON M5V 2H1. (416) 593-0556. FAX: (416) 593-7201. www.compt.com
MANAGER/POST SERVICES
Dave Bruner
OPERATIONS MANAGER
Louis Major
LAB & ADMINISTRATION MANAGER
John Walsh

MULTI-TRACK DIGITAL INC.
793 Pharmacy Ave., Scarborough, ON M1L 3K2. (416) 752-1510. FAX: (416) 752-8684.
CONTACT
Jim Hopkins

NUMBERS
(Edge coding 16-35mm/editing supplies.)
90 Adelaide St. E., Toronto, ON M5C 2R4. (416) 941-9412. FAX: (416) 941-9413.

PANIC & BOB
567 Queen St. W., Toronto, ON M5V 2B6. (416) 504-2020. FAX: (416) 504-0266.
EXECUTIVE PRODUCERS
Janice May
Barbara Rondinelli

PEGASUS PRODUCTIONS, LTD.
11313 - 123 St., Edmonton, AB T5M 0G1. (780) 452-8719.
email: pegasusproduction@compuserve.com
CONTACT
Marke Slipp

PIRATE RADIO & TELEVISION
(Sound/music.)
260 King St. E., Ste. 507, Toronto, ON M5A 1K3. (416) 594-3784. FAX: (416) 360-1789.
PARTNERS
Rick Shurman
Terry O'Reilly
Tom Eymundson
Kerry Crawford
Robert Armes

POST MODERN SOUND INC.
(Audio post/TV & film.)
1720 W. 2nd Ave., Vancouver, BC V6J 1H6. (604) 736-7474. FAX: (604) 738-7768. www.postmodernsound.com
PRESIDENT
David Hoole
VICE PRESIDENT
Mark Scott

PREMIER POST
409 King St. W., Ste. 300, Toronto, ON M5V 1K1. (416) 598-2100. FAX: (416) 598-1496. www.premierpost.com
PRESIDENT
Bill Cooke Jr.
VICE PRESIDENT, VIDEO OPERATIONS
Gord Stoddard
VICE PRESIDENT, AUDIO OPERATIONS
George Novotny
CLIENT LIAISON/SCHEDULING
Marisa DeBartolo

PRISMA-LIGHT, LTD.
762 Queen St. W., Toronto, ON M6J 1E9. (416) 504-4321. FAX: (416) 504- 7325. www.prismalight.com
VICE PRESIDENT, PRODUCTION
Les Zawadzki
POST-PRODUCTION SUPERVISOR
Christiane Galley

PRODUCER'S CHOICE
(Audio post.)
179 John St., Toronto, ON M5T 1X4. (416) 977-1132. FAX: (416) 977-2529. email: producer@netrover.com
PRESIDENT
Steve Hurej
STUDIO MANAGER
Barbara Hurej

RAINMAKER DIGITAL PICTURES
(Lab, post, visual effects, MPEG compression services - film, MOWs, TV, documentaries, commercials.)
50 W. 2nd Ave., Vancouver, BC V5Y 1B3. (604) 872-8700. FAX: (604) 872-1719. www.rainmaker.com
PRESIDENT/CEO
Bob Scarabelli
GENERAL MANAGER
Barry Chambers
DIRECTOR OF OPERATIONS
Katie McFadden
LAB GENERAL MANAGER
Dave Hardon

RED SHIFT PRODUCTIONS INC.
(Translation/Dubbing/Rythmoband/Complete language versioning services.)
225 Mutual St., Toronto, ON M5B 2B4. (416) 977-9740. FAX: (416) 977-7147. email: dubbing@mcclear.com
CONTACT/BOOKINGS
Pamela Brookes

RESTORATION HOUSE FILM GROUP INC.
P.O. Box 298, Belleville, ON K8N 5A2. (613) 966-4076. FAX: (613) 966-8431.
PRESIDENT
Arnold C. Schieman

ROBERT BOCKING PRODUCTIONS, LTD.
(Direct to disc computerized/stereo digital audio editing for any format/stereo digital audio EFX library support/stock shot library/non-linear editing.)
75 Hucknall Rd., Downsview, ON M3J 1W1. (416) 631-9845.
email: 105441.3040@compuserve.com

ROGERS PRODUCTIONS
(Full service film & video production house/post-production services & creative concepts.)
333 Bloor St. E., 7th Fl., Toronto, ON M4W 1G9. (416) 935-4758, (416) 935-4754. FAX: (416) 935-4777.
email: ccrosbie@rci.rogers.com
EXTERNAL CLIENT RELATIONS
Charles Crosbie
SALES & PROMOTIONS
Adam B. Christie

ROSNICK MACKINNON
(Audio production - TV & radio commercials/TV series/films, shorts, documentaries.)
555 Church St., Toronto, ON M4Y 2E2. (416) 323-3511. FAX: (416) 323-3647.
CEO/PRODUCER
Ted Rosnick
PRESIDENT/COMPOSER/PRODUCER
Steve MacKinnon

ROUND SOUND STUDIOS INC.
(Music writing & production/audio post-production/audio-video sync.)
60 Pippin Rd., Unit 44 & 45, Concord, ON L4K 4M8. (905) 660-5815. FAX: (416) 463-8233.
PRESIDENT
Gina Troiano

SIGNAL INC.
(Basic photographic chemicals for B&W and colour processes to processing labs.)
12 Carlaw Ave., Toronto, ON M4M 2R7. (416) 461-8181. FAX: (416) 469-2299.
CONTACT
Stan Picha

SOHO DIGITAL FILM
(Digital film lab/film scanning & imaging/video to film.)
26 Soho St., Toronto, ON M5T 1Z7. (416) 591-8408. (888) SOHO DIG. FAX: (416) 591-3979.
email: inquiries@sohodigital.com
PRESIDENT/DIRECTOR, OPERATIONS
Brian Hunt
VICE PRESIDENT, MARKETING & SALES
Nick Paulozza

SOLARUS
(Post-production & special effects/film editing/digital suite.)
1751 Richardson, Ste. 3147, Montréal, QC H3K 1G6. (514) 932-2980. FAX: (514) 932-7667.

SOUND DOGS
(Sound editing.)
424 Adelaide St. E., Toronto, ON M5A 1N4. (416) 364-4321. FAX: (416) 364-1310.
CONTACTS
Nelson Ferriera
Steve Barden

SPENCE-THOMAS AUDIO POST
320 King St. E., Toronto, ON M5A 1K6. (416) 361-6383. FAX: (416) 361-2970. www.spence-thomas.com
email: info@spence-thomas.com
PRESIDENT
Patrick Spence-Thomas

STARGATE STUDIOS
(Computer animation/Flame/Platinum edit box.)
530 Richmond St. W., Rear Bldg., Toronto, ON M5V 1Y4. (416) 504-2555. FAX: (416) 504-4545.
PRESIDENT
Wayne Trickett
VICE PRESIDENT
Robin Trickett

STUDIO POST
(Film-to-tape/tape-to-tape colour correction; Negative/processing/16mm/Super 16mm/35mm.)
5305 Allard Way, Edmonton, AB T6H 5X8. (780) 436-4444. FAX: (780) 438-8520.
CONTACTS
Bill Hamilton
Dean Langille

STUDIO 306
(Music/effects/dialogue recorded to picture.)
17 Central Hospital Lane, Toronto, ON M5A 4N4. (416) 968-2306. FAX: (416) 968-7641.
CONTACT
Brian Mitchell

SUNDOG FILMS
(Feature films/special effects.)
530 Richmond St. W., Rear Bldg., Toronto, ON M5V 1Y4. (416) 504-5335. FAX: (416) 504-4545.
CONTACT
Robin Trickett

TATTERSALL SOUND
(Audio post/sound design - film/TV/MOWs/documentaries.)
424 Adelaide St. E., Toronto, ON M5A 1N4. (416) 957-6221, (416) 364-4321. FAX: (416) 368-0690. www.tatsound.com
PRESIDENT
Jane Tattersall

THIRD FLOOR EDITING
116 Spadina Ave., Ste. 100, Toronto, ON M5V 2K6. (416) 504-6004. FAX: (416) 504-5650.
OWNER/EDITOR
Richard Unruh
EXECUTIVE PRODUCER
Jane Broadfoot

TOPIX/MAD DOG
(Digital compositing/Design/ special effects/Flame & Inferno.)
35 McCaul St., Ste. 200, Toronto, ON M5T 1V7. (416) 971-7711. FAX: (416) 971-9277. www.topix.com
PRESIDENT
Chris Wallace
EXECUTIVE PRODUCERS
Sylvain Taillon
Anne Deslauriers

TOYBOX
(Visual effects/motion control/editorial/transfer/high-resolution imaging.)
A Division of Command Post & Transfer Corp., 179 John St., 8th Fl., Toronto, ON M5T 1X4. (416) 585-9995. FAX: (416) 979-0428. www.compt.com
PARTNERS
Andy Sykes
Steve Robinson
VISUAL EFFECTS MANAGER
Dennis Berardi
DIRECTOR OF ANIMATION
Derek Grime

WAYNE KOZAK AUDIO PRODUCTIONS
(Audio post/music.)
1525 W. 8th Ave., Vancouver, BC V6J 1T5. (604) 736-8667. FAX: (604) 739-8661.
PRODUCER/OWNER
Wayne Kozak
COORDINATOR
Janice Bulger

VANCOUVER STUDIOS
(Complete audio post.)
3955 Gravely St., Burnaby, BC V5C 3T4. (604) 291-0978. FAX: (604) 291-6909. www.greenhouse-studios.com
email: studios@ greenhouse-studios.com
STUDIO MANAGER
Bruce Levens

WHALLEY-ABBEY DIGITAL STUDIOS,, INC..
(Non-linear digital post-production/Avid suites.)
1303 Greene Ave., Ste. 305, Westmount, QC H3Z 2A7. (514) 846-1940. FAX: (514) 846-1550.
email: andy@painted-house.com
CONTACT
Andrew Kemp

WOLF WILLOW SOUND, INC.
(Complete audio post, location sound.)
#4, 10878 - 97 St., Edmonton, AB T5H 2M5. (780) 448-9653. FAX: (780) 428-3985. www. wolfwillowsound.com
email: contact@wolfwillowsound.com
CONTACTS
Ian Armstrong
John Blerot

ZAZA SOUND PRODUCTIONS, LTD.
322 Dufferin St., Toronto, ON M6K 1Z6. (416) 534-4211. FAX: (416) 534-9520.
CONTACT
Paul Zaza

DISTRIBUTION COMPANIES

ACTION FILM LIMITEE
(35mm/16mm/vidéo.)
467 est boul. St-Joseph, Montréal, QC H2J 1J8. (514) 845-5572. FAX: (514) 286-2313. email: actionfilm@qc.dird.com
PRESIDENT
André Monette

ALLIANCE ATLANTIS MOTION PICTURE DISTRIBUTION
121 Bloor St. E., Ste. 1400, Toronto, ON M4W 3M5. (416) 967-1174. FAX: (416) 967-0044.
CHAIRMAN, MOTION PICTURE GROUP
Victor Loewy - (416) 966-7233
PRESIDENT, MOTION PICTURE DISTRIBUTION
Patrice Theroux - (416) 966-7703
PRESIDENT, ALLIANCE ATLANTIS VIVAFILM
Guy Gagnon - (514) 878-228
PRESIDENT, ODEON FILMS INC.
Brian Gliserman - (416) 966-6955
S.V.P., GENERAL MANAGER, MOTION PICTURE DISTRIBUTION
Jim Sherry (416) 966-7206

ASKA FILM DISTRIBUTION, INC.
1600 ave. de Lorimier, Ste. 211, Montréal, QC H2K 3W5. (514) 521-7103. FAX: (514) 521-6174.
email: askafilm@login.net
CONTACTS
Samuel Gagnon
Natasha Rybina

ATLANTIC THEATRE SERVICES, LTD.
P.O. Box 2419, 114 Dresden Ave., Saint John, NB E2L 3V9. (506) 696-6618. FAX: (506) 696-4472.

AUDIO CINE FILM
(35mm/16mm/video - schools & public performance rights Distributing: Walt Disney, MCA-Universal, Buena Vista, Hollywood, Metro Goldwyn Mayer, United Artists, Orion, Touchstone, Turner Entertainment, France Film, Alliance Vivafilm, Allegro, Action Films, Aska Film, C/FP, Evolution Video, Film Tonic, Lapointe Films, Prima Film/Video, Prisma Films, Mar-An, Melenny, Universal Studios, Paramount Pictures, Polygram Filmed Entertainment, New Line Cinema, Miramax Films.)
8462 Sherbrooke St. E., Montréal, QC H1L 1B2. (514) 493-8887, (800) 289-8887. FAX: (514) 493-9058.
SALES REPRESENTATIVES
Christian Bergeron
J.F. Cormier
Sal Gallo

BACCHUS ENTERTAINMENT, LTD.
(Film and music distribution. Specializing in online distribution.)
402 - 1959 West 2nd Ave., Vancouver, BC V6J 1J2. (604) 728-2522. FAX: (604) 728-2512. email: blakston@direct.ca
PRESIDENT
Penny O. Green

BAYVIEW FILM DISTRIBUTION, INC.
8 Mandel Cr., North York, ON M2H 1B9. (416) 362-5890. FAX: (416) 362-1218.
PRESIDENT
Orval Fruitman

BEVTEL PROGRAMS, INC.
285 Forest Hill Rd., Toronto, ON M5P 2N3. (416) 484-8000. FAX: (416) 484-8001.
PRESIDENT
Beverley Fein
VICE PRESIDENT
Michael J. Taylor

BLACKWATCH RELEASING, INC.
180 Bloor St. West, Ste. 1102, Toronto, Ontario M5S 2V6. (416) 934-9419. FAX: (416) 934-9420 .
EXECUTIVE V.P. & GENERAL MANAGER
Andy Myers
V.P. MARKETING
Robin Smith
DIRECTOR, THEATRICAL DISTRIBUTION
Adrian Herscovici
DISTRIBUTION MANAGER
Jean Paradis
V.P. INTERNATIONAL SALES
Lina Marrone
1410 Stanley, Ste. 606, Montreal, QC H3A 1P8. (514) 844-6655. FAX: (514) 844-6886 .
PRESIDENT
Yves Dion
V.P. MARKETING & DISTRIBUTION
Johanne Pelletier

BONDED SERVICES INTERNATIONAL LIMITED
517 Wellington St. W., Ste. 211, Toronto, ON M5V 1G1. (416) 703-1740. FAX: (416) 703-7075.

BRIGHTSTAR DISTRIBUTION
100 Yonge St., Ste. 1205, Toronto, ON M5C 2W1. (416) 362-5890. FAX: (416) 362-1218.

BUENA VISTA PICTURES DISTRIBUTION CANADA, INC.
(Distributors of Walt Disney Pictures, Touchstone Pictures and Hollywood Pictures.)
Sales: 1235 Bay St., Ste. 901, Toronto, ON M5R 3K4. (416) 964-9275, (800) 263-2853. FAX: (416) 964-8537.
VICE PRESIDENT
Anthony Macina
SALES MANAGER
Tony Schittone
BOOKING/SALES
Karen Burke
MARKETING COORDINATOR
Antonella Zappone

Publicity & Promotions: 21 St. Clair Ave. E., Ste. 701, Toronto ON M4T 1L9. (416) 413-0966, ext 227. FAX: (416) 416-7909.
DIRECTOR, PUBLICITY & PROMOTIONS
Jane Elltoft

Buena Vista Pictures Distribution: 350 S. Buena Vista St., R.O.D. Bldg., Burbank, CA 91521-0021. (818) 567-5000.
PRESIDENT
Chuck Viane
S.V.P. & GENERAL SALES MANAGER
Rod Rodriguez

CAMBIUM RELEASING, INC.
18 Dupont St., Toronto, ON M5R 1V2. (416) 964-8750. FAX: (416) 964-1980.
DIRECTOR, SALES
David Piperni
DIRECTOR, OPERATIONS
Steve Marinelli
CHAIRMAN
Arnie Zipursky
GENERAL MANAGER & GENERAL COUNSEL
Annette Frymer

CANADIAN FILMMAKERS' DISTRIBUTION CENTRE
(35 & 16mm/Video/Super 8: An artist-run organization specializing in the distribution of independently made, primarily Canadian films to the non-theatrical and broadcast markets.)
37 Hanna Ave., Ste. 220, Toronto, ON M6K 1W8. (416) 588-0725. FAX: (416) 588-7956. www.cfmdc.org
email: cfmdc@cfmdc.org
DIRECTOR
Alan McNairn

CANADIAN LEARNING COMPANY, INC.
(Educational film/video/CD-ROM)
95 Vansittart Ave., Woodstock, ON N4S 6E3. (519) 537-2360, (800) 267-2977. FAX: (519) 537-1035. www.canlearn.com
email: info@canlearn.com
CONTACT
Mike Harding

CANAMEDIA
(Series/movies/documentaries - TV worldwide plus pre-sales.)
1670 Bayview Ave., Ste. 408, Toronto, ON M4G 3C2. (416) 483-7446. FAX: (416) 483-7529.
email: canamed@ibm.net
PRESIDENT
Les Harris
SECRETARY/TREASURER
Jane Harris
VICE PRESIDENT, DISTRIBUTION, NORTH AMERICA
David W. Jackson
INTERNATIONAL SALES & ACQUISITIONS
Michèle Dal-Cin

CATALYST DISTRIBUTION, INC.
67 Mowat Ave., Ste. 200, Toronto, ON M6K 3E3. (416) 533-6767. FAX: (416) 533-2070.
email: distribution@catalystdistribution.com
CEO
Charles Falzon
PRESIDENT
Nancy Chapelle
VICE PRESIDENT, GROUP HEAD OF DISTRIBUTION
Jill Keenleyside
HEAD OF INTERNATIONAL SALES
Stephen Kelley

New York: Gullane Pictures, 1133 Broadway, Ste. 1520, New York, NY 10010 USA. (212) 463-9623. FAX: (212) 463-9626
VICE PRESIDENT, DISTRIBUTION
Cindy Bernstein

CBC INTERNATIONAL SALES
P.O. Box 500, Stn. A, Toronto, ON M5W 1E5. (416) 205-3500. FAX: (416) 205-3482. email: cbcis@toronto.cbc.ca
DIRECTOR, INTERNATIONAL CO-PRODUCTIONS, SALES & ACQUISITIONS
Criss Hajek
MANAGER, BROADCAST SALES (TORONTO)
Jennifer Stewart

Los Amgeles: 1950 Sawtelle Blvd., Ste. 333, Los Angeles, CA 90025. (310) 478-0212. FAX: (310) 478-6364.
email: cbcia@ix.netcom.com
HEAD OF SALES & NEW BUSINESS DEVELOPMENT
Sandra Sarciada-Naughton
SALES & ADMINISTRATION COORDINATOR
Aurora Hernandez

London: 43/51 Great Titchfield St., London, UK W1P 8DD. 011-44 207 9200. FAX: 011-44 207 323-5658.
HEAD OF SALES & NEW BUSINESS DEVELOPMENT
Susan Hewitt

CHARLES CHAPLIN ENTERPRISES, INC.
318 Hillhurst Blvd., Toronto, ON M6B 1N2. (416) 781-0131. FAX: (416) 781-0834. email: jeff.carp@path.com
PRESIDENT
Charles S. Chaplin

CHESTNUT PARK PRODUCTIONS
1 Atlantic Ave., Ste. 103, Toronto, ON M6K 3E7. (416) 537-5004. FAX: (416) 537-8984. email: mail@microtainment.com
PRESIDENT/EXECUTIVE PRODUCER
Garry Blye

CINAR CORPORATION
1055 René Lévesque Blvd. E., Montréal, QC H2L 4S5. (514) 843-7070. FAX: (514) 843-7080.

Cinar Europe Inc., 59/61 Kensington High St., London W8 5ED, England. 011 44 171 591 7500.
INTERNATIONAL SALES
David Ferguson

CINE-GROUPE
1151 Alexandre-Desève St., Montréal, QC H2L 2T7. (514) 524-7567. FAX: (514) 524-7354. email: distribution@cinegroupe.ca
S.V.P., DISTRIBUTION & DEVELOPMENT
Derek McGillivray
DIRECTOR, INTERNATIONAL SALES & MARKETING
Sylvie Bélanger

CINEMA ESPERANCA INTERNATIONAL, INC.
96 Spadina Ave., Ste. 301, Toronto, ON M5V 2J6. (416) 703-5000, (877) 525-3776. FAX: (416) 703-5002.
email: jakeprod@on.aibn.com
CHAIRMAN/PRESIDENT/CEO
André Bennett

COLUMBIA TRISTAR FILMS OF CANADA
A Division of Columbia Pictures Industries Inc., 1303 Yonge St., 1st Fl., Toronto, ON M4T 2Y9. (416) 922-5740.
CANADIAN GENERAL MANAGER
Michael Skewes
MANAGING DIRECTOR
Michael Brooker
WESTERN SALES MANAGER
Neil Campbell
EASTERN SALES MANAGER
Bill Robinson
QUÉBEC SALES MANAGER
Claude Chene
WESTERN CANADA SALES REPRESENTATIVE
Denise James
EASTERN CANADA SALES REPRESENTATIVE
Peter Wertelecky
QUÉBEC SALES REPRESENTATIVE
Sylvie Kenny
VICE PRESIDENT, MEDIA
Donna Slack
CANADIAN FIELD DIRECTOR, PUBLICITY/PROMOTIONS
Eliza Fernandes

COMPAGNIE FRANCE FILM, INC.
505 rue Sherbrooke est., Ste. 2401, Montréal, QC H2L 4N3. (514) 844-0680.
PRÉSIDENT/CEO
Pierre René
DIRECTEUR DIV. FILM
Michael Mosca

CREATIVE EXPOSURE
2236 Queen St. E., Toronto, ON M4E 1G2. Tel. & FAX: (416) 690-0755.
PRESIDENT
Tom Litvinskas

CRESWIN FILM DISTRIBUTORS, LTD.
18 Corwin Cr., Downsview, ON M3H 2A1. (416) 633-9079. FAX: (416) 638-5282.
PRESIDENT
Larry Rittenberg

CRITERION PICTURES
(Representing over 90 feature film producers, including: Columbia Pictures Industries Inc., Fox Searchlight, Janus Films, New Yorker Films, Norstar Releasing Inc., Savoy Pictures, Sony Pictures, Sony Classics, Tri-Star Pictures, 20th Century Fox Film Corp. and Warner Bros.)
41 Horner Ave., Unit 3, Toronto, ON M8Z 4X4. (416) 252-4151, (800) 565-1996. FAX: (416) 251-3720.
PRESIDENT
John W. Fisher

7801 Louis-H LaFontaine, Ste. 104, Anjou, QC H1K 4E4. (514) 356-0050, (800) 361-2788.
PROGRAM CONSULTANT
Tony DiPaolo

200 - 5000 Bridge St., Delta, BC V4K 2KT. (604) 940-9540, (800) 663-0991.
PROGRAM CONSULTANT
Carole Burgoyne

CRITICAL MASS PRODUCTIONS
77 Mowat Ave., Ste.110, Toronto, ON M6K 3E3. (416) 538-2535. FAX: (416) 538-3367. email: cmass@netcom.ca
PRESIDENT
Stephen Maynard

CRITICAL MASS RELEASING
77 Mowat Ave., Ste.110, Toronto, ON M6K 3E3. (416) 538-2535. FAX: (416) 538-3367. email: cmass@netcom.ca
PRESIDENT
William Alexander
SALES EXECUTIVE
Lisa-Marie Doorey

DARK HORSE ENT.
102 - 2935 Spruce St., Vancouver, BC V6H 3N3. (604) 734-0390. FAX: (604) 734-0380.
CONTACTS
Janine McCaw
Paul Busch

DISTR'ACTION DISTRIBUTION INTERNATIONALE, INC.
261 rue du St-Sacrement, Montréal, QC H2Y 3V2. (514) 844-5800. FAX: (514) 844-8210. email: kbobby@distraction.com
PRESIDENT
Michel Rodrigue

DISTRIBUTION LA FÊTE
387 Saint-Paul St. W., Montréal, QC H2Y 2A7. (514) 848-0417. FAX: (514) 848-0064. email: info@lafete.com
PRESIDENT
Rock Demers

DOMINO FILM & TELEVISION INTERNATIONAL, LTD.
(Domestic & international distribution of motion pictures and TV programming)
4002 Grey Ave., Montréal, QC H4A 3P1. (514) 484-0446. FAX: (514) 484-0468.
PRESIDENT
Jeanne Ritter

DOOMSDAY STUDIOS LIMITED
212 James St., Ottawa, ON K1R 5M7. (613) 230-9769. FAX: (613) 230-6004.
CONTACTS
Ramona Macdonald
Tony Kelleher

DREAMWORKS DISTRIBUTION CANADA CO.
2 Bloor St. W., Ste. 2510, Toronto, ON M4W 3E2. (416) 513-0312. FAX: (416) 513-0316. www.dreamworks.com
DISTRIBUTION
Don Popow
SALES
Jennifer Hofley
BOOKER
Sandra Reinholds

ELLIS RELEASING
1300 Yonge St., Ste. 300, Toronto, ON M4T 1X3. (416) 924-2186. FAX: (416) 924-6115. email: sales@ellisent.com
CHAIRMAN
Ralph C. Ellis
PRESIDENT
Stephen Ellis
SALES EXECUTIVE
Reg McGuire
MANAGER, CLIENT SERVICES
Grace Lo

ESPRIT FILMS LIMITED
2 Lake St., St. Catharines, ON L2R 5W6. (905) 685-8336

THE FILM CIRCUIT
(The Film Circuit, a division of the Toronto International Film Festival Group, was launched in the fall of 1995 to create a broader-based network for Canadian and significant international films. The Film Circuit has launched multiple successful screenings of such films as The Red Violin, Last Night and The Hanging Garden. These films would not have had the opportunity to be shown in the smaller sized centres of Ontario and British Columbia without the Circuit. The Circuit is proving to be a viable network for helping to deliver Canadian films to a broader public spectrum. Currently The Film Circuit consists of 44 active communities.)
A division of the Toronto International Film Festival Group (TIFFG), 2 Carlton St., Ste. 1600, Toronto, ON M5B 1J3. (416) 967-7371. FAX: (416) 967-9477.
DIRECTOR (TIFFG)
Piers Handling
MANAGING DIRECTOR (TIFFG)
Michèle Maheux
FILM CIRCUIT DIRECTOR
Cam Haynes
FILM CIRCUIT MANAGER
Blair Haynes

FILMOPTION INTERNATIONAL
3401 St-Antoine St. W., Westmount, QC H3Z 1X1. (514) 931-6180. FAX: (514) 939-2034. email: filmopt@total.net
PRESIDENT
Maryse Rouillard
VICE PRESIDENT
Lizanne Rouillard

144 Front St. W., Ste. 760, Toronto, ON M5J 2L7. (416) 598-1557. FAX: (416) 593-0013. email: mrosilio@filmoption.com
SENIOR EXECUTIVE, SALES & CO-PRODUCTIONS
Muriel Rosilio

FILMS TRANSIT INTERNATIONAL, INC.
402 est rue Notre-Dame, Ste. 100, Montréal, QC H2Y 1C8. (514) 844-3358. FAX: (514) 844-7298.
email: filmtran@odyssee.net

FILM TONIC, INC.
5130 boul. St-Laurent, 4e étage, Montréal, QC H2T 1R8. (514) 272-4425. FAX: (514) 274-0214.
CONTACTS
Pierre Latour
Joanne Senécal
Andrew Nobel

FILMWEST ASSOCIATES DISTRIBUTION, LTD.
2399 Hayman Rd., Kelowna, BC V1Z 1Z8. (250) 769-3399. FAX: (250) 769-5599. email: info@filmwest.com
www.filmwest.com
CONTACTS
Merrie Christoff
Lynn D'Albertanson

U.S. Office: 300 W. Second St., Carson City, NV 89703. (775) 883-8090. FAX: (800) 570-5505. email: sales@filmwest.com
CONTACT
George Christoff

FOREFRONT ENTERTAINMENT GROUP
700 - 402 W. Pender St., Vancouver, BC V6B 1T6. (604) 682-7910. FAX: (604) 682-8583. www.shirleyholmes.com
email: generalinfo@forefront-ent.com
CONTACT
Mickey Rogers

FREMANTLE OF CANADA, LTD.
23 Lesmill Rd., Ste. 201, Toronto, ON M3B 3P6. (416) 443-9204. FAX: (416) 443-8685.
CONTACTS
Randy H. Zalken
Marshall B. Kesten

FUNFILM DISTRIBUTION
5146 boul. St-Laurent, Montréal, QC H2T 1R8. (514) 272-4956. FAX: (514) 272-9841.
CONTACT
Robert Meunier

GOLDI PRODUCTIONS, LTD.
1409 Malibou Ter., Mississauga, ON L5J 4B9. (905) 855-1510.
CONTACTS
John Goldi, csc
Joan Goldi

GREAT NORTH INTERNATIONAL
3720 - 76 Ave., Edmonton, AB T6B 2N9. (780) 440-2022. FAX: (780) 440-3400.
CONTACT
Sandra Green

GREYSTONE INTERNATIONAL, INC.
490 Adelaide St. W., Ste. 100, Toronto, ON M5A 1T2. (416) 504-6059. FAX: (416) 504-4843.
CONTACTS
G. Philip Jackson
Daniel D'or

HEARTLAND RELEASING, INC.
1102 - 8th Ave., 3rd Fl., Regina, SK S4R 1C9. (306) 777-0888. FAX: (306) 586-3537.
SALES EXECUTIVE
Brent Evans

IDERA FILM & VIDEO
1037 W. Broadway, Ste. 400, Vancouver, BC V6H 1E3. (604) 732-1496. Film line: (604) 738-8815. FAX: (604) 738-8400.
www.vcn.bc.ca/idera
EXECUTIVE DIRECTOR
Stuart Black
DIRECTOR OF FILM, VIDEO & PROGRAMMING
Karen Weggler

IMAX CORPORATION
(Distributing the largest available library of 15/70 films in the industry, including entertainment, space, science and natural history films.)
2525 Speakman Dr., Sheridan Park, Mississauga, ON L5K 1B1. (905) 403-6500. FAX: (905) 403-6450.
CO-CHAIRMAN & CO-CEO
Bradley J. Wechsler
CO-CHAIRMAN & CO-CEO
Richard L. Gelfond
EXECUTIVE VICE PRESIDENT & COO
John Davison
SENIOR VICE PRESIDENT, FILM
Andy Gellis

INDO CANADIAN FILMS INTERNATIONAL
4500 boul. de Maisonneuve O., bur. 21, Montréal, QC H3Z 1L7. (514) 935-6888. FAX: (514) 935-8588.
email: indocdn.films@ibm.net
PRESIDENT
Gotham Hooja

INTERNATIONAL TELE-FILM
41 Horner Ave., Unit 3, Etobicoke, ON M8Z 4X4. (416) 252-1173, (800) 561-4300. FAX: (416) 252-1676. www.itf.ca
email: info@itf.ca
PRESIDENT
Stuart Grant

KALEIDOSCOPE ENTERTAINMENT, INC.
23 Lesmill Rd., Ste. 201, Toronto, ON M3B 3P6. (416) 443-9200. FAX: (416) 443-8685.
PRESIDENT
Randy H. Zalken
EXECUTIVE VICE PRESIDENT & CEO
Marshall B. Kesten

KENSINGTON COMMUNICATIONS, INC.
20 Maud St., Ste. 402, Toronto, ON M5V 2M5. (416) 504-9822. FAX: (416) 504-3608.
CONTACT
Robert Lang

K FILMS AMERIQUE
P.O. Box 2, Beaubien Postal Office, Montréal, QC H2G 3C8. (514) 277-2613. FAX: (514) 277-3598.
PRÉSIDENT
Louis Dussault

KING MOTION PICTURE CORPORATION
10104 - 103rd Ave., Ste. 1702, Canada Trust Tower, Edmonton, AB T5J 0H8. (780) 424-2950. FAX: (780) 420-0518.
email: kingpict@planet.eon.net
PRESIDENT
Douglas Hutton

LIONS GATE ENTERTAINMENT CORP.
2 Bloor St. W., Ste. 1901, Toronto, ON M4W 3E2. (416) 944-0104. FAX: (416) 944-2212. www.lionsgate-ent.com
PRESIDENT
Jeff Sackman

3 Bentall Centre, Ste. 3123, 595 Burrard St., P.O. Box 49139, Vancouver, BC V7X 1J1. (604) 609-6100. FAX: (604) 609-6149.

3600 boul. Thimens, St. Laurent, QC H4R 1V6. (514) 336-9696. FAX: (514) 336-6606.

561 Broadway, Ste. 12B, New York, NY 10012. (212) 966-4670. FAX: (212) 966-2544.
CO-PRESIDENT OF US RELEASING
Mark Urman

5750 Wilshire Blvd., Ste. 501, Los Angeles, CA 90036. (323) 692-7300. FAX: (323) 692-7373.
PRESIDENT/LIONS GATE INTERNATIONAL
Joe Drake
CO-PRESIDENT OF US RELEASING
Tom Ortenberg

L.M. MEDIA MARKETING SERVICES, LTD.
115 Torbay Rd., Unit 8, Markham, ON L3R 2M9. (905) 475-3750. FAX: (905) 475-3756, (800) 268-2380.
PRESIDENT
C. Lynn Meek
VICE PRESIDENT
Kaye Meek

LYNX IMAGES RELEASING
(Non-theatrical/TV/home video)
P.O. Box 5961, Stn. A, Toronto, ON M5W 1P4. (416) 925-8422. FAX: (416) 925-8352. www.lynximages.com
PRESIDENT
Russell Floren
EDUCATIONAL DIRECTOR
Andrea Gutsche

MARVIN MELNYK ASSOCIATES, LTD.
P.O. Box 220, Queenston, ON L0S 1L0. (416) 262-4964. FAX: (905) 262-4974.
PRESIDENT
Marvin Melnyk

MGM DISTRIBUTION OF CANADA
20 Queen St. W., Ste. 3500, Toronto, ON M5H 3R3. (416) 260-9680.
VICE PRESIDENT & DIVISION MANAGER, CANADA
Marisa Contardi
VICE PRESIDENT MEDIA & CO-OP ADVERTISING
Sandra Crann
BOOKERS
Danish Vahidy
Simone Konieczny

666 Sherbrooke W., Ste. 1002, Montréal, QC H3A 1E7. (514) 284-5113.
DISTRICT MANAGER
Robert Montplaisir

MONGREL MEDIA, INC.
109 Melville Ave., Toronto, ON M6G 1Y3. (416) 516-9775. FAX: (416) 516-0651. email: mongrelmedia@compuserve.com
PRESIDENT
Hussain Amarshi

MOVING IMAGES DISTRIBUTION
(Specializing in the non-theatrical and broadcast distribution of Canadian independent film & video productions since 1979)
402 W. Pender St., Ste. 606, Vancouver, BC V6B 1T6. (604) 684-3014. FAX: (604) 684-7165. TTY: (604) 684-3018.
www.movingimages.bc.ca
email: mailbox@movingimages.bc.ca

THE MULTIMEDIA GROUP OF CANADA
Head office: 261 du St-Sacrement St., Montréal, QC H2Y 3V2. (514) 844-3636. FAX: (514) 844-4990.
email: mgc@the-mgc.com
PRESIDENT
Jacques Bouchard

Toronto office: 2 College St., Ste. 107, Toronto, ON M5G 1K3. (416) 968-2075. FAX: (416) 927-1956. email: themgc@istar.ca
VP, ACQUISITIONS & DEVELOPMENT
David Seeler

NELVANA ENTERPRISES, INC.
32 Atlantic Ave., Toronto, ON M6K 1X8. (416) 588-5571. FAX: (416) 588-5588. www.nelvana.com
CO-CEO
Patrick Loubert
CO-CEO
Michael Hirsh
CO-CEO
Clive Smith

22 Kingly Court, London, UK W1R 5LE. 011 44 207 287-2770. FAX: 011 44 207 287-2740. email: cathyl@uk.nelvana.com
CONTACT
Cathy Laughton

55 rue de Bretagne, Paris, France 75003. 331 42 71 08 28. FAX: 331 42 71 01 44.
CONTACT
Emmanuéle Petry

NORTH AMERICAN RELEASING, INC.
808 Nelson St., Ste. 2105, Vancouver, BC V6Z 2H2. (604) 681-2165. FAX: (604) 681-5538. www.nar.bc.ca
PRINCIPAL
Lloyd A. Simandl
INTERNATIONAL SALES
Sharla Bullard

OASIS PICTURES, INC.
6 Pardee Ave., Ste. 104, Toronto, ON M6K 3H5. (416) 588-6821. FAX: (416) 588-7276. www.oasispictures.com
PRESIDENT
Peter Emerson
VICE PRESIDENT INTERNATIONAL
Valerie Cabrera
INTERNATIONAL SALES & DEVELOPMENT
Steven Murphy
DIRECTOR, OPERATIONS
Liz Bradford
DIRECTOR, ACQUSITIONS & DEVELOPMENT
Mike Soutter
DEVELOPMENT & ACQUISITIONS
Leigh Elliott

OASIS SHAFTESBURY RELEASING
6 Pardee Ave., Ste. 104, Toronto, ON M6K 3H5. (416) 588-6821. FAX: (416) 588-7276.
VICE PRESIDENT, THEATRICAL
Halina Marie Jakowenko
DIRECTOR, MARKETING
Wendy Boylan

ODEON FILMS, INC.
An Alliance Atlantis Company, 121 Bloor St. E., Ste. 1500, Toronto, ON M4W 3M5. (416) 967-1141. FAX: (416) 934-6999.
PRESIDENT
Bryan Gliserman

OPTIMA PRODUCTIONS, INC.
1253 McGill College Ave., Ste. 452, Montréal, QC H3B 2Y5. (514) 397-9988. FAX: (514) 954-1237.
PRÉSIDENT
Jean Zaloum

OWEN-STEWART PERFORMANCE RESOURCES, INC.
(Distributors for CRM films, Video Arts, Charthouse, Fenman, Media Partners, Right Brain, Mentor Media, Telephone Doctor, Video Communicators and many more.)
20 Valleywood Dr., Ste. 100, Markham, ON L3R 6G1. (905) 474-9898, (800) 263-3399. FAX: (905) 474-0834.
email: sales@owenstewart.com

PACIFIC CINEMATHEQUE PACIFIQUE
(16mm)
1131 Howe St., Ste. 200, Vancouver, BC V6Z 2L7. (604) 688-8202. FAX: (604) 688-8204.

PAPILLON PRODUCTIONS
R.R. #2, Priceville, ON N0C 1K0. Tel. & FAX: (519) 369-3494.
email: bluesky@bmts.com
CONTACT
George Ritter

PARAMOUNT PICTURES CANADA
Viacom Enterprises Canada Limited, 146 Bloor St. W., Toronto, ON M5S IM4. (416) 969-9901. FAX: (416) 922-0287.
PRESIDENT
Gino Campagnola
SENIOR VICE PRESIDENT
Chris Sullivan
VICE PRESIDENT/CONTROLLER
Anne Shaw

MOTION PICTURE GROUP
PRESIDENT
Gino Campagnola
SENIOR VICE PRESIDENT
Chris Sullivan
VICE PRESIDENT/CONTROLLER
Anne Shaw

MARKETING
SENIOR VICE PRESIDENT, MARKETING
Greg Ferris
DIRECTOR OF PUBLICITY
Anne Davidson-Muru
DIRECTOR OF ADVERTISING
Leigh Higgins

146 Bloor St. W., Toronto, ON M5S 1M4. (416) 969-9901. FAX: (416) 922-0287.
ALBERTA/BC SALES
Derek Boulet

ONTARIO SALES
Bob Cowan
ATLANTIC CANADA/MANITOBA/SASKATCHEWAN SALES
Jean White

1255 University Ave., Ste. 912, Montréal, QC H3B 9W4. (514) 866-2010. FAX: (514) 866-2411.
MANAGER
Lise Bertrand

Television Group: (416) 969-9901. FAX: (416) 922-4743.
VICE PRESIDENT & GENERAL MANAGER
Bruce Swanson
EXECUTIVE DIRECTOR SALES, CANADA
Kevin Keeley
ADMINISTRATION & DISTRIBUTION SUPERVISOR
Kathy Case

PEERLESS FILMS LIMITED
2277 Noel St., St. Laurent, QC H4M 1S1. (514) 747-2226. FAX: (514) 747-5781.
PRESIDENT/GENERAL MANAGER
Lottie Roher

PICTURE PLANT RELEASING, LTD.
P.O. Box 2465, Halifax, NS B3J 3E4. (902) 455-3901. FAX: (902) 455-5704. www.pictureplant.com
email: pixplant@istar.ca
PRESIDENT
William MacGillivray
VICE PRESIDENT
Terry Greenlaw

RAYMOND INTERNATIONAL
238 Davenport Rd., Ste. 122, Toronto, ON M5R 1J6. (416) 485-3406. FAX: (416) 487-3820.
PRESIDENT
Bruce Raymond

RED SKY ENTERTAINMENT
Ste. 635 - The Landing, 375 Water St., Vancouver, BC V6B 5C6. (604) 899-0609. FAX: (604) 899-0619.
PRESIDENT & CEO
Mike Smallwood
VICE PRESIDENT, MARKETING & CANADIAN FILM DEVELOPMENT
Mary-Pat Gleeson
VICE PRESIDENT, SALES & ACQUISITIONS
Dave Forget
BOOKER
Darryl Croft

REMSTAR DISTRIBUTION
85 St-Paul St. W., Ste. 530, Montréal, QC H2Y 3V4. (514) 847-1136. FAX: (514) 847-1163. email: remstar@remstarcorp.com
PRESIDENT
Julien Rémillard
VICE PRESIDENT
Maxime Rémillard
EXECUTIVE DIRECTOR (ENGLISH CANADA)
Andrew Austin
EXECUTIVE DIRECTOR (FRENCH CANADA)
Armand Lafond

RHOMBUS INTERNATIONAL
489 King St. W., Ste. 102, Toronto, ON M5V 1L3. (416) 971-7856. FAX: (416) 971-9647. email: rhombus@total.net
PRESIDENT
Sheena Macdonald
VICE PRESIDENT
Niv Fichman
VICE PRESIDENT, HEAD OF BUSINESS & LEGAL AFFAIRS
Danny Iron

THE ROKE ENTERTAINMENT GROUP
522 - 11th Ave., S.W., Calgary, AB T2R 0C8. (403) 264-4660. FAX: (403) 264-6571.
CONTACTS
Hector Ross
Frank Kettner
Syd Sniderman
Lloyd Fedor

RON HASTINGS COMMUNICATIONS, LTD.
20 Holly St., Ste. 300, Toronto, ON M4S 3B1. (416) 484-8000. FAX: (416) 484-8001.
PRESIDENT
Ron Hastings

R.S.M. PRODUCTIONS INTERNATIONALES, INC.
720 Montpellier, Ste. 912, Ville St. Laurent, QC H4L 5B5. (514) 748-2678. FAX: (514) 748-7560.
CONTACT
Rafik M. Murad

SALTER STREET FILMS INTERNATIONAL LIMITED
1668 Barrington St., Ste. 500, Halifax, NS B3J 2A2. (902) 420-1577. FAX: (902) 425-8260. www.salter.com
email: salter@salter.com
VICE PRESIDENT, 3RD PARTY & ACQUISITIONS
Liliana Vogt
DIRECTOR OF BUSINESS AFFAIRS
Allison Outhit
SALES EXECUTIVE
Clarence LeBlanc
LATIN AMERICAN SALES
Sonia Ormeachea

SATURDAY PLAYS LIMITED
965 Bay St., Ste. 2409, Toronto, ON M5S 2A3. (416) 964-7284. FAX: (416) 964-7997.
PRESIDENT
Allan King
VICE PRESIDENT
Colleen Murphy
EXECUTIVE ASSISTANT
Elisa Suppa

SEVILLE PICTURES, INC.
147 St. Paul St. W., 2nd Fl., Montréal, QC H2Y 1Z5. (514) 841-1910. FAX: (514) 847-8030.
CONTACTS
David Reckziegle
Pierre Brousseau

2221 Yonge St., Ste. 400, Toronto, ON M4S 2B4. (416) 480-0453. FAX: (416) 480-0501.
CONTACT IN TORONTO
Jeff Grottick

SOCIETE DE DISTRIBUTION CINEMA LIBRE, INC.
460 Ste-Catherine o, bur. 500, Montréal, QC H3B 1A7. (514) 861-9030. FAX: (514) 861-3634. www.cinemalibre.com
email: clibre@cam.org
DIRECTEUR GÉNÉRAL
Claude Forget
DIRECTEUR ADMINISTRATIF
Michel Gélinas

SULLIVAN ENTERTAINMENT INTERNATIONAL, INC.
110 Davenport Rd., Toronto, ON M5R 3R3. (416) 921-7177. FAX: (416) 921-7538.
PRESIDENT
Trudy Grant
DIRECTOR OF HOME VIDEO & ACQUISITIONS
Tara Gascho

TELEGENIC LICENSING, INC.
20 Holly St., Ste. 300, Toronto, ON M4S 3B1. (416) 484-8000. FAX: (416) 484-8001.
PRESIDENT
Michael R. Carlisle

TELEVISION NETWORK MEDIA CORPORATION, INC.
(TV & educational films distribution)
39 Baywood Rd., Toronto, ON M9V 3Y8. (416) 745-6270. FAX: (416) 745-7179.
CONTACT
Ronald Convey

TELEGENIC PROGRAMS, INC.
20 Holly St., Ste. 300, Toronto, ON M4S 3B1. (416) 484-8000. FAX: (416) 484-8001. email: telegenic@aol.com
PRESIDENT/CEO
H. Lawrence Fein
EXECUTIVE VICE PRESIDENT/COO
Michael J. Taylor
PROGRAM CO-ORDINATOR
Linda LePage
CONTROLLER, FINANCE & CONTRACT MANAGEMENT
Aide Smit
BOOKING & PROMOTION
Ronda Fein

THA MEDIA DISTRIBUTORS, LTD.
307 - 1200 West Pender, Vancouver, BC V6E 2S9. (604) 687-4215. FAX: (604) 688-8349. email: tha.sales@thamedia.com
MANAGING DIRECTOR
Roberta Colombin

TVA INTERNATIONAL, INC.
(Formerly Motion International Inc.) 465 McGill St., Montréal, QC H2Y 4A6. (514) 284-2525. FAX: (514) 284-0640.
PRESIDENT, DISTRIBUTION
Stephen Greenberg
VICE PRESIDENT, INTERNATIONAL DISTRIBUTION
Jean Bureau

101 Bloor St. W., Ste. 400, Toronto, ON M5S 2Z7. (416) 968-0002. FAX: (416) 643-3900.
EXECUTIVE V.P., DISTRIBUTION & MARKETING
Daniel Lyon

TWENTIETH CENTURY FOX FILM CORPORATION

33 Bloor St. E., Ste. 1106, Toronto, ON M4W 3H1. Sales: (416) 921-0001, Publicity: (416) 515-3365, (800) 668-9927. FAX: (416) 921-9062.
VICE PRESIDENT/GENERAL MANAGER
Barry Newstead
COMPTROLLER
Rosemarie Marshall
BRANCH MANAGER
Damian O'Regan
SALES MANAGER
Darlene Elson
HEAD BOOKER
Sharon Irwin
ENGLISH MEDIA ADVERTISING
Joanna Smith, (416) 484-5306
FAX: (416) 484-5308
PRINT ADVERTISING/FRENCH MEDIA ADVERTISING
Joanna Smith, (416) 484-5306. FAX: (416) 484-5308.
MANAGER, PUBLICITY & PROMOTION
Julia Perry

UNIVERSAL FILMS CANADA

2450 Victoria Park Ave., Willowdale, ON M2J 4A2. (416) 491-3000. FAX: (416) 502-0323, (416) 494-3587 (Publicity), (416) 491-5180 (Advertising).
VICE PRESIDENT/GENERAL MANAGER
Eugene Amodeo
DIRECTOR, PUBLICITY & PROMOTION
Janice Luke
EXECUTIVE DIRECTOR, ADVERTISING
Janice Doyle
ACCOUNTING, 35MM/16MM
Linda Allen

2450 Victoria Pk. Ave., Willowdale, ON M2J 4A2.
TORONTO/ST. JOHN BRANCH MANAGER
Peter Doody
CALGARY/VANCOUVER/WINNIPEG BRANCH MANAGER
Gail Shiffman

1430 rue Peel, Montréal, QC H3A 1S9. (514) 987-5233. FAX: (514) 849-8270.
MANAGER, 35MM
Louise Palmos

Non-theatrical: Audio Ciné Films, 8462 Sherbrooke E., Montréal, QC H1L 1B2. (514) 493-8887.
REPRESENTATIVE
Benoit Lachance

VIACOM ENTERPRISES CANADA

See Paramount Pictures Canada

VIDEO EL CANADA LIMITED

(Films (35mm)/TV programs/video/Czech & Slovak)
583 William St., London, ON N6B 3E8. (519) 434-9939. FAX: (519) 434-8182. email: joemara@home.com
PRESIDENT
Josef Mara

WARNER BROS. ENTERTAINMENT, INC.

4576 Yonge St., 2nd Fl., North York, ON M2N 6P1. (416) 250-8384. FAX: (416) 250-1898 (Advertising). FAX: (416) 250-8930 (Sales).
PRESIDENT & CANADIAN DIVISION MANAGER
Philip R. Carlton
VICE PRESIDENT, CANADIAN DISTRICT MANAGER
Florent Boulet
SENIOR VICE PRESIDENT, ADVERTISING & PUBLICITY
Dianne Schwalm

4576 Yonge St., 2nd Fl., North York, ON M2N 6P1. (416) 250-8384.

9900 Cavendish, Ste. 205, Ville Saint-Laurent, QC H4M 2V2. (514) 333-6400. FAX: (514) 333-1460.
SALES
Susan Karam

WESTON WOODS CANADA

60 Briarwood Ave., Port Credit, ON L5G 3N6. (905) 278-0566. FAX: (905) 278-2801. email: westonwood@homeroom.ca

WILLIAM F. COOKE TELEVISION PROGRAMS

890 Yonge St., Ste. 800, Toronto, ON M4W 3P4. (416) 967-6141. FAX: (416) 967-5133.
PRESIDENT & CEO
William Cooke
PRESIDENT, TV DISTRIBUTION
Alex McWilliams
CFO
David Fraser

WINNIPEG FILM GROUP DISTRIBUTION OFFICE

304 - 100 Arthur St., Winnipeg, MB R3B 1H3. (204) 925-FILM. FAX: (204) 942-6799. www.winnipegfilmgroup.mb.ca
email: marlene@winnipegfilmgroup.mb.ca
DISTRIBUTION COORDINATOR
Marlene James

EXHIBITORS & EXHIBITION SERVICES

CHIEF EXHIBITION CIRCUITS

ALLIANCE CINEMAS
#200 - 1788 W. 5th Ave., Vancouver, BC V6J 1P2. (604) 734-8700. FAX: (604) 734-7489.
PRESIDENT
Leonard Schein
BRITISH COLUMBIA: VANCOUVER: Fifth Avenue (5), Park (1); VICTORIA: University (4).
ONTARIO: Bayview (4), Beaches (6), Cumberland (4).

AMC THEATRES OF CANADA
1240 Bay St., Ste. 205, Toronto, ON M5R 2A7. (416) 920-8333. FAX: (416) 920-3662.
VICE PRESIDENT, OPERATIONS
Thomas L. Velde
DIRECTOR OF FILM
Eric Bauman
OPERATIONS MANAGER
Larry Whittenberger
DIRECTOR OF BUSINESS AFFAIRS
Cliff Narbey
MARKETING COORDINATOR
Jack Gardner
ONTARIO: Concord: Interchange 30 (30); Kanata: Kanata 24 (24); Oakville: Winston Churchill (24); Scarborough: Kennedy Common (20); Whitby (24).

A THEATRE NEAR YOU, (CANADA) INC.
c/o Dolphin Cinema II, 4555 E. Hastings St., N. Burnaby, BC V5C 2K3. Tel. & FAX: (604) 293-0332.
Head Office: 17215 Smokey Pt. Dr., Ste. B, Arlington, WA 98223. (360) 653-9899. FAX: (360) 653-1720.
CHAIRMAN
Al Dabestani
PRESIDENT
Surinder Uppal

BOULEVARD CINEMA, LTD.
113 Richmond Blvd., Unit 2, Napanee, ON K7R 3Z8. (613) 354-2597. FAX: (613) 354-0441.
PRESIDENT
Diane Remington

CAPRICE SHOWCASE THEATRES, INC.
100 - 560 Beattie St., Vancouver, BC V6B 2L3. (604) 683-8038. FAX: (604) 683-8077
PRESIDENT
Terry Weir
GENERAL MANAGER
Bill Nowrie
HEAD BOOKER & FILM BUYER
Dene Joyal
BRITISH COLUMBIA: Campbell River: Caprice Showcase (5); Courtenay: Caprice Showcase (5), Palace (1); Delta: Caprice Showcase (1); Duncan: Caprice (4); Kelowna: Showcase Grand (10); Langford: Caprice Showcase (3); Nanaimo: Caprice Showcase (2), Showcase Grand (8); Vancouver: Paradise (1); W. Vancouver: Caprice Park Royal (3); Westbank: Caprice Showcase (5); White Rock: Caprice Rialto (2); Caprice Showcase (4)

CARNIVAL CINEMAS
5402 - 47 St., Red Deer, AB T4N 6Z4. (403) 341-6565. FAX: (403) 341-4355.
CEO
Bill Ramji

CINEMA CITY, INC.
Box 172, 9944 - 33rd Ave., Edmonton, AB T6N 1E8. (403) 463-5783. FAX: (403) 463-5893.
CONTACTS
Lamar E. Gwaltney
Lamar A. (Andy) Gwaltney

CINEMA PARALLELE
3668 boul. St-Laurent, Montréal, QC H2X 2V4. (514) 843-4725. FAX: (514) 843-4631.
DIRECTOR
Claude Chamberlan

CINEPLEX ODEON CORPORATION
1303 Yonge St., Toronto, ON M4T 2Y9. (416) 323-6600. FAX: (416) 323-6677.
CHAIRMAN & CEO
Allen Karp
CFO
Michael Brandt
SENIOR VICE PRESIDENT, FILM:
Tony Cianciotta
SENIOR VICE PRESIDENT, MARKETING & COMMUNICATIONS
Marci Davies
SENIOR VICE PRESIDENT, REAL ESTATE
Sam DiMichele
SENIOR VICE PRESIDENT, OPERATIONS
Dan McGrath
VICE PRESIDENT & GENERAL COUNSEL
Karen Hacker
BRITISH COLUMBIA: CLEARBROOK: Clearbrook (6); COQUITLAM: Pinetree (6); KAMLOOPS: Aberdeen Mall (8); Odeon (4); PRINCE GEORGE: Odeon (3); SURREY: Strawberry Hill (12); VANCOUVER: Granville (7), Oakridge (3), Park &Tilford (6), Station Square (5); VICTORIA: Odeon (7).
ALBERTA: CALGARY: Canyon Meadows (10), Crowfoot (10), Eau Claire Market (5), London Town Square (6), Northland Village (5), Northland Village (5), Southlands (4); EDMONTON: Clareview (10), Eaton Centre (9), West Mall 6 (6), West Mall 8 (8), Westmount (4), Whitemud Crossing (8), Twin Drive-In (2); GRANDE PRAIRIE: The Grande (10); LETHBRIDGE: Park Place (6); MEDICINE HAT: The Grande (10) ST. ALBERT: Village Tree (12).
SASKATCHEWAN: REGINA: Coronet (6), Southlands (10); SASKATOON: Centre (7), Pacific (4).
MANITOBA: WINNIPEG: Garrick (4), Grant Park (8), Odeon Drive-In (1).
ONTARIO: AJAX: Ajax (10); BARRIE: The Grande (12); BOWMANVILLE: Clarington Discount (10); BRAMPTON: Centennial Discount (3), 410 & 7 Centre (4), Orion Gate (10); BRANTFORD: Cinemas Brantford (6), Market Square Discount (3); BURLINGTON: Showcase (6); CAMBRIDGE: Cambridge (7); GUELPH: Stone Road Mall (5); HAMILTON: Centre Mall (8), Upper James (7); KINGSTON: Cataraqui (6); KITCHENER: Fairway Centre (7); LONDON: Galleria (6), Huron Market Place (6), Westmount 6 (6); MARKHAM: First Markham Place (10); MISSISSAUGA: Erin Mills (5), South Common Mall Discount (6); NIAGARA FALLS: Niagara Square (10); OAKVILLE: Oakville Mews Discount (5); OTTAWA: Kanata Cineplex (4), Orleans Town Centre (6), St. Laurent (5), Somerset (1), South Keys (12), Vanier Discount (7), Westgate Discount (3), World Exchange (7); RICHMOND HILL: Elgin Mills (10); ST. CATHARINES: Can-View Drive-In (4), Fairview Mall (9); SUDBURY: Odeon (2); THORNHILL: Promenade (6); THUNDER BAY: Cineplex Thunder Bay Discount (8), Cumberland (5); TORONTO: Canada Square (8), Carlton (9), Eaton Centre (16), Fairview (6), 401 & Morningside (11), Humber Discount (2), Hyland (2), Market Square (6), The Grande at Sheppard Centre (10), Scarborough Town Centre Discount (12), Sherway (13), Varsity (8), Warden Woods Discount (8), Woodbine (8), York (2); WELLAND: Seaway (7); WHITBY: Champlain Mall (6); WINDSOR: Glade Place (3), Palace (4).
QUEBEC: BOUCHERVILLE: C.P. Boucherville Drive-In (2); BROSSARD: Brossard (7); CHATEAUGUAY: C.P. Chateauguay Drive-In (3); LAVAL: Carrefour (6), Les Galeries Laval (8), C.P.Laval Drive-In (4); LONGUEUIL: Place Longueuil (5); MONTREAL: Cineplex Centre-ville (9), Complexe Desjardins (4), Côte de Neiges (7), Dauphin (2), Egyptien (3), Le Faubourg (4), Mall Cavendish (8); Place LaSalle (12), Pointe-Claire (6); Quartier Latin (17); St-Bruno (11), QUEBEC CITY: Laurentien (12), Place Charest (8), C.P. Beauport Drive In (3), C.P. De La Colline Drive In (2); TROIS RIVIERES: C.P. Trois Rivieres Drive-In (2); WESTMOUNT: Atwater (3).

EMPIRE THEATRES LIMITED
Head Office, 610 East River Rd., New Glasgow, NS B2H 3S8. (902) 755-7620. FAX: (902) 755-7640.
PRESIDENT
Stuart G. Fraser
Regional Office, 650 Portland St., Dartmouth, NS B2W 6A3. (902) 434-4114. FAX: (902) 434-6933
DIRECTOR, MARKETING
Dean S. Leland

NEW BRUNSWICK: FREDERICTON: Empire Cinemas (10), Take Two Cinemas (2); MONCTON: Crystal Palace Cinemas (8); SAINT JOHN: Exhibition Cinemas (7).

NOVA SCOTIA: AMHERST: Paramount (3); BEDFORD: Empire 6 (6); DARTMOUTH: Empire 6 (6); HALIFAX: Oxford (1), Empire 17 Cinemas (17), Empire IMAX (1); NEW GLASGOW: Aberdeen Cinemas (7), Empire Drive-In (1); NEW MINAS: Empire Cinemas (7); SYDNEY: Empire Cinemas (8); TRURO: Centennial (3); YARMOUTH: Yarmouth (3).

PRINCE EDWARD ISLAND: CHARLOTTETOWN: Charlottetown Mall (8)

NEWFOUNDLAND: CORNER BROOK: Millbrook (2); ST. JOHN'S: Avalon Mall (12), Empire Cinemas (6).

ENCORE CINEMAS, INC.

131 Speers Rd., Oakville, ON L6K 2E8. (905) 337-3717. FAX: (905) 337-0458.
PRESIDENT
Douglas Stoll
VICE PRESIDENT
Jeff Knoll

FAMOUS PLAYERS, INC.

(Famous Players is a part of the entertainment operations of Viacom Inc. and operates 111 theatres with 690 screens and 202,247 seats across Canada).
146 Bloor St. W., Toronto, ON M5S 1P3. (416) 969-7800. FAX: (416) 964-3924.
PRESIDENT
John Bailey
SENIOR EXECUTIVE VICE PRESIDENT & C.F.O.
Ton Kars
SENIOR VICE PRESIDENT, BUSINESS PLANNING
Damien Cheng
SENIOR VICE PRESIDENT & GENERAL MANAGER, THEATRE OPERATIONS & MARKETING
Roger Harris
SENIOR VICE PRESIDENT, DESIGN & CONSTRUCTION
Brian Holberton
SENIOR VICE PRESIDENT, SECRETARY & GENERAL COUNSEL
Michael Scher
SENIOR VICE PRESIDENT, FILM
Joe Strebinger
VICE PRESIDENT, IMAX OPERATIONS & MARKETING
Laura Brillinger
VICE PRESIDENT, NEW THEATRES, CENTRAL OPERATIONS
Nigel Bullers
VICE PRESIDENT, FINANCE & CONTROLLER
Dean Einarson
VICE PRESIDENT, CORPORATE PUBLIC RELATIONS
Dennis Kucherawy
VICE PRESIDENT, MARKETING
Stuart Pollock
VICE PRESIDENT, WEST COAST THEATRE OPERATIONS
David Polny
VICE PRESIDENT, CONCESSIONS
Jeff Rush
VICE PRESIDENT, DESIGN & CONSTRUCTION
Hartmut Sahl
VICE PRESIDENT, HUMAN RESOURCES & INDUSTRIAL RELATIONS
Douglas Smith
VICE PRESIDENT, CORPORATE PUBLIC RELATIONS
Dennis Kucherawy, (416) 969-6506
COORDINATOR, CORPORATE PUBLIC RELATIONS
Karen Bradt, (416) 969-6523. FAX: (416) 969-3924.
DIRECTOR, EASTERN OPERATIONS
Armand Zwibel
EXECUTIVE DIRECTOR, FILM - EASTERN CANADA
John Xinos, (514) 861-6017. FAX: (514) 861-4969.
DIRECTORS, CENTRAL OPERATIONS
Jill Kitson
Brenda Bugg
VICE PRESIDENT, NEW THEATRES, CENTRAL OPERATIONS
Nigel Bullers, (416) 969-7800. FAX: (416) 969-3924.
VICE PRESIDENT, WESTERN OPERATIONS
David Polny, (604) 926-7321. FAX: (604) 926-2553.
ACTING DISTRICT MANAGER, S.W. ONTARIO
Mike Hogan
DISTRICT MANAGER
S. W. Ontario
DISTRICT MANAGER, CENTRAL OPERATIONS
Jim Liolios

BRITISH COLUMBIA: BURNABY: Station Square (7), SilverCity Metropolis (10); COQUITLAM: Eagle Ridge(6), SilverCity Coquitlam (20); GUILDFORD: SilverCity Guildford (12); KELOWNA: Orchard Park (5); LANGLEY: Willowbrook (6), Colossus Langley (18); PRINCE GEORGE: Prince George 6 (6); RICHMOND: Richmond Centre (6), SilverCity Riverport (18); VANCOUVER: Capitol (6), Esplanade 6 (6), Vancouver Centre (2); VERNON: Famous Players Vernon (7); VICTORIA: Capitol (6), University (4).

ALBERTA: CALGARY: Banker's Hall (5), Coliseum Calgary (10), Market Mall (8), Sundridge Cinemas (5), Westhills (10); EDMONTON: Gateway (8), Paramount (1), SilverCity West Mall (17) & Imax 3D (1) Westmount Centre (4); LETHBRIDGE: Centre Cinema (2), Paramount (2); RED DEER: Park Plaza (7).

SASKATCHEWAN: REGINA: Cornwall Centre (4); SASKATOON: Capitol Four (4), Midtown (2) MANITOBA: WINNIPEG: Garden City (2), Kildonan Place (6), Northstar (2), Portage Place (3), SilverCity St. Vital (10).

ONTARIO: BELLEVILLE: Famous Players 8 (8); BRAMPTON: Gateway (6); BURLINGTON: Burlington 8 (8); HAMILTON: Fiesta Mall (4), Jackson Square (6), Lime Ridge Reel Deal (4), SilverCity Ancaster (10); KINGSTON: Capitol (7); KITCHENER: Kings College (4), SilverCity Kitchener (12); LONDON: Capitol (2), Wellington 8(8); MARKHAM: Markville (4); MISSISSAUGA: Coliseum (12) plus a 3D IMAX, SilverCity (10); Sussex Centre (4); NEWMARKET: Glenway (5); OAKVILLE: Town Centre (6); OSHAWA: Centre 8 (8), OTTAWA: Coliseum (12), Rideau Centre (3), Gloucester 5 (5), SilverCity Ottawa (16); PICKERING: Pickering 8 (8); RICHMOND HILL: Parkway 6 (6), SilverCity (14); ST. CATHERINES: Lincoln Mall (3), SilverCity (8); SARNIA: Lambton 5 (5); SUDBURY: City Centre (3), Super Mall (3); THUNDER BAY: SilverCity (12); TORONTO: Backstage (2), Bayview Village (4), Cedarbrae 8 (8), Colossus Toronto (18) plus a 3D IMAX, Coliseum Scarborough (12), Eglinton (1), Paramount Toronto (13) plus a 3d IMAX, Plaza (2), Sheridan North York (4), Uptown (3), Victoria Terrace (6), SilverCity Yonge & Eglinton (9), SilverCity Yorkdale (10); WINDSOR: Devonshire Arts (3), Parkway (5), SilverCity (12).

QUEBEC: DORVAL: Dorval (4); GATINEAU: Les Promenades (4); GREENFIELD PARK: Famous Players Greenfield Park (8); LASALLE: Carrefour Angrignon (10); LAVAL: Cinéma Laval (12); MONTREAL: Centre Eaton (6), Loew's (5), Palace (6), Paramount, Montreal (12) plus a 3D IMAX, Versailles (6), Parisien (7); POINTE-CLAIRE: Famous Players 8 (8); QUEBEC CITY: Les Galéries Capitale (12); SHERBROOKE: Carrefour de l'Estrie (3).

NEW BRUNSWICK: MONCTON: Moncton 8 (8); SAINT JOHN: Paramount (2).

NOVA SCOTIA: DARTMOUTH: Penhorn (5); HALIFAX: Park Lane (8).

FESTIVAL CINEMAS

Head Office: 2236 Queen St. E., Toronto, ON M4E 1G2. (416) 690-0667. FAX: (416) 690-0755.
PRINCIPALS
Tom Litvinskas
Jerry Szczur

GALAXY ENTERTAINMENT, INC.

745 Mt. Pleasant Rd., Toronto, ON M4S 2N4. (416) 481-1186. FAX: (416) 481-5244.
PRESIDENT
Norman Stern
ADMINISTRATION/BOOKING
Shellie Goldberg
ADVERTISING/CONCESSIONS
Cindy Morris
ACCOUNTING/OPERATIONS
Wendy Ciampaglia

ONTARIO: BROCKVILLE: Parkedale (2); CORNWALL: Brookdale (3); GEORGETOWN: Cinema (3); OWEN SOUND: Owen Sound Cinema (5); PETERBOROUGH: Lansdowne (6); SAULT STE. MARIE: Station Cinema (7).

GALLERY CINEMAS, INC.

4351 Morgan Cres., W. Vancouver, BC V7V 2P1. (604) 922-3765. FAX: (604) 922-3725. email: info@gallerycinemas.com www.gallerycinemas.com/canada
PRESIDENT
Chris van Snellenberg

GALLERY CINEMAS (WOODSTOCK) INC.

15 Perry St., Woodstock, ON N4S 3C1. (519) 658-6920.
FILM BUYER
Eric Ball

GOLDEN CLASSICS CINEMA, INC.

186 Spadina Ave., Toronto, ON M5T 2C2. (416) 504-0012. FAX: (416) 504-9869.
PRESIDENT
Jacob Cheung

OLDEN THEATRES, LTD.
c/o Central Parkway Mall Cinemas, 10 - 377 Burnhamthorpe Rd. E., Mississauga, ON L5A 3Y1. Tel. & FAX: (905) 896-7123.

HARRIS ROAD ENTERTAINMENT GROUP, LTD.
19190 Lougheed Highway, Pitt Meadows, BC V3Y 2H6. (604) 465-0528. FAX: (604) 485-0587.
PRESIDENT
Joanne Bondar
GENERAL MANAGER
Paul Bondar
BUSINESS MANAGER
Christine Keenan

LANDMARK CINEMAS OF CANADA, LTD.
522 - 11th.Ave. S.W., 4th Fl., Calgary, AB T2R 0C8. (403) 262-4255. FAX: (403) 266-1529.
DIRECTORS
Hector H. Ross
Philip H. May
Frank Kettner
Charles D. K. May
Barry Myers
Brian F. McIntosh
CHAIRMAN
Hector H. Ross
PRESIDENT
Brian F. McIntosh
SECRETARY
Philip H. May
VICE PRESIDENTS
Frank Kettner
Charles D. K. May
Barry Myers.
MANAGER, CONSTRUCTION & DEVELOPMENT
D.C. (Chuck) Bradley
OPERATIONS MANAGERS
Kevin Graham
Geoff Linquist
MANAGER, FILM BUYING & BOOKING
Kevin Norman
MANAGER, ADVERTISING & CREATIVE SERVICES
Donald D. Langkaas
MANAGER, MARKETING & PROMOTION
Gordon Imlach
ACCOUNTING MANAGER
Ian Harwood
ADMINISTRATION MANAGER
Sherry Chappell

BRITISH COLUMBIA: ABBOTSFORD: Towne Cinema Centre (9); CAMPBELL RIVER: Galaxy (2); CHILLIWACK: Paramount Theatre (2); COURTENAY: Rialto Theatre (4); CRANBROOK: Armond Theatre (2), Columbia Theatre (5); DAWSON CREEK: Centre Cinema (1); FORT ST. JOHN: Lido Theatre (1); KAMLOOPS: Northills Theatre (1), Paramount Theatre (2); KELOWNA: Paramount Theatre (3), Uptown Cinema Centre (2); NANAIMO: Avalon Cinemas (3), The Bay Theatre (2); PENTICTON: Pen-Mar Cinema Centre (4); PORT ALBERNI: Paramount Theatre (1); VICTORIA: Vic Theatre (1).

YUKON: WHITEHORSE: The Qwanlin Cinema Centre (2) The Yukon Theatre (2).

ALBERTA: AIRDRIE: Roxy Theatre (2); BANFF: Lux Cinema Centre (4); BROOKS: Oasis Theatre (1); CALGARY: Globe Cinema (2); EDMONTON: Jasper Cinema Centre (2); EDSON: Nova Theatre (1); GRANDE PRAIRIE: Jan Cinema (3), Lyric Theatre (3); HINTON: Roxy Theatre (1); MEDICINE HAT: Monarch Theatre (1), Towne Cinema Centre (3); REDCLIFF: Gemini Drive-In (1); RED DEER: Uptown Cinema Centre (4); SHERWOOD PARK: Sword & Shield Cinema Centre (4); STETTLER: Jewel Theatre (1).

SASKATCHEWAN: REGINA: Cinema `6' Drive-In (2), WEYBURN: Soo Theatre (1); YORKTON: Tower Theatre (1).

MANITOBA: BRANDON: Capitol Theatre (4), Strand Theatre (1); SELKIRK: Garry Theatre (1); WINNIPEG: Towne 8 (8).

MAGIC LANTERN THEATRES
14306 - 115 Ave., P.O.Box 3707, Stn. D, Edmonton, AB T5L 4J7. (780) 482-1611. FAX: (780) 482-3520.
PRESIDENT
Tom Hutchinson
SECRETARY
Bill Booth

ALBERTA: CAMROSE: Duggan Cinemas (5); EDMONTON: Garneau (1); PEACE RIVER: Cinema 72 (2); ST. PAUL: Elite (3), Princess (2); SPRUCE GROVE: Magic Lantern (1); WHITECOURT: Vista (1).

SASKATCHEWAN: REGINA: Rainbow Cinemas (9); SASKATOON: Rainbow Cinemas (8).

MANITOBA: WINKLER: Southline Cinemas (5).

MAGIC THEATRES, INC.
1564 Wyandotte St. E, Windsor, ON N9A 3L2. (519) 977-7700. FAX: (519) 974-9265.
PRESIDENT
Jim Shaban

MAY THEATRES, INC.
4905 - 50 Ave., Lloydminster, SK S9V 0P7. (306) 825-3884. FAX: (306) 825-6172.
PRESIDENT
Phil May

THE MOVIE MILL, INC.
1710 Mayor Magrath Dr. S., Lethbridge, AB T1K 2R6. (403) 381-1251. FAX: (403) 381-1256. www.moviemill.com
email: themill@moviemill.com
PRESIDENT
Leonard Binning

MULTIPLEX CINEMAS OF CANADA, LTD.
369 Yonge St., Toronto, ON M5B 1S1. (416) 860-2600. FAX: (905) 707-1636.
CONTACT
Marvin Miller

NIAGARA PALACE THEATRES, LTD.
Operating Town Cinemas, 280 St. Paul St., St. Catharines, ON L2R 3M9. (905) 685-3456. FAX: (905) 682-8244.
PRESIDENT
Arthur Lefstein

OAKBURN INVESTMENTS, LTD.
Consky Theatres, 425 Walmer Rd., Unit 6A, Toronto, ON M5P 2X9. (416) 515-8506.
PRESIDENT
Lou Consky

ONTARIO CINEMAS, INC.
745 Mt. Pleasant Rd., Toronto, ON M4S 2N4. (416) 481-1186.
PRESIDENT
Norman Stern (Ext. 300)
FILM OPERATIONS
Dale Doody (Ext. 223)

ONTARIO: COBURG: Coburg (3); LINDSAY: Lindsay (3).

PREMIER OPERATING CORPORATION, LIMITED
1262 Don Mills Rd., Ste. 92, Don Mills, ON M3B 2W7. (416) 443-1645. FAX: (416) 443-1760.
PRESIDENT
Barry Allen

THE PRINCESS CINEMA, INC.
6 Princess St., Waterloo, ON N2L 2X8. (519) 885-2950.
OWNER
John Tutt

RPL FILM THEATRE
Central Library, 2311 - 12th Ave., Regina, SK S4P 3Z5. (306) 777-6104. FAX: (306) 777-6221. www.rpl.regina.sk.ca
PROGRAMMER
Belinda New

SLIDE SCREEN ENTERTAINMENT, INC.
61 Renwick Ave., Cambridge, ON N3C 2T5. Business Office: (519) 658-6920, Sales Office: (519) 496-6920. FAX: (519) 658-5684.
PRESIDENT
Eric Ball

STINSON THEATRES, LTD.
Box 142, Barrie, ON L4M 4S9. (705) 726-8190. (705) 721-9579.
PRESIDENT
Robert Stinson
BOOKER/BUYER
Cathy Watson

ONTARIO: BARRIE: Barrie Triple Drive-In (3), Imperial Cinema 8 (8); CHATHAM: Cinema Six (6); COLLINGWOOD: Cinema Four (4); HUNTSVILLE: Capitol Theatre (2); ORANGEVILLE: Uptown Cinemas (2); ORILLIA: Orillia Cinema Four (4); OWEN SOUND: Twin Drive-In (2); TIMMINS: Cinema Six (6).

TARRANT ENTERPRISES LIMITED
56 Charles St., Newmarket, ON L3Y 3V9. (905) 898-4072. FAX: (905) 898-7629.
PRESIDENT
June Tarrant

ONTARIO: GUELPH: 3-Star (6); NEWMARKET: Film Factory (6); PICKERING: MoVIPlex 9 (9); ST. THOMAS: Capitol (3); TRENTON: Centre (3).

TILLSONBURG BROADWAY CINEMAS, INC.
518 Broadway North, Tillsonburg, ON N4G 3S7. (519) 688-0923. FAX: (519) 688-2362.
PRESIDENT
Cam McKnight

INDEPENDENT BOOKING COMPANIES

ATLANTIC THEATRE SERVICES, LTD.
P.O. Box 2419, 114 Dresden Ave., Saint John, NB E2L 3V9. (506) 696-6618. FAX: (506) 696-4472.

INDEPENDENT BOOKING & THEATRE SERVICES, LTD.
61 Renwick Ave., Cambridge, ON N3C 2T5. (519) 658-6920. FAX: (519) 658-5684.
PRESIDENT
Eric Ball

PRAIRIE ALLIED BOOKING ASSOCIATION
A division of Theatre Agencies Ltd., 522 - 11th Ave. S.W., Calgary, AB T2R 0C8. (403) 264-4660. FAX: (403) 264-6571.
CONTACTS
Frank Kettner
Ellen Smeltzer
Donna Campbell

THUNDER NORTH BROADCAST SERVICES
39 Baywood Rd., Toronto, ON M9V 3Y8. (416) 745-6533. FAX: (416) 745-7179. email: thnorth@aol.com
VICE PRESIDENT
Ronald Convey

WEST COAST THEATRE SERVICE, LTD.
788 Beatty St., Ste. 401, Vancouver, BC V6B 1A2. (604) 669-4738. FAX: (604) 669-9640.
CONTACTS
Doug Isman
Hector Ross

FILM CARRIERS

EMERY WORLDWIDE
Pearson International Airport, 6500 Silverdart Dr., Toronto, ON L5P 1B1. Information: (905) 676-0488. Sales & Administration: (905) 676-8872. FAX: (905) 673-5761.
SALES MANAGER
Barbara Williams

Branches: Calgary (403) 221-1981, Dorval (514) 636-1333, Edmonton (403) 890-4475, Halifax (902) 873-3545, London (519) 452-0088, Ottawa (613) 733-9650, Regina (306) 352-9046, Saskatoon (306) 931-1110, Vancouver (604) 273-9077, Winnipeg (204) 775-2676.

RUSSELL A. FARROW LIMITED
5397 Eglinton Ave. W., Ste. 220, Etobicoke, ON M9C 5K6 (416) 622-3777. FAX: (416) 622-2217.

5200 Miller Rd., Ste. 2040, Vancouver International Airport, Richmond, BC V7B 1K5 (604) 270-3131. FAX: (604) 270-9741.

751 Stewart Graham Blvd. N., Ste. 118, Dorval, QC H4Y 1E7 (514) 636-1941. FAX: (514) 636-3222.

MAVETY FILM DELIVERY
40 Lesmill Rd., Don Mills, ON M3B 2T5. (416) 447-5169.
GENERAL MANAGER
Jim Matsumoto

SAMEDAY RIGHT-O-WAY
6975 Menkes Dr., Mississauga, ON L5S 1Y2. (905) 676-1888 (Pickup), (905) 677-9722 (Customer Service).
VICE PRESIDENT/GENERAL MANAGER
Bob Brogan

VICTORIA FILM SERVICES LIMITED
40 Lesmill Rd., Don Mills, ON M3B 2T5 (416) 449-8597.
PRESIDENT
Paul Wroe
CANADIAN GENERAL MANAGER
Jim Matsumoto

1644 W. 75th Ave., Vancouver, BC V6P 6G2 (604) 263-2551.
MANAGER
Rick Williston

3904 - 1st St. N.E., Calgary, AB T2E 3E3 (403) 276-6696.
MANAGER
Susan Piotrowski

2315 Logan Ave., Winnipeg, MB R2R 2S7 (204) 633-1203.
MANAGER
Ben Adleman

708 rue Walnut, Montréal, QC H4C 2M4 (514) 931-6212.
MANAGER
Marie-Claude Boudreau

55 Bentley St., St. John, NB E2K 1B2 (506) 634-1018.
MANAGER
Kevin McDermott

THEATRE ASSOCIATIONS

ASSOCIATION DES PROPRIETAIRES DE CINEMA ET CINE-PARCS DU QUEBEC, INC.
6727 de Châteaubriând, Montréal, QC H2S 2N9. (514) 278-3458. FAX: (514) 274-7311. email: alexfilm@microtec.net
EXECUTIVE DIRECTOR
Carole Boudreault

ATLANTIC INDEPENDENT THEATRE EXHIBITORS ASSN.
P.O. Box 2419, Saint John, NB E2L 3V9. (506) 696-6618.
PRESIDENT
Don McKelvie

ATLANTIC MOTION PICTURE EXHIBITORS ASSOCIATION
c/o Empire Theatres Limited, 190 Chain Lake Dr., Halifax, NS B3S 1C5. (902) 876-4848. FAX: (902) 876-4849.
PRESIDENT
Dean Leland

MOTION PICTURE THEATRE ASSOCIATIONS OF CANADA
146 Bloor St. W., Toronto, ON M5S 1P3. (416) 969-7057. FAX: (416) 964-5839. www.mptac.ca
email: mptac@inforamp.net
EXECUTIVE DIRECTOR
Dina Lebo
PRESIDENT
Dennis Kucherawy

MOTION PICTURE THEATRE ASSOCIATION OF B.C.
Ridge Theatre, 3131 Arbutus St., Vancouver, BC V6J 3Z3. (604) 732-3352.
PRESIDENT
Ray Mainland

MOTION PICTURE THEATRE ASSOCIATION OF ALBERTA
May Theatres Ltd., 4905 - 50 Ave., Lloydminster, SK S9V 0P7. (306) 825-3884. FAX: (306) 825-6172.
PRESIDENT
Michael May

MOTION PICTURE THEATRE ASSOCIATION OF SASKATCHEWAN
c/o Rainbow Theatres, 3806 Albert St., Golden Mile Centre, Regina, SK S4S 3R2. (306) 359-6353. FAX: (306) 359-6362.
PRESIDENT
Wilf Runge

MOTION PICTURE THEATRE ASSOCIATION OF MANITOBA
c/o Cinema Services, Canada, 31 Parkview Rd, St. Andrews, MB R1A 3B7. (204) 339-9190. FAX: (204) 339-6015.
email: cineserve@escape.ca
PRESIDENT
Florence Watson

MOTION PICTURE THEATRES ASSOCIATION OF ONTARIO
21 Dundas Sq., Ste. 906, Toronto, ON M5B 1B7. (416) 368-1139. FAX: (416) 368-1130.
PRESIDENT
Norman Stern

TRADE ASSOCIATIONS

ACADEMY OF CANADIAN CINEMA AND TELEVISION
Annual Genie, Gemini, and Gémeaux Awards, as well as year-round educational, professional development and promotional services and programs, publications, information and research.
National Office
172 King St. E., Toronto, ON M5A 1J3. (416) 366-2227, (800) 644-5194. FAX: (416) 366-8454. www.academy.ca
PRESIDENT & CEO
Maria Topalovich
MANAGING DIRECTOR
Jeanette Slinger
DIRECTOR OF FINANCE & DEVELOPMENT
Cynthia Dron
MEMBERSHIP MANAGER
Francis Domingue
SENIOR MANAGER, PROGRAMMING
Carmen Celestini
PROGRAM COORDINATOR
Jennifer Enright
SPECIAL PROJECTS COORDINATOR
Christine Maloney

Montreal: 3575 boul. St-Laurent, bur. 709, Montréal, QC H2X 2T7. (514) 849-7448. FAX: (514) 849-5069.
DIRECTOR
Patrice Lachance
AWARDS COORDINATOR
Jocelyne Dorris

Vancouver: 1385 Homer St., Vancouver, BC V6B 5M9. (604) 684-4528. FAX: (604) 684-4574.
MANAGER, WESTERN DIVISION
Judy Jackson-Rink

ACTRA PERFORMERS GUILD (CLC, FIA)
National Office: 2239 Yonge St., Toronto, ON M4S 2B5. (416) 489-1311, (800) 387-3516. FAX: (416) 489-8076.
www.actra.com email: apg@actra.com
NATIONAL EXECUTIVE DIRECTOR
Stephen Waddell
DIRECTOR, FINANCE & ADMINISTRATION
Anna Bucci
DIRECTOR, MANAGEMENT INFORMATION SERVICES
Bernie F. Metzner
NATIONAL PRESIDENT
Brian Gromoff

Union of B.C. Performers, 400 - 856 Homer St., Vancouver, BC V6B 2W5. (604) 689-0727. FAX: (604) 689-1145.

ACTRA Southern Alberta, Mount Royal Place, 1414 - 8th St. S.W., Ste. 260., Calgary, AB T2R 1J6. (403) 228-3123. FAX: (403) 228-3299. www.actracalgary.com
email: actra@telusplanet.net

ACTRA Northern Alberta, 10324-82nd Ave., Edmonton, AB T6E 1Z8. (403) 433-4090. FAX: (403) 433-4099.
email: actraedm@ab.sympatico.ca

ACTRA Saskatchewan, 212 - 1808 Smith St., Regina, SK S4P 2N4. (306) 757-0885. FAX: (306) 359-0044.
email: actrask@sk.sympatico.ca

ACTRA Winnipeg, Phoenix Building, 110 - 388 Donald St., Winnipeg, MB R3B 2J4. (204) 943-1307. FAX: (204) 947-5664.
email: actrawin@mb.sympatico.ca

ACTRA Toronto, 2239 Yonge St., Toronto, ON M4S 2B5. (416) 489-1311. FAX: (416) 489-1435. email: atp@actra.com

ACTRA Ottawa, 1A Springfield Rd., Ottawa, ON K1M 1C8. (613) 742-7720. FAX: (613) 742-8211.
email: actraott@sympatico.ca

ACTRA Montréal, 530 - 1450 City Councillors St., Montréal, QC H3A 2E6. (514) 844-3318. FAX: (514) 844-2068.
email: actramtl@sympatico.ca

ACTRA Maritimes, 103 - 1660 Hollis St., Halifax, NS B3J 1V7. (902) 420-1404. FAX: (902) 422-0589.
email: actramar@ns.sympatico.ca

ACTRA Newfoundland/Labrador, 127 Queen's Rd., P.O. Box 575, St. John's, NF A1C 5K8. (709) 722-0430. FAX: (709) 722-2113. email: actranfld@nf.sympatico.ca

ACTRA Performers' Rights Society (PRS), 2239 Yonge St., Toronto, ON M4S 2B5. (416) 489-1311, (800) 387-3516. FAX: (416) 489-8076. email: prs@actra.com

ACTRA Fraternal Benefit Society, 1000 Yonge St., Toronto, ON M4W 2K2. (416) 967-6600, (800) 387-8897. FAX: (416) 967-4744.
email: benefits@actrafrat.com

ALBERTA MOTION PICTURE INDUSTRIES ASSOCIATION
Ste. 606, Merrill Lynch Tower, Edmonton Centre, Edmonton, AB T5J 2Z2. (780) 944-0707. FAX: (780) 426-3057.
www.ampia.org email: ampia@compusmart.ab.ca
EXECUTIVE DIRECTOR
Leon Lubin
PRESIDENT
Josh Miller

ALBERTA RECORDING INDUSTRIES ASSOCIATION (ARIA)
Ste. 1205 Energy Sq., 10109 - 106 St., Edmonton, AB T5J 3L7. (780) 428-3372, (800) 465-3117. FAX: (780) 426-0188.
www.aria.ab.ca email: albrek@telusplanet.net
EXECUTIVE DIRECTOR
Maryanne Gibson

ALLIANCE FOR CHILDREN & TELEVISION (ACT)
60 St. Clair Ave. E., Ste. 1002, Toronto, ON M4T 1N5. (416) 515-0466. FAX: (416) 515-0467. www.act-canada.com
email: acttv@interlog.com
NATIONAL DIRECTOR
Kealy Wilkinson
DIRECTOR, PROJECTS & OPERATIONS
Rebecca Shay

AMERICAN FEDERATION OF MUSICIANS OF THE UNITED STATES & CANADA (AFM)
75 The Donway West, Ste. 1010, Don Mills, ON M3C 2E9. (416) 391-5161. FAX: (416) 391-5165.
email: afmcan@ican.net
PRESIDENT
Emile Subirana
VICE PRESIDENT, CANADA
David J. Jandrisch

ASIFA-CANADA/ASSOCIATION INTERNATIONALE DU FILM D'ANIMATION
CP 5226, St-Laurent, QC H4L 4Z8. FAX: (514) 496-1895.
PRESIDENT
Marcel Jean
CONTACT
Lucie Charbonneau (514) 283-9806

ASSOCIATION DES PRODUCTEURS DE FILMS ET DE TELEVISION DU QUEBEC (APFTQ)
740 St-Maurice, bur. 400, Montréal, QC H3C 1L5. (514) 397-8600. FAX: (514) 392-0232.
www.quebec.audiovisuel.com/engl/core.asp
PRÉSIDENTE/DIRECTRICE-GÉNÉRALE
Claire Samson

ASSOCIATION DES REALISATEURS ET REALISATRICES DU QUEBEC
3480 rue Saint-Denis, Montréal, QC H2X 3L3. (514) 842-7373. FAX: (514) 842-6789. www.quebec.audiovisuel.com
email: realiser@arrq.qc.ca
PRÉSIDENT
Phillip Bay Laucq

ASSOCIATION OF BRITISH COLUMBIA ANIMATION PRODUCERS (ABCAP)
101-480 Smithe St., Vancouver, BC C6B 5E4. (604) 689-0702. FAX: (604) 689-0715.
PRESIDENT
Mark Freedman
VICE PRESIDENT
Chris Delaney
MEMBER'S LIAISON
Chris Bartelman

ASSOCIATION QUEBECOISE DES CRITIQUES DE CINEMA (AQCC)
C.P. 1134, Succ. Place d'Armes, 435 rue Saint-Antoine Ouest, Montréal, QC H2Z 1H0. (514) 847-0178.
email: phlgaj@odyssee.net
PRESIDENT
Philippe Gajan

BLACK FILM AND VIDEO NETWORK
2 College St., Ste. 213, Toronto, ON M5G 1K3. (416) 925-2407. FAX: (416) 925-7820. www.bfvn.com
email: bfvn@interlog.com
PRESIDENT
David Sealy
EXECUTIVE DIRECTOR
Elizabeth Kerr

CANADIAN ACTORS' EQUITY ASSOCIATION
44 Victoria St., 12th Fl., Toronto, ON M5C 3C4. (416) 867-9165. FAX: (416) 867-9246.
EXECUTIVE DIRECTOR
Susan Wallace

CANADIAN ASSOCIATION OF BROADCASTERS (CAB)
P.O. Box 627, Stn. B, Ottawa, ON K1P 5S2. (613) 233-4035. FAX: (613) 233-6961. www.cab-acr.ca
PRESIDENT & CEO
Michael McCabe

CANADIAN ASSOCIATION OF FILM DISTRIBUTORS AND EXPORTERS/
30 Chemin des trilles, Laval, QC H7Y 1K2. (450) 689-9950. FAX: (450) 689-9822. email: cic@total.net
CO-CHAIRMEN/PRESIDENT
Victor Loewy
Stephen Greenberg
PRESIDENT/CEO
Richard J. Paradis
SECRETARY/SECRÉTAIRE
Helena Cynamon
TREASURER/TRÉSORIER
Michel Mosca

CANADIAN BROADCASTERS RIGHTS AGENCY, INC.
155 Queen St., Ste. 1204, Ottawa, ON K1P 6L1. Mailing address: Box 1196, Stn. B, Ottawa, ON K1P 5R2. (613) 232-4370. FAX: (613) 236-9241. email: tscap@cbra.ca
EXECUTIVE DIRECTOR
Tony Scapillati

CANADIAN BROADCAST STANDARDS COUNCIL (CBSC)
P.O. Box 3265, Stn. D, Ottawa, ON K1P 6H8. (613) 233-4607. FAX: (613) 238-1734. www.cbsc.ca
email: info@cbsc.ca
NATIONAL CHAIR
Ron Cohen

CANADIAN CABLE TELEVISION ASSOCIATION
360 Albert St., Ste. 1010, Ottawa, ON K1R 7X7. (613) 232-2631. FAX: (613) 232-2137. www.ccta.ca
PRESIDENT & CEO
Janet Yale
VICE PRESIDENT, LEGAL & REGULATORY AFFAIRS
Chris Taylor
VICE PRESIDENT, REGULATORY AFFAIRS
Michéle Beck
VICE PRESIDENT, ECONOMIC RESEARCH
Suzanne Blackwell
VICE PRESIDENT, INDUSTRY RELATIONS
Harris Boyd
VICE PRESIDENT, REGULATORY ENGINEERING
Michéle Beck
DIRECTOR, POLICY & REGULATORY RESEARCH
Mary Lemon
DIRECTOR, CONVENTIONS & MEETINGS
Christiane Thompson
MANAGER, RESEARCH
Lisa Pirie
COMMUNITY CHANNEL COORDINATORS
Virginie Mongeon
Raymonde Rochon

Toronto Office: 333 Bloor St. E., 8th Fl., Toronto, ON M4W 1G9. (416) 935-4771. FAX: (416) 935-4773.
EXECUTIVE DIRECTOR
Roy O'Brien

CANADIAN FILM AND TELEVISION PRODUCTION ASSOCIATION (CFTPA)/
151 Slater St., Ste. 605, Ottawa, ON K1P 5H3. (613) 233-1444/(800) 656-7440. FAX: (613) 233-0073.
email: ottawa@cftpa.ca

20 Toronto St., Ste. 830, Toronto, ON M5C 2B8. (416) 304-0280, (800) 267-8208. FAX: (416) 304-0499.
email: toronto@cftpa.ca

BC Producers Branch: 1140 Homer St.. Ste. 250, Vancouver, BC V6B 2X6. (604) 682-8619. FAX: (604) 684-9294.
email: vancouvr.@cftpa.ca

CANADIAN INDEPENDENT FILM CAUCUS (CIFC)
National Office/Toronto Chapter: 337-517 College St., Toronto, ON M6G 4A2. (416) 599-3844. FAX: (416) 599-0187.
email: cifc@tvo.org
EXECUTIVE DIRECTOR
Michale Raske

Quebec Chapter: 201 - 4067 St. Laurent, Montréal, QC H2W 1Y2. (514) 426-1431. FAX: (514) 426-6696.
email: turek@aei.ca
CONTACT
Laura Turek

Atlantic Chapter: 2103 Bauer St., Halifax, NS B3K 3W4. (902) 422-1337. FAX: (902) 422-4586. email: clapp@istar.ca
CO-CHAIRS
Chuck Lapp
Connie Littlefield

B.C. Chapter: 137-2906 West Broadway, Vancouver, BC V6K 2G8. email: cifcvancouver@canada.com
CO-CHAIRS
Brian Hamilton and Cari Green

CANADIAN INDEPENDENT RECORD PRODUCTION ASSOCIATION (CIRPA)
214 King St. W., Ste. 614, Toronto, ON M5H 3S6. (416) 593-1665. FAX: (416) 593-7563. www.cirpa.ca
email: cirpa@cirpa.ca
PRESIDENT
Brian Chater

CANADIAN MEDIA GUILD
144 Front St. W., Ste. 300, Toronto, ON M5J 2L7. (416) 591-5333. FAX: (416) 591-7278. www.cmg.ca
email: guild@interlog.com
PRESIDENT
Lise Lareau
STAFF REPRESENTATIVES
Dan Oldfield
Kathy Viner
Keith Maskell
Bruce May
Glenn Gray
Gabi Durocher
Gerry Whelan

CANADIAN MOTION PICTURE DISTRIBUTORS ASSOCIATION (CMPDA)
22 St. Clair Ave. E., Ste. 1603, Toronto, ON M4T 2S4. (416) 961-1888. FAX: (416) 968-1016.
MEMBER COMPANIES
Buena Vista Pictures Distribution Canada, Inc.
Columbia Pictures of Canada Ltd.
Disney
MGM/UA Entertainment of Canada
Paramount Production Picture Corp. (Canada) Ltd.
Twentieth Century-Fox (Canada) Ltd.
Universal Films (Canada)
Warner Brothers Distributing (Canada) Ltd.
PRESIDENT
Hon. D.C. Frith, P.C.
BOARD OF DIRECTORS
W. Baker
J. Collins
Bernard Mayer
COMMITTEE CHAIRMEN
Phil Carlton
Derek Forster

CANADIAN MUSICAL REPRODUCTION RIGHTS AGENCY (CMRRA)
56 Wellesley St. W., Ste. 320, Toronto, ON M5S 2S3. (416) 926-1966. FAX: (416) 926-7521. www.cmrra.ca
email: inquiries@cmrra.ca
PRESIDENT
David A. Basskin

CANADIAN RETRANSMISSION COLLECTIVE (CRC)/
20 Toronto St., Ste. 830, Toronto, ON M5C 2B8. (416) 304-0290. FAX: (416) 304-0496. www.crc-scrc.ca
email: info@crc-scrc.ca
EXECUTIVE DIRECTOR
Carol J. Cooper

CANADIAN RETRANSMISSION RIGHT ASSOCIATION (CRRA)
c/o CBC/SRC, P.O. Box 3220, Stn. C, Ottawa, ON K1Y 1E4. Law Operations: (613) 724-5373. FAX: (613) 724-5453. Accounting Operations: (613) 737-0648. FAX: (613) 737-0766.
CONTACT
Teresa Mendes

CANADIAN SOCIETY OF CINEMATOGRAPHERS (CSC)
3007 Kingston Rd., Ste. 131, Toronto, ON M1M 1P1. (416) 266-0591. FAX: (416) 266-3996.
PRESIDENT
Joan Hutton, csc
VICE PRESIDENT
Richard Stringer, csc
SECRETARY
David Greene, csc
TREASURER
Joseph Sunday
MEMBERSHIP
Philip Earnshaw, csc
EDUCATION
Harry Lake, csc
PUBLIC RELATIONS
Bill Metcalfe

CANADIAN WOMEN IN COMMUNICATIONS/
67 Yonge St., Ste. 804, Toronto, ON M5E 1J8. (416) 363-1880. FAX: (416) 363-1882. email: cwc.afc@sympatico.ca
PRESIDENT
Stephanie MacKendrick

CASTING DIRECTORS OF CANADA (CDC)
119 Oakwood Ave., Toronto, ON M6H 2W1. (416) 658-8455. FAX: (416) 658-8572.
CO-CHAIRS
Tina Gerussi
Diane Kerbel

COPYRIGHT COLLECTIVE OF CANADA (CCC)
22 St. Clair Ave. E., Ste. 1603, Toronto, ON M4T 2S4. (416) 961-1888. FAX: (416) 968-1016.
VICE PRESIDENT
Susan Peacock

DIRECTORS GUILD OF CANADA
National Office: 1 Eglinton Ave. E., Ste. 604, Toronto, ON M4P 3A1. (416) 482-6640, (888) 972-0098. FAX: (416) 486-6639. Calgary: (403) 244-3456; Vancouver: (604) 688-2976; Atlantic Region: (902) 492-3424; Toronto: (416) 925-8200; Montréal: (514) 844-4084; Regina: (306) 757-8000; Manitoba: (204) 946-0913. www.dgc.ca email: mail@dgc.ca
PRESIDENT
Alan Goluboff

FEMA - FILM & ELECTRONIC MEDIA ASSOCIATION
P.O. Box 308, London, ON N6P 1P9. (519) 850-3000. FAX: (519) 652-1541. www.fema.on.ca email: info@fema.on.ca
PRESIDENT
Wendy Nesseth

THE FILM CREW ASSOCIATION OF NEWFOUNDLAND (FilmCAN)
P.O. Box 1602, Stn. C, St. John's, NF A1C 5P3. (709) 726-1501. FAX: (709) 726-4338. www.newcomm.net/filmcan
email: filmcrew@seascape.com
ADMINISTRATOR
Glenys Moss

FILM PRODUCERS ASSN. OF NEWFOUNDLAND (PAN)
155 Water St., P.O. Box 72, St. John's, NF A1C 5H5. (709) 579-2308. FAX: (709) 579-2386. www.pan.nf.ca
email: pan@nfld.com

THE GUILD OF CANADIAN FILM COMPOSERS
Box 291, 275 King St. E., Toronto, ON M5A 1K2. (416) 484-4091. FAX: (416) 484-7409
PRESIDENT
Paul Hoffert
VICE PRESIDENT
Glenn Morley

IATSE - INTERNATIONAL ALLIANCE OF THEATRICAL STAGE EMPLOYEES, MOVING PICTURE TECHNICIANS, ARTISTS AND ALLIED CRAFTS OF THE UNITED STATES, ITS TERRITORIES AND CANADA
Canadian Office: 258 Adelaide St. E., Ste. 403, Toronto, ON M5A 1N1. (416) 362-3569/ FAX: (416) 362-3483.
INTERNATIONAL VICE PRESIDENT
James B. Wood

INDEPENDENT FILM AND VIDEO ALLIANCE
4550 Garnier, Montréal, QC H2J 3S7. (514) 522-8240. FAX: (514) 522-8011. www.culturenet.ca/ifva
email: ifva@cam.org
NATIONAL CO-ORDINATOR
Peter Sandmark

MANITOBA MOTION PICTURE INDUSTRIES ASSN.
304 - 100 Arthur St., Winnipeg, MB R3B 1H4. (204) 949-8869. FAX: (204) 947-9290. www.mmpia.mb.ca
email: info@mmpia.mb.ca
PRESIDENT
Phyllis Laing
EXECUTIVE DIRECTOR
Richard Horne

MOTION PICTURE THEATRE ASSOCIATIONS OF CANADA
146 Bloor St. W., 2nd Fl., Toronto, ON M5S 1P3. (416) 969-7057. FAX: (416) 969-9852. www.mptac.ca
email: mptac@inforamp.net
PRESIDENT
Ton Kars

MUSIC & ENTERTAINMENT INDUSTRY EDUCATORS ASSOCIATION
451 St-Jean St., Montréal, QC H2Y 2R5. (514) 845-4141.
CONTACT
David Leonard

MUSIC INDUSTRY ASSOCIATION OF NEWFOUNDLAND AND LABRADOR (MIA)
155 Water St., St. John's, NF A1C 1B3. (709) 754-2574. FAX: (709) 754-5758. www.mia.nf.ca
email: dparker@nfld.com
PRESIDENT
Roger Skinner
EXECUTIVE DIRECTOR
Denis Parker

MUSIC INDUSTRY ASSOCIATION OF NOVA SCOTIA (MIANS)
P.O. Box 122 Central, Halifax, NS B3J 2M4. (902) 423-6271, (888) 343-6426. FAX: (902) 423-8841.

NATIONAL ASSOCIATION OF BROADCAST EMPLOYEES & TECHNICIANS/ASSOCIATION OF FILM CRAFTSPEOPLE LOCAL 700 (NABET/AFC)
Toronto: 1179-A King St. W., Studio 102, Toronto, ON M6K 3C5. (416) 536-4827. FAX: (416) 536-0859.
www.nabet700.com
BUSINESS REPRESENTATIVE
Conor O'Sullivan

NEW BRUNSWICK PRODUCERS' ASSOCIATION
140 Botsford St., Ste. 20, Moncton, NB E1C 4X4.
CONTACT & PRESIDENT
Cécile Chevrier, (506) 857-9941
VICE PRESIDENT
Barry Cameron

NORTH AMERICAN BROADCASTERS ASSOCIATION (NABA)
P.O. Box 500, Stn. A, Toronto, ON M5W 1E6. (416) 598-9877. FAX: (416) 598-9774. www.nabanet.com
email: info@nabanet.com
SECRETARY GENERAL
Bill Roberts

NOVA SCOTIA FILM & VIDEO PRODUCERS ASSOCIATION (NSPA)
1496 Lower Water St., Box 36, Brewery Market, Halifax, NS B3J 1R9. (902) 492-7172. FAX: (902) 425-8851.
www.canadaweb.com/nspa email: nspa@ra.isisnet.com

QUICKDRAW ANIMATION SOCIETY
#201 - 351 11th Ave., S.W., Calgary, AB T2R 0C7. (403) 261-5767. FAX: (403) 261-5644. www.awn.com/qas
email: qas@home.com

SASKATCHEWAN MOTION PICTURE ASSOCIATION (SMPIA)
2425 - 13th Ave., Ste. 200, Regina, SK S4P 0W1. (306) 525-9899. FAX: (306) 569-1818. www.smpia.sk.ca
email: smpia@sk.sympatico.ca
EXECUTIVE DIRECTOR
Rob Dewhirst

SOCAN/SOCIETY OF COMPOSERS, AUTHORS AND MUSIC PUBLISHERS OF CANADA
41 Valleybrook Dr., Toronto, ON M3B 2S6. (416) 445-8700, (800) 55 SOCAN. FAX: (416) 445-7108. www.socan.ca
GENERAL MANAGER
Michael Rock
MANAGER, LICENSING
Gina Pollock
MANAGER, MEMBER SERVICES
Lynne Foster

1201 W. Pender St., Ste. 400, Vancouver, BC V6E 2V2. (604) 669-5569, (800) 93 SOCAN. FAX: (604) 688-1142.

600 boul. de Maisonneuve O., bur. 500, Montréal, QC H3A 3J2. (514) 844-8377, (800) 79 SOCAN. FAX: (514) 849-8446.

1145 Weber Centre, 5555 Calgary Trail, Edmonton, AB T6H 5P9. (780) 439-9049, (800) 51 SOCAN. FAX: (780) 432-1555.

45 Alderney Dr., Ste. 802, Queen Sq., Dartmouth, NS B2Y 2N6. (902) 464-7000, (800) 70 SOCAN. FAX: (902) 464-9696.

SOCIETY OF MOTION PICTURE AND TELEVISION ENGINEERS (SMPTE)
SMPTE, Toronto Section: Fred Benedikt , c/o CBC, 250 Front St. W., Toronto, ON M5V 3G5. (416) 205-5787. FAX: (416) 205-8500. email: fred_benedikt@cbc.ca

SMPTE, Ottawa Section: Ross Mutton, c/o Carleton University, Instructional Media Service, Ottawa, ON K1S 5B6. (613) 520-3814. FAX: (613) 520-3928.

SMPTE, Montréal/Québec Section: Michel Yeon, TVA Inc. (514) 598-2855. FAX: (514) 598-6091. email: yeonm@tva.ca

SOCIÉTÉ DES AUTEURS DE RADIO, TÉLÉVISION ET CINEMA (SARTEC)
1229, rue Panet, Montreal, QC H2L 2V6 . (514) 526-9196. FAX: (514) 526-4124. www.micronet.net/sartec
PRESIDENT
Suzanne Aubry

SYNDICAT DES TECHNICIENNES ET TECHNICIENS DU CINEMA ET DE LA VIDEO DU QUEBEC (S.T.C.V.Q.)
4200 boul. St. Laurent, bur. 911, Montréal, QC H2W 2R2. (514) 985-5751. FAX: (514) 985-2227. www.stcvq.qc.ca
PRÉSIDENT
Bernard Aseneau
UNION REPRESENTATIVE
Pierre Lafrance
DIRECTOR
Catherine Louméde

UNION DES ARTISTES (UDA)
Siége Social, 3433 rue Stanley, Montréal, QC H3A 1S2. (514) 288-6682. FAX: (514) 288-1807.
PRÉSIDENT
Pierre Curzi
PREMIER VICE-PRÉSIDENT
Raymond Legault

WOMEN IN FILM AND TELEVISION - TORONTO
(WIFT-T)
2300 Yonge St., Ste. 405, Box 2386, Toronto, ON M4P 1E4. (416) 322-3430. FAX: (416) 322-3703.
EXECUTIVE DIRECTOR
Joan Jenkinson

WOMEN IN FILM & VIDEO VANCOUVER
1431 Howe St., Vancouver, BC V6B 1R9. (604) 685-1152. FAX: (604) 685-1124. www.canadafilm.com/wifvv/
email: wifvv@idmail.com
PRESIDENT
Joyce Thierry

WRITERS GUILD OF CANADA (WGC)
123 Edward St., Ste. 1225, Toronto, ON M5G 1E2. (416) 979-7907, (800) 567-9974. FAX: (416) 979-9273.
www.writersguildofcanada.com
email: info@writersguildofcanada.com
EXECUTIVE DIRECTOR
Maureen Parker

GOVERNMENT AGENCIES

FEDERAL

CANADIAN HERITAGE/LES TERRASSES DE LA CHAUDIÈRE
(The Film, Video and Sound Recording Policy and Program Section provides advice and assistance to the Minister of Canadian Heritage in the formulation and development of policies and programs for the achievement of cultural objectives in the area of film, video and sound recording.)
14 Eddy St., 4th Fl., Hull, QC KIA 0M5. (819) 997-5918. FAX: (819) 997-5709.
DIRECTOR
Jean-François Bernier
SECRETARY
Nathalie DuPont
CHIEF, FILM & VIDEO, FRENCH MARKET
Hélène Asselin

CANADIAN INTERNATIONAL DEVELOPMENT AGENCY (CIDA)
200 Promenade du Portage, Hull, QC K1A 0G4. (819) 997-1663.
DIRECTOR
Paul Turcotte

FOREIGN AFFAIRS AND INTERNATIONAL TRADE
Arts and Cultural Industries Promotion Division (ACA), 125 Sussex Dr., Ottawa, ON K1A 0G2. (613) 992-6104. FAX: (613) 992-5965.
DEPUTY DIRECTOR, CULTURAL INDUSTRIES
Luc Santerre
FILM & TELEVISION OFFICER
Sonya Thissen

THE NATIONAL FILM BOARD OF CANADA
Head Office: Constitution Sq., 360 Albert St., Ste. 1560, Ottawa, ON K1A 0M9.
Operational Headquarters: 3155 Côte de Liesse Rd., Ville Saint-Laurent, QC H4N 2N4.
Postal address: P.O. Box 6100, Stn. Centre-Ville, Montréal, QC H3C 3H5. (514) 283-9246. FAX: (514) 283-8971.
GOVERNMENT FILM COMMISSIONER AND CHAIRPERSON OF THE NFB
Sandra Macdonald, (514) 283-9244
DIRECTOR GENERAL, FRENCH PROGRAM
Andréanne Bournival, (514) 283-9285
DIRECTOR GENERAL, ENGLISH PROGRAM
Barbara Janes, (514) 283-9501

STATISTICS CANADA/STATISTIQUE CANADA
Culture, Tourism and The Centre for Education Statistics, R.H. Coats Building, 17th Fl., Ottawa, ON K1A 0T6. (613) 951-1569.
DIRECTOR
T. Scott Murray
ASSISTANT DIRECTOR
Brad Ruth
CHIEF, CULTURAL INDUSTRIES
John Gordon
RADIO & TV SENIOR ANALYST
Lotfi Chahdi
FILM & VIDEO SENIOR ANALYST
Michael Pedersen

TELEFILM CANADA/TÉLÉFILM CANADA
Head Office/Siège social: 360 St. Jacques St., Ste. 700, Montréal, QC H2Y 4A9. (514) 283-6363. FAX: (514) 283-8212.
www.telefilm.gc.ca
2 Bloor St. W., 22nd Fl., Toronto, ON M4W 3E2. (416) 973-6436. FAX: (416) 973-8606.
1684 Barrington St., 3rd Fl., Halifax, NS B3J 2A2. (902) 426-8425. FAX: (902) 426-4445.
310 - 440 Cambie St., Vancouver, BC V6B 2Z5. (604) 666-1566. FAX: (604) 666-7754.
CHAIRMAN
Laurier L. LaPierre, O.C. (Ottawa)
VICE CHAIRMAN
Jeanine C. Beaubien (Montréal)
OPERATIONS DIRECTOR
Peter Katadotis

PROVINCIAL

ALBERTA

ALBERTA FILM COMMISSION
2526 Battleford Ave. S.W., Ste. 111, Calgary, AB T3E 7J4. (403) 221-7868. FAX: (403) 221-7857.
PRESIDENT
Murray Ord

CALGARY FILM OFFICE
P.O. Box 2100, Stn. M (6), Calgary, AB T2P 2M5. (403) 221-7825. FAX: (403) 221-7857. email: bbasham@ceda.calgary.ab.ca
FILM SERVICES OFFICER
Brenda Basham

BRITISH COLUMBIA

BRITISH COLUMBIA FILM
2225 W. Broadway, Vancouver, BC V6K 2E4. (604) 736-7997. FAX: (604) 736-7290. www.bcfilm.bc.ca
PRESIDENT & CEO
Rob Egan

BRITISH COLUMBIA FILM COMMISSION
375 Water St., Ste. 350, Vancouver, BC V6B 5C6. (604) 660-2732. FAX: (604) 660-4790. www.bcfilmcommission.com
DIRECTOR
Mark DesRochers
LOCATIONS MANAGER
Tom Crowe

GREATER VICTORIA FILM COMMISSION
#210 - 931 Fort St., Victoria, BC V8V 3K3. (250) 386-3976. FAX: (250) 386-3967. www.members.home.net/islandfilm
FILM COMMISSIONER
Kate Petersen

MANITOBA

CITY OF WINNIPEG
Civic Centre, 3rd Fl., Administration Bldg., 510 Main St., Winnipeg, MB R3B 1B9. (204) 986-3058. FAX: (204) 986-3350.
email: kboyce@city.winnipeg.mb.ca
FILM & CULTURAL LIAISON/EPC SECRETARIAT
Kenny Boyce

MANITOBA FILM & SOUND
410 - 93 Lombard Ave., Winnipeg, MB R3B 3B1. (204) 947-2040. FAX: (204) 956-5261. www.mbfilmsound.mb.ca
email: explore@mbfilmsound.mb.ca
CEO AND FILM COMMISSIONER
Carole Vivier
FILM PROGRAM ADMINISTRATOR
Alexa Saborowski
LOCATIONS ASSISTANT
Dani Jubinville

NEW BRUNSWICK

NEW BRUNSWICK FILM/FILM NOUVEAU-BRUNSWICK

P.O. Box 5001, Moncton, NB E1C 8R3. (506) 869-6868. FAX: (506) 869-6840. www.gov.nb.ca/filmnb
email: filmnb@gov.nb.ca
EXECUTIVE DIRECTOR
Ray Wilson
FINANCIAL SERVICES
Ghislain Labbé
ADMINISTRATIVE ASSISTANT
Bernice LeBlanc
LOCATION SERVICES & MARKETING
Margo Flewelling

NEWFOUNDLAND & LABRADOR

NEWFOUNDLAND AND LABRADOR FILM DEVELOPMENT CORPORATION

197-199 Water St., St. John's, NF A1C 1B4. (709) 738-3456. FAX: (709) 739-1680. www.newfilm.nf.net
DIRECTOR OF PROGRAMS
Chris Bonnell

NOVA SCOTIA

NOVA SCOTIA FILM DEVELOPMENT CORPORATION

1724 Granville St., P.O. Box 1047, Halifax, NS B3X 1X5. (902) 424-7177. FAX: (902) 424-0617. www.film.ns.ca
CEO
Ann MacKenzie

PRINCE EDWARD ISLAND

PRINCE EDWARD ISLAND FILM OFFICE

c/o Prince Edward Island Business Development Inc., P.O. Box 910, Charlottetown, PE C1A 7L9. (902) 368-6329. FAX: (902) 368-6301. email: mbwood@gov.pe.ca
FILM COMMISSIONER
Berni Wood

ONTARIO

CITY OF TORONTO

Toronto Film and Television Office, Toronto City Hall, North Rotunda, 100 Queen St. W., Toronto, ON M5H 2N2. (416) 392-7570. FAX: (416) 392-0675. www.torontofilmpermits.com
FILM COMMISSIONER
Rhonda Silverstone

ONTARIO FILM DEVELOPMENT CORPORATION (OFDC)

175 Bloor St. E., North Tower, Ste. 300, Toronto, ON M4W 3R8. (416) 314-6858. FAX: (416) 314-6876. email: mail@ofdc.on.ca

QUÉBEC

MONTREAL FILM AND TV COMMISSION

275 Notre-Dame St. E., Ste. R-100, Montréal, QC H2Y 1C6. (514) 872-2883. FAX: (514) 872-3409. www.quebec-film.com
FILM COMMISSIONER
André Lafond

SOCIETE DE DEVELOPPEMENT DES ENTREPRISES CULTURELLES (SODEC)

215 rue Saint-Jacques, bur. 800, Montréal, QC H2Y 1M6. (514) 841-2200, (800) 363-0401. FAX: (514) 841-8606

SASKATCHEWAN

THE SASKATCHEWAN FILM AND VIDEO DEVELOPMENT CORPORATION

1701 College Ave, Regina, SK S4P 1B8. (306) 347-3456. FAX: (306) 359-7768. email: saskfilm@cableregina.com
ACTING GENERAL MANAGER
Valerie Creighton
DIRECTOR, TAX CREDITS
Louise Usick

YUKON

YUKON FILM COMMISSION

P.O. Box 2703, Whitehorse, YT Y1A 2C6. (867) 667-5400. FAX: (867) 393-6456. www.reelyukon.com
MANAGER
Mark Hill

BRITISH YEAR IN REVIEW

BY NIMRA HANIF

Efforts were made again this year to justify the use of lottery money to finance British films. Less than ten percent of the lottery money spent on backing films has been recouped so far. Out of 140 odd films made with lottery funds less than a dozen have had either critical or box office success. Among them were last year's Ratcatcher, The Ideal Husband, Topsy Turvy, Hideous Kinky and The Land Girls. The biggest turkey this year would have to be The Secret Laughter of Women which won a lottery grant of just under a million but which made a shocking 2,832 pounds at the British box office. It seemed that the members of the board responsible for dispensing the funds inevitably chose to give them to the films that were least likely to succeed at the box office. In May of this year a film council was launched by the culture secretary, Chris Smith, with acclaimed film director Alan Parker as chairperson. This time, the council is determined to make it work. Contrary to the past practice of funding films which would not be able to get mainstream finance, the new council is going to back films which in their opinion will fare well at the box office. The result, they hope, will be fewer films with bigger budgets, the assumption being that bigger budgets will bring higher returns. The council will have an initial budget of 22 million pounds in lottery funds and they intend to spend almost half of that on big, financially viable projects. Approximately 4.2 million will be spent on co-productions with European filmmakers and 5 million invested in offbeat films which are likely to draw audiences. A quarter of the money will also be spent on training screenwriters to develop strong screenplays, the scarcity of which is seen as the major cause of the failure of British films. It remains to be seen whether this new box office driven strategy will bring any more success than backing of the underdog by the previous council. Critics of the new council say that whatever the case, the box office is too fickle a place to bet public funds on.

But the problem might lie in the short-sightedness of the industry, mainly its producers and distributors. Overwhelmed by big American films, financiers and distributors are likely to look for either something that emulates them or go for what in their opinion is a quintessentially British period drama. The success of The Full Monty a couple of years ago should have shown them otherwise but this year the short-sightedness of distributors was clearly displayed when at least two British films fared better outside the country. Saving Grace and Croupier, which were largely ignored by British distributors, did quite well in the United States. Saving Grace made more than three million dollars at the US box office within weeks of its release. Croupier, on the other hand, was grabbed by a Manhattan based distributor, shown at a festival and then given a separate release. To date it has made more than 2 million dollars. One Life Stand was another film that did not get the attention it deserved. A DIY project by director May Miles Thomas is still struggling to get a release in a UK cinema. The film, shot entirely on a Sony VX-1000 camera was hailed by critics and experts as having used technology in a revolutionary new way as well as having a great script and excellent performances by established actors.

Meanwhile British audiences continue to be lured to cinemas by Hollywood releases. This year the big pullers included American Beauty and Toy Story 2 early in the year and Dinosaur released in the fall amidst a giant publicity blitz. Snatch, directed by British director Guy Ritchie, was one exception. It cost 5 million pounds and had record earnings of between 2.8 and 3 million pounds in its first week. Billy Elliot, a purely British product was another. But then again it has had the Hollywood treatment of worldwide distribution and large amounts of publicity. It has several backers, including Working Title, Tiger Aspect Pictures, and Universal as well as the BBC.

TOP UK PERFORMERS BY 2000 CUMULATIVE BOX OFFICE TAKINGS UP TO OCT 15

Film	Distributor	Release Date	Gross
Toy Story 2	Buena Vista	Feb 2000	43,462,228
Gladiator	UIP	May 2000	30,872201
Chicken Run	Pathe	June 2000	28,806,950
Snatch	Columbia	Sep 2000	27,887,202
American Beauty	UIP	Jan 2000	21,030,487
Mission Impossible 2	UIP	Jul 2000	17,275,399
Stuart Little	Columbia	Jul 2000	16,156,301
X-Men	Fox	Aug 2000	14,311,027
The Beach	Fox	Feb 2000	13,282,998
Erin Brokovich	Columbia	Apr 2000	10,482,408

EXHIBITION CIRCUITS

ABBEY FILMS LTD.
135 Upper Abbey Street, Dublin 1. Tel: (353 1) 723 922. FAX: (353 1) 723 687.
MANAGING DIRECTOR
Leo Ward

ABC CINEMAS LTD.
80 Great Portland St., London WN 5PA. Tel: (0207) 291 9000. www.abccinemas.co.uk
CONTACT
Barry Jenkins

APOLLO LEISURE (UK) LTD. - CINEMA DIVISION
7 Palatine Suite, Coppull Enterprise Centre, Mill Lane, Coppull, Chorley PR7 5AN. Tel: (01257) 471 012. FAX: (01257) 470 042.
424 Woolton Road, Liverpool L25 6JQ. Tel: (0151) 708 6672.
CONTACTS
G. S. Lipson
J. Merryweather

ARTIFICIAL EYE COMPANY
14 King Street, London WC2E 8HN Tel: (0207) 240 5353. FAX: (0207) 240 5252.

BELLEVUE CINEMAS
Station Road, Edgeware, London Tel: (0208) 381 2556.
Willesden Green Library Centre, London NW10.

BLOOM THEATRES
37 Museum Street, London WC1A 1LP Tel: (0207) 242 5523.

BROADWAY CINEMAS
Eastcheap, Letchworth. Tel: 01462 681 223.

CAC LEISURE COMPANY
Box 21m, 23-25 Huntley St., Inverness, Scotland 1VI 1LA. Tel: (01463) 237611.
CONTACTS
Cluley, P. Perrins

CALEDONIAN CINEMAS
Ist Floor Highland Rail House, Station Square, Inverness 1V1 1LE. Tel: (01463) 718888 FAX: (01463)718180. www.caledoniancinemas.co.uk
CONTACT
Ivan Cluley

CINE-UK LTD.
Sutherland House, 5/6 Argyll St., London W1V 1AD. Tel: (0207) 494 1394. FAX: (0207) 734 1443.
www.cine-uk.com
MANAGING DIRECTOR
Steve Wiener

CITY SCREEN
86 Dean Street, London W1V 5AA Tel: (0207) 734 4342 FAX: (0207) 734 4027.

DUBLIN CINEMA GROUP LTD
Film House, 35/36 Upper Abbey Street, Dublin 1 Tel: 353 1 872 3922 FAX: 353 1 872 3687.

FILM NETWORK
23 West Smithfield, London EC1A 9HV Tel: (0207) 489 0531 FAX: (0207) 248 5781.

FOCUS CINEMAS LTD.
147-149 Wardour Street, London W1V 3TB. Tel: (0207) 434 1961.

GALLERY CINEMAS
Nightingale House, 65 Curzon Steet, London W1Y 7PE. Tel: (0207) 629 9642.

GCT
Curzon Cinemas, 110 St. Martin's Lane, London WC2 N4AD Tel: (0207) 867 1131.

HOYTS UK CINEMA LTD
27 Southampton Street, London WC2E Tel: (0207) 557 7600

KINE SUPPLIES (BIRMINGHAM) LTD.
Regal Buildings, Augusta Place, Leamington Spa CV32 5EP. Tel: (01926) 22157.

LUX CINEMA
2-4 Hoxton Square, London N1. Tel: (0207) 684 0201. FAX: (0207) 684 1111.

MAINLINE PICTURES
37 Museum Street, London WC1A 1LP. Tel:(0207) 242 5523. FAX: (0207) 430 0170. www.screencinemas.co.uk

THE METRO CINEMA
11 Rupert Street, London W1V Tel: (0207) 437 0747.

METRO TARTAN DISTRIBUTION LTD
79 Wardour Street, London W1V. Tel: (0207) 494 1400. FAX: (0207) 4391922.

NATIONAL AMUSEMENTS (UK)
Showcase Cinema, Redfield Way, Lenton, Nottingham NG7 2UW. Tel: (01159) 862 508. www.nationalamusements.com
CONTACT
J. Bilsborough

OASIS CINEMAS AND FILM DISTRIBUTION LTD
20 Rushcroft Road, Brixton, London SW2 1LA. Tel: (0207) 733 8989. FAX: (0207) 733 8790. email: oasiscinemas@u-net.com

ODEON CINEMAS
Rank Leisure Division, Stafferton Way, Maidenhead, Bucks SL6 1AY Tel: (01628) 504000. FAX: (01628) 504 383.
54 Whitcomb Street, London WC2H 7DN. Tel: (0207) 839 6373. FAX: (0207) 321 0357.www.odeon.co.uk
MANAGING DIRECTOR
Hugh Corrance
CONTACT
Mike Archibald

PANTON CORONET CINEMAS
Notting Hill Gate, London W11 3LB. Tel: (0207) 221 0123.
CONTACT
Denise Dowson

PEPSI LONDON IMAX THEATRE
The Trocadero, 1 Picadilly Circus, London W1R. Tel: (0207) 494 4153. FAX: (0207) 434 0190.

PICTUREDROME THEATRES
1 Duchess Street, London W1N 3DE. Tel: (01372) 460 108.

RECORDED CINEMAS
155-157 Oxford St., London W1R 1TB. Tel: (0207) 734 7477.

ROBINS CINEMAS
Studio 3B, Highgate Business Centre, 33 Greenwood Place, London NW5 1DH. Tel: (0207) 482 3842. FAX: (0207) 482 4141.

SHOWCASE CINEMAS
Redfield Way, Lenton, Nottingham NG7 2UW. Tel: (01159) 862 508. www.showcasecinemas.com
MANAGING DIRECTOR
Duncan Short

TYNESIDE FILM THEATRE
10 Pilgrim Street, Newcastle-Upon-Tyne NE1 6QG. Tel: (0191) 232 8289.

UNITED CINEMAS INTERNATIONAL UK
Lee House, 90 Great Bridgewater Street, Manchester M1 5JW. Tel: (0161) 455 4000. FAX: (0161) 455 4079.
MANAGING DIRECTOR
Steve Knibbs

UGC UK LTD.
(Formerly Lumiere Pictures Ltd.)
24 av Charles de Gaulle, 92522 Neuilly sur Seine, France. Tel: (33 146) 404 400. FAX: (33 146) 243 728.
CHAIRMAN
Alain Sussfeld
EXECUTIVE V.P. (UK)
Louisa Dent

VIRGIN CINEMAS LTD.
Adelaide House, 626 High Road., Chiswick, London W4 5RY. Tel: (0208) 987 5000. FAX: (0208) 742 2998.
COMMERCIAL DIRECTOR
Margaret Taylor
BOOKING MANAGER
Joe Nunes

WARD-ANDERSON CINEMA GROUP
Film House, 35 Upper Abbey Street, Dublin 1, Ireland. Tel: (353 1) 872 3422/3922. FAX: (353 1) 872 3687.

WARNER VILLAGE EXHIBITION
3rd fl. S., Wells Point, 79 Wells St., London W1P 3RD. Tel: (0207) 465 4090 FAX: (0207) 465 4919.
www.warnervillage.com
CONTACTS
S. Wiener
P. Dobson

CIRCUIT MULTIPLEXES

Theatre Name	City	Circuit	Screens
ABC Wester Hailes	Edinburgh	ABC	8
ABC	Mansfield	ABC	8
ABC	Nuneaton	ABC	8
ABC	Rochdale	ABC	9
Apollo	Burnley	Apollo	9
Apollo	Paignton, Torbay	Apollo	9
Cineworld, The Movies	Ashford	Cine UK	12
Cineworld, The Movies	Bexleyheath	Cine UK	9
Cineworld, The Movies	Bristol	Cine UK	14
Cineworld, The Movies	Chesterfield	Cine UK	10
Cineworld, The Movies	Feltham	Cine UK	14
Cineworld, The Movies	Luton	Cine UK	11
Cineworld, The Movies	Shrewsbury	Cine UK	8
Cineworld, The Movies	Stevenage	Cine UK	12
Cineworld, The Movies	Swindon	Cine UK	12
Cineworld, The Movies	Wakefield	Cine UK	12
Cineworld, The Movies	Wolverhampton	Cine UK	14
Hoyts	Bluewater, Dartford	Hoyts	13
Piccadilly	Birmingham	Ind. Avtar Singh	8
Movie House	Belfast	Movie House	14
UCI	Basildon	National Amusements	12
Showcase	Birmingham	National Amusements	12
Showcase	Bristol	National Amusements	14
Showcase Glasgow East	Coatbridge	National Amusements	14
Showcase	Conventry	National Amusements	14
Showcase	Derby	National Amusements	11
Showcase	Leeds	National Amusements	16
Showcase	Liverpool	National Amusements	12
Showcase	Manchester	National Amusements	14
Showcase	Newham	National Amusements	14
Showcase	Nottingham	National Amusements	13
Showcase Phoenix Retail Park	Paisley	National Amusements	14
Showcase	Peterborough	National Amusements	13
Showcase Winnersh	Reading	National Amusements	12
Showcase	Stockton on Tees	National Amusements	14
Showcase	Walsall	National Amusements	12
Odeon	Birmingham	Odeon	8
Odeon	Blackpool	Odeon	10
Odeon	Bridgend	Odeon	9
Odeon	Bromborough	Odeon	11
Odeon	Chelmsford	Odeon	8
Odeon	Coventry	Odeon	9
Odeon	Glasgow	Odeon	12
Odeon	Guildford	Odeon	9
Odeon	Hampstead	Odeon	8
Odeon	Hull	Odeon	10
Odeon	Kettering	Odeon	8
Odeon	Kilmarnock	Odeon	8
Odeon	Leicester	Odeon	12
Odeon	Liverpool	Odeon	12
Odeon Holloway	London	Odeon	8
Odeon	Maidstone	Odeon	8
Odeon	Romford	Odeon	8
Odeon	Sheffield	Odeon	10
Odeon	Southampton	Odeon	13
Odeon	Southend on Ses	Odeon	8
Odeon	Stoke on Trent	Odeon	10
Odeon	Tunbridge Wells	Odeon	9
UCI	Bracknell	UCI	10
UCI	Cardiff	UCI	12
UCI	Cerdy	UCI	10
UCI	Clydebank	UCI	10
UCI	Dudley	UCI	10
UCI	East Kilbride	UCI	9
UCI	Edinburgh	UCI	12
UCI	Gateshead	UCI	11
UCI	Hatfield	UCI	9
UCI	Huddersfield	UCI	9
UCI	Hull	UCI	8
UCI Lee Valley	London	UCI	12
UCI Surrey Quays	London	UCI	9
UCI Whiteleys	London	UCI	8
UCI	Manchester	UCI	20
UCI	Milton Keynes	UCI	10
UCI	North Shields	UCI	9
UCI	Poole	UCI	10
UCI	Preston	UCI	10

Theatre Name	City	Circuit	Screens
UCI	Sheffield	UCI	10
UCI	Solihull	UCI	8
UCI	Swansea	UCI	10
UCI	Tamworth	UCI	10
UCI	Telford	UCI	10
UCI	Thurrock	UCI	10
UCI	Warrington	UCI	10
Virgin	Aberdeen	Virgin	9
Virgin	Balfast	Virgin	10
Virgin	Birmingham	Virgin	9
Virgin Great Park	Birmingham	Virgin	13
Virgin	Boldon	Virgin	11
Virgin	Bolton	Virgin	15
Virgin	Brighton	Virgin	8
Virgin	Crawley	Virgin	15
Virgin	Dundee	Virgin	9
Virgin	Edinburgh	Virgin	13
Virgin	Ipswich	Virgin	11
Virgin	Liverpool	Virgin	8
Virgin	Newport	Virgin	13
Virgin Sixfields Leisure Park	Northampton	Virgin	9
Virgin Valley Park	Rochester	Virgin	9
Virgin	Salford	Virgin	8
Virgin	Sheffield	Virgin	20
Virgin	Slough	Virgin	10
Virgin	Stockport	Virgin	10
Virgin	Wigan	Virgin	11
Omniplex	Lisburn	Ward Anderson	14
Omniplex	Newry	Ward Anderson	9
Warner Village	Bury	Warner Vaiilage	12
Warner Village	Basingstoke	Warner Village	10
Warner Village	Bolton	Warner Village	12
Warner Village	Bristol	Warner Village	12
Warner Village	Cambridge	Warner Village	8
Warner Village	Croydon	Warner Village	8
Warner Village	Dagenham	Warner Village	9
Warner Village	Harrow	Warner Village	9
Warner Village	Leeds	Warner Village	9
Warner Village	Leicester	Warner Village	9
Warner Village Finchley Rd.	London	Warner Village	8
Warner Village No. Finchley	London	Warner Village	8
Warner Village Acton	London	Warner Village	9
Warner Village West End	London	Warner Village	9
Warner Village	Newcastle	Warner Village	9
Warner Village	Plymouth	Warner Village	15
Warner Village	Sheffield	Warner Village	11
Warner Village	Watford	Warner Village	8
Warner Village	York	Warner Village	12

PRODUCERS & DISTRIBUTORS

A1 ENTERTAINMENT
16a South Parade, Chiswick, London, W4. Tel: (0208) 742 1975. FAX: (0208) 742 1980.

AARDMAN ANIMATIONS
Gas Ferry Road, Bristol, BS1 6UN. Tel: (0117) 984 8845. FAX: (0117) 984 8486.
CONTACT
Michael Rose

ABACUS FILM PRODUCTIONS LTD
40 St. Martin's Lane, London WC2N 4ER. Tel: (0207) 240 1277 FAX: (0207) 836 7014
MANAGING DIRECTOR
A. Gache

ABSOLUTELY PRODUCTIONS LTD
8th Floor, Alhambra House, 27-31 Charing Cross Road, London WC2H OAU. Tel: (0207) 930 3113. FAX: (0207) 934 4114. email: info@absolutely-uk.com
www.absolutely-uk.com
MANAGING DIRECTOR
Miles Bullough

ABBEY FILMS LTD.
Film House, 35 Upper Abbey Street, Dublin 1, Ireland. Tel: (353 1) 872 3922. FAX: (353 1) 872 3687.
DIRECTORS
K. Anderson
L. Ward
A. Ryan

ACTIVATE PRODUCTIONS
64 Charlotte Road, London EC2A 3PE. Tel: (0207) 739 9009. FAX: (0207) 739 9559. email: activate.prods@btinternet.com
MANAGING DIRECTOR
Mary Calderwood

ADDICTION LTD.
Third Floor, 6-8 Sedley Place, London W1R 1HG. email: jeremy@addictionltd.demon.co.uk

ADDICTIVE TELEVISION LTD
Canalot Production Studios, 222 Kensal Road, London W10 5BN. Tel: (0208) 960 2233. FAX: (0208) 960 2244.
email: mail@addictive.com
Producer
Nick Clarke

ADN ASSOCIATES/HOLLYWOOD CLASSICS
8 Cleveland Gardens, London, W2 6HA. Tel: (0207) 262 4646. FAX: (0207) 262 3242. www.hollywoodclassics.com
email: hollywoodclassicsuk@compuserve.com
CONTACTS
Pano AlaFouzo
Joe Dreier
John Flynn (USA)

ADVENTURE PICTURES LTD
6 Blackbird Yard, Ravenscroft St., London E2 7RP. Tel: (0207) 613 2233. FAX: (0207) 256 0842.
email: adventurepics@compuserve.com
CONTACT
Sally Potter

AGFA GEVAERT LTD. (MOTION PICTURE DIVISION)
27 Great West Road, Brentford, Middlesex, TW8 9AX. Tel: (0208) 231 4310. FAX: (0208) 231 4315.

ALL AMERICAN LEISURE GROUP INC.
Production Office: 6 Woodland Way, Petts Wood, Kent BR5 1ND. Tel: (01689) 87 1535. FAX: (01689) 87 1519.

ALL FILMS
4th Floor, 9 Carnaby St., London W1V 1PG. Tel: (0207) 437 6667. FAX: (0207) 439 3066. email: Allfilms9@Aol.com

ALLIED VISION LTD.
3 4 Ashland Place, London, W1M 3JH. Tel: (0207) 224 1992. FAX: (0207) 224 0111.
MANAGING DIRECTOR
Peter McRae

AMARANTH FILM PARTNERS LTD
Suite 215, The Linen Hall, 162-168 Regent Street, London W1R 5TB. Tel: (0207) 439 3734. FAX: (0207) 734 6839.
Contacts
Paul Hill
Rosa Romero

AMY INTERNATIONAL PRODUCTIONS
P.O.Box 17, Towcester Northamptonshirem NN12 8YJ. Tel: (01295) 760 256. FAX: (01295) 760 889. email: amyent@compuserve.com
DIRECTORS
Simon MacCorkindale
Susan George

ANGLE FILMS LIMITED
25 Blenheim Crescent, London, W11 2EF. Tel: (0207) 229 6034. FAX: (0207) 727 8498.

ANGLO-FORTUNATO FILMS
170 Popes Lane, London W5 4NJ. Tel: (0208) 932 7676. FAX: (0208) 932 7491.
CONTACT
Luciano Celentino

ANTELOPE FILMS LTD.
2 Bloomsbury Place, London WC1A 2QA. Tel: (0207) 209 0099. FAX: (0207) 209 0098. email: reception@antelope.co.uk
www.teleimages.com/antelope.html
CONTACT
Mick Csaky

ANVIL POST PRODUCTION LTD.
Denham Studios, North Orbital Road, Denham, Uxbridge, Middlesex, UB9 5HL. Tel: (01895) 83 3522. FAX: (01895) 83 5006.
CONTACTS
Ken Somerville
C. Eng. M.I.E.R.E.
Alan Snelling

ARROW FILM DISTRIBUTORS
18 Walford Road, Radlett WD7 8LE, Berkshire. Tel: (1923) 85 8306. FAX: (1923) 85 9673. email: neil@arrowfilms.co.uk
www.arrowfilms.co.uk

ARROWHEAD PRODUCTIONS LTD
Chelsea Wharf, 15 Lots Road, London SW10 OQD. Tel: (0207) 376 8222. FAX: (0207) 376 3345. email:
arrowhead@dial.pipex.com
CHIEF EXECUTIVE
Alan Wright

ARTIFICIAL EYE FILM CO.
13 Soho Square, London W1V 5FB. Tel: (0207) 437 2552. FAX: (0207) 437 2992.
CONTACT
Pamela Engel

ASIAN PICTURES UK LTD
587 High Road, London E11 4PR. Tel: (0208) 539 6529. FAX: (0208) 558 9891.

ATOMIC WORX
15-19 Powis Mews, London W11 1NT. www.atomic-worx.com/
email: nucleus@atomic.worx.com
MANAGING DIRECTORS
Eddy De Vilhena
Sonni Modi

RICHARD ATTENBOROUGH PRODUCTIONS LTD.
Beaver Lodge, The Green, Richmond, Surrey, TW9 1NQ. Tel: (0208) 940 7234. FAX: (0208) 940 4741.
DIRECTORS
Lord Richard Attenborough, CBE
The Lady Attenborough
Richard Blake
Claude Fielding

AUSTRALIAN FILM COMMISSION
Victory House, 99 101 Regent Street, London, WIR 7HB. Tel: (0207) 734 9383. FAX: (0207) 434 0170.
DIRECTOR OF MARKETING
Sue Murray

AUTOCUE LTD.
Autocue House, 265 Merton Road, London, SW18 5JS. Tel: (0208) 870 0104. FAX: (0208) 874 3726.
CONTACTS
Mick Gould
Sarah Lewis

AVTON COMMUNICATIONS AND ENTERTAINMENT, INC.
19 Watford Road, Radlett, Herts., WD7 8LF. Tel: (01923) 85 3255. FAX: (01923) 855757.
CONTACT
Tony Klinger

AVS ROTHMAR
Common Farm, Milton Common, Thames, Oxfordshire OX9 2NU. Tel: (01844) 27 9291. FAX: (01844) 27 9192

JANE BALFOUR FILMS LTD.
Burghley House, 35 Fortress Road, London, NW5 1AD. Tel: (0207) 267 5392. FAX: (0207) 267 4241.
email: jbf@janebalfourfilms.co.uk
CONTACT
Mary Barlow

BASILISK COMMUNICATIONS LTD
31 Percy Street, London W1P 9FG. Tel: (0207) 580 7222. FAX: (0207) 631 0572.

BEACONSFIELD FILMS LTD.
52 Queen Anne Street, London, W1M 9LA. Tel: (0207) 935 1186.
DIRECTORS
Peter Rogers
Mrs. B. E. Rogers
G. E. Malyon

BEAMBRIGHT LTD
Debnershe, The Street, Shalford, Surrey GU4 8BT. Tel: (01483) 539 343. FAX: (01483) 539 343.
email: 113316.777@compuserve.com
CONTACT
Therese Pickard

BFI FILM & VIDEO LIBRARY
21 Stephen Street, London, W1P 1PL. Tel: (0207) 255 1444. FAX: (0207) 436 7950.
HEAD OF DISTRIBUTION SERVICES
Heather Stewart

BLACK AUDIO FILMS
7-12 Greenland Street, Camden, London NW1 2HD. Tel: (0207) 267 0846. FAX: (0207) 267 0845.

BLUE DOLPHIN FILM DISTRIBUTORS LTD.
(Blue Dolphin Film Productions Ltd.)
40 Langham Street, London, W1N 5RG. Tel: (0207) 255 2494. FAX: (0207) 580 7670. email: joseph.dmorais@virgin.net
CONTACT
Joseph D'Morais

BLUE WAND PRODUCTIONS LTD
2nd Floor, 12 Weltje Rd, Hammersmith, London W6 9TG. Tel: (0208) 741 2038. FAX: (0208) 741 2038.
email: bluewandproltd@btinternet.com
CONTACT
Lino Omoboni

BOP MOTION PICTURES LTD.
6 Woodland Way, Petts Wood, Kent BR5 IND. Tel: (01689) 871535/871519. FAX: (01689) 871519.
DIRECTORS
Bachoo Sen
John C. Broderick

BORDEAUX FILMS INTERNATIONAL LTD.
22 Soho Square, London, W1V 5FJ. Tel: (0208) 959 8556. FAX: (0208) 959 0555.
MANAGING DIRECTOR
K. Barakat
CONTACT
Melanie Young

SYDNEY BOX ASSOCIATES, LTD.
52 Queen Anne St., London, W1M 9LA. Tel: (0207) 935 1186.
DIRECTORS
Mrs. B. E. Rogers, G. E. Malyon

BRIGHT STAR
Reuters Television Ltd., 40 Cumberland Avenue, London, NW10 7EH. Tel: (0208) 965 7733. FAX: (0208) 965 0620.

BRITISH LION
Pinewood Studios, Pinewood Road, Iver, Bucks., SL0 0NH. Tel: (01753) 651 700. FAX: (01753) 656 391.
CHAIRMAN & CHIEF EXECUTIVE
Peter R. E. Snell

BRITISH MOVIETONEWS LTD.
North Orbital Road, Denham, Nr. Uxbridge, Middlesex, UB9 5HQ. Tel: (01895) 833071. FAX: (01895) 834893.
www.movietone.com
MANAGING DIRECTOR
Barry S. Florin
LIBRARIAN
Barbara Heavens

BRITISH SKY BROADCASTING LTD.
Grant Way, Isleworth, Middx. TW7 5QD. Tel: (0207) 705 3000. FAX: (0207) 705 3030.
CHIEF EXECUTIVE & MANAGING DIRECTOR
Sam Chisholm
MARKETING DIRECTOR
Jim Hytner

BRITISH SCREEN FINANCE LTD.
14 17 Wells Mews, London, W1P 3FL. Tel: (0207) 323 9080. FAX: (0207) 323 0092. email: info@britishscreen.co.uk
CHIEF EXECUTIVE
Simon Perry

BRITISH UNIVERSITIES FILM & VIDEO COUNCIL
55 Greek St., London, W1V 5LR. Tel: (0207) 734 3687. FAX: (0207) 287 3914.
DIRECTOR
Murray Weston

BROUGHTON HOUSE
6 8 Sackville St., 3rd fl., London W1X 1DD. Tel: (0207) 287 4601. FAX: (0207) 287 9652.

BUENA VISTA PRODUCTIONS LTD.
Beaumont House, Kensington Village, Avonmore Road, London, W14 8TS. Tel: (0207) 605 2400. FAX: (0207) 605 2597.
MANAGING DIRECTOR
David Simon

CALLISTER COMMUNICATIONS LTD
88 Causeway End Road, Lisburn, Co, Antrim BT28 3ED. Tel: (01846) 673 717. FAX: (01846) 673 652.
:email: jcallister@tibus.com
MANAGING DIRECTOR
John Callister

CAPITOL FILMS LTD.
15 Portland Place, London, W1N 3AA. Tel: (0207) 872 0154. FAX: (0207) 636 6691.
CONTACTS
Sharon Harel
Jane Barclay

CARLTON COMMUNICATIONS PLC
25 Knightsbridge, London, SW1X 7R2. Tel: (0207) 663 6363.
CHAIRMAN
Michael Green
MANAGING DIRECTOR
June de Holler

CARLTON FILM DISTRIBUTORS LTD.
127 Wardour St., London W1V 4AD. Tel: (0207) 437 9020. FAX: (0207) 434 3689.
CONTACT
George Helyer

CASTLE COMMUNICATIONS PLC
A29 Barwell Business Park, Leatherhead Road, Chessington, Surrey KT9 2NY. Tel: (0208) 974 1021. FAX: (0208) 974 2674.
CHAIRMAN
Terry Shand
MANAGING DIRECTOR
Geoff Kempin

CASTLE ROCK INTERNATIONAL
8 Queen Street, London, W1X 7PH. Tel: (0207) 409 3532. FAX: (0207) 499 9885/4120.
PRESIDENT
Masamo Grasnsi
V.P., MARKETING & PUBLICITY
Lindsey Shide

CASTLE TARGET INTERNATIONAL
(Castle Premier Releasing Ltd.)
A29 Barwell Business Park, Leatherhead Road, Chessington, Surrey KT9 2NY. Tel: (0208) 974 1021. FAX: (0208) 974 2674.

CATTERMOUL FILM SERVICE
(Cecil Cattermoul Ltd.)
69 New Oxford Street, London, WC1A 1DG. Tel: (0207) 379 4361/379 4038. FAX: (0207 240 4895.
DIRECTOR
Marina Cattermoul (Mrs.)

CAZENZA PRODUCTIONS LTD.
57 Great Cumberland Place, London W1H 7LJ. Tel: (0207) 402 8858. FAX: (0207) 262 4143.
CONTACT
Ann Zahl

CHARGEURS PRODUCTIONS LTD.
Kent House, Market Place, London, W1N 8AR. Tel: (0207) 323 5151. FAX: (0207) 636 7594.
CONTACT
Timothy Burrill

CHEERLEADER PRODUCTIONS
62 Chiswick High Road, Chiswick, London W4 15Y. Tel: (0207) 995 7778. FAX: (0207) 995 7779.

ROGER CHERRILL LTD.
65 66 Dean Street, London W1V 6PL. Tel: (0207) 437 7972. FAX: (0207) 437 6411.
CONTACT
Brian Hickin

CHRYSALIS VISUAL ENTERTAINMENT
13 Bramley Road, London W10 6SP. Tel 0207 465 6208. FAX: (0207) 465 6159.
CONTACT
Jo Wood

CIBY SALES
14 Curzon St, London W1Y 7FH. Tel: (0207) 333 8877. FAX: (0207) 493 2443.
CONTACT
Wendy Palmer

CINE LINGUAL SOUND STUDIOS LTD.
27/29 Berwick Street, London, W1V 3RF. Tel: (0207) 437 0136. FAX: (0207) 439 2012.
DIRECTORS
A. Anscombe
P. J. Anscombe
M. Anscombe
D. J. Old
D. J. Newman

CINE U.K. LTD.
Sutherland House, 5/6 Argyll St, London W1V 1AD. Tel: (0207) 494 1394. FAX: (0207) 734 1443.
MANAGING DIRECTOR
Steve Wiener

CINEMA SEVEN PRODUCTIONS LTD.
Pinewood Studios, Iver Heath, Bucks, SL0 0NH. Tel: (01753) 651700. FAX: (01753) 652525.
www.deluxe-ent.com
DIRECTORS
Cassian Elwes
George Pappas
CONTACT
Chantal Ribeiro

CINEMA VERITY PRODUCTIONS LTD.
The Mill House, Millers Way, 1a Shepherds Bush Road, London, W6 7NA. Tel: (0208) 749 8485. FAX: (0208) 743 5062.
EXECUTIVE PRODUCER
Verity Lambert

CINESOUND EFFECTS LIBRARY LTD.
Imperial Studios, Maxwell Road, Elstree Way, Boreham Wood, Herts. Tel: (0208) 953 5837. FAX: (0208) 207 1728.
CONTACTS
Mike Rogers, Angela Marshall

CLARENDON FILM PRODUCTIONS LTD
7 Trinity Crescent, London SW17 7AG Tel: (0208) 488 9208. FAX: (0208) 488 3959. email: 100532.362@compuserve.com

BRIAN CLEMENS ENTERPRISES LTD.
Park Farm Cottage, Ampthill, Beds. Tel: (01525) 402 215. FAX: (01525) 402 954.

COLSTAR INTERNATIONAL
11 Wythburn Place, London W1H 5WL. Tel: (0207) 437 5725. FAX: (0207) 706 1704.

COLUMBIA PICTURES CORPORATION LTD.
19 23 Wells Street, London W1P 4DH. Tel: (0207) 580 2090. Telex: 263392 COLPIC G. FAX: (0207) 528 8980.
DIRECTORS
Nicholas Bingham
Martin Blakstad
Lester McKellar, J.
Edward Shugrue (USA)
Columbia Tri Star Films (Ireland)

54 Middle Abbey St., Dublin, Ireland. Tel: (353 1) 3872 4151.
BRANCH MANAGER
Gerry Mulcahy

Columbia Tri Star Films (UK)
19/23 Wells Street, London, W1P 4DH. Tel: (0207) 580 2090. Telex: 263392 COLPIC G. FAX: (0207) 436 0323.
MANAGING DIRECTOR, UK
Carmen Menegazzi

COMPLETION BOND CO., INC.
Pinewood Studios, Iver, Bucks., SL0 0NH. Tel: (01753) 651 700, (01753) 652 099.
CONTACT
John L. Hargreaves

CONTEMPORARY FILMS
24 Southwood Lawn Road, Highgate, London, N6 5SF. Tel: (0208) 340 5715. FAX: (0208) 348 1238.
CONTACT
Kitty Cooper

CORI FILM DISTRIBUTORS
19 Albemarle Street, London, W1X 3HA. Tel: (0207) 493 7920. FAX: (0207) 493 8088.
CONTACTS
Marie Hoy
Bob Jenkins

CREWS EMPLOYMENT AGENCY
111 Wardour Street, London, W1V 4AY. Tel: (0207) 437 0350/0810/0721. FAX: (0207) 494 4644.
CONTACTS
Lynda Loakes
Shirley Hinds

CURZON FILM DISTRIBUTORS LTD.
38 Curzon Street, London, W1Y 8EY. Tel: (0207) 465 0565. Telex: 21612. FAX: (0207) 499 2018.
DIRECTORS
R. C. Wingate
G. Biggs
D. Kiernan
J. Gamble
R. Cossey

CYGNET LTD.
Communications Business Centre, Blenheim Road, High Wycombe, Bucks., HP12 3RS.
MANAGING DIRECTOR
D. N. Plunket

DECENT EXPOSURE LTD
8 Duck Lane, London W1V 1FL Tel: (0207) 734 0698 FAX: (0207) 437 2260.
CONTACT
Steven Rosam

DE LANE LEA SOUND CENTRE
75 Dean Street, London, W1V 5HA. Tel: (0207) 439 1721. FAX: (0207) 437 0913.
CONTACT
Richard Paynter

DE WARRENNE PICTURES LTD
2 Queen Victoria Terrace, Sovereign Court, London E1 9HA Tel: (0207) 481 8000 FAX: (0207) 481 8624
CONTACT
Tom Waller

DIGITAL FILM
5 D'Arblay Street, London, W1V 3FD. Tel: (0207) 434 3100. FAX: (0207) 287 3191.
CONTACT
Matthew Holben

DIPLOMAT FILMS LTD
The Carlton Centre , Greenwood Street, Altrincham, Cheshire WA14 1RZ. Tel: (0161) 929 1603. FAX: (0161) 929 1604.
email: 10064.2501@compuserve.com
PRODUCER AND MANAGING DIRECTOR
Keith Thompson

WALT DISNEY COMPANY LTD.
Beaumont House, Kensington Village, Avonmore Road, London, W14 8TS. Tel: (0207) 605 2400. FAX: (0207) 605 2593.
MANAGING DIRECTOR
Etienne de Villiers

DISTANT HORIZON LTD.
84 86 Regent Street, London, W1R 5PF. Tel: (0207) 734 8690. FAX: (0207) 734 8691.

DOGSTAR UK LTD
5 Sherwood Street, London W1V 7RA. Tel: (0207) 287 5944. FAX: (0207) 287 1786. email: mail@dogstar.co.uk
CONTACTS
Liz Barron
Alan Greenspan

DOLBY LABORATORIES INC.
Interface Park, Wootton Bassett, Wiltshire, SN4 8QJ. Tel: (01793) 842100. FAX: (01793) 842101.
CONTACT
Catherine Unwin

DOLPHIN INTERNATIONAL FILM DISTRIBUTORS LTD.
70 71 New Bond Street, London, W1Y 9DE. Tel: (0207) 493 8811. FAX: (0207) 491 2094.

DRUMMER FILMS LTD.
14 Haywood Close, Pinner, Middx. HA5 3LQ. Tel: (0208) 866 9466. FAX: (0208) 866 9466.
PRODUCER & MANAGING DIRECTOR
Martin M. Harris

DUCK LANE FILM PRODUCTIONS LTD.
8 Duck Lane, London, W1V 1FL. Tel: (0207) 439 3912. FAX: (0207) 437 2260.
DIRECTOR
Rigby Andrews

EAST WIND FILMS
Old Rectory Studios, Rosary Road, Norwich, Norfolk NR1 1TA. Tel: (01603) 628 728. FAX: (01603) 664 727. email: gixigzell@netcom.co.uk
CONTACT
Avril Brennan

EATON FILMS
10 Holbein Mews, Lower Sloane Street, London SW1W 8NN. Tel: (0207) 823 6173. FAX: (0207) 823 6017.
CONTACTS
Judith Bland
Liz Cook

EDUCATIONAL AND TELEVISION FILMS, LTD.
247a Upper Street, London, N1 IRU. Tel: (0207) 226 2298.
GENERAL MANAGER
Stanley Forman

ELECTRIC PICTURES
15 Percy Street, London W1P 9FD. Tel: (0207) 636 1231. FAX: (0207) 636 1675.

ENGLISH FILM CO. (EXPORTS) LTD.
6 Woodland Way, Petts Wood, Kent BR5 IND. Tel: (01689) 871 535. FAX: (01689) 871 519.

ENIGMA PRODUCTIONS
13 15 Queen's Gate Place Mews, London, SW7 5BG. Tel: (0207) 581 0238.
CHAIRMAN
Lord David Puttnam
MANAGING DIRECTOR
Steve Norris

ENTERTAINMENT FILM DISTRIBUTORS LTD.
27 Soho Square, London, W1V 5FL. Tel: (0207) 439 1606. Telex: 262428 ENTVIF. FAX: (0207) 734 2483.
DIRECTORS
Michael L. Green
Trevor H. Green
Nigel G. Green

EON PRODUCTIONS, LTD.
138 Piccadilly, London, W1V 9FH. Tel: (0207) 493 7953. Cables: Brocfilm, London, W1. FAX: (0207) 408 1236.
DIRECTORS
M. G. Wilson
J. Higgins, MBE

EUREKA LOCATION MANAGEMENT
51 Tonsley Hill, London, SW18 1BW. Tel: (0208) 870 6569. FAX: (0208) 871 2158.
HEAD OF OPERATIONS
Suzannah Holt

EUROPA FILMS LTD.
Registered Office: Park House 158/160, Arthur Road, Wimbledon Park, London, SW19.
DIRECTORS
Hugh Stewart, Michael M. Stewart

EUSTON FILMS
Pinewood Studios, Iver Heath, Bucks, SL0 0NH. Tel: (01753) 654 321. FAX: (01753) 650 222.
CONTACT
John Hambley

EYE FILM & TELEVISION
The Guildhall, Church St, Eye, Suffolk 1P23 7BD. Tel: (01379) 870083. FAX: (01379) 870987. www.eyefilm.dircon.co.uk
email: eyefilm@dircon.co.uk
CONTACT
Frank Prendergast

EYELINE FILM FACILITIES/VIDEO 77 LTD.
77 Dean Street, London, W1V 6LP. Tel: (0207) 734 3391. Telex: 265361. FAX: (0207) 437 2095.
DIRECTORS
Harold Orton, Jacki Roblin

F.I.L.M.S. LTD.
2 Savile Row, London W1X 1AF. Tel: (0207) 434 0340. FAX: (0207) 434 0442.
DIRECTORS
Jorge Gallegos
Adrian Scrope

FIFTH WHEEL PRODUCTIONS LTD
67-71 Collier Street, London N1 3BE. Tel: (0207) 713 1582. FAX: (0207) 833 9823.
CONTACT
Philip Harrow

FTS BONDED
Heston Industrial Estate, Aerodrome Way, Cranford Lane, Hounslow, Middlesex, TW5 9QN. Tel: (0208) 897 7973. FAX: (0208) 897 7979.
SALES DIRECTOR
John Reeves

FILM AND GENERAL PRODUCTIONS LTD.
10 Pembridge Place, London, W2 4XB. Tel: (0207) 221 1141. FAX: (0207) 792 1167.
DIRECTORS
Clive Parsons
Davina Belling

FILM BOOKING OFFICES LTD.
211 The Chambers, Chelsea Harbour, London, SW10 OXF. Tel: (0207) 734 5298. FAX: (0207) 352 4182.
DIRECTORS
B. G. Sammes
F. B. Perham

FILM FINANCES LTD.
1/11 Hay Hill, Berkeley Square, London, W1X 7LF. Tel: (0207) 629 6557. FAX: (0207) 491 7530. Telex: 298060;
U.S. Office: Suite 1400, 9000 Sunset Boulevard, Los Angeles, CA 90069, U.S.A. Tel: (310) 275 7323. FAX: (310) 275 1706.
DIRECTORS
Richard M. Soames (Pres. Film Finances Inc.)
Graham J. Easton

FILM FOUR INTERNATIONAL
124 Horseferry Road, London, SW1P 2TX. Tel: (0207) 396 4444. FAX: (0207) 306 8361.
DIRECTOR OF SALES
Bill Stephens
FILM SALES MANAGER
Heather Playford Denman

FILMARKETEERS LTD.
81 Piccadilly, London, W1V 9HB. Tel: (0207) 491 2767. Telex: 299565. FAX: (0207) 629 1803.
DIRECTORS
S. Shorr
I. Hamaoui

FILMVERHUURKANTOOR DE DAM B.V.
59 Warwick Square, London, SW1V 2AL. Tel: (0207) 233 6034. FAX: (0207) 233 6036.
CONTACT
Moses Rothman

THE FIRST FILM COMPANY
38 Great Windmill St, London W1V 7PA.
CONTACT
Roger J Randall Cutler

FIRST INDEPENDENT FILMS LTD.
69 New Oxford St., London, WC1A 1DG. Tel: (0207) 528 7767. FAX: (0207) 528 7770.
MANAGING DIRECTOR
Michael Myers

FLASHLIGHT FILMS
10 Golden Square, London W1R 3AF. Tel: (0207) 287 4252. FAX: (0207) 287 4232.
CONTACT
Aaron Simpson

FOCUS FILMS LTD
The Rotunda Studio, 116-118 Finchley Road, London NW3 5HT. Tel: (0207) 435 9004. FAX: (0207) 431 3562.
email: focus@pupix.demon.co.uk

MARK FORSTATER PRODUCTIONS LTD.
Suite 66, Pall Mall Deposit, 124 128 Barlby Road, London, W10 6BL. Tel: (0208) 964 1888. FAX: (0208) 960 9819.
DIRECTOR
Mark Forstater

FORTRESS FILM PRODUCTIONS LTD
9 Goodwins Court, London WC2N 4LL. Tel: (0207) 244 6696. FAX: (0207) 372 1344. email: fortress@dircon.co.uk

FOUR STAR FILMS LTD.
52 Queen Anne Street, London, W1M 9LA. Tel: (0207) 935 1186.
DIRECTORS
N. Butt
G. Golledge

THE FOWLER CHAPMAN CO. LTD.
28 Saint Mary le Park Court, Albert Bridge Road, London, SW11 4PJ. Tel: (0207) 223 0034. FAX: (0189) 278 4023.
MANAGING DIRECTOR
Roy Fowler

FOXWELL FILM PRODUCTIONS LTD.
8 Alexander Place, London, SW7 2SF.
DIRECTORS
Ivan Foxwell, A. G. Cotterell

FREEDOM PICTURES
10 Rylett Crescent, Shepherd's Bush, London W12 9RL. Tel: (0208) 743 5330.

FREEWAY FILMS
67 George Street, Edinburgh, Midlothian EH2 2JG. Tel: (0131) 225 3200, (0207) 937 9114. FAX: (0131) 225 3667. email: 100012.3206@compuserve.com
DIRECTOR
John McGrath

FRONTROOM FILMS LTD.
1 The Barton, Mill Road, Countess Wear, Exeter, Devon EX2 6LD. Tel: (01392) 70985. FAX: (01392) 431 405.
CONTACTS
John Davies
Robert Smith

GFD COMMUNICATIONS LTD.
Unit 15a, Parkmore Ind. Est. Long Mile Road, Dublin 12, Ireland. Tel: (353 1) 569 500. FAX: (353 1) 569 342.
DIRECTORS
C. M. Anderson
R. J. Whitty

G.H.W. PRODUCTIONS LTD.
52 Queen Anne Street, London, W1M 9LA. Tel: (0207) 935 1186.
DIRECTORS
Peter Rogers
Betty E. Box O.B.E.
G. E. Malyon

GAINSBOROUGH (FILM & TV) PICTURES LTD.
8 Queen Street, Mayfair, London, W17 XPH. Tel: (0207) 049 1925. FAX: (0207) 408 2042.

GALA FILM DISTRIBUTORS LTD.
26 Danbury St., Islington, London, N18JU. Tel: (0207) 226 5085. FAX: (0207) 226 5897.
MANAGING DIRECTOR & CHIEF EXECUTIVE
Kenneth Rive

GANNET FILMS LTD.
Eton Cottage, 88 Gresham Road, Staines, Middx. TW18 2AE. Tel: (01784) 453 912.
DIRECTORS
Bob Kellett
Anne Kellett
SECRETARY
B.C. Stebbings

GENERAL SCREEN ENTERPRISES
Highbridge Estate, Oxford Road, Uxbridge, Middlesex, UB8 1LX. Tel: (01895) 231 931. FAX: (01895) 235 335.
DIRECTOR & GENERAL MANAGER
Fred Chandler

WILLIAM GILBERT ASSOCIATES LTD.
16 Brook Mews North, London W23 BW. Tel: (0207) 258 3620. FAX: (0207) 723 5100. Telex: 264826 RKOINT G.
MANAGING DIRECTOR
William G. Gilbert
DIRECTOR
M. Gilbert

GINGER FILMS PRODUCTIONS LTD.
39 41 Hanover Steps, St. Georges Fields, Albion Street, London, W2 2YG. Tel: (0207) 402 7543. Telex: 896559 GECOMS G. FAX: (0207) 262 5736.
CONTACT
Brian Jackson

GLOBAL ENTERTAINMENT MANAGEMENT LTD.
22 Wadsworth Road, Perivale, Middx. NB6 7JD. Tel: (0208) 991 5051. FAX: (0208) 998 3521.
CHIEF EXECUTIVE
Claude Heilman
DIRECTOR
P. Kotak

GOLDCREST FILMS AND TELEVISION LTD.
65 66 Dean Street, London, W1V 6PL. Tel: (0207) 437 8696. Telex: 267458 GOLDCR. FAX: (0207) 437 4448.
CHIEF EXECUTIVE
John Quested

ROBERT GOLDEN PICTURES
9 Doughty Mews, London WC1N 2PG. Tel: (0207) 404 1144. FAX: (0207) 404 1224.

SAMUEL GOLDWYN COMPANY
St. George's House, 14 17 Wells Street, London, W1P 3FP. Tel: (0207) 436 5105. FAX: (0207) 580 6520.
CONTACT
Diana Hawkins

GOSH ENTERTAINMENT LTD
420 Sauchiehall Street, Glasgow, Lanarkshire G2 3JD. Tel: (0141) 353 0456. FAX: (0141) 353 1012. email: gkco@dial.pipex.com, gosh@dial.pipex.com
CONTACT
Garfield Kennedy

GRADE COMPANY
8 Queen Street, London, W1X 7PH. Tel: (0207) 409 1925. FAX: (0207) 408 2042.
CONTACT
Lord Grade

GRANADA GROUP PLC
36 Golden Square, London, W1R 4AH. Tel: (0207) 734 8080. Telex: 27937. FAX: (0207) 734 8080.
CHAIRMAN
Alex Bernstein
CHIEF EXECUTIVE
G. J. Robinson

GREEN UMBRELLA LTD
The Production House, 147A St Michael's Hill, Bristol Co., Bristol BS2 8DB. Tel: (0117) 973 1729. FAX: (0117) 946 7432. www.umbrella.co.uk email: info@umbrella.co.uk
CONTACT
Nigel Ashcroft

GUILD FILM DISTRIBUTION LTD.
Kent House, 14 17 Market Pl., Great Titchfield St., London W1N 8AR. Tel: (0207) 323 5151. FAX: (0207) 631 3568.
CONTACTS
Alexis Lloyd
Nick Hill

HAMMER FILM PRODUCTIONS LTD.
Millennium Studios, Elstree Way, Herts. WD6 1SF. Tel: (0208) 207 401. FAX: (0208) 905 1127.
DIRECTORS
Roy Skeggs
Andrew Mitchell

HAMMERWOOD FILM PRODUCERS AND DISTRIBUTORS
110 Trafalgar Rd. Portslade, Brighton, East Sussex BN41 1GS. Tel: (01273) 277333. FAX: (01273) 705451.
CONTACT
Countess Von Kollman

HANDMADE FILMS (DISTRIBUTORS) LTD.
15 Golden Square, London, W1R 2AG. Tel: (0207) 434 3122. FAX: (0207) 434 3143.
DIRECTORS
Denis O'Brien
Gareth Jones

HARKNESS HALL LTD.
Gate Studios, Station Road, Boreham Wood, Herts., WD6 1DQ. Tel: (0208) 953 3611. Cables: Screens, London. Tel: (0208) 207 3657. FAX: (0208) 207 3657.

HEMDALE COMMUNICATIONS LTD.
21 Albion Street, London, W2 2AS. Tel: (0207) 724 1010. FAX: (0207) 724 9168.
CONTACT
John Smattcombe

JIM HENSON PRODUCTIONS
1 (B) Downshire Hill, Hampstead, London, NW3 1NR. Tel: (0207) 431 2818. FAX: (0207) 431 3737.
CONTACTS
Duncan Kenworthy
Angus Fletcher
Martin Baker

HERO FILMS
34-35 Berwick Street, London W1V 3RF. Tel:(0207) 287 5190, (0207) 734 9903. FAX: (0207) 287 5191.
HEAD OF DEVELOPMENT
Anne Betz

HIGH POINT FILMS & TELEVISION LTD.
25 Elizabeth Mews, London, NW3 4UH. Tel: (0207) 586 3686. FAX: (0207) 586 3117.
MANAGING DIRECTOR
Carey Fitzgerald

HIT AND RUN PRODUCTIONS
25 Ives Street, London SW3 2 ND. Tel: (0207) 590 2600. FAX: (0207) 584 5774.
CHAIRMAN
Tony Smith

HIT ENTERTAINMENT PLC
The Pump House, 13 16 Jacobs Well Mews, London, W1H SPD. Tel: (0207) 224 1717. FAX: (0207) 224 1719.
MANAGING DIRECTOR
Peter Orton

HOLDINGS ECOSSE LTD
9/2 Tweeddale Court, 14 High Street, Edinburgh, Midlothian EH1 1TE. Tel: (0131) 557 2678. FAX: (0131) 557 4954.

GERARD HOLDSWORTH PRODUCTIONS LTD.
140 Buckingham Palace Road, London, SW1W 95A. Tel: (0207) 824 8770. FAX: (0207) 824 8762.
DIRECTORS
P. H. Filmer Sankey
A. M. V. Brunker

HOLMES ASSOCIATES/DEVCO
38-42 Whitfield Street, London W1P 5RF. Tel: (0207) 813 4333. FAX: (0207) 637 9024. email: holmes@dial.pipex.com
MANAGING DIRECTOR
Andrew Holmes

HOT PROPERTY FILMS
27 Newman Street, London W1P 3PE. Tel: (0207) 323 9466. FAX: (0207) 323 9467.
PRODUCER
Janine Marmot

HOURGLASS PRODUCTIONS LTD
4 The Heights, London SE7 8JH. Tel: (0208) 858 6870. FAX: (0208) 858 6870.
MANAGING DIRECTOR, PRODUCER & DIRECTOR
John Walsh

HUDSON FILM LTD
24 St Leonards Terrace, London SW3 4QG. Tel: (0207) 730 0002. FAX: (0207) 730 8033. email: hudsonfilm@aol.com
DIRECTOR
Hugh Hudson

HUNGRY HORSE PICTURES LTD
15 Golden Square, London W1R 3AG. Tel: (0207) 734 7979. FAX: (0207) 434 4588. email: hungryhorse@compuserve.com

IDEAL WORLD PRODUCTIONS LTD
St Georges Studios, 93-97 St Georges Road, Glasgow, G3 6JA. Tel: (0141) 353 3222. FAX: (0141) 353 3221.
EXECUTIVE PRODUCER
Zad Rogers

IMAGE DYNAMIC PRODUCTIONS LTD
Chalk Farm Studios, 10 A Belmont Street, London NW1 8HH. Tel: (0207) 267 0066. FAX: (0207) 485 4255.
email: id@idp.u-net.com
PRODUCER
Patrick Holtkamp

INDEPENDENT IMAGE FILM & TV CO
Teddington Studios, Broom Road, Teddington, Middlesex TW11 9NT. Tel: (0208) 943 3555. FAX: (0208) 943 3646. email: info@kilroy.co.uk
CHAIRMAN
Robert Kilroy-Silk

INDEPENDENTS FILMS AND TV PRODUCTION LTD
Top Floor Suite, 6 Inverleith Avenue, Edinburgh, Midlothian EH3 5PT. Tel: (0131) 551 5725. FAX:(0131) 5511525.
www.independents-ltd.com.uk
email: eg:d.trimibtt@independents-ltd.com.uk
PRODUCER/DIRECTOR
Drew Trimlett

INTERNATIONAL BROADCASTING TRUST
2 Ferdinand Place, London NW1 8EE. Tel: (0207) 482 2847. FAX: (0207) 284 3374. email: ibt@gn.apc.org
www.infilms.co.uk
DIRECTOR
Paddy Coulter

J & M ENTERTAINMENT
2 Dorset Square, London, NW1 6PU. Tel: (0207) 723 6544. Telex: 298538. FAX: (0207) 724 7541.
CONTACTS
Julia Palau

MICHAEL RYAN
Brian Jackson Films Ltd., 39 41 Hanover Steps, St. Georges Fields, Albion Street, London, W2 2YG. Tel: (0207) 402 7543. Telex: 896559 GECOMS G. FAX: (0207) 262 5736.
CONTACT
Brian Jackson

JARAS ENTERTAINMENTS LTD.
Broughton House, 3rd fl., 6 8 Sackville St., London W1X 1DD. Tel: (0207) 287 4601. FAX: (0207) 287 9652.

KAVUR PRODUCTIONS LTD.
14 Lownes Square, London, SW1X 9HB. Tel: (0207) 235 4602. FAX: (0207) 235 5215.

KENILWORTH FILM PRODUCTIONS LTD.
Newhouse, Mersham, Ashford, Kent TW2S 6NQ. Tel: (01233) 503 636. FAX: (01233) 502 244.
DIRECTORS
Lord Brabourne
Richard Goodwin

KENSINGTON FILMS AND TELEVISION
60 Charlotte Street, London W1P 2AX. Tel: (0207) 927 8458. FAX: (0207) 927 8798.

LANDSEER FILM AND TELEVISION PRODUCTIONS LTD
140 Royal College Street, London NW1 0TA. Tel :(0207) 485 7333. FAX: (0207) 485 7573. email: landseerfilms@msn.com
MANAGING DIRECTOR
Derek Bailey

LIBERTY FILMS
4th Floor, The Forum, 74 80 Camden Street, London, NW1 0JL. Tel: (0207) 387 5733. FAX: (0207) 383 95368.
CONTACTS
Teresa Kelleher
John Kelleher

LIMELIGHT FILMS
3 Bromley Place, London, W1P 5HB. Tel: (0207) 255 3939. FAX: (0207) 436 4334.
CONTACT
Sally Woodward

LION'S DEN COMMUNICATIONS MANAGEMENT LTD
Devonshire House, 12 Barley Mow Passage, London W4 4PH. Tel: (0208) 742 0392. FAX: (0208) 742 0393.
email: john@lionsden.co.uk
MANAGING DIRECTOR
John Clare

LITTLE DANCER LTD
Avonway, Naseby Road, London SE19 3JJ. Tel: (0208) 653 9343. FAX: (0208) 653 9343. email: littledancer@compuserve.com
PRODUCER
Robert Smith

LONDON FILM PRODUCTIONS LTD.
Kent House, 14 17 Market Place, Great Titchfield Street, London, W1N 8AR. Tel: (0207) 323 5251. FAX: (0207) 436 2834.
CONTACT
Andrew Luff

LONDON INDEPENDENT PRODUCERS LTD.
52 Queen Anne Street, London, W1M 9LA. Tel: (0207) 935 1186.
DIRECTORS
William MacQuitty
Mrs. B. E. MacQuitty
Ralph Thomas,
Leonora Dossett

LUCIDA PRODUCTIONS LTD.
53 Greek Street, London, WIV 5LR. Tel: (0207) 437 1140. FAX: (0207) 287 5335.
DIRECTORS
Paul Joyce
Chris Rodley

MAINLINE PICTURES
37 Museum Street, London, WC1A 1LP. Tel: (0207) 242 5523. FAX: (0207) 430 0170.
MANAGING DIRECTOR
Romaine Hart

MAJESTIC FILMS AND TELEVISION INTERNATIONAL
P.O. Box 13, Gloucester Mansions, Cambridge Circus, London, WC2H 8XD. Tel: (0207) 836 8630. FAX: (0207) 836 5819. Telex: 46601 BTGKA G.
CHIEF EXECUTIVE
Guy East

MANAGEMENT COMPANY ENTERTAINMENT GROUP INC.
Portobello Dock, 328 Kensal Road, London W10 5XJ. Tel: (0207) 968 8888. FAX: (0207) 968 8537.

MAYFAIR CINEMAS & THEATRES UK LTD.
110 St. Martin's Lane, London, WC2N 4AD. Tel: (0207) 867 1131.

MEDIA RELEASING DISTRIBUTORS LTD.
27 Soho Square, London, W1V 5FL. Tel: (0207) 437 2341. Telex: 943763 CROCOM G (MRD). FAX: (0207) 734 2483.
DIRECTORS
Trevor H. Green
J. Green

MEDUSA COMMUNICATIONS LTD.
Regal Chambers, 51 Bancroft, Hitchin, Herts., SG5 1LL. Tel: (01462) 421 818. FAX: (01462) 420 393.
CHAIRMAN
David Hodgins
EXECUTIVE DIRECTOR
Stephen Rivers

MENINCARTER MEDIA
40 Pursers Cross Road, Fulham, London SW6 4QY. Tel: (0207) 348 3763. FAX: (0207) 384 3763.
email: chrisbirch67@hotmail.com
CONTACT
Chris Birch

MERCHANT IVORY PRODUCTIONS
46 Lexington Street, London W1P 3LH. Tel: (0207) 437 1200. FAX: (0207) 734 1579.
CONTACTS
Ismail Merchant
James Ivory

MERSHAM PRODUCTIONS LTD.
Newhouse, Mersham, Ashford, Kent. TW25 6NQ. Tel: (01233) 503 636. FAX: (01233) 502 244.
DIRECTORS
Lord Brabourne
Michael John Knatchbull
Richard Goodwin

METRO TARTAN LTD.
79 Wardour Street, London, WIV 3TH. Tel: (0207) 734 8508. FAX: (0207) 287 2112.

METROCOLOUR LONDON LTD.
91 95 Gillespie Road, London, N5 1LS. Tel: (0207) 226 4422; 22 Soho Square, London, W1V 5FL. Tel: (0207) 437 7811. FAX: (0207) 359 2353.
DIRECTORS
K. B. Fraser (Managing)
D. A. Compton
C. P. Smith,
C. Young
M. Hillier
E. Senat

METROPOLIS MEDIA
P.O. Box 2875, London, W6 O2X. Tel: (0208) 563 7989. FAX: (0208) 563 8867.
CHIEF EXECUTIVE
Tony Stephens

MIRACLE COMMUNICATIONS LTD.
69 New Oxford Street, London, WC1A 1DG. Tel: (0207) 379 5006. FAX: (0207) 528 7772.

MIRAMAX FILMS (UK)
Prominent Studios, 68A Delancey Street, London, NW1 7RY. Tel: (0207) 284 0242. FAX: (0207) 267 9666.
CONTACT
Anne Greenhalgh

MOLLIKO FILMS (LONDON) LTD.
16 18 New Bridge Street, London, EC4V 6AU. Tel: (0207) 262 0638. Cables: Umeshmalik, London, EC4.
CHAIRMAN & MANAGING DIRECTOR
Umesh Mallik, B.A., India
DIRECTOR PRODUCTION
Bina Chatterjee (Miss)
GENERAL MANAGER IN INDIA
P.C. Mallik, BSC, B.L.
SCRIPT EDITOR
Janet Bennett

MOVING PICTURE COMPANY
25 Noel Street, London, W1V 3RD. Tel: (0207) 434 3100. FAX: (0207) 437 3951.
CONTACT
David Jeffers

MUSEUM OF THE MOVING IMAGE
South Bank, Waterloo, London, SE1 8XT. Tel: (0207) 928 3535. FAX: (0207) 815 1378.
CURATOR
Leslie Hardcastle, OBE

MTM ARDMORE STUDIOS LTD.
Herbert Road, Bray, Co. Wicklow, Ireland. Tel: (353 1) 862971. FAX: (353 1) 861 894. Telex: 91504 PATT E1.

MTV EUROPE
Hawley Crescent, London NW1 8TT. Tel: (0207) 284 7777. FAX: (0207) 284 7788.
DIRECTOR OF CORPORATE COMMUNICATIONS
Monique Amaudry

N.F.H. LTD.
37 Ovington Square, London, SW3 1LJ. Tel: (0207) 584 7561. FAX: (0207) 589 1863.
MANAGING DIRECTOR
Norma Heyman

NAMARA LTD.
51 Beak Street, London, W1R 3LF. Tel: (0207) 437 9524. FAX: (0207) 734 1844.
EXECUTIVE PRODUCER
Naim Attallah

NATIONAL FILM BOARD OF CANADA
1 Grosvenor Square, London, WIX OAB. Tel: (0207) 258 6480. FAX: (0207) 258 6532.
CONTACT
Jane Taylor

NATIONAL SCREEN
15 Wadsworth Road, Greenford, Middlesex, UB6 7JN. Tel: (0208) 998 2851. FAX: (0208) 997 0840.
2 Wedgwood, Mews, 12 13 Greek Street, London, W1V 6BH. Tel: (0207) 437 4851. FAX: (0207) 287 0328.
DIRECTORS
John Mahony
Brian Mcmail
Norman Darkins

NATIVE PRODUCTIONS LTD
6 Brewer Street, London W1R 3FS. Tel: (0207) 287 2433 FAX: (0207) 287 1537. email: nativeproductions@virgin.net
PRODUCERS
Giles Lovell-Wilson
David Tremellen

NELSON ENTERTAINMENT
8 Queen Street, London, W1X 7PH. Tel: (0207) 493 3362. FAX: (0207) 409 0503. Telex: 8950483 NELSON G.

NEW WORLD TRANS ATLANTIC PICTURES (UK) LTD.
27 Soho Square, London, W1V 5FL. Tel: (0207) 434 0497. FAX: (0207) 434 0490.

OASIS FILM DISTRIBUTION
155 157 Oxford Street, London, W1R 1TB. Tel: (0207) 734 7477. FAX: (0207) 734 7470.
MANAGING DIRECTOR
Peter Buckingham

ODEON CINEMAS LTD.
(A subsidiary of the Rank Organisation PLC.)
439 445 Godstone Road, Whyteleafe, Surrey. Tel: (01883) 623 355. FAX: (01883) 626 717. Telex: 262305 088362 6044.
54 Whitcomb Street, London, WC2H 7DN. Tel: (0207) 839 6373. FAX: (0207) 321 0357.
MANAGING DIRECTOR
Hugh Corrance
BOOKING EXECUTIVE
Michael Archibald
MARKETING EXECUTIVE
Stuart Francis

OIL FACTORY, LTD
165 Caledonian Road London N1 OSL. Tel: (0207) 837 0007. FAX: (0207) 837 8449. email: oilfctry@dircon.co.uk
MANAGING DIRECTOR
John Stewart

OPEN EYE PRODUCTIONS
24 Poland Street, London W1V 3DD. Tel: (0207) 287 4177. FAX: (0207) 287 4818. www.openeye.co.uk
CONTACT
Graeme McMurchie

OPTICAL FILM EFFECTS LTD.
Pinewood Studios, Iver Heath, Bucks., SL0 0NH. Tel: (01753) 655 486. FAX: (01753) 656 844.
DIRECTORS
R. W. Field
R. A. Dimbleby

OVERVIEW FILMS LTD.
16 Brook Mews North, London, W2 3BW. Tel: (0207) 258 3620. FAX: (0207) 723 5100. Telex: 2 64826 RKOINT 6.
CONTACT
William G. Gilbert

OXFORD SCIENTIFIC FILMS
Lower Road, Long Hanborough, Oxon OX8 8LL. Tel: (0993) 881 881. FAX: (0993) 882 808.
10 Poland Street, London, W1. Tel: (0207) 494 0720. FAX: (0207) 287 9125.
MANAGING DIRECTOR
Karen Goldie Morrison

PALOMAR PICTURES INTERNATIONAL (UK) LTD.
5 Chancery Lane, Clifford's Inn, London, EC4A 1BU.

DAVID PARADINE PRODUCTIONS LTD.
5 St. Mary Abbots Place, Kensington, London, W86LS. Tel: (0207) 371 3111. FAX: (0207) 602 0411.

PARADOGS LTD
206 Panther House, 38 Mount Pleasant, London WC1X 0AP. Tel: (0207) 833 1009.
EDITOR AND COMPANY DIRECTOR
Duncan Western

PARALLAX PICTURES
Denmark Street, London, WC2H 8LS. Tel: (0207) 836 1478. FAX: (0207) 497 8062.
DIRECTOR
Ken Loach

PARAMOUNT BRITISH PICTURES LTD.
Twickenham Film Studios Ltd., The Barons, St., Margaret's, Twickenham, Middx. TW1 2AW. Tel: (0208) 892 4477. Telex: 8814497. FAX: (0208) 891 0168.

PARAMOUNT PICTURES (UK) LTD.
UIP House, 45 Beadon Road, Hammersmith, London, W6 0EG. Tel: (0208) 563 4220. FAX: (0208) 563 4266.
SENIOR V.P., INTERNATIONAL MARKETING
Leslie Pound

PARK ENTERTAINMENT LTD.
Mortlake Court, 28 Sheen Court, London, SW14 8LW. Tel: (0208) 876 0207. FAX: (0208) 876 4686.

PATHE ENTERTAINMENT LTD.
Kent House, 14-17 Market Place, Great Titchfield, London, W1N 8AR. Tel: (0207) 323-5151. FAX: (0207) 631-3568. www.pathe.co.uk
CONTACTS
Alexis Lloyd
Nick Hill

PBF MOTION PICTURES
The Little Pickenhanger, Tuckey Grove, Ripley, Woking, Surrey GU23 6JG. Tel: (01483) 225179. FAX: (01483) 224118. www.pbf.co.uk email: image@pbf.co.uk
CONTACT
Peter B Fairbrass

PEARL & DEAN LTD.
Woolverstone House, 61 62 Berners Street, London, WIP 3AE. Tel: (0207) 636 5252. FAX: (0207) 637 3191.
MANAGING DIRECTOR
Peter Howard Williams

PHOENIX FILMS LTD.
6 Flitcroft St., London WC2 8DJ. Tel: (0207) 836 5000. FAX: (0207) 836 3060.
DIRECTORS
Lewis More O'Ferrall
Alan Taylor

PICTURE PALACE FILMS
19 Edis Street, London NW1 8LE. Tel: (0207) 586 8763. FAX: (0207) 586 9048. www.picturepalace.com
email: 100444.2737@compuserve.com
CONTACT
Malcolm Craddock

PINEWOOD STUDIOS LTD.
(A subsidiary of the Rank Organisation PLC. Film and TV studios; goods and services.)
Pinewood Road, Iver, Buckinghamshire SL0 ONH. Tel: (01753) 651 700. Telex: 847505. FAX: (01753) 656 844.
MANAGING DIRECTOR
Steve Jaggs

THE PINK FILM COMPANY LTD
8-18 Smith's Court off Great Windmill Street, London W1V 7PF. Tel: (0207) 287 5502. FAX: (0207) 287 5503.
email: pink@pinkfilmco.demon.co.uk
PRODUCERS
Karen Cunningham
Julia Fetterman
Bash Robertson
Dawn Laren

PLATO FILMS LTD.
247a Upper Street, London, N1 1RU. Tel: (0207) 226 2298.
GENERAL MANAGER
Stanley Forman

PLATYPUS PICTURES
33 Endwell Road, London SE24 2NE. Tel: (0207) 207 5187. FAX: (0207) 207 1440. www.platypuspictures.freeserve.co.uk
email: admin@platypuspictures.freeserve.co.uk

POLYGRAM FILMED ENTERTAINMENT
8 St. James Square, London, SW1 4JV. Tel: (0207) 747 4000. FAX: (0207) 747 4499.
CONTACT
Stuart Till

POLYGRAM FILM INTERNATIONAL
76 Oxford St., London W1N 0HQ. Tel: (0207) 307 1300. FAX: (0207) 307 1355.
PRESIDENT
Aline Perry

PORTMAN ZENITH GROUP LTD.
43 45 Dorset Street, London, W1H 4AB. Tel: (0207) 224 3344. FAX: (0207) 224 1057.
DIRECTORS
Victor Glynn
John Hall
John Sivers
Simon Cox
Andrew Warren
Richard Leworthy
Scott Meek
Dorothy Berwin
Ivan Rendall

PORTOBELLO PICTURES
42 Tavistock Road, London W1I 1AW. Tel: (0207) 379 5566. FAX: (0207) 379 5599.
EXECUTIVE PRODUCER/DIRECTOR
Eric Abraham

POST OFFICE FILM & VIDEO UNIT
(Archival Material) 130 Old Street, London EC1V 9PQ. Tel: (0207) 320 7125. FAX: (0207) 320 7209.
CONTACT
Alma Headland

THE PRODUCERS
8 Berners Mews, London W1P 3DG. Tel: (0207) 636 4226. FAX: (0207) 636 4099.
PRODUCER
Jake Lloyd

PROMINENT FEATURES LTD.
Prominent Studios, 68A Delancey Street, London, NW1 7RY. Tel: (0207) 284 0242. FAX: (0207) 284 1004.
DIRECTORS
Steve Abbott
Terry Gilliam
Eric Idle
Anne James
Terry Jones
Michael Palin

PYTHON (MONTY) PICTURES LTD.
Prominent Studios, 68A Delancey Street, London, NW1 7RY. Tel: (0207) 284 0242. FAX: (0207) 284 1004.
DIRECTORS
John Cleese
Terry Gilliam
Eric Idle
Terry Jones

PTV
The Studios, Hornton Place, London W8 4LZ. Tel: (0207) 937 9819. FAX: (0207) 937 4326. email: ptv@easynet.co.uk
MANAGING DIRECTOR
Trevor Rogers

Q FILM PRODUCTIONS LTD.
Rosehill House, Rose Hill, Nr. Burnham, Bucks. SL1 8NN. Tel: (0168) 605 129.
DIRECTORS
I. E. L. Shand
D. J. Bennet
F. Shand

QUAD PRODUCTIONS
26 Kingly Court, London W1R 5LE. Tel: (0207) 494 9191. FAX: (0207) 494 9192.

QUADRIGA PRODUCTIONS LTD
Teddington Studios, Broom Road, Teddington, Middlesex TW11 9NT. Tel: (0208) 614 2339. FAX: (0208) 614 2079.

QWERTYUIOP PRODUCTIONS LTD.
118 120 Wardour Street, London, W1 4BT. Tel: (0207) 437 3224. FAX: (0207) 437 3674.
MANAGING DIRECTOR
David Land

RANK BRIMAR LTD.
(A subsidiary of the Rank Organisation PLC.).
Greenside Way, Middleton, Manchester M24 1SN. Tel: (0161) 681 7072. Telex: 665326. FAX: (0161) 682 3818.
MANAGING DIRECTOR
Dr. Richard Fenby

RANK CINTEL LTD.
(A subsidiary of the Rank Organisation PLC. Manufacturer of equipment for broadcast and film/tape transfer.)
Watton Road, Ware, Hertfordshire SG12 OAE. Tel: (01920) 463 939. Telex: 81415. FAX: (01920) 460 803.
MANAGING DIRECTOR
Jack R. Brittain

THE RANK ORGANISATION PLC
6 Connaught Place, London, W2 2EZ. Tel: (0207) 706 1111. Telex: 263549. FAX: (0207) 262 9886.
CHAIRMAN
Sir Denys Henderson
MANAGING DIRECTOR & CHIEF EXECUTIVE
Andrew Teare
FINANCE DIRECTOR
Nigel V. Turnbull
DIRECTORS
Dr. David V. Atterton
James Daly
Michael Jackaman,
Anthony W. Stenham
Douglas M. Yates
J. F. Garrett,
Peter J. Jarvic
Hugh R. Jenkins

RANK TAYLOR HOBSON LTD.
(A subsidiary of the Rank Organisation PLC. Manufacturer of precision measurement equipment, professional cine lenses.)
P.O. Box 36, 2 New Star Road, Thurmaston Lane, Leicester LE3 7JQ. Tel: (01533) 763 771. FAX: (01533) 740 167.
MANAGING DIRECTOR
Richard Freeman

RANK VIDEO SERVICES LTD.
(A subsidiary of the Rank Organisation PLC. Operation of video and broadcast facilities and video cassette duplication.)
Phoenix Park Great West Road, Brentford, Middlesex, TW8 9PL. Tel: (0208) 568 4311. FAX: (0208) 847 4032.
MANAGING DIRECTOR
Peter Pacitti

RECORDED PICTURE CO. LTD.
8 12 Broadwick St., London, W1V 1FH. Tel: (0207) 439 0607. FAX: (0207) 434 1192.
DIRECTORS
Jeremy Thomas, Hercules Bellville, Chris Auty

RED ROOSTER FILM & TELEVISION ENTERTAINMENT
29 Floral Street, London, WC2E 9DP. Tel: (0207) 379 7727. FAX: (0207) 379 5756.
CHIEF EXECUTIVE
Linda James

REDIFFUSION FILMS LTD.
P.O. Box 451, Buchanan House, 3 St. James's Square, London, SW1Y 4LS. Tel: (0207) 925 0550. Telex: 919673. Cables: Rediffuse. FAX: (0207) 839 7135.

REUTERS TELEVISION LTD.
40 Cumberland Avenue, London, NW10 7EH. Tel: (0208) 965 7733. FAX: (0208) 965 0620.
DIRECTOR
Enrique Jara
HEAD OF NEWS
Stephen Claypole

ROBOT PRODUCTIONS LTD
Unit 121, Battersea Business Centre, 99-109 Lavender Hill, London SW11 2QD. Tel: (0207) 585 0015. FAX: (0207) 585 0014.
DIRECTOR
Simon Cassels

PETER ROGERS PRODUCTIONS LTD.
Pinewood Studios, Iver Heath, Bucks. SL0 0NH. Tel: (01753) 651 700. FAX: (01753) 656 844.
DIRECTORS
Peter Rogers
B. E. Rogers
G. E. Malyon

ROMULUS FILMS LTD.
214, The Chambers, Chelsea Harbour, London, SW10 0XF. Tel: (0207) 376 3791. FAX: (0207) 352 7457.
DIRECTORS
Sir John Woolf (Chairman)
J. C. Woolf
M.A., Lady Woolf
C. E. Fielding

ROYAL SOCIETY FOR THE PROTECTION OF BIRDS (RSPB)
Film and Video Unit, The Lodge, Sandy, Beds. SG19 2DL. Tel: (01767) 680 551. Telex: 82469 RSPB. FAX: (01767) 692 365.
FILM & VIDEO MANAGER
Colin Skevington

SAFIR FILMS LTD.
49 Littleton Road, Harrow, Middlesex HA1 3SY. Tel: (0208) 423 0763. FAX: (0208) 423 7963.
CONTACT
Lawrence Safir

SALAMANDER FILM PRODUCTIONS LTD.
Seven Pines, Wentworth, Surrey. FAX: (01344) 845 174.
DIRECTORS
Bryan Forbes, Nanette Forbes, John L. Hargreaves

THE SALES COMPANY
62 Shaftesbury Ave., London, W1V 7AA. Tel: (0207) 434 9061. FAX: (0207) 494 3293.
CONTACT
Alison Thompson

SAMUELSON PRODUCTIONS
23 West Smithfield, London EC1A 9HY. Tel: (0207) 236 5532. FAX: (0207) 236 5504.
MANAGING DIRECTOR
Marc Samuelson

SANDS FILMS STUDIOS
119 Rotherhithe Street, London SE16 4NF. Tel:(0207) 231 2209. FAX: (0207) 231 2119.
CONTACT
Olivier Stockman

SCALA PRODUCTIONS
15 Frith Street, London W1V 5TS. Tel: (0207) 734 7060. FAX: (0207) 437 3248. email: scalaprods@aol.com
CONTACTS
Nick Powell
Stephen Woolley

SCIMITAR FILMS LTD.
6 8 Sackville Street, London, W1X 1DD. Tel: (0207) 734 8385. FAX: (0207) 602 9217.
DIRECTORS
Michael Winner M.A. (Cantab)
John Fraser, M.A. (Oxon), M.Phil

SCOTT FREE ENTERPRISES LTD.
6 10 Lexington St., London, W1R 36S. Tel: (0207) 437 7426.

SCREEN SCENE PRODUCTIONS LTD
Garden Suite, 51 Goldney Road, London W9 2AR. Tel: (0207) 286 4308. FAX: (0207) 286 3525.
CONTACT
E Joffe

SEPTEMBER FILMS
Silverhouse, 35 Beak Street, London W1R 3LD. Tel: (0207) 494 1884. FAX: (0207) 439 1194. email: september@tcp.co.uk
MANAGING DIRECTOR
David Green

SETAN A STUDIOS LTD.
Ardmore Studios, Herbert Road, Bray, Co. Wicklow, Ireland. Tel: (1) 286 2971. FAX: (1) 286 1894.
CONTACT
Tracey Richardson

SEVENTH HEAVEN PRODUCTIONS
14 Annandale Road, London W4 2HH. Tel: (0208) 696 0377. FAX: (0208) 696 0390.

HASAN SHAH FILMS LTD
153 Burnham Towers, Adelaide Road, London NW3 3JN. Tel: (0207) 722 2419. FAX: (0207) 483 0662.
PRODUCER AND DIRECTOR
Hasan Shah

SHAND PICTURES LTD.
Rosehill House, Rose Hill Nr. Burnham, Bucks SL1 8NN. Tel: (0168) 605129.
DIRECTORS
I. E. L. Shand, D. J. Bennett, F. Shand

SHART BROS LTD
52 Lancaster Road, London N4 4PR. Tel: (0207) 263 4435. FAX: (0207) 436 9233.
PRODUCER
Patrick Shart

SHEPPERTON STUDIOS
Studios Road, Shepperton, Middx. TW17 0QD. Tel: (01932) 562 611. FAX: (01932) 568 989.
CONTACT
Paul Oliver

SIEGE PRODUCTIONS LTD.
17 Adam's Row, London, W1. Tel: (0207) 493 4441.
MANAGING DIRECTOR
Peter Fetterman

SILVER
61 Charlotte Street, London W1P 1LA. Tel: (0207) 208 1520. FAX: (0207) 208 1521. email: enquiries@silver-digital.co.uk
HEAD OF PRODUCTION
Jeff Emerson

SILVER PRODUCTION (LONDON) LTD
29 Castle Street, Salisbury, Wiltshire SP1 1TT. Tel: (01722) 336221. FAX: (01722) 336 227. www.silver-productions.co.uk email: ethem@silver-productions.co.uk
CONTACT
Etham Cetintas

SKREBA FILMS LTD.
5a Noel St., London, W1V 3RB. Tel: (0207) 437 6492. FAX: (0207) 437 0644.

SKYLINE FILMS
P.O. Box 8210, London W4 1WH. Tel: (0208) 354 2236. FAX: (0208) 354 2219. email: sky@easynet.co.uk
MANAGING DIRECTOR
Steve Clark-Hall

SMART EGG PICTURES
62 Brompton Road, London, SW3 1BW. Tel: (0207) 581 1841. Telex: 27786 GZOM G. FAX: (0207) 581 8998.
CONTACT
Tom Stoberg

SOVEREIGN PICTURES INC.
10 Greek Street, London, W1V 5LE. Tel: (0207) 494 1010. FAX: (0207) 494 3949. Telex: 261564 SOVE G.

SPECIFIC FILMS
25 Rathbone Street, London W1P 1AG. Tel: (0207) 580 7476. FAX: (0207) 434 2676. email: specificfilms@compuserve.com
PRODUCERS
Michael Hamlyn
Christian Routh

STARFIELD PRODUCTIONS
1st and 2nd Floors, 50 Chiswick High Road, London W4 1SZ. Tel: (0208) 995 8060. FAX: (0208) 994 1113. email: starfeel@dircon.co.uk

STERLING PICTURES LTD
33 Percy Street, London W1P 0LN. Tel: (0207) 439 4330. FAX: (0207) 287 4323. email: mriley_@hotmail.com
CONTACTS
Michael Riley
Tedi de Toledo

SYNDICATE PICTURES LTD
63-65 Riding House Street, London W1P 7PP. Tel: (0207) 636 6336. FAX: (0207) 636 6226. www.synpics.com/syndicate
email: mailbox@synpics.com/syndicate

TALISMAN FILMS LIMITED
5 Addison Place, London W11 4RJ. Tel: (0207) 603 7474. FAX: (0207) 602 7422. email: email@talismanfilms.com
EXECUTIVE PRODUCER
Alan Shallcross

TAPSON STEEL FILMS
24 Hanway Street, London W1P 9DD. Tel: (0207) 636 0033. FAX: (0207) 636 0043.
PRODUCERS
Charles Steel
Polly Tapson
Nick Love

TKO COMMUNICATIONS LTD.
P.O. Box 130, Hove, East Sussex, BN3 6QV. Tel: (01273) 550 088. FAX: (01273) 540 969.
DIRECTORS
J. S. Kruger
R. Kruger

TARGET INTERNATIONAL LTD.
A 29 Barwell Business Pk., Leatherhead Road, Chessington Castle, Surrey KT9 2NY. Tel: (0208) 974 1021. FAX: (0208) 974 2674.
CHAIRMAN
Terry Shand
MANAGING DIRECTOR
Geoffrey Kerpin

TARTAN FILMS LTD.
40 Bernard St., London, WC1N 1LG. Tel: (0207) 837 3377. FAX: (0207) 833 4102.
CONTACT
Hamish McAlpine

TECHNICOLOR LTD.
(Subsidiary of Carlton Communication PLC.)
Bath Road, West Drayton, Middlesex, UB7 0DB. Tel: (0208) 759 5432. FAX: (0208) 897 2666.
MANAGING DIRECTOR & CEO
Ashley Hopkins

THIN MAN FILMS LTD
9 Greek Street, London W1V 5LE. Tel: (0207) 734 7372. FAX: (0207) 287 5228.
PRODUCER
Simon Channing-Williams
DIRECTOR
Mike Leigh

THE 39 PRODUCTION COMPANY LTD
The Estate Offices, Knebworth House, Knebworth, Hertfordshire SG3 6PY. Tel: (01438) 814150. FAX: (01438) 816909.
CONTACT
Henry Cobbold

TILIRIS FILM PRODUCTIONS
13A Fitzgeorge Ave., London W14 0SY. Tel: (0207) 602 2824. FAX: (0207) 371 4709.

TOTEM PRODUCTIONS
8 York Mansions, Prince of Wales Drive, London SW11 4DN. Tel: (0207) 738 8377. FAX: (0207) 738 8378.
email: 101505.2156@compuserve.com
CONTACT
Francis Gerard

TRING ENTERTAINMENTS
Twickenham Film Studios, St. Margarets, Twickenham, TW1 2AW, Middx. Tel: (0208) 892 4477. FAX: (0208) 891 5574.
DIRECTORS
Maurice Landsberger
Nabil Daou

TROY FILMS, LTD.
Film Rights Ltd., Hammer House, 113 Wardour Street, London, W1V 4EH. Tel: (0207) 437 7151.
DIRECTORS
Michael Anderson
Maurice Lambert

TURNER INTERNATIONAL
19 22 Rathbone Place, London, W1P 1DF. Tel: (0207) 637 6900.
CONTACT
Howard Karshan

TWENTIETH CENTURY FOX FILM CO. LTD.
20th Century House, 31 32 Soho Square, London, W1V 6AP. Tel: (0207) 437 7766. FAX: (0207) 434 2170.
DIRECTORS
S. Moore
P. Livingstone

TWICKENHAM FILM STUDIOS LTD.
St. Margarets, Twickenham, Middlesex, TW1 2AW. Tel: (0208) 892 4477. FAX: (0208) 891 0168.
CONTACT
G. Humphreys

TWO HATS PRODUCTIONS
Unit 20, The Pall Mall Deposit, 124-128 Barlby Road, London W10 6BL. Tel: (0208) 964 2582. FAX: (0208) 964 4614.
email: twohats@virgin.net
PRODUCER
Georgia Dussaud

TYRO PRODUCTIONS
The Coach House, 20 A Park Road, Teddington, Middlesex TW11 0AQ. Tel: (0208) 943 4697. FAX: (0208) 943 4901.
CONTACT
Simon Passmore

UGC UK LTD.
(Formerly Lumiere Pictures Ltd.)
24 av Charles de Gaulle, 92522 Neuilly sur Seine, France. Tel: (33 146) 404 400. FAX: (33 146) 243 728.
CHAIRMAN
Alain Sussfeld
EXECUTIVE V.P. (UK)
Louisa Dent

UNION PICTURES
36 Marshall Street, London, W1V 1LL. Tel: (0207) 287 5100. FAX: (0207) 287 3770.
DIRECTORS
Brad Adams, Franc Roddam, Geoff Deeham
CONTACT
Richard Kalms

UNITED ARTISTS SCREEN ENTERTAINMENT LTD.
84 86 Regent Street, London, W1R 5PF. Tel: (0207) 915 1717. FAX: (0207) 915 1702.
DIRECTORS
Trevor Fetter
Brian Yell
CONTACT
Paul Hudson

UNITED CINEMAS INTERNATIONAL UK LTD.
Lee House, 90 Great Bridgewater Street, Manchester, MI 5JW. Tel: (0161) 455 4000. FAX: (0161) 455 4079.
MANAGING DIRECTOR
Steve Knibbs

UNITED INTERNATIONAL PICTURES
(A subsidiary of United International Pictures B.V., Postbus 9255, 1006 AG Amsterdam, The Netherlands.)
UIP House, 45 Beadon Road, Hammersmith, London, W6 0EG. Tel: (0208) 741 9041. Telex: 8956521. FAX: (0208) 748 8990.
PRESIDENT & CEO
Michael Williams Jones
SENIOR V.P., GENERAL COUNSEL
Brian Reilly
SENIOR V.P., MARKETING
Hy Smith
SENIOR V.P., FINANCE & ADMINISTRATION
Peter Charles
SENIOR V.P., INTERNATIONAL SALES
Andrew Cripps
V.P., PUBLICITY
Anne Bennett
V.P., PROMOTIONS
Mark deQuervain
V.P., SALES, LATIN AMERICA
Michael Murphy
V.P., SALES, EUROPE
Tony Themistocleous
SENIOR EXEC./GENERAL MANAGER-PAY TV GROUP
Andrew Kaza

UNITED INTERNATIONAL PICTURES (UK)
Mortimer House, 37 41 Mortimer Street, London, W1A 2JL. Tel: (0207) 636 1655. FAX: (0207) 637 4043 (Mr. Hedges). FAX: (0207) 636 4118 (Accounts/Sales). FAX: (0207) 323 0121 (Publicity).
MANAGING DIRECTOR
Christopher Hedges
DIRECTOR OF MARKETING
Ken Green

UNIVERSAL PICTURES LTD.
c/o UIP House, 45 Beadon Rd., Hammersmith, London, W6 0EG. Tel: (0208) 563 4329. FAX: (0208) 563 4331.

VICTOR FILMS COMPANY
2B Chandos Street, London, W1M 0EH. Tel: (0207) 636 6620. FAX: (0207) 636 6620.
MANAGING DIRECTOR
Vic Bateman

VIRGIN CINEMAS LTD.
Adelaide House, 626 High Road., Chiswick, London W4 5RY. Tel: (0208) 987 5000. FAX: (0208) 742 2998.
COMMERCIAL DIRECTOR
Margaret Taylor
BOOKING MANAGER
Joe Nunes

VISUAL PROGRAMME SYSTEMS LTD.
Sardinia House, 52 Lincoln's Inn Fields, London, WC2A 2L2. Tel: (0207) 405 0438. FAX: (0207) 831 9668.
CONTACT
Bernard Gilinsky

VIVA FILMS LTD
C/O NLPAC, 76 St James Lane, London N10 3DF. Tel: (0208) 444 5064. FAX: (0208) 444 1074.
email: vivafilms@dial.pipex.com
CONTACT
John Goldshmidt

WALPORT INTERNATIONAL LTD.
(Subsidiary of Novo Communications)
15 Park Road, London, NW1 6XH. Tel: (0207) 258 3977. FAX: (0207) 723 9568.
DIRECTORS
C. Preuster, S. Campion

WANDERING STAR
Strode Manor Farm, Netherbury, Blandford Forum, Dorset DT11. Tel: (01258) 881178. FAX: (01258) 881170.

WARNER BROS. DISTRIBUTORS LTD.
135 Wardour Street, London, W1V 4AP. Tel: (0207) 437 5600. Telex: 22653. FAX: (0207) 465 4869.
DIRECTORS
R. Fox
C. Young
E. Savat
W. Duband
C. Lima

WARNER BROS. OPERATIONAL DIVISION
135 Wardour Street, London, W1V 4AP. Tel: (0207) 734 8400. FAX: (0207) 437 2950.
MANAGING DIRECTOR
Maj Britt Kirchner

WARNER BROS. PRODUCTIONS LTD.
Warner Suite, Pinewood Studios, Iver Heath, Bucks., SL0 0NH. Tel: (01753) 654 545.
MANAGING DIRECTOR
R. D. Button
DIRECTORS
E. H. Senat
A. R. Parsons

WELBECK FILM DISTRIBUTORS, LTD.
52 Queen Anne Street, London, W1M 9LA. Tel: (0207) 935 1186.
DIRECTORS
Mrs. B. E. Rogers
R. P. Thomas
J. Thomas

WEST ONE FILM PRODUCERS LTD.
c/o Cooper Murray, Princess House, 50 60 Eastcastle Street, London, W1A 4BY. Tel: (0207) 436 4773. FAX: (0207) 436 1889.
DIRECTOR
Anthony Simmons

MICHAEL WHITE PRODUCTIONS LTD.
13 Duke St., St. James', London, SW1Y 6DB. Tel: (0207) 839 3971. FAX: (0207) 839 3836.
DIRECTORS
Michael S. White
Louise M. White

THE WICKES COMPANY
169 Queens Gate, London SW7 5HE. Tel: (0207) 225 1382. FAX:(0207) 589 8847.
COMPANY DIRECTOR
David Wickes

WORKING TITLE FILMS LTD.
1 Water Lane, Kentish Town Road, London, NW1 8NZ. Tel: (0207) 911 6100. Telex: 914106. FAX: (0207) 911 6150/1.
CONTACTS
Tim Bevan
Eric Fellner

WORLD FILM SERVICES LTD.
12 14 Argyll Street, London, W1V 1AB. Tel: (0207) 734 3536. FAX: (0207) 437 4098.
CHAIRMAN
John Heyman
MANAGING DIRECTOR
John Chambers

WORLD LEISURE CORP. MOTION PICTURES LTD
102 Dean Street, London W1V 5RA. Tel: (0207) 437 2345. FAX: (0207) 437 2021.
MANAGING DIRECTOR
Andy Grant

WORLDMARK PRODUCTIONS LTD.
The Old Studio, 18 Middle Row, London, W10 5AT. Tel: (0208) 960 3251. FAX: (0208) 960 6150.
DIRECTORS
Drummond Challis
David Wooster

WORLD PRODUCTIONS LTD
17 Golden Square, London W1R 4BB. Tel: (0207) 734 3536. FAX: :(0207) 734 3585. www.world-productions.com

WOT FILMS &TELEVISION LTD
Suite 3, 44 Mortimer Street, London W1N 7DG. Tel: (0207) 323 5901. FAX: (0207) 323 5903.
MARKETING DIRECTOR
Duncan Sibbald

WORLD WIDE GROUP LTD.
21 25 St. Anne's Court, London, W1V 3AW. Tel: (0207) 434 1121. FAX: (0207) 734 0619.
CONTACTS
R. King
R. Townsend
M. Rosenbaum
C. Courtenay Taylor

YELLOWNET FILM AND TV PRODUCTIONS
61 A Camden Road, London NW1 9EU. Tel: (0207) 482 3943. FAX: (0207) 482 3993.
DIRECTOR
Adel Fares

CHRISTOPHER YOUNG, FILMS LTD.
102 Brandon Street, London, SE17 1AL. Tel: (0207) 708 0820.

ZENITH GROUP
43 45 Dorset Street, London W1H 4AB. Tel: (0207) 224 2440. FAX: (0207) 224 3194.
DIRECTOR OF PRODUCTION
Scott Meek.

ZEPHYR FILMS LTD
24 Colville Road, London W11 2BS. Tel: (0207) 221 8318. FAX: (0207) 221 9289. email: user@zephyr-l.dircon.co.uk
PRODUCER
Philip Robertson

ANIMATION

A FOR ANIMATION LTD.
Unit 3A, The Old Malthouse, Little Anne St., Bristol BS2 9EW. Tel: (0117) 955 0611. FAX: (0117) 955 0600.
www.aforanimation.co.uk
email: info@afora.astra.co.uk
CONTACT
Mark Taylor

AARDMAN ANIMATIONS
Gas Ferry Rd., Bristol, Avon BS1 6UN. Tel: (0117) 984 8485. FAX: (0117) 984-8486. www.aardman.com
CONTACT
Lisa Murphy

THE ANIMATION PARTNERSHIP LTD.
77 Dean St., London W1V 5HA. Tel: (0207) 636 3300. FAX: (0207) 580 9153.

THE ANIMATION PEOPLE LTD.
5/7 Kean St., London WC2B 4AT. Tel: (0207) 836 1623. FAX: (0207) 836 4130.
CONTACT
Brian Larkin

ANIMATION SERVICES LTD.
9 Bourlet Close, London W1P 7PJ. Tel: (0207) 436 0426. FAX: (0207) 436 0428.

ANIMATION WORKS
10 Stokes Court, Diploma Ave., London N2 N8X. Tel: (0208) 883 3402.
CONTACT
Lee Stork

ANTICS WORKSHOP
42 Champion Hill, Camberwell, London SE5 8BS. Tel/FAX: (0207) 274 0135.

BARE BOARDS PRODUCTIONS LTD.
Studio 6, Commercial Wharf. 6 Commercial St., Manchester M15 467. Tel/FAX: (0161) 860 5660.
email:
purvesb@chf.co.uk

BERMUDA SHORTS LTD.
1 Lower John St., London W1R 3PD. Tel: (0207) 437 7335. FAX: (0207) 437 7334.
CONTACT
Maria Manton

BOLEXBROTHERS LTD.
3-6 Brunel Lock Development, Cumberland Basin, Bristol BS1 6SE. Tel: (0117) 985 8000. FAX: (0117) 985 8899.

BROOKE EDWARDS ANIMATION
21 Kingly St., London W1R 5LB. Tel: (0207) 734 9384. FAX: (0207) 734 9385. email: beukani@aol.com
CONTACT
Lee Hill

BUMPER FILMS LTD.
Unit 15, Bridgewater Ct., Oldmixon Crescent, Weston-super-Mare, N. Somerset BS24 9AY. Tel: (01934) 418 961. FAX: (01934) 624 494. email: bumper@ibm.net
CONTACT
John Walker

THE CANNING FACTORY
11b Albert Place, London W8 5PD. Tel: (0207) 937 1136. FAX: (0207) 938 1896. email: canningfactory@online.rednet.co.uk
DIRECTOR
Kate Canning

CARTWN CYMRU
Screen Centre, Llantrisant Rd., Cardiff, South Glamorgan CF5 2PU. Tel: (01222) 575 999. FAX: (01222) 575 919.
CONTACT
Naomi Jones

CELL LTD.
28-30 Osnaburgh St., London NW1 3ND. Tel: (0207) 208 1500. FAX: (0207) 208 1501.

CFX ASSOCIATES LTD.
16-18 Ramillies St., London W1V 1DL. Tel: (0207) 734 3155. FAX: (0207) 494 3670.
ANIMATORS
Craig Zerouni
Chris Briscoe

THE COMPUTER FILM COMPANY
19-23 Wells St., London W1P 3FP. Tel: (0207) 344 8000. FAX: (0207) 344 8001.
CONTACT
Rosy Burnie

CONCEPT MEDIA LTD.
Orwell Place, 172 Tunbridge Rd, Wateringbury Kent ME18 5NS. Tel/FAX: (01622) 817 178.
CONTACT
Denise Peckham

TONY CUTHBERT PRODUCTIONS
7A Langley St., London WC2H 9JA. Tel: (0207) 437 8884. FAX: (0207) 734 6579.
CONTACT
Susanna Balson

WALT DISNEY PRODUCTIONS LTD.
Beaumont House, Kensington Village, Avonmore Rd., London W14 8TS. Tel: (0207) 605 2400. FAX: (0207) 605 2795.

DUDOK DE WIT ANIMATION
Studio 153, 31 Clerkenwell Close, London EC1R 0AT. Tel: (0207) 608 1188. FAX: (0207) 608 1188.
www.dudokdewit.demon.co.uk
CONTACT
Michael Dudok De Wit

EALING ANIMATION
302 Canalot Production Studios, 222 Kensal Rd., London W10 5BN. Tel: (0208) 960 8188. FAX: (0208) 964 9917.

EAST ANGLIAN PRODUCTIONS
Frinton-on-Sea, Essex CO13 0AA Tel: (01255) 676 252. FAX: (01255) 850 528.
CONTACT
Ray Anderson

EDITPOINT
SM House, 26-27 West St., Horsham, West Sussex RH20 3BX. Tel: (01403) 241 345. FAX: (01403) 269 264.

ELECTRIC IMAGE LTD.
7-11 Lexington St., London W1R 3HQ. Tel: (0207) 287 8800. FAX: (0207) 287 3750.

FAIRWATER FILMS LTD.
68 Vista Rise, Llandaff, Cardiff CF5 2SD. Tel/FAX: (01222) 578 488.
ANIMATOR
Tony Barnes

ESPRESSO ANIMATION
17-18 Dover St, London W1X 3PB. Tel: (0207) 409 0576. FAX: (0207) 493 1507. email: espressoanimation@compuserve.com
DIRECTOR
Philip Vallentin

FILMFAIR ANIMATION LTD.
106 Gloucester Place,London W1H 3DB. Tel: (0207) 935 1596. FAX: (0207) 935 0229.

FLICKS FILMS LTD.
101 Wardour St., London W1V 3TD. Tel: (0207) 734 4892. FAX: (0207) 287 2307. email: flicks@demon.co.uk
CONTACT
Tracy Cook

FAMOUS FLYING FILMS LTD
Unit 122, 31 Clerkenwell Close, London EC1R 0AT. Tel: (0207) 608 1977. FAX: (0207) 608 1973.
email: famousflyingfilms@btinternet.com
CONTACT
David Johnson

FRAMELINE
33-34 Rathbone Pl., London W1P 1AD. Tel: (0207) 636 1301. FAX: (0207) 436 8878.

FUNNY BUSINESS LTD.
61 Connaught St., London W2 2AE. Tel: (0207) 402 9281. FAX: (0207) 402 2643.

G&M PRODUCTIONS
3 Carlisle St., London W1 5RH. Tel: (0207) 439 6936. FAX: (0207) 439 0280.
CONTACT
Mike Wallis

BOB GODFREY FILMS
199 Kings Cross Rd., London WC1X 9DB. Tel: (0207) 278 5711. FAX: (0207) 278 6809.
CONTACT
Bob Godfrey

GRAND SLAMM PARTNERSHIP LTD.
22 Bloomsbury St., London WC1B 3QJ. Tel: (0207) 436 1982. FAX: (0207) 323 0183.

HIBBERT RALPH ANIMATION LTD.
10 D'Arblay St., London W1V 3FP. Tel: (0207) 494 3011. FAX: (0207) 494 0383. www.hibbert-ralph.co.uk
email: info@hibbert-ralph.co.uk
CONTACTS
Maddy Sparrow
Bernadette Hannon
John Woolley

GRIFFILMS LTD
Cae Llenor, Lon Parc, Caernarfon, Gwynedd LL55 2HH. Tel: (01286) 685304. FAX: (01286) 685301.
email: griffilms@cwmnida.co.uk
DIRECTOR
Hywel Griffith

HELLZAPOPPIN PICTURES LTD
2 Eaton Crescent, Clifton, Bristol, Co Bristol BS8 2EJ. Tel: (0117) 923 7581. FAX: (0117) 923 7810.
email: hellzapoppin@compuserve.com

HONEYCOMB ANIMATION STUDIOS
Bank House, 66 High St, Honiton, Devon EX14 8PD. Tel: (01404) 47077. FAX: (01404) 47066
email: honeycomb@compuserve.com

ICE PICS
111A Wardour St., London W1V 3TD. Tel: (0207) 437 3505. FAX: (0207) 287 0393.
CONTACT
Mike Davis

KING ROLLO PRODUCTIONS
Dolphin Court, High Street, Honiton Devon EX14 8LS. Tel: (01404) 45218 FAX: (01404) 45328.

KLACTOVEESEDSTEENE ANIMATIONS
49/50 Great Marlborough St., 2nd floor, London W1V 1DB. Tel: (0207) 439 1420. FAX: (0207) 434 0410.
email: klacto@klacto.com
CONTACT
Sue Hicks

LEEDS ANIMATION WORKSHOP
45 Bayswater Row, Leeds LS8 5LF. Tel: (0113) 248 4997. FAX: (0113) 248 4997.
CONTACT
Jane Bradshaw

LIQUID TELEVISION GRAPHICS LTD
1-2 Portland Mews, Soho, London W1V 3FL. Tel: (0207) 437 2623. FAX: (0207 437 2618. www.liquid.co.uk
email: info@liquid.co.uk

MAGNETIC IMAGE GRAPHICS
6 Grand Union Centre, West Row, North Kensington, London W10 5AS. Tel: (0208) 964 5000. FAX: (0208) 964 4110.

MATTES AND MINIATURES
Bray Studios, Water Oaklet, Windsor, Berks SL4 5UG. Tel: (01628) 622111, ext. 126. FAX: (01628) 778 872.
CONTACT
Leigh Took

MELENDEZ FILMS
1-17 Shaftesbury Avenue, Picadilly Circus, London W1V 7RL. Tel: (0207) 434 0220. FAX: (0207) 434 3131.

PUSHME PULLYOU ANIMATION
19 Oxford Rd, Teddington, Middlesex TW11 OQA. Tel: (0208) 395 5130. FAX: (0208) 395 5129.
PRODUCER
Harriet Hellman BA (Hons)

TJFX DEPARTMENT
40-41 Great Marlborough St., London W1V 1DA. Tel: (0207) 287 4041. FAX: (0207) 287 8393.
CONTACTS
Dave Levy
Dave Throssell

HILL ROBERTS FILMS
Unit 2, 81 Southern Row, London W10 5AL. Tel: (0208) 964 0234. FAX: (0208) 968 7710.
email:
hillroberts.firms@virgin.net
CONTACT
Julian Roberts

RAY MOORE ANIMATION LTD.
Animation Centre, 113 Humber Rd., London SE3 7LW. Tel: (0208) 853 1164. FAX: (0208) 853 3043.
CONTACT
Ray Moore

NISSELL LTD.
Maxted Close, Hemel Hempstead, Herts HP2 7BS. Tel: (01422) 69101. FAX:(01422) 211 804.

PASSION PICTURES LTD.
25-27 Riding House St. London W1P 7PB. Tel: (0207) 323 9933. FAX: (0207) 323 9030.
CONTACT
Sian Rees

PEARCE STUDIOS LTD.
Old Lodge Farm, Coningsby Lane, Fifield, Maidenhead, Berks SL6 2PF. Tel: (01628) 627032. FAX: (01628) 777 343.
CONTACT
Rod Lord

PICASSO PICTURES LTD.
7 D'arblay St., London W1V 4FD. Tel: (0207) 437 9888. FAX: (0207) 437 9040. email: picasso@dial.pipex.com
CONTACT
Jane Bolton

PIZAZZ PICTURES
30 Berwick St., London W1V 3RF. Tel: (0207) 434 3581. FAX: (0207) 437 2309.
CONTACT
Pam Dennis

PUPPET VISUALS
60 Catton Chase, Old Catton, Norwich, Norfolk NR6 7AS. Tel: (01603) 482513.

RAGDOLL PRODUCTIONS
11 Chapel Street, Stratford upon Avon, Warwickshire CV 37 6EP. Tel: (01789) 262 772 FAX: (01789) 262 773

ROCKY ROAD PRODUCTIONS LTD.
9 Wellington Road, Wimbledon Park London SW19 8EQ. Tel: (0208) 947 2404. FAX: (0208 947 2404.
CONTACT
John Ley

SCENE 2
72 Campbell Rd., Woodley, Reading RG5 3PG. Tel/FAX: (01734) 268144.

SIMONETTI PRODUCTIONS LTD.
18 Leighton Crescent, Kentish Town London NW5 2QY. Tel: (0207) 284 1164. FAX: (0207) 284 1392.
MANAGER
Gina Heffler

SIRIOL PRODUCTIONS
Phoenix Buildings, 3 Mount Stuart Square Butetown, Cardiff CF1 6RW. Tel: (01222) 488400 FAX: (01222)485962
email: siriol@baynet.co.uk

SOHO 601
71 Dean St., London W1V 5HB. Tel: (0207) 439 2730. FAX: (0207) 734 3331.
CONTACT
John Roberts-Cox

SPEEDY FILMS LTD.
8 Royalty Mews, Dean St., London W1V 5AW. Tel: (0207) 494 4043. FAX: (0207) 434 0830.

STARDUST PICTURES
58-59 Highgate, Westhill., London N6 4RT. Tel: (0208).342 9444.
CONTACT
Gayle Martin

BRIAN STEVENS ANIMATED FILMS LTD.
11 Charlotte Mews, London W1P 1LN. Tel: (0207) 637 0535. FAX: (0207) 323 3892.
CONTACT
Brian Stevens

STOP FRAME LTD.
46 Fortrose St., Glasgow, Strathclyde G11 5LP. Tel: (0141) 334 2577. FAX: (0141) 334 8990.
CONTACT
Beart Ross

SUPER-VISIONS 3D COMPUTER ANIMATION
84A Telephone Pl., London SW6 1TH. Tel/FAX: (0207) 385 2848.
CONTACT
Gordon Tait

RICHARD TAYLOR CARTOON FILMS
76 Dukes Ave., London N10 2QA. Tel: (0208) 444 7547. FAX: (0208) 444 7218.

TELLY GRAPHICS LTD.
The Pictures, 5th floor, 41 St. Vincent's Place,.Glasgow G1 2ER. Tel: (0141) 226 2201. FAX: (0141) 248 1022.
CONTACT
David Long

TOUCH ANIMATIONS LTD.
44 Earlham St., London WC2H 9LA. Tel: (0207) 379 6247. FAX: (0207) 379 5210.
CONTACT
Jo Manser

TRIFFIC FILMS
114 High St., Stony Stratford, Milton Keynes, Bucks MK11 1AY. Tel: (01908) 261 234. FAX: (01908) 263 050.
CONTACT
Tim Searle

TV CARTOONS
39 Grafton Way, London W1P 5LA. Tel: (0207) 388 2222. FAX: (0207) 383 4192.
CONTACTS
John Coastes
Claire Jennings

WARDOUR MOTION PICTURES LTD.
Flint Studios Knatts Valley Nr Brands Hatch, Sevenoaks, Kent TN15 6XY. Tel & FAX: (0147) 485 3538

WILL VINTON PRODUCTIONS
10 D'Arblay St., London W1V 3FP. Tel: (0207) 613 3740. FAX: (0207) 494 0383.

WIZARD ANIMATION
Geller House, 51 Hoxton Sq., London N1 6PB. Tel/FAX: (0207) 613 3740.

WOODLAND ANIMATIONS LTD.
58 Queens Gate Mews, London SW7 5QN. Tel: (0207) 589 7584. FAX: (0207) 584 1790.
CONTACT
Mrs JO Wood

Z ANIMATION
8 Royalty Mews, Dean St., London W1V 5AW. Tel: (0207) 439 8653. FAX: (0207) 437 4518.

COSTUME SUPPLIERS

ACADEMY COSTUMES
50 Rushworth Street, London SE1 ORB. Tel: (0207) 620 0771 FAX: (0207) 928 6287. www.academycostumes.co.uk
email: academyco@aol.com

ANGELS & BERMANS
40 Camden Street, London, NW1 0EN. Tel: (0207) 387 0999. FAX: (0207) 383 5603.
119 Shaftesbury Avenue, London, WC2H 8AE. Tel: (0207) 836 5678. FAX: (0207) 240 9527. www.fancydress.com
email: info@angelscos.co.uk
CONTACTS
Tim Angel, Jonathan Lipman

THE ANTIQUE CLOTHING SHOP
282 Portobello Rd., London W10. Tel: (0208) 993 4162.
CONTACT
Sandy Stagg

ARMS & ARCHERY
The Coach House, London Road, Ware, Herts, SG12 9QU. Tel: (01920) 460 335. FAX: (01920) 461 044.
CONTACT
Terry Goulden

THE BUSINESS
Unit F36, The Acton Business Centre, School Road, London NW10 6DT. Tel: (0208) 963 0668. FAX: (0208) 838 0867.
email: bronwen@costume-rental.com
CONTACT
Bronwen Nolan

CARLO MANZI RENTALS
32 33 Liddell Road, London, NW6 2EW. Tel: (0207) 625 6391. FAX: (0207) 625 5386.

CLANCAST
P.O. Box 1305, Glasgow,
Lanarkshire G51 4WE. Tel: 0141 445 5599 FAX: 0141 445 5599. email: clancast@hotmail.com
CONTACT
Helen Craig

COSPROP LTD.
26 28 Rochester Place, London, NW1 9JR. Tel: (0207) 485 6731. FAX: (0207) 485 5942. www.cosprop.co.uk
email: costumes@cosprop.freeserve.co.uk
CONTACT
Bernie Chapman

THE COSTUME STUDIO
Montgomery House, 159-161 Balls Pond Rd., Islington N1 4BS Tel: (0207) 388 4481. FAX: (0207) 837 6576
www.thecostumestudioltd.co.uk
email: costume.studio@easynet.co.uk
CONTACTS
Rupert Clive, Richard Dudley

M.B.A. COSTUMES
Good Year House, 52-56 Osnaburgh St., London NW1 3ND. Tel: (0207) 388 4994. FAX: (0207) 383 2038.
CONTACTS
Noel Howard
Fred Brazier

PULLONS PM PRODUCTIONS
St. Georges Studio, Wood End Lane, Fillongley, Coventry, Warks CV7 8DF. Tel: (01676) 541 390. FAX: (01676) 542 438.

ROYAL NATIONAL THEATRE
1-3 Brixton Rd., London SW9 6DE. Tel: (0207) 820 1358. FAX: (0207) 820 9324.

ROYAL SHAKEPEARE COMPANY
Timothy's Bridge Rd., Sratford Upon Avon, Warks CV37 9UY. Tel: (01789) 25920. FAX: (01789) 205 920.
CONTACT
Alison Mitchell

TORBAY COSTUME HIRE
31 Market St., Torquay, Devon TQ1 3AW. Tel: (01803) 211 930. FAX: (01803) 293 554.
CONTACT
Lionel Digby

EDITING SERVICES

124 FACILITIES
124 Horseferry Rd., London SW1P 2TX. Tel: (0207) 306 8040. FAX: (0207) 306 8041.
CONTACTS
Carolyn Heald, Tracy Smith

ACMADE INTERNATIONAL LTD
Studio No 64, Shepperton Studios, Shepperton, Middlesex TW17 0QD Tel: (01923) 572560 FAX: (01923) 568414
CONTACT
Roger Merrison

BBC RESOURCES SCOTLAND
Broadcasting House, Queen Margaret Dr., Glasgow G12 8DG. Tel: (0151) 338 2020. FAX: (0141) 338 2335.
MARKETING & BUSINESS DEVELOPMENT MANAGER
Jim Douglas

BLUE POST PRODUCTION
58 Old Compton St., London W1V 5PA. Tel: (0207) 437 2626. FAX: (0207) 439 2477. email: sam.greewood@bluepp.co.uk
CONTACT
Samantha Greenwood

CAPITAL TELEVISION
13 Wandsworth Plain, London SW18 1ET. Tel: (0208) 874 0131. FAX: (0208) 877 0234.
CONTACT
Clare Phillips

CFX ASSOCIATES
16-18 Ramillies St., London W1V 1DL. Tel: (0207) 734 3155. FAX: (0207) 494 3670.
CONTACT
Alison Thompson

CHRYSALIS TODD-AO EUROPE
Hawley Crescent, Kindin NW1 8NP. Tel: (0207) 284 7900. FAX: (0207) 485 3667.
CONTACTS
Carolyn McManus
Kerry Aspinal

CUT & RUN LTD
22 Dean Street, London W1V 5AL. Tel: (0207) 434 2244 FAX: (0207) 434 2277. email: info@cutandrun.co.uk
CONTACT
Steve Gandolfi

DIGITAL ARTS
9-11 Richmond Buildings, Dean St., London W1V 5AF. Tel: (0207) 439 0919. FAX: (0207) 427 1146.
CONTACT
Geoff Axtell

EDIT HIRE
Unit7, St Margarets Business Centre. Moor Mead Rd, Twickenham Middlesex TW1 1JS. Tel: (0208) 892 6644. FAX: (0208) 892 5828. email: postmaster@edit-hire.com

ELECTRIC IMAGE
7-11 Lexington St., London W1R 3HQ. Tel: (0207) 287 8800. FAX: (0207) 287 3750.
CONTACT
Jay Williams

ESSENTIAL PICTURES
Canalot Studios, 222 Kensal Rd., London W10 5BN. Tel: (0208) 969 7017. FAX: (0208) 960 8201.
CHIEF EXECUTIVES
John Martineau
Robin Clarkson

THE FILM EDITORS
6-10 Lexington St., London W1R 3HS. Tel: (0207) 437 6409. FAX: (0207) 751 1119
CONTACT
Pam Power

FILM MEDIA SERVICES LTD.
Unit 8, Spacewaye, North Feltham Trading Est., Feltham, Middlesex TW14 0TH. Tel: (0208) 890 8780.
CONTACT
Brian Gilmore

FINAL CUT LTD
Fenton House,55-57 Great Marlbourough St., London W1V 1DD. Tel: (0207) 556 6300. FAX: (0207) 287 2824. email: finalcut@final-cut.co.uk

FOUNTAIN TELEVISION STUDIOS
Cocks Crescent, New Malden, Surrey KT3 4TA. Tel: (0208) 942 6633. FAX: (0208) 949 7911.
CONTACT
Bobbi Johnstone

400 COMPANY
Unit B3, Askew Crescent Workshops, 2a Askew Crescent, Shepherd's Bush, London W12 9DP. Tel: (0208) 746 1400. FAX: (0208) 746 0847. www.the400.co.uk
email: info@the400.co.uk
CONTACT
Mark Sloper

FRONTIER POST
66-67 Wells Street, London W1P 3RB. Tel: (0207) 291 9191. FAX: (0207) 291 9199. www.frontierpost.co.uk
email: info@frontierpost.co.uk
CONTACT
Beth Jefferyes

GENERAL SCREEN ENTERPRISES
Unit 9, Highbridge Estate, Oxford Rd., Uxbridge, Middlesex UB8 1LX. Tel: (01895) 231 931. FAX: (01895) 235 335.
CONTACT
Fred Chandler

HOLLOWAY FILM & TELEVISION
68-70 Wardour St., London W1V 3HP. Tel: (0207) 494 0777. FAX: (0207) 494 0309.
CONTACT
David Holloway

THE LANTREN TWINS
Leory House, 436 Essex Rd, Islington London N1 3QP. email: michael@lantren-twins.co.uk
CONTACT
Michael Whaley

LONDON POST
34-35 Dean St., London W1V 5AP. Tel: (0207) 439 9080. FAX: (0207) 434 0714. email: tim.wilmott@londonpost.co.uk
CONTACT
Tim Wilmot

THE LONDON STUDIOS
The London Television Centre, Upper Ground, London SE1 9LT. Tel: (0207) 261 3473. FAX: (0207) 633 9703.
CONTACT
Charlotte Bernard

THE MILL
40-41 Great Marlborough St., London W1V 1DA. Tel: (0207) 287 4041. FAX: (0207) 287 8393.
HEAD OF PRODUCTION
Derryn Clarke

MOLINARE
34 Fouberts Pl., London W1V 2BH. Tel: (0207) 439 2244. FAX: (0207) 734 6813.
CONTACTS
Kate George
Simon Gosling

OBE PARTNERSHIP LTD.
16 Kingly St., London W1R 5LD. Tel: (0207) 734 3028. FAX: (0207) 734 2830.
CONTACT
Clare House

PARALLAX PICTURES LTD.
7 Denmark St, London WC2H 8LS. Tel: (0207) 836 1478. FAX: (0207) 497 8062.
CONTACT
Angela Murray

PINEWOOD STUDIOS LTD.
Pinewood Rd., Iver, Bucks SL0 0NH. Tel: (01753) 651 700. FAX: (01753) 656 844.
CONTACT
David Lance

PMPP FACILITIES
69 Dean Street, London W1V 5HB. Tel: (0207) 437 0979. FAX: (0207) 434 0386. www.pmpp@dircon.co.uk
email: pmpp@dircon.co.uk
CONTACT
Rosie Beauvais

QUANTEL LTD.
Turnpike Rd., Newbury, Berks RG14 2NE. Tel: (01635) 48222. FAX: (01635) 31776.
CONTACT
Roger Thornton

THE QUARRY
26-28 Brewer Street, London W1R 3FW Tel: (0207) 437 4961. FAX: (0207) 437 1491.
email: postmaster@thequarry.demon.co.uk
CONTACT
Lucy Willcox

RED POST PRODUCTION
Hammersly House, 5-8 Warwick St., London W1R 6JD. Tel: (0207) 439 1449. FAX: (0207) 439 1339.
www.red-post.co.uk
PRODUCER
Carl Grinter

SHEARS POST PRODUCTION SERVICES
Warwick House, Shapone Pl., Dean St., London W1V 5AJ. Tel: (0207) 437 8182. FAX: (0207) 437 8183.
CONTACT
Steve Shears

TANGRAM POST PRODUCTIONS
5 Sherwood St., London W1V 7RA. Tel: (0207) 437 8710. FAX: (0207) 439 0491.

TV MEDIA SERVICES LTD.
3rd floor, 420 Suchiehall St., Glasgow G2 3JD. Tel: (0141) 331 1993. FAX: (0141) 332 9040.
CONTACT
Charles Chalmers

THE WHITEHOUSE POST PRODUCTION
12-13 Kingly St., London W1R 5LD. Tel: (0207) 287 3404. FAX: (0207) 287 9670.

FILM & VIDEO LABORATORIES

BUCKS MOTION PICTURE LABORATORIES LTD.
714 Banbury Avenue, Slough, Berks., SL1 4LH. Tel: (01753) 576 611. FAX: (01753) 691 762.
CONTACTS
Harry Rushton
Mike Bianchi.

COLOUR FILM SERVICES LTD.
22-25 Portman Close, Baker Street, London, W1A 4BE. Tel: (0207) 486 2881. Telex: 24672.
10 Wadsworth Road, Perivale, Greenford, Middx., UB6 7JX. Tel: (0208) 998 2731.

COLOUR VIDEO SERVICES LTD.
10 Wadsworth Rd., Perivale, Greenford, Middlesex UB6 7JX. Tel: (0208) 998 2731. FAX: (0208) 997 8738.

FILMATIC LABORATORIES LTD.
16 Colville Road, London, W11 2BS. Tel: (0207) 221 60208. FAX: (0207) 229 2718.
www.filmatic-lab.com
CHAIRMAN & MANAGING DIRECTOR
D. L. Gibbs
ASSISTANT MANAGING DIRECTOR
I. Magowan

HALLIFORD STUDIOS
Manygate Lane, Shepperton, Middlesex. Tel: (01932) 226 341. FAX: (01932) 246 336.
STUDIO MANAGER
Allan d'Aguiar

THE LANTREN TWINS
Leory House, 436 Essex Rd, Islington London N1 3QP. email: michael@lantren-twins.co.uk
CONTACT
Michael Whaley

METROCOLOR LONDON LTD.
22 Soho Square, London, W1V 5FL. Tel: (0207) 437 7811.
91/95 Gillespie Road, Highbury, London, N5 1LS. Tel: (0207) 226 4422. FAX: (0207) 359 2353.
MANAGING DIRECTOR
K. B. Fraser

PORTLAND RECORDING STUDIOS LTD.
35 Portland Place, London, W1N 3AG. Tel: (0207) 637 2111.

RANK FILM LABORATORIES LTD.
Denham, Uxbridge, Middlesex, UB9 5HQ. Tel: (01895) 832 323. Telex: 934704. FAX: (01895) 833 617.
MANAGING DIRECTOR
T. A. McCurdie
DIRECTOR OF SALES
David Dowler

SOHO IMAGES GROUP LTD.
8-14 Meard Street, London, W1V 3HR. Tel: (0207) 437 0831. FAX: (0207) 734 9471.
MANAGING DIRECTOR
Ray Adams

TECHNICOLOR LTD.
Bath Road, West Drayton, Middx., UB7 0DB. Tel: (0208) 759 5432. FAX: (0208) 897 2666.
MANAGING DIRECTOR
Ashley Hopkins

TWICKENHAM FILM STUDIOS, LTD.
St. Margarets, Twickenham, Middlesex, TW1 2AW. Tel: (0208) 892 4477. FAX: (0208) 891 0168.

UNITED MOTION PICTURES (LONDON) LTD.
3 and 36/38 Fitzroy Square, London, W.1. Tel: (0207) 580 1171, (0207) 388 1234.

WORLD WIDE GROUP
21-25, St. Anne's Court, London, W1V 3AW. Tel: (0207) 434 1121. Telex: 269271. FAX: (0207) 734 0619.

FINANCIAL SERVICES

AON ENTERTAINMENT LTD. INSURANCE SERVICES
9th floor, Minster Court, Mincing Lane, London EC3R 7AA. Tel: (0207) 283 1033. FAX: (0207) 283 1077.

BARCLAYS BANK MEDIA BANKING CENTRE
27 Soho Square, London, W1A 4WA. Tel: (0207) 439 6851. FAX: (0207) 434 9035.
www.barclays.com

COMPLETION BOND COMPANY INC.
Pinewood Studios, Iver Heath, Bucks., SL0 0NH. Tel: (01753) 652 433. Telex: 849003 CPLBND G. FAX: (01753) 655 697.
www.primenet.com

CONSOLIDATED ARTISTS
Strachans Somerville, Phillips Street, St. Helier, Jersey, Channel Islands. Tel: (01534) 71505. FAX: (01534) 23902.

CONTRACTS INTERNATIONAL LTD.
13-14 Golden Square, London, W1R 3AG. Tel: (0207) 287 5800. FAX: (0207) 287 3779. Telex: 295835.

EUROPEAN SCRIPT FUND
39c Highbury Place, London, N5 1QP. Tel: (0207) 226 9903.

F J ASSOCIATES
Little Orchard House, Bears Den, Kingswood, Tadworth, Surrey KT20 6PL. Tel: 01737 830084 FAX : 01737 830063
www.fvam.co.uk email: info@fvam.co.uk

GENERAL ENTERTAINMENT INVESTMENTS
65-67 Ledbury Road, London, W11 2AD. Tel: (0207) 221 3512. Telex: 28604. FAX: (0932) 868 989.

GUARANTORS INTERNATIONAL INC.
5 Carlton Gardens, Pall Mall, London, SW1Y 5AD. Tel: (0207) 839 9355. FAX: (0207) 839 1774.

GUINNESS MAHON & CO. LTD.
32 St. Mary at Hill, London, EC3P 3AJ. Tel: (0207) 623 9333. FAX: (0207) 283 4811.

INTERNATIONAL COMPLETION INC.
Pinewood Studios, Pinewood Road, Iver Heath, Bucks SL0 0NH. Tel: (01753) 651 700. FAX: (01753) 656 564.
www.completioninc.com

KPMG PEAT MARWICK
1 Puddle Dock, Blackfriars, London, EC4V 3PD. Tel: (0207) 236 8000. FAX: (0207) 248 6552.

MEDIA ADVISORY GROUP
5 Elstree Gate, Elstree Way, Borehamwood, Hertfordshire WD6 1JD Tel: (0208) 207 0602 FAX: (0208) 207 6758

MOVING IMAGE DEVELOPMENT AGENCY
109 Mount Pleasant, Liverpool, Merseyside L3 5TF Tel: 0151 708 9858 FAX: 0151 708 9859
email: enquire@mida.demon.co.uk

PARMEAD INSURANCE BROKERS LTD.
Lyon House, 160-166 Borough High Street, London, SE1 1JR. Tel: (0208) 467 8656. FAX: (0208) 295 1659.

PRODUCTION PROJECTS FUND
BFI, 29 Rathbone Place, London, WIP 1AG. Tel: (0207) 636 5587. FAX: (0207) 780 9456.

ROLLINS BURDICK HUNTER (INTERNATIONAL) LTD.
Braintree House, Braintree Road, Ruislip, Middx., HA4 0YA. Tel: (0208) 841 4461. FAX: (0208) 842 2124.

RUBEN SEDGWICK INSURANCE SERVICES
Pinewood Studios, Pinewood Road, Iver, Bucks., SL0 0NH. Tel: (01753) 654 555. FAX: (01753) 653 152

SAMUEL MONTAGU & CO. LTD.
10 Lower Thames Street, London, EC3 R6AE. Tel: (0207) 260 9000. FAX: (0207) 488 1630.

SARGENT-DISC LTD.
Pinewood Studios, Pinewood Road, Iver, Bucks. Tel: (01753) 656 631. FAX: (01753) 655 881.
www.sargent-disc.co.uk

SCOTTISH SCREEN
249 West George Street, Glasgow, Lanarkshire G2 4QE Tel: 0141 302 1700 FAX: 0141 302 1714
www.scottishscreen.com
email: info@scottishscreen.com
CHAIRMAN
James Lee

SPECTRUM ENTERTAINMENT GROUP PLC
The Pines, 11 Putney Hill, London, SW15 6BA. Tel: (0208) 780 2525. FAX: (0208) 780 1671. Telex: 262433.

UNITED MEDIA LTD.
2nd fl., Broadwick House, 8 12 Broadwick St., London, W1V 4EQ. Tel: (0207) 434 3501. FAX: (0207) 734 8893.

WILLIS WRIGHTSON LONDON LTD.
Willis Wrightson House, Wood Street, Surrey KT1 1UG. Tel: (0207) 860 6000. Telex: 929606. FAX: (0208) 943 4297.

PRODUCTION EQUIPMENT AND SUPPLIES

ABEKAS COX ELECTRONICS
Hanworth Trading Estate, Feltham TW13 6DH. Tel: (0208) 894 5622. FAX: (0208) 898 0298.

ACMADE INTERNATIONAL
Studio 64, Shepperton Studios, Studios Road, Shepperton, Middlesex, TW17 QD. Tel: (01932) 562 611. FAX: (01932) 568 414.

ADVANCED VIDEO HIRE LTD.
51 The Cut, London, SE1 8LF. Tel: (0207) 928 1963.

ADVENT COMMUNICATIONS LTD.
Watermeadow House, Watermeadow Chesham, Bucks. HP5 1LF. Tel: (01494) 774 400.

AGFA-GEVAERT (MOTION PICTURE DIVISION)
27 Great West Road, Brentford, Middlesex, TW8 9AX. Tel: (0208) 231 4310. FAX: ((0208)) 231 4315. www.agfa.co.uk
DIVISIONAL MANAGER
Ken Biggins

AMPEX MEDIA EUROPA
Unit 3, Commerce Park, Brunel Road, Reading, Berks, RG7 4AB. Tel: (01734) 302 208. FAX: (01734) 800 521 773.

AMSTRAD PLC
Brentwood House, 169 Kings Road, Brentwood, Essex, CM14 4EF. Tel:(01277) 228888.

ASTON ELECTRONIC DEVELOPMENTS, LTD.
125 Deepcut Bridge Road, Deepcut, Camberley, Surrey. Tel: (01251) 66221.

AUTOCUE LTD.
265 Merton Road, London, SW18 5JS. Tel: (0208) 870 0104. FAX: (0208) 874 3726.
CONTACTS
Sarah Lewis
Mick Gould

AV DISTRIBUTORS (LONDON) LTD.
21 22 St. Albans Place, Upper Street, Islington Green, London N1 0NX. Tel: (0207) 226 1508.

BAL COMPONENTS LTD.
Bermuda Road, Nuneaton, Warwickshire, CV10 7QF. Tel: (01203) 341 111. Telex: 311563.

F. W. O. BAUCH LTD.
49 Theobald Street, Boreham Wood, Herts., WD6 4RZ. Tel: (0208) 953 0091. Telex: 27502. FAX: (0208) 207 5970. www.fwobauch.com

R. R. BEARD LTD.
110 Trafalgar Avenue, London, SE15 6NR. Tel: (0207) 703 3136.

STUART BELL & PARTNERS LTD.
40 Frith Street, London, W1V 5TF. Tel: (0207) 439 2700.

BETTER SOUND LTD.
35 Endell Street, London, WC2. Tel: (0207) 836 0033.

CAMERON VIDEO SYSTEMS LTD.
Burnfield Road, Glasgow G46 7TH, Scotland. Tel: (0141) 633 0077. FAX: (0141) 633 1745.

CANON (UK) LTD.
TV Products Dept., Canon House, 2 Manor Rd., Wallington, Surrey, SM6 0BW. Tel: (0208) 773 3173. FAX: (0208) 773 2851.

CFS EQUIPMENT HIRE LTD.
10 Wadsworth Road, Perivale, Greenford, Middx., UB6 7JX. Tel: (0208) 998 2731. FAX: (0208) 997 8738. www.cfsequipment.co.uk

CINESOUND INTERNATIONAL LTD.
Imperial Studios, Maxwell Road, Boreham Wood, Herts., LWD6 1WE. Tel: (0208) 953 5387. FAX: (0208) 207 1728.
DIRECTORS
Mike Rogers
Angela Marshall

CINETECHNIC LTD.
169 Oldfield Ln., Greenford, Mdsx. Tel: (0208) 578 1011. 35 Briardale Gardens, London, NW3 7PN. Tel: (0207) 435 2289.

CINEVIDEO LTD.
7 Silver Road, White City Industrial Park, Wood Lane, London, W12 7SG. Tel: (0208) 743 3839. FAX: (0208) 743 8417.

DESISTI LIGHTING (UK) LTD.
15 Old Market Street, Thetford, Norfolk IP24 2EQ. Tel: (01842) 752 909. FAX: (01842) 753 746.

DOLBY LABORATORIES INC.
Interface Park, Wootton Bassett, Wiltshire, SN4 8QJ. Tel: (01793) 842 100. FAX: (01793) 842 101.
CONTACT
Catherine Unwin

JOE DUNTON CAMERAS LTD.
Wycombe Road, Wembley, Middlesex, HA0 1QN. Tel: (0208) 903 7933. Telex: 291843. email: dunton@compuserve.com

EDRIC AUDIO VISUAL LTD.
34-36 Oak End Way, Gerrard's Cross, Bucks, SL9 8BR. Tel: (01753) 884 646.

ENGLISH ELECTRIC VALVE COMPANY LTD.
Waterhouse Lane, Chelmsford, Essex. Tel: (01245) 493 493. Telegrams: Enelectico, Chelmsford. Telex: 99103.

ELECTRA FILM & TV LTD
64-66 Glentham Rd. Barnes, London Sw13 9JJ Tel: (0208) 563 7900 FAX: (0208) 563 7601. email: eftv@eftv.demon.co.uk

EXTREME FACILITIES
15-17 Este Rd, London SW11 2TL Tel: (0207) 801 9111. FAX: (0207) 801 9222. www.extremefacilities.com

FAMILY CHANNEL STUDIOS
Vinters Park, Maidstone, ME14 5NZ. Tel: (01622) 691 111. FAX: (01622) 684 456.

FUJI PHOTO FILM (UK) LTD.
Fuji Film House, 125 Finchley Road, London, NW3 6JH. Tel: (0207) 586 5900. FAX: (0207) 722 4259, Telex: 8812995.
DIVISIONAL MANAGER
E. J. Mould

GE THORN LAMPS LTD.
Miles Road, Mitcham, Surrey CR4 3YX. Tel: (0208) 640 1221. FAX: (0208) 640 9760. www.thornlamps.com

GEC LAMPS & LIGHTING LTD.
P.O. Box 17, East Lane, Wembley, Middlesex HA9 7PG. Tel: (0208) 904 4321.

GTE LIGHTING LTD.
Otley Rd., Charleston, Shipley, West Yorkshire. Tel: (01274) 595 921.

HARKNESS HALL LTD.
Gate Studios, Station Road, Boreham Wood, Herts., WD6 1DQ. Tel: (0208) 953 3611. FAX: (0208) 207 3657.

HAYDEN LABORATORIES LTD.
Hayden House, Chiltem Hill, Chalfont St. Peter, Gerrards Cross, Bucks., SL9 9UG. Tel: (01753) 888 447. FAX: (01753) 880 109.

HENDON STUDIO
2 Victoria Road, London, NW4 2BE. Tel: (0208) 203 4206. FAX: (0208) 203 7377. www.hendonstudios.co.uk

HITACHI DENSHI (UK) LTD.
13-14 Garrick Ind. Centre, Irving Way, Hendon, London, NW9 6AZ. Tel. (0208) 202 4311. FAX: (0208) 202 2451.

I.C. EQUIPMENT LTD.
Unit 1 3, The Robert Elliot Center, 1 Old Nichol Street, Shoreditch, London, E2 7HR. Tel: (0207) 739 4800. FAX: (0207) 729 2554.

INTERNATIONAL VIDEO CORPORATION
10 Portman Road, Reading, Berks., RG3 1JR. Tel: (01734) 585 421. Telex: 847579.

ITN LTD.
200 Gray's Inn Road, London, WC1X 8XZ. Tel: (0207) 833 3000. FAX: (0207) 430 4016. Telex: 22101.
CHIEF EXECUTIVE
Stewart Purvis

JVC PROFESSIONAL PRODUCTS (UK) LTD.
Alperton House, Bridgewater Road, Wembley, Middx. HA0 1EG. Tel: (0208) 902 8812. FAX: (0208) 900 0941.

KEM ELECTRONIC LTD
24 Vivian Avenue, Hendon Central, London, NW4 3XP. Tel: (0208) 202 0244. Telex: 28303.

KODAK LTD.
Professional Motion Imaging, P.O. Box 66, Kodak House, Station Road, Hemel Hempstead, Herts., HP1 1JU. Tel: (01442) 61122. FAX: (01442) 844458. www.kodak.co.uk
DIRECTOR & GENERAL MANAGER
John Parsons-Smith
NATIONAL SALES MANAGER
Denis Kelly

LEE COLORTRAN LTD.
Ladbroke Hall, Barlby Rd., London, W10 5HH. Tel: (0208) 968 7000.

LEE FILTERS LTD.
Central Way, Walworth Industrial Estate, Andover, Hants., SP10 5AN. Tel: (01264) 66245.

LEE LIGHTING
Wycombe Road, Wembley, Middlesex, HA0 1QD. Tel: (0208) 900 2900. FAX: (0208) 902 5500. www.lee.co.uk
email: info@lee.co.uk
CONTACT
Martin Maund

LIGHTHOUSE EDITING SYSTEMS LTD.
38 Soho Square, London, W1V GLE. Tel: (0207) 494 3084. FAX: (0207) 437 3570. www.lee.co.uk

LIMEHOUSE TELEVISION LTD.
The Trocadero, 19 Rupert Street, London, W1V 7FS. Tel: (0207) 287 3333. FAX: (0207) 287 1998. www.limehouse.co.uk
CONTACT
A. Goddard

MALHAM PHOTOGRAPHIC EQUIPMENT LTD.
65 67 Malham Road, London, SE23 1AJ. Tel: (0208) 699 0917. FAX: (0208) 699 4291.

MGB FACILITIES
Capital House, Sheepscar Court, Meanwood Rd, Leeds, West Yorkshire LS7 2BB. Tel: (0113) 243 6868 FAX: (0113) 243 8886. www.mgb.tv.co.uk/mgb

THE MINIATURE CAMERA COMPANY
7 Portland Mews, D'Arblay Street, London W1V 3FL Tel: (0207) 734 7776. FAX: (0207) 734 1360. www.skarda.net
email: sales@skarda.net
CONTACTS
John Buckley
John Venables
Dave Palmer

MITCHELL CAMERAS
Wycombe Road, Wembley, Middx. HA0 1QN. Tel: (0208) 903 7933. FAX: (0208) 902 3273.

NEILSON-HORDELL LTD.
Unit 18, Central Trading Estate, Staines, Middlesex, TW18 4XE. Tel: (01784) 456 456. FAX: (01784) 459 657.

OPTEX
22 26 Victoria Road, New Barnet, Herts. EN4 9PF. Tel: (0208) 441 2199. FAX: (0208) 449 3646.

OSRAM (GEC) LTD.
P.O. Box 17, East Lane, Wembley, Middlesex HA9 7PG. Tel: (0208) 904 4321.

OTARI ELECTRIC (UK) LTD.
22 Church Street, Slough, Berks, SL1 1PT. Tel: (01753) 822 381. FAX: (01753) 83707. www.otarielectric.com

PANASONIC BROADCAST EUROPE
117-119 Whitby Road, Slough, Berks, SL1 3DR. Tel: (01753) 692 442. FAX: (01753) 512 705.

PANAVISION (UK)
Wycombe Rd., Stonebridge Park, Wembley, Middx. HA0 1QN. Tel: (0208) 903 7933. FAX: (0208) 902 3273.

PHILIPS LIGHTING LTD.
City House, 420 430 London Road, Croydon, Surrey CR9 3QR. Tel: (0208) 689 2166. FAX: (0208) 665 5102.

PHOENIX VIDEO
Unit 4, Denham Way, Maple Cross, Herts., WD3 2AS. Tel: (01923) 777 782. FAX: (01923) 772 163.

PHOTOMEC (LONDON) LTD.
Valley Road Industrial Estate, St. Albans, Herts, AL3 6NU. Tel: (01727) 501 711. FAX: (01727) 43991.

RADAMEC EPO LTD.
Bridge Road, Chertsey, Surrey, KT16 8LJ. Tel: (01932) 561 181. FAX: (01932) 568 775. Telex: 929945 RADEPOG.

RANK CINTEL
Watton Road, Ware, Herts, SG12 0AE. Tel: (01895) 463 939. Telex: 81415. FAX: (01895) 460 803.
MANAGING DIRECTOR
Jack R. Brittain

RANK TAYLOR HOBSON LTD.
P.O. Box 36, 2 New Star Road, Leicester, LE4 7JQ. Tel: (01533) 763 771. Telex: 342338. Cables: Metrology Lestr. FAX: (01533) 740167.
MANAGING DIRECTOR
Richard Freeman

PHILIP RIGBY & SONS LTD.
14 Creighton Avenue, Muswell Hill, London, N10 1NU. Tel: (0208) 883 3703. FAX: (0208) 444 3620.
www.philip-rigby.com

RONFORD-BAKER
Braziers, Oxhey Lane, Watford, Herts., WD1 4RJ. Tel: (0208) 428 5941. FAX: (0208) 428 4743.

RONFORD LTD.
Shepperton Film Studios, P. O. 30, Studio Road, Shepperton, Middx. TW17 0QD. Tel: (01932) 564 111. FAX: (01932) 561 423.

SAMUELSON FILM SERVICE LONDON LTD.
21 Derby Road, Metropolitan Centre, Greenford, Middx., UB6 8UQ. Tel: (0208) 578 7887. FAX: (0208) 578 2733.

MICHAEL SAMUELSON LIGHTING LTD.
Pinewood Studios, Iver Heath, Bucks. SL0 0NH. Tel: (01753) 631 133. FAX: (01753) 630 485.

SET PARTNERS
13 D'Arblay Street, London, W1V 3FP. Tel: (0207) 734 1067. FAX: (0207) 494 0197.

SHURE ELECTRONICS LTD.
Eccleston Rd., Maidstone, Kent, ME15 6AU. Tel: (01622) 59881.

S & H TECHNICAL SUPPORT GROUP
Unit A, The Old Laundry, Chambercombe Rd, Ilfracombe, Devon EX3 9PH Tel: (01271) 866 832. FAX: (01271) 865 423. www.new-med.co.uk email: shtsg@aol.com

SIGMA FILM EQUIPMENT LTD.
Unit K, Chantry Lane, Industrial Estate, Storrington, West Sussex, RH20 4AD. Tel: (019066) 3382.
www.sigma-film.co.uk

SONY BROADCAST LTD.
Jay Close, Viables, Basingstoke, Hants, RG22 4SB. Tel: (01256) 474 011. FAX: (01256) 474 585.

SOHO IMAGES GROUP LTD.
8-14 Meard Street, London, W1V 3HR. Tel: (0207) 437 0831. FAX: (0207) 734 9471. www.soho-images.com
MANAGING DIRECTOR
Ray Adams

STRAND LIGHTING
Grant Way, Off Syon Lane, Isleworth, Middx. TW9 5QD. Tel: (0208) 560 3171. FAX: (0208) 490 0002.

SYSTEM VIDEO LTD.
Venture House, Davis Rd., Chessington, Surrey KT9 1TT. Tel: (0208) 391 5678. FAX: (0208) 391 5522.

TECHNOVISION CAMERAS LTD.
Unit 4, St. Margaret's Business Centre, Drummond Place, Twickenham, Middlesex, TW1 1JN. Tel: (0208) 891 5961. FAX: (0208) 744 1154.

VARIAN TUT LTD.
P.O. Box 41, Coldhams Lane, Cambridge, CB1 3JU. Tel: (01223) 245 115. FAX: (01223) 214 632.

VIDEO TIME
22/24 Greek Street, London, W1V 5LG. Tel: (0207) 439 1211. Telex: 27256. FAX: (0207) 439 7336.

VIEWPLAN
1 Syon Gateway, Great West Road, Brentford, Middx., TW8 9DD. Tel: (0208) 847 5771.

VINTEN BROADCAST
Western Way, Bury St. Edmunds, Suffolk, IP33 3TB. Tel: (01284) 752 121. FAX: (01284) 750 560. www.vinten.co.uk

WESTAR SALES & SERVICES LTD.
Unit 7, Cowley Mill Trading Estate, Longbridge Way, Uxbridge, Middx., UB8 2YG. Tel: (01895) 34429. Telex: 8954169.

WOTAN LAMPS LTD.
1 Gresham Way, Durnsford Road, London, SW19 8HU. Tel: (0208) 947 1261. FAX: (0208) 947 5132.

ZONAL LTD.
Holmethorpe Avenue, Redhill, Surrey, RH1 2NX. Tel: (01737) 767 171. FAX: (01737) 767 610.

Publicity and Marketing

BLUE DOLPHIN FILMS
40 Langham Street, London, W1N 5RG. Tel: (0207) 255 2494. FAX: (0207) 580 7670.

CONSOLIDATED COMMUNICATIONS MANAGEMENT
1 5 Poland Street, London, W1V 3DG. Tel: (0207) 287 2087. FAX: (0207) 734 0772.

CORBETT & KEENE
122 Wardour St., London W1V 3TD. Tel: (0207) 494 3478. FAX: (0207) 734 2024.

NAMARA COWAN LTD.
45 Poland Street, London, W1V 3DF. Tel: (0207) 434 3871. Telex: 919034. FAX: (0207) 439 6489.
www3.showbizdata.com

CREATIVE PARTNERSHIP
19 Greek Street, London W1V. Tel: (0207) 439 7762. FAX: (0207) 437 1467. www.creativepartnership.co.uk

DENNIS DAVIDSON ASSOCIATES LTD.
Royalty House, 72 74 Dean Street, London, W1V 5HB. Tel: (0207) 439 6391. FAX: (0207) 437 6358.

CLIFFORD ELSON PUBLICITY LTD.
223 Regent Street, London, W1R 7DG. Tel: (0207) 495 4012. FAX: (0207) 495 4175.

EDELMAN PUBLIC RELATIONS
Kings Gate House, 536 Kings Road, London, SW10 0TE. Tel: (0207) 835 1222. FAX: (0207) 351 7676.
www.edelman.com

FEREF ASSOCIATES LTD.
14 17 Wells Mews, London, W1A 1ET. Tel: (0207) 580 6546. FAX: (0207) 631 3156.

MARGARET GARDNER CONSULTANTS
17 Onslow Square, London, SW7 3NJ. Tel: (0207) 584 6700. FAX: (0207) 581 9823.

SUE HYMAN ASSOCIATES LTD.
70 Chalk Farm Road, London, NW1 8AN. Tel: (0207) 485 8489. FAX: (0207) 267 4715.

IMPRESSION MEDIA & PUBLIC RELATIONS
Premier House, 77 Oxford St., London, W1R 1RB. Tel: (0207) 439 1188. FAX: (0207) 734 8367.

INTERMARK PUBLIC RELATIONS LTD.
91 Regent Street, London, W1R 7TB. Tel: (0207) 937 1284. FAX: (0207) 734 1014. URL: http://www.intermark.com

JAC PUBLICITY & MARKETING CONSULTANTS LTD.
36 Great Queen Street, Covent Garden, London, WC2B 5AA. Tel: (0207) 430 0211. FAX: (0207) 430 0222.

CAROLYN JARDINE PUBLICITY
2nd fl., 3 Richmond Bldgs., London, W1V 5EA. Tel: (0207) 287 6661. FAX: (0207) 437 0499.

RICHARD LAVER PUBLICITY
3 Troy Court, High Street Kensington, London, W8 7RA. Tel: (0207) 937 7322. FAX: (0207) 937 8670.

MEDIA RELATIONS LTD.
Glen House, 125 Old Brompton Road, London SW7 3RP. Tel: (0207) 835 1000. FAX: (0207) 373 0265.
www.mediamaven.com

PEARTREE ASSOCIATES LTD.
Cloister Court, 22 Farringdon Lane, London, EC1R 3AV. Tel: (0207) 250 0292. FAX: (0207) 250 3031.

ROGERS & COWAN INTERNATIONAL
43 King Street, Covent Garden, London, WC2E 8RJ. Tel: (0207) 411 3000. FAX: (0207) 411 3020.
CONTACTS
Phillip Symes
Brian Daly.

JUDY TARLO ASSOCIATES
35a Elizabeth Street, London, SW1W 9RP. Tel: (0207) 824 8815. FAX: (0207) 823 6195.

PETER THOMPSON ASSOCIATES
134 Great Portland Street, London, W1N 5PH. Tel: (0207) 436 5991. FAX: (0207) 436 0509.

TOWN HOUSE PUBLICITY
45 Islington Park Street, London, N1 1QB. Tel: (0207) 226 7450. FAX: (0207) 359 6026.

WINSOR BECK PUBLIC RELATIONS
Network House, 29 39 Stirling Road, London, W3 8DJ. Tel: (0208) 993 7506. FAX: (0208) 993 8276.

SOUND SERVICES

APS LTD.
4 Lapwing Lane, West Didsbury, Manchester M20 8WS. Tel: (0161) 448 9990. FAX: (0161) 448 2023.

ABBEY ROAD STUDIOS
3 Abbey Rd., St. John's Wood, London NW8 9AY. Tel: (0207) 266 7000. FAX: (0207) 266 7250.

ADMUSIC
Shepperton Studios, Studio No. 94, Studios Rd., Shepperton, Middlesex TW17 0QD. Tel: (01932) 572 266. FAX: (01932) 572 265. admusic-studios.com

ANVIL FILM & RECORDING GROUP LTD.
Denham Studios, North Orbital Rd., Denham, Nr. Uxbridge, Mdsx UB9 5HL. Tel: (01895) 833 522. FAX: (01895) 835 006.
CONTACT
Ken Somerville

BACKYARD RECORDING STUDIOS
Units 405, Willowbrook Industrial Estate, Crickhowell Rd., St. Mellons, Cardiff. Tel: (01222) 777 739. FAX: (01222) 798 901.

BOUNDARY ROW STUDIOS
1-7 Boundary Row, London SE1 8HP. Tel: (0207) 633 9629. FAX: (0207) 928 6082.

CTS STUDIOS LTD.
Engineers Way, Wembley, Middlesex HA9 0DR. Tel: (0208) 903 4611. FAX: (0208) 903 7130.

CINELINGUAL SOUND STUDIOS
27-29 Berwick St., London W1V 3RF. Tel: (0207) 437 0136. FAX: (0207) 439 2012. www.cinelingual-sound.com

D B POST PRODUCTIONS LTD.
1-8 Batemans Buildings, South Soho Square, London W1V 5TW. Tel: (0207) 434 0097. FAX: (0207) 287 9143.

DE LANE LEA SOUND CENTRE LTD.
75 Dean St., London W1V 5HA. Tel: (0207) 439 1721. FAX: (0207) 437 0913.

DELTA SOUND SERVICES
Shepperton Studios, Studios Rd., Shepperton, Middlesex TW17 0QD. Tel: (01932) 562 045. FAX: (01932) 572 396.

THE DIGITAL AUDIO COMPANY
3 Carleton Business Park, Carleton New Rd., Skipton, North Yorkshire BD23 2AA. Tel: (01756) 797 100. FAX: (01756) 797 101. www.the-digital-audio.co.uk

DIGITAL SOUND HOUSE
14 Livonia St., London W1V 3PH. Tel: (0207) 434 2928. FAX: (0207) 287 9110. www.digital-sound-house.com

THE FACILITY
Ravenhill Business Park, Ravenhill Rd., Belfast BT6 8AW. Tel: (01232) 450 231. FAX: (01232) 459 499.

FLAMINGO PRODUCTIONS
25-26 Poland St., London W1V 3DB. Tel: (0207) 437 2243. FAX: (0207) 437 0410.

FOUNTAIN TELEVISION LTD.
Cocks Crescent, New Malden, Surrey KT3 4TA. Tel: (0208) 942 6633. FAX: (0208) 949 7911. www.ftv.com

GRAND CENTRAL SOUND RECORDING
Ccaven House,25-32 Marshall St, London W1V 1LL. Tel: (0207) 306 5600 FAX: (0207) 306 5616. www.grand-central-studios.com

GWBB AUDIOVISION
2 Silver Rd., White City, London W12 7SG. Tel: (0208) 746 2000. FAX (0208) 746 0180.

G WHIZ TELEPRODUCTION
22 Chervil Way, Burghfield Common, Reading Berks RG7 3YX. Tel: (01734) 832 232. FAX: (01734) 831 295.

GATEWAY AUDIO VISUAL & VIDEO
472 Green Lanes, Palmers Green, London N13 5XF. Tel: (0208) 872 054. FAX: (0208) 882 4131.

HULABALOO STUDIOS
8 Albany Rd, Manchester, Lancashire M21 0AW. Tel: (0161) 882 0007 FAX: (0161) 882 0774.

INDUSTRIAL ACOUSTICS CO. LTD. (STUDIO DIVISION)
IAC House, Moorside Road, Winchester SO23 7US TW18 4XB. Tel: (01962) 873 000. FAX: (01962) 873 111.

INHOUSE PRODUCTIONS LTD.
3rd floor, Canada House, Chepstow St., Manchester M1 6FQ. Tel: (0161) 228 0366. FAX: (0161) 236 3056.

INTERACT SOUND LTD
160 Barlby Rd, London W12 9LB. Tel: (0208) 960 3115 FAX: (0208) 964 3022. www.interacr-sound.com

LANSDOWNE MUSIC PUBLISHING LTD.
Lansdowne House, Lansdowne Rd., London W11 3LP. Tel: (0207) 727 0041. FAX: (0207) 792 8904.

MAGMASTERS POST PRODUCTIONS
20 St. Annes Court, London W1V 3AW. Tel: (0207) 437 8273. FAX: (0207) 494 1281.

MATINEE SOUND & VISION
132 Oxford St., Reading, Berks RG1 7NL. Tel: (0118) 958 4934. FAX: (0118) 959 4936.

MAYFAIR RECORDING STUDIOS
11a Sharpleshall St. London NW1 8YN. Tel: (0207) 586 7746. FAX: (0207) 586 9721. email: bookings@mayfair.co.uk

NINTH WAVE AUDIO
PO Box 5517 Birmingham B13 8QB. Tel: (0121) 442 2276. FAX: (0121) 689 1902. www.ninth-wave-audio.com

OASIS TELEVISION LTD.
6-7 Great Pluteney St, London W1R 3DF. Tel: (0207) 434 4133. FAX: (0207) 494 2843. www.oasistv.co.uk

PERFECT PITCH
39 Landser Rd., London N19 4JU. Tel: (0207) 272 9456.

PINEWOOD SOUND DEPARTMENT
Pinewood Studios, Pinewood Rd., Iver, Bucks SL0 0NH. Tel: (01753) 656 301. FAX: (01753) 656 014.

RED BUS RECORDING & VIDEO STUDIOS LTD
Broadley House, 48 Broadley Terrace, London NW1 6UL. Tel: (0207) 258 0324. FAX: (0207) 724 2361.

THE SOUND COMPANY LTD.
23 Gosfield St., London W1P 7HP. Tel: (0207) 580 5880. FAX: (0207) 580 6454. www.sound.co.uk

THE SOUND DESIGNERS
11 Wardour Mews., London W1V 3FF. Tel: (0207) 437 7161. FAX: (0207) 437 3667.

THE SOUND HOUSE SCOTLAND
Forth House, Forth St., Edinburgh EH1 3LF. Tel: (0131) 557 1557. FAX: (0131) 557 3899. email: lorna@thesoundhouse.com

THE SOUND STUDIO LTD.
17 St. Annes Ct., London W1V 3AW. Tel/FAX: (0207) 734 6198.

THE SOUNDHOUSE LTD.
Unit 11, Goldhawk Industrial Estate, 2A Brackenbury Rd., Shepherds Bush, London W6 0BA. Tel: (0208) 743 2677.

STEREO FILM SOUND
3 Sterndale Rd., London W14 0HT Tel: (0207) 603 7401. FAX: (0207) 359 4027. email: Johnl@alchemea.demon.co.uk

STUDIO SOUND (PART OF IBF)
15 Monmouth Street, London WC2H 9DA. Tel: (0207) 497 1515. FAX: (0207) 379 8562

SYNCHRO SONICS LTD.
5 Richmond Mews, Richmond Building, London W1V 5AG. Tel: (0207) 437 3361. FAX: (0207) 437 0913.

TARAN STUDIOS
Cardiff Workshops, Lews Rd., Cardiff CF1 5EJ. Tel: (01222) 484 298. FAX: (01222) 451 200.

TRIANGLE
81 Whitfield Street, London W1A 4XA. Tel: (0207) 255 5215. FAX: (0207) 255 5215

UNIVERSAL SOUND
16 Aintree Rd., Perivale, Middlesex UB6 7LA. Tel: (0208) 998 1619. FAX: (0208) 991 9461.

VIDEOLONDON SOUNDSTUDIOS
16-18 Ramillies St., London W1V 1DL. Tel: (0207) 734 4811. FAX: (0207) 494 2553. email: info@videolon.ftech.co.uk

VIDEOSONICS LTD.
13 Hawley Crescent, London NW1 8NP. Tel: (0207) 482 2855. FAX: (0207) 482 0849. www.videosonics.com

WARWICK DUBBING THEATRE
111 A Wardour St., London W1V 3TD. Tel: (0207) 437 5532. FAX: (0207) 439 0372.

WILD TRACKS AUDIO STUDIOS LTD
2nd Floor, 55 Greek Street, London W1V 5LR. Tel: (0207) 734 6331 FAX: (0207) 734 6195.

SPECIAL EFFECTS

AARDMAN ANIMATIONS LTD.
Gas Ferry Rd., Bristol, Avon BS1 6UN. Tel: (0117) 984 8485. FAX: (0117) 984 8486. www.aardman.com
email: mail@aardman.com

ALBATROSS MODELS, SETS, EFFECTS
Unit 2, Beckett's Wharf, Lower Teddington Rd., Hampton Wick, Kingston-upon-Thames, Surrey KT1 4ER. Tel: (0208) 943 4720. FAX: (0208) 977 0854.

ANIMATED EXTRAS
Buiding 13/24a, Shepperton Film Studios, Studios Rd., Shepperton, Middlesex TW17 0QD. Tel: (01932) 562 611, ext. 2347. FAX: (01932) 569 605.

ANY EFFECTS
64 Weir Rd., London SW19 8UG. Tel :(0208) 944 0099. FAX: (0208) 944 6989. www.anyeffects.com
email: lisa@anyeffects

ARTEM VISUAL EFFECTS
Perivale Industrial Park, Horsenden Lane, South Perivale, Middlesex UB6 7RH. Tel: (0208) 997 7771. FAX: (0208) 997 1503. www.artem.com
email: info@artem.com

CHRIS CORBOULD
Rustling, 4 Tudor Close, Great Bookham, Surrey, KT23 3DP
Tel/FAX: (01372) 454088

CINE IMAGE FILM OPTICALS
7A Langley St., Covent Garden, London WC2H 9JA. Tel: (0207) 240 6222. FAX: (0207) 240 6242.
www.cineimage.co.uk

CRAWLEY CREATURES
The Lime Studio, East St., Fritwell, Oxon OX6 9QF. Tel: (01869) 345 208 (01296) 336315. FAX: (01869) 345 639
www.crawley-creatures.com

DIGITAL ARTS LTD.
39 Beak Street London W1R 3LD. Tel: (0207) 484 8800. FAX: (0207) 484 8802. www.digital-arts.co.uk
CONTACT
Graham Brown-Martin

THE DEFINITIVE SPECIAL PROJECTS LTD
P. O. Box 169 Stevenage SG2 7SG Tel: (01438) 869 005 FAX: (01438) 869 006. wwwlaserlightshows.co.uk

EFFECTS ASSOCIATES LTD.
Pinewood Studios, Pinewood Rd., Iver Heath, Bucks SL0 0NH. Tel: (01753) 652 007. FAX: (01753) 630 127.
www.cinesite.com email:ea@effectsassociates.co.uk
CONTACTS
Martin Gutteridge
Elaine Wishart

ELECTRIC IMAGE
7-11 Lexington St., London W1R 3HQ. Tel: (0207) 287 8800. FAX: (0207) 287 3750. www.bydeluxe.com

ENTERPRISES UNLIMITED SPECIAL EFFECTS
Unit 6, Cowbridge Business Park, Cowbridge, Boston, Lincs PE22 7DJ. Tel: (01205) 310 440. FAX: (01205) 310 450.
www.snowboy.co.uk

GENERAL SCREEN ENTERPRISES
Denham Media Park North Orbital Road Denham, Middlesex UB9 5HG. Tel: (01895) 831931. FAX: (01895) 835338.

DAVID HARRIS SPECIAL EFFECTS
Shepperton Studios, Studios Rd., Shepperton, Middlesex TW17 0QD. Tel: (01932) 562 611. FAX: (01932) 572 377.

IMAGE ANIMATION
Pinewood Studios, Pinewood Rd., Iver, Bucks SL0 0NH. Tel: (01753) 656 962. FAX: (01753) 630 394.

LASER CREATIONS INTERNATIONAL LTD.
55 Merthyr Terrace, Barnes, London SW13 9DL. Tel: (0208) 741 5747. FAX: (0208) 748 9879. www.lci-uk.com

LIQUID IMAGE
1 Park Circus, Charing Cross, Glasgow, G3 6AX Tel: (0141) 353 2455 FAX: (0141) 353 2466

LYONS MODEL EFFECTS
85 Bell Barn Rd., Stoke Bishop, Bristol BS9 2DF. Tel: (0117) 987 3699. FAX: (0117) 987 3698.

MILL FILMS
Box 42, Shepperton Studios, Studios Rd., Shepperton, Mdsx TW17 0QD. Tel: (01932) 572 424. FAX: (01932) 568 944.
www.millfilms.co.uk

OPTICAL FILM EFFECTS
Pinewood Studios, Pinewood Rd., Iver, Bucks SL0 0NH. Tel: (01753) 655 486. FAX: (01753) 656 844.

OTTER EFFECTS
Pinewood Film studios, Pinewood Rd., Iver, Bucks SL0 0NH. Tel: (01753) 656 430. FAX: (01753) 656 844.

OXFORD SCIENTIFIC FILMS LTD.
Lower Rd, Long Hanborough, Oxford OX8 8LL. Tel: (01993) 881 881. FAX: (01993) 882 808.

PERDIX FIREARMS LTD.
P.O. Box 1670 Sasbury SP4 6QL, Avon BA2 4RL. Tel: (01722) 782 402. FAX: (01722) 782 790
www.perdix.co.uk

QUANTEL LTD.
Turnpike Rd., Newbury, Berkshire RG14 2NE. Tel: (01635) 48222. FAX: (01635) 31776.

BRYAN SMITHIES SPECIAL EFFECTS
No 1Lyne Close Cottages, Lyne Close, Virginia Water Surrey GU25 4EA. Tel: (01344) 843 251. FAX: (01344) 843 337

SNOW BUSINESS
56 Northfield Road, Tetbury, Gloucestershire, GL8 8HQ
Tel/FAX: (01666) 502 857. www.snowfx.com

UNDIVIDED LTD/KIT WEST PRODUCTIONS
12 Gilpin Ave., East Sheen, London SW14 8QY. Tel: (0208) 878 6745. FAX: (0208) 392 2948.

IAN WINGROVE
Park House, Wash Hill, Woburn Green, Bucks HP10 0JA.
Tel/FAX: (016285) 21356.

Studio Facilities

ARDMORE STUDIOS LTD.
Herbert Road, Bray, Co. Wicklow, Ireland. Tel: (0404) 416 2971. Telex: 91504 PATT E1. FAX: (0404) 416 1894. www.ardmorestudios.co.uk

BRAY STUDIOS
Windsor Road, Windsor, Berks SL4. Tel: (01628) 22111. FAX: (01628) 770 381. www.braystudios.com
CAPITAL GROUP STUDIOS
13 Wandsworth Plain, London, SW18 1ET. Tel: (0208) 874 0131. FAX: (0208) 871 9737. www.capital-studios.co.uk

CENTRAL TELEVISION STUDIOS
Lenton Lane, Nottingham NG7 2NA. Tel: (01602) 863 322. FAX: (01602) 435 142. www.centraltv.com

EALING STUDIOS
Ealing Green, Ealing, London, W5 5EP. Tel: (0208) 567 6655. www.ealingstudios.com

FOUNTAIN TELEVISION
128 Wembley Park Drive, Wembley, Middlesex HA9 8HQ. Tel: (0208) 900 1188. FAX: (0208) 900 2860.

GUERILLA FILMS
35 Thornbury Road, Isleworth, TW7 4LQ England. Tel: (0208) 758 1716. FAX: (0208) 758 9364. www.gureilla-u-net.com

HAMPDEN GURNEY STUDIOS LTD.
39/41 Hanover Steps, St. George's Fields, Albion Street, London, W2 2YG. Tel: (0207) 402 7543. FAX: (0207) 262 5736. www.hampden-gurney.com

HILLSIDE STUDIOS
Merry Hill Road, Bushey, Watford WD2 1DR. Tel: (0208) 950 7919. FAX: (0208) 950 1437. www.hillsidesound.com

LEAVESDEN STUDIO
PO Box 300 Leavesden, Hertfordshire. WD2 7LT UK. Tel: (01923) 685 060. FAX (01923) 685061. www.leavesdenstudios.com

LIMEHOUSE STUDIOS
The Trocadero, 19 Rupert Street, London, W1V 7FS. Tel: (0207) 287 3333. FAX: (0207) 287 1998. www.limehousestudio.com

THE LONDON STUDIOS
The London Television Centre, Upper Ground, London SE1 9LT. Tel: (0207) 737 8888. FAX: (0207) 928 8405.

PARAMOUNT CITY TV THEATRE
Great Windmill St., London, W1V 7PH. Tel: (0207) 722 8111.

PINEWOOD STUDIOS
Pinewood Rd., Iver Bucks., SL0 0NH. Tel: (01753) 651 700. FAX: (01753) 656 844. www.creatfx.dircon.co.uk
MANAGING DIRECTOR
Steve Jaggs

PROSPECT STUDIOS LTD.
High Street, Barnes, London, S.W.13. Tel: (0208) 876 6284. www.prospectstudios.co.uk

REEL TV STUDIOS
19 Derry's Cross, Plymouth, PL1 2SP. Tel: (01752) 255 529. FAX: (01752) 255 531. www.reealtvstudios.com
CONTACT
Tim Watson

SHEPPERTON STUDIOS
Studios Road, Shepperton, Middlesex, TW17 0QD. Tel: (01932) 562 611. FAX: (01932) 568 989. www.sheppertonstudios.co.uk

TEDDINGTON STUDIOS
Broom Road, Teddington Lock, Middx., TW11 9NT. Tel: (0208) 977 3252. FAX: (0208) 943 4050. www.teddington.co.uk

TWICKENHAM
St. Margaret's, Twickenham, Middlesex, TW1 2AW. Tel: (0208) 892 4477. FAX: (0208) 891 0168. www.twickenhamstudios.com

WORLD WIDE GROUP
21-25 St. Anne's Court, London, W1V 3AW. Tel: (0207) 434 1121. FAX: (0207) 734 0619.

BRITISH TRADE ORGANISATIONS AND GOVERNMENT UNITS

ADVERTISING FILM AND VIDEOTAPE PRODUCERS'ASSOCIATION
26 Noel Street, London W1V 3 R D TEL: (0207) 434-2651. FAX: (0207) 4349002. email: afvpa@easynet.co.uk www.afvpa@easynet.co.uk
CHIEF EXECUTIVE
Cecilia Garnett

AGENTS ASSOCIATION
54 Keys House, Dolphin Square, London SW1V 3NA Tel: (0207) 821-0261 FAX: (0207) 821 0261. www.agents-uk.com email: association@agent-uk.com

AMALGAMATED ENGINEERING & ELECTRICAL UNION (EETPU SECTION)
Hayes Court, West Common Road, Bromley, BR2 7AU. Tel: (0208) 462 7755. FAX: (0208) 462 4959.
GENERAL SECRETARY
Paul Gallagher

THE ARTISTES ASSOCIATION (GREAT BRITAIN)
54 Keyes House, Dolphin Square, London, SW1V 3NA. Tel: (0207) 834 0515. FAX: (0207) 821 0261.
PRESIDENT
Kenneth Earle
SECRETARY
Ivan Birchall

ASSOCIATION OF PROFESSIONAL RECORDING SERVICES LTD.
2 Windsor Square, Silver Street, Reading, Berks. RG1 2TH. Tel: (0118) 975 6218. FAX: (0118) 975 6216. www.aprs.co.uk
CHIEF EXECUTIVE
Mark Broad

BRITISH ACADEMY OF FILM AND TELEVISION ARTS
195 Piccadilly, London, W1V 0LN. Tel: (0207) 734 0022. FAX: (0207) 734 1792.
PRESIDENT
H.R.H. The Princess Royal
VICE PRESIDENT
David Puttnam, C.B.E.
CHAIRMAN
Tim Angel
CHIEF EXECUTIVE
Jane Clarke

BRITISH ACTORS' EQUITY ASSOCIATION
(Incorporating the Variety Artistes' Federation)
Guild House, Upper St. Martin's Lane, London, WC2 9EG. Tel: (0207) 379 6000. FAX: (0207) 379 7001.
GENERAL SECRETARY
Ian McGarry

BRITISH BOARD OF FILM CLASSIFICATION
3 Soho Square, London, W1V 6HD. Tel: (0207) 439 7961. FAX: (0207) 287 0141. www.bbfc.co.uk email: xandra_barry@bbfc.co.uk
PRESIDENT
Earl of Harewood, KBE
DIRECTOR
James Ferman

BRITISH FEDERATION OF FILM SOCIETIES
BFFS P.O. Box 1DR, London, W1A 1DR. Tel: (0207) 734 9300. FAX: (0207) 734 9093.

BRITISH FILM DESIGNERS GUILD
9 Elgin Mews South, London, W9 1JZ Tel: (0207) 286 6716. FAX: (0207) 286 6716.
EXECUTIVE CONSULTANT
John French

BRITISH KINEMATOGRAPH, SOUND AND TELEVISION SOCIETY
(Publisher of the BKSTS Journal, "Image Technology" and Cinema Technology.)
63-71 Victoria House, Vernon Place, London, WC1B 4DF. Tel: (0207) 242 8400. FAX: (0207) 405 3560.
EXECUTIVE DIRECTOR
Anne Fenton

BRITISH MUSIC INFORMATION CENTRE
(Reference library of works by 20th Century British composers.)
10 Stratford Place, London, W1N 9AE. Tel: (0207) 499 8567. FAX: (0207) 499 4795.

BRITISH SOCIETY OF CINEMATOGRAPHERS LTD.
Tree Tops, 11 Croft Road, Chalfont St. Peter Gerrards Cross, Bucks., SL9 9AE. Tel: (01753) 888 052. FAX: (01753) 891 486. email: britcinematographers@compuserve.com
SECRETARY & TREASURER
Frances Russell

BRITISH VIDEO ASSOCIATION LTD.
167 Great Portland Street, London, W1M 5FD. Tel: (0207) 436 0041. FAX: (0207) 436 0043. email: general@bva.org.uk
DIRECTOR GENERAL
Mrs Lavinia Carey

BROADCASTING ENTERTAINMENT CINEMATOGRAPH AND THEATRE UNION
111 Wardour Street, London, W1V 4AY. Tel: (0207) 437 8506. FAX: (0207) 437 8268. www.bectu.org.uk

CENTRAL CASTING LTD.
(Licensed annually by the Dept. of Employment)
162 170 Wardour Street, London, W1V 3AT. Tel: (0207) 437 1881. FAX: (0207) 437 2614.
DIRECTORS
R. McCallum
T. Burrill
G. Smith
M. O'Sullivan
J. Sargent
B.T. Yeoman
J. Woodward

CHILDREN'S FILM & TELEVISION FOUNDATION LTD.
Elstree Studios, Boreham Wood, Herts., WD6 1JG. Tel: (0208) 953 0844. FAX: (0208) 207 0860.
CHIEF EXECUTIVE & SECRETARY
Stanley T. Taylor, FCIS

CINEMA ADVERTISING ASSOCIATION LTD.
127 Wardour Street, London, W1V 4NL. Tel: (0207) 439 9531. FAX: (0207) 439 2395.
SECRETARY
Bruce Koster

CINEMA AND TELEVISION VETERANS
166 The Rocks Road, East Malling, Kent ME19 6AX. Tel: (01732) 843 291.
PRESIDENT
Robert Bennett
SECRETARY
K.M. Morgan

CINEMA AND TELEVISION BENEVOLENT FUND
22 Golden Square, London, W1R 4AD. Tel: (0207) 437 6567. FAX: (0207) 437 7186.
EXECUTIVE DIRECTOR
S.D. Hunsley
APPEALS & PUBLIC RELATIONS OFFICER
Sandra Bradley

CINEMA EXHIBITORS' ASSOCIATION
22 Golden Square, London, W1R 3PA. Tel: (0207) 734 9551. FAX: (0207) 734 6147. email: cea@cinemauk.ftech.co.uk
(For regional delegates, please contact CEA directly)
CHIEF EXECUTIVE
John Wilkinson, c/o CEA.
VICE PRESIDENTS
Alistair Cameron, Dominion Cinema, Newbattle Terrace, Morningside, Edinburgh EH10 4RT. Tel: (0131) 441 2660.
John Downs, Cosmo Leisure Group, Central Hall, 62-66 Market St., Stalybridge, Cheshire SK15 2AB.
Nick Kilby, Robins Cinemas, 13 New Row, London WC2N 4LF. Tel: (0207) 497 332.
John Merryweather, Apollo Leisure, 199 Glenfield Rd., Leicester LE3 6DL. Tel: (01257) 471 102.
Mike Vickers, Reeltime Entertainment, 6 Ryders Ave., Westgate on Sea, Kent CT8 8LN. Tel: (01843) 834 609.
HONORARY VICE PRESIDENTS
John Bilsborough, National Amusements, 200 Elm St., Dedham, MA 02026. Tel: (617) 461 1600.
Peter Dobson, Warner Bros. International Theatres, 3rd Floor South, Wells Point, 79 Wells St., London W1P 3RD. Tel: (0207) 437 5600..
Barry Jenkins, ABC Cinemas Ltd., 80 Great Portland St., London W1N 5PA. Tel: (0207) 291 9000.
Steve Knibbs, UCI, Lee House, 90 Bridgewater St., Manchester M1 5JW. Tel: (0161) 455 4000.
Gerry Lipson, Apollo Leisure UK, 424 Woolton Rd., Liverpool L25 6JQ. Tel: (0151) 708 6672.

IMMEDIATE PAST PRESIDENT
Bob Warbey, ABC Cinemas Ltd., 80 Great Portland St., London W1N 5PA. Tel: (0207) 291 9000.
HONORARY TREASURER
Brian Bull, Circle Cinemas, 1 Teamans Row, Marganstown, Radyr, Cardiff CF4 8LN. Tel: (01222) 522 606.
CIRCUIT DELEGATES

ABC CINEMAS LTD.
80 Great Portland St., London W1N 5PA. Tel: (0207) 291 9000.
DELEGATES
Alan McCann, Frank Filgate, Barry Jenkins, Adam Johnson, George Rymer, Bob Stanesby, Bob Wallis, Bob Warbey

APOLLO LEISURE UK
424 Woolton Rd., Liverpool L25 6JQ. Tel: (0151) 708 6672.
DELEGATE
Gerry Lipson, Boar's Hill, P.O. Box 16 Oxford OX1 5JB. Tel: (01865) 730 066.
DELEGATE
Paul Greg, 199 Glenfield Rd., Leicester LE3 6DL. Tel: (01257) 471 012.
DELEGATE
John Merryweather, Grehan House, Gersington Rd., Cowley, Oxford OX4 5NQ. Tel: (01865) 281 800.
DELEGATE
David Rogers

CALEDONIAN CINEMAS
16 Locarno Rd., Acton, London W3 6RG. Tel: (0208) 993 1511.
DELEGATE
Ivan Cluley, 203B High St., Elgin Morayshire IV30 1DJ. Tel: (01343) 549 100.
DELEGATE
Jim Davidson, Taylor Clark Leisure plc, 32 Haymarket, London SW1Y 4TP. Tel: (0207) 930 8484.
DELEGATE
Reg Harvey

CINE-UK LTD.
Sutherland House, 5-6 Argyll St., London W1V 1AD. Tel: (0207) 734 1394.
DELEGATE
Ian Johnston

NATIONAL AMUSEMENTS (UK)
200 Elm St., Dedham, MA 02026. Tel: (617) 461 1600.
DELEGATE
John Bilsborough, Showcase Cinema, Redfield Way, Lenton, Nottingham NG7 2UW. Tel: (01159) 862 508.
DELEGATE
Duncan Short

ODEON CINEMAS LTD.
54 Whitcomb St., London WC2H 7DN. Tel: (0207) 839 6373.
DELEGATE
Barry Keward, 439-445 Godstone Rd., Whyteleafe, Surrey CR3 0YG. Tel: (01883) 623 355.
DELEGATES
Tom Allison, Alistair Craig, Tony Giddings, Steve Gosling, Anne Robson, Geoff Sale, Richard Segal, Malcolm Walker

ROBINS CINEMAS
13 New Row, London WC2N 4LF. Tel: (0207) 497 3320.
DELEGATES
Ben Freedman, Nick Kilby

UNITED CINEMAS INTERNATIONAL (UK)
Lee House, 90 Great Bridgewater St., Manchester M1 5JW. Tel: (0161) 455 4000.
DELEGATES
Stuart Boreman, Anne Harper-Smith, Dave Harris, Steve Knibbs, Mark Redding

VIRGIN CINEMAS LTD.
Adelaide House, 626 High Rd., Chiswick, London W4 5RY. Tel: (0208) 987 5000.
DELEGATES
David Alder, Joe Carroll, Joe Nunes, Keith Pullinger, Margaret Taylor

WARNER VILLAGE EXHIBITION
3rd floor South, Wells Point, 79 Wells St., London W1P 3RD. Tel: (0207) 437 5600.
DELEGATES
Malvyn Angell, Rafael Badillo, Derek Cownty, Peter Dobson

COMPOSERS' GUILD OF GREAT BRITAIN
The Penthouse, 4 Brook St, Mayfair, London W1Y 1AA. Tel: (0207) 629 0886. FAX: (0207) 436 1913.
GENERAL SECRETARY
Naomi Maskovic

CRITICS' CIRCLE
4 Alwyne Villas London N1 2HQTel: (0207) 226 2726. FAX:(0207) 354 2574
CHAIRMAN
Christopher Tookey
HON. SECRETARY
Tom Hutchinson

DIRECTORS GUILD OF GREAT BRITAIN
15 19 Great Titchfield Street, London, W1P 7FB. Tel: (0207) 436 8626. FAX: (0207) 436 8646. www.dggb.co.uk
CONTACT
Kate Hillman

EDINBURGH AND LOTHIAN SCREEN INDUSTRIES OFFICE
Filmhouse, 88 Lothian Road, Edinburgh EH3 9BZ, Scotland. Tel: (0131) 228 5960. FAX: (0131) 228 5967.
CONTACTS
George Carlaw
Ros Davis

EUROPEAN SCRIPT FUND
39c Highbury Place, London, N5 1QP. Tel: (0207) 226 9903. FAX: (0207) 354 2706.

FEDERATION AGAINST COPYRIGHT THEFT (FACT)
7 Victory Business Centre, Worton Road, Isleworth, Middx., TW7 6DB. Tel: (0208) 568 6646. FAX: (0208) 560 6364.
DIRECTOR GENERAL
R. Dixon

FILM ARTISTES' ASSOCIATION
111 Wardour Street, London W1V 4AY. Tel: (0207) 937 4567. FAX: (0207) 937 0790.
GENERAL SECRETARY
Spencer MacDonald

FILM CENSOR'S OFFICE
16 Harcourt Terrace, Dublin 2, Republic of Ireland. Tel: (353 1) 676 1985. FAX: (353 1) 676 1898
CONTACT
Sheamus Smith

FILM INSTITUTE OF IRELAND
Irish Film Centre, 6 Eustace Street, Dublin 2, Republic of Ireland. Tel: (353 1) 679 5744. FAX: (353 1) 677 8755.
DIRECTOR
Sheila Pratschke

GUILD OF BRITISH CAMERA TECHNICIANS
5 11 Taunton Road, Metropolitan Centre, Greenford, Middx., UB6 8UQ. Tel: (0208) 578 9243. FAX: (0208) 575 5972.
CONTACT
Maureen O'Grady

GUILD OF BRITISH FILM EDITORS
Travair, Spurlands End Road, Great Kingshill, High Wycombe, Bucks, HP15 6HY. Tel: (01494) 712 313. FAX: (01494) 863 563. email: cox.gbfe@btinternet.com
HON. SECRETARY
Alfred E. Cox
HON. TREASURER
Audrey Cox

GUILD OF FILM PRODUCTION EXECUTIVES
Pinewood Studios, Iver, Bucks. Tel: (01753) 656 428. FAX:(01753) 656 850.
CONTACT
Ann Runeckles

GUILD OF FILM PRODUCTION ACCOUNTANTS AND FINANCIAL ADMINISTRATORS
Pinewood Studios, Pinewood Road, Iver, Bucks. SL0 0NH. Tel: (01753) 656 473. FAX: (01753) 656 850.
www.gfpa.org.uk
VICE PRESIDENT
Michele Tandy

INDEPENDENT FILM DISTRIBUTORS' ASSOCIATION
10A Stephen Mews, London, W1A 0AX. Tel: (0207) 957 8957. FAX: (0207) 957 8968.

INTERNATIONAL ANIMATED FILM ASSOCIATION
61 Railwayside, Barnes, London, SW13 OPQ. Tel: (0208) 878 4040. FAX: (0208) 675 8499.
VICE PRESIDENT
Pat Raine Webb

INTERNATIONAL ASSOCIATION OF BROADCASTING MANUFACTURERS
4B, High St., Burnham, Slough SL1 7JH. Tel: (01628) 667 633. FAX: (01628) 665 882.
SECRETARIAT
Brenda White

INTERNATIONAL VISUAL COMMUNICATION ASSOCIATION (IVCA)
Bolsover House, 5 6 Clipstone Street, London, W1P 7EB. Tel: (0207) 580 0962. FAX: (0207) 436 2606.
CHIEF EXECUTIVE
Wayne Drew

IRISH ACTORS EQUITY GROUP
Liberty Hall, Dublin 1, Republic of Ireland. Tel: (3531) 874 0081. FAX: (353 1) 874 3691.
GROUP SECRETARY
Gerard Browne

MECHANICAL COPYRIGHT PROTECTION SOCIETY LTD. (MCPS)
Elgar House, 41 Streatham High Road, London, SW16 1ER. Tel: (0208) 769 4400. FAX: (0208) 769 8792. Telex: 946792 MCPS G. www.mcps.co.uk
CONTACT
Adrian Crooke

MUSICIANS' UNION
60 62 Clapham Road, London, SW9 0JJ. Tel: (0207) 582 5566. FAX: (0207) 582 9805. email: info@musicunion.org.uk www.musiciansunion.org.uk
CONTACT
Don Smith

PACT LTD.
(Producers Alliance for Cinema and Television)
45 Mortimer Street, London W1N 7 TD. Tel: (0207) 331 6700. FAX: (0207) 233 8935.
CHIEF EXECUTIVE
John Woodward
MEMBERSHIP OFFICER
David Alan Mills

THE PERFORMING RIGHT SOCIETY LTD. (PRS)
29 33 Berners Street, London, W1P 4AA. Tel: (0207) 580 5544.. FAX: (0207) 306 4050.
GENERAL MANAGER
John Axon
PUBLIC AFFAIRS CONTROLLER
Terri Anderson

THE PERSONAL MANAGERS' ASSN. LTD.
Rivercroft, One Summer Road, East Molesey, Surrey KT8 9LX. Tel: (0208) 398 9796. FAX: (0208) 398 9796.
SECRETARY
Angela Adler

ST. PAUL BOOK AND MEDIA CENTRE
5A 7 Royal Exchange Square, Glasgow, G1 3AH, Scotland. Tel: (0141) 226 3391.

SCREEN ADVERTISING WORLD ASSOCIATION LTD.
103A Oxford Street, London, W1R 1TF. Tel: (0207) 734 7621.
SECRETARY GENERAL
Charles Sciberras

SOCIETY OF FILM DISTRIBUTORS LTD.
22 Golden Square, London, W1R 3PA. Tel: (0207) 437 4383. FAX: (0207) 734 0912.
GENERAL SECRETARY
D.C. Hunt
SFD COUNCIL MEMBERS
Buena Vista Int'l (UK) Ltd., Carlton film Distributors Ltd., Columbia Tri Star Films UK, Entertainment Film Dist. Ltd., Film Four Distributors Ltd., First Independent Films Ltd., Gala Film Dist., Pathe Distribution Ltd., Polygram Filmed Entertainment (UK) Ltd., Twentieth Century Fox Film Co. Ltd., United International Pictures (UK), Warner Bros. Distributors Ltd.

SOUND & COMMUNICATIONS INDUSTRIES FEDERATION
4 B High Street, Burnham, Slough SL1 7JH. Tel: (01628) 667 633. FAX: (01628) 665 882.
CHIEF EXECUTIVE
Ken Walker, M.B.E.

VARIETY CLUB OF GREAT BRITAIN
St Martin's House, 139 Tottenham Court Road, LondonW1P 9 LN.
CONTACT
Christian Jenner

WOMEN IN FILM AND TELEVISION
Garden Studios, 11/15 Betterton St., London WC2H 9BP. Tel: (0207) 379 0344. FAX: (0207) 379 1625.
email: wftv@easynet.co.uk
EXECUTIVE DIRECTOR
Kate Norrish

THE WRITERS' GUILD OF GREAT BRITAIN
430 Edgware Road, London, W2 1EH. Tel: (0207) 723 8074. FAX: (0207) 706 2413. email: postie@wggb.demon.co.uk www.writers.org.uk/guild

GOVERNMENT DIVISIONS ON FILM AFFAIRS

AUSTRALIAN FILM COMMISSION
2nd Floor, Victory House, 99 101 Regent Street, London, W1R 7HB. Tel: (0207) 734 9383. FAX: (0207) 434 0170.
CONTACT
Pressanna Vasudevan

BRITISH COUNCIL EVENTS SECTION
Film, TV and Video Department, 11 Portland Place, London, W1N 4EJ. Tel: (0207) 389 3063/4. FAX: (0207) 389 3041. Telex: 8952201 BRICON G.
FESTIVALS OFFICERS
Kevin Franklin
Satwant Gill
OTHER EVENTS
Geraldine Higgins
Jo Maurice

THE BRITISH DEFENCE FILM LIBRARY
SSVC Chalfont Grove, Chalfont St. Peter, Gerrerds Cross, Bucks, SL9 8TN. Tel: (01494) 878 278. FAX: (01494) 878 007.
PATRON
H.R.H. The Princess Margaret
MANAGING DIRECTOR
Air Vice Marshall David Crwys Williams, CB FIPM, FIMGT, RAR
FILM & VIDEO DEPARTMENT
Renate Foster

BRITISH FILM INSTITUTE (BFI)
(The BFI's divisions and departments include: BFI on the South Bank (National Film Theatre, Museum of the Moving Image and London Film Festival); Research (Research and Education, Book Publishing and "Sight and Sound" magazine); the National Film and Television Archive; Exhibition and Distribution; Library and Information Services; Planning Unit; BFI Production.)
21 Stephen Street, London, W1P 1PL. Tel: (0207) 255 1444. FAX: (0207) 436 7950. URL: http://www.bfi.org.uk
DIRECTOR
John Woodward

BRITISH FILM COMMISSION
70 Baker Street, London W1M 1DJ. Tel: (0207) 224 5000. FAX (0207) 224 1013. email: info@britfilmcom.co.uk www.britfilmcom.co.uk
BRITISH FILM COMMISSIONER
Steve Norris
EVENTS AND DEVELOPMENT MANAGER
Krysia Rozanska
INFORMATION MANAGER
Joanna Dewar Gibb
PRESS AND PUBLICATIONS MANAGER
Tina McFarling

BRITISH SCREEN ADVISORY COUNCIL
19 Cavendish Square, London W1M 9AB. Tel: (0207) 304 0040. FAX: (0207) 306 0329. email: bsac@bsacouncil.co.uk
CHAIRMAN
David Elstein
DIRECTOR
Fiona Clarke Hackslor

CENTRAL OFFICE OF INFORMATION
Hercules Road, London, SE1 7DU. Tel: (0207) 261 8500. FAX: (0207) 928 5637.
DIRECTOR OF FILMS, TELEVISION & RADIO DIVISION
Ian Hamilton

DEPARTMENT FOR CULTURE, MEDIA AND SPORT
Media Division, 2-4 Cockspur Street, London, SWIY 5DH. Tel: (0207) 211 6000. FAX: (0207) 211 6249.
CONTACT
Diana Brown

LONDON FILM COMMISSION
20 Euston Centre, Regent's Place, London NW1 3JH. Tel: (0207) 387 8787. FAX: (0207) 387 8788.
CONTACT
Christabel Albery

NATIONAL FILM AND TELEVISION SCHOOL
Beaconsfield Studios, Station Road, Beaconsfield, Bucks., HP9 1LG. Tel: (01494) 671 234. FAX: (01494) 674 042.
CONTACT
Hilary Thomas

THE SERVICES SOUND & VISION CORPORATION
Chalfont Grove, Chalfont St. Peter, Gerrards Cross, Bucks., SL9 8TN. FAX: (01494) 872 982.
PATRON
H.R.H. The Princess Margaret
BOARD OF MANAGEMENT CHAIRMAN
Gen. Sir Geoffrey Howlett, K.B.E. M.C.
MANAGING DIRECTOR
Air Vice Marshal David Crwys Williams, CB FIPM, FIMGT, RAR

EUROPEAN CIRCUIT MULTIPLEXES

Theatre Name	City, Province	Circuit	Screens
AUSTRIA			
Apollo, Das Kino	Vienna	CineInvest	12
Cineplexx	Graz-Puntigam	Cineplexx	11
Cineplexx	Wals	Cineplexx	10
Metropol Tirol	Innsbruck	F. Purner Lichtspiel	8
Hoyts Hollywood Megaplex	Pasching, Linz	Kino Betriebsges	12
Hoyts Hollywood Megaplex	Sankt Polten	Kino Betriebsges	8
Annenhofkino	Graz	UCI	8
UCI Kinowelt	Wien	UCI	9
UCI Kinopalast	Wiener Neudorf, Wien	UCI	9
Kolosseum	Wien	Wr. Stadthalle	8
BELGIUM			
Rialto	Ostend	Cine Rialto	8
Cinecity	Mechelen	Cinecity	12
Carollywood	Charleroi	Empire	14
Euroscoop	Lanaken	Euroscoop	8
Gaumont Cinemas	Antwerp	Gaumont	17
Imagibraine	Braine, L'Allued	Imagibraine	10
Kinepolis	Kortrijk	Kineoplis	10
Metropolis	Antwerp	Kinepolis	24
Kinepolis	Bruxelles	Kinepolis	25
Decascoop	Gent	Kinepolis	12
Kinepolis	Hasselt	Kinepolis	14
Kinepolis	Liege	Kinepolis	14
Eldorado	Namur	La Renaissance	8
Imagimons	Mons	Lumiere	12
UGC Toison d'Or	Bruxelles	UGC	14
UGC De Brouckere	Bruxelles	UGC Belgique	12
CZECH REPUBLIC			
Multi Cinema Galaxie	Praha	Kino 2005	8
Olympia	Brno	Ster Century	14
DENMARK			
Palads Teatret	Copenhagen	Nordisk Film	17
Biocity	Odense	Nordisk Film	9
FINLAND			
Tennispalatsi	Helsinki	Finnkino	14
Plevna	Tampere	Finnkino	10
Kinopalatsi	Helsinki	Sandrew Metro	10
FRANCE			
Carnot	Agen	CGR	8
Mega CGR	Angouleme	CGR	11
Mega CGR	Blagnac, Toulouse	CGR	12
CGR Le Francais	Bordeaux	CGR	14
Mega CGR	Buxerolles, Poitiers	CGR	12
CGR	Chateauroux	CGR	8
Mega CGR	La Rochelle	CGR	12
Mega CGR	Lattes, Montpellier	CGR	12
Mega CGR	Le Mans	CGR	12
Mega CGR	Pau	CGR	12
CGR Rabelais	Poitiers	CGR	8
Mega CGR	Rivesaltes, Perpignan	CGR	12
Mega CGR	Tarbes	CGR	8
Mega CGR	Tours	CGR	12
Mega CGR	Villenave d'Ornon	CGR	15
Cine Cap Vert	Dijon	Cine Cap Vert	12
Casino	Auxerre	Cine Casino	8
Le Mazarin	Nevers	Cine Alpes	8
Ocine	Saint Omer	Coppey	8
Grand Ecron	La Teste	Friedmann	8
Gaumont	Archamps, Annecy	Gaumont	11
Gaumont	Bordeaux	Gaumont	10
Gaumont Celtic	Brest	Gaumont	8
Gaumont Cite Europe	Coquelles, Calais	Gaumont	12
Gaumont Grand, Quevilly	Grand Quevilly, Rouen	Gaumont	16
Gaumont	Labege, Toulouse	Gaumont	15
Gaumont Colisee	Le Havre	Gaumont	8
Gaumont	Lens	Gaumont	12
Gaumont Disney Village	Marne la Vallee, Paris	Gaumont	15
Gaumont	Montpellier	Gaumont	17
Gaumont	Montpellier	Gaumont	8
Gaumont Palace	Mulhouse	Gaumont	9
Gaumont	Nantes	Gaumont	12
Gaumont Aquaboulevard	Paris	Gaumont	14
Gaumont Parnasse	Paris	Gaumont	12
Gaumont	Rennes	Gaumont	8

Theatre Name	City, Province	Circuit	Screens
Gaumont	Saint Etienne	Gaumont	8
Gaumont Stade de France	St Denis	Gaumont	9
Gaumont Wilson	Toulouse	Gaumont	8
Gaumont	Valenciennes	Gaumont	15
Arcades	Dunkerque	Georges Odetto	8
Megarama	Bastide, Bordeaux	Jean Pierre Lemoine	17
Megarama	Villeneuve la Garenne	Jean Pierre Lemoine	17
Kinepolis	Lomme, Lille	Kinepolis	23
Kinepolis	Saint Julien Les Metz	Kinepolis	14
Kinepolis	Thionville	Kinepolis	10
Cezanne	Aix en Provence	Pathe	9
Pathe Cap Sud	Avignon	Pathe	10
Pathe	Echirolles, Grenoble	Pathe	12
Pathe Grand Ciel	La Garde, Toulon	Pathe	12
Pathe	Lyon	Pathe	10
Pathe Madeleine	Marseille	Pathe	8
Pathe Wepler	Paris	Pathe	12
Pathe Plan de Campagne	Pennes Mirabeau	Pathe	16
Pathe Atlantis	Saint Herblain, Nantes	Pathe	14
Pathe	Strasbourg	Pathe	12
Pathe Belle Epine	Thiais, Paris	Pathe	12
Pathe	Tours	Pathe	8
Prado	Marseille	Pradex	11
Olympia	Cannes	Sa Olympia	9
Colisee	Colmar	SNE	9
Horizon les Grands Ecrans	Limoges	Soc. Centrale	11
Sully	Bethune	Soc. Exploitation	8
NEF Scala	Lyon	Societe NEF Scala	9
Cyrano	Versailles, Paris	Socogex	8
Les 3 Palmes	Marseille	Someci	11
Castillet	Perpignan	Someci	8
Rex	Lorient	Soredic	11
UGC	Bordeaux	UGC	15
UGC	Lille	UGC	14
UGC Cine Cite	Lundres, Nancy	UGC	12
UGC Cine Cite	Lyon	UGC	14
UGC Part Dieu	Lyon	UGC	14
UGC Capitole	Marseille	UGC	8
UGC Cine Cite	Marseille	UGC	15
UGC Cine Cite	Mondeville, Caen	UGC	12
Artel Marne la Vallee	Noisy le Grand, Paris	UGC	8
UGC Cine Cite Bercy	Paris	UGC	18
UGC Cine Cite/Les Halles	Paris	UGC	19
UGC George V	Paris	UGC	11
UGC La Defense 4 Temps	Puteaux, Paris	UGC	9
UGC Cine Cite Rosny	Rosny Sous Bois, Paris	UGC	15
UGC Cine Cite Atlantis	Saint Herblain, Nantes	UGC	12
UGC	Toulouse	UGC	9

GERMANY

Theatre Name	City, Province	Circuit	Screens
Kinodrom	Bocholt	Bresser	9
CCC Filmkunst	Berlin	CCC Filmkunst	10
Cineplex	Mannheim	Cineplex	8
Cineplex	Ahaus	Cineplex Paffrath	12
Comet Cineplex	Berlin	Comet	8
Cinedom	Koln	Constantin Kino	14
Flebbe	Krefeld	Flebbe/Politt	10
Cinemaxx Colosseum	Berlin	Flebbe/Sputnik	10
CineStar	Hagen	FTB Buchal (Kieft)	8
Moviedick	Esslingen	FTB Colm	8
Cineplaza	Bayreuth	FTB Thomas	8
Cinemaxx Hohenschohausen	Berlin	H. J. Flebbe	9
Cinemaxx Potsdamer Platz	Berlin	H. J. Flebbe	19
Cinemaxx	Bielefeld	H. J. Flebbe	8
Cinemaxx	Bremen	H. J. Flebbe	10
Cinemaxx	Essen	H. J. Flebbe	16
Cinemaxx	Freiburg	H. J. Flebbe	9
Cinemaxx	Gottingen	H. J. Flebbe	9
Cinemaxx	Halle	H. J. Flebbe	10
Cinemaxx	Hamburg	H. J. Flebbe	8
Cinemaxx	Hanover	H. J. Flebbe	10
Cinemaxx	Kiel	H. J. Flebbe	10
Cinemaxx	Magdelburg	H. J. Flebbe	9
Cinemaxx	Mannheim	H. J. Flebbe	10
Cinemaxx	Muhlheim	H. J. Flebbe	11
Cinemaxx	Regensburg	H. J. Flebbe	8
Cinemaxx	Wuppertal	H. J. Flebbe	9
CineStar	Augsburg	Kieft & Kieft	9
CineStar	Berlin	Kieft & Kieft	12
CineStar	Berlin	Kieft & Kieft	9
Cinestar Luxor	Chemnitz	Kieft & Kieft	12
CineStar	Dortmund	Kieft & Kieft	14
CineStar	Erlangen	Kieft & Kieft	10
CineStar	Jena	Kieft & Kieft	8
CineStar	Siegen	Kieft & Kieft	9
CineStar	Wilhelmshaven	Kieft & Kieft	8
Extra Kinocenter	Koblenz	Mega Extrem Music	9
Movie Town	Brandenburg	P.H. Vollmann	8
Bofimax	Leipzig	Rehs Gruppe	8

Theatre Name	City, Province	Circuit	Screens
UFA Filmpassage	Osnabruck	Rosenhof Und	9
Kinopolis	Bonn Bad Godesberg	Theile	11
Kinopolis	Frankfurt/Sulzbach	Theile	12
Kinopolis	Viernheim/Rhein	Theile	10
Kinopolis	Leverkusen	Theile/Brunotte	8
UCI Kinowelt	Augsburg	UCI	9
UCI Kinowelt	Berlin	UCI	8
UCI Kinowelt Zoo Palast	Berlin	UCI	9
UCI Friedrichshain	Berlin	UCI	8
UCI Kinowelt	Bochum	UCI	18
UCI Kinowelt	Cottbus	UCI	9
UCI Kinowelt	Dresden	UCI	9
UCI Kinowelt	Duisburg	UCI	8
UCI Park	Dusseldorf	UCI	12
UCI Kinowelt	Gera	UCI	8
UCI Kinowelt	Hamburg	UCI	9
UCI Kinowelt Smart City	Hamburg	UCi	10
UCI Kinowelt Hurth Park	Hurth, Koln	UCI	14
UCI Kinowelt	Jena	UCI	8
UCI Kinowelt	Kaiserslautern	UCI	8
UCI Kinowelt	Leipzig	UCI	10
UFA Kosmos	Berlin	UFA	10
UFA Palast Kristall	Dresden	UFA	8
UFA Palast	Dusseldorf	UFA	11
UFA Palast	Dusseldorf, Oberkassel	UFA	9
UFA Palast	Erfurt	UFA	9
UFA Palast	Hamburg	UFA	10
UFA Palast	Koln	UFA	12
Capitol UFA Palast	Plauen	UFA	8
UFA Palast	Stuttgart	UFA	13
Village Cinema	Gelsenkirchen	Village	9
Village Cinema	Hamburg	Village	8
Village Cinema	Magdelburg	Village	9
Village Cinema	Muhlheim	Village	8
Village Cinema	Oberhausen	Village	9
Cinecitta	Nurnberg	Wolfram Weber	13

GREECE

Platia	Thessaloniki	Assos Ster Odeon	8
Village Centre Paradeissos	Athens	Village Roadshow	10
Village Centre	Thessaloniki	Village Roadshow	9

HUNGARY

Hollywood Multiplex	Budapest	Intercom	11
Hollywood Multiplex	Budapest	Intercom	10
Cinema City	Gyor	International	10
Cinema City	Debrecen	International	9

IRELAND

Liffey Valley	Dublin	Ster Century	14
UCI Blancharostown	Dublin	UCI	9
UCI Coolock	Dublin	UCI	10
UCI Tallaght	Dublin	UCI	12
Virgin Multiplex	Dublin	Virgin	9
Santry Omniplex	Dublin	Ward Anderson	10
Galway Omniplex	Galway	Ward Anderson	11
Limerick Omniplex	Limerick	Ward Anderson	12

ITLAY

Oz Il Regno Del Cinema	Brescia	Cin.Cin.	10
Oden	Milano	Cinema 5 Gestione	10
Cineland	Ostia Lido, Roma	Grandi Impianti	14
Cineplex Porto Antico	Genova	Mediaport	9
Ariston	Colleferro, Roma	Multisale Ariston	9
WV Casamassima	Bari	Warner Village	9
WV La Grande	Lugagnano di Sona	Warner Village	8
Warner Village	Montesilvano, Pescara	Warner Village	11
WV Parco de'Medici	Roma	Warner Village	18
WV Le Piramidi	Torri di Quartesolo	Warner Village	9

LUXEMBOURG

Utopolis	Luxembourg	Utopia	10

NETHERLANDS

Pathe Scheveningen	Den Haag	Pathe	8
Pathe	Eindhoven	Pathe	8
Pathe	Groningen	Pathe	9
Movie Palace	Zoetermeer	Polyfilm	8

NORWAY

Konsertpaleet	Bergen	Bergen Kinema	13
Kino 1	Sandvika	Kino 1	8
Filmteatret	Stavanger	Stavanger Kinema	8
Prinsen	Trondheim	Trondheim Kinema	8

Theatre Name	City, Province	Circuit	Screens
POLAND			
Multikino	Poznan	UCI	8
Multikino	Warszawa	UCI	13
PORTUGAL			
AMC Arrabida 20	Vila Nova de Gaia	AMC	20
Amoreiras	Lisboa	Lusomundo AV	10
WL Colombo	Lisboa	Warner Lusomundo	10
WL Gaiashopping	Vila Nova de Gaia	Warner Lusomundo	9
WL Maiashopping	Maia	Warner Lusomundo	11
WL Norteshopping	Matosinhos	Warner Lusomundo	8
WL Vasco da Gama	Lisboa	Warner Lusomundo	10
SPAIN			
Abaco	Albacete	Abacocine	9
Abaco	Burgos	Abacocine	8
Abaco	Camas, Sevilla	Abacocine	12
Abaco	Cartagena	Abacocine	9
Abaco	Castellon	Abacocine	10
Abaco	Jerez de la Frontera	Abacocine	9
Abaco	Valladolid	Abacocine	8
AMC Parc Valles	Barcelona	AMC	24
Zig Zag	Murcia	Carceserna	10
Bilbondo	Basauri	Cin. Basauri	8
Multicines El Centro	Cadiz	Cine City 2000 Sa.	9
Estrella	Villalba, Madrid	Cine Palafox S.A.	8
Broadway	Valladolid	Cinegar	11
Valle Real	Camargo	Cinema Camargo	8
Ideal	Bilbao	Cinema Ideal	8
Lauren	Reus	Cinemes Reus	9
El Ferrol Multicines	El Ferrol	Cines Galicia	8
Van Dyck	Salamanca	Cines Juan Heras	10
Princesa	Madrid	Cines Princesa	8
Cinesa Diagonal	Barcelona	Cinesa	11
Maremagnum	Barcelona	Cinesa	8
Loranca	Fuenlabrada	Cinesa	11
Parque Sur	Leganes	Cinesa	8
Artea	Leioa	Cinesa	9
Levante	Sedavi	Cinesa	8
Augusta	Zaragoza	Cinesa	9
Cines Conquistadores	Badajoz	Cinesur	8
Nervion Plaza	Sevilla	Cinesur	20
Max Center	Barcelona	Coliseo	12
Multicines 8	Bilbao	Coliseo	8
Fuenlabrada	Madrid	Damag	10
Golem	Logrono	Difusora Logrono	8
El Paseo	El Puerto de Santa Maria	Diverfilm	9
Gran Sarria	Barcelona	Empresa Balana	8
Figueres Multicines	Figueres	Espect Emporda	8
Bages Centre	Barcelona	Espectaculos	12
ABC Gran Via	Alicante	Excin	9
ABC Gandia	Gandia	Excin	8
ABC El Saler	Valencia	Excin	9
ABC Marti	Valencia	Excin	8
ABC Gran Turia	Xirivella, Valencia	Excin	11
Larios	Malaga	Finesar Andalucia	10
Centro	Granada	Funcion Privada	8
Reus Palace	Reus	Hermanos Zuniga	8
Kinepolis Madrid	Madrid	Kinepolis	25
Lauren Horta	Barcelona	Lauren	8
Lauren Getxo	Getxo	Lauren	12
Lauren Girona	Girona	Lauren	9
Lauren Valladolid	Valladolid	Lauren	11
Llobregat	Corneilla de Llobregat	M.C. Llobregat	14
Porto Pi	Palma de Mallorca	M.C. Porto	15
Albeniz Multicines	Girona	Multicines Albeniz	10
Arenys Multicines	Arenys de Mar	Multicines Arenys	8
Eix Macia	Sabadell	Multicines Eix Macia	9
Parque Oeste	Alorcon	Multicines Po	9
Mirador	Sevilla	Multicines Sta. Justa	8
Aljarafe	Tomares	Multicines Sta. Justa	10
Cinemax	Tudeia, Navarra	Multicines Tudela	9
Barnasud	Gava, Barcelona	Multiplex Barnasud	10
La Ballena	Las Palmas	OC. De Jesus	10
Parque Corredor	Torrejon de Ardoz	Parque Corredor	9
Abrera Multicines	Abrera	Pryco	8
Acteon	Madrid	Sirvepi	9
La Vaguada	Madrid	Sociedad CC	9
Les Gavarres	Tarragona	Tarragona Cinemes	12
Europa	Andujar	UCC	8
Las Salinas	Chiclana de la Frontera	UCC	10
Arcangel	Cordoba	UCC	10
Alhambra	Granada	UCC	15
Jerez	Jerez de la Frontera	UCC	15
Multicines Tenerife	La Laguna, Tenerife	UCC	18
Rosaleda	Malaga	UCC	12
Las Huertas	Palencia	UCC	8
Al Campo	Savilla	UCC	10
Los Arcos	Sevilla	UCC	12

Theatre Name	City, Province	Circuit	Screens
UGC Cine Cite	Madrid	UGC	12
Kursaal	Cerdanyola del Valles	Vallesvin	11
Aana	San Juan de Alicante	Vicente Espadas	8
WL La Moraleja	Alcobendas, Madrid	Warner Lusomundo	8
WL Majadahonda	Madrid	Warner Lusomundo	12
Warner Lusomundo	San Sebastian	Warner Lusomundo	10
Rosales	A Coruna	Yelmo	13
Baricentro	Barbera del Valles	Yelmo Cineplex	11
Icaria	Barcelona	Yelmo Cineplex	15
Yelmo Lugo	Lugo	Yelmo Cineplex	8
Ideal	Madrid	Yelmo Cineplex	9
Madrid Sur	Madrid	Yelmo Cineplex	9
Yelmo Cineplex	Madrid	Yelmo Cineplex	9
El Ferial	Parla	Yelmo Cineplex	8
Yelmo Sant Cugat	Sant Cugat del Valles	Yelmo Cineplex	9
Sant Feliu	Sant Feliu de Llobregat	Yelmo Cineplex	8
Puente Real	Badajoz	Zojadab	8

SWEDEN

Filmstaden	Goteborg	AB Svensk	16
Filmstaden	Helsingborg	AB Svensk	8
Filmstaden	Karlstad	AB Svensk	8
Filmstaden	Linkoping	AB Svensk	8
Filmstaden	Malmo	AB Svensk	8
Filmstaden	Norrkoping	AB Svensk	8
Filmstaden	Orebro	AB Svensk	10
Filmstaden	Ostersund	AB Svensk	8
Filmstaden Stergel	Stockholm	AB Svensk	14
Filmstaden	Sundsvall	AB Svensk	8
Filmstaden	Umea	AB Svensk	9
Filmstaden	Uppsala	AB Svensk	12
Filmstaden	Vasteras	AB Svensk	8
Biopalatset	Goteborg	Sandrew Metro	10
Biopalatset	Stockholm	Sandrew Metro	10

SWITZERLAND

Cinemax	Zurich	Ascot Elite	10
Galeries	Lausanne	Metrocine	8

TURKEY

Capitol	Istanbul	Metur A.H.	8

THE WORLD MARKET

ALBANIA

Population: 3.5 million.

EXHIBITORS

CINEMA PARIS
'Ish Pallati Kultures "All Kelmendi", Tirana, Albania

ARGENTINA

Population: 37 million.
Ticket Price: $7.00.

DISTRIBUTORS

COLUMBIA TRISTAR FILMS OF ARGENTINA, INC.
Ayacucho 533/37, 1026 Buenos Aires. Tel: (541) 954 3820. FAX: (541) 954 3819.
GENERAL MANAGER
Oscar Scarinci

DISTRIFILMS S. A.
Lavalle 1860, 1051 Capital Federal, Buenos Aires. Tel: (541) 371 3438. FAX: (541) 374 9250.
PRESIDENT
Luis Albert Scalella

UNITED INTERNATIONAL PICTURES
Ayacucho 520, 1026 Buenos Aires. Tel: (541) 373 0261. FAX: (541) 111 303.
MANAGER
Juan Manuel Fascetto

WARNER BROS.
Tucuman 1938, 1050 Buenos Aires. Tel: (541) 372 6094. FAX: (541) 111 3030.
GENERAL MANAGER
Anibal Codebo

EXHIBITORS

HOYTS ARGENTINA
Avda Corriertes 447, 5 Piso, 1043 Buenos Aires.
Number of Theatres: 5
Number of Screens: 52

VILLAGE CINEMAS
Tucuman 2133, Planta 2, 1050 Buenos Aires. Tel: (54) 1 954-6245.
Number of Screens: 47

VILLAGE ROADSHOW, LTD.
(For complete listing see Australian branch.)
206 Bourke St., Melbourne, VIC 3000 Australia. Tel: (613) 96 67 66 66. FAX: (613) 96 39 15 40.
Number of Theatres: 7
Number of Screens: 69

AUSTRALIA

Population: 19.2 million.
Number of Screens: 1,500.

FILM COMMISSIONS

AUSTRALIAN FILM COMMISSION
Level 4, 150 William Street, Woolloomooloo NSW 2011. Tel: (612) 951 6444. FAX: (612) 357 3737. email: info@afc. gov. au
www. afc. gov. au

AUSTRALIAN FILM FINANCE CORP.
Bob Campbell, G. P.O. Box 3886, Sydney NSW 2001; 130 Elizabeth St., Sydney NSW 2001. Tel: (612) 268 2555. FAX: (612) 264 8551.

FILM AUSTRALIA
101 Eton Road, Lindfield NSW 2070, Level 12. Tel: (612) 413 8777. FAX: (612) 416 5672.

N.S.W. FILM & TELEVISION
P.O. Box 1744, Sydney, NSW 2000. Tel: (612) 9380 5599. FAX: (612) 9360 1090.

NEW SOUTH WALES FILM & TV OFFICE
Level 6, 1 Francis St., East Sydney, NSW 2000. Tel: (612) 9380 5599. FAX: (612) 9360 1090, 9360 1095.

PACIFIC FILM & TELEVISION COMMISSION
Level 16, 111 George St., Brisbane, QLD 4000. Tel: (617) 3224 4114. FAX: (617) 3224 4077.

SCREEN WEST
Western Australian Film & TV, Office 4 Catherine Court, 420 Hay St., Subiaco, WA 6008. Tel: (619) 382 2500. FAX: (619) 381 2848.

GOVERNMENT OFFICES

AUSTRALIAN TAXATION OFFICE
GPO Box 4197, Sydney, NSW 2001. Tel: (612) 9374 2111. FAX: (612) 9374 8150.

DEPARTMENT OF ARTS, SPORTS, ENVIRONMENT, TOURISM & TERRITORIES
GPO Box 1920, Canberra City, ACT 2601. Tel: (616) 275 3000. FAX: (616) 275 3819.

FILM AUSTRALIA PTY., LTD.
101 Eton Road, Lindfield, NSW 2070. Tel: (612) 9413 8777. FAX: (612) 9416 9401.

FILM AND LITERATURE BOARD OF REVIEW
Level 1, 255 Elizabeth St., Sydney, NSW 2000. Tel: (612) 9581 7000. FAX: (612) 9581 7001.

NATIONAL FILM & SOUND ARCHIVE
McCoy Circuit, Acton, ACT 2601. Tel: (616) 267 1711. FAX: (616) 247 4651.

SOUTH AUSTRALIAN FILM CORPORATION
3 Butler Dr., Hendon, SA 5014. Tel: (618) 8348 9300. FAX: (618) 8347 0385.

STATE FILM CENTRE OF VICTORIA
17 St. Andrew's Place, East Melbourne, VIC. 3002. Tel: (613) 9651 1301. FAX: (613) 9651 1502.

STATE FILM LIBRARY OF NEW SOUTH WALES
Macquarie St., Sydney, NSW 2000. Tel: (612) 9230 1414. FAX: (612) 9223 3369.

DISTRIBUTORS AND PRODUCERS

ACORN FILM PRODUCTIONS PTY. LTD.
354 Highett St., Richmond, VIC 3121. Tel: (613) 9429 4531. Mobile: (018) 329 646. FAX: (613) 9428 4116.

A COUPLE A COWBOYS
38 Atchinson St., Crows Nest, NSW 2065. Tel: (612) 9438 2044. FAX: (612) 9438 4859.

THE AIREDALE FILM CO. PTY., LTD.
Ste. 4/6 Gurrigal St., Mosmon, NSW 2088. Tel: (612) 9968 4180.

ALCHEMY FILMS
2nd Flr., The Metro Building, 109 Edward St., Brisbane, QLD 4000. Tel: (617) 3221 1487. FAX: (617) 3221 4375.

ALFRED ROAD FILMS
25a Billyard Ave., Elizabeth Bay, NSW 2011. Tel: (612) 9356 3344. FAX: (612) 9358 1613.

ALL MEDIA INTERNATIONAL
643 Chapel St., South Yarra 3141, Victoria. Tel: (613) 926 3637. FAX: (613) 824 0370.

ALMOST MANAGING CO. P/L
192 Elgin St., Carlton, VIC 3053. Tel: (613) 9347 1800. FAX: (613) 9347 0235.

ANJOHN INTERNATIONAL
19/151 Bayswater Rd., Rushcutters Bay 2011, NSW. Tel: (612) 361 6536. FAX: (612) 361 6521.

APOCALYPSE
111-114 Chandos St., Crows Nest, NSW 2065. Tel: (612) 9439 5044. FAX: (612) 9438 2647.

APPALOOSA FILMS
P.O. Box 552, Elsternwick, VIC 3185. Tel: (613) 9699 9722. FAX: (613) 9690 1764.

ARANDA FILM PRODUCTIONS PTY., LTD.
40 Bay St., Brighton, VIC 3186. Tel: (613) 9596 4847. FAX: (613) 596 3580.

ARCHIVE GENERATION FLMS PTY., LTD.
111 Nott St., Port Melbourne, VIC 3207. Tel: (613) 9646 1033. FAX: (613) 9646 2158.

ARTISTRALIA (FILM EXCHANGE SERVICES)
Australia House, 155 Clairebrook Rd., Perth 6000, Western Australia. Tel: (619) 227 1577. FAX: (619) 227 1516.

ATLANTA FILM INTERNATIONAL
95 James Cook Dr., Kings Langley, 2147 NSW. Tel: (612) 838 9210. FAX: (612) 674 5028.

ATLANTIS RELEASING
Ste. 4, 65 Military Rd., Neutral Bay 2089, NSW. Tel: (612) 953 2999. FAX: (612) 953 3248.

AUSTRALIAN FILM THEATRE
114 Glenmore Rd., Paddington, NSW 2021. Tel: (612) 9368 5739. FAX: (612) 9360 1051.

AUSTRALIAN FILM INSTITUTE
49 Eastern Rd., South Melbourne, VIC 3205. Tel: (612) 9332 2111. FAX: (612) 9331 7145. www.afi.org.au
email: afi@vicnet.net.au
CEO
Ruth Jones

AUSTRALIAN SCREEN ASSOCIATES LIMITED
30 Hillview Rd., Mount Lawley, WA 6050. Tel: (619) 370 4822. FAX: (619) 370 4823.

AUSTRALIAN VISUAL PRODUCTIONS
Unit 1, 17 Grosvenor St., Neutral Bay 2096, NSW. Tel: (612) 953 8877. FAX: (612) 953 6221.

AUSTRALIAN WORLD ENTERTAINMENT
202 Tynte St., North Adelaide 5006, SA. (618) 267 3644. FAX: (618) 267 3996.

AUSTRAL VISION
52 Victoria St., North Sydney, NSW 2060. Tel: (612) 9922 4311. FAX: (612) 9922 6956.

AVALON FILMS CORPORATION
9 Albert St., Narranbeen, NSW 2101. Tel/FAX: (612) 9913 1175.

BANSKIA FILM & TV DISTRIBUTION
202 Tynte St., North Adelaide, SA 5006. Tel: (618) 8267 0290. FAX: (618) 8267 3383.

BARRON FILMS
Ste. 7, 85 Forrest St., Cottesloe, WA 6011. Tel: (619) 385 1551. FAX: (619) 385 2299.

BBC ENTERPRISES
11th Fl. 50 Berry St., North Sydney, NSW 2060. Tel: (612) 9957 3777. FAX: (612) 9957 6448.

R. A. BECKER & CO./FREEMANTLE INTERNATIONAL PRODS.
4/21 Chandos St., St. Leonards 2065, NSW. Tel: (612) 438 3377. FAX: (612) 439 1827.

RICHARD BENCE PRODUCTIONS
299 Moray St., South Melbourne, VIC 3205. Tel: (613) 9690 9922. FAX: (613) 9699 1288.

BENDIGO STREET PRODUCTIONS
22 Bendigo St., Richmond, VIC 3121. Tel: (613) 9420 3377. FAX: (613) 9420 3654.

BEYOND FILMS
1st Flr., 53 55 Brisbane St., Surry Hills 2010, NSW. Tel: (612) 281 1266. FAX: (612) 281 9220.

BIG BEAR PICTURE COMPANY PTD., LTD.
1 Simmons Lane, South Belgrave, VIC 3160. Tel: (613) 9754 5548. FAX: (613) 9754 8834.

BILCOCK & COPPING FILM PRODUCTIONS
183 Rouse St., Port Melbourne, VIC 3205. Tel: (613) 9646 0466. FAX: (613) 9646 0282.

BILL BENNETT PRODUCTIONS PTY., LTD.
171 Edinburgh Rd., Castlecrag, NSW 2068. Tel: (612) 9958 3232. FAX: (612) 9958 4816.

BINNABURA FILM CO. PTY., LTD.
P.O. Box 105, Bondi Beach, NSW 2026. Tel: (612) 9362 3923. FAX: (612) 9362 3970.

BIRCH CARROLL AND COYLE THEATRE
418 Adelaide St., Brisbane, QLD 4000. Tel: (617) 3834 0222. FAX: (617) 3832 1101.

BLACK
80 Campbell St., Surry Hills, NSW 2010. Tel: (612) 9281 0088. FAX: (612) 9281 4616.

RICHARD BRADLEY PRODUCTIONS
Ste. 8 / 1st Flr., Sydney, Theatrical Centre, 2-8 Ennis Rd., Milson's Point, NSW 2061. Tel: (612) 9959 3588. FAX: (612) 9955 3808.

BRAY & HAYES
1/1 Ridge St., North Sydney, NSW 2060. Tel: (612) 9957 1559. FAX: (612) 9922 1931.

BRILLIANT FILMS
11/39 Rockley Rd., South Yarra, VIC 3141. Tel: (613) 9826 9682. FAX: (613) 9827 7419.

ROBERT BRUNING
P.O. Box 105, Cremorne Junction, NSW 2090. Tel: (612) 9906 6144, 9953 5867. FAX: (612) 9906 5402, 9953 3184.

BUCKINGHAM PICTURE PRODUCTIONS PTY., LTD.
98 Queens Parade, Newport Beach, NSW 2106. Tel: (612) 9979 9977. FAX: (612) 9979 9279, 9973 1341.

ANTHONY BUCKLEY PRODUCTIONS
P.O. Box 124, Willoughby, NSW 2068. Tel: (612) 9428 2344. FAX: (612) 9427 0247.

BURROWES FILM GROUP
1st Fl., 407 Coventry St., South Melbourne, VIC 3205. Tel: (613) 9690 0388. FAX: (613) 9696 1543.

CALIFORNIA CONNECTION PTY., LTD.
8 Stella Close, East Killara, NSW 2071. Tel: (612) 9498 7697. FAX: (612) 9499 2559.

CASCADE FILM PTY., LTD
117 Rouse St., Port Melbourne, VIC 3205. Tel: (613) 9646 4022. FAX: (613) 9646 6336.

C B FILMS
Level 10, 8 West St., North Sydney, NSW 2060. Tel: (612) 9957 2788. FAX: (612) 9955 5759.

CENTAUR ENTERPRISES PTY., LTD.
89 Eddy Rd. Chatswood, NSW 2067. Tel: (612) 9411 5885. FAX: (612) 9411 1458.

CHRISTIAN TELEVISION ASSOCIATION OF QUEENSLAND
16 Hasp St., Seventeen Mile Rocks, QLD 4073. Tel: (617) 3279 0600. FAX: (617) 3279 0699.

CINEMA CENTRE GROUP
Bunda St., Canberra 2601, ACT. (616) 295 9644. FAX: (616) 295 9694.

CINEMATIC SERVICES PTY., LTD.
Lvl 1/116 Prince Albert St., Mosman, NSW 2088. Tel: (612) 9960 3811.

CINE SERVICE
233-235 Moray St., South Melbourne, VIC 3205. Tel: (613) 9699 6999.

C M FILMS
323 William St., Perth, WA 6000. Tel: (619) 328 8977. FAX: (619) 328 7672.

COLIN MCLENNAN AND ASSOCIATES
13 Napier St., North Sydney 2060, NSW. Tel: (612) 955 5122. FAX: (612) 957 3550.

COLOSIMO FILM PRODUCTIONS
22 Hanover St., Fitzroy, VIC 3065. Tel: (613) 9417 1241. FAX: (613) 9416 1779.

COLUMBIA TRISTAR FILM DISTRIBUTORS INTERNATIONAL
42-26 Longueville Rd., Lane Cove, NSW, 2066. Tel: (612) 911 3377. FAX: (612) 418 6270.
VICE PRESIDENT
Peter Wikinson

CONTINENTAL MOUNTS AUSTRALIA
45 Grafton St., Naremburn, Sydney, NSW 2065. Tel: (612) 9906 4777. FAX: (612) 9436 3553.

CORAL SEA IMAGERY
P.O. Box 2186, Townsville, QLD 4810. Tel: (6177) 211 633. FAX: (6177) 757 851.

CO-PRODUCTIONS AUSTRALIA PTY., LTD.
104 Longwood Rd., Heathfield, North Adelaide, SA 5153. Tel/FAX: (618) 8370 9062.

JANINA CRAIG SCREEN SERVICES PTY., LTD.
16 Bridport St., South Melbourne, VIC 3205. Tel: (613) 9690 1229. FAX: (613) 9699 6986.

BEN CROPP PRODUCTIONS
Shipwreck Museum, Port Douglas, QLD 4871. Tel: (6170) 995 858. FAX: (6170) 994 300.

PAUL DAVIES FILM AND TELEVISION ENTERPRISES
62 South Road, Brighton, VIC 3186. Tel: (613) 9597 0596. FAX: (613) 9598 6853.

DENDY FILMS
34 Louisa Rd., Birchgrove 2041, NSW. Tel: (612) 810 8733. FAX: (612) 810 3228.

DIGITAL ARTS FILM & TELEVISION
1 Ledger Rd., Beverly, SA 5009. Tel: (618) 8347 4691. FAX: (618) 8347 4692.

DISCOVERY INTERNATIONAL
P.O. Box 550, Malvern 3144, Victoria. Tel: (613) 563 9344. FAX: (613) 563 9885.

EASTWAY COMMUNICATIONS
Ste. 109, 6/8 Clarke St., Crows Nest, NSW 2065. Tel: (612) 9437 6155. FAX: (612) 9439 4387.

EDGECLIFF FILMS
25 Suffolk St., Paddington, NSW 2021. Tel: (612) 9331 6277. FAX: (612) 9331 2588.

EMPRESS ROAD PRODUCTIONS PTY., LTD.
1-126 Brighton Rd., Bondi, NSW 2026. Tel: (612) 9365 4073. FAX: (612) 9365 4529.

EN CUE PRODUCTIONS PTY., LTD.
P.O. Box 5291, West End, QLD 4101. Tel: (617) 3844 6242. FAX: (617) 3844 6285.

ENTERTAINMENT MEDIA PTY., LTD.
157 Eastern Rd., South Melbourne, VIC 3205. Tel: (613) 9690 1044. FAX: (613) 9690 1764.

ENTREG PTY., LTD.
1075 High St., Armdale, VIC 3143. Tel: (613) 9822 6999. FAX: (613) 9822 0957.

FAST FORWARD PTY., LTD.
Innovation Hse., Technology Park, The Levels, SA 5095. Tel/FAX: (618) 8260 8139.

FILM & TELEVISION INSTITUTE (WA) INC
92 Adelaide St., Fremantle, WA 6160. Tel: (619) 335 1055. FAX: (619) 335 1283.

FILM ASSOCIATES
22 Lindsay Ave., Murrumbeena, VIC 3163. Tel: (613) 9568 3741.

FILM AUSTRALIA
Eaton Rd., Linfield 2070, NSW. Tel: (612) 413 8777. FAX: (612) 416 5672.

THE FILM BUSINESS & PARTNERS
91 Reservoir St., Surry Hills, NSW 2010. Tel: (612) 9281 8380. FAX: (612) 9281 8155.

FILM CENTRE AUSTRALIA
E270 The Esplanade, Swan Point, TAS 7275. Tel/FAX: (613) 6399 4903.

FILMPARTNERSHIP & ASSOCIATES
12 Fifth St., Black Rock, VIC 3193. Tel: (613) 9589 3622. FAX: (613) 9534 3502.

FILM TAGGS
52a Anzac Ave., West Ryde, NSW 2114. Tel/FAX: (612) 9807 4914.

FIRST CLASS FILMS
40 Osgathorpe Rd., Gladesville, NSW 2111. Tel: (612) 9816 1813. FAX: (612) 9816 5402.

FONTANA FILMS PTY., LTD.
360 Pacific Highway, Crows Nest, NSW 2068. Tel: (612) 9906 2188. FAX: (612) 9906 2337.

FOX TELEVISION
Level 25, 44 Market St., Sydney, NSW 2000. Tel: (612) 9299 2941. FAX: (612) 9290 2623.

FRONTIER FILMS
P.O. Box 294, Harbord, NSW 2096. Tel: (612) 9938 5762.

FUNNY FARM
68 Cecil St., South Melbourne, VIC 3205. Tel: (613) 9690 4466. FAX: (613) 9696 7977.

GARNER MACLENNAN DESIGN
P.O. Box 1418, Crows Nest, NSW 2065. Tel: (612) 9438 1002. FAX: (612) 9439 6710.

GENESIS FILMS PTY., LTD.
82 Eton Rd., Somerton Park, SA 5044. Tel: (618) 8295 5353. FAX: (618) 8295 6898. email: genesisfilm@msn.com

GOLDEN DOLPHIN PRODUCTIONS
P.O. Box 398, Spit Junction, NSW 2088. Tel: (612) 9971 1783. FAX: (612) 9971 2261.

GREAT SOUTHERN FILMS PTY., LTD.
5 Haig St., South Melbourne, VIC 3205. Tel: (613) 9699 6466. FAX: (613) 9699 6400.

GREAT SOUTHERN FILMS (SA) PTY., LTD.
16 Conyngham St., Glenside, SA 5065. Tel: (618) 8388 2811. FAX: (618) 8388 3090.

GREAT SOUTHERN FILMS (SYD) PTY., LTD.
Studio 18, 37 Nicholson St., Balmain East., Sydney 2041. Tel: (612) 9818 3377. FAX: (612) 9818 3378.

GREATER UNION ORGANISATION PTY., LTD.
State Theatre Building, 49 Market St., Sydney, NSW 2000. Tel: (612) 9373 6600. FAX: (612) 9267 5277.

HANNA-BARBERA AUSTRALIA
c/o Southern Star Group, 8 West St., North Sydney, NSW 2060. Tel: (612) 9202 8555. FAX: (612) 9925 0849.

DAVID HANNAY PRODUCTIONS
2 Buckland St. Amend, Broadway, NSW 2007. Tel: (612) 9211 2022. FAX: (612) 9212 2350.

THE HAYDEN GROUP OF COMPANIES
380 Military Rd., Cremorne, NSW 2090. Tel: (612) 9908 1799. FAX: (612) 9908 4238.

HAYDON PRODUCTIONS
P.O. Box 185, Rose Bay, NSW 2029. Tel: (612) 9388 1990. FAX: (612) 9388 1991.

HELICAM
P.O. Box 310, Yandina, QLD 4561. Tel/FAX: (6174) 46 8482.

HOUSE AND MOORHOUSE FILMS PTY.
117 Rouse St., Port Melbourne, VIC 3207. Tel: (613) 9646 4025. FAX: (613) 9646 6336.

HOYTS FOX COLUMBIA TRI-STAR FILMS
490 Kent St., Sydney 2000, NSW. Tel: (612) 261 7800. FAX: (612) 283 2191.

ILLUMINATION FILMS
1 Victoria Ave., Albert Park, VIC 3206. Tel: (613) 9690 5266. FAX: (613) 9696 5625.

INLAND FILMS PTY., LTD.
27 Surfside Ave., Clovelly, NSW 2031. Tel: (612) 9665 2977. Mobile: (018) 259 936. FAX: (612) 9665 7773.

JD PRODUCTIONS
116 Crescent Rd., Newport, NSW 2106. Tel: (612) 9997 1601. FAX: (612) 9979 5083.

J'ELLY BALLANTYNE PRODUCTIONS
119B Old Mt. Barker Rd., Stirling, SA 5152. Tel: (618) 8370 9458 FAX: (618) 8370 9487.

JNP FILMS
87 Alexander St., Crows Nest, NSW 2065. Tel: (612) 9439 5855. FAX: (613) 9436 0583.

JSA PRODUCTIONS PTY., LTD.
16/16 Lyall St., Leichhardt, NSW 2040. Tel/FAX: (612) 9564 1957.

KALEIDOSCOPE PRODUCTIONS
22 Hewlett St., Waverley, NSW 2024. Tel: (612) 9387 7117. FAX: (612) 9387 7156.

KANANGRA FILMS
56 Carranya Road, Lane Cove, NSW 2066. Tel: (612) 9428 4268.

KAVANAGH PRODUCTIONS PTY., LTD.
7/15 South Terrace, Clifton Hill, VIC 3068. Tel: (613) 9481 4312. (613) 9481 4695.

KENNEDY MILLER
Metro Theatre, 30 Orwell St., Kings Cross, NSW 2011. Tel: (612) 9357 2322. FAX: (612) 9356 3162.

KESTREL FILM & VIDEO
367 Bridge Road, Richmond, VIC 3121. Tel: (613) 9429 1688. FAX: (613) 9428 6202.

KOOKABURRA PRODUCTIONS PTY. LTD.
P.O. Box 555, Artarmon, NSW 2064. Tel: (612) 9438 4344. FAX: (612) 9906 1701.

LATENT IMAGE PRODUCTIONS PTY. LTD.
82 Glenmore Rd., Paddingfton, NSW 2021. Tel: (612) 9331 4155. FAX: (612) 9331 4135.

LEA FILMS
P.O. Box 93, North Carlton, VIC 3084. Tel: (613) 9646 9455. FAX: (613) 9646 0220.

LOOK PRODUCTIONS
83 Willoughby Road, Crows Nest, NSW 2065. Tel: (612) 9436 1647. FAX: (612) 9438 3660.

LORI DALE PRODUCTIONS PTY., LTD.
120 Bridport St., Albert Park, VIC 3206. Tel: (613) 9699 8400. FAX: (613) 9699 3048.

LOVELL FILMS
P.O. Box 701, Avalon Beach, NSW 2107. Tel: (612) 9918 2999. FAX: (612) 9918 0883.

PETER LUCK PRODUCTIONS
19 Edward St., East Balmain, NSW 2041. Tel: (612) 9810 2458. FAX: (612) 9818 5325.

LUCKY COUNTRY PRODUCTIONS
Tagallant House, Scotland Island, NSW 2105. Tel: (612) 9977 3405. FAX: (612) 9977 8953.

LUMIERE PRODUCTIONS PTY. LTD.
51 Farnell St., Hunters Hill, NSW 2110. Tel: (612) 9879 6140.

LYONS-SINCLAIR PRODUCTIONS
P.O. Box 83, Toorak, VIC 3142. Tel/FAX: (613) 9827 4641.

MACAU LIGHT CORPORATION LTD.
16 Lang Road, Centennial Park, NSW 2021. Tel: (612) 9361 3961. FAX: (612) 9360 3346.

MARLO AUDIO VISUAL
P.O. Box 50, Belgian Gardens, Townsville, QLD 4810. Tel: (61018) 777 709. FAX: (61018) 180 927.

MASON PICTURE COMPANY
Ste. 3/239 Pacific Hwy., North Sydney, NSW 2060. Tel: (612) 9959 3500. FAX: (612) 9959 3679.

MAX STUDIOS
19-25 Birmingham St., Alexandria, NSW 2015. Tel: (612) 9317 2999. FAX: (612) 9667 4528.

MCA
1st Flr., MCA Universal House, 23 Pelican Street, Sydney 2010, NSW. Tel: (612) 267 9844. FAX: (612) 264 1742.

M. C. STUART AND ASSOCIATES
88 Highett St., Richmond 3121, Victoria. Tel: (613) 429 8666. FAX: (613) 429 1839.

MEANINGFUL EYE CONTACT
18 Moor Ave., West Lindfield, NSW 2071. Tel/FAX: (612) 9416 9662.

MEDIACAST PTY., LTD.
P.O. Box 67, Round Corner, Dural, NSW 2158. Tel: (612) 9651 4219. FAX: (612) 9482 1298.

MEDIA WORLD
278 Gore St., Fitzroy, VIC 3065. Tel: (613) 9417 4888. FAX: (613) 9417 5383.

METRO TELEVISION, LTD.
249 Oxford St. (Cnr Oatley Rd.), Paddington, NSW 2021. Tel: (612) 9361 5318, 9361 3048. FAX: (612) 9361 5320.

MGM/UA
P.O. Box 6125, Shopping World, North Sydney, NSW 2060. Tel: (612) 9966 1711. FAX: (612) 9966 1969.

HARRY MICHAEL PRODUCTIONS
7 McCabe Place, Willoughby, NSW 2068. Tel: (612) 9417 5700. FAX: (612) 9417 5879.

HARRY M. MILLER AND COMPANY MANAGEMENT PTY., LTD.
174 Cathedral St., Woolloomooloo, NSW 2011. Tel: (612) 9357 3077. FAX: (612) 9356 2880.

MILTON INGERSON PRODUCTIONS
2a Torrens St., Linden Park, SA 5065. Tel: (618) 8338 1666. FAX: (618) 8338 2510.

MODERN TIMES PTY., LTD.
P.O. Box 908, Bondi Junction, NSW 2022. Tel: (612) 9365 2416. FAX: (612) 9365 2454.

MURRAY MANCHA PTY., LTD.
199 Richardson St., Middle Park, VIC 3206. Tel: (613) 9690 2510. FAX: (613) 9690 6981.

NALUSA PTY., LTD.
1st Fl., 34 Burton St., Kirribilli, NSW 2061. Tel: (612) 9925 0716. FAX: (612) 9922 3063.

NEW BLOOD & OLD MONEY
28-30 Surrey St., Darlinghurst, NSW 2010. Tel: (612) 9361 5002. FAX: (612) 9361 4701.

NEW VISION FILM DISTRIBUTORS
2nd Flr., 254 Bay St., Port Melbourne 3207, Victoria. Tel: (613) 646 5555. FAX: (613) 646 2411.

N.S.W. FILM & TELEVISION
GPO Box 1744, Sydney, NSW 2000. Tel: (612) 9380 5599. FAX: (612) 9360 1090.

ORACLE PICTURES
St. Dugham St., Level 12, 15/19 Boundary St., Rushcutters Bay, NSW 2011. Tel: (612) 9358 3788. FAX: (612) 9357 1723.

ORANA FILMS PTY. LTD.
133 Dowling St., Woolloomooloo, NSW 2011. Tel: (612) 9356 2266. FAX: (612) 9356 2629.

OPEN EYE (FILM & TV)
1/87 Bent St., North Sydney 2060, NSW. Tel: (612) 954 3626. FAX: (612) 959 3253.

OXFORD FILM SERVICES
Ste. 1, 372 Anzac Pde., Kingsford, NSW 2032. Tel: (612) 9662 8842. FAX: (612) 9662 7663.

PACIFIC LINK COMMUNICATIONS
2A Eltham St., Gladesville 2111, NSW. Tel: (612) 817 5055. FAX: (612) 879 7297.

PALACE ENTERTAINMENT
1/101 Union St., North Sydney 2060, NSW. Tel: (612) 954 3323. FAX: (612) 954 3306.

PARAMOUNT PICTURES
Ste. 3209, Australia Square, Sydney 2000, NSW. Tel: (612) 247 9367. FAX: (612) 251 3251.

DAMIEN PARER PRODUCTIONS
5 Longfellow St., Norman Park, QLD 4170. Tel: (317) 3899 1555. FAX:(317) 3899 1936.

PAVILLION FILM PTY., LTD.
P.O. Box 701, Avalon Beach, NSW 2107. Tel: (312) 9918 2999. FAX: (312) 9918 0883.

PICTURE START
4 Glen St., Milsons Point, NSW 2061. Tel: (612) 9959 5550. Mobile: (0181) 961 013. FAX: (612) 9929 5961.

POLYGON PICTURES
19 Forest Knoll Ave., Bondi, NSW 2026. Tel: (612) 9365 2955. FAX: (612) 9365 2711.

POLYGRAM FILMED ENTERTAINMENT
3 Munn Reserve, Sydney 2000. Tel: (612) 207 0500. FAX: (612) 241 1497.
CONTACT
Richard Sheffield MacClure

PREMIUM FILMS
92 Bay St., Port Melbourne 3207, Victoria. Tel: (613) 645 1612. FAX: (613) 645 1591.

PRO FILMS
Level 2/486 Pacific Highway, St. Leonards, NSW 2065. Tel: (612) 9438 3377. FAX: (612) 9439 1827.

QUANTAS
14 Bourke Rd., Mascot 2020, NSW. Tel: (612) 691 1069. FAX: (612) 691 1865.

QUEST FILMS
4 Marshall Ave., St. Leonards, NSW 2065. Tel: (612) 9436 1970. Mobile: (18) 967 336. FAX: (612) 9436 1970.

REEPRODUCTIONS PTY., LTD.
56 Gipps St., Birchgrove, NSW 2041. Tel: (612) 9818 4908. Mobile: (18) 416 704. FAX: (612) 9810 3086.

REID AND PUSKAR
44 Moruben Rd., Mosman 2088, NSW. Tel: (612) 969 2077. FAX: (612) 960 4971.

R I P PRODUCTIONS
5 Little Chapel St., Prahan, VIC 3181. Tel: (613) 9529 2144. FAX: (613) 9529 6953.

RKA THE ANIMATION STUDIO
21 Harris St., Paddington, NSW 2021. Tel: (612) 9362 4669. FAX: (612) 9362 3711.

ROADSHOW COOTE AND CARROLL PTY.
1st Flr., 608 Harris St., Ultimo, NSW 2009. Tel: (612) 9211 2211. FAX: (612) 9211 2144.

ROGUE PRODUCTIONS
30 South St., Fremantle, WA 6160. Tel: (619) 335 2426.

ROSEN HARPER ENTERTAINMENT
5/2 New McLean St., Edgecliff, NSW 2027. Tel: (612) 9363 5658.

ROSS WOOD PRODUCTIONS
36 Gosbell St., Paddington, NSW 2021. Tel: (612) 9331 5154. FAX: (612) 9360 1583.

SAGITTA FILM PRODUCTIONS
32 Barcoo St., East Roseville, NSW 2069. Tel: (612) 9417 5643. FAX: (612) 9417 6443.

SAMSON PRODUCTIONS
119 Pyrmont St., Pyrmont, NSW 2009. Tel: (612) 9660 3244. FAX: (612) 9692 8926.

SEA FILMS PTY., LTD.
7 Woodsmans Copse, Hallett Cove, SA 5158. Tel/FAX: (618) 8322 3127.

SERIOUS ENTERTAINMENT
P.O. Box 600, North Sydney, NSW 2060. Tel: (612) 9957 5375. FAX: (612) 9955 8600.

SEVEN DIMENSIONS PTY., LTD.
8 Daly St., South Yarra, VIC 3141. Tel: (613) 9826 2277. FAX: (613) 9826 4477.

SHARMILL FILMS
Ste. 4, 200 Toorak Rd., South Yarra 3141, Victoria. Tel: (613) 826 9077. FAX: (613) 826 1935.

SHOT PRODUCTIONS
P.O. Box 305, Darlinghurst, NSW 2010. Tel: (612) 9360 5733. FAX: (612) 9360 5535.

SIMPLE STORIES
RMB 1117A, Wodonga, VIC 3691. Tel: (6157) 545 262. FAX: (613) 699 3123.

SMILEY FILMS
33 Riley St., Woolloomooloo, NSW 2011. Tel: (612) 9361 4164. FAX: (612) 9692 8387.

SOERABAIA PICTURES PTY., LTD.
6 David St., Forest Lodge, NSW 2037. Tel: (612) 9552 2634. FAX: (612) 9692 8387.

SOKOL FILM PRODUCTIONS
P.O. Box 1599, North Sydney, NSW 2059. Tel: (612) 9959 5526. Mobile: (018) 678 792. FAX: (612) 9959 5714.

SORENA
P.O. Box 215, French Forest, NSW 2086. Tel: (612) 9417 8112, 9417 8138.

SOUTH AUSTRALIAN FILM CORPORATION
3 Butler Dr., Hendon, SA 5014. Tel: (618) 8348 9300. FAX: (618) 8347 0385.

SOUTHERN CROSS NETWORK
1-3 Bowen Rd., Moonah, TAS 7009. Tel: (613) 6344 0202. FAX: (613) 6343 0340.

SOUTHERN STAR ENTERTAINMENT
10th Flr., 8 West St., North Sydney, NSW 2060. Tel: (612) 9202 8555. FAX: (612) 9925 0849.

SOUTHERN STAR INTERNATIONAL
10th fl., 8 West St., North Sydney, NSW 2060. Tel: (612) 9202 8555. FAX: (612) 9925 0849.

WILL SPENCER PRODUCTIONS PTY., LTD.
22 Hanover St., Fitzroy, VIC 3065. Tel: (613) 9417 1241. FAX: (613) 9416 1779.

SPOTZ CASTING AGENCIES
10/a 31-37 Thompson St., Bowen Hill, QLD 4006. Tel: (617) 3854 1949. FAX: (617) 3252 7237.

SPROWLES OFF BROADWAY FILMS
8-14 Nelson St., Annandale, Sydney, NSW 2038. Tel: (612) 9550 5599. FAX: (612) 9550 5742.

STRAUSS PRODUCTIONS
P.O. Box 167, Round Corner, NSW 2158. Tel: (612) 9899 1691. Mobile: (018) 222 886. FAX: (612) 9680 2871.

STUART, M C & ASSOCIATES PTY., LTD.
88 Highett St., Richmond, VIC 3121. Tel: (613) 9429 8666. Telex: AA 33147 MCSAA. FAX: (613) 9429 1839.

D. L. TAFFNER AUSTRALIA
Unit 20, Greenwich Square, 130-134 Pacific Highway, Greenwich 2065, NSW. Tel: (612) 439 5699. FAX: (612) 439 4501.

TAFFNER RAMSEY PRODUCTIONS
Ste. 303, 156 Pacific Hwy., Greenwich, NSW 2065. Tel: (612) 9437 5433. FAX: (612) 9437 4501.

WILLIAM THOMAS FILM PRODUCTIONS
10 Carlton Rd., Camden Park, SA 5038. Tel: (618) 8294 4468. FAX: (618) 8294 9434.

TMS DISTRIBUTION
Level 1, 50 King St., Sydney, NSW 2000. Tel: (612) 9299 5788. FAX: (612) 9299 5704.

TROUT FILMS PTY., LTD.
189 St. Georges Rd., North Fitzroy, VIC 3068. Tel: (613) 9489 3127. FAX: (612) 9486 3618. email: troutfilms@ibm.net
DIRECTOR
Chris Warner

ULLADULLA PICTURE COMPANY
Ste. 5, 600 Military Rd., Mosman, NSW 2088. Tel: (612) 9969 7599. FAX: (612) 9969 5011.

UNITED INTERNATIONAL PICTURES
Unit 1, 11 Parkview St., Milton, QLD 4064. Tel: (617) 367 0633. FAX: (617) 367 0688.
208 Clarence St., Sydney 2000, NSW. Tel: (612) 264 7444. FAX: (612) 264 3203.
Unit 4, 113 Adderley St., West Melbourne, VIC 3003. Tel: (613) 9326 6966. FAX: (613) 9329 6247.
MANAGER
Michael Selwyn

VALKYRIE FILMS
166 Glebe Point Rd., Glebe 2037, NSW. Tel: (612) 552 2456. FAX: (612) 552 2457.

VIACOM INTERNATIONAL
Ste. 3501, Level 35s Tower, North Point, 100 Miller St., North Sydney, NSW 2060. Tel: (612) 9922 2322. FAX: (612) 9955 6808.

VICTORIAN COUNCIL FOR CHILDREN'S FILM & TV
41 St. Andrews Place, East Melbourne, VIC 3002. Tel: (613) 9651 1919. FAX: (613) 9651 1238.

VICTORIAN INTERNATIONAL PICTURES
Melbourne Film Studios, 117 Rouse St., Port Melbourne, VIC 3207. Tel: (613) 9646 4777. FAX: (613) 9646 4946.

VIEW FILMS PTY., LTD.
2nd fl., 41 Oxford St., Darlinghurst, NSW 2010. Tel: (612) 283 3066.

VILLAGE ROADSHOW PICTURES
Warner Roadshow Movie World, Studios, Pacific Way, Oxenford, Gold Coast, QLD 4210. Tel: (7) 5588 6666. FAX: (7) 5573 3698.

VILLAGE ROADSHOW PICTURES
4th Flr., 235 Pyrmont St., Pyrmont 2009, NSW. Tel: (612) 552 8600. FAX: (612) 552 2510.

VIRGIN VISION AUSTRALIA
99 Victoria St., Potts Point 2011, NSW. Tel: (612) 368 1700.

VISIONLINK & CULT PRODUCTIONS
44 Sailors Bay Road, Northbridge, NSW 2063. Tel: (612) 9958 2077. FAX: (612) 9958 2974.

WALKER CLANCY
Unit 16, 2 Greenkowne Ave., Potts Point, NSW 2021. Tel: (612) 9358 1163. FAX: (612) 9368 1064.

THE WALT DISNEY COMPANY
149 Castlereagh St., Sydney 2000, NSW. Tel: (612) 268 942. FAX: (612) 264 1289.

WARNER BROTHERS AUSTRALIA
Level 22, 8-20 Napier St., North Sydney, NSW. Tel: (612) 957 3899. FAX: (612) 956 7788.
CONTACT
Fiona Curtis

WESTBRIDGE PRODUCTIONS PTY., LTD.
P.O. Box 219, Port Douglas, QLD 4871. Tel: (6170) 985 577. FAX: (6170) 994 295.

WILD VISUALS PTY., LTD.
133 Dowling St., Woolloomooloo, NSW 2011. Tel: (612) 9331 0877. FAX: (612) 9357 4126. email: info@wildvisuals.com.au

WORLD VISION ENTERPRISES
2nd Flr., 5-13 Northcliff St., Milsons Point 2061, NSW. Tel: (612) 922 4722. FAX: (612) 955 8207.

ZAP PRODUCTIONS PTY., LTD.
24 Calotta St., Artamon, NSW 2064. Tel: (612) 9438 4333. FAX: (612) 9439 5172.

EXHIBITORS

AUSTRALIAN MULTIPLEX CINEMAS (AMC)
P.O. Box 2152, Brookside Centre, QLD 4520. Tel: (617) 33 55 33 53. FAX: (617) 33 54 47 00. email: amc@powerup.com.au
CHAIRMAN
James C. Sourris
CEO
Michael Hawkins

Number of Theatres: 5
Number of Screens: 41
QLD (5); NSW (1).

DENDY CINEMAS
19 Martin Pl., Sydney, NSW 2000. Tel: (612) 92 33 85 58. FAX: (612) 92 32 38 41. email: dendy@dendy.com.au

Number of Theatres: 5
Number of Screens: 9
NSW, QLD, VIC.

GRAND CINEMAS
P.O. Box 2137, Warwick, WA 6024. Tel: (618) 94 n48 31 88. FAX: (618) 92 46 17 55. email: grandcin@wanet.com.au.
CHAIRMAN
Colin Stiles
MANAGING DIRECTOR
Alan Stiles

Number of Theatres: 3
Number of Screens: 19

THE GREATER UNION ORGANISATION
(Including BIRCH CARROLL & COYLE)
49 Market St., Sydney, NSW 2000. Tel: (612) 93 73 66 00. FAX: (612) 93 73 65 32.
MANAGING DIRECTOR
Robert Manson

Number of Theatres: 53 (Australia)
Number of Screens: 386 (Australia)

Greater Union Organisation (GUO)
NSW (3), ACT (2), VIC. (1), SA (3), WA (4), QLD (1).

Birch, Carroll, & Coyle (BCC)
NSW (3), QLD (23), NT (2).

Theatres outside Australia
Germany (30), Poland (1), UAE (1).

HAWTHORNE–BALMORAL CINEMAS
168 Oxford St., Bulimba, QLD, 4171. www.merricum.hotmail.com
OWNER
Family Company
EXECUTIVES
Leo Catalano
Merilyn Catalano

HOYTS CINEMAS PTY., LTD.
6th Flr. 505-523 George St., Sydney, NSW 2000. Tel: (612) 92 73 7373. FAX: (612) 92 73 7356.
CEO
Paul Johnson
CFO
Colin Resnick
COO (Australia & New Zealand)
Roger Eaton

Number of Theatres: 41
Number of Screens: 312 (Australia)
NSW (18), ACT (1), VIC (9), SA (4), WA (5), QLD (4).
Number of Screens outside Australia: 1,648
Mexico (27), Uruguay (1).

Hoyts Argentina
Avda Corriertes 447, 5 Piso, Buenos Aires, Argentina

Number of Theatres: 5
Number of Screens: 52

Hoyts Chile
Roger de Flores #2736, Piso 6
Las Condes, Santiago, Chile

Number of Theatres: 5
Number of Screens: 49

Hoyts Europe
St. Andrews House
22-28 High St., Epsom Surrey, KT19 89H
Austria (4), Germany (8), U.K. (1)

Hoyts New Zealand
44, 47 Wakefield St., Auckland.

Number of Theatres: 15
Number of Screens: 106

NOVA CINEMAS
Lygon Court Shopping Centre, 380 Lygon St., Carlton, VIC. Tel: (613) 93 47 53 31. FAX: (613) 93 47 26 95.
EXECUTIVES
Natalie Miller
Barry Peake
OWNERS
Natalie Miller
Barry Peake
Palace Cinemas

Number of Theatres: 2
Number of Screens: 15

PACIFIC CINEMAS
Logan Hyperdome, Pacific Hwy., Loganholme, QLD 4129. Tel: (617) 38 01 17 88. FAX: (617) 38 01 39 86. email: eatont@tq.com.au
CHAIRMAN
Terri Jackman
GENERAL MANAGER
Pamela Rosenthall

Number of Theatres: 2
Number of Screens: 16
QLD (1), ACT (1).

PALACE CINEMAS
233 Whitehorse Rd., Balwyn, VIC 3103. Tel: (613) 9817 6421. FAX: (613) 9817 4921.
MANAGING DIRECTOR
Antonio Zeccola

Number of Theatres: 16
Number of Screens: 43
NSW (4), SA (1), VIC (7), WA (4).

READING ENTERTAINMENT
6 Bay St., Port Melbourne, VIC 3207. Tel: (613) 9644 1900. FAX: (613) 9646 1185.
email: reading.melbourne@readingaust.com.au
CHAIRMAN
James Cotter
PRESIDENT
Ellen Cotter
CHIEF EXECUTIVE
Neil Pentecost
OWNER
Australian subsidiary of Reading Entertainment, Inc. (U.S.)

Number of Theatres: 10 (Australia)
Number of Screens: 71 (Australia)
Number of Screens outside Australia 12 (New Zealand)

REGENT CINEMA–SOUTH COAST THEATRES PTY., LTD.
197 Keira St., Wollongong, NSW 2500. Tel: (612) 4229-5130.
MANAGING DIRECTOR
Rowena Milgrove

RONIN FILMS
P.O. Box 1005, Civic Square, ACT 2608. Tel: (612) 6248 0851. FAX: (612) 6249 1640.
EXECUTIVES
Andrew Pike
Merrilyn Pike
OWNER
Pike-Fitzpatrick Nominees Pty., Ltd.

Number of Screens: 3

ROSEVILLE TWIN CINEMAS
112 Pacific Hwy., Roseville 2069. Tel: (612) 9416-5988. FAX: (612) 9416-3473.
MANAGER, DIRECTOR & OWNER
Emma van Pinxteren
MANAGER, DIRECTOR & OWNER
Lisa van Pinxteren
MANAGER, DIRECTOR & OWNER
Sue van Pinxteren

VILLAGE ROADSHOW, LTD.
206 Bourke St., Melbourne, VIC 3000. Tel: (613) 96 67 66 66. FAX: (613) 96 39 15 40.
CHAIR
J.R. Kirby
MANAGING DIRECTOR
G.W. Burke
FINANCE DIRECTOR
P.E. Foo
GROUP COMPANY SECRETARY
P. Leggo
CO-CEO (VILLAGE CINEMAS INTL.)
J. Anderson
EXECUTIVE CHAIR & CO-CEO, EXHIBITION
J. Crawford

Number of Theatres: 75 (Australia)
Number of Screens: 517 (Australia)
Theatres in Australia:
NSW (17), VIC (32), TAS (4), QLD (10), WA (7), NT (1), SA (4).

Theatres outside Australia:
Argentina (7), Austria (1), China (1), Fiji (2), France (2), Germany (8), Greece (4), Hong Kong (8), Hungary (4), India (2), Italy (6), Korea (2), Malaysia (40), New Zealand (40), Singapore (9), Switzerland (1), Taiwan (17), U.K. (28).

WALLIS THEATRES
139 Richmond Rd., Richmond, SA 5033. Tel: (618) 8352 1377. FAX: (618) 8352 1865. email: wallis@wallis.com.au
CHAIRMAN
Bob Wallis
PROGRAM MANAGER
Bob Parr

Number of Theatres: 8
Number of Screens: 20

WESTSIDE CINEMAS
P.O. Box 77, Indooroopilly, QLD 4068. Tel: (617) 33 78 15 66. FAX: (617) 33 78 15 04. www.eldorado8.com.au
EXECUTIVES
Ray Roobottom
Judy Roobottom
Paul Roobottom

Number of Theatres: 2
Number of Screens: 10

AUSTRIA

Population: 8.1 million.
Ticket Price: $6.24.
Theatre grosses: $80.9 million.

ASSOCIATIONS & ORGANIZATIONS

AKTION FILM
(Austrian Section of the International Center of Films for Children and Young Children), Neubaugasse 25, Vienna A-1070. Tel: (431) 523 2437. FAX: (431) 523 3971.

ARGE OSTERREICHISCHES DREHBUCHAUTOREN-DREHBUCHFORUM WIEN
Stiftgasse 6, Vienna A-1070. (431) 526 8503 500. FAX: (431) 526 8503 550.

ART DIRECTORS & COSTUME DESIGNERS ASSOCIATION
Siegelgasse 1/16, Vienna A-1030. (431) 523 6085. FAX: (431) 523 6085.

ASIFA-AUSTRIA (INTERNATIONAL ANIMATED FILM ASSOCIATION)
Huttelberggasse 75/1, Vienna A-1140. (431) 914 7797. FAX: (431) 712 0392.

ASSOCIATION OF AUSTRIAN FILM DIRECTORS
Spittelberggasse 3, Vienna A-1070. Tel: (431) 526 0006. FAX: (431) 426 0006 16.

ASSOCIATION OF AUSTRIAN FILM JOURNALISTS
Speisinger Strasse 4, Vienna A-1130. Tel: (431) 804 3561. FAX: (431) 804 1720.

ASSOCIATION OF AUSTRIAN FILM PRODUCERS
Speisinger Strasse 121-127, Vienna A-1230. Tel: (431) 888 9622.

ASSOCIATION OF DISTRIBUTORS
Wiener Hauptstrasse 63, P.O. Box 327, Vienna A-1045. Tel.: (431) 50105 3011. FAX: (431) 50206 376.

AUSTRIA FILMMAKERS CO-OPERATIVE
Wahringer Str. 59, Vienna A-1090. Tel: (431) 408 7627. FAX: (431) 408 7627.

AUSTRIAN ASSOCIATION OF CINEMATOGRAPHERS (AAC)
Karlsplatz 5, Künstlerhaus, Vienna A-1010. Tel: (431) 713 6611. FAX: (431) 587 9665.

AUSTRIAN FILM COMMISSION–AFC
Stiftgasse 6, Vienna A-1070. Tel: (431) 526 3323 200. FAX: (431) 526 6801.

AUSTRIAN FILM FUND
Stiftgasse 6, Vienna A-1070. Tel: (431) 526 9730 406. FAX: (431) 526 9730 440.

AUSTRIAN FILM INSTITUTE
Stiftgasse 6, Vienna A-1070. Tel: (431) 523 9730 400. FAX: (431) 526 9730 440.

AUSTRIAN SOCIETY OF SOUND ENGINEERS
Natteregasse 4, Laxenburg A-2361. Tel: (43) 2236 71307. FAX: (43) 2236 71307.

FEDERATION OF AUSTRIAN FILM PRODUCERS
Neubaugasse 25, Vienna A-1070. Tel: (431) 523 7437. FAX: (431) 526 4302/3.

NATIONAL TOURIST OFFICE
Margaretenstrasse 1, Vienna A-1040. Tel: (431) 588 660. FAX: (431) 588 660.

AUDIENCE RESEARCH

AUSTRIAN SOCIETY FOR FILM SCIENCES, COMMUNICATION & MEDIA STUDIES
Rauhensteingasse 6, Vienna A-1010. Tel: (431) 512 9936. FAX: (431) 513 5330. email: oegfkm@cybertron.at

DISTRIBUTORS

AKTION FILM (AUSTRIAN SECTION OF THE INTERNATIONAL CENTER OF FILMS FOR CHILDREN AND YOUNG PEOPLE)
Neubaugasse 25, Vienna A-1070. Tel: (431) 523 2437. FAX: (431) 523 3971.

ALPHA FILM
Neubaugasse 4, Vienna A-1070. Tel: (431) 523 7660. FAX: (431) 523 7660.

AUSTRIA FILMMAKERS CO-OPERATIVE
Wahringer Strasse 59, Vienna A-1090. Tel: (431) 408 7627. FAX: (431) 408 3871.

BUENA VISTA INTERNATIONAL (BVI)
Hermannagasse 18, Vienna A-1071. Tel: (431) 526 9467. FAX: (431) 526 9468 5.

CENTFOX FILM GMBH
Neubaugasse 35, Vienna A-1070. Tel: (431) 932 2629. FAX: (431) 526 7297.

CINESTAR
Opernring 19, Vienna A-1010. Tel: (431) 587 8406. FAX: (431) 587 5711.

CLASSIC-FILM
Magaretenstrasse 24, Vienna A-1040. Tel: (431) 319 6386.

COLUMBIA TRISTAR
Wallgasse 21, Vienna A-1060. Tel: (431) 597 1515. FAX: (431) 597 1516.

CONSTANTIN FILM
Siebensterngasse 37, Vienna A-1070. Tel: (431) 521 2850. FAX: (431) 521 2860.

CZERNY FILM
Lorgasse 17, Vienna A-1150. Tel: (431) 982 0249. FAX: (431) 982 4081.

EINHORN FILM
Unterfeld Strasse 29, P.O. Box 158, Bludenz A-6700. Tel: (4355) 526 7034. FAX: (4355) 526 3674.

EPO FILM PRODUCTIONS
Edelsinn Strasse 58, Vienna A-1120. Tel: (431) 812 3718. FAX: (431) 812 3718 9.

FILMHAUS STOBERGASSE
Stobergasse 11-15, Vienna A-1050. Tel: (431) 545 3244. FAX: (431) 545 3244.

FILMLADEN
Mariahilferstrasse 58, Vienna A-1070. Tel: (431) 523 4362. FAX: (431) 526 4749.

FLEUR FILM
Stadlgasse 2, Enns A-4470. Tel: (431) 7223 2670. FAX: (431) 7223 2406.

INDEPENDENT MOVIES
Paracelsusgasse 19-21, Gablitz A-3003. Tel: (432) 231 4629.

JUPITER FILM
Neubaugasse 36, Vienna A-1070. Tel: (431) 521 270. FAX: (431) 523 8253.

OEFRAM FILM
Neubaugasse 36, Vienna A-1070. Tel: (431) 523 7611. FAX: (431) 523 3709.

POLYFILM VERLEIH
Margaretenstrasse 78, Vienna A-1050. Tel: (431) 581 3900 20. FAX: (431) 581 3900 39.

SMILE FILM
Lange Gasse 52/2/20, Vienna A-1080. Tel: (431) 408 9843. FAX: (431) 408 9843.

STADTKINO FILMVERLEIH
Spittelberggasse 3, Vienna A-1070. Tel: (431) 522 4814. FAX: (431) 522 4815.

TOP FILM
Lindengasse 56, Vienna A-1070. Tel: (431) 526 1919. FAX: (431) 526 1918.

UNITED INTERNATIONAL PICTURES
Neubaugasse 1, P.O. Box 280, Vienna A-1071. Tel: (431) 523 4631. FAX: (431) 526 7548.

WARNER BROS.
Zieglergasse 10, Vienna A-1072. Tel: (431) 523 8626. FAX: (431) 523 8626 31.

WEGA FILM
Hagelingasse 13, Vienna A-1140. Tel: (431) 982 5742 0. FAX: (431) 982 5833.

PRODUCERS

AICHHOLZER FILM PRODUCTION
Mariahilferstrasse 58, Vienna A-1070. Tel: (4310) 523 4081. FAX: (431) 526 4749.

ALLEGRO FILM PRODUCTIONS
Krummgasse 1A, Stg. 1, Vienna A-1030. Tel: (431) 712 5036. FAX: (431) 712 5036 20.

ARION FILM
Wuerzburgergasse 11, Vienna A-1130. Tel: (431) 804 2000.

CINE CARTOON
Haydngasse 5, Vienna A-1060. Tel: (431) 597 4162 12. FAX: (431) 597 4162 20.

CINECOOP FILM PRODUCTIONS
Mariahilferstrasse 1B, Vienna A-1060. Tel: (431) 587 6735. FAX: (431) 587 6735 20.

CINEDOC FILM PRODUCTION
Hauslabgasse 6-10/1, Vienna A-1050. Tel: (431) 545 6645 90. FAX: (431) 545 6645 90.

CINE-FILM PRODUCTION
Speisingerstrasse 234, Vienna A-1238. Tel: (431) 889 3366. FAX: (431) 889 2831.

CINEMERCURY
Hietzinger Kai 169, Vienna A-1130. Tel: (431) 876 3066. FAX: (431) 876 3099.

DEGN FILM
Konstanze Webergasse 3, Salzburg A-5020. Tel: (43662) 831 992. FAX: (43662) 822 688.

DOR FILM PRODUCTION
Neulerchenfelderstrasse 12, Vienna A-1160. Tel: (431) 403 2138. FAX: (431) 402 2139.

EXTRA FILM
Grosse Neugasse 44/24, Vienna A-1040. Tel: (431) 581 7896. FAX: (431) 587 2743.

FILM & CO.
Lainzerstrasse 71, Vienna A-1170. Tel: (431) 877 7875. FAX: (431) 877 7876.

GOESS FILM & MEDIA
Metternichgasse 2/8, Vienna A-1090. Tel: (431) 713 3905. FAX: (431) 713 2827.

INTERSPOT
Lainzerstrasse 121, Vienna A-1130. Tel: (431) 804 8363. FAX: (431) 804 8363 10.

LOTUS FILM
Sechshauserstrasse 83, Vienna A-1150. Tel: (431) 892 8808. FAX: (431) 892 8809 11.

ADI MAYER FILM
Lindengasse 65, Vienna A-1070, Tel: (431) 523 4788. FAX: (431) 526 6673.

MUNGO FILM
Munichreiterstrasse 18, Vienna A-1130. Tel: (431) 876 3600. FAX: (431) 876 3646.

NEUE STUDIO FILM
Hietzinger Hauptstrasse 11, Vienna A-1130. Tel: (431) 877 6253. FAX: (431) 877 3564.

ODELGA FILM PRODUCTIONS
Landhausgasse 2.37, Vienna A-1010. Tel: (431) 535 0433. FAX: (431) 532 8496.

PAMMER FILM
Neubaugasse 1, Vienna A-1070. Tel: (431) 523 9191. FAX: (431) 523 9192.

PAN FILM
Obkirchergasse 41, Vienna A-1070. Tel: (431) 321 4033. FAX: (431) 325 7169.

MICHAEL PILZ FILM
Teschnergasse 37, Vienna A-1180. Tel: (431) 402 3392. FAX: (431) 408 4649.

PPM FILMPRODUCTIONS
Lerchenfelderstrasse 136, Vienna A-1080. Tel: (431) 408 1630 0. FAX: (431) 408 9243.

SATEL FILM
Computerstrasse 6, Vienna A-1101. Tel: (431) 661 1090. FAX: (431) 667 5650.

SCHOENBRUNN FILM
Neubaugasse 1, Vienna A-1070. Tel: (431) 523 2265. FAX: (431) 523 9568.

SK FILM
Salzachstrasse 15A, Salzburg A-5026. Tel: (43662) 625 969. FAX: (43662) 625 969 22.

STAR FILM
Konstanze Webergasse 3, Salzburg A-5020. Tel: (43662) 831 992. FAX: (43662) 822 688.

TEAM FILM PRODUCTION
Waaggasse 5, Vienna A-1040. Tel: (431) 587 2542 0. FAX: (431) 587 2542 27.

TERRA FILM
Lienfeldergasse 39, Vienna A-1160. Tel: (431) 484 1101 0. FAX: (431) 484 1101 27.

WEGA FILM
Hagelingasse 13, Vienna A-1140. Tel: (431) 982 5742 0. FAX: (431) 982 5833.

EXHIBITORS

VILLAGE ROADSHOW, LTD.
(For complete listing see Australian branch.)
206 Bourke St., Melbourne, VIC, 3000. Tel: (613) 96 67 66 66. FAX: (613) 96 39 15 40.

Number of Theatres: 1
Number of Screens: 8

BAHAMAS

EXHIBITORS

RND CINEMAS LIMITED
P.O. Box EE-17203, Nassau, Bahamas. Tel: (242) 394-6456. FAX: (242) 394-6457.
PRESIDENT
A. Brent Dean
VICE PRESIDENT
Jerome K. Fitzgerald.

BELGIUM

Population: 10.1 million.
Screens: 434.
Admissions: 21 million.
Average Ticket Price: $5.52.

ASSOCIATIONS & ORGANIZATIONS

APEC
Association for the Promotion of Belgian Cinema in Education, 73 Ave. de Coccinelles, Brussels B-1170. Tel: (322) 672 9459.

ASSOCIATION OF DIRECTORS AND PRODUCERS
109 Rue du Fort, Brussels B-1060. Tel: (322) 534 3152. FAX: (322) 534 7637.

CINEMATHEQUE ROYALE DE BELGIQUE
23 Rue Ravenstein, Brussels B-1000. Tel: (322) 507 8370. FAX: (322) 513 1272.

EUROPEAN ACADEMY FOR FILM & TELEVISION
69 Rue Verte, Brussels B-1210. Tel: (322) 218 6607. FAX: (322) 217 5572.

FEDERATION DES CINEMAS DE BELGIQUE
10-12 Ave. L'Montmarts, Brussels B-1140. Tel: (322) 705-0670. FAX: (322) 705-0664.

MINISTERIE VAN DE VLAAMSE GEMEENSCHAP ADMINISTRATIE KUNST BESTUUR MEDIA
29-31 Kolonienstraat, Brussels B-1000. Tel: (322) 510 3565. FAX: (322) 510 3651.

MUSEE DU CINEMA/FILMMUSEUM
9 Baron Horta St., Brussels B-1000. Tel: (322) 507 8370. FAX: (322) 513 1272.

POUR LE CINEMA BELGE
12 Rue Paul-Emile Janson, Brussels B-1050. Tel: (322) 649 5969. FAX: (322) 649 3340.

DISTRIBUTORS AND PRODUCERS

ALAIN KEYTSMAN PRODUCTION
159 Berkendaelstraat, Brussels B-1060. Tel: (322) 347 5710. FAX: (322) 347 2462.

ALCYON FILMS
89 Rue de Lorrian, Brussels B-1210. Tel: (322) 426 7981. FAX: (322) 426 7981.

ALTERNATIVE FILMS
10 Place Colignon, Brussels B-1030. Tel: (322) 242 1930. FAX: (322) 242 0180.

BEECK TURTLE
27F Van Den Bosschestraat, Lennik B-1750. Tel: (322) 582 8318. FAX: (322) 582 8318.

BUENA VISTA INTERNATIONAL
Chausee Romaine, 468 Romeinsesteenweg, 1853 Grimbergen, Brussels. Tel: (322) 263 1700. FAX: (322) 263 1797.

CINELIBRE
270 Chaussee de Haecht, Brussels B-1030. Tel: (322) 245 8700. FAX: (322) 216 2575.

CONCORDE FILM
Terhulpsesteenweg 130, Brussels B-1050. Tel: (322) 675 2050. FAX: (322) 675 3076.

IMAGE CREATION
92 Rue Colonel Bourg, Brussels B-1040. Tel: (322) 733 3451. FAX: (322) 732 6666.

INDEPENDENT FILMS
1 Doornveld, Box 42, Zellik-Asse B-1731. Tel: (322) 463 1130. FAX: (322) 466 9460.

KINEPOLIS FILMS DISTRIBUTION
89 Boulevard du Centenaire, B 1020 Brussels. Tel: (322) 474 2600. FAX: (322) 474 2606. www.kinepolis.com

PROGRES FILMS
243 Rue Royale, Brussels B-1210. Tel: (322) 218 0960. FAX: (322) 218 4354.

UNITED INTERNATIONAL PICTURES
288 Rue Royale, Brussels B-1210. Tel: (322) 218 5206. FAX: (322) 218 7933.

WARNER BROS. BELGIUM
42 Boulevard Brand Whitlock, Brussels B-1200. Tel: (322) 735 4242. FAX: (322) 735 4919.

EXHIBITORS

FED DES CINEMAS DE BELGIQUE
Av. L. Mommaertslaan 10-12, B-1140, Brussels. Tel: (322) 218-1455. FAX: (322) 217-2372.
PRESIDENT
Mrs. Claeys-Vereecke
SECRETARY/GENERAL
Guy Morlion

GAUMONT CINEMAS
(For complete listing see French branch.)
Gaumont NV
Brussels, Belgium

Number of Theatres: 2
Number of Screens: 20

KINOPOLIS GROUP H.V.
Eeuwfeestlaan 20, Brussels, 1020. Tel: (32) 2 47 4 26 00. FAX: (32) 247 22 606.
CEO
Joost Bert
CEO
Florent Gilbels
CFO
Jan Staelens
RESEARCH & DEVELOPMENT OFFICER
Luc Van de Casseye
CORPORATE DIRECTOR, MARKETING & OPERATIONS
Gilbert Deley

Number of Theatres: 16
Number of Screens: 212
Belgium (10), France (5), Spain (1).

UGC BELGIQUE
Av. De La Toison D'or 8, Brussels, B-1050. Tel: (32) 22 89 71 00. FAX: (32) 22 89 71 01.
GENERAL MANAGER
Andre Harvie
SALES & MARKETING MANAGER
Jean-Philippe Van Nyen
PROGRAMMING DIRECTOR
Eric Carvels

Number of Theatres: 2
Number of Screens: 26

BERMUDA

Population: 64 thousand.

EXHIBITORS

THE LIBERTY THEATRE
49 Union Square, Hamilton, HM 12, Bermuda. Tel: (809) 292-7296. FAX: (809) 295-5667.
OWNER
Bermuda Industrial Union
CHAIRMAN & PRESIDENT
Derrick Burgess
GENERAL SECRETARY
Helena Burgess
TREASURER
Cecil Durham
MANAGER & FILM BUYER
Nelda L. Simons

BOLIVIA

Population: 8.2 million.

DISTRIBUTORS

MANFER FILMS S.R.L.
Ave. Montes 768, 4th Flr., Box 4709, La Paz. Tel: (5912) 376 834. FAX: (5912) 391 158.

WAZA FILMS
(Agent for UIP), Edificio Caraas-2do. piso, Avenida 16 de Julio No. 1456, Casilla 2613, La Paz. Tel: (5912) 354 635. FAX: (5912) 354 054.

MARKET RESEARCH

REN
Guachalla, Casilla 9773, La Paz. Tel/FAX: (5912)376 992. Telex: 3317 guatec BV.

BRAZIL

Population: 172.8 million.
Number of Screens: 1,600.
Average Ticket Price: $8.00 (max. $10.00).

DISTRIBUTORS & PRODUCERS

C.E.F. REPRESENTACOES
(Agent for Columbia Tristar)
Rua Aarao Reis 538, S/206 Centro, 3012000-000 Belo Horizonte, Mias Gerais. Tel: (5531) 273 2093.

COLUMBIA TRISTAR
Av. Rio Branco, 277-Sobrejola 101-Centro, 20040-009 Rio de Janeiro. Tel: (5521) 262 0722. FAX: (5521) 262 0675.

DISTRIBUIDORA DE FILMES WERMAR
Rua General Bento Martins 268, 90010-080 Porto Alegre, Rio Grande de Sul. Tel: (5551) 228 6275.

FOX/WARNER BROS. FILM DO BRASIL
Calcada dos Cravos 141, Centro Commercial Alphaville, 06453-000 Barueri, Sao Paulo. Tel: (5511) 725 5999. FAX: (5511) 725 0767.

SETIMA ARTE SERVICOS
Av. Barbosa Lima, 149 S/102, Centro, 50030-330 Recife-Pernambuco. Tel: (5581) 224 3732.

UNITED INTERNATIONAL PICTURES
Rue Desmbargado, Viriato 16, CEP 20030-090, Rio de Janeiro. Tel: (5521) 210 2400. FAX: (5521) 220 9491.
MANAGER
Jorge Peregrino

WARNER BROS. (SOUTH)
Rua Senador Dantas 19-10 Andar, 20031-200 Rio de Janiero. Tel: (5521) 282 1322. FAX: (5521) 262 0195.

EXHIBITORS

PLAYARTE CINEMAS
Avenida Republica do Libano, 2155-04501-003 Sao Paulo SP, Brazil. Tel: (55) 11 575-6996.

Number of Screens: 40

UCI BRAZIL
Rue Mexito, 51-3 Andar, Cinelandia CEP 20031, Rio de Janeiro 144, Brazil. Tel: (55) 21 262-6404.

CHILE

Population: 15.2 million.

DISTRIBUTORS AND PRODUCERS

SILVIO CAIOZZI PRODUCTIONS
Federico Froebel 1755, Santiago. Tel: (562) 209 9031. FAX: (562) 204 8988.
PRESIDENT
Silvio Caiozzi

CHILE INC./WARNER BROS. (SOUTH), INC.
(Columbia Pictures, Tri-Star, Hollywood Pictures, Touchstone Pictures, Orion), Chilefilms, La Capitania 1200, Las Condes, Santiago. Tel: (562) 220 3086

CINE CHILE S. A.
(Umbrella organization of the Association of Producers)
Huerfanos 878, Ste. 918, Santiago. Tel: (562) 633 3948. FAX: (562) 632 5342

ARTHUR EHRLICH
Huerfanos 786, Ste. 210, Santiago. Tel: (562) 633 2503 FAX: (562) 639 7921. Rep. for: Twentieth Century Fox

FILMOCENTRO
Gerona 3450, Santiago. Tel: (562) 225 2203. FAX: (562) 209 1671.
PRODUCER
Eduardo Larrain

UNITED INTERNATIONAL PICTURES
Huerfanos 786, Office 808, Casilla 3462, Santiago. Tel: (562) 639 5005. FAX: (562) 633 0562.
MANAGER
Mario Cuevas

EXHIBITORS

CONATE
La capitania No. 1200, Las Condes, Santiago, Chile. Tel: (562) 212-5071.

Number of Screens: 39

HOYTS CHILE
Roger de Flores #2736, Piso 6
Las Condes, Santiago, Chile

CHINA

Please see Hong Kong in a separate section below.
Population: 1.26 billion.
Number of Screens: 3,300 fixed screens, 180,000 factory-based screens and outdoor theatres.
Admissions: 6 billion.
Average Ticket Price: varies by province, $.47–$1.20.

ASSOCIATIONS & ORGANIZATIONS

CHINA FILM EXPORT & IMPORT CORPORATION
25 Xin Wai St., Beijing 100088. Tel: (861) 225-4488. FAX: (861) 225-1044.

CHINA FILMMAKERS' ASSOCIATION
22 Beisanhuan Donglu, Beijing 100013. Tel: (861) 421-9977. FAX: (861) 421-1870.

DISTRIBUTOR

SONY PICTURES ENTERTAINMENT BEIJING
Ste. 1819, Beijing Asia Jinjiang Hotel, 8 Xinzhong Xi Je, Gongti Bei Lu, Beijing 100027. Tel: (861) 508 9869. FAX: (861) 500 7335.

EXHIBITORS

VILLAGE ROADSHOW, LTD.
(For complete listing see Australian branch.)
206 Bourke St., Melbourne, VIC 3000, Australia. Tel: (613) 96 67 66 66. FAX: (613) 96 39 15 40.

COLOMBIA

Population: 39.7 million.
Admissions: 21 million.

DISTRIBUTORS

AMERICAN FILMS
Av. 2C Norte No, 24 N 40, Cali. Tel: (5723) 685 792.

COLUMBIA TRISTAR FILMS OF COLOMBIA
Carrera 13A, No. 97-23, Bogota. Tel: (571) 610 0149. FAX: (571) 610 0125.

ELEPHANT JOSEPH & CIA
(Agent for Warner Bros.), Calle 96 No. 12-10, Santafe de Bogota, D.C. Tel: (571) 610 2142. FAX: (571) 610 2060.

L.D. FILMS
Calle 23 No. 5-85 Interior 201, Bogota. Tel: (571) 341 7285. FAX: (571) 286 5960.

PROGRAFILMS
Carrera 53 No. 59-77, Edificio Royal Films, Barranquilla. Tel: (5753) 318 520.

UNITED INTERNATIONAL PICTURES
Calle 77 No. 15-09 Paratado Aereo 3450, Bogota. Tel: (571) 256 2139. FAX: (571) 218 6089. Manager: Maitland Pritchett.

EXHIBITORS

CINE COLUMBIA S.A.
Carrera 13, No. 38-85, Santa Fe De Bogota, Columbia, South America. Tel: (57) 1 28 58 431. FAX: (57) 1 28 75 160.

OWNER
Mayaguez Organization
CHAIRMAN
Alvaro Correa Holguin
CEO & FILM BUYER
Munir Falah
MANAGER, DISTRIBUTION
Maria Jose Iragorri
V.P., ADMINISTRATION
Alvaro Beltran
V.P., OPERATIONS
Gilberto Gallego
V.P., FINANCE
Eduardo Medrano

CROATIA

Population: 4.3 million.

DISTRIBUTORS AND PRODUCERS

BLITZ FILM & VIDEO
Sv Mateja 121-04, Zagreb 10000. Tel: (3851) 687 541. FAX: (3851) 692 814.

CONTINENTAL FILM
Sostariceva 10, Zagreb 10000. Tel: (3851) 421 312. FAX: (3851) 428 247.

JADRAN FILM DD
Oporovecka 12, Zagreb 10000. Tel: (3851) 298 7222. FAX: (3851) 251 394.

KINEMATOGRAFI
(UIP), Tuskanac 1, Zagreb 41000. Tel: (3851) 426 305. FAX: (3851) 426 531.
CONTACT
Davor Koracevic

ORLANDO FILM
Nasicka 14, Zagreb 10000. Tel: (2851) 334 587. FAX: (3851) 170 167.

POLYBROS
Draganicka 19, Zagreb 10000. Tel: (3851) 563 236. FAX: (3851) 563 236.

ZAUDER FILM
Jablanicka 1, Zagreb 10040. Tel: (3851) 245 724. FAX: (3851) 245 973.

CZECH REPUBLIC

Population: 10.3 million (1.5 million in Prague).
Number of Screens: 920.

ASSOCIATIONS & ORGANIZATIONS

AUTHORS' PRODUCTION AND DISTRIBUTION
P.O. Box 60, Prague 10 10100. Tel: (422) 729 204. FAX: (422) 725 453.

CZECH FILM SOCIETY
Novotneho Lavka 5, Prague 1 11000. Tel: (422) 298 138.

FILMOVY PODNIK HL. M. PRAHY
Vodickova 30, Prague 1 11000. Tel: (422) 242 16010. FAX: (422) 242 26497.

FILMOVY PRUMYSL (EQUIPMENT)
Krizeneckeho Nam. 322, Prague 5. Tel: (422) 294 510. FAX: (422) 542 539.

FITES-UNION OF TV AND FILM
Pod Nuselskymi Schody 3, Prague 2 12000. Tel: (422) 691 0310. FAX: (422) 691 1375.

MINISTRY OF CULTURE
Valdstejnske Nam 4, Prague 1 11000. Tel: (422) 513 1111. FAX: (422) 536 322.

SLOVENSKA POZICOVNA FILMOV
Priemyselna 1, Bratislava 82460. Tel: (427) 211 301. FAX: (427) 215 685.

DISTRIBUTORS AND PRODUCERS

AVED
Wenzigova 15, Prague 12000. Tel: (422) 299 290. FAX: (422) 297 137.

BONTONFILM
Nardoni Trida 28, Prague 1 11000. Tel: (422) 2422 7644. FAX: (422) 2422 5263.
DIRECTOR
Ales Danielis

CINEMART
Nardoni Trida 28, Prague 1 11121. Tel: (422) 2422 7202. FAX: (422) 2110 5234.

FALCON FILM
Stroupenznickeho 6, Prague 5 15000. Tel: (422) 538 085. FAX: (422) 533 194.
GENERAL MANAGER
Michael Malek

FILMEXPORT PRAGUE
Na Moranhi 5, Prague 5 12800. Tel: (422) 293 275. FAX: (422) 293 312.

GAUMONT CINEMAS
(For complete listing see French branch.)
Bonton Gaumont AS
Prague, Czech Rep.

GEMINI FILMS
V Jame 1, Prague 1 11000. Tel: (422) 2416 2142. FAX: (422) 2422 6562.

GUILD ENTERTAINMENT FILM AND VIDEO
Krliprovo Nam-3, Prague 6. Tel: (422) 328 094. FAX: (422) 311 8852.

GUILD ENTERTAINMENT (FILM DISTRIBUTION)
V Jame 5, Prague 1 11000. Tel: (422) 2421 5738. FAX: (422) 2422 6385.

HEUREKA
Litevska 8, Prague 10 11174. Tel: (422) 6731 5219. FAX: (422) 6731 5221.

LUCERNA FILM
Narodni Trida 28, Prague 111 21. Tel: (422) 2422 7644. FAX: (422) 422 2563.

NATIONAL PRODUCTION
Krizeneckeho Nam 322, Prague 5 15252. Tel: (422) 692 7291. FAX: (422) 2451 0628.

SPACE FILM
Karlovo Namesti 19, 12000 Prague 2. Tel: (422) 249 12937. FAX: (422) 249 11370.

EXHIBITORS

INTERSONIC TAUNUS PROD., LTD.
Stare Grunty 36, 842 25 Bratislava, Slovakia. Tel: (421) 772 2070. FAX: (421) 772 1017.

MULTIKINO 93
Plackeho 8, Prague 1. Tel: (422) 261 134. FAX: (422) 261 134.

DENMARK

Population: 5.3 million.
Screens: 346
Admissions: 10.9 million.
Average Ticket Price: $6.54.

ASSOCIATIONS & ORGANIZATIONS

DANISH FILM DISTRIBUTORS ASSOCIATION
Bulowsvej 50A, Fredericksberg DK-1870. Tel: (45) 3536 5616. FAX: (45) 3135 5758.
DIRECTOR
Anne-Grete Wezelenburg

DANISH FILM INSTITUTE
Miels Hemmingsensgade 20, Bh3, Copenhagen K DK-1153. (45) 3315 6760. FAX: (45) 3391 5242.

DANISH FILM MUSEUM
Store Sondervoldstraede 4, Copenhagen DK-1419. Tel: (45) 3157 6500. FAX: (45) 3154 1312.

DANISH FILM WORKSHOP
Versterbrogade 24, Copenhagen DK-1620. Tel: (45) 3124 1624. FAX: (45) 3124 4419.

DANISH PRODUCERS' ASSOCIATION
Kroprinsensgade (B 3, Copenhagen K DK-1114. Tel: (45) 3314 0311. FAX: (45) 3314 0365.

FILM KONTAKT NORD
Skindergade 29 A, Copenhagen DK-1159. Tel: (45) 3311 5152. FAX: (45) 3311 2152.

NORDIC FILM/TV SOCIETY
c/o MGM Nordisk Film Biografer, Axeltorv 9, Copenhagen DK-1609. Tel: (45) 3314 76906. FAX: (45) 3314 7979.

DISTRIBUTORS AND PRODUCERS

AB COLLECTION
Hirsemarken 3, Farum DK-3520. Tel: (45) 4499 6200. FAX: (45) 4295 1786.

ALL RIGHT FILM DISTRIBUTION
Indiakaj 12, Copenhagen DK-2100. Tel: (45) 3544 1100. FAX: (45) 3543 4008. www.allright-film.dk
CEO
Jesper Boas Smith

BUENA VISTA INTERNATIONAL
Ostergade 24B, 3rd Flr., Copenhagen K DK-1100. Tel: (45) 3312 0800. FAX: (45) 3312 4332.

CAMERA FILM
Mikkel Bryggergade 8, Copenhagen K DK-1460. Tel: (5) 3313 6112. FAX: (45) 3315 0882.

CINNAMON FILM
Brandts Passage 15, Odense C DK-5000. Tel: (45) 6612 1716. FAX: (45) 6612 8082.

CONSTANTIN APS
Skelbaekgade 1, Copenhagen V DK-1717. Tel: (45) 3325 2424. FAX: (45) 3325 0707.

DAN INA FILM
Huset, Radhusstraede 13, 2. Flr., Copenhagen DK-1466. Tel: (45) 33 324077. FAX: (45) 33 325077.

EGMONT AUDIO VISUAL
Skelbaekgade 1, Copenhagen V DK-1717. Tel: (45) 3325 4000. FAX: (45) 3123 0488.

FOX FILM
Skelbaekgade 1, 3, Copenhagen V DK-1717. Tel: (45) 3325 4000. FAX: (45) 3123 0488.

HUSETS BIOGRAF
Huset, Radhusstraede 13, 2nd Flr., Copenhagen K DK-1466. Tel: (45) 3315 2002. FAX: (45) 3332 5077.

KRAK VIDEO
Virumsgardvej 21, Virum DK-2830. Tel: (45) 4583 6600. FAX: (45) 4583 1011.

NORDSIK FILM ACQUISITION
Skelbaekgade 1, Copenhagen DK-1717. Tel: (45) 3123 2488. FAX: (45) 3123 0488. email: nikki@inet.uni-c.dk

PATHE-NORDISK
Skelbaekgade 1, Copenhagen DK-1717. Tel: (45) 3123 2488.

REGINA FILM IMPORT
Bregnegaardsvej 7, Charlottenlund DK-2920. Tel: (45) 3962 9640.

SAGA FILM INTERNATIONAL
Soendergada 5, Hjorring DK-9800. Tel: (45) 9892 2199. FAX: (45) 9890 0439.

SCALA FILM
Centrumpladsen, P.O. Box 215, Svendborg DK-5700. Tel: (45) 6221 8866. FAX: (45) 6221 0821.

SCANBOX DANMARK A/S
Hirsemarken 3, Farum DK-3520. Tel: (45) 4499 6200. FAX: (45) 4295 1786.

SFC
Vestergade 27, Copenhagen P DK-1456. Tel: (45) 3313 2686. FAX: (45) 3313 0243.

SIRIUS FILM
Gammel Kongevej 10, Copenhagen, DK 2200. Tel: (45) 33 117060. FAX: (45) 33 1428 88. URL: www.siriusfilm.dk
CONTACT
Steen Iversen

UNITED INTERNATIONAL PICTURES
Haunchvej 13, Frederiksberg C DK-1825. Tel: (45) 3131 2330. FAX: (45) 3123 3420.

WARNER & METRONOME FILM
Sondermarksvej 16, Copenhagen, Valby DK-2500. Tel: (45) 3646 8822. FAX: (45) 3644 0604.

ZENTROPA PRODUCTION
Ryesdage 106A, Copenhagen DK-2100. Tel: (45) 3542 4233. FAX: (45) 3542 4299. email: zentrop@zentropa-film.com. URL:http://www.zentropa-film.com

EXHIBITORS

NORDISK FILM BIOGRAFER A/S
Axeltorv 9, Copenhagen 1609. Tel: (45) 33 14 76 06. FAX: (45) 33 14 76 06.
CEO
Morten Anker Nielsen
V.P. & CFO
Henrik Pallesen
V.P., FILM & ADVERTISING
Helle Smith
V.P., CONSTRUCTION & EQUIPMENT
Steen Laesen

SANDREW METRONOME FILM AB
Sondermarksve 16, 2500 Valby.

DOMINICAN REPUBLIC

Population: 8.4 million.

EXHIBITORS

REGENCY CARIBBEAN ENTERPRISES, INC.
(d.b.a. Caribbean Cinemas)
Cinema Centro, Avenida George Washington, Santo Domingo, Dominican Repupblic. Tel: (809) 688-8710. FAX: (809) 686-2642.
PRESIDENT
Victor Carrady

CARIBBEAN CINEMAS OF THE VIRGIN ISLANDS, INC.
Centro del Cibao SA, Estrella Sadala No. 20, Santiago, Dominican Republic. Tel: (809) 686-2642. FAX: (809) 971-5991.
ADMINISTRATOR
Amado Perez

ECUADOR

Population: 12.9 million.

EXHIBITORS

MULTICINES
Amazonas y N.N.U.U., C.C.I., Piso 3, Quito, Ecuador. (593) 2265-061. FAX: (593) 225-503.
DIRECTOR, PROGRAMMING
Rafael Barriga
MANAGER
Guillermo Dahik

EGYPT

Population: 68.4 million.
Average ticket price: Varies from E£3.00 to E£7.00.

FREE FILM CENTERS

THE AMERICAN CENTER
Part of the American Embassy, Cairo.

THE BRITISH CENTER
Part of the British Embassy, Cairo.
Both the American and British Centers have film libraries.

THE CATHOLIC FILM CENTER
9, Adly St., Cairo.

CENTER CULTURAL FRANCE
One at Al Mounira, Cairo, and at Hiliopolice.

PRINCIPAL PRODUCTION COMPANIES & DISTRIBUTORS

AFLAM FARID SHAWKI
Farid Shawki 36, Sherif St., Cairo.

AFLAM GALAL
Nader Galal 85, Ramses St., Cairo.

ALAMIA T. V. & CINEMA
Hussein Kalla-41, Guizira Elwosta, Zamalek, Cairo.

AFLAM MISR ALAMIA
Yousef Shahin 35, Champion St., Cairo.

ARTIST UNITY
Farid Shawki 16, Adly St., Cairo

BADIE SOBHI
Badie Sobhi 12, Soliman Elhalabi St., Cairo.

CENTRAL FILM
Nagib Spiro, 85, Ramses St., Cairo.

EL-LEITHY FILMS
Ihab El-Leithy 37, Kasr El-Nil St., Cairo.

GAMAL EL-LEITHY
Gamal El-Leithy 11, Saray El-Azbakia St., Cairo.

HANY FILM
Zaki Guirges 4, Soliman Elhalabi St., Cairo.

KASR EL-NIL INTERNATIONAL AHMED SAMI
(Ahmed Sami & Co.) 4, Hussein Almimar St., Kasr El Nil, Cairo, Tel. (202) 574 5416. FAX: (202) 291 8059.

MANAR FILM
Atef Ibrahim, 11, Saray El-Azbakia St., Cairo.

MASR EL-GUIDIDA
Salah Kharma, 36, Orabi St., Cairo.

MISR EL-ARABIA
Wasef Faiez 12, Soliman Elhalabi St., Cairo.

NASR FILM
Mohamed Hassan 33, Orabi St., Cairo.

OSIRIS FILM
Omran Ali 87, Ramses St., Cairo.

SOAT EL-FANN
D. Abdel Wahab 16, Adly St., Cairo.

TAMIDO FILM
Medhat Sherif 4, Zaki St., Orabi, Cairo.

DISTRIBUTORS AND PRODUCERS

MGM
35 Talaat Harb St., Cairo. Tel: (202) 393 3897. FAX: (202) 392 7998.
MANAGER
Fouad Nader

TWENTIETH CENTURY FOX IMPORT CORP.
11 Saray el Ezbekieh, Box 693, Cairo. Tel: (202) 591 2477. FAX: (202) 591 2829.
MANAGER
Zagloul Gad El Karim Salama

UNITED MOTION PICTURES
(Licensee for Warner Bros.)
7 26th of July St., P.O. Box 923, Cairo. Tel: (202) 591 2477. FAX: (202) 591 2829.
MANAGER
Antoine Zeind

FIJI

Population: 832 thousand.

EXHIBITORS

VILLAGE ROADSHOW, LTD.
(For complete listing see Australian branch.)
206 Bourke St., Melbourne, VIC, 3000, Australia. Tel: (613) 96 67 66 66. FAX: (613) 96 39 15 40.
Number of Theatres: 2
Number of Screens: 10

FINLAND

Population: 5.2 million.

ASSOCIATIONS & ORGANIZATIONS

ASSOCIATION OF FINNISH FILM DIRECTORS
Suomen Elokuva Ohjaajalitto SELO, PI 116, Helsinki 00171. Tel: (3580) 632 108.

ASSOCIATION OF FINNISH FILM WORKERS
Soumen Elokuvaja Videotyontekijain, Litto Set, Metritullinkatu 33, Helsinki 00170. Tel: (3580) 135 6370. FAX: (3580) 135 6658.

ASSOCIATION OF INDEPENDENT PRODUCERS
Suomen Audiovisuaalisen Alan Tuottajatm SATU, Kanavaranta 3 D 31, Helsinki 00160. Tel: (3580) 622 1690. FAX: (3580) 622 1860.

AVEK—THE PROMOTION CENTRE FOR AUDIOVISUAL CULTURE IN FINLAND
Hietaniemenkatu 2, Helsinki 00100. Tel: (3580) 446 411. FAX: (3580) 446 414.

CENTRAL ORGANISATION OF FINNISH FILM PRODUCERS
Kaisaniemenkatu 3 B 29, Helsinki 00100. Tel: (3580) 636 305. FAX: (3580) 176 689.

FINNISH FILM CHAMBER
Kaisaniemenkatu 3 B 29, Helsinki 00100. (3580) 636 305.

FINNISH FILM CONTACT
Annakatu 13 B 11, Helsinki 00120. Tel: (3580) 645 126. FAX: (3580) 641 736.

FINNISH FILM FOUNDATION
Kanavakatu 12, Helsinki 00160. Tel: (3580) 622 0300. FAX: (3580) 6220 3050.

STATE COMMITTEE FOR CINEMA
Valion elokuvataidetoimikunta PL 293, Helsinki 00171. Tel: (3580) 134 171. FAX: (3580) 624 313.

DISTRIBUTORS AND PRODUCERS

ALFA PANORAMA FILM & VIDEO
Laipattie 5, Helsinki 00880. Tel: (3580) 759 2600. FAX: (3580) 755 5460.

ARISTA FILM
Pohjoisranta 11, Box 24, Pori 28100. Tel: (35839) 633 4433. FAX: (35839) 633 4433.

AXEL FILM
Maneesikatu 1-3 J, Helsinki 00170. Tel: (3580) 278 1996.

BUENORAMA PICTURES
Purimiehenkatu 27, Helsinki 00150. Tel: (3580) 2709 0490. FAX: (3580) 622 3855.

CINEMA MONDO
Unioninkatu 10, Helsinki 00130. Tel: (3580) 629 528. FAX: (3580) 631 450.

DADA-FILMI
Kolmas Linja 5, Helsinki 00530. Tel: (3580) 737 788. FAX: (3580) 730 734. email: rile@dada.pp.fi

EL-KO FILMS
Kavallvagen 23A, Grankulla 02700. Tel: (3580) 505 2600.

EUROPA VISION
Koivuvaarankuja 2, Vantaa 01641. Tel: (3580) 852 711. FAX: (3580) 853 2183.

FINNKINO OY
Koivuvaarankuja 2, Vantaa 01641. Tel: (3580) 131 191. FAX: (3580) 1311 9300.

KINOFINLANDIA
Maunnkatuoiu 2, Helsinki 00170. Tel: (3580) 278 1783. FAX: (3580) 278 1763.

KINOSCREEN/KINOPRODUCTION
Katajanokantuu 6, Helsinki 00160. Tel: (3580) 663 217. FAX: (3580) 662 048.

KOSMOFILMI
Steinbackinkatu 8A, Helsinki 00250. Tel: (3580) 477 3587. FAX: (3580) 477 3583.

MIO-FILM
Hiidentie 1 A 7, Oulu 90550. Tel: (35881) 314 1732. FAX: (35881) 314 1730.

OULUN ELEKUVAKESKUS
Torikatu 8, Oulu 90100. Tel: (35881) 881 1292. FAX: (358) 81 881 1290.

SENSO FILMS
Uudenmaankatu 13D, Helsinki 00120. Tel: (358) 0602 810. FAX: (358) 0602 292.

TALENT HOUSE
Tallberginkatu 1 A, loc. 141, Helsinki 00180. Tel: (358) 0685 2227. FAX: (3580) 685 2229.

UNITED INTERNATIONAL PICTURES OY
Kaisaniemenkatu 1C 98, Helsinki 00100. Tel: (358) 0662 166. FAX: (3580) 665 005.

URANIA FILM
Hiidentie 1 A 7, Oulu 90550. Tel: (358) 81 881 1291. FAX: (358) 81 881 1290.

WALHALLA
P.O. Box 1134, Helsinki 00101. Tel: (358) 01311 9365. FAX: (358) 0637 023.

WARNER BROTHERS FINLAND OY
Kaisaniemenkatu 1B A 69, Helsinki 00100. Tel: (358) 0638 953. FAX: (358) 0638 161.

EXHIBITORS

SANDREW METRONOME FILM AB
Kaisaniemenkatu 2B, 00100 Helsinki, Finland

FRANCE

Population: 59.3 million.
Screens: 4,900..

ASSOCIATIONS & ORGANIZATIONS

ACADEMIE DES ARTS ET TECHNIQUES DU CINEMA
19 Ave. du President Wilson, Paris 75116. Tel: (331) 4723 7233. FAX: (331) 4070 0291.

ATELIERS DU CINEMA EUROPEEN
(European Film Studio), 68 Rue de Rivoli, Paris 75004. Tel: (331) 4461 8830. FAX: (331) 4461 8840.

AUXITEC (SOCIETE AUXILIAIRE POUR LE CINEMA ET LA TV)
Ibis Ave. du Roi Albert, Cannes 06400. Tel: (3393) 940777. FAX: (339) 3438 8895.

BUREAU DE LIAISON EUROPEEN DU CINEMA
c/o FIADF, 43 Blvd. Malesherbes, Paris 75008. Tel: (331) 4266 0532. FAX: (331) 4266 9692.

CENTRE FRANCAIS DU COMMERCE EXTERIEUR
10 Ave. d'Iena, Paris Cedex 16 75783. Tel: (331) 4073 3000. FAX: (331) 4073 3979.

CENTRE NATIONAL DE LA CINEMATOGRAPHIE
12 Rue Lubeck, Paris 75016. Tel: (331) 4434 3440. FAX: (331) 4755 0491.

CHAMBRE SYNDICALE DES PRODUCTEURS & EXPORTATEURS DE FILMS FRANCAIS
5 Rue de Cirque, Paris 75008. Tel: (331) 4225 7063. FAX: Tel: (331) 4225 9427.

CICCE
(European Committee Film Industries Commission)
5 Rue du Cirque, Paris 75008. Tel: (331) 4225 7063. FAX: (331) 4225 9427.

CONSEIL SUPERIEUR DE L'AUDIOVISUEL (CSA)
39-43 Quai Andre-Citroen, Paris Cedex 15 75015. Tel: (331) 4058 3800. FAX: (331) 4579 0006.

EUROPA CINEMAS
54 Rue Beaubourg. Paris 3 75003. Tel: (331) 4271 5370. FAX: (331) 4271 4755.

FEDERATION INTERNATIONALE DES ASSOCIATIONS DE DISTRIBUTEURS DE FILMS
43 Blvd. Malesherbes, Paris 75008. Tel: (331) 4266 0532. FAX: (331) 4266 9692.

FEDERATION NATIONALE DES CINEMAS FRANCAIS (FNCF)
10 Rue de Marignan, Paris 75008. Tel: (331) 4359 1676. FAX: (331) 4074 0864.

FEDERATION NATIONALE DES DISTRIBUTEURS DE FILMS
43 Blvd. Malesherbes, Paris 75008. Tel: (331) 4266 0532. FAX: (331) 4266 9692.

FEDERATION OF THEATRE, CINEMA & AUDIOVISUAL UNIONS
14-16 Rue des Lilias, Paris 75015. Tel: (331) 4240 1495. FAX: (331) 4240 9020.

INSTITUT NATIONAL DE L'AUDIOVISUEL
4 Ave. de l'Europe, Bry-Sur-Marne 94366. Tel: (331) 4983 2000. FAX: (331) 4983 3195.

INTERNATIONAL FEDERATION OF FILM PRODUCERS
33 Champs Elysées, Paris 75008. Tel: (331) 4225 6214. FAX: (331) 4256 1652.

INTERNATIONAL UNION OF CINEMAS
10 Rue de Marignan, Paris 75008. Tel: (331) 4359 1676. FAX: (331) 4074 0864.

MINISTERE DES AFFAIRES ETRANGERES
244 Blvd. St. Germaine, Paris 75007. Tel: (331) 4317 9662. FAX: (331) 4317 9242.

SESAM
16 Place de la Fontaine, Aux Lions, Paris 19 75920. Tel: (331) 4715 4905. FAX: (331) 4715 4974.

SOCIETE DES REALISATEURS DE FILMS (SRF)
215 Rue de Faubourg-Honoré, Paris 75008. Tel: (331) 4563 9630. FAX: (331) 4074 0796.

UNIFRANCE FILM INTERNATIONAL
4 Villa Bosquet, Paris 75007. Tel: (331) 4753 9580. FAX: (331) 4705 9655.

UNION DES PRODUCTEURS DE FILMS
1 Place des Deux Ecus, Paris 75001. Tel: (331) 4028 0138. FAX: (331) 4221 1700.

DISTRIBUTORS AND PRODUCERS

AAA DISTRIBUTION
12bis Rue Keppler, Paris 75011. Tel: (331) 4475 7070. FAX: (331) 4705 4554.

AGENCE DU COURT METRAGE
2 Rue de Toqueville, Paris 75017. Tel: (331) 4380 0365. FAX: (331) 4267 5971.

A.I.L.O. PRODUCTIONS
9 Rue Fontaine, St. Denis 93200. Tel: (331) 4813 0666. FAX: (331) 4813 0632.

AMLF
10 Rue Lincoln, Paris 75008. Tel: (331) 4076 9100. FAX: (331) 4225 1289.

ARCHEO PICTURES
9 Rue René Boulanger, Paris 75010. Tel: (331) 4240 4899. FAX: (331) 4239 9413.

FARIANE FILMS
15 Rue de Colonel Pierre Avia, Paris 75015. Tel: (331) 4662 1777. FAX: (331) 4662 1797.

ARP
75 Ave. des Champs Elysées, Paris 75008. Tel: (331) 4359 4330. FAX: (331) 4563 8337.

ARTEDIS CINEMA ARTS ENTERTAINMENT
44 Rue du Colisee, Paris 75008. Tel: (331) 4256 2275. FAX: 33 1 4256 1087.

A.S.P.
23 Rue Raynouard, Paris 75016. Tel: (331) 4224 5050. FAX: (331) 4224 6642.

BAC FILMS
5 Rue Pelouze, Paris 75008. Tel: (331) 4470 9230. FAX: (331) 4470 9070.

CELLULOID DREAMS
24 Rue Lamartine, 75009 Paris. Tel: (331) 4970 0370. FAX:(331) 4970 0371.

CIBY DISTRIBUTION
90 Ave. des Champs Elysées, Paris 75008. Tel: (331) 4421 6417. FAX: (331) 4421 6435.

CINEMADIS FILMS
78 Ave. des Champs Elysées, Paris 75008. Tel: (331) 4562 8287. FAX: (331) 4289 2198.

COLUMBIA TRISTAR FILMS
131 Ave. de Wagram, Paris 75017. Tel: (331) 4440 6220. FAX: (331) 4440 6201.

CONNAISSANCE DU CINEMA
22 Rue du Pont Neuf, Paris 75001. Tel: (331) 4013 0722. FAX: (331) 4026 2544.

CYTHERE FILMS
34 Ave. des Champs Elysées, Paris 75008. Tel: (331) 4289 0767. FAX: (331) 4256 0773.

EUROCINE
33 Ave. des Champs Elysées, 75008 Paris. Tel: (331) 4225 6492. FAX: (331) 4225 7338.

FILMS SANS FRONTIERES
70 Blvd. de Sebastopol, Paris 75003. Tel: (331) 4277 2184. FAX: (331) 4277 4266.

GAUMONT
30 Ave. Charles de Gaulle, Neuilly-sur-Seine 92200. Tel: (331) 46 43 20 00. FAX: (331) 46 43 21 68.

GAUMONT/BUENA VISTA INTERNATIONAL
5 Rue du Clisée, Paris 75008. Tel: (331) 4643 2000. FAX: (331) 4643 2047.

HAUT ET COURT
5 Passage Piver, Paris 75011. Tel: (331) 4338 5300. FAX: (331) 4338 3872.

JECK FILM
5 Rue Rene Boulanger, Paris 75010. Tel: (331) 42 40 78 00. FAX: (331) 48 03 02 64.

K—FILMS
15 Rue Saintonge, Paris 75003. Tel: (331) 4274 7016. FAX: (331) 4274 7024.

LES ACACIAS CINE AUDIENCE
33 Rue Berger, Paris 75008. Tel: (331) 4256 4903. FAX: (331) 4256 0865.

LES FILM DE L'ATALANTE
100 Rue Monfletard, Paris 75005. Tel: (331) 4287 0202. FAX: (331) 4287 0189.

LES FILMS DU LOSANGE
26 Ave. Pierre 1er de Serfie, Paris 75116. Tel: (331) 4720 5412/ 4443 8715. FAX: (331) 4952 0640.

LES FILMS NUMBER ONE
16 Ave. Hoche, Paris 75008. Tel: (331) 4563 4402. FAX: (331) 4289 1921.

LES FILMS SINGULIER
20 Rue Michelet, Montreuil 93100. Tel: (331) 4287 5908. FAX: (331) 4287 0189.

LES GRANDS FILMS CLASSIQUES
49 Ave. Theophile Gautier, Paris 75016. Tel: (331) 45 24 43 24. FAX: (331) 45 25 49 73.

LE STUDIO—CANAL PLUS
17 Rue Dumont D'urville, Paris 75116. Tel: (331) 4443 9800.
COO
Brahin Chioua
HEAD OF INTERNATIONAL SALES
Daniel Marquet

LOGOS
24 Ave. du Recteur Poincare, Paris 75016. Tel: (331) 46 47 97 48. FAX: (331) 46 47 97 58.

METROPOLITAN FILMEXPORT
1 Rue Lord Byron, Paris 75008. Tel: (331) 4563 4560. FAX: (331) 4563 7731.

MK2
55 Rue Traversiere, Paris 75012. Tel: (331) 4467 3000. FAX: (331) 4341 3230.

OUTSIDER DIFFUSION
63 Rue Pascal, Paris 75013. Tel: (331) 43 35 81 74. FAX: (331) 47 07 10 49.

POINT DU JOUR
38 Rue Croix des Petits Champs, Paris 75001. Tel: (331) 47 03 40 00. FAX: (331) 47 03 39 48.

POLYGRAM FILM DISTRIBUTION
107 Blvd. Periere, Paris 75017. Tel: (331) 4415 6666. FAX: (331) 4764 3638.

PRETTY PICTURES
9 Rue Charlot, Paris 75003. Tel: (331) 4029 0044. FAX: (331) 4029 0121.

PYRAMIDE DISTRIBUTION
6 Rue Catulle Mendes, Paris 75017. Tel: (331) 42 67 44 66. FAX: (331) 42 67 80 28.

QUINTA COMMUNICATIONS
16 Ave. Hoche, Paris 75008. Tel: (331) 4076 04540. FAX: (331) 4256 6921.

REVCOM INTERNATIONAL/LES FILMS ARIANE
15 Rue du Colonel Pierre Avia, Paris 75015. Tel: (331) 4662 1777. FAX: (331) 4662 1797.

REZO FILMS
52 Rue Charlot, Paris 75003. Tel: (331) 4027 8525. FAX: (331) 4027 0887.

TWENTIETH CENTURY FOX
8 Rue Bellini, Paris 75116. Tel: (331) 4434 6000. FAX: (331) 4434 6105.

U.F.D.
2 Ave. de Montaigne, Paris 75008. Tel: (331) 5367 1717. FAX: (331) 5367 1700.

UNITED INTERNATIONAL PICTURES
1 Rue Meyerbeer, Paris 75009. Tel: (331) 4007 3838. FAX: (331) 47472 5716.

WARNER BROS.
67 Ave. de Wagram, Paris 75017. Tel: (331) 4401 4999. FAX: (331) 4763 4515.

EXHIBITORS

CINE-ALPES
150, rue Haute Tarentaise, 73700 Bourg Saint Maurice. Tel: (33) 04 79 07 61 40. FAX: (33) 04 79 07 61 41.
PRESIDENT
Gerard Davoine

Number of Theatres: 53
Number of Screens: 110

CINEMA LES ECRANS
9-11, place Denis Dussoubs, 87000 Limoges. Tel: (33) 05 55 77 40 79. FAX: (33) 05 55 79 49 91.
PRESIDENT
Michel Fridemann

Number of Screens: 30

CINEMAS 14 JUILLET
M.K. 2, 55, rue Traversiere, 75012, Paris. Tel: (33) 44 67 30 00. FAX: (33) 43 41 32 30.
PRESIDENT
Marin Karmitz

Number of Theatres: 9
Number of Screens: 44

CIRCUIT GEORGES RAYMOND (CGR)
8, rue Blaise Pascal, Z.I. de Perigny, 17039 La Rochelle Cedex. Tel: (33) 05 46 44 01 76. FAX: (33) 05 46 44 55 85.

Number of Screens: 330

GAUMONT CINEMAS
30, Av. Charles de Gaulle, Neuilly, Sur Seine 92200. Tel: (33) 1 46 43 20 00. FAX: (33) 1 46 43 24 28.
CHAIRMAN, CEO, & PRESIDENT
Nicolas Seydoux
EXECUTIVE V.P. & COO
Patrice Ledoux
V.P., EXHIBITION
Jean-Louis Renoux
DIRECTOR OF DEVELOPMENT
Jean-Yves Rabet.

Number of Theatres: 47
Number of Screens: 365
Foreign Screens: 20
France (40), Belgium (2)

GROUPE AUBERT
5, place de Gaulle, 06400 Cannes. Tel: (33) 4 93 39 38 20. FAX: (33) 4 93 38 01 90.
PRESIDENT
Raoul Aubert

Number of Theatres: 9
Number of Screens: 49

LES IMAGES MEGARAMA
62. rue Grande Rue, 25000 Besancon. Tel: (33) 45 00 01 22. FAX: (33) 45 00 01 99.
GENERAL DIRECTOR
Jean-Pierre Lemoine

Number of Screens: 37

M.K.2
55, rue Traversiere, 75012, Paris. Tel: (33) 44 67 30 00. FAX: (33) 43 41 32 30.
PRESIDENT
Marin Karmitz

Number of Theatres: 9
Number of Screens: 44

PATHE PALACE
21 Rue Francois 1er, 75008 Paris. Tel: (33) 49 24 40 03. FAX: (33) 49 24 45 10.
PRESIDENT, PATHE GROUP
Jerome Seydoux
GENERAL DIRECTOR, CINEMAGRAPHIC EXHIBITION
Thierry Marques

Number of Theatres: 46
Number of Screens: 300

SOCOGEX
7, rue Rameau, 78000 Versailles. Tel: (33) 39 50 78 78. FAX: (33) 39 49 09 67.
ADMINISTRATORS
Francois Dupuy
Jean-Francois Edeline

SOREDIC
3E, rue de Paris - BP 135, 35513 Cesson-Sevigne. Tel: (33) 2 99 83 78 00. FAX: (33) 2 99 83 29 37.
PRESIDENT
Philippe Paumelle

Number of Theatres: 150
Number of Screens: 200

UGC FRANCE
24 ave Charles de Gaulle, 92200 Nuyilly-sur-Seine. Tel: (33) 46 40 44 30. FAX: (33) 46 24 37 28.

VILLAGE ROADSHOW FRANCE
4-6, Rond Point Champs Elysees, 75008, Paris. Tel: (33) 53 93 92 00. FAX: (33) 42 89 20 43.
MANAGING DIRECTOR
Didier Bedin

Number of Theatres: 2
Number of Screens: 11

STUDIOS

ACME FILMS
14 Rue Sthrau, Paris 75013. Tel: (331) 5394 5151. FAX: (331) 4570 7004. www.acme-films.fr

BOULOGNE-BILLANCOURT
2 Rue de Silly, Boulogne 92100. Tel: (331) 4605 6569. FAX: (331) 4825 2347.

CAIMAN
30 Blvd. de la Bastille, Paris 75012. Tel: (331) 4344 1122. FAX: (331) 4344 7930.

PARIS STUDIO BILLANCOURT
50 Quai du Point-du-Jour, Boulogne-Billancourt 9200. Tel: (331) 4609 9324. FAX: (331) 4620 2471.

STUDIOS LA VICTORINE COTE D'AZUR
16 Ave. Edouard Grinda, Nice 06200. Tel: (3393) 725 454. FAX: (3393) 719 173.

GERMANY

Population: 82.8 million.
Screens: 4,760.

ASSOCIATIONS & ORGANIZATIONS

BERLIN PROVINCIAL FILM SERVICE
Bismarckstrasse 80, 1000 Berlin 12. Tel: (4930) 313 80 55.

GERMAN INSTITUTE FOR FILM INFORMATION
Schaumainkai 41, Frankfurt am Main 60596. Tel: (4969) 617 045. FAX: (4969) 620 060.

GERMAN INSTITUTE FOR FILM INFORMATION/FILM ARCHIVE
Kreuzbergerring 56, Wiesbaden 65205. Tel: (49611) 723 310. FAX: (49611) 723 318.

INSTITUTE FOR FILM AND THE VISUAL ARTS IN EDUCATION
Bavariafilmplatz 3, Geiselgaskig 82031. Tel: (4989) 64971. FAX: (4989) 649 7300.

DISTRIBUTORS AND PRODUCERS

ALHAMBRA FILMVERLEIH
Friedrich Ebertstrasse 12, Dusseldorf 40120. Tel: (49211) 352 972.

ARSENAL FILMVERLEIH STEFAN PAUL KG
Neue Strasse 2, Tuebingen 72012. Tel: (497071) 92960. FAX: (497071) 929611.

ATLAS FILM UND AV GMBH & CO. KG
Ludgeristrasse 14-16, Duisburg 47057. Tel: (49203) 378 6222. FAX: (49203) 362 482.

ATLAS INTERNATIONAL
Rumfordstrasse 29-31, Munich D-80469. Tel: (4989) 227 525. FAX: (4889) 224 332.

BAUER FILMVERLEIH-KINO UND GASTRONOMIE
Schmiedingstrasse 19, Postfach 100329, Dortmund 4600. Tel: (49231) 148 078.

BAVARIA FILM GMBH
Bavariafilmplatz 7, Geiselgasteig, Munich D-82031. Tel: (4989) 6499 2681. FAX: (4989) 6499 2240.

BEATE UHSE FILMVERLEIH
Gutenbergstrasse 12, Flensburg 24941. Tel: (49461) 996 6221.

BOJE BUCK PRODS./DELPHI FILM
Kantstrasse 12a, Berlin 10623. Tel: (4930) 313 2200, (4930) 312 6070. FAX: (4930) 312 9996.

BUENA VISTA INTERNATIONAL
P.O. Box 800329, Munich D-81603. Tel: (4989) 9934 0270. FAX: (4989) 9934 0139.

CENTRAL FILMVERTRIEB
(Represents Senator Filmverleih & Jugendfilm), Uhlandstrasse 179/180, Berlin 10263. Tel: (4930) 8842 8570. FAX: (4930) 8842 8512.

CINE INTERNATIONAL
Leopoldstrasse 18, Munich D-80802. Tel: (4989) 391 025. FAX: (4989) 331 089.

CINEMA FILMVERLEIH
Braystrasse 20, Munich D-811677. Tel: (4989) 472 061. FAX: (4989) 474 736.

CINEPOOL
Sonnenstrasse 21, Munich D-80331. Tel: (4989) 5587 6188. FAX: (4989) 5587 6188.

CINEVOX
Bavariafilmplatz 7, Gruenwald 82031. Tel: (4989) 641 8000. FAX: (4989) 649 3288.

COLUMBIA TRISTAR FILM
8 Ickstattstrasse 1, Munich D-80469. Tel: (4989) 230 370. FAX: (4989) 264 380. Sales: Gerd Bender.

CONCORDE—CASTLE ROCK/TURNER FILMVERLEIH
Rosenheimer Strasse 143b, Munich D-81671. Tel: (4989) 450 6100. FAX: (4989) 4506 1010.

CONNEXION FILM VETRIEBS & PRODUKTIONS GMBH
Rothembaumchaussee 80c, Hamburg 20148. Tel: (4940) 419 9750. FAX: (4940) 419 9799.

CONSTANTIN FILM
Kaiserstrasse 39, Munich D-80801. Tel: (4989) 386 090. FAX: (4989) 386 9242.

CONTACT FILMVERLEIH
Huttenstrasse 40, Dusseldorf 40215. Tel: (49211) 374 024. FAX: (49211) 374 025.

DAZU FILM BONN
c/o Daniel Zuta Filmproduktion, Kaiserstrasse 39, Frankfurt am Main D-60329. Tel: (4869) 253 735. FAX: (4989) 239 058.

ENDFILM
Am Vogelherd 4, Bach D-93090. Tel: (4994) 823 377. FAX: (4994) 823 378.

FILMWELT—PROKINO VERLEIHGEMEINSCHAFT
Ismaninger Strasse 51, Munich D-81675. Tel: (4989) 418 0010. FAX: (4989) 4180 0143.

FUTURA/FILMVERLAG DER AUTOREN
Rambergstrasse 5, Munich 80799. Tel: (4989) 381 7000. FAX: (4989) 381 70020.

GERMANIA FILMVERLEIH
Blissestrasse 38-40, Berlin 10713. Tel: (4930) 821 3072.

HIGHLIGHT FILMVERLEIH
Herkomerplatz 2, Munich D-80000. Tel: (4989) 9269 6602. FAX: (4989) 981 543.

HVW FOCUS FILMVERTRIEB
Wurmtalstrasse 125, Munich D-81375. Tel: (4989) 740 9411. FAX: (4989) 740 9319.

JUGENDFILM VERLEIH GMBH
Reichstrasse. 15, Berlin D-14052. Tel: (4930) 300 6970. FAX: (4930) 3006 9711.

KERYX FILM
Immenried 97, Kisslegg D-88353. Tel: (497563) 8372 8147. FAX: (497563) 8372 8217.

KINOWELT FILMVERLEIH
Pfisterstrasse 11, Munich 80331. Tel: (4989) 296 963. FAX: (4989) 221 491.

KIRCHGROUP
Robert-Burklestrasse 2, Ismaning W-8045. Tel: (4989) 9508 8323. FAX: (4989) 9508 8330.

KLASING
Siekerwass 21, Bielefeld 33602. Tel: (49521) 5590. FAX: (49521) 559 113.

KORA FILMVERLEIH
Leopoldstrasse 65, 8000 Munich 40. Tel: (4989) 334 409.

KUCHENREUTHER FILM GMBH
Film Theater Verleih Produktion, Leopoldstrasse 80, Munich 80802. Tel: (4989) 332 224. FAX: (4989) 333 742.

MERCATOR FILMVERLEIH
Postfach 101950, Bielefeld 33519. Tel: (49521) 124 061. FAX: (49521) 131 010.

NEUE CONSTANTIN FILM
Kaiserstrasse 39, Munich 80801. Tel: (4989) 386 090. FAX: (4989) 3860 9242.

PANDORA FILM
Hamburger Allee 45, Frankfurt 60486. Tel: (4969) 779 094. FAX: (4969) 707 4033.

PROGRESS FILMVERLEIH
Burgstrasse 27, Berlin 10178. Tel: (4930) 280 5110. FAX: (4930) 282 9157.

SCOTIA INTERNATIONAL
Possartstrasse 14, Munich 81679. Tel: (4989) 413 0900. FAX: (4989) 470 6320.

SELLENG FILMAGENTUR
Lietzenburgerstrasse 51, Berlin 1000. Tel: (4930) 213 6788.

TIME MEDIENVERTRIEBS
Nymphenburgerstrasse 158, Munich D-80634. Tel: (4989) 160 923. FAX: (4989) 162 056. Distribution: Annette Niehues.

TOBIS FILMKUNST GMBH & CO.
Pacelliallee 47, Berlin 14175. Tel: (4930) 839 0070. FAX: (4930) 890 0765.

TWENTIETH CENTURY FOX OF GERMANY
Hainer Weg 37-53, 70 Frankfurt am Main D-60599. Tel: (4969) 609 020. FAX: (4969) 627 715.

UNITED INTERNATIONAL PICTURES
Hahnstrasse 31-35, Frankfurt am Main D-60528, Tel: (4969) 669 8190. FAX: (4969) 666 6509. Manager: Paul Steinshulte.
Lietzenburger Strasse 51, Berlin 10789. Tel: (4930) 211 2063. FAX: (4930) 213 3148.

WARNER BROS. FILM
Hans-Henny-Jahn-Weg 35, Hamburg D-22085. Tel: (4940) 227 1250. FAX: (4940) 2271 2519. Sales: Hans Hermann Schopen.

WILD OKAPI FILM VERLEIH VERTRIEB
Kreuzbergstrasse 43, Berlin 10965. Tel: (4930) 785 0376. FAX: (4930) 785 9620.

EXHIBITORS

BLUE MOVIE
Gutenbert 12, Flensburg 24941. Tel: (49461) 996 6247. FAX: (49461) 96265.

BROADWAY ENTERTAINMENT GMBH
Merkurstr 9-11, 66849, Landstuhl. Tel: (49) 63 71 93 70 00. FAX: (49) 63 71 93 71 11.
MANAGING DIRECTORS
Renate Goldhammer
Ernst Pletsch

BROADWAY FILMTHEATER, GMBH
Im Feld 53, 51427 Bergisch-Gladbach. Tel: (49) 22 04 65 595. FAX: (49) 22 04 62 450.
MANAGING DIRECTORS
Helmut Brunotte
Claudia Hebbel

BROADWAY FTB GMBH
Paulinstr. 18, 54292 Trier. Tel: (49) 65 1 246 05. FAX: (49) 65 1 261 11.

BROADWAY KINO
Ehrenstrasse 11, Cologne 50672. Tel: (49221) 925 6570. FAX: (49221) 9257 5714.

CADILLAC
Rosenkavalierplatz 12, Munich 81925. Tel: (4989) 912 000. FAX: (4989) 916 390.

CASABLANCA GASTST, KULTUR & KINO GMBH
Johannisstr. 17, 26121 Oldenburg. Tel: (49) 4 41 88 47 57. FAX: (49) 4 41 88 80 72.
MANAGING DIRECTOR
Dr. Detlef Rossman

CINEMAXX H.J. FLEBBE FILMTHEATERBETRIEBE
Mittelweg 176, 20148 Hanburg. Tel: (49) 40450 680. FAX: (49) 40 450 68201.
PRESIDENT & GENERAL MANAGER
Hans-Joachim Flebbe
GENERAL MANAGER & CFO
Michael Pawlowski
DIRECTOR, MARKETING
Jens Thomsen

Number of Theatres: 49
Germany (47), Turkey (1), Switzerland (1).

CITY KINO
Schwanthalerstrasse 7, Munich 80331. Tel: (4989) 598 749. FAX: (4989) 550 2171.

COLM ENTERTAINMENT AG
Alte Poststr 3, 701 73 Stuggart. Tel: (49) 7 11 29 22 45. FAX: (49) 7 11 2 26 3411.
MANAGING DIRECTOR
Roman Colm

COLM FILMTHEATERBETRIEBE
Alte Poststrasse 3, Stuttgart 70197. Tel: (49711) 650 400. FAX: (49711) 657 2530.

COMET FTB-GMBH
Konigstr 20, 41236 Moenchengladbach. Tel: (49) 21 66 94 4050. FAX: (49) 21 66 94 6067.
MANAGING DIRECTOR
H.J. Brandtner

CONSTANTIN KINOTRIEBE GMBH
Cinedom Im Mediapark, 50670 Koln. Tel: (49) 2 21 95 19 51 07. FAX: (49) 2 21 95 51 08.

DELPHI FILMVERLEIH
Kantstrasse 12a, Berlin 10623. Tel: (4930) 313 2200. FAX: (4930) 313 9996.

ECKART AND WOLFRAM WEBER-FTB
Gewerbemuseumpsl 3, 90403 Nurnberg. Tel: (49) 11 20 66 60. FAX: (49) 11 20 66 612.

ERASMUS KINOVERWALTUNG
Grimmstrasse 30A, Stuttgart 70197. Tel: (49711) 650 400. FAX: (49711) 657 2530.

FILMTHEATERBETRIEBE BERLIN
Schuchardtweg 9B, Berlin 14109. Tel: (4930) 805 4829. FAX: (4930) 805 5258.

FILMTHEATERBETRIEBE GEORGE REISS
Sophienstrasse 1, Munich 803333. Tel: (4989) 552 1650. FAX: (4989) 5521 6525.

FILMTHEATER-VERWVLTUNG REHS
44787 Bochum, Viktoriastr. 29. Tel: (49) 34 96 1710. FAX: (49) 34 96 17199.

FREYMUTH SCHULTZ VEREINGTE LICHTSPIELE
Jann-Berghaus-Str. 9, 26757 Borkum. Tel: (49) 22 91 810. FAX: (49) 22 91 8141.

FTB ADRIAN KUTTER
88400 Biberach. Tel: (49) 73 51 7 23 31. FAX: (49) 73 51 1 37 64.

FTB BERLIN
Schuchardtweg 9, 14109 Berlin. Tel: (49) 30 805 48 29. FAX: (49) 30 805 52 58.
MANAGING DIRECTOR
Peter H. Vollman

FTB W. BURTH
88212 Marienpl. 4, Ravensurg. Tel: (49) 7 51 36 14 436. FAX: (49) 7 51 36 14 459.
MANAGING DIRECTOR
Axel Burth

FTB DR. HERIBERT SCHLINKER
34414 Warburg, Johanaistorstr 35. Tel: (49) 56 41 23 63. FAX: (49) 56 41 54 40.

FTB GEORG REISS GMBH
Sophienstr. 1, 80333 Munchen. Tel: (49) 89 55 21 650. FAX: (49) 89 55 21 6525.

FTB HANS-GEORGE SAWATZKI
55543 Bad Kreuznach, Kreuzstr. 57-63. Tel: (49) 06 71 28883.

FTB MANFRED EWERT KG
Moritzstr. 6, 65185 Wiesbaden. Tel: (49) 6 11 30 00 35.

FTB MARTIN OHG
Vogelgesang 1, 36251 Bad Hersfeld. Tel: (49) 66 21 7 70 44. FAX: (49) 66 21 5 14 29.

FTB SPICKERT
Lichtenberger Str. 10, 67059 Ludwigshafen. Tel: (49) 6 21 59 1090. FAX: (49) 66 21 5 14 29.

FUTURA KINOBETRIEBS GMBH
80799 Munchen, Rambergstr. 5. Tel: (49) 89 38 17 000. FAX: (49) 8938 17 0020.

FWU FILM INSTITUTE
Bavaria Film Platz 3, Gruenwald 82131. Tel: (4989) 64970. FAX: (4989) 649 7360.

GILDE DEUTSCHES FILMKUNSTTHEATER
Waldseerstrasse 3, Biberach/Riss 884000. Tel: (4973) 517 2331. FAX: (4973) 511 3764.

THE GREATER UNION ORGANISATION
(including BIRCH CARROLL & COYLE)
49 Market St., Sydney, NSW 2000, Australia. Tel: (612) 93 73 66 00. FAX: (612) 93 73 65 32.
MANAGING DIRECTOR
Robert Manson

Number of Theatres: 30 (Germany)
Number of Screens: 246 (Germany)

HANSEATER FILMTHEATERBETRIEBE
Kurfuerstendamm 33, Berlin 10719. Tel: (4930) 883 6086. FAX: (4930) 883 6520.

HERMANN-CLOSMANN ERBEN D.G. FTB
Biegenstr. 8, 35037 Marburg. Tel: (49) 64 21 17 300. FAX: (49) 64 21 17 30 40.
MANAGING DIRECTOR
Gerhard Closmann

WALTER H. JANN WERBE & FILMBETR. GMBH
Hauptstr. 16, 82319 Starnberg. Tel: (49) 81 51 1 37 92. FAX: (49) 81 51 2 83 20.

KIEFT & KIEFT FILMTHEATER GMBH
Muehlenbruecke 9-11, 23552 Luebeck. Tel: (4517) 030 200. FAX: (4517) 030 222.
MANAGERS
Marlis Kieft
Heiner Kieft

Number of Theatres: 37
Number of Screens: 179

KINEMATOGRAPH FILM GMBH
Biedersteiner Str. 11, 80802 Munchen. (49) 89 55 71 60. FAX: (49) 89 59 45 59.
PRESIDENT & OWNER
Dr. Dieter Buchwald
EXECUTIVE V.P.
Klans Ungerer

KINOCENTER OTTOBRUNN
Ottostrasse 72, Ottobrunn 85521. Tel: (4989) 609 4141. FAX: (4989) 609 9696.

KINOPOLIS MAIN–TAUNUS GMBH & CO.
Main-Taunus-Zentrum, Sulzbach/Hossen, 65843. Tel: (49) 6 39 14 03 80. FAX: (49) 6 93 14 03 899.
MANAGING DIRECTOR
Wolfgang Theile
MANAGER
Hans-Jurgen Jochum

KRUGMANN & WEISCHERMUNDSBURGER
Hamburgerstrasse 152, Hamburg 22083. Tel: (4940) 291 111. FAX: (4940) 291 117.

KUCHENREUTHER FILM
Sonnenstrasse 22, Munich 80331. Tel: (4989) 596 717. FAX: (4989) 596 286.

LISELOTTE JAEGER FILMTHEATERBETRIEBE
Holzgraben 26, Frankfurt 60313. Tel: (4969) 285 205. FAX: (4969) 281 957. Second Address: Zeil 125, 60313 Frankfurt. Tel: (49) 69 28 52 05. FAX: (49) 69 28 19 57.

LUDWIG SCHEER & CO. KG-FTB
Juliuspromenade 68, 97070 Wurzburg. Tel: (49) 93 15 31 31. FAX: (49) 93 15 51 01.

MEGA EXTREM CINEMA GMBH
August-Horch-Str. 2a, 56070 Koblenz. Tel: (49) 2 61 8 09 05 15. FAX: (49) 2 61 8 09 05 30.
MANAGING DIRECTOR
Dieter Tobolik

MUENSTERSCHE FILMTHEATER
Bahnhofstr. 20-22, 48143 Muenster. Tel: (49) 2 515 60 07. FAX: (49) 2 515 60 08.

NEUE CONSTANTIN KINOBETRIEBE
Kaiserstrasse 39, Munich 80801. Tel: (4989) 386 090. FAX: (4989) 3860 9166.

OLYMPIC/HEINZ RIECH & SON
Graf Adolfstrasse 96, Dusseldorf 40210. Tel: (49211) 169 060. FAX: (49211) 169 0633.

OMNIPLEX FILMTHEATERBETRIEBE
30159 Hannover. Luisenstr. 10-11. FAX: (49) 51 132 27 11.

PALAST/SCHMID & THEILE
Lautenschlagerstrasse 3, Stuttgart 70173. Tel: (49711) 225 750. FAX: (49711) 225 7599.

PEP FILMTHEATER GMBH
35757 Driedorf, P.O. Box 1221. Tel: (49) 27 75 95 05 03. FAX: (49) 27 75 95 05 04. email: Plass@gloria.dill.de
MANAGING DIRECTOR
Peter Plass

GERD POLITT FILMTHEATERBETRIEBE
Konigswall 4, 45657 Recklinghausen. Tel: (49) 23 61 93 350. FAX: (49) 23 61 22 287.

POTSDAM FILM MUSEUM
Martsall, Potsdam 14467. Tel: (49331) 271 810. FAX: (49331) 271 8126.

ROLF THEILE FILMTHEATERBETRIEBE
Holdgestrasse 12, Darmstadt 6100. Tel: (49615) 129 780. FAX: (49615) 129 7832.

ROSSLENBROICH-FTB GMBH
Dusseldorfer Str. 2, 40822 Mettman. Tel: (49) 21 04 7 43 66. FAX: (49) 21 04 7 46 34.
MANAGING DIRECTORS
M. Papenhoff
G. Rosslenbroich

ROYAL PALAST
Goetheplatz 2, Munich 80337. Tel: (4989) 533 956. FAX: (4989) 530 9618.

SCALA: FTB GMBH
78462 Konstanz Rosgartenstr. 9. Tel: (75) 31 2 45 22. FAX: (75) 31 1 63 23.
MANAGING DIRECTOR
Kurt Rabe

UFA THEATER AG
Graf-Adolf-Strasse 96, 40210 Dusseldorf. Tel: (49) 211 169 060. FAX: (49) 211 169 0633.
DIRECTOR
Volker Riech
Number of Screens: 500

UNION KG KRUGMANN & WEISCHER
Hamburger St., 152, 22083 Hamburg. Tel: (49) 40 2 07 05. FAX: (49) 40 29 90 71 77.

UNITED CINEMAS INTERNATIONAL MULTIPLEX GMBH
Oskar-Hoffman-Strasse 156, 44789 Bochum. (49) 234 937 190.
Number of Screens: 123

VEREINIGTE LICHTSPIELE
72016 Pf. 2609 Tubingen. Tel: (49) 70 71 2 36 61. FAX: (49) 70 71 2 14 21.

VILLAGE ROADSHOW, LTD.
(For complete listing see Australian branch.)
206 Bourke St., Melbourne, VIC, 3000, Australia. Tel: (613) 96 67 66 66. FAX: (613) 96 39 15 40.
Number of Theatres: 8 (Germany)
Number of Screens: 74 (Germany)

WETTLAUFER KINOBETRIEBS-GESELLSCHAFT MBJ
82456 Garmisch- Partenkirchen, Postfach. 1624. Tel: (49) 88 21 23 70. FAX: (49) 88 21 95 01 44.
EXECUTIVES
Georg Wettlaufer
Nora Wettlaufer

YORK–KINO GMBH-FTB
10789 Rankestrasse 31, Berlin . Tel: (49) 30 2 12 98 00. FAX: (49) 30 21 29 80 99.

GREECE

Population: 10.6 million.
Screens: 200 plus an equal number of open air cinemas open during summer months.

ASSOCIATIONS & ORGANIZATIONS

ASSOCIATION OF TECHINICIANS (ETEKT)
25 Veltetsiou St., Athens 106 80. Tel: (301) 360 2379. FAX: (301) 361 6442.

GREEK ACTORS GUILD
83 Kaningos St., Athens 10677.

GREEK FILM & TV PRODUCERS UNION
1A Egyptou St., Athens. Tel: (301) 883 8460. FAX: (301) 883 8410.

GREEK FILM CENTER
19 Paneoistimiou St., Athens 10671. Tel: (301) 363 4586. FAX: (301) 351 4336.

GREEK FILM DIRECTORS UNION
11 Tositsa St., Athens 10683. Tel: (301) 822 3205. FAX: (301) 821 1390.

MOTION PICTURE DIRECTORATE BY THE MINISTRY OF CULTURE
12 Aristidou St., Athens 105 59.

PANHELLENIC FEDERATION OF FILM EXHIBITORS
96 Academias St., Athens 10677. Tel: (301) 801 1045.

TENIOTHIKI TIS HELLADOS
Greek Film Archives, 1 Kanari St., Athens 10671. Tel: (301) 361 2046. FAX: (301) 362 8468.

THESSALONIKI FILM FESTIVAL
153 Egratias St., Thessaloniki, 36 Sina St., Athens 10672. FAX: (301) 362 1023.

DISTRIBUTORS AND PRODUCERS

AMA FILMS
22 Tositsa St., Athens 10583. Tel: (301) 381 2640. FAX: (301) 384 2559.
GENERAL MANAGER
George Stergiakis

HELLINIKI KINIMSTROGRAFIKI ENOSSI (ELKE)
(Distributes films of Warner Bros, Goldcrest, Carolco, Lorimar, Globe, Rank, Thames International, etc.) 96-98 Academias St., Athens 10677. Tel: (301) 382 3801. FAX: (301) 380 301.
GENERAL MANAGER
George V. Michaelides

NEA KINISSI
9-13 Gravias St., Athens, 10677. Tel: (301) 382 4545. FAX: (301) 383 9008.
GENERAL MANAGER
Antonis Karatzopoulos

ODEON FILMS (ELKE)
96-98 Academias St., Athens 10677. Tel: (301) 382 3801. FAX: (301) 382 3801.

OVO FILMS
27 Themistokleous St., Athens 10677. Tel: (301) 330 4521. FAX: (301) 330 4523.

PROOPTIKI S. A.
(Distributes films of Columbia Pictures, Orion, Touchstone, Walt Disney, Tri Star, Cannon.)
40-42 Koleti St., Athens 10682. Tel: (301) 383 3541. FAX: (301) 381 3762.
GENERAL MANAGER
Pantelis Metropoulos

ROSEBUD MOTION PICTURES ENTERPRISES
(Distributes independent American, European & international films)
96 Academias St., Athens 10677. Tel: (301) 384 4293. FAX: (301) 383 9208.
GENERAL MANAGER
Zenos Panayotides

SPENTZOS FILMS S. A.
(Distributes films of Twentieth Century Fox, New Line Cinema, independent and European films.)
9-13 Gravias St., Athens 10678. Tel: (301) 362 0297. FAX: (301) 382 1438.
GENERAL MANAGER
George Spentzos

UNITED INTERNATIONAL PICTURES (UIP)
(Distributes films of MGM, Paramount, Universal, United Artists.)
4 Gamveta St., Athens 10678. Tel: (301) 381 1472. FAX: (301) 383 5396.
GENERAL MANAGER
John Takaziadis

EXHIBITORS

APOSTOLOS FOUKIS
Messoguion St., Athens 11522.
Theaters: Galaxias, Metropolitan.

ATTICA CINEPLEX
12 Messoguion St., Athens 16231.,
Theaters: Opera I, Opera.

K. GEORGOPOULOS S.A.
109 Kifissias St., Athens 11524.
Theaters: Danos.

HOME VIDEO HELLAS
325 Messoguion St., Athens 15231.
Theaters: Opera I, Opera II, Radio City, Assos Odcon I, Assos Odcon II, Tropical, Havana, Anessis, Assos Odeon Maroussi, Olympion I and Olympion II, Assos Odeon.

IONAIDES FILMS EPE
12 Nikiforou Lytra St., Athens 11474.
Theaters: Astron.

STAVROS ISAAKIDES
26 Velvendous St., Athens 11364.
Theaters: Ilyssia.

KAPSIS HEIRS
14 Kifissias St., Athens.
Theaters: Anessis.

CHRISTOS KARAVIAS & COMPANY
12 Alexandras Ave., Athens.
Theaters: Nirvana.

A KARAVOYKYROS – K. FRANTZIS, S.A.
122 Patrission St., Athens 11257.
Theaters: Athena.

KONTOULIS
152 EL. Venizelos St., Callithea, Athens.
Theatres: Etoile.

FOTIS KOSMIDES
Korae St., Athens 10566.
Theaters: Asty, Hellinis.

VICTOR MICHAELIDES
Theatre Palac, 4 Voukoutestiou St., Athens 10565.

PANAYOTOPOULOS
3 Patriarchou Ioakem, Athens 1-673.
Theaters: Embassy.

D.P. SKOURAS FILMS
19 Stadium St., Athens 10561.
Theaters: Attikon, Apollon.

SPENTZOS FILMS S. A.
9-13 Gravias St., Athens 10678. Tel: (301) 382 0957. FAX: (301) 382 1438.
Theaters: Ideal, Aliki, ABC, Oscar, Ideal Maroussi.

STERIAKIS BROTHERS/AMA FILMS
122 Patrission St., Athens 11257.
Theaters: Athena.

VILLAGE ROADSHOW, GREECE
(For complete listing see Australian branch.)
11 Mistral St., Neo Psyhiko, Athen 15451. Tel: (301) 685 6833. FAX: (301) 685 6830
Number of Theatres: 4 (Greece)
Number of Screens: 44 (Greece)

HONG KONG

Population: 6.3 million.

ASSOCIATIONS & ORGANIZATIONS

EAST ASIA FILM AND VIDEO SECURITY
13/F, Rm B, Lockhart Centre, 301 Lockhart Rd., Wanchai. Tel: (852) 575 7842. FAX: (852) 838 0937.

HONG KONG AND KOWLOON CINEMA AND THEATRICAL ENTERPRISE FREE GENERAL ASSOCIATION
Flat A-B, 9/F, 88 Nathan Rd., Kowloon. Tel: (852) 376 3833. FAX: (852) 721 9225.

KOWLOON & NEW TERRITORIES MOTION PICTURE INDUSTRY ASSOCIATION
319 Beverley Commercial Centre, 87-105 Chatham Rd., Tsimshatsui, Kowloon. Tel: (852) 311 2692. FAX: (852) 311 1178.

FILM DISTRIBUTORS AND PRODUCERS

ATLAS FILM
Rm. 905-6, Winning Commercial Bldg., 46-48 Hillwood Rd., Tsimshatsui, Kowloon. Tel: (852) 367 1057. FAX: (852) 369 0855.

CAPITAL ARTISTS
No. 1, Leighton Rd., Causeway Bay. Tel: (852) 833 9192. FAX: (852) 832 5055.

CITY ENTERTAINMENT
Flat E, 14/F, Tung Nam Bldg., 475 Hennessy Rd., Wanchai. Tel: (852) 892 0155. FAX: (852) 838 4930.

CHINA STAR ENTERTAINMENT, LTD.
Unit 503C, Miramar Tower, 1-23 Kimberley Rd., TST, Kowloon. Tel: (852) 2323 1888. FAX: (852) 2191 9888. email: mal@chinastar.com.hk

CLEVELAND FILM
Imperial Cinema, 29 Burrows St., Wanchai. Tel: (852) 572 0002. FAX: (852) 834 0723.

CONTINENTAL FILM DISTRIBUTORS
Unit 1922, Star House, 3 Salisbury Rd., Tsimshatsui, Kowloon. Tel: (852) 730 4373. FAX: (852) 730 2977.

CRYSTAL CORPORATION
10/F, Lee Kar Bldg., 4-4A Carnarvon Rd., Tsimshatsui, Kowloon. Tel: (852) 367 4077. FAX: (852) 723 3054.

DELON INTERNATIONAL FILM
7B Astoria Bldg., 24-30 Ashley Rd., Tsimshatsui, Kowloon. Tel: (852) 376 1168. FAX: (852) 376 2569.

EKDO FILMS
19/F Fung Hse, 19-20 Connaught Rd., Central. Tel: (852) 523 1152. FAX: (852) 810 6670.

ERA COMMUNICATIONS
Unit 604, Taikoktsui Centre, 11-15 Kok Cheung St., Kowloon. Tel: (852) 787 3612. FAX: (852) 787 4367.

FILM CITY DISTRIBUTION
Flat A-F, 16/F, Marvel Bldg., 25-31 Kwai Fung Cres, Kwai Chung, New Territories. Tel: (852) 423 4272. FAX: (852) 420 0352.

FILM CONSORTIUM
Rm. 1302, 1 Hysan Av., Causeway Bay. Tel: (852) 5760321. FAX: (852) 895 5471.

FOX COLUMBIA TRISTAR
Rm. 1014, World Commerce Centre, 11 Canton Rd., Tsimshatsui, Kowloon. Tel: (852) 736 6277. FAX: (852) 736 3872.

GOLDEN COMMUNICATIONS
8 Hammer Hill Rd., Kowloon. Tel: (852) 726 5541. FAX: (852) 351 1683.

GOLDEN GLOBE FILM
1203 Tak Woo Hse, 17-19 D'Aguilar St., Central. Tel: (852) 576 0321.

GOLDEN HARVEST ENTERTAINMENT CO. LTD.
8 King Tung Street, Hammer Hill Rd., Kowloon. Tel: (852) 2352 8222. FAX: (852) 2351 1683.

GOLDEN PRINCESS AMUSEMENT
6th Flr., 742-744 Nathan Rd., Kowloon. Tel: (852) 391 9988. FAX: (852) 789 1365.

HAPPY INTERNATIONAL ENTERTAINMENT
Rm. 1205, Shun Tak Centre, 200 Connaught Rd., Central. Tel: (852) 559 1051. FAX: (852) 858 2657.

WILLIAM HAY & CO.
5th Flr. Rear, 234 Nathan Road. Central. Tel: (852) 368 8319. FAX: (852) 311 6727.

IMPACT FILMS PRODUCTION
22/F Waterloo Plaza, 53-55 Waterloo Rd., Kowloon. Tel: (852) 332 1762. FAX: (852) 783 8225.

IN-GEAR FILM DISTRIBUTION INTERNATIONAL
14th Flr., 206-208 Prince Edward Rd., Kowloon. Tel: (852) 397 1452. FAX: (852) 380 5216.

INTERCONTINENTAL GROUP HOLDINGS LTD.
(Subsidiaries: Intercontinental Film Distributors, Mini Cinema Ltd., Intercontinental Video, Jesu International Entertainment, Lauro Films, Intercontinental Communications and Perfect Advertising & Production Co.)
27/F Wyler Centre, Phase 2, 200 Tai Lin Pai Rd., Kwai Chung, New Territories. Tel: (852) 2481 6693. FAX: (852) 2481 6377.

JOY SALES FILM & VIDEO DISTRIBUTORS
2/F Hang On Mansion, 239-249 Portland St., Mongkok, Kowloon. Tel: (852) 771 6161. FAX: (852) 770 6218.

KOREAN MOTION PICTURE PROMOTION (HK)
Ste. B1, 14/F, Golden Crown Ct, 68 Nathan Rd., Tsimshatsui, Kowloon. Tel: (852) 369 2789. FAX: (852) 311 3425.

NEWPORT ENTERTAINMENT
19/F, Southland Bldg., 47 Connaught Rd., Central. Tel: (852) 543 6973. FAX: (852) 544 9574.

PARSONS INTERNATIONAL
11J Far East Mansion, 5-6 Middle Rd., Tsimshatsui, Kowloon. Tel: (852) 721 8647. FAX: (852) 311 5383.

SALON FILMS LTD.
6 Devon Rd., Kowloon Tong, Kowloon. Tel: (852) 2338 0505. FAX: (852) 2338 2539.

SAM LOON INTERNATIONAL
12/F, Vincent Commercial Centre, 21 Hillwood Rd., Tsimshatsui, Kowloon. Tel: (852) 723 6239. FAX: (852) 721 4954.

SOUTHERN FILM
1902 Dominion Centre, 37-59 Queens Rd. East, Wanchai. Tel: (852) 527 7282. FAX: (852) 865 1449.

UIP INTERNATIONAL SERVICES
Ste. 1501, Dina Hse., 11 Duddell St., Central. Tel: (852) 526 6841. FAX: (852) 845 9581.

THE WALT DISNEY STUDIOS HONG KONG
15th Flr., Citibank Tower, Citibank Plaza, 3 Garden Rd., Central. FAX: (852) 2536 2453.

WARNER BROS. (FAR EAST)
12/F Siberian Fur Bldg., 38-40 Haiphong R., Tsimshatsui, Kowloon. Tel: (852) 376 3963. FAX: (852) 376 1302.

EXHIBITORS

EDKO FILMS LIMITED
1212 Tower II, Admiralty Centre, 18 Harcourt Rd., Hong Kong. Tel: (85) 2 25 29 3898. FAX: (85) 2 25 29 5277.
EXECUTIVE DIRECTOR
William Kong
THEATRE OPERATIONS
Eric Li
DISTRIBUTION DEPT.
Audrey Lee
ADVERTISING DEPT.
Leung Yuet Ngor
ACCOUNTS DEPT.
Angela Fung
Number of Theatres: 9
Number of Screens: 29
Mongkok (3), Kernhill (3), Tgnen Wan (3), Kwai Fong (5), Kowloon Bay (3), Ynen Long (4), Silvercord (2), Windsor (2), Cinematheque (4).

GOLDEN HARVEST ENTERTAINMENT CO., LTD.
16/F Peninsula Office Tower, 18 Middle Rd., Kowloon. Tel: (852) 2352 8222. FAX: (852) 2353 5989.
EXECUTIVE DIRECTORS
Mr. Chow Ting Hsing
Raymond
Mr. Graham Burke
Mr. C.K. Phoon
Mr. Albert Lee
Mr. Stephen Chu
Mr. Richard Potter
Number of Theatres: 58
Number of Screens: 251
Hong Kong (7), Malaysia (33), PRC (2), Singapore (9), Thailand (7).

GOLDEN VILLAGE
8 Hammer Hill Rd., Kowloon. Tel: (852) 352-8222.
Number of Screens: 14

STUDIO CITY CINEMA HOLDINGS, LTD.
Rm. 409-411, 4/F, World Commerce Centre, 11 Canton Rd., Kowloon. Tel: (85) 27 35 4633. FAX: (85) 23 75 8869.
GENERAL MANAGERS
Bob Vallone
Maureen Koh
Ben Keung
EXECUTIVE DIRECTORS
James Kralik
Hamilton Tang
CHAIRMAN
Ira D. Kaye

UNITED ARTISTS CINEMA CIRCUIT, LTD.
Room 409-410/F, World Commerce Centre, 11 Canton Rd., Kowloon. Tel: (852) 2736-4633.
Number of Screens: 30.

VILLAGE ROADSHOW, LTD.
(For complete listing see Australian branch.)
206 Bourke St., Melbourne, VIC, 3000, Australia. Tel: (613) 96 67 66 66. FAX: (613) 96 39 15 40.
Number of Theatres: 8
Number of Screens: 29

HUNGARY

Population: 10.1 million.

ASSOCIATIONS & ORGANIZATIONS

ASSOCIATION OF CINEMAS OF HUNGARY
Maria u 19, Szolnok H-5000. Tel. (3656) 420 612.

GUILD OF HUNGARY
Varosligeti Fasor 38, Budapest H-1068. Tel: (361) 342 4760. FAX: (361) 342 4760.

HUNGARIAN FILM INSTITUTE & ARCHIVE
Budakeszi u 51B, Budapest H-1021. Tel: (361) 176 0205. FAX: (361) 176 7106.

MOTION PICTURE FOUNDATION OF HUNGARY
Szalaiu 10, Budapest H-1054. Tel. (361) 1126417.

DISTRIBUTORS AND PRODUCERS

BUDAPEST FILM
Batori u 10, Budapest H-1054. (361) 111 6650. FAX: (361) 131 5946.

CINEMAGYAR KFT (HUNGAROFILM EX)
Batori u 10, Budapest H-1054. (361) 111 4614. FAX: (361) 153 1317.

DUNA/UIP DANUBE
Tarogato u 24, Budapest H-1021. Tel: (361) 174 7291. FAX: (361) 176 7291.

EUROFILM STUDIO
Rona u 174, Budapest H-1145. Tel: (361) 252 5069. FAX: (361) 251 3986. email: eurofilm@hungary.net

FLAMEX
Labanc u 22B, Budapest H-1021. Tel: (361) 176 1543. FAX: (361) 176 0596.

FOCUSFILM LTD.
Pasareti ut 122, Budapest H-1026. Tel: (361) 200 6857, (361) 275 2312 . FAX: (200) 200 6858. email: focusflm@mail.matav.hu
MANAGING DIRECTORS
Aron Sipos
Denes Skeres

HUNNIA FILMSTUDIO
Rona u 174, Budapest H-1145. Tel: (361) 252 3170. FAX: (361) 251 6269.

INTERCOM
Karolina ut. 65, Budapest H-1113. Tel: (361) 209 0933. FAX: (361) 209 0930.

MOKEP
Bathori u 10, Budapest H-1054. Tel: (361) 111 2097. FAX: (361) 153 1613.

UIP—DANUBE INTERNATIONAL PICTURES
Tarogato u 2-4/2nd Flr., Budapest H-1021. Tel: (361) 176 7291. FAX: (361) 274 2177.
MANAGER
Peter Balint.

EXHIBITORS

BUDAPEST FILM
Bathori u 10, Budapest H-1054. Tel: (361) 111 2494. FAX: (361) 111 2687.

CORVIN BUDAPEST FILMPALACE
Corvin koz 12, Budapest H-1082. Tel: (361) 303 1500. FAX: (361) 303 2526.

CINEPLEX ODEON INTERNATIONAL MOZI
Polus Centre, Szentmihalyi ut 131, 1153 Budapest. Tel: (361) 419 4223. FAX: (361) 419 4228.
CONTACT
Ana LeRoux
Number of Theatres: 1
Number of Screens: 6

HUNGARIAN FILM INSTITUTE & FILM ARCHIVE
Budakeszi u 51B, Budapest H-1021. Tel: (361) 176 0205. FAX: (361) 176 7106.

VILLAGE ROADSHOW, LTD.
206 Bourke St., Melbourne, VIC, 3000, Australia. Tel: (613) 96 67 66 66. FAX: (613) 96 39 15 40.
(For complete listing see Australian branch.)
Number of Theatres: 4 (Hungary)
Number of Screens: 26 (Hungary)

ICELAND

Population: 276 thousand.
Average Ticket Price: $7.18

ASSOCIATIONS & ORGANIZATIONS

ASSOCIATION OF FILM DISTRIBUTORS IN ICELAND
Stjornubio, Laugaveg 94, Reykjavik 101. Tel: (3541) 551 6500. FAX: (3541) 554 4630.

ASSOCIATION OF ICELANDIC FILM DIRECTORS
Hverfisgata 46, Reykjavik 121. (3541) 562 1850. FAX: (3541) 552 5154.

ASSOCIATION OF ICELANDIC FILM PRODUCERS
Posthusstraeti 13, Reykjavik 101. (3541) 152 8188. FAX: (3541) 162 3424.

DIRECTORS GUILD OF ICELAND
Hverfisgata 46, Reykjavij 101. Tel: (3541) 551 2260. FAX: (3541) 552 5154.

ICELANDIC FILM FUND
Laugavegur 24, Reykjavik 101. (3541) 562 3580. FAX: (3541) 562 7171.

ICELANDIC FILMMAKERS ASSOCIATION
Laugavegur 24, P.O. Box 320, Reykjavik 101. (3541) 562 3225. FAX: (3541) 562 7171.

MINISTRY OF CULTURE & EDUCATION
Solvholsgotu 4, Reykjavik 105. Tel: (3541) 560 9500. FAX: (3541) 562 3068.

DISTRIBUTORS AND PRODUCERS

BERGVIK
Armula 44, Reykjavik. Tel: (3541) 588 7966. FAX: (3541) 588 0288.

HASKOLABIO UNIVERSITY CINEMA
Hagatorg, Reykjavik 107. Tel: (3541) 561 1212. FAX: (3541) 562 7135. email: cinema@centrum.is

ICELANDIC FILM COMPANY
Hverfisgata 46, Reykjavik 101. Tel: (3541) 551 2260. FAX: (3541) 552 5154.

LAUGARASBIO
Laugaras, Reykjavik 104. Tel: (3541) 563 8150. FAX: (3541) 568 0910.

MYNDFORM
Holshraun 2, Hafnarfirdi 220. (354) 565 1288. FAX: (354) 565 0188.

SAM FILM
Alfabakki 8, Reykjavik 109. Tel: (3541) 587 8900. FAX: (3541) 587 8930.

SKIFAN
Skeifan 17, Reykjavik 108. Tel: (354) 525 5000. FAX: (3541) 525 5001.

STJOERNUBIO
Laugavegi 94, Reykjavik 101. Tel: (3541) 551 6500. FAX: (3541) 554 4630.

EXHIBITORS

BORGARBIO
Akuyeri. Tel: (354) 462 3500. FAX: (354) 461 2796.

HASKOLABIO-UNIVERSITY CINEMA
Hagatorg, Reykjavik 107. Tel: (3541) 561 1212. FAX: (3541) 562 7135. email: cinema@centrum.is
DIRECTOR
Fridbert Palsson

LAUGARASBIO
Laugaras, Reykjavik 104. Tel: (3541) 563 8150. FAX: (3541) 568 0910.

REGNBOGINN
Hverfisgata 54, Reykjavik 101. Tel: (3541) 462 3500. FAX: (3541) 461 2796.

SAM FILM
Alfabakka 8, Reykjavik 109. Tel: (3541) 587 8900. FAX: (3541) 587 8930.

STJOERNUBIO
Laugavegi 94, Reykjavik 101. Tel: (3541) 551 6500. FAX: (3541) 554 4630.

INDIA

Population: 1 billion/
Theatres: 13,000.

ASSOCIATIONS & ORGANIZATIONS

CINEMATOGRAPH EXHIBITOR'S ASSOCIATION OF INDIA
Flat 22/23B, 1st Flr., Vellard View, Tardeo Rd., Bombay 400034.

EASTERN INDIA MOTION PICTURE ASSOCIATION
98E Chowringhee Square, Calcutta.

FILM FEDERATION OF INDIA
91 Walkeshwar Rd, Bombay 400006.

INDIAN DOCUMENTARY PRODUCERS ASSOCIATION
305 Famous Cine Bldg., Mahalaxmi, Bombay 400018.

INDIAN FILM EXPORTERS ASSOCIATION
305 Famous Cine Bldg., Mahalaxmi, Bombay 400018.

THE INDIAN MOTION PICTURE DISTRIBUTORS' ASSOCIATION
33 Vijay Chamber, Tribhuvan Rd, Bombay 400004.

INDIAN MOTION PICTURE PRODUCERS' ASSOCIATION
Dr. Ambedkar Road, Bandra (W), Bombay 400050.

SOUTH INDIA'S FILM CHAMBER OF COMMERCE
122 Mount Road, Madras 60002.

PRINCIPAL EXPORTERS

ANAND EXPORTS
730 Chandra Niwas, Annex Shop 2, 11th Rd., Khar, Bombay 400052. Tel: (9122) 646 2755.

CITIZEN INTERNATIONAL
B/6 3rd Flr., Everest, Tardeo Road, Bombay 400034. Tel: (9122) 495 1688.

FAIRDEAL EXPORTS LTD.
10 Kashi Kunj, 2nd Flr., Waterfield Road, Bandra, Bombay 400050. FAX: (9122) 604 2429.

NATIONAL FILM DEVELOPMENT CORP., LTD.
Nehru Centre, Dr. A. Besant Road, Worli, Bombay 400018. Tel: (9122) 495 2662.

NEPTUNE ENTERPRISES
C 8/9 Everest, 4th Flr., Tardeo Rd., Bombay 400034. FAX: (9122) 492 0890.

RAJSHRI PRODUCTIONS LTD.-BHAVNA
1st Flr., Opp Kismat Cinema, Prabhadevi, Bombay 400025. FAX: (9122) 422 9181.

TRIMURTI EXPORTS
B/11 Commerce Centre, Tardeo Road, Bombay 400034. FAX: (9122) 811 667.

PRINCIPAL IMPORTERS

ALLIED ARTS OF INDIA INC.
Metro House, M. G. Road, Bombay 400020.

COLUMBIA TRISTAR FILMS OF INDIA LTD.
Metro House, 1st Flr., M. G. Road, Bombay 400020. Tel: (9122) 201 4264. FAX: (9122) 201 4321.

METRO-GOLDYN-MAYER FILMS OF INDIA LTD.
Metro House, M. G. Road, Bombay 400020.

PARAMOUNT FILMS OF INDIA, LTD.
(Also representing Universal)
Hague Building, Sprott Rd., Bombay 400020. Tel: (9122) 261 3877. FAX: (9122) 261 2856.
MANAGER
Sarabjit Singh

TWENTIETH CENTURY FOX CORP. (INDIA), LTD.
Metro House, 3rd Flr., M. G. Road, Bombay 400020. Tel: (9122) 205 4290. FAX: (9122) 208 9388. Calcutta: Tel: (9133) 249 5623. New Delhi: (9111) 332 0351. Madras: Tel: (9144) 852 0078.
GENERAL MANAGER
Sunder Kimatrai

UNITED ARTISTS CORP.
Metro House, M. G. Road, Bombay 400020.

UNIVERSAL PICTURES INDIA P LTD.
Hague Bldg, Sprott Road, Bombay 400020. Tel: (9122) 266 6146. FAX: (9122) 261 2856.

WARNER BROS (F. D.) INDIA
Eros Theatre Bldg., 42 M. Karve Road, Bombay 400020. Tel: (9122) 285 6557. FAX: (9122) 285 0984.
Leslie House, 19A Jawarharlal Nehru Rd., Calcutta 700087. Tel: (9133) 249 5613.
Dinroze Estate, 69 Mount Rd., Madras 600002. Tel: (9144) 852 5964.
Plaza Thatre Bldg., Connaught Circus, New Delhi 110001. Tel: (9111) 332 1544.
MANAGING DIRECTOR
J. Fernandes

EXHIBITORS

THE BALJI GROUP
8 Thiru-V-Ka Rd., Chennai 600014. Tel: (91) 44 85 24 875, (91) 44 852 3813. FAX: (91) 44 85 21 972.
CONTACT
KR Subramaniam
MANAGING PARTNER
Mr. Vijaykumar

CHAPHALKAR GROUP OF CINEMAS
Mangala Cinema, 111 Shivajinagar, Pune 411005. Tel: (91) 21 2 323468, 323519. FAX: (91) 21 2 323973.
MANAGING DIRECTOR
Ajay Bijlee
CONTACT
D.D. Prakash Chaphalkar

MARIS THEATRES PVT, LTD.
Fort Station Rd., Tiruchirapally 62 0002.

MODI U.A.T.C. (PVT) LTD.
4 Lands End, 54 Byramji Jeetibhoy Rd., Bandra, Bombay 400050. Tel: (9122) 645 0000. FAX: (9122) 645 8282.
CHIEF EXECUTIVE
Rajiv Sahai

PRIYA VILLAGE ROADSHOW LIMITED
Priya Cinema and Anupam Cineplex, 50 W. Regal Bldg., Connaught Pl., New Delhi 110001. Tel: (91) 11 37 32 089 and 334 0605. FAX: (91) 11 374 71 39.

RAJSHRI PICTURES
42 Virsavarkar Rd., Post Box No. 9103, Prabha Devi, Bombay 400025, India. Tel: (912) 422 7705 and 430 7688. FAX: (912) 242 9181.

SHRINGAR CINEMAS PVT., LTD.
B-103, Kailash, Juhu Church Rd., Juhu, Mumbai, 400 049, Maharashtra State. Tel: (91) 22 625-5900. FAX: (91) 22 625-5272.
email: Shrigar001@vsnl.com
DIRECTOR
Shravan Shroff

VILLAGE ROADSHOW, LTD.
(For complete listing see Australian branch.)
206 Bourke St., Melbourne, VIC, 3000, Australia. Tel: (613) 96 67 66 66. FAX: (613) 96 39 15 40.

Number of Theatres: 2 (India)
Number of Screens: 5 (India)

WESTERN INDIA THEATRES LIMITED
Liberty Bldg., 41-42 New Marine Lines, Bombay 400020. Tel: (91) 22 20 1 42 17, (91) 22 20 1 43 18. FAX: (91) 22 20 57 939.
CONTACTS
Roosi K. Modi
Kamal Barjatiya

INDONESIA

Population: 224.7 million.

DISTRIBUTORS

UNITED INTERNATIONAL PICTURES (UIP)
c/o PT Camila Internuse Film, Subentra Bank Building, Ste. 716, Jl. Jend, Gatot Subroto Kaz 21, Jakarta 12930, Indonesia. Tel: (6221) 522 0063. FAX: (6221) 522 0064.
REPRESENTATIVE
Douglas Lee

EXHIBITORS

SUBENTRA GROUP
Subentra Bank Building, 21 Jl. Send, Gatot Subroto, Jakarta 12930. Tel: (6221) 522 0122. FAX: (6221) 522 0078.
MANAGING DIRECTOR, EXHIBITION & DISTRIBUTION
Harris Lasmana

Number of Screens: 500

ISRAEL

Population: 5.8 million.

ASSOCIATIONS & ORGANIZATIONS

ISRAEL FILM CENTRE
Ministry of Industry & Trade, 30 Gershon Agron St., P.O. Box 299, Jerusalem 94190. Tel: (9722) 750 433. FAX: (9722) 245 110.

ISRAEL FILM SERVICE
Ministry of Education & Culture, P.O. Box 13240, Hakirya Romema, Jerusalem 91130. Tel: (9722) 512 248. FAX: (9722) 526 818.

DISTRIBUTORS AND PRODUCERS

ALBERT D. MATALON & CO.
(Agency for Columbia TriStar & Twentieth Century Fox), 13 Yona Hanavi St., Tel Aviv 63302. Tel: (9723) 516 2020. FAX: (9723) 516 1888.
CONTACT
Amnon Matalon

FORUM FILM LTD.
P.O. Box 12598, Herzlia Pituah, Industrial Zone 46766. Tel: (9729) 562 111. FAX: (9729) 561 581.

NACHSHON FILMS
22 Harakeuel St., Tel Aviv 66183. Tel: (9723) 356 40015. FAX: (9723) 350 05112.

NOAH FILMS/UNITED INTERNATIONAL PICTURES (UIP)
10 Glickson St., Tel Aviv 63567. Tel: (9723) 200 221. FAX: (9723) 202 071.
CONTACT
Jonathan Chissick

SHAPIRA FILMS
34 Allenby Rd., P.O. Box 4842, Tel Aviv 63325.

SHOVAL-FILM PRODUCTION
32 Allenby Rd., Tel Aviv. Tel: (9723) 659 288. FAX: (9723) 659 289.

TAMUZ FILMS
5 Pinsker St., Tel Aviv. Tel: (9723) 201 512. FAX: (9723) 528 1564.

EXHIBITORS

TAMUZ FILMS
5 Pinsker St., Tel Aviv. Tel: (9723) 201 512. FAX: (9723) 528 1564.

STUDIOS

G. G. ISRAEL STUDIOS
Communications Centre, Neve Ilan, D. N. Harei, Yehuda 90850. Tel: (9722) 349 111. FAX: (9722) 349 9000.

JERUSALEM CAPITAL STUDIOS
P.O. Box 13172, 206 Jaffa Rd., Jerusalem 91131. Tel: (9722) 701 711. FAX: (9722) 381 658.

ORION FILMS
4 Shamgar St., Jerusalem 90058. Tel: (9722) 238 0221. FAX: (9722) 238 0925.

TEL AD JERUSALEM STUDIOS
20 Marcus St., P.O. Box 4111, Jerusalem Theatre Building, Jerusalem 91040. Tel: (9722) 619 988. FAX: (9722) 611 451.

ITALY

Population: 57.6 million.

ASSOCIATIONS & ORGANIZATIONS

ANICA
Viale Regina Margherita 286, Rome 00198. Tel: (396) 4423 1480. FAX: (396) 440 4128.

CINECITTA INTERNATIONAL
Via Tuscolana 1055, Rome 00173. Tel: (396) 722 2824. FAX: (396) 722 3131.

ENTE AUTONOMO GESTIONE CINEMA
Via Tuscolana 1055, Rome 00173. Tel: (396) 722 861. FAX: (396) 722 1883.

PRESIDENZA DEL CONSIGLIO DEI MINISTRI
Via Della Ferracella in Laterano 51, Rome 00184. Tel: (396) 77321. FAX: (396) 759 2602.

DISTRIBUTORS AND PRODUCERS

AB FILM DISTRIBUTORS
Via Monte Zebio 28, Rome 00195. Tel: (396) 321 9554. FAX: (396) 361 3641.

ACADEMY PICTURES
Via F. Ruspoli 8, Rome 00198. Tel: (396) 884 0424. FAX: (396) 841 7043.

ADRIAN CHIESA ENTERPRISES
Via Barnaba Oriani 24A, Rome 00197. Tel: (306) 807 0400. FAX: (306) 8068 7855.

ARTISTI ASSOCIATI INTERNAZIONALE
Via Degli Scipioni 281-283, Rome 00192. Tel: (396) 321 0367. FAX: (396) 321 7245.

BIM DISTRIBUZIONE
Via G. Antonelli 47, Rome 00196. Tel: (396) 323 1057. FAX: (396) 321 1984.

BUENA VISTA INTERNATIONAL ITALIA
Via Palestro 24, Rome 00185. Tel: (396) 445 2269. FAX: (396) 445 1202.

CDI (COMPAGNIA DISTRIBUZIONE INTERNAZIONALE)
Via Saleria 292, Rome 00199. Tel: (309) 854 8821. FAX: (396) 854 1691.

CECCHI GORI GROUP
Via Valadier 42, Rome 00193. Tel: (306) 324 721. FAX: (306) 3247 2300.

CHALLENGE FILM INTERNATIONAL
Via Lazio 9, Rome 00187. Tel: (396) 481 8117. FAX: (396) 482 4890.

CHANCE FILM
Via G. Mercalli 19, Rome 00197. Tel: (396) 808 5041. FAX: (396) 807 0506.

CIDIF
Via Vicenza 5a, Rome 00185. Tel: (396) 446 9636. FAX: (396) 446 9636.

CLEMI CINEMATOGRAFICA
Via Salaria 292, Rome 00199. Tel: (396) 854 8821. FAX: (396) 841 9749.

COLUMBIA TRISTAR FILMS ITALIA
Via Palestro N. 24, Rome 00185. Tel: (396) 494 1196. FAX: (396) 446 9936.

DELTA
Via Elenora Duse 37, Rome 00197. Tel: (396) 808 4458. FAX: (396) 807 9331.

EAGLE PICTURES
Via M. Buonarroti 5, Milan 20149. Tel: (392) 481 4169. FAX: (392) 481 3389.

EDIZIONI EDEN
Via A. Grandi 1, Mazzo Di Rho, Milan 20017. Tel: (392) 9350 9822.

ENRICO GAMBI
Via C. Sul Clitunno 20, Rome 00181. Tel: (396) 788 7746. FAX: (396) 780 6803.

EUPHON TECHNICOLOUR
Via Po 13-15, San Giuliano Milanes 20098. Tel: (392) 9828 0406.

FILMAURO
Via Della Vasca Navale 58, Rome 00146. Tel: (396) 556 0788. FAX: (396) 559 0670.

FULVIA FILM
Via Bruno Nuozzi 36, Rome 00197. Tel: (396) 808 1575. FAX: (396) 808 1510.

GRANATO PRESS
Via Marconi 47, Bologna 40122. Tel: (3951) 237 737.

GRUPPO BEMA
Via N. Martelli 3, Rome 00197. Tel: (396) 808 8551. FAX: (396) 807 5454.

GRUPPO CURTI COMMUNICAZIONE
Via Domenico Cimarosa 18, Rome 00198. Tel: (396) 854 3382. FAX: (396) 855 8105.

IMPERIAL BULLDOG PRODUCTIONS
Via B. Eustachi 12, Milan 20129. Tel: (392) 2952 2363.

INTERNATIONAL MOVIE COMPANY
Lungotevere Flaminio 66, Rome 00196. Tel: (396) 361 0344. FAX: (396) 361 2676.

ISTITUTO LUCE
Via Tuscolana 1055, Rome 00173. Tel: (396) 722 2492. FAX: (396) 722 2493.

ITALIAN INTERNATIONAL FILM
Via Gian Domenico Romagnosi 20, Rome 00196. Tel: (396) 361 1377. FAX: (396) 322 5965.

KINA
Piazza Duomo 16, Milan 20122. Tel: (392) 8646 4102. FAX: (392) 7200 1817.

LIFE INTERNATIONAL
Via Monte Zebio 43, Rome 00195. Tel: (396) 321 5972. FAX: (396) 361 0036.

LUCKY RED
Via Antonio Baiamonti 10, Rome 00195. Tel: (396) 3735 2296. FAX: (396) 3735 2310.

MARGY FILM
Via Orti 2, Milan 20122. Tel: (392) 551 7545. FAX: (392) 545 9918.

MEDUSA FILM
Via Aurelia Antica 422-424, Rome 00165. Tel: (396) 66301. FAX: (396) 663 960.

MFD
Largo A., Ponchielli 6, Rome 00198. Tel: (396) 854 0542. FAX: (396) 854 1691.

MIKADO FILM
Via Victor Pisani 12, Milan 20124. Tel: (392) 6671 1476. FAX: (392) 6671 1488.

MIMA FILMS
Largo V. Alpini 12, Milan 20145. Tel: (392) 349 2860.

MOVIETIME
Via Nicola Ricciotti 11, Rome 00195. Tel: (396) 322 6709. FAX: (396) 3600 0950.

MULTIMEDIA FILM DISTRIBUTION
Via L. Ximenes 21, Florence 50125. Tel: (3955) 225 622. FAX: (3955) 233 6726.

NEMO DISTRIBUZIONE CINEMATOGRAFICA
Via Livigno 50, Rome 00188. Tel: (396) 331 851. FAX: (396) 3367 9491.

NINI GRASSIA COMMUNICATIONS
Via Velletri 49, Rome 00198. Tel: (396) 855 1745. FAX: (396) 844 3572.

NUOVE INIZIATIVE COMMERCIALI SRL
Via Flaminia 872, Rome 00191. Tel: (396) 333 9416. FAX: (396) 333 6367.

PEGASO INTER-COMMUNICATION
L. Gen. Gonzaga del Vodice 4, Rome 00195. Tel: (396) 360 0830. FAX: (396) 3611 13251.

PENTA DISTRIBUZIONE
Via Aurelia Antica 422, Rome 00165. Tel: (396) 663 901. FAX: (396) 663 9040.

ROYAL FILM ENTERPRISES
Via A. Caroncini 47. Rome 00197. Tel: (396) 808 3506.

SACIS
Via Teulada 66, Rome 00195. Tel: (396) 374 981. FAX: (396) 372 3492.

SIRIO FILM
Viale Parioli 28 Int. 1, Rome 00197. Tel: (396) 808 2144. FAX: (396) 808 8748.

SKORPION
Via L. Caro 12-A, Rome 00193. Tel: (396) 324 2223. FAX: (396) 321 0890.

SO CINEMATOGRAFICA
Lungotevere Delle Navi 19, Rome 00196. Tel: (396) 321 5114. FAX: (396) 361 2852.

STARLIGHT
Via Bellerio 30, Milan 20161. Tel: (392) 646 6441. FAX: (392) 646 6444.

SURF FILM
Via Padre Filippini 130, Rome 00144. Tel: (396) 529 3811. FAX: (396) 529 3816

TWENTIETH CENTURY FOX
Largo Amilcare Ponchielli 6, Rome 00198. Tel: (396) 8530 1060. FAX: (396) 8530 0971.
MANAGING DIRECTOR
Osvaldo De Santis

UNITED INTERNATIONAL PICTURES
Via Bissolati 20, Rome 00187. Tel: (396) 482 0626. FAX: (396) 482 0628.
MANAGER
Richard Borg

VARIETY FILMS COMMUNICATIONS
Via Nomentana 257, Rome 00161. Tel: (396) 3600 1409. FAX: (396) 3600 1022.

VISTARAMA
Via Savoia 72, Italy 00198. Tel: (396) 854 6646. FAX: (396) 8535 0050.

WARNER BROS. ITALIA
Via Varesse 16B, Rome 00185. Tel: (396) 446 3191. FAX: (396) 675 1022.

ZENITH DISTRIBUZIONE
Via Soperga 36, Milan 20127. Tel: (392) 261 3207. FAX: (392) 261 0768.

EXHIBITORS

CECCHI GORI GROUP
Via Valadier 42, Rome 00193. Tel: (396) 3247 2236. FAX: (396) 3247 2300.

Number of Screens: 61

CINEMA 5
Via Aurelia Antica 422, Rome 00165. Tel: (396) 663 901. FAX: (396) 6639 0440.

CIRCUITO GERMANI
Piazza Strozzi 2, Florence 50123. Tel: (3955) 295 051.

ERNESTO DI SARRO
Via Soperga 36, Milan 20127. Tel: (392) 260 3207.

ISTITUTO LUCE
Via Tuscolana 1055, Rome 00173. Tel: (396) 722 2492. FAX: (396) 722 2493.

LORENZO VENTAVOLI
Via Pomba 18, Turin 10123. Tel: (3911) 544 083.

LUIGI DE PEDYS
Via Sorpega 43, Milan 20127. Tel: (392) 284 6756.

DAVID QUILLERI
Via Ville Patrizi 10, Rome. Tel: (396) 884 4731.

RAFFAELE GAUDAGNO
Cinema President, Largo Augusto 1, Milan 20122. Tel: (392) 7602 1410. FAX: (392) 7602 2223.

UCI ITALIA SRL
Via Giarezzo No. 4, Milan 20145. Tel: (392) 4855 9029. FAX: (392) 469 4998.
DIRECTOR
Donna Roberts

UGO POGGI
Via Fiume 11, Florence 50123. Tel: (3955) 218 682.

VILLAGE ROADSHOW, LTD.
(For complete listing see Australian branch.)
206 Bourke St., Melbourne, VIC, 3000, Australia. Tel: (613) 96 67 66 66. FAX: (613) 96 39 15 40.

Number of Theatres: 6 (Italy)
Number of Screens: 60 (Italy)

JAPAN

Population: 125.5 million.
Average Ticket Price: $15.

ASSOCIATIONS & ORGANIZATIONS

HI-VISION PROMOTION ASSOCIATION
1-9-6 Sendagaya, Shibuya-ku 151, Tokyo. Tel: (813) 3746 1125. FAX: (813) 3746 1138.

HI-VISION PROMOTION CENTER
Kowa Kawasaki Nishiguchi Bldg. 4F, 66-2, Horikawa-Cho, Saiwai-ku 210, Kanagawa-Ken. Tel: (8144) 541 6331. FAX: (8144) 541 6335.

UNI JAPAN FILM(ASSOCIATION FOR THE DIFFUSION OF JAPANESE FILMS ABROAD)
Nakamura Bldg., 9-13 Ginza 5, Chuo-Ku, Tokyo 104. Tel: (813) 3572 5106. FAX: (813) 3572 8876.

DISTRIBUTORS AND PRODUCERS

ASCII PICTURES
12 Mori Bldg SF. 1-17-3 Toranomon, Minato-ku, Tokyo 105. Tel: (813) 3581 9501. FAX: (813) 3581 9510.

ASIA COORDINATION
505 Premier Nakano, 2-5-4 Chuou, Nakano-Ku, Tokyo 164. Tel: (813) 3360 0704. FAX: (813) 3360 5956.

BUENA VISTA INTERNATIONAL JAPAN
Roppongi DK Bldg., 7-18-23 Roppongi 106, Minato-ku. Tel: (813) 3746 5009. FAX: (813) 3746 0009.

CHANNEL COMMUNICATIONS, INC.
303 Mitsuai Bldg., Take-Kanta, Minato-Ku, Tokyo 108. Tel: (813) 3280 0971. FAX: (813) 3280 0555.

COMMUNICA FILM CORP.
401, 5-1-25 Minami-Aoyama, Minato-Ku, Tokyo 107. Tel: (813) 3409 0431. Telex: 2423210 EVRGRN J. FAX: (813) 3498 1086.

CREATIVE ENTERPRISE INTERNATIONAL INC. (TOKYO)
Villa Bianca 205, 33-12-2 Cho-Me, Jingu-Mae, Shibuya-Ku, Tokyo 150. Tel: (813) 3403 4893. FAX: (813) 3404 3766.

DAIEI
1-1-16 Higashi Shimbashi, Minato-ku 105-8671, Tokyo. Tel: (813) 3573-8717. FAX: (813) 3573 8720.

DELA CORPORATION
Rozan Bldg. 813, 7-15-13, Roppongi, Minato-ku, 106, Tokyo. Tel: (813) 479 0591. FAX: (813) 479 0602.

EURO SPACE
24-8-601 Sakuragaoka-Cho, Shibuya-ku 150, Tokyo. Tel: (813) 3461 0212. FAX: (813) 3770 1179.

GAGA COMMUNICATIONS
East Roppongi Bldg., 3-16-35 Roppongi, Minato-ku, Tokyo 106. Tel: (813) 5410 3507. FAX: (813) 5410 3558.

IWANAMI PRODUCTIONS INC.
3-19-11 Yushima, Bunkyo-Ku, Tokyo 113. Tel: (813) 5688 3551. FAX: (813) 5688 3566.

KAJIMAVISION PRODUCTION CO. LTD.
6-5-13 Akasaka, Minato-Ku, Tokyo 107. Tel: (813) 3582 6661. FAX: (813) 3588 0883.

KIROKU EIGASHA PRODUCTIONS INC.
2-12-1 Yoyogi, Shibuya-Ku, Tokyo 151. Tel: (813) 3370 3386. FAX: (813) 3370 3469.

MARUBENI CORPORATION
4-2, Ohtemachi 1-Chome, Chiyoda-u, Tokyo. Tel: (813) 282 4136. FAX: (813) 3282 4835.

MEDIA INTERNATIONAL CO., LTD.
Koyo Bldg 2F, 1-37-8 Yoyogi, Shibuya-Ku, Tokyo 151. Tel: (3) 3370 6577. FAX: (3) 3370 0243.

MEDIA INTERNATIONAL CORPORATION
2-14-5 Akasaka, Minato-ku, Tokyo 107. Tel: (813) 5561 9571. FAX: (813) 5561 9550/49.

MITSUBISHI CORPORATION
3-1, Marunouchi 2-Chome, Chiyoda-ku, Tokyo 100-86. Tel: (813) 3210 7795. FAX: (813) 3210 7397.

MOTION PICTURE PRODUCERS ASSOCIATION OF JAPAN INC.
Sankei Bldg., Bekkan, 1-7-2 Otemachi, Chiyoda-Ku, Tokyo 100. Tel: (813) 3231 6417. FAX: (813) 3231 6420.

NEXUS (JAPAN), LTD.
47 Poland St., London W1V 3DF. Tel: (0171) 434 9243. FAX: (0171) 437 3720.

NHK INTERNATIONAL, INC.
Daini Kyodo Bldg., 7-13 Udagawacho, Shibuya-Ku, Tokyo 150. Tel: (813) 3464 1823. Telex: 29518 NHKINT J. FAX: (813) 3770 1829.

OPTO-ELECTRONICS MEDIA DEPT.
New Select, Nakamura Bldg., 7th Flr., 5-9-13 Ginza, Chuo-ku. Tel: (813) 3573 7571. FAX: (813) 3572 0139.

ORIENT FILM ASSOCIATES, INC.
Naoki Bldg., 2-11-14 Minami Aoyama, Minato-Ku, Tokyo 107. Tel: (813) 334 792 340. Telex: 26193. FAX: (813) 334 792 319.

SHIBATA ORGANIZATION
2-10-8 Ginza, Chuo-ku, Tokyo. Tel: (813) 3545 3411. FAX: (813) 3545 3519.

SHOCHIKU COMPANY
13-5, Tsukiji, 1-Chome, Chuo-ku 104, Tokyo. Tel: (813) 3542 5551. FAX: (813) 3545 0703.

SONY PICTURES ENTERTAINMENT, JAPAN
Hamamatsucho-TS Bldg. 5F, 8-14, Chome, Hamamatsucho Minato-ku, Tokyo 105. Tel: (813) 5476 8361. FAX: (813) 5473 8369.

TELECOM JAPAN INTERNATIONAL INC.
80 St. Marks Place, New York, NY 10003. Tel: (212) 254 2845. FAX: (212) 254 7845.

TKK ASSOCIATES INC.
Tokyo Bldg., 2-17-3 Takanawa, Minato-Ku, Tokyo 108. Tel: (813) 3447 5241. FAX: (813) 3441 7826.

TOEI COMPANY
2-17, 3-Chome, GinzaJapan, Chuo-ku 104, Tokyo. Tel: (813) 535 7621. FAX: (813) 535 7622.
CHARIMAN & CEO
Shigeru Okada
PRESIDENT & COO
Tan Takaiwa

TOHO INTERNATIONAL (A DIVISION OF TOHO CO., LTD.)
1-8-1, Yurakucho, Chiyoda-ku, Tokyo 100-0006. Tel: (813) 3213 6821. FAX: (813) 3213 6825.

TOHO SEISAKU CO. LTD.
7-7-4 Akasaka, Minato-ku, Tokyo 107. Tel: (813) 3505 7350. FAX: (813) 3505 7357.

TOHO TOWA COMPANY
6-4, Ginza 2-Chome, Chuo-ku, Tokyo 104. Tel: (813) 3562 0109. FAX: (813) 3535 3656.

TV MAN UNION
30-13 Motoyoyogi-Cho, Shibuya-ku, Tokyo. Tel: (813) 5478 1611. FAX: (813) 5478 8141.

TWENTIETH CENTURY FOX (FAR EAST)
Fukide Bldg. 4-1-13 Toranomon, Minato-ku, Tokyo. Tel: (813) 3436 3421. FAX: (813) 3433 5322.

WARNER BROS. THEATRICAL DISTRIBUTION JAPAN
1-2-4 Hamamatsu-Cho, Minato-ku 105, Tokyo. Tel: (813) 5472 8000. FAX: (813) 5472 8029.

WORLD TELEVISION CORPORATION
6F 8-10 Ban Bldg., 8-10-8 Ginza, Chuo-ku, Tokyo 104. Tel: (813) 3571 8047. FAX: (813) 3572 2307.

EXHIBITORS

SHOCHIKU COMPANY
13-5, Tsukiji, 1-Chome, Chuo-ku 104, Tokyo. Tel: (813) 3542 5551. FAX: (813) 3545 0703.

TOEI COMPANY
2-17, 3-Chome, GinzaJapan, Chuo-ku 104, Tokyo. Tel: (813) 535 4641.

TOHO INTERNATIONAL (A DIVISION OF TOHO CO., LTD)
1-8-1, Yurakucho, Chiyoda-ku, Tokyo 100-0006. Tel: (813) 3213 6821. FAX: (813) 3213 6825.

TOHO TOWA COMPANY
6-4, Ginza 2-Chome, Chuo-ku, Tokyo 104. Tel: (813) 3562 0109. FAX: (813) 3535 3656.

UCI JAPAN KK
4F Izumi Akasaka Building, 2-22-24 Akasak, Minato-ku, Tokyo 107. Tel: (813) 3224 3200. FAX: (813) 3224 3212.
DIRECTOR
Adam Gover

Number of Screens: 27

WARNER MYCAL CORP.
2nd Flr., Izumikan Sanban-cho, Bldg. 3-8, Sanban-cho, Chiyoda-ku, Tokyo 102-0075. Tel: (81) 33 26 20 096. FAX: (81) 35 21 02 552.
CONTACT
Yoji Ikushima

Number of Theatres: 31
Number of Screens: 232

Akashi (7), Chigasaki (60, Ebetsu (8), Ebina (7), Fukushima (7), Higahikishiwada (8), Hirosaki (6), Hiroshima (7), Hofu (7), Ichikawamyoden (9), Ishinomaki (7), Itabashi (12), Kamimine (7), Kanazawa (8), Kenoh (7), Kitakami (7), Kuwana (8), Minatomirai (8), Ohi (7), Ohnojo (8), Okyouzuka (8), Otaru (7), Shinyurigaoka (9), Suzuka (7), Takamatsu (7), Takaoka (6), Tobata (8), Toyokawa (7), Utazu (7), Yonezawa (7), Yukarigaoka (8).

LUXEMBOURG

Population: 437 thousand.

EXHIBITORS

KINEPOLIS GROUP
89 Boulevard du Centenaire, B 1020, Brussels. Tel: (322) 474 2600. FAX: (322) 474 2606.www.kinepolis.com

UTOPIA S.A.
45 avenue J.F. Kennedy, L-1855 Luxembourg. Tel: (352) 42 95 111. FAX: (352) 42 95 1191.
CHAIRMAN & MANAGER
Nico Simon
MANAGER
Luc Nothum
FINANCES
Didier Briere

Number of Theatres: 7
Number of Screens: 48

Luxembourg (3), Belgium (3), France (1).

MALAYSIA

Population: 21.8 million.

STATE ASSOCIATIONS

MALAYSIAN MINISTRY OF INFORMATION
Angkasapuri, 50610 Kuala Lumpur. Tel: (603) 282 5333. FAX: (603) 282 1255.

MINISTRY OF INTERNATIONAL TRADE & INDUSTRY
Block 10, Government Offices Complex, Jalan Duta 50622, Kuala Lumpur. Tel: (603) 254 0033. FAX: (603) 255 0827.

EXHIBITORS & DISTRIBUTORS

(Local addresses and telephone numbers are listed where available, otherwise please contact the corporate headquarters below.)

CATHAY ORGANISATION (M) SDN BHD
1 Jalan SS22/19 Damansara Jaya, 47400 Petaling Jaya, Selangor, Malaysia 47400. Tel: (603) 71 95 666. FAX: (603) 71 92 179. (A branch of Plantations Berhad, 17th Flr., Wisma Jerneh, 38 Jalan Sultan Ismail, 50250 Kuala Lumpur, Malaysia.)
CHAIRMAN
Jen (R) Tan Sri Dato Mohd Ghazali Seth
CHIEF EXECUTIVE
Ong Te Cheong
EXECUTIVE DIRECTOR
Chuah Teong Tor

Number of Theatres: 34
Number of Screens: 47

GOLDEN COMMUNICATIONS
8 Hammer Hill Rd., Kowloon, Hong Kong. Tel: (852) 726 5541. FAX: (852) 351 1683.

TANJONG GOLDEN VILLAGE
Level 1, Bukit Raja Shopping Centre, Persiaran Bukit Raja 2, Bandar Baru Klang, 41150 Klang, Malaysia. Tel: (603) 344-1688.

Number of Screens: 47

TANJONG PLC
17th Flr., Menara Boustead, Jln Raja Chulan, 50200 Kuala Lumpur. Tel: (603) 244 3388. FAX: (603) 244 3388.

TWENTIETH CENTURY FOX FILM
Sendirian Berhad, 22 Jalan Padang Walter Grenier off Jalan Imbi, 55100 Kuala Lumpur. Tel: (603) 242 4396. FAX: (603) 248 3129.

UNITED INTERNATIONAL PICTURES
No. 22 Jalan SS26/6, Taman Mayang Jaya, 47301 Petaling Jaya, Selangor, Malaysia. Tel: (603) 704 4899. FAX: (603) 703 7833.
MANAGER
Nicholas Yong.

VILLAGE ROADSHOW, LTD.
(For complete listing see Australian branch.)
206 Bourke St., Melbourne, VIC, 3000, Australia. Tel: (613) 96 67 66 66. FAX: (613) 96 39 15 40.

Number of Theatres: 40 (Malaysia)
Number of Screens: 145 (Malaysia)

WARNER BROS.
24 Jalan Padang Walter Grenier off Jalan Imbi, 55100 Kuala Lumpur. Tel: (603) 242 3669. FAX: (603) 248 9670.

MEXICO

Population: 100.4 million.
Average Ticket Price: $0.30–$3.95.

DISTRIBUTORS

COLUMBIA TRISTAR FILMS DE MEXICO
Av. Ejercito Nacional, 343-3er Piso, Col. Granada, Delegacion Miguel Hidalgo, Mexico D.F. 11520. Tel: (525) 531 1428. FAX: (525) 545 1986.

UNITED INTERNATIONAL PICTURES
Apartado Postal No. 70 bis, Mexico D.F. 06000. Tel: (525) 255 5727. FAX: (525) 255 5657.

EXHIBITORS

CINEMASTAR LUXURY THEATRES, INC.
12230 El Camino Real, Ste. 320, San Diego, Calif., U.S. 92130. Tel: (619) 509-2777. FAX: (619) 509-9425.
CHAIRMAN & CEO
Jack Crosby
PRESIDENT & COO
Frank Moreno
CFO
Norman Dowling
EXECUTIVE V.P.
Neal Austrian Jr.

Number of Screens: 10

CINEMARK USA, INC.
Lateral Del Rio Churubusco, Esq. Canal De Miramontes, Col. Country Club, Mexico D.F. 0422 011.
7502 Greenville Ave., Ste. 800, Dallas, TX 75231. (214) 860-0823. FAX: (214) 696-3946. International: FAX: (214) 860-0792.
CHAIRMAN & CEO
Lee Roy Mitchell
PRESIDENT
Alan Stock
PRESIDENT, CINEMARK INTERNATIONAL
Tim Warner
DIRECTOR, MEXICO
Enrique Benhumea

Number of Theatres: 14
Number of Screens: 151
Breakdown of screens: Acapulco: Oceanic 2000 (8); Aguascalientes: Expo Plaza (10); Chihuahua: Plaza Hollywood (12); Guadalajara: Plaza Sol (12); Hermosillo: Metro Centro (10); Irapuato: Movies (10); Juarez: Cinemark (10); Mexico City: Centro Cultural (12), Pedregal Plaza Cinemark (10), Rojo Gomez, Villacoapa (15); Monterey: Plaza Le Fe (10); Quertaro: Cinemark (12); Reynosa: Cinemark (10); Tijuana: Minarete (10).

CINEMEX/CADENA MEXICANA DE EXHIBICION S.A. DE C.V. CINEMEX
Blvd. Manuel Avila Camacho No. 40 Piso 16, Col. Lomas de Chapultepec, Mexico 11000 DF. Tel: (525) 201-5800. FAX: (525) 201-5813.
CO-DIRECTOR GENERAL
Matthew Heyman
CO-DIRECTOR GENERAL
Adolfo Fastlicht
CO-DIRECTOR GENERAL
Miguel Angel Davila

COMPANIA OPERADORA DE TEATROS S.A. DE C.V. COTSA
Insurgentes Sur 453, Col. Condesa, Mexico D.F.C.P. 06140. Tel: (525) 264-6010.
GENERAL DIRECTOR
Pablo Hernandez

Number of Theatres: 13
Number of Screens: 64
Mexico City (9), Colima (1), Cordova, Veracruz (1), Jalapa, Vercruz (1), Orizaba, Veracruz (1).

COTSA
Insurgentes Sur #453, 2nd Piso, Mexico DF. Tel: (525) 264-6010.

Number of Screens: 64

ORGANIZACION RAMIREZ S.A. DE C.V. MULTICINEMAS & CINEPOLIS
Avenida Enrique Ramirez Miguel #701, Fraccionamiento Las Americas, Morelia, Michoacan 58270. (524) 3220 526 229, (524) 3220 505. FAX: (524) 3220 511.
PRESIDENT
Enrique Ramirez Villalon
COO
Alejandro Ramirez Magana
CFO
Enrique Ramirez Magana

Number of Screens: 670

NETHERLANDS

Population: 15.9 million.

ASSOCIATIONS & ORGANIZATIONS

AMSTERDAMSE ARTS COUNCIL
Kloveniersburgwal 47, Amsterdam 1011 JX. Tel: (3120) 626 4315. FAX: (3120) 626 7584.

AMSTERDAM FUND FOR THE ARTS
Keizerstraat 223, Amsterdam 1016 DV. Tel: (3120) 624 2443. FAX: (3120) 624 6053.

ASSOCIATION FOR FILM & TELEVISION PROGRAMME MAKERS (NBF)
Jan Luykenstraat 2, Amsterdam 1071 CM. Tel: (3120) 664 6588. FAX: (3120) 664 3707.

ASSOCIATION OF DUTCH FILM THEATRES
2e der Helstraat 38, 1072 PE Amsterdam. Tel: (3120) 671 67 76. FAX: (3120) 673 08 04.

AUDIOVISUAL PLATFORM/MEDIA DESK NETHERLANDS
Postbus 256, Sumatralaan 45, Hilversum 1200 AG. Tel: (3135) 623 8641. FAX: (3135) 621 8541.

CARTOON
E Hoogt 4, Utrecht 3512 GW. Tel: (3130) 233 1733. FAX: (3130) 233 1079.

CIRCLE OF DUTCH FILM CRITICS (KNF)
Snelliuslaasn 78, Hilversum 1222 TG. Tel: (3135) 685 6115.

COMMISSARIAAT VOOR DE MEDIA
Emmastraat 51-53, P.O. Box 1426, Hilversum 1200 BK. Tel: (3135) 672 1721. FAX: (3135) 672 1722.

DUTCH ARTS COUNCIL
RJ Schimmelpennincklaan 3, The Hague 2517 JN. Tel: (3170) 346 9619. FAX: (3170) 361 4727.

DUTCH CULTURAL BROADCASTING PROMOTION FUND
Korte Leidsedwarsstraat 12, Amsterdam 1017 RC. Tel: (3120) 623 3901. FAX: (3120) 625 7456.

DUTCH FILM & TELEVISION ACADEMY
Ite Boeremastratt 1, Amsterdam 1054. Tel: (3120) 683 0206. FAX: (3120) 612 6266.

DUTCH FILM MUSEUM
Vondelpark 3, Amsterdam 1071 AA. Tel: (3120) 589 1400. FAX: (3120) 683 3401.

DUTCH FOUNDATION FOR AUDIOVISUAL CONGRESSES (SAM)
Honongstraat 14B, P.O. Box 262, Hilversum 1200 AG. Tel: (3135) 624 5589. FAX: (3135) 623 8208.

FILM INFORMATION & DOCUMENTATION SERVICE (FID)
Postbus 805, Utrecht 3500 AV. Tel: (3130) 332 328. FAX: (3130) 334 018.

FILM MAKERS SOCIETY OF THE NETHERLANDS (GNS)
P.O. Box 581, Amsterdam 1000. Tel: (3120) 676 5088. FAX: (3120) 676 5837.

HOLLAND FILM PROMOTION
Jan Luykenstraat 2, Amsterdam 1071 CM. Tel: (3120) 664 4649. FAX: (3120) 664 9171.

NEDERLANDS FEDERATION FOR CINEMTOGRAPHY
Jan Luykenstraat 2, P.O. Box 75048, Amsterdam 1070 AA. Tel: (3120) 679 9261. FAX: (3120) 675 0398.

NEDERLANDS INSTITUTE FOR AUDIOVISUAL MEDIA
Neuyskade 94, P.O. Box 97734, The Hague 2509 GC. Tel: (3170) 356 4107. FAX: (3170) 364 7756

THE PRODUCERS WORKSHOP (RBS)
Aalbrechtskade 129, Rotterdam 3023 JE. Tel: (3110) 425 7477. FAX: (3110) 425 7193.

SOURCES
Jan Luykenstraat 92, Amsterdam 1071 CT. Tel: (3120) 672 0801. FAX: (3120) 672 0399.

STICHTING FUURLAND/FILMKRANT
Prinsengracht 770-IV, Amsterdam. Tel: (3120) 623 0121. FAX: (3120) 627 5923.

UNITED AUDIOVISUAL PRODUCTION COMPANIES (UAP)
c/o H. Wennink, Mozartlaan 27, Hilversum 1217 CM. Tel: (3135) 623 8677. FAX: (3135) 623 8674.

VEVAM
P.O. Box 581, Amsterdam 1000 AN. Tel: (3120) 676 5088. FAX: (3120) 676 5837.

DISTRIBUTORS AND PRODUCERS

ARGUS FILM
P.O. Box 18269, Amsterdam 1001 ZD. Tel: (3120) 625 4585. FAX: (3120) 626 8978. email: argusfilm@xs4all.nl

BIOSCOOP EXPLOITATIE MINERVA BV
P.O. Box 7220, Amsterdam 1007 JE. Tel: (3120) 644 6823. FAX: (3120) 644 8946.

BUENA VISTA INTERNATIONAL (NETHERLANDS)
P.O. Box 349, Badhoevedorp 1170 AH. (3120) 658 0300. FAX: (3120) 659 3349.

CINEMA INTERNATIONAL
P.O. Box 9228, Amsterdam 1006 AE. Tel: (3120) 617 7575. FAX: (3120) 617 7434.

CINEMIEN FILM AND VIDEO DISTRIBUTORS
Entrepotdok 66, Amsterdam 1018 AD. Tel: (3120) 625 8857. FAX: (3120) 620 9857.

CNR FILM RELEASING
Amstellandlaan 78, Weesp 1382 CH. Tel: (3129) 446 1800.

COLUMBIA TRISTAR FILMS
Van Eeghenst 70, Amsterdam 1071 GK. Tel: (3120) 673 6611. FAX: (3120) 573 7656.

CONCORDE FILM BENELUX
Lange Voorhout 35, Den Haag 2514 EC. Tel: (3170) 3605810. FAX: (3170) 360 4925.

THE FILM COMPANY AMSTERDAM
Entrepotdok 66, Amsterdam 1018 AD. Tel: (3120) 620 9504. FAX: (3120) 620 9857.

HUNGRY EYE PICTURES
Duivendrechtsekade 82, Amsterdam 1096. Tel: (3120) 668 6126. FAX: (3120) 668 3452.

INTERNATIONAL ART FILM
Vodelpark 3, Amsterdam 1071 AA. Tel: (3120) 589 1418. FAX: (3120) 683 3401.

KINEPOLIS GROUP
89 Boulevard dy Centenaire, B 1020 Brussels. (322) 474 2600. FAX: (322) 474 2606. www.kinepolis.com
DIRECTOR OPERATIONS, NETHERLANDS
Boudewijn Muts

LAVA FILM DISTRIBUTION & SALES
Korte Leidsedwarstraat 12, Amsterdam 1017 RC. Tel: (3120) 625 5442. FAX: (3120) 620 2426.

MELIOR FILMS
Steynlaan 8, Hilversum 1217 JS. Tel: (3135) 624 5542. FAX: (3135) 623 5906.

METEOR/POLYGRAM FILM
P.O. Box 432, Hilversum 1217 JS. Tel: (3135) 626 1500. FAX: (3135) 624 8418.

MOONLIGHT FILMS
Geerdinkhof 236, Amsterdam 1103 PZ. Tel: (3120) 695 3811. FAX: (3120) 588 4343.

THE MOVIES ARTHOUSES & FILM DISTRIBUTION
Haarlemmerdjik 161, Amsterdam 1013 KH. Tel: (3120) 624 5790. FAX: (3120) 620 6758.

NETHERLANDS INSTITUTE FOR ANIMATION FILM
P.O. Box 9358, Tillburg 5000 HJ. Tel: (3113) 535 4555. FAX: (3113) 535 0953.

NFM/IAF
Vondelpark 3, Amsterdam 1071 AM. Tel: (3120) 589 1418. FAX: (3120) 683 3401.

NIS FILM DISTRIBUTION HOLLAND
Abba Paulownastraat 76, The Hague 2518 BJ. Tel: (3170) 356 4208. FAX: (3170) 356 4681.

POLYGRAM FILMED ENTERTAINMENT
P.O. Box 432, Hilversum 1200 AK. Tel: (3135) 626 1700. FAX: (3135) 624 8418.

SHOOTING STAR FILM COMPANY
Prinsengracht 546, Amsterdam 1017 KK. Tel: (3120) 624 7272. FAX: (3120) 626 8533.

STICHTING STEMRA
Prof. E. M. Meijerslaan 3, 1183 AV Amstelveen. Tel: (3120) 5407911. FAX: (3120) 5407496.

THREE LINES PICTURES
Laapersveld 68, Hilversum 1213 VB. Tel: (3135) 623 0555. FAX: (3135) 623 9966.

TWENTIETH CENTURY FOX
Mozartlaan 27, Hilversum 1217 CM. Tel: (3135) 622 2111. FAX: (3135) 623 9966.

TWIN FILM
Sarphatistraat 183, Amsterdam 1018 GG. Tel: (3120) 6228206. FAX: (3120) 6248729.

UNITED DUTCH FILM COMPANY
Jan Luykenstraat 5-7, Amsterdam 1071 CJ. Tel: (3120) 675 7774. FAX: (3120) 675 7754.

UNITED INTERNATIONAL PICTURES
Willemsparkweg 112, Amsterdam 1071 HN. Tel: (3120) 662 2991. FAX: (3120) 662 3240. Manager: Max van Praag.

WARNER BROS.
De Boelelaan 16 3H, Amsterdam 1083 HJ. Tel: (3120) 541 1211. FAX: (3120) 644 9001.

EXHIBITORS

ACTUEEL BIOSCOOPEXPLOITATIE B.V.
Potterstraat 30 - 4611 NJ Bergen, op Zoom, Netherlands. Tel: (31) 16 42 54 886.
Number of Screens: 5

A.E.M.M. KOOPAL-WASKOWSKY
P.O. Box 1194 - 4801 BD Breda.
Number of Screens: 5

ASSOCIATION OF DUTCH FILM THEATRES
2E Der Helstraat 38, Amsterdam 1072 PE. Tel: (3120) 671 6776. FAX: (3120) 673 0804.

A.TH. ABELN
P.O. Box 82 -7890 AB, Klazienaveen. Tel: (31) 59 13 12798. FAX: (31) 59 13 18426.
Number of Screens: 5

BIOSCOOPEXPLOITATIE J.M. PUNT HEERHUGOWAARD B.V.
P.O. Box 2071 - 7500 CB ,Heerhugowaard. Tel: (31) 72 57 43 344. FAX: (31) 72 57 42 437.
Number of Screens: 7

BIOSCOOPEXPLOITATIEMAATSCHAP-PIJ CINEX B.V.
P.O. Box 2071 - 7500 CB, Enschede. Tel: (31) 53 43 23 552. FAX: (31) 53 43 23 562.
Number of Screens: 5

BIOSCOOPONDERNEMING AF WOLFF B.V.
Postbus 777, 3500 AT Utrecht. Tel: (31) 30 233-1312
Number of Screens: 27

B.V. BIOSCOOP EXPLOITATIE MINERVA
Kromme Mijdrechstraat 110 - 1079 LD, Amsterdam. Tel: (31) 20 64 46 823. FAX: (31) 20 64 48 946. email: info@minervagroup.nl
Number of Screens: 43
Arnhem, Alkmaar, Breda, Eindhoven, Deventer,Venlo, Zwolle, Zaandam, Tilburg, Haarlem, Maastricht.

B.V. 'DE NIEUWE BUITENSOCIETEIT'
Stationsplein 1 - 8011 CW Zwolle. Tel: (31) 38 42 60 260. FAX: (31) 38 43 60.
Number of Screens: 7

B.V. UTRECHTSE FILMONDERNEMING UFIO
Postbus 777 - 3500 AT Utrecht. Tel: (31) 30 23 1312. FAX: (31) 30 23 15 2276.
Number of Screens: 12

DE HEER R. VAN STEEN
Binnenwatersloot 1 - 2611 BJ Delft. Tel: (31) 15 21 43 426. FAX: (31) 1521 44 922.
Number of Screens: 5

JOGCHEM'S THEATERS BV
Veenestraat 31, 3751 GE Bunschoten, P.O. Box 127, 3750 GC Bunschoten. Tel: (31) 33 29 84 884. FAX: (31) 33 29 84 908.
MANAGING DIRECTOR & OWNER
J. Van Dommelen
MANAGING DIRECTOR & OWNER
W. Van Dommelen
Number of Screens: 46
Alphen a/d Rijn, Amerefoort, Apeldoorn, Arnhem, Dordrecht, Eindhove, Hilversum, Hertogenbosch, Nijmegen.

THE MOVIES ARTHOUSES & FILM DISTRIBUTION
Haarlemmerdjik 161, Amsterdam 1013 KH. Tel: (3120) 624 5790. FAX: (3120) 620 6758.

NEW GALAXY CINEMAS
P.O. Box 128, Walter Nisbeth Rd., 37, Philipsburg, St. Maarten, Dutch Antilles. Tel: (599) 525 871. FAX: (599) 523 425.
CONTACTS
G. Pelgrum
M. Hodge
T. Heyliger

PATHE CINEMAS
P.O. Box 75948, 1070 AX, Amsterdam. Tel: (31) 20 57 51 751. FAX: (31) 20 57 51 777.
MANAGING DIRECTOR
Lauge Nielsen

Number of Theatres: 12
Number of Screens: 66
Amsterdam (4), Eindhoven (1), Groningen (1), Rotterdam (2), The Hague (3), Utrecht (1).

POLYFILM ALMERE B.V.
P.O. Box 5 - Lelystad 8200 AA. Tel: (31) 320.24 6506. FAX: (31) 320 28 0488.

Number of Screens: 17

UNITED DUTCH FILM COMPANY
Jan Luykenstraat 5-7, Amsterdam 1071 CJ. Tel: (3120) 675 7774. FAX: (3120) 675 7754.

WARNER–MORGAN CREEK–CHARGEURS CINEMAS
De Boelelaan 16, Amsterdam 1083. Tel: (4620) 541 1211. FAX: (4620) 644 9001.

WOLFF CINEMA GROEP
P.O. Box 777 - 3500 AT Utrecht. Tel: (31) 23 32312. FAX: (31) 30 23 15227. email: woff@bioswolff.nl

Number of Screens: 37.
Haarlem, Enschede, Huizen, Tilburg, Groningen, Utrecht, Nieuwegein.

NEW ZEALAND

Population: 3.8 million.
Screens: 265.

ASSOCIATIONS AND ORGANIZATIONS

MANU AUTE
P.O. Box 38-141, Petone, Wellington. Tel: (644) 385 9387. FAX: (644) 384 2580.

NEW ZEALAND FEDERATION OF FILM SOCIETIES INC.
P.O. Box 9544, Te Aro, Wellington. Tel: (644) 385 0162. FAX: (644) 801 7304.

NEW ZEALAND FILM ARCHIVE
Corner Cable St. and Jervois Quay, P.O. Box 9544, Wellington. Tel: (644) 384 7647. FAX: (644) 384 9719.

NEW ZEALAND FILM COMMISSION
Flr. 2, Film Centre, Corner Cable St. and Jervois Quay, Wellington. Tel: (644) 385 9754. FAX: (644) 384 9719.

QE II ARTS COUNCIL OF NZ
Old Public Trust Bldg., P.O. Box 3806, Wellington. Tel: (644) 473 0880. FAX: (644) 471 2865.

DISTRIBUTORS AND PRODUCERS

ENDEAVOUR ENTERTAINMENT
P.O. Box 68-445, Auckland. Tel: (649) 378 1900. FAX: (649) 378 1905.

EVERARD FILMS
P.O. Box 3664, Auckland 1. Tel: (649) 302 1193. FAX: (649) 302 1192.

FIRST TRAINING
P.O. Box 17096, Auckland. Tel: (649) 579 1332. FAX: (649) 579 5113.

FOOTPRINT FILMS
P.O. Box 1852, Auckland. Tel: (649) 309 8388. FAX: Tel: (649) 373 4722.

UNITED INTERNATIONAL PICTURES
P.O. Box 105263, Auckland. Tel: (649) 379 6269. FAX: (649) 379 6271.

WARNER BROS (NZ)
P.O. Box 8687, Mt. Eden, Auckland. Tel: (649) 377 5223. FAX: (649) 309 2795.

EXHIBITORS

EVERARD FILMS
P.O. Box 3664, Auckland 1. Tel: (649) 302 1193. FAX: (649) 302 1192.

HOYTS CINEMAS
(For additional listings, please see Australia, Chile & Belgium)
44, 47 Wakefield St., Auckland. Tel: (649) 303 2736. FAX: (649) 307 0011.
GENERAL MANAGER
Wilfred Steiner

Number of Theatres: 15
Number of Screens: 106

VILLAGE FORCE CINEMAS
82 Symonds St., P.O. Box 2384, Auckland, New Zealand. Tel: (649) 309-9137.

Number of Screens: 70

VILLAGE ROADSHOW, LTD.
(For complete listing see Australian branch.)
206 Bourke St., Melbourne, VIC, 3000, Australia. Tel: (613) 96 67 66 66. FAX: (613) 96 39 15 40.

Number of Theatres: 40 (New Zealand)
Number of Screens: 139 (New Zealand)

WELLINGTON FILM SOCIETY
P.O. Box 1584, Wellington. Tel: (644) 384 6817. FAX: (644) 384 6248.

NORWAY

Population: 4.5 million.
Screens: 630.
Average Ticket Price: $5.62.

ASSOCIATIONS & ORGANIZATIONS

NORSK FILMFORBUND
Storengvn 8 B, Jar N-1342. Tel: (47) 2259 1000. FAX: (47) 2212 4865.

NORSK FILMINSTITUTT
Grev Wedelsplass 1, P.O. Box 482 Sentrum, Oslo N-0105. Tel: (47) 2242 8740. FAX: (47) 2233 2277.

NORSK FILMKLUBBFORBUND
Teatergata 3, Oslo N-0180. Tel: (47) 2211 4217.

NORSK FILMKRITIKERLAG
Norwegian Society of Film Critics, Radhusgata 7, N-0151 Oslo 1. Tel: (47) 2241 9409. FAX: (47) 2242 0356.

DISTRIBUTORS AND PRODUCERS

ACTION FILM
Valerenggata 47, P.O. Box 9343, Valerenga, Oslo N-0610. Tel: (47) 2267 3131. FAX: (47) 2267 3005.

ARTHAUS
Teatergaten 3, Oslo N-0180. Tel: (47) 2211 2612. FAX: (47) 2220 7981.

BV-FILM INTERNATIONAL
N-4262, Avaldnsnes. Tel: (47) 5284 3544. FAX: (47) 5284 3575.

EGMONT FILM
P.O. Box 417, Asker N-1370. Tel: (47) 6690 4121. FAX: (47) 6690 4175.

EUROPAFILM
Stortingsgt 30, Oslo N-0161. Tel: (47) 2283 4290. FAX: (47) 2283 4151, Mobile: 9202 1017.

FIDALGO
P.O. Box 2054 Posebyen, Kristiansand N-4602. Tel: (47) 3802 4004. FAX: (47) 3802 2354.

HOLLYWOOD FILM
Baneviksgt 7, Stavanger N-4014. Tel: (47) 5153 4045. FAX: (47) 5152 7398.

KIKU VISUAL PRODUCTIONS
Gange Rolvsgt 1, Oslo N-0273. Tel: (47) 2244 9650. FAX: (47) 2244 5098, Mobile: 9424 5294.

KOMMUNENES FILM-CENTRAL
Nedre Voligt 9, Oslo N-0158. Tel: (47) 2241 4325. FAX: (47) 2242 1469

NORSK FILM DISTRIBUTION
Stortingsgt 12, Oslo N-0161. Tel: (47) 2242 3600. FAX: (47) 2242 2313.

ROYAL FILM
Hedmarksgt 15, Oslo N-0658. Tel: (47) 2268 5140. FAX: (47) 2219 7393.

SF NORGE
P.O. Box 6868 St Olavs Plass, Grensen 3, Oslo N-0130. Tel: (47) 2233 4750. FAX: (47) 2242 7293.

UNITED INTERNATIONAL PICTURES
Hegdehaugsvn 27, P.O. Box 7134, Homansbyen, Oslo N-0307. Tel: (47) 2256 6115. FAX: (47) 2256 7181.

WARNER BROS (NORWAY)
Oscarsgt 55, P.O. Box 7053, Homansbyen, Oslo N-0258. Tel: (47) 2243 1800. FAX: (47) 2255 4683.

EXHIBITOR ASSOCIATION

NATIONAL ASSOCIATION OF MUNICIPAL CINEMAS
Kongensgt. 23 0153, Oslo 1. Tel: (47) 2233 0530. FAX: (47) 2242 8949.

EXHIBITORS

FREDERIKSTAD KINEMATOGRAFER
Boks 383, 1601 Frederikstad. FAX: (47) 6931 0615.

Number of Theatres: 3

HAUGESUND KINEMATOGRAFER
Boks 488, 5501 Haugesund. FAX: (47) 5271 3986.
Number of Theatres: 5

KRISTIANSAND KINO
Boks 356, 4601 Kristiansand. FAX: (47) 3802 0390.
Number of Theatres: 6

OSLO KINEMATOGRAPHER
P.O. Box 1584, Stortingsgt 16, 0161, Oslo N-0118. Tel: (47) 2242 7154. FAX: (47) 2282 4368.
Number of Screens: 29

SANDNES KINEMATOGRAFER
Boks 14, 4301 Sandnes. FAX: (47) 5566 8872.
Number of Theatres: 3

SANDREW METRONOME FILM AB
P.O. Box 1178, N-0107, Oslo, Norway.

STRAVANGER KINEMATOGRAPHER
Boks 194, 4001 Stravanger. FAX: (47) 5150 7016.
Number of Theatres: 8

TROMSO KINO
Boks 285, 9001 Tromso. FAX: (47) 7768 3570.
Number of Theatres: 2

TRONDHEIM KINO
Prinsensgt. 2B, Trondheim N-7013. Tel: (47) 7254 7369. FAX: (47) 7352 2550.
Number of Theatres: 13

PAKISTAN

Population: 141.5 million.
Average Ticket Price: varies widely between Rs .10—Rs. 50.

ASSOCIATION & ORGANIZATIONS

THE CENTRAL BOARD OF FILM CENSORS
Street No. 55-F, Blue Area, Islamabad. Tel: (9251) 920-4387. FAX: (9251) 920-4338.

THE NATIONAL FILM DEVELOPMENT CORPORATION LTD.
NAFDEC Complex, Blue Area, Islamabad. Tel: (9251) 821 154. FAX: (9251) 221 863.

PAKISTAN FILM DISTRIBUTORS' ASSOCIATION
Geeta Bhawan, Lakshmi Chowk, Lahore. Tel: (9242) 58785.

PAKISTAN FILM EXHIBITORS' ASSOCIATION
National Auto Plaza, C Block, 3rd Flr., Marston Road, Karachi. Tel.: (9221) 772-7764.

PAKISTAN FILM PRODUCERS' ASSOCIATION
Regal Cinema Building, The Mall, Lahore. Tel.: (9242) 322 904.

PAKISTAN MOTION PICTURE INVESTORS' ASSOC.
National Auto Plaza, 3rd Flr., C-Block, Marston Road, Karachi. Tel: (9221) 772 7764.

IMPORTERS

AJRAK ENTERTAINMENT
357 Hotel Metropole, Karachi. Tel: (9221) 567-0313, 567-1046. FAX: (9221) 568 4377.

AL HAVIZ CORPORATION
Al Hafiz Mansion, 11 Royal Park, Lahore. (9242) 636-3484.

CARRY-ON FILMS
Moon Bldg., 4 Royal Park, Lahore. Tel: (9242) 722 2543.

CLASSIC PICTURES
Ismail Building, 5 Royal Park, Lahore. (9242) 637-3018.

CONTINENTAL TRADERS
Ex-Rally Bros. Bldg., Talpur Rd., Karachi. Tel: (9221) 241 3254. FAX: (9221) 243 7451.

EVERLAST PICTURES
Haroon Mansion, Royal Park, Lahore. (9242) 636-3148.

GOLDEN BIRD PICTURES
1, Abbot Road, Lahore. (9242) 722-2138.

GOLDEN EAGLE PICTURES
Shaikh Building, Royal Park, Lahore. (9242) 722-2279.

HEENA FILMS
Dar Chambers, Royal Park, Lahore. (9242) 631-1964.

JAVED PICTURES
Gaba Building, Royal Park, Lahore. (9242) 722-3051.

MANDVIWALA ENTERTAINMENT
Nishat Cinema Bldg., M.A. Jinnah Rd., Karachi. Tel: (9221) 721 9505, 722-3535/6. FAX: (9221) 722 7259.

PAKISTAN INTERNATIONAL CORPORATION
Lyric Cinema Bldg., Garden Rd., Karachi. Tel: (9221) 772 7273.

PARAMOUNT COMMUNICATIONS
Marston Road, Karachi. Tel: (9221) 777 8165. FAX: (9221) 568 0981.

PULSE GLOBAL COMMUNICATION
Plot 12, Block 7 & 8, Tipu Sultan Rd., Karachi. Tel: (9221) 453 5001.

STERLING INTERNATIONAL
Paradise Building, Near Passport Office, Saddar, Karachi. (9221) 566-1412, 526 280.

TEE JEES ENTERPRISES
367 Hotel Metropole, Karachi. Tel: (9221) 522 540.

ZEE RAY ENTERPRISES
209 Hotel Metropole, Karachi. Tel: (9221) 414 089. FAX: (9221) 568 0671.

EXHIBITORS

AFSHAN CINEMA
Marston Rd., Karachi. Tel: (9221) 772 4344.

ALFALAH CINEMA
The Mall, Lahore. Tel: (9242) 630 1551.

ANMOL CINEMA
Lahore. Tel: (242) 511-0615.

BAMBINO CINEMA
Garden Rd., Karachi Tel: (9221) 772 9656.

CAPRI CINEMA
M.A. Jinnah Rd., Karachi. Tel: (9221) 721 9904.

GULISTAN CINEMA
Abbot Rd., Lahore. Tel: (9242) 631 3110.

LYRIC CINEMA
Garden Rd., Karachi. Tel: (9221) 772 7274.

MUBARAK CINEMA
Lahore. Tel: (9242) 630-2308.

NAFDEC CINEMA
Blue Area, Islamabad.

NAGINA CINEMA
Lahore. Tel: (9242) 722-6220.

NISHAT CINEMA
M.A. Jinnah Rd., Karachi. Tel: (9221) 721 9505.

ODEON CINEMA
The Mall, Lahore.

PLAZA CINEMA
Queens Rd., Lahore. Tel: (9242) 630 3122.

RATTAN CINEMA
McLeod Rd., Lahore. Tel: (9242) 724-3383.

REGAL CINEMA
The Mall, Lahore. Tel: (9242) 724 9477.

SANGEET CINEMA
Shadra, Lahore. Tel: (9242) 274-4290/

SHABISTAN CINEMA
Lahore. (9242) 636-0731.

SHABISTAN CINEMA
Muree Road, Rawalpindi. Tel: 70 625.

STAR CINEMA
Garden Rd., Karachi. Tel: (9221) 772 8787.

PANAMA

Population: 2.8 million.

EXHIBITORS

SAVOY LANE FILMS, INC.
Via Espana, Edificio Domino, 1er Piso, Oficina 26, P.O. Box 6-4911, Zona 6, Panama. Tel: (507) 262-6585. FAX: (507) 264-1805.
DIRECTOR
Enrique Martin
GENERAL MANAGER
Lucio Marcon
MANAGER (PANAMA)
Victor Chizmar

PHILIPPINES

Population: 81.2 million.

DISTRIBUTORS & PRODUCERS

COLUMBIA PICTURES INDUSTRIES, INC.
Rooms 306-308, Philippine President Lines Bldg., 1000 United Nations Ave., Ermita, Metro Manila 1000. Tel: (632) 521 1381. FAX: (632) 521 3684. Manager: Victor R. Cabrera

MEVER FILMS, INC.
9th Flr., Ave. Theatre Bldg., Rizal Ave., Manila.

UNITED INTERNATIONAL PICTURES
Room 310, Philippine Presidential Lines Bldg., 1000 United Nations Ave., Ermita Metro Manila 1000. Tel: (632) 509304. FAX: (632) 521 6133.
MANAGER
Tristan Leveriza

WARNER BROS.
Room 311, Philippine Presidential Lines Bldg., 1000 United Nations Ave., Ermita Metro Manila 1000. Tel: (632) 596 991. FAX: (632) 521 2673.
MANAGER
Lucas Pasiliao.

EXHIBITORS

MEDEIA FILMES
Rua Tomas Ribeiro 8-20, 1150 Lisboa, Portugal. Tel: (351) 1317-2029.
Number of Screens: 37

WARNER LUSOMUNDO
Rua Luciano Cordeiro 113, 1150 Lisboa, Portugal. Tel: (351) 1315-0860.
Number of Screens: 80

WEST AVENUE THEATER CORPORATION
The SM City, North Ave. cor. EDSA, Quezon City. Tel: (632) 975 452. FAX: (632) 924 4274.
EXECUTIVE V.P.
Engr. Hans T. Sy
OPERATIONS MANAGER
Ricardo B. David
Number of Screens: 56

POLAND

Population: 38.6 million.
Average Ticket Price: $2.75.

ASSOCIATIONS & ORGANIZATIONS

ASSOCIATION OF POLISH FILM PRODUCERS AND PRODUCTION MANAGERS
Pulawska 61, Warsaw 02595. Tel: (4822) 245 5586.

ASSOCIATION OF POLISH FILMMAKERS
Krakowskie Przedmiescie, Warsaw 00071. Tel: (4822) 227 6785. FAX: Tel: (4822) 263 51927.

COMMITTEE OF CINEMATOGRAPHY
Tel: (4822) 263 449. FAX: (4822) 276 233.
PRESIDENT
Tadeusz Sciborylski

FEDERATION OF FILM TRADE GUILDS
Pulawska 61, Warsaw 02595. Tel: (4822) 628 4855. FAX: (4822) 245 5586.

FEDERATION OF NON-PROFESSIONAL FILM CLUBS
Pulawska 61, Warsaw 02595. Tel: (4822) 245 5382.

FILM ART FOUNDATION
Krakowskie Przedmiescie 21/23, Warsaw 00071. Tel: (4822) 226 1409. FAX: (4822) 635 2001.

POLISH FEDERATION OF FILM SOCIETIES
Plocka 16/34, Warsaw 01138. Tel: (4822) 232 1187.

POLISH FILM AND TV DIRECTOR'S GUILD
Pulawska 67, Warsaw 02595. Tel: (4822) 245 5316. FAX: (4822) 245 5316.

POLISH SCREENWRITERS GUILD
Al. Jerozolimskie 49m 41, Warsaw 00697. Tel: (4822) 262 81158.

PRIVATE FILM PRODUCERS CLUB
Walbrzyska 14/11, Warsaw 02738. Tel: (4822) 243 2861.

SOCIETY OF AUTHORS-ZAIKS
Hipoteczna 21, P.O. Box P-16, Warsaw 00092. Tel: (4822) 227 7950. FAX: (4822) 635 1347.

DISTRIBUTORS AND PRODUCERS

ANWA FILM INTERNATIONAL
Str. Smolensk 27/3, Krakow 31-12. Tel: (4812) 215 634.

BEST FILM
Ul. Twarda 16a, Warsaw 00105. Tel: (4822) 220 1201. FAX: (4822) 220 1201.

BLACK CAT
Magnoliowa 2, Lublin. Tel: (4881) 774 654. FAX: (4881) 774 654.

EUROKADR
Potocka Str. 14, Warsaw 01639.Tel: (4822) 233 2491. FAX: (4822) 233 2491.

FILM ART FOUNDATION
Krakowskie Przedmiescie 21/23, Warsaw 00071. Tel: (4822) 261 409. FAX: (4822) 635 2001.

FILM DISTRIBUTION AGENCY
Trebacka 3, Warsaw 00074. Tel: (4822) 635 2038. FAX: (4822) 635 1543.

FILM STUDIO HELIOS
Przybyszewskiego 167, Lodz 93120. Tel: (4842) 812 196. FAX: (4842) 812 481.

GRAFFITI
Ul, SW. Gertrudy 5, Krakow 31306. Tel: (4812) 214 294. FAX: (4812) 211 402.

IMP
Ul. Hoza 66, Warsaw 00950. Tel: (4822) 6287081. FAX: (4822) 628 7691.

ITI CINEMA POLAND
Marszalkowska 138, Warsaw 00004. Tel: (4822) 640 4447. FAX: (4822) 642 5001.
Wernyhory 14, Warsaw 02727. Tel: (4822) 243 3488. FAX: (4822) 243 4532.

KRAKATAU
Ul, Kaminskiego 29/12, Lodz. Tel: (4842) 788 536.

NEPTUN FILM
Piwna 22, Gdansk 80831. Tel: (4858) 314 876. FAX: (4858) 313 744.

NEPTUN VIDEO CENTRE
Grzybowska Str. 6-10, Warsaw 00131. Tel: (4822) 224 0395. FAX: (4822) 224 5969.

ODRA FILM
Ul. Boguslawskiego 14, Wroclaw 50023. Tel: (4871) 33487. FAX: (4871) 441 088.

SILESIA-FILM
Head Office: Plebiscytowa 46, Katowice 40041. Tel: (483) 251 2284. FAX: (483) 251 2245.

STARCUT FILM-POLAND
6 Wybickiego St, Rumia 84230. Tel: (4858) 219 769.

SYRENA ENTERTAINMENT GROUP
Marsz al kowska 115, Warsaw 00102. Tel: (4822) 827 3500. FAX: (4822) 827 5204.
PRESIDENT
Jerzy Jednorowski
MANAGING DIRECTOR
Levis Minford

VISION
Rydygiera 7, Warsaw 01793. Tel: (4822) 239 0753. FAX: (4822) 239 2575.

WARNER BROS. POLAND
Ul. Palawska 37/39, Warsaw 02508. Tel: (4822) 249 5959. FAX: (4822) 249 3598.

EXHIBITORS

APOLLO-FILM STATE FILM DISTRIBUTOR
Pychowicka 7, Krakow 30960. Tel: (4812) 671 355. FAX: (4812) 671 552.

FILM STUDIO HELIOS
Przybyszewskiego 167, Lodz 93120. Tel (4842) 812 196. FAX: (4842) 812 481.

THE GREATER UNION ORGANISATION
(Including BIRCH CARROLL & COYLE)
49 Market St., Sydney, NSW 2000, Australia. Tel: (612) 93 73 66 00. FAX: (612) 93 73 65 32.
MANAGING DIRECTOR
Robert Manson
Number of Theatres: 1 (Poland)
Number of Screens: 4 (Poland)

IFDF MAX
Jagiellonska Str 26, Warsaw 03719. Tel: (4822) 219 0481. FAX: (4822) 218 1783.

ITI CINEMA POLAND
Marszalkowska 138, Warsaw 00004. Tel: (4822) 640 4447. FAX: (4822) 642 5001.

MULTIKINO
(A joint venture of ITI and United Cinemas International), Tel: (4822) 640 4416. FAX: (4822) 640 4413.
MANAGING DIRECTOR
Aldona Szostakowska

NEPTUN FILM
Piwna 22, Gdansk 80831. Tel: (4858) 313 744. FAX: (4858) 313 744.

SILVER SCREEN/PORTICO DEVELOPMENT
Tel: (4822) 630 7076. FAX: (4822) 630 7077.
MANAGING DIRECTOR
Frank Stork

UCI JOINT VENTURE CO., POLAND
Multiurino Spa, Powsinska 4, Warsaw 02910. Tel: (4822) 2640 4416. FAX: (4822) 2640 4413.
DIRECTOR
Aldona Szostakowsk

PORTUGAL

Population: 10 million.
Average Ticket Price: $2.83

ASSOCIATIONS & ORGANIZATIONS

CINEMA, TELEVISION & VIDEO TRADE UNION
Rua D Pedro V 60, 1 Esq., Lisbon 1200. Tel: (3511) 342 2660. FAX: (3511) 342 6943.

CINEMATICA PORTUGUESA
Rua Barata Salgueiro 39, Lisbon 1200. Tel: (3511) 354 6279. FAX: (3511) 352 3180.

PORTUGUESE FILM INSTITUTE
Rua Sao Pedro de Alcantara 45, 1st Flr., Lisbon 1250. Tel: (3511) 345 6634. FAX: (3511) 347 2777.

SECRETARY OF STATE FOR CULTURE
Palacio Nacional da Ajuda, Lisbon 1300. Tel: (3511) 364 9867. FAX: (3511) 364 9872.

DISTRIBUTORS AND PRODUCERS

COLUMBIA TRISTAR & WARNER FILMES DE PORTUGAL
Av Duque De Loule 90 3 Esq., Lisbon 1000. Tel: (3511) 572 007. FAX: (3511) 315 5389.

FILMES CASTELLO LOPES
Rua de St. Amaro Estrelo 17-A, 5955. Tel: (3511) 395 5955. FAX: (3511) 395 5924.

FILMES LUSOMUNDO S.A.
Praca de Aleguia 22, Apartado 1063, Lisbon 1294. Tel: (3511) 347 4561. FAX: (3511) 346 5349.

MEDIA
Avenida Joao Crisostomo, 38 C-1, Escr. 3, Lisbon 1050. Tel: (3511) 353 1616. FAX: (3511) 353 1636.

UNITED INTERNATIONAL PICTURES
(See Filmes Lusumundo.)

VITORIA FILME
Avenida Duquer de Loul, 75, 3 Dt, Lisbon 1000. Tel: (3511) 546 195. FAX: (3511) 546 195.

EXHIBITORS

AMERICAN MULTI-CINEMA
106 West 14th St., Ste. 1700, Kansas City, Missouri, U.S. 64105. (816) 221 4000.
CHAIRMAN & CEO
Stanley H. Durwood
PRESIDENT & COO
Philip M. Singleton
Number of Theaters: 1 (Porto: Arrabida 20)
Number of Screens: 20

ATALANTA FILMES
Avenida D. Carlos 1, 72 D-3, Lisbon 1200. Tel: (3511) 397 0680. FAX: (3511) 397 4723.

FILMES CASTELO LOPES
Rua de St Amaro Estrelo 17-A, 5955. FAX: (3511) 395 5924.

LUSOMUNDO
Praca da Alegria 22, Lisbon 1294. Tel: (3511) 347 4561. FAX: (3511) 346 5349.

PAULO MARTINS
Avenida Duque de Loul, 75, 3 Dt, Lisbon 1000. Tel: (3511) 546 195. FAX: (3511) 546 195.

WARNER LUSOMUNDO CINEMAS
(Time Warner Co. and Lusomundo Audiovisuals S.A.)
Rua Luciano Cordeiro 113, 10 Lisbon 1150. Tel: (3511) 315 0860. FAX: (3511) 355 7784.
400 Warner Blvd., Bridge Bldg. South, 5th Flr., Burbank, Calif., U.S. 91522. Tel: (818) 954 6014. FAX: (818) 954 6655.
PRESIDENT
Millard Ochs
VICE PRESIDENT
Luis da Silva
MANAGING DIRECTOR
Miguel Tecedeiro
Number of Theaters: 4
Number of Screens: 30
Breakdown of screens: Cascais (7); Colombo (10); Gaia (9); Olivais (4).

RUSSIAN FEDERATION

Population: 146 million.

ASSOCIATIONS & ORGANIZATIONS

COMMITTEE OF CINEMATOGRAPHY OF THE RUSSIAN FEDERATION (ROSKOMKINO)
7 Mal Gnezdnikovsky Ln., Moscow 103877. Tel: (7095) 229 8224. FAX: (7095) 229 4522.

CONFEDERATION OF FILMMAKERS UNIONS
Maly Kozikhinsky Per 11, Moscow 103001. Tel: (7095) 299 7020. FAX: (7095) 299 3880.

FEDERATION OF CINEMA CLUBS
Konstantin Simonov St. 5, Cor 3, Apt. 41, Moscow 125167. Tel: (7095) 255 9105. FAX: (7095) 393 4896.

FILMMAKERS UNION OF REPUBLIC OF BELARUS
5 Karl Marx St., Minsk, Belarus 220050. Tel: (70172) 271 002. FAX: (70172) 271 451.

KAZAKHINO
Abylai Khana St. 93/95, Alma-Ata 480091, Kazakhstan. Tel: (7327) 269 2418.

STATE FILM CONCERN GRUZIA-FILM
Akhmedeli St. 10a, Tbilisi 308059, Georgia. Tel: (99532) 510 627. FAX: (99532) 510 010.

STATE FILM CONCERN MOLDOVA FILM
Enunesku St. 10, Kishinev 277012, Moldova. Tel: (3732) 234 405. FAX: (3732) 234 405.

ST. PETERSBURG CULTURE FUND
Nevsky Prosp. 31, St. Petersburg 191011. Tel: (7812) 311 8349. FAX: (7812) 315 1701.

DISTRIBUTORS AND PRODUCERS

ARGUS
Olypissicis Prospect 16, Moscow 129090. Tel: (7095) 288 4027. FAX: (7095) 288 9147.

ATLANT CO
Kirovogradskaya St. 9A, Moscow 113587. Tel: (7095) 312 5203. FAX: (7095) 312 8127.

EAST WEST CREATIVE ASSOCIATES
Bldg. 4, Stankevich St., Moscow 113587. Tel: (7095) 229 7100. FAX: (7095) 200 4249.

EKATERINBURG ART
Chebyshev St., 5th Flr., Ekaterinburg 620062. Tel: (73432) 442 1120. FAX: (73432) 442 343.

GEMINI FILM
Bldg. 6, Myansnitskaya St. 40, Moscow 101000. Tel: (7095) 921 0854. FAX: (7095) 921 2394.

GORKY FILM STUDIOS
8 Einstein St., Moscow 129226. Tel: (7095) 181 0183. FAX: (7095) 188 9871.

KINOTON
Okruzhnoy Proyezd 16, Moscow 105058. Tel: (7095) 290 3412. FAX: (7095) 200 5612.

KREDO-ASPEK
Novy Arbat St. 11, Moscow 121019. Tel: (7095) 291 7269. FAX: (7095) 219 6880.

MOST MEDIA
Maly Gnezdnikovsky 7, Moscow 103877. Tel: (7095) 229 1172. FAX: (7095) 229 1274.

PARADISE LTD. AGENCY
12a Christoprudny Blvd., Ste. 601, Moscow 101000. FAX: (7095) 924 1331.

RUSSKOYE VIDEO
Malaya Nevka 4, St. Petersburg 191035. Tel: (7812) 234 4207.

SKIP CENTRE
2 Flievskaya St. 7/19, Moscow 121096. Tel: (7095) 145 2459. FAX: (7095) 145 3355.

SOVENTURE
Bolshiye Kamenshchiki 17, Lorpus 1, Moscow 109172. Tel: (7095) 912 3065. FAX: (7095) 911 0665.

SOVEXPORTFILM
14 Kalashny Pereulok St., Moscow 103009. Tel: (7095) 290 2053. FAX: (7095) 200 1256.

TRETYAKOVKA
8 Maly Tolmachevsky per, Moscow 109017. Tel: (7095) 231 0183. FAX: (7095) 231 4857.

SINGAPORE

Population: 4.2 million.

ORGANIZATIONS

MINISTRY OF INFORMATION & THE ARTS
#36-00 PSA Bldg., 460 Alexandra Rd., Singapore. Tel: (65) 279 9707. FAX: (65) 279 9784.

SINGAPORE FILM SOCIETY
Robinson Rd., P.O. Box 3714, Singapore. Tel: (65) 235 2088.

DISTRIBUTORS AND PRODUCERS

ALLSTAR FILM
Block 136, Alexandra Rd., 01-161, Singapore 0315. Tel: (65) 472 7554. FAX: (65) 474 2676.

CATHAY ASIA FILMS
11 Dhoby Ghant #05-00, Cathay Building, Singapore 0922. Tel: (65) 337 6855. FAX: (65) 339 5609.

CINEMA VISION
2 Leng Kee Rd., Singapore 0315. Tel: (65) 472 2233. FAX: (65) 475 3346.

ENG WAH FILM
400 Orchard Rd., 16-06 Orchard Towers, Singapore 0923. Tel: (65) 734 0028.

FAIRMOUNT INTERNATIONAL
200 Jalan Sultan, 08-02 Textile Centre, Singapore 0719. Tel: (65) 296 5904. FAX: (65) 293 4742.

GLOBE FILM DISTRIBUTORS
Block 1, Rochor Rd., Singapore 0718. Tel: (65) 296 6324. FAX: (65) 296 6742.

GOLDEN VILLAGE MULTIPLEX PTE., LTD
2 Handy Rd., #15-04, Singapore 229233. Tel: (65) 334 3766. FAX: (65) 334 8397. email: webmaster@golden-village.com.sg. www.goldenvillage.com.sg
EXECUTIVE DIRECTOR & GENERAL MANAGER
Gerald Dibbayawan

KIM FONG FILM
05-03, Block 8, Lorong Bakur Batu, Singapore 1334. Tel: (65) 7480265. FAX: (65) 7470939.

OVERSEAS MOVIE
#04-21 People's Park Complex, Singapore 0106. Tel: (65) 535 0555. FAX: (65) 535 0783.

SHAW ORGANISATION
Shaw Centre, 1 Scotts Rd., Singapore 0922. Tel: (65) 235 2077. FAX: (65) 235 2860.

TWENTIETH CENTURY FOX FILM (EAST)
400 Orchard Rd., 17-064 Orchard Towers, Singapore 0923. Tel: (65) 723 0952. FAX: (65) 235 4957.

UNITED INTERNATIONAL PICTURES
15-04 Shaw Centre, 1 Scotts Rd., Singapore 0922. Tel: (65) 737 2484. FAX: (65) 235 3667.

WARNER BROS. SINGAPORE
04-02 Midlands House, 122 Middle Rd., Singapore 0718. Tel: (65) 337 5060. FAX: (65) 339 1709.

EXHIBITORS

CATHAY CINEPLEXES PTE, LTD.
11 Unity St., #02-01, Robertson Walk, Singapore 237995. FAX: (65) 732-1944.
CHAIRPERSON
Meileen Choo

Number of Screens: 20

CATHAY THEATRE MANAGEMENT PTE LTD.
2 Handy Rd., Cathay BLDG., #05-00, Singapore 229233. Tel: (65) 337 8181. FAX: (65) 338 2153.
MANAGING DIRECTOR
Choo Meileen

Number of Theatres: 6
Number of Screens: 24

GOLDEN HARVEST ENTERTAINMENT CO., LTD.
(For additional listings see Hong Kong, Thailand & Malaysia.)
8 King Tung St., Hammer Hill Rd., Kowloon. Tel: (852) 2352 8222. FAX: (852) 2351 1683.
EXECUTIVES
Raymond Chow
Leonard Ho
Anthony Chow
Peter Chung
S.Y. Ho

Number of Theatres: 11
Number of Screens: 50

GOLDEN VILLAGE ENTERTAINMENT
68 Orchard Rd., #07-10/14 Plaza Singapura, Singapore 238839. Tel: (65) 334-3766. FAX: (65) 334-8397.
GENERAL MANAGER
Gerald Dibbayawan
OPERATIONS DIRECTOR, ASIA
Marcus Khaw
MARKETING MANAGER
Connie Lai

Number of Theatres: 9
Number of Screens: 64

SHAW ORGANISATION GROUP OF COMPANIES
Shaw Centre, 13th & 14th Storeys, 1 Scotts Rd., Singapore 228208. Tel: (65) 235 2077. FAX: (65) 235 2860.
DIRECTOR, ADMINISTRATION
Vee-Meng Shaw
DIRECTOR, DISTRIBUTION
Harold Shaw
DIRECTOR, OPERATIONS
Vee King Shaw
GENERAL MANAGER
S.Y. Liok
GROUP FINANCIAL CONTROLLER
SAJ Jesuthasan
GROUP SECRETARY
B.S. Yap
MANAGER, CHINESES DISTRIBUTION
Tan Chua
MANAGERS, BOOKING
KS Mak
YT Kwan
MANAGER, CONCESSIONS
Brian Tam

Number of Screens: 41

STUDIO CITY CINEMA HOLDINGS, LTD.
5 Magazine Rd., #03-02, Singapore 059571.
CONTACT
Maureen Koh

Number of Screens: 13

VILLAGE ROADSHOW, LTD.
(For complete listing see Australian branch.)
206 Bourke St., Melbourne, VIC, 3000, Australia. Tel: (613) 96 67 66 66. FAX: (613) 96 39 15 40.

Number of Theatres: 9 (Singapore)
Number of Screens: 64 (Singapore)

SOUTH AFRICA

Population: 43.4 million.
Admission Prices: From approx. $4.00 in Johannesburg to ¢20 in rural areas.

ASSOCIATIONS & ORGANIZATIONS

AFRICAN FILM AND TELEVISION COLLECTIVE
P.O. Box 42723, Fordsbury 2033. Tel: (2711) 804 5186. FAX: (2711) 838 3034.

CINEMA THEATRE AND VIDEO UNION
P.O. Box 81338, Parkhurst 2120. Tel: (2711) 782 4273. FAX: (2711) 492 1221.

DEPARTMENT OF HOME AFFAIRS-FILM DEPARTMENT
Private Bag X114, Pretoria 0001. Tel: (2712) 314 3328.

FILM AND ALLIED WORKERS ORGANISATION
P.O. Box 16939, Doornfontein 2028. Tel: (2711) 402 4570. FAX: (2711) 402 0777.

PROFESSIONAL PHOTOGRAPHERS OF SOUTHERN AFRICA
P.O. Box 47044, Parklands, Johannesburg 2121. Tel: (2711) 880 9110. FAX: (2711) 880 1648.

SOUTH AFRICAN SOCIETY OF CINEMATOGRAPHERS
P.O. Box 17465, Sunward Park 1470. Tel: (2711) 902 2826.

SOUTH AFRICAN FILM AND TELEVISION INSTITUTE
P.O. Box 3512, Halfway House 1685. Tel: (2711) 315 0140. FAX: (2711) 315 0146.

DISTRIBUTORS AND PRODUCERS

ATLAS MOTION PICTURE CORPORATION
P.O. Box 87385, Houghton 2041. Tel: (2711) 728 4912. FAX: (2711) 728 5287.

CONCORD FILMS
P.O. Box 8112, Johannesburg 2000. Tel: (2711) 337 5581. FAX: (2711) 337 3913.

EMS
24 Napier Road, Richmond, Johannesburg. Tel: (2711) 482 4470. FAX: (2711) 482 2552.

ENTERTAINMENT WORKERS' UNION
P.O. Box 81338, Parkhurst 2120. Tel: (2711) 782 4273.

FILM FARE INTERNATIONAL
P.O. Box 24, Crawford 7770. Tel: (2721) 637 8028. FAX: (2721) 637 3138.

GENESIS RELEASING
Charter House, 3 Robertson St. Observatory Ext 2198, Johannesburg. Tel: (2711) 487 1060. FAX: (2711) 487 1040.

JAGUAR FILM DISTRIBUTORS
P.O. Box 53126, Yellowood Park 4011. Tel: (2731) 420 610.

MIMOSA FILM DISTRIBUTORS
P.O. Box 50019, Randburg 2125. Tel: (2711) 787 1075.

SAVAGE EYE FILMWORKS
6A Glade Rd., Rondebosch, Cape Town 7700. Tel: (2721) 686 3858. FAX: (2721) 244 313.

STER-KINEKOR (PTY.) LIMITED
Interleisure Park, 185 Katherine St., Eastgate, Sandton. Tel: (2711) 4457 7300. FAX: (2711) 444 1003.

UNITED INTERNATIONAL PICTURES
Castrol House, 7 Junction Ave., Parktown, Johannesburg 2193. Tel: (2711) 484 4215. FAX: (2711) 484 3339.

STUDIOS

FRAMEWORK TELEVISION
P.O. Box 5200, Horizon 1730. Tel: (2711) 475 4220. FAX: (2711) 475 5333.

SONNEBLOM FILM PRODUCTIONS
P.O. Box 3940, Honeydew 2040. Tel: (2711) 794 2100. FAX: (2711) 794 2061.

SONOVISION STUDIOS
P.O. Box 783133, Sandton 2146. Tel: (2711) 783 1100. FAX: (2711) 883 3834.

TORON INTERNATIONAL
P.O. Box 89271, Lyndhurst 2106. Tel: (2711) 786 2360. FAX: (2711) 440 5132.

SOUTH KOREA

Population: 45.5 million.

DISTRIBUTORS

COLUMBIA TRISTAR FILMS OF KOREA
Songpa Bldg., 505 Shinsa-Dong, Kangnam-Gu, Seoul. Tel: (9822) 545 0101. FAX: (822) 546 0020.

DAEWOO
(Agency for New Line International), 12th Flr., Daewoo Foundation Bldg., 526 5 Ga Namdaemoon Ro, Jung Gu 100-095, Seoul.

TWENTIETH CENTURY FOX KOREA
Asia Cement Bldg., 8th Flr., 726 Yeok Sam-dong, Kangnam-ku, Seoul. Tel: (822) 3452 5980. FAX: (822) 3452 7223.

UIP—CIC FILM & VIDEO DISTRIBUTION
Jang Choong Bldg., 2nd Flr., 120-1, 1Ka, Jang Choong-Dong, Jung-ku, Seoul. Tel: (822) 276 0077. FAX: (822) 273 8208. Manager: H.K. Lee.

WALT DISNEY KOREA
4th Flr., Samboo Bldg., 676 Yeok Sam-dong, Kangam-ku, Seoul. Tel: (822) 527 0400. FAX: (822) 527 0399.

WARNER BROS KOREA
M Bldg., 6th Flr., 221-5 Nonhyun-dong, Kangnam-ku, Seoul. Tel: (822) 547 0181. FAX: (822) 547 8396.

EXHIBITOR

VILLAGE ROADSHOW, LTD.
206 Bourke St., Melbourne, VIC, 3000, Australia. Tel: (613) 96 67 66 66. FAX: (613) 96 39 15 40.
(For complete listing see Australian branch.)

Number of Theatres: 2 (Korea)
Number of Screens: 25 (Korea)

SPAIN

Population: 40 million.
Average Ticket Price: $3.89.

ASSOCIATIONS & ORGANIZATIONS

ASSEMBLY OF SPANISH DIRECTORS & PRODUCERS
San Lorenzo 11, Madrid 28004. Tel: (341) 319 6844.

ASSOCIATION OF NATIONAL FILM DISTRIBUTORS & PRODUCERS
Blanca de Navarra 7, Madrid 28010. Tel: (341) 308 0120. FAX: (341) 319 0036.

FEDERACION ESPANOLA DE PRODUCTORAS DE CINE PUBLICITARIO Y CORTOMETRAJE
Sanchez Pacheco 64 Entreplanta, Madrid 28002. Tel.: (341) 413 2454. FAX: 34 1 519 2019.

FEDERATION OF SPANISH FILM COMPANIES
Velazquez 10 3 deha., Madrid 28001. Tel: (341) 576 9913. FAX: (341) 576 2774.

FEDERATION OF THEATRICAL DISTRIBUTORS
Velazquez 10, 3 deha., Madrid 28001. Tel: (341) 576 0820. FAX: (341) 578 0028.

MINISTRY OF CULTURE
Plaza del Rey 1, Madrid 28071. Tel: (341) 532 0093. FAX: (341) 522 9377.

PROCINE FOUNDATION
Ayala 20-5 B, Madrid 28001. Tel.: (341) 576 6066. FAX: (341) 578 1915.

DISTRIBUTORS AND PRODUCERS

ALAS FILMS
Maestro Guerrero 4, Madrid 28015. Tel.: (341) 547 6664. FAX: (341) 542 7887.

JOSE ESTEBAN ALENDA
Trujillos 7, Madrid 28013. Tel: (341) 541 1838. FAX: (341) 548 3791.

ALTA FILMS
Martin de los Heros 12, Madrid 28008. Tel: (341) 542 2702. FAX: (341) 542 8777.

ARABA FILMS
Dr. Arce 1b, Madrid 28002. Tel: (341) 564 9498. FAX: (341) 564 5738.

BARTON FILMS S.I.
Iturribide 68, Lonja, Bolbao. Tel: (344) 433 7103. FAX: (344) 433 5086.

BRB INTERNATIONAL
Autovia Fuencarral Alcobendas, Km. 12 220 Edificio Auge 1, Madrid 28049. Tel: (341) 358 9596. FAX: (341) 358 9818.

BREPI FILMS
Corredera Baja de San Pablo, 2-30, Madrid 28004. (341) 522 3108. FAX: (341) 522 5721.

BUENA VISTA INTERNATIONAL SPAIN
Jose Bardasano Baos 9-11, Edificio Gorbea 3, Madrid 28016. Tel: (341) 383 0732. FAX: (341) 766 9241.

CINE COMPANY
Zurbano 74, Madriid 28010. Tel: (341) 442 2944. FAX: (341) 441 0098.

CINEMUSSY
Quintana No. 1, 2 B, Madrid 28029. Tel: (341) 542 0036. FAX: (341) 559 9069.

COLUMBIA TRI-STAR FILMS DE ESPANA
c/o Hernandez de Tejada 3, Madrid 28027. Tel: (341) 377 7100. FAX: (341) 377 7128.
Edificio Piovera Azul, Peonias 2, Madrid 28042. Tel: (341) 320 0744. FAX: (341) 320 6105.

DISTRIBUIDORA COQUILLAT
Denia 43, Valencia 46006. Tel: (346) 341 7000. FAX: (346) 380 4270.

ESICMA
Maestro Lasalle 15, 28016 Madrid. Tel: (341) 345 8708. FAX: (341) 355 7991.

FILMAX GROUP
P. San Gervasio 16-20, Barcelona 08022. Tel: (343) 453 0303. FAX: (343) 453 0608.

FILMAYER INTERNATIONAL
Arda Brugos, 8-A Planta 10-1, Madrid 28036. Tel: (341) 383 0265. FAX: (341) 383 0845.

GOLEM DISTRIBUCION
Corezonde Maria 56-9A, Madrid 28002. Tel: (341) 519 1737. FAX: (341) 416 3626.

HISPANO FOXFILM S.A.E.
Avenida de Bourgos 8-A, Planta 18, Madrid 28036. Tel: (341) 343 4640. FAX: (341) 343 4646.

IBEROAMERICANA FILMS INTERNACIONAL
Velazquez 12, 7 & 8, Madrid 28001. Tel: (341) 4314246. FAX: (341) 435 5994.
CONTACT
Andres Vicente Gomez

IMPALA MONTILLA
Manuel Motilla 1, Madrid 28016. Tel: (341) 350 6200. FAX: (341) 345 1948.
CONTACT
Jose Antonio Sainz de Vicuna

KALEKIA
Comino del Obispo 25, Mostoles, Madrid 28935. Tel: (341) 616 3710. FAX: (341) 616 3710.

LAUREN FILM
Tetuan 29-2, Madrid 28013. Tel: (341) 521 8284. FAX: (341) 522 0616.

LECAS FILM DISTRIBUCION
Galileo 82, Madrid 28015. Tel: (341) 447 4657. FAX: (341) 448 8978.

LIDER FILMS
Isla de Fuenteventura No, 21-10, San Sebastian de los Reyes, Madrid 28700. Tel: (341) 663 9000. FAX: (341) 663 9320.

MOVIERECORD
Martires de Alcala 4, Madrid 28015. Tel: (341) 559 9205. FAX: (341) 547 5985.
CONTACT
Jesus Martin Sanz

MULTIVIDEO
La Luna 15, Madrid 28004. Tel: (341) 522 9347. FAX: (341) 532 8695.

MUSIDORA FILMS
Calle Princesa 17, Madrid 28008. Tel: (341) 541 6869. FAX: (341) 541 5482. Contact: Javier de Garcillan.

NEPTUNO FILMS
Cardaire 36-38, Terassa, Barcelona 08221. Tel: (341) 784 1622. FAX: (341) 784 2938.

POLYGRAM FILM ESPANA
Manuel Montilla 1, Madrid 28016. Tel: (341) 350 6200. FAX: (341) 350 1371.

PRIME FILMS
Padre Xitre 5-7C, Madrid 28002. Tel: (341) 519 0181. FAX: (341) 413 0772.

REX FILMS
Provenza 197-199. Barcelona 08008. Tel: (343) 451 3315. FAX: (343) 453 5391.

SOGEPAQ DISTRIBUCION
Manual Montilla 1, Madrid 28016. Tel: (341) 350 6200. FAX: (341) 345 1948.
PRESIDENT
Jose Vicuna

SUCESORES DES JESUS RODRIGUEZ DORESTA
Triana 68-1, Las Palmas de Gran Canaria 35002. Tel: (3428) 371 560. FAX: (3428) 371 560.

SUPER FILMS S.A.
Provenza 197/199, Barcelona 08008. Tel: (343) 451 3315. FAX: (343) 453 5391.

SURF FILMS
Zurbano 74, Madrid 28010. Tel: (341) 442 2944. FAX: (341) 0441 0098.

TRIPICTURES
Doce De Octubre 28, Madrid 28009. Tel: (341) 574 9008. FAX: (341) 574 9005.

U FILMS/UNION FILMS
Maestro Guerrero 4, Madrid 28015. Tel: (341) 547 6664. FAX: (341) 542 7887.

UNITED INTERNATIONAL PICTURES
Plaza del Callao 4-6, Madrid 28013. Tel: (341) 522 7261. FAX: (341) 532 2384.
MANAGER
Gaulberto Bana

VICTORY FILMS
Cuesta de Santo Domingo 11, Madrid 28013. Tel: (341) 541 8734. FAX: (341) 541 4612.

WANDA FILMS
Avenida de Europa 9, Pozuelo, Madrid 28224. Tel: (341) 352 8376. FAX: (341) 345 1948.

WARNER ESPANOLA
Manual Montilla 1, Madrid 28016. Tel: (341) 350 6200. FAX: (341) 345 1948.

EXHIBITORS

ALPHAVILLE
Martin de Los Heros 14, Madrid 28008. Tel: (341) 559 3836. FAX: (341) 541 5482.

ALTA FILMS S.A.
Cuesta de San Vicente 4, 28008, Madrid. Tel: (349) 1542-2702.
Number of Screens: 108

AREA CATALANA D'EXHIBICIO CINEMATOGRAFICA, S.A.
221 Mallorca St., 6th Flr., Barcelona 08008. Tel: (3493) 323 6426. FAX: (3493) 323 7223.
PRESIDENT
Jaime Tarrazon Badia
VICE PRESIDENT
Jaume Camprecios
MANAGER
Francisco Garcia Bascunana
Number of Theatres: 41
Number of Screens: 112
Badalona (2); Cerdanyola (1); Cornella (2); Granollers (4); Igualada (2); Hospitalet (2); Mataro (4); Manresa (2); Mollet (1); Reus (1); Sabadell (5); Tarragona (2); Terrassa (1).

BAUTISTA SOLER
Abada 14, Madrid 28013. Tel: (341) 531 6107. FAX: (341) 522 2202.

CASABLANCA CINEMA
Paseo de Gracia 115, Barcelona 08008. Tel: (343) 218 4345.

CINESA
Floridablanca 135, Barcelona 08011. Tel: (34) 93 228 96 00. FAX: (34) 93 424 38 05.
SENIOR V.P., SOUTHERN EUROPE & BRAZIL
Jose Batle
GENERAL MANAGER & V.P., OPERATIONS
Javier Fernandez
V.P., CONSTRUCTION, SOUTHERN EUROPE
Eduardo Fontcuberta
MARKETING DIRECTOR
Ricardo Gil
FINANCIAL DIRECTOR
Jose Lopez
LEGAL, SOUTHERN EUROPE
Agustoin Sanchez
MIS DIRECTOR
Juan Luis Bernabe
HEAD FILM BUYER, SOUTHERN EUROPE
Juan Antonio Gomez
Number of Theatres: 29
Number of Screens: 167

COLISEO ALBIA
Alameda de Urquijo 13, Bilbao 48008. Tel: (344) 423 2148. FAX: (344) 423 1001.

COMPANIA DE INICIATIVAS Y ESPECTACULOS
Floridablanca 135, 08011 Barcelona. Tel: (349) 3423-2455
Number of Screens: 149

DIFUSARA CULTURAL CINEMATOGRAFICA
Cines Golem, Avenida de Bayona 52, Pamplona 31008. Tel: (3448) 174 141. FAX: (3448) 171 058.

DIFUSORA BURGOS
Avenida Sanjurjo 36, Cines Can Golem, Burgos 09004. Tel: (3448) 174 141. FAX: (3448) 171 058.

DIFUSORA LOGRONO
Cines Golem, Parque de San Adrian s/n, Logrono 26006. Tel: (3448) 174 141. FAX: (3448) 171 058.

EMPRESA BALANA
Provenza 266, 5, Barcelona 08008. Tel: (343) 215 9570. FAX: (343) 215 6740.

FRANCISCO HERAS
Van Dyke Cinema, Van Dyke 59-61, Salamanca 37005. Tel: (3423) 243 538.

IZARO FILMS
Raimundo Fernandez Villaverde 65, Madrid 28003. Tel: (341) 555 8041. FAX: (341) 555 8292.

KINEPOLIS GROUP
89 Boulevard dy Centenaire, B 1020 Brussels. (322) 474 2600. FAX: (322) 474 2606. www.kinepolis.com

LAUREN FILMS VIDEO HAGAR
Balmes 87, Barcelona 08008. Tel: (343) 451 7189. FAX: (343) 323 6155.

PALAFOX CINEMA
Luchana 15, Madrid 28010. Tel: (341) 446 1887. FAX: (341) 447 3441.

PEDRO BALANA
Provenza 266, Barcelona 08008. Tel: (343) 215 9570. FAX: (343) 215 6740.

REAL CINEMA
Plaza de Isabel II 7, Madrid 28013. Tel: (341) 547 4577. FAX: (341) 547 4650.

TABEXSA CINE
Albatros Minicines, Plaza Fray Luis Colomer 4, Valencia 46021. Tel: (346) 369 4530. FAX: (346) 360 1469.

UNION CINE CIUDAD
Alameda de Hercules 9 y 10, Edifico Alameda Multicines, 41002 Sevilla, Spain. Tel: (349) 5437-5900.
Number of Screens: 204

WARNER LUSOMUNDO CINES DE ESPANA, S.A.
(Warner Bros. International Theaters in partnership with Lusomundo SGPS, S.A.)
Miniparc, 1 c/Azalea, No.1, Edificip B, Primera planta, El Soto de la Moraleja Alcobendas, 28109, Madrid.
EXECUTIVE DIRECTORS
Millard Ochs
Luis Silva
Ele Juarez
MANAGING DIRECTOR
Tomas Naranjo

YELMO CINEPLEX DE ESPANA
Princesa 31, 3rd Flr., 28008 Madrid, Spain. Tel: (349) 1758-9600.
Number of Screens: 190

YELMO FILMS
Jacometrezo 4 7 Piso, Madrid 28013. Tel: (341) 523 1560. FAX: (341) 523 1658.

SWEDEN

Population: 8.8 million.
Average Ticket Price: $9.00.

ASSOCIATIONS & ORGANIZATIONS

PRODUCERS CONTROL BUREAU
Box 1147, Solna S-171 23. Tel: (468) 735 9780. FAX: (468) 730 2560.

SVENSKA TEATERFORBUNDET
Hantverkargatan 4, Stockholm S-112 21. Tel: (468) 785 0330. FAX: (468) 653 9507.

SWEDISH DISTRIBUTORS ASSOCIATION
P.O. Box 49084, Stockholm S-100 28. Tel: (468) 785 0400. FAX: (468) 730 2560.

DISTRIBUTORS AND PRODUCERS

BUENA VISTA INTERNATIONAL
Box 5631, Stockholm S-114 86. Tel: (468) 679 1550. FAX: (468) 678 01728.
GENERAL MANAGER
Eric Broberg.

CAPITOL FILM DISTRIBUTION
Sodravagen 12, Kalmar S-392 33. Tel: (46480) 12215. FAX: (46480) 24085.

CINEMA SWEDEN
P.O. Box 20105, Bromma S-161 02. Tel: (468) 280 738. FAX: (268) 299 091.

COLUMBIA TRISTAR FILMS (SWEDEN)
Hornsbruksgatan 19, 1 Tr, P.O. Box 9501, Stockholm S-102 74. Tel: (468) 658 1140. FAX: (468) 841 204.
GENERAL MANAGER
Peter Jansson.

EGMONT FILM
P.O. Box 507, Taby S-183 25. Tel: (468) 5101 0050. FAX: (468) 5101 2046.

FOLKETS BIO
P.O. Box 2068, Stockholm S-103 12. Tel: (468) 203059. FAX: (468) 204023.

FOX FILM
Box 9501, Stockholm S-102 74. Tel: (468) 658 1144. FAX: (468) 841 204.

NORDISK FILM TV DISTRIBUTION
P.O. Box 9011, Soder Malarstrand 27, Stockholm S-10271. Tel: (468) 440 9070. FAX: (468) 440 9080.

PLANBORG FILM
Granhallsvagen 23, Stocksund S-182 75. Tel: (468) 655 80 70. FAX: (468) 655 03 40.

SANDREW FILM & TEATR
P.O. Box 5612, Stockholm S-114 86. Tel: (468) 234 700. FAX: (468) 103 850.

SONET FILM
Tappvagen 24, P.O. Box 20105, Bromma S-161 02. Tel: (468) 799 7700. FAX: (468) 285 834.

SVENSK FILMINDUSTRI
Dialoggatan 6, Stockholm S-12783. Tel: (468) 680 3500. FAX: (468) 710 4460. email: stefan.klockby@sf.se
PRESIDENT
Jan Edholm

SVENSKA FILMINSTITUTET
Filmhuset, Borgvagen 1-5, P.O. Box 27126, Stockholm S-102 52. Tel: (468) 665 1100. FAX: (468) 661 1820.

UNITED INTERNATIONAL PICTURES (SWEDEN)
P.O. Box 9502, Stockholm S-102 74. Tel: (468) 616 7400. FAX: (468) 843 870.

WARNER BROS. SWEDEN
Hornsbruksgatan 19, 4th Flr., Stockholm S-117 34. Tel: (468) 658 1050. FAX: (468) 658 6482.

EXHIBITORS

FILMOVID R REISS
Ralangsvegen 6, Enskede S-120 42. Tel: (468) 910 316. FAX: (468) 910 316.

FOLKETS BIO
P.O. Box 2068, Stockholm S-103 12. Tel: (468) 402 0820. FAX: (468) 402 0827.

SANDREW METRONOME FILM AB
P.O. Box 5612, Stockholm S-114 86. Tel: (468) 762 1700. FAX: (468) 103 850.
PRESIDENT & CEO
Klas Olofsson
HEAD OF EXIBITION
Bo Nilsson
HEAD OF ACQUISITION
Bertil Sandgren
Number of Theatres: 31
Number of Screens: 104

SF BIO AB
S-12783 Stockholm. Tel: (468) 680 3500. FAX: (468) 680 3748.
PRESIDENT & CEO
Jan Bernhardsson
SENIOR V.P., DEVELOPMENT
Johan Wrangel
SENIOR V.P., PROMGRAMMING
Sture Johansson
SENIOR V.P., CONCESSIONS
Steve Sodergren
MEDIA/MARKETING DIRECTOR
Per Rustner

Number of Theatres: 33
Number of Screens: 176

SVENSK FILMINDUSTRI
Dialoggatan 6, Stockholm S-12783. Tel: (468) 680 3500. FAX: (468) 710 4460.
PRESIDENT
Jan Edholm

STUDIOS

EUROPA STUDIOS
Tappvagen 24, P.O. Box 20105, Stockholm S-16102. Tel: (468) 764 7700.

FILM HOUSE STUDIOS
P.O. Box 27 066, Stockholm S-102 51. Tel: (468) 665 1200. FAX: (468) 661 1053.

MEXFILM
P.O. Box 17607, Stockholm S-11892. Tel: (468) 642 0035. FAX: (468) 642 9850.

STUDIO 24
Sibyllegatan 24, Stockholm S-114 42. Tel: (468) 662 5700. FAX: (468) 662 9240.

SWITZERLAND

Population: 7.3 million.
Average Ticket Price: $9.20.

ASSOCIATIONS AND ORGANIZATIONS

CINELIBRE
Swiss Associations of Film Societies and Non-Commercial Screening Organisations, Postfach, CH-4005 Basel. Tel: (4161) 681 3844. FAX: (4161) 691 1040.

FEDERAL DEPARTMENT OF FOREIGN AFFAIRS
Sektion fur internationale kulturelle und UNESCO-Angelegenheiten, Schwarztorstrasse 59, CH-3003 Bern. Tel: (4131) 325 9267. FAX: (4131) 325 9358.

FEDERAL OFFICE OF CULTURE
Sektion Film, Hallwylstrasse 15, CH-3003 Bern. Tel: (4131) 322 9271. FAX: (4131) 322 9273.

SUISSIMAGE
Neuengasse 23, CH-3001 Bern. Tel: (4131) 312 1106. FAX: (4131) 311 2104.

SWISS CINEMATHEQUE
Case Postale 2512, CH-1002 Lausanne. Tel: (4121) 331 0101. FAX: (4121) 320 4888.

SWISS FILM DISTRIBUTORS ASSOCIATION
Effingerstrasse 11. P.O. Box 8175. CH-3001 Bern. Tel: (4131) 381 5077. FAX: (4131) 382 0373.

SWISS FILM THEATRES ASSOCIATION
Effingerstrasse 11. P.O. Box 8175. CH-3001 Bern. Tel: (4131) 381 5077. FAX: (4131) 382 0373.

DISTRIBUTORS AND PRODUCERS

ALEXANDER FILM
Lagernstrasse 6, CH-8037 Zurich. Tel: (411) 362 8443. FAX: (411) 361 1603.

ALPHA FILMS S. A.
4 Place du Cirque, Case Postale 5311, CH-1211 Geneve 11. (4122) 328 0204. FAX: (4122) 781 0676.

BERNARD LANG AG
Dorf Strasse 14D, Freienstein, CH-8427 Zurich. Tel: (411) 865 6627. FAX: (411) 865 6629.

BUENA VISTA INTERNATIONAL (SWITZERLAND) LTD.
Am Schanzengraben 27, CH-8002 Zurich. Tel: (411) 201 6655. FAX: (411) 201 7770. .

COLUMBUS FILM AG
Steinstrasse 21, CH-8036 Zurich. Tel: (411) 462 7377. FAX: (411) 462 0112.

CONDOR FILMS
Restelbergstrasse 107, CH-8044 Zurich. Tel: (411) 361 9612.

FAMA-FILM AG
Balthasarstrasse 11, CH-3027 Bern. Tel: (4131) 992 9280. FAX: (4131) 992 6404.

FILMCOOPERATIVE ZURICH
Fabrikstrasse 21, Postfach 172, CH-8031 Zurich. Tel: (411) 271 8800. FAX: (411) 271 8038. Contact: Wolfgang Blosche.

KINEPOLIS GROUP
89 Boulevard du Centenaire, B 1020 Brussels. (322) 474 2600. FAX: (322) 474 2606. www.kinepolis.com

IMPERIAL FILMS S. A.
Ave. de la Gare 17, CH-1002 Lausanne. Tel.: (4121) 732 1830. FAX: (4121) 738 7882.

MASCOTTE-FILM AG
Dienerstrasse 16-18, CH-8026 Zurich. Tel: (411) 296 9070. FAX: (411) 296 9089.

MONOPOLE PATHE FILMS S. A.
Neugasse 6, CH-8005 Zurich. Tel: (4311) 271 1003. FAX: (411) 271 5643.

REGINA FILM S. A.
4 Rue de Rive, CH-1204 Geneve. Tel: (4122) 310 8136. FAX: (4122) 310 9476.

RIALTO FILM AG
Neugasse 6, CH-8021 Zurich. Tel: (411) 271 4200. FAX: (411) 2714203.

SPIEGEL FILM AG
Ebelstrasse 25, Postfach 179, CH-8030 Zurich. Tel: (411) 252 7406. FAX: (411) 251 1354.

STAMM-FILM AG
Lowenstrasse 20, CH-8023 Zurich. Tel: (411) 211 6615.

TWENTIETH CENTURY-FOX FILM CORPORATION
P.O. Box 1049, CH-1211 Geneva 26. Tel: (4122) 343 3315. FAX: (4122) 343 9255.
MANAGER
Peter Danner.

UNITED INTERNATIONAL PICTURES (SCHWEIZ)
Signaustrasse 6, CH-8032 Zurich. Tel: (411) 383 8550. FAX: (411) 383 6112.
MANAGER
Hans Ulrich Daetwyler.

WARNER BROS. (TRANSATLANTIC)
Studerweg 3, Postfach, CH-8802 Kilchberg. Tel: (411) 715 5911. FAX: (411) 715 3451.
SALES
Richard Broccon.

EXHIBITORS

CINEMAX
Tel: (411) 273 2222. FAX: (411) 273 3354.

CINEMAXX H.J. FLEBBE FILMTHEATERBETRIEBE
Mittelweg 176, 20148 Hanburg. Tel: (49) 40450 680. FAX: (49) 40 450 68201.
PRESIDENT & GENERAL MANAGER
Hans-Joachim Flebbe
GENERAL MANAGER & CFO
Michael Pawlowski
DIRECTOR, MARKETING
Jens Thomsen

Number of Theatres: 1 (Switzerland)
Number of Screens: 8 (Switzerland)

CINEMOBIL OPEN AIR CINEMA
Dorfstrasse 77, CH-8105 Regensdorf. Tel: (411) 840 5342.

CINETYP
Obergrundstrasse 101, CH-6005 Lucerne. Tel: (4141) 422 257. FAX: (4141) 422 746.

ERNO INTERNATIONAL
Niedergaslistrasse 12, CH-8157 Dielsdorf. Tel: (411) 855 5353. FAX: (411) 855 5350.

FILMCOOPERATIVE ZURICH
Fabrikstrasse 21, Postfach 172, CH-8031 Zurich. Tel: (411) 271 8800. FAX: (411) 271 8038.

KITAG KINO THEATER AG
Laupenstrasse 8, 3008 Bern. Tel: (413) 1390-110.

Number of Screens: 29

LIAG CAPITOL
Bergstrasse 42, CH-8032 Zurich. Tel: (411) 251 5228. FAX: (411) 251 4444.

METROCINE
Ch. de Rosenack 6, CH-1000 Lausanne 13. Tel: (4121) 614 3333. FAX: (4121) 614 3399.

QUINNIE CINEMA FILMS, LTD.
Seilestrasse 4, 3011 Bern (Schweiz), Switzerland. Tel: (413) 1381-1721. FAX: (413) 1398-1272.
OWNER
Roland Probst

V ESPOSITO
4 Rue de Reve, CH-1204 Geneva. Tel: (4122) 782 1417. FAX: (4122) 310 9476.

VILLAGE ROADSHOW, LTD.
(For complete listing see Australian branch.)
206 Bourke St., Melbourne, VIC, 3000, Australia. Tel: (613) 96 67 66 66. FAX: (613) 96 39 15 40.

Number of Theatres: 1 (Switzerland)
Number of Screens: 10 (Switzerland)

WALCH KINOBETRIEBS
Steinentorstrasse 8, CH-4051 Basel. Tel: (4161) 281 0908. FAX: (4161) 281 6564.

TAIWAN

Population: 22.2 million.

ORGANIZATION

MOTION PICTURE DEVELOPMENT FOUNDATION
2 Tien-Tsin St., Taipei. 866 2 3516625. FAX: (8862) 341 6252.

DISTRIBUTORS

BUENA VISTA FILM CO. LTD.
4th Flr., No. 1, Hsiang Yang Rd., Taipei. Tel: (8862) 383 6309. FAX: (8862) 382 5348.

COLUMBIA TRISTAR FILMS OF CHINA, LTD.
City Hero Plaza, 8F-A No. 59, Chung-hua Rd., Section 1, Taipei 100. Tel: (8862) 331 9456. FAX: (8862) 381 4492.

PARAMOUNT FILMS OF CHINA, INC.
(Also: MGM of China, Inc., United Artists of China, Inc, Universal Picture Corp of China, Inc.), 2nd Flr., 18 Kwei Yang St., Section 2, Taipei. Tel: (8862) 331 4929. FAX: (8862) 331 1967.

TWENTIETH CENTURY FOX
City Hero Plaza, 8F-A No. 59, Chung-hwa Rd., Section 1, Taipei 100. Tel: (8862) 315 3773. FAX: (8862) 381 4492.

WARNER BROS. VILLAGE CINEMAS
(Warner Bros. International Theatres in association with Village Roadshow International)
P.O. Box 167, Taipei 100. Tel: (8862) 389 0159. FAX: (8862) 311 8526.
4000 Warner Blvd., Bridge Bldg. South, 5th Flr., Burbank, Calif., U.S. 91522. Tel: (818) 954 6014. FAX: (818) 954 6655.
PRESIDENT
Millard Ochs

EXHIBITORS

STUDIO CITY CINEMA HOLDINGS, LTD.
No. 226-1 Cheng Kung, 1st Rd., B1 B2 Flrs., Kaohslung, Taiwan.
CONTACT
Ben Leung

VILLAGE ROADSHOW, LTD.
(For complete listing see Australian branch.)
206 Bourke St., Melbourne, VIC, 3000, Australia. Tel: (613) 96 67 66 66. FAX: (613) 96 39 15 40.

Number of Theatres: 1 (Taiwan)
Number of Screens: 17 (Taiwan)

WARNER VILLAGE CINEMAS
No. 18 Sung Shou Rd., B1 Flr., Taipai. Tel: (886) 287 80 1166.

Number of Screens: 17.

THAILAND

Population: 61.2 million.
Screens: approx. 250.
Average Ticket Price: $2.80.

ASSOCIATIONS & ORGANIZATIONS

AMERICAN MOTION PICTURE ASSOCIATION
Rm. 602, Akane Bldg., 315 Silom Rd., Bangkok 10500. Tel: (662) 234 0240.

MOTION PICTURE EXHIBITORS ASSOC. OF THAILAND
352 Siam Theatre, Tama 1 Rd., Pathumwan, Bangkok 10500.

THAILAND FILM PROMOTION CENTRE
599 Bumrung Muang Rd., Bangkok 10100. Tel: (662) 223 4690. FAX: (662) 253 1817.

THAI MOTION PICTURES PRODUCERS ASSOCIATION
15/79 Soi Chokchairuammit, Viphavadee-Rangsit Rd., Bangkhen, Bangkok 10900. Tel: (662) 275 8833. FAX: (662) 281 8460.

DISTRIBUTORS AND PRODUCERS

APEX INTERNATIONAL CORP.
215 1 6 Rama 1 Rd., Slam Sq., Pathumwa, Bangkok 10500. Tel: (662) 251 8476. FAX: (662) 255 3131.

CINEAD GROUP
40 19 Sol Amonphannivas 4, Vipavadee Rangsit Road, Bangkok 10900. Tel: (662) 561 1965. FAX: (662) 561 1887.

CO BROTHERS ORGANISATION
117/2 Phayathai Rd., Rajthevi, Bangkok 10400. Tel: (662) 251 7163. FAX: (662) 254 7714.

FIVE STARS
31 345 Petchburi Rd., Phayathai, Bangkok 10400. Tel: (662) 215 0704.

GOLDEN TOWN FILM
69/55 Phayathai Atehn Theater Rd., Bangkok 10400. Tel: (662) 251 9168. FAX: (662) 259 3117.

HOLLYWOOD FILM DISTRIBUTION
420 Petchburi Rd., Phayathai, Bangkog 10400. Tel: (662) 251 5211.

MOVIELINK
40/19 Soi Amorn Pannives 4, Vipavadee-Rangsit Rd., Bangkok. Tel: (662) 561 1915.

NONTANUND ENTERTAINMENT
113/10 Suriwong Centre, Suriwong Rd., Bangkok 10500. Tel: (662) 236 7504. FAX: (662) 253 4830.

PYRAMID ENTERTAINMENT
216/1-6 Rama Rd., Siam Square, Bangkok 10500. Tel: (662) 252 7416.

SAHA MONGKOL FILM
1081/5 Phaholyothin Rd., Bangkok 10400. Tel: (662) 279 8456.

TWENTIETH CENTURY FOX/WARNER BROS.
Rm. 603, South East Insurance Bld., 315 Silom Road, Bangkok 10500. Tel: (662) 233 0920. FAX: (662) 236 4384.

UNITED INTERNATIONAL PICTURES (UIP)
Rm. 605, South East Insurance Bldg., 315 Silom Road, Bangkok 10500. Tel: (662) 233 4225. FAX: (662) 236 7597.

EXHIBITORS

ENTERTAIN GOLDEN VILLAGE
110 Moo 9 Petchkasem Rd., Bang Wa, Pasricharowen, Bangkok 10160. Tel: (662) 455-0150.
Number of Screens: 73

GOLDEN HARVEST ENTERTAINMENT CO., LTD.
(For additional listings, see Hong Kong, Singapore & Malaysia)
8 King Tung St., Hammer Hill Rd., Kowloon. Tel: (852) 2352 8222. FAX: (852) 2351 1683.
EXECUTIVES
Raymond Chow
Leonard Ho
Anthony Chow
Peter Chung
S.Y. Ho
Number of Theatres: 13
Number of Screens: 75

VILLAGE ROADSHOW, LTD.
(For complete listing see Australian branch.)
206 Bourke St., Melbourne, VIC, 3000, Australia. Tel: (613) 96 67 66 66. FAX: (613) 96 39 15 40.
Number of Theatres: 17 (Thailand)
Number of Screens: 93 (Thailand)

TURKEY

Population: 65.6 million.

ASSOCIATIONS & ORGANIZATIONS

ISTANBUL FOUNDATION FOR CULTURE & ARTS
Besiktas, Istanbul 80700. Tel: (90216) 259 1738. FAX: (90216) 261 8823.

SOCIETY OF IMPORTERS AND DISTRIBUTORS
Yesilcam Sok 7/1, Beyoglu, Istanbul. Tel: (90216) 249 0986.

SODER, THE SOCIETY OF ACTORS
Mete Cad Yani Prefabrik Binasi, Taksim, Istanbul. Tel: (90216) 252 6566.

DISTRIBUTORS AND PRODUCERS

BARLIK FILM
Ahududu Cad 32/3, Beyoglu, Istanbul 80060. Tel: (90216) 244 1542. FAX: (90216) 251 0386.

KILIC FILM
Yesilcam SK 26/2, Beyoglu, Istanbul 80070. Tel: (90216) 249 5804. FAX: (90216) 244 1612.

UNITED INTERNATIONAL PICTURES
Filmcilik ve Ticaret Ltd. Sti, Spor Cad. Acisu Sok. 1/7-8, Macka, Istanbul 80200. Tel: (90216) 227 8205. FAX: (90216) 227 8207.

WARNER BROS. A.S. TURKEY
Bronz Sokak, Bronz Apt. 3/6, Macka, Istanbul 80200. Tel: (90216) 231 2569. FAX: (90216) 231 7070.

EXHIBITORS

AFM CINEMA GROUP
416 Akmerkez Etiler, Istanbul, 80600. Tel: (90) 212 282 0508. FAX: (90) 212 282 0507. www.afm.com.tr
PRESIDENT
Sedat Akdemir
VICE PRESIDENT
Adnan Akdemir
CHAIRMAN
Yalcin Selgur
GENERAL MANAGER
Agah Tansev
GENERAL COORDINATOR
Gediz Tetik
V.P., FINANCE
Berent Akdemir
Number of Theatres: 19
Number of Screens: 63
Dr.-Ins: 1
Istanbul, Izmir, Bursa, Denizli, Isparta, Corlu.

CINEMAXX H.J. FLEBBE FILMTHEATERBETRIEBE
Mittelweg 176, 20148 Hanburg. Tel: (49) 40450 680. FAX: (49) 40 450 68201.
PRESIDENT & GENERAL MANAGER
Hans-Joachim Flebbe
GENERAL MANAGER & CFO
Michael Pawlowski
DIRECTOR, MARKETING
Jens Thomsen
Number of Theatres 1 (Turkey)
Number of Screens 5 (Turkey)

UNITED ARAB EMERATES (UAE)

Population: 2.4 million.

EXHIBITOR

THE GREATER UNION ORGANISATION
(Including BIRCH CARROLL & COYLE)
49 Market St., Sydney, NSW 2000, Australia. Tel: (612) 93 73 66 00. FAX: (612) 93 73 65 32.
MANAGING DIRECTOR
Robert Manson
Number of Theatres: 1 (UAE)
Number of Screens: 6 (UAE)

U.S. TERRITORIES

PUERTO RICO

Population: 3.8 million.

EXHIBITORS

REGENCY CARIBBEAN ENTERPRISES, INC.
(d.b.a.: Caribbean Cinemas)
1512 Fernandez Juncos, Stop 22-1/2, Santurce. Tel: (809) 727-7137. FAX: (809) 728-2274.

U.S. VIRGIN ISLANDS

Population: 120 thousand..

EXHIBITORS

CARIBBEAN CINEMAS OF THE VIRGIN ISLANDS, INC.
P.O. Box 9700, St. Thomas 00801. Tel: (809) 775-2244. FAX: (809) 724-2274.
ADMINISTRATOR
Jeff McLaughlin
PRESIDENT, CEO & CFO
Victor Carrady
V.P., COO & FILM BUYER
Robert Carrady
THEATRE OPERATIONS
Joe Ramos
Alfredo Morales
EQUIPMENT BUYER
Joel Matos

Website Guide

EXHIBITION CIRCUITS

Ajay Theatres, LLC .... www.movieline.com
Allen Theatres, Inc. .... www.allentheaters.com
AMC Entertainment, Inc. .... www.amctheatres.com
Carmike Cinemas .... www.carmike.com
Century Theatres .... www.centurytheatres.com
Cinema & Grill Systems, Inc. .... www.cinemagrill.com
Cinema Entertainment Corp. .... www.cec.hollywood.com
Cinemark USA, Inc. .... www.cinemark.com
Cinemastar Luxury Theatres, Inc. .... www.cinemastar.com
City Cinemas .... www.city-cinemas.com
Classic Cinemas .... www.classiccinemas.com
Clearview Cinema Corp. .... www.clearviewcinema.com
Dickinson Theatres, Inc. .... www.dtmovies.com
Dipson Theatres, Inc. .... www.dipson.hollywood.com
Douglas Theatre Co. .... www.douglastheatre.com
Eastern Federal Corp. .... www.hollywood.com
Edwards Theatres .... www.edwardscinemas.com
F & F/Value Theatres .... www.valuetheatres.com
GKC Theatres .... www.gkctheatres.com
General Cinema Theatres .... www.generalcinema.com
Goodrich Quality Theatres, Inc. .... www.gqti.com
Kerasotes Theatres .... www.kerasotes.com
Jack Loeks Theatres .... www.bigscreenmovies.com
Loews Cineplex Entertainment Corp. .... www.enjoytheshow.com
Malco Theatres, Inc. .... www.malco.com
Marcus Theatres Corporation .... www.marcustheatres.com
Marquee Cinemas .... www.marqueecinemas.com
National Amusements, Inc. .... www.nationalamusements.com
O'Neil Theatres, Inc. .... www.movie-info.com
Regal Cinemas, Inc. .... www.regalcinemas.com
Silver Cinemas, Inc. .... www.silvercinemasinc.com
United Artists Theatre Circuit, Inc. .... www.uatc.com
Wallace Theatre Corporation .... www.wallacetheatres.com
Wehrenberg Theatres, Inc. .... www.wehrenberg.com

MOTION PICTURE PRODUCERS & DISTRIBUTORS

Abandon Entertainment .... www.abandonent.com
Alliance Atlantis Communications, Inc. .... www.allianceatlantis.com
Altar Rock Films, Inc. .... www.altarrockfilms.com
Amazing Movies .... www.amazingmovies.com
AMC Entertainment Inc. .... www.amctheatres.com
American Zoetrope .... www.zoetrope.com
A Plus Entertainment .... www.aplusent.com
Arama Entertainment .... www.aramaent.com
Mark Archer Entertainment .... www.markarcherentertainment.com
Arrow Entertainment .... www.arrowfilms.com
Artisan Entertainment .... www.artisanent.com
The Artists' Colony .... www.theartistscolony.com
Artistic License Films .... www.artlic.com
Atkinson Way Films .... www.atkinsonway.com
Atlantic Streamline .... www.atlanticstreamline.com
Avenue Pictures .... www.avenue-entertainment.com
The Badham Co. .... www.badhamcompany.com
Baltimore/Spring Creek Pictures, LLC .... www. Levinson.com
Black & Blu Entertainment .... www.hollywoodlitsales.com
Jerry Bruckheimer Films .... www.jbfilms.z.com
Burrud Productions, Inc. .... www.burrud.com
Castle Rock Entertainment .... www.castle-rock.com
Cecchi Gori Pictures .... www.cecchigori.com
Centropolis Entertainment .... www.centropolis.com
The Cinema Guild .... www.cinemaguild.com
Cinevista, Inc .... www.cinevistavideo.com
Crown International Pictures, Inc. .... www.crownintlpictures.com
Crystal Pyramid Productions .... www.crystalpyramid.com
Dark horse Entertainment .... www.dhorse.com
Destination Cinema, Inc. .... www.destinationcinema.com
Digital Domain www.d2.com
Discovery Pictures .... www.discovery.com
The Walt Disney Company .... www.disney.com
Distant Horizon .... www.distant-horizon.com

Eastman Kodak Company	www.kodak.com
Fifty Cannon Entertainment, LLC	www.50cannon.com
Filmworld International, Inc.	www.filmworldinc.com
First Look Pictures/Overseas Film Group	www.ofg.com
First Run Features	www.firstrunfeatures.com
Fox, Inc.	www.fox.com
Full Moon Universe	www.fullmoonpictures.com
General Media International	www.penthouse.com
Good Machine International	www.goodmachine.com
Gotham Pictures	www.resolutionprod.com
Grainy Pictures	www.grainypictures.com
Greenestreet Films, Inc.	www.greenestreetfilms.com
Jim Henson Pictures	www.henson.com
Home Box Office, Inc.	www.hbo.com
Imagine Entertainment	www.imagine-entertainment.com
Imax Corp.	www.imax.com
International Film Circuit	www.winstartelevid.com
Italtoons Corp.	www.italtoons.com
Iwerks Entertainment	www.iwerks.com
Killer Films, Inc.	www.killerfilms.com
Kino International Corp.	www.kino.com
Kushner-Locke Co.	www.kusher-locke.com
Leading Pictures, Inc.	www.alistpictures.com
Leisure Time Features	www.leisurefeat.com
Lions Gate Films	www.lionsgateent.com
RGH/Lions Share Pictures, Inc.	www.lionsharepictures.com
L-Squared Entertainment	www.lsqr.com
Lucasfilm, Ltd.	www.lucasfilms.com
Lucasarts Entertainment Co.	www.lucasarts.com
Lucas Digital, Ltd.	www.ilm.com
Lucid Media	www.loop.com\~macbravo\
Macgillivray Freeman Films	www.macfreefilms.com
Malibu Bay Films	www.andysidaris.com
Marvel Characters, Inc.	www.marvel.com
Merchant Ivory Productions	www.merchantivory.com
Metro-Goldwyn-Mayer Studios, Inc.	www.mgm.com
Miramax Films Corp.	www.miramax.com
The Mount Company	www.hollywoodbroadcasting.com
Moving Pictures, Ltd.	www.movingpics.net
MTV Films	www.mtv.com
Muse Productions, Inc.	www.musefilm.com
National Geographic	www.nationalgeographic.com/main.html
National Lampoon	www.nationallampoon.com
New Concorde Corp.	www.concorde-newhorizons.com
New Line Cinema Corporation	www.newline.com
New Regency Prods.	www.newregency.com
New Yorker Films	www.newyorkerfilms.com
Newstar Media, Inc.	www.newstarmedia.com
New Yorker Films	www.newyorkerfilms.com
No Prisoners	www.noprisoners.com
Nova Large Format Films	www.pba.org/wgbh/nova
NWave Pictures	www.nwave.com
Omega Entertainment, Ltd.	www.omegapic.com
100% Entertainment	www.100percent.com
Orpheus Films	www.orpheusfilms.com
Outlaw Prods.	www.outlawfilm.com
Oxygen Media	www.oxygen.com
Paramount Pictures	www.paramount.com
Phaedra Cinema	www.phaedracinema.com
Picture This Entertainment	www.picturethisent.com
Platonic Films, Inc.	www.platonicfilms.com
Porchlight Entertainment	www.porchlight.com
Pray For Rain Pictures, Inc.	www.toendallwars.com
Edward R. Pressman Films, Ltd.	www.pressman.com
Principal Large Format	www.principalmedia.com
Priviledged Communications	www.thebasket.net
Propaganda Films	www.propagandafilms.com
Rainbow Releasing	www.rainbowfilms.com
Redeemable Features	www.redeemable.com
Regent Entertainment, Inc.	www.regententertainment.com
Revelations Entertainment	www.revelationsent.com
RKO Pictures	www.rko.com
Roxie Releasing	www.roxie.com
Samuel Productions	www.oscarwilde.com
Seventh Art Releasing	www.7thart.com
Shonkyte Productions, Inc.	www.seanyoung.org
The Shooting Gallery, Inc.	www.shootinggallery.com
Showscan Entertainment	www.showscan.com

Silverlight Entertainment	www.silverlightent.com
Alan Smithee Films	www.smithee.com/films
Sony Pictures Entertainment, Inc.	www.spe.sony.com
Spectromedia Entertainment	www.goldcoasthandbook.com
Strand Releasing/New Oz Productions	www.strandrel.com
Stratosphere Entertainment	www.stratospherefilm.com
Sundance Institute	www.sundance.org
Swartwout Enterprises, Inc.	www.supervue.com
Taurus Entertainment Co.	www.taurus-entertainment.com
Telling Pictures	www.tellingpix.com
Bob Thomas Productions, Inc.	www.bobthomasprods.com
Tribeca Productions	www.tribecafilm.com
Trident Releasing	www.tridentreleasing.com
Trimark Pictures	www.trimarkpictures.com
Troma Entertainment, Inc.	www.Troma.com/home
Universal Studios, Inc.	www.unistudios.com
USA Films	www.usafilms.com
Viacom, Inc.	www.viacom.com
View Askew Productions, Inc.	www.viewaskew.com
Warner Bros. Inc.	www.warnerbros.com
West Glen Communications, Inc.	www.westglen.com
Wild Child Entertainment, Ltd.	www.wildchildent.com
Winstar Television & Video	www.winstartelevid.com
Saul Zaentz Film Center	www.zaentz-filmcenter.com
Zeitgeist Films, Ltd.	www.zeitgeistfilm.com
Zide/Perry Entertainment	www.inzide.com
Zollo Productions, Inc.	www.members.aol.com/zpi/index.html

ALPHABETICAL INDEX OF SUBJECTS

This index lists selected companies, agencies and organizations from major sections of the book. If the company you are looking for is not in the index, please find the company in alphabetical order within the relevant section.

A

A & A Special Effects .746
A & B Co. .893
A & C Harbour Lites, Ltd. .724
A & J Recording Studios, Inc. .742
A Band Apart .645
A Plus Entertainment .647
A Retrospect Film Archive .754
A Theatre Near You, (Canada), Inc. .963
A. Karavoykyros - K. Frantzis, S.A. (Greece) .1023
A.C. Nielsen Company .741
A.C. Nielsen Company-EDI .741
A.D.2, Inc. .746
A.E.M.M. Koopal-Waskowsky (Netherlands) .1031
A.J. Productions .633
A.Th. Abeln (Netherlands) .1031
AAMI-TDS (Theatron) .881
Aardman Animations .712
Aargh! Animation, Inc. .712
AASI-TDS (Systems) (Theatron) .881
AASI-TDS-NV .881
AB Audio Design Studios .742
AB-Strakt Pictures .645
ABA Picture Vehicles & Casting Services .721
Abandon Entertainment .645
Abatemarco, Frank, Productions .645
Abbey Films, Ltd. .973
Abby Lou Entertainment .712
ABC Cinemas, Ltd. .973
ABC Costume Shop .726
Abilene Pictures .645
About Face Productions .645
Above The Line Agency .760
Abraham Rugs Gallery .726
Abrams Artists Agency .760
Abrams, Bob, & Associates .706
Abrams, Rubaloff & Lawrence .760
Absher Enterprises, Inc. .771
AC Works .645
Academy Casting .721
Academy of Canadian Cinema & Television .967
Academy Award Winners 1999 .17
1995-1998 .17
Academy of Motion Picture Arts & Sciences .908
Stock Shots .753
Academy Players Directory .931
Acappella Pictures .645
Access Casting .721
Accommodating Ideas, Inc. .724
ACCU-Cast/ACCU-Dent .726
Ace Audio Visual .885
Acme Filmworks .712
Acme Talent & Literary .760
Acorn Entertainment .712
Acorto, Inc. .882
Acoustic & Noise Control .879
Acoustipleat Co. .879
Act III Productions .645
Action America Entertainment .645
Action Sets & Props/Wonderworks .726
Actors Etc., Inc. .760
Actors' Equity Assn. .915
Actra Performers Guild .967
Actueel Bioscoopexploitatie B.V. (Netherlands) .1031
Adam's Stained Glass .726
Adams & Brooks .896
Adaptive Micro Systems .885
Addis, Michael, Films (Gorgon) .645
Address One Post .755
Adele's of Hollywood .726
Adelson, Orly, Productions .645
Admarketing, Inc. .706
Adriaticocinema .632
Adsposure Advertising Specialties .706
Advanced Camera Systems .746
Advanced Fire & Rescue Services .724, 746
Advanced Thermal Technologies .886
Advantage Audio .742
Advertising & Publicity .706
Advertising Age .931
Aerial Focus Productions .724
Aero Mock-Ups .726
AFD/Photograd Film Coating Lab .735
Affiliated Paper Companies, Inc. .897
Affiliated Property Craftsmen, Hollywood .917
Affrime, Mindy, Productions .645
AFI/Los Angeles Intl. Film Festival .633
AFM Cinema Group (Turkey) .1041
AFRA Film Enterprises, Inc .737
Afra-Film Enterprises, Inc. .645
African Film & TV Collective (South Africa) .1036
Afshan Cinema (Pakistan) .1033
Aftershock Digital .755
Agamemnon Films, Inc. .645
Agape Uniform Company .726
Agency 2 Talent Agency .760
Agency for the Performing Arts, Inc. .760
Agency, The .760
Agents for the Arts .760
Ahern Group, The .704
Aidikoff, Charles, Screening Room, The .900
Aim Promotions .726
Air Hollywood .726
Airpower Aviation Resources .726
Aisle & Wall Lighting .879
AIU Media & Entertainment .739
Ajar, Charles, Projector Co., Inc. .900
Akima's Casting & Productions Services .721
Akin, Gump, Strauss, Hauer & Feld .730
AKO Productions .760
Akre, Bryan & Mailan, LP .730
Albania .1007
Albert G. Ruben Insurance Services, Inc. .739
Alchemy Entertainment .646
Alcon Entertainment, LLC .646
Alcops Inc. .891
Alden, Phil, Robinson .679
Alexander Technique/Actor's Movement Specialist .724
Alfalah Cinema (Pakistan) .1033
Alias/Wavefront .746
Alice Entertainment .712
Alive Films .646
All Effects Co., Inc. .726, 746
All Girl Productions .646
All Post, Inc. .742
All-Star Carts & Vehicles, Inc. .882
Allan King Associates Limited .938
Allan Uniform Rental Services, Inc. .726
Allegra Partners .737
Allen Lawrence & Associates .739
Allen Products Co., Inc. .892
Allen Theatres, Inc. .771
Allen, David, Productions .712, 746
Alliance Atlantic Motion Picture Distribution .957
Alliance Atlantis Communications, Inc. .646
Canada .938
Alliance Cinemas .963
Alliance of Motion Picture & TV Producers .908
Alliance Talent, Inc. .760
Allied Entertainment Group .737
Allied Stars .646
Allied/Vaughn's New Independent Lab .735
Allison, Sandy .721
Almost Christmas Propshop .726
Alpern Group, The .760
Alpha Cine Laboratory, Inc. .735
Alphaville .646
Alphaville (Spain) .1038
Alpro Acoustics .879
Alschuler, Grossman, Stein & Kahan, LP .730
Alta Films S.A. (Spain) .1038
Alta-Dena Certified Dairy .897
Altar Rock Films, Inc. .646
Altered Anatomy, Inc. .726
Alterian Studios .746
Altman Luggage .726
Alvarado Manufacturing .884

Alvarado, Carlos, Agency .760
AM Productions & Management .647
Amalgamated Dynamics .746
Amalgamated Incorporated .646
Amato, Michael, Theatrical Agency .760
Amazing Movies .646
Ambergate Associates .706, 737
Ambrosio-Johnston Management .760
AMC Entertainment, Inc.
Distribution .646
Theatres .771
AMC Theatres of Canada .963
AMC Film Marketing, Inc. .646
Amen RA Films .647
America Zoetrope .755
American Archives, Inc. .735
American Assoc. of Advertising Agencies, Inc. .706
American Can Co. .897
American Cinema Editors .915
American Cinema Equipment, Inc. .893
American Cinematheque .908
American Cinematographer, The .931
American Costume Corp. .726
American Entertainment Co. .647
American Express .881
American Federation of Musicians .915
American Film & Tape, Inc. .755
American Film Institute .908
Awards .19
Screening Room .900
Library (Stock Shots) .753
American Film Market .630
American Film Marketing Assn. .908
American Filmworks .647
American First Run Studios .647
American Guild of Musical Artists, Inc. .915
American Guild of Variety Artists .915
American Humane Assn. .908
American Indians In Film .721
American International Talent Agency .760
American Intl. Concession Products Corp. .896
American Licorice Co. .896
American Marketing Association .741
American Multi-Cinema (Portugal) .1035
American New Wave Films .647
American Popcorn Co. .898
American Seating Co. .890
American Society of Cinematographers .915
Awards .19
American Society of Composers, Authors & Publishers .909
American Stock Photography .753
American World Pictures .647
American Zoetrope .647
AMG-Renaissance .760
Amlon Ticket .894
Amorosano Associates .706
Ampac Theatre Cleaning Services .893
Ampas: Academy Little Theatre & Samuel Goldwyn Theatre .900
Amsel, Eisenstadt & Frazier, Inc. .760
Amsell Entertainment, Inc. .647
Ana Special Effects .726
Anatomorphex .726, 746
Anchor Editorial .755
Andaction Corp. .886
Anderson, Beverly .760
Anderson, Craig Productions .647
Anderson, Howard, West .721
Anderson, McCook, White Casting, Inc. .721
Andreadis Talent Agency, Inc. .760
Angel Ark Productions .647
Angel Films .712
Angellotti Company, The .706
Angry Dragon Entertainment .647
Angry Films, Inc. .647
Animal Makers .712, 726
Animal Outfits for People Co. .726
Animatics & Storyboards, Inc. .712
Animation .712
Animation Equipment .712
Anime Comics & Movies .712
Animotion .712
Animus Films .746
Anmol Cinema (Pakistan) .1033
Ann Arbor Film Festival .630
Annecy Intl. Animated Film Festival .632
Annelise Collins Casting .721
Annual Index to Motion Picture Credits .931
Ant Farm .706
Antiquarian Traders .726
Antique & Classic Vehicles .726
Antique Guild .726
Anvil Post Production, Ltd. .976
Aon/Albert G. Ruben Insurance Services, Inc. .739
Aon/Ruben-Winkler Entertainment Insurance .739
APA Studios .746
Apatow Productions .647
Apogee Productions .706
Apollo Leisure (UK), Ltd. - Cinema Division .973
Apollo-Film State Film Distributor (Poland) .1034
Apostle Pictures .647
Apostolos Foukis (Greece) .1023
Appledown Films, Inc. .648
Applied Lighting Systems .879
Aquarius Releasing, Inc./Aquarius Media Corp. .648
Aquavision .726
Aquila, Deborah .721
Arama Entertainment .648
ARC Science Simulations .712
Archer, Mark, Entertainment .648
Archion .755
Architecture, Design, & Construction .880
Archive Films/Archive Photos .753
Arcimage Films .648
Area Catalina D'Exhibicio Cinematografica, S.A. (Spain) .1038
Arenas Group, The .706
Argentina .1007
Aria Model & Talent Management .761
Aries Entertainment, Inc. .648
Arizona Theatre Owners Assn. .905
Armstrong, Hirsch, Jackoway, Tyerman & Wertheimer .730
Arnold & Porter .730
Arrow Entertainment .648
Arrowstreet, Inc. .880
Art Directors, Hollywood .915
Art Directors, Local 876, Hollywood .917
Arteffex .746
Arthouse Entertainment .648
Artificial Eye Co. .973
Artisan Entertainment .648
Artisan Legal .730
Artistic License Films .648
Artists Agency, The .761
Artists Management Agency .761
Artists Network .761
Artists' Colony, The .648
Arts & Crafters, Inc. .726
Artz & Cohen Casting .721
ASC Audio Video Corp. .755
ASC Theatre Equipment Sales .893
Asherson, Klein & Darbinn .730
Ashly Audio, Inc. .892
Ashurst Agency .902
Aspen Filmfest .633
Aspen Shortsfest .631
Assigned Seating & Mfg. Group, Inc. .890
Assistive Listening Systems .881
Assn. des Prop. de Cin. et Cine-Parcs du Quebec, Inc. .966
Assn. of Dutch Film Theatres (Netherlands) .1031
Assn. of Film Commissioners Intl. .909
Assn. of Independent Video & Filmmakers, Inc. .909
Assn. of Talent Agents .916
Assn. Musicians of Greater New York .916
Assn. of National Film Distributors & Producers (Spain) .1037
Associated Actors & Artists of America .916
Associated Booking Corp. .761
Associated Hearing Instruments .881
Associated Media Images, Inc. .753
Associated Production Music .742
Association of Cinemas of Hungary .1025
Asther/Goulg Advertising, Inc. .706
Astor, Richard .761
Astral Media, Inc. .939
Astraltech, Inc. .742
Animation .712
Canada .953
Astro Color Lab .735
Astro Film & Video .900
Astron Films Corporation .648
Asylum, The .648
ATA Trading Corp. .648
Atalanta Filmes (Portugal) .1035
Ateliers du Cinema Europeen (France) .1018
Atkins & Associates .761
Atkinson Way Films .649
Atlantic Independent Theatre Exhibitors Assn. .966
Atlantic Motion Picture Exhibitors Assn. .966
Atlantic Streamline .649
Atlantic Theatre Services, Ltd. .966
Atlas Entertainment .649
Atlas Specialty Lighting .879
Atlas Specialty Lighting Projector Lamps & Lenses .889

Atman Entertainment .649
Atomix, Inc. .712
Attenborough, Richard, Productions, Ltd. .976
Attica Cineplex (Greece) .1023
Audex Assistive Listening Systems .881
Audio Cine Film .957
Audio Department, The .742
Audio Mechanics .742
Audio Services Company .742
August Entertainment .649
Aura Lighting Products .879
Aurora Productions .649
Australia .1007
Australian Film Commission .737, 1007
Australian Film Finance Corp. .1007
Australian Multiplex Cinemas (AMC) .1011
Austria .1012
Authentic Design .755
Authors Guild, Inc. .916
Authors League of America, Inc., The .916
Automatic Bar Controls/Wunder-Bar .882
Automatic Devices Co. .884
Automatic Pictures .649
Automaticket .881
AV Guide: The Learning Media Newsletter .931
Available Light, Ltd. .746, 755
Avalanche Entertainment .649
Avalon Stages .735
Avask .888
Avenue Pictures .649
Aviation In Entertainment Consultants .724
Aviator Films, LLC .649
Avid Technology .742, 755
AVL Systems, Inc. .879
Avnet-Kerner Co. .649
Awards & Polls .13
Axelson-Weintraub Productions .649
Axis Animated Graphic Systems, LLSC .885
Axis Media .706
Ayer, Jane, Public Relations, Inc. .706
Ayer, N.W., & Partners .706

B

B & B Theatres .773
B.D. Fox & Friends, Inc. Advertising .708
B.V. 'De Nieuwe Buitensocieteit' (Netherlands) .1031
B.V. Bioscoop Exploitatie Minerva (Netherlands) .1031
B.V. Utrechtse Filmonderneming UFIO (Netherlands) .1031
Bablove Agency, Inc. .706
Babylon Post .755
Bac Film & Video Festival .631
Backer, Spielvogel, Bates, Inc. .706
Background Animation .712
Badgley/Connor .761
Badham Co., The .649
Baer Animation Company, Inc. .712
Baer Entertainment Group .649
Bagdasarian Productions .713
Bahamas .1014
Baker, Winokur, Ryder .706
Bakery Recording Studio, The .742
Bakula Productions .649
Balana, Pedro, (Spain) .1038
Balji Group, The 9 (India) .1026
Ballantyne of Omaha/Strong Intl. .888
  Projectors .889
Ballard Communications .706
Ballyhoo, Inc. .649
Balsmeyer & Everett, Inc. .746
Baltimore/Springs Creek Pictures, LLC .649
Bambino Cinema (Pakistan) .1033
Bandeira Entertainment .650
Banff Television Festival .632
Bank of America NT & SA/Commercial Banking Ent. Office .737
Bank of California .737
Bank of New York .737
Bank Sumitomo .737
Bankers Trust Co. .737
Banned from the Ranch Entertainment .746
Banner Candy Mfg. Corp. .896
Banner Entertainment .650
Banque Paribas .737
Barab, Kline & Coate, LLP .730
Barclay Communications .706
Barish, Rise, Casting .721
Barnette, Alan, Productions .650
Barnholtz Entertainment .650
Barnstorm Films .650
Baron, Stephen .730
Bartco Co. .888
Bartel Design Group .706
Barton G. Creative Productions .721
Barwood Films .650
Bascom, Fran, & Associates .721
Basker, Pamela .721
Bass Industries .885
Batjac Productions, Inc. .650
Bauer Company, The .650
Baum, Carol, Productions .650
Bauman, Richard & Associates .761
Baumgarten/Prophet Entertainment .650
Bay Films .650
Bayley Silleck Productions, Inc. .650
Baypost Co. .755
BBC Worldwide Americas .713
  BBC Library Stock Shots .753
BBDO .706
Beacon Communications, LLC .650
Bear Advertising, Inc. .706
Bear, Streams & Co., Inc. .737
Beaver Machine Corp. .882
Bedfellows .726
Bedford Falls Co., The .650
Bee People Unlimited .724
Behr & Abramson .730
Behr Browers Architects, Inc. .880
Bel-Air Entertainment .650
Beldock, Levine & Hoffman .730
Belgium .1014
Belisarius Productions .650
Bellevue Cinemas .973
Benchmark Design Group .880
Bender, Goldman & Helper .706
Bender-Spink .651
Benedetti, Robert, Productions, Inc. .651
Bennett Agency .761
Bennett, Sara, Agency, The .761
Bennett, Walter F., Communications .706
Benson, Annette .721
Benton Film Forwarding Co. .735
Berg/Saccani Entertainment .651
Berger, Kahn, Shafton, Moss, Figler, Somon & Gladstone .730
Berkett, Lloyd S., Agency .739
Berkowitz & Associates .730
Berland, Terry, Casting .721
Berlin International Film Festival .630
Berlitz Translation Center .759
Berman, Rick Productions .651
Bermuda .1015
Berner, Fred, Films .651
Bern Levy Associates .889
Berton & Donaldson .730
Berzon Talent Agency .761
Best Shot, Inc. .753
Beth Holmes Casting .722
Beverages .896
BGW Systems .891
BGW Systems Sound Reinforcement .892
Bieber, Rick, Productions .651
Biederman, Kelly & Shaffer, Inc. .706
Bienstock & Clark .730
Bifrost Laserfx .713, 746
Big Bang Films .651
Big Screen Ideas .901
Big Screen Pictures, LLC .878
Big Sky Industries .888
  Projectors .889
  Theatre Equipment .893
Big Time Picture Co. .755, 900
Big Town Productions .651
Bigger Than Life, Inc. .726, 746
Biggs-Adams .724
Bil Mar Foods, Inc. .897
Bill Millar .750
Billboard .931
Billings, Marion, Publicity, Ltd. .706
Billy Sky Productions .746
Bioscoopexploitatie J. M. Punt Heerhugowaard B.V. (Netherlands) .1031
Bioscoopexploitatiemaatschap-PIJ Cinex B.V. (Netherlands) .1031
Bioscooponderneming AF Wolff B.V. (Netherlands) .1031
Biovision .746
Birtcher Construction .880
Bite the Mango Film Festival .632
BJK&E Media Group .741
Black & Blu Entertainment .651
Black Logic .713

Blackstone Magik Enterprises, Inc. .724, 746
Blackwatch Communications .939
Blackwatch Releasing, Inc. .957
Blain & Associates .730
Blair Design & Construction .880
Blanc, Williams, Johnston & Kronstadt .730
Bleecker Street Films .651
Block-Korenbrot Public Relations .706
Blodgett Advanced Cooking Technology/Maytag .882
Bloom at Ford .761
Bloom Theatres .973
Bloom, Hergott, Cook, Diemer & Klein .730
Bloom, J. Michael, & Assoc. .761
Bloomfilm .901
Blooming Paradise Productions .753
Blue Movie (Germany) .1021
Blue Relief, Inc. .651
Blue River Digital .713
Blue Sky Studios .713
Blue Sky/VIFX .746
Blue Tulip Productions .651
Blue Wolf Productions, Inc. .651
Bluefield Music Design .742, 755
Blur Studio, Inc. .713, 746
BMI (Broadcast Music, Inc.) .909
Boardwalk Entertainment .651
Bobtown .713
Bodie, Carol, Entertainment .651
Bodytech .746
Bohbot Entertainment .713
Bohrman Agency, The .761
Bolivia .1015
Bolton, Michelle, & Associates .706
Bona Fide Productions .651
Bonded Film Storage .735
Bonded Services .735
Boneyard Entertainment .651
Bontalent, Inc. .761
Bontonfilm (Czech Republic) .1016
Boom Boom Effects .746
Booz, Allen & Hamilton, Inc. .724
Borgarbio (Iceland) .1025
Borinstein Oreck Bogart Agency .761
Boston Casting .721
Boston Light & Sound, Inc. .878, 893
Bottom Line Studios .755
Boulevard Cinema, Ltd. .963
Bouquet Post .755
Box Office, Concession, & Accounting Systems .881
Boxing Cat Productions .652
Boxoffice .931
Boyd Coffee Co. .896
Boyington Film Productions .713
Bozell Worldwide .706
Brad Barry Co./Caffe D'Vita Cappuccino .896
Bradford Animation Festival .632
Bradford Film Festival .630
Bradley Fixtures Corp. .886
Bragman Hyman Cafarelli .706
Brambles Information Management .735
Bramson & Associates .706, 721, 741
Branam Enterprises, Inc. .746
Brandt Company, The .761
Brass Smith, Inc. .884
Bravo Helicopters .724
Brazil .1015
Bregman Productions .652
Brejtfus Enterprises, Inc. .879
Bresler Kelly & Associates .761
Bret Adams, Ltd. .760
Brevard Talent Group, Inc. .761
Bridgeman Art Library Intl., The .753
Bright & Associates .724
Briles Wing & Helicopter, Inc. .726
Brilliant, Robert A., Inc. .741
Brillstein-Grey Entertainment .652
Brimstone Entertainment .737
Brintons U.S. Axminster .882
Brisbane Intl. Film Festival .632
Bristol Cities .652
Britannica Films Stock Shots .753
British Academy of Film & TV Arts .999
Awards .19
British Actors' Equity Assoc. .999
British Board of Film Classification .999
British Connection .737
British Film Commission .1001
British Film Festival .634
British Film Institute (BFI) .1001
British Movietonews, Ltd. .977
British Screen Finance, Ltd. .977
British Sky Broadcasting, Ltd. .977
British Columbia Production Financing .737
Broadcast (Great Britain) .933
Broadcast Board of Governors .930
Broadcast Business Consultants, Ltd. .724
Broadcasting & Cable, The News Weekly of TV & Radio .931
Broadcasting & Cable Yearbook .931
Broadcasting Studio Employees .916
Broadway Cinemas .973
Broadway Entertainment Group (Germany) .1021
Broadway Filmtheater, GMBH (Germany) .1021
Broadway FTB GMBH (Germany) .1021
Broadway Kino (Germany) .1021
Broadway Screening Room .900
Broadway Video Design .713
Brokaw Company, The .706
Bronston, Paul, M.D. .724
Brooklyn Model Works .746
Brooksfilms, Ltd. .652
Brown, Curtis, Ltd. .761
Brown/West Casting .721
Brubaker Group, The .726, 746
Bruckheimer, Jerry, Films .652
Brussels International Film Festival .630
Brussels Intl. Festival of Fantasy, Thriller & Sci-Fi Films .631
Bryant & Johnsen, Inc. .713
Brymer, Pat, Creations .726
Bubba Scrubba Gum Removal Svc. .893
Bubble Factory, The .652
Buck/Edelman Casting Co. .721
Budapest Film (Hungary) .1025
Budget Films .753
Budgets by Design .724
Buena Vista (also see The Walt Disney Company)
Animation .713
Home Entertainment .657
Home Entertainment International .657
International .657
International Offices (see individual contries in World Market) .1007
Motion Pictures Group .656
Non-Theatrical .704
Pay Television .657
Pictures Distribution Canada, Inc. .656, 957
Pictures Distribution, Inc. .655
Pictures Marketing .656
Special Effects .747
Stock Shots .753
Bumble Ward & Associates .706
Bungalow 78 Productions .652
Bureau of the Intl. Film Festivals/"Festival of Festivals" .632
Burkett Talent Agency .761
Burman Studios, Inc. .747
Burnett, Leo, Company, Inc. .707
Burns, Dott, Talent Agency .761
Burr, Wally, Recording .742
Burrud Productions .652
Burson-Marsteller .707
Burton, Iris, Agency .761
Butchers Run Films .652
Bux-Mont Signs .885
Buying & Booking Agenices .902
Buzzco Associates, Inc. .713
Byk, Jon Advertising, Inc. .707

C

C & S International Insurance Brokers, Inc. .739
C. Cretors & Co. .882
C.J.S. Film Studios .727
C/W Productions .655
CAA/Creative Artists Agency .761
CAC Leisure Co. .973
Cacioppo Production Design, Inc. .747
Caddy Cupholder .886
Cadillac (Germany) .1021
Cagey Costume Source .726
Cal-East Imports .726
Calabash Animation .713
Caledonian Cinemas .973
Caliban Filmworks .755
Calico Entertainment .747
Calico World Entertainment .713
California Art Products Co. .726
California Booking .902
California Communications, Inc. .755
California Historical Group WWII Living History Assn. .724
California Sailing Academy .724, 726

California Seating & Repair Co., Inc. .890
California Stage & Lighting .893
California Surplus Mart .727
California United Bank .737
Call The Cops .724
Calvert Group, The .713
Camatic Seating .890
Cameo Film Library, Inc. .753
Camera Ready Cars .727
Cameron Productions .704
Camille H. Patton .723
Campbell Agency, The .762
Canada .936
Distribution Companies .957
Exhibitors & Exhibition Services .963
Government Agencies .970
Production Companies .938
Production Services .952
Trade Associations .967
Year in Review .936
Canadian Assn. of Film Distributors & Exporters .968
Canadian Film & TV Production Assoc. .968
Canadian Filmmakers' Distribution Centre .957
Canadian Independent Film Caucus .968
Canadian Intl. Development Agency .970
Canadian Media Guild .968
Canadian Motion Picture Distributors Assn. .968
Canadian Society of Cinematographers .968
Canal + (U.S.) .652
Canamedia .957
Canamedia Productions, Ltd. .940
Candace Lake Agency .765
Candy & Confections .896
Cannes Film Festival Awards .20
Canton Company, The .652
Capella Films, Inc. .653
Capella Films, Inc. & Connexion American Media .737
Capitol Studios .742
Cappa Productions .653
Capri Cinema (Pakistan) .1033
Caprice Showcase Theatres, Inc. .963
Capstone Film Co. .707
Caption Center .759
Captionmax .759
Captions, Inc. .759
Cardinal Sound & Motion Picture Systems, Inc. .893
Cardlogix .881
Cargill .898
Caribbean Cinemas of the Virgin Islands, Inc. .1041
Carlton, Cathi, Casting .721
Carlton Communications PLC .977
Carlton Film Distributors, Ltd. .977
Carmike Cinemas .774
Carnival Cinemas .963
Carousel Films, Inc. .704
Carpets .882
Carroll, William, Agency .762
Carson Adler Agency, Inc. .762
Casablanca Gastst, Kulture & Kino GMBH (Germany) .1021
Cassell-Levy, Inc. .762
Castanon, Richard G., M.D., F.A.C.S. .724
Casting 2000/Starcast 2000 .721
Casting Comapny, The .721
Casting Crew, Inc., The .721
Casting Directors .721
Casting Directors of Canada .969
Casting Society of America .721
Castle Hill Productions, Inc. .653
Castle Rock Entertainment .653
Catalina Graphic Films .712
Catania Group, The .707
Cathay Cineplexes Pte., Ltd. (Singapore) .1036
Cathay Organisation (M) SDN BHD (Malaysia) .1029
Cathay Theatre Management Pte., Ltd. (Singapore) .1036
Cavalcade Productions, Inc. .704
Cavaleri & Associates .762
Cawley Co. .886
CBC International Sales .958
CCDA: Commerical Casting Directors Associates .721
Cecchi Gori Group (Italy) .1028
Cecchi Gori Pictures .653
CEG Post .755
Celebrity Eyeworks .727
Celebrity Service Intl. .931
Celestial Lighting Products .879
Celluloid Studios .713
Central Casting .721
Central Casting, Ltd. (UK) .999
Central Properties .727
Central Soya Co., Inc. .898
Central States Theatre Corp. .778
Centre Firearms Co., Inc. .727
Centropolis Entertainment .653
Century Artists, Ltd. .762
Century Theatres .778
Certified Marketing Services, Inc. .741
Certified Reports, Inc. East .741
Certified Reports, Inc. West .741
Cerwin-Vega .892
Chace Productions, Inc .735, 742
Chakeres Theatres .779
Change Ad-Letter Co. .885
Chaphalkar Group of Cinemas (India) .1026
Character Builders, Inc. .712, 713
Character Shop, Inc., The .747
Charisma Design Studio, Inc. .727
Chart Industries/MVE .883
Charter Connection, The .724
Chartoff Productions .653
Chase Productions, Inc. .755
Chase Securities, Inc./Entertainment Group .737
Chasin Agency, The .762
Chenoweth, Bob, Rentals .755
Chequered Flag International, Inc. .724
Cherry Alley Productions .653
Chertok Assoc., Inc. .753
Chicago Alt. Film Festival .632
Chicago Filmmakers .900
Chicago Intl. Children's Film Festival .633
Chicago Intl. Film Festival .633
Chicago Latino Cinema .631
Chicago Lesbian & Gay Intl. Film Festival .634
Chief Exhibition Circuits (Canada) .963
Children's Media Productions .713
Chile .1015
China .1015
China Film Equipment Corp. .889
China Film Export & Import Corporation .1015
China Mist Tea Co. .896
Chiodo Bros. Productions, Inc. .713, 747
Christensen, Miller, Fink, Jacobs, Glaser, Weil & Shapiro .730
Christie, Inc. .878, 889
Christy's Editorial Film & Video Supply .755
Chromacolour International .712
Chubb Group Insurance .739
Chyron Corp. .713
Ciby Distribution (France) .1019
Ciby Sales .978
Cicce (France) .1018
Cienvision Editorial, Inc. .755
Cifex Corporation .704
Cimmelli, Inc. .747
Cinar Films (US), Inc. .713
Cincom-The Megaplex Cinema Specialists .893
Cine Cite Montreal .952
Cine Columbia S.A. .1015
Cine Magnetics Film & Video .735
Cine Motion Picture Service Lab .735
Cine Vegas Intl. Film Festival .634
Cine-Alpes (France) .1020
Cine-UK, Ltd. .973
Cineasia .634
Cinecitta International (Italy) .1027
Cinefex .931
Cinefilm/Cinetransfer .735
Cinegrand .878
Cinema 5 (Italy) .1028
Cinema Booking Service of New England .902
Cinema City, Inc. .963
Cinema Completions International .739
Cinema Concepts .886
Cinema Concepts Theatre Service Co., Inc. .901
Cinema Consultants Group .741
Cinema du Reel .631
Cinema Engineering Co. .712, 747
Cinema Entertainment Corp. .782
Cinema Equipment, Inc. .893
Cinema Exhibitors' Assoc. .999
Cinema Expo Intl. .632
Cinema Film Systems/Rentec, Inc. .889
Cinema Grill .779
Cinema Guild, The .653
Cinema Les Ecrans (France) .1020
Cinema Lighting & Installation .879
Cinema Parallele .963
Cinema Paris (Albania) .1007
Cinema Products Intl. .887, 888
Cinema Services .882, 884
Cinema Seven Productions .653
Cinema Supply Co. .883

Cinema Systems .878
Cinema Talent Agency .762
Cinema Xenon Intl. .889
Cinema, Television & Video Trade Union (Portugal) .1035
Cinemafloat .727
Cinemagic Theatres .783
Cinemanson Marketing & Distribution .653
Cinemark USA, Inc. .780
International Offices (see individual countries in World Market) .1007
Mexico .1030
Cinemart .630
Cinemas 14 Juillet (France) .1020
Cinemascore .741
Cinemaster Luxury Theaters, Inc. .783
Mexico .1030
Cinemateca Uruguaya .631
Cinemaxx H.J. Flebbe Filmtheaterbetriebe
Germany .1021
Switzerland .1040
Turkey .1041
Cinemeccanica U.S., Inc. .889
Cinemex/Cadena Mexicana de Exhibicion S.A. de C.V. Cinemex .1030
Cinemobil Open Air Cinema (Switzerland) .1040
Cinemotion Pictures .713
Cinenet (Cinema Network, Inc.) .747
Cineplex Odeon Corp. .963
Cineplex Odeon Intl. Mozi (Hungary) .1025
Cinequest: The San Jose Film Festival .630
Cinergi Pictures Entertainment, Inc. .653
Cinesa (Spain) .1038
Cinesite Digital Studios .755
Cinesite, Inc. .747
Cinesound .742
Cinetel Films, Inc. .653
Cinetransformer .887
Cinetyp (Switzerland) .1040
Cinetyp, Inc. .759
Cineville International .654
Cinevision Entertainment .747
Cinevision Intl. Film Festival .632
Cinevista, Inc. .654
Cinevox Entertainment .713
Cinnabar .747
Circuit Georges Raymond (CGR) (France) .1020
Circuit Rider Talent & Management .721,762
Circuit Theatres by Market .831
Circuit Theatres by State .819
Circuito Germani (Italy) .1028
CIS Hollywood .747
Citicorp .737
Citigate, Albert, Frank Law, Inc. .707
City Cinemas .782
City Kino (Germany) .1021
City National Bank .737
City Screen .973
Claman, Barbara, Casting .721
Clark Theatres .783
Clark, Margie, Casting .721
Clark, W. Randolph, Company .762
Classic Car Suppliers .727
Classic Cars Leasing Co. .727
Classic Cinemas .783
Classic Films .654
Classic Images .753
Classic Industries .880
Clay Digital Sound .742
Clay Lacy Aviation, Inc. .754
Clean Net USA .893
Clearview Cinema Corp. .784
Clein & White, Inc. .707
Cler, Colleen, Agency .762
Clermont Ferrand Short Film Festival .630
Cleveland International Film Festival .631
Click 3XLA .713
Click Active Media .707
Clinc Talent Agency .762
Clip Joint for Film, The .753, 900
Clock-Wise .707
Cloud Industries, Inc. .884, 888
CMG Worldwide .707
Co-Operative Theatres of Ohio, Inc. .902
Coast to Coast Talent Group, Inc. .762
Cobe, Lori, Casting .721
Coca-Cola Co., The .896
Codikow, Carroll, Guido & Grossman .730
Cohen Pictures .654
Cohen, Herman, Productions/Cobra Media, Inc. .654
Colgate-Palmolive Co. .893
Coliseo Albia (Spain) .1038
Colm Entertainment AG (Germany) .1021
Colm Filmtheaterbetriebe (Germany) .1021
Colombia .1015
Colony West Financial & Insurance .739
Colorado Cinemas .784
Colossal Pictures .713
Colours Talent Agency .762
Columbia Pictures (also see Sony) .686
Corporate History .636
Columbia Pictures Corporation, Ltd. (UK) .978
Columbia Pictures Culver Studios .687
Columbia Tristar Film Distributiors Intl. .687
Columbia Tristar Films De Mexico .1030
Columbia Tristar Films of Canada .958
Columbia Tristar Home Video .687
Columbia Tristar International Television .687
Columbia Tristar Motion Picture Group .686
Columbia Tristar Television .687
Columbia Tristar Television Distribution .687
Comerica Bank, California .737
Comet FTB-GMBH (Germany) .1021
Coming Attractions .931
Coming Attractions, Inc. .785
Commercials Unlimited, Inc. .762
Communication Commission of the National Council of the Churches of Christ in the USA. .909
Communications Corp. Of America .721
Communications Plus, Inc. .707
Community Light & Sound, Inc. .892
Compania de Iniciativas y Espectaculos (Spain) .1038
Compania Operadora de Teatros S.A. de C.V. Cotsa (Mexico) .1030
Complete Booking Service .902
Completion Bonds & Insurance .739
Component Engineering .891
Computer Film Co., The .747
Conate (Chile) .1015
Concept Plus .742, 755
Concession Equipment .882
Concession Suppliers .896
Concession Supply Co. .883
Connecticut Assn. of Theatre Owners .906
Consolidated Advertising Directors, Inc. .707
Consolidated Film Industries .713, 735, 900
Consolidated Theatres .785
Constantin Film Development, Inc. .654
Constantin Kinotriebe GMBH .1022
Construction Solutions/Stadium Seating .880
Consultants & Technical Advisors .724
Consultants for Talent Payment, Inc. .724
Consumers Perspective .741
Contemporary Art Resource .727
Contempory Artists, Ltd. Talent Agency .762
Contemptible Entertainment .654
Continental Film Group, Ltd. .654
Continental Film Labs, Inc. .735
Continental Film Productions Corp. .704
Continental Film Service .902
Continental Scenery .727
Conundrum Entertainment .654
Cooper Film Cars .727
Copeland Creative Talent .722, 762
Coralie Jr. Agency .762
Corelli-Jacobs Recording, Inc. .742
Corn Poppers .899
Corvin Budapest Filmpalace (Hungary) .1025
Cosden Agency, The .762
Costume & Prop Rentals .726
Costume Armour, Inc. .727
Costume Collection .727
Costume Designers Guild Directory .931
Costume Designers Guild. Local 892 .917
Costume Place, The .727
Costume Rentals Co. .727
Cotsa (Mexico) .1030
Council of Consulting Organizations .724
Council on Intl. Non-theatrical Events (C.I.N.E.) .909
Countryman & McDaniel .730
Courtney, Elizabeth, Costumes .727
Cowan, Debaets, Abrahams & Sheppard .730
CPC Entertainment .713
Craig Agency, The .762
Crane, Peter, Assoc. .878
Craven Film Corporation .704
Craven, Thomas, Film, Corp. .654
Craven, Wes, Films .654
Creative Character Engineering .713, 747
Creative Costume Co. .727
Creative Effects, Inc. .747
Creative Entertainment Consultants .902

Creative Group, The .747
Creative Interests .714
Creative Management .737
Creative Media Recording .742
Creative Packaging .897
Creative Productions .707
Creative Resource Maven .707
Creative Visions Miami, Inc. .714
Creative West .755
Creative West, The .901
Credit Card Center .887
Crescendo Studios .742
Crest Audio, Inc. .892
Crest National Digital Media Complex .755, 759
Crest National Viedo Film Labs .735
Crest-Talmadge .887
Criterion Pictures .958
Croatia .1016
Crowd Control .884
Crown Industries, Inc. .884
Crown International Pictures, Inc. .654
Crown Intl. .892
Crown Theatres .785
Crusader Entertainment .654
Cruse & Co., Inc. .714, 747, 901
Crystal Pyramid Productions .654
Crystal Sky, LLC .654
Cubena Research Corp./Digital Resolution .747
Cunningham, Escott, Dipene & Associates .762
Cunningham, Patrick, CSA .722
Curb Entertainment .655
Curious Pictures .714
Curtains & Drapery .884
Curzon Film Distributors, Ltd. .978
Cushman, Aaron D., & Associates, Inc. .707
Custom Characters .727
Custom Color Corp. .886
Custom Films/Video, Inc. .704
Cyber F/X .714
Cyclotron .714
Czech Republic .1016

D

D'Arcy, Masius, Benton & Bowles .707
D-Vision Systems, Inc. .756
D.D.K. .762
Daddy-O Productions .714
Dade/Schultz Associates .762
Daily Variety .931
Daktronics, Inc. .886
Dale System, Inc. .724, 741, 891
Dalta Productions .735
Danbarry Cinemas .785
Dance, Bill, Casting .722
Danger Productions .714
Danjaq, LLC .655
Dark Horse Entertainment .655
Dart Container Corp. .897
Data Display .886
Data Quest Investigations, Ltd. .891
Dave's Marine Services, Inc. .747
Davidson, Dennis, & Associates, Inc. .707
David's Outfitters, Inc. .727
Davis Entertainment Co. .655
Daviselen Advertising, Inc. .707
Day Shades .747
Daybreak Productions .655
Dazu Merchandising, Inc. .707
DB Sound & Music .742
DDB Needham Worldwide, Inc. .707
De Heer R. Van Steen (Netherlands) .1031
De La Mare Engineering, Inc. .747
Dean Pickle & Specialty Products .898, 899
Dean, Samantha, & Associates .707
Deanza Land & Leisure Corp. .786
Deckert, Curt, Associates, Inc. .724
Decolite Products .879
Decoustics Cine-Line .879
Del, Shaw, Blye & Moonves .730
Delancy, Richard, & Associates .722
Delphi Filmverleih (Germany) .1022
Deluxe Laboratories, Inc. .735
Deluxe Toronto (Canada) .954
Dendy Cinemas (Australia) .1011
Denmark .1016
Dennis, Hal, Productions .756
Dentsu, Inc. .707
Denver Intl. Film Festival .633
Department of Agriculture .929
Department of Commerce .929
Department of Defense .929
Department of Education .929
Department of Energy .929
Department of Health & Human Services .929
Department of Housing & Urban Dev. .929
Department of Justice .929
Department of Labor .929
Department of State .929
Department of the Interior .929
Department of Transportation .930
Department of Treasury .930
DES .756
Des Cartes Catering .727
Desert Props .727
Desrochers, Marcel, Inc. .890
Destination Cinema, Inc. .655
DeWitt Stern Group, Inc. .739
DH Talent Agency .762
Di Novi Pictures .655
Diamond Artists Agency, Ltd. .762
Dic Entertainment, L.P. .714
Dick Clark Media Archives .753
Dickinson Theatres, Inc. .786
Difusora Burgos (Spain) .1038
Difusora Cultural Cinematografica (Spain) .1038
Difusora Logrono (Spain) .1038
Digiscope .747
Digiscope Digital Visual Effects .714
Digital Consortium .714
Digital Creative .714
Digital Domain .655, 714, 747
Digital Magic Co. .747, 756
Digital Masters .742
Digital Quest .714, 756
Digital Sound Systems .885
Digital Sparks .885
Digital Technology Systems, Inc. .885
Digital Television Equipment, Inc. .756
Digital Theater Systems .742, 878, 885
Dillingham Ticket Co. .894
Dimension 3 .747
Dimensional Innovations .880
Dinamo Entertainment .655
Dino De Laurentiis Company .655
Dippin' Dots .896
Diprima Casting .722
Dipson Theatres, Inc. .786
Directors Guild of America .900, 916
  Awards .20
Directors Sound & Editorial Service .743
Di Sarro, Ernesto, (Italy) .1028
Discovery Pictures .655
Disney, Walt, Company, The (also see Buena Vista) .655
  Corporate History .637
  Costume & Prop Rentals .727
  Disney Channel .657
  Disney-MGM Studios .712
  Feature Animation .714
  I.D.E.A.S. at the Disney MGM Studios (Sound) .743
  I.D.E.A.S. at the Disney MGM Studios (Special Effects) .747
  Imagineering .658
  Imagineering (Special Effects) .747
  MGM Studios .747
  Motion Pictures Group, The .655
  Post-Production Services .756
  Screening Room .900
  Special Effects .747
  Television Animation .714
Distant Horizon .658
Divisek Casting & Associates .722
Dixon, Pam .722
DLT Entertainment, Ltd. .714
DNA Productions, Inc. .714
Dolby Laboratories, Inc. .743, 878, 885
Dolezal, Josef, Czech Slovak Consulting Services .724
Dominican Republic .1017
Domsey International Sales Corp. .727
Donley, Maureen, Pictures .658
Donner/Shuler Donner Prods. .659
Donovan/Foley Casting .722
Doremus & Company .707
Dorn, Larry, Associates, Inc. .707
Dornstein, Judith C. .731
Douglas Theatre Co. .786
Douglas, Gorman, Rothacker & Wilhelm .762
Doumanian, Jean, Productions .659
Dowd, Mick/Tom Reudy Casting .722

Dozar Office Furniture .727
Dr. Pepper/Seven-Up .896
Dr. Rawstock .736
Dramatists Guild of America, Inc., The .916
Dream Quest Images .714, 747
Dream Theater .714, 747
Dreamworks Distribution Canada Co. .958
Dreamworks SKG .659
Corporate History .639
Feature Animation .714
Dreyer's Grand Ice Cream .897
Dreyfuss/James Productions .659
Du Art Film Laboratories .735
Dublin Cinema Group, Ltd. .973
Dublin Film Festival .631
Dublin Theatre Festival .633
Dubuque Foods, Inc. .897
Duck Soup Studios .714
Dura Engraving Corp. .886
Duraform .887
Durkan Patterned Carpet .882
Durkin Entertainment Group .762
Duva-Flack Associates, Inc. .762
Dynacs Digital Studios .714, 747
Dytman & Associates .762

E

E Squared .707
E. C. 2 Costumes .727
E. Farrell/C. Coulter Talent Agency .763
E=MC2 .727
E=MC2, Inc. .748
Eagle Eye Film Co. .756
East Coast Lamp Sales, Inc. .879
East Coast Post .756
East West Capital Associates .659
Eastern Acoustic Works Speakers .892
Eastern Costume .727
Eastern Federal Corp. .787
Eastman Kodak Company .659, 736, 753
Eaves-Brooks Costume Co., Inc. .727
EAW, Inc. .892
Echo Sound Services, Inc. .743
ECI-www.Ticketing Systems .894
Eckart & Wolfram Weber-FTB (Germany) .1022
Eckholdt, Donna .722
Econo-Pleat/East West Carpet Mills .879
Ecuador .1017
Edelman Public Relations Worldwide .707
Edit Point Post-Production Systems .756
Editcomm, Inc. .954
Editel Los Angeles .748
Editor & Publisher .931
Edko Films Limited (Hong Kong) .1024
Edmonds Entertainment .659
Eds Digital Studios .743, 748
Edwards Theatres .787
Edwards, Blake, Co. .659
Efex Specialists .748
Effective Engineering .748
Effects House, The .748
Efilm .748
Efilm Studio & Editing Equip. Rentals .756
EFX .743
EG & G Opto-Electronics .889
Egg Pictures .659
Ego Film Arts .942
Egypt .1017
Eisen, Max .707
EIMS, Inc. .882
Eisenberg Gourmet Beef Franks .897
El Dorado Pictures .659
El Norte Productions .659
Electric Encore Properties, Inc. .727
Electric Machine Entertainment .714, 748
Electric Picture Solutions .756
Electro-Voice .892
Electrofex .724, 748
Electronic Media .932
Electronics Now .932
Elite Casting .762
Ellis Popcorn Co., Inc. .898
Ellis Props & Graphics .727
Ellis, Alice Casting .722
EMA Multimedia .714
EMA Multimedia, Inc. .708
Emery Worldwide .966
Emmerling, John, Production .708
Empire Theatres, Ltd. .963
Empresa Balana (Spain) .1038
Encore Cinemas, Inc. .964
Encore Enterprises .714
Encore International Group .708
Encore Visual Effects .748
Endeavor Talent Agency, LLC .762
Energy Film Library .748, 753
Engineering Animation, Inc. .714
Enoki Films U.S.A., Inc. .714
Entertainment Group Insurance & Administrators/Near North Entertainment Insurances Services .739
Enterprise Image .756
Entertain Golden Village (Thailand) .1041
Entertainment Brokers International .739
Entertainment Coalition .739
Entertainment Communications Network .708
Entertainment Data, Inc. .659
Entertainment Enterprises .763
Entertainment Industries Foundation .909
Entertainment Industry Mergers & Acquisitions, 1999-2000 .22
Entertainment Lawyers .730
Entertainment Partners .722
Entertainment Post .756
Entertainment Productions, Inc. .659
Envirion Vision .727
Environmental Protection Agency .930
Episcopal Actors Guild of America, Inc. .916
Eprad, Inc. .891
Epstein-Wyckoff & Associates .763
Equinox Entertainment, Ltd. .659
Era Aviation .727
Erasmus Kinoverwaltung (Germany) .1022
Erdek, Steven/Herman, Stacey, Casting .722
Erickson & Halloran .731
Erickson Agency, The .722
Erickson, Eddy G., Booking Service .902
Erno Intl. (Switzerland) .1040
Ervin, Cohen & Jessup .731
ESQ. Management .731
Eternity Pictures, Inc. .659
Ett, Allan, Music Group .743
EUE/Screen Gem Prints .748
Euro RSCG Tatham .708
Euro-American Brands, Inc. .896
Evans & Sutherland .878
Evans, Robert, Co., The .660
Evelyn Hudson Insurance .739
Everard Films (New Zealand) .1032
EVI Audio .892
EVS Broadcast Equipment .888
Executive Yacht Management, Inc./Film Services Division .727
Exhibition Circuits (Great Britain) .973
Exhibition Employees, Local 829, (IATSE), New York .918
Exhibition Facts .770
Exhibitor Organizations .905
Exhibitor Relations Co., Inc. .741
Exhibitor Services .885
Exhibitors & Exhibition Services (Canada) .963
Exploratorium, McBean Theater .900
Explosive Studios Eyemark Entertainment .714
Extras Network Casting .722
Extreme Marine Production Services .727
Extreme Sports For Filming .727
Eyes On Main .727

F

F & F/Value Theatres .788
F-Stop, Inc. .715, 748
F.F. & E. Enterprises, Inc. .893
F.I.L.M. Archives, Inc. .753
Fabrique D'Images Limitee, La .942
Face Productions .660
Faith, Carol, Agency .763
Famous Players, Inc. .964
Fantasporto-Oporto Intl. Film Festival .630
Fantasy Entertainment .887
Fantasy II Film Effects .714, 748
Farber, Russ .715, 748
Farmhouse Films, Inc. .715
Farrow, Russell A., Ltd. .966
Fashion Seal Uniforms .894
Fast Multimedia .756
Fast-Ad, Inc. .886
Favored Artists .763

Fawn Vendors .883
Fax Animation Company .712
Faxon, Donald M. .725
Feature Film Releases, 1999-1998 .530
Fed des Cinemas de Belgique .1014
Federal Communications Commission .930
Federal Government Offices & Film & Media Services .929
Federal Trade Commission .930
Feldman Public Relations .708
Feldman, Edward S., Co. .660
Festival Cinemas .964
Festival de Films de Fribourg .631
Festival Intl. de Programmes Audiovisuels .630
Festival Intl. du Film (Cannes) .632
FGM Entertainment .660
Field Container Co., LP .887, 898
Field-Coch Agency, Inc., The .763
Fiesta Sound .743
Fifty Cannon Entertainment, LLC .660
54th Street Productions .660
Figueras Intl. Seating .890
Fiji .1018
Film & Video Magazine .932
Film & Video Stock Shots, Inc. .753
Film Alternative/Big Muddy Film Festival .630
Film Artists Associates .763
Film Bank .753
Film Bond International .739
Film Canada Yearbook (Canada) .934
Film Capital Corp. .737
Film Carriers (Canada) .966
Film Circuit, The .959
Film Commissions .921
Film Craft Lab .735
Film Distribution in Key Cities .904
Film East .748
Film Emporium .736
Film Exchange Employees, Back Room .916
Film Exchange Employees, Front Office .916
Film Federation of India .1026
Film Finances, Inc. .737
Film Finances Services .739
Film Finances, Ltd. .979
Film Four International .979
Film Journal Intl. .932
Film Music Associates .763
Film Network .973
Film Preservation, Processing & Repair .735
Film Preserve .735
Film Roman, Inc. .715
Film Service Theatre Group .902
Film Society of Lincoln Center .909
Film Society of Miami .630
Film Stock .736
Film Studio Helios (Poland) .1034
Film Technical Services/Special Effects .748
Film Technology Company, Inc. .735
Film Ventures International .715
Film/Video Arts .909
Filmack Studios .735
Filmack Studios .901
Filmcolony, Ltd. .660
Filmcooperative Zurich (Switzerland) .1040
Filmes Castelo Lopes (Portugal) .1035
Filmfestival Mannheim-Heidelberg .633
Filmfestival Max Ophulus Preis .630
Filmlife Inc. American Film Repair Institute .735
Filmmakers Symposium .633
Filmopolis .660
Filmovid R. Reiss (Sweden) .1039
Films Around the World, Inc. .660
Films for Educators/Films for TV .704
Filmtheater-Verwvltung Rehs (Germany) .1022
Filmtheaterbetriebe Berlin (Germany) .1022
Filmtheaterbetriebe George Reiss (Germany) .1022
Filmtreat International Corp. .735
Filmtreat West Corp. .735
Filmtrix, Inc. .748
Filmwerks Digital .756
Filmworld International, Inc. .660
Financial Management Advisors, Inc. .737
Financial Network Investment Corp. .737
Financial Services .737
Fine Art Productions/Tichie Suraci Pictures .748
Fine Line Graphics .748
Finerman, Wendy, Productions .660
Finland .1018
Finnegan-Pinchuk Company .660
Fioritto's, Larry, Special Effects Services .727
Fire Protection Specialists/Dan Gold .725
Fireworks Entertainment/Canwest Entertainment, Inc. .943
First Aid Employees, Local 767, Hollywood .917
First Charter Bank, N.A. .737
First Impressions .880
First Kiss Productions .660
First Light .660
First Look Pictures/Overseas Film Group .660
First Run Features .660
525 Post Production .748
Flamdoodle Animation, Inc. .715
Flashcast Companies, Inc. .722, 763
Flashpoint Entertainment Financing .737
Flat Earth .748
Flavor Wear .894
Fleischer Studios, Inc. .715
Flick East-West Talents, Inc. .763
Flip Your Lid Animation Studios .715
Florida Film Cars/Classic Vehicle Rentals .725
Florida Film Festival .632
Florin-Creative Film Services .902
Flower Films, Inc. .660
Flying Foto Factory, Inc. .715
Foch, Nina, Studios .725
Focus Camera, Ltd. .973
Foley, Morgan Casting .722
Folkets Bio (Sweden) .1039
Folklore Productions, Inc. .763
Folz Vending Co. .896
Foote, Cone & Belding Communications, Inc. .708
Forde Motion Picture Labs .735
Foreign Candy Co., The .896
Foreign Film Releases, 1999-2000 .485
Foreign Language Graphics .759
Fort Lauderdale Intl. Film Festival .633
Fort Lee Film Storage & Service .735
Fortis Films .661
Forty Acres & A Mule Filmworks .661
44 Blue Productions, Inc. .661
Forward Pass, Inc. .661
Fotis Kosmides (Greece) .1023
Foto-Kem Foto-Tronics, Film-Video Lab .735
Foundation of Motion Pictures Pioneers, Inc., The .910
Foundry Film Partners .737
Fountainbridge Films .661
Four Media Company .735, 743
Four Sisters Casting .722
4-Ward Productions .748
Fox, Inc. (also see Twentieth Century Fox)
Animation Studios .715
Filmed Entertainment .661
Fox Searchlight .661
Home Entertainment .662
Interactive .662
Licensing .662
Studio Operations .662
Foy, Eddie, III, Casting .722
FPC, Inc. .756
FPL Energy Services .882
Fragomen, Del Rey & Bernsen .731
France .1018
Franchise Pictures, Inc. .662
Francisco Heras (Spain) .1038
Frankfurt, Garbus, Klein & Selz, P.C. .731
Frazier, Inc. .892
Frederikstad Kinematografer (Norway) .1032
Fredricks & Vonderhorst .731
Freedman & Taitelman, LLP .731
Fremantle of Canada, Ltd. .959
French Film Office/Unifrance Film Intl. .910
Freymuth Schultz Vereingte Lichtspiele (Germany) .1022
Friars Club .910
Friars Club of California, Inc. .910
Fridley Theatres .788
Friendly Productions .663
Friends of the German Film Archive & Intl. Forum of New Cinema .630
Fries Multimedia, Inc. .708
Fries, Chuck, Productions, Inc. .663
Fromson, Dodi .725
Frontier Booking International .763
Frontier Post .756
Fryworks .883
FTB Adrian Kutter (Germany) .1022
FTB Berlin (Germany) .1022
FTB Dr. Heribert Schlinker (Germany) .1022
FTB Georg Reiss GMBH (Germany) .1022
FTB Hans-George Sawatzki (Germany) .1022
FTB Manfred Ewert KG (Germany) .1022
FTB Martin Ohg (Germany) .1022
FTB Spickert (Germany) .1022
FTB W. Burth (Germany) .1022
Fuji Photo Film U.S.A., Inc. .736

Full Moon Universe .663
Fun Antiques & Collectibles .727
Funacho .883, 899
Furthur Films .663
Futura Kinobetriebs GMBH (Germany) .1022
FWU Film Institute (Germany) .1022
FX & Design .748
FX Zone-Special Effects .748

G

G&S Acoustics (Golterman& Sabo), Inc. .879
Gabriella Imports .883
Gage Group, The .763
Gage, Davis & Benjamin, LLP .731
Galaxie Entertainment Co. .715, 748
Galaxy Entertainment, Inc. .964
Galaxy World, Inc. .715
Gallery Cinemas .973
Gallery Cinemas (Woodstock), Inc. .964
Gallup Organization, The .741
Gamble, Jim, Puppet Productions .715
Gamma Technologies .886
Gannet Films, Ltd. .980
Garber Talent Agency .763
Garrick, Dale, International Agency .763
Gary Gang Stables .725, 727
Gati, John, Film Effects, Inc. .748
Gaumont Cinemas (Belgium) .1014
Gaumont Cinemas (France) .1020
GCT .973
Gear Productions .748
Gear Productions/Gear CGI .715
Geddes Agency .763
Gehl's Guernsey Farms, Inc. .896
Gelfand, Newman & Wasserman .739
Gelfond, Gordon Associates .708
Gelula & Co. .756, 759
Gemini, Inc. .886
Gendece Film Co. .663
Gendler & Kelly .731
Gene Kraft Productions .716, 749
Gene Young Effects .752
General Cinema Theatres .789
General Insurance Consultants .739
General Media Intl. .663
George Street Pictures .663
Georgia Theatre Company II .791
Georgopoulos, K., S.A. (Greece) .1023
Gerard Klauer Mattison & Co. .737
Gerber Advertising Agency .708
Gerd Politt Filmtheaterbetriebe (Germany) .1022
Gerdes & Associates .731
Gerler, Don, Talent Agency .763
German Institute for Film Information (Germany) .1020
Germany .1020
Gerrard, Jeff, Casting .722
Gersh Agency, The .763
Geyer, Peter, Action Props & Sets .727, 748
Ghirardelli Chocolate Co. .897
Ghouldardi Film Company .663
Gibson, Dunn & Crutcher, LLP .731
Gilchrist Talent Group, The .763
Gilde Deutsches Filmkunsttheater (Germany) .1022
Gilderfluke & Co., Inc. .748
Gilla Roos, Ltd. .763
Gipson, Hoffman & Pancione .731
GKC Theatres .790
Glass/Schoor Films .901
Glassform .887
Glendale Costumes .727
Glickfeld, Fields & Jaffe .731
Global Cup .883
Global Effects, Inc. .727
Global Language Services .759
Globe Ticket & Label Co. .894
Globus Studios, Inc. .748
Glocom Products, Inc. .712
GMR Productions, Inc. .663
Gnome Productions .743
Goat Cay Productions, Inc. .663
Goatsingers, The .663
Going Postal Productions .756
Golchan, Frederic, Productions .663
Gold Medal Products .883, 899
Gold/Marshak/Liedke Associates .763
Goldberg Brothers, Inc. .887, 888, 889
Golden Candy Co. .897
Golden Classics Cinema, Inc. .964
Golden Communications (Malaysia) .1029
Golden Globe Awards .20
Golden Harvest Entertainment Co., Ltd.
  Hong Kong .1024
  Singapore .1036
  Thailand .1041
Golden Harvest Films, Inc. .663
Golden Parashoot Entertainment .724
Golden Quill .663
Golden Theatres, Ltd. .965
Golden Village (Hong Kong) .1024
Golden Village Entertainment (Singapore) .1036
Golden Village Multiplex PTE., Ltd. (Singapore) .1036
Goldey Company, The .763
Goldman, Danny, & Associates Casting .722
Goldsholl Film Group .704
Goldstein Co., The .663
Goldwyn, Samuel, Company .980
Goldwyn, Samuel, Films, LLC .663
Golin/Harris Communications .708
Good Edit .756
Good Humor .897
Good Machine Intl. .663
Good Wag Merchandising, Inc. .708
Goodrich Quality Theatres, Inc. .791
Gordon Films, Inc. .663
Gordon Rael Company .766
Gordy Co. Media Library .753
Gorfaine/Schwartz Agency, Inc. .763
Goteborg Film Festival .630
Gotham Pictures .663
Gothic Artists Agency .763
Gracie Films .664, 715
Grady, Mary, Agency .763
Grainy Pictures .664
Grakal, Root & Rosenthal, LLP .731
Grammer Cinema Seating .890
Granada Film .664
Grand Cinemas (Australia) .1011
Grandview Productions .664
Graphic Illusions/Hollywood 2000 .727
Graubert, Jeffrey L. .731
Great Britain .972
  Animation .987
  British Trade Organisations & Government Units .999
  Costume Suppliers .989
  Editing Services .990
  Exhibition Circuits .973
  Film & Video Laboratories .991
  Financial Services .992
  Multiplexes .974
  Producers & Distributors .976
  Production Equipment & Supplies .993
  Publicity & Marketing .995
  Sound Services .996
  Special Effects .997
  Studio Facilities .998
Great Waves Film Library .753
Great Western Products Co. .898
Greater Huntington Theatre Corp. .792
Greater Union Organisation, The (Australia) .1011
Greater Union Organisation, The (Germany) .1022
Greater Union Organisation, The (Poland) .1034
Greater Union Organisation, The (United Arab Emirates) .1041
Greatest Tales .715
Greece .1023
Green & Associates .763
Green Grass Blue Sky Company .715
Green Moon Productions .664
Greenberg, Glusker, Fields, Claman & Machtinger, LLP .731
Greenberg, Ira A., Ph.D./Group Hypnosis Center .725
Greenberg, Jeff .722
Greenstreet Films, Inc. .664
Gregory's Tux Shop .728
Grey Advertising, Inc. .708
Grey Entertainment & Media .708
Greycat Films .664
Griffith, Aaron, Casting .722
GRM Productions .743
Grosh Scenic Rentals, Inc. .728, 893
Grossman, Iris .722
Grossman, Larry, & Associates .763
Groupe Aubert (France) .1020
GS Entertainment Marketing Group .708
Guffanti Film Laboratories, Inc. .735
Guide to European Multiplexes .1002
Guilds & Unions .915
Gulf Insurance Group .739
Gulistan Cinema (Pakistan) .1033
Gun for Hire Production Center .756
Gun For Hire Productions .664
Guttman Associates .708
Guyett Booking Service .902

H

H.W.A. Talent West .764
Haagen-Dazs .897
Haas, Richard, Photo Imagery, Ltd. .748
Hafler Professional .892
Halcyon Days Productions .753
Halgo Specialties Co. .885
Hall, Dickler, Kent, Friedman & wood .731
Halliday, Buzz, & Associates .763
Hallmark Entertainment .715
Halsted Pictures .664
Hamilburg Agency .763
Hammer Films .756
Hamptons Intl. Film Festival .633
Hand Prop Room, Inc. .728
Handmade Films (Distributors) Ltd. .980
Hands-on Broadcast .715
Hanna-Barbera Cartoons .704
Hanna-Barbera Productions .715
Hanover Security Reports .741
Hanover Uniform Co. .894
Hanovia .888
Hansard Enterprises, Inc. .748
Hanseater Filmtheaterbetriebe (Germany) .1022
Hansen, Jacobsen, Teller, Hoberman,
Newman & Warren, Hertz & Goldring .731
Hanson & Schwam .708
Harbin, Robert .722
Hardcastle Films & Video .704
Haribo of America, Inc. .897
Harkins Theatres .792
Harkness Hall .890
Harley's House .756
Harmony Gold Preview House .900
Harpo Films, Inc. .664
Harrah's Film Corp. .664
Harrah's Theatre Equipment Co. .878, 894
Harris Road Entertainment Group, Ltd. .965
Hart, Vaughn D. .764
Hartig, Michael .764
Haskolabio-University Cinema (Iceland) .1025
Haugesund Kinematografer (Norway) .1032
Havoc, Inc. .664
Hawaii Intl. Film Festival .634
Hawthorne - Balmoral Cinemas (Australia) .1011
Hayes, Patti .722
Hearst Entertainment, Inc. .715
Heart of Texas Productions .715
Heartland Film Festival .633
Hecht, Beverly, Agency .764
Heel & Toe Films .664
Henderson/Hogan Agency .764
Hennana Blaikie .731
Henry Architects .880
Henry Heide, Inc. .897
Henry J. Kaufman & Associates, Inc. .709
Henson, Jim, Pictures .664
Henson, Jim, Productions .715
Henson's, Jim, Creature Shop .748
Herbert L. Strock Productions .901
Herman Goelitz Candy Co., Inc. .897
Hermann-Closmann Erben D.G. FTB (Germany) .1022
Hershey Foods .897
Herzog, Gary D. .731
HFWD Visual EFX .748
High End Systems, Inc. .880
High Performance Stereo .892
Highland Laboratories .735
Hill & Nolton .708
Hill, John, Music .743
Hirshenson, Janet .722
Hispanic Entertainment Specialist .741
Hispanic Talent Casting of Hollywood .722
Histories of the Motion Picture Studios .636
Hodes, Bernard, Advertising .708
Hofflund Polone .664
Hoffman, Nathalie, & Associates .708
Hoffy .897
Hogan Moorhouse Pictures .665
Hollywood Breakaway .728
Hollywood Central Props .728
Hollywood Creative Directory .932
Hollywood Digital .749
Hollywood Entertainment Labor Council .916
Hollywood Film & Video, Inc. .735
Hollywood Film Co. .735, 756
Hollywood Glass Company .728
Hollywood Independent Film Festival .633
Hollywood Madison Group, The .722
Hollywood Newsreel Syndicate, Inc. .753, 900, 901
Hollywood Picture Vehicles/The Bosews Collection .728
Hollywood Reporter, The .932
Hollywood Software, Inc. .887
Hollywood Toys & Costumes .728
Hollywood Vaults, Inc. .736
Hollywood-Madison Group, The .708
Holmes, Frank, Laboratories .736
Holographic Studios .749
Home Box Office, Inc. (HBO) .665
Animation .715
Studio Productions .748
Home Video Hellas (Greece) .1023
Hong Kong .1024
Hong Kong & Kowloon Cinema & Theatrical Ent. Free General Assoc. 1024
Hong Kong Intl. Film & TV Market (Filmart 2000) .632
Hong Kong Intl. Film Festival (HKIFF) .631
Horizon Media, Inc. .708
Horseshoe Bay Productions .666
Horwitz, Lewis, Organization .737
Hoshizaki North Eastern .883
Hot Cookies Productions .899
Hot Springs Documentary Film Festival .633
House of Costumes, Ltd. .728
House of Movies Capture Studios, LLC .715
House of Props .728
House of Representatives, The .764
Howard A. Anderson Co. (Special effects) .746
Howard A. Anderson, Co. .901
Howard Talent West .764
Hoyts Cinemas Corporation .792
Argentina .1007
Australia .1011
Chile .1015
New Zealand .1032
UK .973
Hoyts Fox Columbia Tri-Star Films (Australia) .1009
Hubley Studio .715
Hudson Valley Film festival .632
Hugarian Film Institute & Film Archive (Hungary) .1025
Hugh & Suzanne Johnston, Inc. .704
Humboldt Intl. Film Festival .631
Hungary .1025
Hunt Wesson .896
Hunter Gratzner Industries, Inc. .749
Hurley Screen Corp. .890
Hussey Seating Co. .890
Hutchins/Young & Rubicam .708
Hyams, Peter, Productions, Inc. .666
Hyde Park Entertainment .666
Hyperion Studios .715

I

I.A.T.S.E. .917
I.A.T.S.E. Official Bulletin .932
IBEW, Local 349 (Film) .918
IBEW, Local 40 (Film) .918
Ice Cream & Frozen Dairy Products .897
Ice Tea Productions .715
Icee USA .896
Iceland .1025
Icelandic Filmmakers Assoc. (Iceland) .1025
Icon Identity Solutions .886
Icon International .882
Icon Productions, Inc. .667
ICS Services, Inc. .736
IF/X Digital, Inc. .743, 749
IF/X Productions, Inc. .715
IFA Talent Agency .764
IFDF Max (Poland) .1034
IFM Film Associates, Inc. .667
Ilford Imaging U.S.A., Inc. .736
Illumilite, Inc. .880
Illusions .749
Illuvatar, LLC .715
Image Analysts All-Media .741
Image Bank, The/The Image Bank West .753
Image Creators, Inc. .749
Image Engineering, Inc. .728, 749
Image National .886
Image Technology (Great Britain) .934
Imagemovers .667
Imagica USA, Inc. .715
Imaginary Forces .708
Imagination Factory .715

Imagine Entertainment 667
Imagine That 749
Imax Corporation (CA) 667
Imax Corporation (Canada) 876
Distribution 959
Production 944
IMI Cornelius, Inc. 883
Immortal Entertainment 667
Imperial Bank 737
In Costume 728
In-Sight Pix 716
Indelible Pictures 667
Independent Booking & Theatre Services, Ltd. 966
Independent Booking Companies (Canada) 966
Independent Feature Film Market 633
Independent Feature Project 632
Independent Feature Project, The 910
Midwest 910
North 910
South 910
West 910
Independent Film Services 902
Independent Film Services Buying & Booking 902
Independent Filmmakers Competition 633
Independent Media West, Inc. 708
Independent Spirit Awards 20
Independent Studio Services 728
Independent Theatre Booking 902
Independent Theatres 848
India 1026
Indiana Cash Drawer Co. 882
Indonesia 1026
Indshare Media 709
Industrial Light & Magic (ILM) 715, 749
Industry Entertainment 667
Industry in Canada, The 936
Industry in Great Britain & Ireland, The 972
Infiniti Pacific Insurance Service 739
Infinity Filmworks 667
Infocomm Asia 633
Infocomm Europe at Photokina 633
Infocomm Intl. 632
Infocomm Japan 630
Informerical Solutions, Inc. 708
Initial Entertainment Group 667, 737
Ink Tank, The 716
Innovative Artists 764
Inside Film Magazine 932
Integrated Food Systems 883
Intelligent Media, Inc. 749
Inter/Media Advertising 708
Interama, Inc. 667
Intercontinental Group Holdings, Ltd. (Hong Kong) 1024
Intergraph Computer Systems 712
Interlock Studios 743
Intermedia Films 667
Intermission Productions 901
International Alliance of Theatrical Stage Employees & Moving Picture Technicians, Artists & Allied Crafts of the U.S., Territories, & Canada 916
International Cinema Equipment 888, 890
International Cinematographers Guild Magazine 932
International Color Stock, Inc. 753
International Communications group, Inc. 708
International Costume 728
International Creative Effects 749
International Creative Management 764
International Documentary Assn. 911, 932
International Film Circuit 667
International Film Festival Rotterdam 630
International Film Festivals & Markets 630
International Film Guarantors 739
International Motion Picture Almanac 932
International Research & Evaluation 741
International Television & Video Almanac 932
International Theatre Equipment Assn. 905
Internet Impact 708
Interscope Communications, Inc. 668
Intersonic Taunus Prod., Ltd. (Czech Republic) 1016
Intersound, Inc. 743
Intervideo, Inc. 753
Interweave Entertainment 743
Intex Audiovisuals 759
Intl. Brotherhood of Electrical Workers 918
Intl. Communications Film & Video Competition 631
Intl. Electrical Wire/Cable 891
Intl. Media & Advertising Group In Ent. (I.M.A.G.E.) 708
Intl. Paper Foodservice 898
Introvision Intl. 749
Invision Entertainment 716
Ionaides Films EPE (Greece) 1023
IRA Tec/Pro Audio 892
Irell & Manella, LLP 731
Irish Dreamtime 668
Iron Mountain Records Management 736
Irwin Seating Co. 890
Isaacman, Kaufman & Painter 731
Isaacson, Donna 722
Isbell, Alec, Casting 722
Island Display Corp. 886
Israel 1026
Israel Film Centre 1026
Istituto Luce (Italy) 1028
It's A Wrap 728
Italtoons Corp. 668
Italy 1027
ITC Entertainment 716
ITI Cinema Poland 1034
Itzawrap, Inc. 716
Iverson, Yoakum, Papiano & Hirsch 731
Iwasaki Images of America 728
Iwerks Entertainment 668, 878, 880, 889
Izaro Films (Spain) 1038
Izquierdo Studios 728

J

J & J Snacks 899
Jackman & Taussig Entertainment 765
Jackson Artists Corp. 765
Jacobson & Colfin, P.C. 731
Jag Entertainment 722
Jalbert Productions, Inc. 753
Jalem Productions, Inc. 668
Jan J. Agency 765
Japan 1028
Japan Society/Film Center 911
Jarco Industires 883
Jay, George, Agency, The 765
JBL Professional 892
Jeffer, Mangels, Butler & Marmaro 731
Jensen Communications, Inc. 708
Jersey Films 668
Jetlag Productions 716
JEX FX 749
JKR Productions, Inc. 756, 901
Jogchem's Theaters B.V. (Netherlands) 1031
Johnson & Rishwain, LLP 731
Johnson Kwick Bag 893
Johnson/Liff Casting 722
Johnson/McKibben Architects 880
Jones Effects Studio, The 749
Jonseisa Productions Internationale, Inc. 716
Jordan, Gill & Dornbaum 765
Judson-Atkinson Candy Co. 897
Juicy Whip, Inc. 896
Jules & Jim Custom Artwork 728
Jumbo Pictures 668, 716
Junction Entertainment 668
Just Born, Inc. 897
Just for Laughs! The Montreal Intl. Comedy Festival 632
Just Imagine Exhibits 886
Just Singer Entertainment 668

K

Kagan, Paul, Associates, Inc. 741
Kaiser Communications, Inc. 708
Kaiser McEuen, Inc. 708
Kaleidoscope Films, Inc. 901
Kaplan-Stahler-guhmer Agency 765
Kapsis Heirs (Greece) 1023
Karavias, Christos, & Co. (Greece) 1023
Katten, Muchin & Zavis 732
Katz, Golden & Sullivan, LLP 732
Katz, Marty, Productions 668
Kaufer Miller Communications 709
Kawasho Intl. 892
Kazarian & Spencer & Associates, Inc. 765
Keeshen, Jim, Productions 716
Kehr, Schiff & Crane 732
Kelman/Arletta Agency 765
Kelmar Systems, Inc. 888
Kemps Film, TV & Video Handbook (Great Britain) 934

Kenimation Animation Services .716
Kennedy-Marshall Company .668
Kenoff & Machtinger .732
Kerasotes Theatres .793
Kesser Stock Library .753
Ketchum Communications, Inc. .709
Kichaven, Jeffrey G. .732
Kidfilm/USA Film Festival, Dallas .630
Kieft & Kieft Filmtheater GMBH (Germany) .1022
Killer Films, Inc. .668
Killer Music .743
Kim & Scott's Gourmet Pretzels .899
Kinderhook research, Inc. .741
Kine Supplies (Birmingham), Ltd. .973
Kinematograph Film GMBH (Germany) .1022
Kinepolis Group (Luxembourg) .1029
Kinepolis Group (Spain) .1038
Kinetics Noise Control .879
Kinetronics .888
Kings Road Entertainment, Inc. .669
Kingsgate Films, Inc. .668
Kino International Corp. .669
Kinocenter Ottobrunn (Germany) .1022
Kinopolis Group H.V. (Belgium) .1014
Kinopolis Main-Taunus GMBH & Co. (Germany) .1022
Kinoton .889
Kinsella, Boesch, Fujikawa & Towle .732
Kirkland & Packard .732
Kirsch & Mitchell .732
Kitag Kino Theater AG (Switzerland) .1040
Kjar, Tyler, Agency .765
Klasky Csupo, Inc. .716
Klass, Eric, Agency, The .765
Kleinberg, Lopez, Lange, Brisbin & Cuddy, LLP .732
Klipsch Professional .890
Klipsch, LLC Speakers .892
Klotz, Jane M., Booking .902
KMD Architects .880
KNB EFX Group, Inc. .749
Kneisley Electric .889
Knight, Eileen .722
Koala Corp. .887
Koch Co., The .669
Kohner, Paul, Agency .765
Koneta/LRV .882
Konigsberg-Smith Co., The .669
Kontoulis (Greece) .1023
Kopelson Entertainment .669
Kouf-Bigelow Productions .669
Kowloon & New Territories Motion Picture Industry Assn. (Hong Kong) .1024
Kraft Foods/Oscar Mayer .897
Kraft-Benjamin Agency, The .765
Kramer & Kaslow .737
Kransy Office, The .765
Kreiss Collection .728
Krikorian Premiere Theatres, LLC .794
Krislin Company, The .716
Krispy Kist Machine Co. .883
Kristiansand Kino (Norway) .1033
Krugmann & Weischermundsburger (Germany) .1022
Kuchenreuther Film (Germany) .1022
Kullman Industries .886
Kurtz & Friends .716
Kurtz, Deborah Casting .722
Kushner-Locke Co. .669
Kuttner Prop Rentals, Inc. .728

L

L-Squared Entertainment .670
L.A. Animation .716
L.A. Eyeworks .728
L.A. Intl. Short Film Festival .633
L.A. Talent .765
L.A. Videograms .749
L.P. Associates, Inc. .889
LA Xcess Insurance Brokers, Inc. .739
Lacy, Ross, Casting .722
Ladd Company, The .669
Laemmle Theatres .795
Laguna Beach Film Festival .633
Lakes & Rivers Cinemas .795
Lakeshore Entertainment Corp. .669
Lally Talent Agency .765
Lamb & Company .716
Lancer Corp., Inc. .883
Landin Media, Inc. .709
Landmark Cinemas of Canada, Ltd. .965
Landmark Entertainment Group .716
Landscape Entertainment .669
Lane, Stacey, Talent Agency .765
Lane, Susan, Model & Talent Agency, Inc. .765
Lanese, Bill, Advertising & Public Relations .709
Language Services, International .759
Laon Intl. Film Festival For Young People .631
Large Format Cinema Association .878
Larger Than Life Productions .669
Largo Construction .881
Largo Entertainment .669
Larry Dorn Assoc., Inc. .753
Larry Fioritto's Special Effects Services .748
Larson Sound Center .743
Lartec Systems .725
Laser Pacific Media Corp. .736, 743, 749, 756
Laser Viedo Titres, Inc. .759
Laugarasbio (Iceland) .1025
Lauren Films Video Hagar (Spain) .1038
Lavezzi Precision, Inc. .888
Lavi Industries .884
Lawrence Metal Products, Inc. .884
LBI/Boyd Wallcoverings .879
Le Film Francais (France) .934
Leading Pictures, Inc. .669
Lear Casting .722
Lee & Associates, Inc. .709
Lee, Buddy, Attractions, Inc. .765
Lehigh Electric Products .880
Leigh, Kathy, Pryor .723
Leisure Time Features .669
Len-D Enterprises .888
Lena Production Services .725
Lennox Industries .887
Lenny, Jack Associates .765
Leonard H. Goldenson Theatre .900
Leonard, Dicker & Schreiber .732
Leprevost Corporation .716
Leprevost Corporation .716
Les Images Megarama (France) .1020
Lesser Theatre Service .902
Levey, John .722
Levin Agency, The .765
Levinson Associates .709
Levy, Robin, & Associates .765
Levy-Gardner-Laven Productions, Inc. .669
Lewis, D'Amato, Brisbois & Bisgaard .732
Lewis, Robert, Company, The .670
Lexington Scenery & Props .725, 728, 749
Liag Capitol (Switzerland) .1040
Lieberman, Jerry, Productions .716
Liberman Patton Casting .722
Liberty International Entertainment, Inc. .716
Liberty Livewire Corporation .670
Liberty Studios, Inc. .749
Liberty Theatre, The (Bermuda) .1015
Liberty Theatrical Decor .893
Library of Congress .930
Library of Moving Images, Inc. .754
Lichter, Grossman, Nichols & Adler .732
Lichtman, Terry, Company .765
Lieberman, Ken, Laboratories, Inc. .736
Lien Cowen Casting .722
Light, Robert, Agency, The .765
Lighthouse Productions .670
Lighting & Electronic Design (LED) .880
Lightmotive, Inc. .670
Lightstorm Entertainment .670
Lightworks .880
Lillian Costume Co. of L.I., Inc .728
Lin-Del Associates .725
Lindner, Ken, & Associates, Inc. .765
Linguatheque of L.A. .759
Linker Systems .712, 716, 749
Lino Sonego & C.S.R.L. .890
Linsey-Fairbanks, Inc. .880, 888
Lion Rock Productions .670
Lion's Den Animation, Inc. .716
Lionel Larner, Ltd. .765
Lions Gate Entertainment Corp. (Canada) .945
Lions Gate Film Production .670
Lippin Group, Inc. .709
Lipsner-Smith Company .736
Liselotte Jaeger Filmtheaterbetriebe (Germany) .1022
Little Gemstone Music/24 Carat Productions .743
Little John, William, Productions, Inc. .716
Litvinoff, Si Productions .670
Live Wire Productions & VFX .716, 749
Liveplanet .670

Lobby Previews .901
Lochland Group, LLP, The .737
Lockhart, Warren, Consulting .725
Lockhart, Warren, Productions, Inc. .716
Loeb & Loeb, LLP .732
Loeks, Jack, Theatres .795
Loeks Star Theatres .795
Loews Cineplex Entertainment Corp. .796
London Film Festival .634
London Independent Producers, Ltd. .981
London Lesbian & Gay Film Festival .631
Longbow Productions .670
Look Talent .765
Look, Inc. .743
Loos, Taweel, & Co. Entertainment .720
Lorenzo Ventavoli (Italy) .1028
Lor, Ted, Entertainment Marketing .709
Los Angeles County Museum of Art .900
Los Angeles Film Critics Awards .20
Los Angeles Theatre .900
Lost Planet Productions .757
Love Spell Entertainment .670
Lovell & Associates .765
Lowell Mfg. Co. .891
Lower East Side Films .670
Lowtech .749
Lowy & Zucker .732
Lucas Digital, Ltd. .671
Lucas Entertainment Company .670
Lucasfilm, Ltd. .736
Production .670
Sound Equipment .891
Special Effects .749
THX Division .743
Lucid Media .671
Ludwig Scheer & Co. KG-FTB (Germany) .1022
Luigi De Pedys (Italy) .1028
Luker, Jana, Talent Agency .765
Lumeni Productions, Inc. .716, 749, 901
Lusomundo (Portugal) .1035
Lutron Electronics .888
Lux Cinema .973
Lux Pictures, Inc. .671
Luxembourg .1029
Lynne & Reilly Agency .765
Lyon Group, Inc., The .709
Lyons/Sheldon Agency, The .765
Lyric Cinema (Pakistan) .1033

M

M&M Mars .897
M.K.2 (France) .1020
M3D Studios, Inc. .717
MacDonald-Bullington Casting .722
Mace Neufeld Productions .674
MacGillivray Freeman Films .671, 754
Macy & Associates .709
Mad Chance .671
Mad Dog Studios & South Lake Stage .743
Made in L.A. .728
Mademoiselle Irene UJDA .725
Maelstrom Entertainment LLC .671
Mag-Tech Environmental, Inc. .890, 893
Magic Casting, Inc. .722
Magic Film & Video Works .757
Magic Lantern Theatres .965
Magic Theatres, Inc. .965
Magical Media Industries, Inc. .749
Magid, Lee, Inc. .743
Magnetic North .954
Magno Sound & Video .736, 757, 900
Magno Visuals .736
Magnum Cinema .878
MAH Communication, Inc. .887
Mainline Pictures .973
Mainstreet Menu Systems .883, 886
Makeup & Effects Laboratories, Inc. (M.E.I.) .749
Makeup & Monsters .749
Malaysia .1029
Malco Theatres, Inc. .799
Mali Finn Casting .723
Malibu Bay Films .671
Malpaso Productions .671
Mambo Kasting .723
Management Brokers Insurance Agency .739
Manatt, Phelps & Phillips, LLP .732
Mandalay Pictures .671
Mandy Films, Inc. .671
Manga Entertainment .716
Manhattan Transfer/Edit/Digital .749
Manifest Film Company .671
Manko Seating Co. .891
Mann Theatres of Minnesota .800
Mannequin Gallery, The .728
Manutech Co. .887
Many, Chris, Music/Silverstorm Studios .744
Marathon National Bank .738
Marble Co., Inc. .888
Marcland International Communications .744, 759
Marcus Advertising, Inc. .709
Marcus Theatres Corp. .800, 902
Marin County National Short Film Festival .632
Marine Corps Public Affairs .930
Maris Theatres Pvt., Ltd. (India) .1026
Mark, Laurence, Productions .671
Markee-Regional America's Mag. for Film & Video Prod. .932
Market Research & Analysis .741
Marketing Communications Services .709
Markham/Novell Communications, Ltd. .709
Marlin Entertainment Group .709
Maroevich, O'Shea & Coghlan .739, 885
Marquee Cinemas .801
Marquee Technical Services .885
Marquees, Signs & Displays .885
Mars Sequel Theater Mgmt. Sys./AOL Moviefone .882
Marsh Risk & Insurance Services .739
Marsh, Sandra, Management .765
Marshall Entertainment Insurance, Inc. .740
Marshall/Plumb Research Associates .725
Martin & Donalds Talent Agency, Inc. .765
Martinelli, Johnnie, Attractions, Inc. .765
Marvel Characters, Inc. .671
Marvel Films Animation .716
Masland Carpets, Inc. .882
Mass-Illusion .749
Mastersfx, Inc. .749
Masterwords .759
Matchframe Video .757
Material .671
Matinee Entertainment .716
Matson Advertising .709
Matte World Digital .749
Matthau Company, Inc., The .671
Matthews Productions .716
Maui Cup .898
Maui Film Festival .632
Maverick Entertainment .672
Mavety Film Delivery .966
Max Ink Café .716, 749
Maxann's Casting Co. .723
May Theatres, Inc. .965
Mayor, Glassman, Gaines & Rapore, LLP .732
Maysville Pictures .672
Mazie & Silverman .732
Maziroff, Ferrar, Associates .763
MBI Products .879
MCA Music Media Studios .744
McAllister Associates, Inc. .882
McCann-Erickson, Inc. .709, 741
McCoury & Robin, Inc. .749
McDermott, Marge .765
McKelvy, Carol L. .732
McLane Co. .897, 898
McQueeney Management, Inc. .765
MDC Wallcoverings .879
MDP Worldwide .672
Meat Products .897
Med + Rent, Inc. .728
Medeia Filmes (Philippines) .1034
Media Access Office IEDD .723
Media Artists Group .765
Media City Sound .744
Media City Teleproduction .725
Media Fabricators, Inc. .750
Media Salles .885
Media Technology Source, Inc. .878, 889, 891
Media Week .932
Medialab Productions .717, 750
Mediamax Productions .717
Mega Entertainment .717
Mega Extrem Cinema GMBH (Germany) .1022
Megasystems .878
Megasystems Projectors .889, 894
Melded Fabrics, Inc. .879
Melendez, Bill, Productions .717

Melrose Titles & Optical Effects .750
Mendel, Barry, Productions .672
Mendelson, Lee, Film Productions .704, 717
Menes Law Corporation .732
Mercantile National Bank .738
Merchant Ivory Productions .981
Merchant-Ivory .672
Merlin Film Group .738
Merrill Lynch .882
Mesbur & Smith Architects .881
Mescop, Inc. .902
Mestres, Ricardo, Productions .672
Metro Cinema, The .973
Metro Tartan Distribution, Ltd. .973
Metro-Goldwyn-Mayer (MGM) .672
Animation .717
Canada .672
Corporate History .639
Distribution .672
Distribution, Canada .960
MGM Pictures .672
Puerto Rico .672
United Kingdom .672
United Artists Intl. .672
Metrocine (Switzerland) .1040
Metrocolour London, Ltd. .982
Metrolight Studios .717, 750, 901
Metropolis Digital .717
Metropolitan Provisions .883
Metropolitan Theatres Corp. .801
Metropolitian Talent Agency .765
Mexico .1030
MHB Paradigm Design .881
Mica Lighting Co., Inc. .880
Michaelides, Victor (Greece) .1023
Michaelo Espresso, Inc. .883
Microlite Lighting Control .880
Mid-Atlantic NATO .906
Mid-States NATO .906
Midem Music Market .630
Military Services .929
Mill Valley Film Festival, The Film Institute of Northern CA .633
Millennium Film Work Shop .736
Miller & Kreisel Sound Corp. .892
Miller Imaging Intl., Inc. .750
Miller, Ann, Casting .723
Milliken Carpet .882
Millimeter Magazine .932
Milne FX .717
Mini Theatres .801
Minneapolis/St. Paul Intl. Film Festival .631
Minutemaid Co., The .899
MIP-DOC .631
MIP-TV .631
MIPCOM Jr. .633
Miracle Entertainment .673
Miracle Pictures .673
Miracle Recreation Equipment Co. .887
Mirage Enterprises .673
Miramar Talent Agency .765
Miramax Films Corp. .673
Miramar Enterprises .725
Mirisch Agency, The .766
Mirisch Corporation of California, The .673
Mirisch, David .709
Miscellaneous Equipment .886
Misco/Minneapolis Speaker Co., Inc. .892
Mitchell Agency, Inc. .766
Mitchell, Patty, Agency .766
Mitchell, Silerberg & Knupp, LLP .732
MJR Theatre Service, Inc. .902
MJR Theatres, Inc. .799
MK2 (France) .1019
Modern Cartoons .717
Modern Props .728
Modi U.A.T.C. (Pvt.), Ltd. (India) .1026
Modular Hardware .887
Modus EFX Productions .750
Mojo Films .673
Momentum International .709, 741
Monkey Boy Productions .717
Monster Cable .891
Monster Mecanix .750
Montage Entertainment .673
Montage Group, Ltd. .757
Montana Artists .766
Montana Assn. of Theatre Owners .906
Montana Edit .757
Monte Carlo Television Film Festival .630
Montecito Picture Company, The .673
Montreal World Film Festival .633
Moon Mesa Media .717
Moonstone Entertainment .673
Moress-Nanas-Hart Entertainment .673
Morgan & Lasky .738
Morgan Creek Productions .674, 717
Moritz, Milton I., Company, Inc., The .672
Morning Sun Animation Group, Inc. .717
Moroch & Associates .709
Morris Projects, Inc. .902
Morrison & Foerster .732
Morrison Farms Popcorn .898
Morse, Richard A., II .732
Moses, Charles A. .741
Moss, David H., & associates .766
Moss, Larry, Speech & Dialect Services .725
Mostow/Lieberman .674
Motion Artists, Inc. .766
Motion City Films .717, 750
Motion Picture & Television Fund .911
Motion Picture & Video Editors Guild, Local 700, L.A. .917
Motion Picture Assn. of America, Inc./Motion Picture Assn. .911
Motion Picture Bond Company, The .740
Motion Picture Corp. of America .674
Motion Picture Costume & Suppliers, Inc. .728
Motion Picture Costumers Local 705, Hollywood .917
Motion Picture Counseling .902
Motion Picture Crafts Service, Local 80, Hollywood .917
Motion Picture Editors Guild, Local 700, New York .917
Motion Picture Exhibitors of WA & AK & OR .906
Motion Picture Laboratories, Inc. .736
Motion Picture Marine .728
Motion Picture Organizations .908
Motion Picture Placement .709
Motion Picture Projectionists
& Video Technicians, Local 110, Chicago .918
Motion Picture Projectionists,
Video Technicians, & Theatre Employees, Local 306, New York .918
Motion Picture Screen Cartoonists, Local 839, Hollywood .917
Motion Picture Script Supervisors
& Production Office Coordinators, Local 161 .917
Motion Picture Set Painters, Local 729, Hollywood .917
Motion Picture Studio Art Craftsmen, Local 790, Hollywood .917
Motion Picture Studio Electrical Lighting Technicians, Local 728 .917
Motion Picture Studio Grips, Local 80, Hollywood .917
Motion Picture Studio Mechanics, Local 476, Chicago .917
Motion Picture Studio Teachers
& Welfare Workers, Local 884, Hollywood .917
Motion Picture Theatre Assn. of Alberta .966
Motion Picture Theatre Assn. of B.C. .966
Motion Picture Theatre Assn. of Manitoba .966
Motion Picture Theatre Assn. of Ontario .966
Motion Picture Theatre Assn. of Saskatchewan .966
Motion Picture Theatre Associations of Canada .966
Motion Picture Year in Review .5
Mount Company, The .674
Mountaintop Productions .738
Move Tech Studios .757
Movie Mill, Inc., The .965
Movie Tech Studios .744, 750
Moviead Corp. .885
Movies Arthouses & Film Distribution, The (Netherlands) .1031
Moving Pictures .674
Moving Pictures, Ltd. .674
Mozark Productions .674
MPO Videotronics .890
Mr. Mudd .674
MTM Enterprises MTV Animation .717
MTV Films .674
Mubarak Cinema (Pakistan) .1033
Muenstersche Filmtheater (Germany) .1022
Multicines (Ecuador) .1017
Multikino (Poland) .1034
Multimedia, Inc. .886
Multiplex Cinemas of Canada, Ltd. .965
Multiplex Co. .883
Munich Film Festival .632
Murphy's Cork Film Festival .633
Muse Productions, Inc. .674
Museum of Modern Art, Dept. of Film & Video .912
Museum of Natural History Film Archives Stock Shots .754
Music Prop Services .728
Music Room Pictures, Productions & Publishing .744
Musivision .717
Mutant Enemy, Inc. .674
Mutant Productions, Inc. .674
Mutual Film Company .674
Muvico Theatres .802
My You Me Productions .757
Myers, Julian, Public Relations .709
Myman, Abell, Fineman & Greenspan .732
Myriad Entertainment .709

N

Nabisco, Inc. Snack Foods .899
NADY Systems, Inc. .881
Nafdec Cinema (Pakistan) .1033
Nagina Cinema (Pakistan) .1033
Namco Cybertainment .887
Namrac Music/Souci Music .744
Nasso Productions .674
Natexis Banque-BFCE .738
Nation Glass & Gate Services, Inc. (N.G.&G.) .887
National Aeronautics & Space Admin. .930
National Alliance for Media Arts & Culture .912
National Amusements (UK) .973
National Amusements, Inc. .803
National Archives & Records Admin. .930
National Asian American Telecomm. Assn. (NAATA) .912
National Assn. of Concessionaires .905
National Assn. of Theatre Owners, Inc. .905
National Assn. of Theatre Owners, Inc. Motion Picture Org. .912
National Assn. of TV Program Exe./
Program Conference & Exhibition (NATPE) .630
National Association of Broadcasters .631
National Board of Review of Motion Pictures, Inc. .912
National Board of review Awards .20
National Captioning Institute .759
National Cinema Network, Inc. .885
National Cinema Service Projection Room Equipment/Film Handling .888
National Cinema Supply Corp. .883
National Educational Media Network .632
National Endowment for the Arts .930
National Endowment for the Humanities .930
National Film Board of Canada, The .970
National Film Preservation Foundation .912
National Geographic .674
Film Library .754
National Helicopter Services .728
National Icee Corp. .896
National Lampoon .674
National Maintenance Supply .893
National Music Publishers' Assn., Inc./The Harry Fox Agency, Inc. .912
National Screen .982
National Screen Service Group, Inc. .901
National Society of Film Critics Awards .21
National Ticket Co. .894
National Video Center .757
Nationwide Advertising Service, Inc. .709
Nationwide Entertainment Services .766
Native Planet Foods .896
NATO
California/Nevada .905
Colorado & Wyoming .906
Florida .906
Georgia .906
Idaho .906
Illinois .906
Michigan .906
New Jersey .906
New York State .906
North & South Carolina .906
Pennsylvania .906
Wisconsin & Upper Michigan .906
Natwest Group/Coutts .738
Nautical Heritage Film Services .728
Navesync Sound .900
Nayor, Nancy .723
NBC News Archives .754
Neale Advertising Associates .709
Near North Insurance Brokerage, Inc. .740
Nelson, Guggenheim, Felker & Levine, LLP .732
Nelvana (Canada) .946
Nelvana Communications, Inc. .717
Nelvana Enterprises, Inc. (Canada) .960
Nemschoff, Louise .732
Neotek, Inc. .728
Neptun Film (Poland) .1034
Nest Entertainment .717
Nestle Ice Cream .897
Nestle USA .897
Netherlands .1030
Netter Digital Entertainment, Inc. .717
Network Art Service .750
Neuberger & Berman .738
Neue Constantin Kinobetriebe (Germany) .1022
Neumade Products Corp. .888
Nevada Casting Group, Inc. .723
New Concorde Corp. .675
New Crime Productions .675
New England Confectionary .897
New England Film & Video Festival .631
New Galaxy Cinemas (Netherlands) .1031
New Hollywood, Inc. .717, 757
New Line Cinema Corporation .675
New Orleans Film & Video Festival .633
New Regency Productions .676
New Wave Entertainment .709
New World Animation .717
New York Film Critics Circle Awards .21
New York Film Festival, The Film Society of Lincoln Center .633
New York Foundation for the Arts, Inc. .912
New York State Council on the Arts (NYSCA) .912
New York Women in Film & Television .912
New Yorker Films .676
New Zealand .1032
New Zealand Film Commission .1032
Newedit, Inc. .757
Newman/Tooley Films .676
Newmarket Capital Group .676
Newmarket Capital Group .738
Newstar Media, Inc. .676
Next Wave Films .738
NFL Films, Inc. .704
Niagara Palace Theatres, Ltd. .965
Nick Mulone & Sons, Inc. .890
Nickelodeon .717
Nickelodeon Movies .676
Nicktoons Animation .717
Nights of Neon .728
Nishat Cinema (Pakistan) .1033
Nitelite Editorial .757
No Prisoners .676
Non-Theatrical Motion Picture Companies .704
Norcon Communications, Inc. .888
Norcostco, Inc. .728
Nordisk Film Biografer A/S (Denmark) .1017
Norris Booking Agency .902
Norsk Filminstitutt (Norway) .1032
Norstar Filmed Entertainment, Inc. .947
Nortel Palm Springs Intl. Film Festival .630
Northern Arts Entertainment .676
Northwest Diversified Entertainment .902
Northwest Film & Video Festival .634
Norway .1032
Norwood Entertainment Group .676
Nova Cinemas (Australia) .1012
Nova Large Format Films .676
Novar Controld Corp. .887
Novastar Digital Sound .744
Novelty Scenic Studios .885
Novian & Novian, LLP .732
Novocom .750
NRD, Inc. .886
NT Audio Video Film Labs .757
NT Audio's Hollywood Telecine Facility .744
Nuance Productions .676
Nutty Bavarian, The .899
Nwave Pictures .676

O

O'Brien Partition Co. .879
O'Connor, David, Casting Company .723
O'Melveny & Myers .732
O'Neil Theatres, Inc. .804
O/Z Films .678
Oakburn Investments, Ltd. .965
Oakview Construction, Inc. .881
Oasis Cinemas & Film Distribution, Ltd. .973
Oasis Pictures, Inc. (Canada) .960
Obituaries .456
Obst, Lynda, Productions .676
Occidental Studios .900
Ocean Avenue Screening Room .900
Ocean Capital Corp. .738
Ocean Pictures .677
Ocelot Films, Inc. .677
OCS/Freeze Frame/Pixel Magic .750
OCS/Pixel Magic .712
OCS/Pixel Magic .717
Oculus .717
Odell's .898
Odense Intl. Film Festival .633
Odeon Cinema (Pakistan) .1033
Odeon Cinemas .973
Odeon Cinemas, Ltd. .982
Odyssey Productions .717
Odyssey Products, Inc. .888

Offroad Entertainment .677
Ogilvy & Mather, Inc. .709
Ojai Film Society .634
Olesk, Jaak .732
Olmos Marketing .709
Olmos Productions, Inc. .677
Olson, Dale C., Associates .709
Olympic/Heinz Riech & Son (Germany) .1022
Omega Cinema Props .728
Omega Entertainment, Ltd. .677
Omega Pattern Works, Inc./Artisans, Inc. .882
OMI Industries .884
Omnibus .677
Omniplex Filmtheaterbetriebe (Germany) .1022
Omniprop, Inc. Talent Agency West .766
Omniterm Data Technology, Ltd. .882
1124 Design Advertising, Inc. .707
100% Entertainment .677
1492 Pictures .661
O'Neil, James, & Assoc. .750
On Stilts Productions .677
On-Time Off-Line Video .757
Ontario Cinemas, Inc. .965
Open Door Entertainment .677
Openden, Lori .723
Operators, Local 150 (IATSE), Los Angeles .918
Opinion Research Corp. International .741
Oppenheim-Christie Associates .766
Oppenheimer & Co. .738
Optic Nerve Studios .750
Optical Effects & Photography .712
Opticam, Inc. .717
Oracle Entertainment .677
Orbit Entertainment Group .677
Orbit Productions .717
Organizacion Ramirez S.A. de C.V. Multicinemas & Cinepolis (Mexico) .1030
Original Film .677
Original Voices, Inc. .677
Orpheus Films .677
Orrick, Herrington & Sutcliffe .732
Oscard, FIFI, Agency .766
Oslo Kinematographer (Norway) .1033
Osram Sylvania, Inc. .890
Otis, Dorothy Day, & Associates .766
Otto Model & Talent Agency .766
Our Secret Creations .728
Out of the Blue Entertainment .678
Outerbanks Entertainment .677
Outlaw Productions .678
Ovation/Animation .717
Overbrook Entertainment .678
Overwise, Jessica .723
Owen Magic Supreme .750
Oxford Scientific Films .982
Oxygen Media .678

P

P & O Nedlloyd .887
P.F.M. Dubbing International .759
P.O.P. Animation .718
P.O.V. .710
P.P.R. Enterprises .881
Pace Films, Inc. .704
Pacer/Cats .882
Pachyderm Entertainment .717
Pacific Century Bank .738
Pacific Cinemas (Australia) .1012
Pacific Coast Studio Directory .932
Pacific Concessions, Inc. .881, 884
Pacific Data Images .678, 717, 750
Pacific Entertainment Group .750
Pacific Film Archive .900
Pacific Motion Pictures .678
Pacific Ocean Post .757
Pacific Theatres .804
Pacific Title & Art Studio .757, 759
Pacific Title Archives .736
Pacific Title Digital .757
Pacific Title Mirage Studio .750
Pacific Title/Mirage .750, 878
Pacifica Entertainment, Inc. .678
Packaging Concepts .884, 898
Packaging Dynamics .884, 898
Pact, Ltd. .1001
Pactive Corp. .898
Padded Cell Productions .757
Pagano/Manwiller Casting .723
Paige, Marvin, Casting .723
Pakistan .1033
Pakula/King & Associates .766
Palace Cinemas (Australia) .1012
Palace Costume & Prop Company .728
Palafox Cinema (Spain) .1038
Palast/Schmid & Theile (Germany) .1022
Palisades Wildlife Library .754
Palm Springs Intl. Short Film Festival .632
Palmer, Dorothy, Talent Agency, Inc. .766
Palomar Pictures .678
Panama .1033
Panasonic .889
Panastereo, Inc. .891
Panayotopoulos (Greece) .1023
Panpipes Magickal Marketplace .725
Panton Coronet Cinemas .973
Paper & Plastic Goods .897
Paradigm A Talent & Literary Agency .766
Paradox Productions, Inc. .678
Paradoxe Casting .723
Paragon Entertainment .717
Paramount Pictures (also see Viacom)
Canada .960
Costume Department .728
Distribution .694
Motion Picture Group .694
Paramount British Pictures, Ltd. .982
Paramount Films of India, Ltd. .1026
Recording Studios .744
Stock Footage Library .754
Television .695
United Kingdom. .982
Parkway Productions .678
Parrot Communications International, Inc. .709
Parrot Ice Drink .896
Pasadena Advertising .709
Pasadena Production Studios .757
Pascotto & Gallavotti .732
Paskal Lighting .880
Passport Intl. Productions .754
Pathe Cinemas (Netherlands) .1032
Pathe Entertainment, Ltd. .982
Pathe Palace (France) .1020
Patriot Cinemas, Inc., The .805
Patriot Pictures .678
Paul Mantell Studio .749
Paulo Martins (Portugal) .1035
Paulson, Daniel L., Productions .678
PB Management/AFT Productions .679
PCNY USA .881
Peak Productions .679
Pearce, Joan, Research Assocs. .741
Peavey Electronics .892
Peavey Electronics Speakers .892
Pelican Pictures .757
Penfield Productions, Inc. .704
Penn's, Zak, Company .679
Pep Filmtheater GMBH (Germany) .1022
Pepsi London Imax Theatre .973
Pepsi-Cola Co. .896
Percenterprises Completion Bonds, Inc. .740
Perennial Pictures Film Corp. .718
Performance Magazine .932
Performance World Special Effects .750
Period Props .728
Permlight, Inc. .880
Permut Presentations .679
Perpetual Motion Pictures .750
Persky, Lester, Productions .679
Pet Fly Productions .679
Peters Entertainment .679
Petersen Aviation .728
Petersen International Underwriters .740
Petrie Jr., Daniel, & Co. .679
Pevner, Stephen, Inc. .679
Pfeffer Film .679
Pfilmco, Inc. .679
Phaedra Cinema .679
Phase I Productions .679
Philadelphia Festival of World Cinema .631
Philbin Cinema Service, Inc. .902
Philippines .1033
Phillips, Linda, Palo .723
Phoenix Entertainment .718
Phoenix Pictures .679
Phonic Ear .881
Photovision, Los Angeles .736
Pico Creek Productions .679
Picture Cars, East, Inc. .728

Picture This Entertainment .679
Picturedrome Theatres .973
Pike Productions, Inc. .901
Pillsbury, Madison & Sutro .733
Pine Mountain Talent Agency .766
Pinewood Studios .983, 998
Pinnacle EFX .718, 750
Pioneer Sales & Marketing: Hunt-Wesson .884
Pirates Cove Entertainment, Inc. .679
Pittard Sullivan .718
Pixar Animation Studios .718
Pixel Liberation Front .718
PLA Media West .709
Planet Video .757
Plastic Reel Corp. of America .888
Platinum Film Investments .738
Platinum Studios, LLC .679
Platonic Films, Inc. .680
Platt, Marc, Productions .680
Playarte Cinemas (Brazil) .1015
Players Talent Agency, The .766
Playhouse Pictures .704, 718
Plaza Cinema (Pakistan) .1033
Plurabelle Films .680
Plus Three Post .744
PMK, Inc. .709
PNC West, Inc. .879
Poblocki & Sons .886
Poirier, Richard, Model & Talent Agency .766
Poland .1034
Polar Technologies USA .750
Poll, Martin, Films, Ltd. .680
Pollack PR Marketing Group, The .710
Polson Theatres .805
Polyfilm Almere B.V. (Netherlands) .1032
Popcorn & Popping Oils .898
Porchlight Entertainment .680, 718
Port Street Films (Spooky House) .680
Porter/Novelli .710
Portman Zenith Group, Ltd. .983
Portugal .1035
Post Consultants Group .757
Post Edge .750
Post Logic Studios .757
Post Production Playground .757
Post Time .757
Post/La Expo .633
Potsdam Film Museum (Germany) .1022
PR Newswire .710
Practical Automation .894
Prairie Allied Booking Assn. .966
Prairie Films .680
Pray For Rain Pictures, Inc. .680
Precision Post .757
Preferred Popcorn, LLC .898
Premier Chemical Products .893
Premier Data Vision (P.D.I.) .741
Premier Operating Corp., Ltd. .965
Premier Seating Co. .891
Premier Southern Ticket Co. .894
Premier Talent Agency .766
Premiere Artists Agency .766
Premiers Plans-Festival D'Angers .630
Preminger, Jim Agency .766
Preminger, Otto, Films, Ltd. .680
Press, The .931
Pressman, Edward R., Film Corp. .680
Preview & Policy Trailers .901
Prime Casting .723
Prime Ticket, Inc. .884
Princess Cinema, Inc., The .965
Principal Large Format .680
Priority Mfg., Inc. .894
Privileged Communications .680
Priya Village Roadshow, Ltd. (India) .1026
Pro Star Industries .893
Pro Vision Intl., Inc. .632
Proctor Companies .881
Proctor Companies .884
Producer's Masterguide .932
Producer-Writers Guild Of America Pension Plan .919
Producers & Distributors .645
Producers Color Service .736
Producers film Center .736
Producers Guild of America .919
Producers Library Service .754
Production Office Coord. & Accountants Guild, Local 717 .917
Professional Force Security Consultants .725
Professional Musicians, Local 47 .919
Professional Research Associates .741
Progressive Artists Agency .766
Projected Sound, Inc. .891
Projection Room & Film Handling Equipment .888
Projector Lamps & Lenses .889
Projectors .889
Promark Entertainment Group .680
Prominent Features, Ltd. .983
Promotion in Motion Co., Inc./Ferrara Pan Candy .897
Promotional Mgmt. Group, Inc. .884
Prop Masters, Inc. .729
Prop Services West, Inc. .729
Prop-Art .729
Propaganda Films .680
Props Displays & Interiors, Inc. .729
Props for Today .729
Protocol .893
Protozoa, Inc. .718
Prufrock Pictures .680
Public Relations Associates .710
Publicists, Local 818, Hollywood .917
Publicity West .710
Puerto Rico .1041
Pullman Group, The .738
Pulse Entertainment .718
Punch Productions .680
Puppet Studio .718
Pure Arts .681
Pyramid Film & Video .754
Pyros Corporation .718
Pyros Pictures .750
Python (Monty) Pictures, Ltd. .983

Q

QSC Audio .891
QSC Audio Products Sound Reinforcement .892
Quantel .718, 750
Quartermaster Uniform Company .729
Quartermoon @ National .757
Quartermoon Productions .901
Quigley Publishing Company .933
Quilleri, David (Italy) .1028
Quince Productions, Inc. .681
Quincy Jones Media Group, Inc. .681
Quinette Gallay .891
Quinnie Cinema Films, Ltd. (Switzerland) .1040
Quinzaine Des Realisateurs (Director's Fortnight) .632

R

R & B Films .718
R & M Casting .723
R/C Models .729, 750
R/C Models Reality Check, Inc. .718
R/C Theatre Management Corp. .805
R/C Theatres Booking Service .902
Radiant Productions .681
Radiant Systems, Inc. .894
Radio & Television Broadcast Engineers, Local 1212 .917
Raffaele Gaudagno (Italy) .1028
Rainbow Casting .723
Rainbow Film Co./Rainbow Releasing .681
Raincity, Inc. .681
Rainmaker Digital Pictures .718, 736, 750
Rainmaker Digital Pictures (Canada) .955
Rainmaker Productions, Inc. .681
Rajshri Pictures (India) .1026
Raleigh Group, The .710
Raleigh Sound .744
Raleigh Studios .757, 900
Ramsey Popcorn Co., Inc. .898
Rando Productions .750
Rank Cintel, Ltd. .983
Rank Organisation PLC, The .983
Rank Taylor Hobson, Ltd. .983
Rank Video Services, Ltd. .983
Rankin/Bass .681, 718
Ransohoff, Martin, Productions, Inc. .681
Rastar Productions .681
Rat Entertainment/RAT TV .681
Rattan Cinema (Pakistan) .1033
Raw Stock .736
Raxxess .887
RDS Data Group .882, 894
Readervision, Inc. .886

Reading Entertainment (Australia) .1012
Real Cinema (Spain) .1038
Real People Casting .723
Recorded Cinemas .973
Recorded Picture Company .681
Red Bird Productions .681
Red Car Los Angeles .757
Red Hour Films .681
Red Mullett, Inc. .681
Red Rose Sales/Marketing .893
Red Wagon Productions .681
Redeemable Features .681
Reel Directory, The .933
Reel Effects .718
Reel EFX .750
Reel Southern Casting .723
Reelistic FX .750
Regal Cinemas, Inc. .806
Regal Cinema (Pakistan) .1033
Regberg & Associates, Inc. .710
Regency Caribbean Enterprises, Inc.
Dominican Rep. .1017
Puerto Rico .1041
Regent Cinema - South Coast Theatres Pty., Ltd. .1012
Regent Entertainment, Inc. .682, 738
Regnboginn (Iceland) .1025
Rehme Productions .682
Reiff, D.R., & Associates .738
Reinert, Rick, Pictures, Inc. .718
Rembrandt Films .718
Remote Control Productions .718
Renaissance .766
Renaissance Pictures .682
Rencher's, Joy, Editorial Service .759
Renegade Animation .718
Renfield Productions .682
Reperage .682
Research Technology, Inc. .736
Response Marketing .710
Retriever Software .882
Reuters Newmedia, Inc. .754
Reveal Entertainment .682
Revelations Entertainment .682
Revolution Media Management .682
Reynolds & Reynolds .740, 885
Rezn8 Productions, Inc. .718
RGB Color Lab .736
RGH/Lions Share Pictures, Inc. .682
Rhythm & Hues .718, 750
Rich Animation Studio .718
Richland Agency, The .766
Richman, Lawrence, Mann, Chizever, Phillips & Duboff .733
Ricos .899
Rio Syrup Co., Inc. .896
River One Films .682
RKO Pictures .682
RMS Service & Electronics, Inc. .893
RND Cinemas, Limited (Bahamas) .1014
RNF Media Corporation, Inc. .710
Ro-Ma Stock Images .754
Roaring Mouse Entertainment .718, 750
Roberts Company, The .766
Robertson, Hugh, Duff .733
Robins Cinemas .973
Robinson, Amy, Productions .682
Robinson/Kirshbaum Industries, Inc. .884
Robson Entertainment .682
Rock & Water Creations, Inc. .729
Rogers & Cowan .710
Rogers Cinema, Inc. .811
Rolf Theile Filmtheaterbetriebe (Germany) .1022
Roll-a-Grill Corp. .884
Rollins & Joffe, Inc. .682
Ronin Films (Australia) .1012
Roscoe Enterprises, Inc. .682
Rose, Proskauer, LLP .733
Rosen, Charles, Casting .723
Rosenberg, Marion, Office, The .766
Rosenfeld, Meyer & Susman, LLP .733
Rosenfield, Stan, Public Relations, Ltd. .710
Rosenman, Howard, Productions .682
Rosenstein, Donna .723
Roseville Twin Cinemas (Australia) .1012
Ross, Herbert, Hera Productions .682
Rosslenbroich-FTB GMBH (Germany) .1022
Rothman Agency, The .766
Roundabout Entertainment .757
Roundtable Ink .683
Roundup Food Equipment .884
Roxie Releasing .683
Roxy Management Co., Inc. .903
Royal Palast (Germany) .1022
Royal Paper Corp. .898
Royal Pictures .683
RPL Film Theatre .965
RSO Films .683
RTAS, LLC .881
Ruben, Albert G. & Co. .738
Rubie's Costume Co., Inc. .729
Rubin, Baum, Levin .733
Ruby-Spears Productions .718
Rudehoney Design Group .710
Rudin, Scott, Productions .683
Runway Editing Services .757
Russian Federation .1035
Russian Hill Recording .744
Ryder Sound Services, Inc. .744
Rysher Entertainment .683

S

S & K Theatrical Draperies .885
S.O.T.A. FX .751
Saatchi & Saatchi Advertising .710
Saatchi & Saatchi/The Saatchi Entertainment Group .710
Saban Entertainment .683, 718
Safari Animation & Effects .751
Sagon-Phior Group .710
Saguaro Film Festival .632
Salibello & Broder .738
Salter Street Films Limited .949
Sam Communications .710
Sam Film (Iceland) .1026
Sameday Right-o-Way .966
Samuel Goldwyn Films .683
Samuelson Productions .683
San Francisco Intl. Asian American Film Festival .631
San Francisco Intl. Film Festival .631
San Francisco Intl. Lesbian & Gay Film Festival .632
Sanders Agancy, Ltd., The .766
Sandnes Kinematografer (Norway) .1033
Sandrew Metronome Film AB
Denmark .1017
Finland .1018
Norway .1033
Sweden .1039
Sanford/Pillsbury Productions .683
Sangeet Cinema (Pakistan) .1033
Sani-Serv .884
Santa Anita Park .725
Santa Clarita Intl. Film Festival .631
Santa Monica Bank .738
Sara Lee/Ball Park Franks .897
Sarabande Productions .683
Sarkissian, Arthur Productions .683
Sarnow Candy .897
Saturn Films .683
Savage Agency, The .766
Savoy Lane Films, Inc. (Panama) .1033
Scala: FTB GMBH (Germany) .1022
Scenic & Title Artists, Local 816, Los Angeles .917
Scenic Highlights .729
Scenic Technologies .751
Schary, Gabrielle, Casting .723
Schecter, Irv, Company .766
Scherick, Edgar J., Associates, Inc. .683
Schiff, Paul, Productions .683
Schill, William, Agency .766
Schindler, Deborah, Productions .683
Schneider Optics, Inc. .890
Schoepfer Studios .729
Scholastic Productions .719
Schroder & Co. .738
Schulller Talent .766
Schult Design & Display .886
Schulze & Associates .738
Schumacher, Joel, Productions .683
Schwartz, Don & Associates .766
Schwartzberg & Co. .751
Schwartzberg & Company .719
Scott Free Productions .684
Screaming Mad George, Inc. .751
Screen Actor/Call Sheet .933
Screen Actors Guild .919
Awards .21
Screen Gems .684
Screening Rooms .900

Screenmusic Studios .744
Screens & Frames .890
Screenvision Cinema Network .710
Script Supervisors & Screen Composers of America .920
Script Supervisors, Local 871, Hollywood .917
Seating & Re-Upholstery .890
Seating Concepts, Inc. .891
Seattle Intl. Film Festival .632
Second Line Search .725, 754
Securities & Exchange Commission .930
Security Service .891
Sedelmaier, J.J., Productions, Inc. .716, 719
Sedona Intl. Film Festival Workshop .631
Segue Productions, Inc. .684
Segura's, Kathryn, Ph.D. Animals .725
Seiler, Tina, Casting .723
Selby Products, Inc. .890
Selik, Lila, Casting .723
Sellers, Dylan, Productions .684
Seltzer, Nancy, & Associates .710
Seltzer, R., Associates .741
Sennheiser Electronic Corp. .881
Series, USA .891, 893
Server Products, Inc. .884
SESAC, Inc. .912
Set Designers & Model Makers, Local 847, Hollywood .917
Sets & Props by Foam-Tec, Inc. .729
Seven Arts Pictures .684
Seven Summits Pictures & Management .766
Seven Torch Music .744
Seventh Art Releasing .684
7th Level, Inc. .719
Seyfarth, Shaw, Fairweather & Geraldson .733
SF Bio AB (Sweden) .1039
SG Cowen .738
SGI Marketing .710
Shabistan Cinema (Pakistan) .1033
Shady Acres Entertainment .684
Shakey's Wigs .729
Shanghai Morning Sun Animation Co., Ltd. .719
Shapira, David, Associates, Inc. .767
Shaw Organisation (Singapore) .1036
Shaw Organisation Group of Companies (Singapore) .1036
Sheffield Systems .887
Sheldon & Mak, Inc. .733
Shelly's Apparel Warehouse .729
Sheppard, Mullin, Richter & Hampton .733
Shepperton Studios .998
Sherer Digital Animation .719
Shevitt, Ava .723
Shindler Perspective, The .738
Shochiku Co. (Japan) .1029
Shoelace Productions, Inc. .684
Shonkyte Productions, Inc. .684
Shoot .933
Shooting From the Hip Casting .723
Shooting Gallery, Inc., The .684
Showbiz East Expo Reed Exhibition Companies .634
Showbiz West Expo Reed Exhibition Companies .632
Showcase Cinemas .973
Showeast .634
Showest .631
Showscan Entertainment .684, 876
Shringar Cinemas Pvt., Ltd. (India) .1026
Shumaker, Sragow & Steckbauer, LLP .733
Shutt-Jones Productions .684
Shyer, Charles, Inc. .684
Sideshow Productions .751
Sidley & Austin .733
Sight Effects .751
Sign Language Company, The .725
Signature Technologies .886
Signature Theatres .811
Silicon Valley Bank .738
Silver Cinemas, Inc. .811
Silver Lion Films .685
Silver Pictures .685
Silver Screen/Portico Dev. (Poland) .1034
Silver, Massetti & Szatmary, Ltd. .767
Silverfilm Productions, Inc. .684
Silverlight Entertainment .685
Silverline Pictures .719
Silverlining Productions .685
Sim EX Digital Studios .719
Simons, Michelson, Zieve, Inc. .710
Simply Done Software .886
Sindell, Richard, & Associates .767
Singapore .1035
Singapore Intl. Film Festival .631
Single Cell Pictures .685
Single Frame Films .719, 751
Sitting Ducks Productions .685
Six Foot Two Productions .719
Skadden, Arps, Slate, Meagher & Flom, LLP .733
Skouras, D.P., Films (Greece) .1023
Sky Pond Productions .685
Skyfish Productions .685
Skylark Entertainment, Inc./R & R Films .685
Skylark Films, Ltd. .685
Skyline Partners .685
Skyview Film & Video .744
Skyview Studios .719, 757
Sladek Entertainment Corp. .685
Slagle Minimotion, Inc. .751
Slate Please Casting .723
Slater, Mary Jo, Casting .723
Slaton, Don, Casting .723
Slessinger, Michael, & Associates .767
Slide Screen Entertainment, Inc. .965
Sloane/Borden Pictures .685
Sloss Law Office .733
Smart Devices, Inc. .891
Smart Products .887
Smart Theatre Systems .892
Smith Affiliated Capital Corp. .738
Smith's, Ron, Celebrity Look-Alikes .723
Smith, Susan, & Associates .767
Smithee, Alan, Films .685
Smithgroup Communications .719, 901
Smithsonian Institution .930
Smoke & Mirrors Public Relations .710
SMPTE Advanced Motion Imaging Conference .630
SMPTE Journal .933
Snack Foods .899
Snackworks, Inc. .899
Snapdragon Films, Inc. .685
Sneak Preview Entertainment, Inc. .685
SNL Studios .685
Snow Leopard Productions .685
Socal Cinemas, Inc. .812
Socan/Society of Composers, Authors & Music Pub. of Canada .969
Society of Composers & Lyricists .912
Society of Film Distributors, Ltd. .1001
Society of Motion Picture & Television Engineers (SMPTE) .913, 969
Socogex (France) .1020
Softni Subtitling & Dubbing International .759
Soldiers of Light Productions .751
Solo Cup .898
Solo One Productions .686
Solothurn Film Festival .630
Soltes, Elan, FX & Design .719
Sommer & Bear .733
Somper Furs .729
Songwriters Guild of America, The .920
Sonics Associates .891
Sony Cinema Products Corp. Sound Systems .885
Sony Pictures Entertainment, Inc. .686
Beijing (China) .1015
Classics .686
Digital Studios Div. & Editing Equip. Rentals .757
International Offices .687
Sony Pictures Family Entertainment Group .687
Sony Pictures Imageworks .687
Sony Pictures Imageworks (Animation) .719
Sony Pictures Imageworks (Special effects) .751
Sony Pictures Releasing .686
Sony Pictures Screen Gems .686
Sony Pictures Sony Digital Studios Division .687
Sony Pictures Studios .744
Sony Pictures Studios Post-Production Facilities .758
Sony Pictures Studios Studio & Editing Equip. Rentals .757
Sony Pictures Studios Wardrobe .729
Soredic (France) .1020
Sound Associates, Inc. .881
Sound Equipment .891
Sound Master Audio/Viedo .744
Sound Reinforcement .892
Sound Related Technologies .893
Sound Studios & Services .742
Sound Thinking Music Research .744
Soundcastle Recording Studio .744
Soundelux Showorks .744
Soundelux/Soundelux Media Labs .744
Soundfold .879
Soundscape Productions .744
Soundz Nu .744
Soundcraft USA .892

Source Stock Footage, The .754
South Africa .1036
South Bay Studios .710
South Central States NATO .906
South Fork Pictures .688
South Korea .1037
South, Leonard, Productions .719, 758, 901
Southern Library of Recorded Music .744
Southfield/J.G. Clark Co. .898
Southwest Cinema Products .890
Spain .1037
Spalla, Rick, Video & Hollywood Newsreel .758
Spanky Pictures, Inc. .688
Spark Factory, The .710
Speakers .892
Speare & Company Insurance .740
Special Effects .746
Special Effects Unlimited, Inc. .751
Special Optics .890
Specialty Exhibitor Equipment & Services .878
Specialty & Large Format Exhibitors .876
Speco .889
Spectak Productions .719, 751
Spectra Cine, Inc. .887
Spectral Communications .754
Spectromedia Entertainment .688
Spectrum Motion Picture Lab .736
Special Effects Systems .751
Spelling Communications .710
Spentzos Films, S.A. (Greece) .1023
Spikings Entertainment .688
Spinelli Cinemas .813
Spirit Dance Entertainment .688
Splash Radio .710
Sporn, Michael, Animation, Ltd. .719
Sports Film Lab .736
Sportsrobe .729
Spumco, Inc. .719
Spyglass Entertainment Group .688
Square H Brands .899
SSA Public Relations .710
SSI Advanced Post Services .901
ST Productions .719, 738
Stage 18 .751
Stage Accompany USA .892
Stage Design .893
Stage Employees
Local 1, New York .918
Local 2, Chicago .918
Local 33, Los Angeles .918
Local 4, Brooklyn .918
Stalmaster, Lynn & Associates .723
Stampede Entertainment .689
Stanbury & Fishelamn, Inc. .733
Stander, Scott, & Associates .767
Stankevich-Gochman, LLP .733
Star Cinema (Pakistan) .1033
Star Cinemas (AGT Enterprises, Inc.) .813
Star Manufacturing Intl. .884
Stardust Film, Inc. .744
Stargate Films, Inc. .719
Starnet Cinemas .813
Startoons International .719
State Street Pictures .689
Statistics .9
Stavros Isaakides (Greece) .1023
Steadi Systems .736
Steamroller Productions .689
Steenbeck, Inc. .758
Stefan Wilcox .729
Stein Industries .884
Stereo Vision Entertainment .738
Steriakis Brothers/AMA Films (Greece) .1024
Stern, Howard, Production Company, The .689
Stern, Neubauer, Greenwald & Pauly .733
Steve Johnson's X/FX, Inc. .749
Steve Wright Digital FX, Inc. .752
Stewart Filmscreen Corp. .890
Sticks & Stones .729, 751
Stiefel Entertainment .689
Stinson Theatres, Ltd. .965
Stipes, David, Productions, Inc. .719, 751
Stjoernubio (Iceland) .1026
Stock House, The .754
Stock Shots .753
Stokes/Kohne Assoc., Inc. .751
Stokes/Kohne Associates, Inc. .719
Stone vs. Stone .689
Storyopolis .719
Strand Releasing/New Oz Productions .689
Stratford, Bert, Productions .719
Stratosphere Entertainment .689
Stravanger Kinematographer (Norway) .1033
Streamline Pictures .719
Stribling Productions .719
Strong International .878, 889
STS Foreign Language Services .759
Stuart Stone Casting .723
Studio & Editing Equipment & Services .755
Studio 56 .745
Studio Analysts, Local 700 (IATSE), Hollywood .917
Studio City .710
Studio City Cinema Holdings, Ltd.
Hong Kong .1025
Singapore .1036
Taiwan .1040
Studio Film & Tape, Inc. .736
Studio Home Entertainment .689
Studio M Productions Unlimited .745
Studio Mechanics
Local 209, Ohio .918
Local 477, N. Miami .918
Local 479, Atlanta .917
Local 480, Santa Fe .918
Local 484, Texas .918
Local 52, New York .918
Local 812, Detroit .918
Studio Picture Vehicles .729
Studio Productions .719, 751
Studio Talent Group .723
Studio Wardrobe Department, The .729
Stuntmen's Assn. .920
Subentra Group (Indonesia) .1026
Subtitles & Captions .759
Sudler & Hennessey, Inc. .710
Suite A. Management .767
Summit Entertainment .689
Sun Agency, The .767
Sunbow Entertainment .719
Sundance Film Festival .630
Sundance Institute .689
Sunnywell Display Systems .886
Sunset Post, Inc. .751
Sunset Sound Recorders .745
Super 8 Sound .736
Supercolor .719
Superior Quartz Products West .890
Superior Quartz Products, Inc. .890
Superloopers .745
Sutton, Barth & Vennari, Inc. .767
Svensk Filmindustri (Sweden) .1039
Swain Film & Video .704
Swank Motion Pictures, Inc. .704
Swartout Enterprises, Inc. .689
Sweden .1039
Sweetheart Cup Co. .898
Switzerland .1039
Sword & The Stone, The .729
Sydney Film Festival .632
Syndicate Theatres, Inc. .813
Systems & Products Engineering Co. .889

T

T & T Optical Effects .751
T. Miller Popcorn Co. .898
T.E.S.T. Kreashens .751
T.G.I.F. Productions .710
T.H.A. Media Distribution, Ltd. .704
Tabexsa Cine (Spain) .1038
Taffetdesign, Inc. .710
Taiwan .1040
Talent Agencies .760
Talent Group, Inc. .767
Talent Trek & Nashville .767
Tanjong Golden Village (Malaysia) .1029
Tanjong PLC (Malaysia) .1029
Tannen, Kathy L. .733
Tantleff Office, The .767
Tanzinite Productions .710, 751
Tape House Toons .720
Tape/Disc Business .933
Taper, Mark, Forum Casting .723
Tapestry Films, Inc. .689
Target Enterprises .710
Tarrant Enterprises, Limited .965

Taste of Nature .899
Taurus Entertainment Co. .689
Taylor & Taylor Associates, Inc. .740
Taylor Co. .884
Taylor Made Films .690
Taylor, Maurice, Insurance Brokers, Inc. .740
Team Todd .690
Technicolor (Screening room) .900
Technicolor Entertainment .885
Technicolor, Inc. .736
Technicolor, Ltd. (UK) .985
Technicreations .751
Technikote Screen Corp. .890
Technology Intl. .889
Teco .889
Tektronix .758
Tel-Air Interest, Inc. .704
Telefilm Canada/Telefilm Canada .970
Telescene Film Group, Inc. .950
Television & Cable Factbook .933
Television Digest with Consumer Electronics .933
Television Quarterly .933
Televisual (Great Britain) .934
Telling Pictures .690
Telluride Film Festival .633
Temecula Valley Intl. Film Festival .633
Tempo Industries, Inc. .880
Ten Thirteen Productions .690
Thailand .1040
Theatre & Video Products .894
Theatre Associations (Canada) .966
Theatre Authority, Inc. .920
Theatre Circuits .771
Theatre Cleaning & Maintenance .893
Theatres Employees
Local B-183, New York .918
Local B-46, Chicago .918
Theatre Equipment & Services .879
Theatre Equipment Dealers .893
Theatre Equipment Suppliers .879
Theatre Management Associates .903
Theatre Management, Inc. (TMI Theatres) .813
Theatre Owners of Indiana .906
Theatre Owners of New England .906
Theatre Service Network .885, 903
Theatre Services .893
Theatre Specialty Co., Inc. .893
Theatrical Wardrobe Attendants, Local 768, L.A. .918
Theatrical Wardrobe Union, Local 764, NY .918
Thelen, Reid & Priest, LLP .733
Third Dimension Effects .751
30 Sixty Design, Inc. .710
Thomas, Bob, Productions, Inc. .690
Thompson, J. Walter, Company .710
3 Arts Entertainment .690
3 Point Digital .758
3 Ring Circus Films .690
Three Strange Angels, Inc. .690
Threshold Entertainment .720
Thrillseekers Unlimited, Inc. .725
Thunder North Broadcast Services .966
THX .885
THX .892
Ticket Pro Systems .894
Ticket.USA, LLC .894
Ticketing Systems.com .882, 894
Ticketpro Systems .882
Tickets & Ticket Stock .894
Tidewater Entertainment, Inc. .690
Tierney & Partners .711
Tig Productions, Inc. .690
Tigermark, The Display Source, Inc. .711
Tillsonburg Broadway Cinemas, Inc. .965
Tisch, Steve, Co., The .690
Tisdale & Nicholson .733
Tisherman Agency, Inc. .767
Title House, Inc. .751, 759
Titra California, Inc. .759
Tivoli Industries, Inc. .880
TK Architects .881
TLC Entertainment/The Mini-Movie Studio .720
TMG International .711
TMS/Kyokuichi Corporation .720
Todd-AO
Digital Images .751
Studios .745
Editworks .745, 758
Toei Animation Co., Ltd. .720
Toei Company (Japan) .1029
Toho International (A Div. of Toho Co., Ltd) Japan .1029
Toho Towa Co. (Japan) .1029
Tom Thumb Music/Ruth White Films .745
Toon Makers, Inc. .720
Tooniversal Company, Inc. The .720
Tootsie Roll Industries, Inc. .897
Toronto Film Studios .952
Toronto Intl. Film Festival .633
Total Creative .711
Total Digital Productions .758
Total Theatre Design .881
Totem Productions .690
Touch Controls, Inc. .889
Toybox .956
TR Productions, Inc. .704
Trackwise, Inc. .736
Tracy-Locke Advertising, Inc. .711
Trane Co. .888
Trans-Lux (Theatre Circuits) .813
Trans-Lux Corp. .886
Travelers Insurance Co. .740
Treasurers & Ticket Sellers
Local 750, Chicago .918
Local 751, NY .918
Local 857, L.A. .918
Tri-Elite Entertainment, Ltd. .711
Tri-Ess Sciences, Inc. .751
Tri-State Theatre Service, Inc. .903
Tristano, Mike, Weapons & Special Effects .729, 751
Triangle Scenery Drapery & Lighting .729, 885
Triangle Theatre Service, Inc. .903
Tribal Scenery .751
Tribeca Film Center .900
Tribeca Productions .690
Tricor Entertainment .690
Trident Releasing .690
Trident Film Financing .738
Trilogy Entertainment Group .690
Trimark Cinemanow .693
Trimark Pictures .693
Troma Entertainment, Inc. .693
Tromso Kino (Norway) .1033
Trondheim Kino (Norway) .1033
Troon, Ltd. .720
Troop, Steuber, Pasich, Reddick & Tobey, LLP .733
Trust Company of the West .738
Try Soundwall Systems .879
Tube Lighting Products .880
Tucker Wayne/Luckie & Co. .711
Tulchin, Harris, & Associates .733
Turbochef Technologies .884
Turbyfill Booking Service .903
Turin Intl. Gay & Lesbian Film Festival .631
Turkey .1041
Turman-Morrissey Company, The .693
Turner Feature Animation .720
Turner, Lawrence J. .733
Turning Point Management Talent Agency .767
TV Guide .933
TVA International, Inc. .961
TVP-Theatre & Video Products .888
Twenieth Century Artists .767
Twentieth Century Fox (also see Fox, Inc.)
Corporate History .641
Distribution .661
Fox Production Services: Wardrobe .729
India .1026
Production .661
Props .729
Television .662
Twilight Entertainment Films .720
Twin States Booking Service .903
Two Headed Monster .751
Two Headed Monster Studio & Editing Equip. Rentals .758
II Jam Productions .722
II Jam Productions .725
2 Match World Sales .738
Tyler, Susan, Casting .723
Tyneside Film Theatre .973
Tyson, David, Lighting, Inc. .879

U

U.S. Air Force, Motion Picture & Television Liaison Office .930
U.S. Coast Guard, Motion Picture & Television Office .930
U.S. Feature Film Releases, 1999-2000 .459
U.S. Film Force .725
U.S. Intl. Film & Video Festival .631

U.S. Intl. Trade Commission .930
U.S. Territories .1041
U.S. Virgin Islands .1041
UCI Brazil .1015
UCI Italia SRL (Italy) .1028
UCI Japan KK .1029
UCI Joint Venture Co., Poland .1034
UCLA Entertainment Symposium .630
UCLA Film & Television Archive .754
UFA Theater AG (Germany) .1023
Ufland Productions .693
UGC
Belgique .1014
France .1020
UK .973
Ugo Poggi (Italy) .1028
UIP International Services (Hong Kong) .1024
Ultimate Effects .751
Ultra Stereo Labs .745, 892
Uniforms .894
Uniforms To You .894
Union Bank of California Entertainment Group .738
Union Cine Ciudad (Spain) .1038
Union KG Krugmann & Weischer (Germany) .1023
United Agencies, Inc. .740
United American Costume .729
United Arab Emerates (UAE) .1041
United Artists Cinema Circuit, Ltd. (Hong Kong) .1025
United Artists Films, Inc. .693
United Artists Theatre Circuit, Inc. .814
United Cinemas Intl. Multiplex GMBH (Germany) .1023
United Cinemas Intl., UK .973
United Dutch Film Co. (Netherlands) .1032
United International Pictures .985
Malaysia .1030
Mexico .1030
United Media .720
United Motion Picture Assn. of Kansas & Missouri .906
United States Catholic Conference,
Dept. of Commun. Office for Film & Broadcasting .913
United Talent Agency .767
United Theatre Service .903
Unitel Video .751, 758
Universal Studios, Inc. .691
Cartoon Studios .720
Cinema Services .888
Corporate History .642
Facilities Rental .729
Television .693
Universal Cinema Services .894
Universal Films Canada .962
Universal Pictures .692
Universal Pictures India, Ltd. .1026
Universal Pictures, Ltd. (UK) .986
Universal Seating/Bass Industries .891
Universal Stock Footage Library .754
Universal Studios .745
Universal Studios Studio & Editing Equip. Rentals .758
UPA Productions of America .693
Animation .720
USA Film Festival, Dallas .631
USA Films .693
Ushist Historical Resources .729
USI Entertainment Insurance Services .740
Utopia S.A. (Luxembourg) .1029

V

V Esposito (Switzerland) .1040
V.A.S.T., Inc. .894
V.C.I. Beverage Co. .896
Valhalla Motion Pictures .693
Van Duren, Annette, Agency .767
Vancouver Intl. Film Festival .633
Vanguard Documentaries .693
Vanguard Productions .711
Vantage Lighting, Inc. .890
Variety .933
Variety Club of Great Britain .1001
Variety Clubs Intl. .913
Vaughan, Suzanne .733
Ventanarosa Productions .693
Ventura Foods .898
Verdon-Cedric Productions .693
Vereinigte Lichtspiele (Germany) .1023
Vermont Intl. Film Festival .634
Vertex Construction, LLC .881
Viacom, Inc. (also see Paramount Pictures) .694
Consumer Products .696
District Branches & Managers, Motion Picture Group .694
Famous Music Publishing .696
New Media .696
Paramount Pictures .694
Victor Products, Inc. .896
Victoria Film Services, Ltd. .966
Vide-U Productions .720, 901
Video Agency, The .751
Video Monitoring Services of America .741
Video Post & Transfer, Inc. .751
Video Store Magazine .933
Video Systems Magazine .933
Video Tape Library, Ltd. .754
Video Week .933
View Askew Productions, Inc. .696
View Point Studios .751
View Studio, Inc. .720, 752
Viewpoint 99, Intl. Documentary Film Festival .631
Viewpoint Data Labs .720, 752
Viewport Images .720, 752
Village Cinemas (Argentina) .1007
Village Force Cinemas (New Zealand) .1032
Village Roadshow
Argentina .1007
Australia .1012
Austria .1014
China .1015
France .1020
Fiji .1018
Germany .1023
Greece .1024
Hong Kong .1025
Hungary .1025
India .1026
Italy .1028
Malaysia .1030
New Zealand .1032
Pictures .696
Singapore .1036
South Korea .1037
Switzerland .1040
Taiwan .1040
Thailand .1041
Vinton, Will, Studios .720
Virgin Cinemas, Ltd. .973
Virtualmagic Animation .720
Vision Art Design & Animation .752
Vision Crew Unlimited .752
Vista Group .711
Vista Manufacturing, Inc. .880
Visteon .891
Visual Concept Engineering .720, 752
Visual FX.com .752
Visual Impulse Productions .720, 752
Visual Services .729
Vitac .759
Vogel Popcorn Co. .898
Voicecaster .723
Voices .745
Voight, Jon, Entertainment .696
Volpe, Brown, Whelan & Co. .738
Vynyl .900

W

W.F. Cinema Holdings, L.P. (Mann Theatres) .818
W.L. Mitchell & Associates .897, 898
W.N.A./Cups Illustrated, Inc. .898
Wabash Associates .741
Wagner Zip Change, Inc. .886
Walch Kinobetriebs (Switzerland) .1040
Wald, Jeff, Entertainment, Inc. .696
Walden Group, The .738
Wall Coverings .879
Wallace Theater Corporation .816
Wallis Theatres (Australia) .1012
Walter H. Jann Werbe & Filmbetr. GMBH (Germany) .1022
Wang & Williams .711
Ward, Vincent, Films, Inc. .696
Ward-Anderson Cinema Group .973
Wardlow & Associates .767

Warner Bros., Inc. .696
Canada (Distribution) .962
Classic Animation .720
Corporate History .643
Consumer Products .698
Distribution .697
Feature Animation .720
International Offices .699
International Theatres .699
Studio Facilities .699
Studios Facilities (Sound Studio & Services) .745
Studios Facilities (Studio & Editing Equip. Rentals) .758
Studios, Facilities/Wig Rentals .729
Telepictures .699
Television .699
Television Animation .720
Theatrical Distribution Japan .1029
United Kingdom .986
United Kingdom (Productions) .986
Warner Hollywood Studios .745
Screening Room .900
Studio Services .758
Warner Lusomundo
Cines de Espana, S.A. (Spain) .1038
Philippines .1034
Portugal .1035
Warner Mycal Corp. (Japan) .1029
Warner Village Cinemas (Taiwan) .1040
Warner Village Exhibition .973
Warner-Morgan Creek-Chargeurs Cinemas (Netherlands) .1032
Warren, A. Chandler, Jr. .733
Waves Sound Recorders .745
Wayne, Don, Magic Effects .752
Wax/Courier, MD, Films .702
Wax, Morton D., Public Relations .711
Weapons Specialists, Ltd. .729
Weaver Popcorn Co., Inc. .898
Webb, Mimi, Miller .723
Website Guide .1042
Weed Road Pictures .702
Wehrenberg Theatres, Inc. .817
Weil, Gotshal & Manges .733
Weinstein & Hart .733
Weird Stuff Designers .729
Weissman, Wolf, Bergman, Coleman & Silverman .733
Weldon Williams & Lick, Inc. .894
Wellington Film Society (New Zealand) .1032
Wells, Bob, Theatre Painting .893
Wesni/Hines III .884
West Avenue Theater Corp. (Philippines) .1034
West Coast Theatre Service, Ltd. .966
West Glen Communications, Inc. .702, 704, 901
West Productions, Inc. .745, 758
Westar Productions, LLC .758
Westar/Int. Cinema Equipment Co. .889
Western Costume Co. .729
Western India Theatres, Ltd. (India) .1026
Western Product Placement .711
Western Security Bank .738
Westlake Audio .745
Westside Cinemas (Australia) .1012
Wettlaufer Kinobetriebs-Gesellschaft MBJ (Germany) .1023
Wexler Film Productions, Inc. .704
Whamo Entertainment .720
Whisper Walls .879
White Wolf Productions .702
WHP Architecture .881
Wiese, Michael, Productions .725
Wild Brain, Inc. .720
Wild Child Entertainment, Ltd. .702
Wildfire, Inc. Lighting & Visual Effects .752
Wildwood Enterprises, Inc. .702
Wildwood Theatres .818
Will Rogers Memorial Fund .914
William Morris Agency .768
William Tuft Corp. .885
Williams Sound Corp. .881
Williamson, J.C., Entertainment, Inc. .738
Wilshire Corp. .884
Wilson Theatre Service .903
Wilson, Elser, Moskowitz, Edelman & Dicker, LLP .733
Winchester Carton .898
Wine Country Film Festival .632
Wing Enterprises .888
Wing Gallery, The .725
Winkler Films, Inc. .702
Winpak Technologies, Inc. .884, 898
Winsome Pictures, Inc. .702
Winstar Television & Video .702
Winston, Stan, Studio .752
Winter, Ralph, Production .702
Wise & Associates, C.S.A. .723
Wish You Were Here Film & Video .754
Witt-Thomas Films .702
Wolf, Fred, Films .720
Wolf Group .711
Wolf, Rifkin & Shapiro .733
Wolfe Merchandising .888
Wolfe, Keith, Casting .723
Wolff Cinema Groep (Netherlands) .1032
Wolper Organization, The .702
Women in Communications .914
Women in Film & Television .1001
Women in the Director's Chair Intl. Film & Video Festival .631
Wonderworks .729, 752
Word of Mouth Creative .711
Word Popcorn Co. .899
Words in Pictures .759
Working Title Films .702
Working Title Films, Ltd. (UK) .986
Workshirt Music .745
World Class Sports .768
World Events Productions, Ltd. .720
World Film Services, Inc. .702
World Market: Europe, Latin America, Asia & the Pacific .1007
Worldfest-Houston Intl. Film Festival .631
Worldview Entertainment, Inc. .702
Worldwide Safe & Vault .891
Worth Mentioning Public Relations .711
Wright Popcorn & Nut Co. .899
Writers & Artists Agency .768
Writers Guild of America, East, Inc. .920
Writers Guild of America, West, Inc. .920
Writers Guild Theater .900
Wunderfilm Design .752
Wyandot, Inc. .899
Wychwood Productions .702
Wyle/Katz Company, The .702
Wyman, Lori, Casting .723
Wyman/Sullivan Productions .703

X Y Z

X-Stream Post (Laube-Roth, Inc.) .752
Xaos .752
Xaos, Inc. .878
Xenotech, Inc. .878
Xetron Division/Neumade Products .889
Xzacto Post & Illusion .758
Y.L.S. Productions .752
Yagher, Kevin, Productions .752
Yak Yak Pictures .703
Yamagata Intl. Documentary Film Festival .634
Yamaha Electronics .892
Year in Review
Canada .936
Great Britain .972
U.S. .5
Yelmo Cineplex de Espana (Spain) .1038
York-Kino GMBH-FTB (Germany) .1023
Yorktown Productions, Inc. .703
Yorktown Productions, Ltd. .951
Yosemite Film Festival .631
Young, Cy, Industries, Inc. .890
Young, Mike, Productions .720
Young & Rubicam, Inc. .711
Young, Robert J. .733
Yu, Helen .733
Yurkiw, Mark, Group, The .749
Zacuto Audio .745
Zaentz, Saul, Film Center .703, 745, 758, 900
Zanuck Company, The .703
Zeitgeist Films, Ltd. .703
Zen Entertainment .720
Zenith Specialty Bag Co., Inc. .898
Zero 2 60 .711
Zide/Perry Entertainment .703
Ziffren & Ziffren .733
Ziffren, Brittenham, Branca & Fischer .733
Zimmerman, Adria .729
Zollo Productions, Inc. .703
Zoom Cartoons Entertainment .720
Zucker Productions .703
Zucker/Netter Productions .703